MSU LIBRARIES

O9-BRY-361

Union list

New Serials Title
+ & Con...
Periodical room

WITHDRAWAL

Who's Who in American Art

THE
AMERICAN
FEDERATION
OF ARTS

Who's Who
in
American Art

EDITED BY

Dorothy B. Gilbert

NEW YORK   *R. R. Bowker Company*   1959

© 1959 BY R. R. BOWKER COMPANY
62 W. 45th St., New York 36, N. Y.
$22.50 non-members AFA—$20.00 members AFA
Library of Congress Card Number 36-27014
Printed and Bound in the
United States of America

115533

Ref
N
6536
W5
1959

Contents

The American Federation of Arts

1083 FIFTH AVENUE, NEW YORK 28, N. Y.

OFFICERS

Robert Woods Bliss, *Honorary President*
Richard F. Bach, *Honorary Vice-President*

Roy R. Neuberger, *President*
George H. Fitch, *First Vice-President*
Lloyd Goodrich, *Second Vice-President*
David M. Solinger, *Third Vice-President*
Alice M. Kaplan, *Secretary*
Lee A. Ault, *Treasurer*

Harris K. Prior, *Director*

A complete list of Trustees and Committee Members of The American Federation of Arts appears in the 1958 edition of the American Art Directory.

The American Federation of Arts

FIFTY YEARS OF SERVICE

TO ART IN AMERICA

1909-1959

"... FOR HALF A CENTURY THE AMERICAN FEDERATION
OF ARTS HAS BEEN A STRONG FORCE BEHIND THE
GROWTH OF ART APPRECIATION IN THE UNITED STATES.
ITS EXHIBITIONS HAVE BROUGHT THE ARTS TO PEOPLE
THROUGHOUT THE NATIONAL COMMUNITY—AND TO
OUR NEIGHBORS ABROAD. ITS STANDARDS OF QUALITY,
FREE OF ANY BIAS, HAVE BEEN AS DEEP AS THE HUMAN
HEART AND AS HIGH AS THE SPIRIT."

Dwight D. Eisenhower

Preface

All living artists entered in the 1956 edition of WHO'S WHO IN AMERICAN ART, who sent in personal data, are included in this 1959 edition, as well as 1,000 new names, making a total of some 7,000 entries for this edition. Those in the 1956 edition who did not return personal data are included with an asterisk following their entry, denoting no answer received to current mailed questionnaires.

Research has again been done to locate persons who did not return information for the 1956 edition and prior. Where addresses were unobtainable through research and postal information, such entries have been eliminated. Reinstatement will gladly be made on receipt of notice to the Editor of proper address of any entry omitted.

For the first time, museum directors, associate and assistant directors, heads of college and university art departments are included. Also, for the first time, a beginning has been made to include artists of the new state of Alaska and this inclusion will be increased for the next edition. Hawaiian artists have long been included.

The information herein has been edited from questionnaires returned by the artists. Women are listed under their professional names with cross reference for married names. Architects, photographers and decorators are not listed unless they are also creative artists in other fields. These groups publish their own membership lists and directories.

The Geographical Index is compiled alphabetically by state and city, with professional classifications. Other sections include Canadian Biographies, Obituaries from 1956 to 1959, and Open Exhibitions.

The Editor expresses her sincere appreciation to the art organizations, gallery directors and to many art and educational leaders throughout the country for their suggestions and assistance in this work. It is important that artists and art organizations keep the Editor informed of changes of address. Corrections and new names will always be welcome.

Dorothy B. Gilbert
Editor

August, 1959

Abbreviations

PROFESSIONAL CLASSIFICATIONS

C.—Craftsman
Cart.—Cartoonist
Comm. A.—Commercial Artist
Cr.—Critic
Cur.—Curator
Des.—Designer

E.—Educator in Col. or Univ.
Eng.—Engraver
Et.—Etcher
Gr.—Graphic Artist
I.—Illustrator
L.—Lecturer

Lith.—Lithographer
P.—Painter
S.—Sculptor
Ser.—Serigrapher
T.—Teacher in Elem. or H.S.
W.—Writer

ADDRESSES AND SYMBOLS

First address is studio or business.
h.—Home address (if more than one address)
s.—Summer address.

w.—Winter address.
*—No information from artist this year.
†—Death notice received too late to omit name.

MUSEUMS

AGAA—Addison Gallery of American Art, Andover, Mass.
AIC—Art Institute of Chicago.
BM—Brooklyn Museum.
BMA—Baltimore Museum of Art.
BMFA—Boston Museum of Fine Arts.
CAL.PLH—California Palace of the Legion of Honor, San Francisco, Cal.
CAM—City Art Museum of St. Louis.
CGA—Corcoran Gallery of Art.
CM—Cincinnati Museum Association.
CMA—Cleveland Museum of Art.
DMFA—Dallas Museum of Fine Arts.
FMA—Fogg Museum of Art.
LC—Library of Congress.

MMA—Metropolitan Museum of Art.
MModA—Museum of Modern Art.
NCFA—National Collection of Fine Art, Washington, D.C.
NGA—National Gallery of Art, Washington, D.C.
PC—Phillips Collection, Washington, D.C.
PMA—Philadelphia Museum of Art.
SAM—Seattle Art Museum.
SFMA—San Francisco Museum of Art.
VMFA—Virginia Museum of Fine Arts, Richmond, Va.
WAC—Walker Art Center, Minneapolis, Minn.
WMA—Worcester Museum of Art, Worcester, Mass.
WMAA—Whitney Museum of American Art.

AAMus—American Association of Museums.

AAPL—American Artists Professional League.

AAUP—American Association of University Professors.

AAUW—American Association of University Women.

A.Dir. Cl.—Art Directors Club, New York, N.Y.

AEA—Artists Equity Association, New York, N.Y.

AFA—American Federation of Arts, New York, N.Y.

AIA—American Institute of Architects.

AID—American Institute of Decorators.

AIGA—American Institute of Graphic Arts.

ANA—Associate of the National Academy of Design, New York, N.Y.

Arch. Lg—Architectural League of New York, N.Y.

ASL—Art Students League of New York, N.Y.

ASMP—American Society of Miniature Painters, New York, N.Y.

AWS—American Watercolor Society of New York, N.Y. (formerly AWCS)

BAID—Beaux-Arts Institute of Design, New York, N.Y.

CAA—College Art Association of America, New York, N.Y.

CUASch—Cooper Union Art School, New York, N.Y.

FAP—Federal Art Project, Works Projects Administration.

GGE1939—Golden Gate Exposition, San Francisco, Cal., 1939.

IDI—Industrial Designers Institute.

IGAS—International Graphic Arts Society.

MIT—Massachusetts Institute of Technology, Cambridge, Mass.

NA—Academician of National Academy of Design, New York, N.Y.

NAC—National Arts Club, New York, N.Y.

NAD—National Academy of Design, New York, N.Y.

Nat. Ser. Soc—National Serigraph Society, New York, N.Y.

NAEA—National Art Education Association.

NAWA—National Association of Women Artists, New York, N.Y.

NSMP—National Society of Mural Painters, New York, N.Y.

NSS—National Sculpture Society, New York, N.Y.

PAFA—Pennsylvania Academy of Fine Arts, Philadelphia, Pa.

PBA—Public Buildings Administration, U.S. Treasury Dept., Washington, D.C.

PIASch—Pratt Institute Art School, Brooklyn, N.Y.

PMSchIA—Philadelphia Museum School of Industrial Art, Philadelphia, Pa. (now PMSchA)

R.I.Sch.Des.—Rhode Island School of Design, Providence, R.I.

SAGA—Society of American Graphic Artists, New York, N.Y. (formerly SAE)

SC—Salmagundi Club, New York, N.Y.

SI—Society of Illustrators.

SSAL—Southern States Art League.

WFNY1939—World's Fair, New York, N.Y., 1939.

GENERAL ABBREVIATIONS

A—Art, Arts, Artist.

AA—Art Association (preceded or followed by city).

AC or A.Cl.—Art Club (preceded or followed by city).

Ann.—Annual.

Arch.—Architect, Architectural.

Assn.—Association

Assoc.—Associate, Associated.

Asst.—Assistant.

B.—Born.

B.A.—Bachelor of Arts.

B.Arch.—Bachelor of Architecture.

Balt.—Baltimore, Md.

B. of E.—Bachelor of Education.

B.F.A.—Bachelor of Fine Arts

B.P.—Bachelor of Painting.

Chm.—Chairman.

Cl.—Club.

Col.—College.

Coll.—Collection.

Com.—Committee.

Comm.—Commission.

Cur.—Curator.

D. or d.—Died.

Dec.—Decorator.

Deg.—Degree.

Dir.—Director.

Ed.—Editor.

Edu.—Educated, Education.

Exh.—Exhibited, Exhibition.

Exec.—Executive.

Exp.—Exposition.

F.—Fellow (used with organizations).

F.A.—Fine Arts.

Fed.—Federation.

Fnd.—Foundation.

Gal.—Gallery.

Gld.—Guild.

Gr.—Graver, Graphic.

Grad.—Graduate, Graduated.

Hon.—Honorary member.

Illus.—Illustrated, Illustration.

Indp.—Independent.

Indst.—Industry, Industrial.

Inst.—Institute.

Instr.—Instructor.

Int.—International.

Let.—Letters.

Lg.—League.

Los A.—Los Angeles, Cal.

M.A.—Master of Arts.

Mem.—Memorial.

M.F.A.—Master of Fine Arts.

Min.—Miniature.

Mod.—Modern.

Mun.—Municipal.

Mus.—Museum.

Nat.—National.

N.Y.—City of New York, N.Y.

Phila.—Philadelphia, Pa.

Publ.—Publication, Publisher.

Pr.M.—Printmakers (preceded or followed by city).

San F.—San Francisco, Cal.

Sc.—Science.

Sch.—School.

Soc.—Society.

Un.—Union, United.

USPO—United States Post Office.

WC—Watercolor.

American Biographies

American Biographies

AARON, MAY TODD (Mrs.)—*Painter, I.*
Allerton Hotel, North Michigan Ave., Chicago, Ill.

B. LaCelle, Iowa. *Studied*: AIC and in Paris, France with Andre L'hote. *Member*: NAWA; Oklahoma AA; AC of Chicago; AIC Alumni; Phila. Pr. Cl. *Work*: PAFA; Univ. Oklahoma; John Vanderpoel Coll. *Exhibited*: AIC; AWS; Audubon A.; Phila. Pr. Cl.; San F. AA; PAFA; Hugo Gal., N.Y.; AC of Chicago; NAWA, in Paris; All. A. Am.; one-man: Philbrook A. Center; Univ. Oklahoma; Paris, France, 1956. Illus. "Wah Kon Tah." Work reproduced in Christian Science Monitor.

AARONS, George—*Sculptor*
35 Coolidge St., Brookline 46, Mass.

B. Russia, Apr. 6, 1896. *Studied*: BMFA Sch.; BAID. *Member*: NSS. *Awards*: prizes, Boston Inst. Contemporary A., 1945; Rockport AA, 1953. *Work*: groups, memorials, monuments, reliefs: Old Harbor Village, Boston; USPO, Ripley, Miss.; Telephone Bldg., Cincinnati; West End House, Boston; Brandeis Univ., Waltham, Mass.; Hillel House, Univ. Connecticut; Baltimore Hebrew Congregation; Hillel House, Boston Univ. *Exhibited*: Inst. Contemporary A., Boston; BMFA; Busch-Reisinger Mus., Cambridge, Mass.; AGAA; WMAA; Sc. Center, New York, N.Y.; PAFA; A. Alliance, Phila., Pa.; PMA, 1940, 1949; DMFA; CMA; AAG; CGA.

ABADI, FRITZIE—*Painter, Gr.*
11 Riverside Dr., New York 23, N.Y.

B. Allepo, Syria, Mar. 10, 1915. *Studied*: ASL, and with Nahum Tschacbasov. *Member*: AEA; Brooklyn Soc. A.; NAWA; ASL. *Awards*: prizes, NAWA, 1949, 1950. *Exhibited*: Univ. Illinois, 1952, 1955; Carnegie Inst., 1950; LC, 1950; BM, 1950, 1951, 1953; NAWA, 1947-1955; WMAA, 1954; City Center Gal., 1958; one-man: Argent Gal., and Van Dieman-Lilienfeld Gal., N.Y., 1947-1949. *Work*: Butler Inst. Am. A.

ABBATE, PAOLO S.—*Sculptor, Mus. Cur., W., L.*
Torrington, Conn.

B. Villarosa, Italy, Apr. 9, 1884. *Studied*: in U. S. & abroad. *Member*: NSS; A. & W. of Conn.; Kent AA. *Work*: mem., monuments: Newburgh, N.Y.; Providence, R.I.; Torrington, Conn.; Fiume, Italy. *Exhibited*: NSS; Arch. L.; PAFA. *Position*: Cur., Torrington Mus. A., Torrington, Conn.

ABBE, ELFRIEDE MARTHA—*Sculptor, Gr., I.*
24 Woodcrest Ave., Ithaca, N.Y.

B. Washington, D.C., Feb. 6, 1919. *Studied*: Cornell Univ., B.F.A.; AIC; Syracuse Univ. *Awards*: med., Cornell Univ., 1938, 1940; Tiffany Fnd. F., 1948. *Work*: statue, WFNY 1939; mem. panels, Ellis Room, Wiegand Herbarium, 1953 and Mann Library, 1955, Cornell Univ.; BMFA Print Collection; port. bust of Liberty Hyde Bailey, Bailey Hortorium, Cornell Univ.; Kerlan Coll.; Rosenwald Coll.; Harvard, Princeton, Wellesley, Swarthmore, Univ. California Colls., and others; wood-cut editions of "Aesop's Fables" and "Rip Van Winkle," 1950 and 1951; "Garden Spice and Wild Potherbs," 1955; I., limited editions of "American Scholar," "Significance of the Frontier," "Seven Irish Tales" for Cornell Univ. Press, 1955-1957. *Position*: Scientific Illustrator, Cornell Univ., 1942-58; Operates private press for hand-printed woodcut books.

ABBEY, RITA DEANIN—*Painter*
1524 Lead St., Southeast, Albuquerque, N.M.

B. Passaic, N.J., July 20, 1930. *Studied*: Goddard Col.; ASL (Woodstock, N.Y.) with Sigmund Menkes; Univ. New Mexico, B.F.A., M.A.; N.Y. Univ.; Hans Hofmann Sch. A. *Exhibited*: PAFA, 1954; N.Y. City Center Gal., 1954; Univ. New Mexico A. Gal., 1952, 1954, 1955; Harwood Fnd., Taos, 1953; Jonson Gal., 1955; Albuquerque Mus. Mod. A., 1954, 1955. *Position*: Asst. Instr., Univ. New Mexico, 1953; Highland H.S., Albuquerque, N.M.*

ABBOT, EDITH R.—*Educator, L., P., W.*
12 East 97th St., New York 29, N.Y.

B. Hartford, Conn. *Studied*: Norwich A. Sch., with Alice V. V. Brown; ASL, and with William M. Chase, Arthur W. Dow. *Exhibited*: NAWA, 1946, 1949; Southern Vermont A., 1941; Argent Gal., 1940, 1942, 1945 (one-man); AAPL; Nat. AA. *Author*: "The Great Painters," 1927. *Positions*: Assoc. Prof., Wellesley Col., 1905-15; Senior Instr., MMA, 1915-41. (Retired.)

ABBOTT, AGNES ANNE—*Painter, E.*
Wellesley College, Wellesley 81, Mass.; h. Bolton Road, Harvard, Mass.

B. Potsdam, Germany, Aug. 19, 1897. *Studied*: Sch. FA & Crafts, Boston, with C. Howard Walker, Katherine B. Child. *Member*: AWS; NAWA; CAA; Pen & Brush Cl. *Work*: BMFA; FMA. *Exhibited*: WMA, 1935; Grace Horne Gal., Boston, 1931, 1937, 1939 (one-man); Margaret Brown Gal., 1946 (one-man); Pen & Brush Cl., 1949 (one-man); Childs Gal., Boston, 1952, 1954 (one-man). *Position*: Assoc. Prof., Art Dept., Wellesley Col., Wellesley, Mass., 1943- .*

ABBOTT, ANNE FULLER (Mrs. A. Lenox Uhler)—*Painter*
2019 Eye St., N. W., Washington, D.C.

B. Brandon, Vt. *Studied*: ASL; Corcoran Sch. A.; NAD, and with William Chase, Douglas Volk, Francis Jones. *Member*: Wash. A. Cl.; Wash. WC Cl.; Wash. SA; AFA; NAC; PBC. *Work*: Navy Dept., Wash., D.C. *Position*: Dir., Abbott Sch. Fine & Commercial A., Washington, D.C.

ABBOTT, EDITH ABIGAIL—*Painter, C., E., Des.*
836 Prospect St., La Jolla, Cal.

B. Randolph, Vt. *Studied*: Univ. Vermont; Mt. Holyoke Col.; T. Col., Columbia Univ., N.Y. *Member*: La Jolla A. Center; Daytona Beach AA. *Awards*: prizes, Clearwater, Fla., 1941; Rockport, 1942; Daytona Beach AA, 1944; AAUW, 1953-1955. *Exhibited*: AAUW; San Diego, Cal., 1952 (one-man), 1954.

ABBOTT, EDWARD ROYDON—*Painter*
1631 N.W. 23rd St., Oklahoma City 6, Okla.

B. Joplin, Mo., Mar. 15, 1897. *Studied*: Kansas City AI; & with Frank von der Lancken. *Member*: Assn. Oklahoma A. *Awards*: prize, Assn. Oklahoma A., 1940-1944. *Exhibited*: Denver A. Mus., 1943; Mississippi AA, 1945; Assn. Oklahoma A., 1936-1958; Ozark Exh., Springfield, Mo., 1941-1944.

ABBOTT, EMILY (Mrs. B. J. O. Nordfeldt)—*Painter*
Wooden's Lane, Lambertville, N.J.

B. Minneapolis, Minn., Oct. 22, 1900. *Studied*: Univ. Minnesota, A.B., M.A.; Minneapolis Sch. A. *Member*: Minnesota AA. *Awards*: prizes, Minnesota State Fair, 1937; Minneapolis Inst. A., 1938, 1944. *Work*: Walker A. Center. *Exhibited*: CGA, 1941; AIC, 1937-1940; 1943; SFMA; Walker A. Center; Univ. Minn.; Minneapolis Inst. A.; St. Paul Gal.; Nebraska AA; Montclair A. Mus., 1953; Harriet Hanley Gal., Minneapolis, 1953 (one-man); PAFA, 1953; Delaware Bookshop, New Hope, Pa., 1954.

ABEL, CHRISTINE JEANNETTE (JEAN)—
Educator, P., S., Des., L.
150 Butterfly Lane, Montecito, Santa Barbara, Cal.

B. Poplar Shade Ranch, Maxwell, Cal. *Studied*: Cal. Sch. FA; Schaeffer Sch. Des., San F.; Chouinard AI; Jepson AI; Columbia Univ.; Univ. Cal., Berkeley; UCLA, and with Armin Hansen, Xavier Martinez, Adolfo Best-Maugard, and others. *Member*: Pacific AA; San F. Soc. Women A.; Glendale AA; Glendale FA Fnd.; N.A.E.A.; So. Cal. A. Teachers Assn.; Santa Barbara AA; Santa Barbara Artists Workshop. *Awards*: Glendale City Schools AA, 1951. *Work*: Long Beach City Schools; Glendale City Schs. *Exhibited*: Glendale AA, 1944, 1951; San F. Women A.; Los A. Mus. A.; San F. AA; Glendale Col. Library, 1950 (one-man); Glendale Library, 1950; Casa Verdugo Library, Glendale; Santa Barbara Women's Club, 1957; Faulkner Gal., 1956-1958; Glendale Independent Gal., 1958. Contributor to Cal. Journal of Secondary Education. Lectures on art subjects to art associations and other organizations. *Position*: A. Instr., Glendale Col., Glendale, Cal. (Retired, 1956).

ABEL, LOUISE—*Sculptor*
c/o Ludwig Abel, 962 North Bend Rd., Cincinnati 24, Ohio

B. Widdern, Wurttemberg, Germany, Sept. 7, 1894. *Studied*: Cincinnati A. Acad.; ASL; Kunstgewerbe Schule, Stuttgart. *Member*: Cincinnati Crafters; Am. Craftsmen's Council, N.Y.; Prof. A., Cincinnati. *Awards*: F., Tiffany Fnd.; Julian Bechtold award, 1955. *Work*: CM; Employees Country Cl., Endicott, N.Y.; Trail Side Mus., Cincinnati. *Exhibited*: CM, 1925, 1945; AIC, 1926, 1940; Nat. Ceramic Exh., 1937, 1941; Getz and Brown Gal., Ohio, 1936; Andrews Gal., 1942; Dayton AI, 1936; Ceramic Gld. of Cincinnati, 1955; Syracuse Mus. A., 1956.

ABELL, MARGARET NOEL—*Sculptor, C., P.*
Ridgefield Rd., Wilton, Conn.

B. New York, N.Y., Dec. 3, 1908. *Studied*: ASL; Breckenridge Sch., Gloucester, Mass., and with Alexander Archipenko. *Member*: AEA. *Exhibited*: Provincetown AA; NAWA; FA Mus., Palm Beach, Fla.

ABISKHAIROUN, NASSAN—*Sculptor, Des.*
Cup of Gold Estates; mail: Box 224, Sedona, Ariz.

B. Assiout, Egypt, Dec. 3, 1915. *Studied*: FA College, Cairo Univ.; Royal Acad. A., Cairo; BMFA. *Member*: Societe des Amis des Arts, Cairo; Salon de Caire, Cairo; Inst. Contemp. A., Boston; Phoenix FA Center, Ariz. *Awards*: prizes, FA College, Cairo, 1933; Salon de Caire, 1936, 1938, 1943; Mod. A. Gal., Cairo, 1940; Inst. Contemp. A., Boston, 1949; Phoenix FA Fair, 1950; scholarship, BMFA, 1946. *Work*: monument for Egyptian Ministry of Agriculture, 1939; commissioned by Egyptian Government to design and execute the Civilization Museum in Cairo, 1942-45; sets for Berkshire Music Center, 1948; also sets for Royal Opera House, Cairo, 1938-41. *Exhibited*: annually, Salon de Caire, 1936-46 (one-man); annually Independent A. Gal., Cairo, 1942-45; BMFA, 1947-50; Inst. Contemp. A., Boston, 1947; Independent A. Gal., Boston, 1948; Arizona State College, Tempe, 1952; Arizona State Fair, 1956; Phoenix A. Center, 1958 (one-man). *Positions*: Instr. A., Cairo FA Sch., 1939-46; privately, 1948-50; Dir. A. Dept., Verde Valley Sch., Sedona, Ariz., 1950-53; Hd., Sc. and Ceramic Dept., Arizona State College, Sedona, 1956-58; Hd., A. Dept., Verde Valley Sch., Sedona, Ariz., 1958-. Des., Partner, Cup of Gold Estates Development, Sedona, Ariz., 1953- .

ABRACHEFF, IVAN—*Educator, L., P.*
410 West 110th St., New York 25, N.Y.

B. Sliven, Bulgaria, Apr. 20, 1903. *Studied*: Nat. Acad. FA-Sofia, Bulgaria & Rome, Italy; & with G. Menato. *Work*: Govt. of Brazil. *Exhibited*: AIC, 1935; Grace Horne Gal., Boston, 1930-34; Indp. Gal. Mod. A., Boston, 1936; Van Diemen-Lilienfeld Gal., N.Y., 1958 (one-man). *Position*: Instr., Abracheff Sch. A.

ABRACHEFF, LIDIA. See Morson, Lidia

ABRACHEFF, NICOLAI—*Educator, W., L., P.*
410 West 110th St., New York 25, N.Y.

B. Sofia, Bulgaria, July 22, 1897. *Studied*: Nat. Acad. FA-Sofia, Bulgaria & Rome, Italy, with Antonio Mancini, Alfons Mucha. *Work*: Govt. of Brazil: Mus. São Paulo; PMA. *Exhibited*: Grace Horne Gal., Boston, 1931-35; Indp. Gal. Mod. A., Boston, 1937; & in Europe & South America, I., books & nat. magazine. *Position*: Dir., Abracheff Sch. A.

ABRAHAMS, JOSEPH B.—*Designer, Gr., I., W.*
Hotel des Artistes, 1 West 67th St., New York 23, N.Y.; h. and studio, Mount Holly, Katonah, N.Y.

B. Grodno, Poland, July 4, 1884. *Studied*: NAD; ASL. *Work*: inscriptions, symbols, Temple Emanuel, N.Y., and many ecclesiastical structures throughout the country; illuminations for citations and awards by educational, communal and religious institutions and public organizations; type faces for Classic Series, Jewish Publication Society of America, Phila., Pa., and for complete Talmud of 30 vols. to be published in Jerusalem; stained glass windows, historic ornaments and decorations for theatres, churches, hotel interiors. Contributor to art journals. *Positions*: Dir., Graphic Arts Studios and Graphic Arts Press, New York, 1910- ; Memb. A. Comm., Educational Art School; Consultant in lettering, industrial and ornamental design.

ABRAMOFSKY, ISRAEL—*Painter, Cr.*
808½ Madison St., Toledo 2, Ohio

B. Kiev, Russia, Sept. 10, 1888. *Studied*: Julian Acad., Paris, with Jean Paul Laurens, Lucien Simon. *Work*: Luxembourg Gal., Salon d'Automne, Nat. Beaux-Arts, Paris; AIC; Toledo Mus. A.; Akron AI; Canton AI; BM; Hillel Fnd., Columbus, Ohio. *Exhibited*: Morgan A. Gal., 1938; Contemporary A. Gal., 1944; Youngstown AI, 1946; Jewish Mus., 1948; State T. Col., Indiana, Pa., 1945.*

ABRAMOWITZ, BENJAMIN—*Painter, Lith., T., L.*
3 L Eastway Rd., Greenbelt, Md.

B. New York, N.Y., July 4, 1917. *Studied*: NAD; George Washington Univ. *Awards*: prizes, Washington A. Fair, 1945; BMA, 1950, 1951. *Work*: Howard Univ.; PMG. *Exhibited*: PMG, 1944, 1945, 1952; U.S. Nat. Mus., 1945; New Sch. for Social Research, 1939; BMA, 1945, 1950, 1951, 1952-1954; Wash. D.C. Pub. Lib., 1945; CGA, 1952, 1953; International House, 1954; Washington T. Col., 1955; one-man: Howard Univ., 1946; Barnet Aden Gal., 1948; CGA, 1950; BMA, 1951; Whyte Gal., 1951; Watkins Gal., American Univ., 1953; Dupont Theatre Gal., 1954; Washington Hebrew Congregation Temple Gal., 1955; District Teachers Gal., 1957; IFA Gal., Wash., D.C., 1958; BMA, 1958 (one-man). *Lectures*: "Development of Modern Art," "Contemporary Thought in Art," "Recent Years of Art." *Position*: Instr., Washington Workshop of the Arts, 1948-; Abramowitz Sch. of Painting, 1951- , Washington, D.C.

ABRAMS, RUTH—*Painter*
205 East 9th St.; h. 18 West 10th St., New York 11, N.Y.

B. New York, N.Y., Mar. 6, 1912. *Studied*: Columbia Univ. (Fine Arts); ASL; New Sch. for Social Research and with Wallace Harrison. *Member*: Artists Cl., N.Y. *Work*: Carnegie Inst., Pittsburgh, Pa.; George Walter Vincent Smith A. Mus., Springfield, Mass., and in private colls. *Exhibited*: CGA, 1949; Camino Gal., 1955; Stable Gal., 1956; Tanager Gal., 1956; RoKo Gal., 1957; Riverside Mus.; Art: USA, 1958, all New York City. One-man: ACA Gal., 1940, 1943, 1949; Artists Gal., Provincetown, Mass., 1954; RoKo Gal., 1956; Camino Gal., 1957.

ABRAMSON, MAURICE—*Painter, L., T.*
938 Boulevard, Bayonne, N.J.

B. Bayonne, N.J., Mar. 4, 1908. *Studied*: NAD. *Awards*: Hallgarten prize, 1937; Jersey City Mus., 1942, 1947, 1954, 1957; Hunterdon A. Center, 1956, 1957; Painters & Sc. Soc. of New Jersey, 1957; Jersey Journal award, 1957; Tinton Falls Assn. award, 1958; Bamberger's permanent coll. award, 1958; Newark Mus. purchase award, 1958. *Work*: mural, Bayonne Pub. Lib. *Position*: Lecturer and teacher, Free Acres Assn., New Jersey.

ABSTETAR, STANLEY F.—*Painter, E., Lith., L.*
720 Broadway, Sheboygan, Wis.

B. Sheboygan, Wis., Nov. 10, 1916. *Studied*: Milwaukee State T. Col.; Central Mich. Col. of Edu. *Exhibited*: AIC, 1941; Wis. P. & S., 1936-1942, 1947-1950; Wis. Exh., Madison, 1936-1940; Wis. State Fair, 1937-1940.

Work: Selected for Wis-Gimbel Centennial coll. and traveling exh. Painting presented by Gimbels to Milwaukee Veterans Mem. Gal., 1955. *Position*: Asst. Supv., Milwaukee Pub. Mus., 1940-41; Wis. Visual-Aids Program, 1941-42.*

ACHESON, ALICE (Mrs. Dean)—Painter, I.
2805 P St., Washington 7, D.C.
B. Charlevoix, Mich., Aug. 12, 1895. *Studied*: Wellesley Col.; BMFA Sch. *Member*: NAWA; Soc. Wash. A.; A. Gld. Wash.; Wash. WC Cl. *Work*: PMG; Watkins Gal., Wash., D.C.; CGA. *Exhibited*: one-man: Wash., D.C., 1924, 1930, 1936, 1939, 1944, 1947, 1954, 1957; New York, 1939, 1942, 1947, 1956; Manatee County A. Center, Bradenton, Fla., 1956. Illustrated "New Road in Old Virginia."

ACHNING, ESTELLYN ALLDAY (Mrs. Walter J.)—
Painter, Lith., I.
534 Geneseo Rd., San Antonio 2, Tex.
B. Atlanta, Tex., June 12, 1909. *Studied*: Colorado Springs FA Center; Univ. New Mexico; and with Andrew Dasburg, Charles Rosen, Henry McFee. *Member*: Texas FA Assn.; NAWA. *Awards*: prizes, Texas FA Assn., 1945; SSAL, 1945. *Exhibited*: NAWA, 1941-1946; Texas FA Assn., 1945, 1946; Denver A. Mus., 1945; Midwestern A., 1942; Caller-Times Exh., Corpus Christi, 1953; local artists exh., 1954. *Position*: Pres., San Antonio A. Lg., 1948-50; Bd. Dir., San Antonio AI, 1947-59.

ACKER, EDNA LEONHARDT—Designer, E., P., L.
413 Vernon Rd., Jenkintown, Pa.; h. The Touraine, 1520 Spruce St., Philadelphia, Pa.
B. Philadelphia, Pa., Jan. 17, 1904. *Studied*: Phila. Sch. Des. for Women; Royal Acad., Victoria & Albert, London, with Prof. Butterfield; Louvre Forney, Paris, France, with Prof. Trulong, and in Germany and Italy. *Member*: Phila. A. All. *Awards*: P.A.B. Widner European Fellowship; La France, Fox, Royle, Lewis, Page and Cohan prizes. *Work*: Styling textiles, Jacquard Fabrics. *Exhibited*: Chicago, Los Angeles, Arizona, New Mexico, Philadelphia. *Position*: Des., Moss Rose Mfg. Co.; Brooks Brothers; Pres. & Dir., Leonhardt Textile Studios; Prof. A., Moore Inst. A., Science & Industry, Philadelphia, Pa.

ACKER, GERALDINE D. N. (Mrs. Ernest R.)—
Portrait Painter
Spring Gable, Poughkeepsie, N.Y.
B. Wassiac, N.Y., June 27, 1895. *Studied*: NAD, with Hinton, Curran; ASL, with DuMond, Luks. *Member*: NAWA; Dutchess County AA; Audubon A. *Exhibited*: NAWA, 1942, 1943, 1946, 1948, 1950, 1951; Syracuse Mus. FA, 1942; Albany Inst. Hist. & A., 1943, 1945, 1946, 1947, 1949, 1951; Poughkeepsie, N.Y., 1940-1946, 1952 (one-man); Argent Gal., 1944; Dutchess County AA, 1947-1952; Terry AI, 1952.*

ACKER, HERBERT V(AN) B(LARCOM)—
Portrait Painter
2293 Country Club Dr., Altadena, Cal.
B. Pasadena, Cal., Oct. 4, 1895. *Studied*: NAD, with Douglas Volk, Francis Jones; ASL, with Frank DuMond, F. Luis Mora; Grande Chaumiere, Academie Colorossi, Paris. *Member*: Laguna Beach AA; Pasadena AI. *Award*: prize, Pasadena AI, 1931. *Exhibited*: Paris Salon, 1924; Salon d'Automne, 1923; Pasadena AI, 1926-1950; Los A. Mus. A., 1936-1938; Pasadena SA, 1925-1950. Portraits in private collections in the U.S., London, England, Buenos Aires, Argentina.

ACKERMAN, FRANK EDWARD—Painter
680 Glenmore Blvd., Glendale 6, Cal.
B. Los Angeles, Cal., Jan. 3, 1933. *Studied*: Sch. All. A.; Chouinard AI; Glendale Col. *Member*: Cal. WC Soc.; Los A. AA; Glendale AA. *Awards*: prizes, Bank of America award, 1951; Gibson award, Long Beach, Cal., 1955. *Work*: Roosevelt H.S., City Hall of Glendale. *Exhibited*: Cal. WC Soc.; Terry AI, 1951; Carnegie Inst. Sch. Corp., 1950; Los A. County Exh., 1950; Glendale Col., 1955; Newport Harbor Exh., 1955; Cal. PLH, 1956; H. M. deYoung Mem. Mus., 1953. *Positions*: Gallery Dir., Glendale AA; Vice-Pres., Glendale AA; Instr. Water Color at Brandt-Dike Schl.

ACKERMAN, MARIE FEATHERSTON (Mrs.)—
Assistant Museum Director
Brooks Memorial Art Gallery; h. 1884 Nelson Ave., Memphis 14, Tenn.
B. Woodbury, Ga. *Studied*: Wesleyan College, and Mercer Univ., Macon, Ga.

ACRUMAN, PAUL—Cartoonist, I., P.
P. O. Box 714, Texarkana, Texas; h. 1011 Hickory St., Texarkana, Ark.
B. Mena. Ark., Aug. 22, 1910. *Studied*: Hendrix Col., Conway, Ark., B.A. *Work*: Cartoons, spot drawings, children's illustrations, scenic designs for leading manufacturers, transportation companies, publishers of trade and national magazines.*

ADAMS, BERTRAND R. (BERT)—Illustrator, C., P.
R. R. #1, Ames, Iowa
B. Webster City, Iowa, Nov. 29, 1907. *Studied*: Federal Schools; Univ. Iowa, B.A. *Member*: AFA. *Work*: murals, USPO, Dubuque and Siloam Springs, Iowa; Equitable Life Bldg., Des Moines, Iowa. *Exhibited*: Iowa State Fair, 1934-36. I., "Manual of Cranial Technique."

ADAMS, CLINTON—Painter, Lith., E., Cr.
University of Florida; h. 1110 N.W. 36th Rd., Gainesville, Fla.
B. Glendale, Cal. Dec. 11, 1918. *Studied*: Univ. Cal., Los Angeles, Ed. B., M.A. *Member*: Cal. WC Soc.; CAA; AAUP. *Awards*: prizes, Cal. WC Soc., 1948, 1950, 1952, 1953, 1957; Cal. State Fair, 1949, 1950; Los A. County Fair, 1953; purchase awards, Univ. Illinois, 1954; SAM, 1954; Chaffey Col., 1954; Louisville A. Center, 1955; Fla. State Fair, 1958. *Exhibited*: nationally, including MMA; MModA; LC; CM; Carnegie Inst.; SFMA; Denver A. Mus.; Los A. Mus. A.; one-man: UCLA, 1950; Landau Gal., 1952, 1955, 1958; Pasadena A. Mus., 1954; Louisville A. Center, 1956; Univ. Texas, 1957. *Position*: Cal. Editor, "Pictures on Exhibit," 1953-54; Vice-Pres., Cal. WC Soc., 1953-54; Asst. Prof. A., UCLA, 1946-54; Instr., Los A. County AI, 1953-54; Prof. A., Hd. A. Dept., University of Kentucky, Lexington, Ky., 1954-1957; Prof. A., Hd. A. Dept., University of Florida, Gainesville, Fla., 1957-. Pres., Southeastern College Art Conference, 1958-59.

ADAMS, FLORENCE BOWMAN—Educator, P., L.
City Centre Bldg., 34 South 17th St., Philadelphia, Pa.; h. 1028 Tatum St., Woodbury, N.J.
B. Philadelphia, Pa., Apr. 10, 1902. *Studied*: with Earl Horter, Lugi Spizzirre, Yarnall Abbott. *Member*: Phila. A. All.; Phila. Plastic Cl.; Woodmere AA; A.T.Assn. *Work*: Lutheran Church, Woodbury, N.J. *Exhibited*: PAFA, 1934, 1935, 1938; DaVinci Exh.; Phila. A. All.; Phila. A.T.Exh.; PAFA, 1951; Phila. Sketch Cl. Lectures on appreciation of art and "The Madonna" in the Italian School of Art. *Position*: Instr., Kensington H.S. for Girls.

ADAMS, HARRIET DYER—Educator, L.
255 West Eleventh St., New York 14, N.Y.
B. Champaign, Ill. *Studied*: Univ. Michigan, A.B.; Radcliffe Col.; N. Y. Univ., A.M. *Author*: "Selective Bibliography of Hispano-Islamic Art in Spain and Northern Africa, 711-1492" (1939). *Lectures*: "Picasso's Recent Painting," with slide illus., given in universities, colleges, schools and clubs. Staff Lecturer at Montclair A. Mus., New Jersey, 1955. Taught Contemporary Art and Modern Painting, Univ. North Carolina, Chapel Hill, N.C.; Survey of Art History, Cranbrook Academy of A., Bloomfield Hills, Mich.*

ADAMS, JEAN CRAWFORD—Painter
5315 Washington Blvd., Chicago 44, Ill.
B. Chicago, Ill. *Studied*: AIC; & with George Bellows, John Vanderpoel. *Member*: Chicago AC; Chicago SA. *Exhibited*: MModA; WMAA, 1932, 1933; Toledo Mus. A.; PMA, 1932; BMA, 1938; Carnegie Inst., 1928-1930; CAM, 1930; AIC, 1930-1945 (one-man); SFMA; Milwaukee AI; Dallas Mus. FA. *Position*: Bd. Dir., Chicago A. Cl.

ADAMS, JOHN SQUIRE—Teacher, P., Comm. A.

6900 Broadway; h. 222 Claywell Dr., San Antonio 9, Tex.

B. Toledo, Ohio, Nov. 28, 1912. *Studied*: Cleveland Sch. A.; Trinity Univ. (B.A.). *Member*: Alamo Heights T. Council; NEA; Contemporary A. Group; San Antonio A. League; Texas WC Soc.; River A. Group. *Awards*: prizes, CMA, 1935; Witte Mem. Mus., 1950, 1957; Arneson Theatre Exh., 1950, 1951, 1957. *Work*: Witte Mem. Mus. *Exhibited*: Alabama WC Soc., 1951; Southwestern Print Exh., 1950; San Antonio, 1947-1958; Texas FA Exh., 1950; Texas WC Exh., 1957, 1958. *Positions*: Instr. A., San Antonio College, Alamo Heights High School, San Antonio, Texas.

ADAMS, KATHARINE LANGHORNE
(Mrs. Benjamin P.)—Painter, L.

225 South Lee St., Alexandria, Va.

B. Plainfield, N.J. *Studied*: ASL. *Member*: Soc. British A. *Awards*: prize, NAWA, 1936; Junior League, Alexandria, Va., 1957. *Work*: AIC; PAFA. *Exhibited*: Century Progress, Chicago; Detroit Inst. A.; CMA; PMA; Albright A. Gal.; AIC; Pittsburgh, Pa.; Plainfield, N.J.; Old Lyme, Conn.; Buenos Aires, Argentina; CGA. *Lectures*: Appreciation of Modern Art.

ADAMS, KENNETH MILLER—Painter, Lith., E.

Cedar St., N.E., Albuquerque, N.M.

B. Topeka, Kan., Aug. 6, 1897. *Studied*: AIC; ASL; & with Kenneth Hayes Miller, George Bridgman; Maurice Sterne, Andrew Dasburg, and in France and Italy. *Member*: ANA; Prairie Pr.M.; AAUP; New Mexico Edu. Assn. *Awards*: prizes, CGA, 1935; Kansas City AI, 1938; IBM, 1940; Phila. Pr. Cl., 1940; Denver A. Mus., 1944; N.M. State Fair, 1944, 1945; Mus. New Mexico, 1950. *Work*: Univ. N.M.; Colorado Springs FA Center; Kansas State Col.; Denver A. Mus.; Los A. Mus. A.; Honolulu Acad. A.; Dallas Mus. FA; N.Y.Pub.Lib.; WMAA; Carnegie Inst.; Lib. Cong.; USPO, Goodland, Kan. *Exhibited*: NAD, 1928-1946; PAFA; San F. AA, 1920, 1932; SFMA, 1942, 1946; AIC; CGA; Dallas Mus. FA; VMA; Kansas City AI; Denver A. Mus.; Carnegie Inst.; Mus. New Mexico, Santa Fe; Harwood Fnd.; Gilcrease Fnd.; Cedar City and Logan, Utah; New Mexico State Mus. *Position*: Prof., Painting & Drawing, Resident Artist, Univ. New Mexico, Albuquerque. N.M.

ADAMS, (MOULTON) LEE—Painter, I., L.

4243 St. Johns Ave.; h. 1436 Avondale Ave., Jacksonville, Fla.

B. Jacksonville, Fla., July 15, 1922. *Studied*: Univ. North Carolina and special work in botany at Rollins Col., A.B. *Member*: Audubon Soc.; Assoc. member, AID. *Work*: many botanical watercolors in private collections; Fairchild Tropical Gardens, Coral Gables; Garden Club of America Headquarters, New York City; United Fruit Co. Murals: St. Vincent's Hospital, River Club, Timuquana Country Club, and Sears Roebuck Co., all Jacksonville, Fla. I., series of prints "Fifty Wildflowers of Northeastern America" (Nat. Audubon Soc., 1951); series of folios illus. tropical fruit of the world (with George Opdyke under direction of David Fairchild). Cover des. for Horticulture magazine and others. Lectures on expeditions made for subject matter. *Exhibited*: nationally; one-man: Mus. Natural History, Buffalo; Baylor Univ.; Cornell Univ.; Fairchild Tropical Gardens, Miami; Garden Club of America, New York; Horticultural Hall, Boston; International House, New Orleans; Los A. Mus. A.; Miami Beach A. Center; Morehead Gal., Univ. North Carolina; N.Y. Botanical Gardens; Phi Beta Kappa Hall, College of William & Mary; Wilmington Soc. Fa.; Univ. Georgia; Garden Symposium, Williamsburg, Va.

ADAMS, MARGARET BOROUGHS (Mrs. Wayman)—Painter, Lith., C., I.

2815 San Gabriel St., Austin 5, Tex.; s. Elizabethtown, N.Y.

B. Austin, Tex. *Studied*: Univ. Texas; Newcomb Col.; Tulane Univ.; Columbia Univ.; N. Y. Sch. F. & App. A. *Member*: Southern Pr. M.; Pen & Brush Cl.; NAWA; AWS; Life Memb. and Bd. Dir., Texas FA Assn.; Fndr. Member and Past Pres., Austin A. League; Founder & Hon. Pres., Heritage Soc., Austin, Tex. *Exhibited*: AWS, 1944; All. A. Am., 1945; PAFA, 1945; one-man: Univ.

Texas, 1936; Grand Central Gal., 1936; CGA, 1939; Harlow-Keppel Gal., 1943; Texas FA Assn.; Dallas Woman's Cl., 1950; Texas Fed. of Woman's Cl., 1950, 1958. Illus. "Stars and Their Stories."

ADAMS, MARJORIE NICKLES (Mrs. Edgar F.)—Painter, C.

Fuller Bldg., Philadelphia, Pa.; h. R. D. 3, Media, Pa.

B. Shippensburg, Pa. *Studied*: Shippensburg T. Col.; PMSchIA; PAFA; Chester Springs Acad. FA. *Member*: Phila. A. All.; Phila. Plastic Cl.; Woman's A. Cl. *Awards*: F.PAFA; prize, PAFA, 1922, 1923; Cresson traveling scholarship for study in Europe, 1924; Phila. Plastic Cl., 1929. *Work*: portraits, Dupont Magazine; many private commissions with work in private colls., in U.S. and abroad.

ADAMS, MARK—Designer, P.

161 Divisadero St., San Francisco 17, Cal.

B. Fort Plain, N.Y., Oct. 27, 1925. *Studied*: Syracuse Univ.; Columbia Univ.; and with Hans Hofmann; Jean Lurcat, France. *Awards*: San F. Art Commission award, 1956. *Work*: Dallas Mus. FA; tapestries: San F. Pub. Lib., Marina Branch. *Exhibited*: Tapestries: Mus. Contemp. Crafts, 1956; "Wall Hangings," 1957; "Patron Church," 1957; AFA traveling Exhs., 1957, 1958; De Young Mus. A., San F., 1953, 1958 (ptgs.); Des.-Craftsmen of the West, 1957; San F. Mus. A, 1953, 1958; one-man: Gumps, San F., 1954; Stanford Univ. A. Gal., 1957; San Diego, 1958.

ADAMS, PHILIP RHYS—Museum Director, L., W.

Cincinnati Art Museum, Cincinnati, Ohio

B. Fargo, N.D., Nov. 19, 1908. *Studied*: Ohio State Univ., B.A.; N.Y. Univ., M.A.; hon. deg., Litt. D., Miami Univ.; D.F.A., Wittenberg Col., Springfield, Ohio; Litt. D., Conservatory of Music, Cincinnati; Princeton Univ.; The Sorbonne, and with Cook, Robinson, Mather. *Member*: Assn. A. Mus. Dir.; Trustee, AFA; AAMus.; Taft Mus. Comm. of the Inst. FA; AID. *Author*: "The Sculpture of Erwin F. Frey," 1940; "Rodin," 1945. Contributor to art magazines. *Position*: Instr., L., Newcomb Col., 1931-34; Asst. Dir., 1934-36, Dir., 1936-45, Columbus (Ohio) Gal. FA; Dir., Cincinnati Mus. Assn., Cincinnati, Ohio, 1945- .

ADAMS, VELMA—Lithographer, Et., Eng., P., S.

714 South Oxford Ave., Los Angeles 5, Cal.

B. Fruita, Colo., April 4, 1902. *Studied*: Los A. County AI; ASL; Grand Central Sch. A., and with George Biddle, F. Tolles Chamberlin, Leo Katz. *Member*: Cal. Pr. M.; Cal. SE; Cal. AC; Women Painters of the West. *Awards*: prizes, Cal. SE, 1939; Ebell Annual, 1939, 1948; Cal. AC, 1940, 1947; Los A. County AI, 1941, 1942, 1943, 1945; Southern Pr. M., 1941; Women Painters of the West, 1944; Nat. Lg. Pen Women, 1949. *Work*: Southwest Mus., Los A.; Appalachian Mus. A., Mt. Airy, Ga.; Los A. Mus. A.; triptych, U.S. Navy. *Exhibited*: GGE 1939; Staten Island Inst.; Fnd. Western A., 1940-1945; Laguna Beach AA, 1949; Los Angeles AA, 1943-1949; Occidental Col., 1946; Fillmore Art Barn, 1941-1943; Pasadena AI, 1949. *Author*: "Southwest Indian Designs." Included in "Prints by California Artists," 1954.*

ADAMS, WALTER BURT—Painter, Cart.

820 Hamilton St., Evanston, Ill.

B. Kenosha, Wis., July 6, 1903. *Studied*: AIC, and with William Owen, Jr., Elmer A. Fosberg, Charles Wilimovsky, Frederick V. Poole, George Oberteuffer. *Awards*: prizes, AIC, 1930; Evanston Women's Cl., 1936, 1938, 1940, 1942, 1944, 1946, 1950, 1952. *Work*: Chicago Public Schools; Evanston Hist. Soc. *Exhibited*: AIC, 1930-1946; PAFA, 1936-1938; Evanston Women's Cl., 1932-1952. Author, Illus., "Infinite Dynamics, The Golden Key to Art." *

ADAMS, WALTER LANGLEY—Painter, L., E.

Circle Dr., Irvington, N.Y.

B. New York, N.Y., May 31, 1897. *Studied*: Sorbonne, Paris; Univ. Pennsylvania; ASL; NAD; & with Ten Brook, Coombs, Metcalf. *Member*: Soc. Am. A.; Albemarle AA; Assn. Contemp. Am. A.; Hudson Valley AA. *Awards*: Whitman Gold Medal, N.Y., 1916. *Work*: Fields Gal.,

Chicago; Hudson Gal., Detroit, and others, and in private colls. *Exhibited*: Sorbonne, Paris, France, 1919, 1950; NAD, 1922-1924; Albemarle AA, 1937-1938; Westchester A. & Crafts, 1942-1946; The Hague, Holland, 1952; Tel-Aviv, Israel, 1954; Rome, Italy, 1955. *Position*: Hd., Adult Painting & Fine Arts, Greenburg School, N.Y.

ADDAMS, CHARLES—*Cartoonist*
c/o New Yorker Magazine, 25 W. 43rd St., New York, N.Y.
Contributor to New Yorker Magazine.*

ADDISON, WILFRED JOHN—*Painter, Lith., Des., I., Comm. A.*
20 Drumlins Terr., Syracuse 10, N.Y.
Studied: Syracuse Univ.; NAD; ASL, with George Bridgman, Frank DuMond, Thomas Fogarty. *Member*: Assoc. A., Syracuse; Syracuse Pr. M.; Syracuse Sketch Cl. *Awards*: prizes, Assoc. A., Syracuse, 1938, 1945; Onandaga Hist. A. Exh., 1942, 1943, 1946, 1948, 1951, 1953; Syracuse Pr. M., 1951. *Exhibited*: Cayuga Mus. Hist. & A., 1942-1946; CAM, 1919; Albright A. Gal., 1921, 1922; Assoc. A., Syracuse, 1927-1953; Onandaga Hist. A. Exh., 1942-1958; Syracuse Mus. FA, 1945 (one-man); Syracuse Pr. M., 1937-1958. Inventor of Aquachrome Printing. *Position*: Dir., Syracuse Sketch Cl., 1933-58; Bd. Dir., Onondaga Hist. Assn.; A. Dir., Crouse-Hinds Co.

ADEN, ALONZO J.—*Museum Director*
127 Randolph Pl., N.W., Washington 1, D.C.
B. Spartanburg, S.C., May 6, 1906. *Studied*: Howard Univ., B.A.; Buffalo Mus. Sc. *Member*: AAMus; AFA. *Awards*: F., AAMus, 1938; Scholarship, Rockefeller Fnd., 1936. Lectures: "Negro in American Art." *Position*: Cur., Howard Univ. Gal. A., 1930-43; Dir., Barnett Aden Gal., Washington, D.C., 1943- .

ADES, HAL—*Painter, I., Comm. A., E.*
21 East 14th St., New York 3, N.Y.
B. Tunbridge Wells, England, Apr. 16, 1888. *Studied*: with George Frederick Watts, R.A.; Torquay A. Sch., England. *Exhibited*: AAPL; Grand Central A. Gal.; WMAA; Fifty Am. A.; Terry AI; Fla. Southern Col.; Schonemann Gal.; Arthur Newton Gal., N.Y.; Asheville, N.C.; Seton Hall Univ., Newark, N.J.; Howard Univ., Wash., D.C.; Pine Bluff, Ark.; Greensboro and Charlotte, N.C.; Oklahoma City, Okla. I., "Short Stories of Famous Men"; "Down to the Sea in Ships," 1946. *Position*: Vice-Pres., AAPL, New York, N.Y.

ADLER, ELMER—*Typographer, E., L., W.*
Erwinna, Bucks County, Pa.
B. Rochester, N.Y., July 22, 1884. *Member*: AIGA; hon. mem., Grolier Cl. *Award*: medal, AIGA, 1947; hon. degree Bucknell Univ., 1955. *Position*: Research Assoc. Gr. A., Princeton Univ. Library; Founder, Pres. & Dir., Pynson Printers to 1940; Editor, The Colophon to 1940; Editor, New Colophon, 1948- ; Prof. Emeritus, Princeton Univ., 1952- ; Dir., Calle del Cristo 255, San Juan, for the Commonwealth of Puerto Rico, 1955.*

ADLER, SAMUEL M.—*Painter, E., L.*
27 East 22nd St. (10); h. 185 McClellan St., New York 56, N.Y.
B. New York, N.Y., July 30, 1898. *Studied*: NAD. *Member*: Woodstock AA; AEA; Audubon A. *Awards*: J. Henry Schiedt Memorial prize, PAFA, 1951; purchase award, Univ. Illinois, 1952 and WMAA, 1952; Audubon A. Patron's Award, 1956. *Work*: Univ. Illinois; Munson-Williams-Proctor Inst.; Clearwater Mus. A.; WMAA; Glicenstein Mus., Safad, Israel. *Exhibited*: AIC, 1948, 1952, 1957; Chicago Soc. for Contemp. Am. A., 1949, 1952; PAFA, 1948, 1951-1953; Nebraska AA, 1949, 1952, 1953; CGA, 1949; NAD, 1949, 1951; Dallas AI, 1949; Dayton AI, 1949, 1950; Univ. Illinois, 1949-1953, 1955, 1957; Des Moines Art Center, 1949, 1954; Museum of Cranbrook Academy, 1949, 1953; MMA, 1950, 1952; WMAA, 1951-1955, 1956; CAM, 1951, 1953; Norton Mus. and Gal. A., 1952, 1955; VMFA, 1954, 1956; Univ. Mississippi, 1953; Sarasota AA, 1952, 1956; Clearwater Art Center, 1953, 1956; Audubon A, 1953, 1954, 1956, 1957; Columbus Gal. FA, 1953; Los Angeles County Mus., 1945; Key West Art

& Hist. Soc., 1952, 1955; Denver A. Mus., 1955, 1956; N. Y. Univ., 1955-1958; Univ. Georgia, 1949, 1953, 1954, 1956; Univ. Washington, 1952; SFMA, 1952; Stanford Univ., 1952; Woodstock AA, 1952, 1953, 1955; Jewish Mus., N.Y., 1949; Telfair Acad., 1953, 1956; Staten Island Inst. A. & Sc., 1956, 1957; DeCordova & Dana Mus., 1955; Illinois Wesleyan Col., 1955; Grand Rapids A. Gal., 1957; "75 Living Americans," France, Italy and Germany, 1956, 1957, and many others. One-man: Luyber Gal., New York City, 1948; Univ. Indiana, 1950; Louisville Art Center, 1950; Mint Mus. A., 1951; Phila. A. Alliance, 1954; Borgenicht Gal., New York City, 1952, 1954. Lectures at art associations, museums and schools. *Position*: Washington Square College of Arts & Sciences, and Div. of General Education, 1948- ; Private Instruction, 1935- ; Adj. Assoc. Prof. FA, New York University, N.Y.

ADLOW, DOROTHY (Mrs. Nicolas Slonimsky)—*Critic, L., E.*
1 Norway St.; h. 295 Beacon St., Boston 16, Mass.
Studied: Radcliffe Col., A.B., A.M. *Awards*: Art critic's award of the American Federation of Arts, 1953; Citation, Boston Univ., 1956. Author "Twentieth Century Highlights of American Painting," catalogue for traveling exhibition organized by the United States Information Agency. *Position*: A. Cr., Christian Science Monitor; L, BMFA.

ADOMEIT, GEORGE G.—*Painter*
2054 East 102nd St., Cleveland 6, Ohio
B. Memel, Germany, Jan. 15, 1879. *Studied*: Cleveland Sch. A. *Member*: Cleveland SA. *Awards*: 24 awards in CMA May Shows, 1920-1958. *Work*: CMA; Ashtabula Lib.; City of Cleveland Collection. *Exhibited*: Detroit Inst. A., 1925, 1926; Toledo Mus. A., 1928, 1929, 1932, 1935; PAFA, 1925-1941; CGA, 1929, 1931, 1933, 1935, 1937; CAM, 1925, 1926; WMAA, 1937; Los A. Mus. A., 1931; AAG, 1928; Carnegie Inst., 1930; AIC, 1941; Newark Mus. A., 1927; Springfield Mus. A., 1954; CMA, 1920-1958; AFA Traveling Exhibitions, 1932, 1934 and others. *Position*: A. Dir., The Caxton Company, Cleveland, Ohio, 1902-1956. (Retired)

ADRIANI, BRUNO—*Writer*
Valley View Ave., Carmel, Cal.
B. Werne, Germany, Aug. 18, 1881. *Studied*: Kiel, Munich, Berlin, Germany. *Member*: CAA. *Author*: "Baudelaire and George," 1939; "Philipp Harth, Sculptor," 1939; "Problems of the Sculptor," 1943; "Pegot Waring, Stone Sculptures," 1945; "Probleme des Bildhauers," 1948; "Los Problemas del Escultor," 1949; "Ueber das Lesen franoesischer lyrischer Dichtungen," 1952.

ADY, MARION—*Educator*
Southern Oregon College; h. 733 Indiana St., Ashland, Oregon
B. Belle Plaine, Iowa, Nov. 21, 1898. *Studied*: Univ. Oregon; T. Col., Columbia Univ.; California Sch. FA. *Member*: NAEA; PAA; Oregon A. All.; Oregon A. Edu. Assn.; College Council of A. Educators of Oregon. *Position*: Chm., A. Dept., Southern Oregon College, Ashland, Ore., 1926- .

AGHA, MEHEMED FEHMY—*Designer, W., L.*
140 West 57th St., New York 19, N.Y.
B. Nikolaieff, Russia, Mar. 11, 1896. *Studied*: Technical College, Emperor Alexander III, Nikolaieff, Russia; Polytechnic Inst., St. Petersburg, Russia; Ecole Nationale des Langues Orientales Vivantes, Paris, France. *Member*: Life member Art Directors Club, N.Y.; AIGA (Hon. member). *Award*: medal, AIGA, 1957. Lectures on Photography, Typography, Design and Color.

AHL, HENRY CURTIS—*Painter, I., W.*
Middle St., Newbury (Rowley, R.F.D.), Mass.
B. Springfield, Mass., Dec. 30, 1905. *Studied*: with Henry Hammond Ahl & Eleanor Curtis Ahl; Harvard Col., A.B. *Member*: North Shore AA. *Work*: Vanderpoel Coll.; Farnsworth Mus., Rockland, Me.; Sweat Mem. Mus.; Bowdoin Art Coll., Brunswick, Me.; Springville (Utah) AA. *Exhibited*: AIC; Springfield (Ill.) AA; Portland (Me.) Mus. A.; Gloucester A. Exh.; Conn. Acad. FA; New Haven Paint & Clay Cl.; Springville (Utah) AA. Author, Illus., booklets on literary shrines, and natural history subjects.

AHNEMAN, LEONARD J.—*Painter, Des., E.*

385 Madison Ave., New York, N.Y.; h. 151 White Oak Terr., Belleville, N.J.

B. New York, N.Y., May 21, 1914. *Studied*: CUASch.; N.Y. Univ., B.S., M.A. *Work*: USPO, Montpelier, Ohio. *Member*: Arch. Lg.; Nat. Soc. Modern A. *Exhibited*: Honolulu Acad. A., 1942; Southwest Pacific Service Exh., 1944; WFNY, 1939; Nat. A. Soc., 1939; CGA, 1939; Saranac A. Lg., 1940. *Position*: Arch. Des., New York City, N.Y., 1946- ; Raymond Loewy Corp., 1952-1954; Webb & Knapp, 1955- .*

AHLSKOG, SIRKKA—*Craftsman, T., S.*

414 East 83rd St., New York 28, N.Y.

B. Finland, Apr. 15, 1917. *Studied*: Suolahden Kansano-pisto (Weaving Sch.), Finland; Crafts Students League, N.Y. *Member*: Pen & Brush Cl. *Awards*: prizes, Pen & Brush Cl., 1957, 1958. *Exhibited*: Pen & Brush Cl.; Women's Intl. Exposition, N.Y.; Augusta, Ga.; one-man: Winston-Salem, N.C., 1956; Norfolk Mus. A.; Manchester Inst. A. & Sc. *Position*: Instr., Tapestry Weaving, Penland School of Handicrafts, 1956-57; L., Tapestry Weaving.

AHRENDTS, HAROLD L.—*Educator*

Nebraska State College, 25th St. at 9th Ave.; h. 2120 9th Ave., Kearney, Neb.

B. Albion, Neb., Aug. 4, 1914. *Member*: AAUP; Am. Speech & Hearing Assn.; Speech Assn. of Am. *Position*: Chm., Div. Fine Arts, Nebraska State College, Kearney, Neb.

AIKEN, CHARLES AVERY—*Painter, Gr.*

58 West 57th St., New York 19, N.Y.; h. 102 Wood-lawn Ave., Wellesley Hills 82, Mass.

B. Georgia, Vt., Sept. 29, 1872. *Studied*: BMFA Sch. *Member*: SC; Wellesley SA; AWS; Phila. WC Cl.; North Shore AA; All.A.Am.; New Haven Paint & Clay Cl. *Awards*: med., All.A.Am., 1945; AWS purchase prize, 1949; Hudson Valley AA, 1953; All.A.Am., Jane Peterson prize, 1953; med., NAC, 1955, 1958. *Work*: BM; WMA; Dallas Mus. FA; Vanderpoel Coll.; NCFA; Yale Univ.; New Haven Paint & Clay Cl.; Wesleyan Col., Macon, Ga.; San Diego FA Soc.; Santa Barbara Mus. A.; Steinert Hall, Boston. *Exhibited*: CGA; PAFA; NAD; Carnegie Inst.; AIC; Pan-Pacific Exp., 1915; WFNY, 1939; Wellesley SA; WMA; Newport AA; San Diego Exp., 1936; All.A.Am., 1953; NAC, 1955; Hudson Valley AA, 1953; Southern Vermont A. Center, Manchester, Vt. *Position*: Dir., All. A.Am., 1958- .

AIKEN, JOHN DARY—*Painter, E., L., Des.*

7 Harcourt St., Boston, Mass.; h. 1 Waldo Court, Linden St., Wellesley 81, Mass.

B. Boston, Mass., Apr. 10, 1908. *Studied*: Vesper George Sch. A.; and with Eliot O'Hara. *Member*: Wellesley SA. *Work*: deCordova & Dana Mus., Lincoln, Mass. *Exhibited*: deCordova & Dana Mus., 1956. *Position*: Instr., 1939- ; Hd., Dept. Appl. Des., at present, Boston Sch. Occupational Therapy, Boston, Mass.

AITKEN, IRENE ANABEL—*Craftsman, E., W., L.*

15314 Macauley Ave., Cleveland 10, Ohio

B. Cleveland, Ohio, Nov. 25, 1907. *Studied*: Western Reserve Univ., A.B.; Ohio State Univ., M.A.; Cleveland Sch. A; & with Russell B. Aitken, Arthur Baggs. *Awards*: Columbus A. Lg., 1937; CMA, 1937, 1939, 1940, 1942; Columbus Gal. FA, 1938; Syracuse Mus. FA, 1939. *Work*: CMA. *Exhibited*: Nat. Ceramic Exh., Syracuse, N.Y., 1933-42. Author: "Methods of Weaving." *

AKED, ALEEN—*Painter, C., S., L.*

s. Quaint Acres, Tyrone, Ont., Canada

B. England. *Studied*: Ontario Col.A.; Ringling Sch. A.; & with Sydney March, Abbott Graves, Robert Brackman. *Member*: Sarasota AA. *Awards*: prizes, Ont. Col. A.; Ringling Mus. A., 1938. *Exhibited*: Canadian Nat. Exh., 1936-1938; Royal Canadian Acad., 1938; All.A.Am., 1939; SSAL, 1938-1940; Sarasota AA; Studio Gld., 1939, 1940; N.Y.Pub.Lib., 1940; St. George Pub. Mus., 1940; Ontario SA, 1938; Toronto Golf Club, 1946-1952 (one-man).*

ALAIN, D. A.—*Cartoonist, W., I.*

Peapack, N.J.

B. Mulhouse, France, Sept. 11, 1904. *Studied*: Ecole des Beaux-Arts, Geneva, Switzerland. Author: "The Elephant and the Flea," 1956. Contributor to: The New Yorker and other periodicals.

ALAJALOV, CONSTANTIN—*Illustrator, P.*

140 West 57th St., New York, N.Y.

B. Rostov, Russia, Nov. 18, 1900. *Studied*: Univ. Petro-grad. *Member*: Phila. WC Cl. *Work*: BM; PMA; Mus. City of New York; MModA; Societe Anonyme.*

ALAN, JAY (J. ALAN KLEIN)—*Cartoonist*

140 East 40th St., New York 16, N.Y.; h. Lower Byrdcliffe Rd., Woodstock, N.Y.

B. Beatrice, Neb., Apr. 24, 1907. *Studied*: Univ. Nebraska; Chicago Acad. FA. *Member*: SI; Nat. Cartoonist Soc. *Exhibited*: Nat. Cartoonist Soc. Exhibition, MMA, 1951. Creator of comic strip "Modest Maidens," syndicated by AP Newsfeatures. *Work*: Albert T. Reid cartoon collection, Journalism Historical Center, Univ. Kansas. Cartoons represented in collection of humorous writing and cartoons "This Is My Best Humor," 1955.

ALBEE, GRACE (THURSTON) (ARNOLD)
(Mrs. Percy F.)—*Engraver, L.*

Springtown, Pa.

B. Scituate, R.I., July 28, 1890. *Studied*: R.I.Sch. Des.; with Paul Bornet in Paris. *Member*: NA; Conn. Acad. FA; Phila. WC Cl.; Albany Pr. Cl.; Print Council of Am.; Audubon A.; Academic A., Springfield, Mass.; Providence A. Cl.; Providence WC Cl.; Boston Pr. M. *Awards*: prizes, NAD; Providence AC; SAGA, 1951; Conn. Acad., 1955, 1958; Hunterdon County A. Center, 1958; Boston Pr. M.; medals: Audubon A.; Artists Fellowship. *Work*: MMA; Carnegie Inst.; CMA; Okla. A&M Col.; John Herron AI; R.I.Sch. Des.; LC; Nat. Mus., Stockholm; NAD; PMA; Cleveland Pr. Cl.; Marblehead AA; N.Y. Pub. Lib.; Newark Pub. Lib.; Boston Pub. Lib.; Culver Military Acad.; Nat. Mus., Israel; Coll. of King Victor Emmanuel, Italy. Frontispiece port. engr., Duc de la Rochefoucauld for "A Little Book of Aphorisms" and frontispiece for "Unicorns and Tadpoles." *Exhibited*: Salon d'Automne, Beaux Arts, Am. Lib., Paris; NAD, 1934-1958; AIC, 1935; PAFA, 1936, 1944; Sweden, 1937; 50 Am. Prints, AIGA, 1945, 1946, 1951; Providence AC; Albany Pr. Cl.; LC; CGA; Carnegie Inst.; Am-British A. Center; New Jersey State Mus.; Phila. Pr. Cl., 1938-1946; CMA, 1943; MMA, 1942; England, France, Austria, Germany, Italy, Switzer-land, Israel, 1953-1958; Indonesia, Iran, Iraq, Pakistan, New Zealand, Australia, 1958-1960.

ALBEE, PERCY F.—*Painter, Gr.*

Hellerstown, R. F. D., Pa., or Springtown, Pa.

B. Bridgeport, Conn., June 26, 1883. *Studied*: PAFA; R.I.Sch. Des. *Member*: ANA; SAGA; Providence AC; Providence WC Cl.; SC; New Hope Hist. Soc. *Awards*: Palm Beach A. Center; AllA.Am., 1937; Conn. Acad. FA, 1942; SC, 1946. *Work*: decorations, Mem. Hall, St. Paul's Chapel, Brown Univ.; Roger Williams Park Mus.; murals, Bridgeham St. Pub. Sch.; Brown & Sharpe Mfg. Co.; triptych: Lady Chapel, St. Stephens Church, Providence, R.I.; lunette: Fort Belin, Salins-les-Bains, France; MMA Print Coll. *Exhibited*: internationally. Seven joint exhibi-tions with Grace Albee, to 1954; Knickerbocker A., Providence AC, SC, all 1958. *Position*: Pres., Salmagundi Club, New York, N.Y., 1948-1952; Bd. Directors, 1952- .

ALBER, ROSE—*Painter, T., Des.*

321 West 78th St., New York 24, N.Y.

B. Stuttgart, Germany, Dec. 7, 1931. *Studied*: Akademie der bildenden Kunst, Stuttgart and with Erich Fuchs and Willi Baumeister. *Work*: Rutgers Univ.; Santa Barbara Mus. A.; Dorr Oliver, Inc., New York; and in private collections. *Exhibited*: Dusseldorf, Germany, 1951; one-man: Stuttgart, Germany, 1952; Van Diemen-Lilienfeld Gal., 1953, 1956, 1958; Rutgers Univ., 1954; Passedoit Gal., 1955; Carl Schurz Mem. Fnd., Phila., Pa., 1957. *Position*: Des. for drapery fabrics; Hd. A. Dept., Dwight School of Engle-wood, N.J., 1954- .

ALBERS, ANNI—*Designer, C., E., W., L.*

8 North Forest Circle, New Haven 15, Conn.

B. Berlin, Germany. *Studied*: A. Sch., Berlin; A. Acad., Hamburg; Bauhaus (Diploma), Weimar & Dessau. *Work*: MMoDA; Busch-Reisinger Mus., Harvard Univ.; Cooper Union, N.Y.; BM; Cranbrook Acad. A.; Currier Gal. A. *Exhibited*: MMoDA traveling exh., 1949-1953; Wadsworth Atheneum, 1953; Honolulu Acad. A., 1954; one-man: MMoDA, 1949. Contributor to art magazines. Lectures and lecture courses at Univ. Hawaii, 1954; SFMA, 1954; de-Cordova and Dana Mus., 1955; Yale Univ., 1955; BM, 1958; Syracuse Univ., 1958. *Position*: Asst. Prof., Black Mountain College, 1933-49.

ALBERS, JOSEF—*Painter, E., Cr., W., L., Gr.*

8 North Forest Circle, New Haven 15, Conn.

B. Bottrop, Germany, March 19, 1888. *Studied*: Royal A. Sch., Berlin; Sch. Appl. A., Essen; A. Acad., Munich; Bauhaus, Weimar. *Member*: Am. Abstract A. *Awards*: Ada Garrett prize, AIC, 1954; William A. Clark prize, CGA, 1957; Officers Cross of the Order of Merit of the German Federal Republic, 1957; D.F.A., University of Hartford, 1958. *Work*: Yale Univ. A. Gal.; AGAA; CM; BM; Springfield (Mass.) Mus.; Busch-Reisinger Mus.; Munson-Williams-Proctor Inst.; Los. A. Mus. A.; NGA; Rosenwald Coll.; Graduate Center, Harvard Univ.; MMA; WMAA; Solomon R. Guggenheim Mus. A.; AIC; Wadsworth Atheneum; Portland (Ore.) A. Mus.; PMA; CGA; Museu de Arte Moderno, Rio de Janeiro, Brazil and in museums in Hagen, Muenster, Ulm and Kaiserslautern, Germany. *Exhibited*: North and South America, Europe, Japan. Various group shows including Sao Paolo, Brazil, 1957; first Biennale, Mexico, 1958; Brussels Worlds Fair, 1958. Lectures extensively in leading universities, colleges and art schools including Mexico, 1949; Cuba, 1952; Chile, Peru, Germany, 1953; Hawaii, 1954; Germany, 1955. *Positions*: Hd. A. Dept., Black Mountain (N.C.) College; Chm., Dept. Design, Yale Univ., New Haven, Conn., 1950-1958; Visiting Critic, Yale Sch. Fine A., 1958- .

ALBERT, ALLEN D.—*Museum Director*

Sheldon Swope Art Gallery, Terre Haute, Ind.*

ALBERT, CALVIN—*Sculptor, E.*

421 Kent Ave.; h. 222 Willoughby Ave., Brooklyn 5, N.Y.

B. Grand Rapids, Mich., Nov. 19, 1918. *Studied*: AIC; Inst. Des., Chicago, with Moholy-Nagy; Archipenko Sch. FA. *Member*: Fed. Modern Painters & Sculptors; Am. Abstract A. *Awards*: prizes, Audubon A., 1955, 1957; American prizewinner "Unknown Political Prisoner" competition, London, 1953; Haas prize, Detroit Inst. A., 1944. *Work*: Detroit Inst. A.; WMAA; MMA; AIC; Univ. Nebraska; Park Ave. Synagogue, New York City; BM; Chrysler Mus.; Temple Israel, Tulsa, Okla. *Exhibited*: AIC, 1941, 1945, 1952, 1954; VMFA, 1946; Detroit Inst. A., 1945; PAFA, 1949, 1953; WMAA, 1953-1955, 1956-1957; Stable Gal., 1953-1955; MMoDA, 1953, 1954, 1956; MMA, 1952; Univ. Nebraska, 1955; Walker A. Center, 1954; Denver A. Mus., 1954; Univ. Illinois, 1957; BM, 1957; one-man: Theobold Gal., Chicago, 1941; Grand Rapids A. Gal., 1943; Puma Gal., 1944; AIC, 1945; Cal. PLH, 1946; Laurel Gal., 1950; Grace Borgenicht Gal., 1952, 1954, 1956, 1957; one-man traveling exh., 1957, to Des Moines A. Center, Univ. Michigan, Grand Rapids A. Gal., Michigan State Univ. *Position*: Assoc. Prof., Pratt Institute, Brooklyn, N.Y. Co-author: "Figure Drawing Comes to Life," 1957.

ALBIN, EDGAR A.—*Educator, P., Eng.*

1216 South Gary Pl., Tulsa 4, Okla.

B. Columbus, Kan., Dec. 17, 1908. *Studied*: Univ. Tulsa, B.A.; Iowa State Univ., M.A.; & with Fletcher Martin, Philip Guston, Donald M. Mattison. *Member*: Prairie WC Painters Assn.; Southwestern AA; Oklahoma AA. *Award*: med., Oklahoma State AA, 1946. *Work*: IBM. *Exhibited*: Tulsa AA, 1936-1939; Philbrook A. Center, 1940, 1944 (one-man); Mus. New Mexico, Santa Fè, 1940; Prairie WC Painters traveling exh., 1940-1946; Tulsa A. Gld.; 1939-1946; Bethany Col., 1941; Northwest Pr.M., 1942; Southern Pr.M. traveling exh., 1942; Texas State AA, 1943; Saranac Lake A. Lg., 1943, 1944; Univ. Kansas, 1944 (one-man). *Position*: Assoc. Prof., A., Univ. Tulsa, Okla., 1943-46.*

ALBRECHT, FREDERICK E.—*Painter, I.*

1070 Lexington Ave., New York 21, N.Y.

B. Seattle, Wash. *Studied*: N. Y. Sch. F. & App. A.; Seattle ASL; ASL, New York, with John Sloan, Jean Charlot. *Member*: AAPL; ASL. *Exhibited*: All. A. Am., 1943, 1954; AWS, 1942; Montross Gal., 1942; Audubon A., 1946, 1951; AAPL, 1948, 1949, 1951, 1954; NAC, 1953.

ALBRIGHT, IVAN—*Painter, S., Lith.*

55 East Division St., Chicago 10, Ill.; s. Three Spear Ranch, Dubois, Wyo.

B. Chicago, Ill., Feb. 20, 1897. *Studied*: AIC; PAFA; NAD. *Member*: NA; Nat. Inst. A. & Lets.; AWS; F., PAFA. *Awards*: prizes, PAFA, 1940, 1942, 1956; AIC, 1928, 1941, 1943, 1945, 1949, 1950; NAD, 1944; Nat. Print Exh., N.Y., 1946; Carnegie Inst., 1950; Northwestern Univ., 1951; MMA, 1952; medals, Chicago Soc. A., 1931; Temple gold medal, PAFA, 1942; MMA, 1942; bronze medal, AIC, 1943; silver medal, CGA, 1955. *Work*: MMA; AIC; MMoDA; BM; Carnegie Inst.; LC; Wadsworth Atheneum; PMA, and in private colls. *Exhibited*: nationally and internationally.

ALBRIGHT, MALVIN MARR (ZSISSLY)—*Sculptor*

Warrenville, Ill.

B. Chicago, Ill., Feb. 20, 1897. *Studied*: BAID; Ecole des Beaux-Arts, Nantes, France; & with Albin Polasek, Charles Grafly. *Member*: NSS; Laguna Beach AA; Chicago Galleries Assn.; Chicago SA. *Awards*: F.PAFA; prizes, AIC, 1929; Chicago SA, 1930, 1934. *Work*: San Diego FA Soc.; Carnegie Lib., Marion, Ill.; Nichols H.S., Evanston, Ill.; Morton H.S., Cicero, Ill.; statues, Omaha, Neb.; Chicago, Ill.*

ALBRIZIO, CONRAD ALFRED—*Painter, E., Des.*

208 Conti St., New Orleans, La.; h. Foley, Ala.

B. New York, N.Y., Oct. 1894. *Member*: New Orleans AA; NSMP. *Awards*: Rosenwald F., 1945-46; Arch. Lg., 1955. *Work*: 14 panels in tempera, Church of St. Cecilia, Detroit, Mich., 1934; Frescos: La. State Capitol; USPO, De Ridder, La.; Russellville, Ala.; State Office Bldg., Baton Rouge, La., 1938; Exposition Bldg., Shreveport, La., 1939; Court House, New Iberia, La., 1940; Waterman Bldg., Mobile, Ala., 1947-49; Pan-American Southern Corp., New Orleans, La., 1950; Union Passenger Terminal, New Orleans, 1951-54; Synagogue B'Nai Israel, Baton Rouge, La., 1954; mosaics: Supreme Court Bldg., New Orleans, La.; Citizens Nat. Bank, Houma, La.; Court House & City Hall, Gretna, La.; Court House & City Hall, Mobile, Ala. *Exhibited*: GGE, 1939; WMAA, 1937, 1944, 1945; Critic's Show, Cincinnati, 1944; Critic's Show, New York, 1945; Univ. Iowa, 1946; Springfield, Mass., 1946; Passedoit Gal., 1946 (one-man); Delgado Mus. A., 1947 (one-man); Contemporary A. Assn., Houston, Tex., 1953; New Orleans A. Lg., 1955. *Position*: Assoc. Prof. FA, Louisiana State Univ., Baton Rouge, La., 1936-1954.

ALBRIZIO, HUMBERT—*Sculptor*

State University of Iowa; h. 512 Clark St., Iowa City, Iowa.

B. New York, N.Y., Dec. 11, 1901. *Studied*: BAID; New Sch. Social Research. *Member*: NSS; S. Gld.; Audubon A. *Awards*: med., NSS, 1940; prizes, Walker A. Center, 1945, 1946, 1951; Des Moines, Iowa, 1946; Denver Mus. A., 1947; Audubon A., 1947; Joslyn A. Mus., 1949. *Work*: Walker A. Center; USPO, Hamilton, N.Y.; State Univ. Iowa; Joslyn A. Mus., Worcester Mus. A.; Iowa State Teachers Col.; Univ. Wisconsin. *Exhibited*: MMA; WMAA; BM; NAD; PMA; Carnegie Inst.; PAFA; Albany Inst. Hist. & A.; AIC. *Position*: Prof. Sculpture, State Univ. Iowa, Iowa City, Iowa.

ALCORN, ROWENA LUNG (Mrs. Gordon D.)— *Educator, P., W.*

3806 North 24th St., Tacoma, Wash.

B. Tacoma, Wash., Mar. 27, 1905. *Studied*: Santa Barbara State Col.; Univ. Idaho; Santa Barbara Sch. A.; & with Colin Cooper, DeWitt Parshall, Albert Herter, Frank M. Fletcher, Ettore Cadorin. *Member*: Nat. Lg. Am. Pen Women (Founder Tacoma Branch, 1956). *Work*: SAM; Ferry Mus. A., Tacoma, Wash.; State Capitol, Boise, Idaho; Tacoma Pub. Lib.; Col. Puget Sound; Santa Barbara Mus. Natural Hist. *Exhibited*: NCFA, 1938; Delaware A. Center, 1939; Spokane A. Mus., 1940; Wash.

State Col., 1943; A. Assn. Gal., Boise, 1945, 1946; Tacoma A. Lg., 1950, 1951; Santa Barbara Mus. A., 1949; State Mus., Nevada, 1949; Southwest Mus., Los A., 1950; State Hist. Mus., Tacoma, Wash., 1955; State Mus., Olympia, Wash., 1955; Walla Walla, Wash., 1955; Chehalis (Wash.) Pub. Lib., 1955; Tacoma A. Lg., 1955; Smithsonian Inst., 1939; Maryhill Mus. FA, 1957 (one-man shows). *Position*: Hd. A. Dept., Grays Harbor Jr. Col., Aberdeen, Wash., 1938-46; Instr., State Adult Education Program, Tacoma, Wash., 1950-.

ALDEN, KATHARINE L.—*Craftsman, Des., E.*
   42 Summer St., Plymouth, Mass.

B. Boston, Mass., Jan. 8, 1893. *Studied*: Mass. Sch. A. *Member*: Boston Soc. A. & Crafts. *Exhibited*: WMA. *Position*: Instr., Plymouth Pottery Sch., 1936- .

ALDRIDGE, C. CLAY—*Museum Director*
   The Joe & Emily Lowe Art Gallery, Coral Gables 46, Fla.

B. Rome, N.Y., Mar. 16, 1910. *Studied*: Cornell Univ., B.A.; Harvard Univ., M.A. *Member*: AAMus; Am. Archaeological Soc. *Position*: Dir., Everhart Mus., Scranton, Pa., 1945-46; Dir., Lowe Gallery, Univ. Miami, Coral Gables, Fla., 1956- .

ALDRIN, ANDERS GUSTAVE—*Painter*
   2858 Allesandro St., Los Angeles 39, Cal.

B. Sweden, Aug. 29, 1889. *Studied*: Otis AI; Santa Barbara Sch. A.; Sch. FA, San Francisco. *Member*: Cal. WC Soc. *Awards*: prizes, Cal. WC Soc., 1946; Pomona Fair, 1941, 1950; Los A. Mus. A., 1942, 1944; Nat. Orange Show, 1949, 1954; South Bay Comm. A., 1955; San Bernardino Orange Show, 1956; Cal. State Fair, 1957. *Exhibited*: MMA, 1950; PAFA, 1946; AIC, 1941; Nat. Exh. Woodcuts & Prints, New York, 1936; Pasadena AI; Santa Barbara Mus. A.; San Diego FA Soc.; Pomona Fair; Los A. Mus. A., and others.

ALEGRE, A. VILLAMOR—*Painter, I.*
   253 West 58th St., New York, N.Y.

B. Philippine Islands, Feb. 19, 1909. *Studied*: AIC; Chicago Acad. FA; Northwestern Univ.; Univ. Chicago; Columbia Univ. *Member*: AEA. *Awards*: prize, Am. Service Forces Exh., London, 1944. *Exhibited*: AIC, 1936, 1937, 1946; Los A. Mus. A., 1939; CGA, 1941.

ALEXANDER, CHRISTINE—*Museum Curator, W., L.*
   Metropolitan Museum of Art; h. 64 East 82nd St., New York 28, N.Y.

B. Tokyo, Japan, Nov. 10, 1893. *Studied*: Cornell Univ., M.A. *Member*: Archaeological Inst. Am.; German Archaeological Inst. *Author*: "Greek Athletics," 1925; "Jewelry, the Art of the Goldsmith in Classical Times," 1928; "Arrentine Relief Ware," 1945. *Contributor* to MMA Bulletin; Am. Journal Archeology. *Lectures*: Greek and Roman Antiquity. *Positions*: Dept. Greek and Roman Art, 1923, Cur., 1948- , MMA, New York, N.Y.

ALEXANDER, (SARA) DORA BLOCK (Mrs. Max)—
Painter
   21218 Providencia St., Woodland Hills, Cal.

B. Suwalki, Poland, July 1, 1888. *Studied*: with Charles Reiffel, Ruby Usher. *Member*: San Diego FA Soc.; San Diego A. Gld.; Women Painters of the West; Cal. A. Cl.; AAPL; Los A. County AA. *Awards*: Women Painters of the West, 1949; gold med., Cal. A. Cl., 1955. *Exhibited*: Denver A. Mus., 1936; Audubon A, 1943, 1944; Argent Gal., 1943 (one-man); San Diego FA Soc., 1930-1940; Los A. Mus. A., 1935, 1938, 1942; Santa Cruz A. Lg., 1946; Oakland A. Mus., 1946; Los A. Ebell Cl., 1948-1956; Friday Morning Cl., 1948-1956; West Side Jewish Community Center, 1955; Greek Theatre, Los Angeles, 1947-1958; Descanso Gardens, 1958; All Art Los Angeles, 1956-1958; Rancho Cl., 1956-1958; Calabasas Art Festival, 1958; Wilshire Savings Galleries, 1958. *Work*: Federated Womens Club Coll., and private colls.

ALEXANDER, FRANCES B. (Mrs.)—*Painter, L., T.*
   Route 2, Lithonia, Ga.

B. Moreland, Ga., June 28, 1911. *Studied*: Univ. Georgia; High Mus. A. Sch., B.F.A., and with Gilmer Petroff,

Dong Kingman. *Member*: Georgia AA; Atlanta AA; Nat. Lg. Am. Pen Women; Atlanta WC Cl. *Awards*: prize, High Mus. A., 1944. *Work*: mural, Grady Hospital, Atlanta, Ga. *Exhibited*: NAWA; Georgia AA, 1950; Robert Vose Gal., Boston, 1949; The Gallery, Atlanta, 1950; NAWA, 1949; Atlanta AA, 1951; Atlanta WC Cl., 1955. *Position*: Owner-Dir., Georgia Art Mart; Instr., Y.W.C.A., Atlanta, 1955- .

ALEXANDER, FRANKLIN O.—*Cartoonist*
   The Evening & Sunday Bulletin; h. 5450 Wissahickon Ave., Philadelphia 44, Pa.

B. St. Louis, Mo., Nov. 3, 1897. *Studied*: Northwestern Univ.; Chicago Acad. FA. *Member*: Phila. A. All.; Am. Assn. of Editorial Cartoonists. *Awards*: Freedom Fnd. awards, 1950, 1951, 1952, 1953, 1954, 1956, 1957; Christopher Award, 1955; Nat. Council Christians & Jews, 1956; Nat. Headliner's award, 1945; Nat. Safety Council award, 1948; Boy Scouts of Am. bronze plaque, 1957; Laymen's Nat. Committee Award of Merit, 1957. *Exhibited*: Nat. Cartoonist Soc., 1951; Univ. Pennsylvania, 1945; Gr. Sketch Cl., 1944. *Contributor* to: Sat. Eve. Post, Christian Herald Magazine. *Position*: Cartoonist of comic strips, "The Featherheads," "Finney of the Force," "Hairbreadth Harry," for Western Newspaper Union and Ledger Syndicate, 1924-31, 1931-37; freelance, 1938-41; del., Cart., The Bulletin, Philadelphia, Pa., and United Feature Syndicate, 1956- .

ALEXANDER, ROBERT SEYMOUR—
Industrial Designer, P., T.
   Art Dept., Michigan State University, East Lansing, Mich.; h. 2703 Lafayette Ave., Lansing 6, Mich.

B. Pittsburgh, Pa., Feb. 1, 1923. *Studied*: Shrivenham Am. Univ., England; Carnegie Inst. Tech.; Univ. Illinois, B.F.A.; Cranbrook Acad. A., M.F.A. *Member*: Industrial Des. Edu. Assn.; IDI. *Awards*: prize, Furnishings-Des. competition, New York, N.Y., 1958; Merit Awards, Design in Leather Competition, 1955, 1956, 1957; other awards in painting and photography. *Work*: Designs and design consultation for business firms including ANSCO, Beaver Furniture, Capitol Storage, Keyworth Boat Co.; Michigan State Univ.; U.S. Air Force; ROTC; Weger Interiors and others. *Exhibited*: Creative Gals., New York, 1952; one-man exhibition of industrial designs at Saginaw Mus. A., 1956; Michigan State Univ. Galleries, 1956; paintings 1956-1958 in Saginaw, Kalamazoo, Detroit and Flint, Michigan, Champaign, Illinois, Bloomfield Hills, Michigan and Pittsburgh, Pa. *Positions*: Des., Ford Motor Co., 1952-1953; Des. Consultant, 1954- ; in charge Indust. Des., Dept. of Art, Michigan State University, East Lansing, Mich., 1954- .

ALEXANDER, JON H.—*Sculptor, I., P.*
   Rochester Museum, 657 East Ave.; h. 150 Beckwith Terr., Rochester 10, N.Y.

B. Rochester, N.Y., Dec. 8, 1905. *Studied*: Mechanics Inst., Rochester; NAD, with Robert Aiken, Charles Hawthorne; Univ. Rochester, Sch. Medicine. *Work*: Ecclesiastical sculptures: Nazareth Col., Pittsford, N.Y., St. Patrick's Church, Rochester, N.Y.; Nave and Narthex, Most Holy Rosary Church, Syracuse, N.Y.; monument: East Avon, N.Y.; reliefs: Eagle's Cl., Tonawanda, N.Y.; East Greenbush, N.Y., Central Sch. *Position*: Diorama A., Anthropology Div., Rochester Mus. A., Rochester, N.Y., 1941- .*

ALFORD, (EDWARD) JOHN (GREGORY)—
Educator, W., L., P.
   The Art Center, Univ. Indiana, Bloomington, Ind.

B. England, Apr. 3, 1890. *Studied*: Cambridge Univ., B.A., M.A. *Member*: CAA; Am. Soc. for Aesthetics. *Exhibited*: London Group, 1930; Canadian WC Soc., 1941, 1943; Canadian Soc. Gr. A., 1941, 1943; Ohio Valley Exh., 1958. *Contributor* to: art magazines & reviews. *Positions*: Prof. FA, Univ. Toronto, 1934-45; Prof. Aesthetics, R.I.Sch.Des., Providence, R.I., 1945-1952; Visiting Prof. Philosophy and Fine Arts, Indiana University, Bloomington, Ind., 1957, 1958.

ALGOREN, LIONEL C.—*Designer*
   620 North Michigan Ave., Chicago 11, Ill.; h. 2200 Lincolnwood Drive, Evanston, Ill.

B. Minneapolis, Minn., Nov. 14, 1896. *Studied*: Minneapolis Sch. FA; Ecole des Bellevue, Paris, with Leslie

Cauldwell; Victoria & Albert Mus., London, with Oliver Brackett. *Member*: F., IDI; Furniture Cl. of America; AIC. *Awards*: Hardwood Industry Exh., Mus. Science & Industry, Chicago, 1953. *Work*: Designer for numerous nationally known furniture and television manufacturers. Author of numerous articles on furniture design for trade journals.

ALLCOTT, JOHN VOLNEY—*Museum Director, E., L.*

Person Hall Art Gallery, University of North Carolina; h. 301 Chase Ave., Chapel Hill, N.C.

B. St. Paul, Minn., May 30, 1905. *Studied*: Univ. Wisconsin, Ph.B., with Hagen; AIC, with Anisfeld & Giesbert; Royal Acad. FA, Florence, Italy; Univ. Chicago, M.A. *Member*: N.C. State A. Soc.; Comm. on A. Edu., MModA., New York, Council Assoc. *Exhibited*: AIC, 1936, 1938. *Position*: Hd., Dept. A., Univ. of N.C.; Dir., Person Hall A. Gal., Chapel Hill, N.C.*

ALLEN, AGNES (OLIVER)—*Painter*

1714 Walnut St., Philadelphia 3, Pa.

B. Philadelphia, Pa., June 22, 1897. *Studied*: PAFA; Univ. Pa., B.F.A.; Barnes Fnd., and with Clinton Peters, Frank Linton, Hobson Pittman. *Member*: AFA; Phila. A. All.; Phila. Plastic Cl. *Awards*: PAFA, 1947; Nat. Lg. Am. Pen Women, 1948, 1953, 1955. *Work*: State portraits in Schuylkill, Pa.; portraits in Andalusia, Pa.; American Oncologic Hospital, Univ. Pa.; Insurance Co. of North America; Drexel Institute and murals in Mask & Wig Club, all in Philadelphia. *Exhibited*: Portraits, Inc., 1945; A. Dir. Cl., 1945; PAFA, 1929, 1934, 1947, 1951; Harcum Col., Bryn Mawr, 1943 (one-man); Smithsonian Inst., Washington, D.C., 1948, 1950, 1956, 1958; Univ. Delaware, 1955; Moore Inst., Phila., 1955, 1958.

ALLEN, ANNA ELIZABETH—*Painter, I.*

200 University Ave., Orange City, Fla.

B. Worcester, Mass., Feb. 18, 1881. *Studied*: Mass. Sch. A.; Ogunquit, Me., with Charles Woodbury; Gloucester, Mass., with Hugh Breckenridge. *Member*: Orlando AA; Fla. Fed. A.; SSAL; Gloucester AA. *Awards*: prizes, Boothbay Harbor, Me.; Daytona Beach, Fla., 1945. *Exhibited*: Fla. Fed. A., 1955; Orlando, Fla., 1955. *Work*: Carnegie Lib., Turner Falls, Mass.; Methodist Church, Titusville, Fla. Illus., "History of Montague."*

ALLEN, CHARLES—*Teacher, Comm. A., Cart.*

33-68 21st St., Long Island City 6, N.Y.

B. June 23, 1921. *Studied*: City Col., New York, B.S.S.; N.Y. Univ.; Columbia Univ. *Position*: Instr. Comm. A., High School of Indst. A., New York, N.Y.; Consultant, production of animated films.

ALLEN, CLARENCE CANNING—

Painter, Des., Cart., I., W., L.

Tulsa World-Tribune; h. 1224 East 21st St., Tulsa 14, Okla.

B. Clermont, Ga. *Studied*: Southeastern State Col.; ASL; San Antonio A. Acad., and with Bridgman, Neilson, Gonzales, Arpa and others. *Member*: AAPL; NSMP; AFA; Southwestern AA; Nat. Cartoonists Soc.; The Mission Group, Tucson. *Awards*: Freedoms Foundation award, 1953; Nat. Freedoms Award, 1954. *Work*: port. of Will Rogers, Mem. Hospital, Saranac Lake, N.Y.; designed New World-Tribune Mechanical Bldg. and murals for same. Mural, Tulsa Press Cl. Author: "Sketching"; "Tulsa Churches"; "Who's Who in Tulsa"; "Are You Fed Up With Modern Art?" etc. Contributor to Editor & Publisher, Southwestern Advertiser, and Advertisers Digest. *Position*: A. Dir., World-Tribune and Cart., for Tulsa Tribune.

ALLEN, COLIN—*Cartoonist, I.*

115 Edmondson St. (P. O. Box 3413), Sarasota, Fla.

B. Hammond, Ore., 1912. *Studied*: Cal. Sch. FA.; ASL; Pratt Inst. *Work*: Magazine and newspaper cartoons and illustrations: N.Y. Times; New Yorker Magazine; Saturday Evening Post, etc. Advertising cartoons and illustrations: General Electric; Gulf Oil; Standard Oil; General Mills; Ciba; Sharpe & Dohme Pharmaceuticals, etc., 1935-1946. Creator of comic "What A Family!," King Features Syndicate. Illus., "Pictorial Review," King Features Syndicate, 1946-1954. Experimental work in plastic, metal, wood and photography, 1954-1958.

ALLEN, COURTNEY—*Illustrator, S., C., Gr.*

County Rd., North Truro, Mass.

B. Norfolk, Va., Jan. 16, 1896. *Studied*: Corcoran Sch. A.; NAD, and with Charles W. Hawthorne. *Member*: Provincetown AA; SI; All.A.Am. *Exhibited*: SI; New Rochelle AA; NAD; All.A.Am.; Provincetown AA; Chrysler A. Mus.; Hudson Valley AA; Mus. A. & Sciences, Norfolk, Va.; Audubon Soc., Boston, Mass. (Last two were exh. of carved miniature waterfowl). Book illustrator, fiction and textbooks. Contributor of illus. to Sat. Eve. Post; Colliers Weekly; Cosmopolitan; American, True, Field & Stream, Outdoor Life, and other national magazines. *Positions*: Pres., Provincetown AA, 1956-58; Trustee, Chrysler A. Mus., Provincetown and of Provincetown, Mass., Arts Festival.

ALLEN, FRANK LEONARD—

Educator, P., Gr., W., L.

17 Parker St., Rockport, Mass.

B. Portland, Me., Nov. 19, 1884. *Studied*: Mass. Sch. A.; BMFA Sch., with Denman W. Ross; Harvard Univ. *Member*: SC; AWCS. *Position*: Instr. FA, PIASch., 1912-30; Cranbrook Acad. A., 1930-32; Hd., Des. Dept., Mass. Sch. A., Boston, Mass., 1934-1954; Hd., Allen Art School, Rockport, 1954- .

ALLEN, GRETA (Mrs.)—*Portrait Painter*

s. West Gouldsboro, Me.; h. 34 Wales St., Boston, Mass.

B. Boston, Mass. *Studied*: Mass. Sch. A., with Joseph DeCamp; BMFA Sch., with Frank Benson. *Member*: Copley Soc. *Exhibited*: Milwaukee AI, 1930 (one-man); Boston AC; Copley Soc.; Irving & Casson Gal.; PAFA; Jordan Marsh Co., 1958.

ALLEN, HAZEL LEIGH—*Sculptor, P., C.*

2756 North Murray Ave., Milwaukee 11, Wis.

B. Morrilton, Ark., Dec. 8, 1892. *Studied*: AIC, and with Ferdinand Koenig. *Member*: Wis. Designer-Craftsmen; Wis. Painters & Sculptors Soc.; Walrus Cl. *Exhibited*: PAFA, 1929; Milwaukee AI, 1923, 1929, 1931, 1933, 1938; Layton A. Gal., 1941, 1949; Milwaukee-Downer Col., 1947-1952; Walrus Cl., Milwaukee, 1946-1952; Wisconsin P. & S. Soc., 1955; Milwaukee A. Center, 1958.

ALLEN, JAMES E.—*Etcher, Lith., P.*

41-A Mayhew Ave., Larchmont, N.Y.

B. Louisiana, Mo., Feb. 23, 1894. *Studied*: AIC; ASL; Grand Central A. Sch.; & with Hans Hofmann, Joseph Pennell, Arshile Gorky. *Member*: SAE; Chicago SE; Phila. SE; New Rochelle AA; SC. *Awards*: prizes, SC, 1932, 1939, 1946; NAC, 1932; Phila. Pr. Cl., 1933; SAE, 1940; Northwest Pr.M., 1942; Oklahoma WPA A. Center, 1942; Fred D. Keithly prize, SC, 1946. *Work*: BM; CM; CMA; SAM; AIC; Montclair A. Mus., Lib. Cong.; N.Y.Pub.Lib.; PMA. *Exhibited*: NAD; PAFA; SAGA; Phila. SE; Phila. Pr. Cl.; Chicago SE, 1932-1946; one-man exh.: Lib. Cong.; New Rochelle Pub. Lib.; Charleston, W. Va., A. Gal., 1944; Rehn Gal., 1950.

ALLEN, JOSEPHINE L. (Mrs. Herbert D.)—

Former Museum Curator

552 Westfield Ave., Westfield, N.J.

B. Cairo, Egypt, July 2, 1893. *Studied*: Wellesley Col., B.A. Contributor to MMA Bulletin. *Position*: Asst. Dept. Paintings, 1919-1927, Asst. Cur., 1928-1949, Assoc. Cur. in Charge of Loans, 1950-1957, Metropolitan Museum of Art, New York, N.Y. (Retired)

ALLEN, JUNIUS—*Painter*

63 East 111th St., New York, N.Y.

B. Summit, N.J., June 9, 1898. *Studied*: N.Y. Sch. F. & App. A.; NAD, and with George Elmer Browne, Charles Hawthorne, George W. Maynard. *Member*: NA; SC; All. A.Am.; Audubon A.; Summit AA; Grand Central Gal. *Awards*: med., Plainfield AA; Montclair AA; AAPL; prizes, Contemporary Gal.; NAD, 1933; SC, 1939, 1941, 1944; All. A. Am., 1943; Vezin-James prize, 1949; Ranger Fund purchase award, NAD, 1955. *Work*: MMA; State T. Col., Trenton, N.J.; Gould Acad., Bethel, Me.; Summit (N.J.) H.S.; Montclair A. Mus.; A. Mus. of the New

Britain Inst. *Exhibited*: NAD; All. A. Am.; Audubon A.; WFNY 1939. *Positions*: Instr., Wayman Adams A. Sch., Elizabethtown, N.Y., 1951; Vice-Pres., NAD and Chm., School Comm., 1952; Chm., A. Comm., and Cor. Sec., Vice-Pres., Salmagundi Club, New York.*

ALLEN, MARGARET PROSSER. See Prosser, Margaret

ALLEN, MARGO (Mrs. Harry Hutchinson Shaw)—
   Sculptor, P., L., W.
   122 Edgewood Terr., Lafayette, La.; s. Cohasset, Mass.

B. Lincoln, Mass., Dec. 3, 1895. *Studied*: BMFA Sch.; Naum Los Sch., British Acad., Rome, Italy. *Member*: NSS. *Awards*: prizes, (2) Delgado Mus. A. *Work*: Port., busts, bas-reliefs: U.S.Frigate "Constitution"; HMS "Dragon"; Cohasset War Mem.; church, Winchester, Mass.; Clearwater A. Mus.; Butler AI; CM; von Pagenhardt Coll.; Mus. New Mexico, Santa Fe; Cal. PLH; Nat. Mus., Mexico; Dallas Mus. FA; First Nat. Bank, Lafayette, La.; New Iberia Bank, La.; Stanford Univ. *Exhibited*: NAD; PAFA; Cal.PLH; Phila. A. All.; AGAA; one-man: Mus. FA of Houston; Dallas Mus. FA; SAM; Joslyn A. Mus.; Currier Gal.; Clearwater A. Mus.; San Diego FA Soc.; DeYoung Mus.; Delgado Mus. A., 1953; Beaumont (Tex.) Mus. A.; Lafayette (La.) Mus. A.; AAUW, Lafayette, La.

ALLEN, MARTHA—Craftsman, S., E.
   Montevallo, Ala.

B. Appleton, Tenn., Sept. 22, 1907. *Studied*: Alabama Col., A.B.; T. Col., Columbia Univ., M.A. *Member*: Birmingham AC; Alabama WC Soc.; Alabama A. Lg. *Exhibited*: Alabama WC Soc.; Birmingham AC; Junior Lg. Gal. *Position*: Assoc. Prof. A., Alabama Col. Montevallo, Ala. 1932- .*

ALLEN, MARY COLEMAN—Painter
   22 West Franklin St., Troy, Ohio

B. Troy, Ohio, Aug. 9, 1888. *Studied*: Cincinnati A. Acad., with Duveneck; Am. Sch. Min. P.; ASL. *Member*: ASMP. *Work*: BM; Dayton AI.

ALLEN, MAX I.—Educator
   Manchester College; h. 607 Miami St., North Manchester, Ind.

B. Markle, Ind., Mar. 19, 1913. *Studied*: Manchester Col., B.S.; AIC, B.F.A.; Indiana Univ., M.F.A. *Member*: CAA; A. Edu. Assn. of Indiana; Western AA. *Exhibited*: Ft. Wayne A. Sch. *Positions*: Assoc. Prof., Manchester Col., North Manchester, Ind., 1937- ; Prof., Indiana Univ. (summer) 1950; Workshop Dir., Goshen & North Manchester, Ind., 1954.*

ALLEN, WILHELMINA FRANCIS. See Minna

ALLEN, PATRICIA (Patricia Burr Bott)—
   Painter, S., T., Gr., W.
   115 West 55th St., New York, N.Y.; h. 151 Carroll St., City Island, Bronx 64, N.Y.

B. Old Lyme, Conn., Mar. 17, 1911. *Studied*: Rollins Col.; ASL, and with George B. Burr, Malcolm Fraser, Ivan Olinsky, Harry Sternberg. *Member*: Fla. Fed. A.; AAPL; Nat. Lg. Am. Pen Women; Orlando AA; AEA; NAWA. *Awards*: med., Fla. Fed. A., 1944. *Exhibited*: Fla. Fed. A., 1934; AEA, 1955; Riverside Mus., 1954; Yonkers Mus., 1953; NAD, 1950; Brygider Gal.; Louisiana State Graphic Exh.; Yorktown Heights. One-man: Orlando, Fla., 1934; Burr Gal., 1955, 1958. *Position*: Dir., Burr Gallery, New York, N.Y., Innovator of Plasmics, a media of plastic, oil and collage.

ALLENBROOK, CHARLES THEADORE—Painter, L.
   w. 313 South Ocean Blvd., Pompano Beach, Fla.; s. Bearskin Neck, Rockport, Mass.

B. London, England, Dec. 9, 1905. *Studied*: St. Martin's Sch. A., Hornsey Sch. A., Cheltenham Sch. A., England. *Member*: New Rochelle AA; Rockport AA. *Awards*: Rockport AA, 1955. *Work*: murals, portraits: U.S. and Europe. *Exhibited*: Am-British A. Center, 1941; AWS, 1945, 1946; New Rochelle Pub. Lib., 1940-1946; one-man: Am. Mus. Natural Hist., 1946; Rockport AA, 1955; St. Petersburg A. Cl., 1956; Tarpon Springs AA, 1956.

ALLER, GLADYS (Mrs. Gladys Aller Farber)—Painter
   11342 Santa Monica Blvd.; h. 12310 Rochedale Lane, Los Angeles 49, Cal.

B. Springfield, Mass., July 14, 1915. *Studied*: Otis AI; Chouinard AI; ASL; & with George Grosz. *Member*: Cal. WC Soc.; AEA. *Awards*: prizes, Cal. WC Soc., 1936; Los A. Mus. A., 1942. *Work*: MMA. *Exhibited*: PAFA, 1937-1940; Los A. Mus. A., 1941-1943; Cal. WC Soc., 1930-1946.

ALLSTON, GEORGE ALCORN—Painter, Et.
   86-06 231st St., Queens Village 27, N.Y.

B. Philadelphia, Pa., July 20, 1913. *Studied*: ASL with Corbino, March, Dickinson, Barnet, Brown, Vytlacil, Zorach and others. *Member*: ASL; Soc. Am. P. & S. *Awards*: prizes, Emily Lowe Award, 1955. *Exhibited*: Chicago Soc. Et., 1949; PAFA, 1953; Audubon A., 1955, 1957; N.Y. City Center Gal., 1956; P. & S. Soc. of New Jersey, 1957; Contemporary Arts Gal., 1954 (one-man); Eggleston Gal., 1955, 1956; Caravan Gal., 1955; Riverside Mus., 1955; A. Lg. of Long Island; Washington Irving Gal., 1958. *Position*: Instr., Painting, Adult Edu., Martin Van Buren H.S., Queens Village and Central H.S., Dist. #2, Garden City, N.Y.

ALLWORTHY, JOSEPH—Portrait Painter
   31 Scott St., Chicago 10, Ill.

B. Pittsburgh, Pa., Sept. 19, 1897. *Studied*: in U.S. & Europe. *Member*: All. Francaise de Chicago; Chicago AC. *Awards*: prize, Mun. A. Lg., 1931, 1935; Chicago Galleries Assn., 1934; med., Findlay Gal., 1935. *Work*: Eastman Mem. Gal., Laurel, Miss.; Union Lg. Cl., Chicago; City of Chicago Mun. Coll.; Universities of Iowa, Georgia, Missouri, and Northwestern Univ., Princeton Univ., Iowa State Col. *Exhibited*: Carnegie Inst.; Chicago Century of Progress, 1933; Tex. Centennial Exp., 1935; Palacio de Bellas Artes, Mexico (one-man). *Position*: Official portrait painter Saddle & Sirloin Club Gallery of Portraits.

ALPERT, ALEXANDER—Painter
   857 Broadway, New York, N.Y.; h. 1042 38th St., Brooklyn 19, N.Y.

B. Lithuania, Mar. 22, 1896. *Studied*: CAD; ASL; Yale Univ. *Member*: Knickerbocker A.; Painters & Sculptors of N.J.; AEA; ASL. *Awards*: prize, Knickerbocker A., 1951. *Exhibited*: NAD, 1951; NAC, 1951; BM; Yale Univ.; Jersey City Mus. A.; Laurel Gal.; Contemporary A. Gal.; Argent Gal., 1951 (one-man).*

ALPS, GLEN—Educator
   University of Washington, Seattle, Wash.

Position: Prof. Graphic Arts, Art Dept., Univ. Washington.*

ALSTON, CHARLES HENRY—Painter, S., T.
   555 Edgecombe Ave., New York 31, N.Y.

B. Charlotte, N.C., Nov. 28, 1907. *Studied*: Columbia Univ., B.A., M.A. *Member*: NSMP. *Awards*: Dow F., Columbia Univ., 1930; Rosenwald F., 1939-40, 1940-41; grant, Nat. Inst. A. & Lets., 1958; prizes, Atlanta Univ., 1941; Dillard Univ., 1942. *Work*: MMA; WMAA; Butler AI; Detroit Inst. A.; Ford Coll.; IBM; murals, Golden State Mutual Life Ins. Co., Los Angeles; Lincoln H.S., Brooklyn, N.Y.; portrait, Louis T. Wright Mem. Lib., Harlem Hospital, N.Y. *Exhibited*: MMA, 1950; WMAA, 1952-1953; PAFA, 1952, 1953, 1954; High Mus. A., 1938; BMA, 1937; Downtown Gal., 1942; MModA, 1937, 1958; Brussels World Fair, 1958; CGA, 1938; ASL, 1950-1952; John Heller Gal., 1953, 1955, 1956, 1958. Illus. for leading publishers. Contributor illus. to Fortune, New Yorker, Reporter, and other magazines. *Positions*: Instr., ASL, New York, N.Y., 1949- ; Joe and Emily Lowe A. Sch., New York, N.Y., 1949- .

ALTSCHULE, HILDA (Mrs. Hilda Altschule Coates)—
   Painter, S.
   220 Highland Parkway, Rochester 20, N.Y.

B. Russia. *Studied*: Hunter Col., B.A.; Cornell Univ., M.A. *Awards*: prizes, Rochester Mem. A. Gal., 1935, 1940, 1942, 1944; Albright A. Gal., 1939; Lillian Fairchild award, Rochester, 1945; Finger Lakes Exh., 1950; N.Y. State Exh., Syracuse, 1950; Cortland Fair, 1953.

Work: Rochester Mem. A. Gal., and in private colls. in U.S. and Canada. *Exhibited*: Rochester Hist. Soc.; Albright A. Gal., 1939, 1952-1955; Finger Lakes Exh., 1929-1958. Lectures for art clubs and study groups. Lectures on Aesthetics at University School, Univ. of Rochester, 1959.

ALTSON, LOUISE (Louise Vandenbergh)—
Portrait Painter
15 Manor Rd., Douglaston, L.I., N.Y.

B. Antwerp, Belgium, July 4, 1910. *Studied*: College Marie Jose, Academie des Beaux-Arts, Antwerp; Polytechnic Sch. A., London, and with Leon Brunin, Abbey Altson. *Awards*: med., for portraiture. *Work*: Community Church, Douglaston, L. I. Many portraits and portrait groups in U.S. *Exhibited*: England, Scotland, Belgium.*

ALTVATER, CATHY (Mrs. Fred L.)—Painter
160-15 Powell's Cove Blvd., Beechhurst 57, N.Y.

B. July 26, 1907. *Studied*: A. Lg. of Long Island; NAD. *Member*: A. Lg. of Long Island (Treas. 1953-1955, Pres., 1955-1957); Hudson Valley AA; AWS; Nat. Lg. Am. Pen Women; AAPL; Catherine Lorillard Wolfe A. Cl. *Awards*: prizes, A. Lg. of Long Island, 1947, 1949, 1950, 1957, 1958. *Work*: A. Lg. of Long Island; murals, Clearview Beach Club and in private homes. *Exhibited*: A. Lg. of Long Island, 1946-1958; AAPL, 1955, 1956; Catherine L. Wolfe A. Cl., 1957; Parrish A. Mus., 1957, 1958; AWS, 1958; Hudson Valley AA, 1950-1958.

ALVAREZ, MABEL—Painter, Lith.
9208 Beverly Blvd., Beverly Hills, Cal.

B. Waialua, Hawaii. *Studied*: with William V. Cahill, S. Macdonald-Wright, Morgan Russell. *Member*: Los Angeles AA; AFA, Los A. Mus. Assn. *Awards*: med., Pan-Cal. Exp., San Diego, 1916; prizes, Cal. AC, 1918, 1919, 1933; Fed. Women's Cl., 1923; Laguna Beach AA, 1928; Ebell Cl., 1933-1935; Honolulu Pr. M., 1939; Oakland A. Gal., 1938; Madonna Festival, Los Angeles, 1954; Palos Verdes Annual, 1957. *Work*: Honolulu A. Acad.; San Joaquin Mus.; Univ. So. Cal. *Exhibited*: AIC, 1923; PAFA, 1923; MMoA., 1933; GGE, 1939; Los A. Mus. A., 1954, 1955, 1957; Oakland A. Gal., 1949, 1950 (one-man); San Diego FA Soc.; Univ. Cal.; Los Angeles AA, 1948-1951, 1953-1957; Springville, Utah, 1950; Cal. State Fair, 1950; San Joaquin Pioneer Mus., 1950 (one-man); Crocker A. Gal., 1951 (one-man); San Bernardino, 1951; Tracy Putnam Fnd., 1952; Chaffey Col., 1957; Mt. St. Mary's Col., 1958.

ALVORD, MURIEL—Painter
Twin Lakes, Salisbury, Conn.; h. 1033 Prospect Ave., Hartford, Conn.

B. Goshen, Conn. *Studied*: Yale Univ., B.F.A., and with Wayman Adams, Arthur J. E. Powell. *Member*: Hartford Soc. Women Painters; New Haven Paint & Clay Cl.; North Shore AA; Academic AA; Kent AA; Hudson Valley AA; NAC; Min. P., S., & Gravers, Wash., D.C. *Awards*: med., BAID; prize, Meriden A. & Crafts Exh., 1944; Salisbury popular prize, 1945. *Exhibited*: All. A. Am. 1944; Min. P & S & Gr., 1944, 1946; North Shore AA; Newport AA; Pa. Soc. Min. P.; New Haven Paint & Clay Cl.; Conn. Acad. FA; Hartford Soc. Women Painters; Kent AA; Hudson Valley AA; NAC; New England Contemp. A.; one-man: Western Col.; Sweet Briar Col.; Argent Gal.; Doll & Richards, Boston, Mass. *Positions*: Sec., Kent AA; Vice-Pres., Academic AA.

AMATEIS, EDMOND—Sculptor, E., W.
R.F.D. 3, Brewster, N.Y.; w. 1650 Morning Dr., Clermont, Fla.

B. Rome, Italy, Feb. 7, 1897. *Studied*: BAID; Julian Acad., Paris; Am. Acad. in Rome. *Member*: NA; NSS; University Cl., Winter Park, Fla.; A. Fellowship; Nat. Inst. A. & Let. *Awards*: F., Am. Acad. in Rome, 1921-1924; prizes, Arch. L., 1929; PAFA, 1933; Morris prize, NSS; Government comp. for Typhus Comm. medal; Government comp. for Asiatic-Pacific Theatre medal. *Work*: Brookgreen Gardens, S.C.; Baltimore & Kansas City war mems.; William M. Davidson Mem., Pittsburgh; USPO, Ilion, N.Y.; Commerce Bldg., Wash., D.C.; portraits: Hall of Am. Artists, New York; reliefs, garden sculpture, portraits, sc. groups, etc.; sc. Rochester Times-Union; private estates; USPO, Philadelphia, Madison Square Branch; Acacia Life Bldg., Wash., D.C.; George Washing-

ton Univ.; Metropolitan Housing Project; Kerckhoff Mausoleum, Cal.; medal for Soc. Medalists; figure, U.S. Government Cemetery Draguignan, France; American Red Cross; "The Polio Wall of Fame," Ga. Warm Springs Fnd., Warm Springs, Ga., 1958, and many others. *Exhibited*: PAFA; NAD; NSS. Author of articles on sculpture.

AMBELLAN, HAROLD—Sculptor, Indst. Des.
324 West 26th St., New York 1, N.Y.

B. Buffalo, N.Y., May 24, 1912. *Member*: S. Gld.; AEA.*

AMBERG, H. GEORGE—Writer, E. L.
University of Minnesota; h. 2208 Irving Ave., South, Minneapolis 5, Minn.

B. Halle, Germany, Dec. 28, 1901. *Studied*: Univ. Munich, Kiel, Cologne, Germany, Ph.D. *Member*: Am. Soc. for Aesthetics; Theatre Lib. Assn.; Committee on Art Education; CAA. Author: "Art in Modern Ballet," 1946; "The Theatre of Eugene Berman," 1947; "Ballet in America," 1949; article on Ballet in Encyclopedia of the Arts; article on Ballet Design in Encyclopedia of the Dance. Lectures: Theatre, Art, Aesthetics, Film. *Position*: Prof., Univ. Minnesota, Minneapolis, Minn.

AMBROSE, CHARLES EDWARD—Painter, E., S.
Mississippi Southern College; h. Box 94, Station A, Hattiesburg. Miss.

B. Memphis, Tenn., Jan. 6, 1922. *Studied*: Univ. Alabama, B.F.A., M.A. *Member*: New Orleans AA; Alabama WC Soc.; Mississippi AA; Mississippi Edu. Assn.; AAUP. *Awards*: prize, New Orleans AA, 1954; Mississippi AA, 1955. *Work*: portraits, Science Hall and Lawrence Hall, William Carey College; Grace Christian School, and Latin Am. Inst., both Hattiesburg; Federal Savings & Loan, First Presbyterian Church, Hattiesburg; portrait plaques: (3) Student Union, Mississippi Southern College. *Exhibited*: New Orleans AA, 1952, 1954, 1957; Mississippi AA, 1953, 1954; Birmingham AA, 1949; Alabama WC Soc., 1955, 1957; one-man: Univ. Alabama, 1950; Lauren Rogers Mus., 1952, 1954; Gulf Coast A. Workshop; Meridian AA. Lecturer, Art History, Art Appreciation and Art Forms. *Position*: Instr. A., Mississippi Southern Col., 1950-51; Asst. Prof. A., 1951- .

AMEN, IRVING—Engraver, P., S.
295 Seventh Ave., New York 1, N.Y.

B. New York, N.Y., July 25, 1918. *Studied*: ASL; PIASch.; Acad. Grande Chaumiere, Paris. *Member*: International Soc. of Wood Engravers; Audubon A; Am. Color Pr. Soc.; Boston Pr. M.; SAGA; AEA. *Awards*: F. H. Anderson Mem. prize, 1950; Erickson award, 1952, 1954. *Work*: MMA; LC; MMoA; Smithsonian Inst.; U.S. Nat. Mus.; PMA; Pennell Collection; N.Y. Pub. Lib.; Bibliotheque Nationale, Paris; Bibliotheque Royal, Brussels; BMA; FMA; CM; Bezalel Nat. Mus., Jerusalem; Stadtische Mus., Wilberfeld, Germany; Victoria and Albert Mus., London, and in many colleges and universities. *Exhibited*: one-man: New York City; Wash., D.C.; Pennsylvania; Cincinnati; Greensboro, N.C.; Los Angeles, Cal. 14 International Group Exhibitions in Europe and the Far East, 1953-1958; National Group shows: MMoA, 1949, 1953; MMA, 1955; Univ. Illinois, 1956; Univ. Wisconsin; Art: U.S.A., New York, 1958. Annual National Group Shows: LC; BM; NAD; Phila. Pr. Cl.; Am. Color Pr. Soc.; Boston Pr. M.; Audubon A.; SAGA. *Position*: Instr., Pratt Institute, Brooklyn, N.Y. Bd. Dirs., N.Y. Chapter, Artists Equity Assn.

AMENDOLA, ROBERT—Sculptor
Frankland Rd., Hopkinton, Mass.

B. Boston, Mass., Apr. 24, 1909. *Studied*: Mass. Sch. A.; Yale Univ., B.F.A.; Am. Acad. in Rome. *Member*: Liturgical A. Soc.; Wellesley SA. *Awards*: med., Mass. Sch. A., 1930; F., Am. Acad. in Rome, 1933. *Work*: Yale Univ. Chapel; church sculpture in Braintree, Gloucester, Boston, Newton, Natick, Mass.; Avon, Conn.; Univ. Connecticut Catholic Chapel; Convent of the Immaculate Conception, Bristol, Conn.; Sanctuary sculptures. O.M.I. Retreat House, Nashua, N.H.; George Washington Carver figure, Carver Houses, New York, N.Y.; sculpture for the SS "United States," in collaboration with Austin Purves, 1930-42. *Position*: Instr., "The Art of Visualization," St. Paul's Rehabilitation Center for Newly Blinded Adults.*

AMES, JEAN GOODWIN—*Craftsman, P., E.*
4094 Olive Hill Dr., Claremont, Cal.

B. Santa Ana, Cal., Nov. 5, 1905. *Studied*: AIC; Univ. Cal. at Los Angeles, B.E.; Univ. So. Cal., M.F.A. *Awards*: prizes, Syracuse Ceramic Exh., 1951; Wichita Ceramic Exh., 1952; California Fashion Creators award for ceramic achievement, 1952; AIA (So. Cal. Branch), 1954, 1958; Los Angeles Times "Woman of the Year in Art," 1958. *Work*: decorations in enamel, ceramics, mosaics: Newport Harbor Union H.S.; Claremont Community Church; Emanuel Temple, Beverly Hills; St. Paul's Church, Westwood, Los Angeles; Guarantee Savings & Loan Assn., Fresno; murals: San Diego Civic Center; North Hollywood First Presbyterian Church; Rose Hills Mem. Park. *Exhibited*: nationally. *Position*: A. T., Scripps and Claremont Colleges, Cal., 1940- .

AMES, LEE J.—*Illustrator*
669 Van Siclen Ave., Brooklyn 7, N.Y.

B. New York, N.Y. *Studied*: Columbia Univ., with Carnohan. Illustrated many juvenile books, 1947-1956, plus many text books, Golden Books, book jackets, etc. Contributor of cartoons and illus. to Boy's Life. Lectures "Book Illustration vs. Comic Books." *Positions*: Instr., Cartoonists & Illustrators Sch., New York, N.Y., 1947-48; A. Dir., Weber Assoc., 1947-52; Pres., Ames Advertising Co., New York, N.Y., 1953-54; Artist-in-Residence, Doubleday & Co., 1957- .

AMES, SCRIBNER—*Painter, S., W., L.*
5834 Stony Island Ave., Chicago 37, Ill.

B. Chicago, Ill. *Studied*: AIC; Univ. Chicago; with Jose de Creeft, Hans Hofmann and with Schwegerle in Munich. *Member*: AEA; Chicago A. Cl.; Chicago Soc. A.; Renaissance Soc. *Work*: Hudson Walker Gal., and in private collections, in U.S. and abroad. Portrait of Cooper D. Schmitt in Schmitt Dormitory, Univ. of Tennessee, 1958. *Exhibited*: One-man exhibitions nationally; Knoedler Gal., N.Y.; Chicago A. Cl.; MModA; Bonestell Gal., 1939; WFNY 1939; Kalamazoo AI, 1939; Puma Gal., 1943; Creative Arts Gal., Charlottesville, Va., 1947; Carroll-Knight Gal., St. Louis, 1948, 1949; WMAA, 1950; Renaissance Soc., Chicago, 1956-1958; Cromer-Quint Gal., Chicago, 1957, 1958; Chicago A. Cl., Chicago Navy Pier Jury Selection, 1958; Illinois State Fair, 1958; one-man exhibitions abroad: Culture Center, N.W.I., 1947; Galerie Chardin, Paris, France, 1949; Esher-Surrey Gal., The Hague, 1950; Cercle Universitaire, Aix-en-Provence, 1950. Contributor of articles to magazines and lectures on art and artists.

AMICK, ROBERT WESLEY—
Painter, E., Comm. A., I.
92 Shore Rd., Old Greenwich, Conn.

B. Canon City, Colo., Oct. 15, 1879. *Studied*: Yale Univ.; ASL. *Work*: in schools, public buildings, and private homes.

AMINO, LEO—*Sculptor, Des., T.*
58 Watts St., New York 13, N.Y.

B. Formosa, Japan, June 26, 1911. *Studied*: N.Y. Univ.; Am. A. Sch. *Work*: Grand Rapids A. Gal.; AGAA; Univ. Nebraska; Texas State Col. for Women; Des Moines A. Center; WMAA; MModA; Massillon Mus., Ohio. *Exhibited*: WFNY 1939; AIC; MMA; MModA; WMAA; PAFA; Worcester A. Mus.; Munson-Williams-Proctor Inst.; Nebraska AI; VMFA; State Univ. Iowa; Grand Rapids A. Gal.; Newark Mus.; Cranbrook Acad.; Columbus Gal. FA; one-man: Montross Gal., 1940; Artists Gal., 1940, 1943; Clay Club Gal., 1941; Bonestell Gal., 1945; Sculptor's Gal., 1946-1949; Grand Rapids A. Gal., 1948; Memphis Acad. A., 1948; Decatur A. Center, 1948; Univ. Nebraska, 1949; Texas State Col. for Women, 1949; Univ. North Carolina, 1949; George Walter Vincent Smith A. Gal., 1949; Cornell Univ., 1949; Indiana State T. Col., 1950; Sculpture Center, 1951, 1952, 1954; Phila. A. All., 1951; Sculpture Center, 1957. *Position*: Instr., Cooper Union A. Sch., New York, N.Y., 1952- .

AMORE, JOHN—*Sculptor, E.*
156 East 39th St., New York 16, N.Y.

B. Genoa, Italy, Feb. 28, 1912. *Studied*: BAID; Fontainebleau Sch. FA; NAD. *Member*: F., Am. Acad. in

Rome. *Awards*: BAID, 1935, Rome prize, 1937. Competition gold medal design for City of New York, 1948; NSS, 1951. *Work*: Zodiacal spheres, lobby of Louisville Times-Courier Journal Bldg.; figures, St. Francis Col., Biddeford, Me.; St. Claire's Hospital, New York; decorations, SS "Independence" and SS "Constitution"; port. tablet for Erie Resistor Co.; "Pioneer Award" for Institute of Radio Engineers; Commemorative medals for Nat. Tuberculosis Assn. and Lincoln Nat. Bank, Ft. Wayne.*

AMOROSO, ANTHONY—*Painter, T.*
47-08 69th St., Woodside 77, L.I., N.Y.

B. Messina, Italy, Aug. 19, 1877. *Studied*: Acad. FA, Messina; Brera Acad. FA, Milan, Italy. *Awards*: Messina, 1900; Milan, 1918. *Exhibited*: CGA, 1935, 1939.

AMOROSO, LOUIS (JACK)—*Painter*
3109 Grand Ave., Coconut Grove, Miami 33, Fla.; h. 5321 Southwest 90th Ct., Miami, Fla.

B. Boston, Mass., Apr. 28, 1930. *Studied*: Sch. Practical A., Boston; Lacedra Sch. FA, Boston. *Member*: AEA; Soc. Florida Pr. M. (Dir.); Miami AA. *Awards*: prizes, Fla. Federation of Art State Exhibition, 1953, 1954; Blue Dome Fellowship, 1953, 1954, 1955; Joe & Emily Lowe Gal., 1954. *Work*: Lowe A. Gal.; Playhouse Gal., Coconut Grove, Fla. Mural, Coconut Grove Playhouse. *Exhibited*: Boston A. Festival, 1954, 1956; Fla. Painters, 1955; BMA, 1955; Soc. Four Arts, 1955, 1956; Houston, Tex., 1956; N.Y. City Center, 1958; Riverside Mus., N.Y., 1958; Inst. Contemp. A., Boston, 1956; Munson-Williams-Proctor Inst., 1956; Patronato de Bellas Artes, Cuba, 1956; Museo Nacionales, Cuba, 1956; Lyceum, Cuba, 1956; Ringling Mus. A., 1955; Mirell Gal., Fla., 1954, 1957; Studio Craft Gal., Coconut Grove, 1955, 1958; Designer's Gal., 1957; Tampa State Fair, 1956; Miami AA, 1955-1957; Miami Beach A. Center, 1956; one-man: Lowe Gal., 1955; Norton A., Palm Beach, 1958. *Positions*: Dir., Owner, Studio Craft Gal., 1954- ; A. Dir., Coconut Grove Playhouse, 1955- ; Dir., Playhouse Gallery, 1958- .

AMYX, CLIFFORD—*Educator, P., W.*
University of Kentucky; h. 321 Dudley Rd., Lexington, Ky.

B. Jackson County, Ky., Jan. 22, 1909. *Studied*: Univ. Kentucky, A.B., M.A.; Univ. California; Ford F., Univ. California, 1952-53. *Member*: CAA; Am. Soc. for Aesthetics. *Exhibited*: San F. AA; CMA; Louisville, Ky. Contributor to Journal of Aesthetics and Art Criticism; College Art Journal; Kenyon Review. *Position*: Asst. Prof., 1946-52, Assoc. Prof., 1952- , Univ. Kentucky, Lexington, Ky.

AMYX, LEON KIRKMAN—*Painter, E.*
Hartnell College; h. 265 San Benancio Rd., Salinas, Cal.

B. Visalia, Cal., Dec. 20, 1908. *Studied*: San Jose State Col., A.B.; Claremont Col., M.A.; Cal. Col. A. & Crafts. *Member*: Cal. WC Soc.; San F. AA; Carmel AA. *Awards*: med., Oakland A. Gal., 1945; prizes, SFMA, 1944; Monterey County Fair, 1949. *Exhibited*: San F. AA, 1933, 1939-1944; AWS, 1943; NAD, San Diego FA Soc., 1941; Oakland A. Gal., 1933-1945; Cal. WC Soc., 1945-1954; Los A. Mus. A.; SFMA; Riverside Mus.; Crocker A. Gal., Sacramento, Cal. *Position*: Instr., History & Painting, Hartnell Col., Salinas, Cal.; Painting & Art Edu., Sacramento State Col., 1949-52 and San Jose State Col., 1953, 1955, 1956 (summers).*

ANDERS, WILLI—*Painter*
15185 West Burleigh Rd., Brookfield, Wis.

B. Hanover, Germany, July 19, 1897. *Studied*: Kunstgewerbe Schule, Hanover, and with Robert von Neumann, Myron Nutting. *Member*: Wisconsin P & S. *Awards*: prizes, Wis. State Fair, 1938, 1939, 1945; Univ. Wisconsin, 1934, 1935, 1938; Milwaukee AI, 1936, 1938, 1951; Mead Pub. Lib., Sheboygan, Wis., 1951; City of Milwaukee purchase award, 1951. *Work*: Milwaukee AI. *Exhibited*: AIC, 1935; PAFA, 1939; Wis. Salon; Wis. P & S; Kansas City AI; Great Lakes Exh., 1938, 1939; Milwaukee Inst., 1944 (one-man). One-man shows, Milwaukee, 1957, 1958.

ANDERSEN, ANDREAS STORRS—*Educator, P.*
University of Arizona; h. 2830 East Third St., Tucson, Ariz.

B. Chicago, Ill., Oct. 6, 1908. *Studied*: Carnegie Inst.; British Acad., Rome, Italy; AIC. *Member*: Am. Assn. Univ. Prof.; Palette & Brush Cl.; Western AA; Nat. Art Edu. Assn. *Work*: IBM; Univ. Arizona. *Exhibited*: GGE 1939; MMA; CGA; Colorado Springs FA Center. *Position*: Prof. A., Hd. Dept. A., Univ. Arizona, Tucson, Ariz.

ANDERSEN, NIELS YDE—*Designer, Et., P., E.*
396 Washington Highway, Snyder 21, N.Y.

B. Copenhagen, Denmark, Mar. 4, 1888. *Member*: SAGA; The Pateran; Buffalo Pr. Cl. *Awards*: prizes, Albright A. Gal., 1936, 1937, 1940; Phila. Pr. Cl., 1941; SAGA, 1943. *Work*: Albright A. Gal.; Moscow Mus. Foreign Art; LC; Carnegie Inst.; Charles Lea Coll., Phila., Pa.*

ANDERSON, ALMA—*Educator, L., P.*
Carmel, Cal.

B. Sweden. *Studied*: Univ. North Dakota, B.A.; Columbia Univ., M.A.; Univ. Iowa; Banff Sch. A.; AIC; Woodstock, N.Y. *Member*: Carmel Craft Gld. *Positions*: Dir. A., City Sch., La Crosse, Wis., 1926-1927; Asst. Prof. A., 1927-1937, Hd. FA Dept., 1937-1955, Northern Illinois State Col., De Kalb, Ill. (Retired)

ANDERSON, ALMA—*Painter*
521 Third Ave., Anchorage, Alaska

Exhibited: Northwest Annual, SAM.

ANDERSON, ARNOLD NELSON—*Etcher, Des.*
12 South 12th St.; 1323 Fillmore St., Philadelphia 24, Pa.

B. Camden, N.J., Aug. 24, 1895. *Studied*: PMSchIA. *Work*: Univ. Nebraska; PMA; Pennsylvania Hist. Soc. *Exhibited*: SAE; Phila. SE; Phila. Pr. Cl.*

ANDERSON, BEATRICE M.—*Craftsman, Textile Des.*
2 Clarendon St., East Gloucester, Mass.

B. Quincy, Mass., Mar. 2, 1910. *Studied*: Boston Univ., B.S.; Handarbetets Vanner, Stockholm, Sweden; Saterglantan Vavskola, Sweden. *Member*: Boston Soc. A. & Crafts; Weavers Gld. of Boston; Mass. Soc. of Handicraft Groups; DeCordova Craftsmen. *Awards*: Master Craftsman, Boston Soc. of A. & Crafts, 1949. *Exhibited*: Fleischman Co., Nat. Carpet Des. Competition, 1951; International Handwoven Textile Competition, Seattle, Wash., 1951; Fiber, Clay & Metal, St. Paul, 1952; Smithsonian Travel. Exh., 1956-57; Boston Soc. A. & Crafts, 1947, 1949, 1951, 1953; DeCordova & Dana Mus., 1952, 1953; WMA, 1952, 1955; Fitchburg A. Mus., 1954; Boston Y.W.C.A., 1955.*

ANDERSON, BRAD(LEY) J.—*Cartoonist*
1 Main St., Brocton, N.Y.; h. Third St., Portland, N.Y.

B. Jamestown, N.Y., May 14, 1924. *Studied*: Syracuse Univ., B.F.A. *Work*: Albert T. Reid Coll.; William Allen White Fnd., Univ. Kansas. *Exhibited*: Punch (British-American Exh.) 1954; Cartoon Exhibition "The Selected Cartoons of 14 Saturday Evening Post Cartoonists." Illus. "Marmaduke," 1955 (a collection of reprints from Anderson's syndicated panel "Marmaduke"). Contributor cartoons to: Sat. Eve. Post; Look; N.Y. Times Book Review; American Weekly and others. "Marmaduke" internationally syndicated in daily newspapers; "Grandpa's Boy" in weekly newspapers. *Position*: A. Dir., Graphic A. Dept., Syracuse Univ., N.Y., 1950-1952.

ANDERSON, C. STEPHEN—*Designer, P.*
64 Wellington Ave., West Orange, N.J.

B. Harrisburg, Pa., Jan. 4, 1896. *Studied*: Am. Acad. A., Chicago; Gettysburg Col.; and with William Mosby, Gillette Elvgren; Lajos Markos. *Member*: Rahway A. Center. Teaches portrait painting in home studio. Designs and publishes the Anderson Historical First-Day Cover Envelopes for philatelists.

ANDERSON, CLARENCE WILLIAM—
Etcher, Lith., I., W.
Ashby Rd., Mason, N.H.

B. Wahoo, Neb., Apr. 12, 1891. *Studied*: AIC. *Member*: SAGA. *Author*, I., "Thoroughbreds," 1942; "Big Red," 1943; "Tomorrow's Champion," 1946; "Horses Are Folks," 1953; "The Smashers," 1954; "Grey, Bay and Chestnut," 1955; "Horse of Hurricane Hill" and "Colts and Champions," 1956; "Afraid to Ride," 1957; "Accent on Youth" and "Pony for Three," 1958.

ANDERSON, CLAUDE J. K.—*Painter, W.*
"Rive Gauche," Riverbank, Riverton, N.J.; s. "Dowhill," Taos, N.M.

B. Hamilton Township, N.J., Feb. 10, 1902. *Studied*: Princeton Univ.; & in Europe. *Member*: Phila. A. All.; AAPL.

ANDERSON, DONALD M.—*Educator, P., Des.*
5750 Elder Place, Madison, Wis.

B. Bridgewater, S.D., Dec. 13, 1915. *Studied*: Univ. Iowa, B.A., M.A., with Fletcher Martin, Jean Charlot, Philip Guston; Mexico City Col. *Awards*: prizes, Midwest Annual, Kansas City, 1940; Old Northwest Territory Exh., 1948; Walker A. Center, 1952; many local and state awards, 1947- . *Work*: Milwaukee AI; Springfield Mus. A.; Univ. Iowa Union; Univ. Wisconsin Mem. Union. *Exhibited*: VMFA, 1941; Northwest Print Exh., 1940; SFMA, 1950, 1952; PAFA, 1952, 1953; Midwest Exh., Kansas City, 1940; Old Northwest Territory Exh., 1948-1951; Walker A. Center, 1949, 1951, 1953; Denver A. Mus., 1949, 1950. *Author*, I., "Creative Design," 1956. *Position*: A. Dir., Adjutant Generals Office, Wash., D.C., 1946; Exhibit Specialist, Civil Aeronautics Authority, Wash., D.C., 1947; Univ. Wisconsin, 1947- ; Assoc. Prof A. Edu., Univ. Wisconsin, Madison, Wis., 1954- .*

ANDERSON, DOROTHY VISJU—*Painter, T., S., W.*
616 North Rossmore Ave., Hollywood 28, Cal.

B. Oslo, Norway. *Studied*: AIC, and with William M. Chase. *Member*: Cal. AC. *Awards*: prize, Springfield, Ill.; med., Los A. Mus. A., 1937. *Work*: Vanderpoel Coll. *Exhibited*: Salon d'Automne, Paris; AIC; San Diego FA Soc.; Tilton Sch., Chicago; Los A. Mus. A., and extensive exhibitions abroad. Among many portraits are those of Pres. Franklin D. Roosevelt; Countess du Nord, Paris, France and Lt. Col. Percy, Chicago; Alice Calhoun, Bel-Air, Cal., Prof. and Mrs. Olav Halvorson, Countess Nicolas Nierotti, and others. *Author*, I., "Norse Fairy-Tales," 1958.

ANDERSON, EMILY DELIA—*Painter, Comm. A.*
10 Russell Ave., Gloucester, Mass.

B. Gloucester, Mass., Sept. 25, 1899. *Studied*: Mass. Sch. A.; Sch. of Practical A., Boston, and with Meyer Both. *Member*: North Shore AA; Rockport AA. *Exhibited*: Boston A. Festival, 1953; Independent A., Boston, 1954-1958; Rockport AA, 1945-1958; one-man exhibitions, North Shore AA.

ANDERSON, ERNFRED—
Sculptor, Mus. Dir., E., L., P.
235 Lake St., Elmira, N.Y.

B. Esperod, Sweden, Aug. 28, 1896. *Studied*: Societe Industrielle de Lausanne. *Member*: Elmira AC. *Awards*: prize, Swedish Cl., Chicago. *Work*: monuments, Elmira, Horseheads, N.Y.; sculpture relief on Fine Arts Bldg., Elmira College, Elmira, N.Y., 1958. *Exhibited*: NSS, 1935-1940; NAD, 1933-1935; Rochester Mem. A. Gal.; Swedish Cl. *Author*: "Public Art in Elmira," 1941. *Position*: Dir., Arnot A. Gal., 1943- ; Instr., Elmira Col., Elmira, N.Y.

ANDERSON, GENEVIEVE DILLAYE—*Painter, C., E.*
25 Atheneum Sq., North; h. 64 Garden St., Hartford 5, Conn.

B. Avon, N.Y., June 15, 1900. *Studied*: Skidmore Col., B.S.; Columbia Univ., M.A.; Hillyer Col. Further grad. work at Columbia Univ., Univ. of Guadalajara, Mexico, Univ. of Hawaii, Alfred Univ., N.Y. *Member*: NAWA; Hartford Soc. of Women Painters; Conn. WC Soc.; Eastern AA; Conn. AA; Conn. Crafts Assn. *Award*: Conn. WC Soc. 1944. *Exhibited*: NAWA, 1943-1950; Hartford Soc.

of Women Painters; Conn. WC Soc. *Position*: Supv. A., Public Schools, Hartford, Conn., 1945- ; Chm. T. Training, Hartford A. Sch. of the Univ. of Hartford and Chm., Scholastic Awards for State of Connecticut, at present.

ANDERSON, GWEN(DOLYN) (ORSINGER)—
Painter, T., Cr., L.

1361 Wisconsin Ave., Georgetown, Washington 7, D.C.; h. 1611 Ivy Hill Dr., McLean, Va.

B. Chicago, Ill., May 31, 1915. *Studied*: UCLA; Univ. Illinois, B.S.; AIC; Norton Gal. & Sch. A.; Corcoran Sch. A., and with Eliot O'Hara. *Member*: Palm Beach A. Lg.; Georgetown A. Group; Corcoran A. Lg.; Charter Memb. Falls Church-Arlington Br., Nat. Lg. of Am. Pen Women (Vice-Pres., 1956-58, Pres., 1958-60). *Awards*: prizes, Norton Gal., 1946; Metropolitan State A. Comp., 1953; Harvest Festival, Alexandria, Va., 1953, 1955, 1957, 1958; Nat. A. Week, 1955; Georgetown A. Group, 1955, 1956; Nat. Fed. Women's Cl., 1953, 1955; Smithsonian Inst., 1956, 1958; Nat. Lg. of Am. Pen Women, 1956, 1958; Md. Religious Show, 1958; Md. Art Festival, 1958. *Exhibited*: AIC; Norton Gal. A.; Palm Beach A. Lg.; Corcoran Gal. A.; Washington WC Cl.; Rehoboth Cottage Tour, 1955; NCFA, 1948, 1949, 1953-1955; Smithsonian Inst., 1956, 1958; Georgetown A. Group, 1956; Nat. Lg. of Am. Pen Women, 1956, 1958; CGA, 1957; Md. Religious Show and Md. A. Festival, 1958. *Position*: Partner, The Artists Mart, Washington, D.C.

ANDERSON, HAROLD N.—*Illustrator*

h. 54 Sound Beach Ave., Old Greenwich, Conn. (Nov.-May); 39 Phillips Rd., Nahant, Mass. (May-Nov.)

B. Boston, Mass., June 26, 1894. *Studied*: Fenway Sch. A. *Member*: SI; A. Gld.; Old Greenwich AA; Westport AA. *Awards*: prizes, A. Dir. Cl., 1937, 1940, 1942, 1946, 1950-51. I., national magazines.

ANDERSON, HOWARD BENJAMIN—
Lithographer, P., Comm. A.

2725 Devon Ave., Chicago 45, Ill.

B. Racine, Wis., June 26, 1905. *Studied*: Univ. Wisconsin, B.S.; AIC with Chapin, Ritman, Kahn; CGA Sch., with Eugen Weiss. *Member*: Chicago Soc. A.; SAGA. *Awards*: Univ. Wisconsin, 1951. *Exhibited*: Univ. Wisconsin, 1950-1954, 1957; Oakland A. Mus., 1948-1952; SAM, 1949-1952, 1954; Wichita AA, 1949, 1950, 1952-1954; Joslyn A. Mus., 1949; Phila. Pr. Cl., 1949, 1952; BM, 1950, 1953; SAGA, 1950-1955, 1956, 1957; Bradley Univ., 1952; AIC, 1948, 1949, 1952; Denver A. Mus., 1951, 1952; PAFA, 1952, 1953, 1957; LC, 1953, 1956; SFMA, 1954; Portland (Me.) Mus. A., 1953, 1955; BMFA, 1954; NAD, 1956; Soc. Washington Pr. M., 1956-1958; Portland (Me.) Mus. A., 1956, 1957; Washington WC Cl., 1956, 1957; Los A. County Fair Assn., 1956; Chicago A., 1957, 1958; one-man: Wustum A. Mus., Racine, Wis.; State T. Col., Kutztown, Pa., 1957.

ANDERSON, JOEL RANDOLPH—
Etcher, Lith., P., Des., T.

46½ Prospect St.; h. 41 Prospect St., Waterbury, Conn.

B. South Britain, Conn., July 13, 1905. *Studied*: ASL, with George Bridgman. *Member*: Conn. Acad. FA. *Work*: MMA. *Exhibited*: NAD, 1941; Lib. Cong., 1943; Conn. Acad. FA, 1940, 1941, 1946.*

ANDERSON, JOHN K.—*Sculptor, P., Arch., Des.*

257 Highland Ave., Buffalo 22, N.Y.

B. Buffalo, N.Y., Dec. 31, 1904. *Studied*: Cornell Univ., Col. Arch. *Member*: Buffalo SA. *Exhibited*: Albright A. Gal., 1937-1944; Buffalo SA, 1942-1946, 1950, 1951.

ANDERSON, LOULIE (RAYMOND)—*Painter, T., C.*

Hobby Shop, Thornwell, Clinton, S.C.

B. Brownsville, Tenn., Mar. 14, 1887. *Studied*: AIC, with Wagner, Inness; Ringling Sch. A., and with Fred Yost. *Award*: Pan-American Committee award. *Member*: Florida Fed. A.; Gulf Coast A. Group; Hon. Life Member, Tampa A. Inst., 1958. *Exhibited*: Gulf Coast A. Group, 1950, 1951; Fla. Southern Col., 1952; Fla. State Fair, 1956; one-man: Shorter Col., Rome, Ga.; Madison Col., Harrison-

burg, Va.; Mary Buie Mus. A.; Montgomery Mus. FA; Belhaven Col.; Tampa AI. *Position*: Instr., A. & Crafts, Thornwell Home & School, Clinton, S.C.

ANDERSON, LYMAN (MATTHEW)—*Illustrator*

Hoyden's Lane, Fairfield, Conn.

B. Chicago, Ill., May 4, 1907. *Studied*: AIC. *Member*: SI; Westport A.A. *Exhibited*: A.Dir. Cl., 1939, 1945. I., fiction, covers, advertising in leading publications.*

ANDERSON, MARTHA FORT (Mrs. Frank H.)—
Painter, C., L.

Mountain Hall, Mt. Airy, Ga.

B. Macon, Ga. *Studied*: Piedmont Col.; BMFA Sch.; ASL; & with Philip Hale, Frank Benson. *Work*: Univ. Alabama; Univ. Pennsylvania; St. Paul's Church, Richmond, Va.; Lakeview Lib., Birmingham, Ala.; Fed. Bldg., Fairfield, Ala.; Fulton County Court House; N.Y. Pub. Lib.; Univ. Georgia. *Exhibited*: NAWA; SSAL, 1919-1938; Assn. Ga. A.; Birmingham A. Cl. *Positions*: A. Instr., Univ. Ala. Sch. FA, 1919-23; Ext. Div., 1934-38; Hd., A. Dept., Piedmont Col., 1948-1954; A. Consultant, N. Georgia Pub. Schs., 1956; L., civic and other groups.*

ANDERSON, RUTH BERNICE—*Painter, Et., T.*

3264 North Pennsylvania St., Indianapolis 5, Ind.

B. Indianapolis, Ind., July 7, 1914. *Studied*: John Herron AI. *Member*: Indiana A. Cl.; Hoosier Salon; The 20 Club; Brown County AA. *Awards*: prizes, All State Exh., Tucson, Ariz., 1937; L. S. Ayers & Co. award, 1954; De Pauw Univ. purchase award, 1954; Edward Gallahue prize, 1955. *Work*: Dailey Mem. Collection, Indiana Univ.

ANDERSON, VERA STEVENS. See *Stevens, Vera*

ANDERSON, VIOLA—*Craftsman, Textile Des.*

2 Clarendon St., East Gloucester, Mass.

B. Quincy, Mass., Apr. 11, 1905. *Studied*: Mass. T. Col.; Boston Univ.; Brunssons Weaving Sch., Stockholm; Saterglantan Weaving Sch., Sweden. *Member*: Boston Soc. A. & Crafts; Weavers Gld., Boston; Mass. Soc. of Handicraft Groups. *Awards*: Master Craftsman, Boston Soc. A. & Crafts, 1948; prize, International Textile Exh., Greensboro, N.C., 1950. *Work*: Womens Col., Univ. North Carolina; Ecclesiastical Handwoven textiles in New England churches. *Exhibited*: International Textile Exh., Greensboro, N.C., 1950; Fleischman Co., Nat. Carpet Des. Comp., 1951; International Handwoven Textile Comp., 1951, Seattle; America House, 1951; Smithsonian Travel. Exh., 1956-57; Boston Soc. A. & Crafts, 1947, 1949, 1951, 1953; deCordova & Dana Mus., 1952, 1953; WMA, 1955; Fitchburg A. Mus., 1954; Boston Y.W.C.A., 1955. *Lectures*: Decorative Arts in Sweden; Weaving.*

ANDERSON, WEB(STER)—*Educator, P., C., Gr.*

855 North Vermont Ave.; h. 817 North Edgemont St., Los Angeles 29, Cal.

B. Constantinople, Turkey, Nov. 13, 1911. *Studied*: Occidental Col.; Univ. California, A.B.; Cal. Col. A. & Crafts; Univ. Cal. at Los Angeles, M.A., and with Vaclav Vytlacil, Worth Ryder, John Haley, and others. *Member*: A. & Sculptors of Hawaii. *Awards*: prize, Honolulu Acad. A., 1950. *Exhibited*: Perls Gal.; Univ. Cal.; Los A. City Col., 1935-1956; Pacific AA, 1952; A. & Sculptors of Hawaii; Los A. County Fair, 1955; American Gal., Los Angeles, 1955. Art Films: "Make a Mobile," 1948; "Exploring in Paint," 1955. *Position*: Instr., Painting & Des., Los Angeles City Col., Los Angeles, Cal.*

ANDRESON, LAURA—*Educator*

Art Department, University California at Los Angeles, 405 Hilgard Ave., Los Angeles 24, Cal.

Position: Chm., Art Dept., Univ. California at Los Angeles.*

ANDREWS, EDNA ROZINA—
Art Educator, I., P., Et., Comm. A.

111 Riviera Dr., Apt. #1, Sarasota, Fla.

B. Pulaski, N.Y., Apr. 6, 1886. *Studied*: Syracuse Univ., B.F.A., M.S. in Edu. *Member*: Assoc. A. Syracuse; Sarasota AA; Bradenton A. Center; Ringling Mus. Assn.; NAWA; Rockport AA; Syracuse Pr. M.; Nat. Lg. Am. Pen Women. *Awards*: prize, N.Y. State A. Exh., Cortland, N.Y., 1945; CGA, 1958. *Work*: Cornell Univ.; Cal. State Lib. *Exhibited*: SAGA, 1945, 1946; NAWA, 1944-1946, and in traveling shows; Assoc. A. Syracuse; Syracuse Pr. M.; Finger Lakes Exh., 1944; Rockport AA; Sarasota AA; Bradenton A. Center; Atlanta, Ga.; Washington, D.C.; Syracuse Daubers Cl. *Position*: Supv. A., Syracuse (N.Y.) Public Schools, 1938-56.

ANDREWS, SPERRY—*Painter*

R. D. 1, Ridgefield, Conn.

B. New York, N.Y., Oct. 5, 1917. *Studied*: NAD; ASL. *Member*: ASL; Audubon A. *Awards*: prizes, NAD, 1950; Silvermine Gld. A., 1950, 1951; St. Lawrence Univ., 1952. *Work*: Mus. New Britain Inst.; Columbus (Ohio) Gal. FA; Am. Acad. A. & Let., (purchase 1952) Wadsworth Atheneum, Hartford, Conn., (purchase 1955); William Bradford Green Mem. award, Conn. Acad. FA, 1954, 1956. *Exhibited*: NAD, 1938, 1940, 1947, 1950-1952, 1958; Ferargil Gal., 1950, 1952 (one-man), 1953 (one-man); Kipnis Gal., Westport, Conn., 1954, 1955; Travel. exh., Conn. Contemporary Painting, 1951; Slater Mem. Mus., Norwich, 1955; Los Angeles County Fair, 1953; Wadsworth Atheneum, Hartford, Conn., 1957.

ANDRUS, J. ROMAN—*Educator, Lith.*

Brigham Young University; h. 1765 North 651 East, Provo, Utah

B. St. George, Utah, July 11, 1907. *Studied*: Otis AI, with Eduard Vysekal, Roscoe Shrader; ASL; Columbia Univ., T. Col.; Brigham Young Univ., M.A.; Colorado Springs FA Center; Univ. Colorado, Ed. D. *Member*: Assoc. Utah A.; Utah State Curriculum Comm.; ASL; Utah Acad. A. Sc. & Let. *Awards*: prizes, Otis AI, 1939; Brigham Young Univ., 1940-1942; Utah State Inst. FA, 1945, 1950. *Work*: Utah State Capitol Coll.; Dixie Jr. Col.; Brigham Young Univ. *Exhibited*: Cal. State Fair, 1939; Otis AI, 1938, 1939; Assoc. Utah A., 1940-1945; Springville Exh., 1939-1955; Cedar City, 1943-1955; Dixie Jr. Col., 1939-1955. *Positions*: Instr. A., 1943-46; Asst. Prof. A., 1947-1952; Assoc. Prof. A., 1952- ; Chm., A. Dept., 1954- , Brigham Young Univ., Provo, Utah.

ANDRUS, VERA—*Painter, Lith., W., T., L., I.*

250 East Main St., Gloucester, Mass.

B. Plymouth, Wis. *Studied*: Univ. Minnesota; Minneapolis Inst. A.; ASL, with Boardman Robinson, George Grosz. *Member*: NAWA; Boston Pr. M; Rockport AA; Cape Ann Soc. Mod. A.; Rocky Neck A. Group (Vice-Pres.); Boston Soc. Indp. A. *Awards*: prizes, Minneapolis Inst. A., 1928; Westchester Fed. Womens Cl., 1954; Albert H. Wiggins Mem. prize, Boston Pr. M., 1953; med., NAWA, 1941; Hudson Valley AA, 1941, 1943, 1944. *Work*: MMA; Minneapolis Inst. A.; LC; Smithsonian Inst.; BMFA; Boston Pub. Lib.; Univ. Minnesota; Univ. Maine. *Exhibited*: WMAA; Carnegie Inst.; PAFA; AIC; MMA; one-man: Smithsonian Inst.; Univ. Maine; Am. Mus. Natural Hist. Author, I., "Sea-Bird Island," 1939; "Sea Dust," 1955. *Positions*: Formerly Staff Member, MMA, 1931-1957; T., City Col., Adult Education Program, New York, N.Y.

ANDRUS, VINCENT D.—*Museum Curator*

Metropolitan Museum of Art, Fifth Ave. at 82nd St., New York 28, N.Y.

Position: Cur., American Wing, Metropolitan Museum of Art, New York, N.Y.•

ANDRUS, ZORAY—*Painter, I., Des., T., S.*

Virginia City, Nev.

B. Alameda, Cal., Apr. 27, 1908. *Studied*: Cal. Col. A. & Crafts, B.A.; Univ. California, with Hans Hofmann; Mills Col., with Alexander Archipenko. *Member*: Cal. WC Soc. *Awards*: prize, Denver A. Mus., 1942. *Exhibited*: Reno, Nev., 1943, 1954, 1955; (2) one-man exhs., 1957 and group show 1958; Virginia City, Nev., 1945; San F. AA, 1943-1945; Denver A. Mus., 1941, 1942; Cal. WC Soc., 1942-1944; Elko, Nev., 1948; Carson City, Nev., 1952; Las Vegas, 1957; Tucson Festival, 1958. *Work*: murals, Veterans Hospital, Reno, Nev.; Illus. for Ford publications, 1956, 1957, 1958. Conducts artist's workshop group, Virginia City, Nev.

ANGEL, JOHN—*Sculptor, C., L.*

Old Mill Rd., Sandy Hook, Conn.

B. Newton Abbott, Devon, England, Nov. 1, 1881. *Studied*: Albert Memorial, Cheltenham, and Royal Acad. Schs., London, England. *Member*: NA; Royal Soc. British Sculptors; A. Workers Gld.; NSS; Arch. Lg. *Awards*: Landseer Scholarship, Diplomas, two Silver Medals, Gold Medal and Traveling Scholarship, 1911; Hon. Litt. D. degree, Columbia Univ., 1936. *Work*: England—War Memorials at Exeter, Bridgewater, and Rotherham. Statues on Reredos Cheltenham Men's College. U.S.A.—sculpture: Cathedral of St. John the Divine, St. Patrick's Cathedral, New York. Panel: East Liberty Presbyterian Church, Pittsburgh, Pa.; sculpture on Princeton Univ. Chapel, St. Paul's Sch., Concord, N.H. Statues: Alexander Hamilton, Lincoln Park, Chicago; Francis Vigo, Vincennes, Ind.; Stephen Austin, Austin, Tex.; William Marsh Rice, Houston, Tex.; Braintree, Mass.; Reredos statuary, St. John's Church, Youngstown, Ohio; statuary: Kirk in the Hills Church, Bloomfield Hills, Mich., National Shrine of the Immaculate Conception, Wash., D.C. Various medals. Four heroic size marble statues of the Evangelists, Cathedral of St. Paul, St. Paul, Minn. Lectures at various universities and schools.

ANGEL, RIFKA—*Painter*

79-81 MacDougal St., New York 18, N.Y.

B. Calvaria, Russia, Sept. 16, 1899. *Studied*: ASL, with Boardman Robinson; Moscow A. Acad. *Member*: AEA. *Awards*: prizes, AIC, 1933; Des. for Democratic Living Exh., 1948; Chicago A. Soc., 1934; CAM, 1945. *Work*: AIC; Honolulu Acad. A.; William Rockhill Nelson A. Gal. *Exhibited*: AIC, 1931, 1933, 1935, 1939; MModA., 1934; WMAA; BM; CAM; one-man: Honolulu Acad. A.; Nelson A. Gal.; Findlay Gal.; Knoedler Gal.; Diana Court Gal.; Breckenridge Gal.; Carl Fischer Gal.; Roullier Gal., Chicago; ACA Gal., 1947; Van Dieman-Lilienfeld Gal., 1954 (Retrospective).

ANGELA, EMILIO—*Sculptor*

68 Hedges Ave., Chatham, N.J.

B. Italy, July 12, 1889. *Studied*: CUASch.; NAD; ASL. *Member*: NSS. *Awards*: prizes, NAD. *Work*: figures, bronzes, fountains, etc., Bryant Sch., Brooklyn, N.Y.; SC; NSS; many private estates in the U.S. and abroad.

ANGELO, EMIDIO—*Cartoonist, P., L.*

1510 Crest Rd., Penn Wynne, Pa.

B. Philadelphia, Pa., Dec. 4, 1903. *Studied*: PMSch. Indst. A. *Member*: Da Vinci All.; PAFA Fellowship; Nat. Cartoonist Soc. *Awards*: PAFA European Scholarships, 1927, 1928; Da Vinci award, 1945, silver medal, 1958; Freedom Fnd. award, 1951. *Work*: cartoon mural, R.D.A. Cl., 1952. *Exhibited*: PAFA; Da Vinci A. All., 1930-1952; Author, I., "Just Be Patient," 1951; Panel strip, "Emily and Mabel" nationally syndicated. Lectures on History of Cartooning. Author of three cartoon books: "Just Be Patient"; "The Time of Your Life"; "Oh, Baby." Producer of abstract animated films.

ANGELO, NICHOLAS JOSEPH—*Painter, Comm. A.*

39 West 67th St., New York 23, N.Y.

B. Plainfield, N.J., June 1, 1921. *Studied*: ASL. *Member*: AWS. *Awards*: prize, NAD, 1958. *Exhibited*: AWS, 1956-1958; NAC, 1958; N.Y. City Center, 1958; Gld. Hall, 1956, 1957. Illus. for: Woman's Home Companion; Good Housekeeping; Charm; Town & Country; Colliers; House Beautiful; Gourmet; Seventeen; Cosmopolitan, and others.

ANGELO, VALENTI—
Illustrator, Eng., Des., P., S., W.

68 Cassilis St., Bronxville 8, N.Y.

B. Massarosa, Italy, June 23, 1897. *Member*: AIGA. *Work*: LC; N.Y. Pub. Lib.; Daniel Estate, Bristol, Va. *Exhibited*: PAFA; Gump's Gal., San F.; Dalzell-Hatfield Gal., Los Angeles; Ferargil Gal. Author, I., "Nino"; "Golden Gate"; "Paradise Valley"; "Hill of Little Miracles"; "Look Out Yonder"; "The Rooster Club"; "The Bells of Bleecker Street"; "The Marble Fountain," 1951; "A Battle in Washington Square"; "Big Little Island," 1955; "The Acorn Tree."

ANNEAR, ROGER—*Painter, T.*

926 North Bourland St., Peoria, Ill.

B. Christopher, Ill., Nov. 8, 1926. *Studied*: Southern Illinois Univ.; Univ. of Colorado, with Max Beckmann, B.F.A.; Univ. of Iowa with James Lechay, Eugene Ludins, Maurice Lasansky. *Awards*: Louis Comfort Tiffany award, 1953; Emily Lowe award, 1953. *Work*: Berkshire Mus. A.; Emily Lowe Coll.; Univ. Iowa. *Exhibited*: Denver Mus. A.; Des Moines, Iowa, Artists; Omaha Mid-West Annual; Kansas City; Central City, Colo., and others. One-man: Galerie Marcel Coard, Paris, France, 1955; Kanegis Gal., Boston, 1955, 1958. *Position*: Instr., Painting & Drawing, Bradley University, Peoria, Ill., 1958-1959.

ANNEN, HELEN WANN (Mrs. Peter J.)—
Educator, P., L., I., W.

83 Education Bldg., University of Wisconsin; h. 2321 Rugby Row, Madison 5, Wis.

B. Fairplay, Mo., Nov. 23, 1900. *Studied*: Univ. Oklahoma, A.B., B.F.A., with Oscar Jacobson; Univ. Wisconsin, M.S.; Cal. Sch. FA; Univ. Chicago; Broadmoor Acad., with Birger Sandzen. *Member*: Madison AA. *Awards*: med., Univ. Oklahoma, 1919, prizes, Madison AA, 1940; Wis. Salon, 1945; grand prize, Wis. State Fair, 1940, 1942, 1943. *Work*: Madison AA; Wis. State Journal Coll. *Exhibited*: Univ. Oklahoma; Univ. Tennessee; Milwaukee AI; Wis. Salon; Instituto Guatemalteco-Americano; AAA; Forum. I., children's books. Lectures on Guatemala, Peru, Europe, Morocco. Contributor to Design; School Arts. *Position*: Prof. A., Univ. Wisconsin, Madison, Wis., 1946- ; Chm. Dept., 1949-1952.

ANNUS, AUGUSTUS—*Painter, E., Des.*

35 Clarkson Ave., Brooklyn 26, N.Y.

B. Latvia, Oct. 27, 1893. *Studied*: Univ. Riga; Univ. St. Petersburg; Acad. FA, Riga. *Member*: Latvian A. Assn., Riga; A. Assn., Munich and Stuttgart; CAA. *Awards*: numerous prizes in European exhibitions. *Work*: Coll. of many museums and galleries of Europe, and in private coll. in U.S. *Exhibited*: Finland, Sweden, Norway, Denmark, Netherlands, France, Germany, etc.; Terry AI, 1952; Reading (Pa.) A. Mus., 1951, 1956-1958; also in New York, N.Y.; Hagerstown, Md.; Cleveland, Ohio; Boston, Mass.; Philadelphia, Pa. (1956-1958). *Position*: Instr., Stained Glass, City College Ext. Div., New York, N.Y.

ANSBACHER, JESSIE—*Painter, T.*

25 East 77th St., New York 21, N.Y.

B. Wilkes-Barre, Pa. *Studied*: N.Y.Sch. A., with Chase, Pennell, McCartain; Hunter College. *Work*: Guggenheim Fnd.; Hudson Gld. *Member*: NAWA; AEA. *Exhibited*: Anderson Gal., 1921; Milch Gal., 1944 (one-man), and other one-man exhs. *Position*: Dir., & T., Jessie Ansbacher A. Sch., 1933- .

ANSHUTZ, ELSA MARTIN—*Painter, T.*

Reed Studios, East Gloucester, Mass.; h. 9 Third St., North, St. Petersburg, Fla. (w)

B. Pittsburgh, Pa. *Studied*: Cleveland Sch. A.; BMFA Sch. *Member*: Florida A. Group. *Exhibited*: Carnegie Inst. A.; A. All. Am. (one-man); St. Petersburg A. Cl. (one-man); Florida Fed. A.; Boston Conservatory (one-man); North Shore AA; Clearwater A. Mus.; Florida A. Group travel. exh.; Cape Ann A. Festival (annually); Rocky Neck, Cape Ann (one-man). *Position*: A. Dir., Sch. Creative Arts, East Gloucester, Mass.

ANTHES, RUDOLF—*Museum Curator, E.*

University Museum, Philadelphia 4, Pa.; h. 203 Rosemary Lane, Philadelphia 19, Pa.

B. Hamburg, Germany, Mar. 1, 1896. *Studied*: Archaeological and other studies in universities of Tubingen, Greifswald, and Berlin (Ph. D.). *Member*: Archaeological Soc.; Deutsches Archaeologisches Institut. *Author*: "Aegyptische Plastik," Stuttgart, 1954, 3rd revised edition of "Meisterwerke aegyptischer Plastik"; "The Head of Queen Nofretete"; Staatliche Museen zu Berlin, 1954, translated by Kathleen Bauer from "Die Büste der Königin Nofretete," 1954; "Werkverfahren aegyptischer Bildhauer" in Mitteilungen des Deutschen Instituts in Kairo, Vol. 10 (1941); "Aegyptische Bildwerke rings um den Gruenen Kopf," in Jahrbuch des Deutschen Archaeologischen In-

stituts, 1939. Lectures on Egyptian Art and Archaeology in U.S. and Europe. *Position*: Dir., Egyptian Museum, Berlin, 1929-1950; Prof. Egyptology, Cur., Egyptian Section, University Mus., Univ. of Pennsylvania, Philadelphia, Pa., 1950- .

ANTHONY, ELISABETH MARY—*Painter, Des., T.*

106 Maple Ave., Hackensack, N.J.

B. New York, N.Y. *Studied*: NAD, with Charles Hawthorne, Ivan Olinsky; N.Y. Univ.; Master Inst. of United Arts. *Member*: Catholic A. Gld. *Work*: Bergen County Hist. Mus.; mural, Pollack Hospital Chapel, Medical Center, Jersey City, N.J., 1955; private collections. *Exhibited*: Ogunquit A. Center; Montclair and Ridgewood A. Mus.; PAFA; Montross Gal.; Contemporary A. Gal.; Barbizon-Plaza Gal.; Plainfield (N.J.) Lib.; one-man: Decorative Cl., and Barbizon-Plaza Gal., 1936, 1939, 1946; Ford Comp. Exh., 1956; Latham Fnd. Intl. Poster Comp., 1958. *Position*: A. T., Benedictine Acad., Paterson, N.J., and privately.

ANTREASIAN, GARO ZAREH—*Painter, Lith., T., L.*

615 North Payton Rd., Indianapolis, Ind.

B. Indianapolis, Ind., Feb. 16, 1922. *Studied*: John Herron AI, B.F.A. *Awards*: prizes, Hoosier Salon, 1944, 1949; Wash. Herald Exh., 1945; Indiana A., 1946, 1949-1951, 1953, 1956-1958; Indiana A. Cl., 1950, 1953; Old Northwest Territory Exh., 1949; Indiana Pr. M., 1948-1950, 1954; Minnesota Pr. Annual, 1950; Indiana State Fair, 1953, 1954, 1955, 1958; Phila. Pr. Cl., 1958; MModA, 1953; Bradley Prints, 1955. *Work*: U.S. Coast Guard, New London, Conn.; John Herron AI; Phila. Pr. Cl.; Bradley Univ.; Univ. Minnesota; L. S. Ayers & Co.; Indiana Univ.; Indiana Nat. Bank; private collections. *Exhibited*: SFMA, 1942; Texas Pr. M., 1942; NAD, 1943; Kansas Pr. M., 1942; Armed Forces Exh., Albany, N.Y., 1944; Ohio Valley WC Soc., 1944; Hoosier Salon, 1944; Indiana A., 1944, 1946, 1949-1953; Indiana A. Cl., 1950, 1953; Old Northwest Territory Exh., 1948, 1949, 1951; BM, 1948-1952; LC, 1949; Indiana Pr. M., 1948-1951, 1954; Life Magazine Exh., MMA, 1950; AFA Traveling Exh., 1950-1952, 1953; BMFA; PMA; N.Y. Pub. Lib.; prints in UNESCO European Traveling Exh. *Position*: Pres., Indiana A. Cl., 1953; Indiana Pr. M., 1952; Instr., A. Sch., John Herron AI., Indianapolis, Ind.

APGAR, NICOLAS ADAM—*Painter*

813 Comstock Ave., Syracuse 10, N.Y.

B. Gaillon, France, Dec. 8, 1918. *Studied*: Syracuse Univ. *Member*: Albany A. Group. *Awards*: prizes, Myers Comp., Albany, N.Y., 1953, 1955; Albany Inst. Hist. & A. (purchase prize), 1953; Cooperstown, N.Y., 1955; Syracuse Mus. A. FA, 1957, 1958; *Exhibited*: Albany Inst. Hist. & A., 1954 (one-man); Birmingham, Ala., 1954; Albany and Utica, N.Y., 1954; Butler AI, 1954; Roberson Mem. Mus., Binghamton, N.Y., 1957; Oneonta State T. Col., 1958 (one-man); Munson-Williams-Proctor Inst., Utica, 1957, 1958; Cooperstown, N.Y., 1955, 1958; Rochester, N.Y., 1957, 1958; N.Y. State Fair, 1957, 1958. *Work*: Syracuse Univ., Munson-Williams-Proctor Inst.

APOSTLE, JAMES—*Painter, I.*

48 Hartford Ave., Thompsonville, Conn.

B. Thompsonville, Conn., Feb. 17, 1917. *Studied*: Am. Int. Col. *Member*: Springfield A. Lg. *Exhibited*: Springfield A. Lg., 1939-1945; A. Gld., 1943-1945; Springfield Mus. FA; G.W.V. Smith A. Gal.; Inst. Contemporary A., Boston; Berkshire Mus., Pittsfield, Mass.; Wadsworth Atheneum; Farnsworth A. Mus.; Worcester A. Mus.; Currier Gal. A.; AEA; Mus. A., R.I. Sch. Des.; NAD; CGA.; one-man: Somers Playhouse Gal.; Little Gal., Springfield, Mass.; Graphic A. Gal.; Swetzof Gal., Boston.*

APPEL, JACK—*Sculptor*

308 West 47th St.; h. 420 East 86th St., New York, N.Y.

B. New York, N.Y., Oct. 28, 1915. *Studied*: N.Y. Univ.; BAID; and with Cecere, Snowden, Manship, Piccirilli. *Member*: NSS; hon. member Australian Fauna Preservation Soc. *Work*: reliefs, Ohio and New Jersey Gun Collectors Assn., 1953-54; monument, Canberra, Australia, National Park. Specializes in sculpture of Australian animals.

APPEL, MARIANNE (Mrs. Marianne Appel Mecklem)—Painter, I.
Woodstock, N.Y.

B. New York, N.Y., May 6, 1913. *Studied*: Woodstock Sch. P., and with Peppino Mangravite, B. W. Tomlin, Henry Lee McFee, Judson Smith. *Member*: Woodstock AA; AEA. *Awards*: Keith Mem., Woodstock AA, 1938; Carville, La., 1940; Dutchess County Fair, 1935. *Work*: MMA; Marine Hospital, Carville, La.; USPO, Middleporte, N.Y.; Wrangell, Alaska. *Exhibited*: CGA, 1940, 1941; WMAA, 1938-1944; AIC, 1938-1942; Carnegie Inst., 1941-1944; AFA traveling exh., 1942; Woodstock AA. I., commercial and art magazines.*

APPLEBEE, FRANK WOODBERRY—Painter, E.
312 Chewacla Dr., Auburn, Ala.

B. Boston, Mass., June 2, 1902. *Studied*: Mass. Sch. A.; Alabama Polytechnic Inst., B.S. in Edu., M.A., and with Ralph M. Pearson, Hans Hofmann. *Member*: Alabama A. Lg.; Alabama WC Soc.; Scarab Cl. *Work*: Montgomery Mus. FA; Alabama Col. for Women; Alabama Poly. Inst. *Exhibited*: Rockefeller Center, N.Y., 1936; Corpus Christi, Texas, 1946; Ala. Col. for Women, 1939; SSAL, 1939, 1945; Ala. A. Lg., 1933-1956. *Position*: Hd., Prof. A., Alabama Polytechnic Inst., Auburn, Ala., 1932- .

ARBEIT, ARNOLD A.—Designer, P., E., Cr., L.
154 Nassau St., New York 38, N.Y.; h. 116 Fox Meadow Rd., Scarsdale, N.Y.

B. New York, N.Y., Oct. 1, 1916. *Studied*: BAID; Columbia Univ.; N.Y. Univ., B.Arch., M.Arch., M.A.; MIT; Georgetown Univ., and with Hale Woodruff, William Armstrong, Lloyd Morgan. *Member*: AIA; N.Y. Soc. Arch.; BAID; CAD. *Awards*: Armstrong Mem. medal. *Exhibited*: N.Y. Univ. traveling exh., 1950-52; CAD, 1951, 1952; Laurel Gal., 1949; Isaac Delgado Mus. A., 1945; Tucson A. Exh., 1949; BM, 1942, 1948; NAD, 1942, 1943; N.Y. Univ., 1948-1952. Contributor to Architectural Forum. Lectures on Art and its Relation to Architecture. *Position*: Instr. & Cr., Senior Arch. Des., The Cooper Union, New York, N.Y., 1947- ; Lt. Col., U.S. Army Res. Civil Affairs Military Govt.; Fine Arts, Monuments & Archives, Chief; Exh., Art Schools U.S.A., 1953.

ARCHER, EDMUND MINOR—Painter, E.
532 20th St., N.W., Washington 6, D.C.; h. 13 South Foushee St., Richmond 20, Va.

B. Richmond, Va., Sept. 28, 1904. *Studied*: Univ. Virginia; ASL with Kenneth Hayes Miller, Allen Tucker; privately with Nora Houston, Adele Clark, Jacques Maroger and in Europe. *Awards*: Clark prize and bronze medal, CGA, 1930; purchase award, VMFA, 1941; prizes, Norfolk Mus. A. & Sciences, 1950. *Work*: BMFA; CGA; WMAA; VMFA; Fisk Univ. Mus.; Univ. Michigan; Princeton Univ.; Univ. of Virginia; Univ. of Richmond; Medical College of Virginia; State Capitol, Richmond, Va.; mural, USPO, Hopewell, Va. *Exhibited*: PAFA; CGA; AIC; WMAA; WFNY 1939; VMFA; NAD; SFMA. *Positions*: Asst. & Assoc. Cur., WMAA, 1930-40; Instr., Corcoran Sch. A. & George Washington Univ., Washington, D.C. at present.

ARCHIPENKO, ALEXANDER—Sculptor, T., L.
1947 Broadway; h. 624 Madison Ave., New York, N.Y.; s. Woodstock, N.Y.

B. Kiev, Ukraine, May 30, 1887. *Studied*: A. Sch., Kiev; L'Ecole des Beaux Arts, Paris. *Work*: monuments, Public Gardens, Cleveland, Ohio, and in museums in Europe, Japan and the United States. *Exhibited*: nationally and internationally in leading museums, colleges and universities, 1910-1956. 115th one-man show opened in Dusseldorf, Germany and will travel throughout Europe. *Position*: Dir., Instr., Archipenko Sch. A., New York, N.Y., and Woodstock, N.Y.

ARCIER, JOSEPH WILLIAM—Painter
Dogwood Lane, New Canaan, Conn.

B. Berkeley, Cal., Nov. 18, 1909. *Studied*: Univ. Pennsylvania, Wharton Sch., M.B.A.; also with Herb Olsen. *Member*: SC; AWS; Conn. WC Soc.; Silvermine Gld. A.; Royal Soc. A., London, England. *Awards*: Zabriskie purchase award, AWS, 1954; Bainbridge award, All. A. Am., 1955; D. H. Tribble award, AWS, 1956; Howard Maeder award, SC, 1956. *Exhibited*: AWS, 1953-1958;

All. A. Am., 1953-1958; New Jersey WC Soc., 1953-1958; Conn. WC Soc., 1955-1958; SC, 1953-1958; Silvermine Gld. A., 1955-1958.

ARENS, EGMONT—Industrial Designer, E., W., L.
480 Lexington Ave., New York 17, N.Y.

B. Cleveland, Ohio, 1889. *Studied*: Univ. New Mexico; Univ. Chicago. *Member*: F. Soc. Indst. Des.; F., Package Des. Council; Int. Soc. Color Council; Soc. of the Plastics Industry. Author: "Consumer Engineering," and articles on design for trade publications. Lectures at N.Y. Univ., Harvard Univ., etc.

ARGALL, CHARLES G.—Painter
9020 Wonderland Ave., Hollywood 46, Cal.

B. San Jose, Cal., Oct. 25, 1892. *Studied*: Col. of the Pacific, San Jose; Chouinard AI; Los A. County AI, and with Ralph Johonnet, Will Foster, F. Tolles Chamberlin. *Member*: Cal. AC; Southland AA; Los A. County AI Alumni Assn., and others. *Awards*: prizes, Los A. County AI; San Fernando Valley Prof. A. Gld., 1950; Cal. AC, 1951; Painters & Sculptors Soc., 1952. *Work*: Los A. Mus. A.; Cal. State Fair, and in private galleries. Numerous portraits of prominent persons.*

ARKUS, LEON ANTHONY—Assistant Museum Director
Carnegie Institute, 4400 Forbes Ave.; h. 513 North Neville St., Pittsburgh 13, Pa.

B. New Jersey, May 6, 1915. Exhibitions and Collections arranged: Retrospective Exhibition of Paintings in Pittsburgh Internationals (1958); Lockhart Collection of Rare Drawings and Prints (1958); Paintings by Alberto Burri (1957); many print shows and one-man exhibitions. *Position*: Asst. Dir., Carnegie Institute Museum, Pittsburgh, Pa.

ARMS, WINIFRED LEFFERTS—Painter, Des.
Blandford, Mass.

B. Newtonville, Mass., Oct. 9, 1903. *Studied*: PIASch; NAD; Tiffany Fnd. *Member*: NAC; All. A. Am.; AWS. *Awards*: Tiffany Fnd F., 1925; prizes, NAC, 1931, 1933, 1936.*

ARMSTRONG, ANDREW F. H.—Designer, P.
5536 Dorchester Ave., Chicago, Ill.

B. Berkeley, Cal., Feb. 8, 1910. *Studied*: Rutgers Univ.; Parsons Sch. Des.; Univ. Chicago, B.A. *Member*: Chicago A. Cl.; A. Dir. Cl. of Chicago. *Exhibited*: Santa Fe, N.M., 1955; New Mexico State Mus., 1955; Rodeo Show, Santa Fe, 1956; Fiesta Show, New Mexico State Mus. 1957. *Position*: Advertising Consultant.

ARMSTRONG, CAROLYN FAUGHT (Mrs. T. M.)—Painter, T.
5130 Wayne Ave., Philadelphia 44, Pa.

B. Asbury Park, N.J., July 9, 1910. *Studied*: PMSchA; PAFA. *Member*: AEA; Woodmere AA; Phila. A. All.; Bd. Mem., F., PAFA; Allen's Lane A. Center. *Work*: PAFA; Springhouse School. *Exhibited*: PAFA, 1940, 1951, 1955-1957; Phila. A. All., 1941, 1949-1958; Woodmere A. Gal., 1941-1958; Phila. Sketch Cl., 1950, 1952, 1956; Phila. Free Lib., 1950, 1952; Wilmington WC Soc., 1950; Nassau, Bahamas, 1950; Wolpert Gal., 1956 (one-man); Phila. Fidelity Annual, 1957; Allen's Lane A. Center, Cape May, N.J., 1951-1958.

ARMSTRONG, ESTELLE (R.) (Manon)—Educator, P.
603 Bloomfield Ave., Nutley 10, N.J.

B. Lincoln, Ill., May 11, 1884. *Studied*: Cal. Sch. Des.; ASL; Sch. F. & App.A; AIC, and in Europe. *Member*: NAWA; N.J. WC Soc.; Montclair AA; St. Joseph A. Lg. *Awards*: BM; Montclair A. Mus.; NAWA. *Work*: Univ. Oklahoma; N.Y. Univ.; Montclair A. Mus. *Exhibited*: NAD; NAWA; AWS; Montclair A. Mus. *Positions*: Instr., Painting, N.Y. Univ., 1927-43; Instr. Painting, Montclair A. Mus., 1943- ; Instr., Kimberley Day Sch., Hd. Dept. A., Montclair, N.J.; Memb. A. Committee, Montclair A. Mus.

ARMSTRONG, ROGER JOSEPH—Cartoonist, P., I.
860 Cress St., Laguna Beach, Cal.

B. Los Angeles, Cal., Oct. 12, 1917. *Studied*: Pasadena City Col.; Chouinard AI, and with Richard Haines, Phil Dike, Dan Lutz, Rex Brandt, Edmund Kuhn. *Exhibited*: Nat. Orange Show, San Bernardino, 1950. *Work*: Comic strip "Ella Cinders," United Features Syndicate; "Napoleon," Times-Mirror Syndicate.

ARNASON, H. HARVARD—
Educator, Mus. Dir., Art Historian, W., L.
Dept. of Art, University of Minnesota; Walker A. Center, 1710 Lyndale Ave.; h. 1719 Bryant Ave., South Minneapolis 3, Minn.

B. Winnipeg, Man., Canada, Apr. 24, 1909. *Studied*: Univ. Manitoba; Northwestern Univ., B.S.; Princeton Univ., M.F.A. *Member*: AAUP; Archaeological Inst. of Am.; CAA; AAMD; AAMus.; AFA (Trustee). *Award*: Fulbright Fellow, 1955-56. *Positions*: Instr., Dept. A., Northwestern Univ., 1936-38; L., Frick Coll., 1938-42; Senior Field Rep., OWI, Iceland, 1942-44; Asst. Deputy Dir. for Europe, OWI, 1944-45; Actg. Chief, Program Planning and Evaluation Unit, Office of International Information and Cultural Affairs, Dept. of State, 1946-47; Alternate U.S. Representative, Preparatory Comm. of UNESCO, London and Paris, 1946; Tech. Adv., to U.S. Delegation, First General Conference of UNESCO, Nov., Dec., 1946; Visiting Assoc. Prof., College of the Univ. of Chicago, 1947; Prof. and Chm., Dept. Art, Univ. of Minnesota, 1947- ; Dir., Walker A. Center, Minneapolis, Minn., 1950- ; Editorial Bd., Art in America. Author: Articles on Medieval and Modern Art.

ARNAUTOFF, VICTOR MICHAIL—Painter, E., Gr.
1007 Washington St., Colma, Cal.

B. Mariupol, Ukraine, Russia, Nov. 11, 1896. *Studied*: Cal. Sch. FA. *Awards*: prizes, San F. AA, 1937, 1938. *Work*: SFMA; Albert Bender Mem. Coll.; Edward Bruce Mem. Coll.; murals, Coit Mem. Chapel, George Washington H.S., San F.; USPO, Linden & College Station, Tex.; Richmond, Cal.; Pacific Grove, Cal. *Exhibited*: GGE 1939; WFNY 1939; San F. AA, 1929-1939; AIC; San F. AA, 1958; Toledo Mus. A.; Artists' Union Hall, Moscow, U.S.S.R., 1958. *Position*: Asst. Prof., Dept. A. & Arch., Stanford Univ., Cal.

ARNDT, PAUL WESLEY—Painter
Woodstock, N.Y.

B. Jacksonville, Ill., Sept. 30, 1881. *Studied*: AIC; J. Francis Smith A. Acad.; Ecole des Beaux Arts, Paris, with Gerome, Ferrier. *Work*: murals for steamships, theatres & public bldgs.*

ARNEST, BERNARD PATRICK—Painter
c/o Kraushaar Gallery, 1055 Madison Ave., New York 22, N.Y.

B. Denver, Colo., Feb. 19, 1917. *Studied*: Colorado Springs FA Center. *Awards*: Guggenheim F., 1940; Chief, War Artists, Hist. Sec., ETO, 1944-45. *Member*: AEA; Assn. Univ. Prof. *Work*: War Dept. Permanent Coll.; murals, private bldgs., Denver, Rocky Ford, Colo.; USPO, Wellington, Tex. *Exhibited*: WMAA, 1948-1951; CGA; Carnegie Inst., 1952; Univ. Minnesota, 1951. *Positions*: Instr., Minneapolis Sch. A., 1947-49; Assoc. Prof. A., Univ. Minnesota, 1949-1957; Prof., Hd. Sch. A., Colorado College & Colorado Springs A. Center, 1957- .

ARNETT, ELEANOR—Painter
1716 Chestnut St. (3); h. The Lenox Apartments, 13th & Spruce Sts., Philadelphia 7, Pa.

B. Philadelphia, Pa., Mar. 13, 1895. *Studied*: PAFA; Hans Hofmann Sch. A., Munich, Germany; Fla. West Coast A. Center, and with Arnold Blanche. *Member*: AEA; Phila. A. All.; F., PAFA; Woodmere AA; Phila. Plastic Cl. *Awards*: prizes, Soc. Four Arts, Palm Beach, Fla.; F., PAFA; gold medal, Phila. Plastic Cl. *Work*: in private colls. *Exhibited*: PAFA; PMA; one-man: New York City, Clearwater, Fla.; Philadelphia, Pa.; Phila. A. All.; Woodmere A. Gal.

ARNHEIM, RUDOLF—Educator, W.
Sarah Lawrence College, Bronxville, N.Y.

B. Berlin, Germany, July 15, 1904. *Studied*: Univ. Berlin, Ph. D. *Member*: CAA; Am. Soc. for Aesthetics; Am. Psychological Assn. *Awards*: Guggenheim F., 1941, 1942. Contributor to Journal of Aesthetics; Psychological Review; "Aspects of Form"; "Poets at Work"; "Essays in Teaching," etc. Author: "Art and Visual Perception"; "Film As Art," 1957. *Position*: Prof., Psychology of Art, Sarah Lawrence Col., Bronxville, N.Y., 1943- ; Visiting Prof., New Sch. for Social Research, New York, N.Y., 1943- ; Trustee, Am. Soc. for Aesthetics.

ARNHOLT, WALDON SYLVESTER—Designer, Lith., P.
Savannah Lake, R.D. 5, Ashland, Ohio

B. Nankin, Ohio, Jan. 1, 1900. *Studied*: with C. Fritz Hoelzer. *Work*: Church murals. *Position*: A. & Lith., A. L. Garber Co., 1941- . Restorer of paintings.*

ARNO, PETER—Cartoonist
c/o New Yorker Magazine, 25 West 43rd St., New York, N.Y.

Contributor cartoons to New Yorker and other magazines.*

ARNOLD, GRANT—Painter, Lith., T., W.
155 Winslow St., Watertown, N.Y.

B. Brooklyn, N.Y., Apr. 24, 1904. *Studied*: ASL, with Max Weber, Kenneth Hayes Miller; Syracuse Univ., B.F.A.; City Col., N.Y., M.S. in Edu. *Member*: ASL; N.Y. State T. Assn. *Work*: LC; N.Y. Pub. Lib.; MMA; commissioned for painting by Watertown Chamber of Commerce and presented to Sec. Dulles. Author: "Creative Lithography," 1941. *Position*: Pres., Watertown H.S. Teachers Assn., 1954-55; Instr., Mech. Drawing, Costume Illus., Painting, Watertown H.S. Consultant for revision of N.Y. State mechanical drawing syllabus, 1957.

ARNOLD, HOWARD WESTON—
Illustrator, Des., P., C., E., I., Comm. A., L.
130 Farley Ave., Fanwood, N.J.

B. Chicago, Ill., July 19, 1904. *Studied*: CUASch.; Grand Central Sch. A; NAD; N.Y. Indst. Sch., and with Harvey Dunn, Ivan Olinsky, Jay Weaver. *Member*: SC; A. Gld. *Awards*: Gold ctf., Int. Packaging Exh., 1936; prizes, Art Center of the Oranges. *Work*: Consulting A. Dir., for manufacturers and advertising agencies; A. Dir., in charge of Naval illus. and special subjects, Jordanoff Aviation Corp., World War II. *Exhibited*: Montclair Mus. A.; Art Center of the Oranges; Newark AC; Montross Gal.; N.Y. WC Soc.; SI; A. Gld., 1937 (one-man). *Position*: Hd., Adv. Dept., day session, & Asst. Dir. of the Sch. of Visual Arts, New York, N.Y., at present.

ARNOLD, NEWELL HILLIS—Sculptor, C., T.
1412 Shands Court, Kirkwood 22, Mo.

B. Beach, N.D., July 10, 1906. *Studied*: Univ. Minnesota, B.A.; Minneapolis Sch. A.; Cranbrook Academy, with Carl Milles. *Member*: St. Louis A. Gld.; Minn. S. Group; AEA; Group 15, St. Louis. *Work*: Walker A. Center; Monticello Col.; Univ. Minnesota; Minn. Dept. Health; USPO, Abingdon, Ill.; World War II Mem., St. Louis; St. Anne's Church, Normandy, Mo.; Resurrection Church and H.S., St. Louis; St. Mary's Church, Hays, Kans.; St. Joseph's Church, Damar, Kans.; Rockhurst Col., Kansas City; St. Mary's Church, Hannibal, Mo.; Greensfelder Mem, Park, Coeur Creve, Mo.; St. Joseph's Church, Yates Center, Kans.; Lutheran Church, Columbus, Ga.; Archbishop's Chapel, St. Louis, Mo.; Interparish H.S., Jefferson City, Mo., and private commissions for homes and gardens. *Exhibited*: Arch. Lg., 1937; WFNY 1939; CAM; Wichita, Kans.; A. Gld. *Position*: Instr., S., ceramics, Monticello College, Godfrey, Ill., 1938- .

ARNOLD, PAUL ?.—Educator, P., Gr.
Allen Art Museum; h. 396 Morgan St., Oberlin, Ohio

B. Taiyuanfu, China, Nov. 24, 1918. *Studied*: Oberlin Col., A.B., M.A.; Univ. Minnesota, M.F.A. *Member*: CAA; Midwest Col. A. Conference. *Work*: Allen A. Mus.; Canton AI; SAM; LC; Univ. Minnesota; Dayton AI; Brooks Mem. A. Gal., Memphis. *Awards*: F., Faculty Fellowship Program, Ford Fnd., 1951-52; purchase prizes, Canton AI, 1951; Joslyn A. Mus., 1952; LC, 1953; Print

Exh., Dallas, Tex.; prizes, Audubon A; Canton AI, 1955; Audubon A., prize, 1956, medal, 1957. *Exhibited*: Portland Soc. A., 1948, 1951, 1953; Ohio WC Soc., 1949-1952, 1956; Midwest A., 1950; Canton AI, 1951, 1953, 1955; Butler AI, 1952; SAGA, 1951, 1953, 1954, 1957; Joslyn A. Mus., 1952; Am. Color Pr. Soc., 1952, 1957; Northwest Pr. M., 1952, 1953, 1957; LC, 1952, 1954; Phila. Pr. Cl., 1952; Audubon A., 1953-1955, 1956, 1957; Ohio Pr. M., 1953, 1955-1957; Albany Pr. Cl., 1953, 1955; Massillon Mus. A., 1953; Ohio State Univ., 1953, 1956 (one-man); Denison Univ., 1954; Youngstown, Ohio, 1954; Dallas, Tex., 1954; Bradley Univ., 1955; Ohio WC Soc., 1956; Phila. A. All., 1957; Silvermine Gld. A., 1958; Pasadena A. Mus., 1958. I., "General Chemistry," 1955; "Laboratory Experiments in General Chemistry," 1955. *Position*: Prof. FA, Oberlin College, Oberlin, Ohio, 1941-42, 1946-51, 1952-1956; Assoc. Prof., 1956- .

ARONSON, BORIS—*Painter, Des., Gr., I., W.*
1 West 89th St., New York 24, N.Y.

B. Kiev, Russia, Oct. 15, 1900. *Studied*: in Russia, Germany, France; State A. Sch., Kiev; special training with Ilya Mashkov, Sch. Mod. Painting, Moscow. *Member*: United Scenic A. Union; German A. Soc. *Awards*: Guggenheim F., 1950; American Theatre Wing award, 1950, 1951. *Work*: sets for more than 70 stage productions including Awake and Sing; Cabin in the Sky; Detective Story; The Crucible; The Rose Tattoo; The Diary of Anne Frank; The Firstborn; J.B., etc. *Exhibited*: AIC; WMAA; MModA; Ross Gal.; Provincetown AA; New School; PMA; Cincinnati Mod. A. Soc.; one-man: New Art Circle; Steimatsky Gal., Jerusalem; Tel-Aviv Mus.; Boyer Gal., Phila.; Babcock Gal.; Stendahl Gal., Los A.; Bertha Schaefer Gal.; Nierendorf Gal., and others. Author: "Marc Chagall," 1923; "Modern Graphic Art," 1924; Illus., "The Theatre in Life"; various children's books. *Position*: Instr., Stage Designing, PIASch., 1957.

ARONSON, DAVID—*Painter*
Sudbury, Mass.

B. Shilova, Lithuania, Oct. 28, 1923. *Studied*: BMFA Sch. *Awards*: prizes, Inst. Mod. A., 1944; VMFA, 1946; Boston A. Festival, 1952-1954; Tupper A. Fund Competition, 1954; grant, Nat. Inst. A. & Lets., 1958. *Work*: VMFA; AIC; Bryn Mawr Col.; Brandeis Univ.; de Cordova & Dana Mus. *Position*: Instr., BMFA Sch. FA, Boston, Mass., 1943-55; Chm., Div. A., Assoc. Prof. A., Sch. Fine & Applied A., Boston University, 1955- .

ARONSON, IRENE—*Designer, P., Gr., T.*
63-20 Haring St., Rego Park, Long Island, N.Y.

B. Dresden, Germany, Mar. 8, 1918. *Studied*: Eastbourne Sch. A. & Crafts, England; Slade Sch. FA., Univ. London; Ruskin Sch. Drawing, Oxford Univ.; Parsons Sch. Des., New York. *Member*: NAWA; AEA; United Scenic A.; Boston Indp. A.; Am. Color Pr. Soc.; Chicago Et. Soc.; Phila. Pr. Cl.; Atelier 17. *Awards*: gold medal, Eastbourne Sch. A. & Crafts; prizes, Slade Sch. Des.; Knickerbocker A., 1958; NAWA, 1954, 1957. *Work*: Mus. City of N.Y.; Ringling Bros. Mus.; N.Y. Pub. Lib.; Mus. A., Providence, R.I.; MModA; MMA; Bezalel Mus., Israel; Bibliotheque Nationale, Paris, France; Royal Lib., Brussels; Benjamin Franklin Lib., Paris France; Free Lib., Phila., Pa. Illus. for Theatre Arts, Country Book, Tomorrow, Encore, and other magazines; Ballet Russe de Monte Carlo "Souvenir Book"; Vienna Choir Boys "Souvenir Book"; jackets and illus. for leading publishers. Costumes for "The Spectacle of Toys," Barnum & Bailey's Circus, 1946; "Front Page" and "Laura." Contributed articles to Design magazine, 1951, 1955. *Exhibited*: Wakefield Gal.; Am.-British A. Center; Bonestell Gal.; MModA; Chicago SE; Univ. So. Cal.; Phila. Pr. Cl.; Creative Gal.; Weyhe Gal., 1952 (one-man); Smithsonian Inst., 1954 (one-man); Brooks Mem. Gal., Memphis, 1955 (one-man); Weyhe Gal., 1956 (one-man); Contemporaries; NAD; PAFA; BMFA; NCFA; BM, 1958; Argent Gal., 1959 (2-man); Rome, Italy. *Position*: Asst. Instr. Painting, Walden School, New York; Instr., A. & Des., Evening Div., City Col. for Adult Edu., New York, 1948-1951; Instr., Painting & Drawing, N.Y. Bd. Edu., Adult Edu., evening classes.

ARONSON, JOSEPH—*Designer, W., L.*
118 East 37th St., New York 16, N.Y.

B. Buffalo, N.Y., Dec. 22, 1898. *Studied*: Univ. Buffalo; Columbia Univ. Sch. Arch., B. Arch. *Member*: ADI;

Arch.L.; Soc. Arch. Hist. Author: "Furniture & Decoration," 1936, (revised, 1952); "Encyclopedia of Furniture," 1938. Contributor to: Popular Science magazine; Dictionary of the Arts; Book of Knowledge. Cr., Design, Pratt Institute, Brooklyn, N.Y.

ARRIOLA, GUS—*Cartoonist*
1022 East Keim Dr., Phoenix, Ariz.

B. Florence, Ariz., July 23, 1917. *Member*: Nat. Cartoonists Soc. Author: "Gordo," published, 1950. Creator of comic strip "Gordo," appearing in newspapers regularly. Cartoon adv. for West Coast agencies. Lectures at Phoenix A. Center and Arizona State Col.

ARTHUR, REVINGTON—*Painter, E., Gr., L.*
Box 276, Glenbrook, Conn.

B. Glenbrook, Conn. *Studied*: ASL; Grand Central Sch. A., with George Luks, George P. Ennis; Eastport Summer Sch. A., with Arshile Gorky; Columbia Univ. Ext. *Member*: Audubon A.; Silvermine Gld. A.; Conn. Acad. FA; New Orleans AA; Conn. WC Soc. *Awards*: prizes, Conn. Acad. FA, 1955; New Haven P. & C., 1948, 1955; Stonehenge award, New England Exh., 1953; Conn. WC Soc., 1951; Silvermine Gld. A., 1944. *Work*: BM; Telfair Acad. A.; Walker A. Center; Wilmington Soc. FA; Fla. Southern Col.; Rollins Col.; Ford Motor Co. *Exhibited*: 16 one-man exhs., New York, N.Y., 1932-1955; 21 one-man exhs., elsewhere, 1947-1955. Lectures: "Art Today and Yesterday," Chautauqua, 1956; "History of Graphics," Silvermine Gld., 1955; "The Art of the World," series of 8 talks, Chautauqua. Lecture-Demonstrations. *Position*: Dir., Chautauqua A. Center, 1944- ; Assoc. Dir., Silvermine A. Sch., 1951- ; Dir., The New England Exh., 1950- ; Dir., 1st Nat. Pr. Exh., Silvermine Gld., 1956- ; Instr., Syracuse Univ. courses at Chautauqua A. Center, 1953- ; Instr., Silvermine Sch. A., 1951- ; Instr., New York Univ. courses at Chautauqua, 1944-1952.*

ARTIS, WILLIAM ELLISWORTH—
Educator, C., S., Lith., L.
Nebraska State College; h. 704 Main St., Chadron, Neb.

B. New York, N.Y., Feb. 2, 1919. *Studied*: N.Y. State Col. of Ceramics, Alfred Univ.; Syracuse Univ.; Nebraska State Col.; Pa. State Univ. *Member*: Am. Ceramic Soc.; NSS; CAA; NAEA. *Awards*: Rosenwald F., 1947; Atlanta Univ. purchase award, 1944, 1945, 1947, 1951, 1952. *Work*: WAC; IBM; Slater Mem. Mus., Norwich, Conn.; Howard Univ.; Trevor Arnett Gal., Wash. D.C., ceramic tile room divider, men's dormitory, Nebraska State Col. *Exhibited*: NAC, 1940; NSS; WMAA; Syracuse Mus. FA, Nat. Ceramic Exh., 1940, 1947-1951. *Position*: Instr., S. Ceramics, A. Hist., Drawing, Painting, Nebraska State Col., Chadron, Neb., at present.

ARTZYBASHEFF, BORIS—*Illustrator, P., Des., W.*
Joshuatown Rd., Lyme, Conn.

B. Kharkov, Russia, May 25, 1899. *Studied*: Tenishev Sch., St. Petersburg, Russia. *Member*: Grolier Cl.; SI; Royal Soc. A., London; Century Cl. *Awards*: prize, children's book, N.Y. Herald Tribune, 1937. Illus. books by Edmund Wilson, Padriac Colum, Tagore, Balzac's "Droll Stories," and others. Edited and illus., "Aesop's Fables"; Painter of portraits, particularly for Time magazine. *Exhibited*: in world wide exhibitions. Author, I., "Seven Simeons," "Poor Shaydula," "As I See," etc. Illus. for Time, Life and Fortune magazines.

ASAWA, RUTH (LANIER)—*Sculptor*
21 Saturn St., San Francisco 14, Cal.

B. Norwalk, Cal., Jan. 27, 1926. *Studied*: Milwaukee State T. Col., with Robert von Neumann; Black Mountain Col., with Josef Albers. *Exhibited*: MModA, 1958; Sao Paulo, 1955; San F. AA, 1952, 1957; WMAA, 1955, 1956, 1958; AIC, 1955, 1957; New Haven, Conn., 1953; Design Research, Cambridge, Mass., 1956; SFMA, 1954 (4-man); Peridot Gal., N.Y., 1954, 1956, 1958 (one-man).

ASCH(EMEIER), STAN(LEY) WILLIAM JOSEPH—
Cartoonist, L.
Apt. 3-C, 362 Riverside Dr., New York 25, N. Y.

B. St. Paul, Minn., Aug. 31, 1911. *Studied*: Mills Acad., St. Paul, Minn. *Member*: Nat. Press Cl. Lectures: Cartooning. Cart., national magazines, 1931-46. *Position*: Instr., Univ. Minnesota, 1934-37; Ft. Jay Regional Hospital, Governors Island, N.Y., 1945-46; Freelance cartoonist at present.

ASCHENBACH, PAUL—*Sculptor*
Charlotte, Vt.

B. Poughkeepsie, N.Y., May 25, 1921. *Studied*: R.I. Sch. Des. *Work*: de Cordova & Dana Mus., Lincoln, Mass.; Fleming Mus., Univ. of Vermont. Sculpture: Trinity College Chapel, Burlington, Vt., and in many private homes. *Exhibited*: AFA traveling exh., 1958; Mus. of Contemp. Crafts; one-man: Fleming Mus., Univ. of Vermont; Moore Gal., Cambridge, Mass.; Sculpture Center, N.Y.

ASCHER, MARY G. (Mrs. David)—*Painter*
336 Central Park West, New York 25, N.Y.

B. Leeds, England, Dec. 24, 1900. *Studied*: Col. City of New York, B.A.; N.Y. Univ., M.A.; N.Y. Sch. App. Des.; Grand Central Sch. A.; Famous Artists Sch.; ASL; Sch. Chinese Brushwork, and with Will Barnet, Morris Davidson, Morris Kantor, Vaclav Vytlacil and George Elmer Browne. *Member*: NAWA; AAUW; ASL; AFA. *Awards*: gold medal of honor, P. & S. Soc. of New Jersey, 1958. *Exhibited*: P. & S. Soc. of New Jersey, 1958; Art: USA, 1958, 1959; NAWA, 1958; Provincetown A. Festival, 1958; N.Y. City Center, 1957, 1958; Bodley Gal., 1958; Sch. Chinese Brushwork, 1958. Author, I., "Poetry-Painting" 1958. *Position*: in N.Y. City schools, Hd. Dept., 1939-46, Dean of Girls, Guidance Dir. & Asst. Principal, 1946-53.

ASHBY, PAUL W(ARREN)—*Graphic Artist, T., P., L.*
Butler, Ind.

B. Gunnison, Colo., Sept. 9, 1893. *Studied*: Indiana Univ., M.S.; Evansville Col., A.B.; Cincinnati Univ.; Ft. Wayne A. Sch. *Member*: Indiana Soc. Pr. M.; Hoosier Salon: Northern Indiana A. Salon. *Awards*: prizes, Indiana AC, 1939; Ft. Wayne A., 1942; A. & Models, 1944; Hoosier Salon, 1944, 1947; Northern Indiana A. Salon, 1946-1950; Indiana Pr. M., 1944, 1945; Indiana State Fair, 1948-1950. *Exhibited*: Wichita AA, 1938; Phila. Pr. Cl., 1938, 1940; Southern Pr. M., 1938-1943; Missouri A., 1945; LC, 1943; Cal. SE, 1945-1950; San F. AA., 1945; Northwest Pr. M., 1946; Laguna Beach AA, 1946-1950; Mint Mus. A., 1946; Albany Inst. Hist. & A., 1945-1947; Am. Monotype Soc., 1940-1942; Indiana A., 1937-1943; Hoosier Salon, 1939-1952; Indiana Soc. Pr. M., 1938-1952; Indiana AC, 1938-1940; Soc. Min. P. & Engravers, 1951. *Work*: Evansville Col.; Indianapolis Methodist Hospital. *Position*: Instr., Public Schools, Butler, Indiana.*

ASHE, EDD(MUND) M., Jr.—*Cartoonist, P., I.*
The Buckingham Place, New Milford, Conn.

B. Norwalk, Conn., Aug. 11, 1908. *Studied*: Carnegie Inst., B.A. *Member*: Nat. Cartoonist Soc.; A. Gld.; Westport AC. *Work*: Father Duffy Mem., 165th Reg. Armory, N.Y.; murals in homes, restaurants and hotels. *Exhibited*: regional and other exhibitions. Illus. of teenage books, biographies. Cartoonist of syndicated strip, "Ted Towers."

ASHER, LILA OLIVER—*Painter, Des., T., S.*
4100 Thornapple St., Chevy Chase 15, Md.

B. Philadelphia, Pa., Nov. 15, 1921. *Studied*: PMSchIA, and with Frank B. A. Linton. *Member*: Soc. Wash. A. *Awards*: prizes, Metropolitan State A. Exh., 1949, 1950; CGA, 1956; Chevy Chase A. Fair, 1957, 1958. *Work*: Howard Univ.; Barnett Aden Gal.; CGA. *Exhibited*: PAFA, 1941; Barnett Aden Gal., 1951 (one-man); Soc. Wash. A., 1949, 1952; CGA, 1947, 1949, 1951; Wash. Ceramic Show, 1948; Am. Vet. Exh., 1948; Metropolitan State A. Exh., 1948, 1950; A. Cooperative, 1948; Whyte Gal., 1949, 1950; Woodmere A. Gal., Phila. Pa., 1949, 1950; Wash. WC Soc., 1949; Soc. Wash. Pr. M., 1949-1951; Wm. C. Blood Gal., 1955, Phila. (one-man); A. Cl., Wash., D.C., 1957 (one-man). Executed 3600 portraits of servicemen in Army & Navy Hospitals for USO. *Position*: Instr., Dept. A., Howard Univ., Washington, D.C., 1948-1951; Instr., Wilson T. Col., Washington, D.C., 1952-1954.

ASHERMAN, DAVID G(UY)—
Painter, L., W., T., Des., Lith.
142 East 18th St., New York 3, N.Y.; h. "River Rock," 22 Grasshopper Lane, Ogunquit, Me.

B. New York, N.Y., July 22, 1917. *Studied*: ASL, with Bridgman, Grosz, Kuniyoshi, Kantor, and others; Univ. Krakow and Warsaw, Poland; Univ. Hawaii; Columbia Univ.; Ogunquit Sch. Painting, with Robert Laurent, William von Schlegell. *Member*: NSMP; NAC; Hawaiian P. & S.; Honolulu Pr. M.; Ogunquit AA; AEA; ASL; Portland (Me.) Soc. A. *Awards*: prizes, John Wanamaker Competition, 1937; NAC, 1938; Honolulu Pr. M.; medal, Royal Drawing Soc., England, 1937; F., Kosciuszko Fnd., 1936. *Work*: Dept. of Defense, Wash. D.C.; murals, Friends Seminary, New York; Univ. Hawaii; Palama Settlement House, Honolulu; Nat. Recreation Assn. *Exhibited*: Ogunquit AA, 1947-1955; Hawaiian P. & S., 1952; Honolulu Pr. M., 1951; Kennebunk Mus. A., 1947-1949; ASL, 1949; NSMP, 1956; NAC, 1937-1939, 1947, 1948. Contributor to art magazines and newspapers. *Position*: Instr., King-Coit Sch., New York, N.Y.; Dept. of Hospitals, N.Y.; NYU-Bellevue Inst. of Physical Medicine & Rehabilitation; Bd., Veterans Affairs Com., ASL, 1949; Com. on Foreign Art Students, Inst. International Edu., 1950; War A. & Combat Observer, 1942-45.*

ASHTON, ETHEL V.—*Painter, Gr.*
2022 Walnut St., Philadelphia 3, Pa.

B. Philadelphia, Pa. *Studied*: Moore Inst. A. Sc. & Indst.; PAFA, *Member*: Phila. A. All.; AEA; F., PAFA; Am. Color Pr. Soc. *Awards*: Phila. Sketch Cl., 1937, 1945; DaVinci All., 1943; F., PAFA, 1943, 1945; gold medal, DaVinci Soc., 1955; Chas. K. Smith prize, Woodmere A. Gal., 1956. *Work*: mural, USPO, Tunkhannock, Pa. *Exhibited*: Carnegie Inst., 1944-1946; Am. Color Pr. Soc., 1943-1955; LC, 1943-1946; NAD, 1946; Northwest Pr. M., 1946; PAFA, 1955; SFMA, 1941, 1946; Phila. A. All., 1930-1955; Phila, Pr. Cl., 1939-1948; DaVinci All., 1939-1955; Phila. Sketch Cl., 1928-1946; Ellen Donovan Gal., 1951, 1952; Pyramid Cl., 1948-1958; Woodmere Gal., 1951, 1955.

ASKENAZY, MISCHA—*Painter*
547 North McCadden Place, Los Angeles 4, Cal.

B. Odessa, Russia, Feb. 22, 1888. *Studied*: NAD; France and Italy. *Member*: Soc. Western Painters; Cal. AC; Los Angeles AA; Laguna Beach AA. *Awards*: prizes, Oakland A. Mus., 1952; M. H. deYoung Mus. A., 1950, 1952, 1955; Laguna Beach AA, 1951-1953; Cal. AC, 1951-1955; Cal. State Fair, 1934, 1936, 1954; medal, Los A. Mus. A., 1939. *Work*: many ports., paintings, in private collections, U.S. and abroad. *Exhibited*: Los A. Mus. A.; M. H. deYoung Mus. A.; Oakland A. Mus.; NAD; PAFA, and others.*

ASKIN, JULES—
Painter, Des., T., L., W., Cr., Restorer
7 South Fullerton Ave.; h. 21 South Mountain Ave., Montclair, N.J.

B. Baltimore, Md. *Studied*: Maryland Inst.; Johns Hopkins Univ.; PAFA; City Col., New York, N.Y.; Mt. Vernon Inst., Baltimore, and with C. Y. Turner, Joseph Lauber, Ephraim Keyser, Charles Grafly, Daniel Garber, Joseph Pierson, Nathan Hale, Robert Vonnoh, Henry McCarter. *Member*: CAA; Montclair AA; Maryland Hist. Soc. *Awards*: Nat. Hon. Certif., Freedoms Fnd., 1955. *Work*: Tropical plants, Nann's Florists, Montclair, N.J.; Hist. bas-reliefs, Temple Sharey Tfilo, East Orange, N.J.; work in private coll., apartments. Many portraits. Contributor to Art, Fashion and Theatre magazines. Lectures: "Art Appreciation," "Children in Art," "Art Past and Present," "Trends in Art," etc., to Service Clubs, Art Associations, Parent-Teacher Associations. Restorer of fine paintings, American and European.*

ASPEN, PHYLLIS CAMPBELL (Mrs.)—
Educator, S., L.
Nebraska State College; h. 805 West 24th St., Kearney, Neb.

B. Broken Bow, Neb., Apr. 30, 1910. *Studied*: Chicago Acad. FA; National Col. of Edu., Evanston, Ill., B.E.; Evanston Acad. FA; Sch. A. & Crafts, Detroit; Univ. Denver; Nebraska State Col., M.A., and with R. Weisenborn, S. Sarkisian, Gwen Lux, Vance Kirkland. *Member*:

NAA; NEA; Eastern AA; WAA. *Awards*: prizes, WAC, 1946, 1947; Ceramic Exh., Wichita, Kans., 1949. *Work*: Joslyn Mem. Mus.; WAC. Many portrait commissions. *Exhibited*: Joslyn Mem. Mus., 1944, 1947, 1948, 1957; Lincoln A. Gld., 1947, 1948; Nebraska AA, 1949; WAC, 1946, 1947, 1951; Sioux City A. Center, 1948; Springfield (Mo.) A. Mus., 1950, 1951; Denver A. Mus., 1948; Wichita, Kans., 1959. *Position*: Instr., A. Dept., Nebraska State College, Kearney, Neb., 1946- .

ATHERTON, J. CARLTON—*Craftsman, E.*
Ohio State University; h. 474 Hutton Place, Columbus 15, Ohio

B. Taylor, Pa., Jan. 17, 1900. *Studied*: Syracuse Univ., with Adelaide Robineau; PIA Sch.; Sevres, France, with Taxile Doat. *Awards*: special certif., Syracuse Univ.; Certif., PIA Sch.; numerous prizes in exhibitions. *Work*: MMA; WMA; SFMA. *Exhibited*: Syracuse Nat. Ceramic Exh., and Traveling Exh. of ceramics, and others. Author: Historical Introduction to "Ceramic Whitewares," by Rexford Newcomb, Jr., 1947. Contributor to Design Magazine; Ceramic Monthly. Lectures on Ceramic Art History, to museums, art schools and university groups. *Position*: Prof., Pottery and Ceramic History, Ohio State Univ., Columbus, Ohio.

ATKIN, MILDRED TOMMY (Mrs. Fisher Winston)—
Painter
895 Park Ave., New York 21, N. Y.

B. New York, N.Y. *Studied*: Metropolitan A. Sch., and with Winold Reiss, Arthur Schweider. *Member*: NAWA; AEA; Brooklyn Soc. A.; P. & S. of New Jersey; Pen & Brush Cl.; N.Y. Soc. Women A.; Nat. Soc. of Painters in Casein. *Work*: Washington County Mus. FA, Hagerstown, Md.; Robert Hull Fleming Mus., Burlington, Vt.; Georgia Mus. A., Athens, Ga. *Exhibited*: Montross Gal., 1935, 1937-1939; Bonestell Gal., 1944, 1945 (one-man); NAD, 1948, 1950-1955; Argent Gal., 1949-1952; Lighthouse, 1951; WMAA, 1951; Ludwig-Baumann Contemp. A. Exh., 1952; Colony Restaurant, 1949-1952 (one-man); Barzansky Gal., 1953-1955; Riverside Mus., 1953; Stedelijke Mus., Amsterdam, Holland, 1956; Brussels, Belgium, 1956; Bern, Switzerland, 1957; Chase Gal., 1957, 1958; and in other museums and universities in U.S. and Europe. *Positions*: Instr., Albert Pels A. Sch., New York, 1952; Dir., N.Y. Chapter, AEA, 1952-1955, 1956-1958; Exec. Bd., NAWA, 1952-1954, 1955-1957, Treas., 1957-1959.

ATKINS, DAVID—*Painter, Lith., L.*
217 West 29th St. (1); h. 850 East 175th St., New York 60, N.Y.

B. Waterbury, Conn., Nov. 28, 1910. *Studied*: ASL, with Kenneth Hayes Miller, William von Schlegel; NAD, with Sidney Dickinson, Leon Kroll; Edu. All. A. Sch., with Abbo Ostrowsky. *Member*: Lg. Present Day A. (Vice-Chm.); Horizon Group (Corr. Sec.). *Awards*: prize, Lg. Present Day A., 1948; Knickerbocker A.; Village A. Center. *Exhibited*: Riverside Mus., 1956, 1957; Regina, Gal., 1956; James Gal., 1957; Kaufman Gal., 1957; Bodley Gal., 1957; Horizon Group, 1958; Village A. Center, 1958, and other galleries in prior years.

ATKINSON, ALICA (Mrs. G. Chychele Waterston)—
Painter, T.
691 Great Pond Rd., North Andover, Mass.

B. Brookline, Mass., Dec. 10, 1905. *Studied*: BMFA Sch.; ASL; Fontainebleau Sch. A. *Awards*: prize Jr. Lg. Exh., Boston, 1931; Fitchburg AA, 1947; South County AA, 1954, 1958; Merrimac Valley Exh., 1953. *Exhibited*: PAFA, 1937; Salon des Beaux-Arts, Paris, 1938; AGAA, 1939, 1944, 1945, 1949-1952; Jordan-Marsh, 1943, 1945, 1952, 1958; South County AA, 1944, 1945, 1949-50, 1954, 1958; Kraushaar Gal., 1949, 1950, 1951; Margaret Brown Gal., 1949, 1950; Boston Soc. Indp. A., 1950, 1958; Copley A. Soc., Boston, 1955 (one-man); Vose Gal., 1955; Newport, R.I., 1955; Fitchburg A. Mus., 1955; Fontainebleau Alumni Exh., New York, N.Y., 1954; Logan Airport, 1958; John Esther Gal., Andover, Mass., 1958 (one-man); Studio Cl., N.Y., 1958 (one-man); St. Gaudens Mem., 1958; A. Center, Marion, Mass., 1959 (one-man); Greenwich (Conn.) AA, 1959 (one-man). *Position*: A. Dir., Brook School, North Andover, Mass., 1936- ; A. Dir., South County AA, Kingston, R.I., 1950-1955.

ATKINSON, RUTH M. (Mrs. F. C.)—*Painter*
Summit, Miss.

B. Hazlehurst, Miss., Feb. 14, 1914. *Studied*: Mississippi State Col. for Women; Southwest Jr. Col., and with Ralph Hudson, Karl Zerbe, Fred Conway, Lamar Dodd, and others. *Member*: New Orleans AA; Mississippi AA; Allison A. Colony. *Awards*: prizes, Allison A. Colony, 1953-1955; Mississippi AA, 1956. *Work*: murals, Church of God, McComb, Miss.; Progressive Bank, Summit, Miss. *Exhibited*: Miss. AA, 1956, 1957; New Orleans AA, 1956-1958; "Mid-South," Memphis, 1956; Allison A. Colony, 1953-1958; Louisiana A. Comm. Gal., 1958; Mississippi State Col. for Women, 1955; 331 Gallery and Circle Theatre, New Orleans, 1958. Co-author: "Camellia Magic," 1950.

ATKYNS, (WILLIE) LEE (JR.)—
Painter, T., Gr., S., L., I.
4712 Wisconsin Ave., Washington 16, D.C.; s. Lee Atkyns Puzzletown Art Studio, Duncansville, Pa.

B., Washington, D.C., Sept. 13, 1913. *Member*: Soc. Wash. A.; Wash. WC Cl.; Puzzletown A. Gld.; All. A. Johnstown; Indiana (Pa.) AA; Wash. AC; Am. A. Lg.; Landscape Cl., Wash. *Awards*: prizes, Soc. Wash. A., 1947, 1954; Wash. AC, 1946; All. A. Johnstown, 1947; 1948, 1949, 1950, 1953; Landscape Cl., Wash., 1954, 1956; Indiana AA, 1954; Interdenominational Religious Exh., Wash., D.C., 1957; Interdenominational AAPL, 1954. *Exhibited*: Butler AI; Carnegie Inst.; Univ. Chicago; AWS; NAD; Wash. AC; Smithsonian Inst.; CGA; Phillips Mem. Gal.; Whyte Gal.; Toledo Mus. A.; Springfield AA; L.D.M. Sweat Mem. A. Mus.; Utah State Inst.; Terry AI; Catholic Univ.; Indiana State T. Col.; BMA, and 23 one-man exhs. to date. *Work*: Phillips Mem. Gal.; Talladega Col., Alabama; All. A. Johnstown; Altoona (Pa.) H.S.; Hospital, Lexington, Ky.; private coll. U.S. and abroad. *Position*: Dir., Lee Atkyns Studio & Sch., Washington, D.C. & Duncansville, Pa.

ATTARDI, THOMAS—*Painter, T.*
R.F.D. #2, Hopewell Junction, N.Y.

B. Italy, Sept. 10, 1900. *Studied*: NAD; ASL; DaVinci Sch. A., with Lockman, Bernecker. *Member*: Springfield A. Lg.; A.Lg.Am.; Fishkill A. Group. *Awards*: prizes, NAD, 1924. *Exhibited*: CGA; WFNY 1939; Springfield A. Mus.; Seligman Gal., 1932; Newark Mus., 1929; Midtown Gal., 1934, 1936; All.A.Am., 1946; Audubon A., 1953, 1954; Bennett Col., Milbrook, N.Y., 1958 (one-man). *Positions*: Lecturer and Demonstrator, Art Life-Craft Studio, New York, 1953-1955; Instr., Adult Edu., Poughkeepsie H.S. and Wappinger Central Sch., 1957-58.

ATTRIDGE, MRS. IRMA GERTRUDE—*Painter*
9450 Cherokee Lane, Beverly Hills, Cal.

B. Chicago, Ill., Nov. 21, 1894. *Studied*: Chouinard AI. *Member*: AEA; Cal. WC. Soc.; Women Painters of the West. *Awards*: prizes, Los A. Mus. A., 1944; Los A. Pub. Lib., 1943, 1946; Whittier AA, 1954; City Hall, Los Angeles, 1953, 1954; Los Angeles Greek Theatre, 1951; Bowers Mem. Mus., 1952; Frye Mus., Seattle, Wash., 1957. *Work*: USO portraits, Army Hospitals, Italy. *Exhibited*: SFMA, 1942; Oakland A. Mus., 1943, 1952-1954; Los A. Mus. A., 1940, 1945, 1954, 1955; Sacramento Mus. Assn.; San Diego FA. Soc.; Santa Barbara Mus. A., 1951; Los A. County Fair, 1951; Pasadena AI, 1953-1955; Denver A. Mus., 1952, 1953. *Position*: Vice-Pres., AEA, So. Cal. Chapter, 1957-58.

ATWATER, MARY MEIGS—*Designer, T., W., L.*
6120 South 23rd East, Salt Lake City 7, Utah

B. Rock Island, Ill., Feb. 28, 1878. *Studied*: AIC; Chicago A. Acad.; Julian Acad., Paris, and with Rafael Collin. Author: "Shuttle-Craft Book of American Hand Weaving"; "Byways for Hand Weavers"; "Guatemala Visited"; pamphlets on weaving and rug making. Conducts weaving institutes at colleges and universities in the U.S. and Canada. Lectures on hand weaving to guilds and university classes.*

AUCELLO, SALVATORE L.—*Painter, S., C., Des.*
30 Beschoff St., Chappaqua, N.Y.

B. Italy, Dec. 12, 1903, *Studied*: NAD, with Hawthorne, Robinson, *Awards*: med., prizes, NAD, 1924, 1926, 1927,

1929. *Member*: Tiffany Fnd., Chicago SA; A. Lg. Am.; Midwest Des. & Craftsmen; AAPL; South Side Community A. Center. *Work*: Mural, Chrysler Bldg., N.Y.; Nelson A. Gal., Kansas City, Mo; ceramics and mosaics in hotels, restaurants and public bldgs. Mosaic panels, Union Station, Chicago; Fred Harvey Shop, Union Station, Chicago; Skokie (Ill.) Shopping Center. *Exhibited*: Oakland A. Gal., 1944, 1945; Milwaukee AI; Findlay Gal., 1945; AIC; Mandel Bros.; Evanston A. Lg.; Oak Park A. Lg.

AUCHMOODY, ELAINE PLISHKER—*Painter, L.*
46-19 259th St., Great Neck, L.I., N.Y.

B. New York, N.Y., Apr. 8, 1910. *Studied*: Traphagen Sch. Des.; Grand Central Sch. A.; ASL. *Member*: NAWA. *Awards*: prizes, Parkersburg FA Center; P.&S. Soc., N.J.; Douglaston A. Lg.; Great Neck AA. *Work*: Dayton AI. *Exhibited*: CGA; Carnegie Inst.; CAM; Butler AI; Chicago AC; Mint Mus. A; Denver A. Mus.; Parkersburg FA Center; Springfield Mus. A.*

AUERBACH-LEVY, WILLIAM—*Etcher, I., L., P., T.*
Kobold, Glendale Rd., Ossining, N.Y.

B. Russia, Feb. 14, 1889. *Studied*: NAD; Julian Acad., Paris, France, with Jean Paul Laurens. *Member*: NA; SC; Chicago SE; SAGA. *Awards*: prizes, NAD, 1921, 1925, Samuel F. B. Morse gold medal, 1958; med., Cal. Pr. M., 1923; SC, 1923, 1952, 1956; PAFA, 1924; Guggenheim F., 1928. *Work*: AIC, BMFA; WMA; N.Y. Pub. Lib.; LC; Honolulu Acad. A; Detroit Inst. A. I., Collier's, New Yorker, and other magazines. Author: "Is That Me?," 1947; "The Art of Caricature," 1951.

AUNIO, IRENE (Mrs. Saasto)—*Painter*
1032 78th St., Brooklyn 28, N.Y.

B. Finland, Mar. 27, 1919. *Studied*: ASL, with Bernard Klonis, Robert Brackman. *Member*: AWS; All. A. Am.; NAWA; Brooklyn Soc. A. *Awards*: prizes, NAWA, 1952, 1958; Pen & Brush Cl., 1953; Ranger purchase prize, NAD, 1953; Catherine L. Wolfe A. Cl., 1955, 1957; ASL, Johnson Merit Scholarship, 1954-55; Michael Engel award 1958; *Work*: ASL; NAD; ETC Gal., Chicago; Seton Hall Univ. *Exhibited*: AWS, 1950-1955; All. A. Am., 1952-1955; Brooklyn Soc. A., 1952-1956; NAWA, 1951-1955; Alabama WC Soc., 1952, 1953; NAC, 1952-1955 (Pen & Brush Cl.) *Position*: Instr. A., Adult Edu. Program.

AURNER, KATHRYN DAYTON (Mrs. Robert R.)—
Painter, Gr., E., W.
Postoffice Box 3434, Carmel, Cal.

B. Iowa City, Iowa. *Studied*: State Univ. of Iowa, B.A.; Carnegie Inst.; Univ. of Wisconsin, and with Charles Cumming, Norwood McGilvary, Barse Miller, and Frederick Taubes. *Exhibited*: Madison and Milwaukee, Wis.; Washington, D.C.; Watsonville, Cal.; Santa Cruz, Cal.; Carmel, Cal.; one-man: Madison, Wis., 1948; Oklahoma City, 1953; Salem, Ore., 1954; Crocker A. Gal., Sacramento, Cal., 1955. *Positions*: Supv. Public School Art, Madison, Wis., to 1940; Dir., Soldier A. Program, Truax Field, Madison, Wis., 1943-1946; Member Bd. Dir., Carmel AA, 1953-1954; Sec. of the Bd., 1956-1957. Contributor to art magazines and newspapers.

AUSTIN, DARREL—*Painter*
c/o Perls Galleries, 1016 Madison Ave., New York 21, N.Y.

B. Raymond, Wash., June 25, 1907. *Studied*: Univ. Oregon. *Work*: MMA; MModA; Detroit Inst. A.; William Rockhill Nelson Gal. A.; Rochester Mem. A. Gal.; Albright A. Gal.; Smith Col. Mus.; BMFA; Clearwater A. Mus.; PMG; mural, Medical Col., Portland, Ore. *Exhibited*: annual national exh., 1941- .*

AUSTRIAN, FLORENCE H(OCHSCHILD)
(Mrs. Charles R.)—Painter
1417 Eutaw Pl., Baltimore 17, Md.

B. Baltimore, Md., Sept. 8, 1889. *Studied*: Goucher Col., A.B., and with Charles Hawthorne, S. Edwin Whiteman, Leon Kroll, John Sloan. *Member*: NAWA; AEA. *Awards*: prizes, med., Maryland Inst., 1931; Mun. Mus., Baltimore, 1945; News Post-Century Theatre prize,

1934; Fed. Women's Cl., 1935. *Work*: Mun. Mus., Baltimore. *Exhibited*: CGA, 1941; PAFA, 1932, 1933; PMG; NAWA; BMA, 1931 (one-man), 1951; Maryland Inst. (one-man); Delphic Studios, N.Y.; College Cl., Baltimore; Peale Mus. A., 1950; Little Theatre, Baltimore, 1951; Contemporary Gal.; Hilltop Theatre, Baltimore, 1954 (one-man); Rehoboth (Del.) A. Lg., 1958 (one-man).

AUVIL, KENNETH WILLIAM—
Serigrapher, Lith., Et., T., P.
4016 Blackford Ave., San Jose 28, Cal.

B. Ryderwood, Wash., Dec. 18, 1931. *Studied*: Univ. of Washington, B.A., M.F.A. *Member*: AEA; Northwest Pr. M. *Awards*: prizes, Wichita AA, 1956; Northwest Pr. M., 1953; Pacific Northwest A. & Crafts Fair, Bellevue, Wash., 1953-1956, 1958; Washington Artists, 1953, 1954. *Work*: prints: U.S. Information Service; Victoria & Albert Mus., London, England; Bibliotheque Nationale, Paris, France; Wichita AA; Henry Gallery, Seattle; Arizona State Col., Tempe, Ariz. *Exhibited*: 4th Biennale, Italy, 1956; SFMA, 1956; Northwest Pr. M., 1953, 1954, 1957; Dallas, Tex., Print Exh., 1953; Art Schools, USA, 1954; Wichita, 1955, 1956; Northwest Pr. M. Regional Exh., 1953-1955; Washington Artists, 1953-1956; Pacific Northwest Arts & Crafts, 1953-1958; Oakland A. Mus., 1958. *Positions*: Instr., Printmaking & Des., San Jose State College, Cal.; Tech. Illustrator, Boeing Aircraft Co., 1953-56; Pres., Northwest Pr. M., 1954-56.

AVERY, FRANCES—*Painter, T.*
67 Seventh Ave., New York 11, N.Y.

B. Kitchner, Ont., Canada. *Studied*: Wicker's Sch. FA, Detroit, Mich.; ASL. *Member*: NAWA; N.Y. Soc. Women A.; AEA. *Awards*: Yolens Interiors award for contemp. oil, Silvermine Gld. A., 1956. *Work*: Georgia Mus. A., Athens. *Position*: Faculty, Bergen Sch., Jersey City, N.J.; Adelphi College, N.Y.; YWCA, Brooklyn, N.Y.

AVERY, MILTON—*Painter*
294 West 11th St., New York 14, N.Y.

B. Altmar, N.Y., Mar. 7, 1893. *Studied*: Conn. Lg. A. Students. *Member*: Fed. Mod. P. & S.; Soc. Indp. A. *Awards*: prizes, Conn. Acad. FA, 1930; AIC, 1932; BMA, 1949; Boston A. Festival, 1958. *Work*: Newark Mus.; BM; PMG; Albright A. Gal.; PAFA; Barnes Fnd.; MMA; WMAA; MMod.A. *Exhibited*: PAFA, 1945; Carnegie Inst., 1944; AIC; CGA; BM; Newark Mus.; Albright A. Gal. Retrospective exhibitions at: BMA; Phillips Coll., Wash., D.C.; Wadsworth Atheneum, Hartford; Lowe Gal. A., Coral Gables; Inst. Contemporary A., Boston. One-man: Borgenicht Gal., New York, 1954, 1958.

AVERY, MYRTILLA—*Museum Director, E.*
425 West 23rd St., New York 11, N.Y.

B. Katonah, N.Y. *Studied*: Wellesley Col., B.A., M.A.; Univ. State of N.Y., B.L.S.; Radcliffe Col., Ph.D. *Member*: Mediaeval Acad. Am.; CAA; Archaeological Inst. Am. Contributor to Art Bulletin; College Art Journal (Rome). *Positions*: Hon. Dir., CAA; Dir., Farnsworth A. Mus., Prof. A., 1913-37, Prof. A. Emeritus, Wellesley Col., Wellesley, Mass., 1937 to date.†

AVERY, RALPH H.—*Painter, Comm. A.*
60 North Fitzhugh St. (14); h. 2 Atkinson St., Rochester 8, N.Y.

B. Savannah, Ga., Sept. 3, 1906. *Studied*: Rochester Inst. Technology; Louis Comfort Tiffany Fnd., Oyster Bay, N.Y. *Member*: ANA; AWS; Rochester A. Cl. *Awards*: Herbert L. Pratt purchase award, AWS, 1954; M. Grumbacher purchase prize and Rudolf Lesch purchase prize, AWS, 1957; Citation, American Artist Magazine, 1954. *Work*: Rochester Mem. A. Gal.; Charles and Emma Frye A. Mus., Seattle, Wash. *Exhibited*: NAD, 1956, 1958; AWS, 1952-1955, 1957, 1958; Roberson Mem. Center, 1957; N.Y. State Fair, 1958; Rochester A. Cl., 1946-1958; Rochester-Finger Lakes Exhs., 1946-1958; one-man: Smithsonian Inst., 1944; Arnot A. Gal., Elmira, N.Y., 1953; Telfair Acad., Savannah, 1952. Cover paintings for Reader's Digest, Mar. & Apr., 1957, Jan. & Apr. & Dec., 1958. Illus., "The Instructor" magazine.

AVISON, GEORGE (ALFRED)—Illustrator, P., W.

21 Woodland Rd., New Canaan, Conn.

B. Norwalk, Conn., May 6, 1885. *Studied*: Chase Sch. A.; N.Y. Sch. A. *Member*: Westport A. Cl.; AAPL. *Awards*: AAPL, 1953, 1956, 1957, 1958. *Work*: mural, New Canaan Town Hall; Roger Ludlowe H.S., Fairfield, Conn.; Norwalk (Conn.) H.S.; Rowayton (Conn.) Lib. *Exhibited*: Argent Gal.; Silvermine Gld. A.; Ogunquit A. Center; Anderson Gal., Riverside Mus.; NAC. I., "Sunflight"; "White Captive of The Sioux"; "Radar Commandos"; "Treasure Beyond Red Mesa," and many others. I., and co-author, with H. D. Nadig, "They Stood Alone," 1955. Author, I., "Uncle Sam's Army," "Uncle Sam's Navy," "Uncle Sam's Marines," "Lone Wagon into Danger." Illus. for "Golden Deeds" in Book of Knowledge, and many others.

AVLON-DAPHNIS, HELEN—Painter, T.

400 West 23rd St., New York, N.Y.

B. New York, N.Y., June 18, 1932. *Studied*: Hunter Col., B.F.A., M.A. *Member*: Com. on A. Edu., MModA. *Awards*: Scholarships, BMSch.; Colo. Springs FA Center. *Exhibited*: Colo. Springs FA Center, 1951; N.Y. City Center, 1952; Contemp. A., 1953; Forum, 1954; Panoras Gal., 1954, 1955; Silvermine Gld., A., 1955; BM, 1953; Provincetown AA; Schenectady Mus. A., 1957; Rochester Mem. A. Gal.; Ohio Univ., Athens, Ohio, 1958; Northern Illinois State T. Col.; Saginaw Mus. A.; Rockford AA; BM, 1958. *Position*: A.T., Adults and children, Painting & Drawing: Sch. Indust. A., Erasmus Hall H.S.; Manual Training H.S.; Washington Irving Adult Art Edu.; BM children's Div.; Horace Mann Sch. and Haaren H.S., New York, N.Y. and Brooklyn, N.Y.

AYER, MARGARET—Illustrator

129 East 10th St., New York 3, N.Y.; s. Westport, Conn.

B. New York, N.Y. *Studied*: PMSchIA, and with Beloul in Paris. *Member*: SI. I., children's books and for magazines.

AYER, RALPH DWIGHT—Painter, T.

14 Cleveland Ave., Woburn, Mass.

B. Woburn, Mass., Apr. 2, 1909. *Studied*: Mass. Sch. A.; BMFA Sch., with Frederick Bosley. *Member*: Boston Soc. Indp. A. *Awards*: medal, Mass. Sch. A., 1930; Palm Beach A. Center, 1933. *Exhibited*: Ogunquit A. Center, 1933, 1934; Irvington A. & Mus. Assn.; 1945; Portland SA, 1949; Phila. Sketch Cl., 1945; Springfield A. Lg., 1945; Yonkers AA, 1945; New England A., 1949; New Hope, Pa., 1956 (one-man). *Work*: murals, Choate Mem. Hospital, Woburn, Mass.

AYMAR, GORDON CHRISTIAN—
Portrait Painter, Des.

Rings End Rd., Noroton, Conn.

B. East Orange, N.J., July 24, 1893. *Studied*: Yale Univ., A.B., BMFA Sch. *Member*: A. Dir. Cl.; Nat. Soc. A. Dir.; AWS. *Awards*: prizes, Nat. Soc. A. Dir., 1951; A. Dir. Cl., 1954; Prout's Neck, Me.; Yale Cl., New York. *Work*: MModA.; Union Theological Seminary; private collections. *Exhibited*: One-man exhs., Dayton, Ohio; Montreal, Canada; Portraits, Inc., New York. Also in Stamford, Greenwich, Noroton, Darien, Conn.; Berkshire, Mass.; Century Assn., New York; AWS.

AYRES, MARTHA OATHOUT—
Sculptor, P., T., W., L.

11147 South Berendo Ave., Los Angeles 44, Cal.

B. Elkader, Iowa, Apr. 1, 1890. *Studied*: Carleton Col., B.A.; AIC. *Member*: Los Angeles AA; Art Section, Women's Cl.; F., Royal Soc. A., London, England; Prof. Artists Roost. *Awards*: prizes, A. Students Lg., Chicago, 1914; Los A. County Fair, 1915. *Work*: statues—Forest Lawn Cemetery, Glendale, Cal.; statues and bas-relief in many high schools, colleges and private homes. *Exhibited*: one-man exhs., Denver, Colo.; Pomona, Long Beach and Los Angeles, Cal.

BAAR, MARION (Mrs. Marion Baar Stanfield)—
Painter, T., W., L., Cr.

123 Compo Rd., Westport, Conn.

B. New York, N.Y., Sept. 22, 1899. *Studied*: ASL, with Frank Dumond, Johansen, Henri; in France, with A. & V. Charreton; College of Mt. St. Vincent, B.A. *Member*: NAWA; AFA; Westport AA; North Shore AA; Women P. & S. Soc. *Awards*: John W. Alexander prize for portraiture; the Johansen and Henri Scholarships. *Exhibited*: Nationally, in group and one-man exhibitions. Lectures on art education, history of art, art appreciation and color in design.

BABCOCK, ELIZABETH JONES (Mrs.)—Painter

172 East 71st St., New York 21, N. Y.

B. Keokuk, Iowa, July 19, 1887. *Studied*: Cincinnati Acad. A.; ASL; Fontainebleau, France; & with Duveneck, Chase, Despujols. *Member*: NSMP. *Work*: murals, Marine Hospital, N.Y.; triptychs, Army & Navy Hospitals, clubs & residences.*

BACA, CATHERINE EATON—Watercolorist

987 Sunnyhills Rd., Oakland 10, Cal.

B. Oakland, Cal., Jan. 18, 1907. *Studied*: Cal. Col. A. & Crafts, and with Phil Paradise. *Member*: Cal. WC Soc.; San F. Women A. *Awards*: prizes, Santa Cruz, Cal., 1948; Oakland A. Gal., 1952. *Exhibited*: AWS, 1949-1950; Audubon A., 1948-1952; PAFA, 1949-1952; NAC, 1951; Cal. WC Soc., 1948-1950; Cal. WC Soc. traveling exh., 1951; deYoung Mem. Mus., 1952; Passadena AI, 1952; Denver A. Mus., 1951, 1952; SFMA, 1952; San F. Women A., 1950-1952; Santa Cruz, Cal., 1948-1952; Oakland A. Gal., 1945-1952, 1953 (one-man).*

BACH, ALFONS—Designer, P.

Ridgeway Center; h. Haviland Rd., Stamford, Conn.

B. Germany, June 19, 1904. *Studied*: European schools. *Member*: F., IDI; Phila. A. All.; Silvermine Gld. A. *Awards*: med., IDI, 1942; prize, Silvermine Gld. A., 1950; des. award, Fifth Ave. Assn., 1954. *Work*: Designs for General Electric Co.; Heywood Wakefield Co.; Bigelow-Sanford Co.; Ridgeway Center; United Merchants Seneca Mills, and others. *Exhibited*: MMA, 1934, 1936, 1938; MModA.; New Jersey State Mus.; Phila. A. Center; Riverside Mus.; Los Angeles AA; Newark Mus. A.; Rockford AA; Babcock Gal., 1948 (one-man); Stamford Mus., 1954 (one-man). Contributor to consumer and trade publications; cover designs for national magazines.

BACH, E(MANUEL) FRANK—
Educator, S., Art Film Producer

Central Washington College; h. 19 Radio Rd., Ellensburg, Wash.

B. Schweidnitz, Germany, May 23, 1914. *Studied*: Colorado State Col. of Edu., B.A., M.A.; AIC, with Albin Polasek; Univ. Denver; grad. study Univ. Washington. *Member*: Univ. Film Producers Assn.; NAEA; PAA. *Work*: 10-13 art films distributed nationally. *Exhibited*: sculpture, Chicago, 1941; Greeley, Colo., 1948-49; Bellevue, Wash., 1951-1952. Contributor to School Arts, Arts & Activities, Educational Screen. *Position*: Asst. Prof. A., Central Washington Coll., Ellensburg, Wash., 1951-54; Asst. Prof. A., Edu. Univ. Wisconsin, Madison, Wis., 1954-1956; Assoc. Prof. A., Central Washington College, Ellensburg, Wash., 1956- ; Pres., Wash. AA, 1957-59.

BACH, OTTO KARL—
Museum Director, P., Cr., E., W., L., C.

Denver Art Museum; h. 1300 Logan St., Denver Colo.

B. Chicago, Ill., May 26, 1909. *Studied*: Dartmouth Col.; Univ. Paris; Univ. Chicago, M.A. *Member*: AA Mus.; Western Assn. A. Mus. Dir.; CAA; International Soc. for the Conservation of Museum Objects. *Awards*: Hon. degree, Doctor of Humanities, Univ. Denver, 1955; Extraordinary Services certif., City and County of Denver, 1955. Author: "A New Way to Paul Klee"; "Life in America"; "Under Every Roof," and others. *Position*: L., Univ. of Denver Sch. A., 1946- ; Dir., Grand Rapids A. Gal., 1934-44; Dir., Denver A. Mus., Denver, Colo., 1944- .

BACH, RICHARD (FRANZ)—
Educational Director, T., L., W.

American Institute of Decorators, New York, N.Y.; h. Grosvenor Ave., Riverdale 71, N.Y.

B. New York, N.Y., June 29, 1887. *Studied*: Columbia Univ., A.B. *Awards*: Friedsam medal, Indst. A., 1930; Cultural Leadership Medal, Sterling Silversmiths Gld., 1958.

Member: Hon.: AIA; Arch. Lg., N.Y.; AID; NSMP; NSS; Am. Craftsmen's Council; Artist-Craftsmen; A. Dir. Cl.; Indst. Des. Inst.; Mus. Council of N.Y.; Svenska Slojdforeningen, Stockholm; Nat. Soc. A. Dir.; also AAMus. Boards & Councils: AFA, Sec., 1937-39, 1954-55, Trustee, 1937 to date, Hon. V-Pres., 1956 to date; Am. Handicraft Council, Trustee, 1939-42; Comm. on Motion Pictures in Adult Edu., 1946-50; N.Y. Adult Edu. Council, Bd. Dir., 1941-50; Sch. A. Lg. of N.Y., Trustee, 1941 to date, Vice-Pres., 1946-51, Pres., 1951-52; Am. Craftsmen's Council, Trustee, 1942-1948; Mus. Contemp. Crafts, Trustee, 1956-1958; CUASch., Advisory Council, 1943- , Chm., 1945-54; Nat. Council Des. Protection, 1933-35; Nat. Ceramic Advisory Council, 1944-53; Nat. Assn. of Schs. of Des., Consultant, 1946 to date; Cooper Union Mus. Advisory Council, 1952- , Chm., 1953- . Dir., Survey Place of Arts in Am. Life, Carnegie Corp., 1924; Member, Hoover Comm. on Int. Exp. of Mod. Dec. & Indst. A., Paris, 1925; Carnegie Corp. & Social Science Research Council, 1931; Pres., Hoover's Research Comm. on Social Trends, 1925; United Nations, Dept. Public Information, Advisor, 1947-52; Bd. of Edu., City of N.Y., Com. on Vocational & Extension Edu., 1948-52; John Wesley Hyatt Award in Plastics, Chm., 1942-53; FA Fed., N.Y., 1946- , Pres., 1948-50, Hon. Vice-Pres., 1952- ; Assoc. Ed., Good Furniture & Decoration, 1916-18; Ed., 1930-31; Assoc. Ed., Magazine of Art, 1930-32; Contributing Ed., Journal of AIA, 1927-28. *Exhibitions:* 15 Am. & international exhs. contemp. indst. arts and crafts at MMA; 72 installations of circulating exhibitions in N.Y. schools and libraries. *Position:* Cur. & Inst., Sch. Arch., Columbia Univ., 1909-19; AFA Extension Sec., 1919-28; MMA, Assoc. in Indst. A., 1918-29, Dir. of Indst. Relations, 1929-41, Dean of Edu. & Ext., 1941-49; Consultant in Indst. A., 1949-52; Edu. Advisor, AID, 1952- .

BACHE, MARTHA MOFFETT (Mrs.)—Painter, T., W.
4532 Macomb St., N.W., Washington 16, D.C.

B. Flint, Mich., Oct. 26, 1893. *Studied:* PIASch., with Ernest Watson; AIC; Chicago Acad. FA, with Lester Stevens, Andrea Zerega; Univ. Michigan. *Member:* Wash. Soc. FA; Min. P. S. & Gravers Soc.; AAPL. *Awards:* prizes, Garfinckels, Wash., D.C., 1936; Georgetown Gal., 1939; AAPL, 1950, 1957 (2); Min. P. S. & Gravers, 1956; Wash. AC, 1956, 1958; Art & Music Center, Bethesda, Md., 1953. *Exhibited:* ASMP; Soc. Wash. A.; CGA; NCFA; Trans-Lux Theatre, Wash., D.C. (one-man); Wash. AC; Georgetown Gal.; Georgetown Theatre, Garden Gate Restaurant, Wash., D.C., Wash. AC (all one-man). *Positions:* T., Wash., D.C. Pub. Sch. & Army hospitals.

BACHMURA, BARBARA LEE (Mrs. Frank T.)—
Painter, Gr., E., C.
108 29th Ave., South, Nashville, Tenn.

B. Detroit, Mich., Mar. 5, 1925. *Studied:* Wayne Univ., B.F.A., M.A.; Univ. Mexico; Mexican Art Workshop; Univ. Oslo and with F. H. Hayward, Carlos Merida and others. *Member:* Detroit Soc. Women P. & S.; Nashville A. Gld.; Michigan WC Soc. *Awards:* Fulbright Award, 1952. *Work:* Wayne Univ.; Denison Univ.; Motive Magazine; Vanderbilt Hospital and Nashville A. Gld., Nashville, Tenn.; Crandall A. Gal., Alliance, Ohio. *Exhibited:* in many Southern and Mid-Western exhibitions; one-man: Centennial Club; Capellan Gal., Oslo, Norway; A. Intl. Assoc., London, England; Detroit A. Market. *Positions:* Instr., Wayne Univ., 1946-47; St. Mary's Hall, Faribault, Minn., 1947-48; Asst. Prof. A., Denison Univ., 1951-55.

BACHRACH, GLADYS WERTHEIM—Painter
c/o Condon Riley Gallery, 24 East 67th St., New York 21, N.Y.

B. New York, N.Y., June 10, 1909. *Studied:* Columbia Univ. *Member:* AEA; Boston Soc. Indp. A.; Provincetown AA. *Awards:* Fla. Southern Col. 1952. *Work:* Fla. Southern Col. and in private collections national and international. *Exhibited:* Norfolk Mus. A. & Sc., 1951, 1952; Fla. Int. Exh., 1952; Ohio Wesleyan Univ., 1950; Gal. St. Etienne, 1951; Berkshire A. Center, 1951, 1952; Shore Studios, Provincetown, 1951, 1952; Cambridge AA, 1951; Contemporaries, 1952; AFI Gal., New York, 1952 (one-man); J. Myers Fnd., 1952; one-man: Gal. St. Etienne, 1949; Mint Mus. A., 1951; Loring A. Gal., Wickford, R.I., 1952; Massillon Mus., (Ohio), 1953; Neville Pub. Mus., Green Bay, Wis., 1953; Cayuga Mus. Hist. & Art, Auburn, N.Y., 1953; South Bend AA, 1954; Univ. Kentucky, 1954; Roosevelt Field A. Center, 1958; Condon Riley Gal., 1958 (one-man).

BACHTEL, CLAYTON—Educator
Cleveland Institute of Art, 11141 East Blvd., Cleveland 6, Ohio

Position: Asst. Dir., Cleveland Institute of Art, Cleveland, Ohio.*

BACIGALUPA, ANDREA—Painter, C.
626 Canyon Rd., Santa Fe, N.M.

B. Baltimore, Md., May 26, 1923. *Studied:* Maryland Inst. FA, with Jacques Maroger; ASL (Woodstock) with Arnold Blanch, Sigmund Menkes; Accademia di Belli Arti, Florence, Italy, with Ottone Rosai; Am. Univ., Biarritz, France, 1945 (U.S. Army sponsorship); Alfred Univ., with Daniel Rhodes. *Awards:* Bronze medallion, Maryland Inst. FA, 1950. *Member:* Santa Fe Assn. Arts. *Work:* murals, St. Stanley Catholic Church, Coatesville, Pa., 1950; ceramic tiles, Santa Fe, 1955. *Exhibited:* All Maryland Exh., 1949; New Mexico Ann., 1945; New Mexico Fiesta Exh., 1955, 1957, 1958; Biarritz, France, 1955; Woodstock, N.Y., 1949; one-man: Mus. New Mexico, 1955; "10 Santa Fe Artists," 1958.

BACKUS, STANDISH, Jr.—Painter, I., Des., Gr.
2626 Sycamore Canyon, Santa Barbara, Cal.

B. Detroit, Mich., Apr. 5, 1910. *Studied:* Princeton Univ., A.B.; Univ. Munich. *Member:* Cal. WC Soc.; AFA; AEA; AWS; Los Angeles AA; F., Intl. Inst. A. & Lets.; Santa Barbara AA. *Awards:* prizes, Cal. WC Soc., 1940; Oakland A. Gal., 1939; Cal. State Fair, 1948, 1949. *Work:* Santa Barbara Mus. A.; Utah State Col.; San Diego FA Soc.; mural, Beckman Instrument, Inc., 1955; Cal. WC Soc.; Los A. Mus. A.; U.S. Navy Dept., Wash., D.C. *Exhibited:* AIC, 1940; Los A. Mus. A., 1938-1940; Navy Combat Exh., 1945, 1946; BM; Denver A. Mus.; one-man: Santa Barbara Mus. A.; Detroit AI, and in Salt Lake City, San Francisco. *Position:* Naval Combat A., Pacific area & Japan, 1945; Instr., Univ. California Extension; official Navy artist, Byrd Expedition to South Pole, 1955-56.

BACON, IRVING R.—Painter, S., W.
4946 Southwest 7th St., Miami 44, Fla.

B. Fitchburg, Mass., Nov. 29, 1875. *Studied:* Gies A. Sch.; Detroit; Chase Sch. A.; Royal A. Acad., Munich, with Heinrich von Zugel, Carl von Marr. *Awards:* med., Royal Acad. A., Munich; prizes, Paris Salon; NAD; PAFA; Western A. *Work:* Louisville A. Gal.; Cody Coll., Cody, Wyo.; Royal Castle Mus., Sweden; Book Tower, Detroit; Edison Inst.; Ford Museum. Executed portraits of Henry Ford, Luther Burbank, Noah Webster, Mark Twain, Dr. George Washington Carver, Stephen Foster, John Burroughs and many others. Reproductions of early Ford inventions in the Ford Collection. *Exhibited:* NAD; PAFA; AIC; Western A.

BACON, PEGGY (BROOK)—
Painter, Gr., I., Cart., W.
20 East 13th St., New York 3, N.Y.

B. Ridgefield, Conn., May 2, 1895. *Studied:* N.Y.Sch. F. & App. A.; ASL. *Member:* NAD; SAGA; Nat. Inst. A. & Let. *Awards:* Guggenheim F., 1934; award, Nat. Acad. A. & Let., 1944. *Work:* MMA; WMAA; BM; MMoDA, etc. *Exhibited:* nationally. Author of 14 books and illustrator of 45 books. Contributor to New Yorker, Town & Country, Vanity Fair and other national magazines.

BADUE, DANIEL SERRA. See Serra, Daniel

BADURA, BERNARD—Painter, C.
North Main St., New Hope, Pa.

B. Milwaukee, Wis. *Studied:* Milwaukee Normal A. Sch., with George Oberteuffer; PAFA, with Arthur Carles, Daniel Garber. *Awards:* Cresson traveling scholarship, PAFA. *Work:* PMA. *Exhibited:* CGA; NAD; CM; VMFA; PAFA; Hartford Mus.; New Haven Mus.

BADURA, FAYE SWENGEL. See Swengel, Faye

BAEB, HENRY R. (HANK)—Cartoonist, Comm. A.
7310 Kentucky St., Dearborn, Mich.

B. Nova Scotia, Canada, Nov. 22, 1922. *Studied:* Sir George Williams Col., Montreal; Valentine Sch. Comm.

A., Montreal. *Exhibited*: Intl. Humor Exh., Bordighera, Italy, 1957 (awarded Golden Palm Trophy). *Work*: "Best Cartoons of 1953-54-55-56-57"; "Treasury of Sports Cartoons," 1957; "Look on the Light Side" (cartoons from Look Magazine), 1957; "One Moment, Sir" (cartoons from Sat. Eve. Post), 1957, and other volumes. Contributor to Sat. Eve. Post; True; Look; and other magazines; King Features Syndicate; McNaught Syndicate. *Position*: A. Dir., Henning & Cheadle, N.Y., 1952-55.

BAEHR, FRANCINE (Mrs.)—Painter
45 Sutton Place, South, Apt. 14K, New York 22, N.Y.

B. Chicago, Ill., July 21, 1897. *Studied*: Univ. Chicago; Julian Acad., Grande Chaumiere, Paris. *Member*: NSMP. *Work*: mural, WFNY 1939; U.S. Public Health Service, Wash., D.C. *Exhibited*: Brooklyn SE; Chicago SE; Los Angeles, Cal.; Philadelphia, Pa.; New York, N.Y.

BAER, HOWARD—Painter, I., Cart.
30 East 14th St., New York 3, N.Y.

B. Finleyville, Pa., Feb. 14, 1906. *Studied*: Carnegie Inst., A.B. *Work*: MMA; Walker Mus., Youngstown, Ohio; Pentagon Archives of War, Wash., D.C., and in private coll. *Exhibited*: Carnegie Inst., 1949; Paris, France, 1950, 1958; CGA, 1949. Illus. children's book on China, and on India. Author, Illus., "Now This Now That," 1957. *Position*: Instr., Drawing and Composition, Henry St. Settlement; Parsons Sch. Des., New York, N.Y.

BAER, JOHN M.—Cartoonist, Des., W., Comm.A.
815 16th St., N.W., Washington, D.C.; h. 3809 East West Highway, Chevy Chase, Md.

B. Blackcreek, Wis., Mar. 29, 1886. *Studied*: Lawrence Col., A.B.; Fed. Sch. A., Minneapolis, Minn.; Nat. A. Sch., Washington, D.C. *Member*: Nat. Press Cl.; Am. Newspaper Gld. *Exhibited*: cartoons in several traveling exhs. Cartoonist for "Labor," weekly newspaper owned by Railroad Brotherhoods.

BAER, MARTIN—Painter, Et.
P.O. Box 2038, Carmel, Cal.

B. Chicago, Ill., Jan. 3, 1895. *Studied*: Smiths A. Acad., Chicago; AIC; State Acad., Munich; Ecole des Beaux-Arts, Paris. *Member*: AAPL; Carmel AA. *Work*: MModA; Los A. Mus. A.; San Diego FA Soc.; Palace Legion Honor; Eastman Mem. Fnd.; Oshkosh Pub. Mus.; Ft. Worth Mus. A.; Luxembourg Mus.; Musee du Jeu de Paume; Casablanca Mus., Morocco. *Exhibited*: Palace Legion Honor, 1943, 1946; one-man exh.: AIC, 1926-1931; Durand-Ruel, Paris, 1926; Galerie Jeune Peinture, Paris, 1928; Newhouse Gal., 1929, 1936, 1941; Santa Barbara Mus. A., 1942; San Diego FA Soc., 1942; Taylor Gal., 1942; Galerie M. Benezit, Paris, 1936.*

BAESEMANN, MARGARET MAASSEN—
Designer, P., E.
320 Macomber St., Chippewa Falls, Wis.

B. Milwaukee, Wis., Oct. 24, 1907. *Studied*: Layton Sch. A. *Member*: Wis. P. & S. *Exhibited*: AIC, 1930, 1934; Layton Sch. A.; Wisconsin P. & S.; Madison Salon; Wisconsin State Fair; Mt. Mary Col.; traveling exh., Milwaukee AI, 1951-52. *Position*: Instr. A., Chippewa Falls Vocational Sch.; Supt. A. & Crafts Dept. of Northern Wisconsin Dist. Fair.

BAGERIS, JOHN—Painter, T.
302 East 56th St., New York 22, N.Y.

B. Fremont, Ohio, May 11, 1924. *Studied*: AIC, B.F.A., M.F.A. (painting with Boris Anisfeld); Acad. FA, Munich, Germany; Univ. Chicago; Wayne Univ. *Awards*: Fulbright Fellowship, 1953-54; Emily Lowe award, 1957; prizes in regional shows; scholarships. *Exhibited*: Fulbright Traveling Exh., Europe, 1954; WMAA, 1958; RoKo Gal., 1957 (oneman); Werbe Gal., Detroit, 1955; Souza Gal., Mexico City, 1958; AIC, 1947, 1948, 1950, 1951; Detroit Inst. A., 1943, 1950, 1951-1953.

BAGLEY, RALPH LEON—Painter, E., L.
Orlando Institute of Art, 2408 East Robinson Ave.; h. 2017 Sycamore Dr., Orlando, Fla.; s. Fontana Village, N.C.

B. Bertrand, Mo., May 14, 1913. *Studied*: Flint AI, with Brozik; ASL, with Lee; CGA. *Member*: Fla. Fed. A.; A. Lg. of Orange County (past pres.); Fla. A. Group; Orlando AA (past pres.). *Awards*: prizes, A. Lg. of Orange County, 1955, 1957, 1958. *Exhibited*: Flint AI, 1931-33; Detroit Inst. A., 1931, 1932; Univ. Tennessee; Manatee A. Lg., Bradenton, Fla.; Morse Gal. A., Winter Park, Fla.; A. Lg. of Orange County; Fla. A. Group; one-man: Fontana Village, N.C.; Winter Park Woman's Cl.; Eola Plaza Gal., Orlando; Univ. of Florida, 1958; Hidden Garden Gal., Winter Park, 1958. *Position*: Dir., Orlando Inst. A.; Instr., Orlando Jr. Col., Fla.; Instr., A. Groups in Leesburg, Mt. Dora and St. Cloud, Fla.; Summer School, Fontana Village, N.C.

BAHM, HENRY—Painter
1247 Commonwealth Ave., Boston, Mass.

B. Boston, Mass., Feb. 26, 1920. *Studied*: Mass. Sch. A., with Ernest Major; BMFA Sch., with Karl Zerbe. *Member*: Inst. Mod. A., Boston. *Exhibited*: SFMA, 1945; Assoc. Am. A., 1946; Inst. Mod. A.; Boris Mirski Gal.; Stuart A. Gal.; Butler AI; Provincetown AA; Boston A. Festival; Columbia Mus. *Work*: Walter Chrysler, Jr., Coll.

BAHNC, SALCIA—Painter, Lith., I., T.
Hotel Ansonia, 73rd St. & Broadway, New York, N.Y.

B. Dukla, Poland. *Studied*: AIC; Chicago Acad. FA. *Member*: Chicago A. Cl. Awards: Armstrong prize, Chicago, 1942. *Exhibited*: AIC, 1919-29, 1942, 1943; Johnson Gal., Chicago, 1925, 1927, 1929, 1931 (one-man); Arch. Lg., 1925; Marie Sterner Gal., 1928; PAFA, 1922; Jeune Peinture Paris, 1934 (one-man); Salon des Tuileries, Paris, 1930-1935; Sur-Indp., Paris, 1929. *Position*: A.T., AIC, Chicago, Ill., 1923-29, 1943-44, 1947-1953; Garrison Forest Sch., Garrison, Md., 1955-1957.

BAHR, FLORENCE RIEFLE (Mrs. Leonard M.)—
Painter, I.
Lawyers Hill, Elkridge 27, Md.

B. Baltimore, Md., Feb. 2, 1909. *Studied*: Dickinson Col.; Maryland Inst. *Member*: Maryland A. Cooperative; Nat. Lg. Am. Pen Women. *Awards*: prize, BMFA, 1953. *Work*: BMA; Johns Hopkins Hospital. *Exhibited*: Maryland Inst., 1936; BMA, 1936-1946, 1947, 1951; Vagabond Theatre, 1950 (one-man), Balt.; Little Theatre, 1952; Eastern Shore Gal., Easton, Md., 1952; Rehoboth A. Lg., 1952; Peale Mus. A., 1952-1954.

BAHR, LEONARD MARION—Painter, T., I., L.
4228 Reistertown Rd., Baltimore 15, Md.; h. Lawyers Hill, Elkridge 27, Md.

B. Baltimore, Md., May 12, 1905. *Studied*: Maryland Inst. *Awards*: prizes, Maryland Inst. traveling scholarship, 1929; CGA, 1958. *Work*: Johns Hopkins Univ.; Univ. Maryland; Md. State T. Col.; Baltimore Aquarium; Fed. Land Bank, Catonsville, Md.; Provident Savings Bank; Maryland Natural Hist. Soc.; Peabody Inst.; Fifth Reg. Armory, Balto.; Baltimore City Col. *Exhibited*: BMA, 1930, 1946, 1952 (one-man); Maryland Inst., 1956; Western Maryland Col., 1956 (one-man). *Position*: Instr., Maryland Inst., Baltimore, 1930-42, 1946-56; Dir., Maryland Inst. Branch, Glen Burnie, Md.; Instr., Metropolitan Sch. A., Baltimore, Md.

BAILEY, BEN P., JR.—Educator, P., S., L., I.
Texas College of Arts & Industries; h. 1209 West Santa Gertrudis St., Kingsville, Tex.

B. Houston, Tex., Dec. 28, 1902. *Studied*: Univ. Texas; Columbia Univ.; Colorado State Col. Edu.; Claremont Grad. Sch., and with Gutzon Borglum, Charles Lawler, Henry Lee McFee, Jean Goodwin Ames. *Member*: Texas FA Soc.; Texas WC Soc.; South Tex. A. Lg. *Awards*: prizes, Texas WC Soc., 1951; GI Exh., San Antonio; Corpus Christi A. Fnd., 1946-48, 1950, 1953, 1954. *Work*: IBM; Texas Mem. Mus., Austin; D. D. Feldman Coll., Dallas; Robert Strauss Coll., Houston. *Exhibited*: Texas WC Soc.; Corpus Christi A. Fnd. I., "The Adventures of Prince Leandro," 1945; "Padre Island," 1951. *Position*: Prof., Texas Col. A. & Indst., Kingsville, Texas.

BAILEY, EARL CLIFFORD—Teacher, P.
Billings Senior High School; h. 1314 Avenue E, Billings, Mont.

B. Havre, Mont., May 30, 1909. *Studied*: Montana State Univ. B.A.; Colorado State Col. Edu., M.A.; ASL, with

Harry Sternberg, Kenneth Hayes Miller. *Awards*: prize, Montana State Univ., 1937; North Montana Fair, 1942. *Exhibited*: Northwest AA, 1944-1946; Yellowstone A. Gal., Billings, 1944; one-man: 1947-1955. *Position*: T., FA & Crafts, Billings H.S., Billings, Mont.

BAILEY, LA FORCE—*Painter, T.*
　　205 West University Ave., Urbana, Ill.
B. Joliet, Ill., Apr. 17, 1893. *Studied*: with William M. Hekking, Charles W. Hawthorne. *Member*: AIA; Provincetown AA; AWCS; Wash. WC Cl.; Phila. WC Cl. *Awards*: med., AWCS, 1934. *Work*: murals, Ill. Century of Progress Exp., 1933. *Position*: Assoc. Prof. A., Univ. Illinois, Urbana, Ill.*

BAILEY, MERRILL A.—*Painter T.*
　　Cazenovia, N.Y.
B. Cazenovia, N.Y., July 21, 1909. *Studied*: PIASch.; Syracuse Univ., B.F.A., and with Ogden Pleissner, Anna Fisher. *Member*: AWS; Assoc. A. Syracuse; Phila. WC Cl. *Awards*: prizes, Syracuse Mus. FA., 1940, 1944, 1952; Rochester Mem. A. Gal., 1944; N.Y. State Fair, 1950; AV 1943. *Work*: Syracuse Mus. FA; Rochester Mem. A. Gal.; Munson-Williams-Proctor Inst.; Toledo Mus. A.; Readers Digest Coll. *Exhibited*: BM, 1941-1945; AIC, 1942-1946; MMA, 1942; Toledo Mus. A., 1945, 1946; AWS, 1940-1946; Assoc. A. Syracuse, 1935-1946; Rochester Mem. A. Gal., 1943, 1944, 1946; Munson-Williams-Proctor Inst., 1951 (one-man); Syracuse Mus. FA, 1953 (one-man); Cazenovia Jr. Col., 1953 (one-man). Contributor to American Artist magazine, 1946, 1956; "Landscape & Seascape," 1955. *Positions*: Visiting Instr., P., Art Workshop, State T. Col., Potsdam, N.Y.; T., Cazenovia Jr. Col., Cazenovia Central Sch.; Syracuse Univ., 1954.

BAILEY, WILLIAM J. (BILL)—*Cartoonist, I., Des.*
　　Cape May Point, N.J.
B. Philadelphia, Pa., May 26, 1902. *Studied*: PMSchIA; Spring Garden Inst. *Position*: Asst. to A. Dir., Saturday Evening Post.

BAILEY, WORTH—*Museum Curator, E., Des.*
　　American Buildings Survey, National Park Service, Washington 25, D.C.; h. 207 Washington Rd., Alexandria, Va.
B. Portsmouth, Va., Aug. 23, 1908. *Studied*: William & Mary Col.; Univ. Pennsylvania, B.A., with Virginia Morris, Glenna Latimer. *Member*: AAMus.; Am. Soc. Arch. Historians. *Awards*: Norfolk Soc. A., 1926-1928. *Work*: Univ. Pennsylvania; Valentine Mus. A.; Col. of William & Mary. *Exhibited*: Norfolk, Williamsburg, Richmond, Va., 1928-1938. Contributor to Encyclopedia Americana and to art, antique and history magazines. Illus., "Christmas with the Washingtons"; "Seaport in Virginia: George Washington's Alexandria." Des., Christmas card series; Alexandria Commemorative Stamp, 1949. *Position*: Cur., Jamestown Archaeological Project, 1933-38; Cur., Mount Vernon, Va., 1938-51; Consultant, "Our Town 1749-1865," special exhn., Alexandria Assn., 1956; Cur., Alexander Hamilton Bicentennial Exhn., U.S. Treasury, 1957; Arch. Hist., Historic American Buildings Survey, National Park Service, Washington, D.C., 1958- . Curatorial Consultant, National Trust for Historic Preservation, Washington, D.C., 1951-56.

BAIN, JOAN *(Mrs. Joan Bain Nicodemus)*—*Painter*
　　2233 East Silver St., Tucson, Ariz.
B. Manila, P.I., Mar. 9, 1910. *Studied*: Newcomb Col., Tulane Univ.; and with Robert Graham, John Lenhardt, Wayman Adams; Corcoran Sch. A. *Exhibited*: South Carolina AA, 1938; VMFA, 1939, 1940; CGA, 1941; James Lee A. Acad., 1941 (one-man); Brooks Mem. Mus. A., 1941, 1942; Am. A. Week, Memphis, Tenn., 1943-1945; Overton Park, Memphis, 1947 (one-man). Port. demonstrations, Am. A. Week, 1942, 1944. *Position*: Instr., James A. Lee Mem. A. Acad., Memphis, Tenn., 1941; private instr., 1942-48.*

BAIRD, JOSEPH A., JR.—*Educator, W., L.*
　　Department of Art, University of California; h. 838 Eureka Ave., Davis, Cal.
B. Pittsburgh, Pa., Nov. 22, 1922. *Studied*: Oberlin Col. (B.A.); Harvard Univ. (M.A., Ph.D.). *Member*: CAA;

Soc. Arch. Historians; Soc. for Aesthetics; Renaissance Soc. of California; Nat. Trust for Hist. Preservation; Friends of Fogg Mus. Photographer: "Los Retablos Dorados de Mexico" (De La Maza); "To the City of the Dead" (Woodcock); "Arquitectura de los Siglos XVII y XVIII" (Kubler). Contributor to Art Bulletin, Journal of the Society of Architectural Historians, Journal of Aesthetics and Art Criticism, Handbook of Latin American Studies. Lectures: Baroque and 18th Century Architecture in Mexico; American Architecture; Research Methods; Oriental Art, at Univ. So. California, University of Mexico, Royal Ontario Mus. of Archaeology. *Positions*: Instr., Art History and Archaeology, Univ. Toronto, 1949-53; Art History, and Curator of Collections, University of California, Davis, Cal., 1953- .

BAIZERMAN, SAUL—*Painter*
　　311 6th Ave., New York, N.Y.*

BAKER, ANNA P.—*Painter, Gr.*
　　Barton, Vt.
B. London, Ont., Canada, June 12, 1928. *Studied*: Univ. of Western Ontario, B.A.; AIC, B.F.A., M.F.A. *Member*: Canadian Painters, Etchers & Engravers. *Awards*: Mr. and Mrs. Frank G. Logan prize and medal, AIC, 1956; prizes, Cleveland Inst. A., 1956, 1958. *Work*: LC; London Pub. Lib. and A. Mus.; CMA. *Exhibited*: Phila. Pr. Cl., 1953-1956; Northwest Pr. M.; Albany Pr. Cl.; Bradley Univ.; Boston Soc. Indp. A.; Portland, Me.; CM, 1954, 1956, 1958; Silvermine Gld. A., 1951; Wichita Print Exh., 1956; Butler Inst. Am. A., 1956; Norfolk Mus. A.; Boston Pr. M.; Alabama WC Soc.; San F. Mus. A.; "Art-USA," 1958; AIC, 1953, 1955, 1956, 1957; Cleveland May Show, 1955, 1956, 1957; Western Ontario, 1952-1958; Young Contemp. of Canada, 1956-1958; Canadian Painters, Etchers & Engravers, 1955-1957.

BAKER, BRYANT—*Sculptor*
　　222 West 59th St., New York 19, N.Y.
B. London, England, July 8, 1881. *Studied*: City & Glds. Tech. Inst.; Royal Acad. A., London, England. *Awards*: med., Royal Acad. A., 1910. *Work*: statues, mem., busts in England & the United States (for list, see WWAA, Vol. 3). *Exhibited*: NAD; PAFA; BMFA; CGA; NCFA; AIC; Paris Salon; Royal Acad., London. Lectures: Contemporary Sculpture.*

BAKER, CHARLES EDWIN—*Editor, W.*
　　New-York Historical Society h. 4652 Manhattan College Parkway, New York 71, N.Y.
B. Harlan, Iowa, Dec. 16, 1902. *Studied*: State Univ. Iowa, B.A., M.A.; Columbia Univ. *Member*: Bibliographical Soc. Am.; Am. Assn. State & Local Hist.; N.Y. State Hist. Assn. Contributor to art magazines; Editor of books on the history of American art. Author: "The American Art Union," 1953. *Position*: Ed., Hist. Records Survey, New York City, 1937-41; New-York Hist. Soc., 1944- .

BAKER, DORIS WINCHELL—*Painter*
　　3108 Strand St., Manhattan Beach, Cal.
B. Washington, D.C., Jan. 7, 1905. *Studied*: Chouinard Inst. A.; Otis AI, and with Marion Kavanagh Wachtel. *Member*: Carmel AA; Women Painters of the West. *Awards*: prizes, Women Painters of the West, 1941, 1946-1949; A. in Nat. Defense, 1943; Palos Verdes, Cal., 1955. *Exhibited*: Carmel AA, 1952 (one-man) and monthly since 1950; A. Gld., Am.; Monterey County Fair, 1950; Palos Verdes A. Gal., 1955.*

BAKER, LAMAR—*Etcher, Lith., P. ,I.*
　　Waverly Hall, Ga.
B. Atlanta, Ga., Sept. 15, 1908. *Studied*: Univ. Georgia, B.S.; High Mus. A.; ASL, with Kenneth Hayes Miller, Harry Sternberg; Hans Hofmann Sch. FA. *Awards*: Rosenwald F., 1942. *Work*: PMA; N.Y. Pub. Lib.; ASL. *Exhibited*: NAD, 1940, 1941, 1943; MMA, 1942; High Mus. A., 1939 (one-man); Weyhe Gal., 1945 (one-man); Univ. Georgia, 1951 (one-man); Castle Gal., Atlanta, 1954 (one-man).

BAKER, LLOYD THERON—Cartoonist, Comm. A.

943 Grange Hall Rd., Cardiff-by-the-Sea, Cal.

B. Rochester, N.Y., Jan. 20, 1922. *Studied*: Univ. Rochester; Hollywood A. Center. *Member*: Carlsbad-Oceanside A. Lg. Contributor to Cosmopolitan, Redbook, Sat. Eve. Post, and other national magazines and foreign publications. Humorous greeting cards for Rust Craft, Gibson, Barker, Volland, etc.

BAKER, MARY HOFSTETTER—Painter, Des.

Pleasant Mills, R.D. 1, Hammonton, N.J.

B. Philadelphia, Pa., Jan. 4, 1913. *Studied*: PAFA; PMSchIA; Barnes Fnd. *Member*: F. PAFA; Phila. WC Cl. *Work*: PAFA, 1942-1944; PAFA, 1942-1944; CGA, 1943-1945; Soc. Four A., 1942; Temple Univ., 1941; DaVinci Gal., 1942; Cape May, N.J., 1941-1945; Plastic Cl.; Phila. A. All., 1939.

BAKER, MILDRED (Mrs. Jacob)—
Associate Museum Director

The Newark Museum, 43-49 Washington St. (1); h. 569 Mt. Prospect Ave., Newark 4, N.J.

B. Brooklyn, N.Y., Aug. 14, 1905. *Studied*: Univ. Rochester. *Member*: CAA; AAMus. *Positions*: Asst. to Exec. Dir., CAA, 1929-32; Asst. to Dir., and Asst. Dir., Federal Art Project, 1935-47; Asst. to Dir., 1944- , Asst. Dir., 1949, Assoc. Dir., 1953- , The Newark Museum, Newark, N.J.; Assembled many important exhibitions including Decorative Arts Today, 1948; annual exhibition of objects of good design and the triennial exhibition of works by New Jersey Artists.

BAKER, M(INNIE) (MITCHELL)—Educator, P., S., L.

Southeastern State College; h. 615 Pine St., Durant, Okla.

B. Ardmore, Okla. *Studied*: Southeastern State Col., B.A.; Univ. Iowa, M.A.; Oklahoma Univ.; Ohio State Univ.; & with Tarbell, Merryman, Guston. *Member*: Oklahoma AA; Oklahoma Edu. Assn.; Nat. Edu. Assn. *Awards*: prizes, Oklahoma State Fair, 1929, 1930, 1931. *Work*: Oklahoma A. Center; Alice Robertson Jr. H.S., Muskogee, Okla. *Work*: Wilburton H.S., Okla.; Southeastern State Col., Durant, Okla. *Exhibited*: CGA; Okla. A. Center; Philbrook A. Center; Interstate A. Soc., Denison, Tex. *Position*: Assoc. Prof. A., Southeastern State Col., Durant, Okla.*

BAKER, RAYMOND NELSON—Designer, P., Gr.

Pleasant Mills, R.D. 1, Hammonton, N.J.

B. Philadelphia, Pa., June 11, 1913. *Studied*: PAFA; PMSchIA. *Member*: PAFA. *Exhibited*: PAFA; Phila. A. All.; Plastic Cl.; Cape May (N.J.) Exh. *Positions*: A. Dir., Webb Mfg. Co., Philadelphia, 1946- ; Bd. Mngrs., F.PAFA, 1946-47.

BAKER, SARAH M.—Educator, P.

1273 New Hampshire Ave., N.W., Washington 6, D.C.

B. Memphis, Tenn., Mar. 7, 1899. *Studied*: Maryland Inst.; Tiffany Fnd.; and in Paris. *Member*: AAUP; CAA; A. Gld. of Wash. (Com. on A. Edu.); F., PAFA. *Awards*: Cresson traveling scholarship, 1922; F., PMG, 1946; prizes, Wash. Soc. Indp. A., 1935; BMA, 1945. *Work*: BM; Am. Univ.; PC; Am. Univ., Watkins Coll.; St. Timothy's Sch. *Exhibited*: 1953-55: CGA; BM; Kenneth Taylor Gal., Nantucket; Watkins Gal.; Franz Bader Gal., Wash., D.C. (2 one-man). *Position*: Instr., Bryn Mawr Sch. for Girls, Baltimore, 1929-37; St. Timothy's Sch., Catonsville, Md., 1931-45; Assoc. Prof., Am. Univ., Washington, D.C., 1945- .*

BAKOS, JOZEF G.—Educator, P.

Santa Fe, N.M.

B. Buffalo, N.Y., Sept. 23, 1891. *Studied*: in New York and Canada. *Member*: Los Cinco Pintores, Santa Fe. *Awards*: prizes, Denver, Colo.; Oakland A. Mus., 1930; Albuquerque State Fair, 1945; Mus. New Mexico, Santa Fe. *Work*: WMAA; BM; Palace Legion of Honor, San F.; Univ. Oklahoma; Denver A. Mus.; Riverside Mus., N.Y.; Smoky Hill Gal., Lindsborg, Kans.; Ford Fnd.; Mill Iron Ranches, Wellington, Tex., and in many private collections. *Exhibited*: CGA, 1941; AIC; Carnegie Inst.; 48 States Comp., 1946; PAFA; Santa Barbara Mus. A., 1945, 1946

(one-man); State Fair, Albuquerque; Mus. of New Mexico, Santa Fe. *Positions*: Prof., Univ. Denver, 1931-33; Santa Fe (N.M.) H.S., 1940- .

BAKOS, TERESA—Painter

P.O. Box 1003, Santa Fe, N.M.

B. Nervi, Italy. *Member*: Santa Fe Women A. Exh. Group (Fndg. Member). *Exhibited*: Rotunda Gal., San F., Cal.; Stanford Univ. A. Gal.; Crocker Gal. A., Sacramento, Cal.; Amarillo (Tex.) Gal.; Mus. New Mexico, Santa Fe; La Fonda Gal., Santa Fe. *Work*: in many private collections, U.S. and abroad.

BALCH, GEORGIA W. (Mrs.)—Painter, C.

Johnson, Vt.

B. Toronto, Canada, Dec. 12, 1888. *Studied*: Kansas City AI, with Charles Wilimovsky, Haley Lever. *Award*: prize, Fed. of Women's Cl., 1954. *Exhibited*: CGA, 1936; Rockefeller Center, 1936; Ogunquit, Me.; Gloucester, Mass.; Burlington, Vt. *Work*: Vermont Soc. A. & Crafts, (reproduction of original painting in new technique of yarn and darning needle).*

BALCH, GERTRUDE HOWLAND—Painter, T., Et.

1314 West 10th St., Wilmington 6, Del.

B. Flushing, N.Y., Dec. 27, 1909. *Studied*: Wilmington Acad. A. *Member*: Wilmington Soc. FA; Phila. Pr. Cl.; Com. on A. Edu., MModA; Delaware Assn. for A. Edu. *Work*: Delaware A. Center. *Exhibited*: Delaware A. Center, 1948-1955; Phila. Pr. Cl., 1948-1953; BMA, 1955; Phila. A. All., 1955. *Position*: A. T., Tatnall Sch., Wilmington, Del.*

BALDINGER, WALLACE SPENCER—
Museum Director, E., Cr., W., L.

1790 Walnut St., Eugene, Ore.

B. Springdale, Pa., Apr. 19, 1905. *Studied*: Oberlin Col., A.B., Ph.D.; PAFA; Univ. Chicago; Univ. Paris.; Univ. Kyoto, Japan. *Member*: CAA; Am. Soc. for Aesthetics; Assn. for Asian Studies. *Awards*: F., Oberlin Col., 1927; Carnegie F., Univ. Paris, 1932; F. Univ. Chicago, 1935-1936; Research Grant, Am. Council of Learned Soc. Contributor to art magazines on history of America and Oriental art. Author: Catalogues and textbook on art appreciation. *Positions*: Visiting L., to Am. and Japanese Univ.; Dir., Mulvane A. Mus., Washburn Col., 1932-40; Prof., Lawrence Col., 1940-44; Assoc. Prof. A., Univ. Oregon, Eugene, Ore., 1944- ; Dir., Mus. A., Univ. Oregon, Eugene, Ore., 1955- ; Prof. A., Univ. Oregon, 1956- ; Hon. Pres. for Life, Oregon A. All., 1955; Sec., Western Assn. A. Mus., 1956-57, Treas., 1957-58.

BALDRIDGE, CYRUS LEROY—
Illustrator, W., P., Des., Gr.

Santa Fe, N.M.

B. Alton, N.Y., May 27, 1889. *Studied*: Frank Holme Sch. A.; Univ. Chicago, Ph.B. Litt. *Awards*: prizes, Chicago SE, 1937; Prairie Pr. M., 1944; various prizes at Mus. New Mexico, Santa Fe. *Work*: Fiske Univ., Nashville, Tenn.; BMFA; N.Y. Pub. Lib.; NGA. I., "First Illinois Cavalryman"; "I Was There" (World War I drawings); "Time and Chance" (autobiography), and 40 additional books. Author: "Americanism—What Is It?". Cartoonist, original Stars & Stripes Staff. Organized "Art Industry of America" for NRA.

BALDWIN, BARBARA (Miss Barbara Baldwin Smith)—
Sculptor, P., W.

93 King St., Groveland, Mass.

B. Portland, Me., Jan. 13, 1914. *Studied*: Portland Sch.FA; PAFA; NAD; ASL, and with Bower, Kroll, DuMond, Laessle, McCartan and others. *Member*: Yonkers AA; Sarasota AA. *Work*: murals, Deering H.S., Portland, Me.; sc., WFNY 1939; Pathe News; sculpture and figurines in private colls. *Exhibited*: L.D.M. Sweat Mem. Mus., 1932-1934; N.Y. Mun. Exh., 1936; Grand Central Palace, 1936; Soc. Indp. A., 1936; Hudson River Mus., 1942; NAD, 1944, 1947; Sarasota AA, 1950; Ogunquit A. Center, 1958.

BALDWIN, CLIFFORD PARK—*Illustrator, P.*

1641 Alvarado St., Oceanside, Cal.

B. Cincinnati, Ohio, Feb. 14, 1889. *Studied*: with George Demont Otis, Jean Mannheim. *Member*: Southwestern Archaeological Soc.; Painters & Sculptors Cl.; Carlsbad-Oceanside AC. *Work*: Southwest Mus., Los A. *Exhibited*: Southwest Mus.; Long Beach, La Jolla, Oceanside and Sacramento, Cal. I., books & periodicals. Illus., "Gypsum Cave"; "Navaho Weaving"; "Masterkey," pub. of Southwest Mus., 1933-1941. *Position*: Staff A., Photographer, Southwest Mus., Los Angeles, Cal., 1933-41. (Retired.)

BALDWIN, FRANCES—*Painter*

1100 Lombard St., San Francisco, Cal.

B. San Francisco, Cal., Oct. 18, 1907. *Studied*: Cal. Sch. FA; ASL, with Kuniyoshi. *Member*: San F. AA; San F. Women A; AEA. *Work*: SFMA. *Exhibited*: San F. AA; San F. Women A.; Rotunda Gal., San F., Cal., 1955 (one-man).

BALDWIN, MURIEL FRANCES—*Former Art Librarian*

321 East 53rd St., New York 22, N.Y.

B. Brooklyn, N.Y. *Studied*: Columbia Univ.; Univ. Wisconsin. *Member*: Special Libraries Assn. Author: Costume section for children, World Book Encyclopedia; contributor to N.Y. Pub. Lib. Bulletin. *Position*: Staff, Frick Art Reference Lib., 1920-26; Asst. A. Div., 1926-52, Chief, A. Div., 1952-1956, New York Public Library, New York, N.Y. (Retired.)*

BALL, KATE KRAUS (Mrs.)—*Painter*

3420 North Stanton St., El Paso, Tex.

B. El Paso, Tex. *Studied*: Univ. California with Eugen Neuhaus; also with Perham H. Nahl and Henry Balink. *Member*: AAPL; Studio Gld., Redding, Conn.; Nat. Soc. A. & Lets., Wash., D.C.; Texas FA Assn.; El Paso AA. *Awards*: prizes in numerous exhibitions. Creator of "Scripture in Color," a collection of parchment scrolls, engrossed and illuminated. Twenty selected for two month exh. at Library of Congress, 1952 and on tour under auspices of Studio Gld., W. Redding, Conn. Among one-man exhs. of these scrolls were: AAPL; Public Libraries of: Utica, N.Y., St. Louis, Mo., Mason City, Iowa, Milwaukee, Wis., East Chicago, Ind., also—Dearborn Hist. Mus.; Oklahoma A. Center; Intl. Mus., El Paso; Mary Buie Mus. A., Oxford, Miss.; Columbus Mus. A., Ga.; Nashville Mus. A.; Hunter Gallery, Chattanooga; Everhart Mus., Scranton, Pa.; Fleming Mus. A., Burlington, Vt., and many others.

BALL, (LE)ROY—*Cartoonist*

12233 Richard Ave., Palos Heights, Ill.

B. La Salle, Ill., July 11, 1901. *Studied*: Chicago Acad. A. Contributor to Cosmopolitan, Town Journal, Farm Journal, Star Weekly, and others.

BALLATOR, JOHN R.—*Painter, E., Lith.*

Hollins College, Va.

B. Portland, Ore., Feb. 7, 1909. *Studied*: Portland Mus. A. Sch.; Univ. Oregon; Yale Univ., B.F.A. *Work*: Murals, USPO, Portland, Ore.; Dept. Justice, Wash., D.C.; Menninger Sanatorium, Topeka, Kan. *Position*: Prof. A., 1938- , Hd. A. Dept., Hollins Col., Va., 1941- ; Memb. Bd., Roanoke FA Center, 1952- ; Assoc. Dir., 1956-57, Dir., 1958-59, Hollins Abroad Program.

BALLINGER, HARRY RUSSELL—*Painter, T., W., L.*

R.F.D., New Hartford, Conn.

B. Port Townsend, Wash., Sept. 4, 1892. *Studied*: Univ. California; ASL; Academie Colorossi, Paris. *Member*: SC; All. A. Am.; Audubon A.; Conn. Acad. FA; Kent AA; AWS; North Shore AA; Rockport AA. *Awards*: prizes, SC, 1944, 1952, 1955, 1956, 1958(2); Hartford Atheneum, 1944; Conn. WC Soc., 1944, 1945, 1955; Meriden A. & Crafts, 1944, 1952, 1957; Springfield, Mass., 1952, 1953, 1955; New Haven Paint & Clay Cl., 1956; Hudson Valley AA, 1958; Rockport AA, 1953, 1955. *Work*: Wadsworth Atheneum; A. Mus. of New Britain; murals: Plant H.S., West Hartford, Conn. *Exhibited*: SC; NAD; Audubon A.; All. A. Am.; Conn. Acad. FA; AWS; Rockport AA, and others. Author: "Painting Sea and Surf." Instr., L., art subjects.

BALLINGER, LOUISE BOWEN (Mrs. Raymond A.)—*Educator*

334 South Camac St., Philadelphia 7, Pa.

B. Palmyra, N.J., Feb. 9, 1909. *Studied*: PMSch.A; Univ. Pennsylvania; Barnes Fnd.; Pendle Hill. *Member*: Phila. A. All.; Nat. A. Edu. Assn.; Committee on A. Edu., New York; Eastern AA. *Position*: Cur., PAFA, 1943-48; Supv., A. Edu., PMSch.A., Philadelphia, Pa., 1948-55; Assoc. Dir., A.T. Edu. Dept., PMA Sch. A., 1955-56; Dir., 1956- .

BALLINGER, MAXIL—*Printmaker, P., W.*

145 East 49th St., New York, N.Y.

B. Walnut Grove, Mo., Mar. 30, 1914. *Studied*: Springfield (Mo.) State Col., B.A.; Harvard Univ.; Univ. North Carolina; Univ. Iowa, M.A. *Member*: Phila. Pr. Cl.; Am. Color Pr. Soc.; Ozark AA. *Awards*: prizes, Phila. Pr. Cl.; BM, 1947; Northwest Pr. M., 1947; Illinois State Fair, 1947; Springfield A. Mus., 1947; Indiana Pr. M., 1947; Albany Pr. M., 1947; Mary S. Collins prize, Phila. Pr. Cl., 1954; purchase prizes, PMA, 1953; LC, 1954; Bradley Univ., 1954. *Work*: MModA; Carnegie Inst.; CAM; PMA; LC; BM; SAM; Springfield A. Mus.; Univ. Iowa; John Herron AI. *Exhibited*: Northwest Pr. M., 1942, 1943, 1946, 1947, 1954; SFMA, 1942; Phila. Pr. Cl., 1942, 1943 1946, 1952-1955; Am. Color Pr. Soc., 1942, 1943, 1946; AIC; Des Moines A. Center; LC; BM, 1947, 1948, 1952; WMAA, 1948, 1949; MModA, 1954; MModA Overseas Am. Show, 1955; Salzburg, 1953; PMA, 1953; SAGA, 1954; IFA Gal., Wash., D.C., 1954; Univ. So. Cal., 1954; Portland (Me.) Mus. A., 1954; Univ. Illinois, 1954.*

BALLOU, BERTHA—*Painter, L., T., S.*

2918 West Sherwood Ave., Spokane 11, Wash.

B. Hornby, N.Y., Feb. 14, 1891. *Studied*: Randolph-Macon Woman's Col.; ASL; CGA; BMFA Sch., and with DuMond, Blumenschein, Tarbell, Merryman and others. *Member*: Wash. AA; F. Tiffany Fnd. *Work*: Eastern Washington Hist. Mus.; Spokane Pub. Lib.; Spokane County Courthouse; Wash. State Col.; First Fed. Savings Loan Bank, Spokane. *Exhibited*: Wash., D.C.; New York, N.Y.; Northwest and Inland Empire Exh.; one-man exh. in Montana and Washington. *Position*: Instr., Holy Names College, Spokane, Wash., 1955-58.

BAMA, JAMES E.—*Illustrator*

150 East 56th St., New York 22, N.Y.

B. New York, N.Y., Apr. 28, 1926. *Studied*: City Col., N.Y.; ASL. *Member*: SI; ASL.*

BANCEL, HENRY A.—*Painter*

125 East 84th St., New York 28, N.Y.

B. New York, N.Y., Nov. 12, 1885. *Studied*: N.Y. Univ. *Member*: AWCS. *Exhibited*: AWCS, 1936-1950.

BANCROFT, ALBERT STOKES—*Painter*

Bailey, Colo.

B. Denver, Colo., May 15, 1890. *Studied*: Cornell Univ., LL.B. *Member*: Denver A. Gld. *Awards*: prizes, Denver A. Gld., 1954, 1955. *Work*: Denver A. Mus.

BAND, MAX—*Painter, W.*

6401 Ivarene Ave., Hollywood 28, Cal.

B. Naumestis, Lithuania, Aug. 21, 1900. *Studied*: Acad. A., Berlin, and in Paris. *Member*: hon. memb., Cal. A. Cl. *Work*: Musée de Luxembourg, Petit Palais, Paris, and other European museums; French AI, Phila.; Riverside Mus.; PMG; Los A. Mus. A.; Mus. Mod. A., Paris; deYoung Mem. Mus., San F.; Cal.PLH; Santa Barbara Mus. A.; Parliament of Israel, Jerusalem. *Exhibited*: extensively in U.S. and Europe; one-man: Wildenstein Gal., 1948; Galerie Delisée, Paris, 1949; Vigiveno Gal., Los Angeles, 1952, 1955; AIC (group), 1954; Musée du Petit Palais, Paris, 1955; Cal.PLH, 1956; also Marlborough Gal., London, 1956; B'nai B'rith Mus., Wash., D.C., 1958. Author: "History of Contemporary Art," 1935.

BANEVER, GILBERT—

Designer, P., I., Comm. A., T., W.

101 Park Ave., New York 17, N.Y.; h. Ansonia Rd., Woodbridge, Conn. (New Haven 15)

B. New Haven, Conn., June 8, 1913. *Studied*: Yale Univ., B.F.A.; F., Am. Acad. in Rome; & with Ferruccio Ferrazzi.

Member: Conn. Acad. FA; Alumni of Am. Acad. in Rome. *Awards*: prizes, Yale Univ., 1933, 1934; med., Alum. Am. Acad. in Rome, 1933, 1934; Prix de Rome, 1934; Tennessee I.B.M. Comp., 1942. *Work*: Yale Univ. A. Gal.; New Haven Bd. of Edu.; I.B.M.; Grand Central A. Gal. *Exhibited*: PAFA, 1940; AIC, 1941; Conn. Acad. FA, 1937-1942; Springfield A. Lg., 1939-1942; SSAL, 1942, 1943. *Position*: T. & Dir., Memphis Acad. A., 1938-43; Des., General Electric Co., 1943-45; MGM, 1945-1946; Instr., Whitney Sch. A., New Haven, Conn., 1950-1952.

BANG, ELEONORE E.—*Craftsman, E., W.*
24 Newtonville Ave., Newton 58, Mass.

B. Copenhagen, Denmark. *Studied*: Sweden; Berlin; Copenhagen A. Soc. *Member*: Boston Soc. A. & Crafts. Author: "Leather Craft for Amateurs." *Position*: Instr., Boston Center for Adult Education.

BANKER, WILLIAM EDWIN—*Designer, I.*
339 East Main St., West Carrollton, Ohio

B. Los Angeles, Cal., June 16, 1908. *Studied*: Dayton AI; Central Acad. Comm. A. *Member*: Dayton A. Center. *Position*: A. Dir., Dancer-Fitzgerald-Sample, Inc., Dayton, Ohio.

BANKS, VIRGINIA—*Painter*
Crescent Rd., Westport, Conn.

B. Norwood, Mass., Jan. 12, 1920. *Studied*: Smith Col., B.A.; Butera Sch. FA; State Univ., Iowa, M.A.; Colorado Springs FA Center. *Awards*: prizes, SFMA, 1947; Wash. State Fair, 1949; Audubon A., 1951; Hallmark award, 1949. *Work*: SAM; IBM; Davenport Mun. Gal.; Plattsburg State Col. *Exhibited*: nationally since 1946, including AIC; PAFA; BM; WMAA; Carnegie Inst.; Audubon A.; NAD; VMFA; MMA; Hallmark; Weyhe Gal.; Alaska; Paris; Tokyo and Osaka, Japan; one-man: Grand Central Moderns, New York, 1950, 1952, 1956; Dusanne Gal., Seattle, 1952. Included in MModA lending service. *Position*: T., Shady Hill Sch., Cambridge, Mass., 1941-51; State Univ. Iowa; Univ. Buffalo; Univ. Washington Ext. Div., 1950; AAG and Cornish A. Sch., Seattle, Wash., 1950-51.*

BANNING, BEATRICE HARPER (Mrs. Waldo)—*Etcher, P.*
Old Lyme, Conn.

B. Staten Island, N.Y., Dec. 5, 1885. *Studied*: CUASch; ASL; NAD; European schools. *Member*: SAGA; Old Lyme AA; NAWA. *Awards*: prize, Conn. Acad. FA, 1944; Bridgeport A. Lg., 1945. *Work*: MMA; N.Y. Pub. Lib.; Lib. Cong. *Exhibited*: NAD, 1946; SAGA, annually; NAWA, 1946; Old Lyme AA, annually; Conn. Acad. FA, 1946; Albright A. Gal.; PAFA; Newport AA; CMA; Lib. Cong., 1946; Women's Int. Exh., London, 1946; WFNY 1939; Royal Soc. P. & Et., London, England, 1954; MMA, (John Taylor Arms Mem. Exh.), 1955; Rome, Italy.

BANTA, E(THEL) ZABRISKIE (SMITH)—*Painter, T.*
406 Inness Dr., Tarpon Springs, Fla.; also 105 Granite St., Pigeon Cove, Mass.

B. Philadelphia, Pa. *Studied*: Cornell Univ.; ASL. *Member*: Florida A. Group; Phila. WC Soc.; Washington WC Soc.; Rockport AA; Bradenton AA; Fed. of Women A.; Maine WC Cl.; Tarpon Springs AA; North Shore AA; Cape Ann Mod. A. *Awards*: prizes, Mineola, N.Y., 1942 (2); Fla. Fed. A., 1954; Mineola, N.Y., 1942, 1943; Pinellas, Fla., 1955, 1956, 1957. *Work*: First Nat. Bank, Tarpon Springs; Pub. Lib., and Woman's Cl., Tarpon Springs, Fla., and Federal Savings & Loan, Tarpon Springs. *Exhibited*: Fla. Artists, 1952-1958; NAD, 1957; Emily Lowe A. Gal., 1955; PAFA, 1947-1951; Sarasota AA, 1950-1952; All. A. Am., 1948, 1949; Wash. WC Cl., 1946-1950; Rockport AA, 1946-1958; North Shore AA, 1946-1950; Cape Ann Mod. A., 1956; Portland Mus., A., 1947-1950; Rockland, Me., 1947-1950; A. All., Rhode Island, 1946, 1947; Fed. Women Painters, 1948, 1949; Elmira, N.Y., 1950; Woodmere A. Gal., Phila. Pa., 1947, 1948; Winter Haven AA, 1954; Vero Beach, Fla., 1955. *Positions*: Pres., Tarpon Springs AA, 1955-56; Dir. of A., Tarpon Springs AA, 1957-58; Dir., Stonehenge Gallery, Pigeon Cove, Mass., 1946- .

BARANCEANU, BELLE—*Painter, Eng., I., T.*
Fine Arts Gallery, Balboa Park, San Diego, Cal.

B. Chicago, Ill., July 17, 1905. *Studied*: Minneapolis Sch. A., and with Anthony Angarola. *Member*: San Diego A. Gld.; La Jolla A. Center. *Awards*: prizes, AIC, 1931. *Work*: San Diego FA Soc.; LC; La Jolla A. Center; murals, USPO, La Jolla, Cal.; La Jolla Jr. H.S., La Jolla, Cal.; Roosevelt Jr. H.S., San Diego, Cal. *Exhibited*: nationally and internationally. Illus., Dr. George Huff's "Gynecology," 1943, "Human Reproduction and Gynecology," 1951. Cover designs for Journal of the American Academy of Applied Nutrition; Southern California Dental Journal. Many port., illus. and cover des. Lectures: "Printmaking"; "Children's Art." *Position*: Instr., Sch. A. & Crafts, La Jolla, Cal.; Fine Arts Gallery and Francis W. Parker Sch., San Diego, Cal.

BARANIK, RUDOLF—*Painter*
152-16 Melbourne Ave., Flushing 67, N.Y.

B. Lithuania, Sept. 10, 1920. *Studied*: AIC; ASL; Academie Julien, Paris; Academie Fernand Leger, Paris. *Member*: AEA. *Awards*: Joseph W. Beatman and Charles Shipman Payson awards, Silvermine Gld. A., 1958. *Work*: Living Arts Fnd. *Exhibited*: PAFA, 1954; Brandeis Univ., 1954; Univ. Nebraska, 1954; MModA circulating exh., 1954-55; Illinois Wesleyan Univ., 1954; Art: USA, 1958; Provincetown A. Festival, 1958; WMAA, 1958; Silvermine Gld. A., 1957, 1958; BM, 1958; Am. Painting & Sculpture, 1958; one-man: ACA Gal., 1953, 1955; RoKo Gal., 1958; Miami, Fla., 1958; Galerie 8, Paris, France, 1951.

BARBARITE, JAMES PETER—*Painter, E.*
9 Grace St., New Canaan, Conn.

B. Brooklyn, N.Y., Feb. 20, 1912. *Studied*: CUASch; Columbia Univ.; NAD, with Jonas Lie, Karl Anderson. *Member*: Silvermine Gld. A. *Awards*: F. Tiffany Fnd., 1939-1942; Prix de Rome, 1942. *Work*: Milch Gal., N.Y. *Exhibited*: BM, 1941; All.A.Am., 1942-1944; New Canaan Lib., 1955. *Position*: Prof., Painting, Biarritz Am. Univ., France, 1945-46; Academie Royal des Beaux-Arts, Brussels, Belgium, 1947-52.

BARBAROSSA, THEODORE COTILLO—*Sculptor*
40 West Eagle St., East Boston, Mass.

B. Ludlow, Vt. Dec. 26, 1906. *Studied*: Yale Univ., B.F.A., and with Cyrus E. Dallin, Heinz Warnecke. *Member*: F., NSS; Audubon A.; All. A. Am.; New England Assn. for Contemp. Sculpture. *Awards*: Med., Mass. Sch. FA, 1927; prizes, Yale Univ., 1931; Nat. Comp. for medal of Golden Anniversary of the City of New York, 1948; Morris mem. prize, Arch. Lg., 1949; med., Rome Collab. Comp., 1931, 1933; med., New Rochelle Art, 1941; All. A. Am., 1952; gold med., 1955. *Work*: reliefs and panels: USPO, Geneva, Oakville, N.Y.; Clinton, Mass; groups: Parkchester Housing, N.Y.; sc. Transfiguration Sch., Tarrytown, N.Y., Church of the Sacred Heart, Yonkers, N.Y.; reliefs: Bd. Edu. Bldg., Methodist Church, both in Nashville, Tenn.; relief, Blessed Sacrament Church, Holyoke, Mass.; Maryknoll, N.Y.; St. Mary's Seminary, Baltimore, Md. *Exhibited*: AIC, 1938; PAFA, 1939; CGA, 1939; NAD, 1935, 1936, 1938; WFNY 1939; Audubon A.; AGAA; Arch. Lg., N.Y.; PAFA; Mint Mus.; All. A. Am., 1953-1955; Boston A. Festival, 1953-1955.*

BARBER, MRS. GEORGE. See *Cresson, Cornelia*

BARBER, GEORGE (RODGERS)—*Painter, T.*
266 West 12th St., New York, N.Y.

B. Philadelphia, Pa., Jan. 6, 1910. *Studied*: Rollins Col.; Black Mountain Col., and with George Grosz, George Luks, Josef Albers, William Palmer. *Member*: Silvermine Gld. A. *Awards*: Gold medal, Audubon A., 1950. *Exhibited*: PAFA, 1941; Carnegie Inst., 1941, 1943, 1955; Audubon A., 1950, 1956; WMAA, 1952; Terry Nat. A. Exh., 1952; BM, 1953; Conn. Acad. FA, 1955; group shows in N.Y. since 1933; one-man: Berkshire Mus. A., 1950. *Position*: Instr., CUASch., New York, N.Y., 1945-47.

BARBER, H. WADDELL—*Painter, T., I., L.*
173 Old Wilmot Rd., Scarsdale, N.Y.

B. Whitwell, Tenn., June 6, 1907. *Studied*: John Herron AI; Louisville Conservatory of Music & Art; NAD; Cincinnati A. Acad.; ASL. *Member*: AEA. *Award*: prize, ACA Gal., 1953. *Exhibited*: BM, 1953; PAFA, 1953; Audubon A., 1953, 1954, 1958; Art:USA, New York, 1958; "An American Group," Rockefeller Center, 1941; Municipal Gal., N.Y., 1941; CM, 1946; ACA Gal., Regional, 1952; ACA Gal., group, 1953; one-man: Panoras Gal., 1958. *Lectures*: Art: Middle Ages to Contemporary, MMA, 1953-58 sponsored by Fine Arts Committees of Scarsdale, Larchmont and Mt. Vernon, N.Y. *Positions*: United Business Publishers, 1929-31; World News of the Week, 1947-51; A. Dir., World News of the Week, 1949-51; Instr. A., various clubs, 1950-58.

BARBER, JOHN—*Painter, Et., I., L.*
    Merion Gardens Apts., Merion, Pa.

B. Galati, Roumania, Oct. 19, 1898. *Studied*: European academies. *Member*: Am.A.Cong. *Work*: Luxembourg Mus., Paris, France. *Exhibited*: Salon d'Automne, 1923-1946; Salon des Tuileries, Paris; NAD, 1938, 1943; Ministry FA, Lisbon, Portugal; WMAA, 1951; Phila. A. All., 1957; group exh., Paris, 1958. Lecturer, Hist. A., colleges, museums and art galleries. Illus., "Carlota," 1944. I., for art magazines. *Position*: Prof. FA, Pres., Harcum Jr. Col., Bryn Mawr, Pa., 1944-46.

BARBER, MURIEL V. (Mrs. J. S. Barber, Sr.)—*Painter, C., S., T., Cr.*
    373 South Ridgeway Rd., South Orange, N.J.

B. West Orange, N.J. *Studied*: Fawcett A. Sch., Newark; Wayman Adams Sch. A., and with Hubert DeGroat Main, Michael Lenson, Stanley Marc Wright, and others. *Member*: AAPL; Bloomfield A. Lg.; Verona-West Essex AA; South Orange-Maplewood AA; Maplewood WC Cl.; Art Center of the Oranges, and others. *Work*: Davis Elkins Coll., W. Va., and in private collections. *Exhibited*: NAC, 1957; New Brunswick Coll., 1957, 1958; Maplewood WC Cl., 1957, 1958 and many others in prior years. *Awards*: Nat. award, AAPL; New Jersey Fed. WC, 1957; Warren Hotel, Spring Lake, N.J., 1957; Maplewood WC Cl., 1958; Glen Ridge WC exh., 1957; Art Center of the Oranges, 1958; 12 one-man exhs. *Position*: State Dir., Am. Art Week, New Jersey, 1957, 1958.

BARD, SARA FORESMAN—*Painter, T.*
    215 West Walnut Lane, Philadelphia 44, Pa.

B. Slippery Rock, Pa. *Studied*: PIASch; Grand Central Sch. A.; AIC. *Member*: AWCS; Wash. WC Cl.; Balt. WC Cl.; Studio Gld.; Springfield A. Lg.; NAWA. *Awards*: Prizes, Balt. WC Cl., 1928; N.Y. WC Cl., 1928, 1929; med., NAWA, 1931; Springfield A. Lg., 1939; Hoosier Salon, 1929, 1931, 1934, 1936; Studio Gld., 1941.

BARE, ARNOLD EDWIN—*Illustrator, P., Des.*
    31 East 65th St., New York 21, N.Y.

B. New York, N.Y., June, 1920. *Studied*: Yale Univ. Sch. FA. *Member*: Knickerbocker A. I., "Pierre Pidgeon," 1943; "Peter Paints the U.S.A." (50 Best Books of the Year, 1948); "Mikko's Fortune," 1955. Author, I., "Mauis' Summer," 1952.*

BARETSKI, CHARLES ALLAN—*Art Librarian, Archivist*
    Newark Public Library, Van Buren Branch, 140 Van Buren St. (5); h. 229 Montclair Ave., Newark 4, N.J.

B. Mount Carmel, Pa., Nov. 21, 1918. *Studied*: N.Y. Univ., with Demetrios Tselos; Newark Univ. (merged with Rutgers), B.A.; Columbia Univ., B.S.L.S., M.S.L.S.; American Univ., Wash., D.C., Archival Dipl. and Dipl., Advanced Archival Admin.; Notre Dame Univ., M.A., Ph.D. *Member*: Am. Soc. for Aesthetics; Soc. of Am. Archivists; Polish A. Cl., Newark; Polish Univ. Cl. of New Jersey. *Awards*: Archival Internship, Natl. Archives, Wash., D.C., 1951; Edna M. Sanderson Scholarship, Columbia Univ., 1945-46; (2) Louise Connolly Scholarships, Newark Pub. Lib., 1945-46; Research F., Univ. Notre Dame, 1956-57. Editor & Compiler: "The Polish Pantheon: A Roster of Men and Women of Polish Birth or Ancestry Who Have Contributed to American Culture and World Civilization," 1958. Contributor to Art in America, College Art Journal, Journal of the American Institute of Architects, School and Society, The Polish Arts Club of Buffalo Bulletin, and others. Lectures on 19th Century American Painting; Historical School of Polish Painting in 19th Century; European Folk Art of 19th and 20th Centuries, etc.

Founded and directed The Institute of Polish Culture, Seton Hall Univ., 1953-54. *Positions*: Sr. Lib. Asst., A. Dept., 1945-47, Sr. Libn., A. Dept., 1948-54, Branch Libn., 1954-56, 1957- , Newark Pub. Library; Archivist, Am. Council of Polish Culture Clubs, 1954- . Research Asst., Univ. Notre Dame, 1956-57.

BARFOOT, DOROTHY—*Educator, P., C., Des., L.*
    Kansas State College; h. 815 Sunset St., Manhattan, Kans.

B. Decorah, Iowa, Oct. 7, 1896. *Studied*: State Univ. Iowa, B.A.; T. Col., Columbia Univ., M.A. *Member*: CAA; NAEA. *Exhibited*: John Herron A. Sch., 1952; NAWA; Kansas Univ., 1957. *Position*: Hd., Art Dept., Kansas State College, Manhattan, Kans.

BARILE, XAVIER J.—*Painter, T., L., Et., W.*
    67 West 67th St., Studio #6; h. 2126 Hughes Ave., New York, N.Y.

B. Tufo, Italy, Mar. 18, 1891. *Studied*: CUASch; ASL, and with Victor Perard, William DeL. Dodge, Luis Mora, John Sloan and others. *Member*: Soc. Indp. A.; FA Soc., Pueblo, Colo.; Am. Monotype Soc.; Audubon A.; St. Augustine AC; AAPL; P. & S. Soc., N.J.; AEA; ASL; Nat. A. Edu. Assn.; SC; Nat. Soc. Painters in Casein. *Exhibited*: NAD, 1943; Am. Monotype Soc. traveling exh., 1940, 1944; Mus. New Mexico, 1944 (one-man); NAC; LC; Soc. Indp. A.; Denver A. Mus.; Colorado Springs FA Center; Audubon A.; Newark Mus. A.; WMAA; Studio Cl.; AAPL; AEA; SC; Nat. Soc. Painters in Casein; New Jersey Soc. P. & S.; Union Square Savings Bank, N.Y., 1958. Illus., magazine stories and covers; portraits of prominent persons. *Position*: Dir., Barile A. Sch., 1919-39; Hd., A. Dept., Pueblo Jr. Col., 1939-45; Instr. St. Augustine, Fla., 1945-46, Pan America A. Sch., 1948-49, Catan Rose Inst. FA., 1948-50; Dir., Instr., Barile Art Group, 67 West 67th St., New York, N.Y., 1950- .

BARKER, GEORGE—*Painter, T., L.*
    535 Alma Real Dr., Pacific Palisades, Cal.

B. Omaha, Neb., Feb. 20, 1882. *Studied*: Grande Chaumiere, Andre L'Hote, Paris, France, and with J. Lawrie Wallace, Edwin Scott. *Member*: Los Angeles AA; Cal. AC; Pacific Palisades AA. *Awards*: prize, Cal. AC, 1951, 1953, 1955, 1956; Pacific Palisades AA, 1956. *Work*: Olympic Lib., Los Angeles; Joslyn A. Mus., Omaha, Neb. *Exhibited*: Greek Theatre, Los A.; Los Angeles AA, 1950, 1951, 1956, 1957; Cal. AC, annually; Pacific Palisades AA, annually, (one-man) 1952; Long Beach Mun. A. Center, 1951; Joslyn A. Mus., 1954; Santa Monica A. Gal.; Santa Monica Lib., 1957; Bakersfield A. Gal., 1958. Lectures: "Explorations in Color"; "Art & Technique of Thomas Eakins; "Velasquez at The Prado," etc.

BARKER, OLIVE (RUTH)—*Painter*
    535 Alma Real Dr., Pacific Palisades, Cal.

B. Chicago, Ill. *Studied*: N.Y.Sch. F. & App. A., Paris Branch; Oberlin Conservatory; and with F. Tolles Chamberlin, Millard Sheets, Paul Sample. *Member*: Cal. WC Soc.; Cal. AC; NAWA; Women Painters of the West. *Work*: Children's altarpiece, St. Matthew's Church School, Pacific Palisades; Bishop Clarkson Mem. Hospital, Omaha, Neb. *Exhibited*: Los Angeles AA; City of Los Angeles exh., 1949; Pacific Palisades AA, 1952; Ebell Salon, 1949, 1958; Long Beach Mun. A. Center, 1951; Riverside Mus., N.Y., 1948; Women Painters of the West, 1949; Pacific Palisades, (Cal.) A. Gal., 1955, 1958 (2-man with George Barker); Santa Monica Pub. Lib., 1956-1958.

BARKER, VIRGIL—*Writer, Cr., L.*
    4225 Lennox Dr., Coconut Grove, Fla.

B. Abingdon, Va., Dec. 11, 1890. *Studied*: Harvard Col.; Corcoran Sch. A. Author: "Pieter Bruegel the Elder: A Study of His Paintings," 1926; "Henry Lee McFee," 1931; "A Critical Introduction to American Painting," 1931; "American Painting: History and Appreciation," 1950. Contributor to The Arts, Creative Arts, The Yale Review, Saturday Review, and Art in America. *Member*: CAA. *Position*: Cur., Carnegie Inst., 1919-20; Dir., Kansas City AI, 1920-21; Memb. Ed. Bd., The Arts, 1923-31; Art in America; Visiting L., Univ. of Nebraska, 1958 (Oct.); Prof. Hist. A., Univ. Miami, Fla., 1931- .

BARKSDALE, GEORGE EDWARD—*Painter*

Route 14, Box 3, Richmond, Va.

B. Charlotte County, Va., Aug. 13, 1869. *Studied*: PAFA, and with William L. Shepherd, Herman Sodersten. *Awards*: F., PAFA, 1953; prize, Am. Medical Assn., Art Div. (historical painting). *Work*: Petersburg Battlefield Mus., Petersburg, Va.; Confederate Mus., Richmond, Va; Halifax Court House, Va. Author of novel "Punch."*

BARLOGA, VIOLA H.—*Painter, T.*

624 Brown Bldg.; h. 1234 National Ave., Rockford, Ill.

B. Camden, N.J., Feb. 21, 1890. *Studied*: AIC; Chicago Acad. FA; ASL; Rockford Col.; & with Sidney Laufman, Oskar Gross, Briggs Dyer. *Member*: NAWA. *Awards*: prizes, Rockford AA, 1941, 1946, 1949; Montclair AA. *Work*: Burpee A. Gal., Rockford, Ill. *Exhibited*: Carnegie Inst.; CGA; AIC; Burpee Gal.; Argent Gal. *Position*: A.T., Burpee A. Gal., Rockford, Ill., at present.*

BARLOW, MARVIN K. (TONY)—*Cartoonist*

622 Pine Ave., Long Beach, Cal.

B. Bellingham, Wash., Apr. 11, 1906. *Studied*: Univ. Washington; AIC; Am. Acad. A.

BARNES, CATHERINE J.—*Illustrator, Des.*

Wenonah Ave., Mantua, N.J.

B. Philadelphia, Pa., June 6, 1918. *Studied*: PMSchIA; ASL; & with Eliot O'Hara. *Member*: Phila. WC Cl.; PAFA; Phila. A. All. *Exhibited*: PAFA; AIC; BM; Montclair A. Mus.; Butler AI; Phila. A. All. (one-man). I., "Favorite Tales," 1945; "Understood Betsy," 1946; & other books. Illus., national travel & fashion magazines.

BARNES, ERNEST HARRISON—*Painter, T.*

676 Chicago Blvd., Detroit 2, Mich.

B. Portland, N.Y. *Studied*: Hillsdale Col., A.M.; AIC; ASL; & with Charles H. Davis, W. H. Foote. *Member*: Scarab Cl.; Boston AC; Conn. Acad. FA; SSAL; All.A.Am. *Awards*: prizes, Detroit Inst. A., 1916, 1922; SSAL, 1928. *Work*: Univ. Michigan; Hillsdale Col.; Vanderpoel Coll.; Detroit Inst. A. *Exhibited*: CGA, 1921, 1923, 1926, 1933; AIC, 1906, 1907, 1932 NAD, 1923, 1925, 1931, 1933; CM, 1909, 1910, 1911; Detroit Inst. A., 1919-1923, 1926, 1928; WFNY 1939; Mystic AA, 1920-1945; Conn. Acad. FA, 1922-1946; SSAL; Ann Arbor AA. *Position*: Asst. Prof., A., Univ. Michigan, 1929-43.*

BARNES, HALCYONE—*Painter*

Summit, Miss.

B. Dallas, Tex., Mar. 31, 1913. *Studied*: Allisons A. Colony, Way, Miss., and with Karl Zerbe, Fred Conway, Lamar Dodd, Richard Zellner, Andrew Bucci, Pat Travigno, and others. *Member*: Mississippi AA; New Orleans AA. *Awards*: prizes, Jackson, Miss., 1957; Nat. WC Show, Jackson, Miss., 1956; Allisons Art Show, 1956, 1957. *Exhibited*: Birmingham WC Soc., 1956, 1957; Mississippi AA, 1956, 1957; Atlanta, Ga., 1958; Delgado Mus. A., New Orleans, 1955-1958; Mid-South Exh., Memphis, Tenn., 1956-1958; Allisons A. Colony, 1955-1958.

BARNES, VIRGINIA (VAE)—*Teacher, P., Ser.*

Montevallo, Ala.

B. Livingston, Ala. *Studied*: Alabama Col., A.B.; AIC; Univ. Georgia; T. Col., Columbia Univ.; Hans Hofmann. *Member*: Alabama A. Lg.; Alabama WC Soc.; Birmingham AC; SSAL. *Work*: Montgomery Mus. FA; Huntington Col.; Alabama State T. Col.; Alabama Col.; Montgomery State Capitol; Montclair Mus. A.; paintings and prints in numerous colleges, universities and public buildings. *Awards*: prizes, Birmingham AC, 1938, 1941; Alabama A. Lg., 1939, 1943, 1949, 1950, 1953, 1954; Alabama WC Soc., 1940, 1954; Art Instruction, 1949, 1951; Grant from Alabama College for experimental work in printing, 1958. *Exhibited*: prints in United States, Europe, South America, Asia; Nat. Exh., Birmingham Mus. A., 1954. Seven one-man exhs. in Western Alabama, 1958. *Position*: Assoc. Prof. A., Alabama Col., Montevallo, Ala., 1947-59.

BARNET, WILL—*Painter, T., Gr.*

215 West 57th St.; h. 60 East End Ave., New York 28, N.Y.

B. Beverly, Mass., May 25, 1911. *Studied*: BMFA Sch.; ASL. *Member*: Phila. Pr. Cl.; Am. Abstract A.; Fed. Modern P. & S.; Audubon A.; SAGA. *Awards*: prizes, Phila. Pr. Cl., 1942, 1945, 1951; BM, 1949, 1952; Provincetown A. Festival, 1958; N.Y. State Fair, 1951, 1958. *Work*: BMFA; WMAA; MMA; FMA; LC; PC; PMA; Carnegie Inst.; SAM; Honolulu Acad. A.; BM; N.Y. Pub. Lib.; Montana State Col. *Exhibited*: CAM, 1951; WMAA, 1952, 1955, 1957; MMA, 1950-1951; AIC, 1950; Univ. Nebraska, 1951, 1955; Univ. Minnesota, 1951; PAFA; BMFA; Am. Abstract A.; Exchange Exh., Mus. Tokyo, Japan, 1955; BM, 1955-56; Yale Univ., 1955; Minneapolis Inst. A., 1945-1957; Retrospective Exh., Tweed Gal. A., Univ. Minnesota, 1958; one-man: Walker A. Center, 1938; Galerie St. Etienne, 1943; Bertha Schaefer Gal., 1948-1951, 1953, 1955; DMFA, 1950; Stephens Col., 1950; AFA traveling exh., 1952-53; Boris Mirskie Gal., Boston, 1954; Esther Robles Gal., 1957; Krasner Gal., 1958. *Position*: Instr., ASL, 1936- ; CUASch., 1945- ; Birch Wathen Sch., 1944- , all in N.Y.; Summer Instr., Montana State Col., 1951; Visiting Cr., Yale Univ., 1952, 1953; Guiding Faculty, Famous Artists Schs., 1954- ; Summer Instr., Univ. Ohio, Univ. Minnesota, Duluth, 1958.

BARNETT, BION—*Painter, L.*

1718 Osceola St., Jacksonville 4, Fla.

B. Jacksonville, Fla., Sept. 18, 1887. *Studied*: ASL, with Bridgman, DuMond; Woodstock, with Harrison and Carlson; Provincetown, Mass., with Charles Hawthorne; Ogunquit, Me., with Joseph Davol; Academie Julian, Academie Colarossi and Academie de la Grande Chaumiere, Paris. *Member*: Societe Nationale des Beaux-Arts; All. A. Am.; Lotos Cl.; SC. *Awards*: Chevalier, Legion d'Honneur, 1937; silver med., Paris Exp., 1937; Bemis award, Palm Beach A. Lg., 1941. *Exhibited*: N.Y. WC Cl., 1910; Mc-Dowell Cl., 1917; 2 one-man exhs., Edinburgh, Scotland, and exhibited with Soc. Scottish Artists; 7 one-man exhs. in Paris. AFA traveling exh., 1917; Salon d'Automne, 1920, 1923; Carnegie Inst., 1922; Beaux-Arts, 1924-1940; Royal Acad., 1928-1934; New English A. Cl., 1935; AAPL (Paris chapter) 1927-1940; Soc. FA, Palm Beach; Palm Beach A. Lg.; Fla. Fed. A.; St. Augustine A. Soc.

BARNETT, HERBERT PHILLIP—*Educator, P., L.*

Art Academy of Cincinnati; h. 3 Moyer Place, Cincinnati 26, Ohio

B. Providence, R.I., July 8, 1910. *Studied*: BMFA Sch., and in Europe. *Awards*: prizes, Manchester, N.H.; PAFA; Hallmark Award. *Work*: WMA; PAFA; Univ. Arizona; Amherst Col.; Randolph-Macon Col.; CM. *Exhibited*: (1952-58)—WMA (one-man); Fleming Mus. A.; Phila. A. All.; Fitchburg A. Center; Grace Horne Gal., Boston; Marie Harriman Gal.; Contemporary A.; Mortimer Levitt Gal., N.Y.; CM, 1952; Wittenberg Col., 1957; Miami Univ., 1957; Interior Valley Exh.; U.S. Exh., France; Corcoran Biennial; Hallmark International. *Positions*: Instr., P., Univ. Vermont 1943; Norfolk A. Sch., Yale Univ., 1948; Dir., Norfolk A. Sch., 1949; Hd., WMA Sch., 1940-51; Assoc. Prof. A. (affiliate) Clark Univ., 1946-51; Dean, Art Acad. Cincinnati, at present.

BARNETT, WILLIAM—*Painter*

4805 York Rd., Philadelphia 41, Pa.

B. Philadelphia, Pa., Feb. 11, 1919. *Studied*: PIASch., B.A.; Temple Univ. *Member*: AEA; Phila. A. All.; Contemporary AA; Cheltenham A. Center. *Awards*: prizes, Cooperative A. Exh., Indiana, Pa., 1948; Cheltenham A. Center, 1949, 1955; PAFA, 1951, 1955; Tri-State Exh., 1955; Woodmere A. Gal., 1955; DaVinci medal; Guggenheim Fellowship, 1958. *Work*: PAFA; PMA; Cheltenham A. Center; murals, Gimbel Bros., Phila., Pa. *Exhibited*: PAFA, 1948-1958; Indiana, Pa., 1948; Phila. Sketch Cl., 1947, 1948; Phila. A. All., 1951-1955; Pyramid Cl., 1951, 1952; Cheltenham A. Center, 1949, 1951-1955; Contemporary AA, 1948-1950; Beach Haven Fnd., 1950, 1955; CGA, 1953; CMA, 1955; BM; AAG; BMA; PMA traveling exh., 1955-56; PMA, 1958; AFA traveling exh., 1953-54; Butler AI traveling exh., nationally & internationally, and oil annual, 1956, 1958; Norfolk Mus. A., 1958; Tri-State Exh., 1955; one-man: Harcum Jr. Col., 1955; PAFA, 1953; Phila. A. All., 1955; Dubin Gal., Phila., 1954. *Position*: Instr., PMA Sch. A., Philadelphia, Pa.

BARNEY, MAGINEL WRIGHT (Mrs.)—Craftsman, I.
16 East 11th St., New York 3, N.Y.

B. Weymouth, Mass., June 19, 1881. *Studied*: AIC. *Work*: Illus. for leading publications including Woman's Home Companion, Ladies Home Journal, Collier's, McCall's and others. Specializes in decorative embroidery, jewelled slippers and painting of landscapes. *Exhibited*: Marie Sterner Gal.; French & Co., New York.

BARR, ALFRED HAMILTON, JR.—
Director of Museum Collections, W.
The Museum of Modern Art, 11 West 53rd St., (19); h. 49 East 96th St., New York 28, N.Y.

B. Detroit, Mich., Jan. 28, 1902. *Studied*: Princeton Univ., A.B., A.M.; Harvard Univ., Ph.D. *Awards*: Princeton Univ., Litt.D., 1949; Bonn Univ., Hon. Ph.D., 1958. Lectures: Mary Flexner Lectures, Bryn Mawr College, 1946, "Programs and Practices in Modern Art." *Member*: Advisory Council, Dept. Art & Archaeology, Princeton, 1946- ; AAMD. Author: "Cubism and Abstract Art," 1936; "What Is Modern Painting?", 1943; "Picasso: Fifty Years of His Art," 1946; "20th Century Italian Art," 1949 (with James Thrall Soby); "Matisse: His Art and His Public," 1951; "Masters of Modern Art," 1954 (Editor); Editor of 32 museum exhibition catalogs. Director or Organizer of some 85 exhibitions for The Museum of Modern Art. *Positions*: Instr., Vassar Col., 1923-24; Harvard Univ., 1924-25; Princeton Univ., 1925-26; Wellesley Col., 1926-29; Trustee, MModA, 1939- ; Member: Advisory Council, Dept. Art & Archaeology, Princeton, 1946- ; Editorial Bd., Art Bulletin, 1956- ; Art Quarterly, 1950- ; Art in America, 1957- ; Visiting Committee, Fogg Museum of Art, Harvard Univ., 1958 ; Dir., MModA, 1929-43; Dir., Research in Painting & Sculpture, MModA, 1944-46; Dir., The Museum Collections, MModA, 1947- .

BARR, ROGER TERRY—Painter, E., Gr.
44 Rue de Seine, Paris VI, France

B. Milwaukee, Wis., Sept. 17, 1921. *Studied*: Univ. Wisconsin; Nat. Univ. of Mexico; Pomona Col., B.A.; Claremont Col., M.F.A.; Jepson AI, with Henry L. McFee, Millard Sheets, Rico Lebrun. *Member*: AEA; San F. AA. *Awards*: prizes, Arizona State Fair, 1948; Cal. WC Soc., 1955; Oakland A. Mus., 1955; Stanford Univ., 1956 (purchase); Catherwood Fnd. F., 1956. *Work*: NAD; Pasadena A. Mus.; Claremont Col.; Los A. AA; Museu del Arte Moderna, Sao Paulo, Brazil; Stanford Univ., and in private colls. *Exhibited*: MMA, 1950; Univ. Illinois, 1948; BMA, 1954; Los A. Mus. A., 1948-1952; Cal. State Fair, 1948, 1952-1955; Santa Barbara Mus. A., 1955; Cal. PLH, 1956; La Jolla A. Center, 1956; Oakland A. Mus., 1956; SFMA, 1956; Downtown Gal., N.Y., 1955; Stockholm, Sweden, 1953; Redfern and Waddington Gals., London, 1957-1959, and in Paris; one-man: Scripps Col., 1949; Landau Gal., Los Angeles, 1952, 1954, 1956; deYoung Mem. Mus., 1956; Galerie Philadelphie, Paris, 1958. *Positions*: Instr., Univ. Cal. at Los Angeles, 1950-52; Cal. Sch. FA, San Francisco, 1954-56; Prof. Painting, Hd. Dept. A., American Students' and Artists' Center, Paris XIV, France, 1958- .

BARRER, GERTRUDE (RUSSELL)—Painter, C.
48-24 65th St., Woodside, L.I., N.Y.

B. New York, N.Y., Mar. 11, 1921. *Studied*: ASL; Iowa State Univ. *Member*: Spiral Group; Soc. Am. Painters. *Work*: Univ. Maine; Riverside Mus., N.Y.; ceramics in private colls., in collaboration with Frank Russell. *Exhibited*: PAFA, 1947; WMAA, 1951, 1952, 1956; BM, 1952; AIC, 1953; Brown Univ., 1954; Univ. Maine, 1956; Jessup Mem. Gal., 1956; Gal. Neuf, 1947; Artists Gal., 1947, 1951, 1956; Riverside Mus.; Washington Irving Gal., 1958; Kootz Gal., N.Y., 1950; Mint Mus. A.; AFA traveling exh.

BARRET, RICHARD CARTER—
Museum Director—Cur., W., L., E.
Bennington Museum of Art; h. "Lemon Fair," Bennington, Vt.

B. White Plains, N.Y., Mar. 19, 1916. *Studied*: Miami Univ.; Univ. Toledo, A.A.; Columbia Univ. Ext.; Univ. Berne, Switzerland; Middlebury Col., B.A. *Member*: F., Intl. Inst. for Conservation of Museum Objects; Early Am. Industries Assn.; Am. Assn. State and Local History; Vermont Hist. Soc.; Bennington Battle Monument & Hist.

Assn. (Sec.-Dir., 1953). *Awards*: Departmental honors in Fine Arts, Middlebury Col., 1950. Author: "Bennington Pottery and Porcelain," 1958. Contributor to "Antiques"; "Vermont Life" publications. Lectures on Bennington Pottery and Porcelain. Arranged and catalogued special exh. of the Spargo Collection of Bennington Pottery and Porcelain. *Positions*: Member, A. Committee, Southern Vermont A. Center, 1956-57; Founder (1954) Dir., Bennington Museum Sch.; Dir., Bennington Museum, Bennington, Vt., at present.

BARRETT, LISBETH S. (Mrs. Albert O.)—
Miniature Painter
Dorset Rd., Devon, Pa.

B. Seattle, Wash., Apr. 2, 1904. *Studied*: Newcomb Col., Tulane Univ.; ASL; Grand Central Sch. A.; Julian Acad., Paris; PAFA. *Member*: Pa. Soc. Min. P.; Am. Soc. Min. P. *Award*: medal of honor, Pa. Soc. Min. P., 1949. *Work*: PMA. *Exhibited*: AFA; Portraits, Inc.; MMA; Smithsonian Inst.*

BARRETT, NEIL (Mrs. Roger W.)—Painter
222 Leicester Rd., Kenilworth, Ill.

B. Milwaukee, Wis., July 2, 1915. *Studied*: N.Y. Sch. F. & Appl. A.; Parsons Sch. Des. (Grad.). *Member*: Chicago AC; Renaissance Soc., Univ. Chicago. *Exhibited*: MModA, 1956; Denver Mus. A., 1956; Butler Inst. Am. A., 1957; Art: USA, 1958; Univ. Illinois, 1959; AIC; one-man exhs. in Illinois since 1954.

BARRETT, OLIVER O'CONNOR—Sculptor, I., E., W.
4205 Washington Rd., West Palm Beach, Fla.

B. London, England, Jan. 17, 1908. *Studied*: Fircroft Col., England. *Member*: S. Gld. *Awards*: prizes, Audubon A., 1948, medal, 1950; medal, Knickerbocker A., 1953. *Work*: Birmingham City Mus., England. *Exhibited*: PAFA, 1945; Royal Acad., London, 1933; Audubon A., 1946, 1948, 1950; New Orleans A. Lg., 1942, 1943; one-man: Sculpture Center, 1953; Potsdam State Univ., 1953; Norton Gal. & Sch. A., 1956; Potsdam Festival of Arts, 1955. Illus. "Anything For a Laugh," "Little Benny Wanted a Pony," 1951. Contributor to Town & Country and other magazines. *Position*: Instr., S., CUASch., MModA., New York, N.Y.; Norton Gal. & Sch. A., West Palm Beach, Fla., at present.*

BARRETT, MRS. RIVA HELFOND. See Helfond, Riva

BARRETT, ROBERT D.—Painter, C., E.
174 East 71st St., New York 21, N.Y.

B. Fulton, N.Y., Nov. 23, 1903. *Studied*: Syracuse Univ., B.F.A. *Member*: All.A.Am.; N.Y.Soc.C. *Awards*: F., Syracuse Univ., 1925. *Exhibited*: NAD, 1932, 1938; AFA (traveling exh.), 1939; All.A.Am., 1936, 1945, 1946; AWCS, 1946; WFNY 1939; El Paso Mus., 1945; Paris Exp., 1937. *Position*: Asst. Prof., Brooklyn Col., N.Y.; Pres., A. Fellowship, Inc.

BARRICK, KENNETH ROBERTS—Painter, E., I.
Star Route, Box 11 A, Las Cruces, N.M.

B. Hudson, S.D., July 15, 1913. *Studied*: Univ. Illinois, B.F.A.; Univ. Iowa, M.A., with Grant Wood. *Member*: AAUP. *Exhibited*: New Mexico Annual, 1949-1955; El Paso Sun Carnival, 1949-1955. *Position*: Instr., A., Otterbein Col., Ohio; Maryville Col., Tenn.; Asst. Prof. A., New Mexico Col. of A. & M.A.*

BARRIE, ERWIN S.—Painter
40 Vanderbilt Ave., New York 17, N.Y.; h. Greenwich, Conn.

B. Canton, Ohio, June 3, 1886. *Studied*: AIC. *Member*: Chicago AC; NAC; Greenwich A. Soc. *Work*: specializes in painting golf courses. In permanent coll. United States Golf Assn., Metropolitan Golf Assn.; private coll.; Pres. D. D. Eisenhower; Robert Jones, Jr.; Richard D. Tufts, Pres. U.S. Golf Assn. Permanent one-man exhibition at Pinehurst, N.C. *Position*: Dir. & Manager, Grand Central A. Gal., New York, N.Y.

BARRITT, ROBERT CARLYLE—*Portrait Painter, T.*

Charlottesville, Va.

B. West Pittston, Pa., June 23, 1898. *Studied*: PAFA; N.Y. Sch. A. *Member*: AAPL; Audubon A.; Wyoming Valley A. Soc.; Albemarle A. Lg.; Am. Veterans Soc. A.; Buck Hill AA. *Awards*: prizes, Wanamaker Exh.; deCordova & Dana Mus. A. *Work*: portraits, Univ. Hospital, Charlottesville, Va.; O. Henry Museum, Greensboro, N.C.; many others in private colls.; murals in churches. *Exhibited*: Audubon A.; Am. Veterans Soc. A.; Univ. Virginia; deCordova & Dana Mus. A.; New Hope, Pa.; Johnstown, Pa.

BARRON, GRACE—*Painter, T.*

27 West 67th St., New York 23, N.Y.

B. Buffalo, N.Y., Dec. 7, 1903. *Studied*: Boston Sch. FA & Crafts; Fontainebleau, France. *Member*: Rockport AA. *Awards*: prizes, Albright A. Gal., 1935, 1941. *Work*: Albright A. Gal. *Exhibited*: Carnegie Inst., 1941; AFA (traveling exh.), 1941, 1942; U.S. Govt. Section FA, 1941; Albright A. Gal., 1933-1944; N.Y. State Exh., Syracuse, 1941; Rockport A.A., 1953-1958. *Position*: Instr. A., Little Red School House, New York, N.Y.

BARRON, HARRIS—*Sculptor, Arch. Des.*

30 Webster Place, Brookline 46, Mass.

B. Boston, Mass., Nov. 15, 1926. *Studied*: Vesper George Sch. A.; Kerr Sch. A.; Mass. Sch. A., B.F.A. *Awards*: prizes, Fiber, Clay & Metal Exh., 1956; Ceramic Natl. Exh., 1956; Portland Mus. A. Festival, 1958. *Work*: Architectural commissions: Choate Sch., Wallingford, Conn.; Temple Adath Yeshurun, Manchester, N.H.; Chapel, B'nai B'rith, Danvers, Mass., and others; AGAA; Portland Mus. A.; St. Paul Gal. A. *Exhibited*: Boston A. Festival, 1955-1957; Ceramic Nat. Exh., 1954, 1956; Silvermine Gld. A., 1957; Smithsonian Inst., 1957; Wichita AA, 1955; America House, 1953, 1955, 1956; St. Paul A. Gal., 1955; Inst. Contemp. A., Boston, 1955; New Hampshire Potters Gld., 1954, 1955; New England Crafts, 1955; deCordova & Dana Mus., 1955; Mass. Crafts of Today, 1953-1955; Brussels World Fair, 1958; Ceramic International, 1958; Arch. Lg., 1958. One-man exhs.: deCordova & Dana Mus., 1956; Bonnier Gal., N.Y., 1956; Kanegis Gal., Boston, 1958; Cummington Sch. A., 1958. *Position*: Instr., Sculpture, deCordova & Dana Mus., Lincoln, Mass., 1954-1958.

BARRON, ROS—*Sculptor, Des.*

30 Webster Place, Brookline 46, Mass.

B. Boston, Mass., July 4, 1933. *Studied*: Mass. Sch. A., B.F.A., and with Carl Nelson. *Awards*: prizes, Fiber, Clay & Metal Exh., 1956; Ceramic Nat., 1956; deCordova & Dana Mus., 1953. *Work*: AGAA; St. Paul Gal. A.; Arch. commissions: Choate Sch., Wallingford, Conn.; Temple Adath Yeshurun, Manchester, N.H.; Chapel B'nai B'rith, Danvers, Mass., and others. *Exhibited*: Boston A. Festival, 1955, 1956, 1957; Ceramic Nat., 1954, 1956; Wichita AA, 1955; America House, 1953, 1955, 1956; St. Paul A. Gal., 1955; Inst. Contemp. A., Boston, 1955; deCordova Mus., 1955; Silvermine Gld. A., 1957; Smithsonian Inst., 1957; Brussels World Fair, 1958; Ceramic International, 1958; Arch. Lg., 1958; one-man: deCordova & Dana Mus., 1956; Bonniers, N.Y., 1956; Kanegis Gal., Boston, 1958; Cummington Sch. A., 1958. *Position*: Instr., deCordova & Dana Mus., Lincoln, Mass., 1956-1958.

BARRY, EDITH CLEAVES—*Painter, S., Des.*

116 East 66th St., New York 21, N.Y.; s. 24 Summer St., Kennebunk, Me.

B. Boston, Mass. *Studied*: ASL; Paris, France; Rome, Italy. *Member*: NAWA; All. A. Am.; NSMP; Conn. Acad. FA; NAC; AAPL. *Work*: portraits in public bldgs., in New Jersey, Massachusetts, Maine. Murals in Maine and New York. *Position*: Founder, Brick Store Museums, Kennebunk, Me.

BARSCHEL, H(ANS) J(OACHIM)—
Advertising Designer

37 Hartfeld Dr., Rochester 10, N.Y.

B. Berlin-Charlottenburg, Germany, Feb. 22, 1912. *Studied*: Mun. A. Sch., Acad. Free & App. A., Berlin, M.A. *Award*: prize, AIGA, 1938. *Work*: MModA.; N.Y. Pub. Lib.; LC. *Exhibited*: AIGA, 1938; A. Dir. Cl., 1938, 1939, 1950; A-D Gal., 1946; Bevier Gal., Rochester Inst. Tech., 1954. Contributor to international art magazines: "Gebrauchs-

graphik," Germany, 1952; "Art & Industry," London, 1954; "Publimondial," Paris, 1955; "Productionwise," New York, 1955. Des. book jackets, covers for Fortune, Steel Horizons, Seminar, Ciba Symposia, Town & Country, etc. Created graphic arts program brochure for Rochester Inst. Tech. *Position*: A. Dir., Dept. Health, New York City, 1950-51; Assoc. A. Dir., Great Lakes Press Corp., Rochester, N.Y., 1952-53; Assoc. A. Dir., John P. Smith Co., Rochester, N.Y., 1953-54; Des., Graphic A. Research Dept., 1954- ; Prof. Advanced Adv. Des. & Creative Dwg., A. Dir., Sch. of Arts & Design, Rochester Inst. of Tech., Rochester, N.Y.

BARTHE, RICHMOND—*Sculptor*

Cole Gate P.O., St. Ann, Jamaica, B.W.I.

B. Bay St. Louis, Miss., Jan. 28, 1901. *Studied*: AIC; ASL; Xavier Univ., M.A.; & with Charles Schroeder. *Member*: S. Gld.; NSS; Audubon A. *Awards*: Rosenwald F., 1930, 1931; Guggenheim F., 1940, 1941; Hoey Award, 1945; med., Audubon A., 1945; grant. Am.Acad.A. & Let., 1946; hon. deg., Doctor of Fine Arts, St. Francis Col., Brooklyn, N.Y., 1947. *Work*: WMAA; Oberlin Col.; PAFA; monuments, "Toussaint L'Ouverture," "General Dessalines," Haitian Government, 1952; VMFA; MMA; N.Y. Univ. *Exhibited*: Harmon Fnd., 1929, 1931, 1933; WMAA, 1933-1936, 1940-1942, 1944; BM, 1935, 1945; CGA, 1936; PAFA, 1938, 1940-1944; Atlanta Univ., 1945, 1946; Audubon A., 1945; Montclair A. Mus., 1946; Hampton Inst., 1944; Carnegie Inst., 1938, 1941; MMA, 1942, etc.*

BARTLETT, FRED STEWART—*Museum Director, T. W.*

30 West Dale St.; h. 41 West Cache La Poudre, Colorado Springs, Colo.

B. Brush, Colo., May 15, 1905. *Studied*: Univ. Colorado, A.B.; Univ. Denver; Harvard Univ. *Member*: AAMus. *Award*: F., Carnegie Inst. *Positions*: Dir. Edu., Asst. to Dir., Denver A. Mus., 1935-43; Cur., Paintings, Colorado Springs FA Center, 1945-55; Dir., 1955- ; Instr., A. History, Colorado College, Colorado Springs, Colo.

BARTLETT, IVAN—*Designer, P., Lith., Ser., I.*

420 East 64th St., New York 21, N.Y.

B. Plainfield, Vt., Feb. 3, 1915. *Studied*: Chouinard AI. *Awards*: prizes, Cal. Festival of All. A., 1935; Long Beach Exh., 1937; Charlot prize, Laguna Beach, 1938; Los A. County Fair, 1938, 1941; A.I.D., 1946. *Work*: Lib. Cong.; Los A. County Fair; USPO, Huntington Park, Redondo Beach, Cal.; Long Beach H.S. *Exhibited*: WFNY 1939; GGE, 1939; SFMA, 1937, 1938; Oakland A. Gal., 1938; Laguna Beach, 1938 (one-man); Los A. Mus. A., 1936-1939; San Diego, 1937-1939; Los A. County Fair, 1938, 1939; Fnd. West A., 1938, 1939; Zeitling Gal., 1938 (one-man); City of Paris, San F., 1944, 1945 (one-man). *Position*: Textile and Wallpaper Des., 1945- .

BARTLETT, PAUL—*Painter, T.*

824 East Kingston Ave., Charlotte 3, N.C.

B. Taunton, Mass., July 8, 1881. *Studied*: Harvard Univ., A.B.; AIC; Julian Acad., Paris, and with John Sloan. *Member*: Gld. of Charlotte A. *Awards*: medal, Chicago Soc. A., 1920; Temple medal, PAFA, 1932. *Work*: Luxembourg Mus., Paris; CMA; WMAA; Mint Mus. A. *Exhibited*: PAFA; CGA; AIC; Carnegie Inst., and many others; one-man: Kraushaar Gal.; Wildenstein Gal., New York; Chester Johnson Gal., Chicago.*

BARTO, EMILY (Mrs.)—*Painter, I., Cr., W.*

402 West 22nd St., New York 11, N.Y.

B. Greenport, L.I., N.Y., Apr. 6, 1886. *Studied*: CUASch.; NAD, and with George Bridgman, Charles Hawthorne, William Dodge. *Member*: AAPL; Gotham Painters; Catherine L. Wolfe A. Cl. I., "The Crooked Man"; "Piper's Son"; "Jack Horner," and others. Teaches watercolor and color theory privately.

BARTON, AUGUST CHARLES—*Designer, P., E., L.*

110 West 40th St., New York 18, N.Y.; h. Louises Lane, New Canaan, Conn.

B. Szekesfehervar, Hungary, Nov. 15, 1897. *Studied*: Royal Hungarian Univ. Tech. Sciences; Royal Hungarian Col. Indst. A.; ASL. *Member*: AWS; Textiles Des. Gld.; Hudson Valley AA; Silvermine Gld. A. *Work*: Fabric Designs, U.S. and Europe. *Exhibited*: AWS; Hudson Valley AA; Silvermine Gld. A.; Bronxville Women's Cl.; Moore Inst., Phila. Contributor to Women's Wear Daily. *Position*: Prof. A., Dress Fabric Des., Moore Inst. A., Indst. & Sciences, Philadelphia, Pa., 1952- ; Member of Faculty of Silvermine Gld. Sch. A., New Canaan, Conn., 1958- .

BARTON, CATHERINE GRAEFF—*Sculptor*
96 Edgemere Rd., Hamden 17, Conn.

B. Englewood, N.J., July 22, 1904. *Studied*: CUASch.; ASL; & with Archipenko; Despiau, Gimond, in Paris. *Member*: New Haven Paint & Clay Cl. Awards: prizes, FA Comm., Wash., D.C., 1930; NAWA, 1931; one of 3 finalists in Miami Univ. Sesqui-centennial Medallion Comp., 1956. *Work*: Dwight Sch. for Girls, Englewood, N.J. *Exhibited*: NAD, 1926; Arch. L., 1926; PAFA, 1927; NSS, 1940; New Haven Paint & Clay C., 1944-1946.

BARTON, ELEANOR DODGE—*Educator*
Sweet Briar College, Sweet Briar, Va.

B. Willsborough, N.Y., Jan. 23, 1918. *Studied*: Vassar Col., B.A.; N.Y. Univ., M.A.; Radcliffe Col. Grad. Sch., Ph.D. *Member*: CAA; Renaissance Soc. of Am.; Archaeological Inst. of Am.; AAUW; AAUP. Contributor to: Marsyas; Collier's Encyclopaedia; Encyclopaedia Britannica; Encyclopedia of World Art. Lectures on Modern and Baroque Sculpture. *Positions*: Teaching F., Instr., Asst. Prof., Smith College, 1942-1953; Prof., Chm. Dept. A., Sweet Briar College, Sweet Briar, Va., 1953- ; Visiting L., Wellesley College.

BARTON, ETHEL ROSE—*Painter, Des.*
18 West 25th St., New York 10, N.Y.; s. Cornish, N.H.

B. Cornish, N.H. *Studied*: CUASch.; NAD; ASL; and with Guy Pene DuBois, Boardman Robinson. *Awards*: med., CUASch. *Exhibited*: AWS, 1927; Carl Fischer Hall, N.Y., 1952; Burr Gal., N.Y., 1957, 1958. *Position*: Comm. work in textile des., paper wrappings, and card des.; Des., greeting cards for The Paramount Line, Inc., Pawtucket, R.I., 1957- .

BARTON, JOHN MURRAY—*Painter, Gr., L.*
222 West 23rd St., New York 11, N.Y.

B. New York, N.Y., Feb. 8, 1921. *Studied*: ASL, with George Bridgman, Frank Dumond, William von Schlegell; Tschacbasov Sch. A. *Member*: Woodstock AA. *Work*: BM; N.Y. Pub Lib.; Newark Pub. Lib.; MMA; Mus. Modern A., Haifa, Israel; murals, Riverdale Jr. H.S., N.Y.; ceramic, Manhattan Pub. Sch. #41. *Exhibited*: one-man: Fantasy Gal., Wash., D.C., 1958; Mack Gal., Philadelphia, Pa., 1957. Lectures to art associations and clubs.

BARTON, LOREN (Mrs. J. Russell Miller)—
Painter, Et., I.
Dalzell Hatfield Galleries, Ambassador Hotel, Los Angeles 5, Cal.; h. 357 South Curson Ave., Los Angeles 36, Cal.

B. Oxford, Mass., Nov. 16, 1893. *Studied*: Univ. So. California. *Member*: AWS; Cal. WC. Soc. *Awards*: NAWA, 1928; Arcadia, Cal., 1924; Pacific Southwest Exh., 1928; Los A. Mus. A., 1937; AWS, 1941; Santa Paula, Cal., 1941, 1947; Cal. WC Soc., 1945; Santa Cruz A. Lg., 1946; Clearwater A. Mus., 1946; Gardena, Cal., 1947, 1950; San Fernando, Cal., 1947. *Work*: AIC; Cal. State Lib.; Los A. Pub. Lib.; N.Y. Pub. Lib.; BM; San Diego FA Soc.; Los A. Mus. A.; MMA; Nat. Lib., France; Wesleyan Col.; Phoenix (Ariz.) Mun. Coll.; VMFA; NGFA. *Exhibited*: NAD, 1945; AIC, 1945. Illus., "The Little House," 1937; "California," 1938; "The Butterfly Shawl," 1940, and others.

BARTON, MACENA ALBERTA—*Painter*
4 East Ohio St., Chicago 11, Ill.

B. Union City, Mich., Aug. 7, 1901. *Studied*: AIC. *Member*: Chicago SA; Chicago P. & S.; Chicago Galleries Assn.; A. Salon of Chicago; AEA; Alumni Assoc. of AIC. *Awards*: prizes, Augustus Peabody prize, AIC, 1927; Chicago Woman's Aid, 1931, 1932; Chicago Galleries, 1945, 1956. *Work*: City of Chicago Coll.; Chicago Pub. Schs.; Vanderpool A. Gal., Chicago. *Exhibited*: AIC, 1927, 1928, 1932, 1933, 1937, 1939, 1941-1943, 1949; VMFA, 1946;

Kansas City AI; Riverside Mus., N.Y.; Carnegie Inst., Pittsburgh; Los A. County Mus.; Minneapolis Inst. A.; and others. One-man: AIC, 1928; Knoedler Gal., Chicago, 1931; Finlay Gal., Chicago, 1933, 1936; Chicago Galleries, 1932, 1936, 1943, 1948, 1951.

BARUCH, ANNE BARBARA—*Painter*
257 Atlantic Ave., Palm Beach, Fla.; h. Mayflower Hotel, Washington, D.C.

B. Boston, Mass., July 21, 1903. *Studied*: R.I. Col. Edu.; & with Bessie Kaufman, Francine Utrecht. *Member*: Soc. Four A.; Palm Beach A. Lg. *Work*: Norton Gal. A. *Exhibited*: AAPL; Soc. Four A.; Palm Beach A. Lg.; Norton Gal. A., 1955; First Nat. Bank, Palm Beach, Fla., 1953. *Position*: T., Mayflower Hotel Progressive A. Sch., Wash., D.C.

BARUZZI, PETER B.—*Painter, C., Gr., T.*
Skidmore College; h. 2 Fifth Ave., Saratoga Springs, N.Y.

B. Fredericktown, Pa., Dec. 3, 1924. *Studied*: Memphis Acad. A., B.F.A.; Memphis State T. Col.; Syracuse Univ., M.F.A.; State Univ. of Iowa, and with Mauricio Lasansky. *Work*: Altar set, St. John's Episcopal Church, Memphis; wall fountain, Fountain Mart, New York, N.Y.; many commissions in jewelry and silver. *Exhibited*: PAFA, 1954; Chicago, Ill., 1954; AGAA, 1954; Memphis, 1948; Joslyn A. Mus., 1951; Va. Intermont Col., 1952; Brooks Mem. Mus., 1948-1954; Union Col., Schenectady, N.Y., 1955. Lectures: contemporary painting, printmaking to art associations, art conferences and student groups. *Position*: Instr., Memphis Acad. A., 1951-54; Asst. Prof. A., Skidmore Col., Saratoga Springs, N.Y., 1954- .

BARZUN, JACQUES—*Writer, T., Hist., Cr., L.*
Columbia University; h. 165 East 83rd St., New York 28, N.Y.

B. Créteil, France, Nov. 30, 1907. *Studied*: Lycee Janson de Sailly, Paris; Columbia Univ., A.M., Ph.D. *Member*: Am. Hist. Assn.; Soc. Am. Hist.; Authors Gld. Am.; Century Assn.; Nat. Inst. A. & Let.; Am. Acad. A. & Sciences; Acad. Delphinale, Grenoble. *Awards*: F. Am. Council Learned Soc., 1933-34; Guggenheim F., 1945; Legion of Honor, 1956. Author: "Of Human Freedom," 1939; "Darwin, Marx, Wagner," 1941; "Romanticism and the Modern Ego," 1943; "Berlioz and the Romantic Century," 1950, and others. *Positions*: Instr., Columbia Col., Columbia Univ., 1928- ; Prof. Columbia Univ., 1945- ; Dean of Faculties and Provost, New York, N.Y., 1958- .

BASHOR, JOHN WILLIAM—*Educator, P.*
Art Department, Bethany College; h. 716 North First St., Lindsborg, Kans.

B. Newton, Kans., Mar. 11, 1926. *Studied*: Washburn Univ., A.B.; State Univ. Iowa, M.F.A., and with Howard Church. *Member*: Kansas SA; Kansas Fed. A. *Awards*: Harrison S. Morgan award, Missouri Valley annual, 1951, 1952; purchase award, Mid-America annual, Nelson Gal. A., 1952; purchase award, Springfield, Mo., 1957; Kansas State Col., 1952, 1956; Kansas State T. Col., 1957; Kansas Free Fair, Topeka, 1952; Iowa A. Salon, Des Moines, 1950. *Work*: State. Univ. Iowa; Kansas State College; Kansas State T. College; Wm. Rockhill Nelson Gal. A.; St. Benedict's Col., Springfield, Mo.; Hutchinson Jr. Col. *Exhibited*: AWS, 1948; Magnificent Mile, 1956; Mid-America Exh., 1952, 1955; Joslyn Mus. A., 1957; Missouri Valley, 1951, 1952; Joslyn Mus. A., Biennial, 1957; Univ. Nebraska, 1957; circulating one-man exh., 1957. *Position*: Hd., Art Dept., Bethany College, Lindsborg, Kans., 1956- .

BASKERVILLE, CHARLES—*Painter*
130 West 57th St., New York 19, N.Y.

B. Raleigh, N.C., Apr. 16, 1896. *Studied*: Cornell Univ.; ASL; Julian Acad., Paris. *Member*: NSMP (Pres., 1957-58); AAPL. *Work*: murals, S.S. "America"; 72 official portraits, AAF, Pentagon, Washington, D.C. Many portraits of noted persons including the King of Nepal and Prime Minister Nehru, 1949. *Exhibited*: Carnegie Inst., 1941; WMAA, 1936; CGA, 1940; Soc. Four A., Palm Beach, Fla., 1938, 1940; NGFA; Albright A. Gal.; deYoung Mem. Mus., San Francisco; MMA; Sitges, Spain, 1958.

BASKIN, LEONARD—Sculptor, Gr.
Fort Hill, Northampton, Mass.

B. New Brunswick, N.J., Aug. 15, 1922. *Studied*: Yale Univ. Sch. FA; The New School; in Paris, and with Maurice Glickman. *Awards*: Tiffany Fnd. F., 1947; Guggenheim F., 1953. *Work*: MMA; MModA.; BM; NGA; FMA; BMFA; WMA; SAM; PMA; CAM; LC. *Exhibited*: BM, 1949, 1952-1955; LC; Phila. Pr. Cl.; SAGA, 1952, 1953; Sao Paulo, Brazil; Musee de L'Art Moderne, Paris; Yugoslavia; Zurich, Switzerland, etc. *Position*: Asst. Prof., S. & Gr. A., Smith College, Northampton, Mass., 1953- .

BASSETT, CHARLES PRESTON—
Designer, P., Lith., S., T., L., C.
Bethel Park, Pa.

B. Pittsburgh, Pa., June 27, 1903. *Studied*: Carnegie Inst., B.A.; & with Wilfred Readio, Joseph Bailey Ellis, Emil Grapin. *Member*: Assoc. A. Pittsburgh; Pittsburgh WC Soc. *Awards*: prizes, Westinghouse Electric Co., 1933; Brunswick-Balke Co., 1934; 1st prize, design for public fountain, Pittsburgh, Pa., 1938. *Exhibited*: Assoc. A. Pittsburgh; Carnegie Inst., 1938-1944; A. & Crafts Center, Pittsburgh, 1945.*

BASSETT, MARGARET GIFFEN (Mrs. Charles P.)—
Painter, T., Des., L., C.
5099 Brightwood Rd., Bethel Park, Pa.

B. Pittsburgh, Pa., Aug. 15, 1904. *Studied*: Carnegie Inst., B.A.; & with Wilfred Readio, Joseph Bailey Ellis, Norwood McGilvary. *Member*: Assoc. A. Pittsburgh. *Exhibited*: Carnegie Inst., 1942-1945; A. & Crafts Center, Pittsburgh, 1945, 1946. Teaching privately 1953-1955, 1956-1958; Sub. A. T., Bethel Jr. & Sr. H.S. 1956-1958; Pittsburgh Pub. Schs., 1957-1958.

BASSFORD, WALLACE—Painter, Des.
115 East 69th St., New York, N.Y.

B. St. Louis, Mo. *Studied*: Washington Univ.; Univ. Missouri, and with Pennell, Hoke, Von Schlegell, Wuerpel, Carpenter, Brown. *Member*: All. A. Am.; Grand Central A. Gal.; Provincetown AA; Cape Cod AA; Audubon A. *Awards*: gold med., Kansas City AI, 1933; prizes, Conn. Acad. FA; Silvermine Gld A.; CAM; St. Louis A. Gld.; Boston Gardens Festival; Cape Cod AA; All.A.Am.; Terry AI. *Work*: Missouri State Capitol, Jefferson City; Univ. Missouri; Susan R. Buder Sch., St. Louis; many portraits of prominent persons. *Exhibited*: CGA; SFMA; NAD; Audubon A.; Cal. PLH; Univ. Illinois; Carnegie Inst.; PAFA; Toledo Mus. A.; Conn. Acad. FA; MMA; Provincetown AA; All. A. Am.; CAM, and others.*

BASSO, TONY—Cartoonist
700 Northeast 15th St., Homestead, Fla.

B. Chicago, Ill., Dec. 27, 1910. *Studied*: Chicago Acad. FA. Contributor to American magazine, Nation's Business, Red Book, Star Weekly (Canada), Saturday Evening Post, Farm Journal, and many other major publications.

BASTIAN, RUFUS A.—Painter, Et., Lith., T., W.
Phoenix, Ariz.

B. Milwaukee, Wis., Dec. 8, 1908. *Studied*: AIC, and abroad. *Member*: A. Dir. Cl.; Nat. Soc. A. Dirs. *Awards*: John Quincy Adams European F. *Exhibited*: Nationally. Contributor to art magazines.

BASTRUP, LEONARD HOLLIS—Designer, P.
19 East 48th St., New York 17, N.Y.; h. Turtleback Rd., Wilton, Conn.

B. St. Louis, Mo., Mar. 15, 1907. *Studied*: Otis AI; AIC; ASL. *Member*: A. Dir. Cl.; SI. *Exhibited*: Silvermine, Conn., 1951; Wilton A., 1952. Contributor to "Advertising Layout," and national magazines. *Position*: Instr., Adv. Des., PIASch., 1946-47; Columbia Univ., New York, N.Y., 1947-48.

BATCHELOR, C. D.—Cartoonist
New York Daily News, 220 East 42nd St., New York, N.Y.

Editorial cartoonist.*

BATE, NORMAN ARTHUR—Etcher, I., W., T.
112 Sagamore Dr., Rochester 17, N.Y.

B. Buffalo, N.Y., Jan. 3, 1916. *Studied*: Buffalo AI; Pratt Inst. A., B.F.A.; Univ. Illinois, M.F.A. *Member*: AAUP; CAA; Print Council of Am. *Awards*: prizes, purchase awards: Youngstown (Ohio) Univ.; Northwest Pr. M., 1957; Boston Soc. Indp. A., 1957, 1958; Paul Sachs award, Boston Pr. M., 1957; Wichita AA, 1957; Silvermine Gld. A., 1958. *Work*: (prints): FMA; Rochester Mem. A. Gal.; Middlebury (Vt.) Col.; deCordova & Dana Mus.; Youngstown Univ.; Northwest Pr. M.; Silvermine Gld. A.; Wichita AA.; IGAS, 1958. *Exhibitions*: AIGA Exh., "50 Best Children's Books," MMA, 1955; BM, 1958; Audubon A., 1958; LC, 1957; Silvermine Gld. A., 1958; Boston Pr. M., 1957, 1958; Wichita AA, 1958; Bay Pr. M. (Oakland, Cal.), 1957; Northwest Pr. M., 1957; Phila. Pr. Cl., 1957, 1958, and others. Author, I., "Who Built the Highway?," 1953; "Who Built the Bridge?," 1954; "Who Fishes for Oil?," 1955; "Who Built the Dam?," 1958. *Position*: Asst. Prof., Nature Structure, The Art Sch., Pratt Institute of Art, Brooklyn, N.Y., 1951-1955.

BATE, RUTLEDGE—Painter, T.
27 School St., Rockport, Mass.

Studied: BMFA Sch., and with Abbott Thayer. *Member*: All. A. Am.; AWS; Boston WC Soc.; Gld. Boston A.; Rockport AA. *Award*: Paige traveling scholarship, BMFA, 1920. *Work*: murals, Naumkeag Trust Co., Salem, Mass., 1954; 1st Nat. Bank, Wellesley, Mass., 1955; portraits: St. Paul's Sch., Garden City, Long Island; Adelphi Col., Garden City. *Exhibited*: NAD; All. A. Am.; AWS; Rockport AA; North Shore AA; Boston WC Soc.; Hartford AA; Springfield AA. *Position*: Instr., Pratt Inst., Brooklyn, N.Y., 1938-45; Vesper George Sch. A., Boston, Mass., 1950-55.*

BATE, STANLEY—Painter, Gr.
R. D. Craryville, N.Y.

B. Nashville, Tenn., Mar. 26, 1903. *Studied*: ASL, with Bridgman; France and Switzerland. *Member*: SI; Berkshire AA (Vice-Pres.); Conn. Acad. FA; Albany Pr. Cl. *Awards*: prizes, BMA; Carnegie Inst.; LC; Soc. Four Arts (6); Munson-Williams-Proctor Inst.; Brooks Mem. Mus.; Conn. Acad. FA (2); Albany Pr. Cl.; Chautauqua AA; Albany Inst. Hist. & A. (2); Berkshire AA (5); Audubon A.; Thursday Morning Cl. *Work*: Albany Inst. Hist. & Art; Albany Pr. Cl.; Carnegie Inst.; LC; Berkshire A. Mus., and in private coll. *Exhibited*: MMA; WMAA; CGA; Butler AI; PAFA; AWS; Wash. WC Cl.; VMFA; Munson-Williams-Proctor Inst.; Silvermine Gld. A.; Pioneer Valley AA. *Position*: A. Dir., Encyclopaedia Britannica, 14th Edition.

BATES, GLADYS EDGERLY—Sculptor
Stonecroft, Mystic, Conn.

B. Hopewell, N.J., July 15, 1896. *Studied*: CGA; PAFA, with Charles Grafly. *Member*: NSS; NAWA; Mystic AA; Pen & Brush Cl.; Conn. Acad. FA. *Awards*: med., PAFA, 1931; NAWA, 1934; prizes, PAFA, 1920; Conn. Acad. FA, 1933; AIC, 1935; Pen & Brush Cl., 1944; NAWA, 1948. *Work*: MMA; PAFA. *Exhibited*: Century Progress, 1934; Texas Cent., 1936; AIC, 1939; Carnegie Inst., 1938; PMA, 1949; AGAA, 1941-1951; NAWA; Conn. Acad. FA; PAFA, 1950 and prior; Lyman Allyn Mus. A., 1952; New Jersey State Mus., 1953; Phila. A. All.; Mystic AA, 1925-1958; Madison A. Gal., 1958. *Position*: Instr. S., Madison A. Sch., 1958 (Summer); West Hartford A. Sch., 1958 (Fall).

BATES, KENNETH—Painter
Stonecroft, Mystic, Conn.

B. Haverhill, Mass., Oct. 28, 1895. *Studied*: ASL; PAFA. *Member*: ANA; New Haven Paint & Clay Cl.; Mystic AA; Conn. Acad. FA. *Awards*: prizes, PAFA, 1920; AIC, 1926; New Haven Paint & Clay Cl., 1929, 1953; Conn. Acad. FA, 1927, 1950; medal, PAFA, 1928. *Exhibited*: WFNY 1939; Carnegie Inst., 1944, 1945; CGA; PAFA; AIC; Toledo Mus. A.; Contemporary A. Gal.; Grand Central A. Gal., (one-man); Conn. Acad. FA, 1951; NAD, 1953-1955, 1958; Grand Central A. Gal., 1958; Mystic AA, 1958; Madison A. Gal., 1958, and others. *Work*: IBM; PAFA. Author: "Brackman, His Art and Teaching," 1951.

BATES, KENNETH FRANCIS—*Craftsman, T., L.*

11441 Juniper Rd., Cleveland, Ohio; h. 7 East 194th St., Euclid 19, Ohio

B. North Scituate, Mass., May 24, 1904. *Studied:* Mass. Sch. A., B.S. in Edu.; and abroad. *Member:* Cleveland Soc. A.; Cleveland AA. *Awards:* prizes, CMA, 1929-1958; Wichita Nat. Ceramic Exh., 1951; Butler AI, 1954. *Work:* CMA; Butler AI; WFNY 1939; ecclesiastical enamels, Wash., D.C., Bethesda, Md., Chagrin, Ohio; murals, Campus Sweater Co., Cleveland. *Exhibited:* Contemp. Am. Ceramics, 1937, 1938, 1940; Syracuse Mus. FA, 1938-1958; Toledo Mus. A.; Akron AI, 1939; Butler AI, 1940, 1955; Phila. A. All., 1941; CMA, 1927-1958; Brussels World's Fair, 1958; Intl. Ceramics Exh., 1958. Author: "Enameling Principles and Practice," 1951, second, third and fourth editions, 1952-1954; articles on ceramics; contributor to Design Magazine, Ceramics Monthly magazine, Encyclopaedia Britannica. *Position:* Instr., Cleveland Inst. A., Cleveland, Ohio, 1927- .

BATTAGLIA, PASQUALE MICHAEL—*Painter, T.*

619 West Hortter St., Philadelphia 19, Pa.

B. Philadelphia, Pa., Jan. 5, 1905. *Studied:* Univ. Pennsylvania, B.S.; PAFA, B.F.A.; PMSchIA. *Member:* Phila. WC Cl.; Phila. A.T. Assn.; Phila. Pr. Cl. *Awards:* prizes, PAFA; Westchester AA; F., PAFA. *Work:* PAFA. *Exhibited:* Pa. Soc. Min. P., 1944-1951; PAFA, 1929-1945; Phila. WC Cl.; Smithsonian Inst.; NCFA, 1944, 1945; Woodmere A. Gal.; Phila. A. All., traveling exh.; Cape May, N.J.; Westchester AA. *Position:* T., Holmes Jr. H.S., Philadelphia, Pa., 1936- ; Chm. A. Dept., Sayre Jr. H.S., Philadelphia, Pa.*

BATZELL, EDGAR A.—*Commercial Artist, P., T.*

227 Juniper Drive, Schenectady 6, N.Y.

B. Pittsburgh, Pa., Nov. 8, 1915. *Studied:* Syracuse Univ., B.F.A., M.A.; ASL, with Morris Kantor, Walt Kuhn, and with Morris Davidson. *Member:* Ogunquit AA. *Awards:* Hazard F., Syracuse Univ., 1938; prizes, Buffalo, N.Y., 1939; Schenectady Merchants Show, 1952, 1953; Schaefer purchase prize, Schenectady Mus., 1954; Brick Store Mus., Kennebunk, Me. *Work:* Schenectady Mus. Assn.; Munson-Williams-Proctor Inst., Utica, N.Y., and in private coll. *Exhibited:* Schenectady Mus., 1945-1955; A. of the Upper Hudson, 1947-1958; Greater Schenectady Show, 1945-1958; Argent Gal., 1951; Ogunquit AA, 1950-1955. *Position:* A., General Electric Co., 1940- ; part-time instr., Schenectady Mus. Assn., 1946-1955.

BAUER, ELI(AS)—*Cartoonist*

2343 Valentine Ave., Bronx 58, N.Y.

B. New York, N.Y., Nov. 17, 1928. *Studied:* Sch. Indst. A. *Awards:* Superman D.C. Cartooning Award, 1947; Ctf. Merit, A. Dir. Cl., 1956. Contributor to American magazine, Fawcett Publications, Park East magazine, 1,000 Jokes magazine. *Position:* Assoc. A. Dir. & Des., Demael Greeting Cards, 1953-54; Freelance for NBC and major art agencies; Des., Ray Patin Productions, Hollywood, Cal., 1956-57; Story Des. & Layout CBS "Terrytoons," New York, N.Y., 1957- .

BAUER, SOL A.—*Sculptor, T.*

3614 Tolland Rd., Shaker Heights, Cleveland 22, Ohio

B. Cleveland, Ohio, Mar. 11, 1898. *Awards:* prizes, CMA, annually. *Work:* CMA; PAFA. *Exhibited:* PAFA, 1933, 1934, 1937, 1938, 1942, 1946, 1950; CMA, 1928-1956; AIC, 1938, 1940; WFNY 1939; Audubon A., 1945; Dayton A. Mus., 1946 (one-man); Ten Thirty Gal., Cleveland, 1948 (one-man).

BAUER, WILLIAM—*Painter, Comm. A., I., Gr.*

7741 General Sherman Lane, Affton 23, Mo.

B. St. Louis, Mo., June 13, 1888. *Studied:* St. Louis Sch. FA. *Member:* AEA; St. Louis A. Gld.; New Orleans AA; St. Louis County AA. *Awards:* prizes, St. Louis A. Gld., 1921, 1923; Kansas City AI, 1924; Missouri State Fair, 1926, 1949-1951; St. Louis A. Lg., 1927; St. Louis Indp. A., 1931; St. Louis County Fair, 1947; Cal. AC, 1948; Missouri Fed. Women's Cl., 1949; Isaac Delgado Mus., 1953, 1956. *Work:* Governor's Mansion, Jefferson City, Mo.; Kansas City AI; St. Louis Pub. Lib.; Waverly (Mo.) Pub. Lib. *Exhibited:* St. Louis A. Gld.; CAM; Carnegie Inst.; Am. A. All.; NAD; Isaac Delgado Mus. A.; Brooks Mem. A. Gal., Memphis; Mulvane A. Center, Topeka; State Fair, Springfield, Ill.

BAUGH, DOROTHY GERALDINE—*Painter*

518 South Madison Ave., Pasadena, Cal.

B. Bath, England, Oct. 2, 1891. *Studied:* Pomona Col. *Member:* Women Painters of the West; Pasadena Soc. A. *Awards:* prizes, Los A. Mus. A., 1942, 1944; Pasadena AI, 1950; Ebell Cl. Los Angeles; Glendale Lib. and Women's Cl.; Pomona Col., 1953; Julia Ford prize, 1953. *Work:* Hamilton Col., Clinton, N.Y. *Exhibited:* Los A. Mus. A.; Pasadena AI; Los A. City Hall; one-man: Bowers Mus., Santa Ana, Cal., 1945; Ebell Cl., 1950; San Gabriel A. Gld., 1945; City of Los Angeles, 1951; San Gabriel Women's Cl., 1951; Sierra Madre A. Gld., 1940; Glendale, 1949; Palos Verdes, Cal., 1949.

BAUM, FRANZ—*Painter, Et., L.*

4691 Branciforte Dr., Santa Cruz, Cal.

B. Wiesbaden, Germany, Jan. 14, 1898. *Studied:* A. Acad., Munich, Germany. *Work:* Stadt Gal., Munich; Kunsthalle, Bremen; SAM. *Awards:* prize, San Mateo County Fiesta, 1953. *Exhibited:* SAM, 1939-1941; SFMA, 1941; Crocker A. Gal., Sacramento, Cal., 1941; Cal. PLH, 1951 (one-man); Montalvo Fnd., Saratoga, Cal., 1956 (one-man); other one-man exhs., in Germany, 1925-1935. *Position:* Instr., A., Adult Edu. Dept., Santa Cruz, Cal., 1949.*

BAUM, MARK—*Painter*

644 Riverside Dr., New York 31, N.Y.

B. Sanok, Poland, Jan. 2, 1903. *Studied:* NAD; Col. City of N.Y. *Member:* Provincetown AA. *Work:* WMAA. *Exhibited:* PAFA; one-man: Laurel Gal.; Perls Gal.; Galerie St. Etienne, N.Y.; Harry Salpeter Gal.*

BAUMANN, GUSTAVE—*Engraver, P., C., W.*

409 C. de los Animas, Santa Fe, N.M.

B. Magdeburg, Germany, June 27, 1881. *Studied:* Kunstgewerbe Schule, Munich; AIC. *Awards:* med., Pan-Pacific Exp., 1915; Fifty Books of the Year, 1940; Los A. Mus. A., 1926; Hon. F., Sch. Am. Research, 1952. *Work:* NGFA; BMFA; Nat. Gal., Toronto, Canada; AIC; MMA. *Exhibited:* CGA, 1930, 1931. Author, I., "Frijoles Canyon Pictographs," 1939.

BAUMANN, KARL HERMAN—*Painter, Des., Lith.*

1207 Clayton St., San Francisco, Cal.

B. Leipzig, Germany, Dec. 26, 1911. *Member:* San F. AA. *Work:* murals, SS "President Hayes." *Awards:* prize, San F. AA, 1949. *Exhibited:* Riverside Mus., 1940; Dayton AI, 1940; Cal.PLH, 1945, 1951; SFMA, 1940, 1942, 1945, 1949; PC, 1949; MMA, 1952; City of Paris, San F., 1952-1956; Cal. State Fair, 1953; one-man: Gump's Gal., San F., 1947; La Jolla A. Center, 1947; SFMA, 1949; City of Paris Gal., 1950, 1956; Labaudt Gal., 1957; Mezzanine Gal., Oakland, 1956. *Position:* Prof. Painting, Cal. Col. of A. & Crafts, Oakland, Cal., 1947-52.

BAUMBACH, HAROLD—*Painter*

1730 47th St., Brooklyn 4, N.Y.

B. New York, N.Y., Sept. 18, 1905. *Studied:* PIASch. *Member:* Fed. Mod. P. & S. *Work:* BM; Albright A. Gal.; Univ. Arizona; Univ. Georgia; Univ. Iowa; R. I. Sch. Des.; Samuel S. Fleischer Mem., Phila., Pa.; Stephen C. Clark Coll. *Exhibited:* PAFA, 1945, 1952; AIC, 1942; Carnegie Inst., 1944, 1945; Univ. Iowa, 1946; Univ. Nebraska, 1952; Univ. Illinois, 1952; Wildenstein Gal.; Contemporary A. Gal., 1952 (one-man); Harry Salpeter Gal., 1954, 1955 (one-man); 2 one-man exhs., Barone Gal., 1956, 1957. *Position:* L., Instr., Vocational Studies, Brooklyn Col., Adult Edu.

BAUMGARTEN, CECIL—*Advertising Designer*

P.O. Box 1387, St. Thomas, Virgin Islands

B. Washington, D.C., June 11, 1903. *Studied:* N.Y. Univ.; Cincinnati Mus. Sch. A.; ASL; Grand Central Sch. A., and with Fred Goudy, George Bridgman. *Member:* A. Dir. Cl.; Nat. Soc. A. Dir.; SI. *Awards:* A. Dir. Cl., 1945. *Exhibited:* A. Dir. Cl., 1945, 1946. Contributor of articles and editorials to "Art Direction." Lectures on Layout and Design of Book Advertising. *Position:* A. Dir., Morse International, Inc., New York, N.Y. (14 years); Green-Brodie Adv., New York, N.Y. (10 years).*

BAUMGARTNER, WARREN W.—*Illustrator, P.*

Box 453, Englewood, N.J.

B. Oakville, Mo., Mar. 15, 1894. *Studied*: AIC, with Wellington J. Reynolds; Grand Central Sch. A., with Pruett Carter; and with Walter Biggs. *Member*: NAD; AWS; SI; Maine WC Soc.; Baltimore WC Soc., North Shore AA; SC. *Awards*: prizes, AWS, 1940, 1946, 1958; AWS purchase prize, 1953; Herman Wick Mem. prize, SC, 1955; Maine WC Soc., 1957. I., books and illus. for national magazines.

BAUMHOFER, WALTER M.—*Illustrator, P., Comm. A.*

56 School St., Northport, L.I., N.Y.

B. Brooklyn, N.Y., Nov. 1, 1904. *Studied*: PIASch. *Member*: SI. *Award*: Suffolk Mus., 1951. *Exhibited*: SI, 1941-1945. I., national magazines.

BAUR, JOHN I. H.—
** *Associate Museum Director, L., W.***

Whitney Museum of American Art, 22 West 54th St., New York, N.Y.; h. Mt. Holly Rd., Katonah, N.Y.

B. Woodbridge, Conn., Aug. 9, 1909. *Studied*: Yale Univ., B.A., M.A. Author: "An American Genre Painter, Eastman Johnson," 1940; "John Quidor," 1942; "Theodore Robinson," 1946; "Revolution and Tradition in Modern American Art," 1951; "American Painting in the Nineteenth Century, Main Trends and Movements," 1953; "Loren MacIver and I. Rice Pereira," 1953; "George Grosz," 1954; "ABC for Collectors of American Contemporary Art," 1954; "The New Decade: 35 American Painters and Sculptors" (ed), 1955; "Charles Burchfield," 1956; "Bradley Walker Tomlin," 1957; "Nature in Abstraction," 1958. Contributor to art magazines. Lectures: American Art. *Position*: Supv. Edu., 1934-36, Cur., Brooklyn Museum of Art, 1936-52; Cur., Whitney Museum of American Art, 1952- ; Visiting L., Yale Univ., 1951-52.

BAVINGER, EUGENE A.—
** *Museum Director, T., Des., P.***

Museum of Art, University of Oklahoma; h. Rt. #4, Norman, Okla.

B. Sapulpa, Okla., Dec. 21, 1919. *Studied*: Univ. Oklahoma, B.F.A. *Awards*: Terry AI, Miami, Fla., 1952; Joslyn Mem. A. Mus., 1950; Denver A. Mus., 1954. *Work*: Springfield A. Mus.; Philbrook A. Center; Fathers of St. Benedicts, Atchison, Kans.; Mulvane A. Center, Topeka; Oklahoma A. Center, Oklahoma City. *Exhibited*: PAFA, 1948; MMA, 1950; Provincetown A. Festival, 1958; Northwest Pr. M., 1948; Denver Mus. A., 1949, 1950, 1954; Missouri Valley Artists, 1949, 1953; Southwestern Art, Santa Fe, 1951, 1957; Mid-America, 1954, 1956-1958; Artists West of the Mississippi, 1948, 1949. I., "Basic Physics." *Positions*: Instr., Drawing, P. & Des., 1947- , Dir., Museum of Art, Univ. Oklahoma, Norman, Okla., at present.

BAYARD, CLIFFORD ADAMS—
** *Painter, Et., Lith., T., L.***

Box 248, Wilmington, Vt.

B. McKeesport, Pa., Dec. 12, 1892. *Studied*: Carnegie Inst., A.B. *Member*: AFA; Assoc. A. Pittsburgh; Springfield AA; Deerfield Valley AA; AEA. *Awards*: prizes, Assoc. A. Pittsburgh, 1922, 1944; Stockbridge AA, 1936. *Work*: Fleming Mus. A., Burlington, Vt.; Latrobe Pub. Sch.; Bennington Mus. A.; Williams Col.; Carnegie Inst.; Pittsburgh Bd. of Edu. *Exhibited*: Carnegie Inst., 1922; AWCS, 1939; NAD, 1938; WFNY 1939; Assoc. A. Pittsburgh; Springfield A. Lg.; Deerfield Valley AA; Albany Inst. Hist. & A.; Southern Vt. A.; AFA (traveling exh.), 1938, 1939; Boston Soc. Indp. A.; deCordova Mus.; Boston Symphony Hall.

BAYARD, DONALD D.—*Designer, P., I.*

3740 North Sheffield St., Chicago, Ill.

B. Duluth, Minn., Nov. 3, 1904. *Studied*: Yale Univ. Sch. FA, B.F.A., with Eugene Savage; Chicago Inst. Des., with Moholy-Nagy. *Awards*: prizes, BAID, 1932; Kimball F., New Haven, Conn., 1932. *Work*: Cleveland Pub. Lib.; Bryant Sch., Cleveland. *Exhibited*: CGA, 1935; Paris Exp., 1937; Butler AI, 1937; White House Exh., 1937. *Position*: Graphic Engineer, Fisher Body Co., 1943-45; Gr. Engineering Service, 1945- ; Raytheon Mfg. Co., 1956; Admiral Corp., 1958.

BAYER, HERBERT—*Painter, Des.*

P.O. Box 128, Aspen, Colo.

B. Haag, Austria, Apr. 5, 1900. *Studied*: The Bauhaus, Weimar, Germany. *Member*: Alliance Graphique Internationale; Am. Abstract A.; Intl. Des. Conference, Aspen, Colo. *Awards*: prizes, U.S. and Europe. *Work*: Paintings: Landes Mus., Linz; Albertina Mus., Vienna; Folkwang Mus., Essen; SFMA; FMA; MMoModA; Smith Col. Mus.; Ft. Worth A. Center, Texas; Denver A. Mus.; Designs: MMoModA and in other museums. Mural, Bauhaus Bldg., Weimar; Commons Bldg., Grad. Center, Harvard Univ.; Elementary Sch., Bridgewater, Mass.; Health Center, Aspen, Colo.; map murals, Colonial Williamsburg, Va.; Sgraffito, Seminar Bldg., Aspen (Colo.) Inst. *Exhibited*: Bauhaus Exh., MMoModA, 1938; Sao Paulo, Brazil, 1957; one-man: London, England, 1937; Dessau Bauhaus, 1931; Nat. Mus., Nurnberg; Die Neue Sammlung, Munich, 1956-57 (Retrospective); Yale Univ., 1940; Willard Gal., N.Y., 1943; Schaefer Gal., N.Y., 1953. Co-Editor: "Bauhaus 1919-1928," 1st ed., 1938, MMoModA, 2nd ed., 1952, Brandord Co., Boston, German ed., 1955; Editor, Des., "World Geo-Graphic Atlas," Container Corp. of Am., 1953. Contributor articles to Gebrauchsgraphik; College Art Journal; Bauhaus Magazine. *Positions*: A. Dir., Vogue, Germany; Dir., Dorland Studio, Berlin; A. Dir., Dorland International, N.Y.; Consultant A. Dir., J. Walter Thompson, N.Y.; Consultant Des., Aspen Inst.; Chm., Dept. Design, Container Corp. of America.

BAZIOTES, WILLIAM A.—*Painter*

c/o Kootz Gallery, 600 Madison Ave.; h. 90 LaSalle St., New York 27, N.Y.

B. Pittsburgh, Pa., June 11, 1912. *Studied*: NAD. *Awards*: prizes, AIC, 1948; Univ. Illinois, 1950. *Work*: WMAA; MMoModA; MMA; BMA; FMA; Harvard Univ.; Newark Mus. A.; Smith Col.; AIC; Art of This Century; Tel Aviv Mus.; Los A. Mus. A.; Washington Univ.; Univ. Illinois; Univ. Oklahoma; Cal. Sch. FA; PMA; Minneapolis Inst. A.; Detroit Inst. A.; Albright A. Gal.; AIC; Carnegie Inst.; Wadsworth Atheneum. *Exhibited*: Maeght Gal., Paris, 1947; MMoModA, 1952, 1954, 1958; WMAA, 1954; Brussels World's Fair, 1958; one-man: Kootz Gal., 1945-1952, 1953, 1954, 1956, 1958.

BEACH, BEATA (Mrs. Vernon C. Porter)—
** *Painter, Des., Et., I.***

Putnam Valley, N.Y.

B. Rome, Italy, May 26, 1911. *Studied*: Julian Acad., Paris; ASL. *Member*: NSMP. *Work*: USPO, Monticello, Ga. *Exhibited*: VMFA, 1939; PAFA, 1939; CAA (traveling exh.), 1935; Riverside Mus.

BEACH, SARA BERMAN—*Painter, Lith.*

3 East 14th St., New York 3, N.Y.; h. 4721-41st St., Sunnyside, L.I., N.Y.

B. Lodz, Poland, Sept. 29, 1897. *Studied*: CUASch; DaVinci A. Sch.; Polish A. Acad. *Member*: A.Lg.Am.; AEA. *Awards*: prize, DaVinci A. Sch., 1927. *Work*: New-Age Gal.; Aviation Cl., N.Y. *Exhibited*: Western Mus., Moscow, 1934; AEA, 1952; Indp. A., 1940-1942; New Sch. Social Research, 1936, 1938; Audubon A., 1946; NAD, 1946; ACA Gal., 1935; A.Cong., 1937; A.Lg.Am., 1945; New-Age Gal., 1945, 1946; Solidarity House, 1948 (one-man); Caravan Gal., 1955, 1956; Ikuf Gal., 1957; Eastside Indp. A., 1958; Abraham Lincoln H.S., 1955.

BEACH, WARREN—*Museum Director, P.*

Fine Arts Gallery of San Diego, Balboa Park; h. 3740 Pio Pico St., San Diego 6, Cal.

B. Minneapolis, Minn., May 21, 1914. *Studied*: Phillips Acad., Andover, Mass.; Yale Univ., B.F.A.; Univ. Iowa, M.A.; Harvard Univ., M.A. *Member*: AGAA; AAMus.; AAMD; Western Assn. Mus. Dir. *Work*: AGAA; Columbus Gal. FA. *Exhibited*: Minneapolis AI; Art & Artists Along the Mississippi, 1941; Minnesota State Fair, 1941; Columbus A. Lg., 1948; one-man: Harriet Hanley Gal., Minneapolis, 1943; Grace Horne Gal., Boston, 1945. *Position*: Dir. Ext. Services, WAC, 1940-41; Asst. Dir., Columbus (Ohio) Gal. FA, 1947-55; Dir., FA Gal. of San Diego, Cal., 1955- .

BEADENKOPF, ANNE—*Painter*

3203 North Charles St., Baltimore 18, Md.

B. Baltimore, Md., Aug. 6, 1875. *Studied*: ASL; also with Henry Roben, Ivan Olinsky. *Member*: NAWA. *Work*:

paintings, City Hall, Peale Mus., Sch. Admin. Bldg., Provident Hospital, American Cancer Soc., Happy Hills Convalescent Home for Children, Urban Lg., Y.M.C.A., Maryland Univ. Hospital, all in Baltimore, Md. *Exhibited*: NAWA, 1943-1945; Am-British A. Center; BMA; NAD; one-man: Argent Gal., 1943; Peale Mus., 1950.*

BEALL, CECIL CALVERT—
Illustrator, P., S., Des., Comm. A., W., L.
200 Davenport Ave., New Rochelle, N.Y.

B. Saratoga, Wyo., Oct. 15, 1892. *Studied*: PIA Sch.; ASL. *Member*: SI; SC; AWS; Hudson Valley AA; New Rochelle AA; Mount Vernon AA. *Work*: Air Force Acad. Mus., Colorado Springs, Colo.; Marine Mus., Quantico, Va.; many covers for Reader's Digest; 25 years of regular illus. for Collier's. Painted the official picture of the Surrender of the Japanese Aboard the Missouri. *Exhibited*: AWS, 1953, 1954 and many local and regional exhibitions. Contributor to: Reader's Digest; Collier's; Cosmopolitan; Woman's Day; Woman's Home Companion; True; Sat. Eve. Post; Family Circle; Successful Farming; This Week; Better Homes & Gardens; also, American Legion; Elks. Lectures: Art in the Magazine, to women's clubs, universities, etc.*

BEALL, LESTER THOMAS—*Industrial Designer, P., I.*
Dumbarton Farm, Brookfield Center, Conn.

B. Kansas City, Mo., Mar. 14, 1903. *Studied*: Lane Technical Sch., Univ. Chicago, Ph.B. *Member*: A. Dir. Cl., N.Y.; AIGA; Chicago Soc. Typographic A.; SI; All. Graphique Internationale. *Awards*: prizes, Chicago Soc. Typographic A., 1934, 1935 (2), 1948; A. Dir. Cl., 1936-1940, 1942, 1948, 1950-1952, 1953, 1955; AIGA, 1939, 1943 (4), 1950 (6), 1951 (5), 1952, 1954; N.Y.Exh. Printing, 1941. *Exhibited*: AIC, 1935-1936, 1948; MModA, 1937-1941; Paris International, 1937; Royal Mus., Kensington, London, 1937; AIGA; A. Dir. Cl.; Phila. A. All.; Los A. A. Center; A-D Gal.; Ferargil Gal.; SI; R. I. Sch. Des.; Sch. Des., Cambridge, Mass., 1951; Package Exh., 1952; traveling package exh., Europe, 1952-53; All. Graphiques Internationale, 1955.*

BEAM, PHILIP CONWAY—*Museum Director, E.*
Bowdoin College; h. 41 Spring St., Brunswick, Me.

B. Dallas, Tex., Oct. 7, 1910. *Studied*: Harvard Col., A.B.; Harvard Univ., M.A., Ph.D.; Courtauld Inst., London. *Member*: Am.Assn. Univ. Prof.; Maine A. Comm., 1946-55, Chm., 1954-55. Contributor to Art Journal; New England Quarterly. Author: "The Language of Art," 1958. *Position*: Dir., Bowdoin Col. Mus. A., Bowdoin Col., Brunswick, Me., 1939; Asst. Prof. A., 1939, Assoc Prof., 1942, Prof. & Chm. Dept. A., 1946- .

BEAN, CAROLINE VAN H.—*Painter, Et.*
309 Vallette Way, West Palm Beach, Fla.

B. Washington, D.C. *Studied*: Smith Col.; & with William M. Chase, B. J. Blommers, John Singer Sargent. *Member*: Soc. Wash. A.; Soc. Wash. Et.; Wash. AC; Palm Beach A. Lg.; West Palm Beach A. Gld. *Work*: Dayton AI. *Exhibited*: High Mus. A.; Closson Gal., Cincinnati, Ohio; Bresler Gal., Milwaukee, Wis.; Milch Gal.; Ferargil Gal.; Ainslee Gal.; Ehrich Gal., N.Y.

BEARD, RICHARD ELLIOTT—*Educator, P.*
Art Department, Maryville College; h. 803 Court St., Maryville, Tenn.

B. Kenosha, Wis., June 13, 1928. *Studied*: Univ. Wisconsin, B.S., M.A., with Dean Meeker, Santos Zingale, Alfred Sessler, Oskar Hagen, James Watrous, John Kienitz. *Member*: CAA; Southeastern College AA; IGAS. *Exhibited*: Univ. Tennessee; Knoxville A. Center; Watkins Inst., Nashville; one-man: Maryville College; Berea College; Univ. Chattanooga; East Tennessee State College. *Position*: Prof. A., Art Dept., Maryville College, Maryville, Tenn.

BEARDEN, EDWARD (CARPENTER)—
Educator, P., Des., I., Comm. A., Lith.
Art Department, Southern Methodist University; h. 3607 Amherst St., Dallas, Tex.

B. Dallas, Tex., Oct. 9, 1919. *Studied*: Southern Methodist Univ., B.A.; Colorado Springs Fine A. Center. *Member*: Dallas-Ft. Worth Men of A. Gld.; Adv. A. of Dallas; Texas FA Assn. *Awards*: prizes, Dallas Painting & Sc.

exh.; Texas Painting Annual; Texas WC Soc.; Dallas-Ft. Worth Men of A. Gld.; Texas Inst. Lets., for best book design, 1956. *Work*: DMFA; D.D. Feldman Coll. of Texas Art; Jefferson (Tex.) Mus. *Exhibited*: Dallas Painting & Sc. exh.; Texas Painting Annual; Texas WC Soc.; Men of A. Gld., San Antonio, Dallas-Ft. Worth; Texas FA Assn.; Southwestern Exh. Adv. & Editorial A.; Dallas Adv. A. Assn. exhs. Contributor illus. to Southwest Review; Southern Methodist Univ. Press. Lectures: series of TV programs for SMU "College of the Air," Dallas. *Position*: Bd. Dir., Dallas Mus. for Contemp. A.; Asst. Prof. A., Southern Methodist University, Dallas, Tex., 1944- .

BEARDEN, ROMARE—*Painter*
243 West 125th St., New York, N.Y.

B. Charlotte, N.C., Sept. 2, 1914. *Studied*: N.Y. Univ.; ASL. *Work*: MMA; MModA. *Exhibited*: WMAA, 1955 and many other museums.*

BEATTY, HETTY BURLINGAME—
Sculptor, Des., I., C., W.
Drumlin Rd., Rockport, Mass.

B. New Canaan, Conn., Oct. 8, 1906. *Studied*: BMFA Sch., and with Charles Grafly, Albert Laessle, George Demetrios. *Member*: Authors Lg. of Am. *Work*: USPO, Farmington, Me. *Exhibited*: PAFA, 1931-1937; AIC, 1935-1937; Macbeth Gal., 1934; WMA, 1941 (one-man); Gloucester Festival A., 1952. Author, I., "Topsy," 1946; "Little Wild Horse," 1948; "Little Owl Indian," 1951; "Bronto," 1952; "Saint Francis and the Wolf," 1953; "Droopy," 1954; "Thumps," 1955; "Bucking Horse," 1957.

BEATTY, RICHARD R.—*Lithographer, T.*
62 West Cedar St., Boston 14, Mass.

B. Wilkensburg, Pa., Jan. 28, 1899. *Studied*: Carnegie Inst.; AIC. *Member*: Cleveland Pr.Cl. *Awards*: Prize, CMA. *Work*: CMA. *Exhibited*: CMA; Ohio Pr. M.; & in Sweden.

BEAUGUREAU, FRANCIS HENRY—*Painter, T.*
6929 East Coronado Rd., Scottsdale, Ariz.

B. Chicago, Ill., Apr. 5, 1920. *Studied*: Mizen Acad.; AIC. *Member*: AWS; Philadelphia WC Cl. *Awards*: Kautsky Mem. Award, AWS, 1955. *Work*: Dept. Air Force; Dept. of the Army; Frye Mus., Seattle; Phoenix A. Center; Illus. for USAF, 1951, 1952. *Exhibited*: CGA, 1951; AWS, 1952-1958, traveling exh., 1954-1957; Phoenix WC exh., 1950, 1953, 1957; Sarasota, Fla., 1953, 1954; Arizona State Fair, 1954, 1955, 1956, 1957; Univ. Arizona, 1955, 1958; Univ. Arizona Traveling exh., 1958; one-man: Frye Mus., A., Seattle, Wash., 1955. *Position*: Consultant to USAF, formulating Art Program and USAF Museum, 1950-1952.

BECK, DUNBAR—*Painter, T.*
2100—22nd St., Sacramento 17, Cal.

B. Delaware, Ohio, Sept. 16, 1902. *Studied*: Ohio Wesleyan Univ.; Northwestern Univ.; Yale Univ., B.F.A.; Am. Acad. in Rome. *Awards*: Prix de Rome, 1927; F., Am. Acad. in Rome. *Work*: Decorations, East Room, White House, Wash., D.C. Altar, church paintings, N.Y., Phila., St. Paul, Sacramento. Des., Sacramento Bee, Modesto Bee Bldgs. (Cal.). *Exhibited*: Sacramento, Cal., 1940, 1945, 1946.*

BECK, GEORGE ANTHONY—*Industrial Designer*
General Electric Co., French Rd., Utica, N.Y.; h. Palmer Rd., R.D. 1, Manlius, N.Y.

B. Maywood, Ill., Mar. 29, 1908. *Studied*: Chicago Acad. FA. *Member*: IDI (Past Pres., Chm. Bd. Trustees at present). *Work*: designed many major and small appliances, refrigerators, trade-marks, radio, television apparatus, studio equipment, etc. Lectures on Industrial Design. *Position*: Mgr., Indst. Des., Light Military Electronics Dept., General Electric Co., Utica, N.Y., at present.

BECK, JAY—*Illustrator, S., C., P., L.*
361 Osage St., Park Forest, Ill.

B. Chicago, Ill., Sept. 20, 1916. *Studied*: Univ. Chicago. *Exhibited*: AIC. I., "Wild Bird Neighbors," 1946. Lectures on and teaches crafts to children.*

BECK, ROSEMARIE (PHELPS)—Painter, T.
Box 382, Woodstock, N.Y.

B. New York, N.Y., July 8, 1923. *Studied*: Oberlin College, B.A.; N.Y. Univ., Inst. FA; Columbia Univ., and with Robert Motherwell. *Work*: WMAA. Mural, Rotron Mfg. Co. *Exhibited*: Kootz Gal., 1950; PAFA, 1954; AIC, 1954-1957; WMAA, 1955, 1957; Univ. Michigan, 1956; Allen A. Mus., Oberlin, 1957; BM, 1957; Abstract Impressionists, England, 1958; one-man: Peridot Gal., 1953, 1956; Vassar Col., 1957. *Position*: Instr., Painting, Vassar College, 1957-1958.

BECKER, CHARLOTTE—Illustrator, P., W.
50 West 67th St., New York 23, N.Y.

Studied: CUASch.; ASL. Author, I., children's books; children's portraits.

BECKER, FRED—Educator, Pr. M.
Washington University, St. Louis, Mo.

Position: Prof. Graphic A., Washington Univ., St. Louis, Mo.*

BECKER, JOSEPH (HUBERT)—
Cartoonist, W., P., Des., C.
3415 East 19th St., Kansas City 27, Mo.

B. Kansas City, Mo., Feb. 17, 1905. *Exhibited*: Kansas City AI, 1945; CAM, 1945; MModA., 1941; Topeka, Kans., 1949, 1950, 1951, 1953; Intl. Exh., Mickiewicz Mus., Warsaw, 1956; Art of Today Gal., N.Y., 1957. *Work*: in private collections.

BECKER, MAURICE—Painter, I.
237 East 10th St., New York 3, N.Y.

B. Russia, Jan. 4, 1889. *Studied*: with Robert Henri, Homer Boss. *Member*: Indp. A.; AEA (Bd. Dir.); Fed. Mod. P. & S. *Awards*: AFA, 1950. *Work*: Woods A. Mus., Montpelier, Vt.; Jefferson Sch. Soc. Science, New York; Holbrook Col.; Univ. Georgia; Ain Harod & Tel Aviv Mus., Israel. Mural, Worcester (Mass.) Acad. *Exhibited*: San F. AA, 1916 (one-man); Whitney Studio Cl., 1924 (one-man); Mexico City, 1922 (with Orozco and Rivera); J. B. Neumann Gal., 1925-1929; Macbeth Gal., 1942, 1945; WMAA, 1924-1939, 1945, 1946; MMA, 1942, 1952, 1953; NAD, 1944, 1945; Carnegie Inst., 1945; Berkshire Mus., 1946 (one-man); AIC; John Heller Gal., 1951; AEA; A. Lg. Am., 1949; Fed. Modern P. & S., 1951-1955; A.F.I. Gal., 1952; Fed. Modern P. & S. traveling exh., 1955-56; Greenwich Gal., N.Y., 1957; One-man: Hartert Gal., 1954, 1955, 1957; Art of Today Gal., 1955.

BECKHOFF, HARRY—Illustrator
Woods Grove, Westport, Conn.

Member: SI.*

BECK-MEYER, RICHARD CHRISTIAN (RICK)—
Painter, T.
1542 North Vista St., Los Angeles 46, Cal.

B. Van Nuys, Cal., Aug. 13, 1930. *Studied*: Glendale Col., A.A., with Jean Abel; Cal. Col. A. & Crafts, B.A. in Edu., with Victor De Wilde; Los Angeles State Col.; San Jose State Col., M.A., with Wendall Gates, Warren Faus. *Member*: Cal. WC Soc.; Carmel AA. *Awards*: Ctf. of Merit, Art News Comp., 1950; Huntington Hartford Fnd. award, 1958. *Exhibited*: Art News Comp., 1950; Cal. WC Soc., 1952; Los A. Mus. A., 1952; Los A. AA, 1949-1952; Santa Paula, Cal., 1949-1951; Carmel AA, 1953-1957; Canyon AI, Los A., 1957; Los A. Mus. A., 1958; Brentwood AA, 1958; Cosmo Alley, Hollywood, 1958; Malibu, Cal., 1958; Monterey County Fair, 1956; Assoc. A. Gal., Carmel, 1956; Los A. Art Festival, 1958; one-man: Glendale Col., 1952; Hill Theatre, Monterey, 1954; Robert North Gal., Chicago, 1955; Wharf Theatre, Monterey, 1956; Charisse Gal., Los A., 1957. *Position*: Instr. A., Carmel Sch. A., Children's A., 1956; Pacific Grove (Cal.) H.S., 1956-57.

BECKWITH, JAMES—Painter, Des.
Bluff Lane, Setauket, L.I., N.Y.

B. Mt. Pleasant, Iowa, Dec. 21, 1907. *Studied*: Yale Univ. Sch. FA; Columbia Univ. *Member*: Nat. Soc. of Painters

in Casein; AWS. *Awards*: American Artists Magazine Citation, 1953. *Work*: Altoona Mus. *Exhibited*: AWS, 1937, 1939, 1940, 1951; BM, 1937; N.Y. WC Cl., 1937-1940; Cal. WC Cl., 1936-1939; CM, 1937; WFNY 1939; PAFA, 1936; Royal Canadian Acad., 1934, 1935; Nat. Gal., Canada, 1934, 1935; Montreal AA; Several one-man exh., New York, Montreal, Florida.*

BEDFORD, HELEN DE WILTON—Educator
Southeast Missouri State College; h. 943 Bellevue St., Cape Girardeau, Mo.

B. Columbia, Mo., Nov. 12, 1904. *Studied*: Univ. Missouri, B.S.; T. Col., Columbia Univ., M.A.; Univ. New Mexico. *Member*: AAUP; Western AA; Missouri State T. Assn.; Missouri State A. T. Contributor to Missouri Art Magazine. *Position*: Dir., Southeast Missouri State Col., Dept. FA, Cape Girardeau, Mo.

BEDFORD, VIRGINIA—Educator
Art Department, Longwood College, Farmville, Va.

Position: Chm., Art Dept., Longwood College, Farmville, Va.*

BEDNO, EDWARD—Designer
879 North State St. (10); h. 1905 Morse Ave., Chicago 26, Ill.

B. Chicago, Ill., Mar. 8, 1925. *Studied*: AIC, B.F.A.; Inst. Des., Chicago, M.S. in Visual Des.; Northwestern Univ.; Univ. Chicago. *Member*: Soc. Typographic A. *Award*: merit award, A. Dir. Cl., Chicago, 1955. *Exhibited*: Palmer House Gal., 1948, Bordelon Gal., 1949, 1950, Riccardo Gal., 1949, Contemp. Gal., 1950, in Chicago; Int. Color Lith. Exh., Cleveland, 1948; Momentum, 1950; AFA traveling exh., 1949-50; A. Dir. Cl., Chicago, 1948, 1949, 1953, 1955-1958; Soc. Typographic A., 1949, 1951, 1952, 1953, 1955-1958; Contemp. Des. Exh., Los Angeles, 1950; Midwest Book Clinic, 1955; AIGA, 1954, 1956, 1957; A. Dir. Cl., N.Y., 1957, 1958; A. Gld., Chicago, 1958 (one-man des. exh.). *Position*: Instr., Northwestern Univ., Evanston, Ill., 1951-52; Instr., Inst. of Design, 1957; Pres., Bedno Associates, Chicago, Ill.

BEDORE, MRS. ANNA LOU MATTHEWS. See Matthews, Lou

BEEM, PAUL EDWARD—Designer, I., P., Gr., S., W.
W. E. Long Co., 188 West Randolph St.; h. 1360 Lake Shore Dr., Chicago 10, Ill.

B. Indianapolis, Ind., Jan. 12, 1908. *Studied*: John Herron AI; AIC, and with Elmer Taflinger, R. L. Coats. *Member*: Soc. Typographic A.; A. Dir. Cl.; Hoosier Salon; AIC. *Awards*: prizes, Herron AI, 1930-1934; CM, 1929; AIC, 1932, 1938. *Work*: John Herron AI; Univ. North Dakota; Indiana Univ.; mural, Orphan's Home, Indianapolis, Ind. *Exhibited*: AIC, 1932, 1938; John Herron AI, 1929-1936; Hoosier Salon, 1929-1940; CM, 1932; Dayton AI, 1932; Detroit Inst. A., 1933; Carnegie Inst., 1934; Delgado Mus. A.; numerous one-man and group shows in Chicago since 1933. Contributor to art magazines and other publications. *Position*: A. Dir., W. E. Long Co., Chicago, Ill.

BEERBOHM, MARVIN—Painter
20201 Gillman St., Livonia, Mich.

B. Toronto, Canada, July 24, 1909. *Studied*: Det. Soc. A. & Crafts, and with Samuel Halpert, John Carroll. *Member*: Scarab Cl., Detroit; AEA; Mich. Acad. Sc., A. & Let. *Awards*: prizes, Det. Inst. A., 1940; Friends of Am. A., 1947; Grand Rapids AI, 1949; Mich. Acad. Sc., A. & Let., 1950; Scarab Cl., Detroit, 1952. *Work*: Detroit Inst. A.; murals, USPO, Knoxville, Iowa; Belding, Mich.; Detroit Pub. Lib.; Rochester, Mich.; Harlan Electric Co., Detroit, Mich. (series 12 paintings "Adventure in Time"); Harlan Elementary Sch., Birmingham, Mich.; Jewish War Veterans Memorial Home, Detroit; des., stained glass windows for Sinai Hospital, Detroit. *Exhibited*: CGA, 1935, 1937; PAFA, 1939; VMFA, 1940; San F. AA, 1940; Carnegie Inst., 1940; San Diego FA Soc., 1942; Milwaukee AI, 1945; Detroit Inst. A., 1932-1942, 1953 (one-man); Univ. Michigan, 1936-1938; Kansas City AI, 1937; Detroit Hist. Mus., 1955 (Adventure in Time),

BEERMAN, HERBERT—Painter, L.

469 Rogers Ave., Brooklyn 25, N.Y.

B. Newark, N.J., Nov. 8, 1926. *Studied*: Rutgers Univ.; Univ. Miami, A.B.; Yale Univ., Sch. Des., with Josef Albers, B.F.A. *Awards*: MacDowell F., 1958. *Exhibited*: Artists Gal., N.Y., 1957 (one-man), 1958; Camino Gal., N.Y., 1957, 1958. Lectures: Contemporary Art, Rutgers Univ.

BEETZ, CARL HUGO—Lithographer, P., E., W.

266 27th Ave.; h. 262 25th Ave., San Francisco 21, Cal.

B. San Francisco, Cal., Dec., 25, 1911. *Studied*: Cal. Sch. FA, with Spencer Macky; ASL, with George Bridgman; Chouinard AI, with Pruett Carter. *Member*: Cal. WC Soc.; Cal. Soc. Et. *Awards*: Redlands A. Gld., 1941. *Work*: SFMA. *Exhibited*: Pomona, Cal., 1937; AIC, 1941; Riverside Mus., 1940, 1944; San Diego, 1941; Lib. Cong., 1944, 1945; Phila. Pr. Cl., 1944; Indianapolis Pr. Show, 1946; Springfield Pr. Show, 1946; Cal. WC Soc., 1937, 1939, 1940, 1942, 1943; San F. AA, 1941, 1943, 1946; Fnd. Western A., Los A., 1937, 1938, 1940, 1942, 1944; Utah State Agri. Col., 1947; Oakland A. Mus., 1950, 1956; SFMA, 1951; Cal. Soc. Et., 1954, 1956; San F., Sacramento, Cal.; one-man: Los A. Mus. A., 1942; M.H. de-Young Mus., 1944, 1957; Jepson AI, 1949; SFMA, 1946 (4-man). *Position*: Instr., Chouinard AI, 1935-44; Cal. Col. A. & Crafts, Oakland, Cal., 1944- ; Acad. Adv. A., San Francisco, 1944-53; Prof. A., Cal. Col. A. & Crafts, Oakland; City Col. of San Francisco, 1945- .

BEGG, JOHN (ALFRED)—Sculptor, P., Des.

Oxford Univ. Press, 417 Fifth Ave., New York 16, N.Y.; h. 137 South Broadway, Hastings-on-Hudson, N.Y.

B. New Smyrna, Fla., June 23, 1903. *Studied*: Columbia Univ., B.S., and with Arthur Wesley Dow, Ossip Zadkine. *Member*: AIGA. *Work*: Indiana Mus. Mod. A.; AGAA; bronze plaque for Readerscope award, 1945. *Exhibited*: WMAA, 1945, 1950; BM, 1935, 1937; Buchholz Gal., 1943, 1945; Wakefield Gal., 1942 (one-man); Nierndorf Gal., 1945; New Sch. Social Research, 1948, 1949; WMA, 1948; AWS, 1952. Author, Technical book reviews; "Form and Format"; "Two Little Tigers and How They Flew." *Position*: E. E., Am. Book Co., 1932-37; Dir. Des. & Production, Oxford Univ. Press, 1939- . L., Typography & Des., N.Y. Univ., 1950- ; A. Dir., "Art in America," 1958- .

BEGGS, THOMAS MONTAGUE—Museum Director, P.

National Collection of Fine Arts, Wash., D.C.; h. Old Dominion Dr., McLean, Va.

B. Brooklyn, N.Y., Apr. 22, 1899. *Studied*: PIASch.; ASL; Yale Univ., B.F.A.; Ecole des Beaux-Arts, Fontainebleau, France. *Member*: AAMus. *Awards*: med., Sch. A. Lg., 1917; BAID, 1923; Carnegie F. to FMA, 1928-1929; Grant from Federal Republic of Germany (for travel in Germany to museums and art schools), 1954. *Work*: Redlands Univ., Redlands, Cal.; murals, H.S., Brooklyn, N.Y.; Pacific Bldg., Miami, Fla. Author, I., magazine and newspaper articles. *Position*: Hd., A. Dept., Pomona Col., 1926-47; Asst. Dir., Nat. Coll. Fine Arts, Smithsonian Inst., Washington, D.C., 1947-48, Dir., 1948- ; Smithsonian Inst. Representative on Cultural Presentations Committee, O.C.B., 1957- .

BEGIEN, JEANNE (Mrs. Jewett Campbell)—Painter, E.

Douglasdale Rd., Richmond 21, Va.

B. Cincinnati, Ohio, Oct. 21, 1913. *Studied*: Richmond Professional Inst.; Colorado Springs FA Center, with Henry Varnum Poor, Boardman Robinson, Karfiol, Blanch, Hans Hofmann. *Awards*: prizes, Acad. Sc. & FA, Richmond, Va., 1939; VMFA, 1940, 1943, 1946; Butler AI, 1942; Mint Mus. A., 1943; Soc. Wash. A., 1940. *Work*: VMFA; Hollins Col.; murals, Church of the Good Shepherd, St. Luke's Episcopal Church, Southern States Co-operative, and others in Richmond, Va. *Exhibited*: VMFA, 1940, 1943, 1946, 1951; Butler AI, 1942; Mint Mus. A., 1943; Soc. Wash. A., 1940; WFNY 1939; Richmond Acad. Sc. & FA, 1939.*

BEHL, WOLFGANG—Sculptor, T.

Hartford Art School, 15 Girard Ave.; h. 179 Kenyon St., Hartford 5, Conn.

B. Berlin, Germany, Apr. 13, 1918. *Studied*: Acad. FA, Berlin, Germany; R.I. Sch. Des. *Awards*: Eisendrath prize, AIC, 1944; Milwaukee AI, 1945; Springfield A. Lg., 1955. *Work*: AGAA; Lowe Gal., Univ. Miami, Fla. Statues: St. Anthony Sch., Bristol, Conn.; relief carving, Universal Life Insurance Co., Virginia; Arch. Sculpture for Willow Lawn Shopping Center. *Exhibited*: Univ. Illinois, 1957; Bertha Schaefer Gal., annually; AIC, 1943, 1944; Milwaukee AI, 1945; Virginia Mus. A., 1947, 1949, 1951; Boston A. Festival, 1946, 1947; Silvermine Gld. A., 1946, 1947. *Position*: Instr., Sc. & Drawing, Layton Sch. A., Milwaukee, 1944-45; Richmond Professional Inst. of the College of William & Mary, 1945-1953; Hartford A. Sch., Hartford, Conn., 1946- .

BEHNCKE, ETHEL BOUFFLEUR (Mrs. Nile J.)—Educator, Des., L.

545 Algoma Blvd., Oshkosh, Wis.

B. Tacoma, Wash. *Studied*: Univ. Washington, B.E.; Univ. Chicago, M.A.; Chicago Acad. FA, and with Nile Behncke, and others. *Awards*: Julia Piatt F., AAUW, for European study. *Member*: AAUW (life); NEA; Wisconsin A. Edu. Assn. Contributor to Design Magazine. Lectures: Modern Art, Interior Design, Art Education, History of Art. *Positions*: Iowa State College, Ames, Iowa; Chm. A. Dept., Assoc. Prof., Wisconsin State College, Oshkosh, Wis.

BEHNCKE, NILE JURGEN—Museum Director, P.

545 Algoma Blvd., Oshkosh, Wis.

B. Oshkosh, Wis., June 4, 1894. *Studied*: Oshkosh State Col.; George Enness A. Sch. *Member*: Wisconsin P. & S.; Bd., Paine A. Center. *Awards*: Wisconsin Fed. Women's Cl.; Wisconsin P. & S.; Wisconsin State prize; Northeast A. *Work*: Madison Pub. Sch.; Nurses Hospital, Victoria, B.C.; Oklahoma A. Center; Neville Pub. Mus.; Kenosha, Wis., A. Gal.; Manitowoc Mus.; Allis A. Lib., Milwaukee; Paine A. Center; Casper (Wyo.) A. Center; Kohler (Wis.) Pub. Sch.; Ripon Col.; Ft. Dodge A. Gal.; AIC; Colburn Co.; Oshkosh Pub. Mus.; Oshkosh State Col.; and in private coll. *Exhibited*: Wisconsin P. & S.; PAFA; AIC; CGA; AWS. *Position*: Dir., Cur. A., Oshkosh Pub. Museum, Oshkosh, Wis.; T., A. & Mus. classes.

BEILER, (IDA) ZOE—Painter, T., L.

Teachers College, Dickinson, N.D.; h. Lock box 105, Elida, Ohio

B. Lima, Ohio. *Studied*: Lima Col., B.A.; Mich. State T. Col.; AIC, B.F.A., M.F.A.; Univ. Chicago, and with Paul Shwab. *Member*: Nat. Edu. Assn.; Nat. Inst. A. & Let. *Awards*: prizes, Fargo, N.D., 1938; med. GGE 1939; AAPL, 1950. *Work*: IBM; FA Cl., Fargo, N.D.; Mayville State Col.; Fargo Agricultural Col.; Dickinson Pub. Lib.; Capitol Bldg., Bismarck; State Col., Dickinson, N.D. *Exhibited*: Nat. Exh. Am. Painting, 1936-1938; CGA, 1942; Chicago World's Fair, 1933; GGE 1939; N.D. State T. Col., 1935, 1936; Aberdeen, S.D., 1937; Fargo, N.D., 1938; Grand Forks, N.D.; Bismarck, 1938, 1943; Glendive, Mont., 1945; Dickinson, N.D., 1933, 1935, 1942, 1945, 1950, 1951; Hartman Gal., Sarasota, Fla., 1954, 1955; Sarasota AA. *Position*: Instr., State T. Col., Dickinson, N.D., to 1953.*

BELCHER, HILDA—Painter

Pittsford, Vt.

B. Pittsford, Vt., 1881. *Studied*: with Chase, Henri, Bellows, Luks. *Member*: NA; AWS; Conn. Acad. FA; Southern Vt. A.; Mid-Vermont A. *Awards*: prizes, Strathmore Comp., 1908; NY WC Cl., 1909, 1915; AWS, 1918; NAD, 1926, 1931; PAFA, 1932; med., Brown-Bigelow Comp., 1925; Phila. WC Cl., 1935; Hon. deg., M.A., Middlebury Col., 1941. *Work*: Montclair Mus. A.; Museum of FA of Houston; Wood Mus. A.; High Mus. A.; Dumbarton House, Wash., D.C.; Vassar Col.; Laurence Mus., Williamstown, Mass.; Am. Unitarian Assn. Hdqts., Boston, Mass.; PAFA; Newark (N.J.) Mus. A.; Maryland Inst.

BELINE, GEORGE—Painter, S.

370 Central Park West, New York 25, N.Y.

B. Minsk, Russia, July 23, 1887. *Studied*: NAD; Lycee Charlemagne, Ecole des Beaux-Arts, Ecole Superieure des

Places de Vosges, Paris, France. *Member*: All. A. Am.; SC; AAPL. *Awards*: prizes, AAPL; SC; medals, NAD. *Exhibited*: NAD; PAFA; Mun. A. Gal.; AAPL; AWS; BM; NAC; PC; Ogunquit A. Center; Springville, Utah; Washington, D.C. Represented in public and private collections.

BELING, HELEN (Mrs. Lawrence R. Kahn)—
Sculptor, T., L.
287 Weyman Ave., New Rochelle, N.Y.

B. New York, N.Y., Jan. 1, 1914. *Studied*: Col. City of N.Y.; NAD; ASL. *Member*: Audubon A.; NAWA; S. Gld.; N.Y. Soc. Women A.; New Rochelle AA; Westchester A. & Crafts Gld. *Awards*: prizes, Audubon A., 1952; NAWA, 1951; Silvermine Gld. A., 1957; Sabena Comp. (Intl.), 1953. *Work*: Butler Inst. Am. A., Youngstown, Ohio; Jewish Community Center, White Plains, N.Y. *Exhibited*: MMA; NAD; PAFA; Audubon A.; NAWA; Syracuse Mus. FA; John Heller Gal.; WMAA; Ohio Univ.; Univ. Illinois; London, England; Brussels, Belgium, 1957. *Position*: Instr., S., Westchester Workshop, White Plains, N.Y.

BELL, CECIL CROSLEY—Painter
17 Tompkins Circle, Staten Island 1, N.Y.

B. Seattle, Wash., July 15, 1906. *Studied*: AIC; ASL. *Work*: WMAA; Howard Univ.; Cooper Union; Childe Hassam Fund, and in private collections. *Exhibited*: CGA, 1937; PAFA, 1938, 1958; WMAA, 1936-1942, 1945; AIC, 1937, 1941, 1943, 1944; Univ. Nebraska, 1943 (one-man), annually, 1944-1948; NAD, 1944-1947, 1957; MMA, 1950; Montclair A. Mus.; one-man: Kraushaar Gal., 1945-1952.

BELL, CLARA LOUISE (Mrs. Bela Janowsky)—Painter
52 West 57th St., New York 19, N.Y.

B. Newton Falls, Ohio. *Studied*: Cleveland Sch. A.; ASL, and with Henry G. Keller. *Member*: ASMP; NAWA; Brooklyn Soc. Min. P.; Studio Cl., N.Y. *Awards*: prizes, CMA, 1919, 1923, 1925, 1926; Studio Cl., 1926, 1928; NAWA, 1949, medals, 1930, 1952. *Exhibited*: ASMP, 1945-1952; MMA, 1950; NAWA, 1928-1958; Argent Gal., 1950; All. A. Am., 1954; Royal Soc. Min. P., London, England, 1958; Greenbriar, White Sulphur Springs, W. Va., 1933 (one-man); Butler Inst. Am. A., 1939; Newport, R.I., 1932; Copley Gal., Boston, 1914 (one-man); Clinton Acad., Easthampton, N.Y. (2-man) 1930. *Work*: MMA; BM; Masonic Temple, Youngstown, Ohio; Butler Inst. Am. A.; Coast Guard Acad., Hamilton Hall, New London, Conn.

BELL, EDITH MARIAN—Painter, T.
5205 North 8th Place, Phoenix 2, Ariz.

B. Cushing, Iowa. *Studied*: NAD; & with Wayman Adams, George Pearse Ennis. *Member*: Iowa A. Gld.; Chicago Galleries Assn. *Awards*: Tiffany Fnd. F., & Pulitzer Award, NAD, 1922; Town & Country A. Cl., Chicago, 1938; Exh. Iowa Paintings, Chicago, 1937. *Work*: State Univ. Iowa; Frances Shimer Col., Mt. Carroll, Ill. *Exhibited*: AWCS, 1934, 1936-1938; N.Y. WC Cl., 1935-1937; Phila. WC Cl., 1937; Wash. WC Cl., 1937, 1938; All.A.Am., 1940, 1941; Chicago Galleries Assn., 1943 (one-man); Dickerson Gal., Frances Shimer Col., 1946; Des Moines A. Center, 1951, 1952; Sioux City A. Center, 1952; Iowa State Col., 1951, 1952, 1956, 1957; State Univ. Iowa, 1952; Tres Palmas Gal., 1951; Iowa A. Gld., Mason City, 1955; one-man: Holland Hall, Tulsa, 1946; Western Col., Oxford, Ohio, 1946; Scottsdale, Ariz., 1954; Younkers Gal., Des Moines, Iowa, 1956, 1958.

BELL, ENID (Mrs. Enid Bell Palanchian)—
Sculptor, C., T., I., W., L.
701 Columbia Ave., North Bergen, N.J.

B. London, England, Dec. 5, 1904. *Studied*: in England & Scotland; & with Sir W. Reid Dick, London; ASL. *Members*: Assoc. A. New Jersey; NSS. *Awards*: Med., Paris Int. Exh., 1937; AAPL, 1934; New Mexico State Fair, 1940, 1941; Newark AC, 1933; N.J.Exh., 1949, 1951. *Work*: Congressional med. for Lincoln Ellsworth; Carved wood murals, Robert Treat Sch., Newark, N.J.; Beth Israel Hospital, Newark, N.J.; USPO, Mt. Holly, Boonton, N.J.; Hereford, Tex.; carved wood portrait reliefs, Armenian Cultural Fnd., Boston. *Exhibited*: PAFA; NAD; WFNY 1939; Paris Int. Exp.; MMA; BM; Mus. New Mexico, Santa

Fé; Ferargil Gal., 1929 (one-man); Arden Gal., 1934, Argent Gal., 1949; NSS; Illinois State Mus., Springfield, 1957 (one-man); Columbus (Ga.) Mus. A. & Crafts, 1957 (one-man). *Author*: "Tincraft as a Hobby"; "Practical Woodcarving Projects"; "Arts and Crafts" filmstrips. *Position*: Instr., S. Newark Sch. F. & Indst. A., Newark, N.J., 1944- .

BELL, PHILIP FLETCHER—Painter
1635 Wisconsin Ave., N.W., Washington 7, D.C.

B. Kirksville, Mo., July 6, 1907. *Studied*: George Washington Univ., B.A.; Yale Univ., B.F.A. *Member*: Georgetown A. Group. *Awards*: prize, D.P.I. exh., Denton, Md., 1958. *Work*: mural, McKinley H.S., Wash., D.C. *Exhibited*: CGA, 1937; PMG; Grand Central A. Gal.; one-man: Whyte Gal., 1947; United Nations Cl., 1949; George Washington Univ., 1950; Artists Mart, 1954. *Position*: Instr., Recreation Assn., Lib. Congress; Dir., Children's A. Gal. & D.C. A. Project, 1938-1941; Assoc. in A., Georgetown Univ., 1938-1941; Actg. Exh. Officer, Lib. Congress, 1945-1955; Owner & Dir., Studio 33 A. Gal., Wash., D.C.

BELLE, CECILE (Mrs. Ralph M. Carson)—Painter
200 East 66th St., New York 21, N.Y.; h. Wing Farm, Quaker Hill, Pawling, N.Y.

B. Verdun, France, July 22, 1900. *Studied*: in Caen and Rouen, France; Oxford Univ.; Sch. FA, Antwerp, Belgium. *Work*: IBM; Coca Cola Company. *Exhibited*: Carnegie Inst., 1944, 1945; Durand-Ruel Gal., 1945 (one-man); Bonestell Gal., 1944 (one-man); Midtown Gal., 1949, one-man, 1953, 1956; VMFA; Des Moines A. Center; Univ. Miami; Butler AI; Ft. Wayne Mus. A.; Dayton AI; Springfield Mus. A.; Montclair A. Mus.; Phila. A. All.; Columbus Mus. FA; PAFA; Southern Mus. Circuit; Univ. So. California, 1957 (one-man); Univ. of Virginia, 1956-57. *Position*: Memb. Advisory Council, Grosvenor Neighborhood House, New York, N.Y.

BELLIN, MILTON ROCKWELL—Painter
303 East 37th St., New York 16, N.Y.

B. New Haven, Conn., June 6, 1913. *Studied*: Yale Univ. Sch. FA, B.F.A. *Awards*: prizes, Springfield AA, 1937; F., Tiffany Fnd., 1938; MModA, 1940; Conn. WC Soc., 1944, 1946; Norwich AA, 1946; A. in Res. award, New Britain T. Col., 1938-39. *Exhibited*: Conn. WC Soc., 1938-1953; MModA, 1940; MMA, 1952; AWS, 1941-1946; Audubon A, 1946, 1947; NAD, 1950; CGA, 1939; Conn. Acad. FA, 1941; Lyman Allyn Mus. A., 1951.*

BELLIS, DAISY MAUDE—Painter, Des., W., L., E.
4275 Knoll Ave., Oakland 19, Cal.

B. Waltham, Mass. *Studied*: Mass. Sch. A.; Univ. Vermont, with Scott Carbee; Montreal A. Gal., with Dioner; with Thurston Topham, Montreal; Andre L'Hote, Paris, France; Breckenridge Sch. Painting, Gloucester, Mass. *Member*: F., Royal Soc. of A., London, England. *Exhibited*: New Haven (Conn.) Pub. Lib.; Copley Gal., Boston; Morency Gal., Montreal; McGill Univ., Montreal; Walker A. Gal., Liverpool, England; A. All., N.Y.; WFNY 1939; Blackstone Lib., Branford, Conn.; Stamford (Conn.) Pub. Lib.; Town House, Berkeley, Cal.; Jackson A. Gal., San F., Cal.; deYoung Mem. Mus., San F., Cal.; Burlington (Vt.) Univ., and in San Jose, Oakland, Cal., and Paris, France. *Lectures*: "Old Masters," "Color." *Positions*: Pub. Sch., Supv., Cincinnati, Ohio; Instr. A., Sch. for Teachers, Univ. of Ohio; Salem College, Winston-Salem, N.C.; Univ. Vermont, Sch. for Teachers.

BELMONT, I(RA) J(EAN)—Painter, W.
160 West 59th St., New York 19, N.Y.

B. Kaunas, Lithuania, June 15, 1885. *Studied*: Konigsberg, Paris, New York. *Work*: BM; Crocker Coll., San F.; Heckscher Fnd.; Univ. Georgia; Musee du Jeu de Paume, Paris; Denver Mus. A.; Tel-Aviv Mus., Israel. *Exhibited*: Bryn Mawr A. Center, 1945; Belmont Gal., 1945; Phila. A. All., 1929; Renaissance Gal., Paris, 1932; Wildenstein Gal. 1933; Mus. Sc. & Indst., 1940; Malvern Festival, England, 1947 (one-man); Closson Gal., Cincinnati, 1951 (one-man). *Author*: "Modern Dilemma in Art," 1944.*

BELMONT, LU—Painter, T.
R.F.D. 5, Ridgefield, Conn.

B. New York, N.Y., June 23, 1907. *Studied*: ASL, with Kenneth Hayes Miller, Kimon Nicolaides. *Member*: Artists of Today; Assoc. A. New Jersey; Audubon A; AEA. *Exhibited*: Contemporary A. Gal.; Ferargil Gal.; NAC; WMAA; BM; Newark Mus. A.; Indianapolis AA; Audubon A.; AWS; J. Seligmann; Galerie Neuf; one-man: Artists of Today, Newark New-Age Gal.; Travel Center Gal., N.Y.*

BELSKIE, ABRAM—*Sculptor*
 New York Medical College, Fifth Ave. at 106th St., New York, N.Y.; h. 38 Brook St., Closter, N.J.

B. London, England, Mar. 24, 1907. *Studied*: Glasgow Sch. A., Scotland, with Alexander Proudfoot, Archibald Dawson; London, Paris, Rome, and with John Gregory, Malvina Hoffman. *Member*: ANA; F., NSS. *Awards*: John Keppie traveling scholarship, Glasgow Sch. A.; prizes, Sir John Edward Burnett prize, Glasgow Sch. A.; NSS, 1951, 1956. *Work*: Brookgreen Gardens, S.C.; Mariners Mus., Newport News, Va.; Am. Mus. Natural Hist., N.Y.; Field Mus., Chicago; Cleveland Health Mus.; N.Y. Acad. Medicine; Jewish Theological Seminary, N.Y.; Park Ave. Synagogue; medal des., 25th Anniversary, Columbia Presbyterian Medical Center, 1953; medallion panel, Col. of Physicians & Surgeons; medallion for Ortho Research Fnd.; medal des., Ben Hogan Medal; Soc. of Medallists, 1954 issue; Endocrine Soc., 1955; Edison Brothers Achievement medal, 1956. *Exhibited*: NAD. Co-author, "Birth Atlas," 1940. *Position*: Faculty, N.Y. Medical College, New York, N.Y.

BELT, A. ELMER—*Library Director*
 The Elmer Belt Library of Vinciana; h. 1893 Wilshire Blvd., Los Angeles 57, Cal.

B. Chicago, Ill., Apr. 10, 1893. *Studied*: Univ. California, B.S., M.S., M.D. *Member*: CAA; AMA; AFA. *Awards*: med., AMA Exh., 1922. Lectures: Leonardo daVinci; "Leonardo daVinci's Anatomical Dissections," Sorbonne, Paris, 1952. Author: "Manuscripts of Leonardo daVinci," 1948; "Leonardo daVinci's Library," 1949; "Leonardo daVinci's Studies of the Aging Process," 1952; "Leonardo, the Anatomist," 1955 (Logan Clendenning lectures on History of Medicine). *Position*: Dir., The Elmer Belt Library of Vinciana, Los Angeles, Cal.

BEMELMANS, LUDWIG—*Painter, Gr., W., I.*
 15 Place Vendôme, Paris 1, France; h. 15 Gramercy Park, New York 3, N.Y.

B. Austrian Tyrol, 1898. *Studied*: Lyceum, Regensburg, Bavaria. Author, I.: adult books, "The Woman of My Life"; "My War With the U.S."; "The High World"; "Now I Lay Me Down to Sleep"; "Dirty Eddy"; "Hotel Splendide"; "My Life in Art"; juveniles: "Madeline"; "Madeline's Rescue"; "Madeline and the Bad Hat." *Exhibited*: Paris, New York and London. *Work*: Represented in most U.S. and European museums and private galleries. Contributor in words and pictures to The New Yorker; Holiday; Vogue; McCall's; Town and Country; Realitées; Sie und Er.

BENDIG, WILLIAM C.—*Painter, T.*
 Hollycroft, Ivoryton, Conn.

B. Corry, Pa., Dec. 1, 1927. *Studied*: Trinity Col., Hartford, Conn.; Univ. London, Chelsea Sch. A., (London) with Ceri Richards; private study in Greece and Italy. *Member*: Essex AA; Mediaeval Acad. of Am. *Work*: Trinity Col. *Exhibited*: Provincetown, Mass., 1957; Ogunquit, Me., 1956; Springfield Mus. A., 1953; Mystic AA, 1957-58; N.Y. City Center, 1957; Lyme AA, 1956; Springfield A. Lg., 1957; Essex AA, 1956, 1957, 1958. Lectures: Art History, Mediaeval Art, Architecture, etc. *Position*: Instr., Painting, Drawing, Art History, Brunswick Sch., Greenwich, Conn.; Cheshire Acad. (Conn.); Publisher of the magazine The Art Gallery, 1957- .

BENDINER, ALFRED—*Architect, P., Gr., Cart. W.*
 Western Savings Fund Bldg.; h. 322 South Camac St., Philadelphia 7, Pa. and R. D. #1, Malvern, Pa.

B. Pittsburgh, Pa., July 23, 1899. *Studied*: PMSchIA; Univ. Pennsylvania, B.Arch., M.Arch., and with Paul Cret. *Member*: F., AIA; Pa. Soc. Arch.; Phila. WC Cl.; Phila. A. All. *Awards*: prizes, PAFA, 1946; Phila. Pr. Cl., 1938, 1944; Concord AA, 1954; Gimbel Comp., 1950; Newspaper Gld., "Front Page" award. *Work*: NGFA; LC; PMA; PAFA; Princeton Univ.; Univ. Pennsylvania Rosenwald Coll.; murals, Byck Bros., Louisville, Ky., Philadelphia Fidelity Bank, Univ. Pennsylvania Mus., Acad. of Music,

Phila., Gimbel Bros., Phila.; Bibliotheque Nationale, Paris; Uffizi Gal., Florence, Italy; Nat. Gal., Oslo, *Exhibited*: nationally since 1929. Contributor to numerous scientific publications. Cartoonist, Phila. Evening Bulletin, 1938-45; Phila. Record, Washington Times Herald. Author, I., "Music to My Eyes," 1952.

BENEDUCE, ANTIMO—*Painter*
 19 East Pearson St., Chicago 11, Ill.

B. St. Antimo, Naples, Italy, Mar. 28, 1900. *Studied*: Cleveland Sch. A.; & with Charles Hawthorne, Henry G. Keller. *Member*: Chicago AC; Phila. WC Cl.; AWCS; Renaissance Soc., Chicago; Cleveland SA. *Awards*: Ill. State Fair, 1955, 1957; Mississippi Valley A. (purchase prize); Chicago SA, 1958; Union Lg. A. Show, Chicago, 1957. *Work*: Akron AI; CM; Vanderpoel Coll.; New Trier H.S., Winnetka, Ill.; Toledo Mus. A.; John Herron AI. *Exhibited*: CGA, 1929 (one-man); Albany Inst. Hist. & A., 1933 (one-man); AIC, 1945; Akron AI, 1939 (one-man); Chicago SA, 1958; Union Lg. A. Show, Chicago, 1957; Illinois State Fair, 1957.

BENEKER, KATHARINE—*Museum Designer Exh., P.*
 American Museum of Natural History; h. 11 St. Luke's Pl., New York 14, N.Y.

B. Brooklyn, N.Y., May 11, 1909. *Studied*: PMSchIA; Mass. Sch. A., and with Richard Miller, Charles W. Hawthorne. *Exhibited*: AWS, 1942-1945; NAWA, 1943, 1944; Provincetown AA, 1938-1941. *Position*: T., Brewster, Mass., 1932-34-36; Supv. Exh., Am. Mus. Natural Hist. New York, N.Y., 1940-52, Hd. Dept. Preparation & Exhibition, 1952- ; Exh. Co-ordinator, 1954- .

BENESCH, OTTO—*Historian, W., L.*
 Spiegelgasse 8, Vienna I, Austria

B. Ebenfurth, Austria, June 29, 1896. *Studied*: Univ. Vienna, Ph.D. *Member*: Austrian Univ. Lg. Am. *Awards*: Guggenheim F. Author, many books on art and artists. Contributor to art magazines and periodicals. Lectures on History of Painting, Drawing & Graphic Arts. *Position*: Dir., Albertina Mus., Vienna; Prof., Univ. of Vienna; formerly, Instr., Harvard Univ.; Research F., FMA.*

BENGTZ, (ERIC ALGOT) TURE—
 Painter, Et., Lith., T., Des., L.
 61 Clifton Park, Melrose 76, Mass.

B. Westansunda, Aland, Finland, Oct. 23, 1907. *Studied*: BMFA Sch. *Member*: Gld. Boston A.; Boston Pr. M. *Awards*: prizes, NAD, 1943; BMFA Sch. traveling scholarship, 1934; Tiffany Fnd., 1939-40; New England A.; LC; Boston Pr. M., 1956. *Work*: Vanner's Coll., Aland, Finland; Wiggins Coll., Boston Pub. Lib.; BMFA; Berkshire Mus., Pittsfield, Mass. *Exhibited*: AIC, 1946; Carnegie Inst.; CGA, 1941; NAD, 1941-1946; Lib. Cong., 1944, 1946; Palace Legion Honor, 1946. *Position*: Hd., Dept. Drawing, Graphic Arts & Anatomy, BMFA Sch., Boston, Mass. Conducted TV lecture program, "Bengtz on Drawing," Boston, Mass., 1956, 1958-59.

BENISOVICH, MICHEL N.—*Writer, T.*
 83 Washington Pl., New York 11, N.Y.

B. Russia, 1891. *Studied*: N.Y. Univ., Inst. FA; Ecole du Louvre, Paris. *Member*: CAA. Contributor to Burlington Magazine, Gazette Beaux-Arts and other publications in France, Holland, Brazil, Denmark, Sweden, Belgium.

BENJAMIN, GERSHON—*Painter*
 328 Emerson Lane, Berkeley Heights, N.J.; h. 310 East 54th St., New York, N.Y.

B. Roumania, Jan. 6, 1899. *Studied*: ASL; Edu. All., N.Y. *Member*: ASL; Fed. Mod. P. & S.; Indp. A. Am. *Awards*: prize, Newspaper Gld., N.Y., 1957. *Exhibited*: BM; AIC; Carnegie Inst.; Contemp. A. Gal. (one-man); Montclair A. Mus., 1955; Fed. Mod. P. & S., 1955, 1956; AFA traveling exh.; Newark Mus. A., 1958; Riverside Mus., N.Y.; Churchill's Gal., N.Y.; 7 American Artists, N.Y.; Silvermine Gld. A.; Newspaper Gld. Press Cl., 1958 (one-man).

BENN, BEN—*Painter, T.*
 206 West 105th St., New York 25, N.Y.

B. Russia, Dec. 27, 1884. *Studied*: NAD. *Member*: AEA; Fed. Mod. P. & S. *Awards*: Schiedt award, PAFA, 1952.

Work: MMA; WMAA; Walker A. Center; Newark Mus. A.; Albany Inst. Hist. & A.; Mus. City of New York; Watkins Gal., American Univ., Wash., D.C. *Exhibited*: PAFA; WMAA; MMA; Butler AI, Youngstown, Ohio; Intl. Assn. of the Plastic Arts, traveling exh., Europe, 1956.

BENNETT, BERTHA (Mrs.)—Painter, Et., Lith.
920 West Craig Place, San Antonio 1, Tex.

B. Eastland, Tex., Mar. 5, 1883. *Studied*: San Antonio Sch. A., with Henry F. McFee; San Antonio AI, with Charles Rosen. *Member*: San Antonio A. Lg.; San Antonio Pr.M.; Texas FA Acad. *Exhibited*: Denver A. Mus.; Texas FA Acad., 1937-1946; Jacksonville, Miss. (one-man); Borglum Studio, San Antonio (one-man).*

BENNETT, MARY ELIZABETH—Painter
53 Home Ave., Middletown, Conn.

B. Coventry, Conn., Sept. 27, 1877. *Studied*: PIASch. *Exhibited*: Hartford Soc. Women Painters. *Position*: T., City H.S., Middletown, Conn., 1899-1944.

BENNETT, RAINEY—Painter, I.
5761 South Dorchester Ave., Chicago 37, Ill.

B. Marion, Ind., July 26, 1907. *Studied*: Am. Acad. A., Chicago; AIC; Univ. Chicago; George Grosz-Maurice Sterne Sch., N.Y. *Member*: AWS. *Awards*: prizes, Tuthill award, Chicago, 1936; Renaissance Soc., Chicago, 1945; Springfield, Ill., 1947; Town & Country award, Chicago, 1950; Bartels award, Chicago, 1952; Clarke award, Chicago, 1956; French medal, Chicago, 1957. *Work*: MMA; MMoDA; BM; AIC; Univ. Illinois; Beloit College; DMFA; Cranbrook Acad. A., and others. Murals: USPO, Dearborn, Mich.; Stevens Store, Circle Restaurant, Chicago; Hibbard, Spencer, Bartlett Co., Evanston, Ill.; Edison Co., Mus. of Sc. & Indstry., Chicago; Watercolor traveling commission, Venezuela for Nelson Rockefeller & Standard Oil of New Jersey, 1939; South America, Nelson Rockefeller, 1941. *Exhibited*: Univ. Illinois, 1949, 1951, 1957; Carnegie Inst., 1951; AIC, 1957; one-man National Exh., MMoDA Art Touring, 1940-1942; one-man, AIC, 1942; AIC, annual, 1944-1958. Author, I., children's book, "What Do You Think?," 1958.

BENNETT, RUTH M.—Craftsman, T., P.
1439 North Stanley Ave., Hollywood 46, Cal.

B. Momence, Ill., Feb. 11, 1899. *Studied*: Pomona Col., B.A.; ASL; Otis AI; Chouinard AI, and with Armin Hansen, John Carlsen, Emily Mocine, George Bridgman, Millard Sheets. *Member*: Cal. WC Soc. *Awards*: prizes, San Diego, Cal., 1927; Arizona State Fair, 1931; Cal. AC, 1926; Los A. County Fair, 1927, 1932, 1933, 1934, 1936, 1937; Los A. Mus. A., 1934; Tri-Craft Gld., 1937. *Exhibited*: Gardena, Cal., 1952, 1953. *Work*: panel, Westchester H.S. Lib. *Position*: Instr., Woodcarving, Los Angeles City & County Sch., 1934- .

BENNEY, ROBERT—Painter, I., W., L.
152 West 57th St., New York 19, N.Y.

B. New York, N.Y., July 16, 1904. *Studied*: CUASch.; ASL; NAD; Grand Central Sch. A., and with Bridgman, Briggs, Dunn, Cornwell. *Member*: SI; AEA; ASL; A. & Writers Assn. *Awards*: prizes, PMA; med., A. Dir. Cl. (Abbott Lab.), 1945; CUASch. *Work*: Shell Oil Co.; RCA-Victor; Abbott Lab.; U.S. Navy; U.S. Army; U.S. Air Force; Standard Oil Co., New Jersey; Chrysler Corp.; United Aircraft Corp.; deYoung Mus. A.; IBM; Am. Sugar Refining Co.; American Tobacco Co.; General Foods Corp.; Western Electric Corp.; SAM; CGA; Mariners Mus., Newport News, Va.; Fort Sam Houston, Tex.; MDW Pentagon, Wash., D.C.; Chaplain Sch., Fort Slocum, N.Y.; Army Medical Center, Fort Totten, N.Y.; produced Visual Story of Sugar. *Exhibited*: NAD; CGA; Currier Gal., 1940; VMFA, 1940; BMFA, 1944; AIC, 1944; Inst. Mod. A.; NGA, 1943, 1945; MMA, 1943; Carnegie Inst., 1945; BM; Montreal AA; deYoung Mem. Mus.; Dallas Mus. FA, 1945; Portland Mus. A., 1945; Arch. Lg., N.Y.; N.Y. Pub. Lib.; Newspaper A. Exh., 1938; San Diego FA Soc.; La Jolla A. Center; SAM; Norfolk Mus. A. & Sc.; Springfield (Mass.) Mus. FA; MMA; SI; U.S.A.F. Acad., Denver; U.S.A.F., Bolling Field, Wash., D.C. Many portraits of prominent persons, I., "Naval Aviation," 1944; Author: "Men Without Guns" (as told to DeWitt Mackenzie). Contributor to "Our Flying Navy"; "Pictures, Painters and You," 1949; Life's Picture History of World War II, 1950;

American Artist magazine, 1956; True Magazine, and others. *Position*: Instr., Sch. for A. Studies, 1948-50; Pratt Institute, Brooklyn, N.Y., 1950- .

BENNO, BENJAMIN G(REENSTEIN)—Painter
5 Great Jones St., New York 12, N.Y.

B. London, England, June 2, 1901. *Studied*: Modern Sch. A., N.Y., with Robert Henri and George Bellows; sculpture at Sch. of Architecture and Beaux Arts, N.Y. with Solon and John Gutzon Borglum and others; study in Europe. *Work*: FMA; BM; BMA; SFMA, and in private collections in U.S. and Europe. *Exhibited*: Whitney Studio Cl., 1916-1922; New Gal., N.Y., 1923 (one-man); New Sch., N.Y., 1931; WMAA, 1933; Vassar College, 1939 (retrospective); SFMA, 1939 (retrospective); Chicago A. Cl., 1939 (retrospective); Norlyst Gal., 1940; Pinacotheca Gal., N.Y., 1940; Passedoit Gal., N.Y., 1941; Riverside Mus., 1943; CGA, 1943; Hillel Fnd. traveling exh., 1953-54; Lotte Jacobi Gal., N.Y., 1954; in many galleries in Paris, London, Norway, Czechoslovakia, Tunis, Africa, 1934-1939.

BENSCO, CHARLES J.—Painter
2214 East Polk St., Phoenix, Ariz.

B. Hungary, Feb. 19, 1894. *Studied*: Royal Acad. FA, Budapest; ASL with Milton Banckroft, George Bridgman, Ernest Blumenschein. *Member*: Cal. AC; AAPL; Artists of the Southwest; Phoenix FA Assn. *Awards*: prizes, Ebell A. Salon, Los Angeles; Gardena (Cal.) H.S.; Josephine Logan medal (2); "American Artist of the Year" title, AAPL, Ariz. Chptr., 1951; Cal. A. Cl., 1955, prize and medal, 1956. *Work*: Gardena H.S.; FA & Crafts Mus., Budapest; mural, Our Lady of Perpetual Help Church, Downey, Cal.; First Fed. Savings & Loan Assn., Phoenix, Ariz.; many portraits of prominent persons. *Exhibited*: Los A. Mus. A., 1932-1945; Ebell A. Salon, 1932-1945; Continuous exh. Paintings of the West, Westward Ho in Phoenix, Ariz.

BENSING, FRANK C.—Portrait Painter, I., Des.
1 West 67th St., New York 23, N.Y.; s. Woodstock, N.Y.

B. Chicago, Ill., Oct. 29, 1893. *Studied*: AIC. *Member*: AWS; A. & W. Gld.; SI; SC; A. Gld.; A. Fellowship. *Exhibited*: NAD; All. A. Am.; SC; AWS. I., national magazines. *Work*: Bryn Mawr Col.; State Office Bldg., Albany, N.Y.; Joseph P. Kennedy Mem. Hospital, Boston, Mass.; Univ. Delaware; Earlham Col., Richmond, Ind.; Univ. Notre Dame; Spaulding House, Harvard Univ.; St. Luke's Hospital, N.Y.; Douglass Col., New Brunswick, N.J.; Union College, Schenectady, N.Y.

BENSON, BEN ALBERT—Engraver, Des., I., Comm. A.
737 North Michigan Ave., Chicago 11, Ill.; h. 4132 Highland Ave., Downers Grove, Ill.

B. Bollnas, Sweden, Jan. 23, 1901. *Studied*: AIC; ASL; Univ. Nebraska, B.F.A. *Member*: Swedish A. of Chicago; The Westerners. *Awards*: prize, Am. Legion, 1925. *Exhibited*: Swedish-Am. A., Chicago, 1946; Northwest Pr. M.; Wichita Pr. Exh.; Joslyn Mem., 1945 (one-man); Swedish Soc. A., Chicago. I., Rotarian Magazine.*

BENSON, EMANUEL—Educator, W., Cr., L.
525 West Arbutus St., Philadelphia 19, Pa.

B. New York, N.Y., Oct. 22, 1904. *Studied*: Dartmouth College, B.A.; Columbia Univ. Contributor to: Parnassus; Saturday Review; N.Y. Sun; Creative Art; American Magazine of Art; monographs on John Marin; Problems of Portraiture. *Position*: Chief, Div. Edu., Philadelphia Museum of Art, 1937-1953; Dean PM Sch. A., 1953- .

BENSON, GERTRUDE A.—Art Critic, Feature Writer
525 West Arbutus St., Philadelphia 19, Pa.

Studied: Hunter Col., B.A.; N.Y. Univ., M.A. *Awards*: Carnegie F., 1929-30, 1930-31. Contributor to Art Bulletin; Parnassus; New York Times; Philadelphia Evening & Sunday Bulletin; Philadelphia Inquirer.

BENSON, HANNAH NICHOLSON (Mrs. Adolph B.)—Painter, W., L.
136 Middletown Rd., Berlin, Conn.

B. Pawtucket, R.I. *Studied*: Brown Univ., B.A.; & with Henry Davenport, C. Gordon Harris. *Member*: Conn.

Acad. FA; New Haven Paint & Clay Cl. *Exhibited*: Conn. Acad. FA, 1934-1952; New Haven Paint & Clay Cl., 1928-1952. Author: "The Craftsman"; "Swedish Weaving." Lectures: Scandinavian Art, Swedish Art.

BENSON, TRESSA EMERSON (Mrs. B. A.)—
Painter, T.
4132 Highland Ave., Downers Grove, Ill.

B. Bucksport, Me., June 28, 1896. *Studied*: Syracuse Univ., B.F.A.; & with Charles Hawthorne, C. Ambrose Webster, and in Europe. *Member*: Lincoln A. Gld.; Chicago SA; NAWA. *Awards*: F., Syracuse Univ., 1923; med., Kansas City AI, 1929; prize, AIC, 1937. *Exhibited*: AIC, 1931-1938, 1941, 1942, 1944; Mandel Bros., Chicago, 1941 (one-man); Joslyn Mem., 1943 (one-man); Chicago Soc. A., 1932-1958; Renaissance Soc., Chicago, 1957; Downers Grove Pub. Lib., 1958 (one-man). *Position*: A. Dir., Avery Coonley Sch., Downers Grove, Ill., 1946-1948; Instr., Adult Edu., Downers Grove H.S., 1950-52; private Instr., 1937- ; Trustee, Downers Grove Pub. Lib., 1950- ; Founder, Downers Grove A. Gld.

BENTLEY, CLAUDE—Painter, Gr., Des., E.
245 West North Ave.; h. 1544 Wieland St., Chicago 10, Ill.

B. New York, N.Y., June 9, 1915. *Studied*: Northwestern Univ.; AIC. *Awards*: Mural comp., Taxco, Mexico, 1949; Univ. Illinois (purchase award) 1949; MMA, 1952; Denver A. Mus., 1954 (purchase); AIC, 1955; Magnificent Mile award, Chicago, 1955; Milwaukee Journal award, 1957. *Work*: Univ. Illinois; MMA; Denver A. Mus.; Fairweather-Hardin Gal., Chicago. *Exhibited*: 1956-58: Duveen-Graham Gal., N.Y. (one-man); CGA; AIC; Univ. Illinois; Butler Inst. Am. A.; Univ. Nebraska; WMAA; Denver A. Mus.; Assn. Francais D'Action Artistique, France. *Position*: Instr., creative painting, Contemporary Art Workshop, Chicago, Ill.

BENTLEY, LESTER (W.)—Painter
610 Lake Ave., Greenwich, Conn.

B. Two Rivers, Wis., Mar. 29, 1908. *Studied*: AIC. *Awards*: 13 awards in nat. competitions. *Work*: Columbia Univ.; Princeton Univ.; Univ. Wisconsin; Geisner Mem. Clinic; Oshkosh Pub. Mus.; Milwaukee Journal Coll.; Neville Pub. Mus.; Roosevelt Hospital, N.Y.; Coast Guard Acad., New London, Conn.; murals, USPOs and many portraits of prominent persons. *Exhibited*: Carnegie Inst.; CGA; VMFA; Golden Gate International; PAFA; AIC; Kansas City. *Position*: Instr., Painting, Briarcliff Jr. Col.*

BENTON, THOMAS HART—Painter, T., W.
3616 Belleview Ave., Kansas City, Mo.

B. Neosho, Mo., Apr. 15, 1889. *Studied*: AIC; & abroad. *Awards*: Med., Arch. L., 1933. *Work*: MMA; Wanamaker Gal. Coll.; MModA; BM; murals, State Capitol, Jefferson, Mo.; Indiana State Univ.; New Sch. Social Research; WMAA. Author: "An Artist in America."*

BENZ, OTTO CHARLES—Designer, P., L.
55 Gionti Pl., North Haledon, Paterson, N.J.

B. Paterson, N.J., Feb. 6, 1882. *Studied*: ASL; & with Harry Emmons, Carl Lenz. *Member*: Ridgewood AA; Paterson AA. *Awards*: prize, Paterson, N.J., 1950, 1953, 1955; med., 1946; Ridgewood, N.J., 1955. *Exhibited*: Montclair, 1948-1950; Glen Rock, N.J., 1949; Millburn, N.J., 1951 (one-man); Paterson, 1950-1952, Newark, 1948, Pompton, 1950-52; Ridgewood, 1957, Paterson, 1958, Haledon, 1958 (last 3 are one-man), all in New Jersey.

BEN-ZION—Painter, Gr., T.
58 Morton St., New York 14, N.Y.

B. Ukraine, Russia, July 8, 1897. *Work*: MModA; Newark Mus. A.; AIC; Phillips Coll.; N.Y. Pub. Lib.; Tel Aviv Mus., Israel; AIC; William Rockhill Nelson Mus. A.; Ball State Col.; Bezalel Mus., Jerusalem. *Exhibited*: PAFA, 1940; Carnegie Inst., 1945; WMAA, 1946; Willard Gal.; Buchholz Gal.; Jewish Mus., N.Y., 1948, 1952; annual exhibition, Bertha Schaefer Gal.; one-man: BMA; Portland (Ore.) Mus.; Taft Mus., Cincinnati; SFMA; Univ. Iowa; CAM; Duveen-Graham Gal., N.Y., and many others. Publications: 3 portfolios of etchings on Biblical Themes—Biblical Themes, Prophets, Ruth, Job, Song of Songs.*

BERARDINELLI, DENNIS—Painter, T., Eng., I.
450 Washington Ave., Kingston, N.Y.

B. Italy, Mar. 25, 1897. *Studied*: with John B. Whittaker, Charles W. Hawthorne. *Awards*: Med., NAD, 1926, 1929. *Exhibited*: AWCS, 1933; Phila. Pr. Cl., 1946; Conn. Acad. FA, 1946; NAD, 1946; Lib. Cong., 1946; New Haven Paint & Clay Cl., 1946; MMA; Northwestern Pr. M.; Buffalo Pr. Cl.; Woodstock, N.Y., 1958.

BERD, MORRIS—Painter, T.
R. D. #2, Media, Pa.

B. Philadelphia, Pa., Mar. 12, 1914. *Studied*: Phila. Graphic Sketch Cl.; PMSch.IA. *Awards*: Gimbel mural comp., 1952. *Exhibited*: PAFA, 1939, 1941, 1946, 1948-1952; Traveling A., Inc.; Phila. A. All.; one-man: Carlin Gal., 1951; PMA Sch. A., 1952; PAFA, 1953; Phila. A. All., 1957. *Work*: Barnes Fnd.; Lyman Allyn Mus. A.; Mus. FA of Houston; PAFA. *Position*: Dir., Painting & Drawing, PM Sch. A., and Instr., Adult Classes, PMA, Philadelphia, Pa.

BERDANIER, PAUL F., SR.—Cartoonist, P., Et.
83-10 35th Ave., Jackson Heights, L.I., N.Y.

B. Frackville, Pa., Mar. 7, 1879. *Studied*: St. Louis Sch. FA, and with Gustav Wolff, Alfred Gihon. *Member*: Chicago Soc. Et.; SAGA; All. A. Am; Hudson Valley AA; P & S. Soc. of New Jersey; A. Lg. of Long Island. *Awards*: prizes, St. Louis A. Lg.; SC; SAGA; P. & S. of New Jersey; Freedom Fnd., 1951, medal, 1952-1955; A. Lg. of Long Island, 1958. *Exhibited*: SC; All. A. Am.; Hudson Valley AA; A. Lg. of Long Island. *Work*: Jefferson Mem., St. Louis, Mo.; Museum Moret, France; Univ. Kansas; Howard Univ.; NGFA; N.Y. Pub. Lib.; SC. *Position*: Cartoonist, United Features Syndicate, New York, N.Y., 1929-1957. (Retired)

BERDICK, VERONICA (VERA)—Painter, Et., Eng., T.
1925 North Hudson St., Chicago 14, Ill.

B. Chicago, Ill., Jan. 18, 1915. *Studied*: AIC, B.A.E. *Awards*: Clyde M. Carr, Pauline Palmer, and the Renaissance Soc. awards, AIC; McFadden Eyre medal, Pennsylvania; LC (2 purchase awards); Northwest Pr. M.; Huntington Hartford study grant, 1955. *Work*: AIC; Univ. Chicago Print Lib.; LC; N.Y. Pub. Lib.; Mus. of Lyon, France; Bibliotheque Nationale, Paris, France; Victoria & Albert Mus., London, England. *Exhibited*: one-man: AIC, 1950; Chicago Pub. Lib., 1954; Main St. Book Store, Chicago, 1954; Cliff Dwellers, Chicago, 1952; Esquire Gal., 1952; group shows: AIC, 1945 and others; Chicago SA, 1946; Chicago Soc. Et., 1950; Bismarck Hotel, 1952; Steven Gross Gal., 1953; Evanston A. Center, 1953; North Shore A. Lg., 1953; Chicago Renaissance Soc., 1954; Faculty exhs., 1955-57; 414 Art Gal., 1957, and others; Print Exhs.: LC; PAFA; Carnegie Inst.; Boston Pub. Lib.; Phila. Pr. Cl.; BM; N.Y. Graphic Soc.; Northwest Pr. M.; Dallas (Tex.) Nat. Pr. Exh.; Midwest Pr. M.; CM; Beirut, Lebanon; 4th Intl. Bordighera Biennale, Italy; Int. Exchange of Prints, France, and others. *Position*: Instr., Intaglio Techniques, Sch. of the Art Institute of Chicago, 1947- ; Instr., of college course on "The Introduction to Prints and Printmakers," Chicago Univ. College, Chicago, Ill., 1954-55.

BERENSTAIN, STANLEY—Cartoonist, W.
644 Stetson Rd., Elkins Park 17, Pa.

B. Philadelphia, Pa., Sept. 29, 1923. *Studied*: PMSch. Indst. A.; PAFA. *Member*: Nat. Cartoonists Soc. Author, I., "Berenstain's Baby Book," 1948; "Sister" (syndicated U.S. & Canada); "Tax-Wi$e," 1952; "Marital Blitz," 1955; "Baby Makes Four," 1956; "Lover Boy," 1958; "It's All in the Family," 1958 (all in collaboration with Janice Berenstain). Contributor to: Look, McCall's, This Week, Sat. Eve. Post, Better Homes and Gardens, True, etc. Cartoons by The Berenstains featured in advertising campaigns and brochures. Monthly cartoon feature, "It's All in the Family," for McCall's.

BERESFORD, HELEN ELIZABETH—Educator, L., Des.
106 Gwynn Hall; h. 306 Frederick Apt., Columbia, Mo.

B. Vinton, Iowa, Jan. 5, 1900. *Studied*: Iowa State Col., B.S.; New York Sch. F. & App. A.; Univ. Iowa, M.A. *Exhibited*: Textile Des. Exh., Univ. Iowa, 1940, 1941; Hist.

of Costumes Exh., Univ. Missouri, 1945, 1946. *Position*: Assoc. Prof., F. & App. A., Univ. Missouri, Columbia, Mo., 1929-47; Prof., Dir. Des., Univ. Vermont, Burlington, 1947-54; Color & Des. Consultant, Giddings Interiors, Colorado Springs, Colo., 1954-56.*

BERGAMO, DOROTHY JOHNSON—
Painter, Lith., T., L.
2927 North 18th St., Phoenix, Ariz.

B. Chicago, Ill., Feb. 1, 1912. *Studied*: Univ. Chicago, Ph.B.; AIC, B.F.A.; Northwestern Univ., M.A.; Arizona State Col.; Univ. Colorado. *Awards*: F., AIC, 1937; prizes, AIC, 1943; Arizona State Fair, 1950, 1952; Texas WC Soc., 1952; Tucson FA Assn., 1955. *Work*: Pub. Health Service Hospital, Lexington, Ky.; Witte Mus. A.; Marion Koogler McNay AI; Agricultural & Tech. H.S., San Antonio, Tex.; Mun. Coll., City of Phoenix, Ariz.; Grand Canyon Col., Phoenix; Olsen Fnd., Cheshire, Conn.; Valley Nat. Bank Coll. of Am. Art. *Exhibited*: AIC; San Antonio A. Exh.; Texas FA Assn.; Contemp. A. Gal.; one-man: Witte Mus. A., San Antonio, 1944; Bright Shawl Gal., San Antonio, 1945; Phoenix Little Theatre, 1951; Phoenix A. Center, 1951; Phoenix Woman's Cl., 1954. *Position*: Instr., San Antonio AI, 1943-46; Jr. Col., Bergen County, N.J., 1946-47; Shurtliff Col., Alton, Ill., 1947-48; Arizona State Col., Tempe, 1948-51; Dir., Phoenix A. Center, Phoenix, Ariz., 1951-56. Hd. A. Dept., Carl Hayden H.S., Phoenix, Ariz., 1957- .

BERGE, (EDWARD) HENRY—*Sculptor*
217 West Lanvale St.; h. 5 Merrymount Rd., Baltimore, Md.

B. Baltimore, Md., May 29, 1908. *Studied*: Maryland Inst.; Rhinehart Sch. S., with J. Maxwell Miller. *Member*: NSS. *Work*: BMA; Zimmerman, Baker, Crozier mem.; McCulloh Homes; Cherry Hill Community Bldg.; War mem., Suffolk, England; Loyola Anniversary plaque, City Hall, Baltimore; Lafayette Courts plaque; St. Francis-Kernan Hospital, Baltimore, Md.; 48 portrait heads for American Waxworks Museum, Washington, D.C. *Exhibited*: NAD, 1933; PAFA, 1933, 1934; Baltimore Mun. AA; Maryland A; A. Un. Baltimore.

BERGER, JASON—*Painter*
51 Albion St.; h. 25 Cortes St., Boston 16, Mass.

B. Malden, Mass., Jan. 22, 1924. *Studied*: BMFA Sch.; Univ. Alabama; Ossip Zadkine Sch. A., Paris, France. *Awards*: BMFA Sch., Paige Scholarship for study abroad; prize, Boston A. Festival, 1955; Traveling F., BMFA Sch. *Work*: MModA; Guggenheim Mus. A. *Exhibited*: Inst. Mod. A., Boston, 1943; Boris Mirsky Gal., Boston, 1943-1947; Downtown Gal., N.Y., 1947; Berkshire Mus. A., 1947; Swetzoff Gal., Boston, 1949-1958; Galerie LeGrip, Rouen, France, 1950; AIC, 1952, 1954; Salon de la Jeune Sculpture, Musee Rodin, Paris, France, 1952; Inst. Contemp. A., Boston, 1952, 1956; Boston A. Festival, 1952-1957; AGAA, 1953-54 (traveling exh., auspices of AFA); Brandeis Univ., 1953; Tufts Col., 1953; Boston Indp. A., 1953; BMFA, 1953-1957; WMA, 1954; Carnegie Inst., 1954; LC, 1954; MModA (toured U.S. and Europe), 1954, drawings, 1957; Deerfield Acad., 1954 (one-man); Silvermine Gld. A.; Collector's Show, Dallas, Tex.; Fitchburg A. Mus., 1955; Swetzoff Gal., 1956 (one-man); Peridot Gal., N.Y., 1956, 1957, 1958 (one-man). Illus., "Foundation Course in French," 1956. *Position*: Instr., Painting, BMFA Sch., Boston, Mass., 1955- ; Painting & Sculpture, Wellesley College.

BERGER, KLAUS—*Educator, W.*
Department Art History, University of Kansas; h. 700 Indiana St., Lawrence, Kans.

B. Berlin, Germany, Mar. 24, 1901. *Studied*: Univs. of Munich, Berlin, Heidelberg, Germany; Univ. Goettingen, Ph.D.; Ecole du Louvre, Paris. *Member*: CAA; Renaissance Soc. Am.; AAUP; Société de l'Histoire de l'Art français. *Awards*: Fulbright F., 1954 (guest Prof. Univ. of Cologne, Germany); Am. Council of Learned Societies, 1958. Author: "Géricault, Drawing and Watercolors," 1946; "French Master Drawings of the Nineteenth Century," 1950 (also German edition); "Géricault and His Work," 1952 (also French & German eds.). Contributor to Art News; Art Quarterly; College Art Journal; Gazette des Beaux-Arts; Renaissance News, and others. Lectures: Forerunners of Impressionism, Odilon Redon, Ingres, Poussin Revival.

Positions: Prof., Northwestern Univ.; Biarritz U.S. Army Univ.; Univ. Kansas City; Univ. of Kansas, Lawrence, Kans., at present.

BERGERE, RICHARD—*Painter, Des., W.*
143-28 Madison Ave., Flushing, N.Y.

B. Chicago, Ill., July 3, 1912. *Studied*: N.Y. Univ., B.S.; Columbia Univ., M.A.; ASL, with George Bridgman. *Awards*: St. Gauden's Med., 1930. *Exhibited*: Assoc. Am. A. Gal.; G Place Gal., 1943; Findlay Gal., 1941; Esquire Gal., 1943 (one-man); CGA, 1937; ASL, 1936; WMAA, 1946; AIC, 1942, 1944; Lib. Cong., 1943; AFA traveling exh., 1948. Illus. "Treasure Island," 1946; "Tree Grows in Brooklyn," 1948.*

BERGIER, ARNOLD HENRY—*Sculptor, Des., C., L.*
131 West 10th St., New York 14, N.Y.

B. Cincinnati, Ohio, Oct. 22, 1914. *Studied*: Ohio Univ.; New Sch. Social Research, and with Joseph Du Be, Robert Gwathmey, Camilo Egas. *Member*: AEA; Sculpture Center. *Work*: U.S. Navy Combat A. Section; portraits of John Dewey, Toscanini, Admirals Halsey, Nimitz and Turner; James Forrestal and others. Sc., in Baltimore Synagogue, 1951; Temple Israel, Canton, Ohio; Church of the Good Shepherd, Bellaire, L.I., N.Y.; Temple Israel, Jamaica, N.Y.; B'nai B'rith Israel, Woodmere, N.Y.; Temple Israel, Lawrence, L.I., N.Y.; Holy Family Church, Brooklyn, N.Y.; Memorial plaque, Washington Square, N.Y. *Exhibited*: NAD; WMAA, 1951; Decatur Mus. Naval Hist. Fnd., Wash., D.C., 1951; Newport AA; Guildhall, East Hampton, L.I., 1948; Jewish Mus., 1952; Newark Mus. A., 1957; Arch. Lg., 1955, 1956.

BERGLING, V(IRGINIA) C.—*Writer*
Mail: P.O. Box 523, Coral Gables 34, Fla.; h. 4101 Southwest 62nd Ave., Miami 43, Fla.

B. Chicago, Ill., Nov. 6, 1908. *Member*: Miami A. Lg.; Heraldry Soc. of Great Britain; Dade Bus. Prof. Women's Cl. *Work*: Bergling publications in leading museum libraries in U.S. and abroad, including Lyon Office Lib., Edinburgh, Scotland; Rome, Italy; Beaux-Arts Mus., Canada. *Exhibited*: 50 Books of the Year, AIGA, 1952; Am. Nat. Retail Jewelers Assn., Waldorf-Astoria Hotel, New York, 1951; Miami A. & Writers Assn., 1952; Int. Inventions & Hobby Show, Miami, 1950; Indst. A. Nat. Exh., Miami, 1950; Miami Mem. Lib., and Flagler Mem. Lib., 1951; Miami Beach A. Center Lib., 1956. Ed., "Heraldic Designs and Engravings," illus. handbook, 1951 (author: the late J. M. Bergling); "Art Monograms and Lettering"; "Ornamental Designs and Illustrations," and others. *Position*: Ed. & Publ., Bergling Technical Art Books, Miami, Fla.

BERGLUND, AMANDA—*Painter*
Evanston Hotel, 840 Forest Ave., Evanston, Ill.

B. Stockholm, Sweden, Jan. 22, 1879. *Studied*: AIC; & with Carl R. Krafft, Increase Robinson. *Member*: Swedish-Am. AA; North Shore AA; Chicago Mun. A. Lg.; Evanston A. Center; AEA. *Exhibited*: AIC; Milwaukee AI; Century of Progress Exp., Chicago.*

BERGMANN, FRANZ W.—*Painter, C., I., W.*
P.O. Box 130, Mill Valley, Cal.

B. Dimling, Austria, Aug. 6, 1898. *Studied*: Nat. Acad. FA, Vienna; Univ. Vienna. *Member*: San F. AA. *Awards*: Med., Palace Legion Honor, 1946. *Work*: SFMA; Mills Col.; Mural, USPO, Stockton, Cal. *Exhibited*: GGE, 1939; AIC; San F. AA; SFMA, 1946. I., "This Way to the Circus," 1938; Author, I., "San Francisco Flips," 1946; & other juvenile books.*

BERKMAN, AARON—*Painter, T., L., W.*
62 East 90th St., New York 28, N.Y.

B. Hartford, Conn., May 23, 1900. *Studied*: Hartford A. Sch.; BMFA Sch. Member: AEA; Audubon A. *Awards*: F., Yaddo Fnd., 1957; Huntington Hartford Fnd., 1958. *Exhibited*: BM, 1941; Avery Mem., Hartford, 1936; AWS, 1944; Audubon A., 1954-1958, and others. One-man: Grace Horne Gal., Boston, 1926, 1927; Wadsworth Atheneum, 1926, 1927; Babcock Gal., 1928, 1951; ACA Gal., 1932, 1934; Erich-Newhouse Gal., 1937; Assoc. Am. A., 1943; Kaufmann A. Gal., 1946, 1950; BM, 1932. Author: "Art and Space," 1949; "The Functional Line in Painting,"

1955. Monthly column "Amateur Standing," in Art News. *Position*: T., Dir., YM-YWHA A. Center, New York, N.Y., 1940- .

BERKMAN, JACK—*Painter*

Route #3, Box 339A, Wilmington, N.C.; h. 501 North Channel Drive, Harbor Island, N.C.

B. Washington, D.C., Apr. 10, 1908. *Studied*: George Washington Univ.; Corcoran Sch. A.; Univ. New Mexico. *Member*: Wash. A. Gld.; Soc. Wash. A. *Awards*: prizes, medals, CGA, 1942, 1943; Mississippi State A., Jackson, 1931, 1941; Soc. Wash. A., 1942, 1943, 1946; New Mexico State Fair, 1947; CGA, 1956; Nat.Lg.Am. Pen Women, 1957; scholarship, Tiffany Fnd., 1937, 1938. *Work*: Barnett Aden Gal.; Hammond Coll. *Exhibited*: CGA, 1941; VMFA, 1940; Soc. Wash. A., 1941-1955; Wash. A. Gld., 1941-1955; Winchester, Mass., 1951; Marblehead, Mass., 1952; Mus. of New Mexico, 1948, 1949; Whyte Gal., 1950; A. Mart, Wash., D.C., 1957; Dickey Gal., Wash., D.C., 1956. Lectures: Contemporary Art. *Position*: Instr., Adult A. Program, Alexandria, Va.

BERKMAN-HUNTER, BERNECE—*Painter, Gr., Des.*

357 West 11th St., New York 14, N.Y.; also, Bridgehampton, N.Y.

B. Chicago, Ill. *Studied*: AIC; New Sch. for Social Research; Hunter Col.; Columbia Univ., and with Rudolph Weisenborn, Stuart Davis, Ralph Mayer. *Member*: NAWA; AEA; Boston Soc. Indp. A. *Awards*: SAM, 1946. *Work*: Evansville State Hospital; Kelly H.S., Chicago; AIC; Carnegie Inst.; SAM; Univ. Iowa; Univ. Michigan; included in "American Prize Prints of the 20th Century." *Exhibited*: Denver A. Mus., 1938; AIC, 1938, 1940, 1941; Springfield Mus. A., 1939; MModA, 1940; MMA, 1942; Carnegie Inst., 1943; Univ. Iowa, 1943; LC, 1945; SAM, 1946, 1952; Illinois State Mus., 1940; Weyhe Gal., 1943; BMFA, 1955; N.Y. City Center Gal., 1954-1955; NAWA, 1954-55; Boston Soc. Indp. A., 1954; AEA, (Riverside Mus.), 1951; BM; Ogunquit A. Cent.*

BERKOFF, BLANCHE—*Illustrator, Des., Comm. A., T.*

1749 Grand Concourse, New York 53, N.Y.

B. Milwaukee, Wis., Sept. 4, 1911. *Studied*: Wisconsin State Col., B.A.; Layton Sch. A.; PIASch. *Member*: SI. *Awards*: First award for design, Box Assn. of Am., 1953. *Exhibited*: Milwaukee AI, 1940. I., "A Complete Guide to Professional Cartooning," 1950; "A Complete Guide to Drawing, Illustration, Cartooning & Painting," 1948. *Position*: Instr., PIA Sch., Brooklyn, N.Y., 1942- .*

BERMAN, ANNI RADIN—*Painter, S.*

308 Kimber Rd., Syracuse, N.Y.

B. New York, N. Y., Feb. 18, 1914. *Studied*: Am. Sch. Des.; Traphagen Sch. Fashion; Am. A. Sch.; and with Raphael Soyer. *Member*: Assoc. A. Syracuse. *Exhibited*: Indp. A.; ASL; Assoc. A. Syracuse; Rochester Mem. A. Mus. *Position*: Dir., Children's classes, Syracuse (N.Y.) Mus. FA, 1939-45.*

BERMAN, ELLIOTT WALTER—*Painter, Eng.*

8446 Temple Rd., Philadelphia 50, Pa.

B. Philadelphia, Pa., June 25, 1913. *Member*: Lehigh A. All. *Award*: F., PAFA; West Oak Lane A. Lg., 1954. *Exhibited*: Laguna Beach AA, 1944; Rittenhouse Square, 1941, 1942, 1944; Allentown Mus. A., 1942, 1943; Lehigh A. All., 1943, 1944; Muhlenberg Col., 1943, 1944; West Oak Lane A. Lg., 1954, 1955; Vernon A. Exh., 1955.

BERMAN, EUGENE—*Painter, Des., Scenic Des., Gr.*

107 Via del Plebicito, Rome, Italy.

B. St. Petersburg, Russia, 1899. *Studied*: Russia, Germany, Switzerland, France and Italy. *Awards*: Guggenheim F., 1947, 1949. *Work*: Musee d'Art Moderne, Paris; Mod. Gal., Venice; Albertina Mus., Vienna; MModA; MMA; AIC; CM; CMA; Hartford Atheneum; CAM; Denver Mus. A.; Smith Col.; FMA; BMFA; Vassar Col.; Univ. Nebraska; Univ. Illinois (Urbana); Columbia Mus. FA; Albright A. Gal.; Univ. Iowa; Santa Barbara Mus. A.; Los A. Mus. A., etc. *Exhibited*: many one-man shows in the U.S. and abroad. Retrospective exh., Inst. Mod. A., Boston, 1941, circulated to leading museums; MModA, 1945. Lithographic work and illus. for numerous books. Scenic work: Music Festival, Hartford Atheneum, 1936; ballets: Ballet Russe

de Monte Carlo; Ballet Theatre; American Ballet Caravan; Sadler's Wells Ballet, London; Scala Ballet, Milan; opera Theatre de l'Etoile, Paris; Metropolitan Opera, N.Y.; New York City Center Opera, 1952; N.B.C. Television premiere, 1951; inauguration of the Italian XVIII century Theatre at Ringling Museum, Sarasota, Fla., 1952.*

BERNARD, DAVID EDWIN—*Lithographer, P., E.*

1725 Fairmont St., Wichita 14, Kans.

B. Sandwich, Ill., Aug. 8, 1913. *Studied*: Univ. Illinois, B.F.A.; Univ. Iowa, M.F.A., and with Mauricio Lasansky, Humbert Albrizio. *Member*: Mid-Am. A.; SAGA. *Awards*: prizes, Veteran's A. Exh., Santa Monica, Cal., 1950; Mid-Am. A., 1950. *Exhibited*: Alabama WC Soc., 1943; LC, 1945, 1946, 1949; Denver A. Mus., 1945; San Antonio, Tex., 1945; Springfield, Mo., 1945; Albany Inst. Hist. & A., 1945; Joslyn A. Mus., 1949; SAGA, 1949; Chicago SE, 1951; Phila. Pr. Cl., 1951; Bradley Univ., 1952; Am. Color Pr. Soc., 1952; So. Cal. Pr. M., 1952; Mid-Am. A., 1952; Wichita AA, 1952. *Position*: Asst. Prof. A., Municipal Univ., Wichita, Kans., 1949-50.*

BERNAT, MARTHA MILIGAN—*Sculptor*

6300 Fulton Ave., Van Nuys, Cal.

B. Toledo, Ohio, Aug. 5, 1912. *Studied*: Cleveland Sch. A.; Syracuse Univ.; Budapest Sch. Indst. A., Hungary, and with Alexander Blazys, Ivan Mestrovic. *Member*: Liturgical A. Soc.; Los. A. Art Assn.; Council All. A. *Awards*: prizes, CMA, 1935; Toledo Mus. A., 1936, 1947; Mansfield FA Gld., 1947, 1948; Rochester Mem. A. Gal., 1948. *Work*: panels, St. Peter's Church, Mansfield, Ohio; in churches in Hollywood, Cal., Pacific Palisades, Cal., Norwalk, Cal. *Exhibited*: CMA, 1935, 1942; Toledo Mus. A., 1936; Los A. Art Assn., 1949, 1950; Greek Theatre, Los. A., 1949, 1950; A. of the Southwest, 1950; Los A. Mus. A., 1950; ann. "Madonna" exh., Los A., 1949, 1950.*

BERND-COHEN, MAX—*Painter, E., W., L., Cr.*

Cowles St., Englewood, Fla.

B. Macon, Ga., May 7, 1899. *Studied*: Columbia Univ., B.A., LL.B.; Ecole Moderne, Paris, France, with Leger, Ozenfant; Grande Chaumiere, Paris, France; Research at British Mus., and The Louvre, Paris. *Awards*: Chester County AA, 1932. *Work*: mural, Florida Bldg., Century of Progress, Chicago; Methodist Church, Canon City, Colo. *Exhibited*: John Herron AI, 1931; PAFA, 1932, 1933; Mus. Modern A., Madrid, Spain, 1930; Ringling Mus. A., Sarasota, Fla., 1932; Delgado Mus. A., 1932; CAA, 1930; Clearwater, Fla., 1932; Tampa AI; Durand-Ruel Gal., N.Y., 1930. Contributor to London Art News. Lectures: Aesthetics. *Positions*: Instr., Ringling Sch. A.; Central Sch. A. & Crafts, London; St. Petersburg, Fla., Jr. College; Prof. A., Hd. A. Dept., Fla. Southern College, etc.

BERNHARD, LUCIAN—*Designer, P.*

36 Central Park South; h. 120 East 86th St., New York 28, N.Y.

B. Stuttgart, Germany, Mar. 15, 1883. *Member*: AIGA; SI; A. Gld. *Position*: Instr., N.Y. Univ.; ASL; Des., "Bernhard Types"; Inventor of "Bernhard Magnet Type" and "Bernhard Phonetic Type."

BERNHARDT, BARBARA—*Painter, Et., Cart., L.*

35 North 10th St., Richmond, Ind.

B. Richmond, Ind., Apr. 22, 1913. *Studied*: Earlham Col.; ASL; & with Diego Rivera, John Sloan. *Awards*: Prizes, Richmond AA, 1922, 1925, 1942, 1952. *Exhibited*: NAWA, 1934; Springfield Mus. A., 1937; Richmond AA, 1922, 1925, 1931, 1932, 1934, 1935, 1936, 1941, 1942, 1943, 1951; Woodstock AA, 1937-1939; Montross Gal.; Argent Gal.; Contemporary A. Center; ACA Gal.*

BERNHARDT, JOHN—*Painter, Gr.*

Salida de Queretard 9, San Miguel Allende, Guanajuato, Mexico.

B. Indianapolis, Ind., Feb. 5, 1921. *Studied*: John Herron AI; Colorado Col.; Colorado Springs FA Center; Columbia Univ. *Awards*: F., Tiffany Fnd., 1951, 1955. *Work*: N.Y. Pub. Lib.; MMA; BMFA; Boston Pub. Lib.; LC; Joslyn A. Mus.; John Herron AI; BM; CM; AGAA; Hartford Atheneum. *Exhibited*: CGA, 1955; McNey Mus. A., San Antonio, 1958 (one-man); Colorado Springs FA Center, 1958 (one-man), and many national print exhs.

BERNHEIMER, FRANZ KARL—Educator, P., S., Cr.

Sweet Briar College, Sweet Briar, Va.

B. Munich, Germany, May 6, 1911. *Studied*: Munich, Hamburg, Rome, Zurich; Yale Univ., M.A., M.F.A. *Member*: CAA. *Exhibited*: Yale Univ., 1944; Univ. Louisville, 1953; Randolph-Macon Col., 1954; Hollins Col., 1955; Intermont Col., 1952; Norfolk Mus. A., 1952; Phila. A. All., 1943; Argent Gal., 1950; Virginia Mus. FA, 1955, 1957, one-man, 1958. *Position*: Asst. Prof., Dept. A., Sweet Briar Col., Sweet Briar, Va., 1946- . (On leave 1958-59.)

BERNHEIMER, RICHARD—Educator, L., W.

255 Roberts Rd., Bryn Mawr, Pa.

B. Munich, Germany, Sept. 30, 1907. *Studied*: Univ. Munich, Ph.D.; Univ. Rome; Univ. Berlin. *Member*: CAA. Author: "Romanesque Animal Sculpture," 1930. "Wildmen in the Middle Ages," 1952. Contributor to: art magazines. *Position*: L., Univ. Pennsylvania, 1933-38; L., Haverford Col., 1937-42; L., Bryn Mawr Col., 1933-37; Asst. Prof., 1938-42; Assoc. Prof., Bryn Mawr Col., 1942-52, Prof., 1952- .*

BERNI, ALAN—Industrial Designer

Penthouse, 580 Fifth Ave., New York 36, N.Y.; h. Mamaroneck, N.Y.

B. New York, N.Y., May 16, 1912. *Studied*: PIASch. *Member*: Package Des. Council (Founder & Dir.); Merchandise Exec. Cl.; N.Y. Sales Exec. Cl. *Awards*: Nat. prizes package des., 1938, 1940, 1941, 1946-1950, 1952, 1955-1958. Author: "Modern Packaging." *Position*: Packaging Panel member, "Printers' Ink," "Variety Merchandiser," "Sales Management." Chm., International Package Des. Council Competition, 1954; Adv. Council, N.Y. Sch. Indst. A. *Exhibited*: Donnell Lib.; AMA. Packaging Exh., N.Y.

BERNSTEIN, GERALD—Painter, Former Mus. Cur., T.

81 New Dorp Plaza, Staten Island 6, N.Y.

B. Indianapolis, Ind., Aug. 25, 1917. *Studied*: John Herron AI; ASL; N.Y. Univ., B.A.; N.Y. Univ. Inst. FA, M.A. *Exhibited*: Staten Island Mus., 1950-1956. Lectures: History of Art, Art Appreciation to associations, clubs, schools and colleges. Mus. Exhs. arranged or assembled: "The Artist Looks at Nature," 1952; "Two Hundred Years of American Art," 1954; "American Art Today," 1954; "Modern Realism," 1956, etc. *Position*: Cur. A., Staten Island Inst. Arts & Sciences, 1950-1956.*

BERNSTEIN, HENRY—Painter

19324 Littlefield St., Detroit 35, Mich.

B. Detroit, Mich., Apr. 1, 1912. *Studied*: Soc. A. & Crafts, Detroit, with John Carroll. *Member*: NSMP. *Work*: Murals, USPO, East Lansing, Frankfort, Midland, Mich.; Mt. Sterling, Ill.; Michigan Sch. for the Blind; des. & illus. Memorial Golden Book, Jewish War Veterans of Michigan, 1955. *Exhibited*: Rockefeller Center, 1936; AIC, 1937; CGA, 1940, 1943; Detroit Inst. A., 1930-1944; Garelicks Gal., Detroit, 1953; ACA Gal., 1954.

BERNSTEIN, KATHRYN. See Kathe, Betty

BERNSTEIN, SYLVIA—Painter

80 Winnebago Rd., Yonkers 7, N.Y.

B. Brooklyn, N.Y., Apr. 11, 1918. *Studied*: NAD, with Arthur Covey, Gifford Beal, Sidney Dickinson. *Member*: AEA; Knickerbocker A.; AWS; NAWA; Young Am. Painters; P. & S. of New Jersey. *Awards*: prizes, Jane C. Stanley Mem. award, NAWA, 1954, 1957; New Haven R.R. Painting Comp., 1956; Grumbacher award, Silvermine Gld. A., 1957; same at Chautauqua, N.Y., 1958; gold medal, NAC, 1957. *Work*: N.Y. Univ. *Exhibited*: Butler Inst. Am. A., 1957, 1958; AWS, 1958; Audubon A., 1957; Portland (Me.) Mus. A., 1957; Columbia (S.C.) Mus. A., 1956; Exchange exh., Berlin, Germany, Galerie Boss-Petrides, Paris, France; Silvermine Gld. A., 1957, 1958; Chautauqua Inst., 1958; Ruth White Gal., N.Y., (one-man).

BERNSTEIN, THERESA F. (Mrs. William Meyerowitz)— Painter, Et., Lith., T., W.

54 West 74th St., New York 23, N.Y.; s. 44 Mt. Pleasant Ave., East Gloucester, Mass.

B. Philadelphia, Pa. *Studied*: PAFA, ASL. *Member*: NAWA; North Shore AA; Audubon A.; Am. Color Pr. Soc.; SAGA; Gloucester Soc. A.; Cape Ann Soc. Mod. A. *Awards*: med., Phila. Plastic Cl.; French Inst. A. & Sc.; prizes, NAWA, 1949, 1951, 1955; SAGA, 1953; LC (purchase), 1953; North Shore AA; Am. Color Pr. Soc.; Phila. Pr. Cl. *Work*: AIC; LC; BM; Princeton Univ.; Harvard Univ.; Dayton AI; WMAA; Bezalel Mus., Jerusalem; Tel Aviv and Ain Harod Mus., Israel; MMA. *Exhibited*: AIC; Carnegie Inst.; MMA; CGA; PAFA; NAD; Dayton AI; WMAA; BMFA; BM; WMA; and others. Contributor to newspapers and museum bulletins. *Position*: Dir., Summer Art Course, East Gloucester, Mass.*

BERRESFORD, VIRGINIA—Painter

Vineyard Haven, R.F.D., Mass.

B. New York, N.Y., 1904. *Studied*: Wellesley Col.; Columbia Univ.; Ozenfant Sch. A., Paris & New York. *Work*: WMAA. *Position*: Dir., Berresford Gallery, Martha's Vineyard, Mass. (July-Aug. only). Private Instr., Menemsha, Mass.*

BERRY, CAMELIA (Mrs. Jack D.)—Painter, I.

South Perkins Rd., Stillwater, Okla.

B. Washington, D.C., Dec. 28, 1918. *Studied*: ASL; Barnard Col.; & with K. Williams, F. Luis Mora. *Member*: Oklahoma AA; Western AA. *Work*: Stillwater (Okla). Lib.; murals, public bldgs. and churches, Stillwater, Okla. *Exhibited*: Norlyst Gal., 1944; Oklahoma A. Center, 1942-1945; Philbrook A. Center, 1945*

BERRY, HELEN MURRIN (Mrs. Helen Berry Shanes)— Painter, C.

Crafts Center, Salisbury, Vt.

B. Philadelphia, Pa., Aug. 25, 1900. *Studied*: PAFA. *Member*: Southern Vermont AA. *Work*: PAFA, and in private coll. *Exhibited*: PAFA; N.Y. WC Cl.

BERRY, RUTH LINNELL—Painter, T.

1088 Massachusetts Ave., Lexington 73, Mass.

B. Watertown, Mass., Feb. 14, 1909. *Studied*: Boston Univ., B.S.; Radcliffe Col., M.A.; & with Leslie Thompson, Richard Lahey. *Member*: New Hampshire AA; Springfield A. Lg.; North Shore AA. *Work*: State House, Concord, N.H. *Exhibited*: Wawasee A. Gal., 1945; Springfield AA, 1956; New Hampshire AA, 1943-1946; Boston AC, 1932, 1933; Jordan-Marsh, 1946; North Shore AA, 1946.*

BERRYMAN, FLORENCE SEVILLE—Critic, W., L.

The Evening Star, 11th & Pennsylvania Ave., N.W. (4); h. 2114 Bancroft Place, N.W., Washington 8, D.C.

B. Washington, D.C. *Studied*: George Washington Univ., A.B. *Member*: Wash. AC; Am. Newspaper Women's Cl. *Awards*: prize, George Washington Univ., 1924; Alumni Achievement award, George Washington Univ., 1957. Author: "Early American Bookplates," monograph, 1925. Contributor of annual review for The American Year Book, 1932-50; "The Year in Art" for the American Art Annual, 1927-48. Illus. lectures: "French Regional Costumes," "Early English Domestic Architecture, Interiors & Furniture," "The Artist Looks at Children," etc. Contributes to newspapers and art magazines. *Position*: Cr., Washington (D.C.) Post, 1924- , Evening Star, 1938- , staff, AFA, 1924-1955.

BERRYMAN, JAMES THOMAS (JIM)— Cartoonist, I., W.

Room 426, Star Bldg.; h. 6633-32nd Place, N.W., Washington 15, D.C.

B. Washington, D.C., June 8, 1902. *Studied*: George Washington Univ.; Corcoran Sch. A. *Awards*: Graphic Arts prize, WFNY 1939; Pulitzer prize, 1950; Freedoms Fnd., gold med., 1949-1951; Nat. Cartoonists Soc. silver T-square, 1950; American Legion DSM, 1950; Headliner's award for cartoon, 1953. *Position*: Cart., Washington Evening Star, King Features Syndicate, 1936- ; Chief Ed. Cart., for Assoc. American Railroads.

BERTOIA, HARRY—*Sculptor, Des., P., C.*
Main St., Bally, Pa.; h. R.D. #1, Barto, Pa.

B. San Lorenzo, Italy, Mar. 10, 1915. *Studied*: A. & Crafts Sch., Detroit; Cranbrook Acad. A. *Awards*: Gold Medal, Arch. Lg.; Gold Medal, AIA; Graham F., 1957. *Work*: MIT Chapel, Cambridge, Mass.; Dallas Pub. Lib.; MGM Technical Center; St. Louis Airport.

BESS, FORREST CLEMENGER—*Painter, L.*
1701 Avenue E, Bay City, Tex.

B. Bay City, Tex., Oct. 5, 1911. *Studied*: Texas A. & M. Col.; Univ. Texas. *Awards*: Prize, Witte Mem. Mus., 1946. *Work*: Museum of FA of Houston; Brandeis Univ. *Exhibited*: CGA, 1940; Mus. FA of Houston, 1939, 1940; San Antonio A., 1946; Dallas Mus. FA, 1946; A. West of the Mississippi, Colo. Springs FA Center; one-man: Mus. FA of Houston, 1951; Dallas Mus. FA, 1951; Witte Mem. Mus., (retrospective); Betty Parsons Gal., 1951; Philbrook A. Center, 1952; Oklahoma A. Center, 1952; Texas Southern Univ., 1951; Mus. Contemp. A., Houston, 1957; Emmerich Gal., Houston, 1958; Stanford Univ., 1958; deYoung Mem. Mus., San F., 1958; Dord Fitz Gal., Amarillo, Tex., 1958. Lectures on Design.

BESSEMER, AURIEL—*Painter, E., I., W., L.*
221 West 82nd St., New York 24, N.Y.

B. Grand Rapids, Mich., Feb. 27, 1909. *Studied*: Western Reserve Acad.; Columbia Univ.; Master Inst.; NAD. *Members*: NSMP; Soc. Wash. A.; Indian Cultural Center, N.Y. *Awards*: Scholarships, Columbia Univ. Cl.; Western Reserve Acad.; Master Inst. *Work*: PC; Western Reserve Acad.; murals: Amalgamated Meat Cutters Exec. ofc., N.Y.; United Wire, Metal & Machine Health Center Fund, N.Y.; Michael's Cl., Wash., D.C.; Citizens Comm. for Army & Navy; Wabash Railroad; Pennsylvania Railroad; Volco Brass & Copper Co.; USPO, Hazelhurst, Miss., Arlington, Va., Winnsboro, S.C.; mosaics: Church of St. Clement, Alexandria, Va.; many portraits, *Exhibited*: PC; CGA; Wash., D.C. Pub. Lib.; one-man: Asheville, N.C.; Raleigh A. Center; Currier Gal., A.; Bowdoin Col.; Springfield (Mo.) State Teachers Col.; St. Louis Pub. Lib., and museums in Ohio, Fla., New York, etc. Lecturer to schools, colleges, women's clubs and art groups. Author, I., "Aurielartograph," 1947.

BESSER, LEONARD—*Painter, T., Gr., I.*
49 Wilton Rd.; h. 341 Wilton Rd., Westport, Conn.

B. Philadelphia, Pa., May 16, 1919. *Studied*: Phila. Gr. Sketch Cl.; Kann Inst., Los Angeles, Cal.; seminars with Dong Kingman, Ben Shahn and Fletcher Martin. *Member*: AWS. *Awards*: prizes, Am. Legion Veterans A. Festival, Los A., 1950, 1951, 1952. *Work*: National Archives, Wash., D.C. *Exhibited*: Audubon A., 1954-1956; AWS, 1954-1957; Los A. Mus. A., 1951, 1952; San Bernardino Orange Show, 1951, 1952; N.Y. City Center, 1953, 1954; Portland AA, 1957. Illus., N.Y. Herald Tribune. *Position*: Asst. Dir., Instruction Dept., Famous Artists School, Westport, Conn.

BESSIRE, DALE PHILIP—*Painter*
Nashville, Ind.

B. Columbus, Ohio, May 14, 1892. *Studied*: Univ. Chicago; John Herron AI. *Member*: Hoosier Salon; Indiana A. Cl.; Brown County A. Colony; Brown County A. Gld.; Florida Fed. A. *Awards*: prizes, Hoosier Salon, 1944, 1952; Indiana A. Cl., 1945, 1946; Indiana State Fair; Fla. Fed. A., 1950; Strauss Centennial Exh. *Work*: Indiana Univ.; DePauw Univ.; Rollins Col.; Ball State Col.; Duncan, Whiting, Gary mem.; Indiana Veterans Home; Gary, Lafayette, Indianapolis pub. sch.; Muncie AA; Bedford (Ind.) Pub. Lib. *Exhibited*: Century of Progress, Chicago; John Herron AI; Hoosier Salon; Chicago Galleries Assn.; Fla. Fed. A.; Palm Beach, Fla.

BETHEA, F. ELIZABETH—*Educator, P.*
Louisiana Polytechnic Institute; h. 709 North Trenton St., Ruston, La.

B. Birmingham, Ala., May 11, 1902. *Studied*: Newcomb Col., Tulane Univ., B. Des.; Columbia Univ., M.A. *Member*: Southeastern AA; AAUP; Com. on A. Edu.; MModA; Int. Des. Conference; NAEA; Am. Studies Assn. *Exhibited*: SSAL; Alabama A. Lg.; New Orleans A. Lg. *Position*: Prof., Hd. Dept. A., Louisiana Polytechnic Inst., Ruston, La., 1926- .

BETSBERG, ERNESTINE (Mrs. Arthur Osver)—*Painter*
50 Victory Blvd., Staten Island 1, N.Y.

B. Bloomington, Ill., Sept. 6, 1909. *Studied*: AIC, with Boris Anisfeld. *Awards*: Raymond Traveling F., AIC. *Exhibited*: AIC, 1936, 1938, 1939, 1941, 1942; VMFA, 1946; NAD, 1945; one-man: Syracuse Univ., 1949; Grand Central Moderns, 1950, 1952; Japan, 1951; Paris, France, 1953; Rome, Italy, 1953, 1958; Univ. Florida, 1955; PAFA, 1951-1953; Univ. Nebraska; Munson-Williams-Proctor Inst., 1955; WMAA, 1955.

BETTELHEIM, (JOLAN) GROSS—*Painter, Et., Lith.*
86-10 34th Ave., Jackson Heights, N.Y.

B. Nitra, Czechslovakia, Jan. 27, 1900. *Studied*: Royal Hungarian Acad. FA; State Acad. FA, Berlin; Grande Chaumiere; Cleveland Sch. A.; & with Orlik, Hofer. *Member*: AFA; SAGA; AEA; Conn. Acad. FA. *Awards*: Prizes, CMA, 1928-1937; Lib.Cong., 1944, 1945; Northwest Pr.M., 1945, 1946; Conn. Acad. FA, 1945. *Work*: Cleveland Pr. Cl.; CMA; Lib.Cong.; SAM; BM; Everhart Mus., Scranton, Pa.; Munson-Williams-Proctor Inst.; PMA; Mus. Western A., Moscow, USSR. *Exhibited*: AIC, 1932, 1934, 1935, 1937; PAFA, 1931, 1933, 1934, 1936, 1941, 1942; NAD, 1943-1946; Santa Barbara Mus. A., 1944; Lib.Cong., 1943-1946; Northwest Pr.M., 1945, 1946; Conn. Acad. FA, 1944-1946; Denver A. Mus., 1944; WMAA, 1942; CGA, 1944; SFMA, 1944; BM, 1945; Montclair A. Mus., 1945; Durand-Ruel Gal., 1945 (one-man); SAGA, 1944-1946, 1950.*

BETTS, EDWARD H.—*Painter, E.*
1009 West Nevada St., Urbana, Ill.; h. 804 Dodds Dr., Champaign, Ill.

B. Yonkers, N.Y., Aug. 4, 1920. *Studied*: Yale Univ., B.A.; Univ. Illinois, M.F.A.; ASL. *Member*: ANA; AEA; AWS; Audubon A.; Cal. WC Soc.; Phila. WC Cl.; CAA; ASL; Ogunquit AA. *Awards*: medal, Audubon A., 1952; AWS, 1953; Phila. WC Cl., 1954, 1955; prizes, NAD, 1953, 1954; Altman award, 1957; Butler AI, 1953 (purchase); AWS, 1950; All. A. Am., 1951; Audubon A., 1951; Cal. WC Soc., 1951, 1954, 1955, 1957 (purchase). *Work*: Univ. Rochester; Davenport Mun. A. Gal.; Springfield (Mo.) A. Mus.; Butler AI; Ball State T. Col.; VMFA; Cal. WC Soc.; Ogunquit A. Mus.; Walter Chrysler, Jr., Collection. *Exhibited*: CGA, 1947, 1951, 1955, 1957; MMA, 1950; BM, 1953, 1955; Univ. Nebraska, 1953, 1955; PAFA, 1953-1955; Denver A. Mus., 1954, 1955, 1957; one-man: New York, N.Y., 1953, 1955, 1956; Chicago, Ill., 1954, 1956, 1957; Phila., Pa., 1955, 1957. *Position*: Asst. Prof. A., Univ. Illinois, 1949- .

BEVELACQUA, SALVATORE—
Industrial Designer, Arch.
19 Via Mizner; h. 239 Australian Ave., Palm Beach, Fla.

B. Italy. *Studied*: Univ. of Rome, Arch. degree; Columbia Univ. *Member*: IDI. *Awards*: med., Arch. Lg., 1922. *Work*: Des. many bldgs., with Warren & Wentmore, including Broadmoor Hotel, Colorado Springs, Colo.; Condado Vanderbilt, San Juan, Puerto Rico; Fox Theatres in New York, St. Louis, Detroit. *Exhibited*: designs, MMA; Arch. Lg.; and in furniture exh. in Chicago, Ill., Grand Rapids, Mich. Contributor of articles to trade and art magazines. Originator of Bucks County Provincial furniture, nationally trademarked.*

BEVERLY-HAYNES, D(OROTHY) F(RANCES)—
Painter, Des., Comm. A.
22 Kenyon St., Hartford 5, Conn.

B. Hartford, Conn. *Studied*: Hartford Sch. A., and with Stanislav Rembski, Joseph C. Chase, H. H. Darnell. *Member*: Hartford Soc. Women P.; Meriden A. & Crafts; Nat. Lg. Am. Pen Women. *Awards*: prizes, Travelers Insurance Co., N.Y. adv. exh.; Conn. General Life Insurance Co., N.Y. adv. exh.; gold award, Ogunquit Nat. Exh., 1953, 1954; prize, Hartford Soc. Women P., 1953. *Work*: U.S. Coast Guard, port., "Sinbad," dog mascot; official drawings of Great Seal, Armorial Bearings, State Flower and Bird, for the State of Connecticut, originals of which are in Conn. State Capitol; Rochester Mus. A., 1955. *Exhibited*: Laguna Beach AA, 1943; AV poster traveling exh.; Conn. Acad. FA; Hartford Soc. Women P.; Meriden A. & Crafts; Terry AI; Capper Fnd., Topeka, Kans.; AIC; Ogunquit A. Center. Specializes in dog portraits. Counselor, Vice-Pres., 1956-58, Hartford Soc. Women A.

BEYERS, MRS. ROBERT A. See *West, Bernice*

BEYNON, WILLIAM—*Painter, Des., Cart., Comm. A.*
Los Angeles Evening Herald-Express; h. 4625 West 64th St., Los Angeles 43, Cal.
B. Springfield, Ohio, May 3, 1917. *Studied*: Univ. Southern Cal.; Trade Tech. Comm. A. Sch., Los A. *Work*: Santa Barbara Mus. A. *Exhibited*: AWS, 1948; Cal. WC Soc., 1945, 1946, 1948, 1950; Assoc. Honolulu A., 1943, 1944.*

BIAMONTE, GRACE HOUSTON (Mrs.)—
Teacher, P., L.
463 Nixon Ave., Indiana, Pa.
B. Marysville, Ohio. *Studied*: Columbus A. Sch.; Ohio State Univ., A.B.; Columbia Univ., M.A.; N.Y. Sch. App. Des.; Carnegie Inst., and with Charles Hawthorne. *Member*: Assoc. A. Pittsburgh; All. A. of Johnstown. *Awards*: prize, All. A. of Johnstown, and others. *Positions*: A. Supv., Pittsburgh Schs., 1916-26; Instr. A., Indiana (Pa.) State T. Col., 1926-39, and other teaching in Pennsylvania schools since retirement.

BIANCO, PAMELA (RUBY) (Mrs. Georg Theo Hartmann)—*Illustrator, P., Lith., W.*
428 Lafayette St., New York 3, N.Y.
B. London, England, Dec. 31, 1906. *Member*: AEA. *Award*: Guggenheim F., 1930. *Exhibited*: Leicester Gal., London, England; Anderson Gal., N.Y.; Print Rooms, San F., Cal.; Knoedler Gal.; Ferargil Gal.; Rehn Gal.; Los A., Cal.; Boston, Mass.; Chicago, Ill. I., "The Skin Horse," 1927; "The Birthday of the Infanta," 1929; "Three Christmas Trees," 1930; "The Easter Book of Legends and Stories," 1947; Author, I., "The Starlit Journey," 1933; "Playtime in Cherry Street," 1948; "Paradise Square," 1950; "Little Houses Far Away," 1951; "The Look-Inside Easter Egg," 1952; "The Doll in the Window," 1953; "The Valentine Party," 1954; "Toy Rose," 1957, and many others. Contributor of "The Velveteen Rabbit" and "The Little Wooden Doll," to Harpers Bazaar, 1921, 1922.

BIBERMAN, EDWARD—*Painter, Ser.*
3332 Deronda Dr., Hollywood 28, Cal.
B. Philadelphia, Pa., Oct. 23, 1904. *Studied*: Univ. Pennsylvania, B.S. in Econ.; PAFA. *Member*: NSMP; AEA. *Awards*: Prize, PAFA, 1931; City of Los Angeles, 1951, 1956; Cal. State Fair, 1952; Los A. Mus. A., 1955; Tupperware prize, Orlando, Fla., 1957. *Work*: PAFA; Houston Mus. FA; Fed. Bldg., Los A., Cal.; USPO, Venice, Cal. *Exhibited*: PAFA, 1930, 1931; WMAA, 1931-1933; MModA, 1930, 1934; SFMA; Los A. Mus. A.; PMA; BMFA (one-man), 1930-1946; Raymond & Raymond, Los A., 1946 (one-man); Frayinot Gal., Los A., 1950 (one-man); Framecraft Gal., Los Angeles, 1953. Author, I., "The Best Untold," 1953 (book of paintings by the author).

BIDDLE, GEORGE—*Painter, S., Gr., W., Cr., L.*
Croton-on-Hudson, N.Y.
B. Philadelphia, Pa., Jan. 24, 1885. *Studied*: Harvard Univ., B.A. *Member*: NSMP; Mural A. Gld.; SAGA; Am. A. Congress; AEA. *Work*: murals: Dept. Justice, Wash., D.C.; Nat. Lib., Rio de Janeiro; Supreme Court, Mexico City; USPO, New Brunswick, N.J.; in collections of: MMA; Mus. Mod. A., Tokyo; Bridgestone Mus., Tokyo; Nat. Mus., Tel-Aviv; WMAA; MModA; PAFA; PMA; BMFA; SFMA; San Diego FA Soc.; Los A. Mus. A.; LC; N.Y. Pub. Lib.; NCFA, Carnegie Inst.; Joslyn A. Mus.; Portland AA; FMA; Museo Arte Moderna, Venice; Kaiser Friedrich Mus., Berlin; Nat. Gal., Canada; more than 80 one-man exhs., U.S. and abroad. Author: "Adolphe Borie"; "Boardman Robinson"; "Green Island"; "Artist at War"; "George Biddle's War Drawings"; "Yes and No of Contemporary Art," etc. Contributor to national magazines. *Position*: Chm., War Dept. A. Com., 1943; A. Memb. Nat. Comm. FA, 1950; Dir., 1950, Nat. Dir., AEA; Pres., NSMP, 1934, Mural A. Gld., 1934-36; Vice-Pres., SAGA, 1935; Nat. Dir., Am. A. Congress.

BIDDLE, MRS. GEORGE. See *Sardeau, Helene*

BIDWELL, WATSON—*Painter, E., Cr., L.*
Bidwell Ranch, Briggsdale, Colo.
B. Kinsley, Kans., Sept. 11, 1904. *Studied*: Univ. Denver, B.F.A.; Colorado State Col. Edu., M.A., and with Cyril Kay-Scott, John E. Thompson, B. J. O. Nordfeldt, Walt Kuhn. *Member*: Western AA; Colorado A. Edu. Assn.; Nat. A. Edu. Assn. *Awards*: prizes, Denver A. Mus., 1933, 1935, 1937; Central City (Colo.) 1955, 1957, 1958; Wichita A. Mus., 1957; Colo. State Fair, 1957, 1958; Las Vegas (Nev.) A. Lg., 1958. *Work*: Denver A. Mus.; Colorado State Col. Edu.; Wichita A. Mus., and in private coll. *Exhibited*: Mid-Am. A., 1951, 1955, 1956; Tri-States Exh., Cheyenne, Wyo., 1955; Colo. State Col. Edu., 1952; Denver A. Mus., 1955, 1958; Wichita, Kans., 1954, 1955; A. of Missouri Valley, Topeka, 1955, 1957; one-man: Marco Polo Gal., Denver; Colo. Women's Col., Denver. *Position*: Docent, 1933-36; Cur. Oriental A., 1936-39, Denver A. Mus.; Hd. A. Dept., East H.S., Wichita, Kans, 1948; Colorado State College, Greeley, Colo., 1958- .

BIEBEL, FRANKLIN MATTHEWS—*Museum Director*
Frick Collection, 1 East 70th St., New York 21, N.Y.
B. La Grange, Ill., Nov. 4, 1908. *Studied*: Col. Wooster, B.A.; Oberlin Col.; Princeton Univ., M.A., M.F.A.; Univ. Paris. *Member*: CAA; Archaeological Inst.; AA Mus.; Assn. A. Mus. Dir. *Awards*: F., Dumbarton Oaks Research Lib. & Coll., Wash., D.C., 1942. Author: "The Mosaics of Gerasa," 1938. Contributor to: Art magazines & periodicals. *Position*: Asst. Cur., CAM, 1935-37; Instr., Princeton Univ., 1937-38; Asst. Prof., Chm. A. Dept., Rutgers Univ., 1938-42; L., 1943, Asst. to Dir., 1944-46, Asst. Dir., 1946-51, Frick Coll., New York, N.Y., Dir., 1951- .

BIEHL, GODFREY F.—*Painter, Gr., C., E., L.*
R.R. 3, Chambersburg, Pa.
B. Pirmasens, Germany, Feb. 11, 1879. *Studied*: Central State Normal Sch., B.S., and with Lucy Drake Marlow, Christian Walter, John Follinsbee, Emil Gruppe, Anthony Thieme. *Member*: Assoc. A. Pittsburgh; Chambersburg AA. *Awards*: prizes, Carnegie Inst., 1936; Chambersburg AA., 1949, 1951. *Work*: Pa. State Univ.; Lockhaven State T. Col.; Southwest Texas State Col.; Pittsburgh Pub. Sch.; Chambersburg Hospital. *Exhibited*: CM; Butler AI; Assoc. A. Pittsburgh; Washington County Mus. FA, Hagerstown; Chambersburg AA.*

BIEHN, IRVING L(EW)—*Painter*
818 West Wisconsin Ave., Milwaukee 3, Wis.
B. Milwaukee, Wis., Aug. 1, 1900. *Studied*: Milwaukee AI; Layton Sch. A.; Chicago Acad. A. *Work*: Milwaukee Pub. Mus.; Milwaukee Grade & H.S. *Exhibited*: Marquette Univ.; Beloit Col.; Milwaukee AI; Layton A. Gal.; Bresler A. Gal.; Allis A. Lib.; Nat. Wildlife Show. *Position*: Assoc. A., Milwaukee Pub. Mus., Milwaukee, Wis.

BIELECKY, STANLEY—*Painter, T.*
328 Wilhelm St., Schererville, Ind.
Studied: Minneapolis Inst. A.; AIC. *Awards*: prizes, John Herron AI, 1939; Detroit Inst., A., 1941; F., Tiffany Fnd., 1938. *Work*: U.S. Pub. Health Service Hospital, Lexington, Ky. *Exhibited*: PAFA, 1941; Grand Rapids, Mich., 1940; SFMA, 1938; Elgin Acad., 1941; AIC, 1935-1941, 1948-1952; Detroit Inst. A., 1941, 1942, 1945; John Herron AI, 1939-1942, 1946, 1957; Valparaiso Univ., 1947-1952; Springfield Mus. FA, 1955; Indiana Univ., 1947-1952, 1955; Mackinac Island, 1956-1958. *Positions*: Instr., Indiana Univ. Ext. Div., 1937-43, 1946-52; Valparaiso Univ., 1941-43, 1946-58.

BIER, ELMIRA—*Assistant to Museum Director*
1600-21st St.; h. 4311 North Glebe Rd., Arlington 7, Va.
B. Baltimore, Md. *Studied*: Goucher Col., A.B.; Harvard Univ.; American Univ.; Univ. Wisconsin. *Position*: Asst. to Dir., Phillips Gal., in charge of music, Washington, D.C., 1923- .

BIER, JUSTUS—*Educator, W., Cr., L.*
University of Louisville, Louisville 8, Ky.; h. Route 1, Box 435, Anchorage, Ky.
B. Nurnberg, Germany, May 31, 1899. *Studied*: Univ. Munich, Erlangen, Jena, Bonn, Zurich, Ph.D. *Member*:

CAA; Chm., Comm. on regional societies, 1951, 1952, mem., nominations com., 1952; Am. Soc. for Aesthetics. Ed. Council, 1952-54, chm. session, 1954; Midwestern Col. A. Conference, Pres., 1951-52; Southeastern Col. A. Conference, Chm. session on A. Hist., 1951, chm. nominations com., 1952; Assoc. memb., Int. Assn. A. Cr., Am. Section; AFA; AAUP; A. Center Assn., Louisville, Ky., memb. Bd. Dir., 1949-53, 1954-56, 1957- ; Prof. Advisor, Junior League of Louisville, 1945- . *Awards*: Albrecht Durer med., City of Nurnberg, 1928; traveling F., publication grant Notgemeinschaft der Deutschen Wissenschaft, 1928, 1930; August Kestner med., Kestner-Gesellschaft, Hannover, 1938; Guggenheim F., 1953-54, 1956-57; Institute for Advanced Study, Princeton, N.J., research grant, 1953-54. Author: Tilmann Riemenschneider (3 vols.) and other books published in Germany and Austria, 1922-1948; contributor to Art Bulletin, Art in America, Art Quarterly, Studio, Gazette des Beaux-Arts, Munchner Jahrbuch der bildenden-Kunst, and others. Lectures: Tilmann Riemenschneider; Franconian Sculpture; Twentieth Century Sculpture. *Positions*: Docent, Instr., A. Hist., Municipal Univ., Nurnberg, 1925-30; Dir., Cur., Kestner-Gesellschaft AI, Hannover, 1930-36; Fnd., Dir., Mus. fur das vorbildliche Serienprodukt, Hannover, 1930-36; Asst. Prof. A. Hist., Actg. Hd., Dept. FA, Univ. Louisville, 1937-41; Assoc. Prof., 1941-46, Prof., 1946- ; Dir., Allen R. Hite AI, 1946- ; Cr. & A. Ed., The Courier-Journal, Louisville, Ky., 1944-53, 1954-56; Visiting Prof., Free University of Berlin, 1956.

BIER, SENTA DIETZEL (Mrs. Justus Bier)—
Educator, W., Cr.
Route 1, Box 435, Anchorage, Ky.

B. Nurnberg, Germany, Oct. 12, 1900. *Studied*: Univ. Munich, Zurich, Bonn, Ph.D. *Member*: Midwestern Col. A. Conference; Southeastern Col. A. Conference; Louisville A. Center Assn.; Louisville Dance Council (Bd. Dir. 1951-55); Arts Cl., Louisville; Ky. A. Edu. Assn., Chm. of session 1955. Author: Furttenbachs Gartenentwurfe. *Positions*: Asst. to A. Libn., Vereinigte Staatsschulen fur freie und angewandte Kunst, Berlin, 1928-29; Asst., Bavarian State Museums, Munich, 1929-31; Cur., Museum fur das vorbildliche Serienprodukt, Kestner-Gesellschaft, Hannover, 1932-36. Lecturer in German, 1946-47, Instr. German, 1947-48, Lecturer in A. Hist., 1948-53, Asst. Prof. A. Hist. (part-time), 1953-54, 1955-58, Univ. of Louisville. Cr. & A. Ed., The Courier-Journal, Louisville, Ky., 1953- . Lecturer in Art History, Bellarmine College, Louisville, Ky., 1958- .

BIGELOW, OLIVE (Mrs. Herbert Pell)—Painter
807 Fifth Ave., New York, N.Y.

B. Mountain Station, N.J., May 12, 1886. *Studied*: ASL, N.Y.; and in Paris, France, with Rafaelle Colin. *Member*: NAWA; Newport AA; SI; Soc. Women P. & S. *Awards*: prizes, Royal Drawing Soc., London, 1902, 1904; Newport AA, Crane prize, 1901, "People's Prize," 1933. *Work*: Providence Mus. A.; Vienna Military Mus.; Norwich Mus. A., England; photographs of portraits Frick Art Reference Lib.; Naval Mus., Annapolis; N.Y. Hist. Soc.; St. John & St. Elizabeth Hospital, London; Palmella Palace, Portugal; Portuguese Embassy, London; Vassar Col., N.Y.; Oakwood Sch., Poughkeepsie, N.Y.; Hungarian Lib., N.Y.; Carnavalet Mus., Paris, France; Leslie Castle, Ireland; Mus. City of N.Y.; executed numerous portraits of officials on War Crimes Comm., London, 1944; paintings, Soc. Prevention Cruelty to Children; Soc. Prevention of Cruelty to Animals; Chinese Embassy, Wash., D.C.; cover des., Vogue, Harper's Weekly and other magazines; magazine illus.; miniatures on ivory. Condensed version King James, Old & New Testaments titled "Olive Pell Bible," 1952-55, now in 6th edition. *Exhibited*: Knoedler Gal., N.Y., 1920; Walker Gal., London, 1922; Ferargil Gal., 1927; Bernheim Jeunne, Paris, 1929; Newport AA, 1943; Lisbon, 1942; Royal Acad., London; Scott & Fowles, N.Y.

BIGGERS, JOHN THOMAS—Painter, S., Lith., I., E.
3527 Ruth St., Houston 4, Tex.

B. Gastonia, N.C., Apr. 13, 1924. *Studied*: Hampton Inst., with Viktor Lowenfeld; Pennsylvania State Univ., M.A., D. Edu.; Univ. So. California. *Member*: NSMP; Com. on A. Edu., MModA, New York. *Awards*: prizes, Atlanta Univ. (purchase), 1953; NSMP, 1955; Mus. FA of Houston, 1950; DMFA, 1952; UNESCO F., to do mural painter's Study of Life in West Africa, 1957; Mural, Science Bldg., Texas Southern Univ., Houston, 1958; mural,

Labor-Longshoreman's Temple, Houston, 1957. *Work*: murals, Naval Training Sch., Hampton, Va.; Eliza Johnson Home, Houston, Tex.; YWCA, Houston, 1954; Carver H.S., Naples, Tex., 1955. *Exhibited*: MModA, 1943; CAM; SFMA; Portland A. Mus.; BMFA; SAM; VMFA traveling exh., 1945, 1946; Brooklyn Pub. Lib., 1946; Petersburg, Va.; Knoedler Gal.; Contemp. A. Mus., Houston, 1953; Mus. FA of Houston, 1954 (2-man); NSMP, 1954-1956. *Position*: Prof., Hd. Dept. A., Texas Southern Univ., Houston, Tex.

BIGGS, GEOFFREY—Illustrator
131 East 47th St., New York, N.Y.; h. Box 22, Palatine Bridge, N.Y.

B. London, England, Apr. 6, 1908. *Studied*: Grand Central Sch. A., with De Feo, Wolfle. *Member*: SI. *Exhibited*: SI; A.Dir.Cl. Illus., magazines & adv. agencies.

BIGGS, WALTER—Painter, I.
Salem, Va.

B. Elliston, Va., June 4, 1886. *Studied*: with Robert Henri, Kenneth Hayes Miller, Edward Penfield, F. Luis Mora. *Member*: NA; AWS; SI; SC; Phila. WC Cl.; All. A. Am. *Awards*: prizes, SC, 1939; A. Dir. Cl., 1939; NAD; New Britain (Conn.) Inst. A.; Chicago, Ill.; Hickory (N.C.) Mus. A.; Montclair Mus. A.; medals, gold & silver, AWS; med. of honor, A. Fellowship. *Work*: Oklahoma A. Center; Davenport (Iowa) A. Mus. *Exhibited*: Nationally. I., national magazines.

BIGLER, MARY JANE WHITE—Painter, E., C.
16708 Rosemont Road, Detroit 19, Mich.

B. Columbia City, Ind. *Studied*: Indiana Univ., A.B.; Wayne Univ., M.A.; Taylor Sch. A.; Brown County Sch. Painting; AIC; Detroit Soc. A. & Crafts. *Member*: Detroit Soc. Women P. & S.; Indiana A. Cl.; Mich. WC Soc.; Detroit A. Market. *Awards*: prizes, Mich. WC Soc., 1946-1958; Mich. A., 1952-1958; Butler Inst. Am. A., 1952, 1958; Detroit Soc. Women P. & S., 1946-1958; Palette & Brush, 1951; Scarab Cl., 1951, 1953; Newberry prize, 1951; Leon Fram prize, 1957; Mich. WC Soc., 1952, 1956; and others. *Exhibited*: Indiana A. Cl., 1940, 1946; Hoosier Salon; Detroit Inst. A.; Detroit A. Market; Syracuse Mus. FA; Wichita Craftsmen; Mich. Craftsmen; Mich. State Fair, 1950-1958; MMA 1952; Michiana Annual, 1954-1958; Scarab Cl.,1942-1958; Detroit Inst. A., 1956; ACA Gal., N.Y.; Univ. Michigan, 1955; Grand Rapids A. Gal., 1957 (3-man); Ball State T. Col., 1957 (one-man); Gal. 4, 1956 (4-man); Indiana A., 1957. *Positions*: Instr., Wayne State Univ., Detroit, Mich., 1943-58; Instr., Detroit Soc. A. & Crafts, 1948-52.

BIGNELL, JAMES F.—Educator
University of Tampa; h. 3101 North Adams St., Tampa 6, Fla.

B. Cedar Bluffs, Neb. *Studied*: Midland Col., Fremont, Neb., B.S.; Univ. Nebraska, M.A.; Escola Technica de Aviacao, Sao Paulo, Brazil. Author, I., "Pictorial Illustrations," 1952, reprint, 1956. *Position*: Hd., Dept. of Art, University of Tampa, Tampa, Fla.

BILL, CARROLL (M.)—Painter, I.
162 Newbury St., Boston, Mass.; h. 596 Commercial St., East Weymouth 89, Mass.

B. Philadelphia, Pa., Dec. 28, 1877. *Studied*: Harvard Univ. *Member*: Boston Soc. WC Painters (Pres.); Copley Soc.; Gld. Boston A.; AWS. *Work*: Hispanic Soc., N.Y.; John Herron AI; Univ. Michigan; BMFA; Farnsworth Mus., Rockland, Me.; MIT; murals: Boston Airport; Bethlehem Ship Co., and in Worcester, Springfield, Manchester, Mass. *Exhibited*: PAFA; AWS; Butler AI; Boston Soc. WC Painters; Gld. Boston A. Author, I., articles in national magazines.

BILLINGS, HENRY—Painter, Des., I., W.
1 West 72nd St., New York, N.Y.

B. Bronxville, N.Y., 1901. *Studied*: ASL. *Work*: WMAA; murals, Music Hall, N.Y.; WFNY 1939; USPO, Lake Placid, Wappinger Falls, N.Y.; Columbia, Tenn.; Medford, Mass.; American Export Lines, 1950. *Exhibited*: Midtown Gal.; NAD; WMAA. *Positions*: Instr., ASL, 1940-41; Pres., AEA, 1951-52; Memb., Nat. Comm. for UNESCO;

I., children's books. *Position*: Vice-Pres., International Assn. Plastic Arts, Paris; Sec., Nat. Council for U.S. Art; Trustee, American Federation of Arts, New York, N.Y.

BILLINGTON, JOHN J. (JULES)—
Painter, T., Lith., Ser., I.
914 North Serrano St., Los Angeles 29, Cal.
B. Meadville, Mo., Feb. 17, 1900. *Studied*: Univ. Misouri; AIC; ASL. *Member*: Cal. WC Soc. *Awards*: Prizes, Laguna Beach AA, 1938; San Diego FA Soc., 1941; Am. A. Cong., 1940; Douglas Aircraft Co., 1943. *Exhibited*: WFNY 1939; CGA, 1939; San Diego FA Soc., 1941; AIC, 1940; Riverside Mus., 1940; Cal. WC Soc., 1945. *Position*: Instr., Grand Central Sch. A., 1929-35; teaching privately at present.

BILLMYER, JOHN EDWARD—*Educator, C., P., Gr.*
1519 East Mexico St., Denver 10, Colo.
B. Denver, Colo., Aug. 17, 1912. *Studied*: Univ. Denver; Kirkland Sch. A.; Western Reserve Univ., B.A., M.A. *Member*: AAUP; Am. Ceramic Soc.; 15 Colorado Artists. *Work*: CMA; Denver A. Mus. *Exhibited*: Syracuse Mus. FA., 1948, 1950, 1952, 1953, 1956; Wichita Mus. A., 1951, 1955, 1957; Denver A. Mus., 1947-1958; Metropolitan Show, Denver A. Mus., 1952-1957; CMA, 1933-1942. *Position*: Assoc. Prof., Ceramics, Graphics, and others, University of Denver, Denver, Colo.

BINDER, JACOB—*Portrait Painter*
24 Gerald Rd., Boston, Mass.
B. Kreslavke, Russia, Dec. 18, 1887. *Studied*: Vilna A. Sch.; Acad. A. Petrograd; & with Joseph DeCamp, John Singer Sargent. *Member*: Boston AC; North Shore AA; Am.A.Lg. *Awards*: Prize, New England A. Exh., 1929. *Work*: BMFA; Harvard Univ.; Northeastern Univ.; Boston Univ.; Pub. Lib. & State House, Boston; Concord (N.H.) State House. *Exhibited*: AIC, 1919-1921; PAFA, 1923, 1924, 1925, 1928; CAM; Indiana AA; Springfield A. Mus.; Copley Soc., Boston; FA Mus., Harrisburg, Pa.; North Shore AA, 1920-1945; East Gloucester AA; Ogunquit AA.*

BINDER, JOSEPH—*Designer*
100 Central Park South, New York 19, N.Y.
B. Vienna, Austria, Mar. 3, 1898. *Studied*: States Sch. App. A. & Crafts, Vienna. *Member*: A. Dir. Cl. *Awards*: prizes, State prize of Austria, 1926; WFNY 1939; A. Dir. Cl., 1939. med., 1943; MModA, 1941. *Work*: BMFA; MMA; MModA; Franklin Inst., Phila., Pa.; American Airlines; U.S. Navy; Am. Red Cross Fund; many ports. of prominent persons. Author: "Color in Advertising." Contributor to art magazines in U.S. and abroad.*

BINDRUM, JOHN I.—*Painter, T., L.*
River Rd., Piermont, N.Y.; s. Rochester, Vt.
B. Brooklyn, N.Y., Jan. 22, 1907. *Studied*: ASL; Brooklyn Inst. A. & Sc., and with J. R. Koopman, Richard Lahey. *Member*: AWS. *Exhibited*: PAFA, 1939, 1941; AIC, 1939, 1941; AWS, 1936-1955; WFNY 1939; BM, 1941, 1955; Vienna, 1939; Toronto, 1939; San Francisco, 1954; Paris, 1954; Boston, 1955; Chicago, 1955; Detroit, 1955; Brooklyn A. Exh., 1940-1946. *Position*: Instr., Brooklyn Mus., 1939-1956; Instr., Brooklyn Col., 1948-1952; Pres. Bd. Edu., Tappan Zee H.S.*

BINFORD, JULIEN—*Painter, S.*
Route 2, Powhatan, Va.
B. Richmond, Va., 1909. *Studied*: Emory Univ., Ga.; AIC. *Awards*: Ryerson F., AIC; F., VMFA, 1940; Rosenwald F., 1943; prize, Buck Hill Falls, Pa.; Va. State Library Natl. Mural Comp.; Springfield Mus. A. *Work*: Shiloh Baptist Church, Fine Creek, Va.; H.S., Richmond, Va.; 57th St. Branch, Greenwich Savings Bank, N.Y.; 14th St. Branch, Greenwich Savings Bank, N.Y.; Jamestown Festival, Jamestown, Va.; PMG; IBM; BMFA; New Britain Mus.; Springfield, Mus. A.; Oberlin College, Ohio; Univ. Nebraska; William Rockhill Nelson Gal. A.; Univ. Georgia; State Mus. of Washington; Munson-Williams-Proctor Inst.; AGAA; VMFA; Mary Washington College; Univ. Virginia. *Exhibited*: Salon d'Automne, Paris; AIC; Carnegie Inst.; and many national exhs. One-man: Galerie Jean Charpentier; Galeries Jeanne Castel, both Paris, France; VMFA;

Midtown Gal., N.Y.; Oberlin College; Univ. Virginia. *Position*: Prof. A., Mary Washington College, Fredericksburg, Va.

BING, ALEXANDER—*Painter*
1155 Park Avenue, New York, N.Y.
B. New York, N.Y., June 2, 1878. *Studied*: City Col., N.Y., B.S.; Columbia Univ., A.M.; Florence Cane A. Sch.; and with Sol Wilson, Abraham Rattner, Hans Hofmann. *Work*: Carnegie Inst.; WMAA; Douglas Col. A. Gal. *Exhibited*: Bertha Schaefer Gal., 1952-1955, (one-man, 1955); H.C.E. Gal., Provincetown, Mass., 1956-1958 (1957 one-man).

BIRCH, GERALDINE (Mrs. G. R. Duncan)—
Painter, Et.
1550 North Garfield Ave., Pasadena 6, Cal.
B. Sussex, England, Nov. 12, 1883. *Studied*: Slade Sch. A., London; Paris, with Georges Desvallieres; London Univ. *Member*: Cal. Pr.M.; Pasadena SA. *Work*: State Library, Sacramento; Episcopal Church, Sierra Madre, Cal.; Oakland A. Gal.; port., Gen. John Cannon, U.S. Airforce Acad., Colorado Springs, Colo.; mural, Fletcher Aircraft Co., Rosemead, Cal. *Exhibited*: Brooklyn SE; Phila. SE; Los A. Mus. A.; Pasadena SA (annually); Roswell (N.M.) Mus. A.

BIRKENBERGER, WILLIAM—*Painter, Des., C.*
189 Wood St., Waterbury, Conn.
B. Germany, Jan. 11, 1903. *Member*: AFA. *Award*: prize, New Haven Paint & Clay Cl., 1935.

BIRMINGHAM, LLOYD PAUL—*Illustrator, Cart., P.*
Signal Hill South, Wilton, Conn.
B. Buffalo, N.Y., Aug. 23, 1924. *Studied*: Brown Univ.; Harvard Univ.; Parsons Sch. Des.; Sch. for A. Studies; ASL. *Member*: SI; Int. House; Westport A. *Exhibited*: U.S. Veterans Exh.; Bodley Gal. (prize, 1957). *Work*: Cart., newspaper comic strip syndicated by General Features Syndicate.

BIRNBAUM, ABE—*Painter, Cart., I.*
Croton-on-Hudson, N.Y.
B. New York, N.Y., June 11, 1899. *Studied*: ASL. *Member*: AEA. *Exhibited*: Carnegie Inst., 1944; Phila. A. All.; PMA, I., "Listen to the Mocking Words," 1945; & for Harper's Bazaar, New Yorker, & other magazines.*

BIRNBAUM, MARTIN—*Writer, Cr., L.*
200 East 66th St., New York 21, N.Y.
B. Miskolcz, Hungary, May 10, 1878. *Studied*: Col. of the City of N.Y., B.A.; Columbia Univ., LL.B., M.A.; Asia Institute, Hon. M.A. *Award*: Commendatore of the Crown of Italy. Author: "Oscar Wilde: Fragments and Memories," 1920; "Arthur Rackham" (with F. Coykendall), 1922; "Beardsley et Wilde," 1939; "John Singer Sargent: A Conversation Piece," 1940; "Vanishing Eden," 1942; "Jacovleff and Other Essays," 1946; "Angkor and the Mandarin Road," 1952; "Romance in the World of Art," 1957. Contributor to Natural History; Asia; International Studio; Art in America, and others.

BIRRELL, VERLA LEONE—*Painter, L., E., W., Des., C.*
University of Utah; h. P.O. Box 952, Salt Lake City, Utah
B. Tacoma, Wash., Nov. 24, 1903. *Studied*: Univ. Utah, B.S.; Claremont Col., M.F.A. *Member*: Assoc. Utah A. *Awards*: prizes, Utah AI; Utah State Fair. *Work*: Ephraim A. Gal.; Utah State Capitol; Cache Valley H.S.; Pleasant Grove H.S.; Univ. Utah; Brigham Young Univ. *Exhibited*: Cal. PLH; regularly in exhs. in Utah, Idaho and Nevada. Lectures: Art and Travel. Author: "Mormon Guide Book"; "Portfolio of Historic Design"; "The Textile Arts." *Position*: Asst. Prof. A., Brigham Young Univ., 1937-48; Asst. Prof. A., in Home Ec., Univ. Utah, 1948- .

BISCHOF, SEVERIN—*Painter, C.*
302 Mertens Ave., Syracuse 8, N.Y.
B. Wenden, Germany, Sept. 24, 1893. *Studied*: Syracuse Univ., A.B., and abroad. *Awards*: prize, Syracuse Mus. FA,

1925, 1940, 1941. *Exhibited*: Rochester Mem. A. Gal.; Indp. A.; Syracuse Mus. FA, 1924-1952; Munson-Williams-Proctor Inst., Utica, N.Y.; Art: USA, 1958, N.Y. *Position*: Past-Pres., Syracuse A. & Crafts Gld.; Trustee, Allied Arts of Syracuse, Inc.

BISCHOFF, ELMER NELSON—*Painter, T.*
California School of Fine Arts; h. 628 Montgomery St., San Francisco, Cal.

B. Berkeley, Cal., July 9, 1916. *Studied*: Univ. California, A.B., M.A. *Member*: San F. AA. *Awards*: prizes, SFMA, 1941, 1946; Richmond (Cal.) A. Center, 1955, 1956; Oakland A. Mus., 1957. *Exhibited*: San F. AA, 1941-1958; AIC, 1947; Los A. Mus. A., 1951; Art: USA, 1957; Am. Paintings, 1945-1957; Minneapolis Inst. A., 1957; New Talent, USA, 1958; AFA "West Coast Artists," 1958. One-man: Cal.PLH, 1947; Paul Kantor Gal., Los A., 1955; San F. AA Gal., 1956. *Position*: Instr. & Chm. FA Dept. & Graduate Program, California School of Fine Arts, San Francisco, Cal., 1956- .

BISCHOFF, ILSE MARTHA—*Illustrator, P., Gr.*
455 East 57th St., New York 22, N.Y.

B. New York, N.Y. *Studied*: ASL; & in Europe. *Awards*: Prizes, Phila. Pr. Cl., 1927; AIGA, 1930; Pepsi-Cola, 1945. *Work*: BMFA; BMA; MMA; N.Y. Pub. Lib. I., children's books.*

**BISHOP, ISABEL (Mrs. Harold G. Wolff)—
*Painter, Et.***
857 Broadway, New York 3, N.Y.; h. 355 West 246th St., Riverdale 71, N.Y.

B. Cincinnati, Ohio, Mar. 3, 1902. *Studied*: ASL; N.Y.Sch. App. Des. *Member*: NA; Nat. Inst. A. & Let.; SAGA; Phila. WC Soc.; Audubon A. *Awards*: prizes, NAD, 1936, 1943, 1945, 1955; SAGA, 1939; Butler AI, 1941; PAFA, 1953; med., CGA, 1945; LC, 1946; Hon. D.F.A., Moore Inst. A., Sc. & Industry, Phila., Pa. *Work*: WMAA; MMA; PAFA; AGAA; Springfield Mus. A.; Butler AI; PMG; BMA; CAM; N.Y. Pub. Lib.; Phillips Acad., Andover, Mass.; LC; CGA; mural, USPO, New Lexington, Ohio; Cranbrook Acad. A.; John Herron AI; Munson-Williams-Proctor Inst.; Newark Mus. A.; New Britain A. Mus.; Tel-Aviv Mus., Israel; Des Moines Art Center. *Exhibited*: Carnegie Inst.; VMFA; CGA; WFNY 1939; GGE 1939; AIC; WMAA; CAM; Berkshire Mus., Pittsfield, Mass., 1957 (one-man); six one-man exhs., New York, and many others. Contributor to art magazines.

BISHOP, MARJORIE (CUTLER)—*Painter, T.*
Setauket, L.I., N.Y.

B. Melrose, Mass., Aug. 23, 1904. *Studied*: ASL; New Sch. Social Research; private instr., and in Paris, France. *Awards*: prize, WAC, 1946. *Work*: WAC. *Exhibited*: PAFA, 1945; Carnegie Inst., 1945; WAC, 1946; ACA Gal., N.Y., 1943; Brandt Gal., N.Y., 1943; Audubon A., 1947, 1951, 1954; Nebraska AA, 1950; St. Paul de Vence, France, 1953; Silvermine Gld. A., 1954, 1955; Parrish Mus., 1958; one-man: Suffolk Mus., 1946, 1953, 1955; New Hope, Pa., 1948; Levitt Gal., N.Y., 1945, 1947; Barzansky Gal., N.Y., 1958; Sunken Meadow Gal., 1959.

**BISSELL, DOROTHY PENDENNIS (Mrs. Lloyd)—
*Sculptor, P., Des.***
80 Cayuga Rd., Williamsville 21, N.Y.

B. Buffalo, N.Y., May 17, 1894. *Studied*: with Arthur Lee. *Member*: Buffalo Soc. A. Specializes in heads of children and animals; des., hooked rugs.

BISSELL, (CHARLES) PHIL(IP)—*Cartoonist, I.*
Boston Globe, Sports Dept., Morrissey Blvd., Dorchester, Mass.; h. 27 Hollett St., North Scituate, Mass.

B. Worcester, Mass., Feb. 1, 1926. *Studied*: Sch. Practical A., Boston; Art Instruction, Minneapolis, Minn. *Position*: Cart., Boston Globe.

BISTLINE, EDNA (MARIAN) (Mrs.)—*Painter*
2245 Afton St., Philadelphia 15, Pa.

B. Elliottsburg, Pa., Aug. 14, 1914. *Studied*: PAFA, with McCarter, Chapin, Watkins; Barnes Fnd. *Member*: F. PAFA; Woodmere A. Gal.; DaVinci All. *Awards*: prize,

DaVinci All., 1944. *Work*: PAFA. *Exhibited*: PAFA, 1945, 1951; Phila. Sketch Cl., 1944-1946; Ragan Gal., 1945; DaVinci exh., 1943, 1944, 1949-1958; Cape May, N.J., 1948-1958; Woodmere A. Gal., 1942-1958.

BISTTRAM, EMIL—*Painter, Des., L., T.*
Box 46, Taos, N.M.

B. Hungary, Apr. 7, 1895. *Studied*: with Howard Giles. *Member*: Phila. WC Cl.; Fnd. Western A. (hon.) *Awards*: prizes, Phila. WC Cl., 1926; AWCS, 1927, 1930, 1931; med., Phila. WC Cl., 1931; Guggenheim F., 1931. *Work*: Albright A. Gal.; Roerich Mus., N.Y.; Taos (N.M.) County Court House; murals, Dept. Justice, Wash., D.C.; USPO, Ranger, Tex. *Position*: Dir., Bisttram Sch. FA, Taos, N.M., at present.*

BITTINGER, CHARLES (Capt., USNR)—*Painter*
3403 O St., N.W., Washington 7, D.C.

B. Washington, D.C., June 27, 1879. *Studied*: ASL; Ecole des Beaux-Arts. *Member*: NA; NAC; All. A. Am.; SC; AFA; The Colorists; Gld. Boston A.; Wash. AC; Soc. Wash. A.; Duxbury AA. *Awards*: Med., St. Louis Exp., 1904; prizes, NAD, 1909, 1912; med., Pan-Pacific Exp., 1915; prize, Duxbury AA, 1919; Soc. Wash. A., 1925; Newport AA, 1938. *Work*: Allegheny Col.; NAC; CAM; MMA; Nat. Acad. Sc., Wash., D.C.; Montgomery (Ala.) Mus. FA; mural, Franklin Inst., Phila., Pa. *Position*: Naval Camouflage, World War I and II.

BITTINGER, ROSS THOMAS (Dr.)—*Educator, C.*
Art Dept., New Mexico Western College; h. 1804 Juniper Rd., Silver City, N.M.

B. Madison, Mich., Nov. 6, 1899. *Studied*: BMFA Sch.; Univ. Michigan, B.S.A., M.A.; Cranbrook Acad. A.; MIT, and with Denman W. Ross. *Member*: New Mexico Edu. Assn.; NEA; New Mexico A. Edu. Assn.; Michigan Union. *Awards*: Fulbright F., 1955-56. *Work*: special commissions for jewelry, silver work and furniture. *Exhibited*: Mus. Mod. A., Santa Fe, 1953-1955; Mus. Four A., Santa Fe, 1952-1955; New Mexico Western Col., 1950-1955. Author, I., "Modern Creative Design and Its Application." Lectures: Pre-Historic to Modern; History of Art of the Southwest; Indian Jewelry of the Southwest. *Position*: Des. Staff, Univ. Michigan, 1926-39; Asst. Dir., Vocational Training, Parkersburg, W. Va., 1939-41; Arch., Harry Ferguson, Inc., Detroit, 1942-45; Asst. Prof., Dept. Engineering, Univ. Michigan, 1945-49; Chm. A. Dept., New Mexico Western Col., 1949- .

BJAREBY, (ALFRED) GUNNAR—*Painter, S., I., C.*
147 Worthington St., Boston 15, Mass.

B. Forslovsholm, Sweden, Feb. 11, 1899. *Studied*: Julian Acad., Paris; BMFA Sch., with L. Thompson, Charles Grafly; Gotthard Sandberg, Sweden. *Member*: North Shore AA. *Awards*: Prize, North Shore AA, 1942, 1951, 1955; medal, Chicago, 1957. *Work*: Murals, St. Joseph's Cathedral, Manchester, N.H.; Parker House, Boston. *Exhibited*: Salon de Printemps, Paris, 1933; Swedish Cl., Chicago, 1946-1955, 1956, 1957; Boston A. Festival, 1956; Gloucester, Mass., 1956-1958; Boston AC, 1933; Jordan-Marsh, 1935-1944, 1946-1951, 1953, 1954, 1956-1958; North Shore AA, 1939-1955; Ogunquit, Me., 1950-1955. Illus. "Comrades in Snow," 1940.

BJERREGAARD-POULSEN, JACOB—*Writer*
Copa-Club, Beverly-Wilshire Hotel; h. 141 South Maple St., Beverly Hills, Cal.

B. Copenhagen, Denmark, July 6, 1890. *Member*: Cal. A. Cl.; Los A. Mus. A. Assn.; Laurel Canyon AA; Scandinavian-American A. Soc. *Awards*: many national and international Orders, Citations and Medals, Diplomas of Honor from Italy, Brazil, France, Belgium, Ecuador, Uruguay, Nicaragua, Bolivia, Mexico, Cuba, U.S. Govt. Treasury Dept., Am. International Acad., etc.*

BJORNCRANTZ, CARL G.—*Industrial Designer*
Sears Roebuck & Co., D/817, 925 South Homan Ave., Chicago 7, Ill.; h. 2212 Pioneer Rd., Evanston, Ill.

B. Grand Rapids, Mich., Aug. 8, 1904. *Studied*: Kendall Mem. A. Sch.; Colgate Univ., A.B. *Member*: IDI (Exec. V.-Pres.). *Position*: Dir., Indst. Des., Sears Roebuck Co., 1943- ; Chm., Annual IDI Design Award.

BJORVAND, HELEN H. (Mrs. Bernt J.)—Teacher, I.

Elmira College; h. Forest Hills Drive, Elmira, N.Y.

B. Hartford, Conn., May 17, 1902. *Studied*: Smith Col., B.A.; Yale Grad. Sch., M.A. Illus., "Lucy Perhaps," 1935. *Position*: Asst. Prof. A., Elmira (N.Y.) Col., 1933-52; Assoc. Prof., 1952- .

BLACK, FREDERICK (EDWARD)—Painter, Lith.

General Delivery, Sandoval P.O., Corrales, N.M.

B. Providence, R.I., May 24, 1924. *Studied*: Univ. Redlands; Univ. New Mexico, B.S., B.A., M.A. *Member*: Sarasota AA; New Mexico A. Lg. *Awards*: Providence Journal scholarship to R.I. Sch. Des.; I.G.A.S.; Providence A. Cl., 1953. *Exhibited*: Providence A. Cl., 1953; Creative Gal., N.Y., 1953, 1954; Sarasota AA, 1954; New Mexico State Fair, 1952-1955; St. Joseph's Col., Albuquerque (one-man); Mus. of New Mexico, 1952-1955; SAGA, 1952, 1953, 1954; SAGA traveling exh., 1953, 1954; "New Mexico Painting Today" and "Avant Garde Painters" exhs., 1955.

BLACK, HAROLD—Painter, Des.

26 West 12th St., New York 14, N.Y.

B. New York, N.Y., Dec. 13, 1913. *Studied*: NAD, and with Leon Kroll, Gifford Beal. *Member*: Audubon A. (Bd. Dir., Chm. Awards); AEA (Cor. Sec., 1951-2; Treas. Bldg. Fund, 1951-2; 1st V.-Pres., 1952-3; Nat. Bd., Dir., 1952-3); Exhibit Producers & Des. Assn. (Treas., 1955). *Awards*: prizes, NAD, 1936; MModA., 1940; 48 States Comp., 1940. *Exhibited*: Arch. Lg., 1942; Poughkeepsie, N.Y., 1950, one-man; Audubon A., 1948-1952; WMAA, 1951; Terry AI, 1952; one-man: Wellons Gal., N.Y., 1954; Tyringham, Mass., 1955. *Work*: murals, Fed. Court House, Salina, Kans. I., "The Kaw," 1943. *Position*: Pres., Manhattan Gallery Group; Pres., Black, Clark & Tunick, Inc.*

BLACK, OSWALD RAGAN (OZ)—
Illustrator, Comm. A., Cart., L., T.

300 Trinity Bldg., 1820 Broadway; h. 2960 Hudson St., Denver, Colo.

B. Neoga, Ill., Oct. 29, 1898. *Studied*: Univ. Nebraska. *Awards*: prize, Nat. Lg. Women Voters, 1924. *Work*: Illus., "Outdoors" and "Minnesota Panorama," 1957. *Positions*: Cart., Lincoln (Neb.) Star, 1921-27; Nebraska State Journal, 1930-40; Minneapolis Tribune, 1940-52; Freelance Comm., Minneapolis, 1952-57; Dir. Pub. Rel., Denver Area Council of Churches, 1957- ; Instr., Cart. & Caricature, Univ. Colorado, Inst. of Adult Learning, Denver, Colo., 1958- .

BLACK, WENDELL—Educator, Pr. M.

Art Department, University of Colorado, Boulder, Colo.

Position: Prof. Graphic A., Univ. Colorado, Boulder, Colo.*

BLACKBURN, MORRIS—
Painter, Et., Eng., Lith., Ser., T.

2104 Spring St., Philadelphia 3, Pa.

B. Philadelphia, Pa., Oct. 13, 1902. *Studied*: PAFA, and with Arthur B. Carles. *Member*: Phila. A. All.; Phila. Pr. Cl.; Nat. Ser. Soc.; Phila. WC Cl.; AWS; All. A. Am.; Audubon A. *Awards*: Guggenheim F., 1952-53; Phila. Pr. Cl.; med., PAFA, and Thornton Oakley prize, 1955. *Work*: PMA; PAFA; Capehart Coll.; U.S. State Dept.; Brooks Mem. A. Gal.; Pa. State Univ.; Fleisher A. Mem.; LC; Woodmere A. Gal.; Phila. Pub. Lib.; Univ. Montana; U.S. Information Service. *Exhibited*: PAFA, 1937-1956; NAD; AIC; WMAA; MMA; Toledo Mus. A.; three exhs. in France, sponsored by U.S. Embassy; Venice Biennale; Santa Barbara Mus. A.; Montclair A. Mus.; Springfield A. Mus.; Gimpel Fils, London; Kunsthaller Gallerie, Zurich; PMA; Phila. Pr. Cl.; Phila. A. All. Author, I., of article in "How Paintings Happen," by Ray Bethers; "The Artist Teacher," AEA Newsletter, 1955. *Position*: Instr., Painting, PMA; Instr., Graphic A., & Painting, PAFA, Philadelphia, Pa.

BLACKETER, JAMES (RICHARD)—Painter, Des.

31652 Jewel St., South Laguna Beach, Cal.

B. Laguna Beach, Cal., Sept. 23, 1931. *Studied*: Santa Ana College, and with Bennett Bradbury. *Member*: Laguna Beach AA; Festival of A. Assn. *Awards*: Nat. Scholastic award, 1950; various prizes and awards, Laguna Beach AA, 1953- . *Exhibited*: Carnegie Inst., 1950; Laguna Beach AA, 1953-1958; Laguna Beach Festival A., 1953-1958; Long Beach A. Mus.

BLACKMAN, LEONARD—Painter, Des., T., L.

456 Beach 127th St., Belle Harbor 94, L.I., N.Y.

B. Brooklyn, N.Y., Oct. 3, 1895. *Studied*: N.Y. Univ., B.C.S., in Journalism, D. Sc.; City Col., N.Y.; ASL, with Ernest Fiene; and with Dong Kingman, Eliot O'Hara, Herb Olsen, John Pellew and E. A. Whitney; BMSch. A., with Kienbusch. *Member*: AAPL (Treas.); ASL; Brooklyn Mus. A. Alumni; SC; N.Y. State A. T. Assn.; F. (Life) Royal Soc. A., London; Hon. memb., Kappa Pi; Nat. Press Cl., Wash., D.C. *Awards*: prizes, New Jersey Creative A., 1952; NAC, 1955. *Work*: Seton Hall Univ.; DAR; Chrysler A. Mus., Provincetown, Mass., and in many private colls. *Exhibited*: AWS, 1955; AAPL, 1952-1955; Washington WC Cl., 1954; Providence A. Cl., 1952; Acad. A., West Berlin, Germany, 1954; Hudson Valley AA, 1955; A. Lg. of Long Island, 1952-1955; NAC; Grand Central A. Gal.; Hudson River Mus.; Knoedler Gal.; Creative A. Gal., N.Y.; Ogunquit A. Center; one-man: to college art depts., 1955-1956; New York, N.Y., 1952, 1954. Lectures: "Color Theories of Prang, Munsell, Ostvald, in Design"; "Importance of Drawing in Industrial Design"; "Perspective of Color and Shadow." *Position*: Dir., Watercolor Workshop, Bd. Edu., Adult Edu. Project, New York, N.Y. Guest Instr., Des., N.Y. Public Library A. Project.

BLACKSHEAR, ANNIE LAURA EVE—Painter, T., W.

165 Wilcox St., Athens, Ga.

B. Augusta, Ga., Oct. 30, 1875. *Studied*: CUASch.; Chase Sch. A.; ASL; PAFA, and with John Twachtman, William Chase, R. Swain Gifford and Breckenridge. *Member*: Assn. Georgia A.; Athens AA; Georgia Patrons of A. *Work*: Georgia Agricultural Ext. Bldg.; Univ. Georgia, Law Sch., Academic Bldg.; Georgia Mus. A.; Piedmont Col., and in many private collections. *Exhibited*: Univ. Georgia A. Mus.; Athens (Ga.) Regional Lib.; Assn. Georgia A.; Houston, Tex.; Atlanta, Ga.; Athens, Ga.; Gainesville, Ga.; Eufala, Ala. Author, I., "Charts for Visual Instruction." Produced a number of historical pageants for Univ. of Georgia, Georgia Fed. Women's Cl., etc. *Position*: Hd. A. Depts. at Piedmont Col.; Ga. Agri. Ext. Service; Nacoochee (Ga.) Inst.; Jones Normal Sch., Eclectic, Ala. (now retired). Chm. Exh. Committee Athens A. Assn., at present.

BLACKSHEAR, KATHLEEN—Painter, C., Gr., E., L.

Art Institute of Chicago; h. 1037 North Rush St., Chicago 11, Ill.

B. Navasota, Tex., June 6, 1897. *Studied*: Baylor Univ. B.A.; AIC, M.F.A.; ASL. *Member*: Chicago SA. *Work*: Mus. FA of Houston. *Exhibited*: Various museums and galleries in the U.S.A.; "An Artist's Calendar," 1937- ; Illus., and designs in Helen Gardner's "Art Through the Ages." *Position*: Prof., Hist. A., Sch. of the AIC, Chicago, Ill., 1926- .

BLACKSTONE, ROZSIKA B.—Craftsman, P., Des.

412 East 84th St., New York 28, N.Y.

B. Hungary. *Studied*: N.Y. Univ., with Elizabeth Buris Meyer; BMSch A., with Ka Kwong Hui, Rolf Key-Oberg. *Member*: Artist-Craftsmen of New York; Am. Craftsmen's Council; BMSch A. Alumni. *Exhibited*: Museum of Natural History; BM; Cooper Union Mus. *Work*: in private collections.

BLACKWOOD, GLADYS ROURKE—Illustrator, Port. P.

Westwood Lane, Freeport, Ill.

B. Sterling, Ill., April 13, 1904. *Studied*: AIC. Illus., "Auno and Tauno," 1940; "The Cocoa Dancer," 1945; "The Eskimo Store," 1948; Author, I., "Whistle for Cindy," 1952. Diorama of Lincoln-Douglas Debate on permanent exh., Freeport Hist. Soc.

BLAGDEN, THOMAS P.—Painter, T.

Lime Rock Rd., Lakeville, Conn.

B. Chester, Pa., Mar. 29, 1911. *Studied*: Yale Col., B.A.; PAFA. *Member*: Conn. WC Soc. *Awards*: prizes, Conn. WC Soc.; Berkshire AA. *Work*: Albany Inst. Hist. & Art;

Wadsworth Atheneum; Berkshire Mus.; Amherst Col.; Univ. Georgia. *Exhibited*: CGA, 1937, 1941; PAFA, 1938, 1940; Albany Inst. Hist. & A., 1939-1955; Conn. WC Soc., 1940-1958; MMA, 1950; one-man: Berkshire Mus., 1950, 1958; Milch Gal., 1951, 1954, 1957.

BLAI, BORIS—Sculptor, E.

Beach & Penrose Aves.; h. Fourth & High Aves., Melrose Park, Philadelphia 26, Pa.

B. Rovnow, Russia, July 24, 1890. *Studied*: Kiev Imperial Acad. FA; Imperial Acad. FA, Leningrad; Ecole des Beaux-Arts, Paris, France; Apprentice to Auguste Rodin; Fla. Southern Col., D.F.A. *Member*: Phila. A. All.; PMA; Grand Central A. Gal. *Work*: Sculpture: PMA; Temple Univ.; Long Beach Island Fnd. A. & Sc.; Lessing Rosenwald Coll.; many portrait commissions; Samuel Fels medal, 1957; Sheerr Mem., Beth Sholom Center, Elkins Park, Pa.; Assoc. with R. Tait McKenzie in work for Canadian Mem., Edinburgh, Scotland and statue of General Wolfe, London; statue of Gen. Meade, New Jersey State Park; statue of Johnny Ring, Temple Univ. *Exhibited*: PAFA, 1924, 1925; Intl. Sculpture Exh., PMA, 1949; Detroit Inst. A., 1934; one-man: Grand Central A. Gal., 1934; Phila. A. All.; Woodmere A. Gal.; AIC; Long Beach Fnd. Contributor to American Magazine; Reader's Digest. Lectures, demonstrations on portrait sculpture, art education, etc. *Positions*: Hd. A. Dept., Oak Lane Sch., 1927-35; Fndr. & Dean, Tyler Sch. FA, Temple Univ., 1935- ; Fndr. & Vice-Pres., Long Beach Island Fnd. for A. & Sc., 1948- .

BLAIN, J(ULIA)—Teacher, P., C., L.

Ship Bottom, N.J.

B. Ozark, Mo., June 3, 1893. *Studied*: Drury Col.; & with Charles Cagle, Omar Lassonde, Antonio Cortizas. *Member*: SSAL. *Exhibited*: SSAL, 1934; Springfield Mus. A. Lectures: Modern Art. *Position*: In charge of Art Classes & Exhibitions, Springfield (Mo.) Art Museum 1944-45.

BLAINE, NELL—Painter, Gr., Des., Comm., T.

153 West 21st St., New York 11, N.Y.

B. Richmond, Va., July 10, 1922. *Studied*: Richmond Professional Inst.; Richmond Sch. A., and with Hans Hofmann. *Member*: Jane St. Group; Am. Abstract A.; F., Macdowell Colony & Yaddo Fnd. *Awards*: F. VMFA, 1943, 1946; Norfolk Mus. A., 1946. *Work*: 2 murals Revlon "Paris Room." Tishman Bldg., New York, N.Y. *Exhibited*: Pasadena AI, 1946; VMFA, 1944 (traveling exh., 1944-46); AIC, 1944; Am. Abstract A., 1945-1957; Art of this Century, 1945; Norfolk Mus. A., 1944-1946; Riverside Mus.; Am-British A. Gal.; traveling exh., sponsored by State Dept., in Paris, Rome, Munich, Copenhagen; Mus. Mod. A., Japan, 1955; Stable Gal., 1954, 1955; AIC; PAFA; MModA, 1956; WMAA, 1956; Spoleto, Italy, 1958 "Festival of 2 Worlds"; MModA (lending); one-man: Jane St. Gal., 1945, 1948; VMFA, 1947; Univ. So. Illinois, 1949; Tibor de Nagy Gal., 1953, 1954; Poindexter Gal., N.Y., 1956, 1958; 3-man: VMFA, 1955. *Book*: "Prints, Nell Blaine—Poems, Kenneth Koch," 1953. *Position*: A. Dir., United Jewish Appeal, 1950; Instr., Painting, Great Neck Pub. Sch., L.I., N.Y., 1956-57, Adult Program.

BLAIR, DOROTHY L(ILLIAN)—
Museum Curator, T., W., L.

University of Michigan Center for Japanese Studies, 363 Minamigata, Okayama City, Japan

B. Webster Groves, Mo., Sept. 10, 1890. *Studied*: Mount Holyoke Col., A.B.; Kyoto Imperial Acad., Japan; Univ. Michigan. *Member*: Soc. Japanese Studies, N.Y.; Japan Soc., London; Japan Soc., N.Y. *Awards*: F., Mount Holyoke Col., 1932, 1933; prize, Int. Essay Contest, conducted by Kokusai Bunka Shinkokai, Tokyo, 1940. *Author*: "Survey of East Asiatic Art in the Museums of Europe," 1937. Contributor to Museum Bulletins and art magazines. Lectures: Arts and Cultures of East Asiatic Countries. *Position*: Asst. Dir., John Herron AI, 1922-26, Asst. Cur., Oriental Art, Toledo (Ohio) Mus. A., 1928-50.*

BLAIR, LAWRENCE EDSON—Teacher, I., W.

University of Wisconsin; h. 605 Sheldon St., Madison 5, Wis.

B. Darlington, Wis., Nov. 17, 1892. *Studied*: AIC. *Work*: Galena Hist. Mus., Ill. Contributor to trade periodicals.

Exhibited: Univ. Cl., Madison, Wis., Northland Col., Ashland, Wis.; Kenosha A. Mus.; Mus. A., Ft. Atkinson, Wis.; Dubuque Pub. Lib.; Wisconsin Fair, Milwaukee; Woman's Cl., Des Moines. *Position*: Arch. Delineator, Wisconsin Hwy. Comm., 1939-1958 (retired).

BLAIR, LEE E.—Painter, Des.

245 West 55th St., New York, N.Y.; h. 110 Beach Rd., Great Neck, L.I., N.Y.

B. Los Angeles, Cal., Oct. 1, 1911. *Studied*: Chouinard AI, Los Angeles. *Member*: AWS; Artists & Writers Soc. *Awards*: prizes, Venice Film Festival, 1956 (best children's films); drawings, 1932 Olympics; Wm. Church Osborn purchase prize, 1946. *Work*: Cal. PLH; Los A. Mus. A.; Cal. WC Soc. *Position*: Motion Picture A. Dir. & Prod. Des., 1946-1958; Walt Disney Prod., 1936-1941; Film Graphics, Inc., at present.

BLAIR, PRESTON E.—Cartoonist, Des., P.

21 Taylor Place; h. 8 Dogwood Lane, Westport, Conn.

B. Los Angeles, Cal., Oct. 24, 1908. *Studied*: Los Angeles AI; Chouinard AI, Los Angeles. *Member*: AWS; Westport A. *Exhibited*: AWS; Laguna Beach AA; Cal. WC Soc. *Author*: "Advanced Animation," 1949. *Positions*: Disney Feature Animator, 1937-1941; Cartoon Dir., MGM, 1942-1947; TV Cartoon Producer, 1948- .

BLAIR, ROBERT N.—Painter, S., Gr., E., I.

R.D. #1, Olean Rd., Holland, N.Y.

B. Buffalo, N.Y., Aug. 12, 1912. *Studied*: BMFA Sch.; Buffalo AI. *Member*: Portland WC Soc.; El Paso AA; Baltimore WC Soc.; AWS; Buffalo Soc. A.; Alabama WC Soc.; Patteran Soc. *Awards*: prizes, Albright A. Gal., 1940, 1944, 1947, 1951; AIC, 1948; Buffalo Soc. A., 1951, 1954, 1955, 1956-1958; Alabama WC Soc., 1947; medal, Buffalo Soc. A., 1947, 1950; Guggenheim F., 1946, 1951; Butler AI, 1953; Baltimore WC Soc., 1953; Silvermine Gld. A., 1955, 1958. *Work*: MMA; Butler AI; Bryn Mawr AA; Ford Motor Co.; Munson-Williams-Proctor Inst.; Colgate Univ.; Dubuque AA; murals, chapel and hospital, Ft. McClellan, Ala.; Bethlehem Steel Co., Lackawanna. Book covers for "St. Lawrence Seaway"; "Under Three Flags." *Exhibited*: BM, 1939; AIC, 1942-1944, 1948; NCFA, 1942; MMA; Riverside Mus.; Albany Inst. Hist. & A., 1934-1946; BMA; Alabama WC Soc.; Albright A. Gal., 1942 (one-man); Buffalo Mus., Sch., 1942 (one-man); Alabama Polytechnic Inst., 1944; Univ. Alabama, 1944; Colgate Univ., 1939, 1941; one-man: Morton Gal., 1939-1941; Ferargil Gal., 1953; Buffalo, N.Y., 1937, 1938, 1945-1948, 1953, 1955. I.; "Captain and Mate," 1940 and other children's books. *Position*: Dir., Buffalo AI, 1946-49; Instr., Univ. Buffalo, Buffalo, N.Y.

BLAIR, STREETER—Painter

209 North Doheny Dr., Beverly Hills, Cal.

B. Cadmus, Kans., July 16, 1888. *Studied*: Univ. Kansas, A.B.; Univ. Chicago. *Member*: Laguna Beach A. Center. *Awards*: certif. of merit, Art News Annual; prizes, San Diego County Fair. *Exhibited*: Art News Annual, 1952; Portland, Me., 1951; William Rockhill Nelson Gal. A., 1951; Shierer Mus., 1951; Ross Mus., Newark, N.J., 1951; Smithsonian Inst. traveling exh., Europe, 1955, U.S.A., 1958-59; Los A. Mus. A., 1953; deYoung Mem. Mus., 1952; La Jolla A. Center, 1952; one-man: Univ. Kansas, 1951; Philbrook A. Mus., 1952; Carlebach Gal., 1950; Galerie St. Etienne, 1953-1954; Kansas State Col., 1958.

BLAIR, CAMILLE—Painter

209 North Doheny Dr., Beverly Hills, Cal.

B. Sabetha, Kans., 1894. *Exhibited*: Kansas State Col., Manhattan, Kans.; FA Gal., San Diego; New School Art, Los Angeles (one-man); Little Gal., Downers Grove, Ill., 1957; Clossen Gal., Cincinnati, Ohio, 1958.

BLAISDELL, ELINORE—Illustrator, T., W.

217 West 14th St., New York 11, N.Y.

B. Brooklyn, N.Y. *Studied*: ASL, and with Naum Los, Robert Brackman. *Member*: SI; A. Gld. *Awards*: Julia Ellsworth Ford Fnd. prize, 1939. *Author, I.*, "Falcon, Fly Back"; I., "Lamb's Tales from Shakespeare"; "Little Women"; "Child's Life of Jesus." *Position*: Staff Artist, Norcross Co., I., for Grolier Soc. and University Soc.*

BLAKE, LEO B.—*Painter, T., L., I.*
Blake Studios, Berkshire, Mass.

B. Galesburg, Ill., July 7, 1887. *Studied*: AIC; & with Alfred East, W. J. Reynolds, Birge Harrison. *Member*: SC; North Shore AA; Conn. Acad. FA; Grand Central A. Gal.; New Haven Paint & Clay Cl. *Awards*: New Haven Paint & Clay Cl., 1942; Conn. Acad. FA, 1939; SC, 1942; Mass. Fed. Women's Cl., 1943, 1944; Meriden A. & Crafts, 1952, 1958 (hon. mention); Jordan Marsh, Boston, 1957. *Work*: Rochester Inst. Tech.; Ill. Acad. FA; Foxhollow Sch.; Bavier Gal. *Exhibited*: AIC, 1910, 1911; Chicago SA; North Shore AA; SC; Syracuse Univ.; Conn. Acad. FA; Williams Col.; Berkshire Mus. A.; Springfield A. Lg.; Phila. A. All; Grand Central A. Gal.; Jordan Marsh Co., Boston, 1957; Meriden A. & Crafts Assn. (Conn.), 1957, 1958. *Position*: Instr. A., Berkshire Mus., Pittsfield, Mass.; Dir., Blake Studios Summer School.

BLAKE, MRS. WILLIAM HAROLD. See Stanton, Elizabeth Cady

BLANC, PETER (WILLIAM PETERS BLANC)—*Painter, E., W.*
161 West 75th St., New York, N.Y.

B. New York, N.Y., June 29, 1912. *Studied*: Harvard Univ., B.A.; St. John's Univ., L.L.B.; Corcoran Sch. A.; American Univ., M.A. *Member*: Spiral Group; AEA; A. Gld., Washington; Soc. Washington A. *Awards*: prizes, CGA, 1949; Soc. Wash. A., 1951; Wash. WC Cl., 1952. *Work*: VMFA. *Exhibited*: WMAA, 1952; CAM, 1951; Nebraska AA, 1951; Wash. WC Cl., 1949, 1951, 1952; CGA, 1948-1951; Riverside Mus., 1950, 1954, 1956, 1958; New Sch. for Social Research, 1950, 1951, 1953, 1955; Springfield Mus. A., 1952; Passedoit Gal., 1951, 1953 (one-man), 1958 (one-man); NCFA, 1953; BMA, 1953; BM, 1955; Colorado Springs FA Center, 1955; La Galeria Escondida, Taos, N.M., 1955 (one-man); Artists Gal., N.Y., 1957; Univ. Nebraska, 1958. *Position*: Instr., American Univ., Washington, D.C., 1950-53.

BLANCH, ARNOLD—*Painter, Gr., I., W., T., L., Des.*
c/o Associated American Artists, 711 Fifth Ave., New York 22, N.Y.; h. Woodstock, N.Y.

B. Mantorville, Minn., June 4, 1896. *Studied*: Minneapolis Sch. A.; ASL. *Member*: Woodstock AA. *Awards*: prizes, San F. A., 1931; Cal. PLH, 1931; Harris prize, Chicago, 1932; med., PAFA, 1938; Guggenheim F., 1933; med., Carnegie Inst., 1938; Domesday Press, 1945; Nat. Ceramic Exh., 1949, 1951. *Work*: WMAA, MMA; CMA; Colorado Springs FA Center; Cal. PLH; Cranbrook Acad. A.; Detroit Inst. A.; Univ. Nebraska; CAM; Denver A. Mus., Butler AI; Encyclopaedia Britannica; Univ. Arizona; PAFA; LC; BM; Carnegie Inst.; Gulf Coast FA Center, Clearwater, Fla.; Univ. Minnesota; murals, USPO, Fredonia N.Y.; Norwalk, Conn.; Columbus, Wis. *Exhibited*: CGA, 1931-1945; WMAA, 1931-1946, 1948-1952; PAFA, 1931-1945, 1948-1952; AIC, 1930-1943; GGE, 1939; WFNY, 1939; MModA; Carnegie Inst.; VMFA; MMA; LC, etc. *Author*: "Methods and Techniques for Gouache Painting," 1946; "The Creative Incentive," 1951, and other books; I., "The Humboldt River," 1943, and other books. *Position*: Instr., Cal., Sch. FA, 1930-31; ASL, 1935-39, summer, 1947-52, summer, Woodstock, N.Y., 1950-1958; Colorado Springs FA Center, 1939-41; Michigan State Univ., 1944; Gulf Coast A. Center, Clearwater, Fla., 1950-51; Ohio Univ., Summer School, 1952, 1956; Visiting Instr., Univ. Minnesota, 1949, 1952; Univ. Hawaii, 1955; Minneapolis A. Sch., 1954; Consultant, Rollins Col., 1950.

BLAND, GARNET WILLIAM—*Designer, P., I., Comm., Cart.*
635 East Elizabeth St., Detroit 1, Mich.

B. Manhattan, Kan., June 9, 1903. *Studied*: Kansas City AI; Wicker Sch. FA; Detroit, Mich.; Federal Sch. A., Minneapolis, Minn. *Member*: Am. Advertising A. & I. *Exhibited*: AIC; PAFA; Detroit Inst. A.; Soc. Indp. A.; MModA.

BLANK, J(OHN) PHILIP—*Designer, P., Cart.*
321 South Iseminger St., Philadelphia 7, Pa.; h. 809 Ridley Creek Dr., Media, R.D. 16, Pa.

B. Philadelphia, Pa., Apr. 8, 1916. *Studied*: PMSchIA; & with H. Clinton Beagary. *Member*: Phila. A. Dir. Cl.;

Phila. Pr. Cl.; Phila. A.All.; Fairmount Park AA; Woodmere A. Gal. *Exhibited*: PAFA, 1940, 1942; Ogunquit, Me., 1946; Cape May, N.J., 1944, 1945; Woodmere A. Gal., 1944-1946; Phila. A. Dir. Cl. *Position*: Asst. A. Dir., Gray & Rogers, Philadelphia, Pa., 1944-46; Freelance A. Dir., 1952- .*

BLANKE, MARIE E.—*Painter*
1718 North La Salle St., Chicago 14, Ill.

B. Chicago, Ill. *Studied*: AIC; Munich & London. *Member*: Chicago Galleries Assn.; Assn. Chicago P. & S.; Chicago AC; Women A. Salon, Chicago. *Awards*: Prize, AIC, 1920, 1922. *Work*: State Mus., Springfield, Ill. *Exhibited*: AIC; Chicago AC; Chicago Galleries Assn.; Women's Salon.

BLASINGHAM, KATHERINE GROH (Mrs. H. E.)—*Painter, T., L.*
2924 Kessler Blvd., East Dr., Indianapolis 20, Ind.

B. Logansport, Ind., Aug. 4, 1893. *Studied*: Indiana State T. Col.; John Herron AI, and with Carl Graf, Wayman Adams, Eliot O'Hara, Francis Chapin. *Member*: Nat. Soc. A. & Let.; Hoosier Salon; Indiana A. Cl.; Indiana Fed. A. Cl.; Brown County A. Gld. *Awards*: prizes, Canton AI, 1936, 1938; Indiana A. Cl., 1941, 1945; Swope Gal. A., 1950, 1954; Hoosier Salon, 1950. *Work*: Canton AI. *Exhibited*: Hoosier Salon; Indiana A. Cl.; John Herron AI; Canton AI; Swope Gal. A.; Butler AI. *Position*: Past Pres., Indiana Chapter, Nat. Soc. A. & Let.

BLASS, CHARLOTTE L.—*Painter*
183 Columbia Heights, Brooklyn 1, N.Y.

B. Orange, N.J., Apr. 21, 1908. *Studied*: NAD, with Charles Hawthorne; ASL, with George Luks. *Member*: McDowell Colony. *Work*: BM; U.S. Military Academy, West Point, N.Y.; T. Col., Columbia Univ., N.Y. *Exhibited*: NAD; AIC; PAFA; Toledo A. Mus.; AWCS; Provincetown AA; BM; New York, N.Y.; St. Thomas, Virgin Islands. *Position*: A. Dir., World Petroleum Magazine, New York, N.Y., at present.

BLATAS, ARBIT—*Painter*
50 West 56th St., New York 19, N.Y.

B. Kaunas, Lithuania, Nov. 19, 1908. *Studied*: Julian Acad., Grande Chaumiere, Paris. *Member*: Salon d'Automne; Fed. Mod. P. & S. *Work*: VMFA; Providence Mus. A.; BM; Wichita Mus. A.; MModA; WMAA; Carnegie Inst.; Newark Mus. A.; Musee de Grenoble, Musee de Jeune Paume, Mus. Mod. A., Paris; Govt. of France; Kaunas Mus.; Jerusalem Mus. A.; Tel-Aviv Mus.; MMA; Beaux Arts de Lausanne; Univ. Illinois; Delgado Mus. A.; Montclair A. Mus.; Reader's Digest and Abbott Colls. *Exhibited*: Salon d'Automne, 1935, 1939; WMAA, 1943-1946; Carnegie Inst., 1943-1945; Critic's Choice, N.Y., 1945; CGA, 1944; VMFA, 1943-1944; Providence Mus. A., 1944; R.I.Sch. Des.; N.Y. City Center, 1958; Hirschl Adler Gal., 1957; Dayton AI; Colo. Springs FA Center; Santa Barbara Mus. A., Portland A. Mus.; Galerie Elysee, Paris, 1945, 1946 (one-man), 1954; Galerie Vallonton-Mouradian, Paris, 1953; Cushman Gal., Houston, Tex., 1956-1958 (one-man); Assoc. Am. A., annually.

BLATT, LOUIS—*Painter, T.*
6309 Strickland Ave., Brooklyn 34, N.Y.

B. Russia, Sept. 24, 1911. *Studied*: NAD; ASL; N.Y. Univ., B.S. in Edu. *Exhibited*: Vendome Gal. (one-man); ACA Gal.; BM; Roerich Mus. A.*

BLATTNER, ROBERT HENRY—*Designer, I., T., P., W., L.*
230 Park Ave., New York, N.Y.; h. Loch Lane, Port Chester, N.Y.

B. Lynn, Mass., Dec. 8, 1906. *Studied*: Mass. Sch. A., B.S. in Edu. *Member*: AIGA; A. Dir. Cl.; SI. I.; Christian Science Monitor, Reader's Digest. *Lectures*: Design; Advertising Illustration. *Position*: A. Dir., Marschalk & Pratt, 1944-45; A. Dir., Domestic Edition, Reader's Digest, 1945- .

BLATTNER, ROSE—*Painter, T., Des., W.*
22 East 29th St., New York 16, N.Y.

B. Pittsburgh, Pa., Mar. 29, 1900. *Studied*: ASL, with Benton, Robinson; & with Leger, Hans Hofmann. *Mem-*

ber: Com. A. Edu., N.Y. *Awards*: medal, BAID, 1934. *Exhibited*: Soc. Women P., 1942, 1943; Am.-British A. Center, 1940, 1942; Lilienfeld Gal., 1943, 1944 (one-man).*

BLAUSTEIN, ALFRED—*Painter, Gr.*
603 Sixth Ave., New York 11, N.Y.

B. New York, N.Y., Jan. 23, 1924. *Studied*: CUASch.; Skowhegan Sch. A. *Awards*: Prizes, Patteran prize, Buffalo, N.Y., 1950; Cortland prize, New York, 1951; Prix de Rome, 1954-1957; LC, 1956; Guggenheim F., 1958; Am. Acad. A. & Lets., 1958. *Work*: WMAA; Everhart Mus., Scranton, Pa.; LC. Mural, South Solon Meeting House, South Solon, Me.; commissioned: drawings of African Life, 1948-1949. *Exhibited*: VMFA, 1948; MMA, 1950; PAFA, 1951; Albright A. Gal., 1952; WMAA, 1953, 1957; Carnegie Inst., 1952; Butler Inst. Am. A., 1952; Univ. Illinois, 1957; AFA "Art in America," 1958; LC, 1956; Acad. A. & Lets., 1957; BM, 1957; Buffalo, N.Y., 1950, 1951, 1952; N.Y. State Fair, Syracuse, 1951; Cortland State Fair, 1951; Downtown Gal., 1956; Am. Acad. in Rome, Italy, 1955-1957. Contributor to The Reporter, Spectrum, Natural History Magazine. *Position*: Instr., Des., Drawing & Painting, Albright A.Sch., Buffalo, N.Y.; CUASch., N.Y.; Yale Summer A. Sch., Norfolk, Conn.

BLAZEY, LAWRENCE—*Designer, C., P., L.*
537 Juneway Dr., Bay Village, Ohio

B. Cleveland, Ohio, Apr. 6, 1902. *Studied*: Cleveland Inst. A.; Univ. London; Slade Sch. A.; Cranbrook Acad. A. *Member*: Cleveland Soc. A.; IDI. Awards: prizes, CMA, 1935, 1946. *Work*: CMA; Mansfield (Ohio) Mus. A. *Exhibited*: PAFA; AIC; CMA, thru 1957; Syracuse Mus. FA; Nat. Ceramic Traveling Exh., 1954. Lectures: Ceramics; Indst. & Arch. Des. *Position*: Indst. & Arch. Des. & Product Development Engineer.

BLEY, ELSA W.—*Painter, T.*
West Rd., Dorset, Vt.; w. 75 Central Park West & 15 W. 67th St., New York 23, N.Y.

B. New York, N.Y., Mar. 10, 1903. *Studied*: ASL; Grand Central Sch. A., and with George Luks, George Pearse Ennis, Wayman Adams, Henry B. Snell. *Member*: Southern Vt. A.; Scarsdale AA; NAWA. *Awards*: med., Sch. A. Lg., 1919; Scarsdale AA, 1936, 1938, 1944, 1945. *Exhibited*: Wash. WC Cl., 1936; AWS, 1931, 1937; Montross Gal., 1933-1942; Scarsdale AA, 1931-1946; NAC, 1936-1939; Southern Vt. A., 1938-1958; NAWA, 1948-1958; Bronxville Pub. Lib., 1956; Stedelijke Mus., Amsterdam, 1956; 3 nat. traveling exhs., and in Canada, 1953-1955; traveling exh., Belgium & Switzerland, 1956-57. *Position*: Founder, Dir., Scarsdale A. Gld., 1934-45; Instr., Southern Vt. A. Center, 1951-1958; Garden City Community Cl., 1957-58.

BLISS, ALMA HIRSIG (Mrs.)—*Painter*
322 East 126th St., New York 35, N.Y.

B. Berne, Switzerland. *Studied*: with Willard Metcalf, B.F.A.; N.Y. Univ. Inst. FA, M.A.; Harvard Univ.; Douglas Volk. *Member*: ASMP; NAWA. *Awards*: prizes, Pa. Soc. Min. P., 1931; ASMP, 1932; NAWA, 1932, 1937, 1941; Cal. Soc. Min. P., 1938. *Work*: CGA; PMA; BM; Norfolk Mus. A.; murals, Wilbraham Acad., Mass. *Exhibited*: NAWA; Cal. Soc. Min. P.; ASMP; PA, Soc. Min. P.*

BLOCH, ALBERT—*Painter, W., L., E., Gr., Cr.*
Lawrence, Kans.

B. St. Louis, Mo., Aug. 2, 1882. *Studied*: St. Louis Sch. FA; Washington Univ., and in New York and Europe. *Work*: PC; AIC; Columbus Gal. FA; Yale Univ.; Univ. Kansas; Kansas State Col.; Baker Univ. *Exhibited*: Cologne, Berlin, Germany; Chicago Worlds Fair; WFNY 1939; one-man: Chicago, St. Louis, New York, Germany, Switzerland, Sweden; retrospective—Univ. Kansas A. Mus., 1955 (followed by wider tour of exh.). Contributor to periodicals in the U.S. and abroad. Lectures: History of Art. *Position*: Instr., Chicago Acad. FA; L., Dir., Dept. Painting, Sch. FA, Univ. Kansas, Prof. Emeritus.

BLOCH, E. MAURICE—*Educator, L., Mus. Cur., W., P.*
10840 Lindbrook Dr., Los Angeles 24, Cal.

B. New York, N.Y. *Studied*: N.Y. Univ. B.F.A.; N.Y. Univ. Inst. FA, M.A., Ph.D.; Harvard Univ.; NAD, with

Gifford Beal, Charles C. Curran; ASL; with Robert Brackman. *Member*: Am. Assn. Univ. Prof.; CAA; Am. Assn. Mus.; Am. Studies Assn.; State Hist. Soc. of Missouri. *Awards*: F., N.Y.Univ., 1944, 1945, 1947; C.R.B. Fellowship, Belgium, 1951; prizes, N.Y. Univ., 1937, 1938. Contributor to art magazines. *Position*: Instr., Univ. Missouri, 1943-44; L., N.Y.Univ., 1945-46, Univ. Minnesota, 1946-47; Asst. Prof., Keeper Drawings & Prints, The Cooper Union Museum, New York, N.Y., 1949-1955; Asst. Prof., Cur. Drawings & Prints, Univ. California, Los Angeles, Cal.

BLOCH, JULIA (Mrs. Gustav Straus)
Printmaker, I., P., W.
501 East Gorgas Lane, Philadelphia 19, Pa.

B. Philadelphia, Pa., Dec. 2, 1903. *Studied*: Phila.Sch. Des. for Women; PAFA; PMSchIA. *Work*: Carnegie Inst. *Exhibited*: PAFA, 1932-1936; Lib.Cong., 1943-1945; Carnegie Inst., 1943-1945; Phila. Pr. Cl., 1935-1941; Albright A. Gal., 1940-1943; Oakland A. Gal., 1936, 1939, 1940; Wichita, Kan., 1936; Phila. A. All., 1934, 1939, 1943. I., "Matilda, the Old-Fashioned Hen," 1936. Contributor to: "Philadelphia Inquirer."*

BLOCH, JULIUS (T.)—*Painter*
10 South 18th St.; h. 6445 North 16th St., Philadelphia, 26, Pa.

B. Kehl, Germany, May 12, 1888. *Studied*: PAFA; PM SchIA. *Member*: Phila. Pr. Cl.; Phila. A. All.; AFA. *Awards*: Prizes, Wanamaker Exh., 1934; WMA, 1933, 1934; Phila. Pr. Cl., 1933; Phila. A. All., 1929. *Work*: MMA; WMAA; PMA; PAFA; CGA; White House, Wash., D.C. *Exhibited*: CGA, 1935; PAFA; WMAA; AIC; Carnegie Inst. *Position*: Instr., Painting, PAFA, Philadelphia, Pa.

BLOCK, ADOLPH—*Sculptor*
400 West 23rd St.; h. 319 West 18th St., New York 11, N.Y.

B. New York, N.Y., Jan. 29, 1906. *Studied*: BAID; Fontainebleau, France, and with Hermon MacNeil, Sterling Calder. *Member*: ANA; F., NSS; All. A. Am.; Arch. Lg.; Fontainebleau Alumni Assn. *Awards*: prizes, BAID (Paris prize), 1927; F., Fontainebleau, 1927; F. Tiffany Fnd., 1926; Fontainebleau Alumni Assn., 1932, 1934, 1938; medal, BAID, 1926; Hon. men., Arch. Lg., 1955, 1956; prize, All. A. Am., 1956, gold med., 1958; NSS, 1958. *Work*: Morris, Bryant H.S., New York; Bayonne (N.J.) Pub. Lib.; Queens Vocational H.S., N.Y.; Beth-El Hospital, Brooklyn, N.Y.; port. busts & medal des., Am. Chemical Soc.; Am. Tel. & Tel. Co.; Am. Inst. of Physics; panels for Nat. Shrine of the Immaculate Conception, Wash., D.C. *Exhibited*: NAD; PAFA; Arch. Lg.; NSS; WMAA; NAC; Argent Gal.; French & Co.; SC; All. A. Am.; Jewish Mus.; religious sculpture: Barbizon Plaza Hotel, N.Y. *Positions*: Vice-Pres., 1958, Chm. Jury of Selection, 1958, All. A. Am.; Rec.-Sec., 1953-1955, Sec., 1956-58, NSS; Ed., Nat. Sculpture Review, 1958; Dir., FA Fed. of New York, 1954-59; Delegate to FA Fed., 1954-60; NSS Delegate, Intl. Council of Plastic Arts, 1958- ; Chm. Memb. Comm., NSS, 1956-58; Memb. Comm. on Awards & Scholarships, Arch. Lg., N.Y., 1958- .

BLOCK, DOROTHY—*Painter, Lith.*
8 Barrow St., New York 14, N.Y.

B. Brooklyn, N.Y. *Studied*: ASL, and with William von Schlegell. *Member*: AEA; Brooklyn Soc. A. *Work*: in several private coll. *Exhibited*: BM, 1952; ACA Gal., 1947; WMAA, 1951; Am-British A. Center; Norlyst Gal., 1949 (one-man); Bordighera, Italy, 1955; Montana Mus. A., 1955; 6th one-man, RoKo Gal., 1958.

BLOCK, JULIAN—*Illustrator, P.*
1 Eve Lane, Rye, N.Y.

B. New York, N.Y., Mar. 8, 1923. *Studied*: ASL; BM Sch. A. *Member*: SI. Illus. in Collier's, True, Argosy, Reader's Digest, Blue Book (covers), and other publications. *Exhibited*: Audubon A., 1958; City Center, N.Y., 1958; Silvermine Gld. A., 1958.

BLOCK, LOU—*Painter, T., I., W., L.*
10 Keller Court, Louisville 8, Ky.

B. New York, N.Y., July 11, 1895. *Studied*: NAD; ASL; and in Europe. *Awards*: purchase prize, Kentucky & So.

Indiana annual, 1952; Evansville Regional exh., 1957, others in local exhs. *Work*: Univ. Louisville; murals in homes, hotels, steamships; Rikers Island, N.Y. (in collaboration with Ben Shahn). *Exhibited*: Evansville, Ind., 1954, 1955; Louisville A. Center, 1952-1958; BM, 1948; Provincetown AA, 1958. Author, I., to H.S. Journal; N.Y. Times; Herald Tribune; Fortune; Harpers; New Republic; Louisville Courier-Journal and others. Lectures: Contemporary Painting; Domestic Crafts; Creative Photography. *Position*: Dir., Mural Div., WPA, 1935-37; Dir., Index of Am. Design, 1937-39; Adv., A. & Crafts, Nat. Youth Admin., 1939-40; Manual Arts Branch, Special Services, Dept. of Army, 1945-46; Instr., Painting, mural painting, Univ. Louisville, Ky.

BLOCK, MAURICE—*Director of Restoration*

Baldwin Casino & Carriage House, Los Angeles State & County Arboretum, 301 North Baldwin Ave., Arcadia, Cal.; h. 625 Westgate St., Pasadena 3, Cal.

B. Galion, Ohio. *Studied*: Cincinnati A. Acad.; AIC; Univ. Chicago, Ph.B. Hon. Degree, D.F.A.; Univ. So. California. Author: "Francois Boucher and the Beauvais Tapestries." *Position*: Asst. Cur., AIC, 1910-20; Dir. & Omaha AI, 1920-26; Cur. A. Coll., Huntington Lib. & A. Gal., San Marino, Cal., 1928-49; Dir., Restoration, as above, 1951- .

BLODGETT, EDMUND WALTON—*Painter*

R.F.D. 2, Stowe, Vt.

B. Cleveland, Ohio, Dec. 23, 1908. *Studied*: with George Luks, George Pearse Ennis. *Member*: AWCS; AEA; Audubon A. *Work*: Zanesville AI; Evansville (Ind.) Pub.Mus. I., Fortune, Scribner's, and other national magazines.*

BLONDHEIM, ADOLPHE (WIENER)—
Painter, Et., Lith., T.

Lahaska, Bucks County, Pa.

B. Baltimore, Md., Oct. 16, 1888. *Studied*: Maryland Inst.; PAFA. *Awards*: Med., NAD, 1918; AIC, 1920; prize, Chicago SE, 1920; med., Kansas City AI, 1926. *Work*: Cal. State Lib.; AIC; NGFA; Vanderpoel Coll.; mural, Missouri State Capitol. *Exhibited*: NAD, 1915, 1918; PAFA, 1919, 1941; CGA, 1921; Kansas City AI, 1926; Milch Gal., 1928; Nierendorf Gal., 1938.

BLOODWORTH, ALVIN HALE—*Cartoonist*

1838 South Euclid Ave., Ontario, Cal.

B. Biloxi, Miss., Oct. 29, 1918. *Studied*: Billy Hon Cartoon Sch., Los Angeles; Chaffey Col., Ontario, Cal. Cartoonist for all drawings in "The Lighter Side," 1952. Contributes to over 300 industrial, trade and professional magazines.

BLOOM, HYMAN—*Painter*

235 Beacon St., Boston, Mass.*

BLOS, MAY—*Illustrator, T., P., C.*

29 Live Oak Rd., Berkeley 5, Cal.

B. Sebastopol, Cal., May 1, 1906. *Studied*: Univ. California, A.B. *Exhibited*: Oakland A. Mus. *Position*: I., Botany & Zoology, Univ. California, 1944-1952. Illus. "Mammals of Nevada"; "Nicotiana," 1955; Cactus & Succulent Journal, 1953-58; Field Museum, 1956; Madroño, 1956.

BLOS, PETER W.—*Painter, C., T.*

29 Live Oak Rd., Berkeley 5, Cal.

B. Munich, Germany, Oct. 29, 1903. *Studied*: with Herman Groeber, Franz von Stuck, in Munich. *Member*: East Bay AA; Soc. Western A.; Oakland Mus. Assn. *Awards*: prize & medal, Oakland A. Mus., 1941, 1951; Western A., 1951; Los Angeles Festival award, 1952; Lafayette, Cal., 1955; popular choice, Soc. Western A., San F., 1955, 1956, 1957; Lodi Grape Festival, 1957, 1958; Jack London Festival, Oakland, 1957, 1958, and others. *Work*: NAD; mural, Calexico, Cal.; portraits throughout the U.S., and paintings in private coll. *Exhibited*: NAD, 1939; Cleveland (Critics Choice), 1945; GGE 1939; Oakland A. Mus., 1935-1946, 1948-1955; Los A. Mus. A., 1942; Univ. Cal., 1944; Springville, Utah, 1950-1955; Maryhill, Wash., 1952; Soc. Western A., 1950-1958; Frye Mus., Seattle, 1958; Claremont Hotel, Oakland, 1958. *Position*: Instr., Peninsula A. & Crafts, Burlingame, Cal., 1956- .

BLOWER, DAVID HARRISON—*Painter*

3504 Glenhurst Ave., Los Angeles 39, Cal.

B. Fontanet, Ind., Sept. 18, 1901. *Studied*: Wicker Sch. FA, Detroit, Mich.; Colorossi & Grande Chaumiere Acads., Paris, France. *Awards*: prizes, Detroit Inst. A., 1930, 1931; Hoosier Salon, 1948, 1949, 1952. *Work*: Sheldon Swope A. Gal., Terre Haute, Ind.; DePauw Univ. *Exhibited*: John Herron AI, 1949; Cal. State Fair, 1951, 1953; Detroit Inst. A., 1931, 1950, 1951; Los A. Mus. A., 1941, 1945, 1950; Hoosier Salon, 1954, 1955; one-man: Gordon Gals., Detroit, 1933; Swope A. Gal., 1957; Brand Lib., Glendale, Cal., 1957.

BLUM, ALEX A.—*Etcher, P.*

287 Rye Beach Ave., Rye, N.Y.

B. Budapest, Hungary, Feb. 7, 1889. *Studied*: NAD; Cincinnati A. Acad. *Awards*: prize, NAD, 1924. *Work*: MMA; LC; Yale Univ.; BMFA; Wesleyan Col.*

BLUMBERG, RON—*Painter, T.*

10930 Le Conte Ave.; h. 3175 Coolidge Ave., Los Angeles 66, Cal.

B. Reading, Pa., May 16, 1908. *Studied*: ASL; NAD; Academie Grande Chaumiere, Paris, France. *Member*: AEA; Cal. WC Soc.; Los A. AA. *Work*: Los A. Mus. A. *Awards*: prizes, Texas State Fair, 1934; Westwood AA, 1953, 1955; Cal. WC Soc., 1954; Los A. Mus. A. purchase prize, 1958. *Exhibited*: PAFA, 1936, 1937; San Bernardino, 1951, 1953-1955, 1956; Cal. State Fair, 1954, 1955, 1956; Los A. Mus. A., 1955-1958, and others. *Position*: Private instruction, 1951- .

BLUMBERG, YULI [Feiga Blumberg-Kopman]—
Painter, Lith., I.

77 West 104th St., New York 25, N.Y.

B. Kaunas, Lithuania, Sept. 4, 1894. *Studied*: in Europe. *Member*: AEA. *Work*: J.B. Neumann Gal.; Tel-Aviv Mus., Israel; PC; Butler Inst. Am. A., and in private coll. *Exhibited*: BM, 1929; Neumann Gal. (one-man); ACA Gal., 1946, one-man: 1948, 1949, 1951; Carnegie Inst., 1948, 1949; WMAA, 1955; Artists Gal., N.Y., 1958.

BLUME, PETER—*Painter*

Sherman, Conn.

B. Russia, Oct. 27, 1906. *Studied*: ASL; Edu. All. Sch. A., N.Y; Beaux-Arts. *Member*: ANA; Nat. Inst. A. & Let. *Awards*: Guggenheim F., 1932, 1936; prizes, Carnegie Inst., 1934; Grant, Nat. Inst. A & Let., 1947. *Work*: BMFA; Columbus Gal. FA; MModA; MMA; WMAA; PMA; Wadsworth Atheneum; Randolph-Macon Col.; Newark Mus. A.; Williams Col.; murals, USPO, Cannonsburg, Pa.; Rome, Georgia; Geneva, N.Y. *Exhibited*: BMFA; WMAA; MMA; MModA and many others.*

BLUMENSCHEIN, ERNEST LEONARD—*Painter, I.*

Taos, N.M.

B. Pittsburgh, Pa., May 26, 1874. *Studied*: CM; ASL; Julian Acad., Ecole des Beaux-Arts, Paris. *Member*: NA; AWS; Audubon A.; Taos AA. *Awards*: med., prizes, NAD, 1914, 1917, 1921, 1925; med., NAC; SC, 1935; med. and prize, AIC, 1917; Grand Central A. Sch.; PAFA, 1910. Hon. degree, M.F.A., Univ. New Mexico. *Work*: MModA; MMA; NAC; CM; Dayton AI; Toronto A. Gal.; BM; NCFA; John Herron AI; Los A. Mus. A.; PIASch.; Milwaukee AI; murals, Missouri Capitol; USPO, Walsenberg, Colo. *Exhibited*: NAD; CGA; Carnegie Inst.; AIC; PAFA; Univ. New Mexico; group and one-man exh., Canada, Europe, South America. I., for books and magazines.

BLUMENSCHEIN, HELEN GREENE—*Painter, I.*

Taos, N.M.

B. New York, N.Y., Nov. 21, 1909. *Member*: Bd., memb., Indiana A. Fund, Santa Fe, N.M. *Awards*: prizes, New Mexico and Arizona State Fairs; PBC. *Work*: N.Y. Pub. Lib.; LC; Newark Pub. Lib.; Carnegie Inst.; CM. *Exhibited*: WFNY 1939; Paris Salon, 1940; NAD, 1933-1946; LC; Carnegie Inst.; Rochester Mus. FA; Wichita Mus. A.; Kansas City, Denver, Santa Fe; Swope A. Gal., Terre Haute, Ind., 1958 (one-man). I., archaeological paintings and watercolors.

BLUMENTHAL, MARGARET M.—*Designer, T.*
    10 West 93rd St., New York 25, N.Y.

B. Latvia, Sept. 7, 1905. *Studied*: in Berlin, with B. Scherz, Bruno Paul. *Exhibited*: Monza, Italy, 1927; MMA, 1930; Pratt Inst. Gal., 1935. *Position*: Indst. & Textile Des., 1943- .

BOAL, SARA (METZNER)—*Painter, T.*
    40 Mount Tom Rd., New Rochelle, N.Y.; h. 246 Corona Ave., Pelham, N.Y.

B. Wheeling, W. Va., Jan. 10, 1896. *Studied*: Wellesley Col., B.A.; Cornell Univ.; T. Col., Columbia Univ., and with Carle Blenner, M. A. Rasko, Dmitri Romanovsky and others. *Member*: Fifty American Artists; NAC; Catherine Lorillard Wolfe A. Cl.; Hudson Valley AA; AAPL; Academic A. of Springfield, Mass.; F., Royal Soc. A., London. *Awards*: prizes, Hudson Valley AA, 1950; AAPL, 1951; Catherine L. Wolfe A. Cl., 1953; Manor Cl., Pelham, N.Y., 1955. *Work*: Starr Mus., Albion, Mich.; Wheeling, W. Va. Pub. Lib.; Barnesville (Ohio) Pub. Lib.; Barbizon Plaza Hotel, N.Y. *Exhibited*: All. A. Am.; Academic A. of Springfield; NAC; Ogunquit A. Center, 1948-1958; AAPL, 1948-1958; Nat. Lg. Am. Pen Women, 1953; Fifty Am. Artists, annually; Fed. Women's Cl. of Westchester County; Mt. Vernon A.; A. Gld., Long Island; Yonkers AA, and many one-man exhs. in U.S.

BOARDMAN, E. T.—*Asst. Museum Director*
    Rochester Museum of Arts & Sciences, 657 East Ave., Rochester 7, N.Y.*

BOARDMAN, NELL—*Painter*
    43 Fifth Ave., New York, N.Y.

B. Calendar, Iowa, Sept. 1, 1894. *Studied*: Iowa State T. Col.; Traphagen Sch. Des.; NAD, and with Victor Pirard, Ivan Olinsky, Alan Swisher. *Member*: Catherine L. Wolfe A. Cl.; Indst. Inst.; All. A. Am.; AAPL; Nat. Lg. Am. Pen Women, Wash. Square Bus. & Prof. Cl. *Awards*: prizes, Indst. Inst., 1947; Wolfe A. Cl., 1948; AAPL, 1955. *Work*: Fla. Southern Col. *Exhibited*: AAPL; Indst. Inst.; Fla. Southern Col., 1952; All. A. Am.; Wolfe A. Cl. *Position*: Chm., Pres., Wash. Square Outdoor Exh., 1947- ; 2nd Vice-Pres., Nat. & State Bds., AAPL; Chm. A. Com., Woman's Press Cl.; Bd. Member, Catherine L. Wolfe A. Cl.*

BOARDMAN, ROSINA COX—*Miniature Painter*
    R.F.D. #3, Huntington, N.Y.

B. New York, N.Y. *Studied*: ASL; N.Y. Sch. App. Des.; Chase Sch. A., with Alice Beckington, William Chase, Vincent Dumond and Luis Mora. *Member*: ASMP; Pa. Soc. Min. P.; NAWA. *Awards*: Boardman prize, N.Y.; Pa. Soc. Min. P., 1949; ASMP, 1952; NAWA, 1932, 1958; medal, Los A. Soc. Min. P.; BMFA, 1952. *Work*: MMA; BM; CAM; CGA; Fairmount Mus. A., Phila., Pa. *Exhibited*: PAFA, 1920-1946; ASMP, 1920-1951; NAWA, 1919-1954; Min. P., S., & Gravers Soc., Wash., D.C., 1946-1955; Cal. Soc. Min. P., 1947, 1949. Author, I., "Lilies and Orchids."

BOAZ, WILLIAM G.—*Teacher, S., P.*
    Murray State College; h. 1409½ Main St., Murray, Ky.

B. Hickory, Ky., July 6, 1926. *Studied*: Murray State College, with Clara Eagle, and others; Univ. Louisville, with Wilkie and Krause; Univ. Georgia, M.A. in Art Edu., with Lamar Dodd, Ferdinand Warren, Sibyl Browne; Hans Hofmann Sch. FA, Provincetown, Mass. *Member*: Southeastern Arts; Kentucky A. Edu. Assn.; AAUP. *Exhibited*: Louisville A. Center, 1952, 1956, 1957; H.C.E. Gal., Provincetown, 1956; Oxford, Miss., 1956-1957; Tri-State exh., Evansville, Ind., 1956-1958; Kentucky Wesleyan Annual, Owensboro, Ky., 1957-58. *Position*: A. Edu., Univ. Georgia, Athens, Ga.; Supv. A., Gainesville, Ga.; Asst. Prof., S. & A. Edu., Murray State College, Murray, Ky., at present.

BOBBITT, VERNON L.—*Painter, T.*
    Albion, Michigan

B. Pella, Iowa, July 27, 1911. *Studied*: State Univ. Iowa, B.F.A., M.A.; Denison Univ.; Columbia Univ. *Member*: Am. Assn. Univ. Prof.; Michigan A. Edu. Assn.; Midwest-

ern Col. AA; CAA. *Exhibited*: nationally. One-man Weyhe Gal., N.Y., 1956. *Position*: Chm., A. Dept., Albion Col., Albion, Mich., 1946- .

BOBBS, RUTH PRATT (Mrs. William C.)—
    Portrait Painter
    160 East 14th St., Indianapolis 2, Ind.

B. Indianapolis, Ind., Sept. 3, 1884. *Studied*: Julien Acad., Paris; Chase Sch. A.; ASL; BMFA Sch., and with Charles Hawthorne. *Member*: Indiana A. Cl.; NAWA; Hoosier Salon; John Herron Mus. A. *Awards*: prizes, John Herron AI; Hoosier Salon; Indiana A. Cl. *Work*: Indianapolis AI; ports. in private collections. *Exhibited*: Hoosier Salon, 1955 and prior.*

BOBLETER, LOWELL STANLEY—
    Painter, E., Gr., L., W.
    School of the Associated Arts; h. 2040 Berkeley Ave., St. Paul 5, Minn.

B. New Ulm, Minn., Dec. 24, 1902. *Studied*: St. Paul Gal. & Sch. A. *Member*: SAGA; Chicago SE; Am. Assn. Mus. Dir.; Am. Assn. Univ. Prof.; Minnesota AA; AFA. *Awards*: Prizes, Minneapolis State Fair, 1931, 1933, 1934, 1935, 1936, 1938; Minneapolis Inst. A., 1933, 1935-1937, 1939, 1940, 1942, 1943, 1945; Minneapolis Women's Cl., 1940, 1941; Prints chosen by Walker A. Center, St. Paul Gal. & Sch. A., Collectors of Am. A., for "Presentation Print Prizes." *Work*: Smithsonian Inst.; Cal. State Lib.; SAGA; Chicago SE; Parkersburg FA Center; Minneapolis Inst. A.; PAFA; N.Y. Pub. Lib.; Lib. Cong.; Walker A. Center; NGA; Flint AI; Hamline Univ.; Minn. Fed Women's Cl.; MMA. *Exhibited*: SAE, 1931-1946; Chicago SE; NAD; Lib. Cong.; PAFA; 50 Prints of the Year; 100 Best Prints; regularly in national and international exhs. Numerous one-man exhs., 1956-58. Lectures: Art History. *Position*: Pres., School of the Associated Arts, St. Paul 1, Minn., 1948- .

BOCCIA, EDWARD EUGENE—*Painter*
    106 Hart Ave., Webster Groves 19, Mo.

B. Newark, N.J., June 22, 1921. *Studied*: PIASch., ASL; Columbia Univ., B.S., M.A. *Awards*: prizes, St. Louis A. Gld., 1952, 1953; Harrison Morgan award, Topeka, Kans., 1953; CAM, 1954-1957; Morton May purchase prize, St. Louis, 1955; Metropolitan Church Fed., St. Louis, 1955; Kansas State College purchase prize, 1956; William Rockhill Nelson Gal. A. Kansas City, purchase prize, 1957. Italian Government Fellowship Award for research and painting in Italy, 1958-1959. *Work*: CAM; St. Louis A. Gld.; Metropolitan Church Federation, St. Louis; Kansas State College; Nelson Gal. A.; Joe & Emily Lowe Gal., Univ. Miami, Fla. *Exhibited*: Columbus (Ohio) Gal. FA, 1948-1950; Univ. Missouri, 1951; CAM, 1951-1958; St. Louis A. Gld., 1951-1955, 1958; Wm. Rockhill Nelson Gal. A., 1951, 1953, 1957, 1958; Mulvane A. Center, 1952, 1953, 1955; Joslyn A. Mus., 1952, 1956; Springfield A. Mus., 1952, 1956; Univ. Chicago, 1952; Beloit Col., 1953; Denver A. Mus., 1952; Concordia Theological Seminary, 1953; Washington Univ., St. Louis, 1953; Springfield AA, 1957; Contemp. A. Center, Cincinnati, Ohio, 1955; Brooks Mem. A. Gal., Memphis, 1956. *Position*: Dean, Columbus A. Sch., Columbus, Ohio, 1948-51; Asst. Dean, Sch. FA, 1951-54, Assoc. Prof. FA, Washington University, St. Louis, Mo., at present.

BOCCINI, MANUEL (FIORITO)—*Painter, S., Et., Lith.*
    349 East 62nd St., New York, N.Y.; h. 470 Midland Ave., Rye, N.Y.

B. Pieve di Teco, Italy, Sept. 10, 1890. *Studied*: Grande Chaumiere, Paris; ASL; Grand Central A. Sch.; & with André Favory, André Derain. *Exhibited*: Anderson Gal., 1927; Gal. Barrero, Paris, 1929, 1930; Salon d'Automne; Boccini Gal., N.Y., 1938; Soc. Indp. A.; Salons Am.

BOCK, VERA—*Illustrator, Des.*
    318 West 105th St., New York 25, N.Y.

B. St. Petersburg, Russia. *Studied*: in Europe. *Exhibited*: N.Y. Pub. Lib., 1942; Woodmere A. Gal., 1946; A. Dir. Cl., 1946; William Farnsworth Mus., Rockland, Me., 1952 (one-man), 1957. Illus., and designs books for leading publishers. I., Life, Coronet magazines.

BODIN, PAUL—*Painter*

210 West 82nd St., New York 24, N.Y.

B. New York, N.Y., Oct. 30, 1910. *Studied*: NAD; ASL, with Boardman Robinson. *Member*: Spiral Group. *Awards*: special distinction award, Art: USA, 1958. *Work*: Dallas AA; Univ. W. Va. *Exhibited*: Audubon A., 1954; MMA, 1952; BM, 1949; Phila. A. All., 1949; Santa Barbara Mus. A., 1949; Ohio Wesleyan Univ., 1949; Yale A. Gal., 1949; Grand Central A. Gal., 1946; Rose Fried Gal., 1958; Am. British A. Center, 1943-1945; Chas. Egan Gal., 1946; Parsons Gal., 1947, 1948; Argent Gal., 1950; Korman Gal., 1955; Spiral Group, 1951-1958; Springfield Mus. A., 1952; Univ. Maine, 1956; one-man: Playhouse Gal., 1936; Kohn Gal., 1937; Artists Gal., 1942; Laurel Gal., 1948, 1950; New Gallery, 1952.

BODKIN, SALLY GROSZ—*Sculptor*

10 Apple Tree Lane, Great Neck, L.I., N.Y.

B. Budapest, Hungary. *Studied*: ASL; Sc. Center, N.Y. *Member*: Sc. Center; NAWA; AEA; AAPL. *Awards*: NAWA, 1949. *Work*: in private collections. *Exhibited*: John Wanamaker, Great Neck, N.Y., 1954; Sc. Center, 1942 (one-man); major museums and galleries in U.S. *Position*: Instr., Great Neck, N.Y., Adult Edu., 1950-56. Teaching privately at present.

BOERNER, EDWARD A.—*Painter, E., S.*

2500 West Oklahoma Ave.; h. 2963 North Frederick Ave., Milwaukee 11, Wis.

B. Cedarburg, Wis., June 26, 1902. *Studied*: Univ. Wisconsin, with Varnum, Colt; Minneapolis Inst. A., with Cameron Booth; Univ. Iowa, M.A., with Grant Wood, L. D. Longman. *Member*: Wisconsin A. Edu. Assn.; Wisconsin P. & S.; Milwaukee A. T. Assn.; Wisconsin WC Soc.; Walrus Cl. *Exhibited*: Wisconsin P. & S.; All-Iowa Exh., 1940; AIC; Wisconsin All. A. Center traveling exh. *Position*: Hd. A. Dept., Rufus King H.S., Milwaukee, Wis.; Asst. Supv. A., Wisconsin State Fair.*

BOGART, STELLA MARSHALL (Mrs.)—*Painter*

48 Beacon St., Boston 8, Mass.

B. Terre Haute, Ind. *Studied*: with E. A. Vysekal; A.D. Gihon, Paris, France; Colorossi, Paris and Schachinger, Vienna. *Member*: AAPL. *Work*: Thomasboro, Ill.; Atlanta Univ., Atlanta, Ga.

BOGATAY, PAUL—*Educator, S., C.*

Ohio State University; h. 45 West Weisheimer Rd., Columbus 14, Ohio

B. Ava, Ohio, July 5, 1905. *Studied*: Cleveland Sch. A.; Ohio State Univ., with Arthur E. Baggs. *Member*: Columbus A. Lg.; Am. Ceramic Soc. *Awards*: F., Ohio State Univ., 1930-1933, Hon. Phi Beta Kappa; Tiffany Fnd. Scholarship, 1928-1930; Fulbright F., 1955; prizes, CMA, 1930, 1931; Syracuse Mus. FA, 1935, 1936, 1940, 1946, 1949; Columbus A. Lg., 1933, 1935, 1936, 1939-1941, 1943, 1946-1951; Nat. Dec. Arts, Wichita, Kansas, 1953 (purchase prize); Alfred F. Binns medal for ceramics; Ohio State Fair, 1957. *Work*: Columbus Gal. FA; IBM; Butler AI; Wichita, Kans.; Springfield, Mo.; Ball State T. Col. *Exhibited*: Syracuse Mus. FA; Phila. A. All.; WMAA; Toledo Mus. A.; AFA, Paris; CAD; Columbus A. Lg.; CMA; Butler AI, etc. *Position*: Prof. A., Ohio State Univ., Columbus, Ohio; Juror, Miami Nat. Ceramic Exh., 1958; Advisory Selection Comm. for A. & Architecture, Fulbright Program, 1958-59.

BOGDANOVICH, BORISLAV—*Painter, W. L.*

175 Riverside Dr., New York 24, N.Y.

B. Ruma, Yugoslavia, Apr. 3, 1899. *Studied*: Prague, and in Paris. *Member*: AEA. *Work*: WMA; Chicago, Ill. and in private colls. U.S. and abroad. *Exhibited*: AIC, 1941; WMAA, 1945; CGA, 1949, 1951; one-man: Van Dieman-Lilienfeld Gal., 1948, 1952.*

BOGGS, FRANKLIN—*Painter, I., Des., E.*

Beloit College; h. R.F.D. #3, Beloit, Wis.

B. Warsaw, Ind., July 25, 1914. *Studied*: Ft. Wayne A. Sch.; PAFA. *Awards*: Two Cresson Scholarships, Chas. Tappan award, PAFA; Gimbels Wisconsin A., prize, 1952; prize, Milwaukee Journal "Freedom of the Press" exh.; Fulbright research grant to Finland, 1958. *Work*:

Abbott Laboratories Coll.; U.S. War Dept.; USPO, Newton, Miss.; murals, A. S. Aloe Bldg., New Orleans, La.; Mayo Clinic, Rochester, Minn., 1953; Corral Restaurant, Beloit, Wis.; Meyer Assoc., Milwaukee; Merchants & Savings Bank, Janesville, Wis.; tryptich, Marquette Univ., Milwaukee, Wis., 1954. *Exhibited*: PAFA, 1939, 1950. Illus., "Men Without Guns." Army medical paintings reproduced in art magazines. Series of paintings for Trostel Tanneries, Brussels, exhibited nationally and published. *Position*: I., T.V.A., 1940-44; War Artist, 1944; Chm. A. Dept., Beloit Col., 1955- ; Artist-in-Residence, Beloit Col., 1945- .

BOHAN, R(UTH) H.—*Painter, Et., Lith.*

420 East Armour Blvd., Kansas City, Mo.

Awards: Med., Mid-Western Exh., Kansas City; prize, Terry AI, 1952. *Exhibited*: NAD; PAFA; CGA; VMFA; CAM; Oakland A. Gal.; Mid-Am. A., 1950; Miami, Fla., 1952. *Work*: Univ. Kansas Hospital; St. Luke's Hospital, Kansas City.*

BOHM, C. CURRY—*Painter, T.*

Nashville, Ind.

B. Nashville, Tenn., Oct. 19, 1894. *Studied*: AIC. *Member*: North Shore AA; Brown County A. Gld.; Indiana AC; Palette & Chisel Acad.; Hoosier Salon; Chicago Galleries Assn.; Rockport AA. *Awards*: prizes, Chicago Mun. A. Lg., 1931; Hoosier Salon, 1934, 1937, 1939, 1941, 1942, 1945, 1946, 1950, 1953-1955, 1957; Rockport AA, 1957; Brown County A. Gal.; Indiana AC, 1945; med., Palette & Chisel Acad. FA, 1931, gold med.; North Shore AA, 1951. *Work*: Chicago Pub. Sch. Coll.; Illinois State Mus.; Swope Gal. A.; Muncie AA; Indiana Univ.; Davenport Mun. A. Gal. *Exhibited*: GGE 1939 (representing State of Indiana, sponsored by IBM); AIC, annually.

BOHNERT, HENRY—*Painter, I., Comm., T.*

243 South Broadway, Hastings-on-Hudson, N.Y.

B. Cleveland, Ohio, May 19, 1890. *Studied*: Cleveland Sch. A. *Member*: Hudson Valley AA; All. A. Am.; AAPL; SI; NAC; Yonkers AA. *Position*: Bd. Dir., Hudson Valley AA, Chm. Exh. Com., NAC, New York, N.Y.*

BOHNERT, HERBERT—*Portrait Painter, T.*

243 South Broadway, Hastings-on-Hudson, N.Y.

B. Cleveland, Ohio. *Studied*: Cleveland Sch. A.; ASL. *Member*: SI; SC; NAC; All. A. Am.; AAPL; Hudson Valley AA; Yonkers AA. *Work*: Bruckner Mus.; Brookgreen Gardens; Hispanic Mus.; Govt. Bldg., of Cuba; Pan American Bldg., Wash., D.C.; White House, Wash., D.C.

BOHNERT, ROSETTA (Mrs. Herbert)—*Painter, W., T.*

243 South Broadway, Hastings-on-Hudson, N. Y.

B. Brockton, Mass. *Studied*: Univ. Rhode Island; Sch. App. Des., N.Y., and with Olaf Olesen, Maud Mason, Walter Farndon. *Member*: NAC; AAPL; Yonkers AA; All. A. Am.; Catherine Lorillard Wolfe A. Cl. *Work*: Bruckner Mus. *Awards*: prizes, Hudson Valley AA; NAC; Wolfe A. Cl., and others. *Exhibited*: traveling exh.; Studio A. Gld. *Position*: Columnist for Westchester Life "Art Notes."

BOHROD, AARON—*Painter*

432 Lorch St., Madison, Wis.

B. Chicago, Ill., Nov. 21, 1907. *Studied*: Crane Col., Chicago; AIC; ASL. *Member*: NA. *Awards*: prizes, AIC, 1933 (2), 1934 (2), 1935, 1937, 1945, 1947; GGE, 1939; Carnegie Inst., 1939; Cal. WC Soc., 1940; PAFA; MMA; CGA, 1943; Ill. State Fair, 1955; Old Northwest Territory Exh., 1954; Guggenheim F., 1936, 1937. *Work*: MMA; WMAA; AIC; BM; BMA; PAFA; CGA; Swope Gal. A.; Walker A. Center; Butler AI; Telfair Acad. A.; Cranbrook Acad. A.; Witte Mem. Mus.; Davenport AI; Springfield Mus. A.; Norton Gal. A.; Universities of Neb., Ariz., Ill., Ohio, Wis., Mo.; ceramics (with F. Carlton Ball) CMA; Detroit Inst. A.; Univ. Illinois; murals, USPO, Vandalia, Clinton, and Galesburg, Ill. *Position*: A.-in-Residence, So. Illinois Univ., 1941-42; A., War Correspondent, Life Magazine, 1942-45; A.-in-Residence, Univ. Wisconsin, 1948- ; Instr., Ohio Univ. (summer), 1949, 1954; Ball State T. Col. (summer), 1952; No. Michigan Col. (summer), 1953.*

BOIME, ALBERT I.—Cartoonist, Comm. A.
P.O. Box 173, Cooper Station, New York 3, N.Y.

B. St. Louis, Mo., Mar. 17, 1933. *Studied*: Los A. City Col.; Cal. Sch. A., and with Hendrik Greis, Richard Swift; Kahn AI; Cartoonists & Illus. Sch., with David Pascal. *Awards*: Cart. & Illus. Sch., 1952. Illus., "Good Times," 1953; "You've Got Me in a Hole," 1954; "The World We Live In," 1954; "Words Fail Me," 1954; "Best Cartoons of the Year," 1954, 1955; "You've Got Me and How," 1955; "Best Cartoons of Sports Illustrated," 1955; "Best Cartoons of Wall Street Journal," 1955; Fantastic, 1955. Contributor to: Sat. Eve. Post; Colliers; American magazine; Esquire; True; Los Angeles Examiner; Boy's Life; Civic Edu. Service, Wall Street Journal. Lectures: Cartooning—Its Functional Purpose. *Position*: Cart., Civic Edu. Service Publications, Washington, D.C.*

BOK, HANNES VAJN—Painter, I., Lith.
Box 137, Cathedral Station, New York 25, N.Y.; h. 116 West 109th St., New York 25, N. Y.

B. Kansas City, Mo. *Exhibited*: LC, 1945, 1946; Assoc. Am. A., 1943; Ferargil Gal., 1945. *Work*: in private collections in Los Angeles, San Francisco, Cal.; Chicago, Pekin, Ill.; River Edge, Paramus, N.J.; Denver, Colo.; Cincinnati, Ohio; New York, N.Y.; Philadelphia, Reading, Pa., and others. Illus., "Dwinkle the Dwarf," 1940; "Go South Young Man," 1946; "The Fox Woman," 1946; "The Black Wheel," 1947; "Lest Darkness Fall," 1948; "Seven Out of Time," 1949; "The Blind Spot," 1950; "The Spot of Life," 1950; "The Crystal Horde," 1951. Illus. in following magazines: Unknown Worlds; Fantasy Fiction; Mystic; Future Fiction; Planet Stories; Super Science; Science Fiction Quarterly; Short Stories, and many others.

BOLLAM, MRS. CATHERINE JONES.
See Jones, Catherine

BOLLIN, LEONE C(OBBUM) (Mrs. Leon E.)—
Painter, T.
1133 Mariana Ave., Coral Gables 34, Fla.

B. Bluffton, Ind., Dec. 8, 1893. *Studied*: Chicago Acad. FA; Am. Acad. A., Chicago. *Member*: Miami A. Lg.; Florida Fed. A.; Blue Dome Fellowship. *Awards*: prizes, Fla. Fed. A., 1940, 1943, 1945; Blue Dome Fellowship, 1951. *Position*: Instr., Associated Art Sch., Miami, Fla., 1940-45; Private Instr., 1945- .

BOLLING, LESLIE G(ARLAND)—Sculptor
509 North 5th St., Richmond 19, Va.

B. Dendron, Va., Sept. 16, 1898. *Studied*: Hampton Inst.; Virginia Union Univ.; & with William E. Young, Berkeley Williams. *Awards*: Prize, Sch. & Mechanic Magazine, 1942. *Work*: VMFA; Valentine Mus. A., Richmond, Va.; State T. Col., Indiana, Pa., 1950.*

BOLOTOWSKY, ILYA—Painter, T.
State University Teachers College; h. 128 Huguenot St., New Paltz, N.Y.

B. Petrograd, Russia, July 1, 1907. *Studied*: Col. St. Joseph, Constantinople, Turkey; NAD. *Member*: Am. Abstract A.; Fed. Mod. P. & S. *Awards*: prize, NAD, 1924-25, 1929-1930; Tiffany & Yaddo Fnd. scholarships, 1929, 1930, 1934; Guggenheim F., 1942; Univ. Wyoming Grad. Sch. Grant, for experimental and creative film work, 1953, 1954. *Work*: PMA; PMG; Guggenheim Mus.; WMAA; Munson-Williams-Proctor Inst.; Yale Univ. Gal. A.; Brandeis Univ.; Frederick Olsen Fnd.; Rock Springs (Wyo.) H.S.; Univ. Wyoming College of Agriculture; murals, Williamsburgh Housing Project; WFNY, 1939; Theodore Roosevelt H.S.; Hospital for Chronic Diseases, N.Y.; Phillips Steel Co., Pittsburgh, Pa. *Exhibited*: Carnegie Inst., 1946-1948; MModA; WMAA, 1938, 1950, 1952-1958; CGA, 1934; SFMA; Riverside Mus.; New Art Circle (one-man), 1946, 1952; Pinacotheca (one-man), 1947; Rose Fried Gal. (one-man), 1950; Grace Borgenicht Gal. (one-man), 1954, 1956, 1958; Realties Nouvelles Salon, Paris, 1947, 1949, 1952; Mus. Mod. A., Tokyo, Japan, 1955; Contemp. Am. Painting, Paris and other cities in France, 1956-57. *Position*: Actg. Hd., Dept. A., Black Mountain Col. (N.C.), 1946-48; Asst. Prof. A., 1948, Assoc. Prof. A., 1953, Univ. of

Wyoming, Laramie, Wyo. (On leave from Univ. Wyoming 1954-56; teaching Brooklyn Col. Dept. A., Brooklyn, N.Y.); Prof. A., State University of New York, State T. College, New Paltz, N.Y., 1957- . Ed. Comm., "World of Abstract Art," 1957.

BOLT, JOSEPH SULLIVAN—
Educator, P., Art Historian
313 Garland Hall, University of Alabama, University, Ala.; h. 5 Riverside Circle, Tuscaloosa, Ala.

B. Laurens, S.C., Jan. 18, 1921. *Studied*: Univ. Georgia, B.F.A., with Jean Charlot, Lamar Dodd; Univ. North Carolina, M.A. in Sociology and M.A. in Art History; Doctoral course work, Harvard Univ., 1952-53, 1955-57. *Member*: CAA; Southeastern College A. Conference. Author: article, "John B. Flannagan," Encyclopaedia Britannica. *Position*: Instr., Art History, Painting, 1949- , Actg. Hd., A. Dept., 1957-58, 1958-59, University of Alabama, University, Ala.

BOLTON, CLARENCE—Lithographer, P., Des.
P.O. Box 175, Woodstock, N.Y.

B. Wallingford, Conn., Sept. 16, 1893. *Studied*: Yale Sch. FA; & with John F. Carlson. *Member*: Woodstock Gld. Craftsmen; New Haven Paint & Clay Cl.; Conn. Acad. FA; Meriden A. & Crafts Soc.; SAGA. *Awards*: Prizes, A. All., 1929; Southern Pr. M.; Oklahoma A. Lg., 1939; New Haven Paint & Clay Cl., 1942. *Exhibited*: NAD; CGA; Phila. Pr. Cl.; Northwest Pr. M.; Woodstock AA; Albany Inst. Hist. & A.; San F. A. Center; Denver A. Mus.; LC; Portland Mus. A., 1958; Springfield Mus. FA, 1958.

BOLTON, MIMI DUBOIS—Painter, L.
3115 Quebec Pl., N.W., Washington 8, D.C.

B. Gravlotte, France, Dec. 12, 1902. *Studied*: Marquette Univ.; Corcoran Sch. A.; Phillips Mem. Gal., and with Richard Lahey, Karl Knaths. *Member*: Wash. Soc. A.; Wash. Gld. A.; NAWA. *Awards*: prizes, Wash. Soc. A., 1952 (2). *Work*: CGA. *Exhibited*: CGA, 1950, 1954, 1955, 1956 (one-man); Butler AI, 1951; BMA, 1952 (one-man), 1955; VMFA, 1950; Audubon A., 1954; New York City Center, 1954; Toledo Mus. A., 1956; BMFA, 1957; AFA traveling exh., 1956-57, and in local exhs., 1938-1958.

BOLTON, THEODORE—Writer, A. Historian
219 East 71st St., New York 21, N.Y.

B. Columbia, S.C., Jan. 12, 1889. *Studied*: Corcoran Sch. A.; PIASch., B.L.S.; N.Y. Univ., M.A.; Columbia Univ., M.F.A. *Member*: Am. Lib. Assn. *Exhibited*: Indp. A., 1917; AIGA, 1917; Brooklyn Soc. Et., 1917-20; Wash. WC Cl.; AWS, 1932, 1933. *Author*: "Early American Portrait Draughtsmen in Crayon," 1923; "American Book Illustrators," 1938; "Ezra Ames, Portrait Painter," (with I.F. Cortelyou), 1955. Translator and I., "Diane de Turgis" (Prosper Merrimee). Contributor of articles on American Art and Architecture to art magazines. *Position*: Librarian, Century Club, New York, N.Y.

BOMAR, BILL—Painter
Hotel Chelsea, 222 West 23rd St., New York, N.Y.*

BONAR, HENRY (H. G. BUETTNER-BONAR)—
Designer
22 West 48th St., New York 36, N.Y.; h. 266 Harrison St., Passaic, N.J.

B. Greiz-Thueringen, Sept. 18, 1896. *Studied*: Acad. Graphic A., Leipzig, Germany. *Member*: A. Gld. Lectures: Type Design; Lettering.

BOND, BYRON L.—Designer, P., Gr., I., Comm., Cart.
211 North 8th St., Richmond, Ind.

B. Richmond, Ind., May 8, 1906. *Studied*: Indiana Univ.; John Herron AI; ASL, with Randolph Coates; Earlham Col. *Exhibited*: Richmond AA; John Herron AI; Hoosier Salon. Des., "Leland Line" bookplates. *Position*: Adv. A., Leland Studios.*

BOND, GWEN(DOLINE) (MAPLESDEN) (Mrs. E. P.)—
Etcher, P., T., W., L., S.
c/o National Arts Club, 15 Gramercy Park, New York
3, N.Y.

B. India, Sept. 3, 1890. *Studied*: Columbia Univ., B.A.,
M.A.; N.Y. Univ., D.Edu.; N.Y. Sch. App. Des.; PAFA,
with Daniel Garber; ASL, with Dumond, Bridgman. *Member*: NAC; AFA. *Exhibited*: NAD, 1944; NAWA, 1946;
NAC; SAGA; N.Y. Soc. C. Lectures: History of Art.*

BOND, LEROY—Educator
Art Department, Oklahoma Baptist University, Shawnee,
Okla.
Position: Hd., Art Department, Oklahoma Baptist University, Shawnee.*

BONELLI, JAMES P.—Painter, Des., T.
832 North 63rd St., Philadelphia 31, Pa.

B. Philadelphia, Pa., Mar. 8, 1916. *Studied*: PAFA; Univ.
Pennsylvania, B.F.A., M.F.A., and with George Harding,
James Chapin, Earl Horter; Ctf. in Teacher Edu. for
Pennsylvania, 1957. *Member*: DaVinci All., Phila., Pa.
Awards: Cresson Traveling Scholarship, PAFA, 1939;
prize, DaVinci All., 1950, 1958. *Work*: Phila. Pub. Lib.;
murals, Wittenberg Col. Chapel, 1955; 34th Ward Cl.,
Phila., Pa.; Savings & Loan Assn., Uniontown, Pa.; paintings & drawings in private coll.; polychrome of reredos
(in collaboration with Louis Ewald), Christiana, Del.
Exhibited: All. A. Am., 1954; Norton Gal. A.; Soc. Four
A., Palm Beach, Cal.; PAFA; Phila. Pr. Cl.; Phila. A.
All.; Gimbels, Phila., Pa.; Phila. A. Festival, 1955; Woodmere A. Gal.; one-man: Lush Gal., Phila., Pa., 1955.
Position: Instr., Drexel Inst. Tech., Phila. Sketch Cl.,
Philadelphia, Pa.

BONGIORNO, LAURINE MACK (Mrs.)—Educator
19 North Park St., Oberlin, Ohio

B. Lima, Ohio, Apr. 17, 1903. *Studied*: Oberlin Col., A.B.;
Radcliffe Col., Ph.D. *Member*: CAA. Contributor to: College Art Bulletin. *Position*: Asst. Prof. A., 1930-42, Assoc.
Prof. A., Wellesley (Mass.) College, 1942-44; Lecturer in
Fine Arts, Oberlin College, 1956- ; Ed., Allen Mem. A.
Mus. "Bulletin," Oberlin, Ohio.

BONN, MARION—Sculptor, C., T.
27 North 3rd Ave., Mt. Vernon, N.Y.; h. McLain St.,
Mt. Kisco, N.Y.

B. Barbados, B.W.I., Apr. 30, 1890. *Studied*: Alfred Univ.
and with Marion Fosdick, Charles Harder, Ruth Yates,
Albert Weems. *Member*: AEA; Silvermine Gld. A.; Knickerbocker A.; New Jersey P. & S.; Audubon A.; AWS; New
Rochelle AA; Mt. Vernon AA; Fed. Women's Cl.; Pen
& Brush Cl.; NAC. *Awards*: prizes, Mt. Vernon AA, 1952,
1953, 1955; New Rochelle AA, 1952, 1953, 1954; Westchester A. & Crafts Gld., 1952-1955; Rye Fed. Women's
Cl., 1954; Mamaroneck Fed. Women's Cl., 1954; Westchester Fed. Women's Cl., 1957; Jr. Lg.; Mt. Kisco, 1957;
Pleasantville Women's Cl., 1956; Honor Roll award,
AAPL, 1956; Contemp. A., Portchester, 1958; New Jersey
P. & S., 1954; Contemp. Cl., Portchester, 1954; Bedford
Hills Community House, 1955. *Work*: in private collections. *Exhibited*: Audubon A., 1952; New Jersey P. & S.,
1954, 1955; Conn. Acad. FA, 1955; Knickerbocker A.,
1955; NAC, 1953-1955; Silvermine Gld. A., 1950-1955; Pen
& Brush Cl., 1950-1955; New Rochelle AA; Mt. Vernon
AA; Westchester A. & Crafts; Hotel Gramatan, Bronxville,
N.Y. *Position*: Co-Chm., Pen & Brush Cl., 1953-54, Chm.,
1954-55.

BONNAR, JAMES KING—Painter, Des.
92 Bowers St.; h. 49 Judkins St., Newtonville 60, Mass.

B. North Adams, Mass., May 12, 1885. *Studied*: Mass.
Sch. A.; & with Joseph de Camp. *Member*: Rockport AA;
North Shore AA; Copley Soc., Boston. *Exhibited*: Rockport
AA, 1940-1946; North Shore AA, 1935-1946; SC at Bethel
Inn. *Work*: Murals, private homes and institutions.

BONSIB, LOUIS WILLIAM—Painter
Bonsib Advertising Agency, 927 South Harrison St.;
h. 4201 Taylor Rd., Ft. Wayne, Ind.

B. Vincennes, Ind., Mar. 10, 1892. *Studied*: Indiana Univ.,
A.B.; Vincennes Univ.; Univ. Illinois; Univ. Cincinnati.

Member: Indiana A. Cl.; Hoosier Salon; Ft. Wayne A.
Sch. & Mus. Assn.; "The Twenty" Club. *Work*: Indianapolis and Ft. Wayne Pub. Schs.; Veterans Hospital, Ft.
Wayne; Indiana Univ.; Hanover Univ.; Fed. Women's
Cl.; Gary (Ind.) Pub. Schs. *Exhibited*: Ogunquit AA, 1949,
1950; Tate Gal., Terre Haute; South Bend AA; Ft. Wayne
AA; Hoosier Salon (over 20 years); No. Indiana A. Salon;
Ft. Wayne Woman's Cl., and many one-man exhs. *Position*:
Pres., Bd. Dir., Ft. Wayne Art School & Museum Assn.,
1949- .

BOOG, CARLE MICHEL—Painter, I.
206 Parkville Ave., Brooklyn 30, N.Y.

B. Lucerne, Switzerland, June 27, 1877. *Studied*: ASL;
Ecole des Beaux-Arts, Paris; & with Leon Bonnat. *Member*:
SC; All. A. Am. *Work*: Mus. City of N.Y.; Univ. Nebraska; Hist. Mus., Bennington, Vt. *Exhibited*: NAD;
PAFA; CGA; Rochester Mem. A. Gal.; AWCS; All. A.
Am.; BM; Société des Artistes Francaise, Paris. I.,
"Leather Stocking Tales"; "How It Came About Stories";
& others.

BOOK, HARRY MARTIN—Painter
1963 Millersville Pike, Rt. 6, Lancaster, Pa.

B. Millersville, Pa., June 27, 1904. *Studied*: Pennsylvania
State. Col., A.B.; Columbia Univ., M.A. *Member*: Phila.
A. All. *Work*: T. Col., Millersville, Pa.; Pa. State Col.
dormitories; Lancaster Y.W.C.A.; Elizabethtown Col. Lib.;
Harrisburg Br., Insurance Co. of North America. *Exhibited*:
Argent Gal., 1939 (one-man); Phila. A. All., 1947 (one-man); annual one-man exh., Mt. Gretna, Pa. Paintings on
loan exh., at Lancaster County Historical Soc., Lancaster,
Pa., June 1, 1957- .

BOOKATZ, SAMUEL—Painter
2700 Que St., N.W., Washington, D.C.

B. Philadelphia, Pa., Oct. 3, 1910. *Studied*: John Huntington Inst., Cleveland, Ohio; Cleveland Sch. A.; BMFASch.;
Grande Chaumiere, Paris; Am. Acad. in Rome. *Member*:
NSMP. *Awards*: F., BMFASch.; prizes, CMA; Hallmark
award, 1949, 1952; CGA, 1952, 1953, 1955; Birmingham
Mus. A., 1956; Butler Inst. Am. A., 1958. *Work*: CGA;
PC; Barnet Aden Gal.; Smithsonian Inst.; CMA; Milwaukee
AI; LC; PAFA; Rochester Mus. A.; Birmingham Mus. A.;
murals & portraits, Navy Hospitals, Phila., Pa., Wash.,
D.C., Norfolk, Va.; Bethesda, Md. Work also in private
coll. & indst. firms. *Exhibited*: CGA, 1944, 1953-1955;
PAFA, 1953 and prior; CMA, 1930-1946; VMFA, 1940;
Univ. Illinois, 1953; Butler AI, 1955; BMA, 1955. *Position*:
Instr., Dir., Samuel Bookatz Sch. & Gal. A., Washington,
D.C.

BOOKBINDER, JACK—Painter, Lith., T., L., W.
323 South Smedley St., Philadelphia 3, Pa.

B. Odessa, Ukraine, Jan. 15, 1911. *Studied*: Univ. Pennsylvania, B.F.A. in Edu.; PAFA, with Henry McCarter,
Daniel Garber; Tyler Sch. FA, M.F.A., and European
study. *Member*: AEA; Phila. A. All.; Phila. WC Cl.;
Phila. Pr. Cl.; NAEA; Eastern AA; Pr. Council of Am.
Awards: F., Barnes Fnd., 1938, 1939; F., Pa. Sch. Social
Work, Univ. Pa., 1935-36; prizes, PAFA, 1947, 1952, 1953;
Tyler Sch. FA, 1950, 1951, 1955; Rochester Pr. Cl., 1948;
Phila. A. T. Assn., 1950; DaVinci All., 1949, silver med.,
1952; Pennell Mem. medal, Phila. WC Soc., 1957; F.,
Tyler Sch. FA, Temple Univ., 1958. *Work*: PAFA; LC;
PMA; Yale Univ.; Tyler Sch. FA; Woodmere A. Gal.; New
Britain Inst.; Lessing J. Rosenwald Coll. *Exhibited*: annually PAFA, 1944- ; annually Phila. A. All., 1948- ; LC,
1945, 1946, 1949, 1951; Phila. Pr. Cl., 1944-1953; DaVinci
All., 1944-1955; Woodmere A. Gal., annually 1944- ; CGA,
1945, 1951, 1953, 1957; Albany Inst. Hist. & A., 1945;
PMA, 1946, 1955; Assoc. Am. A., 1946; Pyramid Cl.,
Phila., Pa., annually 1947- ; SAM, 1947; Rochester Pr. Cl.,
1948; Carnegie Inst., 1949; Phila. Sketch Cl., 1949-1957;
BM, 1949; Phila. WC Cl., annually 1947- ; Contemporary
A. Assn., 1950, 1951; Tyler Sch. FA, annually 1947- ;
Butler AI, 1951, 1956, 1958; AWS, 1956; Traveling Art,
Inc., 1955, 1956, 1957. One-man: PAFA, 1953; Phila. A.
All., 1954; Woodmere A. Gal., 1955; Atlantic City, 1958;
Hager Gal., Lancaster, Pa., 1958. *Position*: L., Barnes Fnd.,
1936-44; Pa. State Col., 1950; Univ. Pa., 1947-1956; PAFA,
1949-1956; Consultant Edu. Div., PMA, 1944-45; Asst. to
Dir. A., Bd. Edu., Phila., Pa., 1945- ; Producer & Moderator of series of television programs on art over Philadelphia stations. Contributor to: Compton's Encyclopedia,

1955; American Artist magazine, AEA Journal, Nat. A. Edu. Assn. Yearbook, Eastern AA Research Bulletin, etc. Author booklets: "Invitation to the Arts," 1944; "The Gifted Child—His Education in the Philadelphia Public Schools"; "Art in the Life of Children," 1957.

BOOTH, CAMERON—*Painter, T.*

3408 47th Ave., South, Minneapolis 6, Minn.

B. Erie, Pa., Mar. 11, 1892. *Studied*: AIC; & with Hans Hofmann, Munich, Germany. *Awards*: Traveling scholarship, AIC, 1917; Guggenheim F., 1942, 1943; Hon. Degree, Dr. Humanities, Hamline Univ., 1949. *Work*: PAFA; Newark Mus.; Minneapolis Inst. A.; PMG; Denver A. Mus.; SFMA; MMA; AIC; Univ. Cal. Mus. A.; Univ. Minnesota. *Exhibited*: Carnegie Inst., 1923, 1924, 1928, 1930, 1943, 1944, 1946; AIC, 1923, 1924, 1931, 1934-1937, 1940, 1942-1944, 1946; PAFA, 1924, 1925, 1943-1946; deYoung Mem. Mus., San F., Cal., 1958 (one-man). *Position*: Instr., ASL, New York, N.Y., 1944-1948. L. Art. Univ. Minnesota, 1950- . Guest Prof. Painting, Univ. California, Berkeley, Cal., 1957-58.

BOOTH, ZADIE CORY—*Sculptor, P., T.*

Box 214, Rt. 4, Ft. Collins, Colo.

B. Crete, Neb., Dec. 7, 1905. *Studied*: Doane Col., A.B.; Univ. Nebraska; Univ. Colorado. *Member*: Am. Assn. Univ. Women; Ft. Collins A. Lg.; NEA. *Exhibited*: Univ. Nebraska, 1942-1951; Joslyn Mus. A., 1940-1951; Springfield (Mo.) A. Mus., 1950; Walker A. Center, 1951; William Rockhill Nelson Gal. A., 1950. *Award*: prize, Univ. Nebraska, 1951. *Position*: Chm., A. Dept., Doane Col., Neb., 1938-51; Instr. A., Lincoln Jr. H.S., Ft. Collins, Colo., 1953-1956.

BOPP, EMERY—*Educator, P.*

Bob Jones University, Greenville, S.C.; s. Hillsdale, Route 2, N.Y.

B. Corry, Pa., May 13, 1924. *Studied*: PIASch.; Yale Univ., Sch. Painting & Design, B.F.A.; N.Y. Univ. *Member*: Gld. South Carolina A. *Position*: Chm., Div. of Art, Bob Jones University, Greenville, S.C., 1955- .

BORATKO, ANDRE—*Painter, S., T.*

2001 Drake Drive, Oakland, Cal.

B. Austria-Hungary, Jan. 5, 1912. *Studied*: St. Paul. Sch. A.; Minneapolis Sch. A., and with Cameron Booth, Nicolai Cikovsky, Robert Brackman, Hans Hofmann. *Awards*: prizes, Minneapolis Inst. A., 1930-1935; Minnesota State Fair, 1931-1939; St. Paul AA, 1935; Lodi (Cal.) Festival, 1951; Sc. Western Hemisphere, 1942. *Work*: IBM; murals, Holy Trinity Church, Richmond, Cal.; Town Hall, Milaca, Minn.; Minnesota Sch. for the Deaf; sculpture, Am. Island Park, Chamberlain, S.D. *Exhibited*: AIC, 1931; SFMA, 1939; GGE, 1939; CGA, 1941, 1942; San F. WC Soc., 1946; Univ. Washington, 1946; Los A. County Fair, 1949; Cal. State Fair, 1949-51. *Position*: Asst. Prof., Cal. Col. A. & Crafts, Oakland, Cal., 1946-54.*

BORCHARDT, NORMAN—*Educator, I., P., Et., L.*

University of Tampa; h. 714 South Blvd., Tampa 6, Fla.

B. Brunswick, Ga., Jan. 21, 1891. *Studied*: AIC, with Norton, Vanderpoel; and with Henri. *Member*: Freelance A. Group, N.Y.; Florida Fed. A.; Tampa AI. *Work*: murals, Univ. Tampa, Fla.; in association with students other work is on display at Tampa Pub. Hospital; Tampa Children's Home; Hillsboro County Hospital, and other buildings and churches. Illus.; Scribner's Red Book, Spur, N.Y. Post, N.Y. Times, World Traveller, Sloan Fnd., McClain's and many others. *Position*: In charge A. Bldg., Florida State Fair, 1938-1953; Hd. Dept. A., Univ. of Tampa, Fla., 1934-1955.

BORGATTA, ISABEL CASE—*Sculptor*

320 Clinton Ave., Dobbs Ferry, N.Y.

B. Madison, Wis., Nov. 21, 1921. *Studied*: Smith Col.; Yale Univ. Sch. FA, B.F.A.; ASL, and with Jose de Creeft. *Member*: NAWA. *Awards*: prizes, Village A. Center, 1946; NAWA, 1952; sc. award, Village A. Center, 1951. *Work*: Wadsworth Atheneum, Hartford, Conn. *Exhibited*: PAFA, 1950-1952, 1954; WMAA, 1954; Audubon A., 1947-1958; NAD, 1949; NAWA, 1952, 1953; Riverside

Mus., 1949, 1950, 1953; Laurel Gal., 1949, 1950; RoKo Gal., 1947-1950; LaVista Gal., 1950; Van Loen Gal., 1950, 1951; Penthouse Gal., 1951; New Haven Paint & Clay Cl., 1943, 1944; Village A. Center, 1946, 1947, 1951; Silvermine Gld. A., 1954, 1955; New Jersey P. & S., 1945, 1947; one-man: Village A. Center, 1947; Peoria (Ill.) Pub. Lib., 1951; Galerie St. Etienne, 1954; Tyringham (Mass.) Gal., 1955. Article & repro. in Life, 1954. *Position*: L., Art Dept., City College of New York, at present.

BORGATTA, ROBERT E.—*Painter, E.*

320 Clinton Ave., Dobbs Ferry, N.Y.

B. Havana, Cuba, Jan. 11, 1921. *Studied*: NAD; N.Y. Univ. Sch. of Architecture & Allied Arts, B.F.A.; Yale Univ. Sch. FA, M.F.A.; N.Y. Univ. Inst. FA. *Member*: F., Intl. Inst. A. & Lets.; AWS; Nat. Soc. Painters in Casein; Brooklyn Soc. A. *Awards*: N.Y. Univ. Chancellor's F., 1939; Tiffany F., 1942; Emily Lowe award, 1957; Chautauqua AA, 1955; Silvermine Gld. A., 1954, 1956. *Work*: Ford Fnd. *Exhibited*: PAFA, 1957; WMAA, 1954; CGA, 1940; All. A. Am., 1946; Audubon A., 1953-1955, 1957; AWS, 1955, 1957; Nat. Soc. Painters in Casein, 1957, 1958; Schettini Gal., Milan, 1957; Associated Gal., Detroit, 1955, 1956; Los A. AA, 1952; Ft. Worth Mus. A., 1950; Riverside Mus., N.Y., 1956, 1958; Kaufman Gal., N.Y., 1955; RoKo Gal., N.Y., 1950; Weyhe Gal., 1945; Chautauqua AA, 1954; Ross Gal., White Plains, N.Y., 1957, 1958; New Sch. for Social Research, N.Y., 1957; one-man: Wellons Gal., 1954; Tyringham (Mass.) Gal., 1954, 1955; Peoria (Ill.) Pub. Lib., 1954. *Position*: Instr., City College of New York; Departmental Rep. at Baruch School, City College of New York.

BORGHI, GUIDO RINALDO—*Painter, S., T.*

117 Carroll St., City Island 64, N.Y.

B. Locarno, Switzerland, Mar. 29, 1903. *Studied*: Europe and New York. *Member*: Soc. Indp. A. *Awards*: prize, Yorktown Heights Exh., 1957. *Work*: mural, Lexington Sch. for Deaf & Dumb Children, N.Y.; Minadoka County Grange, Idaho; Adamo Restaurant, N.Y.; East River Savings Bank; Rockefeller Center Bank. *Exhibited*: CGA, 1939; NAD, 1940; Roerich Mus., 1936; Salon of America, 1934; Boise Mus. A., 1941; Soc. Indp. A., 1937; Mun. A. Gal., N.Y.; Contemporary A. Gal.; Heyburn AI (Idaho); Gramercy Gal.; Hudson (N.Y.) Pub. Lib.; Yonkers Mus. A.; Burr Gal., N.Y. *Position*: Tech. Dir., Hall of Art, 1943-45; Burr Gallery, New York, 1955- .

BORGSTEDT, DOUGLAS—*Cartoonist, W.*

Bryn Mawr, Pa.

B. Yonkers, N.Y., Jan. 3, 1911. *Studied*: Haverford Col.; PMSchIA. *Exhibited*: Berkshire Mus. A. (one-man); MMoMA, MMA traveling shows. I., Saturday Evening Post, Collier's, New Yorker, & newspapers. *Position*: A.Ed., Yank magazine, U.S. Army, 1942-45; Photography Ed., Saturday Evening Post, 1946- .*

BORNE, MORTIMER—*Etcher, P., S., E., W., L.*

107 South Broadway, Nyack, N.Y.

B. Rypin, Poland, Dec. 31, 1902. *Studied*: NAD; ASL; BAID, and with Hinton, Charles Hawthorne, F. Jones. *Member*: SAGA; Audubon A. *Awards*: prizes, SAGA, 1939, 1943. *Work*: LC; MMoMA; NGA; N.Y. Pub. Lib.; Syracuse Mus. FA; Rochester Mem. A. Gal.; N.J. State Mus.; Rosenwald Coll. *Exhibited*: AIC, 1931; AIGA, 1937; Sweden, 1937; WFNY, 1939; 100 Prints, 1940; MMA, 1942; MMoMA, 1940; Royal Soc. Painters, Etchers & Engravers, London, 1954; CGA, 1941 (one-man); Montreal Mus. FA, 1942 (one-man); N.Y. Pub. Lib. (one-man); Grand Central A. Gal., 1943 (one-man); Currier Gal. A., 1945; BM, 1950; Wichita AA, 1952; N.Y. State Fair, 1950, 1951; Carnegie Inst., 1947. Lectures: "Sources and Components of Modern Art." Contributor to: Symposium on Modern Art, 1952. Originator of "Color Drypoint"; "Chromatic Wood Sculpture."

BORONDA, BEONNE—*Animal Sculptor, T.*

P.O. Box 276, Mystic, Conn.

B. Monterey, Cal., May 23, 1911. *Studied*: ASL, with Arthur Lee. *Member*: NSS; Mystic AA; Conn. Acad. FA; All. A. Am. *Awards*: prizes, NAWA, 1938; N.J. Soc. P. & S., 1945, 1946; Pen & Brush Cl., 1945; Norwich AA, 1953; Silvermine Gld. A., 1955. *Exhibited*: Montclair A.

Mus., 1944; WMAA, 1940; Pen & Brush Cl., 1944, 1945; Conn. Acad. FA, 1933-1946, 1949-1951, 1953; PAFA, 1935-1945; NAD, 1935, 1937, 1941, 1944, 1945, 1948-1951; AIC, 1937, 1938, 1940; NAWA, 1932-1946, 1948; WFNY, 1939; MMA, 1942; Mystic AA, 1930-1945, 1948-1951, 1952-1955; Arch. Lg., 1941, 1944; AGAA, 1950; Norwich AA, 1949-1951, 1953; New Britain Inst. A., 1955; Silvermine Gld. A., 1955; Lyman Allyn Mus. A., 1955. *Position*: Instr. S., Montclair A. Mus., 1944-45; Keramic Soc., N.Y., 1953; private instruction, 1954- .*

BORST, GEORGE H.—*Sculptor*

125 Bloomingdale Ave., Wayne, Pa.

B. Philadelphia, Pa., Feb. 9, 1889. *Studied*: PAFA, with Charles Grafly; Julian Acad., Paris. *Awards*: Prizes, PAFA, 1927; F. PAFA; Cresson traveling scholarship, 1928. *Work*: Bronze mem., Acad. Music, Phila., Pa.; sculpture, Plymouth, Pasquaney, Onaway, N.H.; Wayne, Pa. *Exhibited*: PAFA, 1930-1946; NAD; NSS; Phila.A.All., 1937 (one-man); Un.Lg., Phila., 1953.

BORTIN, DORA (Mrs. Dora Bortin Goldberg)— *Painter, T.*

2101 Walnut St., Philadelphia 3, Pa.

B. Ukraine, Mar. 14, 1888. *Studied*: PAFA, and with James Kirk Merrick, Herman Block. *Member*: Phila. A. All.; DaVinci All.; AEA. *Awards*: PAFA, 1954. *Work*: private collections. *Exhibited*: Florida Nat. & International Exhs.; 4 one-man exhs., Phila., Pa.; many group exhs., Pennsylvania and New Jersey.

BORUM, LINWOOD C(LARKE)—*Marine Painter*

s. 84 Shore Rd., Ogunquit, Me.; h. 4809 Laurel Ave., Baltimore 15, Md.

B. Gwynn's, Va., May 20, 1898. *Studied*: Maryland Inst., with Henry Roben; Rockport, Mass., with Harry Ballinger, Emile Gruppe, Stanley Woodward. *Member*: AAPL. *Awards*: Med., Maryland Inst., 1938; prizes, SAM, 1944; NAD, 1945. *Work*: San F. Mus. Sc. & Indst., and in private colls. in U.S., Canada, and abroad. *Exhibited*: SAM, 1944; Los A. Mus. A., 1944; Milwaukee AI, 1944, 1945; Norfolk Mus. A. & Sc., 1944; CGA, 1944; Newark Mus., 1945; BMA, 1945; NAD, 1945; Syracuse Mus. FA, 1945; Buffalo AI, 1945; William Rockhill Nelson Gal., 1945; Speed Mem. Mus., 1945; Atlanta AA, 1945; Morton Gal., 1943; AAPL, 1938; traveling ex., Merchant Seamen of United Nations, 1943-1946.

BORZEMSKY, BOHDAN—*Painter*

211 Oakdene Ave., Teaneck, N.J.

B. Kolomyja, Ukraine, July 7, 1923. *Studied*: CUASch., and in Europe. *Awards*: CUASch., 1949, 1951. *Exhibited*: NAC; LC; Cooper Union; Contemp. A.; one-man: Panoras Gal., N.Y.; Ukrainian National Home; Ukrainian Art Club.

BOSA, LOUIS—*Painter, T.*

1886 East 97th St., Cleveland 6, Ohio

B. Cordoipo, Italy, Apr. 2, 1905. *Studied*: ASL, with John Sloan, and in Italy. *Member*: NA; AEA; Audubon A.; ASL. *Awards*: prizes, Wanamaker, 1938; Pepsi-Cola, 1944, 1945, 1948; NAD, 1945; Rockport AA, 1945; Acad. A. & Lets., 1948; Los A. County Fair, 1948; Univ. Illinois (purchase), 1949; Audubon A., 1951, medal, 1949; Hallmark awards, 1949, 1955, 1957. *Work*: PAFA; Clearwater (Fla.) Mus. A.; Kansas City AI; Wilmington A. Center; Springfield (Mass.) Mus. A.; Pepsi-Cola Coll.; Carnegie Inst.; Encyclopaedia Britannica Coll.; U.S. State Dept.; IBM; WMAA; WMA; Montclair A. Mus.; MMA; VMFA, and many others. *Exhibited*: MMA; MModA; WMAA; Carnegie Inst.; CGA; PMA; BMFA; Toledo Mus. A.; Springfield Mus. A.; Kansas City AI; Delgado Mus. A.; WMA; Montclair A. Mus.; Wilmington FA Center; Audubon A.; and many others. One-man: (8) Kleeman Gal., N.Y.; others, Springfield Mus. A.; Coy Gal., Miami, Fla.; Oehlschlaeger Gal., Chicago; Cleveland Inst. A.; in Brazil, and also a traveling exh. through Europe. *Position*: Instr., ASL, 1944-46; Cape Ann A. Sch., Rockport, Mass., 1943-46; Instr., Advanced Painting, Cleveland Inst. A., Cleveland, Ohio, at present.

BOSCH, GULNAR KHEIRALLAH—*Educator*

Fine Arts Department, Louisiana State University; h. 834 Magnolia Woods Dr., Baton Rouge, La.

B. Lake Preston, S.D., Oct. 31, 1909. *Studied*: AIC, B.A. in Edu.; N.Y. Univ., M.A.; Oriental Inst., Univ. Chicago, Ph.D. *Member*: CAA; Southeastern College Art Conference (Vice-Pres., 1956-57, Pres., .1957-58). Contributor to Journal of Near Eastern Studies; Islamic Review; Muslim Digest; Art Bulletin. Lectures: Islamic Art and Contemp. Art: "Booktrade Practices Indicated by Islamic Bookbindings of the 14th and 15th Centuries"; "Space in Persian Miniature Painting," etc. *Positions*: (Art History)—Asst. Prof., Florida State College for Women; Prof., Wesleyan College, Macon, Ga.; Prof., Louisiana State Univ., Baton Rouge, La.; Research Asst. at Oriental Inst., Univ. Chicago; Hd. A. Dept., Wesleyan College; Chm. Art. Dept., Louisiana State University, at present.

BOSE, NORMA—*Painter, T.*

Rt. 1, Box 100, McLean, Va.

B. San Francisco, Cal. *Studied*: George Washington Univ., A.B.; Columbia Univ., M.A.; & with Henry McFee, Paul Sample. *Member*: Soc. Wash. A.; Wash. WC Cl. *Exhibited*: PAFA, 1934-1937, 1940; AWCS; Wash. WC Cl., 1931-1946; Soc. Wash. A., 1926-1946. *Position*: T., Roosevelt H.S., Washington, D.C.*

BOSIN, F. BLACKBEAR—*Painter*

1032 Parker St., Wichita, Kans.

B. Cement, Okla., June 5, 1921. *Studied*: with J. Havard McPherson, Spencer Asah. *Member*: Wichita A. Gld. *Awards*: prizes, Philbrook A. Center, 1953-1955; deYoung Galleries, 1953; Denver A. Mus., 1953 (purchase, 1954); Santa Fe, N.M., 1958; Am. Research Fnd. award, Gal. of Indian Art, 1958. *Work*: Philbrook A. Center; Gilcrease Fnd.; Wichita AA; and in private coll. *Exhibited*: Philbrook A. Center (one-man); Gilcrease Fnd.; J. Graham Gal.; deYoung Gal; Denver A. Mus.; Wichita AA (one-man); Smithsonian Inst. *Position*: A. Dir., Training Aids, Div. of Graphic Arts, McConnell Air Force Base, Wichita, Kans., 1951- .

BOSSERT, EDYTHE HOY—*Painter, T.*

Mill Hall, Pa.

B. Pennsylvania, July 18, 1908. *Studied*: Carnegie Inst.; Lock Haven State T. Col. *Member*: NAWA; Lock Haven AC. *Exhibited*: NAD, 1944; Lock Haven Exh., 1946; North Shore AA, 1943, 1944; NAWA, 1945, 1953; Parkersburg FA Exh., 1942, 1943; Bucknell Univ., 1951; Terry AI, 1952; Ogunquit, Me., 1954; Lock Haven (Pa.) State T. Col., 1955 (one-man).*

BOSTELMAN, ELSE W. von ROEDER— *Painter, C., Des., I., Comm., W.*

15 Apple Tree Lane, Darien, Conn.

B. Leipzig, Germany. *Studied*: Univ. Leipzig; Acad. FA, Germany, and with Sasha Schneider, H. Giles, Bernard Klonis. *Member*: Soc. Women Geographers. *Awards*: prizes, Pen & Brush Cl., 1953, 1954. *Work*: Four oceanographic expeditions with Zool. Soc. Tropical Research, under direction of Dr. William Beebe. Executed over 300 plates of deep-sea and shore fish, published in Nat. Geographic magazine; series of floral watercolors, Nat. Geographic magazine. *Exhibited*: Argent Gal.; Biltmore A. Gal.; Palm Beach, Fla.; Pen & Brush Cl.; NAC, 1952; AAPL, 1951; one-man exhs., in Germany, Florida and Conn. Author: "Sea Horse Adventures." I., numerous books for children. Contributor to national magazines.

BOSTICK, WILLIAM ALLISON— *Painter, C., Cart., I., Lith., L., E., W.*

The Detroit Institute of Arts; h. 9340 West Outer Dr., Detroit 19, Mich.

B. Marengo, Ill., Feb. 21, 1913. *Studied*: Carnegie Inst. of Tech., B.S.; Cranbrook Acad. A., with Zoltan Sepeshy; Wayne Univ., M.A. *Member*: Scarab Cl., Detroit. *Awards*: prizes, Detroit Inst. A., 1943, 1945. *Work*: Cranbrook Acad. A.; Detroit Inst. A. *Exhibited*: Audubon A., 1945; Detroit Inst. A., 1936-1958; Detroit WC Cl., 1946; Domesday Press Exh., 1945. Author, I., "England Under G.I.'s Reign," 1946; I., "Art in the Armed Forces"; Des. & Illus., "Mysteries of Blair House," 1948; Des., "For Modern Living" catalogue. Contributor articles to Navy publications. *Position*: Sec., Detroit Inst. A.; Exec. Sec., Detroit Mus. A. Founders Soc.; Bd. Memb., Scarab Cl.; Past Pres., Midwest Museums Conference; Ed., Midwest Museums Quarterly; Bd. Memb., The Book Club of Detroit; Regional Vice-Pres., AIGA.

BOSWELL, NORMEN GOULD—
   Painter, Des., S., I., T., W., Gr.
   Box 379, Vallejo, Cal.

B. Halifax, N.S., Canada, Sept. 10, 1882. *Studied*: Victoria Sch. A. & Des., Halifax; Otis AI, Los A.; & with H. W. Cannon. *Work*: mural, Rosicrucian Oriental Mus., San Jose, Cal. *Exhibited*: Santa Cruz, Cal.; Hollywood Pub. Lib.; Los A. A. Lg.; Soc. Western A.; NSS. I., "Illuminations, Tibetan Teachings on the Short Path"; "Art's Jewels" and "Isis Illuminated."

BOTHWELL, DORR—*Painter, Gr., Des., T.*
   s. 716 Montgomery St., San Francisco 11, Cal.

B. San Francisco, Cal., May 3, 1902. *Studied*: Cal. Sch. FA; Univ. Oregon. *Member*: San F. AA; Nat. Ser. Soc. *Awards*: prizes, San F. Soc. Women A., 1929, 1942; San Diego A. Gld., 1932; San F. AA, 1944; Rosenberg Traveling Scholarship, 1949-50; Cal. PLH; Nat. Ser. Soc., 1952, 1955; BM, 1948. *Work*: San Diego FA Gal.; Los A. Mus. A.; SFMA; Crocker A. Gal., Sacramento; San Diego A. Mus. A.; MModA; BM; Nelson Gal. A.; Univ. Wisconsin; WMAA; MMA; FMA. *Exhibited*: GGE, 1939; Cal. PLH, 1946-1952; SFMA, 1940-1951; Los A. Mus. A., CGA, NGA, San F. Soc. Women A.; San Diego A. Gld; San Diego FA Soc.; Denver A. Mus.; WMAA; Foundation des Etats-Unis, Paris, 1949; U.S.I.S., American Embassy, Paris, 1950, 1951; Universidad de Chile, 1950; Circulo de Bellas Artes, La Palma, Mallorca, 1952; Carnegie Inst., 1952, 1955; Museu de Arte Moderna, Sao Paulo, Brazil, 1955; Art: USA, 1958; Smithsonian Inst., 1952; one-man: Rotunda Gal., San F., 1946, 1949, 1952; Cal.PLH, 1947; Serigraph Gal., N.Y., 1948, 1952; Nat. Serigraph Soc., 1954; deYoung Mem. Mus., 1957; Meltzer Gal., N.Y., 1958. *Position*: Instr., Color & Design, Cal. Sch. FA, San Francisco, Cal., (summers).

BOTKE, JESSIE ARMS—*Painter*
   Route 1, Box 285, Santa Paula, Cal.

B. Chicago, Ill. *Studied*: AIC, with John Johanson, Charles Woodbury. *Member*: Cal. WC Soc.; Cal. AC; NAWA; AWS; Fnd. Western A. *Awards*: prizes, AIC, 1917-1919, 1926; NAWA, 1925, 1933; Western Acad. Painters, 1935, 1936; Sanity in Art, 1938; Chicago Galleries Assn., 1951; Cal. State Fair, 1947; med., Peoria Soc. All. A., 1918; Southwest Exp., 1928. *Work*: AIC; Nebraska AA; Santa Paula, Bakersfield, Gardena (Cal.) H.S.; Mills Col.; Swope Gal. A.; Norton Gal. A.; Los A. County Coll.; murals, Univ. Chicago; I. Magnin Co., Los A.; Woodrow Wilson H.S., Oxnard, Cal.; Ojai, Cal. *Exhibited*: AIC, 1916-1925; NAD; PAFA; CGA; Los A. Mus. A.; GGE, 1939; Cal.PLH; Paris Salon.

BOTKIN, HENRY—*Painter, Cr., W., L.*
   56 West 11th St., New York 11, N.Y.

B. Boston, Mass., April 5, 1896. *Studied*: Mass. Sch. A.; ASL, and abroad. *Member*: AEA. *Awards*: prizes, Audubon A., 1945, 1950; Pepsi-Cola, 1947. *Member*: Fed. Mod. P. & S.; Audubon A.; Provincetown AA; FA Assoc. Gal. *Work*: MMA; MModA; PMG; Univ. Nebraska; Newark Mus. A.; Univ. Oklahoma; Walker A. Center; Denver A. Mus.; Akron AI; BM; Modern Mus., Munich, Germany; Rochester Mem. A. Gal.; Riverside Mus.; Walter Chrysler, Jr., Coll.; Norton Gal. A.; DMFA; BMFA; WMAA; Smith Col.; Tel-Aviv Mus. A., and in private coll. in U.S. and abroad. *Exhibited*: CGA; PAFA; Carnegie Inst.; AIC; WMAA; GGE, 1939; WFNY, 1939; MMA; BMA; Denver A. Mus.; Harriman Gal. (one-man); Los A. Mus. A.; SFMA; Chicago AC; PMG; BMFA; Kansas City AI; Downtown Gal., N.Y.; 29 one-man exhs. *Position*: Organized many art exhs. U.S. and abroad, including first American abstract show in Japan; Pres., Am. Abstract A., 1954-55; Pres., AEA, 1951-52; Pres., Fed. Mod. P. & S., 1957-58.

BOTT, EARLE WAYNE—
   Painter, Des., Lith., Eng., I., Cart., L., Comm., Gr.
   Artist Acres, R.R. 5, Brazil, Ind.

B. Indianapolis, Ind., Jan. 1, 1894. *Studied*: John Herron AI; A. Acad., Cincinnati; AIC; & with Forsythe Hopkins.

Member: Indiana A. Cl. *Awards*: Prizes, Indiana State Fair, 1921. *Work*: Am. Legion, Kokomo, Ind. *Exhibited*: Hoosier Salon, 1925, 1933; John Herron AI, 1914, 1921, 1922, 1923, 1932, 1957; Indiana A. Cl., 1922, 1933, 1935; Richmond AA, 1922-1924; Indiana A., 1932-1934; Indiana State Fair, 1950; Swope A. Gal., 1948, 1951, 1958; Terry AI, 1952. Lectures: Lithography.

BOTT, MABEL SIEGELIN (Mrs. Earle W.)—
   Teacher, C., P., Des.
   Artist Acres, R.R. 5, Box 124, Brazil, Ind.

B. Clay County, Ind., Sept. 12, 1900. *Studied*: John Herron AI. *Member*: Indiana A. Cl.; Indiana Fed. A. Cl.; Soc. A. & Crafts, Boston. *Awards*: Prizes, Indiana State Fair, 1924-1940; Kentucky State Fair, 1927, 1932; med., Indiana Fed. A. Cl., 1936. *Exhibited*: Hoosier Salon; Marshall Field Gal., 1926; John Herron AI, 1926, 1927, 1929, 1930, 1957; Indiana A. Cl., 1933, 1935, 1936; Indiana State Fair, 1951; Terry AI, 1952. *Position*: A.T., Van Buren Township H.S., Clay County, Ind., 1944-56.

BOTT, PATRICIA BURR. See Allen, Patricia

BOTTO, OTTO—*Painter, I., T., L.*
   214 East 59th St., New York 22, N.Y.; h. 426 78th St., North Bergen, N.J.

B. Ragaz, Switzerland, July 15, 1903. *Studied*: in Switzerland. *Member*: Fed. Mod. P. & S. *Work*: Textile H.S., N.Y.; Brooklyn Lib. *Exhibited*: PAFA, 1941; MModA, 1938; WMAA, 1939; BM, 1941, 1943, 1945; AIC, 1942, 1943, 1944; Carnegie Inst., 1946; La Tausca Pearl Exh., 1946; Fed. Mod. P. & S., annually; American Univ., Wash., D.C., 1947; Salpeter Gal., 1948; Univ. Illinois, 1952; AFA traveling exh., 1955-57; "Faces in the Arts" exh., MMA, 1957, traveling AFA, 1958; Audubon A., 1952; one-man: Gal. Secession, 1934; Contemporary A. Gal., 1937; Egan Gal., 1946; New Gal., 1951; Tamimen A. Gal., 1956; Women's City Cl., 1958. *Position*: Instr., BM Sch. A., Brooklyn, N.Y.; Vice-Pres., Fed. Mod. P. & S., 1951-55, 1956-1958. Instr., N.Y. Adult Edu. Program.

BOTTORF, EDNA ANNABELLE—*Educator, P., W., L.*
   State Teachers College; h. 215 East Walnut St., Lock Haven, Pa.

B. Lock Haven, Pa., Jan. 30, 1901. *Studied*: Lock Haven State T. Col.; N.Y. Univ.; Snow-Froelich Sch. Indst. A.; Pennsylvania State Col., B.S., M.A., D.Edu.; Ohio Univ. *Member*: Am. Assn. Univ. Prof.; Nat. Edu. Assn.; NAWA; Eastern AA; Johnstown AA. *Awards*: prizes, New Jersey P. & S., 1955; Milford, Conn., 1955. *Exhibited*: Butler AI; Parkersburg, W. Va.; CM; Bucknell Univ.; Ohio Univ.; Audubon A.; A. Lg. of Long Island; Knickerbocker A.; Springfield (Mass.) A. Lg.; Portland (Me.) Soc. A.; Johnstown AA; Milford, N.J.; Jersey City Mus.; Morris Gal., N.Y., 1956, 1958 (one-man). Contributor to educational magazines and journals. *Position*: A. Dir., State T. Col., Lock Haven, Pa., 1935- .

BOTTS, HUGH—*Printmaker, P., Des., S., C., I., W.*
   203 West 78th St., New York 24, N.Y.

B. New York, N.Y., Apr. 19, 1903. *Studied*: Rutgers Univ.; NAD; ASL; BAID, and with Hinton, Curran, Hawthorne. *Member*: ANA; SC; AAPL; Phila. WC Cl.; Princeton Pr. Cl.; SAGA; AEA; Am. Color Pr. Soc.; ASL; Conn. Acad. FA; Chicago SE; New Jersey P.&S.; New Haven Paint & Clay Cl.; NSS; Audubon A.; Northwest Pr. M.; North Shore AA; Springfield A. Lg.; New England Pr. Assn. *Awards*: F., Yaddo Fnd., 1929; prizes, Arch. Lg., 1934; BAID, 1937; SC, 1943; New Jersey State Exh., Montclair A. Mus., 1942-1944, med., 1941; New Jersey P. & S., 1946; AAPL; Carnegie Inst.; N.Y. Pub. Lib.; LC. *Work*: MMA; FMA; BM; Boston Pub. Lib.; CM; Newark Mus. A.; Montclair A. Mus.; SAM; Queens Col.; Naval Hospital, N.Y.; N.Y. Pub. Lib.; U.S. Nat. Mus.; Carnegie Inst.; Princeton Univ.; Mus. Natural Hist.; Rutgers Univ.; Rochester Mem. A. Gal.; Pa. State Col.; Syracuse Univ. *Exhibited*: MMA, 1940, 1943; WMAA, 1941; Carnegie Inst., 1941; CGA, 1939-1942; AIC, 1938; LC, 1941-1943; MModA, 1942; NAD, 1936-43; WFNY 1939; Phila. Pr. Cl., 1936-1946; Conn. Acad. FA, 1936-1946; SAGA, 1936-1943; Oakland A. Gal., 1941-1943; Southern Pr. M., 1936-1940; 100 Prints, 1938-1941; AEA; LC; All. A. Am.; Audubon A.; SC; Medallic A.; NSS; Am. Color Pr. Soc.; Phila. WC Cl.; PAFA; Northwest Pr. M.; Chicago SE;

Syracuse State Fair; Albany Pr. Cl.; Laguna Beach AA; Wichita AA; Syracuse Univ.; Springfield A. Lg.; New Haven Paint & Clay Cl., etc. One-man: Smithsonian Inst.; U.S. Nat. Mus.; Rutgers Univ. Contributor to craft, technical and trade publications with articles and illus. *Position*: Dir., Audubon A. Membership Committee.

BOUCHE, LOUIS—*Painter, T.*
20 West 10th St., New York 11, N.Y.; s. Old Chatham, N.Y.

B. New York, N.Y., Mar. 18, 1896. *Studied*: Grande Chaumiere, Ecole des Beaux-Arts, Paris; ASL. *Member*: Nat. Inst. A. & Let.; NA. *Awards*: Guggenheim F., 1933; med., PAFA; Altman prize, NAD, 1956; Art:USA, 1958. *Work*: MMA; WMAA; PMG; WMA; Blandon Mem. Gal.; PAFA; Univ. Nebraska; Des Moines A. Center; Columbus (Ohio) Mus. A.; CM; Los A. Mus. A.; U.S. State Dept.; Univ. Oklahoma; Cranbrook Acad. A.; New Britain Mus. A.; Am. Acad. A. & Lets.; Lehigh Univ.; Wichita Mus. A.; murals, Dept. Interior, Justice Bldgs., Wash., D.C.; USPO, Ellenville, N.Y.; Pennsylvania R.R. lounges; Radio City Music Hall lounge; Eisenhower Mus., Abilene, Kans. *Exhibited*: CGA, 1937, 1939; NAD; PAFA, 1941, 1942, 1945. *Position*: Instr., NAD A. Schl., New York, N.Y.

BOUDREAU, JAMES CLAYTON—
Educator, Lith., L., W.
421 Woodlawn Ave., Belleair, Fla.

B. Framingham, Mass., Dec. 25, 1891. *Studied*: Mass Sch. A., B.S. in Edu.; Columbia Univ.; Alfred Univ.; Univ. Pittsburgh; Colorossi, Paris, France; PIASch., D.F.A. *Member*: Nat. Edu. Assn.; Eastern AA; Western AA; A.Dir.Cl.; AFA; SI. *Exhibited*: one-man: St. Augustine, St. Petersburg, Belleair, Fla. Author: "History of Coastal Patrol Base No. 17," 1944; "Art Education in Elementary Schools"; "Junior High School Art Education." Lectures: History of Art, Camouflage, Aviation. *Position*: Dir. A., Pittsburgh Pub. Schs., 1920-28; Dean, PIASch., Brooklyn, N.Y., 1928-56. L., Gulf Coast A. Center, Belleair, Fla.

BOUGHTON, CLETA OLMSTEAD ROBBINS—*Writer*
4625 Corkwood Lane, Beaumont, Tex.

B. Columbia, Mo., Feb. 15, 1915. *Studied*: Univ. Chicago, A.B., M.A.; Bryn Mawr Col., Ph.D.; Am. Sch. Oriental Research, Jerusalem; Am. Sch. Classical Studies, Athens. *Awards*: Ryerson F.; Riegel F.; Belgian-American Grant. *Positions*: Instr., Univ. Rochester; Assoc. Prof., Florida State Univ.; A. Ed., Journal of Human Ecology. Contributor to College Art Journal and others.

BOUGHTON, WILLIAM HARRISON—*Painter, T.*
4625 Corkwood Lane, Beaumont, Tex.

B. Dubuque, Iowa, Feb. 19, 1915. *Studied*: Univ. Iowa, B.A. with Grant Wood, Fletcher Martin; Univ. California, M.A., with Erle Loran, Shaeffer Zimmern. *Member*: AAUP; CAA; AEA; Nat. Ser. Soc. *Awards*: Phelan Scholar, Univ. California, 1945-46. *Exhibited*: SFMA, 1945; Serigraphies Americaines, Paris, France; 10 Am. Painters of Today, France; American Watercolorists, France; Salade Exposiones de La Universidad de Chile; Student Union, Lamar State College. *Position*: Prof., Hd. Dept. A., Lamar State Col., Beaumont, Texas.

BOULTON, JOSEPH L.—*Sculptor, T.*
Florida Hill Rd., Ridgefield, Conn.

B. Fort Worth, Tex., May 26, 1896. *Studied*: NAD; ASL; BAID; with H.A.MacNeil. *Member*: All. A. Am.; Phila. A. All.; SC; New Jersey P. & S. Soc.; Hudson Valley AA; NSS. *Awards*: prizes, NAD, 1921, 1953 (med.); Hempstead, L.I., 1945; Hudson Valley AA, 1951, med., 1953, 1955; med., All. A. Am., 1948, 1952, 1955. *Work*: D.A.R., Ft. Worth, Tex.; Detroit Inst. A.; Ft. Worth Mus. A.; Phila. Acad. Medicine; Huntington Mus.; Brookgreen Gardens, S.C.; Boulder (Colo.) Mus. A.; Starr Commonwealth Mus., Albion, Mich. *Exhibited*: NAD, 1921-1944; All. A. Am., 1926-1945; PAFA, 1927-1940; Danbury, Norwalk, Bridgeport, Conn.

BOUNDEY, BURTON S(HEPARD)—*Painter, T., Gr.*
P.O. Box 1188, Monterey, Cal.

B. Oconomowoc, Wis., Feb. 2, 1879. *Studied*: AIC; Smith A. Sch., Chicago, with Robert Henri. *Member*: Carmel

AA. *Awards*: prizes, Santa Cruz A. Lg., 1933; Cal. State Fair, 1937, 1940; AV, Carmel, 1943; Monterey County Fair, 1956. *Work*: murals, Monterey, Pacific Grove H.S.; Cal. Custom House, Monterey. *Exhibited*: San F. AA, 1935, 1937; Oakland A. Gal., 1937, 1938, 1940, 1941, 1946; Cal. State Fair, 1937-1941, 1951-1953; Santa Cruz A. Lg., 1935-1950; Dayton AI, 1943; GGE 1939; Carmel AA (annually); A. Gld. of Am. (Carmel, Cal.) annually.

BOURGEOIS, LOUISE—*Sculptor, Eng.*
435 West 22nd St., New York 11, N.Y.

B. Paris, France, Dec. 25, 1911. *Studied*: Ecole des Beaux-Arts, Paris; ASL, and with Fernand Leger. *Awards*: prize, MModA, 1943. *Work*: Albright A. Gal.; MModA; WMAA. *Exhibited*: MModA, 1941, 1951; LC; MMA; WMAA, 1945, 1946, 1953-1955; Los A. Mus. A., 1943; SFMA, 1944; Cal. PLH, 1950; Walker A. Center, 1954; Univ. Illinois, 1954; Boston A. Festival, 1955.

BOURNE, GERTRUDE B. (Mrs. Frank A.)—*Painter*
130 Mt. Vernon St., Boston, Mass.

B. Boston, Mass. *Studied*: with Henry B. Snell, Henry W. Rice. *Member*: AWS; Wash. WC Cl. *Exhibited*: Boston, Washington, D.C., New York.*

BOVE, RICHARD JOHN—*Painter, Et., E.*
241 Ryerson St., Brooklyn 5, N.Y.

B. Brooklyn, N.Y., Oct. 21, 1920. *Studied*: PIASch., B.F.A.; ASL; Brera Acad. FA, Milan, Italy. *Member*: Brooklyn Soc. A.; SI; ASL (Bd. Control); Assoc., Inst. of International Edu.; AAUP. *Awards*: prizes, NAD, 1949, 1953; Emily Lowe award, 1950, 1952; ASL scholarship; Brooklyn Soc. A.; Tiffany F., 1948, 1953; Fulbright F. (Italy), 1951-52. *Exhibited*: 1950-55: Audubon A.; NAD; PAFA; Rome, Italy; BM; Riverside Mus.; MMA; BMFA; WMAA; CGA; Universities of Miami, Syracuse and Cornell. *Position*: Instr., PIASch., Brooklyn, N.Y. and ASL, New York, N.Y.*

BOWDEN H(ARRY)—*Painter, Des.*
Box 534, Sausalito, Cal.

B. California, Feb. 9, 1907. *Studied*: Univ. California; Los Angeles AI; NAD; ASL, and with Hans Hofmann. *Exhibited*: SMFA, 1945, 1950; Am. Abstract A., 1937-1939; Cal. Sch. FA, de Young Mem. Mus., 1948; Artists' Gal., N.Y., 1949; Los A. Mus. A., 1949; Gump's Gal., San F., 1951, 1952; one-man: East & West Gal., San F., 1955; Cal. PLH, 1955; George Eastman House, Rochester, N.Y., 1957; Galerie du Quartier, San Francisco, 1958. Portfolio of recent works for UCLA Lib., 1944.

BOWER, HELEN LANE—*Painter, Des.*
284 Bay 10th St., Brooklyn 28, N.Y.

B. Lanesville, N.Y., Dec. 16, 1898. *Studied*: PIASch.; & with George Pearse Ennis, Oscar Julius. *Member*: PBC; Wolfe AC; Gotham Painters. *Awards*: Prize, Wolfe AC, 1939, 1944. *Exhibited*: NAWA; PBC; 8th St. Gal.*

BOWERS, BEULAH SPRAGUE—*Painter, C., S., T., L.*
High School Annex; h. 514 East Main St., Meriden, Conn.

B. Everett, Mass., Nov. 5, 1892. *Studied*: MIT, with W. F. Brown; South Boston A. Sch.; Mass. Sch. A., B.S. in Edu.; M. in Edu.; CUASch; Univ. New Hampshire. *Member*: Meriden A. & Crafts Assn.; Conn. AA. *Awards*: prizes, A. & Crafts Assn., Meriden, Conn. *Exhibited*: Meriden A. & Crafts Assn., 1939-1946; Kansas WC Soc.; Kansas AA; A. Gld.; Meriden, Wallingford, Conn., and Boston, Mass., annually. Lectures: Color, Design. *Position*: Asst. Prof. A., Univ. Wichita, 1929-37; Supv. A., Meriden, Conn., 1939-1959.

BOWLING, JACK (FRANK)—*Engraver, Lith., C., I.*
1920 Ringgold Place, Philadelphia 46, Pa.

B. Bonham, Tex., July 5, 1903. *Studied*: U.S. Naval Acad. *Member*: Honolulu Pr. M.; Newport AA. *Awards*: John Poole Mem. prize, Honolulu, 1934. *Work*: LC; Mus. Art, Colombo, Ceylon; Honolulu Acad. A.; chalice, St. Columba's Episcopal Church, Wash., D.C.; chalice and Cross, Church of The Holy Trinity, Phila., Pa. *Exhibited*: Honolulu Pr. M.; SAGA; So. Cal. Pr. M.; Southern Pr.

M.; one-man: Newport AA, 1945; Colombo, Ceylon, 1946; Singapore, 1946; Manila, P.I., 1946; Honolulu Acad. A., 1934; Lawrence Gal., Dallas, 1937. I., "Book of Navy Songs"; "U.S. Naval Institute Proceedings," and others. *Position*: Owner "Two Star Studio" & "Society Hill Silver Workshop," Philadelphia, Pa. Rear Admiral, U.S.N., Ret.

BOWMAN, DOROTHY (LOUISE)
(Mrs. Howard Bradford)—Serigrapher, P.
Big Sur, California

B. Hollywood, Cal., Jan. 20, 1927. *Studied*: Chouinard AI, with Dan Lutz, Richard Haines, Jean Charlot; Jepson AI, with Rico Le Brun. *Member*: Western Serigraph Inst.; Am. Color Pr. Soc. *Awards*: prizes, Los A. County Fair, 1952, 1953; purchase prizes: Nat. Ser. Soc., 1952; BM, 1954; LC, 1954; Univ. Illinois, 1956; Boston Pr. M., 1956, 1958; California A., 1957; Wichita, Kans., 1957. *Work*: N.Y. Pub. Lib.; Immaculate Heart Col., Los Angeles; BM; Crocker A. Gal., Sacramento, Cal.; MMA; LC; San Jose State College; BMFA; deCordova & Dana Mus.; Boston Pub. Lib.; Rochester Mem. A. Gal.; Univ. Wisconsin, Milwaukee. IGAS commission for 210 serigraphs, 1957. *Exhibited*: BM; 1950-1956, 1958; Nat. Ser. Soc., 1950, 1951, 1953, 1954; LC, 1951-1953, 1955-1958; AFA traveling exhs., 1955-1958; Los A. Mus. A., 1947-1953, 1957.

BOWMAN, JEAN (JEAN ELEANOR BOWMAN MAC-KAY-SMITH)—*Painter, I.*
Lucky Hit Farm, White Post, Va.; Studio: 33 W. 67th St., New York 23, N.Y.

B. Mt. Vernon, N.Y., Sept. 27, 1917. *Studied*: Grand Central A. Sch.; NAD; Scott Carbee Sch. A., and with Jonas Lie, Jerry Farnsworth, Leon Kroll. *Member*: Grand Central A. Gal. *Awards*: prize, Grand Central A. Sch., 1936. *Work*: many equestrian portraits for private collectors; port. in permanent exh. at National Museum of Racing. *Exhibited*: Knoedler Gal., 1949; one-man: Scott & Fowles, 1952; Vose Gal., 1940; Grand Central A. Gal., 1953, 1954; Nat. Museum of Racing, 1958. I., for various equestrian publications including British Race Horse, The Blood Horse; covers for The Chronicle, a weekly horse publication on hunting, steeple chasing, racing & polo. Commissions in England and Ireland, 1958.

BOYCE, GERALD GLADWIN—*Educator, P., C.*
Indiana Central College, 4001 South Otterbein Ave.; h. 1260 Morgan Dr., Indianapolis 27, Ind.

B. Embarrass, Wis., Dec. 29, 1925. *Studied*: Milwaukee State T. Col.; Milwaukee AI; State Univ. of Iowa; Indiana Univ.; Americano-Guatemalteco Instituto, Guatemala City. *Member*: CAA; Mid-west College A. Conference; Indiana College AA. *Awards*: numerous awards in competitions. *Work*: MModA and in private colls. *Exhibited*: AIC; Toledo Mus. A.; Wadsworth Atheneum; Los A. Mus. A.; Colo. Springs FA Center; J.B.Speed Mus. A.; SFMA; MModA; Wichita A. Mus.; Des Moines A. Center; St. Paul Gal. A.; Ball State T. Col.; Bradley Univ.; Indiana Univ.; South Bend A. Center; Univ. Iowa; Univ. Michigan; Ohio State Univ.; Univ. Wisconsin; Milwaukee AI; Wisconsin State Col.; Univ. Illinois. *Position*: Prof. A., Indiana Central College, Indianapolis, Ind., 1950- .

BOYD, E. (Miss)—*Writer, Mus. Cur., P., L.*
Museum of New Mexico, Santa Fe, N.M.

B. Philadelphia, Pa., Sept. 23, 1903. *Studied*: PAFA. *Member*: Intl. Inst. for Conservation of Museum Objects; Spanish Colonial A. Soc.; New Mexico Archaeological Soc. *Work*: renderings of regional folk art, Index of American Design; restoration and preservation of interior paintings of regional colonial churches; conservation of altarpieces, in missions at Laguna Pueblo, N.M.; Ranchos de Taos; San Miguel, Santa Fe; San Jose Church, Hernandez, N.M. Author: "Saints and Saintmakers," 1946; Section on New Mexican Spanish colonial material in "The Concise Encyclopedia of American Antiques," 1958. Contributor to Arts & Architecture; Antiques; Hobbies; House & Garden; Southwest Review and other publications. Lectures on New Mexican arts and crafts. Arranged rooms, DMFA, "Religious Art of the Western World," 1958; "Primitive American Art" (Santos), Kleijkamp & Monroe Coll., Santa Barbara, Pasadena, Cal., and Los A. Mus. A.; Catalogued Alfred I. Barton coll., 1951 (publ.); Santo colls. at Santa Barbara A. Mus.; Taylor Mus., Colorado Springs and various private colls. *Position*: Project Supv.,

New Mexico Div. of Index of American Design (FAP). Registrar, Los A. Mus. A., 1949-51; Cur., Spanish Colonial Dept., Museum of New Mexico, Santa Fe, 1951- .

BOYD, FISKE—*Painter, Gr.*
Plainfield, N.H.

B. Philadelphia, Pa., July 5, 1895. *Studied*: PAFA; ASL. *Member*: NAD; Audubon A; SAGA; Boston Pr. M. *Awards*: prizes, Phila. Pr. Cl., 1931; NAD, 1955; John Taylor Arms Mem. award, SAGA, 1954; BM (purchase prize), 1953. *Work*: MMA; PMA; N.Y. Pub. Lib.; LC; BM; murals, USPO, Summit, New Jersey. *Exhibited*: nationally.

BOYD, MOREON BEURNERE—*Painter, W.*
P.O. Box 281, Hartsdale, N.Y.; h. South Newbury, Vt.

B. France, July 26, 1902. *Studied*: Univ. Innsbruck; ASL. *Member*: AEA. *Exhibited*: CGA; Wash. WC Cl.; AWS; Ridgewood AA; NAD; AEA. *Work*: Cuban Embassy; All Souls Convent, Cal.; St. Patrick's Cathedral, N.Y.*

BOYD, MRS. W. A., JR. See Wickham, Nancy

BOYER, HELEN KING—*Engraver, Des., P., Et., C.*
258 Broad Ave., Leonia, N.J.

B. Pittsburgh, Pa., Dec. 16, 1919. *Studied*: with Samuel Rosenberg, Wilfred Readio, Boyd Hanna. *Member*: SAGA. *Awards*: prizes, SAGA, 1943; LC, 1943; Tiffany Fnd. grant, 1949; N.J. Fed. Women's Cl., 1952, 1953, 1954. *Work*: LC; Carnegie Inst.; MMA; Miniature Pr. Soc. Presentation Print, 1953; mural on silk, Henning Co., 1955. *Exhibited*: Buffalo Pr. Cl., 1943; Laguna Beach AA, 1945, 1946; LC, 1933, 1934; NAD, 1942, 1943; Northwest Pr. M., 1941, 1944; Oakland A. Gal., 1941-1943; PAFA, 1941, 1942; SAGA, 1940-1944; Southern Pr. M., 1942; Pittsburgh Assoc. A., 1942-1945; Pittsburgh A. & Crafts Center, 1951 (one-man); all major print exhs.; SAGA exh. to England. *Position*: Des., Tiesilks Co., 1954; Des., stuffed toys, My-Toy Co., New York, N.Y., 1954- .*

BOYER, JACK K.—*Museum Director, Cur.*
Kit Carson Home & Museum, Kit Carson St.; h. Canon Rd., Taos, N.M.

B. Van Houten, N.M., Sept. 2, 1911. *Member*: AAMus.; Archaeological Soc. of New Mexico; New Mexico State Hist. Soc.; Clearing House for Western Museums. Contributor to newspapers and other publications. Collected and arranged all exhibits in the Kit Carson Home & Museum. *Position*: Dir., Cur., Kit Carson Home & Museum, Taos, N.M., 1954- .

BOYER, LOUISE (RIVE-KING) (MILLER)—
Engraver, P., Des., L., T., C.
258 Broad Ave., Leonia, N.J.

B. Pittsburgh, Pa., Oct. 30, 1890. *Studied*: Carnegie Inst., B.A.; & with Henry Keller, Arthur Sparks, Charles Hawthorne. *Member*: SAGA. *Awards*: Prizes, Assoc. A. Pittsburgh; John Herron AI, 1946. *Work*: Lib.Cong.; MMA; Carnegie Inst.; Richard C. du Pont mem.; Aluminum Co. of Am. *Exhibited*: Lib.Cong., 1943, 1944; SAGA, 1940-1945, 1953-1955; Northwest Pr.M., 1941-1945; SFMA, 1943-1945; Pittsburgh Assoc. A., 1928-1945; NAD, 1942-1946; MMA, 1942, 1955; Carnegie Inst., 1941, 1944; Laguna Beach AA, 1945, 1946; PAFA, 1941, 1942; Wash. Soc. Min. P., 1942; Wash. WC Cl., 1942; Southern Pr.M., 1942; Am. Prints Today, Indianapolis, 1946; Montclair A. Mus., 1955; Montpelier, Vt., 1955; SAGA Rotary. Lectures: Etchings and Drypoints.*

BOYLE, KEITH—*Painter, T.*
c/o Feingarten Galleries, 58 East Walton St., Chicago, Ill.

Studied: Univ. Iowa; Ringling Sch. A., Sarasota, Fla. *Awards*: purchase awards, Indiana State T. Col.; Univ. Pennsylvania; Dept. Edu., State of Iowa; Springfield (Mo.) Mus. A.; prizes, Logan award, AIC, 1958. *Exhibited*: Mid-America annual; WAC; Des Moines A. Center; Springfield Mus. A.; Ringling Mus. A.; Mulvane A. Mus., Topeka; Joslyn A. Mus.; PAFA, 1958; Art:USA, 1958, New York; 2-man exh., Feingarten Gal., Chicago, 1958. *Position*: Instr. A., Lake Forest College, Ill., 1956-57; Instr. A., Barat College, Lake Forest, Ill., at present.

BOYNTON, JAMES W.—*Painter*

4037 Browning St., Houston 5, Tex.

B. Ft. Worth, Tex., Jan. 12, 1928. *Studied*: Texas Christian Univ., Ft. Worth, Tex., B.F.A., M.F.A. *Awards*: purchase awards and prizes, Denver Mus. A., 1952, 1954, 1958; Texas FA Assn., 1952, 1957; Texas State Fair, 1953; Ft. Worth, 1951, 1952, 1954, 1955; Houston, Tex., 1955; Texas WC Soc., 1951, 1953-1955; Underwood-Neuhaus Comp., 1957; Butler Inst. Am. A., 1957. *Work*: DMFA; Mus. FA, Houston; Witte Mem. Mus.; Texas FA Assn.; Ft. Worth A. Center; Butler Inst. Am. A.; Inland Steel Co., Chicago; Underwood-Neuhaus, Houston; Denver Mus. A.; WMAA, and in many private colls. *Exhibited*: Ft. Worth annuals, 1950-1955; DMFA and circuit, 1950-1958; Texas WC Soc., 1951-1956; Texas FA Assn., 1951, 1952, 1954, 1957; Mus. FA, Houston, 1955, 1957; Mus. New Mexico, Santa Fe, 1957; Knoedler Gal., N.Y., 1952; SFMA 1952; Delgado Mus. A., 1951, 1952, 1954, 1958; Colorado Springs FA Center, 1953, 1954, 1957; Denver A. Mus., 1952, 1954-1956, 1958; Guggenheim Mus., N.Y., 1954; Carnegie Inst., 1955; MMoA., 1956; Mus. FA, Houston, 1956, 1957; AFA circulating exh., 1956, 1957; Columbia Mus. A., 1957; DMFA & AFA circulating exh., 1957; Butler Inst. Am. A., 1957; Mus. Contemp. A., Houston, 1957; WMAA, 1957; AIC, 1957, 1958; Stanford Univ., 1958; VMFA, 1958; Brussels World's Fair, 1958; one-man: Ft. Worth A. Center, 1955; La Galeria Escondido, Taos, N.M., 1956; Emmerich Gal., Houston, 1957; Fairweather-Hardin Gal., Chicago, 1958; Barone Gal., N.Y., 1958 and other regional and national shows.

BRACKEN, CHARLES W.—*Designer, I., P., S.*

646 North Michigan Ave., Chicago 11, Ill.

B. Corry, Pa., Dec. 21, 1909. *Studied*: Univ. Washington, B.A.; Chicago Acad. FA. *Member*: A. Gld. of Chicago; Soc. Typographic A.; 27 Designers. *Exhibited*: AIC, 1946; SAM, 1938; Univ. Wash., 1930, 1931, 1946. *Position*: A.Dir., Bracken-Tyler, Chicago, Ill., 1943-48; A.Dir., Owner, Chas. W. Bracken Studio, Chicago, Ill., 1948- .

BRACKMAN, ROBERT—*Painter*

Noank, Conn.

B. Odessa, Russia, Sept. 25, 1898. *Studied*: Francisco Ferrer Sch.; NAD, and with George Bellows, Robert Henri. *Member*: NA; All. A. Am.; Audubon A.; Conn. Acad. FA; Int. Soc. A. & Lets.; Mystic AA; New Haven Paint & Clay Cl.; AWS. *Awards*: Thomas B. Clarke prize, 1932; AIC, 1929; NAD, 1941; Noel Flagg prize, 1936; Conn. Acad. FA, 1947; gold medal, NAC, 1950; prize, Laguna Beach A. Festival, 1952; med., All. A. Am., 1952; Beck gold med., PAFA, 1958. *Work*: BM; R.I.Sch. Des.; Conn. Agricultural Col.; Honolulu Acad. A.; Pasadena AI; MMA; Newark Mus. A.; Montclair A. Mus.; High Mus. A.; New Haven (Conn.) Lib.; Wilmington Soc. A.; Minneapolis Inst. A.; Canajoharie Mus.; Norton A. Gal.; Rockford AA; Encyclopaedia Britannica; IBM; New Britain Inst.; Mus. FA of Houston; Brooks Mem. Gal.; Univ. Georgia; Davenport Mem. A. Gal.; Toledo Mus. A.; Yale Univ.; Princeton Univ.; Harvard Coll.; Pentagon Bldg., Wash., D.C.; U.S. State Dept.; West Point Acad.; Conn. Life Insurance Co.; Bryn Mawr Coll.; Rochester Mem. A. Gal.; Milton Acad.; Dupont Coll.; Colonial Williamsburg; many portraits of prominent persons. *Exhibited*: nationally and internationally. *Position*: Instr., ASL, 1934- ; American A. Sch., New York, N.Y., 1951- ; Guest Instr., Minneapolis AI.

BRADBURY, C. EARL—*Portrait Painter, E., W., I., L.*

1501 Grand View Dr., Champaign, Ill.

B. North Bay, N.Y., May 21, 1888. *Studied*: Syracuse Univ., B.P., M.F.A.; Julian Acad., Paris, France and study and travel elsewhere in Europe. *Awards*: F., Syracuse Univ., 1911; scholarship, ASL, 1911. *Work*: many portraits, Univ. Illinois and community; others in Onarga Military Sch.; Wabash Col.; Southern Illinois Univ.; Syracuse Univ.; Southwestern Univ. (Memphis); USAF Acad., Colorado Springs, Colo.; ports. in private colls. in U.S. and Canada. *Exhibited*: Salon des Beaux Arts, 1927; PAFA, 1924; Lotos Club, N.Y., 1955; Syracuse Univ., 1956; Univ. Illinois, 1916-1956; one-man: Univ. Illinois, 1927, 1956; Syracuse Univ., 1929; Quincy, Decatur and Bloomington, Ill., 1955-1956. Lecture-demonstrations of port. painting, municipal and art organizations. Author, I., "Anatomy and Construction of the Human Figure"; I., "Canoes the World Over." *Positions*: Set Des., Motion Pictures, 1912-13; Instr.,

1913-16, Assoc., 1916-21, Asst. Prof., 1921-29, Assoc. Prof., 1929-41, Prof. A., 1941-56, Prof. Emeritus, 1956- , Univ. Illinois, Urbana, Ill.

BRADBURY, EDITH M.—*Educator, P.*

75½ Franklin St., Waterloo, Iowa

B. Onawa, Iowa, Feb. 22, 1910. *Studied*: State Univ. Iowa, B.A.; AIC. *Exhibited*: Waterloo AA; Cedar Falls A. Gal.; State Univ. Iowa; Iowa WC Soc. *Position*: Dir. A., Waterloo Pub. Sch., Waterloo, Iowa, 1937- .

BRADFIELD, EDWARD (ORR)—*Painter, Eng.*

1636 Amelia St., New Orleans, La.; h. 913 Crawford St., Vicksburg, Miss.

B. Vicksburg, Miss., June 1, 1902. *Studied*: with Mary Clare Sherwood. *Member*: AEA; AAPL; New Orleans AA; Southwestern AA; Philbrook AA; Assoc. A. Philbrook; Mississippi AA; New Orleans A. Lg.; AFA. *Awards*: prizes, Miss. AA, 1939, 1944. *Exhibited*: Miss. AA, 1939-1945; Shreveport AC, 1941, 1942; New Orleans A. Lg., 1942-1944; SSAL, 1943, 1945; Howard Mitchum Gal., Provincetown, Mass.; Philbrook Mus., 1954, 1955; Sun Ray Oil Co. exh., 1955; Brown Duncan Dept. Store, Tulsa, Okla., 1955 (one-man).*

BRADFIELD, MARGARET (JEWELL) [Mrs. John]—*Painter, I., L., W.*

Ann Arbor, Mich.

B. Danville, Ill., June 2, 1898. *Studied*: Northwestern Univ.; Columbia Univ., B.S.; AIC; Detroit Soc. A. & Crafts, with John Carroll. *Member*: Detroit Soc. Women Painters; NAWA. *Awards*: prizes, Detroit Soc. Women Painters; Ann Arbor A. Exh.; Gov. Carville Comp., 1941. *Exhibited*: PAFA, 1943; Mus. City of N.Y., 1942; All. A. Am., 1942; Detroit Inst. A., 1925-1945. Illus.: "Mr. Plum and the Little Green Tree," 1946; "Dr. Trotter and His Big Gold Watch," 1948; "900 Buckets of Paint," 1949; "A Whistle for Tootles," 1955; "Suzy and the Dog School," 1953; "Mr. O'Riley and Brownie," 1950; "Mr. Pudgins," 1951. Wrote and produced over 100 full color film-strips for school use.

BRADFORD, FRANCIS SCOTT—*Mural Painter*

15 West 67th St., New York, N.Y.; h. River Rd., Cornwall Bridge, Conn.

B. Appleton, Wis., Aug. 17, 1898. *Studied*: Lawrence Col., Wis.; Univ. Wisconsin; NAD; Fontainebleau Sch. A., France; Am. Acad. in Rome, Italy. *Member*: ANA; F., Am. Acad. in Rome; NSMP; Arch. Lg.; Century Assn. *Awards*: Prix de Rome, 1923; med., Arch. Lg., 1954; New Haven Paint & Clay Cl., 1935; hon. degree, Lawrence Col., Dr. FA, 1934. *Work*: portrait, State Lib., Hartford, Conn.; NAD coll.; murals: Milwaukee County Court House, Milwaukee, Wis.; Hooker Electro Chemical Co., Niagara Falls, N.Y.; WFNY 1939 (10); Outagamie Court House, Appleton, Wis.; Nat. City Bank, N.Y.; First Nat. Bank, Glens Falls, N.Y.; U.S. Govt. Military Cemetery, Cambridge, England (ceiling and apse); Altar piece, Christ Church, Cranbrook, Mich.; Ideal Clamp & Tool Co., Brooklyn, N.Y., and many murals in private homes. *Exhibited*: PAFA; NAD; New Sch. for Social Research; Arch. Lg.; Century Assn.; New Haven Paint & Clay Cl., and others. *Position*: Instr., mural painting, CUASch., 1930-32; NAD, 1932-38; Yale Univ. Sch. FA, 1938; Trustee, Am. Acad. in Rome, 1937-47; Pres. Alum. Assn., Am. Acad. in Rome, 1938-47.

BRADFORD, HOWARD—*Serigrapher, P., T.*

Big Sur, California

B. Toronto, Ont., Canada, July 14, 1919. *Studied*: Chouinard AI; Jepson AI, with Rico LeBrun. *Member*: Am. Color Print Soc. *Awards*: purchase awards and prizes, SFMA, 1950; Los A. Mus. A., 1950; Bradley Univ., 1951; Serigraph Soc., N.Y., 1951, 1952; Am. Color Pr. Soc., 1951, 1952; Northwest Pr. M., 1951; LC, 1951, 1956, 1957; Print Exh., Pomona, Cal., 1951; Cal. State Fair, 1951, 1952, 1956; Nat. Pr. Exh., Peoria, Ill., 1952; Pacific A. Festival, Oakland, Cal., 1952; New Britain Pr. annual, 1953; Los A. Art Festival, 1953; Nat. Pr. annual, Dallas, 1953; Graphic A. Exh., Wichita, Kans., 1955; Univ. Illinois, 1957. *Work*: paintings—Los A. Mus. A.; Cal. State Fair Coll.; serigraphs—DMFA; MMoA.; SAM; LC; FA Center, San Diego; N.Y. Pub. Lib.; Crocker A. Gal.,

Sacramento; MMA; High Mus. A., Atlanta; New Britain Mus. A. (Conn.); BMA; PMA; Univ. Wisconsin; Univ. Illinois; Bradley Univ.; Univ. New Hampshire; Norton Gal. A., Palm Beach, Fla. and others. *Exhibited*: Dallas Pr. Soc.; MModA., 1953; U.S. Information Service, Europe, 1956-1958; 60 American Printmakers, Europe, 1956; Nat. Pr. Exh., Pomona, Cal., 1948-1953; SFMA, 1950, 1956; Northwest Pr. M., 1951; Bradley Univ., 1951, 1952; LC, 1951-1955, 1957, 1958; BM, 1950-1952, 1954, 1955, 1958; Boston Pr. M., 1956, 1957; AIC, 1956; Santa Barbara Mus. A., 1955, 1957; Los A. Mus. A., 1950-1953; Cal. State Fair, 1950-1958; Am. Printmakers, Bordighera, Italy, 1957; AIC, 1957; Univ. Illinois, 1956; Denver A. Mus., 1958, and others. *Position*: Instr., Lith., Painting, Ser., Jepson AI, Los Angeles, Cal., 1950-53; summer Guest Instr., Univ. Utah, 1958.

BRADFORD, MRS. HOWARD.
See Bowman, Dorothy Louise

BRADFORD, MYRTLE TAYLOR—*Painter*, W., L., T.
249 Northeast 17th Terrace, Miami 36, Fla.

B. Indianapolis, Ind., Aug. 22, 1886. *Studied*: Harvard Univ., B.F.A., and with Lena Hinman; and in Germany with Aulick; in Italy with Campania. *Member*: AAPL; Miami A. Lg.; SSAL; Blue Dome Fellowship (Hon. Pres.). *Awards*: medal, Miami Woman's Cl.; AAPL, 1951; plaque, 1952, Miami, Fla.; Citation, Fla. Southern Col., 1950; med., AAPL, 1952, citation, 1958. Dedicated the American Wing, Palace of Fine Arts, Havana, Cuba, 1955; Citation "Women of Achievement," 1958, Fla. Fed. Business & Prof. Women's Cl.; Citation, "Contribution to Art and Culture," Miami-Dade County Chamber of Commerce, 1958. Contributor to Biographical Dictionary of American Poets. Author: "Ulilah," the Pocohontas of Florida; many folklore stories of the Caribbeans. *Position*: State A. Dir., Florida.

BRADISH, ETHELWYN—*Painter*, W., L.
155 East 93rd St., New York 28, N.Y.

B. Springfield, Ill., June 3, 1882. *Studied*: T. Col., Columbia Univ., B.S., and in Paris. *Member*: AAPL. *Exhibited*: Ogunquit AA, 1948-1958; Illinois State Mus.; NAC, 1952-1958; Argent Gal., 1940-1950 (one-man); AWS; Phila. WC Cl.; AFA traveling exh.; one-man: Springfield AA and State Mus., 1940-1950. Lectures: MMA, 1923-1945 on Art Edu.

BRADLEY, ANNE CARY—*Painter*
Fryeburg, Me.

B. Fryeburg, Me., Aug. 19, 1884. *Studied*: Sch. F. & App. A., Portland, Me.; & with George Elmer Browne, Henry Poore, Michel Jacobs. *Member*: Soc. Indp. A.; Salons of Am. *Awards*: prizes, County Fair, Rochester, N.H., and Fryeburg, Me. *Exhibited*: Ogunquit A. Center, 1946, 1951; Portland SA, 1946, 1950.*

BRADLEY, CHARLES B.—*Educator*, W., L., C., P.
The Wood Lot, Liebler Rd., Boston, N.Y.

B. Binghamton, N.Y., Feb. 11, 1883. *Studied*: PIASch.; Cornell Univ.; State T. Col., Buffalo, B.S. in Edu. *Member*: Eastern AA; Am. Assn. Univ. Prof. *Awards*: Certificate of Service, Eastern AA, 1945. Author, I., "Design in the Industrial Arts," 1946. Lectures: Art History and Appreciation. *Position*: Dir. & Prof. A. Edu., State T. Col., Buffalo, N.Y., 1918-46; Part-time Lib., Boston Free Library, Boston, N.Y., 1946- .

BRADSHAW, ALEXANDRA CHRISTINE (Mrs. C. B. Hoag)—*Painter*, E., Lith., L.
11 Acorn Rd., Wakefield Mass.; Three Arch Bay, South Laguna, Cal.

B. Nova Scotia, Canada. *Studied*: Stanford Univ., A.B.; Univ. California (Los A.); Columbia Univ., and with W.T. Hedges, Hans Hofmann, André L'Hote. *Member*: Pacific AA; Cal. WC Soc.; Laguna Beach AA; Boston Soc. WC Painters; Cambridge AA. *Awards*: prizes, San F. Soc. Women A., 1932; Laguna Beach AA, 1941, 1942, 1948. *Work*: Fresno State Col.; East Bakersfield H.S. *Exhibited*: BMFA, 1953-1955, 1956, 1958; Laguna Beach AA, 1949-1952, 1956, 1958; one-man: San Diego Gal. FA, 1955; City of Paris, San Francisco, 1955; Little Gal, Bos-

ton, 1955; Pasadena AI; Lucius Beebe Mem. Lib., Wakefield, Mass., 1958. *Position*: Former Prof., Hd. A. Dept., Fresno State Col., Fresno, Cal.

BRADSHAW, GEORGE A.—*Etcher*, P., T.
597 Parkway Ave., Trenton 8, N.J.

B. Trenton, N.J., Oct. 15, 1880. *Studied*: Trenton Sch. Indst. A. *Member*: SAGA; Chicago SE; Southern Pr.M; North Shore AA; Conn. Acad. FA; SC. *Awards*: Med., Montclair A. Mus., 1935, prize, 1936; Phila. Sketch Cl., 1956. *Work*: NGA; N.Y. Pub.Lib.; Vanderpoel Coll.; Montclair A. Mus.; MMA; Wadsworth Atheneum; New Britain (Conn.) Mus. A.; Pa. State Col.; Newark Mus.; Univ. Nebraska. *Exhibited*: Los A. Mus. A., 1926; NAC, 1924, 1926, 1927, 1929, 1930; MMA, 1942; SAGA, 1923-1956; Chicago SE, 1926-1956; North Shore AA, 1956; Montclair A. Mus., 1932-1946; Mint Mus. A., 1943-1946; Conn. Acad. FA, 1943-1946; Lib. Cong., 1943-1945; NAD, 1942, 1943, 1946; Buffalo Pr. Cl., 1936-1943; Audubon A., 1945; Southern Pr.M.; SC, 1944-1946; Phila. SE, 1930, 1934, 1937. Illus., Pictorial history books on New Jersey.

BRADSHAW, GLENN RAYMOND—*Educator*, P.
h. 1005 Crestwood Dr., Urbana, Ill.; (studio) 1009 West Nevada St., Urbana, Ill.

B. Peoria, Ill., Mar. 3, 1922. *Studied*: Kenyon Col.; Illinois State Normal Univ., B.S.; Univ. Illinois, M.F.A. *Member*: Cal. WC Soc.; Mississippi AA; Western AA; AWS; Illinois A. Edu. Assn. *Awards*: prizes, Alabama Nat. WC Exh., 1949, 1956; Mississippi Nat. WC Exh., 1950, 1955, oil exh., 1954; Mid-Am. A., 1950; Hallmark award, 1953; Delgado Mus. A., 1957; Ill. State Fair, 1955; NAD, 1955, 1957. *Work*: Alabama WC Soc.; William Rockhill Nelson Gal. A.; Jackson (Miss.) A. Mus.; Illinois State Normal Univ. *Exhibited*: Mississippi AA, 1948-1955; Audubon A, 1948, 1955; Swedish-Am. Exh., 1949, 1953, 1955; Alabama WC Soc., 1949-1954; Cal. WC Soc., 1951, 1952; Cal. WC Soc. traveling exh., 1952; PAFA, 1950; Northwest Territory Exh., 1948, 1954; Springfield Mus. A., 1949; Denver A. Mus., 1948, 1950, 1952, 1958; Butler AI, 1950, 1955-1958; Mid-Am. A., 1950, 1951; Univ. Wisconsin, 1954; NAD, 1955, 1957, 1958; AWS, 1955-1958; CM, 1955; Ohio Valley, 1955; Delgado Mus. A., 1956-1958; Swedish-Am. Exh., 1957; CM, 1958; Flint A. Center, 1956; Pittsburgh "Plan for Art," 1956; Ill. State Fair, 1957, 1958; one-man: Schermerhorn Gal., Beloit, Wis., 1956; Flint A. Center, 1958. *Position*: Cr., A.T., Univ. Illinois, 1947-50; Instr. A., Iowa State T. Col., 1950-52; Assoc. Prof. A., Univ. Illinois, 1952- .

BRADSHAW, ROBERT GEORGE—*Educator*, P.
Douglass College, Rutgers University, New Brunswick, N.J.; h. 48 Hilltop Blvd., Milltown, N.J.; s. West Wharf Studios, Gloucester, Mass.

B. Trenton, N.J., Mar. 13, 1915. *Studied*: Princeton Univ., A.B.; Columbia Univ., M.A. *Member*: CAA; Cape Ann Soc. Mod. A.; New Jersey WC Soc.; Rocky Neck A. Group (Pres.); New Brunswick A. Center (Exec. Bd.). *Awards*: honors, Art & Archaeology, Princeton Univ., 1937. *Exhibited*: AWS, 1955; NAC, 1952, 1953, 1955; BMFA, 1954; Princeton A. Mus., Alumni Exhs.; Newark Mus. A.; N.J. State Mus.; Montclair A. Mus.; New Brunswick A. Center; Morrisville-Trenton A. Group; New Jersey P. & S.; North Shore AA; Cape Ann Festival; Cape Ann Soc. Mod. A.; one-man: Contemporary Cl.; Univ. Vermont; Douglass Col. Gal. Lectures: Art Appreciation and History. *Position*: Assoc. Prof., Douglass Col. of Rutgers Univ., Art Dept., 1946- .

BRADWAY, FLORENCE DELL—*Painter*, T.
654 Wyncote Ave., Philadelphia 38, Pa.

B. Philadelphia, Pa., Oct. 16, 1897. *Studied*: Phila. Sch. Des., and with Henry B. Snell, Leopold Seyffert. *Awards*: prizes, Moore Inst., 1934, 1955. *Exhibited*: NAD, 1931; CGA, 1931; PAFA, 1917-22, 1926, 1938, 1940, 1951; Terry AI, 1952, and in many other museums, college and university galleries. *Position*: Instr., Moore Inst. A. & Indst., 1918-55, Prof. A., 1955-.*

BRAGA, ALFRED MAYNARD—*Painter*, T., Indust. Des.
102 Washington St., Hudson, Mass.

B. Hudson, Mass., May 3, 1911. *Studied*: Vesper George Sch. A.; Harvard Univ.; WMA Sch.; & with Eliot O'Hara.

Member: North Shore AA; Rockport AA; AAPL. *Awards*: F., Tiffany Fnd., 1938. *Exhibited*: NAD, PAFA, 1939.

BRALL, RUTH—Sculptor, T.
67 West 67th St.; h. 45 Park Terrace, West, New York 34, N.Y.

B. New York, N.Y., Dec. 3, 1906. *Studied*: Columbia Univ., and with Charles Hafner, Joseph Nicolosi, Oronzio Maldarelli. *Member*: All. A. Am.; New Jersey P. & S. Soc.; Pen and Brush Cl.; Hudson Valley AA; AEA; AAPL. *Awards*: prizes, New Jersey P. & S. Soc.; med., Wanamaker bronze med.; Hudson Valley AA; Pen and Brush Cl. *Work*: Columbia Univ.; N.Y. Soc. Social Work; Paine Col., Atlanta, Ga. *Exhibited*: numerous national and regional exhibitions, one-man shows. *Position*: Bd. Dir., Pen & Brush Cl.*

BRAINARD, OWEN D.—Educator, P., Ser.
Kresge Art Center, Michigan State University; h. 3508 Daisy Lane, East Lansing, Mich.

B. Kingston, N.Y., Sept. 6, 1924. *Studied*: Syracuse Univ., B.F.A., M.F.A.; Columbia Univ.; N.Y. State Univ., Col. for Teachers, Albany, N.Y., and with Stephen Peck, Dong Kingman. *Member*: CAA; AEA; AAUP; NAEA; Western A. Edu. Assn. *Awards*: prizes, Des Moines A. Center, 1953, 1955; Northeast Iowa A. Exh., Cedar Falls, 1957; Des Moines Women's Club, 1956; Iowa State Fair, 1953, 1955, 1957 (purchase). *Work*: Ford Coll. Am. Art; Iowa A. Edu. Assn.; Ford Times. *Exhibited*: PAFA, 1953; LC, 1958; Art:USA, 1958; Nelson Gal. A., Kansas City, 1952, 1955; Hudson Valley, 1950; Schenectady, N.Y., 1950; WAC, 1953; Joslyn A. Mus., 1953, 1956; AEA traveling exh., 1956; Regional Art Today, Joslyn Mus. A., 1957; Univ. Nebraska Gal., 1957; Cornell College, 1952; Sioux City A. Center, 1952, 1954; Kansas City AI, 1953; Central Col., 1953; Grinnell Col., 1954; Univ. Nevada, 1955; Midland, Mich., 1957; Little Gallery, Jackson, Mich., 1957; one-man: Albany Inst. Hist. & Art, 1951; Schenectady A. Mus., 1951; Des Moines A. Center, 1955. *Positions*: Supv., Elem. Art, Bethlehem Central Schs., Delmar, N.Y., 1949-51; Asst. Prof., Drake Univ., Dept. Art, 1952-57; Asst. Prof., Michigan State Univ., East Lansing, Mich., 1957- .

BRANDT, REX(FORD)—Painter, I., W., L., T., Des.
405-407 Goldenrod Ave., Corona del Mar, Cal.

B. San Diego, Cal., Sept. 12, 1914. *Studied*: Univ. California, A.B.; Stanford Univ.; Redlands Univ. *Member*: ANA; San F. AA; Cal. A. Cl.; Laguna Beach AA; AWS; Phila. WC Cl.; San Diego FA Soc.; Cal. WC Soc.; Riverside FA Gld.; hon: Cal. Color Soc.; Glendale Gal.; Pomona Valley AA; Desert A. Center. *Awards*: prizes, Los A. Mus. A., 1937, 1945; Oakland A. Mus., 1937, 1942; San Diego FA Gal., 1939, 1942; So. Cal. Fair, 1936-1939; Laguna Beach, 1936, 1937, 1941, 1944, 1948, 1949, 1952; Cal. WC Soc., 1938, 1941, 1945, 1952; Orange Show, 1949; Cal. State Fair, 1934; Univ. Cal., 1935; Univ. Cal., Berkeley, 1936; Los A. County Fair, 1936-1939; Ebell Cl., Los A., 1938; Santa Paula, 1943; Riverside FA Gld., 1941, 1943; Newport H.S., 1946; San Dimas, Cal., 1946; AWS, 1952; Paramount H.S., 1952; de Young Mem. Mus., 1953; medals, Oakland A. Mus., 1940, 1942; City of Los Angeles, 1951; citation, A. Dir. Cl., Los A., 1955. *Work*: Los A. Mus. A.; Crocker A. Gal.; San Diego FA Soc.; Chaffey AA; Cole of California; Riverside Polytechnic H.S.; Fort Motor Co.; Newport Union H.S.; Bonita H.S.; Paramount H.S.; Automobile Cl. of So. Cal.; U.S. Maritime Service; Orange Coast College; U.S. Treasury Dept.; SFMA; murals, San Bernardino and Chemawa H.S. *Exhibited*: AIC; CGA; Chaffey AA; Los A. AA; AGAA; Haggin Mem. Gal.; NCFA; Chicago A. Cl.; St. Paul Acad. (Minn.); DMFA; Los A. County Fair; Denver A. Mus.; San Diego FA Gal.; Currier Mus. A.; Faulkner Gal. A.; Monticello Col.; Univ. So. Cal.; Riverside Mus.; Laguna Beach AA; Yellowstone A. Center; John Herron AI; Pasadena AI; Long Beach A. Center, and many others; one-man: Cal. PLH; Crocker A. Gal.; Santa Barbara Mus. A.; Los A. Mus. A.; Coronado AA; Fleming Mus. A.; So. Methodist Univ.; Univ. of Redlands; Pasadena Col.; Padua Hills Gal.; Chaffey Col.; Courvoisier Gal., San F.; Allan Hancock Col., and others. I., Fortune and Life magazines. Author: "Watercolor Technique in Fifteen Lessons"; "Watercolor Landscape in Fifteen Lessons." *Position*: Co-Dir., Brandt-Dike Sch., Corona del Mar, Cal., 1946-56; Dir., Rex Brandt Sch., Corona del Mar, Cal., 1956- ; Instr., Chouinard AI, Los Angeles, Cal., 1947- .

BRANDT, WARREN—Educator, P.
Department of Art, University of Mississippi; mail: Box 7, University 1, Miss.

B. Greensboro, N.C., Feb. 26, 1918. *Studied*: PIASch.; ASL; Washington Univ., St. Louis, Mo., B.F.A.; Univ. North Carolina, M.F.A. *Member*: Southeastern Col. Assn. *Awards*: John T. Millikin Traveling F., Washington Univ., 1948. *Position*: Hd., Dept. Art, Salem College, Winston-Salem, N.C., 1949-50; Instr., Pratt Institute Art Sch., Brooklyn, N.Y., 1950-52; Chm., Dept. Art, Univ. of Mississippi, University, Miss., 1957- .

BRANNAN, SOPHIE MARSTON—Painter, S.
1301 Leavenworth St., San Francisco, Cal.

B. Mountain View, Cal. *Studied*: Mark Hopkins Inst. A., and in Paris. *Member*: AWS; Conn. Acad. A.; AFA; N.Y. Soc. Women Painters; Soc. Medalists. *Awards*: prizes, NAWA; Conn. Acad. FA; McMillan prize, N.Y. Soc. Women Painters. *Work*: NAD; CGA; AIC; Syracuse Mus. FA; PAFA; Mus. FA, Toronto, Canada; Nebraska AA; Kansas AA; BM; Vanderpoel Coll.; AWS; Union Lg.; N.Y. WC Cl.; Wesleyan Col., Macon, Ga.; Macbeth Gal.; Maryland Inst. A. & Sc.; and in South America. *Exhibited*: AWS; Syracuse Mus. FA; AIC; Nebraska AA; PAFA; CGA; Macbeth Gal.; BM; Toronto, Canada, etc.

BRANNER, MARTIN M.—Cartoonist
Owsegatchie, Waterford, Conn.*

BRANSBY, ERIC JAMES—Painter, I., T.
Fine Arts Center; h. Lytle Star Route, Colorado Springs, Colo.

B. Auburn, N.Y., Oct. 25, 1916. *Studied*: Kansas City AI, with Thomas Hart Benton, Fletcher Martin; Colorado Springs FA Center, with Boardman Robinson, Jean Charlot; Colorado Col., B.A., M.A.; Yale Univ., M.F.A. *Member*: NSMP. *Awards*: Abbey Fnd. F., 1952; Teaching F., Yale Univ., 1949-50. *Work*: Nelson Gal., Kansas City, Mo.; Princeton Univ.; Oklahoma A. Center; Brigham Young Univ.; murals, Command & Genl. Staff Sch., USA, Ft. Leavenworth, Kans.; Colorado Col.; USAF, Colorado Springs, Colo.; Hq. NORAD, Colo. Springs; Brigham Young Univ., Provo, Utah; Medical Center, Colorado Springs; Univ. Illinois. *Exhibited*: Assoc. Am. A., 1941; Kansas City AI, 1940; Joslyn A. Mus., 1940; Oakland A. Mus., 1940; Oklahoma A. Center, 1945 (one-man); Denver A. Mus., 1951; LC, 1951; Colorado Springs FA Center, 1951. *Position*: Instr., Univ. Illinois, 1950-52; Summer Sch., Brigham Young Univ., 1956; Instr., Colorado Springs FA Center (evening) 1958; Dir., Creative Illus., USAF Air Defense Command, 1954-58.

BRANSOM, (JOHN) PAUL—Painter, I., Et.
15 West 67th St., New York 23, N.Y.

B. Washington, D.C., July 26, 1885. *Member*: AWS; SC; Audubon A.; AAPL. Illus., forty-five books, including, "The Call of the Wild," "The Wind in the Willows," "An Argosy of Fables," "Animals of American History," "Hunters Choice," "Wilderness Champion," "Wahoo Bobcat," "Phantom Deer," "Zoo Parade," and others.

BRAUGHT, ROSS—Painter, Lith., T.
4415 Warwick Blvd., Kansas City, Mo.

B. Carlisle, Pa., Aug. 6, 1898. *Studied*: PAFA, and in Europe. *Work*: PAFA; William Rockhill Nelson Gal. A.; WMAA; murals, Music Hall, Kansas City, Mo.; San Juan, Puerto Rico. *Position*: Instr. Kansas City AI, 1931-36, 1948- .

BRAUNER, ERLING B.—Educator, P.
Michigan State University, East Lansing, Mich.

B. Ithaca, N.Y., Apr. 16, 1906. *Studied*: Cornell Univ., B.F.A., M.F.A. *Member*: Mich. Acad. A., Sc. & Let. *Work*: Denison Univ. Lib. *Exhibited*: Flint AI, 1950, 1952; Birmingham Little Gal.; Detroit Inst. A., 1953; South Bend AA, 1954; Ohio State Univ., 1956; Wooster College, 1956; Detroit Inst. A., 1956; Grand Rapids AI, 1956; Saginaw Mus. A., 1958. *Position*: Instr., 1935-40, Asst. Prof., 1940-42, Assoc. Prof., 1942-58, Prof., 1958- , Michigan State Univ., East Lansing, Mich.

BRAZEAU, WENDELL PHILLIPS—*Painter, Gr., T.*
University of Washington; h. 2631 29th Ave., West, Seattle 99, Wash.

B. Spokane, Washington, May 19, 1910. *Studied*: Univ. Washington, B.A., M.F.A.; Archipenko Sch. FA. *Member*: AEA; Am. Soc. for Aesthetics. *Awards*: prizes, Northwest WC Exh., 1950; Henry Gal., 1952; Western Wash. Fair. *Exhibited*: SAM, annually; Northwest Pr.M.; Oakland A. Gal.; Portland (Ore.) A. Mus.; Kaufman Gal., N.Y.; Northwest WC Soc.; Henry Gal. (one-man). *Position*: Assoc. Prof. A., Univ. Washington, Seattle, Wash.

BRCIN, JOHN DAVID—*Sculptor, T.*
4 East Ohio St., Chicago, Ill.

B. Yugoslavia, Aug. 15, 1899. *Studied*: AIC, B.F.A.; Univ. Chicago; Chicago Acad. FA; Ohio State Univ., M.A., and with Albin Polasek. *Member*: NSS. *Awards*: prizes, Traveling F., AIC, 1920; AIC, 1923, 1926; Hoosier Salon, 1920, 1936; Mun. A. Lg., 1945. *Work*: Mun. A. Lg.; Witte Mem. Mus.; Washington & Lee Univ.; Joslyn Mus. A.; Washington Blvd. Hospital, Chicago; des., Herring medal for Am. Soc. Civil Engineers; Henry Horner monument, Chicago; Stephen Decatur monument, Decatur, Ill.; portrait, U.S. Naval Academy, Annapolis.

BREASTED, JAMES H(ENRY), JR.—*Lecturer, Hist.*
Kent School, Kent, Conn.; Mail: P.O. Box 276, Kent, Conn.

B. Chicago, Ill., Sept. 29, 1908. *Studied*: Princeton Univ., A.B.; Heidelberg Univ.; Oxford Univ.; Univ. Chicago, A.M.; Inst. for Advanced Study, Princeton. *Member*: Archaeological Inst. Am.; CAA; Officier de l'Academie Francaise. *Author*: "Arab Nationalism in the Near East," in publ., Africa, The Near East and The War, 1943; Egyptian Servant Statues (Bollingen Fnd., 1948). *Contributor* to professional journals. *Positions*: Instr., A. & Archaeology, Colorado College, Colorado Springs, 1937-39; Visiting L. in Art Hist., Hunter College, N.Y., 1941; Asst. Prof., Art Hist., UCLA, Los Angeles, Cal., 1941-46; Dir., Los A. Mus. A., 1946-51; L., Art Hist., and Master, Kent Sch., Kent, Conn., 1952-. Memb. Screening Comm., 3rd Intl. Art-film Festival, MMA, 1957.

BRECHER, SAMUEL—*Painter, T.*
124 West 23rd St.; h. 425 East 78th St., New York 21, N.Y.

B. Austria, July 4, 1897. *Studied*: CUASch.; NAD, and with Charles Hawthorne. *Member*: Audubon A.; AEA; Nat. Soc. Casein Painters; All. A. Am; Phila. WC Cl.; Painters & Sc. of New Jersey. *Awards*: prizes, SC, 1950, 1951; N.Y.State Fair, 1951; Fla. Southern Col., 1952 (citation); A. Lg. Long Island, 1954; Audubon A., 1953, 1956. *Work*: MMA; Walker A. Center; Newark Mus. A.; Tel-Aviv and Ain Harod Mus., Israel; Fla. Southern Col. *Exhibited*: WFNY 1939; GGE 1939; PAFA, 1936, 1943, 1957; Phila. WC Cl., 1958; Silvermine Gld. A., 1958; Butler Inst. Am. A., 1958; NAD, 1924, 1927, 1931, 1936, 1937, 1945, 1946; Carnegie Inst., 1941, 1944; AIC, 1936, 1938; AFA, 1931, 1944; Walker A. Center, 1943; Dayton AI, 1936, 1951, 1952; VMFA, 1944; BM, 1944; CM, 1939; SFMA, 1942; N.Y.State Fair, 1951; Rochester Mem. A. Mus., 1951-1955; Fla. Southern Col., 1952; Riverside Mus., 1954; CGA, 1953; P.&S. Soc., N.J., 1952; New Britain A. Mus., 1951; Staten Island Mus. A. & Sc., 1956; one-man: ACA Gal., 1935; Hudson Walker Gal., 1938, 1940; Kraushaar Gal., 1942, 1944; Babcock Gal., 1949, 1951. *Position*: Instr., Painting, Newark Sch. F. & Indst. A., Newark, N.J.; Bd. Dir., AEA, 1956-59; All. A. Am., 1958-59.

BREESKIN, ADELYN DOHME (Mrs.)—*Museum Director*
Baltimore Museum of Art, Wyman Park; h. 1521 Northwick Rd., Baltimore 18, Md.

B. Baltimore, Md., July 19, 1896. *Studied*: Bryn Mawr Col.; Radcliffe Col.; Sch. FA, Crafts & Dec. Des., Boston. *Awards*: Doctor of Letters, Goucher Col., 1953; "Star of Solidarity," Italian Government, 1954, for promoting intercultural betterment. *Author*: "The Graphic Work of Mary Cassatt," 1948; Baltimore Museum "News" articles, and contributor to other art publications. Lectures in U.S. and abroad. Television and radio, U.S.A. *Positions*: Staff, Johns Hopkins Univ., McCoy College, Art Dept., 1937-1950; Dir. & Cur. Graphic Art, Baltimore Museum of Art; Sec.-Treas., 1953-1956, Pres., 1956-1957, Assn. of Art Museum Directors; Committee on Ethics, Intl. Graphic

Arts Soc., 1958-1959; Memb. American Jury of Selection, 1955- ; Member Steering Committee, Museum Exhibition Assn., 1956- ; Sec., Print Council of America, 1956- ; Dir., Baltimore Museum of Art, Baltimore, Md., 1956- ; has served on many juries of selection for exhibitions shown in U.S. and abroad.

BREGER, DAVE (DAVID)—*Cartoonist*
King Features Syndicate, New York, N.Y.; h. 217 Fountain Rd., Englewood, N.J.

B. Chicago, Ill., Apr. 15, 1908. *Studied*: Univ. Illinois; Northwestern Univ., B.S. *Member*: Nat. Cartoonists Soc.; Newspaper Comics Council; Soc. Technical Writers & Editors. *Awards*: Award of Merit, Northwestern Univ., 1946; Certif. of Honor, Am. Nat. Red Cross, 1947; Award of Merit, U.S. Treasury Dept., 1950, 1958. *Author*: "Private Breger," 1942; "Private Breger's War," 1944; "Private Breger in Britain," 1944; "G.I. Joe," 1945; creator syndicated cartoon, "Mr. Breger"; Editor, "But That's Unprintable," 1955.

BREGLER, CHARLES—*Painter, W.*
4935 North 11th St., Philadelphia 41, Pa.

B. Philadelphia, Pa. *Studied*: PAFA, and with Thomas Eakins. Contributor to art magazines. *Author*: "Thomas Eakins as a Teacher."*

BREHM, GEORGE—*Illustrator, P.*
Chilmark, Martha's Vineyard, Mass.

B. Anderson, Ind., Sept. 30, 1878. *Studied*: ASL, with Twachtman, DuMond, Bridgman; Indiana Univ. *Member*: SI. Illustrations and portraiture.

BREHME, CLAIRE—*Painter, I., L., T., W.*
"Sunnyside," Church Rd., Glenside, Pa.

B. Berlin, Germany, May 16, 1886. *Studied*: with Franz von Skarbina. *Member*: AAPL. *Exhibited*: one-man: Glenside Pub. Lib.; Carl Schurz Fnd., Phila. Pa. *Author*: "Woman of Two Countries," 1936, and many articles on art.

BREININ, RAYMOND—*Painter, S., T.*
126 West 21st St., New York 11, N.Y.

B. Vitebsk, Russia, Nov. 30, 1910. *Studied*: Chicago Acad. FA; and with Uri Penn. *Awards*: prizes, AIC (7); MMA; PAFA (2); Univ. Illinois; Ecclesiastical A. Gld., Detroit; Art:USA, 1958; Bloomington AA. *Work*: MMA; MModA; BM; AIC; PC; BMFA; FMA; SFMA; San Diego FA Soc.; Newark Mus. A.; Cranbrook Acad. Art; Zanesville A. Mus.; John Herron AI; Williams Col.; Univ. Illinois; Am. Acad. A. & Lets.; State Dept., U.S. Govt.; Encyclopaedia Britannica; Capehart Coll.; E. Lilly Co.; Nat. Gal., Scotland; costumes and settings for Ballet Theatre's "Undertow"; murals, Winnetka (Ill.) H.S.; State Hospital, Elgin, Ill.; USPO, Wilmette, Ill.; Pump Room, Ambassador East Hotel, Chicago; Jade and Emerald rooms Sherman Hotel, Chicago. *Positions*: A-in-Res., Univ. Southern Illinois; Instr. A., Univ. Minnesota; Breinin Sch. A., Chicago, Ill.

BREITENBACH, EDGAR—*Chief, Print Division*
Library of Congress, Washington, D.C.

Position: Chief, Prints and Photograph Division, Library of Congress, Washington, D.C.*

BRENNAN, ANN SCHABBEHAR. See Schabbehar, Ann

BRENNAN, DEAN—*Painter*
526 N St., Anchorage, Alaska

Exhibited: nationally, U.S.A., especially on the West Coast.

BRENNAN, HAROLD JAMES—*Educator, C., L., W.*
School for American Craftsmen of the Rochester Institute of Technology, 65 Plymouth Ave., South, Rochester 8, N.Y.; h. 920 Lake Rd., Webster, N.Y.

B. Indianapolis, Ind., Oct. 25, 1903. *Studied*: Carnegie Inst., B.A., M.A.; Harvard Univ.; Univ. of Paris. *Member*: Com. on A. Edu.; Am. Inst. AA; Midwest Des-Craftsmen. *Awards*: Scholarship, Inst. of International Edu., Univ.

Paris, 1938; Grogan prize, Assoc. A. of Pittsburgh, 1938. *Exhibited*: Assoc. A. Pittsburgh. Contributor to Craft Horizons; Handweaver & Craftsman; Journal of Am. Indst. AA. Lecturer, Arts Program of the Assn. of Am. Colleges, 1934-53, on "Contemporary Design for Living"; "The Designer-Craftsman in Modern Society," etc. *Position*: Prof. A., 1933-46, Chm. Div. of the Arts, 1946-48, Westminster Col.; Dir., SFMA. for Am. Craftsmen, Rochester Inst. Tech., 1948- ; Chm. Div. Arts, 1953- .

BRENSON, THEODORE—*Painter, Gr., E., L., W.*
51 West 81st St., New York 24, N.Y.

B. Riga, Latvia, Nov. 27, 1893. *Studied*: Beaux-Arts; Petrograd; Univ. Riga, Arch. deg. *Member*: SAGA; CAA; AAUP; Am. Abstract A.; Fed. Mod. P.&S. *Awards*: Decorated by French State, "Officier d'Academie," 1938; Scholarship, Direction Generale pour les Relations Culturelles, Paris; prizes, BM (purchase); Pennell Fnd. (purchase); Channing Hare award. Soc. Four Arts, Palm Beach, Fla.; Prix de la Critique, 1957; Prix Suisse de peinture Abstraite, 1958. *Work*: Nat. Mus., Stockholm; LC; Dumbarton Oaks Fnd.; N.Y. Pub. Lib.; MMA; French Inst. in the U.S.; Carnegie Inst.; Bibliotheque Nationale, Paris; BM; Contemp. A. Soc., London; WMAA, and in museums in Milan, Rome, Florence, Riga, Paris. *Exhibited*: SAGA; NAD; LC; AIC; PAFA; MMA; WMAA; Phila. Pr. Cl.; Inst. Contemp. A., Boston; CAM; Salon d'Automne, Salon des Indp., Petit Palais, Bibliotheque Nationale, Salon des Realites, Paris, France; Tate Gal., London; Wittenborn Gal.; Newcomb-Macklin Gal.; SFMA; FMA; Harvard Univ.; Roullier Gal.; N.Y. Pub. Lib.; Lyman Allyn Mus.; Currier Gal. A.; CAM; BM; Soc. Four Arts; Douglass Col. A. Gal.; Rutgers Univ.; The Contemporaries; Stable Gal.; Rochester Mus. A.; DMFA; N.Y. City Center Gal.; Univ. Minnesota; Mint Mus. A.; Bradley Univ.; Wichita AA.; Galerie du Haut Pave, Paris; Galerie St. Laurent, Brussels; New Vision Centre Gal., London; Drian Gal., London. Author, I., books on art and education. Contributor to national magazines in U.S. and abroad. *Position*: Prof. A., Rutgers Univ.; Chm., Dept. A., Douglass Col., New Brunswick, N.J.

BRENT, ADALIE MARGULES—
Teacher, Comm. A., I., Des., P.
3043 Eastland, Baton Rouge, La.

B. Dallas, Tex., Nov. 27, 1920. *Studied*: Univ. Texas; Univ. California at Los A., B.E., B.A., M.A., with Alexander Hogue. *Awards*: prize, Dallas Mus. FA, 1943; La. A. Comm., 1956, 1958. *Exhibited*: Texas General, 1942, 1945; Oklahoma General, 1944; Houston All. A., 1944; Ney Mus. A., 1941, 1944; Univ. California, 1945; Witte Mem. Mus., 1941, 1943, 1945; Louisiana A. Comm., (one-man) 1955 & prior; Terry AI, 1952. Author, Correspondence Courses in A. Edu., Correspondence Course Instr.; Instr., Louisiana State Univ., Baton Rouge, La.; Instr., St. Joseph's Acad., Baton Rouge, La.

BRESSLER, HARRY S.—*Painter, L.*
521 Ogden Ave., West Englewood, N.J.

B. Austria, Jan. 7, 1893. *Studied*: ASL; NAD, and with George Bridgman, Robert Brackman, Frank DuMond, Leon Kroll, Emile Gruppe. *Member*: North Shore AA; Southern Vermont AA; ASL; Bergen County A. Gld.; SC; Ridgewood (N.J.) AA. *Exhibited*: NAC, 1952-1955; So. Vermont AA, 1950, 1951; Bergen County A. Gld., 1949-1955; New Jersey State Exh., 1953, 1954; one-man: Teaneck (N.J.) Pub. Lib., 1954; N.Y. Pub. Lib. Branches, 1954; seascape exh., Teaneck, N.J., Pub. Lib., 1955. Lecturer: "Sketching Out of Doors," N.Y. Pub. Lib., 1956; Fairleigh-Dickinson Univ., 1958. *Position*: Chm., Cart. Council, Nat. Com. Infantile Paralysis; Cart., King Features, 1920-28; Dayton, Ohio, Daily News and Cox papers, 1929-32; N.Y. Daily Mirror, 1933-35; Ed., Bressler Ed. Cartoons, Inc., 1935-47; Pres. & Ed. Dir., 'Incentiv-Aids' series of posters for industry and armed forces, World War II.

BRETSNYDER, ARNO—*Painter*
9706 Longwood Dr., Chicago 43, Ill.

B. Chicago, Ill., July 13, 1885. *Studied*: Francis A. Acad., Chicago; AIC; & with John Vanderpoel. *Member*: Illinois Soc. F. *Awards*: Med., AIC, 1939; prize, Galesburg, Ill., 1938; Logan Prize, 1938; All-Illinois Prize, 1952.*

BRETT, DOROTHY EUGENIE—*Painter, W.*
Taos, N.M.

B. London, England, Nov. 10, 1883. *Studied*: Slade Sch. A., London. *Exhibited*: MMA, 1950; Univ. Illinois, 1953; Am-British A. Center, 1950; DMFA, and throughout Texas. Contributor to New Yorker magazine.*

BREUL, HAROLD (G.)—*Designer, Cart., I., P.*
48 Custom House St., Providence 3, R.I.; h. 185 Brown St., Providence, R.I.

B. North Providence, R.I., May 6, 1889. *Studied*: R.I.Sch. Des.; PAFA. *Member*: Providence AC; Providence WC Cl.; AWS. *Awards*: Cresson traveling scholarship, PAFA, 1912. *Exhibited*: AWS, 1942, 1944, 1945, 1946; Providence AC, 1956, 1957; Providence WC Cl., 1957, 1958.

BREWER, FLOYD E.—
Mural Tapestry Des., P., T., L.
1121 Thomas Ave., St. Paul 4, Minn.

B. Coin, Iowa, Apr. 24, 1899. *Studied*: Minneapolis Sch.A.; St. Paul Sch. A., and with Hans Hofmann, Fernand Leger, Wassily Kandinsky, Diego Rivera. *Member*: Minnesota AA (hon.); AEA; St. Paul Assn. of P. & S.; St. Paul Council of A. & Sc. *Awards*: prizes, AFA; Minneapolis Inst. A., 1947, 1950; Minnesota State Fair, 1949. *Work*: Walker A. Center; Treasury Dept., Wash., D.C.; Minneapolis Inst. A. *Exhibited*: AIC, 1931-1938; SFMA; Milwaukee AI; Macalester Col., 1957; Mus. Contemp. Crafts, N.Y., 1956; Kansas City AI; one-man: mural tapestries, World Theatre Gal., St. Paul, 1954; St. Paul Gal., 1955, Am-Mexican Inst. of Culture, Mexico City, 1953, Winona Pub. Lib. Gal., 1954; 16 paintings, "Uncle Sam's Children," Minnesota State Capitol, 1954; Coffman Union, Univ. Minnesota, 1956; paintings, Westgate Theatre A. Gal., Minneapolis, 1954; Davenport Mun. A. Gal., 1951; St. Thomas Col., St. Catherine's Col., St. Paul, 1951; Hamline Univ., 1952; Walker A. Center, 1952. *Position*: Pres., Minnesota AA, 1951-52, 1952-53; Pres. St. Paul Assn. P. & S., 1954-58; Dir., Campus Theatre A. Gal., Minneapolis; Bd. Dir., St. Paul Council of A. & Sc.

BREWINGTON, MARION VERNON—
Museum Curator, W.
The Peabody Museum; h. 6 Hamilton St., Salem, Mass.

B. Salisbury, Md., June 23, 1902. *Studied*: Univ. Pennsylvania, B.S. *Member*: Soc. for Nautical Research; Salem Marine Soc.; Mass. Hist. Soc. *Awards*: Guggenheim F., 1958. Author: "Chesapeake Bay, A Pictorial Maritime History," 1953. Contributor of many articles to The American Neptune; Maryland Magazine of History; Pennsylvania Magazine of History; U.S. Naval Inst. Proceedings, etc. *Positions*: Cur., Naval Hist. Fnd., 1946-48; Cur., Maritime History, Md. Hist. Soc., 1954-55; Cur., The Kendall Whaling Mus., 1956- ; Asst. Dir. & Cur., Maritime History, The Peabody Mus., Salem, Mass., 1956- .

BREZEE, EVELYN—*Painter, E.*
2716 Shasta Rd., Berkeley 8, Cal.

B. Seattle, Wash., Sept. 27, 1912. *Studied*: Univ. California, A.B., M.A. *Member*: San F. AA. *Exhibited*: SFMA, 1936-1946; Oakland A. Gal., 1945. *Position*: A.T., El Cerrito H.S., El Cerrito, Cal., 1944- ; Instr., California Col. A. & Crafts, Oakland, Cal., 1945-1950 (summer 1956).*

BRICE, WILLIAM—*Painter, E.*
427 Beloit St., Los Angeles 49, Cal.

B. New York, N.Y., Apr. 23, 1921. *Studied*: Chouinard AI; ASL. *Member*: AEA. *Awards*: Los Angeles, 1947; Los Angeles City Exh., 1951. *Work*: MMA; WMAA; MModA; Los A. Mus. A.; Santa Barbara Mus. A. *Exhibited*: Carnegie Inst., 1948, 1949, 1954; WMAA, 1947, 1950, 1951; Santa Barbara Mus. A., 1945; Los A. Mus. A., 1947-1951; Cal. PLH, 1951-1952; Sao Paulo, Brazil. *Position*: Assoc. Prof., Dept. A., Univ. California at Los Angeles, 1953- .*

BRIDAHAM, LESTER BURBANK—
Museum Director, E., W., L., P., Eng.
Strathmont Museum, Elmira, N.Y.

B. Denver, Colo., Aug. 30, 1899. *Studied*: MIT, B.S., M.S.; Harvard Univ.; ASL, with Kenneth Hayes Miller, K. Nicolaides. *Awards*: Am. Field Service Fnd., F., 1931, 1932, in France & Morocco. *Exhibited*: GRD Gal., N.Y., 1932; AIC, 1946, 1948; AEA, 1951, 1952. Author: "Gargoyles, Chimeres and the Grotesque in French Gothic Sculpture," 1930. Contributor to Art in America, 1951. Lectures on Gothic and Modern Art; Morocco; Spain. *Position*: Pub. Relations Counsel, AIC, 1938-42; U.S.Navy Instr., 1942-45; Sec., AIC, Chicago, Ill., 1945-54; Dir., Louisiana State Museum, New Orleans, La., 1954-58; Dir., Strathmont Museum, Elmira, N.Y., 1958- .

BRIDGE, EVELYN—Etcher, W., P., I., Gr.
19 East 54th St., New York 22, N.Y.

B. Chicago, Ill., June 16, 1872. *Studied*: AIC; College de France, Sorbonne, Academie Colorossi, Paris. *Member*: Chicago Soc. Et. *Work*: NGA; N.Y. Pub. Lib.; MMA; Carnegie Lib., Wash., D.C. *Exhibited*: Salon d'Automne, 1932, 1933 (miniatures); AIC; PAFA; Southern Pr. M.*

BRIDGES, GEORGES—Sculptor, Des.
214 Edgewood Blvd., Birmingham 9, Ala.

B. Chattanooga, Tenn., Mar. 31, 1899. *Studied*: Cincinnati Acad. A.; & abroad. *Work*: IBM; Univ. Alabama; monuments, Atlanta, Ga., Birmingham, Ala.; Arch. Sculptures, public bldgs. in Ala., Ga., La., and Eglin Field, Fla. Many portraits in bronze and marble. *Exhibited*: CGA; Birmingham Mus. A., 1955 (one-man).

BRIGANTE, NICHOLAS P.—Painter
2620 Rutherford Dr., Los Angeles 28, Cal.

B. Naples, Italy, June 29, 1895. *Studied*: ASL of Los A., with Rex Slinkard, Val Costello. *Member*: Cal. WC Soc.; San Diego A. Gld. *Award*: Prizes, med., Los A. Fiesta Exh., 1929; prizes, Cal. WC Soc.; San Diego A. Gld., 1939. *Exhibited*: BM, 1924; AIC, 1924; Cal. WC Soc.; Riverside Mus.; GGE 1939; San F. AA; Los A. Mus. A.; Santa Barbara Mus. A., 1942 (one-man); Los A. AA, 1946.*

BRIGGS, AUSTIN—Illustrator
Redding, Conn.

Member: SI; Players Cl.; Co-Founder, Member, Famous Artist Schools, Westport, Conn. Illus. for Saturday Evening Post; Good Housekeeping; Look, and many other publications. Author articles on art for current periodicals. Former Pres., Westport A. Cl.

BRIGGS, BERTA N. (Mrs. William H.)—Painter, W., L.
49 East 96th St., New York 28, N.Y.

B. St. Paul, Minn., June 5, 1884. *Studied*: ASL, with Kenyon Cox, George Breck; PIASch; Columbia Univ.; Minneapolis Craft Sch., with Ernest Batchelder. *Member*: NAWA; Sch.A.Lg. *Awards*: Med. of Honor, NAWA, 1954. *Work*: Wesleyan Col., Macon, Ga. *Exhibited*: NAWA, 1927-1945; Women's Int. A., London, 1931; Palace Legion Honor, 1931; Argent Gal., 1932, 1934, 1936, 1939, 1943 (one-man); Currier Gal. A., 1943; Whyte Gal., 1944; Cosmopolitan Cl., N.Y., 1958; Burr Gal., N.Y., 1958. Lectures: History of Painting, Architecture, Romanesque Sculpture. Author: "Charles Willson Peale, Artist and Patriot," 1952; "To the Shores of Tripoli," 1955. *Position*: Hon. Trustee, Sch.A.Lg., New York, N.Y., 1955- .

BRIGGS, JUDSON REYNOLDS—Painter, Eng., T., L.
c/o ACA Gallery, 63 East 57th St., New York 22, N.Y.

B. Philadelphia, Pa., May 17, 1906. *Studied*: with Charles Schroeder. *Awards*: prizes, A. Dir. Cl., 1945; Palacio de Bellas Artes, Mexico, D.F.; Treasury Dept., Wash., D.C.; Carillon Mus., Va.; MModA; Portland Mus. A. *Exhibited*: PAFA, 1946, MModA; WFNY 1939; MMA; Galeria Reger, 1952, San Carlos Acad., 1949, Galeria Mont Orendain, 1949, 1950, all in Mexico, D.F.; Casa de los Intellectuales, Madrid, Spain. *Work*: Prado Mus., Madrid; Maison de Culture, Paris; U.S. Embassy, Mexico City.*

BRIGHAM, GERTRUDE RICHARDSON—
Art School Director
East Boothbay, Me.

B. Boston, Mass. *Studied*: Mass. State A. Sch.; George Washington Univ., A.B., M.A., Ph.D.; Anson Cross A. Sch. *Member*: SSAL; Georgia AA. *Work*: Cross A. Sch.

Coll. *Exhibited*: SSAL; Georgia AA; Cross A. Sch. Author: "How to Draw and Paint—The New Vision Training Method," 1945, 2nd ed., 1958, & other books on art. Contributor to: Art magazines & periodicals. Lectures: Art & travel. *Position*: Dir., Cross A. Sch., East Boothbay, Me.

BRIGHAM, WILLIAM EDGAR—Craftsman, T., Des.
460 Rochambeau Ave., Providence 6, R.I.

B. North Attleboro, Mass., July 29, 1885. *Studied*: Harvard Univ., with Denman Ross; R.I.Sch.Des., with Henry Hunt Clark. *Member*: Providence AC; Boston Soc. A. & Crafts. *Awards*: Med., Boston Soc. A. & Crafts, 1936; Int. Exp., Paris, 1937; R.I.Fed. Garden Cl., 1939. *Work*: R.I.Sch.Des.; Cleveland Sch. A. *Exhibited*: WMA, 1943; Phila. A. All., 1945; America House, N.Y., 1944. Lectures: Design and Color.

BRIGHT, BARNEY—Sculptor, T., Des.
2031 Frankfort Ave.; h. 37 Claremoor Dr., Anchorage, Ky.

B. Shelbyville, Ky., July 8, 1927. *Studied*: Davidson Col.; Louisville A. Center, with Romauld Kraus; Univ. Louisville. *Member*: Louisville Sc. Soc.; Louisville A. Center Assn. *Awards*: prizes, Ky. & So. Indiana Exh., 1948; Louisville A. Center, 1949, 1955; Kentucky State Fair, 1956, 1957, 1958. *Work*: Children's Hospital, Louisville; First Christian Church, Shelbyville, Ky.; bronze figure, Citizen's Fidelity Bank, Louisville, Ky.; many port., reliefs, medals, etc., in private coll. *Exhibited*: Ky. & So. Indiana Exh., 1948-1950; Louisville A. Center, 1953-1955; Evansville Mus. A., 1955.

BRINDESI, OLYMPIO—Sculptor, T.
27 West 15th St., h. 201 Prince St., New York 12, N.Y.

B. Abruzzi, Italy, Feb. 7, 1897. *Studied*: ASL; BAID; & with Chester Beach, A.P. Proctor. *Member*: Arch.L.; NSS; Am. Veterans Soc. A. *Award*: Prize, Arch.L., 1927; A. & Crafts Assn., Meriden, Conn., 1958. *Work*: Lincoln Lib., Shippensburg, Pa. *Exhibited*: Arch. L., NSS; PAFA; AIC; Hispanic Soc.; BMA; Rochester Mem. A. Gal.; BM; WMAA. *Positions*: Inst., Cornell Univ., 1924-25, 1926-27; Instr., Modelling, drawing, St. Paul's Sch., Concord, N.H., 1930-31; CUASch., New York, N.Y., 1931.

BRINDLE, MELBOURNE—Commercial Artist, I.
Bridgewater, Conn.

B. Melbourne, Australia, Nov. 18, 1904. *Awards*: prizes, A. Dir. Cl., 1935, 1938, 1942, 1946. *Exhibited*: nationally and internationally. I., for national magazines.*

BRINLEY, D(ANIEL) PUTNAM—Painter, I., C.
231 South Main St., New Canaan, Conn.

B. Newport, R.I., Mar. 8, 1879. *Studied*: Dwight Sch.; ASL, and in Europe. *Member*: ANA; NAC; Arch. Lg.; NSMP; Silvermine Gld. A. *Awards*: med., Arch. Lg., 1932. *Work*: murals, Brooklyn Savings Bank; Met. Life Ins. Bldg.; Community Church, New Canaan; St. Paul's Church, Norwalk; St. George's Church, Bridgeport; Liberty Memorial, Kansas City, Mo.; USPO, Blakeley, Ga.; Hudson Motor Co. Stained glass, Fordham Lutheran Church; St. Mark's Church, New Canaan. Terrestrial Globe, Daily News Bldg., N.Y. *Exhibited*: Paris Salon; PAFA; Carnegie Inst.; NAD; Arch. Lg.; Silvermine Gld. A. I., travel books including 100 watercolors and crayon sketches of Canadian scenes published in books by Gordon Brinley.*

BRISAC, EDITH MAE—
Educator, Des., P., C., Comm., L.
Texas State College for Women; h. 528 Roberts Rd., Denton, Tex.

B. Walton, N.Y. *Studied*: PIASch; Columbia Univ., B.S., M.A.; Ecole des Beaux-Arts, Paris; Cranbrook Acad. A. *Member*: Texas FA Assn.; SSAL. *Awards*: Prizes, West Texas Exh., 1938, 1940, 1944, 1946; Dallas Mus. FA, 1941; med., Univ. California, 1942. *Work*: Dallas Mus. FA; Cranbrook Acad. A. *Exhibited*: Lib.Cong., 1944, 1945, 1946; BM, 1939; Carnegie Inst., 1944; Laguna Beach AA, 1945; WFNY 1939; Dallas Pr. Cl., 1938-1946; Texas FA Assn., 1937-1946; SSAL, 1939-1945; Kansas City AI, 1935-1941; Texas General Exh., 1939-1946. Lectures: Design;

Interior Decoration. *Position*: Prof. FA, Alabama College for Women, 1929-33; Texas Woman's University, Denton, Tex., 1934- .

BRITSKY, NICHOLAS—Painter, E.
University of Illinois, Champaign, Ill.; h. 1410 South Vine St., Urbana, Ill.

B. Weldirz, Ukraine, Russia, Dec. 11, 1913. *Studied*: Yale Univ., B.F.A.; Columbia Univ.; Syracuse Univ. *Member*: CAA. *Awards*: Traveling F., Yale Univ., 1938; Fulbright F., 1956-57; prizes, Ohio Univ., 1951; Old Northwest Territory Exh., 1954. *Work*: Bell Telephone Bldg., Waterloo, Iowa; Illinois State Mus.; Galesburg Jr. H.S. Contributor to Encyclopaedia Slovanica. Lectures: Contemporary Art; Mural Decoration. *Exhibited*: Butler AI, 1953, 1955; Old Northwest Territory Exh., 1953, 1954, 1958; AWS, 1958; Illinois State Mus., 1958. *Position*: Assoc. Prof. A., Univ. Illinois, 1946- ; A. Dir., Garrard Press, Champaign, Ill.

BRITTON, EDGAR—Sculptor, P., L., C.
1947 Mesa Rd., Colorado Springs, Colo.

B. Kearney, Neb., Apr. 15, 1901. *Studied*: Univ. Iowa; Univ. Kansas, and with Karl Mattern, Albert Bloch. *Member*: Colo. Springs A. Gld. *Awards*: prizes, Denver A. Mus., 1944; Pasadena AI, 1946; Colo. Springs FA Center, 1946. *Work*: AIC; Colo. Springs FA Center; Pasadena AI; Univ. Nebraska; USPO, East Moline, Ill.; Dept. Interior Bldg., Wash., D.C.; sc. for U.S. Nat. Bank, Colorado Springs, 1955 (including 3 bronze doors). *Exhibited*: Denver A. Mus., 1943-1945; Pasadena AI, 1946; Univ. Nebraska, 1945; Colo. Springs FA Center, 1945, 1946, 1953, 1955; Des Moines A. Center, 1949, 1950, 1952. Lectures: Fresco Painting. *Position*: Instr., Des Moines A. Center, 1948-49; Colo. Springs FA Center, 1949-50.*

BRIXIUS, DOROTHY ANN—Designer, P., I.
810 South 28th St., Manitowoc, Wis.

B. Yankton, S.D., Jan. 30, 1916. *Studied*: Federal Sch. A.; Layton Sch. A. (maj. indst. des.). *Awards*: nat. winner painting, U.S.Navy recruiting, 1944. *Position*: Engineering Dept., Allis Chalmers Mfg. Co., 1942-44; Indst. I., 1953-55, A. Dir., 1955- , Manitowoc Engineering Corp., Manitowoc, Wis.

BROADD, HARRY ANDREW—Educator, P., L., A. Hist.
University of Tulsa; h. 2424 East 40th St., Tulsa 5, Okla.

B. Chicago, Ill., Feb. 17, 1910. *Studied*: Univ. Chicago, Ph.B.; Columbia Univ., A.M.; Univ. Michigan, Ph.D.; Northwestern Univ.; AIC. *Member*: AAUP; CAA; NAEA. *Exhibited*: AIC, 1932, 1933, 1936, 1937; Laguna Beach AA, 1945; Univ. Chicago, 1932, 1933; Century Gal., Chicago, 1935; Detroit Inst. A., 1946; Philbrook A. Center, 1947-1958. Contributor to Design Magazine; articles on art to World Book Encyclopedia, 1958. *Lectures*: History of Art, Philbrook A. Center, 1950-54. *Position*: Instr., Indiana Univ., 1935-37; Asst. Prof. A., Mich. State Normal Col., Ypsilanti, Mich., 1937-1947; Assoc. Prof. A., 1947-54, Prof. A., 1954- , Univ. Tulsa, Tulsa, Okla.

BROCK, EMMA L.—Writer, I.
3719 Bryant Ave., S., Minneapolis 9, Minn.

B. Fort Shaw, Mont. *Studied*: Univ. Minnesota, B.A.; Minneapolis Sch. A.; ASL, with Bridgman, Robinson, Pennell. *Member*: Authors Lg. Am.; A. Gld.; Minnesota AA. *Exhibited*: Minnesota AA; AWS; Brooklyn Soc. Et. Author, I., "Kristie and the Colt," 1949; "Three Ring Circus," 1950; "Kristie's Buttercup," 1952; "Ballet for Mary," 1954; "Plug Horse Derby," 1955; "Come on-along, Fish," 1957.

BROCKDORFF, HERMAN—Sculptor, P., T.
Cocoa, Fla.

B. Copenhagen, Denmark, Oct. 21, 1907. *Member*: A. Lg. Am. *Awards*: prizes, Merchant Seamen Exh., 1943-45. *Exhibited*: Merchant Seamen Exh., 1943-1945; LC, 1945, 1946; NAD, 1946; Phila. Pr. Cl., 1946; Northwest Pr. M., 1946 (one-man); New-Age Gal., 1944-1946, 1948-1952; Research Studios, Maitland, Fla., 1949 (one-man); Contemporary Interiors, Miami Beach, 1951 (one-man). *Work*: carved tile front, Florida Power & Light Co., Cocoa, Melbourne, Fla.*

BROCKHURST, GERALD L.—Painter
Ewing Ave., Franklin Lakes, N.J.*

BRODEUR, CLARENCE A.—Painter, W., L.
77 Avon St., New Haven 11, Conn.

B. Westfield, Mass., Oct. 18, 1905. *Studied*: Harvard Univ., A.B.; Yale Univ., Sch. FA, M.A.; Fontainebleau Sch. FA; Norfolk Sch. A. *Member*: New Haven Paint & Clay Cl.; Conn. WC Soc.; Conn. Acad. A. & Sc.; Norwich AA; Essex AA. *Awards*: prizes, Norwich, Conn., 1951, 1954; New Haven Paint & Clay Cl., 1952. *Work*: FMA; Yale Univ.; Fla. Southern Col. *Exhibited*: NAD, 1943; Albany Inst. Hist. & A., 1949, 1951; Conn. Acad. FA, 1948-1954; PAFA, 1946, 1952; New Haven Paint & Clay Cl., 1944-1958; Silvermine Gld. A., 1950-1958; New Hampshire AA, 1949-1951; WMAA, 1952; Essex AA, 1954-1958; Eastern States Exh., 1957; Mystic AA., 1958. *Position*: Instr., Asst. Prof., Vassar Col., 1936-41; PIASch., 1945-51; Trustee, Fontainebleau FA & Music Fnd., 1947- , Vice-Pres., 1953- ; Pres., New Haven Paint & Clay Cl., 1952-54; Dir., Conn. WC Soc., 1954-56.

BRODHEAD, QUITA [Mrs.]—Painter, T.
Box 165, Atlee Rd., Wayne, Pa.

B. Wilmington, Del. *Studied*: PAFA; Grande Chaumiere, Paris, and with McCarter, Alexander Archipenko, Arthur B. Carles. *Member*: A. All. Am.; AEA; Group 55. *Awards*: F., PAFA; prize and medal, Wilmington AA, 1941, 1942; Ohio Univ., Col. FA, 1947. *Exhibited*: PAFA, 1939-1943; Am. Soc. Women P. & S., 1936; Bryn Mawr, Pa., 1944, 1959; Salon d'Automne, Paris, 1951; Delgado Mus. A., 1948; Butler AI, 1948, 1949; A. All. Am., 1945; one-man: New York, 1939, 1940, 1941, 1947, 1949, Pittsburgh, Pa., 1939; Philadelphia, Pa., 1953; Wilmington, Del., 1954; Dubin Gal., Phila., Pa., 1956. *Work*: Creuze Gal., Paris; many portraits of prominent people. *Position*: Instr., Painting, Bryn Mawr A. Center, Pa.

BRODNEY, EDWARD—Painter
196 Boylston St., Boston 16, Mass.; h. 15 Clark St., Newton Centre 59, Mass.

B. Boston, Mass., Apr. 15, 1910. *Studied*: Yale Sch. FA, B.F.A.; BMFA Sch.; Mass. Sch. A. *Work*: murals, Mass. State Capitol; Newton City Hall. *Position*: Dir., Brodney A. Gal., Boston, Mass.*

BRODY, PHILIP MORTON—Designer, Gr., P., L.
170 Boulevard, Scarsdale, N.Y.

B. New York, N.Y., April 22, 1905. *Studied*: Harvard Col., B.S.; ASL; Real Academia di Belle Arte, Florence, Italy; Ecole de l'Art Contemporain, Paris. *Member*: IDI; Scarsdale AA; Westchester A. & Crafts Gld. *Exhibited*: AIC, 1938; Sarasota AA, 1937; Ferargil Gal., 1938; Michigan State Col., 1939; Los A. Mus. A., 1943. Lectures in museums, women's clubs, universities on art and color. *Position*: Chm. Program Committee, Nat. Soc. for Dec. Des.

BROEMEL, CARL W.—Painter
10 Carrigan Ave., White Plains, N.Y.

B. Cleveland, Ohio, Sept. 5, 1891. *Studied*: Cleveland Sch. A.; ASL; Royal Sch. App. A., Munich, Germany. *Member*: SI (Bd. Memb., Com. Chm.). *Awards*: prizes, CMA, 1920-1929; AWS, 1942. *Work*: CMA; BM. *Exhibited*: AIC; WFNY 1939; CMA, 1953, 1955; Air Force Art Show, Pentagon, Wash., D.C., 1955. Selected as one of group sent to the Arctic to make pictorial records for the U.S. Air Force. Lectures on Arctic travel and painting in the Arctic.

BROGDEN, ROBERT B.—Cartoonist
417 Riverside Dr., New York 25, N.Y.

B. Winter Haven, Fla., Apr. 2, 1924. *Studied*: Ringling Sch. A.; A. Career Sch.; ASL. Contributor of cartoons to Collier's, American, True, This Week, Argosy, American Legion, Parents, American Mercury, Seventeen, Cue, Parade, True Detective, Successful Farming, Family Circle, Adventure, Dell Publ. Co., Chilton Publ. Co., N.W. Ayer Co., Best Cartoons of the Year, and others.

BRONER, ROBERT—Etcher, Eng., P., T., Cr.
18981 Greenlawn St., Detroit 21, Mich.

B. Detroit, Mich., Mar. 10, 1922. *Studied*: Wayne Univ., B.F.A., M.A.; Detroit Soc. A. & Crafts, with Sarkis Sar-

kisian; Atelier 17, with S. W. Hayter. *Awards*: Wayne
Univ. Scholarship. *Work*: MModA; BM; N.Y. Pub. Lib.
Exhibited: MModA, 1954; MMA, 1953; BM, 1951, 1953,
1958; Phila. Pr. Cl., 1958; Silvermine Gld. A., 1958; Oak-
land Mus. A., 1958; Detroit Inst. A., 1943, 1945, 1950-
1954, 1956; one-man: Phila. A. All., 1956; Wellons Gal.,
N.Y., 1955; Werbe & Garelicks Gal., 1953, 1957; Michigan
State Univ., 1957. Contributor to Detroit Times; Art in
America; Art in Industry. *Positions*: Instr., Alabama Poly-
technic Inst., 1948-1949; Dir., Montclair Sch. Fine &
Comm. A., 1951-52; Instr., Etching, Robert Blackburn's
Creative Graphics, New York, N.Y., 1953-56; Instr.,
Graphics, Detroit A. Sch. of the Soc. of A. & Crafts.

BROOK, ALEXANDER—*Painter*
"Point House," Sag Harbor, L.I., N.Y.

B. Brooklyn, N.Y., July 14, 1898. *Member*: NAD; Nat.
Inst. A. & Let. *Awards*: Med. & prize, AIC, 1929; Carnegie
Inst., 1930, 1939; med., PAFA, 1931; Guggenheim F., 1931;
WMA; gold med., PAFA, 1948; Los A. Mus. A., 1934;
med., Paris Exp., 1937; med., San F. AA, 1938; 2nd Alt-
man prize, NAD, 1957. *Work*: MMA; WMAA; MModA;
BM; Newark Mus.; AIC; Albright A. Gal.; CGA; Nelson
Gal. A.; Toledo Mus. A.; SFMA; Univ. Nebraska; BMFA;
Detroit Inst. A.; CAM; Carnegie Inst.; Wadsworth Athe-
neum, Hartford, Conn.; Michigan State Univ.; deYoung
Mem. Mus., San Francisco, etc.

BROOK, MRS. ALEXANDER. See *Knee, Gina*

BROOKS, CHARLES M., JR.—*Educator*
Art Department, Lawrence College, Appleton, Wis.
Position: Hd., Art Dept., Lawrence College, Appleton,
Wis.*

BROOKS, ERICA MAY—*Lecturer, P., C., Gr., E.*
180 Washington Ave., Albany, N.Y.

B. London, England, July 9, 1894. *Studied*: with Myra K.
Hughes, Norman Garstin, Charles Woodbury. *Member*:
Royal Drawing Soc., London (hon.); Royal Soc. T.
Awards: prizes, Altamont (N.Y.) Fair, 1955; Chautauqua,
N.Y., 1956; Albany, N.Y., 1956; Albany Pr. Cl., 1956;
Southall prize, 1948; Albany A. Group, 1958. *Exhibited*:
Barnard Cl., 1932; 8th St. Gal., 1939, 1947; Albany Inst.
Hist. & A., 1950; Albany A. Group, 1948-1958; Sche-
nectady Mus. A., 1951 (one-man); Ganso Gal., 1934;
SFMA, 1936; Nat. Print Exh., 1955. Contributor to English
and American educational magazines.

BROOKS, HOWARD (GRIGGS)—*Painter, Des., C., T.*
230 West 139th St., New York 30, N.Y.

B. Staunton, Va., Mar. 21, 1915. *Studied*: West Virginia
State Col., B.S.; PIASch; T. Col., Columbia Univ.; Cran-
brook Acad. A., M.F.A.; Parsons Sch. Des., and with
Jo Mielziner. *Awards*: prize, Solomon Islands A. Show;
Textile Des. Comp. *Work*: murals, West Va. State Col.;
U.S. Navy; Am. Red Cross; Desert Inn, Las Vegas, Nev.
Exhibited: CAM, 1940; CGA, 1940; VFMA, 1944.*

BROOKS, JAMES—*Painter, T.*
500 West Broadway, New York 12, N.Y.

B. St. Louis, Mo., Oct. 18, 1906. *Studied*: Southern Metho-
dist Univ.; ASL, with K. Nicolaides, Boardman Robinson.
Awards: prizes, Carnegie Inst., 1952; Logan prize, AIC,
1957. *Work*: BM; WMAA; MModA; Albright A. Gal.,
Buffalo, N.Y.; MMA. *Exhibited*: Univ. Nebraska, 1951,
1952; Univ. Minnesota, 1951, 1957; BM, 1951; WMAA,
1950-1952, 1953, 1955-1958; "Vanguard American Painters,"
Japan, 1950, Paris, 1951; Univ. Illinois, 1952, 1953, 1955;
Guggenheim Mus., 1954; Carnegie Inst., 1952, 1955;
MModA, 1951, 1956; Sidney Janis Gal., 1950; "New
American Painting," Basle, Milan, Brussels, Barcelona,
Paris, London and Berlin, 1958; Sao Paulo, 1957; CGA,
1958; Carnegie Inst., 1958; Tokyo, 1958; one-man: Peridot
Gal., 1949-1951; Miller-Pollard Gal., Seattle, 1952; Grace
Borgenicht Gal., 1954; Stable Gal., N.Y., 1956, 1959.
Position: Instr., drawing, Columbia Univ., 1946-48; Instr.,
Lettering, PIASch., 1948- ; Visiting Cr., Yale Univ., 1955-
56, 1957-58.

BROOMHALL, VINCENT—*Craftsman, Des.*
Box 292; h. Andrews Pl., East Liverpool, Ohio

B. East Liverpool, Ohio, Oct. 3, 1906. *Studied*: Carnegie
Inst., B.A. *Member*: Am. Ceramic Soc. Contributor to:
Trade publications. Lectures: Ceramic Art & History. *Posi-
tion*: A.Dir., Edwin M. Knowles Co.; Pres., Des., Con-
tinental Kilns, Inc.; Sales Mgr. & A.Dir., Steubenville
Pottery Co.; Des. Dir., Harker Pottery Co., East Liverpool,
Ohio, at present.

BROSSARD, RAYMOND—*Painter*
43 East 59th St. (22); h. 118 East 93rd St., New York
28, N.Y.

B. Irvington, N.J., Jan. 15, 1915. *Member*: NSMP.
Awards: prizes, GI watercolor exh., Wash., D.C., 1943;
Bodley drawing comp., N.Y., 1958. *Work*: Cal. PLH;
murals: University de Bellas Artes, San Miguel De Allende,
Mexico; Pentagon Bldg., Wash., D.C.; Luz Electrical Bldg.,
Caracas, Venezuela. *Exhibited*: one-man, Hollywood (Cal.)
Gal., 1934, 1936; Cultural Inst., Mexico, 1948; Inton Falls,
N.J., 1954; Cal. PLH, 1957; Bodley Gal., N.Y., 1958.

BROUDO, JOSEPH DAVID—*Educator, C., P., L.*
Endicott Junior College; h. 5 Gary Ave., Beverly,
Mass.

B. Baltimore, Md., Sept. 11, 1920. *Studied*: Alfred Univ.,
B.F.A.; Boston Univ., M. Edu. *Member*: Boston Soc. A.
& Crafts; Boston Soc. Indp. A.; New England Craft Coun-
cil; Eastern AA; Gld. of Beverly A.; Mass. Assn. Handi-
craft Groups. *Awards*: prizes, Eastern States Expo. (ceram.),
Storrowton, Mass., 1946; Sarasota, Fla., 1953; DeCordova
& Dana Mus. (ceramics), 1954; Lowe Gal. A. (ceramics),
1955. *Work*: International Mus. Ceramics, Faenza, Italy.
Exhibited: Syracuse Mus. A., 1947, 1950, 1954, 1956; East-
ern States Exh., 1946, 1947; Lowe Gal. A., 1955, 1957;
Nat. Dec. A. & Ceramics, Wichita, Kans., 1955; America
House, N.Y., 1950; Boston A. Festival, 1952, 1953, 1955,
1956, 1957; Sarasota A. & Crafts, 1953; Doll & Richards
Gal., Boston, 1952, 1956 (one-man); Roka Gal., Newton,
Mass., 1951 (one-man); Marblehead AA, 1953, 1957;
WMA, 1948, 1952; BMFA, 1952-1954; DeCordova Mus.,
1953, 1954; Inst. Contemp. A., Boston, 1955; G. W. V.
Smith Mus., 1955; New England Crafts, 1955; Berkshire
Mus., Pittsfield, Mass., 1958 (one-man); Marblehead A.
Gld., 1958 (one-man). Contributor to A. Edu. Bulletin;
Eastern A. Assn.; Mass. Craft Bulletin. *Position*: Bd. Dir.,
Mass. Assn. of Handicraft Groups, 1955-56; Pres. Gld. of
Beverly A., 1949-51, Bd. Dir., 1952-57; Craftsmen Rep.,
Council Boston Soc. A. & Crafts, 1955; Mass. Rep., on
New England Craft Council, 1955-56; Hd. Dept. A., Endi-
cott Junior Col., Beverly, Mass., 1946- ; Instr., State
Adult Edu. Program; Summer Dir., Ceramic Workshop,
Lenox, Mass.; Member Statewide Adv. Committee on Craft
Edu., 1955, 1958- ; Member Boston A. Festival Committee
on Crafts, 1957- .

BROUDY, MIRIAM L.—*Painter*
Cloverly Circle, East Norwalk, Conn.

B. Altoona, Pa., Sept. 30, 1905. *Studied*: PIASchA.;
Academie Colorossi, Paris; ASL with Kuniyoshi. *Member*:
Silvermine Gld. A. (Exec. V.P., 1957-58); NAWA; Meri-
den A. & Crafts; AEA. *Awards*: prizes, Penrose award,
Conn. Acad. FA, 1956; New England Exh., 1957; bronze
medal, Silvermine Gld. A., 1958. *Exhibited*: NAWA, 1952-
1956, 1958; Silvermine Gld. A., 1950-1958; Terry AI, 1952;
Riverside Mus., 1949; Meriden A. & Crafts, 1952; New
Haven Paint & Clay Cl., 1954-1958; BMA, 1954; NAD,
1953, 1956; Conn. Acad. FA, 1954, 1956; Chautauqua,
N.Y., 1955; New England Exh., 1957; Art:USA, 1958;
Springfield Mus. A., 1958; Silvermine Gld. A., 1958; one-
man: Silvermine Gld. A., 1951, 1954, 1957.

BROUGH, RICHARD BURRELL—
Educator, P., Des., Comm. A.
Art Department, University of Alabama; h. 17 Elmira
Dr., Tuscaloosa, Ala.

B. Salmon, Idaho, May 31, 1920. *Studied*: Grande Chau-
miere, Paris; San Antonio AI; Chouinard AI. *Member*:
Texas WC Soc.; AAUP; Cal. WC Soc.; Alabama WC
Soc.; Mississippi AA; New Orleans AA; Soc. Graphic Des.;
Birmingham AA. *Awards*: prizes, Mississippi AA, 1954;
Alabama A. Lg., 1954; Texas WC Soc. *Work*: Mississippi
AA; Birmingham AA; murals, Service Cl., Sheppard Field,
Texas. *Exhibited*: Mississippi AA, 1947, 1948, 1951-1955;

Cal. WC Soc., 1947-1949, 1951; Alabama WC Soc., 1948-1958; BMA, 1949, 1950; Butler AI, 1952; Oakland A. Mus., 1950, 1951; MMA, 1950; Audubon A., 1951; Birmingham AA, 1949-1955; New Orleans AA, 1949, 1950; Southeastern Ann., 1949-1952, 1955; Alabama A. Lg., 1949-1952; Texas WC Soc., 1950, 1951; DMFA, 1952. I., for Ford Motor Co. Publications; Birmingham News Sunday magazine; jacket des., Univ. Alabama Press, 1953-1955. *Position*: Assoc. Prof. A., Univ. Alabama, at present. A. Dir., Colonial Press, Birmingham, Ala.

BROWN, AARON I.—*Painter*
   17 Gramercy Park, New York 3, N.Y.; h. 26 Euclid Ave., Mount Vernon, N.Y.

B. New York, N.Y., July 8, 1904. *Studied*: with Walter Farndon. *Member*: SC; Hudson Valley AA; New Rochelle AA; Mt. Vernon AA; AAPL. *Awards*: prizes, Westchester Fed. Women's Cl., 1958; Bronxville Exh., 1958. *Work*: Children's Pavilion, Presbyterian Hospital, New York, N.Y. *Exhibited*: AAPL, 1957, 1958; All. A. Am., 1953, 1955, 1956; NAC, 1952, 1953, 1955, 1956; SC, 1957, 1958; Mt. Vernon AA, 1953-1958.

BROWN, ANNE R. (Mrs. C. W.)—*Painter*, C.
   827 Northeast 21st Dr., Wilton Manors, Ft. Lauderdale, Fla.

B. Des Moines, Iowa, July 23, 1891. *Studied*: Drake Univ.; State T. Col., Albany, N.Y. *Member*: Albany A. Group; AAPL. *Exhibited*: Albany Inst. Hist. & A., 1941-1949; Munson-Williams-Proctor Inst., 1944; Schenectady AI, 1947-1949; Miami Univ., 1952; Ft. Lauderdale, Fla., 1951; Boca Raton, Fla., 1956-1958; Instr. Textile painting.

BROWN, ARTHUR WILLIAM—*Illustrator*
   33 West 67th St.; h. 159 East 64th St., New York 21, N.Y.

B. Hamilton, Ontario, Canada, Jan. 26, 1881. *Studied*: ASL. *Member*: SI (Hon. Pres.); Nat. Cartoonists Soc.; A. Gld.; Artists & Writers Cl. I., for leading national magazines. Illus., stories by O. Henry, F. Scott Fitzgerald, Booth Tarkington, Ring Lardner, Irvin S. Cobb, Clarence Buddington Kelland. Best known pictorial characters, "Ephriam Tutt," in Sat. Eve. Post, and "Claudia," in Red Book.

BROWN, BO (ROBERT FRANKLIN)—*Cartoonist*
   218 Wyncote Rd., Jenkintown, Pa.; s. South Hero, Vt.

B. Philadelphia, Pa., July 2, 1906. *Studied*: Univ. Pennsylvania, A.B. *Member*: Nat. Cartoonists Soc.; Phila. Sketch Cl. *Exhibited*: Treasury Dept., 1948; A. Dir. Exh., Phila., 1943-1947. Author, I., "Bo Brown Abroad." *Work*: cartoons in leading U.S. and foreign magazines.

BROWN, BRADFORD—*Museum Director*, P., T.
   Portland Museum of Art, 111 High St.; h. 548½ Congress St., Portland, Me.

Studied: Sch. F. & App. A., and with Alexander Bower. *Member*: Maine WC Soc.; SC; Nat. Committee on A. Edu. *Work*: Bowdoin Col. Mus. FA, and in private coll. *Exhibited*: Portland Mus. A. (annually); State of Maine Regional Exhs., Portland Mus. A. *Position*: Mus. Attendant, 1935-40, Cur., 1940-50, Actg. Dir., 1950-51, Dir., 1951- , Portland Mus. A., Portland, Me.

BROWN, CARLYLE—*Painter*
   Via Cecilia Metella 10, Appia Antica, Rome, Italy.*

BROWN, DAN(IEL) Q(UILTER)—*Cartoonist*
   108 East Madison St., Sandusky, Ohio

B. Fremont, Ohio, Oct. 17, 1911. *Exhibited*: Am. Soc. Magazine Cart. War Show, 1943; Butler AI, 1940; Mansfield (Ohio) A. Cl., 1941; Sandusky, Ohio, 1944. Contributor cart., Sat. Eve. Post, American Weekly, Wall Street Journal, King Features Syndicate, Phila. Inquirer, Ladies Home Journal, Town Journal, and many other publications.

BROWN, DOROTHY (WOODHEAD)—
   Painter, E., W., L., Cr.
   University of California at Los Angeles; h. 31000 Broad Beach Rd., Malibu, Cal.

B. Houston, Tex., Mar. 13, 1899. *Studied*: Stanford Univ., A.A.; Univ. California, B.A., and with Henry Lee McFee. *Member*: Cal. WC Soc. (2nd Vice-Pres., 1955-56, Pres., 1958-59); Santa Monica A. Gal. (Bd. Memb.). *Awards*: prizes, San Diego FA Soc., 1955; Cal. WC Soc., 1953; Los A. Mus. A., 1958; La Jolla A. Center. *Exhibited*: Cal. WC Soc., 1950-1955; SFMA; Mod. Inst. of Beverly Hills; Western Assn. A. Mus. Dir., traveling exh., 1950-1952; San Diego FA Soc., 1955; Canadian-Cal. Int. Exh., 1955, 1956; Denver Mus. A., 1955; Los A. Mus. A., 1955; one-man: U.C.L.A. A. Gal. (15 one-man exhs.); San Diego State Col.; Santa Barbara Mus. A., 1954; Stanford Research Inst., 1954; Pasadena Mus. A., 1956; Crocker A. Gal., Sacramento, 1954; Ruth White Gal., N.Y., 1958; Robles Gal., Los Angeles, 1958; Texas Western State Col., 1956. *Work*: U.C.L.A. coll.; La Jolla A. Center, Stanford Research Inst; Long Beach Mus. A. *Position*: Assoc. Prof. A., Univ. California, Los Angeles, Cal., 1945- .

BROWN, MRS. ELEANOR DE LAITTRE. See *deLaittre, Eleanor*

BROWN, ELMORE J.—*Painter*, I.
   80 Palmer Ave.; h. 56 Northway, Bronxville, N.Y.

B. Buchanan, Mich., July 7, 1899. *Studied*: AIC. *Member*: A. & Writers Assn. *Work*: Pentagon, Wash., D.C. *Exhibited*: Turf & Field Cl., Belmont Park, N.Y., 1955; Fairfield Hunt Cl., 1955; USAF Exh., Pentagon, Wash., D.C. I., National magazines.*

BROWN, FRANCIS F.—*Educator*, P.
   612 Ashland Ave., Muncie, Ind.

B. Glassboro, N.J., Jan. 19, 1891. *Studied*: John Herron AI; Ball State T. Col., B.S.; Ohio State Univ., M.A. *Awards*: prizes, Richmond AA, 1922; John Herron AI, 1922; Hoosier Salon, 1923-1940. *Work*: John Herron AI; Ball State T. Col.; Richmond AA, and in various schools and libraries in Indiana. *Exhibited*: Hoosier Salon, 1922-1945; CMA, 1922-1925; PAFA, 1922, 1923. *Position*: Prof., Ball State T. Col., Muncie, Ind., 1925-1957 (Retired); Prof. Emeritus, 1957- .

BROWN, GERTRUDE G.—*Painter*, C., E.
   4424 P St., N.W., Washington 7, D.C.

B. Malden, W. Va., May 9, 1880. *Studied*: Maryland AI; Columbia Univ., in Europe, and with Henry B. Snell. *Member*: AWS; Washington AC. *Position*: Instr., A., Washington, D.C., H.S., 1924-48.*

BROWN, GRACE EVELYN—*Painter*, W., L., T.
   57 B Longwood Ave., Brookline 46, Mass.

B. Beverly, Mass., Nov. 24, 1873. *Studied*: Mass. Normal Sch. A., and with Joseph DeCamp, Albert Munsell, Armand Clement, Frank M. Rines. *Member*: Ogunquit A. Center; All. A., Boston; Brookline Soc. A.; Boston Soc. Indp. A.; Copley Soc.; Springfield A. Lg. *Exhibited*: PAFA, 1929; Boston A. Cl., 1936-1946; Springfield A. Lg., 1941-1946, 1948-1955; Copley Soc., 1933 (one-man), 1948-1953; Ogunquit A. Center, 1948-1955; Boston Center for Adult Edu., 1950; Boston Soc. Indp. A., 1950-1953; Brookline Soc. A., 1953-1955. Contributor to poetry magazines and anthologies.*

BROWN, JAMES M. III—*Museum Director*
   Corning Glass Center, Centerway; h. 106 East Fifth St., Corning, N.Y.

B. Brooklyn, N.Y., Oct. 7, 1917. *Studied*: Amherst Col., B.A., M.A. (hon.); Harvard Univ., M.A *Member*: Council, AAMus.; CAA; AFA. *Awards*: Hon. degree, Amherst Col., 1954. Contributor to: College Art Journal; Saturday Review. Lectures: "French Impressionist Painting"; "Survey of Glass History"; "John Marin," etc. *Position*: Asst. to the Dir., Inst. Contemp. A., Boston, Mass., 1942; Asst. to Dir., Dumbarton Oaks Research Lib. & Coll., Wash., D.C., 1946; Asst. Dir., Inst. Contemp. A., Boston, 1946-48; Dir., William A. Farnsworth Mus., Rockland, Me., 1948-51; Dir., Corning Glass Center, Corning, N.Y., 1951- ; Vice-Pres., Council of Am. Assn. of Museums.

BROWN, JOSEPH—*Sculptor, E.*

Princeton University; h. 34 Edwards Pl., Princeton, N.J.

B. Philadelphia, Pa., Mar. 20, 1909. *Studied:* Temple Univ., B.S., and with R. Tait McKenzie. *Member:* NSS; AAUP; Franklin Inn Cl. *Awards:* med., Montclair A. Mus., 1941; prize, NAD, 1944. *Work:* MacCoy Mem., Princeton, N.J.; Leroy Mills Mem.; Rosengarten Trophy; Firestone Lib.; PAFA; Clarence Irvine Mem., Collingwood, N.J.; Lehigh Univ.; A.A.U. Swimming Monument, Yale Univ.; St. Barnabas, Phila., Pa.; Crucifix, Trinity Church, Princeton, N.J. Many portraits of prominent persons. Designer of Play Communities in London, Tokyo, Phila., Pa., N.J. Neuro-Psychiatric Inst. Contributor to Architectural Record; Editorial-Domus; Home Economics Journal, and others. *Exhibited:* NAD, 1934, 1935, 1940, 1944; AIC, 1941; PAFA, 1934-1944; Arch. Lg., 1935, 1937; Montclair A. Mus., 1941, 1942; Phila. Pub. Lib., 1949-1951; PMA, 1949; Firestone Lib., Princeton, N.J.; Woodmere A. Gal., 1950; one-man: Yale Univ.; Univ. Virginia; Bucknell Univ.; Lehigh Univ.; Univ. Bridgeport; Springfield Col. Lectures in universities, colleges and museums. Radio-TV programs. *Position:* Assoc. Prof., S. & Arch., Princeton Univ., Princeton, N.J., 1939- .

BROWN, M(AY) (MORGAN) (Mrs. Everett S.)—Painter

2576 Devonshire Rd., Ann Arbor, Mich.

B. Hartwell, Ohio. *Studied:* Univ. Michigan. *Member:* Ann Arbor AA; Detroit Soc. Women Painters; Michigan Acad. Sc., A. & Let. *Awards:* prizes, Detroit Inst. A., 1938; Detroit Soc. Women Painters, 1943. *Exhibited:* NAC, 1928; CGA, 1941; Milwaukee AI, 1946; Ann Arbor AA, 1923-1955; Detroit AA, 1929-1949; Detroit Soc. Women Painters, 1933-1952; Michigan Acad., 1943-1958.

BROWN, MARY CHALMERS—*Designer, E.*

Apt. F-1, Greenwood Terr., Jenkintown, Pa.

B. Sydney, N.S., Canada, July 12, 1915. *Studied:* Moore Inst. A. Sc. & Indst.; Pennsylvania State Univ. *Awards:* California Good Design, 1955. *Exhibited:* Nat. Glass & Pottery Assn., 1952-1955. *Position:* Instr., Textile Des. Dept., Moore Inst. A. Sc. & Indst.; Des., Barton Studio, New York, N.Y., 1947-51; Castleton China, New Castle, Pa., 1952; (Franciscan) Gladding McBean & Co., Los Angeles, Cal., 1953-55.*

BROWN, OZNI (Mr.)—Painter, E.

Marymount College, Tarrytown, N.Y.

B. Owatonna, Minn. *Studied:* Macalester Co., St. Paul; Minneapolis Inst. A.; ASL; Grand Central Sch. A. *Member:* SI; SC. Specializes in painting horses and horsemen with emphasis on fox hunting and hunters. *Position:* Instr., Painting, Marymount Col., Tarrytown, N.Y.*

BROWN, (HOWARD) SCOTT—*Cartoonist*

555 West 4th St.; h. 143 Rae Ave., Mansfield, Ohio

B. Mechanicsburg, Ohio, Dec. 25, 1909. *Studied:* AIC. I., Collier's, American, & other national magazines & newspapers. Represented in cartoon anthologies, books and collections.*

BROWN, WILLIAM ALDEN—*Painter*

80 Benefit St., Providence 4, R.I.

B. Providence, R.I., Mar. 15, 1877. *Studied:* R.I. Sch. Des.; & with John F. Carlson. *Member:* St. Petersburg AC; Providence AC; Providence WC Cl.; Conn. Acad. *Exhibited:* Albright A. Gal.; Baltimore WC Cl.; Denver SA; Conn. Acad. FA; Providence AC; New Haven Paint & Clay Cl.; R.I. Sch. Des.; Newport AA; William Hall Library, Edgewood, R.I., and in Miami, St. Petersburg, Fla.

BROWN, W(ILLIAM) F(ERDINAND) II—*Cartoonist*

Grahampton Lane, Greenwich, Conn.

B. Jersey City, N.J., Apr. 16, 1928. *Studied:* Montelair, N.J. Acad.; Princeton Univ., A.B. *Member:* Acad. Television A. & Sc. *Work:* in many cartoon anthologies. Author, I., "Tiger, Tiger," 1950. Contributor cartoons to: Sat. Eve. Post, Collier's, True, Look, Sports Illustrated, American Weekly, American Legion, Parade, Argosy, Field & Stream, Outdoor Life, Sports Afield, Sport, and other publications.

BROWN, W(ILLIAM) NORMAN—*Educator, W., L.*

University of Pennsylvania, Philadelphia 4, Pa.; h. Rose Valley, Moylan, Pa.

B. Baltimore, Md., June 24, 1892. *Studied:* Johns Hopkins Univ., A.B., Ph.D. *Member:* Am. Oriental Soc. (Ed. Journal, 1926-41, Pres., 1942); Am. Linguistic Soc.; Am. Philosophical Soc.; Assn. for Asian Studies; Linguistic Soc. of India; Royal India, Pakistan and Ceylon Soc. *Awards:* Litt. D., Univ. Madras, 1957; Hon. F., Royal Asiatic Soc. (London). Author: articles in journals of oriental studies; books on Indian culture, including The Story of Kalaka, Washington: Smithsonian Inst., 1933; Miniature Paintings of the Jain Kalpasutra, Washington, Smithsonian Inst., 1934; A Pillared Hall from Madura, Philadelphia: Univ. Pa. Press, 1940; Manuscript Illustrations of the Uttaradhyayana Sutra, New Haven: Am. Oriental Soc., 1941; The Saundaryalahari, Boston, Harvard Univ. Press, 1958. Lectures: Art of India. *Position:* Prof. Sanskrit, Univ. Pennsylvania, 1926- ; Cur., Indian Art, PMA, 1930-54; Cur., Oriental Section, Univ. Pennsylvania Mus., Phila., Pa., 1942-1948; Chm., South Asia Regional Studies, Univ. Pennsylvania, 1947- .

BROWN, WILLIAM JOSEPH—*Craftsman, Des., T.*

Craft Center, 25 Sagamore Rd.; h. 22 Burncoat St., Worcester, Mass.

B. Flint, Mich., Mar. 10, 1923. *Studied:* Western Michigan Col. of Edu.; Cranbrook Acad. A., B.F.A., M.F.A.; Univ. Michigan. *Member:* Michigan Acad. A., Science & Lets. *Awards:* prizes, Flint Inst. A., 1948; Cranbrook Acad. A., 1949; Michigan Acad. A., Science & Lets., 1950. *Exhibited:* Flint Inst. A., 1946, 1948, 1950, 1951; Cranbrook Acad. A., 1947-1950; Delaware A. Center, 1951-1954; Detroit Inst. A., 1949, 1955; Univ. Delaware A. Gal., 1954; WMA, 1955, 1958; Craft Center, Worcester, Mass., 1958; Arch. Lg., N.Y., 1957. *Position:* Asst. Dir., Flint Inst. A., 1950-51; Instr., Des. & Crafts, Univ. Delaware, 1951-55; Des. Instr., Haystack Mountain Sch. of Crafts, 1950-58; Assoc. Prof. Des., N.Y. State Univ., Oswego, N.Y., 1956-57.

BROWNE, ALDIS B., II—*Painter*

Essex, Conn.

B. Washington, D.C., Aug. 2, 1907. *Studied:* Westminster Col.; Yale Univ., B.F.A. *Work:* murals, U.S. Coast Guard Acad.; USPO, Oneonta, Ala.

BROWNE, BYRON—*Painter*

216 East 15th St., New York 3, N.Y.

B. Yonkers, N.Y., June 26, 1907. *Studied:* NAD. *Member:* Am. Abstract A.; AEA; Audubon A. *Awards:* prizes, NAD, 1928; LaTausca Exh., 1947; Univ. Illinois, 1951. *Work:* murals, Mun. Broadcasting Station, N.Y.; WFNY 1939; coll. of WMAA; Newark Mus. A.; MModA; Butler AI; Univ. Georgia; Dallas Mus. FA; Tel-Aviv Mus.; San Angelo AA; IBM; Rio de Janeiro; Roswell Mus.; Univ. Minnesota; Cornell Univ.; Northeastern Univ.; Brown Univ.; New Sch. for Social Research, N.Y.; Univ. Arizona; Walter Chrysler, Jr. Coll.; mosaic, U.S. Passport Office, N.Y. *Exhibited:* NAD, 1928, 1929; Carnegie Inst., 1946; Audubon A, 1945; CGA, 1928; PAFA, 1930, 1936, 1946; WMAA, 1935, 1937, 1939, 1946; MModA, 1939; AIC, 1928, 1935, 1946; twenty-one one-man exh., to date. *Position:* Instr., ASL, New York, N.Y., 1948- .

BROWNE, DIK—*Cartoonist*

Rivergate Park, Wilton, Conn.*

BROWNE, MARGARET FITZHUGH—*Painter, T.*

30 Ipswich St., Boston 15, Mass.

B. Boston, Mass., June 7, 1884. *Studied:* Mass. Normal A. Sch.; BMFA Sch.; & with Frank Benson. *Member:* All. A. Am.; NAWA; North Shore AA; Gld. Boston A; Grand Central A. Gal.; Audubon A.; Academic A.; Rockport AA; Copley Soc.; AAPL; Newport AA. *Awards:* prizes, North Shore AA, 1925; BM, 1928; Ogunquit A. Center, 1941; Rockport AA, 1955; Conn. Acad. FA. *Work:* MIT; Boston Univ.; Harvard Univ.; Bureau Standards, Wash., D.C.; Powers Sch., Boston; Springfield AA; Buckley Sch., N.Y.; Driscoll Sch., Brookline, Mass. *Exhibited:* CGA, 1924, 1926, 1930 (one-man), 1937; PAFA, 1925, 1931; AIC, 1914; Conn. Acad. FA, 1916-1955, Newport AA, 1916-1955 (one-man, 1950); All.A.Am.; NAWA; Copley Soc., 1950,

1955 (one-man); North Shore AA, 1924-1958; Rockport AA, 1952-1958; Gld. Boston A., 1953, 1957 (one-man). Author: "Portrait Painting."

BROWNE, SYD—*Painter, Lith., Et., T.*
Winter Harbor, Me.

B. Brooklyn, N.Y., Aug. 21, 1907. *Studied*: ASL, and with Eric Pape, Frank DuMond. *Member*: ANA; AWS; SAGA; Southern Pr. M.; SC; Audubon A; Baltimore WC Cl.; All.A.Am.; Conn. Acad. FA; ASL; Phila. WC Cl.; Grand Central A. Gal. *Awards*: Conn. Acad. FA; SC; Audubon A; AWS; med., All.A.Am. *Work*: N.Y. Hist. Soc.; N.Y. Univ.; LC; New Britain Inst; Staten Island Inst.; Prentiss Hall Coll. *Exhibited*: Paris Int. Exp., 1937; WFNY 1939; AIC, 1939; NAD; PAFA; CGA; Montclair A. Mus.; New Britain Inst.; Sweat Mem. Mus.; Farnsworth Mus. A. *Position*: Instr., Newark Sch. F. & Indust. A., Newark, N.Y., 1946- ; Guest Instr., Norton Gal. & Sch. A., West Palm Beach, Fla., 1956.

BROWNING, COLLEEN—*Painter, I.*
2310 Second Ave., New York 35, N.Y.

B. Fermoy, County Cork, Eire, May 16, 1925. *Studied*: Slade Sch. A., London, England. *Awards*: Anna Lee Stacey Scholarship; Tupperware; prizes, Slade Sch. A.; Carnegie Inst., 1952; NAD; Butler AI, 1954; AWS, 1953; Nat. Inst. A. & Let.; Emily Lowe award; Rochester Fingerlakes Exh.; Metamold, Cedarburg, 1953; Edwin Austin Abbey Scholarship; F.; MacDowell & Yaddo Fnds.; Los A. County Fair; Stanford Univ. *Work*: Cal. PLH; Butler AI; Williams Col.; Detroit Inst. A.; Rochester Mem. A. Gal.; Spaeth Fnd.; Trinity Col.; Friends of Am. A. Assn.; Williamstown (Mass.) Mus. A.; Columbia (S.C.) Mus. A.; murals, Grinkle Hall, Yorkshire, England; Services Canteen, Salisbury, England; Sibley, Lindsay & Curr, Rochester, N.Y. *Exhibited*: WMAA; MModA; Carnegie Inst.; Nat. Inst. A. & Let.; AIC; Butler AI; Walker A. Center; Brandeis Univ.; Flint Inst. A.; Rochester Mem. A. Gal.; AWS; Wisconsin Union; WMA; NAD; Springfield Mus. A.; DMFA; Audubon A.; Univ. Illinois; Cortland Fair; N.Y. State Fair; Easthampton Religious A. Exh.; Metamold Exh.; and in England; one-man: Little Gal., London, 1949; Edwin Hewitt Gal., 1952, 1954; Lane Gal., Los Angeles; Rochester, N.Y. Illus., Doubleday Junior DeLuxe Editions.

BRUCE, MARJORIE MACKENZIE—*Designer, C.*
43 Babcock St., Brookline, Mass.

B. Shelburne, N.S., Canada, Dec. 25, 1895. *Studied*: Boston Sch. FA & Crafts; & with C. Howard Walker. *Member*: Boston Soc. A. & Crafts.*

BRUCKER, EDMUND—*Painter, T.*
John Herron Art School; h. 3502 North La Salle St., Indianapolis 18, Ind.

B. Cleveland, Ohio, Nov. 20, 1912. *Studied*: Cleveland Inst. A., and with Henry G. Keller, Rolf Stoll. *Member*: Indiana A. Cl.; Brown County A. Gal. Assn.; Hoosier Salon. *Awards*: prizes, CMA, 1937-1939, 1942, 1945, 1948, 1951; Hoosier Salon, 1939, 1940, 1944, 1946, 1947, 1949, 1951, 1952, 1955; John Herron AI, 1941-1943, 1946-1948, 1953-1955; Butler AI, 1937; Indiana A. Cl., 1941, 1945-1950, 1953-1957; Indiana State Fair, 1939-1941, 1946-1951, 1953-1958; Illinois State Fair, 1953, 1958; Indiana Pr. Exh., 1945-1947, 1951; Michiana regional, 1955, 1957, 1958; Chicago Magnificent Mile, 1955; L.S. Ayers Exh., 1947. *Work*: City of Cleveland Coll.; John Herron AI; CMA; Butler AI; Dartmouth Col.; U.S. Govt.; De Pauw Univ. *Exhibited*: CMA, 1948-1958; Hoosier Salon, 1948-1958; PAFA; Univ. Illinois; Butler AI, 1948, 1958; Ohio Valley A., 1950, 1951, 1953-1955; John Herron AI, 1953-1958; Michiana regional 1954, 1955; MMA; Carnegie Inst.; MModA; NAD; LC. *Position*: Instr., Cleveland Inst. A., 1936-38; Instr., John Herron A. Sch., Indianapolis, Ind., 1938- .

BRUCKNER, WILLIAM—*Painter, Des., Comm., T.*
34 Dickinson Ave., Nyack, N.Y.

B. Vienna, Austria, Dec. 1, 1915. *Studied*: AIC; Barnes Fnd., and with Theodore Saunders, Rudolph Sheffler Valley. *Member*: Rockland Fnd. *Awards*: prize, South Side A., Chicago, 1947. *Work*: U.S. Army coll., Wash., D.C.; many portraits of prominent persons; portraits also in Court House, Rockland County, N.Y.; CIO Bldg., Wash., D.C.; Presbyterian Church, Bryn Mawr, Pa. *Exhibited*: Nyack, N.Y. (one-man), 1953. Contributor to Rockland County Journal News. *Position*: A., U.S. Air Force Hdqtrs., Europe, stage sets, murals, publications. Teaching portraiture privately at present.

BRUESTLE, BERTRAM G.—*Painter*
Old Lyme, Conn.

B. New York, N.Y., Apr. 24, 1902. *Studied*: NAD, with Charles C. Curran, Francis Jones. *Member*: SC; Lyme AA; New Haven Paint & Clay Cl. *Work*: Ames Mem. Gal., New London, Conn. *Exhibited*: Lyme AA; SC; New Haven Paint & Clay Cl.

BRULE, ELMO A. (AL)—*Painter, T., Comm., I.*
551 Fifth Ave., New York, N.Y.; h. New Hempstead Rd., Spring Valley, N.Y.

B. Alameda, Cal., Apr. 17, 1917. *Studied*: Sacramento Col., with H. Ward, J. B. Matthew; Chouinard AI, with H. Jepson; Otis AI, with Alexander Brook, Paul Clemens. *Member*: SI; Ten A. Cl., Sacramento, Cal. *Work*: in private collections. *Awards*: Chicago Outdoor Adv. Exh., 1953. *Exhibited*: Crocker A. Gal., 1934, 1935, 1936, 1938, 1940; Oakland A. Mus., 1936, 1938; Los A. Mus. A., 1936-1938, 1940; one-man: Crocker A. Gal., 1940; Geitlan's Gal., Los A., 1941; Wolmer Gal., N.Y., 1946. I., "The Lord's Prayer," 1956. Contributor of illus., to Colliers, American, Woman's Home Companion, Today's Woman, Family Circle, Argosy, American Weekly, Esquire, People's Book Club, Doubleday & Co., and others. *Position*: Animated Cart., Warner Bros. Studios, Hollywood, 1937-38; Illus., Adv. & Editorial, Chas. E. Cooper Studios & Fredman-Chaite Studios, N.Y., 1944-53; Freelance A., 1953- .*

BRUMBAUGH, R. NICKEY—*Educator, P., Des.*
Coker College; h. Rt. 3, Hartsville, S.C.

B. Columbia City, Ind., Sept. 25, 1918. *Studied*: DePauw Univ., A.B.; Western Reserve Univ., M.A.; Ohio Univ., M.F.A. *Member*: CAA. *Exhibited*: Florence (S.C.) Mus. A., 1954 (one-man); High Mus. A., 1954; Gibbes Gal., 1955; Studio Gld. Group Show. *Position*: Prof., Hd., Dept. A., Coker Col., Hartsville, S.C., 1944- .

BRUMBAUGH, THOMAS B.—*Educator, L.*
Emory University, Box 872, Atlanta 22, Ga.

B. Chambersburg, Pa., May 23, 1921. *Studied*: State T. Col., Indiana, Pa., B.S.; Biarritz American Univ.; Univ. Iowa, M.A.; Ohio State Univ., Ph.D.; Harvard Summer Sch. *Member*: Am. Soc. for Aesthetics; AAUP; CAA; Archaeological Inst. Am.; Atlanta AA. Contributor to Emory Quarterly; Virginia Magazine of History & Biography; Art Quarterly; Accent; Commentary; American-German Review, and other publications. Lectures 19th Century Art to art organizations and study groups. *Positions*: Actg. Hd., A. Dept., Hood College, Frederick, Md., 1950-53; Instr., Ohio State Univ., 1953-54; Asst. Prof. A., Emory Univ., Atlanta, Ga., 1954- .

BRUMME, C(ARL) LUDWIG—*Sculptor, P., W., Cr.*
c/o Hacker Gallery, 57 W. 54th St., New York, N.Y.

B. Bremerhaven, Germany, Sept. 19, 1910. *Studied*: with Leo Amino. *Exhibited*: Massillon Mus. A., 1942-1945; Mus. Non-Objective Painting, 1943, 1944; Pinacotheca, 1944, 1945; Dartmouth Col., 1944; WMAA, 1947-1951; Worcester A. Mus., 1951; Delaware A. Center, 1948; Munson-Williams-Proctor Inst., 1947; Fairmount Park, Phila., 1949; PAFA, 1949; Am-British A. Center, 1947; Sculpture Center, N.Y., 1945-1951; l'Institut Endoplastique, Paris, France, 1952.*

BRUNELL, RICHARD H.—*Educator*
Atlanta Art Institute, 1262 Peachtree St., Atlanta, Ga. *Position*: Dir., Atlanta Art Institute.*

BRUNER, LOUISE (Mrs. Raymond A.)—*Critic*
Toledo Blade (4); h. 2244 Scottwood Ave., Toledo 10, Ohio

B. Cleveland, Ohio, June 13, 1910. *Studied*: Denison Univ., B.A.; Western Reserve Univ. *Member*: Toledo A. Cl.; Ohio Newspaper Women's Assn. *Awards*: prize (first) for critical reviews in any Ohio Newspaper, 1955, 1957; Ohio

Newspaper Women's Assn., 1942-1951. Contributor to art magazines. Author: "Directory of Museums and Art Exhibits," Toledo Blade, 1956. *Position*: Critic, Cleveland (Ohio) News, 1942-52; Toledo Blade, 1955- .

BRUNET, ADELE LAURE—*Painter, T., Des., Cr., L., I.*
3011 Fairmount St., Dallas 4, Tex.

B. Austin, Tex. *Studied*: Univ. Texas; ASL; AIC, and with George Bridgman, Henry Rittenberg. *Member*: Dallas AC; Interstate A. Soc.; Fed. Dallas A. *Work*: murals, Newman Club Hall, Austin, Tex.; Parkland Hospital, Dallas, Tex. *Awards*: prizes, Fed. Dallas A., 1948-1951, 1953-1955. *Exhibited*: Mus. of New Mexico, Santa Fé, 1930; Dallas Mus. FA; NAWA; SSAL; Texas FA Assn.; Laguna Gloria Mus., 1950; Texas A. & M. Col., 1951; Interstate A. Soc., 1948-1951; Fed. Dallas A., 1948-1951; Sartor Gal., Dallas, 1952-1955; Reaugh A. Cl.; Klepper A. Cl.

BRUNETTIN, ALFRED JOSEPH—*Sculptor, C., Des.*
3518 South 58th Ave., Cicero 50, Ill.

B. Chicago, Ill., Aug. 28, 1917. *Studied*: AIC, with Cheuseng, Wallace; Minneapolis Sch. A.; Cranbrook Acad. A., with Carl Milles. *Awards*: Minneapolis Inst. A., 1939, 1940; Prix de Rome, 1940; F., Cranbrook Acad. A., 1941; Allied Forces Exh., Algiers, 1943; AIC, 1956; Linde Air Products award, 1957. *Work*: paintings, St. Francis of Rome Church, Cicero, Ill.; St. Finbarr Church, Chicago; Law Bldg., Chicago; bronze plaque of Naval Mem. Monument of Pearl Harbor, 1955; numerous bronze ports. for public bldgs. and monuments, 1948-1955. *Exhibited*: 1956-58: New York; Ravinia, Ill.; AIC; Chicago Pub. Lib. (one-man); Hyde Park A. Center, Chicago; Contemp. Am. A. Exh., Chicago. *Position*: Instr. S., Hyde Park A. Center, Chicago, Ill., 1956-57.

BRUNS, EDWIN JOHN—*Painter, I., Comm. A.*
246 15th St., N.W., Cedar Rapids, Iowa

B. Manistee, Mich., Dec. 12, 1898. *Studied*: AIC, and with Leon Kroll, George Bellows. *Member*: Cedar Rapids AA. *Awards*: prizes, Iowa State Fair; Iowa State Women's Cl. *Work*: Univ. Iowa; Cedar Rapids AA; Governor's Home, Des Moines, Ia.; Murals, Western Bohemian Frat. Assn. *Exhibited*: AIC; Iowa State Women's Cl., and in regional exhibitions. Contributor to Design magazine. Des. and illus., "Seven Ages of a City: A Pictorial History of Cedar Rapids," 1957.

BRUSKIN, KATHLEEN (SPENCER) (Mrs. Robert)—*Painter*
102 Ichabod Pl., Falls Church, Va.

B. Omaha, Neb., Dec. 28, 1911. *Studied*: PAFA, and with William C. McNulty, Jon Corbino, Louis Bosa. *Member*: Soc. Washington A. *Work*: mural, Unitarian Church, Arlington, Va. *Exhibited*: CGA, 1945, 1951, 1955-1957; NAC, 1945; Soc. Wash. A., 1944, 1946, 1948, 1957; AAPL (NCFA), 1944-1946, 1948, 1949, 1954, 1956; in Germany, 1953. *Position*: Hd. A. Dept., National Cathedral Sch., Washington, D.C., 1957- .

BRUSSEL-SMITH, BERNARD—*Printmaker*
210 East 40th St., New York, N.Y.*

BRUTON, DAVID THOMAS—*Painter, Lith., T.*
1718 Holly St., Kansas City, Mo.

B. Kansas City, Mo., Dec. 20, 1927. *Studied*: Kansas City AI, B.F.A., M.F.A., and with Bruce Mitchell. *Member*: AEA; Mid-Am. A. *Awards*: prizes, Kansas City AI, 1949, 1952; Missouri State Fair, 1951. *Work*: William Rockhill Nelson Gal. A.; murals, Boy's Cl., Kansas City; Western Highlands Presbyterian Church, Kansas City. *Exhibited*: Butler AI, 1952; Norfolk Mus. A. & Sc., 1951; Huckleberry Mountain, Tenn., 1951; CAM, 1950; Mid-Am. A., 1951; Denver A. Mus., 1952; Springfield Mus. A., 1949-1951; Peoria, Ill., 1952.*

BRY, EDITH—*Painter, Lith.*
211 Central Park West, New York 24, N.Y.

B. St. Louis, Mo., Nov. 30, 1898. *Studied*: in Europe, with Herman Struck; ASL; & with Alexander Archipenko, Charles Locke. *Member*: Fed. Mod. P.&S.; NAWA. *Work*: MMA; N.Y. Pub.Lib.; Lib.Cong.*

BRYAN, ALDEN—*Painter*
Bryan Gallery, Gloucester, Mass.; h. Windridge Farms, Jeffersonville, Vt.

Studied: Harvard Univ., A.B. *Member*: Gld. Boston A.; SC; Copley Soc., Boston; North Shore AA; Rockport AA; All. A. Am. *Awards*: prizes, North Shore AA, 1955; Rockport AA, 1956; SC, 1958; Silvermine Gld. A., 1955. *Exhibited*: All. A. Am., 1954-1958; NAD, 1958; annually—Gld. Boston A.; SC; Grand Central A. Gal.; Copley Soc., Boston; North Shore AA; Rockport AA.

BRYAN, MARY (TAYLOR LEWIS)—*Painter*
Windridge Farms, Jeffersonville, Vt.; s. Rocky Neck, Gloucester, Mass.

B. Carlsbad, N.M., Jan. 15, 1907. *Studied*: Eliot O'Hara Sch. Watercolor, and with Emil Gruppe. *Member*: AWS; Gld. Boston A.; Phila. WC Cl.; Copley Soc., Boston; NAWA; North Shore AA; F., Intl. Inst. A. & Lets. *Awards*: prizes, AWS, 1953, 1955; Women's National, 1954; North Shore AA, 1949, 1951, 1954; Rockport AA, 1956; Silvermine Gld. A., 1954, 1955; Fleming Mus. A., 1958. *Exhibited*: AWS, 1952-1958; NAWA, 1954-1958; All. A. Am., 1954, 1955, 1957, 1958; Audubon A., 1952, 1955; all regional shows, Gloucester, Rockport, Boston, since 1949.

BRYAN, WILHELMUS B.—*Educator*
Minneapolis School of Art, 200 East 25th St., Minneapolis 4, Minn.; h. Route 1, Box 206, Hopkins, Minn.

B. Washington, D.C., Oct. 9, 1898. *Studied*: Princeton Univ., B.A., M.A.; Univ. Minnesota; Macalester Col., L.H.D. *Member*: Nat. Assn. of Schs. of Design (Vice-Pres.); Soc. A. & Art Dir.; Minnesota A. Edu. Exchange. Lectures to schools, colleges, church and art education groups. *Position*: Dean, Macalester College, St. Paul; Dir., Blake School, Minneapolis; Dir., Westminster Fnd., Princeton Univ.; Dir., Minneapolis Sch. A., Minneapolis, Minn., at present.

BRYANS, JOHN ARMOND—*Painter, T.*
2264 North Vernon St., Arlington, Va.

B. Marion, Ohio, July 21, 1925. *Studied*: Ringling Sch. A.; Farnsworth Sch. A., Sarasota, Fla.; Burnsville, N.C., with Edward Shorter and Frank S. Herring. *Member*: Washington WC Cl. *Awards*: prizes, AAPL, 1953; Soc. Wash. A., 1954. *Work*: mural, Parkway Playhouse, Burnsville, N.C. *Exhibited*: Wash. WC Cl., 1952-1958; CGA, 1952, 1953, 1955, 1957; BMA, 1957; Soc. Wash. A., 1952-1958; Newport AA, 1957; Ringling Mus. A., 1948-1950.

BRYSON, ROBERT ALEXANDER—*Painter*
North East, Md.; h. 205 Atkins Ave., Wilmington 5, Del.

B. Marshallton, Del., Sept. 19, 1906. *Studied*: Maryland Inst. *Awards*: Prize, Wilmington Soc. FA, 1934.

BRZOSTOSKI, JOHN—
Painter, Gr., T., L., Mus. Consultant
587 West Front St., Red Bank, N.J.

B. Newark, N.J., July 1, 1926. *Studied*: Newark Sch. F. & Indst. A., with R. Nakian; Rutgers Univ.; Syracuse Univ., B.F.A., M.F.A.; New Sch. Social Research. *Member*: CAA; Artmakers Group; Assoc. A. of New Jersey. *Awards*: scholarship, New Sch. Social Research (Japanese Studies), 1955; prize, Nat. Print Show, Seton Hall Univ., 1956. *Work*: prints: Newark Publ. Lib.; Roswell (N.M.) Mus. & A. Center; Parrish A. Mus., Southampton, N.Y.; Syracuse Univ.; Univ. of Philippines. Woodcut edition of "Collectors of American Art," 1955. *Exhibited*: BM, 1953; PAFA, 1949; Phillips Acad., 1949; Portland A. Mus., 1955; Farnsworth Mus., 1957; Univ. Ontario, 1955; Univ. British Columbia, 1955; Univ. Saskatchewan, 1956; Univ. Regina, 1956; McGill Univ., 1956; Newark Mus. A., 1952-1955, 1958; Trenton Mus. A., 1953; Montclair A. Mus., 1952-1957; one-man: Montclair State T. Col., 1957; Artists Gal., N.Y., 1957; Univ. Philippines, 1957; Newark Pub. Lib., 1947, 1950. Author, I., "Yanks in Krautiania," 1946; "Isle of DRDL," 1949; "The Kiss and 32," 1951. Assembled and arranged exhibit "Ukiyo-E," Parrish Mus. A., 1955; "Japanese Prints," Montclair A. Mus., 1956; Catalogued Print Coll., Parrish Mus. A., 1958.

BUCCI, ANDREW A.—*Painter, Gr.*

mail: NAWAC, U.S. Weather Bureau, Washington 25, D.C.; h. 1209 First North St., Vicksburg, Miss.

B. Vicksburg, Miss., Jan. 12, 1922. *Studied:* Louisiana State Univ., B.S.; AIC, M.F.A. *Member:* Mississippi AA; New Orleans AA; Alabama WC Soc. *Awards:* prizes, Brooks Mem. Gal., 1948, 1956; Mississippi AA, 1954-1956; New Orleans AA, 1955, 1956; Gld. South Carolina A., 1956 (purchase). *Exhibited:* Mississippi AA, 1950-1958; Brooks Mem. Gal., 1956, 1957; Butler Inst. Am. A., 1955, 1956; Columbia Mus. A., 1957; Wash. WC Cl., 1956-1958; Soc. Wash. A., 1957; Atlanta Southeastern annual, 1948-1955; Alabama WC Soc., 1952-1957; Memphis, 1948, 1950, 1952, 1955; New Orleans AA, 1948, 1949, 1951, 1954-1958; Mun. A. Gal., Jackson, 1949, 1952 (one-man), 1955 (3-man); PAFA, 1953; Phila. Pr. Cl., 1955; Mandel Bros., Chicago, 1954 (4-man), 1956 (3-man); Greenville (S.C.) A. Gal., 1956 (one-man); Lauren Rogers Lib. & Mus., Laurel, Miss., 1952 (one-man); Delgado Mus. A., 1955 (2-man); Miss. State Col. for Women, 1952 (one-man).

BUCHANAN, LAURA—*Painter*

3638 Colonial Ave., Dallas 15, Tex.

B. Waxahachie, Tex. *Studied:* with Frank Reaugh, John Knott. *Member:* Texas FA Assn.; Fed. Dallas A.; Dallas AA. *Awards:* prizes, Fed. Dallas A., 1954, 1955. *Work:* Waxahachie H.S.; Elisabet Ney Mus. A.; Parkland Hospital, Dallas.*

BUCHHOLZ, EMMALINE (HARDY) (Mrs. F. W.)— *Painter, I., T.*

Rocky Point, Gainesville, Fla.

B. Ormondsville, N.C. *Studied:* Randolph-Macon Col.; PAFA; AIC. *Member:* Gainesville Assn. FA; Florida Fed. A.; Nat. Lg. Am. Pen Women. *Work:* Florida State Col. for Women; Univ. Florida; State Lib., Tallahassee; State Mus. A. I., "Growing English." *Position:* A.T.; Dir., Antique & Art Studio, Gainesville, Fla.; Historian, Gainesville Little Theatre; Pres., Gainesville Br., Nat. Lg. Am. Pen Women.

BUCHHOLZ, FREDERICK—*Painter*

19 Bethune St., New York 14, N.Y.; s. Lyme, Conn.

B. Springfield, Mass., Aug. 5, 1901. *Studied:* ASL. *Member:* Essex AA; Creative A. Assn; Lyme AA. *Exhibited:* Springfield Inst. A., 1922-1944; Newhouse Gal., 1934 (one-man); Decorator's Cl., 1938 (one-man); Am-British A. Center, 1943; Chappelier Gal., 1944; AWS, 1946, SFMA, 1946; Jackson, Miss., 1946; Riverside Mus., 1946, 1950, 1951, 1953, 1956; NAC, 1949; Essex (Conn.) AA, 1951-1958; Lyme AA, 1951-1958; G.W.V. Smith Mus., 1954 (one-man); Attleboro (Mass.) Mus. A., 1957; State Col. A. Gal., Willimantic, Conn., 1957; Fremont Fnd., Fremont, Mich., 1958; State Col. Gal., La Crosse, Wis., 1958; County Lib., Mason City, Iowa, 1958; Bethany Col., Bethany, Okla., 1958; Condon Riley Gal., N.Y., 1959. *Lectures:* "A New Pastel Method."

BUCHTA, ANTHONY—*Painter, Et., T., Cr.*

3824 North Clark St., Chicago 13, Ill.

Studied: Chicago Acad. FA; AIC; and with Charles Schroeder, Leslie F. Thompson. *Member:* Chicago Galleries Assn.; Chicago P. & S.; Hoosier Salon; Brown County A. Gld. *Awards:* prizes, Hoosier Salon; Palette & Chisel Cl., Chicago. *Work:* Sheldon Swope Gal. A. *Exhibited:* Chicago Galleries Assn.; Chicago Acad. FA; Little Gal., Cedar Rapids, Iowa.*

BUCK, CLAUDE—*Painter, T.*

128 Rankin St., Santa Cruz, Cal.

B. New York, N.Y., July 3, 1890. *Studied:* NAD, with Emil Carlsen, Kenyon Cox, George deForrest Brush. *Member:* Carmel AA; Soc. Western A.; Santa Cruz A. Lg.; Chicago Galleries Assn.; Grand Central A. Galleries. *Awards:* prizes, Chicago Galleries Assn., 1926-1928, 1930-1932, 1935; AIC, 1929, 1932 (3); Chicago P.&S., 1932; All-Ill. Soc. FA, 1934; Cal.PLH, 1944; Oakland A. Gal., 1945; Santa Cruz County Fair, 1947, 1949, Statewide Exh., 1954, 1957; Soc. Western A, 1948, 1952. *Work:* Eastman Mem. Fnd.; Univ. Chicago; Vanderpool Coll.; Swope A. Mus.; Santa Cruz A. Gal.; Roycemore Sch. for Girls, Evanston, Ill.; Elgin (Ill.) A. Mus.; LaGrange (Ill.) Pub.

Sch.; Congregational Church, Chicago; Midway Sch., Chicago; Des Moines Pub. Lib. *Exhibited:* AIC; NAD; Grand Central A. Gal.; Purdue Univ.; John Herron AI; Brooks Mem. A. Gal.; Crocker A. Gal.; Cal. PLH; Oakland A. Gal.; deYoung Mem. Mus.; Laguna Beach AA; Santa Cruz A. Gal.; Carmel AA; Swope Gal. A.; CAM; State Mus.; Springfield, Ill.; Art:USA, 1958, etc.

BUCK, HENRY BENNETT—*Painter*

Monk Road, Old Saybrook, Conn.

B. Syracuse, N.Y., Dec. 8, 1900. *Studied:* BMFA Sch., and in Paris. *Member:* Essex AA; Conn. WC Soc. *Award:* prize, Conn. WC Soc., 1946. *Work:* Syracuse Mus. FA. *Exhibited:* SAGA; MMA; Essex A. Gal.; and in Puerto Rico.

BUCK, LESLIE (BINNER) (Mrs. Claude)—*Painter*

128 Rankin St., Santa Cruz, Cal.

B. Chicago, Ill. *Studied:* AIC, Studio Sch. A., Chicago, and with Claude Buck. *Member:* Carmel AA.; Chicago Galleries Assn.; Soc. Western A.; Santa Cruz A. Lg. *Awards:* prizes, Sanity in Art, Chicago, 1938; Santa Cruz A. Lg., 1944; Santa Cruz County Fair, 1947, 1950; Chicago Galleries Assn., 1941, 1944; Cal. PLH; Oakland A. Gal., 1947, 1948; Santa Cruz State Exh., 1953, 1955. *Work:* Vanderpool Coll.; Pub. Sch., LaGrange, Ill. *Exhibited:* Cal. PLH, 1944, 1945; Santa Cruz, 1944-1958; Carmel AA, 1946-1958; Oakland A. Gal., 1945-1952; Chicago Galleries Assn.; AIC, 1935, 1937, 1939, 1941; Crocker A. Gal.; Swope Gal. A.; deYoung Mem. Mus.; Rosicrucian Mus., 1957; Burr Gal., N.Y., 1958.

BUCK, RICHARD DAVID—*Museum Conservator, L.*

Intermuseum Laboratory, Dudley Peter Allen Memorial Art Museum; h. Oberlin, Ohio

B. Middletown, N.Y., Feb. 3, 1903. *Studied:* Harvard Univ., S.B., A.M. *Member:* Int. Inst. for Conserv. of Mus. Objects; Contributor: Studies in Conservation, Museum. *Position:* Dept. Conservation, Fogg Mus. A., Harvard Univ., 1937-52; Conservator, 1949-52; L., in FA, 1950-52; Advisor on Conservation, Nat. Gal., London, 1949-50 (on leave from Fogg Museum); Chief Conservator, Intermuseum Conservation Assn., & Dir., Intermuseum Laboratory, Lecturer, Allen Mem. A. Mus., Oberlin, Ohio, 1952- .

BUCKLEY, CHARLES E.—*Museum Director*

Currier Gallery of Art, 192 Orange St., Manchester, N.H.

Position: Dir., Currier Gallery of Art.*

BUCKLEY, JEAN—*Sculptor, P., C., Lith., T.*

7811½ Melrose Ave., Los Angeles 46, Cal.

B. Sacramento, Cal., Mar. 10, 1925. *Studied:* Sacramento Col.; Chouinard AI; ASL; Cal. Col. of A. & Crafts; Univ. So. California. *Member:* Cal. WC Soc.; Los A. AA; So. Cal. Des-Craftsmen; Southwest Mus. Assn. *Awards:* prizes, Cal. WC Soc., 1952; Unitarian Exh., Los A., 1954; Cal. State Fair, 1955 (purchase); Orange County Nat. Exh., 1957 (purchase); Los A. Art Festival, 1957 (purchase); Des.-Craftsmen Exh., Los A., 1957 (purchase); Unitarian A. Festival, 1958. *Work:* sc., Cal. State Coll., Sacramento; Immaculate Heart Col.; Grant Beach Sch. of A. & Crafts; Dept. Recreation, Oakland, Cal. (mural). *Exhibited:* Wichita, Kans., 1954-1955; Young Americans, N.Y., 1955; Univ. So. Cal., 1953; Cal. WC Soc., 1952-1958; Cal. State Fair, 1954-1957; Los A. Mus. A., 1952, 1956-1958; Orange Show, 1954-1955; Heilborn Gal., Los A., 1953 (one-man); Denver A. Mus., 1958; Pasadena Mus. A., 1957, 1958; Los A. Mus. A., 1958; Santa Monica, Cal., 1957; Mt. St. Mary's Col., Los A., 1957 (7-man); Pasadena Mus. A., 1958 (2-man). Contributor to National Craft Magazine, 1954-1955. *Position:* Gal. Asst., Crocker A. Gal., Sacramento, Cal., 1943; Dir., Studio One Workshop & Gal., Oakland, Cal., 1947-49; Dir., A. & Crafts, Special Services, U.S. Army (Europe), 1949-50; Treas., Cal. WC Soc.; Assoc., College of Appl. Arts, UCLA, Los Angeles, Cal., 1958.

BUCKNER, MELVIN D.—*Painter, Des., T., Comm. A.*

American Chemical Society; h. 800 Emerson St., N.W., Washington 11, D.C.

B. Washington, D.C., Mar. 28, 1915. *Studied:* Carnegie Inst.; ASL; George Washington Univ., B.A. in Edu.; Univ.

Puerto Rico, and with Isabel Bishop, Raphael Soyer. *Member*: Soc. Wash. A.; Wash. A. Gld.; Assoc. A. Pittsburgh. *Awards*: med., CGA, 1940, prize, 1954; Creative Gal., N.Y., 1953; Univ. Puerto Rico, 1945; Soc. Wash. A., 1952. *Work*: Des. productions, "Six Characters in Search of an Author," and others. *Exhibited*: CGA, 1941, 1946, 1949, 1950, 1953-1955; WFNY 1939; Assoc. A. Pittsburgh, 1937-1939; Soc. Wash. A., 1941, 1942, 1946; PMG; Univ. Puerto Rico; Hudson Walker Gal.; The Ateneo, San Juan, P.R.; BMFA; Smithsonian Inst., 1950-1955; Creative Gal., 1953. *Position*: A. Dir., American Chemical Society, Wash., D.C.; Vice-Pres., Soc. Wash. A., 1957-58.

BUDELL, ADA—*Painter, I.*
627 Fourth Avenue, Westfield, N.J.

B. Westfield, N.J., June 19, 1873. *Studied*: ASL, with Bridgman, DuMond, Pennell. *Member*: NAWA; AAPL; Westfield AA; Plainfield AA. *Awards*: prizes, A. Center of the Oranges, 1927, 1931; Westfield AA, 1932, 1933, 1935, 1936, 1940, 1952; Plainfield AA, 1941, 1950, 1951; NAWA, 1952. *Work*: Asbury Park Mus.; State House, Trenton, N.J.; Beckley Company, Garwood, N.J. *Exhibited*: NAD, 1930; AWCS, 1909, 1916, 1927, 1935, 1945, 1946; Arch. L., 1904, 1905; NAWA, 1922-1946; Montclair A. Mus.; AAPL; SAE, 1905, 1906; NAC; NAWA, 1922-1946. Illus., stories, textbooks & music books for children. Former Dir., Budell A. Sch., Westfield, N.J.

BUDELL, (EMILY) HORTENSE—*Painter*
627 Fourth Ave., Westfield, N.J.

B. Lyons, France, Mar. 23, 1884. *Studied*: with John Carlson, Henry B. Snell, George Elmer Browne. *Member*: All.A.Am.; NAWA; Conn. Acad. FA; AAPL; Westfield AA; Plainfield AA. *Awards*: Prizes, A. Center of the Oranges, 1926, 1931, 1953; NAWA, 1931; med., Plainfield AA, 1931, 1938; Contemporary Gal., N.J., 1933, 1935, 1936, 1938, 1941; Montclair A. Mus.; 1936; Spring Lake AA, 1939; Irvington A. & Mus. Assn., 1944, 1949; Rahway A. Center, 1953; Westfield AA. 1940, 1950, 1952, 1953, 1955, 1957. *Work*: Asbury Park Mus. *Exhibited*: NAD, 1927, 1928; All. A.Am., 1927-1945, 1946-1952; AWS, 1948; NAWA, 1926-1945, 1952; Conn. Acad, FA, 1927, 1928, 1931, 1932, 1936, 1938, 1940, 1941, 1945; Phila. A. Cl., 1925; AAPL, 1939, 1942, 1943, 1944; Montclair A. Mus.; NAC. *Position*: Former A.T., Adult Edu., Schools in Westfield & Cranford, N.J.

BUECHNER, THOMAS S.—*Museum Director*
Corning Museum of Glass, Corning, N.Y.
Position: Dir., Corning Museum of Glass.*

BUELL, ALICE STANDISH—*Etcher*
11 Bryant Crescent, White Plains, N.Y.; s. Woodstock, Vt.

B. Oak Park, Ill. *Studied*: Oberlin Col., A.B.; ASL; & with Martin Lewis. *Member*: SAGA; NAWA; PBC; ASL; So. Vermont A.; Westchester A. & Crafts Gld. *Awards*: prizes, SSAL, 1931; Southern Pr.M., 1938; Phila. Pr. Cl., 1939; Pen & Brush Cl., 1953. *Work*: Lib.Cong.; Dartmouth Col.; Univ. Wisconsin; Montclair A. Mus.; ASL. *Exhibited*: SAGA, 1931-1934, 1943, 1945, 1947, 1948; PBC, 1945, 1946, 1953, 1954; Lib.Cong., 1944; Carnegie Inst., 1944; WFNY 1939; AIC, 1938; Cal.Pr.M., 1935; Phila. Pr. Cl., 1931, 1939, 1941; AV, 1942; NAD, 1943, 1946; NAWA, 1941-1949, 1953-1955; Phila. SE, 1931, 1934, 1937, 1938; Wash. WC Cl., 1936; Northwest Pr.M., 1935, 1938; SSAL, 1931; Vermont A., 1938-1940, 1950; Southern Pr.M., 1938.*

BUFANO, BENIAMINO—*Sculptor*
San Francisco Press Club, San Francisco, Cal.

B. San-Fele, Italy, Oct. 14, 1898. *Studied*: NAD; BAID; ASL; & with Paul Manship, James L. Fraser, Herbert Adams. *Awards*: Prizes, WMAA, 1917; ASL, 1916. *Work*: MMA; SFMA; Palace Legion Honor; Sun Yat Sen statue, St. Mary's Park, San F.; Peace mem., San F., & others. *Position*: A. Commissioner, City of San Francisco, Cal.

BUFF, CONRAD—*Painter, Lith., I., Des.*
414 Mooresque Dr., Pasadena 2, Cal.

B. Speicher, Switzerland, Jan. 15, 1886. *Studied*: in Europe. *Awards*: prizes, Los A. Mus. A., 1924, 1934; San Diego

FA Soc., 1925; AIC; Santa Paula Cal., 1944; Los A. County Mun. Exh., 1948; Commonwealth Cl., 1950. *Work*: Encyclopaedia Britannica Coll.; MMA; NGA; BMFA; AIC; Detroit Inst. A.; Palace Legion Honor; CMA; Los A. Mus. A.; Los A. Pub. Lib.; San Diego FA Soc.; murals, Nat. Bank, Phoenix, Ariz.; Edison Co., Los A.; Barlow Medical Lib., Los A., Cal. I., "Dancing Cloud," & other juvenile books.

BUGBEE, HAROLD DOW—*Illustrator, P.*
Clarendon, Tex.

B. Lexington, Mass., Aug. 15, 1900. *Studied*: Clarendon Col.; Texas A.&M. Col.; Cumming Sch. A.; & with Herbert Dunton. *Work*: murals, Panhandle Plains Hist. Soc. Mus., Canyon, Tex.; Hall of State, Dallas, Tex.; Amarillo Army Air Field, Amarillo, Tex. I., Western books & short stories; Illus. for The Cattleman, Country Gentleman, Field and Stream and other national magazines. *Position*: Cur. A., Panhandle Plains Hist. Mus., Canyon, Tex., at present.

BUGBIRD, MARY BAYNE (Mrs. Herbert C.)—
Painter, T.
28 Overhill Rd., Tall Oaks, Summit, N.J.

B. Richmond, Va., Sept. 18, 1889. *Studied*: ASL, with George Bellows, Kenneth Hayes Miller, Joe Jones. *Member*: NAWA; Summit AA; Staten Island Inst. A.&Sc.; Assoc. A. of New Jersey. *Awards*: prizes, Whitney Studio Cl.; Newark A. Cl., 1940; NAWA, 1955; Verona-West Essex AA, 1957. *Exhibited*: Audubon A., 1953, 1954, 1957; VMFA, 1955; Montclair A. Mus., 1955-1957; Montclair Women's Cl., 1955 (one-man); NAWA, 1955 and prior; Summit AA; N.J. State Mus.; Newark Mus. A., 1958; YM-YWCA, Newark, 1958 (one-man); Art:USA, 1958. *Position*: A.T., Summit AA.

BUHOLZ, FRANCES—*Painter, I., T.*
142 East 18th St., New York 3, N.Y.

B. Red Wing, Minn., Sept. 23, 1896. *Studied*: Minneapolis Sch. A. *Member*: Minnesota AA. *Awards*: prize, Minneapolis Inst. A., 1935. *Exhibited*: PAFA; AIC; NAD; Minneapolis Inst. A. I., "Say It In Spanish." *Position*: Former Instr. Illus., Minneapolis Sch. A.; Cooper Union, N.Y.*

BUK. See Ulreich, Eduard Buk

BULLER, AUDREY (Mrs. Audrey Buller Parsons)—
Painter, Des.
West Rd., Little Compton, R.I.

B. Montreal, Canada. *Studied*: ASL. *Member*: AEA; NAWA. *Awards*: prizes, NAD, 1937; Pepsi-Cola Comp.; NAWA, 1953. *Work*: MMA; WMAA. *Exhibited*: CGA; AIC; NAD; PAFA; Carnegie Inst; MMA, 1950; BM, 1951; Mus. A., R.I. Sch. Des., 1954.

BULLER, CECIL (Mrs. Cecil T. Murphy)—
Wood Engraver, P.
355 East 86th St., New York 28, N.Y.

B. Montreal, Canada. *Studied*: Montreal A. Sch., and with Noel Rooke, London; Maurice Denis, Paris. *Member*: SAGA; Audubon A.; NAD. *Awards*: Pennell prize, LC, 1945; Audubon A., 1947, gold med., 1953; NAD, 1949. *Work*: British Mus., London; Nat. Gal., Canada; LC; Bibliotheque Nationale, Paris; N.Y.Pub.Lib.; Montreal Mus. FA; Royal Mus. A., Exeter, England. *Exhibited*: Carnegie Inst., 1941, 1945, 1947, 1949; LC, 1945-1949, 1952; NAD, 1940, 1941, 1943, 1946, 1948, 1949, 1952, 1956; BM, 1947, 1950; Oxford, England, 1951; Montreal Mus. FA, 1957; SAGA, 1957. Illus., "Le Cantique des Cantiques," publ. Paris, France.

BULLOCK, MARY JANE MC LEAN (Mrs. Kenneth K.)
—Painter, C., T.
Winton Terrace East, Fort Worth, Tex.

B. Fort Worth, Tex., Apr. 10, 1898. *Studied*: Texas Christian Univ.; AIC; & with Joseph Fleck, Frank Klepper. *Member*: AAPL; SSAL; Texas FA Assn.; Ft. Worth AA. *Awards*: prizes, SSAL, 1936, 1938, 1946. *Work*: Women's Cl., Tyler, Tex. *Exhibited*: SSAL, 1936, 1938, 1946; Texas

FA Assn., 1936, 1937, 1938, 1940; Ft. Worth AA, 1946; Civic A. Exhs. *Position*: Instr. P. & Crafts, Camp Wanaka for Girls, Woodland Park, Colo., summers.*

BULL-TEILMAN, GUNVOR (Mrs.)—
Painter, S., I., W., L., C.
3 Washington Square, North, New York 3, N.Y.

B. Bodoe, Norway, Mar. 14, 1900. *Studied*: Grande Chaumiere, Julian Acad., Paris; Acad. FA, Leipzig, with A. Lehnert, A. Müller, André L'Hote, Paris. *Awards*: prizes Albany Inst. Hist. & A., 1935; Salon d'Automne, Paris, 1926; Germanic Mus., Harvard Univ., 1933; Am-Scandinavian A. Group, 1936. *Work*: murals, Waldorf-Astoria Hotel, N.Y.; U.S. Time Corp., Waterbury, Conn. (ceramics). *Exhibited*: Europe: 1922-1956; Bernheim-Jeune, 1949; Paris, France; U.S.: Ferargil Gal., 1943; BM; WMAA; Passedoit Gal.; Serigraph Gal., 1953; NAC, 1957; Meltzer Gal., N.Y., 1958. Illus., Undset's "Sigurd and His Brave Companions," 1943. Contributor to magazines with articles on art. Lectures: "Art in Occupied Norway."

BUNCE, LOUIS—*Painter, Gr., T.*
10270 Southwest Boones Ferry Rd., Oswego, Ore.

B. Lander, Wyo., Aug. 13, 1907. *Studied*: Portland Mus. A. Sch.; ASL. *Member*: Portland AA; AEA. *Awards*: SAM, 1936, 1952 (purchase); Portland A. Mus., (purchase), 1951, 1954; Oregon Pr. Ann., 1951-1954 (purchase); Northwest Pr. M., 1948. *Work*: Portland A. Mus.; SAM; WMAA; Munson-Williams-Proctor Inst.; Butler AI; Colo. Springs FA Center; Hollins Col.; PMA; AAUW; Springfield (Mo.) Mus. A.; Univ. Michigan; Univ. Washington; Am. Acad. A. & Let.; U.S. Treasury Dept. (mural); Grants Pass, Ore., Federal Bldg. *Exhibited*: AIC, 1947; WMA, 1949; WMAA, 1951, 1953, 1954; CGA, 1953; Toledo Mus. A., 1953; VMFA, 1954; Nebraska AA, 1954; PAFA, 1954; Carnegie Inst., 1955; Sao Paulo, Brazil, 1955; MMA, 1950; Colo. Springs FA Center, 1951, 1953, 1955; Portland A. Mus. Ann., 1950-1955; SAM, 1951, 1955. *Position*: Instr. Painting, Portland (Ore.) Mus. A. Sch.; Drawing, Pacific Univ., Forest Grove, Ore., Painting & Drawing, Grants Pass (Ore.) A. Lg.*

BUNN, WILLIAM EDWARD LEWIS—
Painter, Des., C., W., T.
P.O. Box 479; h. High Point, Fort Madison, Iowa

B. Muscatine, Iowa, May 29, 1910. Studied: Univ. Iowa, B.A., M.A.; & with Grant Wood. *Awards*: prize, Davenport, Iowa, 1941. *Work*: murals, USPO, Dubuque, Hamburg, Iowa; Minden, Neb.; Hickman, Ky. *Exhibited*: NAD, 1937, 1941, 1945; CGA, 1939-1941; VMFA, 1942; PAFA, 1941; AIC, 1937, 1942; Kansas City AI, 1938; Davenport A.Mus., 1940, 1941; traveling exh., 1948-49. *Position*: Indst. Des., Barnes & Reinecke, Chicago, 1944-45; Manager, Indst. Des. Dept., Sheaffer Pen Co., Fort Madison, Iowa, 1946- .

BUONGIORNO, NICK—*Painter, Et., Lith.*
2108 Second Ave., New York 29, N.Y.

B. New York, N.Y., Sept. 17, 1908. *Studied*: Leonardo da Vinci A. Sch., with Michael Falanga; NAD, with Leon Kroll; N.Y. Univ., B.A., M.M.A. *Awards*: DaVinci Traveling F., 1925-1929. *Work*: portraits in private collections. *Exhibited*: NAD, 1942-1945, 1947-1951; AEA; Pepsi-Cola exh., 1947; Burr Gal., N.Y., 1956, 1957; one-man: Union Square Savings Bank, 1957.

BURCAW, G. ELLIS—*Museum Director*
Neville Public Museum, 129 South Jefferson St., Green Bay, Wis.*

BURCHESS, ARNOLD—*Painter, T., Comm. A.*
211 East 79th St., New York, N.Y.; h. 147-23 Willets Point Blvd., Whitestone, L.I., N.Y.

B. Chicago, Ill., June 7, 1912. *Studied*: City Col., N.Y., B.S.S., and with George W. Eggers, Robert Garrison. *Member*: Alabama WC Soc.; Springfield A. Lg.; New Orleans AA; Cal. WC Soc. *Awards*: prize, Birmingham Mus. A., 1954. *Work*: Sc., with Robert Garrison, walls of Radio City (Music Hall Bldg.), 1934-35. *Exhibited*: Riverside Mus., 1955; AWS, 1955-1958; Butler AI, 1955; G.W.V. Smith Mus., Springfield, Mass., 1955; Contemp. A. Gal., 1955; Birmingham Mus. A., 1955; Cal. WC Soc., 1955; Assoc. Am. A., 1955; Delgado Mus. A., 1957; West-

chester A. Center, 1958; U.S. Natl. Mus., 1958; PAFA, 1958; N.Y. City Center, 1958; MMoDA, 1958; Audubon A., 1956-1958; NAC, 1956-1958; Howard Col., 1957; Long Beach (Cal.) Mun. A. Center, 1957; Cal. PLH, 1957; Mobile AA, 1957; Shorter Col., 1957; Alabama Polytechnic Col., 1957; Alabama State T. Col., 1957; Jacksonville (Fla.) Mus. A., 1957; Lauren Rogers Mus. A., Laurel, Miss., 1957. Lectures: Sculpture; Shapes in Clay, etc. *Position*: Instr., Sch. Indst. A., New York, N.Y., 1937- .

BURCHFIELD, CHARLES E.—*Painter*
c/o Rehn Galleries, 683 Fifth Ave., New York 22, N.Y.; h. 3574 Clinton St., Gardenville, N.Y.

B. Ashtabula, Ohio, Apr. 9, 1893. *Studied*: Cleveland Sch. A. *Member*: Am. Acad. A. & Lets.; N.A. *Awards*: prizes, Cleveland SA, 1921; PAFA, 1929, 1940, 1946, 1949; Carnegie Inst., 1937; Newport AA, 1938; San Diego FA Soc., 1940; AIC, 1941; Univ. Buffalo, 1944; Hon. Degree, L.H.D., Kenyon Col., Gambier, Ohio; Hon. Degrees, Art D., Harvard Univ.; Art D., Hamilton Univ.; L.H.D., Valparaiso Univ. *Work*: FMA; BMFA; Detroit Inst. A.; R.I. Sch. Des.; Syracuse Mus. FA; Univ. Nebraska, and many others. *Exhibited*: MMA; Newark Mus.; R.I.Sch.Des.; BMFA; FMA; Albright A. Gal.; CMA; PMG; BM; WMAA; MMoDA; John Herron AI, 1929-1946; PAFA, 1946, and many others. Retrospective exh. covering 40 years of work, WMAA, 1956. "Charles Burchfield," by John I. H. Baur, 1956.

BURCHFIELD, LOUISE H.—
Former Museum Assoc. Curator
2085 Cornell Rd., Cleveland 6, Ohio

B. Akron, Ohio, Aug. 9, 1898. *Studied*: Western Reserve Univ. *Member*: Hon. memb., Royal Soc. Min. P.S.&Engravers, London, 1949. *Awards*: Guggenheim F., 1952. Contributor to Museum Bulletins; compiled catalogue "Portrait Miniatures, The Edward B. Greene Collection," 1951. *Position*: Asst. Cur., Paintings, CMA, Cleveland, Ohio, 1941-50; Assoc. Cur., 1950-1954. (Retired.)

BURCK, JACOB—*Cartoonist*
Chicago Sun-Times, Chicago, Ill.
Position: Editorial Cart., Chicago Sun-Times.*

BURDETTE, DOROTHY MAY—*Painter*
2508 North Penn Road, Independence, Kans.

B. Arkansas City, Kans., May 11, 1893. *Studied*: State Col., Pittsburgh, Kans.; Scranton, Pa. *Member*: Mid-America A.; AAPL. *Exhibited*: Whistler House, Lowell, Mass.; Ogunquit A. Center; Mid-America A.; Crippled Children's Exh., Topeka, Kans.; Verdigris Valley A. Center.*

BURDOIN, JULIET (HOWSON)—*Painter*
70 Silver St., Dover, N.H. s. Gloucester, Mass.

B. Toronto, Canada, Feb. 21, 1873. *Studied*: Ontario A. Sch.; Academie Julian, with Bougereau, Ferrier; also studied in Holland. *Member*: Gloucester AA; Rockport AA. *Work*: in private colls. U.S. and Canada.

BURG, COPELAND CHARLES—*Painter, T., L., Cr.*
1544 Wieland St., Chicago 10, Ill.

B. Livingston, Mont., Feb. 18, 1895. *Studied*: Univ. Washington. *Awards*: prizes, Portland (Ore.) A. Mus., 1939; PAFA, 1940; AIC, 1941, 1942, 1943, 1947, 1948; San F. AA, 1941, 1942; Palace Legion Honor; Milwaukee AI, 1946; purchase prize, Union League, Chicago, 1956. *Work*: AIC; PAFA. *Exhibited*: WMAA, 1945; Carnegie Inst., 1943, 1944; CGA; VMFA; PAFA; San F. AA; MMA, 1943; Santa Barbara Mus. A., 1945, 1946 (one-man); de Young Mem. Mus. 1945, 1946 (one-man); Chicago Pub. Lib., 1945, 1946 (one-man); AIC Navy Pier Exhs., 1957, 1958. *Position*: Instr. Painting, Old Town A.Sch., Chicago, Ill., 1957-58.

BURGDORFF, FERDINAND—*Painter, Gr., C.*
Pebble Beach, Cal.

B. Cleveland, Ohio, Nov. 7, 1883. *Studied*: Cleveland Sch. A., B.A.; in Paris, with Menard. *Member*: Carmel AA. *Work*: SFMA; CMA; Fort Ord, Monterey; U.S. Navy Post-Grad. Sch., Monterey; Cottonwood (Ariz.) Hospital;

Ganado (Ariz.) Mission Hospital; Carmel (Cal.) Hospital; Ross General Hospital, San Rafael, Cal.; 36 paintings given to six U.S. Air Force Hospitals in the Arctic; U.S. Air Force Acad., Denver, Colo.; Salinas Valley Mem. Hospital, Salinas, Cal. *Exhibited*: CGA; Las Vegas (Nev.) AA, 1958 (one-man).

BURGESS, JOSEPH (E.)—Painter, I.
344 West 72nd St., New York 23, N.Y.
B. Dansville, N.Y., Mar. 28, 1890. *Studied*: Syracuse Univ., B.F.A., and with George Bridgman, Harvey Dunn. *Member*: SC. Portraits, Figure Illus.

BURKE, (E.) AINSLIE—Painter
P.O. Box 91, Bearsville, N.Y.
B. Omaha, Neb., Jan. 26, 1922. *Studied*: Maryland Inst. A.; Johns Hopkins Univ., McCoy Col.; ASL; San Miguel Allende, Mexico. *Member*: ASL; Woodstock AA. *Awards*: prizes, Baltimore Sun award, 1947; Woodstock Fnd.; Fulbright F., 1957-58. *Work*: Columbia Univ., Student Center; Springfield Mus. A. *Exhibited*: BM, 1947, 1953; Toledo Mus. FA, 1950; Springfield Mus. A., 1951; PAFA, 1957; Nebraska AA, 1958; WMAA, 1958; N.Y. State Fair, 1957; VMFA; Galleria Schneider, Rome, Italy, 1958; AAA Gal., N.Y., 1951, (one-man).

BURKE, WILLIAM LOZIER MUNRO—Historian
Department of Art, University of Iowa, Iowa City, Iowa
B. Brooklyn, N.Y., May 26, 1906. *Studied*: Princeton Univ., A.B., M.A., M.F.A.; Univ. Hamburg. *Member*: AAUP; CAA; Medieval Acad. Am. Contributor to The Art Bulletin. *Position*: Assoc. Prof. A., State Univ. Iowa, Iowa City, Iowa, 1951- .

BURKENROAD, FLORA SALINGER—Painter
5214 Prytania St., New Orleans, La.
B. Lafayette, Ind., Mar. 31, 1873. *Studied*: NAD; & with Thomas Eakins, Will H. Low, C. Y. Turner; André L'Hote, Paris. *Exhibited*: NAWA; Delgado Mus. A.; New Orleans A. & Crafts Cl.

BURKHARDT, HANS GUSTAV—Painter
1914 Jewett Dr., Los Angeles 46, Cal.
B. Basel, Switzerland, Dec. 20, 1904. *Studied*: CUASch.; Grand Central Sch. A., and with Gorky. *Member*: AFA; Los A. AA, Westwood AA. *Awards*: prizes, Los A. Mus. A., 1946, 1954, 1957; Cal. State Fair, 1954, 1958; Terry AI, 1951; Los Angeles All-City Exh., 1957; Santa Barbara Mus. A., 1957. *Work*: Los A. Mus. A.; Santa Barbara Mus. A.; City of Los Angeles Coll.; Pasadena Mus. A.; Columbia (S.C.) Mus. A.; Emily & Joe Lowe A. Gal., Coral Gables, Fla.; Mus. Mod. A., Eilat, Israel; Mus. A., Tel-Aviv. *Exhibited*: Los A. Mus. A., 1945, 1946, 1953-1955, 1957; Cal. State Fair, annually; Cal. PLH, 1946, 1947; deYoung Mem. Mus., San Francisco, 1950; SFMA, 1955-1957; Santa Barbara Mus. A., (Pacific Coast Biennial, on tour), 1957; Denver Mus. A., 1949, 1953, 1954; Univ. Nebraska, 1957; Nat. Orange Show annually; "Art of Southern California, II," on extended tour at present; AIC, 1947, 1951; Univ. Illinois, 1951; PAFA, 1951-1953; MMA, 1951; Terry AI, 1951; Butler Inst. Am. A., 1955; Art:USA, 1958; United Nations Tenth Anniversary, San Francisco, 1955; WMAA, 1951, 1955, 1958; CGA, 1947, 1951, 1953; AFA circulating exh., 1951-52; Sao Paulo Biennial, 1955; one-man: Yearly at Los Angeles galleries since 1939; Los A. Mus A., 1945; Univ. Oregon, 1948; Mus. of Guadalajara, Mexico, 1950; Occidental Col., Los A., 1955; Instituto Allende, Mexico, 1956; Pasadena Mus. A., 1958.

BURKHART, EMERSON C.—Painter, T., L.
223 Woodland Ave., Columbus 3, Ohio.
B. Kalida, Ohio, Jan. 30, 1905. *Studied*: Ohio Wesleyan Univ., B.F.A.; NAD, and with Charles W. Hawthorne. *Member*: Columbus A. Lg. *Awards*: prizes, Columbus A. Lg., 1940-1946, 1949, 1952; Ohio WC Soc., 1951; Butler AI, 1950, 1955 (purchase); Columbus Gal. FA, 1955 (purchase); AIC, 1955; Ohio State Fair, Governor's award, 1955. *Work*: Columbus Gal. FA; Walter Chrysler, Jr., Coll.; murals, Ohio State Univ.; Butler AI; port. private coll. *Exhibited*: AIC, 1932, 1933, 1955; PAFA, 1932, 1933, 1936; CGA; CM, 1932, 1937, 1938; Butler AI, 1946, 1955;

WMAA, 1946, and later; Carnegie Inst., 1946; Columbus Gal. FA, 1931-1946, 1952, 1955, 1957, 1958; Dayton AI, 1951 (one-man); Inst. A. & Let.; Univ. Cl., Detroit; Ohio State Fair, 1955; PMA, 1958; Detroit Inst. A., 1958.

BURLIN, PAUL—Painter, Lith.
54 West 74th St., New York 23, N.Y.
B. New York, N.Y., Sept. 10, 1886. *Studied*: in England. *Awards*: prizes, Pepsi-Cola, 1945. *Work*: MModA; WMAA; BM; Newark Mus. A.; Encyclopedia Britannica; Washington Univ.; Univ. Minnesota; IBM; Wichita Mus. A.; Alabama Polytechnic Inst.; Lamont Mus., Exeter, N.H. *Exhibited*: Carnegie Inst., 1936-1946; WFNY 1939; AIC, 1935-1945; MModA, 1945; one-man: Downtown Gal.; Stable Gal., 1954; Cal. PLH, 1954; FA Soc. San Diego, 1954; Univ. So. California, 1954; Louisiana State Univ., 1954; Washington Univ., St. Louis, 1954; Union Col., Schenectady, N.Y., 1954; Poindexter Gal., N.Y., 1958; Univ. Mississippi, 1958; State T. Col., New Paltz, N.Y., 1958. *Position*: L., Painting, Washington Univ., 1949-54; John Hay Whitney Fnd.; Visiting Prof., Union Col., Schenectady, N.Y., 1954-55.

BURLINGAME, SHEILA ELLSWORTH—Sculptor, P., Des.
202 Bradford St., Provincetown, Mass.
B. Lyons, Kans., 1905. *Studied*: AIC; ASL; Grande Chaumiere, Paris; Kalamazoo Col. *Member*: NSS; Arch. Lg.; Audubon A.; AAPL. *Awards*: prizes, St. Louis A. Gld.; Pen & Brush Cl.; AAPL; NAWA; Artists for Victory; med., Kansas City. *Work*: figures and reliefs in churches in Mo., Ark., Colo., Mont.; Vanderpoel Coll.; Leonberger Davis Coll.; Kroeger Mem., St. Louis. *Exhibited*: Fairmount Park, Phila., Pa., 1950; PAFA; NAD; AIC; Buffalo, N.Y.; Denver, Colo.; Wichita, Kans.; Audubon A.; Provincetown AA; Hyannis AA; Colo. Springs FA Center; Arch. Lg., N.Y. Des., "Sarah Lee" doll.

BURLIUK, DAVID—Painter, L., W.
Hampton Bays, L.I., N.Y.
B. Kharkov, Russia, July 22, 1882. *Studied*: A. Schs. in Kazan, Odessa, Munich, Paris & Moscow. Founder-Member: "De Blaue Reiter" and "Sturm" together with Picasso, Kandinsky, F. Mark, 1910-14; with Mayakovsky and Kamiensky "Cubo-Futurism," 1911. *Work*: MMA; WMAA; BM; BMFA; PC; Yale Univ.; ACA Gal.; PMA, and others throughout the U.S. *Exhibited*: nationally and internationally. One-man: Societe Anonyme, 1924; J.B. Neumann Gal., 1927; Morton Gal., 1928; Dorothy Paris Gal., 1933-35; Cal. PLH, 1931; Philip Boyer Gal., 1935-1939; PC, 1937; ACA Gal., 1941-1955; Havana, Cuba, 1955. Co-publisher (with Mary Burliuk), art magazine "Color and Rhyme," 1930- ; Author, special research on "Van Gogh in Arles," 1949-50. Pres., Burliuk A. Gal., Hampton Bays, L.I., N.Y., Marussia Burliuk, A.Dir. (June, July & Aug.).

BURNETT, CALVIN—Graphic Artist, P., T.
10 Kings St.; h. 12 King St., Cambridge 40, Mass.
B. Cambridge, Mass., July 18, 1921. *Studied*: Boston Univ.; BMFA Sch. A.; Mass. Sch. A., B.S., in Edu. *Member*: Inst. Contemp. A., Boston; Cambridge AA; Boston Pr. M. (Bd. Dir.). *Awards*: prizes, Atlanta Univ., 1947, 1948, 1956; Cambridge Centennial Exh., 1946; Cambridge AA, 1949; Germanic Mus., Cambridge, 1946; Wharton Settlement, Phila., Pa., 1953 (purchase); Busch-Reisinger Mus., 1949; Howard Univ., 1949 (purchase). *Work*: Howard Univ.; Wharton House, Phila., Pa.; Atlanta Univ.; Lewis Sch., Boston; Nat. Bezalel Mus., Jerusalem; Inst. Contemp. A. (AEA slide coll.); Boston Pr.M. Presentation Print, 1958; BMFA; Fogg Mus.A.; Boston Pub.Lib. *Exhibited*: Inst. Mod. A., Boston, 1943, 1944; Boris Mirski Gal., 1943-1953; Int. Pr. Soc., N.Y., 1944; Oakland Mus A., 1944; NAD, 1944-1946; Jordan Marsh Co., 1944, 1947, 1949, 1954, 1955, 1958; Wellesley Col., 1944, 1950; Atlanta Univ., 1944-1953, 1956-1958; Boston Pub. Lib., 1944-1955; AFA traveling exh., 1945-1948, 1956-1957; Kiel Auditorium, St. Louis, Mo., 1946; San F. AA, 1946; Taller de Graphico, Mexico; Mass. Sch. A., 1946-1948, 1954, 1955; Cambridge AA, 1946-1955; Downtown Gal., 1946-1955; Children's A. Center, Boston, 1947, 1953; State Dept. traveling exh., 1957-58; Inst. Contemp. A., 1955; LC, 1948, 1949; Howard Univ., 1949; Boston Univ., 1951, 1953; Arthur Wood Gal., Boston, 1954, 1955 and many others. One-man: Boris Mirski Gal., 1946; Cambridge AA, 1953; Children's A. Gal., 1947, 1953; Lewis Sch. FA,

1950; Arthur Wood Gal., 1955; Marlboro Col., 1955; Gropper Gal., 1956; Village Studio, 1957; AGAA, 1955 (traveling, 1955-56). *Position*: Comm. & Ed. Illus. & Adv. Art for many firms and publications; Instr., Gr. A., deCordova & Dana Mus., Lincoln, Mass., 1953-56; Instr., Mass. Sch. A., Boston, Mass., 1956- .

BURNETT, E. K.—*Museum Director*
Museum of the American Indian, Broadway at 155th St., New York 32, N.Y.*

BURNETT, LOUIS ANTHONY—*Painter, T.*
322 West 72nd St., New York 23, N.Y.

B. New York, N.Y. *Studied*: ASL. *Member*: ASL (Bd. Control); AEA; AAPL. *Awards*: prizes, Village A. Center, 1948, 1949; Washington Square Outdoor Show, 1949; Madison Square Garden, 1952. *Work*: in private coll. U.S., Canada, and South America; Friars Cl., N.Y. *Exhibited*: WMAA; Riverside Mus.; Jersey City Mus. A.; NAD; NAC; New Jersey P. & S.; Long Island A. Lg.; Portraits, Inc.; All. A. Am.; Town Hall Cl., N.Y.; Gloucester, Mass., and others.

BURNETT, MRS. LOUIS A. See Moore, Martha E.

BURNHAM, ANITA WILLETS—*Painter, W., L., T., Et.*
1407 Tower Rd., Winnetka, Ill.

B. Brooklyn, N.Y., Aug. 22, 1880. *Studied*: ASL; PAFA; & with Chase, Freer, Vanderpoel, DuMond. *Member*: North Shore AA; Chicago SA; Chicago AC. *Awards*: prizes, AIC, 1903, 1905, 1916; North Shore AA, 1936. *Work*: Pub. Sch., Children's Hospital, Chicago; Beloit Col. *Exhibited*: San Diego FA Soc. (one-man). Author, I., "Around the World on a Penny"; "Fourth of July in Old Mexico."*

BURNHAM, CAROL-LOU—*Painter, T., I., L.*
1407 Tower Rd., Winnetka, Ill.

B. Chicago, Ill., Feb. 22, 1908. *Studied*: Fontainebleau Sch. FA; AIC, B.A.E.; and with Fernand Leger, Amedee Ozenfant, Andre L'Hote, Nancy Coonsman Hahn, Paul Baudouin. *Member*: Fontainebleau Alumni Assn.; AIC; North Shore A. Lg. *Work*: Decatur A. Center. *Exhibited*: AIC, 1923, 1924, 1935, 1943; Ill. Soc. Et., 1928; A. of Chicago, 1925, 1927, 1928, 1938; Chicago World Fair, 1933; Mid-west Col. Conf., Kansas City, 1953; Faculty Exh., Layton Sch. A., 1954; one-man: Grand Central A. Gal., 1931; Layton A. Gal., 1949. I., "Around the World on a Penny," 1933. *Position*: Instr., Peninsula Sch., 1946-47; Layton Sch. A., 1947-54; Milwaukee-Downer Seminary, Milwaukee, Wis., 1955- .*

BURNHAM, ROGER NOBLE—*Sculptor, T., L.*
615 South Virgil Ave., Los Angeles 5, Cal.

B. Hingham, Mass., Aug. 10, 1876. *Studied*: Harvard Univ., A.B., and with Caroline Hunt Rimmer. *Member*: AFA; Cal. AC; P.&S. Cl.; Am. Numismatic Soc. *Awards*: prizes, Arch. L., 1904; Univ. Cal., 1911; Long Beach Int. Exp.; SFMA; Los A. Mus. A., 1944. *Work*: Boston City Hall; mem., Atlanta, Ga.; Memphis, Tenn.; Honolulu, T.H.; Chapel Hill, N.C.; Valentino Mem., Hollywood, Cal.; BMFA; Harvard Univ.; Univ. So. Cal.; Cal. State Bldg., Los Angeles; Oxford Univ.; Will Rogers mem. tablet, 20th Century-Fox Studios, Los Angeles; statue of Gen. MacArthur, MacArthur Park, Los Angeles. *Exhibited*: Arch. Lg.; PAFA; Los A. Mus. A.; SFMA; Long Beach AA; Laguna Beach AA; and in Paris, Rome, Ghent, Hawaii. Lectures: sculpture.

BURNHAM, WILBUR HERBERT—*Craftsman, Des., P.*
1126 Boylston St., Boston, Mass.; h. 14 Overlook Rd., Melrose Highlands, Mass.

B. Boston, Mass., Feb. 4, 1887. *Studied*: Mass. Sch.A.; in Europe, and with Joseph DeCamp, Albert Munsell. *Member*: Boston Soc. A. & Crafts (Master Craftsman); AFA; Mediaeval Acad. Am.; Copley Soc.; Stained Glass Assn. Am.; F., Royal Soc. A. *Awards*: med., Boston Tercentenary, 1930; Paris Exp., 1937; gold med., AIA, 1947. *Work*: Windows, St. John the Divine, Riverside, Calvary churches, N.Y.; Rollins Col.; American church, Paris; Washington Cathedral; St. Mary's of Redford, De-

troit; Chapel at St. Paul's Sch., Concord, N.H.; Chancel window, Chapel of Milton Acad., Mass.; East Liberty Presbyterian church, Pittsburgh; Church of St. Vincent dePaul, Los A.; First Presbyterian church, Evanston, Ill.; Our Lady of Peace, Cleveland; murals and windows, St. Mary's Cathedral, Peoria, Ill.; Princeton Univ. Chapel, and others. Contributor to architectural and craft magazines.

BURNLEY, J(OHN) EDWIN—
Educator, P., Des., Comm. A., I.
Burnley School of Professional Art, 905 East Pine St. (22); h. 2503 Nob Hill Ave., Seattle 9, Wash.

B. Victoria, B.C., Canada, Oct. 4, 1896. *Studied*: Univ. Alberta; Toronto Sch. FA. *Member*: Seattle A. Dir. Soc.; Puget Sound Group of Men Painters; Northwest WC Soc.; Washington AA; Seattle Acad. A. & Sciences. *Work*: SAM. *Exhibited*: SAM, annually; Northwest WC Soc., many invitational exhs. *Position*: Dir.-T., Comm. A., Edison Vocational Sch., Seattle, Wash., 9 years; Dir.-Owner, Burnley Sch. Professional A., Seattle, Wash., at present.

BURNO, MRS. R. H. See Seaver, Esther Isabel

BURNS, PAUL CALLAN—*Painter, Des., I., Comm. A.*
67 Bergen St., Westwood, N.J.

B. Pittsburgh, Pa., April 28, 1910. *Studied*: PMSchIA; PAFA, and in Europe. *Member*: Phila. WC Cl.; SC; SI. *Awards*: prizes, Montclair A. Mus.; NAD. *Work*: Collingswood Lib.; U.S. Court House, Phila., Pa. *Exhibited*: NAD, 1936-1942; PAFA, 1934-1942; Wilmington Soc. FA, 1939-1941; AIC; BM; John Herron AI; Phila. Sketch Cl.; SC; Milch Gal. Illus., for Good Housekeeping, Ladies Home Journal, Cosmopolitan magazines; Adv. Des., in national magazines. *Positions*: Formerly taught at PMSch.A., Philadelphia, Pa.; Wilmington (Del.) Acad. A.; Rosemont Col., Rosemont, Pa.

BUROS, LUELLA [Mrs. Oscar K.]—*Painter, Des.*
220 Montgomery St., Highland Park, N.J.

B. Canby, Minn. *Studied*: Rutgers Univ.; T. Col., Columbia Univ.; Ohio State Univ. *Member*: AEA; Assoc. A. New Jersey; NAWA; New Brunswick A. Center; New Jersey WC Soc.; Phila. WC Cl. *Awards*: prizes, Columbus A. Lg., 1935; AAPL, 1938, 1940; Asbury Park Soc. FA, 1938; New Jersey Gal., 1938, 1940; Montclair A. Mus., 1938, 1940-1; Springfield A. Lg., 1941; Norfolk Mus. A. & Sc., 1944, 1945; Wash. WC Cl., 1945; A. Council New Jersey, 1949, 1952; Plainfield AA, 1950-1951; Rahway A. Center, 1951-1952; Newark A. C., 1940, 1953; NAWA (med. honor), 1953; Old Mill Gal., 1954; Hunterdon County A. Center, 1955. *Work*: Montclair A. Mus.; Newark Mus. A.; City of Cape May. *Exhibited*: AIC; CGA; Nat. Exh. Am. A.; GGE, 1939; MMA; Stedelijke Mus., Amsterdam, Holland; AWS; NAWA; Audubon A.; NAC; All. A. Am.; Phila. WC Cl.; Wash. WC Cl.; Montclair A. Mus.; Newark Mus. A.; New Jersey State Mus.; St. Botolph Cl, Boston; Butler AI; traveling exhs., AFA, AIC, NAWA, Montclair A. Mus. in U.S. and abroad. Des., "Mental Measurements Yearbooks."

BURR, FRANCES—*Portrait Painter, I.*
Landing Ave., Smithtown Branch, L.I., N.Y.

B. Boston, Mass., Nov. 24, 1890. *Studied*: ASL; Provincetown Sch. A., with Charles Hawthorne, William M. Chase; Fontainebleau Sch., and with George Bridgman, Eliot O'Hara, Howard Giles. *Member*: AAPL; NSMP; Fontainebleau Alumni Assn. *Exhibited*: MMA; Ehrich Gal.; Anderson Gal.; John Herron AI; Rochester Mem. A. Gal.; Minneapolis Inst. A.; Milwaukee AI; Arch. Lg.; BM; AIC; one-man: Suffolk Mus. at Stony Brook, L.I., N.Y., 1949, 1950, 1955. Originated new method of emphasizing mountains on aeronautical charts known as the Burr Three-Dimensional Charts, widely used by U.S. Govt.; also new type of Celestial Chart.

BURR, (HAROLD) SAXTON—*Painter, T.*
Old Lyme, Conn.

B. Lowell, Mass., Apr. 10, 1889. *Studied*: Yale Univ., Ph.D. *Member*: Lyme AA; New Haven Paint & Clay Cl. *Exhibited*: Lyme AA, 1926-1946; New Haven Paint & Clay Cl., 1930-1946. *Position*: E. K. Hunt, Prof. Emeritus, Anatomy, Yale Univ. Sch. Medicine, 1933- ; L., Yale Univ. Sch. FA, 1939-49, New Haven, Conn.

BURRAGE, JANE B. (Mrs. William S.)—
Museum Director, W., L.
Sheldon Museum; h. 1 South St., Middlebury, Vt.

B. Jamaica Plain, Mass., Sept. 19, 1911. Contributor to
Antiques Magazine. Lectures: Furniture, China, Silver, to
organizations and student groups. *Position*: Dir., Sheldon
Museum, Middlebury, Vt.

BURRAGE, MILDRED GIDDINGS—Painter, Mus. Dir.
Wiscasset, Maine

B. Portland, Me., May 18, 1890. *Studied*: Academie Color-
ossi, Grande Chaumiere in Paris. *Awards*: Int. A. Un.,
Paris, 1912. *Work*: murals, Bryn Mawr Science Lib. *Ex-
hibited*: PAFA, 1911, 1913, 1928, 1931, 1935; AIC; BMFA;
Montclair A. Mus.; Detroit Inst. A., 1927; Arch. Lg., 1921;
Maine A. Gal., 1958; Boston A. Festival, 1958; one-man:
Sweat Mem. Mus., 1934, 1936; AGAA, 1931; Univ. Maine,
1951; BMFA, 1952; Currier Gal. A., 1955. *Position*: Dir.,
Lincoln County Museum, Wiscasset, Me.; Pres., Lincoln
County Cultural & Hist. Assn.

BURROUGHS, BETTY (Mrs. Betty Burroughs Wood-
house)—Teacher, S.
Rhode Island School of Design, Providence, R.I.; h.
Little Compton, R.I.

B. Norwich, Conn., Aug. 17, 1899. *Studied*: ASL, and
abroad. *Member*: NSS; CAA. Ed., "Vasari's Lives of the
Painters," 1946. *Position*: Asst., Dept. Edu., L., Hist. of
A., Instr., Adult Classes, R.I.Sch. Des. Mus. Providence,
R.I.*

BURROUGHS, EDWARD R.—Painter, E., Des., Gr.
Forest & Riverview Aves.; h. 542 Kenwood Ave.,
Dayton 6, Ohio

B. Portsmouth, Va., Aug. 17, 1902. *Studied*: Maryland
Inst., and with Elizabeth Shannon, Henry Roben, Charles
Walther. *Member*: Ohio WC Soc.; Dayton SE. *Awards*:
prizes, Butler AI, 1941; Dayton AI, 1943-1946, 1948, 1952;
Springfield AA, 1950-1952; Ohio WC Soc., 1946; med.,
Maryland Inst., 1932. *Work*: Dayton AI; Butler AI; Day-
ton Pub. Sch. *Exhibited*: AIC, 1941, 1943; CAA, 1937;
MMA, 1944; CM, 1933-1938; AFA, 1945; LC, 1943-1945;
PAFA, 1946; Butler AI, 1939-1946; Dayton Soc. Painters,
1936-1946; Dayton AI, 1948, 1952; Ohio Pr.M., 1953;
Springfield AA, 1950-1952. *Position*: Dean, Sch. of Dayton
AI, 1938- ; Asst. Prof. A., Univ. Dayton, 1940- , Dayton,
Ohio.

BURROUGHS, LOUISE (Mrs. Bryson)—Writer
110 Elmhurst Rd., Baltimore, Md.

B. Allentown, Pa. *Studied*: Cedar Crest Col., B.A., Litt.
D.; Lib. Sch., N.Y. Pub. Lib. Contributor to MMA Bulletin; Creative Art; The Art Quarterly; Art News; and other
art magazines. Author: "Rembrandts in the Metropolitan"
and "Great Drawings in the Metropolitan" (both in MMA
Miniatures series). *Position*: Former Assoc. Cur., Paintings,
MMA, New York, N.Y.

BURROWS, PEARL (Mrs.)—Painter, L.
Texhoma, Okla.

B. Shoals, Ind., Mar. 3, 1916. *Studied*: BMFA Sch.; Har-
vard Univ. *Member*: Taos AA; Southern AA, Dallas, Tex.;
Pen & Brush Cl. *Work*: Court House, Dalhart, Tex.; Pub.
Lib., La Junta, Colo.; A & M Col., Goodwell, Okla.
Exhibited: Pen & Brush Cl., 1941; Amarillo AA, 1939;
Santa Fé Exh., 1936; Pen & Brush Cl. (one-man), 1947.*

BURRUSS, GARLAND (GARLAND BURRUSS PETERSON)
—Painter, Et., T.
North Beach, Md.

B. Norfolk, Va., Jan. 28, 1919. *Studied*: Col. William &
Mary; Univ. North Carolina, B.A.; ASL, with Will Barnet.
Member: Lg. Present Day A.; ASL. *Exhibited*: Va. Artists,
1945; Ward Eggleston Gal., 1947; Carolina Artists, 1948;
Burliuk Gal., 1951; Riverside Mus., 1951, 1953; New
School for Social Research, 1955; ANTA Playhouse, 1952.
Position: T., A. & Crafts, Chesapeake Beach, Md.*

BURT, MARIE HAINES (Mrs. Frederick A.)—
Painter, C.
123 Union St., Bennington, Vt.

B. Cincinnati, Ohio. *Studied*: Cincinnati A. Acad.; PMSch
IA; AIC; NAD; ASL. *Member*: So. Vermont A.; Berkshire
AA. *Awards*: prizes, SSAL, 1930, 1937. *Work*: Mus. New
Mexico, Santa Fe; Texas A. & M. Col.; Austin H.S., Bryan,
Tex.; Ehlinger-Grant Clinic, Bryan, Tex.; port., Vt. Su-
preme Court Justice; Blackmer Mem. Law Lib., Bennington
County Court House; other ports. in private collections.
Exhibited: Mus. New Mexico; So. Vermont A., 1953-1955;
Northern Vermont A., Univ. Vt., 1953-1955; Berkshire
AA. Lectures: "Building a Picture" to women's clubs.

BURTON, NETTA M.—Painter, C., T., Des., Gr.
112 Moore Ave., Mt. Kisco, N.Y.

B. Scott, Pa. *Studied*: Columbia Univ., B.S., M.A. *Mem-
ber*: NAWA. *Awards*: prizes, NAWA; Ossining AA; West-
chester A. Gld., 1940-1951, 1953; All. A. Am.; Pleasant-
ville A. Cl., 1954. *Exhibited*: NAWA, 1954, 1955 and prior;
Mus. Non-Objective Painting, 1946; Alabama WC Cl., 1945;
Irvington AA, 1945; Pleasantville AA, 1946-1951, 1954;
Bedford Hills AA, 1955; Ann Ross Gal., White Plains,
N.Y., 1955.*

BUSA, PETER—Painter, E.
Address unknown

B. Pittsburgh, Pa., June 23, 1915. *Studied*: Carnegie Inst.;
ASL; Hans Hofmann; Yaddo Fellowship. *Exhibited*: WFNY
1939; Carlebach Gal.; Bertha Schaefer Gal.; PAFA; AAG;
"Young Painters USA," sponsored by AFA; WMAA, etc.
Position: Former Instr., CUASch., New York, N.Y.; New
York Univ.; Prof. A., Buffalo State T. Col., Buffalo, N.Y.*

BUSCH, ELIZABETH W. (Mrs. W. H.)—
Painter, Lith., Ser.
137 Odlin Ave., Dayton 5, Ohio

B. Dayton, Ohio, Feb. 6, 1897. *Studied*: Stout Inst.,
Menomonie, Wis.; Dayton AI. *Member*: Tri-Arts Cl.; Dayton Soc. P. & S. *Awards*: prizes, Springfield AA, 1955;
Dayton, Ohio, 1954; Little Jury award, 1957; Ohio Valley,
1957. *Exhibited*: Ohio Valley, 1948, 1954; Dayton AI,
1948, 1950, 1952-1955; Dayton Artists, 1948, 1950, 1952-
1955, 1958; Springfield AA, 1950-1955, 1956; Ohio Pr. M.,
1953; Blowing Rock, N.C., 1950; Ohio WC Soc., 1956;
Dayton & Vicinity Exh., 1956.

BUSH, LUCILE ELIZABETH—Educator, P.
Wheaton College, Norton, Mass.; h. 425 North Mays-
ville St., Mt. Sterling, Ky.

B. Mt. Sterling, Ky., July 26, 1904. *Studied*: Univ. Kentucky, A.B.; T. Col., Columbia Univ., M.A.; Columbia
Univ., Ph.D.; ASL, and with Leger, L'Hote and Marcoussis, Paris, France. *Member*: CAA; AAUP; Mediaeval
Acad.; Renaissance Soc. *Awards*: Carnegie Scholarship,
1930; Elizabeth Avery Colton F., 1945-46, AAUW. *Work*:
Skidmore Col., Saratoga Springs, N.Y.; portraits in private
colls. *Exhibited*: one-man exhs. in Saratoga Springs, Schenectady and Glens Falls, N.Y. Author: "Bartolo di Fredi,
Sienese Painter of the late 14th Century," 1950 (microfilm
only). Lectures, Modern Painting. *Position*: Instr. A., Skidmore Col., 1928-43; Instr., A. Dept., Chm. A. Dept.,
Wheaton Col., Norton, Mass., 1947- .

BUSH, RUTH C. (Mrs.)—Museum Director
Memphis Museum, 233 Tilton Road, Chickasaw Gardens, Memphis, Tenn.*

BUSH, WILLIAM BROUGHTON—Painter, I.
2010 North Levert Dr., Mobile 20, Ala.

B. Summit, N.J., Sept. 20, 1911. *Studied*: Univ. Alabama,
A.B.; Anson J. Cross A. Sch.; ASL, with DuMond. *Mem-
ber*: Mobile AA; Alabama A. Lg.; Alabama WC Soc.
Awards: prize, Ala. WC Soc. *Exhibited*: Mobile AA,
1944-1946; Montgomery Mus. FA, 1946. I., "Ghosts of Old
Mobile," 1946. *Position*: Instr. A., Univ. Alabama, Mobile
Center, 1950- .*

BUSHMILLER, ERNEST PAUL (ERNIE)—Cartoonist

United Features Syndicate, 220 East 42nd St., New York, N.Y.; h. Haviland Rd., Stamford, Conn.

B. New York, N.Y., Aug. 23, 1905. *Studied*: NAD. *Member*: SI; Nat. Cartoonists Soc.; Dutch Treat Cl.; A. & Writers Assn. Author, I., several books on comic strip "Nancy." *Position*: Cart., comic strip "Nancy" and Sunday comic "Fritzi Ritz," syndicated by United Features.

BUTERA, JOSEPH CHARLES—Educator, L., Restorer

111 Beacon St., Boston 16, Mass.

B. Italy, May 8, 1905. *Studied*: Child Walker Sch. *Member*: Inst. Contemp. A., Boston; BMFA; Northeastern Soc. Indp. A. (Dir.); Copley Soc. (Treas. 1956, Gov. 1949-53); Boston Soc. Indp. A. (Vice-Pres. 1955-56, Dir., 1947-53); Advertising Cl.; A. Dir. Cl., Boston. *Awards*: European traveling scholarship, 1926-29; prize, G.W.V. Smith Gal. A., 1941. *Work*: BMFA; LC; White House, Wash., D.C.; Smith Mus. A.; Springfield Pub. Lib. (purchase); Northeastern Univ. *Exhibited*: Inst. Mod. A.; WMA; NAD; Carnegie Inst. *Position*: Founder & Dir., Butera Sch. A.; Prof. Painting & Restoration, Avon Univ., 1954-56; Asst. Dept. Conservation & Restoration, FMA, Cambridge, Mass.*

BUTLER, JOHN (DAVIDSON)—
Craftsman, T., Gr., P., L.

Philadelphia Museum School of Art, Broad & Pine Sts., Philadelphia, Pa.; h. Ossipee, N.H.

B. Mauston, Wis., Jan. 17, 1890. *Studied*: Univ. Washington, B.F.A.; Univ. Pennsylvania; PMSchIA; Alfred Univ.; Sorbonne and with Renard Taylor Despujol. *Member*: Wash. Soc. A.; Wash. WC Cl.; Pa. Gld. Craftsmen; Phila. A. All.; New Hampshire Lg. A. & Crafts. *Position*: Instr., Philadelphia Museum School of Art, Philadelphia, Pa.

BUTLER, JOSEPH G.—Museum Director, E., P.

The Butler Institute of American Art, 524 Wick Ave., Youngstown 2, Ohio; h. 161 Walker Mill Rd., Poland, Ohio

B. Youngstown, Ohio, Sept. 5, 1901. *Studied*: Dartmouth Col. *Member*: Ohio WC Soc.; AEA. *Awards*: prizes, Massillon Mus. A., 1941; Arizona State Fair, 1946; Mississippi AA, 1948-49; Ohio State Fair, 1949, 1950, 1956; Ohio WC Soc., 1952; A. Festival, Bloomfield, Mich., 1954-55; Canton AI, 1957. *Exhibited*: CM, 1938, 1941; Midyear Show, Youngstown, Ohio, 1938-1952, 1954-1958; Portland Mus. A., 1940-1944, 1946, 1947; Denver Mus. A., 1940, 1942; AIC, 1941; Baltimore WC Cl., 1942, 1949; Jackson, Miss., 1942, 1946, 1947; All. A. Am., 1942, 1945, 1949, 1957; Mint Mus. A., 1946; P. & S. Soc. of New Jersey, 1946, 1948, 1951; Newport AA, 1946, 1947, 1949, 1950; Mississippi AA, 1948-1951, 1953, 1956; New Orleans A. & Crafts, 1948; Alabama WC Soc., 1949; AWS, 1949-1953; PAFA (WC), 1949, 1953 (oils), 1950, 1952, 1953; Oakland Mus. A., 1950; Flint Inst. A., 1957; Illinois State Fair, 1957; Audubon A., 1947, 1948, 1950; Massillon Mus. A., 1940-1943, 1945, 1946, 1948-1953, 1957; Conn. Acad. FA, 1941, 1942; New Haven Paint & Clay Cl., 1942; Ohio WC Soc., 1942, 1946-1948, 1950, 1952, 1953, 1955; Ohio Valley, Athens, Ohio, 1944, 1946-1949, 1952, 1954; Arizona State Fair, 1946, 1949; Ohio State Fair, 1948-1951, 1953, 1956, 1958; Old Northwest Terr. Exh., 1948. Arranged Nat. Annual Midyear Shows, 1938- ; "Ohio Painters of the Past"—David G. Blythe, 1947, Wm. T. Richard and Anna Richards Brewster, 1954. *Position*: Dir., Butler Inst. American Art, Youngstown, Ohio.

BUTLER, JOSEPH THOMAS—Museum Curator, W.

Sleepy Hollow Restorations, Tarrytown, N.Y.; h. 269 Broadway, Dobbs Ferry, N.Y.

B. Winchester, Va., Jan. 25, 1932. *Studied*: Univ. Maryland, B.S.; Ohio Univ., M.A.; Univ. Delaware, M.A. *Member*: AFA; CAA. *Awards*: Winterthur F., 1955-57. Contributor to Antiques; Encyclopaedia Britannica, articles on various aspects of the American decorative arts with emphasis on 19th Century. Lectures: 17th, 18th and 19th century decorative arts to museum groups. Conducted rearrangement of interiors of "Sunnyside," home of Washington Irving, 1957-58. *Position*: Curator, Sleepy Hollow Restorations, Tarrytown, N.Y., 1957- .

BUTT, GAIL HAMMOND, JR.—Painter, E.

Art Dept., University of Nebraska; h. 344 North 21st St., Lincoln, Neb.

B. Zanesville, Ohio, May 19, 1924. *Studied*: Ohio State Univ., B.S., B.F.A., M.A. *Member*: Midwest Col. A. Conference; AEA. *Awards*: purchase awards, Ohio Pr. M.; Butler Inst. Am. A.; Atkins-Nelson Gal., 1958; Univ. Minnesota Gal., 1958; Kansas State Univ., 1958. *Work*: Butler Inst. Am. A.; Atkins-Nelson Gal.; Univ. Minnesota; Ohio Pr. M.; Univ. Nebraska Gal.; Kansas State Univ.; Oakwood Col., Huntsville, Ala.; WAC. *Exhibited*: WAC, 1953, 1956; Denver A. Mus., 1952, 1954, 1958; Colorado Springs FA Center, 1953, 1957; Atkins-Nelson Gal., 1951, 1952, 1957, 1958; CAM, 1952, 1954; Columbus Mus. A., 1953, 1955, 1957; Butler Inst. Am. A., 1953, 1955; Joslyn Mus. A., 1950-1957; AIC, 1953, 1954; Kansas State Univ., 1957, 1958; Mulvane Mus. A., 1957; Wooster Col., 1956; Univ. Washington, 1956; Univ. Kansas City, 1957; Springfield Mus. A., 1953, 1957; Santa Monica, Cal., 1957; SFMA, 1955; one-man: Univ. Minnesota, 1957; Cornell Col., 1958; Concordia Col., 1958; Univ. Nebraska, 1953, 1957. *Position*: Asst. Prof. A., Art Dept., Univ. Nebraska, Lincoln, Neb., 1949- .

BUTTERWORTH, ROD—Advertising Designer

698 West End Ave., New York 25, N.Y.

B. Newark, N.J., July 27, 1901. *Studied*: Pratt Inst. A.; ASL. *Member*: AIGA; SI; A. & W. Gld.; A. Dir. Cl.

BUTTRICK, SUE K(INGSLAND) (Mrs.)—
Craftsman, L., Des.

Cragsmoor, N.Y.

B. Mt. Vernon, N.Y. *Studied*: PIASch; & with Arthur W. Dow. *Member*: PBC; N.Y. Ceramic Soc. *Exhibited*: WFNY 1939; Cornell Univ.; N.Y. Ceramic Soc., 1921-1945; Syracuse Mus. FA, 1930-1940; PBC; PIASch; MMA; Phila. A. All.; NAC; Pen & Brush Cl.; Cragsmoor Cooperators in Crafts, 1957. Lectures: Pottery.

BUTTS, PORTER FREEMAN—
Museum Director, E., W., L.

Memorial Union Bldg.; h. 2900 Hunter Hill, Shorewood Hills, Madison 5, Wis.

B. Pana, Ill., Feb. 23, 1903. *Studied*: Univ. Wisconsin, B.A., M.A. *Member*: Madison AA. Author: "Art in Wisconsin: The Art Experience of the Middle West Frontier," 1936. Editor, "Bulletin of Assn. of College Unions," 1934- ; script for color-sound film, "Arts Center and Living Room of the University." Contributor to: art magazines. Lectures: Art in Wisconsin. Planning Consultant, Milwaukee War Mem. Cultural Center and 75 college community centers in U.S. and Puerto Rico. *Position*: Dir., Mem. Un. Gal., Univ. Wisconsin, 1928- ; Exec. Com., Wisconsin Centennial A. Program, 1946-48.

BUZEK, IRENE M.—Painter, Indst. I.

2036 Griffith St., Philadelphia 15, Pa.

B. Camden, N.J., Oct. 8, 1891. *Studied*: PAFA; Tyler Sch. FA. *Member*: AAPL; Woodmere AA; Cheltenham AA. *Awards*: F., PAFA; prizes, Montclair AA, 1943; Woodmere AA, 1944. *Exhibited*: Montclair A. Mus., 1939-1945; Sketch Cl., 1940-1946; PAFA, 1940-1945; DaVinci All., 1941-1943; Woodmere A. Gal., 1942-1946, 1953-1955. *Position*: Tech. Indst. I., Atlantic Refining Co.; Tech. Indst. I., Navigation Computer Corp., Philadelphia, Pa., at present.

BUZZELLI, JOSEPH ANTHONY—
Painter, Lith., Ser., C., T., L., Enamelist.

400 West 57th St., New York 19, N.Y.

B. Old Forge, Pa., May 6, 1907. *Studied*: ASL; Univ. So. California; Columbia Univ.; Beaux-Arts and Grande Chaumiere, Paris, France. *Member*: ASL; AEA; N.Y. Am. Friends. *Awards*: prizes, Butler AI, 1940, 1941; Parkersburg FA Center, 1945 1946; All. A., Johnstown, 1941; Advertising Cl., N.Y., 1942; Emily Lowe Award, Eggleston Gal., 7th annual. *Work*: N.Y. Mem. Hospital; Holy Cross & St. Benedict's churches, N.Y.; Wiltwyck Sch., Esopus, N.Y. *Exhibited*: San Diego FA Soc.; AIC; Denver A. Mus.; LC; Carnegie Inst.; Syracuse Mus. FA; Phila. A. All.; SAM; Everhart Mus. A.; WMAA; Birmingham Mus. A.; Atlanta AA; Columbia (S.C.) Mus. A.; Columbus (Ga.) Mus. A.; Sioux City A. Center; Davenport Mun. A.

Gal.; Lowe Gal.; Tannenbaum Gal., N.Y.; America House, N.Y.; Univ. Delaware; Massillon Mus. A.; Philbrook A. Center; Jacksonville A. Mus.; Univ. Georgia; Guild Hall, East Hampton, N.Y.; Cultural Inst., Guadalajara, Mexico; Hammer Gal., N.Y.; Sagittarius Gal., N.Y.; Ruth White Gal., N.Y.; Hampton Gal., Amagansett, N.Y.; and many others including one-man exhs.; MMA; CM; CMA; Butler AI; Ferargil Gal.; AWS; San F. AA; Rochester Mem. A. Gal.; Dartmouth Col.; Currier Gal. A.; Sweat Mem. Mus.; Kent State Col.; Akron AI; Dayton AI; CAM; William Rockhill Nelson Mus. A.; New Haven Paint & Clay Cl.; Oklahoma A. Center. *Position:* Founded Vendome A. Gal., 1936-43; Established Long Beach A. Center, 1939; Dir., Jabu Enamel Art Gal., New York, N.Y.

BYE, ARTHUR EDWIN—*Craftsman, P., W., L.*
Old Congress, Holicong, Pa.

B. Philadelphia, Pa., Dec. 18, 1885. *Studied:* PMSchIA; Princeton Univ., M.A., Ph.D. Contributor to: Art magazines & periodicals. Lectures: History of Art. *Position:* Cur., PMA, 1922-30; Tech. Advisor, Princeton Univ., 1926-46; Restorer of paintings, 1930- .

BYE, RANULPH (de BAYEUX)—*Painter*
Buckingham, Pa.

B. Princeton, N.J., June 17, 1916. *Studied:* PMSchIA; ASL, with Earl Horter, Henry C. Pitz. *Member:* Phila. WC Cl.; SC; AWS. *Exhibited:* Grand Central A. Gal., 1953 (one-man), 1956, 1958; Doll & Richards, Boston, 1955; Audubon A.; 1954; Phila. WC Cl., 1953-1955. Contributor to American Artist magazine. Included in "Watercolor Seascapes and Landscapes," 1956. *Work:* Am. A. Group; Ford Motor Co.; Munson-Williams-Proctor Inst. A., Utica, N.Y.; Am. Colortype Co.; Kipe Offset Process Co.; BMFA; Bucks County Circulating Lib. *Position:* Asst. Prof., A. Moore Inst. A., Philadelphia, Pa.

BYRD, D(ECATUR) GIBSON—*Painter, T.*
Art Education Dept., University of Wisconsin; h. 5905 Hammersly Rd., Madison, Wis.

B. Tulsa, Okla., Feb. 1, 1923. *Studied:* Univ. Tulsa, B.A.; State Univ. of Iowa, M.A. *Awards:* prizes, Oklahoma A., 1950, 1951, 1952; Tulsa A., 1950, 1951; Delgado Mus. A., 1952; Denver A. Mus., 1952; 1953 (purchase). *Work:* Philbrook A. Center. *Exhibited:* New Orleans AA, 1951, 1952; Mid-West, 1952, 1954; Denver A. Mus., 1952, 1953; Mid-America A., 1952; Oklahoma A., 1950-1952, 1954; Michigan A., 1952, 1954; Wisconsin Salon, 1955; one-man: Philbrook A. Center, Beloit Col., Univ. Wisconsin, Univ. of Tulsa. Lectures: 19th & 20th Century Art. *Position:* T., & Dept. Chm., Central H.S., Tulsa, 1950-52; Dir., Kalamazoo A. Center, 1952-55; Asst. Prof., A. Edu., Univ. of Wisconsin, Madison, Wis., 1955- .

BYRNES, (EU)GENE—*Cartoonist, W., I.*
570 Park Ave., New York 21, N.Y.

B. New York, N.Y., Mar. 18, 1889. *Member:* Nat. Cartoonists Soc. *Exhibited:* MMA traveling exhibition. Author: "A Complete Guide to Drawing, Illustration, Cartooning and Painting." Contributor to Ladies Home Journal. *Work:* Syndicated cartoon, "Reg'lar Fellers."*

BYRNES, JAMES BERNARD—*Museum Director*
North Carolina Museum of Art, Raleigh, N.C.; h. Boxwood, R.F.D. #1, Wake Forest, N.C.

B. New York, N.Y., Feb. 19, 1917. *Studied:* Univ. Perugia, Italy; T. Col., Columbia Univ.; Am. Mus. Natural Hist. (Mus. Edu. Methods); ASL; Am. A. Sch.; NAD. *Member:* Western Assn A. Mus. Dirs.; Am. Mus. Assn.; Am. Soc. for Aesthetics; Spanish Colonial Arts Soc.; Southeastern A. Mus. Dirs. Assn. (Council Memb.); Committee Memb., for Standards for Small Museums, Southeastern Mus. Conference. Author various museum catalogs, monographs, popular and scholarly articles on painting and sculpture. *Positions:* Mus. Docent, Field Activity Program, N.Y.C. Board of Edu., 1935-40; Indst. Des., 1940-41; Draftsman-Expediter, H. Newton Whittlesey, Naval Architects, N.Y.C., 1941-42; U.S. Navy, Audio-Visual Training Aids Specialist, 1942-45; Docent, in Art, and Cur., Los A. Mus. A., 1946; Cur., Los A. Mus. A., 1946-53; Dir., Colorado Springs FA Center, 1954-Oct. 1955; Assoc. Dir., 1955-1957, Acting Dir., 1957- , North Carolina Mus. A., Raleigh, N.C.

BYRUM, RUTHVEN HOLMES—*Educator, P., W., L.*
517 Walnut St., Anderson, Ind.

B. Grand Junction, Mich., July 10, 1896. *Studied:* Indiana Univ., A.B.; AIC; Grande Chaumiere, Paris; & with Hans Hofmann. *Member:* AFA; CAA; Indiana A. Cl.; Hoosier Salon; Anderson (Ind.) SA. *Awards:* prizes, John Herron AI, 1943; Hoosier Salon, 1942; Indiana State Fair, 1932; Indiana A. Cl., 1942; Ft. Wayne A. Mus., 1953, 1954. *Work:* Swope A. Gal.; Richmond AA; Indiana Univ.; murals, Pub. Sch. & Churches, Anderson, Ind. *Exhibited:* CGA, 1932; AIC, 1931, 1939; Hoosier Salon, 1928-1946, 1954; Indiana A. Cl., 1928-1946; Anderson (Ind.) SA, 1925-1946. I., "Mr. Noah's ABC Book." Contributor to: Art magazines. *Position:* Instr., Anderson College, Ind., 1936-1947; Asst. Prof. A., Chm. A. Dept., 1947- .*

BYWATERS, JERRY—*Museum Director, E., W., P., L.*
Dallas Museum of Fine Arts; h. 3625 Amherst St., Dallas 5, Tex.

B. Paris, Tex., May 21, 1906. *Studied:* Southern Methodist Univ., A.B.; ASL. *Awards:* prizes, Dallas Mus. FA, 1933, 1937, 1939, 1942; Houston Mus. FA, 1940; Corpus Christi, 1947. *Work:* Dallas Mus. FA; Texas State Col. for Women; Southern Methodist Univ.; Princeton Univ. Pr. Cl.; OWI; murals, USPO, Houston, Farmersville, Trinity, Quannah, Tex. Lecturer: American and Mexican subjects. Contributor to: Art in America, 1955; Southwest Review (A.Ed.); Ed., "Twelve From Texas," 1952. *Position:* Assoc. Prof. A., Southern Methodist Univ., Dallas, Tex., 1936- ; A. Cr., Dallas News, 1933-39; Dir., Dallas Mus. FA, 1943- .

BYXBE, LYMAN—*Etcher*
Box 456, Estes Park, Colo.

B. Pittsfield, Ill., Feb. 28, 1886. *Member:* Chicago SE. *Work:* Smithsonian Inst.; Lib. Cong. *Exhibited:* SAE; Northwest Pr. M.; Int. Pr. M.; Kansas City AI; Lib. Cong.; Chicago SE; Grand Central A. Gal.; Smithsonian Inst., 1937.*

CABANISS, LILA MARGUERITE—*Teacher, P.*
118 East 31st St., Savannah, Ga.

B. Savannah, Ga. *Studied:* Columbia Univ.; Syracuse Univ.; ASL; & with Hilda Belcher, Eliot O'Hara, William Chadwick. *Member:* Wash. WC Cl.; Savannah AC (Hon. Pres.); Assn. Georgia A.; SSAL; AAPL. *Award:* prize, SSAL. *Work:* Hospitals in Frankfort, Ky., and in private colls. *Exhibited:* PAFA, 1926; CGA; SSAL; Assn. Georgia A.; Savannah AC; AAPL. *Position:* Supv. A., High Schools, Savannah, Ga. (Retired).

CABOT, HUGH, III—*Painter*
202 East El Paso St., Fort Stockton, Tex.; h. Boston, Mass.

B. Boston, Mass., Mar. 22, 1930. *Studied:* Vesper George Sch. A.; BMFA Sch. A.; Mexico City Col. *Member:* Assoc. Am. A. *Work:* Official Navy Combat Artist, Korean War, with work in the Navy Office of History & Records. Specializing at present, in oil field industrial painting with many commissions. Presently engaged in series of 30 paintings depicting the ranch of L. G. McCormick, Midland, Tex. *Exhibited:* First Exh. combat art, Navy sponsored, Tokyo, 1953; eight one-man exhs. past two years. Combat art "Korea by Cabot," 1953. Illus. for Nippon Times, and Boston Globe. *Position:* Instr., Hugh Cabot Studio, Ft. Stockton, Tex.; Asst. A. Dir., Boston Mus. of Science, Boston, Mass., 1949-50.

CADMUS, PAUL—*Painter, Et.*
5 St. Luke's Pl., New York 14, N.Y.

B. New York, N.Y., Dec. 17, 1904. *Studied:* NAD; ASL. *Member:* SAGA. *Awards:* prize, AIC, 1945. *Work:* MMoDA; Sweet Briar Col.; Am. Embassy, Ottawa, Can.; MMA; WMAA; AGAA; Cranbrook Acad. A.; Lib. Cong.; AIC; BMA; N.Y. Pub. Lib.; SMA; Wadsworth Atheneum; Williams Col.; Milwaukee AI, and others; mural, Parcel Post Bldg., Richmond, Va. *Exhibited:* WMAA, 1934, 1936-1938, 1940, 1941, 1945; BM, 1935; AIC, 1935; London, Eng., 1938; SAE, 1938; GGE, 1939; PAFA, 1941; Carnegie Inst., 1944, 1945; MMoDA, 1942, 1943, 1944 and many others; Am. Exh., Florence, Italy.

CADORET, MICHEL (de l'EPINEGUEN)—
Painter, Gr., I.
59 West 9th St., New York, N.Y.

B. Paris, France, Sept. 7, 1912. *Studied*: Ecole Nationale Superieure des Beaux Arts, Paris; Ecole Nationale Superieure des Arts Decoratifs, Paris. *Member*: Salon de Tuileries; Salon de Surindependants. *Awards*: prize, Govt. of France; MacDowell F., 1957. *Work*: in many museums and colls. in France; frescoes: Banco del Atlantico, Mexico City; and in churches of Mexico. *Exhibited*: Musee France D'Outremer, 1939; Galerie Contemporaine, Paris, 1942; Galerie Rouxhentschell, Paris, 1947; Exh. "France Comes to You," Boston, San Francisco, Los Angeles, New Orleans, Houston; other exhs., The Contemporaries, N.Y., 1955; Galerie Furstenberg, Paris, 1956; Caracas, Venezuela, 1956; Galerie Chalette, N.Y., 1957. I., Kolnischer Kunstverein, 1958; Antigone et Euridyce, 1946.

CADY, HARRISON—Illustrator, Et., P.
27 West 67th St., New York 23, N.Y.

B. Gardner, Mass., June 17, 1877. *Member*: SI; Audubon A.; AWS; North Shore AA; Rockport AA; Century Cl.; SC; Illustrator's Cl., N.Y. *Awards*: prizes, NAD, 1945; SC, 1944; Rockport AA; All. A. Am., 1945. *Work*: N.Y. Pub. Lib.; LC; Univ. Nebraska; New Britain Inst.; MMA, and many others. *Exhibited*: nationally. One-man: Macbeth Gal.; Kleeman Gal.; Currier Gal. A.; Smithsonian Inst., and others. Author: "Caleb Cottontail"; "Animal Alphabet" and various short stories. Illus., Thornton Burgess nature stories. Illus., for many national magazines including Life, Good Housekeeping, St. Nicholas, Ladies Home Journal, etc.

CAESAR, DORIS—Sculptor
Litchfield, Conn.

B. New York, N.Y., 1893. *Studied*: ASL; Archipenko Sch. A., and with Rudolph Belling. *Member*: Sculptor's Gld.; NAWA; N.Y. Soc. Women A.; Audubon A.; Arch. Lg.; Fed. Mod. P. & S. *Work*: sc., Utica Pub. Lib.; AGAA; Newark Mus. A.; WMAA; Connecticut Col.; Ft. Worth AA; Univ. Iowa, Minnesota and Delaware; Wadsworth Atheneum; Dayton AI; Minneapolis Inst. A.; Chapin Sch.; Chapel of Our Redeemer, Chappaqua, N.Y.; PMA; PAFA; Albion Col.; Farnsworth Mus. A.; Wellesley Col.; Atlanta AA. *Exhibited*: nationally & internationally. One-man: Buchholz Gal., 1943; Wayne Gal., 1933, 1935, 1937, 1947, 1953; Petit Palais, Paris, France, 1950.*

CAFARELLI, MICHELE A.—Painter
324 Francis St., Teaneck, N.J.

B. Laurenzana, Italy, Jan. 5, 1889. *Studied*: ASL. *Member*: Bergen County A. Gld.; ASL; Amal. Lithographers of America. *Work*: Paterson (N.J.) Court House; Jersey City Pub. Lib.; Borough of Lodi, N.J.; City of Newark; Bayonne, N.J. *Exhibited*: MMA, 1942; PAFA, 1932-1934; WFNY 1939; NAD; Newark Mus. A., 1958 and prior; Montclair A. Mus., 1955, 1956, 1957 and prior; WMA; Ridgewood AA; Riverside Mus., 1952.

CAIN, JOSEPH A.—Painter, T., Cr.
1042 Wilshire Pl., Corpus Christi, Tex.

B. Henderson, Tenn., May 27, 1920. *Studied*: Tennessee State Col.; Univ. California, B.A., M.A. *Member*: Cal. WC Soc.; New Orleans AA; Texas WC Soc.; South Texas A. Lg.; Corpus Christi A. Fnd. (Critic); Wash. (D.C.) WC Cl.; Texas FA Assn.; NEA; Texas Classroom T. Assn.; AFA. *Awards*: prizes, South Texas A. Lg., 1948-1958; Corpus Christi A. Fnd., 1948-1959; South Texas Fair, 1949; Texas WC Soc., 1951, 1958; Texas FA Assn., 1954, and many others. *Work*: Marine Corps Combat Art Coll., Wash., D.C.; Seton Hall Univ.; Ford Times; Goliad Lib., Goliad, Tex., and in many private colls. *Exhibited*: Radio City Music Hall, Marine Combat Art, 1952; Grand Central A. Gal., 1955, 1956; Los A. Mus. A., 1955; Santa Barbara Mus. A., 1955; DMFA, annually; Witte Mem. Mus., annually; Butler Inst. Am. A., 1957; Ball State T. Col., 1957, 1958; Denver Mus. A., 1955, 1958; Brooks Mem. A. Gal., 1956-1958; St. Augustine AA; Richmond (Cal.) A. Center, 1951; Saranac Lake, N.Y., 1958; Laguna Gloria Gal., Austin, Tex., annually; Centennial Mus., Corpus Christi, annually; D. D. Feldman Coll. Contemp. Texas Art, Dallas and national circuit; Grumbacher Coll. Am. Watercolors; Delgado Mus. A., annually; Alabama WC Soc.; Texas WC Soc., 1950-1958; Wash. WC Cl., 1952, 1953; Cal. WC

Soc., 1953-1958; South Texas A. Lg.; Corpus Christi A. Fnd., 1949-1958; Beaumont (Tex.) Mus.; El Paso AA; Mus. New Mexico, 1957; Seton Hall Univ., 1958; Provincetown A. Festival, 1958; Petite Gal., N.Y., 1957; one-man: Texas Col. of A. & Indst., Kingsville, 1953; Little Theatre, Corpus Christi, 1955; Rosenberg Gal., Galveston, 1955; Connors Jr. Col., Okla., 1955; Univ. Corpus Christi; Laguna Gloria A. Gal., 1957; Parkdale Grill, Corpus Christi, 1958 and others.

CAIN, JO(SEPH) (LAMBERT)—Painter, E., Lith.
University of Rhode Island, Kingston, R.I.

B. New Orleans, La., Apr. 16, 1904. *Studied*: Chicago Acad. FA; AIC; ASL; & in Paris. *Member*: Am. Assn. Univ. Prof.; Contemporary A. Group. *Awards*: F., Carnegie Inst.; F. & med., Tiffany Fnd. *Work*: murals, N.Y. State Training Sch., Warwick, N.Y. *Exhibited*: PAFA; NAD; AGAA; Fleming Mus.; R.I. Sch. Des.; WMAA; MModA. *Position*: Prof., Hd. A. Dept., Univ. Rhode Island, Kingston, R.I.

CAIN, MRS. JO. See Rachotes, Matene

CAIN, THERON IRVING—Painter, E., Des., W., L.
15 Candia St., East Weymouth 89, Mass.

B. South Braintree, Mass., Dec. 16, 1893. *Studied*: Mass. Sch. A., B.S.; Harvard Univ.; Boston Univ.; BMFA Sch. A.; & with Aldro T. Hibbard. *Member*: Copley Soc., Boston; Am. Soc. for Aesthetics. Contributing Ed. to Encyclopaedia of the Arts, 1946; articles to Journal of Aesthetics & Art Criticism; Am. Journal of Psychology. *Position*: Assoc. Prof., Massachusetts Sch. A., Boston, 1921-1957.

CAJORI, CHARLES—Painter, T.
315 East 10th St., New York 9, N.Y.

B. Palo Alto, Cal., Mar. 9, 1921. *Studied*: Colorado Springs FA Center; Cleveland Sch. A.; Columbia Univ. *Member*: CAA. *Awards*: Fulbright F., 1952-53. *Exhibited*: CGA, 1959; WMAA, 1957; Univ. Nebraska, 1958; Vanguard A., WAC, 1955; one-man: New York City, 1956, 1958; Wash., D.C., 1955; Stable Gal., 1954-1957. *Positions*: Instr. Painting, Notre Dame of Maryland, 1949-1955; American Univ., 1955, 1956; PMA Sch. A., 1956; CUASch., 1956- .

CALCIA, LILLIAN ACTON—Educator
301 Rea Ave. Extension, Hawthorne, N.J.

B. Paterson, N.J., Mar. 28, 1907. *Studied*: Montclair State Normal; Columbia Univ., T. Col., B.S., M.A.; N.Y. Univ., Sch. Edu., Ed. D. *Member*: NEA (Life); New Jersey Edu. Assn.; Assn. Supv. & Curriculum Dirs.; New Jersey A. Edu. Assn.; Eastern AA.; Nat. A. Assn.; CAA. *Positions*: Instr. A. Elementary, Passaic, N.J., 1925-28; A., Elem. & Jr. H.S., Paterson, N.J., 1928-35; A., Newark State T. Col., 1935-55; A., Montclair State Col., 1955- ; Chm. A. Dept., Newark State T. Col., 1949-55; Chm. A. Dept., Montclair State Col., 1955- .

CALAPAI, LETTERIO—Painter, Eng., Et., L.
160 West 73rd St., New York 3, N.Y.

B. Boston, Mass., Mar. 29, 1904. *Studied*: Mass. Sch. A.; Sch. FA & Crafts; ASL; Am. A. Sch., and with Robert Laurent, Ben Shahn, Stanley Hayter. *Member*: NSMP; Atelier 17, New York & Paris; Western N.Y. Pr. M.; SAGA; AIGA; AEA; Phila. Pr. Cl.; Boston Pr. M. *Awards*: prizes, Am. in the War Exh., 1943; Fifty Prints of the Year, AIGA, 1944; Boston Pr. M., 1948; LC, 1950, 1951. *Work*: MMA; FMA; BMFA; BM; Houghton Lib., Harvard Univ.; LC; N.Y. Pub. Lib.; Bibliotheque Nationale, Paris; Princeton Univ. Lib., and in coll. in the U.S. and abroad. *Exhibited*: Smithsonian Inst., 1947; Kenyon Col., 1948; Boston Pub. Lib., 1948; Univ. Maine, 1951; Petit Palais, Paris, 1949; London (England) Gal., 1948; Mus. FA, Zurich, 1949; Berlin Festival, 1951; Royal Ontario Mus., 1952; LC, 1948-1952; Carnegie Inst., 1950, 1951; AIC; CGA; BM; CM; DenverA.Mus.; Stanford Univ.; SFMA; Honolulu Acad A.; VMFA; N.Y. Pub. Lib.; Phila. Pr. Cl.; SAGA; Boston Pr. M.; Northwest Pr. M.; Western N.Y. Pr. M.; traveling exh.: America in the war exhs., 1944; AIGA European exh., 1945-1946; OWI, European tour of prints, 1944-45; Paris, Exp. Int. de la Gravure Contemporaine, 1949-50, 1951-52; one-man: Montross Gal., 1934; Tricker Gal., 1939; Norlyst Gal., 1945; George Binet Gal., 1946. *Position*: Hd., Gr. A. Dept., Albright A. Sch., 1949-52; L., Univ. Buffalo.*

CALDER, ALEXANDER—*Sculptor, P., I.*
Roxbury, Conn.

B. Philadelphia, Pa., July 22, 1898. *Studied*: Stevens Inst. Technology, M.E.; ASL. *Awards*: prizes, Plexiglas Comp., 1938; AV, 1942. *Work*: MModA; MMA; Berkshire Mus. A.; Smith Col.; Wadsworth Atheneum; Chicago AC; Mus. Western A., Moscow; Washington Univ.; CAM; PMA; Paris Exp., 1937. I., "Fables of Aesop," 1931; "Three Young Rats," 1944.*

CALDER, JAMES JOHN—*Painter*
2906 East Jefferson St., Detroit 7, Mich.

B. Detroit, Mich., Mar. 29, 1907. *Studied*: Detroit Soc. A. & Crafts, and with Samuel Halpert, John Carroll. *Awards*: prizes, Detroit Inst. A., 1932, 1936; 48 States Comp., FAP, 1938; Michigan A., 1951, 1954; Maiullo prize, 1955, 1957; Garelick Mus. Purchase prize, 1957. *Work*: murals, USPO, Grand Ledge, St. Clair, Rodgers City, Mich. *Exhibited*: PAFA, 1938; GGE, 1939; WFNY 1939; CGA, 1939; WMAA, 1939; Los A. Mus. A., 1945; Detroit Inst. A., 1931-1951; J. L. Hudson Gal., 1952 (one-man); Detroit A. Market, 1954 (one-man); ACA Gal., 1954; Magnificent Mile Exh., Chicago, 1955; Provincetown A. Festival, 1958.

CALDWELL, HENRY BRYAN—*Museum Director*
Fort Worth Art Center, 1309 Montgomery St. (7); h. 409 Crestwood Dr., Fort Worth, Tex.

B. Larchmont, N.Y., June 22, 1918. *Studied*: Harvard Univ., A.B.; N.Y. Univ., M.A. *Position*: Asst. Dir., Corcoran Gal. A., Washington, D.C., 1950-54; Dir., Fort Worth A. Center, Fort Worth, Tex., 1955- .

CALFEE, WILLIAM H.—*Sculptor*
Dorset, Vt.; also 4817 Potomac Ave., N.W., Washington, D.C.

B. Washington, D.C., Feb. 7, 1909. *Studied*: Ecole des Beaux-Arts, Paris, with Paul Landowski; Cranbrook Acad. A., with Carl Milles. *Member*: Wash. A. Gld. *Work*: PMG;; MMA; Cranbrook Acad. A.; Philbrook A. Center; BMA; murals, public bldgs. *Exhibited*: PAFA; MMA; Whyte Gal., Wash., D.C., 1952 (one-man); Weyhe Gal., 1950 (one-man); Bader Gal., Wash., D.C., 1955 (one-man); Graham Gal., N.Y. (one-man). Collaborator on and Introduction to: "Tradition and Experiment in Modern Sculpture," text by Charles Seymour. *Position*: Chm. Dept. Painting & Sculpture, American Univ., Wash., D.C., 1945-1953; Co-Owner, Jefferson Place Gallery, Washington, D.C.

CALIFANO, MICHAEL—*Portrait Painter*
225 West 86th St., New York 24, N.Y.

B. Naples, Italy, Nov. 8, 1890. *Studied*: Royal Acad. FA, Naples, Italy; & with Antonio Mancini, Paul Vetri. *Awards*: Med., Int. Exp., Tampa, Fla.; med., Bologna, Italy. *Work*: Columbia Univ.; many portraits of national & military figures of the U.S.; mural, Village Temple, N.Y. *Exhibited*: All. A. Am.

CALKIN, CARLETON IVERS—*Educator, P.*
Art Dept., Purdue University, Lafayette, Ind.; h. 604 Robinson St., West Lafayette, Ind.

B. Grand Rapids, Mich., July 27, 1914. *Studied*: Univ. South Dakota, B.F.A.; Minneapolis Inst. A. Sch.; Choulnard A. Inst.; Ohio Univ., M.A.; Univ. California, Ph.D.; Univ. Michoacan, Mexico; Inter-Am. Univ., Panama. *Member*: CAA; Am. Archaeological Soc. *Work*: Ports. of Indian Chiefs, So. Dakota Hist. Mus., Vermillion, S.D.; ports., Texas Christian Univ., Ft. Worth; Hist. mural, Ohio Univ.; War murals, Rio Hato Air Base, Panama. *Exhibited*: Regional exhs., Ft. Worth, Tex.; Local, regional and State Fair Shows, Indiana. Contributor, Latin American Art section to Encyclopaedia Britannica, 1957. Lectures: Pre-Columbian, Latin American Archaeology; Colonial and Contemp. Latin American Art. *Positions*: Instr., A., Ohio Univ.; Univ. California, Texas Christian Univ.; Hd., A. Dept., Purdue Univ., Lafayette, Ind., 1955- .

CALKINS, LORING GARY—*Bookplate Designer, Et., I.*
3712 West 59th St., Los Angeles 43, Cal.

B. Chicago, Ill., June 11, 1887. *Studied*: Yale Univ., Ph.B.; AIC; & with Vanderpoel, Duveneck, Freer. *Member*: ASL of Chicago; P. & S. Cl. of Los A.; Soc. Am. Bookplate Des. *Awards*: Los A. P. & S. Cl., 1947, 1948.

Work: Yale Univ.; Yale Univ. Lib. (10 bookplate drawings); Rye Pub. Lib.; Lake Mills (Wis.) Pub. Lib.; Huntington Mus. A.; Yale Cl., N.Y. *Exhibited*: AIC, 1902-1920; Laguna Beach Nat. Pr. Exh.; San Gabriel AA; Lib. Cong., 1944, 1945; Chicago SE, 1919, 1952; Brooklyn SE, 1922-1927; NAC, 1926, 1927; Long Beach AA, 1945, 1946; SAE, 1944; P. & S. Cl. of Los A., 1945, 1946; Cal. SE, 1945; Los A. Mus. A.; Montclair A. Mus.; AA of Los A. County. Illus., "The Land and Sea Mammals of Middle America and the West Indies," 1904, Pub. by Field Mus., Chicago; article on Bookplates & repro. of plates in Annual of Am. Soc. Bookplate Des. & Coll., 1949.

CALLAHAN, JACK—*Portrait Painter*
Bearskin Neck, Rockport, Mass.

B. Somerville, Mass. *Studied*: Vesper George Sch. A.; Mass. Sch. A.; ASL. *Member*: Portraits, Inc., N.Y.; Portrait A. of New England; Copley Soc., Boston; Springfield AA; Rockport AA; North Shore AA. *Awards*: Carl Matson Mem. Award, Rockport AA. *Work*: Portraits in oil and pastel in many private collections.

CALLAHAN, KENNETH—*Painter, W.*
1138—17th St., North, Seattle 2, Wash.

B. Spokane, Wash., Oct. 30, 1906. *Studied*: Univ. Washington. *Member*: Puget Sound Group; AEA. *Awards*: Guggenheim F., 1954-55. *Work*: SAM; SFMA; MModA; MMA; PAFA; PMA; BM; AGAA; Wichita Mus. A.; Phelps Mem. Gal.; Walker A. Center; Am. Acad. A. & Let.; Springfield Mus. A.; Portland A. Mus.; Henry Gal., Seattle; murals, USPO, Anacortes, Centralia, Wash.; Rugby, N.D.; Marine Hospital, Seattle, Wash. *Exhibited*: WMAA; MMA; MModA; PAFA; Maynard Walker Gal., N.Y., 1948, 1952 (one-man). *Position*: Cur., SAM, Seattle, Wash., 1932- .*

CALLCOTT, FRANK—*Educator, P., Gr.*
P.O. Box 62, Georgetown, Tex.

B. San Marcos, Tex., May 28, 1891. *Studied*: Southwestern Univ., A.B.; Columbia Univ., A.M., Ph.D.; ASL, with George Bridgman, Nicolaides. *Member*: Audubon A.; Conn. Acad. FA; Studio Gld.; ASL; Am. Veterans Soc. A.; AAPL. *Awards*: Southern Pr. M., 1939; Conn. A. Gld., 1940. *Work*: MMA; Columbia Univ.; DMFA; Southwestern Univ.; Texas Tech. AI; Texas State Col.; Texas Senate; Scudder Sch., N.Y.; Lubbock A. Mus.; Frye Mus. A., Seattle, Wash.; Adirondack Mountain Cl.; altar-piece, Kimble County Hospital, Junction, Tex.; North Shore Unitarian Soc., Port Washington, N.Y. *Exhibited*: NAD, 1939; VMFA, 1940; Conn. Acad. FA, 1938-1947; All. A. Am., 1938, 1940, 1951, 1954-1955; Southern Pr. M., 1936-1941; Audubon A., 1948, 1951-1956; Columbia Univ. Faculty Show, 1948-1956; Am. Vet. Soc., 1948-1956; Studio Gld. traveling exh., 1948-1958; MMA, 1950; one-man: Riverside Church, 1950; Studio Gld., 1939; Woman's Grad. Cl., Columbia Univ., 1935; Playhouse A. Gal., N.Y., 1937 and five one-man exhs. in Texas, 1957, 1958. Author: "When Spain Was Young"; several Spanish textbooks. *Position*: Instr., 1920-23, Asst. Prof., 1923-44, Assoc. Prof., 1944-50, Prof., 1950- , Columbia Univ., New York, N.Y.

CALLERY, MARY—*Sculptor*
R.D. 2, Huntington, L.I., N.Y.

B. New York, N.Y., June 19, 1903. *Studied*: ASL. *Member*: AEA. *Work*: MModA; Toledo Mus. A.; SFMA; AGAA; CM; Detroit Inst. A.; Aluminum Co. of America; Roosevelt P.S., N.Y.; Wingate P.S., Brooklyn, N.Y., and in private collections. *Exhibited*: one-man: Curt Valentin Gal., 1944, 1947, 1949, 1950, 1952, 1955; Galleria Mai, Paris, 1949; A. Cl., Chicago, 1945; Margaret Brown Gal., Boston, 1951; Brussels World's Fair, 1958; Knoedler Gal., 1957.

CALLICOTT, BURTON (HARRY)—
Painter, E., Calligrapher
Memphis Academy of Arts, Overton Park; h. 3395 Douglass Ave., Memphis 11, Tenn.

B. Terre Haute, Ind., Dec. 28, 1907. *Studied*: Cleveland Sch. A. *Work*: murals, Memphis Mus. Natural History. *Exhibited*: WFNY 1939; numerous local and regional exhs., 1939- ; Circle Gal., Detroit, 1952. *Position*: Instr., Memphis Acad. A., 1936- .

CALNEK, LOUIS HERMANN—
Commercial Artist, Cart.
153 East 18th St., New York 3, N.Y.

B. Manchester, Mass., Mar. 7, 1922. *Studied*: Mass. Sch. A.; PIA Sch., and with William Auerbach-Levy. Contributor cartoons to: Sat. Review; Sat. Eve. Post; Collier's; True; Nation's Business.*

CALVERT, MELVINA (Melvina Calvert Schworm)—
Painter, Gr.
1432 McCausland St., St. Louis 17, Mo.

B. Carterville, Mo., Sept. 7, 1908. *Studied*: Washington Univ.; St. Louis Sch. FA. *Member*: St. Louis A. Gld. (Bd. Governors); Soc. Indp. A., St. Louis; AEA. *Awards*: prizes, CAM, 1951, 1952, 1954, 1955; St. Louis A. Gld., 1954. *Exhibited*: Cal. WC Soc. 1952, 1954; BMA, 1953, 1955; CAM, 1946, 1948, 1949, 1955; St. Louis A. Gld., 1947-1952, 1954; Joslyn A. Mus., 1947-1950, 1952, 1954; Davenport Mun. A. Gal., 1950; Springfield Mus. A., 1949, 1954.*

CAMERO, BLANCHE GONZALEZ—*Painter, Et., T.*
6018 Columbia Ave., Philadelphia 31, Pa.

B. New York, N.Y., Nov. 3, 1894. *Studied*: PMSchIA; PAFA; & with Earl Horter, Arthur Carles, Morris Blackburn. *Member*: Phila. WC Cl.; Phila. A. All.; Phila. A. T. Assn. *Awards*: F. PAFA; prizes, PMSchIA, 1916, 1918. *Work*: Shoemaker Jr. H.S., Phila., Pa.; Overbrook H.S., Phila., Pa. *Exhibited*: PAFA, 1931, 1933, 1934, 1937, 1943, 1944; Phila. Pr. Cl., 1934; Phila. WC Cl., annually; Phila. A. T. exh., 1922-1952; Cape May (N.J.), 1955, 1956; Engineers Cl., Phila., Pa., 1953, 1957, 1958. *Position*: A.T., Overbrook H.S., Philadelphia, Pa., 1926-1957 (Retired).

CAMERON, JOSEPHINE ELAINE—*Painter, Eng.*
3427 Northwest Franklin Ct., Portland 10, Ore.

B. Portland, Ore., Oct. 31, 1925. *Studied*: Portland Mus. A. Sch.; Marylhurst (Ore.) Col.; Seattle Col., and with Mark Tobey. *Member*: AEA; Portland A. Mus.; A. All. of Oregon; Alaskan Contemp. A. *Awards*: prizes, Alaskan Exh., 1957; Anchorage, Alaska, 1957. *Work*: Airport Heights Elem. Sch., Anchorage, Alaska; Henry Gal., Univ. Washington; mural, Sandy (Ore.) H.S. Lib.; Sandy Union H.S.; private portrait commissions. *Exhibited*: SAM, 1948; Portland A. Mus., 1948-1958; Henry Gal., Univ. Washington, 1950-1957; Reed Col., Portland, 1955; one-man: Portland A. Mus., 1954; Anchorage, Alaska, annual prints and oils. Contributor to Anchorage Daily Times; Anchorage Daily News.

CAMERON-MENK, HAZEL—*Painter, S., W.*
839 Highland Dr., Sarasota, Fla.

B. St. Paul, Minn., Nov. 3, 1888. *Studied*: Ringling Sch. A.; George Washington Univ.; Corcoran Sch. A., and with Eugene Weiss, Richard Lahey, Heinz Warneke. *Member*: Sarasota AA; Lg. Am. Pen Women; Woman's Cl., Sarasota. *Awards*: prizes, Lg. Am. Pen Women, 1933, 1935-1937; med., Soc. Indp. A., 1933; Arlington Women's Cl., 1934. *Work*: Clarendon Lib., Arlington, Va. *Exhibited*: Sarasota AA, 1953-1955; Gulf Stream Gal.; Terry AI, 1952; Grumbacher Traveling Exh.*

CAMFFERMAN, MARGARET GOVE (Mrs. Peter)—
Painter
Brackenwood, Langley, Wash.

B. Rochester, Minn. *Studied*: Minneapolis Sch. FA; N.Y. Sch. Des., and with Robert Henri; Andre L'Hote, Paris, France. *Member*: Women Painters of Wash.; Nat. Lg. Am. Pen Women. *Awards*: prizes, Women Painters of Washington, 1942, 1944, 1945, 1951; Nat. Lg. Am. Pen Women, 1947, 1952, 1954, 1955. *Work*: SAM. *Exhibited*: N.Y. Mun. Exh., 1936; Cal. PLH, 1933; Portland (Ore.) Mus. A., 1929; Spokane AA, 1945; Northwest A., 1932-1946, 1947-1951; Women Painters of Wash., 1932-1952; Lg. Am. Pen Women, 1946, 1952, 1954, 1955; SAM, 1952, 1954, 1956, 1958; Seligmann Gal., Seattle, 1955; Woessner Gal., Seattle, 1955; Smithsonian traveling exh., 1958; Alpha Tau Omega, Seattle, 1958; Frye Mus. A., Seattle, 1958; one-man: SAM, 1935; Hathaway House, 1952.

CAMPANELLA, VINCENT RICHARD—*Painter, E., L.*
3414 Karnes Blvd., Kansas City 11, Mo.

B. New York, N.Y., Jan. 9, 1915. *Studied*: DaVinci A. Sch.; NAD; Univ. Kansas City, A.B., M.A. *Member*: AWS; Phila. WC Cl.; Mid-Am. A. *Awards*: prizes, San F. AA, 1941; Denver A. Mus., 1941; Mid-Am. A., 1951. *Work*: SFMA; Rock Springs AA; Toledo Mus. A.; Newark Mus. A.; Univ. Tennessee; Am. Acad. A. & Let. *Exhibited*: BM, 1934, 1946, 1947, 1955; AWS, 1933, 1944, 1946, 1947, 1951; Roerich Mus., 1935; SFMA, 1939-1942, 1947, 1948; AIC, 1941, 1948; Carnegie Inst., 1941, 1947; Denver A. Mus., 1939, 1941, 1946; PAFA, 1946, 1947; CAM, 1942; MMA, 1941; San Diego FA Soc., 1941; Colo. Springs, 1945, 1955; CGA, 1947; John Herron AI, 1947; WMAA, 1939, 1949; Univ. Tennessee, 1947 (one-man); Cal. PLH, 1949; Santa Barbara Mus. A., 1948; SAM, 1947; VMFA, 1948; Univ. Nebraska, 1946-1949; Mulvane A. Center, 1950, 1951; Encyclopaedia Britannica, 1948; Nelson Gal. A., 1949-1951, and many others. One-man: Univ. Alabama, 1948; Univ. Nebraska, 1950; Kansas City AI, 1950; Frank Rehn Gal., N.Y., 1947, 1951, 1954, 1956; Mulvane A. Center, 1956; Univ. Kansas City, 1954, etc. *Positions*: Instr., L., Columbia Univ. Sch. Painting, 1947-49; Artist-in-Residence, Kansas City AI, Kansas City, Mo., 1949-52; Assoc. Prof., Chm. A. Dept., Park Col. 1952- .

CAMPBELL, C. ISABEL—*Painter*
714 Roberts Ave., Drexel Hill, Pa.

B. Brooklyn, N.Y. *Studied*: Phila. Sch. Des. for Women; & with Daniel Garber, Henry B. Snell, Samuel Murray, Elliot Daingerfield. *Member*: Plastic Cl. *Awards*: Med., Sesquicentennial Exp., Phila., Pa., 1926; Moore Inst., 1948; F., Phila. Sch. Des. for Women. *Work*: murals, dioramas, Phila. Commercial Mus., Philadelphia, Pa.

CAMPBELL, CORA A.—*Painter, Et., C., T., I., L.*
1927 North Broad St., Philadelphia 22, Pa.

Studied: PSchIA; Pa. State Col.; Cornell Univ., and with Charles Hawthorne, W. C. Copeland, Henry C. Pitz. *Member*: Phila. A. All.; Phila. Plastic Cl.; Phila. A.T. Assn. *Awards*: prizes, Phila. Plastic Cl. *Exhibited*: Phila. Plastic Cl., 1922-1955; Phila. A. All., 1944-1955; Cape May (N.J.) A. Lg., 1945-1955; Pa. State Col.; Women's Univ. Cl., 1952. *Position*: Supv. A., Pub. Sch., Philadelphia, Pa., 1922-42; Cor. Sec., Phila. Plastic Cl., 1942-55.*

CAMPBELL, HARRIET (Mrs. W. D.)—*Painter, Des.*
3000 West Broad St., Columbus 4, Ohio

B. Columbus, Ohio. *Studied*: Columbus A. Sch.; Ohio State Univ.; ASL, with Bridgman, Dow, Henri, Chase; Thurn Sch. A., and with McNulty. *Member*: Columbus A. Lg.; Ohio WC Soc. *Awards*: prizes, Columbus A. Lg., 1920, 1921, 1923, 1927, 1933, 1935; Ohio WC Soc., 1950, 1952. *Exhibited*: AWS, 1934; Boston A. Cl., 1934; Phila. WC Cl., 1935; AIC, 1935; Columbus A. Lg.; Ohio WC Soc.; Little Gal., 1938 (one-man), and others. *Work*: Univ. Ohio, Athens, Ohio.*

CAMPBELL, H(ELENA) E(ASTMAN) OGDEN (Mrs.)—
Painter, T.
280 Marbledale Rd., Tuckahoe, N.Y.

B. Eastman, Ga. *Studied*: with William M. Chase, Robert Henri, Lucien Simon. *Member*: AAPL; Catherine Lorillard Wolfe A. Cl.; Hudson Valley AA; Mt. Vernon AA; Knickerbocker A.; Southern Vermont A. *Awards*: citation and award, Wesleyan Col., Macon, Ga. (Procured gift coll. of contemp. art Wesleyan Col.); citation, Phi Mu Fraternity, 1954; prizes, Crestwood Woman's Cl., 1954; New Rochelle Woman's Cl., 1955; Londonderry (Vt.) 1956, 1957; Honor Roll & Citation, AAPL, 1957. *Work*: Columbia Univ. State T. Col., Upper Montclair, N.J.; Wesleyan Col.; Mid-Valley Hospital, Pa.; Mus. City of N.Y.; Hist. Dept., U.S. Navy; Pub. Lib., Boonville, N.Y.; Am. Mathematical Soc., Columbia Univ. *Exhibited*: AAPL; NAD; NAWA; All. A. Am.; Yonkers AA; Knickerbocker A.; Manchester (Vt.) A. Center; Ogunquit A. Center; West River AA, Londonderry, Vt.; Crestwood Woman's Cl.; New Rochelle Woman's Cl.; Westchester A. & Crafts Gld.

CAMPBELL, I(SABELLA) F. (Mrs. W. T. B.)—*Painter*
7021 Lanewood Ave., Los Angeles 28, Cal.

B. Rockford, Ill., Nov. 11, 1874. *Studied*: AIC; ASL, and with Joseph De Camp, William Chase, George Otis. *Mem-*

ber: Cal. AC; Laguna Beach AA; Women Painters of the West; A. of the Southwest. *Awards*: prizes, Women Painters of the West, 1940; AAPL, 1949; Lg. Am. Pen Women, 1949. *Work*: Hollywood Congregational Church. *Exhibited*: Santa Cruz, Cal., 1938, 1943, 1945, 1946; Oakland A. Gal., 1938, 1945, 1946; Cal. PLH, 1940, 1942, 1944, 1945; Laguna Beach AA; A. of the Southwest, Greek Theatre, Los Angeles, 1948-1958; Arizona State Fair; Cal. State Fair, 1951; Woman's Cl., Hollywood, 1958; Cal. AC, 1958.

CAMPBELL, JEWETT—*Painter*
> Douglasdale Rd., Richmond 21, Va.

B. Hoboken, N.J., Aug. 10, 1912. *Studied*: ASL, with Curry, DuBois, Miller, Poor and Hofmann. *Awards*: prizes, VMFA, 1941; Va. Acad. Sc. & FA, 1942. *Work*: MMoDA; VMFA. *Exhibited*: VMFA, 1941; NGA, 1942. *Position*: Inst., Univ. Richmond, Richmond Prof. Inst., Richmond, Va.*

CAMPBELL, MRS. JEWETT. *See Beglen, Jeanne*

CAMPBELL, MARJORIE DUNN—*Educator, P.*
> Arts & Industries Bldg., Iowa State Teachers College; h. 713 Main St., Cedar Falls, Iowa

B. Columbus, Ohio, Sept. 14, 1910. *Studied*: Ohio State Univ., B.S. in Edu., M.A.; Claremont Col. Grad. Inst. A.; T. Col., Columbia Univ., and with Hans Hofmann, Emil Bisttram, Millard Sheets. *Member*: A. Edu. of Iowa; Intl. Soc. for Edu. through Art; Western AA; Nat. A. Edu. Assn. *Position*: Instr., App. A., Univ. Missouri, 1942-45; Asst. Prof. FA, Ohio State Univ., 1945-49; Asst. Prof. A., Iowa State T. Col., Cedar Falls, Iowa, 1949- .

CAMPBELL, ORLAND—*Portrait Painter*
> 1 West 67th St., New York 23, N.Y.

B. Chicago, Ill., Nov. 28, 1890. *Studied*: George Washington Univ.; Corcoran A. Sch.; PAFA, with Henry McCarter. *Member*: Century Assn. *Work*: U.S. Capitol Bldg., Wash., D.C.; Canajoharie Mus.; U.S. Military Acad., West Point, N.Y.; MIT; Univ. Chicago; Rensselaer Polytechnic Inst.; Mus. City of N.Y.; Southern Vermont A. Center. *Exhibited*: CGA, 1923; CAM, 1924; Arch. L., 1926; Knoedler Gal.; Wildenstein Gal. Contributor to American Heritage, 1958.

CAMPBELL, RICHARD H.—*Painter*
> 16551 Sunset Blvd., Pacific Palisades, Cal.

B. Marinette, Wis., Jan. 11, 1921. *Studied*: Cleveland Sch. A.; A. Center, Los Angeles. *Member*: Cal. WC Soc.; Los A. AA. *Awards*: prizes, Los A. City Exh., 1951; CMA, 1954; Los A. Festival A., 1958. *Exhibited*: Butler AI, 1954, 1955, 1957, 1958; Denver A. Mus., 1951; Oakland A. Mus., 1954; Cal. WC Soc., 1955; CMA, 1939, 1954; Los A. Mus. A., 1952, 1958; Northwest Territory Exh., 1954; Los A. AA, 1950, 1957, 1958; Cal. State Fair, 1955, 1957; one-man: deYoung Mem. Mus., 1945; Santa Monica A. Gal., 1958. *Position*: Bd. Dir., Santa Monica A. Gal.

CAMPBELL, SARA WENDELL (Mrs.)—
> 645 Madison Ave., New York 22, N.Y.

B. St. John, N.B., Canada. *Studied*: Eric Pape Sch. A., Boston; Chase Sch. A., and with Pape, Chase, Penfield, Miller. *Exhibited*: A. Dir. Cl.; SI; Gld. Freelance A.; NAD; Waldorf-Astoria Hotel; Kennedy Gal.; N.Y. Pub. Lib. *Work*: Art work in Scribner's, McCall's, national women's magazines; cover designs for Packard, Dennison, Hudnut, Nestles, Waltham watches, and other leading companies. I., "Bible Stories"; children's books.

CAMPBELL, SHIRLEY ALEY—*Painter*
> 472 North Rocky River Dr., Berea, Ohio

B. Cleveland, Ohio, Mar. 26, 1925. *Studied*: Cleveland Inst. A.; ASL; PIASch. *Awards*: prizes, Agnes Gund Scholarship, Cleveland Inst. A., 1947; CMA, 1956, 1957, 1958; Ohio State Fair; Jay Show awards, Cleveland, 1957, 1958; Fashion Group award, Cleveland, 1958. *Work*: CMA. *Exhibited*: CMA traveling exhs., 1955-1958; Butler Inst. Am. A., 1954-1956, 1958; All. A. Am., 1952, 1957; Chautauqua, N.Y., 1956; Audubon A., 1948-1950, 1952; Evansville Mus. A. & Sc.; CMA, 1954-1958; Cleveland Jay Shows, 1956-1958; one-man: Karamu House, Cleveland. *Position*: Instr., Cleveland Inst. A., Cleveland, Ohio.

CAMPBELL, W(ILLIAM) ADDISON (JR.)—*Painter, E.*
> 551 Davis St., San Francisco, Cal.

B. New York, N.Y., June 18, 1914. *Studied*: Cal. Sch. FA, with Maurice Sterne. *Member*: San F. AA. *Work*: Crocker A. Gal.; Chappell House, Denver, Colo. *Exhibited*: San F. AA, 1938-1946; AFA, 1938-1942. *Position*: Instr., A. Sch. Center, San F., 1938-1942; Cal. Col. A. & Crafts, Oakland, Cal., 1946- .*

CAMPBELL, WILLIAM P.—*Museum Curator*
> National Gallery of Art, Washington, D.C.

Position: Cur., Paintings, National Gallery of Art, Washington, D.C.*

CAMPRUBI, LEONTINE (Mrs. Leontin Camprubi Tintner)—*Painter*
> 830 Hodge Ave., Ames, Iowa

B. Caldwell, N.J., Jan. 6, 1916. *Studied*: ASL; Colorado Springs FA Center, and in Switzerland. *Exhibited*: CGA, 1941; Contemporary A. Gal., 1946 (one-man), traveling exh. 1947; Pinacotheca; Springfield A. Mus., 1944; La Grange (Ga.) Col.; Univ. Chattanooga; Shorter Col.; Univ. Georgia; Limestone Col., Gaffney, S.C.; Univ. North Carolina; Museo Nationale, Rio de Janeiro; Prestes Meier Gal., Sao Paulo, Brazil; one-man: Iowa State Col., 1950; Des Moines A. Center, 1952.*

CANDELL, VICTOR—*Painter, T.*
> 23 East 9th St., New York 3, N.Y.

B. Budapest, Hungary, May 11, 1903. *Studied*: in Paris, Budapest, New York. *Member*: Audubon A. (Dir.); AEA. *Awards*: prizes, MMoDA, 1940; Treas. Dept., U.S. Govt., 1942; Brooklyn Soc. A., 1946, 1950; Audubon A., 1951, 1952; Emily Lowe award, 1956. *Work*: WMAA; MMA; Nat. Inst. A. & Let.; Montclair A. Mus.; Univ. Nebraska; Carnegie Inst.; Munson-Williams-Proctor Inst.; Brandeis Univ. *Exhibited*: WMA, 1945; Audubon A., 1945-1952; Everhart Mus. A., Scranton, Pa., 1944 (one-man); Brooklyn Soc. A., 1946, 1950; Grand Central Moderns, 1952 (one-man), 1954 (one-man); MMA, 1950; WMAA, 1952; AIC, 1952; Univ. Illinois, 1952; CGA; Carnegie Inst.; Des Moines A. Center, 1948-1952; PAFA, 1948-1952; Phila. A. All., 1958 (one-man). *Position*: Instr., Brooklyn Mus. Sch. A., 1946-54; Cooper Union A. Sch., New York, N.Y., 1954- .

CANFIELD, LILLIAN CAROLINE—*Museum Curator*
> Institute of Social Studies, Molenstraat 27, den Haag, The Netherlands

B. Columbus, Ohio, Feb. 1, 1911. *Studied*: Johns Hopkins Univ., M.A.; Univ. Munich; Univ. Berlin; Radcliffe Col.; Univ. California. *Awards*: F., Univ. Pennsylvania, N.Y. Univ., Univ. Chicago. Former Prof. A. Hist., Florida State Col., Univ. Missouri, Univ. Texas. Ed., articles in Harper's Art History Encyclopedia. *Position*: Former Cur., Oakland A. Mus., Oakland, Cal.; Hist. Research, Inst. of Social Studies, den Haag, Netherlands at present.

CANIFF, MILTON A.—*Cartoonist, I., W., L.*
> New City, Rockland County, N.Y.

B. Hillsboro, Ohio, Feb. 28, 1907. *Studied*: Ohio State Univ., B.A.; Atlanta Law Sch., Hon. LL.D.; Rollins Col., Hon. D.F.A. *Member*: Natl. Cartoonists Soc.; Natl. Press Cl.; Overseas Press Cl.; Aviation Writers Assn.; Players Cl.; SI; Newspaper Comics Council; Military Collectors & Historians; Rockland County Civil Air Patrol (Hon.). *Awards*: Billy DeBeck Mem. award, 1947; Sigma Delta Chi Distinguished Service award, 1949; Air Force Assn. Medal of Merit, 1952; Air Force Assn. A. & Lets. Trophy, 1953; Treasury Dept. Citation, 1953; B'nai B'rith's Philadelphia Lodge Americanism award, 1953; Ohio Career Medal, 1954; USAF Exceptional Service award, 1957; Ohio Governor's award for outstanding Ohioan, 1957; Aviation Man of the Month, Natl. Aviation Cl., 1958. *Work*: Producing features "Dickie Dare" and "Gay Thirties" for Assoc. Press, N.Y., 1932; created "Terry and The Pirates," Chicago Tribune-N.Y. Daily News Syndicate, 1934; started "Steve Canyon" strip for Chicago Sun-Times Syndicate in 1947; weekly GI strip "Male Call" for service publications, WW II.

CANNARD, RUTH E. (HINTZ)—
Educator, L., Mus. Dir.
28 Peck St., Attleboro, Mass.

B. Green Bay, Wis., Sept. 23, 1912. *Studied*: Layton Sch. A. *Exhibited*: Milwaukee AI; Univ. Wisconsin; Neville Pub. Mus., Green Bay, Wis. Lectures: Early American Silver; Paintings in the Collection of the Neville Pub. Mus. *Position*: Cur. A., Neville Pub. Mus., Green Bay, Wis., 1936-45; Dir. Attleboro Mus., Attleboro, Mass., 1950.

CANNON, FLORENCE V.—*Painter, Gr., E., L.*
576 Benson St., Camden 3, N.J.

B. Camden, N.J. *Studied*: PMSchIA; PAFA; Grande Chaumiere, Paris. *Member*: NAWA; Phila. Pr. Cl.; AEA; Phila. A. All.; Northwest Pr. M.; AAPL; Springfield AA; Wash. WC Cl.; Southern Pr. M.; Baltimore WC Cl.; Woodmere AA; Am. Color Pr. Soc. (Founder); Marblehead AA; Color Block Pr. M.; Phila. Plastic Cl.; Phila. WC Cl.; F. PAFA. *Awards*: Cresson traveling scholarships, PAFA, 1928, 1929; Toppan award, 1930; prizes, Northwest Pr. M., 1933; NAWA, 1936; Southern Pr. M., 1937; med., Plastic Cl., 1943; F., PAFA; med., Camden H.S., Camden, N.J. *Work*: PAFA; Phila. A. All.; Harcum Jr. Col., Bryn Mawr, Pa.; PMA; Woodmere A. Gal.; Northwest Pr. M.; Southern Pr. M. *Exhibited*: Denver A. Mus.; PAFA; Phila. Pr. Cl.; NAWA; Montclair A. Mus.; CGA; AFA; AIC; Laguna Beach AA; Oakland A. Gal.; Northwest Pr. M.; AWCS; Balto. WC Cl.; Trenton Mus. A.; Wash. WC Cl.; Cal. Pr. M.; Portland Soc. A.; Wichita A. Mus.; Newark Mus.; Southern Pr. M.; Phila. A. All.; Ogunquit AA; Phila. AC; Phila. Sketch Cl.; one-man: Women's A. Cl., Camden, 1958; Walt Whitman Hotel, Camden, 1958. *Position*: Dir., Cannon A. Sch., Camden, N.J., 1930-1954.

CANTARELLA, MARIA BOVERI—*Painter*
2901 Grand Concourse, Bronx, N.Y.

B. New York, N.Y. *Studied*: CUASch.; N.Y. Univ.; NAD, with Louis Bouche; Col. of the City of N.Y., and with Ralph Fabri, Alfred Crimi, and Ada Cecere. *Member*: NAWA; AAPL; Pen & Brush Cl.; All. A. Am.; Grand Central A. Gal.; Knickerbocker A.; A. Lg. of Long Island; Audubon A. *Awards*: prizes, Am. Women's Cl., 1941; NAWA, 1948; AAPL, 1951, 1954 (2); Margaret Arlen prize, 1952; medal, NAC, 1951; NAD; 1956 (3); Catherine L. Wolfe prize, 1957; Buck Hill AA, 1956; A. Lg. of Long Island, 1956, 1957; Knickerbocker A. Medal, 1956; Amita award, 1957; citation, Am. Bill of Rights Day Assn., 1957. *Exhibited*: Studio Gld.; Soc. Indp. A.; Pen & Brush Cl.; AAPL; NAC; Audubon A.; Hudson Valley AA; All. A. Am.

CANTER, ALBERT M.—*Painter, T.*
12 Dawson Ave., West Orange, N.J.

B. Norma, N.J., June 1, 1892. *Studied*: PMSchIA; PAFA; Grande Chaumiere, Paris; Rutgers Univ.; N.J. State T. Col. *Awards*: F., PAFA; prizes, Montclair A. Mus., 1936; Paris Salon, 1931. *Work*: Phila. Sketch Cl.; Orange H.S., Orange, N.J. *Exhibited*: AWCS, 1918; Phila. WC Cl., 1917; Montclair A. Mus., 1933, 1936, 1944, 1945; Paris Salon, 1931; Newark Mus., 1939; N.Y. Mun. Gal., 1938, 1939. *Position*: Instr., Drawing & Indst. A., West Paterson (N.J.) Pub. Schs.

CANTIENI, MARGARET BALZER (Mrs. Joseph F.)—
Painter
43 South 13th St., Allentown, Pa.

B. Newton, Kans., Apr. 30, 1914. *Studied*: Carleton Col., B.A.; AIC, and with Lyonel Feininger, Josef Albers, William Stanley Hayter. *Awards*: med. & prize, AIC, 1946; prize, Intermont Col., Bristol, Va., 1945. *Exhibited*: AIC, 1944, 1946; Lincoln A. Gld., 1941; Intermont Col., 1944, 1945; Ohio Valley A., 1944, 1945; Berea Col., 1946; Univ. Louisville, 1946; Carleton Col., 1946; BM, 1947; Lehigh Univ., 1949, 1952. *Position*: Asst. Dir. A., Berea Col., Berea, Ky., 1937-45; Instr. A., Swain Sch. A., 1948-50.*

CANTOR, ROBERT LLOYD—
Educator, Des., C., Cr., W., L.
15 Gulf Rd., Lawrence Brook, East Brunswick, N.J.

B. New York, N.Y., Aug. 14, 1919. *Studied*: N.Y. Univ., Ph. D. *Member*: Eastern A.; Nat. Edu. Assn.; Indst. A. Assn.; Com. on A. Edu., MModA; Soc. Plastic Engr. *Exhibited*: Charleston A. Gal. (one-man). Author: "His-

tory of Art Workbook"; "Plastics for the Layman"; also training film scenarios, manuals, textbooks. Contributor to art, educational and political journals; New Leader, etc. *Position*: Prof. F. & Indst. A., West Virginia Inst. Tech., Montgomery, W. Va.; Exec. Dir., AEA, New York; Ed. Dir., Am. Craftsman Sch., New York, N.Y.; Instr., N.Y. Univ., City Col., Columbia Univ., New York, N.Y.

CANTRALL, HARRIET M.—*Educator, P.*
853 MacArthur Blvd., Springfield, Ill.

B. Cantrall, Ill. *Studied*: PIASch; Univ. Oregon, B.S., M.F.A.; & with Woodbury, Dow, Townsend. *Member*: Illinois Edu. Assn.; Nat. Edu. Assn.; Western AA; NAWA; St. Louis AC; Springfield AA. Co-Author: "Art in Daily Activities." (Retired.)

CANZANI, JOSEPH V.—*Educator*
Columbus Art School of the Columbus Gallery of Art, 44 North 9th St., Columbus 15, Ohio

Position: Dean, Columbus Art School.*

CAPARN, RHYS (Mrs. Rhys Caparn Steel)—*Sculptor*
939 8th Ave.; h. 333 West 57th St., New York 19, N.Y.

B. Onteora Park, N.Y., July 28, 1909. *Studied*: Bryn Mawr Col.; Archipenko Sch. FA; and in Paris with Navellier. *Member*: Fed. Mod. P. & S.; Sculptor's Gld.; Am. Abstract A.; New Sculpture Group; New York Six; AEA; NAWA. *Awards*: prizes, NAWA, 1944, 1945; MMA, 1951. *Work*: Brooklyn Botanical Gardens; WMAA; Fogg Mus. A.; CGA; Colo. Springs FA Center; CAM; reliefs & designs lobby of library, Barnard College. *Exhibited*: MMA; PMA; BM; WMAA; MModA; Petit Palais, Paris, 1950; Fed. Mod. P. & S.; Sculptor's Gld.; one-man: Delphic Studios, 1933, 1935; Arch. Lg., 1941; Bronx Zoo, 1942; Mus. of Tacoma, Wash., 1943; Wildenstein Gal., 1944, 1947; Dartmouth Col., 1949; Meltzer Gal., 1956 (one-man); Tate Gal., London, 1953; John Heller Gal., 1953; PAFA, 1951-1953; Art Colony Gal., Cleveland, Ohio, 1955; "Eight Americans," USIA, on tour of Europe & Asia, 1957, 1958. *Position*: Instr., Sculpture, Dalton Sch., New York, N.Y., 1946-1955.

CAPLANE, FELICE—*Painter*
424 East Fifth St., Mt. Vernon, N.Y.

B. Hamburg, Germany, Dec. 5, 1912. *Studied*: Acad. A., Hamburg, Germany, and with Salvatore Lascari. *Member*: AEA; Knickerbocker A.; Mt. Vernon AA. *Work*: Fla. Southern Col. *Exhibited*: New Jersey Soc. P. & S., 1946, 1947; WMAA, 1951; Fla. Southern Col., 1952.*

CAPOLINO, J(OHN) JOSEPH (Lt. Col.)—*Painter, E.*
Marine Corps, Navy Publicity Bureau, 25th & Locust Sts., h. 8105 Navajo St., Philadelphia 18, Pa.

B. Philadelphia, Pa., Feb. 22, 1896. *Studied*: PAFA; & abroad. *Member*: Phila. WC Cl.; Da Vinci All. *Awards*: F., PAFA; traveling scholarships, PAFA, 1917-1918, 1924; prizes, PAFA, 1918, 1924; Woodmere A. Gal., 1940; med., Sesqui-Centennial Exp., Phila., 1926; Spring Garden Inst., 1936; Citation, Am. Legion "Marine of the Year;" 1950; gold med., Phila. Printing Industries, 1955. *Work*: murals, USMC, Phila.; Jenks Sch., Phila.; Phila. Pub. Lib.; USMC Mus., Quantico, Va.; Mun. Court Bldg., Phila.; Navy Bldg., Wash., D.C.; St. Joseph's Convent, Phila.; USMC Quartermaster's Depot, San F., Cal. Many official portraits of military figures. Also work in State Capitol, Del.; Woodmere A. Gal.; Valley Forge Hist. Mus.; des., USMC flag. *Position*: Dir., Spring Garden Inst. & Chestnut Hill A. Center, Phila., Pa.; Cur., Woodmere A. Gal., Philadelphia, Pa.*

CAPONI, ANTHONY—*Educator, S.*
Art Department, Macalester College; h. Rt. #1, Pilot Knob Rd., St. Paul 11, Minn.

B. Pretare, Italy, May 7, 1921. *Studied*: Univ. Flore, Italy; Cleveland Sch. A.; Walker A. Center; Univ. Minnesota, B.S., M. Ed. *Member*: AEA; Soc. Minn. Sculptors; AAUP. *Awards*: prizes, Minneapolis Inst. A., 1947, 1948, 1949, 1953; Minnesota State Fair, 1948, 1950, 1955; St. Paul Gal. A., 1949, 1955. *Work*: Minneapolis Inst. A.; sc., columns, figures: St. Joseph Sch., Red Lake Falls, Minn.; St. Mary's Church, Warroad, Minn.; St. Johns Church, Rochester, Minn.; Trinity Lutheran Church, Rochester; Immaculate Conception Church, Minneapolis, Minn. *Exhib-*

ited: WAC, 1947-1958; Iowa State T. Col., 1958; St. Paul Gal. A., 1947-1958; Minneapolis AI, annually. Co-Dir., film "Sculpture in Minnesota," 1950. *Positions:* Pres., Minn. Sculpture Group, 1952; Vice-Pres., Minn. Soc. Sculptors, 1958; Prof. A., Hd. A. Dept., Macalester College, St. Paul, Minn., 1958- .

CAPPS, CHARLES MERRICK—Etcher, Lith.
   1424 Fairmount Ave., Wichita 14, Kan.

B. Jacksonville, Ill., Sept. 14, 1898. *Studied:* Chicago Acad. FA; PAFA. *Member:* SAE; Prairie Pr. M.; Cal. Pr. M.; Chicago SE; *Awards:* Prizes, Northwest Pr. M., 1930; Rocky Mountain Pr. M., 1934; Chicago SE, 1936, 1937, 1950; Kansas City AI, 1935, 1937, 1940; LC, 1941, 1948; Carnegie Inst., 1948; New Orleans AA, 1950. *Work:* Philbrook A. Center; Swedish Nat. Mus., Stockholm; Carnegie Inst.; Joslyn A. Mus.*

CAREWE, SYLVIA—Painter, Pr. M., Tapestry Des.
   1626 York Ave.; h. 544 East 86th St., New York 28, N.Y.

B. New York, N.Y., Feb. 22, 1914. *Studied:* Columbia Univ. *Member:* AEA; Brooklyn Soc. A.; AWS; Springfield AA; Phila. Pr. Cl.; N.Y. Soc. Women A.; NAWA; Atelier 17. *Work:* Brandeis Univ.; Butler AI; Howard Univ.; Musee de l'Arte Moderne, Paris, France; Richmond (Ind.) AA; Tel-Aviv Mus.; MModA Rental Lib., and in private collections. *Awards:* ACA Gal. Comp., 1947. *Exhibited:* MModA.; WMAA; BMFA; Audubon A.; BM; Brooklyn Pub. Lib.; Riverside Mus.; Vassar Col.; Phila. Pr. Cl.; Smith Mus., Springfield, Mass.; Columbia Mus. A. (S.C.); Georgia Mus. A., Athens; High Mus. A., Atlanta, Ga.; Colo. Springs FA Center; one-man: Three Arts, Poughkeepsie, N.Y., 1947, 1952, 1954, 1958; ACA Gal., 1947, 1953, 1954 (4-man), 1956, 1958; Barnett Aden Gal., Wash., D.C., 1950; Richmond AA, 1955; Univ. Indiana, 1955; Ball State T. Col., Muncie, 1955; Terza Karlis Gal., Westport, Conn., 1955; Decatur A. Center, 1955; Butler AI, 1955; Galerie Granoff, Paris, France, 1957; Univ. North Carolina, 1958; Winston-Salem Col., 1958; North Carolina Col. Union, Raleigh, 1958.

CAREY, CHARLES (CHRISTOPHER)—Etcher, P.
   222 Fairview Ave., Elmhurst, Ill.

B. Chicago, Ill., Oct. 29, 1894. *Studied:* AIC. *Member:* Oak Park, River Forest A. Lg.; Elmhurst A. Gld. *Awards:* prize, Elmhurst A. Gld., 1957. *Work:* Elmhurst (Ill.) Lib. *Exhibited:* Phila. A. All., 1930; NAC, 1930; Phila. Pr. Cl., 1930; Chicago SE, 1931; Cleveland Pr. M., 1931; Cal. Pr. M., 1932; SAE, 1932; Lib. Cong., 1944; Mills Col., Cal.; Elmhurst, Ill. Lectures: Prints.

CAREY, JAMES SHELDON—Educator, C.
   University of Kansas; h. 2122 Owens Lane, Lawrence, Kans.

B. Bath, N.Y., July 28, 1911. *Studied:* N.Y. State Col. of Ceramics, Alfred Univ., B.S. in Ceramic Art; T. Col., Columbia Univ., A.M. in F. & Indst. A. *Member:* Am. Ceramic Soc.; AAUP; Am. Craftsmen's Council; Sertoma Intl. *Awards:* prize, 9th Ann. Exh., Hendersonville, N.C., 1951; CAM, 1952, 1955; Kansas Free Fair, 1952, 1958; Nat. Ceramic exh., Wichita, 1958. *Exhibited:* Syracuse Mus. FA, 1938, 1941, 1947-1954, 1956, 1958; GGE 1939; Wichita Nat. Ceramic Exh., 1948-1951; Am. Craftsmen's Gld., 1951; PMA; Grace Horne Gal., Boston, 1939; Andre Seligmann Gal., 1941; R.I. Sch. Des., 1942; Univ. Kansas, 1944; Denver A. Mus.; Nelson Gal. A., 1946; Philbrook A. Center, 1947; Colo. A. & M. Col.; Joslyn Mus. A., 1950; Smithsonian Inst. traveling exh.; Cranbrook Acad. A.; Miami Nat. Ceramic, 1956; AIC, 1957; Nat. Dec. A. & Ceramic exh., Wichita, 1956-58; Fiber, Clay & Metal Comp., St. Paul, 1957; Joslyn A. Mus., 1958; one-man: Spooner Mus., Univ. Kansas, 1958. Contributor to Am. Ceramic Soc. Bulletin; Edu. & Tech. Des. Magazine; Arts & Activities. Lectures and demonstrations, TV, 1956-58. *Position:* Instr. Ceramics, T. Col., Columbia Univ., 1940-42; R.I. Sch. Des., 1942-43; Univ. Kansas, 1944-45; Asst. Prof., Univ. Kansas, 1945-48; Assoc. Prof. Ceramics, 1948-53, Prof., 1953- ; Adv. Ed., Ceramics Monthly, 1953-55.

CAREY, JOHN T.—Educator
   Northern Illinois University, De Kalb, Ill.
Position: Chm., Dept. Fine Arts, Northern Illinois University.*

CARIANI, VARALDO J.—Painter
   Nashville, Ind.

B. Renazo, Italy, Feb. 8, 1891. *Studied:* NAD; ASL, with Frank V. DuMond. *Member:* Springfield A. Lg.; Hoosier Salon; Indiana A. Cl.; Brown County A. Gld. *Awards:* F., Tiffany Fnd., 1920; prizes, Springfield A. Lg., 1923; Hoosier Salon, 1933, 1934, 1936, 1938, 1947, 1948, 1955; Brown County A. Gal., 1943; Indiana A. Cl., 1945, 1955. *Work:* Indiana Univ.; Indianapolis Pub. Sch.; State House, Indiana; Glen Park Sch., Gary, Ind.; Tipton (Ind.) AA; Hanover Col., Hanover, Ind.; Mishawaka (Ind.) H.S.; Cook County Hospital, Chicago, Ill.; Gary County Hospital, Gary, Ind.

CARISS, MARGUERITE (Mrs. Walter L.)—Painter
   801 North 41st St., Philadelphia, Pa.

B. Green Tree, Pa., Aug. 16, 1883. *Studied:* PMSchIA; & with Ludwig Faber, A. Margaretta Archambault. *Member:* Phila. A. All. *Work:* PAFA; PMA; NCFA. *Exhibited:* CGA; NCFA; PAFA.*

CARLIN, JAMES—Painter, T.
   73 Cathedral Ave., Nutley, N.J.

B. Belfast, North Ireland, June 25, 1909. *Studied:* Belfast Mun. Col., Ireland, and with Beaumont, in London, England. *Member:* AWS; Phila. WC Cl.; SC; N.J. WC Soc.; Audubon A.; All. A. Am. *Awards:* AWS, 1943, 1947; Audubon A., 1947; Montclair A. Mus., 1941, 1942, 1946, 1949; All. A. Am., 1945; P. & S. Soc., N.J., 1946; A. Council of N.J., 1948; SC, 1950; N.J. State Exh., 1952; SC, 1952; NAD, 1951. *Work:* stained glass windows (in collaboration) Londonderry Guild Hall; memorial windows in several churches in Ireland. *Exhibited:* PAFA; NAD; MMA; BM; Denver A. Mus.; N.Y. Hist. Soc.; Newark Mus.; one-man: Grand Central A. Gal.; Miami Beach A. Center. *Position:* Hd. Dept. FA, Newark Sch. F. & Indst. A., Newark, N.J.

CARLSEN, DINES (Mr.)—Painter
   Rt. 1, Box 23, Falls Village, Conn.

B. New York, N.Y., Mar. 8, 1901. *Member:* NA. *Awards:* prizes, NAD, 1919, 1923. *Work:* CGA; John Herron AI; Sweat Mem. Mus. *Exhibited:* CGA, 1923, 1935; Carnegie Inst., 1920-1923, 1925, 1930; PAFA, 1917-1932; NAD, 1915-1946; AIC, 1919, 1925, 1927; CAM, 1919, 1921, 1923, 1926, 1927-1929; Detroit Inst. A., 1920, 1923-1928; Grand Central A. Gal.

CARLSON, OSCAR A.—
   Painter, Des., Et., Eng., C., Lith.
   Box 42, Merrimack, N.H.

B. Glencoe, Ill., Jan. 20, 1895. *Studied:* AIC; & with Charles Curtis Allen. *Exhibited:* Jordan-Marsh, Boston; New Hampshire AA; North Shore AA; Swedish Cl., Chicago.*

CARLSON, MRS. VALERIE KLEE—Painter
   120 East 36th St., New York 16, N.Y.

B. Cincinnati, Ohio, July 4, 1907. *Studied:* Cincinnati A. Acad.; Frankfurt, Germany; Westminster Sch. A., London, England; Acad. FA, Munich, Germany. *Member:* Chamber of Art, Munich; 3-Arts Cl., Cincinnati. *Awards:* prizes, CM, 1945; Cincinnati Woman's Cl., 1949, 1950. *Exhibited:* CM, 1945-1947; Ogunquit A. Center, 1948-1950, 1958; NAC, 1954, 1955; one-man: Loring Andrews Gal., Cincinnati, 1946, 1948, 1950, 1955; Town Cl., Cincinnati, 1953.

CARLSSON, OSCAR T.—Painter, Gr., C.
   Dublin, N.H.

B. Hedemora, Sweden, Sept. 23, 1893. *Studied:* WMA Sch.; NAD; ASL, and with John Sloan, G. L. Nelson, Eugene Fitsch. *Member:* ASL; AEA; AAPL. *Exhibited:* BM; WMA; Los A. Mus. A.; Germanic Mus., Boston; CAA; Staten Island Mus. A.; Riverside Mus.; Botanical Gardens, N.Y.; FA Bldg. Gal., N.Y.; Grand Central Palace; Argent Gal.; Squibb & Anderson Gal., N.Y.; Gotenburg, Sweden; one-man: Norheim Gal., Brooklyn; Bonnier Gal., N.Y.

CARMACK, PAUL R.—*Cartoonist*

1 Norway St., Boston 16, Mass.; h. Longwood Towers, Brookline 46, Mass.

B. Madisonville, Ky., Dec. 18, 1895. *Studied*: AIC. *Award*: Freedom Fnd. Hon. Medal, 1951. Author, I., "The Diary of Snubs, Our Dog" (4 vols.); I., "Huttee Boy, the Elephant." Lectures: newspaper cartoons and comic strips. *Position*: Staff Cart., The Christian Science Monitor, 1925- .*

CARMICHAEL, IDA BARBOUR (Mrs.)—
Teacher, C., L., W., P.

308 Amazon Ave., Cincinnati 20, Ohio

B. Windham Center, Ontario, Canada, Nov. 1, 1884. *Studied*: Emory Univ.; Cincinnati A. Acad.; Univ. Cincinnati, B.S., M.A.; Univ. Oregon, D. Edu. *Member*: Nat. Edu. Assn.; Ohio Edu. Assn.; T. Assn., Ceramic Gld., Crafters Cl., Woman's A. Cl., Mus. Assn., all of Cincinnati; Mod. A. Soc. *Exhibited*: CM, 1938-1940, 1943, 1946, 1948-1951, 1955; Woman's A. Cl., 1931-1957; Dayton AI, 1955; Cincinnati Crafters Cl., Ohio Valley A., 1948; Cincinnati Ceramic Gld., 1955-1957; Massillon Mus. A., 1948; Butler AI, 1948; one-man: Loring Andrews Gal., Cincinnati, 1951; Closson's Gal., 1952, 1955. Author: "Consumer Education Through Art." *Position*: Formerly T., Dept. Ceramics, Walnut Hills H.S., Cincinnati, Ohio; Adult Edu., ceramics & painting, Cincinnati, Ohio, at present; Hd., A. Studio, Dayton, Ohio.

CARMICHAEL, JAE (Jane Grant Giddings)—
Painter

985 San Pasqual St., Pasadena, Cal.; also 21032 Eastman Way, Laguna Beach, Cal.

B. Hollywood, Cal., Aug. 22, 1925. *Studied*: Univ. So. California, B.A., with Francis deErdely; Claremont Col., M.F.A., with Millard Sheets, Phil Dike; Mills Col., with Roi Partridge, Raymond Puccinelli, Dong Kingman, William Gaw. *Member*: Cal. WC Soc.; Pasadena Soc. A.; Women Painters of the West; Laguna Beach AA. *Awards*: prizes, Pasadena Soc. A., 1955; Orange County Fair, 1955 (3); Pasadena A. Mus., 1954; Julia Ellsworth Ford award, 1956; Laguna Beach A. Festival, 1957. *Work*: Mills Col.; Scripps Col.; mural, Crippled Children's Soc., Conoga Park, Cal., 1955. *Exhibited*: Pasadena A. Mus., 1956; Cal. WC Soc., 1953, 1955, 1956; Los A. AA, 1956-1958; Pasadena Soc. A., 1950-1958; Women Painters of the West, 1956-1958; Pasadena Public Lib., 1956-1958; Los A. Mus. A., 1957; Madonna Festival, Adrian, Mich., 1958; Bodley Gal., N.Y., 1958; Newport Beach, Cal., 1954, 1958; AWS, 1958; Ligoa Duncan Gal., N.Y., 1958; Denver A. Mus., 1953, 1958; Butler Inst. Am. A., 1958; Cal. WC Soc., 1958; Prix de Paris Exh., Duncan Gal., N.Y., 1958; Scripps Col., 1958; Laguna Beach A. Gal., 1958; one-man: Pasadena A. Mus., 1955; Palos Verdes Gal., 1954, 1955 (2-man), 1958 (2-man); La Canada (Cal.) Lib., 1956; Westridge Sch., Pasadena, 1957. *Positions*: Instr., Jr. Mus., Pasadena A. Mus., 1953- ; Pasadena Sch. FA, 1953, 1955, 1957; adult classes, Pasadena A. Mus., 1956-57, Sch. FA, 1956-58; Seymour Sch., Pasadena, 1957; Westridge Sch. for Girls, 1957-58.

CAROTHERS, SARAH PACE (Mrs. W. Allen Rhode)—
Etcher, P., T.

13 Overbrook Rd., Catonsville 28, Md.

B. Baltimore, Md., Jan. 15, 1910. *Studied*: Maryland AI; ASL. *Member*: Nat. Lg. Am. Pen Women. *Awards*: prizes, A. Fnd., Maryland, 1945; State Exh., Annapolis, 1954 (2), 1956 (2); BMA, 1946. *Exhibited*: Southern Pr. M., 1942; Phila. Pr. Cl., 1943; SAGA, 1942-1944, 1947; LC, 1944, 1951; Mint Mus. A., 1946; Laguna Beach AA, 1946; Whyte Gal., 1942, 1943; PMG, 1941; NAD, 1944; BMA, 1941-1951; Mun. Mus. Baltimore, 1943-1952; CGA, 1951, 1952, 1956, 1957; Baltimore A. Festival, 1952-1958; Peale Mus. A., 1952-1958; Sessler Gal., Phila., Pa., 1955; one-man: Contemporary Gal., 1944; Denues Studio, 1946; Goucher Col., 1949; Vagabond Theatre, 1950, 1955 (one-man). *Position*: Instr., Garrison Forest Sch., 1952-55.

CARPENTER, FRED GREEN—*Painter, T., C.*

416 Woodlawn Ave., St. Louis 19, Mo.

B. Nashville, Tenn. Studied: St. Louis Sch. FA; Julian Acad., Paris; & with Laurens, Baschet, Royer. *Member*: St. Louis A. Gld. *Awards*: Med., Pan-Pacific Exp., 1915; St. Louis A. Gld., 1920, 1922, 1925, 1929, 1932, 1945,

1954; St. Louis State Fair, 1927, 1940; citations of merit, Washington Univ., 1955, 1957. *Work*: John Herron AI; CAM; PAFA; St. Louis hospitals, schools, libraries; USPO, Paris, Ill.; murals, Missouri State Capitol Bldg. *Exhibited*: PAFA, 1912-1936; CAM, 1912-1952; Kansas City AI; AIC. *Position*: Instr. A., St. Louis Sch. FA, Washington Univ., St. Louis, Mo., 1904-52, Emeritus, 1952- .

CARPENTER, JAMES M.—*Educator, Mus. Cur.*

Colby College; h. 1 Edgewood St., Waterville, Me.

B. Glens Falls, N.Y., Dec. 7, 1914. *Studied*: Harvard Univ., A.B., Ph.D. Contributor to The Art Bulletin. Lectures: French Painting, 1850-1950 on TV. *Position*: Instr., Colby College, Waterville, Me.

CARPENTER, MILDRED BAILEY (Mrs. Fred G.)—
Painter, W., I., T., L.

416 Woodlawn Ave., St. Louis 19, Mo.

B. St. Louis, Mo. *Studied*: St. Louis Sch. FA; Univ. Madrid; Provincetown, Mass.; Puerto Rico. *Member*: St. Louis A. Gld.; Woman's Adv. Cl.; NAWA. *Awards*: prizes, St. Louis A. Gld., 1919-1946, 1954, 1957; med., Kansas City AI; AIC; St. Louis Woman of Achievement, 1947 (1 of 3). *Work*: Christian Orphans Home, St. Louis; murals, St. Louis pub. schs., and hotels. *Exhibited*: Kansas City AI; AIC; CAM; St. Louis A. Gld.; Milwaukee AI; Springfield (Ill.) A. Mus.; Int. WC Exh. I., Children's books. *Position*: Port. Painter, Army & Navy Hospitals, USO, N.Y., 1945-49; Instr., Washington Univ. Sch. A., St. Louis, Mo.

CARRINGTON, OMAR RAYMOND—*Painter, Gr., I., E.*

Travelers Insurance Co., Washington, D.C. & Corcoran School of Art; h. 3107 Taylor St., Chevy Chase, Md.

B. Philadelphia, Pa., Oct. 16, 1904. *Studied*: Univ. Maryland, A.B.; American Univ.; Corcoran Sch. A.; PAFA; Hill Sch. A. *Member*: A. Gld. of Washington; Soc. Wash. A.; Wash. WC Cl.; Wash. SE; Landscape Cl., Wash.; Baltimore WC Cl.; AEA; Baltimore A. Union; F., PAFA. *Awards*: F., Tiffany Fnd., 1937; med., Landscape Cl., 1943, 1944, 1948, 1952; prizes, Wash. A. Cl., 1944; Soc. Wash. A., 1945, 1948, 1950; SSAL, 1945, 1947; All Maryland A. Exh., 1947, 1948. *Work*: Dallas Mus. FA.; Mint Mus. A.; BMA, and many private colls. *Exhibited*: Wash. A. Cl., 1941-1945; New Haven Paint & Clay Cl., 1936, 1950; Soc. Wash. A., 1935-1952; Wash. WC Cl., 1936-1946; Landscape Cl., 1935-1952; Wash. SE, 1937, 1938, 1941; SSAL, 1945, 1947; CGA, 1946, 1947-1950; MMA, 1950; American Univ.; Catholic Univ. Am., and in France and Switzerland. One-man: Wash. A. Cl., 1944; Mint Mus. A., 1948; BMA, 1949; Chequire House, 1949; Dupont Gal., Wash., D.C., 1950. I., Univ. Maryland publications and Naval Acad. Yearbook, 1942. *Position*: Asst. Ed., Asst. Prof., Univ. Maryland Ext. Service, 1928-42; Hd., Dept. Publ., Univ. Maryland, 1942-44; Instr., Corcoran Sch. A.; Project Dir., Graphics Branch, U.S. Dept. State, 1950-1953; Travelers Insurance Co., 1953- .*

CARROLL, JOHN—*Painter*

East Chatham, N.Y.

B. Kansas City, Kan., Aug. 14, 1892. *Studied*: with Frank Duveneck. *Awards*: prizes, PAFA, 1922, 1924; Pan-Am. Exh., 1924; med. & prize, AIC, 1927; prize, Cal. Pr. Cl., 1929; Guggenheim F., 1927; prize, Detroit Inst. A., 1935; med., Scarab Cl., 1936. *Work*: PAFA; Los A. Mus. A.; John Herron AI; Joslyn Mem.; Detroit Inst. A.; Newark Mus.; Toledo Mus. A.; WMAA; Honolulu Acad. A.; AGAA.*

CARROLL, NELLIE—*Cartoonist, Des.*

8826 Sunset Strip, Los Angeles 46, Cal.

B. Zillah, Wash., Apr. 3, 1923. *Studied*: A. Center Sch., Los Angeles. *Work*: greeting card designer; studio cards, drawings and captions distributed through gift and department stores. *Position*: A. Dir., Nellie Card Co., Los Angeles, Cal.

CARROTHERS, GRACE NEVILLE (Mrs.)—
Painter, E., Lith., T.

1315 South Norfolk St., Tulsa 5, Okla.; s. Bellaire, Mich.

B. Abington, Ind. *Studied*: with John Carlson, Anthony Thieme. *Awards*: Med., Okla. State Exh., 1938. *Work*:

N.Y.Pub.Lib.; Gibbes A. Gal., Charleston, S.C.; NGA; British Mus.; Lib. Cong.; Royal Ontario Mus., Toronto; Bibliotheque Nationale, Paris, France; Philbrook A. Center. *Exhibited*: Phila. Pr. Cl., 1932; Hoosier Salon, 1932; Northwest Pr.M., 1932; Kansas City AI, 1933; N.Y.Mun.Exh., 1937; Lib.Cong., 1936; Philbrook A. Center, 1931-1938, 1940 (one-man); Junior League Gal., Tulsa, Okla., 1932 (one-man). *Position*: Instr., Landscape Painting, Philbrook A. Center, Tulsa, Okla., 1940-52; Hd., Grace Neville Carrothers Sch. Landscape Painting, 1932-52.

CARRY, MARION KATHERINE—*Painter, T., Lith.*

Art Association, 76 Bellevue Ave.; h. 12 Friendship St., Newport, R.I.

B. Newport, R.I., Jan. 30, 1905. *Studied*: R.I.Sch.Des.; ASL. *Member*: Newport AA. *Awards*: Traveling scholarship, Newport AA, 1939, People's Prize, 1950, 1955. *Work*: R.I.Sch.Des.; many portraits in private collections. *Exhibited*: WFNY 1939; Providence AC; Newport AA; R.I.Sch.Des.; Boissevain Gal., N.Y., 1956. *Position*: Hd., Sch. A., Newport AA, Newport, R.I., 1945- .

CARSON, FRANK—*Painter, T., Cr., W.*

483 Tremont St., Boston 16, Mass.

B. Waltham, Mass., Sept. 8, 1881. *Studied*: Mass. Normal A. Sch.; Fenway A. Sch.; ASL; Boothbay (Me.) A. Colony. *Awards*: prize, Boston AC, 1924. *Work*: Berkeley (Cal.) FA; Vanderpoel Coll. *Exhibited*: PAFA; BM; Berkeley (Cal.) Lg. FA; Buffalo FA Acad.; Newport AA; Detroit Inst. A.; Provincetown AA; Gloucester SA; Boston Soc. Indp. A.; Toledo Mus. A.; Providence AC; Providence WC Cl.; BMFA; Wash. AC (one-man); Univ. Washington (one-man); Copley Soc. (one-man).

CARSON, MRS. RALPH M. *See Belle, Cecile*

CARSON, SOL KENT—*Painter, E.*

8211 MacArthur Rd., Philadelphia 18, Pa.

B. Philadelphia, Pa., June 7, 1917. *Studied*: Barnes Fnd.; Temple Univ., B.F.A., B.S. in Ed., M.Ed.; Zecker-Hahn Acad., Phila., Pa. *Member*: Eastern AA; NAEA. *Awards*: Scholarships, Tyler Sch. FA, Temple Univ.; Zecker-Hahn Acad. *Work*: Free Lib., Phila., Pa.; Temple Univ., Tyler Gal.; Temple Univ., Sch. Theology; Cornwells Heights, Pa. *Exhibited*: WFNY, 1939; MModA; Dubin Gal.; Federal A. Gal.; PAFA; Cheltenham AA; Woodmere A. Gal.; Free Lib., Phila., Pa.; Temple Univ., Tyler Gal.; Eastern AA traveling exh.; Oklahoma A. Center. Lectures: Art; Restorative Art; Color Concepts to educational clinics, State Boards and other groups. *Position*: Dir., Dept. Restorative Art, Temple Univ. Community College, 1946-1955; A. Consultant, A. Supv., Bristol Township Sch. System, at present.

CARSTENSON, CECIL C.—*Sculptor, T.*

1018 West 38th St., Kansas City, Mo.

B. Marquette, Kans., July 23, 1906. *Studied*: Kansas City AI; Omaha A. Sch. *Member*: AEA; Mid-Am. A. *Awards*: prizes, Mid-Am. A., 1950; Joslyn Mus. A.; Univ. Kansas, 1955. *Work*: Kansas City Pub. Lib.; Univ. Kansas; Salina (Kans.) Pub. Lib.; Holy Rosary Col., Chicago; Bethany Col.; St. Benedict's Col., Atchison, Kans. *Exhibited*: Denver A. Mus., 1951, 1952; Joslyn Mus. A., 1946-1952; CAM, 1948-1952; Creative A. Gal., 1951; one-man: Joslyn Mus. A., 1952; Univ. Kansas City, 1951, 1957; Mulvane A. Center, 1954; Bethany Col., 1953; Kansas City AI, 1955; Lawrence Gal., 1956; Bates Gal., 1958.

CARTER, ALBERT JOSEPH—*Museum Curator, T.*

1016 K St., Northeast, Washington 2, D.C.

B. Washington, D.C., Apr. 20, 1915. *Studied*: Howard Univ., B.S.; Columbia Univ., T. Col., M.A. in art and art edu. Exhibitions assembled & arranged: Ceramics, Textiles, Metals & Wood, 1947-48; Japanese Wood Block Color Prints, 1947-48; Contemporary Indian Paintings, 1947-48; Expressionism in Graphic Arts, 1948-49; Miniatures for Illuminated Books of the Middle Ages, 1949-50; Contemporary American Paintings, 1949-50. *Position*: Cur., Howard Univ. Art Gallery, Washington, D.C.; Instr. Comm. A., G.I. Sch., Letchers A. Center, Washington, D.C., 1946- .

CARTER, BETTY M.—*Painter, Des., T.*

Hotel New Weston, 34 East 50th St., New York 22, N.Y.

B. New York, N.Y. *Studied*: Parsons Sch. Des.; & with George Pearse Ennis, Howard Giles. *Member*: AWCS; NAWA. *Exhibited*: PAFA, 1932, 1934, 1936; AIC, 1935, 1937, 1940; BM, 1935, 1939; WFNY 1939; NAWA; AWCS; SSAL; Wash. WC Cl.; Phila. WC Cl.; Conn. Acad. FA; Palm Beach A. Center. Lectures: Painters of the Italian Renaissance. *Position*: Asst. Hd., Dept. Advertising Des., 1936-46; Hd. Dept., 1946-1954; Dir. Evening Classes, 1954- ; Instr. Painting, European branch, 1949- ; Parsons Sch. Des., New York, N.Y.; Instr., Painting, French Sch., New York, N.Y.*

CARTER, CLARENCE HOLBROOK—
Painter, E., L., Des.

Spring Mills, Milford, N.J.

B. Portsmouth, Ohio, Mar. 26, 1904. *Studied*: Cleveland Sch. A., and with Hans Hofmann. *Member*: ANA; AWS. *Awards*: prizes, Cleveland A. & Crafts, 1927-1939; Cleveland Pr. M., 1931; Butler Inst. Am. A., 1937, 1940, 1943, 1946; Carnegie Inst., 1941, 1943, 1944. *Work*: MMA; MModA; IBM; San Diego FA Gal.; Upjohn Mus., Kalamazoo, Mich.; WMAA; BM; FMA; CMA; Toledo Mus. A.; Butler Inst. Am. A.; Oberlin Col.; Nelson Gal. A.; Swope A. Gal.; Rochester Mem. A. Gal.; Arnot A. Gal.; Wooster Col. Mus.; Univ. Ohio; City of Portsmouth, Ohio; Univ. Nebraska; Lehigh Univ.; Jefferson Sch., Maplewood, N.J.; Pittsburgh Pub. Schs.; USPO, Portsmouth, Ravenna, Ohio; Cleveland Pub. Auditorium. *Exhibited*: Carnegie Inst.; PAFA; CGA; AIC; BM; CMA; VMFA; Detroit Inst. A.; Toledo Mus. A.; Nebraska AA; Nelson Gal. A.; Swope A. Gal.; DMFA; GGE, 1939; deYoung Mem. Mus.; Cal. PLH; WMAA; MModA; MMA; Arch. Lg.; Albright A. Gal.; Ft. Worth A. Center; Montclair Mus. A.; Musee de Moderne Arte, Paris; Zurich, Switzerland; Museo di Moderno Arte, Rome; Tate Gal., London; Museo de Arte Moderno, Barcelona; Belgrade, Yugoslavia and in many South American and Canadian museums; one-man: Butler Inst. Am. A.; Finley Gal.; Milwaukee A. Inst.; Sarasota AA; Grand Central A. Gal.; Ferargil Gal.; Suffolk Mus., Stony Brook, L.I.; Cleveland Inst. A.; Minneapolis Inst. A.; "Clarence Carter Week," Portsmouth, Ohio, 1950; Univ. Louisville; Arnot A. Gal.; High Mus. A., 1957; Palm Beach, Fla., 1957; New Brunswick, N.J., 1957; New Hope, Pa., 1958; Buffalo, N.Y., 1958. *Positions*: Asst. Prof., Carnegie Inst., 1938-44; Dir. A., Chautauqua Inst., N.Y. Univ., 1943; Dir., FAP for Northeastern Ohio, 1937-38; Guest Instr., Ohio Univ.; Cleveland Inst. A.; Minneapolis Sch. A.; Lehigh Univ.; Guest Instr., Atlanta A. Inst.; lectures on art in museums, colleges and art schools.

CARTER, DEAN—*Sculptor*

Virginia Polytechnic Institute; h. Blacksburg, Va.

B. Henderson, N.C., Apr. 24, 1922. *Studied*: Corcoran Sch. A.; American Univ., B.A.; Univ. Indiana, M.F.A.; Ogunquit Sch. P. & S.; Ossip Zadkine Sch. A., Paris, France. *Member*: Soc. Wash. A.; So. Highlands Handicrafts Gld.; Indianapolis AA; Blacksburg AA; Springfield A. Lg.; P. & S. of New Jersey; Boston Soc. Indp. A. *Awards*: Scholarship, American Univ., 1941; Sleicher award, 1947; Brick Store Mus., 1948; Detroit Inst. A., 1949; Huckleberry Mountain, N.C., 1950; Winston-Salem Gal.; P. & S. of New Jersey, 1951; Wash. Sculptors Group, 1951; Santa Monica, Cal., 1951; Wichita AA, 1953 (purchase). *Work*: Mary Baldwin Col.; Radford Col.; Student Union Bldg., Univ. Indiana; Cranbrook Acad. A.; Hollins Col.; Wichita AA. *Exhibited*: Wash. Sculptors Group, 1948-1955; Virginia Highlands Festival, 1954; Springfield Mus. A., 1953; BMFA, 1953; PAFA, 1954; Carnegie Inst., 1955; Sculpture Center, 1955; one-man: Hunter Gal., Chattanooga; Schneider Gal., Rome, Italy; Blacksburg, Va.; Weatherspoon Gal., Greensboro, N.C.; Univ. Virginia; The Contemporaries, N.Y.C.; Artists Mart, Wash., D.C.; Washington & Lee Univ.; Workshop Originals; Albuquerque, N.M.; New Mexico Mus. FA; Taos, N.M.; Mary Baldwin Col., Staunton, Va. *Position*: Asst. Prof., Va. Polytechnic Inst., Blacksburg, Va., 1950- .

CARTER, DUDLEY C.—*Sculptor, T.*

P.O. Box 655, Bellevue, Wash.

B. New Westminster, B.C., Canada, May 6, 1891. *Member*: SAM; Northwest Acad. A.; AEA; Northwest Inst. Sculpture. *Awards*: prizes, Music & Art Fnd., Seattle, 1956;

Bellevue A. Fair, 1956. *Work*: SAM; GGE, 1936-39; San F. Jr. Col.; Pacific Nat. Bank, Bellevue, Wash.; Lake Wilderness, Wash.; Bon Marche, Spokane; Shell Oil Co., Seattle; Wash. State Parks; Schafer Bros., Aberdeen, Wash.; Metropolitan Hotel, Denver, Colo.; Shell Refinery, Anacortes, Wash.; Bon Marche, Seattle; Golden Gate Park, San F.; Henry Gal., Seattle; Nat. Bank of Commerce, Seattle. *Exhibited*: SAM, 1932-1947, 1957; SFMA, 1936; GGE, 1939; California Centennial, 1949; Univ. Washington, 1945, 1950; Eugene, Ore., 1955; Vancouver (B.C.) A. Gal., 1956

CARTER, ESTHER FLINT (Mrs. Charles W., Jr.)— Painter, C., L., T.
140 West 16th St., New York 11, N.Y.; also Brookfield Center, Conn.

B. Winchester, N.H., Mar. 31, 1895. *Studied*: Radcliffe Col., A.B.; Univ. Minnesota; New Sch. Des., Boston, and with Guy Pene du Bois. *Member*: AEA; AAPL; Washington (Conn.) AA. *Work*: Illuminated manuscripts in private collections; easel paintings and portraits in U.S. and Japan. Port. commissions, 1937-58. *Exhibited*: Arthur Newton Gal., 1947; Munson-Williams-Proctor Inst., 1949; Ogunquit A. Center, 1954; Cayuga A. Mus.; Town Hall Cl., N.Y.; and other group shows. One-man: Springfield Mus. A., 1938; Argent Gal., 1944, 1945; Arthur Newton Gal., 1948; Danbury Mus. A., 1950; Newtown (Conn.) Lib., 1951, 1954; Ridgefield Playhouse, 1951; Brookfield Center Lib., 1952; R.F.D. Gal., Brookfield, 1958; Middle East House, N.Y.C., 1954; Jefferson Hotel, Wash., D.C., 1955; Burr Gal., 1959. Lectures on art to women's groups.

CARTER, HELENE—Illustrator
453-C Franklin Delano Roosevelt Dr., New York 2, N.Y.

B. Toronto, Canada. *Member*: A. Gld.; SI; Women's Nat. Bk. Assn.

CARTER, MARC (MARCELLUS CARTER)— Painter, S., Cart., C., Des., T., Comm. A.
31 Rosemont Blvd., White Plains, N.Y.

B. North Tarrytown, N.Y., Mar. 19, 1918. *Studied*: ASL; Westchester Workshop, and with Ruth Nickerson, Ruth Yates. *Member*: ASL; AEA; Westchester A. & Crafts Gld. *Work*: Altoona Mus. A. *Exhibited*: one-man: Wellons Gal., 1951, 1953, 1954; Arthur Brown Gal., 1951; Ann Ross Gal., 1954, 1955; Westchester A. & Crafts Gld., 1947-55. *Position*: Pres., Westchester A. & Crafts Gld., 1956-58; Instr. life drawing, Westchester County Center; A. Dir., Teleregister Corp.

CARTER, WILLIAM SYLVESTER—Painter, I.
3831 Michigan Ave.; h. 2967 Michigan Ave., Chicago, Ill.

B. St. Louis, Mo., May 5, 1909. *Studied*: AIC; Univ. Illinois. *Awards*: prizes, CAM, 1940; Atlanta Univ., 1942; South Side Community A. Center, 1943. *Work*: Atlanta Univ.; South Side Community A. Center; Barnett Aden Gal. *Exhibited*: CAM, 1940; Atlanta Univ., 1942; AIC, 1940; McMillen A. Gal., 1940; St. Louis Urban Lg., 1940-1946; South Side Community A. Center, 1941. *Position*: Instr., South Side Community A. Center, Chicago, Ill.*

CARVER, MABEL MACDONALD (Mrs. Walter L.)— Painter, Gr.
2 West 15th St.; h. 39 Fifth Ave., New York, N.Y.

B. Forest, Ill., Oct. 11, 1891. *Studied*: Wicker Sch. FA, Detroit, Mich.; Grande Chaumiere, Paris, France. *Member*: Pen & Brush Cl.; NAWA; Nat. Lg. Am. Pen Women. *Awards*: prizes, Pen & Brush Cl., 1951; Village A. Center, 1949. *Work*: St. Basil's Cathedral. *Exhibited*: NAWA; NAD; Argent Gal.; one-man: Eighth St. Gal.; Argent Gal.; Barbizon-Plaza; Pen & Brush Cl.; Village A. Center.*

CARVALLO, SUZANNE (Mrs. Julius W.)—Painter
41 West 83rd St., New York 24, N.Y.

B. Paris, France, July 1, 1883. *Exhibited*: Salon des Tuilleries; Salon d'Automne, Paris. One-man: Carstairs Gal., New York. Portraits: Alfred Steiglitz, Thomas Mann, Bruno Walter and others.

CASARELLA, EDMOND—Educator, Pr. M.
Brooklyn Museum School, Brooklyn, N.Y.
Position: Prof. Graphic Arts, Brooklyn Museum School.*

CASCIANO, AUGUST—Painter
108 Carpenter St., Providence 3, R.I.

B. Providence, R.I., July 13, 1910. *Studied*: Rhode Island Sch. Des. *Awards*: prizes, R.I. Sch. Des., 1927, 1930. *Exhibited*: Art of this Century, 1944; Lib.Cong., 1945; GGE, 1939; Providence Mus. A., 1940; Brown Univ., 1939

CASE, ANDREW—Painter, Comm., E., W.
826 West Beaver Ave., State College, Pa.

B. Tipton, Ind., July 19, 1898. *Studied*: PIASch; Pennsylvania State Univ., B.S., M.A. *Member*: Scarab Cl.; AAUP; Catholic A. Soc.; CAA; Catholic Comm. on Intellectual & Cultural Affairs. *Exhibited*: Nationally; one-man: Warwick Gal., Phila., Pa. Contributor to America; Amer-Ecclesiastical Review; Catholic Digest; Catholic World; The Lamp. *Position*: Prof. FA, Pennsylvania State University, University Park, Pa.

CASEAU, CHARLES H(ENRY)—Designer, P.
133 East 34th St., New York 16, N.Y.

B. Boston, Mass., May 2, 1880. *Studied*: BMFA Sch.; Harvard Col., with Denman Ross; ASL. *Exhibited*: Boston A. Cl.; AIC; N.Y. WC Cl.; AFA; AWS. Illus. for Mickiewicz Centenary Comm., Wash., D.C. *Position*: Indst. Des. & Advertising Illus.

CASEBIER, CECIL LANG—Painter
8134 Broadway; h. 107 Calumet Pl., San Antonio, Tex.

B. Fort Stockton, Tex., Mar. 2, 1922. *Studied*: Univ. So. California, B.F.A.; Univ. Texas, with Dan Lutz, Everett Spruce. *Member*: San Antonio A. Lg.; Texas WC Soc.; Cal. WC Soc.; CAA. *Awards*: Texas Annual, 1949, 1950, 1954, 1957, 1958; Texas WC Soc., 1950-1952, 1953, 1955, 1957; All-Texas General, 1952; San Antonio, 1952. *Work*: Ft. Worth AA; Witte Mem. Mus.; DMFA; Texas FA Assn.; stained glass windows, St. Lukes, San Antonio; Keesler USAF Hospital, Chapel, Miss.; Student Chapel, Univ. Oklahoma; Tulsa Mem., Okla. *Exhibited*: New Orleans AA, 1951; Mississippi WC Soc., 1951; Terry AI, 1952; Cal. WC Soc., 1950; Springfield WC Soc., 1949; Texas Annual, 1941-1951, 1955; Texas FA Assn., 1951; All-Texas General, 1952; CGA, 1955-1957; Butler AI, 1955; WMAA; Denver A. Mus.; Stanford Univ.; DMFA; Stained Glass Assn., Wash., D.C.

CASEY, ELIZABETH T.—Museum Curator
Rhode Island School of Design Museum of Art, 224 Benefit St., Providence, R.I.
Position: Cur., Oriental Art, Rhode Island School of Design Museum.*

CASH, HAROLD—Sculptor
Wildwood, Ga.

B. Chattanooga, Tenn., Sept. 26, 1895. *Studied*: Stanford Univ.; Univ. Virginia, B.A.; N.Y.Sch. F. & App.A; BAID. *Member*: NSS; S.Gld. *Awards*: Guggenheim F., 1930, 1931. *Exhibited*: PAFA, 1941-1943; WMAA, 1935; MModA, 1930-1934; AIC, 1932-1938; BM, 1931; SFMA; MMA.

CASS, KATHERINE DORN (KAE) (Mrs. Harry B.)— Teacher, P., L.
Cleveland Institute of Art, 11141 East Boulevard, Cleveland 6, Ohio; h. Aintree Park, Mayfield Village, Lyndhurst P.O., Cleveland 24, Ohio

B. Cleveland, Ohio, May 15, 1901. *Studied*: Cleveland Inst. A.; Julien Acad., Paris, France. *Member*: Cleveland Woman's A. Cl.; NAWA. *Work*: Mun. Coll., City of Cleveland; CMA. *Exhibited*: CMA, 1926-1958; Ohio WC Soc., 1935-1955; Women's A. Cl., 1923-1955; Cleveland Inst. A., 1940-1955. *Position*: Instr., Cleveland Inst. A.; Ashtabula A. Center; special classes, Lake Erie Col., Painesville, Ohio.

CASSADY, EDITHE JANE—Painter, T.
4940 East End Ave., Chicago 15, Ill.

B. Chicago, Ill., Aug. 22, 1906. *Studied*: Chicago Acad. FA; AIC, B.A., M.A. in Edu., and with Frederic M.

Grant, Ruth Van Sickle Ford, Guy Wiggins. *Member*: Assn. Chicago P. & S.; Conn. Acad. FA; Women's A. Salon, Chicago; A. Cl. of Chicago; Chicago Soc. A.; Ill. A. Edu. Assn.; AEA. *Awards*: prizes, Union Cl., Chicago; Conn. Acad. FA, 1947; South Side AA, 1944, 1946, 1947; Magnificent Mile Exh., Chicago, 1952; bronze med., All-Illinois Soc. FA, 1933; gold med., Assn. Chicago P. & S., 1948. *Work*: Bd. Edu., Chicago; City of Chicago Coll. *Exhibited*: AIC, 1931-1937, 1941, 1943, 1944, 1949, 1950, 1952, 1955, 1956, 1957; NAD, 1934-1936, 1938, 1944, 1945; Conn. Acad. FA, 1930-1945, 1947-1949, 1951; PAFA, 1933-1940; CGA, 1941; Women's A. Salon, 1937-1945; Assn. Chicago P. & S. 1934-1958; All-Illinois Soc. FA, 1928-1937; South Side AA, 1928-1947; Chicago Soc. A., 1948-1958; AIC, 1949, 1951; South Bend AA, 1948; Findlay Gal., 1945, 1946, 1948, 1950; Riverside Mus., 1951; Butler AI, 1953; A. Cl. of Chicago, 1938-1958; Ill. State Mus., 1941-1943, 1949-1958; North Shore A. Lg., 1954-1957. *Position*: Instr., Professional Day Sch., Hd. Jr. Sch. of the Art Inst. of Chicago, Chicago, Ill.

CASSARA, FRANK—*Painter, Pr. M.*
1122 Pomona Rd., Ann Arbor, Mich.

B. Partinico, Italy, Mar. 13, 1913. *Studied*: Detroit Sch. A.; Colorado Springs FA Center; Univ. Michigan. *Member*: Michigan Acad. A., Sc. & Let.; Michigan Pr. M.; Ann Arbor AA. *Awards*: prizes, Bay Pr. M., Berkeley, Cal., 1957; Boston Pr. M., 1957; Wichita AA, 1958; Washington (D.C.) Pr. M., 1958; South Bend AA, 1958; Western Mich. A. Exch., Grand Rapids, 1958. *Work*: Detroit Inst. A.; LC; murals: Thompson Sch., Detroit; Water Plant, East Lansing, Mich.; USPO, Sandusky, Mich.; East Detroit, Mich. *Exhibited*: AIC, 1939; Detroit Inst. A.; Rackham Gal., Ann Arbor, 1955; Michigan Pr. M. traveling exh., 1945-55; Univ. Seattle, 1955; LC, 1957; Hunterdon County A. Center, Clinton, N.J., 1958. *Position*: Asst. Prof., Univ. Michigan, Ann Arbor, Mich.; Pres., Ann Arbor AA, 1956-57.

CASSEL, JOHN HARMON—*Cartoonist, I.*
2 West 67th St., New York 23, N.Y.; s. Silvermine, Conn.

B. Nebraska City, Neb. *Studied*: Doane Col.; AIC. *Member*: SI; SC; A. Gld. I., national magazines.*

CASSIDY, INA SIZER *(Mrs. Gerald)*—
Writer, C., S., T., L.
924 Canyon Rd., Santa Fe, N.M.

B. Sizers Ranch, Bent Co., Colo., Mar. 4, 1869. *Studied*: Columbia Univ., and privately. *Member*: Spanish Colonial A. Soc.; Nat. Fed. Press Women; Nat. Lg. Am. Pen Women; Mus. New Mexico-Sch. Am. Research. *Awards*: prizes, Nat. Fed. Press Women, 1954; Child Art, 1953; New Mexico Press Women. *Work*: Writings: New Mexico Hist. Lib., Southwest Mus., Los A., Cal.; Huntington Lib., Pasadena, Cal.; Univ. New Mexico Lib., Albuquerque. *Exhibited*: Oshkosh Mus.; Oakland A. Mus.; Woman's Cl., Denver; Mus. New Mexico, 1928-1954 (one-man, 1954); New Mexico State Fair, Albuquerque, 1930-1953. Author: "This is Santa Fe" (History of Art in Santa Fe), 1955. Contributor: column: Art & Artists; New Mexico Hist. Review; New Mexico Folklore; Folksay, Norman, Okla.; New Mexico newspapers and other publications; many poetry anthologies. Lectures: Indian Art; Art in New Mexico. *Position*: Sec., Santa Fe A. Sch., 1929-31; State Pres., New Mexico Folklore Soc., 1948-49; Pres., Woman's Board, School of American Research & Museum, Santa Fe, 1946-47.*

CASSON, MEL—*Cartoonist*
435 West 23rd St., New York 11, N.Y.

B. Boston, Mass., July 25, 1920. *Studied*: ASL. *Member*: Nat. Cartoonists Soc. *Work*: Reid Col.; Univ. Kansas. *Exhibited*: MMA, 1951, 1953. Author: "Ever Since Adam and Eve." Creator: "Angel," for Chicago Sun-Times Syndicate and "It's Me, Dilly!" for Hall Syndicate.

CASTALDO, AMAYLIA *(Mrs. Amaylia C. Trebilcock)*
—*Portrait Painter*
44 West 77th St., New York 24, N.Y.

B. New York, N.Y., Aug. 12, 1906. *Studied*: ASL; & with Leon Kroll, Boardman Robinson.

CASTANO, GIOVANNI—*Painter*
71 Newbury St., Boston, Mass.; h. 245 Hunnewell St., Needham, Mass.

B. Gasperina, Calabria, Italy, Oct. 2, 1896. *Studied*: BMFA Sch., with Philip L. Hale, Leslie P. Thompson, Huger Elliott, Henry James, and others. *Member*: Boston AC; Cincinnati AC. *Work*: Brockton (Mass.) Pub. Lib.; Springfield AA; murals, First Baptist Church, Covington, Ky.; St. Peter's Church, Boston; Mercy Acad., Cincinnati, Ohio; scenic des., Cincinnati & Boston Opera House; Town Hall, Peterborough, N.H., many portraits of prominent persons. *Position*: Instr., Anatomy, BMFA Sch., Boston, Mass.

CASTEEL, HOMER, JR.—*Painter*
1408 16th St., Meridian, Miss.

B. Canton, Miss., July 25, 1919. *Studied*: George Washington Univ.; Univ. Mississippi, B.A.; AIC, M.F.A.; Escuela Pintura y Escultura. *Work*: murals: Continental Trailways; Coyoacan, Mexico; bas-relief, College Park Auditorium, Jackson, Miss. *Exhibited*: one-man, Chicago, Ill.; Mexico City; Jackson, Miss. Author, I., "The Running Bulls." *Position*: Hd. A. Dept., Meridian Jr. College, Meridian, Miss.

CASTELLON, FEDERICO—*Painter, Gr., I., T., L.*
48 Sidney Place, Brooklyn 1, N.Y.

B. Almeria, Spain, Sept. 14, 1914. *Member*: ANA; SAGA. *Awards*: F., Spanish Republic, 1934-36; Guggenheim F., 1941, 1950; Nat. Inst. A. & Let. Grant, 1950; prizes, AIC, 1938; PAFA, 1940; Assoc. Am. A., 1946; LC, 1949. *Work*: WMAA; PAFA; MModA; PMA; MMA; BM; AIC; N.Y. Pub. Lib.; LC; Newark Pub. Lib.; Princeton Univ. *Exhibited*: Weyhe Gal., 1934, 1936-1940; AFA traveling exh., 1937; AIC, 1937-1940; WMAA, 1938-1945; PAFA, 1938-1942; Carnegie Inst., 1942; one-man: Assoc. Am. A., 1952; Paris, France, 1952; Bombay, India, 1952; in 1953: Venezuela, Colombia, Peru, Chile, Bolivia, Uruguay, Argentina, Paraguay, with lectures in each under auspices of State Dept. Specialist Div. of I.E.S. I., "Shenandoah," 1941; "I Went into the Country," 1941; "Bullfinch's Mythology," 1948; "The Story of Marco Polo," 1954; "The Man Who Changed China," 1954; "The Story of J. J. Audubon," 1955; "The Little Prince," 1954; "The Life of Robert L. Stevenson," 1954. Reproduction of paintings on "The Sumerian Civilization" for Life's series "The Epic of Man," 1956, and others. *Position*: Instr., T. Col., Columbia Univ., New York, N.Y., 1948-56; Pratt Inst., Brooklyn, N.Y., 1952-56.*

CASTERTON, EDA NEMOEDE *(Mrs. W. J.)*—*Painter*
201 First National Bank Bldg., 110 South Higgins Ave., Missoula, Mont.

B. Brillion, Wis., Apr. 14, 1877. *Studied*: Minneapolis Sch. A.; AIC; Chicago Acad. FA; and in Paris, France. *Member*: ASMP; Chicago Soc. Min. P. *Awards*: Med., Pan-Pacific Exp., 1915; med., Sesqui-Centennial Exp., Phila., Pa., 1926; prize, Evanston Woman's Cl., 1942, 1944, 1946. Lg. Am. Pen Women, 1949-1951. *Work*: Smithsonian Institution; BM; Illinois State Mus. *Exhibited*: Paris Salon, 1907; Century of Progress, Chicago, 1933; Grand Central A. Gal., 1934 (one-man); CGA, 1934 (one-man).

CATAN-ROSE, RICHARD—
Painter, T., Et., Lith., S., L., I.
72-72 112th St., Forest Hills, L.I., N.Y.

B. Rochester, N.Y., Oct. 1, 1905. *Studied*: Royal Acad. FA, Italy, M.F.A.; CUASch; & with Pippo Rizzo, Antonio Quarino, J. Joseph, A. Shulkin. *Member*: AAPL; Our Lady Queen of Martyrs Church, Forest Hills, L.I., N.Y.; Royal Acad. FA, Italy; murals, Trabia, Sicily. *Exhibited*: All.A.Am., 1939, 1940; Vendome Gal., 1939, 1940, 1941; Forest Hills, L.I., N.Y., 1944-1946 (one-man); Argent Gal., 1946 (one-man); & in Europe. *Position*: Pres., Catan-Rose Inst. FA, 86-19 150th St., Jamaica 35, L.I., N.Y.

CATER, HAROLD DEAN—*Museum Director, W.*
Sleepy Hollow Restorations, Inc., Tarrytown, N.Y.; h. 429 Bellwood Ave., North Tarrytown, N.Y.

B. Syracuse, N.Y., Aug. 5, 1908. *Studied*: Syracuse Univ., A.B.; Columbia Univ., Ph.D. *Member*: Nat. Assn. State & Local History; Nat Assn. Preservation of Historic Sites & Buildings. Author: "Modern Study Guide for American

History," 1942; "Henry Adams and His Friends," 1947. *Positions*: Hist. Div., War Dept. Spec. Staff, 1946-48; Dir., Minnesota Historical Soc., 1948-55; Dir., Sleepy Hollow Restorations, Inc., Tarrytown, N.Y., 1955- .

CATLIN, STANTON L.—Asst. Art Gallery Director
Yale University Art Gallery, 1111 Chapel St., New Haven, Conn.*

CATOK, LOTTIE MEYER—Painter
45 Mayfair Drive, Longmeadow 6, Mass.
B. Hoboken, N.J. *Studied*: N.Y. Sch. F. & Appl. A.; and with Guy Wiggins; W. Lester Stevens and Jane Freeman. *Member*: Springfield Academic A.; 50 American Artists. *Awards*: prizes, Springfield A. Gld., 1932; Springfield A. Lg., 1942. *Work*: Florida Southern Col.; ports. of prominent Springfield persons in public buildings and schools. *Exhibited*: Grand Central A. Gal., 1955, 1957; Springfield Mus. FA, annually; Conn. Acad. FA, annually. One-man: Hartford, Conn., 1937; Boston, Mass., 1938; Springfield, Mass., 1940; Westfield, Conn., 1941.

CAVALLI, DICK—Cartoonist
Sleepy Hollow Rd., New Canaan, Conn.
B. New York, N.Y., Sept. 28, 1923. *Member*: Nat. Cartoonists Soc. *Exhibited*: Punch exh. of Humor, London, England, 1953. Contributor to: Sat. Eve. Post, Collier's, Look, This Week, True, Wall Street Journal, Sports Illustrated, American Weekly and to many foreign magazines. Cartoons have appeared in numerous books, anthologies and cartoon collections. NEA Service syndicated comic strip, "Morty Meekle." Assisted in preparation of text books for Famous Cartoonists Course, Famous Artists Schools.

CAVALLITO, ALBINO—Sculptor
261 Mulberry St., New York, N.Y.
B. Cocconato, Italy, Feb. 24, 1905. *Studied*: Trenton (N.J.) Sch. Indst. A.; BAID; Fontainebleau Sch. FA, and with Jose de Creeft. *Member*: F., NSS; S. Gld.; Audubon A.; All.A.Am. *Awards*: prizes, Nat. Inst. A. & Let., 1953; NAD, 1954; Arch. Lg., 1954; Hudson Valley AA, 1955; NSS, 1957; Audubon A., 1956; gold med., All. A. Am., 1954. *Work*: AGAA; mural, USPO, Kenovia, W. Va. *Exhibited*: NAD; AIC; WMAA; DMFA; BM; MMA; S. Gld.; Nat. Inst. A. & Let.; Arch. Lg.; Hudson Valley AA; Audubon A.; All. A. Am.

CAVANNA, ELISE (Mrs. James B. Welton)— Painter, I.
2847 Effie St., Los Angeles 26, Cal.
B. Philadelphia, Pa. *Studied*: PAFA. *Awards*: prize, Ebell Cl., Los A. *Work*: Los A. Mus. A.; USPO, Oceanside, Cal. *Exhibited*: WFNY 1939; 50 Prints of the Year, 1933-1935; WMAA, 1955; Sao Paulo, 1956; one-man: Antheil Gal., Hollywood, Cal.; Forsyte Gal., Hollywood, Cal.; John Heller Gal., N.Y.. I., "Valdemar," 1938; "Fit for a King," 1939; "Elise"; "Looking Backward," 1941; Author, I., (with James B. Welton) "Gourmet Cookery for a Low Fat Diet."

CAWEIN, KATHRIN—Etcher, Eng., Lith.
35 Mountain Rd., Pleasantville, N.Y.
B. New London, Conn., May 9, 1895. *Studied*: ASL, with George Bridgman, Allen Lewis, Harry Wickey. *Member*: SAGA; Chicago Soc. Et.; NAWA; Northwest Pr. M. *Awards*: prizes, SAGA, 1936; Village A. Center, 1944; NAWA, 1947; Pleasantville Woman's Cl., 1949, 1953; Westchester Fed. Women's Cl., 1950. *Work*: MMA; Pa. State (Mack Mem. Coll.); St. Mark's Church, Van Nuys, Cal. (Book of Remembrance). *Exhibited*: SAGA; NAWA; national print shows in U.S. and in Milan, Paris, London and South America; SAGA rotary exh., England, 1954.

CECERE, ADA RASARIO—Painter, T.
436 West 38th St.; h. 240 Waverly Pl., New York 14, N.Y.
B. New York, N.Y. *Studied*: ASL; NAD; BAID. *Member*: NAWA; AWS; Audubon A.; Arch. Lg.; Pen & Brush Cl.; All. A. Am.; Knickerbocker A. *Awards*: Treas. Dept. mural for S.S. Pres. Jackson, 1941; prizes, NAWA, 1943,

1946, 1950, 1951, 1953, 1958 and med. hon., 1955; Pen & Brush Cl., 1950, 1951, 1953, 1955. *Work*: murals, Hyde Park Restaurant; Broadway Central Hotel; Hotel Newton, etc. *Exhibited*: BM, 1936; AWS, 1928-1933, 1946, 1952-1958; NAWA, 1930-1958; Arch. Lg., 1928-1933; Ferargil Gal.; Argent Gal., 1930-1958; Newport AA, 1944; Dayton AI, 1945; Audubon A., 1948-1955; Albright A. Gal., 1951; Pen & Brush Cl., 1953, 1955, 1958. Represented in many private collections.

CECERE, GAETANO—Sculptor, E., L.
436 West 38th St.; h. 240 Waverly Pl., New York 14, N.Y.
B. New York, N.Y., Nov. 26, 1894. *Studied*: NAD; BAID; Am. Acad. in Rome. *Member*: NA; NSS. *Awards*: prizes, NAD, 1924; AIC, 1927; PAFA, 1930; Garden Cl. of Am., 1929, 1930; NSS, 1935; F., Am. Acad. in Rome. *Work*: MMA; Numismatic Mus., N.Y.; plaques, U.S. Capitol, Wash., D.C.; reliefs, Fed. Reserve Bank, Jacksonville, Fla.; Brookgreen Gardens, S.C.; Norton Gal., West Palm Beach, Fla.; War mem., Clifton, Plainfield, Princeton, N.J.; port. monuments, Lincoln Mem. Bridge, Milwaukee, Wis.; State of Texas; State of Montana. *Exhibited*: NAD, 1924-1958; PAFA, 1924-1958; AIC, 1924-1927; WMAA, 1934; MMA, 1935, 1951; CAM, 1942-1946; Arch.L., 1924-1933; NSS, 1924-1958. Lectures: Contemporary & Ecclesiastical Sculpture. *Position*: Assoc. Prof., A., Mary Washington Col., Fredericksburg, Va.

CELENTANO, DANIEL RALPH—Painter, Des.
P.O. Box 94, Farmingdale, N.Y.; h. North Chestnut St., Massapequa, N.Y.
B. New York, N.Y., Dec. 21, 1902. *Studied*: Parsons Sch. Des.; NAD; & with Charles Hawthorne, Howard Giles, Ivan Olinsky. *Awards*: prize, Nassau County A. Lg., 1934. *Work*: WMAA; murals, Flushing Lib.; P.S. No. 150, Sunnyside, L.I., N.Y.; USPO, Vadalia, Ga.; Grumman Aircraft Corp., Bethpage, L.I., N.Y. *Exhibited*: BM, 1935; CGA, 1937-1939; Detroit Inst. A., 1937; PAFA, 1936-1942; AIC, 1937-1942; Carnegie Inst., 1937; WMAA; GGE, 1939; CAM; VMFA; Inst. Mod. A., Boston; Walker A. Center, 1939 (one-man); Ferargil Gal.*

CERVANTEZ, PEDRO L.—Painter, Comm. A.
821 West 5th St., Clovis, N.M.
B. Wilcox, Ariz., May 19, 1915. *Studied*: Eastern New Mexico Univ.; Phillips Comm. Sch.; Hill & Canyon Sch. A.; and with R. V. Hunter. *Member*: Eastern N.M. Univ. A. Cl.; Clovis A. Lg.; Roosevelt County FA Soc. *Awards*: prizes, MModA, 1938; Paris Int. Exh., 1939; Stanford, Cal., 1952; Roswell Mus., 1953; Clovis, N.M., 1953. *Work*: MModA; DMFA, and in private colls. *Exhibited*: Latham Fnd., 1952; Terry AI, 1952; MModA, 1938; WFNY 1939; Eastern N.M. Univ., 1956, 1957; Roosevelt County Mus.; DMFA; WMAA; Colorado Springs FA Center; Albuquerque State Fair; Roswell Mus.; Mus. New Mexico, 1956-1958; Art:USA, 1958.

CHACE, DOROTHEA (Mrs. Peter Dalton)— Painter, T.
114 River Rd., Nyack, N.Y.
B. Buffalo, N.Y. *Studied*: Albright A. Gal. Sch.; ASL. *Member*: NAWA; Woodstock AA. *Awards*: prizes, Wichita A. Mus., 1937; NAWA, 1935. *Work*: in private colls. *Exhibited*: GGE, 1939; MMA, 1942; Carnegie Inst., 1941; CGA, 1937, 1939; AIC, 1938-1944; NAD, 1939, 1940, 1942, 1944; PAFA, 1938; VFMA, 1938, 1940, 1942; Portraits, Inc., 1946; Toledo Mus. A., 1938-1940; CM, 1939; Levitt Gal.; Woodstock A. Gal. *Position*: Instr. A., Bennett Jr. Col., Millbrook, N.Y., 1920-45.

CHACE, LESTER MERTON, JR.—Portrait Painter
314 West 107th St., New York 25, N.Y.
B. Pekin, Ill., Sept. 22, 1925. *Studied*: Columbia Col., A.B.; Columbia Sch. P. & Sc. *Work*: Columbia Univ. Cl. *Exhibited*: Portraits, Inc., annually. Lectures: Development of Techniques in Portrait Painting.

CHADBOURN, ALFRED CHENEY—Painter
Pond Rd., Wilton, Conn.
B. Smyrna, Turkey, Oct. 5, 1921. *Studied*: Chouinard AI, Los Angeles; Ecole des Beaux-Arts, Paris, France; Acad-

emie de la Grande Chaumiere, Paris, France. *Work*: Los A. Mus. A.; AIC; BMFA. *Exhibited*: Les Independents, Paris, 1950, 1951; Salon d'Automne, Paris, 1950, 1951; PAFA, 1953; BMFA, 1954; Los A. Mus. A., 1956; AIC, 1956; NAD, 1954-1956; Wadsworth Atheneum, 1957; Butler Inst. Am. A., 1958; Portland (Me.) Mus. A., 1958; one-man: Galerie Creuze, Paris, 1951; deCordova & Dana Mus. A., 1952; Kipnis Gal., Westport, Conn., 1952, 1954; Grand Central Moderns, N.Y.C., 1954; Obelisk Gal., Wash., D.C., 1958. *Positions*: Instr. Painting, Queens Col., New York, N.Y.; Famous Artists Schs., Westport, Conn.

CHAET, BERNARD R.—*Painter, E.*
885 Indian Hill Rd., Orange, Conn.

B. Boston, Mass., Mar. 7, 1924. *Studied*: BMFA Sch.; Tufts Col., B.S. in Edu. *Awards*: Anonymous award, Boston, for European study, 1949-50; Silvermine Gld. A., 1955; New Haven A. Festival, 1958; Sharon (Conn.) A. Fnd., 1958. *Exhibited*: Los A. Mus. A., 1945; Inst. Mod. A., Boston, 1943; Detroit Inst. A., 1949; Springfield Mus. A., 1950; Univ. Illinois, 1951, 1953; Cornell Col., 1951; Ft. Worth Mus. A., 1951; MIT, 1951; Inst. Contemp. A., Boston, 1954, 1957; MModA, 1956; Univ. Arkansas, 1955; BM, 1955, 1957; one-man: Boris Mirski Gal., N.Y., 1946, 1951, 1955, 1957; Bertha Schaefer Gal., 1954. Lectures: "Expressionism," Boston Univ.; "Landscape Space," Smith Col. Catalogue and Selection for "20th Century Drawings"—An Exhibition, Yale Univ. A. Gal., 1955. *Position*: Asst. Prof. Drawing & Painting, Dept. A., Yale Univ., New Haven, Conn., 1951- ; Contributing Editor, Arts magazine, monthly column, 1956- .

CHALIAPIN, BORIS—*Painter*
38 Central Park South, New York 19, N.Y.
Member: SI.

CHAMALIAN, LILLIAN—*Illustrator*
500 East 80th St., New York 21, N.Y.

B. New York, N.Y. *Studied*: ASL; Parsons Sch. Des. *Member*: A.Gld.; Newspaper Gld. Illus., The New Yorker, Harper's Bazaar, Vogue, & other magazines. *Work*: N.Y. Pub. Lib.

CHAMBERLAIN, SAMUEL—*Etcher, Lith., W., E., L.*
5 Tucker St., Marblehead, Mass.

B. Cresco, Iowa, Oct. 28, 1895. *Studied*: Univ. Washington; MIT; Royal Col. A., London; & with Edouard Leon, Paris. *Member*: NA; SAGA; Am. Acad. A. & Sc.; Chicago SE. *Awards*: Guggenheim F., 1926; Kate W. Arms prize. *Work*: Lib.Cong.; N.Y.Pub.Lib.; MMA; BMFA; AIC; British Mus., London; Victoria & Albert Mus., London; Bibliotheque Nationale, Paris. *Exhibited*: NAD, annually; various etching exh. Author, I., "France Will Live Again," 1940; "Fair is Our Land," 1942; "Bouquet de France," 1952; "Soft Skies of France," 1954; "Nantucket," 1952; "Italian Bouquet," 1958. Contributor to Antiques Magazine. Lectures: Technique of Etching, Drypoint, Softground Etching.

CHAMBERLAIN, WYNN—*Painter*
14 East 52nd St., New York 22, N.Y.

B. Minneapolis, Minn., May 19, 1929. *Studied*: Minneapolis Sch. A.; Univ. Idaho, B.A.; Univ. Wisconsin, M.S. *Work*: Sarah Roby Fnd.; WMAA. *Exhibited*: PAFA, 1953; Walker A. Center, 1951, 1954; WMAA, 1955; Edwin Hewitt Gal., 1954, 1957 (one-man); DeCordova & Dana Mus., 1954; Colorado Springs FA Center, 1955; Denver A. Mus., 1955; Yale Univ. Gal., 1955, 1957; Phila. A. All.; Lane Gal., Los Angeles; R.I. Sch. Des.; Deerfield Acad.; Provincetown A. Festival; Spoleto Festival of Two Worlds, Spoleto, Italy, 1958.

CHAMBERLIN, F(RANK) TOLLES—*Painter, S., Et., T.*
223 South Catalina Ave., Pasadena 5, Cal.

B. San Francisco, Cal., Mar. 10, 1873. *Studied*: ASL; & with Dwight W. Tryon, George Bridgman, George de Forest Brush. *Member*: BAID (hon.); Gld. Book Workers (hon.); Cal. AC; Cal. WC Soc.; Cal. Pr. M.; Pasadena SA. *Awards*: Prix de Rome, 1909-1912; F., Am. Acad. in Rome, 1911; prizes, Arch. L., 1914; Pasadena AI, 1934; Acad. Western Painters, 1935; Terry AI, 1952; Soc. A. of the Southwest, Los A., 1940. *Work*: Peabody Inst., Balti-

more; New Rochelle Pub. Lib.; Detroit Inst. A.; McKinley Jr. H.S., Pasadena, Cal.; Los A. Mus. A. *Exhibited*: Arch. Lg., 1913, 1914, 1920; NAD; PAFA; AIC; Pan-Pacific Exp., 1915; GGE, 1939; Palace Legion Honor, 1929; Pasadena SA, 1924-1946; Pasadena AI, 1934; Fnd. Western A., 1935-1940; Cal. AC; Cal. WC Soc.; Scripps Col., Claremont, Cal., 1937. Lectures: Italian Renaissance. *Position*: Former Instr., BAID, Columbia Univ., Univ. So. Cal., Chouinard AI and others.*

CHAMBERLIN, HELEN—*Illustrator, P.*
34-24 82nd St., Jackson Heights 72, N.Y.

B. Grand Rapids, Mich. *Studied*: AIC, and with Charles Hawthorne. *Member*: ASL; Knickerbocker A.; AAPL; Catherine Lorillard Wolfe A. Cl.; Jackson Heights A. Cl. *Awards*: prize, Knickerbocker A., 1952. *Exhibited*: Barbizon Hotel, 1948, 1955-1958 (one-man); Audubon A., 1954; Knickerbocker A., 1953-1958; AAPL, 1957, 1958; Catherine L. Wolfe A. Cl., 1957, 1958; NAC, 1956, 1957. Illus., "Princess Hildegarde"; "English Fairy Tales"; "French Fairy Tales," and others.

CHAMBERLIN, KATHARINE BEECHER STETSON.
See Stetson, Katharine Beecher

CHAMBERS, ROBERT L.—*Illustrator*
232 East 40th St., New York 16, N.Y.
Member: SI.*

CHAMPANIER, ABRAM AUGUST—*Painter, Des., T., L.*
Woodstock, N.Y.

B. Jan. 4, 1899. *Studied*: with Kenneth Hayes Miller, F. Luis Mora, George Bridgman. *Member*: NSMP; Woodstock AA; AFA. *Work*: murals, Wanamakers, Phila., Pa.; Cotton Exchange Bldg., N.Y.; Int. Tel. & Tel. Bldg., N.Y.; Breakers Hotel, Palm Beach, Fla.; Roxy Theatre, N.Y.; Nat. City Bank, N.Y.; Paramount Theatre, N.Y.; St. James Theatre, N.Y.; N.Y. Athletic Cl.; DeWitt Clinton Hotel, Albany, N.Y.; Children's Ward, Gouvernour Hospital, N.Y.; Spanish Bldg., WFNY 1939; and many murals and portraits in private collections. *Exhibited*: Whitney Cl., 1926-1929; Highland Park Mus., Dallas, Tex., 1930; Woodstock AA, 1926- ; Montclair Mus. A.; one-man: Morton Gal., 1928, 1930. *Position*: Dir., Owner, Saxton Fells Sch. A.; Child-Life Wallpaper Co.*

CHAMPLAIN, DUANE—*Sculptor*
North Main St., Essex, Conn.

B. Black Mountain, N.C., Apr. 20, 1889. *Studied*: with A. A. Weinman, I. Konti, A. Stirling Calder, Hermon A. MacNeil. *Member*: F., NSS; Lyme AA; Essex AA. *Awards*: prize, NAD, 1913; med., Pan Pacific Exp., 1915; BAID. *Work*: Mem. tablet, Peekskill, N.Y., Jamaica, L.I., N.Y.; USPO, Forest City, N.C.*

CHANASE, DANE—*Painter, Eng.*
3844 Atlantic Ave., Brooklyn 24, N.Y.

B. Italy, Oct. 21, 1896. *Studied*: with George Bridgman, Paul Baudouin. *Member*: AEA. *Awards*: med., French Govt., 1930; prizes, Int. Aeronautical A. Exh., 1937; Am. A. Group, 1950. *Work*: Mun. A. Coll., Paris; Los A. Mus. A.; Bezalel Nat. Mus., Palestine; BM; LC; N.Y. Pub. Lib.; murals, Sch. Aviation Trades; Welfare Hospital, N.Y. *Exhibited*: Paris, France, 1931 (one-man); Arch. Lg.; NSMP; BM; SAGA; WMAA; Art:USA, 1958.

CHANDLER, JOHN WILLIAM—*Educator*
2 Coolidge Ave., Concord, N.H.; w. Lycoming College, Williamsport, Pa.

B. Concord, N.H., Sept. 28, 1910. *Studied*: Exeter Sch. A., Boston; Manchester (N.H.) Inst. A. & Sc.; St. Anselm's Col., A.B.; Boston Univ., M.E.; further study at Harvard, Columbia Univs., and abroad; and with Aldro T. Hibbard. *Member*: New Hampshire AA; Pa. Gld. of Craftsmen; CAA. *Award*: prize, Currier Gal. A., 1947. *Exhibited*: Pasadena AI, 1946; New Hampshire AA, 1941-1945; New England Prep. Schools, 1950-51; Keene T. Col., Keene, N.H., 1951 (one-man); Jordan-Marsh, Boston, 1944, 1945; Currier Gal. A., 1947; de Cordova & Dana Mus., 1952; Symphony Hall, Boston; Bucknell Univ.; BMFA; Nebraska Wesleyan, 1958; Everhart Mus. A., 1958. Lectures on Design; Folk Art, to civic and church groups. Contributor articles to Hobbies magazine. *Position*: Instr. & Exec. Dir., 1933-46, Dept. FA, Manchester Inst. A. & Sc., Manchester, N.H.; Acting Dir., Currier Gal. A., 1946; Asst. Prof., Dept. A., Lycoming Col., 1952- .

CHAPEL, GUY M.—Painter
3919 North Kenneth Ave., Chicago 41, Ill.

B. Detroit, Mich., Jan. 30, 1871. *Studied*: with George E. Hopkins. *Member*: Palette & Chisel Acad. FA, Chicago, Ill. *Work*: Vanderpoel Coll.; Chicago Pub. Schs.*

CHAPIN, CORNELIA VAN AUKEN—Sculptor, L.
Wells Hill Rd., Lakeville, Conn.

B. Waterford, Conn., Aug. 7, 1893. *Studied*: with Mateo Hernandez, in Paris. *Member*: NA; NSS; All. A. Am.; NAC; Salon d'Automne, Paris. *Awards*: prizes, NAWA, 1936; Paris Int., 1937; AAPL, 1939; Pen & Brush Cl., 1942-1945; All. A. Am., 1941-1945; Meriden, Conn., 1951. *Work*: S., Cathedral St. John the Divine, N.Y.; Rittenhouse Square, Phila., Pa.; IBM; Dumbarton Oaks, Wash., D.C.; Brookgreen Gardens, S.C.; CGA; BM; Springfield A. Mus.; PAFA; Nat. Zoological Gardens, Wash., D.C. *Exhibited*: WFNY 1939; GGE, 1939; Paris Salon, 1937; PMA, 1939, 1949; PAFA, 1938-1946; NAD, 1933-1945; Los A. Mus. A.; SFMA; Montclair A. Mus., 1940-1944; WMAA, 1940-1942; MMA, 1942; Washington (Conn.) A. Group; Kent (Conn.) AA; Springfield A. Mus., and others, 1952-58. Lectures: Aspects of Modern Sculpture. *Position*: Sculptor Member, N.Y. City Art Commission, 1951-53.

CHAPIN, FRANCIS—Painter, Lith.
347 Menomonee St., Chicago 14, Ill.

B. Bristol, Ohio, Feb. 14, 1899. *Studied*: Washington & Jefferson Col., B.S.; AIC. *Member*: NAD. *Awards*: CGA, 1952; PAFA, 1949, 1953; Bryan Lathrop F., AIC; prizes and medal, AIC, 1933, 1945, 1950. *Work*: AIC; PAFA; Norton Gal. A.; Phillips Acad.; BM; MMA; PMA; John Herron AI; Notre Dame, Oregon and Syracuse Univs., and others. *Exhibited*: Salon d'Automne, Paris; MModA, 1942; AIC; Carnegie Inst.; PAFA; CGA. *Position*: Faculty, AIC, 1929-46; Dir., AIC Summer Sch., 1941-46; Res. A., Univ. Georgia, 1951-53; Visiting Artist, Atlanta AI, 1954, John Herron AI, 1938, 1958.

CHAPMAN, CHARLES SHEPARD—Painter, Lith., L., T.
156 Sylvan Ave., Leonia, N.J.

B. Morristown, N.Y., June 2, 1879. *Studied*: with William Chase, W. Appleton Clark. *Member*: NA; SC; NAC. *Awards*: Prizes, NAD, 1917, 1921, 1924, 1938; SC, 1910, 1911, 1917, 1920, 1921-1925, 1929; Montclair A. Mus., 1935, 1936, med., Paris Exp., 1937. *Work*: NGA; MMA; CMA; Amherst Col.; murals, USPO, Holidays Cove, W. Va.; M.E., Church, Leonia, N.J.; Roosevelt Sch., Englewood, N.J.; Am. Mus. Natural Hist., N.Y. *Exhibited*: NAD, annually; PAFA; Lib.Cong.; N.Y.Pub.Lib.; Montclair A. Mus.; Newark Mus.; Ridgewood AA; CGA; CMA; NGA. Illus., "T. Tembarom"; & other books. Lectures: Fundamentals of Art & Reproduction.*

CHAPMAN, DAVE—Industrial Designer
420 North Michigan Ave.; h. 568 Hawthorne Pl., Chicago 13, Ill.

B. Gilman, Ill., Jan. 30, 1909. *Studied*: Armour Inst. Tech., B.S. in Arch. *Member*: F., Am. Soc. Indst. Des. (Bd. Dirs., Past Pres.); 27 Designers; AIC (Life). *Awards*: Des. award medal, IDI, 1954. *Exhibited*: Phila. A. All., 1945, 1946. Lectures on phases of industrial design. *Position*: Hd., Products Des. Div., Montgomery Ward & Co., 1934-36; Pres., Dave Chapman, Inc., Industrial Design, 1936- ; Pres., Design Research, Inc., 1955- .

CHAPMAN, EDMUND HAUPT—Educator
Western Reserve University, Cleveland 6, Ohio; h. R.D. #1, Chardon, Ohio

B. New Haven, Conn., Aug. 14, 1906. *Studied*: Yale Univ., M.A., Ph. B.; N.Y. Univ., Ph. D. *Member*: CAA; Soc. Architectural Historians; AAUP. Contributor to College Art Journal; Journal of the Soc. of Arch. Historians. *Positions*: Instr., A. Hist., Univ. Colorado, 1930-37; Goucher Col., 1938-41; Prof., Western Reserve Univ., Cleveland, Ohio, 1946- .

CHAPMAN, FREDERICK T.—Illustrator
Mahwah, N.J.

B. Windsor, Cal. 1887. *Studied*: ASL, with George Bridgman. *Member*: F., Military Collectors & Hist. *Work*: Smithsonian Inst.; dioramas of battle scenes, West Point Military Acad. Mus. Illustrations for national magazines, adult and children's books, and textbooks for leading publishers; illus. for History of Virginia, for Va. State Bd. of Edu., 1957.

CHAPMAN, HOWARD EUGENE—Cartoonist, P.
10 Wingfield Place, Alexandria, Va.

B. Martinsburg, W. Va., Dec. 20, 1913. *Studied*: Corcoran Sch. A., with Richard Lahey; George Washington Univ., B.S. in Edu.; Tiffany Fnd., with Hobart Nichols. *Member*: Landscape Cl., Wash. *Awards*: bronze med., Wash. A. Cl., 1948; scholarship, Tiffany Fnd.; prize, Washington County Mus. FA, Hagerstown, Md., 1939. *Work*: CGA. *Exhibited*: CGA, 1948-1951; Smithsonian Inst., 1948; Wash. A. Cl., 1948; Arlington Jewish Civic Center, Arlington, Va., 1952 (one-man). *Positions*: A.Dir., Congressional Quarterly News Features, Wash., D.C.; Creator-A. Dir., Agri-Graphics; Creator, Dir., Association Art Aids, Wash., D.C.; Ed. Cartoons for major farm publications; Des., Consultant, trade association communications.

CHAPMAN, KENNETH M(ILTON)—
Educator, W., I., L., P.
Laboratory of Anthropology; h. P.O. Box 789, Santa Fé, N.M.

B. Ligonier, Ind., July 13, 1875. *Studied*: AIC; ASL. *Awards*: Hon. deg., Litt. D., Univ. Arizona, 1951; L. H. D., Univ. New Mexico, 1952; D.F.A., Art Inst. Chicago, 1953. *Member*: Am. Assn. for Advancement of Sc.; Archaeological Inst. Am.; Am. Anthropological Assn.; Soc. for Am. Archaeology. *Work*: murals, St. Francis auditorium, Mus. of New Mexico, Santa Fé. Author, I., "Pueblo Indian Pottery," Vol. I, 1933, Vol. II, 1936; "The Pottery of Santo Domingo Pueblo," 1936. Contributor to: Art and Archaeology, School Arts, & other publications. Lectures: Arts of the American Indians. *Position*: Sec., Cur., Asst. Dir., Mus. of New Mexico, 1909-29; Sec., Cur., Acting Dir., Dir., Research Assoc., Laboratory of Anthropology, Santa Fé, N.M., 1929- ; Instr., Prof., Prof. Emeritus, of Indian Art, Univ. New Mexico, Santa Fé, 1926- .

CHAPMAN, WILLIAM McKISSACK—
Consultant on Art Films, W., L., Editor
420 Lexington Ave., New York, N.Y.; h. New Hope, Pa.

B. New York, N.Y., Aug. 9, 1905. Produced film "Lascaux, Cradle of Man's Art," 1949. Lectures on Lascaux, art schools and museums. Conducted special course at New School for Social Research, New York, N.Y., entitled "Art in Motion," 1952, 1953. Founder of first Art Film Festival, Woodstock, N.Y., 1951; Hunter College, 1953. *Positions*: Paris Correspondent for Time and Life magazines, 1946-47; European Ed., Life magazine's Western Civilization series, 1947-48; V.Pres., First Int. Art Film Congress, Paris, France, 1948; Ed., Films on Art, 1952; Cur., Art Film Library, AGAA, Andover, Mass.; Sr. Editor, House & Garden, 1955- .*

CHAPPELL, WARREN—Illustrator, Des., Gr.
James St., Norwalk, Conn.

B. Richmond, Va., July 9, 1904. *Studied*: Univ. Richmond, B.A.; ASL; Colorado Springs FA Center, and in Germany. With Boardman Robinson and Rudolf Koch. Author: "The Anatomy of Lettering," 1935; Illus., "Tom Jones"; "The Tragedies of Shakespeare"; "The Complete Novels of Jane Austen," and others. Contributor to The Dolphin; Virginia Quarterly Review. Designer: Lydian and Trajanus type.

CHARLES, CLAYTON (HENRY)—Sculptor, E., P., L.
University of Miami, Coral Gables, Fla.; h. 5835 Southwest 87th Ave., Miami 43, Fla.

B. Goodman, Wis., Sept. 11, 1913. *Studied*: Univ. Wisconsin, B.A., M.A., with Wolfgang Stechow, Oskar Hagen, John Kienitz, James Watrous. *Member*: AEA. *Awards*: Milwaukee AI, 1950; Wisconsin Salon, 1947; Wisconsin Ann., 1939. *Work*: IBM; City of Milwaukee; Univ. Wisconsin; Beloit Col.; Gimbel's Wisconsin Coll.; North Carolina State A. Soc.; arch. sc., South Florida State Hospital. *Exhibited*: Grand Central A. Gal., 1947; AIC, 1949; Wis. Salon, 1939-1942, 1948-1950; Milwaukee AI, 1939-1942, 1947; Gimbels, 1949. *Positions*: Edu. Dir., Milwaukee AI, 1946-47; Assoc. Prof., 1947-49, Chm. Dept. A., 1949-51, Beloit Col.; Prof., Chm. Dept. A., Univ. Miami, Coral Gables, Fla., 1951- .

CHARLES, SAM—*Painter*
228 Grove St., Wellesley 81, Mass.

B. Agawam, Mass., May 18, 1887. *Member*: Inst. Mod. A., Boston. *Exhibited*: Inst. Mod. A., 1945, 1946; AGAA, 1943; PAFA, 1937, 1941, 1942; Ogunquit AA; Gloucester Soc. A.; Provincetown AA; Boston A. Cl.; Grace Horne Gal.; Marie Sterner Gal.; Doll & Richards, Boston, 1950, 1953, 1954, 1956; Kenneth Taylor Gal., Nantucket, Mass.

CHARLOT, JEAN—*Painter, Gr., E., I., W., L.*
University Hawaii Art Department; h. 5002 Kahala Ave., Honolulu, Hawaii

B. Paris, France, Feb. 7, 1898. *Studied*: Lycee Condorcet, Paris. *Member*: AIGA; AEA; P. & S. of Hawaii; SAGA; Pr. M. of Hawaii. *Awards*: Guggenheim F., 1945-1947; Hon. Deg., D.F.A., Grinnell Col., 1946; Hon. Deg. LL.D., St. Mary's Col., 1956; Ryerson L., Yale Univ., 1948; prizes, Los A. County Fair, 1949; Honolulu Acad. A., and many others. *Work*: MModA; Rochester Mem. A. Gal.; DMFA; SMFA; Honolulu Acad. A.; MMA; AIC; San Diego FA Soc., and abroad; frescoes: Mexican Govt.; Church of St. Bridgit, Peapack, N.J.; Univ. Georgia FA Bldg.; Arizona State Col.; Univ. Hawaii; Bishop Bank, Waikiki, Hawaii; churches in Kohala, Honolulu, Lincoln Park, Mich.; two series of The Way of the Cross in tile, in churches in Honolulu and Kauai, Hawaii; frescoes, FA Bldg., St. Mary's Col., Notre Dame, Ind., Univ. Notre Dame, South Bend, Ind.; murals, Des Moines FA Center; St. Catherine's Church, Kauai; Hawaiian Village Hotel, Waikiki; St. Leonard Friary, Centerville, Ohio. *Exhibited*: principal museums in the U.S. and abroad. Author: "Art from the Mayans to Disney"; "Charlot Murals in Georgia"; "Dance of Death"; "Art-Making From Mexico to China." Illus., "Book of Christopher Columbus"; "Characters of the Reformation"; "Pageant of the Popes"; "Carmen"; "El Indio"; "Henry the Sixth," Part 3; "Conversational Hawaiian"; children's books: "Sun, Moon and Rabbit"; "Tito's Hats"; "Two Little Trains"; "Fox Eyes"; "Secret of the Andes"; "A Hero by Mistake"; "Martin de Porres, Hero"; "The Poppy Seeds"; "Our Lady of Guadalupe"; "Sneakers"; "Dumb Juan," and many others. Portfolios of lithographs and woodcuts published. I., Sheed and Ward's "Own Trumpet" (quarterly). *Position*: Prof., Dept. A., Univ. Hawaii, Honolulu, Hawaii.

CHARMAN, (FREDERICK) MONTAGUE—
Educator, P., Des., L., W.
Syracuse University; h. 571 Cumberland Ave., Syracuse 10, N.Y.

B. London, England, Apr. 6, 1894. *Studied*: London, England with Sidney Haward. *Member*: AWS; Phila. WC Cl.; Assoc. A. Syracuse; Audubon A.; F., Intl. Inst. A. & Lets., 1958. *Awards*: prizes, Syracuse Mus. FA, 1929; Assoc. A. Syracuse, 1935, 1945; Syracuse Hist. Soc., 1943. *Work*: Syracuse Mus. FA; Solvay H.S., N.Y.; Springville (Utah) A. Soc.; Salt Lake City Mun. Coll.; Syracuse Univ.; Brigham Young Univ.; Agricultural Col., Cedar City, Utah; Brooks Mem. Mus., Memphis, Tenn. *Exhibited*: Phila. WC Cl., annually; AWS, annually; Phila. A. All.; Baltimore WC Cl.; AIC; Audubon A.; Syracuse Mus. FA; Rochester Mem. A. Gal.; Arnot A. Gal.; Lowe A. Gal., Syracuse, N.Y.; Munson-Williams-Proctor Inst.; Syracuse Univ.; Binghamton Mus. A.; Springville AA; Cedar City AA; Ogden, Utah; N.Y. State Fair; one-man: Syracuse Univ.; 2-man: Salt Lake City, Utah. *Position*: Prof., Syracuse Univ., Syracuse, N.Y., 1923- .

CHARPIOT, DONALD—*Painter, S., T., L.*
2916 Harper St., St. Louis 7, Mo.

B. St. Louis, Mo., Jan. 3, 1912. *Studied*: Music & Art Col., St. Louis, B.A. *Member*: St. Louis A. Gld.; Missouri Fed. A. & Crafts (Pres.). *Exhibited*: Carnegie Inst.; MMA; Mint Mus. A.; Kansas City AI; Joslyn Mus. A.; CAM; St. Louis A. Gld.; Indp. A. of St. Louis. *Lectures*: Art of the Blind. *Position*: Instr., Missouri School for the Blind, St. Louis, Mo.

CHARRY, JOHN—*Sculptor, T.*
West State & Willow Sts., Trenton 8, N.J.; h. New Hope, Pa.

B. Trenton, N.J., Dec. 24, 1909. *Studied*: Sch. Indst. A., Trenton, N.J.; BAID; Inst. Des., Chicago, Ill., with Moholy-Nagy. *Exhibited*: NAD, 1933; PAFA, 1944, 1952; Contemp. Cl., Trenton, N.J., 1946; Phillips Mill, New Hope, Pa., 1935, 1936, 1946-1951; Pickett Gal., 1938; Morrisville-Trenton A. Group, 1939; Princeton Univ.; Delaware River A., 1937; N.J. State Mus.; Montclair A. Mus., 1947. *Position*: Instr., Trenton Junior Col. & Sch. Indst. A., Trenton, N.J., 1939.*

CHASE, ALICE ELIZABETH—*Educator, L.*
Yale University Art Gallery; h. 324 Willow St., New Haven 11, Conn.

B. Ware, Mass., Apr. 13, 1906. *Studied*: Radcliffe Col., B.A., with G.H.Edgell, P.J. Sachs; Yale Univ., M.A., with Henri Focillon, Sumner Crosby, G.H.Hamilton. *Member*: CAA. Lectures: "Christmas Story in Art"; "The Passion in Art," and other history of art subjects. Author: "Famous Paintings, An Introduction to Art for Young People," 1951. *Position*: Docent, 1931- ; Asst. Prof., Hist. A., 1946- , Yale Univ., New Haven, Conn. Cur. Edu., Brooklyn Museum, 1946-47.

CHASE, EDWARD LEIGH—*Painter, W.*
R.F.D., Woodstock, N.Y.

B. Elkhart, Wis., Aug. 3, 1884. *Studied*: ASL. *Exhibited*: Portraits, Inc., 1945; St. Louis, Mo.; Springfield, Ill. Author, I., "Intelligent Drawing," 1946; "Big Book of Horses," 1951. Many portraits of famous horses and their owners.

CHASE, JESSIE KALMBACH (Mrs. W. E.)—
Painter, Des., Ser.
54 North 8th Ave., Sturgeon Bay, Wis.

B. Baileys Harbor, Wis. *Studied*: AIC. *Member*: AAPL. *Awards*: Prizes, Milwaukee AI, 1925; Madison A. Gld., 1928. *Work*: H.S. & Bank of Sturgeon Bay, Wis.; H.S. Madison, Wis. *Exhibited*: Wisconsin P.&S., 1914-1936; Neville Mus. A., Green Bay, Wis., 1955 (one-man-serigraphs); Peninsula AA, 1956, 1957, 1958.

CHASE, JOSEPH CUMMINGS—
Portrait Painter, W., L.
2228 East Woodstock Place, Milwaukee, Wis.

B. Kents Hill, Me., May 5, 1878. *Studied*: PIA Sch; PAFA; Julian Acad., Paris. *Member*: AAPL; NAC. *Awards*: Prizes, Grunwald Poster Comp., Paris, 1904; AIGA. *Work*: U.S. Nat. Mus., Wash., D.C. (Official port. painter, World War I & II, & Korea, with 189 ports. of Generals and Medal of Honor heroes now in U.S. Nat. Mus.); Mus. City of N.Y. *Exhibited*: PAFA; Paris Salon; Los A. Mus. A., 1943 (one-man). Author, I., "An Artist Talks About Color," 1930; "Creative Design," 1934; & others. Contributor to: national magazines. Lectures: "The Part Design Plays in Art." *Position*: Prof. Emeritus, Chm., Dept. A., Hunter Col., New York, N.Y.

CHASE, MARION (CROUZE) (Mrs. Philip H.)—
Painter, Gr.
1032 27th Ave. North, St. Cloud, Minn.

B. New York, N.Y., Aug. 17, 1926. *Studied*: Skidmore Col., B.S.; Univ. Colorado, M.F.A. *Member*: Studio A. Cl., Skidmore Col.; AAUW. *Awards*: prize, Canyon City A. Festival, 1955 (purchase). *Work*: Canyon City A. Mus. *Exhibited*: Joslyn Mus. A., 1953; Wichita AA, 1952; Canyon City A. Festival; College A. Print Show traveling exh., 1954-55; one-man: Panoras Gal., N.Y., 1956; Sioux Falls (S.D.) Col., 1958. Lectures on Modern Art to various civic groups.

CHATTERTON, C(LARENCE) K.—*Painter, E.*
2 De Garmo Pl., Poughkeepsie, N.Y.

B. Newburgh, N.Y., Sept. 19, 1880. *Studied*: Newburgh Acad.; N.Y. Sch. A., and with DuMond, Henri, Chase, Mora. *Awards*: prize, SC. *Work*: BM; Hackley A. Gal.; Canajoharie Mus.; Vassar Col.; mural, Poughkeepsie Savings Bank. *Exhibited*: AIC; SC; Toledo Mus. A.; MacDowell Cl.; Carnegie Inst.; PAFA; CGA; NAD; Dutchess

County AA; one-man; Wildenstein Gal.; Macbeth Gal., Vassar Col. *Position*: Prof. A., Vassar Col., Poughkeepsie, N.Y., 1915-48, Emeritus, 1948- .

CHAUDHRY, ALOYS SACKSTEDER—Ceramist, E.
1512 Barker St., Sandusky, Ohio

B. Dayton, Ohio, Sept. 8, 1911. *Studied*: Cleveland Sch. A.; Kent State Univ., B.S. in Edu.; Ohio State Univ., M.A.; Univ. So. California; Sophia Univ., Tokyo, Japan. *Awards*: prize, Syracuse Mus. FA, 1937. *Work*: Syracuse Mus. FA. *Exhibited*: Syracuse Mus. FA, 1936-1941, 1947, 1948; Paris Salon, 1937; GGE, 1939; Columbus A. Lg., 1937-1940; NAC, 1940; Phila. A. All., 1937, 1939; Ohio-Pennsylvania Exh., 1938. *Position*: Asst. Prof. A., Indiana State T. Col., Terre Haute, Ind., 1938-48; U.S. Armed Forces Inst., Information and Edu., Tokyo, Japan, 1948-51; Prof. A. & Crafts, Teacher Training Col., Harar, Ethiopia, 1952- .*

CHAVEZ, EDWARD ARCENIO—Painter, Lith., T.
Woodstock, N.Y.

B. Santa Fé, New Mexico, Mar. 14, 1917. *Studied*: with Frank Mechau, Boardman Robinson, Peppino Mangravite. *Member*: NSMP. *Awards*: Tiffany F.; 1948; Fulbright Award, 1951. *Work*: MModA; Newark Mus.; Roswell Mus. A.; Watkins Mem. A. Gal.; Mus. of New Mexico; murals, USPO, Center, Tex.; Geneva, Neb.; Glenwood Springs, Colo.; West H.S., Denver, Colo. *Exhibited*: WFNY 1939; AIC, 1939, 1940, 1942, 1943, 1946; PAFA, 1942, 1952, 1954; NAD, 1943; Carnegie Inst., 1942; SFMA, 1940, 1941, 1944, 1945; Los A. Mus. A., 1944, 1945; WMAA, 1950, 1953; MMA, 1950; Univ. Illinois, 1952, 1954; VMFA, 1954; Mus. New Mexico, 1955; AFA traveling exh., 1955. *Position*: Instr., ASL, New York, N.Y.

CHEEK, LESLIE, JR.—Museum Director
Virginia Museum of Fine Arts, Boulevard & Grove Ave. (20); h. 35 Westmoreland Place, Richmond 26, Va.

B. Nashville, Tenn., Oct. 28, 1908. *Studied*: Duncan Sch., Nashville; Harvard Univ., S.B.; Yale Univ., B.F.A. (Dept. Arch.); Peabody Col.; Columbia Univ. *Member*: A. Comm., State of Va.; AID; Am. Assn. of A. Mus. Dir.; CAA; AFA (Trustee, 1940-42 and 1950-); Soc. Arch. Hist. (Dir. 1952-); Yale Univ. Council; Century Assn.; Rotunda Cl., Richmond (Bd., 1954-); Yale Cl., N.Y. and Richmond (Pres. 1952-54); Harvard Cl., Richmond (Dir. 1953-55). *Awards*: Hon. deg., D.F.A., Univ. Richmond, 1955; medal from 4 Scandinavian countries for organizing "Design in Scandinavia" exh., 1954. Contributor articles to: Architectural Forum; House Beautiful; Town & Country; Craft Horizons; New York Times magazine; Theatre Arts; Baltimore Mus. A. catalogs and bulletins; VMFA catalogs and bulletins; camouflage manuals of U.S. Army. Co-author "Ten Talents in the American Theatre," 1957. Lectures: "Organizing a Museum"; "The Artmobile"; "The Brussels Fair: Installing Art Objects, Planning a Museum." Exhibitions arranged: "Work of Carl Milles," 1940, "Scenery for Cinema," 1942, BMA; "Home & The Machine," 1951, "Healy's Sitters," 1950, "Furniture of the Old South," 1952, "Habiliments for Heroines," 1952, "Design in Scandinavia," 1953-54, "The Architecture of Skidmore, Owings & Merrill," 1958, all at VMFA. Installations: permanent display, "Work of Faberge," VMFA. *Position*: Assoc. Prof., Hd. FA Dept., Col. of William & Mary, 1931-35; Dir., BMA, 1939-42; Assoc. Ed., Architectural Forum, 1945-47; Ed. (Arch.), House Beautiful, 1947-48; Hd., Camouflage Sect., Ft. Belvoir; Office Strategic Services Sch.; President's A. Comm., "People to People" program; A. Adv., Comm., U.S. Air Force Acad.; A. Comm., U.S. Commission, Brussels Fair, 1958; Dir., Virginia Museum of Fine Arts, Richmond, Va., 1948- .

CHEFFETZ, ASA—Engraver, I.
182 State St.; h. 484 White St., Springfield, Mass.

B. Buffalo, N.Y., Aug. 16, 1896. *Studied*: BMFA Sch.; NAD. *Member*: NA; Phila. WC Cl.; Audubon A.; F., Intl. Inst. A. & Lets.; Nat. Com. of Engraving. *Awards*: Prizes. PAFA, 1928, 1939, 1940; AIC, 1930, 1932; Los A. Mus. A., 1934; Diploma of Honor, Warsaw, Poland, 1936; Phila. Pr. Cl., 1935; Chicago World's Fair, 1934; Nat. Exh. Prints, N.Y., 1946 (purchase); Lib. Cong., 1943-1945 (purchase). *Work*: Lib. Cong.; CMA; PAFA; BMA; State of Israel Coll.; Wesleyan Univ.; Univ. Pennsylvania; BMFA; MMA; N.Y. Pub.Lib.; AIC; Los A. Mus. A.;

NCFA; Princeton Univ.; Carnegie Inst.; Newark Mus.; Honolulu Acad. A.; Am. Antiquarian Soc. Springfield (Mass.) Mus. A.; BMFA; Boston Pub. Lib., etc. Des., official bookplate Lib. Cong. *Exhibited*: Royal Acad., London, 1929; Victoria & Albert Mus., London, 1929; WFNY 1939; PAFA, 1928-1945; AFA, 1929-1931; Cal. Pr.M., 1929-1938; AIC, 1929-1932, 1934, 1936, 1937, 1939; Cleveland Pr. Cl., 1931; Phila. Pr. Cl., 1931, 1932, 1934-1946; Bookplate Exh., Los A., 1932-1934; NAD, 1934-1939, 1941; BM, 1939; Princeton Univ., 1941; MMA, 1942; AIGA, 1944; Carnegie Inst., 1944, 1945; Lib.Cong., 1943-1946, Warsaw, Poland, 1936; South America, Denmark, Sweden, etc.

CHEN, CHI—Painter
23 Washington Square North, New York 11, N.Y.

B. Wusih, Kiangsu, China. *Studied*: in China. *Member*: ANA; AWS; Audubon A.; All. A. Am.; SC; Phila. WC Cl.; Intl. Inst. A. & Lets. *Awards*: prizes, AWS, 1955; NAD, 1955; Butler Inst. Am. A., 1955; Chautauqua AA, 1954; Phila. WC Cl.; gold med. (2) NAC; gold med., Knickerbocker A.; Medal of Honor, Audubon A., 1956; prize, New England Exh., 1957. *Exhibited*: AWS, 1948-1958; MMA, 1952; NAD, 1954, 1955, 1956-1958; WMAA, 1954; CGA; Butler Inst. Am. A., 1957 and prior; "Sport in Art" (American coll. assembled for an Olympic Year); Audubon A., 1956, 1957, 1958; All. A. Am., 1956-1958; PAFA, 1956-1958; Phila. WC Cl.; Knickerbocker A.; SC; NAC; NAD, 1956-1958; Provincetown A. Festival, 1958; Univ. Illinois, 1957; one-man: Grand Central A. Gal., 1956, 1958, and others. On juries of awards and selections, AWS; NAD; Phila. WC Cl.

CHENEY, PHILIP—Lithographer, P.
P.O. Box 1065, Warrenton, Va.

B. Brookline, Mass., Dec. 29, 1897. *Studied*: Harvard Col., B.S.; Am. Sch.; Fontainebleau, France. *Member*: Phila WC Cl. *Work*: Valentine Mus., Richmond, Va.; Honolulu Acad. A.; Yale Univ.; Phila. SE.; N.Y.Pub.Lib.; Detroit Inst. A.; IBM; LC; BMFA. *Exhibited*: LC, 1948, 1952; Burlington, Vt., 1948; Wichita, Kans., 1948; Southern Vt. Artists, 1949; Phila. WC Cl., 1950; PAFA, 1950; Silvermine Gld. A., 1950; Wash. Pr.M., 1951.

CHENEY, SHELDON—Writer, Cr.
Stoney Hill Rd., New Hope, Pa.

B. Berkeley, Cal., June 29, 1886. *Studied*: Univ. California, A.B.; Cal. Col. A. & Crafts. *Member*: Authors Lg. Am.; Soc. Am. Hist. *Awards*: Hon. F., Union College, 1937-40; F., Royal Soc. A., London. *Author*: "The Story of Modern Art," 1941; "Men Who Have Walked with God," 1945; "A New World History of Art," 1956; and other books. Contributor to art magazines and Encyclopaedia Britannica, etc.

CHENEY, WARREN—Sculptor, W., L., E., Cr.
58-29 187th St., Flushing, L.I., N.Y.

B. Paris, France, Sept. 19, 1907. *Studied*: Univ. California, B.A.; Columbia Univ., M.A.; Ecole des Beaux-Arts, Paris, and with Hans Hofmann. *Work*: Sculpture, SFMA; Teamster's Union Bldg., Oakland, Cal.; Marie Sterner Coll., and in private homes. *Exhibited*: Gumps Gal., San F., 1934 (one-man); Marie Sterner Gal., 1936 (one-man); MMA, 1934; Weyhe Gal., 1934-1936; SFMA, 1936, 1937; PMA, 1940. Contributor to art and architectural magazines. Stage sets: "Le Sacre du Printemps," 1938; "Liliom" and "The Mad Hopes," 1938; Army Training Films, 1951. Illus., "The Theatre"; "A World History of Art." Lectures, History of Modern Art. *Positions*: Instr., S. & Des., Univ. California, Los Angeles, Cal., 1937-38; Chm. A. Dept., Adjunct Prof. A., Randolph-Macon Women's Col., 1939-40; City Col. of N.Y., 1947-48. Civil Defense Ed., Film News Magazine, 1951- .*

CHENNEY, STANLEY JAMES, JR.—
Painter, I., W., T., Des.
2037 West 29th St., Cleveland 13, Ohio

B. Cleveland, Ohio, Nov. 10, 1910. *Studied*: John Carroll Univ.; Louisiana State Univ., B.S.; Cleveland Col.; Huntington Polytechnic Inst., and with Rolf Stoll, Clarence Carter. *Member*: Cleveland A. Cl.; Kokoon A. Cl. *Awards*: prizes, CMA, 1936; Latham Fnd.; 1948; NSS, 1949; Kokoon A. Cl., 1939; Cleveland A. Cl., 1936, 1937, 1945.

Exhibited: Cleveland A. Cl., 1948; Kokoon A. Cl., 1949, 1950; Polish-Am. Exh., 1951, 1952; Canton AI, 1952; Mc-Candlish Poster Exh., 1950, 1952; Latham Fnd., 1950. *Position*: Instr., University Settlement, Cleveland, Ohio.*

CHERNER, NORMAN—*Designer, T., L., I., W.*
666 Fifth Ave., New York 19, N.Y.

B. New York, N.Y., June 7, 1920. *Studied*: N.Y.Sch. F. & App. A.; Columbia Univ., B.S., M.A. *Exhibited*: Four one-man exhs., American House, New York, N.Y.; travel-ing exhibition sponsored by Am. Craftsmen's Assn., at present; Good Design Exh., 1951-1953; MModA; Inst. Con-temp. A., Boston; Akron AI; Mus. FA of Houston; BMA; work selected by Interiors magazine as one of best com-mercial interiors of the year. Author: "Make Your Own Modern Furniture"; "How To Build Children's Toys & Furniture," 1954; "How To Build Under $5,000," and "Fabricating Houses from Component Parts," 1957. Lec-turer, City Col. and N.Y.Pub. Lib. *Position*: Des. Con-sultant for W. H. Gunlocke Chair Co.; Instr., MModA. & Fieldston Sch. Indst. Des., 1946-49; T. Col., Columbia Univ., 1949-1953; Dir. Norman Cherner Associates, New York, N.Y., and Norwalk, Conn., 1946- ; Des. Consultant, C. & S. Construction Co., Housing Development, 1955; Des. House for Intl. Trade Fair, U.S. Dept. Commerce in Vienna, 1958; Des. Consultant, Remington-Rand Lib. Bureau.

CHERNEY, MARVIN—*Painter*
126 East 16th St.; h. 112 East 17th St., New York 3, N.Y.

B. Baltimore, Md., Nov. 1, 1925. *Studied*: Maryland Inst. A.; Sch. for A. Studies. *Member*: AEA; Audubon A. *Awards*: prizes, Silvermine Gld. A., 1958; BMA, 1951, 1953, 1955; BM, 1954, 1955. *Exhibited*: PAFA, 1957; Butler Inst. Am. A., 1956-1958; Audubon A., 1956-1958; Univ. Nebraska, 1957; Birmingham Mus. A., 1957; Ball State T. Col., 1957, 1958; Norfolk Mus. FA, 1956; NAD, 1956; Wichita AA, 1957, 1958; John Herron AI, 1957; Spring-field Mus. A., 1955-1957; BMA, 1953, 1955, 1957; BM, 1954, 1956, 1958; Silvermine Gld. A., 1958; Great Eastern States Exh., 1957; one-man: AFI Gal., N.Y., 1953; Carl Schurz Fnd., Phila., Pa., 1954-1956; Babcock Gal., N.Y., 1958. *Position*: Instr., Painting, Edu. Dept., Brooklyn Mus.; South Shore A. Workshop, Rockville Centre, N.Y.

CHERRY, HERMAN—*Painter, T.*
10 Cooper Square, New York 3, N.Y.

B. Atlantic City, N.J., April 10, 1909. *Studied*: Los A. County A. Sch.; ASL, and in Europe. *Exhibited*: MMA; Los A. Mus. A.; SFMA; Denver Mus. A.; Cal. PLH; PAFA; WMAA; MModA; one-man: Weyhe Gal.; Los Angeles, Cal.; Stable Gal., 1955. Lectures on Modern Art. *Position*: Chm., Nat. A. Conference, Bd. of "Contemporary Slides," Woodstock, N.Y., 1947, 1948.*

CHESNEY, LEE (R., Jr.)—*Graphic-Printmaker, P., E.*
Graphics Workshop, Dept. of Art, University of Illi-nois; h. 207 West Vermont St., Urbana, Ill.

B. Washington, D.C., June 1, 1920. *Studied*: Univ. Colo-rado, B.F.A., with James Boyle; State Univ. of Iowa, M.F.A., with Mauricio Lasansky, James Lechay; Universi-dad de Michoacan, Mexico, with Alfredo Zalce. *Member*: Midwest Col. AA; CAA; SAGA. *Awards*: prizes, PMA, 1953; DMFA, 1953; John Taylor Arms award, 1955; LC, 1954, 1958; purchase awards: BM, 1953, 1956; Univ. So. California, 1953, 1954; DMFA, 1953, 1954; Denver Mus. A., 1954; Bradley Univ., 1953; Youngstown Col., 1954; Washington Univ., 1955; Texas Wesleyan Univ., 1955; Michigan State Univ., 1956; Oakland A. Mus., 1957; Ful-bright award, 1956-57. *Work*: prints—Mus. Mod. A., Tokyo; Tokyo Univ. of Arts; Nat. Gal. A., Stockholm, Sweden; Tate Gal., London, England; MModA; BM; LC; PMA; Denver A. Mus.; DMFA; Oakland A. Mus.; Illinois Mus. Natural History; USIA (State Dept.); Albion Col.; Bradley Univ.; Illinois Wesleyan Univ.; Michigan State Univ.; Texas Wesleyan Univ., and others. *Exhibited*: BM, 1948, 1950, 1952-1956, 1958; LC, 1950, 1954, 1956, 1958; Phila. Pr. Cl., 1947, 1949, 1950, 1953-1955, 1958; SAM, 1947-1951, 1953-1956; SFMA, 1949, 1950, 1953, 1954; Bradley Univ., 1950, 1952-1955; plus many other national annuals and group shows; paintings—Denver A. Mus., 1949, 1952, 1955, 1956; Des Moines A. Center, 1947-1950; WAC, 1949; 1st Biennial, Tokyo, Japan, 1957; 4th Biennial,

Bordighera, Italy, 1957. Arranged the following biennial national print exhs. for Univ. Illinois: "Graphic Arts—USA," 1954; "50 Contemporary American Printmakers," 1956; "Recent American Prints," (1947-1957), 1958. *Posi-tion*: Assoc. Prof. A., Univ. of Illinois, Urbana, Ill., 1950- .

CHETCUTI, JOHN—*Painter, T.*
Rockport, Mass.

B. Malta, Jan. 25, 1900. *Studied*: Florence Col., Malta; BM Sch. A.; ASL, with George Bridgman. *Member*: AWS; Audubon A.; North Shore AA; Rockport AA. *Awards*: medal, All. A. Am., 1947; prizes, Miami, Fla.; St. Augus-tine, Fla.; Ridgewood, N.J.; North Shore AA; Rockport AA; Hayward Neidringhaus award, 1956; A. Carl Britman award, 1958. *Work*: many in private collections. *Exhibited*: AWS; Audubon A.; All. A. Am., and others; one-man: Bermuda A. Gal., Hamilton, Bermuda; Grand Central A. Gal.; Ferargil Gal., N.Y. Lectures, watercolor demonstra-tions: BMFA; North Shore AA; Rockport AA; Bermuda AA; Bedford AA, etc. *Position*: Instr. A., Rockport, Mass.

CHEW, PAUL ALBERT—*Museum Director*
Westmoreland County Museum of Art, 221 North Main St.; h. 208 North Maple Ave., Greensburg, Pa.

B. Norristown, Pa., Apr. 22, 1925. *Studied*: Univ. Pitts-burgh, B.A., M.A.; Manchester Univ., England, Ph. D. *Member*: CAA; AAMus.; Soc. Arch. Historians. *Awards*: Fellowship, Univ. Manchester, 1955-56, 1957-58; Grad. Assistantship, Henry Clay Frick FA Dept., Univ. Pitts-burgh, 1950-51. Genl. Editor, "250 Years of Art in Penn-sylvania," Univ. Pittsburgh Press, 1959. Contributor to Carnegie Magazine; Journal of the School of Architecture, Univ. Manchester, England; Perspectives, Washington Univ. Lectures: l. ..tory of Art. *Positions*: Exec. to the Dir., Circulating Exhibitions, MModA; Asst. Dir., Stable A. Gallery, N.Y.; Dir., Westmoreland County Mus. A., Greensburg, Pa., at present.

CHILDS, GEORGE HENSHAW—
Craftsman, P., ~art., W.
American Museum of Natural History, Central Park West at 77th St., New York 24, N.Y.; h. 79 State St., Brooklyn 2, N.Y.

B. Minneapolis, Minn., Dec. 20, 1890. *Studied*: Univ. Minnesota, A.B., M.A., Ph.D. *Member*: Am. Veterans Soc. A. *Work*: Am. Mus. Natural Hist., N.Y.; Natural Hist. Mus., Univ. Minnesota. *Exhibited*: Am. Veterans Soc. A. Contributor to: "Natural History," official organ of Am. Mus. Natural Hist., N.Y. Specializing in miniature habitat groups and figurines. *Position*: Scientific A., 1923-38; Asst. Cur., 1938-43; Temporary Chm., Invertebrate Dept., 1943-45; Assoc., Preparation Dept., 1945-46, Am. Mus. Natural Hist., New York, N.Y.*

CHILLMAN, JAMES, JR.—*Educator, L.*
2242 Stanmore Dr., Houston 19, Tex.

B. Philadelphia, Pa., Dec. 24, 1891. *Studied*: Univ. Penn-sylvania, B.S. in Arch., M.S. in Arch.; PAFA; Am. Acad. in Rome. *Member*: F., AIA; Am. Assn. Univ. Prof.; AA Mus.; Texas FA Assn. *Awards*: F., Am. Acad. in Rome, 1919-1922; F., Univ. Pennsylvania, 1913, 1914; F., Carl Schurz Fnd., 1936. Contributor to: Encyclopedia of the Arts; art & architectural magazines. Lectures: Western Art & Architecture. *Position*: Instr., Asst. Prof., Prof. Arch., The Rice Inst., Houston, Tex., 1916-19, 1923- ; Dir., Mus. FA of Houston, 1924-53, Dir. Emeritus, 1953- ; Chm., Arch. Com., Texas Medical Center, Houston, Tex.*

CHINN, YUEN YUEY—*Painter, Gr.*
Kraushaar Galleries, 1055 Madison Ave., New York 21, N.Y.

B. Kwantung, China, Dec. 24, 1922. *Studied*: Columbia Univ., B.F.A., M.F.A. *Member*: CAA. *Awards*: Brevoort Eickemeyer F., Columbia Univ., 1952-53; Fulbright Award, 1954-55; John Hay Whitney F., 1956-57. *Work*: Columbia Univ. *Exhibited*: BMFA, 1954; Young American Print-makers, 1953; CGA, 1957; LC, 1958; WMAA, 1958; one-man: Numero Gal., Florence, Italy, 1955; Galleria D'Arte, Ascona, Switzerland, 1955; Gallerie Arnaud, Paris, France; Gallery Beno, Zurich, Switzerland, 1956; Franz Bader Gal., 1957. Kraushaar Galleries permanently.

CHIPMAN, C. DEAN—*Museum Director, E.*

Elgin Academy Art Gallery; h. 322 Kimball St., Elgin, Ill.

B. La Porte, Ind., June 6, 1908. *Studied*: Northwestern Univ., B.S.; Columbia Univ., M.A.; Kunstgewerbe Schule, Vienna, Austria. *Member*: Nat. Edu. Assn.; Nat. A. Edu. Assn.; AAMus. *Exhibited*: Fox Valley AA, Elgin, Ill., annually. *Position*: Instr., A., Monticello Col., Godfrey, Ill., 1935-40; Instr. A., Dir. A. Gal., The Elgin Academy, Elgin, Ill., 1940- .

CHIU, ALFRED KAIMING—*Librarian, Mus. Consultant*

Boylston Hall 13, Harvard University; h. 30 Mellen St., Cambridge 38, Mass.

B. Ningpo, China, Mar. 11, 1898. *Studied*: Boone Col., A.B.; N.Y. Pub.Lib.Sch.; Harvard Univ., A.M., Ph.D. *Member*: Far Eastern Assn.; Chinese Lib. Assn. Contributor to: library journals, bulletins & art magazines. *Position*: Cur., Oriental Coll., Harvard Col. Lib., 1927-30; Research F., Social Sciences Research Inst., Academia Sinica, 1930-31; Libr., Harvard-Yenching Inst., Harvard Univ., 1931- ; L., Dept. Far Eastern Languages, Harvard Univ., Cambridge, Mass., 1936- ; Consultant to Am. Lib. Assn. Special Com. on Cataloging Oriental Materials, 1954- .*

CHIU, TENG H.—*Painter, Des., Lith.*

Grand View St., Pownal, Vt.

B. Amoy, China. *Studied*: BMFA Sch. A.; London Univ. and Royal Acad., London, England; Ecole des Beaux-Arts, Paris, France. *Member*: Assoc., Royal Soc. British Artists. *Awards*: prize, All. A. Am., 1946; silver med., Royal Acad., 1928; gold med., London, England, 1929. *Exhibited*: Royal Acad., London; Paris Salon; Dayton A. Inst.; Carnegie Inst.; John Herron AI; BMFA; Knoedler Gal., N.Y.; NAD; MMA, and others.

CHOATE, NAT(HANIEL)—*Sculptor, C.*

73 Third Ave., New York 3, N.Y.

B. Southboro, Mass., Dec. 26, 1899. *Studied*: Harvard Univ., A.B.; Julian Acad., Grande Chaumiere, Paris, France. *Member*: NA; NSS; Arch. Lg.; N.Y. Ceramic Soc.; Century Assn. *Awards*: med., Arch. Lg. *Work*: Brookgreen Gardens, S.C.; Harvard Univ.; USPO, Pitman, N.J.; battle monument, Luxembourg.*

CHODOROW, EUGENE—*Serigrapher, S., P.*

1725 Redcliff St., Los Angeles 26, Cal.

B. Ukraine, Mar. 15, 1910. *Studied*: Edu. All., N.Y., and with Ossip Zadkine, Paris, France. *Member*: Western Serigraph Soc.; AEA; N.Y. Graphic Soc. *Work*: LC; murals, Greenpoint Hospital, N.Y.; Floyd Bennett Airport, N.Y.; Naval Hospital, Oceanside, Cal. *Exhibited*: mosaic sc., Pomona Fair, 1955. Work reproduced in "Prints of California Artists."

CHOUINARD, MRS. NELBERT M.—*Educator*

Chouinard Art Institute, 743 South Grand View, Los Angeles 57, Cal.

Studied: PIASch. *Awards*: "Woman of the Year," Los Angeles Times, 1956. *Position*: Fndr., Pres., Chouinard Art Institute, Los Angeles, Cal., 1921- .

CHRISSINGER, MARY HELEN—*Painter*

38 Wayside Ave., Hagerstown, Md.

B. Hagerstown, Md., Oct. 29, 1877. *Studied*: Kee Mar Col., B.A.; Maryland Inst. A.; Rinehart Sch. S.; Columbia Univ., B.S., M.A., and with Albert Heckman, Charles Martin. *Member*: Alumni, Md. Inst. A. *Awards*: prizes, Rinehart Sch., S.; Wash. County Mus. FA; gold medal, for oil painting and Medal of Honor for 4 yr. course, Md. Inst. A. *Work*: Wash. County Mus. FA. *Exhibited*: N.Y. A. All.; BMA; Wash. County Mus. FA; Md. Inst. A. Alumni exhibition; Art:USA, 1958; Am. A. Week, AAPL, 1958; one-man: Wash. County Mus. FA, 1955-56. *Positions*: Assisted in assembly of annual exh. of School Art at Wash. County Mus. FA, 1932-46; Dir., A. Edu., Hagerstown & Washington County, Md.; Chm. A. Section, Maryland State T. Assn. (Retired).

CHRISTALDI, ANGELINE A.—*Painter*

1863 Wynnewood Rd., Philadelphia 31, Pa.

B. Philadelphia, Pa. *Studied*: Univ. Pennsylvania, B.S.; Tyler Sch. FA, Temple Univ., M.F.A.; PAFA, and with

Earl Horter, Umberto Romano. *Member*: DaVinci All.; Phila. WC Cl.; Phila. A. All. *Awards*: prize, Cape May, N.J.; medals, Plastic Cl. *Exhibited*: PAFA; Phila. Plastic Cl.; Phila. WC Cl.; Phila. A.T. Assn.; Montclair A. Mus.; Tyler Alumni exh.; eight one-man exh. in Phila., Pa.

CHRISTENSEN, ERWIN OTTOMAR—
   Museum Curator, E., W., L.

National Gallery of Art, Washington 25, D.C.; h. Lanham, Md.

B. St. Louis, Mo., June 23, 1890. *Studied*: Univ. Illinois, B.S.; Harvard Univ., M. Arch., M.A.; AIC. Contributor to psychological and art journals. Lectures: American (U.S.) Folk Art; History of European Art; History of Architecture, etc. Author: "Popular Art in the United States," 1948; "The Index of American Design," 1950; "Early American Wood-carving," 1952; "Primitive Art," 1955; "A History of Western Art," 1959, and others. *Positions*: Instr., Syracuse Univ., 1934-36; Univ. Pennsylvania, 1937-39; Carl Schurz Fnd., 1939-40; Cur., Index of Am. Des. & Dec. A., NGA, Washington, D.C., 1946- .

CHRISTENSEN, ETHEL MADILL (Mrs.)—*Painter, T.*

512-A Kenwood Ave., Delmar, N.Y.

B. Glendive, Mont., Feb. 28, 1926. *Studied*: Univ. Minnesota, B.S., M. Ed., and with Walter Quirt, Kyle Morris, Cameron Booth, Jo Rollins. *Member*: AFA; NAEA; Eastern AA; NEA. *Awards*: Mulvane A. Center, Topeka, 1956 (purchase); Boston & Maine Railroad award, Berkshire Mus., Pittsfield, Mass., 1958. *Work*: Mulvane A. Center and in many private collections. *Exhibited*: Delgado Mus. A., 1957; Art:USA, 1958; WAC, 1951 (one-man); Univ. A. Center, Fayetteville, Ark., 1954 (2-man); WAC regional, 1951; CAM, 1956; Mid-America annual, Kansas City, 1956, 1957; Missouri Valley Artists, Topeka, 1956; Berkshire Mus. A., 1957, 1958; Albany Inst. Hist. & A., 1958. Co-author: "Children's Art Education," 1957. Contributor to School Arts magazine. *Positions*: A.T., Hamagrael & Clarksville, N.Y., Elem. Schs.; Minneapolis Pub. Schs.; Hackett Jr. H.S., Albany, N.Y., and others.

CHRISTENSEN, GARDELL DANO—*Designer, S., I., P.*

7 East 75th St., New York, N.Y.

B. Shelley, Idaho, Aug. 31, 1907. *Studied*: sculpture with Alice Craze, Max Kalish. *Member*: AAMus. *Work*: African Hall, North American Hall and Boreal Hall, of the American Mus. Natural Hist., N.Y.; Mus. of Okmulgee Nat. Park, Macon, Ga.; Custer Battle Field, Montana; Colonial Mus., Nairobi, British East Africa. *Exhibited*: NAD; Georg Jensen Co., 1939. Illus. "Wapiti the Elk," "Animals of the World," "Monkeys," "Big Cats"; Author, I., "The Fearless Family." Contributor of articles and illus. to Era, Audubon and other nature magazines. *Position*: Exhibits Des., Am. Mus. Natural Hist., 1928-41; Asst. Prod. Mngr., McArthur 3-Dimensional Adv. Corp., 1947-49; Sculptor, Nat. Park Mus. Laboratories, 1950-51; Exh. Des., Montana Historical Soc., 1952-53.*

CHRISTENSEN, HANS (JORGEN)—
   Craftsman, Des., T.

School for American Craftsmen, Spring St.; h. 119 Faircrest Rd., Rochester 23, N.Y.

B. Copenhagen, Denmark, Jan. 21, 1924. *Studied*: Denmark and Norway. *Member*: Am. Craftsmens Council. *Awards*: prizes, Copenhagen, 1954; Huntington (W. Va.) Gal., 1955; Wichita, Kans., 1955; Finger Lakes Exh., Rochester Mem. A. Gal., 1955; two silver med. & traveling scholarship, Europe. *Exhibited*: Copenhagen, Denmark, 1954; Huntington Gal., 1955; Wichita, Kans., 1955; Rochester, N.Y., 1955. *Position*: Silversmith, Georg Jensen's Solvsmedie, Copenhagen, Denmark, 1944-52; Instr., Kunsthaandverkerskolen, Copenhagen, 1952-54, Instr., Metalcraft, Sch. for Am. Craftsmen, Rochester Inst. Tech., Rochester, N.Y., 1954- .

CHRISTENSEN, RALPH A.—
   Painter, C., S., Des., I., T., L.

Wilmot Apts., 805 Connecticut Ave., Bridgeport 7, Conn.

B. Chicago, Ill., Apr. 4, 1897. *Studied*: AIC, B.S., with Vanderpoel, Spaulding; Yale Univ., B.S.; New Britain T. Col., B.S. *Member*: Connecticut Printing House Craftsmen. *Awards*: Col. Elmer Havens and Edward Payton

Bullard, Jr. bronze plaques, 1952. Author, I., "The Art of Printing Layout," 1938. Contributor to Printers Ink. *Position*: Instr., Bullard-Havens Tech. Sch., Bridgeport, Conn.

CHRISTENSON, JOHN LEONARD—Painter, C.
　230 West Montecito St., Sierra Madre, Cal.

B. Gilmore City, Iowa, Jan. 27, 1922. *Studied*: Long Beach City Col.; Long Beach State Col.; Univ. So. California. *Member*: Cal. WC Soc. *Award*: prize, Cal. WC Soc., 1954. *Exhibited*: Cal. WC Soc., 1951, 1954, 1956, 1958; Los A. County Fair; Nat. Orange Show; Long Beach AA; Allied Craftsmen Gld., San Diego, 1952; A. of Los A. and Vicinity, 1953; Fresno A. Center, 1955; San Marino, Cal., 1955 (one-man); Exodus Gal., San Pedro, 1956, 1957; Wichita A. Mus., 1957; Ball State T. Col., 1957; Pasadena A. Mus., 1957; Oakland A. Mus., 1958.

CHRISTIANA EDWARD I. —Painter, T.
　310 Genesee St., Utica, N.Y.; h. 21 Oakdale Circle, Whitesboro, N.Y.

B. White Plains, N.Y., May 8, 1912. *Studied*: PIASch; Munson-Williams-Proctor Inst., with William C. Palmer; Utica, Sch. A. & Sc. *Member*: Cooperstown AA; AWS. *Awards*: prizes, Utica, N.Y., 1945; Cortland, N.Y., 1947, 1950, 1951; AWS, 1949, 1952; Cooperstown AA, 1953, 1954; Syracuse Ann., 1954, 1956; Albany Inst. Hist. & A., 1956. *Work*: Munson-Williams-Proctor Inst.; Manchester (N.H.) Mus. A. *Exhibited*: AIC, 1942, 1944; Mississippi AA, 1946; AWS, 1945-1947, 1949-1951; Munson-Williams-Proctor Inst., 1939-1958; Cortland, N.Y., 1947-1951; BMA, 1949; N.Y.State Fair, 1950, 1951, 1957, 1958; Audubon A., 1950; PAFA, 1952; Assoc. A. Syracuse, 1952; one-man: Munson-Williams-Proctor Inst., 1946, 1955, 1957; Cazenovia Jr. Col., 1949; Colgate Univ., 1946; Utica Pub. Lib., 1950; Utica Col., 1951; Syracuse Mus. FA, 1939; Cooperstown, N.Y., 1957; Cushman Gal., Houston, Tex., 1957; Albany Inst. Hist. & A., 1956, 1958. *Position*: Instr., children's classes, Munson-Williams-Proctor Inst., 1941-46, and Instr. Ptg., Drawing & Des., 1954- ; Instr., Cazenovia Jr. Col., 1948-49; Utica Col., 1953-54; A. Dir., Cooperstown AA.

CHRIST-JANER, ALBERT WILLIAM—Educator, W. P.
　Pratt Institute of Arts, Brooklyn, N.Y.

B. Appleton, Minn., June 13, 1910. *Studied*: St. Olaf Col., B.A.; AIC, B.F.A.; Yale Univ., M.A.; Harvard Univ.; Lake Erie Col., D.F.A. *Awards*: Guggenheim F., 1950; Rockefeller Award, 1955. *Exhibited*: CAM; Detroit Inst. A.; Kansas City AI; AIC; BM; NAD; etc. *Author*: "George Caleb Bingham," 1940; "Boardman Robinson," 1946; "Eliel Saarinen," 1948. *Position*: Hd. A. Dept., Stephens Col., 1936-41; Michigan State Univ., 1942-45; Dir., Cranbrook Acad. Mus. & Lib., 1945-47; Dir., Humanities Div., Univ. Chicago, 1947-52; Dir., Arts Center, New York Univ., 1952- ; Dir., Sch. A., Pennsylvania State Univ., 1956-58; Dean, A. Sch., Pratt Inst., Brooklyn, N.Y., 1958- .

CHRYSTIE, MARGARET H.—Painter, Lith., T.
　15 Arthur Rd., Rosemont, Pa.

B. Bryn Mawr, Pa., July 23, 1895. *Studied*: PAFA; Phila. Sch. Occupational Therapy; & with Hobson Pittman, Henry McCarter. *Awards*: F., PAFA; Chester County AA, 1953. *Work*: PAFA; Woodmere A. Gal.; Allentown Mus. *Exhibited*: CGA, 1937; CM, 1941; Phila. Sketch Cl.; Friends Central Sch., Overbrook, Pa.; PAFA, 1931, 1938, 1940-1945, 1955, 1956-1958; Butler AI, 1939, 1941, 1945; Woodmere A. Gal., 1956-1958; Phila. AC; DaVinci All.; Bryn Mawr, Pa. (one-man); Women's Univ. Cl., Phila., Pa.; Chester County AA, 1955-1958; Temple Univ., 1953 (one-man); PMA, 1955; Wayne A. Center, 1956-1958; Traveling Art, Inc., 1956-1958. *Position*: T., Wayne A. Center, Wayne, Pa.

CHUBB, FRANCES FULLERTON—Educator, P., S., Gr.
　College of Puget Sound; h. 3905 North 35th St., Tacoma 7, Wash.

B. St. Mary's, Idaho, Oct. 6, 1913. *Studied*: Col. Puget Sound, B.F.A.; Univ. Washington, M.F.A., and with George Z. Heuston. *Member*: Tacoma A. Lg.; Women Painters of Washington; Washington AA. *Awards*: prize, Olympia Ann., 1953, 1957; Tacoma AA, 1940. *Exhibited*: SAM, 1939, 1941, 1942; Tacoma AA, 1939-1945; Tacoma A. Lg., 1952, 1953, 1956, 1957. *Illus*., "Lumber Industry in Washington," 1939. *Position*: Instr., A., A. Appreciation, Painting, A. Hist., Col. Puget Sound, Tacoma, Wash., 1942-53, Asst. Prof., 1953-58, Assoc. Prof., 1958- .

CHUMLEY, JOHN WESLEY—Painter
　Tazewell Pike, Knoxville, Tenn.

B. Rochester, Minn., Sept. 12, 1928. *Studied*: Univ. Kentucky; Ringling Sch. A., Sarasota, Fla.; PAFA. *Member*: AWS; Phila. WC Cl. *Awards*: prizes, Florida Fed. A., 1954; Manatee A. Lg., 1954; Knoxville A. Center, 1955; Phila. WC Cl., 1957; Audubon A., 1957. *Work*: PAFA; N.Y. Hospital; Utica (N.Y.) Hospital. *Exhibited*: AWS, 1957, 1958; Audubon A., 1957; PAFA, 1957, 1958; Fla. Fed. A., 1954; Ft. Lauderdale Fnd., 1955; Knoxville A. Center, 1955; Atlanta, Ga., 1954; Alabama WC Soc., 1954; Sarasota AA, 1954, 1955; Manatee A. Lg., 1954, 1955. *Position*: Instr., Ft. Worth (Tex.) A. Center, at present.

CHURCH, C. HOWARD—Educator, P., Lith.
　Michigan State University; h. 313 Lexington Ave., East Lansing, Mich.

B. Sioux City, Neb., May 1, 1904. *Studied*: AIC, B.F.A., with Boris Anisfeld; Univ. Chicago, B.A.; Ohio State Univ., M.A.; and with John Norton, William P. Welsh. *Member*: CAA; Mich. A. Edu. Assn.; Mich. Acad. Sc., A. & Let. (Art Program Chm., 1953-54, 1954-55, Chm. FA Section, 1956-59). *Awards*: prizes, Joslyn A. Mus., 1941, 1942. *Work*: murals, 1932-36, Morgan Park Military Acad., Chicago. *Exhibited*: widely since 1932. One-man: Mulvane A. Mus.; Thayer Mus. A.; Univ. Nebraska; Joslyn A. Mus. *Position*: Dir., Morgan Park Sch. A., Chicago, Ill., 1933-36; Dir., Mulvane A. Mus., Hd. A. Dept., Washburn Univ., Topeka, Kans., 1940-45; Hd. A. Dept., Michigan State Univ., East Lansing, Mich., 1945- .

CHURCH, FREDERIC E.—Painter
　15 West 67th St.; h. 655 Park Ave., New York 21, N.Y.

B. Brooklyn, N.Y., Oct. 25, 1876. *Studied*: Columbia Univ. *Member*: SC; Audubon A.; All. A. Am. *Awards*: Clark prize, NAD. *Work*: N.Y. Genealogical Soc. *Exhibited*: PAFA; CGA; AIC; Detroit Inst. A.; NAD, and many other national exhibitions.

CHURCH, ROBERT M.—Educator, Mus. D.
　University of Arizona, Art Gallery, Tucson, Ariz.

B. Junction City, Kans. *Studied*: Univ. Michigan; Univ. California, B.A.; Notre Dame Univ.; Columbia Univ.; Cornell Univ. *Member*: CAA; AAMus. *Work*: SFMA; Philbrook A. Center. Contributor to College Art Journal, Western Arts Quarterly, San F. AA Bulletin, and others. Lectures on Art History, Contemporary Art and Architecture. *Position*: Asst. Cur., Cur., SFMA, 1945-50; Dir., Philbrook A. Center, Tulsa, Okla., 1950-1955; Asst. to the President, Cal. Col. of Arts & Crafts, Oakland, Cal, 1955-1957; Dir., A. Gal., Univ. Arizona, Tucson, Ariz., 1957- .

CHURCHILL, ROSE—Painter
　1 Norton Lane, Farmington, Conn.

B. New Britain, Conn., June 3, 1878. *Studied*: with Xavier Gonzalez, Charles Martin, Eliot O'Hara, Guy Wiggins. *Member*: NAWA; Conn. WC Soc.; Hartford Soc. Women Painters. *Awards*: prizes, NAWA, 1946; Hartford Soc. Women Painters, 1944, 1946. *Work*: New Britain A. Mus. *Exhibited*: NAWA, 1944-1953; All.A.Am., 1938, 1941, 1942; Conn. WC Soc., 1938-1953; New Haven Paint & Clay Cl., 1942, 1954; Hartford Soc. Women Painters, 1939-1946.

CIAMPA, EMILIUS ROGERS—Sculptor
　Caproni Galleries, 8 Newcomb St., Boston 18, Mass.; h. 10 Blueberry Lane, Lexington 73, Mass.

B. Taurasi, Italy, Jan. 25, 1896. *Studied*: DeBenedictis A. Sch., Boston; Belle A. Sch., Boston, Mass. *Member*: North Shore AA. *Work*: World War I and II memorials, Medford, Mass.; War Mem., City of Boston, 1955; bas-relief port. of Arthur Fiedler, Esplanade, Boston, Mass.

CIAMPAGLIA, CARLO—Mural Painter, T.
　Middle Valley, N.J.

B. Italy, Mar. 8, 1891. *Studied*: CUASch; NAD; Am. Acad. in Rome. *Member*: ANA; All.A.Am. *Awards*: Prix de Rome, 1920-1923; Plainfield, N.J., 1951. *Work*: murals & decorations, Cranbrook Acad. A.; Anzio Mem., Anzio, Italy; Slovak Girls Acad., Danville, Pa.; Masonic Temple, Scranton, Pa.; Fairmount Mausoleum, Newark, N.J.; Court

House, Sunbury, Pa. *Exhibited*: NAD. Contributor to: Arch. magazines, newspapers & Encyclopaedia Britannica. *Position*: Instr., Life Drawing, Traphagen Sch. Fashion, New York, N.Y.*

CIANFARANI, ARISTIDE BERTO—*Sculptor, Des.*
104 Butler Ave., Providence 6, R.I.
B. Italy, Aug. 3, 1895. *Studied*: R.I.Sch. Des., with Arthur William Heintzelman, and in Italy, with Dazzi, Zanelli, Selva. *Member*: Providence A. Cl.; Arch. Lg.; SC; All.A. Am.; Audubon A; Int. AA; Rome. *Awards*: prizes, Arch. Lg., 1942; Madonna Festival, Los Angeles; All. A. Am.; med., Bologna, Italy. *Work*: Brown Univ.; war mem., Meriden, Conn.; Northborough, Mass.; Ogden, Utah; Fall River, Mass.; Providence, R.I.; statues, Muhlenberg Col., Pa.; Our Lady of Providence Seminary, R.I.; Worcester, Mass.; Kansas State Col.; Angell Mem. Hospital, Boston; Elks Nat. Fnd., Chicago. *Exhibited*: PAFA; WMAA; WFNY 1939; Audubon A; Arch. Lg.; Ogunquit AA; Contemp. Am. A.; Providence A. Cl.; Newport AA; R.I.Sch. Des.; All.A.Am; Los Angeles Festival; Rockefeller Center.

CICERO, CARMEN LOUIS—*Painter*
68 Lehigh Ave., Newark 8, N.J.
B. Newark, N.J., Aug. 14, 1926. *Studied*: Newark State T. Col., B.S.; Hunter Col., and with Hans Hofmann, Robert Motherwell. *Awards*: Guggenheim F., 1958. *Work*: Newark Mus. A.; Guggenheim Mus.; MModA; Toronto Mus. A.; BM; WMAA, and in many private collections. *Exhibited*: CGA, 1953; WMAA, 1955, 1957; MModA, 1953, 1955; AFA traveling exh., 1956; Stable Gal., 1956; Nebraska AA, 1957; AIC, 1957; Rome, Italy, 1958; WMA, 1958, and others.

CIKOVSKY, NICOLAI—*Painter, Lith., T.*
500 West 58th St., New York 19, N.Y.
B. Russia, Dec. 10, 1894. *Studied*: in Vilna, Penza, Moscow. *Awards*: med. & prize, AIC, 1931, 1932; prize, WMA, 1933, 1937; Soc. Wash. A., 1941. *Work*: MModA; BM; AIC; PAFA; CAM; WMA; Los A. Mus. A.; PC; Nelson Gal. A.; WMAA; murals, Dept. Interior, Wash., D.C.; USPO, Towson, Silver Spring, Md. *Exhibited*: Toledo Mus. A.; MModA; AIC; Newark Mus. A.; Glasgow Mus.; Walker A. Center; Carnegie Inst.; PC; CGA; BM; BMFA; PMA; WMA; CAM; Los A. Mus. A., and others.

CILFONE, GIANNI—*Painter, T., L.*
4 East Ontario St., Chicago 11, Ill.
B. San Marco, Italy, Jan. 20, 1908. *Studied*: Chicago Acad. FA; AIC, and with Wellington J. Reynolds, Carl Scheffler. *Member*: Brown County AA; Audubon A; All.A. Am.; Hoosier Salon; Chicago Soc. A. *Awards*: prizes, Chicago Galleries Assn., 1941, 1943, 1945, 1953; SC, 1943, 1944; Mun. A. Lg., Chicago, 1946, 1949, 1953; Hoosier Salon, 1950-1952, 1956. *Work*: Michigan City (Ind.) Lib.; Hawthorn Sch., Elmhurst, Ill.; Mormon Church, Salt Lake City; Midwest A. Coll., Chicago; Swedish Cl., Chicago; Indiana Univ. *Exhibited*: AIC, 1928, 1929; Chicago Galleries Assn., 1940-1952; SC, 1940-1952; Audubon A., 1947-1952; All. A. Am., 1951; Hoosier Salon, 1949-1952.

CIMOTTI, GUSTAVE—*Painter, T.*
144 Bleecker St., New York, N.Y.
B. New York, N.Y., Nov. 10, 1875. *Studied*: ASL; Julian Acad., Delacluse Acad., Paris. *Member*: SC. *Awards*: Prize, NAD, 1929. *Work*: Newark Mus.

CIRINO, ANTONIO—*Painter, C., W., T., Des.*
56 Granite St., Rockport, Mass.; h. 1 Broadview Rd., East Providence 14, R.I.
B. Serino, Italy, Mar. 23, 1888. *Studied*: T. Col., Columbia Univ., B.S. in Edu. *Member*: Eastern AA; Rockport AA; Audubon A; All.A.Am.; North Shore AA; Providence AC; SC; Springfield A. Lg.; Conn. Acad. FA. *Awards*: Prizes, Springfield A. Lg., 1920; Providence AC, 1930, 1931; Ogunquit A. Center, 1931, 1951; Rockport AC, 1932, 1937, 1944, 1949, 1958. *Work*: Rhode Island Sch. Des. *Exhibited*: NAD; PAFA; Conn. Acad. FA; Ogunquit AA; Rockport AA; North Shore AA; Terry AI; Springville (Utah) AA; SC; Providence AC; R.I.Sch. Des. Co-Author: "Jewelry Making & Design." Contributor to: Art magazines.

CITRON, MINNA (WRIGHT)—*Painter, Gr., T., W., L.*
32 Union Square; h. 21 East 9th St., New York 3, N.Y.
B. Newark, N.J., Oct. 15, 1896. *Studied*: Brooklyn Inst. A.&Sc.; N.Y.Sch. App. Des.; ASL; Col. City New York; and with K. Nicolaides, Kenneth Hayes Miller, and abroad. *Member*: SAGA; AFA; A. Lg. Am.; NAWA; Audubon A; ASL; Boston Pr. M.; Am. Color Pr. Soc.; AEA; Assoc. A. of New Jersey; Soc. Indp. A., Boston; Provincetown AA; West Palm Beach AA; Fla. Fed. A.; Pan-Am. Cultural Soc. *Awards*: prizes, N.Y.Sch. App. Des., 1926; SAGA, 1942, 1943; Am. Color Pr. Soc., 1948, 1950; Norton Gal. A., 1948; Phila. Pr. Cl., 1948; Boston Soc. Pr. M., 1949; Boston Soc. Indp. A., 1949; Brooklyn Soc. A., 1950; Soc. Four A. 1951; DMFA, 1953; Cal. Soc. Pr. M., 1956. *Work*: MMA, WMAA; Norfolk Mus. A. & Sc.; Newark Mus. A.; CGA; AIC; LC; N.Y. Pub. Lib.; New Jersey Pub. Lib.; Detroit Inst. A.; MModA; Worcester A. Mus.; R.I.Sch.Des.; Howard Univ.; FMA; BMA; Rosenwald Coll.; NGA; murals, USPO, Manchester and Newport, Tenn., etc. *Exhibited*: CGA; WMAA; Newark Mus. A.; Carnegie Inst.; PAFA; AIC, and abroad. One-man: ACA Gal., 1944, 1946, 1947; Midtown Gal., 1935, 1937, 1939, 1941, 1943; Lynchburg, Va., 1938; Havana, Cuba, 1949, 1952; Smithsonian Inst., 1949; Galerie Conti, Paris, 1947; Salon des Realites Nouvelles, 1947-48; Van Dieman-Lilienfeld Gal., 1950; Delgado Mus. A., 1947; Howard Univ., 1947; Museu de Arte Moderna, Sao Paulo, Brazil, 1952; Rio de Janeiro, 1952; San Miguel de Allende, Mexico, 1955. Lecturer. *Position*: Instr., Brooklyn Mus., Brooklyn, N.Y., 1943-46; Paris correspondent, Iconograph magazine, 1946- ; Lecturer, (tour), South America, 1952.

CLAD, JEAN DAVIES—*Painter*
93 Avenue B (9); h. 23 Leroy St., New York 14, N.Y.
B. Alexandria, Minn., Nov. 30, 1925. *Studied*: Univ. California, B.A.; Andre L'Hote, Paris, France. *Exhibited*: Carnegie Inst., 1958; Provincetown A. Festival, 1958; Phila. Pr. Cl., 1955; Hebrew Univ., 1958; Wagner Col., 1957; Premio di Bolzano, Italy, 1951; one-man: Camino Gal., N.Y., 1957; Labaudt Gal., San F., 1953; Galleria Scorpione, Italy, 1951; Stubing-Greenfield Gal., White Plains, N.Y., 1958; Camino Gal. 1957 (3-man).

CLANCY, JOE WHEELER—*Painter, Lith., Des., T., L.*
2915 16th Way, Homewood, Ala.
B. Birmingham, Ala., Apr. 16, 1896. *Studied*: Alabama Polytechnic Inst. *Member*: Birmingham AC; Alabama A. Lg. *Work*: Montgomery Mus. FA; Huntington Col.; Eastern State T. Col., Charleston, Ill.; Seton Hall, Decatur, Ala. *Exhibited*: CM, 1935-1937; Albany Inst. Hist. & A., 1939; VMFA, 1940; WFNY 1939; SFMA, 1940; Birmingham AC, 1935-1952; Alabama A. Lg., 1936-1952; SSAL, 1934-1938; Mt. Holyoke Col., 1939. Lectures: Lithography.

CLAPP, FREDERICK MORTIMER—
Former Museum Director, L., Cr., W.
530 East 86th St., New York 28, N.Y.
B. New York, N.Y., July 26, 1879. *Studied*: Col. City of N.Y., B.A.; Yale Univ., M.A.; Univ. Lausanne. *Member*: Socio dell Accademia di San Luca, Rome; CAA; Assn. A. Mus. Dir. (V. Pres., 1946-47). *Awards*: Docteur (ès lettres) de l'Univ. de Paris, 1914; Hon. Deg., LL.D., Univ. Pittsburgh, 1937; Harris medal, 1942; F., Yale Univ. Author: "Les Dessins de Pontormo," 1914; "Jacopo Carucci, His Life and Works," 1916; various articles on history of art; Ed., folio cat. Frick Coll. *Position*: Instr., Greek, City Col.; L., Univ. California, 1906-14; Hd. Dept. FA, Univ. Pittsburgh, 1926-37; Advisor, 1931-32, Organizing Dir., 1933-35, Dir., 1936-50, Frick Collection, New York, N.Y.

CLAPP, MARCIA—*Portrait Sculptor, L.*
Bushkill, Pa.; h. 172 East 75th St., New York, N.Y.
B. Hartsville, Ind., Dec. 7, 1907. *Studied*: John Herron A. Sch.; Butler Univ., B.F.A.; ASL. *Awards*: Prize, John Herron AI, 1931; F., Tiffany Fnd., 1932; Griffith F., for study abroad. *Exhibited*: NAD, 1931, 1932, 1934; Hoosier Salon, 1931, 1932; CM, 1931; PAFA, 1932; Indianapolis, Ind., 1934 (one-man). Lectures: History of Fashions, at Women's clubs and colleges.

Clark

CLARK, BENTON HENDERSON—*Painter, I.*
420 West 24th St., New York, N.Y.

B. Coshocton, Ohio, July 25, 1900. *Studied*: NAD; AIC. *Awards*: prizes, AIC. *Work*: murals in Chicago, Ill.; Columbus, Ohio. Illus. for Sat. Eve. Post; Cosmopolitan, Red Book and other leading magazines.*

CLARK, CLAUDE—*Painter, E., Gr.*
557 66th St., Apt. A, Oakland 9, Cal.

B. Rockingham, Ga., Nov. 11, 1915. *Studied*; PMASch. A., with Franklin C. Watkins, Earl Horter, Eliot O'Hara; Barnes Fnd.; Alfred Univ.; Sacramento State Col. *Member*: AAUP; N.A.A.C.P. *Work*: PMA; LC; Atlanta Univ.; Barnes Fnd.; Talladega Col.; Phila. Orchestra Assn. *Exhibited*: PAFA, 1939, 1940; Phila. Pr. Cl., 1939-1942; traveling exh. to U.S. colleges, universities and museums, 1954-1958; Phila. Sketch Cl., 1940-1942; Woodmere A. Gal., 1942; Audubon A., 1946; Ruthermore Gal., San F., 1958. *Position*: Instr., Phila. Pub. Schs., 1945-48; Asst. Prof. A., Talladega Col., Alabama, 1948-55.

CLARK, ELIOT (CANDEE)—*Painter, W., L., E., Cr.*
19 East 94th St., New York 28, N.Y.

B. New York, N.Y., Mar. 27, 1883. *Studied*: ASL; & with John Twachtman, Walter Clark. *Member*: NA; NAC; Intl. Inst. A. & Lets.; NSS (hon.); SC (hon.); Century Assn.; Conn. Acad. FA; AWS; All. A. Am. *Awards*: Prizes, NAD; Witte Mem. Mus., San Antonio, Tex.; All. A. Am., 1950. *Work*: NAD; NAC; Dayton AI; Muncie (Ind.) AA; MMA; Witte Mem. Mus.; Ft. Worth AA; Wichita Falls, Ft. Worth, San Antonio Women's Clubs. *Exhibited*: NAD; CGA; Carnegie Inst.; PAFA; Albright A. Gal.; CAM; R.I. Sch. Des.; AIC; VMFA; NAC; SC; AWCS. *Author*: "Alexander Wyant," 2 vols., 1916; "John Twachtman," 1924; "J. Francis Murphy," 1926; "History of the National Academy of Design," 1954. Contributor to: Art magazines; cr., Studio of London (reviews of N.Y. Exhs.). *Position*: Bd. Governors, NAC, 1943- ; Member, Council, NAD, 1945- , First Vice-Pres., 1955, Pres., 1958- , Bd. Dir., N.Y. City Center Gal.; Staff L., Asia Inst., New York, N.Y.; Trustee (ex-officio) MMA.

CLARK, G. FLETCHER—*Sculptor*
72-11 110th St., Forest Hills 75, N.Y.

B. Waterville, Kans., Nov. 7, 1899. *Studied*: Univ. California, B.A.; BAID, and in Europe. *Work*: in public and private collections in the U.S. and abroad.

CLARK, FREEMAN—*Painter*
Holly Springs, Miss.

B. Holly Springs, Miss. *Studied*: ASL; Chase Sch. A.; & with Irving R. Wiles. *Awards*: Prize, Chase Sch. A. *Work*: Brooks Mem. A. Gal., Memphis, Tenn.; N.Y. Pub. Lib. *Exhibited*: NAD; PAFA; Carnegie Inst.; Boston AC; Detroit Inst. A.; Albright A. Gal.; CAM; SAM; Pan-Pacific Exp., 1915; Men's City Cl., N.Y. (one-man).*

CLARK, ISAAC CARPENTER—*Etcher*
Litchfield Rd., Norfolk, Conn.

B. Grand Island, Neb., Aug. 25, 1892. *Member*: Boston AC; New Haven Paint & Clay Cl.

CLARK, LOUISE BENNETT (Mrs.)—
Museum Director, L.
Brooks Memorial Art Gallery; h. 230 Hawthorne St., Memphis, Tenn.

B. Memphis, Tenn. *Studied*: Ward Belmont Sch. A.; Dana Hall, Wellesley, Mass.; Ecole du Pantheon, Paris. *Member*: AAMus; AAPL; Memphis Biennial Assn.; Memphis A. Lg.; Southeastern Mus. Conference; Memphis Glass Collectors Cl.; Antiquarians. *Position*: Asst. Dir., 1932; Dir., 1933- , Brooks Mem. A. Gal., Memphis, Tenn.

CLARK, MABEL BEACH—*Painter*
710 South Kingsley Drive, Los Angeles 5, Cal.

B. San Rafael, Cal. *Studied*: privately. *Member*: Southland AA; Cal. A. Cl.; A. of the Southwest; East Los A. A. Center. *Awards*: prizes, Los A. Mus. A., 1943-1945; Friday Morning Cl., 1943, 1945, 1953; medal, Cal. A. Cl., 1955; AAPL. *Exhibited*: Cal. PLH, 1942-1948; Barn Gal.,

St. Louis, Mo., 1948; State Fair, Phoenix, Ariz., 1941; Los A. Women's Cl., 1942-1955; Laguna Beach AA, 1954; Occidental Col., 1946; Los A. Mus. A., 1943-1945; Bakersfield, Cal., to 1951; Cal. A. Cl., 1948-1955; A. of the Southwest, 1948-1955; Los A. City Hall, 1947, 1948; Los A. City Libraries; Kern County, Cal., 1949; AAPL; Ebell Cl., 1942-1955, 1957; Friday Morning Cl., 1942-1955, 1957; Beverly Hills Cl., 1942-1955; Santa Cruz A. Lg., 1942; Barnsdale Gal., 1955; Palos Verde Gal., 1955; Greek Theatre, Los A., 1956-1958; Pasadena Lib., 1958; Duncan Vail Gal., 1957, 1958; Altadena Gal., 1958; Lynwood Women's Cl., 1958, and others.

CLARK, MRS. ORTON LORING. See Coulter, Mary J.

CLARK, VIRGINIA KEEP (Mrs. Marshall)—*Painter, I.*
"Tree Tops," 1280 Park Ave., Winter Park, Fla.

B. New Orleans, La. *Studied*: Indiana Sch. A., with William Forsyth; ASL with Kenyon Cox, Carroll Beckwith; & in Spain. *Member*: NAWA. *Awards*: Prizes, AIC, 1923; St. Paul, Minn., 1924. *Work*: John Herron AI. Many portrait commissions, 1918-1946. *Exhibited*: AIC; PAFA; CGA; Montross Gal. (one-man); NAWA; Exh. ports. & drawings, Winter Park, Fla., 1953. I., "Live Doll Series"; & short stories.

CLARKE, CARL DAME—
Medical Illustrator, E., W., L.
School of Medicine, University of Maryland, Baltimore 1, Md.; h. Butler, Md.

B. Danville, Va., Apr. 25, 1904. *Studied*: Yale Univ. Sch. FA; Johns Hopkins Univ. Sch. Medical A.; Maryland Inst.; Am. Int. Acad., A.M., Ph.D. *Awards*: med., Maryland Inst., 1929. Author, I., "Molding and Castings," 1938; "Facial and Body Prosthesis," 1945; "Illustration, Its Technique and Application to the Sciences," 1940; "Metal Casting of Sculpture," 1948; "Paintings, Their Preservation and Restoration," 1959. Contributor to medical periodicals. *Position*: Assoc. Prof., Dept. A. as Applied to Medicine, Sch. of Medicine, Univ. Maryland, Baltimore, Md.

CLARKE, RENE—*Painter, Des.*
587 Palisade Ave., Yonkers, N.Y.

B. Eustis, Fla., Feb. 4, 1886. *Member*: AWS; Phila. WC Cl.; SI. *Awards*: Bok gold med., Harvard; A. Dir. gold med. (4).*

CLAWSON, REX MARTIN—*Painter*
413 West 39th St., New York, N.Y.

B. Dallas, Tex., Nov. 2, 1930. *Studied*: Colorado Springs FA Center, with William Johnstone. *Awards*: Texas F., 1948; prize, DMFA, 1951. *Exhibited*: DMFA, 1947-1951; Texas Ann., 1951-1953; Knoedler Gal., 1952; Edwin Hewitt Gal., 1955 (one-man).*

CLAXTON, WAYNE L.—*Educator*
Wayne State University, Detroit, Mich.
Position: Chm., Art Dept., Wayne State University.*

CLAXTON, WILLIAM ROCKLIFF—
Designer, I., P., Cart., C., Comm. A.
Stony Brook Rd., Darien, Conn.

B. New York, N.Y., July 13, 1903. *Studied*: ASL; Grand Central A. Sch.; Johns Hopkins A. Sch., San F., Cal. *Member*: SI; Westport AA. *Position*: A. Dir., Ruthrauff & Ryan, 1942-45.*

CLAYPOOL, NAOMI—*Educator*
Morehead State College, Morehead, Ky.
Position: Hd., Art Dept., Morehead State College.*

CLEAR, CHARLES VAL—
Museum Consultant, E., Des., Cr., P., L., W.
109 Southwest 4th Ave., Miami 36, Fla.; h. 3143 South Indian River Dr., Ft. Pierce, Fla.

B. Albion, Ind., Nov. 3, 1910. *Studied*: John Herron A. Sch.; Indiana Univ.; Corcoran Sch. A.; Velsey Studio of Sculpture; Fla. Southern Col., B.S. *Member*: AAMus.; AFA; Southeastern A. Conf.; Fla. Hist. Soc.; AID, and others. *Work*: Phillips Mem. Gal.; John Herron A. Mus.;

Mt. Ranier (Md.) Pub. Lib.; Greenfield and Albion (Ind.) Pub. Libs.; Soc. Wash. A. *Positions*: Gal. Guide, John Herron A. Mus., 1929-31; Asst. Dir. Edu., Phillips Mem. Gal., 1931-33; Dir., Art. Lg. Wash., 1933-36; Dir., Oregon A. Center, 1938-42; Dir. A. & Hd. Pub. Rel., Hackley Sch., Tarrytown, N.Y., 1942-45; Dir., Akron Art Inst. (Mus. & Sch.), 1945-49; Dir., Clearwater A. Mus. & Fla. Gulf Coast A. Center, 1949-52; Dir., Reorganization, Sioux City A. Center, 1955; Spec. Consultant, City of Tampa, Fla., 1957; Dir., "House of Refuge" Mus. and Martin County Hist. Soc., Stuart, Fla., 1955-58; Dir., Jupiter Island A. Cl., Hobe Sound, Fla., 1956-57; Permanent Consultant, Sioux City (Iowa) A. Center, and "House of Refuge" A. Mus.; Advisor on Community Culture to cities' and states' agencies and Consultant to Public Museums, at present.

CLELAND, T(HOMAS) M(AITLAND)—
Illustrator, Des., P., C.
R.F.D. 2, Danbury, Conn.

B. Brooklyn, N.Y., Aug. 18, 1880. *Member*: Arch. Lg.; SI; Boston Soc. A. & Crafts; AIGA; SC; Century Cl.; Double Crown Cl., London, Eng., (hon.). *Awards*: med., Boston Soc. A. & Crafts, 1920; AIGA, 1921, 1940; A. Dir. Cl., 1940. Author: "Harsh Words," 1940; "J. B. Bodoni"; "Progress in the Graphic Arts"; I., "Jonathan Wild," "Tristram Shandy," "Tom Jones," 1952. *Exhibition*: Comprehensive of work in all fields, Newberry Lib., Chicago, 1948. Lectures: Book Decoration, MMA.

CLEMENS, PAUL LEWIS—*Painter.*
620 North Beverly Dr., Beverly Hills, Cal.

B. Superior, Wis., Oct. 29, 1911. *Studied*: Univ. Wisconsin, B.A.; AIC. *Member*: AEA; Cal. A. Cl. (hon.). *Awards*: med., Milwaukee AI, 1937; NAD (Altman prize), 1942; NAD, 1944; Milwaukee Journal purchase prize, 1937. *Work*: MMA; Univ. Nebraska; Milwaukee AI; Los A. Mus. A.; Nelson Gal. A.; Clark Mus., Williamstown, Mass.; Butler AI; many portraits of prominent persons. *Exhibited*: Carnegie Inst., 1938, 1944-1946; CGA, 1944, 1947; WFNY 1939; GGE, 1939; AIC, 1937, 1938, 1943, 1945; NAD, 1942-1944, 1946; PAFA, 1938; WMAA, 1938, 1940; Los A. Mus. A., 1954 (Juror).

CLEMENT, SHIRLEY—*Painter, T.*
3955 Redrock Lane, Sarasota, Fla.

B. New York, N.Y., July 7, 1922. *Studied*: Ringling Sch. A.; Amagansett A. Sch. *Member*: AWS; Fla. Fed. A.; Sarasota AA; Fla. A. Group; Manatee A. Lg.; Clearwater A. Group. *Awards*: prizes, Fla. Fed. A., 1948, 1949; special jurors award, Fla. Fed. A., St. Petersburg, 1950; Pinellas Lumber award, Tampa, 1952; Grumbacher award, 1952; Ringling award, 1954; Lykes purchase award, Tampa, 1956; Clearwater, Fla., 1952; bronze medal, Sarasota, 1953. *Work*: Univ. Florida. *Exhibited*: AWS, 1948, 1949, 1951, 1953-1955; NAWA, 1949; Southeastern annual, 1949, 1950; All Florida Exh., 1950; Fla. Intl. Exh., 1952; Soc. Four Arts, 1954; Fla. A. Group, 1950, 1952, 1953, 1955, 1956; Fla. Gulf Coast Group, 1948, 1949; Clearwater A. Group, 1950, 1952, 1953; Fla. Fed. A., 1948-1952, 1956, 1957; Rowland Traveling Exh., 1957-1958; Manatee A. Lg., 1953-1957; Sarasota AA, 1946-1958.

CLENDENIN, EVE—*Painter, C.*
150 Central Park South, New York 19, N.Y.; s. Provincetown, Mass.

B. Baltimore, Md. *Studied*: Banff Sch. FA., with H. G. Glyde, and with Eliot O'Hara, Hans Hofmann. *Member*: NAWA; Am. Abstract A.; Provincetown AA; Cape Cod AA. *Awards*: prizes, NAWA, 1957; BMA, 1958. *Exhibited*: New York City Center, 1953; Eola Gal., Orlando, Fla., 1954 (one-man); Cape Cod AA, 1953-1958; NAWA traveling exh., 1953-54, 1955; NAWA, 1954; NAD, 1953, 1954; Provincetown AA, 1946-1957; Riverside Mus., 1954; Realites Nouvelles, Paris, 1955; Nat. Mus. Mod. A., Tokyo, Japan, 1955; Gallery 251, Provincetown, 1954; H-C Gal., Provincetown, 1955; Provincetown AA, 1946-1957; Argent Gal., N.Y., 1945 (one-man); Eola Gal., Orlando, Fla., 1945 (one-man); Vose Gal., Boston, 1946; Seligmann Gal., N.Y., 1946; Dayton AA, 1947; Am. Abstract A., 1953-1958; New York City Center, 1953; Soc. Four Arts, 1957; James Gal., N.Y., 1957, 1958; Art:USA, 1958; BMA, 1958; NAWA print exh., 1957; Stedelijk Mus., Amsterdam, 1956; Maison des Arts, Brussels, 1956; Kunst Mus., Bern, Switzerland, 1957; Cianu Gal., Lugano, Switzerland, 1957.

CLIFFORD, HENRY—*Museum Curator*
Philadelphia Museum of Art, Philadelphia, Pa.; h. Radnor, Pa.

B. Newcastle, Me., May 24, 1904. Arranged and organized exhs.: Mexican Art Today, 1943; Jose Maria Velasco, 1944; Henri Matisse, Retrospective Exh. of Paintings, Drawings and Sculpture (in collaboration with the artist), 1948; Toulouse-Lautrec, 1955; Picasso, 1958. *Position*: Cur. Painting, Philadelphia Museum of Art, Philadelphia, Pa.

CLEPHANE, ROSEBUD (Mrs. Carlton Hurst)—*Painter*
2301 Columbus Blvd., Coral Gables, Fla.

B. Atlanta, Ga. *Studied*: George Washington Univ.; Corcoran Sch. A., and with Charles Hawthorne, Wayman Adams, Henry Hensche. *Member*: Palm Beach A. Lg.; Blue Dome F., Miami, Fla.; Lg. Am. Pen Women. *Awards*: prizes, Fla., 1936; Lg. Am. Pen Women, 1939; Palm Beach AA, 1940. *Work*: Children's Home, Miami, Fla. *Exhibited*: Soc. Wash. A.; CGA; Wash. A. Cl.; Adirondacks AA; Soc. Four A Gal.; Ringling Mus. A.; and in Miami Beach, Orlando, Jacksonville and Tampa, Fla., Jamaica and Haiti. Lectures on art.*

CLIFFORD, LOIS IRENE—*Craftsman, T.*
5607 Elmer St., Pittsburgh 32, Pa.

B. Providence, R.I., Dec. 15, 1892. *Studied*: Carnegie Inst.; Penland Inst.; & with Florence Newcomer. *Member*: Weaver's Gld., Craftsmen's Gld., A. & Crafts Center, all of Pittsburgh. *Exhibited*: Contemporary Am. Handwoven Textiles Exh., 1945, 1946; Women's Int. Inst., N.Y., 1941; Phila. A. All., 1946; Assoc. A. Pittsburgh, 1938-1941; St. Louis Weaver's Gld., 1942; Pittsburgh Weaver's Gld.; Pittsburgh Craftsmen's Gld. Lectures: Weaving & Crafts. Author: "Card Weaving." *Position*: Occupational Dir., West Pennsylvania Sch. for Blind Children, Pittsburgh, Pa., 1930-1958; Instr., Weaving, Adult Edu., Carnegie Inst. Mus.; Sec., Exec. Bd., A. & Crafts Center, 1944- , Pittsburgh, Pa.

CLINEDINST, M(AY) S(PEAR)—*Painter, T.*
1851 Second Ave., North, St. Petersburg 3, Fla.

B. Brooklyn, N.Y., Aug. 12, 1887. *Studied*: Cornell Univ.; Brooklyn Inst. A. & Sc., and with John Carlson, Stanley Woodward, Anthony Thieme, Umberto Romano. *Member*: NAWA; AAPL; North Shore AA; Brooklyn Soc. A.; St. Petersburg A. Cl.; Clearwater A. Group; Gulf Coast A. Group; Catherine L. Wolfe A. Cl.; Fla. A. Group; St. Petersburg A. Lg. *Awards*: prizes, NAC, 1951; St. Petersburg A. Cl.; Tampa, Fla., 1953; Largo, Fla., 1954. *Exhibited*: CGA, 1941; NAWA, 1950-1955 (traveling exh., 1955-56); Brooklyn Soc. A., 1950-1955; North Shore AA, 1950-1955; Fla. Fed. A., 1950-1955; AAPL, 1950-1955; St. Petersburg A. Lg., 1954, 1955; NGA, 1953. Other exhs. prior to 1950. *Positions*: Publ. Chm., 1950-51, Cor. Sec., 1952, 1953, Rec. Sec., 1954, St. Petersburg A. Cl.; St. Petersburg A. Lg., 1955-57.*

CLOAR, CARROLL—*Painter, Lith.*
75 South Prescott St., Memphis 11, Tenn.

B. Earle, Ark., Jan. 18, 1913. *Studied*: Southwestern Col., A.B.; Memphis Acad. A.; ASL. *Member*: AEA. *Awards*: prizes, McDowell F., 1940; Guggenheim F., 1946; LC; Rochester Mem. Gal.; BM; Butler Inst. Am. A., 1956. *Work*: MMA; MMoDA; BM; Newark Mus. A.; Butler Inst. Am. A.; LC; Brooks Mem. A. Gal.; Columbia (S.C.) A. Mus.; Brandeis Univ.; Abbott Labs. *Exhibited*: Carnegie Inst., 1955, 1958; Univ. Illinois, 1957; WMAA; PAFA; Butler Inst. Am. A., 1956; Univ. Nebraska, 1958; Mid-South Exh., Memphis, 1956; one-man: Brooks Mem. A. Gal., 1955, 1957; Little Rock Mus. A., 1956; Alan Gal., N.Y., 1954, 1956, 1958. Contributor to Life, Horizon magazines. *Position*: Instr. Painting, Memphis Acad. A., 1956.

CLOETINGH, JAMES H.—*Painter, Des.*
1141 Mishawaka Ave.; h. 1601 East La Salle St., South Bend 17, Ind.

B. Muskegon, Mich., July 3, 1894. *Studied*: with Raymond Weir, England; Harry Muir Kurtzworth, Emil Jacques, Belgium. *Member*: AAPL. *Exhibited*: Hoosier Salon, 1939-1941; Northern Indiana A., 1940, 1941; Hackley A. Gal., 1943 (one-man); Wawasee A. Gal., 1938-1940; Royal Acad. (photos), London, England.*

CLUNIE, ROBERT—*Painter*

Box 191, Rt. 1, Bishop, Cal.

B. Eaglesham, Scotland, June 29, 1895. *Studied*: in Scotland. *Member*: Cal. A. Cl. *Awards*: prizes, Acad. Western Painters, 1936, 1937; Gardena, Cal., 1936; Cal. State Fair, 1938, 1955; Heyburn (Idaho) Pub. Sch., 1939, Chamber of Commerce, 1948; Santa Paula H.S. (purchase), 1955, and others. *Work*: Pub. Schs., Gardena, Santa Paula, Cal., Ogden, Utah, Heyburn, Idaho, Bishop, Cal. *Exhibited*: Cal. State Fair, 1955; Chamber of Commerce, Santa Paula, 1955.

COATES, MRS. HILDA ALTSCHULE.

See Altschule, Hilda

COATES, ROBERT M.—*Writer, Cr.*

New Yorker Magazine, 25 West 43rd St., New York, N.Y.; h. Old Chatham, N.Y.

B. New Haven, Conn., Apr. 6, 1897. *Studied*: Yale Univ., B.A. *Author*: "The Eater of Darkness," 1929; "The Outlaw Years," 1930; "Yesterday's Burdens," 1933; "All The Year Round," 1943; "The Bitter Season," 1946; "Wisteria Cottage," 1948. *Position*: A. Cr., W., New Yorker Magazine.

COBHAM, ETHEL RUNDQUIST—*Illustrator, Comm. A.*

400 Riverside Dr., New York 25, N.Y.

B. Minneapolis, Minn. *Studied*: AIC. *Member*: Gld. Freelance A. I. Vogue, McCall's, American, & other national magazines.

COBURN, RUTH WINONA—*Educator*

Arts and Crafts Service, State Department of Education, Montpelier, Vt.; h. 134 Caroline St., Burlington, Vt.

B. St. Albans, Vt., July 3, 1904. *Studied*: Massachusetts Sch. A., B.S. in Edu.; Univ. Vermont. *Member*: Eastern AA, (Loan Service Com., 1954-56); Nat. A. Edu. Assn. (A. Edu. in Rural Areas Com., 1955-57). *Position*: Supv. A. Pub. Sch., Exeter, N.H., 1927-1929, Rutland, Vt., 1929-1934, Burlington, Vt., 1934-1945; Dir., Arts & Crafts Service, State Dept. Edu., Montpelier; Vt., 1945- .*

COCHRAN, DEWEES (Mrs. Dewees Cochran Helbeck) —*Painter-Craftsman, Des., P., S., T.*

Main St., Norwich, Vt.

B. Dallas, Tex., Apr. 12, 1902. *Studied*: PMSchIA; Univ. Pennsylvania; PAFA, with Henry McCarter. *Member*: Am. Craftsmen's Edu. Council; Doll Collectors of Am. (hon.); United Fed. Doll Clubs; Soc. Vermont Craftsmen. Creator of the "Portrait Doll," "The Look-Alikes," "The Grow-Up Dolls." *Awards*: Award of Merit, 14th ann. doll exh., Bowers Mem. Mus., Santa Ana, Cal., 1954; Goodwill Industries, San Diego, Cal., 1955. *Exhibited*: Marie Sterner Gal., 1931; Phila. Pr. Cl., 1931; Carpenter A. Gal., Dartmouth Col., 1952; exhs. Portrait Dolls, Vermont Development Center, 1956; Rockefeller Center, 1956; Bowers Mem. Mus., Santa Ana, Cal., 1956, 1957. *Des.*, executed six full-color historical maps of Dartmouth College for building promotion program, circulating U.S. for 2 yrs., 1957-58. Contributor to craft magazines. *Position*: Des. Dir., Instr., Sch. for Am. Craftsmen, Hanover, N.H., 1945-46; Dir., Dewees Cochran Dolls, Norwich, Vt.

COCHRAN, GIFFORD (ALEXANDER)—*Painter*

R.F.D. #2, Lamoine, Me.; also, Oviedo, Fla.

B. New York, N.Y., Dec. 4, 1906. *Studied*: Yale Univ.; and in Munich, Germany with Hans Stangl. *Member*: AAPL. *Work*: Hudson River Mus., Yonkers, N.Y. *Exhibited*: WFNY, 1939; traveling exhs. nationally; Farnsworth Mus.; Hudson River Mus.; five one-man exhs. New York City.

COCKING, GRETTA—*Painter, E., W., L.*

Spearfish, S.D.

B. Mineral Point, Wis., Aug. 11, 1894. *Studied*: Univ. Nebraska, B.S.; Univ. Oregon, M.F.A.; State Col. Edu., Greeley, Colo.; Montana State Col., and art with Eugene Steinhof, Otis Dozier. Sponsor of local chapter, Kappa Pi; Fndr., Rapid City Paint & Sketch Cl., 1950; Fndr., Spearfish Paint & Palette Cl., 1954; Delta Kappa Gamma (hon. in teaching). *Awards*: Black Hills Regional Exhs., 1935-1955. *Work*: murals, Univ. Oregon. *Exhibited*: AAUW, 1953; Black Hills, S.D., 1953-1955, 1958; Rapid City, 1955, 1958; Spearfish Little Gal., 1955 (one-man). Lectures on art and art education. *Position*: Pres. A. Section, South Dakota Edu. Assn., 1950; Dir., Black Hills A. Center, Spearfish, 1935- ; Pres., local chptr. AAUW, 1938-40; State A. Chm., AAUW, 1947-48; Hd. A. Dept., Black Hills T. Col., Spearfish, S.D., 1935- .

COCKRELL, DURA BROKAW (Mrs. E. R.)—*Educator, P., W.*

Winslow Heights, Winslow, Ark.

B. Liscomb, Iowa, Feb. 16, 1877. *Studied*: Drake Univ., A.B.; Texas Christian Univ., A.M.; ASL, with Kenneth Hayes Miller, F. Luis Mora, Robert Henri; William Chase A. Sch., and abroad. *Awards*: Med. Woman's Forum, Dallas, Tex., 1919; Dallas Mus. FA, 1926. *Member*: Southern AA. Author: "Introduction to Art," 1930. Preparing script for Masterpieces of Painting with Religious Subjects for Yale Divinity School.

CODMAN, RUTH (Mrs. David)—*Painter*

2239 Primrose Ave., Monrovia, Cal.

B. New York, N.Y., Aug. 11, 1920. *Studied*: Pasadena Sch. FA, with Frode N. Dann; Pasadena City Col. *Member*: Cal. WC Soc.; Women Painters of the West; AEA; Los A. AA; Pasadena AA. *Awards*: prizes, Los A. All-City Exh., 1953; Santa Paula Chamber of Commerce, 1955; Pasadena A. Mus.; San Gabriel Valley Exh., 1955; Nat. Pr. Exh., Pasadena, 1958; Los A. City Hall, 1956-1958. *Work*: Pasadena A. Mus.; Santa Paula Chamber of Commerce; Long Beach Mus. A.; Home Saving & Loan Assn. *Exhibited*: Los A. Mus. A. Rental Gal., 1955; Los A. Mus. A., 1956, 1957; Cal. PLH, 1955; Pasadena A. Mus., 1953-1958; San Diego FA Gal., 1954; Sacramento State Fair, 1954-1958; Nat. Orange Show, 1955-1958; Los A. City Hall, 1953, 1956-1958; WMFA, 1957, 1958; Jack Carr Gal., 1956, 1958 (one-man); Long Beach Mun. A. Center, 1955.

COE, HELEN STOTESBURY (Mrs. Arthur Paul)—*Painter, T.*

4806 Little Falls Rd., Arlington, Va.

B. New York, N.Y. *Studied*: Grand Central A. Sch.; ASL, and with Eliot O'Hara, Wayman Adams. *Member*: NAWA; A. Cl. of Wash.; A. Lg. of Northern Virginia (Pres., 1956-57). *Exhibited*: Pen & Brush Cl., 1936-1946; NAWA, 1938-1946; Rockport AA, 1934-1937, 1939, 1942, 1943, 1945; Salons of Am., 1936; All. A. Am., 1937, 1938, 1943; Portland Soc. A., 1940; Wash. WC Cl., 1942; AWS, 1946; Morton Gal., 1939, 1944 (one-man); Argent Gal., 1942; A. Cl. of Wash.; A. Lg. of No. Virginia; CGA, 1949.

COE, (MATCHETT) HERRING—*Sculptor*

2554 Gladys St., Beaumont, Tex.

B. Loeb, Tex., July 22, 1907. *Studied*: Lamar Col.; Cranbrook Acad. A., with Carl Milles. *Awards*: prize, All-Texas Exh., 1952. *Work*: portrait busts, panels, statues, memorials in Beaumont, Houston, Sabine Pass, New London, Texas; animal figures for entrance to zoo at Herman Park, Houston, Texas; St. Mary's Seminary, Houston; Lamar Inst. of Technology, Beaumont; First Methodist Church, Ganado, Tex.; U.S. Navy Mus., Port Hueneme, Cal. *Exhibited*: NSS, 1950, 1952; Nat. Cathedral, Wash., D.C.

COE, ROLAND (RAE)—*Cartoonist*

Middle St., Amherst, Mass.

B. Havana, Ill., May 24, 1906. *Member*: Nat. Cartoonists Soc. Author, I., "Coe's Crosstown Carnival"; "Little Scouts in Action." Contributor to Collier's, Sat. Eve. Post, American, This Week, Esquire magazines. *Position*: Batten, Barton, Durstine & Osborn Adv., 1929-34; New York Post, 1934-42; freelance, Bell Syndicate, 1942- .*

COE, THEODORE (DEMEREST)—*Landscape Painter*

30-16 Villa Rosa Park, Tampa 6, Fla.

B. Suffern, N.Y., Apr. 13, 1865. *Studied*: NAD; & with Menard, Paris; John Twachtman. *Member*: Boston AC. *Exhibited*: NAD; Phila. A. Cl.; Soc. Am. A.; Doll & Richards Gal., Boston, 1920-1926 (one-man); A. Center, N.Y., 1925-1929 (one-man).*

COES, KENT DAY—*Painter, Des., I.*
330 West 42nd St., New York 36, N.Y.; h. 22 Seymour St., Montclair, N.J.

B. Chicago, Ill., Feb. 14, 1910. *Studied*: N.Y. Univ.; Grand Central A. Sch., with George Ennis, Grant Reynard, Edmund Greacen and others; ASL, with Frank DuMond, George Bridgman. *Member*: AWS; New Jersey WC Soc. (Fndr.-Memb.); All. A. Am.; SC; Academic A. Assoc.; Montclair AA; Hudson Valley AA; Baltimore WC Cl. *Awards*: prizes, All. A. Am., 1954; Academic A. Assoc., 1954, 1956; Kresge award, New Jersey WC Soc., 1954; Balt. WC Cl., 1958; American Artist Magazine, medal of honor, 1957; SC, 1956; Hudson Valley AA, 1955. *Work*: Montclair A. Mus.; Univ. Pennsylvania; Frye Mus. A., Seattle, Wash. *Exhibited*: AWS, 1948-1958; All. A. Am., 1950-1958; Audubon A., 1950-1957; NAD, 1950, 1957; Academic A. Assoc., 1953-1958; New Jersey State Exh., 1930-1957; New Jersey WC Soc., 1939-1958. *Position*: Asst. Instr., Painting, Montclair A. Mus. Sch., Montclair, N.J., 1954-55.

COFFEY, KATHERINE—*Museum Director*
Newark Museum, 43-49 Washington St. (1); h. 569 Mt. Prospect Ave., Newark 4, N.J.

B. New York, N.Y. *Studied*: Barnard Col., Columbia Univ., A.B. *Member*: AAMus.; Council of AAMus.; Am. Assn. A. Mus. Dir.; Mus. Council of New Jersey; AFA; CAA. *Awards*: Degree, M.A., Rutgers Univ., State Univ. of New Jersey. *Position*: Newark Mus. Staff, 1923-24; Exec. Sec., Barnard Col. Alumnae Assn., 1924-25; Dir., Apprentice Training Course, 1925-42, Cur., 1931-47, Asst. Dir., 1947-49, Dir., 1949- , Newark Museum, New Jersey.

COGSWELL, DOROTHY McINTOSH—
Educator, P., L., I.
Mount Holyoke College; h. 23 Jewett Lane, South Hadley, Mass.

B. Plymouth, Mass., Nov. 13, 1909. *Studied*: Yale Sch. FA, B.F.A., M.F.A. *Member*: AEA; Springfield A. Lg; CAA. *Awards*: prizes, Eastern States Exh, 1941; Fulbright Grant for Lectureship, National A. Sch., Sydney, Australia, 1957-58. *Work*: Springfield A. Mus.; mural, Mt. Holyoke Col. *Exhibited*: WFNY 1939; AWS, 1933, 1934, 1941; New Haven Paint & Clay Cl., 1930-1952; Conn. Acad. FA, 1937, 1940-1945; Springfield A. Lg., 1940-1954; Albany Inst. Hist. & A., 1941-1946; Elmira Col., 1950, 1952; Univ. Massachusetts, 1951; Rutgers Univ., 1952; Boston Soc. Indp. A., 1946-1954; one-man: Smith Mus., Springfield; Oklahoma A. & M. Col., 1953; Nebraska State Col., 1954; Coker Col. (S.C.), 1954; Georgia Mus. A., Columbus, Ga., 1955; State Colleges of New York at Fredonia and Oswego, 1956. Illus., "Doctor in Homespun," 1941. Lectures: Modern Painting at Sydney Univ. and Nat. A. Gal. of New South Wales, Australia; Mexican Art at Univ. of New South Wales. *Positions*: Instr. A., 1939-44, Asst. Prof., 1944-47, Assoc. Prof., 1947- , Mount Holyoke Col., South Hadley, Mass.; Chm., Mount Holyoke Friends of Art, 1948- .

COHEE, MARION M.—*Painter, T.*
5134 Castor Ave., Philadelphia 24, Pa.

B. Baltimore, Md., Dec. 11, 1896. *Studied*: Univ. Pennsylvania, B.S.; Temple Univ., M.F.A.; & with Earl Horter, Arthur B Carles, Ernest Thurn, Hans Hofmann. *Member*: Phila. A. T. Assn.; Phila. WC Cl.; Plastic Cl.; Phila. A. All.; Woodmere AA. *Awards*: Plaque, Phila. A. T. Assn.; gold and silver medals, Plastic Cl., 1945, 1951, 1957; silver med., DaVinci All., 1951. *Work*: Tyler Sch. FA, Temple Univ. *Exhibited*: PAFA; Phila. Plastic Cl.; Phila. A. All.; Sketch Cl.; Woodmere A. Gal.; one-man: Women's City Cl., Phila., 1955; Phila. A. All., 1955.

COHEN, ESTHER SIMA—*Ceramist, E.*
203 Church St., Willimantic, Conn.

B. New York, N.Y., Dec. 29, 1913. *Studied*: ASL, with Sternberg; Alfred Univ., with Harder, Merritt; New York Univ., B.S., M.A., with Woodruff, Baziotes. *Member*: N.Y. Soc. C.; Eastern AA; AEA; Nat. Edu. Assn.; Nat. A. Edu. Assn.; Conn. Edu. Assn.; Conn. A. Assn.; Com. on A. Edu. *Exhibited*: Univ. Minnesota, 1946; America House, 1944-1946; WFNY 1939; NAC; Argent Gal.; Phila. A. All.; Barbizon-Plaza Gal.; Hartford Atheneum; Norwich A. Sch., 1953 (one-man); Mystic AA, 1958; Brentano, N.Y., 1958. Lectures: The Art of Ceramics; Crafts as a Hobby. Contributor to: Teacher Education Quarterly; Connecticut

Teacher; School Arts Magazine; Connecticut Craftsman. *Position*: Dir., Lenox Hill Pottery, 1934-45; Instr., N.Y. Univ., 1947-49; Prof. A. & Crafts, Herzilah Teachers Inst., New York, N.Y., 1944-1952; Asst. Prof. A. Edu., Willimantic State T. Col., Willimantic, Conn., 1949- .

COHEN, H. GEORGE—*Painter, Des.*
Hillyer Bldg., Smith College; h. 15 Washington Ave., Northampton, Mass.

B. Worcester, Mass., Sept. 14, 1913. *Studied*: WMA Sch.; Inst. Des., Chicago, and with Herbert Barnett, Kenneth Shopen. *Member*: Springfield A. Lg.; Worcester Soc. A. & Craftsmen; Com. on A. Edu.; CAA; Provincetown AA. *Awards*: prizes, Springfield A. Lg., 1945-1949, 1951-1958; Columbia (S.C.) Mus. A., 1957; Conn. WC Soc., 1957; Macdowell F., 1958. *Exhibited*: NAD, 1943; AWS, 1942-1944; AIC, 1945, 1954; SFMA, 1944; Springfield A. Lg., 1942-1958; WMA, 1940, 1941, 1943, 1944, 1946, 1950; Boston Arts Festival, 1954, 1955, 1956, 1957; MMA, 1952; Provincetown AA, 1948-1955; Mt. Holyoke Col., 1954; Smith Col. Mus., 1955, 1958; Deerfield Acad., 1953, 1957 (one-man); G.W.V. Smith Mus. (one-man); AFA traveling exh., 1953-54; Ford Motor Co. traveling exh., 1952-53, 1954-55, 1955-56; Boris Mirski Gal., 1955-56, 1957 (one-man); Wadsworth Atheneum; Radcliffe Grad. Center, 1958; Columbia (S.C.) Mus. A., 1957. *Work*: Smith Col. Mus.; Ford Motor Co., Dearborn, Mich. Lectures: Modern Painting. Contributor to Lincoln Times; Ford Times (illus.). *Position*: Instr., 1942- , Prof. A., 1946- , Smith Col., Northampton, Mass.

COHEN, HAROLD LARRY—*Educator, Des., L.*
Dept. Design, Southern Illinois University; h. 515 North Oakland St., Carbondale, Ill.

B. Brooklyn, N.Y., May 24, 1925. *Studied*: PIASch.; Northwestern Univ.; Inst. Design, B.A. in Product Des. *Member*: Indst. Des. Assn.; Am. Assn. for the Advancement of Science. *Awards*: winner of five Good Design Awards, with Davis Pratt; MModA, 1949-1953; Des. of chair selected by U.S. Govt. for traveling exh. of one hundred leading U.S. products. Lectures: "Educating the Architect"; "On Furniture"; "Creative Thinking", etc. *Position*: Prof. Des., Dept. Des., Southern Illinois Univ., Carbondale, Ill.

COHEN, HY—*Painter*
166 West 72nd St., New York 23, N.Y.

B. London, England, June 13, 1901. *Studied*: Col. of the City of N.Y., B.S.; NAD. *Member*: AWS; AEA. *Exhibited*: BM; PAFA; AIC; WAC; Butler Inst. Am. A.; CGA, and others; one-man: ACA Gal., N.Y., 1932-1936, 1940, 1942, 1945, 1952, 1958. Organized and conducted weekly radio program "Let's Talk About Art," WNYC, 1945-46.

COHEN, NESSA—*Sculptor, P.*
107 Clinton Ave., Newark 2, N.J.

B. New York, N.Y. *Studied*: with James E. Fraser, New York; Despiau, Charles Malfrey, Paris. *Member*: NAWA; Soc. Indp. A. *Awards*: Med., 9th Olympiad, Amsterdam, Holland, 1928. *Work*: Am. Mus. Natural Hist.; Sch. Arch. & All. A., Portland, Ore.; Stanford Univ. *Exhibited*: AAPL, 1956-58.

COHN, MAX ARTHUR—*Painter, Ser., W.*
258 West 17th St., New York 11, N.Y.

B. London, England, Feb. 3, 1904. *Studied*: ASL, with Boardman Robinson, John Sloan. *Member*: ASL; Nat. Ser. Soc.; Delaware Valley A. *Work*: MMA; PMA; Albany Inst. Hist. & A.; Nelson Gal. A.; Howard Univ.; DMFA. *Exhibited*: BM, 1939; LC, 1945; MModA, 1936, 1941, 1942; Milford, N.J., 1946-1957; DMFA; one-man: New Sch. for Social Research, N.Y., 1932; ACA Gal., 1934; Delphic Studios, 1936. Author: "Silk Screen Stenciling as a Fine Art," 1942. Treas., Delaware Valley AA.

COLBURN, FRANCIS PEABODY—*Painter, L.*
University of Vermont; h. College & Willard Sts., Burlington, Vt.

B. Fairfax, Vt., Oct. 20, 1909. *Studied*: Univ. Vermont, Ph.B.; ASL, with Raphael Soyer, Harry Sternberg. *Member*: Fleming Mus. A. Assn. (Pres.). *Awards*: prizes, Springfield

Mus. FA, 1941; Fed. Women's Cl., Vermont, 1933, 1934; med., Palace Legion Honor, 1946; Inst. Contemp. A., 1949. *Work*: Fleming Mus. A.; Bennington Mus.; Oklahoma Univ.; Univ. Utah; Middlebury Col. *Exhibited*: WFNY 1939; Contemporary Am. A., 1939; AIC, 1941; Springfield A. Lg., 1941-1943; CGA, 1941; Conn. Acad. FA, 1941; Carnegie Inst., 1941, 1946; Pasadena AI, 1946; Palace Legion Honor, 1946; WMAA, 1945-1949; Knoedler Gal. (one-man); Grace Horne Gal. (one-man); Smith Col. (one-man); Macbeth Gal., 1951 (one-man); Univ. Maine (one-man); Dartmouth Col.; Audubon A.; Boston Arts Festival. Contributor of: critical articles to newspapers. *Position*: A. in residence, Prof. FA., Chm. A. Dept., Univ. Vermont, Burlington, Vt., 1942- .

COLBY, MRS. JOHN STITT. See George, Dorothy

COLBY, VICTOR—Educator, S.
Franklin Hall, Cornell University, Ithaca, N.Y.; h. R. D. #1, Groton, N.Y.

B. Frankfort, Ind., Jan. 5, 1917. *Studied*: Corcoran Sch. A., with Robert Laurent; Indiana Univ., A.B.; Cornell Col., M.F.A., with Kenneth Washburn. *Work*: Munson-Williams-Proctor Inst. A., Utica, N.Y.; Phillips Hall, Cornell Univ. *Exhibited*: N.Y. State A., 1950-1956; one-man: Cornell Univ., 1952; Hewitt Gal., N.Y.C., 1957; Munson-Williams-Proctor Inst. A., 1955. *Position*: Prof. Sculpture, Cornell Univ., Ithaca, N.Y.

COLE, ALPHAEUS P.—Painter, I., T., Des., W.
360 West 22nd St., New York 11, N.Y.

B. Hoboken, N.J., July 12, 1876. *Studied*: Julien Acad., Paris; Ecole des Beaux-Arts, Paris, and with Benjamin Constant, Jean Paul Laurens. *Member*: NA; SC; NAC; AWS; All. A. Am.; Hudson Valley AA. *Awards*: prizes, SC, 1943; NAC, 1934, 1937, 1939; med., AAPL, 1934; Conn. Acad. FA, 1920; Montclair Soc. A., 1934; Hudson Valley AA, 1956-1958. *Work*: Nat. Port. Gal., London; BM; Univ. Virginia; Univ. Alabama; Fordham Univ. Law Sch.; Univ. Col., London, England; Museum of Art, Newcastle-on-Tyne, England. *Exhibited*: Paris Salon, 1900, 1901, 1903; Royal Acad., London, 1904-1910; NAD, 1910-1919, 1953-1955; AWS, 1953-1955 and prior; All. A. Am., 1953-1955; Hudson Valley AA, 1953-1955; NAC, 1953-1955; SC, 1953-1955. Co-author (with Margaret Cole) "Timothy Cole, Wood Engraver."

COLE, ANN—Painter, C., S., Des., T., L.
284 Whitford Ave., Nutley 10, N.J.

B. Brooklyn, N.Y., Feb. 12, 1903. *Studied*: PIASch.; ASL; Montclair Mus. A. Sch. *Member*: New Jersey WC Soc.; NAWA. *Awards*: prizes, Audubon A., 1957; NAWA, 1955; Montclair A. Mus.; Essex WC Cl.; AAPL (several); New Jersey WC Soc., and others. *Work*: paintings in private collections; mosaic column & fountain, 1957; textile mural, 1958; tile interiors and other commissions. *Exhibited*: Audubon A.; Albright A. Gal.; All. A. Am.; Phila. A. All.; AWS; Rochester Mem. A. Gal.; Riverside Mus.; CGA; NAWA; CMA; Portland Mus. A.; Montclair A. Mus.; Trenton Mus. A.; Newark Mus. A.; Princeton Univ.; Jersey City Mus. A. *Positions*: Instr., Newark Sch. FA; Nutley Sch.; Bloomfield, N.J.; Passaic, N.J.; Camp Dir., A. & Crafts, 1956-58.

COLE, GAIL (SHEPARDSON)—Painter, T.
5421 Anza St., San Francisco 21, Cal.

B. San Diego, Cal., Apr. 27, 1914. *Studied*: Stanford Univ., with George Post, Victor Arnautoff; Cal. Sch. FA, with Maurice Sterne, Otis Oldfield, Spencer Macky, William Gaw. *Member*: Cal. WC Soc.; AEA; San F. AA; San F. Women Artists. *Awards*: prizes, San Francisco A. Festival, 1951; San F. Women Artists, 1952; Cal. State Fair, 1952; Hallmark award, 1953; 10th & 12th ann. San F. A. Festival, 1956, 1958. *Exhibited*: Cal. WC Soc., 1943, 1944, 1948, 1952, 1954, 1955, 1956; Western Assn. Mus. Dirs., traveling exh., 1954-55; AWS, 1948; Assoc. Am. A. Gal., N.Y., 1947; Los A. AA, 1945, 1946; Denver A. Mus., 1952-1954; Hallmark Awards, 1953-54; SFMA, 1952-1956, 1958; deYoung Mem. Mus., 1953; Cal. State Fair, 1951-1954; Studio 44, San F., 1955; Richmond A. Center, 1954, 1956, 1958; San F. AA, 1953, 1956, 1957; one-man: Biltmore A. Gal., Los A., 1942; British Colonial Hotel, Nassau, Bahamas, 1946; Moseley Gal., Nassau, 1947; Cal. PLH, 1957; IBM, San Jose, Cal., 1958. *Position*: private classes, 1952-58; Discussion leader, Univ. Cal., Ext. Div., 1958.

COLE, JACK R.—Cartoonist
R. D. #2, New Milford, Conn.

B. New Castle, Pa., Dec. 14, 1914. Contributor to Playboy, True, Look and many other magazines since 1942.*

COLE, THOMAS CASILEAR—Painter, L.
939 Eighth Ave., New York 19, N.Y.

B. Staatsburgh, N.Y., July 23, 1888. *Studied*: BMFA Sch., with Philip Hale, Frank W. Benson; Julian Acad., Paris, with Laurens. *Member*: Rockport AA; Am. Veterans Soc. A. *Work*: Fed. Court, N.Y.; Vt. State Capitol; N.Y. Bar Assn.; Brooklyn Pub. Lib.; Battle Abbey Mus., Richmond, Va.; U.S. Naval Acad.; Queens Pub. Lib., L.I., N.Y.; Mass. Supreme Court; L.I. Col. Hospital; Duke Univ.; Tennessee Supreme Court, etc. *Exhibited*: NAD; PAFA; BMFA; AIC; Albright A. Gal.; All. A. Am.; Paris Salon, 1923; Knoedler Gal. (one-man). Lectures on art. *Position*: Former Instr. port. painting, Phoenix Sch. A., Traphagen Sch. A., Sch. F. & Indst. A., all New York, N.Y.

COLEMAN, LAURENCE VAIL—Writer, Mus. Dir.
American Association of Museums, Smithsonian Institution, Washington 25, DC.; h. 1500 Massachusetts Ave., N.W., Washington 5, D.C.

B. Brooklyn, N.Y., Sept. 19, 1893. *Studied*: Col. City of N.Y., B.S.; Yale Univ., M.A.; Harvard Univ. *Member*: Hon. F., British Mus. Assn.; Hon. F., Rochester Mus. A. & Sc.; Hon. memb., Midwest Mus. Conference; Life memb., AAMus.; memb. of many nat. & intl. bodies. *Awards*: AAMus., 1940; med., Col. City of N.Y., 1933, 1944; Townsend Harris med., 1944. Author: "The Museum in America," 3 vols., 1939; "College and University Museums," 1942; "Museum Buildings," vol. 1, 1950, and other books on museums. Contributor to educational magazines in U.S. and Europe. *Position*: Exec. Sec., 1923-27, Dir., 1927-58, Dir. Emeritus, 1958- , American Assn. of Museums.

COLEMAN, LORING W(ILKINS) JR.—Painter, T.
Concord Rd., Sudbury, Mass.

B. Jamaica Plain, Mass., Apr. 27, 1918. *Studied*: with H. Dudley Murphy, Charles Curtis Allen; Scott Carbee Sch. A., Boston, with Bernard Keyes. *Member*: AWS; All. A. Am.; SC; Knickerbocker A.; Boston Soc. WC Painters; Gld. Boston A.; St. Botolphs Cl., Boston; North Shore AA. *Awards*: prizes, All. A. Am., 1951, 1952; Boston A. Festival, 1955; gold med., Jordan Marsh Co., Boston, 1953, 1954, 1956, 1957; medal of honor, AWS, 1956; Ranger purchase prize, NAD, 1958. *Work*: Maryhill Mus., Maryhill, Wash.; BMFA; Parrish Mus., Southampton, L.I., N.Y. *Exhibited*: All. A. Am., 1951-1958; NAC, 1952; AWS, 1954-1957; NAD, 1956-1958; Boston A. Festival, 1952-1958. *Position*: Instr., Vesper George Sch. A., Boston, 1949-51; A. Dir., Publications Dept., Emory Univ., 1946-48; Instr. deCordova & Dana Mus., Lincoln, Mass., 1953-58; Supv. A. for Pub. Schs., Sudbury, Mass., 1949-57; Instr., Middlesex Sch., Concord, Mass., 1949-56, Chm. A. Dept., 1957- .

COLEMAN, RALPH PALLEN—Painter, I.
568 Baeder Rd., Baederwood, Jenkintown, Pa.

B. Philadelphia, Pa., June 27, 1892. *Studied*: PMSchIA. *Member*: Woodmere A. Gal.; NSMP; Old York Rd. A. Gld., Jenkintown, Pa. *Work*: Paintings and murals for churches in Jenkintown, Lancaster, Montoursville, Pa.; Wilmington, Del., and a series of paintings on the life of Christ in the George Washington Memorial Park, White Marsh, Pa.; 42 paintings for Coleman edition of "Hurlbuts' Story of the Bible"; 55 paintings for "The Way, The Truth and the Life"; Portraits in 103rd Engineers Armory, Phila., Pa.; New Haven Hospital; Old York Rd. Country Club. Illus. in leading national magazines. Illus. stories by Somerset Maugham, Rex Beach, Clarence Buddington Kelland, Louis Bromfield, Temple Bailey, 17 paintings for "Life of Christ," by Donald F. Irvin. Lectures: "The Life of Jesus Through an Artist's Brush," with color slides of Coleman's paintings, to churches & organizations, and others.

COLEMAN, VERNON HERBERT—
     Educator, P., Des., I., Cart., Comm. A.
Lake Dr., Wequaquet Lake, Centerville, Mass.

B. Norwich, Conn., Apr. 28, 1898. *Studied*: Corcoran Sch. A., with M. Messer, Burtis Baker; Washington Sch. A., with Will Chandlee. *Member*: Cape Cod A. Cl. *Awards*:

prizes, N.Y. Soc. A. & Sc., 1935, 1936. *Work*: murals, Maritime Col., Hyannis, Mass.; Pub. Sch., Barnstable, Mass.; Cape Cod Hospital; restaurants and private homes. *Position*: A. Supv., Barnstable, Mass., Pub. Schs., 1944-1956; Dir., Cape Cod AA.; Tech. Dir., Mary Young Theatre.*

COLER, STELLA C. (Mrs.)—Painter, T., L.
543 Givens St., Sarasota, Fla.

B. Grand Rapids, Mich. *Studied*: Univ. Michigan, A.B.; John Herron AI, and with Jerry Farnsworth, Aaron Bohrod, Hilton Leech, Will Barnet. *Member*: Indiana A. Cl.; Sarasota A.A; Pen & Brush Cl.; Fla. A. Group; Manatee A. Center. *Awards*: prizes, John Herron AI, 1942; Hoosier Salon, 1946, 1953, 1955, 1956; Indiana A. Cl., 1946, 1950, 1951, 1953, 1954, 1957; Sarasota AA, 1951; Fla. Southern Col., 1952; Manatee A. Center, 1958; one-man: Hoosier Salon Gal., 1947, 1952, 1956; Goddard Gal., Sarasota, 1953; Manatee A. Center, 1957. *Positions*: Instr., Summer Classes, Indianapolis A. Lg., 1953, 1955-1958; Pres., Sarasota AA, 1955; Vice-Pres., Fla. A. Group, 1958-59.

COLES, ANN (CADWALLADER)—Painter
1520 Senate St., Columbia 1, S.C.

B. Columbia, S.C., Aug. 4, 1882. *Studied*: Converse Col.; ASL, and with F. Luis Mora, Vincent Tack, Harry Sternberg. *Member*: AEA; Gld. South Carolina A. *Work*: portraits, Univ. North Carolina Lib.; Yale Univ. Lib.; Parish House, Charlotte, N.C.; Columbia Mus. A.; port., South Carolina Supreme Court, State Capitol (S.C.); Winthrop Col., Rock Hill, S.C.; ports. Fndr. and Dirs. The State-Record, Columbia, S.C. *Exhibited*: PAFA; AIC; Columbia A Lg.; Charlotte Woman's Cl.; one-man: Columbia Mus. A.; Florence (S.C.) Mus. A.; Converse Col., Spartanburg, S.C.

COLESCOTT, WARRINGTON—Painter, Ser., E., Et.
Art and Art Education Dept., University of Wisconsin, Madison, Wis.

B. Oakland, Cal., Mar. 7, 1921. *Studied*: Univ. California, A.B., M.A.; Grande Chaumiere, Paris, France. *Member*: Am. Color Pr. Soc.; Nat. Ser. Soc. *Awards*: prizes, Wisconsin Salon, 1949, 1951, 1955; Am. Color Print Soc., 1951, 1952, 1956; Nat. Ser. Soc., 1957; Wisconsin Pr. M., 1957; Wisconsin State Fair, 1958; Gimbel's Coll., 1951, 1953; SFMA, 1954; BM, 1955 (purchase). *Work*: Univ. Wisconsin; N.Y. Pub. Lib.; Gimbel Coll.; U.S. Information Service; MMA; MModA.; Univ. Nebraska; Smith Col.; BM. *Exhibited*: PAFA, 1950, 1952; Carnegie Inst., 1952; Walker A. Center, 1949, 1953, 1957; BM, 1953, 1957; Am. Color Pr. Soc., 1953-1956; MModA, 1953; Univ. Illinois; WMAA, 1954, 1956, 1957; Pasadena A. Mus., 1957; Denver A. Mus., 1958; Silvermine Gld A., 1957; one-man: The Contemporaries, 1956. *Position*: Chm. Dept. A. & A. Edu., Univ. Wisconsin, Madison, Wis., 1949- .

COLETTI, JOSEPH ARTHUR—Sculptor, L., W.
Fenway Studios, 30 Ipswich St., Boston 15, Mass.

B. San Donato, Italy, Nov. 5, 1898. *Studied*: Harvard Univ., A.A.; Am. Acad. in Rome, and with John Singer Sargent. *Member*: F., NSS; Mass. State A. Comm.; North Shore AA; Medieval Acad. Am. *Awards*: Traveling scholarship, FMA, 1923, 1924-1925; F., Harvard Univ.; med., Boston Tercentenary FA Exh., 1932; hon. Phi Beta Kappa, Harvard Univ., 1948. *Work*: FMA; Lyman Allyn Mus.; Brookgreen Gardens, S.C.; Gagnon Mem., Quebec, Canada; Quincy (Mass.) Pub. Lib.; Harvard Glee Club medal; Deedy Mem., Mass. State House; Gagnon Mem., Lafayette Park, Manchester, N.H.; Lafayette Park, Salem, Mass.; sculpture on Facade and 11 panels for interior of Cathedral of the Assumption, Balt., Md.; Boston A. Festival medal; Nat. Gal. Contemp. A., Florence, Italy; Sen. Walsh statue, Esplanade, Boston; Gen. Logan statue, Logan Airport, East Boston; Father McGivney statue, Waterbury, Conn. *Exhibited*: Cal. PLH, 1929; PAFA, 1929-1931; MModA, 1933; WFNY 1939; PMA, 1939; MMA, 1942; WMAA, 1940; FMA, 1928 (one-man); Boston Inst. Mod. A., 1940-1942; Audubon A., 1946. Lectures: Contemporary Sculpture. Author: Foreword to catalog "Maillol," Inst. of Modern Art, Boston.

COLL, FRANCIS A.—Artist-Craftsman
212 South Gray Ave., Wilmington 5, Del.

B. Center Port, L.I., N.Y., Sept. 12, 1884. *Studied*: Graphic Sketch Cl., Phila., Pa., and with Frederic Nunn; wood carving with Frederic Harer. *Exhibited*: Wilmington Soc. FA.; Phila. A. Cl.; Tricker Gal. *Position*: Des. & maker of hand carved gold leaf picture frames and ecclesiastical work; restorer of paintings. Executed gold embossing of Figure of Christ by N. C. Wyeth now in Nat. Cathedral, Wash., D.C. Restorer of paintings and gold leaf work, George Hardcastle & Sons, Wilmington, Del.*

COLLEY, JAMES F.—Museum Curator, P., T.
University of Oregon Museum of Art; h. 55 Prall Lane, Eugene, Ore.

B. Claresholm, Alta., Canada, Mar. 30, 1914. *Studied*: Univ. Minnesota; Oregon Col. of Edu.; Univ. Oregon, B.S. in A. Edu., M.A. *Member*: Oregon A. All.; Oregon WC Soc.; Cascade Artists; AAUP; Western Assn. A. Mus. *Exhibited*: regularly in Oregon, Washington and California. Lectures on Oriental Art to study groups, classes, and others. Arranged, assembled exhs.: Japanese Gardens, 1957; "Kodo," 1957; Tom Hardy, 1958; Chou-Ling Fang, 1958; "Aegis Collection of Egyptian Art," 1958; French Prints, 1957; English Prints, 1958; Italian Prints, 1958; "Framing —Right and Wrong," 1957; Museum of Art Gift Show, 1958; Oregon A. All. annual exhibitions, 1958 and numerous local art exhs. *Position*: Cur., Museum of Art, Univ. Oregon, Eugene, Ore., 1955- .

COLLIER, NATHAN LEO (NATE)—Cartoonist, W.
618 New St., River Vale, N.J.

B. Orangeville, Ill. *Studied*: Acme Sch. Drawing; Lockwood A. Sch.; & with J. H. Smith, G. H. Lockwood. I., "Illiterate Digest," 1927; Co-Author, I, "Breaks," 1932. Contributor to: national magazines & newspapers.

COLLINS, HAROLD DEAN—
Painter, I., Des., Comm. A.
64 Blade Ave., Frankfort, Ky.

B. Lexington, Ky., Sept. 20, 1908. *Studied*: Chicago Acad. FA; Am. Acad. FA; BMFA Sch.; & with Herbert Barnett. *Member*: Louisville AC; Frankfort AC. *Work*: Ky. Hist. Soc. Mus.; Mansion Mus., Harrodsburg, Ky.; Court House, Louisville, Ky.; Court House, Paris, Ky.; Univ. Louisville; Federal Bldg., Louisville, Ky. and Cincinnati, Ohio; Kentucky State Capitol; State Capitol Annex, Frankfort, Ky.; des., Gibson greeting cards; new official seal for Kentucky; uniforms for Ky. State Police; des. plans for Econ. Sec. Bldg., Frankfort, Ky.; four police barracks in Ky. *Exhibited*: Louisville AC, 1938; one-man: Kentucky Hist. Soc., 1956. I., "Capt. John Fowler," 1942.

COLLINS, KREIGH—Illustrator
Ada, Mich.

B. Davenport, Iowa, Jan. 1, 1908. *Studied*: Cincinnati A. Acad.; Cleveland A. Sch. *Work*: murals, East Grand Rapids H.S., Ottawa Hills H.S., East Congregational Church, all in Grand Rapids, Mich. *Exhibited*: Grand Rapids A. Gal., 1930, 1933. I., "Marconi," 1943; "Perilous Island," 1942; "World History," 1946; & others. Creator Sunday feature, "Kevin the Bold."

COLLINS, LOWELL DAUNT—
Painter, E., L., Gr.
1001 Bissonnet St. (5); h. 3303 Drexel St., Houston 6, Tex.

B. San Antonio, Tex., Aug. 12, 1924. *Studied*: Mus. FA Sch., Houston, with Ruth Uhler, Robert Preusser; Colorado Springs FA Center, with Boardman Robinson; ASL, with Harry Sternberg; Univ. Houston, B.F.A., M.L. *Awards*: prizes, Texas FA Assn., 1948; Houston A. Exh., 1952, 1957 (purchase); Feldman A. Exh., Dallas, 1956; Easter A. Exh., Houston, 1954, 1957. *Work*: U.S. Information Service; Nelson Fnd.; Mus. FA of Houston. *Exhibited*: New Zealand Exchange Exh., 1948; Houston Intl. Exh., 1956; AFA exh., Dallas, 1948, 1957; Knoedler Gal., 1952; Downtown Gal., 1952; Nat. WC Exh., Jackson, Miss., 1956; Columbia Biennial, 1957; Metzler Gal., 1957; Provincetown A. Festival, 1958; Houston A. Exh., 1947-1958; Texas FA Assn., 1948, 1949, 1957; D. D. Feldman Exh., 1956, 1958; Texas Print & Drawing, Dallas, 1957; Texas WC., Dallas, 1957; Texas Painting & Sc., 1958; one-man: Mus. of FA, Houston, 1952; Stephen F. Austin Col.; Cushman Gal., Houston, 1958. Illus., "Houston, Land of the Big Rich," 1951. Position: Instr., Drawing & Painting, Mus. FA, Houston; Des. & Painting, Univ. Houston; Dean, A. Sch., Mus. FA, Houston, Tex.

COLLINS, MRS. LOYD A. *See Logan, Elizabeth D.*

COLLINS, MARY SUSAN—Painter, C., T.
122 South 11th St., Easton, Pa.

B. Bay City, Mich., June 1, 1880. *Studied*: AIC; BMFA Sch.; ASL; T. Col., Columbia Univ.; & with Charles Hawthorne. *Member*: AAPL; Lehigh A. All.; AFA. *Awards*: prizes, CMA, 1921, 1922, 1924, 1925, 1929, 1936; Eastern Areas Exh., 1957. *Work*: CMA; Cleveland Pub. Sch.; Cleveland Mun. Coll. *Exhibited*: PAFA, 1925, 1928, 1930, 1932; AFA, 1922, 1924; All. A. Am.; 1925; CMA, 1919-1945; Detroit Inst. A., 1926, 1928, 1930, 1931; Great Lakes Exh., 1938, 1939; Lehigh A. All.; Easton, Pa. (one-man). *Position*: A.T., East H.S., Cleveland, Ohio, 1911-45.

**COLLISON, MARJORY (Mrs. R. J. Nelms)—
Illustrator, P., Lith., Des., Comm. A.**
736 James Dr., Richardson, Tex.

B. Washington, D.C., Aug. 17, 1902. *Studied*: PAFA; & with George Harding, Henry McCarter, A. Carles. *Awards*: Cresson traveling scholarship, 1924-1925; prizes, SSAL, 1927; Book of the Month award, 1944. *Exhibited*: Weyhe Gal.; Gibbes A. Gal., Charleston, S.C. Illus., "Penny and the White Horse," 1944; "Sibby Botherbox," 1945; "Water Babies," 1946; "Alice in Wonderland"; "Through the Looking-Glass"; Terry Toons Animation Cartoons, 1949-54.

COLMAN, BLANCHE EMILY—Painter, Et., Des.
28 School St., Rockport, Mass.

B. Somerville, Mass. *Studied*: BMFA Sch.; Am. Acad. in Rome; Boston Univ.; & with Charles Woodbury, Harry Leith-Ross. *Member*: Boston Soc. A. & Crafts; Copley Soc.; NAWA; Wash. WC Cl.; Conn. Acad. FA; North Shore AA; Rockport AA. *Work*: BMFA. *Exhibited*: NAWA, 1936-1946; Conn. Acad. FA, 1935, 1946; All. A. Am., 1945; North Shore AA, 1926-1946; Rockport AA, 1926-1946; Doll & Richards Gal., 1941, 1948; Copley Soc., 1942; Jordan-Marsh, 1945, 1951; Marblehead AA, 1945. *Position*: Fnd., Dir., A. Dept., Boston Univ., 1919-32.*

COLMAN, CHARLES C.—Designer, Et., I., W.
1836 Euclid Ave.; h. 2525 Kemper Rd., Shaker Heights, Cleveland 20, Ohio

B. Cleveland, Ohio, July 23, 1890. *Studied*: Cornell Univ., B. Arch.; Fenway Sch. A.; Cleveland Sch. A.; John Huntington Polytechnic Inst., Cleveland. *Member*: AIA; Arch. Soc. of Ohio. *Awards*: Med., Cleveland Chamber of Commerce, 1926, 1935; CMA, 1921, 1922, 1931, 1932. *Work*: CMA.*

COLMORGAN, PAUL—Designer, P., T.
333 North Michigan Ave., Chicago 11, Ill.; h. 700 Echo Lane, Glenview, Ill.

B. Piqua, Ohio, Aug. 20, 1903. *Studied*: Chicago Acad. FA; Cleveland Sch. A.; AIC. *Member*: Soc. Typographic A.; A. Gld. of Chicago. *Exhibited*: AIC; Glenview (Ill.) A. Exh. *Position*: T., Layout, Central YMCA Col., Chicago, Ill.

COLT, MARTHA COX—Painter, S., Mus. Asst.
5 West Green St., Shiremanstown, Pa.

B. Harrisburg, Pa., Sept. 16, 1877. *Studied*: Moore Inst.; PAFA; Univ. Pennsylvania; & with Kenneth Hayes Miller, Henry B. Snell, Calder Penfield. *Member*: Harrisburg AA; Plastic Cl., Phila., Pa. *Work*: PMA; Univ. Pennsylvania; Pa. State Museum. *Exhibited*: Plastic Cl.; Harrisburg AA. Lectures: "Portrait Relief during the Middle Ages." *Position*: Dir., Central Pennsylvania A. Sch., Harrisburg, Pa., 1929-34; State Dir., Mus. Extension Project, FAP, 1935-41; A.-Illus., Carlisle Barracks & Mechanicsburg Naval Supply Depot, 1944-48; A., Pa. State Mus., Harrisburg, 1952-58.

**COLT, PRISCILLA C.—
Museum Research & Program Assistant**
330 West Schantz Ave., Dayton 19, Ohio

B. Kalamazoo, Mich., Oct. 15, 1917. *Studied*: Kalamazoo Col., A.B.; Western Reserve Univ., M.A.; Harvard Univ., Inst. FA; New York Univ. *Member*: AAMus.; Am. Soc. for Aesthetics. Lectures: European and American Painting & Sculpture; Northwest Coast Indian Arts, etc. Arranged

special exhibitions and conducted research on collections, Portland A. Mus. *Positions*: Asst., Junior Mus., MMA, 1943-44; Asst. & Cur., Edu., VMFA, 1944-1947; Ed., Cur., Minneapolis Inst. A., 1948-49; Research Asst., Portland A. Mus., Portland, Ore., 1949-56.*

COLT, THOMAS C., JR.—Museum Director
Dayton Art Institute (5); h. 330 West Schantz Ave., Dayton 19, Ohio

B. Orange, N.J., Feb. 20, 1905. *Studied*: Dartmouth Col., B.S.; Columbia Univ.; Cambridge, England. *Member*: AAMus.; Assn. Art Mus. Dir.; Am. Soc. for Aesthetics. Ed., "C.S. Price, 1874-1950"; "Prehistoric Stone Sculpture of the Pacific Northwest"; "Samuel H. Kress Collection of Paintings of the Renaissance," and others. *Award*: Star of Solidarity, Italian Govt., 1953. *Positions*: Dir., VMFA, Richmond, Va., 1935-42; Armed Forces, 1942-45; Resumed Directorship, VMFA, 1945-48; Dir., Portland (Ore.) A. Mus., 1948-56; Dir. Dayton Art Institute, Dayton, Ohio, 1957- .

COLTON, HAROLD S.—Museum Director
Museum of Northern Arizona, Fort Valley Road, Flagstaff, Ariz.

Position: Dir., Museum of Northern Arizona.*

**COLTON, MARY-RUSSELL FERRELL (Mrs. Harold S.)
—Painter, S., C.**
Coyote Range, Flagstaff, Ariz.

B. Louisville, Ky., Mar. 25, 1889. *Studied*: Moore Inst.; Phila. Sch. Des. for Women. *Member*: NAWA; AAPL; Phila. WC Cl.; AWCS; Wash. WC Cl. Author: papers on "Indian Art and Folk Lore"; "Truth of a Hopi" (Ed.); "Art for the Schools of the Southwest," an outline for public and Indian schools. Contributor to: "Plateau" published by Mus. Northern Arizona. *Position*: Cur., Mus. Northern Arizona, Flagstaff, Ariz., 1928-46; Chm. A. Com., Bd. Trustees, Northern Arizona Soc. of Science & Art, 1946- .

COMBS, ALEX—Craftsman, P., T.
Box 80, Anchorage, Alaska

Director A., Anchorage Independent School District; Instr., Anchorage Community College, Univ. Alaska.

**COMES, MARCELLA (Mrs. Randolph Winslow)—
Painter, W.**
3106 P. St., Northwest, Washington 7, D.C.

B. Pittsburgh, Pa. *Studied*: Carnegie Inst., with Alexander Kostellow, Karl Knath, and in Europe. *Member*: Assoc. A. Pittsburgh; Women's Com., CGA; AEA; Wash. Soc. A.; Wash. A. Gld. A.; Wash. Chptr., Nat. Soc. A. & Let. *Awards*: prizes, Assoc. A. Pittsburgh, 1929; Carnegie Inst., 1936, 1941; Soc. Wash. A., 1946; Georgetown A., 1955. *Work*: murals, Pittsburgh Pub. Lib.; U.S. Military Acad., West Point, N.Y.; Pittsburgh Pub. Sch.; Pittsburgh Parochial Sch. (painting); mural, Stone Ridge Convent of the Sacred Heart. *Exhibited*: CGA; Assoc. A. Pittsburgh, 1929-1952; Wash. Soc. A., 1938-1952; Baltimore, 1952; one-man: Whyte Gal., 1948; Brooks Mem. Mus., 1941; Chequire House, Alexandria, Va., 1950; 4 Washington Artists Exh., CGA, 1957; portraits of authors reproduced in New York Times. Contributor critical reviews to Carnegie Magazine and other university publications.

COMFORT, BARBARA—Painter, I.
21 Perry St., New York 14, N.Y.

B. Nyack, N.Y., Sept. 4, 1916. *Studied*: NAD; ASL; Ecole des Beaux-Arts. *Awards*: prize, AAPL, 1942; Audubon A., 1954. *Exhibited*: Audubon A., 1950-1952; N.Y. WC Cl., 1947; AIC, 1945; one-man: 460 Park Ave. Gal., 1942; Scranton Mus. A., 1949; Creative A. Gal., 1946; Guild Gal., 1951; Argent Gal., 1951; Maui Gal., Hawaii, 1948; one-man: So. Vermont A. Center, 1955; Argent Gal., 1955. Illus., "Tower by the Sea," 1950.*

COMITO, NICHOLAS U.—Painter, Lith., T.
1747 Burnett St., Brooklyn 29, N.Y.

B. New York, N.Y., Sept. 30, 1906. *Studied*: N.Y. Univ., B.S. in Edu.; NAD, and in Italy. *Member*: Brooklyn Soc. A.; SC; Southern Vermont A.; Audubon A.; AWS; Cal.

Soc. Et.; Am. Veterans Soc. A. *Awards*: prizes, NAD, 1940; Wawasee A. Gal., Syracuse, Ind., 1944, 1945; Jersey City A. Mus., 1945; Irvington, N.J., 1946. *Work*: N.Y. Univ. *Exhibited*: NAD, 1940-1944; Phila. WC Cl., 1941; AWS, 1945; Carnegie Inst., 1943-1945; Wash. WC Cl., 1944; LC, 1944-1946; BM, 1941-1945; Currier Gal. A., 1941.

COMPTON, CAROLINE RUSSELL—*Painter*
2408 Drummond St., Vicksburg, Miss.

B. Vicksburg, Miss., Jan. 10, 1907. *Studied*: Sweet Briar Col., B.A., with Virginia McLaws; Grand Central A. Sch.; and with Grant Reynard, Wayman Adams, George Pearse Ennis, George Luks. *Member*: Mississippi AA; Allison A. Colony. *Awards*: prize and med., Mississippi AA, 1933, 1934, 1954. *Work*: 19 portraits for "River Hall of Fame" Mus., on "The Sprague," steamboat at Vicksburg, Miss.; Miss. AA; Miss. State Col. for Women. *Exhibited*: Am. A., New York, 1937, 1938; Miss. AA, 1926-1955; Delgado Mus. A., 1931-1937; High Mus. A., 1936; Davenport, Iowa, 1940, 1941; Vicksburg, Jackson, Oxford, Miss. (one-man); Sweet Briar Col.; Allison A. Colony, 1950, 1952, 1954 (one-man); Columbus, Miss., 1952 (one-man); Delta AA, Greenwood, Miss., 1954 (one-man).

CONANT, HOWARD S.—*Educator, W., L., P.*
New York University, New York, N.Y.; h. New Rochelle, N.Y.

B. Beloit, Wis., May 5, 1921. *Studied*: Univ. Wisconsin, Milwaukee, B.S. in Edu.; ASL, with Yasuo Kuniyoshi; Univ. Wisconsin, Madison, M.S. in A. Edu.; Univ. Buffalo, Ed. D. *Member*: Am. Assn. Univ. Prof.; Nat. Committee on A. Edu.; NAEA; Eastern AA; N.Y. State A.T. Assn. *Awards*: prizes, Wisconsin State Fair, 1943, 1946. *Work*: Hartland, Wis., Pub. Sch.; Winneconne, Wis., Pub. Sch.; and in private coll. *Exhibited*: Milwaukee AI, 1943, 1946, 1947, 1951; Layton A. Gal., 1945; NAD, 1946; SFMA, 1946; Albany Inst. Hist. & A., 1947; Hofstra Col., 1949; Ithaca (N.Y.) AA, 1950; State Univ. of N.Y. traveling exh., 1951-52, 1954-55; one-man: International Gal., Wash., D.C., 1945, 1946; Alexandria Pub. Lib., 1946; Wash., D.C. Pub. Lib., 1946; New-Age Gal., 1948; Junior League, Buffalo, 1955; College Union, Buffalo, 1955. Author: "Art as the Communication of Human Values" (Chap. 6, 1953 Yearbook) of NAEA; "Art in Education" (with Arne Randall), 1959; "Masterpieces of the Arts," New Wonder World Encyclopedia, Parents Magazine, 1959; "Art Workshop Leaders Planning Guide," 1959. Contributor of articles to art and educational publications. Lectures; Moderator of TV program "Fun to Learn" series, 1951-55. Color telecast on Modern Art, 1955; A. consultant & program participant to NBC—TV, "Adventuring in the Hand Arts," 1958-59. *Position*: Chm., Dept. A. Edu., N.Y. Univ., 1955; Adv. Ed, School Arts magazine.

CONDER, JACQUES—*Painter, T.*
Box 773, Anchorage, Alaska

Position: Instr., Anchorage Community Col., at present.

CONDIT, (ELEANOR) LOUISE
(Mrs. Frederic G. M. Lange)—*Museum Supervisor*
Metropolitan Museum of Art, Fifth Ave. & 82nd St., New York 28, N.Y.; h. 1203 Emerson Ave., Teaneck, N.J.

B. Baltimore, Md., May 7, 1914. *Studied*: Vassar Col., A.B.; Columbia Univ., M.A. *Member*: AAMus.; N.Y. Film Council; Nat. Committee on A. Edu.; Councillor, AAMus., 1957- ; Incorporator, Bergen Community Mus., 1956. *Awards*: Carnegie Grant, 1939. Author: "Paul Revere," Metropolitan Museum Picture Book, 1944 and articles in professional journals. *Position*: Supv. Edu., Brooklyn Children's Mus., 1935-42; Supv., The Junior Museum, MMA, New York, N.Y., 1943- .

CONDIT, WALTER D.—*Painter, T., Comm. A.*
7800 Gettysburg Rd., Philadelphia 28, Pa.

B. Passaic, N.J., Mar. 30, 1918. *Studied*: PAFA; Univ. Pennsylvania, B.F.A., M.F.A.; Barnes Fnd. *Member*: Phila. A. All.; Norristown A. Lg.; Woodmere A. Gal.; Manayunk A. All. *Awards*: Cresson traveling F., PAFA, 1940, prize, 1941; Vernon Park drawing exh., 1958; Phila. Regional Exh., 1958. *Exhibited*: Phila. Sketch Cl.; Woodmere A. Gal., annually; Norristown A. Lg.; Manayunk A. All.; one-man: Phillips Gal. (2).

CONDON, GRATTAN—*Painter, E.*
100 Orchard Rd., Piqua, Ohio

B. Eugene, Ore., June 10, 1887. *Studied*: Los A. Sch. A. & Des.; and with Walter Biggs, Lewis Daniel. *Member*: SC. *Position*: Former Instr., Parsons Sch. Des., City Col., New York, N.Y. and Newark Sch. F. & App. A.; Instr., Piqua Studio, Piqua, Ohio.

CONE, MARVIN—*Painter, E.*
1721 5th Ave., S.E., Cedar Rapids, Iowa

B. Cedar Rapids, Iowa, Oct. 21, 1891. *Studied*: Coe Col., B.S.; AIC; Ecole des Beaux-Arts, France. *Member*: Am. Assn. Univ. Prof. *Awards*: prizes, Davenport Mun. A. Gal., 1940; Joslyn Mem., 1944, 1945; Chicago Gal. Assn., 1940; D.F.A., Cornell Col., Mt. Vernon, Iowa. *Work*: Cedar Rapids AA; Norton Gal., West Palm Beach, Fla.; Art Festival, Chicago, 1955; Joslyn Mem.; Des Moines A. Center (purchase award); Mulvane A. Mus.; Davenport Mun. A. Gal.; Walker A. Center. *Exhibited*: PAFA, 1936, 1937, 1941, 1942; CGA, 1937, 1942; AIC, 1938, 1939-1945, 1951; VMFA, 1940, 1942, 1946; NAD, 1941, 1943-1945, 1956; WFNY 1939; Carnegie Inst., 1941, 1943, 1951; Colorado Springs FA Center, 1945, 1946; Toledo Mus. A., 1941, 1944; Swope Gal. A., 1942; MMA, 1942; Denver A. Mus., 1940-1945; Joslyn Mem., 1943-1945; Walker A. Center, 1951, 1952, 1954; Des Moines A. Center, 1955 (one-man & group); Mid-Am. exh., Kansas City, 1954, 1958; Chicago, 1955; State Univ., Iowa, 1955; Butler Inst. Am. A., 1957; Kansas State Col., 1958. *Position*: Prof. A., Coe Col., Cedar Rapids, Iowa.

CONGDON, WILLIAM—*Painter*
64 Angell St., Providence 6, R.I.

B. Providence, R.I., Apr. 15, 1912. *Studied*: Yale Univ., B.A.; Demetrios Sch. Sc.; Cape Sch. A., with Henry Hensche; PAFA. *Awards*: Temple gold med., PAFA, 1951; prizes, R.I. Mus. A., 1949, 1950; CGA, 1953; Univ. Illinois, 1952 (purchase). *Work*: CAM; Univ. Illinois; Detroit Inst. A.; R.I. Mus. A.; BMFA; PC; AGAA; Wadsworth Atheneum; Rochester Mem. Mus.; Iowa State T. Col.; MModA; WMAA; MMA; Toledo Mus. A. *Exhibited*: NAD, 1939; PAFA, 1937-39, 1950; Carnegie Inst., 1940, 1952, 1958; WMAA, 1941, 1951, 1952, 1955; R.I. Mus. A., 1948, 1949; AGAA, 1941; AIC, 1952; Toledo Mus. A., 1952; Albright A. Gal., 1952; Cal. PLH, 1952; Contemp. A., Boston, 1951; Univ. Michigan, 1951; Univ. Illinois, 1952; Los A. Mus. A., 1951; Venice Biennale, 1952, 1958; MMA, 1950; Wildenstein Gal., 1952; Hallmark Comp., 1955; one-man: Betty Parsons Gal., 1949, 1950, 1952-1954, 1956 (and group shows); Margaret Brown Gal., 1951, 1956; Duncan Phillips Gal., 1952; Contemp. A., 1951; Chicago A. Cl., 1954; Obelisco Gal., Rome, Italy, 1954, 1958; Arthur Jeffress Gal., London, 1958. Contributor of articles to Italian magazines "Ovest," "Botteghe Oscure." Illus. for Life magazine and others.

CONNAWAY, JAY HALL—*Painter, T., L.*
Connaway Art School, Dorset, Vt.; h. Pawlet, Vt.

B. Liberty, Ind., Nov. 27, 1893. *Studied*: ASL, with Bridgman, Chase; Julien Acad., Paris, with Laurens; NAD; Ecole des Beaux-Arts, Paris. *Member*: NA; All. A. Am.; SC; NAC; Audubon A.; CAA; Meriden A. & Crafts. *Awards*: prizes, Hoosier Salon, 1926, 1947; Ogunquit A. Center, 1949; Meriden A. & Crafts, 1950; NAD, 1926; NAC, 1928; New Haven Paint & Clay Cl., 1944; All. A. Am., 1945; Boothbay Harbor, Me., 1947. *Work*: John Herron AI; Sweat Mus. A.; Canajoharie A. Mus.; Springville (Utah) A. Gal.; Charleston AA; BMFA; New Haven Paint & Clay Cl.; Farnsworth Mus.; So. Vermont A.; Indiana Univ. *Exhibited*: CGA; PAFA, 1926-1943; NAD, 1924-1946; AIC, 1928-1946; Toledo Mus. A., 1937; Clearwater, Fla., 1939, 1940; All. A. Am.; Albright A. Gal.; Macbeth Gal.; Grand Central A. Gal.; one-man: Macbeth Gal., 1926-1940; Milch Gal., 1929, 1941, 1944, 1949; Vose Gal., Boston, 1940, 1948; Doll & Richards Gal., 1948, 1949, 1951, 1953, 1954; Oberlin Col., 1939; Dayton AI, 1939; John Herron AI, 1939; Currier Gal. A.; Montclair A. Mus., 1946; Manchester, Vt., 1951, 1952; So. Vermont A., 1953-1957; Cayuga Mus. A., 1955; Utica Pub. Lib., 1955; Westerly, R.I., 1956; Kennedy Gal., N.Y., 1957, and many others. Lectures & demonstrations: Techniques and Art History at museums and art centers. *Position*: Instr., Dir., Connaway A. Sch., Dorset, Vt.; Trustee, Southern Vt. A. Center, 1954- .

CONNELLY, BRIAN—*Painter*

Belden Hill, Wilton, Conn.; also 38 Central Park South, New York 19, N.Y.

B. Roseburg, Ore., June 27, 1926. *Studied*: Univ. Oregon; ASL, and in Europe. *Awards*: prizes, Carnegie Inst., 1952; A. Dir. Cl., 1953 (DeBeers coll.). *Work*: AIC. *Exhibited*: Carnegie Inst., 1952, 1955; one-man: Am-British A. Center, 1950, 1951; Santa Barbara Mus. A., 1954; Cal. PLH, 1954; SAM, 1954; Los A. Mus. A., 1954; Long Beach A. Center, 1954; Mus. FA of Houston, 1955; Syracuse Mus. FA, 1956; Dayton AI, 1956.

CONNELLY, GEORGE L.—*Illustrator*

Street Rd., Westtown, Pa.

B. Philadelphia, Pa., Mar. 3, 1908. *Studied*: PMSchIA; & with Franz De Merlier, Belgium. *Member*: Phila. A. Dir. Cl.; Phila. Sketch Cl.; Chester County AA. *Awards*: prizes, Phila. A.Dir.Cl., 1943. *Exhibited*: Phila.A.Dir.Cl. Exh.; West Chester AA. I., magazines & journals.

CONNERY, RUTH (McGRATH)—*Painter, T., L.*

570 Shore Acres Drive, Mamaroneck, N.Y.

B. New York, N.Y., Mar. 2, 1916. *Studied*: Mills Col.; ASL, with Frank DuMond, William von Schlegell. *Member*: NAWA; Mamaroneck A. Gld. *Awards*: prizes, New Rochelle AA, 1954, 1955; Larchmont AA, 1954; Mamaroneck AA, 1955. *Work*: in private colls. *Exhibited*: NGA, 1951; NAWA, 1952, 1954; Mamaroneck AA; Anne Ross Gal., White Plains, N.Y.; Westchester A. & Crafts; New Rochelle AA. *Position*: Instr., The Art Barn Studio of Mamaroneck A. Gld.*

CONSTABLE, WILLIAM GEORGE—

Museum Advisor, A. Hist.

Museum of Fine Arts, Boston, Mass.; h. 23 Craigie St., Cambridge, Mass.

B. Derby, England, Oct. 27, 1887. *Studied*: Cambridge Univ., M.A.; Slade Sch., London, with Wilson Steer, Hadvard Thomas. *Member*: F. Soc. Antiquaries; A. Workers Gld., London; Goldsmiths Co., London; Am. Acad. A. & Sc.; F., Int. Inst. Conservation (Pres.); Royal Acad. A. & Sc., Belgium (Hon.); Chevalier, Legion of Honor; Commendatore of the Crown of Italy; Officier, Ordre des Arts et Lettres, France. Author: "Flaxman: English Painting 17th & 18th Centuries"; "Richard Wilson"; "The Painters Workshop"; "Canaletto," & others. Contributor to: Art magazines & bulletins. *Position*: Asst. Dir., Nat. Gal., London; Dir.; Courtauld Inst. A. Univ. London; Slade Prof., Univ. Cambridge; Cur. Paintings, BMFA, Boston, Mass.; L., Yale Univ., New Haven, Conn.

CONSTANT, GEORGE—*Painter*

187 East Broadway, New York 2, N.Y.

B. Greece, Apr. 17, 1892. *Studied*: Washington Univ., St. Louis, Mo.; AIC, and with Charles Hawthorne, George Bellows. *Member*: Fed. Mod. P. & S.; Audubon A. *Awards*: Scholarship, 1917, prize and med., 1943, AIC; Schilling purchase prize, 1939, 1945; LC, 1947 (purchase); Audubon A., 1946; Parrish Mus., Southampton, L.I., 1950, 1951. *Work*: MMA; BM; Detroit Inst. A.; Dayton AI; SFMA; Walker A. Center; Delgado Mus. A.; LC; Stedelijk Mus., Amsterdam, Holland; Alabama Polytechnic Inst.; AGAA; Tel-Aviv Mus., Israel; State Dept., Wash., D.C.; PAFA. *Exhibited*: CGA; Carnegie Inst.; AIC; MMA; BM; WMAA; MModA; PAFA; SFMA; Los A. Mus. A.; Rollins Col.; Amsterdam, Holland; VMFA; Wadsworth Atheneum; Musee d'Arte Moderne, Paris, France; Munich, Germany; Victoria & Albert Mus., London; Mexico Univ., Mexico City; CAM; Cultural Div., U.S. Embassy, Paris, 1954-55 and many others. Over 31 one-man exhs., U.S. and abroad. Reproductions in "The Art Museum in America," Walter Pach; "The Naked Truth and Personal Vision," Bartlett H. Hayes, Jr.; "Twentieth Century Highlights of American Painting," State Dept. USIA.

CONTI, GINO EMILIO—*Painter, S., T., C., L.*

21 Planet St., Providence 3, R.I.

B. Barga, Italy, July 18, 1900. *Studied*: R.I.Sch.Des.; Ecole des Beaux-Arts, Julian Acad., Paris. *Member*: R.I. Sch. Des. Mus.; Providence A. Cl.; Providence WC Cl.; Botolph Group, Boston. *Awards*: various prizes in U.S.

exhs. *Work*: murals, R.I. State Col.; R.I.Pub.Sch.; St. Francis Church, Wakefield, R.I.; Bishop Chapel, Providence, R.I. *Exhibited*: Paris, 1925; Italy; Arch. Lg., 1929, 1930; NAD, 1929; PAFA, 1929; CAM, 1930; Providence Mus. A.; WMA; CM; Newport AA; Doll & Richards, Boston; Argent Gal., 1950, 1951; Providence A. Cl., 1950, 1951; Des Moines A. Center, 1951; AGAA, 1951; Wadsworth Atheneum, 1950; Silvermine Gld. A., 1952; Ogunquit A. Center, 1951, 1952; Springfield Mus. A., 1952. *Positions*: Fndr., Dir., Penelope Court A. Sch., Providence, R.I.; Instr., Gordon School, Providence, R.I.

CONVERSE, LILY S.—*Lithographer, P.*

1900 Locust St., Philadelphia, Pa.

B. St. Petersburg, Russia, Oct. 14, 1892. *Studied*: PAFA; ASL, in Paris with Andre L'Hote, and with Kenneth Hayes Miller, Robert Henri and others. *Member*: NAWA; AAPL; Phila. Pr. Cl.; Phila. A. All. *Awards*: prizes, Wilmington Soc. FA, 1940; Chester County (Pa.) AA, 1941; Springfield AA; P. & S. Soc., New Jersey; Clearwater Mus. A.; VMFA. *Work*: MMA; PMA; BMFA; Detroit Inst. A.; Phila. Pr. Cl.; North Carolina State Mus.; N.Y.Pub.Lib.; Nat. Mus., Wash., D.C.; Berkshire Mus. A.; BM; British Mus., Victoria & Albert Mus., London; Bibliotheque Nationale, Paris. *Exhibited*: LC; CGA; NAD; PAFA; AIC; PMA; Phila.Pr.Cl.; Los Angeles AA; Provincetown AA; North Shore AA; and in London and Paris. One-man: Nat. Mus., Wash., D.C.; Berkshire Mus. A.; Mus. of New Mexico; NAWA; Sarasota AA; Palm Springs Cl., Fla.*

CONWAY, FRED—*Painter, E., L.*

Washington University, Art School, St. Louis, Mo.

B. St. Louis, Mo., 1900. *Studied*: St. Louis Sch. FA; Julian Acad., Acad. Moderne, Paris, France. *Member*: St. Louis A. Gld. *Awards*: prizes, CAM, 1944, 1945, 1949; St. Louis A. Gld., 1928-1931, 1938-1948; Joslyn Mem. A. Mus., 1947; Univ. Illinois, 1949; CGA, 1949; Hallmark Comp., 1949; Springfield, Mo., 1944; Rolla, Mo., 1940; Y.M.H.A., St. Louis, 1941, 1942; Pepsi-Cola Exh., 1945, 1947, 1948; 48 States Comp., 1940; Denver A. Mus., 1947; Mulvane A. Mus., 1947, 1949; gold medal, Arch. Lg., 1956. *Work*: CAM; Pepsi-Cola Co.; Springfield Mus. A.; Univ. Missouri; Denver A. Mus.; Joslyn Mem. A. Mus.; Univ. Illinois; CGA; Mulvane A. Mus.; Hallmark Coll.; Illinois Wesleyan Univ.; Washington Univ.; IBM; murals, First Nat. Bank, Tulsa, Okla.; Mayo Clinic, Rochester, Minn.; Barnes Hospital, St. Louis, Mo.; Brown Shoe Co., St. Louis, Mo.; Peabody Coal Co., St. Louis; Ch. 9, T.V., St. Louis, Mo. *Exhibited*: CAM; St. Louis A. Gld.; Denver A. Mus.; NAD; VMFA; PAFA; AIC; Carnegie Inst.; CMA; AGAA; Rochester Mem. Mus.; Toledo Mus. A.; WMAA; Butler AI; Wildenstein Gal.; Philbrook A. Center; Los A. Mus. A.; Des Moines A. Center; Univ. Oklahoma; Bowdoin Col.; Utica Pub. Lib.; and many others including numerous one-man exhibitions. *Position*: Instr., Painting, Washington Univ., St. Louis, Mo.

CONWELL, AVERIL COURTNEY (Mrs. L. D.)—*Painter*

Upper Jay, N.Y.

B. Belvidere, Ill. *Studied*: AIC, B.F.A.; Chicago Acad. FA; & with Edmund Giesbert, Jon Corbino, John Vanderpoel, John Norton. *Member*: NSMP; Chicago AC; Assn. Chicago P.&S.; Chicago SA; Austin, Oak Park & River Forest A. Lg. *Awards*: Prizes, Chicago Gal. Assn., 1941; Austin Oak Park & River Forest A. Lg., 1943-1945; CM, 1945; Albany Inst. Hist. & Art, 1958. *Work*: murals, Mirror Lake Inn, Lakeside Inn, Lake Placid, N.Y.; Whiteface Inn, Whiteface, N.Y. *Exhibited*: CM, 1945; AIC, 1931, 1932, 1935, 1937, 1941, 1944; Findley A. Gal., 1938, 1941 (one-man); Lake Placid Club, 1951, 1956-1958 (one-man); Albany Inst. Hist. & Art, 1954, 1956, 1958.

COOK, ALMA MAY—*Educator, Cr.*

Herald & Express, 1243 Trenton St.; h. 1810 Avalon St., Los Angeles 26, Cal.

B. Los Angeles, Cal., Sept. 30, 1891. *Studied*: Univ. So. California, Col. of FA; Univ. So. California, Col. of Liberal A., B.F.A. *Member*: Cal. A. Cl. (hon. Life). Contributor art criticism and feature stories, Los A. Herald & Express. Lectures: Art in California; Art in History; Art in Our Lives.

COOK, AUGUST—Educator, P., Eng.

Converse College; h. 438 South Fairview Ave., Ext., Spartanburg, S.C.; s. Bethel, Vt.

B. Philadelphia, Pa., Mar. 15, 1897. *Studied*: Harvard Univ.; PAFA, and with Garber, Hale, Carles. *Member*: Boston Pr. M.; Gld. of South Carolina A; F. PAFA. *Awards*: prizes, Cresson traveling scholarship and Toppan prize, PAFA; Mint Mus. A.; Gibbes A. Gal.; Gld. South Carolina A. *Work*: Carnegie Inst.; Gibbes A. Gal.; LC; Furman Univ., Greenville, S.C.; Bethel (Vt.) Pub. Lib. *Exhibited*: BM; Carnegie Inst.; LC; Boston Pr. M.; Albany Inst. Hist. & A.; Buffalo Print exh.; SAGA; Audubon A.; Bradley Univ.; Phila. Pr. Cl.; Univ. California; Gibbes A. Gal.; Laguna Beach AA; New Britain Mus.; Newport, R.I.; Northwest Pr. M., etc. *Position*: Prof. A., Converse Col., Spartanburg, S.C.

COOK, BLANCHE McLANE (Mrs. Harry C.)—
Painter, T.

915 Pleasant Ave., Yakima, Wash.

B. Moulton, Iowa, July 1, 1901. *Studied*: Phila. Sch. Des.; Central Washington Col. of Edu. *Member*: Nat. Lg. of Am. Pen Women; Larson Gal. Gld.; Washington State AA; SAM; Yakima Valley AA; Women Painters of Wash.; Woessner Gal. *Awards*: prizes, Wash. State Fair, 1930, 1931; F., Phila. Sch. Des.; Spokane 5-State Comp., 1954. *Exhibited*: SAM, 1945; Cal. PLH, 1946; Pacific Northwest Exh., Seattle, 1944; Spokane 5-State Exh., 1954; Coliseum Gal., Spokane, 1955; Larson Gal., 1956-1958; Woessner Gal., Seattle, 1955, 1956; Women Painters of Wash. (annually); Yakima Valley A.; F & N Little Gallery, Seattle, 1956; Frye Mus. A., 1957; Spokane Art Board, 1955; Chinook Hotel, Yakima, 1957, 1958; one-man: Larson Gal., Yakima, 1933. *Position*: Instr. A., Yakima Jr. Col., 1933-48, part-time, 1958; freelance commercial artist and portrait painter.

COOK, GLADYS EMERSON—
Illustrator, P., Et., W., L.

41 Union Square, West; h. Hotel Wolcott, 4 West 31st St., New York 1, N.Y.

B. Haverhill, Mass. *Studied*: Skidmore Col., B.S.; Univ. Wisconsin, M.S.; ASL, with Anthony Thieme, Yarnall Abbott. *Member*: F., Royal Soc. A., London; SAGA; SI; AAUW; Wisconsin Alumni Assn. *Awards*: Artist of the Year, Albany Pr. Cl. *Work*: CM; N.Y.Pub.Lib.; MMA; PMA; LC. Created print "Queenie and Her Cubs," Ringling Bros. *Exhibited*: NAD, 1943, 1944, 1945; LC, 1943-1945; N.Y. Pub. Lib., 1942; NAC; SI, 1945 (one-man); Grand Central Gal., 1946; MMA; Bronx Zoological Park, 1941 (one-man). Author, I., "Hiram and Other Cats," 1941; "American Champions," 1945; "How to Draw the Cat"; Portfolio of Champion Dogs; Portfolio of Cats; "How to Draw Horses"; "Circus Clowns on Parade"; "How to Draw Dogs," and others. I., "We Lived with Peter"; "My Dog," and others. Motion picture work on "The Yearling," "Thunderhead," "Rhubarb"; "Douglas—a Labrador Retriever." Contributor to newspapers with animal illus. Carter's Ink cat advertisements.

COOK, GRETCHEN—Teacher, P.

Boston Museum of Fine Arts, Huntington Ave., Boston, Mass.; h. 100 Boylston St., Chestnut Hill 67, Mass.

B. Newton Centre, Mass. *Studied*: BMFA Sch.; & with Aldro Hibbard. *Member*: Copley Soc.; Newton AA. *Exhibited*: BMFA; Portland, Me.; New Haven, Hartford, Conn. *Position*: A.T., BMFA, Boston, Mass., 1927- ; Boston H.S., 1944- .

COOK, HOWARD—Painter, Gr., E., S., L.

c/o Grand Central Moderns Gallery, 1018 Madison Ave., New York, N.Y.; h. Ranchos de Taos, N.M.

B. Springfield, Mass., July 16, 1901. *Studied*: ASL, and in Europe. *Member*: ASL; NAD "Graphics Class." *Awards*: Guggenheim F., 1931-32, 1934-35; gold med., Arch. Lg., 1937; AV, 1942; Tucson A. Festival, 1958; DMFA; Mus. New Mexico; NAD. *Work*: MModA; MMA; WMAA; Santa Barbara Mus. A.; deYoung Mem. Mus.; PMA; Minneapolis Inst. A.; Denver A. Mus.; Dartmouth Col.; murals, Fed. Bldgs., Springfield, Mass.; Pittsburgh, Pa.; San Antonio, Tex.; Corpus Christi, Tex.; Mayo Clinic, Rochester, Minn. *Exhibited*: WMAA; AIC, 1934-1946; BM;

Cal. WC Soc.; Springfield Mus. A.; Phila. Pr. Cl.; Phila. A. All.; Weyhe Gal. (4 one-man shows); Rehn Gal., 1945, 1949; Kennedy Gal., 1945; Grand Central Moderns, 1951, 1952, 1956. Author, I., "Sammi's Army," 1943. Contributor to art magazines. *Position*: Guest Prof. A., Univ. Texas, 1942-43; Minneapolis Sch. A., 1945, 1950; Univ. California, Berkeley, 1948; Scripps Col., 1951; Washington Univ., St. Louis, Mo., 1954; Highlands Univ., N.M., 1957- .

COOK, JOHN—Cartoonist, I.

c/o Alexander, 50 East 42nd St., New York 17, N.Y.; h. 2322 Larkin St., San Francisco 9, Cal.

B. Yreka, Cal., Jan. 14, 1904. *Studied*: Univ. California, A.B.; ASL; San Francisco Sch. FA. Cart. I., Life, Judge, Collier's, San Francisco Chronicle, Ladies Home Journal.

COOK, OTIS—Painter

Bearskin Neck, Rockport, Mass.

B. New Bedford, Mass., July 27, 1900. *Studied*: Swain Sch. Des., New Bedford, Mass., and with Emil Gruppe, Gloucester, Mass. *Member*: SC; Gld. Boston A.; Rockport AA; North Shore AA; Academic A., Springfield; Copley Soc., Boston. *Awards*: prizes, Jordan-Marsh Co. gold medal and prizes, 1952-1955, 1958. *Work*: Springfield Mus. A.

COOK, PETER GEOFFREY—Painter

Heathcote Farm, Kingston, N.J.

B. New York, N.Y., June 10, 1915. *Studied*: Princeton Univ., A.B.; NAD, with Gifford Beal, Leon Kroll. *Member*: Century Assn. *Awards*: Pulitzer traveling scholarship, 1939; prize, NAD, 1944; Ogunquit A. Center, 1951; bronze medal, NAC, 1956; Century Assn. medal, 1956; prize, Portland (Me.) A. Festival, 1957; Boston A. Festival, 1957. *Work*: Princeton Univ.; Wells Col.; Clearwater Mus. A. *Exhibited*: NAD, 1940, 1944, 1945, 1957, 1958; Woodmere A. Gal., Phila., 1956 (with John Folinsbee); one-man: Vose Gal.; Boston; Princeton, N.J.

COOK, WALTER W. S.—Educator

17 East 80th St., New York 22, N.Y.

B. Orange, Mass., Apr. 7, 1888. *Studied*: Harvard Univ., A.B., A.M., Ph.D.; Princeton Univ. *Member*: Hispanic Soc. Am.; F., Mediaeval Acad. Am.; Assoc. member, N.Y. Hist. Soc.; Corr. member: Institute d'Estudis Catalans, Barcelona; Sociò/Corrisponde, Accademia Senese degli Intronati (Siena, Italy); Real Acádemia de Bellas Artes de Santa Isabel de Hungria de Sevilla (Seville); Real Acádemia de Buenas Letras (Barcelona); Real Acádemia de San Fernando (Madrid); Acádemia de la Historia (Madrid); Real Acádemia de Cordoba; Centro de Cultura Valenciana (Valencia); Sociedad Arqueológico Luliana (Palma de Mallorca). Patronato del Instituto Amatller de Arte Hispanico (Barcelona); Associé Correspondant Etranger, Société Nationale des Antiquaries de France (Paris). *Awards*: F. Archaeological Inst. Am.; Research F., CAA, 1927-29, 1930, 1932; Order of Isabela la Catolica by Spanish Govt.; Medal of A. & Lit., Hispanic Soc. Am. Special research in Mediaeval Spanish Art. Author of many writings for art and educational publications. Author: "Pintura e Imagineria Romanicas," 1950, Madrid; "La Pintura Romanica En España," 1952; "La Pintura Mural Románica en Cataluña," 1956; "Prologue of Spain: Romanesque Paintings," text by Juan Ainaud, UNESCO, Paris, 1957. *Position*: Prof. FA, Hd. Dept. FA, Dir. Inst. FA, N.Y. Univ., 1932-1953; Pres., 1938-39, Dir., 1939; Hon. Dir., 1947- ; Prof. Emeritus FA, N.Y. Univ., 1953- ; Ed. Bd., Art in America; Bd. Dir., The Spanish Inst., Inc., New York, N.Y.; Dir., Research Fund of Art & Archaeology in Spain, of the Spanish Institute, Inc., New York, N.Y.

COOKE, C. ERNEST—Educator, W., Cr., L., P.

502 Harmeling St.; h. Virginia Intermont College, Bristol, Va.

B. Owensboro, Ky., June 3, 1900. *Studied*: Univ. Richmond, A.B.; Harvard Univ., M.A.; Oxford & London Univ.; & with Robert Brackman. *Exhibited*: Norfolk Mus., 1945-1956; Intermont Exh., 1945-1956. Lectures: Renaissance & Contemporary Art. *Position*: Hd., Hist. A. Dept., Virginia Intermont Col., Bristol, Va., 1940- ; Instr., A. Hist., King Col., Bristol, Va., 1948- .

COOKE, DONALD EWIN—Writer, I., Des., L.

John C. Winston Co., 1010 Arch St., Philadelphia 7, Pa.; h. 1605 Lynnewood Dr., Havertown, Pa.

B. Philadelphia, Pa., Aug. 5, 1916. *Studied*: PMSchIA, with Henry C. Pitz. *Member*: Phila. Sketch Cl.; Pa. Hist. Soc.; Pen & Pencil Cl. *Exhibited*: PAFA. I., "The Nutcracker of Nuremberg," 1938; "The Firebird," 1939; "The Sorcerer's Apprentice," 1946; "Story-Teller Poems," 1948; "Miss Pickett's Secret," 1952; "Island Fortress," 1952, and others. Author: "Little Wolf Slayer," 1952; "Powder Keg," 1953; "The Narrow Ledge of Fear," 1954; "Johnny-on-the-Spot," 1955; "Valley of Rebellion," 1955; "Color by Overprinting," 1955; "The Romance of Capitalism," 1958; Author-I., "The Silver Horn of Robin Hood," 1956. Illus. of children's stories for "Child Life," "Jack and Jill," etc. *Position*: Mng. Ed., Trade Books, John Winston Co.

COOKE, EDNA (Mrs. Edna Cooke Shoemaker)—Illustrator

620 Manchester Ave., Media, Pa.

B. Philadelphia, Pa., June 19, 1890. *Studied*: PAFA, with Breckenridge, McCarter. *Member*: Phila.A.All. *Exhibited*: PAFA, Illus., "Hans Brinker," "Heidi," "Mother Goose," & other children's books. Contributor of: stories and articles for children to national magazines. Lectures: Development of Children's Books. Creator, "Rose Tree Marionettes" theatre, for colleges, schools, art centers.

COOKE, HEREWARD LESTER, JR.—Museum Curator, W., P.

National Gallery of Art, Washington, D.C.

B. Princeton, N.J., Feb. 16, 1916. *Studied*: Oxford Univ., England, M.A.; ASL, with George Bridgman; Yale Univ. Sch. FA; Princeton Univ. Grad. Sch., Ph.D. *Member*: CAA. *Awards*: Yates-Thompson award, England, 1935; prize, Beaux-Arts Comp., 1941; F., Princeton Univ., 1947-48; Fulbright award, France, 1951-52; Prix de Rome, 1952-53, 1953-54; F., Am. Philosophical Soc., 1954. *Exhibited*: nationally. One-man: Philadelphia, Princeton and Washington, D.C. Contributor articles on art to American and foreign journals. *Position*: Museum Curator, National Gallery of Art, Wash., D.C., 1954- .

COOLEY, RUTH PATTON—Painter

240 Panama St., Philadelphia, Pa.

B. Philadelphia, Pa., Feb. 4, 1901. *Studied*: PAFA, with Daniel Garber, ASL; and with Nicolaides. *Member*: Provincetown AA; Boston AC; Phila. A. Gld. *Work*: murals, Babcock Sch., Cambridge, Mass. *Exhibited*: PAFA, 1935; Mass. Women's Professional Cl., 1932; Provincetown AA, 1942-1945. *Position*: I., children's stories.*

COOLIDGE, JOHN PHILLIPS—Museum Director

Fogg Art Museum, Harvard University; h. 24 Gray Gardens West, Cambridge 38, Mass.

B. Cambridge, Mass., Dec. 16, 1913. *Studied*: Harvard Univ., A.B.; New York Univ., Ph.D. *Member*: CAA; Soc. Arch. Historians; Am. Acad. A. & Sciences. Author: "Mill and Mansion," 1943. *Position*: Dir., Fogg A. Mus., Harvard Univ., Cambridge, Mass.; Trustee, BMFA, 1948- ; Asst. Prof. FA, Univ. Pennsylvania, 1946-47; Prof. FA, Harvard Univ., 1947- .

COOLIDGE, ROSAMOND—Portrait Painter

30 Ipswich St., Boston 15, Mass.; h. 206 Belmont St., Watertown 72, Mass.

B. Watertown, Mass., May 18, 1884. *Studied*: Mass. Sch. A., with Anson K. Cross, Wilbur Dean Hamilton; BMFA Sch., with Edmund C. Tarbell. *Member*: AAPL; North Shore AA; NAWA; Copley Soc. *Awards*: gold med., Jordan-Marsh Co., 1947; prize, Nat. Lg. Am. Pen Women. *Work*: Framingham Normal Sch.; Harvard Univ.; Masonic Temple and Channing House, Boston; First Parish and Phillips Sch., Watertown; Jackson Col., Tufts Univ.; and in many private colls. *Exhibited*: AAPL; Nat. Lg. Am. Pen Women; CGA; AIC; NAD; PAFA; Jordan-Marsh Co.; North Shore AA; Ogunquit A. Center; Newport AA.

COONEY, BARBARA (Mrs. J. Talbot Porter)—Illustrator

Pepperill, Mass.

B. Brooklyn, N.Y. *Studied*: Smith Col.; ASL. *Awards*: Caldecott Medal, 1959. *Work*: Illus. for various magazines

and anthologies and in the past eleven years, illus. thirty-five books. Caldecott Medal was awarded for "Chanticleer and the Fox."

COOPER, ANTHONY J.—Painter

1960 Leland Ave., Chicago 40, Ill.

B. Chicago, Ill., Feb. 28, 1907. *Studied*: AIC. *Member*: Chicago A. Lg.; All-Illinois Soc. F.A. *Awards*: Traveling scholarship, AIC, 1931. *Work*: Illinois State Mus., Springfield. *Exhibited*: NAD, 1945, 1947; CGA, 1943, 1945; Chicago Century of Progress, 1934; AIC, 1934-1957; Ohio Univ., 1945; Illinois State Fair, 1947; Union League, Chicago, 1957; Lithuanian A. Exh., Chicago, 1957; All-Illinois Soc. FA, 1957, 1958; AIC art rental & sales div., 1957, 1958.

COOPER, BROTHER ETIENNE—Sculptor, P., T.

Holy Cross High School, Flushing, L.I., N.Y.

B. Altoona, Pa., July 11, 1915. *Studied*: Univ. Notre Dame, A.B.; Catholic Univ. *Exhibited*: Mus. Sc. & A., Evansville, Ind., 1954. *Work*: murals, Children's Room, Sts. Peter and Paul Cathedral, Indianapolis, Ind.; mural & chapel dec., St. Joseph's Novitiate, Rolling Prairie, Ind. *Position*: A. T., Holy Cross H.S., Flushing, L.I., N.Y.*

COOPER, EDWARD J. W.—Painter, T., Cr., L.

14 Little's Point Rd., Swampscott, Mass.

B. England, Oct. 10, 1914. *Studied*: City of London Col.; Campion House Col., Central Sch. A., London, England; Grande Chaumiere, Paris, France. *Member*: Brookline Soc. A. (Pres. 1952-54); Cambridge AA; Palette & Chisel Acad., Chicago. *Exhibited*: Royal Scottish Acad., 1942, and others in England and Scotland; Galeria della Ghiacciaie, Florence, Italy, 1954; De Cordova & Dana Mus., 1953; Boston Soc. Indp. A. traveling exh., 1954; Inst. Contemp. A., Boston, 1955; Cambridge AA, annually; one-man: Boston Univ., 1955; Little Gallery, Chicago, 1949; Galerie de Baune, Paris, 1956; Paul Schuster Gal., Cambridge, 1957; Marblehead AA, 1953, 1958. *Position*: A. Cr., Boston Univ. Radio Station WBUR, 1952- .

COOPER, FRED G.—Cartoonist, Des.

Cooper Rd., Fanwood, N.J.

B. McMinnville, Ore., Dec. 29, 1883. *Member*: SI; A. Gld. Author: Munsell Book of Color.*

COOPER, LEONE—Painter, E., L., Gr., I.

140 North Rock Hill Rd., Webster Groves (St. Louis) 19, Mo.

B. St. Louis, Mo., Mar. 30, 1902. *Studied*: Harris T. Col. *Member*: St. Louis A. Gld. *Work*: Bristol Sch., Edgar Road Sch., Douglass Sch., Sigma Nu House (Washington Univ.), St. Louis; Central Lib., Carondelet Lib., St. Louis; Webster Groves H.S., and in private colls. *Exhibited*: LC; CAM; VMFA; William Rockhill Nelson Mus.; Six States Exhibit; Midwest A.; Springfield A. Mus.; St. Louis A. Gld.; Joslyn A. Mus.; Laguna Beach AA; Mid-South Exh.; East St. Louis A. Center. Lectures: "Water Color Sketching"; lectures, demonstrations before women's clubs, college groups and organizations in Missouri and Illinois. *Position*: Instr., Webster Col., 1947-48; Dir., Leone Cooper A. Sch., Webster Groves, Mo., 1949- .

COOPER, MARIO—Painter, S., E., I.

25 Oakland Drive, Port Washington, L.I., N.Y.

B. Mexico City, D.F., Nov. 26, 1905. *Studied*: Otis AI; Chouinard AI; Grand Central Sch. A.; Columbia Univ. *Member*: NA; AWS; Audubon A.; All. A. Am.; Knickerbocker A.; Brooklyn Soc. A.; Cal. WC Soc.; Texas WC Soc.; New Jersey P.&S.; A. Lg., Long Island; SI; NSS; N.Y. Artists Gld. *Awards*: prizes, med., Knickerbocker A., 1952, 1955; A. Lg., Long Island, 1950; New Jersey P.&S., 1949; Nassau A. Lg., 1949; prizes, All. A. Am., 1950, 1956; Hendersonville, N.C.; Indiana (Pa.) State T. Col.; AWS, 1955, 1956; Brooklyn Soc. A., 1955; NAD, 1956. *Work*: Coll. of U.S. Air Force; Processional Cross, Chapel of Intercession, and St. Martin's, New York, N.Y.; Butler Inst. Am. A.; St. Lukes Hosp., Denver, Colo.; painting of Atlas ICBM and planes, USAF, Marianas Hall, Armed Services Staff Col., Norfolk, Va. Illus., short stories of P.G. Wodehouse, Quentin Reynolds, Gouverneur Morris, Clarence Buddington Kelland, Eric Remarque's "Arch of Triumph," and others. Represented in "Forty Illustrators and How They Work"; "Introduction to Cartooning and Illustrating." *Exhibited*: PMA, 1949; BM, 1952; NAD, 1947, 1948, 1950, 1951; PAFA, 1948, 1951, 1952; Indiana (Pa.) State T. Col.; Arch. Lg., 1951; AWS; Cal. WC Soc.; Audubon A.; All. A. Am.; WFNY 1939; Sarasota AA; Conn. Acad. FA; one-man: New York, N.Y., 1953; Phila., Pa., 1953, and others. Contributor to national magazines. *Position*: Delegate to U.S. Comm. for IAPA, 1954- ; Pres., Audubon A., 1954- ; Official A., for paintings of opening of U.S. Air Force Acad., in Far East, 1954; temp. duty, Alaska, USAF, 1956; in charge of team of four artists to Japan, Korea, Okinawa, 1956, for USAF; in charge team of five artists to Japan, 1957, for USAF. Instr., ASL, 1957- .

COOTES, F(RANK) GRAHAM—
Portrait Painter, Comm. A.
630 Park Ave., New York 21, N.Y.

B. Staunton, Va., Apr. 6, 1879. *Studied*: Washington and Lee Univ.; Univ. Virginia, B.A., M.A.; Chase A. Sch. *Work*: White House, Wash., D.C.; Liberty Mem., Kansas City, Mo.; Virginia State Capitol; Univ. Virginia; Univ. Delaware; Stuart Hall, Staunton, Va.; Woodrow Wilson Fnd., N.Y.; Woodrow Wilson Shrine, Staunton, Va. (U.S. 7¢ postage stamp carries reproduction of Graham Cootes' port. of Wilson). The State of Virginia has given a bronze tablet of Woodrow Wilson, taken from Wilson's port. painted by F. Graham Cootes, installed on the facade of the Palais de Chaillot on Avenue Pres. Wilson, in Paris, Oct., 1958. I., leading magazines, books and advertising.

COPE, LESLIE—*Painter, Et., Des.*
Roseville, Ohio

B. Stoke-on-Trent, England, Aug. 10, 1913. *Member*: SAGA; Prairie Pr. M.; Cal. Soc. Et.; Ohio WC Soc.; Soc. Academic A.; Columbus A. Lg. *Awards*: prizes, SAGA, 1950, 1952. *Work*: Zanesville AI; MMA; Pa. State Univ.; LC; Carnegie Inst.; murals, New Lexington, Ohio; Roseville (Ohio) Federal Savings & Loan Assn. *Exhibited*: SAGA, 1949, 1950, 1952, 1953; BM, 1949; NAD, 1948, 1949; LC, 1948, 1950; Carnegie Inst., 1949; Northwest Pr. M., 1949; Smithsonian Inst., 1949 (one-man); Prairie Pr. M., 1948-1952; Cal. Soc. Et., 1948-1952; Columbus, Ohio, 1948, 1950 (one-man).

COPELAND, LAWRENCE G.—*Craftsman, Des., E.*
94 Palamino Drive, Rochester 23, N.Y.

B. Pittsburgh, Pa., Apr. 12, 1922. *Studied*: Royal F., Univ. Stockholm; Ohio State Univ., B.F.A., and with Baron Eric Fleming, Stockholm, Sweden; Emeric Gomery, Paris, France; Cranbrook Acad. A., M.F.A. *Member*: Shop One; York State Craftsmen. *Awards*: med., Cranbrook Acad. A., 1951; Court of Honor, York State Crafts Fair, 1955; Purchases by U.S. State Dept. for U.S. Int. Exh., 1953. *Work*: NGA; altar silver, Grace Presbyterian Church, Rochester, N.Y. *Exhibited*: Wichita Nat., 1950-1952; Finger Lakes Exh., 1952-1955, 1958; Mus. Contemp. Crafts, 1956-1958; York State Craft Fair, 1955; one-man: Davidson A. Center, Middletown, Conn., 1955; Essex AA, 1955. Contributor to Craft Horizons. Lectures: Metalcraft, to craft and school groups. *Position*: Instr., metal crafts and Counselor, Sch. for Am. Craftsmen, Rochester Inst. Tech., Rochester, N.Y., 1951- .

COPELAND, LILA—*Painter*
14 East 9th St., New York 3, N.Y.

B. Rochester, N.Y. *Studied*: ASL. *Member*: AEA; ASL; Provincetown AA; Woodstock AA. *Awards*: bronze med., AIC. *Exhibited*: AIC; Dayton AI; GGE, 1939; Flint Inst. A.; WMAA; Lenox Gal.; Riverside Mus.; Greenwich Gal., 1958; Provincetown AA, 1958; Downtown Community School, 1958; one-man: Ward Eggleston Gal., 1958, and others.

COPELIN, JEANNETTE KNOWLES—*Painter, T.*
1140 Fifth Ave., New York 28, N.Y.

B. New York, N.Y., December, 1902. *Studied*: Parsons Sch. Des.; NAD; ASL, and with Robert Brackman, Harry Sternberg. *Member*: Lyme AA; Clinton AA; Guilford AA (all Conn.). *Awards*: prize, NAD, 1950. *Work*: Many portraits in private colls. *Exhibited*: Audubon A.; NAC; NAD; Lyme AA; Clinton AA; Guilford AA; Ivoryton AA; Studio Gld. traveling exhs. *Position*: Instr. A., children and adult classes, Mamaroneck, N.Y., 1938-42; Madison, Conn., 1954-57.

COPLAN, KATE M.—*Library Exhibits Division*
400 Cathedral St.; h. 3404 Rosedale Rd., Baltimore 15, Md.

B. Baltimore, Md., Dec. 25, 1901. *Studied*: Johns Hopkins Univ. *Member*: Maryland Lib. Assn.; Lib. Pub. Relations Council; Am. Lib. Assn.; Baltimore Pub. Relations Council. *Awards*: prize, Putnam's "Boys Books for Boys" window display comp., 1927; gold, silver & bronze meds., "Display Worlds" International window display comp., 1950, 1955. Contributor to Library Journal, Publisher's Weekly. Author: "Effective Library Exhibits: How to Prepare and Promote Good Displays," 1958. *Position*: Chief, Exhibits & Publ., Enoch Pratt Free Pub. Library, Baltimore, Md., 1935- .

COPP, GERTRUDE M.—*Craftsman, P., T., Des.*
2449 North Downer Ave., Milwaukee 11, Wis.

B. Lawrence, Mass., Mar. 26, 1874. *Studied*: BMFA Sch.; T. Col., Columbia Univ.; Parsons Summer Sch.; Provincetown Summer Sch., and with Charles Hawthorne. *Member*: Copley Soc.; Boston A. & Crafts Soc.; Wisconsin Des-Craftsmen. *Awards*: prizes, Milwaukee AI; Boston Soc. A. & Crafts; Wisconsin Des-Craftsmen; Laconia, N.H. *Exhibited*: Boston Soc. A. & Crafts; Milwaukee AI; AIC; Laconia, N.H. *Position*: Dir. A., Girls Trade & Tech. H.S., Milwaukee, Wis., 1913- . (Now retired from teaching.)

COPPIN, JOHN STEPHENS—*Painter, Comm., W.*
4301 Echo Rd., Bloomfield Hills, Mich.

B. Mitchell, Ontario, Canada, Sept. 13, 1904. *Studied*: Stratford Collegiate Inst., Ontario, Can.; John P. Wicker A. Sch., Detroit, Mich., and in Europe. *Member*: Detroit Scarab Cl. *Awards*: Prizes, Detroit Inst. A., 1933, 1939, 1946; Hartwig prize, 1937; Field prize, 1945, 1950; Clarke prize, 1953; gold med., Scarab Cl., 1940, 1944, 1946. *Work*: Capitol Bldg., Lansing, Mich.; County Bldg. & City Hall, Detroit; Edison Co.; Rackham Bldg., Detroit; Ann Arbor Lib.; Detroit Hist. Mus.; Automobile Club; Central H.S., Detroit; Detroit Gas Co.; Detroit Inst. A.; Mich. State Univ.; Acanthus Cl., Prismatic Cl., and St. Dunstan's Gld., all Cranbrook, Mich. Many portraits of prominent persons.

COPPOLINO, JOSEPH—*Sculptor, Des.*
Veteran's Administration, 252 Seventh Ave., New York, N.Y.; h. 217-09 120th Ave., St. Albans 11, N.Y.

B. New York, N.Y., Nov. 3, 1908. *Studied*: CUASch; BAID; NAD, and with Piccirilli, Lee Lawrie, Gaetano Cecere; indst. des. with Dreyfuss, Barnhardt. *Awards*: prizes, BAID, 1929, 1935; CUASch; Prix de Rome, 1937, 1938. *Position*: Prosthetic work wtih Veteran's Administration, New York, N.Y., 1946- .

CORASICK, WILLIAM W.—*Painter, T.*
4368 Woodland Ave., Drexel Hill, Pa.

B. Philadelphia, Pa., July 9, 1907. *Studied*: Temple Univ., B.S. in Edu.; Univ. Pennsylvania. *Member*: Phila. A. All.; Phila. A. T. Assn. *Awards*: Prizes, Phila. A. T. Assn., 1944, 1945. *Exhibited*: PAFA, 1936, 1944, 1951; NAD, 1943; Phila. A. All (one-man), 1953; Galerie Neuf, 1945 (one-man); Butler AI, 1944; PMA, 1950; Phila. Pyramid Cl., 1957. *Position*: A.T., Philadelphia, Pa., Pub. Sch.

CORBETT, EDWARD M.—*Educator, P.*
Mount Holyoke College; h. 8 Park St., South Hadley, Mass.

B. Chicago, Ill., Aug. 22, 1919. *Studied*: California Sch. FA. *Awards*: Rosenberg F., 1951-52. *Work*: AIC; MMoDA; WMAA; SFMA. *Exhibited*: CGA, 1955; WMAA, 1953-1955; Sao Paulo, 1954; Univ. Illinois, 1955; Carnegie Inst., 1955; MMoDA, 1952; AIC, 1948, 1953, 1954; MMoDA traveling exh., Paris & Grenoble, France, 1954; Stable Gal., 1954, 1955. *Position*: Instr., Cal. Sch. FA, 1947-50; Asst. Prof., Mount Holyoke Col., South Hadley, Mass., 1953- ; Dir., Taos Field Sch. of A., Univ. New Mexico, 1955.*

CORBETT, OLIVER J.—Painter

907 East Loren St., Springfield, Mo.

B. Meridan, Iowa, July 21, 1886. *Studied*: AIC; PMSchIA, and with John Eliot Jenkins. *Member*: Ozark AA; SSAL. *Awards*: prizes, Ozark Empire Fair; Springfield A. Mus.; William Rockhill Nelson Gal. A.; Governor's Mansion, Mo. *Work*: 12 murals for St. Louis-San F. R.R. Co.; Masonic Temple, High St. Baptist Church, Jewel Theatre, Springfield; Rolla (Mo.) Pub. Sch.; Springfield A. Mus.; port. purchased by Dem. Central Comm. for gift to Harry Truman; mural, St. Agnes Cathedral and Seminole Baptist Temple, Springfield, Mo.; Paintings in Carnegie Lib. and City Council Chamber, Monett, Mo.; Handley Mem. Hospital. *Exhibited*: Nelson Gal. A., 1938; one-man: Springfield A. Mus., 1940, 1951; Robertson Gal., 1954.

CORBINO, JON—Painter, T.

c/o Rehn Gallery, 836 Fifth Ave., New York, N.Y.; h. 5 Marmion Way, Rockport, Mass.

B. Vittoria, Italy, Apr. 3, 1905. *Studied*: PAFA; ASL; Ethical Culture Sch. *Member*: NA; F., PAFA. *Awards*: Guggenheim F., 1936-37, 1937-38; prizes, AIC, 1937, 1944; BMA, 1938; NAD, 1938, 1944, 1945; Lotos Cl., 1939; Nat. Inst. A. & Let., 1941; SC, 1945; PAFA, 1938; DaVinci All., 1942 (silver med.); Pepsi-Cola Comp., 1945; La Tausca Exh., 1946; Niedringhaus prize, 1950; med., Audubon A., 1945; NAC, 1950. *Work*: MMA; Carnegie Inst.; WMAA; BM; Toledo Mus. A.; PAFA; WMA; ASL; IBM; Ripon Col.; Soc. Liberal A., Omaha; Maryville (Mo.) State T. Col.; Walker A. Center; Montclair A. Mus.; Brooks Mem. A. Gal.; NAD; Butler AI; Muncie Univ.; Amherst Col.; Canajoharie A. Gal.; Brigham Young Univ.; Mt. Holyoke Col.; AGAA; Pittsburgh Univ. Tech.; Pasadena AI; New Britain A. Mus.; Kalamazoo Inst. A.; Mun. Univ., Omaha; San Diego FA Soc.; Lotos Cl.; AIC; Nelson Gal. A.; Sweet Briar Col.; Ball State T. Col.; Norton Gal. A.; Encyclopaedia Britannica. *Exhibited*: annually in national exhibitions in leading museums. I., Swift's "Gulliver's Travels," 1945; "Marco Polo," 1948. *Position*: Instr., NAD, 1945; ASL, New York, N.Y., 1938- .*

CORCOS, LUCILLE—Painter, I., Des., Cart.

South Mountain Rd., New City, N.Y.

B. New York, N.Y., Sept. 21, 1908. *Studied*: ASL. *Member*: Audubon A. *Awards*: Pepsi-Cola, 1944; Grumbacher award, 1956. *Work*: WMAA; U.S. Gypsum Co.; Upjohn Pharmaceutical Co.; Columbia Broadcasting System; Mus. A., Tel-Aviv; mural, North Shore Hospital, Manhasset, N.Y.; Life Magazine; mural, Waldorf-Astoria, New York. *Exhibited*: WMAA, 1936, 1938, 1939, 1941, 1942, 1944 1947, 1949-1954; AIC, 1939-1944; BM; MMA, 1941, 1942, 1950, 1951; Carnegie Inst., 1941, 1944, 1945, 1946, 1948, 1949; Rockland Fnd., 1954 (one-man); PMG, 1942; Audubon A., 1946-1957; Columbus Gal. FA, 1952; Grand Central Moderns, (one-man) annually; traveling exh., South America, Great Britain; Exchange Exh., Paris, 1953-54; Am-Embassy, Paris, 1954; U.S.I.S., Rome, Italy, The Netherlands, 1957. I., "Treasury of Gilbert & Sullivan," 1941; "Chichikov's Journey," 1944; "Treasury of Laughter," 1946; "Little Lame Prince," 1946; "Follow the Sunset," 1952; Limited Editions Club, "The Picture of Dorian Gray," 1957; Author, I., "Joel Gets a Haircut," 1952; "Joel Spends His Money," 1954; "Joel Gets a Dog." 1958. Work reproduced in American Weekly, 1957, 1958; Life, 1954; Fortune, 1955-1958.

CORDREY, EARL (SOMERS)—Illustrator

429 South Belardo Rd., Palm Springs, Cal.

B. Piru, Cal., Sept. 6, 1902. *Studied*: Chouinard AI; Grand Central Sch. A. *Member*: SI. I., for Cosmopolitan, Collier's, American, & other magazines. *Position*: Instr., A. Center Sch., Los Angeles, Cal.*

CORMIER, ROBERT JOHN—Painter

30 Ipswich St., Boston 15, Mass.

B. Boston, Mass., May 26, 1932. *Studied*: R. H. Ives Gammell Studios. *Member*: Provincetown AA; AAPL; 50 American A.; Academic A.; Copley Soc., Boston. *Awards*: prizes, All. A. Am., 1955; Northeast A. Contemp. Show, 1957; Ogunquit, Me., 1957; AAPL, 1958; Ogunquit AA nat. exh., 1958. *Work*: Boston College Lib., and in private colls. *Exhibited*: All. A. Am., 1955; Ogunquit A. Center, 1956-1958; NAC, 1958; AAPL, 1958; New England A., 1956-1958; Academic A., 1957; Chrysler Mus. A., 1958;

Copley Soc., 1957, 1958; Concord AA, 1957; Maryhill (Wash.) Mus., 1958; Oregon Soc. A., 1958; Wash. State Hist. Mus., Tacoma, 1958; Walla Walla, Wash., 1958; Everett, Wash., 1958; SAM, 1958 and other West Coast exhs.

CORNELIUS, FRANCIS DuPONT—Conservator, P.

Colorado Springs Fine Arts Center; h. 1601 Cresta Rd., Colorado Springs, Colo.

B. Pittsburgh, Pa., Oct. 19, 1907. *Studied*: Univ. Pennsylvania, B. Arch.; Univ. Pittsburgh, M.A. *Member*: AAMus.; F., Int. Inst. for the Conservation of Mus. Objects. *Exhibited*: Assoc. A. Pittsburgh, annually. Author: "Frick Pieta Panels." Lectures, "Conservation Methods," at universities and colleges. *Position*: Research F., in Conservation, 1944-45; F., in Conservation, MMA, 1945-52; Tech. Advisor, 1952-55, Restorer, 1955- , Colorado Springs FA Center; Conservator, Mus. New Mexico A. Gal., 1955- ; private studio for preservation of works of art, Colorado Springs, Colo., 1952- . Participated in British Council course on Conservation, London, 1956. Research findings on surface films and disintegration of canvas supports exhibited at ICOM meeting, Amsterdam, Holland, 1957.

CORNELIUS, MARTY (Miss)—
Painter, Des., T., I., W., L.

724 College Ave., Pittsburgh 32, Pa.

B. Pittsburgh, Pa., Sept. 18, 1913. *Studied*: Carnegie Inst., B.A., and with Reginald Marsh, Alexander Kostellow. *Awards*: prizes, Assoc. A. Pittsburgh, 1939, 1945, 1953; Martin Leisser Sch. Des., 1946-1949; Allegheny County, 1947, 1948, 1955; Butler Inst. Am. A., 1948; CGA, 1941, 1947; Kappa Kappa Gamma, 1952. *Exhibited*: Carnegie Inst., 1946-1949; WMAA, 1949; CGA, 1941, 1947; N.Y. Mun. Exh., 1936; Cal. PLH, 1946; Assoc. A. Pittsburgh, 1936-1946, 1953; Univ. Ohio, 1957; Ogunquit A. Center, 1957. *Work*: Mercy Hospital, Pittsburgh; Latrobe (Pa.) H.S.; Pittsburgh Pub. Schs.; 2 illus. in "The Story of Pittsburgh," Stefan Lorant, 1958. *Position*: Instr. A., Veteran's Hospitals, Pittsburgh, Pa.; A. Des., Aluminum Co. of Am., New Kensington, Pa., 1950-51; Instr. Drawing, Carnegie Inst. Tech., FA College, Pittsburgh, Pa., at present.

CORNIN, JON—Painter, Des., E.

2912 Newbury St., Berkeley 3, Cal.

B. New York, N.Y., Mar. 24, 1905. *Studied*: N.Y. Univ.; ASL, and with Raphael Soyer. *Member*: AEA; San F. AA; East Bay AA. *Exhibited*: Univ. Seattle; Gump's Gal., San F.; St. Botolph's Cl., Doll & Richards, Boston; Arizona State Fair; Montgomery Mus. A.; Cal. PLH; NAD; SFMA; Irvington A. & Mus. Assn.; Cal. State Fair; Pasadena AI; Oakland A. Gal.; Cal. WC Soc., traveling exh.; Univ. Alabama; Alabama WC Soc., traveling exh; Laguna Beach A. Gal.; Albright A. Gal.; Fresno A. Lg.; Denver Mus. A.; Los A. Mus. A.; Phila. Pr. Cl.; Kennedy Gal.; J. B. Speed Mus. A.; deYoung Mem. Mus.; Philbrook A. Center; Montross Gal.; Mus. New Mexico; Flint Inst. A.; Saginaw (Mich.) Mus. A.; Michigan State Col.; Slaughter Gal., San F. (one-man); Terry AI; Portland (Me.) Mus. A.; Henry Gal., Seattle; Laguna Beach A. Festival; San Joaquin & Haggin A. Gal., Stockton, Cal.; Butler Inst. Am. A.; SFMA; Oakland A. Mus.; Art:USA, 1958; Frye Mus. A., Seattle, and many others. *Work*: in many private colls. *Position*: Instr., Painting & Drawing in own school, Berkeley, Cal.

CORNISH, NED A.—Museum Director

Kalamazoo Institute of Arts, 421 West South St., Kalamazoo, Mich.

Position: Dir., Kalamazoo Institute of Arts.*

CORNWELL, DEAN—Mural Painter, I.

33 West 67th St., New York 23, N.Y.

B. Louisville, Ky., Mar. 5, 1892. *Studied*: with Harvey Dunn, Charles A. Chapman. *Member*: NA; NSMP (Pres., 1953-56); SI; NAC; Century Assn. *Awards*: med., All. A. Am.; Wilmington Soc. A.; gold med., Arch. Lg.; prize, SC. *Work*: murals, Los A. Pub. Lib.; Lincoln Memorial Shrine, Redlands, Cal.; County Court House, Nashville, Tenn.; State Office Bldg., Nashville, Tenn.; Eastern Airlines Bldg., N.Y.; USPO, Chapel Hill, Morgantown, N.C.; Raleigh Room, Hotel Warwick, N.Y.; General Motors Bldg., WFNY 1939; New England Tel. & Tel. Co., Boston; Bethlehem Steel Co., Bethlehem, Pa.; Springfield (Mass.)

Fire Ins. Co.; murals, Gomper's Room, Int. Labor Office, Geneva, 1955; 3 murals, inlaid marble, Battle Monument, American Cemetery, Neuville-en-Condroz, Belgium, 1958; 2 murals, Mfrs. Nat. Bank, Lewiston, Me., 1958-59.

CORR, MRS. PHILIP J. See Snow, Mary Ruth

CORRELL, GRACE VAN NORMAN (Mrs.)—
Designer, P.
2622 Linn St., Peoria, Ill.

B. Peoria, Ill., Nov. 15, 1912. *Studied:* Bradley Polytechnic Inst., B.S., M.F.A., with P. R. McIntosh, Edward Nicholson. *Member:* Peoria Lg. A.; Peoria A. Center. *Awards:* Prize, Textile des., A. Instruction Sch., Minneapolis, Minn., 1943; Peoria A. Center, 1955. *Work:* murals, private homes, Gardenia & Peoria, Ill.; Fannie May Candy Co., La Grange, Sheridan Village and Skokie, Ill.; Illus. in children's publications. *Exhibited:* CGA, 1941; Decatur A. Center, 1945; Peoria Lg. A.; Pere Marquette Gal. (oneman); Peoria A. Center, 1951, 1955. *Position:* Des., Forster Textile Mills, Inc.; Fabric Des.; Part-time Instr., Costume Des., Int. Dec., Bradley Univ.

CORRINGTON, VERONICA E. (Mrs. Julian D.)—
Painter
1306 Madrid St., Coral Gables 34, Fla.

B. Chicago, Ill., Feb. 5, 1891. *Studied:* PIASch.; and with Eliot O'Hara. *Member:* Miami A. Lg.; Wilmington A. Center; Blue Dome Fellowship; Miami WC Soc.; Fla. Fed. A. *Awards:* prizes, Miami A. Lg., 1947, 1949, 1950; Poinciana Festival, Miami, 1948; Coral Gables Jubilee, 1949; Miami Women's Cl., 1949, 1952; Blue Dome Fellowship, 1950 (2); Lowe Gal. A., 1953. *Exhibited:* Soc. Four Arts, Palm Beach; Alabama WC Soc.; High Mus. A., Atlanta; Norton Gal. A., 1952; Lowe Gal. A., 1953; Lakeland, Fla., 1952; Wilmington A. Center; Chestertown, Md.; Washington Col., Chestertown; Miami Beach A. Center (6 one-man); Miami Woman's Cl.; Miami Beach Woman's Cl.; Miami Boat Show; Coral Gables Country Cl.; Miami Poinciana Exh.; Fla. Fed. A.

CORTESE, EDWARD FORTUNATO—
Illustrator, Des., Comm. A.
Lake Villa Drive, Kresson, (Marlton P.O.), N.J.

B. Philadelphia, Pa., Jan. 11, 1922. *Studied:* Graphic Sketch Cl., Phila., Pa.; PMA Sch. A., B.F.A.; Temple Univ., and with Robert Susan, Henry C. Pitz, Donald E. Cooke. *Exhibited:* (books) Book Fair, PAFA, 1955; Free Lib. of Philadelphia, 1955; Color by Overprinting. Illus., "A Boy for a Man's Job," 1952; "Lost Colony," 1953; "Bonny's Boy Returns," 1953; "The New Wonder Book Cyclopedia of World Knowledge," 1954; "Quest of a Hemisphere," 1954; "To the Shores of Tripoli," 1955; "Color by Overprinting," 1955. Contributor to Baptist Leader; Young People; Graphic Arts Review. *Position:* Book Des., and Illustrator, John C. Winston Book Publ. Co., Philadelphia, Pa., 1951- .*

CORTIGLIA, NICCOLO—Painter, T.
89 North Franklin St., Wilkes-Barre, Pa.; s. R.D. 1, Noxen, Pa.

B. New York, N.Y., Apr. 7, 1893. *Studied:* John Herron AI; Royal Acad. FA, Florence, Italy. *Awards:* Prize, Soc. FA, Florence, Italy, 1920. *Exhibited:* NAD. *Position:* Instr., Drawing & Painting, Cortiglia A. Sch., Wilkes-Barre, Pa.*

CORTLANDT, LYN—Painter, Lith., Ser.
1070 Park Ave., New York 28, N.Y.

B. New York, N.Y., Jan. 7, 1926. *Studied:* Chouinard AI; Jepson AI; ASL; PIASch.; Columbia Univ. Sch. Painting & Sculpture; Hans Hofmann Sch. A.; China Inst. in America. *Member:* F.; Intl. Inst. A. & Lets.; F., Royal Soc. A., London, England; All A. Am.; P. & S. Soc. of New Jersey; Phila. WC Cl.; Pen & Brush Cl.; NAWA; North Shore AA; AEA. *Awards:* prizes, NAWA, 1957; Pen & Brush Cl., 1958, and others. *Work:* MMA; BMFA; FMA; AIC; BM; Boston Pub. Lib.; BMA; CAM; Springfield Mus. A.; Stedelijk Mus., Amsterdam, Holland and in private colls. *Exhibited:* PAFA; BM; AWS; and in many other national exhs.; also in Belgium, Greece, Holland, Switzerland. One-man: Ruth White Gal., N.Y., 1957. Moderator radio panel forums: "Where is Abstract Art Leading Us?" and "Contemporary Styles of Painting."

CORTOR, ELDZIER—Painter, Lith., Eng.
c/o Niveau Gallery, 962 Madison Ave., New York, N.Y.; h. 126 Baruch Pl., New York 2, N.Y.

B. Richmond, Va., Jan. 10, 1916. *Studied:* AIC; Inst. Des., Chicago; Columbia Univ. *Awards:* Rosenwald F., 1944, 1945; AIC, 1945, 1946; Guggenheim F., 1949; Carnegie award, Carnegie Inst. *Work:* Bd. Edu., Chicago; Whyte Gal.; South Side Community A. Center; Howard Univ.; AFA; IBM; Gothic Press, Chicago; Musée du Peuple Hatien, Haiti; Univ. Illinois; Bacardi, Santiago, Cuba; LC; Jackson Gal., N.Y. *Exhibited:* VMFA, 1941; Atlanta Univ., 1943; Lib. Cong., 1940; Whyte Gal., 1940; Downtown Gal., 1941; Smith Col., 1943; Inst. Mod. A., Boston, 1943; BMA, 1944; Albany Inst. Hist. & A., 1945; Minneapolis Inst., A., 1944; Rochester Mem. A. Gal., 1945; Carnegie Inst., 1945; AFA, 1945; Howard Univ., 1945; AIC, 1941-1946; Milwaukee AI, 1944; Univ. Illinois, 1950; Univ. Michigan, 1956.

COSGRAVE, JOHN O'HARA, II—
Illustrator, P., Gr., W.
26 Orange St., Brooklyn 1, N.Y.

B. San Francisco, Cal., Oct. 10, 1908. *Studied:* Univ. California; Cal. Sch. FA, and with Andre L'Hote, in Paris. *Awards:* prize, Brooklyn Soc. A., 1941. *Member:* SI; Dutch Treat Cl. *Exhibited:* Paris Salon; AWS; PAFA; AIC; BM; SFMA; Brooklyn Soc. A. *Work:* Illus. & covers for Life, Fortune and Yachting magazines. I., "Wind, Sand and Stars," 1939; "The Salt Rivers of the Massachusetts Shore," 1950; "The Monitor and The Merrimac," 1951; "The Monongahela," 1952; "Carry On Mr. Bowditch," 1955; "Come In," 1942 (Poems by Robert Frost); "Let the Best Boat Win," 1957; "Tall Ships," 1957; "Flashing Harpoons," 1958; "Sailing the Seven Seas," 1958. Reproduction of painting of Yacht America, Encyclopaedia Britannica.

COSTIGAN, JOHN EDWARD—Painter, Et.
Orangeburg, N.Y.

B. Providence, R.I., Feb. 29, 1888. *Member:* NA; NAC; SC; SAGA; AWS. *Awards:* prizes, NAD (purchase) 1955 and prior; AIC; SC, 1954 and prior; NAC (gold med., 1954 and prior); med., AWS, prize, 1958; SAGA; LC, 1942, 1944, 1946; Ogunquit A. Center, 1955. *Work:* N.Y. Pub. Lib.; Brigham Young Univ.; Rochester Mem. A. Gal.; MMA; AIC; Los A. Mus. A.; Cranbrook Acad. A.; LC; Davenport Mun. A. Gal.; Frye Mus. A., Seattle; Utah State Univ.; murals, USPO, Girard, Ohio; Rensselaer, Ind.; Stuart, W. Va. *Exhibited:* nationally.

COTSWORTH, STAATS—Painter, I.
360 East 55th St., New York 22, N.Y.

B. Oak Park, Ill., Feb. 17, 1908. *Studied:* PMSchIA, and with Thornton Oakley, Herbert Pullinger. *Member:* Phila. WC Cl.; Am. Soc. Painters in Casein; AWS. *Awards:* prizes, Conn. Acad. FA, 1954; Knickerbocker A., 1955. *Work:* murals in private homes and public buildings. *Exhibited:* PAFA; CGA; Phila. WC Cl.; NAC; Am-British A. Center, 1948 (one-man); WMAA, 1955; Hammer Gal., 1953 (one-man). I., "A Bacchic Pilgrimage"; "Deep Water Days."

COTT, PERRY BLYTHE—Museum Curator
National Gallery of Art; h. 4201 Massachusetts Ave., N.W., Washington, D.C.

B. Columbus, Ohio, Mar. 27, 1909. *Studied:* Princeton Univ., A.B., Ph.D.; Univ. Paris. *Member:* CAA. *Awards:* Med., CAA, 1929. *Author:* "Siculo-Arabic Ivories," 1939. Contributor to: Art magazines. *Position:* Chief Cur., National Gallery of Art, Washington, D.C.

COTTON, LILLIAN—Painter
30 East 67th St., New York 21, N.Y.

B. Boston, Mass. *Studied:* Andre L'Hote Acad., Paris; ASL, with Robert Henri, George Bellows. *Member:* NAWA; N.Y. Soc. Women A.; PBC; Société Nationale des Beaux-Arts, Paris; Knickerbocker A. *Awards:* Prize, NAWA, 1946, 1953; New England Exh., 1954; Pen & Brush Cl., 1955. *Work:* Fla. Southern Col.; Seton Hall Univ., Jersey City, N.J.; Staten Island Mus. A. & Sc. *Exhibited:* PAFA, 1930; CGA, 1930; Paris Salon; NAD; NAWA; N.Y. Soc. Women A.; PBC, 1946; All. A. Am.; Audubon A.; Silvermine Gld. A.

COULTER, DORIS MARY—*Designer, C., E.*

Art Dept., University of Texas; h. 6 Happy Hollow Lane, Austin 3, Tex.

B. New Berlin, Ill., Aug. 25, 1917. *Studied*: Ill. State Normal Univ., B. of Edu.; Northwestern Univ.; Univ. of Michigan; Penland Sch. of Handicrafts (N.C.); Cranbrook Acad. A., M.F.A., with Marianne Strengell. *Member*: Am. Craftsmen's Council; Contemporary Handweavers of Texas; Texas Designer-Craftsmen; Swedish Soc. Indst. Des. *Awards*: prizes, Texas Crafts Exh., Dallas, 1951; Int. Textile Exh., 1952; Texas State Ceramics & Textile Exh., San Antonio, 1952; Texas FA Exh., Austin, 1952; Contemp. Handweavers of Texas, Beaumont, 1952; Fort Worth, 1957; Contemp. Handweavers of Texas, 1953; Texas Crafts, Dallas, 1954; Contemp. Handweavers of Texas, 1954; Texas FA Exh., Austin, 1955; A. & Crafts Fiesta, Austin, 1957, 1958; Lincoln, Neb., 1957; Women's Nat. Exh., N.Y., 1958. *Exhibited*: Int. Textile Exh., 1949, 1950, 1952; Des-Craftsmen, U.S.A., 1953; Young Designers, 1954; Rochester Mem. A. Gal., 1949; Michigan A. & Craftsmen, Detroit, 1949, 1950; Cranbrook Acad. A., 1950, 1951; Phila. A. All., 1950; Miami Univ., Oxford, Ohio, 1950; Springfield, Ill., 1950; Contemp. A. Assn., 1951, 1953; Texas Crafts Exh., Dallas, 1951, 1953, 1954, 1955; Texas Ceramic & Textile Exh., San Antonio, 1952; Texas FA Assn., 1952, 1953, 1955; Contemp. Handweavers, 1952-1957; Ft. Worth, 1953, 1955; Texas State Fair, 1954, 1955; High Mus. A., Atlanta, 1955 (2-man); Denver A. Mus., 1952; Milwaukee AI, 1956; Wichita, Kans., 1954, 1956; Southwest Craft Exh., Dallas, 1957; Mint Mus. A., (2-man), 1957; Texas Des-Craftsmen, Austin, 1957, 1958; Episcopal Seminary, Austin, 1958; San Antonio, 1958; Del Mar Col., Corpus Christi, 1958; Tulane Univ., 1958, and others. *Position*: Dir., Crafts, Nat. Music Camp., Interlochen, Mich., 1949-50; Instr., Weaving, Summer Sch., Cherokee Hist. Assn., 1953- ; Asst. Prof. A., Weaving & A. Edu., Art Dept., Univ. Texas, Austin, Tex., 1954- .

COULTER, MARY J. (*Mrs. Orton Loring Clark*)— *Etcher, P., L., W.*

c/o First National Bank & Trust Co., Santa Barbara, Cal.; h. 74 College St., Amherst, Mass.

B. Newport, Ky. *Studied*: Cincinnati A. Acad.; AIC; Univ. Chicago, Ph. B.; abroad; and with Frank Duveneck, Lionel Walden, Charles Hawthorne. *Member*: San F. AA; AAMus.; AFA; AAPL; Cal. SE; Cal. AC; NAWA; Friends of the Huntington Lib. *Awards*: Medal, Lewis & Clark Exp., 1905; Pan-Pacific Exp., 1915; prizes, AIC, 1909; Los A. Mus. A.; F. and Reader, Huntington Lib. & Art Gal., San Marino, Cal. *Work*: Chalcographie du Louvre, Paris, France; British Mus., London, England; Huntington Lib. & Art Gal.; John Herron AI; Cal. State Lib., Sacramento; Univ. Cl., San Diego; Cal. Soc. of Pioneers, San Francisco; 168 etchings for Matson Navigation Co.; Cooke Gal., Honolulu, Hawaii; NGA; LC; AIC; BMFA; MMA, and in many important private collections U.S. and abroad. *Exhibited*: Uffizzi Gal., Florence, Italy; Bibliotheque Nationale, Paris, France; Victoria & Albert Mus., London, England; one-man: Cal. PLH; deYoung Mem. Mus.; Los A. Mus. A. *Position*: Former Cur. Prints, AIC, Chicago, Ill.; Asst. Dir., San Diego FA Gal., San Diego, Cal.

COUNSEL, FREDERICK ALAN—*Painter, T.*

"Rose Ledge," R.D. 2, Box 230, Altoona, Pa.

B. Eldorado, Pa., Jan. 8, 1913. *Studied*: PMSchIA; PAFA; Parsons Sch. Des. (N.Y. & Paris, France), & with Thornton Oakley, John J. Dull. *Member*: All. A. of Johnstown, Pa.; Blair County (Pa.) A. Lg.; Pa. State Edu. Assn.; Pa. Art Edu. Assn. *Awards*: prizes, Johnstown, Pa., 1938; Blair County A. Lg., 1942; Wisconsin AA, 1944, 1945; Army A. Show, Baltimore, Md., 1945. *Work*: Pub. Lib., Wash., D.C.; Detroit Pub. Sch.; Altoona Pub. Sch.; murals, Bradley Field, Conn.; Truax Field, Wis.; Langley Field, Va.; Peterson Field, Colo.; Camp Grant, Ill. *Exhibited*: PAFA, 1934, 1935; Johnstown All. A., 1937, 1938; Phila. A. All., 1938, 1939; New Haven Paint & Clay Cl., 1941; Georgetown Gal., Wash., D.C., 1940 (one-man); No. 10 Gal., 1941, 1942; Soldier Show, Baltimore, Md., 1945; Madison AA, 1944, 1945; Colorado Springs FA Center, 1945; Camp Grant, Ill., 1945; Ferargil Gal., 1950; Ogunquit A. Center, 1955; Boulevard Hotel, Altoona, Pa., 1954 (one-man); Pa. State Univ. (Altoona campus), 1958 (one-man). *Position*: A. Supv., Pub. Sch., Central Cove Dist., Martinsburg, Pa.; A.T., Pa. State Univ., Altoona campus evening classes.

COUSINS, CLARA LEA (*Mrs.*)—*Sculptor, P., T., L.*

Bremo Bluff, Va.

B. Halifax County, Va., Apr. 6, 1894. *Studied*: Cincinnati A. Acad., with Kate Miller, Clement J. Barnhorne; Corcoran A. Sch., with M. M. Leisenring, Burtis Baker; PAFA; Grand Central A. Sch., with Ennis, George Lober, Snell, and with Cecilia Beaux. *Work*: Stratford Col., Danville, Va. *Exhibited*: Danville A. Cl.; Richmond Acad. A. & Sc.; Richmond A. Center; Morton Gal.; Buchanan Gal.; SSAL; Witte Mem. Mus.; Mississippi AA; Delgado Mus. A.; NGA; Irene Leach A. Gal., Norfolk, Va. Lectures: Garden Sculpture.*

COVEY, ARTHUR—*Painter, Lith.*

201 Lake Blvd., Tarpon Springs, Fla.

B. Bloomington, Ill., June 13, 1877. *Studied*: AIC; Royal Acad. A., Munich, Germany. *Member*: NA; SC; NSMP; Arch. Lg.; AWS. *Awards*: Med., Arch. L., 1925; prizes, Florida Gulf Coast Group, 1946; SC. *Work*: murals, Norton Hall, Worcester, Mass.; LaGuardia Field, N.Y.; sc. bas-relief, Kohler Co.; vaulted ceiling, Lutheran Church, Worcester, Mass. *Exhibited*: AV; NAD; Audubon A.; Gulf Coast Group, Fla.*

COVEY, MRS. ARTHUR. See *Lenski, Lois*

COVI, DARIO A.—*Museum Curator, E.*

University of Louisville; h. 1361 South 4th St., Louisville 8, Ky.

B. Livingston, Ill., Dec. 26, 1920. *Studied*: Eastern Illinois State T. Col., B.Ed.; State Univ. of Iowa, M.A.; Warburg Inst., Univ. London; N.Y. Univ., Ph.D., and in Italy. *Member*: CAA; Renaissance Soc. of Am.; AAUP. *Awards*: Fulbright award, 1949-50; Metropolitan Mus. A. F., 1951-52; Brussels Seminar F., 1952. Contributor to Marsyas; Renaissance News; MMA Bulletin. Lectures: Lettering in the Inscriptions of Florentine Painting to art associations and colleges. *Position*: Cur., Univ. A. Collections & Exhibitions, Univ. Louisville, Louisville, Ky., 1957- .

COWAN, (MARY) ELIZABETH (*Mrs. James A.*)— *Craftsman, Des., S., W., L., P.*

8 West 8th St.; h. 35 West 9th St., New York 11, N.Y.

B. Atlanta, Ga., July 31, 1915. *Studied*: Randolph-Macon Women's Col., and with Winold Reiss, Victor Raffo, Albert Jacobson. *Member*: Keramic Soc., N.Y.; Pen & Brush Cl.; Ga. Hist. Soc.; Oyster Ponds Hist. Soc. *Awards*: prizes, Pen & Brush Cl., 1957. *Work*: Fashion, Home & Apparel des. for Burlap Council & Assn. Jute Mills of India and for Pakistan Consulate in N.Y., and Embassy in Wash., D.C. *Exhibited*: ceramics, MMA, 1942; burlap des., Pakistan Int. Trade Show, 1955; Palette A. Gal., N.Y.; Pen & Brush Cl., 1948-1958; N.Y. Soc. Ceramic A., 1954; How-To-Do-It Show, N.Y., 1955. Contributor to McCall's Needlework and Craft publications, 1950-1958; "How To" articles for N.Y. Herald Tribune and Assoc. Press; leaflets, "How To" directions and des., for various manufacturers; Radio-TV "How To" demonstrations and talks. *Position*: Pres., Keramic Soc., 1948- ; Treas., Pen & Brush Cl., 1950-58; Chm., Craft Section, Pen & Brush Cl., 1952-1957; Publ. Chm., N.Y. Soc. Ceramic A., 1955-56.

COWAN, WOOD—*Cartoonist, L., W.*

Godfrey Rd., Weston-Westport, Conn.

B. Algona, Iowa, Nov. 1, 1889. *Studied*: Univ. Iowa; AIC, with Vanderpoel, Dunn. *Member*: A. & W. Assn.; Westport A. Cl. Contributor to: New Yorker, Argosy, & other magazines of cartoons, comics. Lectures: Cartooning; Cartoon History. *Position*: Cart., for newspapers in Chicago, Wash., D.C., & others. *Position*: Pres., Artists & Writers Service, Westport, Conn.; Ed. Cart., Bridgeport (Conn.) Post.

COWDREY, (MARY) BARTLETT— *Historian, W., Cr., Mus. Dir., Archivist*

Archives of American Art; h. 33 Randolph St., Passaic, N.J.

B. Passaic, N.J., June 16, 1910. *Studied*: Rutgers Univ., A.B.; Research student, London Univ., 1934-35. *Member*: AAMus.; Am. Studies Assn.; CAA; N.Y. Hist. Soc.; N.Y. State Hist. Assn.; SAH. Author: "National Academy of

Design Exhibition Record, 1826-1860," 2 vols. 1944; "George Henry Durrie," 1947; "The Mount Brothers," 1947; "Winslow Homer: Illustrator," 1951; "American Academy of Fine Arts and American Art Union, 1816-1852," 2 vols. 1953. Co-author: "William Sidney Mount, 1807-1868. An American Painter," 1944. Contributor to American Collector; Antiques; Art Bulletin; Dictionary of American Biography; Art in America; Art News; Gazette des Beaux Arts; New York Hist. Soc. Quarterly; New York History; Panorama; Portfolio; William and Mary Quarterly; Wisconsin Magazine of History. *Positions*: Registrar, BM, 1940-42; Cur. Prints, N.Y. Hist. Soc., 1943; Cur. Paintings, H.S. Newman Gal., New York, 1943-49; Cur., 1949-52; Asst. Dir., 1952-55, Actg. Dir., 1954-55, Smith Col. Mus. A.; Archivist, New York Area, Archives of Am. A., (Detroit Inst. A.), 1955- ; Asst. Archivist, NAD, 1951-55, as compiler of NAD Exhibition Record, 1861-1890; Hon. Cur., Paintings and Prints, Long Island Hist. Soc., N.Y., 1958- .

COWELL, JOSEPH GOSS—*Painter, E., S., L., W.*
424 South St., Wrentham, Mass.

B. Peoria, Ill., Dec. 4, 1886. *Studied*: Univ. Illinois; George Washington Univ.; BMFA Sch.; Bradley Univ., B.S.; ASL; Julian Acad., Paris, and with George Bridgman, William Chase. *Work*: murals, churches in Waltham, Whitman, Mass.; South Orange, N.J.; Peoria, Ill.; State House, Richmond, Va.; Wrentham, Mass., Pub. Lib.; Boston Clerical Sch.; Cambridge City Hospital; Self Revelation Temple, Wash., D.C.; National Cathedral, Washington, D.C.; Sevayatan Temple, Midnapur, India; sc., Mem. Park, Wrentham, Mass. *Exhibited*: Paris Salon, 1920; Arch. Lg., 1923, 1924, 1931; Boston A. Cl., 1922-26; Rockport AA, 1939. Contributor to Mass. State Bulletin on Art Therapy. Illus.; Gray's Anatomy. Lectures: Art Therapy. *Position*: Instr., Mass. Sch. A., 1922-27; Boston Des. A. Sch., 1927-33; Dir. A. Therapy & Research, Boston State Hospital, 1933-39; Dir. National A. Sch., Washington, D.C., 1940-48 (now Dir. Emeritus).

COWLES, RUSSELL—*Painter*
c/o Kraushaar Gallery, 1055 Madison Ave., New York, N.Y.; h. New Milford, Conn.

B. Algona, Iowa, Oct. 7, 1887. *Studied*: Dartmouth Col., A.B.; NAD; ASL; Am. Acad. in Rome; Century Assn. *Awards*: Med., AIC, 1925; Hon. Deg., D.H.L., Dartmouth Col., 1951; D.F.A., Grinnell Col., 1945; D.F.A., Cornell Col., 1958; prizes, Denver A. Mus., 1936; Santa Barbara Mus. A., 1943. *Work*: Denver A. Mus.; Terre Haute Mus.; Encyclopaedia Britannica Coll.; Murdock Coll., Univ. Wichita; Dartmouth Col.; Minneapolis Inst. A.; PAFA; Des Moines A. Center; Blanden Mem. A. Gal.; AGAA; VMFA. *Exhibited*: CGA; PAFA.

COWLEY, EDWARD P.—*Educator, P.*
New York State College for Teachers, Albany, N.Y.; h. Altamont, N.Y.

B. Buffalo, N.Y., May 29, 1925. *Studied*: Albright A. Sch.; Buffalo State T. Col., B.S.; Columbia Univ., M.A. *Awards*: Ford Fnd. F., for study in Ireland, 1955. *Work*: paintings: Smith Col. Mus.; Berkshire Mus. A.; Albany Inst. Hist. & A.; Colgate Univ. Gal.; Schenectady Mus. A.; Munson-Williams-Proctor Inst. *Position*: Assoc. Prof. A., N.Y. State Col. for Teachers, Albany, N.Y.

COX, ALLYN—*Painter, T., L., W.*
207 East 17th St., New York 3, N.Y.; s. Essex, Mass.

B. New York, N.Y., June 5, 1896. *Studied*: NAD; ASL; Am. Acad. in Rome. *Member*: ANA; NSMP; FA. Fed. of N.Y.; Mun. A. Soc.; AAPL; Arch. Lg. *Awards*: Prix de Rome, 1916; med., Los A. Mus. A., 1926; gold med., Arch. Lg., 1954; AAPL, 1945. *Work*: Princeton Mus.; Parrish Mus. A., Southampton, N.Y.; murals, Clark Mem. Lib., Los A., Cal.; Univ. Virginia; Dumbarton Oaks; George Washington Masonic Nat. Mem., Alexandria, Va.; S.S. "America"; Norfolk Naval Hospital; rotunda frieze, Nat. Capitol, Wash., D.C. *Exhibited*: NAD; AAPL; Arch. Lg., and others. Lectures. Contributor of articles to various publications. *Position*: Pres., NSMP, 1942-46; Nat. Pres., AAPL, 1952-54.

COX, GARDNER—*Painter*
88 Garden St., Cambridge, Mass.

B. Holyoke, Mass., Jan. 22, 1906. *Studied*: Harvard Col.; MIT; BMFA Sch. *Member*: Century Assn.; Boston Soc. Indp. A. *Awards*: prizes, Inst. Mod. A., Boston, 1945; AIC,

1949, 1951. *Work*: Harvard Univ.; BMFA; AGAA; Wadsworth Atheneum; Yale Univ.; Wabash Col.; Wellesley Col.; Univ. Michigan; U.S. Dept. State; U.S. Army; Dept. Defense, U.S. Army; NGA. *Exhibited*: Carnegie Inst., 1941; VMFA, 1946; Inst. Contemp. A., Boston; MMA; AIC; Univ. Illinois, 1950, 1951; Pepsi-Cola, 1948. *Position*: Hd. Dept. Painting, Boston Mus. FA. Sch., 1954- .

COX, J. HALLEY—*Painter, E.*
University of Hawaii; h. 3020 Manoa Rd., Honolulu, Hawaii

B. Des Moines, Iowa, May 20, 1910. *Studied*: San Jose State Col., A.B.; Univ. California, M.A. *Member*: Pacific AA; Hawaii P. & S. *Awards*: prizes, Honolulu Pr. M., 1951, 1955; A. of Hawaii, 1951, 1952. *Work*: BMFA; Honolulu Acad. A.; Univ. Hawaii. *Exhibited*: Cal. PLH, 1945 (one-man); San F. AA, 1939-1945; SFMA, 1949; Honolulu Acad. A., 1948-1952; Honolulu Pr. M., 1948-1955; one-man: Gump's Gal., San F., 1949, 1951; Honolulu Acad. A., 1951; The Gallery, Honolulu, 1956; Santa Barbara Mus. A., 1955. *Position*: Assoc. Prof. A., Univ. Hawaii, Honolulu, Hawaii; Exhibit Des., Bishop Mus., Honolulu, Hawaii; Pres., Hawaii P. & S. Lg., 1958-59. Lectures: Hawaiian Sculpture; Hawaiian Petroglyphs—An Artist's Interpretation.

COX, JOHN ROGERS—*Painter, T.*
4 East Ohio St. #19, Chicago 11, Ill.

B. Terre Haute, Ind., Mar. 24, 1915. *Studied*: PAFA; Univ. Pennsylvania B.F.A. *Awards*: Med., AV, 1942; prizes, Carnegie Inst., 1943, 1944; A.Dir.Cl., 1944. *Work*: CMA; Encyclopaedia Britannica Coll.; Abbott Laboratories; Springfield (Mass.) Mus. A., and in private colls. *Exhibited*: Carnegie Inst., 1941, 1943-1946; PAFA, 1944; WMAA, 1943; AIC, 1944, 1945; John Herron AI, 1944; Dallas Mus. FA, 1944; Toledo Mus. A., 1944; Nebraska AA, 1944-1946; Pepsi-Cola, 1946; Encyclopaedia Britannica traveling exh., 1946. Contributor to American Artist, Life magazine, Figure Photography Annual. *Position*: Instr., AIC, Chicago, Ill., 1948- .

COX, JOSEPH H.—*Painter, E.*
School of Design, North Carolina State College, Raleigh, N.C.

B. Indianapolis, Ind., May 4, 1915. *Studied*: John Herron AI, B.F.A., with Donald Mattison, Eliot O'Hara; Univ. Iowa, M.F.A., with Jean Charlot, Philip Guston. *Awards*: prizes, Indiana A., 1939; Hoosier Salon, 1942; Memphis Biennial, 1951; Knoxville A. Center, 1952; Atlanta Paper Co., "Painting of the Year" Exh., 1955; Southeastern Exh., Atlanta, 1956; purchase award, Norfolk Mus. A., 1957. *Work*: Atlanta Paper Co. Coll.; Ford Motor Co. Coll. (with reproductions in Ford Times); murals, USPO, Garret, Ind.; Alma, Mich.; six murals for TVA, Tenn., 1948-53; exterior murals, Carousel Theatre, Knoxville; North Greenville Jr. Col., Tigerville, S.C.; mosaic, Am. Oil Co., Yorktown, Va.; Catholic Church, Lexington, N.C.; mural, Woman's College, Greensboro, N.C. *Exhibited*: Carnegie Inst., 1941; VMFA, 1942; Indiana A., 1938, 1939; Hoosier Salon, 1940, 1942; Kansas City AI, 1942; Univ. Iowa; Univ. Illinois; Joslyn A. Mus.; Weyhe Gal.; Denver A. Mus.; traveling exh. "10 Southern Artists"; High Mus. A., 1950, 1952-54; John Herron AI; Memphis, Tenn., 1951, 1953; Univ. Kentucky; State A. Exh., Raleigh, N.C.; Norfolk Mus. A.; High Mus. A., and others. *Position*: Instr. A., to 1942, Asst. Prof., Univ. Iowa; Univ. Tennessee, 1948-54; Assoc. Prof. Des., Sch. Des., North Carolina State Col., Raleigh, N.C., 1954- .

COX, J(OHN) W(ILLIAM) S(MITH)—*Painter, T.*
19 T Wharf St., Boston 10, Mass.

B. Yonkers, N.Y., May 18, 1911. *Studied*: PIASch; Academie Colorossi, Paris, with Othon Friesz; Boston Univ.; Eliot O'Hara Sch. A. *Member*: AWS; F., Intl. Inst. A. & Lets.; Lindau-Bodensee, Germany. *Awards*: Scholarship, O'Hara Sch. A.; prizes, Rockport, Mass., 1951; Wash. WC Cl., 1957. *Work*: BMFA; Ford Publications. *Exhibited*: Audubon A.; AWS; Alabama WC Soc.; Mississippi WC Soc.; Springfield A. Lg.; BM; Wash. WC Cl.; Rockport AA (annually); L.D.M. Sweat Mem. Mus.; Boston A. Festival; Marblehead AA, 1958; Golden Cod Gal., 1958; Cox Gal., 1958; deCordova & Dana Mus., 1955 (one-man); WAC, 1957 (2-man); New Britain Mus., 1958 (one-man). Contributor articles and illus. to Christian Science Monitor. *Position*: Dir. of Training, New England Sch. of Art, 1954-1958.

COX, THEODOSIA—*Editor and Librarian*

3023 14th St., N.W., Washington 9, D.C.

B. Cameron, W. Va., Nov. 26, 1892. *Studied*: Vassar Col., A.B.; Univ. Virginia; Cornell Univ.; Columbia Univ. Compiler of "List of Museum Periodicals for the United States," publ. by AAMus. *Position*: Libr., Ed., AAMus., 1934-1958.

COX, WARREN EARLE—

Craftsman, P., C., Des., W., L., T., Cr.

6 East 39th St.; h. 140 East 40th St., New York 16, N.Y.

B. Oak Park, Ill., Aug. 27, 1895. *Exhibited*: NAD. Contributor to national art magazines. Lectures: Decorations & Craftsmanship. Author: "Pottery & Porcelain"; "Chinese Ivory Sculpture"; "Lighting and Lamp Design"; "Some Master Painters of Early Chinese Ceramics," Connoisseur Year Book, 1955. *Position*: Pres., Warren E. Cox Associates, New York, N.Y.; A.Dir., A. Ed., 14th Edition, Encyclopaedia Britannica, 1929-1939.*

COY, C. LYNN—*Sculptor, Des., W.*

4 East Ohio St., Chicago 11, Ill.

B. Chicago, Ill., Oct. 31, 1889. *Studied*: AIC; & with Albin Polasek, Lorado Taft. *Member*: Chicago A. Cl.; Chicago P. & S.; Chicago AA. *Work*: Vanderpoel Coll.; Munroe Mem., Joliet, Ill. *Exhibited*: AIC, 1915, 1917, 1919, 1921; Chicago P. & S., 1950-1958; Chicago A. Cl., 1952-1958.

COYE, LEE BROWN—*Sculptor, P., C., Eng., I.*

305 Academy Pl., Syracuse, N.Y.

B. Syracuse, N.Y., July 24, 1907. *Member*: Onondaga A. Gld. *Awards*: prizes, Syracuse Assoc. A., 1937, 1938, 1944-1946; Rochester Mem. A. Gal., 1955; Cooperstown AA, 1955. *Work*: Syracuse Mus. FA; MMA; Univ. North Carolina. *Exhibited*: GGE, 1939; Pepsi-Cola, 1946; MMA, 1950, 1951; Syracuse Assoc. A., 1936-1946; WMAA, 1939-1941; Contemp. A., 1944; Cayuga Mus. Hist. & A., 1941; Syracuse Mus. FA, 1939, 1955 (both one-man); Skidmore Col., 1940 (one-man); Colgate Univ. (one-man); 1956-58: Oswego State T. Col. (one-man); Syracuse Mus. FA; Rochester Mem. A. Gal. I., "Scylla the Beautiful," 1939; "Sleep No More," 1944; "The Night Side," 1947; "Who Knocks," 1946; "The Art of Bundling," 1938. *Position*: Sec. Syracuse All. A., 1956-58.

COZE, PAUL (JEAN)—*Painter, W., I., L., T.*

4040 East Elm St., Phoenix, Ariz.

B. Beirut, Lebanon, July 29, 1903. *Studied*: Lycee Janson de Sailly; Ecole des Arts Decoratifs, Paris, France; and with J. F. Gonin. *Member*: Societe Nationale des Beaux-Arts; Societe des Peintres et Sculpteurs de Chevaux; Societe des Artistes Independants; Pasadena Soc. A.; Pasadena A. Assoc.; Arizona A. Gld.; Phoenix FA Assn.; Heard Mus., etc. *Awards*: Chevalier de la Legion d'Honneur; prizes, Pasadena; Arizona State Fair, etc. *Work*: Victoria Mus., Ottawa, Canada; Southwest Mus., Los A., Cal.; Heard Mus., Phoenix; Mesa Verde Mus. (Colo.); Casa Grande Mus. (Ariz.); Montezuma Castle (Ariz.); Koshares Mus., La Junta, Colo.; many nat. monuments in Arizona and New Mexico; murals, in pub. bldgs., Arizona. *Exhibited*: Pasadena AI; Los A. Mus. A., Mus. New Mexico, Santa Fé; Tucson & Phoenix, Ariz., and in France and Canada. Author: "Moeurs et Histoire des Peaux-Rouges"; "Quatre Feux" and other books. W., I., "L'Illustration," "Les Enfants de France," "Tatler," "Arizona Highways Magazine, Nat. Geographic Magazine," and other publications. *Position*: Instr. A., Pasadena AI, 1942-46; Dir., Studio Workshop, Pasadena, 1944-51; Tech. Dir., Twentieth Century Fox, Universal and Warner Bros. Studios, Hollywood, Cal.; Dir., Expedition for Musee de l'Homme, Paris, in North Canada; conducted TV program and art column; Dir., "Miracle of the Roses," Scottsdale, Ariz.; French Republic Consular Agent for Arizona; Dir., Studio Paul Coze, Phoenix, Ariz.

COZZENS, EVANGELINE CHAPMAN—*Painter*

Allerton House, 130 East 57th St., New York 22, N.Y.

B. New York, N.Y., June 13, 1895. *Studied*: Halsted Sch., Yonkers, N.Y.; Capen Sch., Northampton, Mass. *Member*: Martha's Vineyard AA. *Work*: MMA. *Exhibited*: AWS, 1932, 1934, 1935; CAA, 1934; N.Y. WC Cl., 1935; Toledo Mus. A., 1935; Kraushaar Gal., 1935, 1939; Int. A. Center,

N.Y., 1936; MMA, 1942; BM, 1943; Wakefield Gal., 1944; Martha's Vineyard AA, 1939- ; Weyhe Gal., 1955; N.Y. Pub. Lib., 1957, 1958.

CRAFT, JOHN RICHARD—*Museum Director*

Columbia Museum of Art, Senate & Bull Sts.; h. 1407 Wellington Dr., Columbia, S.C.

B. Uniontown, Pa., June 15, 1909. *Studied*: Yale Univ.; ASL; Sorbonne, Paris; Am. Sch. Classical Studies, Athens; Johns Hopkins Univ., M.A., Ph.D. *Member*: AAMus. *Position*: Dir., Washington County Mus. FA, Hagerstown, Md., 1940-1950; Dir., Columbia Mus. A., Columbia, S.C., 1950- ; Pres., Southeastern Museums Conference, 1953-55; Chm., Southern Art Mus. Dir. Assn., 1955-1956.

CRAFT, PAUL—*Painter, T.*

1914 Kemper Lane, Cincinnati 2, Ohio

B. Leavittsburg, Ohio, Mar. 3, 1904. *Studied*: Hiram Col. (Ohio), A.B.; Cincinnati A. Acad. *Member*: Cincinnati Indp. A.; Ohio A. Edu. Assn.; Cincinnati Mod. A. Soc.; Dayton AI; Contemp. A. Center. *Awards*: prizes, Butler AI; Ohio WC Soc.; Ohio State Fair, 1958. *Work*: CM; IBM; Walnut Hills H.S., Cincinnati; Dayton A. Center. *Exhibited*: Cincinnati Mod. A. Soc.; CM; Butler AI; Ohio Univ.; Canton AI, 1955; Akron AI, 1955; Massillon A. Mus., 1955; A. of Cincinnati and Vicinity, 1954, 1955; Dayton AI, 1954-55; one-man: Closson A. Gal., Cincinnati, 1948, 1953; Hiram Col., 1950. *Position*: Instr. A., Cincinnati Pub. Schs.; Hughes H.S., 1954- .

CRAIG, MARTIN—*Sculptor, T., Des.*

235 7th Ave. (11); h. 305 East 10th St., New York 9, N.Y.

B. Paterson, N.J., Nov. 2, 1906. *Studied*: Col. City of N.Y., B.S. *Member*: S. Gld.; A. Cl. *Awards*: prizes, MModA, 1940, 1955. *Work*: sc., Temple Mishkan Tefila, Newton, Mass.; Fifth Avenue Synagogue, N.Y.; Federal Housing Comm.; WFNY 1939. *Exhibited*: Salon de Mai, Paris, 1952-1954; Salon de la Jeune, Paris, 1950-1954; U.S. Embassy, Paris, 1953; Summer A. Festival, Belgium, 1952; MModA, 1955; WMAA; Mus. Contemp. A., Houston, Tex.; Stable Gal., N.Y.; Matisse Gal., N.Y.; one-man: Galerie du Siecle, Paris, 1949; Galerie Colette Allendy, Paris, 1954.

CRAIG, NANCY ELLEN—*Painter*

9 Vine St., Bronxville, N.Y.

B. Bronxville, N.Y., Feb. 7, 1927. *Studied*: Sweet Briar Col.; Bennington Col.; ASL; Farnsworth Sch. A.; Academie Julien, Paris; Taubes-Pierce Sch. A.; Hans Hofmann. *Member*: All. A. Am.; NAWA. *Awards*: prizes, Hudson Valley AA, 1951; NAWA, 1953, 1954, 1956; NAD, 1954 (purchase), 1957; Audubon A., 1955; gold medal, All. A. Am., 1956. *Work*: MMA; New Britain (Conn.) Mus. A. *Exhibited*: NAD; Audubon A.; All. A. Am.; NAWA; N.Y. City Center; one-man: Bronxville, N.Y., 1952, 1954, 1957; Scarborough, N.Y., 1954; Greenwich, Conn., 1955; Grand Central A. Gal., 1955.

CRAIG, ROBERT—*Painter, Et., Lith.*

#1 High St., Eastport, Me.

B. Spencer, Ind. *Studied*: Bradley Polytechnic Inst.; Columbia Univ., B.S. *Member*: AWS; PAFA; AWS; LC; Carnegie Inst.; BM; John Herron AI. *Work*: State House, Augusta, Me.; Calais (Me.) Mem. Hospital.

CRAMER, A(BRAHAM)—*Cartoonist, Comm., P.*

1909 Quentin Rd., Brooklyn 29, N.Y.

B. Russia, Aug. 25, 1903. *Studied*: Kiev Sch. FA, Russia; Acad. FA., Mexico City, Mexico. *Work*: murals and portraits in Mexico City and private colls. *Exhibited*: Soc. Indp. A. Contributor cartoons to: Sat. Eve. Post, Colliers, American magazine, Red Book, New Yorker, Cosmopolitan, Ladies Home Journal, King Features Syndicate, Phila. Enquirer, Esquire, and others.

CRAMER, CARL—*Sculptor, L., T.*

P.O. Box 815, Covington, La.

B. Cleveland, Ohio, Apr. 19, 1927. *Studied*: Cleveland Inst. A.; Cranbrook Acad. A. (Asst. to Carl Milles). *Member*: New Orleans AA; St. Tammany AA; Louisiana

Hist. Soc. (Co-Organizer & Fndr.); Louisiana State A. Comm. (Contrib. memb.) *Work*: Ft. Benning, Ga.; Cabildo-Louisiana State Mus.; Intl. Trade Mart, Hotel Roosevelt, Hall of Philosophy, Goldring's, Art Assn. Gld. Gal., St. Augustine's Episcopal Church, St. Martin's, Celotex Corp., Lighthouse for the Blind, all in New Orleans; Covington Country Club; Broadwater Beach Hotel, Biloxi, Miss.; St. Charles Seminary, Grand Coteaux, La.; Ballet Alonzo, Havana, Cuba, and numerous heads and busts sculptures of prominent persons. *Exhibited*: Cleveland May Show, 1945-1947; Detroit Inst. A., 1947; Ft. Benning AA, 1950; New Orleans AA, 1955; Louisiana State A. Comm., 1959. Lectures on art history. *Positions*: Art Ed., Louisiana Historical Society Quarterly; Instr. S., St. Martin's Sch.; New Orleans AA; Base Hospital, Ft. Benning; St. Tammany AA, Covington, etc.

CRAMER, FLORENCE BALLIN—*Painter, C.*

P.O. Box 193, Woodstock, N.Y.

B. Dec. 13, 1884. *Studied*: ASL, with Burroughs, Cox, Harrison, DuMond. *Member*: Woodstock AA; Nat. Assn. Women P. & S. *Exhibited*: Woodstock AA; Rudolph Gal. (one-man); Marie Harriman Gal.; PMA; CGA; WMAA; PAFA; CAA traveling exh.

CRAMER, KONRAD—*Painter, Gr., Des., I., L., C.*

Woodstock, N.Y.

B. Wurzburg, Germany, Nov. 9, 1888. *Studied*: Acad. FA, Karlsruhe, Germany. *Work*: MMA; WMAA; MModA. *Exhibited*: CGA, 1938, 1939; Carnegie Inst., 1937, 1938; WMAA, 1946; PAFA, 1936; AFA traveling exh., 1946; Woodstock AA; Woodstock, N.Y., 1952 (one-man); Long Island Univ., 1958 (one-man). I., Ed., "Indian Arts in North America." Contributor to: Graphic Graphlex; Leica Magazine. *Position*: Instr., Photography, Bard Col., 1940; Fndr., Woodstock Sch. of Photography, 1936.

CRANDALL, NORRIS INGERSOLL—*Educator, Arch.*

1117 Madison Lane, Alexandria, Va.

B. Hornell, N.Y., Aug. 17, 1891. *Studied*: Cornell Univ., B. Arch., M. Arch.; MIT. *Member*: AIA; Cornell Cl., Wash., D.C.; Am. Assn. Univ. Prof. *Awards*: Columbus Mem. Lighthouse Comp.; med., Cornell Univ.; Soc. Beaux Arts Arch. *Position*: Asst. Prof. Arch. Des., Univ. Illinois, 1921-22; Prof. Arch., Hd. Dept., Univ. Puerto Rico, 1922-23; Prof. Arch., Hd. Dept., 1923-28, Dir., Div. FA, 1928-37, Exec. Officer, Dept. A., 1937-1954; Prof. A., 1954-1957; Prof. Emeritus, 1957- , George Washington Univ., Washington, D.C.

CRANDELL, BRADSHAW—*Portrait Painter*

400 East 52nd St., New York 22, N.Y.; h. Madison, Conn. (Box 173)

B. Glens Falls, N.Y., June 14, 1896. *Studied*: Wesleyan Univ.; AIC; ASL. *Member*: AAPL; Grand Central A. Gal.; SI. *Work*: Illustrations for national magazines and national advertisers, 1930-1950. *Exhibited*: Grand Central A. Gal.; Wisconsin State Capitol; Pennsylvania State Capitol; Cornell Univ.; Syracuse Univ.

CRANE, ALAN (HORTON)—*Painter, Lith., I., W.*

Country Club Rd., Rockport, Mass.

B. Brooklyn, N.Y., Nov. 14, 1901. *Studied*: PIASch., and with Winold Reiss. *Member*: SC; Phila. WC Cl.; Rockport AA; North Shore AA; Prairie Pr. M.; Audubon A.; SAGA; Albany Pr. Cl.; Gld. Boston A.; Soc. Wash. Pr. M. *Awards*: prizes, Rockport AA, 1941, 1945, 1952; LC, 1943, 1945; SC, 1943, 1944, 1952; Meriden, Conn., 1949; Corpus Christi, Tex., 1950; SAGA, 1955; BM, 1947. *Work*: LC; N.Y. Pub. Lib.; CGA; Princeton Pr. Cl.; Carnegie Inst.; Trinity Univ.; Lawrason Brown Mus., Saranac Lake; MMA; BM; Univ. Pennsylvania; Wesleyan Univ.; Inst. A. & Lets. *Exhibited*: LC; PAFA; Carnegie Inst.; NAD; Conn. Acad. FA; MMA; North Shore AA; Northwest Pr. M.; Mint Mus. A.; Laguna Beach AA; Audubon A; SAGA; Albany Pr. Cl., annually; one-man: Rockport AA, 1951; Univ. Maine, 1952; Fitchburg A. Mus., 1948; Gld. Boston A., 1954; Northwestern Oklahoma A. & M. Col., 1956. Author, I., "Gloucester Joe," 1943; "Nick and Nan in Yucatan," 1945; "Pepita Bonita," 1941; Illus., "A Carpet of Flowers," 1956; Illus. for American Home Magazine.

CRANE, JAMES—*Educator, P., Gr., Cart.*

Wisconsin State College; h. 121 West 6th St., River Falls, Wis.

B. Hartshorne, Okla., May 21, 1927. *Studied*: Albion Col., B.A.; Univ. Minnesota; Univ. Michigan; State Univ. Iowa, M.A. *Awards*: prizes, Western Michigan A., 1955; Grand Rapids A. Gal., 1955; Kalamazoo Inst. A., 1955. *Work*: Albion Col. print coll.; Joslyn A. Mus.; Iowa State T. Col. *Exhibited*: PAFA, 1954; Albion Col., 1952, 1954 (one-man); Iowa State T. Col., 1958; Michigan A., 1953, 1954; Michigan Acad. FA, 1955; Western Michigan A., 1955; Michiana, 1955; Joslyn A. Mus., 1958; Wisconsin Salon, 1958. Author, I., "What Other Time?" (a book of satirical cartoons), 1953. Participant CBS-TV "The Creative Response," 1958. *Position*: Chm. A. Dept., Wisconsin State College at River Falls, Wis., 1958- .

CRANE, ROY—*Cartoonist*

c/o King Features Syndicate, 235 East 45th St., New York 36, N.Y.*

CRANE, ROY(STON) (CAMPBELL)—*Cartoonist, W.*

P.O. Box 250, Orlando, Fla.

B. Abilene, Tex., Nov. 22, 1901. *Studied*: Hardin-Simmons Univ.; Univ. Texas; Chicago Acad. F.A. *Member*: SI; Cart. Cl. *Awards*: Cited, U.S. Navy, as War Correspondent, 1946; "Cartoonist of the Year," 1950, Nat. Cart. Soc.; Hon. Deg., Doctor of Humane Letters, Rollins Col., 1957; U.S. Navy gold medal for Distinguished Public Service, 1957. *Position*: A., W., NEA Service, newspaper strip "Wash Tubbs," "Captain Easy," 1924-1943; King Features Syndicate, newspaper strip "Buzz Sawyer," 1943- .

CRANE, STANLEY WILLIAM—*Painter, Des.*

Box 248, Woodstock, N.Y.

B. La Porte, Ind., Nov. 14, 1905. *Member*: Grand Central A. Gal. *Awards*: prizes, Hoosier Salon, 1928; Albany Inst. Hist. & A., 1940, 1942; MModA, 1942; Carnegie Inst., 1948; Grand Central A. Gal., 1952; Terry AI, 1952; Miami, Fla., 1952; Stanley Allyn prize, 1952; med., NAD, 1945. *Work*: Albany Inst. Hist. & A. *Exhibited*: AIC, 1938; VMFA, 1940; Carnegie Inst., 1941, 1949; NAD, 1942, 1944, 1945; PAFA, 1938, 1940-1942; Ogunquit A. Center, 1952; Terry AI, 1952; Albany Inst. Hist. & A., 1940, 1945, 1946; Univ. Illinois, 1950; Grand Central A. Gal., 1950-1952 (one-man).

CRATHERN, HELEN GOODWIN—*Teacher, P., L.*

18984 Oak Dr., Detroit 21, Mich.; s. Coach House Workshop, Mason, N.H.

B. Mason, N.H., Jan. 17, 1896. *Studied*: WMA Sch.; Wayne Univ., B.S., M.A.; Columbia Univ.; AIC. *Member*: Soc. Women P.&S., Detroit; Copley Soc., Boston; Michigan Acad. Sc., A. & Let.; Am. Assn. Univ. Women; Michigan Edu. Assn.; Detroit T. Assn. *Exhibited*: Soc. Women P.&S., Detroit; Fitchburg A. Center; Michigan Acad. Sc., A. & Let.; Scarab Cl., Detroit. Contributor to: School Arts magazine. Lectures: "Community Workshops." *Position*: Dir., A. & Skills Corps, Am. Red Cross, Lovell General Hospital, Ft. Devens, Mass., 1944-45; Founder, Dir., Coach House Workshop, Mason, N.H., 1940- ; Founder, Coach House Fellowship, 1941; Hd., FA Dept., Hutchins Intermediate Sch., Detroit, Mich.; Asst. Prin., Jackson Intermediate Sch., Mich.*

CRAVATH, RUTH (Mrs. Ruth Cravath Wakefield)— *Sculptor, T.*

716 Montgomery St., San Francisco 11, Cal.

B. Chicago, Ill., Jan. 23, 1902. *Studied*: AIC, Grinnell Col.; Cal. Sch. FA. *Member*: San F. Soc. Women A.; AEA; Liturgical A. Soc. *Awards*: prizes, San F. AA, 1924, 1927; San F. Soc. Women A, 1934, 1940. *Work*: SFMA; Stock Exchange, San F.; Vallejo, Cal.; Chapel at the Archbishop Hanna Center for Boys, Sonoma, Cal.; marble group, Starr King Sch., San F. *Exhibited*: San F. AA, 1924, 1926-1928, 1930, 1932, 1935, 1937; SFMA, 1941; WFNY 1939; Raymond & Raymond Gal., San F.; SAM, 1929; Stockton Mus., 1934; Denver A. Mus., 1944; San F. Soc. Women A., 1926-1928, 1932, 1934, 1938-1941, 1944; Catholic Art Forum traveling exh., 1953-55; Bay Area S., Seattle, Spokane, Wash., Vancouver, B.C., 1953. Lectures: Contemporary Sculpture. *Position*: Instr. A., Dominican Convent, San Rafael, Cal., 1943-49; Mills Col., summer sessions, 1945-46, Oakland, Cal.; Sculptor Memb., San Francisco Art Comm., 1937-42.*

CRAVEN, EDGAR MALIN—*Painter*
Intervale Rd., Mountain Lakes, N.J.

B. Paterson, N.J., Apr. 4, 1891. *Studied*: Grand Central Sch. A., and with George E. Browne. *Member*: SC; All. A. Am. *Awards*: prizes, Morris County AA, 1944, 1948, 1954; Spring Lake Annual, 1947, 1951. *Exhibited*: All. A. Am., 1946-1949, 1951, 1953, 1954; Audubon A., 1946; SC; Spring Lake; Jersey City Mus., 1946; Montclair A. Mus., 1945-1950, 1953; New Jersey P. & S. Soc., 1947; Trenton State Mus., 1950; Palm Beach A. Lg., 1951; Irvington A. & Mus. Assn., 1948, 1949. 1951.

CRAVEN, ROY C., JR.—*Painter, E., Des.*
Department of Art, University of Florida; h. 413 Northwest 36th Dr., Gainesville, Fla.

B. Cherokee Bluffs, Ala., July 29, 1924. *Studied*: Univ. Chattanooga, B.A.; ASL, with Kuniyoshi, Grosz, Browne, Piening; Univ. Florida, M.F.A. *Member*: Southeastern College AA. *Awards*: prizes, VMFA, 1950 (purchase); AIGA, 1950; Brooks Mem. A. Gal., 1952. *Work*: VMFA; Esso Standard Oil Co. of N.J. *Exhibited*: MMA, 1952; AFA traveling exh., 1956-58; Soc. Four Arts, 1956, 1957; Sarasota AA, 1956, 1957; Southeastern annual, Atlanta, 1953, 1957; Painting of the Year, Atlanta, 1956, 1958; Lowe Comp., N.Y., 1950; New Orleans AA, 1957; Norfolk Mus. A., 1954; Director's Choice, 1956, 1957, and others. Lectures: Contemporary Painting; Indian Art. *Position*: Asst. Prof. A., Univ. Florida, Gainesville, Fla., 1954- .

CRAVER, MARGRET—*Craftsman*
Middle Rd., West Newbury, Mass.

B. Pratt, Kan. *Studied*: Univ. Kansas; & with Baron Erik Fleming, Stockholm, Sweden. *Awards*: prizes, Phila. A. All. *Exhibited*: GGE 1939; Phila. A. All.; Currier Gal. A.; Zanesville (Ohio) AI; George Walter Vincent Smith A. Mus.; Springfield, Mass.; Illinois State Mus.; Philbrook A. Center; Decorative-A.-Ceramic Exh., Wichita, Kan.; Des.-Craftsmen: USA, 1953; Mus. Contemp. Crafts, N.Y., 1957, 1958; Boston A. Festival, 1958; DMFA, 1958. *Position*: Hd. Craft Dept., Wichita AA Sch., 1935-44; Former Consulting Silversmith, Hospital & Craft Service Dept., Edu. booklets and films, Handy & Harman, New York, N.Y.

CRAWFORD, BARBARA (Mrs. Samuel L. Feinstein)—*Writer, P., E.*
2008 Chancellor St., Philadelphia 3, Pa.

B. New Castle, Pa., Feb. 16, 1914. *Studied*: PMSchIA. *Work*: PMA. Author: "Day of the Circus," 1954. *Position*: Hd. A. Dept., Chestnut Hill Academy, Dir. A. Gal., Chestnut Hill Academy, Philadelphia, Pa.

CRAWFORD, EARL—*Painter*
6837 Thomas Blvd., Pittsburgh 8, Pa.

B. Johnstown, Pa., June 5, 1891. *Studied*: Carnegie Inst.; Univ. Pittsburgh; & with Christian J. Walter. *Member*: Assoc. A. Pittsburgh; Golden Triangle A. *Awards*: Prizes, Golden Triangle A., 1946; State T. Col., Indiana, Pa., 1945. *Work*: Pennsylvania State Col.; State T. Col., Indiana, Pa.; Latrobe (Pa.) H.S.; Manor Sch., Manor, Pa. *Exhibited*: Golden Triangle A., 1936-1946; Assoc. A. Pittsburgh, 1936-1946; Butler AI, 1944, 1945; Indiana State T. Col., 1945, 1946; Parkersburg, W. Va., 1945, 1946; Newport, R.I., 1947-1949; Sarasota, Fla., 1953; Assoc. A. of Pittsburgh, 1954, 1956-1958.

CRAWFORD, LESLEY—*Painter, Lith.*
24 Ridge Rd., Summit, N.J.

B. New York, N.Y. *Studied*: Vassar Col.; ASL. *Member*: So. Vermont A.; Assoc. A. of New Jersey; NAWA; Pen & Brush Cl.; SAGA. *Awards*: prizes, NAWA, 1948, med., 1950; Pen & Brush Cl., 1951, 1955 (2), 1957. *Work*: MMA; Collectors of Am. A., 1956. *Exhibited*: Carnegie Inst., 1948; LC; BM; MMA; CAM, 1952; Newark Mus. A., 1952-1954, 1955; Montclair A. Mus., 1955; Smithsonian Inst., 1956.

CRAWFORD, RALSTON—
Painter, Lith., Photog., I., T., L.
240 East 20th St.; h. 60 Gramercy Park, New York 10, N.Y.

B. St. Catherines, Ontario, Canada, Sept. 25, 1906. *Studied*: Otis AI; PAFA; Barnes Fnd.; Breckenridge Sch.; Columbia

Univ., and in Europe. *Awards*: Wilmington Soc. FA, 1933; F., Tiffany Fnd., 1931; MMA, 1942. *Work*: MMA; WMAA; Albright A. Gal.; PMG; LC; Mus. of FA of Houston; Flint Inst. A.; CM; Toledo Mus. A.; Walker A. Center; Univ. Minnesota; Honolulu Acad. A.; Univ. Oklahoma; Howard Univ.; Butler AI; MacMurray Col.; Hamline Univ.; Louisiana State Univ.; Louisiana State A. Comm.; Hofstra Col.; MMoodA; Univs. of Georgia, Nebraska, Alabama, Illinois, Michigan; Alabama Polytechnic Inst.; Vassar Col.; Duke Univ., and many others. *Exhibited*: CGA; MMA; WMAA; AIC; CM; PMG; PAFA; Albright A. Gal.; Cal. PLH; Dallas Mus. FA; Denver A. Mus.; Cornell Univ.; Lafayette Col.; Univ. Indiana; Rochester Mem. A. Gal.; Santa Barbara Mus. A.; deYoung Mem. Mus.; SAM; Portland (Ore.) A. Mus.; Downtown Gal.; CAM; Univ. Minnesota; Louisiana State Univ.; Univ. Colorado; AIC; Grace Borgenicht Gal.; Weyhe Gal., and many others in U.S. and abroad. 36 one-man exhibitions. Illus. "Stars: Their Facts and Legends," 1940; covers and articles for Fortune magazine, 1944-46. A. Press Rep., at Bikini Atom Bomb test, 1946; photographs in Le Figaro, British Jazz Journal, Le Jazz Hot, Modern Photography and other publications. Lectures: Modern Art. *Position*: Instr., Cincinnati A. Acad., 1940, 1949; Buffalo Sch. FA, 1941-42; Guest Dir., Honolulu Sch. A.; A. Sch. of BM, 1948; Univ. Minnesota, 1949; Louisiana State Univ., 1950; Univ. Colorado, 1952, 1958; New Sch. for Social Research, New York, 1952-1957.

CRAWFORD, WILLIAM H. (BILL)—*Cartoonist, S., I.*
Newark Evening News, 215 Market St., Newark, N.J.; h. Prospect Rd., Atlantic Highlands, N.J.

B. Hammond, Ind., Mar. 18, 1913. *Member*: Nat. Cartoonists Soc. (Vice-Pres.). *Studied*: Chicago Acad. FA; Ohio State Univ., B.A.; Grande Chaumiere, Paris. *Awards*: Prize, CMA, 1934. I., "Barefoot Boy with Cheek," 1943; "Zebra Derby," 1946; & others. Contributor to national magazines. *Position*: Ed. Cart., Newark (N.J.) Evening News, 1938- .

CREEKMORE, RAYMOND L.—*Illustrator, Lith., Et., T.*
2440 Inagua Ave., Miami 33, Fla.

B. Portsmouth, Va., May 5, 1905. *Studied*: Maryland Inst. *Awards*: Med., Maryland Inst., 1934; prize, Baltimore Sun, 1936, 1937; Friends of Art med., 1938. Author, I., "Lokoshi," 1946, "Little Fu"; "Ali's Elephant"; "Little Skipper," and others.

CREESE, WALTER LITTLEFIELD—*Educator*
Department Architecture, University of Illinois, Urbana, Ill.

B. Danvers, Mass., Dec. 19, 1919. *Studied*: Brown Univ., A.B.; Harvard Univ., M.A., Ph.D.; Columbia Univ. European study. *Member*: Soc. Architectural Hist. (Pres., 1958-59); CAA. *Awards*: Arch. Lg., 1951; Faculty F., Am. Council of Learned Soc., 1951-52; Fulbright F., in Planning, Univ. Liverpool, England, 1955-56. *Position*: Instr. & Teaching F., Harvard Univ., 1944-45; Instr., Wellesley Col., 1945; Instr., 1946-47, Asst. Prof. 1947-52, Assoc. Prof., 1952-55, Prof., 1956-58, Univ. Louisville, Ky.; Chm., Louisville & Jefferson County Planning & Zoning Com., 1954-55; Ed., Journal of Soc. Arch. Hist., 1950-53; Ed. Advisor, College Art Journal. Prof., Univ. Illinois, Urbana, Ill., 1958- .

CREIGHTON, BESSY—*Painter, W.*
9 Goodwin's Court, Marblehead, Mass.

B. Lynn, Mass., April 21, 1884. *Studied*: BMFA Sch. *Member*: Marblehead AA; Cape Ann Soc. Mod. A.; Cambridge AA; St. Augustine A. Gld.; Boston Soc. Indp. A.; Copley Soc., Boston. *Exhibited*: VMFA, 1938; AIC, 1932, 1935; Phila. A. All., 1939; BM, 1931; BMFA, 1945; PAFA, 1935; Gloucester AA; Marblehead AA; Copley Soc., Boston; Logan Airport and other exhs. in Mass. and Fla. one-man: Boris Mirski Gal., Boston; Farnsworth Mus. A.; Marblehead AA; Cambridge AA (two-man). Author, I., "Adventures of the Wandies," 1925.

CRESPI, PACHITA—*Painter, I., Des., L., W.*
33 West 67th St., New York 23, N.Y.

B. Costa Rica, Aug. 25, 1900. *Studied*: N.Y. Sch. F. & App. Des.; ASL, with Henri, Luks. *Member*: NAWA; Pan-Am. Women's Soc.; Lg. Present-Day A. *Work*: WMAA; Univ. Arizona. *Exhibited*: one-man exh.: Beaux-Arts, London, England, 1934; Univ. Panama, 1943; Nat. Theatre, Costa Rica, 1945; Milch Gal., 1931; Morton Gal., 1929; Pinacotheca, 1942; Argent Gal., 1945; Nat. Mus., Wash., D.C., 1942; BMA, 1945; group exh.: Mem. Mus., Memphis, Tenn., 1943; Four Arts Cl., Palm Beach, Fla., 1943; Am.-British A. Center, 1943, 1944; Wildenstein Gal., 1943; NAWA, 1943-1946; Lg. Present-Day A., 1945. Author, I., "Manulito of Costa Rica," 1940; "Cabita's Rancho," 1942; "Wings Over Central America"; "Mystery of the Mayan Jewels"; "Gift of the Earth." Contributor to: The Horn Book; Holiday magazine. *Position*: Dir., Pachita Crespi A. Gal., 232 E. 58th St., New York, N.Y.

CRESS, GEORGE AYRES—Painter, E.
University of Chattanooga; h. Wilson Rd., Signal Mountain, Tenn.

B. Anniston, Ala., Apr. 7, 1921. *Studied*: Emory Univ.; Univ. Georgia, B.F.A.; M.F.A. *Member*: Southeastern College Conference; CAA. *Awards*: prizes, Univ. Georgia, 1941; High Mus. A.; Assoc. Ga. A., 1943, 1954; A. of Chattanooga and Vicinity, 1952-1954; Alabama WC Soc., 1953; Southeastern A., 1954; Memphis Biennial, 1955; Mid-South Annual; Birmingham Mus. A. *Work*: Emory Univ.; Univ. Georgia; High Mus. A.; murals, TVA, Tenn. *Exhibited*: Jackson Mun. A. Gal., 1943; Assoc. Ga. A., 1940-1943, 1954; Denver A. Lg., 1942; Mint Mus. A., 1942; Va-Intermont annual; CGA; BMA; Nashville AA; Delgado Mus. A.; Norfolk Mus. A.; Alabama WC Soc.; AGAA; Southeastern "Painting of the Year" exh., 1955; Columbia Biennial; Provincetown Annual; one-man: Atlanta, Savannah, Knoxville, Washington, Staten Island and Chattanooga; Grand Central Moderns, N.Y. *Position*: Instr., Judson Col., Marion, Ala., 1945-46; Mary Baldwin Col., Staunton, Va., 1946-47; Univ. Maryland, 1947-48; Univ. Georgia, 1949; Univ. Tenn., 1949-51; Hd., A. Dept., Univ. Chattanooga, 1951- .

CRESSON, CORNELIA (Mrs. Cornelia Cresson Barber) —Sculptor, Eng.
496 Avenue of the Americas; h. 266 West 12th St., New York 14, N.Y.

B. New York, N.Y., Feb. 15, 1915. *Studied*: with Genevieve Karr Hamlin, Mateo Hernandez. *Exhibited*: All. A. Am., 1938; AIC, 1940; Ellen Phillips Samuel Mem., Phila., Pa., 1940; WMAA, 1940; MMA, 1942; Grand Rapids A. Gal., 1940; Albany Inst. Hist. & A., 1939, 1940; Mun. A. Gal., N.Y., 1938; ACA Gal., 1943; Riverside Mus., 1946; PAFA, 1947; Silvermine Gld. A., 1952; AEA, 1952.

CRESSON, MARGARET FRENCH—Sculptor, W.
"Chesterwood," Stockbridge, Mass.

B. Concord, Mass. *Member*: ANA; NSS; Arch. L. *Awards*: prizes, NAD, 1927; Stockbridge A. Exh., 1929; med., Soc. Wash. A., 1937; Dublin Hill A. Exh., 1939, 1944. *Work*: Berkshire Mus., Pittsfield, Mass.; CGA; Yale Univ.; Monroe Shrine, Fredericksburg, Va.; Rockefeller Inst.; Mass. State Normal Sch.; Prince Mem., Harvard Medical Lib.; etc. *Exhibited*: NAD, 1921, 1924, 1926, 1927, 1929, 1936, 1940, 1941, 1943, 1944; PAFA, 1922, 1925, 1927, 1928, 1929, 1937, 1940, 1941, 1942; AIC, 1928, 1929, 1937, 1940; Paris Salon, 1938; WFNY 1939; Carnegie Inst., 1941; Concord AA, 1923; Phila. A. All., 1927, 1928; WMAA, 1940. Contributor to: N.Y. Times, American Artist, American Heritage, Readers Digest, articles on art & war memorials. Author: "Journey into Fame," life of Daniel Chester French; "Laurel Hill." Vice-Pres., Arch. Lg., 1944-46; Sec., NSS, 1941-42.

CRICHLOW, ERNEST—Illustrator, P., Lith., T.
692 Park Place, Brooklyn 16, N.Y.

B. New York, N.Y., June 19, 1914. *Studied*: Comm. Illus. Sch. A.; ASL. *Awards*: Atlanta Univ., 1952 (purchase). *Exhibited*: ACA Gal., N.Y., 1953 (one-man) and group exhs. Illus. "Two Is a Team," 1945; "Twelve O'Clock Whistle," 1946; "Freedom Train," 1954; "How Green is My Prairie," 1956; "Captain of the Planter," 1958; "Mary Jane," 1958-59. *Position*: Instr., Drawing & Painting, Workshop Sch. of Editorial Art.

CRIMI, ALFRED DI GIORGIO—Painter, T., I.
227 West 13th St.; h. 1975 Bathgate Ave., New York 57, N.Y.

B. San Fratello, Italy, Dec. 1, 1900. *Studied*: NAD; Beaux-Arts Inst.; Scuola Preparatoria alle Arti Ornamentali,

Rome. *Member*: Arch. Lg.; NSMP; AWS; Audubon A; CAA; SC; AEA; A. Fellowship (Bd. Dir.); All. A. Am.; New York City A. Commission, 1958-61. *Awards*: medal, All A. Am., 1946, 1949; gold medal, NAC, 1954; silver medal, A. Lg. of Long Island, 1954; prizes, N.Y. State Fair, 1951; All. A. Am., 1956, 1957; A. Lg. of Long Island, 1956; Emily Lowe award, 1956; Knickerbocker A., 1957. *Work*: murals, Forbes Lib., Northampton, Mass.; Aquarium, Key West, Fla.; Harlem Hospital; Rutgers Presbyterian Church, Christian Herald Bldg., all of New York. USPO, Northampton, Mass., Washington, D.C., Wayne, Pa. *Exhibited*: NAD; Audubon A; BM; MMA; WMAA; Acad. A. & Lets.; AIC; and in Paris; Rome and Bologna, Italy. One-man: Babcock Gal., 1928; Portland (Ore.) Mus. A., 1932; de Young Mem. Mus., 1932; Binet Gal., 1947; Ferargil Gal., 1949; Ward Eggleston Gal., 1957. Contributor articles on fresco and mural techniques to art magazines including American Artist and Liturgical Arts magazines. *Position*: Instr., Pratt Inst., Brooklyn, N.Y., 1948-49; City Col. of N.Y., 1948-1956; private classes.

CRISP, ARTHUR—Mural Painter
Fortunes Rock, Biddeford, Me.

B. Hamilton, Canada, Apr. 26, 1881. *Studied*: ASL. *Member*: NA; AWCS; NSMP; Arch. L.; All. A. Am.; Century Assn.; NAC. *Awards*: prizes and gold med., Arch L., 1914, 1920; med., Pan-Pacific Exp., 1915; prize, NAD, 1916. *Work*: Many panels & murals in theatres, hotels, clubs, schools, public buildings. Painting in Nat. Gal. of Canada Coll.; Hamilton (Can.) A. Gal.; murals, House of Parliament, Ottawa; State Capitol of Ohio; Law & Medical Lib., N.Y. State Edu. Bldg., Albany, N.Y.

CRISS, H. FRANCIS—Painter
440 West 57th St., New York 19, N.Y.; s. Spring Valley, N.Y.

B. London, England, Apr. 26, 1901. *Studied*: PAFA; ASL; & with Jon Matulka. *Member*: An Am. Group; F., PAFA. *Awards*: Cresson traveling scholarship, PAFA; Guggenheim F., 1934. *Work*: NGA; WMAA; PMA; Kansas City AI; La France Inst., Phila., Pa. *Exhibited*: CGA, 1939; PAFA, 1939, 1941, 1943, 1945; Carnegie Inst., 1944, 1945; WMAA, 1936, 1937, 1938, 1940, 1942, 1951; AIC, 1942, 1943; MMA, 1941; South America, 1939; Paris, France, 1937; Phila. A. All., 1953-54 (one-man). *Positions*: Instr., Painting, BM Sch. A.; Albright A. Gal.; ASL; Cart. & Illus. Sch.*

CRIST, RICHARD—Painter, I., W.
Woodstock, N.Y.

B. Cleveland, Ohio, Nov. 1, 1909. *Studied*: Carnegie Inst. Tech.; AIC. *Member*: Assoc. A. Pittsburgh; Woodstock AA (Exec. Bd.). *Awards*: American Traveling Scholarship, AIC; prizes, Carnegie Inst. 1940; Assoc. A. Pittsburgh; Berkshire Mus. A., 1957, and others. *Work*: Mineral Industries College; Pa. State Univ.; Public Schools colls., Pittsburgh, Somerset and Latrobe, Pa. Mural, Prospect Sch., Pittsburgh, Pa. *Exhibited*: AIC, 1934; MModA, 1934; CM, 1935, 1936; WFNY 1939; Butler Inst. Am. A., 1941; Carnegie Inst. 1941; PAFA, 1947, 1949; Guggenheim Mus. A., 1950; WMAA, 1956, 1957; CGA; Assoc. A. Pittsburgh, annually; Phila. A. All.; New Hope, Pa.; Somerset, Pa.; Johnstown, Pa.; Berkshire A.; Pittsfield, Mass.; Woodstock, N.Y.; Albany Inst. Hist. & A., 1957; N.Y. State Col. for Teachers, Albany, 1957; Pa. State Univ.; one-man: Washington Irving Gal., N.Y., 1958. Author, I., "Excitement in Appleby Street," 1950; "Chico," 1951 (award, Best Designed Book); "Good Ship Spider Queen," 1953; "The Cloud Catcher," 1956; "Secret of Turkeyfoot Mountain," 1957 (Jr. Literary Gld. Selection). Illus. in Natural History Magazine.

CRISTINA, S. ALFIO—
Graphic-Printmaker, P., S., Des., T.
89 Oakland Ave., Tuckahoe, N.Y.

B. New Orleans, La., May 11, 1909. *Studied*: with J. Alessandra, F. Riccardi, Alexandre Zeitlin; BMSch A, with Gabor Peterdi, Manfred Schwartz and Victor Candell. *Awards*: prizes, Florida Intl. Exh., 1952; Sea Cliff, L.I., A. Festival, 1950; New Rochelle Woman's Cl., 1956. *Work*: Graphics: LC; Hudson River Mus.; East Central Mus., Ada, Okla.; Manchester Col.; St. Vincent's Col., Latrobe, Pa.; Peoria (Ill.) A. Center. Private commissions for sculpture. *Exhibited*: LC, 1952-1955 and traveling exhs.; BM, 1951-1953; SAGA, 1952; Am. Color Pr. Soc., 1951-1952 and traveling exhs.; All. A. Am., 1951; Boston

Pr. M., 1951-1953; Audubon A., 1952, 1953; Wichita AA, 1952, 1953; Buffalo Pr. Exh., 1951; Portland Soc. A., 1952; Bradley Univ., 1952; Newport, R.I., 1951; Florida Intl. Exh., 1952; Graphic A. Exh., Portland, Me., 1958, and others. One-man: Sea Cliff, L.I., A. Gal., 1950-1952; Tuckahoe, N.Y., Lib., 1956; New Rochelle AA, 1957; Hudson River Mus., 1957, 1958; Wisconsin State Col., 1958; Manchester Col., North Manchester, Ind., 1958; Platteville State Col. (Wis.), 1958; Meade Lib., Sheboygan, Wis., 1958, and others. 2-man: St. Vincent's Col., Latrobe, Pa., 1957; Milwaukee City Cl., 1957; Fremont (Mich.) Fnd., 1957; East Central Mus., Ada, Okla., 1957; State Col. Lib., Bowling Green, Ky., 1958; Wustum Mus. A., 1958; Bethany (Okla.) Col. Gal., 1958; Cottey Col., Nevada, Mo., 1958; Peoria A. Center, 1958.

CRITE, ALLAN ROHAN—*Painter, I., L., W., C.*
2 Dilworth St., Boston 18, Mass.

B. Plainfield, N.J., Mar. 20, 1910. *Studied*: BMFA Sch.; Mass. Sch. A.; Boston Univ., C.B.A. *Member*: Boston Soc. Indp. A.; Boston Inst. Mod. A.; Alum. Bd., BMFA Sch.; Archaeological Inst. Am. *Awards*: BMFA Sch.; Seabury Western Theological Seminary, 1952. *Work*: BMFA; Spellman Col., Atlanta, Ga.; PMG; AGAA; Marine Hospital, Carville, La.; Villanova Col. (Pa.); Smith Col.; Mount Holyoke Col.; Newton Col. of Sacred Heart; churches, Wash., D.C.; Boston, Roxbury, Mass.; Norwich, Vt.; Detroit, Mich.; Sterrs, Conn.; Brooklyn, N.Y.; mural, Grace Church, Martha's Vineyard, Mass.; Stations of the Cross, Holy Cross Church, Morrisville, Vt., 1957, and many others. *Exhibited*: CGA; AIC; WFNY 1939; Boston Soc. Indp. A.; Boston Inst. Mod. A.; Boston Pub. Lib.; New England Contemporary A.; one-man: Grace Horne Gal.; Margaret Brown Gal.; Children's A. Center, Boston; BMFA; FMA; Farnsworth Mus. A.; Bates Col.; Topeka A. Cl.; Concord AA; libraries in Concord, Andover, Mass.; Nashua, N.H.; St. Augustine Col.; Univ. Maine; Boston Atheneum, etc. Author, I., of many religious books and articles; contributor to magazines and bulletins. Lectured on Christian Art, Oberlin (Ohio) Col., 1958.

CROCKER, DICK—*Painter*
94 South Munn Ave., East Orange, N.J.

B. Newark, N.J., Oct. 7, 1891. *Studied*: ASL; Newark Sch. Fine & App. A., and with Henry Gasser. *Member*: SC; AWS; All. A. Am.; Audubon A; New Jersey WC Soc.; Baltimore WC Cl. *Awards*: gold med., All. A. Am., 1944; prizes, Montclair A. Mus., 1947; Jersey City Mus., 1948; AWS, 1954; Baltimore WC Cl., 1955. *Exhibited*: AWS; Audubon A; All. A. Am.; New Jersey WC Soc.; Baltimore WC Cl.; and many local and regional exhibitions.

CROFT, LEWIS SCOTT—*Painter*
651 West 171st St., New York 32, N.Y.

B. Chester Basin, N.S., Canada. *Studied*: with M. Denton Burgess; A. W. Allen, Vancouver, B.C., and with William S. Schwartz, Chicago. *Member*: AAPL; Nova Scotia Soc. A.; Creative A. Group of Tampa Bay, Fla. *Awards*: prizes, A. Festival Exh., Fla., 1958 and in regional shows. *Exhibited*: AAPL, 1957, 1958; ACA Gal., N.Y.; Collectors Gal., N.Y.; Little Studio, N.Y.; Brooklyn Soc. A.; Tampa AI; Fla. State Fair; Contemp. A. Gal., Fla., and widely in Canada.

CROMWELL, JOANE (Mrs.)—*Painter, Comm. A.*
1774 Palm Dr., Temple Hills, Laguna Beach, Cal.

B. Lewistown, Ill. *Studied*: AIC; Otis AI; & with Edgar Allwyn Paine, Jack Wilkinson Smith. *Member*: Laguna Beach AA; Desert A. Center Assn.; Laguna Beach Festival A. Assn. *Work*: murals, Hollywood Park, Cal., 1941; Santa Anita Race Course, Cal., 1939; St. George (Utah) H.S.; Millersburgh Military Inst., Ky. *Exhibited*: Laguna Beach A. Gal., 1922-1958; Los A. Mus. A.; Balboa Park A. Gal.; Palm Desert A. Gal., Palm Springs, Cal.; AIC, and others. Artist on syndicated feature "Romance of Flowers," 1956-58.

CRONBACH, ROBERT M.—*Sculptor, E., L.*
170 Henry St., Westbury, L.I., N.Y.

B. St. Louis, Mo., Feb. 10, 1908. *Studied*: St. Louis Sch. FA; PAFA; & in Europe. *Member*: S. Gld.; AEA; Arch. Lg.; N.Y. Soc. Ceramic A. *Awards*: Cresson traveling scholarship, PAFA, 1929, 1930; prizes, Rosenthal Potteries,

1931; FAP, 1940. *Work*: sculptural decorations, CAM; Social Security Bldg., Wash., D.C.; St. Louis Mun. Auditorium; Willerts Park Housing Project, Buffalo, N.Y.; Hollenden Hotel, Cleveland; fountain, 240 Central Park South, New York; bronze screen, Dorr-Oliver Bldg., Stamford, Conn., 1958; PMA. *Exhibited*: PMA, 1940; Hudson Walker Gal., 1940 (one-man); S. Gld., 1938, 1939, 1941, 1942, 1948, 1950-1955; PAFA; WMAA; ACA Gal.; Springfield (Mass.) Mus. A.; MModA; CAM; Bertha Schaefer Gal.; Mus. FA of Houston; Denver A. Mus. *Position*: Asst. Prof., Adelphi Col., Garden City, N.Y.

CROOKS, FORREST C.—*Designer, C., P., Comm. A.*
R.D. 2, Doylestown, Pa.

B. Goshen, Ind., Oct. 1, 1893. *Studied*: Carnegie Inst., A.B.; ASL. *Work*: stained glass in churches in Phila., Pittsburgh, Pa., Los Angeles, Cal., Cincinnati, Ohio, Cleveland, Ohio; Syracuse, N.Y.; murals, YMCA, Millville, N.J.; St. Gregory's Church, Los Angeles, Cal.

CROSBY, SUMNER McKNIGHT—*Educator*
Yale University, New Haven, Conn.; h. Fairgrounds Rd., Woodbridge 15, Conn.

B. Minneapolis, Minn., July 29, 1909. *Studied*: Yale Univ., B.A., Ph.D.; Univ. Paris. *Member*: AFA; CAA; Archaeological Inst. Am.; Mediaeval Acad. Am.; Century Assn.; Grolier Cl.; Membre Correspondent, Société Nationale des Antiquaires de France, 1946- ; Chevalier, Legion d'Honneur, 1950. *Author*: "The Abbey of St.-Denis" Vol. 1, 1942; "L'Abbaye Royale de Saint-Denis," 1952. Contributor to art magazines. *Lectures*: Mediaeval Art. *Positions*: Dir. Excavations in Abbey Church of Saint-Denis, France, 1938, 1939, 1946-48; Pres., 1941-45, Bd. Dir., 1940-45, 1946-51, CAA; Bd. Trustees, 1941-44, 1947-1955, AFA; Adv. Com., AGAA, 1946- ; Trustee, Textile Mus., Wash., D.C., 1943-47; Chm., Hist. A. Dept., 1947-53, Chm. Audio-Visual Center, 1950- , Cur., Medieval A., 1947- , Yale Univ., New Haven, Conn.

CROSMAN, ROSE—*Engraver, P., C., Comm. A.*
201 East Ontario St., Chicago 11, Ill.

B. Chicago, Ill. *Studied*: PAFA; AIC. *Member*: Chicago SE. *Exhibited*: Chicago SE, & national etching shows.

CROSS, LOUISE—*Sculptor, W.*
505 East 82nd St., New York 28, N.Y.

B. Rochester, Minn., Nov. 14, 1896. *Studied*: Wellesley Col., B.A.; Minneapolis Sch. A.; AIC; Univ. Chicago, M.A., and with Harriet Hanley. *Member*: S. Gld. *Awards*: prizes, Minneapolis Inst. A. *Work*: Mem. reliefs, Minnesota State Capitol; Todd Mem. Hospital, Univ. Minnesota. *Exhibited*: PMA, 1934, 1940; WFNY 1939; MMA, 1942; NSS; WMAA; AEA; S. Gld. traveling exh., 1940, 1941; Franklin Inst., Phila., Pa. Contributor to: Art magazines. *Lectures*: Sculpture.

CROSS, WATSON, JR.—*Painter*
Chouinard Art Institute, 743 South Grand View St.; h. 16064 Queenside Dr., Covina, Cal.

B. Long Beach, Cal., Oct. 10, 1918. *Studied*: Chouinard AI, with Henry Lee McFee, Rico Lebrun. *Member*: Cal. WC Soc. *Exhibited*: San F. AA, 1946; Los A. Mus. A., 1945, 1952; Laguna Beach AA, 1945; Cal. WC Soc., 1941-1952; Riverside Mus., 1944-1946. *Position*: Instr. A., Chouinard AI, Los Angeles, Cal., 1944-1956.*

CROSSGROVE, ROGER LYNN—*Painter, E.*
171 Steuben St., Brooklyn 5, N.Y.

B. Farnam, Neb., Nov. 17, 1921. *Studied*: Kearney State T. Col.; Univ. Nebraska, B.F.A.; Univ. Illinois, M.F.A.; Universidad de Michoacan, Mexico. *Member*: CAA; AAUP; Brooklyn Soc. A. *Awards*: Des Moines A. Center, 1953 (purchase); prize, Emily Lowe award, Ward Eggleston Gal., 1951; Brooklyn Soc. A., 1957; Silvermine Gld. A., 1957; Village A. Center, 1958; Yaddo F., 1957, 1958. *Exhibited*: Terry AI, 1952; Fla. Southern Col., 1952; Joslyn A. Mus., 1949; A. West of the Mississippi, 1951; Nebraska AA, 1950; BM, 1952, 1958; WMAA, 1956; Ward Eggleston Gal., 1951, 1953-1958; Nebraska A. Gld.; Brooklyn Soc. A., 1955; Des Moines A. Center, 1953, 1958; Springfield (Mo.) A. Mus., 1953. *Position*: Asst. Prof., Painting, Pratt Inst., Brooklyn, N.Y., 1952- .

CROWDER, CONRAD WILLIAM—*Sculptor, L., E.*
P.O. Box 9147, Chicago 4, Ill.

B. Hanford, Cal., Apr. 3, 1915. *Studied*: Riverside Col., Cal.; & abroad. *Member*: AFA. *Award*: Latham Fnd. Poster Prize, 1930. *Work*: Wisconsin State Mem. to Major Richard Bong, State Capitol, Madison, Wis.; portrait busts of prominent Army & Navy officers; bronze statue of Sir Alexander Fleming, 1956. Lectures: Art in the Vatican. *Position*: Dir., S., Virginia Sch. of Prosthetics, Alexandria, Va., 1947-48.

CROWE, AMANDA MARIA—*Sculptor, C., T.*
P.O. Box 630, Cherokee, N.C.

B. Cherokee, N.C., July 16, 1928. *Studied*: AIC; Instituto Allende San Miguel, Mexico; De Paul Univ., Chicago. *Member*: North Carolina A. Soc.; AIC; Southern Highland Gld. *Awards*: John Quincy Adams traveling scholarship, AIC, 1952; AIC scholarship, 1946. *Work*: sc., Container Corp. of Am.; Cherokee Indian Sch. (N.C.); Mus. of the Cherokee Indian (N.C.), and work in private coll. *Exhibited*: Am. Indian Art, Chicago, Ill., 1950; Atlanta A. Mus., 1955; North Carolina A., 1950; Evanston A. Center, 1949; Winston-Salem A. Center, 1946; Ashville, N.C.; one-man: Winston-Salem, 1946, 1948; Children's Mus., Nashville, Tenn., 1954. *Position*: Instr., Cherokee Indian Sch., Cherokee, N.C., 1953- .*

CROWELL, LUCIUS—*Painter*
Mounted Route, Phoenixville, Pa.

B. Chicago, Ill., Jan. 22, 1911. *Studied*: PAFA; Barnes Fnd., and with Franklin Watkins, Arthur B. Carles. *Member*: Phila. A. All. *Awards*: prizes, Chicago, Tribune Comp.; Chester County AA; medal of honor, Concord Mus., 1954. *Work*: BMFA; PAFA; PMA. *Exhibited*: AIC, 1931; WMAA, 1933; Univ. Michigan, 1934; PAFA, 1933-1958; NAD, 1958; Concord Mus., 1958; Newport, R.I., 1954; one-man: Ferargil Gal., 1950, 1951, 1954; Sagittarius Gal., N.Y., 1958; Vose Gal., Boston, 1951, 1954; Bryn Mawr A. Center; Penn Valley Women's Cl.; Phila. A. All., 1958; PAFA, 1954; Beloit Col., and others.

CROWN, KEITH (ALLAN) JR.—
Painter, E., Gr., W., I., L.
3518 University Ave., Los Angeles 7, Cal.; h. 872 Fifth St., Manhattan Beach, Cal.

B. Keokuk, Iowa, May 27, 1918. *Studied*: AIC, B.F.A. *Member*: AEA; Cal. WC Soc. (1st V. Pres., 1958-59). *Awards*: Kuppenheimer Scholarship, AIC; bronze star, U.S. Army, 1945; prize, AEA, 1952; Cal. WC Soc., 1956; Cal. State Fair, 1957. *Exhibited*: AEA, 1952; Cal. WC Soc., 1947-1951, 1953, 1955; Los A. Mus. A., 1947-1949; Orange County Exh., 1949, 1951, 1955; Cal. State Fair, 1951, 1953, 1955; Cal.-Canadian Exh., 1955; Palos Verdes Exh., 1953; one-man: paintings: Pasadena AI, 1953; Oakland A. Mus., 1954; Orange Coast Col., 1954; Stanford Research Inst., 1953; war drawings: Los A. Mus. A., 1954; M. H. deYoung Mem. Mus., 1947; AIC, 1943, 1944. *Position*: Instr., Luther Col., Decorah, Iowa, 1940-41; AIC, 1946; Assoc. Prof. FA, Univ. Southern California, 1946- .

CROWTHER, ROBERT W.—*Illustrator*
32 Linden Ave., Pitman, N.J.

B. Philadelphia, Pa., Dec. 20, 1902. *Studied*: PMSch.A.; PAFA. *Awards*: F., PAFA. I., national magazines.

CRUMMER, MARY WORTHINGTON—*Painter, C., Et.*
302 Suffolk Rd., Guilford, Baltimore 18, Md.

B. Baltimore, Md. *Studied*: Maryland Inst.; Rinehart Sch. S., with Denman W. Ross; Harvard Univ. *Member*: Baltimore WC Cl.; Maryland Hist. Soc.; AFA. *Awards*: prizes, Peabody Inst., 1923; Maryland State Fair, 1928; BMA, 1939.*

CRUMP, KATHLEEN WHEELER. See *Wheeler, Kathleen*

CRUZE, CHARLES—*Industrial Designer*
2340 West Third St., Los Angeles 5, Cal.

B. Wichita, Kans. *Member*: Soc. Indst. Des. Advisor on industrial design problems to Western Electric Co.; Gladding McBean Corp., and others. Conducted lecture courses

at Univ. Southern California and Cal.-Tech. Contributor of articles to national publications. *Position*: Dir., Charles Cruze Industrial Design Co.; Pacific Coast Chm., Soc. Industrial Designers.

CSOKA, STEPHEN—*Etcher, P., E.*
c/o Contemporary Arts, 106 East 57th St., New York 22, N.Y.; h. 349 Evergreen Ave., Brooklyn 21, N.Y.

B. Gardony, Hungary, Jan. 2, 1897. *Studied*: Budapest Royal Acad. A. *Member*: NA; SAGA; Audubon A; Soc. Brooklyn A. *Awards*: med., Barcelona Int. Exh., 1929; City of Budapest, 1930, 1933; SAGA; 1942, 1945, 1952; LC, 1944, 1946; Soc. Brooklyn A., 1944, 1949; Phila. WC Cl., 1945; La Tausca Pearls Comp., 1945; PAFA, 1945; Assoc. Am. A., 1947; Am. Acad. A. & Let., 1948; NAD, 1950. *Work*: Budapest Mus. A.; LC; British Mus. A.; Encyclopaedia Britannica Coll.; Princeton Pr. Cl.; N.Y. Pub. Lib.; Dayton AI; Columbus Mus. FA.; IBM; Delgado Mus. A.; Carnegie Inst. *Exhibited*: CGA, 1945; Carnegie Inst., 1943-1945; NAD, 1940-1945; Contemporary A., 1940, 1943, 1945 (one-man); Phila. A. All., 1943 (one-man); Minnesota State Fair, 1943 (one-man). *Position*: Instr., A., Hunter Col., New York, N.Y.; Parson Sch. Des., New York, N.Y.

CSOSZ, JOHN—*Painter, I., Et., Des., T.*
3711 Euclid Ave., Cleveland 15, Ohio

B. Budapest, Hungary, Oct. 2, 1897. *Studied*: Cleveland Sch. A., with Frederick C. Gottwald, Henry G. Keller. *Work*: Univ. Cl., Akron, Ohio; Treasury Bldg., Wash., D.C.; Pub.Sch., Medical Lib., Collinwood H.S., USPO, all in Cleveland, Ohio. *Exhibited*: Cleveland A., 1920-1931; Cleveland SA, 1920-1946. I., "Good Ship Mayflower," 1933; "Costume Through the Ages"; "Art Through the Ages"; The How and Why Books.

CULLER, GEORGE D.—*Associate Museum Director*
San Francisco Museum of Art, Civic Center, San Francisco, Cal.*

CULVER, CHARLES—*Painter*
21547 Homer St., Dearborn, Mich.

B. Chicago Heights, Ill., May 30, 1908. *Studied*: Wicker Sch. FA, Detroit, Mich. *Awards*: Detroit Inst. A., 1935, 1936, 1940, 1942, 1944, 1946, 1948-1950, 1952, 1955; Old Northwest Territory Exh., 1950; Michigan State Fair, 1950, 1953; Ill. State Mus., 1950; Michigan WC Soc., 1954; Kirk of the Hills Exh., 1955; gold med., Audubon A., 1951. *Work*: Detroit Inst. A.; WMAA; New Britain Inst.; WMA; Flint Inst. A.; Cranbrook Acad. A.; Illinois State Mus.; Middlebury Col.; IBM; Lever Bldg., New York; Albion Col.; Kalamazoo AI, and in many private coll. in the U.S. and abroad. *Exhibited*: nationally and internationally since 1937; many one-man exhibitions. Contributor to Ford Publications and art magazines.*

CULVERWELL, MRS. ANNABELL. See *Krebs, Columba*

CULWELL, BEN(NIE) L(EE)—*Painter*
5841 Martel St., Dallas, Tex.

B. San Antonio, Tex., Sept. 8, 1918. *Studied*: Southern Methodist Univ.; Columbia Univ.; Colgate Univ.; Cornell Univ. *Work*: MModA; Dallas Mus. FA. *Exhibited*: MModA, 1946; Dallas Mus. FA, 1945 (one-man).*

CUMING, BEATRICE—*Painter, E.*
130 State St., New London, Conn.; h. Massapeag Rd., Uncasville, Conn.

B. Brooklyn, N.Y., Mar. 25, 1903. *Studied*: PIASch; and in France. *Member*: AWS; Mystic AA; Conn. WC Soc.; Essex AA. *Awards*: prizes, Hartford, Conn., 1939, 1941; Springfield, Mass., 1936; Bok Fnd. F., 1939, 1940; F., MacDowell Colony, N.H., 1934, 1938, 1943, 1944, 1946, 1952; F., Yaddo Fnd., 1950-51, 1953, 1955; Huntington Hartford Fnd., 1953, 1956. *Work*: Lyman Allyn Mus.; Syracuse Mus. FA; LC. *Exhibited*: CGA, 1937; PAFA, 1932; AIC, 1930, 1942; WMAA, 1938; WFNY 1939; Syracuse Mus. FA, 1945; Four Arts Cl.; Springfield Mus. FA, 1946; Hartford Atheneum, 1939, 1940; Mystic AA; Lyman Allyn Mus.; Univ. Nebraska, 1946, 1948; WMA, 1946; Silvermine Gld. A., 1951, 1952, 1953, 1955; Univ. Nebraska, 1946, 1948; one-man: Guy Mayer Gal., 1942; Contemporary A., 1946; Lyman Allyn Mus., 1952; New Gal., 1952; Westerly, R.I., 1954; Norwich (Conn.) Theatre, 1954; Springfield State Fair, 1957; New Haven Festival A., 1958; Mystic AA, 1956 (one-man); Hartford Audio Workshop, 1955. *Position*: Dir., Young People's A. Program, Lyman Allyn Mus., New London, Conn.; Vice-Pres., Mystic AA, 1955.

CUMMING, ALICE McKEE (Mrs. Charles A.)—
Painter, L., E.
2904 Kingman Blvd., Des Moines 11, Iowa

B. Stuart, Iowa, Mar. 6, 1890. *Studied*: State Univ. Iowa; Cumming Sch. A. *Member*: Iowa A. Gld.; Soc. for Sanity in Art; Des Moines A. Forum. *Awards*: Med., Iowa State Fair; prize, Des Moines Women's Cl., 1925; med., AIC, 1942. *Work*: Des Moines Women's Cl.; State Hist. Gal., Des Moines. *Exhibited*: Soc. for Sanity in Art, Chicago, 1941; Ogunquit AA, 1943-1946; Des Moines A. Forum, 1945, 1946; Iowa A. Gld. traveling exh. *Position*: Pres., Dir., Cumming Sch. A., Des Moines, Iowa, 1937-1954. (Now closed).*

CUMMING, GEORGE BURTON—
Editor Art Books, T., L., W.
95 East Putnam St., Greenwich, Conn.; h. Westport, Conn.

B. Waterbury, Conn., Oct. 12, 1909. *Studied*: Amherst Col., A.B.; Harvard Univ. Grad. Sch. FA. *Awards*: Sachs F., 1939-40. Lectures, radio and TV programs on art. Catalogues: "John Stuart Curry," 1946; "Six States Photography," 1950; "Highlights of American Painting," 1954. Contributor of articles on art to magazines and newspapers. *Positions*: Instr., Institut du Rosey, Rolle, Switzerland, 1932-33; South Kent (Conn.) Sch., 1933-38; Asst. Dir., Albany Inst. Hist. & A., 1940-42; Dir., Milwaukee AI, 1942-43; Lt. U.S.N.R., 1943-46; resumed Directorship, Milwaukee AI, 1946-50; Dir., American Federation of Arts, Washington, D.C. and New York City, 1951-54; Dir., La Napoule A. Fnd., 1955; Dir. of Publications, New York Graphic Soc., Greenwich, Conn., 1956- ; Memb., Advisory Council, New York City Center Gal., 1956- ; Memb., Amherst Col. Advisory Comm. on Modern Art, 1956- .

CUMMING, ROBERT HOMER—*Painter, Mus. D., E., W.*
30 Ipswich St., Boston 15, Mass.

B. Boston, Mass., May 10, 1927. *Studied*: Vesper George Sch. A.; Cape Sch. A., Provincetown, Mass.; Academie Julien, Paris, France, and with R. H. Ives Gammell. *Member*: All. A. Am.; AAPL (Nat. Adv. Bd.); NSMP; Academic A.; Copley Soc., Boston; Fifty Am. A.; North Shore AA; Provincetown AA; AAMus. *Awards*: Elizabeth T. Greenshields Mem. Fnd. Grant, 1955-1958; Pierson prize, Ogunquit A. Center, 1954, 1958; Medal of Honor, Concord AA, 1957; Academic A., 1957. *Work*: murals, Federal Home Loan Bank, Boston, Mass.; Worcester Federal Savings Assn., Springfield, Mass.; Lynn Savings Bank, Lynn, Mass. *Exhibited*: nationally. *Position*: Dir., The Rushford Collections, Salem, Mass., 1953- ; Instr., Vesper George Sch. A., Boston, Mass., 1954-55.

CUMMINGS, HAROLD W.—*Craftsman*
475 Francisco St., San Francisco 11, Cal.; h. P.O. Box 1, Belvedere, Cal.

B. Hampton, Iowa, Jan. 5, 1897. *Studied*: Iowa State Col., and in Europe. *Member*: Stained Glass Assn. Am. *Work*: Stained glass memorials: Presbyterian church, San Rafael, Cal.; All Saints Episcopal Church, Carmel, Cal.; College of the Holy Names, Oakland, Cal.; St. John's Church, Folsom, Cal.; 1st Church of Christ Scientist, Belvedere, Cal.; Church of the Precious Blood, Los Angeles, Cal.; Presidio, San F., Cal.; Col. of Pacific, Stockton, Cal.; Loyola Univ., Los A., Cal.; Univ. Seattle; Iowa State Col.; Col. of St. Albert, Oakland, Cal.; Trinity Episcopal Cathedral, Sacramento, Cal. *Exhibited*: deYoung Mem. Mus.; Oakland A. Mus. Contributor to: Liturgical Arts, Stained Glass, Architect & Engineer, & other magazines. Lectures: Stained Glass.

CUMMINGS, MARY BARRETT (Mrs. Walter P.)—
Craftsman, Des., T.
227 Haven Ave., New York 33, N.Y.

B. Montclair, N.J., Aug. 5, 1897. *Studied*: Craft Students Lg.; T. Col., Columbia Univ., with William Sioni; Inwood

Pottery, with Trygve Hammer. *Member*: Artist-Craftsmen of N.Y.; Eastern AA; Nat. AA; Long Island A.T.; N.Y. State A.T. Assn.; Com. on A. Edu., MModA. *Exhibited*: Syracuse Mus. FA; N.Y. Soc. Ceramic A., 1945-1956; N.Y. Soc. Craftsmen, 1940-1956; WFNY 1939; MMA. Lectures on art to many women's clubs and art organizations. *Position*: Instr., Edu. Dept. Workshop, Adelphi College; formerly Dir., Pottery, Lenox Hill Neighborhood House; Craft Students League and Nassau County Ext. Service.

CUMMINGS, WILLARD WARREN—*Painter, T.*
R. F. D. 4, Skowhegan, Me.

B. Old Town, Me., Mar. 17, 1915. *Studied*: Julien Acad., Paris; Yale Sch. FA; ASL, and with Wayman Adams, Robert Laurent. *Award*: prize, Oakland A. Mus., 1940. *Work*: War Dept., Wash., D.C. *Exhibited*: AIC, 1941; CGA, 1940; Oakland A. Mus., 1940; MModA, 1938-1942; Smith Col. Mus., 1940 (one-man); Sweat A. Mus., 1940; Marie Harriman Gal., 1939; Margaret Brown Gal., Boston, 1951 (one-man); WMAA, 1954, 1955; Katonah Gal., 1956 (one-man); Maynard Walker Gal., 1957 (one-man). *Position*: Dir. & T., Painting, Skowhegan Sch. Painting & Sculpture, Skowhegan, Me.

CUNEO, GEORGE HUMBERT—*Educator, P., E.*
University of Maryland, College Park, Md.; h. 15118 Fairlawn Ave., Silver Spring, Md.

B. Carlstadt, N.J., Feb. 11, 1898. *Studied*: BAID; PAFA; Univ. Kentucky; Univ. Grenoble, France; Columbia Univ., B.S., M.A. *Member*: AAUP; CAA; Soc. Typographic A. *Exhibited*: Assoc. Am. A., 1954 (one-man); Univ. Maryland, 1958 (one-man); regularly to group shows and annually at BMA. *Position*: Assoc. Prof. A., Univ. Maryland, College Park, Md.

CUNLIFFE, MITZI—*Sculptor, Des., L.*
18 Cranmer Rd., Didsbury, Manchester 20, England

B. New York, N.Y., Jan. 1, 1918. *Studied*: Columbia Univ., B.S., M.A.; ASL; & with Oronzio Maldarelli, Anne Goldthwaite, & others. *Awards*: prizes, Smith A. Gal., Springfield, Mass., 1940, 1943, 1945; Widener gold med., PAFA, 1949; Irvington (N.J.) Pub Lib., 1944. *Exhibited*: Syracuse Mus. FA; Phila. A. All.; deYoung Mem. Mus.; Kleemann Gal.; Hanover Gal., London, 1951; Milwaukee AI; Brooks Mem. A. Gal. *Public Commissions*: Festival of Britain, 1951; Univ. Liverpool, 1953; Manchester H.S. for Girls, 1953; Univ. Leeds, 1956; Inlet Well House, Manchester, 1955; Childwall County Col., Liverpool, 1954; Wythenshawe Secondary Tech. Sch., Manchester, 1957; Lewis's, Liverpool, 1957. Lectures: Sculpture Throughout the Ages, Sculpture for Architecture. Contributor to Building magazine. Progressive Architecture.

CUNNINGHAM, CHARLES C.—
Museum Director, W., L.
75 Bloomfield St., Hartford, Conn.

B. Mamaroneck, N.Y., Mar. 7, 1910. *Studied*: Harvard Col., A.B.; London Univ., B.A.; Harvard Univ. *Member*: AFA; CAA; AAMus.; A. Mus. Dir. Assn.; Am. A. Research Council; Conn. Hist. Comm.; Archeological Soc. Am.; F., Int. Inst. A. & Lets.; Hon. Memb., AIA. Ed., "Art in New England," 1939. Lectures: American Painting; French Painting 19th & 20th Century; Dutch and Flemish Painting, 17th Century. Contributor to: Art magazines, Mus. Bulletins and Catalogues. *Position*: Asst. Cur., BMFA, 1935-41; Dir., Wadsworth Atheneum, Hartford, Conn., 1946- .

CUNNINGHAM, JOHN—*Painter, T., Des.*
Box 9, Carmel, Cal.

B. New Jersey, Apr. 5, 1906. *Studied*: Univ. California, A.B., M.A., and with Hans Hofmann, Munich, Germany and at the Univ. of Munich; Andre L'Hote, Paris, France. *Position*: Pres., Dir., Carmel Art Inst., Carmel, Cal., 1941- .*

CUNNINGHAM, PATRICIA—*Painter, T., Des.*
Box 9, Carmel, Cal.

B. California. *Studied*: Univ. California, A.B., M.A., and with Hans Hofmann, Andre L'Hote. *Awards*: F., Univ. California. *Exhibited*: one-man: (circulated by Western Assn. A. Mus. Dir.)—Cal. PLH, Santa Barbara Mus. A.,

Portland (Ore.) A. Mus., Richmond A. Center, Washington State Col., Salt Lake City Mus. A., etc.; other one-man: Carmel AA; All. A. Am.; Pebble Beach A. Gal.; Gump's Gal., San F. *Position*: Instr., Carmel AI, Carmel, Cal., 1941- ; Pres., Carmel AA, 1954.*

CUNNINGHAM, PHELPS—
Designer, Eng., P., I., Gr.
1421 Schofield Bldg., Cleveland 15, Ohio; h. 15016 Grandview Terr., East, Cleveland 12, Ohio

B. Humboldt, Kan., Aug. 24, 1903. *Studied*: Univ. Kansas, B.S. in Arch.; & with Joseph M. Kellogg, Raymond Eastwood, Rosemary Ketcham. *Member*: AIA. *Awards*: prizes, CMA, 1934, 1937, 1941; John Herron AI, 1944. *Work*: CMA; Swedish Nat. Mus.; Lib. Cong.; Cleveland Pub. Lib.; John Herron AI; Print Cl., Cleveland, Ohio. *Exhibited*: PAFA, 1931-1934, 1937; SAE, 1933, 1937; Swedish Nat. Mus., 1938; Wichita AA, 1933, 1934; Woodcut Soc., Kansas City, Mo., 1934 (traveling exh.); Phila. Pr. Cl., 1934; CMA, 1931-1934, 1937, 1939, 1941, 1948, 1949, 1951; Ohio Pr. M., 1933, 1934, 1938, 1939; Kansas City AI, 1932, 1935; WMAA, 1937. Lectures: "Woodcuts as a Print Process."

CUNNINGHAM, THEODORE SAINT-AMANT—Painter
Box 6232, West Asheville, N.C.

B. Ennis, Tex., Oct. 5, 1899. *Studied*: AIC; NAD, and with E. J. F. Timmons, and in Europe. *Work*: Swiss Legation, Wash., D.C.; Tennessee State Capitol Bldg.; Am. Embassy, Canberra, Australia. *Exhibited*: NAD; PAFA; Woodmere A. Gal., Phila., Pa. *Position*: Instr., Painting, Fredericksburg, Tex. and Williams Bay, Wisconsin.

CURREY, RUTH DUNLOP—Craftsman, Des., P., T.
Pine Village, Indiana

B. Chicago, Ill. *Studied*: Beloit Col.; Northwestern Univ.; Clark Univ.; Sch. for Am. Craftsmen, Rochester Inst. Tech., B.F.A.; Univ. Oregon, M.F.A. *Member*: Weavers Gld. (in several states). *Exhibited*: Smithsonian Inst. traveling exh., 1956; Dec. A. and Ceramics Exh., Wichita, Kans., 1954, 1955; Montana Crafts Exh.; Fiber, Clay & Metal Exh., St. Paul, Minn., 1956, 1957; Northwest Craftsmens Exh., 1958; New England Craft Exh., 1955; Mass. Craft Exh., 1954-1956; Univ. Kansas, 1957; Univ. Oregon, 1958. Contributor to Handweaver & Craftsman. Lectures: Techniques of Weaving; Demonstrations in Loom Preparation; Natural & Synthetic Fibers for Handweaving, etc. *Position*: Instr., Handweaving, Chicago, Mass., Montana, and at Craft Center, Worcester, Mass.; Instr., Handweaving, Dept. Indus. & Develop., Fredericton, N.B., Canada, 1958-59.

CURRIER, ALLEN DALE—Painter, E., L., Comm. A.
31 Hawthorn St.; h. 408 Arnold St., New Bedford, Mass.

B. Everett, Mass., Oct. 21, 1893. *Studied*: Boston Univ.; Harvard Univ. *Member*: AAUP. *Positions*: Pub. Rel., Swain Sch. Des., New Bedford, Mass.; Chm. Faculty of App. A., Prof., Boston Univ. Sch. F. & App. A., Boston, Mass., 1946-1958, Prof. Emeritus, 1958- .

CURTIS, CONSTANCE—Portrait Painter
150 East 73rd St., New York 21, N.Y.

B. Washington, D.C. *Studied*: ASL, with William Chase. *Member*: All.A.Am.; NAWA; AAPL; Audubon A.; ASL. *Awards*: prizes, NAC, 1922; NAWA, 1935; AAPL, 1944. *Exhibited*: Paris Expo., 1900; St. Louis World's Fair, 1904; WFNY 1939; CGA, 1923; PAFA, 1921, 1923, 1924; NAD, 1923, 1927, 1933; Boston AC, 1928, 1932; AIC, 1924, 1925; NAWA, 1922, 1925, 1926, 1929, 1933-1941; All.A.Am., 1935-1942; AAPL, 1940, 1944; Stockbridge AA, 1923-1938; Carnegie Hall Gal., 1933-1941.

CURTIS, FLOYD EDWARD—Painter, Gr., W.
17315 Madison Ave., Cleveland 7, Ohio

B. Cleveland, Ohio, Oct. 20, 1894. *Studied*: Pickering Col. *Member*: Ohio WC Soc.; AAPL; Cleveland Soc. A. *Exhibited*: NAD, 1944; A. Gal., Toronto, Canada, 1939; Los A. Mus. A., 1938; Albright A. Gal., 1938, 1940; CMA, 1935, 1936, 1939; Ohio Pr. M., 1940-1945; Toledo Mus. A., 1939, 1944; CM, 1941, 1942, 1944, 1946; Dayton AI, 1940-1945; Indiana Soc. Pr. M., 1944, 1945; LC, 1949; Carnegie

Inst., 1949; CMA, 1948, 1949; Dayton AI, 1949, 1950; Ohio Univ., 1950; Richmond (Ind.) AA, 1950; Massillon Mus. A., 1950; Antioch Col., 1950; Zanesville AI, 1951. *Work*: CMA. Co-Author: "Over the Sea."*

CURTIS, LELAND—Painter
2313 Lake Shore Ave., Los Angeles 39, Cal.; s. Moose, Wyo.

B. Denver, Colo., Aug. 7, 1897. *Member*: A. of the Southwest; Laguna Beach AA. *Awards*: bronze and silver med., Los Angeles P. & S. Cl.; prizes, Cal. State Fair, 1926, 1934, 1948-49, 1954; Los Angeles County Fair, 1926; Oakland A. Gal.; Los A. Mus. A. *Exhibited*: NAD; Toledo Mus.; Cal. PLH; Los A. Mus. A. *Work*: City of Los Angeles Coll.; Dept. Interior, Washington, D.C. Official A., U.S. Antarctic Expedition, 1939-40; "U.S. Navy Operation Deepfreeze, III," Antarctica, 1957.

CUSHING, GEORGE—Industrial Designer, L., T.
101 Park Ave., New York 17, N.Y.; h. 9 Burnside Dr., Short Hills, N.J.

B. Plainfield, N.J., Oct. 14, 1906. *Studied*: Rutgers Univ.; N.Y. Univ. *Member*: IDI; Soc. Industrial Des. *Awards*: Modern Plastic Award, 1939; Electrical Manufacturing Award, 1940; IDI, 1951. (These awards received in collaboration with Thomas G. Nevell, partner). Lectures: Industrial Design at N.Y. Univ.; Pratt Inst.; Newark Sch. F. & Indst. A.; Museum of the City of New York. *Position*: Partner, Cushing & Nevell, 1933- , Partner, Cushing & Nevell, Ltd., Toronto, Canada.

CUSHING, VAL MURAT—Craftsman, T.
3 West University St., Alfred, N.Y.

B. Rochester, N.Y., Jan. 28, 1931. *Studied*: N.Y. State College of Ceramics, Des. Dept., Alfred, N.Y., B.F.A., M.F.A. *Member*: York State Craftsmen; Am. Craftsman's Council. *Awards*: prizes, Nat. Armed Forces Exh., 1953, 1954; Young Americans Exh., 1958; Rochester Finger Lakes Exh., 1958; N.Y. State Fair, 1958. *Work*: AGAA. *Exhibited*: Armed Forces Exh., 1953, 1954; Syracuse Mus. FA, 1956; Miami Nat., 1957; Wichita, 1956; Young Americans, 1957, 1958; Buffalo State T. Col., 1956; James Gal., N.Y., 1956; Elmira Mus. A., 1956; Binghamton Mus. A., 1956; Glidden Gal., Alfred, N.Y., 1956, 1958; Syracuse Intl., 1958; Albright Gal. A., 1955; Rochester Finger Lakes Exh., 1956, 1958; Midwest Des.-Craftsmen, Chicago, 1957; one-man: Lincoln Col., Lincoln, Ill., 1957; Univ. Illinois, 1957. Lectures on Contemporary Crafts. *Position*: Instr., Pottery, Univ. Illinois, Urbana, Ill.; Instr., Design, New York State College of Ceramics, Alfred, N.Y., at present.

CUSTER, BERNADINE—Painter, I., W.
c/o Midtown Galleries, 17 East 57th St., New York 22, N.Y.; s. Londonderry, Vt.

B. Bloomington, Ill. *Studied*: AIC. *Work*: MMA; Detroit Inst. A.; BM; AGAA; murals, Treasury Dept., Wash., D.C.; WMAA; Williams Col., and in private colls. *Exhibited*: AIC; CGA; CM; PAFA; R.I.Sch.Des.; BM; Phila. WC Cl.

CUSTIS, ELEANOR PARKE—Painter, Et., I.
626 East Capitol St., Washington, D.C.; s. 115 B Mt. Pleasant Ave., Gloucester, Mass.

B. Washington, D.C. *Studied*: Corcoran A. Sch.; & with Henry B. Snell. *Member*: AWCS; NAC; Wash. WC Cl.; Soc. Wash. A.; North Shore AA; New Haven Paint & Clay Cl. *Work*: Pub. Lib., New Haven, Conn.; Adams Sch., Wash., D.C. I., children's books, & for national magazines. *Author*: "Composition and Pictures."*

CUSTIS, MRS. JOHN KEITH. See Holt, Naomi

CUSUMANO, STEFANO—Painter, T.
170 West 73rd St., New York 23, N.Y.

B. Tampa, Fla., Feb. 5, 1912. *Studied*: Metropolitan A. Sch., and with Arthur Schwieder. *Work*: Univ. Illinois; Wesleyan Univ. Drawings for Menotti's "The Consul." *Exhibited*: WMAA, 1947, 1948; Carnegie Inst., 1949; Univ. Illinois, 1950; PAFA, 1951, 1952; CGA, 1951; Univ. Nebraska, 1956; Nat. Inst. A. & Lets., 1952; Munson-Williams-Proctor Inst., 1955; Smithsonian Inst., 1956; MModA.,

1956; Galleria Schettini, Milan, Italy, 1957; Bayonne Jewish Community Center; one-man: Montross Gal., 1942; Binet Gal., 1946, 1947, 1948, 1950; Passedoit Gal., 1953, 1956, 1957; Phila. A. All., 1948; Woodmere A. Gal., 1950; Tampa AI, 1949; Oregon State Col., 1951; Washington Univ., 1951. *Position*: Instr., N.Y. Univ., and Cooper Union A. Sch., New York, N.Y.

CUTHBERT, VIRGINIA (Mrs. Philip C. Elliott)—
Painter, T., Cr., Comm. A.
147 Bryant St., Buffalo 22, N.Y.
B. West Newton, Pa., Aug. 27, 1908. *Studied*: Syracuse Univ., B.F.A.; Carnegie Inst.; Chelsea Polytechnical Inst.; Univ. London, and with George Luks. *Member*: The Patteran, Buffalo, N.Y. *Awards*: F., Syracuse Univ., for European study; prizes, Carnegie Inst., 1934, 1935, 1937; Assoc. A. Pittsburgh, 1938, 1939; Butler AI, 1940; Albright A. Gal., 1944, 1946; Pepsi-Cola, 1946; Cortland State Fair, 1949, 1951, 1953; Albright A. Gal., 1950, 1952, 1955, 1958; Nat. Inst. A. & Let. grant, 1954; Chautauqua, N.Y., 1955; Buffalo, N.Y., 1956, 1957. *Work*: Albright A. Gal.; Syracuse Univ.; One Hundred Friends of Pittsburgh Art. *Exhibited*: Carnegie Inst., 1937-1940, 1943-1945, 1949; VMFA, 1940, 1942, 1946; PAFA, 1935, 1941, 1942, 1944, 1948-1952, 1953, 1958; MMA, 1943, 1944, 1951; Pepsi-Cola, 1946; AIC, 1938-1940, 1942, 1946, 1950, 1951, 1953; WMAA, 1946, 1948, 1950, 1953; GGE, 1939; Butler AI, 1938 (one-man); 1940, 1941, 1954, 1955, 1957, 1958; R.I. Sch. Des., 1945; AFA traveling exh., 1937-1938, 1950-1951; Syracuse Mus. A., 1939 (one-man); Syracuse Univ., 1944 (one-man); Contemporary A. Gal., 1945, 1949, 1953 (all one-man); Albright A. Gal., 1942-1946, 1948-1958; A. Dir. Cl. traveling exh., 1952-53; Carnegie Inst., 1952; CGA, 1949, 1951; Univ. Illinois, 1951; Cal. PLH, 1950, 1951; Walker A. Center, 1949, 1954; Nebraska Exh., 1949, 1950; Cortland State Fair, 1949, 1951; N.Y. State Fair, 1951, 1958; AIC, 1953, 1957; Western N.Y. exh., 1953-1955; A. Dir. Cl., 1953; Am. Acad. A. & Let., 1954; VMFA, 1954; Des Moines A. Center, 1954; Chautauqua A. Center, 1955, 1958; MModA, 1956; Rehn Gal., 1956-1958; DMFA, 1957; WMA, 1957; CMA, 1957; Provincetown A. Festival, 1958, and many others. *Positions*: Instr., Painting, Albright A. Sch., 1948- ; N.Y. State T., Col., Buffalo, N.Y., 1950-52; L., Instr., Univ. Buffalo, 1948-52; L., Instr., Albright A. Sch. of Univ. Buffalo, 1954- .

CUTLER, CHARLES GORDON—Sculptor
South Brooksville, Me.; h. 66 East Hollister St., Cincinnati, Ohio
B. Newton, Mass., Jan. 17, 1914. *Studied*: BMFA Sch. *Work*: AGAA; IBM; Fitchburg A. Center; Springfield Mus. A.; VMFA; CMA. *Exhibited*: PAFA, 1942, 1946; AIC, 1942; Buchholz Gal., 1943; New England S., 1942; R.I.Sch. Des., 1938; Fitchburg A. Center, 1946; WMAA; FMA; New London, Conn.; WMA; CGA; one-man: Grace Horne Gal.; Vose Gal., Boston; CM; Detroit Inst. A.; Framingham, Mass. *Position*: Hd., Sculpture Dept., Cincinnati A. Acad., 1952- .

CUTROW, LEONARD A.—Painter, T., Des., Comm. A.
1007 Clark St., Los Angeles 46, Cal.
B. Russia, Dec. 10, 1910. *Studied*: A. Center Sch., Los A. *Member*: AEA; Cal. WC Soc. *Awards*: Huntington Hartford F., 1951; gold medal, AWS, 1950; Cal. State Fair, 1958. *Work*: Encyclopaedia Britannica Book of the Year. *Exhibited*: AWS, 1950; Cal. WC Soc., 1948-1951; Denver A. Mus., 1949; Los A. Mus. A., 1949, 1951; San F. AA, 1950; Orange County exh., 1951; Cal. State Fair, 1950-1952; Chouinard AI, 1955 (one-man). *Position*: Instr., A. Center Sch., and Kann Inst. A., Los Angeles, Cal.; Chouinard AI, 1955; Univ. So. California, Los Angeles, Cal., 1955-1958.

CUTTLER, CHARLES DAVID—Historian, P.
311 Grand Ave., Iowa City, Iowa
B. Cleveland, Ohio, Apr. 8, 1913. *Studied*: Ohio State Univ., B.F.A., M.A.; N.Y. Univ.; in Europe, Ph.D. *Member*: CAA; AAUP; C.R.B. F., Brussels, Belgium, 1953-54. *Exhibited*: PAFA; CMA; Columbus A. Lg. Author (in part) of "An Introduction to Literature and the Fine Arts," Mich. State Univ. Press, 1950. Contributor to Marsyas; Art Quarterly; Art Bulletin. *Position*: Asst. Prof., Michigan State Univ., Dir. A. Gal., East Lansing, Mich., to 1958; Assoc. Prof., State Univ. of Iowa, 1958- .

CZURLES, STANLEY A.—
Educator, P., W., L., Des., Et.
244 Wardman Rd., Kenmore 17, N.Y.
B. Elizabeth, N.J., Sept. 14, 1908. *Studied*: Syracuse Univ., B.F.A., M.F.A.; Univ. Iowa, Ph.D. *Member*: Nat. Edu. Assn.; Eastern AA. *Exhibited*: Albright A. Gal., 1931-1942; Syracuse Mus. FA; Buffalo Town Cl. (one-man). Contributor to: Art education magazines & bulletins. *Position*: Asst. Prof. A., 1941-46; Dir. A. Edu., Prof., 1946- , Dir. Visual Edu., 1943- , State Teachers Col., Buffalo, N.Y.*

DABO, LEON—Painter
315 West 106th St., New York, N.Y.*

DACEY, WILLIAM—Painter, W., T., L.
Box 445, Bar Harbor, Me.
B. Providence, R.I., Oct. 10, 1907. *Studied*: R.I. Sch. Des., B.F.A.; Clark Univ., M.A.; Harvard Univ. Sch. FA. *Member*: Clark Univ. Scientific Soc. *Work*: Brown Univ. *Exhibited*: PAFA, 1941; All. A. Am., 1941; Vendome Gal.; WMA; Fitchburg A. Mus.; Artists Gal., New York, 1950 (one-man). Author: "Geographic Origins of Art," 1946.*

da COSTA, ANTONIO—Sculptor
5530 Netherlands Ave., New York 71, N.Y.
B. Lisbon, Portugal, Sept. 26, 1899. *Studied*: FA Superior Sch., Lisbon, and with Simoes d'Almeida, Antoine Bourdelle. *Member*: Societe Nationale de Beaux-Arts, Paris; Sociedade Nacional de Belas Artes, Portugal; NSS. *Awards*: medals, Rio de Janeiro; Seville, Spain; Lisbon, Portugal. *Work*: Sculptures in Portugal; Azores; Goa, India; Amagola, Africa; France; Spain; Argentina; Brazil; Cuba; Dominican Republic; Mus. of State Dept., Rio de Janeiro; Mus. Contemp. A., Lisbon; Mus. City of Lisbon; Mus. of Setubal, Portugal. Many monuments, statues, groups, reliefs and busts in public bldgs., churches, public gardens and private homes; statue of stallion, "Bull Lea," Calumet Farms, Ky. *Exhibited*: Paris Salon; Salon d'Automne; Intl. Exh., Paris, France; Int. Exh., Brazil; Rio de Janeiro (one-man); Int. Exh., Seville, Spain; many exhs. in Portugal; So. Vermont A., 1949, 1950, 1952; NSS, 1956.

D'AGOSTINO, VINCENT—Painter
621½ North Sycamore Ave., Los Angeles 36, Cal.
B. Chicago, Ill., April 7, 1898. *Studied*: AIC, and with Charles Hawthorne, George Bellows. *Member*: AEA; NSMP; Assoc., Los A. Scenic A. *Awards*: Tiffany Fnd. scholarship. *Work*: WMAA; Tilden H.S., Brooklyn, N.Y.; murals, USPO, Gloucester, N.J.; Mt. Loretto Inst., Staten Island, N.Y.; Riccardo's Restaurant, Chicago, Ill. *Exhibited*: PAFA, 1931; Newark, N.J.; AIC, 1934, 1935; WFNY 1939; Whitney Studio, 1929 (one-man); Milwaukee AI; Riccardo's Restaurant, Chicago; Oshkosh Mus. A.; Univ. Oklahoma; Mus. FA of Houston, 1934; Anthan Gal., Los A., 1950; Pasadena AI, 1951; Los A. Home Show, 1953; Los A. County Fair, 1953; Los A. Mus. A., 1954.

DAHLBERG, EDWIN LENNART—Illustrator, P.
424 Madison Ave., New York 17, N.Y.; h. 2 South Boulevard, Nyack, N.Y.
B. Beloit, Wis., Sept. 20, 1901. *Member*: AWS. *Studied*: AIC. *Awards*: Adams traveling scholarship, AIC, 1924; Ranger Purchase award (NAD) AWS exh., 1958. *Exhibited*: AIC; PAFA; AWS, 1954, 1955-1958, traveling exh. 1956. *Position*: Freelance, 1930- .

DAHLER, WARREN—Painter, S., C.
Wolfpit Hill, Norwalk, Conn.
B. New York, N.Y., Oct. 12, 1897. *Studied*: NAD; Univ. Chicago; & with George Grey Barnard. *Member*: Silvermine Gld. A.; NSMP. *Awards*: prize, Arch. L., 1915. *Work*: murals, Capitol Bldg., Missouri; St. Francis Hotel, San F., Cal.; Somerset Va. Stage sets for Broadway plays. *Exhibited*: NAD, 1920, 1922; Silvermine Gld. A., 1932 (one-man).*

DAHLIN, ED—Cartoonist
4 West 40th St.; h. 45-26 44th St., Sunnyside, L.I., N.Y.
B. Chicago, Ill., Oct. 7, 1928. *Studied*: Chicago Acad. FA. *Work*: in "Best Cartoons of the Year," 1956, 1957, 1958;

"Cartoon Laffs for TRUE," 1958; "The Saturday Evening Post Carnival of Humor," 1958; "Best Cartoons from ARGOSY"; "You've Got Me in the Nursery," 1958; "A Treasury of Sports Cartoons," 1957. Contributor to: Saturday Evening Post; True; Ladies Home Journal; American Legion; Better Homes and Gardens; Successful Farming; King Features Syndicate; McNaught Syndicate; American Weekly; Sport; Argosy; Wall Street Journal; Parade; Cavalier; Christian Science Monitor and in worldwide foreign publications.

DAILEY, JOSEPH CHARLES—
Painter, Des., Ser., C., Mus. Asst. Dir.
Sioux City Art Center, 5th Fl., Commerce Bldg.; h. 622 Jackson St., Sioux City 1, Iowa

B. Reynoldsville, Pa., Mar. 4, 1926. *Studied*: Youngstown Univ., A.B., with Margaret Evans, David P. Skeggs, John Naberezny and Robert Elwell. *Member*: Youngstown Expermentalists; AEA. *Awards*: prizes, Mahoning County, 1951; Trumble County, 1950; Youngstown College Purchase award, 1952. *Work*: Youngstown College; Westmar College; Missouri Synod; Sioux City Lib., and in numerous private colls. *Exhibited*: Butler Inst. Am. A., 1952, 1953; Massillon Mus. A., 1953; Canton AI; Akron AI; Siouxland WC Exch., 1955-1957; Six-State Exh., 1955-1958; Springfield Mus. A., 1956; Life of Christ Show (Iowa), 1957, 1958; Des Moines A. Center; Univ. Nebraska; Blanden Mem. Mus.; Univ. Kansas City; Stephens Col.; Cedar Falls AA; Sanford Mus., Cherokee, Iowa; Iowa State Fair, 1955, 1956; Little A. Gal., Spearfish, S.D.; Sioux City A. Center; one-man: Youngstown College; Youngstown Lib., 1953; Westmar College, 1951; Morningside College, 1957; Sioux City Lib., 1957; Iowa Unitarian Convent, 1956. Des. and Edited numerous brochures, catalogs, publications for Sioux City A. Center; art reviews for Sioux City Journal; TV art education series. *Position*: Des., Crest Johnson Studios, Youngstown, Ohio, 1953; Staff Artist, Warren, Ohio, 1954; Asst. Dir., Sioux City A. Center, 1957- .

DAINGERFIELD, MARJORIE (Mrs. J. Louis Lundean)—
Sculptor, T., L.
1 West 67th St., New York 23, N.Y.; s. Blowing Rock, N.C.

B. New York, N.Y. *Studied*: Sch. Am. S.; Grand Central Sch. A.; & with Solon Borglum, James Fraser, Edmond Amateis. *Member*: NSS; Pen & Brush Cl. *Awards*: Huntington award, Pen & Brush Cl., 1956. *Work*: Sch. Tropical Medicine, San Juan, Puerto Rico; Hobart Col., Geneva, N.Y.; Ovens Auditorium and Queens Col., Charlotte, N.C.; statuette-emblem for Girl Scouts of America; bronze head of Dr. Bailey K. Ashford, Georgetown Univ., 1957; many portrait heads. *Exhibited*: NAD, since 1920; Arch. L., 1945; NSS, 1944, 1945; Mint Mus. A.; Norton A. Gal.; Wildenstein Gal.; Grand Central A. Gal.; Duke Univ.; Audubon A.; Pen & Brush Cl. Lectures: Sculpture—modelling heads. Pres., Blowing Rock AA, 1958.

DALE, MRS. FRANK K. See Hamlin, Edith

d'ALESSIO, GREGORY—Cartoonist, P., I.
8 Henderson Place, New York 28, N.Y.

B. New York, N.Y., Sept. 25, 1904. *Studied*: ASL. *Member*: Nat. Cartoonists Soc.; SI. *Exhibited*: MMA, 1942; Los A. Mus. A., 1943; OWI. Author: "Welcome Home," 1945. I., Cart., national magazines; creator of "These Women," syndicated cart. feature. Lectures: Cartooning.

DALRYMPLE, LUCILE STEVENSON (Mrs. Frederic)—
Painter
4212 Greenwood Ave., Chicago 15, Ill.

B. Sandusky, Ohio, Oct. 29, 1882. *Studied*: J. Francis Smith Acad., Chicago; AIC. *Member*: Pa. Soc. Min. P.; AAPL; All-Illinois Soc. FA; Mun. A. Lg.; Chicago Galleries Assn. *Awards*: prizes, Ill. Acad. FA, 1930, 1940. *Work*: Wabash Univ.; Marietta Univ.; Univ. Illinois; Illinois Acad. FA; Vanderpoel Coll. *Exhibited*: PAFA, 1941-1945, 1950, 1951; NCFA, 1943, 1944; All-Illinois Soc. FA, 1945, 1946; Grand Central A. Gal.; BM; Los A. Mus. A.; AIC; Cordon Gal.; Chicago Galleries Assn., 1951, 1952.*

DALTON, FRANCES L.—Painter, T.
70 Chestnut St., Andover, Mass.

B. Amesbury, Mass., Dec. 28, 1906. *Studied*: BMFA Sch., with Philip Hale. *Member*: AAPL; Boston Soc. Indp. A.; Andover A. Group; Mass. State Group on Nat. A. Exh.; North Andover FA Soc.; Alumni Assn., BMFA. *Awards*: prize and med., Jordan Marsh Co., 1944; traveling scholarship BMFA Sch.; Lawrence (Mass.) Centennial Exh., 1953. *Exhibited*: Jordan Marsh Co., 1954; Whistler House; Springfield Mus. A.; Woodstock A. Gal.; AGAA; Terry AI, 1952; Silvermine Gld. A.; Boston Soc. Indp. A.; Boston A. Festival, 1955; traveling exh., Boston Soc. Indp. A., 1954; John Ester Gal., Andover, 1955; Brooks Sch., No. Andover, 1954; Copley Soc., Boston, 1957; Portland A. Mus., 1957; Andover Inn, 1958; St. Gaudens Mem., Cornish, N.H., 1958; H.S. Art Festival, 1958; Andover FA Soc., 1956-1958. *Position*: Supv., Creative A., Pub. Sch., Andover, Mass.; Chm. Am. A. Week, 1958.

DALTON, PETER—Sculptor
114 River Rd., Grandview-on-Hudson, N.Y.

B. Buffalo, N.Y., Dec. 26, 1894. *Studied*: ASL; BAID; NAD. *Member*: NA; NSS; Audubon A.; Century Assn.; Nat. Inst. A. & Let. *Awards*: med., All. A. Am., 1935; Grant, Am. Acad. A. & Let., 1945; gold med., NAD, 1950, 1951. *Work*: USPO, Carthage, Miss. *Exhibited*: PAFA, 1936, 1941, 1943, 1945, 1950, 1951; Fairmount Park, Pa.; Carnegie Inst., 1941; MMA, 1951; NAD, 1950, 1951.

DALTON, WILLIAM BOWER—Painter, W., C.
298 Ocean Drive, East, Stamford, Conn.

B. Wilmslow, Cheshire, England, Feb. 29, 1868. *Studied*: Royal Col. A., London; Dalhousie Univ., Halifax, N.S.; CUASch. *Member*: A. Workers Gld., London; Far Eastern Ceramic Group (U.S.A.); Assoc., ARCA. *Awards*: gold med., Int. Expo., Paris, 1937. *Work*: Victoria & Albert Mus., London; Royal Ontario Mus., Canada; South London A. Gal. *Exhibited*: Wolfville Univ., Nova Scotia; New Britain A. Gal., Conn.; Royal Acad. A., London. Author: "Craftsmanship and Design in Pottery," publ. London, 1956, in "Notes from a Potter's Diary." Author, I., "Ceramic Age."

DALY, NORMAN DAVID—Painter, E.
426 East Seneca St., Ithaca, N.Y.

B. Pittsburgh, Pa., Aug. 9, 1911. *Studied*: Univ. Colorado, B.F.A.; Ohio State Univ., M.A.; N.Y. Univ. *Awards*: prizes, White Mus. A., Cornell Univ., 1955, 1958 (both purchase); Everson Mem. prize, Syracuse Mus. FA, 1958. *Work*: Oberlin Mus. FA; Wooster Col.; Munson-Williams-Proctor Inst.; White Mus. A., Cornell Univ.; St. Paul's Gal. A.; Univ. Washington. *Exhibited*: WMAA, 1947, 1948, 1950; Carnegie Inst., 1948, 1949; AIC, 1943, 1944, 1951; PAFA, 1948-1950; Univ. Illinois, 1950; Walker A. Center, 1950; VMFA, 1948; BMA, 1948; Toledo Mus. A., 1949; CAM, 1951; MMA, 1952; one-man: Durand-Ruel Gal., 1947; Bertha Schaefer Gal., 1950. *Position*: Assoc. Prof. FA, Cornell Univ., Ithaca, N.Y., 1942- .

DALY, THOMAS F.—Painter, T.
1055 West North Shore Ave., Chicago 26, Ill.

B. Chicago, Ill., Nov. 5, 1908. *Studied*: Georgetown Univ., A.B.; AIC, B.F.A., with Louis Ritman. *Awards*: Raymond traveling scholarship, AIC, 1934. *Exhibited*: nationally.

DAME, LAWRENCE—Critic, W.
Herald-Tribune; h. 1504-A Gulf View Dr., Sarasota, Fla.

B. Portland, Me., July 2, 1898. *Studied*: Harvard Univ.; Univ. of Paris; Univ. Grenoble, France; Instituto de Burgos, Spain. Author: "New England Comes Back," 1940; "Yucatan," 1941. Contributor to Saturday Evening Post; Reader's Digest; American Mercury; Magazine Digest; Arts magazine, etc. Lectures: Trends in Modern Art; Mayan Art, to art associations, New England and Florida. *Positions*: Dir., News Office, Harvard Univ., 1943-44, 1950-53; A. Editor, Boston Herald, 1944-54; Contrib. Ed., Art Digest, 1950-54; Contrib. Columnist, Rome (Italy) Daily American, 1955; A. Ed., Herald-Tribune, Sarasota, Fla., 1955- .

D'AMICO, VICTOR E.—*Educator, W., L.*

Museum of Modern Art, 11 West 53rd St., New York 19, N.Y.; h. 65 West 2nd St., Mt. Vernon, N.Y.

B. New York, N.Y., May 19, 1904. *Studied:* PIASch; CUASch; Columbia Univ., B.A., M.A. Chm., Com. on A. Edu. Author: "Creative Teaching in Art," 1942; Ed., "Visual Arts in General Education," 1940. Contributor to: Art & theatre magazines. Lectures: Art Education. *Position:* Hd. FA Dept., Fieldston Sch., N.Y., 1929-1948; Dir., Edu. Program, MModA, 1937-1948; Survey of Art for General Edu. Bd., 1934; Dir., War Veterans A. Center, MModA, 1944-1948; Dir., Dept. Edu. & People's A. Center, MModA, New York, N.Y., 1948- .

DANA, EUGENE—*Educator, P., Des., Film-Maker*

6717 South Jeffery Blvd., Chicago 49, Ill.

B. Marengo, Ill., June 27, 1912. *Studied:* Univ. Wisconsin, B.S.; Univ. Michigan, M. Des., and with Josef Albers, Cameron Booth. *Exhibited:* AIC, 1951. *Position:* Hd. A. Dept., Drake Univ., 1945-46; Brooklyn Col., 1946-47; Assoc. Prof., Chm., Foundation Course, Inst. Des., Illinois Inst. Technology, Chicago, Ill., 1947- .

d'ANDREA, ALBERT PHILIP—*Educator, S., Eng.*

2121 Bay Ave., Brooklyn 10, N.Y.

B. Benevento, Italy, Oct. 27, 1897. *Studied:* Col. City of N.Y., A.B.; Univ. Rome. *Member:* Brooklyn Soc. A.; Audubon A.; CAA; F., Royal Soc. A., England; Hon. Academician, Accademia di Belle Arti, Perugia. *Awards:* prizes, Col. City of N.Y., 1933; LC, 1944; med., Ingenieurs professionels Francais, 1954; Townsend Harris award, N.Y., 1957. *Work:* LC; City Col. of N.Y.; Mus. City of N.Y.; N.Y. Hist. Soc.; Smithsonian Inst.; Accademia di Belle Arti, Bologna; Biblioteca Apostolica Vaticana; Royal Soc. A.; Bibliotheques Nationale, Dept. des Medailles; Hyde Park Mem. Lib. *Exhibited:* NSS, 1951, 1952, 1957; NAD; Audubon A., 1953, 1954, 1956-1958. *Position:* Dir. Arch. & Engineering Unit of Bd. Edu., New York, 1947-51; Prof. A., Chm., Dept., Dir., Planning & Des., City Col. of New York, 1945- ; Asst. Ed., Theatre Annual, 1946- . Creator of the following medals, 1954: David B. Steinman, Bernard M. Baruch, Jonas E. Salk, George M. Sarton, Morton Wollman.

d'ANDREA, BERNARD L.—*Illustrator, Comm. A.*

136 East 57th St., New York, N.Y.; h. 4 Kings Terrace Rd., Kings Point, L.I., N.Y.

B. Buffalo, N.Y., Aug. 13, 1923. *Studied:* PIASch, with Will Burtin. *Member:* SI; MModA. *Exhibited:* SI; A. Dir. Cl.; Arch Lg. Illus. for Sat. Eve. Post; Woman's Home Companion; American; Good Housekeeping; McCalls; Red Book and other national magazines. Lectures: "Commercial Art—Its Creation—Use—Its Value."*

DANE, WILLIAM JERALD—*Art Librarian*

Newark Public Library; h. 763 Bloomfield Ave., Montclair, N.J.

B. Concord, N.H., May 8, 1925. *Studied:* Univ. New Hampshire, B.A.; Drexel Inst. Technology, M.L.S.; Harvard Univ.; N.Y. Univ. Inst. FA; Univ. Paris (Sorbonne); Univ. Nancy, France. *Position:* Prin. A. Libr., Newark Public Lib., Newark, N.J.

DANES, GIBSON—*Educator, L., Cr.*

School of Art & Architecture, Yale University; h. 148 Cold Spring St., New Haven, Conn.

B. Starbuck, Wash., Dec. 13, 1910. *Studied:* Univ. Oregon, with Michael Mueller; AIC, B.F.A., with Boris Anisfeld; Northwestern Univ., B.S., M.A.; Yale Univ., Ph.D. *Member:* CAA (Bd. Dir.); Hon. Memb. Conn. Chptr. AIA. *Awards:* F., Northwestern Univ., 1937; Carnegie Scholarship, 1938; F., Yale Univ., 1946; Rockefeller Post-War F., 1946; Ford Fnd. F., 1951. *Exhibited:* Missouri State Exh., Jefferson City; Univ. Exh., Austin, Tex.; South County AA, Kingston, R.I. Contributor to art magazines, college journals. Author: "Looking at Modern Painting." *Position:* Prof. A., Univ. Texas, Austin, Tex.; Prof. A., Ohio State Univ., 1948-52; Chm. Dept. A., Univ. California, Los Angeles, Cal., 1952-58; Dean, Sch. A. & Architecture, Yale Univ., New Haven, Conn., 1958- .

DANIELS, ELMER HARLAND—*Sculptor, Indst. Des.*

3382 Washtenaw Rd.; h. 2405 Londonderry Ave., Ann Arbor, Mich.

B. Owosso, Mich., Oct. 23, 1905. *Studied:* Grand Rapids Col.; John Herron AI; BAID; T. Art Center Sch., Indianapolis, and in Europe. *Member:* Soc. Indst. Des.; NSS; Arch. Lg.; Indiana A.; P. & S. of New Jersey; Indiana Lincoln Un.; Lincoln F., of So. California (hon.); Mich. Acad. A. Sc. & Let.; Pasadena AA. *Awards:* Harry Johnson award, 1931; Indiana A., 1938; C. V. Hickox prize, 1942. *Work:* Indiana Univ.; Turkey Run Park; Indianapolis State Lib.; Indianapolis State Capitol Bldg.; Ball State T. Col.; Lincoln mem., Lincoln City, Ind.; 3 figures, St. Joseph Church, Jasper, Ind.; mem., Demopolis, Ala.; war mem., Bay City, Mich.; portraits of prominent persons. Indst. Des. for Henry Kaiser Co.; Graham-Paige Motors; Haywood Wakefield Co.; Plomb Tool Co. Consultant-Des., Steelcase, Inc., Grand Rapids, Mich.; Bear Archery Co., Grayling, Mich.

DANN, FRODE—*Painter, T., C., W., L.*

314 South Mentor Ave., Pasadena, Cal.

B. Jelstrup, Havbro, Denmark, Sept. 10, 1892. *Studied:* Danish Tech. Trade Sch.; Univ. & Royal Acad., Copenhagen. *Member:* Cal. WC Soc.; Pasadena Soc. A.; Pasadena AA. *Exhibited:* PAFA, 1938; Santa Barbara Mus. A., 1944; Los A. Mus. A.; San Diego FA Soc.; SFMA. *Position:* Dir., Instr., Pasadena Sch. FA, Pasadena, Cal.

DANNER, SARA KOLB (Mrs. W. M.)—*Painter*

1555 Alameda Padre Serra, Santa Barbara, Cal.

B. New York, N.Y. *Studied:* Phila. Sch. Des. for Women; Univ. California at Santa Barbara; Cal. Col. A. & Crafts; PAFA Summer School. *Member:* Cal. A. Cl.; Phila. A. All.; Santa Barbara AA; Women Painters of the West; Phila. Plastic Cl. *Awards:* prizes, Hoosier Salon, 1928, 1951; Women Painters of the West, 1942, 1943; Cal. A. Cl., and others. *Exhibited:* Woodmere A. Gal.; Los A. Mus. A.; Cal. State Fair; Hoosier Salon; Women Painters of the West; Cal. A. Cl.; one-man: Phila. A. All., 1953; Santa Barbara A. Mus. (3). Author: "Gallery Tour," 1952 (poetry). Contributor poetry to Sat. Review.*

DANSON, EDWARD B.—*Assistant Museum Director*

Museum of Northern Arizona, Fort Valley Road, Flagstaff, Ariz.*

DANTE, GIGLIO RAPHAEL—*Painter, S.*

15 West 28th St.; h. 23 Jones St., New York 14, N.Y.

B. Rome, Italy, Sept. 4, 1916. *Studied:* Acad. of Rome, Italy. *Awards:* Mitton award, 1950; Pitkin F., 1954. *Work:* Springfield Mus. A.; Savoy Coll., Naples; Michelangelo Auditorium, Boston; Lawrence Mus. A.; BMFA; Fitchburg Mus. A.; Rome, Italy, and in private colls. *Exhibited:* CM, 1945; PAFA, 1934-1936; GGE, 1939; Boris Mirski Gal., 1944, 1946 (one-man); Brandt Gal., 1945, 1946 (one-man); MModA, 1954; BM, 1950-1955; Santa Barbara Mus. A., 1954; other one-man: Betty Parsons Gal., 1947, 1950; Bayne Gal., Los Angeles, 1954; Contemp. A. Gal., Chicago, 1948, 1952, 1955.

DANYSH, JOSEPH A.—*Educator, P.*

California College of Arts & Crafts, 5212 Broadway, Oakland, Cal.

Position: Pres., California College of Arts & Crafts.*

DAPHNIS, NASSOS—*Painter*

400 West 23rd St., New York 11, N.Y.

B. Krokeai, Greece, July 23, 1914. *Member:* Am. Abstract A. *Work:* BMA; Albright A. Gal.; Providence Mus. A.; Tel-Aviv Mus., Israel. *Exhibited:* Carnegie Inst., 1946, 1947, 1952, 1955, 1958, 1959; Am. Abstract A., 1958; Salon de Mai, Paris, 1951; one-man: Contemp. A., 1938, 1947, 1948; Mint Mus. A., Charlotte, N.C., 1949; Galerie Colette Allendy, Paris, France, 1950. *Position:* Instr., Horace Mann Sch., New York, N.Y., 1953- .

DARAIO, INNOCENZO—*Painter*

439 Beverwil Dr., Beverly Hills, Cal.

B. Potenza, Italy, Apr. 26, 1903. *Studied:* Mechanics Inst., New York, N.Y. *Member:* Cal. AC; P.&S.Cl., Los A.;

AAPL; A. of the Southwest; Laguna Beach AA; San Fernando A. Gld. *Awards*: many awards in local and national exhibitions. *Work*: decorations in 14 churches in California; work with major movie studios.

D'ARISTA, ROBERT—*Painter*
149 East 97th St., New York, N.Y.

B. New York, N.Y., July 2, 1929. *Studied*: N.Y. Univ.; Columbia Univ.; Am. A. Sch.; Grande Chaumiere, Paris, France. *Awards*: Fulbright award, 1955. *Work*: Toledo Mus. A., and in private collections. *Exhibited*: PAFA, 1954; Solomon Guggenheim Mus., 1954; WMAA, 1954, 1955, 1957, 1958; Munson-Williams-Proctor Inst., 1955; Carnegie Inst., 1955, 1958; Univ. Illinois, 1955; Univ. Nebraska, 1955-1957; AIC; BM, 1957; DMFA; Illinois Wesleyan Univ., and others; one-man: Alan Gal., N.Y., 1955, 1956.

DARNAULT, FLORENCE MALCOLM—*Sculptor*
Hotel Chelsea, 222 West 23rd St., New York 11, N.Y.

B. New York, N.Y., Dec. 24, 1905. *Studied*: Radcliffe Col.; NAD; ASL; in Europe, and with Daniel Chester French. *Member*: Pen & Brush Cl.; NAC; AAPL. *Awards*: prizes, Pen & Brush Cl.; NAC; All. A. Am.; Redding Ridge, Conn. *Work*: U.S. Naval Acad.; Col. City of N.Y.; N.Y. Post-Graduate Hospital; Am. Inst. Engineers; Whitehead Metals Co.; N.Y.Univ. Medical Sch.; Am. Tel. & Tel. Co.; Harvard Univ.; Verdi Cl.; Army Officer's Cl., Governor's Island, N.Y.; Statue, Mexico City; Colombian Govt., Cartagena, Colombia. *Exhibited*: Pen & Brush Cl.; NAC; NAD; All. A. Am.; AAPL, 1955.*

DARR, HAROLD WINFRED—*Designer, C., Et., E., L.*
5 East 22nd St.; h. 4400 West 50th St., Minneapolis 10, Minn.

B. Rockford, Ill., Mar. 10, 1905. *Studied*: Carleton Col.; Minneapolis Sch. A.; PAFA, and with Henry Varnum Poor, Daniel Garber, Albert Laessle. *Member*: Am. Soc. Indst. Des.; IDI; Soc. Plastic Engineers. *Work*: Columbus Gal. FA; Illuminated plastic map mural, Rochester State Hospital. *Exhibited*: traveling exh., Am. Soc. Indst. Des.; IDI; Phila. A. All., 1948 (one-man); Carleton Col., 1949; Minneapolis Inst. A., 1950, 1953; Minneapolis Sch. A., 1954; Columbus Gal. FA. Author, I., "Steel Horizons." *Position*: Chm., Indst. Des. Dept., Minneapolis Sch. A.; Partner, Harold W. Darr Assoc., Minneapolis, Minn., 1945.

DARROW, PAUL GARDNER—*Painter, Gr., T., Cart.*
628 Blanchard St., Claremont, Cal.

B. Pasadena, Cal., Oct. 31, 1921. *Studied*: A. Center, Los Angeles; Colo. Springs FA Center, with Boardman Robinson; Claremont Grad. Sch., with Millard Sheets, Sueo Serisawa, Henry Lee McFee, Howard Cook. *Member*: Cal. WC Soc.; Los A. AA. *Awards*: prizes, Los A. Mus. A., 1954; Pasadena A. Mus., 1954; Cal. State Fair, 1950; Nat. Orange Show, 1953; Fresno, Cal., 1952. *Work*: Pasadena A. Mus.; Palos Verdes AA; murals, Richmond Youth Center, 1952; Convair Aircraft, San Diego, 1953; Nat. Am. Insurance Co., Los A., 1954; Kaiser Aluminum, Disneyland, Cal., 1955; Broadway Dept. Stores, Anaheim and Van Nuys, Cal., 1955; Gourmet Shop, Hollywood, 1955, and others. *Exhibited*: Sao Paulo, Brazil, 1955; Smithsonian Inst. traveling exh., 1955-56; PAFA, 1954; Los A. Mus. A., 1951-1954; Denver A. Mus., 1954; Butler AI, 1953, 1954; CMA, 1954; Univ. Vienna, 1951; Downtown Gal., 1955; SFMA, 1952, 1953; SAM, 1953; Santa Barbara, Chaffey Nat., 1953-1955; Palos Verdes, 1952-1955; Cal. WC Soc., 1953-1955; Santa Barbara Mus. A., 1952; Oakland A. Mus.; Newport Beach; Laguna Beach, and others. Contributor cartoons to N.Y.Times, Sat. Review, Ladies Home Journal; Fawcett Publ.; Hearst Publ.; etc. *Position*: Instr., Brigham Young Univ., 1954; Coronado Sch. FA, 1953, 1955; Scripps Col., 1954-55; Asst. A. Dir., Los Angeles County Fair, 1952-1955.*

DARROW, WHITNEY, JR.—*Cartoonist*
Newtown Turnpike, Weston, Conn.

B. Princeton, N.J., Aug. 22, 1909. *Studied*: Princeton Univ., A.B.; ASL, and with Thomas Benton, Kimon Nicolaides. Author, I., "You're Sitting on My Eyelashes," 1943; "Please Pass the Hostess," 1949, collected cartoons; "Hold It Florence," collected cartoons, 1954; "Stop Miss!," collected cartoons, 1957. Contributor to New Yorker and other magazines; cartoons for national advertisers. Contributor: Famous Artists Schools Cartoon Course.

DASBURG, ANDREW MICHAEL—*Painter, T.*
Ranchos de Taos, N.M.

B. Paris, France, May 4, 1887. *Studied*: ASL. *Awards*: prizes, Pan-Am. Exp., 1925; Carnegie Inst., 1927, 1931; Guggenheim F., 1932. *Work*: WMAA; Denver A. Mus.; Los A. Mus. A.; Cal. PLH; Dallas Mus. FA; CM; MMA.

DATUS, JAY—*Painter, T., W.*
3801 North 30th St., Phoenix, Ariz.

B. Jackson, Mich., Mar. 24, 1914. *Studied*: Worcester Mus. Sch.; Yale Univ. Sch. FA. *Member*: Phoenix FA Assn. (Bd. Trustees & 1st V.-Pres.). *Work*: Univ. Wisconsin; Beloit Col.; Arizona State Capitol Bldg. Murals, Arizona State Capitol Bldg.; 1st Natl. Bank, Phoenix; Southern Arizona Bank & Trust Co., Tucson, Ariz. *Exhibited*: AIC; O'Brien Gal., Chicago (one-man); Phoenix FA Center (one-man). Author: "The Paint Box" art column in Arizona Republic newspaper. *Position*: Dir. & Fndr., Kachina School of Art, Phoenix, Ariz., 1948- .

DATZ, A. MARK—*Painter, Et., S.*
50 East 56th St., New York 22, N.Y.

B. Russia, Oct. 27, 1889. *Studied*: CUASch.; NAD; BAID. *Member*: Fed. Mod. P. & S.; Atlanta AA; SAGA. *Work*: WMAA; Rochester Mem. A. Gal.; Oshkosh Mus. A.; Los A. Mus. Hist., Sc. & A.; N.Y. Pub. Lib.; Tel-Aviv Mus. Israel; WMA; PC; Atlanta AA; Newark Mus. A., and in private colls. *Exhibited*: one-man: A. Center, N.Y., 1926; New Sch. for Social Research, 1927; J. B. Neumann Gal., 1928; 8th St. Gal., 1934; Dorothy Paris Gal., 1936; Passedoit Gal., 1938; Montross Gal., 1941; Binet Gal., 1946; Hartert Gal., 1952.

DAUGHERTY, JAMES HENRY—
Painter, Lith., W., I., L.
Westport, Conn.

B. Asheville, N.C., June 1, 1889. *Studied*: Corcoran Sch. A.; PAFA. *Member*: Silvermine Gld. A. *Awards*: Newbery med., 1939. *Work*: Yale Mus. FA; N.Y.Pub.Lib.; Wilmington Pub. Lib.; Achenbach Fnd.; Cal. PLH; murals, Stamford H.S.; Loew's Theatre, Cleveland, Ohio. *Exhibited*: Silvermine Gld. A.; Macbeth Gal.; Arch. Lg.; Bridgeport A. Lg. Author, I., "Daniel Boone"; "Poor Richard"; "Andy and the Lion"; "Marcus and Narcissa Whitman," 1953, & others. Contributor to: magazines & periodicals.

d'AULAIRE, EDGAR PARIN—*Painter, Et., Lith.*
Lia Farm, Wilton, Conn.

B. Camp Blenie, Switzerland, Sept. 30, 1898. *Studied*: Academi Scandinave; Academie Moderne, Paris; art schools in Florence and Rome; and with Andre L'Hote, Hans Hofmann. *Awards*: Caldecott medal, 1940. *Work*: many books in coll. of LC; The White House, Wash., D.C., and in European and American schools, libraries and print rooms. *Exhibited*: BMFA graphic art traveling exhibition; in Italy and major cities of U.S.A. Lectures: Art and literature for children on Radio and TV. Books in collaboration with Ingri Parin d'Aulaire: Magic Rug; Ola, Ola and Blakken; Conquest of the Atlantic; Lord's Prayer; George Washington; East of the Sun, West of the Moon; Children of the Northlights; Don't Count Your Chicks; Star Spangled Banner; Animals Everywhere; Wings for Per; Pocahontas; Too Big—Two Cars; Benjamin Franklin; Lief the Lucky; Nils, Buffalo Bill; Columbus; Magic Meadow. Books translated into German, French, Norwegian, Turkish, Japanese, Korean, Burmese and also in Braille.

d'AULAIRE, INGRI MORTENSON PARIN—
Writer, I., Lith., P.
Lia Farm, Wilton, Conn.

B. Kongsberg, Norway, Dec. 27, 1905. *Studied*: Kunsindustriskolen, Oslo, Norway; Hans Hofmann, Munich; Andre L'Hote, Per Krogh, Acadamie Moderne, Paris. *Award*: Caldecott medal, 1940. *Work*: many books in coll. of LC; The White House, Wash., D.C., and in European and American schools. (For list of books, in collaboration with Edgar Parin d'Aulaire, see entry above.)

DAVENPORT, CARSON S.—*Painter, Gr.*
823 North Main St., Danville, Va.

B. Danville, Va., Feb. 14, 1908. *Studied*: Ringling Sch. A.; Parsons Sch. Des., and with George Pearse Ennis, Wayman

Adams. *Member*: Wash. WC Cl. *Awards*: F., VMFA, award and Ctf. of Distinction, 1956; Bristol, Va. regional, 1957; purchase award, Univ. of Virginia, 1958; Natl. Exh., Clinton, N.J. *Work*: murals, USPO, Greensboro, Ga.; Chatham, Va.; VMFA; Rosenwald Coll.; Knoedler Gal. *Exhibited*: one-man: VMFA; Ferargil Gal.; group shows: CGA; AAA Gal. *Position*: Dir. A., Averett Col., Danville, Va., 14 yrs.

DAVENPORT, ETHEL (Mrs. Don A.)—
  Craftsman, Des., W.
  Lambertville, N.J.

B. Philadelphia, Pa. *Studied*: PMSchIA; & in Europe. *Member*: Assoc. Hand Weavers. *Exhibited*: Paris Exp., 1938; MMA. Contributor to: art and crafts magazines.

DAVENPORT, JANE (Mrs. Jane Davenport de Tomasi)
  —Painter, S., T., C., I.
  Laurel Hill Rd., Cold Spring Harbor, L.I., N.Y.

B. Cambridge, Mass., Sept. 11, 1897. *Studied*: Univ. Chicago; ASL; Grande Chaumiere, Paris. I., "Scrimshaw" Folk Art of the Whales. *Position*: Instr., West Side Sch., New York; Private Classes, Asst., Whaling Mus., Cold Spring Harbor, N.Y., at present.

DAVEY, RANDALL—Painter, Et., Lith., E.
  Canyon Rd., Santa Fé, N.M.

B. East Orange, N.J., May 24, 1887. *Studied*: Cornell Univ.; in Europe; & with Robert Henri. *Member*: NA; Nat. Assn. Port. P.; Taos SA; New Mexico SA. *Awards*: prizes, NAD, 1915, 1938, 1939; Grand Central AA, 1939. *Work*: AIC; CGA; WMAA; Montclair A. Mus.; Kansas City AI; CMA; Detroit Inst. A.; U.S. Navy Dept.; USPO, Vinita, Claremore, Okla.; Will Roger's Shrine, Colorado Springs, Colo. *Exhibited*: Extensively in U.S. & Europe.*

DAVID, LORENE—Painter, E., Gr., L.
  650 College St.; h. 5670 Hooks Ave., Beaumont, Tex.

B. Independence, Mo., May 31, 1897. *Studied*: T. Col., Columbia Univ., M.A., with Charles Martin, Arthur Young; ASL, with Robert Laurent; & with Eliot O'Hara; Kansas City AI; Int. Sch. A., and with George Ennis. *Member*: NAWA; SSAL; New Orleans AA; Pr. M.Gld.; Western AA; Southern Pr.M.; Tex. FA Assn. *Awards*: prizes, NAWA, 1936; New Orleans AA, 1939, 1943; Southern Pr.M., 1940; Texas Pr. Exh., 1941, 1942. *Work*: Southern Louisiana Inst.; Pennsylvania Elem. Sch., Beaumont, Tex.; Dallas Mus. FA; Tex. Tech. Inst.; Southern Methodist Univ.; Mus. New Mexico; State T. Col., Huntsville, Tex. *Exhibited*: AWCS, 1936-1938; CAA, 1936; NAWA, 1936-1939, 1942, 1943; Oakland A. Gal., 1936; Denver A. Mus., 1936, 1938; PAFA, 1936, 1937; Phila. Pr. Cl., 1942, 1943; Northwest Pr.M., 1942, 1943; MMA, 1943; NAD, 1943; Lib.Cong., 1943, 1945; SSAL, 1936-1952; Nelson-Atkinson Mus., 1937, 1938, 1941, 1942; Dallas Mus. FA, 1937; Southern Pr.M., 1937, 1941; Wash. WC Cl., 1937-1939; Delgado Mus. A., 1940 (one-man); Mus. FA of Houston, 1937-1939, 1948; Texas General, 1940; Pr. M. Gld., 1941-1951. *Position*: Supv. A. Edu., Beaumont City Sch., Tex. 1944- .

DAVIDSON, BERNICE—Museum Curator
  Rhode Island School of Design Museum of Art, 224 Benefit St., Providence, R.I.

Position: Chief Cur., Rhode Island Sch. Des. Museum of Art.*

DAVIDSON, LILLIAN MARGARET (Mrs. Frank B.)—
  Painter
  Box 147, Highland Shores, Ellenton, Fla.

B. Canton, Ohio, 1896. *Studied*: John Herron AI; ASL; Chester Springs, Pa., and with George Jo Mess, Edwin Fulwider, Aahron Bohrod, Charles Burchfield, Paul Chidlaw, Edmund Brucker. *Member*: Indiana A. Cl.; Brown County A. Gal. Assn.; Bradenton AA; Sarasota AA; NAWA. *Awards*: prizes, Whitney McGuire purchase prize, Richmond; Lucretia Carr prize, Richmond; Indianapolis, Ind.; Tri Kappa prize, Richmond; Ft. Wayne, Ind. *Exhibited*: Champaign, Decatur, Bloomington, Ill.; throughout state of Indiana; Phila., York, Pa.; Miami, Fla.; Athens & Oxford, Ohio; NAD; Univ. Indiana, Ohio and Miami; Culver Military Acad.

DAVIDSON, MARSHALL BOWMAN—
  Editor of Publications, W., L.
  Metropolitan Museum of Art, Fifth Ave. at 82nd St.; h. 308 East 79th St., New York 21, N.Y.

B. New York, N.Y., April 26, 1907. *Studied*: Princeton Univ., B.S. *Awards*: Carey-Thomas award for creative publishing ("Life in America," 1951). *Work*: MMA. Contributor to art magazines and MMA Bulletin. Lectures: American Decorative, Graphic and Fine Arts. Author: "Life in America," 1951. *Position*: Asst. Cur., 1935-41, Assoc. Cur., 1941-47, Am. Wing.; Ed. Publications, 1947- , MMA, New York, N.Y.

DAVIDSON, MORRIS—Painter, W., L., T.
  65 West 56th St., New York 19, N.Y.; h. 7 Orchard Terrace, Piermont, N.Y.

B. Rochester, N.Y., Dec. 16, 1898. *Studied*: AIC, and in Paris. *Member*: Fed. Mod. P. & S.; Provincetown AA. *Work*: BMA. *Exhibited*: one-man: San Diego Mus. A.; BMA; Passedoit Gal., and many others in New York. Author: "Understanding Modern Art," 1931; "Painting for Pleasure," 1938; "An Approach to Modern Painting," 1948. L., PMA; Carnegie Inst.; New Sch. Soc. Research. *Position*: A. Consultant, Schenectady Pub. Sch.; Dir., Morris Davidson Sch. Modern Painting, New York and Provincetown, 1935- .

DAVIDSON, ROBERT—Sculptor, E.
  Skidmore College, Saratoga Springs, N.Y.; h. Rock City Falls, N.Y.

B. Indianapolis, Ind., May 13, 1904. *Studied*: John Herron AI; AIC; Sch. Am. Sculpture, N.Y., and in Germany. *Member*: Portfolio Cl., Indianapolis. *Work*: John Herron AI; Skidmore Col.; Minneapolis Inst. A.; Munson-Williams-Proctor Inst.; war mem., Schenectady, N.Y.; bronze port. head, Administration Bldg., Saratoga Spa, N.Y. *Exhibited*: WMAA, 1944; AIC, 1934; PAFA, 1937; John Herron AI, 1928-1950; SFMA, 1928; Albany Inst. Hist. & Art, 1953; Syracuse Mus. FA, 1953; Munson-Williams-Proctor Inst., 1954, 1955; Skidmore Col., 1955; Union Col., Schenectady, 1955 (one-man), and abroad. *Position*: Asst. Prof. FA, Skidmore Col., Saratoga Springs, N.Y., 1933-1956.*

DAVIES, ELTON MORROW—Painter, Gr., T.
  1715 La Loma Ave., Berkeley 9, Cal.

B. Poughkeepsie, N.Y., July 14, 1907. *Studied*: Columbia Univ., B.A.; Univ. Southern Cal., M.F.A., and with Francis de Erdely, Rico Le Brun. *Member*: Am. Soc. for Aesthetics; Cal. WC Soc.; CAA. *Exhibited*: Cal. PLH; SAGA; Oakland A. Gal., annually; Cal. State Fair, 1951; Cal. WC Soc., annually.*

DAVIES, KEN(NETH) (SOUTHWORTH)—
  Painter, Comm. A., I.
  376 Valley Brook Rd., Orange, Conn.

B. New Bedford, Mass., Dec. 20, 1925. *Studied*: Mass. Sch. A.; Yale Sch. FA, B.F.A. *Member*: Silvermine Gld. A.; Conn. Acad. FA. *Awards*: Tiffany Scholarship, 1950; Springfield Mus. A. purchase award. *Work*: Wadsworth Atheneum; Springfield Mus. A.; Univ. Nebraska; Detroit Inst. A. *Exhibited*: London, England, 1950; Carnegie Inst., 1952; PAFA, 1950; NAD, 1950; Univ. Illinois, 1951, 1952; WMA, 1952; Univ. Nebraska, 1953; Detroit Inst. A., 1952; WMAA, 1952, 1953; Toledo Mus. A., 1953; Conn. Acad. FA; Silvermine Gld. A.; New York, N.Y., 1951 (one-man). Contributor advertising illus., to Life, Time, Fortune, Sat. Eve. Post, Look, Collier's, and other national magazines; covers for Fortune, Collier's, Family Circle. *Position*: Instr., Paier Sch.A., New Haven, Conn.

DAVIS, ALICE—Educator, P.
  Iowa State College; h. 810 Gaskill Drive, Ames, Iowa

B. Iowa City, Iowa, Apr. 1, 1905. *Studied*: Univ. Iowa, B.A., M.A.; NAD. *Member*: CAA; Mid-West Col. Art Assn. *Exhibited*: Kansas City AI; Joslyn A. Mus. *Position*: Prof. A., Hd. Dept., Lindenwood Col., St. Charles, Mo., 1945-47; Asst. Prof. A., Grinnell Col., Grinnell, Iowa, 1947-51; Asst. Prof. App. A., Iowa State Col., Ames, Iowa, 1951- .

DAVIS, EDWARD MORRIS, III—*Museum Director*

The Valentine Museum, 1015 East Clay St., Richmond 19, Va.

B. Wyncote, Pa., Mar. 7, 1904. *Studied*: Univ. Virginia, B.S. in Arch. *Member*: Scarab Cl. *Exhibited*: VMFA, 1941. Contributor to: Virginia Magazine of History; American Collector. *Position*: Asst. Cur., CAD, New York, N.Y., 1933-34; Cur., Decorative A., VMFA, Richmond, Va., 1935-46; Dir., Norfolk Mus. A., 1946-49; Cur. Navy Dept., Dir., Truxton-Decatur Naval Mus., Washington, D.C., 1949-1953; Dir., Valentine Mus., Richmond, Va.

DAVIS, ELISABETH LOGAN (Mrs. Chester M.)—
Painter, W., L.

552 Union St., Rahway, N.J.

B. Shelbyville, Ky., April 22, 1886. *Studied*: AIC, and with Ivanowski, Margery Ryerson. *Member*: AAPL; N.J. Art Council. *Awards*: prizes, N.J. Woman's Cl., 1945, 1955; Rahway Woman's Cl., 1945; AAPL, 1951. *Exhibited*: Southern Vermont A., 1935-1954; East Orange A. Cl., 1945; Spring Lake Exh., 1945; Morton Gal., 1946; Waldorf-Astoria Hotel, 1952; Montclair, N.J., 1951; State Mus., Trenton, N.J.; ports. of Mothers of the Year, for past 10 yrs., exhibited as a collection at the Waldorf-Astoria Hotel, New York, N.Y.; Author: "Mothers of America," "Fathers of America," 1958. *Position*: Dir., Rahway (N.J.) A. Center.

DAVIS, ELIZABETH UPHAM (Mrs. Carl H.)—
Painter, E., L., C.

157 South Prospect Dr.; h. Coconut Grove 33, Fla. (Box 43)

B. Milwaukee, Wis., Aug. 19, 1890. *Studied*: Milwaukee-Downer Col., B.S.; and with Edward Thatcher, Jerry Farnsworth, Robert Brackman. *Member*: NAWA; AEA; Nat. Lg. Am. Pen Women. *Awards*: prizes, Miami A. Lg., 1952, 1954; Blue Dome, 1955; Miami Beach A. Center, 1957. *Work*: portrait commissions. *Exhibited*: NAWA, 1956, 1957; Florida A. Group; Fla. State Fed. A.; Delaware A. Center; Miami A. Lg.; Blue Dome Fellowship, Miami; One-man: Miami Beach A. Center, 1957; 2-man: Brooks Mem. A. Gal., 1951; Washington Gal., Miami Beach, 1950; Chapman Mem. Gal., Milwaukee-Downer Col., 1951; Studio Cl., Wilmington, Del., 1950. Lectures: Modern Concepts in the Ancient Art Traditions, to art groups and women's clubs. *Positions*: Prof. & Dir. A. Dept., Milwaukee-Downer Col., 1912-17; Co-Dir., Wilmington Acad. A., 1940-41; Fed. Bd. for Vocational Edu., Wash., D.C., 1917-19.

DAVIS, EMMA EARLENBAUGH (Mrs. William J.)—
Painter, I.

826 Waverly Rd., Bryn Mawr, Pa.

B. Altoona, Pa., Sept. 8, 1891. *Studied*: PMSchAI; PAFA; & with Wayman Adams, Maurice Molarsky, Beatrice Fenton. *Member*: Phila. A. All. *Exhibited*: PAFA; Phila. A. All. (one-man); Phila. Sketch Cl.; McClees Gal. (one-man); Eaglesmere, Pa. (one-man); Bryn Mawr A. Center; Bala-Cynwyd Cl. I., national magazines. Many portraits, including numerous sketches of patients, in Valley Forge General Hospital, Phoenixville, Pa., 1945-46.

DAVIS, EMMA LU—*Painter, S., T.*

6905½ Sepulveda Blvd., Van Nuys, Cal.

B. Indianapolis, Ind., Nov. 26, 1905. *Studied*: Vassar Col., A.B.; PAFA. *Member*: AEA. *Awards*: prize and traveling scholarship, PAFA, 1930; purchase award, Intl. Folk Art Mus., Santa Fe, N.M., 1958. *Work*: WMAA; MModA; IBM; Beloit Col.; reliefs, Social Security Bldg., Wash., D.C. *Exhibited*: PAFA, 1931, 1933; MModA, 1942; WMAA, 1951; Raleigh, 1950, 1952; Charlotte, 1950, 1951; Greensboro, 1952; Chapel Hill, 1949, 1950; Terry AI, 1952; Fla. Southern Col., 1952; Studio Gal., Taos, 1954; Harwood Fnd., Taos, 1955; New Mexico Annual, 1955; Mus. New Mexico, Santa Fé, 1955 (one-man); Studio Gal., 1955 (4-man); Canyon City, Colo., 1958 (one-man). *Position*: Judge, Canyon City (Colo.) Annual Exh., 1954, Colorado State Fair, A. Sect., 1956. Visiting Instr. S., Univ. North Carolina, 1949-53.

DAVIS, FAITH HOWARD—*Painter, S., T.*

89 Getzville Rd., Snyder 21, N.Y.

B. Chicago, Ill., July 29, 1915. *Studied*: Sarah Lawrence Col., A.B.; & with Peppino Mangravite, Bradley Tomlin,

Kurt Roesch. *Member*: The Patteran. *Awards*: prize, Buffalo, N.Y., 1946; James Carey Evans prize, Western N.Y. Exh., 1955. *Exhibited*: Albright A. Gal., 1939-1955; The Patteran, traveling exh. *Position*: Pres., Patteran Soc., 1954-55.*

DAVIS, GEORGE—*Cartoonist, I.*

106 Charles St., New York 14, N.Y.

B. Newark, N.J., Feb. 6, 1914. Contributor cartoons to Collier's, Sat. Eve. Post, Look, American, Cavalier, Kings Features, Today's Health, Medical Economics, True, Best Cartoons of 1955, 1956, Extension, Ladies Home Journal, McNaught Syndicate, Wall St. Journal, Boy's Life, Cosmopolitan, Argosy and other national magazines and European publications. *Position*: Medical & Scientific Illus., Medical Illustration Div., Veteran's Admin., 1950-52.

DAVIS, GERALD VIVIAN—*Painter, E.*

86 Elm St., Summit, N.J.

B. Brooklyn, N.Y., Sept. 8, 1899. *Studied*: Ecole des Beaux-Arts, Julian Acad., Paris, France. *Member*: Mid-Am. A.; Kansas Fed. A.; Prairie WC Soc.; Societe Nationale Independents; Assoc. A., New Jersey; Arch. Lg. *Exhibited*: London, England; Copenhagen, Denmark; Salon Nationale des Beaux-Arts, Paris, 1929-1939; Salon d'Automne, 1930-1939; Soc. Gr. A., London, England, 1938, 1939; NAD, 1941, 1946; AIC; AWS, 1941, 1942, 1946; All. A. Am., 1940, 1941; Montclair A. Mus., 1957, 1958 and prior; Riverside Mus.; Newark Mus. A., 1958 and prior; Princeton Univ.; Univ. Illinois; Nelson Gal. A.; Mulvane A. Mus.; one-man: Marquie Gal., 1941; Little Gal., Kansas City, 1952; Topeka A. Gld., 1952; Univ. Kansas; Arch. Lg., 1954. *Position*: Asst. Prof. A., Univ. Kansas, Lawrence, Kans., 1948-51.

DAVIS, GLADYS ROCKMORE—*Painter, W.*

1 West 67th St., New York, N.Y.

B. New York, N.Y., 1901. *Studied*: AIC, with John Norton. *Awards*: prizes, CGA, 1939; med., AIC, 1937; prizes, VMFA, 1938; PAFA, 1938, gold medal, 1952; NAD, 1944; gold medal, 1955; Pepsi-Cola, 1946. *Work*: MMA; PAFA; Swope A. Gal.; Nebraska AA; Toledo Mus. A.; Butler AI; Encyclopaedia Britannica Coll.; Cranbrook Acad. A.; Dayton AI; Nelson Gal. A.; Univ. Nebraska; BMA; DMFA; Univ. Arizona; Cranbrook Acad. A.; San Diego FA Soc.; Kent State Univ.; Miami Univ.; Atlanta Mus. A.; Davenport Mun. Mus.; Birmingham Mus. A. *Exhibited*: CGA; AIC; VMFA; PAFA; Pepsi-Cola, 1946; Swope A. Gal.; NAD; Nebraska AA; NAC; CAM; San Diego FA Soc.; Akron AI; Currier Gal. A.; American Embassy, Madrid, Spain, 1952. Author, I., "Pastel Painting," 1943.

DAVIS, HARRY ALLEN—*Painter, T.*

201 South Green St., Brownsburg, Ind.

B. Hillsboro, Ind., May 21, 1914. *Studied*: John Herron AI, B.F.A., with Donald Mattison, Hendrik Mayer; Acad. in Rome. *Member*: Indianapolis AA; Am. Acad. in Rome; Indiana A. Cl.; Grand Central A. Gal. *Awards*: Prix de Rome, 1938; F., Am. Acad. in Rome, 1941; prizes, John Herron AI, 1944, 1946, 1954; Hoosier Salon, 1948-1950, 1952, 1955; Indiana A. Cl., 1946-1949, 1952, 1953, 1955-1957; Bd. Dirs. prize, Indiana A., 1958; Indiana State Fair, 1957. *Work*: Hist. Properties Sect., Wash., D.C.; DePauw Univ.; Univ. Indiana; John Herron AI; Union City Lib.; murals, Am. Acad. in Rome; French Lick Springs Hotel. *Exhibited*: VMFA, 1937, 1940, 1946; Grand Central A. Gal., 1938; Beloit Col., 1941; John Herron AI, 1938-1955; Hoosier Salon, 1948-1955; Indiana A. Cl., 1948-1955; PAFA, 1950; NCFA, 1949; Old Northwest Territories Exh., 1947, 1950, 1954; Magnificent Mile, Chicago, 1955; Interior Valley, 1955; Michiana, 1955; Casein Painters, 1958; Art:USA, 1958. *Position*: Instr., A., Beloit Col., 1940-41; Combat A., 5th Army Hist. Sect., 1945-46; Instr. A., John Herron AI, Indianapolis, Ind., 1946- .

DAVIS, HELEN S.—*Sculptor*

Reed Studios, East Gloucester, Mass.

B. Philadelphia, Pa. *Studied*: PAFA; ASL; CUASch; & with Anshutz, Tefft, Brewster, Laurent. *Member*: Plastic Cl.; NAWA; North Shore AA; Gloucester SA; Catherine Lorillard Wolfe AC. *Awards*: prizes, CUASch. *Work*: Community House, Coral Gables, Fla.; San F., Cal.; Daytona Beach, Fla.; St. Petersburg A. Cl.; Fla. Fed. A. *Exhibited*: St. Petersburg, Fla., 1950-1952.

DAVIS, HUBERT—*Painter, Lith., Et., I., W.*
290 Sixth Ave., New York 14, N.Y.; s. R. D. #1, New Tripoli, Pa.

B. Milton, Pa., Mar. 15, 1902. *Studied*: PMSchIA; ASL; Julian Acad., Paris. *Member*: SAGA. *Awards*: prizes, PAFA, 1946 (purchase). *Work*: MMA; WMAA; PMA; PAFA; Columbus Gal. FA; Newark Pub. Lib.; LC. *Exhibited*: nationally and internationally. Books: Symbolic Drawings of Hubert Davis for An American Tragedy by Theodore Dreiser, 1930. Contributor to national and international publications.

DAVIS, JACK (C.)—*Painter, E.*
Hood College; h. 502 Valley St., Frederick, Md.

B. Sonora, Cal., Sept. 25, 1923. *Studied*: Univ. California, Berkeley, B.A., M.A.; and with Fernand Leger, Paris, France. *Member*: AAUP. *Exhibited*: SFMA, 1948, 1952, 1954, 1955; Denver A. Mus., 1948; Salon de Art Libre, Paris, 1950; Salon de Realites Nouvelles, Paris, 1950; Salon de Mai, Paris, 1951; U.S. Embassy, Paris, 1951. One-man: San Francisco area, 1949, 1952-1954; New York City, 1958. *Positions*: Instr. A., Cal. Sch. FA, San Francisco, 1951-54; Assoc. Prof. A., Hood College, Frederick, Md., 1955- .

DAVIS, JAMES EDWARD—*Film-Maker, S., P., E.*
30 Nassau St., Princeton, N.J.

B. Clarksburg, W. Va., June 4, 1901. *Studied*: Princeton Univ., A.B., and with Andre L'Hote, Paris. *Awards*: for films: "Light Reflections," Brussels, 1949; "Analogies No. 1," Am. Film Assembly, 1954; "Color Dances No. 1" and "Reflections No. 11," Salerno, Italy, 1954; Graham Fnd. F. grant, Chicago, 1957 for work in experimental films. *Work*: numerous experimental films including "Analogies No. 1," 1953 (on program "50 Annees de Cinema Americain," sent to Paris, 1955, by MMoDA); "Shadows and Light Reflections," 1948, circulated by MMoDA, and other films on John Marin and Frank Lloyd Wright; film "Evolution," 1956, in MMoDA film library; two films shown at Intl. Festival of Experimental Films, Brussels Fair, 1958; Still color photographs used by Steichen in lecture "Experimental Color Photography," MMoDA., 1957; plexiglas des. for terrace, Plaza Hotel, Cincinnati, Ohio; AGAA; Yale Univ.; MMoDA; Princeton Univ.; films: Kansas City Pub. Lib.; AGAA; U.S. State Dept., Wash., D.C. *Exhibited*: plastic sc., Walker A. Center, 1947; AGAA, 1949, 1954; Princeton Univ., 1949; Los A. Mus. A., 1950; SFMA, 1950; Phila., Pa., 1952; Univ. Iowa, 1952; paintings: MMoDA; 67 Gal., 1945 (one-man); Ferargil Gal., 1945 (one-man). Lectures: "Film as an Art Medium." *Position*: Instr., Lawrenceville Sch., 1933-36; Asst. Prof., Princeton Univ., Dept. A. & Archaeology, 1936-42.

DAVIS, JESSIE (FREEMONT) (SNOW)—
Painter, S., T.
4216 Travis St., Dallas 5, Tex.

B. Williamson County, Tex., Feb. 22, 1887. *Studied*: ASL, with George Bridgman, John Knott, Frank Reaugh. *Member*: SSAL; NAWA; Dallas AA; Dallas C. Gld. *Awards*: prizes, Dallas Mus. FA, 1948, 1949; San Antonio C. Gld., 1948; Oak Cliff Soc. FA, Dallas, Tex. *Work*: Dallas Mus. FA; Oak Cliff Gal.; Tech. H.S., Dallas; San Angelo (Tex.) Pub. Lib. *Exhibited*: NAWA, 1944; Mus. FA of Houston, 1945; Dallas All. A., 1943, 1946; SSAL, 1946. *Position*: Instr. A., Dallas (Tex.) Pub. Evening Sch.*

DAVIS, LEW E.—*Painter*
Rte. #2, Box 347, Scottsdale, Ariz.

B. Jerome, Ariz., Nov. 2, 1910. *Studied*: NAD. *Awards*: Tiffany F., 1931; prizes, Denver A. Mus., 1938, 1940; Cal. WC Soc., 1941; Pasadena AI, 1946; Hallmark, 1953; Arizona State Fair, 1955. *Work*: Newark Mus. A.; IBM; Pasadena AI; Mus. Northern Arizona; Encyclopaedia Britannica; Santa Barbara Mus. A.; Ariz. State Col.; murals, USPO, Los Banos, Cal.; Marlow, Okla.; State Capitol, Phoenix. *Exhibited*: NAD, 1932; WMAA, 1937, 1938, 1940, 1941; AIC, 1937, 1938, 1941; SFMA, 1938, 1940; VMFA, 1940; CM, 1939; Denver A. Mus., 1938-1940; Los A. Mus. A., 1938; Colorado Springs FA Center, 1938-1940 (one-man); Santa Barbara Mus. A., 1942 (one-man); Dallas Mus. FA, 1947. *Position*: Dir., Ariz. A. Fnd., Scottsdale, Ariz.; L., Arizona State Col., Tempe, Ariz.

DAVIS, MARGUERITE—*Illustrator, P.*
Mail: c/o New England Trust Co., 135 Devonshire St., Boston 7, Mass.

B. Quincy, Mass., Feb. 10, 1889. *Studied*: Vassar Col., A.B.; BMFA Sch.; & with William Paxton, Philip Hale, Gerry Peirce, Henry Hunt Clark. I., "Sugar and Spice"; "Trudy and the Tree House"; "Magical Melons"; & other juvenile books; Illus. for "Treasure Trails," The Children's Hour, Chicago, Ill., 1952- .

DAVIS, MARIAN B.—*Educator*
2517½ Harris Blvd., Austin 3, Tex.

B. St. Louis County, Mo., Sept. 24, 1911. *Studied*: Washington Univ., A.B., M.A.; Radcliffe Col., M.A., Ph.D. *Member*: CAA; Am. Assn. Univ. Prof.; Soc. Arch. Hist.; Renaissance Soc. Am. *Awards*: Carnegie scholarship, 1937; F., Radcliffe Col., 1939; Univ. Texas, 1951. *Position*: Asst. FA, Radcliffe Col., 1939-40; Instr., WMA, 1941-44; Asst. Prof. A., 1946-50, Assoc. Prof., 1950- , Univ. Texas, Austin, Tex.; Dir., CAA, 1951-55; Ed. Bd., College Art Journal, 1955- .

DAVIS, MATHILDE SCHAEFER.
See Schaefer, Mathilde

DAVIS, NELL—*Art Librarian*
Lauren Rogers Library & Art Museum, 5th Ave. at 7th St.; h. 2118 Fifth Ave., Laurel, Miss.

B. Laurel, Miss., Oct. 7, 1911. *Studied*: Southwestern Univ., Memphis, B.A.; Univ. of Illinois, B.S. in L.S. *Member*: Mississippi Lib. Assn. *Position*: Hd. Librn., Lauren Rogers Mus. A., Laurel, Miss.

DAVIS, RANICE (Mrs. Ranice W. V. Birch Davis)—
Medical Illustrator, E.
Johns Hopkins Medical School, 5613 Lothian Rd.; h. 876 Benninghaus Rd., Baltimore 2, Md.

B. Regina, Saskatchewan, Canada, Apr. 26, 1915. *Studied*: Connecticut Col., A.B.; Johns Hopkins Medical Sch., with Max Broedel; and with Robert Brackman. *Member*: Assn. Medical Illustrators; AAUP. Illus., medical textbooks. Contributor of: illus. for Medical Journals. *Position*: A. to Dr. N.J. Eastman, Johns Hopkins Hospital; Asst. Prof. & Dir., Dept. A. as applied to Medicine, Johns Hopkins Medical Sch., Baltimore, Md.

DAVIS, RICHARD ALLEN—*Museum Curator, Gr., T.*
Staten Island Institute of Arts & Sciences, 146 Stuyvesant Pl.; h. 559 Castleton Ave., Staten Island 1, N.Y.

B. Binghamton, N.Y., Apr. 15, 1923. *Studied*: Albion Col., A.B.; State Univ. Iowa, M.F.A.; Univ. Michigan, Postgrad., and with Mauricio Lasansky, Emil Weddige. *Awards*: prize, Michigan A., 1951. *Work*: Detroit Inst. A.; Albion Col.; Univ. Maine; Saginaw Mus. A. *Exhibited*: SAGA, 1950; BM, 1954; Arizona State Fair, 1949; Grand Rapids A. Gal., 1950; Michigan A., 1951; Albion Col., 1954 (one-man); Univ. Maine, 1955 (one-man); Mich. State Univ., 1956 (one-man); Wagner Col., Staten Island, 1958 (one-man). Lectures: Modern Painting; Origin of the Graphic Arts, to club groups and art societies. Prepared exhibition and catalogs: "Illustrated Books of the 20th Century," 1958; "Oriental Art from the John M. Crawford, Jr., Collection," 1957-58; "The Prints of Yasuo Kuniyoshi," complete graphic work, catalog, in prep. *Positions*: Dir., Saginaw Mus. A., Saginaw, Mich., 1953-56; Cur. A., The Staten Island Mus. A. & Sciences, 1956- .

DAVIS, RICHARD S.—*Museum Director*
Minneapolis Institute of Arts, 201 East 24th St., Minneapolis 4, Minn.
Position: Dir., Minneapolis Institute of Arts.*

DAVIS, ROBERT ALLEN—*Painter, I., Gr., C., E., L.*
Ridgecroft, Tarrytown, N.Y.

B. Chicago, Ill., Jan. 1, 1912. *Studied*: ASL; & with George Bridgman, Robert Brackman. *Member*: SI; SC; A.Gld.; Hudson Valley AA. *Exhibited*: SI, annually; Hamilton, Ontario, Canada, 1946 (one-man); SI; SC; Hudson Valley AA. Lectures: Anatomy; Composition; Color. *Position*: Instr., Fashion Acad., New York, N.Y., 1940-42, 1945-46; Instr., Marymount Col., Tarrytown, N.Y., 1946- ; Marymount Col., New York, N.Y., 1949- .*

DAVIS, ROBERT TYLER—*Educator*
5791 Southwest 62nd Terr., Miami 43, Fla.

B. Los Angeles, Cal., Aug. 11, 1904. *Studied*: Univ. California at Los Angeles; Harvard Col., A.B.; Harvard Univ., M.A. *Member*: AAMus.; CAA. *Positions*: Instr. A., Univ. Rochester, 1929-33; Dir. Edu., Albright A. Gal., 1934-39; Dir. Portland (Ore.) Mus. A., 1939-47; Dir., Montreal Mus. FA, Montreal, Canada, 1947-52; Prof. FA, McGill Univ., Montreal, 1947-52; Interim Dir., Lowe Gal., Univ. Miami, Coral Gables, Fla., 1955-56; Dir., Vizcaya-Dade County A. Mus., Miami, Fla., 1953-1957. Teaching 19th and 20th Century European Art, Honors Course in Humanities.

DAVIS, STUART—*Painter, Gr., W., L.*
15 West 67th St., New York 23, N.Y.

B. Philadelphia, Pa., Dec. 7, 1894. *Studied*: Henri Sch. A. *Member*: Nat. Inst. A. & Let. *Awards*: prizes, Carnegie Inst., 1944; PAFA, 1945; AIC, 1951; Guggenheim F., 1952-53; first prize, Nat. Comp. for mural, Conference Room, Gen. Assembly Bldg., United Nations, 1955. *Work*: WMAA; MMoDA; MMA; Guggenheim Mus. A.; PAFA; Washington Univ.; PMG., etc.; murals, Heinz Research Center, Pittsburgh, Pa., 1957; Radio City Music Hall; Radio Station, WNYC; Indiana Univ.; Drake Univ.; Des Moines. *Exhibited*: nationally; retrospective exh., MMoDA, 1945-46; retrospective exh., WMAA, 1957; one-man: Venice Biennale, 1952. Contributor to art magazines.

DAVIS, WILLIAM STEEPLE—*Painter, Gr.*
King St., Orient, L.I., N.Y.

B. Orient, N.Y., May 7, 1884. *Member*: AAPL; NAC; Photog. Soc. Am. *Work*: U.S. Naval Acad. Mus.; Toledo Mus. A.; Los A. Mus. A.; CMA; Parrish Mus. A.; Hiram Col., Ohio; LC; Denison Univ. *Exhibited*: Oyster Ponds Hist. Soc., Orient, N.Y., 1954 (one-man); Parrish A. Mus., Southampton, N.Y., 1954; AAPL, 1954; Royal Inst., London, England, 1953, 1955; NAC, 1957 (one-man), and nationally.

DAVISON, AUSTIN L.—*Decorative Designer, I., T.*
Windy Moor, Stockton, N.J.

B. Center Bridge, New Hope, Pa. *Studied*: State T. Col., Edinboro, Pa. *Work*: Index of Am. Design, NGA; Tech. Illus. for RCA Victor; Longines-Wittnauer Watch Co.; Johns Hopkins Univ.; mural, Atwater Kent Mus., Phila., Pa. Work reproduced in following publications: Index of American Design; Pennsylvania German Folk Art; Folk Art of Rural Pennsylvania; Decorative Arts of Victoria's Era; Pennsylvania German Art, and other books. *Position*: Instr., New Orleans Acad. Adv. A.; Instr., private studio at present.*

DAVY, JAMES BENJAMIN—*Etcher, S., P.*
1226 Ortega St., San Francisco 22, Cal.

B. San Francisco, Cal., Feb. 25, 1913. *Studied*: Rudolph Schaeffer Sch. Des. *Exhibited*: GGE, 1939; San F. AA, 1941, 1942, 1945; Oakland A. Gal., 1943, 1944; Lib. Cong., 1943.

DAWES, DEXTER B.—*Painter*
221 Lydecker St., Englewood, N.J.

B. Englewood, N.J., June 15, 1872. *Studied*: ASL. *Member*: Ridgewood AA; Bergen County A. Gld.; NAC; Ogunquit AA. *Awards*: prizes, Newark AC; Fitzwilliam, N.H., 1939; Montclair A. Mus., 1933.*

DAWSON, BESS PHIPPS—*Painter*
Summit, Miss.

B. Tchula, Miss., Nov. 25, 1916. *Studied*: Belhaven Col., Jackson, Miss., and with Ralph Hudson, Karl Zerbe, Fred Conway, Lamar Dodd, Stuart Purser and others. *Member*: New Orleans AA; Mississippi AA; Allison's A. Colony, Way, Miss. *Awards*: prizes, Allison's A. Colony, 1953-1958; Mississippi AA, 1957. *Work*: murals, Church of God, McComb, Miss.; Progressive Bank Bldg., Summit, Miss. *Exhibited*: Mississippi AA, 1954, 1956-1958; McComb, Miss., 1953 (3-man); Southwest Miss. Jr. Col., 1954; Mississippi State Col. for Women, 1955; Allison's Wells, Way, Miss., 1955; 331 Gallery, New Orleans, 1957; Art Commission Gal., Baton Rouge, 1958; New Orleans

AA, 1955, 1957, 1958; Southeastern annual, Atlanta, Ga., 1956. Lectures: Contemporary Art. *Position*: Bd. Dirs., Allison's A. Colony, Way, Miss., 1953- .

DAY, CHON (CHAUNCEY ADDISON)—*Cartoonist*
22 Cross St., Westerly, R.I.

B. Chatham, N.J., Apr. 6, 1907. *Studied*: ASL, with Boardman Robinson, John Sloan. *Member*: Nat. Cartoonists Soc. *Awards*: Best Gag Cartoonist of 1956, Nat. Cartoonists Soc. *Exhibited*: MMA, 1942; PAFA. Author, I., "I Could Be Dreaming," 1945; "What Price Dory," 1955; "Brother Sebastian," 1957. Contributor cartoons to New Yorker, Sat. Eve. Post, Look, Collier's, This Week, Sports Illustrated.

DAY, HORACE TALMAGE—*Painter, E.*
306 Sherwood Ave., Staunton, Va.

B. Amoy, China, July 3, 1909. *Studied*: ASL; Tiffany Fnd. *Work*: VMFA; AGAA; Yale Univ. A. Gal.; Canajoharie A. Gal.; King Col., Bristol, Va.; Nelson Gal. A.; Fleming Mus. A., Burlington, Vt.; Univ. of Virginia; Longwood College, Va.; mural, USPO, Clinton, Tenn.; Western State Hospital, Staunton, Va. *Exhibited*: WMAA, 1944, 1945; Carnegie Inst., 1941; Pepsi-Cola, 1943; VMFA, 1942-1944, 1949 (one-man); 1954; Macbeth Gal. (one-man); Gibbes Mus. A., 1954; Telfair Acad., 1954; Memphis Acad. A., 1954; Bodley Gal., N.Y., 1958 (one-man). Work reproduced in "Art in the Armed Forces," 1944; folio of drawings, "Staunton in the Valley of Virginia," publ. *Position*: Dir., Herbert Inst. A., Augusta, Ga., 1936-41; Prof. A., Mary Baldwin Col., Staunton, Va., 1941- .

DAY, LAURENCE JAMES (LARRY)—*Painter, Gr., T.*
301 West Johnson St., Philadelphia, Pa.; h. 310 Myrtle Ave., Cheltenham, Pa.

B. Philadelphia, Pa., Oct. 29, 1921. *Studied*: Tyler Sch. FA of Temple Univ. *Member*: AEA. *Work*: PMA. *Exhibited*: PAFA; Phila. A. All.; Phila. Pr. Cl.; PMA; Stanford Univ.; Pa. State Univ.; Dubin Gal., Phila.; Parma Gal., N.Y. *Position*: Instr., P. & Drawing, Phila. Mus. Sch. A.; Public School System, 1951, 1953.

DAY, MARTHA B. WILLSON—*Painter, Miniaturist*
88 Congdon St., Providence 6, R.I.

B. Providence, R.I., Aug. 16, 1885. *Studied*: R.I.Sch.Des.; Julian Acad., Paris; & with Lucia F. Fuller. *Member*: Providence AC; ASMP; Pa. Soc. Min. P. *Award*: prize, PAFA, 1932. *Work*: PMA. *Exhibited*: ASMP, annually; Pa. Min. Soc. P., annually. Lectures: Miniatures.

DAY, ROBERT JAMES—*Cartoonist*
11 Cornwell St., Rockville Centre, N.Y.

B. San Bernardino, Cal., Sept. 25, 1900. *Studied*: Los Angeles County AI. *Exhibited*: Many cartoon exhibitions throughout U.S. and in Europe. Author, I., "All Out for the Sack Race," 1945 (book of Cartoons); Illus., "We Shook the Family Tree," 1946; Reader's Digest "Fun Fare," 1949; Arthur Godfrey's "Stories I Like to Tell," 1952; "Little Willie," 1953; "Any Old Place With You," 1957; "Seen Any Good Movies Lately?," 1958. Contributor to New Yorker, This Week, Sat. Eve. Post, Sports Illustrated.

DAY, WORDEN (Miss)—*Painter, Gr.*
209 West Mt. Ida St., Alexandria, Va.

B. Columbus, Ohio, June 11, 1916. *Studied*: Randolph-Macon Col., B.A.; ASL, and with Maurice Sterne, Vaclav Vytlacil, Stanley William Hayter, and others. *Member*: SAGA; 14 Painters-Pr. M. *Awards*: Traveling F., VMFA, 1940-42; Rosenwald F., 1942-44; Guggenheim F., 1952-53; prizes, VMFA, 1943; Norfolk Mus. A., 1944; CAM, 1948; BM, 1949, 1950. *Work*: VMFA; NGA; MMoDA; Univ. of Minnesota; Mills Col.; Albion Col.; Bradley Univ.; Brooks Mem. Gal.; LC; MMoDA; CAM; Yale Univ.; BM; PMA; Univ. Louisville; MMA; BMA; Carnegie Inst.; N.Y. Pub. Lib. Sao Paulo Mus. Mod. A. *Exhibited*: Phila. A. All., 1937; VMFA, 1942, 1944; Perls Gal., 1940; WMAA, 1941, 1948, 1952; LC, 1945, 1950; PMG, 1944; AIC, 1946-1948, 1951; SFMA, 1946; CAM, 1946, 1951; Bertha Schaefer Gal., 1947, 1948, 1951; BM, 1948-1952; AFA, 1948-1952; MMoDA, 1951; MMA, 1950; Univ. Illinois, 1950; SAM, 1949, 1950; Clearwater Mus. A., 1951-52; Carnegie Inst.;

Stable Gal.; Kraushaar Gal.; Zabriskie Gal. traveling exh. nat. & intl.; Paris Exp., 1951-52, and other national and international shows. One-man: Perls Gal., 1940; VMFA, 1940; Bertha Schaefer Gal., 1948, 1951; Smithsonian Inst., 1951; Phila. A. All., 1954; Norfolk Mus. A.; Ohio Univ., Athens; Chautauqua AA. *Position*: Asst. Prof. Gr. A., Univ. Wyoming, Laramie, Wyo., 1949-51; Instr., PIA Sch., Brooklyn, N.Y. Lectures: "New Expressions in Printmaking," at Catholic Univ., Wash., D.C., and Randolph-Macon Univ.

DEACHMAN, NELLY *(Mrs. William J. Kerr)*—
Painter, L., W.
   1743 East 71st St.; h. 2454 East 74th St., Chicago 49, Ill.

B. Prescott, Ark., Aug. 13, 1895. *Studied*: Arkansas State T. Col.; Univ. Chicago; AIC, B.A., M.F.A. *Member*: All-Illinois Soc. FA; Nat. Lg. Am. Pen Women; AIC Alumni Assn.; AAPL. *Awards*: prizes, Nat. Lg. Am. Pen Women, 1950, 1951, 1954, 1955, 1956-1958; Ill. Fed. Music Cl. 1955. *Work*: Capitol Bldg., Little Rock, Ark.; State T. Col., Conway, Ark.; Hendrix Col.; KFPW Gal., Ft. Smith, Ark. *Exhibited*: Arkansas Mus. FA, 1942, 1943; All-Illinois Soc. FA; Nat. Lg. Am. Pen Women, 1949-1951, 1954, 1955; NGA; AIC; Mandel Bros. Gal., 1950; Findlay Gal., 1948, 1949; CAM; Quincy (Ill.) Mus. A.; Cordon Cl., Chicago, 1954 (one-man); Catherine L. Wolfe A. Cl., 1954; AAPL, 1957; Ill. State Fair, 1956-1958. *Position*: Instr. A., Elmhurst (Ill.) A. Lg., 1949-1952.

DEAK-EBNER, ILONA (ILONA E. ELLINGER)—
Educator, P., L.
   Trinity College, Michigan Ave., N.E.; h. 2800 Woodley Rd., N.W., Washington 8, D.C.

B. Budapest, Hungary, June 12, 1913. *Studied*: Royal Hungarian Univ. Sch. A., M.F.A.; Royal Swedish A. Acad.; Johns Hopkins Univ., Ph.D., with David M. Robinson, W. F. Albright; Univ. Freiburg, Germany. *Member*: Soc. Wash. A.; Archaeological Inst. Am. *Exhibited*: PAFA, 1942; Whyte Gal., 1944 (one-man); Soc. Wash. A.; Am.-British A. Center, George Washington Univ., 1950 (one-man); Silver Spring A. Gal, 1951; CGA, 1958. *Position*: Prof., Hd. A. Dept., Trinity Col., Washington, D.C., 1943- .

DEAN, ABNER—*Cartoonist, I.*
   320 East 57th St., New York 22, N.Y.

B. New York, N.Y., Mar. 18, 1910. *Studied*: NAD; Dartmouth Col., A.B. *Member*: Nat. Cartoonists Soc.; SI. Author, I., "It's a Long Way to Heaven," 1945; "What Am I Doing Here?," 1947; "And on the Eighth Day," 1949; "Come As You Are," 1952; "Cave Drawings for the Future," 1954; light verse & cartoons: "Wake Me When It's Over," 1955; "Not Far from the Jungle," 1956. *Position*: Illustrator for magazines, newspapers and advertising.

de ANGELI, MARGUERITE LOFFT—*Illustrator, W.*
   1227 Panama St., Philadelphia 7, Pa.

B. Lapeer, Mich., Mar. 14, 1889. *Member*: Phila. A. All.; Pa. Hist. Soc. *Awards*: Newbery medal, 1950; Citation for "Bright April," both from Am. Lib. Assn.; Citation for "Yonie Wondernose," from Assn. for Childhood Edu.

DE BAUN, ETTA V.—*Painter*
   45 East Main St., Ramsey, N.J.

B. Kripplebush, N.Y., May 17, 1902. *Studied*: with George Elmer Browne. *Member*: AAPL; Ridgewood AA; Provincetown AA. *Award*: prize, Ridgewood AA, 1945, 1949. *Exhibited*: NAD, 1941, 1943, 1944; All.A.Am., 1940-1946; N.J. State Mus., 1938-1946; N.Y. State Exh., 1940, 1944; N.J. P.&S. Soc., 1945; Ridgewood AA, 1938-1946; Provincetown AA, 1945.*

de BORHEGYI, STEPHAN—*Museum Director, E.*
   Stovall Museum, University of Oklahoma; h. 517 South Lahoma St., Norman, Okla.

B. Budapest, Hungary, Oct. 17, 1921. *Studied*: Peter Pazmany Univ., Budapest, Ph.D.; Yale Univ., Post doctoral research F. *Member*: Am. Anthropological Assn.; Soc. for Am. Archaeology; AAMus.; Spanish Colonial Arts Soc.; Royal Anthropological Soc. of Great Britain and Ireland

(F.); Oklahoma Anthropological Soc.; Mountain Plains Mus. Assns.; Oklahoma Acad. Science, and many others. *Awards*: Diploma of Merit by the Guatemalan Govt. for reorganization of the Guatemalan National Museum, 1951. Articles contributed: "Installation of Archaeological and Ethnological Material in the Guatemalan National Museum" in "Museum," a quarterly publ. by UNESCO, 1954; "American University Museums," Museums Journal, 1956; "The Spanish Colonial Art Museum of Guatemala," "Museum," 1956; "The Public Relations Function in American Colleges and University Museums," The Museologist, 1956; "Aqualung Archaeology," Natural History Magazine, 1958, and others. Lectures: Pre-Columbian Art; Folk Art; Maya Art and Architecture. Arranged exhibitions: Cyprus Exhibit, Hungarian Nat. Mus., 1947; Maya Art & Archaeology Exh., Guatemalan Nat. Mus., 1950; Spanish Colonial Art, Colonial Art Mus., Guatemala, 1951; American Handicrafts (U.S. State Dept.), Guatemala City, 1950; Primitive Art, Univ. Oklahoma, 1957; African Art, Univ. Oklahoma, 1957, etc. *Positions*: Asst. Cur., Hungarian Nat. Mus. of Science & History, 1947-48; Prof. Anthropology, San Carlos Univ., Guatemala, 1949-51; Dir., Stovall Mus., Univ. Oklahoma, Norman, Okla., 1954- ; Asst. Prof. Anthropology, Univ. Oklahoma, 1954- .

deBRUYN, ERICH C.—
Commercial Artist, Des., T., P.
   205 Blumenthal Bldg., Pioneer Plaza; h. 3807 Waymore St., El Paso, Tex.

B. Dusseldorf, Germany, Aug. 24, 1911. *Studied*: Carnegie Tech; Texas Western Col.; Famous Artists, and with Eliot O'Hara. *Exhibited*: N.Y. State Exh.; Assoc. A. Syracuse; Carlsbad (N.M.) Mus.; New Mexico State Exh.; Texas Western Col.; Del Norte Exh., Sun Carnival, Texas Western Col. Contributor to Life; Better Homes & Gardens; Western magazines, newspapers, trade publications. *Position*: Owner-Dir., deBruyn Adv., El Paso, Tex.

de CAMP, HAROLD SYDNEY—*Painter, C.*
   686 Westfield Ave., Westfield, N.J.

B. Philadelphia, Pa., Feb. 27, 1903. *Studied*: with Molly W. Hand, Leslie Crump, Ada Budell, Hortense Budell. *Member*: AAPL; Westfield AA; Plainfield AA. *Exhibited*: Newark AC; Newark Mus.; Westfield AA; Plainfield AA; Spring Lake Exh.

de CARMEL, ANNE (GUTMAN)—*Craftsman*
   51 East 65th St., New York 21, N.Y.

B. Vienna, Austria, Jan. 26, 1902. *Studied*: in Europe. *Member*: Artist-Craftsmen of New York. *Awards*: prizes, N.Y. Soc. Craftsmen, 1940; N.Y. Soc. Ceramic A., 1946. *Work*: Cooper Union Mus. *Exhibited*: Syracuse Mus. FA, Nat. Ceramic Exh., 1947-1950; Artist-Craftsmen of N.Y., annually.

deCELLE, EDMOND CARL—*Painter, Des.*
   1006 Dauphin St.; h. 2008 Old Shell Rd., Mobile, Ala.

B. New York, N.Y., Sept. 26, 1889. *Studied*: with A. S. Hartrick, Reginald Savage, Walter Bayes, in London, England. *Member*: SSAL; Mobile All.A.Gld.; Gulf AA; New Orleans AA; Alabama A. Lg.; Mobile Opera Gld.; Pub. Schs. A. Council; Un. Scenic A. of Am.; Mobile AA. *Awards*: gold palette, Mobile WC Soc. *Work*: Brighton Mus. A., England; Montgomery (Ala.) Mus. FA; Dept. Interior, Wash., D.C.; Mobile Pub. Lib.; murals, Murphy H.S., Mobile; Mobile Mus. FA; many churches & libraries, England. *Exhibited*: Soc. Indp. A., 1917; A.All., 1918; Delgado Mus. A., 1921; Salons of Am., 1922; SSAL, 1923; Biloxi City A. Gal., 1930; Montgomery Mus. FA, 1929; Witte Mem. Mus., 1929; Birmingham Pub. Lib., 1929; Telfair Acad., 1931; CGA, 1934; Nat. Exh. Am. A., 1936-1938; Salon du Printemps, Paris; Royal Acad. & New English A. Cl., England.

DE CESARE, SAM—*Painter, S., C., T.*
   9-05 150th St., Whitestone 57, N.Y.

B. New York, N.Y., May 31, 1920. *Studied*: New York Univ., B.S. in Ed., M.A. in Admin.; and with Ruth Canfield, Oliver Connor Barrett. *Member*: Indst. Arts, N.Y. (Chm.); Assn. Supv. & Administrators. *Awards*: Soc. of Four Arts, Palm Beach, 1944; Springfield Mus. A., 1945 (purchase). *Work*: Springfield (Mo.) Mus. A. *Exhibited*: Springfield Mus. A., 1945; Conn. Acad. FA, 1945; All. A.

Am., 1947, 1948; Audubon A., 1952; Soc. Four Arts, 1944; Pan-American Gal., N.Y., 1946; YMHA, N.Y., 1947, 1948; Laurel Gal., N.Y., 1949; ACA Gal., N.Y., 1949-1951; one-man: Panoras Gal., N.Y., 1944, 1952, 1959. Co-Author technical manuals for USNR, 1942-45; General Crafts Course of Study, N.Y. Bd. Edu., 1948. Lectures on Sculpture; Art Appreciation. *Positions*: Instr., A. & Crafts, New York Secondary Schools; Tech. Advisor (Des.), Yorkville Housing Comm., N.Y., 1956-57; Memb. Comm. on Indst. Arts, Bd. Edu., N.Y., 1957-58.

DECKER, RICHARD—*Illustrator, Cart.*
Lockwood Rd., Route 1, Riverside, Conn.

B. Philadelphia, Pa., May 6, 1907. *Studied*: PMSchIA. Contributor to New Yorker magazine, illus., "How to Lay a Nest Egg."*

de COUX, JANET—*Sculptor*
Gibsonia, Pa.

B. Niles, Mich. *Studied*: Carnegie Inst.; N.Y. Sch. Indst. Des.; R.I.Sch. Des.; AIC, with C. P. Jennewein, A. B. Cianfarani, Alvin Meyer, James Earl Fraser. *Member*: ANA; NSS; Pittsburgh Assoc. A. *Awards*: Guggenheim F., 1938-39, 1939-40; Widener med., 1942; Carnegie award, Pittsburgh; prize, NSS; Am. Acad. A. & Let. grant. *Work*: Col. of New Rochelle; Soc. Medalists; USPO, Girard, Pa.; St. Mary's Church, Manhasset, N.Y.; Sacred Heart Sch., Pittsburgh; Liturgical A. Soc.; St. Vincent's, Latrobe, Pa.; St. Scholastica, Aspinwall, Pa.; Crucifixion Group, Lafayette, N.J.; doors, St. Ann, Palo Alto, Cal.; altar, St. Margaret's Hospital Chapel, Pittsburgh; Christ King Church of Advent, Pittsburgh; Charles Martin Hall Mem., Thompson, Ohio; Brookgreen Gardens, S.C. *Exhibited*: one-man: Carnegie Inst.; Pittsburgh A. & Crafts Center. *Position*: Res. A., Cranbrook Acad. A., 1942-45.

deCREEFT, JOSE—*Sculptor, T.*
551 Hudson St.; h. 79 Barrow St., New York, N.Y.

B. Guadalajara, Spain, Nov. 27, 1884. *Studied*: Julian Acad., Ecole des Beaux-Arts, Maison Greber, Paris, and in Madrid. *Member*: ANA; Palm Beach A. Lg.; AEA; Audubon A.; NSS; S. Gld.; Fed. Mod. P. & S.; Nat. Inst. A. & Let. *Awards*: prizes, Julian Acad., 1906; MMA, 1942; PAFA, 1945; gold med., Audubon A., 1953. *Work*: MMA; WMAA; MMoDA; Wichita Mus. A.; Norton Gal. A.; Univ. Nebraska; BM; IBM; Fairmount Park, Phila., Pa.; Munson-Williams-Proctor Inst.; PMA; war. mem., Sauges, France; 200 pieces of sculpture at Fortress in Majorca, Spain; commissioned—"Alice in Wonderland," Central Park, New York City, 1959. *Exhibited*: Salon d'Automne, Salon de Tuileries, Salon des Artistes Independents, Societe Nationale des Beaux-Arts, France; MMA, 1942; PAFA, 1945-1955; WMAA; Antwerp, Belgium, 1949; Mus. Sao Paulo, Brazil, 1950; AIC, 1951; 17 one-man shows in U.S. since 1929. *Position*: Instr., ASL; New Sch. for Social Research, New York; Skowhegan (Me.) A. Sch., 1948-49; Norton Gal. A., West Palm Beach, Fla., 1948-52. Contributor article on sculpture to "7 Arts."

deCREEFT, MRS. LORRIE. See *Goulet, Lorrie*

DEDEAUX, HELEN—*Painter*
2125 Ames St., Los Angeles 27, Cal.

B. Niles, Cal., Jan. 19, 1915. *Studied*: Univ. So. California, B.F.A., M.F.A., and with Paul Sample, Dan Lutz, Merrell Gage, Jean Ames, Glen Lukens. *Member*: Cal. WC Soc.; Los A. AA. *Awards*: prize, Pomona Fair, 1942. *Exhibited*: Pomona Fair; Cal. WC Soc. traveling exh.; Santa Paula, Cal.; Los A. Mus. A.*

de DIEGO, JULIO—*Painter, Gr., I., C., T.*
65 West 56th St., New York 19, N.Y.

B. Madrid, Spain, May 9, 1900. *Studied*: in Madrid. *Awards*: prizes, AIC, 1935, 1940, 1944; Milwaukee AI, 1944; New Orleans, La., 1948; Birmingham Mus. A., 1954. *Work*: Walker A. Center; Encyclopaedia Britannica; IBM; AIC; Milwaukee AI; SFMA; Santa Barbara Mus. A.; MMA; PC; U.S. State Dept.; Montclair A. Mus.; San Diego FA Soc.; Washington Univ., St. Louis; Abbott Laboratories; Capehart Coll.; Newark Mus. A.; Birmingham Mus. A.; Univ. Denver; Clearwater, Fla., etc.; des. many shows and decorations for hotels and clubs. *Ex-*

hibited: AIC; Mulvane A. Mus.; Cal. WC Soc.; WFNY 1939; WMAA; Culver Military Acad.; Bonestell Gal.; Nierndorf Gal.; PAFA; CGA; Carnegie Inst.; Inst. Mod. A., Boston; Durand Ruel Gal.; VMFA; CAM; Univ. Iowa; CM; MMoDA; Tate Gal., London; Passedoit Gal.; John Heller Gal.; Assoc. Am. A.; Philbrook A. Center; AFA traveling Exh.; MMA, and others. Many one-man shows. I., "Rendezvous with Spain"; many paintings and cover designs for national magazines.

DEDINI, ELDON—*Cartoonist*
P.O. Box 1630, Monterey, Cal.

B. King City, Cal., June 29, 1921. *Studied*: Chouinard AI. *Member*: Nat. Cartoonists Soc. *Work*: Story Dept., Walt Disney Studios. Contributor to Esquire, New Yorker and other national magazines.

de ERDELY, FRANCIS—*Painter, E.*
5471 Eagle Rock View Dr., Los Angeles 41, Cal.

B. Budapest, Hungary, May 3, 1904. *Studied*: Royal Acad. A., Budapest. *Member*: Cal. WC Soc.; AWS; Audubon A; Am. Assn. Univ. Prof.; Los Angeles AA; All. A. Am. *Awards*: prizes, Budapest, Hungary, 1925; Detroit Inst. A., 1940-1944; Denver A. Mus., 1945, 1952; Cal. WC Soc., 1945, 1946, 1949, 1957; Pasadena Soc. A., 1946, 1947, 1949; City of Los Angeles, 1946, 1948, 1953, 1956; Oakland A. Gal., 1949, 1950; Nat. Orange Show, 1949, 1950; Arizona State Fair, 1949; med., Scarab Cl., 1942, 1943; prize, 1944; gold med., Audubon A., 1954, 1955; prize, Los A. Mus. A., 1955; Cal. State Fair, 1956; AWS, 1958. *Work*: Detroit Inst. A.; Los A. Mus. A.; deYoung Mem. Mus.; Pasadena AI; Denver A. Mus.; Nat. Gal. of Victoria, Melbourne, Australia; Oakland A. Gal.; Mus. of Cranbrook Acad. A.; SAM; Univ. Utah; Long Beach A. Mus.; College of So. Utah; Salt Lake City Lib.; Ball State T. Col., and in museums abroad. *Exhibited*: PAFA, 1941; AIC, 1942-1945, 1952; VMFA, 1942; CGA, 1943; Denver A. Mus., 1945-1949, 1952, 1956, 1958; San F. AA, 1945-1947, 1949, 1950; Cal. PLH, 1946, 1947; Laguna Beach AA, 1945, 1948, 1956-1958; Los A. Mus. A., 1944-1949, 1951, 1952, 1954, 1955, 1957; Cal. WC Soc., 1945-1947, 1949-1955, 1956-1958; Pepsi-Cola, 1946-1948; Carnegie Inst., 1946-1948; Detroit Inst. A., 1940-1944, 1948; Scarab Cl., Detroit, 1942-1944; Grand Rapids A. Gal., 1942; Pasadena Soc. A., 1945-1951; Los Angeles AA, 1945, 1946, 1950-1955, 1956, 1958; Oakland A. Gal., 1947-1951, 1952, 1953, 1955; Butler AI, 1951, 1953, 1955, 1958; John Herron AI, 1949; Crocker A. Gal., 1948; Haggin Mem. A. Gal., 1950; Toledo Mus. A., 1947-1948; Pasadena AI, 1945-46, 1948, 1950, 1953, 1954; Sao Paulo, Brazil, 1955; AWS, 1955, 1956-1958; Audubon A., 1954, 1955, 1956-1958; SFMA, 1954, 1956; SAM, 1954; Santa Barbara Mus. A., 1955; MMA, 1952; deYoung Mem. Mus., 1944, 1946, 1952, 1953; San Diego FA Gal., 1950. *Position*: Prof. FA, Univ. Southern Cal., Los Angeles, Cal., 1945- .

DEERING, ROGER (L.)—*Painter, L., T.*
Ocean Ave., Kennebunkport, Me.

B. East Waterboro, Me., Feb. 2, 1904. *Studied*: Grad. Sch. FA, Portland Soc. A.; and with Wayman Adams, Penrhyn Stanlaws, Aldro Hibbard, Anson Cross, George Elmer Browne, Jay Connaway. *Member*: Portland Soc. A.; Grand Central A. Gal.; Copley Soc., Boston; SC; AAPL. *Awards*: prizes, Portland Soc. A., 1924; Brick Store Mus., 1945, 1958. *Work*: Gorham (Me.) State T. Col.; Woodsfords Congregational Church, Portland, Me.; murals, Portland, Scarboro Beach, Sanford, Me.; Ennis Lib., Farmington, Me. *Exhibited*: L.D.M. Sweat Mus. A., 1926-1954; SC, 1952-1958; NAC, 1953, 1954; AAPL, 1953-1958; Copley Soc., 1956-1958; Farnsworth Mus. A., 1958; Brick Store Mus., 1946-1958 (one-man, 1947); Gorham State T. Col.; WFNY 1939; Montclair Woman's Cl., 1946 (one-man); Nasson Col., Springvale, Me., 1950 (one-man); traveling exh., Florida, 1955 (one-man). Lectures: Marine Painting, Past and Present. *Position*: Maine State Chptr. Chm., AAPL, 1938- , Memb. Adv. Bd.; Dir., T., Roger Deering Outdoor Painting Class.

DEFENBACHER, DANIEL S.—*Educator, W., L.*
Victor Gruen Associates, 971 Sutter St., San Francisco, Cal.; h. 6259 Girvin Dr., Oakland, Cal.

B. Dover, Ohio, May 22, 1906. *Studied*: Carnegie Inst.; Indiana Univ. *Awards*: F., Carnegie Inst., 1929-1930; Hon. deg., D.F.A., Lawrence Col., 1950. Ed., "American Watercolor and Winslow Homer," 1945; "Jades," 1944; Author,

"Watercolor—U.S.A." Contributor to: School Arts; Better Design; Everyday Art Quarterly. Lectures: Modern Art; Museum Administration; etc. *Position*: Asst. to Nat. Dir., FAP, 1936-39; Dir., Walker A. Center, Minneapolis, Minn., 1939-51; Dir., Fort Worth (Tex.) A. Center, 1951-54; Exec. Com., Int. Des. Conference, 1951- ; Pres., Cal. Col. A. & Crafts, Oakland, 18, Cal., 1954-1957; Mgmt. Consultant in Des., Associate, Victor Gruen Assoc., Architect, Beverly Hills, Cal., 1957- .

DE FILIPPO, ANTONIO—*Sculptor*
39-64 52nd St., Woodside, L.I., N.Y.

B. Italy, Feb. 22, 1900. *Studied*: BAID; Tiffany Fnd.; Am. Acad. in Rome. *Member*: NSS. *Award*: Scholarship to Am. Acad. in Rome, Italian Am. A. Soc., 1925. *Work*: S., mem., Winthrop Park, Brooklyn, N.Y.; tablet, Bryant H.S., Bronx, N.Y.; mem., Southampton, N.Y.; Princeton Univ.; & many portrait busts.*

DE FOREST, JULIE MORROW (Mrs. Cornelius W.)—
Painter
National Arts Club, 15 Gramercy Park, New York, N.Y.; h. 3731 Earls Court View, Cincinnati 26, Ohio

B. New York, N.Y. *Studied*: Wellesley Col., A.B.; Columbia Univ., A.M.; & with Jonas Lie, Charles Hawthorne, John Carlson. *Member*: All.A.Am.; NAC; Professional A. of Cincinnati; Cincinnati Mus. Assn.; AAPL. *Award*: Medallion, Women's Theodore Roosevelt Mem. Assn.; 2 poetry awards, College Cl., Cincinnati; prize, CM, 1958. *Work*: Farnsworth Mus., Wellesley Col.; Am. Fed. Women's Cl. *Exhibited*: CGA; CM, 1958; PAFA; NAD; All.A.Am.; NAC; WFNY 1939; Professional A., Cincinnati; BM; Kansas City AI; Staten Island Mus. A.; Ohio State Fair; one-man exh.: Marie Sterner Gal.; Milch Gal.; Farnsworth Mus.; Jersey City Mus. Assn.; Loring Andrews Gal., Cincinnati; Woman's A. Cl., Cincinnati; Newhouse Gal., New York.

de FRANCESCO, ITALO L.—*Educator, P.*
State Teachers College, Kutztown, Pa.

B. Rome, Italy, Nov. 11, 1901. *Studied*: Univ. Pennsylvania, B.S., M.S. in Edu.; N.Y. Univ., Ed.D. *Member*: Eastern AA; Nat. Edu. Assn.; Pa. S.E.A. *Award*: Carnegie scholarship, Harvard Univ., 1933. *Exhibited*: Reading (Pa.) Mus., annually; Lehigh A. All., annually. *Author*: "The Education of Teachers and Supervisors of Art," 1942; "Art Education—Its Means and Ends," 1958. Ed., "Art Education" (N.A.E.A.), 1948-52. Lectures: American Art Today; From Giotto to Picasso; etc. *Position*: Past Pres., Eastern Arts Assn., 1946-47; Sec.-Treas., Nat. A. Edu. Assn.; A. Dir., State Teachers College, Kutztown, Pa., at present.

de FRANCISCI, ANTHONY—*Sculptor, T.*
246 West 80th St.; h. 230 West End Ave., New York 23, N.Y.; s. Rockport, Mass.

B. Palermo, Italy, June 13, 1887. *Studied*: CUASch.; NAD; ASL, and with G. T. Brewster, Francis Jones, J. E. Fraser. *Member*: NA; Am. Numismatic Soc.; NSS; Rockport AA; Audubon A; All. A. Am. *Awards*: prizes, All. A. Am., 1932, 1958; med., Am. Numismatic Soc., 1937; PAFA, 1936; gold med., All. A. Am., 1950; NAD, 1939; Medal of Honor, NAC, 1956. *Work*: mem., Union Square, N.Y.; Allegorical group, Eli Lilly Co., Indianapolis; 50th Anniversary medal for Ford Motor Co.; CM; designed U.S. Silver Dollar; U.S. Veterans discharge button, World War II; des., Congressional Medal awarded to Gen. Pershing; sc., Am. Numismatic Soc.; MMA; CM; Mus. of French Mint, Paris; Brookgreen Gardens, S.C. *Position*: Rec. Sec., NAD, New York, N.Y.

DEGEN, IDA DAY—*Sculptor, Des., T., L.*
1375 Warm Springs Rd., Glen Ellen, Cal.

B. San Francisco, Cal., Oct. 10, 1888. *Studied*: Cal. Sch. FA; ASL; & with Ralph Stackpole, William Zorach. *Member*: San F. AA; NAWA; San F. Women A.; Marin SA; Nat. Lg. Am. Pen Women; AEA. *Awards*: prizes, Marin Co. Garden Center, 1948, 1950, 1952; Frances Young Gal., 1949, 1950, 1951; San Rafael, Cal., 1941; Oakland A. Gal., 1942, 1946, 1955; SFMA, 1942, 1943, 1950, 1951, 1955; Nat. Lg. Am. Pen Women, 1957, 1958; Santa Rosa, Cal., 1958. *Work*: S. Grace Cathedral; deYoung Mem.

Mus.; Palace Legion Honor, Bohemian Cl., all in San F., Cal. *Exhibited*: SFMA, 1941-1945; Conn. Acad. FA, 1942; Denver A. Mus., 1941, 1943, 1945; PAFA, 1942, 1952; NAWA, 1942, 1943, 1945, 1946; Pomona, Cal., 1941; Delgado Mus. A., 1942, 1956; Oakland A. Gal., 1941, 1942, 1944, 1946; San F. Women A., 1941-1946; Grace Cathedral, San F., 1957; Cal. PLH, 1949; Cal. State Fair, 1950; Crocker A. Gal., Sacramento, Cal., 1958; Smithsonian Inst., 1958 (Nat. Lg. Am. Pen Women). *Position*: Instr. Sculpture, Santa Rosa Jr. Col., Santa Rosa, Cal., 1955- . Pres. Sonoma County Br. Nat. Lg. Am. Pen Women, 1958.

DEGENHART, PEARL C.—*Painter, T., W.*
Arcata, Cal.

B. Philipsburg, Mont. *Studied*: Univ. Montana, B.A.; Columbia Univ., M.A.; Univ. California; Univ. Oregon; Univ. New Mexico. *Award*: prize, Univ. Montana, 1919. *Exhibited*: San F. AA, 1932, 1937, 1940; Contemporary A. Gal., 1939; Spokane, Wash., 1948; Oakland A. Gal., 1948; Topeka, Kans., 1950; Denver, Colo., 1938; Humboldt State Col., 1935, 1945, 1948, 1954, 1956 (one-man); Stafford Inn, 1954 (one-man). Contributor to: School Arts magazine, on arts & crafts. *Position*: Chm. A. Dept., Arcata H.S., Arcata, Cal., 1928-46.

de GERENDAY, LACI—*Sculptor*
39-55 Greenpoint Ave., Long Island City 4, N.Y.

B. Budapest, Hungary, Aug. 17, 1911. *Studied*: NAD; South Dakota Mines State Col.; Ursinus Col.; Shrivenham Univ., England. *Member*: F., NSS. *Awards*: prizes, NAD, 1947; NSS, 1955; citation, City of New York, 1948. *Work*: Mus. Africa, Algiers; reliefs, USPO, Tell City, Ind.; Court House, Aberdeen, S.D.; Killearn Gardens, Fla., and many medals and portraits; des. for carved glass, Steuben Glass Co., N.Y. *Exhibited*: NAD, 1940, 1941-1947, 1951, 1956-1958; PAFA, 1947, 1949, 1950; PMA, 1951; New Britain Mus., 1950; Arizona, 1949; SFMA, 1949; NSS, 1949-1958; All. A. Am., 1956-1958; Nat. Acad. A. & Let., 1949; French & Co., 1950; Medallic A., 1952; Ferargil Gal., 1948; Barbizon Plaza, N.Y., 1953.

de GHIZE, ELEANOR—*Painter*
1401 Canyon Rd., Santa Fe, N.M.

B. New York, N.Y., Nov. 18, 1896. *Studied*: Maryland Inst.; & with Maurice Denis, Paris; Leon Kroll, John Sloan, New York. *Member*: Balt. A. Cl. *Awards*: Wilson Smith prize, 1931; med., BMA, 1939. *Work*: BMA. *Exhibited*: WFNY 1939; BMA, annually, 1945 (one-man); New Mexico All. for A., 1952; Mus. New Mexico, Santa Fe, 1952-1955; Burro Alley Gal., Santa Fe, 1956 (one-man).*

DE GRAFF, STANLEY (CONRAD)—
Printmaker, P., C., T.
Rt. #1, Box 62, Eau Gallie, Fla.

B. Ludington, Mich., July 21, 1892. *Work*: Detroit Inst. A.; Hackley A. Gal.; Grand Rapids A. Gal. *Exhibited*: Lib. Cong., 1943-1945; Phila. Pr. Cl., 1943, 1944; Laguna Beach A. Lg., 1943, 1944; Mus. FA of Houston, 1942, 1943; Detroit Inst. A., 1934-1945; Grand Rapids A. Gal., 1933-1945; Hackley A. Gal., 1935-1941; Grand Rapids Pub. Lib., 1934 (one-man); A. Center Gal., Grand Rapids, 1940, 1942 (one-man); Trade Winds Cl., 1953 (one-man); Bahama Beach Cl., 1954-56 (one-man); Fla. Fed. A., 1953-1958. *Position*: Instr. Printmaking, A. Center Gal. Sch. Grand Rapids, Mich., 1939-43; Pres., Melbourne AA, 1954-56; Dir., Melbourne AA Gal., 1956- .

de GROOT, ADELAIDE MILTON—*Painter*
21 West 58th St., New York 19, N.Y.

B. New York, N.Y., Mar. 25, 1876. *Studied*: ASL; in Nice, France, and with Frederic Taubes. *Member*: AFA. *Work*: MMA; BMFA; PMA; Zanesville (Ohio) Mus. A.; Columbus Gal. FA; Musee de Nice, France; N.Y. Hist. Soc.; Springfield (Mass.) Mus. FA. *Exhibited*: Galerie des Independents, Paris; Artistes Français, Paris; Tuileries, Paris; Century of Progress, Chicago; Springfield Mus. FA; CM; VMFA; Leger & Sons, London, England; Durand Ruel Gal., N.Y.; Valentine Gal., N.Y.; Midtown Gal., N.Y.; Ferguson Lib., Stamford, Conn.; Rhode Island Mus. A., Providence, and others.

D'ELIA, TERESA ILDA—*Painter, Gr., C., Comm., T.*
19 Woodland Dr., Greenwich, Conn.

B. Greenwich, Conn., Nov. 18, 1918. *Studied*: ASL; New Sch. for Social Research; & with Simkovitch, Charlot, Yasuo Kuniyoshi, Picken. *Member*: Springfield A. Lg. *Awards*: Med., San F. AA, 1943; prizes, Douglas Aircraft Exh., 1943; Springfield A. Lg., 1945, 1946. *Exhibited*: PAFA, 1942; AAPL, 1942; SFMA, 1943; Northwest Pr.M., 1943; Phila. Pr. Cl., 1945; Los A. Mus. A., 1945; Springfield A. Lg., 1945, 1946, 1953; Greenwich SA, 1945; Douglas Aircraft Exh., 1943; Palace Legion Honor, 1946. *Position*: Comm., newspaper adv., 1954; des. wire & papier-mache sculpture for window displays, 1953-54.*

d'HARNONCOURT, RENE—*Museum Director*
Museum of Modern Art, 11 West 53rd St.; h. 333 Central Park West, New York 25, N.Y.

B. Vienna, Austria, May 17, 1901. *Studied*: Univ. Graz, Austria. *Member*: Bd. Member, AFA. *Award*: Doctor of Humane Letters, *honoris causa*, Columbia Univ., 1958. Author: "Mexicana"; Co-Author: "Indian Art of the United States," MModA; Co-I: "The Painted Pig," 1930; Co-Ed.: "Arts of the South Seas," MModA. Contributor to art magazines. Lectures: Primitive Art; Architecture of Installation. *Position*: Dir., Radio program "Art in America," 1933-34; Instr., Hist. A., Sarah Lawrence Col., 1934-36; Sr. Counselor, UNESCO Preparatory Comm., 1946; Chm., Indian Arts & Crafts Bd., Dept. of Interior, Wash., D.C.; Chm. Comm. on Manual Industries, Inter-Am. Development Comm., Wash., D.C., 1942; Actg. Dir., Section of A., Office of Inter-Am. Affairs, Wash., D.C., 1943; Dir., Museum of Modern Art, New York, N.Y., at present.

de HELLEBRANTH, BERTHA—*Sculptor, P.*
109 South Frankfort Ave., Ventnor, N.J.

B. Budapest, Hungary. *Studied*: Budapest Acad. FA; Julian Acad., Grande Chaumiere, Paris, France. *Member*: Hungarian AA; CAA; Audubon A; Phila. WC Cl.; AEA; AWS. *Awards*: prize and med., Budapest, 1938; AAPL, 1938; Montclair A. Mus., 1941, 1956; All. A. Am., 1948; gold med., Audubon A., 1946; citation of merit, Fla. Southern Col., 1951. *Work*: BM; Fordham Univ.; Scranton Univ.; Fla. Southern Col.; Cistercian Abbey, Trappist, Ky., and in private collections. *Exhibited*: Stockholm, Konsthall, 1928; BM, 1929; NGA, 1935; MMA, 1942; PAFA, 1941, 1942, 1946; AIC, 1944; Phila. A. All., 1955; CAA traveling exh.; Amherst Col.; Springfield (Mass.) Mus. A.; Goucher Col.; DMFA; Illinois State Mus.; Worcester A. Center; Appleton, Wis.

de HELLEBRANTH, ELENA MARIA—
Painter, T., L., W., Cr.
109 South Frankfort Ave., Ventnor, N.J.

B. Budapest, Hungary. *Studied*: Acad. FA, Budapest; Julian Acad., Grande Chaumiere, Paris, France. *Member*: AWS; AEA; Audubon A; Wash. WC Cl.; Atlantic City A. Center; New Jersey P. & S. Soc.; AFA; AAPL; CAA; Hungarian AA. *Awards*: prize and med., Budapest, Hungary; Audubon A. (purchase prize); Ogunquit A. Center; citation, Fla. Southern Col.; Jersey City Mus. A.; Montclair A. Mus., 1956. *Work*: IBM; BM; Fla. Southern Col.; Scranton Mus. A.; Ventnor (N.J.) Hospital; Scranton Univ.; Hungarian Legation, Wash., D.C., and in private collections. *Exhibited*: AFA; WMA; Springfield Mus. A.; BM; Silberman Gal.; PAFA; Grand Rapids A. Gal.; NAD; All. A. Am.; AIC; Montclair A. Mus.; New Jersey State Mus.; U.S. Nat. Mus. Wash., D.C.; WFNY 1939; Toledo A. Mus.; Stockholm A. Mus.; St. Botolph Cl., Boston; Audubon A.; Ogunquit A. Mus.; Riverside Mus.

DEHN, ADOLF ARTHUR—*Painter, Lith.*
230 East 15th St., New York 3, N.Y.

B. Waterville, Minn., Nov. 22, 1895. *Studied*: Minneapolis Sch. A.; ASL. *Member*: ANA. *Awards*: Guggenheim F., 1939, 1951; prizes, AIC, 1943; Phila. A. All., 1936; Phila. Pr. Cl., 1939; Lib.Cong., 1946. *Work*: MMA; MModA; WMAA; N.Y. Pub. Lib.; BM; AIC; BMFA; CMA; Minneapolis Inst. A.; CAM; U.S. Navy; Standard Oil Co., etc. *Exhibited*: MMA; MModA; N.Y. Pub. Lib.; BM; AIC; BMFA; CMA; WMAA, etc. Author: "Watercolor Painting," 1945; "How to Draw and Print Lithographs," 1950; "Watercolor, Gouache and Casein Painting," 1955. Contributor of: illus. to Life Magazine, 1941. *Position*: Adv. Instr., Famous Artists School.*

DEHNER, DOROTHY (Mrs. Ferdinand Mann)—
Painter, Pr. M.
Finney Farm, Croton-on-Hudson, N.Y.

B. Cleveland, Ohio, Dec. 23, 1908. *Studied*: Univ. California at Los Angeles; ASL; Skidmore Col., B.S., and with Kenneth Hayes Miller, Jan Matulka, Boardman Robinson. *Member*: Phila. Pr. Cl.; SAGA; S. Gld.; Fed. Am. P. & S. *Awards*: prize, Audubon A., 1947. *Work*: MModA; MMA; Munson-Williams-Proctor Inst.; U.S. Embassies abroad and in private colls. *Exhibited*: Audubon A., 1945, 1947; SFMA, 1944; Albany Inst. Hist. & A.; Butler Inst. Am. A.; Carlebach Gal.; Delius Gal.; WMAA; MModA; BM, 1954-1955; BMA; Colorado Springs FA Center; Skidmore Col.; SAM; Willard Gal.; Stable Gal., 1957; Mus. Contemp. A., Houston, Tex.; Des Moines A. Center, 1957; nationally and with traveling exhs. of U.S. State Dept. in U.S. and abroad, 1954-1958; one-man: Rose Fried Gal., 1952; traveling exh., 1952-1954; AIC, 1955; Wittenborn Gal., 1956; Skidmore Col., 1958; Glens Falls, N.Y., 1954. *Position*: Instr. A., Barnard Sch. for Girls, New York, N.Y.

DEHNER, WALT(ER) LEONARD—*Painter*
Whitehouse, Ohio

B. Buffalo, N.Y., 1898. *Studied*: Univ. Michigan; Univ. Illinois; Univ. Ohio; Harvard Univ.; Columbia Univ.; ASL, with Bellows, Rosen, Speicher, Sternberg, Grosz; PAFA with Breckenridge, Garber. *Awards*: Hassam Fund purchase award, NAD. *Work*: Colorado Springs FA Center; Wichita Mus. A.; Toledo Mus. A. *Exhibited*: AIC; MMA; WMAA; CGA; BM; Clearwater, Fla.; AWS; Kraushaar Gal. *Position*: Dir. A., Univ. Puerto Rico, 1928-48; A.-in-Res., Bowling Green State Univ. (Ohio), 1946.

DEIKE, CLARA L.—*Painter, W., L., T.*
1222 Arlington Rd., Lakewood 7, Ohio

B. Detroit, Mich. *Studied*: Cleveland Sch. A.; in Munich, Germany and Capri, Italy; & with Henry G. Keller, Hugh Breckenridge, Hans Hofmann. *Member*: Cleveland FA Assn. *Awards*: prizes, CMA, 1922, 1923, 1925-1928, 1940, 1957; Halle Bros., Cleveland, 1928. *Work*: CMA; Pub. Sch., Cleveland, Ohio. *Exhibited*: CMA, 1918-1946, 1947, 1948, 1955; Great Lakes Exh., 1937; Wash. AC, 1924; Ohio WC Soc.; Dayton AI, 1931; YWCA, Boston, 1943; Korner & Wood Gal., Cleveland; Gloucester (Mass.) A. Festival, 1953-1955.

DEINES, E(RNEST) HUBERT—*Engraver, Des.*
621 East 31st St., Kansas City 9, Mo.

B. Russell, Kan., Mar., 1894. *Studied*: Kansas City AI; Julian Acad., Paris, France. *Member*: ANA; SC; Audubon A.; Prairie Pr.M.; Northwest Pr.M.; Woodcut Soc.; Soc. Pr. Connoisseurs; AAPL; AFA; MacDowell Colony; Albany Pr. Cl.; Phila. WC Cl.; SAGA; NAC; AIGA. *Awards*: prizes, CAM; Phila. Pr. Cl.; Northwest Pr.M.; Lib. Cong., 1943, 1946; Huntington Hartford Fnd. Grant, 1955; SC, 1958; Wash. WC Cl. at U.S. Nat. Mus., Wash., D.C., 1958. *Work*: State Hist. Soc., Missouri; Kansas State Hist. Soc.; Kansas City Pub. Lib.; William Rockhill Nelson Gal. A.; Cleveland Pr.M.; PMA; Vanderpoel Coll.; CAM; MMA; Pa. State Univ.; Lib. Cong.; Phila. Pr. Cl.; Northwest Pr.M.; Albany Inst. Hist. & A.; Univ. Glasgow, Scotland. *Exhibited*: Kansas City AI; CAM; Kansas City Pub. Lib. (book des. & illus.); Kansas City SA; Women's City Cl., Kansas City (one-man); & principal museums in U.S. & abroad.

de JONG, GERRIT, JR.—*Educator, W.*
Brigham Young University; h. 640 North University Ave., Provo, Utah

B. Amsterdam, Holland, Mar. 20, 1892. *Studied*: Univ. Munich, Germany; Univ. Utah, A.B., A.M.; Nat. Univ. of Mexico, Mexico City; Stanford Univ., Ph.D. *Member*: Utah Acad. Sciences, Arts & Lets.; Am. Musicological Soc.; Internationale Gesellschaft für Musikwissenschaft. *Awards*: Distinguished Service award, Utah Acad. Sciences, Arts & Lets., 1953; Univ. F., Stanford Univ., 1931-32. Contributor article in *Brazil, Portrait of Half a Continent*, "Brazilian Music and Art," 1951. Lectures: "An Approach to Modernity in Art" and "Candido Portinari," Utah Acad. Sciences, Arts & Lets., 1950. Also lectures on Aesthetics. *Position*: Organized the College of Fine Arts at Brigham Young Univ., Provo, Utah, and is Dean at present.

de KOONING, ELAINE MARIE CATHERINE—*Painter*

791 Broadway, New York 3, N.Y.

B. New York, N.Y., Mar. 12, 1920. *Studied*: Leonardo Da Vinci A. Sch.; Am. A. Sch.; and with William de Kooning. *Exhibited*: Carnegie Inst., 1956; Kootz Gal., N.Y., 1950; Stable Gal., N.Y., 1952, 1956; one-man: Stable Gal., 1952, 1956; Tibor de Nagy Gal., 1958. Author: "Painting, Sculpture and Architecture: A Study in Integration," 1952. *Position*: Instr. A., Univ. New Mexico, Albuquerque, N.M., 1958.

DELACOUR, JEAN T.—*Museum Director*

Los Angeles County Museum, Exposition Park; h. 923 South Longwood Ave., Los Angeles 19, Cal.; also: Château de Cleres, Seine-Maritime, France

B. Paris, France, Sept. 26, 1890. *Studied*: Universities of Paris and Lille, France. *Member*: AAMus. *Awards*: Officier de la Legion d'Honneur; Commander Corona d'Italia. Author: ca. 20 books of Natural History; Ed., L'Oiseau, La Revue Française d'Ornithologée, Paris, 1920-40. *Position*: Dir., Los Angeles County Museum of Art, Los Angeles, Cal.

de LAGERBERG, MRS. LUCY WALLACE. See Wallace, Lucy

de LAITTRE, ELEANOR (*Mrs. Eleanor de Laittre Brown)***—***Sculptor, P.*

Higley Hill, Wilmington, Vt.

B. Minneapolis, Minn., Apr. 3, 1911. *Studied*: BMFA Sch.; & with George Luks, John Sloan. *Member*: Am. Abstract A.; Fed. Mod. P.&S.; AEA. *Work*: PMG; Walker A. Center; Univ. Minnesota. *Exhibited*: Am. Abstract A., annually; WMAA; AIC; PAFA; Boston A. Festival; VMFA; Minneapolis Inst. A.; Fed. Mod. P.&S., annually; Am. Abstract A., traveling exh., 1955-56; Fed. Mod. P. & S., traveling exh. (AFA), 1955-56; one-man: Chicago, Ill., 1938; New York, N.Y., 1939, 1943; Santa Barbara Mus. A., 1957; WAC, 1958.

de LANGLEY, MRS. RUFFIN. See Haas, Helen

DELARUE, ALLISON—*Writer*

Wagon House, Box 526, Princeton, N.J.

Studied: Princeton Univ., M.A.; Oxford Univ., M.A. *Member*: Theatre Lib. Assn.; Friends of Princeton Univ. Lib.; Princeton Cl. Contributor to Antiques; American Collector; Dance Index; Princeton Univ. Lib. Chronicle; Dance News. Formerly staff member, CUASch., New York, N.Y.; now on staff of Princeton Univ. McCarter Theatre.

DELAVAN, NELSON B., JR.—*Painter, C., T.*

33 Center St., Berea, Ky.

B. Seneca Falls, N.Y., Apr. 10, 1925. *Studied*: Bard Col., A.B., with Stefan Hirsch; Cranbrook Acad. A., M.F.A., and with Zoltan Zepeshy, Wallace Mitchell. *Member*: CAA; Kentucky A. Edu. Assn. *Exhibited*: Norfolk Mus. A., 1956; Louisville A. Center, 1955; Virginia Intermont Col., 1955; Univ. Kentucky; Vassar Col.; Des Moines A. Center, 1953 (one-man), and others. *Position*: Instr. and in charge of exh. program, Berea Col., A. Dept., Berea, Ky., 1952- .*

DELBOS, JULIUS—*Painter, T.*

167 East 61st St., New York 21, N.Y.

B. London, England, July 22, 1879. *Member*: NA; AWS; NAC; Century Cl. *Awards*: prizes, several from AWS, and others. *Work*: N.Y. Pub. Lib. *Exhibited*: nationally and internationally.

DE LEEUW, CATEAU—*Writer, L., P., I.*

1024 Park Ave., Plainfield, N.J.

B. Hamilton, Ohio, Sept. 22, 1903. *Studied*: Metropolitan A. Sch.; ASL; Grande Chaumiere, Paris. *Member*: PBC; Plainfield AA (Hon.); AAPL. *Award*: Citation, Ohioana Library, for distinguished service to Ohio through writings for children, 1958. *Exhibited*: AWCS, 1931; NAWA, 1933, 1934; Maplewood (N.J.) Woman's Cl.; Montclair A. Mus., 1933, 1934, 1944; New Britain Inst., 1930 (one-man);

New Jersey Col. for Women, 1938, 1942 (one-man); New Jersey State Mus., 1953, 1954. Author: numerous books including "The Dutch East Indies & the Philippines," 1943; "Portrait by Kathie," "From This Day Forward," "Mickey the Monkey," "Make Your Habits Work For You," 1952*; "This My Desire," 1952; "Hideaway House," 1953; "Bright Gold," 1953; "To Have and Not Hold," 1954; "The Expandable Browns," 1955;* "William Tyndale," 1955; "Not For One Alone," 1955; "Showboat's Coming," 1956*; "The Proud Air," 1956; "The Caboose Club," 1957*; "Breakneck Betty," 1957*; "The Strange Garden," 1958.* (* in collaboration with Adele De Leeuw), and others; I., "Gay Design," 1942; "Linda Marsh," 1943; "Future for Sale," 1946; & others. Contributor to: Travel & juvenile magazines. Lectures: Art of Batik; Women in Art, etc.

de LEON, AMANDA—*Painter*

165 Boulevard, Pelham, N.Y.

B. Madrid, Spain, Apr. 19, 1908. *Studied*: San Jose de Tarbes Convent, Caracas, Venezuela. *Member*: NAWA; New Rochelle AA; AEA. *Work*: Musee d'Art Moderne, Paris; Nat. Gal. Mod. A., Rome; Glasgow A. Gal., Scotland; Mus. Mod. A., Barcelona; Musee des Beaux Arts, Lausanne; Mun. Gal. Mod. A., Dublin; Mun. Gal. Mod. A., Genoa; A. Gal. of Toronto, Canada; Denver Mus. A.; Butler AI; Univ. California; Mus. Mod. A., Sao Paulo, Brazil; Nat. Gal. Mod. A., New Delhi, India; Nat. Mus. Mod. A., Tokyo; Mun. A. Mus., Dusseldorf, Germany; Neue Galerie der Stadt Linz, Austria; Hamburger Kunsthalle, Germany, and many others in U.S. and abroad. *Exhibited*: nationally and internationally.

de LEMOS, PEDRO J.—

Designer, I., P., C., L., Mus. Dir.

100 Waverly Oaks, Palo Alto, Cal.

B. Austin, Nev., May 25, 1882. *Studied*: with Arthur Mathews, George Bridgman, Arthur Dow, H.S. Fonda. *Member*: Cal. SE; Carmel AA; F.R.S.A., London, England. *Awards*: Med., Cal. State Fair, 1916. *Work*: State Lib., Sacramento, Cal.; City Lib., Monterey, Cal. Author: "Applied Art"; "Artists Scrap Book"; "Block Printing," etc.*

de LESLIE, ALEXANDRE—*Portrait Painter*

Vergennes, Gloucester, Va.

B. Dec. 14, 1893. *Studied*: Institut Chone, Lycee Henry IV, Paris; ASL; NAD; and with George Bridgman, William Chase, George Bellows and others. Lectures on the Technique of Old Masters. Author: "Fine Pen Drawing"; I., "How France Built Her Cathedrals"; "A Childhood in Brittany."*

DELLARIPA, FILOMENA JOAN—*Painter, Lith., T.*

1731 Pine St.; h. 1922 Mifflin St., Philadelphia 45, Pa.

B. Philadelphia, Pa., Feb. 16, 1922. *Studied*: Moore Inst. A. Sc. & Indst.; PAFA; Barnes Fnd., and abroad. *Member*: Phila. WC Cl.; F., PAFA; Phila. A. All.; AEA; AWS. *Awards*: F., PAFA; Cresson scholarship, 1944, 1945; scholarship, Barnes Fnd., 1944, 1945; prizes, Graphic Sketch Cl., 1940; Ramborger prize, 1943; DaVinci All.; med., Phila. Plastic Cl. *Work*: Fleisher A. Mem., Phila., Pa. *Exhibited*: PAFA, 1944, 1945 (one-man); DaVinci All., 1943; Phila. A. All., 1943, 1957 (one-man); Temple Univ., 1951 (one-man); Phila. Plastic Cl.; Woodmere A. Gal.; Phila. Lib.; Graphic Sketch Cl., 1944; Pyramid Cl.; LC, 1957; NAD, 1957; Harcum Jr. Col.; Hill Sch. for Boys, Pottstown, Pa.; Fleisher A. Mem.; Phila. Sketch Cl.; Gimbels, Phila., Pa.; Strawbridge & Clothier, Phila., Pa., and others. *Position*: Instr. A., Graphic Sketch Cl., 1943- ; Instr., Junto Adult Sch., 1957- .

De LUCE, OLIVE S.—*Educator, P.*

Northwest Missouri State College; h. 928 College Ave., Maryville, Mo.

B. Owego, N.Y., July 27, 1898. *Studied*: T. Col., Columbia Univ., B.S., A.M.; Wayne Univ.; NAD; ASL; Sorbonne, Andre L'Hote, George Goetz, Academie de la Grande Chaumiere, Ecole du Louvre, Paris, France. *Member*: CAA; Midwest AA; Midwest Col. A. Assn.; N.A.E.A.; AAPL; Northwest Mo. Assoc. A.; Missouri State T. Assn.; AAUW. *Awards*: Jenkins Scholar, T. Col., Columbia Univ. *Work*: Northwest Missouri State Col.; Cottey Col. *Exhibited*: AIC; Kansas City Midwestern A.; Kansas City

AI; St. Louis A. Lg.; Indp. A., N.Y. Author: "Northwest Missouri State Teachers College Studies"; "Percival De Luce and His Heritage." Lectures: Greek and Mediaeval Art. *Position*: State Treas., State A. Chm. (3 terms), Regional A. Chm., AAUW; Pres., Northwest Missouri AA; Pres., Dept. A. Edu., NAEA; Instr., FA, Ohio Univ., 1914-15; Prof. FA, Chm. Dept. FA, Northwest Missouri State Col., Maryville, Mo., 1915- .*

DEL MAR, FRANCES—*Painter, L., W., Et.*
140 West 57th St., New York 19, N.Y.

B. Washington, D.C. *Studied*: Univ. Col., London; Sorbonne, Julian Acad., Paris; & with Raphael Colin, Julius Rolshoven. *Member*: SSAL; A.R.P.L. *Work*: murals, Caroline Rest Hospital; Heckscher Fnd.; Musée de la Guerre à Vincennes, France. *Exhibited*: Paris Salon; Nat. Soc. British A.; & in U.S. Author: "A Year Among the Maoris." Contributor to: The International Studio; Asia magazines. Lectures: Polynesian Art.*

DE LUE, DONALD—*Sculptor*
225 East 67th St., New York 21, N.Y.

B. Boston, Mass., Oct. 5, 1900. *Studied*: BMFA Sch. *Member*: ANA; NSS; Nat. Inst. A. & Lets.; Arch. Lg. *Awards*: prizes, Arch. Lg., 1942, gold medal, 1951; NSS, 1942, 1946; Guggenheim F., 1943-44; Nat. Inst. A. & Lets. Grant, 1945; gold medal, All. A. Am., 1946; prize, Meriden, Conn., 1953, 1957, and other awards: *Work*: panels, fountains, memorials, figures, medals: Court House, Phila., Pa.; Univ. Pennsylvania; American Exporter Mem., New York, N.Y.; chapels at West Point and Arlington, Va.; Harvey Firestone Mem.; Fed. Reserve Bank, Boston and Phila.; U.S. Military Cemetery Mem., Omaha Beach, St. Laurent, Normandy, France; Science & Eng. Bldg., Carnegie Tech., Pittsburgh; Mem. chapel, Va. Polytechnic Inst., Blacksburg, Va.; Loyola Jesuit Seminary, Shrub Oak, N.Y.; U.S. Naval Acad., Annapolis, Md.; Sacred Heart Shrine, Hillside, Ill.; Brookgreen Gardens, S.C.; City Hall, Stockholm, Sweden; Anniversary Medal in Bibliotheque Nationale, Paris, France, and many others.

DE LUNA, FRANCIS P.—*Sculptor*
11 West 29th St., New York 1, N.Y.

B. New York, N.Y., Oct. 6, 1891. *Studied*: NAD; BAID; CUASch. *Member*: NSS.

de MARCO, JEAN—*Sculptor, C., Gr., T.*
131 Christopher St., New York 14, N.Y.

B. Paris, France, May 2, 1898. *Studied*: Ecole Nationale des Arts Decoratifs, Paris. *Member*: ANA; NSS; Audubon A; Fed. Mod. P. & S.; All. A. Am.; Nat. Inst. A. & Let. *Awards*: med., New Rochelle AA, 1940; Am. Acad. A. & Lets., 1958; NAD, 1946; Arch. Lg.; 1958; NSS, 1954; prizes, NSS, 1945, 1948; Audubon A., 1948; Nat. Inst. A. & Let., 1950; NAD, 1956. *Work*: Whitemarsh Park Mem., Prospectville, Pa.; War Dept., Bldg., Wash., D.C.; USPO, Weldon, N.C.; Danville, Pa.; U.S. Capitol, Wash., D.C.; Joslyn Mem. Mus.; Mem., Notre Dame Univ.; MMA; reliefs, Cathedral of the Assumption, Baltimore, Md.; S., war mem., Presidio, San Francisco. *Exhibited*: PAFA, 1938, 1940, 1942-1946; AIC, 1938, 1941-1943; NAD, 1942, 1944, 1945; WFNY 1939; Fairmount Park, Phila., Pa., 1940; MMA, 1942; S. Gld., annually; Marie Sterner Gal., 1936; Buchholz Gal., 1941, 1943, 1945; one-man: Boyer Gal., 1940; Clay Cl., New York, 1946; Phila. A. All., 1948; BMFA Sch., 1948. *Position*: Instr., S., BMFA Sch., Boston, Mass., 1948-52; summers—Columbia Univ., New York, N.Y., Treas., S. Gld., 1940-51.

DE MARTELLY, JOHN STOCKTON—
Painter, Gr., E., I., Cart.
c/o Associated American Artists, 711 Fifth Ave., New York 22, N.Y.

B. Philadelphia, Pa., Sept. 10, 1903. *Studied*: PAFA, with Garber, Spencer, Breckenridge; in Florence, Italy; Royal Col. A., England. *Member*: AEA. *Awards*: Lighton prize, 1937; med.; A. Dir. Cl., 1942; MMA; WMAA; prize, Phila. Pr. Cl., 1938, 1939; prize, Oklahoma A. Center, 1940. *Work*: Victoria & Albert Mus., London, England. Contributor: essays to art magazines. I., "Sextant and Sails," 1941; "Green Mansions," 1942; "American River

Series—The Wabash." 1939. *Position*: Instr., Graphic A., Kansas City AI; artist-in-residence, Michigan State Col., East Lansing, Mich., 1944.*

DE MARTINI, JOSEPH—*Painter*
96 Fifth Ave., New York 11, N.Y.

B. Mobile, Ala., July 20, 1896. *Member*: ANA; Audubon A. *Awards*: prize, Pepsi-Cola, 1944; Univ. Illinois, 1948 (purchase); Guggenheim F., 1951; prize, NAD, 1950; gold med., PAFA, 1952. *Work*: PMG; AGAA; CAM; BMFA; MModA; MMA; Brooks Mem. Mus., Memphis, Tenn.; Univ. Arizona; Walker A. Center; Rochester Mem. Mus.; Farnsworth Mus., Rockland, Me.; Wichita A. Mus.; New Britain Inst.; Canajoharie A. Gal.; State Dept., Wash., D.C.; Pepsi-Cola Coll.; IBM; Nebraska AA; WMAA. *Exhibited*: MModA, 1941-1943; Carnegie Inst., 1941, 1943, 1944, 1946; WMAA, 1934, 1942-1945; CGA, 1941, 1943, 1945; CAM, 1938, 1941, 1942, 1946; PAFA, 1940, 1942-1945; AIC, 1941, 1942; WFNY 1939; WMA, 1945; de Young Mem. Mus., 1941, 1943; PMG, 1942, 1943; Critics Choice, New York, N.Y., 1945; VMFA, 1942, 1944, 1946; Colorado Springs FA Center, 1942; BM, 1943; John Herron AI, 1945; Nebraska AA, 1945, 1946. *Position*: A.-in-Res., Univ. Georgia, 1952-53.*

de MERLIER, FRANZ—*Painter, T., W., L.*
Bryn Mawr Art Center, Haverford, Pa.; h. 936 North 7th St., Philadelphia, Pa.

B. Ghent, Belgium, Oct. 28, 1878. *Studied*: in Belgium. *Member*: Chester County AA; Delaware Soc. FA; Reading A. All. *Awards*: prizes, West Chester, Pa., 1937, 1940, 1944; Wilmington, Del., 1935; A. Acad., Bruges, Belgium, 1894; Acad. Ghent, 1895; Brussels, Belgium, 1897. *Work*: West Chester (Pa.) A. Center; Wilmington Soc. FA; West Chester Lib.; 4 panels, Arthur Murray Studios, Phila., Pa.; West Chester (Pa.) Pub. Sch. (permanent exh. of the "Saga of Brandywine Valley: The House of Tanguy"). Cheney (Pa.) State T. Col.; Reading YMCA. *Position*: Instr., Bryn Mawr Art Center, Haverford, Pa.

DEMONET, INEZ (MICHON)—
Painter, Medical I., Et.
National Institutes of Health, Bethesda 14, Md.; h. 2925 43rd St., N.W., Washington, D.C.

B. Washington, D.C., April 25, 1897. *Studied*: Corcoran Sch. A.; PMSchIA; Nat. Sch. F. & App. A., and with Charles Hawthorne, Benson B. Moore. *Member*: Wash. WC Cl.; Assn. Medical Illustrators; Am. Soc. Tropical Medicine & Hygiene; Soc. Wash. Pr. M. (Treas.). *Awards*: med., Corcoran Sch. A., 1915; prizes, Soc. Wash. Pr. M., 1935; Wash. WC Cl., 1946; Nat. Mus., Wash., D.C., 1935. *Exhibited*: Soc. Wash. Pr.M.; Nat. Institutes of Health, Med. exh.; Am. Acad. of Ophthalmologists & Otolaryngology; Am. Medical Assn.; W. Va. State Med. Soc.; Wash., D.C. Med. Soc.; Am. Col. Surgeons; Am. Acad. of Neurology; Nat. Soc. for Prevention of Blindness. *Position*: A. Dir., Medical A. & Exhibits.

DENGHAUSEN, FRANZ H.—*Sculptor*
31 Phillips Ave., Rockport, Mass.

B. Boston, Mass., Apr. 8, 1911. *Studied*: BMFASch., with Charles Grafly; Child-Walker Sch. Des., with Arnold Geissbuhler. *Member*: Inst. Contemp. A.; Copley Soc.; Cambridge AA; Rockport AA (Pres. 1952-54); New England Sculptors Assn.; AEA. *Awards*: MacDowell Colony F., 1947; Silvermine Gld. A., 1955. *Exhibited*: PAFA, 1931; NAD, 1931; CM, 1935; WFNY 1939; Inst. Mod. A., 1943; AGAA, 1939, 1951; Boston A. Cl.; North Shore AA; Rockport AA; Provincetown AA; Wadsworth Atheneum, 1951; Boston Soc. Indp. A.; Cambridge AA; de-Cordova & Dana Mus.; Boston A. Festival, 1954; Silvermine Gld. A., 1955 and elsewhere.

DENGROVE, IDA L(EIBOVITZ)—*Painter, Gr., T.*
314 Grassmere Ave., Interlaken, Asbury Park, N.J.

B. Philadelphia, Pa., Sept. 21, 1918. *Studied*: Phila. Graphic Sketch Cl.; Moore Inst.; Barnes Fnd. *Member*: NAWA; Phila. Pr. Cl. *Award*: Traveling F., Moore Inst. A. Sc. & Indst. *Work*: U.S. Govt. *Exhibited*: Lib. Cong., 1943; PAFA, 1937; NGA, 1941; Carlen Gal. (one-man); Phila. Pr. Cl. (one-man); St. Petersburg, Fla.; Phila. A. All.; N.J. State Mus., Trenton, 1951-1954; YM-YWHA, Phila., Pa., 1952; Norton A. Gal.; NAWA, 1956-1958. *Position*: Pres., Asbury Park FA Soc.

DENIS, LEONARD—Commercial Artist, W., Cr.

"Kenilworth," Alden Park, Germantown, Philadelphia, Pa.

B. Detroit, Mich. *Studied*: PMSchIA; & with Paul Honore. *Member*: Phila. Sketch Cl.; Phila. Pr. Cl.; Stagecrafters; All. Francais. *Exhibited*: Detroit Inst. A., 1938; Scarab Cl., 1939; Woodmere A. Gal., 1946-1958; Phila. Sketch Cl., 1945, 1946; A. Gal., Phila., Pa., 1946 (one-man); Everyman's Gal., Phila., 1957 (one-man); Phila. Sketch Cl., 1947 (one-man); Phila. Pr. Cl., 1952; Phila. A. All. Des., "Seaweed Their Pasture," Folio Club Books; Contributor to Ford Times, 1956; "Wissahickon Paper" (article for the Paper Maker). *Position*: Contributor, A. Ed., Cr., Philadelphia Herald, Philadelphia, Pa.; Chm., Rittenhouse Square Outdoor Exh., Phila., Pa.

DENNEY, GLADYS A.—Painter, C., T., Des.

Emmerich Manual Training High School, 2405 Madison Ave. (25); h. 6179 North Park Ave., Indianapolis 20, Ind.

B. Portland, Ind., Sept. 21, 1898. *Studied*: CUASch.; PMSchIA; John Herron AI, B.A. in Edu., M.A. in Edu.; Univ. Colorado, and with Edward Warwick, James Boule. *Member*: NAWA. *Awards*: prizes, CUASch., 1925; Indiana State Fair, 1937-1940, 1946-1949; Hoosier Salon, 1946-1948. *Exhibited*: PAFA, 1937; NAWA, 1942-1944; John Herron AI; Hoosier Salon, 1946-1958; Indiana State Fair, 1937-1949; Muncie AA; one-man: Argent Gal., 1943; Hoosier Salon; Portland, Ind., 1947; Indiana State Lib.; Franklin Col., and others. *Position*: Instr., FA, Emmerich H.S., Indianapolis, Ind., 1930- .

DENNEY, IRENE—Painter

34 South 17th St.; h. 1231 South 52nd St., Philadelphia 43, Pa.

B. Philadelphia, Pa. *Studied*: PAFA. *Member*: AEA. *Awards*: Cresson award, PAFA; Smith award, PAFA, 1938. *Work*: PAFA. *Exhibited*: DaVinci A. All., 1951-1955; PAFA, 1936, 1938, 1945, 1946, 1951, 1956; Pyramid Cl., Phila., 1953-1955, 1956-1958; F., PAFA, 1955, 1956, 1957, 1958.

DENNIS, CHARLES H.—Cartoonist

P.O. Box 816; h. 1831 Magnolia Way, Walnut Creek, Cal.

B. Springfield, Mo., Nov. 11, 1921. *Studied*: San Francisco Acad. Adv. Art; A. Lg. of California. *Member*: Craftsmen's Gld. Am.; Am. Cartoonists Assn. Contributor cartoons to Look, True, Blue Book, Esquire, Playboy, Christian Science Monitor, Successful Farming and other national publications.

DENNIS, CHARLES WARREN—Painter, I.

9 Birds Hill Ave., Needham 92, Mass.

B. New Bedford, Mass., Feb. 25, 1898. *Studied*: Swain Sch. Des.; Fenway Sch. Illus.; BMFA Sch. *Work*: Tufts Col.; Masonic Temple, Boston, Mass. I., Saturday Evening Post (covers). *Position*: Port. & Miniature Painter with Bachrach, Inc., 33 years.

DENNIS, (BURT) MORGAN—Etcher, I., W., L., P.

Shoreham, Long Island, N.Y.; w. "Sea Dog" Houseboat, Key West, Fla.

B. Boston, Mass., Feb. 27, 1892. *Studied*: Am. Sch. Des., Boston, and with W. H. W. Bicknell, Stanhope Forbes. *Member*: Author's Lg. *Work*: murals, "The Dog House" bar and lounge, Sheraton-Russell Hotel, New York, N.Y. *Exhibited*: Ft. Myers, Fla., 1951; Key West, Fla., 1956-1958; Long Island, N.Y., 1957, 1958; Clarke Univ., Worcester, Mass., 1956. *Author*, I., "Pup Himself," 1943; "Burlap," 1945; "Morgan Dennis Dog Book," 1946; "Skit and Skat," 1951; "Pure Breds," 1953; "Himself and Burlap" on TV, 1954; "The Sea Dog," 1958. Illus., "Pete"; "Cat Who Went to College"; "Every Dog Has His Say"; "The Little Fox"; "Rags the Firehouse Dog"; "The Dog Next Door"; "Yipe"; "The Dog Who Could Swim Under Water," and others. *Position*: Artist—Black & White Whiskey advertisements (22nd year).

DENNIS, ROGER WILSON—
Painter, Lith., T., Conservator

Gallup Lane, Waterford, Conn.

B. Norwich, Conn., Mar. 11, 1902. *Studied*: ASL, and with

Guy Wiggins, Allen Cochran, Emile Gruppe, Robert Brackman. *Member*: Lyme AA; Conn. Acad. FA. *Awards*: prize, Meriden, Conn. *Exhibited*: Conn. Acad. FA; Lyme AA; North Shore AA; Gloucester, Mass. *Position*: Conservator, Lyman Allyn Mus. A., New London, Conn., 1950- .

DENSLOW, DOROTHEA HENRIETTA—Sculptor, T.

167 East 69th St., New York 21, N.Y.

B. New York, N.Y., Dec. 14, 1900. *Studied*: ASL. *Member*: Conn. Acad. FA. *Work*: Mem. plaque, Beth Moses Hospital, Brooklyn, N.Y.; Brookgreen Gardens, S.C. *Exhibited*: Syracuse Mus. FA, 1938; Conn. Acad. FA, 1914-1944; BM, 1936; Springfield (Mass.) Mus. FA, 1936; Rochester Mem. A. Gal., 1940; Plainfield AA, 1943; Newark Mus., 1944; Clay Cl., 1934, 1949; Berkshire Mus. A., 1941; Lyman Allyn Mus., 1939; Sculpture Center, 1953. *Position*: Founder & Dir., Sculpture Center, New York, N.Y., 1928 to present.

DENTZEL, CARL SCHAEFER—
Museum Director, W., L.

Southwest Museum, Highland Park, Los Angeles 42, Cal.; h. Box 101, Northridge, Cal.

B. Philadelphia, Pa., Mar. 20, 1913. *Studied*: Univ. California at Los Angeles; Univ. Berlin; Univ. Mexico. *Member*: Univ. Cal. at Los Angeles A. Council; Los A. Mus. A., Exec. Com., Mus. Assn. Lectures: "American Frontier Art"; "California Artists"; "Pre-Columbian Art"; "Aboriginal American Art"; "Art Aesthetics and Americans"; Art of the Southwest and Mexican 19th Century Art; Southwest Mus.; Pomona Col., Claremont, Cal. Author: "The Drawings of John Woodhouse Audubon, Illustrating His Adventures Through Mexico and California, 1849-50," 1957; "A Note on the Kicking Bear Pictograph of the Sioux Encounter at the Battle of the Little Big Horn with the 7th Cavalry Regiment under Lt. Colonel George Armstrong Custer," 1957; "Diary of Titian Ramsay Peale; Oregon to California, Overland Journey September and October, 1841" (Introduction & Bibliography by Carl Dentzel), 1957. *Position*: Pres., Los A. County Museum Assn.; Memb. Bd., U.C.L.A. Art Council; Pres., Western Mus. Conf., 1957-58; Dir., Southwest Museum, Los Angeles, Cal.

deORLOV, LINO S. LIPINSKY. See Lipinsky, Lino S.

DE PAUW, VICTOR—Painter, C., Lith., W.

East Hampton, L.I., N.Y.

B. Belgium, Jan. 22, 1902. *Studied*: Cal. Sch. FA; ASL. *Work*: MModA. *Exhibited*: one-man: Clayton Gal.; Morgan Gal.; Fifteen Gal.; Passedoit Gal.; 1954. *Position*: Instr., ASL; Peoples A. Center, MModA.; Country Art Sch., Westbury, N.Y., and privately in own studio. Art reviews for Westbury Times and Easthampton Star.

DE POL, JOHN—Printmaker, I., Des.

35-35 82nd St., Jackson Heights 72, N.Y.

B. New York, N.Y., Sept. 16, 1913. *Studied*: ASL; Sch. of Tech., Belfast, Ireland. *Member*: ANA; ASL (Life); SAGA (memb. Council); Albany Pr. Cl. *Awards*: prizes, Richard Comyn Eames purchase prize, 1952; Kate W. Arms Mem. prize, 1955-56. *Work*: LC; MMA; Montclair A. Mus.; CM; N.Y. Pub. Lib., and others. Major coll. of prints and books, Syracuse Univ. Lib. Executed Presentation Prints for: Woodcut Soc., 1952; Miniature Print Soc., 1953; Albany Pr. Cl., 1958. *Exhibited*: LC, 1947, 1948, 1951-1953, 1956; NAD, 1956, 1958; SAGA, 1947, 1950-1957; Oakland A. Mus., 1947; BM, 1950; Boston Soc. Indp. A., 1951; Wichita AA, 1948; Newport AA, 1947; Carnegie Inst., 1948, 1951; PAFA, 1947, 1949, 1950; Royal Soc. Painters, Etchers & Engravers, 1954; one-man: Albany Pr. Cl., 1957; Lycoming College, 1958. Illus., "Two Lovely Beasts," 1950; "Way to Wealth," 1953; "Trusting and the Maimed," 1955; "Anna, Anna," 1955; "Sermon on the Mount," 1955; "Art of Virtue," 1955; "Apology for Printers," 1955; "The Yalu Flows," 1956; "B. Franklin," 1956; "B. Franklin, Wit," 1957; "Bulmer and Shakespeare Press," 1957; "On True Happiness," 1958, and others. Numerous limited editions and ephemera for private presses, principally Pickering; Hammer Creek; Golden Hind; Between-Hours, and others.

DE'PREY, JUAN—*Painter, Muralist*
44 Hicks St., Brooklyn Heights, N.Y.

B. Puerto Rico, Apr. 26, 1906. *Exhibited*: Washington Square Outdoor Exh.; WMAA; Riverside Mus.; Eighth St. Gal.; Galerie St. Etienne, 1942, 1944, 1955 (all one-man); Mount Holyoke Col.; Univ. Puerto Rico; Galeria Sud-americana, 1957, 1958, and others.

de RIVERA, JOSE—*Sculptor*
440 East 59th St., New York 22, N.Y.

B. New Orleans, La., Sept. 18, 1904. *Member*: S. Gld. *Work*: monuments, El Paso, Tex.; Newark Airport, Newark, N.J. *Award*: Nat. Inst. A. & Let. grant, 1959. *Exhibited*: AIC, 1930, 1931; MMoAA, 1938-1940, 1942, 1951; WMAA, 1935-1938, 1940, 1941, 1948-1952; Harvard Univ., 1945; Yale Univ., 1946; BM, 1938; Willard Gal., 1941; Buchholz Gal., 1942; Mortimer Levitt Gal., 1946; PAFA, 1938; MMA, 1951, 1956; Newark Mus. A., 1956; Grace Borgenicht Gal.*

DER HAROOTIAN, KOREN—*Sculptor, P.*
R.F.D. 9-W, Castle Rd., Orangeburg, N.Y.

B. Ashodavan, Armenia, Apr. 2, 1909. *Studied*: WMA Sch. *Member*: S. Gld.; Fed. Mod. P. & S. *Awards*: prize, Springfield A. Lg., 1945; Audubon A., 1950, med., 1949; gold med., PAFA, 1954; Am. Acad. A. Let. grant, 1954. *Work*: MMA; WMA; PAFA; Arizona State Col. Mus., Tempe; marble eagle, U.S. Pavilion, Brussels World's Fair, 1958, and in private colls.; Fairmount Park Assn., Phila., Pa. *Exhibited*: Leicester Gal., Goupils Gal., Zwemmer Gal., London, England, 1938-39; WMAA, 1956 (and prior); PAFA, 1946-1956; AIC, 1951; Univ. Nebraska; Cranbrook Acad. A.; Univ. Iowa; Des Moines A. Center; Fairmount Park; PMA, 1949; one-man: Caz-Delbos Gal., N.Y.; WMA; Morton Gal.; Mus. of Jamaica, B.W.I., 1942; Kraushaar Gal., 1945; Washington Square, 1948; Phila. A. All., 1950.

DERN, CLAUDE—*Painter, T.*
Dorset, Vt.

B. Desertines, Allier, France, Mar. 4, 1906. *Studied*: ASL, with George Bridgman; Grand Central Sch. A., with Ivan Olinsky, Luis Mora; and in France. *Member*: All. A. Am.; SC; So. Vermont A. *Awards*: prizes, A. Center of the Oranges, 1950; AAPL, 1940. *Work*: Bennington Mus., Vt. *Exhibited*: All. A. Am., 1946-1954; Montclair A. Mus., 1948, 1949, 1951-1953; Argent Gal., 1956 (one-man); So. Vermont A., 1936-1955; Bennington Mus., 1940 (one-man); So. Vermont A., 1953 (one-man). *Position*: Instr., Newark (N.J.) Sch. Fine & Indst. A., 1946-54; East Orange, South Orange, Maplewood and Montclair (N.J.) Adult Schs., 1946-54; Vice-Pres., New Jersey P. & S., 1951; Instr. A., Manchester, Vt., A. Center.

DER NERSESSIAN, SIRARPIE—*Educator, W., L.*
Dumbarton Oaks, 3101 R St., N.W., Washington, D.C.; h. 120 Avenue de Versailles, Paris XVI, France

B. Constantinople, Turkey, Sept. 5, 1896. *Studied*: License es Lettres, Diplome d'Etudes Superieures, Diplome de l'Ecole des Hautes Etudes, Docteur es Lettres, at Sorbonne, Paris, France. *Member*: Soc. Byzantine Studies; CAA; Mediaeval Acad. Am.; Archaeological Inst. Am.; AAUW. *Awards*: Prix Foulds, Inst. de France; Prix de l'Association des Etudes Grecques. Author: Many articles and books on Mediaeval & Byzantine Art. Lectures: Coptic Paintings, Byzantine Manuscripts, etc.*

de ROSEN, JOHN HENRY—*Painter, E.*
3440 34th Place, N.W., Washington 16, D.C.

B. Warsaw, Poland, Feb. 25, 1891. *Studied*: Univ. Lausanne, Switzerland, B.Sc.; Univ. Paris & Munich; & with Jan de Rosen, Luc Oliver Merson, Emile Male, Hugo von Tschudi. *Member*: NSMP; Polish Inst. A. & Sc. *Awards*: Legion of Honor, France; award, Polish Acad. of Literature, 1938; Doctor of Humane Letters, Catholic Univ. of America, 1957; Citation, Arch. Lg., 1958. *Work*: murals, cathedrals in Poland, Vienna, Castelgandolfo; Wash., D.C.; Toledo, Ohio; New Wesley Mem. Hospital, Chicago, Ill.; Grace Cathedral, San F.; St. John's, Memphis, Tenn.; Pittsburgh, Pa.; Hollywood, Cal.; Pasadena, Cal.; Buffalo, N.Y., and others. *Exhibited*: WFNY 1939; & abroad. Lectures: History of Liturgical Art. *Position*: Former Research Prof. in Liturgical Art, Catholic Univ. of Am., Washington, D.C., 1939-49; Consultant to the Bishops of U.S. on Iconography of Nat. Shrine of Immaculate Conception, Wash., D.C.

DERUJINSKY, GLEB W.—*Sculptor, C.*
14 West 68th St., New York 23, N.Y.

B. Smolensk, Russia, Aug. 13, 1888. *Studied*: Univ. & FA Acad., Petrograd. *Member*: NA; NSS; Arch. L. *Awards*: Med., Russia, 1916; Phila. Sesquicentennial G., 1926; World's Fair, Paris, 1937; NAD, 1938; Lindsay Mem. prize, 1954; Meriden AA, 1954; AAPL, 1957, 1958; Daniel French prize, All. A. Am., 1958. *Work*: MMA; busts, New Sch. for Social Research; Hyde Park, N.Y.; Cranbrook Acad. A.; USPO, Wash., D.C.; group, Brookgreen Gardens; Stations of the Cross, Cardinal Spellman's private chapel; figures & mem. in San Diego, Cal.; Toledo, Ohio; Pittsburgh & Philadelphia, Pa. *Exhibited*: PAFA; MMA; Royal Acad., England; Royal Acad., Belgium; Knoedler Gal., London, 1928 (one-man).

DESKEY, DONALD—*Industrial Designer*
630 Fifth Ave.; h. 222 Central Park South, New York 19, N.Y.

B. Blue Earth, Minn., Nov. 23, 1894. *Studied*: Univ. California; Mark Hopkins A. Sch.; AIC; Grande Chaumiere, Paris, France. *Member*: BAID; F., Soc. Indst. Designers; A. Dir. Cl. *Awards*: Med. for Indst. Des., Paris Exp., 1937; prizes, Pittsburgh Plate Glass Co. *Exhibited*: MMA, 1931, 1934, 1940; BM, 1931; Detroit Inst. A.; Chicago World's Fair, 1933; WFNY 1939; Paris Exp., 1937; Phila. A. All., 1945; Am. Des. Gal., 1929, 1930; MMoAA, 1937; N.Y. A. All., 1927-1930. Lectures: Industrial Design. *Position*: Senior Member, Donald Deskey Assoc., Indst. Des. Consultants, 1927- ; Pres., Shelter Industries, Inc., 1939- .*

DESMOND, ALICE CURTIS (Mrs. Thomas C.)—*Writer, P.*
P.O. Box 670, Newburgh, N.Y.

B. Southport, Conn., Sept. 19, 1897. *Studied*: Parson's Sch. Des., and with private art teachers. *Member*: Nat. Lg. Am. Pen Women; Soc. Women Geographers; Pen & Brush Cl., Albany A. Group; Hudson Valley AA; Am. Assn. Univ. Women; N.Y. State Hist. Assn.; Royal Photographic Assn., London. *Awards*: F., Soc. Am. Hist.; Litt. D., Russell Sage Col.; Nat. Lg. Am. Pen Women; med., photography, Amsterdam, Holland, 1951. *Exhibited*: Hudson Highlands AA, 1942-44; Albany Inst. Hist. & A., 1943-45; Pen & Brush Cl., 1945-52; Ogunquit A. Center, 1950-52; Hudson Valley AA, 1950-52; St. Augustine AA, 1951; Terry AI, 1951; Nat. Lg. Am. Pen Women, 1952; Lake Placid Cl., 1958. Author: "Far Horizons," 1931; "Soldier of the Sun," 1939; "Sea Cats," 1944; "Alexander Hamilton's Wife," 1952; "Barnum Presents: General Tom Thumb," 1954; "Bewitching Betsy Bonaparte," 1958, and others.

de TOLNAY, CHARLES—*Educator, W.*
Murray Place, Princeton, N.J.

B. Budapest, Hungary, May 27, 1899. *Studied*: Univ. Vienna, Ph.D., and in Germany. *Member*: CAA; Atheneum. *Awards*: Laureat de l'Academie des Inscriptions et Belles-Lettres, Institute de France, 1937; Bollingen F.; Guggenheim F. Author: "History and Technique of Old Master Drawings," 1943; "The Sistine Ceiling," 1945, and many other books on art. *Position*: Memb., Inst. for Advanced Study, Princeton, N.J., 1938-48; Visiting Prof., Columbia Univ., New York, N.Y., 1953- .*

de TOMASI, MRS. JANE DAVENPORT. See Davenport, Jane

DEUEL, THORNE—*Museum Director*
Centennial Bldg.; h. 2150 Illini Rd., Springfield, Ill.

B. Millbrook, N.Y., Dec. 15, 1890. *Studied*: U.S. Military Acad., B.S.; Columbia Univ.; Univ. Chicago, Ph.D. *Member*: Am. Anthropological Assn.; Soc. for Am. Arch.; Ill. Acad. Science; Missouri Archaeological Soc. Co-Author: "Rediscovering Illinois"; Author: "Hopewellian Dress in Illinois"; "Hopewellian Communities in Illinois"; "American Indian Ways of Life"; Ed., Contributor: "Man's Venture in Culture"; contributor to Anthropological and archaeological publications. Taught: Archaeological Field Methods, Univ. Chicago; Anthropology & Ethnology, Syracuse Univ. *Position*: Research Assoc. & Field Dir. in Archaeology, Univ. Chicago; Asst. Prof. Sociology, Syracuse Univ.; Dir., Illinois State Mus. of Natural Hist. & A., Springfield, Ill., at present.

DEUTSCH, BORIS—Painter, Et., Lith., T.
850 South Gramercy Pl., Los Angeles 5, Cal.

B. Krasnagorka, Lithuania, June 4, 1892. *Studied*: in Europe: *Member*: Cal. WC Soc.; All. A. of Los A. *Awards*: prizes, San Diego FA Soc., 1930; Los A. Mus. A., 1932; Oakland A. Gal., 1931, 1939, 1940; Pomona (Cal.) Fair, 1938; 1st prize, Pepsi-Cola, 1946. *Work*: murals, USPO, Reedley, Cal.; Los A. Terminal Annex PO; Hot Springs, N.M.; Palace Legion Honor; Mills Col.; Portland (Ore.) Mus. A.; Carnegie Inst.; Denver A. Mus. *Exhibited*: Univ. California, 1926, 1942; Los A. Mus. A., 1926, 1929, 1941; East-West Gal., San F., 1929; Cal. AC, 1929; Mills Col., 1929; SAM, 1930; San Diego FA Soc., 1930; Denver A. Mus., 1931; Portland (Ore.) Mus. A., 1931; Cal. PLH, 1931; Dallas Mus. FA, 1932; Jacques Seligmann Gal., 1933; Oakland A. Gal., 1936, 1940; Stockton (Cal.) Mus. A., 1940; Sacramento Mus. A., 1940; Scripps Col., 1946 (all one-man exh.).

DE VINNEY, LAURA LAURETT—
    Educator, P., C., Gr., C., L.
40 Day St., Fredonia, N.Y.

B. Howe, Ind. *Studied*: Western State T. Col.; T. Col., Columbia Univ., B.S., M.A.; Fontainebleau, France. *Member*: Buffalo SA; The Patteran; Eastern AA; Nat. Edu. Assn.; Com. A. Edu., MModA; Chautauqua County Soc. A.; Dunkirk-Fredonia Br. of AAUW (Chm.A.). *Awards*: prizes, Buffalo SA, 1935; Chautauqua County SA, 1938. *Exhibited*: Buffalo SA; The Patteran; Albright A. Gal.; Fredonia, N.Y., (one-man). Contributor to: Design Magazine; Everyday Art; & others. *Position*: Dir., A. Dept., Fredonia State T. Col., Fredonia, N.Y., 1925-51.*

DE VITIS, THEMIS—Painter, Des., T., Cr.
111 Bank St., New York 14, N.Y.

B. Lecce, Puglia, Italy, Nov. 3, 1905. *Studied*: Acad. Beaux-Arts, Rome, Venice and Milan, Italy. *Member*: AEA. *Awards*: Scholarship, Lecce, Italy, 1922; Nat. award, Beaux-Arts, Venice, 1927. *Work*: Mus. A., Province Bldg., and Municipal Bldg., Lecce, Italy; Univ. of Ciudad Trujillo, Dominican Republic, and in private collections; murals, port., des., for Thibaut, Renverne Originals, Louis Bowen and others; murals in Italy. *Exhibited*: Bari, Italy, 1930 (one-man), and other one-man exhs. in Italy and France; Palais d'Exposition, Rome, 1931; Salon des Tuileries, Paris, 1931, 1934, 1935; Beaux-Arts, Florence, Italy, 1933; Salon des Independents, Paris, 1935; Salon Art des Murals, Paris, 1935; NAC, 1940; A. Gal., N.Y., 1940, 1955; AEA, 1951, 1952, 1954; AFA, 1955. Contributor art criticisms to French and Italian publications. Memb. Welfare Com., AEA, N.Y. Chptr., 1952- .

DEVLIN, HARRY (ARTHUR)—Cartoonist, I., Port. P.
443 Hillside Ave., Mountainside, N.J.

B. Jersey City, N.J. *Studied*: Syracuse Univ., B.F.A. *Member*: SI; Nat. Cartoonists Soc.; Artists & Writers Assn. *Work*: political cartoons for Collier's; mural, City Savings Bank, Elizabeth, N.J. *Exhibited*: MMA, 1947, 1951. Author, I., Standard Text Book on Cartooning, Minneapolis Sch. A. Comic strip "Raggmopp." *Position*: Pres., Nat. Cartoonist Soc., 1956-57.

DEVREE, HOWARD—Art Critic
5 Gramercy Park, New York, N.Y.

Position: Art Critic, New York Times.*

DEW, HENRIETTA (Mrs. Edgar H.)—Craftsman, T.
422 North Charles St. (1); h. 119 Oak Dr., Catonsville 28, Md.

B. Winona, Minn. *Studied*: Milwaukee Sch. F. & App. A.; Columbia Univ. *Member*: Balt. Mun. A. Soc. *Position*: Hd. Craft Dept., Maryland Inst., Baltimore, Md., 1922-1952.

De WALD, ERNEST THEODORE—Museum Director, E.
The Art Museum, Princeton University; h. 76 Library Place, Princeton, N.J.

B. New Brunswick, N.J., Sept. 18, 1891. *Studied*: Rutgers Univ., A.B., L.H.D.; Princeton Univ., A.M., Ph.D. *Awards*: Chevalier de la Couronne de Belgique, 1937; Order of the British Empire, 1946; Legion of Merit, 1946; Stella della Solidarieta, Italian Govt., 1951; Guggenheim F., 1927; Fulbright F., 1952; F., Medieval Acad. Am. *Member*: CAA; Archaeological Assn. Am. Author: "Pietro Lorenzetti," 1930; "The Stuttgart Psalter," 1930; "The Illustrations of the Utrecht Psalter," 1932. Contributor to Art and Archaeological journals. Co-Editor, Contributing Author: Princeton's corpus of Illustrations of Manuscripts of the Septuagint, 1941- . *Position*: Instr., New Jersey Col. for Women, 1920-33; Asst. Prof., Columbia Univ., 1923-25; Assoc. Prof., Princeton Univ., 1925-38; Dir. Art Museum, Princeton Univ., New Jersey, 1947- .*

de WELDON, FELIX WEIHS—Sculptor, P., T., L.
219 Randolph Pl., N.E.; h. 2132 Bancroft Pl., N.W., Washington 8, D.C.; s. "Beacon Rock," Harrison Ave., Newport, R.I.

B. Vienna, Austria, Apr. 12, 1907. *Studied*: Marchetti Col., B.A.; Univ. Vienna, M.A., M.S., Ph.D.; & in Italy, France, England. *Member*: AFA; Sc. Memb., Nat. Comm. FA, appt. by President, 1950, re-appt. by Pres. Eisenhower, 1955. *Awards*: prizes, Vienna, Austria, 1925, 1927; St. Andrews, Canada, 1939. *Work*: busts, King George V & King George VI, London; Mus. City of Vienna; Nat. Port. Gal., London; American Embassy, Canberra, Australia; Naval War Col., Newport, R.I.; White House, Wash., D.C.; State Capitol, Little Rock, Ark.; Dallas, Tex.; St. Augustine, Fla.; Mus., Brisbane, Australia; U.S. Naval Acad., Annapolis, Md.; many port. busts of prominent officials in Scotland, England & U.S. Groups, mem., monuments, reliefs: U.S. Marine Corps War Mem., Wash., D.C.; Commodore Perry statue, Tokyo, Japan; Marine mon., Belleau Wood, France; Iwo Jima Flag Raising statue, Quantico, Va.; Dealey mon., Dallas, Tex.; fountain, Ottawa, Can.; George Washington bust, Canberra, Australia; bronze statue of Speaker Rayburn, Bonham, Tex.; equestrian statue, Bolivar, Wash., D.C.; Red Cross Monument, Wash., D.C.; Monument to Admiral Richard E. Byrd, Arlington, Va.; equestrian statue, of Garcia, Havana, Cuba. *Exhibited*: Vienna, 1925-1928; Paris Salon, 1929, 1930; Cairo, Egypt, 1932, 1933; Royal Acad., London, 1934-1937; Montreal Mus. A., 1938; Arch. L., N.Y., 1939. Lectures: History of Painting, 12th to 19th Century; etc. *Position*: Dir., Newport Acad. FA.

de WITT, CORNELIUS HUGH—Illustrator, Gr., P.
c/o Artists & Writers Press, 630 Fifth Ave., New York 10, N.Y.

B. Cassel, Germany, June 6, 1905. *Studied*: in Germany & France. *Work*: murals, Calvert Distilleries. *Exhibited*: MMA; Norton A. Gal. Illus. "Regions of America" series; "The Golden Encyclopaedia"; "History of the U.S. for Young People"; "The Golden Geography"; "The Golden History of the World"; "My First Geography of the Pacific," etc. Lectures: Lithography in Children's Books.

DE WITT, JESSIE R.—Painter
520 South Pacific St., Oceanside, Cal.

B. De Queen, Ark. *Member*: San Diego AA; Women Painters of the West; Laguna Beach AA; La Jolla A. Gld.; Carlsbad-Oceanside A. Lg. *Awards*: prizes, Los A. Mus. A.; Laguna Beach AA; San Diego County exh., Vista, Cal.; Carlsbad-Oceanside annual. *Exhibited*: Festival A., Laguna Beach; Women Painters of the West; Vista, Cal.; Carlsbad-Oceanside A. Lg., annually.*

DEY, MAURICE ROBERT—Printmaker, C., S., P.
Scotch Rd., Trenton 8, N.J.

B. Ballaigues, Switzerland, May 15, 1900. *Studied*: with Harry Wickey. *Member*: Hudson Highlands AA. *Work*: Rochester Mem. A. Gal.; USPO, Albany, N.Y.; Cornwall (N.Y.) H.S. *Exhibited*: PAFA, 1936, 1937; Fed. A. Gal., 1938, 1939; NAD, 1941, 1942; Syracuse Mus. FA, 1941; Williams Col., 1940; Hudson Highlands AA, 1935-1939; Southern Pines & Pinehurst, N.C., 1946; Am. A. Group; Woodstock, N.Y., 1953; Trenton, N.J., 1955, 1958; Princeton, N.J., 1958; Clinton, N.J., 1955; Lausanne, Switzerland, 1953.

de ZORO—dei CAPPELLER, (ETTORE) E.—Sculptor
800 Riven Rock Rd., Santa Barbara, Cal.

B. Cibiana, Italy, Jan. 27, 1894. *Studied*: Moci Col., Italy; Imperial A. Acad., Germany; Andhra Research Univ., India, D.F.A. *Member*: Los Angeles AA; Cal. A. Cl.; Societe Academique d'Histoire Int.; Col. Heraldique de France; Atheneum National Sc. & A., Mexico; Hon. Comite Cultural, Argentina; Academia Hispano-Americana de Ciencias y Artes, Spain; Soc. FA, Brazil. *Awards:* Cross Academic Honor, Int. Academic Council, Wash., D.C., 1938; med., Hispano-Americana Acad. Sc. & A., Spain, 1932; Grand Prix, Belgium, 1937; med., GGE, 1939; Aeronautical Int. A. Exh., 1937; Pacific Int. Exp., 1935; Santa Barbara, Cal., 1955, etc. *Work:* Busts, figures, reliefs, San F.; Carmel, Cal.; Univ. Southern California; Mus. of Pieve di Cadore, Italy; Ecuador, Bulgaria, Mexico, Wash., D.C., etc. *Exhibited:* Pacific Int. Exp., 1935; GGE, 1939; Los A. Mus. A.; Palos Verdes, Cal., 1935-1937; Cal. A. Cl., 1936; Santa Barbara, Cal., 1935-1938; Ebell Salon, Los A., 1940, 1941.*

di BENEDETTO, ANGELO—*Painter, C.*

64 Jasper St., Paterson, N.J.

B. Paterson, N.J., June 19, 1913. *Studied:* CUASch.; BMFA Sch.; & with Alexandre Jacoveloff. *Awards:* prize, Montclair A. Mus., 1938. *Work:* Encyclopaedia Britannica Coll. *Exhibited:* CGA, 1941; Pepsi-Cola, 1942, 1943, 1944, 1946; Carnegie Inst., 1941; PAFA, 1941; AIC, 1940; WMAA, 1941; Montclair A. Mus., 1938, 1939; Univ. Colorado, 1945 (one-man). Illus., "Twin Rivers," 1942; "Haitian Folk Lore," 1946.*

DICE, ELIZABETH JANE—*Educator, C., P.*

Box 1094, Mississippi State College for Women, Columbus, Miss.

B. Urbana, Ill., Apr. 3, 1919. *Studied:* Univ. Michigan, B. of Des., M. of Des.; Int. Sch. A., Mexico; Instituto Allende, Mexico; T. Col., Columbia Univ.; Norfolk A. Sch., and with Jerry Farnsworth. *Member:* Miss. AA; New Orleans AA; Southeastern AA; AAUP. *Awards:* prizes, Jackson, Miss., 1946, 1951; Memphis, Tenn.; Canton H.S. (Miss.), 1955 (purchase). *Exhibited:* Nat. WC Show, Jackson, 1951; SAGA, 1951; Nat. Crafts Exh., Wichita, 1950; Mississippi AA, 1948-1951; Friends of Am. A., Grand Rapids, 1950; Memphis Garden Cl., 1952; Starkville (Miss.) Craft Exh., 1954; New Orleans AA, 1955; oneman: Allison's Wells, Miss., 1953, 1958; Miss. State Col. for Women, 1953; Jackson AA, 1958; Meridian AA, 1958. *Position:* Vice-Pres., 1954, Pres., 1955, Mississippi Edu. Assn.; Chm., State Pres., Southeastern AA, 1954-55; Assoc. Prof. A., Miss. State Col. for Women, Columbus, Miss., 1945- .

DICK, JOHN HENRY—*Painter*

Dixie Plantation, Meggett, S.C.

B. New York, N.Y., May 12, 1919. *Studied:* Yale Univ. Sch.F.A. *Work:* Specializes in bird paintings, with numerous commissions and card designs for Nat. Audubon Soc. *Exhibited:* Nat. Audubon Soc., 1950, 1957; Gibbes A. Gal., Charleston, 1951; Columbia Mus. A., 1952; La. State Univ., 1952; Norfolk Div., Col. of William & Mary, 1955; Am. Mus. of Nat. History, N.Y., 1958. I., "South Carolina Bird Life," 1949; "Florida Bird Life," 1954; "The Warblers of America," 1957. Executed Duck Stamp for Fish & Wildlife Service, 1952-53.

DICKERSON, GRACE LESLIE—*Painter, S., C., T.*

R.R. #5 Bass Rd., Fort Wayne 8, Ind.

B. Fort Wayne, Ind. *Studied:* Fort Wayne A. Sch.; Instituto Allende, Mexico, M.F.A.; AIC, and with Guy Pène DuBois; St. Francis Col., Fort Wayne, B.A. *Member:* Hoosier Salon; Fort Wayne A. Sch. Alumni Assn. *Awards:* prizes, Indiana State Fair, 1940, 1946, 1953, 1954, 1957; Fort Wayne Woman's Cl., 1953-1957; Hoosier Salon, 1954; South Bend Ceramic Exh., 1953 (purchase); Northern Indiana A. Salon, Hammond, Ind., 1955, 1956; local exhibitions, 1938, 1940, 1944, 1946, 1948, 1952, 1953, 1957; degree, Fort Wayne Univ., 1950. *Work:* Cathedrals, in Fort Wayne, South Bend, Evansville and Indianapolis; Fort Wayne schools; Keenan Hotel, etc. *Exhibited:* local exhs., 1953-1958; Woman's Cl., 1953, 1958; Michiana A. Exh., 1953; John Herron AI, 1953, 1955, 1957; Kirk o' the Hills, Bloomfield, Mich., 1953; Springfield, Ill., 1953, 1954; Indiana State Fair, 1953, 1954, 1956, 1957; South Bend Ceramic Exh., 1953-1957; Hoosier Salon, 1954, 1955-1958; Northern Indiana A., 1954-1958; Fort Wayne A. Sch. Alumni Exh., 1954; Ohio Univ., Athens, 1954; Montpelier, Ohio, 1954-55; Outdoor Alumni Exh., 1955 and others. *Position:* Instr., Harmar Sch., 1950-51, Arcola Sch., 1955, Fort Wayne, Ind.

DICKERSON, WILLIAM J.—*Painter, Lith., T.*

401 North Belmont St.; h. 509 North Martinson St., Wichita 12, Kan.

B. El Dorado, Kan., Oct. 29, 1904. *Studied:* AIC; & with Bolton Brown, B.J.O. Nordfeldt. *Member:* Prairie Pr.M.; Prairie WC Painters; Wichita A. Gld.; Cal. Soc. Pr.M.; Soc. Canadian Painters, Etchers & Engravers. *Awards:* prizes, Kansas City AI, 1939, 1940; Joslyn Mem., 1944. *Work:* Wichita AA; Kansas State Col.; Kansas Univ.; Wichita Univ. *Exhibited:* AIC, 1931, 1932; PAFA, 1937, 1940; Rockefeller Center, 1936, 1937; Lib.Cong., 1943; Palace Legion Honor, 1946; Kansas City AI, 1930-1950; Joslyn Mem., 1944-1946, 1951; MMA, 1952. *Position:* Dir., Sch. of the Wichita AA, Wichita, Kan., 1930- .

DICKINSON, DAISY OLIVIA—*Sculptor, C., P., L.*

3442 Encinal Ave., La Crescenta, Cal.

B. Bellingham, Wash. *Studied:* Chouinard AI; Santa Barbara Sch. FA; & with F. Tolles Chamberlin, S. MacDonald-Wright, F. M. Fletcher. *Member:* Am. Ceramic Soc. of Southern Cal.; All. A. of Los A. *Award:* prize, Los A. County Fair, 1941. *Exhibited:* Los A. Mus. A., 1929, 1933, 1939, 1940; Pasadena AI, 1930, 1931; Cal. State Fair, 1930, 1931, 1934. Lectures: History & Design of Ceramic Art.*

DICKINSON, EDWIN—*Painter, T.*

420 West 119th St., New York 27, N.Y.

B. Seneca Falls, N.Y., Oct. 11, 1891. *Studied:* PIASch; ASL; & with William M. Chase, Charles W. Hawthorne. *Member:* Fed. Mod. P.&S.; NAD; Patteran Soc., Buffalo; Nat. Inst. A. & Let.; Century Assn.; ASL. *Awards:* prize, NAD, 1929, 1949; med., Century Assn., 1955; Nat. Acad. A. & Lets. grant, 1954. *Work:* MMA; Albright A. Gal.; Bowdoin Col.; Cornell Univ.; Springfield (Mass.) Mus. FA. *Exhibited:* BMFA; MMoDA; WMA; PMA; VMFA; Witte Mem. Mus.; FA of Houston: Pasadena AI; Los A. Mus. A.; SFMA; Portland (Ore.) Mus. A.; CAM; AIC; Toledo Mus. A.; Albright A. Gal.; Luxembourg Mus., Paris; Carnegie Inst.; Rochester Mem. A. Gal.; NAD; Soc. Indp. A., and other leading museums and organizations, since 1916. One-man: Albright A. Gal.; Rochester Mem. A. Gal.; Farnsworth Mus.; Wellesley Col.; MMoDA; Passedoit Gal. *Position:* Instr. A., ASL, 1922-23, 1945- ; CUASch, New York, N.Y., 1945- ; BM, 1949- .*

DICKINSON, MRS. NEVILLE S. See *Feldman, Hilda*

DICKINSON, ROSS EDWARD—*Painter, I., T.*

3442 Encinal Ave., La Crescenta, Cal.

B. Santa Ana, Cal., Apr. 29, 1903. *Studied:* Chouinard AI; Grand Central Sch. A.; NAD; Santa Barbara Sch. FA; & with Hawthorne, Fletcher, Costigan, Ennis. *Award:* prize, Cal. State Fair, 1935, 1939. *Work:* murals, Little Theatre, Santa Barbara Sch. FA; Jefferson, George Washington H.S., Los A.; mosaic, King Jr. H.S., Los A., Cal. *Exhibited:* Los A. Mus. A., 1925, 1926, 1928, 1929, 1931-1933, 1935, 1945, 1951; Cal. State Fair, 1928-1940; Oakland A. Gal., 1937; Santa Cruz A. Lg., 1937. *Position:* Instr. A., Santa Barbara Sch. FA, Santa Barbara, Cal.; A. Center Sch., Los Angeles, Cal.*

DICKINSON, SIDNEY E.—*Painter*

Carnegie Hall, West 57th St., New York 19, N.Y.

B. Wallingford, Conn., Nov. 28, 1890. *Studied:* with Bridgman, Volk, Chase. *Member:* NA; Century Cl.; All. A.Am. *Awards:* prizes, NAD, 1917, 1924, 1933, 1938; PAFA, 1923, 1924, 1931; CGA, 1924; All.A.Am., 1930, 1937; NAC, 1932. *Work:* CGA; AIC; CAM; Mus. FA of Houston; Mun.A.Gal., Davenport, Iowa.*

DICKSON, HAROLD EDWARD—*Educator, W.*

206 Hartswick Ave., State College, Pa.

B. Sharon, Pa., July 18, 1900. *Studied:* Pennsylvania State Univ., B.S.; Harvard Univ., M.A., Ph.D. *Member:* CAA; Am. Assn. Univ. Prof.; Soc. Arch. Hist.; Scarab Cl. Ed., "Observations on American Art; Selections from the Writings of John Neal (1793-1876)," 1943. Contributor to: Art magazines with articles on American art. Author: "A Working Bibliography of Art in Pennsylvania," 1948; "John Wesley Jarvis, American Painter," 1949; "A Hundred Pennsylvania Buildings," 1954; "Pennsylvania Painters," 1955. *Position:* Prof. Hist Art, Pennsylvania State Univ., Pa., 1923- .

DI CRISPINO, MARY REINA—Painter
2703 Keyworth Ave., Baltimore 15, Md.

B. Catania, Italy, Dec. 29, 1900. *Studied*: Maryland Inst., and with Herman Maril. *Member*: A. Un., Baltimore; Balt. Mun. A. Soc.; Nat. Lg. Am. Pen Women; AEA. *Awards*: prizes, Balt. Mun. A. Soc., 1941; Peale Mus. A., 1943, 1945; Nat. Lg. Am. Pen Women. *Exhibited*: NCFA, 1946; CGA, 1945; Peale Mus., 1939-1945, 1948-1952; BMA, 1937, 1939-1946; BMA traveling exh., 1941, 1942; A. Un. Balt., 1937, 1953, 1955; Notre Dame Col., Baltimore, 1944; Contemp. Gal., Baltimore, 1944, 1945; NGA, 1948, 1950, 1952; Playhouse, Balt. (one-man); Balt. A. Week annually; Balt. A. Festival, 1952. *Work*: Peale Mus.; Balt. Friends of Art, and in private collections.

DIDDEL, NORMA L.—Educator, P., Gr.
Nebraska State Teachers College, Peru, Neb.

B. Denver, Colo., Jan. 25, 1901. *Studied*: Univ. Denver, A.B.; Univ. California at Los A.; Colorado State Col. of Edu., M.A.; Harvard Univ. *Member*: Nat. Edu. Assn.; Nebraska Edu. Assn.; Am. Assn. Univ. Women; Am. Assn. Univ. Prof. *Exhibited*: Joslyn A. Mus., 1931-1954; Lincoln A. Gal., 1935-1954. Contributor to: Educational publications. *Position*: Assoc. Prof. A., Nebraska State Teachers Col., Peru, Neb., 1929- .

DIENES, SARI—Painter, Gr., Des., T.
58 West 57th St., New York 19, N.Y.

B. Hungary, Oct. 8, 1899. *Studied*: Ozenfant Sch. FA; and with Andre L'Hote, Fernand Leger in Paris; Henry Moore in London. *Awards*: F., MacDowell Colony, 1952-1954; Yaddo Fnd., 1953. *Work*: BM, and in many private collections. *Exhibited*: BM A. Sch., 1946-1948; BM, 1948; Salon des Realities Nouvelles, Paris, 1951; Ninth St. Exh. P. & S., 1951; WMAA, 1952; Univ. Illinois, 1953; MModA, 1954; AFA traveling exh., 1953-1955; one-man: New Sch. for Social Research, 1942; Parsons Sch. Des., 1944; Carlebach Gal., 1948; Wittenborn Gal., 1949; Univ. Montana, 1952; Mills Col., N.Y., 1955, 1956; Betty Parsons Gal., 1950, 1954, 1955. *Position*: Asst. Dir., Ozenfant Sch. FA, 1936-41; Instr. Parsons Sch. Des., 1944-45; Instr., BM A. Sch., 1946-49; Teaching in own studio, 1940-52.

DIETRICH, GEORGE ADAMS—Sculptor, P., Des., L., E.
2035 North Lake Drive, Milwaukee 2, Wis.

B. Clark County, Ind., Apr. 26, 1905. *Studied*: Layton Sch. A.; AIC; Ohio State Univ. *Member*: Wisconsin P. & S. *Awards*: prizes, Hoosier Salon, 1927-1931; Milwaukee AI, 1929. *Work*: Layton A. Gal.; mem., City of Milwaukee; U.S. Naval Acad., Annapolis; Corpus Christi, Tex.; Whitnall, Washington, Kletsch Parks, Milwaukee; O'Hare Airport, Chicago; Mitscher Field, San Diego; mural, USPO, Lake Geneva, Wis.; fountain, Univ. Wis., Campus (Madison), 1958. *Exhibited*: nationally and internationally, 1930-1955. *Position*: Hd. Dept. S., Layton Sch. A., 1929-37; Prof. S. & Painting, Univ. Michigan, 1937-38; Instr., Indst. Des., Milwaukee Sch. Engineering, 1939-43; U.S. Navy, 1943-46; Hd. S. Dept. & A. Edu., Prof., Univ. Wisconsin, 1946-53; Lt.-Commander, USNR, Air Tech-Tr. Officer, Glenview, Ill.

DIETRICH, JOHN FRANKLIN—Educator, C., Des., P.
Eastern Montana College of Education; h. 2716 Custer St., Billings, Mont.

B. Wayzata, Minn., Aug. 7, 1909. *Studied*: State T. Col., Superior, Wis.; Univ. Iowa; Univ. Chicago, Ph.B., M.A.; Ohio State Univ., Ph.D. in Appl. Des. *Member*: NEA. *Work*: Mus. New Mexico, Santa Fe. *Positions*: Hd. Dept. A. & Crafts, Western Univ., Silver City, N.M., 1945-46; Hd. Dept. A. & Crafts, Dir. A. Edu., New Mexico Highlands Univ., Las Vegas, N.M., 1946-53; Edu. A. & Crafts Specialist for Intl. Co-operation Admin. (Point 4) to establish nation-wide A. & Crafts Program in the schools of Ethiopia, 1953-56; Prof. A., Eastern Montana Col. of Edu., Billings, Mont., 1957- .

DIETRICH, THOMAS MUELLER (TOM)—Painter, E.
Lawrence College; h. 621 North Sampson St., Appleton, Wis.

B. Appleton, Wis., Jan. 20, 1912. *Studied*: Univ. Wisconsin Experimental Col.; Cincinnati A. Acad.; Minneapolis Sch. A. *Member*: Wisconsin A. Fed.; Wisconsin WC Soc.; Am. Assn. Univ. Prof. *Awards*: F., Tiffany Fnd., 1938; prizes, AIC, 1941; Madison AA, 1940; Wis. P.&S., 1942, 1950, 1952, 1958; Wisconsin State Exh., 1948; Gimbel Bros. Exh., 1948, 1950; Wis. State Fair, 1949; Wisconsin Salon, 1949. *Work*: AIC; Wisconsin Union; Rockford (Ill.) AA; Madison AA; Milwaukee Journal Coll.; Milwaukee AI; Lawrence Col.; Appleton H.S.; Wilson Jr. H.S., Appleton; Gimbel Coll.; Marquette Univ.; Rufus King H.S., Milwaukee; Clintonville H.S.; Roosevelt Jr. H.S., Appleton; mural, Lutheran Bldg., Appleton, Wis.; U.S. Maritime Comm. mural on S.S. President Van Buren; Children's Hospital, Milwaukee. *Exhibited*: AIC, 1938, 1941, 1946; Phila. WC Cl., 1938, 1940-1945; CMA, 1939; All. A. Am., 1945; Wisconsin P. & S., 1936-1958; Wisconsin Salon, 1943-1958; Walker A. Center, 1949, 1950; Minnesota Centennial, 1949; Ill. State Fair, 1950, 1951; Exh. Momentum, Chicago, 1952. *Position*: Artist-in-Res., Lawrence Col., Appleton, Wis., 1944- .

DIETSCH, C. PERCIVAL—Sculptor, P.
330 Peruvian Ave., Palm Beach, Fla.; Ayers Point, Old Saybrook, Conn.

B. New York, N.Y., May 23, 1881. *Studied*: N.Y.Sch.A.; Am. Acad. in Rome; & with William M. Chase, Beckwith, Attilio Piccirilli. *Member*: Arch.L.; NSS; Soc. Four Arts, Palm Beach, Fla. (Vice-Pres.); Norton Gal. A. (Hon.). *Awards*: F., Am. Acad. in Rome, 1906-10; prize, Am. Acad. in Rome, 1906; Soc. Four Arts; Norton Gal. *Work*: Peabody Inst., Baltimore, Md.; Rice Inst., Houston, Tex.; Lighthouse for Blind, New York, N.Y.; Besso Lib., Rome, Italy; Soc. Four Arts; war mem., Deep River, Conn. *Exhibited*: PAFA, 1907; Am. Acad. in Rome, 1906-1910; NAD; Fla. Fed. A.; Soc. Four Arts; Norton Gal.

DIETZ, CHARLES—Museum Director
Art Institute of Zanesville, Maple Ave. at Adair St., Zanesville, Ohio

Position: Dir., Art Institute of Zanesville.*

di GIOIA, FRANK—Painter
77 Washington Pl., New York 11, N.Y.

B. Naples, Italy, Dec. 18, 1900. *Studied*: CUASch; ASL, and abroad. *Work*: Univ. Arizona; PMG; AIC; Albright A. Gal.; Norfolk Mus. Sc. & A.; Fla. State Col.; Washington County Mus., Hagerstown, Md.; New Britain (Conn.) Mus. *Exhibited*: AIC, 1942-1946; Marie Harriman Gal. (4 one-man exh.); Argent Gal., 1945 (one-man); WMAA, 1939, 1945; WFNY 1939; PMG, 1938; AV 1942; BM, 1945; Milch Gal. (5 one-man exhs.); Carnegie Inst.; Norfolk Mus. Sc. & A.; PAFA; CGA; MMA; Art:USA, 1958, and others. I., art and theatre magazines.

DIKE, PHIL(IP) (LATIMER)—Painter, Des., C., E.
157 East 10th St., Claremont, Cal.

B. Redlands, Cal., Apr. 6, 1906. *Studied*: Chouinard AI, with Chamberlin, Hinkle; ASL, with DuMond, Luks, Bridgman; Am. Acad., Fontainebleau, with St. Hubert. *Member*: NA; Cal. WC Soc.; Phila. WC Cl.; Fnd. Western A.; California Group; AWS. *Awards*: prizes, Cal. WC Soc., 1931, 1935, 1939, 1945, 1946, 1952, 1953, 1956; Los A. Mus. A., 1931, 1934, 1945, 1947; Pasadena AI, 1933; NAD, 1950, 1958; Cal. State Fair, 1933, 1948, 1951, 1955, 1956; GGE, 1939; Arizona State Fair, 1931, 1950; Santa Cruz A. Lg., 1932, 1934; Los A. County Fair, 1932, 1949; Ebell Cl., 1933; Los A. Nat. Exh., 1934; Newport Harbor H.S., 1948; Coronado A. Fair, 1949; San Gabriel Valley A., 1951; Nat. Orange Show, 1951; med., Pepsi-Cola, 1947; Southwest Expo., 1928. *Work*: Wood Mus., Montpelier, Vt.; MMA; Santa Barbara Mus. A.; Andrew M. Dike Mem. Chapel, Redlands, Cal. *Exhibited*: Carnegie Inst.; Paris Salon; AIC; NAD; Phila. WC Cl.; Ferargil Gal.; Los A. Mus. A.; Fnd. Western A.; San Diego FA Soc.; Cal. PLH; Biltmore Gal., and others. I. & contributor to national magazines. *Position*: Instr., Chouinard AI, Los Angeles, Cal., 1929-30, 1931-34, 1937-38, 1945-50; Instr., Color and Composition, Walt Disney Productions, 1935-45; Rex Brandt-Phil Dike Summer Sch., Corona del Mar, Cal., 1947-55; Asst. Prof. A., Scripps Col. and Claremont Grad. Sch., Claremont, Cal., 1950-58.

DILLENBACK, L. C.—Educator
College of Fine Arts, Syracuse University, Syracuse, N.Y.

Position: Dean, College of Fine Arts, Syracuse University.*

DILLER, MARY BLACK—*Painter, I., W., Des., T.*

220 Cabrini Blvd., New York 33, N.Y.

B. Lancaster, Pa. *Studied*: Carnegie Inst., with Petrovits; PAFA, with McCarter, Garber, Carles; ASL, with Thomas Fogarty; Metropolitan A. Sch., with Jacobs. *Member*: Audubon A.; Lancaster County AA (Fndr. & 1st Pres., 1937-39); Eastern AA; Tiffany Fnd.; AAPL; Heights AC; Studio Cl. *Awards*: prizes, Studio Cl., 1923; Lancaster, Pa., 1925; Ogunquit A. Center, 1940. *Work*: Albany Inst. Hist. & A.; Tiffany Fnd.; Fla. Southern Col. *Exhibited*: Audubon A., 1940-1952; PAFA, 1939-1941 (traveling exh.); ASL Veteran's Exh., 1944; Tiffany Fnd.; Newhouse Gal.; Am-British A. Center; Number 10 Gal.; N.Y.Pub.Lib. (one-man); Reading & Lancaster, Pa. (one-man). Author: "Drawing for Children"; "A Child's Adventures in Drawing"; special contributor of "How To Draw," Book of Knowledge, 1955; "Holiday Drawing Book," 1954; "Drawing for Young Artists," 1955; "Young Artists Go to Europe," 1958. Contributor to: newspapers & magazines; contributing editor to Every Childs Magazine; Design magazine; Lancaster (Pa.) Sunday News. *Position*: Pennsylvania State Dir., Am. A. Week.

DILLON, JOHN K(NOX)—*Painter*

20 Bayside Pl., Amityville, L.I., N.Y.

B. Kansas City, Mo., Nov. 17, 1903. *Studied*: ASL; NAD; and with Ivan Olinsky, Sidney Dickinson, Robert Phillip, Frank J. Reilly. *Member*: ASL; AAPL; SC. *Awards*: prizes, Oakland, Cal., 1949; AAPL, 1954; Washington Square Exh., 1956 and traveling exh., 1957 and traveling exh., 1958. *Exhibited*: Oakland A. Mus., 1949, 1951; Cal. Centennial, 1949; AAPL, 1954; Crocker A. Gal., Sacramento, 1949; Berkeley Pub. Lib., 1949; Washington Square Exhs., 1954-1958; AAPL regional, 1954-1958; SC; Westhampton, L.I., 1957; Knickerbocker A., 1958.

DILLON, MILDRED MURPHY (Mrs. James F.)—
Printmaker, Et., Ser.

728 East Dorset St., Philadelphia 19, Pa.

B. Philadelphia, Pa., Oct. 12, 1907. *Studied*: PMSch. A.; PAFA; Barnes Fnd., with Earl Horter, and in Europe. *Member*: Am. Color Pr. Soc.; Phila. Pr. Cl.; Phila. A. All.; F., PAFA. *Awards*: prize, PAFA, 1953; Am. Color Pr. Soc., 1955 (Presentation Print). *Work*: PMA; Canadian P. & Et.; Phila. Pr. Cl.; Barnes Fnd.; Atwater Kent Mus.; Phila. Free Library. *Exhibited*: PAFA; NAD; Nat. Ser. Soc.; Phila. Pr. Cl.; Bradley Univ.; Wichita AA; Miami Beach A. Cl.; LC; DMFA; Smith Mus., Springfield; Phila. A. All.; Laguna Beach AA; Royal Ontario Mus., Canada. Exhibition Lecture, PAFA, 1955; demonstration, "Making a Serigraph," Phila. Pr. Cl., 1951. *Position*: Pres., Phila. A. Lg., 1940-46; Pres., Am. Color Pr. Soc., 1950-52; Vice-Pres. in charge of traveling exhibits, Am. Color Pr. Soc., Philadelphia, Pa., 1952- ; Chm. Rittenhouse Square Outdoor A. Exh., Phila., Pa., 1958- .

DIMAND, MAURICE S.—*Museum Curator, W.*

Metropolitan Museum of Art; h. 1150 Park Ave., New York 28, N.Y.

B. Austria, Aug. 2, 1892. *Studied*: Univ. Vienna, Ph.D.; & with Josef Strzygowski. *Member*: Am. Oriental Soc.; Hajji Baba Cl. *Awards*: Research F., Univ. Vienna. Author: "A Handbook of Muhammadan Art," "The Ballard Collection of Oriental Rugs in the Art Museum of St. Louis," 1935. Contributor to: Ars Islamica, CAA Bulletin, MMA Bulletin, etc., with articles on Near Eastern Art. Lectures: Coptic, Sasanian & Islamic Art. *Position*: Asst. & Asst. Cur., Dept. Decorative A., 1923-30, Assoc. Cur., 1930-33, Cur., Near Eastern Art, 1933- , MMA, New York, N.Y.

DINCKEL, GEORGE WILLIAM—*Painter, T., L.*

7 High St.; h. 6 High St., Rockport, Mass.

B. Cincinnati, Ohio, Aug. 19, 1890. *Studied*: Cincinnati A. Acad., with Frank Duveneck, L.H. Meakin, Herman Wessel. *Member*: Rockport AA; North Shore AA; Marblehead AA; Tile Cl., Toledo. *Awards*: prizes, Toledo, Ohio, 1939, 1946. *Work*: numerous H.S. in Cincinnati, Ohio, Sandusky, Ohio; Toledo Univ.; Bowling Green State Col.; Heidelberg Univ. (Tiffin, Ohio); Scott H.S., Toledo, Ohio. *Exhibited*: North Shore AA; Rockport AA; Marblehead AA; Toledo Mus. A.; Toledo AA.

DI NEGRO, PAUL GWYNN—*Painter, Et., C.*

614 Francis St., Key West 5, Fla.

B. Key West, Fla., Sept. 5, 1900. *Member*: Key West AA. *Work*: U.S. Naval Station, Marine Mus., Key West, Fla. *Exhibited*: Ringling Sch. A.; Univ. Florida; Univ. Alabama; Key West, Fed. Gal.

DINNEEN, ALICE (Mrs. Allan Gould)—*Painter, Des.*

Scarborough, N.Y.

B. New York, N.Y., Feb. 23, 1908. *Studied*: N.Y. Sch. App. Des. for Women; ASL; & with Nicolaides, Furlong. *Work*: Carville, La.; La Fortaleza, San Juan, Puerto Rico; New York Hospital; mural, USPO, Warrenton, N.C.; Corbin, Ky.; Dept. Labor, Wash., D.C. *Exhibited*: T.R.A.P. nat. traveling exh., 1935; CMA; WMAA; PAFA; Carnegie Inst.; PAFA, 1949, 1950; Kennedy & Co., New York, 1949 (one-man); Woodstock AA.

DIODA, ADOLPH—*Sculptor*

14148 Birwood Ave., Detroit, Mich.

B. Aliquippa, Pa., Sept. 10, 1915. *Studied*: Carnegie Inst.; Cleveland Sch. A.; Barnes Fnd., and with John B. Flanagan. *Awards*: Guggenheim F., 1945; med., PAFA, 1946; Phila. A. All., 1952. *Exhibited*: WMAA, 1939; PMA, 1940; Carnegie Inst., 1941; AIC, 1940; PAFA, 1946; Assoc. A. Pittsburgh, 1941-1945; Chicago A. Cl., 1951; one-man: Phila. A. All., 1951; Carlen Gal., Phila., Pa., 1951; 2-man exh. with William Kienbusch, Carnegie Inst., 1953.*

DIRK, NATHANIEL—*Painter, T., W., L.*

54 West 74th St., New York, N.Y.

B. Brooklyn, N.Y., Dec. 21, 1895. *Studied*: AIC; ASL, with Max Weber, Kenneth Hayes Miller, Boardman Robinson. *Member*: Audubon A.; Cape Ann Soc. A. *Awards*: prize, Audubon A, 1948, 1954, 1958. *Work*: WMAA; BM. *Exhibited*: Carnegie Inst., 1930, 1931; AIC, 1932-1934, 1936, 1938, 1942; BM, 1935-1941; WMAA, 1933-1940; CGA, 1934; NCFA, 1941; Audubon A., 1945, 1959; MMA, 1941; ASL, 1942, 1944, 1947-1951; Wellons Gal., 1956 (one-man). Lectures: Color Construction & Harmonies.

DIRNFELD, FREDERICK ARNOLD—*Painter, Et.*

140 West 16th St., New York 11, N.Y.

B. Budapest, Hungary, Feb. 1, 1889. *Studied*: NAD; & with Edgar Melville Ward, G.T. Turner. *Member*: Pr. Council of Am. *Work*: Boys Town. *Exhibited*: Anderson Gal., 1931; SAGA, 1932, 1933, 1935, 1939, 1946; NAC, 1932, 1933, 1935, 1939, 1946; NAD, 1932, 1933, 1935, 1938, 1942, 1946, 1948; Cal. Pr. M., 1934; CMA, 1935; PAFA, 1938; LC, 1948.

DI SPIRITO, HENRY—*Sculptor*

1008 Blanding St., Utica, N.Y.

B. Castleforte, Italy, July 2, 1898. *Studied*: Munson-Williams-Proctor Inst., and with Richard Davis. *Awards*: prize, Cooperstown AA, 1947, 1948, 1950, 1951; Syracuse Mus. FA, 1954; Nat. Inst. A. & Lets. grant, 1956; Ringling Mus. A., 1956. *Work*: Munson-Williams-Proctor Inst.; Sherburne (N.Y.) Pub. Lib.; AGAA; Syracuse Mus. FA; Colgate Univ.; Wadsworth Atheneum. *Exhibited*: WMAA, 1951; AIC, 1951, 1953; MModA, 1951; Sculpture Center, 1949, 1956, 1958 (three-man); Cortland State Fair, 1948; Cooperstown AA, 1947-1951; Albany Inst. Hist. & A., 1951; St. Lawrence Univ., 1952; AGAA, 1952; Des Moines A. Center, 1953; PAFA, 1954, 1955; Silvermine Gld. A., 1954; Springfield (Mass.) A. Lg., 1955; Sarasota Mus. A., 1955; one-man: Colgate Univ., 1947; Munson-Williams-Proctor Inst., 1949, 1957; Cazenovia Jr. Col., 1949; Sherburne Pub. Lib., 1950; Syracuse Mus. FA, 1953; Lawrence Mus. A., Williamstown, Mass., 1955; Utica Col., 1955.

DIUGUID, MARY SAMPSON—*Painter*

218 Warwick Lane, Lynchburg, Va.

B. Lynchburg, Va., May 29, 1885. *Studied*: PAFA; PMSchIA, and with Henry B. Snell, George Pearse Ennis. *Member*: NAC. *Exhibited*: NAC; Mus. A., Tampa, Fla.; Terry AI; Lynchburg A. Center.

DIXON, FRANCIS STILWELL—*Painter*

1349 Lexington Ave., New York 28, N.Y.

B. New York, N.Y., Sept. 18, 1879. *Studied*: ASL, with Robert Henri, Charles W. Hawthorne. *Member*: All. A. Am.; Conn. Acad. FA; SC. *Work*: Morgan Mem., Hartford, Conn.*

DLUGOSZ, LOUIS FRANK—*Sculptor*

162 Cleveland Ave., Lackawanna 19, N.Y.

B. Lackawanna, N.Y., Nov. 21, 1915. *Studied*: in Paris, France. *Member*: The Patteran, Buffalo, N.Y. *Awards*: Alexander Reed Mem. prize, Buffalo, N.Y., 1940, 1947; Chamber of Commerce gold key award, Lackawanna, N.Y., 1941. *Work*: MModA.; Smith Col. Mus.; Albright A. Gal.; St. Luke Church, Cheektowaga, N.Y.; and in private colls. *Exhibited*: Albright A. Gal., 1936-1938; The Patteran, 1939; Nierendorf Gal., 1940; Paris A. Exh., 1946; Assn. France-Amerique Gal., Paris, 1955 (one-man); Lowe Gal. A., Miami, 1953; Lackawanna Mem. Hall, 1956 (one-man).

DOANE, PELAGIE (Mrs. Pelagie Doane Hoffner)—
Illustrator, W.

1513 Hamilton Rd., Belmar, N.J.

B. Palmyra, N.J., Apr. 11, 1906. *Studied*: Sch. Des., Phila., Pa. Author, I., "A Small Child's Bible," 1946; "Littlest Ones," 1956; "The First Day," 1956; "One Rainy Night," 1957; "The Story of Moses," 1958; "The Big Trip," 1958; I., "A Small Child's Book of Verse," 1948; "The Boy Jesus," 1953; "Bible Children," 1954; "Poems of Praise," 1955, and others. Contributor to: Juvenile magazines.

DOBKIN, ALEXANDER—*Painter, I., W., L., Gr., T.*

737 Greenwich St., New York 14, N.Y.

B. Genoa, Italy, May 1, 1908. *Studied*: Col. City of N.Y., B.S.; T. Col., Columbia Univ., M.A.; ASL. *Member*: AEA. *Award*: Purchase award, Am. Acad. A. & Lets., 1957. *Work*: U.S. Govt., Wash., D.C.; LC; Butler Inst. Am. A.; Newark Mus. A.; Tel-Aviv Mus., Israel; Phoenix FA Assn.; PMA. *Exhibited*: AIC; BM; CGA; PAFA; MModA; Carnegie Inst.; ACA Gal. (6 one-man). Illus., "Child's Garden of Verses," 1945; "Two Years Before the Mast," 1946; Whitman's "Selected Poems," "King Arthur and His Knights"; "Songs for Patricia." Author: "Principles of Figure Drawing." Contributor to: N.Y. Times with art criticisms. Lectures: Appreciation & History of Art. *Position*: Dir., Art Sch. of the Educational Alliance, New York, N.Y., at present.

DOCKSTADER, FREDERICK J.—*Assistant Museum*
Director, C.

Museum of the American Indian, Broadway at 155th St.; h. 790 Riverside Dr., New York 32, N.Y.

B. Los Angeles, Cal., Feb. 3, 1919. *Studied*: Arizona State Col., A.B., M.A.; Western Reserve Univ., Ph.D. *Awards*: prizes, CMA, 1950, 1951; F., Cranbrook Inst. Science. *Work*: Silversmithing, CMA. *Exhibited*: CMA, 1949-1951; Cranbrook Acad. A., 1948. Author, I., "The Kachina and the White Man"; "American Indian Art," in press. Contributor articles on Arts and Crafts to various publications. Lectures: Silversmithing; American Indian Art; Arts and Crafts. Specialized in exhibit installation and reorganization at Cranbrook Inst. Science, Dartmouth College Mus., Mus. of the American Indian. *Positions*: Staff Ethnologist, Cranbrook Inst. Science, Bloomfield Hills, Mich., 1946-53; Cur. Anthropology, Dartmouth College Mus., 1953-56; Asst. Dir., Mus. of the American Indian, New York, N.Y., 1956- ; Commissioner, U.S. Indian Arts & Crafts Board, 1956- .

DODD, ED(WARD) (BENTON)—*Cartoonist*

Lost Forest, Sandy Springs, Ga.

B. La Fayette, Ga., Nov. 7, 1902. *Studied*: Georgia Inst. Tech.; ASL; and with Daniel Beard. *Member*: Outdoor Writers of Am.; Nat. Cartoonists Soc.; Nat. Press Cl.; Izaak Walton Lg. *Awards*: Service to Conservation, Am. Forestry Assn., 1951; Outstanding cartoon strip, Sigma Delta Chi, 1948; Service to Wildlife Conservation, Wisconsin Humane Soc., 1949; Hon. Chm., Nat. Wildlife Week, 1952-1954; Conservation Education award, Detroit Sportsmen's Congress, 1950; Nat. award, Nat. Assn. of Conservation Edu. and Publicity, 1951. Author, I., "Mark

Trail's Book of North American Mammals," 1955; Cart., "Back Home Again," 1930-45; "Mark Trail," 1946- ; "Mark Trail's Outdoor Tips," 1956- (hunting and fishing column).

DODD, LAMAR—*Painter, E., L.*

University of Georgia; h. 590 Springdale Ave., Athens, Ga.

B. Fairburn, Ga., Sept. 22, 1909. *Studied*: Georgia Inst. Tech.; ASL, with Boardman Robinson, George Bridgman, John Steuart Curry, Jean Charlot, George Luks, and others. *Member*: ANA; CAA; Com. on A. Edu.; Southeastern AA; Assn. Georgia A.; Athens AA; Atlanta AA; Audubon A.; Georgia Edu. Assn.; A. Comm., of Georgia; Athens Rotary. *Awards*: prizes, SSAL, 1931, 1940; Alabama A. Lg., 1936; AIC, 1936; WFNY 1939; IBM; Telfair Acad., 1941; Pepsi-Cola, 1947, 1948; Assn. Georgia A., 1941, 1948, 1953; VMFA, 1948; Southeastern AA, 1949, 1953; PAFA (purchase), 1958; WMAA (purchase), 1958; Nat. Inst. A. & Let., 1950; Fla. International, 1951; Terry AI, 1951; NAD, 1953; NAC, 1954. *Work*: Atlanta AI; AIC; IBM; MMA; Montclair A. Mus.; Telfair Acad.; PAFA; WMAA; Univ. Georgia; Rochester Mem. A. Gal.; VMFA; Wilmington Soc. A.; Cranbrook Acad. *Exhibited*: Am. Acad. A. & Let.; AFA; AIC; AWS; BM; CGA; Delaware A. Center; NAD; N.Y. WC Cl.; PAFA; Syracuse Mus. FA Walker A. Center; WMAA; PC; Audubon A.; MMA; Dayton A. Center; Delgado Mus. A.; Grand Central A. Gal.; John Herron AI; Montclair A. Mus.; Univ. Illinois; MModA; NAC; Univ. Nebraska; Philbrook A. Center; Santa Barbara A. Mus.; CAM, Toledo Mus. A., etc. Illus. (Rivers of America Series), The Savannah and The Santee. Contributor to College Art Journal, Book of Knowledge, and other publications; Lectures: USA; Denmark; Germany; Turkey; Italy; Austria; Greece. *Position*: Regents Prof. A., Hd. Dept. of A., Univ. Georgia, Athens, Ga. Pres., CAA, 1954-56; Memb. U.S. Dept. of State Com. on the Arts Tour of India, Belgium, Japan, Korea, Manila, etc., 1958.

DODDS, PEGGY—*Painter, W., L.*

300 East 35th St., Paterson, N.J.; s. Woodstock, N.Y.

B. Paterson, N.J., July 22, 1900. *Studied*: Collegiate Inst., Paterson, N.J.; ASL. *Member*: NAWA; N.J. WC Cl.; Mod. A. of N.J.; Montclair AA; Woodstock AA; AAPL. *Awards*: prize, NAWA, 1944, 1945; Montclair A. Mus., Nat. Lg. Am. Pen Women, 1950, 1952. *Exhibited*: PAFA; WMAA; Woodstock AA; AIC; Paterson AA; NAWA; NAD; Ridgewood AA; Woodstock AA; Montclair A. Mus.; Newark Mus.; Albany Lib. *Position*: A. Ed., Paterson Morning Call, Paterson, N.J.*

DODDS, ROBERT E.—*Painter, T., W,. L.*

Davis High School, Gramatan Ave., Mt. Vernon, N.Y.; h. 140 Norman Rd., New Rochelle, N.Y.

B. Guzneh Mersine, Turkey, Aug. 31, 1903. *Studied*: PIASch; Columbia Univ., B.S., M.A.; Geneva Col., D.F.A. & with Anna S. Fisher, George Elmer Browne, George Pearse Ennis. *Member*: SC; Westchester A. & Crafts Gld.; Hudson Valley AA; Mt. Vernon AA; All.A.Am. *Awards*: prizes, Beaver County, Pa., 1937, 1938, 1939; All.A.Am., 1945; Westchester A. & Crafts Gld., 1945, 1946; New Rochelle AA, 1947; Mt. Vernon AA, 1948; New Rochelle Women's Cl., 1947, 1948; Hudson Valley AA, 1950; Ford Fnd. F., 1953-54. *Work*: State T. Col., Fairmont, W. Va.; A. B. Davis H.S., Mt. Vernon, N.Y.; Fairmount (W. Va.) State T. Col. *Exhibited*: AWCS; Phila. WC Cl.; All.A.Am.; Assoc. A. Pittsburgh; SC; Grumbacher traveling exh. Author, I., "Handicrafts as a Hobby," 1939. Lectures: N.Y. Botanical Gardens and in schools. *Position*: Hd. Dept. A., Davis H.S., Mt. Vernon, N.Y., 1930- .

DODGE, ERNEST STANLEY—*Museum Director, W., L.*

Peabody Museum, 161 Essex St., Salem, Mass.; h. 260 Maple St., Danvers, Mass.

B. Trenton, Me., Mar. 18, 1913. *Studied*: Harvard Univ. *Member*: Am. Acad. A. & Science; Am. Anthropological Inst.; Mass. Hist. Soc.; Colonial Soc. of Mass.; Club of Odd Volumes; Am. Folklore Soc.; Am. Ethnological Soc. *Work*: Peabody Mus. of Salem. Author: "Gourd Growers of the South Seas"; Editor: The American Neptune (Quarterly Journal of Maritime History); Contributor of many articles to learned publications. Lectures: Primitive Art;

Art of the North American Indians and of the South Seas. *Position*: Mus. Asst., 1931, Asst. Cur., 1937, Cur., 1943, Asst. Dir., 1946, Dir., 1950- , Peabody Museum of Salem, Mass.

DODGE, F(RANCES) FARRAND (Mrs. A. C.)—

Painter, Et., L.

Deep Water Point, Easton, Md.

B. Lansing, Mich., Nov. 22, 1878. *Studied*: Michigan State Univ.; Syracuse Univ.; Cincinnati A. Sch.; ASL. *Member*: Chicago P.&S.; Chicago SE; Cincinnati Woman's AC. *Awards*: prize, Minnesota State Fair. *Work*: Cincinnati Pub. Sch. Coll.; Chicago Pub. Sch. Coll.; Nebraska State Univ. *Exhibited*: PAFA, 1914, 1915; AIC; Cincinnati Inst. FA. Lectures: Etching. Vice-Pres., Easton (Md.) Acad. A., 1958-59.

DODGE, JOSEPH JEFFERS—

Painter, Museum Cur., Cr., W., L., T.

Hyde Collection, 101 Warren St.; h. 32 Harrison Ave., Glens Falls, N.Y.

B. Detroit, Mich., Aug. 9, 1917. *Studied*: Harvard Univ., B.S.; Wayne Univ. *Exhibited*: PAFA, 1945; Detroit Inst. A., 1945; So. Vermont annual; A. of the Upper Hudson; Hewitt Gal., N.Y.; Albany Inst. Hist. & A., 1943, 1944, 1946, 1949 (one-man); Katrina Trask Gal., Saratoga Springs, N.Y., 1943-1946; Brandt Gal.; Munson-Williams-Proctor Inst., 1951; One-man: Wildenstein Gal., 1952; others, 1956-58, Albany Inst. Hist. & A.; Schenectady A. Mus.; Willard Sch., Troy, N.Y.; Glens Falls H.S.; Crandall Lib., Glens Falls; Ft. Edward A. Center. Contributor to: Art Quarterly. Lectures: History of Art; Modern Art; Religious Art. *Position*: Cur., Hyde Collection, Glens Falls, N.Y., 1941- .

DODGE, MRS. OZIAS—Museum Director

Slater Memorial Museum, Converse Art Bldg., Norwich, Conn.

Position: Dir., Slater Memorial Museum.*

DOGGETT, JEAN—Painter, L.

4840 Rubio Ave., Encino, Cal.

B. New York, N.Y., Nov. 28, 1902. *Studied*: Columbia Univ.; ASL. *Member*: Women Painters of the West; A. of the Southwest; San Fernando Valley AA. *Awards*: prizes, San Fernando A., 1949 (2), 1950 (3), 1951 (2), 1954; Sherman Oaks Bus. & Prof. Women's Cl., 1950; Women Painters of the West, 1951. *Exhibited*: Pasadena AI; Los A. Pub. Lib.; Women Painters of the West; Bowers Mus., Santa Ana, Cal. Lectures: on Art Appreciation.

DOHANOS, STEVAN—Illustrator, Gr.

Box 112, Westport, Conn.

B. Lorain, Ohio, May 18, 1907. *Studied*: Cleveland Sch. A. *Member*: SI. *Awards*: med., Phila. WC Cl., 1934; A. Dir. Cl., 1936; prize, Cleveland Pr. M., 1934. *Work*: WMAA; Cleveland Pr. Cl.; Avery Mem., Hartford, Conn.; New Britain Inst.; Dartmouth Col.; murals, Charlotte Amalie, St. Thomas, Virgin Islands; Forest Service Bldg., Elkins, W. Va.; USPO, West Palm Beach, Fla. I., national magazines. *Position*: Faculty member, Famous Artists Sch., Westport, Conn.*

DOLBIN, B. F.—Painter, I., W., Cart., Cr.

37-46 85th St., Jackson Heights, N.Y.

B. Vienna, Austria, Aug. 1, 1883. *Awards*: Diploma of Honor, Int. Exh., Moscow & Leningrad, 1928. *Work*: Hamline Univ.; Mus. City of Vienna; Kunstgewerbe Mus., Moscow; MModA and in private colls. *Exhibited*: BM, 1937; Dance International, N.Y., traveling exh., A. Gal.; 1937; WFNY 1939; NAC, 1940; Friendship House, N.Y., 1941 (one-man); Am.-British A. Center, 1942-1944; Tribune A. Center, 1946 (one-man). I., many books published in Europe, including "Musica Nova" and "Magie des Taktstocks" (Ullstein-Verlag, Berlin); national magazines in U.S.*

DOLE, GEORGE. See La Mendola, George

DOLE, MARGARET FERNALD—Painter, L.

Ritch Ave., Byram, Conn.; s. Chatham, Mass.

B. Melrose, Mass., May 5, 1896. *Studied*: Radcliffe Col.; BMFA Sch., and with Philip Hale, Charles Woodbury. *Member*: Providence A. Cl.; Phila. A. All.; NAWA; NAC; Pen & Brush Cl.; Nat. Lg. Am. Pen Women; Gld. of Greenwich A.; AAPL (Nat. Bd.). *Work*: Riverdale Sch. for Girls; Riverdale Sch. for Boys. *Awards*: prizes, Hudson River Mus., 1957; AAPL, 1957; Nat. Lg. Am. Pen Women, 1957, 1958; Greenwich Soc. A., 1957. *Exhibited*: CGA; PAFA; AAPL, 1953, 1954; NAD; Paris Salon; All. A. Am.; Ogunquit A. Center; Smithsonian Inst., 1957; Providence A. Cl.; one-man: Argent Gal., 1940; Port. Painters Gal., N.Y., 1944; Stamford Mus., 1954. *Position*: Instr., Riverdale Sch. for Girls (3 yrs.); Vice-Pres., Conn. Chaptr. AAPL; Chm. A., N.Y. Branch, Nat. Lg. Am. Pen Women.

DOLE, WILLIAM—Painter, E.

29 Calle Crespis, Santa Barbara, Cal.

B. Angola, Ind., Sept. 2, 1917. *Studied*: Olivet Col., A.B.; Univ. California, M.A. *Member*: Cal. WC Soc. *Work*: Santa Barbara Mus. A.; Mills Col.; Rockefeller Inst. *Exhibited*: Cal. PLH, 1947, 1952; SFMA, 1948-1951; PAFA, 1950; Hallmark award, 1953; Cal. WC Soc., 1950-1952; Denver A. Mus., 1948; Cal. State Fair, 1950, 1951; Los A. County Fair, 1951; Santa Barbara Mus. A., 1955, 1957; Los A. Mus. A., 1958; one-man: Santa Barbara Mus. A., 1951, 1958; deYoung Mem. Mus., 1951; Mills Col., 1951; Geddis-Martin Studios, Santa Barbara, 1952; La Jolla A. Center, 1954; Rotunda Gal., San F., 1954; Galerie Springer, Berlin, 1956; Locke Gal., San F., 1956; Sagittarius Gal., Rome, 1957; Duveen-Graham Gal., N.Y., 1958; Univ. California A. Gal., Santa Barbara, 1958. *Positions*: L., Univ. California, 1947-49; Instr. A., 1949-51, Asst. Prof. A., 1951- , Univ. California, Santa Barbara, Cal. (mail: Goleta, Cal.).

DOLEY, PETER—Teacher, Des., P.

67 Parkside Dr., Gaspee Plateau 5, R.I.

B. New Haven, Conn., June 20, 1907. *Studied*: PIASch; Boston Univ., B.S.; R.I.Sch.Des. *Member*: Providence AC; Providence WC Cl.; AAPL; Rhode Island A.T. Assn. *Work*: R.I. State Col.; Nathaniel Greene Sch.; mural, St. Michael's Church, New Haven, Conn. Reproductions of paintings, Publ. 1950-52. *Exhibited*: PAFA, 1936; Providence AC, 1935-1946; Providence WC Cl., 1932-1946. *Position*: A. Instr., Providence R.I., Pub. Sch., 1930-1955; Instr. A., Warwick H.S. & Adult Edu., Warwick, R.I.*

DOLMITH, REX—Painter, T., L.

Taos, N.M.

B. Canton, Ohio, Jan. 22, 1896. *Studied*: AIC; Chouinard AI; Otis AI; Cal. Col. A. & Crafts, and with Robert Graham, Sidney Bell. *Exhibited*: All. A. Am.; Studio Gld., N.Y.; Soc. Indp. A.; Conn. Acad. FA; Arizona State Fair; New Mexico State Fair; Mus. of New Mexico; Denver A. Mus.*

DOLPH, CLIFFORD R.—Museum Director

Maryhill, Wash.

B. Chicago, Ill., July 29, 1901. *Studied*: Univ. Chicago; Univ. Colorado. *Member*: Western Assn. A. Mus. Dir. Editor, general & special exhibition catalogs, Maryhill Mus. FA. *Position*: Dir., Maryhill Mus. FA, Maryhill, Wash., 1938- .

DOMAREKI, JOSEPH T.—Painter, S.

1482 Fox Trail, Mountainside, N.J.

B. Newark, N.J., May 17, 1914. *Studied*: Faucett A. Sch., Newark; Newark Sch. Fine & Indst. A.; Newark State Col., B.A.; Univ. Iowa, M.A.; N.Y. Univ. (grad. work in A. Edu.). *Member*: Audubon A.; Nat. Soc. Painters in Casein (Bd. Dir.); Assoc. A. of New Jersey; N.J. WC Soc.; Hunterdon AA; New Jersey A. Edu. Assn.; Knickerbocker A. *Awards*: prizes, Hunterdon AA, 1957; N.J. WC Soc., 1954; Montclair A. Mus.; Newark A. Cl.; A. Center of the Oranges; medal, Knickerbocker A., 1955. *Work*: Univ. Iowa; Pentagon Bldg., Wash., D.C.; Columbia (S.C.) Mus. A.; Newark State T. Col.; N.Y. Univ., A. Dept.; Columbia H.S., Maplewood, N.J. *Exhibited*: Butler Inst. Am. A., 1950-1952; NAD, 1949, 1953; AWS, 1952; Audubon A., 1949, 1950, 1952; Knickerbocker A., 1954-

1956; Pittsburgh Plan for Art, 1957; Univ. Iowa, 1957; Art:USA, 1958; Univ. Nebraska, 1952; Newark Mus. A., annually; Nat. Soc. Painters in Casein, 1955-1957; Montclair A. Mus., annually; Trenton State Mus.; Festival of A., Princeton; one-man: Louisiana State Mus., 1954; Contemporary Arts, New York, N.Y., 1949, 1952, 1954, 1957. *Position*: Combat A., U.S. Navy, Pacific Area; Instr., South Orange, N.J. Pub. Schs.; A. Center of the Oranges, etc.

DOMBEK, BLANCHE—*Sculptor*

310 West 99th St., New York 25, N.Y.

B. New York, N.Y., June 30, 1914. *Studied*: Grad. Training Sch. for Teachers, and with Zeitlin and Amino. *Member*: Am. Abstract A.; S. Gld. *Awards*: F., MacDowell Colony, 1957; Huntington Hartford Fnd., 1958. *Work*: BM; Randolph-Macon Woman's Col.; and in private colls. *Exhibited*: WMAA, 1947, 1948, 1950, 1952, 1955; BM, 1947; PAFA, 1947; PMA, 1949; WMA, 1951; S. Center, 1946-1950; Tanager Gal., Camino Gal., The Contemporaries, Am. Abstract A., S. Gld., Riverside Mus., all New York City; Scarborough-on-Hudson, 1958, and group shows in France and Germany; one-man: Pinacotheca Gal., 1945; Wellons Gal., N.Y.; Colette Allendy Gal., Paris, France, 1954.

DOMINIQUE, JOHN A.—*Painter*

216 N. Pueblo Ave., R.R. 3, Ojai, Cal.

B. Sweden, Oct. 1, 1893. *Studied*: Cal. Sch. Des.; Van Sloun Sch. Painting, San Francisco, and with Colin Campbell Cooper. *Member*: Cal. A. Cl.; Glendale AA. *Awards*: prizes, Oregon State Fair, 1940, 1941; Glendale AA, 1950. *Exhibited*: Portland (Ore.) A. Mus., 1936; Oakland A. Mus., 1941; Los A. Mus. A., 1944; Cal. A. Cl., 1950, 1955, 1956, 1957, 1958; Santa Paula Chamber of Commerce, 1950, 1951.

DOMVILLE, PAUL—*Educator, P.*

311 Hilldale Rd., Villanova, Pa.

B. Hamilton, Canada, June 16, 1893. *Studied*: Hamilton Collegiate Inst.; Hamilton A. & Tech. Sch., Hamilton, Canada; Univ. Pennsylvania; PAFA. *Member*: NSMP; Phila. WC Cl. *Awards*: Med., Univ. Pennsylvania, 1920. *Work*: murals, St. Luke's Church; Seaman's Church Inst.; Mutual Trust Co.; City Nat. Bank, all in Philadelphia, Pa. *Exhibited*: PAFA, 1923, 1926, 1937, 1938, 1943, 1944; Arch. L., 1924, 1928. *Position*: Prof. Drawing, Chm. Dept. Des., Sch. FA, Univ. Pennsylvania, 1922-1951; Instr. Drawing, Moore Inst., Philadelphia, Pa., 1938-1945.

DONAHUE, KENNETH—*Museum Director*

Ringling Museum of Art, Sarasota, Fla.

Position: Dir., John & Mable Ringling Museum of Art.*

DONAHUE, WILLIAM HOWARD—*Painter*

461 Ave. of the Americas, New York 11, N.Y.; s. Lyme, Conn.

B. New York, N.Y., Dec. 21, 1891. *Studied*: with Everett Warner and John Noble. *Member*: All. A. Am.; Creative A. Assoc.; Lyme (Conn.) AA. *Exhibited*: CGA, 1924; PAFA, 1925; NAD, 1930; Los A. Mus. A., 1924; BM, 1918; Riverside Mus., 1942, 1944, 1946, 1947-1951, 1953-1956; Am.-British A. Center, 1943; Chappelier Gal., 1944; Lyman Allyn Mus., New London, Conn., 1945; Swope A. Mus., 1950, 1951.

DONALDSON, ELISE—*Painter, Lith.*

1350 Virginia Way, La Jolla, Cal.

B. Elkridge, Md. *Studied*: Bryn Mawr Col., A.B.; AIC; abroad with Andre L'Hote. *Member*: San Diego A. Gld.; La Jolla A. Center. *Awards*: prizes, AIC, 1934; San Diego A. Gld., 1954; San Diego FA Soc., 1956. *Work*: San Diego FA Soc.; Davenport Mun. A. Gal. *Exhibited*: AIC; PAFA; Carnegie Inst.; BM; Riverside Mus.; Mandel Bros., Chicago, 1953; Davenport Mun. A. Gal., 1953; Des Moines A. Center, 1953; Grinnell Col., 1953; SFMA; San F. AA; LC; Laguna Beach AA, 1945, 1946; Cal. WC Soc.; BM; San Diego FA Soc., 1944 (one-man), 1956; La Jolla A. Center, 1956 (one-man) & prior; Los A. Mus. A., 1952; Little Gal., Boston, 1955 (one-man); Fresno State Col., 1955 (one-man).

DONATO, LOUIS NICHOLAS—*Painter, Des., T.*

170-09 84th Rd., Jamaica 32, L.I., N.Y.

B. New York, N.Y., Oct. 23, 1913. *Studied*: CUASch. *Member*: AEA; A. Dir. Cl. *Work*: PMG; Exhibited: WFNY 1939; PMG, 1940; BM, 1941; PAFA, 1941, 1942, 1946, 1954; Carnegie Inst., 1941, 1945; CGA, 1943, 1945; VMFA, 1942, 1946; AFA, traveling exh., 1943-1944, 1955-56; Lilienfeld Gal. (one-man); Am.-British A. Center; Artists Gal. (one-man) 1955; Art:USA, 1958. *Position*: A. Dir., Will, Folsom & Smith, New York, N.Y., 1944- ; Instr. CUASch., New York, N.Y.; Chm., Edu. & Scholarship Com., A. Dir. Cl. Lecture series, Young & Rubicam, New York, N.Y.

DONELSON, EARL TOMLINSON—*Painter, Lith.*

Linden Ave., R.D. 2, Morrisville, Pa.

B. Scranton, Pa., July 19, 1908. *Studied*: Trenton Sch. Indst. A.; PAFA; & with Joseph T. Pearson. *Awards*: F., PAFA; prizes, PAFA, 1927, 1928; Cresson award & prizes, 1929, 1930; New Jersey Gal., Newark, 1934, 1936, 1937. *Work*: N.J. Fed. Women's Cl.; PMA; N.J. State Mus. *Exhibited*: PAFA, 1932-1935, 1937, 1938, 1940; AIC, 1932; NAD, 1933; PMA, 1936; VMFA, 1938; BMA, 1932; Soc. FA & Hist., Evansville, Ind., 1932; Hackley Gal. A., 1932; Montclair A. Mus., 1933; Phila. A. All., 1935; Wanamaker Exh., 1935; Newark AC, 1933, 1934, 1936, 1938, 1940; Phila. AC, 1936; N.J. State Mus., 1935, 1937, 1940; N.J. Gal., 1933, 1934, 1936-1940. Lectures: "Trends in Poster Art." *Position*: Hd., Dept. Des., New Jersey A. & Crafts, 1940-42; A. Advisor, FA & Monuments Section, Allied Military Govt., Munich, Germany, 1945; A. Dir., Paterson Parchment Paper Co., Bristol, Pa., 1948- .

DONELSON, MARY HOOPER (Mrs. P. T. Jones)—*Sculptor, P.*

Route 1, Old Hickory, Tenn.

B. Hermitage, Tenn., Jan. 3, 1906. *Studied*: Vanderbilt Univ.; AIC; & with Albin Polasek, Emil Zettler, Guy Pène DuBois. *Member*: Nashville Studio Cl.; Nashville A. Gld. *Awards*: Med., AIC, 1928; Procter & Gamble Comp., 1928; Public Health Assn., 1929. *Work*: Tennessee State Capitol; Univ. Tennessee; Davidson County Court House; many mem. tablets. *Exhibited*: PAFA, 1931; NAD, 1938; AIC, 1930; SSAL, 1934; Studio Cl.; Nashville Mus. A., 1945; Ward Belmont Col., 1945; Nashville A. Gld.; Centennial Cl.; Tennessee State Fair.

DONNELL, EDNA B.—*Museum Curator, W.*

520 East 77th St., New York 21, N.Y.

B. Paterson, N.J., June 3, 1891. *Studied*: Smith Col., A.B.; N.Y. Univ., M.A.; & abroad. Contributor to: Art magazines & museum bulletins. Author: "A. J. Davis and the Gothic Revival"; "The Creators of the Chippendale Style" (with Fiske Kimball). *Position*: Asst. Cur. Prints, MMA, 1927-46; Keeper of Prints & Drawings, Cooper Union Mus., New York, N.Y., 1946-49. Freelance Research, Art, Americana, 1950- .

DONNELLY, MARY E.—*Painter*

Tarpon Springs, Fla.

B. New York, N.Y., Apr. 18, 1898. *Studied*: Hunter Col.; Columbia Univ. *Member*: Mod. A. of N.J. *Awards*: prizes, N.J. Gal., 1939; Bell System Exh., 1946. *Exhibited*: NAD, 1939-1941; Montclair A. Mus.; RoKo Gal., 1943; AWS; DeMotte Gal., 1948; New Hope, Pa., 1951-52; Tarpon Springs AA, 1955; Fla. State Exh., 1953.*

DONNELLY, THOMAS—*Painter, T.*

44 Howard Ave., Valhalla, N.Y.

B. Washington, D.C., Feb. 25, 1893. *Studied*: Corcoran Sch. A.; ASL, with John Sloan, Boardman Robinson. *Member*: Whitney Studio Cl.; Salons of Am.; ASL. *Award*: prize, Westchester A. & Crafts Gld., 1951; Valhalla, N.Y., 1953. *Work*: WMAA; Dartmouth Col.; White House, Wash., D.C.; Pub. Lib., Larchmont, N.Y.; Pub. Lib., Ossining, N.Y.; murals, USPO, Mt. Kisco, N.Y.; Ridgefield Park, N.J.; Attica, N.Y.; Clyde, N.Y. *Exhibited*: WMAA, 1931-1934, 1936-1942, 1944, 1949; Carnegie Inst., 1929; AIC, 1929, 1937; CGA, 1930; PAFA, 1940-1942; WFNY 1939; ASL, 1950; CM, 1934; Berkshire Mus., 1935; Denver A. Mus., 1938; WMA, 1940; Portland (Ore.) A. Mus., (one-man); Marie Harriman Gal. (one-man), 1938.

DONOVAN, CECIL VINCENT—*Educator, P.*

311 Architecture Bldg., University of Illinois; h. 1306 South Carle Ave., Urbana, Ill.

B. Homer, N.Y., June 23, 1896. *Studied*: Syracuse Univ., B.P., M.F.A. *Work*: Bloomington AA, Bloomington, Ill. *Exhibited*: GGE, 1939. *Position*: Prof. A., Univ. Illinois, Urbana, Ill., 1922-46; Cur., Univ. A. Gal., Univ. Illinois; Chm., Univ. Ill. Nat. Biennial Exh. of Contemp. Am. Painting & Sculpture.*

DONOVAN, ELLEN (Mrs. L. V. Heilbrunn)—
Painter, T., L., Lith.

4411 Osage Ave., Philadelphia 4, Pa.; s. Woods Hole, Mass.

B. Philadelphia, Pa. *Studied*: PMSchIA; Barnes Fnd., and with Morris Davidson. *Member*: Phila. WC Cl.; Phila. Pr. Cl., Cape Cod AA; Phila. A. All.; AEA. *Awards*: med., Plastic Cl., 1930. *Work*: PAFA. *Positions*: Instr., Agnes Irwin Sch., Phila., Pa., 1926-32; Fndr., Woods Hole A. Sch., 1934; Dir., Ellen Donovan A. Gal., Phila., Pa., 1950-54.

DONSON, JEROME ALLAN—
Museum Director, S., T., Cr.

Long Beach Museum of Art, 2300 East Ocean Blvd., Long Beach 3, Cal.

B. New York, N.Y., Mar. 20, 1924. *Studied*: City Col., N.Y.; Univ. So. Cal., B.A., M.S.; American Graduate Sch., Denmark; Univ. California, Berkeley, M.A.; New Sch. Social Research, N.Y. *Member*: Nat. Com. on A. Edu.; AAMus.; Western Assn. A. Mus. Dir.; CAA; Am. Anthropological Assn.; Soc. for Am. Archaeology; Am. Ethnological Soc.; Long Beach AA (Hon.); Gld. South Caroline A. (Adv. Bd.); Florence (S.C.) Arts Council (Bd. Memb.); NEA. *Awards*: prizes, Gld. South Carolina A., 1955; AAPL, 1954, 1955; Scholarship to Am. Graduate Sch., Denmark. Contributor to Florence Morning News and other South Carolina newspapers, 1954-56; weekly column on museum news, 1953, "A Technique of Numbering and Storing Archaeological Specimens in the Museum." Occasional TV programs; Hd., Univ. California Extension Course "Looking at Modern Painting." Exhibitions arranged: Traveling exh. series on Arts of Southern California: I: Architecture; II: Painting; III: Art in Film; IV: Indian Art, 1958. Also, Fifteen American Painters, 1957; Art in Long Beach Private Collections, 1957; Art of the Sepik River, 1957. *Positions*: Archaeologist-Art Hist., Nat. Mus., Copenhagen, Denmark, 1950-51; Preparator, Mus. Anthropology, Univ. California, Berkeley, 1953-54; Dir., Florence (S.C.) A. Mus., 1954-56; Dir. Long Beach Mus. A., Long Beach, Cal., 1956- .

DOOLEY, HELEN BERTHA—*Educator, L., P., W.*

College of the Pacific; h. 1107 Longview Ave., Stockton 4, Cal.

B. San Jose, Cal., July 27, 1907. *Studied*: San Jose State Col.; Chouinard AI; Claremont Col., and with Maurice Sterne, Millard Sheets. *Member*: Soc. Western A.; Pacific AA; NAEA; Carmel AA; Stockton A. Lg.; AAUP. *Awards*: prizes, Monterey County Fair, 1951, 1955; de Young Mem. Mus., 1951, 1956; Mother Lode AA, 1956, 1958; Kingsley A. Cl., 1956; Stockton A. Lg., 1951-1954, 1956, 1957; No. California A., 1955. *Exhibited*: Cal. State Fair; Cal. PLH; Oakland A. Mus.; PAFA, 1938, 1943, 1945; Madonna Festival, Los A., 1952; Carmel A. Gld.; Pebble Beach, Cal.; Sonora A. Lg.; Kingsley A. Show, Sacramento, 1955; 15 California Painters, Monterey, 1956; Laguna Beach Festival of A., 1956, 1957; Lodi A. Lg., 1958; Carmel AA, 1955-1958; one-man: San Jose State Col.; San Jose State Col. Lib., 1955; Haggin Mem. Mus., 1951; Bakersfield AA, 1945; Lanai Gal., Sacramento, 1955; Carmel A. Gld., 1955, 1958. Author: "Art for Elementary Schools," 1942; Teaching Charts on Figure Drawing, Lettering, Color Illus., Laurel Handwriting Series, 1935. *Position*: Prof. A. Edu., College of the Pacific, Stockton, Cal.

DOOLEY, WILLIAM GERMAIN—*Educator, Cr.*

Museum of Fine Arts, Boston 15, Mass.; h. 9 Doane St., Cambridge 38, Mass.

B. Boston, Mass., July 6, 1903. *Studied*: Harvard Col. Contributor to: New York Times Book Review; N.Y. Herald Tribune Books. *Position*: A. Cr., Boston Transcript, 1932-41; Assoc. Ed., 1938-41; Hd. Div. Mus. Extension, BMFA, 1941; Hd. Div. Edu., BMFA, Boston, Mass., 1942- ; Chm. Mass. State Art Comm., 1951- ; Chm., A. Com., Harvard Club of Boston, 1952- .*

DOOLITTLE, HAROLD L.—*Etcher, Lith.*

1520 Rose Villa St., Pasadena 4, Cal.

B. Pasadena, Cal., May 4, 1883. *Studied*: Cornell Univ., M.E. *Member*: Pasadena SA; Chicago SE; SAGA; Cal. Pr. M. *Awards*: prize, Chicago SE, 1938, 1947. *Work*: Los A. Pub. Lib.; N.Y. Pub. Lib.; Cal. State Lib.; San Diego FA Soc.; Brooks Mem. Gal.; Lib. Cong.; Dayton AI. *Exhibited*: Pasadena SA; Chicago SE; SAGA; Cal. SE; Cal. Pr. M.; Phila. WC Cl.; NAD; Smithsonian Inst.; Cal. State Fair; Oakland A. Mus.

DOOLITTLE, WARREN FORD, JR.—*Educator, P.*

115 West Pennsylvania Ave., Urbana, Ill.

B. New Haven, Conn., April 3, 1911. *Studied*: Yale Sch. FA, B.F.A.; Syracuse Univ., M.F.A. *Member*: Audubon A.; Midwestern Col. AA; Am. Assn. Univ. Prof. *Award*: Ford Fnd. F., 1953-54. *Exhibited*: AIC, 1944, 1946; Cal. PLH, 1946; Northwest Pr. M., 1946; Pepsi-Cola, 1946; Arizona A. Exh., 1946; CGA, 1947; MMA, 1950; Springfield, Ill., 1950, 1951; Univ. Washington (D.C.), 1951; Butler AI, 1952; Denver A. Mus., 1955; Conn. Acad. FA, 1954; one-man: Urbana, Ill., 1954; Bloomington, Ill., 1955; Decatur, Ill., 1956; Univ. Illinois, 1958. *Position*: Prof. A., Dir., Painting Option & Chm. Grad. Programs in Art, Art Dept., Univ. Illinois, 1948- .

DORA (MRS. DORA MATHIEU)—*Illustrator, T.*

39 Gramercy Park, North, New York 16, N.Y.

B. Schenectady, N.Y., Oct. 20, 1909. *Studied*: PIASch. *Member*: ASL; SI. *Exhibited*: one-man: Sheldon Swope Mus. A.; SI. Illus. for national advertising and magazines. *Positions*: Instr., ASL, 1945-52; PIASch., 1957-59.

DOREY, ELSIE (Mrs. Elsie Dorey Upham)—*Painter*

P.O. Box 433, Naples, Fla.

B. Newark, Ohio, Jan. 31, 1907. *Studied*: Denison Univ.; Columbus Sch. A.; Dayton AI; Ohio State Univ., B.S. in Edu., and with Guy Wiggins. *Awards*: prize, Naples (Fla.) AA, 1956-1958; Fla. Fed. Women's Cl., 1957. *Exhibited*: Old Lyme, Conn., 1934; Columbus A. Lg., 1932, 1935, 1942, 1949, 1952; Butler AI, 1938, 1939; Hartford, Conn.; Naples AA, 1955; A. Lg. of Manatee County, Bradenton, Fla., 1957; one-man: Zanesville Gal. FA; Gambier, Ohio; Naples, Fla.; New York, N.Y.

DORFA (DORIS KATHRYN FANKBONNER)—*Craftsman*

1024 Hardesty Blvd., Akron 20, Ohio

B. Akron, Ohio, Mar. 10, 1909. *Studied*: Univ. Akron; Ohio State Univ., with Marshall Fredericks; Cranbrook Acad. A., with William Sommers. *Member*: Designer-Craftsmen. *Awards*: prize, Akron AI, 1947, hon. men., 1954, prize, 1957. *Work*: ceramics, Georg Jensen, New York; ceramics and jewelry, 1030 Gal., Cleveland; Textile des., Plastic Film Corp., Akron, Ohio. *Exhibited*: Ohio A. & Craftsmen, Massillon, Ohio, 1951; Butler AI, 1953, 1954, 1957; Akron AI, 1933-1954, 1956, 1957 (2-man, 1958); Women's City Cl., 1958 (one-man). *Position*: A.T., Akron Pub. Sch., 1934-39; Private studio (ceramics), 1946-50; Dir., Occupational Therapy, Edwin Shaw Sanatorium, Akron, Ohio, 1948- .

DORNE, ALBERT—*Painter, I., T., W., L.*

322 East 57th St., New York 22, N.Y.

B. New York, N.Y., Feb. 7, 1904. *Member*: A. Dir. Cl., New York; A. & W. Assn.; Dutch Treat Cl. (Bd. Dir.); Players Cl.; SI (Pres.) 1947-48; Co-founder, Joint Ethics Com. covering Fair Practice for Field of Illustration. *Award*: gold medal, A. Dir. Cl. for Distinguished Career, 1953; Hon. Degree, D.F.A., Adelphi Col., 1958. *Exhibited*: one-man exhibitions in major cities and museums. Illustrations and covers for national magazines and national advertisers. Principal author and editor of textbooks to the Famous Artists Schools. *Position*: Founder & Pres., Famous Artists Schools, Westport, Conn.

DORRA, HENRI—*Assistant Museum Director*

The Corcoran Gallery of Art (6); h. 3830 39th St., N.W., Washington 16, D.C.

B. Jan. 17, 1924. *Studied*: London Univ., B. Sc.; Harvard Univ., M.S., M.A., Ph.D. *Awards*: Bowdoin prize, Harvard Univ., 1949; MMA Student F., 1951-52. *Author*: "Gauguin," MMA, 1953. Contributor to: Gazette des Beaux-Arts; MMA Bulletin; Smith Col. Mus. Bulletin; Art News, Art Digest, etc. *Lectures*: Art History. Exhibitions organized: "Three Designers for the Contemporary Stage," FMA, 1950; "Visionaries and Dreamers," "The American Stage," "Living Today," CGA, 1955-57. *Position*: Student F., MMA, 1951-52; A. Dir., Soc. Four A., Palm Beach; Assoc. Dir., Ringling Mus., Sarasota; Asst. Dir., Corcoran Gal. A., Washington, D.C., 1954- .

DORSEY, THOMAS—*Designer, I., L., Comm. A.*

10 Prospect Ave., Hackensack, N.J.

B. Onondaga, N.Y., Feb. 2, 1920. *Studied*: Albany Inst. Hist. & A., with Herbert Steinke. *Award*: prize, 1st Nat. Exh. Indian Painters, Philbrook A. Center, 1946. *Work*: Albany Inst. Hist. & A.; Philbrook A. Center; Thomas Gilcrease Fnd.; Mus. Am. Indian; Am. Mus. Natural Hist. *Exhibited*: Albany Inst. Hist. & A.; Am. Mus. Natural Hist.; AFA traveling exh.; Philbrook A. Center; Gilcrease Fnd.; Mus. Am. Indian. Contributor to: "Indians at Work," publ. by Interior Dept., Wash., D.C.; Illus., "Masks and Men," booklet for Am. Mus. Natural Hist.; children's books: "Lightfoot"; "Little Boy Navajo"; "Eagle Feather"; "The Whirly Bird"; "Ginger's Cave." Des. textiles for: Fuller Fabrics; Wesley Simpson; Textron, etc.; greeting cards; advertising des. Exhibit design and installation: Consul General of Pakistan; Montclair A. Mus.; James Graham Gal. (All work of an Am. Indian nature under the name of Tom Two Arrows). *Lectures*: American Indian songs, arts & crafts, etc. *Position*: Staff A., Dept. Edu., Am. Mus. Natural Hist., New York, N.Y., 1946-49.*

DOSSERT, NORMA BARTON (Mrs. F. C.)—
Designer, C., P.

Chazy, N.Y.

B. Willsboro, N.Y., Feb. 22, 1893. *Studied*: BMFA Sch. *Member*: A.F.A. *Exhibited*: PAFA, 1939; Albany Inst. Hist. & A., 1940; Plattsburg A. Gld., 1936-1942; Saranac A. Gld., 1940; Champlain Col., 1950, 1951.

DOUB, JANET ANN (Mrs. Evarts C. Erickson)—
Textile Designer, Gr., P., E.

State University of New York, College for Teachers, Buffalo, N.Y.; h. 359 Hampshire St., Buffalo 13, N.Y.

B. Hagerstown, Md., June 29, 1924. *Studied*: Mary Washington Col.; Mass. Sch. A., B.F.A. *Member*: Boston Pr. M.; Boston Soc. Indp. A.; Buffalo Craftsmen; York State Craftsmen. *Awards*: Tiffany award for textile des., 1955; Young Americans, 1954; deCordova Craftsmen, 1955. *Work*: BMFA; Wadsworth Atheneum; Berkshire Mus.; drapery des., for numerous colleges; mural, Tufts Univ. *Exhibited*: Nationally. One-man: Rockland, Me.; Cambridge, Mass.; Boston, Mass.; Wellfleet, Mass.; Buffalo, N.Y. *Lectures*: Textile Design and Blockprinting. *Position*: Instr., Willimantic (Conn.) Summer Arts & Crafts Workshop; Asst. Prof. A., State Univ. of N.Y., Col. for T., Buffalo, N.Y., 1955-59.

DOUCETTE, AIME HENRI—*Educator, C.*

Art Department, Edinboro State Teachers College; h. 36 Water St., Edinboro, Pa.

B. Laconia, N.H., Aug. 28, 1899. *Studied*: Mass. Normal A. Sch.; Univ. Pittsburgh; Mass. Sch. A., B.S.; Boston Univ., Ed. M.; BMFA Sch.; Tiffany Fnd. *Member*: NEA; NAEA; Eastern AA; Pa. Assn. A. Edu. *Work*: St. Francis Majella medal, 1946; Benedictine medal, 1948; Vanadium Steel Corp. (pocket piece), 1947. *Lectures*, art education, art supervision, arts & crafts in pub. sch. art, etc. *Positions*: Inst., A. Dept., George Peabody Inst., Nashville, Tenn.; Univ. West Virginia, Morgantown; Hd., Art Dept., Edinboro State T. Col., Edinboro, Pa., at present.

DOUDNA, WILLIAM L.—*Critic*

c/o Wisconsin State Journal (1); h. 222 South Owen Dr., Madison 5, Wis.

B. Dodgeville, Wis., Feb. 21, 1905. *Studied*: Stevens Point (Wis.) State T. Col.; Univ. Wisconsin. *Position*: A. Ed., Wisconsin State Journal, Madison, Wis., 1934- .

DOUGHERTY, BERTHA HURLBUT—
Printmaker, E., P., I., L.

211 South St. Asaph St., Alexandria, Va.

B. Plainfield, N.J., May 13, 1883. *Studied*: Vassar Col.; Fawcett A. Sch.; N.Y. Sch. Des. for Women. *Awards*: prizes, Smithsonian Inst., 1952; Fairfax (Va.); Montclair A. Mus.; Nat. Lg. Am. Pen Women, 1956, 1957. *Member*: Soc. Wash. Pr. M.; Wash. WC Soc.; Nat. Lg. Am. Pen Women; SAGA. *Exhibited*: SAGA, 1943, 1944; Wash. WC Cl., annually; Wash. SE, 1945; Lib. Cong., 1944; Newport AA; Montclair A. Mus., 1940, 1941; Old Lyme AA; Smithsonian Inst. (one-man); Wash. A. Cl.; New Haven, Conn.; and others; Vassar Col., 1944; Alexandria (Va.) Lib., 1941-1945; N.Y. Pub. Lib., 1944; traveling exh., Germany and Austria, sponsored by State Dept. Illus., for own feature articles in Christian Advocate, Antiques Journal; I., of pamphlets "Port of Alexandria," "Gadsby's Tavern," both by Kabler; "Guide Book to Alexandria, Va." by Somerville.

DOUGLAS, CHESTER—*Designer, P., T., I., Comm. A.*

1 Neptune St., Newburyport, Mass.

B. Lynn, Mass., Oct. 6, 1902. *Studied*: Mass. Sch. A., B.S. in Edu.; & with John Sharman. *Member*: Eastern AA; Marblehead AA. *Work*: Reading (Pa.) Mus. A. *Exhibited*: AIC; NAD; PAFA; BMFA; WMA; Springfield (Mass.) Mus. A. *Position*: Instr. Lynn (Mass.) Pub. Schs., 1952- .

DOUGLAS, LAURA GLENN—*Painter, L., T.*

Winnsboro, S.C.

B. Winnsboro, S.C. *Studied*: Col. for Women, Columbia, S.C., B.F.A.; Corcoran Sch. A.; ASL, with Bridgman; NAD, with Hawthorne; abroad. *Member*: South Carolina AA; Wash. A. Gld.; AFA. *Awards*: prizes, MMA, 1926; AIC, 1942. *Work*: PMG; Rochester Mem. A. Gal.; Gibbes A. Gal.; U.S. Treasury Dept., Wash., D.C.; USPO, Camilla, Ga. *Exhibited*: PAFA, 1935; WFNY 1939; Salons of Am., 1935; AIC, 1942, 1943; CGA, 1936; Soc. Wash. A., 1939-1946; Wash. A. Gld., 1939-1946; Whyte A. Gal., 1939-1946; PMG, 1939-1946 (one-man, 1944); Gibbes Mem. A. Gal., 1935-1946; Albany Inst. Hist. & A., 1936; Smithsonian Inst., 1939-1945; Caresse Crosby Gal., Wash., D.C.; Rochester Mem. A. Gal.; Fontainebleau Alum. Assn.; Argent Gal.; Bonestell Gal.; Salon d'Automne, Grand Palais, Salon des Tuileries, etc., Paris; Joslyn Mem.; Minneapolis Inst. A.; Milwaukee AI; BMA; Carnegie Inst., etc.*

DOUGLAS, LESTER—*Designer, W., L.*

21 Duvall Dr., Washington 16, D.C.

B. New York, N.Y., July 27, 1893. *Studied*: PIASch; ASL; Columbia Univ. *Member*: AIGA; Am. Hist. Assn.; Soc. Am. Hist.; Newcomen Soc. of England; A.Dir.Cl.; The Typophiles. *Work*: Book des., Lib. Cong.; Columbia Univ. Lib.; Princeton Univ. Lib. *Exhibited*: 50 Books of the Year Exh., AIGA; Printing for Commerce Exh., AIGA. *Author*: "Color in Modern Printing"; "Modernizing Business Print"; "The Battle of the Fifty Books." Contributor to: The Printing Art; The American Printer; Nation's Business. *Lectures*: Typography; Book & Magazine Design.*

DOUGLASS, HELEN WRIGHT—*Designer,*
Port. P., Et., L.

3413 Bath Rd., Akron 13, Ohio

B. Pottsville, Pa., May 20, 1910. *Studied*: Cleveland Sch. A.; John Huntington Polytechnic Inst., Cleveland; & with Henry G. Keller. *Member*: Akron Women's A. Lg.; Ohio WC Soc.; ADI. *Awards*: prizes, Akron AI, 1930; Canton (Ohio) A. Mus., 1944. *Exhibited*: Phila. A. All., 1936, 1937; AIC, 1936, 1939; Wash. WC Cl., 1936-1940; AWCS, 1938; N.Y. WC Cl., 1937, 1938; Phila. WC Cl., 1936, 1937; Laguna Beach AA, 1938; CM, 1937, 1938; Butler AI, 1938, 1939; Ohio WC Soc., 1935-1937; Akron AI, 1930-1933, 1935, 1944; Harrisburg (Pa.) AA, 1935; Canton Mus. A., 1944. *Lectures*: Design in Industry. *Position*: Indst. Des., B. F. Goodrich Co., 1929-44; Freelance Indst. & Arch. Des., 1945- ; Pres. Women's A. Lg., 1958-59.

DOUGLASS, RALPH WADDELL—
Educator, P., Gr., Des., Cart.

3308 Loma Vista Place, Albuquerque, N.M.

B. St. Louis, Mo., Dec. 29, 1895. *Studied*: Monmouth Col., B.A.; Julian Acad., Paris; AIC; ASL. *Member*: AEA; New

Jersey P. & S. Soc.; New Mexico A. Lg. *Awards*: prizes, N.M. State Fair, 1939, 1940, 1946, 1947, 1950, 1956 (purchase); hon. deg., DFA, Monmouth Col., 1953, and others. *Work*: Coronado Lib., Univ. N.M.; Am. Univ., Cairo, Egypt; Highland H.S., Albuquerque, and in private coll. *Exhibited*: nationally; one-man: Mus. N.M., 1941, 1946, 1958; Monmouth Col., 1946; Univ. New Mexico, 1948, 1955; Univ. Maine, 1950; Jonson Gal., Albuquerque, 1952; Roswell Mus., 1956; Griegos Lib., Albuquerque, N.M., 1957. Des., I., Mesaland Series of Juveniles for Univ. N.M. Press, 1943-49; Des., "Masked Gods," 1950. Author: "Calligraphic Lettering," 1949 (2nd printing), 1955. *Position*: Instr., Am. Univ., Cairo, Egypt, 1920-23; Cart. & Staff A., Chicago Daily News, 1924-29; Instr., Prof. A., 1929- ; Hd. Dept., 1936-46, Univ. New Mexico, Albuquerque, N.M.

DOUGLASS, ROBERT W.—*Painter, I.*

156 East 39th St. (16); h. 441 East 20th St., New York 10, N.Y.

B. Kansas City, Kans., Aug. 6, 1918. *Member*: SI. *Work*: Pan-American Coffee Bureau. *Exhibited*: Univ. Kansas, 1951; Kansas City AI, 1951. Author, I., "Sketch in Recognition," 1944 (used as text in all Naval Pre-Flight, and all C.A.A. Pre-Flight Schools). Illus. for: Good Housekeeping; Cosmopolitan, McCalls, Sat. Eve. Post; American; Woman's Day; Red Book; This Week; Life magazine and others.*

DOW, WILLIAM JAMES—*Painter, Des., T.*

233 Pine St., South Portland, Me.

B. Cape Elizabeth, Me., July 5, 1891. *Studied*: Eric Pape Sch. A., Boston; Sch. Fine & Appl. A., Portland, Me.; PAFA; Harvard Univ., and with Eric Pape, Henry McCarter, Philip Hale, Joseph T. Pearson, Daniel Garber and others. *Member*: SC; Copley Soc., Boston; Portland Soc. A.; Maine WC Soc.; Hayloft Soc., Portland, Me.; Maine Soc. A. & Crafts. *Awards*: Cresson Traveling Scholarship, PAFA. *Exhibited*: Sweat Mem. Mus., 1946 (one-man); Copley Soc., Boston, 1947 (one-man); AWS; Grand Central A. Gal.; NAD; SC; Bowdoin Col.; Farnsworth Mus. A.; Portland A. Soc., annually and others. *Position*: Instr. A., summer classes, Sch. Fine & Appl. A., Portland, Me.; South Portland H.S., and private classes (summers) Prouts Neck, Scarboro, Me.

DOWDEN, RAYMOND BAXTER—*Educator, Des., P.*

205 West 15th St., New York 11, N.Y.

B. Coal Valley, Pa., Dec. 25, 1905. *Studied*: Carnegie Inst. B.A.; Tiffany Fnd. F. *Awards*: prize, Assoc. A. Pittsburgh, 1934. *Work*: murals, Children's Aid Soc. Playground, N.Y. *Exhibited*: AIC, 1932, 1935, 1936; WMAA, 1936; Assoc. A. Pittsburgh; Carnegie Inst., 1930-1934; covers & format for art magazines. *Position*: Instr., 1936-40, Asst. Prof. Des., 1940-46, Prof. Des., 1946- , Hd. Dept. Des., 1956- , Ed., CUASch., New York, N.Y.; Dir., Yale Univ. Summer Art Sch., 1952- .

DOWLING, COLISTA (Mrs. E. H.)—*Painter, I.*

2146 S.E. Belmont St., Portland 15, Ore.

B. Waverly, Kan. *Studied*: Oregon State Col.; ASL. *Member*: Oregon SA. *Work*: portraits in pub. bldgs.; murals in churches. *Exhibited*: Seattle, Spokane, Wash.; Salem, Portland, Ore. Illus., "Six Feet"; "Thunder Hill"; "Muslin Town"; "Trundle Tales"; "Peaceful Conquest," & other books.

DOWLING, JACQUES MacCUISTON (Mrs.)—
Sculptor, P., L., T.

8003 Inwood Rd., Dallas 9, Tex.

B. Texarkana, Tex., Oct. 19, 1906. *Studied*: NAD; ASL, and with Finn Haakon Frolich, Robert Aitken, Robert Laurent, William Zorach, Nicolaides, R. Jerome Hill and others. *Member*: Fed. Dallas A.; Dallas AA; Texas FA Soc.; AFA; Frank Reaugh A. Cl. *Awards*: prizes, All. A. Exh., 1933; Sartors Gal., 1950-1954; Fed. Dallas A., 1950-1954; Southwest Ceramics Exh. (sweepstakes & 1st in sc.) 1954. *Work*: many sculptured portraits of prominent persons, as well as animal groups, reliefs, etc. *Exhibited*: Fed. Dallas A., Sartor's Gal., 1950-1958; DMFA, 1948, 1950, 1951, 1956; Oak Cliff Soc. FA, 1951-1954; Reaugh A. Cl., 1951-1955, 1956, 1958; Ney Mus. A., 1951; Fed.

Dallas A., 1951 (one-man); Telenews Lounge, 1950-1952; Southwest Ceramics, 1954; Fed. Dallas A. annuals, 1952-1954; Rush A. Gal., 1953, 1958 (one-man); Mus. New Mexico, 1957; Artists & Craftsmen traveling exh., 1957-58; Aunspaugh A. Cl., 1957, 1958.

DOWNING, GEORGE ELLIOTT—*Educator, P.*

Brown University; h. 144 Power St., Providence 6, R.I.

B. Marquette, Mich., June 19, 1904. *Studied*: Univ. Chicago, Ph.B.; Harvard Univ., M.A., Ph.D. *Position*: Instr. A., Univ. Chicago, 1926-30; Asst. Prof. A., 1932-46, Assoc. Prof. A., 1946-1953, Prof. A., 1953- , Brown Univ., Providence, R.I.*

DOWNS, MRS. W. FINDLAY. See Howell, Felicie

DOWS, OLIN—*Painter, Lith., Eng., W., L.*

144 East End Ave., New York 28, N.Y.; also Rhinebeck, N.Y.

B. Irvington-on-Hudson, N.Y., Aug. 14, 1904. *Studied*: Harvard Univ.; Yale Sch. FA, with C. K. Chatterton, Eugene Savage, Edwin C. Taylor. *Member*: NSMP; Dutchess County AA; Wash. A. Gld.; SAGA. *Work*: N.Y. Pub. Lib.; PC; murals, USPO, Rhinebeck, N.Y., Hyde Park, N.Y. Murals, screens and other work in private colls. Author, I., "Franklin Roosevelt at Hyde Park," 1949; "His Messengers Went Forth," 1949. *Positions*: Nat. Bd., AEA; Trustee, Chaloner Prize Fnd.

DOYLE, JERRY—*Cartoonist, T.*

6 Beth Lane, Malvern, Pa.

B. Philadelphia, Pa., Nov. 15, 1898. *Member*: Pen & Pencil Cl. *Awards*: Headliners Award, Mercantile Library Award, N.Y. Newspapermen's Cartoon Award, 1938. Author: "According to Doyle," cartoon history of World War, 1943. Contributor: cart. to national magazines.

DOZIER, OTIS—*Painter, Lith.*

8019 Dellrose Drive, Dallas 14, Tex.

B. Forney, Tex., Mar. 27, 1904. *Awards*: Dallas All. A., 1932, 1946; Southwestern AA, 1948; New Orleans A. & Crafts, 1948; Denver A. Mus., 1943. *Work*: Univ. Nebraska; Dallas Mus. FA; Denver A. Mus.; MMA; Wadsworth Atheneum; Newark Mus.; murals, USPO, Arlington, Giddings, Fredericksburg, Tex. *Exhibited*: WMAA, 1945; Carnegie Inst., 1946; Pasadena, Cal., 1946; Dallas All. A., 1946; Witte Mem. Mus., 1948 (one-man); DMFA, 1956 (one-man). *Position*: Instr., Dallas Mus. FA, Dallas, Tex., 1945- .*

DRABKIN, STELLA (Mrs.)—
Painter, Mosaicist, Gr., Des.

2404 Pine St., Philadelphia 3, Pa.

B. New York, N.Y., Jan. 27, 1906. *Studied*: NAD; Phila. Graphic Sketch Cl., and with Earl Horter. *Member*: SAGA; AEA; Phila. A. All.; Am. Color Pr. Soc.; Audubon A.; Phila. Pr. Cl. *Awards*: prizes, Am. Color Pr. Soc., 1944; Phila. Pr. Cl., 1955. *Work*: PAFA; PMA; NGA; MMA; Pa. State Col.; LC; Phila. A. All.; Atwater Kent Mus.; Tel-Aviv Mus., Israel; Dagania Mus., Bezalel Mus., Jerusalem and in many private colls. *Exhibited*: nationally and internationally. Included in Am. A. Festival, Berlin, 1951; one-man: Carlen Gal., 1938, 1939; Mus. New Mexico, 1947; Phila. A. All., 1944, 1950; PAFA, 1952. *Position*: Chm., Pr., Phila. A. All.; Sec., Phila. Chptr., AEA, 1951-52, Bd., 1953, 1955; Ed., AEA "Newsletter"; Council, Am. Color Pr. Soc.

DRAKE, WILLIAM A.—*Etcher, Lith., P., C., T.*

328 West 39th St., New York 18, N.Y.; h. 14 Garden St., Bergenfield, N.J.

B. Toronto, Canada, Nov. 7, 1891. *Studied*: Ontario Col. A., Toronto, Canada. *Member*: NSMP; A. & Let. Cl., Toronto. *Work*: A. Gal. of Toronto; PMA; Montclair A. Mus.; Princeton Pr. Cl.; Nat. Gal. of Canada. *Exhibited*: Royal Canadian Acad.; Lib. Cong.; Ontario (Canada) SA; Laguna Beach AA; Montclair A. Mus.; Venice Biennale, 1940. *Position*: Instr., Scenic Painting, Yale Univ.; Consultant & A. Dir. for scenic studios, producing scenery for theatre and television.*

DRALLE, ELIZABETH M.—
Industrial Designer, Comm., I.
20 West 8th St., New York 11, N.Y.

B. Schenectady, N.Y., May 16, 1910. *Studied*: PIASch., B.F.A.; PIASch. Indst. Des.; N.Y. Univ.; Univ. Colorado; Univ. Chicago. *Member*: IDI (Nat. Bd. Trustees, 1955-61, Nat. Sec., 1955, Exec. Com., N.Y. Chptr., 1954-58). *Exhibited*: Nat. Home Furnishings Show, 1955, 1956; Nat. Hardware Show, 1956; Nat. Housewares Show, 1957, 1958.

DRAPER, ROBERT SARGENT—*Painter, L., W.*
7719 Southwest 69th Ave., South Miami 43, Fla.

B. Rutland, Vt., Feb. 15, 1920. *Studied*: Univ. Florida, B.A.; Norton Sch. A. and with Hans Hofmann. *Member*: Palm Beach A. Lg.; Miami AA; AEA; Miami A. Lg.; Fla. A. Group. *Awards*: prizes, Miami A. Lg., 1948, 1950, 1951, 1955; A. & W. Soc., 1949; Soc. Four A., 1954; AAPL, 1955. *Work*: Lowe Gal. A., Coral Gables, Fla.; Norton Gal. A.; Maitland (Fla.) Research Center, and in private colls. *Exhibited*: Soc. Four A., 1950-1952; Miami A. Lg., 1947-1951; Sarasota AA, 1950; Florida Fed. A., 1947, 1948, 1951; Norton Gal. A., 1947, 1948, 1950, 1951; Tucker Gal., 1949-1958; AAPL, 1950, 1951, 1955; Mirell Gal., Coconut Grove, Fla., 1954 (one-man); Mayfair Art Theatre, 1954; Ringling Mus. A., 1955; Pensacola A. Center, 1956; High Mus. A., 1956; Riverside Mus. A., 1958; one-man: Miami Beach A. Center, 1956; High Mus. A., 1957; Norton Gal. A., 1958; Maitland Research Center, 1958. *Position*: Organizer & 1st Pres., Miami AA, Coral Gables, Fla., 1954-55; Pres., Miami AA, 1957-58; Chm., Blue Dome Fellowship, 1957-58; Memb. Com., AEA, 1958.

DRAPER, WILLIAM FANKLIN—*Painter*
535 Park Ave.; h. 160 East 83rd St., New York, N.Y.

B. Hopedale, Mass., Dec. 24, 1912. *Studied*: Harvard Univ.; NAD; ASL; & with Jon Corbino, Leon Kroll, Zimmerman. *Member*: SC; Century Assn. *Work*: U.S. Navy, combat art; ports., Harvard Univ.; Vassar Col.; Phillips Exeter Acad.; Lawrenceville Sch.; murals, U.S. Naval Acad., Annapolis, Md.; portraits of prominent naval commanding officers. *Exhibited*: NAD, 1934, 1941; AIC, 1941; MMA, 1945; NGA, 1945; CGA, 1943; Inst. Mod. A., Boston, 1940; BMFA, 1942; Nat. Gal., London, 1944. *Author*: "The Navy at War," 1943 (illus. by combat artists); Illus., "5000 Miles to Tokyo." *Contributor*: war paintings to Nat. Geographic magazine; Collier's; American Magazine.

DREISBACH, C(LARENCE) I(RA)—*Painter, Des., T.*
916 North St. Lucas St., Allentown, Pa.

B. Union Hill, Pa., Jan. 28, 1903. *Studied*: Baum A. Sch., Allentown, Pa., and with Orlando G. Wales. *Member*: AAPL; Lehigh A. All.; St. Augustine AA; Lancaster County AA; Woodmere A. Lg.; Lansdale A. Lg.; Buck Hill AA; Pocono Mt. A. Group. *Awards*: prizes, St. Augustine AA, 1953, 1956; Lansdale AA, 1935; Call-Chronicle exhs., 1954, 1955; Pocono Mt. regional. *Work*: Allentown A. Mus.; Reading Pub. Mus.; Raub Jr. H.S.; Bethlehem H.S.; Bucks County Pub. Schs.; Call-Chronicle Pub. Co.; Quakertown H.S., and others. *Exhibited*: Fla. Southern Col., 1952; St. Augustine AA, 1953-1958; Ogunquit A. Center, 1955, 1957; Buck Hill AA, 1949-1951, 1957; Boston Soc. Indp. A.; AAPL, 1957, 1958; Allentown A. Mus.; Pa. State Mus.; Reading Pub. Mus.; Lehigh Univ.; Woodmere A. Gal.; one-man: Allentown A. Mus., 1949; Lancaster County AA, 1958; Bucks County Sch. Service Center, 1957. *Contributor* illus. to Ideals. *Positions*: Instr., Baum A. Sch., Allentown Community College and private classes; Trustee, Allentown A. Mus.

DRERUP, KARL—*Craftsman, P., E., Gr.*
Thornton, N.H., P.O. Campton, N.H.

B. Borghorst-Westphalia, Germany, Aug. 26, 1904. *Studied*: in Germany and Italy. *Awards*: prizes, Syracuse Mus. FA; Wichita, Kans., Nat. Decorative A. Exh. *Work*: BMA; CM; DMFA; Los A. Mus. A.; Manchester, N.H.; Newark Mus. A.; MMA; San Diego FA Soc.; WMA. *Exhibited*: Brussels World's Fair, 1958; Syracuse Mus. FA; Wichita, Kans.; Designer-Craftsmen Exh., and others; one-man: DMFA; Tulsa, Okla.; Detroit Inst. A.; San Diego FA Soc.; Manchester Mus. A.; Springfield (Mass.) Mus. A.; Palm Beach, Fla.; New England Crafts, WMA, 1955. Illus., "Carmen," 1930. *Position*: Prof. FA, Plymouth T. Col., Plymouth, N.H., 1947- .

DRESSEL, FRANNIE—*Printmaker, Des., Comm. A., C.*
206 Coventry Place, Edwardsville, Ill.

B. Edwardsville, Ill., June 29, 1921. *Studied*: AIC. *Awards*: prize, CAM, 1947; citation of merit for fabrics, AID. *Work*: Block printed fabrics, Springfield Mus. A., and in many college colls. Drapery for churches incl. private chapel of Archbishop Ritter, St. Louis, Mo. *Exhibited*: Int. Textile Exh., 1945-1948; LC, 1947, 1952, 1954-1956; and traveling exh., 1956; CAM, 1944-1957; Carnegie Inst., 1947; SFMA, 1948, 1949; PAFA, 1947, 1948; SAGA, 1948, 1952-1955; CAM, 1947-1951; Central States Gr. A., 1949; Northwest Pr. M., 1948.

DRESSER, LOUISA—*Museum Curator, L., W.*
Worcester Art Museum, 55 Salisbury St. (8); h. 65 Wachusett St., Worcester 9, Mass.

B. Worcester, Mass., Oct. 25, 1907. *Studied*: Vassar Col., B.A.; FMA Sch.; Courtauld Inst., Univ. London. *Author*: "Seventeenth Century Painting in New England," 1935; "Early New England Printmakers," 1939; "Likeness of America," 1949. Contributor to Art in America (monographs on Christian Gullager, 1949, and Edward Savage, 1953); WMA Annual and Bulletin; Antiques magazine. John Simon Guggenheim F., 1956-57. *Position*: Assoc. in Decorative A., Cur., Decorative A., 1932-49; Acting Dir., 1943-46; Cur., 1949- ; WMA, Worcester, Mass.

DREW, DOROTHY HART—*Painter*
80 West 40th St., Studio 10 W, New York 18, N.Y.

B. Macon County, Mo. *Studied*: with George Bridgman, Alexander Abels, Raymond Nelson, Sidney Dickinson, Ivan Olinsky. *Member*: AAPL; Grand Central A. Gal. *Work*: Portraits in private coll. and public bldgs. *Exhibited*: NAD. Illus., covers for Literary Digest, Vision and Time magazines.

DREWELOWE, EVE—*Painter, S.*
2025 Balsam Ave., Boulder, Colo.

B. New Hampton, Iowa. *Studied*: Univ. Iowa, A.B., A.M.; Univ. Colorado. *Member*: Boulder A. Gld.; Prairie WC Assn. *Awards*: prize, Colorado State Fair, 1934, 1950; Springfield Mus. A., Denver A. Mus., 1932; Tri-State Exh., Cheyenne, Wyo., 1958. *Work*: Univ. Iowa; Univ. Colorado; Crippled Children's Sch., Jamestown, N.D.; Harkness House, London, Eng.; H.S., Agricultural Col., Cedar City, Utah. *Exhibited*: Nat. Exh. Am. A., N.Y., 1938; WFNY 1939; PAFA, 1936; AIC, 1939; NAWA, 1939-1944, 1946; Denver A. Mus., 1926, 1931, 1933, 1936, 1938, 1941, 1945; Univ. Colorado, 1937; Cornell Univ., 1942; Henderson Gal., 1943, 1949 (one-man); Univ. Oklahoma, 1935; Kansas City A'I, 1935, 1937, 1940, 1942; Joslyn Mem., 1934, 1936-1939, 1942, 1944, 1956; Boulder A. Gld., 1925-1958; Prairie WC Assn., 1936-1958; Boulder A. Gld. traveling exh., 1954-1958; Arizona State Fair, 1950; Cedar City, Utah, 1944-1958; UNESCO traveling exh., England, 1949; Central City Opera Festival, 1957, 1958. Illus. in "Denim and Broadcloth," 1953.

DREWES, WERNER—*Painter, Gr., E.*
School of Fine Arts, Washington University; h. 7135 Northmoor, St. Louis, Mo.

B. Canig, Germany, July 27, 1899. *Studied*: in Germany, with Klee, Kandinsky. *Member*: Am. Color Pr. Soc. *Awards*: prizes, MModA, 1939; Topeka, Kans., 1948; Springfield, Mass., 1952; Textile Comp., Mus. Costume A., N.Y., 1941; 50 Best Prints of the Year, 1932, 1944; several prizes in midwestern shows, 1946-55. *Work*: MModA, Honolulu Acad. A.; City of Frankfurt, Germany; FMA; AGAA; AIC; PAFA; SFMA; CAM; SAM; BM; Springfield, Mo.; Springfield, Ill.; State Mus., Trenton, N.J.; WMA; BMA; Guggenheim Mus., N.Y.; Rosenwald Mus., Jenkintown, Pa.; R.I. Sch. Des.; Wash. Univ., St. Louis; Univ. Urbana, Ill.; Bennington Col.; Wells Col.; Mills Col.; Oakland, Cal.; Yale Univ.; Univ. Alabama; LC; Newark Pub. Lib.; Boston Pub. Lib.; N.Y. Pub. Lib. *Exhibited*: Carnegie Inst.; AIC; MMA, and many other group shows in U.S., and traveling exhs. abroad. One-man: New York, N.Y., 1932-1950 including the following galleries: Morton, Argent, Artists Gal.; Van Dieman-Lilienfeld; Kleemann; Nierndorf; Sch. for Social Research; also, Smithsonian Inst., and in Europe and South America. *Position*: Instr. A., Columbia Univ., 1936-39; Dir., Graphic A. Project, U.S. Federal A. Program, 1940-41; Instr., Brooklyn Col., 1944; Inst. Des., Chicago, 1945; Instr., Des., & Dir. First Year Program, Sch. FA, Washington Univ., St. Louis, Mo., 1946- .

DREYFUSS, HENRY—*Designer, E., W., L.*

4 West 58th St., New York 19, N.Y.; h. 500 Columbia St., South Pasadena, Cal.

B. New York, N.Y., Mar. 2, 1904. *Studied*: with Norman Bel Geddes (stage design). *Member*: Am. Soc. Indst. Des. (Co-Fndr., past Pres., F.); Arch. Lg.; Nat. Council on the Arts & Government. *Awards*: Lord & Taylor Des. award, 1939; Arch. Lg. gold medal, 1951; Order of Orange-Nassau (Netherlands), 1952; Hon. D. Sc., Occidental Col., California, 1953; AIGA, 1953; Progressive Arch. award, 1954; Arch. Lg. gold medal, 1954; Neiman-Marcus Fashion award, 1955; Arch. Lg. gold medal, 1956; Indst. Des. Council of Canada award, 1956; PMSch. A., 1958. *Work*: interiors, equipment, homes and industry: S.S. Constitution, Independence and other liners; Bell Telephone Co.; Cities Service Co.; Esterbrook Pen Co.; Walter Kidde & Co.; Lockheed Aircraft; Mergenthaler Linotype Co.; N.Y. Central System; RCA; U.S. Armed Forces, and many others. *Exhibited*: special exh., Triennale di Milano, 1957; Artisans-Techniciens aux Etats Unis, Paris, 1958, trade fairs in Italy, France, Yugoslavia, Japan, etc. Author: "Designing for People," 1955. Contributor to N.Y. Times Magazine; Harvard Business Review; Industrial Design; American Fabrics, and other publications. *Position*: Faculty, California Inst. Tech., Univ. California at Los Angeles; Lecturer, Harvard, Yale, Mass. Inst. Tech., and other colleges and universities. Hd., Henry Dreyfuss Co., New York and California.

DRIESBACH, DAVID FRAISER—
Educator, P., Gr., L., Cr.

Art Department, Millikin University; h. 1164 West North St., Decatur, Ill.

B. Wausau, Wis., Oct. 7, 1922. *Studied*: Univ. Illinois; Beloit Col.; Univ. Wisconsin; PAFA; State Univ. of Iowa, B.F.A., M.F.A. *Awards*: prizes, Iowa State Fair, 1950; Yonkers prize, Des Moines, Iowa, 1950; All Arkansas annual, 1952; Memphis, Tenn., 1953; Sioux City, Iowa, 1953; All Iowa annual, 1953; Central Ill. Valley, 1955; Oakland A. Mus., 1958. *Work*: State Univ. Iowa; Des Moines A. Center; De Pauw Univ.; Starr King Sch., Oakland, Cal. Private port. commissions. *Exhibited*: Butler Inst. Am. A., 1950; WAC, 1950-1952; AIC, 1951; Denver A. Mus., 1951, 1958; MMoA, 1952; MMA, 1952; SAM, 1953; Oakland A. Mus., 1958; Burpee Gal. A., Rockford, Ill., 1947-1949; Iowa State Fair, 1950-1952; Central Ill. Valley, 1954-1957. *Positions*: Chm. A. Dept., Hendrix College, 1952-53; Instr., Graphics, Iowa State T. College, 1953-54; Chm., A. Dept., Prof. A., Millikin Univ., Decatur, Ill., 1954- .

DRIPPS, CLARA REINICKE (Mrs.)—
Painter, C., Comm. A.

3816½ College Ave., Culver City, Cal.

B. Amelia, Ohio, July 3, 1885. *Studied*: Otis A. Sch., Los A.; Corcoran Sch. A. *Member*: Women Painters of the West; Las Artistas A. Cl.; Cal. A. Cl. *Awards*: prizes, Women Painters of the West; Las Artistas, 1944, 1946; Am. Artist Magazine, 1952; Odessa, Tex., 1954. *Exhibited*: Hermosa Beach AA; Redondo Beach AA; Greek Theatre, Los Angeles.

DRISKELL, DAVID CLYDE—*Painter, E.*

Art Department, Talladega College; h. 709 Cruickshank St., Talladega, Ala.

B. Eatonton, Ga., June 7, 1931. *Studied*: Howard Univ., Wash., D.C., A.B. in Fine Arts; Catholic Univ., with Alexander Giampietro; Skowhegan (Me.) Sch. of Painting & Sculpture, with Jack Levine and Henry Varnum Poor. *Member*: CAA; Ala. State T. Assn. *Awards*: Bocour award, Skowhegan, Me., 1953; Charles Allen award, Wash., D.C., 1953, 1954, 1955; Skowhegan Fellowship, 1953; Scholastic award in Fine Arts, Howard Univ., 1953, 1954, 1955. *Work*: Barnett Aden Gal., Howard Univ., Catholic Univ., all Wash., D.C.; Skowhegan Sch. A.; Savery Coll., Talladega College. *Exhibited*: Soc. Washington A., 1954, 1955; one-man: Talladega Col.; Barnett Aden Gal. Lectures: Italian Renaissance and Its Influence on Modern Art; Art and Appreciation, etc. Arranged and directed exhibitions: "Modern Masters," 1956 (Guggenheim Mus. loan); "26 Prints by Modern Masters," 1959 (Guggenheim Mus. loan); and others from Nat. Gallery of FA, Georgia Mus., etc. *Position*: Asst. to Curator, Howard Univ. Gallery; Asst. Prof. A., 1955- , Hd. Dept. of Art, Talladega College, Alabama, at present.

DROSTE, HOWARD MEYER—*Painter, T.*

517 College Drive, Jamestown, N.D.

B. Fairmont, Minn., July 12, 1921. *Studied*: Univ. Washington, B.A., M.F.A. *Awards*: Univ. Washington, 1953. *Exhibited*: North Dakota annuals. *Position*: Asst. Instr., Univ. Washington, Seattle, Wash., 1953-54; Asst. Prof. A., Jamestown Col., Jamestown, N.D., 1954- .*

DRUCKER, BORIS—*Cartoonist, Comm., Des.*

2207 Rittenhouse Square, Philadelphia 3, Pa.

B. Philadelphia, Pa., May 22, 1920. *Studied*: PMIA Sch. *Member*: Phila. A. Dir. Cl.; Nat. Soc. A. Dir. *Awards*: gold medals, Phila. A. Dir. Cl., 1947, 1950, 1954 (2), 1957. *Work*: Cartoons for advertising campaigns (newspaper, magazine, poster, etc.): Electric Companies, 1950, 1953, 1955, 1957, 1958; Insurance Co. of North America, 1952; A. T. & T. Co., 1954-1958; Phila. Saving Fund Soc., 1950-1958; Bell Tel. Co., Pa., 1950-1958; First Pennsylvania Co., 1954-1958; Yellow Cab Co., 1954. *Exhibited*: A. Dir. Cl., N.Y., 1947, 1955; Phila. A. Dir., 1947-1958. Cartoons included in: Sat. Eve. Post Cartoons, 1950; Collier's Kids, 1952; Cartoon Treasury, 1955. Contributor to: Sat. Eve. Post, Collier's, This Week, True, Look, Holiday, Sports Illustrated.

DRUDIS, JOSE—*Painter, L.*

740 North LaBrea Ave. (38); h. Ambassador Hotel, Los Angeles, Cal.

B. Alvinyo, Spain, Dec. 15, 1890. *Studied*: Sch. FA, Barcelona; Univ. Barcelona. *Awards*: prizes, Barcelona, Spain; Traditional A. Exh., 1955; Friday Morning Cl., Los A., 1955; Pacific Coast Cl., Long Beach, Cal., 1955; gold med., Cal. A. Cl., 1955 (2); Ebell Cl., Los A., 1956; Les Palmes Academiques, Republic of France; Commander Cross, Grand Prix Humanitaire Belge, Belgium; gold medal, City of Mataró, Spain; Medal of Honor, Scandinavian-American A. Soc., Los Angeles. *Work*: Los A. Mus. A.; Royal Palace Mus., Madrid; Phoenix A. Center; Los A. City Hall Mus.; Pasadena A. Mus.; Los A. Mus. A.; Circulo de Bellas Artes de Madrid; Carson Estates; Del Amo Fnd., Los A.; Clarethian Seminary, Compton, Cal., and in private colls. U.S. and abroad. *Exhibited*: one-man: Los A. Mus. A.; Univ. Cal. at Los Angeles; Middlebury Univ., Vt.; Ralston A. Gal., N.Y.; City Cl., Boston; Arch. Cl., Boston; O'Bryan A. Gal., Chicago, Ill.; J. J. Guillespie Gal., Pittsburgh; Santa Barbara A. Lg.; Evanston (Ga.) Hotel; Dalzell Hatfield Gal., 1958; Whittier (Cal.) A. Mus., and others. *Position*: Dir., Cal. A. Cl.; Fndr. & Pres., Drudis Foundation, Los Angeles, Cal.

DRUMMOND, MRS. CHARLES HAWKINS. See Grafly, Dorothy

DRURY, HOPE CURTIS (Mrs. William H.)—*Painter*

Paradise Rd., Newport, R.I.

B. Pawtucket, R.I., June 14, 1889. *Studied*: R.I. Sch.Des. *Member*: Providence AC; Providence WC Cl.; Newport AA. *Exhibited*: Providence AC; Newport AA.

DRURY, WILLIAM H.—*Painter, Et.*

Paradise Rd., Newport, R.I.

B. Fitchburg, Mass., Dec. 10, 1888. *Studied*: R.I. Sch.Des.; BMFA Sch.; & with Tarbell, Woodbury. *Member*: Providence AC; Providence WC Cl.; Newport AA; SAGA. *Awards*: prize, Newport AA, 1916. *Work*: R.I. Sch.Des.; NGA; BM; Cal. State Lib.; Los A. Mus. A.; LC; Victoria & Albert Mus., London. *Position*: Pres. Newport AA, 1953- .

DRYFOOS, NANCY PROSKAUER—*Sculptor*

454 Third Ave.; h. 139 East 35th St., New York 16, N.Y.

B. New Rochelle, N.Y. *Studied*: Sarah Lawrence Col.; Columbia Univ. Ext.; ASL, and with Jose de Creeft. *Member*: NAWA; Knickerbocker A.; Brooklyn Soc. A.; All. A. Am.; Silvermine Gld. A.; Lg. of Present Day A.; N.Y. Soc. Women A.; P. & S. Soc. New Jersey. *Awards*: prizes, NAC, 1947; New Jersey P. & S. Soc., 1950, 1957; Village A. Center, 1950; Westchester A. & Crafts Gld., 1950, 1951; Knickerbocker A., 1953, 1958; NAWA, 1953; Hudson Valley AA, 1953; Silvermine Gld. A., 1953; gold medal, All. A. Am., 1953; Brooklyn Soc. A., 1955. *Exhibited:* PAFA; Syracuse Mus. FA; BM; Riverside Mus.; Jersey City Mus. A.; NAD; Westchester County A. Center; Silvermine Gld. A.; NAC; Phila. A. All.; DMFA; CGA; Albright Gal. A.; YMHA, N.Y., 1952, and others. One-man: Contemporary A., 1952; Silvermine Gld. A., 1954; Wellons Gal., 1956; Bodley Gal., 1958. Des. and executed medal for Am. Jewish Tercentenary, 1954; medallion, Dickenson College; 12 brass plaques for Kingsbridge House.

DUBIN, RALPH—*Painter, T., Gr.*

1780 76th St., Brooklyn 14, N.Y.

B. New York, N.Y., Sept. 2, 1918. *Studied:* City Col., N.Y.; BMSch. A.; and with Hans Hofmann, Ben Shahn, Moses Soyer, James Lechay, Robert Gwathmey, Stuart Davis, Louis Schanker. *Member:* AEA. *Work:* PAFA. *Exhibited:* WMAA, 1948; AIC, 1954; VMFA, 1954; Am. Inst. A. & Let., 1955; Butler Inst. Am. A., 1956; MModA, 1956; Springfield Mus. FA, 1956; Dayton AI, 1956; AFA traveling exh., 1958; BM, 1958; Provincetown A. Festival, 1958; one-man: RoKo Gal., 1947; Charles Fourth Gal., 1948, 1949; Kraushaar Gal., 1954, 1957.

DUBLE, LU—*Sculptor*

16 West 10th St., New York 11, N.Y.

B. Oxford, England, Jan. 21, 1896. *Studied:* ASL; NAD; CUASch., and with Archipenko, deCreeft, Hofmann. *Member:* ANA, NSS; S. Gld.; Audubon A. *Awards:* Guggenheim F., 1937, 1938; F., Inst. Int. Edu.; prize, NAWA, 1937; Audubon A., 1950, gold medal, 1958; Nat. Acad. A. & Let., 1952; med., Audubon A, 1947. *Work:* Newark Mus. A.; WMAA. *Exhibited:* PMA, 1940; Carnegie Inst.; Montclair A. Mus., 1941; MMA, 1942, 1952; PAFA, 1942-1946; WMAA, 1946, 1947; NAD, annually; Audubon A. annually; S. Gld.; NAWA, annually; Marie Sterner Gal., 1938 (one-man); Toledo Mus. A., 1939; Riverside Mus. *Position:* Vice-Pres., Audubon A., 1950-55; Instr. S., Greenwich House, New York, N.Y., at present.

DUCASSE, MABEL LISLE—*Painter*

48 Aberdeen Rd., East Providence 15, R.I.

B. La Porte, Colo., Mar. 3, 1895. *Studied:* ASL; PIASch.; Univ. Washington, B.F.A., M.F.A. *Member:* R.I. WC Cl. *Awards:* prizes, Seattle FA Soc., 1918, 1923, 1925.

DUCKETT, ALBERT—*Cartoonist, P.*

301 Kensington Drive, Biloxi, Miss.

B. Springfield, Ill., Oct. 28, 1907. *Studied:* Studio Sch. A., Chicago, with John Norton, John Chapin; Nat. Acad. A., Chicago; Detroit Soc. A. & Crafts, with Sarkis Sarkisian. *Exhibited:* Detroit Inst. A., 1943, 1944. *Position:* Cart., Hearst Newspapers, 1926-45; A.Ed., Detroit Times, 1935-46 (Retired).

DUDLEY, FANNY—*Craftsman*

Old Lyme, Conn.

B. Brooklyn, N.Y. *Studied:* with Adolph Cuzin, Emil Maylander, Henry Noulhac, Paris. *Member:* Gld. of Book Workers, N.Y. *Award:* Med., Pan-Pacific Exp., 1915. *Work:* Service book, St. John's Church by the Sea, Newport, R.I.; J. P. Morgan Lib. Specialist in hand bookbinding, tooling, etc.

DUDLEY, VIRGINIA (EVELYN)—
Enamelist, P., S., Gr., T., L., C.

"Rising Fawn Enamels," Rising Fawn, Ga.

B. Spring City, Tenn., Dec. 10, 1913. *Studied:* Univ. Chattanooga; ASL; Atelier 17, with Stanley Hayter; New Sch. for Social Research; New Mexico State Col.; Claremont Grad. Sch., M.F.A. *Member:* SAGA; Southern Highland Handicraft Gld.; Chattanooga AA; NAEA; Eastern AA; New Orleans AA; *Awards:* Rosenwald F., 1943-44; prizes, Ceramic Lg., Miami, 1954, 1955; Craftsman's Fair, Asheville, N.C., 1953; Pacific Nat. Exh. ceramics, Vancouver, B.C., 1953; Syracuse Mus. FA, 1956; scholarships to Univ. Chattanooga, ASL, Cranbrook Acad. A., Claremont Grad. Sch. *Work:* MMA; Pennell Coll., LC; SAGA; Universities of Pennsylvania, Tennessee, Chattanooga and Georgia. *Exhibited:* ASL, 1940-1942; Albright A. Gal., 1942; ACA Gal., 1942; SMFA, 1942; SAGA, 1942, 1943, circ. exh. to England, 1954; NAD, 1942, 1943; Phila. Pr. Cl., 1941-1943; MMA, 1943, 1955, 1958-1959; LC, 1942,

1943; Los Angeles County Fair, 1948-1955; AFA traveling exh., 1943-1945; Syracuse Mus. FA, 1950-1952, 1956, 1958; Univ. Chattanooga, 1938-1940, 1943 (one-man), 1950, 1951; Brooks Mem. Gal., 1943; SSAL, 1943; Scripps Col., 1948-1950; Chaffey Col., 1949, 1950; Shorter Col., Rome, Ga., 1952 (one-man); Hunter Gal., Chattanooga, 1952-1955; ceramics, Smithsonian Inst., 1953, 1955, traveling exh., 1957-1959; Intl. Ceramic Exh. joint show with Kiln Club members, 1957; Cooper Union, 1954; Pacific Nat., Vancouver, B.C., 1952-1954; Sioux City A. Center, 1954; Craftsman's Fair, Asheville, 1952-1955; Am. Craftsmen's Edu. Council Gal., 1955; A. Festival, Atlanta, 1954; High Mus. A., 1955; Delgado Mus. A., 1955; circulating exhs.: Studio Gld., West Redding, Conn., 1955-56; Ceramic Lg. Miami, 1955-56; Univ. Illinois, 1953-55, 1955-57; Southern A. Mus. Dir. Assn., 1955-57; Huntington (W. Va.) Mus., 1955-56; BMFA, 1958; East Tennessee T. Col., 1958; one-man: Hunter Gal., Chattanooga, 1953; Georgia Mus. A., Atlanta, 1954. Contributor to Craft Horizons and Design Quarterly. *Position:* Instr. Painting, Univ. Chattanooga, 1956-57; Hunter Gal. A., Chattanooga, 1956-57; Instr., Painting, S., Enameling, Fort Monroe, Va., 1957-58.

DUER, BEN F.—*Painter, Des., E., I., W., L.*

220 South Grand Ave., Los Angeles 12, California

B. Brooklyn, N.Y., April 28, 1888. *Studied:* PIASch.; NAD; ASL; Bisttram Sch. A., and with George Bridgman, Emil Bisttram. *Member:* Hollywood FA Fnd.; P. & S. Cl., Los A.; Los Angeles A.T. Assn. *Exhibited:* Oakland A. Gal., 1948; Taos, N.M., 1950; Bisttram Sch. A., 1949; Los Angeles AA, 1951; Greek Theatre, Los A., 1951. *Position:* Instr., Bisttram Sch. A., Los Angeles, Cal., 1949-51.*

DUFFY, (EDMUND)—*Cartoonist*

253 East 61st St., New York 21, N.Y.

B. Jersey City, N.J., Mar. 1, 1899. *Awards:* Pulitzer Prize, cartoons, 1931, 1934, 1940. *Work:* BMA; BM; Princeton Lib.; WMAA; Huntington Coll. Contributor to national magazines. *Position:* Cart., Baltimore Sun, 1924-48; Ed. Cart., Sat. Eve. Post, 1948- .*

DUGAN, IRVIN—*Cartoonist, I., P.*

2004 Enslow Blvd., Huntington 1, W. Va.

B. Huntington, W. Va., Feb. 8, 1892. *Studied:* Chicago Acad. FA; Fenway Sch. Illus., Boston, Mass.; New Sch. Des., with Vesper George, Douglas Connah. *Awards:* Citation from U.S. Treasury Dept. for cartoons in war bond drives. *Work:* Huntington Lib., San Marino, Cal.; Princeton Univ. Lib.; Univ. Kansas. *Position:* Ed. Cart., Hunt Publishing Co., 1927- .*

DUGOSH, RUBY EVELYN—*Teacher, P., L., Des., I.*

Jefferson High School; h. 359 Larchmont Dr., San Antonio 9, Tex.

B. San Antonio, Tex., Feb. 8, 1907. *Studied:* Texas State Col. for Women, B.S. in Edu.; Columbia Univ., M.A. *Member:* SSAL; San Antonio A. Lg.; Provincetown AA; NEA; Texas FA Assn. *Awards:* prizes, San Antonio A., 1937; Southeast Tex. A., 1939. *Exhibited:* Tex. Centennial, Dallas, 1936; Witte Mem. Mus., 1938; Mus. FA of Houston, 1938, 1939; Tex. State T. Col., 1938 (one-man); Lady of the Lake Col., San Antonio, 1939 (one-man); Jr. League Mus., San Antonio, 1958 (one-man). *Position:* Dir., A. Dept., Jefferson H.S., San Antonio, Tex.; A. Counselor, Famous Artists Course, Westport, Conn.

DUHME, H. RICHARD, JR.—*Sculptor, E.*

St. Louis School of Fine Arts, Washington University; h. 8 Edgewood Rd., St. Louis 24, Mo.

B. St. Louis, Mo., May 31, 1914. *Studied:* PAFA; Univ. Pennsylvania; Barnes Fnd.; Washington Univ., B.F.A.; Am. Sch. Classical Studies, Athens, Greece. *Member:* Phila. A. All.; Group 15; NSS. *Awards:* Cresson award, PAFA, 1935; Rome prize, 1937; Ware F., 1938; Hon. mention, Prix de Rome, 1939; PAFA, 1941; A. Gld., St. Louis, 1948; Vassar Col., 1949; St. Louis Festival of Religion & the Arts, 1955. *Work:* Fountain, Overbrook, Pa.; port. mem., Centralia, Mo.; Granite City, Ill., St. Louis, Mo.; Graham Medal; fountain, Clayton (Mo.) YWCA; figure, St. Louis Priory Sch., 1957; Aviation Safety award, Monsanto Chemical Co., 1958; Plaque, Ralston Purina Co., 1958. *Exhibited:* PAFA, 1938-1941, 1950; MMA, 1942; CAM, 1936-1939, 1947-1952; St. Louis A. Gld., 1948, 1949; Cosmopolitan

Cl., Phila., 1940; Phila. A. All., 1939-1941; People's A. Center, St. Louis, 1952; All. A. Am., 1956; NAD, 1957; Providence A. Cl., 1958; Chautauqua A. Center, 1958. *Position*: Instr. Sculpture, Washington Univ., St. Louis, Mo., 1947- ; Instr. (summer) Syracuse Univ., Chautauqua Center, N.Y., 1953- .

Du JARDIN, GUSSIE (Gertrude Rogers Schooley)—
Painter, S., Gr.
Montezuma, N.M.

B. San Francisco, Cal., Feb. 19, 1918. *Studied*: Univ. Colorado, B.F.A.; State Univ. Iowa, M.A. *Awards*: Roswell Mus., A., N.M. *Work*: New Mexico Highlands Univ. (Collaborated) fresco, Las Vegas (N.M.) Hospital. *Exhibited*: Mus. of New Mexico traveling exh., 1953, 1954, 1956, 1957; annual graphic art exh., Mus. New Mexico, 1952-1955; New Mexico A., 1953, 1954; New Mexico State Fair, 1951-1954; Fiesta Exh., 1951, 1952. *Position*: Instr., Robertson H.S., Las Vegas, N.M.

DULAC, MARGARITA WALKER (Mrs.)—
Painter, S., Comm. A., I., W., T.
152 East 33rd St., New York 16, N.Y.

B. Asheville, N.C., Sept. 12, 1922. *Studied*: Northwestern Univ., B.S.; Univ. Chicago, M.A.; AIC; Academie Andre L'Hote, Paris, and with Leger. *Member*: Author's Gld. *Awards*: prizes, Univ. Chicago, 1942; Evanston Artists, 1942; Wooley F. in Painting to Paris, 1938-39; F. at Northwestern Univ., Univ. Chicago, Univ. Iowa and N.Y. Univ. *Work*: Northwestern Univ., and in Italy. Murals, Northwestern Univ.; Stevens Store, Chicago; ports. *Exhibited*: AIC, 1938; CGA, 1944; Salon des Tuileries, Paris, France, 1939, 1950; Hoosier Salon, 1937; Marshall Fields Gal.; Delphic Studios, 1940; Bodley Gal., N.Y., 1958; Burr Gal., N.Y., 1958; one-man: Deering Lib., Northwestern Univ., 1937. Contributor poetry to magazines and newspapers. *Positions*: Hd. A. Dept., De Kalb (Ill.) H.S.; Asst., Leger Academie, Paris, 1949-50; Instr., Painting, Heidelberg Univ., Germany, 1947-49; Freelance display work.

DUMLER, MARTIN GEORGE—*Painter*
Arbor Pl., Hyde Park; h. 1607 Dexter Ave., Cincinnati 6, Ohio

B. Cincinnati, Ohio, Dec. 22, 1868. *Studied*: with E. H. Potthast, Martin Rettig, Richard Busebaum. *Member*: SC; Cincinnati AC. *Work*: Xavier Univ.; The Cincinnati Cl. *Exhibited*: CM; SC.

DUNBAR, DAPHNE FRENCH—
Lithographer, Des., P., T.
26 Greenleaf St., Boston 15, Mass.

B. Port Colban, Canada, Sept. 27, 1883. *Studied*: BMFA Sch.; & with Denman Ross, Homer Boss, Karl Zerbe, Kenneth Hayes Miller. *Awards*: San Diego, Cal., 1941; Inst. Mod. A., Boston, 1945. *Work*: Colorado Springs FA Center; BMFA; AGAA; Los A. Mus. A.; Detroit Inst. A.; Lib. Cong.*

DUNBIER, AUGUSTUS WILLIAM—*Painter, L.*
914 North 49th Ave., Omaha 32, Neb.

B. Osceola, Neb., Jan. 1, 1888. *Studied*: Royal Acad., Dusseldorf, Germany; AIC. *Awards*: prize, Nebraska Exp., 1922. *Work*: Omaha Pub. Lib.; Joslyn Mem.; Governor's Mansion, Lincoln, Neb.; Howard Univ., Wash., D.C.

DUNCALFE, W. DOUGLAS—*Painter, T.*
117 West 13th St., New York 11, N.Y.

Studied: ASL; Shaw Sch. of Toronto, Can.; New Sch. Social Research, and with Robert B. Hale. *Exhibited*: SFMA, 1942, 1943; Oakland A. Mus., 1942; Vancouver (B.C.) A. Gal., 1934, 1938; ACA Gal., 1947; AWS, 1946, 1947; Audubon A., 1947, 1948; MMA, 1948; WMAA, 1948; Fairleigh Dickinson Col., Rutherford, N.J., 1953 (one-man); City Col. of N.Y., 1953; Little Gal., Hudson Park Branch of N.Y. Pub. Lib., 1955 (one-man); pictures and textile exh., of City College at N.Y. Pub. Lib., 1955, and others. *Position*: Instr., Art Career Sch., N.Y., 1947-55; City Col. of Traphagen Sch. of Fashion, N.Y., 1947-55; City Col. of New York, Ext. Div., 1951-54; Jamesine Franklin Sch. Prof. A., N.Y., 1952-55; Pratt Inst., Brooklyn, N.Y., 1953- .

DUNCAN, MRS. G. R. See Birch, Geraldine

DUNCAN, JEAN—*Painter, T., L.*
482 Laurel Ave., St. Paul 2, Minn.

B. St. Paul, Minn. *Studied*: Vassar Col., A.B.; Univ. Minnesota, M.A.; ASL, and with Hans Hofmann, Walt Killam, Eliot O'Hara. *Member*: Minnesota AA; Lg. Am. Pen Women; AEA; Minneapolis Inst. A. *Awards*: prizes, Minneapolis Inst. A., 1925; Club Montparnasse (St. Paul), 1934; Minneapolis Women's Cl., 1944, 1949; Nat. Lg. Am. Pen Women, 1942. *Work*: Minneapolis Inst. A.; St. Paul Gal. & Sch. *Exhibited*: Nat. Lg. Am. Pen Women; Kansas City AI; Soc. Indp. A.; Minneapolis Inst. A.; Walker A. Center; Minnesota State Fair; St. Paul Pub. Lib.; Univ. Minnesota; Wash. WC Cl.; PAFA; CGA; Nat. Mus., Wash., D.C.; Rockford Women's Cl.; Iowa State Fair. *Positions*: Asst. Prof., Rockford Col., 1931-32; Dir. A., Northrop Collegiate Sch., 1932-47; Instr., Minneapolis Sch. A., 1948-50; Instr. A., Univ. Minnesota, 1949-51.*

DUNKELBERGER, RALPH D.—*Painter, T., I.*
3807 Stoudt's Ferry Bridge Rd., Riverview Park, Reading, Pa.

B. Reading, Pa., Aug. 16, 1894. *Studied*: PMSchIA, and with Schearer, Oakley. *Work*: Pub. Mus. & A. Gal., Reading, Pa.; Pa. State Univ.; Valley Forge, Pa.; Albright Col., Reading; Berks County Court House, Reading; Mun. Mus., City Hall, Reading, England; murals, Berks County Hist. Soc. Mus.; Wyomissing H.S. *Exhibited*: Wyomissing Sch. FA; Pa. Dutch Folklore Festival, Kutztown; Reading Pub. Mus. & A. Gal. *Position*: Instr., Wyomissing Sch. FA, Pa.

DUNLAP, MRS. WILLIAM. See Sargent, Mary F.

DUNN, ALAN (CANTWELL)—*Cartoonist, I., W., P.*
c/o New Yorker Magazine, 25 West 43rd St., New York 36, N.Y.

B. Belmar, N.J., Aug. 11, 1900. *Studied*: NAD; Tiffany Fnd.; Fontainebleau, France; Columbia Univ.; Visiting F., Am. Acad. in Rome. *Member*: Author's Gld. of the Author's Lg. *Work*: Mus. City of N.Y.; Harry Truman Lib., Independence, Mo.; Murdoch Coll., Wichita Mus. A. *Author*: "Rejection," 1932; "Who's Paying for this Cab?," 1945; "The Last Lath," 1947; "East of Fifth," 1948; "Should It Gurgle?," 1957. *Position*: Staff Contributor to New Yorker and Architectural Record magazines. Contributes to other magazines and newspapers.

DUNN, CAL(VIN) (E.)—*Painter, Cart., Comm. A.*
Cal Dunn Studios, 159 East Chicago Ave., Chicago 11, Ill.; h. 329 Ridge Rd., Kenilworth, Ill.

B. Georgetown, Ohio, Aug. 31, 1915. *Studied*: Cincinnati A. Acad.; Central Acad. Comm. A. *Member*: AWS; Chicago A. Gld.; Am. A. Group. *Awards*: prizes, Chicago A. Gld., 1948-1951, 1955; Chicago "Magnificent Mile" A. Festival, 1952, 1953; Union Lg., Chicago, 1955; Visual Presentation Comp. (Sales Motion Picture), 1956; bronze medal, American Artist Magazine, 1956; TV Commercial exh., Chicago A. Gld., 1957; Nat. Offset & Litho. Comp., 1957; Defensive Driving Series (six, 10 min. motion pictures), Nat. Comm. for Films on Safety Comp., 1957; bronze plaque (10 min. animated motion picture), Nat. Comm. for Films on Safety, 1957, and others. *Work*: Ford Motor Co. coll.; Allstate Insurance Co., Am. A. Group and in many private colls. Watercolor story assignments, Ford Times magazine, 1950-58. *Exhibited*: AWS, annually; Butler Inst. Am. A., 1954-1958; AWS traveling exh., 1957; Ford Times traveling exh., 1950-1958; Des Moines Assn. FA, 1939; Cornell Col., 1940; Davenport A. Gal., 1939; Am.-British A. Center, N.Y., 1941; Cincinnati Mod. A. Soc., 1941, 1942; Riverside Mus., 1942; AIC, 1946, 1950, 1951; CM, 1941, 1942; Union Lg., Chicago, 1955, 1956; Lake Geneva, 1954-1956; Magnificent Mile, 1952-1954; Chicago A. Gld., 1942-1958; one-man: Davenport, Iowa, 1940; Cincinnati, Ohio, 1942; Chicago, Ill., 1952-1954; Evanston, Ill., 1956. *Positions*: Cartoons for Esquire, Ford Times, New Yorker, Post, Life, etc.; Animation A. Dir., Training Films, USAF, Wright Field, Dayton, Ohio, 1944-47; A. Dir., Sarra, Inc., Training Films, U.S. Navy; Dir., Cal Dunn Studios, producing cartoons for advertising, slidefilms and motion pictures for sales and training and TV commercials, at present.

DUNN, MARJORIE CLINE—*Portrait Painter,* **S.**
611 Thalia St., Laguna Beach, Cal.

B. El Dorado, Kans., Sept. 7, 1894. *Studied*: Los Angeles Sch. A. & Des., and with Prof. Wolf, Ella Shephard Bush, S. MacDonald-Wright. *Member*: Cal. Soc. Min. P.; Nat. Lg. Am. Pen Women. *Work*: many portraits and miniatures of prominent persons. *Exhibited*: AIC; PAFA; CGA; Los A. Mus. A.; GGE, 1939; Smithsonian Inst.; Laguna Beach A. Gal., 1952 (miniatures).*

DUNN, MONTFORT—*Gallery Director*
Marine-on-St. Croix, Minn.

B. St. Paul, Minn., May 15, 1907. *Studied*: Yale Col., B.A.; & with Cameron Booth, Amedée Ozenfant, Louis Marcoussis. *Position*: Gallery Dir., St. Paul Gallery & Sch. of Art, St. Paul, Minn., 1939-46; Asst. to Dir., Univ. Gal., Univ. Minnesota, 1948-49, Actg. Dir., 1955-56.

DUNN, NATE—*Painter,* **T.**
490 Carley Ave., Sharon, Pa.

B. Pittsburgh, Pa., July 4, 1896. *Studied*: Carnegie Inst. Tech., and with Arthur Sparks, G. Sotter, C. J. Taylor and others. *Member*: Buckeye A. Cl., Youngstown, Ohio. *Awards*: prizes, Butler Inst. Am. A., 1952; Conneaut Lake, Pa. *Work*: Pa. State Col., and in many private colls. *Exhibited*: Mid-year and New Year exhs., Butler Inst. Am. A.; Assoc. A., Pittsburgh; Conneaut Lake, Pa.; one-man: Playhouse, Pittsburgh, 1958; Butler Inst. Am. A.

DUNN, ROBERT—*Painter*
1669 Macomb's Rd., New York 53, N.Y.

B. New York, N.Y., Feb. 17, 1932. *Exhibited*: PAFA, 1957; Springfield Mus. A., 1957; Pyramid Cl., 1957; Provincetown A. Festival, 1958; Univ. Illinois, 1958; N.Y. City Center, 1956, 1957.

DUNWIDDIE, CHARLOTTE—*Sculptor*
c/o Betty Smith Associates, 15 East 48th St. (17); h. 35 East Ninth St., New York, N.Y.

B. Strasbourg, France, June 19, 1907. *Studied*: with Dr. Wilhelm Otto, Acad. Art, Berlin; Mariano Benlliure y Gil in Spain, and with Alberto Lagos, Buenos Aires. *Member*: NSS; NAC; Pen & Brush Cl.; Catherine Lorillard Wolfe A. Cl.; Soc. Women Geographers. *Awards*: prizes, Pen & Brush Cl., 1958 (2). *Work*: Marine Corps Mus., Wash., D.C.; Church of Santa Maria, Cochabamba, Bolivia (monument); Church of the Good Shepherd, Lima, Peru (monument); Throne Room of the Cardinal's Palace, Buenos Aires (port. bust); Bank of Poland, Buenos Aires (bas relief). Sculpture of many top-ranking horses in Europe, South America and the United States; many private sculpture commissions. *Exhibited*: Salon des Bellas Artes, Mexico City, 1940-1945; NAC, 1956-1958; Pen & Brush Cl., 1956-1958; Kennedy Gal., N.Y., 1957-58 (one-man); Woodmere Gal. A., Philadelphia, Pa., 1959.

Du PEN, EVERETT GEORGE—*Sculptor,* **E.**
University of Washington (5); h. 1231 20th Ave., North, Seattle 2, Wash.

B. San Francisco, Cal., June 12, 1912. *Studied*: Univ. So. California; Chouinard AI; Yale Univ., Sch. FA, B.F.A., and with Gage, Lukens, Sample, Snowden, Fulop. *Awards*: Tiffany scholarship, 1935-36; European F., 1937-38; Music & Art Fnd. Award, 1950; Univ. Washington Grad. Sch. Grant, 1954; gold med., NAD, 1954. *Member*: AEA; Research Soc. of Univ. Wash.; A. Commission of City of Seattle; All. A. Am.; Northwest Sculpture Inst. (Pres., 1957). *Work*: bronze fountain, State Lib., Olympia, Wash., 1958. *Exhibited*: Am. Acad. in Rome, 1937; NAD, 1943, 1949, 1954, 1956-1958; CAM, 1939-1942; San F. AA, 1943, 1954; Northwest Annual, 1945-1955; NSS, 1949; PAFA, 1950, 1958; Sculpture Center, 1951-1953; SAM, 1952 (one-man), 1956-1958; Detroit Inst. A., 1958; Portland A. Mus. 1958; Bellevue (Wash.) A. & Crafts exh., 1957. *Work*: arch. sc., and reliefs, Univ. Washington; arch. sc., for churches; private comm. for gardens. Lectures: History of Sculpture and Contemporary Sculpture. *Position*: Assoc. Prof. Sculpture, Univ. Washington, 1954- .

DUPHINEY, WILFRED I.—*Painter,* **T., L.**
7 Thomas St., Providence 3, R.I.; h. 11 Lake View Ave., Johnson 9, R.I.

B. Central Falls, R.I., Sept. 16, 1884. *Studied*: R.I.Sch. Des., with William C. Loring; ASL, with George Bridgman,

Guy Pène du Bois. *Member*: Providence AC; Providence WC Cl. *Award*: prize, Providence AC. *Work*: State of Rhode Island; City of Providence; Univ. Rhode Island; Brown Univ.; Providence Col.; R.I. Hospital; St. Joseph's Hospital; Roger Williams Hospital. *Exhibited*: PAFA, 1929-1933; New Haven, Conn.; Springfield, Boston, Mass. Illus.; "First Lesson in French," 1922; "Rainbow Gold," 1924. Lectures: "Human Head and Figure." *Position*: Instr. A., Rhode Island Sch. Design, Providence, R.I.

DUPONT, ALFRED—*Painter,* **Comm. A., I., W., T.**
1021 Gaviotta St., Laguna Beach, Cal.

B. Orange, N.J., June 6, 1906. *Studied*: Univ. California; Cal. Sch. A. & Crafts; Mark Hopkins Inst., San F., and in Bremen, Germany. *Member*: Desert AA; Laguna Beach AA; Phoenix FA Assn. *Awards*: prizes, Western AA, 1958; Laguna Beach AA. *Work*: Bank of America, Huntington, Cal.; U.S. Navy Combat Illus. Coll.; Hearst Estate, San Simeon, Cal.; murals, Pan-American Airways; United Airlines. *Exhibited*: widely on the West Coast and at Honolulu Acad. A. Illus., "How to Paint Seascapes," by Walter Foster.

DU PRE, GRACE ANNETTE—*Portrait Painter*
15 Gramercy Park, New York 3, N.Y.

B. Spartanburg, S.C. *Studied*: Converse Col.; Grand Central A. Sch., and with Wayman Adams, Frank DuMond. *Member*: All. A. Am.; NAC; Grand Central A. Gal.; AAPL (Nat. Bd.); Carolina AA; Portraits, Inc.; Catherine L. Wolfe Cl. *Awards*: prizes, Ogunquit A. Center, 1951; AAPL, 1953; Wolfe A. Cl., 1955, and others. *Work*: White House; U.S. Supreme Court, Wash., D.C.; ports. ten active Judges: U.S. Court of Appeals, 7th Circuit, Chicago; State Capitol, S.C.; Law Bldg., Univ. Indiana; Law Lib., Columbia Univ.; Lib. Univ. of the South, Tenn.; Medical Col. & City Hall A. Gal., Charleston, S.C.; other Federal courts and pub. bldgs.; Clemson Col. (S.C.); The Citadel, Charleston; State Sch. for the Deaf and Blind, S.C.; port. coll., The Church of the Ascension, New York, N.Y.; official port. coll., New York City Main Post Office. *Exhibited*: nationally; many one-man exhs.

DUQUETTE, MAE—*Painter,* **S., T.**
6015 North Muscatel Ave., San Gabriel, Cal.

B. Boomer Township, Iowa, Jan. 30, 1892. *Studied*: with Augustis Dunbier and Will Foster, and others. *Member*: Cal. A. Cl.; Soc. Western A.; Pasadena AA; Whittier A. Cl.; Highland Park A. Cl. *Awards*: prizes, Omaha, Neb., 1938; Whittier, Cal., 1945, 1946, 1956; A. of the Southwest, 1955; Compton, Cal., 1956; Southland AA, 1957; Highland A. Gld., 1958; Montebella Taylor Ranch A. Center, 1958 (4). *Exhibited*: PAFA; Kansas City AI; Joslyn A. Mus.; Greek Theatre, Los A.; deYoung Mem. Mus.; Cal. State Fair; Nat. Orange Show; Soc. Western A., and many others.

DUREN, TERENCE ROMAINE—*Painter,* **I.**
Shelby, Neb.

B. Shelby, Neb., July 9, 1907. *Studied*: AIC; Fontainebleau, France; & in Vienna. *Member*: NSMP. *Awards*: prizes, AIC, 1928; CMA, 1933, 1934, 1936; Joslyn Mem., 1943; Springfield (Mass.) Mus. A.; Pepsi-Cola, 1946; Terry AI, 1952; Fla. Southern Col., 1952; Franklin County (Neb.), 1952; Lincoln A. Gld., 1952. *Work*: AIC; CMA; CGA; Carnegie Inst.; Joslyn Mem.; Butler AI; murals, Pub. Bldgs., Cleveland, Columbus, Ohio. *Exhibited*: AIC, 1927, 1928; CMA, 1930-1941; Joslyn Mem., 1942-1946; Carnegie Inst., 1945, 1946; Los A. Mus. A., 1945; SFMA; Dallas Mus. FA; New Orleans, La.; Prairie WC Painters, 1944-1946; Cowie's Gal., Los A., 1952 (one-man); Grand Central A. Gal., 1945, 1946, 1950, 1955; Art:USA, 1958. I., cover drawings for "Panoramic Review," World Herald, Omaha, Neb.; Fortune & other publications; Illus. for "The American West" (Lucius Beebe), 1955.

DURFEE, M(ILDRED) LUCILLE—*Educator,* **P.**
1400 Teakwood St.; h. 3032 South B St., Oxnard, Cal.

B. Mt. Pleasant, Mich., Dec. 12, 1908. *Studied*: Central Col. of Edu., Mt. Pleasant, Mich., B.S.; Am. Acad. A., Chicago; Arizona State Col., Tempe; Univ. California; Peabody Col., M.A. *Member*: So. Cal. A. Edu. Assn.; Cal. Sch. Supv. Assn.; Nat. A. Edu. Assn.; Pacific AA. Contributor to: Arts and Activities magazine; School Arts;

Everyday Art. *Exhibited*: Phoenix Pub. Lib., 1957. *Position*: A. Dir., Phoenix Pub. Sch., Phoenix, Ariz., 1940-56; Part., Advertising Artists & Designers, Phoenix, Ariz., 1956-57; A. Consultant, Hueneme Sch. Dist., at present.

DURHAM, ISAIAH DAVIS—*Teacher, P.*

College of William & Mary (Norfolk Div.); h. 1650 West 49th St., Norfolk 8, Va.

B. Augusta, Ga., Sept. 3, 1913. *Studied*: Univ. South Carolina, A.B.; Univ. Georgia, M.F.A., and with Lamar Dodd, Ferdinand Warren, Frances Chapin. *Exhibited*: Art: USA, 1958; AWS, 1958; Gibbes Gal. A., Charleston; Traveling exh. Georgia A.; Southeastern A. Exh., Atlanta; Irene Leach Mem. Mus.; Columbia, S.C.; Tidewater A., Norfolk. *Position*: Instr. A., College of William & Mary, Norfolk, Va.

DURIEUX, CAROLINE (Mrs.)—*Lithographer, P.*

772 West Chimes St., Baton Rouge 2, La.

B. New Orleans, La., Jan. 22, 1896. *Studied*: Newcomb Col., Tulane Univ., B.A.; Louisiana State Univ., M.A.; PAFA with Henry McCarter. *Member*: Phila. WC Cl.; New Orleans AA; Audubon A. *Awards*: prizes, Delgado Mus. A., 1944; LC (purchase) 1944, 1946, 1952; 50 Prints of the Year, 1944; 50 Books of the Year, 1949. *Work*: MMoDA; Delgado Mus. A.; PMA; N.Y.Pub.Lib.; VMFA; Bibliotheque Nationale, Paris; Gibbes A. Gal.; Brooks Mem. Gal.; AGAA; Atomic Mus., Oak Ridge, Tenn. *Exhibited*: MMA; PMA; NAD, and others; one-man: Galleria Central, Mexico City; Marie Sterner Gal., N.Y.; Delgado Mus. A.; VMFA; Witte Mem. Mus.; Mus. FA of Houston; Univ. Tulsa; Univ. Florida; FA Club of Chicago; Burlington Mus. A.; Univ. Georgia; Univ. Alabama; Louisiana State Univ.; Newcomb Col., and others. Developed "Electron Printing" from radioactive drawing in collaboration with Dr. Harry Wheeler. *Position*: Prof. FA, Louisiana State Univ., Baton Rouge, La.

DURLACHER, RUTH (Mrs. I. Seymour Wolper)— *Painter*

29 Chesterfield Rd., Scarsdale, N.Y.

B. Springfield, Mass., Jan. 11, 1912. *Studied*: Ecole des Beaux-Arts, Fontainebleau, with Jean Despujols; Yale Sch. FA, with Richard Rathbone, Lewis York, Deane Keller. *Member*: New Haven Paint & Clay Cl.; New Haven Brush & Palette Cl.; Springfield A. Lg.; Academic A.; Westchester AA; Hudson Valley AA; Scarsdale AA; AEA; Fontaine-bleau Alumni Assn.; Portraits, Inc. *Awards*: prizes, Brush & Palette Cl.; Meriden, Conn.; Scarsdale AA. *Work*: Sch. for the Deaf, N.Y.; Springfield Hospital; port. of H.R.H. Princess Margaret, Government House, Nassau, B.W.I., and in private colls. *Exhibited*: All. A. Am.; Springfield A. Lg.; WFNY 1939; Scarsdale AA, and others.*

DURST, DAVID—*Painter, E., Mus. D.*

857 Fairview, Fayetteville, Ark.

B. Springfield, Mo., Aug. 19, 1911. *Studied*: AIC; Univ. Iowa, M.A., M.F.A. *Member*: AEA; CAA; AAUP. *Work*: Univ. Iowa; Springfield Mus. A.; Little Rock Mus. A., and in private collections. *Exhibited*: CAM; Denver A. Mus.; VMFA; DMFA; Delgado Mus. A.; Bertha Schaefer Gal., N.Y. *Position*: Pres., Midwestern Col. A. Conference (1956-57); Bd. Dir., Council of Ozark A. & Craftsmen; Prof. A., A. Dept., Dir., A. Center Gal., Univ. Arkansas, Fayetteville, Ark.

DURY, LORAINE LUCILLE—*Painter, T.*

Franklin Junior High School; h. 316 South Oakland Ave., Green Bay, Wis.

B. Green Bay, Wis. *Studied*: Milwaukee T. Col.; Univ. Minnesota, B.S.; Columbia Univ., M.A.; & with Lou Matthews Bedore. *Member*: Green Bay A. Colony; Am. Assn. Univ. Women. *Awards*: prize, Green Bay A. Colony, 1935; Northwestern Wisconsin Exh.; 1st prize in color photography, Green Bay Camera Cl., 1958. *Work*: Roi-Porlier-Tank Cottage Mus., Green Bay, Wis.; Green Bay Bd. Edu. *Exhibited*: Green Bay A. Colony, annually; Univ. Wisconsin, 1937-1944, 1947; Northeastern Wisconsin A., annually. I., "It Happened Here," publ. by Wis. Hist. Soc. Lectures: Mexican Art. *Position*: A.T., Franklin Jr. H.S., Green Bay, Wis.; Memb., Wisconsin Co-operative Edu. Planning Program; State Publicity Chm. for Delta Kappa Gamma, 1955-59.

d'USSEAU, LEON—*Painter, S., C.*

702 Iris St., Corona del Mar, Cal.

B. Los Angeles, Cal., Mar. 21, 1918. *Studied*: with Merrill Gage and Archipenko; Chouinard AI. *Work*: Marshall Field, Chicago; Palmer House, Chicago; J. L. Hudson Co., Detroit; deYoung Mem. Mus.; Findlay Gal., Chicago; DMFA. *Exhibited*: MMA; Audubon A.; Cal. PLH; Cal. WC Soc.; Los A. Mus. A.; Westwood, Cal.; Dubois Gal., Los A. (one-man), 1954; Laguna Beach A. Festival, 1958.

DUTCH, GEORGE SHELDON—*Educator, W.*

2304 Oxford Rd., Nashville 12, Tenn.

B. Chelsea, Mass., Aug. 16, 1891. *Studied*: Mass. Normal A. Sch. with Joseph DeCamp. *Member*: Western AA (Sec.-Treas.) Ed. Bd. Author: "Art in American Life and Education," 1941. *Position*: Prof. A., George Peabody Col. for T., Nashville, Tenn., 1918-1956; Prof. Emeritus, 1956- .

DUTTON, BERTHA P.—*Museum Curator, E., W., L.*

Museum of New Mexico (Box 1727), Santa Fe, N.M.

B. Algona, Iowa, Mar. 29, 1903. *Studied*: Univ. Nebraska; Univ. New Mexico, B.A., M.A.; Columbia Univ., Ph.D. *Member*: F., Am. Anthropological Assn.; Soc. for Am. Archaeology; Sociedad Mexicano de Antropologia; Congress of Americanista (Intl.). *Awards*: Alice Fletcher Traveling Fellowship, 1935; Sch. of Am. Research Scholarship, 1936; Sch. Am. Research Grant-in-Aid, 1950; AAUW Fellowship, 1953-54. Author, I., "Leyit Kin, a Small House Ruin, Chaco Canyon, N.M.," 1938; "Excavations at Tajumulco, Guatemala" (with H. R. Hobbs), 1943; "The Pueblo Indian World" (with E. L. Hewett), 1945; Ed., "Pajarito Plateau and Its Ancient People," 1953; "Indians of the Southwest," 1958, plus other monographs and articles (some 140 titles in all). Contributor to: El Palacio; Archaeology; American Antiquity; New Mexico Quarterly; Santa Fe New Mexican, etc. Lectures: Archaeology and Ethnology; Indian Arts & Crafts, to schools, clubs, civic organizations, etc. Planned and supervised remodeling of a building which became the Hall of Ethnology, Mus. of N.M., and prepared and installed all exhibitions. Exhibits deal with the arts, crafts and related subjects and the interpretation thereof, primarily with the Indians of the Southwest, but also includes cultural expressions from over the world. *Positions*: Instr., Anthropology, Univ. New Mexico TV course and adult classes at Taos, N.M., 1947-57; Dept. Sec., Dept. of Anthropology, Univ. New Mexico, 1933-36; Cur., Ethnology, Museum of New Mexico, Santa Fe., N.M., 1938- .

DU VAL, FLORA (Mrs. John)—*Painter*

1521 Glen St., Shreveport, La.

B. Haskell, Okla., Apr. 22, 1906. *Studied*: ASL, with Morris Kantor, Vaclav Vytlacil, and others. *Member*: Louisiana A.; Texas FA Assn.; Contemp. A. Group of Shreveport; New Orleans FA Assn. *Awards*: prizes, Shreveport A. Cl. at La. State Mus., 1956; Louisiana A. Gld., 1956. *Exhibited*: Provincetown A. Festival, 1958; Delgado Mus. A., 1958; Delta A. Annual, Little Rock, Ark., 1958; La. State Mus., 1956-1958; Texas State Mus., 1956-1958; Beaumont, Tex.; Shreveport, La.; Contemp. A. Group, Shreveport.

DUVOISIN, ROGER A.—*Illustrator, W.*

Gladstone, N.J.

B. Geneva, Switzerland, Aug. 28, 1904. *Studied*: Col. Moderne, Ecole des Arts et Metier, Ecole des Beaux-Arts, Geneva, Switzerland. *Awards*: AIGA, 50 Best Books of the Year, 1933, 1938, 1939, 1948, 1950, 1957; 50 Best Children's Books, 1945-1950, 1953, 1954; Caldecott med.; 1948; Herald Tribune award, 1944-1952; N.Y. Times (Ten Best), 1954, 1955; West Germany Govt. first prize for Juvenile Books, 1956. *Exhibited*: MMoDA; Phila. A. All.; WMA; Mus. City of N.Y.; in various museums and colleges, and abroad. Author, I., 20 juvenile books; I., 60 juvenile & adult books. Contributor to New Yorker and other magazines.

DWIGHT, EDWARD H.—*Museum Director*

Milwaukee Art Center, Milwaukee 2, Wis.

B. Cincinnati, Ohio, Aug. 2, 1919. *Studied*: Yale Univ.; Cincinnati A. Acad.; St. Louis Sch. FA. Contributor to Print; Antiques; Art in America. Exhibitions arranged: "Juan Gris," 1948; "Paintings by the Peale Family," 1954;

"Rediscoveries in American Art," 1955; "Still Life Painting Since 1470," 1956; "El Greco, Rembrandt, Goya, Cézanne, Van Gogh, Picasso," 1957; "Ralston Crawford," 1958. *Position*: Dir., Cincinnati Mod. A. Soc., 1947-49; Cur. Am. Art, Cincinnati A. Mus., 1954-55; Dir., Milwaukee A. Center, & Cur. Layton Coll., at present.

DYCK, PAUL—*Painter*

Camp Verde, Ariz.

B. Chicago, Ill., Aug. 17, 1917. *Studied*: Munich Acad., with Johann Skramlik; in Prague, Paris, Rome, Florence. *Exhibited*: one-man: Cowie Gal., Los Angeles, 1955, 1956, 1957; O'Brien Gal., Phoenix, Ariz., 1955, 1956, 1957, 1958; Rosequist Gal., Tucson, Ariz., 1956, 1958; Stuttman Gal., New York, 1958.

DYCZKOWSKI, EUGENE M.—
Painter, Des., Cart., I., T.

1110 Elmwood Ave., Buffalo 22, N.Y.; h. East River Rd., Grand Island, N.Y.

B. Philadelphia, Pa., May 1, 1899. *Studied*: Albright A. Sch.; & with John Rummell, Arthur Lee, Eliot O'Hara. *Member*: Buffalo Soc. A.; The Patteran, Buffalo, N.Y.; Kenmore (N.Y.) A. Soc.; Grand Island (N.Y.) A. Cl. *Awards*: prizes, Old Fort Niagara Assn., 1953; Buffalo Soc. A., 1954, 1955; med., Buffalo Soc. A., 1937, 1953; Cambridge Springs, Pa., 1950. *Work*: Officer's Cl., Ft. Niagara, N.Y.; Burgard Vocational H.S., Buffalo. *Exhibited*: Albright A. Gal., 1935-1946 (traveling exh., 1946); Buffalo Soc. A., 1924-1955; The Patteran, Buffalo, N.Y.; Old Fort Niagara Assn., 1953.

DYER, BRIGGS—*Painter, Lith., T.*

634 Briar Place, Chicago 14, Ill.

B. Atlanta, Ga., Sept. 18, 1911. *Studied*: Univ. Georgia; Cincinnati A. Acad.; AIC. *Awards*: prizes, AIC, 1942, Brower prize, 1954; Minneapolis Inst. A., 1946. *Work*: PC; Univ. Arizona; Minneapolis Inst. A.; AIC; Newark Mus. A. *Exhibited*: MMA; Carnegie Inst.; PAFA; CGA; VMFA; SFMA; AIC; Denver A. Mus.; Minneapolis Inst. A.; BM; Milwaukee A. Center; Univ. Illinois; Joslyn Mus. A.; Toledo Mus. A.; Univ. Iowa; Nelson Gal. A.; Philabrook A. Center; Currier Gal. A.; Soc. Four Arts; Ferargil Gal., N.Y.; Colorado Springs FA Center; WMAA; Detroit Inst. A.; Toronto (Canada) A. Gal.; Contemporary Arts, N.Y. (one-man, 1942, 1946); Connecticut Acad. FA; Kansas City AI; Faulkner Mem. Lib., Santa Barbara; Portland (Ore.) A. Mus.; Phila. A. All.; MModA; CAM; Cal. PLH; Dartmouth Col.; NGA; WAC; Butler Inst. Am. A.; CM; CMA; SAM; Los A. Mus. A.; and many others. *Positions*: Instr., AIC, 1939-42, 1947- ; Dir., Rockford AA, 1938-39; Instr., Univ. Michigan, 1941; Instr., Minneapolis Sch. A., 1945-47; Instr., Katharine Lord's Studio, Evanston, Ill., 1948-54, Dir., 1952-54.

DYER, HERRMANN—*Painter, Lith., T.*

634 Briar Place, Chicago 14, Ill.

B. Wichita, Kan., Apr. 29, 1916. *Studied*: Univ. Chicago; AIC. *Awards*: prizes, AIC, 1939, 1943. *Work*: PAFA. *Exhibited*: Minneapolis Inst. A., 1939-1942; PAFA, 1941-1943; CGA, 1941; SFMA, 1940; Carnegie Inst., 1939, 1941-1943; MMA, 1942; Palace Legion Honor, 1946; VMFA, 1942, 1944, 1946; PMG, 1942; Denver A. Mus., 1941, 1946; CAM, 1939, 1942, 1943; Rochester Mem. A. Gal., 1939, 1943; Kansas City AI, 1938, 1942; MModA, 1943; AIC, 1938-1945. *Position*: Dir., The Studio School, Chicago, Ill., 1954-58.

EAGLE, CLARA M.—*Educator*

Murray State College, Murray, Ky.

Position: Chm., Dept. of Art, Murray State College.●

EAMES, JOHN HEAGAN—*Etcher, P.*

Boothbay Harbor, Me.

B. Lowell, Mass., July 19, 1900. *Studied*: Harvard Col., B.A.; Royal Col. A., London, and with Robert Austin, Malcolm Osborne. *Member*: ANA; SAGA. *Awards*: prizes, SAGA, Kate W. Arms award, 1952, 1954, 1957; John Taylor Arms award, 1953; Henry B. Shope award, 1957; purchase prize, Albany Inst. Hist. & Art, 1957. *Work*: LC; MMA, and in private colls. *Exhibited*: Venice, Italy, 1940;

Royal Acad., London, 1940; PAFA, 1940; NAD, annually; AAPL, 1940, 1941; LC, 1942, 1945; Carnegie Inst., 1945; East Hampton, N.Y., 1946; Albany Inst. Hist. & A., 1949, 1957; BM, 1950; Albright A. Gal., 1951; Sweat Mus. A., 1952, 1957; SAGA, annually; Am. Acad. A. & Let., 1953; Smithsonian Inst. traveling exh., 1954; SAGA exchange exh., England, 1954; Oakland (Cal.) Mus. A., 1958.

EAMES, MRS. RICHARD COMYN. See *Parish, Betty Waldo*

EARLE, EDWIN—*Painter, Eng., T., I.*

Derby Line, Vt.

B. Somerville, Mass., Dec. 9, 1904. *Studied*: Mass. Sch. A.; ASL; Grand Central Sch. A., with Carter. *Member*: Nat. Comm. on A. Edu. I., "Hopi Kachinas," 1938 (28 color plates).

EARLE, EYVIND—*Designer, P., Comm. A., I.*

17740 Parthenia St., Northridge, Cal.

B. New York, N.Y., Apr. 26, 1916. *Studied*: A. Center Sch., Los Angeles, with Lorsen Feitelsen. Also with Ferdinand Earle. *Member*: Cal. A. Cl. *Awards*: MMA, 1940; Probst award, 1949. *Work*: mural, U.S. Navy, Jacksonville, Fla., and in private homes. *Exhibited*: Los A. Mus. A., 1948; Boise, Ida., 1938; Nat. Orange Show, 1957; Cal. A. Cl., 1945, 1948, 1949; one-man: Charles Morgan Gal., N.Y., 1937, 1938, 1939; also in Los Angeles, 1935, 1936, 1938, 1940, 1948, 1949-1957. Illus., "In Norway," 1948; "Peter Pan," 1952. Des., several hundred cards for Am. A. Group, N.Y. *Positions*: A. Dir., Color Stylist, Walt Disney Studios, 1953-57; A. Dir., John Sutherland Prod., 1958.

EARLE, ROBERT MAXWELL—*Designer, P., C., T.*

823 Lexington Ave., New York, N.Y.

B. Syracuse, N.Y., May 23, 1918. *Studied*: Syracuse Univ., B.A. *Member*: Assoc. A. Syracuse; Un. Scenic A. *Awards*: prize, N.Y. State Exh., Syracuse, 1941. *Work*: Syracuse Mus. FA; mural panels, interior, Chateau Henry IV, N.Y. *Exhibited*: Assoc. A. Syracuse; Barbizon Plaza Gal., 1946 (one-man); A. Inst., Buffalo (one-man). *Position*: Des. for television and theatres; Scenic A., NBC, 1951- .

EARLEY, MARY—*Painter*

1 West 85th St., New York 24, N.Y.; s. Woodstock, N.Y.

B. St. Louis, Mo., July 8, 1900. *Studied*: ASL, with Kimon Nicolaides, William C. Palmer. *Member*: AEA; Woodstock AA. *Awards*: prize, 48 States Comp., 1939. *Work*: murals, USPO, Delhi, N.Y.; Middleburg, N.Y.; paintings in private colls. *Exhibited*: Carnegie Inst., 1941; Pepsi-Cola, 1st Annual Exh.; NAD, 1946; Woodstock Gal., Rudolph Gal., Woodstock, 1958; Soc. of Four Arts, Palm Beach, 1957.

EAST, PATTIE RICHARDSON (Mrs.)—*Painter, C.*

2208 Edgewood St., Ft. Worth 3, Tex.

B. Hardesty, Okla., Mar. 6, 1894. *Studied*: AIC; Broadmoor A. Acad.; & with Birger Sandzen, Joseph Fleck. *Member*: Texas FA Assn.; Dallas AA. *Work*: mural, Shady Oaks Country Club, Ft. Worth, Tex. *Exhibited*: SSAL; Texas FA Assn.; Mus. FA of Houston; Abilene, Tex.

EASTMAN, ALVAN C(LARK)—
Orientalist, W., Mus. Dir.

89 Rawson Rd., Brookline, Mass.

B. Munich, Germany, Jan. 10, 1894. *Studied*: Harvard Univ., A.B., A.M., M.A.; N.Y. Univ., A.M., M.A. *Member*: Am. Oriental Soc.; Boston Authors Cl. Cataloguer of Goodnow collection Chinese bronzes, BMFA; Ficke collection Japanese art, Davenport (Iowa) Pub. Mus. Author numerous articles on Near Eastern and Oriental art. Contributor articles to Journal of Am. Oriental Soc.; Parnassus; Journal Near Eastern Studies, and others. Monograph: "The Nola-Damayanti Drawings in American Museums," BMFA, 1959. *Position*: Asst., Oriental Div., BMFA, 1923; Cur., Oriental Art, Detroit Inst. A., 1925-29; Dir., Pub. Mus., Evansville, Ind., 1947-48; Pasadena AI, 1948-50; Dir., Winnipeg Art Gallery, Winnipeg, Man., 1950-53; engaged in research and publication, art of the Near East, 1954- .

EASTMAN, CHARLOTTE FULLER (Mrs. Guy W.)—
Painter, I., E.
Coit Lane; h. Norwich Town, Conn.

B. Norwich, Conn. *Studied*: Norwich A. Sch.; BMFA Sch.; AIC; ASL; PAFA, and with Wayman Adams, Henry McCarter. *Member*: Mystic AA; Conn. WC Soc.; Norwich AA. *Exhibited*: Salon d'Automne, 1928; Wash. WC Cl., 1939, 1940; AWS, 1939; Mus. A. & Sc., Albany, N.Y., 1945; Mystic AA, 1939-1954; Conn. WC Soc., 1946-1953; Lyman Allyn Mus., 1945, 1951; Slater Mem. Mus., 1939-1951; Traveling exh. to Universities, 1950-1951; Doll & Richards, Boston, 1939; Univ. Conn., 1939. Covers, layouts, des., F. J. Quimby Co., Boston; Univ. Press, Chicago; A. C. McClurg Co., Chicago; portrait comm. Collector, Ed., Margaret Fuller's "Sonnets and Songs." *Position*: Dir., Norwich A. Sch., Norwich, Conn., 1910-43; Councillor, Norwich AA.

EASTWOOD, RAYMOND J.—Painter, E.
University of Kansas; h. 1609 Louisiana St., Lawrence, Kans.

B. Bridgeport, Conn., May 25, 1898. *Studied*: Yale Sch. FA; ASL. *Member*: All. A. Am.; Mid-Am. A.; ASL; Scarab Cl. *Award*: prize, Mid-Am. A., 1952. *Work*: Philbrook A. Center; Wichita AA; Tulsa Univ.; Univ. Kansas; Baker Univ.; Cornell Univ. *Exhibited*: NAD; PAFA; Mid-Am. A.; Missouri Valley A.; Kansas Painters. *Position*: Chm., Dept. Drawing & Painting, Univ. Kansas, Lawrence, Kans.

EATON, ALLEN HENDERSHOTT—Writer, E., L.
171 Hollywood Ave., Crestwood, N.Y.

B. Union, Ore., May 10, 1878. *Studied*: Univ. Oregon, A.B., LL.D. *Award*: hon. deg., D.H.L., Berea Col., Ky., 1955. *Member*: AIGA; AFA; Lg. New Hampshire A. & Crafts (Consultant); Southern Highland Handicraft Gld. (Consultant); Typophiles; Nat. Audubon Soc.; Nat. Parks Assn.; Japan Soc.; Am. Forestry Assn.; Am. Craftsmen's Edu. Council; Am. Pioneer Trails Assn. (Fndr.); Early Am. Industries. Author: "Immigrant Gifts to American Life," 1932; "Handicrafts of the Southern Highlands," 1937; "Rural Handicrafts in the United States" (Bulletin U.S. Dept. Agriculture); "Handicrafts of New England," 1949; "Beauty Behind Barbed Wire," 1951. (Arts of the Japanese in Relocation Camps.); "Survey of Handicrafts of Barbados, West Indies," for Dept. of State, Intl. Co-op Admin., 1958; "Beauty for the Sighted and the Blind," 1959. Contributor to educational magazines with articles on arts and crafts, folk, rural and immigrant arts. *Position*: Comm. to German Govt., ECA, Advisor Handicrafts Refugee Problems, 1950; Instr., L., Work Shop, Univ. Tennessee, 1947-50; Member Staff, Dept. Surveys and Exhibits, 1920-41; Dir., Dept. A. & Social Work, Russell Sage Fnd., 1941-48; Vice-Pres., Am. Folk Arts Center; Adv., U.S. Dept. Agriculture on Rural Arts Program, 1930- ; Adv. Handicrafts, Intl. Country Women of World, Wash., D.C., 1930; Am. Mission from E.C.A. to German Govt., 1950.

EATON, DOROTHY—Painter
Petersham, Mass.

B. East Orange, N.J. *Studied*: Smith Col.; Columbia Univ.; ASL, with Kenneth Hayes Miller. *Member*: NAWA; N.Y. Soc. Women A.; Pen & Brush Cl.; ASL; AEA. *Awards*: prizes, NAWA, 1944. *Work*: Smith College. *Exhibited*: CGA, 1930; AIC, 1931; WMA, 1933, 1935; Acad. All. A., 1934; Carnegie Inst., 1941; NAD, 1943, 1945; Montross Gal., 1936, 1938, 1940; Argent Gal., 1945; NAWA Traveling Exh., 1947; Pen & Brush Cl., 1952, 1954-1958, and prior; Ogunquit A. Center, 1948, 1954, 1955; NAWA (Mass.), 1954; AEA, Boston; N.Y.Soc. Women A., 1953, 1954-1957.

EATON, MYRWYN L.—Educator, P., L., W.
New York University, 100 Washington Square (12); h. 171 West 79th St., New York 24, N.Y.

B. Strawberry Point, Iowa, July 30, 1904. *Studied*: State Univ. Iowa, B.A.; Harvard Univ., M.A.; Chicago Acad. A.; AIC, and special training with Arthur Pope, Harvard Univ. *Member*: AAUP. Awards: Harvard Univ. Scholarships: Townsend, 1930-31; Bacon, 1933-34; European Travel Grant, 1938. *Exhibited*: WMAA, 1952; Carnegie Inst., 1955; Nat. Soc. Painters in Casein; Riverside Mus.; Town Hall, N.Y.; Contemporary A. Gal., N.Y.; one-man: Laguna Beach, 1947; George Binet Gal., N.Y., 1947, 1948, 1950; United Nations Cl., Wash., D.C., 1950; Andre Maurice

Gal., Paris, 1949; Worth Gal., Palm Beach, 1952; Suffern, N.Y., 1953; Hofstra Col., 1948; Houston, Tex., 1957. Book reviews for Saturday Review; articles in Design magazine. Lectures: Modern Art; Teaching Techniques. *Positions*: Instr. A., North Dakota State Col.; Harvard Univ.; Radcliffe Col.; Prof. A., New York Univ., New York, N.Y., 1938- .

EATON, SIDNEY LOVETT—Painter, T.
481 Washington St., Dedham, Mass.

B. Syracuse, N.Y., May 1, 1906. *Studied*: Harvard Univ., A.B.; Syracuse Univ., A.M. *Member*: Dedham A. & Craftsmen; Copley Soc. *Work*: BMFA; FMA. *Exhibited*: L.D.M. Sweat Mem. Mus., 1949, 1950, 1953-1955; Silvermine Gld. A., 1951; Kraushaar Gal., 1951, 1952; Jordan Marsh Co., 1952; FMA, 1952; BMFA, 1953; Canton (Ohio) Mus. A., 1955; one-man: Bluehill, Me., 1949, 1950; Syracuse Mus. FA, 1949; DeCordova & Dana Mus., 1951; Town & Country Cl., Hartford, 1951; Loomis Sch., Windsor, Conn., 1952; Castano Gal., Boston, 1952; Princeton Univ., 1954; Scranton Univ., 1954; Univ. Maine, 1955; William Farnsworth Mus., 1955; Copley Soc., Boston, 1956 (one-man). *Position*: Instr., Noble and Greenough Sch., Dedham, Mass., 1942- .

EAVES, WINSLOW BRYAN—Sculptor, C., Des.
West Andover, N.H.

B. Detroit, Mich., Sept. 8, 1922. *Studied*: Cranbrook Acad. A., with Marshall Fredericks, Carl Milles; ASL, with William Zorach; Academie Beaux-Arts, Paris, France. *Awards*: prizes, Rome Comp., 1942; Fulbright grant, 1949-50; Syracuse Mus. FA, 1947; Manchester (N.H.) A. Festival, 1954. *Work*: Cranbrook A. Mus.; Northwestern H.S.; Munson-Williams-Proctor Inst.; Dartmouth Col.; Univ. New Hampshire; Syracuse Univ.; monument, Melvin Village, N.H.; Syracuse Univ.; Eagle Mountain House, Jackson, N.H. *Exhibited*: WMAA, 1948, 1949; MMA, 1951; Phila. A. All., 1947; Syracuse Mus. FA. ceramic exh., 1947-1950; Michigan A., 1940-1942; A. of Central N.Y., 1946-1949, 1956; one-man: Utica, N.Y.; 3 in New York City and 1 in France. *Position*: Instr., S., & Ceramics, Munson-Williams-Proctor Inst., Utica, N.Y., 1946-49; Visiting Sculptor, Dartmouth Col., 1953-55; Instr., S., Syracuse Univ., N.Y., 1955-1958.

EBERHARD, ROBERT GEORGES—
Educator, S., L., C., Mus. Cur.
"Norohaven," River Rd., Newcastle, Me.

B. Geneva, Switzerland, June 28, 1884. *Studied*: Lycee Montaigne, Ecole des Beaux-Arts, Paris; PIASch; Yale Univ., B.F.A., M.A. *Member*: NSS. *Awards*: Lissignol F., 1907-08; Decorations, Kim Tiem 1st class, Annam, 1913; Officer d'Academie, France, 1926; Officer, Instruction Publique, France, 1929; Herbert Adams Mem. medal, NSS, 1952. *Work*: A. Mus., Geneva, Switzerland; Palace Legion Honor, San F., Cal. Lectures: Sculpture. *Position*: Prof. Yale Sch. FA, 1917- , Chm. Dept. S., Cur. S., Yale Univ. Gal. FA, New Haven, Conn.; Prof. Emeritus, 1952- .

EBERLE, MERAB (Miss)—Critic
Dayton Journal-Herald; h. 522 Grand Ave., Dayton 5, Ohio

B. Mattoon, Ill. *Studied*: Oxford Col., Oxford, Ohio, B.A. *Position*: A.Ed., Dayton Journal-Herald, 1927- .

EBERMAN, EDWIN—Designer, E., P.
Famous Artists Schools, Westport, Conn.; h. Wahackme Rd., New Canaan, Conn.

B. Black Mountain, N.C., Feb. 20, 1905. *Studied*: Carnegie Inst., B.A. *Member*: A. Dir. Cl.; SI; AIGA. Co-author: "Technique of the Picture Story," 1945; Author, I., "Nantucket Sketch Book," 1946. Contributor to Arts & Decoration and Look magazines. *Position*: A. Dir., Lord & Thomas Adv. Agency, 1937-41; Look Magazine, 1941-47; Sec. & Dir., Famous Artists Schools, Westport, Conn., 1947- .

EBERSOLE, MABEL HELEN—Painter
718 Orleans Ave., Keokuk, Iowa

B. Keokuk, Iowa. *Studied*: AIC, with Buehr, Norton, Oberteuffer. *Awards*: prize, SSAL, 1930. *Work*: Mus. FA,

Little Rock, Ark. *Exhibited*: Rockefeller Center, 1936; SSAL; Six States Exh., Omaha, Neb.; AIC Alumni Exh., 1957 and prior; Joslyn Mem. Mus., 1954 and prior; All-Iowa Exh., 1941, 1951-1958; All-Illinois Soc. FA, 1937, 1938, 1940; Iowa A. Salon, 1949; Quincy, Ill., 1954-1957.

EBERT, CHARLES H.—*Painter*

Old Lyme, Conn.; s. Monhegan Island, Me.

B. Milwaukee, Wis., July 20, 1873. *Studied*: Cincinnati A. Acad.; ASL; Julian Acad., Paris. *Member*: AWCS; Conn. Acad. FA; Lyme AA. *Awards*: Med., Int. Exp., Buenos Aires, 1910; Pan-Pacific Exp., 1915. *Exhibited*: extensively in U.S. & abroad.*

EBERT, MARY ROBERTS (Mrs. Charles H.)— *Painter, C.*

Old Lyme, Conn.

B. Titusville, Pa., Feb. 8, 1873. *Studied*: ASL; & with Twachtman, Hunt. *Member*: AWCS; Lyme AA.*

ECKE, GUSTAVE—*Museum Curator*

Honolulu Academy of Arts, 900 South Beretania St., Honolulu, Hawaii

Position: Cur., Chinese Art, Honolulu Academy of Arts.*

ECKELS, ROBERT JEVERT—*Painter, C., Gr., T.*

Northland College; h. 719 3rd Ave., West, Ashland, Wis.

B. Wolf Creek, Wis., Oct. 18, 1922. *Studied*: Univ. Illinois. B.F.A.; Colorado Springs FA Center; Central Sch. A. & Crafts, London, England; New Mexico Highlands Univ., M.A. *Member*: SI; N.E.A.; Wisconsin Des.-Craftsmen; Am. Craftsmen's Council. *Awards*: scholarships, Colo. Springs FA Center; Central Sch. A. & Crafts; prizes, Wisconsin Des.-Craftsmen, 1958; Mus. New Mexico, 1956 (purchase); Roswell Mus., 1954. *Work*: Mus. New Mexico, Santa Fe. *Exhibited*: Wichita, Kans., 1954, 1956; Mus. New Mexico, 1955, 1956 (traveling crafts exh., 1953); Mus. Intl. Folk Art, Santa Fe, 1955; Roswell Mus., 1954; Miami, Fla., 1956; Wis. Des.-Craftsmen, 1957. *Position*: Instr., Ceramics, S. & Des., Chicago Park Distr., 1952-53; Instr., A. & Crafts, New Mexico Highlands Univ., Las Vegas, N.M.; Dir., A. & Crafts, Student Industry, Northland College, Ashland, Wis., at present.

ECKERT, E(VELYN) E.—*Illustrator, Comm., P.*

2420 16th St., N.W., Apt. 708, Washington 9, D.C.

B. Opdyke, Ill., Jan. 12, 1915. *Studied*: Univ. Illinois. *Member*: AAPL. *Exhibited*: WFNY 1939; Soc. Indp. A., 1941, 1942; Acad. All. A., 1940; Mun. Auditorium, St. Louis, Mo., 1941, 1942; CAM, 1940-1942. *Position*: I., U.S. Dept. of Labor, visual aids & training films, 1950- .

ECKERT, WILLIAM DEAN—*Educator, P., Gr.*

200 North 21st St., Newark, Ohio

B. Coshocton, Ohio, Oct. 10, 1927. *Studied*: Ohio State Univ., M.A., B.A., B.F.A.; State Univ. Iowa; New Sch. for Social Research, N.Y. *Member*: Sarasota AA; Ridge AA, Winter Haven, Fla. *Awards*: prizes, Akron AI, 1954 (2); Ohio State Fair, 1956. *Work*: Butler Inst. Am. A. *Exhibited*: Sarasota AA, 1956, 1957; Ringling Mus. A., 1956; Ohio State Fair, 1956; Fla. Fed. A., 1956; Ohio Univ., Athens, 1957; State Univ. Iowa, 1958. *Positions*: Instr. A., College of Wooster, Wooster, Ohio, 1953-54; Fla. Southern College, Lakeland, 1954-57; Grad. Asst., State Univ. Iowa, 1957- .

ECKERT, MRS. WILLIAM STANLEY. See Seymour, May Davenport

ED, CARL—*Cartoonist*

Chicago Tribune Syndicate; h. 7914 Kolmar Ave., Skokie, Ill.

B. Moline, Ill., July 16, 1890. *Studied*: Augustana College, Rock Island, Ill. *Member*: Press Veterans of Chicago. *Work*: Creator of comic strip "Harold Teen" which has appeared in hundreds of newspapers for past 40 years; two motion pictures made by Warner Bros. under title "Harold Teen," a silent version, 1928 and in sound, 1933. On radio, 1928, 1933.

EDE-ELSE—*Painter*

s. Lyme, Conn.; h. 19 Bethune St., New York 14, N.Y.

B. East Orange, N.J. *Studied*: ASL. *Member*: Creative A. Assoc.; Essex AA. *Exhibited*: SFMA, 1946; Am.-British A. Center, 1943; Chappelier Gal., 1944; NAC, 1949; Essex A. Gal., 1951-1958; Lyme AA, 1951, 1953-1955, 1958; Riverside Mus., 1946, 1950, 1951, 1953, 1956; Wells Turner Gal., Glastonbury, Conn., 1957; Univ. Connecticut, 1957; Attleboro Mus. A., 1957; Thiel Col., 1958; Lincoln Univ., Jefferson City, Mo., 1958; Little Studio, N.Y., 1958; Condon Riley Gal., N.Y., 1958.

EDGERLY, BEATRICE (Mrs. J. Havard Macpherson)— *Painter, Lith., I., T., Cr., W.*

Pima Ave. & Wilmot Rd.; (mail) P.O. Box 4182, University Station, Tucson, Ariz.

B. Washington, D.C. *Studied*: Corcoran Sch. A.; PAFA; & abroad. *Member*: Phila. A. All.; NAWA; Mystic AA; Author's Gld.; Tucson Press Cl. *Awards*: F., PAFA; prizes, PAFA, 1921; NAWA, 1937; Tucson FA Assn., 1938, 1939. *Work*: PAFA. *Exhibited*: PAFA; NAD; CGA; Tucson FA Assn.; Mystic AA, 1953 (2-man exh. with J. Havard Macpherson); Tucson, Ariz., 1954 (one-man); Milwaukee Pub. Lib., "Music & Art Exh.," 1954 (book & illus. of "From the Hunter's Bow"); Arizona State Col., 1955. Author, I., "Ararat Cocktail," 1939; "From the Hunter's Bow," 1942. Contributor to American Artist magazine; Arizona Highways magazine. *Position*: Co-Dir., Founder, Instr., So. Arizona Sch. A., Tucson, Ariz.; Cr., A. Columnist, Arizona Daily Star, Tucson, 1954- .

EDIE, STUART CARSON—*Painter, E.*

111 South Summit St., Iowa City, Iowa

B. Wichita Falls, Tex., Nov. 10, 1908. *Studied*: Kansas City AI; ASL. *Member*: An Am. Group; Woodstock AA. *Work*: MMA; WMAA; BM; Syracuse Mus. FA; Newark Mus.; Univ. Iowa; Univ. Georgia; mural, USPO, Honeoye Falls, N.Y.; Toledo Mus. A.; Joslyn Mem. Mus.; Kansas City AI; ASL; Des Moines A. Center. *Exhibited*: MMoA; Carnegie Inst.; WMAA; PAFA; NAD; AIC; BM; John Herron AI. *Position*: Prof. Painting, Univ. Iowa, Iowa City, Iowa.

EDMONDSON, LEONARD—*Painter, Et., E.*

714 Prospect Blvd., Pasadena, Cal.

B. Sacramento, Cal., June 12, 1916. *Studied*: Univ. California, Berkeley, A.B., M.A. *Member*: AEA; California WC Soc.; CAA; Bd. Memb., Pasadena A. Mus. *Awards*: Tiffany Fnd. grant, 1952, 1955; prizes, SFMA, 1946, 1949, 1951-1953, 1957; Los A. Mus. A., 1957; Los A. County Fair, 1950-1953, 1956; James Phelan awards, San F., 1951, 1953; Cal. State Fair, 1951, 1952; BM, 1951, 1956; SAM, 1952-1954; Oakland A. Mus., 1952-1955, 1958; Pasadena A. Mus., 1952, 1954, 1957, 1958; Bradley Univ., 1952, 1955; MMA, 1952; Cal. WC Soc., 1953, 1955-1958; Univ. Illinois, 1954, 1955; DMFA, 1954; SAGA, 1957; LC, 1957; Am. Color Pr. Soc., 1954, 1955; VMFA, 1958. *Work*: SFMA; State of California; SAM; N.Y. Pub. Lib., UCLA; Pasadena A. Mus.; Univ. Illinois; LC; DMFA; Oakland A. Mus.; PMA; MMA; VMFA. *Exhibited*: AIC, 1948, 1957; MMA, 1952; Los A. Mus. A., 1947-1958; BM, 1950-1958; Denver A. Mus., 1947-1958; PAFA, 1951-1958; WMAA, 1952, 1953, 1955, 1956, 1958; Univ. Illinois, 1953-1958; Sao Paulo, Brazil, 1955; Guggenheim Mus., 1954; Carnegie Inst., 1955; VMFA, 1958; CGA, 1953, 1956; one-man: deYoung Mem. Mus., 1952; Pasadena A. Mus., 1953; Santa Barbara Mus. A., 1953; Cal. Sch. FA, 1956; Landau Gal., Los Angeles, 1950-1953, 1955, 1958. *Position*: Instr., Pasadena City Col., 1947-54, 1956- ; Hd. Des., Los Angeles County AI, 1954-56; Instr., Summer Session, Univ. So. California, 1957.

EDMUNDSON, CAROLYN— *Painter, Des., I., Comm., T.*

c/o Mrs. Eva Heap, 900 Meadow St., Reno, Nev.

B. Pittsburgh, Pa., Dec. 20, 1906. *Studied*: Carnegie Inst., Col. FA, B.A.; Columbia Univ.; N.Y. Univ. *Member*: Nevada AA; Soc. Western A. *Awards*: prizes, Nevada AA, 1952; Soc. Western A., 1954. *Work*: Nevada State Mus., Carson City; port., figure, still life painting, advertising illus. Illus. for Cannon Mills, Forstmann Woolens. Yardley of London, DeBeers Consolidated Mines, Hudson Motors, Libby McNeill & Libby, Lederle Laboratories and others. *Exhibited*: PAFA; NAD; All. A. Am.; Nevada AA. 1952-1954; Soc. Western A., 1953-1955. *Position*: Staff A., Vogue magazine, 1929-30; Harper's Bazaar, 1930-37; Ed. & Cover illus., leading national magazines, 1929-52; Instr., Dept. Adult Edu. Reno H.S., 1953- .*

EDROP, ARTHUR—
Illustrator, Comm., W., L., P., Cart.
Radnor Inn, Radnor, Pa.

B. Birmingham, England. *Studied*: PIASch.; Brooklyn Sch. A. *Member*: Wayne A. Center (Bd. Dir.); The Footlighters (Wayne, Pa.). *Exhibited*: A. Dir. Cl., Phila., Pa.; Wanamakers Gal.; McClees Gallery; Wayne A. Center. Illus., "The Texans Ride North" and other books; book of poems, "The Wind Carved Tree" (Esther Wood). Contributor illus., cartoons to national magazines. Lecturer, writer (papers, and booklets on military uniforms). A. Consultant, A. Dir., to adv. agencies and advertisers.

EDSALL, MABEL MEEKER—*Painter, T., Cart.*
755 South Price Rd., Clayton, Mo.; h. 7013 Oleatha St., St. Louis 9, Mo.

B. Bay City, Mich. *Studied*: ASL; & with DuMond, Chase, Hawthorne. *Member*: St. Louis A. Gld.; Progressive Edu. Assn.; Nat. Edu. Assn.; Western AA; Missourians; County A. T. Assn., Mo. *Awards*: prizes, St. Louis A. Gld.; St. Louis A. Lg., 1927; prize for painting for church chapel given by Eden Publ. House and Concordia Publ. House, 1957. *Work*: mural, Dr. Albert Schweitzer Organ Studio, Green Lake, Wis.; YWCA, St. Louis. *Exhibited*: PAFA, 1914; Arch.L.; NAD; CAM, 1926-1940, 1945, 1956, 1957; St. Louis A. Gld., 1920-1946; Witte Mem. Mus., 1953 (one-man); Midwestern Univ. Mus., Wichita Falls, Tex., 1955; Assoc. Press Exh., 1944. *Position*: Hd., Painting Dept., John Burroughs Sch., Clayton, Mo., 1931-1953.

EDSON, GUS—*Cartoonist*
c/o Chicago Tribune-N.Y. News Syndicate, Inc., 220 East 42nd St., New York 17, N.Y.; h. 149 Weed Ave., Stamford, Conn.

B. Cincinnati, Ohio, Sept. 20, 1901. *Studied*: PIASch.; ASL. *Member*: Nat. Cartoonists Soc.; SI; Westport A.; A. & Writers Assn.; Banshees; Nat. Comics Council. Author, I., "The Gumps," appearing in 329 newspapers; Author-Creator of new strip "Dondi," 1955.

EDWARDS, ELEANOR—*Painter*
Maverick Rd., Woodstock, N.Y.

B. St. Louis, Mo., Oct. 31, 1906. *Studied*: Iowa Wesleyan Col.; Stephens Col. *Member*: Woodstock Fnd. (Sec.); Woodstock Gld. Craftsmen. *Exhibited*: AIC, 1938; BM, 1939; Morton Gal.; Contemporary A. Gal.; Seven Arts Cl.; Woodstock A. Gal.; Bard Col.; Stephens Col., 1949; All-Missouri Exh., 1951; Woodstock Gal.; W. & J. Sloane Gal., N.Y.; Sculptors Gal., Woodstock; Guild Gal., Woodstock.

EDWARDS, EMMET—*Painter*
Woodstock, N.Y.

B. Mt. Pleasant, Iowa, Oct. 11, 1906. *Studied*: AIC. *Work*: FAP Nat. Exh., Wash., D.C.; Mus. Non-Objective Painting; VMFA; U.S.Govt. *Exhibited*: AIC, 1928, 1930, 1935, 1937; CAA traveling exh.; 1934; BM, 1935; MModA, 1936, 1940 (traveling exh.) 1937-38; WFNY 1939; Mus. Non-Objective Painting, 1942-1946, 1947-1952; FAP traveling exh., 1936-1940; Assoc. Am. A., 1936; Inst. Mod. A., Boston, 1947; Palais des Beaux-Arts, Paris, 1946; Salon des Nouvelles Realities, Paris, 1947; Kunsthaus, Zurich, Switzerland, 1947; Robinson Gal., Chicago; Ferargil Gal.; Passedoit Gal.; Assoc. Am. A.; Am.-British A. Center, N.Y.

EDWARDS, KATE F(LOURNOY)—*Portrait Painter*
The Darlington, Apt. 1105, 2025 Peachtree Rd., Northeast, Atlanta 9, Ga.

B. Marshallville, Ga. *Studied*: AIC; Grande Chaumiere, Paris, and with Charles Hawthorne. *Member*: Assn. Georgia A.; Atlanta AA. *Awards*: prizes, Southeastern Fair Exh., 1916; Atlanta AA, 1921. *Work*: The Capitol, Wash., D.C.; Georgia Sch. Tech.; Mercer Univ.; Wesleyan Col., Macon, Ga.; Univ. Georgia; Wake Forest (N.C.) Col.; Governor's Palace, Puerto Rico; Court House, Atlanta, Ga.; High Mus. A.; Headquarters Bldg., Ft. Benning, Ga.; City Lib.,

Dayton, Wash.; Westminster Sch., Atlanta, Ga.; Fourth Nat. Bank, Columbus, Ga.; Court House, New Bern, N.C.; Univ. Illinois; Federal Reserve Bank, Atlanta; Calhoun Mem. Lib., Atlanta; Johnson Sch., Columbus, Ga.; Decatur-DeKalb Lib., Decatur, Ga.; Columbia Theological Seminary, Decatur; McCall Hospital, Rome, Ga.; Tinsley School, Macon, Ga.; Georgia Indst. Home, Macon; Georgia Federated Mutual Ins. Bldg., Atlanta; Oglethorpe Univ., Atlanta; Rome Bank & Trust Co., Rome, Ga.; Davenport House, Savannah; Willingham Sch., Macon; Telephone Bldg., Dalton, Ga.

EDWARDSON, LAURENCE CHRISTIE—*Painter*
964 High Rd., Kensington, Conn.

B. Waltham, Mass., July 21, 1904. *Studied*: Hartford A. Sch.; & with Gifford Beal. *Member*: Conn. Acad. FA; New Britain A. Lg. *Awards*: prize, Conn. Acad. FA, 1945. *Exhibited*: Conn. Acad. FA, 1930-1946; New Haven Paint & Clay Cl., 1941; New Britain Inst., 1942-1946.*

EGAN, ELOISE—*Painter*
140 West 57th St., New York, N.Y.; h. Compo Rd., Westport, Conn.

B. Ithaca, N.Y. *Member*: NAWA; NAC; All. A. Am. *Exhibited*: NAWA; NAD.*

EGAN, JOSEPH BYRON—*Illustrator, P., Cart., Gr.*
1027 Cathedral Square, Cleveland 14, Ohio; h. 2948 Coleridge Rd., Cleveland Heights 18, Ohio

B. Cleveland, Ohio, Apr. 22, 1906. *Studied*: Cleveland Sch. A.; John Huntington Polytechnic Inst.; Univ. Kansas. *Awards*: prizes, CMA, 1929, 1931-1934. *Work*: CMA; Cleveland Mun. Coll.; BM; Cleveland Pr. Cl.; FAP mural, St. James Church, Lakewood, Ohio; mural, Carmelite Monastery, Holy Hill, Wis. *Exhibited*: CAA, 1932; CMA, 1929-1935; Dayton AI; Butler AI; BM; Ohio State Fair, 1932; AIC, 1934. I., "Those Were the Days"; "The Devil You Say," 1952. *Position*: Ed. Artist, Catholic Press Union.

EGAS, CAMILO—*Painter, S., Et., Lith., T.*
248 West 14th St., New York, N.Y.; h. R.F.D. 1, Orwigsburg, Pa.

B. Quito, Ecuador, Dec. 10, 1899. *Studied*: Academia de las Bellas Artes, Ecuador; Royal Inst. des Beaux-Arts, Rome; San Fernando Academia de Bellas Artes, Madrid. *Awards*: Fellowships to Rome and Paris from Ecuador; prize, Int. Exh., Quito. *Work*: MModA; Newark Mus. A.; IBM; Nat. Mus., Ecuador; Museo de Bellas Artes, Caracas, Venezuela; murals, WFNY 1939; New School for Social Research, N.Y.; Jijon Lib., Quito. *Exhibited*: Salon d'Automne, Salon de Tuileries, Salon des Independents, all in Paris; Galeria Nacional de Rome; Salon del Retiro, Madrid. *Position*: Dir., A. Dept., New Sch. for Social Research, New York, N.Y.

EGBERT, LYN (Mrs. Lawrence D.)—
Designer, C., Gr., E., W.
1647 35th St., Northwest, Washington 7, D.C.

B. Oakland, Cal. *Studied*: Univ. California, A.B.; AIC; PAFA; Abbott Sch. A.; Univ. North Carolina, M.A. in A. Edu.; and abroad. *Member*: Wash. WC Cl.; Wash. Soc. Printmakers; Miniature Painters, Sculptors & Gravers Soc. *Exhibited*: Wash. WC Cl.; Wash. Soc. Min. P. S. & Gravers; Wash. Soc. Printmakers (all annually); Wash. A. Cl.; Smithsonian Inst.; CGA; Wichita, Kans. Author: "Free Brush Designing," 1955. *Position*: Dir., Cherry Tree Textile Designers; Dir., Des. Workshop, Wash., D.C.; Bd. Dir., Wash. WC Cl.; Instr., Textile Des., T. Workshops, American Univ., Wash., D.C.

EGRI, TED—*Sculptor, P., L.*
Taos, N.M.

B. New York, N.Y., May 22, 1913. *Studied*: Master Inst., Roerich Mus., N.Y.; Phillips Mem. A. Sch.; Ozenfant Sch. A.; Hans Hofmann Sch. A. *Member*: AEA; Taos AA. *Awards*: prizes, Audubon A., 1946; Nat. Comp. Jewish Community Center, Scranton, Pa., 1955; New Mexico State Fair. *Work*: William Rockhill Nelson Gal. A.; Mus. of New Mexico, Santa Fe; Jewish Community Center, Scranton, Pa. (facade dec.); Baylor Theatre, Waco, Tex. *Exhibited*: PAFA, 1953; Birmingham, Ala., 1954; Univ. Illinois, 1952, 1953, 1955; Denver A. Mus., 1949, 1953, 1954;

Colorado Springs FA Center, 1950, 1952; Mus. New Mexico, 1951-1958; Santa Barbara Mus. A. *Lectures*: Understanding Modern Art. *Position*: Instr., Kansas City AI, 1948-50; Taos AA, 1953-55; Philbrook A. Center, Tulsa, Okla., 1956-57; Lubbock, Tex., 1957- .

EHRENREICH, EMMA—*Painter, Wood Eng.*

65 West 36th St. (18); h. 55 Park Ave., New York 16, N.Y.

B. New York, N.Y., Sept. 19, 1906. *Studied*: NAD; BMSch.; New Sch. for Social Research; City Col., N.Y.; Long Island Univ.; Grad. Sch., Hunter Col., and with Abraham Rattner, Morris Davidson. *Member*: NAWA; AEA; N.Y. Soc. Women A.; Brooklyn Soc. A.; Nat. Soc. Painters in Casein; Silvermine Gld. A.; Provincetown AA. *Awards*: prizes, NAWA, 1950, 1955; Brooklyn Soc. A., 1951, 1952, 1954, 1957. *Work*: Denver A. Mus.; Dayton Inst. A.; Brandeis Univ.; Governours Hospital and in private collections. *Exhibited*: Brooklyn Soc. A., 1951, 1952; BM, 1953, 1957; Butler AI, 1954, 1957, 1958; Denver A. Mus., 1955; Fed. Mod. A. traveling exh., 1954, 1958; Nat. Exh., Jewish Tercentenary, 1955; BM, 1955; CGA; PAFA; Dayton Inst. A.; NAWA traveling exh., Greece, Belgium, 1958, Holland, Sweden, 1956-57; one-man: Silvermine Gld. A., 1958; in many museums in U.S. and New York galleries; one-man: Contemporary A., 1953, 1955.

EHRICH, WILLIAM E.—*Educator, S., C.*

Fauver Hall, University of Rochester; h. 49 Klink Rd., Rochester 10, N.Y.

B. Koenigsberg, Germany, July 12, 1897. *Studied*: State A. Sch., Koenigsberg, Germany, and with Stanislaus Cauer, Erich Schmidt-Kestner, Franz Thryne. *Member*: The Patteran; The Arena Com., Rochester. *Awards*: prizes, Albright A. Gal.; Rochester Mem. A. Gal. *Work*: Albright A. Gal.; Rochester Mem. A. Gal.; Univ. Rochester. *Exhibited*: Finger Lakes Exh., Rochester; Albright A. Gal.; Syracuse Mus. FA. *Position*: Asst. Prof., Univ. Rochester and Mem. A. Gal., Rochester, N. Y.

EICHENBERG, FRITZ—

Printmaker, Eng., Lith., I., T., W.

69 Oakland Ave., Yonkers, N.Y.

B. Cologne, Germany, Oct. 24, 1901. *Studied*: State Acad. Graphic A., Leipzig, and with H. Steiner-Prag. *Member*: SAGA; NA; AEA; AIGA; Phila. WC Cl. *Awards*: prizes, LC, 1943-1948, 1951; PAFA, medal, 1944; NAD, 1946; Distinguished service award, Limited Editions Cl., 1950. *Work*: N.Y.Pub.Lib.; LC; AIC; Univ. Minnesota Lib.; Rosenwald Coll.; Carnegie Inst.; BM. *Exhibited*: PAFA, 1940-1952; NAD, 1938-1952; LC, 1943-1952; Carnegie Inst., 1943-1952; AIGA, 1938, 1940, 1944; one-man: N.Y.Pub. Lib., 1949; Phila. A. All., 1949; New School, 1949; Univ. Maine, 1950. Illus., "Richard III"; "Eugene Onegin"; "War and Peace"; "Brothers Karamazov," 1949; "Jane Eyre" and "Wuthering Heights," 1943; "Crime and Punishment," 1938-48; "Reynard the Fox"; "The Idiot"; Author-I., "Ape in a Cape"; "Dancing in the Moon," and many other children's books. Author: Pendle Hill pamphlet "Art and Faith." Contributor to Horn Book, Print Magazine, Graphis Magazine; Penrose Annual, etc. Lectures: Art and Religion; Book Illustration; Graphic Arts at various schools and colleges. *Position*: Instr., Gr. A., New School for Social Research, 1935-40; Prof. A., Chm. Dept. Illus., PIASch., Brooklyn, N.Y., 1948- ; Memb. Council, NAD, 1953-56; Dir., Pratt Inst. Contemporaries Graphic A. Centre, 1956- ; Contributing Ed., American Artist magazine, 1956- .

EIDE, PALMER—*Educator, Des., C., S.*

2025 Austin Drive, Sioux Falls, S.D.

B. Minnehaha County, S.D., July 5, 1906. *Studied*: Augustana Col., B.A.; AIC; Harvard Univ.; Yale Univ.; Cranbrook Acad. A. *Member*: AAUP; Com. on A., Nat. Council of Churches of Christ in America; CAA; Am. Oriental Soc. *Awards*: Scholarships, Harvard Univ., 1936-1937; F., Yale Univ., 1940, 1941. *Work*: S., City Hall, Broadcasting Station KSOO, Sioux Falls, S.D.; Trinity Lutheran Church, Rapid City, S.D.; etc. *Position*: Prof. A., Augustana Col., Sioux Falls, S.D., 1931- .

EISELEY MABEL L.—*Assistant Museum Director*

Pennsylvania Academy of Fine Arts, Broad & Cherry Sts., Philadelphia, Pa.

Position: Asst. Dir., Pennsylvania Academy of Fine Arts.*

EISENDRATH, WILLIAM NATHAN, JR.—

Asst. Museum Director, Hist.

City Art Museum of St. Louis (5); h. 4969 Pershing Place, St. Louis 8, Mo.

B. Chicago, Ill., Mar. 4, 1903. *Studied*: Yale Univ., B.A.; Northwestern Univ. (residency for M.A.). *Member*: AAMus.; AFA. Contributor numerous articles for City Art Museum Bulletin; exhibitions assembled and arranged: "Claude Monet," 1957; "Contemporary Italian Art," 1955; Assisted in assembling "Westward the Way," 1954. *Positions*: Dir. Exhs., Arts Club of Chicago, 1940-52; Asst. Dir., City Art Museum of St. Louis, at present.

EISENLOHR, EDWARD G.—*Painter, Lith., L.*

324 North Eads Ave., Dallas 3, Tex.

B. Cincinnati, Ohio, Nov. 9, 1872. *Studied*: with Frank Reaugh, R. J. Onderdonk, Birge Harrison; & in Germany. *Member*: SC; Dallas AA; Texas FA Assn.; SSAL; AFA; AAPL. *Awards*: prizes, Dallas AA, 1931, 1932, 1948; San Antonio A. Lg., 1927, 1928; SSAL, 1920; Tex. Fed. Women's Cl. *Work*: Dallas Mus. FA; Elisabet Ney Mus. A.; Delgado Mus. A.; Witte Mem. Mus.; Mus. FA, Abilene, Tex.; Mus. FA of Houston. *Exhibited*: CGA, 1917; NAD, 1920; Pan-Pacific Exp., 1915; Albany Inst. Hist. & A., 1941; WFNY 1939; AFA rotary exh.; Witte Mem. Mus., 1948; SC, 1948, 1951; Corpus Christi AA, 1948; College Station, Tex., 1950; Elisabet Ney Mus., 1950; Mus. New Mexico, 1951; & in many cities of Texas. *Position*: Bd. Trustees, Dallas Mus. FA, Dallas, Tex.

EISNER, ANNE—*Painter, L., W.*

5 Minetta St., New York, N.Y.

B. Newark, N.J., Apr. 13, 1911. *Studied*: N.Y. Sch. F. & App. A.; ASL. *Member*: Pen & Brush Cl.; Fed. Mod. P. & S.; NAWA. *Awards*: prizes, NAWA, 1940, 1944. *Exhibited*: WFNY 1939; MModA; Inst. Mod. A., Boston; AIC; Riverside Mus.; Norlyst Gal., 1944 (one-man). Author-I., "Madami" (with Allan Keller), 1954; "Eight Years Among Congo Pigmies," 1955. Lectures: Collecting African Art; Eight Years in Central Africa. Contributor to Art Digest; Readers Digest.*

EISNER, DOROTHY (Mrs. Dorothy Eisner McDonald)—

Painter

3 East 14th St.; h. 46 Morton St., New York 14, N.Y.

B. New York, N.Y., Jan. 17, 1906. *Studied*: ASL. *Member*: Fed. Mod. P. & S.; NAWA. *Awards*: prizes, Dance International, 1936; NAWA. *Exhibited*: CGA, 1938; PAFA, 1935, 1946; VMFA, 1944; WFNY 1939; AIC.*

EISNER, MRS. WILLIAM J. See Rensie, Florine

EITEL, CLIFFE D.—*Designer, P., I., Gr.*

8 South Michigan Ave., Chicago 3, Ill.; h. 1819 Oakwood Rd., Northbrook, Ill.

B. Salt Lake City, Utah, June 18, 1909. *Studied*: with Hubert Ropp, Gyorgy Kepes, Joseph Binder. *Awards*: prizes, A. Gld. of Chicago, 1945. *Exhibited*: Phila. Pr. Cl., 1946; NAD, 1946; LC, 1946; Mint Mus. A., 1946; Laguna Beach AA, 1946; AIC, 1945-1947; Chicago A. Gld., 1945; Cliff Dwellers Cl., Chicago, 1946; Akron AI, 1952; in Germany with State Dept. Exh., 1951. *Work*: ceramic murals, Mercy Hospital, Canton, Ohio; Tampa Municipal Hospital, Fla.; Mary Queen of Heaven Church, Elmhurst, Ill.; Augustinian Seminary, Olympia Fields, Ill.; Ravenswood Tile Co., Chicago, Ill.; El Lago Apts., Chicago, Ill.; mural, Meat Products Industry, Northfield, Ill. Contributor to American Artist Magazine.

EKDAHL, ANNE ANDERSON (Mrs.)—*Etcher, P.*

206 South Harvard Ave., Villa Park, Ill.

B. Elgin, Ill. *Studied*: Chicago Acad. FA; AIC; & with Charles Hawthorne, Hugh Breckenridge, Richard Miller. *Member*: Chicago SE. *Work*: NGA; Vexsjo, Sweden.

EKDAHL, KURT—*Educator, C.*

College of Ceramics, Alfred University, Alfred, N.Y.*

ELDER, INEZ STAUB—*Painter, T., L.*
3339 Gibsondell St., Dallas 11, Tex.

B. Kosuth, Ohio, Jan. 16, 1894. *Studied*: A. Acad. Cincinnati; New Sch. Des., Boston; ASL; Otterbein Col. *Member*: SSAL. *Awards*: prizes, All. A., Dallas, Tex., 1931, 1933, 1948; SSAL, 1936; Dallas Mus. FA, 1942. *Exhibited*: Texas Centennial, 1936; Pan.-Am. Exp., Dallas, 1937; Texas All. A., 1928-1946; Mus. FA of Houston, 1937-1945; SSAL, 1932-1934; Texas State Fair, 1933, 1934; Ft. Worth, Tex., 1937-1945; Fed. Dallas A., 1947-1951, 1954, 1955; Texas General, 1950; Texas A. & M. Col., 1951; Austin, Tex., 1950; Topeka, Kans., 1950; Frank Reaugh A. Cl., 1953-1957; Klepper A. Cl., 1953-1958; Otterbein Col. Soc. FA, 1953-1955; one-man, Dallas, Tex., 1949-1951; Oak Cliff FA Soc., 1956-1958.

ELIAS, ARTHUR (LOUIS)—*Painter, T.*
462 Third Ave., New York 16, N.Y.

B. McKeesport, Pa., Nov. 24, 1925. *Studied*: Carnegie Inst. Tech., B.F.A.; Univ. Pittsburgh, M.A.; Col. of the City of N.Y.; N.Y. Univ. (summer). *Work*: Smith Col. Mus. A., and in private colls. *Exhibited*: Salon de Mai, 1951; Salon des Réalités Nouvelles, 1951; Salon d'Art Libre, 1951; Salon d'Automne, 1952, all Paris, France; PAFA, 1954; Univ. Colorado, 1956; Assoc. A. Pittsburgh, 1947-1949; Illinois Wesleyan, 1956; Stable Gal., N.Y., 1956, 1957; one-man: Peridot Gal., N.Y., 1954, 1955, 1956, 1958.

ELIAS, HAROLD JOHN—*Painter, C., Des., T., L.*
Rt. #2, Watervliet, Mich.

B. Cleveland, Ohio, Mar. 12, 1920. *Studied*: AIC, B.F.A., with John Rogers Cox, Kathleen Blackshear; De Paul Univ. *Member*: Mich. Acad. Science, A. & Let.; Mich. WC Soc.; Cultural Com., Univ. Michigan; Chicago Soc. A. *Awards*: prizes, Magnificent Mile, Chicago, 1952; Western Mich. A., 1953. *Work*: Univ. Idaho, Moscow, Idaho; Ill. State Mus.; Massillon Mus. A., and in private colls. *Exhibited*: Alabama WC Soc., 1950; PAFA, 1950, 1952; Exh. Momentum, 1950, 1951, 1952; Creative Gal., N.Y., 1950; Esquire Theatre exh. of Chicago Art, 1950; MMA, 1950; NAD, 1951; Denver A. Mus., 1951; Magnificent Mile, 1951, 1952; Grand Rapids A. Gal., 1950-1952, 1954; Univ. Michigan, 1952; Michigan State Fair, 1952, 1954; Artists, Des., & Manufacturers Exh., Grand Rapids, 1952; BMFA, 1952; Detroit Inst. A., 1952; Sabena's sculpture comp., Brussels, 1953; Springfield, Ill., 1954; Massillon Mus. A., 1954; Michiana, 1955; one-man: Esquire Theatre, Chicago, 1951; Hackley A. Gal., 1951; Albion Col., 1953; Saginaw Mus., 1953; Univ. Mich., 1953; Neville Pub. Mus., 1953; Univ. Tulsa, 1953; Univ. Idaho, 1954; Univ. New Mexico, 1954; Racine AA, 1954; Olivet Col., 1954; State Col. Wash., 1954; Univ. Oklahoma, 1954; Kenosha Pub. Mus., 1954; Ball State T. Col., 1955; Oklahoma A. & M., 1955; Texas Christian Univ., 1955; Eastern N.M. Univ., 1955; Lafayette (Ind.) AA, 1955; Oklahoma A. Center, 1955; Stephen Austin State Col., 1955; Coos Bay A. League (Ore.), 1955; Sanford Mus., Cherokee, Iowa, 1955; Western Mich. Univ., 1958; Central Mo. State Col., 1958; East Carolina Col., 1958; Cornell Col., Mt. Vernon, Iowa, 1958; City Lib. Assn., Springfield, Mass., 1958; one-man traveling exh., 1956-57 to major colleges, libraries, galleries and museums. Smithsonian Inst. traveling exh. "Midwest Designers," 1958. *Position*: Instr., Muskegon Community Col., Adult Edu., 1952- ; Asst. to Dir., Hackley A. Gal., Muskegon, Mich.; Chief Tech. Illus., Clark Equipment Co., Benton Harbor, Mich.; Instr., Adult Edu., St. Joseph, Mich.

ELIAS, LEE (LEOPOLD)—*Cartoonist, I., T.*
9 Robin Lane, South Farmingdale, N.Y.

B. Manchester, England, May 21, 1920. *Studied*: CUASch.; ASL, and with William McNulty, Robert Brackman, Jon Corbino. *Member*: Nat. Cartoonists Soc. *Exhibited*: MMA, 1951. Co-Creator of comic strip, "Beyond Mars," New York News. Contributor to national magazines and New York Sunday News. *Position*: Instr., Cartooning & Illus. Sch.; Asst. to Al Capp on "Lil' Abner."

ELIASOPH, PAULA—*Painter, Gr., C., W., L., T.*
148-25 89th Ave., Jamaica 35, L.I., N.Y.

B. New York, N.Y., Oct. 26, 1895. *Studied*: PIASch.; ASL; Columbia Univ. *Member*: AWS; Nat. Lg. Am. Pen Women; ASL; Long Island A. Lg.; Fed. Mod. P. & S. *Awards*: prizes, Queensboro YWCA, 1943; med., Long Island A. Lg., 1950. *Work*: BM; MMA; LC; Wash. (D.C.) Pub. Lib.; F. D. Roosevelt Lib.; N.Y. Pub. Lib.; murals,

Hillside Hollis Center, Jamaica, L.I.; YMHA, Jamaica, L.I. *Exhibited*: LC, 1943; SAGA, 1944; Phila. Soc. Et.; AIC, 1931; BM, 1931; deYoung Mem. Mus.; AFA traveling exh., 1955-1957; Fed. Mod. P. & S., 1948, 1955; NAC, 1949-1951; PAFA; NAD; AWS; Wadsworth Atheneum; Riverside Mus., 1955; Inst. Mod. A., Boston; Rochester Mem. A. Gal., 1946; Riverside Mus., 1957-1959; Grand Central A. Gal., 1956; Art:USA, 1958; Silvermine Gld. A., 1958; Assoc. Am. A., 1955, and others. One-man: Clayton Gal., N.Y.; BM; Belle & Fletcher Gal., Boston; Kew Gardens A. Center, L.I., 1952; Forest Hills, N.Y., 1952; Guild Hall, East Hampton, L.I.; Montross Gal.; Argent Gal., etc. Author: "Etchings and Drypoints of Childe Hassam." Contributor to art magazines. *Position*: Chm., Queens Botanical Gardens A. Festival, 1949-1955; A. Chm. Golden Jubilee, Queens; A. Supv., Instr., Yeshiva of Central Queens, Elem. & Jr. H.S., 1949- ; Instr., Adult Sch. of Study, Forest Hills, N.Y., 1951- ; Lecturer, Queens Col.

ELIOT, LUCY—*Painter*
131 East 66th St., New York 21, N.Y.

B. New York, N.Y., May 8, 1913. *Studied*: Vassar Col., B.A.; ASL, with George Bridgman, Morris Kantor, William von Schlegell. *Member*: AEA. *Awards*: prize, Rochester Mem. A. Gal., 1946; Silvermine Gld A., 1957. *Work*: Rochester Mem. A. Gal.; Munson-Williams-Proctor Inst. *Exhibited*: PAFA, 1946, 1948, 1949, 1950, 1952; CGA, 1947, 1951; VMFA, 1948; Art:USA, 1958; one-man: Rochester Mem. A. Gal., 1946; Syracuse Mus. FA, 1947; Wells Col., Aurora, N.Y., 1953. Instr., Painting, Red Cross Occupational Therapy Dept., Bronx Veterans Hospital, 1950-52.

ELISCU, FRANK—*Sculptor*
Croton Dam Rd., Ossining, N.Y.

B. New York, N.Y., July 13, 1912. *Studied*: BAID; Pratt Inst. *Member*: F., NSS; ANA; Arch. Lg. *Awards*: prizes, Bennet prize for sculpture, 1953, Moore prize, 1950; Arch. Lg., 1955; silver medal, 1958. *Work*: busts, Aeronautical Hall of Fame; fountain, Brookgreen Gardens, S.C.; fountain, 100 Church St., New York, N.Y.; "Atoms for Peace" figure, Ventura, Cal.; war mem., Cornell Medical Col. *Exhibited*: NAD, 1935-1955; PAFA; Conn. Acad. FA; CMA; Springfield Mus. A.; Detroit Inst. A.; one-man in Mexico, sponsored by U.S. Govt. *Position*: Instr., Sculpture, Sch. of Indst. A., New York, N.Y.; Vice-Pres. for sculpture, Arch. Lg., 1958; 1st Vice-Pres., NSS, 1958.

ELISE (*Elise Rosen***)—***Painter, Gr., I., Des.*
110 Seaman Ave., New York 34, N.Y.

B. Vienna, Austria. *Studied*: Sch. Graphic A., Vienna; City Col., New York. *Member*: Nat. Serigraph Soc.; Amalgamated Lithographers of Am. *Awards*: Diplome de Medaille d'Argent, Paris. *Exhibited*: Ser. Soc., 1952-1955; Roerich Gal., N.Y., 1957. Paris, France and Vienna, Austria.

ELLINGER, ILONA E. *See Deak-Ebner, Ilona*

ELLIOTT, ETHEL M. (*Mrs. E. H.***)—***Painter*
11527 MacGovern St., Downey—Cal.

B. Iowa City, Iowa, Aug. 6, 1908. *Studied*: with Christian Von Schneidau, Leon Franks, Will Foster, E. Withers, Arla Franklin. *Member*: Nat. Soc. A. & Let.; California A. Cl.; Las Artistas; Southland AA; Community A. Lg. *Awards*: prizes, Los A. City Hall, 1951; Community A. Lg., 1952, 1955; Southeast Los A. Community Fair; Los A. Exposition Park, 1951; Cal. Fed. Women's Cl., 1950-1952; Southland AA, 1958; Downey Mus. A., 1958. *Work*: port., West Branch (Iowa) Pub. Lib.; also in Southgate, Downey, Santa Cruz, San Diego, Cal.; painting, San Fernando H.S. *Exhibited*: Madonna Festival, Los A., 1950, 1951; Las Artistas, Greek Theatre, 1952; Cal. A. Cl., 1950-1955; Mid-Cities AA, 1955; 8 one-man local exhs.

ELLIOTT, FRANCES GRAY—*Painter*
3 Marietta Ave., Athens, Ohio

B. East Liverpool, Ohio, Sept. 4, 1900. *Studied*: Ohio Univ., B.S. in Edu., A.M. in Edu. *Member*: Ohio WC Soc.; Columbus A. Lg.; Huntington (W. Va.) Gal. *Awards*: prizes, Huntington Gal., 1954, 1955; Ohio Univ., 1954, 1955. *Work*: Phila. A. All.; Ohio Univ. *Exhibited*: Ohio WC Soc.; Columbus A. Lg.; Huntington, W. Va., Gal.; Ohio State Fair; Ohio Univ. Des. & Creator of the Elliott Dolls.

ELLIOTT, PHILIP CLARKSON—*Painter, E.*

147 Bryant St., Buffalo 22, N.Y.

B. Minneapolis, Minn., Dec. 5, 1903. *Studied*: Univ. Minnesota; Yale Univ., B.F.A. *Member*: The Patteran. *Awards*: Chaloner Fnd. Paris prize, 1929-1933; Pepsi-Cola, 1948; Albright A. Gal., 1949, 1952. *Work*: murals, Univ. Pittsburgh; Albright A. Gal. *Exhibited*: PAFA, 1944; Carnegie Inst., 1943, 1945; Albright A. Gal.; MModA., 1952; Pepsi-Cola, 1948. Lectures: Techniques of Painting. *Position*: Assoc. Prof. FA, Univ. Pittsburgh, 1934-40; Dir., Albright A. Sch., Buffalo, N.Y., 1941-54; Prof. A., Chm. A. Dept., Univ. Buffalo, 1954- .

ELLIOTT, MRS. PHILIP. See *Cuthbert, Virginia*

ELLIOTT, RONNIE—*Painter*

316 East 58th St., New York 22, N.Y.

B. New York, N.Y. *Studied*: N.Y. Univ.; Hunter Col.; ASL; & with William Zorach, Alexander Brook, Hans Hofmann, Francis Luna. *Member*: A. Lg. Am. *Exhibited*: PAFA, 1933, 1934, 1939; Honolulu Acad. A., 1936; GGE, 1939; WFNY 1939; Carnegie Inst., 1941; CGA, 1939; NAD, 1941; Bennington Col., 1943; SFMA, 1945, 1946; Western Col., Oxford, Ohio, 1945; Marquie Gal., 1942, 1944 (one-man); Art of this Century, 1943-1945; MMA, 1942; Mus. Non-Objective Painting, 1946, 1947; Norlyst Gal., 1947; Carlebach Gal., 1947; MModA., 1948; Galerie Creuze, Paris, 1948 (one-man), 1957; Réalités Nouvelles, Paris, 1948-1951; La Galerie Colette Allendy, Paris, 1952 (one-man); Galerie Arnaud, Paris, 1954; Rose Fried Gal., 1956-1958 (one-man, 1957); Mus. Contemp. A., Houston, Tex., 1958; AFA exh., Zabriskie Gal., 1958.

ELLIOTT, RUTH CASS—*Painter, Des., Gr.*

435 South Curson Ave., Los Angeles 36, Cal.

B. Los Angeles, Cal., July 22, 1891. *Studied*: Univ. California, Los A.; Los A. A. Center; Otis AI, and with Millard Sheets. *Member*: Women Painters of the West; Los Angeles AA; Pacific Palisades AA. *Exhibited*: 1955-58:— Orange Show, San Bernardino; Pasadena AI; Los Angeles City Hall; Los Angeles AA; Oakland A. Mus.; Henry A. Gal., Univ. Washington; Stockton, Cal.; Los A. Mus. A.; La Jolla A. Center (one-man); Sierra Madre Gal. (one-man); Santa Monica, Cal.; Bay Cities Jewish Community Center; A. Gld. of Am., Carmel, Cal.; Rotunda Gal., San F.; Bakersfield A. Gal.; Ojai A. Gal.; Ebell Cl., Los A., and many exhs. prior to 1955.

ELLIS, EDWIN CHARLES—*Educator, Gr.*

207 Broad St., Warrensburg, Mo.

B. Iowa City, Iowa, May 29, 1917. *Studied*: State Univ. Iowa, B.F.A., M.A., M.F.A. *Member*: AAUP; NEA; Missouri State T. Assn. *Position*: Hd., Dept. A., Central Missouri State College, Warrensburg, Mo.

ELLIS, FREMONT F.—*Painter*

Hacienda de San Sebastian, Santa Fe, N.M.

B. Virginia City, Mont., Oct. 2, 1897. *Studied*: ASL. *Awards*: prize, Los A. Mus. A., 1924; bronze med. & prize, Oakland A. Mus., 1953; purchase award, Springville (Utah) A. Mus., 1958. *Work*: Mural, S.S. America.

ELLIS, HARRIET A.—*Painter, Ser.*

158 Sherman St., Springfield 9, Mass.

B. Springfield, Mass., Apr. 4, 1886. *Studied*: PIASch; & with Charles Hawthorne, Ralph Johonnot, Cecelia Beaux, Robert Brackman, Walter Kamys, Mabel Welch. *Member*: A. Lg.; A. Gld., of Springfield. *Work*: Nat. Hist. Mus., Springfield; Arthur B. Talmadge Sch.; Springfield A. Lg. *Exhibited*: PAFA; Jones Lib., Amherst, Mass. (one-man); Mus. FA (1956-58 and prior), Pub. Lib., A. Lg., A. Gld., all of Springfield; G. W. V. Smith Mus.; Storrs Lib., Longmeadow.

ELLISON, J. MILFORD—*Teacher, P., L., Gr., C.*

2335 Chatsworth Blvd.; h. 3940 Gresham St., San Diego 9, Cal.

B. Sioux City, Iowa, Sept. 16, 1909. *Studied*: Chicago Acad. FA; Am. Acad. A., Chicago; Chouinard AI; San Diego State Col., A.B.; Univ. Colorado; Univ. So. California; Banff Sch. FA. *Member*: Laguna Beach AA; San Diego T. Assn.; Cal. T. Assn.; Nat. Edu. Assn.; La Jolla AA; San Diego A. Edu. Assn.; San Diego Men's AI; Foothills AA; San Diego Art Mart Assn. *Awards*: prizes, Army Spec. Services A. Exh., Paris, 1945; Banff Sch. FA, 1949; San Diego A. Gld., 1951; San Diego County Fair, 1951, 1954, 1955; San Diego Men's AI, 1954, 1955. *Work*: San Diego FA Gal.; San Diego Men's AI. *Exhibited*: AWS, 1946; San Diego Int. Exh., 1935; San Diego A. Gld., 1931-1946; San Diego FA Soc., 1944-1946, 1948-1952; La Jolla A. Center, 1945, 1952, 1954, 1955; Laguna Beach AA, 1946, 1948-1955; Oakland A. Gal., 1946; New Orleans AA, 1946; City of Paris Gal., San F., 1946; San Diego County Fair, 1954, 1955; Foothills AA, 1953-55. *Position*: Instr., Univ. Ext., Univ. California, 1950-55; Chm. A. Dept., Point Loma H.S., San Diego, Cal.; Instr. A., Cal.-Western Univ., San Diego, Cal.*

ELLSWORTH, CHERYL (LAWTHER)—*Sculptor*

10 Mitchell Place, New York 17, N.Y.

B. Dubuque, Iowa, July 1, 1911. *Studied*: Univ. Wisconsin, B.A. *Member*: NAWA; N.Y. Soc. Ceramic A. *Exhibited*: PAFA, 1949; NAWA, 1951; N.Y. Soc. Ceramic A., 1949-1951; Clay Cl.; Sculpture Center.*

ELLSWORTH, CLARENCE ARTHUR—*Illustrator, P.*

2017 Griffith Park Blvd., Los Angeles 39, Cal.

B. Holdrege, Neb., Sept. 23, 1885. *Member*: Los A. A. Cl.; The Westerners. *Work*: Southwest Mus., Los A. Cal. *Exhibited*: Southwest Mus., 1941, 1942, 1944; Charles W. Bowers Mus., Santa Ana, Cal., 1945 (all one-man); I., "Cottonwood Yarns," 1935; "Dickon Among the Lenape Indians," 1938; magazine covers & book illus. Illus., The Westerner's "Brand Book."

ELSHIN, JACOB ALEXANDER—*Painter, I., T.*

1529 East 105th Place, Seattle 55, Wash.

B. St. Petersburg, Russia, Dec. 30, 1892. *Studied*: in Russia, with Zemin of the Russian Imperial Acad. *Member*: Northwest Acad. A.; AEA; SAM. *Awards*: prizes, Northwest WC Soc., 1946; Studio Gal., Northwest annual, 1945, 1946, 1948; Western Wash. Fair Assn. A., Puyallup, 1933, 1935, 1940, 1946, 1951; Pacific Lutheran Col., 1953. *Work*: SAM; Seattle Pub. Sch.; Smithsonian Inst., Wash., D.C.; murals, USPO, Renton, Wash.; Univ. P.O., Seattle, Wash. *Exhibited*: San Diego FA Soc., 1941; Palace Legion Honor, 1946; Denver A. Mus., 1946, 1952, 1953, 1958; MMA, 1950; Pomona Fair, 1949; Univ. Nebraska, 1952; WMA, 1952; PAFA, 1953; Univ. Illinois, 1952; CAM, 1951; Oakland A. Mus., 1951, 1954; SFMA, 1955; Portland A. Mus., 1955; Vancouver (B.C.) A. Gal., 1958; annually: SAM, Spokane & Portland, Ore.; Sao Paulo, Brazil, 1955; one-man: SAM, 1934, 1943, 1956 (retrospective); Seligmann Gal., N.Y., 1955, 1958; Salpeter Gal., N.Y., 1951.

ELSKUS, ALBINAS—*Painter, Des., C.*

53-31 82nd St., Elmhurst 73, N.Y.

B. Kaunas, Lithuania, Aug. 21, 1926. *Studied*: Inst. A., Kaunas, Lithuania; Ecole des Arts et Metiers, Freiburg, Germany; Ecole des Beaux-Arts, Paris and with John von Wicht, N.Y. *Work*: stained glass, St. Sylvester's Church, Brooklyn, N.Y.; St. Anthony's Convent, N.Y.; Providence Hospital, Holyoke, Mass. *Exhibited*: Contemp. Religious Art Exh., Chicago, 1952; Knickerbocker A., 1954; Audubon A., 1955; Painters in Casein, 1955; New York City Center Gal., 1955, 1957, 1958; Art:USA, 1958; Riverside Mus., 1958; one-man: Picwood Gal., N.Y.; 2-man: Panoras Gal., 1955.

ELTONHEAD, FRANK—*Art Editor, E.*

Good Housekeeping Magazine, Hearst Magazine Bldg., 57th St. & 8th Ave., New York, N.Y.; h. Hatboro, Pa.

B. Philadelphia, Pa., Oct. 17, 1902. *Studied*: PMSchIA. *Member*: A. Dir., Phila., Pa.; New York, N.Y.; SI. *Position*: A. Ed., Ladies Home Journal, 1932-48; Cosmopolitan Magazine, 1948-52; Consulting A. Dir., Bonnier Publ., Stockholm, Sweden, 1953; A. Ed., Good Housekeeping Magazine, 1954-55; Faculty memb., Phila. Mus. Sch., Philadelphia, Pa.; A. Dir., Triangle Publication TV Guide, Radnor, Pa., 1956-58.

ELY, FANNY G.—*Painter*

121 East 91st St., New York 28, N.Y.

B. New York, N.Y. *Studied*: with William Robinson, Cullen Yates, Frank DuMond. *Member*: NAC; All. A. Am.; Long Island AA; AAPL; Buck Hill AA. *Exhibited*: Lyme AA; AAPL; NAC; NAD; Miami, Fla.; Ogunquit A. Center; Long Island AA; Westchester AA; and others.

ELY, WOLCOTT—*Painter*

General Delivery, Taos, N.M.; h. 100 West 20th St., Hutchinson, Kans.

B. Hutchinson, Kans., Jan. 1, 1923. *Studied*: Kansas City AI; Univ. Illinois, B.S.; Inst. Des., Chicago; Northwestern Univ.; Colorado Springs FA Center. *Member*: CAA. *Awards*: prizes, Wichita A. Mus. *Work*: Wichita A. Mus. *Exhibited*: William Rockhill Nelson Gal. A., 1954; Wichita A. Mus., 1954; Colorado Springs, 1955; Denver A. Mus., 1955; Mus. of New Mexico, Santa Fe, 1955-1958; MMoA, 1956; Univ. Utah, 1957. *Position*: Instr., Taos Inst. Creative Orientation, 1958.

EMEREE, BERLA IONE (Mrs. William Henry Emery)— *Painter, T., C., L.*

2417 Louisville St. & Scenic Dr., El Paso, Tex.

B. Wichita, Kan., Aug. 7, 1899. *Studied*: San Antonio A. Sch.; & with Frank Linton, Jose Arpa, Xavier Gonzales. *Awards*: prize, Boerne, Tex. *Work*: Bowie H.S., El Paso, Tex.; Officer's Cl., Biggs Field, Ft. Bliss, Tex. *Exhibited*: Int. Mus., El Paso, 1944, 1945; Texas FA Assn., 1946; Recreation Center, USO Cl., El Paso, 1946. *Lectures*: Art of Today. *Position*: Dir., Berla Ione Emeree School of Painting, El Paso, Tex., 1924- .*

EMERSON, ARTHUR WEBSTER—*Painter, Gr., W.*

842 Ocean View Dr., Honolulu 16, Hawaii

B. Honolulu, Hawaii, Dec. 5, 1885. *Studied*: Stanford Univ.; ASL; T. Col., Columbia Univ., B.S.; and with John C. Johansen, Charles Hawthorne, E. A. Webster. *Member*: Assn. Honolulu A. *Awards*: prizes, Honolulu A. Soc., 1932; Honolulu Acad. A., 1935. *Work*: mural, Honolulu Sch. for Deaf and Blind; Lib. of Hawaii, Honolulu; port., Capitol, Territory of Hawaii. *Exhibited*: PAFA; N.Y. WC Cl.; AWS; NAC; Assn. Honolulu A.; WFNY 1939.

EMERSON, EDITH—*Painter, I., L., W., Mus. Cur., T.*

Woodmere Art Gallery, 9201 Germantown Ave. (18); h. St. George's Rd., Philadelphia 19, Pa.

B. Oxford, Ohio. *Studied*: AIC; PAFA; & with Cecilia Beaux, Hugh Breckenridge, Emil Carlsen, Violet Oakley, Henry McCarter. *Member*: NSMP; Phila. WC Cl.; F., PAFA; Am. Soc. Bookplate Collectors & Designers. *Awards*: F., PAFA; Cresson traveling scholarships, PAFA, 1914, 1915; prizes, PAFA, 1919; Bryn Mawr Col., 1920. *Work*: murals, Plays & Players Theatre, Phila.; Chapel, Sisters of St. Joseph Convent; Church of the Nativity of the Blessed Virgin, Phila., Pa.; Temple Keneseth Israel, Elkins Park, Pa.; Haverford Prep Sch., Pa.; Bryn Mawr Col.; Vanderpoel Coll.; Army & Navy triptychs; Woodmere A. Gal. *Exhibited*: PAFA, 1916-1957; CGA, 1924; AIC; NAD; Newport AA, 1941; PMA; Hartford Atheneum; Carnegie Inst.; Florence, Italy; Conn. Acad. FA, 1938; Arch L.; Woodmere A. Gal., 1940-1958; Phila. Pr. Cl.; Phila. A. All. Illus., "The Song of Roland," 1938; "The Pageant of India's History," 1948. *Contributor to*: Art magazines & newspapers. *Lectures*: History of Art. *Position*: Instr. A., Agnes Irwin Sch., 1916-27; PMSchIA, 1929-36; Cur., Woodmere A. Gal., 1946- ; all in Philadelphia, Pa.; Chm., Regional Council of Community Art Centers (13 groups, 5000 members), 1950- . Chm., Regional Groups, Philadelphia A. Festival, 1959.

EMERSON, STERLING DEAL—*Museum Director*

Shelburne Museum, Inc., Shelburne, Vt.

B. St. Albans, Vt., May 21, 1917. *Studied*: Champlain College. *Member*: Nat. Trust for Historic Preservation in the U.S.; Early Am. Industries Assn. (Dir.); Vermont Hist. Soc.; Green Mountain Folklore Soc.; Newcomen Soc. in North America; AAMus.; New York Vermont Interstate Commission—Historic Sites. *Lectures*: museum collections; Historical meetings throughout New England. *Dir.* of cataloguing Shelburne Mus. collections; with Staff assembled exhibitions of the collections. *Position*: Dir., Shelburne Museum, Shelburne, Vt.

EMERSON, SYBIL (DAVIS)— *Painter, I., E., W., Des., C.*

809 Blain St., McMinnville, Ore.

B. Worcester, Mass. *Studied*: Ohio State Univ., B.A., B.Sc.; ASL, and in Paris. *Member*: Eastern AA; Nat. A. Edu. Assn.; Com. on A. Edu. *Exhibited*: Albany Inst. Hist. & A., 1943, 1947, 1949; San F. AA, 1947; Albany Pr. Cl., 1949; PAFA, 1949; Phila. Pr. Cl., 1951; Cal. Col. A. & Crafts, 1955. *Author*, I., "Jacques at the Window," 1936; "Pigeon House Inn," 1939; "Design—A Creative Approach," 1953. *Des.* & executed the dossal for the Helen Eakin Eisenhower Mem. Chapel, Pennsylvania State Univ. *Lectures*: Problems in Teaching Design. *Position*: Assoc. Prof., A. Edu., Pennsylvania State Univ., University Park, Pa., 1942-56; Prof. Emerita, 1956- .

EMERY, MRS. WILLIAM HENRY. *See Emeree, Berla Ione*

EMMERICH, IRENE HILLEBRAND—*Painter, Comm. A.*

118 Siwanoy Blvd., Tuckahoe, N.Y.

B. New York, N.Y., 1906. *Studied*: CUASch.; Traphagen Sch. Fashion; ASL. *Member*: Hudson Valley AA; AAPL; Yonkers AA; Mamaroneck A. Gld. *Awards*: prizes, Crestwood Women's Cl., 1949, 1950, 1952; Hudson Valley AA, 1950; Bronxville Women's Cl., 1953, 1954, 1956; Westchester Women's Cl., 1955, 1956; Fed. Women's Cl., 1956. *Exhibited*: White Plains, N.Y., 1957 (one-man).

EMPIE, HAL H.—*Cartoonist, I., P., T., W., L.*

Duncan, Ariz.

B. Safford, Ariz., Mar. 26, 1909. *Studied*: with Frederic Taubes. *Member*: El Paso Sketch Cl.; Arizona A. Gld. *Award*: prize, Beaumont (Tex.) A. Mus., 1955. *Work*: panels, Methodist Church, Duncan, Ariz.; Duncan Sch.; Eastern Ariz. Jr. Col. *Exhibited*: MMoA; Pepsi-Cola, 1944, 1945; Cal. WC Soc., 1945; El Paso, Tex.; Polish Embassy; one-man: Falls Civic A. Center, Cuyahoga Falls, Ohio; Canton AI; Massillon, Ohio. *Contributor* illus., cartoons, to Western magazines; cover and illus., to Horse Lovers magazine.

ENGEL, GEORGE LESLIE—*Painter, I., C.*

B. A. Ruegnitz Laboratories; h. 2088 Lincoln Ave., Dubuque, Iowa

B. Baltimore, Md., June 5, 1911. *Studied*: Maryland Inst.; Vocational Sch., Balt. *Awards*: med., Maryland Inst., 1936; prize, Maryland Alumni Assn., 1937. *Work*: U.S. Govt.; Maryland Inst. Illus. in Army manuals, text books, and training publications. *Exhibited*: Washington County Mus. FA, 1934; BMA, 1936, 1937, 1939 (one-man), 1946, 1948, 1950; VMFA, 1938; PAFA, 1939; Galena, Ill.; Dubuque, Ill.; Elkader, Ill.; CGA, 1939, 1940. *Position*: Instr. A., Maryland Inst., 1935-40, 1948-53; Asst. A., I., U.S. Army, 1940-43; A., Des., U.S. Army, 1946; Adv. Dir., A., B. A. Ruegnitz Laboratories, Dubuque, 1953-58; Chm. Exh. Com., Dubuque AA, 1956-58.

ENGEL, HARRY—*Painter, E. L.*

Indiana University, Bloomington, Ind.

B. Roumania, June 13, 1901. *Studied*: Notre Dame Univ., A.B.; Columbia Univ., and in Paris, with Maurice Denis. *Member*: Indiana A. Cl.; Assoc. Am. A. Cl.; CAA. *Awards*: Carnegie F., 1929; prizes, Hoosier Salon, 1931, 1950; Indiana A. Cl., 1931, 1945, 1946; Milwaukee AI, 1946; Audubon A.; John Herron AI, 1951, 1952, 1954, 1955-1958. *Work*: Indiana Univ. Union Bldg., Indiana Univ. Union Club; John Herron AI. *Exhibited*: PAFA, 1939, 1950, 1952; AIC, 1940; Detroit Inst. A., 1936; Milwaukee AI, 1946; John Herron AI, 1933 (one-man), 1951, 1952; Audubon A., 1950, 1952; WMAA, 1948-1951; Indiana A., 1948-1952; Provincetown AA, 1948-1952, 1955; Franz Bader Gal., Wash., D.C., 1958 (one-man); Provincetown A. Festival, 1958; retrospective exh., Indiana Univ., 1955. *Position*: Prof. Painting & Drawing, Indiana Univ., Bloomington, Ind.

ENGEL, MICHAEL M., Sr.—*Art Publicist, W., L., I.*

460 West 34th St., 5th floor, New York, N.Y.

B. Hungary, Apr. 22, 1894. *Studied*: CUASch., with Dielman, Cedarstrom, Harting. *Member*: Nat. Assn. Pub. Relations Counsel; Am. Pub. Rel. Soc.; Publicity Cl.; Life F.,

Royal Soc. A., England; Audubon A. (Founder); A. Gld.; Eastern AA; Lancaster County AA (Life). *Awards*: Med., Mark Twain Centennial Assn., 1935; Hon. degree, LL.D., Fla. Southern Col., 1952, Hon. Chancellor, 1952. I., "Three Centuries Delaware"; & numerous children's books. Contributor to: Art Digest, Design, Texas Artist, Western Artist, Southern Artist magazines. Lectures: Historical & art subjects. *Position*: Nat. Vice-Chm., Nat. A. Week, AAPL, N.Y., 1935-36; Dir. A. Lecture Bureau, Isochromatic Exh., 1936-37; Aqua-Chromatic Exh., 1937-38; Miniature Palette Exh., Grumbacher Research Lab., 1938-39; A. Publicity Advisor, Fla. Int. Exh., 1952. Organized perm. Coll. Fine Arts, Fla. Southern Col., 1951.

ENGEL, MICHAEL (MARTIN) II—
Painter, Des., Lith., W.
22 Lee St., Huntington, L.I., N.Y.

B. New York, N.Y., Mar. 20, 1919. *Studied*: ASL. *Member*: P. & S. Soc. of New Jersey; Huntington (L.I.) A. Lg.; ASL; Audubon A. *Work*: Antioch Col.; Fla. Southern Col. *Exhibited*: Audubon A., annually; Newhouse Gal.; Huntington A. Lg. *Position*: Vice-Pres. (1958-59), Historian, Audubon A., New York, N.Y.; Awards Com. & Public Relations Com., Audubon A., New York, N.Y.

ENGEL, WILHELMINA (Mrs.)—Painter, T.
1111 Rutledge St., Madison, Wis.

B. Middleton, Wis., July 1, 1871. *Studied*: AIC, with Frederic Fursman; Colt Sch. A., and in Europe. *Member*: Madison A. Gld.

ENGLAND, PAUL—Painter, S., Ser., Cr., W.
91 Christopher St., New York 14, N.Y.; also, 1181 North Boston Ave., Tulsa, Okla.

B. Hugo, Okla., Jan. 12, 1918. *Studied*: Univ. Tulsa; Carnegie Inst., A.B.; ASL, with George Grosz, William Zorach, Cameron Booth, Morris Kantor, Jose de Creeft, and in Paris, with Ossip Zadkine. *Member*: AEA; ASL. *Awards*: Philbrook A. Center, 1957, 1958; Joslyn A. Mus., 1957. *Exhibited*: ACA Gal., 1945, 1946; PAFA, 1947, 1952, 1953; Contemporary A. Gal., 1944-1946; Philbrook A. Center, 1943-1958; one-man: Le Centre d'Art, Port-au-Prince, Haiti, 1947; RoKo Gal., 1948; Galerie Creuze, Paris, 1949; Bodley Gal., 1950; Hugo Gal., 1951; La Galeria, Torremolinos, Spain, 1955; Grand Central Moderns, N.Y., 1955; Philbrook A. Center, 1958. *Work*: Williams Col. A. Mus.; Philbrook A. Center; Joslyn Mus. A. Contributor to New Yorker magazine. *Position*: A. Cr., France-Amerique, New York, N.Y., 1955-57.

ENGLANDER, GERTRUD—Craftsman, T.
84-51 Beverly Rd., Kew Gardens 15, N.Y.

B. Germany. *Studied*: Cologne, Germany; Craft Students Lg., N.Y.; N.Y. Univ. *Member*: N.Y. Soc. Craftsmen; N.Y. Soc. Ceramic A. *Work*: Bertha Schaefer Gal.; America House; Rosenthal-Schwadron, New York, N.Y. *Exhibited*: N.Y.Soc. Craftsmen, 1950-1955; N.Y. Soc. Ceramic A., 1950-1955. *Position*: Instr. Ceramics, Craft Students League, N.Y., 1952- .*

ENGLE, ROBERT—Educator
Lyon Art Hall, Ohio Wesleyan University, Delaware, Ohio*

ENRIGHT, WALTER J.—Writer, Cart., I.
Delray Beach, Fla.

B. Chicago, Ill. *Studied*: AIC; Armour Inst., Chicago. *Member*: SI. *Awards*: med., Freedom Fnd., 1950, 1951. Author, I., "Al Alligator"; "Sailor Jim's Cave."

ENSER, GEORGE—Designer, T., L., I.
110 Park Ave., Tuckahoe 7, N.Y.

B. New York, N.Y., Nov. 16, 1889. *Studied*: Columbia Univ.; CUASch.; Mechanics Inst. *Work*: Alabama State Capitol; Waldorf-Astoria Hotel, N.Y.; West Va. State Capitol; U.S. Supreme Court, Wash., D.C.; Chamber of Commerce, Wash., D.C.; in private homes, and work in Cuba and Brazil. Articles & lectures on Good Furniture & Decorations; Interior Architecture. *Position*: Instr., Furniture Design, N.Y. Evening H.S. (retired). Des. interiors, furniture, radio & television installations.

ENTE, LILY (Mrs.)—Sculptor, Et., T.
400 Riverside Drive, New York 25, N.Y.

B. Ukraine, May 6, 1905. *Studied*: in Europe. *Member*: NAWA; AEA; Silvermine Gld. A.; Contemp. A.; Brooklyn Soc. A.; P. & S. Soc. of New Jersey; N.Y.Soc. Women A. *Awards*: BM, 1954; NAWA, 1953; medal, P. & S. Soc. of New Jersey. *Exhibited*: NAWA; BM; N.Y. Soc. Women A.; P. & S. Soc. of New Jersey, and others.

ENTENMANN, RAYMOND TAYLOR—
Museum Curator, E., L.
Pennsylvania Academy of the Fine Arts, Broad & Cherry Sts. (2); h. 1708 De Lancey Place, Philadelphia 3, Pa.

B. Philadelphia, Pa., Dec. 7, 1920. *Studied*: Pa. State Univ.; Harvard Univ., M.A., and Master of City Planning. *Member*: Am. Inst. Planners; AFA; CAA. *Positions*: Instr., Syracuse Univ., 1948-51; Consultant in City Planning & Landscape Arch., 1951-53; Cur. of Schools, Pennsylvania Academy of the Fine Arts, Philadelphia, Pa., 1953- .

ENTERS, ANGNA—Writer, P., I., Gr., S., Cart.
c/o Newhouse Galleries, 15 East 57th St., New York, N.Y.

B. New York, N.Y., Apr. 28, 1907. *Studied*: in U.S., Europe, Greece, Egypt, Near East. *Awards*: Guggenheim F., 1934, 1935. *Work*: MMA; Honolulu Acad. A.; mural, Penthouse Theatre, Univ. Washington. *Exhibited*: Newhouse Gal., 1933-1958 (20th successive exh. at Newhouse Gal., 1958); Warren Gal., London, England; Foyle Gal., London, 1956; MMA, 1943; Honolulu Acad. A.; Rochester Mem. A. Gal.; WMA; Minneapolis Inst. A.; Detroit Inst. A.; R.I. Sch. Des.; SFMA; Wadsworth Atheneum; Renaissance Soc., Univ. Chicago; BMA; Bloomington (Ill.) A. Mus.; Los A. Mus. A.; Colorado Springs FA Center; Denver A. Mus.; Albany Inst. Hist. & A.; Pasadena AI; Santa Barbara, Mus. A.; AGAA; Los A. Mus. A., 1945; AIC, 1949; Mus. FA of Houston, 1950; Brook A. Gal., London, England, 1950; 10th London season of 2 weeks repertory of solo mime theatre, 1956; MModA, 1933, 1944; AIC, 1939-1941. Author, I., "First Person Plural," 1937; "Love Possessed Juana," 1939; "Silly Girl," 1944; "Among the Daughters," 1955; "Artist's Life," 1958; I., "Best American Short Stories of 1945." Contributor to: Art & theatre publications, on painting & arts. Represented Am. Theatre, Int. Berlin A. Festival, 1951. Des. settings & costumes and directed Garcia Lorca's "Yerma," presented to date at Denver, Colo., 1958 and Ithaca Col., N.Y., 1958.

EPPENS, WILLIAM H.—Painter, Des., Gr., I., Comm.
7010 Oglesby Ave., Chicago 49, Ill.

B. Lincoln, Neb., Dec. 25, 1885. *Studied*: AIC; Chicago Acad. FA. *Member*: Chicago P. & S.; All-Illinois Soc. FA. *Work*: Vanderpoel Coll.; Univ. Church, Chicago Pub. Lib. Des., testimonials and scrolls in illuminated manuscript technique. *Exhibited*: AIC; Chicago P. & S., 1945, 1955; All-Illinois Soc. FA, 1927-1955; one-man and group exhs. regularly.*

EPPENSTEINER, JOHN J(OSEPH)—Painter, I.
722 Chestnut St.; h. 3831 Nebraska Ave., St. Louis 18, Mo.

B. St. Louis, Mo., Feb. 14, 1893. *Studied*: St. Louis Sch. FA, Washington Univ. *Awards*: prizes, St. Louis A. Gld., 1923, 1924, 1926, 1929, 1930, 1932; Kansas City AI, 1927, 1929, 1932 (incl. 3 medals); St. Louis Post Dispatch, 1929; Christian Herald, 1929; poster awards and medals, 1944, 1949, 1952-1957; Chicago A. Dir. Cl., 1946, 1952-1954. *Exhibited*: A. Dir. Cl., Chicago, 1946, 1952-1956; PAFA; 1926, 1927; Toledo Mus. A., 1927; Kansas City AI, 1928, 1929, 1931, 1932; St. Louis A. Lg., 1921, 1923, 1928, 1930, 1932; St. Louis A. Gld., 1921, 1923, 1924, 1926, 1928, 1930, 1932; CAM, 1922-1924, 1927, 1928, 1931. I., Portfolio of Drawings: "Domestic Animal Studies in the Modern Manner," 1930.

EPPING, FRANC (DOROTHY)—Sculptor, T.
75 Cliffwood St., Lenox, Mass.

B. Providence, R.I., June 27, 1910. *Studied*: Otis AI, Los Angeles; Corcoran Gal. A., Wash., D.C.; Acad. Fine Arts, Munich, Germany, with Joseph Wackerle and Bernhard Bleeker. *Member*: S. Gld.; Fed. Mod. P. & S. *Awards*:

prizes, Acad. FA Munich, Germany, 1933; Conn. Acad. FA, 1954; Silvermine Gld. A., 1955. *Work*: Washington Col.; Nebraska AA; Berea Col.; High Mus. A., Atlanta, Ga.; Public Bldgs. Admin., Wash., D.C.; USPO, Alabama City, Ala.; Oakmont, Pa. *Exhibited*: Los A. Mus. A., 1930., 1952; NGA, 1931; PC, 1932; CGA, 1937; Smithsonian Inst., 1937; Lehigh Univ., 1938; AIC, 1938, 1940, 1941, 1943; WMAA, 1938, 1939; MModA, 1939-1944; Grand Rapids A. Gal., 1940; Smith Col., 1940; Rochester Mem. A. Gal., 1941; AFA traveling exh., 1941; MMA, 1942; Fairmont Park, Pa., 1940, 1949; PAFA, 1938-1940, 1953; Acad. FA, Hartford, Conn., 1954-1956; G.W.V. Smith Mus. A., Springfield, Mass., 1952, 1955; Silvermine Gld. A., 1954-1956; Deerfield Acad., 1956; Providence A. Cl., 1958; S. Gld., since 1939; Fed. Mod. P. & S., 1939-1958; Berkshire Mus. A.; Bonestell Gal., N.Y., 1940; Knoedler Gal., 1941; Seligmann Gal., 1943. *Positions*: Instr., S., Berkshire Mus., 1942-48; Fndr., Dir., Sculpture Workshop, Lenox, Mass., 1948- .

EPPINK, HELEN B. (Mrs. N. R.)—Painter, Des.
912 Union St., Emporia, Kans.

B. Springfield, Ohio, Aug. 19, 1910. *Studied*: Cleveland Sch. A.; John Huntington Polytechnic Inst. *Member*: Kansas State A. T. Assn.; Kansas Fed. A.; Kansas Soc. A. *Awards*: CMA, 1933, 1935; Kansas City AI, 1939; Prairie WC Painters, 1954; Wichita, 1956. *Work*: Kansas Fed. Women's Cl; Wichita A. Mus. *Exhibited*: Oklahoma A. Center, 1940; CMA, 1932-1938; Kansas City AI, 1939, 1940, 1942; Butler AI, 1941; Kansas A., 1949, 1951, 1952; Prairie WC Soc., 1947-1949, 1953, 1954; Kansas Printmakers, 1949; Derby, England, 1948; Kansas Painters, 1949, 1951, 1952, 1956, 1958; Nelson Gal. A., 1949; Mulvane Mus. A. (2-man), 1954; Mid-Am. A., 1954, 1955; Wichita, Kans., 1955; Hutchinson AA, 1955; Topeka A. Gld., 1953, 1955, 1956; Manhattan, Kans., 1952, 1954-1956; Prairie WC Painters, 1954; Kansas State T. Col., 1957 (one-man); Joslyn A. Mus., 1956. *Position*: Instr. A., Ottawa Univ., Ottawa, Kans., 1948-51; Instr., A. Dept., College of Emporia, Kans., 1944-48, 1949-53; Kansas State T. Col., 1951, 1952.

EPPINK, NORMAN R.—Painter, Gr., L., E.
912 Union Ave., Emporia, Kans.

B. Cleveland, Ohio, July 29, 1906. *Studied*: Cleveland Sch. A., B.E.A.; John Huntington Polytechnic Inst.; Western Reserve Univ., M.A. *Member*: Am. Assn. Univ. Prof.; Kansas State A. T. Assn.; Kansas Fed. A.; Kansas Soc. A. *Awards*: CMA, 1931, 1932, 1934, 1935, 1936, 1953-1955; Kansas City AI, 1938; Kans.Pr.M., 1947; Manhattan, Kans., 1952; Kansas Painters, Pittsburgh, 1949, 1951, 1952; Wichita, 1955; Prairie WC Painters, 1954; Hutchinson AA, 1955; Topeka A. Gld., 1953, 1955, 1956. *Work*: CMA; Cleveland Mun. Coll.; Mansfield (Ohio) Pub. Lib.; Kansas Fed. Women's Cl.; Emporia Women's City Cl.; Manhattan State Col.; Pittsburg State T. Col.; Ft. Scott H.S.; Wichita A. Mus. *Exhibited*: Oklahoma A. Center, 1940; AFA traveling exh., 1941; CMA, 1927, 1939, 1942; Kansas City AI, 1938-1942; Butler AI, 1941; Topeka, 1942 (one-man); Wichita A., 1944 (one-man), 1947; Pittsburg, Kans., 1949, 1951, 1952; Manhattan, Kans., 1952, 1954, 1956; Kansas Pr. M., 1947; Prairie WC Soc., 1947, 1948; Mulvane Mus., 1947, 1951, 1954 (2-man); Kansas Fed. A., 1948, 1949; Denver A. Mus., 1953, 1955; Walker A. Center, 1954; CM, 1953; Derby, England, 1948; Nelson Gal. A., 1949; Mid-Am. A., 1951, 1955; Joslyn A. Mus., 1956; SAGA, 1954, 1955. *Lectures*: Prints and Printmaking. *Position*: Prof. A., Hd. Dept., Kansas State T. Col., Emporia, Kans., 1937- .

ERDMANN, RICHARD F.—Portrait Painter
360 East Main St., Chillicothe, Ohio

B. Feb. 12, 1894. *Studied*: ASL, with Luks, DuMond, Rittenberg; NAD, with Curran; Cincinnati A. Acad., with Herman Wessel, James R. Hopkins, John Weis, and others. *Awards*: prizes, Chillicothe, Ohio; Ohio State Fair, Columbus. *Exhibited*: Mus. of New Mexico, Santa Fé; Myles Standish Gal., Boston; Columbus A. Mus.; Dedham, Mass.; Little A. Gal., New York; White Plains, N.Y.; Chillicothe Hist. Mus.

ERESCH, JOSIE—Lithographer, Et., P., W., I., L., C.
502 North Campbell St., Beloit, Kan.

B. Beloit, Kan., Apr. 13, 1894. *Studied*: N.Y. Sch. F. & App. A.; Fed. Sch. A.; St. Mary-of-the-Woods Col.; in Japan & China; & with Birger Sandzen, Caroline Arming-

ton. *Member*: Kansas Authors Cl.; Lg. Am. Pen Women; Prairie Pr. M.; Ex Libris Soc., Austria. *Awards*: prizes, Lg. Am. Pen Women, 1937, 1938. *Exhibited*: Lg. Am. Pen Women; Kansas City AI; Wichita AA. Author, I., "Elegant Amusement (Flower Arrangement)," 1937; "Come Up and See My Etchings," 1938. Contributor to: Kansas Magazine. Lectures: Etching; Prints and Printmaking.

ERICKSON, MRS. EVARTS C. See Doub, Janet Ann

ERICKSON, MRS. LENORE ALT. See Erik-Alt, Lenore

ERICSON, BEATRICE—Painter
14 Watkins Ave., Middletown, N.Y.

B. Paris, France, Oct. 26, 1909. *Studied*: with Morris Davidson. *Member*: Dutchess AA; Woodstock AA; Provincetown AA; Creative Contemporaries. *Exhibited*: Provincetown AA, 1952-1955; Contemporary A. Gal., N.Y., 1954, 1955; City Center, N.Y., 1956, 1958; Caravan Gal., N.Y., 1953; Dutchess AA, 1953-1958; Albany Inst. Hist. & Art, 1952-1955; Woodstock AA, 1955; Parnassus Gal., 1953, 1954; Berkshire Mus., 1953; Knickerbocker A., 1954; one-man: Albany Inst. Hist. & Art, 1955; Panoras Gal., N.Y., 1957.

ERICSON, ERIC—Cartoonist
144 East 45th St., New York 17, N.Y.; h. 1801 Albany Ave., Brooklyn 10, N.Y.

B. East Orange, N.J., Feb. 14, 1914. *Studied*: PIASch., with Maitland Graves; ASL, with William McNulty, Robert Hale. *Member*: SI; Cart. Soc.; Am. Television Soc. Contributor to: New Yorker, Collier's, Esquire, & other national magazines. Lectures: Cartooning. *Position*: Syndicate cart. with King Features; radio & television writer.†

ERICSON, ERNEST—Illustrator, Des., P., E.
Kenyon & Eckhardt, 247 Park Ave.; h. 510 East 85th St., New York, N.Y.

B. Boston, Mass. *Studied*: BMFASch.; AIC; ASL; Grande Chaumiere, Paris. *Member*: SI. *Exhibited*: Detroit Inst. A.; N.Y. WC Soc.; PAFA; SI. *Position*: Instr., Adv. A., Workshop Sch. Adv. A., 1947-49; Instr., Adv. Layout & Des. Dept., School of Visual Arts, New York, N.Y., 1956- ; Television A. Dir., Kenyon & Eckhardt, New York, N.Y., 1955- .

ERIK-ALT, LENORE (Mrs. Lenore Alt Erickson)—Painter, Gr., S., T., L.
196A Connecticut St., San Francisco, Cal.

B. Cadillac, Mich., June 21, 1910. *Studied*: AIC, with Boris Anisfeld. *Member*: AEA; Minnesota AA. *Work*: Veteran's Hospital, Carville, La.; St. Charles Sch. for Boys, Maywood, Ill. *Exhibited*: AIC, 1936, 1941; Twin City Exh., St. Paul, 1942-1945, 1952; Twin City Exh., Minneapolis, 1945, 1949-1951; Detroit Inst. A., 1935, 1938; Paul Theobold's, Chicago, 1942 (one-man, ceramics); Nat. WC Exh., Wash., D.C., 1941; one-man: Walker A. Center, 1951, 1953; St. Catherine's Col., 1952; N.Y. State Col., New Paltz, N.Y., 1953; Harriet Hanley Gal., Minneapolis, 1953; Walnut Creek, Cal., 1954; Radio Station KPFA, Berkeley, Cal. *Position*: Asst. Prof. A., Macalester Col., St. Paul, Minn., 1947-53; Lecturer, Instr., Univ. California, Design Dept., Berkeley, Cal., 1955.*

ERLANGER, ELIZABETH N.—Painter, Lith., T.
156 West 86th St., New York 24, N.Y.

B. Baltimore, Md., Oct. 23, 1901. *Studied*: with Ralph M. Pearson, Umberto Romano, Jean Liberte, Hans Hofmann. *Member*: NAWA; Audubon A.; N.Y. Soc. Women A.; Nat. Soc. Painters in Casein. *Awards*: prizes, NAWA, 1952, 1953, 1956; Brooklyn Soc. A., 1953, 1955, 1958; Village A. Center, 1953, 1955, 1956. *Work*: Fla. Southern Col.; Univ. Maine; Colby Col.; N.Y. Pub. Lib.; Evansville (Ind.) Mus. A., and in private colls. *Exhibited*: NAWA, 1946-1958; Audubon A., 1949-1958; Brooklyn Soc. A., 1950-1958; Nat. Soc. Painters in Casein, 1953-1958; Wash. Pr. M., 1958; Phila. Pr. Cl.; Pasadena A. Mus.; Delgado Mus. A.; BM; one-man: Mus. New Mexico, 1948; New York, N.Y. (4), 1948, 1949, 1951, 1957; Three Arts Gal., Poughkeepsie, N.Y., 1949; Goshen (N.Y.) Pub. Lib., 1953; Univ. Maine, 1955; Traveling exhs., U.S. and Europe; NAWA, 1953-1958; Brooklyn Soc. A., 1950-1958; and others. *Positions*: Vice-Pres., NAWA; Brooklyn Soc. A.; Chm. Public Relations, Audubon A.; Memb. Exec. Bd., Nat. Soc. Painters in Casein; Delegate to Intl. Organization of Plastic Arts. Lectures to women's clubs and art associations. Private instruction since 1948.

ERNST, JAMES—Painter, E., L.
110 Riverside Dr., New York 24, N.Y.

B. New York, N.Y., Aug. 5, 1916. *Studied*: PIASch.; Grand Central A. Sch. *Member*: CAA; A. Gld.; Hudson Soc. Indp. A.; Adult Edu. Assn. of U.S.; Alumni Assn., Pratt Inst. *Exhibited*: AWS, 1953-1955; Hudson Valley AA, 1947; Hudson Soc. Indp. A., 1947, 1948; Faculty Exh., City Col., N.Y., 1950-1956; one-man: Barzansky Gal., 1950-1958; Tedesco Gal., Paris, France, 1952, 1955; Smith Gal., Charlotte Amalie, St. Thomas, V.I., 1953. Lectures and demonstrations, City Col. and N.Y.Pub. Lib. *Position*: Asst. Supv. N.Y.Pub. Lib. A. Project, New York, N.Y., 1951-1956, Assoc. Supv., 1957-58; Instr., City College of New York, 1950-58; Staff A., Batten, Barton, Durstine & Osborn, N.Y., 1951-58.

ERNST, JIMMY—Painter
7 Harstrom Place, Rowayton, Conn.

B. Cologne, Germany, June 24, 1920. *Studied*: Cologne-Lindenthal Real-Gymnasium; Altona A. & Crafts Sch. *Awards*: prizes, Norman Wait Harris award, AIC, 1954; Creative Arts award, Brandeis Univ., 1957. *Work*: MMA; WMAA; BM; Wadsworth Atheneum; AIC; Solomon Guggenheim Mus. A.; Albright A. Gal.; Toledo Mus. A.; Mus. of FA, Houston; VMFA; Toronto (Canada) A. Mus.; Munson-Williams-Proctor Inst.; Univ. Colorado; Washington Univ.; Lehigh Univ.; Cranbrook Acad. A.; Am. Acad. A. & Lets.; Pasadena A. Mus.; Exec. dining room, G.M. Tech. Center, 1956; painting, Abbott Laboratories, 1955; painting, Fortune Magazine, 1955; sculpture, N.B.C. Producer's Showcase, 1954; murals: USS Adams, 1956; Continental Bank, Lincoln, Neb., 1958-59. *Exhibited*: AIC, 1954, 1956; BM, 1952-1956; Univ. Illinois, 1952, 1953, 1957; WMAA, 1953-1958; PAFA, 1953, 1955, 1957; Carnegie Inst., 1955; Univ. Nebraska, 1953-1957; Venice Biennale, 1956; American Painting, Japan, 1955; American Drawing, Europe, 1954; American Bldg., Brussels World Fair, 1958. Lectures: Contemporary Art. *Positions*: Visiting Artist, Univ. Colorado, 1954, 1956; Mus. FA, Houston, Tex., 1956; Asst. Prof., Dept. Art, Brooklyn College, 1951- .

ERSEK, JOSEPH FRANCIS—Painter, Indst. Des.
10706 Manor Ave., Cleveland 4, Ohio

B. Cleveland, Ohio, Sept. 10, 1912. *Studied*: John Huntington Polytechnic Inst.; ASL, and with Grant Wood. *Awards*: prize, CMA. *Work*: murals and designs executed for: Cleveland Metropolitan Housing Bldg.; Sunny Acres Inst.; John Hay H.S.; Am. Bowling Congress; Super Market Inst.; Kolcast Corp.; Am. Mining Congress; Nat. Railroad Show; Am. Red Cross; United Auto Works CIO; Am. Fed. Churches; Capital Airlines; Nat. Air Races Assn.; Interlake Yachting Assn.; Thompson Products. *Position*: Dir., Industrial Des., United Tube Corp.*

ESCHMANN, JEAN CHARLES—Craftsman
11000 Euclid Ave., Cleveland 6, Ohio; h. RFD #2, Willoughby, Ohio

B. Basel, Switzerland, Jan. 23, 1896. *Studied*: in Switzerland. *Member*: Bookworkers of Am. *Awards*: prize, CMA, 1936-1939; med., Paris Exp., 1937. *Exhibited*: Paris Exp., 1937; GGE, 1939; CMA, 1936-1939; Int. Exh. Mod. Bookbinding, N.Y., 1935. *Position*: Instr., Bookbinding, Cranbrook Acad. A., 1929-1933; Armed Forces Medical Lib., 1943-55 (restoring rare book coll.); Cleveland Medical Lib., at present.

ESHERICK, WHARTON—Sculptor, Des., C., Gr.
Paoli, Pa.

B. Philadelphia, Pa., July 15, 1887. *Studied*: PMSchA.; PAFA. *Member*: AEA. *Awards*: prizes, PAFA, 1951; PMSchA., 1957; one of eleven winners in Intl. Sculpture Comp., for "The Unknown Political Prisoner" (awarded 2 prizes); gold medal, Arch. Lg., 1954. *Work*: PAFA; WMAA; PMA; Univ. Pennsylvania; Hedgerow Theatre. Moylan, Pa. *Work*: woodcut illus., "Song of Solomon";

"Song of the Broad Axe." *Exhibited*: WFNY, 1939; 20th Cent. Sculpture Show, 1952-53; Mus. Contemp. Crafts, N.Y., 1957; Brussels World Fair, 1958; PMA; PAFA; WMAA; Phila. A. All.; MModA, 1953; Tate Gal., London, England, 1953.

ESMAN, BETTY (Betty Esman Samuels)—Painter
1230 Park Ave., New York 28, N.Y.

B. New York, N.Y. *Studied*: Syracuse Univ. Col. FA; NAD; Ecole des Beaux-Arts, Paris, and elsewhere in Europe and South America. *Member*: NAWA; Brooklyn Soc. A.; AEA. *Awards*: prizes, NAWA, 1955; Brooklyn Soc. A., 1955. *Work*: Fla. Southern Col.; Brandeis Univ., and in private coll. *Exhibited*: AIC; SFMA; Albright A. Gal.; CGA; Mus. FA of Houston; Wildenstein Gal.; Miami Univ.; Univ. Cincinnati; PAFA, 1952; NAWA, annually; Brooklyn Soc. A., 1954, 1955; U.S. Embassy, Paris, France; Museé des Beaux Arts, Dijon, France, 1954; Museé Ingres, Montauban, France; Sallé Franklin Bordeaux, Musee Paul Dupuy, Toulouse, France.*

ESTHER, SISTER (NEWPORT)—Educator, P., L., W.
St. Mary-of-the-Woods College; h. Foley Hall, St. Mary-of-the-Woods, Ind.

B. Clinton, Ind., May 17, 1901. *Studied*: AIC, B.A. in Edu.; St. Mary-of-the-Woods Col., A. B.; Syracuse Univ., M.F.A. *Awards*: LL.D., St. Mary's College, Notre Dame, 1956; prize, Hoosier Salon, 1937, 1939, 1942. *Exhibited*: MMA (illuminated mss.), 1944; Lakeside Press Gal., (book illus.), 1933; Hoosier Salon, 1933, 1937, 1939, 1940, 1942; John Herron AI, 1938; Int. Exp. of Sacred Art, Rome, 1950; Contemporary Religious Art, Tulsa, Okla., 1949. Contributor to Liturgical Arts magazine; Journal of Arts & Letters, St. Paul; Catholic Art Quarterly; Church Property Administration; The Catholic Educator, and other magazines. Author: 90 picture studies for Barton Cotton's Picture Series; Jr. A. Hist. section of CAA Course of Study for Art in Elementary Grades. Lectures: Modern, Creative, Plastic Art and Art Edu. *Position*: Founder, Catholic AA, 1936; Dir., 1936-40, Bd. Advisors, 1940-58; Founder, Ed., Catholic Art Quarterly, 1937-40; Hd. A. Dept., St. Mary-of-the-Woods, 1937- ; Assembled U.S. Section of Int. Exp. Sacred Art, Rome, 1950; Chm., U.S. Comm. for the Holy Year Exhibit, 1949-51; Dir., A., Workshop, Catholic Univ., 1954, 1958, Staff, 1952-57. Ed., "Creative Art," 1955. Author: Art Section of "Report of Everett Curriculum Workshop," 1956, Art Consultant, 1956, and Nat. Liturgical Week, 1957. Collecting Committee for Children's Art Exh. for Vatican Pavillion, Brussels World Fair, 1958. Fndr.; Gen. Chm., Conf. of Catholic A. Educators, 1958; Dir. A. Sect. of Nat. Catholic Charities Jubilee Program, 1958-60.

ESTIN, PETER (GEORGE)—Cartoonist, I., Comm. A.
Close Rd., Greenwich, Conn.

B. Prague, Czechoslovakia, June 10, 1927. *Studied*: Dartmouth Col., B.A.; Harvard Univ., M.A. *Exhibited*: J. Walter Thompson, Inc., one-man exh. cartoons, 1954; Perrot Mem. Lib., Old Greenwich, Conn., 1955. Illus., "How to be a Winner at Chess," 1954; "Careers in Book Publishing," 1955; "Chess Made Easy," 1955; "How to Get More Out of Chess," 1957; Adv. cartoons for: Shell Chemical Corp.; Johns-Manville Corp.; Budge-Wood Services; Sugarbush Valley Corp., and others. Represented in anthologies: "This Is My Best Humor," 1955; "Cartoon Treasury," 1955. Contributor of cartoons to The New Yorker, Sat. Eve. Post, Colliers, True, American, Playboy magazine, American Weekly, Saturday Review, etc.

ETCHISON, BRUCE—Museum Director, P., T., Gr.
Washington County Museum of Fine Arts; h. 219 North Colonial Drive, Hagerstown, Md.

B. Washington, D.C., Dec. 19, 1918. *Studied*: American Univ., B.A.; Yale Univ. Sch. FA, B.F.A., M.F.A. *Member*: F., Intl. Inst. for the Conservation of Museum Art Objects; Torch Club Intl.; State of Maryland A. Comm. *Work*: mural, Tortuga Restaurant. *Exhibited*: Terry AI, 1952; Wash. WC Cl., 1948; one-man: Bridgeport, Conn., 1949. Lectures: How to Paint in Oil; Development of Sculpture; Symbolism in Religious Art; Modern Art; Far Eastern Art, to local and regional clubs, church groups, etc. Exhibitions arranged: "Romance of the West," 1954; "Medieval and Renaissance Arms and Armour," 1955; "25th Anniversary Exhibition, European Masterpieces," 1956; "Sister City Exhibition from Hagerstown, Md. to

Wesel, Germany," 1955; "Norman Rockwell Exhibition," 1957; "Stained Glass by Frederic Kurtz," 1957; "Tradition and Pageantry in Britain," by Molly Guion, 1958; "Latvian Art and Handicraft," 1958. *Position*: Instr. A. Appreciation, Hagerstown Jr. Col.; Television teacher for 5th and 6th grade art via Wash. County closed circuit, Washington County Bd. Edu.; Dir., Washington County Museum of Fine Arts, Hagerstown, Md., 1950- .

ETNIER, STEPHEN MORGAN—*Painter*
c/o Milch Gallery, 21 East 67th St., New York, N.Y.; h. Old Cove, South Harpswell, Me.

B. York, Pa., Sept. 11, 1903. *Studied*: Yale Sch. FA; PAFA. *Awards*: prize, Butler AI; gold medal, NAD, 1955, 1956. *Member*: NA. *Work*: MMA; BMFA; Vassar Col.; PAFA; PC; New Britain Mus. A.; Farnsworth Mus. A.; Wadsworth Atheneum; Toledo Mus. A.; Bowdoin Col.; IBM; Brooks Mem. Mus.; Gettysburg Col.; DMFA; Marine Mus., Searsport, Me.; Los A. Mus. A.; Parrish A. Mus., Southampton, N.Y.; Fairleigh Dickinson Col., Rutherford, N.J.; York (Pa.) Hist. Soc.; Butler AI; Martin Mem. Lib., York, Pa.; murals, USPO, Everett, Mass.; Spring Valley, N.Y. *Exhibited*: nationally.

ETS, MARIE HALL *(Mrs. Harold)—Illustrator, W.*
c/o Viking Press, 18 East 48th St., New York, N.Y.; h. Morningside Gardens, 501 West 123rd St., (Apt. 20-E), New York 27, N.Y.

B. North Greenfield, Wis., Dec. 16, 1895. *Studied*: N.Y. Sch. F. & App. A.; Univ. Chicago, Ph.B.; AIC; & with Frederick V. Poole. *Awards*: Hans Christian Andersen award for "Play With Me," Stockholm, Sweden, 1956; also for same book, AIGA, 1958. *Exhibited*: AFA 1st annual exh. selected books for children, 1945. *Author*, I., "Mister Penny," 1935; "The Story of a Baby," 1939; "In the Forest," 1944; "Oley, the Sea Monster" (Herald-Tribune prizewinner) 1947; "Mr. T. W. Anthony Woo," 1951; "Beasts and Nonsense," 1952; "Another Day," 1953; "Play With Me," 1955; "Mr. Penny's Race Horse," 1956; "Cow's Party," 1958, and others. Co-Author: "My Dog Rinty," 1946.

ETTENBERG, EUGENE M.—
Book & Adv. Designer, T., W., L., Cr.
c/o Gallery Press, 225 Varick St. (14); h. 450 West 24th St., New York 11, N.Y.

B. Westmount, Quebec, Canada, Oct. 21, 1903. *Studied*: PIASch. *Member*: AIGA; Type Dir. Cl.; Authors Lg.; Columbia Faculty Cl.; Typophiles; AAUP. *Exhibited*: AIGA, 1935-1941, 1948-1952; Morgan Lib., 1940. *Author*: "Type for Books and Advertising," 1937. Ed., "Advertising and Production Year Book," 1936-1940; "News Letter" of AIGA, 1935-1941, 1948-1952; Morgan Lib., 1940. *Author*: "Print," Gazette des Beaux-Arts (Paris), "Art of the Book," Publisher's Weekly, Times Literary Supplement (London), and other trade publications. Lectures: Typography. *Position*: A. Dir. & Typographer, Publishers Printing Co., 1932-44; Manager, A. Dir., Typographer, The Gallery Press, New York, N.Y., 1945- ; Instr., Typography, Publ. Des., Adv. Des., PIASch., 1947- ; Dir. & V. Pres., AIGA, 1950- ; Tech. Ed., American Printer, 1950- ; Ed., "Portfolio," 1950- . Contr. Ed., American Artist magazine, 1951- ; Lecturer, Columbia Univ. Dept. Gr. A., 1952- ; Oklahoma State Univ. Sch. of Journalism, 1958- .

ETTING, EMLEN—*Painter, Des., I., E., W., L.*
c/o Midtown Galleries, 17 East 57th St., New York 23, N.Y.; h. 1922 Panama St., Philadelphia 3, Pa.

B. Philadelphia, Pa., 1905. *Studied*: Harvard Univ.; Acad. de la Grande Chaumiere, Paris, and with Andre Lhote, Paris. *Work*: WMAA; PAFA; Atwater Kent Mus.; AGAA; murals, Market St. National Bank and Italian Consulate, Philadelphia. *Awards*: Italian Star of Solidarity. *Exhibited*: Fla. Southern Col.; VMFA; NAD; Audubon A.; PAFA; CAM; Phila. AA; Butler AI; Dayton AI; Bloomington AA; Illinois Wesleyan Univ.; GGE 1939; CGA; Norton Gal. A.; one-man: Midtown Gal.; Inst. Contemp. A., Boston, and in Cleveland, Philadelphia and abroad. Translator: Paul Valery's "Cimetiere Marin," 1932. Author: "Drawing the Ballet," 1944; Illus., "Amerika" by Kafka, "Ecclesiastes." Contributor to Art News, Fortune, Town & Country, Atlantic Monthly, This Week. Recording: The Liberation of Paris. *Position*: Instr., PMASch. A., Philadelphia, Pa.; Hon. Pres., Artists Equity Assn.; Pres., Alliance Française of Phila., Pa.

ETTINGHAUSEN, RICHARD—
Museum Curator, W., L., Historian
Freer Gallery of Art, Washington 25, D.C.

B. Frankfort-on-Main, Germany, Feb. 5, 1906. *Studied*: Univ. Frankfort, Ph.D.; & in England. *Member*: CAA; Am. Oriental Soc.; Ed.; Ars Islamica, 1938-1951; Co-Ed., Ars Orientalis, 1951-1958; ed. bd., Art Bulletin; Kairos. *Author*: Studies in Muslim Iconography. Contributor to: Ars Islamica, Ars Orientalis, Bulletin of Iranian Institute, Gazette des Beaux-Arts. Lectures: Persian Miniatures; Art of the Islamic Book; Near Eastern Pottery; The Arts of the Muslim East, etc. *Position*: Research Assoc., Iranian Inst., N.Y., 1934-37; L., N.Y. Univ., 1937-38; Assoc. Prof. Hist. of Islamic A., Univ. Michigan, 1938-44; Assoc. in Near Eastern A., Freer Gal. A., Washington, D.C., 1944-1958, Cur. Near Eastern Art, 1958- ; Research Prof. Islamic Art, Univ. Michigan, 1948- .

ETTL, ALEX J.—*Sculptor, Des.*
38 East 30th St., New York 16, N.Y.; h. Princeton, N.J.

B. Fort Lee, N.J., Dec. 12, 1898. *Studied*: NAD; Columbia Univ.; Col. City of N.Y. *Member*: F., NAD. *Work*: mem. monument, East Rutherford, N.J.; Katrina Spencer Trask and George Foster Peabody memorials, Saratoga Springs, N.Y.; Allan Jacobs and Rennold Wolf mem., Friars Cl., N.Y.; Award Medallion, Interracial Cooperation Organization, Atlanta, Ga.; mem., Hist. Soc. Bergen County, Hackensack, N.J.; Nat. Breweries, Ltd., Canada; Elsie the Borden Cow, 1945, and work for numerous industries in the U.S.

EULER, REEVES—*Painter, S.*
Brewster St., Provincetown, Mass.

B. De Lamar, Nev., Dec. 28, 1896. *Studied*: Corcoran Sch. A.; NAD; & with Charles W. Hawthorne. *Exhibited*: CGA; NAD; NGA; Provincetown AA; Univ. Illinois; Univ. Nebraska; Boise (Idaho) Gal. A.; Papermill Playhouse, Short Hills, N.J.; Amherst Col. *Position*: Pres. Provincetown AA., 1954-55, 1955-56.

EUSTON, JACOB HOWARD—*Etcher, P.*
105 South LaSalle St., Chicago 3, Ill.

B. Lebanon, Pa., Oct. 4, 1892. *Studied*: Univ. Illinois, B.S.; Cleveland Sch. A., with A. R. Dyer; AIC, with J. Allen St. John; & with Alfred de Sauty. *Member*: Cliff Dwellers, Chicago; Chicago SE; Indiana Soc. Pr.M.; AAPL. *Awards*: Indiana Soc. Pr.M., 1949; Hoosier Salon, 1937. *Work*: NGA. *Exhibited*: AIC, 1936; NGA, 1935; Chicago SE, 1935-1955; Northwest Pr.M., 1935; Southern Pr.M., 1937-1941; Phila. Pr. Cl., 1933; Chicago Galleries Assn.; Indiana Soc. Pr.M., 1934-1955; Hoosier Salon, 1931-1940. Lectures: Techniques in Print Making; Appreciation of Prints. *Position*: Dir., Chicago Soc. Etchers.

EVANS, MRS. FREDERICK W. See *Keyes, Emilie*

EVANS, NAOMI T. *(Mrs. Roy K.)—Painter, T., L.*
1745 El Rito St., Glendale 8, Cal.

B. Santa Ana, Cal., Nov. 29, 1902. *Studied*: Otis AI and with Sam Hyde Harris, Ralph Holmes. *Member*: Glendale AA; Cal. A. Cl.; Laguna Beach AA; Valley A. Gld.; A. of the Southwest; Desert A. Center; Nat. Soc. A. & Let.; Pasadena. *Awards*: prizes, Cal. A. Cl., 1950, 1953; Glendale AA, 1951, 1954, 1958; Placer Col., 1953; Placer Union H.S.; Auburn A. Festival, 1953, 1954; Mother Lode AA, Sonora, Cal., 1953; Greek Theatre, Los A., 1957, 1958; Duncan-Vail Gal., 1954. *Exhibited*: Soc. A. & Let., 1955; Cal. A. Cl., 1950-1955; Friday Morning Cl., 1953-1955; Santa Cruz, 1950-1955; Nat. Orange Show, 1954; Laguna Beach AA; A. of the Southwest; Valley A. Gld.; Desert A. Center, Palm Springs, 1954, 1955; Santa Barbara, Cal.; many one-man exhs., and participation in local and regional shows, 1950-1955. *Position*: Dir. Gal., 1950-51, Bd. Dir., 1951-52, 1953-54, Glendale AA.

EVANS, RUDULPH—*Sculptor*
1121 Arlington Blvd., Arlington, Va.

B. Washington, D.C., Feb. 1, 1878. *Studied*: Corcoran Sch. A.; ASL; Julian Acad., Ecole des Beaux-Arts, Paris, and with Rodin. *Member*: NA; Nat. Inst. A. & Let.; NSS. *Awards*: med., Paris Salon, 1914; NAD,

1920; Legion of Honor, Paris; Crown of Italy, Rome. *Work*: statues: Capitols of U.S.; Luxembourg Mus.; MMA; CGA; Detroit Inst. A.; Colorado Springs FA Center; N.Y. Univ.; Princeton Univ.; U.S. War Col., Wash., D.C.; Pan-American Union; Nelson A. Gal.; Wooley Mem., Detroit; Huntington Coll., S.C.; McKinney Mem., Greenwich, Conn.; Kiernan Mem., Greenbay, Wis.; Jefferson Mem., Wash., D.C.; many sculptured portraits in the U.S. and abroad. *Exhibited*: extensively in U.S. and abroad.*

EVANS, VIRGINIA BARGAR—Designer, P., T.

1018 Tomlinson Ave., Moundsville, W. Va.

B. Moundsville, W. Va. *Studied*: Carnegie Inst.; PAFA; Fontainebleau, France; Tiffany Fnd.; & with George Oberteuffer. *Position*: Glass and Pottery Des.*

EVATT, HARRIET (TORREY) [Mrs. William]—
Painter, I., W.

74 East Kanawha Ave., Columbus 14, Ohio

B. Knoxville, Tenn., June 24, 1895. *Studied*: Columbus (Ohio) A. Acad.; & with Charles Rosen, Alice Schille, Robert Chadeayne. *Member*: Columbus A. Lg.; Ohio WC Soc.; Lg. Am. Pen Women. *Awards*: prize, Columbus Gal. FA, 1946; Ohioana award for best juvenile book, 1946. Author, I., "The Red Canoe," 1940; "The Snow Owl's Secret," 1946; "The Mystery of the Alpine Castle," 1951; "The Papoose Who Wouldn't Keep Her Stockings On"; "Big Indian and Little Bear"; "Davy Crockett, Big Indian and Little Bear"; "The Secret of the Ruby Locket"; "Mystery of the Creaking Windmill"; "The Secret of the Singing Tower"; "Mystery of the Alpine Castle"; "The Secret of the Whispering Willows," and many other books. Contributor to: Children's Activities Magazine; The Pen Woman.

EVERETT, ELIZABETH RINEHART—Painter, C., S., L.

602—36th Ave., North, Seattle 2, Wash.

B. Toledo, Ohio. *Studied*: PIASch.; Univ. Washington, B.A., and with Derbyshire, Mark Tobey, Walter Isaacs, Everett Du Pen. *Member*: Women Painters of Wash. (Pres.); Seattle Photographic Soc. *Awards*: prizes, Western Wash. Fair, 1920; Women Painters of Wash., 1933. *Exhibited*: Marshall Field, Chicago, Ill., 1946; SAM, 1952 and prior; Frederick & Nelson, Seattle, Wash.; Woessner A. Gal., 1953; SAM, 1956; Frye A. Mus., Seattle, 1958; Woman's Univ. Cl., 1955 (one-man).

EVERGOOD, PHILIP—Painter, Gr., W., L., Des., I.

c/o ACA Gallery, 63 East 57th St., New York 22, N.Y.

B. New York, N.Y., Oct. 26, 1901. *Studied*: Cambridge Univ., Slade Sch., England; ASL; Julian Acad., Paris. *Member*: An Am. Group; AEA; Nat. Inst. A. & Let. *Awards*: prizes, AIC, 1935, 1946; AV, 1942; Pepsi-Cola, 1944; Carnegie Inst., 1945; Schilling Purchase Award, 1946; La Tausca Comp., 1949; Hallmark Award, 1950; Carnegie Inst., 1950; CGA, 1951; Terry AI, 1952; Gold Med., PAFA, 1950. *Work*: Encyclopaedia Britannica Coll.; Pepsi-Cola Coll.; MMA; MModA; WMAA; BMFA; Arizona State Univ.; Denver A. Mus.; BMA; BM; Kalamazoo AI; Nat. Gal., Melbourne, Australia; Geelong Gal., Victoria, B. C.; Los A. Mus. A.; FMA; AIC; murals, Richmond Hill (L.I., N.Y.) Pub. Lib.; USPO, Jackson, Ga.; Kalamazoo Col. *Exhibited*: Carnegie Inst., 1938, 1939; La Pintura Contemporanea Norte Americana, 1941; WFNY 1939; WMA, 1942; Am-British Goodwill Exh., 1944; loan exh., Tate Gal., London, England, 1946, etc. I., Fortune, Time magazines. Illus., Short Stories by Gogol, 1950. Lectures: Art & Aesthetics.*

EWALD, LOUIS—Painter, Des.

Fetters Mill Rd., Bryn Athyn, Pa.

B. Minneapolis, Minn., Dec. 19, 1891. *Studied*: Minneapolis Sch. A.; PMSchIA. *Member*: Church Arch. Gld. of Am.; NSMP. *Work*: paintings and dec. work in churches in Philadelphia, New York, Baltimore, Washington, D.C., York, Pa.; paintings and polychrome on altar reredos in St. Andrews R.C. Church, Drexel Hill, Pa.; ceiling and reredos in Chapel of the Christ Child, Christ Church, Wilmington, Del.; mural and inscriptions in chapel at Wittenberg Col., Springfield, Ohio; color and ornament painting in Grace Lutheran church, Pottstown, Pa.; decorative pages in Bibles publ. by Winston Publ. Co.; inscriptions, gilding and polychrome work in more than forty churches.

EWING, CHARLES KERMIT—Educator, P., C., Lith.

University of Tennessee, Art Dept., Knoxville, Tenn.

B. Bentleyville, Pa., May 27, 1910. *Studied*: Carnegie Inst., B.A., M.A., with Alexander Kostello; Iowa Univ., with Jean Charlot; Harvard Univ. *Member*: Assoc. A. Pittsburgh (Pres.). *Awards*: prizes, Assoc. A. Pittsburgh, 1940, 1943, 1945, 1956; Parkersburg, W. Va., 1942, 1943; Springfield, Mass., 1941. *Work*: Pittsburgh Pub. Sch.; State Col., Pa.; Univ. Pittsburgh. *Exhibited*: NAD, 1938; Butler AI, 1939-1943, 1945; Carnegie Inst., 1945, 1946; Parkersburg, W. Va., 1942, 1943; All.A. Philadelphia, 1941; Assoc. A. Pittsburgh, 1938-1946; State T. Col., Indiana, Pa., 1946; Pepsi-Cola, 1946.*

EWING, EDGAR—Painter

University of Southern California; h. 4222 Sea View Lane, Los Angeles 65, Cal.

B. Hartington, Neb., Jan. 17, 1913. *Studied*: AIC, with Boris Anisfeld; Univ. Chicago, and in Europe. *Member*: Cal. WC Soc.; Am. Assn. Univ. Prof.; AFA; Pacific AA; Los A. County AI Assn.; Los Angeles AA. *Awards*: Ryerson F., 1935-37; Tiffany Fnd. grant, 1948-49; prizes, AIC, 1943; City of Los Angeles, 1950; Arizona State Fair, 1950; Chaffey Community AA, 1951; Los A. Mus. A., 1952; Cal. WC Soc., 1952-1955; Nat. Orange Show, 1953; Long Beach Mus. A., 1955; Cal. State Fair, 1956; San Jose State Col., 1957; Sierra Madre AA; Samuel Goldwyn award, Los A. Mus. A., 1957. *Work*: Exeter Acad.; Los A. Mus. A.; Santa Barbara Mus. A.; Univ. Syracuse, and others. *Exhibited*: AIC, 1943-1957; VMFA, 1940; Nebraska AA, 1948; Pepsi-Cola, 1948; Los A. Mus. A., 1947-1958; Fresno A. Lg., 1949; Cal. State Fair, 1949-1957; Los A. County Fair, 1949; Carnegie Inst., 1949, 1955; Denver A. Mus., 1950-1957; Oakland A. Gal., 1950, 1951; San F. AA, 1950, 1951; Cal. WC Soc., 1951-1952; UCLA, 1950; City of Los Angeles, 1950-1952; Chaffey Community AA, 1951; Nat. Orange Show; CGA, 1951; AFA traveling exh., 1951-1952; PAFA, 1952, 1958; MMA, 1952; one-man: Tretyakov Gal., Chicago, 1939; Mandels, Chicago, 1941; Syracuse Univ., 1946; Exeter Acad., 1946; Univ. So. Cal., 1946; Pepsi-Cola Gal., 1947; Stanford Univ., 1948; de-Young Mem. Mus., 1948, 1955; Palos Verdes, Gal. 1949; Col. Puget Sound, Wash., 1949; Univ. of Redlands, 1950; Chabot Gal., Los A., 1950; Los A. Medical Assn., 1951; Santa Barbara Mus. A., 1951-1958; Pasadena AI, 1952; Sao Paulo, Brazil, 1955; SFMA, 1951-1957; NAD, 1948; Milwaukee A. Center, 1948; Univ. Illinois, 1957; Detroit Inst. A., 1958. More than 18 one-man exhs. since 1948. *Positions*: Instr., AIC, 1937-43; Prof. FA, Univ. Southern California, Los Angeles, Cal., 1946- .

FABER, EUGENE JAMES—
Painter, Des., C., W., L., T.

2823 North Cramer St., Milwaukee 11, Wis.

B. Milwaukee, Wis., July 13, 1910. *Studied*: Milwaukee State T. Col., B.E. in A. Edu. *Member*: Wis. P.&S. Assn. *Awards*: prize, Milwaukee AI, 1935; med., Good Housekeeping magazine, 1934. *Work*: Wis. pub. bldgs. *Exhibited*: AIC, 1934, 1936; CGA, 1934, 1937; Milwaukee AI, 1933-1941; Univ. Wisconsin, 1935-1937, 1939; Layton A. Gal., 1934, 1939. Contributor to: School Arts; Design magazines. *Position*: Hd. A. Dept., Kilbourn Jr. Trade Sch., Milwaukee, Wis., 1935-42; Staff Officer, Combat Engineers, 1944-45; Chief of Military Personnel, Great Lakes Div. Engineers, 1945-46; Hd. Interior Dec., Ed. Schuster & Co., Milwaukee, Wis.; 1949-56; Chm. com. on study of Interior Dec. in Pub. Schs.; Instr., Int. Dec., West Allis Sch. of Voc. & Adult Edu., 1941-42, 1949-50; Shorewood Opportunity Sch., 1951- ; Fox Point Sch. Adult & Vocational Edu., 1955-1957.

FABION, JOHN—Painter, S.

156 West Chestnut St., Chicago 10, Ill.

B. Vienna, Austria, Oct. 31, 1905. *Studied*: AIC, with Boris Anisfeld; & abroad. *Member*: AEA. *Awards*: prizes, AIC, 1933, 1936. *Work*: S.; Statler Hotel, Wash., D.C.; Los A., Cal.; U.S. Naval Acad.; St. Mary's Hospital, Anderson, Ind.; USPO, Bedford, Ind.; monument, Chopin Sch., Chicago, Ill. *Exhibited*: AIC; GGE 1939; Nat. Mus., Wash., D.C. *Position*: Instr., AIC, 1939; 1946- .*

FABRI, RALPH—*Painter, Et., W., Cr., E.*
54 West 74th St., New York 23, N.Y.

B. Budapest, Hungary, April 23, 1894. *Studied*: Royal State Gymnasium, B.A.; Royal Inst. Technology, Royal Acad. FA, M.A., Budapest. *Member*: NA (Council, 1949-52; Rec. Sec., 1952-53); SAGA; Brooklyn Soc. A.; CAA; Wash. Pr. M.; Audubon A.; Casein S (Pres. 1955-56); Boston Pr.M.; Knickerbocker A.; Providence WC Cl.; A. Lg. of Long Island; AAUP; Art Comm. City of N.Y.; Hon. Life Pres., Audubon A., Nat. Soc. Painters in Casein; Chicago Soc. Et.; F., Royal Soc. A., London. *Awards*: John Taylor Arms prize, 1942; AV, 1943; LC, 1943-1945; Denver A. Mus., 1944; Conn. Acad. FA, 1945; NA, 1950; Fla. Southern Col., 1950; Applebaum prize, N.Y., 1952. *Work*: LC; Honolulu Acad. A.; Vanderpoel Coll.; Newark Pub. Lib.; Univ. Maine; Rochester Mem. Mus.; Budapest; MMA; NAD; Smithsonian Inst.; Currier Gal. A.; N.Y. Pub. Lib.; Massillon Mus. A.; Attleboro Mus. A., etc. *Exhibited*: NA, since 1936; SAGA, 1935-1956; SFMA, 1944, 1945; Northwest Pr.M., 1941-1952; Oakland AA, 1941-1951; AIC, 1932, 1935, 1939; PAFA, 1941, 1942, 1950, 1951; AWS, 1941, 1957; Conn. Acad. FA, 1942-1956; Audubon A., since 1945; LC, 1943-1952; Carnegie Inst., 1949, 1950, 1951; Wichita AA, 1951; Albany Pr. Cl., 1951; Newport AA, 1948-1951; Brooklyn Soc. A., since 1950; U.S.A. Print Exh., France, 1951-52; Portland Soc. A., 1952, etc. One-man: Smithsonian Inst., 1942; Honolulu Acad. A., 1943; Phila, A. All., 1943-44; New York, 1945, 1947, 1949, 1952-1955, 1957; Univ. Maine, 1948, 1951; Newark Pub. Lib., 1951; Internationally: Italy, France, England, Scotland, Sweden, Norway, Belgium, Hungary, Turkey, India, etc. Author: "Learn to Draw," 1945; "Oil Painting, How-to-do-it," 1953. *Position*: Instr., City College of N.Y.; Cr., "Pictures on Exhibit"; Staff writer for "Today's Art."

FACCI, DOMENICO (AURELIO)—*Sculptor, C., Des.*
248 West 14th St.; h. 144 West 11th St., New York 11, N.Y.

B. Hooversville, Pa., Feb. 2, 1916. *Studied*: Roerich Acad. A., and with Pietro Montana, Louis Slobodkin. *Member*: AEA (Bd. Dir., 1956-57, V.Pres., 1958-59); Knickerbocker A.; Brooklyn Soc. A.; Silvermine Gld. A.; P. & S. Soc. of New Jersey; Village A. Center (Council); Audubon A.; Lg. of Present Day A. *Awards*: prizes, Village A. Center, 1949-1953, 1955, 1956; Silvermine Gld. A., 1953-1955 (one-man), 1956, 1958; Brooklyn Soc. A., 1955, 1957; P. & S. Soc. of New Jersey, medal, 1955; Fla. Southern Col., 1951, 1952; Audubon A., 1956; Knickerbocker A., 1959. *Work*: Fla. Southern Col.; Am. Cyanamide Co.; Bd. Edu., N.Y.; B'nai B'rith. *Exhibited*: AEA, 1950; WMAA, 1951; Village A. Center, 1949-1955; NAD, 1936, 1944, 1953, 1954; ACA Gal., N.Y., 1952; BM, 1953; Silvermine Gld. A., 1953, 1954, 1955 (one-man); 1958; Pittsburgh A. & Crafts Center, 1954, 1955; Audubon A., 1955-1958; Brooklyn Soc. A., 1955-1958; Knickerbocker A., 1955-1958. *Positions*: Instr. S., Roerich Acad. A., 1939-41; City Col. of N.Y., Ext. Div., 1953-54.

FAGG, KENNETH S.—*Illustrator, P., Comm. A.*
c/o Charles E. Cooper, 136 East 57th St., New York 22, N.Y.; h. Chappaqua, N.Y.

B. Chicago, Ill., May 29, 1901. *Studied*: Univ. Wisconsin, B.A.; AIC; ASL. *Member*: SI; AWCS. *Exhibited*: AWCS, 1942, 1944-1946, 1952. I.; Holiday, Sat. Eve. Post.*

FAGGI, ALFEO—*Sculptor, L.*
Woodstock, N.Y.

B. Florence, Italy, Sept. 11, 1885. *Studied*: Academia Belle Arti, Florence, Italy. *Awards*: prize & med., AIC, 1942. *Work*: AIC; AGAA; WMAA; Mus. New Mexico, Santa Fé; Phillips Acad.; BM; Univ. Chicago; Rosary Col., River Forest, Ill.; Ogunquit Mus. A.; PAFA; Princeton Univ.; High Mus. A.; Scott Mem. Gal., Atlanta; Minneapolis Inst. A.; SAM; Albright A. Gal.; Columbus (Ohio) Mus. A.; PMG; Michigan State Univ.; St. Thomas Church, Chicago; mem. & busts, New York, N.Y., Wash., D.C., Chicago, Ill., etc. *Exhibited*: AIC, 1942, 1943; Albright A. Gal., 1941 (one-man); Fairmount Park AA (Phila.), 1940, 1949; WMAA, 1942, 1943; PAFA, 1943, 1948-1951, 1955-1957; SAM; Honolulu Acad. A.; PMG; BM; Gulf Coast A. Center; Argent Gal., 1944; Woodstock AA; Little Gal., Woodstock, N.Y., 1946; Univ. Chicago; Weyhe Gal., 1951, 1954 (one-man), 1957 (one-man); Atlantic City, 1951 (one-man); Ft. Worth A. Center, 1954; AFA traveling exh.; Christ Church, Greenwich, Conn., 1957, 1958; AGAA; Southern Ill. Univ., Carbondale, 1953 (one-man). Lectures: "The Sculptor."

FAILING, FRANCES E(LIZABETH)—*Painter, T.*
1010 Rural Rd. (Apt. 8), Tempe, Ariz.

B. Canisteo, N.Y. *Studied*: PIASch.; Western Reserve Univ., B.S.; Columbia Univ., M.A.; Rochester Inst. Technology; Alfred Univ. *Member*: Plymouth (England) A. Cl.; NAWA; Nat. Lg. Am. Pen Women; Arizona A. Gld.; Phoenix AA; NAEA. *Awards*: prizes, Indiana AA, 1934, 1951, 1952; Hoosier Salon, 1947; NAWA, 1937; Arizona State Fair (purchase), 1956, 1957, 1958. *Exhibited*: CM, 1934, 1936, 1937; PAFA, 1936; AIC, 1937; BM, 1937; NAWA, 1936-1938, 1941; CGA, 1937; N.Y. WC Cl., 1936; John Herron AI, 1933-1935, 1937, 1938, 1940-43, 1951; Hoosier Salon, 1934-1936; Indiana A. Cl., 1932-1934, 1936; Univ. Nevada, 1958; Phoenix Gal., 1956-1958; Kansas City AI, 1938; one-man: Witte Mem. Mus., 1936; Dallas Mus. FA, 1938; Mus. FA of Houston, 1939; Baylor Univ., 1938; Ball State A. Gal.; Indiana State T. Col., 1952; Phoenix, Ariz., 1956; Ariz. State Col., 1956, and abroad. *Position*: Chm., Dept. A., Washington H.S., Indianapolis, Ind., 1935-56; Asst. Prof. A., Arizona State College, Tempe, Ariz., at present.

FAIRBANKS, AVARD (Tennyson)—
Sculptor, E., Des., L.
University of Utah, Salt Lake City, Utah

B. Provo, Utah, Mar. 2, 1897. *Studied*: ASL; Ecole des Beaux-Arts, Grande Chaumiere, Ecole Moderne, Paris; Yale Univ., B.F.A.; Univ. Washington, M.F.A.; Univ. Michigan, M.A., Ph.D. *Member*: NSS; Arch. L.; Circolo Degli Artisti, Florence, Italy. *Awards*: Guggenheim F., 1927-1928; prize, Am. Physicians AA, San F., Cal. 1937; med., Michigan Acad. FA, 1946. *Work*: Public monuments & fountains in many cities of the U.S.; also medals, emblems, & awards for societies and industries. *Exhibited*: Paris Salon, 1914; NAD; Pan-Pacific Exp., 1915; Arch.L.; NSS; AIC; Albright A. Gal.; Carnegie Inst.; Detroit Inst. A.; Honolulu Acad. A.; Honolulu AA; CAM; SFMA; Univ. Oregon; Univ. Michigan; Century of Progress, Chicago; etc. Lectures: Sculpture; Automotive Body Design & Styling. *Position*: Asst. Prof. A., Hd. Dept. S., Univ. Oregon, 1920-27; Instr., Seattle Inst. A., 1928-29; Resident A., Assoc. Prof. S., Univ. Michigan, Ann Arbor, Mich.; Univ. of Utah, Salt Lake City, Utah.*

FAIRBANKS, RICHARD (RICHINGS)—*Craftsman, T.*
Art Department, Drake University; h. 1361 27th St., Des Moines 11, Iowa

B. Yakima, Wash., Oct. 27, 1929. *Studied*: Univ. Washington, B.A., with Paul Bonifas; Mills Col., M.A., with Antonio Prieto. *Awards*: prizes, Cal. State Fair, 1954; Iowa State Fair, 1958. *Work*: numerous jewelry, ceramic commissions. *Exhibited*: Syracuse Mus. FA, 1954, 1956; Scripps Col., 1954-1956; "Young Americans," N.Y., 1955; Wichita Mus. A., 1954; Los A. County Fair, 1956; Cal. State Fair, 1954; Iowa State Fair, 1957, 1958; Iowa AA, 1957, 1958; one-man: Yakima, Wash., 1954, 1955; Marshalltown, Iowa, 1958; Pella, Iowa, 1958. *Position*: Instr. Crafts, Drake Univ., Des Moines, Iowa, 1956- .

FAIRCHILD, ELIZABETH NELSON—*Painter*
939 Eighth Ave., New York 19, N.Y.; h. Rhinebeck, N.Y.

B. Yonkers, N.Y. *Studied*: ASL, and privately. *Work*: NGA; Univ. Wisconsin Lib.; F. D. Roosevelt Mus., Hyde Park, N.Y. *Exhibited*: All. A. Am.; Am. Soc. Min. P.; Catherine Lorillard Wolfe A. Cl.; Ogunquit A. Center. I., "True Story of Fala."*

FAIRCHILD, HURLSTONE—*Painter*
4001 Calle de Jardin, Tucson, Ariz.

B. Danville, Ill., Jan. 30, 1893. *Studied*: Univ. Illinois; Univ. Michigan; Missouri Sch. Mines, Rollo, Mo. *Member*: SC; F., Royal Soc. A., London, England; Fifty Am. A.; Soc. Western A. *Work*: Denver A. Mus.; Grand Canyon Nat. Park coll.; Rio de Janeiro, Brazil, and in private coll. *Exhibited*: one-man: La Jolla A. Center, 1942; Frances Webb Gal., Los A.; Anderson Gal., Chicago, 1933; Oklahoma A. Center, 1950; Shreveport (La.) Mus. A.; Blair Gal., Claremore, Okla., 1942; O'Brien Gal., Phoenix, Ariz.; Biltmore Gal., Phoenix; Orr Gal., San Diego, 1942; Springville, Utah, annually; Gilcrease Mem. Inst., Tulsa, 1958, and others. Author, I., "An Artist's Notebook," 1950; "Grand Canyon Sketches & Verse."

FAIRCHILD, MAY (Mrs.)—Painter
939 Eighth Ave., New York 19, N.Y.; h. Rhinebeck, N.Y.

B. Boston, Mass. *Studied*: ASL; Cowles A. Sch., Boston; & in Paris. *Work*: many portraits & miniatures in public & private collections.*

FAISON, S(AMSON) LANE, JR.—
Educator, W., L., Cr.
Lawrence Art Museum; h. College Place, Williamstown, Mass.

B. Washington, D.C., Nov. 16, 1907. *Studied*: Williams Col., A.B.; Harvard Univ., M.A.; Princeton Univ., M.F.A. *Member*: CAA (Pres. 1952-54, Dir., 1952-56). *Awards*: Chevalier de la Legion d'Honneur. Author: "Daumier's Third Class Carriage," 1946; "Manet," 1953; "Great Paintings of the Nude," 1953; "A Guide to the Art Museums of New England," 1958. Contributor to N.Y. Times; Sat. Review; The Nation (A. Cr., 1952-55); Art Bulletin; Art in America; College Art Journal. Lectures: Contemporary Painting; German Baroque Architecture; Manet; Daumier; Nazi Art Looting Activities. *Position*: Instr., Asst. Prof., Yale Univ., 1932-36; Dir., Central Collecting Point, Munich (State Dept.), 1950-51; Exec. Sec., Com. on Visual Arts, Harvard Univ., 1954-55; Asst. Prof., Renaissance & Modern A., 1936- , Chm. Dept. A., 1940- , Dir., Lawrence A., Mus., 1948- , Williams College, Williamstown, Mass.

FALETTI, VINCENT—Cartoonist
321 North Washington Ave., Saginaw, Mich.

B. Mohawk, Mich., Dec. 29, 1916. *Studied*: Chicago Acad. FA, with Vaughn Shoemaker; Cartoonist & Illus. Sch., N.Y., with Jack Markow. *Member*: Cartoonists Gld. of America. Contributor of cartoons to New Yorker; Sat. Eve. Post; Collier's; American, Redbook, Argosy, Sat. Review, etc.*

FALLS, C(HARLES) B(UCKLES)—
Illustrator, P., Des., Gr.
153 East 18th St., New York 3, N.Y.; s. Falls Village, Conn.

B. Fort Wayne, Ind., Dec. 10, 1874. *Member*: SI; A.Gld. *Awards*: Med., PAFA. *Work*: murals, Am. Radiator Bldg.; General Electric Co.; Ford Motor Co.; Warren Paper Co.; General Mills Co.; The Players Club. I., "Falls ABC Book"; "Tom Sawyer"; "Huckleberry Finn"; "The First 4000 Years," & many other books. Illus., for national magazines.

FALTER, JOHN—Illustrator
Perkasie, Pa.

B. Plattsmouth, Neb., Feb. 28, 1910. *Studied*: Kansas City AI; ASL; Grand Central Sch. A. *Member*: SI; NAC; A. & W. Cl. Illus., "A Ribbon and a Star," 1946; "The Horse of Another Color," 1946. Contributor of: covers to Saturday Evening Post.*

FANKBONNER, DORIS KATHRYN—See Dorfa

FANNING, RALPH—Educator, W., L., P.
512 Roanoke Ave., Riverhead, L.I., N.Y.

B. Riverhead, N.Y., Nov. 29, 1889. *Studied*: Cornell Univ., B.Arch.; Univ. Illinois, M.S., M. Arch. *Award*: Fulbright Award, 1954 (Cairo, Egypt). *Work*: Columbus Gal. FA; Ball State T. Col. Mus.; Columbia Univ. *Exhibited*: Ohio WC Soc.; Columbus A. Lg. Author: "Survey Outline of Art History." Contributor to: American Architect, Architectural Record. *Position*: Prof. Emeritus, Ohio State Univ., 1956- .

FARBER, MRS. GLADYS ALLER. See Aller, Gladys

FARKAS, GEORGE B.—Industrial Designer, Arch.
954 41st St., Miami 40, Fla.; h. 3547 St. Gaudens Rd., Coconut Grove 33, Fla.

B. Budapest, Hungary, July 24, 1905. *Studied*: Beaux-Arts, Vienna; Hungarian Indst. A. Col., Budapest, and with the late Andrew Farkas. *Member*: IDI; Mod. Arch. Research Soc., London; AID; Fla. Friends of Contemp. A. *Awards*: prizes, Triannale, Milan, Italy, 1936; Diplome de Medaille D'Or, Paris (with Andrew Farkas); Citation of Merit, 1948; Univ. Miami, 1949. *Work*: Univ. Miami Recreation Center (535 Housing Units and Dormitories); Esso Club, Aruba, Netherlands, West Indies. *Exhibited*: Good Design Show, Lowe Gallery, Univ. Miami, 1951. Co-Contributor: "E. Farkas-Architektur 'Innenr' a' aume Film." Lectures: Design and Architecture. *Position*: Advisory Bd., Florida Architecture, 1949, Design Plus, 1950.*

FARMER, EDWARD McNEIL—Educator, P., Eng., L.
Room 315, Art Bldg., Stanford University; h. 512 Gerona Rd., Stanford, Cal.

B. Los Angeles, Cal., Feb. 23, 1901. *Studied*: Stanford Univ., A.B., M.A.; Rudolph Schaeffer Sch. Des.; ASL. *Member*: Soc. Arch. Historian (Pres. Pacific Section, 1956-57); CAA; Col. Art Administrators Assn. (permanent Sec., Pres., 1954-55). *Exhibited*: AIC; Riverside Mus.; N.Y. WC Cl.; AWS; GGE 1939; CM; California State Fair; PAFA; CGA; Grand Central A. Gal.; and in local exhs. Lectures: Painting & Architecture; Development of the American House; The Arts at Mid-Century. *Position*: Actg. Instr., Graphic A., 1923-25, Instr., 1925-32, Actg. Asst. Prof., 1932-36, Asst. Prof., 1936-40, Assoc. Prof., 1946, Prof., A. & Arch., 1946- , Stanford Univ., Stanford, Cal.; in Germany, Beutelsbach bie Stuttgart, West Germany, 1958. Ed., Stanford Art Series; Native Arts of the Pacific Northwest; 45 Contemporary Mexican Artists, 1951.

FARNDON, WALTER—Painter
129 Ridge Rd., Douglaston, N.Y.

B. Coventry, England, Mar. 13, 1876. *Studied*: NAD. *Member*: NA; AWCS; NAC; All.A.Am.; SC; AAPL. *Awards*: prizes, SC, 1919, 1926, 1929; NAC, 1939, 1957; AWCS, 1925; AAPL, 1944; All.A.Am., 1940, 1944; Westchester AA, 1952, special exh., Citation & gold medal, 1958; NAD, 1930, 1944. *Work*: BM; NAC; SC. *Exhibited*: Extensively in museums of U.S.; annually with NAD.

FARNSWORTH, MRS. HELEN SAWYER.
See Sawyer, Helen

FARNSWORTH, JERRY—Painter, T.
3482 Flamingo, Sarasota, Fla.

B. Dalton, Ga., Dec. 31, 1895. *Studied*: Corcoran Sch. A.; & with Charles W. Hawthorne. *Member*: NA; NAC; SC; Wash. Soc. A.; Provincetown AA. *Awards*: prize, NAD, 1925, 1927, 1933, 1935, 1952, med., 1936, prize, 1938; NAC, 1941; Los A. Mus. A., 1945; High Mus. A., 1946; Grand Central Gal., 1928. *Work*: Mus. FA of Houston; Toledo Mus. A.; PAFA; New Britain Mus.; MMA; Dayton AI; Vanderpoel Coll.; Delgado Mus. A.; WMAA, etc. *Exhibited*: nationally & internationally. Author: "Painting with Jerry Farnsworth"; "Learning to Paint in Oil." *Position*: A. in Residence, Univ. Illinois, 1942-43; Dir., Farnsworth Sch. A., Sarasota, Fla.

FARNUM, ROYAL BAILEY—Educator, W., C.
Hampton, Conn.

B. Somerville, Mass., June 11, 1884. *Studied*: Mass. Sch. A.; Univ. Upsala, Stockholm, Sweden; Cleveland Sch. A., M.E.A. (Hon.); Brown Univ., Art D. (Hon.); State Col. Edu., Providence, R.I., Ed. D. (Hon.); Univ. Rhode Island, LL.D. (Hon.). *Member*: F., Royal Soc. A., London; Nat. Edu. Assn.; Eastern AA; Providence A. Cl.; Century Assn.; AIA (Hon.); A. Adv. Council, CUASch.; Consulting Member, Nat. Assn. Sch. Des.; Hon. Nat. Chm., Scholastic Awards, 1927- . *Awards*: med., Arch. Lg., 1942; A. Edu. Assn., 1938. Author, I., "Decoration for Rural Schools," 1914; "Fine and Applied Arts" (monograph), 1958; "Learning More About Pictures," 1957. Contributor to educational magazines and reviews. *Position*: Specialist, Drawing & Manual Training, N.Y. State Edu. Dept., 9 yrs.; Prin. & State Dir., A. Edu., Mass. Sch. A., Boston, 8 yrs.; Dir. Edu., 8 yrs., Exec. V. Pres., 9 yrs. to 1946, Rhode Island Sch. Design; Dir., T. Film Custodians, 1937- ; Trustee, Munsell Color Fnd., 1945- ; Chm. U.S. Delegates, Int. A. Congress, Paris, 1925, Prague, 1928, Brussels, 1935, Paris, 1937.

FARR, DORATHY—*Painter, C., T.*
57 Jane St., New York 14, N.Y.

B. St. Louis, Mo., Sept. 8, 1910. *Studied*: Portland (Ore.) A. Mus. Sch.; Am. A. Sch.; New School for Social Research, and with Wallace Harrison. *Member*: AEA; Oregon AA. *Work*: murals, Social Security Bldg., Wash., D.C.; SS Argentina, and in private hotels and homes. *Exhibited*: one-man: Bertha Schaefer Gal.; Kharouba Gal., Portland, Ore.; Fabrics, Chicago, Ill., and in numerous traveling exhibitions.

FARR, FRED WHITE—*Sculptor, C., S., T.*
628 Hudson St.; h. 258 9th Ave., New York 1, N.Y.

B. St. Petersburg, Fla., Aug. 9, 1914. *Studied*: Portland (Ore.) A. Mus. Sch.; Univ. Oregon; ASL. *Awards*: prize, Portland A. Mus., 1949; silver med., Port-au-Prince, 1950. *Work*: Portland A. Mus.; Ball State T. Col.; Detroit Inst. A.; PMG; mural, Social Security Bldg., Wash., D.C.; SS Argentina. *Exhibited*: extensively in museums throughout the U.S. Stable Gal., 1954, 1955; Bertha Schaefer Gal., 1955 (one-man); Paul Rosenberg Gal., N.Y., 1957-1959 (one-man). Author: "Jewelry," Collier's New Encyclopaedia. *Position*: Instr., BMSch.A., Brooklyn, N.Y.

FARRIS, JOSEPH G.—*Cartoonist, P.*
Long Meadow Lane, Bethel, Conn.

B. Newark, N.J., May 30, 1924. *Studied*: ASL; Biarritz Univ.; Whitney Sch. A. Contributor cartoons to Stars & Stripes; Sat. Eve. Post; Collier's; True; American Legion; American; American Weekly; Ladies Home Journal; This Week; Redbook; Look; Esquire; New Yorker; Punch, and other national magazines. Illus. "Slave Boy in Judea"; book jackets for others.

FARROW, W(ILLIAM) M(ACKNIGHT) SR.— *Painter, Gr., Des., E., W., L.*
6038 South Racine Ave., Chicago 36, Ill.

B. Dayton, Ohio, Apr. 13, 1885. *Studied*: AIC, and with Clarkson, Norton, Buehr. *Member*: AIC Alumni; Soc. for Sanity in Art; Chicago A. Lg.; A. & Crafts Gld. *Awards*: prizes, Lincoln Exp., Chicago, 1915; Chicago A. Lg., 1928, 1929. *Work*: Western Springs (Ill.) Women's Cl.; Roosevelt H.S., Gary, Ind.; N.Y. Pub. Lib.; Ft. Huacaca, Ariz.; in Chicago: Provident Hospital, Kimball Piano Co., Wabash YMCA, Lincoln Church, Chicago Temple, and in many public schs.; murals, St. Aloysius Church, Calmar, Iowa; St. Joseph's Parish, Bellevue, Iowa; Underwood Chapel, Youngstown, Ohio, and in many homes and public bldgs. *Exhibited*: AIC, 1923, 1929; Chicago A. Lg., 1922-1936; Century of Progress, 1933-1934; Harmon traveling exh., 1929, 1931, 1933; NAD, 1944; Albright A. Gal., 1944; Terry AI, 1953; one-man: N.Y. Pub. Lib.; Nolan Chapel, 1925; Hull House, 1948. *Position*: Instr., Comm. & Adv., Schurz Evening Sch., Chicago, 1926-48; Dir., Loop Art Studios, Chicago, Ill., 1945-56. Author: "Easy Steps to Commercial Art," 1931; "Practical Use of Color," 1933; "Figure Drawing and Construction," 1935.

FARRUGGIO, REMO MICHAEL—*Painter*
47 West 28th St., New York 1, N.Y.

B. Palermo, Italy, Mar. 29, 1906. *Studied*: NAD; Edu. All. Indst. A. Sch., with Bogdonov. *Member*: AEA. *Award*: prize, Detroit Inst. A., 1946; Butler Inst. Am. A., 1956. *Work*: MMA; Portland (Ore.) A. Mus.; Butler AI; St. Paul Mus. A.; DMFA; Mus. of New Mexico, Santa Fé. *Exhibited*: MMA; WMAA; VMFA; Detroit Inst. A.; PAFA; CAM; Univ. Illinois; Delgado Mus. A.; BM.

FASANO, CLARA—*Sculptor, T.*
131 Christopher St., New York 14, N.Y.

B. Castellaneta, Italy, Dec. 14, 1900. *Studied*: CUASch.; ASL; Adelphi Col., Brooklyn, N.Y. *Member*: F., NSS; Audubon A.; S.Gld.; NAWA. *Awards*: Scholarship abroad, 1922-1923; prize, NAWA, 1945, 1950, medal, 1955; Audubon A., 1952; Medal of Honor, 1956; Nat. Inst. A. & Let., 1952. *Work*: S. reliefs, USPO, Middleport, Ohio; Technical H.S., Brooklyn, N.Y.; Port Richmond, Staten Island, N.Y., H.S.; many ports. of prominent persons. *Exhibited*: PAFA, 1940, 1942-1946; AIC, 1941, 1942; NAD, 1935, 1939, 1941, 1943; WMAA, 1940, 1946; WFNY 1939; Fairmount Park AA, 1940; AV, 1941; Audubon A., 1950; Arch. Lg., 1954; NSS, 1955; NAWA, 1945, 1946; Buchholz Gal., 1941, 1943, 1945; S. Gld., 1941, 1942; in Italy, France & England and major museums in U.S.A. *Position*:

A. Instr., Dalton Sch., New York, N.Y. 1940; Former Instr., Sc., Adult Edu., Bd. Edu., New York, N.Y.; Instr. Sc., Manhattanville College, Purchase, N.Y., at present.

FASBENDER, WALTER—*Museum Executive Director*
Vanderbilt Museum, Centerport, N.Y.

Position: Exec. Dir., Vanderbilt Museum.*

FAULKNER, BARRY—*Painter, T.*
137 East 66th St., New York 21, N.Y.; h. Keene, N.H.

B. Keene, N.H., July 12, 1881. *Studied*: Harvard Univ.; Am. Acad. in Rome. *Member*: NA; NSMP; Nat. Inst. A. & Let.; Century Assn.; Am. Acad. & Let.; Am. Acad. in Rome (life). *Award*: Med., Arch.L., 1914. *Work*: murals, State House, Concord, N.H.; Elliot Community Hospital, Keene, N.H.; maps, Cunard Bldg., N.Y.; Eastman Sch. Music, Rochester, Mass.; decorations, Univ. Illinois Lib.; Phillips Acad., Andover, N.H.; Radio City, N.Y.; Archives Bldg., Wash., D.C.; mural, State Capitol, Salem, Ore.; nat. cemeteries in France, Italy; John Hancock Bldg., Boston; Keene Nat. Bank and Cheshire County Savings Bank, Keene, N.H.*

FAULKNER, HENRY LAWRENCE—*Painter, T.*
Egypt, Ky.

B. Franklin, Ky., Jan. 9, 1928. *Studied*: Los A. County AI, with Millard Sheets, Margaret Montgomery, Pierre Sicard, and others. *Award*: Silver medal, Burr Gal., 1958. *Work*: Univ. Kentucky; Los A. County AI; CM. *Exhibited*: Burr Gal., N.Y., 1958; Little Studio, N.Y.; Univ. Kentucky; ACA Gal., N.Y.; Duncan Gal., N.Y.; Raymond Duncan Gal., Paris, France.

FAULKNER, KADY B.—*Painter, Et., Lith., Ser., E.*
Kemper Hall, Kenosha, Wis.

B. Syracuse, N.Y., June 23, 1901. *Studied*: Syracuse Univ., B.F.A., M.F.A.; ASL; & with Hans Hofmann, Boardman Robinson, Henry Varnum Poor. *Member*: Nat. Serigraph Soc.; Phila. Color Pr. Soc.; NAWA; Prairie Pr.M.; AEA; Lincoln A. Gld.; Northwest Pr.M. *Awards*: prizes, Joslyn Mem., 1945; Springfield, Mo., 1946; Madison, Wis., 1953. *Work*: IBM; mural, USPO, Valentine, Neb.; altar piece, St. Mary's Episcopalian Church, Mitchel, Neb.; mural, Chapel Union Col., Lincoln, Neb. *Exhibited*: NAWA, 1940-1943, 1953-1957; AWCS, 1944, 1945; Springfield, Mo., 1945, 1946; Phila. Color Pr. Soc., 1944-1946; SFMA, 1945, 1946; Lincoln A. Gld., 1940-1946; Joslyn Mem., 1940-1945; Denver A. Mus., 1943, 1944; Racine A.; Wisconsin annuals, 1953-1955-1958; Norfolk Mus. A., 1958; Ball State T. Col., 1958. *Position*: Hd. A. Dept., Kemper Hall, Kenosha, Wis.

FAULKNER, PAUL W.—*Painter*
4617 North 29th St., Milwaukee 9, Wis.

B. North Platte, Neb., Apr. 2, 1913. *Studied*: Univ. Nebraska, B.F.A.; AIC. *Awards*: F., Univ. Nebraska, 1937. *Work*: murals, USPO, Kewaunee, Wis.; Clarion, Iowa; WFNY 1939; GGE, 1939; assisted with murals for Dept. Interior Bldg., Wash., D.C. and USPO, Decatur, Ill.; State of Illinois Fed. A. Project, Chicago. *Exhibited*: Pan-American A. Exh.; U.S. Treasury Dept. traveling exh.; CGA; Wisconsin State Centennial Exh.; annuals of Wis. P. & S.; Wis. Designers-Craftsmen. Exhibited widely in U.S. and Canada. *Position*: Instr., Layton Sch. A., Milwaukee, Wis., 1950- .*

FAULKNER, RAY (NELSON)—*Educator, W., Mus. Dir.*
Department of Art & Architecture, Stanford University, Stanford, Cal.

B. Charlevoix, Mich., June 3, 1906. *Studied*: Univ. Michigan, A.B.; Harvard Univ., M.L.A.; Univ. Minnesota, Ph.D. *Member*: CAA; Eastern AA; Am. Soc. for Aesthetics. *Awards*: prize, Sch. Arch., Harvard Univ., 1929. *Exhibited*: Minneapolis Inst. A., 1935-1937; Ohio WC Soc., 1932. Co-Author: "Art Today," 1949; "Teachers Enjoy the Arts," 1943; "Inside Today's Home," 1954. Contributor to: Educational journals with articles on various aspects of college teaching of art. Lectures: Contemporary American Art. *Position*: Instr., Assoc. Prof. A., Univ. Minnesota, 1932-39; Hd., Dept. F. & Indst. A., Prof. FA, T. Col., Columbia Univ., New York, N.Y., 1939-1946; Exec. Hd., Dept. A. & Arch., and Dir. A. Gal. and Mus. Stanford Univ., Stanford, Cal., 1946- .

FAUNTLEROY, MARTHA LORIMER—*Painter*
106 North Mulberry St., Richmond 21, Va.

B. Yakima, Wash. *Studied*: ASL, with Kimon Nicolaides, Kenneth Hayes Miller, Harry Sternberg; William & Mary Col., B.F.A.; Alfred Univ., and with Theresa Pollack, Marion Junkin, Charles Renick. *Member*: Richmond AA.

FAURE, MRS. RENE B.—*See Greacen, Nan*

FAUSETT, (WILLIAM) DEAN—*Painter, Et., Lith.*
1 West 67th St., New York 23, N.Y.; h. Hill Rd., Dorset, Vt.

B. Price, Utah, July 4, 1913. *Studied*: Brigham Young Univ.; ASL; BAID; Colorado Springs FA Center. *Member*: NSMP; Southern Vermont AA. *Awards*: F., Tiffany Fnd., 1932, 1933, 1935; prizes, Carnegie Inst., 1942; Durand-Ruel Gal., 1944; Guggenheim F., 1943-1944-1945; prize, NSMP, 1945; SC, 1946. *Work*: murals, USPO, Augusta, Ga.; West New York, N.J.; Rosenburg, Tex.; Grant's Tomb, N.Y.; YM-YWHA, Pittsburgh; Bldg. for Brotherhood, New York, N.Y.; Randolph Field, Tex.; U.S. Air Acad., Colorado Springs, Colo. Also represented in MMA; MModA; WMAA; Toledo Mus. A.; New Britain Mus.; WMA; Bennington Mus. A.; Witte Mem. Mus.; AIC; Univ. Nebraska; Univ. Arizona; Brigham Young Univ.; White House, Wash., D.C.; Williams Col.; Princeton Univ.; Am. Acad. A. & Let. *Exhibited*: WMAA, 1932, 1940, 1941, 1943-1946; Carnegie Inst., 1941-1946; AIC, 1935, 1943-1945; CGA, 1941, 1942, 1944, 1945; MMA, 1941; VMFA, 1942, 1944, 1946; NAD, 1944-1946; BM, 1935, 1941; Toledo Mus. A., 1939, 1940; Durand-Ruel, 1943; Witte Mem. Mus., 1943-1945; John Herron AI, 1945, 1946; Southern Vermont A., 1940-1943, 1954-55 (one-man); Univ. Utah, 1940.

FAUSETT, LYNN—*Painter, Ser.*
1105 Parkway Ave., Salt Lake City 5, Utah

B. Price, Utah, Feb. 27, 1894. *Studied*: Brigham Young Univ.; Univ. Utah; ASL; & in France. *Member*: NSMP. *Work*: murals, City Hall, Price, Utah; Univ. Wyoming; White Pine H.S., Ely, Nev.; L.D.S. Ward Chapel, Farmington, Utah and Salt Lake City; Kennecott Copper Corp., New York, N.Y.; Harmon Cafe, Salt Lake City, Utah (5 murals); Utah State Pioneer Park, Salt Lake. *Exhibited*: Univ. Utah (one-man).

FAWCETT, ROBERT—*Illustrator*
Ridgefield, Conn.

B. London, England, Feb. 26, 1903. *Studied*: Slade Sch., London. *Member*: SI. *Exhibited*: Phila. Pr. Cl., 1938; All-Illinois Soc. FA Exh., 1938. I., "Epitaph," by Dreiser.*

FAX, ELTON CLAY—*Illustrator*
51-28 30th Ave., Woodside 77, N.Y.

B. Baltimore, Md., Oct. 9, 1909. *Studied*: Crouse Col., Univ. Syracuse, B.F.A. *Member*: Museo de la Caricatura Severo Vaccaro, Buenos Aires, Argentina. *Awards*: gold med., Cooperative Women's Civic Lg., Baltimore, 1932, 1933. *Work*: Virginia State Col.; Museo de la Caricatura, Buenos Aires. *Exhibited*: CGA; NGFA. Books illus.: "Famous Harbors of the World," 1953; "Trumpeter's Tale," 1955; "Genghis Khan and The Mongol Horde," 1954; "Sitting Bull," 1946; "Melinday's Medal," 1945; "Terrapin's Pot of Sense," 1957. *Positions*: Faculty, City Col. of New York (Ext. Div.); Specialist Grantee of Intl. Exchange Div., U.S. State Dept., 1955.

FAYSASH, JULIUS F.—*Painter, Des., I., T., Gr.*
737 Perkins Park Drive, Akron 20, Ohio

B. Budapest, Hungary, Apr. 11, 1904. *Studied*: Univ. Dubuque; Univ. Akron; Cleveland Inst. A., and with Wayman Adams, Henry G. Keller, Sandor Vago. *Member*: Akron Soc. A.; Buffalo Soc. A.; AWS; Ohio WC Soc. *Awards*: Akron AI, 1927, 1932, 1933, 1937, 1941, 1942-1946, 1950, 1953-1955; Canton AI, 1944, 1946, 1948-1950; Cuyahoga Falls Civic A. Cl., 1945-1947, 1954, 1955; Buffalo Soc. A., 1940, 1946, 1948-1950; Tri-City A. Cl., 1939. *Work*: Akron AI, Canton AI; Massillon Mus. A.; Allison-James Sch., Santa Fé, N.M.; Shaw Sanatorium, Springfield Lake, Ohio; YWCA, Akron; Cornland (Ill.) Pub. Sch. *Exhibited*: Rockport AA, 1930; AWS, 1940; Akron AI, 1923-1955; Buffalo Soc. A., 1940-1950; Butler AI, 1935-1954; Massillon Mus. A., 1935-1955; Canton AI, 1940-1955; Ohio WC Soc., 1940,

1942, 1943, 1945, 1946, 1949, 1950, 1952, 1955; Little Rock Mus. A., 1937; Mus. New Mexico, 1937; Milwaukee AI, 1946; Ohio Univ., 1940-1955; Northwest Territory exh., 1942; Miami Beach A. Cl., 1948; Dayton AI, 1939; Kent State Univ., 1946-1948; Miami Univ., Oxford, O., 1940; North Canton A. Cl., 1939, 1940; Ohio State Fair, 1933-1937, 1954. *Position*: I., Firestone Tire & Rubber Co.*

FEARING, KELLY—*Painter, Et., E.*
University of Texas; h. Austin, Tex.

B. Fordyce, Ark., Oct. 18, 1918. *Studied*: Louisiana Polytechnic Inst., B.A.; Columbia Univ., M.A. *Member*: CAA; NEA; N.A.E.A.; Western AA; Texas FA Assn.; Texas State T. Assn. *Awards*: prizes, Texas Annual, 1953-1955; Texas FA Assn., 1953-1955; Texas State Fair purchase award, 1956; D. D. Feldman award, 1956, 1958. *Work*: Fort Worth A. Mus.; Louisiana Poly. Inst.; DMFA; Vancouver (B.C.) A. Mus.; Texas FA Assn., and in private coll. *Exhibited*: Perls Gal., Los A., 1953; Santa Barbara Mus. A., 1953 (one-man); SFMA, 1953; Miami A. Center, 1953; PAFA, 1954; DMFA, 1953; Margaret Brown Gal., Boston, 1954; Catholic Univ., Wash., D.C., 1954; Texas Annual, 1953-1955; Texas FA Assn., 1953-1955; Mus. FA of Houston, 1955 (2-man); Henry Clay Frick Mem. Gal., Univ. Pittsburgh, 1955 (one-man); Univ. Pittsburgh, 1955; AFA Traveling Exh., 1953-54, 1955-56; Fort Worth A. Center, 1955 (2-man); Carnegie Inst., 1955; Hewitt Gal., N.Y.; Valley House, Dallas; McNey AI; Witte Mem. Mus.; Univ. Illinois. *Position*: Assoc. Prof. A., Univ. Texas, Austin, Tex.

FEHRER, OSCAR—*Painter*
c/o National Arts Club, 15 Gramercy Park, New York 3, N.Y.; h. Lyme, Conn.

B. Brooklyn, N.Y., Jan. 21, 1872. *Studied*: NAD; Royal Acad., Munich, Germany; Julian Acad., Paris, France; Univ. Munich. *Member*: SC; Conn. Acad. FA; Springfield A. Lg.; NAC; All.A.Am.; Brooklyn SA. *Awards*: med., NAD. *Work*: Mem. Gal., Lowell, Mass.; Vanderpoel Coll.; Lyman Allyn Mus. A.; Wadsworth Atheneum.*

FEIGIN, DOROTHY LUBELL (Mrs.)—
Painter, Et., Lith., T.
99 East 4th St., New York 3, N.Y.

B. New York, N.Y., Mar. 8, 1904. *Studied*: ASL, with John Sloan, George Luks. *Member*: Fed. Mod. P.&S.; N.Y. Soc. Women A.; NAWA. *Awards*: prizes, NAWA, 1947, 1951. *Work*: LC; MMA. *Exhibited*: PAFA, 1940-1945; AIC, 1938; Toledo Mus. A.; SFMA, 1938; Carnegie Inst., 1934; Lib. Cong., 1944; Wildenstein Gal., 1941-1946; NAD, 1946. *Position*: Dir., N.Y. Soc. Women A.; Treas., Fed. Mod. P.&S.

FEININGER, T. LUX—*Painter, T.*
6 Holly Ave., Cambridge, Mass.

B. Berlin, Germany, June 11, 1910. *Studied*: in Germany. *Member*: AEA. *Work*: MModA; FMA; Busch-Reisinger Mus., Harvard Univ. *Exhibited*: Carnegie Inst., 1932, 1933, 1935, 1936, 1938, 1946, 1947, 1948; AIC, 1940; MModA, 1943; Julien Levy Gal., 1947; U.N. Cl., Wash., D.C., 1949; Hewitt Gal., 1950; Behn-Moore Gal., Cambridge, 1955 (all one-man); WMAA, 1951; BM, 1951; Mass. Inst. Tech., 1953-54; Mint Mus. A., Charlotte, N.C. (with Lyonel Feininger), 1955-56; Sao Paolo Biennale, 1957. *Positions*: Instr., Des., Sarah Lawrence Col., New York, N.Y., 1950-52; Fogg Mus. Fellow and Lecturer & Instr., Drawing & Painting, Harvard Univ., Cambridge, Mass., at present.

FEINSTEIN, BARBARA CRAWFORD.
See Crawford, Barbara

FEINSTEIN, SAM(UEL) LAWRENCE—
Painter, T., Cr., Gr., I., W., L.
57 West 25th St., New York 10, N.Y.; h. 2008 Chancellor St., Philadelphia 3, Pa.

B. Russia, Feb. 27, 1915. *Studied*: PMSchA.; New Sch. for Social Research, and with Franklin Watkins, William Hayter, Hans Hofmann, Meyer Schapiro. *Member*: Phila. A. All.; Phila. Pr. Cl.; Group 55, Phila.; Provincetown

AA; Artists Cl., N.Y. *Awards*: prizes, Phila. Pr. Cl., 1946, 1953; medal, Phila. Sketch Cl., 1936. *Work*: PMA; Walter Chrysler, Jr., Coll.; Chestnut Hill Acad., and in private coll. *Exhibited*: PAFA, 1933, 1934, 1936, 1953; Provincetown AA, 1952-1955; Phila. Sketch Cl.; PMA; Binet Gal., 1952; Phila. Pr. Cl.; DaVinci All.; Phila. A. All.; Chestnut Hill Acad.; Dubin Gal., 1955; Group 55, 1956; Friends Central Sch., 1954-1956; Stable Gal., 1957; Dubin Gal., 1958 (one-man). Contributing Ed., The Arts Digest, Los Angeles Daily News. Lectures: European and American Art from Renaissance to Contemporary. Assembled exhs. in edu. dept. of PMA; Supv., classes, PMA, 1947-48; Art & Animation Dir., 1948-57.

FEITEL, ARTHUR HENRY—*Former Museum President*
820 Carondelet Bldg.; h. 515 St. Ann St., New Orleans 16, La.

B. New Orleans, La., June 3, 1891. *Studied*: Tulane Univ., B.Arch.; Ecole Nationale des Beaux-Arts, Paris, France, A.D.G.F. *Member*: Palmes Academiques; FAIA; BAID; Louisiana Arch. Assn. *Exhibited*: New Orleans AA; New Orleans A. & Crafts Cl. Contributor to: Pencil Points. *Position*: Former Pres., Delgado Mus. A. & New Orleans AA, and Former Dir., Delgado Mus. A. Bd. memb. of both at present.

FELDMAN, GEORGE (DR.)—*Painter, C.*
139 East 35th St., New York 16, N.Y.

B. New York, N.Y., Oct. 13, 1897. *Studied*: N.Y.Univ. *Member*. AWCS. *Exhibited*: WFNY 1939; AWCS, 1939-1941, 1944-1946; BM; Morton Gal., 1939 (one-man); Chautauqua, N.Y., 1945 (one-man).*

FELDMAN, HILDA (Mrs. Neville S. Dickinson)—*Painter, T.*
507 Richmond Ave., Maplewood, N.J.

B. Newark, N.J., Nov. 22, 1899. *Studied*: Fawcett Sch., Newark, N.J.; PIASch., with Anna Fisher. *Member*: AWS; NAWA; Pen & Brush Cl.; Gal. of So. Orange & Maplewood, N.J.; N.J. WC Soc. *Awards*: prizes, NAWA, 1955, 1958. *Exhibited*: AWS, 1929, 1930, 1932, 1936, 1938, 1939, 1943-1946, 1947-1949, 1953; N.Y. WC Cl., 1935; NAWA, 1930, 1931, 1936, 1937, 1939, 1941-1946, 1947-1951, 1954, 1955; Irvington AA; AAPL; Newark A. Cl.; Essex WC Cl.; 15 Gal.; Rabin & Krueger Gal.; Univ. Newark (one-man); Orange Women's Cl.; Maplewood (N.J.) Women's Cl.; Argent Gal. (one-man); in Belgium, Holland and Switzerland, and others in U.S. and Canada. *Position*: Instr. A., Hd., Des. Dept., Newark Sch. F. & Indst. A., Newark, N.J., 1923- ; Instr., Milburn Adult Sch., Milburn, N.J., 1946- ; Exec. Bd., 1953- , Chm. WC Jury, 1955-57, NAWA.

FELDMAN, WALTER—*Painter, E., Gr.*
Art Department, Brown University; h. 71 Elmgrove Ave., Providence, R.I.

B. Lynn, Mass., Mar. 23, 1925. *Studied*: BMFASch.; Yale Univ. Sch. FA, B.F.A.; Yale Sch. Des., M.F.A., and with Abraham Rattner, Wilhelm DeKooning. *Awards*: prizes, New Haven Paint & Clay Cl., 1948; Alice K. English traveling fellowship, Yale Univ., 1950; MMA, 1952; Fulbright Award, 1956-57; Gold Palette Award, Milan, Italy, 1957; Am. Color Pr. Soc., 1958. *Work*: Yale Univ. Gal.; Princeton Univ.; Brown Univ.; Hebrew T. Col., Boston; Immaculate Heart Col., Los A.; Univ. Wichita; MMA; LC; Lehigh Univ.; MMA; mosaics, Temple Beth-El, Providence, R.I. *Exhibited*: PAFA, 1954; LC, 1954; BM, 1953, 1954; SAM, 1952, 1953; MMA, 1952; MModA, 1954; Bradley Univ., 1953; Norfolk Mus. A., 1953; Inst. Contemp. A., Boston, 1949; R.I. Sch. Des., 1955; A. Festival, Boston, 1953-1955; Dey Gosse Gal., Providence, 1954 (one-man); Artists Gal., 1952 (one-man); Kraushaar Gal., 1953-1955, and in numerous nat. exhs. *Position*: Instr., Yale Sch. Des.; Brown Univ., Providence, R.I.

FELIX, FRANZ—*Portrait Painter*
116 Willow St., Brooklyn 1, N.Y.

B. Vienna, Austria, Sept. 18, 1892. *Studied*: in Vienna, and with Arthur DeFarraris. *Member*: AAPL. *Work*: Nyack, N.Y. Hospital; Dutch Reformed Church, Spring Valley, N.Y.

FELL, AMY WATSON WELLS—
Painter, Des., L., T., E., Gr.
1105 West State St., Trenton 8, N.J.

B. Lynchburg, Va., Dec. 21, 1898. *Studied*: Sch. Indst. A., Trenton, N.J.; PAFA; T. Col., Columbia Univ.; Chicago Sch. Des.; & with Hans Hofmann, Charles Hawthorne. *Member*: Morrisville-Trenton A. Group. *Awards*: F., Barnes Fnd. *Work*: Longfellow Sch., Phila., Pa.; IBM Coll.; State Capitol, Trenton, N.J. *Exhibited*: Montclair A. Mus., 1945; Morrisville-Trenton A. Group, 1945; one-man exh.: Contemporary Cl., Trenton, N.J., 1946. *Position*: Instr., L., Trenton Jr. Col. & Sch. Indst. A., Trenton, N.J., 1930- ; Supv. Young People's Saturday Classes, Sch. Indst. A.*

FELS, C(ATHERINE) P(HILLIPS)—
Painter, Gr., T., C.
2456 Hermosa Ave., Hermosa Beach, Cal.

B. Kirksville, Mo., Aug. 29, 1912. *Studied*: Ball State T. Col., Muncie, Ind.; Mayville State T. Col., North Dakota; Univ. California, B.F.A., M.F.A., and with Margaret Peterson. *Member*: San F. Soc. Women A.; New Orleans AA; So. Cal. Pr.M. *Work*: SFMA; mural, San F. Russian Relief Hdqtrs.; Civic Center, San F.; Univ. Washington. *Exhibited*: Northwest Pr.M., 1948; Oakland A. Gal., 1948; Fraymart Gal., Los A., 1950; Fisher Gal., Los A., 1950; BM, 1951; Los A. Mus. A., 1952; So. Cal. Pr.M., traveling exh., 1948-52.*

FENERTY, AGNES LAWSON—*Painter*
Ogden Dunes, Box 955, Gary, Ind.

B. Louisville, Ky., May 14, 1885. *Studied*: AIC; Univ. Chicago; Chicago Acad. FA; Columbia Univ. *Member*: AIC Alumni; Gary A. Lg. *Awards*: prizes, Davenport Mun. A. Gal.; South Side A.; Gary A. Lg., 1954. *Work*: Englewood H.S., Chicago. *Exhibited*: Assoc. Am. A., 1950; Renaissance Soc., 1952; A. of Pacific Northwest; Tri-City A., Chicago; Gary A. Lg., 1953-1955; Northern Indiana A. Salon, 1954; Southern Shores Exh., 1958.

FENICAL, MARLIN EDWARD—*Painter, Comm. A., I.*
Department of the Army, The Pentagon, Washington, D.C.; h. 3192 Key Blvd., Arlington 1, Va.

B. Harrisburg, Pa., July 22, 1907. *Studied*: Wellfleet Sch. A., and with Xavier Gonzales, Ben Wolff. *Member*: Soc. Wash. A.; Wash. WC Cl.; Landscape Cl., A. Cl., Wash.; Rehoboth A. Lg. *Awards*: prizes, Washington A. Fair, 1946; AAPL, 1956, 1957; Wash. WC Cl., 1953; A. Lg. of Northern Virginia, 1958; Wash. Landscape Cl., 1955; Chevy Chase, Md., 1958. *Work*: Univ. Detroit; Rehoboth A. Lg. *Exhibited*: Wash. WC Cl., 1953-1958; Wash. A. Fair, 1946; CGA, 1955, 1956; Soc. Wash. A., 1957; A. Lg. of Northern Virginia, 1954, 1958; AAPL, 1956, 1957; Rehoboth Cottage Inn, 1956; one-man: Wash. A. Cl., 1956; Roumanian Inn, Wash., D.C., 1958; Chevy Chase, Md., 1958. Illus., U.S. Army training, technical and recruiting publications. *Position*: Pres., Landscape Cl. of Washington, 1958-59; Treas., Wash. A. Cl., 1957; Chief A. Dir., Dept. of the Army, Washington, D.C., 1947- .

FENTON, BEATRICE—*Sculptor*
621 Westview St., Philadelphia 19, Pa.

B. Philadelphia, Pa., July 12, 1887. *Studied*: PAFA; PMSchIA. *Member*: Phila. A. All.; NSS. *Awards*: F., PAFA; Cresson traveling scholarship, 1909-10; med., PAFA, 1922; Plastic Cl., 1922; Sesquicentennial Exp., Phila., 1926; Hon. deg., D.F.A., Moore Inst. A., Sc., & Indst., 1954. *Work*: fountains, tablets, memorials, groups: Fairmount Park, Wister Park, Phila.; Danbury Park, Wilmington, Del.; Brookgreen Gardens, S.C.; Acad. Music, Phila.; Children's Hospital, Phila.; Penn Club., Phila.; Johns Hopkins Univ., Baltimore; Univ. Pennsylvania; Hahnemann Medical Col., Phila.; Pratt Free Lib., Balt.; Rittenhouse Square, Phila.; winning design for Alben W. Barkley Congressional Medal. *Exhibited*: Phila. A. All., 1924-1952, 1957; F. PAFA, 1920-1952, 1956; PAFA, 1948, 1951, 1952, 1954; NSS; Woodmere A. Gal., 1958; DaVinci All., 1957. *Position*: Instr. S., Moore Inst. A., Sc. & Indst., Philadelphia, Pa., 1942-53.

FENTON, HOWARD C.—*Educator*
University of California, Goleta, Cal.

Position: Chm., Dept. Art, Univ. California, Goleta Campus, Goleta, Cal.*

FENTON, JOHN NATHANIEL—*Painter*
19 William St., Mt. Vernon, N.Y.

B. Mountaindale, N.Y., June 29, 1912. *Studied*: ASL, with Kenneth Hayes Miller, Allen Lewis, Samuel Adler. *Awards*: Joseph Isador gold medal, NAD, 1958. *Exhibited*: NAD, 1958; Columbus Mus. FA, 1958; Butler Inst. Am. A., 1958; Illinois Wesleyan Univ., 1958; Babcock Gal., N.Y., 1955, 1958. *Positions*: Instr. A., Adult Edu., N.Y. Univ.; Goddard Col., Plainfield, Vt.; Scarsdale (N.Y.) H.S. and Adult Edu. Program.

FERBER, HERBERT—*Sculptor, P., C.*
454 Riverside Dr., New York 27, N.Y.

B. New York, N.Y., Apr. 30, 1906. *Studied*: Col. City of N.Y.; Columbia Univ., B.S. *Awards*: prize, MMA, 1942. *Work*: MMA; WMAA; Williams College; Detroit Inst. A.; Cranbrook Acad. A.; Albright A. Gal. *Exhibited*: WMAA, 1941-1946; PAFA, 1943, 1945; BMFA, 1945.

FERDON, EDWIN NELSON, JR.—
Associate Museum Director
Museum of International Folk Art; h. 111 Malaga Rd., Santa Fe, N.M.

B. St. Paul, Minn., June 14, 1913. *Studied*: Marietta Col.; Univ. New Mexico, A.B.; Univ. Southern California, M.A.; Univ. Michigan. *Position*: Assoc. Dir., Mus. of International Folk Art, Santa Fe, N.M.

FERGUSON, AGNES HOWELL (Mrs. R. M.)—*Painter*
RR No. 3, Grand Detour, Dixon, Ill.

B. Dixon, Ill., Feb. 6, 1895. *Studied*: BMFA Sch.; Chicago Acad. FA; & with John T. Nolf, George Elmer Browne. *Member*: Rockford AA. *Award*: prize, Rockford AA. *Work*: Lee County Circuit Court, Dixon, Ill.; Dixon Pub. Hospital; Community A. Gal., Dixon, Ill.; Girls Cl., Boston. *Exhibited*: AIC, 1934, 1936; All-Illinois Soc. FA; Frances Shimer Col.; Davenport A. Gal., 1941; Beloit Col.; Sycamore, Sterling, Morrison, Ill.; Clinton, Iowa; Ogunquit A. Mus.; Davenport Mun. A. Gal., 1957 (3-man); Rockford AA Gal., 1958 (one-man).

FERGUSON, EDWARD R., JR.—*Painter, Gr.*
Ferguson Art Shop, Buckham & West 2nd St., Flint 3, Mich.; h. G8052 North Bray Rd., Mt. Morris, Mich.

B. Pueblo, Colo., Mar. 21, 1914. *Studied*: Flint Inst. A. *Awards*: prizes, Flint Inst. A., 1955, 1958. *Work*: Detroit Inst. A.; Flint Inst. A.; ports., Genessee County Court House, and in private coll. *Exhibited*: Flint Inst. A., 1933-1942, 1953, 1954, 1956, 1958; PAFA, 1941; Phila. A. All., 1940; Oklahoma A. Center, 1940, 1941; Detroit Inst. A., 1934-1941, 1955, 1956; Wichita AA, 1955, 1956, 1958; LC, 1956-1958; Phila. Pr. Cl., 1957; Portland (Me.) Mus. A., 1958; South Bend AA, 1957, 1958.

FERGUSON, NANCY MAYBIN—*Painter*
53 West Tulpehocken St., Germantown, Philadelphia 44, Pa.

B. Philadelphia, Pa. *Studied*: Phila. Sch. Des.; PAFA, and with Daingerfield, Breckenridge, Hawthorne. *Member*: Phila. A. All.; Provincetown AA; F., PAFA; *Awards*: F., PAFA; traveling scholarships, PAFA and Phila. Sch. Des.; prizes, PAFA; Phila. Sketch Cl.; NAWA; Germantown A. Exh.; Moore Inst. A., Sc. & Indst.; Gimbel Bros. Exh.; Reading Mus. A.; Woodmere A. Gal. *Work*: Friends Central Sch., Overbrook, Pa.; Reading Mus. A.; Barnes Fnd.; Phila. A. All.; Woodmere A. Gal.; PAFA; Moore Inst. A. & Sc.; Sellersville (Pa.) A. Mus., and others. *Exhibited*: Toledo Mus. A., 1927, 1936, 1938, 1944; PAFA, 1945-1952, 1955; CGA; Carnegie Inst.; AIC; Detroit Inst. A.; Reading Mus. A.; Provincetown AA; Milwaukee AI; Buffalo FA Acad.; Columbus Gal. FA; Rochester Mem. A. Gal.; Wilmington Soc. FA; Univ. Illinois; Arch. Lg.; NAD; City Cl., Phila. (one-man); Paris Salon; Miami, Fla.; Woodmere A. Gal.; Park Mus., Phila.

FERGUSON, THOMAS REED, JR.—*Educator, P.*
Pennsylvania State University, State College, Pa.; h. 512 West Hillcrest Ave., State College, Pa.

B. Lancaster County, Pa., May 11, 1915. *Studied*: Pennsylvania State Univ., B.S. in A. Edu.; Univ. Pennsylvania;

Harvard Univ.; and with Charles W. Dawson. *Exhibited*: Lehigh Univ., 1945; Lehigh County AA, 1945; Pa. State Univ. summer exh. *Position*: Asst. Prof., Pennsylvania State Univ., State College, Pa., 1946- ; Dir., Univ. Relations, 1958- .

FERGUSON, VAN HOOD—*Painter*
231 Tharpe St., Tallahassee, Fla.

B. Florida, Aug. 2, 1903. *Studied*: Emory Univ., Atlanta, Ga., B.S.; Jacksonville (Fla.) A. Acad.; ASL. *Awards*: prizes, State of Florida, 1937; Tallahassee, Fla., 1940. *Exhibited*: Rockefeller Center, 1937; Acad. All. A., 1943; Am.-British A. Center, 1943, 1945; Tallahassee, Fla., 1940, 1941.

FERNE, HORTENSE—*Painter, Et., Lith.*
Greens Farm Rd., Westport, Conn.

B. New York, N.Y., Dec. 14, 1890. *Studied*: NAD; T. Col., Columbia Univ. *Member*: NAWA; SAE; Wash. SA; Wash. WC Cl.; North Shore AA. *Awards*: Med., Plastic Cl., 1937; prize, Wash. SA, 1940; Springfield AA, 1939. *Work*: Tuskegee Inst.; N.Y. Pub.Lib.; BMA; Am. Indian Mus.; Hudson River Mus.; Republican Cl., N.Y.; Westport Pub. Sch.; New Era Boys Cl.; Gr. Sketch Cl., Phila., Pa. *Exhibited*: Newman Gal., Phila.; Warwick Gal., Phila.; Milwaukee AI; Currier Gal. A.; Westfield (Mass.) Atheneum; Albany Inst. Hist. & A.; Everhart Mus.; Grosvenor Lib., Buffalo, N.Y.; Utica Pub. Lib.; Westerly (R.I.) Pub. Lib.; Washburn Col.; Mass. State Col.; Hood Col.; Women's Cl., Westport; Westport Playhouse (all one-man).

FERNOW, BERNICE PAUAHI ANDREWS (Mrs. B. E.)
—*Painter, T.*
Clemson College, Clemson, S.C.

B. Jersey City, N.J., Dec. 17, 1881. *Studied*: ASL; Cornell Univ.; & with Olaf M. Brauner, Theodora Thayer. *Work*: MMA. *Exhibited*: NAD; N.Y. WC Cl.; ASMP; PAFA; Montclair A. Mus.; WMA; AIC; Wisconsin P.&S.; Reinhardt Gal.; CGA; High Mus. A.; Gibbes A. Gal.; Mint Mus. A.; WFNY 1939; GGE, 1939; Int. Exp., Rome, Italy.

FERON, LOUIS—*Craftsman, S., Des., E.*
139 West 54th St. (19); h. 239 East 79th St., New York 21, N.Y.

B. Rouen, France, Aug. 16, 1901. *Studied*: Mun. A. Sch. of City of Paris; Ecole Nationale des Arts et Metiers, Paris, France. *Member*: NSS; Saint Luke's A. Gld., Whitestone, N.Y. *Awards*: Ordre du Travail, Sorbonne, Paris, 1933; medal, France; gold medal, International FA Soc., New York, N.Y., 1955; many prizes in Europe. *Work*: gold and silver religious articles—Canterbury Sch., New Milford, Conn.; Portsmouth (R.I.) Priory; Dominican Retreat House, Elkins Park, Pa.; Lauelle Sch. for the Blind, New York, N.Y.; Bellarmine Col., Plattsburgh, N.Y.; many sc. busts, ports, bas-reliefs, etc. in private collections in Europe, U.S., and South America. *Position*: Prof. Painting, Dec. Arts, Pub. Works Schs., Costa Rica, 1935; Organized and Directed Apprenticeship Sch. of Pub. Works for the Govt. of Costa Rica, 1936.

FERREN, JOHN—*Painter, S., Des., Gr., T.*
15 West 73rd St., New York 23, N.Y.; h. 11606 Chenault St., Los Angeles 49, Cal.

B. Pendleton, Ore., Oct. 17, 1905. *Studied*: Sorbonne, Paris; Univ. Florence, Italy; Univ. Salamanca, Spain. *Work*: MMoDA; WMAA; Univ. Nebraska; Yale Univ.; George Washington Univ.; Wadsworth Atheneum; PMA; SFMA; Detroit Inst. A.; Scripps Col.; Guggenheim Mus., N.Y. *Awards*: prize, Provincetown A. Festival, 1958. *Exhibited*: CGA, 1937; PAFA, 1937, 1940, 1945; Cal. PLH, 1945, 1949, 1952; Detroit Inst. A., 1946; CAM, 1946; Kleemann Gal., 1947-1949; Mus. New Mexico, 1950; Santa Barbara Mus. A., 1952; SFMA, 1952; Stanford Univ., 1952; one-man: Matisse Gal., 1936-1938; Willard Gal., 1941; Minneapolis Inst. A., 1936; SFMA, 1937; Putzel Gal., Hollywood, Cal., 1936; Iolas Gal., 1953; Stable Gal., 1954, 1955, 1957, 1958; Pasadena Mus. A., 1955. Contributor to Arts & Architecture; Art News. *Position*: Instr., Queens Col., New York, N.Y.

FERRIS, EDYTHE (Mrs. Raymond H.)—
Painter, C., Gr., T., W., L.
240 South 45th St., Philadelphia 4, Pa.

B. Riverton, N.J., June 21, 1897. *Studied*: Phila. Sch. Des. for Women; and with Henry B. Snell. *Member*: AWS; Phila. Pr. Cl.; Am. Color Pr. Soc. (Council memb.); Soc. Canadian P. & Et. *Awards*: Morris F., 1919, 1920; J. Lessing Rosenwald prize, 1955; med., Gimbels, 1932. *Work*: Phila. Sch. Des. for Women Alumnae Coll.; St. Luke's Church, Kensington, Phila.; PMA; Free Lib. of Phila.; Soc. Canadian P. & Et. *Exhibited*: NAD; PAFA; AWS; Phila. WC Cl.; NAWA; Wash. WC Cl.; prints widely exhibited U.S. and Canada. Contributor to School Arts & Crafts; Am.-German Review magazines; lecturer: Art Appreciation. *Position*: Art Advisor, Carl Schurz Mem. Fnd., 1953- .

FERRISS, DOROTHY—Painter
35 East 9th St., New York 3, N.Y.

B. New York, N.Y. *Studied*: AIC; Cranbrook Acad. A., and with Robert Henri. *Member*: NAWA; Pen & Brush Cl. *Awards*: prizes, NAWA, 1952, 1957; Pen & Brush Cl., 1948. *Exhibited*: NAWA, 1948-1957; Pen & Brush Cl., 1944-1958; Argent Gal., N.Y., 1952-1957.

FERRY, FRANCES—Painter
2115 P St., Northwest, Washington 7, D.C.

B. Salt Lake City, Utah. *Studied*: Univ. Washington, A.B., M.F.A., with John Butler, Walter Isaacs, Ambrose Patterson, Paul Guston; in Europe with Jean Despujols, Andre Lhote, Ozenfant; Alfred Univ., N.Y., with Kathryn Nelson. *Member*: A. Gld. of Wash.; Wash. Soc. A. *Exhibited*: Paris Salon; Dupont Theatre, Wash., D.C.; CGA; Smithsonian Inst.; Am. Inst. Arch.; Whytes Book Store & Gal.; Wash. Workshop; Friendship House; Wilson T. Col.; one-man: A. Gal., N.Y.; Jacques Seligmann Gal.; Midtown Gal.; ACA Gal.; Contemporary Arts; Seattle Pub. Lib.; SAM; Henry Gal., Univ. Wash.; Fine Arts Cl., Playhouse Theatre, Garden Gate Restaurant, Nat. Cathedral Sch., all in Wash., D.C.; also in traveling exhs. *Position*: Instr. A., Univ. Washington, 1940-41; Instr. Hist. A., Grad. Sch., Dept. of Agriculture, Wash., D.C., 1944-45; Washington Workshop.*

FESSENDEN, DeWITT HARVEY—
Etcher, P., Des., W., Cr.
99 Joralemon St., Brooklyn 1, N.Y.

B. Waverly, N.Y., Sept. 25, 1884. *Studied*: Cornell Univ., (Arch. & Landscape Arch.), and in Paris, France. *Exhibited*: Columbia Univ.; Avery Mem. Lib.; Arch. Lg. Publisher and Founder of Sketch Book Magazine, 1923-1937; Publ. "The Life and Works of Claude Deruet, Court Painter," 1952; Author, I., "Pageant of French Architecture," 1935. Contributor to International Studio, Design, Arts & Decoration, House & Garden, Architectural Record, and other national publications.

FIELD, BEATRICE (Mrs. David P.)—Painter, L., T.
200 Lawrence St., Leominster, Mass.

B. Jacksonville, Ill., Mar. 11, 1888. *Studied*: Smith Col. Grad. Sch. Arch. and Landscape; The Cambridge Sch.; Vassar Col. *Member*: Min. P., S. & Gravers Soc., Wash., D.C. *Exhibited*: one-man: Smithsonian Inst.; Vassar Col. A. Gal.; Boston Public Lib., and others. Also in numerous group exhibitions. Lectures on Landscape Design and Civic Planning.

FIELDS, MITCHELL—Sculptor
3 Great Jones St.; h. 38 Morton St., New York 14, N.Y.

B. Belcest, Rumania, Sept. 28, 1901. *Studied*: NAD; BAID. *Member*: ANA; NSS. *Awards*: Guggenheim F., 1932, 1935; prizes, NAD, 1929, 1950; medal, PAFA, 1930; Watrous gold medal, NAD, 1949, 1955; Tiffany Fnd. award, 1955. *Work*: BM; Gorki Literary Mus.; Mus. Western A., Moscow. *Exhibited*: MMoDA; WMAA; BM; MMA; NAD; PAFA; Nat. Inst. A. & Lets., 1957. Taught and lectured on American Sculpture, Tel Aviv, Israel, 1957-58.

FIENE, ALICIA—Painter
331 East 55th St., New York 22, N.Y.

B. Chicopee, Mass., April 23, 1918. *Studied*: ASL; Colorado Springs FA Center; Warsaw A. Acad., Poland. *Mem*-ber: AEA; ASL; NAWA. *Awards*: Kosciuszko Fnd. F., 1937; Tiffany Fnd. grant, 1948, 1949. *Work*: mural, USPO, Mooresville, N.C. *Exhibited*: Carnegie Inst., 1941, 1946-1949; PAFA, 1948, 1949; NAD, 1949; Terry AI, 1951; Michigan A., 1934-1948; Conn. Painters, 1948; Polish-American A., 1948-1950; Portraits in Review, N.Y., 1950-1952.*

FIENE, ERNEST—Painter, Et., Lith., T.
331 East 55th St., New York 22, N.Y.

B. Elberfeld, Germany, Nov. 2, 1894. *Studied*: NAD; BAID; ASL, and in France, Germany and Italy. *Member*: F., Intl. Inst. A. & Let.; NAD; ASL (Life). *Awards*: Guggenheim F., 1932; prizes, AIC, 1937, 1940; LC, 1940, 1944, 1946; CGA, 1938; prize, med., Carnegie Inst., 1939, 1940, 1941. *Work*: MMA; MMoDA; BMFA; AIC; Detroit Inst. A.; CM; Los A. Mus. A.; Newark Mus. A.; Encyclopaedia Britannica Coll.; WMAA; Cal. PLH; BM; CAM; Cal. PLH; Denver A. Mus.; PMG; Swope Gal. A.; N.Y. Pub.Lib.; Ohio, Columbia, Yale Universities; murals, USPO, Canton, Mass.; Dept. Interior Bldg., Wash., D.C.; Needle Trades H.S., N.Y.; Abraham Lincoln H.S., N.Y. *Exhibited*: CGA, 1931-1945; Carnegie Inst., 1930-1945; AIC, 1930-1933, 1936-1945; PAFA, 1930-1945; WMAA, 1930-1945; and abroad. *Position*: Instr., ASL, 1938- ; Fashion Inst., 1944-46; Supv. Faculty, Famous Artists Schools; Lectures and Seminars, Greensboro College, 1958. Hon. Pres. AEA; Cor. Sec., NAD.

FIERO, EMILIE L(OUISE)—Sculptor
242 East 19th St., New York 3, N.Y.

B. Joliet, Ill. *Studied*: AIC; and in France and Italy. *Member*: NSS. *Work*: fountains, CMA; Eccleston, Md.; triptych, Calvary Episcopal Church, Gramercy Park, New York, N.Y. *Exhibited*: MMA; NAD; NSS; Arch.L.; PAFA.

FIESCHI, GIANNETTO—Educator, P., Gr.
University of the South, Sewanee, Tenn.

B. Zogno, Italy, June 10, 1921. *Studied*: Ecole des Beaux-Arts, Paris; Accademia Ligustica and Universota degli Studi, Genoa, with Bevilacqua, Gagliardo; ASL, with Sternberg. *Awards*: Ministry of Pub. Edu., Italy, 1947, 1956; French Govt. grants, 1951-53; Spanish Govt. grant, 1952; Fulbright award, 1953, and others. *Work*: MMA, and in Europe. *Exhibited*: Venice Biennale, 1948, 1950, 1954; Italia-Francia, 1953; Florence, Italy, 1955; UNESCO, Rome, 1955; Nantes, 1954; Italian Printmakers, Rome, 1955; Sindicato Regionale Belle Arti, Genoa, 1948-1957; one-man: Turin, 1947; Genoa, 1948; Paris, 1953; Melbourne, 1956; Milan, 1958; Williamsburg, Va., 1953. *Positions*: Dir., Art Scial., "San Matteo," Genoa; Counselor, Sindicato Belle Arti, Genoa; Fndr., Associazione Artisti, Genoa; Hd., Dept. FA, Univ. of the South, Sewanee, Tenn., at present.

FIFE, MARY E. (Mrs. Edward Laning)—Painter, T.
82 State St., Brooklyn 1, N.Y.

B. Canton, Ohio. *Studied*: Carnegie Inst., A.B.; NAD; CUASch.; ASL, and in Paris. *Member*: NAWA. *Awards*: prizes, Butler AI, Youngstown, Ohio. *Exhibited*: AIC; Carnegie Inst.; PAFA; WMAA; Butler AI; Pepsi-Cola Exh.; CAM; William Rockhill Nelson Gal. A.; New York City Center; NAWA, and others. *Position*: Instr., drawing, Art Workshop, New York, N.Y.

FILMUS, TULLY (Mr.)—Painter, L., T.
37 East 13th St., New York, N.Y.; h. 17 Stuart St., Great Neck, N.Y.

B. Otaki, Russia, Aug. 29, 1903. *Studied*: PAFA; N.Y. Univ.; ASL. *Member*: AEA; Audubon A.; A. Lg. Am. *Awards*: Cresson traveling scholarship, PAFA, 1927, prize, 1948. *Work*: WMAA; N.Y. Hist. Soc.; Kings County Hospital; Temple Beth-El, New York, N.Y.; Tel-Aviv Mus., Ein-Herod Mus., Israel; many portraits of Army and Navy officials and of prominent citizens; murals, Brookwood, N.Y. (6). *Exhibited*: WMAA, 1940-1946; CGA, 1942; PAFA, 1941-1946; AIC, 1941; Denver A. Mus., 1942; Carnegie Inst., 1941-1946; Am. A. Congress, 1935-1939; Audubon A., 1945; Phila. A. All., 1935; Toledo Mus. A.; BM; North Shore AA, 1957; Hirschel Adler Gal., N.Y., 1958. *Position*: A. Instr., CUASch., New York, N.Y., 1938-1949.

FILTZER, HYMAN—*Sculptor*

Metropolitan Museum of Art, New York 28, N.Y.; h. 1639 Fulton Ave., Bronx 57, N.Y.

B. Zitomir, Russia, May 27, 1901. *Studied*: Yale Sch. FA; BAID; & with Gutzon Borglum, Paul Manship. *Member*: All. A. Am.; F., NSS. *Awards*: prize, Nat. Aeronautic Assn., Wash., D.C., 1922. *Work*: S., Pub. Sch., N.Y., Bronx, & Queens; Bellevue Hospital, N.Y.; Ft. Wadsworth, N.Y.; Russell Sage Fnd.; U.S. Army Soldier's Trophy. *Exhibited*: NAD, 1926, 1936, 1940; PMA, 1940; WFNY 1939; Arch.L., 1938; WMAA, 1940; MMA, 1942; N.Y. Hist. Soc., 1943; PAFA, 1953; All. A. Am., 1953-1955. *Position*: Senior Restorer of Sculpture, MMA, New York, N.Y., 1945- .

FINCH, KEITH—*Painter*

702 North La Cienega St., Los Angeles 46, Cal.

B. Holyoke, Colo., Nov. 15, 1920. *Awards*: prizes, California State Fair, 1950; Hallgarten prize, NAD, 1954; Los A. Mus. A. (purchase), 1950, 1953. *Exhibited*: Sao Paulo, Brazil, 1955; Carnegie Inst., 1956; PAFA, 1954; MMA, 1952, 1954; WMAA, 1955; NAD, 1954; Los A. Mus., A., 1950-1955; Cal. State Fair, 1950-1955; Santa Barbara Mus. A., 1955; Nat. Orange Show, San Bernardino, Cal.*

FINCK, FURMAN J.—*Painter, T.*

356 West 22nd St., New York, N.Y.; h. R.F.D. 3, Saint Johnsbury, Vt.

B., Chester, Pa., Oct. 10, 1900. *Studied*: PAFA; Ecole des Beaux-Arts, Academie Julien, Paris, France. *Member*: SC; AEA. *Awards*: Hon. deg., D.F.A., Muhlenberg Col., Allentown, Pa., 1954; Cresson traveling scholarship, PAFA, 1924; Carnegie award, NAD, 1943; prizes, WMA, 1945; SC, 1954; NAD, 1955. *Work*: Univ. Vermont; Lyman Allyn Mus. A.; Yale Univ.; State Capitol, Hartford, Conn.; Nat. Democratic Cl., N.Y.; Long Island Univ.; Toledo Mus. A.; Abington Mem. Hospital, Abington, Pa.; Muhlenberg Col.; Union League, Phila.; Temple Univ.; Phila. Col. Pharmacy; Wyeth Laboratories, Wayne, Pa.; Farragut Medical Bldg., Wash., D.C.; Univ. North Carolina; Univ. Georgia; Fla. Southern Col.; Univ. Iowa; Univ. Utah; Univ. Washington, Seattle, and in private colls. Many portraits of government officials and a series of ports. of Deans of the colleges of pharmacy throughout U.S.; Author of articles: "The Artist and the Architect," Journal of American Architecture; "The Meaning of Art in Education," Columbia Univ. Press; "The Artist as Teacher," Century-Crofts. Series of Medical Portraits including "The Babcock Clinic" containing 34 portraits and "The Chamberlain Clinic," with 7 portraits. *Exhibited*: nationally and internationally. *Position*: Prof. Painting, Tyler Col. FA, Temple Univ., Philadelphia, Pa.

FINCK, HAZEL (Mrs. William C.)—*Painter*

143 Elmer St., Westfield, N.J.

B. New Haven, Conn., Feb. 5, 1894. *Studied*: with Guy Wiggins, Sigismund Ivanowski. *Member*: NAWA; Irvington A. & Mus. Assn.; ASL; Westfield AA (Pres.); AAPL. *Awards*: prizes, AAPL, 1948; Westfield AA, 1949, 1950; N.J. Gal. A., 1937, 1938, 1939, 1941; Newark AC, 1939; Irvington A. & Mus. Assn., 1940, 1943; Plainfield (N.J.) AA, 1941, 1942, 1950. *Work*: State T. Col., De Kalb, Ill. *Exhibited*: NAWA, 1938-1945, 1949, 1951 (traveling exh.); WFNY 1939; NAC; Contemporary A. Gal.; Argent Gal.; Studio Gld.; Conn. Acad. FA, 1937-1939; Montclair A. Mus., 1938-1945; Newark Mus.; N.J. State Mus., Trenton, N.J.

FINDLEY, ILA B. (Mrs. Preston S.)—*Painter*

2626—7th St., Tuscaloosa, Ala.

B. Birmingham, Ala., Dec. 18, 1900. *Member*: Birmingham AC; Alabama A. Lg. *Awards*: prizes, Birmingham AC, 1943. *Exhibited*: Birmingham Pub. Lib., 1942 (one-man); Montevallo Col., 1943 (one-man); Mary Buie Mus. FA, Oxford, Miss., 1945 (one-man); Univ. Alabama, 1945 (one-man); Alabama A. Lg.; Birmingham AC; Tuscaloosa County Lib., 1959 (one-man).

FINE, PERLE—*Painter, T., Gr., L., W.*

51 West 8th St., New York 11, N.Y.; and The Springs, Easthampton, L.I., N.Y.

B. Boston, Mass., May 1, 1908. *Member*: Fed. Mod. P. & S.; Am. Abstract A.; Provincetown AA; 14 Painter-Printmakers. *Work*: WMAA; Smith Col. Mus.; Rutgers Univ.; Munson-Williams-Proctor Inst.; Los A. Mus. A.; Guggen-heim Mus. A.; The Miller Company Coll.; Brandeis Univ.; BM; and in private colls. *Exhibited*: Illinois Annual of Am. A., 1951; AIC; VMFA; SFMA; BM; MModA; MMA; Inst. Contemp. A., Boston; Univ. North Carolina; WMAA; AGAA; Los A. Mus. A.; Réalités Nouvelle, Paris; Tanager Gal.; Stable Gal.; Guild Hall, Easthampton; Carnegie Inst., 1958-59; Signa Gal., Easthampton; six one-man exhs., Parsons Gal.; Tanager Gal. (2 one-man). Monographs in the "New Iconograph": Challenge of Modern Art; Painting Towards Architecture; Michel Seuphor's "Dictionary of Abstract Art" and "Piet Mondrian"; John I. H. Baur's "Nature Abstracted"; "The World of Abstract Art"; "Contemporary American Painting," Univ. Illinois.

FINE, STAN(LEY) M.—*Cartoonist*

1128 Vernon Rd., Philadelphia 50, Pa.

B. Pittsburgh, Pa., May 24, 1922. *Studied*: Dobbins Art Vocational Sch., Phila., Pa.; PMSchIA. *Awards*: top ten Look Magazine, 1956-57; Better Homes & Gardens, 1957-58. *Exhibited*: Mt. San Antonio Col., Pomona, Cal., 1956. Contributor to: Best Cartoons of the Year, 1956-58; "Fun in the Rough," 1957; "Family Book of Humor," 1957; "Youve Got Me in the Nursery," 1958; "A Treasury of Sport Cartoons," 1958; "Look on the Light Side," 1958; "You've Got Me in the Suburbs," 1957; "You've Got Me Behind the Wheel," 1958, and others. Participated in "Confidence in America" campaign under the auspices of The Advertising Council, Inc., 1958. Cartoons to: Colliers; American; Look; Better Homes & Gardens; Redbook; Ladies Home Journal; Sat. Eve. Post; American Legion; American Weekly; Country Gentleman; Pathfinder; Successful Farming; Household; Esquire; Parade; True; Town Journal; This Week; King Features Syndicate; McNaught Syndicate. Cartoon Illus. for Advertising Specialty Gld. of America, 1958.

FINGESTEN, PETER—*Sculptor, E., W., L.*

Pace College, 41 Park Row; h. 36 West 86th St., New York 24, N.Y.

B. Berlin, Germany, Mar. 20, 1916. *Studied*: FA Col., Berlin, M.F.A.; PAFA. *Member*: CAA; Am. Soc. for Aesthetics. *Awards*: Tiffany Fnd. grant, 1948; prize, Milan, 1938. *Work*: port., Glycerine Corp. of America. *Exhibited*: PAFA; Audubon A., 1952; Argent Gal., 1951; Lehigh Univ., 1957 (one-man); ten one-man exhs., U.S. and 23 in Europe. Author: "East is East," 1956; "Private Dictionary of the Arts," 1958 (limited, illus. edition). Contributor to College Art Journal; Sat. Review; Art Quarterly; American Artist magazines. Lectures: Magic and Art; Prehistoric Art; Modern Art, etc. *Position*: Instr., Hist. of Art & Arch., Manhattan Col., 1946-50; Asst. Prof. A., Pace Col., New York, N.Y., 1950- .

FINKLE, MELIK—*Sculptor, C., Des.*

144 East 22nd St., New York 10, N.Y.

B. Roumania, Oct. 12, 1885. *Studied*: Cincinnati A. Acad. *Work*: USPO, Sylvania, Ohio; CM; Col. Dental Surgery, Cincinnati, Ohio; Col. City of N.Y.

FINLAYSON, DONALD LORD—*Educator*

216 Overlook Rd., Ithaca, N.Y.

B. Rye, N.H., Sept. 20, 1897. *Studied*: Dartmouth Col., B.S.; Brown Univ., M.A.; Harvard Univ.; Princeton Univ., Proctor F. Author: "Michelangelo the Man," 1935. *Member*: Soc. A. Historians. *Position*: L., Conductor of European tours for Bureau of Univ. Travel, 1923- ; Instr., Hist. A., Wells Col., 1925-28; Elmira Col., 1938-1952; Instr., 1928- , Prof., 1935- , Cornell Univ., Ithaca, N.Y.; Cur., Chapman & Clark Collections, 1952-55; Trustee, Brick Store Museum, 1956- .

FINLEY, DAVID E.—*Former Museum Director*

3318 O St., Washington 7, D.C.

B. York, S.C., Sept. 13, 1890. *Studied*: Univ. South Carolina, A.B.; George Washington Law Sch., LL.B. *Member*: AAMus. (Pres. 1945-49); Chm., U.S. National Comm. on International Cooperation Among Museums, 1945-49; V. Pres., Int. Council of Mus., 1946-49; V. Chm., American Comm. for Protection and Salvage of Artistic and Historic Monuments in War Areas, 1943-46; Smithsonian A. Comm. *Awards*: hon. deg., Doctor FA, Yale Univ., 1946; D.Litt., Univ. South Carolina, 1950. *Position*: Dir., National Gallery of Art, Washington, D.C., 1938-July 1, 1956; Chm., Commission of Fine Arts; Chm., National Trust for Historic Preservation (retired).

FINLEY, MARY L. (Mrs. Irvin C. Thomas)— Painter, Gr., E., I., Des.

3610 Berry Drive, Studio City, Cal.

B. San Francisco, Cal., Nov. 28, 1908. *Studied*: Univ. California, A.B., M.A., and with Hans Hofmann. *Member*: Cal. WC Soc. (2nd V.P., 1948-49, 1st V.P., 1954-55). *Awards*: prizes, Cal. State Fair, 1947, 1950; New Mexico State Fair, 1944; A. Fair, Wash., D.C., 1947; Cal. WC Soc., 1946; Hermosa (Cal.) A. Fair, 1950; Wilmington, Cal., 1952. *Exhibited*: Cal. WC Soc., 1939-1955; AIC, 1939, 1940; PAFA, 1941, 1946-1948; San Diego FA Soc., 1934, 1940; Audubon A., 1944; SFMA, 1939; Oakland A. Mus., 1940; Conn. Acad. FA, 1939; AWS, 1944; Los A. Mus. A., 1932, 1935, 1940, 1941, 1950; Mus. New Mexico, 1945; Wash. WC Cl., 1947; Santa Paula, Cal., 1947; LC, 1948; Carnegie Inst., 1948; Los A. County Fair, 1950, 1951; Cal. State Fair, 1947, 1949, 1950; AIGA, 1913-1947; Palos Verdes, Cal., 1948, 1952; Santa Maria, Cal., 1952; Los Angeles AA, 1947, 1950, 1952; Greek Theatre, Los A., 1951; Mira Loma H.S., 1953-1955; Santa Monica A. Gal., 1955. Illus., "American Indian Songs," 1950; "Very Easy Descants," 1951; "More Descants & Easy Basses," 1951. *Position*: Instr., Los Angeles City Col., 1930-32; Univ. of Cal., Berkeley, 1932; Long Beach City Col., 1935-42; Univ. Cal., at Los Angeles, 1950; Univ. California Ext. Div., 1948-53; Occidental Col., 1950-51; Chouinard AI, Los Angeles, Cal., 1956- .

FINN, KATHLEEN MACY (Mrs.)—Etcher, L.

Southport, Conn.

B. Feb. 1, 1896. *Studied*: with F.G.Hall, George Senseney, George Bridgman, Joseph Pennell, and others; ASL. *Member*: SAGA; NAWA; Am. Color Pr. Soc.; Pen & Brush Cl.; ASL; New Haven Paint & Clay Cl.; Nat. Lg. Am. Pen Women; Chicago Soc. Etchers; Academic A.; AAPL. *Work*: Smithsonian Inst.; Irvington (N.Y.) Pub. Lib.; Lenox (Mass.) Pub. Lib.; Pa. State Univ.; MMA. *Exhibited*: SAGA; Am. Color Pr. Soc.; Chicago Soc. Et.; NAWA; Portland Soc. A.; Albany Pr. Cl.; Min. P., S. & Gravers, Wash., D.C.; Conn. Acad. FA; New Haven Paint & Clay Cl.; Exh. de Cents Unes, Paris; Academic A.; Pa. State Univ.; MMA; Royal Soc. Etchers, London; Stedelijke Mus., Amsterdam. Etching demonstrations: WFNY 1939; SAGA; NAWA. Lecture-demonstrations: Print Club, Albany, N.Y., 1958, and at various schools and women's clubs.

FINNEY, BETTY (MORRIS)—Painter

1578 Queens Rd., Hollywood 46, Cal.

B. Sydney, Australia, Feb. 20, 1920. *Studied*: Royal A. Soc., Sydney; Academie des Beaux-Arts, Brussels; Otis AI, and with Paul Clemens, Ejnar Hansen, Norman Rockwell, Pruett Carter, Dan Lutz, and others. *Member*: Cal. A. Cl. *Awards*: Scholarship, Royal A. Soc., Sydney; prizes, Los Angeles, Stacy award, 1952; Friday Morning Cl.; Traditional Art Show, Hollywood, 1955. *Exhibited*: Cal. A. Cl.; Friday Morning Cl.; Hollywood, Cal., 1955; Beverly Hills Women's Cl., 1955.

FIRTH, KARL W.—Painter, Des., Cart.

2761 East Jefferson Ave.; h. 254 Ridgemont, Grosse Pointe Farms 30, Mich.

B. Kansas City, Mo., Jan. 1, 1911. *Studied*: Cleveland Sch. A.; & with Henry G. Keller, Paul Travis, Willard Combes. *Member*: Scarab Cl.; A.Dir.Cl.; Detroit, Mich. *Awards*: prizes, CMA, 1942; Butler AI, 1939; Detroit Inst. A., 1950, 1953, 1954, 1956; A. Dir. Cl., 1954; Scarab Cl., 1955. *Work*: Marine Hospital, Carville, La. *Exhibited*: PAFA, 1938-1940; Phila. Rotary Exh., 1939, 1940; Cal. WC Cl., 1940; CMA, 1936-1940, 1942; N.Y. WC Cl., 1940, 1941; AIC, 1941, 1942; Detroit Inst. A., 1941-1943, 1945, 1946. *Position*: A.Dir., Maxon Inc. (advertising), 1935-42, 1945-55; cartoons for television.

FISCHER, ANTON OTTO—Illustrator

Woodstock, N.Y.

B. Munich, Germany, Feb. 23, 1882. *Studied*: in Bavaria; Julian Acad., Paris, France. *Member*: SI. Illustrator of sea stories for: Saturday Evening Post since 1910; Life Magazine; Adventure Magazine. Author: "Focs'le Days." Books illustrated: "Moby Dick"; "Treasure Island"; "Black Hawk"; "Twenty Thousand Leagues Under the Sea."

FISCHER, HENRIETTA C.— Craftsman, Des., T., Gr., L.

3460 Oxford Terrace, Cincinnati 20, Ohio

B. Cincinnati, Ohio, Oct. 26, 1881. *Studied*: Cincinnati A. Acad.; Columbia Univ.; Harvard Univ.; Univ. Cincinnati, & with Arthur Dow, Denman Ross, R. H. Johonnot, Theodore Pond and Mrs. Nieder Caudu. *Member*: CM; Cincinnati Crafters; Cincinnati Women's A. Cl.; AFA; Am. Assn. Univ. Women. *Exhibited*: Ohio Pr. M., 1939, 1940; Saranac Lake A. Lg., 1943; CGA, 1943; Phila. A. All., 1933; Contemporary Crafts Exh., 1933; Cincinnati Women's Art Cl., 1916-1953 (one-man, 1952); CM, 1936, 1938; Cincinnati Crafters; Ohio State Fair, 1933; Town Club Gal., Cincinnati, 1959 (one-man); Ohio Mechanics Inst.; Taft Mus. Lectures on Design, Symbolic Design, Silversmithing, and Art.

FISCHER, HULDA ROTIER—Painter, Gr., T., L.

7261 North Seneca Ave., Milwaukee 17, Wis.

B. Milwaukee, Wis., July 28, 1893. *Studied*: Milwaukee, Wis.; Chicago, Ill.; New York, N.Y.; Provincetown, Mass. *Member*: Wisconsin P.&S.; Milwaukee Pr. M. *Awards*: prizes, Milwaukee P. & S., 1936-1946; Women Painters of Am., 1938; Madison (Wis.) AA, 1938; Wis. State Fair, 1938-1946, 1947; Milwaukee AI, 1946. *Work*: Lib. Cong.; Milwaukee AI; John Herron AI; Winneconni Sch., Wis.; Am.Lib. Color Slides; Merrill (Wis.) H.S.; Boys' Therapeutic Sch., Iron Mountain, Mich.; Wood (Wis.) Veteran's Hospital. *Exhibited*: Women Painters of Am., Wichita, Kan., 1938; Oklahoma A. Center, 1939-1941; Blue Ridge A. Col., N.C., 1941; Lib.Cong., 1943-1946; John Herron AI, 1946; Mississippi AA, 1946; Milwaukee AI, 1935-1951, 1957; Madison AA, 1935-1954, 1957; Kenosha AI, 1938; AIC, 1940-1943; Wisconsin State Fair, 1938-1944; Superior State T. Col., 1946 (one-man); Walker A. Center, 1947; Minnesota Centennial, 1948; Wustum Mus. FA, 1950; 34 one-man exh., 1938-1958. *Position*: A. Instr., Shorewood (Wis.) H.S.

FISCHER, MARTIN (HENRY)—Painter, W., L.

107 Physics Bldg., University of Cincinnati (21); h. 2236 Auburn Ave., Cincinnati 19, Ohio

B. Kiel, Germany, Nov. 10, 1879. *Member*: Duveneck Soc. Painters; Cincinnati AC; AAPL; AFA. *Award*: gold med., AAPL, 1947; bronze med., 1955. *Work*: murals, Col. of Medicine, Col. of Pharmacy, Cincinnati, Ohio. Author: "The Permanent Palette," 1930. Contributor of: technical booklets for AAPL & various journals. Lectures: "Technique of the Fine Arts."

FISCHER, WILLIAM LEE—Painter

328 West Jefferson St. (2); h. 1931 Eastview St., Louisville 5, Ky.

B. Louisville, Ky., Nov. 2, 1918. *Studied*: Univ. Louisville A. Center Assn., Louisville; Bellas Artes and Instituto Allende, Mexico. *Member*: Louisville A. Cl. (Pres. 1954); A. Center Assn. (Dir.). *Awards*: prizes, Louisville Women's Cl., 1951, 1952; Devoe & Raynolds award, 1951. *Work*: Joseph E. Seagram & Sons, and in private collections. *Exhibited*: Magnificent Mile, Chicago, 1955; Dayton AI, 1955, 1956; Ky. & So. Indiana exh., 1950-1955; Interior Valley Exh., Cincinnati, 1955; Cincinnati Contemp. A. Center, 1956; Louisville A. Cl., 1958 (one-man). *Position*: Staff A., Louisville Courier Journal, 1937-46; Instr., Painting, Adult evening class, Jewish Community Center, Louisville, Ky.

FISHER, ANYA—Painter

2989½ West Pico Blvd., Los Angeles 6, Cal.

B. Odessa, Russia, Sept. 1, 1905. *Studied*: Jepson AI, with Rico Lebrun; Academie Grande Chaumiere, Paris, France. *Exhibited*: Greek Theatre, Los Angeles, 1948, 1949; Webb Gal., Los Angeles, 1949; Santa Barbara Mus. A., 1949; San Antonio, Tex., 1949; Orange Show, Pomona, 1949; Assoc. Am. A. Gal., Los Angeles, 1950; Claremont Col., 1954; Little Studio, Beverly Hills, 1955; Esther Robles Gal., Los Angeles, 1956; one-man: Forsythe Gal., Los Angeles, 1950; Anthes Gal., 1951; Pasadena Mus. A., 1958; Long Beach A. Center, 1959. *Work*: Pasadena A. Mus.; Long Beach A. Center.

FISHER, ETHEL—Painter, Et., Lith.
4750 Southwest 82nd St., Miami 43, Fla.

B. Galveston, Tex., June 7, 1923. *Studied*: Univ. Texas, with Howard Cook, Everett Spruce, B.J.O. Nordfelt; Washington Univ., with Fred Conway; ASL, with Morris Kantor, Will Barnet. *Member*: AEA; Fla. A. Group; Miami AA. *Awards*: prizes, Lowe Gal. A., Coral Gables, Fla., 1953; Fla. A. Group, 1956, 1957; Harry Rich Exh., 1957. *Work*: Norton Gal. A., West Palm Beach; Lowe Gal. A. *Exhibited*: Art:USA, 1958; Sarasota AA, 1957; Four Arts Soc., 1955, 1956; Phila. Pr. Cl., 1944; Fla. A. Group nat. circuit, 1956 and 1957; one-man: National Mus., Havana, Cuba, 1957; High Mus. A., Atlanta, 1958; Norton Gal. A., 1958; Riverside Mus., 1958; Mirell Gal., 1954; Lowe Gal. A., 1954; Miami Beach A. Center, 1956; Washington Fed. Bank, 1956. *Position*: Pres., Fla. Chptr. AEA, 1958; Sec.-Treas., Miami AA, 1955-56.

FISHER, ORR CLEVELAND—Painter, Cart., W.
1125 Santa Ana St., Fresno 4, Cal.; h. Woodstock, N.Y.

B. Delphos, Iowa, Nov. 27, 1885. *Studied*: Drake Univ.; Cumming Sch. A. *Member*: Iowa AC; Soc. Western A., San Francisco and Fresno, Cal. *Work*: murals, Mt. Ayr, Forest City, Iowa; Assembly of God Church, St. Joseph, Mo.; also work in Pony Express Mus., San Francisco, and in private colls.

FISHER, REGINALD—
Museum Director, W., L., E., Des.
Museum of New Mexico; h. Cerro Gordo, Santa Fe, N.M.

B. Lawton, Okla., Apr. 19, 1906. *Studied*: Univ. New Mexico, B.Sc., M.A.; Univ. So. California, Ph.D. *Member*: AFA. Co-Author (with the late Edgar L. Hewett) "Mission Monuments of New Mexico," 1943; "Sacred Paintings on Skin" (with E. Boyd, Marie Schmitt Ely, Martha Ann Wallser), 1944. Compiled & Edited, "Art Directory of New Mexico," 1947. Co-Author "A New Mexico Version of the Way of the Cross" (with Ralph Douglass and Frank J. Vergara), 1958. Author of numerous art and archaeological publications. Contributor to museum bulletins and journals. *Position*: Research Assoc., Sch. Am. Research, Mus. N.M., 1929-31; Asst. Dir., 1931-33, 1938-41, Mus. N.M. and Sch. Am. Research; Instr., Univ. N.M., 1929-33; Teaching F., Univ. Southern California, 1933-34; Asst. Prof. Archaeology, Univ. N.M., 1934-38; Assoc. Dir., Mus. N.M., and Sch. Am. Research, 1941-45; Hd. Mus. N.M. Extension Service, 1945- ; Hd. Assoc., Sch. Am. Research and Hd. FA, Mus. N.M., 1947- ; Exec. Sec., Science Comm., N.M., 1931- ; Chm., Mountain and Plains Regional Comm. on Creative Arts, UNESCO, 1947-49; Chm., Comm. on Church Art and Ornamentation, Episcopal Diocese of New Mexico and Southwest Texas, 1952- ; Sec., Comm. on Southwestern Episcopal-Indian Relations, Nat. Council of Episcopal Church, 1953- ; Founding Memb. of Mesilla Design Center, 1958. Lectures: "Three Centuries of Art in New Mexico"; "Art of the Victorian Era in New Mexico"; "Baroque in the Rio Grande Valley"; "Spanish Colonial Painting in the Rio Grande Valley"; "Contemporary Art Situation in New Mexico"; "Culture History of the Rio Grande Valley"; "The Meaning of Liberal Education."

FISHER, STOWELL LE CAIN
(Mrs. Stowell Le Cain Smith)—Painter
Box 474, Ogunquit, Me.

B. Wellsville, N.Y., July 18, 1906. *Studied*: ASL; & in Paris, France. *Member*: Barn Gallery Assoc., Ogunquit. *Exhibited*: NAWA, 1941, 1942; Portland SA, 1946; N.Y. State Exh., 1941; Hyde Park Lib., 1942; Dutchess County Group, 1941; Five Painters Exh., N.Y., 1942, 1945; Boston, Mass.; Kennebunk, Me.; Ogunquit A. Center; PAFA, and others.

FISHER, WILLIAM—Painter, L., T., S.
Box 89, Kennebunkport, Me.

B. Brooklyn, N.Y., June 17, 1890. *Studied*: PIASch; ASL. *Member*: SC; Conn. Acad. FA; AAPL; Springfield A. Lg.; North Shore AA; Ridgewood AA. *Awards*: prizes, Asbury Park, N.J., 1938, 1941; All-Jersey Exh., 1939, 1940; Newark AC, 1942; Springfield A. Lg., 1944; Pepsi-Cola, 1945. *Work*: Haddonfield Woman's Cl.; New Haven Paint & Clay Cl.; Mun. Bldg., Ridgewood, N.J.; Contemporary

Women's Cl., Newark, N.J.; Presbyterian Church, Garfield, N.J. *Exhibited*: NAD, 1938, 1943, 1945; PAFA, 1936; Pepsi-Cola, 1945; Springfield A. Lg., 1944; Conn. Acad. FA, 1942-1946; New Haven Paint & Clay Cl., 1944-1946; Montclair A. Mus., 1938-1946; Ridgewood AA; Currier Gal. A., 1943; N.Y. WC Cl., 1936; Brick Store Mus., 1958. Author, "Oil Painting Outdoors." *Position*: Instr., William Fisher A. Sch., Kennebunkport, Me., L., Art Societies, New Jersey.

FISKE, GERTRUDE—Painter
Weston, Mass.

B. Boston, Mass., Apr. 16, 1879. *Studied*: with Tarbell, Benson, Hale, Woodbury. *Member*: NA; Boston Gld. A.; Concord AA; Conn. Acad. FA; New Haven Paint & Clay Cl.; AFA. *Awards*: Med., Pan-Pacific Exp., 1915; prizes, Conn. Acad. FA, 1918, 1926; Wilmington Soc. FA, 1921; NAD, 1922, 1925, 1929, 1931, 1935; NAWA, 1925; New Haven Paint & Clay Cl., 1925, 1929; Springfield A. Lg., 1925, 1931; Ogunquit A. Center, 1932. *Work*: PAFA; John Herron AI; Detroit Inst. A.

FITE, HARVEY—Sculptor, E., L., W.
High Woods, Saugerties, N.Y.

B. Pittsburgh, Pa., Dec. 25, 1903. *Studied*: St. Stephen's Col., and with Corrado Vigni, Florence, Italy. *Member*: Woodstock AA; Yaddo Fnd., 1954; Asia Fnd. grant for Cambodia, 1956. *Work*: in public and private colls. in U.S. and private colls. abroad. *Exhibited*: nationally and internationally with one-man shows in Rome, Paris, and New York. Reconstructor of Mayan Sculpture, Copan, Honduras, for Carnegie Inst. of Washington. Lectures: History and Theory of Sculpture during Italian Renaissance and Mayan Civilization; The Art of the Maya; Hindu and Khmer Stone Carving. *Position*: Prof. Sculpture, Bard College, Annandale-on-Hudson, N.Y., 1933- .

FITZ-GERALD, BOYLAN—Painter, W., L., T., Lith.
306 West 11th St., New York 14, N.Y.; h. 78 Lake Drive, Mountain Lakes, N.J.

B. Maplewood, N.J., Mar. 21, 1909. *Studied*: Lafayette Col., B.A.; Columbia Univ., M.A.; Drew Univ., B.D., Ph.D.; Newark Sch. F. & Indst. A.; and with Junius Allen, Leonard Richmond. *Member*: NAC (Pres.); AAPL (former Natl. Pres.); SC (Bd. Dir.); All. A. Am.; Hudson Valley AA. *Awards*: prizes, SC, 1953; many awards from AAPL; Medal of Honor, Seton Hall Univ., 1955; prize, Knickerbocker A., 1959. *Exhibited*: All. A. Am., 1953-1958; AAPL, 1951-1958; AAPL, New Jersey Chptr., 1950-1958; Art Center of the Oranges, 1949-1958; one-man: Art Center of the Oranges, 1952; NAC, 1954, 1957. *Position*: Contrib. Ed., 1954-55, Assoc. Ed., 1955-58, Editor, 1958- "The Artist" Magazine (Ed. American Edition).

FITZGERALD, EDMOND JAMES—Painter
94 The Post Rd., Larchmont, N.Y.

B. Seattle, Wash., Aug. 19, 1912. *Studied*: Cal. Sch. FA, and with Eustace Paul Ziegler. *Member*: NSMP; AWS (1st Vice-Pres.); A. Fellowship (Vice-Pres.); SC; All. A. Am.; Grand Central A. Gal. *Awards*: prizes, NSMP, 1946; SC, 1950; med., Hudson Valley AA, 1952; grand prize, Art: USA, 1958; All. A. Am., 1957; gold medal, Hudson Valley AA, 1958. *Work*: Nat. Mus., Wash., D.C.; SAM; IBM; Wash. State Col.; Sheldon Swope A. Gal.; Mus. New Britain Inst.; George Washington Univ.; State T. Col., New Paltz, N.Y.; murals, USPO, Ontario, Ore.; Colville, Wash.; Preston, Idaho; Am. Mus. Nat. Hist.; Seaman's Church Inst., N.Y.; Freeport Sulphur Co.; Chrysler Bldg., N.Y.; White Laboratories, Kenilworth, N.J. *Exhibited*: AWS; CGA; NAD; SFMA; Portland (Ore.) Mus. A.; SAM; Audubon A.; Hudson Valley AA. Author: "Painting and Drawing in Charcoal and Oil."

FITZPATRICK, DANIEL R.—Cartoonist
1111 Olive St.; h. 501 Clara Ave., St. Louis 12, Mo.

B. Superior, Wis., Mar. 5, 1891. *Studied*: AIC. *Awards*: prize, PAFA, 1924; Pulitzer cartoon prize, 1926, 1955; Sidney Hillman Fnd. award, 1955. *Exhibited*: CAM; Assoc. Am. A Contributor to: St. Louis Post-Dispatch; Collier's. Author: "As I Saw It," 1953. *Position*: Ed. Cart., St. Louis Post-Dispatch, 1913-1958 (retired). Ed. Cart., Collier's, 1926-1949.

FITZPATRICK, JOSEPH LLOVERAS—Painter, Des., W.
1011 South Fifth St.; h. 1909 Dorothy Ave., Louisville, Ky.

B. Louisville, Ky., Dec. 11, 1925. *Studied*: Univ. Louisville, B.S. in FA; Cincinnati A. Acad.; Xavier Univ.; Academie Grande Chaumiere, Paris; AIC; Univ. Chicago; Univ. New Mexico. *Member*: Louisville A. Center Assn.; Soc. for the Arts, Louisville. *Awards*: prizes, New Mexico Annual, 1953; Allan R. Hite A. Scholarship, Univ. Louisville, 1954. *Work*: Contemp. A. Soc., CAM. *Exhibited*: A. of Cincinnati, 1947; A. Center, Louisville, 1948, 1949, 1951, 1954, 1955; Groupe du Centre, Paris, 1950; Mus. New Mexico, 1953; J. B. Speed Mus. A., 1955; Interior Valley Exh., Cincinnati, 1955; Col. A. Assn., Chattanooga, 1955. *Position*: Dept. A. Edu., Univ. Louisville, 1955; Instr., Carriage House A. Sch., 1954-55; Sch. for the Arts, 1955- ; Instr., A. Appreciation, Bellarmine Col., 1955; Editor-in-Chief, "Arts in Louisville"; A. Ed. & Ed. Bd., "Views."*

FJELDE, PAUL—Sculptor, E.
140 East 32nd St., New York 16, N.Y.; h. 161 Emerson Place, Brooklyn 5, N.Y.

B. Minneapolis, Minn., Aug. 12, 1892. *Studied*: Minneapolis Sch. A.; ASL; BAID; Royal Acad., Copenhagen; Grande Chaumiere, Paris, France. *Member*: F., NSS; NA; Eastern AA. *Awards*: F., Am.-Scandinavian Fnd.; AAPL; All. A. Am.; NSS. *Work*: monuments, Lier & Oslo, Norway; Hillsboro, N.D.; Madison, Wis.; St. Paul Hist. Soc.; arch. s., schools & bldgs., Pittsburgh, Pa.; New York, N.Y.; Boston, Mass.; Springfield, Mass.; Brookgreen Gardens, S.C.; Mus. of Hispanic Soc., N.Y.; numerous medals designed; mem. tablets and busts; Wendell Willkie memorials in State House, Indianapolis, Ind., and Bryant Park, New York, N.Y. *Position*: Prof. A., PIASch., Brooklyn, N.Y., 1929- , Prof. Emeritus (Retired); Sec. NSS, 1950-53; Editor, Nat. Sculpture Review, 1951-55.

FLANAGAN, ALBERT E.—Etcher, Arch.
301 East 38th St., New York 16, N.Y.

B. Newark, N.J., 1884. *Studied*: Columbia Univ. Sch. Arch., and with Edouard Leon. *Member*: SAGA. *Exhibited*: LC, 1933, 1935, 1937.

FLANIGEN, JEAN NEVITT—Painter, I.
Georgia Agricultural Extension Service, Univ. Georgia, College of Agriculture; h. 221 University Drive, Athens, Ga.

B. Athens, Ga., Feb. 7, 1898. *Studied*: PAFA, with Henry McCarter, Daniel Garber, Hugh Breckenridge. *Member*: Phila. WC Cl.; SSAL; Assoc. Ga. A. *Exhibited*: PAFA, 1926-1940, 1943; Wash. WC Cl.; SSAL; Assoc. Ga. A.; BMA.

FLECK, JOSEPH AMADEUS—Painter, Lith.
Taos, N.M.

B. Vienna, Austria, Aug. 25, 1893. *Studied*: Royal Acad. FA; Sch. Graphic Indst. A., Vienna. *Member*: Taos AA. *Awards*: Med., Kansas City AI, 1923, 1929; prize, AIC, 1927; Rosenwald award, 1928. *Work*: William Rockhill Nelson Gal. A.; Oklahoma City Mun. Coll.; Breckenridge Mus., San Antonio, Tex.; Mus. FA of Houston; Carnegie Mus. FA, Ft. Worth, Tex.; murals, USPO, Raton, N.M.; Hugo, Okla., Univ. Kansas City. Altar piece, Our Lady of Refuge Church, Refugio, Tex. (Reproduction & article in "Widening Horizons"). *Exhibited*: CGA, 1935; Carnegie Inst., 1930; PAFA, 1936; AIC, 1924, 1927, 1933, 1936; NAD, 1926, 1929, 1935; GGE, 1939; Bernheim Jeune, Paris, 1932; WFNY 1939; William Rockhill Nelson Gal. A., 1944 (one-man); Mus. New Mexico, Santa Fé: Lectures: El Greco; Spanish Art. *Position*: Instr., A., A. in Residence, Univ. Kansas City, Mo., 1943-46.

FLECK, ROBERT JOHN—Painter, T., L.
503 Dahlia Ave., Ontario, Cal.

B. Wyomissing, Pa., Mar. 7, 1918. *Studied*: PMSch.A., B.A.; Univ. Colorado, M.F.A., with Paul Burlin, Ben Shahn. *Member*: Cal. WC Soc. Exhibited: Univ. Mississippi, 1951; Nat. Orange Show, 1954; Cal. WC Soc., 1954, 1955, 1957; Los A. Mus. A., 1955, 1956; Newport (Cal.), 1955, 1956, 1957; Cal. State Fair, 1955, 1956; Los A. AA, 1955; A. Festival, Laguna Beach, 1955; Frye Mus. A., Seattle, 1958. Lectures: Art History-Ancient Through Contemporary. *Position*: Instr., Phila. Mus. Sch. A., 1947-50;

Sioux Falls (S.D.) Col. 1952; San Bernardino Valley Col., 1952-54; Mt. San Antonio Col., Pomona, Cal., 1954-1956; Chaffey Col., Ontario, Cal., 1956- .

FLECKENSTEIN, OPAL (Mrs. Fred)—Painter, T., C.
820 South Cochran St., Spokane 44, Wash.

B. Macksville, Kans., Nov. 19, 1912. *Studied*: Univ. Washington; Washington State Col.; Eastern Washington Col. of Edu., B.A., B.A. in Edu., M. Edu. *Member*: Washington AA. *Awards*: prize, SAM, 1943. *Exhibited*: Denver A. Mus., 1943-1946; SAM, 1940-1951 (one-man, 1950); Henry A. Gal., Seattle, 1950-1952. *Position*: Instr., Painting & Crafts, North Idaho Jr. Col., Coeur d'Alene, Idaho, 1944-50; Instr. in A., Eastern Washington Col. of Edu., Cheney, Wash., 1949- ; Guest Instr. A. Edu., Univ. Saskatchewan, Canada, summers 1957, 1958.

FLEISCHMANN, ADOLF RICHARD—Painter
1482 First Ave., New York 21, N.Y.

B. Esslingen, Germany, Mar. 18, 1902. *Studied*: in Stuttgart and Munich, Germany. *Work*: Farnsworth Mus. A., Rockland, Mass.; Carnegie Inst.; Busch-Reisinger Mus., and in France and Germany. *Exhibited*: CGA; AIC; Yale Univ.; FA Center of Houston; one-man: Rose Fried Gal., N.Y., 1955, 1957; and in Stuttgart, Germany, Paris, France and Basel, Switzerland. Work reproduced in art publications abroad.

FLEISCHMANN, GLEN—Illustrator
59 Locust Ave., New Rochelle, N.Y.

B. Manley, Neb., Feb. 23, 1909. *Studied*: Vogue Sch. A., Chicago, Ill. *Member*: SI. *Exhibited*: Sat. Eve. Post traveling exhibition. Contributor to national magazines, including Colliers, American, Good Housekeeping, This Week, Sat. Eve. Post, etc. Covers for Nation's Business. Advertising illustrations for leading manufacturers.

FLEMING, FRANK—Painter, Des., I.
Wilton, Conn.

B. Brooklyn, N.Y., July 16, 1888. *Studied*: ASL. *Work*: mural, Town Hall, Wilton, Conn. I., national magazines & advertising illus. pertaining to furniture, home decorations, etc.

FLERI, JOSEPH C.—Sculptor
461 Sixth Ave., New York 11, N.Y.

B. Brooklyn, N.Y., June 20, 1889. *Member*: NSS. *Work*: Church sculpture, Philadelphia, Bethlehem, Northampton, Pa.; Baltimore, Md.; York, Pa.; Stonehurst, Pa.; garden sculpture, Syosset, L.I., N.Y.; Mattapan, Mass.; Greenville, Del.; statues, Brookgreen Gardens, S.C.; Iona Col., New Rochelle, N.Y., plaque, Newtown, L.I., H.S.*

FLETCHER, CALVIN—Educator, P.
Utah State Agricultural College; h. 166 South 4th East, Logan 1, Utah

B. Provo, Utah, June 24, 1882. *Studied*: PIASch.; Columbia Univ.; AIC; Central Sch. A. & Crafts, London, England; Paris, France; & with Ralph Stackpole, Otis Oldfield, Birger Sandzen, B.J.O. Nordfeldt, Lee Randolf. *Member*: Col. & Univ. Prof.; San F. AA; Utah Creative A. Assn.; Utah AI; CAA. *Awards*: prize, Utah State Inst. FA; Sunset A. Soc. of Kansas; Utah State Fair. *Work*: Logan Temple, Logan, Utah; Utah State Fair Coll.; Student Union Bldg., Logan, Utah; Vanderpoel Coll. *Exhibited*: San F. AA, 1936, 1937; Oakland A. Gal. *Position*: Prof. A., Utah State Agricultural Col., Logan, Utah, 1915-1952; Prof. Emeritus, 1952- ; Pres., Logan A. Group.*

FLEXNER, JAMES THOMAS—Writer, Cr., L.
530 East 86th St., New York 28, N.Y.

B. New York, N.Y., Jan. 13, 1908. *Studied*: Lincoln Sch.; T. Col., Columbia Univ.; Harvard Col., B.S. *Member*: Assn. Am. Historians; Soc. for Am. Studies; Authors Lg. Am.; P.E.N. Cl. (Pres. 1954-55). *Awards*: Lib. Cong. Grant-in-Aid for Studies in the History of Am. Civilization, 1945; Life in America prize, Houghton Mifflin, 1946, Lowell Lecturer, 1952. Lecturer, Columbia Univ., 1955. Author: "Doctors on Horseback," 1937; "America's Old Masters," 1939; "Steamboats Come True," 1944; "American Painting: First Flowers of Our Wilderness," 1947; "John Singleton

Copley," 1948; "A Short History of American Painting" (also publ. as the Pocket History of American Painting), 1950; "The Traitor and the Spy," 1953; "American Painting: The Light of Distant Skies," 1954; "Gilbert Stuart," 1955; "Thomas Eakins," 1956. Co-Author: "William Henry Welch and the Heroic Age of American Medicine," 1941. Contributor of: Articles, book reviews, criticisms, stories to national, art & historical magazines. Lectures: "American Colonial Portraiture"; "Gilbert Stuart," etc.

FLIEGEL, LESLIE—*Painter, T., L.*
24-58 77th St., Jackson Heights 70, L.I., N.Y.

B. New York, N.Y., Jan. 27, 1912. *Studied*: CUASch.; Sch. for Art Studies, and with Faust Azzeretti. *Member*: All. A. Am.; New Jersey Soc. P. & S.; Nat. Soc. Painters in Casein; Audubon A.; AEA; SC; Newark A. Soc.; Am. Veterans Soc. A.; Long Island A. Lg. *Awards*: prizes, Long Island A. Lg., 1952, 1954, 1955; Emily Lowe award, 1950-51, 1951-52, 1953-54, 1955-56; All. A. Am., 1953; med., Long Island A. Lg., 1951; Kew Forest AA, 1953; Am. Veterans Soc. A., 1955; Winsor-Newton award, 1956, 1958; Morilla award, 1958. *Work*: murals, Fort Leonard Wood, Mo. *Exhibited*: Audubon A.; AWS; All. A. Am.; Newark A. Cl.; SC; Long Island A. Lg.; Am. Veterans Soc. A.; CAM; WMAA; NAC; Nassau A. Lg.; Lowe Gal., Univ. Miami; Art:USA, 1958; Allis Gal., Milwaukee, Wis., 1958; Syracuse Univ.; Trinity Col.; Denver A. Mus., 1955; Kew Forest AA, 1953; one-man: Hofstra Col.; People's A. Center, St. Louis; Fort Leonard Wood, Mo.; Ward Eggleston Gal., N.Y. *Position*: Instr., Newark Sch. F. & App. A., Newark, N.J., 1948- ; Dir. & Instr., Art Corner Gal. & Sch., Bayside, L.I., N.Y.; Bd. Dirs., AEA, 1957-58; Membership Com., Audubon A., 1958.

FLINT, BETTY NAGELVOORT. See Nagelvoort, Betty

FLINT, LEROY W.—*Museum Director, T., P., Et.*
The Akron Art Institute, 69 East Market St., Akron 8, Ohio; h. 2910 14th St., Cuyahoga Falls, Ohio

B. Ashtabula, Ohio, Jan. 29, 1909. *Studied*: Cleveland Inst. A.; Cleveland College; Western Reserve Univ.; Univ. Minnesota. *Member*: AAMus.; Am. Soc. for Aesthetics; Akron Soc. A.; Designer-Craftsmen Assoc. *Awards*: prizes, Cleveland Inst. A., 1936, 1937, 1939, 1941, 1947, 1950, 1954, 1955, 1956. *Work*: CMA; Akron AI; Butler Inst. Am. A.; Columbus Mus. A.; CM; LC; murals, Cleveland Metropolitan Housing Authority; Cleveland Heights Pub. Schs.; Akron Pub. Lib.; stained glass window, Fairview Park Hospital, Cleveland. *Exhibited*: Columbus, Ohio, 1953; Houston, Tex.; Butler Inst. Am. A.; CMA, 1936-1941, 1947-1956; Akron Art Inst., 1951-1958. *Positions*: Instr., CMA Edu. Dept.; Akron AI Sch. Des., 1950-53; Cur. Edu., Akron AI, 1954-56; Dir., The Akron Art Institute, Akron, Ohio, at present.

FLOCH, JOSEPH—*Painter*
1947 Broadway; h. 139 Payson Ave., New York 34, N.Y.

B. Vienna, Austria, Nov. 5, 1895. *Studied*: State Acad. FA, Vienna. *Member*: Fed. Mod. P. & S.; AFA. *Awards*: prize, PAFA, 1944; Nat. Inst. A. & Let., 1951; Brevoort-Eickmeyer prize, Columbia Univ., 1955; med., Intl. Exh., Paris, France, 1937. *Work*: museums in U.S., France, Austria. *Exhibited*: Assoc. Am. A.; WMAA, 1945; PAFA, 1944; Wash. County Mus. FA, 1945; Toledo Mus. A., 1942; CGA, 1945; AIC, 1943; Carnegie Inst., 1943-1951. Contributor articles and reproductions in leading newspapers in U.S. and Europe.

FLOETHE, RICHARD—*Illustrator, Des., Gr.*
1391 Harbor Dr., Sarasota, Fla.

B. Essen, Germany, Sept. 2, 1901. *Studied*: in Germany. *Member*: Sarasota AA. *Awards*: prizes, Limited Editions Club, 1934 ("Tyl Ulenspiegl"); 1936 ("Pinocchio"). Illus., "Street Fair," 1936; "Circus Shoe," 1939; "Smoky House," 1940; "Robinson Crusoe," 1945; "Picture Book of Astronomy," 1945; "Valley of Song," 1952; "Mr. Bell Invents the Telephone," 1953; "Picture Book of Electricity," 1953; "Family Shoes," 1954; "Venus Boy," 1955; "Ting-a-Ling Tales," 1955, and many others. In collaboration with Louise Lee Floethe: "If I Were Captain," 1956 (Junior Literary Club selection); "The Farmer and His Cows,"

1957; "The Winning Colt," 1956; "A Year to Remember," 1957; "Terry Sets Sail," 1958. *Work*: PMA; MMA; CAM; N.Y. Pub. Lib.; LC; Univ. Minnesota. *Exhibited*: Sarasota AA, 1955. Contributor to the Horn Book. Note on illustrating "All's Well That Ends Well," Limited Editions Club. *Position*: Former Instr., Comm. Des., CUASch.; Instr., Comm. Des., Ringling Sch. A., Sarasota, Fla.

FLOHERTY, JOHN J., JR.—
Illustrator, Comm., Des., Cart., P.
Waterside & Locust Rds., Northport, L.I., N.Y.

B. New York, N.Y. *Studied*: Columbia Univ.; ASL, with George Bridgman; Grand Central Sch. A., with Harvey Dunn; & abroad. *Member*: SI; SC; Dutch Treat Cl. *Exhibited*: Stephens Gal.; Radio City, N.Y.; U.S. Coast Guard Navy exh. in principal cities of U.S.; Phila. Pr. Cl.; SI; SC (all one-man). Illus., "Where Away," 1945; cover for "G.I. Sketchbook"; advertising illus. for leading manufacturers, & illus. for national magazines. U.S. Coast Guard Combat A., Iwo Jima, Okinawa; awarded Govt. contract for U.S. Coast Guard recruiting posters, 1958; posters for important motion pictures; travel brochures; illus. for books for boys.

FLORIAN, GORDON WILLIAM—*Designer, P., L.*
97 Argonne St., Bridgeport 4, Conn.

B. Bridgeport, Conn., Nov. 25, 1909. *Studied*: Grand Central Sch. A.; Yale Sch. FA, and with Guy Wiggins, Anthony Thieme. *Member*: Am. Soc. Indst. Des.; Silvermine Gld. A.; Conn. WC Soc. *Awards*: prizes, Sterling House, Stratford, Conn.; Contemp. A. & Crafts, 1951, 1953. *Exhibited*: All A. Am.; New Haven Paint & Clay Cl.; Munson Gal., New Haven, Conn.; Bridgeport A. Lg.; Triennale, Milan, Italy, 1951, 1957 (designs); Contemp. A. & Crafts; Silvermine Gld. A.; Bridgeport Pub. Lib.; Wadsworth Mus. A., Hartford, Conn.; Brussels World's Fair, 1958 (designs); Essex AA; Milford A.Lg.; Fairfield Pub. Lib.; New Britain Mus. A.; Contemp. AA., Houston, Tex.; Intl. Trade Fair, Liége, Belgium; Barcelona, Spain; Akron AI. Lectures on Industrial Design. Work reproduced in Industrial Design and Product Engineering magazines. *Position*: Des., 1935-40, Asst. Dir. Des., 1940-44, General Electric Co.; Dir. Des. Reeves-Ely Sound Lab., 1945, 1946; Asst. Prof., Indst. Des., Hd. Des. Dept., Univ. Bridgeport, Bridgeport, Conn., 1950-52; Lecturer, MIT, 1950-52, 1954.

FLORSHEIM, RICHARD A.—*Painter, Gr., E., L.*
Studio F, 5 East Ontario St., Chicago 11, Ill.; s. 651 Commercial St., Provincetown, Mass.

B. Chicago, Ill., Oct. 25, 1916. *Studied*: Univ. Chicago, and with Aaron Bohrod. *Member*: Woodstock AA; AEA. *Awards*: prizes, Chicago Newspaper Gld., 1946; Esquire Exh., 1950. *Work*: Musee du Jeu de Paume, Paris; Mills Col., Oakland, Cal.; AIC; MModA; Birmingham Mus. A.; Univ. Minnesota; MMA; PMA; N.Y. Pub. Lib.; Dartmouth Col.; Idaho State Col.; Bibliotheque Nationale, Paris; La Napoule A. Fnd.; Musee Nationale d'Art Moderne, Paris; Victoria & Albert Mus., London; Royal Scottish Mus., Edinburgh; Glasgow A. Gal.; National Mus., Stockholm; Museo de Arte Moderna, Milan; Palacio de Bellas Artes, Mexico City; National Gal. of Canada; National Lib. of Ireland, Dublin, and in many other museums in U.S., Europe and South America. *Exhibited*: AIC; MModA; Birmingham Mus. A.; SAGA; Univ. Illinois; Wm. R. Nelson Gal. A.; BM; CAM; LC; Des Moines A. Center; Dayton AI; Columbus Mus. A.; Hunter Gal. A., Chattanooga; NAD; CGA; Butler Inst. Am. A.; DMFA; NGA; Norton Gal. A.; Universities of Chicago, Minneapolis, Columbia, Princeton, Cornell and others; Rochester Mem. A. Gal.; PAFA; SFMA; Phila. Pr. Cl.; Delgado Mus. A.; Chicago Pub. Lib.; Milwaukee AI; WMAA; PC, and many others. One-man: Nelson Gal., Chicago, 1953; The Contemporaries, N.Y., 1953; Galerie Gerald Cramer, Geneva, Switzerland, 1953; Landau Gal., Los A., 1954; Jacques Seligmann Gal., 1955, 1957; Phila. A. All., 1955; Ohio State Univ., 1957; AIC, 1958, and many others in prior years. Illus., "Exploring Life Through Literature," 1951. Contributor to College Art Journal; Art League News; Chicago Sun-Times. Lectures universities and colleges; Adult Edu. Council of Greater Chicago, 1949- . *Position*: Instr., Layton Sch. A., Milwaukee, Wis., 1949-50; Pres. AEA, 1954-55; Instr., Painting, Contemporary Art Workshops, Chicago, Ill., 1953- .

FLORY, ARTHUR L.—*Graphic, P., T., I.*

1814 Beech Ave., Melrose Park, Pa.

B. Lima, Ohio, Aug. 14, 1914. *Studied:* PMSchIA; NAD. *Member:* Phila. Pr. Cl.; AEA; Phila. WC Cl.; Am. Color Pr. Soc.; Phila. A. All. *Awards:* prizes, AEA, Phila., 1951; Albany Pr. Cl., 1951; Ohio Pr. M., 1955; medal, Phila. WC Cl., 1955. *Work:* U.S. Marine Hospital, Carville, La.; Wm. R. Nelson Gal. A.; Albany Inst. Hist. & A.; PMA; Bibliotheque Nationale, Paris; Dayton AI; Butler AI; Phila. Pub. Lib.; Princeton Univ.; New Britain Mus.; Phila. Pr. Cl.; Logan County Schs., Logan, W. Va.; PAFA; NGA; Rosenwald Coll.; Tel-Aviv Mus. A. *Exhibited:* PAFA; Syracuse Mus. FA, Phila. Pr. Cl.; Nat. Ser. Soc.; Terry AI; Albany Pr. Cl.; Phila. A. All.; Buffalo Pr. Cl.; AWS; Massillon Mus. A.; Bradley Univ.; Portland Soc. A.; SAGA; Chicago Soc. Et.; BM; Pr. M. of So. Cal.; Ohio Pr. M. and many others, including national print shows, and in France and North Africa. Author, I., "Where Are the Apples?" 1945; "Animal Mother Goose," 1946; "Our Daily Bread," 1946; Co-Author: "Cow in the Kitchen," 1946, and other children's books. *Position:* Hd. Graphics Dept., Stella Elkins Tyler Sch. FA, Temple Univ., Philadelphia, Pa.

FLORY, GAYLORD—*Painter, T.*

319 St. Johns Place, Brooklyn 38, N.Y.

B. Woodland, Mich., Dec. 7, 1919. *Studied:* Meinzinger A. Sch., Detroit; ASL; Hans Hofmann Sch. A.; Grande Chaumiere, Paris, and in Italy. *Member:* Brooklyn Soc. A.; Brooklyn Mus. Assn.; ASL. *Awards:* prizes, Life Magazine "Art of the Armed Forces," 1942; Western Mich. annual, 1949; Emily Lowe award, 1952, 1953. *Work:* Life Magazine Coll.; mural and port., Ft. Sill, Oklahoma. *Exhibited:* NGA, 1944; NAD, 1946, 1948; VMFA, 1948; Detroit Inst. A., 1948; Grand Rapids, Mich., 1949; Jacques Seligmann Gal., 1949; Laurel Gal., 1949; PAFA, 1952, 1954; Ward Eggleston Gal., 1951, 1952; Audubon A., 1952; BM, 1951, 1954; Contemporary A. Gal., 1952; N.Y. City Center, 1954, 1955; PAFA, 1952, 1954; Butler Inst. Am. A., 1955; Nat. Soc. Painters in Casein, 1958, 1959; one-man: Ward Eggleston Gal., 1953, 1955; BM, 1954.

FOGARTY, FRANK JOSEPH—*Cartoonist, Des., P.*

115 Webster Ave., Manhasset, L.I., N.Y.

B. New York, N.Y., Sept. 18, 1887. *Studied:* N.Y. Sch. FA; ASL, with Robert Henri, Kenneth Hayes Miller, George Bridgman, and Jane Peterson. *Member:* Nat. Cartoonists Soc. *Work:* Scrolls, for N.Y. Critic's Awards for motion pictures, domestic and foreign, 1948-1951; Pres. Dwight D. Eisenhower. *Exhibited:* Nat. Cartoonists Soc., MMA, 1951. *Position:* A. Dir., N.Y. Sun; Warner Bros.; Selznick Pictures; Johnson Features Syndicate; Cart., N.Y. Herald Tribune.

FOGEL, SEYMOUR—*Painter, Muralist, W., L.*

"Southwind," 2411 Kinney Rd., Austin 4, Tex.

B. New York, N.Y., Aug. 25, 1911. *Studied:* NAD. *Member:* F., Intl. Inst. A. & Lets. *Awards:* Winner, 48 State Comp., 1940; Social Security Bldg., Comp., 1941; prizes, Texas FA Assn., 1952; Mus. of FA of Houston, 1953; Dallas State Fair, 1955; Feldman Coll. award, 1955, 1956, 1958; Gulf Caribbean Intl., 1956; silver medal, Arch. Lg., 1958. *Work:* DMFA; Mus. FA of Houston; Edward Bruce Mem. Coll.; murals, Am. Nat. Bank, Austin; Univ. Texas Dental Branch, Houston; First Nat. Bank, Waco, Tex.; Abraham Lincoln H.S., N.Y.; Federal Bldg., Safford, Ariz.; Social Security Bldg., Wash., D.C.; USPO, Cambridge, Minn.; Baptist Youth Center, Austin; Petroleum Cl., Houston, Tex.; First Christian Church, Houston. *Exhibited:* WMAA, 1940, 1941, 1945, 1949, 1952, 1955; GGA, 1939, 1955, 1957; Arch. Lg.; Nat. Gal., Canada; MModA; Springfield Mus. A., 1943, 1946; PAFA, 1940, 1946; Univ. Iowa, 1946; Mortimer Levitt Gal., 1946, 1949 (one-man); MMA, 1950; CAM, 1952; AFA, 1950; DMFA; Knoedler Gal. 1952; Delgado Mus. A.; WMA; Boston A. Festival, 1955; Denver A. Mus., 1955; Carnegie Inst., 1958-59, and others. One-man: Kendall Gal., San Angelo, Tex., 1954; Betty MacLean Gal., Dallas, 1954; Ft. Worth A. Mus., 1955; Headliner's Cl., Austin, 1955; Laguna Gloria Mus., Austin, 1956; Duveen-Graham Gal., N.Y., 1956; Mus. FA Houston, 1951; Santa Barbara Mus. A., 1957; McNay AI, 1958; Knoedler Gal., 1958. Contributor to College Art Journal. *Position:* Asst. Prof., Univ. Texas, Austin, Tex., 1946-54.

FOLDS, THOMAS McKEY—*Educator, L., Des.*

Art Department, College of Liberal Arts, Northwestern University; h. 9403 Lincolnwood Dr., Skokie, Ill. (Evanston P.O.)

B. Connellsville, Pa., Aug. 8, 1908. *Studied:* Yale Col., B.A.; Yale Sch. FA, B.F.A. *Exhibited:* Traveling exh., "Painting a Mural," 1940-43; "Modern Advertising Art," 1942 (prepared in collaboration with AGAA for AFA). Author articles on art and other subjects in various magazines. Lectures on painting, architecture and design; Design Consultant. Author-I. books for children. *Position:* A. Dir., Phillips Exeter Acad., Exeter, N.H., 1935-46; Prof. A., Chm. A. Dept., Northwestern Univ., Evanston, Ill., 1946- .

FOLINSBEE, JOHN (FULTON)—*Painter, T.*

New Hope, Pa.

B. Buffalo, N.Y., Mar. 14, 1892. *Studied:* ASL; & with Birge Harrison, John Carlson, Frank DuMond, Jonas Lie. *Member:* NA; NAC; Century Assn.; Conn. Acad. FA. *Awards:* prizes, NAD, 1916-1918, 1921, 1923, 1926, 1936, 1941, 1949, 1950, 1952; AIC, 1918; PAFA, 1931; CGA, 1921; Newport AA, 1917; NAC, 1922; SC 1924, 1926, 1930; Sesquicentennial Exp., Phila., 1926; med., Century Assn., 1951. *Work:* New Britain Inst. (Conn.); Grand Rapids AA; CGA; PAFA; NAD; Phila. AC; murals, USPO, Freeland, Pa.; Burgettstown, Pa.; Paducah Court House, Ky. *Exhibited:* CGA; PAFA; NAD; Carnegie Inst.; & others, from 1920-1952.*

FOLLETT, JEAN FRANCES—*Painter, S.*

55 Bond St., New York 12, N.Y.

B. St. Paul, Minn., June 5, 1917. *Studied:* St. Paul Sch. A., with Cameron Booth; Univ. Minnesota, A.A.; Hans Hofmann Sch. FA; Grande Chaumiere, Paris, and with Fernand Leger. *Member:* Sc. Group. *Award:* Scholarship, St. Paul Sch. A. *Exhibited:* Guggenheim Mus., 1954; Minneapolis Inst. A., 1938-1940; Stable Gal., N.Y., 1957; Jewish Mus. A., N.Y., 1957; Cal. PLH, 1957; S. Group, 1957, 1958; Mus. Contemp. A., Houston, Tex., 1957; Art:USA, 1958; Provincetown A. Festival, 1958; Carnegie Inst., 1958; one-man: Hansa Gal., N.Y., 1953, 1954, 1956, 1957.

FOLLRATH, DARWIN—*Painter, C., T.*

429 Benton St., Anoka, Minn.

B. Arlington, Minn., Sept. 16, 1909. *Studied:* Minneapolis Sch. A.; Univ. Minnesota, B.S. *Member:* Minn. AA; Minn. S. Group; Nat. Edu. Assn.; Minn. Edu. Assn.; Minneapolis Soc. FA. *Awards:* prizes, Minn. State Fair, 1934, 1938, 1940, 1943; Minneapolis Inst. A., 1936, 1939, 1940, 1942; Minneapolis Woman's Cl., 1941; St. Paul Winter Carnival, 1951, 1952. *Exhibited:* AIC, 1937, 1938; Portland (Ore.) Mus. A., 1938, 1939; Carnegie Inst., 1941; Oakland A. Gal., 1944-1946; CGA, 1939; SFMA, 1946; Albany Inst. Hist. & A., 1945; Kansas City AI, 1937; Davenport, Iowa, 1940, 1941; Milwaukee AI, 1944; Minneapolis Inst. A., 1931-1953; Minneapolis Woman's Cl., 1935-1955; Minn. State Fair, 1932-1955. *Position:* Supv. A., Anoka, Minn., Pub. Sch.

FONTANINI, CLARE—*Educator, S., Des., I., W., L.*

Catholic University of America; h. 1029 Perry St., Northeast, Washington 17, D.C.

B. Rutland, Vt., Mar. 18, 1908. *Studied:* Col. of St. Catherine, St. Paul, Minn., A.B.; Columbia Univ., M.A., and with Oronzio Maldarelli, Joseph Albers. *Member:* AAUP; Am. Soc. for Aesthetics; CAA; Liturgical Arts Soc.; Soc. Washington A.; Washington A. Gld.; Washington Sculptors Group. *Awards:* prizes, Soc. Washington A., 1947, 1957; CGA, 1955; Univ. Wisconsin Christian Arts Festival, 1956, 1957; Archdiocese of Washington first annual Arts Festival, 1958; Bruce Fnd. award, 1958; medals, Soc. Washington A., 1942, 1952, 1955, 1957. *Work:* sculpture—St. Mary's Church, Winnsboro, La.; Gibbons Hall, Catholic Univ. of America; private Chapel of Archbishop of Washington; Trinity Col., Wash., D.C.; Home for the Aged, Wash., D.C., and others. *Exhibited:* CGA; NCFA; Mint Mus. A.; VMFA; WAC; Univ. Illinois; Watkins Mem. Gal., Wash., D.C.; St. John's Univ., Collegeville, Minn.; Univ. Wisconsin; College of St. Catherine, St. Paul. *Position:* Assoc. Prof. A. and Hd. Art Div., Catholic University of America, Washington, D.C.

FOORD, FRITZ (FREDERICK A.)—Industrial Designer
Snow Dr., Mahwah, N.J.

B. Boston, Mass., July 9, 1899. *Studied*: N.Y. Sch. F. & App. A. *Member*: IDI. *Position*: A. Dir., Paramount Pictures, 1924-29; Freelance Des. 1930-45; Partner, Scott Wilson & Fritz Foord, 1945-54. Freelance at present.*

FOOTE, DAVID S.—Assistant Museum Director
Springfield Museum of Fine Arts, 49 Chestnut St., Springfield, Mass.*

FORBES, EDWARD WALDO—Museum Director, E., L.
Fogg Museum of Art; Gerry's Landing, Cambridge 38, Mass.

B. Naushon Island, Wood's Hole, Mass., July 16, 1873. *Studied*: Harvard Univ., A.B.; New Col., Oxford. *Member*: Am. Acad. A. & Sc.; Archaeological Inst. Am.; Assn. Mus. Dir.; Century Assn. *Awards*: Hon. degree, A.M., 1921, Art D., 1942, Harvard Univ.; LL.D., Univ. Pittsburgh, 1927; Chevalier Legion d'Honneur, 1937. Co-Author: "Medieval and Renaissance Paintings," FMA, 1919. Contributor to: Art in America. Lectures: History of the methods and materials used in painting. *Position*: Dir., 1909-44; Dir. Emeritus, 1944- , FMA, Cambridge, Mass.; Trustee, BMFA, 1903- ; Hon. Dir., Wadsworth Atheneum, Hartford, Conn., 1927- ; Trustee, Reservations of Massachusetts, 1899- .

FORBES-OLIVER, HARRIETTE—Painter, S., L.
250 River Rd., Nyack 9, N.Y.

B. Atlanta, Ga., May 24, 1908. *Studied*: Lucy Cobb Inst.; Newcomb Col., Tulane Univ., and privately in N.Y. *Member*: AEA; NAWA. *Exhibited*: NAD, 1948-1951; BM, 1948; Contemp. A., 1948; Carlebach Gal., 1948; Hofstra Col., 1949; Rockland Fnd., 1949-1952; A. Gal., 1950, 1951, 1955; NAWA traveling exh., Canada, 1951, 1958, Paris, 1954, Amsterdam, 1956, U.S.A., 1951-1958; Berne, 1957; Athens, 1957; Salonika, 1958; Brussels, 1958; Provincetown AA, 1951, 1952; Hyannis, 1952; Ogunquit A. Center, 1951; Mint Mus. A., 1947; Rochester Mem. A. Gal., 1946; Riverside Mus., 1952; one-man: Norlyst Gal., 1945; Crespi Gal., N.Y., 1953; Ramapo-Suffern, N.Y., 1953; Nyack (N.Y.) Pub. Lib., 1954.

FORD, CHARLES HENRI—Painter, W.
13, Quai d'Anjou, Paris IV, France

B. Mississippi, 1913. Editor, Blues Magazine, 1929-31; View, 1941-47. Co-author (with Parker Tyler) "The Young and Evil," 1933. Author: "The Overturned Lake"; "Garden of Disorder"; "Sleep in a Nest of Flames." *Exhibited*: Galerie du Dragon, Paris, 1956-1958; Salon du Mai, 1958.

FORD, DALE VINTON—Designer, E.
601 Fifth St., Northwest; h. 2590 Lake Drive, Southeast, East Grand Rapids, Mich.

B. Grand Rapids, Mich., Apr. 4, 1919. *Studied*: Kendall Mem. Sch. Des.; Univ. Michigan, Sch. Arch. *Member*: Archaeological Inst. Am.; IDI; Furniture Des. Assn. *Position*: Monuments, FA & Archives Specialist Officer, U.S. Army, 1945-46; Pres., Edu. Dir., Kendall Sch. & Gilbert Sch. of Advanced Des., Grand Rapids, 1946-52; Bd. Trustees, Grand Rapids A. Gal.; Chief of Design, John Widdicomb Co. & Wm. A. Berkey Co., Grand Rapids, Mich., 1952- .

FORD, EDWIN JOSEPH—Illustrator, Des., P.
720 High St., Des Moines, Iowa; h. Lacona, Iowa

B. Milo, Iowa, Aug. 1, 1914. *Studied*: Cumming Sch. A.; Drake Univ., B.S. in A. *Awards*: prizes, All-Iowa Exh., Ft. Dodge, 1940; Sioux City, 1940; Cedar Rapids, 1941; Joslyn Mem., 1939, 1940, 1941. *Exhibited*: NGA, 1942; Joslyn Mem., 1939-1941; All-Iowa Exh., 1940, 1941. Author: "The Dairy," 1938; "Coal Industry," 1938; I., "The Post Office," 1940; & others. *Position*: U.S. Army, 1941-1945; Advertising Des., R. H. Cary Advertising, Des Moines, Iowa, 1945-48; Comm. Printing Div., Register and Tribune, 1948-58.

FORD, RUTH VAN SICKLE—Painter, T.
720 North Rush St., Chicago, Ill.; h. 404 Edgelawn Rd., Aurora, Ill.

B. Aurora, Ill., Aug. 8, 1897. *Studied*: Chicago Acad. FA; ASL; & with George Bellows, Guy Wiggins, John Carlson.

Member: Chicago P. & S.; AWS; FIAL. *Awards*: prizes, AIC, 1931; Chicago Woman's Aid, 1932; Conn. Acad. FA, 1932; Prof. A. Show, Springfield, Ill., 1958. *Exhibited*: NAD, 1933; AIC, annually; Conn. Acad. FA, 1932; Grand Central Gal., annually. *Position*: Instr., 1921- ; Pres. & Dir., 1937- , Chicago Acad. FA, Chicago, Ill.

FORDHAM, ELWOOD JAMES—Painter, T.
2407 Glencoe St., Venice, Cal.

B. Long Beach, Cal., Dec. 8, 1913. *Studied*: A. Center Sch., Los A.; Kansas City AI; Univ. California at Los A., B.A., M.A. *Member*: Fnd. Western A. *Exhibited*: PAFA, 1940; VMFA, 1940; NAD, 1940; Kansas City AI, 1939; Portland (Ore.) Mus. A., 1939; Los A. Mus. A., 1940, 1941, 1950; Oakland A. Mus., 1940, 1941; SFMA, 1940, 1941; Portland (Me.) Soc. A., 1940; Fnd. Western A., 1940-1946; Los A. AA, 1946; Pasadena AI, 1946; Cal. State Fair, 1950; Los A. County Fair, 1951; Allen Hancock Col., Santa Maria, Cal., 1955. *Position*: Instr., Kann AI, 1947-52; Beverly Hills Adult Edu., 1948-53.*

FORMAN, HENRY CHANDLEE—
    Educator, W., L., P.
Easton, Md.; h. Baltimore, Md.

B. New York, N.Y., 1904. *Studied*: Princeton Univ., A.B.; Univ. Pennsylvania, M.Arch. in F.A., Ph.D.; PAFA. *Member*: AIA; Soc. Preservation Md. Antiquities (Dir.); Balt. WC Cl.; CAA. *Awards*: prize, Princeton Univ., 1926; Research Grants in Art & Archaeology, Am. Council of Learned Soc., 1938, 1940; Am. Philosophical Soc., 1940; Univ. Center, Ga., 1946. *Exhibited*: Univ. Pennsylvania Sch. FA, 1946; Enoch Pratt Lib., Baltimore, 1941; Univ. Cl., Balt., 1934 (all one-man); Alabama WC Soc.; St. Augustine AA; BMA. Author, I., "Jamestown and St. Mary's: Buried Cities of Romance," 1938; "The Turner Family," 1931; "The Architecture of the Old South," 1948 & others. Contributor to: educational & art publications. *Position*: Lecturer: FA, Haverford Col., 1937-38; Holder of Comer Chair FA, Wesleyan Col., 1941-45; Prof., Hd. A. Dept., Agnes Scott Col., Decatur, Ga., 1945-1951.*

FORREST, JAMES TAYLOR—
    Museum Director, W., Hist
Thomas Gilcrease Institute of American History & Art, 2401 West Newton St.; h. 2491 West Newton St., Tulsa, Okla.

B. New Castle, Ind., Sept. 22, 1921. *Studied*: Hanover (Ind.) Col.; Univ. Wisconsin, B.S., M.S., and work toward Ph.D. *Member*: AAMus.; AFA; Am. Assn. for State and Local History. Author: "Old Fort Garland" (booklet), 1954. Contributor to Art In America; Ford Times; Montana, Magazine of History. Lectures: The American Artist; The West in Art; History of the Frontier to club and school groups and museum audiences. Arranged several special exhibits including: Paintings of Thomas Moran; Alfred Jacob Miller; George Catlin; William de la Montaigne Cary plus Representational Art Annual (a national competition, first held in 1958). *Positions*: Cur. State Museums; State Hist. Soc. of Colorado, Denver; Research Assoc., Wisconsin State Hist. Soc.; Dir., Thomas Gilcrease Institute of American History & Art, Tulsa, Okla.

FORST, MILES—Painter
167 Crosby St.; h. 301 West 53rd St., New York 19, N.Y.

B. Brooklyn, N.Y., Aug. 18, 1923. *Studied*: Hans Hofmann Sch. A.; ASL, and in Mexico. *Award*: Larian award, 1954. *Work*: MModA. *Exhibited*: Guggenheim Mus., 1954; Stable Gal., 1955, 1956, 1957; James Gal., 1957, 1958; Landau Gal., Los A., 1957, 1958; Carnegie Inst., 1959; Cornell Univ., 1958; Zabriskie Gal., 1958; Rutgers Univ., 1958; Knoedler Gal., 1958; one-man: Hansa Gal., 1953-1955, 1958; Univ. Colorado; Univ. Minnesota; Univ. Illinois; Univ. Washington; Univ. Arkansas. *Position*: Instr. Painting, Adult Edu. Program, Great Neck, N.Y.

FORSYTH, CONSTANCE—Etcher, Lith., P., E.
Department of Art, University of Texas; h. Austin 12, Texas.

B. Indianapolis, Ind., Aug. 18, 1903. *Studied*: Butler Univ., B.A.; John Herron A. Sch.; PAFA; Broadmoor A. Acad. *Member*: Indiana Soc. Pr. M.; NAWA; Texas Pr. M. *Awards*: prizes, Dallas Pr. Soc., 1945; Indiana Soc. Pr.

M., 1953; Texas FA Soc., 1954; NAWA, 1955. *Work*: John Herron AI; Ball State T. Col.; Manual Training H.S., Indianapolis; DMFA; Texas FA Assn.; State of Indiana Coll.; Scottish Rite Cathedral, Indianapolis; Witte Mem. Mus.; Joslyn A. Mus. *Exhibited*: John Herron AI, PAFA; Phila. A. All.; SFMA; CM; Hoosier Salon; Phila. Pr. Cl.; Indiana Pr. Cl.; Indiana Pr. M.; WFNY 1939; Dallas Pr. Soc.; NAD; Mus. FA of Houston; Dallas Mus. FA; Texas FA Assn.; Kansas City AI; Lib. Cong.; Denver A. Mus.; SAM; NAWA; Texas WC Soc.; SAGA; BM; Texas Western Col.; NAWA Exh., Berne, Switzerland; Univ. Utah. Color illus. for "The Friends." *Position*: Instr., John Herron AI, 1931-33; Instr., Western Col., Oxford, Ohio, 1939; Assoc. Prof. A., Univ. Texas, Austin, Tex., 1940- .

FORSYTH, WILLIAM H.—
Museum Associate Curator, W.
    Metropolitan Museum of Art; h. 1105 Park Ave., New York 28, N.Y.

B. Chicago, Ill., May 21, 1906. *Studied*: Hotchkiss Sch.; Princeton Univ., B.A., M.F.A.; & with C. R. Morey, A.M. Friend, F. Stohlman. Contributor to: Metropolitan Museum Studies; Art Bulletin; MMA Bulletin, with articles on mediaeval art. *Lectures*: Mediaeval Tapestries and Sculpture. *Position*: Asst., Mediaeval Dept., 1934-36; Asst. Cur., 1936-41; Assoc. Cur., 1941- , MMA, New York, N.Y.; Assoc. Cor. Member, Société des Antiquaires de France; Société Archeologique du Limousin.*

FORTESS, KARL EUGENE—*Painter, Lith., T.*
    96 Bay State Rd., Boston 15, Mass.; h. Plochman Lane, Woodstock, N.Y.

B. Antwerp, Belgium, Oct. 13, 1907. *Studied*: AIC; ASL; Woodstock Sch. Painting. *Member*: Woodstock AA; AEA; CAA. *Awards*: prize, Woodstock, N.Y.; Carnegie Inst.; Guggenheim F., 1946; Childe Hassam Fund, 1951. *Work*: Univ. Arizona; Rochester Mem. Gal.; BM; Montpelier Mus.; Butler Inst. Am. A.; MMoDA; Newark Mus. A.; and in private colls. *Exhibited*: PAFA; AIC; CGA; WMAA; MMoDA; VMFA; Carnegie Inst.; Boston Univ.; Boston A. Festival; Boris Mirski Gal.; NAD; WFNY 1939; GGE, 1939; MMA; Univ. Iowa; Univ. Illinois; one-man: Bucknell Univ.; Ganso Gal.; Univ. Georgia; Louisiana State Univ.; Assoc. Am. A.; Vose Gal., Boston. Author of chapter on landscape painting in The Art of the Artist, 1951. *Position*: Instr., Am. A. Sch., ASL, Brooklyn Mus. Sch., Louisiana State Univ.; Boston Univ., 1955- .

FOSBURGH, JAMES WHITNEY—*Painter, T., W., L.*
    203 East 60th St., New York 22, N.Y.

B. New York, N.Y., Aug. 1, 1910. *Studied*: Yale College, B.A., M.A.; Univ. Rome. *Work*: MMA; Toledo Mus. A.; PAFA, and other museums. *Exhibited*: CGA; PAFA. Contributor to: Art News; Harper's Bazaar. Lectures on various subjects pertaining to art history at Frick Museum; MMA; NGA.

FOSS, FLORENCE WINSLOW—*Sculptor, E.*
    Mount Holyoke, South Hadley, Mass.

B. Dover, N.H., Aug. 29, 1882. *Studied*: Mt. Holyoke Col., B.A.; Wellesley Col., M.A.; Univ. Chicago; Radcliffe Col. *Member*: Am. Assn. Univ. Prof.; Conn. Acad. FA; Springfield A. Lg. *Awards*: prizes, Springfield AA, 1941, 1943; Soc. Wash. A., 1936. *Exhibited*: PAFA, 1935-1938; NAD, 1937; AIC, 1936, 1941; Soc. Wash. A., 1936, 1937; Conn. Acad. FA, 1936-1946; New Haven Paint & Clay Cl., 1940, 1944; Springfield A. Lg., 1937-1944; AGAA, 1942; Amherst Col., 1940; Mt. Holyoke Col., 1936-1946; Deerfield Valley AA, 1937-1940. *Position*: Prof. A., Emeritus, Mt. Holyoke Col., South Hadley, Mass.

FOSSUM, SYD(NEY) (GLENN)—*Painter, Gr., E., L.*
    115 Collingwood St., San Francisco 14, Cal.

B. Aberdeen, S.D., Nov. 13, 1909. *Studied*: Northern Normal & Indst. Sch.; Minneapolis Sch. A.; Universidad Michoacana, Mexico. *Member*: Nat. Ser. Soc.; AEA. *Awards*: prizes, Minneapolis Inst. A., 1939, 1941, 1947, 1950, 1954; SAM, 1942; Denver A. Mus., 1943, 1947; Nat. Ser. Soc., 1953; Sioux City A. Center, 1954; Walker A. Center, 1947; Kansas City AI, 1957. *Work*: MMoDA; Walker A. Center; Minneapolis Inst. A.; Newark Mus. A.; Univ. Minnesota; SAM; Univ. Montana; Wichita AA; Des Moines A. Center; Joslyn A. Mus.; Albright A. Gal.; New Britain A. Mus.; N.Y. Pub. Lib.; Springfield A. Mus.; Univ. Wisconsin; Univ. Michoacana; Sioux City A. Center. *Exhibited*: nationally. *Position*: Instr., Minneapolis Sch. A., 1945-50; Univ. Colorado; Washington Univ., St. Louis, 1950-51; Des Moines Art Center, Des Moines, Iowa, 1953-1957; Univ. Nevada, summers, 1957, 1958.

FOSTER, BETTY (ELIZABETH JANE)—
Teacher, Des., L., P.
    526 Deming St., Terre Haute, Ind.

B. Columbus, Ind., July 16, 1910. *Studied*: Indiana Univ., B.S., M.S., D. Edu.; John Herron A. Sch.; AIC, and in Cambridge, England. *Member*: Indiana A. Cl.; NAC; Am. Soc. Bookplate Des. & Collectors; Nat. Lg. Am. Pen Women. *Awards*: prizes, Indiana A. Cl., 1944, 1945. *Work*: bookplates, LC. *Exhibited*: NAC; Hoosier Salon; John Herron AI; Indiana A. Cl. *Lectures*: Color; Travel. *Position*: A. Cr., Indianapolis News, 1939-41; Assoc. Prof. A., Consultant in A. Edu., Indiana State T. Col., Terre Haute, Ind.*

FOSTER, ETHEL ELIZABETH—*Painter*
    2915 Connecticut Ave., Washington 8, D.C.

B. Washington, D.C. *Studied*: AIC; T. Col., Columbia Univ.; & with Denman Ross, Henry Snell, George Pearse Ennis. *Member*: Wash. AC; Twenty Women Painters of Wash.; AAPL. *Position*: Hd. A. Dept., Western H.S., Washington, D.C. (Retired).*

FOSTER, FRANCIS—*Painter, S., Gr.*
    113 West Great Falls St., Falls Church, Va.

B. Neuilly-sur-Seine, France, June 16, 1920. *Studied*: Black Mountain (N.C.) Col., A.B.; Columbia Univ.; Harvard Univ. grad. work; Univ. Oregon, M.S. *Work*: private colls. New York and Washington. *Exhibited*: 4 one-man exhs., New York, N.Y., 1949, 1952, 1955, 1957; numerous group shows.

FOSTER, HOLLAND—*Painter, S., T.*
    Country Club Lane, Woodstock, N.Y.

B. Caledonia, Iowa, Feb. 15, 1906. *Studied*: NAD, with Charles Hinton, Alice Murphy, Raymond Nielson, John Carlson; State Univ. Iowa with George Ennis, Wayman Adams; Univ. Iowa, B.A., M.A. *Work*: Iowa State College, Ames, Iowa, and in private colls.

FOSTER, JAMES W.—*Museum Director*
    201 West Monument St.; h. 203 Oakdale Rd., Baltimore 10, Md.

B. The Plains, Va., Aug. 10, 1890. *Studied*: Univ. Virginia, B.A., M.A. *Member*: Am. Hist. Assn.; Am. Assn. for State & Local Hist.; Am. Antiquarian Soc. Ed., Maryland Historical Magazine, 1938-1949; Ed., Md. Hist. Notes, 1943- . *Position*: Assoc. Hd., Maryland Dept., Enoch Pratt Free Lib., Baltimore, Md., 1935-41; Dir., Maryland Hist. Soc., 1942- ; Trustee, Baltimore Mun. Mus., 1940-1944; Dir., Soc. for Preservation of Maryland Antiquities.

FOSTER, JAMES W., JR.—*Museum Director*
    Santa Barbara Museum of Art, 1130 State St.; h. 2044 Garden St., Santa Barbara, Cal.

B. Baltimore, Md., Jan. 4, 1920. *Studied*: Corcoran Sch. A.; Johns Hopkins Univ.; George Washington Univ.; American Univ., Wash., D.C., B.A., and with William H. Calfee. *Member*: AAMus.; Assn. A. Mus. Dirs.; Western AAMus. *Positions*: Asst. Dir., Baltimore Mus. A., 1947-57; Dir., Santa Barbara Mus. A., Santa Barbara, Cal., 1957- .

FOSTER, JUDITH—*Painter, Gr.*
    509 West 59th St., New York 19, N.Y.

B. Three Rivers, Mich., Sept. 28, 1930. *Studied*: PIASch., B.F.A. *Member*: Hunterdon County A. Center. *Awards*: purchase prize, PMA, 1958. *Work*: PMA. *Exhibited*: Silvermine Gld. A., 1956; SAGA, 1956; NAD, 1956; Soc. Washington Pr. M., 1957, 1958; PAFA, 1957; Hunterdon County A. Center, 1957; Boston Pr. M., 1957; Albany Pr. Cl., 1957; Phila. Pr. Cl., 1958; Art:USA, 1958; Panoras Gal., N.Y., 1957 (2-man).

FOSTER, KENNETH E.—*Museum Director*
Museum of Navajo Ceremonial Art, Santa Fe, N.M.
Position: Dir., Museum of Navajo Ceremonial Art.*

FOSTER, (B) NORTON—*Painter*
Manasota Key, Englewood, Fla.
B. Block Island, R.I., May 27, 1899. *Studied*: R.I. State
Col.; Brown Univ.; Columbia Univ.; Anson Cross Sch.
A.; ASL. *Member*: AAPL; Mid-Vermont A; New Hamp-
shire AA; Montclair AA; Sarasota AA; A. Lg. of Manatee
County; Village A. Cl.; ASL. *Awards*: prize, Anson K.
Cross Alumni, 1946; Kappa Pi one-man show award, 1958.
Exhibited: New Hampshire AA, 1942, 1944, 1946; traveling
exh., Mid-Vermont A., 1946; Doll & Richards Gal., Boston,
1953, 1954; Keene (N.H.) T. Col., 1946; Sarasota AA,
1948, 1949; one-man: Norlyst Gal., 1944, 1945; Upper
Montclair Woman's Cl., 1946; Montclair First Baptist
Church A. Gal., 1942, 1944, 1946, 1947; Contemp. A. Gal.,
Pinellas Park, Fla., 1957; Tampa A. Mus., 1957, 1958;
Sarasota, 1958; Daytona Beach A. Cl., 1957; A. Cl. of St.
Petersburg, 1957; Fla. Southern Col., 1958; Ridge AA,
Winter Haven, Fla., 1958; Palm Beach, 1958; Camden,
Me., 1958.

FOSTER, ROBERT—*Graphic Designer*
14 Sutton Pl., South, New York 22, N.Y.
B. State College, Pa., June 11, 1895. *Studied*: Pennsylvania
State Univ., B.S., M.E. *Member*: SI; A.Dir.Cl.; Typophiles.

FOULKE, VIOLA—*Painter, L.*
215 East Providence Rd., Aldan-Clifton Heights P.O.,
Pa.
B. Quakertown, Pa. *Studied*: PMSchIA; Univ. Pennsyl-
vania, B.F.A. in Edu., M.S.; Alfred Univ.; & with George
Walter Dawson, Earl Horter. *Member*: Phila. A. All.;
Phila. WC Cl.; Phila. Plastic Cl.; PMA; Woodmere A.
Gal. Lecturer, PMA, assigned by Phila. Bd. Edu.*

FOWLER, ALFRED—*Writer, Cr.*
1829 M St., Washington 6, D.C.
B. Paola, Kan., Dec. 1, 1889. *Member*: Pr. Collector's Cl.,
London, England. Ed., "The Romance of Fine Prints,"
1938; "The Print Collector's Quarterly," 1937; & other
periodicals. *Position*: Dir., The Soc. of Print Collectors.

FOWLER, CONSTANCE—*Educator*
Art Department, Albion College, Albion, Mich.*

FOX, LORRAINE (D'ANDREA)—*Commercial Artist, I.*
136 East 57th St., New York, N.Y.; h. 4 Kings Terrace
Rd., Kings Point, L.I., N.Y.
B. New York, N.Y., May 22, 1922. *Studied*: PIASch., with
Will Burtin. *Member*: SI. *Awards*: A. Dir. Cl., N.Y.; gold
medal, A. Dir. Cl., Phila. Pa. *Exhibited*: SI; A. Dir. Cl.,
N.Y. and Phila. Pa.; Arch. Lg. Illus., Better Homes &
Gardens Baby Book, 1951. Contributor illus. to: Woman's
Day; Seventeen; Redbook; McCalls; Good Housekeeping;
Woman's Home Companion; Parents; House Beautiful;
Better Homes & Gardens; Mademoiselle; Charm; Bride-to-
Be. Lectures: Commercial Art.*

FOX, MILTON S.—*Painter, Lith., T., W., L.*
224 Nelson Rd., Scarsdale, N.Y.
B. New York, N.Y., Mar. 29, 1904. *Studied*: Cleveland
Sch. A.; Julian Acad., Ecole des Beaux-Arts, Paris; Western
Reserve Univ., M.A. *Member*: CAA; Renaissance Soc.
Awards: prizes, CMA, 1927, 1928, 1933. *Work*: CMA;
murals, Cleveland Pub. Auditorium. *Exhibited*: CMA, an-
nually, 1927-1935. Contributor to: Art magazines & educa-
tional publications; Art Appreciation. Ed., Assoc. Publ.,
Abrams Art Books, publ. by Harry N. Abrams, New York
& Amsterdam.

FOX, ROY C.—*Etcher, Eng., P.*
152 West 5th St., Elmira, N.Y.
B. Oneonta, N.Y., April 14, 1908. *Studied*: with Ernfred
Andersen. *Member*: Elmira A. Cl.; Print Council of Am.
Work: Elmira Col.; Arnot A. Gal.; Fla. Southern Col. *Ex-
hibited*: Audubon A., 1942-1944; Saranac Lake A. Lg.,
1943, 1944; Northwest Pr. M., 1944-1946, 1947, 1948;
Wawasee A. Gal., 1944, 1945; Laguna Beach AA, 1944,
1945; Oakland A. Gal., 1944, 1945; SAGA, 1944, 1946;
Phila. Pr. Cl., 1946; Arnot A. Gal., 1936-1955; Finger
Lakes Exh., Rochester, N.Y., 1938-1949; Elmira Col., 1943,
1957 (one-man); Albany Pr. Cl., 1947; Grand Central
Gal., 1946; Cal. Soc. Et.; Cooperstown AA, 1957, 1958;
Soc. Min. P., S. & Gravers, 1956-1958; Horseheads, N.Y.,
1958 (one-man); Burr Gal., N.Y., 1958.

FOXLEY, GRIFFITH—*Illustrator*
8 Crimmins Rd., Darien, Conn.
Member: SI.*

FOY, EDITH C. GELLENBECK—*Painter*
6322 Grand Vista Ave., Cincinnati 13, Ohio
B. Cincinnati, Ohio, Oct. 9, 1893. *Studied*: Cincinnati A.
Acad., with Weiss, Wessel; PAFA, with Garber, Pierson;
Farnsworth Sch A. *Member*: Womens A. Cl. of Cincin-
nati; Boca Raton A. Gld; Sarasota AA. *Work*: Deer Park
H.S., Cincinnati; Sacred Heart Acad., Cincinnati. *Ex-
hibited*: CM, 1957; Baldwin Gal., Cincinnati, 1956; Boca
Raton A. Gld., 1958; Town Cl., Cincinnati, 1958, and
other exhs. prior.

FRACASSINI, SILVIO CARL—*Painter, E., Des.*
State University of Iowa, 911 Iowa Ave.; h. 101 West
Broad St., Mt. Pleasant, Iowa
B. Louisville, Colo., Nov. 4, 1907. *Studied*: Univ. Denver,
B.F.A.; AIC; Santa Fe Sch. A.; Univ. Iowa, M.F.A.;
Scripps Col., and with Walt Kuhn, John Edward Thomp-
son, Cyril Kay-Scott. *Member*: CAA; Kappa Pi; N.A.E.A.;
Midwest A. Conf.; Am. Soc. Aesthetics; AAUP. *Awards*:
prizes, Univ. Denver, 1931; Denver A. Mus., 1931, 1943;
Chappell Sch. A., 1931; Sioux City, Iowa, 1948; Iowa A.
Show; Des Moines A. Center, 1955, 1958. *Work*: Denver
A. Mus.; Sioux City A. Center; mural, Southern Hotel,
Durango, Colo. *Exhibited*: Denver A. Mus., 1931-1934,
1936, 1937, 1939, 1940, 1941, 1943; Univ. Kansas; Joslyn
Mus. A., 1940, 1949, 1950, 1957; Denver A. Gld., 1931,
1932, 1934, 1935, 1937-1947; AWS, 1949; William Rockhill
Nelson Gal., 1950; Des Moines A. Center, 1952; Am.
Color Pr. Soc., 1952; Colo. Springs FA Center; Springfield
A. Lg., 1954; Alabama WC Soc., 1954, and others; one-
man: Denver A. Mus., 1941; Univ. Denver, 1942; Sioux
City, 1949; Des Moines A. Center, 1955. *Position*: Assoc.
Prof. A., State University of Iowa, Iowa City, Ia., at
present.

FRAIN, N(ELLIE) M. (Mrs.)—
Medical Illustrator, W., P.
53 West Burton Rd., Chicago 10, Ill.
B. Furnesville, Ind. *Studied*: AIC; Northwestern Univ.
Member: Renaissance Soc., Univ. Chicago. *Work*: ports,
Northwestern Univ. Lib.; Presbyterian Hospital; Univ. Illinois Col. of Dentistry; and in many private colls. *Exhibited*: AIC; Century of Progress, Chicago. Illus. many
medical books & publications.

FRAME, WALTER KEITH—
Printmaker, P., Comm., Gr., I.
Sheffield, Mass.
B. Oneida, Ill., Dec. 14, 1895. *Studied*: Carnegie Inst.;
ASL, and with Lewis C. Daniel, Jerry Farnsworth. *Mem-
ber*: SAGA. *Awards*: med., A. Dir. Cl., 1930; SAGA;
Berkshire AA, 1954, 1955; Denver A. Mus.; Phila. Pr. Cl.
Work: LC; N.Y. Pub. Lib.; Westchester Inst. FA; WMAA;
MMA. *Exhibited*: LC; N.Y.Pub.Lib.; SAGA; Northwest
Pr.M.; Phila. Pr. Cl.; NAD; PAFA; BM.*

FRANCES, GENE (Mrs. Francis McComas)—
Painter, W.
1101 Franklin St., Monterey, Cal.
B. San Francisco, Cal. *Studied*: Berkeley Sch. A. & Crafts;
& with Xavier Martinez, Francis McComas. *Member*: San
F. AA; Carmel AA; NSMP. *Work*: Bender Coll., San F.;
Oakland A. Gal.; Mills Col.; mural, Del Monte Lodge,
Cal.; Spreckels Sugar Co., San Francisco; Monterey Penin-
sula Herald Bldg. *Exhibited*: GGE, 1939; MModA, 1940;
Rouillier Gal., Chicago, 1939 (one-man); Palace Legion
Honor, 1940; Sacramento Jr. Col., 1940; AIC, 1940; one-
man, 1943; one-man: New York, N.Y., 1940; deYoung
Mem. Mus., 1952; Pasadena AI, 1954; Carmel AA, 1955.
Writer for Oakland Tribune, Oakland, Cal.

FRANCIS, HENRY SAYLES—*Museum Curator*
County Line Rd., Gates Mills, Ohio

B. Boston, Mass., Mar. 4, 1902. *Studied*: Harvard Univ., A.B. Contributor to: Art Quarterly; Gazette des Beaux Arts; Print Collector's Quarterly, etc. *Position*: Asst., Dept. Prints, BMFA, 1924-27; Cur., Prints & Drawings, CMA, 1927-29; Asst. to Dir., FMA, 1929-31; Cur., Paintings, Prints & Drawings, CMA, Cleveland, Ohio, 1931- .

FRANCIS, MURIEL (WILKINS)—
Teacher, P., C., Comm. A.
1920 6th Ave.; h. 1910 6th Ave., Ft. Worth 10, Tex.

B. Longview, Tex., Oct. 25, 1893. *Studied*: with Frederic Taubes, John Erickson, William Schemmill, Alexander Archipenko, and others. *Member*: Ft. Worth AA; Ft. Worth A. Center; Texas FA Assn. *Awards*: prizes, Ft. Worth AA; Ft. Worth A. Center; Taos, N.M.; Woman's Cl., A. Dept. *Exhibited*: Texas General; Ft. Worth AA; Texas FA Assn.; Austin, Tex.; and in traveling exhs. *Position*: Instr. A., Carswell Air Force Base, Tex.; and privately.

FRANCK, FREDERICK S. (DR.)—*Painter, I., Des., W.*
105 West 55th St., New York 19, N.Y.

B. Maastricht, Holland, Apr. 12, 1909. *Studied*: Belgium, England, U.S. *Member*: AEA; Assoc. A. Pittsburgh. *Awards*: prizes, Carnegie Inst., 1946, 1948, 1950; purchase, Am. Acad. A. & Lets., 1955; purchase, Univ. Illinois, 1950; Maastricht Mus., Holland; Living Arts Fnd., purchase, 1958. *Work*: Univ. Pittsburgh; Latrobe A. Fund; Hundred Friends of Art Coll.; Shell Oil Co.; Musee Nationaux de France; Univ. Illinois; Stedelijk Mus., Holland; Eindhoven Mus., Holland; Santa Barbara Mus. A.; SFMA; MModA; Carpenter A. Gal., Dartmouth Col.; N.Y. Pub. Lib.; Seattle Pub. Lib.; Honolulu Acad. A.; Cornell Univ.; WAC; Achenbach Fnd.; Texas Wesleyan Col.; Intl. Graphic A. Soc.; murals, Temple Beth-El, Elizabeth, N.J.; stage des. for off-Broadway shows. *Exhibited*: Carnegie Inst., 1942-1946; PAFA, 1944; Butler Inst. Am. A., 1944; Cal. PLH, 1946; Univ. Illinois, 1950-1952; CGA, 1951; Univ. Minnesota, 1952; Buffalo, N.Y., 1952; WMAA, 1950, 1951, 1958; MMA, 1950; John Herron AI, 1957; BMA, 1959; Wadsworth Atheneum, Hartford, 1959; Am. Acad. A. & Lets., 1959; Art:USA, 1959; AFA traveling exh., 1959, and others. One-man: Van Dieman-Lilienfeld Gal., 1949, 1952; Drouant-David, Paris, 1951; Benador, Geneva, Switzerland, 1951; Van Leir Gal., Amsterdam, 1951; Contemp. A. Gal., 1942; Passedoit Gal., 1954, 1958; Mus. FA of Houston, 1953; Santa Barbara Mus. A., 1953; SFMA, 1953; exh. drawings done at Albert Schweitzer Hospital, Lambarene, Fr. Africa (1958), Assoc. Am. A. Gal., N.Y., 1958; and many exhs. in Holland, Belgium, France and England. Author: "Modern Dutch Art," 1943; "Open Wide, Please," 1957; "Au Pays du Soleil," 1958; "Days With Albert Schweitzer," 1959; "The Lambarene Landscape," 1959.

FRANCKSEN, JEAN EDA—*Painter, E., Des.*
320 South Camac St.; h. 5410 Baltimore Ave., Philadelphia 43, Pa.

B. Philadelphia, Pa., May 9, 1914. *Studied*: Univ. Pennsylvania, B.F.A. in Edu.; PMSchIA; Barnes Fnd., and with Benton Spruance, Arthur B. Carles, Stanley William Hayter. *Member*: Phila. A. All.; Phila. Pr. Cl. *Work*: LC; PMA; murals, St. Joseph's Hospital, Carbondale, Pa.; Jewish Community Center, Scranton, Pa. (wall); dec.; Community Bldg., Phila. Pr. *Exhibited*: PAFA, 1938-1952; Phila. Pr. Cl., 1939-1952; LC, 1943, 1944; Phila. A. All.; Everyman's Gal.; Mus. New Mexico, 1941, and abroad. *Position*: Asst. Prof. A., Beaver Col., Jenkintown, Pa., 1938- ; Instr. A., Swarthmore Col., Pa., 1944-46; Instr. Adv. Des., L., PMSchIA, Philadelphia, Pa., 1947- ; Freelance Des-Consultant, Bellante & Clauss, Architects.*

FRANK, BENA VIRGINIA (Mrs. Bena Frank Mayer)—
Painter, T.
240 East 20th St., New York 3, N.Y.

B. Norfolk, Va. *Studied*: ASL; CUASch; & abroad. *Member*: N.Y. Soc. Women Painters; NAWA; AEA; Brooklyn Soc. A.; ASL. *Awards*: Med., CUASch, 1916, 1917; prize, NAWA, 1951. *Work*: Hunter Col.; Nassau County Hospitals, N.Y.; Roosevelt H.S., N.Y.; Brooklyn Pub. Lib.; N.Y. Pub. Lib. *Exhibited*: ASL, Woodstock, N.Y.; N.Y.

Soc. Women A.; NAWA; AEA; Carnegie Inst. *Position*: Pres., N.Y. Soc. Women Painters, 1952-53; Vice-Pres., Inst. A. Technology; Dir., New York Soc. Women A.

FRANK, EMILY (SHAPIRO)—*Painter, Des.*
43 Fifth Ave., New York 3, N.Y.

B. New York, N.Y., July 28, 1906. *Studied*: N.Y. Univ.; ASL, with Kuniyoshi, Sternberg. *Work*: in private colls. *Exhibited*: Ward Eggleston Gal.; Salpeter Gal.; Miami Beach, Fla.; Sartor Gal., Dallas, Tex.; Frances Webb Gal., Los Angeles; Bodley Gal., N.Y., 1958 (one-man), and others.

FRANK, HELEN—*Painter, Des., I.*
241 Lexington Ave., New York 16, N.Y.

B. Berkeley, Cal. *Studied*: Cal. Col. A. & Crafts; ASL, and with Glenn Wessels, Hamilton A. Wolf, Joseph Paget-Fredericks, Sheldon Cheney. *Awards*: scholarships, Cal. Col. A. & Crafts; ASL. *Work*: Crocker A. Gal., Sacramento, Cal.; Templeton Crocker Coll., and in private coll. New York, Cal., Texas and abroad. *Exhibited*: East-West Gal., 1932; Second Progressive Show, 1934; Gump's Gal., 1937 (all in San F.); SFMA, 1937, 1939, 1942; Oakland A. Gal., 1938, 1940, 1942; Newport AA, 1944; AIC, 1944; Los A. Mus. A., 1945; New-Age Gal., 1950, 1951; Fla. Southern Col., 1952; Milwaukee AI, 1954; deYoung Mem. Mus., San Francisco, 1957; one-man: Neighborhood Playhouse, San F., 1935; Crocker A. Gal., 1942; Pinacotheca, N.Y., 1943; Santa Barbara Mus. A., 1947; SFMA, 1947; Vancouver (B.C.) A. Gal., 1947; Curacao Mus., N.W.I., 1949; Parson's Gal., London, England 1954; Chase Gal., N.Y., 1958. Des., costumes for modern dance. I., series of text books, 1947-49; music books for children, 1944-45; "Mozart," 1946; Illus. for Sat. Review of Literature, New York Times, Harpers.

FRANKENSTEIN, ALFRED VICTOR—*Critic, W., L., T.*
c/o San Francisco Chronicle, 5th & Mission Sts., San Francisco, Cal.

B. Chicago, Ill., Oct. 5, 1906. *Studied*: Univ. Chicago, Ph. B. *Member*: Newspaper Gld.; CAA; Am. Studies Assn. *Awards*: Guggenheim F., 1947. Author: "After the Hunt," 1953. Contributor to Art in America; Art Bulletin; N.Y. Times; Herald Tribune and other magazines and newspapers, with critical reviews. Lectures on Music and Art. *Position*: Music & Art Cr., San Francisco Chronicle. 1934- ; Lecturer, American Art, Univ. California, 1950- ; L., American Art, Mills Col., Oakland, Cal., 1955- .

FRANKENTHALER, HELEN (MOTHERWELL)—*Painter*
1682 Third Ave.; h. 173 East 94th St., New York 28, N.Y.

B. New York, N.Y., Dec. 12, 1928. *Studied*: Bennington Col., B.A., and with Rufino Tamayo, Hans Hofmann. *Work*: paintings in the colls. of MModA; WMAA; BM; Albright A. Gal.; Carnegie Inst.; tapestries, Temple of Aaron, St. Paul, Minn. *Exhibited*: Carnegie Inst., 1955, 1958; WMAA, 1955, 1957, 1958; Univ. Illinois, 1959; Jewish Mus., N.Y., 1957; Univ. North Carolina (Raleigh and Greensboro), 1956; Minneapolis Inst. A., 1957; DMFA, 1958; Women's Col. of the Univ. North Carolina, 1958; Boulder, Colo., 1958; Landau Gal., Los Angeles, 1957; Univ. Nebraska, 1958; AFA traveling exh., 1957; MModA traveling exh., 1957 (Japan).

FRANKFORTER, W. D.—*Museum Director*
Sanford Museum, 117 East Willow St., Cherokee, Ind.*

FRANKLE, PHILIP—*Painter, I., T., L.*
43 Elmridge Rd., Kings Point, L.I., N.Y.

B. New York, N.Y., June 29, 1913. *Studied*: N.Y. Univ.; Brooklyn Col., A.B.; Columbia Univ., M.A. *Member*: A.T. Assn. *Exhibited*: NGA, 1943-1945; Mississippi AA, 1946; Mint Mus. A., 1946; NAC, 1946; Nat. Gal., London, England, 1944; BM, 1941-1945; Bd. Edu. Gal., N.Y., 1945, 1946 (one-man); Lincoln Gal., Brooklyn, N.Y., 1941, 1946. I., "G.I. Sketch Book," 1944; "Art in the Armed Forces," 1944. Contributor to: The Artist Teacher. *Position*: Instr., WC Painting & Oil Painting, Brooklyn Col., Brooklyn, N.Y.; Pres., A.T. Assn., 1940-41, 1950-51; Chm. A. Dept., Bayside (L.I.) H.S.; A. Dir., Bayside Community Center, 1955- ; Consultant to N.Y.C. Bd. of Edu. A. Dept., 1953- .

FRANKLIN, ARLA (Mrs.)—Painter, T.
 4500 Lennox Blvd., Lennox, Cal.; h. 3933 South Flower Dr., Los Angeles 37, Cal.

B. Florence, Wis., May 9, 1897. *Studied*: Chicago Acad. FA; Ecole des Beaux-Arts, Paris; Univ. So. California; LaFayette Col., Easton, Pa. *Member*: Cal. A. Cl.; Prof. A. Gld. *Awards*: medals, Greek Theatre, Los A., 1948, 1949. *Work*: in private collections. *Exhibited*: AAPL; one-man: Hollywood Woman's Cl., 1950; Westchester Woman's Cl., Los A., 1948, 1956; Inglewood, Cal., 1947; Glendale AA, 1950. *Position*: Instr., Centenella Union Valley H.S., Inglewood, 1945- , Centenella Union Valley H.S., Lennox, Cal., 1954- .*

FRANKLIN, IONE—Sculptor, E., C.
 1635 West Summit Ave., San Antonio, Tex.

B. Texas. *Studied*: Texas State Col. for Women, B.S.; Columbia Univ., M.A.; ASL; & with William Zorach, William Palmer. *Member*: SSAL; Texas S. Group; San Antonio River A. Group. *Awards*: prizes, SSAL, 1936, 1946; Texas General Exh., 1941, 1945. *Work*: Dallas Mus. FA. *Exhibited*: SSAL, 1936, 1942, 1944, 1946; Kansas City AI, 1942; Texas General Exh., 1941, 1944; San Antonio A. Lg.; River Art Group, 1956-1958. *Position*: Hd. A. Dept., East Texas State T. Col., Commerce, Tex. (Retired).

FRANKS, SEYMOUR—Painter, Des.
 300 West 10th St., New York 14, N.Y.

B. New York, N.Y., May 12, 1916. *Studied*: NAD. *Exhibited*: PAFA, 1944; WMAA, 1946-1948, 1950; BM, 1949, 1951; Univ. Nebraska, 1951; Univ. Illinois, 1952; one-man: Peridot Gal., 1948, 1950, 1951, 1952, 1954, 1955.*

FRASCH, MIRIAM R.—Painter
 7710 North High St., Worthington, Ohio

Studied: St. Lawrence Univ., B.Sc.; Columbus A. Sch.; Ohio State Univ., M.F.A. *Exhibited*: CGA, 1937; PAFA, 1937; Butler AI; Parkersburg, W. Va.; Columbus A. Lg.

FRASCONI, ANTONIO—Painter, Des., T., Gr., I.
 20 Dock Rd., South Norwalk, Conn.

B. Montevideo, Uruguay, Apr. 28, 1919. *Studied*: Circulo de Bellas Artes, Montevideo; ASL. *Awards*: scholarship, ASL; New School for Social Research; Guggenheim F., 1952-54; grant, Nat. Inst. A. & Let., 1954. *Work*: MMA; MModA; BM; N.Y. Pub. Lib.; PMA; FMA; R.I. Mus. A.; Williams-Munson-Proctor Inst.; Santa Barbara Mus. A.; San Diego Soc. FA; Princeton Univ.; Honolulu Acad. A.; Univ. Michigan; LC; CAM; BMA; Detroit Inst. A.; Wadsworth Atheneum; AIC; Museo Municipal, Montevideo; A. Council of Great Britain. *Exhibited*: 37 one-man shows in U.S., Mexico City and Montevideo; traveling exh. in Europe circulated by Smithsonian Inst. Author: I., "12 Fables of Aesop," 1954; "See and Say," 1955; "Frasconi Woodcuts," 1958; "The House that Jack Built," 1958.

FRASER, JOSEPH T., JR.—Museum Director, Arch.
 Pennsylvania Academy of the Fine Arts, Broad & Cherry Sts.; h. 330 South Camac St., Philadelphia 7, Pa.

B. Philadelphia, Pa., Sept. 15, 1898. *Studied*: Univ. Pennsylvania, B.Sc. in Arch. *Member*: Am. Sculpture Soc. (Hon.); Am. Assn. Mus. Dir.; AAMus; AFA; AIA; Fairmount Park AA (Dir.); MMA; MModA; Pa. Hist. Soc.; Univ. Pennsylvania Mus.; Phila. A. All. (Dir.); Woodmere A. Gal. (Dir.); PMA. *Position*: Dir. & Sec., PAFA, Philadelphia, Pa., at present.

FRASER, LAURA GARDIN (Mrs. James E.)—Sculptor
 290 North Ave., Westport, Conn.

B. Chicago, Ill., Sept. 14, 1889. *Studied*: ASL. *Member*: F., Intl. Inst. A. & Lets.; NA; NSS; Nat. Inst. A. & Let. *Awards*: prizes, NAD, 1916, 1919, 1924, 1927, 1931; Am. Numismatic Soc., 1926; NAWA, 1929. *Work*: Equestrian statue, Baltimore, Md.; Brookgreen Gardens, S.C.; & many medals, portraits, etc. *Exhibited*: NAD; & in Paris, France.

FRASER, MARY ALDRICH—Sculptor
 42 East Concord Ave., Orlando, Fla.; s. 107 Salisbury Ave., Garden City, N.Y.

B. New York, N.Y., Feb. 22, 1884. *Studied*: with William

Ordway Partridge, Georg Lober. *Awards*: prizes, Central Fla. Exp., Orlando, Fla. *Work*: s., National Cathedral, Wash., D.C.; St. John's Cathedral, New York, N.Y.; Garden City Cathedral, L.I., N.Y.; St. Luke's Cathedral, Orlando, Fla.; mem. statues in churches and fountains in private gardens. *Exhibited*: Argent Gal.; NAC; Studio Gld.; St. Hilda's Gld.; Orlando AA; Central Florida Exp.; Intl. Flower Show.

FRAZER, MABEL PEARL—Educator, P., L.
 328 University St., Salt Lake City 2, Utah

B. West Jordan, Utah, Aug. 28, 1887. *Studied*: Univ. Utah, B.A.; ASL; & in Italy. *Member*: Am. Assn. Univ. Prof.; Utah Creative A. *Work*: State of Utah; mural, Latter Day Saints Temple, Salt Lake City; Beaver, and Granite H.S., Utah. *Exhibited*: Montross Gal., 1930; San F. AA, 1935; one-man: Beaver (Utah) Centennial, 1956; Public Lib., and Craft House, Salt Lake City, 1956; Univ. Utah; & in Italy. *Position*: Assoc. Prof. A., Univ. Utah, Salt Lake City (Retired).

FRAZIER, BERNARD—Sculptor, L., C.
 Box 1152, Tulsa, Okla.

B. Athol, Kansas, June 30, 1906. *Studied*: Univ. Kansas, B.F.A.; NAD; AIC, and with Lorado Taft. *Member*: NSS. *Awards*: prizes, Syracuse Mus. FA, 1941, 1949; Chicago Galleries, 1943; Wichita AA, 1949, 1950; Delgado Mus. A., 1948; Joslyn Mus. A., 1952; Springfield, Mo., 1944; Kansas City AI, 1936, 1938, 1941; Andrew Carnegie grant, 1938, 1939. *Work*: s., Syracuse Mus. FA; Joslyn Mus. A.; IBM; Philbrook A. Center; Univ. Kansas A. Mus.; Springfield Mus. FA; Dyche Mus.; Mulvane A. Mus.; monumental, architectural, portraits, statues, etc.; Jefferson City, Mo.; Univ. Kansas; Temple Israel, Tulsa; Church of the Reformation, Wichita; Will Rogers H.S., Tulsa; Admin. Bldg., Univ. Tennessee Medical Sch., Memphis; Holy Cross Church, Wichita; Kansas State Office Bldg., Topeka; Republic Nat. Bank, Dallas, Tex.; White Eagle Oil Co., Tulsa. Lectures: "Sculpture for Architecture"; "Contemporary Sculpture"; "The Art of Primitive Man"; "American Indian Painting," and others, to universities, colleges, civic groups, etc. *Position*: Mus. Tech. Des., Dyche Mus., 1935-38; Sculptor-in-Res., Univ. Kansas, 1938, 1939; Faculty, Univ. Kansas, 1940-44; Dir., Philbrook A. Center, Tulsa, Okla., 1944-50; Professional S., 1950- .*

FRAZIER, JOHN ROBINSON—Educator, P.
 Rhode Island School of Design, 2 College St.; h. 37 Charles Field St., Providence, R.I.

B. Stonington, Conn., July 28, 1889. *Studied*: Rhode Island Sch. Des.; ASL; Cape Cod Sch. A., Provincetown, Mass. *Member*: Providence A. Cl. *Awards*: prizes, Phila. WC Cl., 1920; Jones prize, Baltimore, 1922; Kansas City AI purchase prize, 1923; BM purchase prize, 1924; Greenough prize, Newport, 1930; Dana Gold Medal, PAFA, 1921; Logan Medal, AIC, 1922; Hon. degree, D.F.A., Brown University, 1957. *Work*: Kansas City AI; BM; AIC; Rhode Island Sch. Des.; John Singer Sargent Coll.; Brown Univ.; Univ. Rhode Island; Bradley Univ.; Wheaton Col. *Positions*: Instr., Bradley Univ., 1912-17; Asst. Prof., Assoc. Prof., Prof. & Hd. Dept. A., Univ. Kansas, Sch. FA, 1917-23; Asst. to Dir., Dir., Cape Cod Sch. A., 1919-39; Chm., Div. FA, 1923-55, Pres., Rhode Island School of Design, Providence, R.I., 1955- .

FREBAULT, MARCELLE—Art Librarian
 371 Lake St., Newark 4, N.J.

B. Lyon, France, Nov. 18, 1890. *Studied*: Lycee de Lyon; N.Y. Lib. Sch. Author: Contributions to professional publications. *Position*: Supv. A. & Music Librarian, Newark Public Library, Newark, N.J. (Retired).

FREBORG, STAN(LEY)—Painter
 6 Cook St., Provincetown, Mass.

B. Chicago, Ill., Aug. 6, 1906. *Studied*: AIC, and with John Norton, Hans Hofmann. *Member*: Provincetown AA; Cape Cod AA. *Work*: Walter Chrysler Coll.; Univ. Mississippi. *Exhibited*: Provincetown A. Festival, 1958; Provincetown AA, 1957, 1958; Cape Cod AA, 1958; James Gal., N.Y., 1957, 1958; Martha Jackson Gal., Provincetown, 1958.

FREDERICK, CARROLL GLENN—*Cartoonist*
364 Adelphi St., Brooklyn 38, N.Y.

B. Columbia, S.C., July 21, 1905. *Studied*: N.Y. Univ.; ASL; & with E. Simms Campbell. Contributor to: Saturday Evening Post, New Yorker, King Features Syndicate.*

FREDERICKS, MARSHALL M.—*Sculptor*
4113 & 4131 North Woodward Ave., Royal Oak, Mich.; h. 875 Waddington Rd., Birmingham, Mich.

B. Rock Island, Ill., Jan. 31, 1908. *Studied*: John Huntington Polytechnic Inst.; Cleveland Sch. A.; Cranbrook Acad. A., and in Munich, Paris, London; Carl Milles Studio, Stockholm. *Member*: Michigan Acad. Sc., A. & Let.; Arch. Lg., N.Y.; Hon. Memb., Mich. Soc. Architects; AIA. *Awards*: Matzen Traveling European F.; prizes, CMA, 1931, 1933; Detroit Inst. A., 1938, 1949; Barbour Mem. Nat. Comp.; gold medal, Michigan Acad. Sc. A. & Let., 1953; AIA. *Work*: WFNY 1939; Rackham Mem. Bldg., Detroit; Veteran's Mem. Bldg., Detroit; Univ. Michigan; Louisville-Courier Journal Bldg.; Fort Street Station, Detroit; Eaton Mfg. Co., war mem.; Cranbrook Acad. A.; City of Detroit Coll.; Detroit Inst. A.; Cleveland Sch. A.; Jefferson Sch., Wyandotte, Mich.; Holy Ghost Seminary, Ann Arbor, Mich.; Ohio State Univ.; Natl. Exchange Cl., Toledo; Ford Auditorium, Detroit; Dallas (Tex.) Pub. Lib.; Detroit Zoological Park; Indian River (Mich.) Catholic Shrine; Beaumont Hospital, Detroit; Michigan Horticultural Soc.; General Motors Corp.; Chrysler Corp.; Dow Chemical Corp.; City of Grand Rapids Coll., and others. *Exhibited*: Carnegie Inst.; CMA; PAFA; AIC; WMAA; Detroit Inst. A.; John Herron AI; NSS; AIA; Cranbrook Mus. A.; Arch. Lg.; Michigan Acad. Sc. A. & Let., and in many other museums and galleries in U.S. and abroad. *Position*: Instr., Cranbrook Acad. A., Bloomfield Hills, Mich., 1933-42.

FREDMAN, HARRY (HOMER)—*Commercial Artist, I.*
25 Hemlock Lane, Roslyn, L.I., N.Y.

B. Kansas City, Mo., Sept. 21, 1923. *Studied*: Kansas City AI, with Richie Cooper, Fletcher Martin, John De Martelli; Mizen Illustration Acad., with Frederick Mizen. *Member*: SI. *Awards*: prizes, Missouri State Fair, 1941; Iowa State Fair, 1941; A. Dir. Illus. Show, Chicago, 1944 (3); 100 Best Posters, 1947. *Work*: National ads for Schlitz Brewing Co.; Beautyrest; T.W.A.; Nescafe; Pullman; Pall Mall cigarettes, Samsonite Luggage and many others. Illus., Good Houskeeping; Collier's; American; Woman's Home Companion; Cosmopolitan; Ladies Home Journal; McCall's; Redbook and other national magazines.*

FREE, MARY ARNOLD (Mrs. R. C.)—*Educator, P., Lith.*
San Antonio Vocational & Technical School, 637 Main St.; h. 707 Westwood Dr., San Antonio 12, Tex.

B. Pleasant Hill, Mo., Nov. 6, 1895. *Studied*: T. Col., Columbia Univ., B.S.; Southwest Texas T. Col., M.A.; Kansas City AI; Univ. Toledo; Univ. Texas; San Antonio AI; Instituto de Allende, Mexico, and with Snell, Wilomovski, Braught, Etienne Ret. *Member*: Am. Assn. Univ. Women; Nat. A. Edu. Assn.; Western AA; Texas A. Edu. Assn.; Texas WC Soc.; San Antonio A. Lg.; Nat. Edu. Assn.; Texas State T. Assn.; Nat. Vocational Assn.; Texas Vocational Assn.; San Antonio River A. Group; San Antonio T. Council; San Antonio Indst. A. & Vocational T. Cl. *Exhibited*: Toledo Mus. A., 1934 (one-man); Witte Mem. Mus., 1935; Kansas City AI; River A. Group, 1955 (one-man). *Position*: A.T. San Antonio Vocational & Technical Sch., 1935- ; San Antonio Col., 1945- ; Chm., Bexar County (Tex.) Jr. Red Cross Int. Sch. A. Project, 1950- . Contributor to School Arts and Texas Outlook magazines.

FREED, ERNEST BRADFIELD—*Etcher, Eng., P., E.*
Los Angeles County Art Institute, 2401 Wilshire Blvd., Los Angeles, Cal.

B. Rockville, Ind., July 20, 1908. *Studied*: Univ. Illinois, B.F.A.; PAFA; Univ. Iowa, M.A., and with Grant Wood, Philip Guston, Mauricio Lasansky. *Member*: SAGA; Chicago Soc. Et. *Awards*: Tiffany F., 1936, 1939; prizes, Indiana State Fair, 1936-1938; BM, 1948; Northwest Territory Exh., 1947, 1950; Sao Paulo Mus., 1955; PAFA, 1953 (medal); Univ. So. Cal., 1954; MMA, 1954; SAGA, 1954. *Work*: Cranbrook Acad. A.; BM; MMA; Sao Paulo Mus. A.; Univ. Iowa; Univ. Illinois; BMA. *Exhibited*: PAFA, 1937; Univ. Illinois, 1948, 1954, 1956; LC, 1946-1952; BM, 1948-1952; SAGA, 1947-1952; Audubon A, 1952;

Phila. Pr. Cl., 1948, 1950, 1951; Northwest Pr.M., 1948-1951; Chicago Soc. Et., 1948-1951; Laguna Beach, 1948, 1949; Indiana A, 1949-1951; Univ. Kentucky, 1956; Wash. Univ., 1956; Royal Painters-Printers, 1953; MMA, 1953; Sao Paulo Mus., 1955; Denver A. Mus., 1946; Corpus Christi, Tex., 1949; Youngstown, Ohio; one-man: Ferargil Gal., 1936; Univ. So. Cal., 1948; Winnipeg Mus. A., 1948; Cranbrook Acad. A., 1950; Bradley Univ., 1950; Pittsburgh A. & Crafts Soc., 1949, and others. *Position*: Hd. Graphic A., Los Angeles County Art Inst., Los Angeles, Cal.

FREED, WILLIAM—*Painter*
750 Beck St., Bronx 55, N.Y.

B. Poland, July 6, 1904. *Studied*: Edu. All. Sch.; ASL; Hans Hofmann Sch. FA. *Member*: AEA. *Awards*: prize, Cape Cod AA, 1957. *Work*: Jewish Mus., N.Y. *Exhibited*: Audubon A., 1949, 1950, 1952; North Carolina Mus. A., 1936; Govt. WC Comp., Wash., D.C., 1938; Provincetown AA, 1945-1958; Cape Cod AA, 1947-1957; Gallert Gal., Provincetown, 1956-1958; Boston A. Festival, 1958; WMA, 1958; Walter P. Chrysler, Jr., Mus. A., 1958; Burliuk Gal., 1950; Riverside Mus., 1950, 1952, 1954, 1956; Edu. All. Alumni Exh., 1950; John Meyers Fnd., 1951; Esther Stuttman Gal., 1957, 1958; Sidney Kaufman Gal., 1950; New Sch. Social Research, 1951; Art:USA, 1958; one-man: James Gal., 1954, 1956, 1958.

FREEDMAN, MAURICE—*Painter*
121 Edgars Lane, Hastings-on-Hudson, N.Y.

B. Boston, Mass., Nov. 14, 1904. *Studied*: Mass. Normal Sch. A.; BMFASch.; Andre Lhote, Paris, France. *Work*: Carnegie Inst.; A. Center of La India; Milwaukee AI; Los A. Mus. A.; Tel-Aviv Mus., Israel; PAFA; Lambert Coll.; CAM; Denver A. Mus. *Exhibited*: CGA; VMFA; Carnegie Inst.; MModA; WMAA; BM; CAM traveling exh.; PAFA; Dayton AI; AIC; Walker A. Center; Audubon A.; NAD; Illinois Wesleyan Univ.; Syracuse Mus. FA; one-man: Midtown Gal.

FREELON, ALLAN RANDALL—*Printmaker, P.*
"Windy Crest," Telford, Pa.

B. Philadelphia, Pa., Sept. 2, 1895. *Studied*: PMSchIA; Univ. Pennsylvania, B.S. in Edu.; Tyler Sch. FA, M.F.A. *Member*: Phila. A. T. Assn.; Lansdale A. Lg. (Bd. Memb.); Soc. New Jersey A; Eastern AA; AEA; Phila. A. Festival Committee, 1958-59; Lehigh A. All. *Work*: PMA; Tyler Sch. FA, Elkins Park, Pa.; Cooke & Smith Schools, Phila.; Phila. Bronze Corp.; Bartlett Jr. H.S., Gloucester, N.J. *Exhibited*: Tyler Sch. FA, 1946; Phila. Pr. Cl., 1946; PAFA, 1951; Lehigh A. All.; Anthracite Indst. Exh., 1954; Temple Univ., 1940 (one-man). *Position*: Special Asst. F. & Indst. A., Phila. Schools, 1936- ; Instr., Print Processes, PMA, 1940-46; Tech. Advisor in Lith., Phila. Pr. Cl., 1946-1947; Adult classes in painting, Windy Crest Studios, Telford, Pa.

FREEMAN, A. ALBERT—*Designer, E., W., L.*
305 East 46th St., New York 17, N.Y.; h. 111-12 75th Rd., Forest Hills 75, N.Y.

B. New York, N.Y., Nov. 15, 1905. *Studied*: N.Y. Univ.; Univ. State of New York. *Member*: AIGA; Direct Mail Adv. Assn.; Nat. Graphic A. Edu. Assn.; N.Y. Cl. of Printing House Craftsmen. *Exhibited*: Arch. Lg. Author feature articles on Copy Preparation in trade magazines. Prepared exhibit of American books by offset for tour through Great Britain, Belgium, Holland and Sweden, 1949. *Position*: Pres., Visualart, 1930- ; Consultant to Lithographic Technical Fnd., 1944-50; Exec. Dir. of Books by Offset Lithography, 1945-50; Instr., Copy Requirements for Offset Lithography, N.Y. Trade Sch., 1945-50; A. & Copy Consultant, N.Y. Lithographing Corp. and Noble & Noble Publishers, 1949-54; A. & Production Consultant, Rapid Typographers, New York, N.Y., 1954- .*

FREEMAN, DON—*Painter, I., Gr.*
625 Locust Rd., Sausalito, Cal.

B. San Diego, Cal., 1908. *Studied*: ASL, with John Sloan, Harry Wickey, and with Kathryn Cherry. *Awards*: prize, Phila. Pr. Cl. *Work*: WMAA. *Exhibited*: AIC; WMAA; PAFA; CGA. I., "Human Comedy" (Saroyan); "White Deer" (Thurber); "Once Around the Sun" (Atkinson). Author: "Come One, Come All." Author, I. (in collaboration with Lydia Freeman), "Chuggy and the Blue Caboose"; "Pet of the Met" and other children's books.*

FREEMAN, JANE—*Painter, T.*
403 Van Dyke Studios, 939 8th Ave., New York 19, N.Y.

B. Newton, Derbyshire, England, Feb. 11, 1885. *Studied:* ASL, with DuMond, Chase, Henri; Grande Chaumiere, Paris, France. *Member:* All.A.Am.; Rockport AA; North Shore AA. *Awards:* prizes, All. A. Am., 1944; Springville (Utah) A. Center, 1944; NAWA; Hudson Valley AA, 1953-1958; Rockport AA, 1958. *Work:* Springville AA.

FREEMAN, MARGARET B.—*Museum Curator*
The Cloisters, Fort Tryon Park, New York 33, N.Y.
Position: Cur., The Cloisters.*

FREEMAN, MARK—*Lithographer, T., Comm. A., P.*
307 East 37th St.; h. 117 East 35th St., New York 16, N.Y.

B. Austria, Sept. 27, 1908. *Studied:* Columbia Col., A.B.; Columbia Univ., B. Arch.; Sorbonne, Paris; NAD. *Member:* Boston Pr. M.; Wash. WC Cl.; Easthampton Gld. Hall. *Work:* LC; Parrish Mus., Southampton, L.I.; De Hengelose Kunstzaal, Holland, and in private collections. *Exhibited:* NAD, 1928-1934; WFNY 1939; CM, 1952, 1954; N.Y. City Center, 1954; Parrish Mus., 1954-1958; Portland Mus. A., 1954, 1956; Wichita AA, 1954; Boston Pr. M., 1954-1958; Wash. WC Cl., 1953-1958; Knickerbocker A., 1954-1958; Audubon A., 1954, 1955, 1957; AWS, 1955, 1958; PAFA, 1957. Covers and drawings for Architectural Forum, Pencil Points magazines. *Position:* Instr., Lithography, T. Col., Columbia Univ., 1932-34; Owner, Allied Arts Guild, 1934- .

FREEMAN, PAUL K.—*Painter, C., Des., Comm. A., I.*
300 Riverside Drive, New York 25, N.Y.

B. Brooklyn, N.Y., Jan. 22, 1929. *Studied:* Community Col., N.Y.; BM; City Col. of N.Y.; Hunter Col. *Exhibited:* Gallerie Philadelphi, Paris, France, 1957; N.Y. City Center, 1956-1958; Contemp. Americans Gal., 1958; Art:USA, 1958; AFA traveling exh., 1958; one-man: traveling exh., Israel, 1957. Illus. & Des., "Israel Today" (by Ruth Gruber); Des., writer, animator films for Omnibus.

FREEMAN, RICHARD B.—*Educator, Mus. Cur.*
University Art Gallery, University of Kentucky, Lexington, Ky.

B. Philadelphia, Pa., Oct. 7, 1908. *Studied:* Yale Univ., A.B.; Harvard Univ., A.M. *Member:* AFA; Southeastern Col. AA (Vice-Pres., 1951-52, Pres., 1952-53); CAA. Author: "Ralston Crawford," 1953. *Position:* Registrar, FMA, 1936-38; Asst. Cur., CM, 1938-41; Dir., Flint Inst. A., Flint, Mich., 1941-47; Asst. Dir., SFMA, San Francisco, Cal., 1947-50; Cur., Univ. A. Mus., Univ. Alabama, University (Tuscaloosa), Ala., 1950-56; Dir., Hartford A. Sch., Hartford Conn., 1956-57; Visiting Prof., Hamilton Col., Clinton, N.Y., 1958; Hd., A. Dept., Cur. Univ. A. Gal., Univ. Kentucky, Lexington, Ky., 1958- .

FREER, HOWARD MORTIMER—*Painter, Des., T., I.*
Freer Galleries, Berlin, Conn.

B. Jackson, Mich., Oct. 25, 1904. *Studied:* Chicago Acad. FA; John Huntington Polytechnic Inst. *Member:* Phila. WC Cl.; Conn. WC Soc. *Awards:* prize, Detroit Inst. A., 1936; Conn. WC Soc., 1946; Dixie award, 1951. *Exhibited:* PAFA, 1932-1936; AWCS, 1934-1936, 1940-1946; AIC, 1934-1939, 1941, 1942, 1944, 1946; Detroit Inst. A., 1932-1934, 1936-1938; GGE, 1939; Palace Legion Honor; CM, 1934-1936, 1938; AIC traveling exh., 1941. Author: "You Can Paint with a Pencil," 1951.*

FREIGANG, PAUL—*Craftsman*
138-07—90th Ave., Jamaica 35, N.Y.

B. Elsterwerda, Germany, Mar. 25, 1886. *Member:* Ceramic Soc. of N.Y. *Awards:* Med., Paris Salon, 1937. *Exhibited:* MMA, 1940; Paris Salon, 1937.

FREILICHER, HY—*Sculptor, C., T.*
2514 Ave. M, Brooklyn 10, N.Y.

B. Northumberland, Pa., Apr. 13, 1907. *Studied:* Col. City of N.Y., B.S.; BAID. *Member:* S. Gld. *Exhibited:* S. Gld., annually; AFA traveling exh.; Carnegie Inst.; BM; MMA, and many others throughout U.S. Lectures: Sculpture History, Aesthetics, Technique. *Position:* Instr. S., Abraham Lincoln H.S., Brooklyn, N.Y.

FRENCH, HAZEL BLAKE—*Craftsman*
Main St., Sandwich, Mass.

B. Brockton, Mass., Aug. 21, 1890. *Studied:* BMFA Sch.; & with C. Howard Walker, Huger Elliot, George Hunt. *Member:* Boston Soc. A. & Crafts. *Exhibited:* Paris Salon, 1937; Phila. A. All., 1937, 1938, 1940-1943, 1945; WMA, 1943; America House, 1944.

FRENCH, JAMES C.—*Museum Curator, W., L.*
Rosicrucian Egyptian Museum; h. 1471 McDaniel St., San Jose 26, Cal.

B. Hayward, Wis., Sept. 16, 1907. *Studied:* Minneapolis Col. of Music & Art, B.A., M.A.; MacPhail Col. of Music & Art. *Member:* AAMus.; AFA; Intl. Inst. Conservation of Museum Objects. Contributor to Rosicrucian Digest. *Position:* Cur., Rosicrucian Egyptian, Oriental Museum and Art Gallery, San Jose, Cal., 1951- .

FRENCH, JARED—*Sculptor, P., Et.*
5 St. Luke's Pl., New York 14, N.Y.; s. Hartland, Vt.

B. Ossining, N.Y., Feb. 4, 1905. *Studied:* Amherst Col., B.A.; ASL. *Work:* WMAA; Baseball Mus., Cooperstown, N.Y.; BMA; murals, USPO, Richmond, Va.; Plymouth, Pa. *Exhibited:* Chicago AC; MModA; CGA; PAFA; WMAA; Carnegie Inst.; AIC; SFMA; NAD; Walker A. Center.

FRENCH, MRS. JARED. See Hoening, Margaret

FRENCH, JOHN E.—*Educator*
San Jose State College, San Jose, Cal.
Position: Hd. A. Dept., San Jose State College.*

FRENKEL, NORA—*Painter*
24 East 97th St., New York 29, N.Y.

B. Shanghai, China, July 14, 1931. *Studied:* CUASch.; Cranbrook Acad. A.; Smith Col., B.A. *Awards:* prize, Springfield (Mass.) Mus. A., 1951. *Work:* Smith Col. Mus. *Exhibited:* Springfield Mus. A., 1951, 1952; Cranbrook Acad. Mus., 1951; New York, N.Y., 1953; Paris, France, 1954; Panoras Gal., 1956 (one-man).*

FREUND, ELSIE MARIE—*Craftsman, P., Lith., T.*
Stetson University, Deland, Fla.

B. Taney County, Mo., Jan. 23, 1912. *Studied:* Kansas City AI; Colorado Springs FA Center; Wichita AA. *Member:* Fla. A. Group; Fla. Craftsmen; Fla. Fed. A.; AWS. *Exhibited:* NAD; PAFA; Assoc. Am. A.; LC; CAM; Brooks Mem. Mus.; Little Rock Mus. FA; Joslyn A. Mus.; DMFA; SAM; Wichita AA; Springfield A. Mus., various schools and colleges. *Position:* Instr., Hendrix Col., 1941-46; A. Sch. of the Ozarks, 1941-48; Instr., Des. & Crafts, Stetson Univ., 1949-51; Community Crafts, Deland, Fla.; Owner "Elsaramic Jewelry" shop at present.

FREUND, HARRY LOUIS—*Painter, E., I.*
Stetson University, Art Department, Deland, Fla.

B. Clinton, Mo., Sept. 16, 1905. *Studied:* Missouri Univ.; St. Louis Sch. FA; Princeton Univ.; Colorossi Acad., Paris; Colorado Springs FA Center. *Member:* Fla. A. Group; Fla. Fed. A.; Fla. Craftsmen; NSMP. *Awards:* St. Louis Sch. FA traveling scholarship, 1929; Carnegie F., 1940; Carnegie grant, 1950. *Work:* Springfield (Mo.) Mus. A.; Little Rock Mus. A.; Pub. Schs. in Missouri, Kansas & Arkansas; murals, USPO, Herington, Kans.; Windsor, Mo.; Idabel, Okla.; Pocahontas & Heber Springs, Ark.; Camp Robinson, Camp Chaffee, Ark.; Hendrix Col.; paintings: Govt. offices and hospitals, Wash., D.C.; Pentagon Bldg.; IBM; St. Louis Sch. FA; LC; Kansas City Pub. Schs.; Univ. Arkansas; Independence (Mo.) Court House; Hendrix Col. *Exhibited:* Denver A. Mus.; CMA; Kansas City AI; Arkansas A.; Ozark A.; WFNY 1939; IBM; NAD; PAFA; Carnegie Inst.; LC; CGA; CM; CAM; Springfield A. Mus.; Little Rock Mus. A.; Philbrook A. Center; Brooks Mem. A. Gal.; DMFA; Joslyn A. Mus.; SAM; Wichita AA; Univ. Illinois, and others. *Position:* Res. A., 1939-41, Hd. A. Dept., 1941-42, 1945-46, Hendrix Col., Conway, Ark.; A. Res., 1949-51, Hd. A. Dept., 1951- , Stetson Univ., Deland, Fla.; Illus., for Ford Motor Co. Publications, 1948- .

FREUND, WILLIAM F.—*Painter, C., E.*

123 Cliff Drive, Columbia, Mo.; s. Watersmeet, Mich.

B. Jan. 20, 1916. *Studied*: Univ. Wisconsin, B.S., M.S.; Univ. Missouri. *Awards*: F. and prize, Tiffany Fnd., 1940, 1949; prizes, Mid-Am. A., 1950; Madison A. Salon; Milwaukee AI; AGAA, 1945, 1946; Denver A. Mus.; Mulvane Mus. A.; William Rockhill Nelson Gal.; CAM; Joslyn A. Mus., 1952, 1953; New Talent, U.S.A., 1956. *Work*: Univ. Nebraska. *Exhibited*: Madison Lib.; Wisconsin Union; Milwaukee AI; CAM; Nelson Gal. A.; Springfield A. Mus.; Joslyn Mus. A.; Mulvane Mun. A. Gal.; Denver A. Mus.; NAD; St. Louis Central Lib. Gal. (one-man); Butler AI; Univ. Indiana; Univ. Kansas City; AGAA; Detroit Inst. A.; J. L. Hudson Co., Detroit; Jackson, Miss.; Sioux City, Iowa; Magnificent Mile, Chicago; Provincetown, Mass.; Gilcrease Inst. Am. Hist. & Art, Tulsa, Okla.; Morris Gal., N.Y. *Position*: Instr., Stephens Col., Columbia, Mo., 1946- .

FREUNDLICH, AUGUST L.—*Educator, P.*

George Peabody College for Teachers; h. 3605 Hampton St., Nashville 12, Tenn.

B. Frankfurt, Germany, May 9, 1924. *Studied*: Antioch Col., A.B.; T. Col., Columbia Univ., M.A.; Hill & Canyon Sch. A.; N.Y. Univ. *Member*: Western AA (Pres.); Nat. Comm. on A. Edu., MModA; Michigan Acad. A. Sc. *Exhibited*: Ohio WC Soc.; Michigan Acad.; Arkansas Annual, etc. Contributor to Art Digest (now Arts magazine); Junior Arts & Activities; School Arts; NAEA Journal; Michigan Edu. Journal; Arkansas Edu. Journal. Lectures: Art Education. *Position*: Dir. Arts, George Peabody College for Teachers, Nashville, Tenn., at present.

FREY, ERWIN F.—*Sculptor, E., W.*

School of Fine & Applied Arts, Ohio State University; h. 4837 Olentangy Blvd., Columbus 14, Ohio

B. Lima, Ohio, April 21, 1892. *Studied*: Lima Col.; Cincinnati A. Acad; ASL; BAID; Julian Acad., Paris, with Henri Bouchard, Paul Landowski. *Member*: NSS; Columbus A. Lg. *Awards*: gold med., Ohio State Univ., 1950. *Work*: Ohio State Univ.; Columbus Gal. FA; Fairmount Park, Phila., Pa.; State Mus., Columbus, Ohio; CM. *Exhibited*: CM, 1918; Paris Salon, 1923; PAFA, 1929; AIC, 1928; Cal. PLH, 1930; Arch. Lg., 1925; NAD, 1930; Columbus Gal. FA, 1940 (one-man); DeMotte Gal., N.Y., 1949; PMA, 1943, 1950. Contributor to Journal of Higher Education, Liturgical Arts Quarterly, College Art Journal. *Position*: Asst. Medalist, U.S. Mint, Phila., Pa., 1920; Prof. FA, Ohio State Univ., Columbus, Ohio, 1925- ; Trustee, Columbus Gal. FA, 1952.

FRICK, JOHN LAWRENCE (LARRY)—*Cartoonist, Comm. A.*

323 East 88th St., New York 28, N.Y.

B. York, Pa., Apr. 18, 1918. *Studied*: Chicago Acad. FA; ASL. Contributor cartoons to Sat. Eve. Post; American; Collier's; Phila. Inquirer; Christian Science Monitor; American Legion magazine; various syndicates; Argosy; cartoon anthologies; etc. Formerly cartoonist for Macon (Ga.) Telegraph & News. *Position*: Cart., I., for advertising companies, 1941, 1946-48; A. Dir., training charts & manuals, Robins Field, Ga., during war years; Instr., cartooning, Cartoonists & Illustrators Sch., New York, N.Y. to 1954.*

FRICKE, DELLA EMELIA—*Educator*

200 Northwest 7th St., h. 2138 East Chandler Ave., Evansville 14, Ind.

B. Cincinnati, Ohio, Jan. 28, 1900. *Studied*: Indiana Univ., A.B.; Chicago Sch. App. A.; Columbia Univ.; Evansville Col. *Member*: Western AA; Indiana Edu. Assn.; Com. on A. Edu.; A.N.E.A.; Classroom T. Lectures: Child Art; Philosophy of Art Education. *Position*: A. T., Evansville (Ind.) School Corporation, and Dir. A. Edu.

FRIED, ALEXANDER—*Critic*

San Francisco Examiner, 3rd & Market Sts.; h. 22 Crown Terrace, San Francisco 14, Cal.

B. New York, N.Y., May 21, 1902. *Studied*: Columbia Col., A.B.; Columbia Univ., M.A. Contributor: news correspondence for Christian Science Monitor. *Position*: A. Ed., San Francisco Chronicle, 1930-34; A. Ed., San Francisco Examiner, 1934- .

FRIED, THEODORE—*Painter*

400 West 23rd St., New York 11, N.Y.

B. Budapest, Hungary, May 19, 1902. *Studied*: in Europe. *Member*: Fed. Mod. P. & S. (Vice-Pres.). *Work*: Walker A. Center; Butler AI; Albertina Mus., Vienna, Austria; Musée Nationale d'Arte Moderne, Paris, France; Kunsthalle, Jena, Germany. *Exhibited*: Vienna, 1924, 1925; Paris, 1928-1935; Prague, 1934; Amsterdam, 1938; Toulouse, 1942; Carnegie Inst., 1943, 1949; Albright A. Gal., 1946; NAD, 1944; Fed. Mod. P. & S., 1943-1955; New Sch. for Social Research, 1952; since 1956: Riverside Mus.; Silvermine Gld. A.; New Canaan, Conn.; Greenwich Gal., N.Y. *Position*: Instr., Hudson Guild, N.Y.

FRIEDENBERG, ELIZABETH Z.—*Painter, Gr., T., L.*

461 Ratcliff St., Shreveport 53, La.

B. New York, N.Y., Dec. 1, 1908. *Studied*: Centenary Col., B.A.; ASL; Cornell Univ.; Tschacbasov Sch. A., Woodstock, N.Y. *Member*: ASL; New Orleans AA; CAA; Louisiana Artists; Shreveport A. Cl.; New Orleans A. Assoc. *Awards*: prizes, Louisiana State Mus., 1949, 1957; Louisiana A. Comm., 1948; Baton Rouge, La., 1951; Donaldsonville, La., 1955; Jackson, Miss., 1957. *Exhibited*: Mississippi AA, 1953, 1955; Beaumont AA, 1955; Louisiana A. Comm., Baton Rouge, 1951, 1953-1955; Shreveport, State Exh., 1947-1954; Art:USA, 1958; Delgado Mus. A., 1958. Lectures: Contemporary Art. *Position*: Instr. A., Centenary Col., Shreveport, La.; Series of TV lectures, 1958.

FRIEDENSOHN, ELIAS—*Painter, T.*

601 West 149th St., New York 31, N.Y.

B. New York, N.Y., Dec. 12, 1924. *Studied*: Tyler Sch. FA, Temple Univ.; Queens Col., N.Y., A.B.; N.Y. Univ., and with Gabriel Zendel, Paris, France. *Member*: AEA. *Awards*: prizes, Emily Lowe Fnd., 1951; Fulbright grant, 1957-58. *Work*: Univ. Illinois. *Exhibited*: Am. Jewish Tercentenary, 1955; Phila. A. All., 1955; Rochester Mem. A. Gal., 1955; DMFA, 1955; CMA, 1955; Albright A. Gal., 1955; R.I. Sch. Des., 1956; WMAA, 1957, 1958; Univ. Illinois, 1957; AIC, 1957; Audubon A., 1957; AFA traveling exh., 1957; Fulbright Annual, Galeria Schneider, Rome, 1958; Galeria Attico, Rome, 1958; Spoleto, Italy, 1958; one-man: RoKo Gal., 1951; Edwin Hewitt Gal., N.Y., 1956, 1957; Vassar Col., 1957. Taught: Queens College; Tobe-Coburn Sch.; Craft Students League, all New York.

FRIEDLANDER, ISAC—*Engraver, Et.*

905 West End Ave., New York 25, N.Y.

B. Mitau, Latvia, Apr. 22, 1890. *Member*: SAGA; AEA; Cal. Soc. Et.; Boston Pr. M. *Awards*: prize, Phila. Pr. Cl., 1934, 1940, 1943; BM, 1942; SAM, 1945; Audubon A., 1948; N.Y. State Fair, 1950, 1951; Cong. for Jewish Culture, 1954; Cal. Soc. Et., 1956. *Work*: Galleria Corsini, Rome, Italy; LC; Jewish Mus., Paris; SAM; Smithsonian Inst.; MMA; Bibliotheque Nationale, Paris; Mus. A., Israel; Newark Mus. A. *Exhibited*: CAA, 1931; Weyhe Gal., 1931, 1941; Phila. Pr. Cl., 1930, 1946, 1954; Roerich Mus. A., 1932; BM, 1943, 1944; Lib.Cong., 1943-1946; SFMA, 1942; SAM, 1943-1946; AV, 1942; Boston Pub. Lib., 1953; SAGA, 1954 (London); Boston Pr. M., 1954-55; traveling exh., France, 1952-54, 1956-58; Italy, 1954-55; DMFA, 1953; Portland Mus. A., 1954-55; Wichita AA, 1953-1955; MMA, 1955; one-man exh.: Kleemann Gal., 1930, 1943; Stendahl Gal., Los A., Cal., 1931; New Sch. Social Research, 1933; Phila. Pr. Cl., 1937; Eaton Gal., Montreal, Canada, 1937 & in Europe.

FRIEDLANDER, LEO—*Sculptor*

Hartsdale Rd., West, White Plains, N.Y.

B. New York, N.Y., July 6, 1890. *Studied*: ASL; Ecole des Beaux-Arts, Brussels and Paris. *Member*: NA; F., NSS; Arch. Lg.; Nat. Inst. A. & Let.; F., Am. Acad. in Rome. *Awards*: prizes, Prix de Rome, 1913; NAD, 1918, 1924; medals, Phila., Pa., 1926; Arch. Lg., 1933; NSS, 1951, 1955. *Work*: sculptures, figures, reliefs, panels, groups: Washington Mem. Arch., Valley Forge, Pa.; Eastman Sch. of Music and Eastman Mem., Rochester, N.Y.; Masonic Temple, Detroit; Nat. Chamber of Commerce, Wash., D.C.; Mus. City of N.Y.; Jefferson County (Ala.) Court House; Genesee Valley Trust Co., Rochester; N.Y. Tel. Co., Buffalo; Goldman Mem., Brooklyn, N.Y.; RCA Bldg.,

N.Y.; Arlington Mem. Bridge, Wash., D.C.; Oregon State Capitol; WFNY 1939; Mus. of Univ. Oregon; Rhode Island State Bldg.; USPO, Ayres, Mass.; Nashville Fed. Court House; Congressional Chamber, Wash., D.C.; Victoria (Tex.) Bank; Nat. Bank of Houston, Tex.; Virginia World War II Mem., and many others throughout U.S.; des., medals for N.Y. Chaptr. AIA; Soc. Medalists.*

FRIEDLANDER, MAURICE—Painter, Des., I., Gr.
22 West Monroe St.; h. 5649 Blackstone Ave., Chicago 37, Ill.

B. Blue Island, Ill., May 3, 1899. *Studied*: AIC; Chicago Acad. FA; Archipenko Sch. A. *Member*: Chicago Soc. A.; Renaissance Soc., Univ. Chicago. *Work*: mural, Servicemen's Center, Chicago. *Exhibited*: PAFA, 1946; Univ. Chicago, 1946; AIC, 1943, 1944, 1946, 1952; Illinois State Mus., 1943, 1951; Mandel Bros. A. Gal., 1950; Milwaukee AI, 1944. I., series of five books, "Child's World," 1949.*

FRIEDMAN, BURR LEE. See Singer, Burr

FRIEDMAN, MARK—Sculptor, C., T.
35 West 92nd St., Apt. 8-C, New York 25, N.Y.

B. Brooklyn, N.Y., Dec. 19, 1905. *Studied*: BAID; ASL; Julian Acad., Paris; & with Jean Bouchard, Paul Landowski. *Member*: Soc. des Artistes Francais; S. Gld.; AEA. *Awards*: prizes, BAID, 1926; Salon d'Automne, 1931; Salon de Printemps, Paris, 1932. *Work*: S., Good Samaritan Hospital, N.Y.; Columbia Univ.; Brooklyn State Hospital; schools in Brooklyn & New York, N.Y. *Exhibited*: NAD, 1932, 1933, 1935, 1938; S. Gld., annually; BM, 1938; Columbia Univ., 1939; N.Y. Mun. A. Exh.; CGA; PAFA; Newark YMHA (one-man); Bonestell Gal., 1944, 1946 (one-man). Lectures: Techniques and Use of Sculptural Media.*

FRIEDMAN, MARTIN—Painter
530 West 113th St., New York, N.Y.

B. Budapest, Hungary, Apr. 26, 1896. *Studied*: NAD. *Member*: Fed. Mod. P. & S.; Audubon A. *Awards*: prize, BM, 1950, 1952; Nat. Soc. Painters in Casein, 1958; medals, Audubon A., 1951, 1954, 1955. *Work*: Rochester Mem. A. Gal.; Univ. Arizona; Tel-Aviv Mus., Israel; Brandeis Univ., and in private collections. *Exhibited*: Am. A. Cong., 1938; WFNY 1939; CGA, 1935, 1939, 1947; PAFA, 1940, 1951; WMAA, 1947-1949; WMA, 1947; Nebraska AA, 1948-1950; Toledo Mus. A., 1947, 1948; Clearwater, Fla., 1947, 1950; Carnegie Inst., 1948, 1949; Univ. Illinois, 1948-1950, 1953, 1955; VMFA, 1948; DMFA; Richmond, Va.; A. Gal., 1955; one-man: Brownell-Lambertson Gal., N.Y., 1932; A. Gal., 1942, 1944; Perls Gal., 1946; Phila. A. All., 1946; Babcock Gal., 1951, 1955; Cowie Gal., Los A., 1951.

FRIEDMAN, MARTIN L.—Museum Curator
Walker Art Center, 1710 Lyndale Ave.; h. 725 Vineland Place, Minneapolis 5, Minn.

B. Pittsburgh, Pa., Sept. 23, 1925. *Studied*: Univ. Pennsylvania; Univ. Washington, B.A.; Univ. California at Los Angeles, M.A.; Columbia Univ.; Univ. Minnesota. *Awards*: BM Fellowship, 1956-57; Belgian-American Edu. Fnd. Fellowship, 1957. Arranged "Art of the South Pacific" (permanent installation, BM, 1957); at Walker Art Center: "Sculpture of Germaine Richier," 1958 and "Modern European Masters," 1959. *Position*: Cur., Walker Art Center, Minneapolis, Minn.

FRIEDMAN, WILLIAM—Designer, E., Mus. Cur.
Albright Art Gallery, Buffalo 22, N.Y.

B. New York, N.Y., July 9, 1909. *Studied*: N.Y. Univ.; Atelier Whitman-Goodman, N.Y.; Col. City of N.Y.; Univ. Minnesota. *Position*: Chm. Faculty, Laboratory Sch. Des., New York N.,Y., 1937-40; Hd. Des. Dept., Iowa A. Program, 1940-41; Asst. Dir., Walker A. Center, Minneapolis, 1944-51; Assoc. Dir., 1951-52; Consultant on Des. Research, Stanford Research Inst., 1953; Consultant on Des. & Industry, AIC, 1953-54; Assoc. Prof. in charge Des., Indiana Univ., Bloomington, Ind., 1955-1958; Visiting Cur. of Design, Albright Art Gallery, Buffalo, N.Y., 1958-59.

FRIEND, DAVID—Painter
327 East 75th St., New York 21, N.Y.

B. Glasgow, Scotland, Sept. 6, 1899. *Studied*: in France, Italy, Holland, Spain, and with Walter Farndon. *Member*: All. A. Am.; AAPL; North Shore AA; AEA. *Exhibited*: All. A. Am., 1939-1952; NAD, 1944; North Shore AA, 1944-1948; AAPL, 1944-1948; Gld. Hall, Easthampton, L.I., 1944, 1945; Springville (Utah) A. Mus., 1947; WMAA, 1951; Y.M.H.A., New York, 1952; Galerie Neuf, N.Y., 1947; one-man: Saratoga, Cal., 1953; deYoung Mem. Mus., 1954.*

FRISMUTH, HARRIET W.—Sculptor
Silvermine Ave., Norwalk, Conn.

B. Philadelphia, Pa., Sept. 17, 1880. *Studied*: in Europe & U.S. *Member*: NA; NSS; Arch. Lg.; All. A. Am. *Awards*: Med., prizes, NAD, 1922, & others. *Work*: MMA; Los A. Mus. A.; mus. in Ohio, New Hampshire, Georgia, New Jersey, John Herron AI, etc.; mem., Hackensack, N.J.; Englewood, N.J.; Philadelphia, Pa., etc. *Exhibited*: Nationally since 1910.

FRITZ, HENRY EUGENE—Educator, W., L., P., I., Gr.
217 Spring House Lane, Merion, Pa.

B. Germany, Oct. 12, 1875. *Studied*: CUASch.; NAD; ASL; Ringling A. Sch., Sarasota, Fla.; Columbia Univ.; N.Y. Univ., B.S., Ph.D., and in Germany. *Member*: N.Y. WC Soc.; Sarasota AA; N.Y.Lecturers Assn. *Work*: Mennonite Church, Sarasota, Fla. *Exhibited*: Sarasota AA; T. Col., Boone, N.C. Author: "Education of Gifted Children," Bd. Edu. Publication, 1938. Contributor to newspapers and educational publications. *Position*: Supv., T., F. & Indst. A., New York City Public School System, 1904-40.*

FROELICH, PAUL—Painter, Des., Gr., Comm., I.
Meetinghouse Rd., New Hope, Pa.

B. Philadelphia, Pa., Sept. 5, 1898. *Studied*: Tadd Sch., Phila., Pa.; PAFA. *Member*: Phila. A. All.; AEA; Phila. Pr. Cl. *Awards*: scholarship to PAFA; 2 Cresson awards, PAFA; F., PAFA; prizes, New Orleans, La.; PAFA; Cheltenham A. Center, Phila.; Pennell gold medal, PAFA. *Work*: Delgado Mus. A.; PMA; Dartmouth Col.; Ogunquit A. Center; Rosenwald Coll., Jenkintown, Pa.; stained glass, Bryn Athyn Cathedral, and work in private collections. *Exhibited*: PAFA, annually; Independents, N.Y.; AIC; BM; CMA; Carnegie Inst.; CGA; Phila. Pr. Cl.; Weyhe Gal.; CM; Delgado Mus. A.; Albright A. Gal.; Gimbels, Phila.; Woodmere A. Gal.; Pa. Mus. Sch. FA.; one-man: New Orleans A. & Crafts Gld.; PAFA; Phila. A. All.; Dartmouth Col.; PMSch.A. *Position*: Assoc. Dir., Drawing & Painting, Phila. Mus. Sch. FA, Philadelphia, Pa., 1948- .

FROLA, JOSEPH R.—Painter
Wild Winds Farm, R.D. #4, Latrobe, Pa.

B. Irwin, Pa., Dec. 6, 1904. *Studied*: Pittsburgh A. Lg.; Carnegie Inst. *Member*: Greensburg (Pa.) A. Cl.; Assoc. A. Pittsburgh; All. A. Johnstown. *Awards*: prizes, Greensburg A. Cl., 1936, 1938, 1941, 1943, 1944, 1945, 1947-1949, 1952; Assoc. A. Pittsburgh, 1937, 1942; All. A. Johnstown, 1945; Butler AI, 1946; State T. Col., Indiana, Pa., 1948. Special awards, Greensburg A. Cl., 1945, 1955. *Work*: Latrobe H.S. *Exhibited*: Greensburg A. Cl., 1936-1939, 1941-1945, 1947-1955; Assoc. A. Pittsburgh, 1937, 1938, 1940, 1942-1946, 1947-1952, 1953; Butler AI, 1939-1943, 1946; Parkersburg (W.Va.) A. Center, 1941; State T. Col., Indiana, Pa., 1944-1946, 1947, 1951; All. A. Johnstown, 1945.

FROMBERG, GERALD—Painter, E.
Bradley University, School of Art; h. 2006 South Mahark Lane, Peoria, Ill.

B. Brooklyn, N.Y., July 19, 1925. *Studied*: Brooklyn College, B.A., with Gyorgy Kepes, Serge Chermayeff; New Sch. for Social Research, with Alexy Brodovitch; BMA. Sch., with Reuben Tam; Univ. New Mexico, M.F.A. *Awards*: prizes, Pacific Northwest A. & Crafts Fair, 1952-1954; Peoria A. Center, 1957; medal, Audubon A., 1957. *Work*: Univ. New Mexico; Jonson Gal., Albuquerque, N.M. *Exhibited*: New Orleans AA, 1954, 1955, 1957; Audubon A., 1957; Butler Inst. Am. A., 1958; SAM, 1953;

Denver A. Mus., 1958 and others at Decatur, Peoria, Ill.; Beaumont, Tex.; Fresno, Cal.; one-man: New Mexico State Mus., 1951; Univ. New Mexico, 1951; Henry Gal., Seattle, 1953; 2-man exhs. (with Laverne Fromberg): Dillard Univ., New Orleans, 1954; 331 Gallery, New Orleans, 1954; Contemp. A. Gal., Peoria, Ill., 1956; Barone Gal., N.Y., 1957. *Positions*: Instr. A., Univ. Washington, Seattle, 1952-53; Dillard Univ., New Orleans, 1953-55; Prof. A., Bradley Univ., Peoria, Ill., 1955- .

FROMBERG, LAVERNE RAY—*Painter, T., Gr.*
2006 South Mahark Lane, Peoria, Ill.

B. Duvall, Wash., May 6, 1930. *Studied*: Univ. Washington, B.A., M.F.A.; Univ. New Mexico; ASL. *Member*: Peoria A. Center; New Orleans AA. *Awards*: Ruth Nettleton Mem. award, 1952; Carnegie Hall Art Award, 1952; Northwest A. Fair, 1951-1954; New Orleans AA, 1955; Peoria A. Center, 1957, 1958; Central Illinois Valley Exh., 1958; Illinois Fair, 1958. *Work*: New Orleans AA, and in private colls.; Illinois Mutual Life & Casualty Co. *Exhibited*: Univ. Washington, 1952; 331 Gal., New Orleans, 1954; Norman Vowles Gal., Seattle, 1953; Dillard Univ., 1954; Barone Gal., N.Y., 1957; SAM, 1951; New Orleans AA, 1954, 1955; Phila. Pr. Cl., 1954; Audubon A., 1956; Bradley Univ., 1955; Painting in Peoria Exh., 1957; Denver A. Mus., 1956, 1958; Butler Inst. Am. A., 1958 and in local exhs. at Springfield, Decatur and Peoria. *Position*: Instr. Painting, Dillard Univ., Eve. Sch., 1953-54; Bradley Univ. (part-time), 1955-56; Peoria A. Center, 1956- .

FRUDAKIS, EVANGELOS W(ILLIAM)—*Sculptor*
1621 Sansom St., Philadelphia 3, Pa.

B. Rains, Utah, May 13, 1921. *Studied*: Greenwich Workshops, N.Y.; BAID; PAFA, with C. Rudy, Walker Hancock, Paul Manship and others; Am. Acad. in Rome. *Member*: F., PAFA; NSS; F., Am. Acad. in Rome. *Awards*: prizes, PAFA, 1946-1949; NAD, 1948, 1956; Tiffany Fnd., 1949; Woodmere A. Gal., 1955; medals, PAFA, 1949, 1954, 1955; DaVinci A. All., 1955; Tiffany Fnd. grant, 1949; Demarest Trust Fund, Pittsburgh, 1949; Prix de Rome, 1950-1952. *Work*: PAFA; Allentown Mus. and in private collections. *Exhibited*: PAFA, 1941-1955; NAD, 1948, 1949, 1953, 1955; S. Gld., 1941; Am. Acad. in Rome, 1951-1953; Pyramid Cl., Phila., 1948, 1949; DaVinci A. All., 1955; Phila. A. All., 1955; PMA, 1954; Saxtons River, Vt., 1953 (one-man). *Position*: Instr., Allen Lane A. Center, Woodmere A. Gal., Philadelphia, Pa.

FRY, GUY EDGAR—*Designer, I., E.*
1810 Rittenhouse Square, Philadelphia 3, Pa.; h. Newtown, Pa.

B. Milton, Pa., Aug. 5, 1903. *Studied*: PMSchA. *Member*: Phila. WC Cl.; Phila. A. All. *Exhibited*: Phila. WC Cl., 1934, 1935, 1945, 1950. I., "Christmas Everywhere," 1932; "Victor Herbert Songs for Children," 1943. Lectures on Advertising Art. *Position*: Pres., A. Dir. Cl., Phila. Pa., 1946-47; Dir., PMSchA, 1946-50; Pres., Nat. Soc. A. Dir., 1949-50; Chm. Bd. Governors, PMSchA, 1951-52; Bd. Trustees, PMA, 1951-52; Consulting A. Dir., Philadelphia, Pa. at present.*

FRY, ROWENA—*Painter, Ser.*
4 East Ohio St., Chicago 11, Ill.

B. Athens, Ala. *Studied*: Watkins Inst., Nashville, Tenn.; AIC; Ropp Sch. A. *Member*: Chicago SA; Chicago A. Cl. *Awards*: Chicago Soc. A., 1959. *Work*: Abbott Laboratories Coll. *Exhibited*: AIC, 1928, 1930, 1933, 1935, 1936, 1938, 1944 (one-man), 1946; Chicago SA, 1935-1958; Chicago A. Cl., 1948-1958; Chicago Women's Aid, 1936. Block Print Calendar, 1937-59, published by Chicago SA.

FULLER, ALFRED—*Painter, T., Lith.*
Monhegan Island, Me.

B. Deerfield, Mass., Jan. 8, 1899. *Studied*: Amherst Col., A.B. *Member*: SC; All. A. Am.; Southern Pr. M. *Awards*: prize, Washington (Conn.) AA. *Exhibited*: NAD, 1945, 1946; AWS, 1939-1946; Wash. WC Cl., annually; All. A. Am.; MMA, 1944; PAFA; Grand Central Gal.; Kent AA; Washington AA; Kennedy Gal.; Robinson Gal.; Moyer Gal., Hartford, Conn.; Soc. Four A., Palm Beach, Fla. *Position*: Instr., Marine & Landscape Painting, Monhegan Island, Me.

FULLER, ANDREW DANIEL, JR.—
    Educator, L., W., Cr., Des., P.
9 Park St., Boston, Mass.; h. 1284 Beacon St., Brookline, Mass.; w. Fairfax Hall, Harvard Square, Mass.; s. Nahant and Truro, Mass.

B. Wakefield, Mass., Nov. 1, 1903. *Studied*: Harvard Univ., Grad. Sch. FA; Avon Univ., and with Langefeld, George Parker Winship, J.C. Butera and others. *Member*: Acad. A.; Authors' Cl. of London. *Awards*: Master Writer, 1937; A.E.D., Avon Univ., 1954. *Work*: mural design, Avon Univ. *Exhibited*: BMFA. Contributor to Massachusetts, Its People and Places, with essays on art and history. Ed., Des.: Contemporary Paintings, 1932-33; Catalogues of Paintings, Banyan-Tree Press; Art and Civilization (Studies from Brooks Adams); Education in Arts and Sciences, Avon Univ. Lectures: Artistic Greatness; The Touch of Genius; Modern and Academic Art; Revival of Style and Beauty in Architectural Design. *Positions*: Trustee, Academy of Artists, 1933-35; Governor, New England Soc. Contemp. A., 1932-50; Arts Foundation, Boston; Mod. Sch. Fashion & Des.; Prof. Aesthetics, Dean of Faculty, College of FA, Avon Univ., 1953- ; Pres., Avon Univ., 1954- .

FULLER, ARTHUR D.—*Illustrator, P.*
Saugatuck Shores, Westport, Conn.

B. Exeter, N.H., Sept. 1, 1889. *Studied*: Harvard Univ., A.B.; Fenway Sch. of Illustration, Boston; Harvey Dunn Sch. A.; Chicago Academy FA. *Member*: SC; SI; Westport A. Illus.: "Longshore" by Joel Barber, 1939; "Tranquility Series" by Col. H.P. Sheldon, 1945; "Sporting Days" by John Taintor Foote, 1937, and other books. Contributor illus. to: Saturday Evening Post; Collier's; Harper's Monthly; Field & Stream, etc.

FULLER, META VAUX WARRICK—*Sculptor, T., L.*
31 Warren Rd., Framingham, Mass.

B. Philadelphia, Pa., June 9, 1877. *Studied*: PMSchIA, with Paul Lachenmeyer; PAFA, with Charles Grafly; in Paris, with Rollard, Injalbert, Gauqui; and with Rodin. *Work*: CMA; N.Y. Pub. Lib.; Garfield Sch., Detroit, Mich. *Exhibited*: CMA; SFMA; Garfield Sch., Detroit; N.Y. Pub. Lib. Lecturer, Livingstone Col., Salisbury, N.C.; Howard Univ., Wash., D.C.*

FULLER, RICHARD EUGENE—*Museum Director*
Seattle Art Museum, Volunteer Park; h. 3801 East Prospect St., Seattle, Wash.

B. New York, N.Y., June 1, 1897. *Studied*: Yale Univ.; Univ. Washington, B.S., M.S., Ph.D. *Member*: Western Assn. A. Mus. Dir.; Chinese A. Soc. Am.; AAMus. (Council, 1954-61); Am. Assn. A. Mus. Dir. (Vice-Pres., 1956-57); U.S. Nat. Com. ICOM, 1958-61. *Awards*: Hon. Deg., LL.D., Washington State Col.; AIA. Lectures: History of Oriental Art. *Position*: Co-Donor, with mother, the late Mrs. Eugene Fuller, of Seattle Art Museum, 1933, and the Eugene Fuller Memorial Collection; Research Prof. Geology, Univ. Washington, 1940- ; Pres., Western Assn. A. Mus. Dir., 1935-37; Pres., Dir., Seattle Art Museum, Seattle, Wash., 1933- .

FULLER, SUE—*Painter, S., Gr., E., W., L.*
44 East 63rd St., New York, N.Y.

B. Pittsburgh, Pa., Aug. 11, 1914. *Studied*: Carnegie Inst., B.A.; T. Col., Columbia Univ., M.A. in FA Edu. *Member*: SAGA. *Awards*: prizes, Assoc. A. Pittsburgh, 1941, 1942; Northwest Pr. M., 1946; Phila. Pr. Cl., 1944, 1946, 1949; Tiffany Fnd. F., 1947; Guggenheim F., 1948; Nat. Inst. A. & Let., 1950; N.Y. State Fair, 1950. *Work*: N.Y. Pub. Lib.; LC; Harvard Univ. Lib.; Carnegie Inst.; PMA; BMA; WMAA; Ford Fnd.; AIC; SAM; MModA; MMA; BM; NAD, and in private colls. *Exhibited*: PAFA, 1944-1946; NAD, 1944, 1945; LC, 1944-1946; Laguna Beach AA; Butler AI; Assoc. A., Pittsburgh, 1936-1944; Tokyo, Japan, 1954; BM, 1955; WMAA Traveling exh., 1955; Newport AA; AIC, 1957; BMFA, 1956; AFA traveling exh., 1957, and in Paris, France, 1950, 1952; Bienal de Sao Paulo, Brazil, 1951; Salzburg, Germany, 1952; one-man: Bertha Schaefer Gal., 1949, 1950, 1953, 1956; CGA, 1951; A. & Crafts Center, Pittsburgh, 1951; Ft. Wayne Mus. A., 1951; Univ. Georgia, 1952; Milwaukee-Downer Col., 1952; Currier Gal. A., 1956; Fort Worth, Tex., 1956; McNay AI, 1956; Wesleyan Univ., 1956; Univ. Delaware, 1956. Contributor to Craft Horizons, Arts magazines, 1954-55. *Posi-*

tion: 1st V.Pres., SAGA, 1949-50; Member Council, 1948-49; Member Council Comm. on A. Edu., MMA, 1950-53; Des., Raymond Loewy Corp., 1955-57; Instr., A. Center of Northern New Jersey, 1957-58.

FULTON, DOROTHY—*Painter, S., C., T., L.*

217 Redmond St., New Brunswick, N.J.

B. Uniontown, Pa., Oct. 23, 1896. *Studied*: PAFA; Columbia Univ.; PMSchIA; Univ. Southern California; Univ. Kansas; Univ. Pennsylvania, B.F.A., M.Sc. in A. Edu., and with Albert Laessle. *Award*: F., PAFA. *Work*: Mulvane A. Mus., Topeka, Kan.; Washburn Col.; Linden Hall, Lititz, Pa., and in private colls. *Exhibited*: Lancaster (Pa.) AA, 1937-1941; Kansas City AI, 1933; PAFA, 1935, 1936-1938, 1940, 1945; Ferargil Gal., 1937; Newman Gal., Phila., 1936 (one-man); Mulvane A. Mus., 1930-1932 (one-man); Franklin Marshall Col., 1940 (one-man). *Position*: Hd. A. Dept., Linden Hall, Lititz, Pa., 1936-52; Instr., New Jersey Pub. Schs., 1953- .

FULTON, ELLEN (M.)—*Writer*

125 Maron St., Snell Isle, St. Petersburg, Fla.

B. Scranton, Pa., June 15, 1887. *Studied*: Wellesley Col. *Member*: Lg. Am. Pen Women. *Position*: A. Ed., St. Petersburg Times, 1944-46; Pres., Nat. Lg. Am. Pen Women (St. Petersburg Branch), 1950-52.*

FULTON, W. JOSEPH—*Museum Director, E., W.*

5 Linden St., Cambridge 38, Mass.

B. Longmont, Colo., Apr. 8, 1923. *Studied*: Univ. Colorado, B.F.A.; Harvard Univ. (Fogg A. Mus.), A.M. *Member*: CAA; AAMus.; Soc. Arch. Historians; AAUP; Harvard Cl. of So. Cal. *Awards*: Joint-Honor Scholarship, Univ. Colorado, 1940-44; James Rogers Rich & Townsend Scholarships, Harvard Univ., 1945-46; Grad. F., Harvard Univ., 1946-47; F., Belgian American Edu. Fnd., 1951; Fulbright F., for France, 1953-54. Contributor art criticism to Norfolk (Va.) Virginian-Pilot; Pasadena Star News. Lectures: The Museum and the Community; 19th & 20th Century Art, to clubs and civic groups; other lectures to colleges and universities. Arranged exhs.: "Pioneer American Moderns," Norfolk (Va.) Mus., 1953; "California Design," Pasadena A. Mus., 1954; "The Blue Four" (coll. catalog and exh.) Pasadena A. Mus., 1955. *Position*: Instr., Humanities in the College, Univ. Chicago, 1948-51; Asst. Dir., Norfolk Mus., 1951-53; Dir., Pasadena A. Mus., Pasadena, Cal., 1953-1957; Writing & Research, 1958- .

FULWIDER, EDWIN L.—*Painter, E., Gr., Des.*

101 East Central Ave., Oxford, Ohio

B. Bloomington, Ind., Aug. 15, 1913. *Studied*: John Herron A. Sch., B.F.A. *Awards*: Traveling F., John Herron AI, 1936; prizes, Herron AI, 1940, 1943, 1945; Massillon A. Mus., 1956; Dayton AI, 1953. *Work*: Herron AI; Dayton AI; LC; SAM. *Exhibited*: CM, 1939, 1941, 1956-1958; AIC, 1940, 1941; John Herron AI, 1936-1946, 1957; LC, 1957; Butler Inst. Am. A., 1958; Dayton AI, 1956, 1958; Massillon A. Mus., 1956. *Position*: Instr., John Herron A. Sch., Indianapolis, Ind., 1945-47; Cornish Sch., Seattle, Wash., 1947-49; Prof., Dept. A., Miami Univ., Oxford, Ohio, at present.

FUNSCH, EDYTH (Mrs. V. S. Trowbridge)—*Illustrator, Des., P.*

511 North Taylor St.; h. 5872 Cates Ave., St. Louis 12, Mo.

B. St. Louis, Mo., Feb. 25, 1905. *Studied*: Washington Univ. A. Sch.; & with Nicholson, Oskar Gross. *Member*: Soc. Indp. A., St. Louis. *Awards*: prizes, Soc. Indp. A., 1940, 1946. *Exhibited*: Soc. Indp. A., 1940, 1942, 1944; CAM; 1945, 1946, 1952. I., for book publishers.*

FURLONG, CHARLES WELLINGTON—*Writer, E., L., I., P.*

"Eight Gables," Old Oaken Bucket Rd., Scituate, Mass.

B. Cambridge, Mass., Dec. 13, 1874. *Studied*: Mass. Normal A. Sch.; AIC; Cornell Univ.; Harvard Univ.; Ecole des Beaux-Arts, Julian Acad., Paris, France. *Member*: F., Royal Geographical Soc., London; Explorer's Club, N.Y.; F., Harvard Travelers Cl., Boston; French Acad., Officier de l'instruction publique (for beaux arts, belles lettres). *Awards*: Prix de Concours; medals, Greece,

Arabia, Montenegro, Italy. *Work*: paintings of Fuegian and Patagonian tribes on permanent exh., Smithsonian Inst. *Exhibited*: PAFA; NAD; SC; Boston A. Cl.; Copley Soc.; Norwell AA. Author, I., "Gateway to the Sahara," 1909, 2nd ed., 1912; "Let'er Buck" (basic principles of freehand drawing), 4 editions; tactical field handbooks on Siberia, Russia and Mexico, 1918. I. (several hundred botanical drawings), for Bailey's "Cyclopaedia of Horticulture." Contributor to Harpers, Scribners, Travel, Blue Book and others. Lectures on Art, explorations, and world affairs to Nat. Geographic Soc.; Royal Geographic Soc., and other scientific societies, universities, schools and clubs throughout U.S., Canada and England. Taught at Cornell Univ., Clark Univ., Boston Univ.

FUSSINER, HOWARD ROBERT—*Painter, T., W.*

(mail): Colby Junior College, New London, N.H.; h. Twin Lake Rd., New London, N.H.

B. New York, N.Y., May 25, 1923. *Studied*: American People's Sch., with C.G. Nelson; ASL, with Sternberg, Vytlacil, Blanch; CUASch., with Gwathmey, Ferren; Hans Hofmann Sch. FA; N.Y. Univ., B.S., M.A. *Member*: CAA; Nat. Com. A. Edu., MModA; ASL. *Work*: Staten Island Inst. Mus.; Everhart Mus. A., Scranton, N.Y.; mural, N.Y. Univ. Edu. Bldg. *Exhibited*: College Art Exh., 1949-50; Woodstock Conf. Exh.; one-man: Morehouse Col., Atlanta, 1954; Peter Cooper, N.Y., 1955; Everhart Mus., 1957; Panoras Gal., 1958; group exh. in New York City: ACA Gal.; RoKo Gal.; Contemp. A. Gal.; Laurel Gal.; N.Y. City Center, etc. Contributor to College Art Journal; Phylon. *Position*: Instr., A. Dept., Colby Junior College, New London, N.H.

FYFE, JOHN HAMILTON—*Painter, Cart., I.*

Chambliss Rd., Whitehaven, Tenn.

B. Gilby, N.D., Aug. 10, 1893. *Studied*: AIC, B.F.A.; SI Sch., N.Y. *Member*: Tennessee Edu. Assn.; Nat. Edu. Assn.; Memphis Palette & Brush; Mid-South AA; Southern Group; Tennessee Vocational Assn.; Am. Vocational Assn. *Awards*: prize, Brooks Mem. A. Gal., 1952. *Exhibited*: Mid-South AA; Memphis Palette & Brush; Brooks Mem. A. Gal.; Memphis Biennial. *Work*: murals, USPO, Camden, Tenn.; Magnolia, Miss. *Position*: A. Instr., Whitehaven, Tenn., 1937-52; A. Supv., Shelby County, Tenn., 1939-46; Chm., West Tenn. Edu. Assn., Art Section, 1951.*

GABO, NAUM—*Sculptor, E., P., Eng.*

Breakneck Hill, Middlebury, Conn.

B. Briansk, Russia, Aug. 5, 1890. *Studied*: Univ. Munich, Germany. *Awards*: Logan medal, AIC, 1954; Guggenheim Fellowship, 1954. *Work*: Tate Gal. London; Hanover Mus., Germany; Moscow Inst. A. & Culture; Yale Univ. A. Gal.; MModA; Solomon R. Guggenheim Mus.; BMA; bas-relief, lobby of U.S. Rubber Co. Bldg., New York City; sculpture, Rotterdam, Holland. *Exhibited*: nationally. Taught Design at Harvard Grad. Sch., 1953-54; conducted Mellon Lectures, National Gallery of Art, Wash., D.C., 1959.

GABRIEL, ADA V.—*Painter, Lith., Des.*

2 West 67th St., New York 23, N.Y.

B. Larchmont, N.Y., July 28, 1898. *Studied*: Barnard Col.; N.Y. Sch. Des., and with Erich Gletter in Munich; Emil Ganso, New York. *Awards*: prizes, Albany Inst. Hist. & Art, 1949; NAWA, 1950; Nat. Acad. A. & Let., 1950, 1954. *Work*: NAWA; N.Y. Pub. Lib.; LC; Toledo Mus. A. *Exhibited*: CGA, 1935; PAFA, 1936, 1937; AIC, 1937; WMAA; CAA; Putnam County AA, 1939, 1940; NAD, 1944; Allison Gal., N.Y., 1941, 1944 (one-man), 1947, 1949, 1956 (one-man); 50 Prints of the Year, 1936; Albany Inst. Hist. & A., 1949; NAWA, 1950; Nat. Acad. A. & Let., 1950. Des. book jackets for publishers.*

GABRIEL, ROBERT A.—*Craftsman, S., T.*

Carnegie Institute of Technology; h. 802 Maryland Ave., Pittsburgh 32, Pa.

B. Cleveland, Ohio, July 21, 1931. *Studied*: Cleveland Inst. A.; Skowhegan Sch. P. & S. *Member*: Assoc. A. of Pittsburgh. *Awards*: Mary Page traveling scholarship, Cleveland Inst. A., 1954; prize, Wichita, Kans., 1953. *Exhibited*: PAFA, 1953; Wichita Dec. A. & Crafts Exh., 1953; Huntington AA, 1953; Texas State Fair, 1953; CMA, 1953-1955; Western Pa. Sculpture Exh., 1955, 1956; Faculty Exh., Allegheny Col., 1955. *Position*: Instr., Design, Carnegie Inst. Tech., Pittsburgh, Pa.; Instr. A., Allegheny Col., 1954.

GABRIELE, GABRIELLE (Mrs. Gustav A. Miller)—
Painter, C.
235 99th St., Stone Harbor, N.J.; w. 15 Sea Horse
Lane, Vero Isles, Vero Beach, Fla.

B. Philadelphia, Pa., Dec. 24, 1906. *Studied*: PAFA;
PMSchIA. *Member*: Phila. Plastic Cl.; Cape May County
A.Lg.; Lg. of So. Jersey A. *Awards*: F., PAFA. *Exhibited*:
Phila. Plastic Cl.; Palm Beach A. Lg.; Soc. Four A.;
Atlantic City, 1954.

GADBURY, HARRY LEE—Painter, Et., T.
32 South Jefferson St.; h. 1245 Wabash Ave., Dayton
5, Ohio

B. Greenfield, Ohio, June 5, 1890. *Studied*: Cincinnati
A. Acad.; AIC. *Member*: Dayton Soc. Et. *Exhibited*:
NAD; Dayton AI. *Position*: Instr., Drawing, Dayton Art
Institute, Dayton, Ohio.

GAGE, GEORGE W.—Painter, T.
Central Park Studios, 15 W. 67th St., New York 23,
N.Y.

B. Lawrence, Mass., Nov. 14, 1887. *Studied*: BMFA Sch.;
PAFA, and with Philip Hale, Frank W. Benson, William
M. Chase, Howard Pyle. *Member*: New Rochelle AA; A.
Gld. *Awards*: prizes, BMFA; A. Gld., 1954. *Work*: Pa.
State Col.; Martha Berry Col., Rome, Ga.; Am. Red
Cross, Chattanooga, Tenn.; Univ. Kansas Medical Center;
Charles Moser Lib., Southbury, Conn.; Mabel Dean Bacon
Sch., N.Y.; N.Y. Medical Col., Brooklyn, N.Y.; Veterans
Admin. Hospital, Bronx, N.Y.; Butler Mem. Lib., Cam-
bridge, Neb.; Univ. of the South, Sewanee, Tenn.; NAD;
Am. Nat. Bank & Trust Co., Chattanooga. *Exhibited*:
NAD; All. A. Am.; BM; BMFA; Berkshire A. Mus.;
Fairleigh Dickinson Col., Rutherford, N.J.; Woman's Cl.,
Montclair, N.J.*

GAGE, HARRY LAWRENCE—
Typographic Designer, W., P., L., Gr.
16 River Rd., Annisquam, Gloucester, Mass.

B. Battle Creek, Mich., Nov. 20, 1887. *Studied*: AIC;
abroad, and with Gerry Peirce. *Member*: AIGA; North
Shore AA; Edu. Council of Graphic A. Indst.; Boston Soc.
Pr. M.; Copley Soc. of Boston; Cape Ann Arts Council.
Awards: Friedman med., in Graphic A. Edu., gold med.,
AIGA, 1951. *Exhibited*: North Shore A.; Copley Soc.,
Boston; Ogunquit A. Center. *Author*: "Applied Design for
Printers"; "Composition Manual—Machines in the Com-
posing Room." *Contributor* to graphic arts magazines.
Lectures on Typographic Design and Graphic Arts Tech-
niques. *Position*: Prof. Graphic A., Carnegie Inst., 1913-
1919; Sec., Bartlett-Orr Press, 1919-1931; Consultant on
Typography, 1919-31, V.Pres., 1932-47, Consultant in
Graphic A., 1947- , Mergenthaler Linotype Co., Brooklyn,
N.Y.

GAGE, JANE (Mrs. Clifton Brigham)—Painter
4124 Hampton St., Western Springs, Ill.

B. La Grange, Ill., Jan. 1914. *Studied*: Rockford (Ill.)
Col.; Am. Acad., Chicago; & with Sterba, Gunther, George
Elmer Browne. *Member*: NAWA; La Grange A. Lg.
Awards: prize, Rockford AA, 1946. *Exhibited*: All. A.
Am., 1942, 1943; AWCS, 1945; NAWA, 1942; AIC, 1941-
1944; Rockford AA, 1946; Mississippi Valley A., Spring-
field, Ill., 1941.*

GAGE, MERRELL—Sculptor, E., L.
456 Mesa Rd., Santa Monica, Cal.

B. Topeka, Kan., Dec. 26, 1892. *Studied*: ASL; Henri Sch.
A.; BAID; & with Gutzon Borglum. *Member*: NSS; Cal.
AC; P. & S. Cl. *Awards*: Med., Kansas City AI, 1923;
Southwestern Int. Exp., Long Beach, Cal., 1928; prize, Los
A. Mus. A., 1933. *Work*: Statues, mem., fountains,
Topeka, Kan.; Kansas City, Mo.; Los A., Beverly Hills,
La Jolla, Cal.; Long Beach, Redlands, Cal.; Indiana State
Capitol; Pacific Palisades, Cal.; San Antonio, Tex.; San
Diego Mus. A.; & other public bldgs.; Am. Numismatic
Soc.; Mulvane Mus. A. "The Face of Lincoln," film award
for Best Short Subject, Acad. Motion Picture Arts & Sc.,
1955; series of 10 films for Nat. Edu. TV and Radio
Center, Ann Arbor, Mich., 1958. *Exhibited*: WFNY 1939;
GGE, 1939; MMA (AV); NSS; Cal. A. Cl.; P. & S. Cl.;

Los A. Mus. A., 1945 (one-man); Santa Barbara Mus. A.,
1945 (one-man). *Lectures*: "The Face of Lincoln." *Position*: Prof. FA, S., Univ. Southern California, Los Angeles,
Cal., 1925-58; Prof. Emeritus, 1958- .

GAHMAN, FLOYD—Painter, Et., L., C., Gr., E.
Ogontz Center, Pa. and Morrisville, Vt.; h. 550 Riverside Drive, New York 27, N.Y.

B. Ohio, Oct. 14, 1899. *Studied*: Valparaiso (Ind.) Univ.;
Columbia Univ., B.S., A.M., and with Hobart Nichols,
Henry Varnum Poor. *Member*: ANA; Audubon A.; SC;
All. A. Am. *Awards*: F., Tiffany Fnd.; prizes, All. A.
Am., 1942; SC, 1941, 1942. *Exhibited*: NAD annually;
SC, annually; Montclair A. Mus.; Pa. State Univ., 1955;
Indiana Univ., 1958. *Lectures*: Contemporary Painting.
Position: Asst. Prof. A., Pennsylvania State Univ., Uni-
versity Park, Pa.

GAINES, NATALIE EVELYN—Sculptor
2956 Glendale Ave., Detroit, Mich.

B. Detroit, Mich. *Studied*: Detroit Soc. for A. & Crafts;
Greason Sch., Detroit. *Awards*: prizes, Crespi Gal., 1958;
Temple Emanu-El, N.Y., 1959. *Exhibited*: Detroit Inst. A.,
1949, 1950; Wayne County A., 1950; Creative Gal., N.Y.,
1951; Kirk-in-the-Hills A. Festival, Detroit, 1952; Crespi
Gal., 1958, 1959; All. A. Am., 1958; Women's Intl. Exh.,
N.Y., 1958; Temple Emanu-El Exh., 1959; one-man: Crespi
Gal., 1958.

GAITHER, MRS. DAVID S. See Markham, Kyra

GALBRAITH, (WILLIAM GALBRAITH CRAWFORD)—
Cartoonist, I.
1456 Giddings St., Southeast, Grand Rapids 7, Mich.

B. Salt Lake City, Utah, Jan. 21, 1894. *Studied*: Brigham
Young Univ.; Univ. Mexico; ASL. *Member*: SI; Cartoonist
Soc. *Contributor* to Sat. Eve. Post; New Yorker; Stage;
Harper's Bazaar; Cosmopolitan, and other national maga-
zines. *Position*: Creator, I., panel cartoon, "Side Glances,"
NEA Service.

GALE, JANE GREENE—Painter, E.
Fresno State College; h. 651 Cambridge Ave., Apt. 3,
Fresno 4, Cal.

B. Leipzig, Germany, July 18, 1898. *Studied*: Minneapolis
Sch. A.; ASL; Duluth State T. Col.; T. Col., Columbia
Univ., B.S., M.A., and with Charles J. Martin, Jean
Charlot, Hans Hofmann, Dong Kingman, Yasuo Kuniyoshi.
Member: Cal. WC Soc.; San Diego A. Gld.; A. Lg. of
Fresno. *Awards*: prizes, Cal. State Fair, 1949; Newport,
Cal., 1951; San Diego A. Gld., 1947-1951, 1953; A. Lg.
of Fresno, 1948-1950, 1954, 1955. *Work*: San Diego FA
Gal.; Newport Harbor H.S. *Exhibited*: Cal. WC Soc.,
1950-1954 and prior from 1941; Inst. Contemp. A., Boston,
1955; AWS, 1951; A. Lg. Fresno, 1948-1950, 1954, 1955;
Cal. State Fair, 1947-1949, 1951-1955; San F. AA, 1948,
1950, 1951 and prior; Walnut Creek, Cal., 1951; Santa
Barbara Mus. A., 1942; San Diego FA Soc., 1945, 1952
(both one-man); La Jolla A. Center, 1946; Laguna Beach,
1948. *Position*: Instr., Univ. Miami, Oxford, Ohio, 1928-
1930; Lake Erie Col., Painesville, Ohio, 1930-35; Fresno
State Col., Fresno, Cal., 1935- .*

GALE, WALTER RASIN—Educator, P., I.
Homewood Apts., Baltimore 18, Md.

B. Kent County, Md., Jan. 17, 1878. *Studied*: Maryland
Inst.; Johns Hopkins Univ.; N.Y. Univ.; Univ. Chicago,
and with Henry Turner Bailey, Walter Sargent, Henry
Parton Haney, David M. Robinson. *Member*: Balt. WC
Cl.; Eastern Shore Soc.; Hist. Soc., Mus. A., all of Balti-
more. *Exhibited*: BMA; Balt. WC Cl.; Maryland Inst.
Alumni Assn. *Position*: Instr., A. Dept., Baltimore City
Col., 1905-1948 (Retired).

GALOS, BEN—Painter, T., I.
216 East 15th St., New York, N.Y.

B. Russia, 1889. *Studied*: Vilna A. Sch.; NAD. *Member*:
All. A. Am. *Awards*: prizes, NAD; Washington Square
exh., 1937; Pepsi-Cola, 1948. *Work*: N.Y. Hist. Soc.;
Brooklyn Col.; Brooklyn Tech. H.S.; Erasmus H.S.; Has-

brouck Heights (N.J.) Pub. Lib.; Mem. Hospital, Oneonta, N.Y.; Dept. Health, Albany, N.Y.; Farm Colony Hospital, Staten Island, N.Y.; Haaren H.S., N.Y.; Ain Harod Mus., Israel; murals, St. Monica's Church, N.Y.; Daly's Theatre, N.Y., and work in private colls. *Exhibited*: NAD, 1942, 1945, 1949; Audubon A., 1946-1948; All. A. Am., 1949-1955, 1956, 1957; WFNY 1939; MMA, 1952; AAPL; ACA Gal., 1949; Gramercy Gal., 1947 (one-man).

GAMBEE, MARTIN—*Painter, Lith., C.*
Instituto Allende, San Miguel de Allende, Gto., Mexico

B. Newark, N.J., April 10, 1905. *Studied*: with Howard Giles, Gustave Cimiotti, James Pinto, and with Andre L'Hote, in Paris; PIASch. *Member*: AWS; SC; Audubon A.; Cal. WC Soc.; Silvermine Gld. A.; All. A. Am.; A. Fellowship. *Awards*: prizes, Albany Inst. Hist. & A., 1937; SC, 1938, 1940, 1943; Santa Cruz, Cal., 1943; Oakland A. Mus., 1943; Santa Monica, Cal., 1953, 1958. *Work*: Phila. A. All.; Albany Inst. Hist. & A., Mus. New Mexico. *Position*: Instr., Instituto Allende, San Miguel, Mexico, at present.

GAMBLE, KATHRYN ELIZABETH—*Museum Director*
The Montclair Art Museum, 3 South Mountain Ave. at Bloomfield Ave., Montclair, N.J.

B. Van Wert, Ohio, Aug. 19, 1915. *Studied*: Oberlin Col., A.B.; N.Y. Univ. Grad. Sch. FA, M.A.; Newark Mus. Apprentice Course (Certif.), 1941. *Member*: AAMus.; Northeast Mus. Conference; Museums Council of New Jersey. *Author*: Thesis: "The Mother and Child in Egyptian Art"; "Methods and Materials of the Painter" (exh. catalogue for traveling show); numerous exhibition catalogues and bulletins compiled, introductions written, etc. Art Survey lectures. Exhibitions arranged: Pennsylvania German Arts and Crafts, 1952; Masks: Rites and Revelry, 1954; Methods and Materials of the Painter (assembled 1954 traveling through Canada for 18 month tour). Organized New Jersey art for Canadian request; American Illustration, 19th Century: Charles Parsons and his Domain, 1958. *Position*: Asst. to the Dir., 1944-52, Dir., Montclair Art Museum, 1952- .

GAMBLE, ROY C.—*Painter*
5726—14th Ave., Detroit 8, Mich.

B. Detroit, Mich., June 12, 1887. *Studied*: Detroit Acad. FA; ASL; Julian Acad., Paris; & with John Wicker, William Chase, Robert Henri, Laurens. *Member*: Scarab Cl. *Awards*: prizes, Detroit Inst. A., 1914, 1920, 1926, 1928, 1942; Scarab Cl., 1957. *Work*: PAFA; Detroit Inst. A.; State Capitol, Lansing, Mich.; Wayne County circuit courts; Univ. Michigan; Princeton Univ.; Mich. Supreme Court; Federal Court, Bay City, Mich., 1958; port. John Lord Booth, Booth Coll., Detroit, 1958; Wayne Univ.; Mich. State Univ.; Detroit Pub. Lib.; murals, Detroit Free Press Bldg.; Michigan mural for Century of Progress, Chicago, 1933. *Exhibited*: Paris Salon, 1910, 1911; PAFA, 1920, 1921; CGA, 1921; Detroit Inst. A., 1911-1956; Univ. Pennsylvania, 1956; Woman's City Cl., Detroit, 1956; Prismatic Cl., Detroit, 1956; Roy Davis Gal., New York City, 1958 (one-man).

GAMBLE, WILLIAM SYLVESTER—
Painter, E., Gr., Comm., I.
Michigan State University, Department of Art; h. 627 Cherry Lane, East Lansing, Mich.

B. Fox Lake, Mich., Mar. 3, 1912. *Studied*: Univ. Washington, B.A., M.F.A., with Johannes Molzahn, Amadee Ozenfant; Michigan State Col.; T. Col., Columbia Univ. *Member*: AAUP; Alabama WC Soc.; Northwest Pr. M.; Com. on A. Edu.; Michigan Pr. M. *Awards*: prizes, Northwest Pr. M., 1936, 1946; Montgomery, Ala.; Milwaukee, Wis.; Grand Rapids, Mich. *Work*: SAM; Grand Rapids A. Gal. *Exhibited*: Northwest Pr. M., 1934, 1938, 1939, 1941-1943, 1945, 1947, 1949, 1951; LC, 1946, 1948, 1949; BM, 1948-1950; Cincinnati, Ohio, 1950; Wichita, Kans., 1946; Laguna Beach, Cal., 1949; Mich. Pr. M., 1953-1955; SAM, 1937-1939, 1946, 1948, 1949; Riverside Mus., 1945; Atlanta, Ga., 1947; Marshall Fields, Chicago, 1946; Ala. WC Soc., 1947, 1948; Grand Rapids A. Gal., 1949, 1950, 1953; Detroit, Mich., 1953; Midwest Col. Conf., Kansas City, 1953. Illus. "Sometime Again," 1945. *Position*: Instr., Seattle Pub. Schs., 1940-46; Univ. Washington, 1944-45; Univ. Alabama, 1947-48; Michigan State Univ., East Lansing, Mich., 1948- . Author, Producer, half-hour film "Children Create," with original music.

GAMMELL, R(OBERT) H(ALE) IVES—*Painter, W.*
30 Ipswich St., Boston 15, Mass.

B. Providence, R.I., Jan. 7, 1893. *Studied*: with William Paxton. *Member*: Providence AC; NSMP; N.Y.Soc. Painters; All. A. Am. *Awards*: prizes, Newport AA, 1936; All. A. Am., 1941. *Work*: murals, Toledo Mus. A.; Women's Cl., Fall River, Mass.; Newark Pub. Lib.; Oxon Hill Manor, Oxon Hill; Industrial Nat. Bank, Providence, R.I.; paintings, Maryhill (Wash.) Mus. FA. *Author*: "Twilight of Painting," 1946; "Dennis Miller Bunker"; "A Pictorial Sequence based on 'The Hound of Heaven,' by Francis Thompson."

GAMMON, ESTELLA—*Painter, Des., T.*
2103 Navarro Ave., Altadena, Cal.

B. Pasadena, Cal., June 25, 1895. *Studied*: Pomona Col., B.A.; T. Col., Columbia Univ., M.A., and with Anna Hills, Charles Reiffe, Orin White, and others. *Member*: Women Painters of the West. *Exhibited*: Women Painters of the West; one-man: Albee's Print Room, La Jolla, Cal.; Padua Hills, Claremont; Mountain View A. Gal., Altadena, 1957; Altadena Lib.; Claremont Lib.; Long Beach Women's Cl. Lectures on Art Appreciation.

GANINE, PETER—*Sculptor, Indst. Des.*
2289 El Contento Dr., Hollywood 28, Cal.

B. Tiflis, Russia, Oct. 11, 1900. *Studied*: Corcoran Sch. A.; and in Russia. *Member*: Cal. A. Cl.; Soc. for Sanity in Art. *Awards*: prizes, CGA, 1932; Cal. A. Cl., 1934, 1936; San Diego FA Soc., 1938; Ebell Salon, 1939, 1945; Soc. for Sanity in A., 1946; Syracuse Mus. FA, 1940; Los A. Mus. A., 1945. *Work*: Syracuse Mus. FA; San Diego FA Soc. *Exhibited*: GGE, 1939; San Diego FA Soc.; Los A. Mus. A.; Syracuse Mus. FA 1958 and prior; Mus. of Industry and Commerce, Chicago (chess set, reproduced in Life magazine).

GANNAM, JOHN—*Illustrator*
33 West 67th St., New York 23, N.Y.

Member: N.A.; SI; A. & Writers; AWS. *Awards*: Two Merit Awards, 1944, medal, 1944, Chicago A. Dir. Cl.; Merit awards, 1948, 1954, 1955, N.Y. A. Dir. Cl.; medal, SI, 1947; medal, 1953, two hon. mentions, 1950, Cleveland A. Dir. Cl.

GANNETT, RUTH CHRISMAN—*Illustrator*
Cornwall, Conn.

B. Santa Ana, Cal., Dec. 16, 1896. *Studied*: Univ. California, A.B., A.M. *Member*: SAGA. I., "Tortilla Flat," 1935; "Hi-Po the Hippo," 1939; "Miss Hickory," 1946; "My Father's Dragon," 1948 (New York Herald-Tribune prize); "Cream Hill," 1949, and other books.

GANNON, CLELL GOEBEL—*Painter, Comm., W., L.*
912 Mandan St., Bismarck, N.D.

B. Wisner, Neb., Jan. 10, 1900. *Studied*: AIC, with Vanderpoel, Forsberg, Lorado Taft, George Bellows, Joseph Pennell. *Member*: North Dakota Hist. Soc. (life). *Awards*: "Artists of the Year," North Dakota, 1948; award of merit, Nat. Lg. Am. Pen Women. *Work*: Bismarck Pub. Lib.; murals, Burleigh County Court House; Bismarck H.S. Lib.; N.D. Hist. Soc. Artist for 2 maps of North Dakota, one historical, one pictorial; covers for publications of Oscar H. Will Co., (25 yrs.). *Exhibited*: New York, N.Y.; Philadelphia, Baltimore, 1954; North Dakota State exhibitions annually. *Author*, I., "Songs of the Bunch Grass Acres"; "How Christmas Came to North Dakota." Lectures: Karl Bodmer, Artist of the Upper Missouri. *Position*: Staff A., Provident Life Ins. Co., Bismarck, N.D., 1937- .

GANSER, IVAN L(AURENCE)—*Sculptor, C.*
Pioneer Lodge, Forsyth, Mo.

B. Eugene, Ore., June 10, 1906. *Studied*: Kansas City AI, B.F.A., M.F.A. *Awards*: prizes, Midwestern A. Exh., 1935, 1937; Kansas City Soc. A., 1936; Missouri State Fair, 1939. *Exhibited*: Univ. Women's Cl., Kansas City, 1958. *Position*: Restorer, sc. & ceramics, William Rockhill Nelson Gal. A., Atkins Mus., 1933-38, 1945-56; Hd. Dept. Ceramics, Kansas City AI, Kansas City, Mo., 1950- .

GARBELY, EDWARD—*Painter*

245½ South 19th St., Newark 3, N.J.

B. Newark, N.J., Aug. 15, 1909. *Studied*: Newark Sch. F. & Indst. A.; & with Grabach, Trouck. *Member*: P. & S. Soc. of N.J.; East Orange A. Center; Irvington A. & Mus. Assn. *Work*: Newark Univ.; Newark City Hall; Rutherford (N.J.) Town Hall; Marlboro State T. Col. *Exhibited*: Newark AC; Montclair A. Mus.; NAD; Newark Mus.; Irvington A. & Mus. Assn.; WFNY 1939; Audubon A.; East Orange A. Center.

GARCIA, ANTONIO E.—*Painter, T.*

2818 Bagnall Drive, Corpus Christi, Tex.; h. San Diego, Tex.

B. Monterrey, Mexico, Dec. 27, 1901. *Studied*: AIC, and with Wayman Adams, Boris Anisfeld, Frederic Taubes, Getlar Smith. *Member*: South Texas A. Lg. (Chm.); Texas FA Assn. (Trustee); Corpus Christi A. Gld.; Texas WC Soc.; Soc. Pastel Painters (Pres.). *Awards*: prizes, AIC, 1929; Kingsville (Tex.) Col. A., 1940; Corpus Christi Mus., 1939-1941. *Work*: Texas Fed. Women's Cl. headquarters; Corpus Christi Mus.; Kingsville A. & Indst. Col. Mus.; pub. schs. of Texas; frescoes, Sacred Heart Church, Corpus Christi; La Bahia Mission, Goliad, Tex.; murals, Our Lady of Texas, McCook, Tex.; Wilson Bldg., Corpus Christi; San Diego, Tex., Sch. *Exhibited*: DMFA; Texas FA traveling circuit; Texas General circuit; Port Arthur Lib. *Position*: Instr. Painting, Del Mar College, Corpus Christi, Tex.*

GARDNER, B(EATRICE) STURTEVANT—*Painter, T., L.*

210 Meads Rd., Woodstock, N.Y.

B. Westtown, N.Y., May 12, 1893. *Studied*: Columbia Univ., B.S., M.A.; Ecole des Beaux-Arts, Paris. *Member*: Woodstock AA; AAUW; Canal Zone A. Lg. *Awards*: prizes, Am. A. Week, Balboa, C.Z., 1941-1955; Fla. Int. Exh., 1952. *Work*: mural, St. Luke's Cathedral, C.Z.; wall dec., Hotel Bout de L'ile, Canada. *Exhibited*: Philadelphia, New York, Baltimore, Canal Zone, Panama, Peru, Woodstock, N.Y.; Honolulu Lib., 1957. Organized Canal Zone A. Lg. (Pres.); arranged exhs. for JWB Gal., Balboa, C.Z.; directed Annual Community Art Exh., C.Z. Contributor art reviews and articles for newspapers and magazines of Panama. Pres., Woodstock Gld. of Craftsmen Shop, 1958. Instr., Adult Edu., Onteora Central Sch.

GARDNER, GERTRUDE GAZELLE—*Painter, T.*

605 Brooks St., Laguna Beach 7, Cal.

B. Fort Dodge, Iowa, Oct. 26, 1878. *Studied*: Ecole des Beaux-Arts, Fontainebleau, France; PIASch.; and with Henry B. Snell, Eliot O'Hara. *Member*: Laguna Beach AA; Nat. Lg. Am. Pen Women. *Awards*: prizes, Pen & Brush Cl., 1941; Laguna A. Festival, 1957; Nat. Lg. Am. Pen Women, 1954, 1958. *Work*: in private colls. *Exhibited*: Assoc. Am. Women A., 1930-1942; Pen & Brush Cl., 1935-1942; AWS, 1920-1942; N.Y. WC Cl.; Blanden Mem. A. Gal., Ft. Dodge (one-man); Smithsonian Inst., Wash., D.C.

GARDNER, PAUL—*Former Museum Director*

Las Milpas, San Patricio, N.M.

B. Boston, Mass., Oct. 20, 1895. *Studied*: George Washington Univ., A.B., M.A.; MIT; Harvard Univ.; Univ. Paris. *Member*: A. Mus. Dir. Assn.; CAA; AAMus. Contributor to Print Collector's Quarterly. *Positions*: Dir., Nelson-Atkins Mus., Kansas City, Mo., 1933-53; Officer, Monuments and FA Comm., Italy, 1943-45.*

GARDNER, WALTER HENRY—*Painter*

5437 Morris St., Philadelphia 44, Pa.

B. Liverpool, England, May 7, 1902. *Studied*: PAFA; Tyler Sch., Temple Univ.; & with Breckenridge, Carles, Garber. *Awards*: Cresson traveling scholarships, PAFA, 1924; F., PAFA, 1938; prize, Wanamaker Exh., 1934. *Work*: murals, USPO, Phila., Pa.; Honesdale, Pa.; Bern, Ind.; Mun. Court, Phila. *Exhibited*: PAFA, 1934-1936, 1938, 1939, 1942, 1943; WMAA, 1936; Detroit Inst. A., 1937; CGA, 1937; AIC, 1936; VMFA, 1939; MMA (AV), 1942.

GAREL, LEO—*Painter, Cart., I.*

Piney Point Rd., Mt. Tremper, N.Y.

B. New York, N.Y., Oct. 8, 1917. *Studied*: Parsons Sch. F. & App. A.; ASL, with George Grosz, Vaclav Vytlacil. *Exhibited*: Mortimer Levitt Gal.; Blue Door A. Gal., N.M.; Zabriskie Gal., N.Y.; Mus. of New Mexico, Santa Fé. I., "Quiz Book of Seven Arts," 1948; "Bridegrooms Only," 1950; "How to Audition," 1949. Contributor cartoons to Sat. Eve. Post; Wall St. Journal; Christian Science Monitor; Esquire; N.Y. Times; Cosmopolitan, etc.

GARFIELD, MARJORIE S.—
Painter, Des., E., L., Gr., W.

Iowa State College; h. 535 Hayward Ave., Ames, Iowa

B. Boston, Mass., Nov. 30, 1903. *Studied*: Syracuse Univ., B.F.A., M.F.A., and with Henry B. Snell, Henry W. Rice, Albert R. Thayer, George Pearse Ennis. *Member*: AWS; Wash. WC Cl.; Assoc. A. Syracuse; Syracuse Pr. M.; Rockport AA; Lg. Am. Pen Women. *Awards*: prizes, Catherine Lorillard Wolfe A. Cl., 1930; Lg. Am. Pen Women, 1936, 1946; Assoc. A. Syracuse, 1936, 1937. *Work*: Syracuse Mus. FA; Dwight A. Gal., Mt. Holyoke; Univ. Manitoba, Canada. *Exhibited*: one-man: Syracuse Mus. FA, 1935, 1939; Wash. A. Cl.; Mint Mus. A.; Univ. Virginia; Rutgers Univ.; Telfair Acad. A. & Sc.; Moore Inst. Des.; Potsdam (N.Y.) Normal Sch.; Mt. Holyoke Col.; Univ. Manitoba; Iowa State Col.; Marshalltown, Iowa, 1950; Des Moines A. Center, 1951; Nat. A. Week, Ames, Iowa, 1952. *Position*: Prof., Head Dept., Int. Des., Syracuse Univ., 1928-48; Prof. Applied A. Hd. Dept. A., Iowa State Col., Ames, Ia., 1948- . Nat. Chm. A., Am. Home Economics Assn., 1955-57.*

GARNSEY, CLARKE HENDERSON—
Painter, Et., C., E., L.

4305 Andrews St., Amarillo, Tex.

B. Joliet, Ill., Sept. 22, 1913. *Studied*: Cleveland Sch. A.; Western Reserve Univ.; Daytona Beach A. Sch., with Don Emery. *Member*: Daytona Beach A. Lg.; West Texas A. Guild; Amarillo Connoisseur Soc.; CAA. *Awards*: prizes, Fla. Fed. A., 1936; Daytona Beach A. Lg., 1932, 1935-1937. *Exhibited*: Fla. Fed. A., 1933-1938; Cleveland, Ohio, 1949. *Position*: Chm. A. Dept., Amarillo Col., Amarillo, Tex.*

GARNSEY, JULIAN ELLSWORTH—*Painter*

10 Newlin Rd., Princeton, N.J.

B. New York, N.Y., Sept. 25, 1887. *Studied*: Harvard Univ., B.A.; ASL; Julian Acad., Paris. *Member*: Arch. Lg.; Cal. A. Cl.; BAID; Inter-Soc. Color Council; Century Assn. *Awards*: prizes, AIA, 1927, 1930. *Work*: Los A. Pub. Lib.; Hotel Del Monte; Los A. Stock Exchange; Univ. California at Los A.; WFNY 1939; Oregon "Journal," Portland; Metropolitan Life & Equitable Life Ins. housing projects. Contributor of articles on color to AIA Journal, Arch. Record, Retailing, and other publications.

GARRETT, ADAMS WIRT—*Painter*

26 Leland Ave., Plainfield, N.J.

B. Forney, Tex., June 23, 1908. *Studied*: T. Col., Columbia Univ., M.A.; ASL. *Awards*: prize, Pepsi-Cola, 1945; Montclair A. Mus., 1957. *Work*: AGAA; Fitchburg Mus. A.; BMA; Smithsonian Inst. *Exhibited*: Carnegie Inst., 1941-1943; AIC, 1945; Pepsi-Cola, 1945; Newark Mus. A., 1958; one-man: 8th St. Gal., 1939; Phila. A. All., 1945; ACA Gal., 1946; Feigl Gal., 1951. *Position*: Instr. Gr. A., ASL, New York, N.Y., 1947-51; Seton Hall University, 1954-57.

GARRETT, PRISCILLA LONGSHORE—*Painter, L.*

12 Forge Rd., Bridgeport, Pa.

B. Chatham, N.J., Mar. 29, 1907. *Studied*: Phila. Sch. Des. for Women; Drexel Inst.; PAFA, with George Harding. *Member*: PAFA; Phila. A. All.; AAPL. *Awards*: F., PAFA; prize, Lackawanna County A. All., 1939; Chester County AA, 1939; med., Plastic Cl., 1940. *Work*: PAFA. *Exhibited*: Butler AI, 1939, 1944, 1945; PAFA, 1933; Springfield A. Lg.; Everhart Mus., Scranton, Pa., 1940, 1945 (one-man). *Lectures*: Contemporary American Art. Cover des. for volume poetry by Helen Brooks, 1955.

GARRISON, EVE—*Painter*

9201 South Clyde Ave., Chicago 17, Ill.

B. Boston, Mass. *Studied*: AIC. *Member*: AEA; AIC Alumni Assn.; Renaissance Soc., Chicago. *Awards*: gold medal, CGA, 1933. *Work*: Univ. Illinois, Urbana; U.S. Treasury Dept., Wash., D.C., and in private colls. *Exhibited*: Wichita AA; Los A. County Fair; Oakland A. Mus.; Portland (Ore.) A. Mus.; NAD; PAFA; Albany Inst. Hist. & A.; Kansas City AI; Contemp. A., N.Y.; AIC; VMFA; CGA; Conn. Acad. FA; Nat. Mus., Wash., D.C.; Albright A. Gal.; Detroit Inst. A.; Butler AI; Alabama WC Soc.; Portland Soc. A.; Springfield A. Mus.; Woodstock AA; one-man: Arthur Newton Gal., 1950; Rafilson A. Gal., Chicago, 1953; Creative Gal., N.Y., 1953; Mandel Bros., 1954; Anna Werbe Gal., Detroit, 1954; Milwaukee AI, 1955; Well-of-the-Sea Gal., Chicago, 1955; Chicago Pub. Lib., 1957; Exhibit A. Gal., Chicago, 1958. Founder of Exhibit A. Gal., Chicago, a Chicago Artists' Co-operative gallery, 1957.

GARTH, JOHN—*Painter, W., L., Cr., T., Gr.*

Studios, 2155 26th Ave., San Francisco 16, Cal.

B. Chicago, Ill., Dec. 21, 1894. *Studied*: AIC; Yale Col., B.A.; Yale Sch. FA, B.F.A.; ASL; & in London, Paris, Florence. *Member*: NSMP; Cal. Soc. Mural P.; AAPL; F., Royal Soc. A., London, England; Soc. Western A. *Awards*: Med., Palace Legion Honor; traveling scholarship, Yale Sch. FA. *Work*: murals, Univ. California; Cal. State Indst. Comm.; Wine & Grape Pavilion, Lodi, Cal.; General Electric Co.; San F. Arch. Cl.; Pacific Marine Contractors; Masonic Temple (mural restoration); Woodlawn Mem. Park (triptych); Fairmont, Somerton, Sir Francis Drake Hotels, all in San F.; Miami Univ., Oxford, Ohio; Redding, Cal. *Exhibited*: Local & national exh., annually. *Position*: Dir., John Garth Sch. A.; A. Ed., The Argonaut, San Francisco, Cal., 1941- ; A. Chm., San F. Press-Union Lg.; Artist-Painter memb. San Francisco Art Comm., 1956- ; Admissions Bd., Huntington Hartford Fnd., 1949- ; Fnd., Past Pres., Soc. Western A., 1939- ; A., San F. Rotary Cl.

GARVER, JACK—*Painter, T.*

502 Tahoe Place, Northeast, Albuquerque, N.M.

B. Larned, Kans., June 11, 1921. *Studied*: Hays Kansas State Col.; Univ. New Mexico, B.F.A. *Member*: New Mexico Edu. Assn.; New Mexico A. Edu. Assn. (Council). *Awards*: prizes, N.M. State Fair, 1950; Albuquerque A., 1954-1956; Mus. New Mexico, Santa Fe. *Work*: Jonson Gal.; Univ. N.M.; Univ. Maine; Eaton W. Tarbell & Assoc., Bangor, Me.; Flatow-Moore-Fairburn-Bryan, Archs., Albuquerque. *Exhibited*: Pasadena Mus. A.; Mus. of New Mexico. *Position*: Arch. Draftsman, 1948-49, 1951-52; Instr. A. & Crafts, Rio Grande H.S., Albuquerque, N.M., 1958-59.

GASKINS, LETHA (HECKMAN)

(Mrs. O. K. Gaskins)—Painter

7 East Westfield Blvd., Indianapolis 20, Ind.

B. Indianapolis, Ind., Oct. 31, 1900. *Studied*: John Herron AI; DePauw Univ.; Butler Univ.; Ohio Univ., with Eliot O'Hara, Hilton Leech, Charles Burchfield. *Member*: Indiana A. Cl.; Brown County A. Gal. Assn. *Awards*: prizes, Indiana A. Cl., 1956; Michiana Regional, South Bend, 1957. *Work*: Butler Univ., and in elementary schools. *Exhibited*: Sarasota, Fla., 1956; Ohio Valley, 1957; Michiana, 1957; Neville Mus. A., Green Bay, Wis., 1951; Hoosier Salon, 1941, 1943, 1944; John Herron AI, 1942, 1946, 1950, 1957; Indiana A. Cl., 1941-1957.

GASPARD, MRS. LEON. See Kaminsky, Dora

GASPARO, ORONZO VITO—*Painter, Des., C.*

167½ East 115th St., New York 29, N.Y.

B. Rutigliano-Prov., Bari, Italy. Oct. 16, 1903. *Studied*: NAD, and with Preston Dickinson. *Member*: AEA; Village A. Center. *Awards*: prizes, Village A. Center, 1951, 1958; Huntington Hartford Fnd. Grant, 1956-57. *Work*: MModA; MMA; WMAA; Four Arts, Palm Beach; Palm Beach A. Cl. *Exhibited*: MModA, 1936; AIC; PAFA, annually; CGA, 1939; WFNY 1939; GGE, 1939; WMAA, 1938-1941, 1944, 1946; CAM, 1945; Carnegie Inst., 1941, 1945; Riverside Mus., 1945, 1952; RoKo Gal., 1952; Little Studio, 1952; Fisher Gal., 1952; one-man: Tilden & Thurber Gal.,

Providence, R.I., 1928; Woodstock, N.Y., 1929; Pinacotheca, 1941; Ferargil Gal., 1942-1944, 1948; Mortimer Levitt Gal., 1945-1954; Gal. Neuf, 1946; Mus. New Mexico, 1949; Village A. Center, 1949-1958; Rutigliano, Italy, 1955-56; Bari, Italy, 1956; Schneider Gal., Rome, 1956; Crespi Gal., N.Y., 1957 (one-man). Dir., Oronzo's Studio Gallery, New York, N.Y.

GASPARRO, FRANK—*Sculptor, T.*

216 Westwood Park Drive, Havertown, Pa.

B. Philadelphia, Pa., Aug. 26, 1909. *Studied*: PAFA, and with Charles Grafly. *Member*: Soc. Medalists; F., PAFA; AEA. *Awards*: Cresson Traveling Scholarship, PAFA, 1930, 1931. *Work*: Designed and executed Stroud Jordan Medal, 1953; U.S. Coast Guard Commendation Medal, 1953; U.S. Central Intelligence Medal, 1955; Philadelphia Medal of Honor, 1955; U.S. Sec. of Treasury Robert B. Anderson Medal, 1958. *Exhibited*: PMA sculpture exh., 1940; PAFA, 1946; medals at French Mint, Paris, France, 1950; Spanish Intl. Medallic Art Exh., Madrid, 1952; Recipient Diploma Citation as Exhibitor. *Position*: Instr., Fleisher A. Sch., Phila., Pa., 1946- ; Sculptor-Engraver, United States Mint, Philadelphia, Pa., 1942- .

GASSER, HENRY MARTIN—*Painter, Des., T., W., L.*

654 Varsity Rd., South Orange, N.J.

B. Newark, N.J., Oct. 31, 1909. *Studied*: Newark Sch. F. & Indst. A.; ASL, and with Brackman, Grabach. *Member*: Conn. Acad. FA; AWS; Phila. WC Cl.; Wash. WC Cl.; New Jersey WC Cl.; Baltimore WC Cl.; SC; All. A. Am.; Audubon A; Mississippi AA; Assoc. A. New Jersey; New Haven Paint & Clay Cl.; SSAL; AAPL; Springfield A. Lg.; NAD; Cal. WC Cl.; NAC; ASL. *Awards*: prizes and medals, Smithsonian Inst., 1941; Montclair A. Mus., 1941, 1943, 1945, 1946; Balt. WC Cl., 1942, 1950; Alabama WC Cl., 1943, 1945, 1946, 1953; NAD, 1944; Oakland A. Gal., 1943, 1952; Springfield A. Lg., 1943, 1945; New Haven Paint & Clay Cl., 1944; Wash. WC Cl., 1945, 1946, 1948; New Orleans AA, 1945, 1946; Phila. WC Soc., 1945; State T. Col., Indiana, Pa., 1946; SSAL, 1946; AWS, 1943, 1944, 1947, 1948; SC, 1947, 1949, 1951; Corpus Christi Mus., 1947; Cal. WC Soc., 1948; Am. Veterans Soc. A., 1949; All. A. Am., 1950; Peale Mus. A., 1950; Conn. Acad. FA, 1951, 1952; Audubon A., 1952; AAPL, 1953; Rockport AA, 1953; Butler AI, 1954; NAC, 1954; New Jersey State Exh., 1954; AWS, 1955; NAC, 1955; SC, 1955; Balt. WC Cl., 1955; Palm Beach, Fla., 1955. *Work*: PMA; New Haven Paint & Clay Cl.; Newark Mus. A.; Springfield (Mo.) Mus. A.; Washington State Col.; Dallas Mus. FA; Irvington A. & Mus. Assn.; Mint Mus. A.; IBM; Montclair A. Mus.; New Britain Inst.; PMA; Syracuse Univ.; BMFA; SAM; Amherst Col.; Canajoharie Mus. A.; NAC; Staten Island Inst. A. & Sc.; U.S. War Dept.; SAM and many others. *Exhibited*: Carnegie Inst.; NAD; AIC; AWS; Phila. WC Cl.; Wash. WC Cl.; All. A. Am.; SFMA; Audubon A.; Albany Inst. Hist. & A.; Texas Int. Exh.; Cal. PLH; Denver A. Mus.; Mississippi AA; Oakland A. Gal.; Alabama WC Soc.; Smithsonian Inst.; Montclair A. Mus.; Balt. WC Cl.; New Haven Paint & Clay Cl.; New Orleans AA; High Mus. A.; Guatemala Nat. Fair; CGA; and in many other national museums. *Position*: Dir., Newark Sch. F. & Indst. A., Newark, N.J., 1946-1954; Hon. Pres. A. Council of New Jersey. Author: "Casein Painting: Methods and Demonstrations"; "Oil Painting: Methods and Demonstrations"; "Watercolor—How to do it."*

GATCH, (HARRY) LEE—*Painter*

Coon Path, Lambertville, N.J.

B. Baltimore, Md., Sept. 10, 1902. *Studied*: Maryland Inst. FA; Am. Sch., Fontainebleau, France; Academie Moderne, Paris, and with Andre Lhote, Kisling. *Work*: MMA; MModA; WMAA; PMA; PC; CAM; Los A. Mus. A. *Exhibited*: PAFA, 1945; Munich, Berlin, Germany, 1950; Italy, 1950; Frankfort, Germany, 1951; Carnegie Inst., 1950, 1952, 1955; Vienna, 1951; Los A. Mus. A., 1951; MMA, 1952; WMAA, 1953; Univ. Illinois, 1953 and many others.

GATES, JOHN MONTEITH—*Architectural Designer*

718 Fifth Ave., New York 19, N.Y.; h. Locust Valley, L.I., N.Y.

B. Elyria, Ohio, June 25, 1905. *Studied*: Harvard Col.; Columbia Univ., B.A. in Arch. *Member*: AIA; F., Royal Soc. A. *Awards*: prize, Swedish Int. Comp., 1933. *Work*:

Steuben Glass des. in several U.S. museums (Toledo, Chicago, Kansas City, etc.). *Exhibited*: FA Soc., London, 1935; WFNY 1939; Paris Salon, 1937. *Position*: Vice-Pres., in charge of des. for Steuben Glass, Inc.*

GATES, MARGARET (CASEY) [Mrs. Robert F.]—
Painter
R.F.D. #2, Box 542, McLean, Va.

B. Washington, D.C. *Studied*: Corcoran A. Sch.; Phillips Mem. Gal. A. Sch.; Colorado Springs FA Center, and with C. Law Watkins, Henry Varnum Poor. *Member*: A. Gld. of Washington. *Awards*: Med., Soc. Wash. A., 1945; CGA, 1953. *Work*: PC; mural, USPO, Mebane, N.C. *Exhibited*: VMFA; Critics Choice, CM, 1945; Pepsi-Cola, 1946; CGA, 1947, one-man 1948; PC; Whyte Gal., 1946 (one-man); Bader Gal., Wash., D.C., 1954, 1955. *Position*: Exec. Sec., Phillips Mem. Gal. A. Sch., 1933-46; Admin. Staff, Watkins Gal., American Univ., Wash., D.C., 1948-53.*

GATH, ETHEL ROBERTSON—*Painter*
410 Leroy St., Fenton, Mich.

Studied: Flint Inst. A. Sch., with Jaroslav Brozik; Corcoran Sch. A., with Richard Lahey, Eugen Weisz, Heinz Warneke, Peggy Bacon. *Member*: Soc. Wash. A. *Awards*: prizes and medals, Flint Inst. A., 1937-1939; Art Fair, Wash., D.C., 1944-1947; SSAL, 1947; Soc. Wash. A., 1943, 1944. *Work*: VMFA; CGA. *Exhibited*: Grand Rapids, Mich., 1940; CGA, 1945; VMFA, 1946; Rockefeller Center, 1936; Detroit Inst. A., 1934, 1935, 1937, 1938, 1949; Ann Arbor, Mich., 1935; Detroit Scarab Cl., 1936-1940; Flint Inst. A., 1933-1941; Soc. Wash. A., 1943-1948; PMG, 1942-1944; Detroit Soc. Women Painters, 1937-1940; AAPL, 1944, 1945-1947; Min. P. S. & Gr., 1944; Pub. Lib., Wash., D.C.; Swope Gal. A., 1945; CGA, 1945; VMFA, 1946, 1948; Boston Soc. Indp. A., 1948; NAD, 1948; one-man: Flint, Mich., 1937; Alexandria, Va., 1945; Wash. A. Cl., 1945; CGA, 1948; Silver Spring, Md., 1948.*

GATRELL, MARION THOMPSON—*Painter, Gr., E.*
School of Fine and Applied Arts, Ohio State University; h. 1492 Perry St., Columbus 1, Ohio

B. Columbus, Ohio, Nov. 13, 1909. *Studied*: Ohio State Univ., B.Sc. in Edu., M.A. *Member*: Columbus A. Lg.; Ohio WC Soc. *Awards*: prizes, Columbus A. Lg., 1939, 1945, 1949, 1951, 1954; Ohio State Fair, 1938, 1939, 1941, 1950, 1951, 1953, 1955; Ohio Valley exh., Athens, 1943, 1948, 1949; Butler AI, 1950, 1957. *Work*: Univ. Sch., Columbus; Butler Inst. Am. A. *Exhibited*: Audubon A., 1945; Ohio Valley exh., 1943-1946, 1948-1955, 1957; Butler AI, 1945, 1950-1952; Union A. Exh., 1957; Parkersburg, W. Va., 1942; Toledo Mus. A., 1939-1945; Columbus A. Lg., 1937-1958; Ohio WC Soc., 1939-1956; Columbus Gal. FA, 1957; Ohio Wesleyan Univ., 1957; Ohio State Fair, 1938-1941, 1949-1957; Massillon Mus. A., 1950-1957; Ohio Pr. M., 1951-1956; Union annual art exh., 1957, 1958. *Position*: Assoc. Prof., Sch. FA, Ohio State Univ., Columbus, Ohio, at present.

GATRELL, ROBERT M.—*Painter, Gr., E.*
School of Fine & Applied Arts, Ohio State University; h. 1492 Perry St., Columbus 1, Ohio

B. Marietta, Ohio, May 18, 1906. *Studied*: Ohio State Univ., B.Sc. in Edu.; M.A. *Member*: Ohio WC Soc.; Columbus A. Lg.; Art section Ohio Edu. Assn. *Awards*: prizes, Ohio State Fair, 1938-1941, 1949-55, 1957; Governors Award, 1939, 1952; Ohio WC Soc., 1942-1944, 1954, 1956; Parkersburg, W. Va., 1942; Columbus A. Lg., 1938, 1941, 1943, 1947-1951, 1953-1955; Ohio Valley Exh., 1944, 1948, 1953; Veterans A. Exh., 1951; Canton, Ohio, 1952; Union Annual Exh., 1955; Northwestern Pr. M., 1956; Ohio Pr. M., 1956; College Print Exh., 1956; AWS, 1958. *Work*: Dunbar Mus., Dayton, Ohio; Dennison Univ.; Ohio Northern Univ.; Ohio State Univ.; Massillon Mus. A.; Canton Mus. A.; Otterbein College; Columbus Gallery of Fine Arts; University School, Columbus, Ohio; B'nai B'rith Hillel Foundation, Columbus, Ohio; Butler Inst. Am. A.; Technological Col., Lubbock, Tex. *Exhibited*: VMFA, 1938; AWS, 1942, 1943, 1950, 1955, 1958; Audubon A., 1945, 1948, 1950; Oklahoma A. Center, 1941; Columbus A. Lg., 1929-1958; Parkersburg FA Center, 1942, 1943; Ohio WC Soc., 1940-1956; Butler AI, 1938, 1942, 1948, 1950-1953, 1955, 1957; Ohio Valley, 1943, 1944, 1946, 1948-1955; Ohio Pr. M., 1939, 1947, 1956; SAGA, 1947, 1948, 1950, 1951, 1954; BM, 1949; PAFA, 1949; Phila., Pr. Cl.,

1949, 1951, 1952, 1954; Northwest Pr. M., 1948, 1956; Terry AI, 1952; Fla. Southern Col., 1952; Wichita A. Mus., 1952, 1953, 1956; Northwest Territory Sch., 1948; Nat. Ser. Soc., 1951, 1952, 1954; Massillon Mus., 1949-1956; Canton Mus. A., 1951-1953, 1955, 1956; MMA, 1952; Inner Valley Exhib., 1955; Tri State Jury Show, Chautauqua, N.Y., 1955; LC, 1955; Magnificent Mile Art Festival, Chicago, 1955; Union Annual Exh., 1955, 1956, 1958. *Position*: Prof., Sch. FA, Ohio State Univ., Columbus, Ohio, at present.

GAUG, MARGARET ANN—*Etcher, Des.*
1909 Irving Park Rd., Chicago 13, Ill.

Member: SAGA; Chicago Soc. Et.; Prairie Pr. M.; Cal. Pr. M. *Awards*: prize, Chicago Soc. Et., 1950, 1955. *Work*: NGA; Illinois State Lib.; Smithsonian Inst.; Brussels Mus. FA, Belgium; MMA. *Exhibited*: one-man: Smithsonian Inst., 1941. Des. & Publ. greeting cards.

GAUGLER, JOSEPH P.—*Painter, Des., T., W., L.*
Color Helm, Inc., Saddle River, N.J.; h. "Rising Mists," Saddle River, N.J.

B. Paterson, N.J., Mar. 17, 1896. *Studied*: ASL; in France, England, and with Wayman Adams, George Pearse Ennis. *Member*: AWS; Inter-Soc. Color Council; Ridgewood AA. *Awards*: Ridgewood AA, 1935; Rockport AA; med., Montclair A. Mus., 1936. *Exhibited*: AWS; N.Y. WC Cl.; SC; Guild Hall, Easthampton (one-man); Montclair A. Mus.; Ridgewood AA. Lectures: Color in Industry; Merchandising & the Fine Arts. *Position*: Pres., Color Helm, Inc., Dir., American Color Trends, New York, N.Y.

GAVENCKY, FRANK J.—*Painter, T.*
P.O. Box 175, Ramona, Cal.

B. Chicago, Ill., June 10, 1888. *Studied*: AIC, Chicago Acad. FA. *Member*: Bohemian AC; Show Case of Arts, Northern San Diego County (Bd. Dir.). *Awards*: Med., Palette & Chisel Cl., 1925; prize, AIC, 1930. *Work*: City of Chicago; Eastern Star Home, Rockford, Ill.; Western Illinois T. Col., McComb, Ill. *Exhibited*: Pasadena AI, 1932; AIC, 1931; Toman Lib., Chicago, 1934 (all one-man).

GAW, WILLIAM A.—*Painter, E., L.*
1409 Edith St., Berkeley 3, Cal.

B. San Francisco, Cal., Nov. 26, 1891. *Member*: San F. AA. *Awards*: prizes and medals, Cal. PLH, 1932; Oakland A. Gal., 1933, 1934, 1939; Los A. Mus. A., 1935; Bay Region AA, 1936; San F. AA, 1936; Fnd. Western A., 1937; SFMA, 1937, 1938; Cal. State Fair, 1939, 1940. *Work*: MModA; SFMA; Cal. PLH; San F. AA; San Diego FA Soc. *Exhibited*: MModA, 1933; AIC, 1936; WMAA; Colorado Springs FA Center; deYoung Memorial Mus.; Cal. PLH, 1935, 1945, 1946, 1949 (one-man), 1951, 1952, 1953 (one-man); MMA, 1942, 1952; CGA, 1939, 1941, 1949; Los A. Mus.; San Diego FA Soc.; SFMA; Mills Col. A. Gal.; Carnegie Inst., 1941; GGE, 1939; WFNY 1939; CM; Tacoma A. Lg., 1948; Everhart Mus., 1948; BMA, 1948; J.B.Speed Mus. A., 1948; Springfield AA, 1948; Oakland A. Gal., 1949; Santa Cruz, Cal., 1949; San F. Art Festival, 1950, 1951; Richmond (Cal.) A. Center, 1951, 1952; Walnut Creek, Cal., 1949, 1950, 1955; PMG, 1947; Rochester Mem. A. Gal., 1947; Paintings of the Year, N.Y., 1947; Earlham Col., 1957, 1958; Pa. State Univ., 1958, and many others. Lectures: Techniques, Science of Color. *Position*: Acting Dir., Cal. Sch. FA, San F., Cal., 1941-45; Chm. Dept. A., Mills Col., Oakland, Cal., 1942-1957; Prof. Emeritus, 1957- ; Chm. Creative A. Workshop, Mills Col., 1943-56; Dir., AEA, Northern Cal., Chapter, 1950, 1951; John Hay Whitney Visiting Prof., Earlham Col., Richmond, Ind., 1957-58.

GAY, RUTH A. [Mrs. Harry Haven]—
Sculptor, P., T.
2928 Ridge Rd., Lewiston, N.Y.

B. Ontario, Canada, Nov. 30, 1911. *Studied*: Syracuse Univ.; ASL; & with Alexander Brook, Henry Varnum Poor, Charles Cutler. *Member*: The Patteran. *Awards*: prizes, Albright A. Gal.; Western N.Y. exh., 1948, 1949. *Exhibited*: Riverside Mus.; Grand Central A. Gal.; AFA; WMA, 1938; Syracuse Mus. FA; Rochester Mem. A. Gal.; Univ. New Mexico; MacMurray Col. (one-man): Decatur, Ill.; Albright A. Gal.; Western N.Y. exh., 1948, 1949, 1951. *Position*: Prof. A., Hd. A. Dept., MacMurray Col., Jacksonville, Ill., 1938-46.

GAYNE, CLIFTON ALEXANDER, JR.—*Educator*

Art Education Department, University of Minnesota, Minneapolis, Minn.; h. 1415 North Cleveland Ave., St. Paul 8, Minn.

B. Watertown, Mass., July 13, 1912. *Studied*: Massachusetts Sch. A., B.S.; Univ. Minnesota, M.A., Ph.D., and widely in Europe. *Member*: NEA; Minnesota Edu. Assn.; Minnesota A. Edu. Assn.; Western AA; NAEA; Intl. Soc. for Edu. Through Art; Comparative Edu. Soc.; AAUP. Contributor articles to professional journals. *Positions*: for Western AA: Council Memb., 1948-49, Chm., College T. of A. Edu. Section, 1952-56; Chm., Publications Com., 1952-54; Editor, Western Arts Bulletin, 1952-54; for NAEA: Chm., Nomination Com., 1949-51; Chm., Constitutional Revision Com., 1953-55; Chm., Accreditation Com., 1955-59; Rep. to NEA Comm. on T. Edu. and Prof. Standards, 1950, 1958; Chm., Com. on Standards for Preparation of A. Teachers of the NAEA College T. of A. Edu., 1953- ; for Minnesota State Dept. of Edu.: Consultant in A. Edu., 1945-48; Chm., Com. on Evaluation in Art, Dramatics and Music, 1955- ; Memb. Bd. Dir., Intl. Inst. of St. Paul, 1953- ; Bd. Dir., St. Paul Council on Arts & Sciences, 1956- ; Comm. which est. the St. Anthony Park Community Interest Center, 1951-53; Chm., Dept. Art Edu., Univ. of Minnesota, Minneapolis, Minn. at present.

GAZZETTA, MARY A.—*Painter, T.*

100 Main St.; h. 312 Main St., Penn Yan, N.Y.

B. Newark, N.J., Aug. 17, 1911. *Studied*: PIASch.; Leonardo de Vinci A. Sch.; ASL, with Cusumano, McNulty, Brackman, DuMond, Warshaw. *Member*: ASL; AAPL; N.Y. State A.T. Assn.; N.A.E.A.; Artmobile, Inc. *Work*: Soldiers and Sailors Mem. Hospital, Pub. Lib., Penn Col., all in Penn Yan, N.Y.; Am. Export Lines, and in private colls. *Exhibited*: Acad. All. A., 1939; Argent Gal., 1947; Portraits, Inc.; Queensboro Soc. A.; ASL; Am. A. Week, 1954, 1955; Hall of Art, 1942-1944; NAC. *Position*: Asst. A., Portraits, Inc., 1947-50; A. Instr., Penn Yan H.S., 1953- ; Yates County A. Chm., Am. A. Week; A. Instr., Adult Edu. Classes.

GEBHARD, DAVID—*Museum Director, E.*

Roswell Museum, Roswell, N.M.

B. Canon Falls, Minn., July 21, 1927. *Studied*: Univ. Minnesota, B.A., M.A., Ph.D. *Member*: CAA; Soc. Arch. Historians; Soc. for Am. Archaeology; Archaeological Soc. New Mexico (Trustee); Southwest Des. Council (Sec.). *Author*: "Purcell & Elmslie, Architects," Walker A. Center, 1953; "Petroglyphs of Wyoming: A Preliminary Paper," El Palacio, Mar. 1951. Lectures: History of American Architecture from 1890-1920; North American Indian Art; "Cave Paintings of the Lower Pecos River." *Position*: Instr. A. & Arch. Hist., Univ. New Mexico, 1953-55; Dir., Roswell Museum, Roswell, N.M., 1955- .

**GEBHARDT, ANN STELLHORN (Mrs. Bruce)—
*Painter, E.***

Queens College; h. 2500 Sherwood Ave., Charlotte 7, N.C.

B. Leavenworth, Kans., Mar. 13, 1916. *Studied*: Lake Erie Col. for Women; Ohio State Univ., B.F.A., M.A., with Carolyn G. Bradley, James R. Hopkins, Alice Schille. *Member*: Charlotte A. Gld. *Exhibited*: Mint Mus. A., 1951 (two-man). *Position*: Asst. Prof. A., and Dean of students, Queens College, Charlotte, N.C.

GEBHARDT, C. KEITH—*Painter, S., Des., L., W., I.*

5821 West Trenton Pl., Milwaukee 13, Wis.

B. Cheboygan, Mich., Aug. 14, 1899. *Studied*: Univ. Michigan; AIC. *Work*: murals, paintings, sculpture, Milwaukee Pub.Mus. *Position*: Dir., Winnipeg Sch. A., Canada, 1924-29; Assoc. A., 1932-40, Chief A., 1940-1953, Milwaukee Pub. Mus., Milwaukee, Wis.

GEBHARDT, HAROLD—*Sculptor T.*

721 Country Club Dr., Burbank, Cal.

B. Milwaukee, Wis., Aug. 21, 1907. *Studied*: Layton Sch. A. *Awards*: prizes and medals, Wisconsin Un., 1936; Wisconsin P. & S., 1937; Milwaukee AI, 1937; Los A. Mus. A., 1946, 1950; City of Los Angeles, 1948. *Work*: Milwaukee Pub. Lib.; State T. Col., Milwaukee; Los A. Mus. A., and in private colls. *Exhibited*: Los A. Mus. A., 1939-1946, 1950; AIC; Milwaukee AI; Univ. Wisconsin; Univ.

Minnesota; Santa Barbara Mus. A.; Scripps Col.; Cal. State Fair; Los Angeles County Fair; Chaffey Col.; Pasadena AI; Sao Paulo, Brazil; Greek Theatre, Los A. *Position*: Instr., S., Occidental Col.; Prof. S., Univ. Southern California; Instr., S., U.C.L.A., Los Angeles, Cal.

GEBHART, PAUL—*Advertising Designer*

1375 Euclid Ave., Cleveland 15, Ohio; h. 281 East 320th St., Willowick, Ohio

B. Greenville, Pa., Jan. 2, 1890. *Studied*: Cleveland Inst. A. *Position*: A. Dir., Stouffer Corp.; Cleveland, Ohio.

GECK, FRANCIS JOSEPH—*Designer, P., E.*

University of Colorado; h. 407 16th St., Boulder, Colo.

B. Detroit, Mich., Dec. 20, 1900. *Studied*: N.Y.Sch. F. & App. A.; Syracuse Univ., M.F.A.; in Paris, and with John P. Wicker. *Member*: Boulder A. Gld.; Boulder Hist. Soc.; Assoc., AID; AAPL. *Awards*: gold med., AAPL, 1953. *Exhibited*: Boulder A. Gld., 1934; Denver A. Mus., 1932, 1933, 1938; Kansas City AI, 1933; Soc. Indp. A., 1934; Joslyn A. Mus., 1947; Michigan WC Soc., 1949; Wash. WC Cl., 1950; Fla. Southern Col., 1952. *Author*: "Introduction to Interior Decoration," 1951. *Position*: Assoc. Prof. FA, Cur. Exhs., Univ. Colorado, Boulder, Colo. 1930-1957; Dir. Exhibits, Pioneer Mus., Boulder, Colo., 1957- .

GEE, JOHN—*Illustrator, Lith., T., W.*

Sarasota, Fla.; s. Southbridge, Mass.

B. Southbridge, Mass. *Studied*: AIC, and with V. L. George, Thornton Oakley, J. Allen St. John. *Member*: AFA; Sarasota AA. *Awards*: prizes, CMA, 1929, 1930. *Work*: CMA. Author, I., "Bunny Bear"; Timbertoes Series, child readers, & other children's books. *Position*: Freelance illus. children's books; A. Consultant, Contributor, "Highlights for Children," "Treasure Trails" magazines, Columbus, Ohio.*

GEE, YUN—*Painter, T.*

51 East 10th St., New York 3, N.Y.

B. Canton, China, Feb. 22, 1907. *Studied*: Cal. Sch. FA. *Member*: AAPL. *Work*: MModA, Paris, France; Lutheran Church, Bronx, N.Y.; Univ. Missouri, and in private colls. *Position*: Fndr., Sch. of Diamondism; Gr. Engineer, Sperry Gyroscope Co.; Research Engineer, I., War Dept., Wash., D.C.; Inventor: Lunar Tube; English Speech Correction Device; Pres., Tri-King Corp., New York, N.Y. (mfgrs. of checker and chess board for 2, 3 or 4 players, created by Yun Gee).

**GEERLINGS, GERALD K.—
*Industrial Designer, Et., Lith., W., Arch.***

115 East 40th St., New York 17, N.Y.; h. 57 Laurel Rd., New Canaan, Conn.

B. Milwaukee, Wis., April 18, 1897. *Studied*: Univ. Pennsylvania, B.A., M.A. in Arch.; Royal Col. of A., London, England. *Member*: Arch. Lg., N.Y.; Chicago Soc. Et.; AIA; SAGA. *Awards*: Woodman traveling F., Univ. Pennsylvania, 1924-25; prize, NAC, 1930; Chicago Century of Progress, 1933; gold med., PAFA, 1931; Societe des Architects Diplomes par le Gouvernement Francais, 1922. *Work*: MMA; Victoria and Albert Mus., London; LC. *Exhibited*: Royal Acad., London; Paris Salon, 1937; WFNY 1939; NAC; NAD; PAFA; BM; AIC; Fine Prints of the Year, London. Author, I., "Color Schemes of Adam Ceilings," 1928; "Wrought Iron in Architecture," 1929; "Metal Crafts in Architecture," 1929.

GEESLIN, LEE GADDIS—*Painter, Gr., E.*

Sam Houston State College; h. 1909 Avenue Q, Huntsville, Tex.

B. Goldthwaite, Tex., June 28, 1920. *Studied*: Univ. Chicago, B.F.A.; AIC, M.F.A., and with Xavier Gonzales, Paul Ninas, Enrique Alfarez, Boris Anisfeld. *Member*: CAA; Texas WC Soc.; Texas FA Assn. *Exhibited*: Texas annual, 1947, 1949; Texas FA Assn., 1947-1950; Dallas Mus. FA, 1947, 1949; Witte Mem. Mus., 1947, 1949; Corpus Christi, Tex., 1947; Ft. Worth, 1947, 1948. I., "Tools of the Earth Mover," 1951. *Position*: Assoc. Prof., Dept. A., Sam Houston State Col., Huntsville, Tex., 1949- . Ed., "Paint Rag," Texas magazine of Art, 1953-54; Summer Art Colonies; Brownsville Mus., 1953-55, Lufkin A. Lg., 1954; Central Texas A. Colony.*

GEHR, JAMES L.—Sculptor, Des.
521 West Bridge St., Cedarburg, Wis.

B. Green Bay, Wis., Dec. 8, 1906. *Studied*: Layton Sch. A.; Goodyear Tech. Inst.; Frank Lloyd Wright F., Taliesin, Spring Green, Wis. *Member*: NSS; Wisconsin P.&S.; Seven A. Soc., Milwaukee, Wis. *Awards*: prizes, Milwaukee AI, 1938, 1940. *Work*: animal sculpture groups, Milwaukee, Wis., parks; Milwaukee Pub. Mus. *Exhibited*: Howard Univ., 1941; Wis. P. & S., annually. Indst. Des. & Packaging Consultant.*

GEHRING, C. F.—Assistant Museum Director
Los Angeles County Museum, Exposition Park, Los Angeles, Cal.*

GEIKEN, ELIZABETH MOELLER (Mrs. Martin H.)—
Museum Director, P., E.
Davenport Municipal Art Gallery, 120 West Fifth St.; h. 1117 West Locust St., Davenport, Iowa

B. Davenport, Iowa, Apr. 18, 1906. *Studied*: State Univ. of Iowa, B.A., M.A.; PAFA. *Awards*: prizes, Davenport Mun. A. Gal., 1934, 1936; Laura Spellman Rockefeller Grad. F., State Univ. Iowa. *Work*: Rock Island (Ill.) Pub. Sch. *Position*: Instr. A., Univ. Iowa Experimental Sch., 1928-31; Chm. A. Dept., Shimer Col., Mt. Carroll, Ill., 1931-34, 1936-38; Instr. A., Montana State Normal Col., Dillon, 1934-36; Gal. Dir. & Lecturer in A. Hist., Davenport Mun. A. Gal., 1938- ; Visiting Instr. A., Augustana Col., Rock Island, Ill., 1955- .

GEISER, BERNARD—Painter
2169 North West Northrup St., Portland 10, Ore.

B. Geuda Springs, Kans., Mar. 28, 1887. *Studied*: PAFA; Univ. Oregon; Portland Mus. Sch. A. *Member*: AEA. *Awards*: Carnegie F., Univ. Oregon. *Work*: SAM; St. Andrew's Church, St. Mark's Church, Portland, Ore.; churches in Gunnison, Colo.; Denver, Colo.; Long Beach and Ilwaco, Wash.; Portland (Ore.) A. Mus. *Exhibited*: SAM, 1939-56; Portland A. Mus., 1939-57; Butler AI, 1941.

GEISSBUHLER, ARNOLD—Sculptor, T.
4 Grove Court, New York 14, N.Y.

B. Delemont, Switzerland, Aug. 9, 1897. *Studied*: Julian Acad., Grande Chaumiere, Paris; Zurich, Switzerland. *Member*: Sculptors Gld. *Work*: A. Mus., Berne, Switzerland; FMA; war mem., Somloire, France; arch. sc., Switzerland, France, U.S.A. *Exhibited*: WFNY 1939; Salon des Tuileries, Paris, France; PMA; Inst. Contemporary A., Wash., D.C.; WMAA; MMA; Sculptors Gld.; one-man: Farnsworth Mus. A.; Dennis (Mass.) A. Center, and others in the U.S. and abroad. *Position*: Instr., Drawing & Sculpture, Wellesley Col., Wellesley, Mass., 1937- .*

GEISSMANN, ROBERT—Illustrator, Des., P.
150 East 47th St. (17); h. 2 Beekman Place, New York 22, N.Y.

B. New Washington, Ohio, Aug. 18, 1909. *Studied*: Ohio State Univ., Dept. FA. *Member*: SI; Air Force Hist. Fnd. *Awards*: many graphic art prizes; Governor's Award, State of Ohio, 1954; U.S. Air Force Service Award for establishing AF art program. *Exhibited*: Wildenstein Gal., 1955. Contributor to American Artist Magazine; Holiday; Coronet magazines. *Position*: Vice-Pres., 1951, 1952, Pres., 1953-55, Society of Illustrators.*

GELB, JAN—Painter, Et., T.
8 East 18th St. (3); h. 966 Third Ave., New York 22, N.Y.

B. New York, N.Y., July 18, 1906. *Studied*: Yale Sch. FA; ASL, with Sigurd Skou. *Member*: AEA; SAGA; 14 Painter-Printmakers; Provincetown AA. *Award*: prize, Boston A. Festival, 1953. *Exhibited*: Weyhe Gal., 1948, 1950 (one-man); BM, 1955; Phila. Pr. Cl. 1958; WMAA, 1951, 1953, 1954-1957; PAFA, 1952, 1957; MMA, 1952; Kraushaar Gal., 1954-1957; Ganso Gal., 1954 (one-man); Ruth White Gal., 1957, 1959 (both one-man); Boston A. Festival, 1953; Am. Acad. A. & Lets., 1957; NAD; Butler Inst. Am. A.; Provincetown A. Festival, 1958; PMA; MModA; BMA; Abbott Acad.; Univ. Delaware. *Work*: MMA, and in private colls.

GELLMAN, BEATRICE (McNULTY)
(Mrs. William C.)—Painter, S., T., W., L.
Rockport, Mass.

B. Philadelphia, Pa., Nov. 20, 1904. *Studied*: Univ. Pennsylvania, B.S. in Edu.; ASL, with William C. McNulty, Morris Kantor, Robert Beverly Hale, Kenneth Hayes Miller. *Member*: Rockport AA. *Work*: in private collections. *Exhibited*: Y.W.C.A., Germantown, Pa.; Rockport AA (one-man and group shows). Lectures: "Styling and Design Principles in the Works of Masters of Painting" to Fashion Acad., New York, N.Y. *Position*: Artist Advisor to Fashion Staff, Fernfield Assoc., 1957-58.

GELTMAN, LILY—Painter
252 Fulton St.; h. 200 Clinton St., Brooklyn 25, N.Y.

B. New York, N.Y., Nov. 25, 1903. *Studied*: Hunter Col., B.A., and with Camilo Egas, Moses Soyer, Morris Davidson. *Member*: NAWA; Brooklyn Soc. A.; Cape Cod AA; Provincetown AA; Audubon A. *Awards*: prizes, NAWA, 1949, 1954; Brooklyn Soc., 1955. *Exhibited*: Audubon A, 1951, 1952; NAWA, 1949-1952; Provincetown AA, 1950, 1952; Cape Cod AA, 1952; Galerie Bose-Petride, Paris, 1950; Argent Gal., 1949-1952; traveling exh., Canada and the U.S.*

GENAUER, EMILY—Critic, W., L.
c/o New York Herald-Tribune, 230 West 41st St.; h. 312 East 52nd St., New York 22, N.Y.

B. New York, N.Y. *Studied*: Hunter Col.; Columbia Univ. Sch. Journalism, B.Litt. *Member*: N.Y. Newspaper Women's Cl.; Int. Assn. of A. Critics. *Awards*: N.Y. Newspaper Women's Cl., annual award for outstanding column in any specialized field, 1935, 1948, 1956. Author: "Labor Sculpture," 1937; "Modern Interiors," 1940; "Best of Art," 1948; Metropolitan Museum monograph on "Toulouse-Lautrec," 1954, "Chagall," 1956. Regular contributor articles on art to major national magazines. Lectures: "American Art Today"; "Functions of Art Criticism," etc. Annual lecturer on art at Town Hall, New York. *Position*: A. Cr., A. Ed., New York World-Telegram, 1932-1948; A. Cr., Columnist, New York Herald-Tribune, 1948- .

GENDERS, RICHARD ATHERSTONE—Painter
Rm. 1533, Main Navy Dept., Washington 25, D.C.; h. 10709 Maybrook Ave., Kensington, Md.

B. London, England, Aug. 3, 1919. *Studied*: John Herron AI, and with John W. Taylor, Edwin L. Fulwider, Donald M. Mattison. *Member*: Indiana A. Cl.; Tidewater AA. *Exhibited*: Indiana State Fair; John Herron AI; Indiana A. Cl.; Ohio Valley Exh.; Am. A. Week Exh., New Castle, Ind.; Officers Cl., U.S. Naval Air Station, Norfolk; Tidewater AA; Norfolk Mus. A. & Sciences; Navy YMCA Exh.; one-man: Seattle Seafair, Seattle, Wash., 1955; Nat. Bank of Commerce, Norfolk, Va., 1957. Continually represented in "Operation Palette," traveling exh., U.S. Navy coll. of selected paintings from Combat Art Section. *Awards*: prizes, Indiana State Fair; John Herron AI; Ohio Valley Exh., Athens, Ohio. *Work*: Many paintings of U.S. Fleet for U.S. Naval Historical Records. *Position*: Official U.S. Navy Combat A., 1953- .

GENIUS, JEANNETTE M. (Mrs. Hugh F. McKean)—
Painter
231 North Interlachen Ave., Winter Park, Fla.

B. Chicago, Ill. *Member*: NAWA (Hon. Vice-Pres.); Pen & Brush Cl.; AEA; Fla. Fed. A.; Fla. A. Group; New Hampshire AA; NAC. *Awards*: prizes, Fla. Fed. A., 1948; Soc. Four A., 1949, 1950, 1954; Pen & Brush Cl., 1953; Cervantes medal of Hispanic Inst. in Fla., 1952; Dec. Honor, Rollins Col., 1943; Sullivan medallion, 1954. *Work*: Georgia Mus. A., Univ. Georgia; Columbus Mus. A. & Crafts, and in private colls. *Exhibited*: All. A. Am.; Pen & Brush Cl.; NAC; Studio Gld., N.Y.; Norton Gal. A., Palm Beach; Soc. Four A.; Jacksonville A. Cl.; Currier Gal. A.; Delgado Mus. A.; NAWA; Contemporary A. Gal., N.Y.; Butler AI; one-man: Research Studios, Maitland, Fla., 1951; Contemp. A. Gal., 1953, 1956; A. Lg. of Manatee County, Bradenton, Fla., 1955. *Position*: Trustee, Rollins Col.; Dir., Exhibitions, The Morse Gallery of Art, Rollins Col., Winter Park, Fla.

GENTILE, EDWARD—*Designer, P.*

832 Wisconsin St., Oak Park, Ill.

B. Chicago, Ill., July 20, 1890. *Studied*: AIC. *Member*: AIGA; Illinois State Hist. Soc. *Exhibited*: AIC; Marshall Field Gal.; All-Illinois Soc. FA.; Chicago Galleries (one-man). Specializes in illuminated manuscripts. Work reproduced in "Inland Printer" magazine. Exh. in Chicago by U.S. Treasury Dept.

GENTRY, HELEN—*Book Designer*

c/o Holiday House, 8 West 13th St., New York 11, N.Y.

B. Temecula, Cal., Nov. 21, 1897. *Studied*: Univ. California, A.B. *Member*: AIGA. *Work*: Book des. for various publishers. *Exhibited*: 50 Books of the Year, AIGA, 1931-1946; AIGA, 1939 (one-man). Co-Author: "Chronology of Books and Printing," 1936. Contributor to Publisher's Weekly, The Horn Book, with articles on book design, production, and reviews of book shows.*

GEOGHEGAN, WALTER B.—*Art Director, Des.*

Calkins & Holden, 247 Park Ave., New York 17, N.Y.

B. Berlin, Conn., Jan. 22, 1904. *Studied*: ASL. *Member*: SI; A. Dir. Cl.; New Rochelle AA. *Position*: Advisory Bd., PIASch.; N.Y.Sch. Indst. A.*

GEORGE, DOROTHY (Mrs. John Stitt Colby)—
Painter, T., L.

Estate Cane Bay, Christiansted, St. Croix, Virgin Islands

B. Manchester, N.H., 1898. *Studied*: State T. Col., Framingham, Mass.; Simmons Col., Boston, Mass.; Univ. California. *Member*: Boston A. Cl.; St. Croix Mus.; Cruzian A. Cl. *Awards*: prize, St. Croix, V.I. (for photography). *Exhibited*: Honolulu Acad. A. (one-man); Boston, Mass. (one-man); St. Croix and Barbados; St. Thomas, V.I., 1958. *Position*: Pres., Dir., Vesper George Sch. A., Boston, Mass., 1924-52 (Retired).

GEORGETTI, WEDO—*Painter, Gr.*

40 Cazneau Ave., Sausalito, Cal.

B. Italy, May 19, 1911. *Awards*: prize, Cal. Soc. Et. *Exhibited*: SFMA, 1943, 1945, 1946, 1948; SAGA, 1944; LC, 1946; Oakland A. Gal., 1942-1944; deYoung Mem. Mus., 1945; Crocker A. Gal., Sacramento, Cal., 1944; Paul Elder Gal., San F.; Col. Puget Sound, Tacoma, Wash., 1944; SAM, 1948; Sam F. Art Festival, 1950.*

GERARD, ALLEE WHITTENBERGER (Mrs.)—
Painter, T.

R.F.D. #2, Country Club Drive, Warsaw, Ind.; also 540 Northwest 49th St., Miami, Fla.

B. Rochester, Ind., Feb. 9, 1895. *Studied*: Ft. Wayne A. Sch.; Miami A. Sch., and with Homer Davisson, Clinton Sheperd, Curry Bohm, Robert Connavale. *Member*: Miami A. Lg.; Indiana A. Cl.; Nat. Lg. Am. Pen Women; AAPL; Blue Dome Fellowship. *Awards*: prizes, Hoosier Salon, 1944; Int. Exh., Miami, 1948-1951; Walter's award, 1950; Northern Indiana Salon, 1944; Ft. Wayne, 1954; Lg. Am. Pen Women, 1956. *Work*: Indiana Univ.; Hoosier Salon; YWCA, Logansport, Ind.; Warsaw (Ind.) H.S. *Exhibited*: Hoosier Salon, 1944-1946, 1948-1951, 1958, one-man: 1956, 1957; Coral Gables Country Club, 1956; DePauw Univ., 1958; Gary, Ind., 1948-1951; Smithsonian Inst., 1949; Miami Int. Exh., 1948-1952; Indiana A. Cl., 1956-1958; Ft. Wayne Women's Cl., 1956-1958; Ft. Wayne A. Mus., 1957, 1958; Miami Beach A. Center, 1956-1958; Metropolitan Flower Show, Miami, 1952; one-man: Franklin, Ind., Col., 1948; Hoosier Salon, 1948; Sheldon Swope A. Gal., 1956; Frankfort, Ind., 1949; Anderson, Ind., 1950; Miami Beach A. Center, 1950.

GERARD, DAVID CHARLES (DAVE)—*Cartoonist*

13 Mills Place, Crawfordsville, Ind.

B. Crawfordsville, Ind., June 18, 1909. *Studied*: Wabash Col., A.B.; Univ. Arizona. *Member*: Nat. Cartoonist Soc. Creator: "WILL-YUM," daily newspaper comic strip and Sunday page syndicated by National Newspaper Syndicate, and "WILL-YUM" comic book; "City Hall," daily and Sunday comic strip syndicated by National Newspaper Syndicate.

GERARD, PAULA—*Painter, Gr., T.*

2211 North Burling St., Chicago 14, Ill.

Studied: AIC, and abroad. *Member*: Renaissance Soc.; Univ. Chicago. *Work*: LC. *Exhibited*: Phila. Pr. Cl., 1937, 1941; Los A. Mus. A., 1937; AIC, 1937, 1946, 1948, 1949, 1955; San F. AA, 1938, 1945; Phila. A. All., 1938; NAD, 1945; Denver A. Mus., 1944, 1950; Milwaukee AI, 1946; Renaissance Soc., 1949-1958; Mississippi Valley A.; Springfield, Ill., 1949; Wichita AA, 1958; one-man: Layton A. Gal., 1945, 1948; AIC, 1947; State T. Col., Terre Haute, 1947; Earlham Col., 1948; Woman's Cl., Milwaukee, 1956. Contributor to American Peoples Encyclopedia. Lecturer & Docent, AIC, 1940-46. *Position*: Instr. A., Layton Sch. A., Milwaukee, Wis., 1945- . Visiting Instr., Graphics, Univ. Chicago, summers, 1956, 1958.

GERARDIA, HELEN—*Painter, Gr.*

246 West 80th St., Studio 12 B; h. 490 West End Ave., New York 24, N.Y.

B. Ekaterinislav, Russia, Dec. 25, 1903. *Studied*: BM; ASL, and with Hans Hofmann, Charles Seide, Adams Garret, Nahum Tschacbasov. *Member*: Rudolph Gal., Woodstock, N.Y. and Coral Gables, Fla.; Brooklyn Soc. A.; ASL; NAWA; Creative A.; Lg. Present Day A.; AEA; Silvermine Gld. A.; Woodstock AA; Am. Color Print Soc.; Soc. Am. A.; Pr. Cl. *Awards*: prizes, Boston Soc. Indp. A., 1952, 1956, 1957; Village A. Center, 1952, 1954, 1955; F., Research Studios, Maitland, Fla., 1952-53; F., Yaddo Fnd., 1955; Woodstock AA, 1956; Abraham Lincoln H.S. purchase; Silvermine Gld. A.; NAWA, 1958. *Work*: Univ. Illinois; Smith Col.; Univ. Maine; Dartmouth Col.; Colby Col.; Lincoln H.S.; Yeshiva Col., and others. FMA; CM; Butler AI; Research Studios A. Center. *Exhibited*: Contemporary A., 1950-1952; BM, 1951; NAWA, 1950-1952; Village A. Center, 1949, 1952, 1954, 1955; ACA Gal., 1950; RoKo Gal., 1950-1952, 1955; WMAA, 1951, 1952; AEA, 1951, 1953, 1955; Arthur Brown Gal., 1951; Parrish Mus., 1950; Rudolph Gal. N.Y., 1952, Fla., 1952; CM, 1953 (and on tour No. Africa and Europe); Berlin Acad., Germany, 1954; Amsterdam, Holland, 1956; Am. Jewish Tercentenary traveling exh., 1954-55; Soc. Young Am. A.; SAGA, 1954; Sweat Mem. Mus., 1952-1955; Northwest Pr. M., 1954; Ser. Gal., 1953; Contemporaries, 1954, 1955; New Sch. Social Research, 1954-1956; Panoras Gal., 1955; City Center Gal., 1953-1955; Southwest Pr. M., 1955; Albany Inst. Hist. & A., 1955; Woodstock Playhouse, 1955, and others, 1956-1958; one-man: 8th St. Playhouse, 1951; Research Studios, 1953, 1957; Univ. Maine, 1957; Bodley Gal., 1957; St. Louis Pub. Lib., 1957; Nashville Mus. A., 1957; Colby Col., 1958; Dartmouth Col., 1958; Mus. Nat. Hist. & Art, Holyoke, Mass., 1958; Utica Pub. Lib., 1958; Zanesville AI, 1958, and others; Rudolph Gal., Woodstock, N. Y., 1953, 1955; Albany Inst. Hist. & A., 1955. *Position*: Chm., Lg. Present Day A., 1954-55; Bd., Chm. travel exhs., Brooklyn Soc. A., 1955-56; Alternate, Bd. Gov., Woodstock AA, 1956; Nat. Memb. Com., AEA, 1955-56.

GERASSI, FERNANDO—*Painter*

215 East 57th St., New York 22, N.Y.; h. Putney, Vt.

B. Constantinople, Turkey, Oct. 5, 1899. *Studied*: Univs., Berlin, Freiburg, Munich, Germany; and in Paris. *Work*: Butler AI, and in private collections in U.S., Europe and Latin America. *Exhibited*: one-man: Barcelona, Madrid, Spain; Paris, France; London, England; New York, N.Y.; Brattleboro, Vt., 1957; Cambridge, Mass., 1957; Northport, N.Y., 1957; Kalamazoo Inst. A., 1957; Dartmouth Col., 1958. *Position*: Dir., Gerassi A. Sch., Putney, Vt.

GERBERG, MORRIS—*Cartoonist, P.*

37 Brighton 11th St., Brooklyn 35, N.Y.

B. Russia, Mar. 23, 1893. *Studied*: Warshawsky A. Sch.; CUASch.; Brooklyn Mus. A. Sch. *Member*: Independent AA. *Work*: Maryhill (Wash.) Mus. FA. *Exhibited*: Independent AA, 1917-1932.

GERBINO, ROSARIO URBINO—*Painter*

132 East 28th St., New York 16, N.Y.

B. Sicily, Italy, Nov. 23, 1900. *Studied*: NAD, with George W. Maynard, Charles L. Hinton, Ivan Olinsky, Charles Hawthorne. *Member*: Audubon A.; SC; All. A. Am.; Grand Central Gal.; AFA. *Awards*: prizes, All. A. Am.; SC; Ogunquit A. Center, 1950, 1951; Int. World's Fair, Naples, 1952. *Work*: Mem. Lib., Georgetown Univ.; U.S. Treasury Dept. *Exhibited*: Jacques Seligmann Gal. (one-man); Chinese Gal.; DaVinci All.; Grand Central Gal. (one-man); Assoc. Am. A.; Ferargil Gal.; CGA; NAD; PAFA; AIC; All. A. Am.; Ogunquit A. Center; SC. Contributor cover des. to Italian magazine, "Divagando."

GERLACH, ALBERT A.—*Designer, C., P., L., Cr.*
2232 Southeast 57th Ave., Portland 15, Ore.

B. Chicago, Ill., Oct. 26, 1884. *Studied*: AIC. *Member*: Oregon Ceramic Soc.; Oregon Soc. A.; Stained Glass Assn. Am.; Hon. Assoc., AIA. *Work*: stained glass, mosaics, ports., Temple Beth Israel, First Baptist Church, St. Andrew's, Valley Community United Presbyterian, Augustana Lutheran, St. Paul's Lutheran, St. Stephen's Catholic churches, all in Portland, Ore.; Our Lady of the Lake, Oswego, Ore.; Benton Park Mem. Mausoleum, Corvallis, Ore.; Elsinore Theatre, Salem, Ore. Lectures on Stained Glass with kodachrome slides to church groups, college and high school students.

GERNAND, JOHN—*Painter*
1600 21st St., N.W.; h. 13 Hillyer Court, Northwest, Washington 8, D.C.

B. Washington, D.C., Oct. 19, 1913. *Studied*: Univ. Illinois; PMG. A. Sch. *Member*: A. Gld. of Wash. *Work*: PMG. *Position*: Staff, PMG, Washington, D.C., 1938- .*

GERSHOY, EUGENIE—*Sculptor, P., Gr., T., Des.*
31 Alta St., San Francisco 11, Cal.

Studied: ASL; Cal. Sch. FA.; in Europe, and with Robinson, Sloan, Miller, Calder. *Member*: An Am. Group; S. Guild; San F. Assn. Women A; AEA; Cal. T. Assn. *Awards*: St. Gaudens med.; prize, Red Cross Nat. Comp., 1941; AV, 1942; MMA, 1943 (purchase prize); Rotunda Gal., San F., 1950; F., Yaddo Fnd., 1951 (also 1940-41). *Work*: S., Astoria Pub. Lib., N.Y.; Biggs Mem. Hospital; WMAA; MMA; AIC. *Exhibited*: MMA (AV), 1942; WMAA, 1931-1946; PAFA, 1940; AIC; Delgado Mus. A., 1941; GGE, 1939; WFNY 1939; BM; MModA; Robinson Gal., N.Y., 1940 (one-man); Raymond & Raymond Gal., San F., 1943 (one-man); Gumps Gal., San F., 1946 (one-man), 1955; Downtown, Weyhe, Midtown, Delphic, ACA, Rehn, Milch, Bonestell, Washington Irving Gal. A., N.Y., 1958, & other N.Y. galleries; San F. AA; Rotunda Gal., San F. *Position*: Instr., S. & Ceramics, Adult Edu. Program, San F. Bd. Edu., 1949- .

GERVASI, FRANK—*Painter*
333 East 41st St., New York 17, N.Y.

B. Palermo, Italy, Oct. 5, 1895. *Studied*: N.Y. Sch. Indst. A.; ASL, with Frank DuMond, George Bridgman, Robert Henri. *Member*: ANA; SC; All. A. Am.; AWS; Balt. WC Cl.; Audubon A. *Awards*: prizes, SC, 1945, 1952; All. A. Am., 1945, med., 1950; Hudson Valley A., 1953; Baltimore WC Cl., 1953; AWS, 1955. *Exhibited*: NAD, 1938; All. A. Am., 1942-1946; Albany Inst. Hist. & A., 1936-1946. *Position*: Vice-Pres., Audubon A.; Past Pres., All. A. Am., New York, N.Y.; Vice-Pres., SC.

GESKE, NORMAN ALBERT—*Museum Director, E., L.*
209 Morrill Hall, University of Nebraska; h. 344 North 21st St., Apt. B, Lincoln 8, Neb.

B. Sioux City, Iowa, Oct. 31, 1915. *Studied*: Univ. Minnesota, B.A.; Inst. FA, N.Y. Univ., M.A. *Member*: CAA; AAMus.; AFA. *Positions*: Asst. Dir., Univ. Nebraska Art Galleries, 1950-53; Actg. Dir., 1953-56, Dir., 1956- .

GEST, MARGARET—*Painter*
34 South 17th St.; h. 5620 City Ave., Overbrook, Philadelphia 31, Pa.

B. Philadelphia, Pa., July 27, 1900. *Studied*: PMSchIA; PAFA; & with Hugh H. Breckenridge. *Member*: Phila. WC Cl. *Awards*: F., PAFA; Cresson traveling scholarship, PAFA, 1927, 1928. *Work*: PAFA; Phila. WC Cl.; F., PAFA; Friends Central Sch.; Penn Charter Sch. *Exhibited*: PAFA, 1928-1953; Phila. Plastic Cl.; Phila. WC Cl.; Phila. A. All. Author: "The House of Understanding," 1954.

GETZ, MRS. ARTHUR. See Gibbons, Margarita

GETZ, DOROTHY—*Educator, S., Comm. A.*
Art Department, Ohio Wesleyan University; h. 52½ West Winter St., Delaware, Ohio

B. Grand Junction, Iowa, Sept. 7, 1901. *Studied*: Ohio State Univ., B.A., M.A.; Hans Hofmann Sch. FA. *Awards*: prizes, Ohio State Fair, 1953, 1958; Columbus A. Lg., 1956, 1957. *Exhibited*: Syracuse Mus. FA, 1952, 1954, 1956; Butler Inst. Am. A., 1954, 1955, 1957; Ball State T. Col., 1954, 1955; Ohio State Fair, 1953, 1955, 1958; Columbus A. Lg., 1953-1957. *Positions*: Instr., Fashion Illus., Columbus (Ohio) A. Sch., 1952- ; Prof. FA, Ohio Wesleyan Univ., Delaware, Ohio, at present.

GETZ, ILSE—*Painter*
178 East 95th St., New York, N.Y.

B. Nurnberg, Germany, Oct. 24, 1917. *Studied*: ASL, with Morris Kantor, George Grosz. *Member*: AFA. *Work*: Carnegie Inst., Pittsburgh, Pa., and in private collections. *Exhibited*: Bertha Schaefer Gal., 1953-1959; 7 one-man exhs., New York, San Francisco, Boston, Switzerland, Italy. Other exhs., in U.S. museums and in France and Holland.

GEYER, HAROLD CARL—*Etcher, W., L.*
237 West 14th St. (11); h. 200 East 66th St., New York 21, N.Y.

B. Cold Spring, N.Y., Aug. 16, 1905. *Studied*: Yale Col., B.A.; Yale Sch. Architecture, B.F.A.; Ecole Americaine des Beaux-Arts, Fontainebleau, France. *Member*: SAGA; ANA; Societe Academique de l'Aube. *Awards*: purchase prize, LC, 1945. *Work*: LC; Bibliotheque Nationale, Musee de la Ville de Troyes, France. *Exhibited*: LC, 1945; NAD, 1945, 1946; SAGA, 1943-1953. Author, I., "All Men Have Loved Thee," a Song of France, 1941; "The Long Way Home," a Song of France, 1949.

GHOLSON, SAMUEL CREED—*Painter, T., S.*
Art Department, Monmouth College; h. 710 East Archer Ave., Monmouth, Ill.

B. Holly Springs, Miss., July 15, 1919. *Studied*: Washington & Lee Univ.; PAFA; Univ. Pennsylvania, B.F.A., and with Wayman Adams, Arthur Carles, Hans Schuler, Jr. *Member*: F., PAFA; NAC. *Awards*: Cresson traveling scholarship, PAFA, 1942. *Work*: paintings: Univ. Pennsylvania; N.Y. Law Sch.; Army Medical Center; Icelandic Embassy, Wash., D.C.; Liberian President's Mansion, Monrovia, Liberia; First Baptist Church, Wash., D.C.; Laird Mem. Hospital, Montgomery, W. Va., and many private portrait commissions. *Exhibited*: CGA; Smithsonian Inst.; one-man: Brooks Mem. A. Gal., 1952; Mary Buie Mus.; Univ. Miss., 1952, and others. *Positions*: Instr., Maryland Inst., 1956-57; Hd., Art Dept., Monmouth College, Monmouth, Ill., 1957- .

GIACOMANTONIO, A. A.—*Sculptor*
Box 809, Sparta, N.J.

B. Jersey City, N.J., Jan. 17, 1906. *Studied*: DaVinci A. Sch.; Acad. FA, Rome, Italy; & with Onorio Ruotolo, Vincenzo Gemito. *Member*: NSS; All. A. Am.; Lotos Cl. *Awards*: Med., Montclair A. Mus., 1936; NAD. *Work*: Lincoln H.S., Moore Sch., Jersey City, N.J.; State House, Trenton, N.J.; Bayview, N.J., cemetery; monuments, Hoboken, N.J.; Hazleton, Pa.; Baltimore, Md.; Nashville, Tenn.; Union City, N.J.; Jersey City, N.J.; & in Rome; bust of Pres. Eisenhower, West Point Acad.; War College, Wash., D.C.; bust of Harry Truman, Truman Lib., Independence, Mo.; Granite Madonna, Handl Mem., Holy Rude Cemetery, Long Island, N.Y.; bronze door, Rea Mausoleum, Fairview Cemetery, Fairview, N.J.

GIANNINOTO, FRANK A.—*Industrial Designer, L.*
133 East 54th St., New York 22, N.Y., and 9046 Sunset Blvd., Los Angeles, Cal.; h. Mohawk Hill, R.D. 1, Redding, Conn.

B. Sicily, Italy, Jan. 6, 1903. *Studied*: ASL; CUASch.; Sch. F. & App. A. *Member*: IDI; Package Des. Council (Fnd., Pres.); Sales Exec. Cl. *Awards*: Wolff awards of Am. Management Assn. *Work*: for General Foods; Borden's; Holgate Toys; Seagram Distillers; Diamond Match; P. J. Ritter & Co.; J. A. Folger Co.; Brown & Williamson Tobacco Co.; Chesebrough-Ponds, Inc.; Foremost Dairies; Kaiser Industries; Thomas J. Lipton Co.; Johnson's Wax;

Philip Morris; Dole; Crown Zellerbach, and many other leading manufacturers. *Exhibited*: N.Y. Nat. Home Furnishings Show, 1950, 1951; IDI traveling exh., 1951, 1952. Contributor of articles to trade papers and design magazines. Lectures on Industrial Design in U.S. and Europe. *Position*: A. Dir., Batten, Barton, Durstine & Osborn, 1928-30; Pres., Frank Gianninoto & Assoc., 1931- ; Frank Gianninoto & Assoc. of California, Inc., 1957- .

GIBBERD, ERIC WATERS—*Painter, T., L.*
Calle Valverde, Taos, N.M.

B. London, England, Feb. 26, 1897. *Studied*: with Oscar Van Young, Ejnar Hansen, and in Barcelona, Spain. *Member*: Taos AA; New Mexico A. Lg.; A. Cl., London; Royal A. Cl., Barcelona. *Award*: prize, New Mexico A. Lg., 1957-58. *Work*: Pasadena A. Mus.; St. Paul's Sch., London; Wadham Col., Oxford; Mus. of New Mexico; Ateno Scientifico, Balearic Islands. *Exhibitied*: extensively in U.S. and Europe; one-man: Landau Gal., Los A., 1951; Galerie Henri Trouche, Paris, 1952; El Ateneo, 1952; Kensington Gal., London, 1952; Sala Vayreda, Barcelona, 1953; Kunstzaal Van Lier, Amsterdam, 1953; Pasadena A. Mus., 1954; Mus. New Mexico, Santa Fe, 1956; Denver A. Mus., 1957; San Angelo, Tex., 1958; Canon City, Colo., 1958; Santa Fe, 1958, and others.

GIBBONS, MARGARITA *(Mrs. Arthur Getz)*—*Painter*
2 West 15th St., New York 11, N.Y.; h. Sherwood Drive, Westport, Conn.

B. New York, N.Y., Aug. 18, 1906. *Studied*: ASL; PIASch; & abroad. *Member*: AEA; NAWA; N.Y. Soc. Women A. *Exhibited*: ACA, Norlyst, Newhouse, RoKo Galleries, N.Y.; Argent Gal., 1946 (one-man).

GIBSON, GEORGE—*Painter, Des., I., L.*
MGM Studios, Culver City, Cal.; h. 12157 Leven Lane, Los Angeles 49, Cal.

B. Edinburgh, Scotland, Oct. 16, 1904. *Studied*: Edinburgh Sch. A.; Glasgow Sch. A.; with William E. Glover, Scotland; Chouinard AI, and with F. Tolles Chamberlain. *Member*: ANA; AWS; Cal. WC Soc. *Awards*: prizes, Santa Paula, Cal., 1946; City of Los Angeles, 1946, 1947, 1949; Santa Cruz annual, 1946-1948, 1950; Arizona State Fair, 1948, 1949; Montgomery, Ala., 1949; Westwood (Cal.) AA, 1951, 1952; Cal. WC Soc., 1953; Newport Beach, 1953; Oakland A. Mus., 1945; Birmingham, Ala., 1950; Phila. Pa., 1948; Orange County Fair, 1950. *Work*: San Diego FA Center; Los A. Mus. A.; AIC; Laguna Beach A. Gal. *Exhibited*: AWS, 1945-1958; Cal. WC Soc., annually and traveling exhs.; and in other galleries and museums in U.S.; one-man: Chabot Gal., Los A., 1950; Long Beach, Cal., 1950; Laguna Beach AA, 1951; Santa Barbara Mus. A., 1952; Santa Monica Lib., 1958; St. Mary's Col., 1958. Lectures on Scenic Art in Theatre and Motion Pictures. *Position*: Scenic A. Dir., Hd. Scenic A. Dept., MGM Studios, 1934- .

GIBSON, LOUISE BLINN *(Mrs. Thomas L.)*—*Illustrator, P., Des.*
2883 Ziegle Ave., Cincinnati 8, Ohio

B. Glendale, Ohio. *Studied*: PIASch.; Cincinnati A. Acad.; Ecole des Beaux-Arts, Fontainebleau, France. *Member*: Cincinnati Women's A. Cl.; Professional A. of Cincinnati; Cincinnati MacDowell Soc. *Work*: murals, Cincinnati Pub. Sch.; Christ Church, Cincinnati; Pleasant Ridge Church, Cincinnati.

GIESBERT, EDMUND W.—*Painter, E., W., Des., L., I.*
6016 South Ingleside St., Chicago, Ill.

B. Neuwied, Germany, June 1, 1893. *Studied*: AIC; Acad. FA, Vienna; & with George Bellows, Andre L'Hote. *Awards*: prize, Acad. FA, Vienna, 1927; med., AIC, 1929; A.Dir.Cl., 1944. *Work*: Univ. Chicago; AIC; Dayton AI & many ports. in universities, colleges and private colls. *Exhibited*: BM; AIC; & abroad. Illus., College Art Journal book reviews. Lectures: "Problems of the Portrait Painter," etc. *Position*: Prof., Drawing & Painting, AIC, 1929- ; Assoc. Prof. A., Univ. Chicago, 1928- .

GIKOW, RUTH—*Painter, I., Ser.*
160 West 95th St., New York, N.Y.

B. Russia. *Studied*: CUASch. *Awards*: F., Yaddo Fnd.,

1943; Nat. Inst. A. & Let. grant, 1959. *Work*: MMA; MModA; PMA; WMAA; Brandeis Univ.; Springfield Mus. A.; Am. Acad. A. & Let.; murals, Bronx Hospital; Rockefeller Center, N.Y. *Exhibited*: Weyhe Gal., 1946 (one-man); Nat. Ser. Soc., 1947 (one-man); Grand Central Moderns, 1949, 1951; Phila. A. All., 1950; Ganso Gal. (one-man), 1952, 1954, 1956; Rehn Gal., 1958, and in national exhs. Illus., "Crime and Punishment," 1946.

GILBERG, ROBERT GEORGE—*Painter, T.*
312 Commercial St.; h. Rt. 1, Box 188 B, Nevada City, Cal.

B. Oakland, Cal., Apr. 25, 1911. *Studied*: Sierra Col., Auburn, Cal., and with Joseph Sheridan. *Award*: purchase prize, Cal. State Fair, 1957. *Exhibited*: Oakland A. Mus., 1940-1942, 1947, 1948, 1953; SFMA, 1940, 1941, 1946, 1954; Albany Inst. Hist. & A., 1949; Cal. WC Soc., 1942, 1948-1950, 1952; Auburn A. Festival, 1949-1958; Kingsley A. Cl., 1950-1958; Fresno A. Lg., 1949; Cal. State Lib., 1953; Newport Harbor, 1954; Northern Cal. A., 1954; Cal. State Fair, 1951-1957. Illus. "The Greatest Fun," 1943. *Position*: Instr., Nevada County Union H.S.; Sacramento State Col., Sacramento, Cal., summer session.

GILBERT, ARTHUR HILL—*Painter*
Box 775, Monterey, Cal.

B. Chicago, Ill., June 10, 1894. *Studied*: Northwestern Univ.; Univ. California. *Member*: Carmel A. Cl.; Bohemian Cl., San F.; ANA. *Awards*: prizes, Hallgarten, Murphy and Ranger prizes, NAD; Santa Cruz A. Lg. *Work*: Springville, Utah Coll.; Mission Inn, Riverside, Cal.; Riverside Woman's Cl. *Exhibited*: NAD; PAFA; AIC, and widely in California.

GILBERT, CREIGHTON—*Art Historian, E.*
Department of Fine Arts, Indiana University, Bloomington, Ind.

B. Durham, N.C., June 6, 1924. *Studied*: Duke Univ.; Johns Hopkins Univ.; N.Y. Univ., B.A., Ph.D.; Columbia Univ., with L. Venturi, W. Friedlander, Offner, Lehmann and others. *Member*: CAA; Am. Soc. for Aesthetics; AAUP; FA Comm., John Herron AI; Editorial Council, Journal of Aesthetics and Art Criticism; AAUP. *Awards*: CAA grant-in-aid, 1943-44, 1944-45; F., N.Y. Univ., 1944-45; Fulbright award, 1951-52. Lectures on Research in Renaissance Painting at Harvard Univ., Tulane Univ., CM, Ringling Mus., etc. Contributor to: Marsyas, Art Bulletin, Burlington Magazine, Gazette des Beaux-Arts, Commentari, Encyclopaedia Britannica, and other publications. Author, booklets: "Paintings by Raphael" (MMA, 1956); "Drawings of the Italian Renaissance" (Indiana Univ., and others, 1957). *Positions*: Chm. Jury, Mather Citation, 1954; Instr. FA, Emory Univ., Atlanta, Ga., 1946-47; Univ. Louisville, 1947-55, Asst. Prof., 1955-56; Asst. Prof., 1956- , Indiana Univ., Bloomington, Ind.; Visiting Prof., Univ. Rome, 1951-52; N.Y. Univ. Inst. FA, 1956 (summer).

GILBERT, LOUISE LEWIS *(Mrs. John)*—*Painter, Et.*
Frederick & Nelson, Little Gallery; h. 1943 Clise Pl., Seattle 99, Wash.

B. Detroit, Mich., Mar. 9, 1900. *Studied*: Univ. Washington. *Member*: AEA; Women Painters of Wash.; Northwest WC Soc. *Awards*: prizes, Women Painters of Wash., 1941, 1942, 1944. *Work*: SAM. *Exhibited*: SAM, 1933-1952, 1955; Portland (Ore.) A. Mus., 1936, 1939; Oakland A. Gal., 1934; PAFA; Spokane, Wash., annually; Western Wash. Fair, 1951; Riverside Mus., N.Y.; Henry A. Gal., Seattle; Northwest WC Soc.; Dusanne Gal., 1955 (one-man). *Position*: Dir., Frederick & Nelson Little Gallery, Seattle, Wash.*

GILBERT, MICHEL G.—*Painter, I., L.*
939 8th Ave., New York 19, N.Y.

B. Paris, France, May 23, 1914. *Studied*: Lycee Louis-le-Grand, Beaux-Arts, Paris, with Simon. *Member*: Phila. WC Cl. *Awards*: prize, Concours General, Paris; silver medal, Menton, France, 1957. *Work*: Petit Palais, Paris; French Govt. *Exhibited*: NAC, 1942; Wildenstein Gal., 1949; Cal. PLH, 1952; Parrish Mus., Southampton, 1947; PAFA, 1949; Audubon A., 1953; Dickinson Col., Carlisle, Pa., 1956; Salon d'Automne, Paris, 1956; Cardo-Matignan, Paris, 1957 (one-man); IV Biennale Intl., Menton, France, 1957; Nice, France, 1958.

GILCHRIST, AGNES ADDISON (Mrs. John M.)— Architectural Historian, W., L.

286 East Sidney Ave., Mount Vernon, N.Y.

B. Philadelphia, Pa., Dec. 25, 1907. *Studied*: Wellesley Col., B.A.; Univ. Pennsylvania, M.A., Ph.D.; and in Europe. *Member*: CAA; Soc. Arch. Historians (Sec.-Treas., 1950-51, V. Pres., 1952); Phila. A. All. *Awards*: Carnegie scholarship, Paris, Harvard Univ., 1934, 1935, 1940; Am. Philosophical Soc., 1941. *Exhibited*: Phila. A. All.; Phila. Women's Univ. Cl. Author: "Romanticism and the Gothic Revival," 1938; "Early American Gothic," 1940; "Pennsylvania Portraits," 1940; "William Strickland," 1950. Contributor book reviews and articles to art magazines. *Positions*: Instr., Texas State Col. for Women, 1931-32; Univ. Pa., 1934-41; Prof., Randolph-Macon Col., 1941-42; Lecturer, N.Y. Univ., New York, N.Y., 1948-49; Pres., 1954, Dir., 1955, Soc. Arch. Historians; Arch. Hist., National Park Service, Phila., Pa., 1957-58.

GILES, CHARLES—Painter, S., C., L., E.

Art Department, University of Tampa; h. 104 Adriatic Ave., Tampa 6, Fla.

B. Arlington, Mass., Dec. 1, 1914. *Studied*: Vesper George Sch. A., with Lincoln Vesper George, Harold Lindergren, Fletcher Adams, Dwight Shepler, Nelson Chase, Dean Cornwell, and others; Massachusetts Sch. A., with Frank Rines; N.Y. Univ.; Univ. North Carolina; Rutgers Univ.; Boston Univ.; Florida Southern Col., B.S., M.A.; Univ. Florida, D. Edu. *Member*: AAPL; Creative A. Group, Tampa Bay; Silvermine Gld. A.; Am. Council on Indst. A. T. Edu.; Fla. Fed. A.; Fla. Indst. AA; Fla. A. T. Assn.; Intl. Hon. Soc. Indst. A.; Edu. Research & Scholastic Fraternity (Hon. Grad.); AAUP; Professional A., Boston; Gld. Printing House Craftsmen. *Awards*: prizes, Florida State Fair, 1948, 1949. *Positions*: Instr., Comm. A., Essex County Voc. & Tech. H.S., Newark, N.J., 1940-42; Asst. Prof. A., Fla. Southern Col., 1946-51; Instr. A. & Voc. Edu., Univ. Florida, 1951-53; Asst. Prof. FA, Univ. Tampa, 1956-57; Assoc. Prof. FA & Indst. A., University of Tampa, Fla., 1957- .

GILES, FREDERIC PARKER—Educator, C., P., L.

Eastern Kentucky State College; h. 323 South 2nd St., Richmond, Ky.

B. Anna, Tex., Mar. 1, 1894. *Studied*: Southern Methodist Univ.; North Texas State Col., A.B.; Peabody Col., M.A., Ph.D., and with Olive Donaldson, Carl Gasslander, George Dutch. *Member*: Southeastern AA; NAEA (Council Memb., 1956-58); Western AA (Council Memb., 1956-60). *Awards*: L.R. Collins award, 1921; A.S. Sullivan prize, 1941. *Exhibited*: DMFA; Ft. Worth A.; A. of Kentucky. Contributor to Peabody Journal of Education. Lectures: Egyptian, Gothic, Renaissance and Greek Art. *Position*: Prof. A., Hd. FA Div., Eastern Kentucky State Col., Richmond, Ky.

GILKEY, GORDON WAVERLY—Etcher, Eng., E., W., L.

Art Department, Oregon State College; h. 350 North 35th St., Corvallis, Ore.

B. Linn County, Ore., Mar. 10, 1912. *Studied*: Albany (Ore.) Col., B.S.; Univ. Oregon, M.F.A.; Lewis & Clark Col., Arts D. *Member*: F. Intl. Inst. A. & Lets.; SAGA; Am. Soc. for Aesthetics; Officier d'Academie, France. *Awards*: Palmes Academique, France, 1947; gold medal, Centro Internazionale d'Arte e di Culture, Bordighera, Italy, 1957. *Work*: prints: MMA; N.Y. Pub. Lib.; LC; Nat. Mus., Wash., D.C.; SFMA; Portland (Ore.) A. Mus.; SAM; British Mus.; Victoria & Albert Mus., London; Bibliotheque Nationale, Paris; Bibliotheque Royale, Brussels; Koninklyk Huis Archief, The Hague; Bordighera Mus., Italy. *Exhibited*: Northwest Pr. M., 1950-1955; LC, 1955-1957; Pr. M. of So. Cal., 1952, 1953; SFMA, 1957; Phila. Pr. Cl., 1954, 1955, 1957, 1958; SAGA, 1952, 1954-1957; Bay Pr. M. Soc., 1956; Butler Inst. Am. A., 1954; Silvermine Gld. A., 1958; Bordighera, Italy, 1957; USIA European traveling exh., Europe, 1956-1958; Turin, Italy, 1957; Centre Culturel Americaine, Paris, 1958; Bath Acad. A., 1958; South Africa, 1958; Portland A. Mus., 1949-1958; Northwest Pr. M. regional, 1953-1957; one-man: Kennedy Gal., N.Y., 1939; St. Louis A. Center, 1940; Portland A. Mus., 1953; Spokane A. Center, 1958. Author, I., "Etchings Showing Construction Progress, Univ. Oregon Library," 1936; "Etchings New York World's Fair," 1939. Contributor to "Impression," Magazine of Graphic Arts. *Positions*: Hd., War Dept. Special Staff A. Projects in Europe,

1946-47; Consulente Artistico in Stati Uniti, IV Bordighera Biennale, Italy, 1956-57; Dir., Intl. Exchange Print Exhibits: from U.S.A., 1956, France, 1956, Italy, 1957, Great Britain, 1958, Norway, 1958; Prof., Hd. A. Dept., Oregon State College, Corvallis, Ore., 1947- .

GILL, BERNIECE CRAM (Mrs. John J.)—Writer, Cr.

Guy Gannett Publishing Co., 390 Congress St., Portland, Me.; h. Shore Acres, Cape Elizabeth, Me.; w. Eastland Hotel, Portland, Me.

B. Scarborough, Me., Nov. 30, 1903. *Studied*: Portland Sch. F. & App. A., with Alexander Bower and with Eliot O'Hara, Bradford Brown, John Muench. *Member*: Am. Newspaper Gld.; Portland Soc. A.; Portland Sch. F. & App. A. Alumni. *Position*: A. Columnist, "Brush Strokes," Portland Sunday Telegram; Ed., Journal for Juniors (children's drawings and writings, Telegram); State Society Ed., Portland Sunday Telegram.

GILL, FREDERICK JAMES—Painter, T., L., Lith.

164 West Hortter St., Philadelphia 19, Pa.

B. Philadelphia, Pa., May 30, 1906. *Studied*: PMSchIA; Univ. Pennsylvania, B.F.A., and with Charles Woodbury, Cesare Ricciardi; Tyler Sch. FA, M.F.A. *Member*: AEA; Phila. A. All.; Phila. WC Cl.; AWS. *Awards*: prizes, Chester County AA, 1938, 1939; Phila. A.T. Assn., 1943-1945, 1949, 1951, 1954-1957; AWS, 1948; Audubon A., 1950; PAFA, 1955; Woodmere A. Gal., 1955, 1958; Tyler Alumni exh., 1956, 1958. *Work*: PMA; Jefferson Hospital, Phila.; Millersville (Pa.) State T. Col.; Lehigh Univ.; Temple Univ.; Harcum Col.; Woodmere A. Gal, and others. *Exhibited*: nationally; one-man: group and traveling exhs. Lecturer, demonstrations. Contributor to American Artist, School Arts magazines. *Position*: A.T., Central H.S., 1930- ; PMSchA., Philadelphia, Pa., 1954- ; T. Summer Workshop (Phila.), 1956- .

GILL, SUE MAY (Mrs. Paul)—Painter, S., T.

639 English Village, Wynnewood, Pa.

B. Sabinal, Tex. *Studied*: PAFA. *Member*: PMA; Phila. A. All.; F., PAFA; Phila. Plastic Cl.; Woodmere A. Gal.; NAWA. *Awards*: prizes, F., PAFA; Cresson traveling scholarship, PAFA, 1922, prize, 1923, 1933; NAWA, 1932; Women's Achievement exh., Phila., 1933; Phila. Sketch Cl., med., 1942, prize, 1943; Phila. Plastic Cl., 1943, 1944, med., 1942; Nat. Assn. Women P. & S., 1933. *Work*: sc., West Point Military Acad.; numerous fountain sculptures in private gardens. *Exhibited*: Phila. A. Cl.; Women's City Cl., 1951; Phila. A. All., 1950; Ferargil Gal.; Syracuse Mus. FA; Wash. A. Cl.; Davenport, Iowa; Denver AA; Denver Lib.; New Orleans AA; Instituto San Miguel Allende, Mexico, 1952; one-man: Miami Beach A. Center, 1955; Oklahoma City A. Center, 1955; Wichita Falls, Tex., 1955. *Position*: Instr., painting, Syracuse Univ. summer sessions. Lectures on painting, PAFA and to private clubs.

GILLESPIE, JESSIE (Miss Jessie Gillespie Willing)— Designer, I., W., Comm. A.

7 Lexington Ave., New York 10, N.Y.

B. Brooklyn, N.Y. *Studied*: PAFA. *Member*: NAC; AIGA. *Positions*: A. Ed., Keystone Pub. Co., Phila., Pa., 1922-31; A. Ed. & covers for Jewelers' circular, 1933-39; Direct mail advertising, J. E. Caldwell & Co., Philadelphia, Pa., 1938- ; Publicity for Children's Aid Soc.; Boys' Club, New York; Peabody Home; Chapin Home; Nat. Council of Protestant Episcopal Churches, etc.

GILLOOLY, WILHELMINA R.—Designer, P.

Beaver Brook Rd., Lincoln Park, N.J.

B. Providence, R.I., Aug. 23, 1895. *Studied*: R.I.Sch. Des.; BMFA Sch., and with Denman Ross. *Member*: Boston Soc. A. & Crafts. Specializes in illumination, and recent works include 65 page World War II book for St. Thomas' Church, N.Y., 1954; Mass Cards for High Altar of Newark Cathedral, 1955.

GILMAN, ESTHER MORGANSTERN—Painter, Lith., I.

47 East 88th St., New York 28, N.Y.

B. Cleveland, Ohio, Aug. 13, 1922. *Studied*: Cleveland Sch. A.; Univ. Wisconsin; Univ. Michigan; ASL. *Awards*: prizes, P. & S. Soc. of New Jersey, 1956, 1958. *Work*:

MModA; NAD; Riverside Mus. *Exhibited*: Northwest Pr. M., 1954; RoKo Gal.; Laurel Gal.; Panoras Gal.; Contemporaries, all N.Y.; Woodstock AA; P. & S. Soc of New Jersey, 1956, 1958; N.Y. City Center, 1957; AWS, 1958; Knickerbocker A., 1957.

GILMORE, ETHEL (Mrs. Charles J. Romans)—
Painter, Gr., T.
1033 New York Ave., Cape May, N.J.
B. New York, N.Y. *Studied*: Hunter Col., B.A.; Columbia Univ., M.A. and with A. Dasburg, C.J. Martin, Oliver Chaffee, Aldro Hibbard, and others. *Member*: Prof. A. of So. New Jersey; NAWA; All. A. Am.; P. & S. Soc. New Jersey; Gotham Painters; Hudson Valley AA; Hudson A. of New Jersey. *Awards*: prizes, Kearney Mus., 1947; P. & S. Soc., New Jersey, 1947; A. Council of New Jersey, 1948, 1950; Gotham Painters, 1948; Jersey City Mus. Assn. 1949, 1951, 1953; All. A. Am., 1951; Hudson A., 1953. *Exhibited*: NAWA, 1938-1955; All. A. Am., 1939-1958; Audubon A., 1945; P. & S. New Jersey, 1945-1958; Argent Gal., 1938-1946; Gotham Painters, 1944-1954; High Mus. A., 1943; Manchester (N.H.) Mus. A., 1940; Montclair A. Mus., 1947-1949; AFA traveling exh., 1939-40; Hudson Valley AA, 1952-1954; Hudson A. of New Jersey, 1953-1955. *Position*: Rec. Sec., 1950-55, Cor. Sec., 1954-55, All. A. Am.; Trustee, Jersey City Mus. Assn., 1953-55.

GINNO, ELIZABETH de GEBELE—Etcher, Lith.
1814 Pacific Ave., San Francisco 9, Cal.
B. London, England, July 8, 1911. *Studied*: Mills Col.; Cal. Col. A. & Crafts; San F. Sch. FA, and with John Winkler. *Member*: Boston Pr. M.; Cal. Soc. Et.; San F. Women A. *Work*: Mills Col.; deYoung Mem. Mus.; Cal. State Lib.; Achenbach Coll. *Exhibited*: Chicago Soc. Et.; San F. Women A.; San F. AA; Boston Pr. M.; Cal. Soc. Et.; SAGA; Cal. PLH; Oakland AA; Northern California AA. One-man: Gump's, San F.; Kennedy & Co., N.Y.; deYoung Mem. Mus.; Cal. State Lib.; 2-man: deYoung Mem. Mus., 1954. *Position*: Vice-Pres., Cal. Soc. Et., San Francisco, Cal.

GINSBURG, ABRAHAM—Painter, T.
939 8th Ave. (19); h. 245 West 107th St., New York 25, N.Y.
B. Odessa, Russia, Oct. 15, 1891. *Studied*: NAD, and with Ivan Olinsky. *Member*: All. A. Am. *Awards*: med., NAD; Pulitzer scholarship, 1918. *Work*: Frick Mus. A. *Exhibited*: NAD; All. A. Am.; Newman Gal. (one-man).*

GIORGI, CLEMENT C.—Ceramist
12720 Triskett Rd.; h. 14537 Alger Rd., Cleveland 11, Ohio
B. Massachusetts, Sept. 30, 1911. *Studied*: Cleveland Inst. A. *Awards*: prizes, BMA, 1946, 1950, 1953; Canton AI, 1956, 1957. *Work*: CMA; Canton AI. *Exhibited*: Delgado Mus. A., 1946, 1948, 1957; Wichita A. Mus., 1950-1953; Arizona State Fair, 1949; Phila. AA, 1947; Columbus Mus. A., 1958; CMA, 1946-1958; Butler Inst. Am. A., 1950, 1954, 1956, 1957; Ohio Artist-Craftsmen, 1953, 1954, 1956, 1957; Canton AI, 1956, 1957, and one-man exhs.

GIORGI, FERN M.—Ceramic Craftsman, P., L.
12720 Triskett Rd.; h. 14537 Alger Rd., Cleveland 11, Ohio
B. Lakewood, Ohio, Aug. 30, 1914. *Studied*: John Huntington Polytechnic Inst.; Cleveland Inst. A. *Member*: Am. Craftsmen's Edu. Council; Am. Ceramic Soc.; Nat. Lg. Am. Pen Women. *Awards*: prizes, Massillon Mus. A., 1955; Canton AI, 1957; CMA, 1946, 1947, 1949, 1950, 1951, 1958. *Work*: CMA; Canton AI; Massillon Mus. A.; First Methodist Church, Midland, Mich., and private commissions. *Exhibited*: Delgado Mus. A., New Orleans, 1946, 1948; Wichita A. Mus., 1951; Arizona State Fair, 1949; North Shore AA, 1950-1952; Butler Inst. Am. A., 1952; Phila. AA, 1947; CMA, 1946-1958; Massillon Mus. A., 1953, 1954, 1955; Canton AI, 1956, 1957; Michigan Artist-Craftsmen; Nat. Lg. Am. Pen Women; Ohio WC Soc., 1951, 1952, 1954; Ohio State Univ., 1955, 1956, and one-man exhs.

GIRONA, JULIO—Painter
53 Genesee Ave., Teaneck, N.J.
B. Manzanillo, Cuba, Dec. 29, 1914. *Studied*: Academia

San Alejandro, Havana; Academie Ranson, Paris, France; ASL. *Awards*: prizes, Nat. Exp. of Cuba, 1952, 1956. *Work*: Palacio de Bellas Artes, Havana; Museo de Buenos Aires; Chicago A. Cl.; Newark Mus. A.; murals, Colegio Medico, Havana. *Exhibited*: MMA, 1943; BM, 1949; PAFA, 1953; SFMA, 1944; Chicago A. Cl., 1957; Nebraska AA, 1958; Denver A. Mus., 1957; Mus. FA of Houston; Zabriskie Gal., N.Y., 1941; MModA European traveling exh., 1957; Mus. A. & Crafts, N.Y.; Stable Gal., 1957; Newark Mus. A., 1958; one-man: Havana, Cuba, 1934, 1939, 1947, 1954, 1958; Artists Gal., N.Y., 1954; Bertha Schaefer Gal., N.Y., 1956, and in Germany, 1958.

GIUSTI, GEORGE—Advertising Designer
Mendham, N.J.
B. Milan, Italy, Oct. 1908. *Studied*: Milan, Italy. *Awards*: numerous prizes in Phila., Pa.; New York, N.Y.; Chicago, Ill., since 1941; "Art Dir. of the Year," 1958, Nat. Soc. A. Dirs. *Work*: Advertising des. for major advertising agencies and manufacturing firms. Cover des. for Fortune, Holiday, Interiors, Graphis and other publications. Book jackets for publishers. *Exhibited*: MModA, 1941; A. Headquarters, N.Y., 1945; A-D Gal., 1945; A. Dir. Cl., N.Y. & Phila., Pa., 1941-1945. Author, I., "Drawing Figures," 1944.

GIVLER, WILLIAM HUBERT—Painter, Et., Lith., T.
2343 North West Irving St., Portland 10, Ore.
B. Omaha, Neb., Mar. 17, 1908. *Studied*: Portland (Ore.) Mus. A. Sch.; ASL. *Member*: Oregon Gld. P. & S. *Awards*: prizes, SAM, 1939; Portland A. Mus., 1938; Topeka, Kan., 1940; Northwest Pr.M., 1940, 1941. *Work*: Portland A. Mus.; PMA; SAM. *Exhibited*: WFNY 1939; PAFA, 1941; NAD, 1940; SFMA, 1940-1946; WMA, 1941, 1942. *Position*: Instr. A., 1931-44; Dean, 1944- , Mus. A. Sch., Portland, Ore.

GLACE, MARGARET F. S.—Educator
Maryland Institute, Mt. Royal & Lanvale Sts., Baltimore, Md.
Position: Dean, Fine Arts, Maryland Institute.*

GLANNON, EDWARD J.—Painter, T.
1621 Northern Blvd., Roslyn, L.I., N.Y.
B. Pittsburgh, Pa., Oct. 2, 1911. *Position*: T., Painting, Fieldston Sch., Riverdale, N.Y., 1937- .

GLARNER, FRITZ—Painter
R.D. #2, Huntington, L.I., N.Y.
B. Zurich, Switzerland, July 20, 1899. *Studied*: Royal Inst. FA, Naples, Italy. *Award*: prizes, CGA, 1957. *Work*: Yale Univ.; PMA; MModA; WAC; Kunsthaus Zurich, Zurich, Switzerland; BMA; WMAA. *Exhibited*: Albright A. Gal., 1931; Am. Abstract A., 1938-1944; Gal. St. Etienne, 1940, 1957; N.Y. Univ., 1941; David Porter Gal., Wash., D.C., 1945; AIC, 1947, 1958; Toronto A. Gal., 1949; VMFA, 1950, 1958; Cal. PLH, 1950; WMAA, 1950, 1951, 1953-1955; MModA, 1951, 1952, 1954, 1955 (New York, Paris, Zurich, Barcelona), 1956; Sao Paulo, Brazil, 1951; BM, 1951; Univ. Illinois, 1952; Univ. Minnesota, 1951; Univ. Nebraska, 1955; Wildenstein Gal., 1952; Carnegie Inst., 1952, 1958; John D. Rockefeller Guest House, N.Y., 1954; CGA, 1955, 1957; Kassel, Germany, 1955; Solomon Guggenheim Mus. A., 1954; Tokyo, Japan, 1953; Kunsthaus, Zurich, Switzerland, 1956; Musee Neuchatel, 1957; Kunstverein Winterthur, 1958; Congresshalle, Berlin, 1958, and others; one-man: Kootz Gal., 1945; Rose Fried Gal., 1949, 1951; Galerie Louis Carre, Paris, 1952, 1955.

GLASCO, JOSEPH—Painter, S.
Ottsville, Bucks County, Pa.
B. Paul's Valley, Okla., Jan. 19, 1925.

GLASELL, CRISS (Christine Albertina Rosner Glasell)
—Painter, C., L.
Dubuque, Iowa
B. Vienna, Austria, July 8, 1898. *Studied*: AIC; & with Grant Wood, Francis Chapin, Adrian Dornbush. *Member*: NAWA. *Awards*: prizes, Iowa A. Salon, 1931-1934, 1938, 1939, 1941. *Work*: Dubuque AA; USPO, Leon, Iowa. *Exhibited*: PAFA, 1934; CGA, 1934; Joslyn Mem., 1934;

Kansas City AI, 1935, 1936; CM; WFNY 1939; Iowa A. Salon, 1931-1941; NAWA, 1945; Argent Gal., 1946; one-man exh.: Des Moines, Mason City, Cedar Rapids, Sioux City, Bloomfield, Dubuque, Iowa. *Position*: Program Dir., Dubuque AA.*

GLASS, HENRY P(ETER)—*Designer, T.*
666 Lake Shore Dr.; h. 245 Dickens Rd., Northfield, Ill.

B. Vienna, Austria, Sept. 24, 1911. *Studied*: Technical Univ., Vienna; Master Sch. for Arch., with Theiss. *Member*: F., IDI. *Award*: gold med., IDI, 1952; Fine Hardwoods Assn. award, 1955. *Work*: Furniture, Product, commercial interiors display & arch. des. Contributor to: Interiors, Plastics & other trade magazines with articles on problems of design. *Position*: Chief Des., Morris B. Sanders, N.Y., 1940-41; Hd., Arch. Des. Dept., W. L. Stensgaard, Chicago, 1942-45; Chm. Chicago Chapter, IDI, 1957-59; Prof. Indst. Des., AIC, Chicago, Ill., at present.

GLASSER, HANNELORE—*Museum Curator*
Virginia Museum of Fine Arts, Grove Ave. & The Boulevard, Richmond, Va.

Position: Cur. of Collections, Virginia Museum of Fine Arts.*

GLEASON, (JOE) DUNCAN—*Painter, I., W.*
2411 Edgemont St., Los Angeles 27, Cal.

B. Watsonville, Cal., Aug. 3, 1891. *Studied*: Mark Hopkins Inst., San F.; AIC; ASL; San Carlos Acad., Mexico City. *Member*: P. & S. Cl. (Past Pres.); Santa Monica AA (Past Pres.); Valley A. Gld.; A. of the Southwest (Pres.); Los Fiesteros. *Awards*: prizes, Clearwater, Gardena, Dana, Mira Costa H.S.; Madonna Festival, Los A.; Greek Theatre, Los A.; medal, San Diego, Cal.; P. & S. Cl., 1956, 1957; Cal. State Fair. *Work*: F.D. Roosevelt Mem., Hyde Park, N.Y.; marine murals, Hotel Clark, Los A. *Exhibited*: NAD; Arch. Lg. Author, I., "Windjammers"; "Islands of California"; "Islands and Ports of California." Illus., Autobiographies of Admiral Schley and Admiral Dewey. Contributor to national magazines.

GLEESON, CHARLES K.—*Etcher, P.*
East Haddam, Conn.

B. St. Louis, Mo., Mar. 5, 1878. *Studied*: ASL; St. Louis Sch. FA; Grande Chaumiere, Paris; & with Renard, Steinlen, Chase, Mora. *Awards*: prizes, St. Louis A. Gld., 1925, 1927, 1929, 1930. *Work*: CAM; Toledo Mus. A.; AIC; N.Y.Pub. Lib.; Lib.Cong. *Exhibited*: AIC; SAGA; Chicago SE; WFNY 1939; St. Louis A. Gld., all from 1914-1943; Conn. Acad. FA. and one-man shows, 1944-1958.

GLEITSMAN, RAPHAEL—*Painter, T.*
345 Diagonal Rd.; h. 531 Fernwood Dr., Akron 20, Ohio

B. Dayton, Ohio, June 11, 1910. *Member*: Audubon A.; Phila. WC Cl.; AWS; AEA. *Awards*: prizes, PAFA, 1945; Carnegie Inst., 1948; NAD, 1949; Butler AI, 1950. *Work*: Newark Mus. A.; PAFA; Massillon Mus. A.; Butler AI; U.S. War Dept.; Syracuse Mus. FA; Wichita Mus. A.; New Britain Inst.; Akron AI. *Exhibited*: VMFA, 1940; MMA, 1942; PAFA, 1944, 1945, 1949, 1951; Carnegie Inst., 1943-1950; CAM, 1946; CM, 1941; SFMA, 1941; Butler AI, 1940-1943, 1950; Massillon Mus., 1941-1945; NAD, 1948-1951; Univ. Iowa, 1948; Univ. Illinois, 1949, 1950; Univ. Nebraska, 1949; Toledo Mus. A., 1948-1951; Walker A. Center, 1950; CGA, 1951. *Position*: Instr., Painting, Akron AI, Akron, Ohio.*

GLENN, SALLY (Mrs.)—*Painter*
500 Arroyo Drive, South Pasadena, Cal.

B. Los Angeles, Cal., Apr. 25, 1917. *Studied*: Univ. California at Los A., B.A. *Member*: Cal. WC Soc.; Women Painters of the West; Los A. AA. *Awards*: prizes, Santa Paula, Cal., 1954; Pasadena Soc. A.; San Gabriel Playhouse Exh. *Work*: Santa Paula, Cal., and in private colls. *Exhibited*: Los A. Mus. A., 1949, 1951-1954, 1956; Cal. WC Soc., 1952-1955, 1958; Greek Theatre, Los A.; Santa Paula, Cal.; Oakland A. Mus.; AWS, 1954, 1955; Palos Verdes, Cal.; Nat. Orange Show, 1953, 1958.

GLICKMAN, MAURICE—*Sculptor, P., T., W.*
2231 Broadway (24); h. 2230 University Ave., New York 53, N.Y.

B. Iasi, Romania, Jan. 6, 1906. *Studied*: ASL; Edu. All. Sch., and abroad. *Member*: Sculptors Gld. *Awards*: Guggenheim Fellowship, 1934. *Work*: sculpture, bas-reliefs, Dept. Interior, Wash., D.C.; Howard Univ.; Roberson Mem. A. Center, Binghamton, N.Y.; Tel-Aviv Mus., Israel; N.Y. Bd. Edu.; USPO, Northampton, Pa.; South River, N.J. *Exhibited*: WMAA, 1937, 1951; PAFA, 1939, 1950; PMA, 1940, 1950; MMA, 1935; S. Gld., 1938-1955; Art:USA, 1958; one-man: Morton Gal., 1931; North Carolina Woman's Col., 1941. Contributor to Architectural Record, Coronet, American Artist and Design magazines. *Positions*: Instr., School for Art Studies, N.Y., 1945-55; Dir., 1945-55; Exec. Sec., Sculptor's Gld., 1954-55.

GLINSKY, VINCENT—*Sculptor, Et., Lith., P. T.*
2 West 15th St.; h. 9 Patchin Place, New York 11, N.Y.

B. Russia, Dec. 18, 1895. *Studied*: Columbia Univ.; City Col., N.Y.; BAID. *Member*: NSS; S. Gld.; Audubon A.; Arch. Lg. *Awards*: Widener gold medal, PAFA, 1935; Guggenheim Fellowship, 1935-36; grant, Am. Acad. A. & Lets., and Nat. Inst. A. & Lets., 1945; Medal of Honor, NAC, 1958; prizes, PAFA, 1948; Arch. Lg., 1956; Adelphi Col., 1956. *Work*: Brookgreen Gardens Outdoor Mus.; S. dec., French Bldg., N.Y.; Public bldgs., Detroit; New Orleans; Bethesda, Md.; Health Center; Sun & Surf Cl., Atlantic Beach, N.Y.; USPO, Hudson, N.Y. and Weirton, W. Va.; Lady of Lourdes Shrine, St. Paul's Col., Wash., D.C.; medal for U.S. Navy; mem. plaque, Bd. Edu., New York City; Carol Lane Safety Award Trophy, and many private commissions. *Exhibited*: Paris, France, 1932; AIC; GGE 1939; WFNY 1939; PMA, 1940, 1949; Carnegie Inst., 1941; Contemp. Am. A., London, 1941; NAD, 1945; MMA; BM; WMAA; MModA, and others. Traveling group shows. *Position*: S. Instr., BAID, 1938-40; Brooklyn Col., 1949-55; Columbia Univ., 1957-58; N.Y. Univ., Div. General Edu., 1950- .

GLUCKMANN, GRIGORY—*Painter*
c/o Dalzell Hatfield Galleries, Ambassador Hotel, Box K, Los Angeles 5, Cal.; h. 400 South Hauser Blvd., Los Angeles 36, Cal.

B. Moscow, Russia, Oct. 25, 1898. *Studied*: Ecole des Beaux-Arts, Paris, France. *Member*: Salon d'Automne, Salon National des Beaux-Arts, Salon des Tuileries, Paris, France; F., Royal Soc. A., London. *Awards*: Med., Paris Salon, 1937; prize, AIC, 1938, 1945. *Work*: Luxembourg Mus.; Petit Palais, Paris, France; Museum de la Ville de Havre, France; AIC; San Diego FA Soc.; Encyclopaedia Britannica Coll.; Charles & Emma Frye Mus., Seattle, Wash. *Exhibited*: John Levy Gal.; Schneider-Gabriel Gal.; Bignou Gal., N.Y.; Chicago AC; Milch Gal.; Drouet Gal.; Drouant-David Gal., Paris; Dalzell Hatfield Gal.; Leicester Gal.; Arthur Tooth Gal., London; Charpentier Gal., Allard Gal., Paris, France. Illus., "Salvador Rosa"; "Nuits Florentines"; "Manon Lescaut"; "Malentendu"; for "L'Illustration."*

GLUSHAKOW, JACOB—*Painter*
5708 Oakshire Rd., Baltimore 9, Md.

B. July 23, 1914. *Studied*: ASL, and with Kenneth Hayes Miller, Alexander Brook, Charles Locke. *Awards*: Tiffany Fnd. grant, 1949; prizes, Peale Mus. A., 1949, 1951; BMA, 1946. *Work*: Balt. Friends of Art Coll.; BMA; PMG. *Exhibited*: NGA, 1942; BMA, 1948-1952; VFMA, 1948; NAD, 1949, 1950; CGA, 1951, 1953; St. John's Col., Annapolis, Md., 1951 (one-man); Peale Mus. A., annually; Western Md. Col., Westminster, Md., 1955 (one-man). *Position*: Instr., Painting & Drawing, Jewish Community Center, Baltimore, Md., at present.

GODFREY, ROB. W.—*Painter, Lith., Des.*
Route 2, Lowell, Mich.

B. Jackson, Mich., July 22, 1910. *Studied*: Am. Acad. A.; ASL, with Bridgman, Lahey. *Member*: Kent A. Group. *Work*: MMA; Albion Col., Mich.; Grand Rapids A. Gal.; mural, Fifth Ave., Presbyterian Church, Newark, N.J. *Exhibited*: NAD, 1936; Springville, Utah, 1937, 1938; Grand Rapids A. Gal., 1940; Detroit Inst. A., 1939, 1940; Roerich Mus., 1935, 1936; one-man exh., New York, California, South Carolina, etc.*

GODWIN, BLAKE-MORE—Museum Director
Toledo Museum of Art; h. The Woods, Harroun Rd., Sylvania, Ohio

B. Clinton, Mo., Jan. 13, 1894. *Studied*: Univ. Missouri, B.A.; Princeton Univ., M.A. *Member*: AAMus.; Mus. Dir. Assn.; CAA; Archaeological Inst. Am.; Mediaeval Acad. Am.; Conseil de Direction, Gazette des Beaux-Arts; Comm. on Church Architecture, Episcopal Diocese of Ohio. *Awards*: Hon. memb. Faculty FA, Univ. Chile, 1943; Hon. D.F.A., Univ. Toledo, 1952, Bowling Green State Univ., 1954, Univ. Missouri, 1955; F., Mus. Assn., Great Britain; Chevalier Legion of Honor, 1950; officer, Order of Nassau-Orange, 1954; Commander, Order of Merit, Chile, 1943. *Work*: designer of Gothic Hall, Cloister and other features of Toledo Mus. A. Author: "European Paintings in the Toledo Museum of Art," 1939; Contributor, biographies of American Painters and Sculptors in Allgemeines Kunstler Lexikon, and articles on art for periodicals. *Position*: Asst., Classical Archaeology & Hist. A., Univ. Missouri, 1912-15; F., A. & Archaeology, Princeton Univ, 1915-16; Rep. of U.S. Mus. to 400th Anniversary Exh. of Chilean Art, Santiago, 1941; Trustee, Toledo Univ., 1919-30, Northwestern Ohio Hist. Soc., 1930-40, Toledo Pub. Health Assn., 1943 (Pres. 1953-55); Pres., Toledo Citizens Plan Assn., 1936-44; Chm., Museum Endowment Fund; Cur., 1916-26, Dir., 1927- , Toledo Museum of Art, Toledo, Ohio.

GODWIN, FRANK—Painter, I., Cart., Et., Des.
Honey Hollow Rd., New Hope, Pa.

B. Washington, D.C., Oct. 20, 1889. *Studied*: Corcoran Sch. A.; & with J. M. Flagg. *Member*: SC; SI. *Work*: murals, Kings County Hospital, Brooklyn, N.Y.; Riverside Yacht Cl., Greenwich, Conn. I., magazines & newspapers.†

GODWIN, MRS. FRANK.
See Harbeson, Georgianna Brown

GOETHE, MRS. JOSEPH A.
See Miller, Dorothy Elizabeth

GOETHE, JOSEPH ALEXANDER—
Sculptor, P., C., Gr.
706 Grove Acre Ave., Pacific Grove, Cal.

B. Ft. Wayne, Ind., Mar. 1, 1912. *Studied*: Dayton AI; PMG. *Member*: Santa Monica A. Gld. *Awards*: F. Huntington Hartford Fnd., 1952; Cal. State Fair, 1957; Monterey County Fair, 1958. *Work*: PC; VMFA; Columbia (S.C.) Mus. FA; St. Mary's Col., Notre Dame, Ind.; Evansville Pub. Mus.; Washington County Mus. FA; Brooks Mem. Mus.; SFMA; s. figures, Langston Terrace Housing Project, Wash., D.C.; USS "President Monroe"; USS "African Meteor." *Exhibited*: CM; AIC; PAFA; Los A. Mus. A., 1956; Los A. AA, 1956; NAD; Hoosier Salon; Chicago Soc. Indp. A.; Wash. A. Cl.; PMA; traveling exh. of wood sculptures to museums and universities, 1955-57, 1957-58; many one-man exhs. nationally. Author: "Handbook of Commercial Woods," 1938, 2nd ed., 1954. Contributor to Craft Horizons.

GOETSCH, GUSTAV F.—Painter, E.
Washington University, St. Louis, Mo.; h. 20 Elm Ave., Glendale 22, Mo.

B. Gaylord, Minn., Mar. 15, 1877. *Studied*: Minneapolis Sch. A.; N.Y.Sch. A.; Julian Acad., Colorossi, Paris, France. *Member*: St. Louis A. Gld.; Chicago Soc. Et.; St. Louis A. All.; A. Lg., N.Y. *Awards*: prizes, Minneapolis Inst. A., 1917; St. Louis A. Gld., 1918, 1920, 1922, 1926, 1928, 1957; St. Louis AA, 1956-1958; med., Kansas City AI, 1924. *Work*: Washington Univ.; Univ. Missouri; Concordia Seminary, St. Louis; AIC; St. Louis Pub. Sch.; Minneapolis Inst. A.; CAM; Masonic Temple, Wash., D.C.; Kirkwood (Mo.) Pub. Schs.; Kappa Alpha Theta Sorority and Kappa Alpha Fraternity, Washington Univ., St. Louis; WMA; LC, and in private homes. Lectures: Painting and Etching. *Position*: Instr. A., Washington Univ., St. Louis, Mo.; former instr., Minneapolis Inst. A., and ASL.

GOETZ, ESTHER BECKER—Painter, I.
339 East 58th St., New York 22, N.Y.

B. Buffalo, N.Y., Aug. 7, 1907. *Studied*: ASL. *Work*: Albright A. Gal. *Exhibited*: PAFA, 1934; AIC, 1935; BM, 1935; WMAA, 1938; Mus. City of N.Y., 1944, 1945 (one-

man); Albright A. Gal., 1945 (one-man); Galerie Moderne, N.Y., 1953 (one-man) group, 1955; Mus. City of N.Y., 1954, Illus., "Mr. Nosey," 1945. Des. Christmas cards for Hallmark.

GOETZ, OSWALD H.—Lecturer, W.
Parke Bernet Galleries, 980 Madison Ave.; h. 788 Riverside Dr., New York, N.Y.

B. Hamburg, Germany, Nov. 23, 1896. *Studied*: Universities of Kiel, Frankfurt, Munich; & with R. Kautzsch, H. Wolfflin, P. Frankl. *Member*: CAA. Author: "The Rembrandt Bible," 1941; Co-Author, AIC publications, "Medals and Plaquettes from the S. Morgenroth Collection," 1944, "Buckingham Medieval Collection," 1945. Contributor of: Articles for art history periodicals and museum bulletins. Lectures: Art of the Middle Ages, Renaissance and following periods in Continental Europe. *Position*: Assoc. Cur., Medieval & Renaissance A., AIC, Chicago, Ill., 1940-51; Hd. Painting Dept., Parke Bernet Gal., New York, N.Y., 1951- .*

GOFF, HARRY (SHARP) (JR.)—Cartoonist, I.
19 Rolling Hill Dr., Chatham, N.J.

B. Haddon Heights, N.J., Aug. 4, 1905. *Studied*: PMSch IA. I., for True, Sports Afield, Farm Journal, Mechanix Illustrated, and other national magazines.

GOFF, LLOYD LOZES—Painter, I., Gr., W., E.
20 West 69th St., New York 23, N.Y.

B. Dallas, Tex., Mar. 29, 1917. *Studied*: ASL; Univ. New Mexico, and with Nicolaides, Locke, Sternberg. *Member*: AEA; ASL. *Work*: LC; WMAA; MMA; Univ. Vermont; Wadsworth Atheneum; Herbert Mem. Mus., Augusta, Ga.; DMFA; Federal Bldg., Cooper, Tex.; Federal Bldg., Hollis, Okla.; Museo Nacionale de Bellas Artes, Mexico City; Instituto Anglo-Mexicano de Cultura, Mexico City; Instituto Mexicano-Norteamericano, Mexico City. *Exhibited*: WMAA, 1937, 1938, 1942, 1943; NAD, 1937, 1938; PAFA, 1936, 1938; AIC, 1936-1938; WFNY 1939; San F. AA, 1941-1943; Mus. New Mexico, Santa Fé, 1940-1946, 1958 (one-man); Dallas Mus. FA, 1940, 1946; Galeria de Arte Mexicano, D.F., 1951 (one-man); AFA, 1951; Nat. Inst. A. & Let., 1954, 1955; Am. Inst. A. & Lets., 1954-55; Botts Mem. Hall, Albuquerque, 1955, 1957 (one-man). Contributor to: Magazines & newspapers with art reviews & critical essays. I., "New Mexico Village Arts," 1949. Author, I., "Run Sandpiper, Run," 1957 (Boy's Clubs of America award); "Fly Redwing Fly," 1959. *Position*: Asst. Prof. A., 1943-45, Actg. Hd. Dept. FA, Univ. of New Mexico, 1944-45.

GOFF, SUDDUTH—Portrait Painter
33 West 67th St., New York 23, N.Y.; also 417 Morrison Ave., Lexington, Ky.

B. Eminence, Ky., Aug. 6, 1887. *Studied*: Kentucky Univ. (now Transylvania Col.); Cincinnati A. Acad.; BMFA Sch. *Member*: Louisville A.C.; BMFA Sch. Alumni Assn. *Awards*: D.F.A., Transylvania Col., 1948; Prizes, BMFA Sch., 1915; gold med., A. Colony, Louisville, Ky., 1923; prize, Chicago Galleries Assn., 1930, 1931. *Work*: Many portraits of prominent military & professional persons; Hist. Soc., Frankfort, Ky.; State Capitol, Ky.; Univ. Kentucky; SC; Lord, Abbett Co., N.Y. *Exhibited*: CGA, 1929; AIC, 1934, 1935; SC, 1945, 1946; NAC, 1946; Assoc. Chicago P. & S., 1933-1943; Chicago Galleries Assn., 1931-1941; CM; one-man exh., Tudor Gal., Chicago; Brooks Mem. Gal., Memphis, Tenn.; J. B. Speed Mem. Mus., Louisville, Ky.; Newton Gal., N.Y., 1945; Pub. Lib., Lexington, Ky., 1948. *Position*: Instr., Louisville Sch. A,. 1923-25; Louisville Sch. Painting & Drawing, 1925-27; Am. Acad. A., Chicago, Ill., 1928-36.

GOITEIN, OLGA—Sculptor
New Haven Ave., Orange, Conn.

B. Vienna, Austria. *Studied*: Scuola Rossi, Paris; BMFA Sch.; BM Sch. A. *Member*: NAWA; Brooklyn Soc. A.; AEA; New England Contemp. S.; New Haven Paint & Clay Cl. *Awards*: prizes, Brooklyn Soc. A., 1949, 1951; New Haven Paint & Clay Cl., 1949, 1951, 1952; Essex AA, 1952. *Work*: Bezalel Mus., Jerusalem. *Exhibited*: NAWA, 1950-1952; New Haven Paint & Clay Cl., 1949-1952; Silvermine Gld. A., 1951, 1952; Brooklyn Soc. A., 1949-1951; George Walter Vincent Smith Mus., 1952; Conn. Acad. FA, 1950, 1952; DeCordova Mus. A., 1952; Este Gal., N.Y., 1953; PAFA, 1954.*

GOLBIN, ANDREE (Mrs.)—Painter

32 East 22nd St., New York 10, N.Y.

B. Leipzig, Germany, June 4, 1923. *Studied*: with Henri Bercher, in Switzerland; N.Y. Sch. F. & Appl. A.; ASL; Hans Hofmann Sch. A. *Member*: 8th St. A. Cl. *Awards*: prizes, NAWA, 1950; Grumbacher prize, Laurel Gal., 1950. *Exhibited*: NAWA, 1950; Los A. Mus. A., 1947; Los A. AA, 1947; Esther Robles Gal., Los A.; RoKo Gal., 1950; N.Y. City Center Gal., 1955; James Gal., 1957; one-man: Fitzsimmons Gal.; Camino Gal., N.Y., 1956, 1958. Contributor illus. to Mademoiselle, Junior League magazines.

GOLD, ALBERT—Painter, Gr., I., T., W., L.

6814 McCallum St., Philadelphia 19, Pa.

B. Philadelphia, Pa., Oct. 31, 1916. *Studied*: PMSchIA, with Franklin Watkins, Earl Horter, Henry C. Pitz; Graphic Sketch Cl., Phila. *Member*: Phila. WC Cl.; Phila. Pr. Cl.; Phila. A. All.; AEA. *Awards*: prizes, Phila. Pr. Cl., 1939; Prix de Rome, 1942; Order of the British Empire, 1947; Phila. A. All., 1953, 1955; AWS, 1953, 1955; Tiffany Fnd. grant, 1947, 1948; gold med., PAFA, 1950. *Work*: PAFA; N.Y. Pub. Lib.; LC; PMA; Ford Motor Co.; Pentagon Bldg., Wash., D.C.; U.S. War Dept.; Abbott Laboratories Coll. *Exhibited*: PAFA, 1938-1942, 1944, 1945, 1948, 1952; CGA, 1939; WFNY 1939; AIC, 1939, 1941, 1942, 1943; Carnegie Inst., 1942, 1943; Nat. Gal., London, 1944; Musee Galliera, Paris, 1945; NAD; Audubon A; Gimbel Bros., traveling exh.; one-man: PAFA, 1948; Phila. A. All., 1951; Lehigh Univ., 1948; Woodmere A. Gal., Phila., Pa., 1948. Illus., "The Commodore," 1954; "The Lamp," 1958 (Standard Oil Co.); jacket, illus., "Our Philadelphia," 1948. *Position*: Instr., PMASch., Philadelphia, Pa.

GOLDBERG, MRS. DORA BORTIN. See Bortin, Dora

GOLDBERG, ROBERT I.—
Industrial Designer, E., W., L.

284 Fifth Ave., New York 1, N.Y.; h. 29 Lawrence St., New Hyde Park, L.I., N.Y.

B. Brooklyn, N.Y., Dec. 30, 1919. *Studied*: Brooklyn Col., B.A.; Columbia Univ., M.A. *Member*: Package Des. Council (Exec. Bd.); IDI (Exec. Bd.); Inter Society Color Council; Am. Marketing Assn.; Soc. Automotive Engineers. *Exhibited*: IDI traveling exh., 1951-52; Nat. Home Furnishings Show, 1949, 1950; Springfield Mus. FA, 1956; Nat. Packaging Expo., Chicago, 1955; Package Des. Council, N.Y., 1955; AIGA, 1955. Contributor to trade magazines. Lectures on Industrial Design and General Package Designs. *Position*: Instr., Indst. & Package Des., Brooklyn Col., 1950-51; N.Y. Univ., 1952- ; Dir. Workshop in Package Des., PIASch.; Ed., "Design Digest," 1950-51; Adv. Bd., Nat. Home Furnishings Show, 1950-52; Chm., 10th annual Package Des. Seminar, N.Y., 1st annual New England Seminar, 1956; Chm., Dir., annual color seminar, N.Y. Univ., 1955- ; Chm., Dir., N.Y. seminar in Package Des., Consultant & Partner, Robert I. Goldberg Assoc., 1946-56; Assoc. Industrial Designers, 1956- .

GOLDBERG, RUBE—Cartoonist, I.

88 Central Park West, New York 23, N.Y.

Member: SI.*

GOLDEN, CHARLES O.—Painter, Lith., S., T.

P.O. Box 4182, University Station, Tucson, Ariz.

B. Upshur County, W. Va., Feb. 3, 1899. *Studied*: Corcoran Sch. A.; PAFA; & with J. J. Gould, Charles D. Mitchell. *Member*: Phila. Sketch Cl.; Phila. WC Cl.; Wash. WC Cl.; Tucson Press Cl.; Mystic AA. *Exhibited*: PAFA; CGA; NAD; AIC; Mystic AA; Tucson, Ariz.; Ariz. State Col., Tempe, 1955. Illus., "Moby Dick"; "The Cruise of the Cachelot." I., national magazines. Demonstration: Painting a Watercolor Portrait, Am. Artist magazine, 1957. *Position*: Founder, Co-Dir., Instr., Watercolor painting, Southern Arizona Sch. A., Tucson, Ariz.

GOLDMAN, ALBERT MARTIN—Painter

708 Canyon Rd., Santa Fé, N.M.

B. New York, N.Y., June 12, 1924. *Studied*: NAD; Am. A. Sch.; Columbia Univ., B.F.A. *Awards*: Brevoort-Eickmeyer F., Columbia Univ., 1951-52; prize, Norton Gal. A., 1954; Alfred Morang Mem. Award, Santa Fé, 1958. *Work*: Columbia Univ.; MMA; murals, Palm Beach Towers; Gonzales Elem. Sch., Santa Fé, N.M. *Exhibited*: widely in New York, Florida, New Mexico; one-man: Prang Gal., N.Y., 1952; Norton Gal. A., 1954; Mus. New Mexico, 1954, 1958.

GOLDMAN, HERBERT—Sculptor, C., T.

816 13th St., Northwest; h. 5302 Edith Blvd., Northeast, Albuquerque, N.M.

B. Detroit, Mich., Mar. 8, 1922. *Studied*: Detroit Soc. A. & Crafts; Wayne Univ.; Univ. New Mexico, B.F.A., and with Samuel Cashwan. *Member*: New Mexico A. Lg.; Mus. Mod. A., Albuquerque (Bd. Memb.). *Work*: Medical Arts Square, Bank of New Mexico, Temple Albert, Veterans Admin. Bldg., St. Francis Xavier Church, Church of the Holy Rosary, LaFonda Hotel, Monroe Jr. H.S., Rio Grande Park Zoo, Motorsport Corp., all in Albuquerque; State Sch. for the Retarded, Los Lunas, N.M. *Exhibited*: San F. AA, 1950, 1951, 1953; Denver A. Mus., 1950; Detroit Inst. A., 1949, 1950; Mus. New Mexico, 1951; Univ. New Mexico; Botts Mem. Gal.; one-man: Albuquerque and in Dallas, Tex. *Position*: Instr., Sculpture, Albuquerque Mus. Mod. A.; Univ. New Mexico Evening College.

GOLDMAN, JULIA—Painter, L., T., Des.

22 East 38th St., New York 16, N.Y.

B. Boston, Mass. *Studied*: Mass T. Training Col.; N.Y. Sch. F. & App. A.; T. Col., Columbia Univ.; Harvard Univ.; Courtauld Inst. A., Univ. London, and with Charles Hawthorne, Denman Ross. *Member*: Am. Assn. Univ. Women; Chinese A. Soc. Am.; China Inst. *Awards*: traveling scholarship, N.Y. Sch. F. & App. A. *Exhibited*: New York, Paris, London, San Francisco, Honolulu. Lectures on the Art of the Orient.*

GOLDMAN, ROBERT DOUGLAS—Painter, E., L., W.

Lincoln High School, Rowland & Ryan Sts., Philadelphia 36, Pa.; h. 817 Rowland St., Cheltenham, Pa.

B. Philadelphia, Pa., Jan. 24, 1908. *Studied*: PMSchIA; Rutgers Univ., B.S. in Edu.; Columbia Univ., M.A.; ASL; Temple Univ.; Colorado Springs FA Center, with Boardman Robinson. *Member*: NAEA; Eastern AA; Am. Indst. AA; Mechanic A.T. Assn.; Am. Vocational Assn.; AEA; Am. Council of Indst. A. Supv.; Phila. A. All.; Assn. for Supervision and Curr. Development; PAFA; Com. on A. Edu.; Planning Com., Regional Indst. A. Awards, 1951-56. *Awards*: prizes, Elizabeth (N.J.) Soc. A., 1934; Nat. Army Exh., 1945; Regional Council of Community A. Centers, 1952; Phila. A.T. Assn., 1952, 1954, 1957; plaque, A.T. Assn., 1953, 1955, 1956. *Work*: Elizabeth YMHA; Phila. YMHA; Springhouse Schl., and in numerous collections. *Exhibited*: PAFA, 1928-1931, 1934, 1951, 1952; Oklahoma A. Center, 1941; Cheltenham A. Center, 1940, 1949, 1952; Bd. Edu., Phila., 1941; Phila. A.T., 1951, 1952; Phila. A. All., 1951, 1952; Rochester Mem. A. Gal., 1955; Lafayette (Ind.). AA, 1955; Butler AI, 1955; Stephens Col., 1955; Florence (S.C.) Mus. A., 1955; Canton AI, 1955; Univ. So. Carolina, 1955; Mills Col., Oakland, Cal., 1955; Univ. New Mexico, 1955; PMA; Dubin Gal., 1955; Tyler Sch. FA; Cheltenham Township A. Center; and others. Contributor to educational magazines and bulletins. *Position*: Dept. Hd., F. & Indst. A., Lincoln H.S., Philadelphia, Pa.; Instr., T. Col., Columbia Univ.; Pa. State Univ. Center; In-Service Instr., So. Jersey Indst. A. T.; Chm., Curriculum Com., Am. Indst. AA; Chm., Research Com., Eastern AA; Assoc. Ed., School Arts Magazine; Pres., Industrial Arts Assn. of Pennsylvania.

GOLDRING, MILTON—Painter

172 Bleecker St., New York 12, N.Y.

B. Brooklyn, N.Y., Feb. 11, 1918. *Studied*: BMSch. A.; Academie Julian, Paris, France; Academie Fernand Leger, Paris, France. *Awards*: prizes, Salon de Arte Moderna, Rio de Janeiro; New Talent, 1958; Provincetown A. Festival, 1958. *Work*: Mus. Modern A., Rio de Janeiro; Toledo Mus. A.; WMA, and others. Stained glass window for synagogue, Rio de Janeiro. *Exhibited*: Dayton AI, 1956; AIC, 1957; CGA, 1957, Toledo Mus. A., 1957; Mary Washington Col., 1957; Carnegie Inst., 1958; Sao Paulo, Brazil, 1951, 1953; Venice, Italy, 1954; Rome, 1954; WMAA, 1957; one-man: Rio de Janeiro, 1952, 1954; Sao Paulo, Brazil, 1953; New York City, 1956-1958.

GOLDSTEIN, GLADYS—*Painter*

3216 Milford Ave., Baltimore 7, Md.

B. Newark, Ohio, Dec. 11, 1918. *Studied*: Maryland Inst.; Pa. State Univ.; Columbia Univ. *Member*: AEA. *Awards*: prizes, Pa. State Univ. purchase award, 1954; Berney Mem. Award, Maryland, 1956; Nat. Lg. Am. Pen Women, 1956; Rulon-Miller award, Baltimore, 1957. *Work*: Pa. State Univ.; BMA; Univ. Arizona; Univ. Pennsylvania, and in private colls. *Exhibited*: CGA, 1957; PAFA, 1954, 1957; Butler Inst. Am. A., 1955, 1957, 1958; Wash. WC Cl., 1958; BMA, 1955; Am. Jewish Tercentenary, 1954; Univ. Nebraska; AIC; DMFA; Rochester Mem. A. Gal.; Phila. A. All.; Albright A. Gal.; Atlantic City, N.J., Paris, France, and others. One-man: BMA, 1956; Western Maryland Col., 1957; Duveen-Graham Gal., N.Y., 1957; Goucher Col., 1958; Paris, France, 1958-59.

GOLDSTEIN, MILTON—*Etcher, P., T., L.*

56-16 219th St., Bayside 64, N.Y.

B. Holyoke, Mass., Nov. 14, 1914. *Studied*: ASL, and with Harry Sternberg, Homer Boss, Morris Kantor. *Member*: SAGA; ASL; AEA; Am. Color Pr. Soc. *Awards*: prizes, Springfield (Mass.) Mus. FA, 1946; PMA, 1949, 1952; Phila. Pr. Cl., 1952; Guggenheim F., 1950; N.Y. State Fair, 1950; LC, 1952; purchase awards: DMFA; Brooks Mem. Mus.; PMA; Univ. Delaware; Albion Col.; Smithsonian Inst.; LC; Louisiana A. Comm. *Work*: Springfield Mus. FA; MModA; PMA; MMA; Univ. Pa.; Univ. Nebraska; Princeton Univ.; LC; SAGA; Univ. Maine; Des Moines A. Center. Color etchings in 210 Prints Editions, Int. Graphic A. Soc., 1952. *Exhibited*: J. B. Speed A. Mus., 1949; Pr. Cl. of Albany, 1949; Wichita AA, 1949; BM, 1947, 1949, 1952; PAFA, 1947, 1950; Carnegie Inst., 1947, 1950; LC, 1947, 1949, 1952; Phila. Pr. Cl., 1948-1952; SAGA, 1947-1952; Am. Color Pr. Soc., 1951, 1952; WMA, 1951; Phila. A. All., 1951; Univ. Maine; Univ. Utah; Cornell Univ.; Indiana Univ., 1951; Univ. Nebraska, 1952; Springfield Mus. FA, 1946-1949; MModA traveling exh. to Europe, 1951-52; traveling group show, Italy and Norway. One-man: Weyhe Gal., 1954; Smithsonian Inst.; Louisiana A. Comm. Illus. educational film, "How to Make an Etching." Lectures on Color Etchings. *Position*: Asst. Prof. A., Adelphi College, Garden City, N.Y.

GOLDWATER, ROBERT—

Museum Director, W., Cr., L., E.

The Museum of Primitive Art, 15 West 54th St. (19); h. 435 West 22nd St., New York 11, N.Y.

B. New York, N.Y., Nov. 23, 1907. *Studied*: Columbia Col., A.B.; Harvard Univ., M.A.; N.Y. Univ., Ph.D. *Member*: Am. Assn. Univ. Prof.; CAA (Dir. 1956-). *Awards*: Guggenheim F., 1944-1945; Fulbright F., 1950-51. Author: "Primitivism in Modern Painting," 1938; "Artists on Art," 1945; "Rufino Tamayo," 1947; "Modern Art in Your Life," 1949; "Jacques Lipchitz," 1954; "Paul Gauguin," 1957. Contributor to: Art magazines with historical and critical articles on modern art. Lectures: 19th & 20th century American and European Art. *Position*: Instr., History of Art, New York Univ., 1934-39; Asst. Prof., History of Art; Assoc. Prof., 1948-55, Prof., 1955-1957, Queens Col., Flushing, L.I., N.Y.; Prof., New York University, 1957- ; Dir., Museum of Primitive Art, New York, N.Y., 1957- ; Ed., Magazine of Art, 1947-53.

GOLINKIN, JOSEPH WEBSTER—*Painter, Lith.*

Centre Island, Oyster Bay, N.Y.

B. Chicago, Ill., Sept. 10, 1896. *Studied*: AIC; ASL. *Member*: AWCS. *Awards*: Med., Int. Exh. Art in Relation to Sport, 1936 Olympiad, Berlin. *Exhibited*: Carnegie Inst.; Ferargil Gal. (one-man); NAD; Macbeth Gal. (one-man); AIC; Sporting Gal., N.Y. (one-man); PAFA; Albright A. Gal.; Mus. City of N.Y.; CGA; Gump's, San F.; R.&R. Gal., Beverly Hills; Century Assn. Illus., Co-Author: "New York is Like This," 1929; "American Sporting Scene," 1941. I., national magazines.*

GOMBERG, STAN (STAG)—*Cartoonist, Des.*

535 East 14th St., New York 9, N.Y.

B. New York, N.Y., May 6, 1927. *Studied*: Brooklyn Col.; Am. Sch. A.; Sch. Visual Arts. *Awards*: Nat. Offset Lithographic award, 1958. Contributor cartoons to: Sat. Eve. Post; American; McNaught Syndicate, and to pharmaceutical house organs. *Position*: A. Dir., Central Printing Co., New York, N.Y.; Unger & Fruhling Advtg.; Consulting A. Dir. & Des., at present.

GONZALES, BOYER—*Painter, E.*

School of Art, University of Washington (5); h. 6525 51st St., Northeast, Seattle 15, Wash.

B. Galveston, Tex., Feb. 11, 1909. *Studied*: Univ. Virginia, B.S. in Arch.; and with Henry Lee McFee, Yasuo Kuniyoshi. *Member*: CAA; Scarab Cl. *Awards*: prizes, So. States A. Lg., 1939; Texas FA Assn., 1950, 1952; Texas A. & Crafts Fair, 1953; Dealy prize, Texas Exh. Painting & Sculpture, 1953; SAM, 1955, 1956. *Work*: Rochester Mem. A. Gal.; Elisabet Ney Mus. A., Austin, Tex.; DMFA; SAM. *Exhibited*: CGA, 1935, 1939, 1951; PAFA, 1936, 1951; WFNY 1939; GGE 1939; Univ. Illinois, 1947; NAD, 1954; Colorado Springs FA Center, 1957; Santa Barbara Mus. A., 1957; Stanford Univ. A. Gal., 1958. *Positions*: Instr., A., Univ. Texas, 1939-54; Chm., A. Dept., Univ. Texas, 1946-48; Dir., Sch. A., Prof. A., University of Washington, Seattle, Wash., 1954- .

GONZALES, CARLOTTA (Mrs. Richard Lahey)—

Painter, S., T., I.

R.F.D. 4, Vienna, Va.; s. Ogunquit, Me.

B. Wilmington, N.C., Apr. 3, 1910. *Studied*: PAFA, with Laessle; NAD, with Aitken; ASL, with Laurent, Karfiol. *Member*: Soc. Indp. A.; Ogunquit AA. *Exhibited*: CGA, 1939, 1950, 1951; Montclair A. Mus., 1952; NAD, 1931. Illus., "Stars in the Heavens"; "U.S.A. and State Seals." *Position*: Instr. S, Goucher Col., 1940-42; CGA, 1940; A., Nat. Geographic Magazine, Washington, D.C., 1943- .

GONZALEZ, XAVIER—*Painter, S.*

27 West 67th St., New York 23, N.Y.

B. Almeria, Spain, Feb. 15, 1898. *Member*: NA; Century Assn.; Audubon A. *Awards*: Grant, Am. Acad. A. & Lets.; Guggenheim Fellowship, 1947. *Work*: in many museums and private collections. *Exhibited*: nationally and internationally. Author: "Notes About Painting," 1955. *Positions*: Instr. A., Sophie Newcomb College, New Orleans, La.; Brooklyn Mus. Sch.; Artist-in-Residence, Western Reserve Univ., 1953-54; Dir., Summer Sch. of A., Wellfleet, Mass.

GOO, BENJAMIN—*Sculptor, Des., E.*

Art Department, Arizona State College; h. 508 Encanto Drive, Tempe, Ariz.

B. Honolulu, Hawaii, July 12, 1922. *Studied*: Honolulu Acad. A.; Univ. Hawaii; State Univ. Iowa, B.F.A.; Cranbrook Acad. A., M.F.A.; Brera Acad. FA, Sch. of Marino Marini, Milan, Italy. *Member*: NAEA; Pacific AA; AAEA. *Awards*: "Institutions" magazine award of honor for furniture and interior des. of Memorial Union Bldg., Arizona State College, 1956; Jay Sternberg Mem. award, Arizona, 1957; St. Francis Xavier Religious Art purchase prize, 1957; Circle Art Exh. purchase prize, New Mexico, 1957; Arizona State Fair, 1957; Fulbright Fellowship to Italy, 1954-55. *Work*: Cranbrook Acad. A.; Museum and A. Center, Roswell, N.M.; State Univ. of Iowa; St. Francis Xavier Parish Coll. of Religious Art; interior des. of main lounge, St. Augustine Episcopal Church, Arizona, 1958, and sculpture and garden sculpture in private homes and collections. *Exhibited*: Wichita A. Center, 1957; PAFA, 1958; Ball State T. Col., 1957; Des Moines A. Center, 1957; Sculpture Center, 1954-1958; Fulbright Designers Show, Mus. Contemp. Crafts, N.Y., 1958; Denver A. Mus., 1958; Santa Fe, N.M., 1957; Roswell, N.M., 1957, 1958; Tucson, Ariz., 1957; Phoenix, Ariz., 1957; Arizona State Fair, 1955-1957.

GOOCH, DONALD B.—*Designer, I., E.*

Department of Art, College of Architecture & Design, University of Michigan; h. 1633 Leaird St., Ann Arbor, Mich.

B. Bloomingdale, Mich., Oct. 17, 1907. *Studied*: Western Michigan Univ.; Univ. Michigan, B.S., M. Des.; Detroit A. Acad.; Am. Sch. Painting, Fontainebleau, France. *Member*: Detroit Mus. A. Fndrs. Soc.; AFA; Adcraft Cl. of Detroit; AAUP. *Awards*: Alumni prize, Am. Acad. in Rome, 1935; Detroit Inst. A. Fndrs. award, 1947; Michigan WC Soc., 1948. *Work*: 1948-59: Advertising & Publication Design, Young & Rubicam; Kenyon & Eckhardt; Benton & Bowles; Univ. Michigan; Allied A., Detroit; Calvillo Studios, Detroit; Educational Radio and TV Center, and others; painting & illus.: Ford Publications; Ford Motor Co.; Young America Films; McGraw-Hill Co.; Michigan Consolidated Gas Co.; Univ. Michigan Union. *Exhibited*: PAFA; Pepsi-Cola; SFMA; Detroit Inst. A., and others.

Editor, "Advertising to the American Taste," 1956; Designer: "The Story of Willow Run," "Mammals of the Great Lakes Region," 1957; Designer: "Your Copy into Type," Michigan Typesetting Co., 1947. *Positions*: Conf. Chm., Univ. Michigan Advertising Conferences, 1956, 1959; Prof. Des., Art Dept., College of Arch. & Des., University of Michigan, Ann Arbor, Mich., 1951- .

GOOD, LEONARD—*Educator, P., Cr., L., W.*
Drake University; h. 750 34th St., Des Moines, Iowa
B. Chickasha, Okla., June 25, 1907. *Studied*: Univ. Oklahoma, B.F.A. in A. Edu.; ASL, with Kimon Nicolaides; Univ. Iowa, with Jean Charlot. *Member*: Prairie WC Soc.; Assn. Okla. A.; SSAL; Madison AA. *Awards*: med., Oklahoma Univ., 1927; prizes, Tulsa AA, 1939, 1941; Assn. Okla. A., 1942, 1949, 1953; Gimbel Bros., Milwaukee, 1951, 1952; Iowa State Fair, 1954; Kansas Fed. A., 1955. *Work*: Oklahoma Hist. Mus.; Governor's Mansion, Des Moines, Iowa; Des Moines A. Center; murals, Gardner Co., Madison, Wis.; Taft Jr. H.S., Oklahoma City. Illus., Instructional manuals for Army Air Corps, 1943, 1944. Author: Correspondence course for U.S. Armed Forces Inst. on Art, 1952. *Position*: Cur. Paintings, Prof. A., Univ. Oklahoma, 1930-50; Univ. Wisconsin, 1950-52; Hd. A. Dept., Drake Univ., Des Moines, Iowa, 1952- ; Nat. Pres., Delta Phi Delta, honor art fraternity, 1958- .

GOODALL, DONALD B.—*Educator*
Department of Fine Arts, University Southern California, University Park, Los Angeles 7, Cal.; h. 2494 Boulder Road, Altadena, Cal.
B. Los Angeles, Cal. *Studied*: Univ. Oregon, A.B.; AIC; Univ. of Chicago, A.M.; Harvard Univ. *Member*: CAA; So. California A. Hist.; Am. Studies Soc. Contributor to College Art Journal; Arts Digest magazine. *Positions*: Dir., Utah A. Center, 1938-42; Chm. Dept. A., Univ. Texas, 1945-46; Actg. Dean, Div. Edu., Toledo Mus. A., 1946-47; Chm., Dept. FA, University of Southern California, 1948- .

GOODELL, WILLIAM NEWPORT—
Painter, Ser., C., T., I.
Crestline, Cal.; h. 7124 Country Club Dr., La Jolla, Cal.
B. Philadelphia, Pa., Aug. 16, 1908. *Studied*: Univ. Pennsylvania, B.A., M.A.; PAFA. *Member*: F., PAFA; San Diego A. Gld. *Awards*: prizes, NAD, 1933; Woodmere A. Gal., 1942; Nat. Ser. Soc., 1948. *Exhibited*: PAFA; NAD; CGA; VMFA; AIC; GGE 1939; Phila. Pr. Cl.; Nat. Ser. Soc.; Laguna Beach, Cal.; Los A. Mus. A.; Woodmere A. Gal.; San Diego FA Gal.; Nat. Orange Show. *Position*: A.T., Germantown Friends Sch., 1936-42, 1946; USNR, 1942-46; Instr., Moore Inst. A., Phila. Pa., 1946-51; Supervisory Scientific Illustrator, Naval Electronics Laboratory, San Diego, Cal., 1951- .

GOODELMAN, AARON J.—*Sculptor, T., L.*
68 West 238th St., Bronx 63, N.Y.
B. Attaki, Bessarabia, Russia, Apr. 1, 1890. *Studied*: CUASch.; NAD; Ecole des Beaux-Arts, Paris; BAID; & with Jo Davidson, Gutzon Borglum, J. MacNeil, etc. *Member*: S.Gld.; Audubon A; AEA; P. & S. Soc. of New Jersey. *Awards*: Med., CUASch., 1910-1913; BAID, 1914-1916; Audubon A., 1955. *Work*: Eastern Mus., Russia; Jewish Theological Lib., N.Y.; Lib. Jefferson Sch. Social Science; Project Houses, Wash., D.C.; Ein-Harod, Tel-Aviv Mus., Israel; many mem., monuments, busts & arch. sculptures. *Exhibited*: MMoDA; WMAA; WFNY 1939; BM; Carnegie Inst.; PMA; AIC; MMA; S.Gld., annually; 8th St. Gal., 1933 (one-man); ACA Gal., 1942, 1946 (one-man), 1956-1958; S.Gld.; Audubon A, annually; Art:USA, 1958; AEA, and many national group shows. I., for newspapers & journals, children's textbooks; lectures on sculpture to educational groups. Contributor of sculpture photographs to "Sculpture in Wood," by John Rood; "Jewish Sculptors," by Carl Schwartz.

GOODENOW, EARLE—*Painter, I.*
108 East 30th St., New York 19, New York, N.Y.
B. Chicago, Ill., July 13, 1913. *Studied*: NAD; ASL. *Member*: Audubon A. *Exhibited*: CGA; W. Va. Biennial Exh., 1940; Carnegie Inst., 1941; PAFA, 1942; Audubon A., 1945; Galerie de l'Elysee, Paris, 1947. Illus., "Arabian Nights," 1946; Author, I., "The Cow Concert," 1951; "The Cow Voyage," 1953; "The Lazy Llama," 1954; "The Peevish Penguin," 1955; "Angelo Goes to the Carnival," 1955; "The Bashful Bear," 1956; "Angelo Goes to Switzerland," 1956.

GOODMAN, ANN TAUBE—*Painter*
203 West 4th St.; h. 1422 West Market St., Bethlehem, Pa.
B. Newark, N.J., May 8, 1905. *Studied*: with Walter Emerson Baum, Philip Evergood. *Member*: WC Cl.; Plastic Cl.; A.All., all of Phila. *Awards*: Med., PAFA, 1944. *Work*: Lehigh Univ. *Exhibited*: PAFA, 1943-1945; Butler AI, 1943-1946; Conn. Acad. FA, 1942-1945; Montclair A. Mus., 1944; AIC, 1941; Phila. Sketch Cl., 1939-43; Lehigh Univ.; Muhlenberg Col.*

GOODMAN, BERTRAM—*Painter, Gr.*
74 Grove St.; h. 299 West 12th St., New York 14, N.Y.
B. New York, N.Y., Sept. 21, 1904. *Studied*: ASL; Sch. Am. Sculpture, and with Thomas Benton, Mahonri Young, Harry Wickey. *Member*: SAGA; Brooklyn Soc. A.; AEA. *Awards*: prizes, Screen Publicists Gld.; Emily Lowe award, 1955; Abraham Lincoln Gal. *Work*: LC; Abbott Laboratories; Butler AI; Tennessee Wesleyan Col.; N.Y.Pub. Lib.; Julien Levy Coll.; Mus. City of N.Y. *Exhibited*: AWS, 1922, 1923, 1927, 1948; PAFA, 1923, 1927, 1929, 1933, 1937-39, 1944; BM, 1925, 1929, 1933, 1939, 1947; AIC, 1926, 1929, 1931, 1940; WMAA, 1935, 1939, 1942, 1943, 1945; Carnegie Inst., 1941, 1950; SAGA, 1947, 1948, 1951; Kansas City AI, 1951; CAM, 1952; Mus. New Mexico, 1952, and others; one-man: Midtown Gal.; Julien Levy Gal.; Laurel Gal.; Butler AI; Research Studio, Maitland, Fla.; Delgado Mus. A., New Orleans, 1952; Artisan's Gal., 1953; Ward Eggleston Gal., 1956.

GOODNOW, CATHERINE SPENCER—
Portrait Painter
Greenbush, Mass.
B. Passaic, N.J., Jan. 17, 1904. *Studied*: ASL; Bradford, (Mass.) Acad.; Smith Col., B.A.; BMFA Sch. *Work*: many portrait commissions; Scituate H.S. *Exhibited*: PAFA; AWS; Boston Soc. WC Painters; Copley Soc., 1959 and prior; MIT; Bradford Jr. Col.; Vose Galleries, (5 exhs.); Ogunquit A. Center; North Shore AA; Jordan-Marsh Co., Boston, Brockton Pub. Lib., 1953, 1955; Milton Pub. Lib., 1954; watercolors "The Early Train" and "The Five O'Clock Tide" exhibited N.Y., New Haven & Hartford Railroad Station, Greenbush, Mass.

GOODRICH, GERTRUDE—*Commercial Artist, Des., P.*
92 Jane St., New York 14, N.Y.
B. New York, N.Y., Oct. 5, 1914. *Work*: murals, USPO, Buchanan, Mich.; Social Security Bldg., Wash., D.C. *Exhibited*: WFNY 1939; AIC; Santa Barbara, Cal.; WMAA. Contributor illus., to Seventeen; Mademoiselle; Living; Harper's Bazaar. *Position*: Asst., A. Dept., Charm Magazine, New York, N.Y.*

GOODRICH, LLOYD—*Museum Director, W., L.*
Whitney Museum of American Art, 22 West 54th St., New York 19, N.Y.
B. Nutley, N.J., July 10, 1897. *Studied*: ASL, with Kenneth Hayes Miller; NAD. Author: Books on American Artists, "Thomas Eakins," 1933; "Winslow Homer," 1944; "Yasuo Kuniyoshi," 1948; "Max Weber," 1949; "Edward Hopper," 1950; "John Sloan," 1951, and others. Ed., Research in American Art, 1945. Contributor to leading art magazines. Lectures on American Art. *Positions*: Assoc. Ed., The Arts, 1925-27, 1928-29, European Ed., 1927-28, Contributing Ed., 1929-31; Member N.Y. Regional Comm., Public Works of Art Project, 1933-34; Research Cur., WMAA, 1935-46, Assoc. Cur., 1946-48, Assoc. Dir., 1948-58, Dir., 1958- ; Dir., American Art Research Council, 1942- ; Member Ed. Bds., Art Bulletin, Art in America; Chm., Com. on Govt. & Art; Member, Smithsonian Art Commission; Ed., "The Museum and the Artist," 1958; Contributor, "New Art in America," 1957; Trustee & Vice-Pres., AFA; Sec., Sara Roby Fnd.; Co-Chm., Joint Artists-Museums Com.; Memb. Adv. Bd., Carnegie Study of American Art; Memb., Conseil Scientifique International, Encyclopedia dell'Arte; Fellow, Am. Acad. A. & Lets.

GOODRIDGE, ELINOR—*Painter*

64 West Cedar St., Boston 38, Mass.; h. 1705 Massachusetts Ave., Cambridge 38, Mass.

B. Cambridge, Mass., Dec. 9, 1886. *Studied*: BMFA Sch. with Umberto Romano, Prescott Jones; Smith Col., A.B., and with Philip Hicken. *Member*: AEA; Cape Ann Soc. Mod. A. *Exhibited*: PAFA, 1936; BM, 1937; Univ. Minnesota, 1937; AWCS, 1936-1938; Rockport AA; Charles Smith Gal., Boston, 1950; Gloucester SA; Cambridge AA, 1954, 1955, 1957, 1958; Busch-Reisinger Mus., 1957; Cape Ann Soc. Mod. A., 1958. Illus., "Children of the Lighthouse," 1924.

GOODSON, HOWARD—*Educator*

Art Department, University of Alabama, University, Ala.*

GOODWIN, GILBERTA D. (Mrs.)—*Educator, P.*

Centenary Junior College, Hackettstown, N.J.

B. Burlington, Vt., Aug. 20, 1890. *Studied*: Yale Sch. FA; ASL; T. Col., Columbia Univ., B.S., M.A. *Member*: AWS; NAWA; Conn. Acad. FA; New Haven Paint & Clay Cl.; Martha's Vineyard AA; CAA. *Awards*: prizes, Pen & Brush Cl., 1943, 1944. *Exhibited*: PAFA, 1930; Arch. Lg., 1913; AWS, 1916-1955; Audubon A., 1951-1953; NAWA, 1952-1955; Pen & Brush Cl., 1951-1955; Martha's Vineyard AA, 1940-1955; one-man: Argent Gal., 1954. *Position*: Supv. A., Richardson Park Sch., Wilmington, Del., 1940-44; Sec., Martha's Vineyard AA, 1940- ; Prof. A., Hd. A. Dept., Centenary Jr. Col., Hackettstown, N.J., 1944- .*

GORDIN, SIDNEY—*Sculptor*

108 Fourth Ave., New York 3, N.Y.

B. Cheliabinsk, Russia, Oct. 24, 1918. *Studied*: CUASch. *Member*: Fed. Mod. P. & S.; Am. Abstract A.; S. Gld. *Awards*: prizes, MModA, 1954 (playground sculpture); Bloomingdale Exh., 1955. *Work*: WMAA; AIC. *Exhibited*: WMAA, 1952-1955; MMA, 1951; AIC, 1954; Nebraska AI; one-man: Bennington Col., 1951; Peter Cooper Gal., 1951; Borgenicht Gal., 1953, 1955. *Position*: Instr., Des., Pratt Inst., Brooklyn, N.Y., 1955.*

GORDON, ELISABETH (CHANDLER)—*Sculptor*

15 Gramercy Park, New York 3, N.Y.; h. Mitchell Road, Hadlyme, Conn.

B. St. Louis, Mo., June 10, 1913. *Studied*: The Lenox Sch.; sculpture with Walter Russell, Edmondo Quattrocchi. *Member*: NSS; Pen & Brush Cl.; All. A. Am.; NAC; Catherine Lorillard Wolfe A. Cl.; Old Lyme AA; AAPL. *Awards*: prizes, Brooklyn War Mem. Comp., 1945; Catherine L. Wolfe A. Cl., 1951, 1958; Pen & Brush Cl., 1954; Proctor prize, NAD, 1956; gold medal, Hudson Valley AA, 1956; Medal of Honor, Pen & Brush Cl., 1957. *Work*: The Lenox Sch., N.Y.; Aircraft Carrier "U.S.S. Forrestal"; James L. Collins Parochial Sch., Texas; Woodstock Cemetery; Kensico Cemetery, N.Y.; James Forrestal Research Center, Princeton Univ., and in private collections. "Barkers for Britain" medal, 1941; Forrestal Mem. Medal, 1954; Timoshenko Medal for Applied Mechanics, 1957, etc. *Exhibited*: NAD, 1950-1952, 1956, 1957; NSS, 1953-1957; All. A. Am., 1952-1957; Pen & Brush Cl., 1950-1958; AAPL, 1950, 1951, 1953, 1954, 1957; NAC, 1948-1958; Catherine L. Wolfe A. Cl., 1951, 1954-1958; Hudson Valley AA, 1956; Old Lyme AA, 1956-1958; Mattituck Mus., Waterbury, Conn., 1953.

GORDON, JOHN—*Museum Curator*

The Brooklyn Museum, Eastern Parkway (38); h. 32 Remsen St., Brooklyn 1, N.Y.

B. Brooklyn, N.Y., Jan. 20, 1912. *Studied*: Dartmouth Col., A.B. *Member*: Adv. Bd., Village A. Center; Adv. Bd., New York City Center Gal. Contributor to Art in America; Brooklyn Museum Bulletin. Arranged exhs.: International Watercolor Exhibition, 1953, 1955, 1957; 14 Painter-Printmakers, 1955; Face of America, 1957. *Positions*: Asst. Dept. Circulating Exhibitions, MModA, 1944-46; Sec., 1946-52; Cur., Paintings and Sculpture, 1952- , The Brooklyn Museum of Art, Brooklyn, N.Y.

GORDON, MAXWELL—*Painter*

200 East 26th St., New York 10, N.Y.

B. Chicago, Ill., Sept. 4, 1910. *Studied*: Cleveland Sch.

A.; John Huntington Polytechnic Inst., Cleveland. *Member*: AEA; Audubon A. *Awards*: prizes, Butler AI, 1947; Springfield (Ill.) Mus. A., 1947, 1949; medal, Audubon A., 1954; CGA, 1947; CMA, 1931. *Work*: Brandeis Univ.; Ein Harod, Israel. *Exhibited*: PAFA; CMA; BM; MModA; Colorado Springs FA Center; BMA; SAM; Butler AI; Pepsi-Cola; CGA; WMAA; Univ. Illinois; Audubon A.; one-man: Pinacotheca Gal., 1943-44; ACA Gal., 1948-1950, 1953, 1959.

GORE, SAMUEL M.—*Educator*

Art Department, Mississippi College, Clinton, Miss. *Position*: Chm., Art Dept., Mississippi College.*

GORES, WALTER W. J.—*Designer, C., W., L., E.*

College of Architecture & Design, University of Michigan; h. 715 South Forest Ave., Ann Arbor, Mich.

B. Los Angeles, Cal., Jan. 23, 1894. *Studied*: Stanford Univ., A.B., M.A.; Ecole du Louvre; Univ. Paris; & with Henry Varnum Poor, Louis Hourticq, Francois Benoit, and others. *Member*: CAA; Ann Arbor AA. *Awards*: Am. Field Service F., to French Univ., 1921-24; prize, Ann Arbor AA, 1945, 1946 (ceramics). *Work*: mural, Am. Univ. in Europe, Paris, France. *Exhibited*: Ann Arbor AA, 1930, 1940-1946; Michigan A. & Craftsmen's Exh., 1946. *Author*: "Manual of the Visual Arts," 1940. Lectures: Function in Art; 20th Century Ceramics. *Position*: Prof. Des., Chm. Des., Col. Arch. & Des., Univ. of Michigan, 1929- ; Exec. Com., Univ. Council, etc., Univ. of Michigan, Ann Arbor, Mich.*

GORIANSKY, LEV VLADIMIR—*Painter, Des., T., W.*

148 Main St., Andover, Mass.

B. Russia, Feb. 11, 1897. *Studied*: MIT, B.S., M.Arch.; Harvard Univ., M.A., and with Carlu, Denman Ross. *Member*: Hon. F., Andrha Research Univ., India. *Awards*: prizes, med., MIT, 1923, 1925; La Merite Francais, Paris, 1938; Cross of Academic Honor, Int. Academic Council, Wash., D.C., 1939. *Work*: BMFA; FMA; Farnsworth Mus.; WMA; War Mem. Church, Seattle, Wash. *Exhibited*: Wellesley Col., 1937-1946; Soc. Indp. A.; Gloucester Soc. A., 1937-1940; Milch Gal.; Contemporary A. Gal.; AGAA; MIT; AEA; Inst. Mod. A., Boston; Silvermine Gld. A.; Bar Harbor, Me.; Stewart Gal., Boston, 1947 (one-man); Portland Mus. A., 1955.

GORMAN, WILLIAM D.—*Painter, I.*

752 Hudson Blvd., Bayonne, N.J.

B. Jersey City, N.J., June 27, 1925. *Studied*: Newark Sch. F. & Indst. A. *Member*: P. & S. Soc. of New Jersey (2nd Vice-Pres.); Am. Veterans Soc. A.; New Jersey WC Soc. (Pres.); Essex WC Cl.; Hudson Valley AA (Co-Fndr.); Group 13; Jersey City Mus. Assn. (Trustee). *Awards*: prizes, Audubon A., 1957; Knickerbocker A., 1957, 1959; P. & S. Soc., 1955, 1957; Ford Motor Comp., 1956; Jersey City Mus., 1956; N.J. Art Council State Exh., 1954; N.J. WC Soc., 1956-1958; Hudson Valley AA, 1953, 1954, 1956, 1958; Essex WC Cl., 1956-1958; Rahway (N.J.) State Exh., 1954. *Exhibited*: Audubon A., 1957, 1958; AWS, 1956, 1957; P. & S. Soc. of New Jersey, 1955-1958; All. A. Am., 1957; Knickerbocker A., 1956-1958; Am. Veterans Soc. A., 1956, 1957; Soc. Painters in Casein, 1957; Newark Mus., 1955-1958; Montclair A. Mus., 1955-1957; Jersey City Mus., 1956; N.J. WC Soc., 1955-1958; Art Council of New Jersey, 1953-1955; Bamberger Annual, 1957, 1958; A. Center of the Oranges, 1955-1957; Rabin & Krueger Gal., Newark, 1957 (2-man); Hudson Valley AA, 1953-1958; Contemp. A. Gal., 1953, 1956, 1957; Seton Hall Univ., 1954; Paterson State T. Col., 1956; Upsala Col., 1953. Contributor to N.Y. Times; Harpers Magazine; The Reporter; Westpark Publications.

GORSLINE, DOUGLAS WARNER—*Painter, I., Gr., T.*

Western Highway, Blauvelt, N.Y.

B. Rochester, N.Y., May 24, 1913. *Studied*: Yale Sch. FA; ASL. *Member*: ANA; SAE. *Awards*: prizes, PAFA, 1942; Lib.Cong., 1942, 1946; NAD, 1942, 1944. *Work*: Lib. Cong.; Univ. Rochester; New Britain Mus.; Hamilton Col. *Exhibited*: Carnegie Inst.; PAFA; CGA; AIC; WMAA; NAD. Illus., "Look Homeward, Angel"; "Compleat Angler"; "Little Men"; Author, I., "Farm Boy"; "What People Wore" (a history of costume).*

GOSS, JOHN—Illustrator, P., Lith., T.

44 Plimpton St., Walpole, Mass.

B. Lewiston, Me., Sept. 19, 1886. *Studied*: R.I.Sch. Des.; Eric Pape Sch. A. *Member*: AWS; Audubon A.; Copley Soc., Boston; Providence A. Cl. *Work*: J.B.Speed Mus. A.; Beal Collection, exh. at Carnegie Inst., 1957. *Exhibited*: Maine Mus. A., Wiscassett, Me. Illus. "English is Our Language," 1950. Contributed illus. to "America, Land of Freedom," 1952; Illus. to "Reading Roundup," Book I, 1954, II, 1955; "Speaking Spanish," 1955. *Position*: Instr., R.I.Sch. Des., Providence, R.I., 1929-51.

GOTH, MARIE—Portrait Painter

State Rd. 135, Nashville, Ind.; h. 2055 Ruckle St., Indianapolis 2, Ind.

B. Indianapolis, Ind. *Studied*: ASL, with DuMond, Chase, Mora. *Member*: Brown County A. Gld.; Indiana AC; Hoosier Salon. *Awards*: prizes, NAD, 1931; Hoosier Salon, 1926-1929, 1932, 1934-1942, 1945, 1946, 1948, 1949, 1951, 1952, 1957, 1958; Brown County A. Gal., 1933; Indiana AC, 1935, 1939, 1944, 1945, 1956; Evansville (Ind.) Mus. A. & Hist., 1939. *Work*: Hanover Col.; Franklin Col.; Purdue Univ.; Indiana Univ.; Butler Col.; port., James A. Allison Pub. Sch., all in Indiana; John Herron AI; Fla. State Univ., Tallahassee; John Howard Mitchell House, Kent, England; Honeywell Mem. Community Center, Wabash, Ind.; port. former Gov. Schricker, lobby of Service Area, No. Indiana Toll Road; Miami Univ., Oxford, Ohio. *Exhibited*: Cincinnati A.Cl.; Hoosier Salon; Indiana A. Cl.; Brown County A. Gld.; Swope Mem. A. Mus.

GOTTLIEB, ADOLPH—Painter

27 West 96th St., New York 25, N.Y.

B. New York, N.Y., Mar. 14, 1903. *Studied*: ASL; and in Paris, France, Berlin, Germany. *Member*: CAA; NSMP. *Awards*: Dudensing Comp., 1929; U.S. Treasury Comp., 1939; prize, Brooklyn Soc. A., 1944. *Work*: WMAA; MModA; Univ. Nebraska; AGAA; Tel-Aviv Mus.; BM; Butler AI; Detroit Inst. A.; Soc. Four A.; San Jose Pub. Lib.; Ball State T. Col.; PC; Univ. Illinois; Guggenheim Fnd.; Delgado Mus. A.; Smith Col.; Univ. Miami; MMA; Yale Univ.; Cornell Univ.; murals, USPO, Yerrington, Nev.; tapestries, Temple B'nai Israel, Milburn, N.J.; Temple Beth El, Springfield, Mass. *Exhibited*: nationally. Also, London, 1946; Paris, 1947, 1952; Tokyo, 1952, 1955; retrospective exhs., Bennington Col., 1954; Williams Col.; 15 year retrospective exh., Jewish Mus., N.Y., 1957. Contributor articles to College Art Journal; Art in America. Des., stained glass facade, Milton Steinberg house, N.Y. *Position*: Instr., Abstract Painting, Pratt Inst., Brooklyn, N.Y.

GOTTLIEB, HARRY—Painter, Ser.

176 West 87th St., New York 24, N.Y.

B. Bucharest, Romania, Sept. 25, 1895. *Studied*: Minneapolis Inst. A. *Member*: A.Lg. Am.; An Am. Group; AEA (Nat. Bd.). *Awards*: Guggenheim F., 1932-1933; prize, NAD, 1935; med. PAFA, 1934; Phila. WC Cl., 1942. *Work*: WMAA; Berkshire Mus.; Univ. Nebraska; Univ. Arizona; Univ. Georgia MMA; BM; Newark Mus.; Springfield (Mass.) Mus. A. *Exhibited*: Carnegie Inst.; CGA; PAFA; WMAA; & other national exh.; Retrospective exh. of 35 years, ACA Gal., 1956. Lectures: Art & Education, etc.

GOULD, MRS. ALLAN. See Dinneen, Alice

GOULD, MRS. IRVING. See Kappel, R. Rose

GOULET, LORRIE (Mrs. Lorrie deCreeft)— Sculptor, P.

171 Sullivan St., New York, N.Y.

B. Riverdale, N.Y., Aug., 17, 1925. *Studied*: Inwood Studios; Black Mountain Col., and with Jose deCreeft, Josef Albers. *Member*: AEA; Audubon A.; S. Center; S. Gld. *Awards*: Norton Gal. A., 1950, 1951; Soc. Four A., 1950. *Work*: ceramic relief for grand concourse, N.Y. Pub. Lib., 1958. *Exhibited*: PAFA, 1949-1952, 1953, 1954; WMAA, 1949-1951, 1953-1955; Fairmount Park, Phila., 1950; Audubon A., 1950-1952; Riverside Mus., 1950; Phila. A. All., 1950; Palm Beach A. Lg., 1949-1951; Soc. Four

A., 1949-1951; S. Center, 1948-1952; one-man: Clay Cl., 1948; Sculpture Center, N.Y., 1955. *Position*: Instr., MModA, and Scarsdale (N.Y.) Studio Workshop.

GOVAN, FRANCIS HAWKS (FRANK)— Educator, P., C., Des., L.

Marianna, Ark.

B. Marianna, Ark., Dec. 19, 1916. *Studied*: Hendrix Col., B.A. in Humanities; Art Inst. of the South, Memphis; Univ. Wisconsin; Layton Sch. A.; Columbia Univ., M.A., and in Mexico. *Member*: Southeastern AA; Com. on A. Edu., MModA. *Awards*: Carnegie Research grant, 1950. *Exhibited*: Wisconsin Salon, 1940-1942; Wisconsin Des-Craftsmen, 1943, 1944; SSAL, 1945; Memphis Biennial, 1946; Arkansas annual, 1944-1953; Am. Watercolor Exh. circulated in France, 1953-1955; one-man: Mus. FA. Little Rock, 1944; Univ. Arkansas, 1944; Little Rock Pub. Lib., 1952; Serigraph Gal., N.Y., 1953; Feigl Gal., 1954-1955, 1956; Kunst uit Amerika, 1957-58; retrospective exh., Brooks Mem. A. Gal., 1957. *Position*: Instr., Witte Voc. Sch., Wisconsin Rapids, Wis., 1941-43; Milwaukee Univ., Creative Writing, co-ord. Publ. Performances, 1943-45; Asst. Prof. A., Hendrix Col., 1945-52; Occupational Therapy Instr., Rockland State Hospital, Orangeburg, N.Y., 1952-54; Edu. Dir., Brooks Mem. A. Gal., Memphis, Tenn., 1955-56; Asst. Prof. A., Memphis State University, Memphis, Tenn., 1956- .

GOWANS, ALAN—Educator, W.

Art Department, University of Delaware; h. 37 East Park Place, Newark, Del.

B. Toronto, Ont., Canada, Nov. 30, 1923. *Studied*: Univ. Toronto, B.A., M.A.; Princeton Univ., M.F.A., Ph.D. *Member*: Soc. Arch. Hist. (Dir., 1957-); CAA. Author: "Church Architecture in New France," 1955; "Looking at Architecture in Canada," 1958. Contributor articles to The Art Bulletin; College Art Journal; Journal of the Soc. of Arch. Historians; Journal of Architectural Education, etc. *Positions*: Dir., Fleming Mus. A., Univ. Vermont, 1954-56; Chm. Dept. Art, University of Delaware and Prof. A. History in the Winterthur Program, 1956- .

GOYA-LUKICH, JORGE—Painter, Lith.

56 Third Ave., New York 3, N.Y.

B. Linndale, Ohio, Jan. 15, 1924. *Studied*: Western Reserve Univ.; Univ. Michigan; Cal. Sch. FA.; San Francisco State Col., B.A.; Univ. Oregon, M.F.A., and with Clyfford Still, Mark Rothko, S. W. Hayter. *Awards*: prize, SFMA, 1951. *Exhibited*: BM, 1948, 1950, 1951; Cal. PLH; 1950; M. H. de Young Mem. Mus., 1950; SFMA, 1948, 1950-1952; Oakland Mus. A., 1948, 1951; Univ. Washington, 1951; Univ. Oregon, 1952; Portland A. Mus., 1951; Camino Gal., N.Y., 1957, 1958; Columbia Univ., 1958. Contributor to Reviewer; Arts magazine. *Positions*: Instr., A., Univ. Oregon, 1952-53; Tech. Adv., Blackburn Litho Workshop, N.Y., 1955; Graphics, Rattner Sch. A., N.Y., 1955; Instr. Mathematics, Staten Island Acad. A. & Sc., 1956-57, Fieldston Sch., N.Y., 1958-59.

GRABACH, JOHN R.—Painter, S.

915 Sanford Ave., Irvington 11, N.J.

B. Greenfield, Mass. *Studied*: ASL. *Member*: Knickerbocker A.; SC; Audubon A.; Phila. WC Cl.; Irvington A. & Mus. Assn. *Awards*: prizes, AIC; Los A. Mus. A.; gold medal, PAFA; William Clark prize & medal, IBM; prize & medal, Audubon A.; medal, Knickerbocker A. *Work*: AIC; Vanderpoel Coll.; John Herron AI; IBM; Biro Bidjan Mus.; Phila. A. All.; Norton Gal. A.; CGA. *Exhibited*: CGA; AIC; Montclair A. Mus.; PAFA; Audubon A; Knickerbocker A. Author: "How to Draw the Human Figure." *Position*: Instr. A., Newark Sch. F. & Indst. A., Newark, N.J.; Dir., Irvington A. & Mus. Assn.

GRAFLY, DOROTHY (Mrs. Charles Hawkins Drummond)—Writer, Cr., L.

131 North 20th St., Philadelphia 3, Pa.

B. Paris, France, July 29, 1896. *Studied*: Wellesley Col., B.A.; grad. work, Radcliffe Col. *Member*: Phila. A. All.; Phila. WC Cl. (hon.); F., PAFA (hon.); Int. A. Cr. Assn.; Charter memb., Phila. Altrusa Cl. Has contributed to Magazine of Art, Art News, American Artist, Design

Magazine, Camera, and other leading publications. Lectures on contemporary American painting, prints, sculpture. *Positions*: W., Cr., Phila. North American, 1920-25; A. Cr., Public Ledger, 1925-34; Phila. Record, 1934-42; Dir. A. & Research, Philip Ragan Assoc., 1942-46; Corr., Art Digest, 1949-53; Corr., Christian Science Monitor, 1920- ; Cur., Coll., Drexel Inst., 1934-45; Contributing Ed., American Artist, 1946-56; L., Temple Univ., 1938-39; Drexel Inst., 1940-42; Ed. Publ., Art in Focus, The Evening and Sunday Bulletin, Phila., Pa., 1956- .

GRAHAM, BILL (WILLIAM KARR)—Cartoonist
Arkansas Gazette; h. 5208 West 24th St., Little Rock, Ark.

B. Coshocton, Ohio, Dec. 14, 1920. *Studied*: Centenary Col., B.S. *Member*: Nat. Cartoonists Soc.; Assn. of Am. Editorial Cartoonists. *Work*: murals, Camp Beauregard, La. *Exhibited*: Nat. Cartoonists Soc. traveling exh. in conjunction with U.S. Treasury Dept., 1950; MMA, 1951; Liverpool, England, Press Cl. exh., 1951. *Position*: Ed. Cart., Arkansas Gazette, 1948- .

GRAHAM, JOHN MEREDITH, II—
Director and Curator of Collections
Colonial Williamsburg, Inc.; h. Duke of Gloucester St., Williamsburg, Va.

B. Mount Berry, Ga., Dec. 23, 1904. *Studied*: Lehigh Univ.; & abroad. Contributor to: Antiques, American Collector magazines. Lectures: American Decoration & Architecture; American glass, silver, pewter. *Position*: Cur., American Decorative Arts, BM, Brooklyn, N.Y., 1938-50; Director and Cur. Coll., Colonial Williamsburg, Williamsburg, Va. 1950- .

GRAHAM, MRS. JOHN R. See Ray, Ruth

GRAHAM, LAURA MARGARET—Painter
10 Washington Sq., North, New York 3, N.Y.

B. Washington, Ind., May 29, 1912. *Studied*: ASL; Traphagen Sch. Des.; & with Bridgman, DuMond, Rittenberg, Schaeffer. *Member*: All. A. Am.; NAWA; AAPL; PBC; NAC; Boston AC; Conn. Acad. FA. *Awards*: prizes, Studio Cl., 1932, 1935, 1937, 1938; NAC, 1939, 1940, 1942; All.A.Am., 1943, 1948; Terry AI, 1952. *Exhibited*: NAD, 1932, 1944; PAFA, 1943; WFNY 1939; John Herron AI; Montclair A. Mus.; Conn. Acad. FA; Ogunquit A. Center; Boston AC; N.Y.Hist.Soc.; PBC; All.A.Am., annually; Terry AI, 1952; Newport AA, 1947-1948; New Britain A. Mus., 1953, 1955; Manchester (Vt.) A. Mus., traveling exhs. to South & Midwest; Catherine L. Wolfe A. Cl., 1954; AAPL annually; exhs. annually with NAWA, Pen & Brush Cl.; NAC, Boston A. Cl., and others.

GRAMATKY, HARDIE—Illustrator, P., W.
Roseville Rd., Westport, Conn.

B. Dallas, Tex., April 12, 1907. *Studied*: Stanford Univ.; Chouinard AI, and with Clarence Hinkle, Pruett Carter, F. Tolles Chamberlin, Barse Miller. *Member*: NA; SI; SC; Audubon A.; AWS; Cal. WC Soc. *Awards*: prizes, AIC, 1942; AWS, 1942, 1952; Cal. WC Soc., 1943; Los A. Mus. A., 1931, 1934; Cal. State Fair, 1933; Audubon A., 1945, 1952; SC, 1952. *Work*: AIC; Toledo Mus. A.; BM. *Exhibited*: AIC, WMAA, 1939-1941; BM, 1938-1940; Audubon A.; AWS; Cal. WC Soc.; Los A. Mus. A.; SC. Author, I., "Hercules," 1940; "Loopy," 1941; "Little Toot"; "Creeper's Jeep," 1946; "Sparky," 1952. Illus. for True, Today's Woman; Collier's; Woman's Day; American, and other national magazines.*

GRANDY, JULIA SELDEN—Painter
110 South Wickham Rd., Baltimore 29, Md.

B. Norfolk, Va., Apr. 3, 1903. *Studied*: Grand Central A. Sch., with Edmund Greacen, Leonard Bahr. *Member*: Lg. Am. Pen Women; Norfolk A. Corner. *Awards*: prize, BMA, 1942. *Exhibited*: Norfolk Mus. A. & Sc., 1940 (oneman); Norfolk A. Corner; BMA, 1939-1945; VMFA, 1944.

GRANOWITTER, JULES—
Illustrator, P., Des., Cart., Comm. A.
115 West 11th St., New York, N.Y.

B. Brooklyn, N.Y., Dec. 28, 1930. *Studied*: Sch. Indst. A.; CUASch.; ASL, with John Ferren, Marsicano, Kantor.

Member: Cooper Union Alumni Assn. *Exhibited*: Peter Cooper Gal., 1954, 1955. Illus. for N.Y. Times; N.Y. Post; Herald Tribune; Motor America. *Position*: A. Dir., Dobbs Co. (3 years); A. Dir., Friend Reiss Adv. Agcy., at present.*

GRANT, EDWARD LYNAM—Designer, P., T.
319 Springhill Ave., Hillcrest, Wilmington, Del.

B. Wilmington, Del., Jan. 13, 1907. *Studied*: PMSchIA; Wilmington Acad. A. *Awards*: prize, Delaware A. Center, 1950. *Work*: Delaware A. Center; murals, Emerson Hotel, Balt.; Smyrna, Del., Pub. Sch.; Georgetown, Del., Pub. Sch. *Exhibited*: Delaware A. Center, 1940-1952; Wilmington Soc. FA, 1936, 1937, 1939, 1940; Univ. Delaware, 1951 (one-man); Delaware State Mus., 1952 (one-man). *Position*: Mngr., Advertising Services, Hercules Powder Co., Wilmington, Del., 1942- ; Instr., Delaware A. Center, 1942-51; Memb. Bd. Dir., Wilmington Soc. FA, 1954.

GRANT, GORDON (HOPE)—Painter, Et., Lith.
137 East 66th St., New York 21, N.Y.

B. San Francisco, Cal., June 7, 1875. *Studied*: Lambeth & Heatherley A. Sch., London, England. *Member*: NA; All.A.Am.; SAE; Chicago SE; AWCS; Phila. WC Cl.; Cal. Pr.M.; SC. *Awards*: prizes, SC, 1929, 1931; AWCS, 1933; NAD, 1926; All.A.Am., 1942; Chicago SE, 1935; LC; med., Paris Salon, 1937. *Work*: MMA; N.Y. Pub. Lib.; Joslyn Mem.; Richmond (Ind.) Mus. A.; Brooks Mem. A. Gal.; Davenport (Iowa) Mus. A.; New Britain Mus. A.; Lib. Cong.; Annapolis Naval Acad.; White House, Wash., D.C.; mural, USPO, Kennebunkport, Me. *Exhibited*: Lib. Cong., 1944-1946; NAD; AIC, 1927, 1933; AWCS; All. A. Am. Author, I., "Ships Under Sail," 1941. "The Secret Voyage," 1943; & other marine stories.

GRANT, J. JEFFREY—Painter
333 North Michigan Ave.; h. 3635 West Cermak Rd., Chicago 23, Ill.

B. Aberdeen, Scotland, Apr. 19, 1883. *Studied*: in Aberdeen, Scotland; Munich, Germany. *Member*: Assn. Chicago P.&S.; Palette & Chisel Acad.; Chicago AC; North Shore AA. *Awards*: prizes, AIC, 1922, 1924, 1926, 1927; med., prize, Mun. A. Lg., 1934, 1936; med., Palette & Chisel Acad., 1917, silver medal, 1956, award, 1958; Illinois State Fair, 1956; Galena Fair, 1958. *Work*: Springfield Mus. A.; Mun. A. Lg., Chicago; Lawrence Col.; Concordia Col. *Exhibited*: NAD, 1932-1935, 1943; CGA, 1930, 1932, 1934; PAFA; AIC, 1918, 1919, 1921-1927, 1932, 1936, 1939, 1942; Currier Gal., 1936 (one-man); AIC, 1927, 1935, 1944 (one-man).

GRANT, VERNON—Illustrator, W., Des., L.
145 East 26th St., New York 10, N.Y.; h. Rock Hill, S.C.

B. Coldridge, Neb., Apr. 26, 1902. *Studied*: Univ. Southern California; AIC. *Member*: SI; A.Gld. Author, I., children's books. I., covers for national magazines.

GRASS, MRS. FRANK. See Patterson, Patty

GRASSO, DORIS ELSIE—Painter, C., Des., Et., I., T.
88 West 32nd St., Bayonne, N.J.

B. Sullivan County, N.Y., May 3, 1914. *Studied*: Edu. All. A. Sch., with Moses Soyer, Alexander Dobkin; Newark A. Center; North Bergen A. Sch., with Fabian Zaccone. *Member*: AAPL; Hudson Valley AA; Essex WC Cl.; Mt. Vernon AA; Sarasota AA; Edu. All.; Jersey City Mus. Assn. *Awards*: prizes, Knickerbocker A., 1958; Jersey City Mus., 1957; Talens & Son award, 1956; Hudson Valley AA, 1956; State Fed. Women's Cl., 1957. *Exhibited*: AAPL, 1954-1958; Burr Gal., N.Y., 1956-1958; Knickerbocker A., 1958; P. & S. Soc. of New Jersey, 1956, 1958; Terry AI, 1952; New Jersey WC Soc., 1957; Seton Hall Univ., 1955-1957; Newark Mus. A., 1958; Montclair A. Mus., 1956; Old Mill Gal., 1955-1958; Papermill Playhouse, 1958; Edu. All., 1958; Monmouth A. Fnd., 1958; Newark Pub. Lib., 1956-1958; Jersey City Mus., 1955-1958; A. Center of the Oranges, 1955-1958; Bambergers, 1956-1959; Hunterdon A. Center, 1956-1958; Newark A. Cl., 1950-1956; Fed. Women's Cl., 1957; Upsala Col., 1957; Rutgers Univ., 1953-1956; NAC, 1954-1958, and others; one-man: Burr Gal., N.Y., 1959. *Position*: Trustee, Jersey City Mus.; Cor. Sec., Pub. Rel., Essex County WC Cl.; Treas. N.J. Chaptr., AAPL, etc.

GRATHWOL, RAY ANTHONY—*Painter*

1342 Forest Glen Dr., Cuyahoga Falls, Ohio

B. Sandusky, Ohio, July 17, 1900. *Awards*: prizes, Akron, AI, 1940, 1941, 1944, 1945, 1948, 1953, 1955, 1956; Canton AI, 1945, 1950; Parkersburg FA Center, 1945; Cuyahoga Falls A. Center, 1957. *Work*: Massillon Mus.; Ohio Univ.; Canton AI; West H.S.; Youngstown Pub. Sch.; Akron AI; Pomroy (Ohio) H.S. *Exhibited*: WFNY 1939; Carnegie Inst., 1941, 1943, 1944; Pepsi-Cola, 1946; Springville, Utah, 1941, 1946; Milwaukee, Wis., 1946; Butler AI, 1937-1953.

GRAUBARD, ANN WOLFE. See *Wolfe, Ann*

GRAUBART, Z. PETER—*Educator*

Manchester Institute of Arts & Sciences, 148 Concord St., Manchester, N.H.

Position: Exec. Dir., Manchester Institute of Arts & Sciences.*

GRAUEL, ANTON C.—*Sculptor*

1110 Eaton Ave., Beloit, Wis.

B. Bad Soden/Salmuenster, Germany, Jan. 25, 1897. *Studied*: in Germany, Paris, Switzerland and Italy. *Awards*: prizes, Berlin and Frankfurt, Germany. *Work*: National Gal., Berlin; Prussian Acad. FA, Berlin; monuments in churches and schools, U.S.A. and Germany. *Exhibited*: NSS; Univ. Illinois; AIC; one-man: Milwaukee A. Center, 1951; Beloit Col., 1952; Rockford AA, 1952; Univ. Wisconsin, 1953; Carl Schurz Mem. Fnd., Phila., Pa., 1954, and in Germany.

GRAUER, WILLIAM C.—*Painter, Et.*

Western Reserve University, Cleveland, Ohio; s. East Claridon, Ohio

B. Philadelphia, Pa., Dec. 2, 1895. *Studied*: PMSchIA. *Awards*: prizes, CMA, 1953, 1955. *Work*: murals, Kansas City (Mo.) City Cl.; Cadillac Lounge, Cleveland, Ohio; Virginia Room, President's Cottage, White Sulphur Springs, W. Va.; Fed. States Bldg., Century Progress, Chicago; Laird Mem. Coll., Montgomery, W. Va.; CMA; Springfield Mus. A.; Norton Gal. A., West Palm Beach; Melbourne, Australia. *Exhibited*: PAFA; CMA; WMAA; WFNY 1939; VMFA; CAM; Rochester Mem. A. Gal.; Syracuse Mus. FA. *Position*: Assoc. Prof. A., Western Reserve Univ., Cleveland, Ohio, 1948- .

GRAVES, MAITLAND—*Painter, T., W.*

25 Tudor City Pl., New York 17, N.Y.

B. New York, N.Y., June 27, 1902. *Studied*: ASL; Grand Central A. Sch.; Brooklyn Polytechnic Inst. *Awards*: prizes, NAC, 1930, 1932, 1935, 1936; European traveling scholarship, 1936. *Work*: NAC. *Exhibited*: NAD, 1928; NAC, 1930, 1932, 1935; Newark Mus., 1934; All. A.Am., 1934, 1935; Arch. L., 1936. Author: "The Art of Color & Design," 1941, second ed., 1951; "Color Fundamentals," 1952; "Design Judgment," 1948. Contributor to: national magazines. Lectures: Color & Design. *Position*: Assoc. Prof., Painting, Color, Des., PIASch., Brooklyn, N.Y.

GRAVES, MORRIS—*Painter*

c/o Willard Gallery, 23 West 56th St., New York, N.Y.

B. Fox Valley, Ore., 1910. *Member*: Nat. Inst. A. & Lets. *Awards*: prizes, SAM, 1933; AIC, 1948; Univ. Illinois, 1955; medal, AIC, 1947; Guggenheim F., 1946; grant, Nat. Inst. A. & Lets., 1956; Windsor award, 1957. *Work*: SAM; MModA; PC; Albright A. Gal.; WMAA; Pasadena AI; CMA; Milwaukee AI; Nat. Inst. A. & Let.; Detroit Inst. A.; A. Gal. Toronto; CAM; AIC; Ft. Wayne A. Sch.; MMA; Univ. Illinois; Wadsworth Atheneum; WMA; Wilmington AA; BMA. *Exhibited*: USIS "8 American Artists," Korea, Japan, Australia and Europe, 1957; Brussels World's Fair, 1958; one-man: SAM, 1936; MMoaA, 1942; Willard Gal., 1942, 1944, 1945, 1948, 1953, 1954; Chicago A. Cl., 1943; Univ. Minnesota, 1943; Detroit Inst. A., 1943; PC, 1943, 1954; Phila. A. All., 1946; Cal. PLH, 1948; Santa Barbara Mus. A., 1948; Los A. Mus. A. 1948; AIC, 1948; Beaumont A. Mus., 1952; Oslo, Norway, 1955; retrospective, 1956, WMAA and various cities in U.S.; Bridgestone Gal., Tokyo and Kyoto, 1957.

GRAY, CHRISTOPHER—*Educator*

Johns Hopkins University (18); h. 17 Elmwood Rd., Baltimore 10, Md.

B. Milton, Mass., June 22, 1915. *Studied*: Harvard Col., B.S.; Univ. California, Berkeley, M.A.; Harvard Univ., Ph.D. *Member*: CAA; Archaeological Inst. of Am.; Am. Soc. for Aesthetics. Author: "Cubist Aesthetic Theories," 1953. "Cubist Concepts of Reality"; "Marie Laurencin and Her Friends." *Positions*: Instr., 1947-51, Asst. Prof., 1951- , Johns Hopkins University, Baltimore, Md.

GRAY, CLEVE—*Painter, W.*

Cornwall Bridge, Conn.

B. New York, N.Y., Sept. 22, 1918. *Studied*: Phillips Acad.; Princeton Univ., and with Jacques Villon, Andre Lhote. *Work*: MMA; Columbus Mus. FA; AGAA; Univ. Illinois; Univ. Nebraska; Princeton Univ. Mus. FA and others. *Exhibited*: nationally since 1947. Contributor articles to Perspectives (Ford Fnd.); College Art Journal.

GRAY, MARY CHILTON—*Painter, I.*

Colorado Museum of Natural History; h. 1337 South Fillmore St., Denver, Colo.

B. Philadelphia, Pa. *Studied*: John Herron AI. *Member*: Taos AA. *Work*: murals, Denver A. Mus.; Hall of Man. *Exhibited*: NAWA, 1943, 1944; AWCS, 1942; Hoosier Salon, 1931, 1933; one-man exh.; New York, N.Y., 1942; Columbus, Ohio, 1931; Indianapolis, Ind., 1931; Stables Gal., Taos; Turner Gal., Denver. Illus. "Prehistoric Indians of the Southwest," "Ancient Man in North America."*

GRAY, ROBERT W.—*Educator, C.*

Craft Center, 25 Sagamore Rd., Worcester 8, Mass.; h. 7 Carol Dr., Boylston, Mass.

B. Tallahassee, Fla. *Studied*: Univ. Florida; Tri-State Col. (Ind.); Sch. for Am. Craftsmen, Alfred, N.Y. *Exhibited*: WMA; Eastern States Fair; Mass. Assn. Handicraft Groups. *Position*: Coordinator, Craft Program, Old Sturbridge Village, 1951; Memb., Old Sturbridge Village Bd. of Managers, 1951; Memb., Mass. Statewide Advisory Com. on Crafts, 1953-54; Sec., New England Craft Council, 1953-55, Chm., 1957-58; Memb. Adv. Bd., of "Cross-Country Craftsmen"; Co-Dir., New England Craft Exh., 1955; Dir., Worcester Craft Center, Worcester, Mass., 1951- ; New England Rep. to "First National Craftsmen's Conference," Asilomar, Cal., 1957; Coordinator, Nat. Adv. Bd., Am. Craftsmen's Council Conf., Lake Geneva, Wis., 1958; juror for many craft exhs., in Mass. and other states.

GRAY, VERDELLE (Mrs. Robert W.)—*Craftsman*

Craft Center, 25 Sagamore Rd., Worcester 8, Mass.; h. 7 Carol Dr., Boylston, Mass.

B. Pomona, Cal., Nov. 9, 1918. *Studied*: Univ. California at Santa Barbara; Sch. for Am. Craftsmen, Alfred, N.Y. *Member*: Mass. Assn. of Handicraft Groups. *Exhibited*: Syracuse Mus. FA, 1949; Miami, Fla. ceramic exh., 1954, 1955, 1956; St. Paul Gal. A., 1955; WMA, 1952, 1955; deCordova & Dana Mus., 1953; Fitchburg A. Mus., 1954; George W. V. Smith Mus. A., 1955; Va. Highlands Festival A. & Crafts, 1950; Eastern States Fair, Springfield, 1950; Worcester County Exh., 1950; Am. Craftsmen's Edu. Council, 1950; Inst. Contemp. A., Boston, 1954; Dey Gosse Gal., Providence, R.I., 1955; Boston Festival A., 1956, 1958; Craft Center Instructor's Exh., WMA, 1958; Ceramic exh. for Art Assn. of New England Prep. Schs., 1958. *Position*: Instr., Pottery, Adult Edu., Alfred, N.Y., 1948; Worcester Craft Center, Worcester, Mass., 1951- .

GRAY, WILLIAM J. (BILL)—

Commercial Artist, T., W., Des.

71 Woodside Drive, Red Bank, N.J.

B. Allentown, Pa., Sept. 28, 1913. *Studied*: Pa. State Univ.; ASL, with McNulty, Trafton; N.Y. State Univ. *Member*: AIGA; Screen Process Printing Assn. Author: "Tips on Gag Cartooning," 1954; "Tips on Lettering," 1956. Illus. for Girl Scouts of America; Nat. Publicity Council. Contributor cartoons for Sat. Eve. Post; Redbook; Better Homes & Gardens; King Features Syndicate; Look, and other national magazines. *Position*: Instr. Adv. Des., Newark Sch. F. & Indst. A., Newark, N.J.; Compton Adv. Agcy., 1946-49; Freelance, Lettering & Typographic Design Studio, 1950- .

GRAZIANI, SANTE—*Painter, Des., T.*

Worcester Art Museum, Worcester, Mass.; h. 2 Eastwood Rd., Shrewsbury, Mass.

B. Cleveland, Ohio, March 11, 1920. *Studied*: Cleveland Sch. A.; Yale Univ. Sch. FA, B.F.A. *Member*: NSMP. *Awards*: Pulitzer scholarship, 1942; Edwin Austin Abbey award, 1948; gold med., Arch. Lg., N.Y., 1950; gold medal, Boston A. Dir. Cl., 1954. *Work*: murals, USPO, Bluffton, Ohio; Columbus Junction, Iowa; Holyoke (Mass.) Pub.Lib.; Springfield Mus. FA; Burncoat Sch., Worcester, Mass.; 2 large murals, American Battle Monument in Henri-Chapelle, Belgium, 1955-58. *Exhibited*: MMA, 1942; Carnegie Inst., 1941; NAD, 1942; CMA, 1937-1941; WMA, 1957 (one-man). *Positions*: Officer in Charge, A. & Crafts, Pacific Theatre, 1945-46; Instr., Drawing & Painting, Yale Univ. Sch. FA, 1946-51; Dean, Whitney Sch. A., New Haven, Conn., 1950-51; Hd., Worcester A. Mus. Sch., Worcester, Mass., at present.

GRAZIOTTI, UGO ADRIANO—*Sculptor, P., E., L., W.*

1254 Market St., San Francisco 2, Cal.

B. Brescia, Italy, May 7, 1912. *Studied*: Brescia and Monza, Italy; Royal Acad. FA, Florence and Rome, Italy; Western Reserve Univ., M.A., and in Czechoslovakia. *Member*: Leonardo da Vinci Soc., and Il Cenacolo Cl., San Francisco; Nat. Fed. of A. & Professionists, Italy. *Awards*: Scholarships, Carpenedolo, Italy, 1928-32; Consorzio Provinciale Istruzione Tecnica, Brescia, Italy, 1932-1947; Govt. Scholarship, 1938-39, 1939-40; Ministry Edu., traveling scholarship, 1941-42; financial subsidy, Royal Acad. S., Lets. & A., Italy, 1940-41; Hartford Fnd., 1953-54; Instituto de Allende, Mexico, 1954; John F. and Anna Lee Stacey award, 1958-59, and others; prizes, Florence, Italy, 1937; Acad. St. Luke's, Rome, 1940; Oakland A. Mus., 1955; Sacramento State Fair, 1956. *Work*: CMA; Italian Consulate, Cleveland; Milan, Ohio; many in Italy; and in Argentina. *Exhibited*: Quadriennale d'Arte Nazionale, Rome, 1947; one-man: Cleveland Inst. A., 1948; Taos, N.M., 1951; Ten-Thirty Gal., Cleveland, 1952; Saratoga, Cal., 1954; San Jose, Cal., 1954; deYoung Mem. Mus., 1953, etc. Many group shows in U.S. and Europe. *Positions*: Co-Dir., Il Circolo Artistico Internazionale, Rome, 1945-46; Asst. Prof. A., Royal Acad. FA, Rome, 1945-47; Prof., Institute Beato Angelico, Rome, 1947-48; Prof., Notre Dame Col., Cooper Sch. A. and Cleveland Inst. A., 1949-52; Asst. Prof., Cal. Col. A. & Crafts, Oakland, 1954; Dir., Prof. A., Graziotti Studio FA, San Francisco, 1955- ; Assoc. Prof. A., Univ. San Francisco, 1958- .

GREACEN, JENNIE RUTH. See *Nickerson, Ruth*

GREACEN, NAN (*Mrs. Rene B. Faure*)—*Painter*

Harwood Bldg.; h. 36 Mt. Joy Ave., Scarsdale, N.Y.

B. Giverny, France. *Studied*: Grand Central Sch. A. *Member*: ANA; All. A. Am.; Scarsdale AA; Audubon A.; Hudson Valley AA; Grand Central A. Gal.; Portraits, Inc.; Yonkers AA; Westchester A. & Crafts Gld. *Awards*: prizes, NAD; NAWA; All. A. Am., 1953; medal, NAC; Montclair A. Mus.; Hudson Valley AA; Albers Mem. medal, 1954. *Exhibited*: NAD, 1933-1955; CGA; All. A. Am. *Position*: Instr., port. & still life, privately.

GREASON, DONALD CARLISLE—

Painter, E., Cr., L., Des., Comm. A.

P.O. R.F.D. No. 1, Bernardston, Mass.; h. Greener Pastures, East Colrain, Mass.

B. Brooklyn, N.Y., July 14, 1897. *Studied*: ASL, and in Paris, France. *Member*: AEA; Deerfield Valley AA. *Work*: BMFA; Lawrence A. Mus., Williams Col.; Rollins Col.; AGAA; Amherst Col.; murals, Lovell General Hospital, Fort Devens; Ciba Pharmaceutical Co.; Channing Betz, Inc. *Exhibited*: 46 one-man exhs. in museums and college art galleries. *Positions*: Res. Instr., AGAA, Andover, Mass., 1933; Norfolk (Conn.) A. Sch., Yale Univ., 1951; Res. A., Deerfield Acad., Deerfield, Mass., 1941-46; Prof. A., Rollins Col., Winter Park, Fla., 1946-49.

GREATHOUSE, WALSER S.—*Museum Director*

Frye Museum of Art, 704 Terry Ave., Seattle, Wash.

Position: Dir., Frye Museum of Art.*

GREBANIER, JOSEPH PHILIP—*Craftsman, T.*

1866 East Fourth St., Brooklyn 23, N.Y.

B. Denver, Colo., Feb. 23, 1912. *Studied*: Brooklyn Col., B.A.; N.Y. Univ. Grad. Sch., M.A., and with Paul Holleman. *Member*: Artist-Craftsmen of N.Y. *Exhibited*: Syracuse Mus. FA, 1954, 1956, 1958, and traveling exh.; N.Y. Soc. Ceramic A., 1954, 1955. *Position*: Instr., Midwood H.S., Brooklyn, N.Y.; Exec. Bd., N.Y. Soc. Ceramic A., 1954-55.

GREEN, DAVID (OLIVER) (JR.)—

Sculptor, Des., Gr., E., L.

176 West Jaxine Dr., Altadena, Cal.

B. Enid, Okla., June 29, 1908. *Studied*: Am. Acad. A.; Nat. Acad. Chicago, and with Carl Hoeckner, Charles Wilimovsky. *Member*: Pasadena Soc. A.; AEA. *Awards*: prizes, Los A. Mus. A., 1946; Greek Theatre, Los A., 1948; Pasadena AI, 1950, 1951; Pomona (Cal.) Fair, 1952; Los A. Municipal Exh., 1957. *Work*: Los A. Mus. A.; Pasadena A. Mus.; Shopping Center, San Mateo; Hillel Council Bldg., Univ. So. Cal.; Arcadia Civic Center. *Exhibited*: City of Los A., 1948, 1949; San Gabriel Valley A., 1948, 1950, 1955; Los A. County Fair, 1949, 1951; Pasadena Soc. A., 1950; Cal. State Fair, 1950, 1954; Chaffey Col., 1948, 1949, 1951, 1955; Los Angeles AA, 1948; Pasadena AI, 1950; Beverly-Fairfax Jewish Center, 1951; Ebell Cl., Los A., 1953; San Diego FA Gal., 1950; Santa Barbara Mus. A., 1951; Los A. Mus. A., 1956, 1957; Los A. Municipal A. Exh., 1957. *Position*: Instr., Los Angeles County AI; South Pasadena A. Center.

GREEN, DORINNE TRAULSEN—*Educator, P., Gr., C.*

Walker Junior High School; h. 4700 West Oklahoma Ave., Milwaukee 19, Wis.

B. Milwaukee, Wis., May 12, 1929. *Studied*: Univ. Wisconsin, B.S.; Layton Sch. A.; Wisconsin State Col. *Member*: Milwaukee A. T. Assn. *Work*: Univ. Wisconsin Union. *Exhibited*: Wisconsin Salon; NAD; Wisconsin State Fair; Milwaukee Pr. M. *Position*: Instr., A. & Crafts, Walker Jr. H.S., Milwaukee, Wis.

GREEN, EDWARD ANTHONY—*Painter, Des., Gr., E.*

Milwaukee Public Museum (3); h. 4700 West Oklahoma Ave., Milwaukee 19, Wis.

B. Milwaukee, Wis., Apr. 20, 1922. *Studied*: Univ. Wisconsin, B.S., M.S.; Layton Sch. A. *Member*: Midwest Mus. Conference; Wisconsin P.&S. (Pres.) *Awards*: prizes, Wis. Salon A., 1957 (2). *Exhibited*: Wisconsin Pr. M.; Wisconsin State Fair; Wisconsin P. & S.; Wisconsin WC Soc. One-man: Lawrence Col., 1957; Kenosha Pub. Mus., 1958. *Position*: Staff A., Milwaukee Public Mus.; Instr., Univ. Wisconsin, Milwaukee, Wis., 1956- .

GREEN, GEORGE ALAN—*Designer, Gr., C., P., E.*

Carl Nelson Associates, 525 East Michigan Ave. (3); h. 3826 West National Ave., Milwaukee 15, Wis.

B. Milwaukee, Wis., Mar. 2, 1933. *Studied*: Univ. Wisconsin, B.S., M.S. *Awards*: prizes, Wisconsin State Fair, 1956, 1957. *Exhibited*: Wisconsin P. & S.; Wisconsin Designer-Craftsmen; Wisconsin WC Soc.; Wisconsin State Fair; Wisconsin Pr. M. *Position*: Instr., University of Wisconsin, Milwaukee, Wis., 1958- ; A. Dir., Carl Nelson Assoc., Milwaukee, Wis.

GREEN, HERBERT LEWIS—*Cartoonist*

12 Harold St., Cos Cob, Conn.

B. Kansas City, Kans., Mar. 1, 1927. *Studied*: Kansas City (Kans.) Jr. Col. Assn. A.; Univ. Missouri, B.A. Contributor cartoons to: Time; Sat. Eve. Post; Colliers; Redbook; Look; True; Esquire; American, and many other national magazines with many reprints abroad; King Features Syndicate. Editor, "The Cartoonist," official publ. of Nat. Cartoonists Soc.

GREEN, JAMES LEAHAN—*Painter, T.*

Principia College, Elsah, Ill.

B. Ware, Mass., June 18, 1911. *Studied*: Mass. Sch. A.; Univ. Vermont, with Barse Miller; Otis AI, with Paul

Clemens. *Member*: Cal. WC Soc.; Group 15, St. Louis, Mo. *Awards*: prizes, PAFA, 1944-1946; CAM, 1945, 1950, 1953, 1958; F., PAFA. *Work*: CAM; Palm Beach, Fla. *Exhibited*: Cal. WC Soc., 1937-1941; PAFA, 1939-1946; AIC, 1939-1944; Oakland A. Gal., 1941-1946; CAM, 1941-1946; Dallas, Tex., 1957 (one-man). *Position*: Prof. A., Principia Col., Elsah, Ill., 1941- .

GREEN, MYRA (Mrs. Joshua)—*Painter, L., T.*
156 Glenway St., Jackson, Miss.

B. Fayetteville, Tenn., Nov. 28, 1924. *Studied*: Virginia Intermont Col., and with Karl Wolfe, Mildred Nungester, Marie Hull. *Member*: Mississippi AA; New Orleans AA; Allison's Wells A. Colony. *Exhibited*: Miss. AA; New Orleans AA; Allison's Wells A. Colony; Jackson Junior League exh.

GREEN, RENA (Mrs.)—*Painter*
131 East Ridgewood St., San Antonio, Tex.

B. Sedalia, Mo., Feb. 10, 1874. *Studied*: with Charles Martin, Maurice Sterne. *Member*: Texas A. Group; Texas WC Soc. *Awards*: prize, SSAL, 1940; San Antonio, Tex. *Work*: Witte Mem. Mus., San Antonio, Tex.*

GREEN, ROBERT BERKELEY—*Painter, E.*
University of Kansas; h. 2121 Tennessee St., Lawrence, Kans.

B. Pittsburgh, Pa., July 28, 1909. *Studied*: Carnegie Inst., B.A.; Yale Univ., B.F.A.; Am. Acad. in Rome. *Member*: Mid-Am. A.; F., Am. Acad. in Rome; Prairie WC Soc.; AAUP. *Awards*: prizes, Prix de Rome, 1935-37, 1937-38; Prairie WC Soc., 1946; Topeka A. Gld., 1953-1955; Air Capitol annual, Wichita, 1955; Am. Acad. in Rome. *Work*: Kansas Fed. Women's Cl.; Atchison (Kans.) H.S.; Pa. State Univ.; Baker Univ., Baldwin, Kans. *Exhibited*: Butler AI, 1952; Mid-Am. A.; Kansas Fed. A.; Prairie WC Soc.; A. West of the Mississippi; Missouri Valley Painters; Kansas Painters, 1949-1952; CAM, 1950, 1951; Topeka A. Gld.; Air Capitol Exh.; Omaha, Neb.; Manhattan, Kans.; Mulvane A. Center; Baker Univ. (one-man). *Position*: Asst. Prof., 1946-53, Assoc. Prof., Dept. Painting, 1953- , Univ. Kansas, Lawrence, Kans.*

GREEN, ROSALIE B.—*Historian, E.*
Index of Christian Art, Princeton University; h. 76 Harris Road, Princeton, N.J.

B. Yonkers, N.Y., Aug. 20, 1917. *Studied*: PIASch.; Univ. Chicago, A.B., A.M., Ph.D. *Member*: CAA; Mediaeval Acad.; Société française d'archéologie; AAUW; AAUP. Contributor numerous articles and reviews to art publications. *Positions*: Prof. Hist. A., L., Rutgers University, 1950- ; Book Review Ed., The Art Bulletin, 1955- ; Dir., Index of American Art, Princeton University, 1951- .

GREEN, RUSSELL—*Educator*
Stephens College, Columbia, Mo.

Position: Hd., Art Dept., Stephens College.*

GREEN, SAMUEL M.—*Educator, P.*
256 Meriden Rd., Middletown, Conn.

B. Oconomowac, Wis., May 22, 1909. *Studied*: Harvard Col., B.A.; Harvard Univ., M.A., Ph.D.; PAFA. *Work*: FMA; LC; Smith Col. Mus. A.; Dartmouth Col. *Position*: Prof. & Chm., A. Dept., Wesleyan Univ., Middletown, Conn.

GREENAMYER, LEAH J.—
Painter, C., Des., L., W., T., Et.
Market St. Ext., Box 45, North Lima, Ohio

B. Ashtabula, Ohio. *Studied*: PAFA; Youngstown Col. *Member*: Youngstown A. All.; Gulf Coast AA; Ohio WC Soc.; Fla. East Coast AA; Clearwater AI. *Awards*: prizes, Butler AI, 1939, 1946; Ohioana Lib. Assn., 1956. *Work*: Mahoning County Court House, and in private collections. *Exhibited*: Butler AI; Canfield (Ohio) Fair; Nat. Craft Exh., Phila., Pa., and in many national and regional exhs. Lectures on painting and crafts to civic and church groups.

GREENBAUM, DOROTHEA S.—*Sculptor*
104 Mercer St., Princeton, N.J.

B. New York, N.Y., June 17, 1893. *Member*: S. Gld. (Fndr.); AEA; NAWA; Audubon A. *Awards*: Med., PAFA, 1941; Soc. Wash.A., 1941; prizes, IBM, 1941; Audubon A., 1954; Grant, Am.Acad.A. & Let., 1947; med., NAWA, 1952, 1954. *Work*: WMAA; Lawrence Mus., Williamstown, Mass.; Oberlin Col.; Fitchburg (Mass.) A. Center; Huntington Mus.; Brookgreen Gardens, S.C.; Newark Mus. A.; BMA; Mus. Moscow, Russia; Puerto Rico; Ogunquit Mus. A., and in private colls. *Exhibited*: nationally and internationally; one-man: Weyhe Gal., 1934; SFMA, 1942; Lawrence Mus., Williams Col., 1943; Cal. PLH, 1950; Santa Barbara Mus. A., 1950; Pomona Col., 1950; San Diego FA Center, 1950; Sculpture Center, 1951, 1958.

GREENBERG, CLEMENT—*Writer, Cr., P.*
90 Bank St., New York 14, N.Y.

B. New York, N.Y., Jan. 16, 1909. *Studied*: ASL; Syracuse Univ., A.B. *Member*: Intl. A. Cr. Assn. *Exhibited*: Stable Gal., N.Y., annually. Contributor to: The Nation; Partisan Review; Horizon (England); Art News; Arts; N.Y. Times Book Review. Author: "Joan Miro," 1948; "Matisse," 1953; "Selected Essays," 1959. Gave a Christian Jauss Seminar in Criticism, Princeton University, 1958.

GREENBERG, JOSEPH J., JR.—*Sculptor*
222 South Van Pelt St., Philadelphia 3, Pa.

B. Philadelphia, Pa., Nov. 10, 1915. *Studied*: MIT; Tyler Sch. FA, Temple Univ., B.S. in Edu., B.A. *Member*: Phila. A. All.; AEA. *Awards*: prize, MMA, 1951; gold medal, DaVinci All., 1947. *Work*: PAFA; Temple Univ.; Lehigh Univ.; Lincoln Univ.; Phila. Zoo; Carnegie Endowment for Intl. Peace. *Exhibited*: PAFA, 1942, 1952, 1954; NAD, 1941; MMA, 1951; PMA, 1940, 1949, 1955; Venice Biennale, 1952; Jewish Tercentenary, 1954; Nat. Inst. A. & Let., 1953; one-man: Phila. A. All., 1957; Lehigh Univ., 1957. *Position*: Instr. S., New Hope (Pa.) FA Workshop; PMA, Fleisher Mem.; Pres., Phila. Chaptr., AEA, 1954-56.

GREENBOWE, F(REDERICK) DOUGLAS—*Painter*
Woodburn Rd., R.D. #3, Sussex, N.J.

B. Bayonne, N.J., Sept. 19, 1921. *Studied*: ASL, with Frank DuMond. *Member*: AWS. *Awards*: medal, NAC, 1953. *Work*: Butler AI; Dayton AI; Am. Acad. A. & Let.; SAM; Phoenix Mus. A.; AIC. *Exhibited*: AWS, 1948-1950, 1952, 1954; BM, 1949; PAFA, 1949; Am. Acad. A. & Let., 1950; AIC, 1949; Butler AI, 1948, 1953; Milch Gal., 1947, 1949, 1956.*

GREENBURG, SAMUEL—*Painter, Gr., T., W., L.*
929 West Argyle St., Chicago 40, Ill.

B. Uman, Ukraine, Russia, June 23, 1905. *Studied*: Univ. Chicago, A.B., A.M., and abroad. *Member*: Chicago Soc. A.; Chicago T. Un.; AEA; Renaissance Soc.; Chicago A. Edu. Soc. *Awards*: prize, AIC, 1942; Am. Jewish A. Cl., 1954, 1956; Illinois State Fair, 1956. *Work*: Mus. Mod. A., Tel-Aviv, Palestine; Bezalel Mus., Israel; LC. *Exhibited*: PAFA, 1935; LC, 1943, 1946, 1948; WFNY 1939; NGA, 1943; Carnegie Inst.; 1943; AFA traveling exh., 1943-1945; AIC, 1931, 1933, 1935, 1936, 1940-42, 1946, 1949; Chicago Soc. A., 1936-1952; Riverside Mus., 1939, 1941, 1945, 1951; Illinois State Mus., 1940; one-man: Delphic Studios, 1934; Chicago Women's Aid, 1939; AIC, 1947; Creative Gal., 1951, 1953. Author, I., "Making Linoleum Cuts," 1947; Co-Author: "Arts and Crafts in the Jewish School," 1952. *Positions*: Instr. A., Tuley H.S., Chicago, Ill.; Supv. A., Chicago Bd. of Jewish Edu., 1949-51.

GREENE, BALCOMB—*Painter, E.*
Montauk, L.I., N.Y.

B. Niagara Falls, N.Y., May 22, 1904. *Studied*: Syracuse Univ.; Univ. Vienna; Columbia Univ.; N.Y. Univ., A.B., M.A. *Member*: CAA; Fed. Mod. P. & S.; Am. Abstract A.; Assoc. A. Pittsburgh; Am. Soc. Aesthetics. *Work*: MMoDA; WMAA; Walker A. Center; MMA; Carnegie Inst.; Univ. Nebraska; Mus. Non-Objective Painting. *Exhibited*: WMAA; MMoDA; PAFA; Carnegie Inst.; SFMA; Bertha Schaefer Gal.; Palace Legion Honor; AIC; Am. Abstract A.; South America; France; Germany; Italy. Ed., "American Abstract Artists Annual," 1938. Contributor to College Art Journal; Art News. *Position*: Prof., History of Art, Carnegie Inst. of Technology, Pittsburgh, Pa.*

GREENE, ELMER WESTLEY—*Painter*
Hotel des Artistes, 1 West 67th St., New York, N.Y.; h. Nantucket, Mass.

B. Boston, Mass., July 24, 1907. *Studied*: Mass. Sch. A., B.S. in Edu.; BMFA Sch. *Member*: Gld. Boston A. *Awards*: medal & prize, Jordan Marsh Gal., 1932, 1933, 1935, 1936, 1939, 1946. *Work*: murals, Bridgewater Normal Sch.; Mass. State Col.; Sch. Practical Arts, Boston; State T. Col., Framingham, Mass.; Univ. Chicago; Maryland Casualty Co., Baltimore; U.S. Fidelity & Guaranty Co., Baltimore; Marine Ins. Co.; Algoma Steel Co.; United Shoe Machine Co.; Northwestern Nat. Bank, Minneapolis; Peerless Woolen Mills; N.Y. Airbrake Co.; Ford Motor Co.; Kellogg Co.; Portraits in: State Capitol, Boston; Dartmouth Col.; Kansas State Col.; Archdiocese of N.Y.; Cooperstown Hospital; Presbyterian Hospital, N.Y.; Roselawn Seminary, Chicago; Exeter Acad.; Pentagon Bldg. (U.S.Navy); First Unitarian Church, Brooklyn; Capitol Hill Cl., Wash., D.C.; Down Town Cl., N.Y.; Am. Tobacco Co.; Northwest Mutual Ins. Co., and in private colls. in U.S. and abroad.*

GREENE, FRANCINA—*Museum Curator*
The Textile Museum, 2320 S St., Northwest; h. 2401 Calvert St., Northwest, Washington, 8, D.C.

B. Alabama, 1899. *Studied*: Alabama State T. Col. *Member*: Centre International d'Etude des Textiles Anciens; CGA; Intl. Inst. for the Conservation of Museum Objects; AFA. Contributor to Textile Museum Workshop Notes. *Position*: Curator-Preparator, Textile Museum, Washington, D.C.

GREENE, J. BARRY—*Painter, Et., T.*
14580 Greenleaf St., Sherman Oaks, Cal.

B. New York, N.Y., June 27, 1895. *Studied*: N.Y. Sch. F. & App. Des.; ASL; NAD; Grande Chaumiere, Acad. Colorossi, Paris, France. *Member*: AAPL; All. A. Am.; Am. Veterans Soc. A.; Salon des Artistes Francaises; Audubon A.; Soc. Western A.; Laguna Beach AA; Los A. AA; Cal. A. Cl.; AEA; Rockport AA. *Awards*: Pulitzer prize, 1919; Guggenheim F., 1929; medals, All. A. Am., 1942; Cal. A. Cl., 1953-1955, 1956; prizes, Laguna Beach AA, 1953, 1955; San Fernando A. Cl., 1951-1953; State Exh., Santa Cruz, 1958; Laguna Beach A. Festival, 1952. *Work*: Ain Harod Mus., Israel. *Exhibited*: Paris Salons, 1919-1939; NAD; CGA; VMFA; All. A. Am.; Am. Veterans Soc. A.; Howard Young Gal., 1923-1925; 1928, 1933, 1935 (all one-man); Newhouse Gal., 1939 (one-man); Audubon A.; Los A. Mus. A.; Palos Verdes, Santa Cruz, Cal.; Chaffee Col.; deYoung Mem. Mus.; Frye Mus. A., Seattle; Bakersfield AA; Sacramento State Fair; A. of the Southwest; other one-man: New Sch. for Social Research, 1949; Doll & Richards Gal., Boston, 1948, 1949; San Fernando A. Cl., 1952; Long Beach, 1953; Glendale AA, 1954; Laguna Beach, 1955.

GREENE, LeROY E.—*Painter*
2009 Virginia Lane, Billings, Mont.

B. Dover, N.J., Nov. 25, 1893. *Studied*: with Roscoe Schrader, Edouard Vysekal, Wayman Adams, George Elmer Browne. *Member*: AEA; SC. *Work*: IBM; Montana State Hist. Soc.; Parmley Cl., Billings, Mont.; Univ. Nebraska; Anaconda (Mont.) Pub. Sch.; Deer Lodge, Mont.; Woman's Cl. Bldg., Bozeman; Heyburn, Ida., Community A. Coll. *Exhibited*: Mun. Exh., N.Y., 1937, 1938; SAM, 1935-1937, 1939, 1941; WFNY 1939; SC; IBM; AWS, 1940; San F. AA, 1941; Oakland A. Gal., 1946; Univ. Idaho, 1935; Portland (Ore.) A. Mus., 1939; Festival of Nations, Red Lodge, 1951, 1952, 1953; Spokane, Wash., 1949-1953; Springville, Utah, 1948-1958; Heyburn, Idaho, 1949-1953; Rigby, Idaho, 1951.

GREENE, LUCILLE BROWN (Mrs. Roy)—
Painter, T., W.
Santa Monica High School, 7th & Pico St., Santa Monica, Cal.; h. 3733 Cedar Ave., Long Beach 7, Cal.

B. Los Angeles, Cal. *Studied*: UCLA, B. Edu., and with S. MacDonald Wright, Millard Sheets, Richard Haines. *Member*: Cal. WC Soc.; Women Painters of the West; Los A. AA; Long Beach AA; Westwood AA; NEA. *Awards*: medal, Cal. A. Cl., 1951, 1953; prizes, Westwood AA, 1954; Women Painters of the West; Long Beach AA purchase award, 1957, and many prizes in other regional shows. *Work*: Santa Monica H.S.; Utah State Agr. Col.,

Logan; Dixie Col., St. George, Utah; Long Beach A. Center. *Exhibited*: Laguna Beach, 1951; Cal. WC Soc., 1952, 1954, 1956, 1958; All. A. Am., 1955; Los A. Mus. A., 1952; Denver A. Mus., 1952, 1953; Nat. Orange Show, 1952, 1953, 1957; ACA Gal., N.Y., 1955; Los A. Flower Show, 1955; Inst. Am. A., 1958; Pittsburgh Plan for Art, 1958; one-man: Long Beach, 1953, 1957; Santa Monica A. Gal., 1958; Los A. Women's Univ. Cl., 1956. Contributor to Cal. Journal of Secondary Education, 1953. *Position*: A.T., 1928-54, Chm. A. Dept., 1954- , Santa Monica H.S., Santa Monica, Cal.

GREENE, MARIE ZOE—*Sculptor*
1232 East 57th St., Chicago 37, Ill.

B. 1911. *Studied*: Radcliffe Col.; New Bauhaus, Chicago; and in France, Italy, Mexico. *Member*: AEA (Vice-Pres., Chicago Chptr., 1957-58). *Work*: Roosevelt Univ., Chicago; Southwest Missouri State Col., and in private collections throughout U.S. *Exhibited*: s., reliefs, drawings, etc., Salon des Beaux-Arts, Salon des Independants, Paris, France; Royal Inst. Gal., London; Inst. Contemporary A., Boston; BMFA; Busch-Reisinger Mus. FA; Harvard Univ.; Royal Canadian Acad.; Montreal Mus. FA; AIC; NAC; ANTA Playhouse, N.Y.; Chicago Chptr., AIA; 10 one-man exhs. Author: "Masterpieces of Italian Art in Painting and Sculpture: A Workbook for Children," and "A Gallery Book for Children," for the Dept. Edu., Art Inst. of Chicago.

GREENE, STEPHEN—*Painter, E.*
Valley Cottage, N.Y.

B. New York, N.Y., Sept. 19, 1918. *Studied*: NAD; ASL; Col. William and Mary; State Univ. Iowa, B.F.A., M.A. *Awards*: prizes, VMFA, 1946; Prix de Rome, 1949-50; Cal. PLH, 1947; Milwaukee AI, 1946; Ohio Univ., 1946; John Herron AI, 1946; Joslyn Mus. A., 1941; Delgado Mus. A., 1958. *Work*: VMFA; AIC; Vassar Col.; WMAA; Detroit Inst. A.; Nelson Gal. A.; CAM; Wadsworth Atheneum; FMA; AGAA; Santa Barbara Mus. A.; Univ. Illinois; Indiana Univ.; Princeton Univ. Mus.; Brandeis Univ.; Isaac Delgado Mus. A. *Exhibited*: WMAA, 1945, 1946, 1955; MModA, 1956; VMFA, 1946; NAD, 1945, 1946; AIC, 1946; Univ. Iowa, 1946; Los A. Mus. A., 1945; Cal. PLH, 1946; Milwaukee AI, 1946; Carnegie Inst., 1953; John Herron AI; Butler AI, 1946; "Drawings in the U.S.," European exh., 1953-54, and in many nat. exhs. One-man: Durlacher Bros., N.Y., 1947, 1949, 1952; Borgenicht Gal., N.Y., 1956, 1958; Retrospective exhs., DeCordova & Dana Mus., 1953; Princeton Univ., 1957. *Position*: Instr., Parsons Sch. Des.; N.Y. University, New York, N.Y.; Artist-in-Res., Princeton University, 1956- .

GREENE, VERNON VAN ATTA—*Cartoonist, L., T.*
235 East 45th St., New York, N.Y.; h. 275 Newtown Rd., Wyckoff, N.J.

B. Battle Ground, Wash., Sept. 12, 1908. *Studied*: Univ. Toledo; Columbia Univ., B.S., and with Henry G. Keller, Oronzio Maldarelli, Peppino Mangravite, Dong Kingman, and others. *Member*: Nat. Cartoonists Soc.; Newspaper Comics Council. *Exhibited*: Nat. Comic Strip Exh., 1942; MMA, 1951; LC, 1956; Detroit Inst. A., 1957; Brussels World's Fair, 1958. Author, I., "Charlie Conscript," Pic magazine. Illus. lectures for schools, churches and clubs. Cartoon shows for USO and Dept. of Defense in Alaska, Germany, Korea, France, England, etc. *Positions*: Ed. Cart., Portland (Ore.) Telegram, Central Press Int. News; Sports Cart., Toledo Blade; Comic strip "Ghost," King Features; Created comic strips, "The Shadow," "Bible Bee," Des Moines Register-Tribune; artist of comic strip "Bringing Up Father" (since death of George McManus, 1954). Teaching, Seminar, FA, Wyckoff, N.J.; Lectures to many college groups, teachers groups, art associations, women's clubs, etc.

GREENFIELD, MACCABI—*Painter, Gr., T.*
605 West 151st St., New York 31, N.Y.; h. 101 Harding Ave., White Plains, N.Y.

B. Bargusine, Siberia, Nov. 24, 1918. *Studied*: ASL; Grand Chaumiere, Paris, France. *Member*: Soc. Young Am. Painters (Exec. Com.); ASL (Bd. Control). *Awards*: McDowell scholarship, 1949; Emily Lowe award, 1954. *Exhibited*: SAGA, 1952; MModA, 1953-1954; LC, 1954; N.Y. City Center, 1954, 1956; Riverside Mus., 1955; Jewish Mus., 1952, 1955, 1956; SAM, 1951; Ohio Wesleyan Univ., 1952; Bradley Univ., 1952; Univ. Virginia, 1952; Hunter

Gal., Chattanooga, 1952; Herbert Inst., Augusta, 1952; Univ. Mississippi, 1952; also in N.Y. galleries: Argent, Laurel, RoKo, Contemporary A., Ward Eggleston, Gallery East, Peter Kolean Gal., Bertha Schaefer, Panoras, Regina, and others; one-man: Galerie 8, Paris, 1950; ASL, 1951; Columbia Univ., 1953; Kolean Gal., 1954; Artists Gal., 1956. *Position*: Instr., Master Inst. United Arts, 1955-56; Instr. A., Hawthorne Cedar Knolls Sch., 1956-58; Rec. Sec., ASL, 1957- .

GREENLEAF, ESTHER (Mrs. Robert)—Painter, C., T.
27 Woodcrest Ave., Short Hills, N.J.

B. Ripon, Wis., Oct. 17, 1904. *Studied*: Univ. Minnesota, B.S. in Arch.; and with Andre Lhote, Paris, France. *Member*: Artist-Craftsmen of N.Y.; Pen & Brush Cl.; NAWA; Summit AA; N.J. Des-Craftsmen; Millburn-Short Hills A. Center. *Awards*: prizes, Minneapolis, Minn., 1944; Millburn-Short Hills A. Center, 1947, 1955, 1958; Summit AA, 1958; NAWA., 1956; Pen & Brush Cl., 1955. *Exhibited*: NAWA, 1954-1957; Artist-Craftsmen of N.Y., 1955, 1956; Millburn-Short Hills A. Center, 1942-1956; A. Center of the Oranges, 1955, 1956; Summit AA, 1954-1956, 1957 (one-man); P. & S. Soc. of New Jersey, 1957; Pen & Brush Cl., 1954-1958; Montclair A. Mus., 1955-1957; Morris Plains, N.J., 1954 (one-man). *Position*: Instr., Painting, Millburn-Short Hills A. Center, 1957-58.

GREENLEAF, JACOB I.—Painter, Des., T.
212 Friend St., Boston 14, Mass.; h. 28 South Rd., Bearskin Neck, Rockport, Mass.

B. Reval, Estonia, Mar. 2, 1887. *Studied*: in Europe. *Member*: Conn. Acad. FA; New Haven Paint & Clay Cl.; North Shore AA; Rockport AA; Copley Soc.; AAPL. *Awards*: prizes, Mint Mus. A., 1943; Paasche Comp., 1945; Woodrow Wilson H.S., Phila., Pa., 1950; Academic A., Springfield, 1953. *Exhibited*: NAD, 1943; Mint Mus., 1943, 1944; Portland (Me.) Soc. A., 1944-1946; St. Petersburg A. Cl., 1941; North Shore AA, 1942-1955; Copley Soc., 1933-1955; New Haven Paint & Clay Cl., 1941-1955; Conn. Acad. FA, 1945-1955; Jordan Marsh Gal., 1939-1958.

GREENMAN, FRANCES CRANMER—
Painter, Cr., W., L., T.
Hampshire Arms, Minneapolis 4, Minn.

B. Aberdeen, S.D., June 28, 1890. *Studied*: Corcoran Sch. A.; ASL; BMFA Sch.; Grande Chaumiere, Paris; & with Chase, DuMond, Henri. *Member*: Soc. Wash. A.; Minnesota AA. *Awards*: Med., Corcoran Sch. A.; Minneapolis Inst. A.; Minn. State Fair. *Work*: New York Univ.; Ohio State Univ.; Univ. Minnesota; Hamline Univ.; Cornell Col.; NAD; Minneapolis Pub. Lib.; Lawrence, Col.; Aberdeen (S.D.) Pub. Lib.; Neville Mus.; Minneapolis Inst. A. *Exhibited*: World's Fair, Chicago, 1933, 1934; Carnegie Inst.; PAFA, 1923, 1926, 1935; AIC; NAD; Detroit Inst. A.; Minneapolis Inst. A., etc. Author: "Higher Than the Sky," 1954. *Position*: A. Columnist & Cr., Minneapolis Sunday Tribune; Instr. A., Minneapolis (Minn.) Sch. A., 1941-43; AIC, 1942 (summer). Lectures to many women's clubs.

GREENOUGH, MRS. CHARLES PELHAM III.
See Sandzen, Margaret

GREENWOOD, MARION—Painter, Lith., I., T., L.
60 West 9th St., New York 11, N.Y.; also, Woodstock, N.Y.

B. New York, N.Y., 1909. *Studied*: ASL; Grande Chaumiere, Paris, France. *Member*: ANA. *Awards*: prizes, Carnegie Inst., 1944; John Herron AI, 1946; PAFA, 1951; NAD, 1952; Butler Inst. Am. A. purchase prize, 1956. *Work*: PAFA; Univ. Arizona; Encyclopaedia Britannica; MMA; Newark Mus. A.; Smith Col.; LC; Yale Univ.; Univ. Georgia; Abbott Laboratories; N.Y. Pub. Lib.; Bibliotheque Nationale, Paris; Bloomington (Ill.) AA; murals, Univ. Tennessee; Univ. San Nicolas Hidalgo; Civic Center, Mexico City; Community Hall, Camden, N.J.; Red Hook Community Bldg., N.Y., Housing Authority; USPO, Crossville, Tenn. *Exhibited*: MMA; WMAA; BM; Carnegie Inst.; CGA; AIC; PAFA; NAD; Am. Acad. FA; one-man: Assoc. Am. A.; Bloomington (Ill.) Univ. *Position*: Visiting Prof. FA, Univ. Tennessee, 1954-55.

GREGG, LEWIS C.—Portrait Painter
30 Polo Dr., N.E., Atlanta 9, Ga.

B. Atlanta, Ga., Oct. 9, 1880. *Studied*: ASL; & in Paris, France. *Work*: Trust Co. of Georgia; Coca-Cola Co., Atlanta, Ga.; Univ. Georgia; Georgia Sch. Tech.; Emory Univ.*

GREGG, RICHARD NELSON—
Museum Curator, Des., W., L., E.
The Toledo Museum of Art, Monroe St. at Scottwood Ave., Toledo 2, Ohio

B. Kalamazoo, Mich., Sept. 4, 1926. *Studied*: Western Michigan Univ.; Cranbrook Acad. A., B.F.A., M.F.A. *Member*: Council on Art Edu. *Awards*: prize, Detroit Inst. A., 1951. Originated exhibition of International Kites, circulated nationally by AFA, 1957-58. Contributor to the museum magazine "Curator." *Position*: Instr., Cranbrook Sch. for Boys; Instr., Des., WMA; Dir., Kalamazoo Inst. A.; Curatorial Asst., Toledo Museum of Art, Toledo, Ohio, at present.

GREGOROPOULOS, JOHN—Painter, T.
Art Department, University of Connecticut, Storrs, Conn.

B. Athens, Greece, Dec. 16, 1921. *Studied*: Athens, Greece; Univ. Connecticut, B.A. Philosophy. *Awards*: prizes, Springfield A. Mus., 1956, 1958; Norwich AA, 1951-1956, 1958; Silvermine Gld. A., 1953; Essex AA, 1954; Mystic AA, 1955; Ball State T. Col., 1955. *Work*: Ball State T. Col.; Ball Brothers Fnd.; USIA Coll. *Exhibited*: WMAA, 1955; Boston A. Festival, 1954, 1955; Wadsworth Atheneum, 1951-1954; Springfield A. Mus., 1955, 1956; Delgado Mus. A., 1948, 1949, 1951; Albany Inst. Hist. & A., 1949; deCordova & Dana Mus., 1954-1956; Lyman Allyn Mus. A., 1955; BMFA, 1954; Slater Mus. A., 1951-1956; Rosicrucian Egyptian Mus., 1955; Univ. Connecticut, 1950, 1954, 1955; Conn. Col., 1955; Howard Univ., 1955; Fla. State Univ., 1955; Ball State T. Col., 1955; ACA Gal., 1954; Duveen-Graham Gal., 1955; Alan Gal., 1955; Chase Gal., 1956; Pan Hellenic Salon of Greek Art, Athens, 1956; Art:USA, 1958; Provincetown A. Festival, 1958; Nexus Gal., Boston, 1958 (one-man); work circulated by USIA abroad, and numerous regional exh. *Position*: Instr., Norwich A. Sch., Norwich, Conn., 1951-53; Univ. Connecticut, Storrs, Conn., 1953- .

GREGORY, ANGELA—Sculptor, P., L.
630 Pine St., New Orleans 18, La.

B. New Orleans, La., Oct. 18, 1903. *Studied*: N.Y. State Col. Ceramics, Alfred, N.Y.; Newcomb Col., B. Des.; Tulane Univ., M.A.; Parsons Sch., Paris, and in Italy; Grande Chaumiere, Paris, and with Antoine Bourdelle. *Member*: F., NSS; New Orleans AA; Orleans Cl.; Landmarks Soc. (Fndr., Bd. Memb.); Le Petit Salon (Hon. Life memb.). *Awards*: scholarship, Newcomb Col.; prizes, SSAL, 1930, 1931; Louisiana P. & S., 1929. *Work*: IBM; Delgado Mus. A.; Louisiana State Mus.; s., Criminal Courthouse, New Orleans, and Courthouse, Opelousas, La.; Louisiana State Univ.; Louisiana State Capitol; Tulane Univ.; Howard-Tilton Mem. Lib.; La Tour Carree, Septmonts, France; s. murals, La. Nat. Bank, Baton Rouge; mem., plaques, Boston Cl.; Charity Hospital, New Orleans; Silver-Burdette Publ. Co., N.Y.; Louisiana State Univ., Baton Rouge; St. Gabriel Church, St. Gabriel, La.; monuments: McDonogh monument, Civic Center, 1938, Bienville monument, 1955, New Orleans, La., and many others. *Exhibited*: Salon des Tuileries, 1928, 1932; Salon d'Automne, Paris, 1930; SFMA; WMAA; U.S. Nat. Mus.; Wash. A. Cl.; Balt. Charcoal Cl.; Cal. PLH; MMA; one-man: New Orleans A. & Crafts Cl.; Mus. of FA of Houston; Delgado Mus. A. *Positions*: Instr., 1935-37, A.-in-Res., 1940-41, Newcomb Col.; State Supv., WPA Project, 1941-42; Asst. Engineer, Camouflage Sect., Corps of Engineers, New Orleans Dist., 1942-43; Dir. A., Gulfpark Col., Gulfport, Miss., 1958-59.

GREGORY, BARBARA DELLE SIMMONS
(Mrs. Henry W., Jr.)—Painter
Arbor Dell, Rte. 7, Box 218; h. 900 Country Club Lane, Pine Bluff, Ark.

B. Fordyce, Ark., Dec. 31, 1914. *Studied*: Hollins Col.; Allison's Wells A. Colony, and with Louis Freund, Fred Conway, Karl Wolfe, Peter Baruzzi, Pat Travigno.

Awards: prizes, All-Arkansas Competition, 1954, 1957; Allison's Wells, 1953, 1954. *Exhibited*: Brooks Mem. Mus., 1955; All-Arkansas Exh., Little Rock Mus. FA, 1953-1955; Allison's traveling exh., Delgado Mus. A., 1955.

GREGORY, DOROTHY LAKE

(Mrs. Dorothy Gregory Moffett)—Painter, L., I.
Commercial St., Provincetown, Mass.

B. Brooklyn, N.Y. *Studied*: Packer Inst.; PIASch.; ASL, and with Henri, Bellows. *Member*: Cape Cod AA; Provincetown AA. *Awards*: prizes, Terry AI, 1952; Hallmark award, 1953; Cape Cod AA, 1954. *Work*: LC; BMFA. *Exhibited*: NAD; MMA; BM; AIC; LC; Living Arts Fnd. Illus. of several books. Trustee, Provincetown AA.

GREGORY, JOHN WORTHINGTON—

Lithographer, W., L., Photog.
72 Commercial St., Provincetown, Mass.

B. Brooklyn, N.Y., Mar. 14, 1903. *Studied*: ASL, with John Sloan, Charles Locke, Alan Lewis, Harry Wickey. *Awards*: 2 scholarships, ASL. *Work*: BMFA; Springfield Mus. A.; CMA; Harvard Univ.; Wheaton Col.; Boston Pub. Lib.; Williams Col.; Smithsonian Inst. (photographs), and in private colls. *Exhibited*: AIC; Faulkner Mem. Gal.; Santa Barbara, Cal.; Warwick Gal., Phila.; Boston A. Cl.; Wheaton Col.; Morton Gal., N.Y.; Univ. Illinois; G.W.V. Smith Mus.; Central Mich. State Col. of Edu.; one-man: 47 pictorial photographs, Smithsonian Inst., 1948, and work shown in Intl. Salons. Contributor magazine articles on the art of Drawing on Stone. Former Instr., Hunter Col., Butera Sch. A., Boston, Mass.; Photographer, Time magazine.

GREGORY, WAYLANDE—Sculptor, Des., W., L., P.

Mountain Top Studios, Bound Brook, N.J.

B. Baxter Springs, Kan., June 13, 1905. *Studied*: Kansas State T. Col.; Univ. Chicago; Kansas City AI; & in Europe. *Member*: NSS; Soc. Designer-Craftsman. *Awards*: Med., Alfred Univ., 1939; Paris Exp., 1937; Syracuse Mus. FA, 1933, 1937, 1940; prize, Arch.L., 1936; CMA, 1929, 1931; gold medal, United Ceramic Glass Corp. *Work*: S., District Bldg., Wash., D.C.; fountain, Roosevelt Park, N.J.; Syracuse Mus. FA; Cranbrook Mus.; CMA; General Motors Corp.; sc. groups, Theological Seminary Bldg., Chicago; sc. wall, Municipal Center, Wash., D.C.; group, Bound Brook, N.J. Numerous ports. of prominent persons; Coll. ports., Hungarian Freedom Fighters, 1958. *Exhibited*: WMAA; MMA; AIC; Montclair A. Mus.; WMA; CAM; Richmond Acad., A. & Sc.; San Diego, Cal.; CMA; Toledo Mus. A.; Los A. County Fair; Cranbrook Fnd.; State Mus., Trenton, N.J.; Tiffany's, N.Y.; Morgan's, Montreal; W.J. Sloane A. Gal., Beverly Hills; Shreve, Crump & Low, Boston; Brussels World's Fair, 1958; America House; Watts Gal., Milwaukee; special exh. "Sculpture in Wire," State Mus., Trenton, N.J., 1958; many one-man shows in leading museums, & in Europe. Contributor to: Art & national magazines. Lectures: Ceramic Art, etc. 20 TV shows "Creative Arts," NBC.

GRELL, LOUIS—Painter, T.

617 North State St.; h. 3 East Ontario St., Chicago 11, Ill.

B. Council Bluffs, Iowa, Nov. 31, 1887. *Studied*: Sch. App. A., Hamburg, Germany; Royal Acad. FA, Munich; Univ. Munich. *Member*: Chicago Galleries Assn.; NSMP; Chicago P. & S. *Award*: prize, Mun. A. Lg., Chicago, 1936. *Work*: murals, Bank of Detroit, Mich.; Union Station, St. Louis; Fort Hayes Hotel, Columbus, Ohio; Northwestern Military and Naval Acad., Geneva, Wis.; Mark Twain Hotel, St. Louis; Manufacturers Bank & Trust Co., St. Louis; Paramount Theatre Lobby, Toledo, Ohio; Heidelberg Hotel, Baton Rouge, La.; Raleigh Hotel, Waco, Tex.; Congress Hotel, Chicago; Roosevelt Hotel, Pittsburgh; Eldorado Hotel, New York City; Netherland Plaza Hotel, Cincinnati; portraits, paintings, Mayflower Hotel, Wash., D.C.; Pompeian dining room and murals for lobby of Congress Hotel, Chicago; Hotel Oliver, South Bend, Ind.; Gulf Mobile & Ohio Station, Springfield, Ill.; decorations for numerous churches. *Position*: Instr., Chicago Acad. FA, Chicago, Ill., at present.

GREPP, JOHN—Educator

Franklin College, Franklin, Ind.
Position: Hd., Art Dept., Franklin College.*

GREYWACZ, KATHRYN BURCH—Museum Director

New Jersey State Museum, Department of Education of New Jersey, Trenton 25, N.J.; h. 429 Latona Ave., Trenton 8, N.J.

B. Philadelphia, Pa., Nov. 26, 1893. *Member*: AAMus.; Mus. Council of New Jersey (Exec. Com.); Archaeological Soc. New Jersey (Organizer & Sec. 1931-); Eastern States Archaeological Fed. (Sec. 1934-); New Jersey A. Edu. Assn. (Hon. memb.); New Jersey Hist. Soc.; New Jersey Edu. Assn. *Awards*: Hon. Degree, M.A., Rutgers Univ., 1952; New Jersey History award, 1958. Exhibitions arranged: Retrospective: John Marin, 1950-51 (catalog); Work of Living New Jersey Artists: Oils, 1954, watercolors, 1956; James Chapin, 1955; Nature in Sculpture, 1957-58; Early New Jersey Arts and Crafts: Silver, Glass, Paintings, Pewter, Furniture, 1952, 1953; Potter's Art, 1955-56 (catalog); New Jersey's Place in Cultural History, 1956-57 (catalog); History in Miniature Figures, 1957-58; 30 Paintings from the Delaware Valley, 1958, and many others. *Position*: Mus. Cur., Dept. Conservation & Development, 1925-45; Dir., New Jersey State Mus., Dept. Education, Trenton, N.J., 1945- .

GRIER, HARRY DOBSON MILLER—

Assistant Museum Director
The Frick Collection, 1 East 70th St.; h. 59 East 80th St., New York 21, N.Y.

B. Philadelphia, Pa., Jan. 23, 1914. *Studied*: Pa. State Univ., B.S. in Arch.; Princeton Univ.; Univ. of Paris, Inst. d'Art et d'Archeologie. *Member*: CAA; AAMus.; Museums Council of New York City, etc. Contributor to Metropolitan Museum Bulletin; Minneapolis Inst. Arts Bulletin; Parnassus; College Art Journal; Museum (UNESCO). Lectures on Painting and Architecture, Mediaeval to Modern, museums and professional organizations. Television: CBS, NBC; Radio: WNYC. *Positions*: Asst. to Dean, L., MMA, 1938-41; U.S. Army, 1941-46; Chief, Monuments, Fine Arts & Archives, Office of Military Government, U.S. (Berlin), 1945-46; Asst. Dir., Minneapolis Inst. A., 1946-51; Asst. Dir., The Frick Collection, New York, N.Y., 1951- .

GRIFFIN, NINA K(ICKBUSCH)—Painter

3000 Sheridan Rd., Chicago 14, Ill.

B. Wausau, Wis., April 13, 1894. *Studied*: AIC, and with Victor Higgins, Charles Rosen, Arnold Blanche, Wayman Adams, and others. *Member*: Chicago Galleries Assn.; Chicago A. Cl.; NAWA; NAC; Wash. WC Cl.; College Cl. of Chicago; All. A. Am.; N.Y. Art Cl.; Rockport AA; New Orleans AA; AEA; Renaissance Soc., Univ. Chicago. *Awards*: silver med., AIC; prize, Chicago Galleries Assn. *Work*: Wausau H.S.; Milwaukee-Downer Col.; Wellesley Col.; Illinois Veterans Orphanage. *Exhibited*: AIC; All. A. Am.; NAWA; Wash. WC Cl.; NAC; Chicago A. Cl.; Rockport AA; AEA; Terry AI; Ogunquit A. Center; Renaissance Soc.; NAD; one-man: Chicago Galleries Assn.; Wash. A. Cl.; Galena (Ill.) A. Cl.; Bismark Hotel, Chicago, 1957; Wausau, Wis., 1957; Los Angeles; Knox Col., Galena, and others.

GRIFFIN, WORTH DICKMAN—Painter, E., L.

Washington State College; Box 1862 C.S., Pullman, Wash.

B. Sheridan, Ind., Dec. 15, 1892. *Studied*: Oklahoma Christian Univ.; John Herron AI; AIC, and with Harry Walcott, George Bellows, Charles Hawthorne, Wayman Adams. *Work*: Washington State Col. Coll. (97 portraits). *Member*: Western Col. AA; Am. Soc. for Aesthetics; Washington AA. *Exhibited*: SFMA, 1940, 1942, 1945; Oakland A. Gal., 1939, 1940; SAM, 1935-1944. Contributor articles to College Art Journal; Research Studies, State Col. of Washington. *Positions*: Magazine Illus. & Coml. A., Chicago, 1918-24; Chm. FA Dept., 1932-51; Prof. FA, 1945-58; Prof. FA Emeritus, 1958- , Washington State College, Pullman, Wash.; Staff, Lewiston (Idaho) Tribune, 1958- .

GRIFFING, ROBERT PERKINS, JR.—

Museum Director, L.
Honolulu Academy of Arts, 900 South Beretania St.; h. 3887 Owena St., Honolulu 15, Hawaii

B. Riverhead, L.I., N.Y., Mar. 27, 1914. *Studied*: Phillips Acad., Andover; Yale Univ., B.A.; Princeton Univ., M.F.A.; Univ. of Paris, France. *Member*: Am. Assn. A.

Mus. Dir.; AAMus.; Intl. Council of Museums; CAA; Social Science Assn. Contributor articles to: Art Bulletin; Bulletin of the Honolulu Acad. Arts; Architectural Record; Museum, etc. Arranged exhibitions: Buddhist Art, 1952; Treasures from Japan, 1954; Japanese Folk Art, 1953; Korean Art, 1954; Arts of the Pacific, 1951; U.S. Art Today, 1950, and many others. *Position*: Instr., European & U.S. Art & Arch., Princeton Univ., 1937-39; Johns Hopkins Univ., 1939-41; Dir. Edu., 1946-47, Dir., 1947- , Honolulu Acad. A., Honolulu, Hawaii.

GRIGAUT, PAUL L.—*Museum Curator*
Detroit Institute of Arts, 5200 Woodward Ave., Detroit 2, Mich.
Position: Cur., Oriental Art, Asst. to the Dir., Detroit Institute of Arts.*

GRILLEY, ROBERT L.—*Painter, E.*
University of Wisconsin, Madison, Wis.; h. 319 South Page St., Stoughton, Wis.
B. Beloit, Wis., Nov. 14, 1920. *Studied*: Univ. Wisconsin, B.S., M.S. *Awards*: prizes, Univ. Illinois, 1953 (purchase); Wisconsin Salon (5 times). *Work*: Univ. Illinois; Univ. Wisconsin; Wisconsin Union. *Exhibited*: AIC, 1951; Univ. Illinois, 1953; Walker A. Center; Univ. Nebraska, 1955, 1956; Des Moines A. Center, 1955; Santa Barbara Mus. A., 1956; Denver A. Mus., 1956; Mus. FA of Houston, 1956; AFA traveling exh., 1957; Intl. A. Festival, Spoleto, Italy, 1958; Flint Mus. A., 1958; one-man: Chicago, Ill., 1952; Lawrence Col., 1953; Milwaukee AI, 1954; Univ. Wisconsin, 1956; Hewitt Gal., N.Y., 1957. Lectures: American Painting in the 20th Century. *Position*: Assoc. Prof. A., Univ. Wisconsin, Madison, Wis. (on Staff since 1945).

GRILLO, JOHN—*Painter*
500 Third Ave., New York, N.Y.
B. Lawrence, Mass., July 4, 1917. *Studied*: Hartford A. Sch.; Cal. Sch. FA; Hans Hofmann Sch. FA. *Member*: Abstract A. Group; A. Cl. *Awards*: prizes, Albert M. Bender grant, San Francisco, 1947-48; Sacramento State Fair. *Work*: Olsen Fnd., Guilford, Conn.; Smith Col. Mus.; Hartford Atheneum; WMAA. *Exhibited*: Provincetown A. Festival, 1958; MMA, 1952; WMAA, 1952; Berkeley, Cal., 1947; one-man: Artists Gal., N.Y., 1948; Bertha Schaefer Gal., N.Y., 1953, 1958.

GRIMES, FRANCES—*Sculptor*
229 East 48th St., New York 17, N.Y.
B. Braceville, Ohio, Jan. 25, 1869. *Studied*: PIASch.; & with Herbert Adams, Augustus St. Gaudens. *Member*: NA; NSS. *Awards*: Med., Pan-Pacific Exp., 1915; prize, NAWA, 1916. *Work*: S., Toledo Mus. A.; MMA; Hall of Fame, N.Y.Univ.; Grace Church, N.Y.; Washington Irving H.S., New York; 2 bronze port. bas-reliefs, Town Hall, N.Y. *Exhibited*: NSS: NAD; Soc. Am. A.

GRIPPE, FLORENCE—*Craftsman, P., S., Des.*
108 Second Ave., New York 3, N.Y.
B. New York, N.Y., Jan. 6, 1912. *Studied*: Edu. All.; Henry St. Settlement, with Hale and Soini. *Member*: Artist-Craftsmen of N.Y. *Exhibited*: NYC Council for A. Week, 1942; Syracuse Mus. FA; Orrefors Gal.; Georg Jensen; America House; Argent Gal.; NAC; Laurel Gal.; RoKo Gal.; Mus. Natural Hist., N.Y.; BM; Borgenicht Gal.; Betty Parsons Gal.; Morris Gal.; Zabriskie Gal.; Pyramid Gal., all NYC. Contributor to Ceramic Age. *Position*: Instr., United Art Workshop of Brooklyn Neighborhood Houses, 1947-54; Brooklyn Mus. A. Sch., 1951-57.

GRIPPE, PETER—*Sculptor, Gr., P.*
108 Second Ave., New York 3, N.Y.
B. Buffalo, N.Y., Aug. 8, 1912. *Studied*: Albright A. Sch.; Buffalo AI, and with E. Wilcox, Edwin Dickinson, William Ehrich. *Member*: Fed. Mod. P. & S.; Am. Abstract A. *Awards*: prizes, BM; MMA; Phila. Pr. Cl.; Boston A. Festival; United Nations Sculpture Competition. *Work*: MModA; Albright A. Gal.; AGAA; Toledo Mus. A.; Rosenwald Coll.; BM; N.Y. Pub. Lib.; Univ. Michigan; Tel-Aviv Mus. A.; Providence, R.I. Mus. A.; Georgia Mus. FA; Phila. Pr. Cl.; Univ. Washington, St. Louis, Mo.; Milwaukee-Downer Col.; PMA; Brandeis Univ.; LC;

WMAA; Blanden Mem. Mus., Ft. Dodge, Iowa; MMA. *Exhibited*: MMA, 1942, 1943, 1947, 1951, 1952; WMAA, 1944-1957; LC, 1946, 1947; Detroit Inst. A., 1945, 1947; PAFA, 1946, 1952; Albright A. Gal., 1935-1939; Willard Gal., 1942, 1944-1948; Wildenstein Gal., 1944, 1945; Am. Abstract A., 1946; Am.-British A. Gal., 1946; Carnegie Inst., 1946; BM, 1947-1949, 1952, 1953, 1956, 1958; SAM, 1947; AIC, 1947, 1948; Univ. Minnesota, 1948, 1956; WMA, 1948; N.Y. Pub. Lib., 1948; Munson-Williams-Proctor Inst., 1949; Seligmann Gal., 1949; French Govt. sponsored exh., France and Germany, 1949; PMA, 1949; State Univ. Iowa, 1949; MModA, 1949, 1951, 1952; Univ. Chicago, 1950; AFA traveling exh., 1950-1953, 1956-1958; Smith Col., 1951; Phila. Pr. Cl., 1946, 1949, 1952, 1956, 1958; Washington Univ., St. Louis; United Nations Sculpture Comp.; Boston A. Festival; Boston Pub. Lib., 1952; AGAA, 1956; VMFA, 1956; Douglass Col., 1957; Peridot Gal., 1957; deCordova & Dana Mus., 1958; Pasadena A. Mus., 1958; Boston A. Festival, 1955, 1958; Carnegie Inst., 1958, and many others. One-man: Orrefors Gal., 1942; Willard Gal., 1944, 1945, 1946, 1948; Brandeis Univ., 1958, etc. *Positions*: Instr., S., Black Mountain Col. (N.C.), 1948; Instr., Drawing & Des., PIASch., 1949-50; Instr. S., Smith Col., 1951-52; Dir., Atelier 17, New York, N.Y., 1951-53; Instr., S. & Gr., Brandeis Univ., Waltham, Mass., 1953- .

GRIPPI, SALVATORE (WILLIAM)—*Painter, Gr., T.*
192 Eighth Ave., New York 11, N.Y.
B. Buffalo, N.Y., Sept. 30, 1921. *Studied*: ASL; MModA Sch.; Instituto Statale de'Arte, Florence, Italy. *Member*: ASL; CAA. *Awards*: Fulbright Fellowship, 1953-54; renewal, 1954-55. *Work*: N.Y. Pub. Lib.; MModA; MMA; Milwaukee-Downer Col. *Exhibited*: CGA, 1959; Carnegie Inst., 1958; WMAA & Smithsonian Inst., Fulbright Exh., 1958; LC, 1956; MMA, 1952; Univ. Nebraska, 1958; Texas Western Col., 1956; Phila. Pr. Cl., 1956; PAFA, 1952; Wash. WC Cl., 1952; Univ. So. Cal., 1952, 1953; Friends of the Whitney Mus., 1958; Fieldston Exh., 1958; Stable Gal., 1952, 1957; Zabriskie Gal., 1955; Camino Gal., 1956; Tanager Gal., 1953, 1958; Amherst Col., 1953; Milwaukee-Downer Col., 1953; Fourth St. Print Shop, N.Y., 1952; one-man: N.Y. Univ., 1958; Zabriskie Gal., 1956; Milwaukee-Downer Col., 1956; and in Rome, Florence, Milan, Italy.

GRISCOM, LLOYD C.—*Painter*
Syosset, L.I., N.Y.
B. Riverton, N.J., Nov. 4, 1872. *Studied*: Chateau de Lancy, Geneva, Switzerland; Univ. Pennsylvania, Ph.B., L.L.B. *Member*: AWS. Author: "Diplomatically Speaking."*

GRISWOLD, VIRGINIA—*Painter*
25 Clark St., Brooklyn 1, N.Y.
Studied: ASL; Univ. Geneva; Acad. Colorossi, Paris, and with George Elmer Browne, Arthur Guptill, Eliot O'Hara, Harry Ballinger. *Member*: NAC; Pen & Brush Cl. *Exhibited*: AWS; All. A. Am.; NAC; NAD; CGA; Adelphi Col.; BM; N.Y. Pan Hellenic, Women's Univ. Cl.

GROCE, GEORGE C.—*Art Historian, W., Cr., L.*
2500 Wisconsin Ave., Northwest, Washington 7, D.C.
B. Waxahachie, Tex., Sept. 20, 1899. *Studied*: Trinity Univ., A.B.; Univ. Texas, A.M.; Columbia Univ., Fayerweather Hall, Ph.D., and abroad. Author: "William Samuel Johnson," 1939; co-author, "New York Historical Society Dictionary of Early American Artists, 1564-1860," 1957. Ed., "Early American Portrait Painters," 1940. Contributor to art magazines with book reviews, historical articles. Lectures for U.S. Information Agency, "American Painting, 1861-1913."

GROFF, JUNE—*Designer, P., Ser.*
1605 Sansom St. (3); h. 862 North 19th St., Philadelphia 30, Pa.
B. North Lawrence, Ohio, June 26, 1903. *Studied*: PAFA; Barnes Fnd., and with Henry McCarter. *Awards*: Traveling scholarship, PAFA, 1935; F., PAFA, 1944; prizes, Women's Col., Greensboro, N.C. Intl. Textile Exh., 1947, 1953, 1954, 1956; MModA, Textile Exh., 1947. *Work*: Barnes Fnd.; PAFA; Pa. State Univ.; PMA; MModA traveling coll., 1947-52; Friends Central coll., Phila., Pa., and

in private collections; fabric des., Harper's Bazaar, Hattie Carnegie, Clare Potter, and others. *Exhibited*: PAFA, 1936-1945, 1954; Harvard Univ., 1954; AWS, 1935, 1936, 1939, 1940; CGA, 1941 & traveling exh.; F., PAFA, annually; Phila. A. All.; Carlen Gal., Phila.; Little Art Gal., Canton, Ohio (one-man) of textiles which later circulated one year. *Position*: Des., Textiles, Jack L. Larsen, Inc., New York, N.Y., 1953-58. Conducts private des. & textile business, 1958- .

GROOM, EMILY (PARKER)—*Painter, T.*

Genesee Depot, Route 1, Box 96, Waukesha, Wis.; h. 1903 North Cambridge Ave., Milwaukee 2, Wis.

B. Wayland, Mass., Mar. 17, 1876. *Studied*: AIC; BMFA Sch.; in London; & with John Vanderpoel, Birge Harrison, Frank Benson, Frank Brangwyn, & others. *Member*: Phila. WC Cl.; AWCS; Wis. P. & S.; Wis. WC Soc. *Awards*: Med., St. Paul Inst. A., 1917; Milwaukee AI, 1920, 1925, 1926, 1931, 1946. *Work*: St. Paul Inst. A.; Milwaukee AI; Gimbel Bros. Coll., Wisconsin. *Exhibited*: NAD; PAFA; AIC; Milwaukee AI; & in Oshkosh, Beloit, Racine, Fond du Lac, Green Bay, Wis., 1946. *Position*: A. in Res., Milwaukee-Downer Col., Milwaukee, Wis.

GROOMS, REGINALD L.—*Educator, P., Lith., L.*

297 Southern Ave., Cincinnati 19, Ohio

B. Cincinnati, Ohio, Nov. 16, 1900. *Studied*: A. Acad. of Cincinnati; Julian Acad., Paris, and with Pages, Royer, Laurens. *Member*: Cincinnati A. Cl.; Scarab Cl.; Cincinnati Professional A.; Am. Soc. for Aesthetics; Ohio WC Soc. *Awards*: prize, Ohio WC Soc., 1948. *Work*: Univ. & pub. sch. in Cincinnati; Ball State T. Col. *Exhibited*: CM, 1923-1944, 1948, 1949, 1953-1955; Butler AI, 1936-1945; PAFA, 1935, 1936; GGE, 1939; WFNY 1939; AIC, 1936, 1937; Kearney Gal., Milwaukee, 1946; Closson Gal., Cincinnati (one-man) 1953; Ball State T. Col., 1948 (one-man); Ohio WC Soc., 1948, 1953, 1954. *Position*: Instr., 1925-45, Asst. Prof., 1945-46, Assoc. Prof., 1951, Prof. A., 1955- , Univ. Cincinnati; Instr., A. Acad. of Cincinnati, Ohio, to 1953.

GROPPER, WILLIAM—*Painter, Lith., I., W.*

Mt. Airy Rd., Croton-on-Hudson, N.Y.

B. New York, N.Y., Dec. 3, 1897. *Studied*: NAD; Ferrer Sch.; N.Y. Sch. F. & App. A. *Member*: AEA; SAGA. *Awards*: Collier prize, 1920; Harmon prize, 1930; Guggenheim F., 1937; Young Israel prize 1931; AV, 1942; Los A. Mus. A., 1945; Lib.Cong., 1915. *Work*: MMA; MModA; WMAA; Mus. Western A., Moscow, Russia; Wadsworth Atheneum; PMG; Newark Mus.; CAM; Walker A. Center; Univ. Arizona; PAFA; FMA; AIC; Univ. Maine; Nat. Museums of Warsaw, Prague and Sofia; Encyclopaedia Britannica Coll.; Abbott Laboratories Coll.; murals, USPO, Freeport, L.I., N.Y.; Northwestern Station, Detroit, Mich.; Interior Bldg., Wash., D.C.; Schenley Corp. *Exhibited*: CGA; PAFA; VMFA; AIC; Carnegie Inst.; WMAA; NAD; WFNY 1939; many one-man exhs., traveling exh., nat. & international; recent one-man: traveling, England, 1958; U.S.A., 1958; Univ. of Miami, Fla., 1958. Author: "The Golden Land," 1927; "American Folklore," 1953; "The Little Tailor," 1955; "Capricios," limited ed. lithographs, 1957, & other books; I., "Lidice," 1942; "The Crime of Imprisonment," 1945; & others. Illus., for national magazines.

GROSS, CHAIM—*Sculptor, T.*

48 Horatio St.; h. 30 West 105th St., New York 25, N.Y.; s. Provincetown, Mass.

B. Kolomaya, Austria, Mar. 17, 1904. *Studied*: ASL; BAID; Edu. All. A. Sch. *Member*: S. Gld.; AEA; An Am. Group; Edu. All. A. Sch. Alumni; Cape Cod AA; Provincetown AA; Audubon A. *Awards*: prizes, FAP, 1936; AV, 1942; Cape Cod AA, 1951; med., Paris Salon, 1937; MMA, 1942; Art Festival, Boston, 1954; Audubon A., 1955. *Work*: USPO, Wash., D.C.; Irvin, Pa.; Queens Col., L.I., N.Y.; Fed. Trade Bldg., Wash., D.C.; MMA; WMAA; Newark Mus. A.; MModA; AGAA; H.S., Bronx, Brooklyn, N.Y.; BM; Norton Gal. A.; Ogunquit A. Center; Brandeis Univ.; Smith Col.; Haifa Mus., Israel; Jewish Mus., N.Y.; WMA; Massillon Mus.; AGAA; Tel-Aviv, Ein-Harod Mus., Chaim Weizmann Inst., Israel. *Exhibited*: S. Gld., 1938-1940, 1942; WMAA, biennially; Carnegie Inst., 1938, 1940; PAFA, 1943, 1945, 1946; BM, 1940; AIC, 1938-1942; MModA., 1940, 1951-1953 (traveling exh.); one-man: Assoc. Am. A., 1952; State T. Col.,

New Paltz, N.Y., 1952; Phila. A. All., 1952; South America, 1951. Contributor to art magazines; art film "Tree Trunk to Head" (with Louis Jacobs). *Position*: Instr. S., BM Sch. A. & Edu. All. A. Sch.; woodcarving & modelling, New School for Social Research; People's A. Center, MModA; Five Town Music & A. Center, Woodmere, L.I., N.Y.*

GROSS, EARL—*Painter, I., T., Cr., W., L.*

Stevens-Gross Studios, 620 North Michigan Ave., Chicago, Ill.

B. Pittsburgh, Pa., 1903. *Studied*: Westminster Col.; Carnegie Inst. *Member*: AWS; All-Illinois Soc. FA; Phila. WC Cl.; SC; Madison AA; Chicago A. *Awards*: prizes, Butler AI; Chicago A. Gld., 1942, 1944, 1950, 1952; Cosmopolitan Illus. Comp. *Exhibited*: PAFA, 1937; Wash. WC Cl., 1939; AIC, 1940, 1949 (both one-man); Macbeth Gal., 1941; Assoc. Am. A., 1946; Wustum Mus. A.; Springfield AA; MMA. Lectures in many universities, art centers and schools. Contributor articles to American Artist Magazine; Studio Magazine (London). Included in "Seascapes & Landscapes," 1956. U.S. Air Force Combat A., sent to Formosa, 1958. *Position*: Pres., A. Dir., Stevens-Gross Studios, Chicago, Ill.

GROSS, SIDNEY—*Painter*

54 West 74th St., New York, N.Y.

B. New York, N.Y., Feb. 9, 1921. *Studied*: ASL. *Member*: Audubon A.; Fed. Mod. P. & S.; AEA. *Awards*: Scholarships, ASL, 1939-40; Schnackenberg Scholarship, 1940-41; Tiffany Fnd. F., 1949; grand prize, Art:USA, 1958. *Work*: WMAA; Univ. Georgia; Univ. Omaha; Mt. Holyoke Col.; Butler AI; Lempert Inst., N.Y.; Am. Acad. A. & Let; Brandeis Univ.; Cornell Univ. *Exhibited*: WMAA, 1945-1949; Carnegie Inst., 1946-1949; PAFA, 1948-1952; NAD, 1947, 1949, 1950; Albright A. Gal., 1946; BM, 1945; Armory Show, 1945; Toledo Mus. A., 1947; VMFA, 1948; Univ. Illinois, 1949; Illinois Wesleyan Col., 1949; Walker A. Center, 1948; Univ. Nebraska, 1948; Audubon A, 1947-1952; MMA, 1950; Hallmark exh., 1949; Fla. State Univ., 1951; Fed. Mod. P. & S., 1947-1952; Pepsi-Cola, 1946-1948, and others. One-man: Contemporary Arts Gal., 1945, 1946; Rehn Gal., 1949, 1950, 1953, 1954, 1956, 1958; Minneapolis Inst. A., 1946. *Positions*: Instr., Parsons Sch. Des., New York, N.Y.; ASL, summer, 1958.

GROSSE, GARNET DAVY—*Painter, Des., W., L., Cr.*

Rancho Brandon, Rt. 1, Box 1067, Scottsdale, Ariz.

B. Kansas City, Kans. *Studied*: Woodbury Col.; Univ. California; NAD, and in Paris with Rene T. duQuillan, Charles Bensco. *Member*: All. A. Am.; AFA; Western Acad. A.; Nat. A. Soc.; AAPL; Gen. Fed. Women's Cl. (Chm., Nat. FA Bd.); Scottsdale A. Colony (Founder, Pres. Emeritus). *Awards*: F., Col. FA, Univ. So. California, 1935; AAPL, 1942, 1944, 1945, 1947, 1949, 1952, 1953; Am. Fed. Women's Cl., 1934; Western Fed., 1937; SC; med., Scottsdale Soc. A., 1937; Arizona Mus. A., 1938. *Work*: figures, paintings, murals, Tiffany's, N.Y.; Arizona Mus. A.; Whistler House, Lowell, Mass.; YWCA, New York; Col. FA, Tempe, Ariz.; U.S.Govt.; and many portraits and paintings in private coll. *Exhibited*: SC, 1950; PAFA; AAPL, N.Y., 1951; AAPL, Arizona, 1950-1952; Phoenix FA Assn., 1952; NAC, 1951; Douglas Bank, Scottsdale, 1952; one-man: Paris, France, 1950; Arizona Mus. A., 1949; Friday Morning Club, Los A., 1949; Goldwaters, Phoenix, 1951; Townsend's, Prescott, Ariz., 1948; Phoenix A. Center, 1954. Contributor of articles to Gen. Fed. Women's Clubs "Club-woman." *Position*: Nat. Exec. Com., AAPL; Nat. Pres., Nat. A. Soc.; Nat. Art Week (Fndr.).

GROSSMAN, JOSEPH B.—*Painter*

1720 Chestnut St., Philadelphia 3, Pa.

B. Latvia, 1889. *Studied*: PAFA. *Awards*: Cresson traveling scholarship, PAFA, 1911; F., PAFA. *Work*: Pennsylvania State Col.; Free Lib.; Graphic Sketch Cl., Bartram H.S., all of Phila., Pa. *Exhibited*: PAFA, 1935; WMAA, 1934; AIC, 1938; PMA, 1933, 1935; Phila. AC, 1940.

GROSSMANN, EDWIN BOOTH—*Painter*

Avenue Farm, Fishkill, N.Y.; s. Ogunquit, Me.

B. Boston, Mass., Apr. 9, 1887. *Studied*: in Paris; & with William Chase, Robert Henri. *Member*: AEA. *Exhibited*: Société des Artistes Francais, Paris, 1910; NAD, 1914,

1915, 1920, 1927, 1929; AIC, 1914, 1915, 1927, 1928; Pan-Pacific Exp., 1915; Carnegie Inst., 1931-1945; CGA, 1931; IBM, 1952; AEA, 1951; PAFA, 1915, 1916, 1930, 1933; CAM; Sweat Mem. Mus., 1939; Montross Gal.; Salons of Am.; WMAA; New Art Circle (one-man); Marie Harriman Gal., 1941 (one-man); Lilienfeld Gal., 1945 (one-man); Ogunquit A. Center, 1953, 1954; Portland Mus. A., 1953.*

GROTELL, MAIJA—*Craftsman, T.*
Cranbrook Academy of Art, Bloomfield Hills, Mich.

B. Helsingfors, Finland, Aug. 19, 1899. *Studied*: in Finland. *Member*: Mich. Acad. Sc., A. & Let. *Awards*: Barcelona, Spain, 1929; med., Paris Salon, 1937; prizes, Syracuse Mus. FA, 1936, 1946, 1949; Wichita AA, 1947, 1951; Michigan A.-Craftsman, 1949-1951; Michigan Acad. Sc., A. & Let., 1949-1951, 1956; Detroit Inst. A., 1953, 1955 (purchase). *Work*: Ceramics, MMA; AIC; Ball State T. Col.; Central Mich. Col. Edu.; General Motors Tech. Center; Flint (Mich.) Journal Bldg.; Detroit Inst. A.; Springfield Mus. A.; Cranbrook Mus.; IBM; Syracuse Mus. FA; CMA; Toledo Mus. A.; Walker A. Center; Univ. Gal., Minneapolis; Univ. Michigan; Univ. Nebraska; Univ. Wisconsin; Children's Mus., Detroit; Wichita AA. *Exhibited*: Syracuse Mus. FA, 1932-1955, 1956, 1958; MMA, 1940; Portland A. Mus., 1942; Nelson Gal. A., 1945; AIC, 1946; Wichita AA, 1947-1952; Newark Mus. A., 1948; Scripps Col., 1949-1951; Wash. Kiln Cl., 1951, 1952, 1957; Detroit Inst. A., 1949, 1956, 1958; WMA, 1951; Univ. Gal., Minneapolis, 1951; Univ. Wisconsin, 1952; Des-Craftsman, U.S.A., 1953-1955; Univ. Illinois, 1953; Iowa State T. Col., 1953; Univ. Chicago, 1954; Cannes, France, 1955; State Univ. Iowa, 1955; Sioux City A. Center, 1955; Mus. Contemp. Crafts, 1956, 1958; Butler Inst. Am. A., 1956. *Positions*: Instr., Ceramics, Henry St. Crafts Sch., New York, N.Y., 1929-38; Instr., Res. Asst., Rutgers Univ., 1937-38; Dir., Dept. Ceramics, Cranbrook Acad. A., Bloomfield Hills, Mich., 1938- .

GROTENRATH, RUTH *(Mrs. Ruth Grotenrath Lichtner)*—*Painter, Ser., Eng., C.*
2626A North Maryland Ave., Milwaukee 11, Wis.

B. Milwaukee, Wis., Mar. 17, 1912. *Studied*: State T. Col., Milwaukee, Wis., B.A. *Awards*: prizes, med., Milwaukee AI, 1934, 1940, 1944; Madison AA, 1935; AIC, 1936, 1944; Grand Rapids A. Gal.; Dayton Company, Minneapolis; Ser. Soc., N.Y. *Work*: Madison Un.; Milwaukee AI; IBM Coll.; Wisconsin State T. Col.; murals, USPO, Hart, Mich.; Hudson, Wis.; Wisconsin State T. Col. *Exhibited*: CGA, 1939; AIC, 1942; GGE, 1939; MMA (AV), 1942; SFMA, 1946; Milwaukee AI, 1937 (one-man); Wustum Mus., Racine, Wis.; Layton A. Gal.; State Hist. Soc.; Wis. State Fair; Madison Un.; Renaissance Soc., Chicago; VMFA; Cal. PLH; Walker A. Center; 2-man: Layton A. Gal., 1953; Lawrence Col.; Cardinal Stritch Col., 1954; (with Schomer Lichtner) Milwaukee, 1957; Frank Ryan Gal., Chicago, 1958; BM, 1958.

GROTH, JOHN—*Painter, I., Gr., T., L., Cart., W.*
61 East 57th St., New York 22, N.Y.

B. Chicago, Ill., Feb. 26, 1908. *Studied*: AIC; ASL, and with Todros Geller, Arnold Blanch, George Grosz. *Member*: ANA; AWS; Audubon A.; Overseas Press Cl.; SAGA; Am. Newspaper Gld.; SI. *Work*: MMoDA; LC; MMA; AIC; NGA; WMAA; Smithsonian Inst.; Mus. Western A., Moscow, Russia. *Exhibited*: nationally. Contributor to Vogue, Esquire, Collier's, and other magazines. Lectures: War Art. Illus., "Grapes of Wrath," 1947; "Men Without Women," 1946; "War and Peace." Author, I., "Studio: Europe," 1945; "Studio: Asia," 1952; Contributor to Life; Sports Illustrated; Look; Esquire and other national magazines. *Position*: A. Dir., Esquire magazine, 1933-37; Parade Publ., 1941-44; War Correspondent, Chicago Sun, 1944; American Legion magazine, 1945; Instr. A., ASL, New York, N.Y.; Pratt Inst., Brooklyn, N.Y.; Parsons Sch. Des., N.Y.; War Correspondent, Korea and Indo-China, 1951; Asia, 1954, 1956; Europe, 1955, 1957; Arctic, 1958.

GROVE, RICHARD GEORGE—*Museum Director, W.*
Wichita Art Museum, 619 Stackman Drive; h. 1126 West Murdock St., Wichita 3, Kans.

B. Lakewood, N.J., Feb. 7, 1921. *Studied*: Mexico City Col., B.A., M.A. *Member*: AAMus. Author: "Guide to Contemporary Mexican Architecture," 1952; "Mexican Pop-

ular Arts Today," 1954. Contributor articles to Art News; Craft Horizons; Frontier; Colorado Magazine; Brand Book (with George Mills); Clearing House for Western Museums (with George Mills). *Positions*: Assoc. Cur., Taylor Mus. of the Colorado Springs FA Center, 1953-58; Dir., Wichita A. Mus., Wichita, Kans., 1958- .

GROW, LOTTIE LYONS *(Mrs. Walter S.)*—*Painter, Et., W., L.*
"Deer Lick," Nashville, Ind.; h. 4240 Park Ave., Indianapolis 5, Ind.

B. Hymera, Ind., July 22, 1884. *Studied*: St. Louis AI; John Herron Inst. A.; Marian Col.; and with Harold West, Edward K. Sitzman. *Member*: Brown County AA; Indiana A. Cl.; AAPL; Nat. Lg. Am. Pen Women; Fed. Women's Cl. Contributor to Indiana Fed. Club magazine with art column, for 8 years; News Week; Baton Magazine; Art Digest; AAPL. *Work*: Riley Hospital for Crippled Children. *Positions*: Presented first art program on television and radio in Indiana; A. Dir., State of Indiana, Nat. A. Week, 1936-51; A. Dir., State Fed. of Clubs, 1938-43; A. Chm., Woman's Dept. Cl., 1936-38; Sec. Program and Social Chm., Indiana A. Cl.; Judge, in numerous Art Awards Contests.

GRUBER, SHIRLEY EDITH MOSKOWITZ.
See Moskowitz, Shirley

GRUBERT, CARL ALFRED—*Cartoonist, Comm. A.*
Woodlawn Ave., Des Plaines, Ill.

B. Chicago, Ill., Sept. 10, 1911. *Studied*: Univ. Wisconsin, B.S.; Chicago Acad. FA. *Member*: Nat. Cartoonists Soc. *Awards*: U.S.Treasury award of merit, 1950; Freedom's Fnd. medal, 1950. *Exhibited*: Nat. Cartoonists Soc. exh., 1950, 1951; MMA, 1951; LC, 1949. *Position*: Creator, Cart., "The Berrys," internationally syndicated cartoon, 1942- ; Staff A., Great Lakes Bulletin and Public Information, 9th Naval Dist., 1944-45.

GRUDIN, SHIM—*Painter*
74 Grove St., New York 14, N.Y.; h. 518 Park Ave., Huntington, N.Y.

B. New York, N.Y., Jan. 1, 1913. *Studied*: Col. City of New York, B.B.A.; New School for Social Research. *Member*: AEA (Bd. Dir.). *Awards*: Hecksher Mus. A., 1957, 1958. *Exhibited*: Jewish Tercentenary, 1955; Riverside Mus.; Phila. A. All.; DMFA; CMA; AIC; Contemporary A.; Adelphi Col.; New Gal., 1951; one-man: Chinese Gal., 1942; New Gal., 1951, 1953; Artisans Gal., 1954; Wellons Gal., 1957.

GRUPPE, EMILE ALBERT—*Painter, T.*
32 Rocky Neck Ave.; h. 9 Wonson St., East Gloucester, Mass.

B. Rochester, New York, Nov. 23, 1896. *Studied*: ASL; NAD; abroad, and with John F. Carlson, Richard Miller, George Bridgman. *Member*: SC; North Shore AA; Rockport AA; All. A. Am.; Longboat Key AA; Sarasota AA; Grand Central A. Gal.; Rockport AA; Audubon A.; Meriden A. & Crafts; St. Augustine AA; Academic A., Springfield, Mass. *Awards*: prizes, Springville, Utah, 1928, 1946; New Haven Paint & Clay Cl., 1933, 1938-1940; North Shore AA, 1939, 1958; Guilford, Conn., 1939; Bridgeport AA, 1940; All. A. Am., 1944; Ranger Fund purchase, 1949, 1953; Academic A., Springfield, 1953; Hollywood, Cal., 1955; Rockport AA, 1956, 1957; SC, 1941, 1953; Ogunquit A. Center, 1941; Champlain Valley Exh., 1949; med., prize, Jordan Marsh, 1943; Meriden A. & Crafts, 1939, 1946. *Work*: Los A. Mus. A.; Witte Mem. Mus.; Univ. Idaho; Webber Col.; Smith Col.; New Haven Paint & Clay Cl.; deCordova and Dana Mus.; White House, Wash., D.C.; Silverman Col., Montreal, Canada; Montclair A. Mus.; Mechanics Inst., Rochester, N.Y.; Greenbrier Col., Lewisburg, W. Va.; Springville, Utah; J.B.Speed Mus. A.; Butler AI; Swope Gal. A.; Rockford (Ill.) H.S. *Exhibited*: NAD, 1916-1938; All. A. Am., 1934-1952; AIC, 1920; Audubon A., 1944-1952; North Shore AA, 1922-1952; Conn. Acad. FA, 1913-1952; Rockport AA, 1925-1952; New Haven Paint & Clay Cl., 1935-1952; SC, 1916-1952; Miami Beach A. Center, 1952; Findlay Gal., Chicago, 1946, 1948, 1950, 1951; Lieber Gal., Indianapolis, 1950; J.L.Hudson Gal., Detroit, 1948, 1950; Brodhead Gal., Rochester, N.Y., 1948; McNichols Gal., Naples, Fla.

GRUPPE, KARL H.—*Sculptor*
138 Manhattan Ave., New York 25, N.Y.

B. Rochester, N.Y., Mar. 18, 1893. *Studied*: Royal Acad., Antwerp, Belgium; ASL; & with Karl Bitter. *Member*: NA; Century Assn.; NAC (life); NSS. *Awards*: prizes, Arch. Lg., 1920; NAD, 1926; AAPL, 1955; gold med., 1952. *Work*: Adelphi Col., Brooklyn, N.Y.; Curtis Inst. Music, Phila.; Brookgreen Gardens; Henry Hudson mem., Spuyten Duyvil Hill, N.Y.; Numismatic Soc., N.Y.; garden figures, portrait busts privately commissioned. *Exhibited*: NSS, 1923; NAD, 1926, 1928, 1929, 1945; Arch. Lg.; WMAA, 1940; WFNY 1939; etc. *Position*: S. Member, N.Y. Art Comm., 1943-47; A. Comm. Assoc., 1948; Pres., NSS, 1950-51; 2nd Vice-Pres., NAD, 1955, 1st Vice-Pres., NAD, 1957-58.

GRUSHKIN, PHILIP—*Designer, T., Calligrapher*
86 East Linden Ave., Englewood, N.J.

B. New York, N.Y., June 1, 1921. *Studied*: CUASch. *Member*: AIGA; Book Jacket Des. Gld.; Soc. for Italic Handwriting. *Awards*: Certif. of Excellence, Printing for Commerce Exh., 1950. *Exhibited*: Book Jacket Des. Gld., 1948-1952; Lettering & Calligraphy in Current Advertising and Publishing exh., 1945; Printing for Commerce, 1950; Victoria and Albert Mus., London, 1949; Cooper Union A. Sch. Instr. Exh., 1951; Gld. of Bookworkers, AIGA, 1954; Graphic Des., Peter Cooper Gal., 1954. I., Calligrapher of "Aesop's Fables," 1946; "Christmas Carols," 1948; calligraphy represented in "Bouquet for Bruce Rogers," 1950 and "Calligraphics," 1955. *Position*: Cartographer, U.S. Geological Survey, 1942-43; Office of Strategic Services, U.S.Army, 1943-45; Instr., Lettering, Calligraphy and Illustration, CUASch., New York, N.Y., 1946- ; Des., The World Publishing Co., New York, N.Y., 1955-56; Des., Harry N. Abrams, Inc., N.Y., 1957- ; Freelance Des., 1946- .

GUACCERO, I. VINCENT—
Educator, Des., Gr., C., P., S.
Box 9026, University Station, Baton Rouge, La.

B. Italy. *Studied*: T. Col., Columbia Univ. B.S., M.A. *Member*: Eastern AA; Soc. for Advancement of Edu.; Am. Assn. Univ. Prof. Lectures: Art Education. *Position*: Asst. Prof. FA & A. Edu., Louisiana State Univ., Baton Rouge, La.; Chm., Southeastern Area A. Comm. for Int. Sch. A. Program; Assoc. Council memb., Comm. on A. Edu.*

GUALTIERI, JOSEPH PETER—*Painter, T.*
120 Platt Ave., Norwich, Conn.

B. Royalton, Ill., Dec. 25, 1916. *Studied*: Norwich A. Sch.; AIC. *Member*: Mystic AA; Norwich AA. *Awards*: Traveling scholarship, AIC, 1939, med. & prize, 1941; prizes, PAFA, 1948, 1951; Wadsworth Atheneum, 1950, 1954, 1956, 1957; Springfield Fair, 1951; Terry AI, 1952; New Haven Paint & Clay Cl., 1954; Slater Mus. A., 1954, 1955, 1956, 1957; Mystic AA, 1957; Silvermine Gld. A., 1954, 1957; Essex AA. *Work*: Slater A. Mus., Norwich, PAFA, 1942, 1948, 1951; Audubon A., 1945; AIC, 1940-Conn.; PAFA; Lyman Allyn Mus. A.; R.I. Sch. Design. *Exhibited*: NAD, 1945; CGA, 1941; SFMA, 1941, 1942; 1943; Lyman Allyn Mus. A., 1944, 1945; Wadsworth Atheneum, 1950, 1954; New Haven Paint & Clay Cl., 1954; Slater Mus. A., 1954, 1955; Silvermine Gld. A., 1954. *Position*: Instr., Drawing & Painting, Norwich A. Sch., Norwich, Conn.

GUCK, EDNA—*Painter, S.*
433 West 18th St., New York 11, N.Y.

B. New York, N.Y., Mar. 17, 1904. *Studied*: ASL, and in Paris, France. *Work*: SAM; BM; Queens Col.; Nat. Hospital for Speech Disorders; Halloran Hospital; N.Y. Pub. Sch.; N.Y. Housing Projects. *Award*: prize, Essex AA, 1951. *Exhibited*: Riggs-Sarent, Mexico, D.F., 1952; Galerie San Angel, Mexico, D.F., 1954; Panoras Gal., 1954; Essex AA, 1950-1951; Carlebach Gal., 1950; Centre d'Art, Haiti, 1949; Bonestell Gal., 1939-1946; Am-British A. Center, 1942; AID, 1941; MMA, 1941; WFNY 1939; New Sch. Social Research, 1940; Ferargil Gal., 1939; N.Y. Soc. Women A., 1935-1938; Newark Mus. A., 1936; Newton Gal., 1935; Jersey City Mus., 1935; CGA, 1935; Providence AA, 1930; Salon d'Automne, Paris, 1928. *Position*: Instr., River Edge Adult Edu., New Jersey, 1951-58; Jewish Community Center of the Rockaways, New York, 1951-1958; Adult Sch. of Englewood, 1956-58.

GUENTHER, PEARL HARDER—*Painter*
4900 Pacific Blvd.; h. 3659 Fairway Blvd., Los Angeles, Cal.

B. Winnipeg, Manitoba, Canada, Oct. 10, 1882. *Studied*: with M. DeNeale Morgan; Evylena Nunn Miller. *Member*: Paint & Palette Cl.; Women Painters of the West (Sec.-Treas.). *Awards*: prizes, Los A. Mus. A., 1943; Greek Theatre, Los A., 1952. *Exhibited*: Los A. State Bldg., 1935, 1936; Oakland A. Gal., 1944; Los A. Mus. A., 1943; Ebell Salon, 1949, 1953; Santa Paula Annual, 1949-1952; Pasadena AI, 1951; Laguna Beach AA, 1952-1954; La Jolla A. Center, 1951, 1954, 1955 and prior; Santa Cruz Gal. A.; Stanford Univ. Gal.; one-man: J.W.Robinson Co., 1942; Frances Webb Gal.; Oceanside, Cal.*

GUERIN, JOHN WILLIAM—*Painter, E.*
Department of Art, University of Texas (12); h. Route 7, Box 9, Austin, Tex.

B. Houghton, Mich., Aug. 29, 1920. *Studied*: Am. Acad. A., Chicago; ASL; San Miguel de Allende, Mexico; Colorado Springs FA Center. *Member*: ASL; Texas FA Assn. *Awards*: Ranger purchase award, NAD, 1958; prize, Texas P. & S. Exh., 1955. *Work*: DMFA; Mus. FA of Houston; Witte Mem. Mus.; Laguna Gloria Mus., Austin; and in many group colls. *Exhibited*: MMA, 1953; WMAA, 1956; AIC, 1957; Univ. Illinois, 1957; Colorado Springs FA Center, 1955; PAFA, 1958; Denver A. Mus., 1957; Time & Life Bldg. Exh., 1957; Nat. Inst. A. & Lets., 1957; DMFA, 1956; Survey of Texas Painting, 1957; Cushman Gal., Houston, 1957; Contemporary A. Gal., Dallas, 1957. *Positions*: Instr. Painting, DMFA, 1950-52; Asst. Prof. Painting, University of Texas, Austin, Tex., 1953- .

GUERIN, JOSEPH—*Painter*
142 Columbus Heights, Brooklyn, N.Y.

B. Ennis Clare, Ireland, Feb. 6, 1889. *Studied*: with G.A. Hays, Jonas Lie, John Singer Sargent. *Member*: AWS; All. A. Am.; SC. *Exhibited*: PAFA, 1948; BM, 1949; Providence A. Cl., 1948; Scranton Mus. A., 1948; Westchester A. Gld., 1949; NAC, 1951; Bronx A. Gld., 1950; AWS, 1950.*

GUERRERO, JOSE—*Painter*
424 West 18th St., New York 11, N.Y.

B. Granada, Spain, Oct. 27, 1914. *Studied*: in Granada and Madrid, Spain; Ecole des Beaux-Arts, Paris, France. *Awards*: Scholarships, Acad. de San Fernando, Madrid, 1944; French Ministry of Edu.; Graham Fnd. for Advanced Study in the Fine Arts Fellowship, 1958-59. *Work*: paintings, French Ministry of Nat. Edu., Paris; Belgian Ministry of Nat. Edu., Brussels; Beloit Col.; Solomon Guggenheim Mus. *Exhibited*: Solomon Guggenheim Mus., 1954; Galerie Creuze, Paris, 1957; Salon des Realites Nouvelles, Musée de l'Art Moderne, 1957; WMA, 1958; Dallas Mus. Contemp. A., 1958; WMAA, 1958; Carnegie Inst., 1958; Rome-New York Fnd., Rome; one-man: Galeria Secolo, Rome, 1948; Lou Cosyn Gal., Brussels, 1948; St. George's Gal., London, 1949; Buchholz Gal., Madrid, 1950; Smithsonian Inst., 1952; Betty Parsons Gal., 1954, 1957, 1958; A. Cl. of Chicago (2-man with Joan Miro), 1954; 10 Jeune Peintres de l'Ecole de Paris, Galerie de France, Paris, 1956.

GUGGENHEIMER, RICHARD H.—*Painter, T., W., L.*
1025 Fifth Ave., New York 28, N.Y.; also, Old Mill River Rd., Pound Ridge, N.Y.

B. New York, N.Y., Apr. 2, 1906. *Studied*: Johns Hopkins Univ., A.B.; Sorbonne, Grande Chaumiere, Paris, France; & with Picart le Doux, Morrisset, Coubine. *Member*: Am. Soc. for Aesthetics. *Exhibited*: CGA; PAFA; NAD; WMAA; AFA; one-man exh.: Van Diemen-Lilienfeld, Macbeth, Georges Seligmann galleries; Maryville Col.; Norfolk Mus. A.; & in Paris. *Author*: "Sight and Insight, A Prediction of New Perceptions in Art," 1945; "Creative Vision, in Artist and Audience," 1950; Article, "Promising Expansions in the Fine Arts," for Art Education magazine. Numerous lectures at colleges and universities. *Position*: Dir., A. Dept., Briarcliff Col., Briarcliff Manor, N.Y.

GUILLAUME, HARRY GEORGE—*Educator, C.*
Department of Art, Iowa State Teachers College; h. 1803 Clay St., Cedar Falls, Iowa

B. Buffalo, N.Y., Feb. 5, 1915. *Studied*: T. Col., Columbia Univ., B.S., M.A., D.Ed.; Fredonia (N.Y.) State T. Col.

Member: Western AA; NAEA; NEA; Iowa Edu. Assn.; A. Educators of Iowa; CAA. *Exhibited*: Grout Mus.; Black Hawk County Exh.; Cedar Falls AA. Lectures: Art Education; Art in Public Schools. *Positions*: Instr. Crafts, especially jewelry; Instr., Pub. Schs., 1936-37, 1939-45; Hd. Dept. A., Iowa State Teachers College, Cedar Falls, Iowa, 1948- .

GUILLE, PETER—*Museum Director*
Sterling & Francine Clark Art Institute, South St., Williamstown, Mass.*

GUIMARD, A(DELINE) O.—*Painter*
37 East 64th St., New York 21, N.Y.

B. New York, N.Y. *Studied*: ASL, and abroad with Albert Maignan, Joseph Bail, Henri Levy. *Member*: ASL; Artistes Francais. *Awards*: Fla. Southern Col.; Medaille de la Reconnaissance Francaise. *Work*: LC; Fla. Southern Col.; Musee St. Pierre, Lyons, France, and in private coll. *Exhibited*: Paris Salon, 1899-1933; NAD; AWS and others.*

GUION, MOLLY—*Portrait Painter*
c/o Portraits, Inc., 136 East 57th St., New York, N.Y.*

GULICK, HENRY T.—*Painter*
Middletown, N.J.

B. Manolapan, N.J., Aug. 1, 1872. *Work*: Newark Mus. A. *Exhibited*: Montclair A. Mus.; Tinton Falls, N.J.; Newark Mus. A.; PAFA; Trenton, N.J.; one-man: Clinton, N.J.; Bloomsbury, N.J.; Newark, N.J.*

GUMMO, BLANCHARD (STANLEY)—
Painter, E., L., Gr., W.
219 Market St., Lewisburg, Pa.; h. 220 North Fairview St., Lock Haven, Pa.

B. Lock Haven, Pa., Feb. 3, 1906. *Studied*: Yale Col., B.A.; Yale Sch. FA, B.F.A., and with Hobson Pittman, Alexander Brook. *Member*: AEA; Harrisburg (Pa.) AA; Central Pennsylvania AA; Conn. Acad. FA. *Awards*: med., Soc. Wash. A., 1934; prizes, Harrisburg AA, 1939, 1941, 1951, 1952; State T. Col., Indiana, Pa., 1949, 1951. *Work*: PAFA. *Exhibited*: AIC, 1935, 1936; CM, 1935-1938; Soc. Wash. A., 1934, 1937; CGA, 1939; PAFA; 1936, 1937, 1940, 1941, 1947, 1949; Conn. Acad. FA, 1935, 1936, 1938-1946, 1948, 1950-1952; All. A. Am., 1936-1938; Springfield A. Lg., 1937, 1938, 1940, 1941, 1943, 1945, 1948; New Haven Paint & Clay Cl., 1939; Butler AI, 1938-1941, 1943-1945; State T. Col., Indiana, Pa., 1944-1946, 1948-1951; Pepsi-Cola, 1945; Terry AI, 1952; Fla. Southern Col., 1952; Audubon A., 1952. Contributor to art magazines and articles on American artists to Encyclopaedia Americana, 1952. *Positions*: Instr. A., 1931-34, Asst. Prof. A., 1934-39, Assoc. Prof. A., 1939-46, Prof. A., 1948- , Bucknell Univ., Lewisburg, Pa.*

GUNDLACH, HELEN FUCHS (Mrs. Emanuel G.)—
Painter, C., S.
4378 Seneca St., Ebenezer, N.Y.

B. Buffalo, N.Y., Feb. 9, 1892. *Studied*: Syracuse Univ.; PMSchIA; Albright A. Sch. *Member*: Buffalo Soc. A.; Lg. Am. Pen Women; AAPL; Catherine L. Wolfe A. Cl. *Awards*: prizes, Lg. Am. Pen Women, 1950; Buffalo Soc. A., 1946. *Work*: designed Zonta Club insignia now used internationally. *Exhibited*: traveling exh. of caseins, circulated by Studio Gld., Reading, Conn., 1954-56.*

GUNKEL, VIRGINIA P.—*Painter, T.*
449 East 58th St., New York 22, N.Y.

B. Chicago, Ill., June 30, 1916. *Studied*: Univ. Illinois Sch. Arch.; Northwestern Univ.; AIC; ASL, and with Andrene Kaufman, Charles Reinecke. *Member*: Boston Soc. Indp. A.; Pen & Brush Cl.; NAWA; AWS; Soc. Painters in Casein; Intl. Plastic Arts Council; New Orleans AA. *Awards*: prizes, New Jersey P. & S. Soc., 1948; Manhasset AA, 1953; Long Island A. Soc., 1952, 1953; Jane Stanley Price award, NAWA, 1956. *Work*: in collections in the U.S. and abroad. *Exhibited*: NAD; NAWA, 1951-1958, traveling exh., 1956-1958; Pen & Brush Cl., 1951-1954; All. A. Am., 1949; Boston Soc. Indp. A., 1951-1954; New Jersey P. & S. Soc., 1948, 1950, 1951; Terry AI, 1952; L.D.M. Sweat Mus. A., 1949; Alabama WC Soc.,

1949; Corpus Christi, Tex., 1948; Old Northwest Territory Exh., 1949; Delgado Mus. A., 1951; Norton Gal. A., 1949, 1950; State T. Col., Indiana, Pa., 1949, 1950; BMFA, 1953; Amsterdam, Holland, 1956; Brussels, Antwerp, and Ostend, Belgium, 1956; Bern and Lugano, Switzerland, 1956; Athens, Greece, 1957; Salonica, Greece and Brussels, 1958; one-man: Argent Gal.; Little Gal., N.Y. *Position*: Chm., Foreign Exhs., NAWA, 1953-56; Chm. Publicity, Pen & Brush Cl., 1954-56; Asst. Treas., Pen & Brush Cl., 1955-58; Pres., NAWA, 1957-59; Bd. Memb., U.S. Committee, Intl. Plastic Arts Council.

GUNN, PAUL JAMES—*Educator, P., Gr.*
Art Department, Oregon State College; h. 1440 Kings Road, Corvallis, Ore.

B. Guys Mills, Pa., June 21, 1922. *Studied*: Edinboro (Pa.) State T. Col., B.S. in A. Edu.; Cal. Col. A. & Crafts, Oakland, Cal., M.F.A. *Member*: AAUP; Portland AA. *Awards*: prizes, Oregon A. print exh., Portland A. Mus., 1950; SAM, 1954; Pacific Northwest A., Spokane, Wash., 1954, 1956. *Work*: Portland A. Mus.; SAM; City of Spokane Coll. *Exhibited*: Oakland A. Mus., 1951, 1956; Bordighera, Italy, 1956; Denver A. Mus., 1951; Portland A. Mus., 1950-1958; SAM, 1951, 1954, 1956; Spokane, Wash., 1954, 1956, 1958; one-man: Portland A. Mus., 1953. *Position*: Assoc. Prof. A., Oregon State College, Corvallis, Ore.

GUNTER, FRANK ELLIOTT—*Painter*
7612 Fifth Ave., South, Birmingham, Ala.

B. Jasper, Ala., May 8, 1934. *Studied*: Univ. Alabama, B.F.A. *Work*: Milton Bradley Co.; Grumbacher Co.; Higgins Co.; Birmingham Mus. FA; Mississippi Mus. FA. *Exhibited*: Birmingham Mus. FA, 1956; Jackson, Miss., 1955; Forum Gal., N.Y., 1956; Birmingham Festival of A., 1953.*

GUNTHER, FLOYD THEODORE (TED)—
Commercial Artist, I.
200 Cabrini Blvd., New York 33, N.Y.

B. London, Ont., Canada, July 21, 1907. *Studied*: London Tech. A. Sch.; Wicker Sch. FA, Detroit, Mich. *Member*: Scarab Cl., Detroit; SI. *Exhibited*: Detroit Inst. A., and in private galleries. *Position*: A. Dir., Morris Press, Detroit, Mich.; A. Dir., Bulova Watch Co., New York, N.Y., 1937-58; Freelance Illustrator, 1958- .

GUNTRUM, EMILIE IDA—*Painter*
471 Madison Ave., Elizabeth, N.J.

B. Brooklyn, N.Y. *Studied*: N.Y. Sch. App. Des. for Women; ASL; NAD; & with Charles Hawthorne, George Luks, George Bridgman, Hans Hofmann. *Member*: AAPL. *Exhibited*: PAFA, 1938; AWCS, 1939; Montclair A. Mus.; WFNY 1939; Newark Mus.; Montross Gal.; Contemporary A. Gal.

GURDUS, LUBA (Mrs.)—*Painter, I., Hist.*
French & Company, 978 Madison Ave.; h. 246 West End Ave., New York 23, N.Y.

B. Bialystok, Poland, Aug. 1, 1914. *Studied*: A. Sch., Lausanne, Switzerland; Acad. A., Warsaw, Poland; Inst. FA, N. Y. Univ., B.A., M.A., and in Germany. *Member*: N.Y. Univ. Alumni Assn. *Award*: prize, Warsaw Acad. A., 1938. *Work*: Tel-Aviv, Israel, Mun. Coll.; Howard Univ.; Jewish Mus., N.Y.; Israeli Consulate; Stephen Wise House, N.Y. *Exhibited*: one-man—Bezalel Mus., Jerusalem; Katz Gal., Tel-Aviv, 1947; ACA Gal., N.Y., 1948; Barbizon-Plaza Gal., 1948, 1952; Stephen Wise House, 1953; Jewish Mus., 1957. Illus. for Hebrew books and publications; The Congress Weekly, N.Y.; "Bluszcz" Publications, Warsaw; "L'Ischa" magazine, Tel-Aviv. *Position*: Hd. Research & Libn., French & Co., New York, N.Y., 1956- .

GURNEY, EDITH B.—*Art Librarian*
Rochester Public Library; h. 178 Wellington Ave., Rochester 11, N.Y.

B. Binghamton, N.Y., Jan. 5, 1905. *Studied*: Elmira Col., A.B.; Columbia Univ., Sch. Lib. Service, B.S. *Member*: York State Craftsmen; Am. Lib. Assn.; N.Y. State Lib. Assn. *Position*: Hd., A. Div., Rochester (N.Y.) Pub. Lib., 1932- ; Sec., Rochester Pr. Cl., 1955-56, 1956-59.

GURR, LENA—*Painter, Ser., Lith.*

2 West 15th St., New York 11, N.Y.; h. 71 Remsen St., Brooklyn 12, N.Y.

B. Brooklyn, N.Y., Oct. 27, 1897. *Studied*: Brooklyn Training Sch. for T.; Edu. All.; ASL, with John Sloan, Maurice Sterne. *Member*: NAWA; N.Y. Soc. Women A.; Brooklyn Soc. A.; Audubon A.; AEA; Soc. Painters in Casein; Am. Color Pr. Soc.; SAGA; Silvermine Gld. A.; P. & S. of New Jersey; Cape Cod AA; Provincetown AA. *Awards*: prizes, NAWA, 1937, 1947, 1950, 1952, medal, 1954, 1956 (2), 1957; Comm. for Democratic Living, 1951; Brooklyn Soc. A., 1943, 1951, 1954, 1955; Nat. Ser. Soc., 1949; Albany Pr. Cl., 1955 (purchase); P. & S. of New Jersey, 1956; Silvermine Gld. A., 1957; Audubon A., 1958. *Work*: Biro Bidjan Mus., Russia; LC; Univ. Wisconsin; AAUW; Tel-Aviv Mus.; Ain-Harod Mus., Israel; N.Y. Pub. Lib.; Cal. State Lib.; Kansas State Col.; Brandeis Univ.; VMFA; Howard Univ.; Butler Inst. Am. A.; Staten Island Mus. A. & Sc. *Exhibited*: PAFA, 1938, 1952-54; NAD, 1944-46, 1951; Carnegie Inst., 1945; VMFA, 1946; BM, 1936, 1954, 1956, 1958; Brooklyn Soc. A., 1941, 1943-1958; ACA Gal., 1935, 1939, 1945, 1947, 1950, 1953, 1959 (all one-man); MMA, 1942, 1952; WMAA, 1953; Oklahoma A. Center; Wichita AA; Syracuse Mus. FA; Riverside Mus.; Paris, France; Canada and Latin America; Am. Acad. A. & Lets., 1958, and others. *Positions*: Bd. Dirs., Brooklyn Soc. A., 1950-53, 1955-57; Audubon A., 1946; NAWA, 1950; AEA, 1949-50, 1950-51, 1952-53; Soc. Painters in Casein, 1957, 1958, and others.

GURREY, HARTLEY FLETCHER (Mrs. Richard B.)— *Lithographer, P., Des., T.*

3704 Via Palomino, Palos Verdes Estates, Cal.

B. Bloomington, Ill. *Studied*: Washington State Col., B.A.; Univ. Oregon; ASL, and with Wayman Adams, Louis Bouche, Jean Charlot. *Member*: New England Pr. M.; Southern Pr. M.; Honolulu Pr. M.; Hawaii P. & S. *Work*: Honolulu Acad. A. (doc. record Army activities in Hawaii); murals, Service Women's Center; Hawaiian Islands Flower Bldg.; textile des., Hawaiian Garment Mfgrs. *Exhibited*: AIC; CM; PAFA; SFMA; Sydney, Australia; Portland (Ore.) Mus. A.; SAM; Northwest Pr. M.; New England Pr. M.; Southern Pr. M.; Honolulu Pr. M.; traveling exhs., Honolulu Acad. A. *Position*: Instr., P., Des., Washington State Col., 1932-36; Pa. State Univ., 1937-41; Pres., Honolulu Pr. M., 1951-53, Bd., 1943-54.

GUSSOW, BERNARD—*Painter, Lith., T.*

Newark School of Fine & Industrial Arts, 550 High St., Newark, N.J.; h. 855 West End Ave., New York 25, N.Y.

B. Russia, 1881. *Studied*: Col. City of N.Y.; ASL; NAD; Ecole des Beaux-Arts, Paris, with Bonnat. *Member*: AEA. *Work*: WMAA; Newark Mus.; Barnes Fnd.; MMoDA; Los A. Mus. A.; U.S. Marine Hospital, La.; USPO, East Rochester, N.Y. *Exhibited*: Int. Armory Show, 1912; Luxembourg Mus., Paris, 1919; AIC, 1930-1932; NGA, 1938; Lib. Cong., 1944-1946; Carnegie Inst., 1944; WMAA, 1930-1936; Assoc. A. New Jersey; Mun. Exh., Rockefeller Center, 1937; WFNY 1939. *Position*: Instr. A., Newark Sch. F. & Indst. A., Newark, N.J., 1912- .*

GUSSOW, ROY—*Sculptor, E., Des.*

110 Cox Ave., Raleigh, N.C.

B. Brooklyn, N.Y., Nov. 12, 1918. *Studied*: Chicago Inst. Des., B.A. Products Des.; and with Moholy Nagy, Archipenko. *Awards*: prizes, Exhibition Momentum, Chicago, 1948; North Carolina State A. Mus., Raleigh, 1952, 1957; PAFA, 1958. *Work*: s., North Carolina State A. Mus.; Lenoir Rhyne Col., Hickory, N.C.; North Carolina State Col., Sch. Des.; numerous residential commissions. *Exhibited*: AIC, 1947-1949; Oakland A. Mus., 1949, 1950; PAFA, 1951-1954, 1958; SFMA, 1951; N.Y. Metropolitan Sculpture Exh., 1951; Sabena Intl., 1953; Birmingham, Ala., 1954; Denver A. Mus., 1949-1951; Omaha, Neb., 1949, 1950; Kansas City AI, 1950; N.C. State A. Mus., 1952-1955, 1957; Univ. Florida, 1953; AFA traveling exh., 1956; WMAA, 1956. *Position*: Instr., S. Ceramics, Des., Bradley Univ.; Colorado Springs FA Center; Prof. Des., North Carolina State Col., Raleigh, N.C., 1952- .

GUSTAFSON, DWIGHT LEONARD—*Educator*

Bob Jones University, Greenville, S.C.

B. Seattle, Wash., Apr. 20, 1930. *Studied*: Bob Jones Univ., B.A., M.A. *Position*: Dean, Sch. FA, Bob Jones University, Greenville, S.C., 1954- .

GUSTEN, THEODORE J. H.—*Art Director*

International Graphic Arts Society, 65 West 56th St., New York 19, N.Y.*

GUSTON, PHILIP—*Painter, T.*

112 E. 18th St., New York, N.Y.

B. Montreal, Canada, June 27, 1912. *Studied*: Otis AI. *Awards*: prizes, WFNY 1939; Carnegie Inst., 1945; med., prize, VMFA, 1946; Guggenheim F., 1948; Prix de Rome, 1948; grant, Am. Acad. A. & Let., 1948. *Work*: CAM; WMAA; PC; Albright A. Gal.; Wash. Univ., St. Louis; VMFA; Illinois Wesleyan Univ.; Univ. Iowa; MMA; Univ. Illinois; MMoDA; Munson-Williams-Proctor Inst.; WMA; Iowa State Col.; murals, Queensbridge Housing Project, N.Y.; Social Security Bldg., Wash., D.C. *Exhibited*: Midtown Gal., 1945 (one-man); BMFA, 1946 (one-man); Carnegie Inst., 1941-1945, 1951, 1955; PAFA, 1944, 1945; CGA, 1943, 1944, 1955; VMFA, 1946; WMAA, 1941-1955; AIC, 1942-1945; AFA traveling exh., 1942; Peridot Gal., 1952 (one-man); MMoDA, 1951, 1956; Guggenheim Mus., 1954, traveling exh., 1955-56; Galerie de France, Paris, 1952; Musee Moderne, Paris, 1955; Rome, 1955; Museo de Arte Moderna, Barcelona, 1955; Tate Gal., London, 1956; Sao Paulo, Brazil, 1957; "New American Paintings," Rome, Milan, London, Paris, Basel, Madrid, 1958-59; Mexico City, 1958; one-man: Egan Gal., 1953; Janis Gal., N.Y., 1956, 1958. Contributor to art magazines with articles and illus. *Position*: Instr. A., Washington Univ., St. Louis, Mo., 1945-47; Instr., N.Y. Univ., at present.

GUTE, HERBERT JACOB—*Painter, E.*

92 Norton St., New Haven 11, Conn.

B. Jeffersonville, N.Y., Aug. 10, 1907. *Studied*: Yale Univ.; & abroad. *Member*: Audubon A.; AWCS; SC; Phila. WC Cl.; Silvermine Gld. A. *Awards*: prizes, Alvord prize, 1932; AWCS, 1940, 1942; Wash. WC Cl., 1943; Conn. Contemporary Painting; Hallmark award; New England A. Exh.; Boston A. Festival, 1956. *Work*: Yale Univ.; Dept. Interior, Wash., D.C.; IBM; Cambridge, England; Jewish Mus., N.Y.; New Britain Mus.; New London Mus. A.; Wadsworth Atheneum; Submarine Base, New London, Conn. *Exhibited*: Audubon A.; AWCS; Phila. WC Cl.; NAD; Wash. WC Cl. I., "Rise of American Democracy," 1942; & other books. Contributor to: American Artist magazine. *Position*: Asst. Prof. A., Yale Univ., New Haven, Conn.; Univ. Virginia; Consultant, Art as Therapy, Conn. State Hospital; Staff A., Yale Univ. and French Acad. Expedition to Dura-Europos, Syria.

GUTMANN, JOHN—*Educator, P., Gr.*

San Francisco State College; h. 80 Fairmont Drive, Daly City, Cal.

B. Breslau, Germany, May 28, 1905. *Studied*: State Acad. A. & Crafts, B.A., Breslau, Germany; State Acad., Berlin. *M.A. Member*: Am. Assn. Univ. Prof.; CAA. *Work*: San Diego FA Soc.; deYoung Mem. Mus.; MMoDA; Mills Col., Oakland, Cal. *Exhibited*: SFMA, 1935, 1939, 1942; deYoung Mem. Mus., 1938, 1941, 1948; New York, N.Y., 1938; Detroit, Mich., 1938; & abroad. Contributor to: Life, Time, Asia, Sat. Eve. Post, & other national magazines. Produced and photographed 2 documentary films on China, 1950. *Position*: Prof. A., San F. State Col., San Francisco, Cal., 1938- .

GWATHMEY, ROBERT—*Painter, Ser., T.*

144 Waverly Place, New York 14, N.Y.

B. Richmond, Va., Jan. 24, 1903. *Studied*: North Carolina State Col.; Maryland Inst.; PAFA. *Member*: An Am. Group; AEA. *Awards*: Cresson traveling scholarship, PAFA, 1929, 1930; prizes, 48 States Comp., 1939; ACA Gal., 1939; PM Artist as Reporter, 1940; Carnegie Inst., 1942; San Diego FA Soc., 1941; Pepsi-Cola, 1946; Rosenwald F., 1944; Grant, Am. Acad. A. & Let., 1946; Birmingham Mus. A., 1956; CGA, 1957. *Work*: BMFA; BM; Birmingham Mus. A.; Butler AI; Mus. Mod. A., Sao Paulo, Brazil; Carnegie Inst.; IBM; Los A. Mus. A.; PAFA; Rochester Mem. Mus.; San Diego FA Gal.; Springfield (Mass.) Mus. A.; Telfair Acad.; Brandeis Univ.; Univ. Nebraska; Univ. Georgia; Univ. Illinois; Univ. Oklahoma; Univ. Texas; Alabama Inst. Tech.; VMFA; WMAA; Cal. PLH. *Exhibited*: nationally. *Position*: Instr., CUASch., New York, N.Y., 1942-52.

GYERMEK, STEPHEN A.—*Museum Director, P., E., C.*
Gerrer Museum of Art; h. 1007 Jefferson Place, Shawnee, Okla.

B. Budapest, Hungary, Nov. 9, 1930. *Studied*: in Amsterdam, Holland, and with Heinrich Campendonck. *Awards*: prizes, Van Alabbe award, Amsterdam, Holland, 1952, and other prizes. *Work*: murals in convent at Madrid, Spain, 1955; U.S. Embassy, Spain, 1955. *Exhibited*: Amsterdam, 1952, 1953; Madrid, 1954. Lectures: Painting Methods; Religious Art. Exhibitions arranged: Archaeology, Europe, Near and Far East, Egypt; American Indians & Central and South American Ethnology; Paintings from the Italian Renaissance; 19th Century American Paintings, and others. *Position*: Dir., Gerrer Museum & Art Gallery, Shawnee, Okla., 1957- .

GYRA, FRANCIS JOSEPH, JR.—*Painter, I., T., L.*
6 Linden Hill, Woodstock, Vt.

B. Newport, R.I., Feb. 23, 1914. *Studied*: R.I. Sch. Des.; Parsons Sch. Des.; Univ. Hawaii; McNeese State Col., Lake Charles, La.; Brighton Col. A. & Crafts, England; Froebel Inst., Roehampton, England, and in France, and Italy. *Member*: NAEA; Eastern AA; Vermont A. T. Assn. *Awards*: prize, Newport AA; Fulbright T. Exchange, 1952-53; State of Rhode Island scholarship, 1931-1935; Frank A. Parsons Mem. scholarship, 1935, 1937. *Work*: Providence Mus. A. *Exhibited*: AIC; Phila. WC Cl.; AFA traveling exh., 1940; one-man: Wash. A. Cl.; Newport AA; L.D.M.Sweat Mus. A.; Robert Vose Gal., Boston. I., "Letters of Father Page"; "A New Italian Reader for Beginners." Lectures: "Developing Creative Expression in the School," to colleges, universities and museums in U.S., Great Britain, Hawaii, South Wales. *Position*: Supv. A., Woodstock (Vt.) Pub. Schs.; Chm., Vermont Edu. A. Program, 1952; Sec.-Treas., Vermont A. T. Assn., 1957-58.

HAAS, CLARA *(Mrs. George C.)*—*Painter*
"Fernbrook," Tripp St., Mt. Kisco, N.Y.

B. New York, N.Y., Apr. 3, 1895. *Studied*: ASL, and with Jerry Farnsworth; Jonas Lie; Xavier Gonzalez. *Member*: Pen & Brush Cl.; NAC; Silvermine Gld. A.; AEA; NAWA. *Awards*: prizes, Village A. Center, 1954, 1955; AAPL, 1956; Westchester A. & Crafts, 1956; Silvermine Gld. A., 1956; Pen & Brush Cl., 1957. *Exhibited*: Audubon A., 1952, 1957; AWS, 1956; N.Y. City Center Gal., 1956, 1957; PAFA, 1957; NAC, 1956, 1957; Pen & Brush Cl., 1956-1958; Silvermine Gld. A., 1956, 1957; Nat. Soc. Painters in Casein, 1957; NAWA, 1951, 1958; Art:USA, 1958.

HAAS, HELEN *(Mrs. Ruffin de Langley)*—*Sculptor*
28 East 73rd St., New York 21, N.Y.

B. Brooklyn, N.Y., Sept. 20, 1904. *Studied*: in France, and with Antoine Bourdelle. *Member*: Salons Artistes Francaises, de Printemps, d'Automne, des Tuileries, Paris, France; NSS. *Work*: Luxembourg Mus., Paris; Port Sunlight Mus., London; N.Y. Mus. Nat. Hist., and in private colls. in U.S., England, France, Italy and Spain. Many port. busts of prominent persons in U.S. and abroad. *Exhibited*: Paris Salons annually, 1926-1939; Tokyo, Japan, 1935; one-man: Charpentier Gal., Paris; Knoedler Gal., London; Leicester Gal., London; Jacques Seligmann Gal., N.Y.; NSS, 1950, 1953.*

HAAS, LEZ (L.)—*Painter, E.*
University of New Mexico; h. 2809 Tennessee St., Northeast, Albuquerque, N.M.

B. Berkeley, Cal., Mar. 10, 1911. *Studied*: San Francisco State T. Col.; Univ. California, Berkeley, A.B., M.A.; Hans Hofmann Sch. A. *Member*: AAUP; AEA; Archaeological Inst. Am.; San F. AA; CAA; NEA; Pacific AA; Albuquerque Comm. A. Gld. *Awards*: prize, Mus. New Mexico, 1957. *Work*: Cedar City, Utah; paintings in private colls. *Exhibited*: SFMA, 1938-1940; GGE, 1939; BMA, 1955; New Mexico State Fair; Mus. New Mexico, Santa Fe, 1957; Roswell Mus. A.; Stanford Univ., 1958. Lectures: History of American Indian Art; Design; Painting. *Position*: Asst. Prof., 1946-47, Assoc. Prof., Chm. Dept. A., 1947-53, Prof., 1953- ; Acting Dean, College of FA, 1947-48, 1954-1955, Univ. New Mexico, Albuquerque, N.M.; Dir., Taos Field Sch., Taos, N.M., 1947-48.

**HAASE, MADELINE F. *(Mrs. Robert Paul Fockens)*
*Painter, Gr., C., T.***
4648 Kester Ave., Sherman Oaks, Cal.

B. Los Angeles, Cal., Jan. 31, 1931. *Studied*: Mount St. Mary's Col., Los A.; Immaculate Heart Col., Los A., B.A., and in Europe. *Member*: Cal. WC Soc. *Award*: prize, Nat. Orange Show, San Bernardino, 1953. *Work*: VMFA; Oregon State Col., and other university colls.; Achenbach Fnd., Cal. PLH. *Exhibited*: BMA, 1953; VMFA, circulating exh., 1953-1955; Cal. Intl. Flower Show Art Exh., 1955; Los A. Mus. A., 1954-1958; National Orange Show, 1953, 1957; San Diego FA Center, 1957; Long Beach Mun. A. Center, 1958; Cal. WC Soc., 1952-1957; Western Assn. Mus. Dirs. traveling exh., 1955-1959; de Young Mem. Mus., 1952; Cal. State Fair, 1953; Santa Cruz A. Lg., 1955. Contributor of reproductions to Fortnight, Arts & Architecture; Design magazines.

HADEN, E(UNICE) (BARNARD)—*Painter, I.*
5112 Connecticut Ave., Washington 8, D.C.

B. Washington, D.C., Oct. 21, 1901. *Studied*: Oberlin Col., B.A.; Abbott Sch. A., with Hugo Inden; and with Eliot O'Hara. *Member*: Min. P. S. & Gravers Soc. (Treas.); A. Cl. of Wash.; St. Augustine (Fla.) AA. *Awards*: prize, A. Cl. of Wash., 1956. *Work*: in private collections. *Exhibited*: St. Augustine AA, 1952; Min. P. S. & Gravers Soc., 1939, 1940, 1946-1958; CGA, 1955; NCFA, 1953-1956; Garden Gate Restaurant, Wash., D.C., 1957; Colony Restaurant, 1958; one-man: A. Cl. of Wash., 1956; Silver Spring (Md.) A. Gal., 1953, 1956; Napoli Restaurant, Wash., D.C., 1958. *Positions*: A. Cl. of Wash. Exh. Comm. Chm., 1956-57, Vice-Chm., 1957-58, Vice-Chm. Program Comm., 1956-59; Chm., Metropolitan State A. Contest (sponsored by AAPL), 1957.

HADER, ELMER (STANLEY)—*Illustrator, W.*
55 River Rd., Grand View-on-Hudson, N.Y.

B. Pajaro, Cal., Sept. 7, 1889. *Studied*: Cal. Sch. Des.; Academie Julian, Paris, France. *Awards*: Caldecott medal (with Berta Hader), 1949. *Work*: San F. AA. *Exhibited*: NAD, 1920; Salon des Artistes Francaise, Paris. Author, I., more than thirty story and picture books for children, 1927-1958. Illus. for McCall's, Pictorial Review, Good Housekeeping, Century magazines and for Christian Science Monitor.

HADLEY, MARY ALICE—*Designer*
1570 Story Ave.; h. 1638 Story Ave., Louisville 6, Ky.

B. Terre Haute, Ind., Oct. 5, 1911. *Studied*: De Pauw Univ.; Indiana State Col.; Columbia Univ.; Univ. Louisvlile; A. Center, Louisville. *Member*: A. Cl. of Louisville; Advertising Cl.; A. Center Assn., Louisville. *Awards*: "Good Design" award, MModA, 1952. *Work*: mural, Louisville YWCA. *Exhibited*: MModA, 1952; Syracuse Mus. FA, 1945; America House, 1946; Morehead (Ky.) State Col., 1949; Massillon Mus. A., 1950; North Canton Little Gal., 1951; Swope Gal. A., Terre Haute, 1951. Lectures: History of Pottery & Porcelain. *Position*: Des., Hadley Pottery, 1940- .

**HADLOCK, WENDELL STANWOOD—
*Museum Director, E., W., L.***
Rockland, Me.

B. Islesford, Me., May 12, 1911. *Studied*: Univ. Maine, A.B.; Univ. Pennsylvania, M.A.; Am. Mus. Nat. Hist., N.Y. (training). *Member*: Maine Hist. Soc.; Am. Folklore Soc.; Am. Archaeological Soc.; F., Am. Anthropological Soc.; Colonial Soc. of Mass. Contributor to: American Folklore; American Anthropologist; American Antiquity. Lectures: Folklore; History; Ethnology. *Position*: Cur., Robert Abbe Mus., Bar Harbor; Admin. Asst., Peabody Mus., Salem, Mass.; Dir., William A. Farnsworth Lib. & A. Mus., Rockland, Me., at present.

**HAENIGSEN, HARRY—
—*Illustrator, Cart., Comm. A., W.***
145 West 44th St., New York, N.Y.; also, New Hope, Pa.

B. New York, N.Y., July 14, 1900. *Studied*: ASL. *Member*: SI; Nat. Cartoonists Soc. (Exec. Bd.); PAFA; MModA. *Work*; N.Y. Evening World and World Syndicate, daily cartoon on news events, 1919-31; King Features Syndicate with same feature, 1932-37; Created "Our Bill," comic page, Herald-Tribune Syndicate, 1939; Created "Penny," comic strip for Herald-Tribune Syndicate, 1943; ("Penny" published U.S., Canada, South America, Australia, Europe, etc.). Contributor to leading magazines including Life, New Yorker, Saturday Evening Post, McClures, etc. Extensive advertising comic art, numerous radio, television and lecture appearances. Faculty of Famous Artists Cartoon Course. Author, I., books: "Our Bill, His Life and Times"; "Penny"; "Penny's Party Book." Theatre: "Penny," Robert Montgomery's Television Theatre.

HAFNER, CHARLES ANDREW—Sculptor, T., P.
112 West 54th St., New York 19, N.Y.

B. Omaha, Neb., Oct. 28, 1888. *Studied:* BMFA Sch.; ASL; BAID, and with Edmund C. Tarbell, Philip Hale, Solon Borglum, and others. *Member:* Am. Veterans Soc. A. (Fndr.-Memb.). *Work:* Theatre sculpture in New York City, Brooklyn, N.Y.; medals, Numismatic Mus.; Engineers Cl., N.Y.; N.Y. Univ.; Chatauqua, N.Y.; Rangeley Lake, Me.; Rockefeller Center; sc., busts, Orange, N.J.; Lafayette Col., Easton, Pa.; Metropolitan Opera House, N.Y., and in private colls. *Exhibited:* annually, Am. Veterans Soc. A. Five one-man exhs. of paintings, including Charlotte Amalie, St. Thomas, Virgin Islands.

HAGEN, ETHEL HALL—Painter, C.
4407 Highland Drive, Carlsbad, Cal.

B. Cleveland, Ohio, Jan. 2, 1898. *Studied:* NAD; PIA Sch.; CGA; and with Eliot O'Hara, Richard Lahey, Weiss. *Member:* Laguna Beach AA; La Jolla AA; Carlsbad-Oceanside A. Lg.; San Diego County Fed. Art Assn. *Awards:* prizes, Fed. Womens Cl., 1950, 1952; San Diego Men's AI, 1955; Carlsbad-Oceanside A. Lg., 1956, 1958. *Work:* port. Gen. Merritt Edson, U.S. Destroyer "Edson," 1958. *Exhibited:* San Diego Men's AI; Vista Gld.; Carlsbad-Oceanside A. Lg.; Am. Mus. Nat. Hist.; Smithsonian Inst. *Position:* Sec.-Treas., 1955-56, Pres., 1958, Carlsbad-Oceanside A. Lg.

HAGERT, HENRY—Industrial Designer
205 Pinehurst Lane, Moorestown, N.J.

B. Summit, N.J., May 3, 1895. *Studied:* Univ. Pennsylvania, B.S. *Member:* Phila. A. All.; F., IDI. *Exhibited:* Paris Expo., 1932; IDI, 1951, 1952. Contributor to N.Y. Times. *Position:* Partner, Lee Hagert Assoc., Ecclesiastical Des.

HAGGART, WINIFRED (WATKINS)—Educator, P.
Lorraine Court, Berea, Ky.; also, 438 Cochran Rd., Pittsburgh 28, Pa.

B. Albany, N.Y., Nov. 19, 1911. *Studied:* Syracuse Univ., B.F.A.; PAFA; Univ. Pennsylvania, M.F.A.; Univ. Pittsburgh. *Member:* CAA; AAUW; Assoc. A. Pittsburgh. *Awards:* PAFA, Thouron prize. *Work:* One Hundred Friends of Pittsburgh Art; Univ. North Carolina Law Lib.; Southern Seminar & Jr. Col. *Exhibited:* Va. Intermont Col.; Carnegie Inst.; Assoc. A. Pittsburgh. *Position:* Prof. A., Sch. A., Richmond Professional Inst., of the Col. of William & Mary, 1947-50; Hd. A. Dept., Southern Seminary & Jr. Col., Buena Vista, Va., 1942-46, 1956- ; Assoc. Prof. A., Hd. A. Dept., Georgetown Col., Georgetown, Ky., 1950-52.

HAGGETT, HIRAM ROCKWELL—
Educator, Des., Comm., L.
121 Cottage St., New Bedford, Mass.

B. Lynn, Mass., Jan. 22, 1921. *Studied:* Mass. Sch. A., B.S. in A. Edu.; Boston Univ., M.E. *Member:* AFA; Eastern AA; NAEA; AAUP. *Awards:* Seklemian award for adv. des., 1951; Vincent Edwards award for adv. des., 1953. Lectures: Color Theory; Careers in Art; Design for Everyone, to art and civic organizations. *Position:* Adv. Des., Creative Printmakers, N.Y., 1946-47; Instr., Boston Univ., 1947-53.*

HAGGLUND, IRV(IN) (ARVID)—Cartoonist
RFD #2, Hendersonville, N.C.

B. Holt, Minn., Mar. 11, 1915. *Exhibited:* Cartoon exh., N.Y., 1941; Huckleberry Mt. Workshop, 1951-1954; No. Cal. Cartoon & Humor Assn. Exh., San Mateo, Cal., 1957.

Cartoons included in: "You've Got Me in Stitches," 1954; "You've Got Me on the Hook," 1954; "You've Got Me and How," 1955; "Happy Holiday," 1956; "You've Got Me on the Rocks," 1956; "You've Got Me in the Suburbs," 1957; "You've Got Me in the Nursery," 1958; "For Stags Only," 1954; "Words Fail Me," 1954; "Auto Antics," 1955; "Klever Kid Kartoons," 1955; Best Cartoons of the Year, 1956, 1957; A Treasury of Sports Cartoons, 1957, and many others. Contributor cartoons to: New Yorker; Look; True; Collier's; Toronto Star; American; King Features Syndicate; Better Homes & Gardens; Nation's Business; Parade; Chatelaine; Gourmet; Elks; Sat. Eve. Post; Cosmopolitan; Holiday; London's Tit Bits; Am. Legion; Argosy; Boston Post; McNaught Syndicate; Etude; Canadian Home Journal; Sports Afield, and others.

HAHN, JOSEPH (FREDERIC)—Painter
855 East 14th St., Brooklyn 30, N.Y.

B. Czechoslovakia, July 20, 1917. *Studied:* Oxford Univ., England; ASL. *Awards:* scholarships, Oxford Univ.; ASL. *Exhibited:* AIC, 1952; Oxford Soc., Oxford, England, 1945; WMAA, 1953; one-man: Artists Gal., N.Y., 1954, 1958.

HAHN, NANCY COONSMAN—Sculptor, T.
370 Walnut St., Winnetka, Ill.

B. St. Louis, Mo. *Studied:* Washington Univ.; St. Louis Sch. FA; & with George Zolnay, Charles Grafly, Eberle. *Member:* St. Louis A. Gld.; North Shore AA. *Awards:* Med., St. Louis Sch. FA; St. Louis A. Gld.; Kansas City AI. *Work:* S., CAM; CMA; mem., St. Louis, Mo.; Mo. State Mem., in France; Sears Sch., Kenilworth, Ill.; Rosehill Cemetery, Chicago; Culver, Ind.; Memphis, Tenn.; fountain, Frederick, Md.; New London, Mo.; Chicago, Ill.; Clayton, Mo.; & others. Ports. in private colls. *Exhibited:* PAFA, 1916, 1918, 1920-1924; Arch. L., 1916-1918, 1920; NAD, 1916, 1918; Pan-Pacific Exp., 1915; Albright A. Gal.; CGA; AIC, 1916-1918, 1920, 1922, 1924, 1944, 1946, 1948, 1949; Kansas City AI, 1921, 1922; St. Louis A. Gld., 1915-1926; Missouri State Exh., 1923-1925; Oklahoma State Exh., 1924, 1925; North Shore A. Lg., 1948-1952; Evanston Woman's Cl., 1948-1952; Ravinia (Ill.) Woman's Cl., 1950.

HAINES, MARIE B. See Burt, Marie Haines

HAINES, RICHARD—Painter, Des., Lith., E.
247 South Amalfi Drive, Santa Monica, Cal.

B. Marion, Iowa, Dec. 29, 1906. *Studied:* Minneapolis Sch. A.; Ecole des Beaux-Arts, Fontainebleau, France. *Member:* Cal. WC Soc.; Audubon A. *Awards:* prizes, Los A. Mus. A., 1944, 1945, 1951; Cal. State Fair, 1948, 1951; CGA, 1951; Cal. WC Soc., 1948, 1949, 1952; Los Angeles County Fair; SFMA, 1948; Soc. Et. & Lith., N.Y., 1948. *Work:* MMA; Los A. Mus. A.; Cal. State Fair Coll.; Los Angeles County Fair Coll.; Cal. WC Soc.; DMFA; CGA; Wm. Rockhill Nelson Gal. A.; Univ. Arizona; Santa Barbara Mus. A.; Rosenwald Coll., and in private collections; murals, Ft. Snelling, Roun Tower, Minn.; Sebeka (Minn.) H.S.; Willmar (Minn.) Auditorium; New Diagnostic Clinic, Mayo Clinic, Rochester, Minn. (one of 9 artists); panels facade of Music Bldg., Univ. Cal. at Los A.; des. and supv., silk screen printing of "World Map" mural for airlines of Lockheed Super Constellation planes. *Exhibited:* Los A. Mus. A., 1944-1955; Cal. State and County Fairs; Cal. WC Soc., 1948-1955; MMA, 1951; CGA, 1951; PAFA, 1951-1953; Denver A. Mus., 1952, 1953; Santa Barbara Mus. A., 1955; Encyclopedia Britannica, 1947; SFMA, 1948, 1949, 1951; Sao Paulo, Brazil, 1955; Oakland A. Mus., 1947; Walnut Creek, Cal., 1950. *Position:* Instr., Painting, Minneapolis Sch. A., 1941-42; Hd. Painting Dept., Chouinard AI, 1945-54; Los A. County AI, Los Angeles, Cal., 1954- .

HAKE, OTTO EUGENE—Painter, T., Gr.
1012 North Dearborn St., Chicago, Ill.

B. Ulm, Germany, Dec. 17, 1876. *Studied:* AIC; & in France, Germany. *Member:* Assn. Chicago P. & S.; Palette & Chisel Acad. *Awards:* prizes, Mun. A. Lg., Chicago, 1927; med., Palette & Chisel Acad., 1935. *Work:* murals, Lake Shore Cl.; Mus. Sc. & Indst., Chicago; Pub. Lib., Wheaton, Ill. *Exhibited:* Chicago Gal. Assn.; AIC, All-Illinois Soc. *Position:* Instr., Palette & Chisel Acad., Chicago, Ill., 1935- .

HALBERSTADT, ERNST—*Painter, S.*
543 Boylston St., Boston 16, Mass.

B. Budingen, Germany, Aug. 26, 1910. *Awards*: prizes, OEM Comp., 1941; Pepsi-Cola, 1946. *Member*: A. Dir. Cl., Boston. *Awards*: A. Dir. Cl., medal, 1956. *Work*: New Britain Mus. FA; Univ. Georgia; AGAA; FMA; murals, State Bd. of Housing (Mass.); Fortress Monroe, Va.; USPO, Chicopee Falls, Mass.; Club House Rockingham Park, Salem, N.H. *Exhibited*: Kraushaar Gal., 1946 (one-man); Inst. Contemp. A., Boston, 1950 (one-man); Art:USA, 1958; Springfield (Mass.) Fair, 1958. *Illus.*, "I Heard Them Sing"; "Three White Horses." *Position*: Hd. Fresco Div., Dept. Painting, BMFA Sch., Boston, Mass., 1947-50.

HALE, LILIAN WESTCOTT—*Painter*
2004 Lewis Mountain Rd., Charlottesville, Va.

B. Hartford, Conn., Dec. 7, 1881. *Studied*: BMFA Sch.; Hartford A. Sch.; & with Tarbell, Hale, Chase. *Member*: NA; Conn. Acad. FA; Gld. Boston A. *Awards*: prizes & med., Pan-Pacific Exp., 1915; Phila. AC, 1919; AIC, 1920; PAFA, 1923; NAD, 1924, 1927; Concord AA, 1925; North Shore AA, 1941; Contemporary A., New England, 1945. *Work*: PAFA; PMG; CGA; Phila. AC; MMA; Concord AA; BMFA.*

HALE, ROBERT BEVERLY—*Museum Curator, E., W., L.*
Metropolitan Museum of Art, Fifth Ave. at 82nd St.; h. 1200 Fifth Ave., New York, N.Y.

B. Boston, Mass., Jan. 29, 1901. *Studied*: Columbia Univ., A.B.; Columbia Sch. Arch.; Fontainebleau, France; ASL, with George Bridgman, William C. McNulty. *Member*: Century Assn.; ASL (life); AAMus.; Fontainebleau Assn. *Author*: "One Hundred American Painters of the 20th Century," 1950; Article on Drawing, Encyclopaedia Britannica, 1957. Contributor to Art News; American Artist; New Yorker; MMA Bulletin; Craft Horizons. *Lectures*: American Painting. *Exhibitions arranged*: "American Artists Under 36," 1950; "American Painting Today," 1950; "20th Century Painters," 1950; "American Sculpture," 1951; "Edward Root Collection," 1953; "Whistler, Sargent, Cassatt," 1954; Art Students League 75th Anniversary Exh., 1951; "14 American Masters," 1958; "Winslow Homer," 1958, and many others. *Position*: Instr., Drawing, ASL, 1942- ; Lecturer, 1943- ; Prof. Drawing, Columbia Univ., 1946- ; Assoc. Ed., Art News, 1941-49; Ed. Bd., Craft Horizons; Trustee, Am. Fine Arts Soc.; Vice-Pres., Tiffany Fnd.; Cur., American Painting, Metropolitan Mus. A., New York, N.Y., 1949- .

HALEY, JOHN (CHARLES)—*Painter, E.*
University of California, Berkeley, Cal.; h. 771 Ocean Ave., Richmond 3, Cal.

B. Minneapolis, Minn., 1905. *Studied*: Munich, Paris, Ravenna. *Awards*: prizes, San F. AA, 1936, 1939, 1944, 1951, 1956; Cal. WC Soc., 1949; Cal. State Fair, 1950, 1951; Richmond (Cal.) A. Center, 1956. *Work*: PMG; SFMA; IBM; Mills Col. A. Gal. *Exhibited*: MMA; PMG; Univ. Illinois; Cal. PLH; AIC; CAM; Watkins Gal., American Univ.; SFMA; Colorado Springs FA Center; Los A. County Fair; PAFA; Sao Paulo, Brazil, 1955; Dallas Mus. FA; Denver A. Mus.; Des Moines A. Center; Cal. WC Soc.; San F. AA; Mortimer Levitt Gal., 1949, 1952 (one-man); Richmond A. Center, 1954 (one-man). *Position*: Prof. A., Univ. California, Berkeley, Cal.

HALEY, SALLY (Mrs. Sally Haley Russo)—
Painter, T.
17243 Northeast Couch St., Portland, Ore.

B. Bridgeport, Conn., June 29, 1908. *Studied*: Yale Sch. FA, B.F.A.; T. Col., Columbia Univ., and in Munich, Germany. *Member*: AEA. *Awards*: prizes, Mattatuck Hist. Soc., Waterbury, Conn., 1945, 1946; San Francisco, Pacific A. Festival. *Work*: mural, USPO, McConnellsville, Ohio; many private port. commissions. *Exhibited*: CGA; ASMP, 1944-1946; Wadsworth Atheneum, 1944-1946; Mattatuck Hist. Soc., 1944-1946; Portland (Ore.) A. Mus. 1958 and prior; SFMA; Denver A. Mus.; Walker A. Center; one-man exh.: Hartford, Conn., 1935; Zanesville, Ohio, 1944; Waterbury, Conn., 1942-1944; Bridgeport, Conn., 1939-1946.

HALL, ARTHUR WILLIAM—*Etcher, P.*
Alcalde, N.M.

B. Bowie, Tex., Oct. 30, 1889. *Studied*: AIC. *Member*: SAGA; Chicago SE; Cal. Pr. M.; Prairie Pr. M. *Awards*: prizes, Kansas City AI, 1929, 1932, 1933; Cal. Pr. M., 1930; SAGA. *Work*: Smithsonian Inst.; Lib. Cong.; Cal. State Lib.; Bibliotheque Nationale, France.*

HALL, CARL A.—*Painter, Gr., Cr., T.*
Route 3, Box 895, Salem, Ore.

B. Washington, D.C., Sept. 17, 1921. *Studied*: Meinzinger A. Sch., Detroit, Mich., with Carlos Lopez. *Awards*: prizes, Detroit Inst. A., 1940, 1941; Sarah Sheridan prize, 1947; Newberry prize, 1949; Portland (Ore.) A. Mus. purchase prize, 1949; grant, Nat. Inst. A. & Lets., 1949. *Work*: Swope A. Gal.; BMFA; Springfield Mus. A.; Detroit Inst. A.; Portland A. Mus.; WMAA. Mural, Commercial Bank of Salem, Ore., 1956. *Exhibited*: AIC, 1941, 1946, 1947; CGA, 1941; Univ. Illinois, 1948, 1950, 1951; Cal. PLH, 1948-1951; Carnegie Inst., 1947-1949; Denver Mus. A., 1949, 1953; WMAA, 1946-1952, 1955, 1956; MMA, 1950; Des Moines A. Center, 1951; Phila. WC Cl., 1950; Butler Inst. Am. A., 1958; Detroit Inst. A., 1939-1941, 1945, 1947, 1949; Portland A. Mus., annually; SAM, 1956. *Positions*: Dept. Asst., All-Oregon Exh., Oregon State Fair, 1957-58; Artist-in-Res., Willamette Univ., Salem, Ore.

HALL, DORIS (Mrs. Doris Hall Kubinyi)—*Enamelist, P.*
203 Western Ave., Gloucester, Mass.; w. 94 Beacon St., Boston, Mass.

B. Lakewood, Ohio, Feb. 5, 1907. *Studied*: Cleveland Inst. A. *Member*: AEA; NSMP. *Awards*: Horace Potter Mem. award, 1952; prizes, Syracuse Mus. FA, 1948; CMA; special award, enameling on metal, 1946-1949, 1953; mural dec., 1952; silver medal, Arch. Lg., 1953. *Work*: CMA; Syracuse Mus. FA; Cranbrook Mus. A.; murals, Mich. State Univ. *Position*: A. Dir., Mural Enamelist, Bettinger Corp., Waltham, Mass.

HALL, EDITH E. (Mrs.)—*Painter*
533 Boulevard, Westfield, N.J.

B. Seymour, Wis., Oct. 10, 1883. *Studied*: with Ivanowski, George Elmer Browne, John Carlson. *Member*: Westfield AA; Plainfield AA; AAPL. *Awards*: prizes, Raritan Valley AA, 1942; Plainfield AA, 1943, 1945, 1951, 1952; Newark, N.J., 1938; Millburn-Short Hills A. Center, 1946; Papermill Playhouse, 1956 (one-man). Conducts painting classes privately.

HALL, HELEN BENEDICT—*Museum Curator*
Museum of Art, University of Michigan; h. 715 South Forest St. Ann Arbor, Mich.

B. Urbana, Ill., Apr. 15, 1905. *Studied*: Univ. Michigan, A.B., A.M.; Univ. Paris. *Member*: AA Mus.; CAA. *Awards*: Franco-Am. Exchange Scholarship, Inst. Int. Edu., 1924-1925; Carnegie scholarship to Univ. Paris, 1933. *Position*: Cur., Inst. FA, Univ. Michigan, 1930-46; Cur., Mus. A., Univ. Michigan, Ann Arbor, Mich., 1946- .*

HALL, LINDSLEY FOOTE—*Museum Research Fellow*
1925 Southwest Main St., Portland 5, Ore.

B. Portland, Ore., Dec. 21, 1883. *Studied*: MIT. I., "Red-Figured Athenian Vases in the Metropolitan Museum of Art," 1936. Contributor of: illus. to the MMA Bulletin. *Position*: Senior Research F., Egyptian Dept., MMA, 1942-1949 (Retired).

HALL, LOUISE—*Educator*
6636 College Station, Durham, N.C.

B. Cambridge, Mass., July 23, 1905. *Studied*: Wellesley Col., B.A.; MIT, S.B. in Arch.; Univ. Paris; Harvard Univ. Grad. Sch. Des. (Radcliffe Col. degree, Ph.D., 1954). *Member*: AIA; CAA; AAUP; AAUW; Soc. Arch. Hist. (Sec.-Treas., 1949, Vice-Pres., 1951). *Awards*: grants, scholarships, Carnegie to Univ. Paris (twice); Carnegie & AIA for Harvard Univ. (twice); LC for studies in Hist. of Am. Civ.; F., AIA, 1950; F., AAUW, 1957. *Position*: Instr. FA, 1931-36, Asst. Prof. FA, 1936-48, Assoc. Prof. Arch., 1948- , Duke Univ., Durham, N.C.

HALL, NORMA BASSETT—*Painter, Eng.*
Rancho del Rio, Alcalde, N.M.

B. Halsey, Ore., May 21, 1890. *Studied*: Portland (Ore.) AA Sch.; AIC; & in London. *Member*: Prairie Pr. M.; Pr. M. Soc., California. *Awards*: prizes, Southern Pr. M., 1938; Kansas State Fed. A., 1937. *Work*: Brooklyn Pub. Lib.; Doctors Hospital, Wash., D.C.; Smithsonian Inst.; Honolulu Acad. A.; Cal. State Lib.; Univ. Tulsa; Wichita AA; Univ. Wichita; Currier Gal. A.*

HALLADAY, MILTON RAWSON—*Cartoonist*
Newfane, Vt.

B. East Dover, Vt., Dec. 16, 1874. *Studied*: Mass. A. Sch., with William Bartlett. *Member*: Providence AC; Providence WC Cl. *Position*: Cart., Providence Journal Co., Providence, R.I., 1900-1947 (Retired).

HALLMAN, H. THEODORE, JR. (TED)—*Craftsman, T.*
Harleysville Pike, Souderton, Pa.

B. Quakertown, Pa., Dec. 23, 1933. *Studied*: Cranbrook Acad. A., M.F.A. in painting and M.F.A. in textiles; Fontainebleau Sch. FA, with Jacques Villon; Tyler Sch. FA, B.S. in Ed., B.F.A. *Awards*: prizes, textiles, 1958; Temple Israel, Detroit, 1958; Pew prize for study in Fontainebleau, 1955; Joy Griffin West scholarship to Cranbrook Acad A., 1956. *Work*: screens, Sara Lee Baking Co., Chicago; screens and textiles commissioned in Detroit, Toledo, New York City and Philadelphia. *Exhibited*: AFA Wall Hanging Exh., 1958; Young Americans, 1958; Midwest Designer-Craftsmen, 1957; Michigan Craftsmen, 1957; Woodmere A. Gal., 1955-1958; Bertha Schaefer Gal., 1958; Miami Episcopal Church Art. Exh., 1958; Design Center, 1958; Temple Israel, Detroit, 1957; Left Bank Gal., Flint, Mich., 1958. Contributor to Craft Horizons. *Positions*: Instr., Weaving, Textile Des., Cranbrook Acad. A., Detroit Inst. A., Tyler Sch. FA.

HALM, ROBERT J.—*Museum Director, P., Gr., E.*
Fort Dodge Community College; h. 1517 3rd Ave., North, Fort Dodge, Iowa

B. Saginaw, Mich., June 9, 1922. *Studied*: Michigan State Univ., B.A.; State Univ. of Iowa, M.F.A., and with Lasansky, Edie, Ludins. *Member*: A. Educators of Iowa; NEA. *Awards*: prize, Iowa State Fair, 1950. *Work*: State Univ. of Iowa. *Exhibited*: SAGA, 1951; Terry AI, 1952; Iowa A., 1951, 1954, 1955. *Positions*: Hd. A. Dept., Fort Dodge Community College; Dir., Blanden Mem. A. Gallery, Fort Dodge, Iowa, 1954- .

HALPER, ESTELLE (L.) (Mrs. Lewis A.)—
Craftsman, Des., S., E., L.
96 Park Drive, Eastchester, N.Y.

B. White Plains, N.Y., Apr. 19, 1918. *Studied*: Westchester Workshop with Lucille Holding, Juanita Brailsford, Ilse Rothmer; Greenwich House Pottery, with James Crumrine. *Member*: N.Y. Soc. Ceramic A.; Artist-Craftsmen of N.Y.; York State Craftsmen; Am. Edu. Council; Westchester A. & Crafts Gld. *Exhibited*: N.Y. Soc. Craftsmen, 1953, 1954; N.Y. Soc. Ceramic A., 1953, 1954; Mus. Natural Hist., 1953; Cooper Union Mus., 1954-1957; Barbizon Gal., 1953; Rabun Gal., 1953-1958; Tuckahoe Lib., 1958; Mt. Vernon Lib., 1958; Westchester A. & Crafts Gld., 1952-1958; Syracuse Mus. FA, 1956. *Positions*: Bd. Memb., Westchester A. & Crafts Gld., 1956-58, Vice-Pres., 1958, Co-Chm. annual exh., 1958, Chm. Crafts Sect., 1954, 1956, 1957; Instr. Ceramics, Westchester Workshop, 1956-58; Summer Ceramic Workshop, 1957-58; Junior Workshop, 1958; Halkiln Ceramics, Eastchester, N.Y.

HALPERT, A.—*Cartoonist*
19 West 44th St., New York 18, N.Y.

Member: SI; A. Dir. Cl., New York, N.Y. *Exhibited*: SI; A. Dir. Cl.*

HALSETH, ODD S(IGURD)—
Museum Director, E., Cr., W., L.
Pueblo Grande Museum, 4619 East Washington St., Phoenix, Ariz.

B. Moss, Norway, May 19, 1893. *Studied*: Sch. Am. Research, Santa Fe, N.M.; San Diego Col., Univ. So. Cal.;

Univ. So. California, M. Sc. *Member*: F., Am. Anthropological Assn.; Soc. Am. Archaeology; Arizona A. Gld. (Hon.); Phoenix FA Assn. (Hon.). Contributor articles to International Studio; Design; Arizona Highways; Arizona Woman; San Diego Union (art notes); Arizona Republic (art notes), and numerous museum publications. Lectures: Primite Art; Indian Arts & Crafts; Ecclesiastical Art in the New World. *Positions*: Judge & Chm., Gallup Ceremonial Indian Arts & Crafts Exhs., 1927-56; Cur. A., San Diego Mus., 1922-23; Dir., Arizona Mus., 1927-29; City Archaeologist and Supt., Div. Archaeology, City of Phoenix, 1929- ; Dir., Pueblo Grande Museum, Phoenix, Ariz.

HALSEY, WILLIAM MELTON—*Painter, T., I.*
38 State St., Charleston, S.C.

B. Charleston, S.C., Mar. 13, 1915. *Studied*: Univ. South Carolina; BMFA Sch., with A. Jacovleff, Karl Zerbe. *Awards*: traveling F., BMFA Sch., 1939-1941; Hughes F., 1950-1951, 1951-1952; prizes, South Carolina Annual, 1947-1949, 1951, 1952, 1956, 1957; Gld. South Carolina A., 1951, 1953, 1955, 1956, 1957. *Work*: Telfair Acad. A.; Gibbes A. Gal.; BMA; Container Corp. Am.; Ball State T. Col.; Furman Univ.; Univ. Georgia; frescoes, Berkshire Mus., Pittsfield, Mass.; murals, Beth Elohim Synagogue, Charleston; Baltimore Hebrew Congregation Temple; Sears Roebuck & Co. Bldg., Charleston. *Exhibited*: AIC, 1939, 1941, 1943, 1954; PAFA, 1943, 1950; Pasadena AI, 1946; Santa Barbara Mus. A., 1948; BMA, 1949; VMFA, 1949-1951; BMFA, 1951; Denver A. Mus., 1952; Jewish Mus., N.Y., 1952; WMAA, 1953, 1954; BM, 1953, 1955, 1957; Columbia Mus. A., 1954; Bertha Schaefer Gal., 1951, 1953, 1955, 1958. *Position*: Asst. Instr., A., BMFA Sch., 1938-39; Dir. A., Telfair Acad. A., 1942-43; Instr. A., Gibbes A. Gal., Charleston, S.C., 1945-53; Instr., Charleston A. Sch., 1953- ; Dir., Castle Hill Art Center, Mass., 1956.

HALSEY, MRS. WILLIAM. See McCallum, Corrie

HALVORSEN, RUTH ELISE—*Educator, P.,*
631 North East Clackamas St.; h. 422 North East Going St., Portland 11, Ore.

B. Camas, Wash. *Studied*: Portland Mus. A. Sch.; PIASch; Univ. Oregon; Columbia Univ., B.S., M.A.; & with Walter Beck, Charles Martin, Jean Charlot. *Member*: AAPL; CAA; Pacific AA; Nat. A. Edu. Assn.; Professional Women's Lg.; Oregon A. & S. Gld. *Work*: Univ. Oregon; Ft. Sumner Marine Hospital, New Mexico. *Exhibited*: SFMA, 1939; Wash., D.C., 1938; Portland Mus. A.; Oakland A. Gal.; Henry Gal., Univ. Wash. (one-man); Reed Col.; traveling exh. on year's tour of Army bases; Lincoln County, Ore. (one-man). Contributor of articles to Education, Junior Arts & Activities; Art Education (Journal of the NAEA); NEA Journal. *Position*: A. Supv., Portland Pub. Sch., Portland, Ore.; Instr., Univ. Oregon Ext.; Pres. Pacific AA; Memb. Council, NAEA; Com. on A. Edu.; MModA; Bd. Dir., Oregon Ceramic Studios.

HALVORSON, ELMER HALFDAN—*Painter, T.*
Wheelock, N.D.

B. Wheelock, N.D., Dec. 10, 1916. *Studied*: State T. Col., Minot, N.D., B.S. in Edu.; Concordia Col., B.A., with C.M.Running. *Member*: AAPL; AFA; North Dakota Inst. for Regional Studies. *Award*: AAPL, 1952. *Work*: in private collections. *Exhibited*: Williston, N.D.; AFA traveling exh.; Fargo, N.D.; North Dakota Inst. Reg. Studies, 1952; Bismarck, N.D. Contributor illus. to Ford Times. Lectures: "North Dakota and the Artist"; "Public School Art"; "North Dakota Landscape, An Inspiration to the Artist." Instr., Adult Evening Classes, Williston, N.D.

HAMAR, IRENE—*Painter, S.*
125 East 81st St., New York 28, N.Y.

B. Sao Paulo, Brazil, May 23, 1915. *Studied*: in Brazil and France. *Member*: S. Gld.; Arch. Lg.; Audubon A.; AEA; NAWA. *Awards*: gold medal, Rio de Janeiro; silver medal, Sao Paulo, Brazil. *Work*: MMA; William Rockhill Nelson Gal. A.; and in museums in Argentina, Brazil, The Hague, Holland, Paris, France; murals in Brazil and U.S.; monument, Univ. Rio de Janeiro, Brazil. *Exhibited*: 18 one-man exhs., South America, Europe and U.S.A. (8).

HAMBLETT, THEORA—*Painter*

619 Van Buren Ave., Oxford, Miss.

B. Paris, Miss., Jan. 15, 1895. *Studied*: Univ. Mississippi, with Charles Mussett; Famous Artists Course. *Work*: MModA. *Exhibited*: Brooks Mem. Mus., 1956, 1957; Birmingham Mus. A., 1956; Atlanta, 1958; Mississippi AA, 1955; Miss. State Col. for Women, 1957; MModA, 1956; one-man: Univ. Mississippi A. Center, 1955; Brooks Mem. Mus., 1956; Miss. State Col. for Women, 1957; Betty Parsons Gal., N.Y., 1958; Lauren Rogers Mem. A. Gal., 1957; Allison's Wells A. Colony, 1958.

HAMILL, MILDRED—*Painter*

Box 943, Anchorage, Alaska

Studied: AIC, and with Mark Tobey. Specializes in the Alaskan scene.

HAMILTON, GEORGE HEARD—*Museum Curator, E.*

Yale University Art Gallery, New Haven, Conn.

B. Pittsburgh, Pa., June 23, 1910. *Studied*: Yale Univ., B.A., M.A., Ph.D. *Member*: CAA. Contributor to: Art magazines, museum bulletins & reviews. Lectures: Modern & French art. Author: "Manet and His Critics," 1954; "Art and Architecture of Russia," 1954; "From the Green Box" (tr.), 1957. *Position*: Research Assoc., Walters A. Gal., 1934-36; Instr., 1936-43, Asst. Prof., Hist. A., 1943-1947, Assoc. Prof., 1947-56, Prof., 1956- , Yale Univ.; Cur., Mod. A., 1941- , Yale Univ. A. Gal., New Haven, Conn.

HAMILTON, HILDEGARD—*Painter*

100 South East 11th St., Fort Lauderdale, Fla.

B. Syracuse, N.Y., Sept. 11, 1908. *Studied*: Julian Acad., Ecole des Beaux-Arts, Paris; ASL; John Herron AI; Cincinnati A. Acad.; Syracuse Univ. *Member*: NAC; PBC; Wash. AC; Lg. Am. Pen Women. *Work*: Wesleyan Col., Ga.; Hall of Art, N.Y.; Evergreen Sch., Plainfield, N.J.; Eaton Gal., N.Y.; Nassau, Bahamas. *Exhibited*: NAC; Ainsley Gal. (one-man); Vendome Gal.; Syracuse Mus. FA; Univ. Kentucky; Univ. Georgia; Ogunquit A. Center, 1944; Soc. Indp. A., 1944; Barbizon A. Gal., 1945; Pen & Brush Cl., 1959; Lucerne Hotel, Nassau, 1959, & abroad. Author, I., "Human Bits."

HAMILTON, THOMAS H.—*Educator, W., Cr.*

900 East Euclid St., Monmouth, Ill.

B. Reinbeck, Iowa, Jan. 24, 1887. *Studied*: Monmouth (Ill.) Col., A.B.; Columbia Univ.; Univ. North Carolina, M.A.; Harvard Univ.; & in Paris. *Position*: Prof., Hist. A., Monmouth Col., Ill., 1932-1957; Emeritus, 1957- ; A. Cr., Monmouth Daily Review Atlas.

HAMLIN, EDITH (Mrs. Frank K. Dale)—*Painter*

Route 5, Box 663, Tucson, Ariz.

B. Oakland, Cal., June 23, 1902. *Studied*: Cal. Sch. FA., and with Maynard Dixon. *Work*: SFMA; San Diego FA Gal.; murals, Mission H.S., San F., Cal.; USPO, Tracy, Cal.; Coit Mem. Tower, San F.; Santa Fe R.R. ticket office, Chicago and Los A. (in coll. with Maynard Dixon); Arizona Biltmore Hotel, Phoenix; Plains Hotel, Cheyenne, Wyo.; Jacome's Dept. Store, St. Ambrose Church, Old Pueblo Club, all in Tucson, Ariz. *Exhibited*: San F. AA, annually; SFMA, 1924-1937; San Diego FA Gal., 1927-1929; Dayton AI, 1942, 1943; Delphic Studios, 1929, 1930; Biltmore Gal., Los A., 1940-1946; Gump's, San F., 1945, 1946; Dallas Mus. FA, 1932; deYoung Mem. Mus.; Stendahl Gal., Los A.; Rotunda Gal., San F., 1950-1952; Arizona Mus.; Tucson FA Assn., 1949-1952; Desert Gal., Tucson, 1950-1952; Camelback Gal., Phoenix, 1947, 1948.*

HAMLIN, GENEVIEVE KARR—*Sculptor, T., C., L.*

Hilltop Studio, Harpursville, N.Y.

B. New York, N.Y., July 1, 1896. *Studied*: Vassar Col.; & with Eberle, Henry Dropsy, Andre L'Hote, in Paris. *Member*: S.Gld. *Awards*: F., Cranbrook Acad. A. *Work*: Joslyn Mem., Omaha, Neb.; medals for Am. A. Dealer's Assn.; Antique & Decorative A. Lg. *Exhibited*: PAFA, 1923-1938; NAD, 1923-1938; AIC, 1926; Oneonta Community A. Center; S. Gld., N.Y.; AFA traveling exh.,

1943; PMG; Outdoor Sculpture Exh., 1938-1940; WFNY 1939; Rehn Gal., 1931 (one-man); Fifteen Gal., 1936-1938 (one-man). Lectures: Appreciation of Sculpture. *Position*: Instr., S., Newark Sch. F. & Indst. A., Newark, N.J., 1926-43; Instr., S. & Pottery, Oneonta H.S. to 1958; Trustee Oneonta Community A. Center.

HAMLIN, JAMES BETTS—*Craftsman, Des., T.*

North Bridgton, Maine

B. Thacker, W. Va., Sept. 18, 1897. *Studied*: Bates Col.; Bridgton Acad.; CUASch. Ext.; Craft Students Lg.; PIA Sch., and with Laurits Eichner, Silversmith. *Member*: Artist-Craftsmen of N.Y.; Maine A. & Crafts, Inc. *Exhibited*: WFNY 1939; Smithsonian Inst. traveling exh., 1955-56, 1956-57; Craft Students Lg., 1935-1954; Staten Island Mus., 1939; N.Y. Soc. Craftsmen, 1939-1955; Cooper Union Mus., 1940, 1941; Phila. A. All., 1948 (two-man); Plainfield AA, 1950; Colby Col., 1954; WMA, 1955; Portland Mus. A., 1955; Bates Col., 1957 (one-man). Demonstrations of silversmithing to clubs, schools and groups. *Position*: Hd. metal work, Craft Students Lg., N.Y., 1944-53; Private classes at present.

HAMLIN, TALBOT—*Educator, W., L., Cr.*

Avery Hall, Columbia University, New York, N.Y.

B. New York, N.Y., June 16, 1889. *Studied*: Amherst Col., B.A.; Columbia Univ., B. Arch.; Dickinson Col., D. Sc. (hon.). *Member*: F., AIA; N.Y. Hist. Soc. (hon.). *Awards*: Alice Davis Hitchcock medallion, Soc. Arch. Hist., 1956. *Work*: Dormitory and Science Bldg., Col., New Rochelle, N.Y.; St. Thomas Chapel, N.Y. *Exhibited*: Contemporary A., 1941; N.Y. WC Cl., 1936. Author: "American Spirit in Architecture"; "Some European Libraries"; "Architecture Through the Ages"; "Greek Revival Architecture in America"; "Architecture—An Art for All Men"; "Benjamin Henry Latrobe"; Co-Author, I., "We Took to Cruising"; Ed., "Forms and Functions of Twentieth Century Architecture." Lectures: "Latrobe and His America"; "The Place of Tradition in Modern Design." *Position*: Ed. Bd., Magazine of Art, 1943-52; Trustee, Am. Scenic & Hist. Preservation Soc.; Prof. Emeritus, Arch., Columbia Univ., New York, N.Y.*

HAMMARGREN, FREDERICK—*Sculptor*

6909 Bonita Terrace, Los Angeles 28, Cal.

B. Orebro, Sweden, Apr. 7, 1892. *Studied*: Goteborg, Sweden; Nat. Acad., Copenhagen, Denmark, and with Antoine Bourdelle, Paris, France. *Member*: NSS. *Awards*: Swedish Govt. award, 1917, 1919; Hartford Acad. A., 1926; Chicago Swedish Cl., 1932; medals, bronze medal, Newark A. Cl., 1934; bronze medal, 1947, gold medal, 1950, silver medal, 1955, Cal. A. Cl. *Work*: Orebro, Sweden park; BM; Newark Mus. A.; John Morton Mem. Mus., Phila., Pa.; Nilsson Mem., Orebro, Sweden; plaque, Texas Hist. Soc.; monument, Port Arthur, Tex., and other arch. & port. sculpture in the U.S.; Bronze Medal for Lief Erikson Fnd. annual award, 1958. *Exhibited*: NAD; PAFA; BM; Palm Beach Soc. A.; Newark A. Mus.; Mus. FA of Houston; Los A. Mus. A.; AIC, and others.

HAMMER, VICTOR KARL—

Painter, C., S., Des., E., Gr., W.

220 Market St., Lexington, Ky.

B. Vienna, Austria, Dec. 9, 1882. *Studied*: Acad. FA, Vienna, and with Camillo Sitte. *Award*: Ritter des Franz Joseph Ordens. *Work*: Albertina Mus., Vienna; Neue Pinakothek, Munich. Portraits in Austria, France, England, Italy, U.S.; triptych, Lexington, Ky. *Exhibited*: Vienna; Munich; Paris; Brook St. A. Gal., Burlington House, London; Carnegie Inst.; Feigl Gal., N.Y.; Renaissance Soc., Chicago; Biennale, Venice; Univ. Louisville; Univ. Kentucky. Architect & builder of stone chapel in Kolbsheim, France, 1935; now contains Crucifix painted for it in 1958; all sculpture done for chapel; monument in Salzburg Festspielhaus of Hugo von Hofmannsthal (destroyed by Nazis in 1939); a brass cast of the head is now owned by Univ. of Kentucky Library. Author: Ost Blätter, No. 2, Victor Hammer, 1936; A Theory of Architecture, 1952; Four Dialogues, 1957. Contributor to Liturgical Arts; Catholic Arts Quarterly. *Position*: Prof., A. Dept., Wells Col., Aurora, N.Y., 1939-48; Transylvania Col., Lexington, Ky., 1948-53.

HAMMON, BILL J.—
   Painter, C., S., Des., T., Gr., I., L.
   Studio 9, Aquila Court, Omaha 2, Neb.

B. Oklahoma City, Okla., Oct. 3, 1922. *Studied*: Oklahoma Art Center; Colorado Springs FA Center; Kansas City AI; Academia de San Carlos, Mexico City, and with Boardman Robinson, Arnold Blanch, Edward Laning, Thomas H. Benton. *Member*: AEA; Assoc. A. Omaha (Chm. Bd., 1951-56, 1958). *Awards*: prizes, Omaha, Neb., 1954; McDowell award, 1947; Assoc. A. Omaha, 1948-1955; purchase prize, Joslyn Mem. A. Mus., 1955. *Work*: dioramas, murals, sc., mosaics, etc., State Hist. Soc., Omaha; Athletic Cl., Omaha; Clarkson Mem. Hospital, Lincoln Auditorium, both Omaha; Doane Col.; Okla. Chamber of Commerce; Okla. A. Center; Joslyn A. Mus.; Lincoln Airport; James Head Co., Birmingham; SAC Headquarters, Omaha; Nichols Business Equipment Co., Syracuse, N.Y.; Creighton Univ.; many churches, etc. *Exhibited*: Joslyn A. Mus., 1948, 1950, 1952, 1954; Walker A. Center, 1952, 1954; William Rockhill Nelson A. Gal., 1946, 1947, 1952, 1953; Mulvane A. Center, 1950-1952, 1954; Denver A. Mus., 1951-1953; Okla. A. Center; Philbrook A. Center; CAM; DMFA; Sioux City A. Center; Des Moines A. Center, and others. Contributor articles to Ford Motor publications. *Position*: A. Dir., Omaha A. Sch., 1949-52; Freelance artist for business firms; Instr., Joslyn Mem. A. Mus.

HAMMOND, JOHN HAYS, JR.—*Museum Director*
   Hammond Museum, Hesperus Ave., Gloucester, Mass.*

HAMMOND, MILDRED WELSH—*Painter, T.*
   Kansas City Art Institute, 4415 Warwick Ave.; h. 4328 Walnut St., Kansas City 2, Mo.

B. Red Oak, Mo., Feb. 25, 1900. *Member*: AEA; Mid-Am. A. *Awards*: Hon. M.F.A., Kansas City AI, 1950; gold medal, Midwest Exh., 1932, 1935. *Work*: murals, Kansas City Southern R.R.; Kansas City Pub. Service, and in numerous hotels and restaurants. *Exhibited*: WFNY 1939; Mid.-Am. A.; Joslyn A. Mus.; Mulvane A. Mus.; Sarasota, Fla. (one-man); Woman's City Cl., Kansas City (one-man); Alden Gal., Kansas City. *Position*: Instr., Design, Kansas City AI, Kansas City, Mo., 1929- .*

HAMMOND, NATALIE HAYS—*Painter, W., Mus. Dir.*
   "Argaty," Deveau Rd., North Salem, Westchester, N.Y.

B. Lakewood, N.J., Jan. 6, 1905. *Member*: AFA; NAWA; Am. Medieval Acad.; Am. Union Dec. A. & Crafts; Assoc., Royal Min. Soc. of London. *Work*: French Govt.; Pittsfield Mus. A., and in private coll. *Exhibited*: Grieves Gal., London; PAFA; BM; one-man: Dunthorne Gal., Wash., D.C., 1927; Rochester Mem. A. Gal., 1928; Palette Francaise, Paris, 1929; Provincetown A. Gal., 1930; Roerich Gal., 1930; CGA, 1931; Marie Sterner Gal., 1932, 1934, 1936; Phila. A. All., 1933; Grace Horne Gal., Boston, 1938; Park Ave. Gal., 1939; Gal. on the Moors, Gloucester, Mass., 1939; Vose Gal., 1944; Arch. Lg., 1945; French & Co., New York, 1946; Seligmann-Helft Gal., New York, 1948; Hewitt Gal., N.Y., 1952. Author, I., "Elizabeth of England"; 1936; "Anthology of Patterns," 1949. *Position*: Fndr., Dir., Hammond Museum, North Salem, N.Y.

HAMMOND, RUTH EVELYN (Mrs. Edward S.)—
   Painter, T., W.
   9 Thompson St., Brunswick, Me.

B. West Haven, Conn., Mar. 19, 1894. *Studied*: Mt. Holyoke Col., B.A.; Yale Grad. Sch., and with Dante Ricci in Rome, Italy. *Member*: Portland Soc. A.; Rockport AA; Springfield A. Lg.; Maine WC Cl.; Ogunquit AA; Copley Soc., Boston. *Awards*: prizes, St. Petersburg A. Cl.; Soc. Four A.; St. Augustine A. Cl.; Brick Store Mus., Kennebunk, Me. *Work*: Bowdoin Col.; Walker A. Gal., Brunswick, Me.; William Farnsworth Mus., Rockland, Me.; Ford Motor Coll. *Exhibited*: PAFA, 1943; All. A. Am., 1944; NAWA, 1943-1945; Sweat Mem. Mus., 1942-1945; North Shore AA; Rockport AA, annually; St. Augustine A. Cl.; Soc. Four A.; New Haven Paint & Clay Cl., 1943; Walker A. Gal.; Deerfield Acad., 1946, 1958; Mt. Holyoke Col. Mus.; Boston Soc. Indp. A., 1952; Boston A. Festival, 1952, 1958; Cape Ann Soc. Mod. A.; Boston, Mass., 1958 (one-man); Ogunquit AA; Brick Store Mus.

HAMPTON, PHILLIP JEWEL—*Painter, E., Lith.*
   Savannah State College, Box 183, Savannah, Ga.

B. Kansas City, Mo., Apr. 23, 1922. *Studied*: Kansas State Col., with John F. Helm; Drake Univ.; Kansas City AI, B.F.A., M.F.A.; Kansas City Univ. *Member*: CAA; AAUP. *Work*: mural, Home Economics Bldg., Savannah State Col.; W. Va. State Col. *Exhibited*: Mid-Am. A.; William Rockhill Nelson Gal. A.; Newport AA; Kirk-in-the-Hills A. Festival, Bloomfield Hills, Mich., 1955; W. Va. State Col., 1957; Atlanta Univ., 1957. *Position*: Prof. FA, Savannah State Col., Savannah, Ga.

HANAN, HARRY—*Cartoonist*
   342 Edgewood Ave., Westfield, N.J.

B. Liverpool, England, Dec. 14, 1916. *Studied*: Liverpool Sch. A. *Member*: Nat. Cartoonists Soc. *Exhibited*: MModA, 1951; Walker A. Gal., Liverpool, England, 1936, 1937. *Work*: Daily comic strip, "Louie," in newspapers in U.S. and abroad. *Position*: Ed. Cart., Liverpool Evening Express, 1936-40; Ed. Cart., "The People," 1946-48; Cart., "Louie," 1947- .

HANCHEY, ORVILLE JAMES—*Painter, C., Des., E.*
   207 Whitfield Dr., Natchitoches, La.

B. DeRidder, La., Mar. 30, 1913. *Studied*: Northwestern State Col., A.B.; Louisiana State Univ., M.A.; Univ. Chicago, Ph.D. *Member*: Louisiana Edu. Assn.; Central Louisiana AA; Southeastern AA (Chm. La. Div.). *Awards*: prizes, Louisiana Art Comm., 1939; Univ. Chicago, 1945. *Work*: Ford Times; All State Insurance Co. *Exhibited*: New Orleans AA, 1950; Ford Motor Co. Exh., 1956; Louisiana T. Faculty Show, 1955; one-man: Louisiana A. Comm., 1949. Contributor illus. to Ford Times and All State Insurance Co. publications. *Position*: Assoc. Prof., Northwestern State Col., 1934-49; Prof. A., Hd. Dept. A., Louisiana Col., 1949-51; Assoc. Prof., Louisiana Inst., 1951-53; Prof. A., Hd. Dept. A., Northwestern State Col., Natchitoches, La., 1953- .*

HANCOCK, JAMES CARL—*Etcher, Des., P., Comm. A.*
   Galloway Pike, North Little Rock, Ark.

B. Springville, Tenn., May 10, 1898. *Work*: Pub. Lib., New Orleans, Monroe, La.; Mun. A. Gal., Jackson, Miss.; Cossitt Lib., Memphis, Tenn.; Pub. Lib., Ft. Smith, Little Rock, Ark.; Beaumont, Tex.; Lake Charles, La.; Tulane Univ.; Louisiana State Univ. *Exhibited*: Little Rock (Ark.) Mus. FA, 1947. Author, I., "New Orleans," etching, dry points & sketches; "Seeing New Orleans." Des. special Xmas cards.

HANCOCK, WALKER (KIRTLAND)—*Sculptor, T.*
   Lanesville, Gloucester, Mass.

B. St. Louis, Mo., June 28, 1901. *Studied*: St. Louis Sch. FA, Washington Univ. D.F.A.; Univ. Wisconsin; PAFA; Am. Acad. in Rome. *Member*: NA; NSS; Arch.L.; Smithsonian A. Comm.; Nat. Inst. A. & Let. *Awards*: prize, PAFA, 1921, med., 1925; F., PAFA, 1932; Cresson traveling scholarship, 1922, 1923; Prix de Rome, 1925; NAD, 1935, 1950, medal, 1953; Saltus award, NSS, 1942, 1954; Phila. A. All., 1953; Arch. Lg., 1955. *Work*: S., PAFA; John Herron AI; CGA; CAM; Brookgreen Gardens, S.C.; Parrish A. Mus., Southampton, N.Y.; Girard Col.; City Hall, Kansas City, Mo.; NGA; Am. Acad. A. & Let.; LC; Eisenhower Inaugural Medal; Kansas City War Mem.; St. Louis Soldier's Mem. Bldg.; Hall of Fame, N.Y. Univ.; Mun. Court Bldg., Phila., Pa.; Pa.R.R. Mem., 30th St. Station, Phila., Pa.; U.S. Air Mail Flyers Med. Honor; Army & Navy Air Med.; Medalist Soc.; John Paul Jones, Fairmount Park, Phila., Pa.; Founders' Mem., Bell Telephone Co. of Canada, Montreal. *Exhibited*: nationally and internationally. Contributor to: College Art Journal. Lectures: Sculpture. *Position*: Instr., S., PAFA, Philadelphia, Pa., 1929- .

HANDVILLE, ROBERT TOMPKINS—
   Painter, Comm. A., I.
   Charles E. Cooper, Inc., 136 East 57th St., New York 22, N.Y.; h. 99 Woodland Drive, Pleasantville, N.Y.

B. Paterson, N.J., Mar. 23, 1924. *Studied*: PIASch. *Member*: SI; AWS. *Work*: U.S. Air Force. *Exhibited*: AWS, 1948-1950, 1952, 1954, 1956-1958; Audubon A., 1954, 1957; Butler AI, 1953; Northern Westchester A., 1954, 1955-1958. Contributor advertising illus. to Sat. Eve. Post; Look; Life, and other national magazines and newspapers.

HANKINS, VINA S. (Mrs.)—Painter, T.
1858 Buena Vista Way, Carlsbad, Cal.

B. Chicago, Ill. *Studied*: AIC. *Member*: Women Painters of the West; La Jolla FA Assn.; Carlsbad-Oceanside A. Lg. *Awards*: Poland award, 1944; Palm Springs, 1949; La Jolla AA, 1955; Carlsbad-Oceanside A. Lg., 1955. *Exhibited*: Los Angeles, San Diego, Carlsbad, Palm Springs, Cal. Arranged art exh. and classes for USO programs; Organized Women Painters of San Diego County, 1957.

HANNA, BOYD—Illustrator, Eng.
1069 Findley Drive, Pittsburgh 21, Pa.

B. Irwin, Pa., Jan. 15, 1907. *Studied*: Univ. Pittsburgh; Carnegie Inst. *Member*: SAGA. *Work*: MMA; LC; Carnegie Inst.; N.Y. Pub. Lib.; Dist. Print, Min. Pr. Soc., 1951. *Exhibited*: SAGA, 1950-1955; Min. Pr. Soc., 1951. I., "Longfellow's Poems," 1944; "The Compleat Angler," 1947; "Dreamthorp," 1947; "The Greatest Thing in the World," 1949; "The Story of the Nativity," 1949; "Leaves of Grass," 1952; "Sayings of Buddha," 1957; "Sayings of Mohammed," 1958; "The Hound of Heaven," 1958.

HANNA, EDITH MARGARET—Educator, C., P., S.
Mary Hardin-Baylor College, Faculty Apts., Belton, Tex.; studio: Box 531, Baylor Station, Belton, Tex.

B. Chico, Tex., Aug. 28, 1895. *Studied*: North Texas State Univ., B.S., M.S., with Octavio Medellin; Colorado State Col. Edu.; Columbia Univ., with Ralph Pearson and others; Southwest Texas State T. Col. *Member*: Texas State AA; Texas FA Assn.; NAEA; Western AA; AAUW; AAUP; Nat. Assn. for Student Teaching Supv. *Exhibited*: Texas FA Assn.; San Marcos, Tex. Contributor to Texas Display Magazine; Texas Outlook; Texas Trends. Lectures: Contemporary Art. *Positions*: Hd. Dept. A., Mary Hardin-Baylor College, Belton, Texas, 1955- ; Summer Session Instr., North Texas State, 1940, West Texas State, 1944-45, South West Texas State, 1943, 1954, Hardin Simmons Univ., 1949-50.

HANNA, KATHERINE—Museum Director
The Taft Museum, 316 Pike St.; h. Hotel Alms, Victory Parkway, Cincinnati 6, Ohio

B. Cleveland, Ohio, Jan. 25, 1913. *Studied*: Sweet Briar Col.; Oberlin Col.; Bryant & Straton, Boston. *Member*: Assn. Mus. Dirs.; AAMus.; AFA Mid-west Museum Conf. Hon. member: AID; Cincinnati Print & Drawing Circle; Cincinnati Contemp. A. Soc. Editor, Taft Museum Catalog, 1957; contributor to Museum Bulletins, Art Magazines and newspapers. Lectures: Art, Architecture and Decorative Arts, 19th Century; French Renaissance; Chinese Porcelains; History of Art; Appreciation of the Arts. *Positions*: President's Adv. Council, Univ. Cincinnati; Dean's Adv. Comm., Evening Col., Univ. Cincinnati; Fine Arts Commission, City of Cincinnati; Chm., Visual Arts Sect., UNESCO, 1955; Art Panel, Biennial Symposium, Oberlin College; Cincinnati American Red Cross, Arts and Skills Corps; Cur., 1941-52, Dir., 1952- , The Taft Museum, Cincinnati, Ohio.

HANNAH, MURIEL—Painter, I., Gr.
136 West 65th St., New York 23, N.Y.

B. England. *Studied*: BMFA Sch.; ASL, and with Philip Hale, William James, Robert Henri. *Member*: NSMP. *Exhibited*: WFNY 1939; NSMP, 1940; BMA; A. Gal., Santa Barbara, Cal.; exh. of Alaska mural at Dept. Interior, Wash., D.C., 1950; Field Mus., Chicago, 1951; Ohio State Col.; Fargo, N.D., 1951; Hist. Mus., Seattle, Wash., 1952; Anchorage, Alaska, 1955; Wailuku, Maui, Hawaii, 1955. I., "People of Poros," 1942. I., for national magazines.*

HANSCOM, TRUDE (Mrs.)—Painter, Et., E.
431 Naomi Ave., Arcadia, Cal.

B. Oil City, Pa., Dec. 6, 1898. *Studied*: Syracuse Univ.; Univ. California; Univ. So. California; Otis AI; Scripps Col. *Member*: SAGA; Pr. M. of Cal.; Cal. A. Cl.; Women Painters of the West; Glendale AA; Pasadena Soc. A. *Awards*: prizes, A. Festival, Arcadia, 1951; A. Festival, San Gabriel, 1951-1955; Pr. M. of Cal., 1952; Pasadena Mus. A., 1953. *Work*: LC; NAD; MMA; Pa. State Univ.; Cal. State Lib. *Exhibited*: Royal Acad., Lon-

don, and in local, regional and national exhibitions. Contributor to Prints by California Artists; Christian Science Monitor. *Position*: Instr. A., Alhambra and Glendale (Cal.) H.S.*

HANSEN, DOUGLAS REID—Painter, E.
Department of Art, University of Missouri; h. 607 Rockhill Rd., Columbia, Mo.

B. Jersey City, N.J., July 15, 1900. *Studied*: NAD; Corcoran Sch. A.; Broadmoor A. Acad.; Fontainebleau, France; Austrian State Sch. A. & Indst., Vienna. *Member*: CAA. *Work*: Portraits; paintings for Ford Motors; Hotel Playa de Cortez, Guaymas, Mex., etc. *Exhibited*: Toledo Mus. A.; Kansas City AI; CAM. *Position*: Instr., 1934-45, Prof. A., 1945- , Chm. Dept. A., 1938-1955, Univ. Missouri, Columbia, Mo.; A.-in-Res., La Napoule A. Fnd., France, 1955.

HANSEN, EJNAR—Painter, Lith., S., T.
238 Wyoming St., Pasadena 3, Cal.

B. Copenhagen, Denmark, Jan. 9, 1884. *Studied*: Royal Acad. FA, Copenhagen, Denmark. *Member*: Cal. WC Soc.; Cal. A. Cl.; Pasadena Soc. A. *Awards*: prizes, Los A. Mus. A., 1927, 1945, 1946, 1954; Fnd. Western A., 1934; San Diego FA Soc., 1941; Los A. A. Cl., 1941; Pasadena AI, 1943, 1953, 1955; Cal. WC Soc., 1944, 1952, 1955; Pasadena Soc. A., 1947, 1951, 1955; State A. Coll., 1948, 1949; Nat. Orange Show, 1951; Laguna Beach AA, 1951, 1952, 1954, 1955, 1957; Newport Beach Union H.S., 1952; Palos Verdes Annual, 1952; Friday Morning Cl., Los A., 1954, 1955; Baldwin Park Chamber of Commerce, 1955; Cal. State Fair, 1956; Scandinavian-American A. Soc., 1958. *Work*: Los A. Mus. A.; San Diego FA Soc.; Pasadena AI; Pomona, Cal. Mun. Coll.; Cal. State Fair Coll.; Nat Orange Show; Springville, Utah, Coll.; Santa Paula, Cal., Mun. Coll.; N.Y. Pub. Lib.; mural, USPO, Lovelock, Nev. *Exhibited*: WFNY 1939; GGE, 1939; CGA, 1943; CM, 1945; AIC, 1945, 1946; Los A. Mus. A., 1954; NAD, 1946; Pasadena AI, 1955, one-man, 1952; MMA, 1952; Cal. WC Soc., 1952, 1955; San Gabriel Valley, 1953; Laguna Beach, 1955. *Position*: Instr., Los A. County AI; Instr., A., Pasadena City College & Pasadena Sch. FA, Pasadena, Cal.

HANSEN, FLORENCE FRONEY—Painter
1834 North Alexandria Ave., Los Angeles 27, Cal.

B. Sheboygan, Wis., Jan. 25, 1892. *Studied*: AIC; Chicago Acad. FA; Academie Julien, Paris. *Member*: Cal. A. Cl.; A. of the Southwest; Societe des Artistes Francaises; Acad. FA, London. *Awards*: gold medal, Miniature Soc., London, 1925; gold medal, Acad. FA, Paris, 1927; silver medal, Acad. FA, London, 1928. *Work*: Stendahl A. Gal., Los A.; Ebell A. Salon; AIC; Am. Acad. in Rome; Acad. FA, London. *Exhibited*: nationally and internationally.

HANSEN, FRANCES FRAKES—Educator, P., Des.
1800 Poplar St.; h. 700 Pontiac St., Denver 20, Colo.

B. Harrisburg, Mo., Dec. 3, 1919. *Studied*: Univ. Denver, B.F.A., with John Edward Thompson; AIC; Colorado State Col. Edu., M.A.; grad. study, Univ. So. California; Fontainebleau Sch. FA, France. *Member*: CAA; Delta Phi Delta. *Exhibited*: Denver A. Mus.; Joslyn Mus. A.; William Rockhill Nelson Gal.; Central City (Colo.) Festival; Colorado Women's Col. *Position*: Instr. A., Univ. Denver, 1942-47 (part time); Prof. A., 1942-58, Dir. A. Dept., 1944-58, Colorado Women's Col., Denver, Colo.

HANSEN, GAYLEN CAPENER—Painter, I., T.
Art Department, Washington State College, Pullman, Wash.

B. Garland, Utah, Sept. 21, 1921. *Studied*: Otis AI; Univ. Utah; Utah State Agr. Col.; Univ. So. California. *Member*: Wash. A. & Crafts Assn. (Bd. Trustees, 1957-60). *Awards*: prizes, Utah State Fair, 1944; Utah State Inst. FA, 1945; Pacific Coast Biennial, 1957; Tacoma, Wash., 1957; Woessner Gal., Seattle; A. of Los A. and Vicinity, 1954. *Work*: Utah State Inst. FA. *Exhibited*: Texas Annual P. & S.; Denver A. Mus., 1951; Kansas City AI; Cal. WC Soc., 1954; Charles & Emma Frye Mus. A., Seattle, 1955. Illus., Biology textbooks and for scientific publications. *Position*: Asst. Prof., Washington State College, Pullman, Wash.

HANSEN, JAMES LEE—*Sculptor*
4115 Q St., Vancouver, Wash.

B. Tacoma, Wash., June 13, 1925. *Studied*: Portland A. Mus. Sch. *Member*: AEA; Northwest Inst. of Sculptors. *Awards*: prizes, San F. AA, 1952, 1956; Am. Trust Co. award. *Work*: Portland A. Mus.; SAM; SFMA. *Exhibited*: WMAA, 1953; SFMA, 1952, 1956; Kraushaar Gal., N.Y., 1952-53; SAM, 1952-1957; Denver A. Mus., 1952; Portland A. Mus., 1951-1958; Henry Gal., Univ. Wash.

HANSEN, JOANNE MARGARETHE—
Educator, L., Des., C.
927 Brookridge St., Ames, Iowa

B. Agtrup, Denmark, Mar. 18, 1880. *Studied*: PIASch.; Iowa State T. Col., B.A.; Columbia Univ., M.A.; ASL, with Bridgman; N.Y.Sch. F. & App. A.; Intl. Sch., Mexico, and in Guatemala. *Member*: Iowa Fed. Women's Cl. (art sect.); Iowa State T. Assn. (Chm. A. Sect.). *Awards*: prizes, Iowa Fed. Women's Cl.; Penny Art Fund purchase; Iowa Art Salon; Joslyn Mem. Mus., and others. *Exhibited*: AFA traveling exh.; AIC; Minneapolis Centennial Exh.; Iowa Artists, many other exhs. in U.S., Europe and South America. Contributor art section, "Rural Life in America." Illus. children's books; lectures to women's clubs, Colleges and Universities, art groups. *Positions*: Supv. A., Sioux City, Iowa, 1905-16; Prof., Hd. Appl. A. Dept., Iowa State Col., Ames, Iowa, 1920-41.

HARARI, HANANIAH—*Painter, I., Ser.*
34 Prospect Pl., Croton-on-Hudson, N.Y.

B. Rochester, N.Y., Aug. 29, 1912. *Studied*: Syracuse Univ.; Fontainebleau, and with Leger, L'Hote, Gromaire, in Paris, France. *Member*: AEA. *Awards*: prizes, NAD, 1941; Audubon A., 1945; medal, A. Dir. Cl., Chicago; prizes, Ossining, N.Y., 1953, 1955, 1957; Mt. Kisco, N.Y., 1955. *Work*: WMAA; Univ. Arizona; PMA; MMoDA; Albright A. Gal.; SFMA; Rochester Mem. A. Gal.; Iowa State Univ. *Exhibited*: MMoDA, 1941, 1943; WMAA, 1942, 1944; Univ. Arizona; MMA, 1943; NAD, 1941, 1942; CM, 1940; Conn. Acad. FA, 1941, 1942; AIC, 1940; PAFA, 1946, 1949; NGA, 1945; Finger Lakes Exh., 1941, 1943, 1946, 1949, 1950; A. Dir. Cl., 1948, 1950, 1952; one-man: Laurel Gal., 1948, 1950.

HARBART, GERTRUDE F. (Mrs. Frank)—*Painter, T.*
2201 Maryben Ave., Long Beach, Michigan City, Ind.

B. Michigan City, Ind. *Studied*: Univ. Illinois; Univ. California; AIC; Ohio Univ., and with Charles Burchfield, Hans Hofmann, Arnold Blanch, Paul Sample and others. *Member*: South Bend AA; Northern Indiana A.; Gary A. Lg.; Northern Indiana A. Patron's Assn. *Awards*: prizes, John Herron AI, 1958; South Bend AA, 1954, 1956, 1957; Old Northwest Territory Exh., Springfield, Ill., 1954, 1956; Ohio Valley, 1955; Hoosier Salon, 1958. *Work*: South Bend AA; St. Mary's of Notre Dame, South Bend; Michigan City H.S. *Exhibited*: CGA, 1957; Butler Inst. Am. A., 1955-1957; Nat. Soc. Painters in Casein, 1956; Provincetown A. Festival, 1958; Art:USA, 1958; Terry AI, 1952; Springfield, Ill., 1953, 1958; Michigan Regional, 1951-1958; Southern Shores, 1956, 1958; Ohio Valley, 1953, 1955; Northern Indiana A., 1958; Hoosier Salon, 1951-1958. Contributor to Art News; School Arts. *Positions*: Instr., Niles, Mich., Adult Edu. classes; Long Beach, Michigan City, Ind.; Beverly Shores and Pub. Schs.; La Porte, Ind., Adult Edu.

HARBAUER, HAZEL JACOBY—*Painter, Gr., C., L.*
2600 Erie Road, Temperance, Mich.

B. Toledo, Ohio, Jan. 20, 1908. *Studied*: Toledo Univ.; Cleveland Sch. A.; AIC. *Member*: Palette Cl.; Toledo Women A.; Ohio WC Soc. *Exhibited*: Butler AI, 1939-1941, 1943; LC; Toledo Mus. A., 1941, 1944 (both one-man); in Mexico, 1946; Town Gal., Toledo, Ohio.

HARBESON, GEORGIANA BROWN (Mrs. Frank Godwin)—*Painter, Des., C., W., L.*
New Hope, Pa.

B. New Haven, Conn., May 13, 1894. *Studied*: PAFA; Moore Inst. A. Sc. & Indst.; N.Y. Sch. Des.; N.Y. Univ.; PMSchIA. *Member*: NAWA; N.Y. Soc. Craftsmen; Phila. WC Cl.; Pen & Brush Cl.; Women's Press Cl.; Needle & Bobbin Cl. *Awards*: prizes, PAFA; N.Y. Women's Exp. A. & Indst.; N.Y. A. All. *Work*: Honolulu Acad. A.;

awarded des. commission in Nat. Comp. for Designers, for decorations, altar rail, cushions, stalls and kneelers to be completed in needlepoint for St. Joseph's Chapel, Wash., D.C. (juried by Nat. Gal. A. for the Wash. Cathedral), 1956; needlepoint for 40 kneelers, Bishop's Chapel, St. Paul's, Cincinnati, Ohio, 1958. Contributor articles on Furniture Decoration and Designs; Authentic Early American stencilling and Patterns to McCall's Annual of Arts and to McCall's Needlework magazine. Author: "American Needlework 17th Century to Contemporary." Articles published in "Studio," London and American Artists magazine.

HARCOFF, LYLA MARSHALL—*Painter*
220 East Pueblo St., Santa Barbara, Cal.

B. Lafayette, Ind. *Studied*: Purdue Univ., B.S.; AIC; & in Paris, France. *Awards*: prize, Santa Barbara Mus. A., 1944. *Work*: LaFayette (Ind.) A. Mus.; Santa Barbara Mus. A.; Santa Fé R.R.; U.S. Govt. *Exhibited*: Santa Barbara Mus. A., 1944, 1949 (one-man); San F., Cal., 1944; San Diego, Cal.; Los A., Cal., Chicago, Ill.; de Young Mem. Mus.*

HARDER, CHARLES MABRY—*Craftsman, Des., E.*
New York State College of Ceramics, Alfred, N.Y.

B. Birmingham, Ala., Nov. 23, 1899. *Studied*: AIC; Alfred Univ., B.S.; & with Charles F. Binns, Hans Hofmann, Ernest Thurn. *Member*: Am. Ceramic Soc. *Awards*: prizes, Syracuse Mus. FA, 1932, 1935, med.; 1937; med., Paris Salon, 1937. Contributor to: Journal and Bulletin, Am. Ceramic Soc.; articles on Ceramic Glazes, Colors, Textures. *Position*: Emeritus Prof., Ceramic Design, State Univ. of N.Y. College of Ceramics, Alfred Univ., Alfred, N.Y.

HARDIN, ADLAI S.—*Sculptor*
90 Brookside Rd., Darien, Conn.

B. Minneapolis, Minn., Sept. 23, 1901. *Studied*: AIC; Princeton Univ., A.B. *Member*: ANA; F., NSS (Pres., 1957-58). *Awards*: prizes, Arch. Lg., 1941; NSS, 1950, Lindsey Morris prize, 1956; Anna Hyatt Huntington prize, Hudson Valley AA, 1957; medal, NAD, 1945. *Work*: PAFA; IBM; Moravian Church, Bethlehem, Pa.; Stamford (Conn.) Hospital; stone figures, Princeton Univ. store, 1958; Congregational Church, Darien, Conn., 1958. *Exhibited*: NAD; PAFA, annually.

HARDING, DOROTHY STURGIS—(Mrs. Lester W.)—
Designer
Little Harbor Rd., Portsmouth, N.H.

B. Boston, Mass., July 28, 1891. *Studied*: BMFA Sch. *Member*: Am. Soc. Bookplate Collectors & Designers. *Awards*: Med., Boston Tercentenary, 1930. *Work*: bookplates: MMA; Am. Antiquarian Soc., Worcester, Mass.; Phila. Pr. Cl.; Boston Soc. A. & Crafts; British Mus., London. *Exhibited*: Phila. Pr. Cl.; Junior Lg. Gal., Boston. *Position*: Draftsman, Portsmouth Naval Shipyard, 1942-1957 (Retired).

HARDING, GEORGE—*Painter*
1231 Montgomery Ave., Wynnewood, Pa.

B. Philadelphia, Pa. *Studied*: PAFA. *Member*: NA; Pennsylvania A. Comm. *Awards*: prize, gold medal, PAFA; gold medal, Arch. Lg.; FA award, Phila. chapter, AIA. *Work*: murals, USPO, Admin. Bldg., Wash., D.C.; Federal Bldg., WFNY 1939; Mun. Court Parkway, U.S. Customs House, First Nat. Corn Exchange Bank, Common Pleas Court, all in Phila., Pa.; Montgomery County Court House; John James Audubon Mus., Montgomery Co., Pa. *Exhibited*: Carnegie Inst.; PAFA; CGA. *Position*: Cr., Mural Dept., PAFA, Philadelphia, Pa.; Dir., Abbey Scholarship Fnd.*

HARDING, G. POWELL (Mrs.)—*Painter, L.*
44678 San Juan Ave., Palm Desert, Cal.

B. San Leandro, Cal., Jan. 11, 1892. *Studied*: Univ. California; Cal. Sch. FA; Columbia Univ. *Member*: Cal. WC Soc.; Los A. AA; Women Painters of the West. *Awards*: prizes, Cal. WC Soc. *Exhibited*: Oakland A. Mus., 1932-1940; SFMA, 1927, 1928; Los A. Mus. A., 1952, 1953, 1955, 1958; San Diego FA Soc., 1937; Riverside Mus., 1946; GGE, 1939; Los A. AA, 1946, 1948-1952, 1958;

Cal. A. Cl., 1936-1938, 1940; High Mus. A.; Grand Central A. Gal.; Santa Barbara Mus. A.; Cal. PLH, 1952; Cal. WC Soc. traveling exh., 1952-1955; Pasadena AI, 1948-1955; Cal. WC Soc., 1953-1955 (annuals); deYoung Mem. Mus., 1952, 1954, 1955; Santa Monica City Gal., 1958 (one-man). *Position*: Chm., Exec. Bd., Santa Monica City A. Gal., 1955.

HARDY, THOMAS AUSTIN (TOM)—
Sculptor, T., Lith.
Address Unknown

B. Redmond, Ore., Nov. 30, 1921. *Studied*: Oregon State Col.; Univ. Oregon, B.S., M.F.A. *Member*: Oregon Ceramic Studio; Portland A. Mus. *Awards*: prizes, Oregon Ceramic Studio, 1951; Portland A. Mus., 1951, 1952; SAM, 1951; SAGA, 1952. *Work*: Portland A. Mus.; Springfield (Mo.) A. Mus.; SAM; Univ. Oregon; Oregon Ceramic Studio, and in private collections. *Exhibited*: Sao Paulo, Brazil, 1955; WMAA, 1954, 1955; MMA, 1953; CM, 1952; SAGA, 1952; Bradley Univ., 1952; SFMA, 1953, 1955; Denver A. Mus., 1953; SAM, 1947, 1951, 1952, 1954, 1955; Wichita AA, 1947; Syracuse Mus. FA, 1952; Portland A. Mus., 1936, 1941, 1952-1955; Oregon Ceramic Studio, 1951-1953; AFA, 1955; one-man: Kraushaar Gal., 1953; Stanford Univ., 1954; SAM, 1954; Oregon State Col., 1953; Univ. British Columbia, 1955; Univ. So. California, 1954; Kasper Gal., San F., 1954. *Position*: Instr., Univ. Oregon, 1952; Oregon State System of Higher Edu., Adult Edu., 1953- ; Sculpture, Univ. British Columbia (summer), 1955; Coos A. Lg. (Ore.) Summer Art Workshop, 1954-55.*

HARE, CHANNING (WEIR)—*Painter*
1 Sutton Pl., South, New York 22, N.Y.; 319 El Vedado Rd., Palm Beach, Fla.; Wonderlea, Ogunquit, Me.

B. New York, N.Y. *Studied*: ASL, and with Robert Henri, George Bellows, William Zorach. *Member*: Soc. Four A., Palm Beach, Fla. *Awards*: prizes, Soc. Four A., 1942, 1943, 1944. *Work*: Virginia Hist. Soc.; BMFA; PAFA; Colorado Springs FA Center; Davenport Mun. A. Gal.; IBM. *Exhibited*: WMA, 1935; BMA, 1936; John Herron AI, 1943; one-man: New York, N.Y.; Boston, Mass.; Palm Beach, Fla.; Lowe Gal. A., 1955; Grand Central Moderns, 1956; also exhibited at Carnegie Inst., 1950; MMA, 1952; Univ. Illinois, 1952.

HARGENS, CHARLES (W.) (JR.)—*Illustrator*
R.F.D. 2, Carversville, Pa.

B. Hot Springs, S.D., Aug. 30, 1893. *Studied*: PAFA; & with Breckenridge, Garber, McCarter, Chase, Carlson, Beaux. *Member*: SI; Phila. Sketch Cl. *Awards*: F., PAFA; Cresson traveling scholarship, PAFA, 1915. I., Western stories & hist. books for leading publishers and national magazines. *Position*: Guest Instr., Illus., PAFA, Philadelphia, Pa.*

HARKAVY, MINNA—*Sculptor*
Hotel Ansonia, 2109 Broadway, New York, N.Y.

Studied: ASL; and in Paris with Antoine Bourdelle; Hunter Col., B.A. *Member*: AEA; Fed. Mod. P. & S.; S. Gld.; Assoc. Memb., Intl. Inst. A. & Let. *Awards*: prizes, NAWA, 1940, 1941; Nat. Exh. Am. Sc., MMA, 1951; Project award, U.S. Treasury. *Work*: WMAA; MModA; Musee Municipal, St. Denis, France; Mus. Western A., U.S.S.R.; Tel-Aviv, Ain Harod Mus., Israel; USPO, Winchendon, Mass., and in many private collections U.S. and abroad. *Exhibited*: SFMA; AIC; PAFA; Albright A. Gal.; Munson-Williams-Proctor Inst.; WMAA; MModA; MMA; Univ. of Nebraska, Iowa, Virginia, etc.; Salon d'Automne, Salon des Tuileries, Jeu de Paume, Paris, France; Petit Palais; Toronto, Can.; Sao Paulo, Brazil; One-man: Paris, France; R.I. Sch. Des. Mus. A., 1956. Contributor articles to magazines.*

HARLAN, ROMA CHRISTINE—*Portrait Painter*
The Woodner, A-734, 3636 16th St., Northwest, Washington 10, D.C.

B. Warsaw, Ind., June 23, 1912. *Studied*: Purdue Univ.; AIC, with Constantine Pougialis, Francis Chapin; and with Ralph Clarkson, Marie Goth. *Member*: Wash. A. Cl.; Indiana Fed. A. Clubs; Lafayette (Ind.) AA. *Work*: St. Joseph's Col., Rensselaer, Ind.; Purdue Univ.; PEO Home,

Mt. Pleasant, Iowa; Lake Shore Cl. of Chicago; Francis Hammond H.S., Alexandria, Va.; Nat. Guard Bldg., Wash., D.C.; Nat. Bus. & Prof. Women's Fnd. Bldg., Wash., D.C. Many ports. of prominent persons. Author essay "Rembrandt" published in Congressional Record, 1957. *Exhibited*: Hoosier Salon, 1940; All-Illinois Soc. FA, 1940-1942; Kaufmann's Gal., Chicago, 1942; Lafayette AA; Wash. A. Cl., 1958; one-man: Lake Shore Cl., Chicago; Little Gal., Chicago; Purdue Univ.

HARLOW, HARRY MERRICK SUTTON—
Painter, Des., Gr., L.
294 Dennett St., Portsmouth, N.H.

B. Haverhill, Mass., July 19, 1882. *Studied*: Eric Pape Sch. A. *Member*: AAPL. *Work*: paintings, Trinity Church, Haverhill, Mass.; St. Augustine & St. Martin Mission Church, Boston, Mass.; Chapel of the Soc. of the Divine Compassion, N.Y.C.; Christ Church, New Franklin Sch., Masonic Home, Portsmouth, N.H.; Haverhill Hist. Soc.; bookplates, Los A. Mus. A. Lectures: "Colonial Doorways, Houses, Ships."

HARLOW, ROBERT ELSING, JR.—
Painter, Ser., C., W.
R.F.D. 3, Princeton, N.J.

B. Philadelphia, Pa., Mar. 20, 1914. *Studied*: Univ. Pennsylvania, B.F.A.; PAFA; Columbia Univ. *Awards*: NAD, 1946. *Work*: Albany Inst. Hist. & A.; Dumbarton Oaks Coll. *Exhibited*: CGA, 1937; VMFA, 1938; NAD, 1941, 1942; Carnegie Inst., 1942; MMA (AV), 1942; Albany Inst. Hist. & A., 1941-1943; Hartford Atheneum, 1941-1943; Conn. Acad. FA, 1940-1942.

HARMAN, FRED—*Illustrator*
Red Ryder Ranch, Pagosa Springs, Colo.

Member: SI.

HARMON, LILY—*Painter, Lith.*
151 Central Park West, New York 23, N.Y.

B. New Haven, Conn., Nov. 19, 1913. *Studied*: Yale Univ. Sch. FA; ASL, and in Paris, France. *Member*: NAWA; A. Lg. Am.; AEA (Nat. Bd. Dir.; Chm. Fund Com.). *Work*: Encyclopaedia Britannica; Butler AI; Tel-Aviv, Ain Harod Mus., Israel; Newark Mus. A.; mural, Port Chester (N.Y.) Jewish Community Center. *Exhibited*: nationally and internationally. Illus. "Pride and Prejudice," 1945.*

HARPER, E(DWIN) L(AURENCE)—
Cartoonist, Des., P., I., T., W.
1215 Colonial Ave., Alexandria, Va.

B. Alexandria, Va., Apr. 27, 1883. *Studied*: Maryland Inst.; NAD; ASL; T. Col., Columbia Univ.; in Paris and Brussels. *Member*: AAPL; Dynamic Realists of Wash. *Exhibited*: AAPL; Smithsonian Inst.; Wash. WC Cl. Cartoons in leading magazines and newspaper syndicates.*

HARRIS, ALEXANDRINA ROBERTSON—
Miniature Painter
193-02 100th Ave., Hollis 23, L.I., N.Y.

B. Aberdeen, Scotland, July 11, 1886. *Studied*: Adelphi Col., Brooklyn, N.Y.; ASL; Am. Sch. Min. P.; Fontainebleau, France, with Despujols. *Member*: NAWA; ASMP (Pres. 1947-1958); Portraits, Inc.; Grand Central Gal.; Pa. Soc. Min. P.; Brooklyn Soc. A.; AWS; Royal Soc. Min. P., London, England (hon.). *Awards*: prizes, Balt. WC Cl.; ASMP, prize & medal, 1954; NAWA, 1935, med., 1944, 1951, Medal of Honor, 1958; Cal. Soc. Min. P., 1941, 1947; med., Pa. Soc. Min. P., 1950. *Work*: PMA; CGA; Butler AI; The Hermitage Mus., Norfolk, Va.; Dept. Archives, State Capitol, Alabama; BMA. *Exhibited*: CGA, 1940; PAFA, 1920-1945; BM, 1936; Century of Progress, Chicago, 1933; High Mus. A., 1944; Royal Soc. Min. P., London, 1924, 1958; WFNY 1939; MMA; Los A. Mus. A.; BMA.

HARRIS, CARYL—*Painter*
80 Park Ave., New York 16, N.Y.

B. Walton, N.Y., Mar. 31, 1884. *Studied*: Yale Univ., B.A. *Exhibited*: Vendome Gal., 1939; All. A. Am. 1939,

1941; Oakland A. Mus., 1940, 1944; Town Hall Cl., N.Y., 1945; North Salem (N.Y.) Lib., 1949; Suffolk Mus., Stony Brook, N.Y., 1950.

HARRIS, CHARLES GORDON—*Painter*
    1699 Louisquisset Pike, Lincoln, Saylesville R.F.D. 1, R.I.

B. Providence, R.I., Oct. 17, 1891. *Studied*: R.I. Sch. Des.; & with Cyrus Farnum, Stacy Tolman, George A. Hays. *Member*: Providence AC; Providence WC Cl.; South County AA. *Awards*: prizes, Attleboro Mus. A.; South County AA; Providence A. Cl. *Exhibited*: Providence AC; Providence WC Cl.; South County AA.*

HARRIS, JOSEPHINE MARIE—*Educator*
    Wilson College; h. 756 Philadelphia Ave., Chambersburg, Pa.

B. Webster Groves, Mo., Jan. 20, 1911. *Studied*: Washington Univ., St. Louis, B.A., M.A., Ph.D.; Am. Sch. of Classical Studies, Athens, Greece; Dumbarton Oaks Research Lib. & Coll. *Member*: Archaeological Inst. Am.; Am. Philological Assn.; CAA; AAUP. Contributor to American Journal of Archaeology. *Positions*: Prof., Hist. of Art, Medieval, Renaissance and Modern, Smith College, 1945-46; Wilson College, Chambersburg, Pa., 1946- .

HARRIS, JULIAN HOKE—*Sculptor, E., W., L.*
    177 Fifth St., Northwest, Atlanta, Ga.

B. Carrollton, Ga., Aug. 22, 1906. *Studied*: Georgia Inst. Tech., B.S.; PAFA. *Member*: NSS; AIA; Atlanta AA (Vice-Pres. 1953-55); Assoc. Georgia A. *Awards*: prizes, Tri-County Exh., Atlanta, 1940; IBM, 1942; Assoc. A. Georgia,, 1951; medal, AIA, 1954. *Work*: Des. & executed sc. on 28 public bldgs., and 24 mem. and portrait comm. including: Ga. State Office Bldg., Atlanta; Coca-Cola Bottling Co., Atlanta; Atlanta Constitution Bldg.; Uncle Remus Lib., Atlanta; Grant Park Zoo, Filtration Plant, Augusta; First Nat. Bank, Decatur, Ga.; 4 bldgs. at Georgia Tech.; Fulton County Health Center, Atlanta; State Agricultural Bldg., Medical Research Bldg., F.W. Olin Indst. Ed. Bldg., Grady Hospital, all in Atlanta, and others. Commemorative medals and medallions for Rich's, Atlanta; Mandeville Mills, Carrollton, Ga. Contributor to architectural magazines including Journal of the AIA. *Exhibited*: nationally. Lectures: "Sculpture and Architecture" at principal colleges in the Southeast. *Position*: Prof. Dept., Arch., Georgia Inst. Tech., Atlanta, Ga.*

HARRIS, LAURENCE W. (LARRY)—*Cartoonist*
    634 Bonair St., La Jolla, Cal.

B. Perrysburg, Ohio, July 17, 1908. *Studied*: Toledo Univ.; Toledo Mus. Sch. A.; Keane's A. Sch., with Theodore J. Keane. Contributor of cartoons to Sat. Eve Post; Look and other national magazines.

HARRIS, LOUIS—*Painter, T.*
    203 Bleecker St., New York 12, N.Y.

B. St. Louis, Mo., Nov. 7, 1902. *Studied*: ASL, with Kenneth Hayes Miller, Max Weber. *Member*: Fed. Mod. P. & S. *Work*: Brandeis Univ. Illus. "The Time of the Calliope." Instr., A., Manhattan Day School.

HARRIS, MARGIE COLEMAN—
    Painter, E., S., Et., W., L., Cr., Gr., C.
    1005 Hoffman Ave., Scalp Level, Pa.

B. Washington, D.C., Mar. 30, 1891. *Studied*: Carnegie Inst.; Univ. Pittsburgh; Univ. Chicago; Pa. State Col. *Member*: Assoc. A. Pittsburgh; All. A. Johnstown; Phila. Pr. Cl.; Johnstown A. Lg.; Cambria County AA. *Awards*: prizes, Ebensburg Fair, 1935; All. A. Johnstown, 1933-1937, 1951, 1952; Garden Cl., 1938-1945. *Work*: Cambria Lib.; All. A. Johnstown; Veteran's Hospital, Aspinwall, Bethlehem, Pa.; State T. Col., Indiana, Pa.; D.A.R., Johnstown; Chamber of Commerce, Johnstown; State Mus., Harrisburg; Bethlehem Steel Co.; Mem. Hospital, Johnstown. *Exhibited*: Indiana, Pa., 1944-1946; Assoc. A. Pittsburgh, 1924-1955; All. A. Johnstown, 1933-1955; Ebensburg, Pa., 1932-1941; Phila. Pr. Cl., 1950-1952; Irvington Pr. Cl., 1950-1952; New Jersey P. & S. Soc., 1952; Norton Gal. A., 1952; Puzzletown Gld., 1950-1952; AIC; Mem. Hospital, Cambria County Assn. for Crippled Chil-

dren; Christian Home for Children; Mountain Playhouse, 1950-1955; Ogunquit A. Center, 1954; Kirk-of-the-Hills, Wis., 1953-1955; one-man: Art Inst., Johnstown, 1953; Pa. Hist. & Mus. Comm. Gal., Harrisburg, 1953. Contributor to School Arts magazine, 1955. *Position*: Instr. A., Pa. State Col., 1919-38; T., L., Art Inst., Johnstown, Pa., 1935-55; State T. Col., 1939; Treas. Pa. A. Edu. Assn., 1952-53; Dir., A. & Crafts, Church of the Brethren Home, Scalp Level, Pa.

HARRIS, MARGO LIEBES—*Sculptor*
    96 Fifth Ave. (11); h. 360 Cabrini Blvd., New York 40, N.Y.

B. Frankfurt, Germany, Oct. 17, 1925. *Studied*: in Germany and Italy; ASL, with William Zorach. *Member*: AEA; NAWA; ASL. *Work*: in private colls. *Exhibited*: Audubon A., 1951, 1953, 1954, 1957; PAFA, 1953; Boston A. Festival, 1957; WMAA, 1951; NAWA, 1958; Brick Store Mus., Kennebunk, Me.; Portland (Me.) Mus. A.; Wellons Gal., N.Y.

HARRIS, MRS. MASON DIX—*Museum Director*
    Fitchburg Art Museum, 25 Merriam Parkway, Fitchburg, Mass.*

HARRIS, PAUL STEWART—*Museum Director, L., W.*
    J. B. Speed Art Museum, 2035 South Third St. (8); h. 60 Eastover Park, Louisville 6, Ky.

B. Orange, Mass., Mar. 7, 1906. *Studied*: Antioch Col., B.S.; Harvard Col., S.B.; N.Y. Univ. Grad. Sch. *Member*: AA Mus.; CAA. Contributor to museum bulletins. *Positions*: Asst. Cur., Dept. Mediaeval A., & the Cloisters, MMA, 1933-38; Dir., Sec., Des Moines Assn. FA, Des Moines, Iowa, 1938-40; Senior Cur., Minneapolis Inst. A., Minneapolis, Minn. 1941-42, 1946; Dir., J. B. Speed Art Mus., Louisville, Ky., 1946- .

HARRIS, ROBERT GEORGE—
    Illustrator, Comm. A., P., L.
    5720 North Saguaro Road, Scottsdale, Ariz.

B. Kansas City, Mo., Sept. 9, 1911. *Studied*: Kansas City AI, with Monte Crews; Grand Central Sch. A., with Harvey Dunn; ASL, with George Bridgman. *Member*: SI; Phoenix FA Assn. *Exhibited*: SI; A. Dir. Cl., 1943-1946; Westport A. Group. I., Ladies Home Journal; McCall's; Sat. Eve. Post, and other national magazines. Lectures: Modern Magazine Illustration; Story and Advertising.

HARRIS, SAMUEL HYDE—*Painter*
    16 Champion Place; h. 222 North Hidalgo St., Alhambra, Cal.

B. Brentford, England. *Studied*: ASL, Los Angeles, and with Hanson Puthuff, Will Foster. *Member*: Cal. A. Cl.; Pasadena Soc. A.; Laguna Beach AA; A. of the Southwest; Whittier AA. *Awards*: prizes, Cal. A. Cl., 1941; Ebell Cl., 1942; Whittier AA, 1942; Los A. AA, 1944; Cal. PLH, 1944; Friday Morning Cl., 1947, 1949, 1951, 1952; Glendale AA, 1951; San Gabriel Festival A., 1954; Laguna Beach AA, 1952; A. of the Southwest, 1955; medal, A. of the Southwest, 1940. *Work*: Gardena, Clearwater, San Pedro, Santa Paula, Alhambra, Berendo high schools; Dixie Col., Utah; Pierce Jr. Col., Canoga Park, Cal.; murals, Santa Barbara, Cal; Southern Pacific Co., Santa Ana, Cal. *Position*: Instr. Painting, Business Men's AI, Los Angeles, Cal., 1945- .*

HARRISON, CLEOBELLE—*Educator*
    Northern Michigan College; h. 115 West Magnetic St., Marquette, Mich.

B. Athens, Mich., Aug. 10, 1907. *Studied*: Western Michigan Col., A.B.; Am. Acad. A., Chicago; Wayne Univ., M.A.; Univ. Michigan, Ed. D.; Chicago Acad. A.; Northwestern Univ.; Ray Sch. Adv. A.; AIC. *Member*: Michigan Edu. Assn.; Michigan Art Edu. Assn.; NEA; AAUW. *Work*: student exh., Detroit Inst. A. Contributor to School Arts magazine. *Positions*: Instr. A., Lansing, Saginaw, Marquette, Mich.; Charleston, Oak Park, Ill.; A. in Audio-Visual Aids, IBM, Endicott, N.Y., 1944-45; Hd., A. Dept., Northern Michigan College, Marquette, Mich., at present.

HARRISON, DOROTHY—Painter, T.
257 West 86th St., New York 24, N.Y.

B. New York, N.Y. *Studied*: T. Col., Columbia Univ., B.S., M.A. *Member*: NAWA; Brooklyn SA. *Exhibited*: BM, 1935; AWCS, 1933-1940; Decorator's Cl., 1940; High Mus. A., 1944; NAWA; Brooklyn SA; Argent Gal., 1939 (one-man).*

HARRISON, ROBERT RICE—Educator, P., W.
1595 Hewitt Ave., St. Paul 4, Minn.

B. Detroit, Mich., May 5, 1908. *Studied*: AIC; Wayne State Univ., B.F.A.; N.Y. Univ.; Iowa Univ., M.A., Ph.D. *Exhibited*: VMFA, 1947, 1949; Contemp. Va. & North Carolina Exh.; Minneapolis Inst. A. *Position*: Assoc. Prof. A., Hd. Dept. A., Hamline Univ., St. Paul, Minn., 1954- .

HARRISON, WILLIAM SHERMAN, JR. (BILL)—
Cartoonist
636 Patton Ave.; h. 28 Cranford Rd., Asheville, N.C.

B. Asheville, N.C., Feb. 17, 1927. *Studied*: Clemson Col.; Univ. North Carolina, A.B. *Member*: Nat. Cartoonists Soc. Contributor cartoons to Sat. Eve. Post; Look; Better Homes & Gardens; Cosmopolitan; Ladies Home Journal; Redbook, and other national magazines.

HARRITON, ABRAHAM—Painter, T.
66 West 9th St., New York 11, N.Y.

B. Bucharest, Roumania, Feb. 16, 1893. *Studied*: NAD, with George DeForest Brush, Emil Carlsen, Kenyon Cox, George Maynard. *Member*: AEA; Audubon A. *Work*: WMAA; Newark Mus. A.; AGAA; Oakland A. Mus.; Tel-Aviv and Ain Harod Mus., Israel; State T. Col., Indiana, Pa.; Queens Col., N.Y.; Fordham Univ.; Samuel Tilden H.S., N.Y.; mural, USPO and Agricultural Bldg., Louisville, Ga.; Living Arts Fnd. *Award*: Hallgarten, Saltus and Suydam prizes, NAD Sch A. *Exhibited*: Carnegie Inst.; MMA; BM; Newark Mus. A.; CGA; PAFA; CAM; VMFA; WMAA; Provincetown A. Festival, 1958; Goodwill Exh. in England & Scotland; ACA Gal., N.Y. (12 one-man exhs. to date). Contributor of article and reproductions to Esquire and American Artist magazines. Author: "Theory and Practice of Underpainting and Glazing."

HARRITON, DAVID M.—Designer, C., P., S., L.
Minisink Hills, Pa.

B. Roumania, Apr. 8, 1895. *Studied*: NAD; ASL. *Awards*: gold and silver medals, Paris Expo., 1937. *Member*: Soc. Des.-Craftsmen (Pres. 1944-48). *Work*: carved glass ceiling, Clark Mem., Vincennes, Ind.; war mem., Worcester, Mass.; Federal Reserve Bldg., Wash., D.C.; U.S. Bureau of Shipping, N.Y.; ceilings, Senate and House, Wash., D.C.; carved decorative glass, ballroom, SS "United States." Lectures: Carved Glass.

HARSANYI, CHARLES—Painter
Stephentown, N.Y.

B. Tapolcza, Hungary, Nov. 21, 1905. *Studied*: Royal Acad. FA, Budapest, Hungary, with A. Benkhard. *Member*: All. A. Am.; Conn. Acad. FA; Audubon A.; SC. *Awards*: prizes, Washington County Mus. FA, 1938, 1939, 1941, 1943, 1946, 1954; Conn. Acad. FA, 1945, 1953, 1955; All. A. Am., 1944, 1953 (medal); Long Island A. Lg., 1954; SC, 1945, 1951; Cumberland Valley A., 1950, 1952. *Work*: MMA; U.S. Govt.; Wash. County Mus. FA; Elmhurst Col. *Exhibited*: CGA, 1935, 1941, 1947, 1951; VMFA, 1942, 1946; PAFA, 1933-1935, 1942, 1948, 1949; AIC, 1941-1944; CM, 1941; WFNY 1939; NAD, 1933, 1934, 1936, 1938, 1940-1952, 1955; All. A. Am., 1935-1952; BM, 1934; Denver A. Mus., 1937-1939; Wash. County Mus. FA, 1937-1946; BMA, 1939; SC, 1946, 1951; Conn. Acad. FA, 1942, 1943, 1945; Audubon A., 1945-1952; Mint Mus. A., 1946; Springfield Mus. A., 1947-1950; Farnsworth Mus., 1950; AFA traveling exh.; Butler AI, 1953.

HARSHMAN, ARTHUR L.—Designer, P., S., Gr.
Indiana Glass Co.; h. South Main St., Dunkirk, Ind.

B. Dunkirk, Ind., Dec. 28, 1910. *Member*: IDI; A. Dir. Cl. of Indiana; Indiana A. Soc.; Indianapolis AA; Indiana Soc. Pr. M.; Southern Pr. M. *Work*: MModA; Ball State

T. Col. Gal., Muncie, Ind. *Exhibited*: LC, 1946; Laguna Beach AA, 1947, 1948; Mint. Mus. A., 1946, 1947; IDI, Good Design Exh., Chicago, 1950; IDI, New York, 1951; Indiana A., 1947-1949; Tri-State Pr. Exh., 1946; Ohio Valley A., 1949. *Position*: Assoc., Russel Wright Assoc., N.Y., 1957; P. & I. Design, Dunkirk, Ind., 1958- ; Dir. Des., Indiana Glass Co., 1958- .

HART, AGNES—Painter, T.
30 East 14th St., New York 3, N.Y.; h. Maverick Rd., Woodstock, N.Y.

B. Connecticut, Jan. 4, 1912. *Studied*: Ringling Sch. A., and with Josef Presser, Lucile Blanch, Paul Burlin. *Member*: Woodstock AA; Kaaterskill Group (Fnd. memb.). *Awards*: Scholarship, Yaddo Fnd., 1947, 1948. *Exhibited*: MMA, 1950, 1952; NAD, 1951; PAFA, 1952; Toledo Mus. A., 1945; AIC; VMFA; New Haven Paint and Clay Cl.; Woodstock AA, 1947-1952; one-man: New York City, 1948, 1954; Woodstock, N.Y., 1951.

HART, DRENNAN WILSON—Advertising Designer
Drennan W. Hart & Co., Illinois Bldg.; h. 4117 Sun Meadow Lane, Indianapolis 8, Ind.

B. Indianapolis, Ind., Mar. 13, 1914. *Member*: A. Dir., Cl., Chicago; Nat. Soc. A. Dir.; Soc. Typographic A., Chicago. *Exhibited*: A. Dir., Cl., 1944; Hoosier Salon, 1945, 1947. *Positions*: Asst. A. Dir., Keeling & Co., 1942-48; Owner, Drennan W. Hart & Co., Indianapolis, Ind., 1951- .

HART, MARVELL ALLISON—Museum Curator
Honolulu Academy of Arts, 900 South Beretania St., Honolulu, Hawaii

Position: Keeper of Collections, Honolulu Academy of Arts.*

HARTELL, JOHN ANTHONY—Painter, T.
Department Painting & Sculpture, Cornell University; h. 319 The Parkway, Ithaca, N.Y.

B. Brooklyn, N.Y., Jan. 30, 1902. *Studied*: Cornell Univ.; Royal Acad. FA, Stockholm, Sweden. *Awards*: prizes, Univ. Nebraska (purchase), 1955; Rochester Mem. A. Gal., 1953, 1954. *Exhibited*: WMAA, 1953; AIC, 1953; PAFA, 1954; Munson-Williams-Proctor Inst., 1953, 1954; Rochester Mem. A. Gal., 1953, 1954; Gulf Coast Mus., 1953; Albany Inst. Hist. & A., 1953; Joslyn A. Mus., 1954; Montclair Mus. A., 1954; John Herron AI, 1954; Univ. Nebraska, 1954, 1955; Birmingham Mus. A., 1955; Mus. FA of Houston, 1955; White A. Mus., Cornell Univ., 1954, 1955; Univ. Colorado, 1958; Andrew Dickson White Mus., Cornell Univ., 1956-1958; one-man: Kraushaar Gal., 1953, 1957; Rochester Mem. A. Gal., 1955; Wells Col., 1955. *Position*: Chm., Dept A., Cornell Univ., Ithaca, N.Y.

HARTER, TOM J.—Educator, P., Des., I.
Arizona State College; h. Southern Ave. & 56th St., Tempe, Ariz.

B. Naperville, Ill., Oct. 8, 1905. *Studied*: Arizona State Col., B.A.; Univ. Oregon, M.F.A.; ASL; Grand Central A. Sch. *Member*: Cal. WC Soc.; Am. Assn. Univ. Prof. *Awards*: prizes, Arizona State Fair, 1955; Maricopa County Fair, 1956-1958. *Work*: Ariz. State Col.; mural, Univ. Oregon. *Exhibited*: BM, 1935; AWS, 1937, 1938; Mus. New Mexico; Southwest A., 1941-1946; Cal. WC Soc., 1945, 1950, 1955, 1956; Arizona State Fair, 1937-1957; Cal. State Fair, 1951; Dallas Mus. FA, 1952; Tucson Festival A., 1958; Univ. Arizona, 1954-1957. I., "Game in the Desert," 1939; "Hunting in the Southwest," 1946; "Arizona: The History of a Frontier State," 1950. *Position*: Instr. A., 1937-41, Asst. Prof., 1941-45, Assoc. Prof. 1946-51, Prof., 1952- , Arizona State Col., Tempe, Ariz.

HARTGEN, VINCENT ANDREW—
Painter, E., Des., Mus. Cur.
Art Department, University of Maine, Orono, Me.

B. Reading, Pa., Jan. 10, 1914. *Studied*: Univ. Pennsylvania, B.F.A., M.F.A. *Member*: CAA; Am. Assn. Univ. Prof.; Audubon A.; Alabama WC Soc.; Maine WC Soc.; Canadian Soc. P. Et. & Engravers (hon.). *Awards*: prizes,

BAID, 1935; Soldier Art, 1945; Audubon A., 1950; F., Univ. Pa. Sch. FA, 1941. *Work*: Howard Univ.; Brooks Mem. A. Gal.; Kutztown State T. Col.; Univ. Maine; Everhart Mus. A.; BMFA; Smith Col.; Colby Col. *Exhibited*: Audubon A., 1946-1952; AWS; Boston Soc. Indp. A.; Alabama WC Soc.; one-man: Maryland Inst.; George Binet Gal.; Howard Univ.; Everhart Mus. A.; N.Y. State Univ.; Summit (N.J.) AA; Rochester Mem. A. Gal.; Benedict Col.; Claflin Univ., Orangeburg, S.C.; Chico State T. Col., Cal.; Col. of the Pacific; Univ. Idaho; Bryn Mawr A. Center; Pa. State Col.; Green Mt. Jr. Col., and others. *Positions*: Traveling Cur., Anna Hyatt Huntington Exh. Sculptures, 1937-39; Dir., Univ. Maine A. Gal., 1946- ; Prof. A., Hd. Dept. A., Univ. Maine; Orono, Me., 1946- .*

HARTLEY, HARRISON SMITH—
Painter, Des., Cart., L., I., Comm. A.
402½ Felix St.; h. Route 2, Huntoon Rd., St. Joseph, Mo.

B. Savannah, Mo., Nov. 9, 1888. *Studied*: Kansas City AI; Chicago Acad. FA; AIC; Cumming Sch. A., Des Moines, Iowa, and with J. Wellington Reynolds. *Member*: Greater Kansas City AA. *Exhibited*: WFNY 1939; Nelson Gal. A., 1943, 1948-1950; Joslyn Mus. A., 1945-1950, 1958; NAC, 1955; Plaza A. Fair, Kansas City, 1950-1955; Holly St. Studio, Kansas City, 1955; Kansas City AI, 1957; K.C. Outdoor Exh.; one-man: Springfield AA; St. Louis Barn Gal., 1949; Hax A. Center, St. Joseph, 1957. *Awards*: F., Huntington Hartford Fnd., 1956. Contributor watercolors to Ford Times. *Position*: Former Cart. with J.N. Darling, Des Moines, Iowa; A. Dir. in Chicago, Kansas City and St. Joseph; freelance at present.

HARTMAN, BERTRAM—*Painter*
8 West 13th St., New York 11, N.Y.

B. Junction City, Kan., Apr. 18, 1882. *Studied*: AIC; & abroad. *Work*: MMA; WMAA; BM; Wichita A. Mus.; Randolph-Macon Col. for Women; murals, Homer Folks Mem. Hospital, Oneonta, N.Y.; N.Y. Univ.; USPO, Dayton, Tenn. *Exhibited*: Pan-Pacific Exp., 1915; Carnegie Inst., 1933; AIC, 1926-1934; PAFA; CGA; WMAA, annually; MMA; BM; Grand Central Palace; & in South America, 1940.

HARTMAN, GERTRUDE—*Craftsman*
115 East 89th St., New York 28, N.Y.

B. San Francisco, Cal. *Studied*: Univ. California, B.S.; Mills Col., Oakland, Cal.; Cal. Sch. FA, with Carlton Ball; and with Hans Hofmann, James Billmyer. *Member*: N.Y. Soc. Ceramic A. (Pres.). *Awards*: prizes, SFMA, 1945. *Exhibited*: Syracuse Mus. FA, 1943-1945; San F. Women A., 1941-1948; San F. Potters Assn., deYoung Mem. Mus., 1945, 1946; Marin Soc. A., 1941, 1942; N.Y. Soc. Ceramic A., 1954; Cooper Union Mus., 1955.*

HARTMANN, GEORG T.—*Painter, Et.*
430 Lafayette St., New York 3, N.Y.

B. Hoboken, N.J., Nov. 1, 1894. *Studied*: NAC; with Homer Boss. *Member*: Audubon A.; AEA. *Awards*: prizes, N.Y. State Fair, 1950, 1951; Audubon A., 1954. *Exhibited*: Whitney Studio Cl., 1927, 1928; Contemporary A., 1947; NAC, 1945, 1946, 1952; PAFA, 1945, 1946, 1952; CGA, 1951; Audubon A., 1945-1951, 1954-1956; Laguna Beach AA, 1948.*

HARTMANN, MRS. GEORG THEO. See *Bianco, Pamela*

HARTMETZ, HERRICA H.—*Painter*
240 Hacienda Drive, Arcadia, Cal.

B. Oakland, Cal., June 3, 1925. *Studied*: Univ. So. California; Chouinard AI; Pasadena AI. *Member*: Cal. WC Soc.; Los A. AA; Women Painters of the West. *Awards*: prizes, Women Painters of the West, 1955; Tri-State Exh., Evansville, Ind., 1949. *Work*: Evansville Mus. *Exhibited*: de Young Mem. Mus., San F., 1952; Pomona Fair, 1948; Los A. Mus. A., 1950; Cal. WC Soc., traveling exh., 1955-56; one-man: Evansville Mus., 1952; Palos Verdes Lib., 1954.*

HARTNETT, EVA VALKER *(Mrs.)*—
Educator, C., Cr., L.
Box 1855, Minot, N.D.

B. Wahpeton, N.D., Dec. 10, 1895. *Studied*: Univ. Minnesota, B.S. in A. Edu.; Univ. Oregon, M.F.A. *Member*: Nat. Com. on A. Edu.; NEA; NAEA; Western AA; North Dakota Edu. Assn. Co-author: "Handbook to Picture Study." Conducts tours for State T. Col., Minot, N.D., U.S., Canada, Mexico and abroad. *Position*: Asst. Prof. A., State T. Col., Minot, N.D., 1927- .

HARTWIG, CLEO—*Sculptor, T.*
2 West 15th St.; h. 9 Patchin Place, New York 11, N.Y.

B. Webberville, Mich., Oct. 20, 1911. *Studied*: Western Mich. Univ., A.B., M.A. (hon.). *Member*: Audubon A.; S. Gld.; NSS. *Awards*: prizes, Detroit Inst. A., 1943; NAWA, 1945, 1951; N.Y. Soc. Ceramic A., 1945; Audubon A., 1952. *Work*: Newark Mus.; Detroit Inst. A.; PAFA; Montclair A. Mus.; Mt. Holyoke Col.; Western Mich. Univ. *Exhibited*: NAD; PAFA; MMA; PMA; WMAA; AIC; Phila. A. All.; Detroit Inst. A.; Nebraska AA; Denver A. Mus.; Newark A. Mus.; Montclair A. Mus.; Am. Acad. A. & Lets.; Nat. Inst. A. & Lets.; one-man: Sculpture Center, 1943, 1947. *Position*: Instr. S., Montclair A. Mus., Montclair, N.J., 1945- .

HARVEY, JACQUELINE—*Painter*
5 Clent Rd., Great Neck, L.I., N.Y.

B. Lille, France, Feb. 2, 1927. *Studied*: with Morris Davidson; Fernand Leger and Leopold Survage, Paris; William Hayter. *Work*: in private colls. *Exhibited*: Great Neck, L.I.; Panoras Gal., 1955 (one-man); Eola Gal., Orlando, Fla., 1957 (one-man); North Shore A. Festival, 1957; Art:USA, 1958.

HARVEY, JAMES V.—*Painter*
337 East 90th St., New York 28, N.Y.

B. Toronto, Ont., Canada, Mar. 9, 1929. *Studied*: AIC, B.F.A. *Awards*: Fulbright Fellowship, 1953-1954. *Exhibited*: MMA, 1952; WMAA, 1952; WMAA Fulbright Exh., 1958; one-man: RoKo Gal., N.Y., 1953; Parma Gal., N.Y., 1956, 1958; Cairo, Egypt, 1954.

HARVEY, LAURA CORNELL *(Mrs. Stewart)*—*Painter*
Box 2038, Santa Fe, N.M.

B. New York, N.Y. *Studied*: Hunter Col., B.A.; NAD; ASL. *Member*: Santa Fe Women's Exh. Group. *Awards*: prize, Mus. N.M., Santa Fe, 1958. *Exhibited*: Mus. New Mexico, Santa Fe, 1930-1944, 1953; Lake Forest (Ill.) Acad., 1946; Springfield Mus. A., 1947; Mandel Bros., 1948-1952; 1020 A. Center, Chicago, 1953; Stevens-Gross Gal., 1954; Knopp Hunter Gal., Santa Fe, 1956; one-man: Mus. New Mexico, 1958; Barat Col., 1958.

HARVEY, SARA EDITH—*Educator, P.*
Stetson University; h. 303 North Boulevard, Deland, Fla.

B. Rome, Ga. *Studied*: Shorter Col., Rome, Ga.; Peabody Col., B.S.; Columbia Univ., M.A., and with Charles Martin. *Member*: Southeastern AA; Fla. Fed. A.; Fla. A. T. Assn. *Award*: prize, Fla. Southern Col., 1951. *Exhibited*: Stetson Univ. Faculty Exh., 1951-1955; Fla. Southern Col., 1952; Volusia County A., 1950-1955. *Position*: Hd. A. Dept., 1935-52; Prof. A., J.B.Stetson Univ., Deland, Fla., 1952-58 (Retired).

HASELTINE, HERBERT—*Sculptor*
200 Central Park South, New York 19, N.Y.

B. Rome, Italy, Apr. 10, 1877. *Studied*: Royal Acad., Munich, Germany; Julian Acad.; & with Aime Morot. *Member*: NA; NSS; Nat. Inst. A. & Let. *Awards*: prize, NAD, 1934. *Work*: Field Mus., Chicago; MMA; WMAA; BM; AGAA; NGA; VMFA; R.I. Sch. Des.; Tate Gal., London, England; etc.*

HASELTINE, JAMES—*Painter, Gr.*
2100 Southwest Crest Drive, Oswego, Ore.

B. Portland, Ore., Nov. 7, 1924. *Studied*: Reed Col., Portland; Portland A. Mus. Sch. A.; AIC; BMSch. A.

Member: AEA; Portland AA. *Awards*: prizes, Portland A. Mus., 1953 (purchase); SAM, 1957. *Work*: Portland A. Mus.; Oakland Mus. A. *Exhibited*: BM, 1951, 1952; LC, 1950; SFMA, 1953, 1954; Northwest A., SAM, 1952, 1953, 1957; A. of Oregon, Portland A. Mus., 1951-1958. *Position*: Pres., Ore. Chptr. AEA, 1953-54, Dir., 1958; Sec., Portland AA, 1952-53; Trustee, Portland AA, 1953-55, Memb. A. Com., 1953-58, Chm. Sch. Com., 1954-55; Vice-Pres., Ore. A. All., 1954-56; Nat. Dir., AEA, 1955-56.

HASELTINE, MARGARET WILSON (MAURY)—
Painter, C., T.
2100 Southwest Crest Drive, Oswego, Ore.

B. Portland, Ore., May 7, 1925. *Studied*: Reed Col.; Portland Mus. A. Sch.; Eastern New Mexico Univ., and with Frederick Littman. *Member*: AEA; Portland AA (artist memb.). *Exhibited*: Portland A. Mus., 1948, 1953-1958; SAM, 1953; Oregon A., 1953-1958; Wash. AA, 1958; Coos Bay A. Festival, 1957.

HASSELMAN, ANNA—Museum Curator, P., E.
121 West 41st St., Indianapolis 8, Ind.

B. Indianapolis, Ind., Jan. 12, 1871. *Studied*: AIC; ASL; T. Col., Columbia Univ.; & with Chase, Hawthorne, O'Hara. *Member*: Indiana AC; Indianapolis AA; AWCS. *Work*: John Herron AI. *Exhibited*: AWCS; Indiana A., annually. *Position*: Instr., Hist. A., Herron AI, 1925-35; Cur., Herron AI, Indianapolis, Ind., 1930-1952 (Retired).

HASSELRIIS, MALTHE C. M.—Painter, I., Comm. A.
52 Seasongood Rd., Forest Hills 75, N.Y.

B. Skive, Denmark, Jan. 16, 1888. *Studied*: with Schroder, Nielsen, Hansen, in Copenhagen, Denmark. *Member*: Am. Soc. Min. P.; Grand Central A. Gal. *Awards*: medals of honor: Am. Soc. Min. P., 1948, 1956; Pa. Soc. Min. P., 1940; Brooklyn Soc. Min. P., 1934; Cal. Soc. Min. P., 1949; King Christian X Liberty Medal, 1946. *Exhibited*: Annually, Am. Soc. Min. P.; Pa. Soc. Min. P., Portraits, Inc.; Grand Central A. Gal.; WFNY 1939; MMA, 1950. I., "Tales of a Chinese Grandmother," 1945; Eugene Fields Poems, 1940; "The Ugly Duckling," 1932. Contributor Illus. to Ladies Home Journal; Ladies Home Companion; McCall's and other national magazines.

HASTINGS, ALIX LEE (Mrs. F. Murray)—
Portrait Painter
5415 Grafton Ave., Cincinnati 37, Ohio

B. New York, N.Y. *Studied*: NAD; Loos Sch. Painting; Academie Julien, Paris, France. *Work*: pastels of children, U.S. and England. *Exhibited*: Asheville A. Gld., 1954; Cincinnati, Ohio, 1956. Specializes in pastel portraits of children.

HASWELL, ERNEST BRUCE—Sculptor, W., L., T.
105 East Third St.; h. 2106 Sinton Ave., Cincinnati 6, Ohio

B. Hardinsburg, Ky., July 25, 1889. *Studied*: Cincinnati A. Acad.; Academie Royale des Beaux Arts, Brussels, Belgium. *Member*: Cincinnati AC. *Awards*: prize, Academie Royale des Beaux Arts, 1912; med., Cincinnati MacDowell Soc., 1939. *Work*: Brookgreen Gardens, S.C.; LaCrosse, Wis.; Salina Cathedral, Kansas City; CM; mem., Springfield, Ill.; St. Paul's Cathedral, Cincinnati, Ohio; Univ. Cincinnati; Miami Univ., Oxford, Ohio; Middletown, Ohio; portrait, Princeton Univ.; etc. *Exhibited*: NSS. Author: "Carving as an Aid to Rehabilitation," 1946. Lectures and articles on art. *Position*: Assoc. Prof., Col. App. A., Univ. Cincinnati, Ohio.

HATCH, EMILY NICHOLS—Painter, Gr., W., L., T.
34 LeGrande Ave., Tarrytown, N.Y.

B. Newport, R.I. *Studied*: with Walter Shirlaw, William Chase, Charles Hawthorne, George Wharton Edwards, and in Paris with Eugene Paul Ullman. *Member*: NAWA; Pen & Brush Cl.; Hudson Valley AA; Westchester Gld. A.; N.Y. Soc. Painters. *Awards*: prizes, NAWA, 1942; Pen & Brush Cl., 1930, 1934; Hudson Valley AA, 1941, 1946; Westchester A. & Crafts Gld., 1950. *Work*: Richmond (Ind.) A. Mus.; U.S. Nat. Mus., Wash., D.C. *Exhibited*: Carnegie Inst., 1913, 1914; NAD, 1913, 1915, 1916, 1932; NAWA, annually; BM; CAM; All. A. Am., 1935, 1936;

N.Y. Soc. Painters; CGA; AWS; Hudson Valley AA, 1948-1952; Westchester Gld. A., 1948-1952; Westchester A. & Crafts Gld., 1948-1952; Detroit Inst. A.; AIC; Hackley Sch., Tarrytown, N.Y., 1949 (retrospective); Pen & Brush Cl., 1953-1955; Catherine L. Wolfe A. Cl., 1954. *Positions*: Pres., NAWA, 1922-26; Pres., Hudson Valley AA, 1939-41; Chm. Com. Painting, MacDowell Cl., N.Y., 1939-45.

HATCH, JOHN DAVIS, JR.—Museum Director, E.
Norfolk Museum of Arts & Sciences; h. 700 Raleigh Ave., Norfolk 10, Va.

B. Oakland, Cal., June 14, 1907. *Studied*: Univ. California; Harvard Univ.; Yale Univ.; Princeton Univ. Author: "Reproductions of Paintings in the Isabella Stewart Gardner Museum." *Positions*: Dir., SAM, 1928-30; Dir. U.S. Art Projects, New England States, 1933-34; Ed., "Parnassus," 1937-39; Founder, Am. Art Depository, 1938; Asst. Dir., Isabella Stewart Gardner Mus., 1932-35; Founder, Am. Drawing Annual, 1940; Dir., Albany Inst. Hist. & Art, 1940-48; Visiting Prof., Univ. Oregon, 1948-49; Univ. California, 1949 (summer); Dir., Norfolk Mus. A. & Sc., Norfolk, Va., 1950- .

HATGIL, PAUL PETER—Educator, C.
Art Department, University of Texas; h. 3201 Cherry Lane, Austin, Tex.

B. Manchester, N.H., Feb. 18, 1921. *Studied*: Mass. Sch. A., Boston, B.S.; Columbia Univ., M.F.A. *Member*: NAEA; Texas FA Soc.; Southwest Ceramic Soc. *Work*: ceramics, sculpture, Laguna Gloria Mus., Austin, Tex.; Witte Mem. Mus. *Exhibited*: Intl. Exh., Wash., D.C., 1954, 1956, 1958; Wichita, Kans., 1953-1958; Mus. FA of Houston, 1956-1958; DMFA, 1952-1958; Texas FA Assn., 1951-1958; Syracuse Mus. FA, 1956; Delgado Mus. A., 1953; Miami, Fla., 1956; Intl. Exh., Mus. FA of Houston, 1956; Community Lutheran Church, Victoria, Tex., 1957. Contributor to Ceramic Monthly; Craft Horizons; Ceramic Age; School Arts magazines. *Position*: Assoc. Prof. A., Univ. Texas, Austin, Tex., 1951- .

HATHAWAY, CALVIN S.—Museum Director
Cooper Union Museum, Cooper Sq., New York 3, N.Y.

Studied: Princeton Univ., A.B.; Harvard Univ.; N.Y. Univ. *Awards*: Traveling F., Am.-Scandinavian Fnd., 1935. *Member*: Cor. Memb., Centre International d'Etude des Textiles Anciens; AAMus.; Assn. A. Mus. Dir.; Inter-Society Color Council (Vice-Pres.); Intl. Inst. for Conservation of Mus. Objects (Assoc.). *Positions*: Asst. Dept. Dec. A., 1930, Sec. to Dir., Ed., 1931-32, in charge Dept. Dec. A., Ed., 1932-33, PMA; Asst. Cur., 1933-34, Assoc. Cur., 1934-42, Cur., 1946-51, Dir., Cooper Union Museum, New York, N.Y., 1951- . Monuments, Fine Arts and Archives Officer, Europe, 1943-46 (Bronze Star medal).

HATLO, JIMMY—Cartoonist
P.O. Box 565, Pebble Beach, Cal.

B. Providence, R.I., Sept. 1, 1897. *Studied*: Cal. Sch. FA. *Member*: Bohemian Cl.; SI; Lambs Cl.; Nat. Cartoonists Soc.; Press & Union Lg. Clubs; Dutch Treat Cl.; Silurian Cl., etc. *Awards*: Banshees award, 1950 for Best Cartoonist; Nat. Cartoonists award 1957 best cartoon panel. *Positions*: Sports & Editorial cartoonist, Los Angeles Times, 1914-18; San Francisco Call-Bulletin and editorial features, Hearst Newspapers, 1924-39; Independent contractor producing features "They'll Do It Every Time" and "Little Iodine" since 1939; cartoons syndicated in about 650 newspapers.

HATTON, CLARA ANNA—Educator, C., Gr., P.
Colorado State College of Agriculture & Mechanic Arts; h. 416 South Grant Ave., Ft. Collins, Colo.

B. Bunker Hill, Kan., Oct. 19, 1901. *Studied*: Univ. Kansas, B. Des., B.F.A.; Royal Col. A., London; AIC; Cranbrook Acad. A., M.F.A.; & with John Frazier, Albert Bloch, Aldro Hibbard, Robert Austin. *Work*: Smithsonian Inst.; Cranbrook Mus. *Exhibited*: SAE; Syracuse Mus. FA; Cranbrook Acad. A., 1945; Denver, Colo., 1946; Tulsa, Okla., 1946; Dec. A. & Ceramics, 1954; Amarillo, Tex., 1945; Lawrence, Kan., 1945. *Position*: Prof., Hd. Dept. A., Colorado A. & M. Col., Ft. Collins, Colo., 1936-56.*

HATTORF, ALVIN—*Painter*
4313 Stuart Ave., Richmond 21, Va.

B. Newport News, Va., May 13, 1899. *Studied*: ASL, with Morris Kantor; Colorado Springs FA Center, with Vaclav Vytlacil, and with Henry Hensche, Hans Hofmann. *Member*: SC. *Work*: Univ. Virginia; Valentine Mus. A. *Exhibited*: VMFA, 1938, 1939, 1940, 1941 (one-man), 1942, 1944, 1946-48, 1953, 1957 (one-man); Butler AI, 1942, 1946; Richmond Acad. A. & Sc., 1936-1940; Valentine Mus. A., 1952-1954, 1956-1958.

HATTORF, HELEN KING. See *King, Helen*

HAUN, ROBERT CHARLES—*Painter, Des.*
209 Norwood Ave.; h. 42 Sea View Ave., Edgewood 5, R.I.

B. Boston, Mass., Dec. 31, 1903. *Studied*: Massachusetts Sch. A. *Member*: NSMP. *Award*: medal, Utopian Club (Mass.-R.I.), 1958. *Work*: Veterans' Mem. Auditorium; R.I. State Capitol; Sheraton Biltmore Hotel; Poughkeepsie Inn; Bristol County Trust Co., Taunton, Mass.; Pacific Nat. Bank, Nantucket, Mass.; R.I. Hospital Trust Co., Providence; Military Installations: U.S. Navair Station, Quonset Pt., R.I.; U.S. Naval Base and Naval War College, Newport, R.I.; U.S. Navphibase, Little Creek, Norfolk, Va.; also work in civic and public bldgs., residences including murals and interior design 100 churches throughout New England. *Exhibited*: Boston, New York and Washington; one-man: Wellington, N.Z.; Melbourne, Australia. *Position*: Staff Artist, Task Force 43, Operation Deepfreeze I, 1955-56.

HAUPERS, CLEMENT (BERNARD)—
Painter, Gr., S., L., T.
377 Ramsey Hill, St. Paul 2, Minn.

B. St. Paul, Minn., Mar. 1, 1900. *Studied*: Minneapolis Sch. A.; & with L'Hote, Bourdelle, Jacovleff, in Paris. *Member*: Minnesota AA. *Awards*: prizes, Minn. State Fair, 1925; Minneapolis Inst. A., 1928. *Work*: BM; N.Y. Pub. Lib.; PMA; Minneapolis Inst., A.; San Diego Soc. FA; Dallas Mus. FA. *Exhibited*: AIC; WFNY 1939; Milwaukee AI; Minnesota State Fair; Minneapolis Inst. A.; Walker A. Center; Atlanta Mus. A.; San Antonio Mus. A.; Norton Gal., North Palm Beach, Fla. *Position*: Supt., FA Dept., Minn. State Fair, 1930-41; Instr., St. Paul Sch. A., 1931-36; State Dir., Regional Dir., Asst. to Nat. Dir., FAP, 1935-42; Instr., St. Paul Gal. & Sch. A., St. Paul, Minn.

HAUPT, ERIK GUIDE—*Portrait Painter*
1 Gramercy Park, New York 10, N.Y.; h. South Egremont, Mass.

B. Cassel, Germany, Aug. 7, 1891. *Studied*: Maryland Inst.; & in Europe. *Work*: Johns Hopkins Univ. & Hospital; Shepard-Pratt Hospital, Baltimore, Md.; Court House, Wilmington, Del.; Vassar Hospital, Poughkeepsie, N.Y.; Berkeley Col.; Washington & Lee Univ. *Exhibited*: Peabody Inst., Balt., Md.; BMA; CGA; PAFA; NAD.*

HAUSER, ALONZO—*Sculptor*
2810 Dodd Rd., St. Paul 7, Minn.

B. La Crosse, Wis., Jan. 30, 1909. *Studied*: Layton Sch. A.; Univ. Wisconsin; ASL, with William Zorach. *Member*: An Am. Group; S. Gld.; Minnesota AA; Minnesota S. Gld. *Awards*: prizes, Wis. P. & S., 1940-1942; IBM, 1941; Minnesota Regional Sculpture Award, 1946. *Work*: IBM; Wustum Mus. A., Racine, Wis.; St. Paul's Church, St. Paul, Minn.; Milwaukee AI; Walker A. Center; reliefs, USPO, Park Rapids, Minn.; Arch. S., St. Paul's Evangelical & Reformed Church; St. Francis Cabrini Church; Blessed Virgin Parish Church; Arlington Lutheran Church. *Exhibited*: WMAA; BM; WFNY 1939; S. Gld.; Minn. Regional Sculpture Exh.; one-man exh.: ACA Gal., 1938; Layton A. Gal., 1941; Walker A. Center, 1946; St. Paul Gal. A., 1946. *Position*: Instr. S., Layton Sch. A., 1940-42; Carleton Col., 1944-45; Hd. A. Dept., Macalester Col., St. Paul, Minn., 1945-1949; Instr. Architecture, Univ. Minnesota, at present.

HAVEN, MRS. HARRY. See *Gay, Ruth A.*

HAVENS, JAMES DEXTER—*Graphic Artist, P.*
66 Crossover Rd., Fairport, N.Y.

B. Rochester, N.Y., Jan. 13, 1900. *Studied*: Univ. Rochester; Rochester Inst. Tech., and with Thomas Fogarty, Troy Kinney, Charles H. Woodbury, John E. Costigan. *Member*: ANA; Rochester A. Cl.; Rochester Pr. Cl.; Am. Color Pr. Soc.; Academic A.; Albany Pr. Cl.; AWS; Wash. WC Cl.; Boston Soc. Indp. A.; Soc. Wash. Pr. M.; Boston Pr. M.; SAGA. *Awards*: prizes, Rochester Pr. Cl., 1936, 1939, 1949, 1951; Univ. Rochester, 1939; Albright A. Gal., 1945; BM, 1947; Rochester Mem. A. Gal., 1949; SAGA, 1955; Pasadena A. Mus., 1958. *Work*: BM; Lyman Allyn Mus. A.; MMA; Rochester Mem. A. Gal.; William Smith Col., Geneva, N.Y.; Arnot A. Gal.; Rochester Inst. Tech.; Arlington (Mass.) Pub. Lib.; Montclair A. Mus.; N.Y. Pub. Lib.; Univ. Maine; Pasadena A. Mus.; G.W.V. Smith Mus. A.; LC; Rochester Pr. Cl. *Exhibited*: AWS, 1938, 1941; Denver A. Mus., 1935, 1936, 1938; LC, 1949, 1951, 1953; PAFA, 1941; Los A. Mus. A., 1934-1936, 1938; Audubon A., 1945, 1947, 1948, 1953; NAD, 1942, 1944, 1952-1955; Phila. Pr. Cl., 1934-1943, 1946-1948; Rochester A. Cl., annually; Rochester Pr. Cl., annually; Rochester Mem. A. Gal.; Albright A. Gal.; SAGA, 1947, 1950-1952, 1955. Executed color woodcuts for Membership Prints for Prairie Pr. M., 1948; The Woodcut Soc., 1949; Am. Color Pr. Soc., 1950; Pr. Cl. of Rochester, 1949.

HAVENS, MURRAY P.—*Designer, T.*
Bob Jones University, Greenville, S.C.

B. Elmira, N.Y., Jan. 21, 1922. *Studied*: Bob Jones Univ., B.A.; Columbia Univ. *Member*: Gld. South Carolina A.; Intl. Inst. for Conservation of Museum Objects. *Awards*: prize, Bob Jones Univ., 1946. *Work*: Bob Jones Univ.; scenic des. for "Wine of Morning," prize winning color film shown at Cannes Festival, 1958. *Exhibited*: Faculty art, Civic Gal., Greenville, 1954; Gld. South Carolina A., 1957. Lectures: Renaissance Art; Symbolism; Religious Art. Installed Bob Jones Univ. permanent coll., 1951; Dir. renovation of Biblical Museum, 1958; Assembled the Hammer Coll., 1957; Instr., Bob Jones University, at present.

HAVLENA, JARI (Miss)—*Painter, T., L.*
4312 Oak St., Kansas City 11, Mo.

B. Grand Forks, N.D., July 17, 1923. *Studied*: Abbott Sch. FA, Wash., D.C.; De Paul Univ., Chicago; AIC, B.F.A., B.A.E., M.F.A.; Univ. Kansas City, and with Paul Wiegert, Robert von Neumann, Max Kahn. *Member*: AEA; Mid-Am. A. *Awards*: Vandergritt scholarship, AIC; prize, Kansas Des-Craftsmen, 1954. *Exhibited*: Univ. Kansas City, 1951; Mid-Am. A., 1952-1954; Better Homes Exh., Kansas City, 1951, 1952; Kansas Des-Craftsmen, 1954, 1955; Walker A. Center, 1954; Evanston, Ill., 1954; one-man: Creative A. Studio, Chicago, 1950; Broadway Gal., 1952; Mid-Am. Gal., 1952; Lawrence Gal., 1954; National Col., Kansas City, 1955. *Work*: Quigley Music Studio, Kansas City. *Position*: Pr. & Drawing Dept. Archives, AIC; Asst. Dir. Edu., William Rockhill Nelson Gal. A.; 1952-53; L., College of St. Theresa, Kansas City; Instr., Adult Edu. Program, College of St. Theresa, 1953-55; L., A. Appreciation, National Col., Kansas City, 1954-55 (part time).*

HAWKINS, ARTHUR, JR.—
Designer, Consulting A. Dir., P.
396 Allaire Ave., Leonia, N.J.

B. Cumberland, Md., Apr. 9, 1903. *Studied*: Univ. Virginia, B.S.; ASL, with Kimon Nicolaides, Kenneth Hayes Miller. *Member*: A.Dir. Cl.; SI; Nat. Soc. A.Dir.; Consulting A.Dir. Assn.; Hon. Member: A. Dir. Clubs of Rochester, N.Y., Seattle, Wash., Dallas, Tex., Ft. Worth, Tex., Richmond, Va. *Awards*: prizes, book jacket des., AIGA, advertising des., 1946; booklet des., Direct Mail Advertising Assn., 1944, 1945; poster des., 1940; prize, A.Dir.Cl., 1946, 1948. *Exhibited*: AIGA, 1932, 1937; A. Dir. Cl., 1946, 1948, 1949, 1952. *Position*: Pres., A.Dir. Cl., 1945-46; Sec-Treas., Nat. Soc. A. Dir., 1945-52 (Adv. Bd., 1946-); Adv. Council, 1952- ; Adv. Bd., CUASch., New York, N.Y., 1952-55; Pres., Consulting A.Dir. Assn., 1954- .

HAWKINS, BENJAMIN F.—*Sculptor*
35 Grandview Ave., Pleasantville, N.Y.

B. St. Louis, Mo., June 17, 1896. *Studied*: St. Louis Sch. FA; ASL. *Member*: NSS. *Awards*: prize, Arch. Lg., 1933.

Work: Univ. Michigan; U.S. Military Acad., West Point, N.Y.; USPO, Albany, N.Y., Hyannis, Mass., Penns Grove, N.J.; Brookgreen Gardens, S.C.; City Bank Farmers Trust, East River Savings Bank, N.Y.; Colorado Springs Day Nursery; Federal Bldg., St. Louis, Mo.; War Mem., Milwaukee, Wis.; Wisconsin Commemorative Half-Dollar.*

HAWKS, RACHEL MARSHALL—Sculptor

Ruxton 4, Md.

B. Port Deposit, Md., Mar. 20, 1879. *Studied*: Maryland Inst.; Rinehart Sch. S. *Work*: S., Maryland Casualty Co., Mem. Hospital, City Hall, all of Baltimore, Md.; fountain figures, Hockiday Sch., Dallas, Tex.; tablet, U.S. Naval Acad., and numerous portrait busts. *Exhibited*: Grand Central A. Gal.; Houston, Tex.; Biltmore Forest, N.C., 1938; one-man, sculptured port. heads of children, Rehoboth A. Lg., 1954. Lectures: Garden Sculpture to schools and garden clubs.*

HAWLEY, MARGARET FOOTE—Painter

137 East 66th St., New York 21, N.Y.

B. Guilford, Conn., June 12, 1880. *Studied*: Corcoran A. Sch.; & with Howard Helmick; Academie Colorossi, Paris, France. *Member*: ASMP; Pa. Soc. Min. P.; Brooklyn Soc. Min. P.; Boston Gld. A.; New Haven Paint & Clay Cl.; AFA; Concord AA; Wash. AC. *Awards*: med., PAFA, 1918, 1920; prize, Balt. WC Cl., 1926; med., Sesqui-Centennial Exp., Phila., 1926; Brooklyn Soc. Min. P., 1931; NAWA, 1931. *Work*: MMA; BM; Concord AA; CGA.

HAY, VELMA (MESSICK)—Painter

133 St. Joseph Ave., Long Beach 3, Cal.

B. Bloomington, Ill., July 14, 1912. *Studied*: Otis AI, Los Angeles; Chouinard AI, Los Angeles, and with Ben Messick, Emil Bisttram, Dong Kingman. *Member*: Long Beach AA; Cultural A. Center Assn., Long Beach. *Award*: Seton Hall Univ., 1958. *Work*: Seton Hall Univ. Coll. *Exhibited*: San Diego FA Center, 1944; Santa Monica AA, 1945; Long Beach AA, 1946, 1953-1958; Grand Central A. Gal., 1957; 2-man: Bellflower (Cal.) \, 1955; E.B. Crocker A. Gal., Sacramento, 1957; Pac' ⌐oast Cl., Long Beach, 1956; 3-man: Palos Verdes A. ⌐., 1954; Fresno A. Center, 1957.

HAYDON, HAROLD—

Painter-Educator, I., Gr., L., W., S.

5009 Greenwood Ave., Chicago 15, Ill.

B. Fort William, Canada, Apr. 22, 1909. *Studied*: Univ. Chicago, Ph.B., M.A.; AIC. *Member*: Chicago Soc. A.; AEA; AAUP. *Awards*: prize, Univ. Chicago, 1945. *Work*: Mus. Science & Indst., Chicago; Bobs Roberts Mem. Hospital, Chicago; mural, Pickering Col., Newmarket, Ontario, Canada; Temple Beth Am, Chicago. *Exhibited*: United States and Canada since 1933. Illus. many educational books, monographs, etc. Contributor to art and educational magazines, journals and bulletins. *Position*: A. in Res., Pickering Col., Canada, 1932-33; Asst. Prof. A., George Williams Col., Chicago, 1933-44; Instr., Asst. Prof. A., Univ. Chicago, Ill., 1944-48; Assoc. Prof., 1948- ; Dean of Students, 1957- ; Nat. Dir., Pres., Chicago Chptr. AEA, 1951-52, 1955, 1958.

HAYES, BARTLETT HARDING, JR.—

Museum Dir., E., L., W.

Addison Gallery of American Art, Phillips Academy; h. off Phillips St., Andover, Mass.

B. Andover, Mass., Aug. 5, 1904. *Studied*: Phillips Acad.; Harvard Univ., A.B. *Member*: F., Am. Acad. A. & Sc.; Col. Soc. Mass.; AFA; CAA; AAMus.; Assn. A. Mus. Dir.; Mus. Assn., England; Am. Soc. Arch. Hist.; Early Am. Indst. Assn.; Eastern AA; Comm. A. Edu. (MModA); New England Sculptors Assn.; Adult Edu. Assn.; AID. Author: "Naked Truth and Personal Vision"; TV series (NET): "Intent of Art"; AGAA monographs; Co-Author: "Layman's Guide to Modern Art." *Positions*: Bd. Bd., John Harvard Lib., 1958- ; Ed. Bd., Art in America, 1944- ; Adv. Comm., Handicraft Edu., Commonwealth of Mass., 1944- ; Adv. Comm., E. W. Root A. Center, Hamilton Col., 1958- ; Art Acq. Comm., Brandeis Univ., 1957- ; Art Comm., Smithsonian Inst., 1954- ; Bd. Dir., Print Council Am., 1956- ; CAA, 1957; Mem. Corp. Ogunquit A. Mus., 1957- ; Trustee: Soc. for Preservation

of New England Antiquities, 1956- ; AFA, 1940- ; Boston A. Festival, 1952- ; BMFA, 1949- ; Old Sturbridge Village, 1950- ; member various regional and national juries; Instr. A., Phillips Acad., 1933- ; Asst. Cur., 1933-40, Dir., 1940- , Phillips Acad., Andover, Mass.

HAYES, MARIAN—Educator, L.

9 Bridgman Lane, South Hadley, Mass.

B. Grand Rapids, Mich., May 23, 1905. *Studied*: Mount Holyoke Col., B.A.; Univ. Wisconsin; N.Y. Univ., M.A.; Rockford Col.; Radcliffe Col., M.A., Ph.D.; Western Michigan State T. Col., Kalamazoo. *Member*: Soc. Arch. Historians; Archaeological Inst. Am.; Am. Assn. Univ. Prof.; CAA; Mediaeval Acad. Am.; Conn. Antiquarian & Landmarks Soc.; Phi Beta Kappa. *Awards*: F., Mt. Holyoke Col., 1928-1929; Univ. F., N.Y. Univ., 1928-1929; Carnegie Grant to Radcliffe Col., 1929-1930; & study in Europe, 1930-1931. *Contributor*: Numerous reviews of exhibitions for "Springfield Sunday Union Republican," and for the "Mt. Holyoke Alumnae Quarterly." *Position*: Asst., Dept. A., 1925-28; Instr., 1932-37; Asst. Prof., 1937-45; Assoc. Prof., 1945-54, Prof., 1954- , Chm. A. Dept., 1948- , Mt. Holyoke Col., South Hadley, Mass.

HAYES, WILLIAM CHRISTOPHER—Associate Curator

Metropolitan Museum of Art; h. 216 East 49th St., New York 22, N.Y.

B. Hempstead, L.I., N.Y., Mar. 21, 1903. *Studied*: Princeton Univ., B.A., M.A., M.F.A., Ph.D. *Member*: Athenaeum, New York, N.Y.; Am. Oriental Soc. Author: "Glazed Tiles from the Palace of Rameses II at Kantir," 1937; "Ostraka and Name Stones from the Tomb of Sen-Mut, no. 71, at Thebes." 1942; & other writings on Egypt. Contributor to: Archaeological & geographic journals. Lectures: Prehistoric Egypt; "The First Pharaoh," & others. *Position*: Asst. Cur., 1937-45, Assoc. Cur., 1945- , Egyptian Dept., MMA, New York, N.Y.*

HAYTER, STANLEY WILLIAM—

Painter, Gr., T., W., L.

7 rue Joseph Bara, Paris 6, France; h. 737 Washington St., New York 14, N.Y.

B. London, England, Dec. 27, 1901. *Studied*: King's Col., Univ. London. *Member*: SAGA; AEA (V-Pres.); Salon d'Automne; London Group. *Awards*: Chevalier de la Legion d'Honneur. *Work*: NGA; MModA; BM; CAM; AIC; SFMA; VMFA; FMA; British Mus.; Victoria & Albert Mus.; Bibliotheque Nationale; Gothenburg Mus., Sweden; Tate Gal., London; Grenoble Mus.; Bibliotheque Royale, Brussels; Albertina Mus., Vienna. *Exhibited*: Carnegie Inst., 1945, 1955; WMAA, 1945; LC, 1942-1946; SAGA, 1942-1945; NAD, 1943-1946; CMA, 1946; CAM, 1944; PAFA, 1943-1946; Oslo, Norway, 1955; Salon de Mai, Paris, 1951-1955, and in other exhs., in U.S., England, France, Germany, Switzerland, Belgium, Denmark, Italy and Mexico. Contributor to Art News, Transformation, Graphis, Documents and other publications. Author: "New Ways of Gravure," 1949; "George Routledge," London, 1949. Lectures: Slade School and Royal College of Art, London. *Position*: Asst. Prof., Brooklyn Col., Brooklyn, N.Y., 1949-50; Dir., Atelier 17, Paris & London.*

HAYWARD, MILDRED (Mrs. John B.)—Painter, W.

8 East 96th St., New York 28, N.Y.; also, 400 Coconut Row, Palm Beach, Fla.

B. Chicago, Ill., Jan. 23, 1889. *Member*: Pen & Brush Cl. *Work*: MMA, and in private colls. *Award*: prize, Norton Gal. A., West Palm Beach, Fla. *Exhibited*: nationally and internationally including Milch Gal., N.Y.; Vose Gal., Boston; India Consulate, N.Y.; Korean Embassy, Wash., D.C.; Whitaker Mus., Palermo, Sicily, and under USIS sponsorship in Rome, Athens and Madrid, 1955; Carnegie Endowment Center, 1957; Audubon House, N.Y., 1958. Author: "Christ Appears"; "Light Breaking Through"; "Miracle at Sea"; "The Forgotten Message"; "While Jesus Walked on Earth."

HAZELET, SALLY POTTER—Painter

111 East 10th St., New York 3, N.Y.

B. Evanston, Ill., June 4, 1924. *Studied*: Rollins Col.; Columbia Univ., B.S.; Univ. Louisville, M.A.; Inst. Des., Chicago; Illinois Inst. Tech. *Awards*: Fulbright award, 1952. *Work*: Univ. Louisville. *Exhibited*: Fulbright Artists

Exh., Rome, 1953; Bordighera, Italy, 1953; Kentucky-Indiana Exh., 1952, 1955; Virginia Intermont Col., 1952; Stable Gal., 1956, 1957; one-man: Louisville, Ky., 1952; New York City, 1954; Tanager Gal., 1957.

HEALEY, RUTH LEYDEN—*Educator*
Russell Sage College, Troy, N.Y.

B. Lawrence, Mass. *Studied*: Mass. Sch. A., Boston, B.A.; Columbia Univ., M.A.; ASL. *Member*: CAA; AFA. *Position*: Hd. A. Dept., Russell Sage Col., Troy, N.Y., 1948- (on leave 1958-59).

HEALY, ARTHUR K(ELLY) D(AVID)—
Painter, Arch., W., L.
RD #2 Middlebury, Vt.

B. New York, N.Y., Oct. 15, 1902. *Studied*: Princeton Univ., A.B., M.F.A.; Univ. Pennsylvania; Fontainebleau Sch. FA, France, and with Eliot O'Hara. *Member*: Boston Soc. WC Painters; Boston Soc. Indp. A.; Baltimore WC Cl.; Wash. WC Cl.; AEA; AWS; Audubon A.; Phila. WC Cl.; Mid-Vermont A.; SC; Springfield AA; No. Vermont A.; Southern Vt. A.; Yaddo Fnd. *Work*: Harvard Univ.; Fleming Mus. A., Burlington, Vt.; FMA; Canajoharie A. Gal.; Kansas City AI; Sweat Mem. Mus.; New Britain Mus. A. *Awards*: prizes, AWS, 1936; Stockbridge AA, 1936-1938; Springfield AA, 1951; Boston Soc. Indp. A., 1952. *Exhibited*: 1936-52: AWS; Phila. WC Cl.; Boston Soc. Indp. A.; Audubon A.; Boston WC Cl.; WMAA; one-man: Ferargil Gal.; Vose Gal., Boston; Margaret Brown Gal.; Grace Horne Gal.; Macbeth Gal.; Galleria di Pincio, Rome, Italy; Middlebury Col. I., "Two Journey-men Painters." *Position*: Prof., Hd. A. Dept., Middlebury Col., Middlebury, Vt., 1946- .

HEALY, MARION MAXON (Mrs. Rufus Alan)—
Painter, Et., Lith.
203 Hill Top Lane, Cincinnati 15, Ohio

B. Mobile County, Ala. *Studied*: Cincinnati A. Acad.; ASL; PAFA. *Member*: Woman's A. Cl.; Cincinnati A. Mus. Assn. *Exhibited*: SSAL; Loring-Andrews Gal., Cincinnati (one-man shows annually); Butler Inst. Am. A., 1957; Hoosier Salon, 1958; Dayton AI, 1958; CM, 1958; Interior Valley Comp., 1958; 3-man: Argent Gal., N.Y., 1959. Lectures on Etching.

HEATH, HOWARD—*Painter, Gr., Des., I., T.*
3 Heathwood Lane, Westport, Conn.

B. Boulder, Colo., Oct. 2, 1879. *Studied*: AIC; ASL; & with Frank DuMond. *Member*: Silvermine Gld. A.; Westport A. Group. *Work*: murals, Town Hall, Hurlburt Sch., Wesport, Conn.; Children's Hospital, Phila., Pa., and in private colls. *Exhibited*: Macbeth Gal.; Hartford Atheneum; Lib.Cong., 1944; N.Y. WC Soc. I., books, newspapers, & national magazines.

HEATH, PEARL B.—*Educator*
Oregon College of Education, Monmouth, Ore.
Position: Chm., Art Dept., Oregon College of Education.*

HEATON, MAURICE—*Craftsman*
Old Mill Rd., Valley Cottage, N.Y.

B. Neuchatel, Switzerland, Apr. 2, 1900. *Studied*: N.Y. Ethical Culture Sch.; Stevens Inst. Tech. *Member*: Artist-Craftsmen of N.Y.; York State Craftsmen; Rockland Fnd.; Boston Soc. A. & Crafts. *Award*: medal, Boston Soc. A. & Crafts, 1956. *Work*: MMA; Newark Mus. A.; Corning Glass Mus.; Cooper Union Mus. A.; murals, Rockefeller Center; Polygraphic Co. of America. *Exhibited*: Syracuse Mus. FA, 1948, 1951, 1956, 1958; MMA, 1950-1952; Wichita AA, 1950, 1951, 1953, 1954, 1956-1958; Royal Ontario Mus., 1952; State Dept. Traveling exh., 1952; Smithsonian Inst., traveling exh., 1955; MMoAA traveling exh., 1952; Guggenheim Mus. A., 1952; Phila. A. All., 1951; N.Y.Soc. Ceramic A., 1949-1954; Ceramic Lg., Miami, 1954; York State Craftsmen, 1954; Hampton Gal., 1954; Assoc. Am. A., 1953, 1954; Mayo Hill Gal., 1954; NGA, 1956; Brussels World's Fair, 1958. Lectures: Crafts; Glass, to art and craft organizations.

HEATON, WILLIAM—*Painter, S.*
General Delivery, Taos, N.M.

B. Dallas, Tex., July 16, 1918. *Studied*: Dallas AI; DMFA. *Member*: Taos AA. *Awards*: prizes, DMFA, 1954; Mus. New Mexico, Santa Fé, 1955. *Work*: wall sc., Dallas Athletic Cl. and Country Cl.; metal mosaic painting, Republic Bank Bldg.; Longview Country Cl.; State Fair of Texas, and in many private colls. *Exhibited*: Mus. FA of Houston, 1954; DMFA, 1954; Neiman-Marcus mosaic exh., 1954; Mus. New Mexico, Santa Fé, 1955; one-man: Swedish Moderns, Dallas, 1952; Texas State Col. for Women, Denton, Tex., 1953; Cooks Modern Exh., Dallas, 1953. Developed new techniques in metal repousse and process of metal mosaic and lead drawing.*

HEBALD, MILTON ELTING—*Sculptor, C., T.*
2 West 67th St., New York, N.Y.

B. New York, N.Y., May 24, 1917. *Studied*: ASL; NAD; BAID. *Member*: S. Gld.; An Am. Group. *Awards*: prizes, Am. A. Cong., 1937; Shilling award, 1947; Brooklyn Soc. A., 1948; PAFA, 1949; Audubon A., 1949; Bronx, N.Y., Tuberculosis Hospital Comp. for Sculpture, 1952; Prix de Rome, 1955-58. *Work*: WMAA; PMA; Tel-Aviv Mus.; murals, USPO, Tom's River, N.J.; des., Thunderbolt Trophy, 1st Fighter Air Force; port. comm., Am. Acad. A. & Lets., 1957; Albert Gallatin Soc. medal; sc., Airport, Puerto Rico; bronze frieze, Pan-American Terminal, Idlewild Airport, N.Y., 1959. *Exhibited*: WMAA, 1937-1945; S. Gld., 1937-1944; WFNY 1939; PMA; one-man: Schneider Gal., Rome, Italy, 1957. *Position*: Hd. S. Dept., Skowhegan Sch. A., Skowhegan, Me., 1951-53.

HEBB, MATHILDE M. MYLANDER—*Sculptor*
Butler, Md.

B. Baltimore, Md., Nov. 16, 1911. *Studied*: Goucher Col., A.B.; Maryland Inst.; Rinehart Sch. S. *Awards*: Med., Maryland Inst., 1934; Rinehart Sch. S., 1935; traveling scholarship, Rinehart Sch. FA, 1936; med., BMA, 1936. *Work*: S., figures, fountains, Balt., Md., parks. *Exhibited*: WFNY 1939; BMA, 1935-1938, 1940; Hood Col.; Goucher Col.*

HEBERT, MARIAN—*Painter, Et., C., Des., E.*
414 East Sola St., Santa Barbara, Cal.

B. Spencer, Iowa, June 5, 1899. *Studied*: Univ. Montana, B.A.; Univ. California, B.A.; Univ. Boston, M.A.; Santa Barbara Sch. A., and with Belmore Brown, Edward Borein, Frank Fletcher, Maurice Lasansky, Eliot O'Hara. *Member*: SAGA; CAA; Santa Barbara AA; Chicago Soc. Et.; Cal. Soc. Et.; Cal. Pr. M.; Lg. Contemp. A., Temple, Tex.; Texas FA Assn. *Awards*: prizes, SAGA, 1938; LC, 1948. *Work*: LC; Santa Barbara City Sch.; SAGA; Chicago Soc. Et.; Univ. Nebraska; Santa Barbara Pub. Lib.; Veteran's Mem. Bldg., Carpinteria, Cal.; BMFA; Mary Hardin-Baylor Col.; Univ. Boston; Beaux-Arts Cl., Clarendon, Tex. *Exhibited*: NAD, 1934-1941; SAGA, 1932-1957; Chicago Soc. Et., 1939-1957; Cal. Pr. M., 1943-1952; Phila. Pr. Cl., 1936-1942; Southern Pr. M., 1939-1942; Paris Salon, 1937; Santa Barbara Mus. A. (one-man); Aberdeen, Wash. (one-man); Greenville (S.C.) A. Center, 1950 (one-man); GGE, 1939; WFNY 1939; London, England, SAGA exh., 1954; Phila. Sketch Cl., 1955; Mary Hardin-Baylor Col., 1957 (one-man). *Position*: Prof. A., Hd. A. Dept., Mary Hardin-Baylor Col., Belton, Tex., 1945-1957.

HECHENBLEIKNER, LOUIS—*Teacher, Gr.*
1181 Madison Ave., New York 28, N.Y.

B. Innsbruck, Austria, Oct. 29, 1893. *Studied*: Royal Acad., Düsseldorf; Munich A. Acad., Germany. *Awards*: prizes, Phila. Pr. Cl., 1943, 1948; LC, 1945, 1948. *Work*: MMA; PMA; LC; CM; Rochester Mem. A. Gal. *Exhibited*: WMAA, 1939; MMA, 1942; Phila. Pr. Cl., 1940-1958; BM, 1953; Carnegie Inst., 1949, 1950; BMFA, 1954; CM, 1953; NAD, 1944, 1945; SAGA Intl. Exh., 1950, 1953, 1958. *Position*: Assoc. Prof., A. Dept., Queens Col., New York, N.Y., 1939- .

HECHT, ZOLTAN—*Painter, E.*
473 West End Ave., New York, N.Y.

B. Hungary, June 24, 1890. *Studied*: Cleveland Sch. A. *Awards*: prize, Audubon A., 1957. *Work*: Syracuse Mus. FA; Newark Airport; Brooklyn Pub. Lib.; Brooklyn Col.; United Hospital Fund (5 paintings), and in many private colls. *Exhibited*: Babcock Gal.; BM; WMAA; CM; Toledo Mus. A.; PAFA; Walker A. Center; BMA; Butler Inst. Am. A., 1957; Nat. Soc. Painters in Casein, 1956-1958; New School Assoc., 1957; Art:USA, 1958; Provincetown A. Festival, 1958; Springfield, Mass., 1958; Artists Gal., N.Y., and other national galleries; one-man: Aquavella Gal., 1943; New-Age Gal., 1950, 1952, 1953; Roosevelt House, 1954; AEA, 1955; Audubon A., 1956, 1957, 1958; Collectors Gal., 1957. *Position*: Instr., People's A. Center, MModA, 1948- .

HEDDINS, TINCIE H(UGHS) (Mrs. Earl)—
Painter, Lith., T.
1409 South Monroe St., San Angelo, Tex.

B. San Angelo, Tex., Dec. 4, 1909. *Studied*: Univ. Texas, B.F.A.; New Mexico Highlands Univ., M.F.A., and with Xavier Gonzales. *Member*: San Angelo A. Cl.; Texas FA Assn.; West Texas AA; AAUW. *Awards*: prizes, Texas General, San Angelo, 1952, 1953; West Texas AA, 1956. *Work*: mural, Church of Christ, San Angelo. *Exhibited*: Texas FA Assn.; West Texas AA; one-man: Elisabet Ney Mus. and Laguna Gloria Mus., Austin, 1954; Helen King Kendall A. Gal., 1956; Hardin-Simmons Col. A. Dept., 1956; Texas A. & M., A. Dept., 1957; Men of Arts Gld., 1957; Bright Shawl Gal., San Antonio, 1957. *Position*: Instr. Painting, San Angelo Col., San Angelo, Tex.

HEERMANN, NORBERT LEO—Painter, W., L., Cr.
Woodstock, N.Y.

B. Frankfurt-on-Main, Germany. *Studied*: in Europe; & with Chase, Duveneck. *Member*: Woodstock AA; Audubon A. *Work*: CM; Wellesley A. Mus.; CMA; Northeastern Univ. Lib.; Frankfort, Ky., State House. *Exhibited*: PAFA; WMAA, 1945; AIC; CGA; WMA; CM (one-man); Phila. A., All.; Boston AC; Wellesley Mus. Author: "Frank Duveneck"; catalog for Duveneck Exh., WMAA, 1938; critical reviews for art magazines & newspapers. Lectures: Portrait Painting, etc.

HEIDEL, FREDERICK (H.)—Painter, E.
Portland State College (1); h. 932 Northwest Summit Ave., Portland 10, Ore.

B. Corvallis, Ore., Dec. 29, 1915. *Studied*: Univ. Oregon, B.S., with Andrew Vincent, David McCosh; AIC, B.F.A., with Boris Anisfeld. *Member*: Portland AA; Oregon A. All. *Awards*: Anna Louise Raymond Foreign Traveling Fellowship, AIC, 1942; prizes, Cal. WC Soc., 1947; SFMA, 1948; Oakland A. Mus., 1950; Portland A. Mus., 1952, 1954; Oregon State Fair, 1957. *Work*: Portland A. Mus. *Exhibited*: Intl. Print Show, 1947; MMA, 1951; DMFA, 1954; United Nations, San Francisco, 1955; Sao Paulo Biennial, 1956; Denver A. Mus., 1958; Oakland A. Mus., 1950-1955; Oregon Annuals, Portland A. Mus., 1950-1958; Cal. WC Soc., 1946-1949; SFMA, 1947, 1948, 1952; SAM, 1951, 1955-1957. *Positions*: Instr. A., Biarritz Am. Univ. (Army), 1945; Long Beach City Col., 1946-1949; Univ. Oregon, 1949-1953; Assoc. Prof. A., Hd. A. Dept., Portland State College, Portland, Ore., 1953- .

HEIL, DR. WALTER—Museum Director
M. H. de Young Museum, Golden Gate Park; h. 2674 Broadway, San Francisco, Cal.

B. Oppenheim, Germany, Nov. 10, 1890. *Studied*: Univ. Munich, Ph.D.; Sorbonne, Paris, France; Univ. Frankfurt, Germany. *Member*: Bohemian Cl. *Awards*: Chevalier Legion of Honor, 1937; Italian Star of Solidarity, 1952; Ritter Deutsches Verdienstkreuz, 1957. Contributor of numerous articles to European and American art magazines. Arranged many special exhibitions in M.H. de Young Mus. & Cal. PLH, particularly in the field of old and modern painting. Dir., European Art Div., GGE, 1939. *Position*: Asst. Cur., Bavarian State Galleries, Munich, 1922-24; F., Inst. A. Hist., Florence, 1924-26; Cur., European A., Detroit Inst. A., 1924-26; Dir., Cal. PLH, San Francisco, 1933-40; Dir., M. H. de Young Mus., San Francisco, Cal. 1933- ; Regional Dir., PWA, 1933-34; Chm., San F., Com., Sec. Painting & Sculpture, Pub. Works Br., U.S. Treasury Dept.; Regional Dir., Treasury Relief A. Project; Memb., F. & App. A. Com. on WPA, Federal Govt.

HEILBRUNN, MRS. L. V. See Donovan, Ellen

HEILEMANN, CHARLES OTTO—
Commercial Artist, I., Des., P., T.
400 East 59th St., New York 22, N.Y.

B. Brooklyn, N.Y., May 16, 1918. *Studied*: Parsons Sch. Des., N.Y., Paris, Italy; Croydon Sch. A., England. *Member*: SI. *Exhibited*: Yale Univ., 1955. Contributor illus. to: Vogue, House & Gardens, McCalls, Woman's Home Companion, Good Housekeeping and other national magazines. *Position*: Indst. Des., Joseph B. Platt Assoc., New York, N.Y., 1938-41; freelance at present.*

HEILOMS, MAY—Painter, T., L.
1915 Morris Ave., New York 53, N.Y.

B. Russia. *Studied*: ASL. *Member*: NAWA; AEA; New Jersey P. & S.; ASL; Knickerbocker A.; Audubon A.; Nat. Soc. Painters in Casein; N.Y. Soc. Women A.; Brooklyn Soc. A.; Silvermine Gld. A.; Young Am. A.; Alabama WC Soc.; Manhattan Gal. Group; Creative A. Assoc. *Awards*: prizes, med., New Jersey P. & S., 1952-1955, 1956; AEA, 1952; Jersey City Mus. Assn., 1950, 1951, 1958; Brooklyn Soc. A., 1958; NAWA, 1954, 1958. *Work*: PMA; Samuel S. Fleisher Mem. A. Fnd.; Collectors of Am. A., and in many private colls. *Exhibited*: PAFA, 1953, 1954; Jersey City Mus., 1950-1952, 1956-1958; BM, 1954; Birmingham Mus. A., 1955, 1956, 1957; Tyringham Gal. (Mass.), 1954, 1955; Silvermine Gld. A., 1954, 1955, 1956-1958; Audubon A., 1952-1958; Kaufman Gal., 1952, 1955; Long Island A., 1949, 1950; Assoc. Gal. A., Detroit, 1955; Argent Gal., 1952, 1953; John Myers Fnd., 1953; Riverside Mus., 1953-1958; traveling exhs. to CGA; traveling exh., Portugal, Italy, Greece, Belgium; Albright Gal. A.; CMA; DMFA; Rochester Mem. A. Gal.; Phila. A. All.; Butler Inst. Am. A.; Denver A. Mus., and in other museums and universities. *Positions*: Pres., Jersey P. & S.; Treas., Manhattan Gal. Group; Dir., Nat. Soc. Painters in Casein.

HEIM, NARA—Painter, S.
165 Boulevard, Pelham, N.Y.

B. Caracas, Venezuela, Oct. 27, 1921. *Studied*: NAD; ASL; Sculpture Center, N.Y. *Member*: Sc. Center; Westchester A. & Crafts Gld.; New Rochelle AA; Mount Vernon AA. *Awards*: prizes, New Rochelle AA, 1952; Manor Cl., 1952; Westchester A. & Crafts Gld., 1955; Mount Vernon AA, 1955. *Work*: Everhart Mus. A., Scranton, Pa.; Lyman Allyn Mus.; Howard Univ.; Farnsworth Mus. A., Wellesley, Mass.; Georgia Mus. A., Athens; Hickory Mus. A., N.C.; Mills Col., Oakland, Cal. *Exhibited*: Sculpture Center, 1955; Carlebach Gal., 1950; New Rochelle AA, 1952, 1954; Manor Cl., 1952, 1953, 1954; Westchester A. & Crafts, 1954, 1955; Mount Vernon AA, 1955.

HEINE, MARC K.—Painter, I., Des., T., Comm. A.
325 Riverside Drive, New York 25, N.Y.

B. Leipzig, Germany, May 11, 1919. *Studied*: Ecole des Arts Decoratif; Univ. Paris; Indiana Univ.; ASL. *Member*: Brooklyn Soc. A.; AEA; ASL; Lg. Present-Day A. *Exhibited*: Audubon A., 1952; Lg. Present-Day A., 1951; Contemp. A.; RoKo Gal.; Kaufmann Gal., 1953; Brooklyn Soc. A., 1955. *Awards*: prizes, Kaufmann A. Gal., 1953; Brooklyn Soc. A., 1955. Illus., "The Mastery of Reading," 1951; Illus. for N.Y. Times; Sat. Review; Reporter. *Position*: Instr., Adult Edu., Bd. of Edu., New York, N.Y.

HEINO, OTTO—Craftsman, E.
Briar Hill Rd., Hopkinson, N.H.

B. East Hampton, Conn., Apr. 20, 1915. *Studied*: New Hampshire Lg. A. & Crafts; Chouinard AI. *Member*: N.Y. Soc. Ceramic A.; Phila. A. All.; N.H. Lg. A. & Crafts; So. Cal. Des. Section, Am. Ceramic Soc. *Work*: Altar vases, Lutheran Church, Bristol, Conn.; pottery for 20th Century-Fox (751 pieces), 1954. *Exhibited*: Currier Gal. A., 1950; Syracuse Mus. FA, 1950, 1954; St. Paul Gal. A., 1953, 1955; Wichita Dec. A. Exh., 1953-1955; N.Y.Soc. Ceramic A., 1950-1952; Cannes Intl. Ceramic, 1955; Scripps Col., 1953-1955; WMA, 1955; Pacific Coast Ceramic Exh., 1952-1955; one-man: Currier Gal. A., 1951; Phila. A. All., 1955; Sharon A. Center, Peterborough, N.H., 1953. *Position*: Instr., Pottery, Univ. Col., Univ. So. California, Los Angeles, Cal., 1953-55.*

HEINO, VIVIKA (Vivien Place)—Craftsman, Des., E.
Briar Hill Rd., Hopkinton, N.H.

B. Caledonia, N.Y., June 27, 1910. *Studied*: Colorado Col. Edu., A.B.; Cal. Sch. FA, with Marian Hartwell, Manuel Jalonovich; N.Y.State Col. Ceramics, Alfred, N.Y., M.A.; Univ. So. California. *Member*: Phila. A. All.; N.Y.Soc. Ceramic A.; New Hampshire Lg. A. & Crafts; Des. Div. Am. Ceramic Soc. *Awards*: Syracuse Mus. FA; Pacific Coast Ceramic Exh., 1944 (purchase); N.Y. Soc. Ceramic A., 1945. *Work*: Altar vases, Lutheran Church, Bristol, Conn.; pottery, 20th Century-Fox (751 pieces). *Exhibited*: Syracuse Mus. FA, 1941, 1946, 1947, 1949, 1950, 1954; St. Paul Gal. A., 1953, 1955; Wichita Dec. A., 1946, 1947, 1953-1955; N.Y.Soc. Ceramic A., 1945-1948, 1950, 1952; WMA, 1955; Cannes Intl. Exh., 1955; Scripps Col., 1953-1955 Pacific Coast Ceramic, 1942, 1944, 1952-1955; New Hampshire Crafts, 1950; one-man: Currier Gal. A., 1951; Phila. A. All., 1955. Lectures: Decorative Treatment—Pottery. *Position*: Instr. Pottery, New Hampshire Lg. A. & Crafts, 1947-1952; Univ. So. California, Los Angeles, 1952-1955.*

HEINTZELMAN, ARTHUR WILLIAM—
Etcher, Mus. Cur., W., L.
Boston Public Library, Boston 17, Mass.; h. 29 Front St., Marblehead, Mass.

B. Newark, N.J., Nov. 22, 1890. *Studied*: R.I.Sch.Des.; & abroad. *Member*: NA; Am. Assn. Mus. Dir.; Royal Soc. A., London; Societe Nationale des Beaux-Arts, Societe de la Gravure Originale en Noir, Paris; Am. Nat. Com. of Engraving; SAE; Chicago SE; Cal. Pr.M.; Marblehead AA (Hon. Pres.); Officer, Legion of Honor; F. (Life) MMA; F., Am. Acad. A. & Sc. *Awards*: prize, med., Chicago SE, 1915, 1920, 1925; Cal. Pr. M., 1934; SAE, 1920, 1924; Cal. SE, 1921; Phila. SE, 1924; Phila. Pr. Cl., 1925; Intl. Exh., Paris, 1938; Soc. for Sanity in Art, 1939; AAPL, 1939, 1945; Southern Pr.M., 1940; Northwest Pr.M., 1941; New England Women's Cl., 1940, 1945; Lib. Cong., 1945; Wichita AA, 1946; Montclair A. Mus., 1939. *Work*: MMA; BMFA; Boston Pub. Lib.; British Mus., London; Victoria & Albert Mus.; Musee du Luxembourg; Nat. Coll., Jerusalem; Bibliotheque Nationale, AIC; N.Y. Pub.Lib.; Lib. Cong.; CGA; Honolulu Acad. A.; Toledo Mus. A.; Milwaukee AI; Los A. Mus. A.; Detroit Inst. A.; R.I.Sch. Des., etc. *Exhibited*: NAD, annually since 1933; Paris, Milan, Rome, Geneva, Lausanne, London, 1925-1935; nationally since 1917. Author: monthly Lib. publication "More Books," Boston Pub. Lib.; exh. catalogs, art periodicals, special articles on graphic artists. Author: "Watercolor Drawings of Thomas Rowlandson"; "One Hundred Unpublished Drawings by Toulouse-Lautrec." Lectures: Graphic Arts. Arranges special exh. for Boston Pub. Lib. *Position*: Keeper of Prints, Boston Pub. Lib., Boston, Mass.; Pres., Nat. Alum. Assn., R.I.Sch.Des.; member A. Comm., State of Massachusetts; Bd. Trustees, R.I.Sch.Des., 1946-52; Pennell Com., Lib. Congress, 1955- ; Pres., Children's A. Center, Boston; Council Fed. South End Settlements, Boston; Dir., Print Council of Am.; Print Com., BMFA; Trustee, R.I.Sch.Des.

HEITLAND, W. EMERTON—Painter, I., T., L.
1414 Spruce St., Philadelphia 2, Pa.

B. Superior, Wis., July 5, 1893. *Studied*: PAFA; ASL, and in Paris. *Member*: AWS; NA; Phila. A. All.; AEA; Phila. WC Cl.; Audubon A.; SI; A. Gld. *Awards*: prizes, PAFA, 1913; Cresson traveling scholarship, 1913; AIC, 1923, 1924; Phila. WC Cl., 1924, 1925, med., 1954; Balt. WC Cl., 1925; Audubon A., 1951; AWS, 1930, 1936, 1954, med., 1955; med., A.Dir. Cl., 1921; Phila. WC Cl., 1922; Phila. A. Week, 1925; medal, All. A. Am., 1956; NAC, 1958. *Work*: BM; AIC; PMA; Lowe Gal. A.; NAD; Columbus Gal. FA; Amherst Col.; Wash. County Mus. A., Hagerstown, Md.; Brooks Mem. A. Gal.; Des Moines A. Center; AGAA; Manchester (Vt.) A. Center; Vanderpoel Coll., Chicago; Davenport Mun. A. Gal. *Exhibited*: Rehn Gal.; Arden Gal.; Macbeth Gal.; Marie Sterner Gal.; Hudson Walker Gal.; O'Brien Gal., Chicago; Findlay Gal., Chicago; Miami Beach A. Center; O'Brien Gal., Arizona; Woodmere A. Gal., Phila., Pa.; Grand Central A. Gal. Contributor to national magazines. I., "Ambling Through Acadia." *Position*: Instr. A., ASL, PAFA, PMSchIA.; Dir., Eagle's Mere A. Center.

HELANDER, LILLIAN VALBORG MARIEA—Designer
International Silver Co., 500 South Broad St.; h. 53 Washington St., Meriden, Conn.

B. Providence, R.I., Feb. 27, 1899. *Studied*: R.I.Sch. Des., and in Europe. *Member*: IDI; Meriden A. & Crafts Assn.; R.I.Sch. Des. Alum. Assn. *Award*: New England Mfg. Jewelers & Silversmiths Assn., 1924. *Positions*: Des., Jewelry, Irons & Russell Co., Providence, 1926-28; Silverware Des., Gorham & Co., 1925-26; Wm. Rogers, Ltd., 1928-30; Oneida Community Silver Co., 1930-31; Chief Des., International Silver Co., Meriden, Conn., 1932- .

HELBECK, MRS. DEWEES COCHRAN. See Cochran, Dewees

HELCK, C. PETER—Illustrator, P., Gr., T.
10 East 53rd St., New York 22, N.Y.; h. Boston Corners, N.Y.

B. New York, N.Y., June 17, 1893. *Studied*: with George Bridgman, Sidney Dickinson, Frank Brangwyn, Harry Wickey, Lewis Daniel. *Member*: NA (Council Member); AWS; Phila. WC Cl.; All. A. Am.; Audubon A.; Columbia County A. Gld.; SI; A. Dir. Cl. *Awards*: Pennell medal, PAFA, 1936; All. A. Am. medal, 1938; Rochester Medal for Lithography, 1941; Phila. Pr. Cl., 1938, 1939; A. Dir. Cl., Detroit, 1950, 1951; A. Dir. Cl., New York, 1931, 1936, 1941, 1944, 1951; awards in Illustration and Advertising: Harvard award, 1929; Phila. Adv. Art Annual, 1939, 1940; Chicago A. Dir. Cl. medal, 1947; Detroit A. Dir. awards, 1950, 1952, 1953 and medals, 1946, 1954; Cleveland A. Dir., 1951. Illus. & Adv. a. for: Saturday Evening Post; True; Esquire; The Lamp; General Electric; General Motors; National Steel and other industrials. Author & Illus. of historic motoring articles published in Speed Age, Sports Car Illustrated, Antique Automobile, Bulb Horn, 1942-1958. *Positions*: Fndg. Faculty member and teacher, Famous Artists Schools, Westport, Conn.; Art Editor, of both Antique Automobile and Bulb Horn.

HELD, ALMA M.—Painter, T.
623 West 8th St., Waterloo, Iowa

B. Le Mars, Iowa. *Studied*: State Univ, Iowa, B.A., M.A.; NAD, and with Hawthorne, Cumming, Dickinson. *Member*: Waterloo AA; Cedar Falls AA. *Awards*: prizes, Iowa State Fair, 1925, 1926, 1928, 1929; Cedar Falls, Iowa, 1943, 1945, 1948, 1951. *Work*: Ft. Dodge Pub. Sch. *Exhibited*: Joslyn Mus. A., 1932, 1934, 1946; Kansas City AI, 1935; Sioux City A. Center, 1951, 1954; Little Gal., Cedar Rapids; Blanden Mem., Ft. Dodge; Mem. Union, Iowa City; Davenport Mun. A. Gal.; Des Moines Pub. Lib.; Clark Col., Dubuque; Drake Univ., Des Moines; Younkers, Des Moines, 1955; Northeast Iowa Exh., Cedar Falls, 1955; Allen Mem. Hospital Gal., Waterloo, 1956 (one-man); Waterloo AA (3-man), 1956; Cedar Falls AA, 1957; Black Hawk County Exh., Waterloo, 1958.

HELDER, Z. VANESSA (Mrs. Zama Vanessa Helder Paterson)—Painter, C.
3827 Ronda Vista Pl., Los Angeles 27, Cal.

B. Lynden, Wash., May 30, 1904. *Studied*: Univ. Washington; ASL, with Robert Brackman, George Picken, Frank DuMond. *Member*: AWS; NAWA; Pen & Brush Cl.; Glendale AA; Balt. WC Soc.; Cal. WC Soc. *Awards*: prizes, Pacific Coast P.&S., 1936, 1939; Women Painters of Wash., 1937; SAM, 1936, 1939; NAWA, 1942; Women Painters of the West, 1946; Pen & Brush Cl., 1947; Greek Theatre, Los A., 1948; Nat. Orange Show, 1949; Ramona H.S., 1953; Glendale AA, 1955; Cal. State Fair, 1949. *Work*: SAM; Newark Mus.; High Mus. A.; IBM; Am. Acad. A. & Let.; Eastern Washington State Col.; Lynden (Wash.) Pub. Lib.; Spokane A. & Hist. Mus.; Coulee Dam Bldg.; Glendale AA. *Exhibited*: NAWA, 1936-1951; AWS, 1936-1958; Cleveland Pr. Cl.; Hartford Atheneum; Phila. WC Soc.; PAFA; Cal. WC Soc., 1939-1958; Denver A. Mus., 1938, 1940; Oakland A. Gal., 1938, 1940, 1941, 1943; MModA, 1943; BM, 1941; MMA, 1942, 1954; WMAA, 1945; Macbeth Gal.; SAM, 1936-1938, 1940, 1941; San Diego FA Soc., 1941; SFMA, 1936, 1937; Portland (Ore.) A. Mus., 1936; Pacific Coast P.&S., 1936, 1939; Women Painters of Wash., 1936-1938; Women Painters of the West, 1945, 1946; Long Beach, Cal., 1947, 1952; Los A. Mus. A., 1945-1948; Birmingham, Ala., 1947; Cal. State Fair, 1953; Newport Beach, 1954; Pasadena, Cal., 1949, 1953, and many others. One-man: SAM, 1939; Spokane A. Center, 1940; Macbeth Gal., N.Y., 1944; Los A. Mus. A., 1945; Spokane Mus. A., 1946, 1957; Long Beach A. Gld., 1951; Glendale Pub. Lib., 1953; Swains Gal., Glendale, 1954, 1955; Beverly Hills, 1958; Kramer Gal., Los A., 1958, and others. *Position*: Instr., Los A. County AI, 1952-55; Dir. A. Research Studies, 1957- .

HELENE, SISTER—*Craftsman, S., P., Gr., W.*

Studio Angelico; h. Siena Heights College, Adrian, Mich.

B. Alameda, Cal. *Studied*: Siena Heights Col., A.B.; Claremont Grad. A. Seminar; Cranbrook Acad. A., M.F.A., and abroad. *Member*: Mich. Acad. Sc., A. & Let. *Work*: bronze doors, figures, stained glass and murals for churches. *Exhibited*: Inst. Mod. A., Boston, 1944; Detroit Inst. A., 1939, 1942, 1945; Catholic AA, 1938-1942; Cranbrook Mus.; Des Moines A. Center; Springfield Mus. A.; Saginaw Mus. A.; Sioux City A. Center. Contributor to Catholic Art Quarterly; Stained Glass Quarterly; American Apostolate, research film strip for metal designers; edu. film strips. *Position*: Dir., Studio Angelico, Adrian, Mich., 1935- ; Comm. of the Arts, Assn. Am. Col., 1945-52, Faculty Visitor, 1952- .*

HELFOND, RIVA (*Mrs. Riva Helfond Barrett*)—
Lithographer, Ser., P.

218 East Front St., Plainfield, N.J.; h. Bayside Dr., Atlantic Highlands, N.J.

B. New York, N.Y., Mar. 8, 1910. *Studied*: ASL. *Member*: Nat. Ser. Soc.; A. Lg. Am.; AEA; Am. Color Pr. Soc.; Nat. Assn. Women P. & S.; Assoc. A. of New Jersey; Audubon A. *Awards*: prizes, MMoDA, 1942; Montclair A. Mus., 1944, 1955; LC, 1950, 1954, 1955; BM, 1948; CM, 1950, 1952; SAGA, 1954. *Work*: MMA; MMoDA; Los A. Mus. A.; Cornell Univ.; Princeton Univ. *Exhibited*: NAD 1945, 1946; PAFA, 1944; SFMA, 1944; Carnegie Inst., 1942; LC, 1943-1946; CM, 1950, 1952; Newark Mus., 1952. Lectures: Lithography; Serigraphy.*

HELIKER, JOHN EDWARD—*Painter, T.*

20 Cornelia St., New York 14, N.Y.; h. 42 Ravine Ave., Yonkers, N.Y.

B. Yonkers, N.Y., Jan. 17, 1909. *Studied*: ASL; & with Kimon Nicolaides, Kenneth Hayes Miller, Boardman Robinson. *Awards*: prizes, CGA, 1941; Pepsi-Cola, 1946; F., Am. Acad. in Rome, 1948; Guggenheim F., 1951; Nat. Inst. A. & Lets., 1957. *Work*: CGA; WMAA; New Britain Mus.; Telfair Acad.; Walker A. Center; Univ. Nebraska; FMA; AGAA; SFMA; MMA; PMA. *Exhibited*: CGA, 1941, 1943, 1945; WMAA, 1941-1946, 1955, 1956, 1957; Carnegie Inst., 1943-1945; Toledo Mus. A., 1942, 1943, 1945; VMFA, 1942; AIC, 1942, 1943, 1945; MMA, 1942; WMA, 1945; PAFA, 1944, 1946; CAM, 1946; Pepsi-Cola, 1946; Maynard Walker Gal., 1938, 1941 (one-man); Kraushaar Gal., 1945, 1951, 1954 (one-man); Brussels World's Fair, 1958. *Position*: Instr., Columbia Univ., 1948- .

HELLER, MAXWELL L.—*Teacher, P., W., L.*

940 Grand Concourse, New York 51, N.Y.

B. New York, N.Y., Mar. 17, 1881. *Studied*: Col. City of N.Y., B.A.; N.Y. Univ., M.A., LL.B.; Parson's Sch. Des., with Howard Giles, Aldro Hibbard, Sigurd Skou, Albert Thayer, Abraham Shulman. *Member*: Rockport AA; Am. Veteran's A. Soc.; A.T. Assn. *Work*: Seward Park H.S., N.Y.; YM & YWHA, Bronx, N.Y.; Temple Rodolph Sholem, N.Y. *Exhibited*: NAD, 1938; AFA, 1932, 1938; All. A. Am., 1940-1944; Rockport AA, 1927-1957; Am. Veteran's Soc. A., 1943-1958; Soc. Indp. A.; Bronx A. Gld.; Springfield A. Lg.; and in New York art galleries. *Author*: "New Standard Letterer"; "How to Letter," and other books. Contributor to national trade publications. Lecturer with museum visits and field work on A. Appreciation and Gr. A., 1950-58. *Position*: Hd. FA Dept., Seward H.S., New York, N.Y., 1935-46; William Howard Taft H.S., 1946-51.

HELM, JOHN F., JR.—*Educator, Gr., P.*

Department of Architecture, Kansas State College; h. 1841 Fairchild St., Manhattan, Kansas

B. Syracuse, N.Y., Sept. 16, 1900. *Studied*: Syracuse Univ., B.D.; and with Charman, Sandzen. *Member*: Prairie WC Painters; Midwestern Col. A. Conference; Prairie Pr. M.; CAA. *Awards*: prizes, Kansas City AI, 1937; D.F.A., Bethany Col., 1951; Kansas State Fed. A., 1953; Faculty Lectureship, Kansas State Col., 1955. *Work*: Kansas State Col.; Bethany Col.; McPherson (Kan.) Sch.; Cal. State Lib.; Tulsa AA; Salina (Kan.) AA; Hutchinson Pub. Sch.; Kansas State Fed. Women's Cl.; Derby Mus., Derby, England. Lectures: Graphic Arts; The Changing Symbol in Painting. *Position*: Prof., Drawing & Painting,

Dept. Arch., Kansas State Col., Manhattan, Kans., 1924- ; Dir., Kansas State Fed. A., 1935-53; A. Ed., Kansas Magazine, 1933- ; Dir., Friends of Art, Kansas State Col., 1954; Chm., Festival A., 1949-51, 1953, 1955, 1957, 1958; Regional Exh., 1950-52, 1954, 1956, 1958; Sec., Delta Phi Delta, 1956- ; Chm., Rural A. Program, 1952- .

HELM, MacKINLEY—*Writer*

1201 Las Alturas Rd., Santa Barbara, Cal.

B. Duluth, Minn., July 4, 1896. *Studied*: Univ. Idaho, B.A., D.Litt.; Cambridge Univ.; Princeton Univ.; Harvard Univ., Th. D. *Author*: "Modern Mexican Painters," 1941; "Journeying Through Mexico," 1948; "John Marin," 1948; "Spring in Spain," 1952; "Man of Fire: Jose Clemente Orozco," 1953.

HELWIG, ARTHUR LOUIS—*Painter, Gr., T.*

Cincinnati Art Academy; h. 192 North Bend Rd., Hebron, Ky.

B. Cincinnati, Ohio, Apr. 22, 1899. *Studied*: Cincinnati A. Acad.; Julian Acad., Paris; & with Marchand. *Member*: AAPL; Cincinnati AC; Cincinnati Crafters. *Awards*: prizes, Dayton AI, 1934; Women's City Cl., Cincinnati, 1937; Denver A. Mus., 1935; Cincinnati Garden Cl., 1945. *Work*: Denver A. Mus.; CM; Cincinnati Women's Cl.; Western Hills H.S.; East End Pub. Sch., Cincinnati; murals, churches in Covington, Ky.; Norwood, Ohio; indst. mural, Cincinnati Milling Machine Co.; Norwood Pub. Sch. *Exhibited*: Rockefeller Center, N.Y., 1937; AIC, 1938; SFMA, 1937-1939; WFNY 1939; CM, 1935-1942; Dayton AI, 1945; Butler AI, 1939; Toledo Mus. A., 1945-1946 (traveling exh.) AFA traveling exh., 1950, 1952, 1954-55; traveling exh. to Europe circulated by U.S. Govt., 1954-55. *Position*: Instr., Drawing & Painting, 1929, Graphic A., 1943-46, Cincinnati A. Acad., Cincinnati, Ohio.

HENDERSON, LESLIE (*Mr.*)—*Painter, Et., T.*

210 Lincoln Dr., Philadelphia 44, Pa.

B. Philadelphia, Pa., Nov. 20, 1895. *Studied*: PMSchIA. *Member*: Phila. Sketch Cl.; Woodmere A. Gal.; Phila. A. T. Assn. *Position*: A.-Illus., Bd. of Edu., Philadelphia, Pa.

HENDERSON, TOM—*Cartoonist, Comm. A.*

Mariomi Rd., New Canaan, Conn.

B. Terre Haute, Ind., Oct. 12, 1920. *Studied*: Wabash Col.; Chicago Acad. FA, with Ruth Van Sickle Ford, Vaughn Shoemaker. *Member*: Nat. Cartoonists Soc. *Awards*: Top cart. in point of sales to America's five largest magazines, 1946. Contributor cartoons to Best Cartoons of the Year, 1945-1947; "Funny Business"; Cartoons 1950; "Honey, I'm Home," 1954; Look cartoon book, 1957; Saturday Evening Post Carnival of Humor, 1958; work for many business firms including General Electric, Shell Oil Co., American Express, Yale & Towne, Mennen, Pennsylvania Tire Co., Johnson & Johnson, etc. Created weekly feature "Major Fanfare," This Week Magazine, 1956. *Exhibited*: British-American Humor Exh., England, 1954. Contributor to Sat. Eve. Post; Collier's; Look; This Week; Popular Science; Chicago Tribune; N.Y. News Syndicate, and many others.

HENDRICKS, GEOFFREY—*Educator, P., Gr.*

Douglass College, Rutgers University, New Brunswick, N.J.; h. 338 West 24th St., New York 11, N.Y.

B. Littleton, N.H., July 30, 1931. *Studied*: Amherst Col., B.A.; Yale Univ., Norfolk A. Sch.; CUASch. *Member*: CAA; Print Council of Am. *Awards*: Yale-Norfolk A. Sch. Fellowship, 1953; MacDowell Colony Fellowship, 1955; prizes, Amherst, Mass., 1953; Springfield A. Mus., 1953; Champlain Valley Exh., 1950. *Work*: Springfield A. Mus.; mural, Amherst College. *Exhibited*: Southern Vermont A., 1949, 1950; Champlain Valley Exh., 1950; Springfield A. Mus., 1952, 1953; RoKo Gal., N.Y., 1956; Newark. N.J., 1957; Douglass Col. A. Gal., 1957; A. Dept. Exhs., 1957, 1958; Newark Mus., 1958; one-man: Dartmouth Col., 1951; Amherst Col., 1953; The Putney Sch., Vermont, 1956; Douglass Col. A. Gal., 1957, 1958. *Position*: Instr. A. Dept. A., Douglass College, Rutgers Univ., New Brunswick, N.J., 1956- .

HENDRICKSON, DAVID—*Illustrator*

Potrero, San Diego County, Cal.

B. St. Paul, Minn., Feb. 4, 1896. *Studied*: St. Paul Inst. A.; Ecole des Beaux-Arts, France; Cal. Sch. FA; Grand Central A. Sch.; ASL, and with George Bridgman, Dean Cornwell, Harvey Dunn. *Member*: SAGA. *Exhibited*: Brooklyn Soc. Et., 1926, 1928; Soc. Am. Et., 1932; SI, 1937, 1942; A. Dir. Cl., N.Y. and San F.; Palo Alto A. Cl.; MMA, 1955. Illus., "American Heartwood," 1949; "Time to Remember," 1950; "Andrew Jackson," 1953; Cal. State Dept. of Edu. textbooks on Mexico, 1955-58; "Luis of Guadalajara"; "The People of Mexico"; "Adventures of Nicolas" (1955-58), and other textbooks for national publishers.

HENKEL, AUGUST—*Serigrapher, Cart., P.*

103-04 217th Lane, Queens Village 9, N.Y.

B. Philadelphia, Pa., July 31, 1880. *Studied*: PAFA; & with William M. Chase, Thomas Anschutz. *Member*: A.Lg. Am.; Nat. Serigraph Soc. *Work*: MMA; Lib.Cong.

HENNINGS, E. MARTIN—*Painter*

Box 32, Taos, N.M.

B. Pennsgrove, N.J., Feb. 5, 1886. *Studied*: AIC; Nat. Acad., Munich, Germany. *Member*: Taos AA. *Awards*: prizes, AIC, 1922, 1923, 1926, 1927; PAFA, 1925; NAD, 1926 (gold medal); Acad. Western Painters, 1938; Texas Wild Flower Exh., 1929 (first prize). *Work*: Mus. FA of Houston; Harrison Gal., Los A.; Chicago Mun. Coll.; PAFA; Illinois State Coll.; Vanderpoel Coll.; Gilcrease Fnd.; Colorado Col. Edu.; Stark Col., Orange, Tex. *Exhibited*: NAD; CGA; NAFA; AIC; Carnegie Inst., and many local and regional exhs.

HENOCH, HANLEY—*Painter, Des.*

418 East 50th St., New York 22, N.Y.

B. La Porte, Ind., Dec. 10, 1886. *Studied*: AIC; PIASch.; Parsons Sch. Des., Paris, and in London. *Member*: NSMP. *Work*: in many private homes.

HENRICH, MRS. JEAN MacKAY—
Sculptor, T., L., P.

155 St. James Pl., Buffalo 22, N.Y.

B. Halifax, N.S., Canada, Sept. 19, 1909. *Studied*: Antioch Col., B.A.; AIC; AI of Buffalo; Univ. Buffalo, M.A. in A. Edu., and abroad. *Member*: The Patteran; CAA; Albright A. Gal. (Adv. Council). *Work*: LC; Veteran's Mem., Geneva, N.Y.; Arch. Sc., Chautauqua County Jail, Mayville, N.Y. *Exhibited*: PAFA; Butler AI; SAM; SFMA; Denver A. Mus.; Albright A. Gal., 1936-46; Crane Lib., 1958. *Position*: Instr. S., AI of Buffalo, N.Y., 1937-43, 1944-46; Hd. A. Dept., Buffalo Seminary, 1946- . L., "Working in Clay."

HENRICKSEN, RALF CHRISTIAN—*Painter, E.*

Michigan State University; h. 619 Division St., East Lansing, Mich.

B. Chicago, Ill., June 22, 1907. *Studied*: AIC, B.F.A.; Instituto de Allende, Mexico, M.F.A. *Member*: Mich. Acad. Sc. A. & Lets.; AAUP. *Awards*: prizes, AIC, 1933; Detroit Inst. A., 1952; South Bend AA, 1957. *Work*: murals, U.S. Treasury Dept., 1938-41; USPO, Monroe, Mich.; Staunton, Ill. *Exhibited*: Pomona, Cal., 1956; AIC, 1942; Butler Inst. Am. A.; Phila. WC Soc., 1954; AIC, 1947-1957; Detroit A. Market, 1957, 1958; Michigan A., 1958; Michigan State Univ., 1947-1958; South Bend AA, 1956, 1957. *Position*: Prof. A. Dept. A., Michigan State University, East Lansing, Mich., 1946- .

HENRICKSON, PAUL ROBERT—*Educator, P., Gr.*

Art Department, State Teachers College; h. 340 9th Ave., Northwest, Valley City, N.D.

B. Boston, Mass., Dec. 25, 1928. *Studied*: R.I. Sch. Des., B.F.A.; State T. Col., Boston, M. Ed.; and in Norway. *Member*: NEA; North Dakota Edu. Assn.; AAUP. *Exhibited*: Providence A. Cl., 1948-1950; R.I. Lg. for A. & Crafts, 1949, 1951, 1953; Mus. New Mexico, Santa Fe, 1951, 1952; Univ. Puerto Rico, 1952; Sioux City A. Center, 1957. Contributor to North Dakota Teacher. *Positions*: Instr. A., Hill & Canyon Sch. A., Santa Fe, 1951-52; Instr. & Supv. A., Tantasqua H.S., Sturbridge, Mass., 1954-56; Prof. A., Hd. A. Dept., State T. Col., Valley City, N.D., 1956- .

HENRY, CHARLES TRUMBO—*Painter, T., L.*

803 South Mansfield St., Los Angeles 36, Cal.

B. Niagara Falls, N.Y., Feb. 17, 1902. *Studied*: Northeast Missouri State T. Col., B.S. in Edu.; ASL; & with Benton, Robinson, Grosz. *Member*: ASL. *Awards*: F., Tiffany Fnd., 1929. *Work*: mem., Kirksville, Mo.; Northeast Missouri State T. Col.; Tiffany Fnd.; murals, Dept. Labor Bldg., Wash., D.C.; USPO, Cornelia, Ga. *Exhibited*: WMAA, 1937, 1943, PAFA, 1934, 1937; NAD, 1940, 1942; Carnegie Inst., 1940; AFA traveling exh., 1940, 1941; BM, 1937, 1939, 1943; San Diego FA Soc., 1940; MMA (AV), 1942; AWCS, 1941; CGA, 1934, 1937; Kansas City AI, 1937; one-man exh.: High Mus. A., 1939; New Orleans AA, 1955; Univ. Georgia, 1939; Northeast Missouri State T. Col., 1935; Los A. Mus. A., 1950; Nat. Orange Show, 1950; Laurel Gal., 1949; Chabot Gal., Los A., 1951; Havenstrite Gal., Los A., 1949; Artists Gal., Geneva, Ill., 1956; Wellington, N.Z., 1956; Mun. A. Gal., Los Angeles, 1957.

HENRY, COAH—*Painter, T.*

5125 Swope Parkway, Kansas City 30, Mo.

B. Hamilton, Mo., Aug. 14, 1878. *Studied*: Kansas City AI; Chicago Acad. FA; N.Y. Sch. F. & App. A.; Colorado Univ.; & with Henry B. Snell, Frank Swift Chase, Ralph Pearson, Eliot O'Hara. *Work*: Newark Mus. *Exhibited*: NAWA; AIC; N.Y. WC Cl.; Wash. WC Cl.; Chapel House, Denver, Colo.; Kansas City AI.

HENRY, H. RAYMOND—*Painter, W., Cr.*

630 Anita St., Laguna Beach, Cal.

B. Woodson, Ill., Mar. 21, 1882. *Studied*: St. Louis Acad. A.; Saugatuck, Mich., with J.G. Johnsen. *Member*: P. & S. Soc., Los Angeles. *Awards*: prizes, Greek Theatre, Los A.; Los A. Women's Cl. *Exhibited*: Los A. Mus. A.; AIC, and others. Conducted art column, Hollywood Citizen.

HENRY, NATALIE S(MITH)—*Painter, Gr.*

4 East Ohio St., Chicago 11, Ill.

B. Malvern, Ark., Jan. 4, 1907. *Studied*: AIC; Ropp Sch. A., Chicago. *Member*: Chicago SA. *Work*: mural, USPO, Springdale, Ark. *Exhibited*: AIC, 1935-1938, 1941, 1944; Chicago SA, 1944- .

HENRY, STUART (COMPTON)—
Museum Director, P., Des.

Berkshire Museum; h. 127 Appleton Ave., Pittsfield, Mass.

B. Tufts College, Mass., 1906. *Studied*: Phillips Acad., Andover, Mass.; Harvard Col., B.S. *Member*: AAMus. *Work*: FMA, and in private colls. *Exhibited*: Pittsfield A. Lg.; one-man: FMA; Berkshire Mus.; Symphony Hall, Boston. Author of catalogues of exhibitions, collections, guides to collections, etc., Berkshire Mus. *Position*: Dir., Berkshire Mus., Pittsfield, Mass.*

HENSCHE, MRS. ADA RAYNER. See *Rayner, Ada*

HENSCHE, HENRY—*Painter, L., T.*

Provincetown, Mass.

B. Chicago, Ill., Feb. 20, 1901. *Studied*: AIC; NAD; ASL; BAID; & with Hawthorne, Bellows. *Member*: SC. *Awards*: Prize, NAD, 1930. *Work*: Harvard Cl., N.Y.; Boston Univ.; Conn. Agricultural Col.; Mint Mus. A.; H.S., Warrenton, N.C.; Provincetown, Mass.; Kenyon Col.; Walter Chrysler, Jr., Coll.; Scottish Rite Cathedral, Ft. Wayne, Ind. *Exhibited*: NAD; PAFA; CGA; Carnegie Inst.; AIC; Provincetown AA; Mint Mus. A.; Jordan-Marsh, Boston, Mass. Lectures: History of Painting. *Position*: Dir., Instr., Cape Cod. Sch. A., Cape Cod, Mass.

HENSEL, HOPKINS—*Painter*

Ogunquit, Me.

B. New York, N.Y. *Studied*: Yale Univ. *Work*: BMFA; Mus. FA of Houston; Toledo Mus. A.; IBM. *Exhibited*: Grand Central Moderns; Margaret Brown Gal., Boston; and in national exhibitions.

HENTSCHEL, ALZA STRATTON. See *Stratton, Alza*

HENTSCHEL, WILLIAM E(RNST)—
Painter, T., Des., C.
Cincinnati Art Academy, Eden Park, Cincinnati, Ohio;
h. April Hill Farm, Burlington, Ky.

B. New York, N.Y., June 15, 1892. *Studied*: Cincinnati A. Acad.; ASL; Columbia Univ. *Work*: IBM; Smithsonian Inst.; MMA; CM; Western and Southern Life Ins. Bldg., Cincinnati (mural). *Exhibited*: Syracuse Mus. FA; CM; CGA; U.S.Nat. Mus.; AIC; Marshall Field & Co.; Monticello Col.; Shimer Jr. Col.; Illinois State Fair, 1951; Indiana Univ.; Ft. Wayne Mus. A.; John Herron AI; Ball State Col.; Swope A. Gal.; Univ. Kentucky; Delgado Mus. A.; Newcomb Col.; WMA; Cranbrook Acad. A.; Flint Inst. A.; Univ. Minnesota; Kansas City AI; Nelson Gal. A.; Currier Gal. A.; Newark Mus.; Albright A. Gal; MMA; WMAA; Rochester Mem. A. Gal.; Munson-Williams-Proctor Inst.; Canton AI; Carnegie Inst.; CMA; Columbus Gal. FA; Butler AI; Portland (Ore.) A. Mus.; PMA; SAM; Milwaukee AI, and others; one-man: Norton Gal. A., 1944; Taft Mus. A., 1945; J.B.Speed Mus. A., 1951; Miami Beach A. Center. *Position*: Instr., Des., Comm. A., Cincinnati A. Acad., 1921-1957 (Retired).

HERBERT, JAMES DRUMMOND—*Teacher, P., S.*
21 Meeting St. (3); h. 70 Barnes St., Providence 6, R.I.

B. New York, N.Y., Dec. 26, 1896. *Studied*: Columbia Univ., A.B.; ASL; Julien Acad., Paris. *Member*: NSS; A. Dir. Cl.; ASL; SI; Providence A. Cl.; Providence WC Cl.; Contemp. A.; Newport AA. *Awards*: A. Dir. Cl.; Providence A. Cl. *Work*: bronze port., Mus. Nat. Hist., N.Y. *Exhibited*: NAD; PAFA; AIC; Arch. Lg.; A. Dir. Cl.; AWS; Salon d'Automne, Paris; Mystic AA; Boston A. Festival, 1955. *Position*: Pres., R.I. Fed. A.; Chm. Exec. Council of "Meeting Place," non-profit picture lending gallery. Taught Columbia Univ. Sch. Arch.; PIASch.; R.I.Sch. Des.; Newport Acad. FA.

HERBERT, V(IRGINIA) (B.)—*Painter*
2606 Washington Ave., Cairo, Ill.

B. Cairo, Ill., Sept. 7, 1912. *Studied*: AIC, B.F.A., with Boris Anisfeld; Univ. Colorado, with James Ernst. *Awards*: prize, Nat. WC exh., Jackson, Miss., 1946. *Work*: Marine Hospital, Lexington, Ky. *Exhibited*: AIC, 1941; AFA traveling exh., 1941-43; MMA, 1943; Mississippi AA, 1946; All-Illinois exh., 1940; CAM, 1942, 1944; Atkins Mus., 1945; Ohio Valley exh., 1945; A. & Crafts Cl., New Orleans, 1948; So. Illinois A. Gld., traveling exh., 1950; Cape Girardeau, Mo., 1951; one-man: Carbondale, Ill., 1944; Cairo, Ill., 1945, 1948; Malden, Mo., 1948; Joliet A. Lg., 1949.

HERDLE, ISABEL C.—*Associate Museum Director*
Rochester Memorial Art Gallery, 490 University Ave., Rochester 7, N.Y.

Position: Assoc. Dir., Rochester Mem. A. Gal.*

HERING, HARRY—*Painter, Gr., C.*
172 West 79th St., New York 24, N.Y.

B. New York, N.Y., Jan. 12, 1887. *Member*: Audubon A.; AEA; All. A. Am. *Awards*: prizes, All. A. Am., 1939; Mineola Fair. *Work*: WMAA; Newark Mus. A.; MMA; Tel-Aviv Mus., Israel, and in private colls. *Exhibited*: PAFA; NAD; Carnegie Inst.; WMAA; AIC; Detroit Inst. A.; CGA; CMA; WMA; BM; Toledo Mus. A.; one-man: Rehn Gal., 1926, 1928, 1937, 1939; Milch Gal., 1941, 1944, 1945; Toledo Mus. A., 1946; Cowie Gal., Los A., 1947, 1949, 1955; Lenox Gal., 1952-1954; Miami Beach A. Center, 1956; Roosevelt Field A. Gal., 1958; Miami Beach, 1959.

HERMAN, VIC—*Cartoonist, Des., I., W.*
104 East 40th St., New York 16, N.Y.; h. 32 Glenbrook Dr., New Rochelle, N.Y.

B. Fall River, Mass., 1919. *Studied*: ASL, with George Bridgman; N.Y. Comm. Illus. Sch. *Member*: Am. Soc. Magazine Cartoonists; Nat. Cartoonists Soc.; Am. Soc. Training Dirs.; Chicago Press Cl.; N.Y.Sales Exec. Cl. *Awards*: Army medal for creation of "Winnie the Wac," 1945; N.Y. City citation for posters, 1945; Direct Mail award, 1952; Citation from United Defense Fund for programs created 1954. *Exhibited*: O.W.I. Conservation exh., 1945; Greek War Relief, Cartoon and Illustration exh.,

1947; Handicapped Children's Cartoon exh., 1947; Am. Soc. Magazine Cartoonists exh., 1947; Fresh Air Fund exh., 1948. Represented in "Best Cartoons of the Year," 1943-51; Sat. Eve. Post's "Laugh It Off," 1944; "Funny Business," 1945. Author, I., "Winnie, the Wac," 1945; I., "Fat Boy," 1952. *Position*: A.-War Correspondent, "Army Motors Magazine"; A. Dir., "Wac News Letter"; Freelance I., Cart., for advertising agencies and magazines, 1937-47; Illus. stories for N.Y. Times and "Pictorial Review"; Pres., Vic Herman Productions, Inc., New York, N.Y.; Training Consultant to Corporations nationally.

HERMANSADER, JOHN B.—*Painter, Des.*
720 Fifth Ave., New York 19, N.Y.; h. 7 Bly Court, Great Neck, L.I., N.Y.

B. Reading, Pa., Nov. 1, 1915. *Studied*: Memphis Acad. A.; New Sch. for Social Research, and with Robert Motherwell. *Award*: prize, Long Island A. Lg., 1951. *Work*: Wake Forest (Ill.) Col.; Schwenkfelder A. Mus., Pa., and in private colls. *Exhibited*: Art:USA, 1958; Panoras Gal., 1956; Gal. Contemp. A., Sunken Meadow, L.I., 1958.

HEROLD, DON—*Cartoonist, W., Des.*
155 East 42nd St., New York, N.Y.; h. Vero Beach, Fla.

B. Bloomfield, Ind., July 9, 1889. *Studied*: Indiana Univ., A.B.; AIC. Author, Cart., "Doing Europe and Vice Versa," 1931; "Love That Golf," 1952, and others. Contributor to national magazines.

HEROLD, DONALD G.—*Museum Director*
Davenport Public Museum, 704 Brady St., Davenport, Iowa.*

HERPST, MARTHA (JANE)—*Portrait Painter*
122 East Main St., Titusville, Pa.

B. Titusville, Pa. *Studied*: PAFA, with Wayman Adams, Edmund Greacen, Harvey Dunn, Guy Pène du Bois. *Member*: AAPL; NAC. *Work*: Titusville Recreation Center; Masonic Lodge, Woman's Cl., U.S. Marine Corps Lg., YWCA, all in Titusville, Pa.; NAC. *Exhibited*: NAC, 1933-1958; Butler AI; Ogunquit AA, 1951-1953; Catherine L. Wolfe A. Cl., 1954-1958; AAPL, 1953-1958. *Position*: Instr. A., St. Joseph's Acad. H.S., Titusville, Pa.

HERRIC, PRU (PRUDENCE C. HERRIC)—*Illustrator*
Pratt Institute, Brooklyn, N.Y.; h. 7112 Boulevard East, North Bergen, N.J.

B. Kodaikanal, India, May 14, 1897. *Studied*: Mount Holyoke Col., B.A.; PIASch., and with Charles Hawthorne. *Work*: N.Y.Hospital, New York, N.Y. *Exhibited*: Mount Holyoke Col.; Studio Gld., traveling exh., 1949-1951. Illus., "Todd's Snow Patrol," 1955; "Bats and Gloves of Glory," 1956, and other children's books. Many textbooks including series on Natural Science for Puerto Rican elementary schools and for other textbook publishers.

HERRIN, M. H.—*Painter, W.*
3912 Thirteenth St., South, Arlington, Va.

B. Moss Point, Miss., Nov. 1, 1897. *Studied*: Eastman Col.; PIASch., and with Nicholas F. Riley. *Member*: AFA; Composers, Authors & Artists of Am.; AAPL. *Awards*: Int. Mark Twain Soc. (hon. life). *Work*: Ballard Mem. Sch., Bradenton, Fla.; Will Rogers Mem. Hospital, Saranac Lake, N.Y.; Modern Indst. Bank, N.Y.; American Officers' Cl., London; Comptroller General's Office, Wash., D.C., and in private coll. in U.S. and abroad; ports. of prominent persons. *Exhibited*: Rockefeller Center, N.Y.; Brentanos; Canadian Pacific Railways Cook's Travel Bureau, N.Y. Author, I., "The Creole Aristocracy."*

HERRING, JAMES VERNON—*Educator, L., C., P.*
127 Randolph Pl., Washington 1, D.C.

B. Clio, S.C., Jan. 7, 1887. *Studied*: Howard Acad.; Crouse Col. FA; Syracuse Univ., B. Ped. in Art; Carnegie Scholar, Harvard Univ.; Columbia Univ. *Member*: CAA (life); AFA; AAMus.; Am. Assn. Univ. Prof. Lectures: "American Art." *Positions*: Prof., Hd. Dept. A., (Emeritus) Howard Univ., Washington, D.C., 1921- ; Dir. College A. Service; Chm. Council of A. Mus. in Dist. of

Columbia, 1949- ; Assembled Contemporary American Painting, Howard Univ., 1958-59; Exh. of Japanese Woodblock Prints, 1957-58; A.-in-Res., Talladega (Ala.) Col., 1957-58; St. Augustine's Col., Raleigh, N.C., 1958-59.

HERRMANN, E. ADELE—*Painter, T.*
    119 North Third Ave., Highland Park, N.J.

B. North Plainfield, N.J. *Studied*: T. Col., Columbia Univ. M.A.; ASL. *Member*: New Brunswick AA; Phila. Plastic Cl.; New Jersey P. & S. Soc.; AAPL. *Awards*: prizes, Huckleberry Mountain exh., 1949; gold med., Phila. Plastic Cl., 1952; N.J. Art Council, 1952; Warren prize; Middlesex County, 1957; AAPL, 1958. *Exhibited*: N.J. State Mus., Trenton; Montclair A. Mus.; Newport AA; Provincetown AA; All. A. Am.; Smithsonian Inst.; PAFA; Huckleberry Mountain; NAC; Audubon A.; Middlesex County, 1957; AAPL, 1958.

HERRON, JASON (Miss)—*Sculptor, W., L.*
    1525 McCollum St., Los Angeles 26, Cal.; s. 1425 Nathan Lane, Ventura, Cal.

B. Denver, Colo., Sept. 11, 1900. *Studied*: Stanford Univ.; Los A. County AI; & with Merrell Gage, F. Tolles Chamberlin. *Member*: Los A. AA. *Awards*: prizes, Los A. County Fair, 1934; Los A. AA.; med., Soc. for Sanity in A., 1945; Cal. AC, 1946. *Work*: Los A. Mus. A.; Browning Mus., London, England; South Pasadena H.S.; Belmont Sch., Los A.; Santa Monica (Cal.) H.S. *Exhibited*: Palace Legion Honor, 1929; NAD, 1944, 1945; CGA, 1944; Medalic A. Soc., 1938; AIC; Los A. Mus. A., 1925, 1928-1932, 1937, 1940, 1943; Cal. AC, 1926-1935, 1938, 1943, 1944; Greek Theatre, Los A., Cal., 1946-1949; San Diego FA Soc.; Santa Barbara Mus. A., 1949; Los A. Art Assn. 1948-1950; Madonna Festival, Los A., 1949-1954; NAD, 1947; Pomona Fair, 1949. *Position*: Chm., Southern Cal. Nat. A. Week, 1941- ; Sec., Civic Com. for Los A. County A. Projects, 1945-50; Bd. Gov., Los A. County AI, 1952; Acting Dir., 1952, Los A. County AI; re-appt. Bd. Gov., 1954; Bd. Memb., Los A. AA, 1948- .

HERSEY, CARL KENNETH—*Educator*
    160 Chelmsford Rd., Rochester 18, N.Y.

B. Sanford, Me., Oct. 27, 1904. *Studied*: Bowdoin Col., A.B.; Harvard Univ., M.A., Ph.D. *Member*: CAA; Am. Soc. Arch. Hist.; Archaeological Inst. Am. *Award*: Guggenheim F., 1947. Author: "The Salmantine Lanterns," 1937; "The Church of Saint-Martin at Tours," (Art Bulletin, 1943); "Early Romanesque Church Towers of Touraine," (Journal Am. Soc. Arch. Hist., 1944); "Current Research on the Church of Saint-Martin at Tours," Journal of Soc. Arch. Hist., Vol. VII, 1948.*

HERSHEY, SAMUEL F.—*Educator, Des., P.*
    132 Bowen St., Providence 6, R.I.

B. Peru, Ind., Aug. 10, 1904. *Studied*: MIT; PAFA; BMFA Sch. *Member*: Rockport AA; New Haven Paint & Clay Cl.; Providence A. Cl.; Univ. Cl. *Exhibited*: CGA; NAD; PAFA; Rockport AA; North Shore AA; New Haven Paint & Clay Cl.; Hoosier Salon; Boston, Springfield, Mass.; Hartford, Conn. *Position*: Instr. Design, Harvard Univ., 1937-42; Chm., Freshman Fnd., R.I.Sch.Des., Providence, R.I., 1946- .

HERZ, NORA (EVELYN)—*Sculptor, C., T., W.*
    425 Ridge Rd., Apt. 1-J, North Arlington, N.J.

B. Hipperholme, England, May 13, 1910. *Studied*: PIASch.; Sculpture Center, and in Germany. *Member*: Artist-Craftsmen of N.Y.; AEA; Assoc. A. New Jersey; New Jersey Des.-Craftsmen; Hunterdon County A. Center. *Awards*: prizes, Village A. Center, 1949, 1951; Montclair A. Mus., 1956; Pen & Brush Cl., 1956; Hunterdon County A. Center, 1957; Bamberger Co., 1957, 1958. *Work*: Bavarian Nat. Mus., Munich, Germany; Athens, Ga. *Exhibited*: Audubon A., 1946, 1947, 1950, 1952; NAD, 1949-1951; Union Theological Seminary, 1952; PAFA, 1950, 1952, 1953; MMA, 1951; Arch. Lg., 1944; Sculpture Center, 1941-1944, 1949, 1950; Saranac Lake, 1948; N.Y.Soc. Ceramic A., 1944-1957; NSS, 1952; Phila. A. All., 1948; Wash. A. Cl., 1950; Newark Mus. A., 1953-1958; Montclair A. Mus., 1953-1956; Syracuse Mus. FA, 1956; Miami, Fla., 1956; Mus. Contemp. Crafts, 1957; one-man: Gallerie Neuf, 1945; Village A. Center, 1952. Contributor to "Ceramic Age." *Position*: Instr., Pottery & Sc., Newark Mus. A., 1950-55; Summit AA, & West Orange Adult Sch., 1957- .

HESKETH—*Sculptor*
    Bluehills Studio, Kempton 1, Pa.

B. Maine. *Studied*: with John Flannagan, Ahron Ben-Schmuel. *Member*: AEA. *Work*: Ferargil Gal.; Egan Gal.; SFMA; AGAA; Atlanta Mus. A. *Exhibited*: Detroit Inst. A., 1946 CAM, 1946; PMA, 1940; Carnegie Inst., 1941; AIC, 1942; PAFA, 1943; MMA, 1943; DeMotte Gal.; Egan Gal.; J. B. Neumann Gal.; one-man: SFMA, 1943; SAM, 1943; Ferargil Gal., 1942, 1943, 1945; Cosmopolitan Cl., Phila., Pa., 1946; WMAA; AGAA.

HESS, EMIL JOHN—*Painter, S.*
    130 West 10th St., New York 14, N.Y.

B. Willock, Pa., Sept. 25, 1913. *Studied*: Duquesne Univ.; A. Inst. Pittsburgh; ASL; Brooklyn Mus.A.Sch. *Work*: Pa. State Mus.; MModA. *Exhibited*: NAD, 1950; Pa. State Mus., 1950; ASL, 1947-1950; BM; 1951; one-man: Betty Parsons Gal., 1951, 1952.

HESS, LOWELL FRANCIS—*Designer, Comm. A., I.*
    Grant's Corners, Ossining, N.Y.

B. Thomas, Okla., Feb. 7, 1921. *Studied*: Univ. Oklahoma Sch. A.; PIASch. *Member*: SI. Illus., "Exploring the Moon," 1955; "Exploring Mars," 1956; "Exploring the Universe," 1956 (awarded Thomas Alva Edison prize); "Exploring the Weather," and four Golden Books of Fairy Tales. Contributor illus. to American, Colliers, Woman's Home Companion, Boy's Life, Argosy magazines.

HESS, SARA—*Painter*
    4334 Valle Vista St., San Diego, Cal.

B. Troy Grove, Ill., Feb. 25, 1880. *Studied*: AIC; Julian Acad.; Paris, France; & with Richard Miller, Henry Hubbel. *Member*: NAWA; San Diego A. Gld.; Laguna Beach AA; La Jolla AC. *Awards*: prizes, Am. Women A., Paris, France; Ridgewood AA. *Work*: Oshkosh Mus. A.; Vanderpoel Coll.; Gary Mem. Gal., Gary, Ind.; Ridgewood (N.J.) Women's Cl. *Exhibited*: NAWA; Laguna Beach AA; San Diego FA Soc.; Ridgewood AA; La Jolla A. Center.

HEUERMANN, MAGDA—*Painter, W., L., T., Des.*
    783 East Eastwood St., Marshall, Mo.

B. Galesburg, Ill. *Studied*: AIC; & with F. H. C. Sammons, von Lenbach, Roth, Max Doerner. *Member*: Chicago SA; Chicago Soc. Min. P.; Chicago AC; NAC; Chicago No-Jury Soc. *Awards*: Med., prizes, Phila., Pa., 1935; New Orleans, La.; Atlanta, Ga., etc. *Work*: Carnegie Lib., Joliet, Ill.; Univ. Iowa; Beloit Col.; Vanderpoel Coll.; Winfield, Scott Schley Sch., Chicago; Carnegie Lib., Nashville, Tenn.; Springfield (Ill.) Acad. FA; Victoria & Albert Mus., London; many portrait miniatures. Personal coll. of 80 miniatures presented to Art Dept., Illinois Inst. Tech., Chicago; fine glassware coll. dating from 1596 presented to Illinois State Mus.; fine paintings to Blosser Home for Crippled Children, Marshall, Mo. *Exhibited*: extensively in U.S. & abroad.

HEUSSER, ELEANORE ELIZABETH—*Painter*
    Columbia University, New York, N.Y.; h. Roosevelt Ave., North Haledon, N.J.

B. North Haledon, N.J. *Studied*: CUASch.; Columbia Univ. *Award*: Fulbright F., 1952-54. *Work*: Newark Mus. A. *Position*: Instr., Painting & Sculpture, Columbia Univ., New York, N.Y., 1945-52.*

HEWETT, EDWARD WILSON—*Painter, T.*
    309 East 16th Ave., Columbus, Ohio

B. Los Angeles, Cal., July 12, 1926. *Studied*: Cincinnati A. Acad.; Univ. Louisville, B.S., M.A. *Member*: Columbus A. Lg. *Awards*: Wilder traveling scholarship, Cincinnati A. Acad., 1949; Allen R. Hite Scholarship, Univ. Louisville, 1952, 1953; Fulbright F., 1954-1955; prizes, Ky.-Southern Indiana Exh., 1952; Interior Valley Exh., Cincinnati, 1955; Columbus A. Lg., 1957; Union County Exh., 1958. *Work*: J.B.Speed Mus., Louisville; murals, Christ Church Cathedral, Louisville; Watterson Hotel, Louisville; Shiloh Methodist Church, Shiloh, Ky.; Aetna Oil Co.; Walter Chrysler, Jr., Coll. *Exhibited*: Paris, France, 1950; Cincinnati A., 1950; Ky.-So. Indiana Exh., 1952, 1954; Norfolk, Va., 1954; Va. Intermont Col., 1954; CM,

1955; Mostra dell' Art Cl., Rome, 1955; AGAA, 1955; regional shows: Ky., Ohio, Virginia, 1952-58; Provincetown A. Festival, 1958. *Position*: Instr., Painting & Drawing, Murray State Col., 1952-53; Ohio State Univ., Columbus, Ohio, 1955- .

HEWITT, DONALD C.—*Illustrator, Comm. A.*
    145 East 26th St., New York 10, N.Y.; h. R.D.#3, Flemington, N.J.

B. Northampton, England, Aug. 12, 1904. *Studied*: AIC; Am. Acad., Chicago; ASL; Grand Central Sch. A. *Member*: SI.*

HIBBARD, A(LDRO) T(HOMPSON)—*Painter, T.*
    Legendsea, Rockport, Mass.

B. Falmouth, Mass., Aug. 25, 1886. *Studied*: Mass. Normal A. Sch.; BMFA Sch., and with E.L. Major, De Camp, Tarbell. *Member*: NA; Gld. Boston A.; North Shore AA; Rockport AA; SC; All. A. Am.; 50 Am. Artists; Audubon A.; Conn. Acad. FA; New Haven Paint & Clay Cl.; Copley Soc., Boston; So. Vermont A.; Academic A., Springfield. *Awards*: prizes, NAD, 1921, 1927, 1931; med., PAFA, 1922, prize, 1927, 1931; Springfield A. Lg., 1931; New Haven Paint & Clay Cl., 1933, 1941; Conn. Acad. FA, 1937; GGE, 1939; Springfield Acad. A., 1958; IBM, 1940; All. A. Am., 1943, 1946; SC, 1932, 1944; Academic A., 1953; Jordan Marsh, Boston, 1938; Palm Beach A. Center, 1936; North Shore AA 1956 and prior; Rockport AA, 1942, 1948, 1954, 1957. *Work*: MMA; BMFA; Portland Mus. A.; AGAA; Currier Gal. A.; Rochester Atheneum; San Diego FA Soc.; IBM; Chandler Sch. for Women; Roosevelt H.S., Phila., Pa.; Newton (Mass.) H.S.; Milton Acad. *Exhibited*: CGA; PAFA; AIC; NAD; and many other national exhibitions throughout the U.S. Pres., Gld. Boston A.; Bd. Mngrs., North Shore AA, Rockport AA.

HIBBARD, ELISABETH HASELTINE (Mrs. Frederick C.)—*Sculptor, E., L.*
    923 East 60th St.; h. 1201 East 60th St., Chicago 37, Ill.

B. Portland, Ore., Sept. 25, 1894. *Studied*: Portland (Ore.) A. Sch.; Univ. Chicago, Ph.B.; AIC; Grande Chaumiere, Paris; & with Polasek, Bourdelle, Navellier, deCreeft. *Member*: NAWA; Chicago Galleries Assn.; Women's A. Salon, Chicago; Renaissance Soc.; Univ. Chicago. *Awards*: French mem. scholarship for foreign travel, AIC, 1925; prizes, Chicago Gal. Assn., 1929, 1930, 1932; NAWA, 1937. *Work*: S. Illinois State Mus., Springfield; Vanderpoel Coll.; Univ. Chicago; Norton Mem. Hall., Chautauqua, N.Y.; Jackson Park, Chicago. *Exhibited*: NAWA, 1937-1939, 1946; AIC, 1924-1931, 1935-1940, 1943; PAFA, 1928, 1929, 1936, 1942; BM, 1930; Paris Salon, 1927; Chicago Gal. Assn., 1927-1932, 1934; Chicago Arch. L., 1929; Illinois Acad. FA, 1931; Women's A. Salon, Chicago, 1943-1945; Dayton AI, 1930; Albany Inst. Hist. & A., 1939; Portland A. Mus., 1925, 1930; one-man exh.: Studio Mus., Bellingham, Wash., 1936; Evanston A. Center, 1939; Univ. Chicago, 1940; St. Catherine's Col., St. Paul, Minn., 1946. *Position*: Asst. Prof. A., Univ. Chicago, Chicago, Ill., 1943- .*

HIBEL, EDNA—*Painter*
    180 Clark Rd., Brookline 46, Mass.

B. Boston, Mass., Jan. 13, 1917. *Studied*: BMFA Sch.; and with Jacovleff, Carl Zerbe. *Member*: AEA. *Work*: BMFA; Harvard Univ.; Boston Univ.; Norton Gal. A. *Award*: prize, Boston A. Festival, 1956. *Exhibited*: PAFA, 1936-1938, 1941, 1943; AIC, 1942, 1943; AWS, 1946; Vose Gal., 1940-1944; Smith Gal., 1944-1946; Inst. Mod. A., Boston, 1943; Shaw Gal., 1945; John Levy Gal., N.Y., 1948-49 (one-man); DeCordova & Dana Mus., 1951, 1952, 1954; Symphony Hall, Boston; Terry AI, 1952; Vose Gal., Boston, 1954; Neptune Gal., 1955, 1957, 1958; AFA traveling exh., 1956-1958; Lee Gal., 1955.

HICKEN, PHILIP BURNHAM—*Painter, Ser., T.*
    108 Morse St., Newton, Mass.

B. Lynn, Mass., June 27, 1910. *Studied*: Mass. Sch. A. *Member*: F., Royal Soc. A., England; Am. Color Print Soc.; Boston Soc. WC Painters; Boston Pr. M.; Nat. Ser. Soc. *Awards*: prizes, Black Mountain (N.C.) A. Cl., 1943; Springfield, Mass., Soldier Art, 1944; New England

Soldier Art, 1944; San F., Cal., 1945; Mint Mus. A., 1946; Boston Pr. M., 1949; Cambridge AA, 1953; New England Art, Boston, 1954; BM, 1958; Nantucket AA, 1958. *Work*: MMA; PMA; U.S. State Dept.; Springfield Mus. A.; Berkshire Mus.; Univ. Iowa; Am. Assn. Univ. Women; Princeton Pr. Cl.; Northfield (Mass.) Seminary; BM; BMA; Ohio Univ.; Marshall Col.; VMFA; Howard Univ.; Univ. Mississippi; Kansas State Col.; Univ. Wisconsin; Bezalel Mus., Israel; Albright A. Gal.; mural, Ft. Warren, Boston. *Exhibited*: LC, 1944, 1946; Wichita, Kans., 1946; Pittsfield A. Lg., 1942; Mint Mus. A., 1946; BM, 1958; Nantucket AA, 1958; USIS traveling exh., France, 1956-1958; Kansas City USO, 1944; 9th Service Command exh., Cal., 1945. *Position*: Instr., Harvard Grad Sch. Des., 1950-53; Chm. Dept. Des., 1957- ; Sch. Practical A., Boston.

HICKEN, RUSSELL BRADFORD—*Museum Director, T., L.*
    Jacksonville Art Museum, 1550 Riverside Ave.; h. 5959 Terry Parker Drive, North, Jacksonville 4, Fla.

B. Jacksonville, Fla., Dec. 24, 1926. *Studied*: Florida State Univ., B.S.; grad. study, Univ. Florida. *Member*: AAMus.; Southeastern Mus. Conf.; Fla. Fed. A.; Class Room T. Assn. Lectures on art and artists to art associations, women's clubs and gallery audiences. *Position*: Dir., Jacksonville Art Museum, Jacksonville, Fla.

HICKEY, ROSE VAN VRANKEN—*Sculptor, Et., Lith.*
    1112 East Court St., Iowa City, Iowa

B. Passaic, N.J., May 15, 1917. *Studied*: Pomona Col., B.A.; ASL; Univ. Iowa, M.A., and with George Bridgman, William Zorach, Robert Laurent. *Member*: Pasadena Soc. A.; ASL; NAWA. *Awards*: prizes, Los A. Mus. A., 1944; Oakland A. Gal., 1945, 1946; Pasadena AI, 1945, 1951; Joslyn Mus. A., 1950; Walker A. Center, 1951; Des Moines A. Center, 1953; NAWA, 1952. *Exhibited*: CGA, 1943; Elisabet Ney Mus., 1943; SAM, 1943; Denver A. Mus., 1943, 1952; SFMA, 1943; Oklahoma A. Center, 1942; Oakland A. Gal., 1944-1946; Nat. A. Week, Los A., 1945, New York, 1941; Pasadena Soc. A., 1944-1946, 1957; Los A. Mus., A., 1944; Laguna Beach AA, 1945, 1946; San Diego FA Soc., 1945; Pasadena AI, 1943-1946, 1951; Walker A. Center, 1947, 1948, 1951, 1952, 1954; NAD, 1947, 1952; Bradley Univ., 1952; Wichita AA, 1951; Joslyn Mus. A., 1950, 1956; NAWA, 1953, 1956 traveling exh. to Europe, and 1957; Iowa State Fair, 1953-1955; Des Moines A. Center, 1953, 1954, 1956.

HICKS, ELIZABETH—*Painter*
    Tolland, Conn.

B. New York, N.Y., Feb. 1886. *Studied*: N.Y. Univ., and with Robert Henri, William Chase, John LaFarge, Kenyon Cox. *Member*: NAC; NAWA. *Work*: Univ. Connecticut. *Exhibited*: NAD, 1927; All. A. Am.; NAC; Ogunquit A. Center.*

HIGDON, HAL—*Cartoonist, Comm. A., I., W.*
    6933 Crandon Ave., Chicago 49, Ill.

B. Chicago, Ill., June 17, 1931. *Studied*: Carleton Col., B.A., with Alfred Hyslop, Dean Warnholtz; Univ. Chicago, with Edmund Giesbert; Chicago Acad. F. Contributor cartoons to Argosy, True, This Week and other national magazines.*

HIGGINS, CARDWELL S.—*Illustrator, Des., P.*
    Wrights Lane, West Nyack, N.Y.

B. East Orange, N.J., July 7, 1902. *Studied*: NAD; ASL. *Work*: mural, U.S. Army Air Base, Richmond, Va. Advertising I. for national magazines & leading corporations. I., "Joe and Bob on Northland Trails."

HIGGINS, MOLLIE (SMITH) (Mrs.)—*Painter, W., T.*
    Woodstock, N.Y.

B. Bar Harbor, Me., Sept. 29, 1881. *Studied*: ASL, with Mahonri Young, Boardman Robinson, John Sloan; Academie Julien, Paris, France; Academie Ranson, and with Fernand Leger, Paris, France; in Woodstock with Henry Mattson and others. *Member*: Woodstock AA; Woodstock Gld. Gal.; Parnassus Square Gal., Woodstock. *Exhibited*: Woodstock AA annually; Woodstock Gld. Gal., annually. *Positions*: A. Ed., Woodstock News; Ulster County News; News Leader and for Ulster Press (recently retired).

HILDEBRANDT, CORNELIA E. (Mrs.)—Painter, L.
   Huckleberry Hill Rd., R.R. 2, Box 36, New Canaan, Conn.

B. Eau Claire, Wis. *Studied*: AIC; in Paris, France; & with Augustus Koopman, Virginia Reynolds. *Member*: ASMP; NAWA; Pa. Soc. Min. P. *Awards*: med., ASMP, 1941; NAWA, 1946; Pa. Soc. Min. P., 1947 (medal), 1948. *Work*: CGA; MMA; PMA. *Exhibited*: ASMP; NAWA; Pa. Soc. Min. P. Lectures: "The History and Development of the Portrait Miniature."

HILDEBRANDT, WILLIAM ALBERT, JR.—
   Painter, S., E., I.
   Turner Rd. & Baltimore Pike, Media, Pa.

B. Philadelphia, Pa., Oct. 1, 1917. *Studied*: Tyler Sch. FA, Temple Univ., B.F.A., B.S. in Edu., M.F.A.; PM SchIA. *Member*: Phila. A.T.Assn.; Pa. State Edu. Assn.; NEA; Temple Univ. Alumni Assn.; Tyler A. Sch. Alumni Assn.; Assn. Prof. Supv. of Phila. Pub. Schs. *Awards*: prizes, Temple Univ., 1948; Tyler A. Sch. Alumni, 1950; Phila. A.T.Assn., 1949, 1950; Phila. Book Show, 1953 (for illus.). *Exhibited*: PAFA, 1941; Temple Univ., 1946 (one-man); Woodmere A. Gal., 1943-1946; Phila. A.T. Assn., 1946-1958; Ragan Gal., 1946; DaVinci A. All., 1948-1958; Friends Sch., 1950-1952; Phila. Book Show, 1953. Illus. "The Keystone State," 1953. *Position*: A. Supv., Sharon Hill, Pa., 1939-44; T., A. Supv., Upper Darby Pub. Sch., 1944-52; A. Supv., Tyler Sch. A., 1944-47; A. Consultant, Franklin Inst. Lab. for Research & Development, 1947- ; A., Winston Publ. Co., 1952-54; A. Supv., Phila. Pub. Schs., 1954- .

HILER, HILAIRE—Painter, C., Des.
   349 West 22nd St., New York 11, N.Y.

B. St. Paul, Minn., July 16, 1898. Studied: Univ. Pennsylvania; Univ. Denver; Univ. Paris, France; Golden State Univ., Los A., A.B.; National Col., Ontario, Canada, M.A. *Member*: F., Royal Soc. A., London, England; New Mexico Archaeological Assn.; Inter-Soc. Color Council; NSMP; SAGA; Am. Soc. for Aesthetics, and others. *Awards*: medals, Academie Latine; Soc. Acad. d'Hist. Internationale, France. *Work*: Musee du Luxembourg; Cal.PLH; Santa Barbara Mus. A.; Mus. New Mexico; MModA; Veteran's Mem. Mus., San F.; Los A. Mus. A.; Commonwealth (Ark.) Col.; Mus. Living Art, N.Y., etc. Book in "Vault of Significant Literature," Harvard Univ.; murals, Aquatic Park Casino, San F.; Grand Duc, Le Jockey, College Inn, Plantations restaurants in Paris, France; Maryland Cl. Gardens, Benning, Md.; Hotel Lafayette Game Room, N.Y.; and others. *Exhibited*: Salon des Independents; Salon d'Automne, Paris; GGE, 1939; Am. Artists European traveling exh., 1947; CAA traveling exh., 1934; Leicester Gal., London, 1926-1932; Ecole de Paris, 1929; AIC, 1946; New Mexico traveling exh., 1949; Japanese exh. of Am. Painters, 1949-50; Pittsburgh, Pa., 1926, and many others; one-man: New Gal., 1926; Dover Gal., London, 1926; Ferargil Gal., 1928; New Art Circle, 1930; Georges Petit Gal., Paris, 1932; Mellon Gal., Phila., Pa., 1932; Milwaukee AI (with Carl Holty), 1937; Veteran's Mem. Mus., San F., 1937; City of Paris Gal., San F., 1938; Cal. Inst. Tech., 1942; Argent Gal., 1942; Perls Gal., Hollywood, 1942; Santa Barbara Mus. A., 1944; Mus. New Mexico, 1945; Univ. New Mexico, 1946; Carlebach Gal., 1947; Georg Jenson, 1948; Vesuvio Gal., San F., 1949; Newark AI, 1950; L'Abbaye, Paris, 1950; Mansard Gal., London, 1955; Société de Arquitectos Mexicanos, Casa del Arquitecto, Mexico City, 1956; Galerie de l'Institut, Paris, 1957; Collectors Gal., N.Y., 1958; Provincetown A. Festival, 1958. *Position*: Hd., Dept. Des., Newark AI, Newark, N.J., 1958-59. Author: "Notes on the Technique of Painting"; "Painter's Pocket Book"; "Bibliography of Costume" (with Meyer Hiler); "Color Harmony and Pigments"; "Why Abstract?"; and others. Contributor to art and aesthetics magazines.

HILL, DOROTHY KENT—Museum Curator
   Walters Art Gallery; h. 259 West 31st St., Baltimore 11, Md.

B. New York, N.Y., Feb. 3, 1907. *Studied*: Vassar Col., A.B.; Johns Hopkins Univ., Ph.D.; Am. Sch. Classical Studies, Athens. *Member*: Archaeological Inst. Am.; CAA; Am. Oriental Soc. Contributor to: American Journal of Archaeology; College Art Journal; Journal of the Walters Art Gallery (Classical Archaeology). Author: Catalogue of Classical Bronze Sculpture in the Walters Art Gallery,

1949. Lectures: Greek, Etruscan & Roman Art. *Position*: Research Assoc., 1934-37; Assoc. Cur., Ancient Art, 1937-40; Cur., Ancient A., 1941- , Ed., Bulletin, 1948- , Walters A. Gal., Baltimore, Md.

HILL, GEORGE SNOW—Painter
   s. Box 82, Highlands, N.C.; h. 2233 Green Way South, St. Petersburg 5, Fla.

B. Munising, Mich., Nov. 13, 1898. *Studied*: Academie Colorossi, Paris, France; Mercersburg (Pa.) Acad.; Lehigh Univ.; Syracuse Univ., B.P. *Awards*: Hazard F., 1923; prizes, Clearwater Mus., 1945, 1946. *Work*: Louisville Mus.; Syracuse Mus. FA; Athens Mus. (Univ. Georgia); murals, Clearwater Mun. Auditorium; Gulfport Mun. Auditorium; USPO, Perry, Madison, Milton, Fla.; Tampa Airport; St. Petersburg City Hall; U.S. Coast Guard Station, St. Petersburg, Fla.; stained glass, St. Bartholomew Church, St. Petersburg; Methodist Church, Tarpon Springs, Fla., and paintings in many private colls. *Exhibited*: nationally & internationally. One-man: Simonson Gal., Paris, 1924; Ferargil Gal., 1927, 1929; Syracuse Mus. FA, 1927-1932; Brooks Mem. Gal., 1928; J.B. Speed Mus. A., 1928; St. Petersburg, Clearwater, Fla.; Miami Beach A. Center regularly; and others. *Position*: Dir., George S. Hill Studios (A.Sch.), St. Petersburg, Fla.; Fndr., Dir., "New Concept in Art" Gal., St. Petersburg, Fla.

HILL, HEDLEY—Associate Museum Director
   Portland Art Museum, S.W. Park at Madison St., Portland, Ore.*

HILL, HOMER—Illustrator, Comm. A., Des., P.
   564 Main St., Chatham, N.J.

B. Newark, N.J., Apr. 4, 1917. *Studied*: Parsons Sch. F. & App. A. *Member*: SI; New Jersey WC Soc; Assoc. A. of New Jersey. *Awards*: Agnes B. Noyes award, 1953; Kresge award; New Jersey WC Soc. *Work*: Newark Mus. A. *Exhibited*: Montclair A. Mus.; Riverside Mus.; AWS; Newark Mus. A.; SI, 1953 (one-man); A. Dir. Cl., N.Y. and San F. Contributor illus. to Good Housekeeping, Herald Tribune, Today's Living, Sports Afield, Woman's Home Companion, Woman's Day and other national magazines. Adv. A., for Shell Oil Co.; Nat. City Bank; RCA-Victor; Seagram, and others. Des. Minnesota Statehood Stamp for U.S. Govt.

HILL, POLLY KNIPP (Mrs. George S.)—Etcher, P., I.
   2233 Green Way South, St. Petersburg, Fla.

B. Ithaca, N.Y., Apr. 2, 1900. *Studied*: Univ. Illinois; Syracuse Univ., B.P. and with Carl Hawley, George Hess, Jeannette Scott. *Member*: Chicago Soc. Et.; Fla. Fed A.; Cal. Pr. M.; St. Petersburg A. Cl.; SAGA; Prairie Pr. M. *Awards*: prizes, SAGA 1929, 1948; Brooklyn Soc. Et., 1930-1933; Fla. Fed. A., 1933, 1944, 1950; SSAL, 1943; Gulf Coast Group, 1946; Phila. Pr. Cl., 1941; Phila. Sketch Cl., 1957; Fla. A. Group, 1951; LC, 1950. *Work*: LC; Tel-Aviv Mus., Israel; Syracuse Mus. FA; MMA; J. B. Speed Mem. Mus. and many ports. & paintings in private colls. *Exhibited*: NAD, 1927, 1929, 1935, 1940, 1944, 1946; SAGA, 1929-1944, 1948-1952; Chicago Soc. Et., 1930, 1932, 1938-1946, 1948-1952; Phila. Pr. Cl., 1930-1942; LC, 1944, 1945, 1949-50; SSAL, 1940-1946; Fla. Fed. A., 1932-1934, 1942-1945, 1948-1951; one-man: Smithsonian Inst.; Ferargil Gal., 1927, 1930; Newhouse Gal.; Syracuse Mus. FA; Speed Mem. Mus.; Brooks Mem. Mus.; Clearwater Mus. A.; Dayton AI; Miami Beach A. Center; and others; also extensively abroad. *Position*: Instr., George S. Hill Studios, St. Petersburg, Fla. and in summer at Hill Studio, Box 82, Highlands, N.C.

HILLSMITH, FANNIE—Painter, Et., Eng.
   915 Second Ave., New York 17, N.Y.

B. Boston, Mass., Mar. 13, 1911. *Studied*: BMFA Sch.; ASL, with Alexander Brook, Kuniyoshi, Zorach and Sloan; Atelier 17 with Stanley Hayter. *Member*: Am. Abstract A.; Fed. Mod. P. & S.; Berkshire AA; New Hampshire AA; AEA. *Awards*: prizes, Currier Gal. A., 1952; Berkshire Mus., 1956, 1957; Boston A. Festival, 1957; Portland Mus. A., 1958; BMFA Sch. Alumni Traveling Scholarship, 1958. *Work*: MModA; BMFA; Currier Gal. A.; Gallatin Coll.; N.Y. Pub. Lib.; FMA; AGAA. *Exhibited*: Am Abstract A., 1946-1958; Fed. Mod. P. & S., 1956-1958; AIC, 1947, 1948, 1954; VMFA, 1948; WMAA, 1949-1951, 1955; WAC, 1953, 1954; Solomon Guggenheim Mus., 1954;

Carnegie Inst., 1955; CGA, 1957; Phila. Pr. Cl.; BM; PC, 1955; Inst. Contemp. A., Boston, 1954; Dayton AI, 1954; Springfield Mus. A., 1954; Boston A. Festival, 1950-1954, 1956-1958; New Hampshire AA, 1952-1958; Berkshire AA, 1956, 1957; Univ. Illinois, 1955, 1957; USIS traveling exh., Europe, 1957; one-man: Norlyst Gal., 1943; Egan Gal., 1949, 1954; Peridot Gal., 1957; Colby Col., 1950; Milton Acad., 1952; Deerfield Acad., 1953; Currier Gal. A., 1954; Swetzoff Gal., Boston, 1949, 1950, 1957.

HILPERT, JOSEF—*Museum Director, P., L.*
de Saisset Art Gallery, University of Santa Clara, Santa Clara, Cal.

B. Kollit, Yugoslavia, Mar. 16, 1893. *Studied*: in Hungary. *Member*: Associacion de Bellas Arts, Havana, Cuba. *Work*: 200 portraits of famous men of history, de Saisset A. Gal., Univ. Santa Clara, Hall of Fame. *Exhibited*: National Exh., Toronto, Canada, 1935 (world's smallest portrait). Author: "My Life in Art," 1935; with Hall of Fame, 1957. Lectures with color slides "World Peace Through Art," "The Magnificence of the Northern Lights." *Position*: Dir., de Saisset A. Gal., and Hall of Fame, Univ. Santa Clara, Santa Clara, Cal.

HILTON, ROY—*Painter, E.*
19 Forsyth Rd., Pittsburgh 20, Pa.

B. Boston, Mass., Feb. 24, 1891. *Studied*: Pape Sch. A.; Fenway Sch. Boston; & with Charles Woodbury. *Awards*: prizes, Assoc. A. Pittsburgh, 1932, 1941. *Work*: murals, USPO, Westfield, N.J.; Rockymount, Va. *Exhibited*: Carnegie Inst., 1948, 1949; Univ. Illinois, 1952; Denver A. Mus., 1952. *Position*: Instr., Carnegie Inst. Tech., Pittsburgh, Pa. (retired 1957).

HIMLER, MARY MARTHA—*Painter, Ser., T., L., Cr.*
10 North Ligonier St., Latrobe, Pa.

B. Greensburg, Pa., June 28, 1890. *Studied*: Pa. State Univ.; T. Col., Indiana, Pa.; Univ. Pittsburgh; Carnegie Inst.; Columbia Univ., & with Leon Winslow, Edmund Ashe, Frank Bicknell. *Member*: Nat. Edu. Assn. *Awards*: prizes, Assoc. A. Pittsburgh, 1934; Greensburg AC, 1935-1939, 1943, 1946; All. A. of Johnstown, 1946; Ebensburg Fair, 1939. and others. *Work*: Pub.Lib., High Sch., Latrobe, Pa.; Assoc. A. Pittsburgh; Pennsylvania State Univ. *Exhibited*: Assoc. A. Pittsburgh, 1925-1957; Butler AI, 1937, 1943, 1945, 1946; All. A. Johnstown, 1946; Greensburg AC, 1934-1957; Indiana (Pa.) State T. Col., 1943-1946. *Position*: Hd. A. Dept. (Emeritus), Latrobe Pub. Sch., Latrobe, Pa. (Retired). A. T., Latrobe Recreation Bd. Adult Edu.

HIMMEL, KALMAN EDWARD—*Painter, E.*
371 Forest St., Park Forest, Ill.

B. Chicago, Ill., Oct. 13, 1903. *Studied*: AIC. *Award*: prize, AIC, 1946; Greater No. Michigan Exh., 1956. *Exhibited*: AIC, 1934, 1940-1952, 1954, 1955; Mississippi Valley A.; Illinois State Mus., 1940; Milwaukee AI, 1946; Univ. Colorado, 1949; Univ. Kansas City, 1949; Rochester Mem. A. Gal., 1947, 1949; J. B. Speed Mem. Mus., 1949; Carnegie Inst., 1949; Univ. Indiana, 1949; Currier Gal. A., 1949; Munson-Williams-Proctor Inst., 1949; Dayton AI, 1949; Swope Gal., A., 1946; Dallas Mus. FA, 1947; Dartmouth Col., 1947; Western Col., Oxford, Ohio, 1948; Rochester Pub. Lib., 1948; BMA, 1948; Hamline Univ., 1948; Beloit Col., 1948; Renaissance Soc., Univ. Chicago, 1946, 1948-1951, 1953-1955; Illinois State Fair, 1950, 1951. *Position*: Instr. Painting, AIC Sch. A., Chicago, Ill.

HIMMELFARB, SAMUEL—*Painter, Des., L.*
4132 West Belmont St., Chicago 41, Ill.; h. Winfield, Ill.

B. Latvia, July 4, 1905. *Studied*: Wisconsin Sch. FA; Univ. Wisconsin; NAD; ASL. *Awards*: prizes, Wisconsin State Fair; Milwaukee AI (purchase); AIC. *Work*: Milwaukee AI. *Exhibited*: AIC, 1938-1957; Chicago A. Cl., 1952-1955; AFA; Old Northwest Terr., Springfield, 1953; Navy Pier Show, 1957 now on tour in France; one-man: Milwaukee AI; Esquire Theatre, Chicago.

HINCKLEY, LAWRENCE BRADFORD—*Painter, L., Des.*
416 Bard St., Fillmore, Cal.

B. Fillmore, Cal., Nov. 29, 1900. *Studied*: Otis AI. *Member*: Cal. WC Cl.; Laguna Beach AA; Santa Bar-

bara AA; 29 Palms A. Gld. *Awards*: prizes, Cal. State Fair, 1940-1947; Otis AI, 1941; San Fernando Valley AA, 1944. *Work*: Santa Barbara Mus. A.; Santa Paula (Cal.) H.S.; Santa Paula City Coll. *Exhibited*: GGE, 1939; Laguna Beach AA; San Diego FA Soc., 1941; Los A. Mus. A.; Cal. WC Soc., traveling exh., 1948; Santa Cruz, 1948; one-man: Stendahl Gal., Los A., 1939; Scripps Col., 1939; Padua Hills, Cal., 1940; Laguna Beach AA, 1940-1942; Santa Barbara Mus. A., 1951. *Position*: Founder, Dir., Artists' Barn and A. Center, Fillmore, Cal., 1936- .

HINKHOUSE, FOREST MELICK—*Museum Director*
Phoenix Art Museum, 45 East Coronado St.; h. 146 East Coronado St., Phoenix, Ariz.

B. West Liberty, Iowa, July 7, 1925. *Studied*: Coe Col., A.B.; Univ. Mexico; Harvard Univ. (Fogg Mus. Research); N.Y. Univ., Inst. FA, M.A.; Univ. Madrid, Ph.D. *Member*: del Claustro Extraordinario, Madrid; CAA; AAMus. Author, A. Cr., Buffalo Evening News; Arizona Republic; Phoenix Gazette. Lectures: Spanish Painting; Mediaeval Art; Art of the Far East; Contemporary Art. Assembled exhs.: "Industrial Gouaches of John Hultberg," 1957; "Paintings & Portraits by Frank Mason," 1958; "Contemporary Arizona Painting," 1958; "Festival of Arts," 1958. *Positions*: Pub. Rel., International House Assn., New York; Asst. Prof., Albright A. Sch., Univ. Buffalo, 1956-57; Dir., Phoenix A. Mus. & Phoenix FA Assn., 1957- .

HINKLE, CATHERINE (Mrs. Richard Koppe)—*Painter, Des., I.*
Scott, Foresman & Co., 433 East Erie St.; h. 4144 North Clarendon Ave., Chicago 13, Ill.

B. St. Joseph, Mich., Jan. 20, 1926. *Studied*: Kalamazoo Col.; Inst. Design, Chicago, B.A.; and with Lazlo Moholy-Nagy; Alexander Archipenko; Richard Koppe; Emerson Woelffer. *Exhibited*: BM, 1951; SAM, 1951; Serigraph Gal., N.Y., 1951, 1952; Exhibition Momentum, Chicago, 1950, 1952-1954; AIC, 1952, 1955-1958; one-man: Well of the Sea Gal., Chicago, 1950, 1951; 750 Studio, Chicago, 1952.

HINKLE, CLARENCE—*Painter, T.*
1415 Hillcrest Rd., Santa Barbara, Cal.

B. Auburn, Cal., June 19, 1880. *Studied*: PAFA. *Awards*: Cresson award, 1906; prizes, Cal. AC, 1944; med., Oakland A. Gal., 1945; Los A. Mus. A., 1945. *Work*: San Diego FA Soc.; Los A. Mus. A.; Santa Barbara Mus. A.; de Young Mem. Mus.; Crocker A. Gal., Sacramento, Cal.; Encyclopaedia Britannica Coll. *Exhibited*: Carnegie Inst., 1944, 1945; Santa Barbara Mus. A., 1944 (one-man), 1952.*

HINSHAW, BERNARD—*Educator*
Lewis & Clark College, Portland, Ore.

Position: Chm., Art Dept., Lewis & Clark College.*

HINTERMEISTER, HY (HENRY)—*Comm. A., I., P.*
9 Warren Ave., Tuckahoe 7, N.Y.

B. New York, N.Y., June 10, 1897. *Studied*: PIASch.; ASL. *Member*: AWS.

HIOS, THEO(DORE)—*Painter, Gr.*
347 West 29th St., New York 1, N.Y.

B. Sparta, Greece, Feb. 2, 1910. *Studied*: Am. A. Sch.; ASL. *Member*: Fed. Mod. P. & S. *Award*: prize, Silvermine Gld. A., 1952. *Work*: Parrish Mus.; Tel-Aviv Mus., Israel; North Carolina State A. Gal.; and in private colls. *Exhibited*: Critics' Show, 1946; BM, 1947; Traveling exh. U.S. Marines at War, U.S. and England; Traveling exh., AFA, 1954-1956; Fed. Mod. P. & S., 1950-1958; Gld. Hall, Easthampton, N.Y., 1949-1958; Parrish Mus., 1949-1958; Audubon A., 1947; Terry AI, 1951; Toledo Mus. A., 1946; one-man: Silvermine Gld. A., 1949, 1952; North Carolina State A. Gal., 1947; Weatherspoon Gal., 1947; Contemporary A. Gal., N.Y., 1946, 1947, 1950; Chase Gal., N.Y., 1957; Hudson Gld., 1949, and others.

HIROTA, SUSUMU—*Painter*
163a Granite St., Rockport, Mass.

B. Hane, Kochi, Japan, Dec. 18, 1898. *Member*: Rockport AA, 1941; New Haven Paint & Clay Cl., 1946.

Awards: Rockport AA, 1941, 1946, 1951; New Haven Paint & Clay Cl., 1946. *Work*: BMFA. *Exhibited*: AIC, 1936, 1940, 1941; CGA, 1939, 1941; WFNY 1939; PAFA, 1941, 1942; Inst. Mod. A., Boston; Bowdoin Col.; Univ. Utah; R.i.Sch.Des.; Toledo Mus. A.; All. A. Am.; Boston A. Festival.

HIRSCH, DAVID W. (DAVE)—*Cartoonist*
150-29 72nd Rd., Flushing 67, L.I., N.Y.

B. New York, N.Y., Dec. 26, 1919. *Studied*: Brooklyn Col.; ASL; Grand Central A. Sch.; Cartoonists & Illus. Sch. *Member*: Nat. Cartoonists Soc. Contributor cartoons to Sat. Eve. Post; Look; Christian Science Monitor; Argosy; American Legion Magazine; U.S. Inf. Agency Russian publication "America"; True; Ladies Home Journal; American Weekly; Sports Illustrated; Wall St. Journal; King Features Syndicate; MacNaught Syndicate.

HIRSCH, JOSEPH—*Painter, Lith.*
90 Riverside Drive, New York 24, N.Y.

B. Philadelphia, Pa., Apr. 25, 1910. *Studied*: PMSchIA, and with George Luks, Henry Hensche. *Member*: NA; Phila. WC Cl.; AEA. *Awards*: prizes, PAFA, 1934; F., Inst. Intl. Edu., 1935, 1936; WFNY 1939; Guggenheim F., 1942-43, 1943-44; LC, 1944, 1945; Grant, Am. Acad. A. & Let., 1947; Fulbright F., 1949; MMA, 1950; AIC, 1951; gold medal, Alumni Assn. of PMSch.A., 1958; Carnegie Inst., 1947. *Work*: WMAA; MModA; PMA; BMFA; CGA; AGAA; LC; Univ. Arizona; Encyclopaedia Britannica; IBM; Walker A. Center; DMFA; Nelson Gal. A.; Dartmouth Univ.; Springfield Mus. A.; Am. Acad. A. & Lets.; Chrysler Corp.; Brown Univ.; Utah State Agricultural Col.; Univ. Oklahoma; Univ. Georgia; Mus. Military History, Wash., D.C.; MMA; murals, Benjamin Franklin H.S., Phila., Pa.; Amalgamated Clothing Workers Bldg., Phila., Pa.; Phila. Mun. Court Bldg.; Documentary Paintings, U.S. Govt. *Exhibited*: nationally since 1934. *Position*: Instr., Am. A. Sch., New York, N.Y.; Instr., Painting, Seminar, Univ. Utah, 1959 (June, July).

HIRSCH, RICHARD—*Museum Director, T., Gr.*
Pensacola Art Center, 407 South Jefferson St., Pensacola, Fla.

B. Denver, Colo., Sept. 12, 1914. *Studied*: Ecole du Louvre, Ecole des Beaux-Arts, Ecole des Arts Decoratifs, all Paris, France. *Member*: Southern A. Mus. Dir. Assn. (Chm.); Southeastern Mus. Conf. (council memb.); AAMus.; AFA; Print Council of Am.; Fla. Pub. Rel. Assn. *Work*: engravings & etchings: Cabinet des Estampes, Bibliotheque Nationale, Paris; Musee de Versailles; Norton Gal. A., West Palm Beach. *Engravings*: Tricentenary of Louis XIV, Versailles, 1938; Salon de la Signature, Gallerie Doree, Versailles, 1939; Stage settings for the Theatre des Ambassadeurs; Les Compagnons de Jeux; Theatre Michel; Theatre de Versailles, 1932-38; stained glass designs, wood cut illus. for gospels: Atelier de l'Eau Vive, Versailles, 1936-39; mural, Pensacola Quadricentennial Historical Exh., 1958. Research and Collaboration: "Romance of French Weaving," Paul Rodier, 1930; "Reasons for France," John Brangwyn. Art lectures to college seminars, professional groups, TV, museum conferences, etc. Organizes about twelve shows a year for Pensacola Art Center. *Positions*: Freelance graphic arts, 1934-38; Publisher of Graphics, 1937-39 & 1945-46, Paris; A. Ed. for many periodicals; Dir., Pensacola Art Center, Pensacola, Fla., at present.

HIRSCH, STEFAN—*Educator, P., Gr., L.*
Bard College, Annandale-on-Hudson, N.Y.

B. Nuremberg, Germany, Jan. 2, 1899. *Studied*: Univ. Zurich, Switzerland, and with Hamilton Easter Field. *Member*: NSMP; Brooklyn Soc. A.; Am. A. Cong.; AFA; Audubon A; Am. Assn. Univ. Prof.; CAA; Am. Soc. for Aesthetics; Comm. on A. Edu. *Awards*: Fulbright Fellowship, Univ. of Baroda, India, 1956-57. *Work*: WMAA; Newark Mus.; WMA; PMG; Harrison Gal., Los A. Cal.; Dartmouth Col.; Milwaukee AI; SAM; MMA; Municipal Mus., Ahmenabad, India; murals, Auditorium, Lenox Hill Assn.; U.S. Court House, Aiken, S.C.; USPO, Booneville, Miss. *Exhibited*: Soc. Indp. A., 1919, 1920; Salons of Am., 1921-1930; Carnegie Inst.; CGA; PAFA; WMAA; AIC; WFNY 1939; Manchester, Vt., 1935-1939. Lectures: "An Appraisal of Modern Art Education"; "What Should the College Expect of the High School?"; "Painting and the Graphic Arts"; "Art as Communication." *Positions*:

Bd. Dir., CAA; Ed. Bd., College Art Journal; Instr. FA, Chm. A. Div., Bennington Col., Vt., 1934-40; Instr., ASL, New York, N.Y., 1940-42; Asst. Prof., 1942-44, 1944-45, Assoc. Prof., 1945-46, Prof. A., Chm. A. Div., Bard Col., Annandale-on-Hudson, N.Y., 1946- .

HIRSCH, WILLARD—*Sculptor, L.*
17 Exchange St.; h. 207 Broad St., Charleston, S.C.

B. Charleston, S.C., Nov. 19, 1905. *Studied*: Col. of Charleston; BAID; NAD. *Member*: AEA; South Carolina A. Gld. *Awards*: prizes, South Carolina A. Gld., 1951, 1955. *Work*: Lincoln Hospital, New York; IBM; Columbia (S.C.) Mus. A.; relief, Nat. Guard Armory, Mullins, S.C.; Clemson Col.; Richland County Pub. Lib., Col. of S.C.; Home Fed. Savings & Loan Co. and American Mutual Fire Ins. Co., both Charlotte, S.C., and work in private homes. *Exhibited*: Syracuse Mus. FA, 1948; NAD, 1935, 1942; PAFA, 1942, 1952; Fairmount Park, Phila., 1949; WMAA, 1950; Wichita AA, 1949; South Carolina A., Gibbes A. Gal., 1947-1952; one-man: Columbia Mus. A., 1952; Gibbes A. Gal., 1943, 1945, 1946, 1951; Telfair Acad., 1953; Florence (S.C.) Mus. A., 1954; Mint Mus. A., Charlotte, N.C., 1957. *Position*: Instr., S., Charleston A. Sch., Charleston, S.C.

HIRSCHFELD, ALBERT—*Caricaturist, I., W., Gr.*
122 East 95th St., New York 28, N.Y.

B. St. Louis, Mo., June 21, 1903. *Studied*: NAD; London County Council; ASL. *Member*: SI. *Work*: MMA; FMA; N.Y. Pub. Lib.; Mus. City of New York; CAM; BM; Musee d'Art Populaire Juif, Paris; Habima Mus., Israel; MMod.A; Roosevelt Mem., Hyde Park, N.Y.; Baseball Mus., Cooperstown, N.Y.; murals, Fifth Avenue Playhouse, N.Y.; Eden Roc Hotel, Miami, Fla.; Sardi's East, N.Y.; Manhattan Playbill Room; American Pavilion, World's Fair, Brussels, 1958. *Exhibited*: nationally and internationally. Author, I., "Manhattan Oases," 1932; "Harlem," 1941; "Show Business is No Business," 1951; "Westward Ha!" with S. J. Perelman, 1948. Author, Cart., I., to N.Y. Times; Colliers; Holiday; Life magazines. *Position*: Theatre Caricaturist, New York Times, 1926- .

HIRSCHFIELD, HARRY—*Illustrator*
122 East 42nd St., New York 17, N.Y.
Member: SI.*

HISE, ALBERT E.—*Museum Curator*
Massillon Museum, 212 Lincoln Way East, Massillon, Ohio*

HITCHCOCK, HENRY-RUSSELL—
Educator, Historian, Cr., Mus. Dir.
Smith College Museum of Art, Northampton, Mass.; h. 111 South St., Northampton, Mass.

B. Boston, Mass., June 3, 1903. *Studied*: Harvard Col., A.B.; Harvard Grad. Sch., M.A. *Member*: Am. Soc. Arch. Hist. *Awards*: F., Harvard Univ., 1924-1925; Carnegie traveling F., 1928-1929; Guggenheim F., 1945-1946; Hon. Corres. Member, Royal Inst. British Arch., 1946. Author: "In the Nature of Materials, the Buildings of Frank Lloyd Wright," 1942; "Early Victorian Architecture in Britain," 1954; "Architecture: 19th and 20th Centuries," & many other books on architecture. Contributor to: Journals, bulletins, newspapers & magazines, with articles & reviews of art & architecture. Lectures at univ., col., & museums. *Position*: Asst. Prof. A., Vassar Col., 1927-28; Asst. Prof. A., 1929-40, Assoc. Prof. A., 1940- , Wesleyan Univ., Middletown, Conn.; L., MIT, 1946-1949; Yale Univ., 1951-52; Prof. A., Smith Col., 1948- ; Dir., Smith Col. Mus. A., 1949-55; Pres. Soc. Arch. Hist., 1952-54; Hon. Corresponding Member, Royal Inst. British Arch., 1950- .

HITCHCOCK, HOWARD GILBERT—*Educator, S.*
Union College, Barbourville, Ky.

B. Ava, Mo., Aug. 20, 1927. *Studied*: College of Puget Sound, B.A.; Univ. Washington, M.F.A., and with Archipenko. *Member*: Kentucky A. Edu. Assn.; Western AA; NAEA. *Awards*: prizes, Northwest Painters scholarship award, Seattle, 1952; ceramic purchase prize, Louisville, Ky., 1954. *Work*: ceramic sc., J.B. Speed A. Mus. *Exhibited*: Louisville A. Center, 1954, 1955. Contributor to Intercollegian and Motive magazines, with reproduction of work. *Position*: Instr. A. & Crafts, Sue Bennett Col., London, Ky., 1953-54; Asst. Prof. A., Union Col., Barbourville, Ky., 1954- .*

HOAG, MRS. C. B. *See Bradshaw, Alexandra Christine*

HOBBIE, LUCILLE—Painter, Lith., T.
Talmadge Road, Mendham, N.J.

B. Boonton, N.J., June 14, 1915. *Member*: AWS; New Jersey WC Soc. *Awards*: prizes, Montclair A. Mus., 1951, 1952, 1953; Seton Hall Univ., 1954; NAC, 1958; Newark A. Cl., 1954; Irvington Mus., 1951, 1952; New Jersey WC Soc., 1956; silver medal, New Jersey WC Soc., 1958. *Work*: Montclair A. Mus.; Williamsburg Fnd., Va. *Exhibited*: NAD, 1956; Audubon A., 1953, 1955, 1957; Trenton State Mus., 1956; Montclair A. Mus., 1947, 1950-1953, 1956, 1958; NAC, 1958; Seton Hall Univ., 1954, 1956, 1958; Nat. Soc. Painters in Casein, 1956, 1958; Jersey City Mus., 1948, 1949; Irvington Mus. A., 1947-1949; Riverside Mus., 1951; Newark A. Cl.; New Jersey WC Soc.; Knickerbocker A.; AAPL; Catherine L. Wolfe A. Cl., and others.

HOBSON, KATHERINE THAYER—Sculptor
27 West 67th St., New York 23, N.Y.

B. Denver, Colo., April 11, 1889. *Studied*: ASL, and in Europe; sculpture with Walter Sintenis, Dresden. *Member*: NSS; All. A. Am.; Arch. Lg.; Hudson Valley AA; Pen & Brush Cl.; AAPL. *Work*: statues, Bahnhofsplatz, Gottingen; Univ. Konigsberg and Gottingen; Sch. Tech., Dresden; Univ. Lib., Gottingen; St. James Church, New York, N.Y. *Exhibited*: Salon de Artistes Francaises, Paris, 1914; NAD, 1942-1944, 1949, 1951, 1952, 1954, 1955; All. A. Am., 1946, 1949-1955; Audubon A., 1945, 1952; NAWA, 1944-1950; Pen & Brush Cl., 1947-1955; Princeton, N.J., 1933; Cooperstown, N.Y., 1948-1951; NSS, 1950-1952, 1954; AAPL. Lectures on Roman and Gothic Sculpture. *Position*: Sec., FA Assn., New York, N.Y., 1952-58.

HOCKER, TREW—Painter, Des., Gr.
174 Bleecker St., New York 12, N.Y.; h. Byram Lake Rd., Mount Kisco, N.Y.

B. Sedalia, Mo., June 17, 1913. *Studied*: Univ. Missouri; Kansas City AI; Grande Chaumiere, Paris, and with Othon Friesz, Fernand Leger, Andre L'Hote, Thomas Benton. *Member*: AEA; United Scenic A.; Nat. Soc. Interior Des. *Work*: USPO, St. Louis, Mo. NBC Staff Des. of Scenery for TV productions. *Exhibited*: Kansas City AI, 1938; NGA, 1945; NAD, 1948; BM, 1950.

HODGE, STUART—Educator, P., Et.
Art Department, Michigan State University; h. 1625 Ann St., East Lansing, Mich.

B. Worcester, Mass. *Studied*: Yale Sch. FA, B.F.A.; Cranbrook Acad. A., M.F.A.; State Univ. of Iowa, Ph.D. *Member*: CAA; Mich. Acad. Sc., A. & Lets. *Exhibited*: in Missouri, Michigan and Western Michigan Annuals; oneman: Paris, France, 1953. *Position*: Prof. A., A. Dept., Michigan State University, East Lansing, Mich.

HODGELL, ROBERT OVERMAN—
Printmaker, Des., P., I., C., Comm. A.
Rt. 2, Waunakee, Wis.

B. Mankato, Kans., July 14, 1922. *Studied*: Univ. Wisconsin, B.S., M.S.; Dartmouth Col.; State Univ. of Iowa; Univ. Illinois; Universidad Michoacana, Mexico. *Member*: SAGA; Madison AA; Soc. Typographic A.; Intl. Des. Conference; FA Comm. of Nat. Council of Churches; Kansas State Fed. A.; Des Moines A. Center. *Work*: Joslyn A. Mus.; Dartmouth Col.; Wisconsin Union; Topeka A. Gld.; Kansas State T. Col.; Kansas State Col.; LC; Des Moines A. Center; Rochester Mem. A. Gal.; MMA. *Exhibited*: Albany Pr. Cl., 1947, 1951; SAGA, 1947, 1950-1955-1957; Wash. WC Cl., 1948; Northwest Pr. M., 1949, 1953; Phila. Pr. Cl., 1950, 1953; Portland Soc. A., 1950; Butler AI, 1951; BM, 1951, 1953; Wichita, Kans., 1951, 1953; Soc. Wash. Pr. M., 1951, 1956; Wis. State Fair, 1947, 1957; Ball State T. Col., 1957; Bradley Univ., 1952, 1953; Nat. Ser. Soc., 1952, 1953; LC, 1948, 1952, 1957; Western A., 1948, 1953; Kansas Painters, 1949-1953, 1957; Mid-Am. A., 1950, 1951, 1955; Walker

A. Center, 1951; Wisconsin Salon, 1942, 1953, 1955-1957; Kansas Fair, 1935-1943, 1947; Six States Exh., 1943, 1944, 1946, 1947; Topeka A. Gld., 1947, 1949, 1950, 1953; Madison AA, 1948-1953, 1957, 1958; Audubon A., 1953; Springfield A. Mus., 1953; DMFA, 1953; Decatur A. Mus., 1955-1957; Illinois State Fair, 1953, 1954, 1956, 1957. Illus., "Caboose on the Roof," 1956; "The Buzzing Bees," 1957; "Tree House at Seven Oaks," 1957; textbooks for USAFI; Motive Magazine; Playboy Magazine. *Position*: Instr., Des Moines A. Center, Des Moines, Iowa, 1949-53; Asst. A. Dir., in charge of Illus., "Our Wonderful World," Champaign, Ill., 1953-56; A. Dir., Editorial & Communication Services, Ext. Div., Univ. Wisconsin, Madison, Wis., 1957- .

HODGIN, MARSTON DEAN—Educator, P.
Miami University; h. 210 Tallawanda Rd., Oxford, Ohio

B. Cambridge, Ohio, Dec. 3, 1903. *Studied*: Earlham Col., A.B.; Indiana Univ.; Univ. Chicago, and with J.R. Hopkins, Charles Hawthorne. *Member*: Richmond AA; Provincetown AA. *Awards*: prizes, Dayton AI, 1953, 1954; Richmond AA, 1952, 1955. *Work*: Dayton AI; Earlham Col.; Richmond AA. *Exhibited*: Butler AI, 1948; Richmond AA, 1922-1958; Provincetown AA, 1948-1958; CM, 1949-1952; Old Northwest Territory Exh., 1951. *Position*: Hd. A. Dept., Miami Univ., Oxford, Ohio, 1927- .

HOE, MABEL KENT—Painter, S.
211 Miln St., Cranford, N.J.

B. Cranford, N.J., Jan. 27, 1880. *Studied*: ASL; & with Archipenko, Arthur Lee, Bridgman, Miller, Nicolaides. *Member*: NAWA; Asbury Park Soc. FA. *Awards*: prize NAWA, 1936. *Exhibited*: NAWA; Montclair A. Mus.; AAPL; & in Asbury Park, Spring Lake, Newark, N.J. Instr. Painting, VA Hospitals.

HOECKNER, CARL—Painter, Gr.
352 East 86th St., New York 28, N.Y.

B. Munich, Germany, Dec. 19, 1883. *Studied*: in Germany. *Member*: Chicago Soc. Et.; AEA. *Awards*: prizes, AIC. *Work*: LC; murals, Portland, Ore.; Coonley Sch., Downers Grove, Ill. *Exhibited*: NAD; AIC, and other national exhibitions.*

HOEFLICH, SHERMAN CLARK—Designer, T., P.
4 South 15th St. (2); h. 2316 Delancey Place, Philadelphia 3, Pa.

B. Philadelphia, Pa., Mar. 1, 1913. *Studied*: PAFA; PMSch.A., with Henry Pitz; Univ. Pennsylvania; Grande Chaumiere, Paris. *Member*: Nat. Soc. A. Dir.; A. Dir. Cl., Phila.; Phila. A. Gld. (Bd. Dir.). *Exhibited*: A. Dir. Cl., 1953, 1954, 1956-1958; Phila. A. All., 1955, 1958.

HOEHN, HARRY—Painter, Des., Gr.
24 Compass Lane, Levittown, N.Y.

B. New York, N.Y., Sept. 30, 1918. *Studied*: Atelier 17; ASL, and in Mexico. *Awards*: prizes, BM; Phila. Pr. Cl. *Work*: BM; PMA; MModA. *Exhibited*: WMAA; MModA; BM, and in other museums and colleges. Author, I., "The Man Who Stood on His Hands," 1953.

HOENING, MARGARET [Mrs. Jared French]—
Painter, Et.
5 St. Luke's Place, New York 14, N.Y.

B. Hoboken, N.J. *Studied*: Smith Col., B.A.; ASL, with Allen Lewis, Harry Wickey, Charles Locke, William von Schlegell. *Work*: Lib. Cong. *Exhibited*: SAGA; NAD; AIC.

HOERGER, D. ADELBERT—Designer, P.
Roman Bronze Corp., 96-18—43rd Ave., Corona, N.Y.; h. 130-23—224th St., Laurelton 13, L.I., N.Y.

B. Philadelphia, Pa., Apr. 21, 1899. *Studied*: Temple Univ.; Queen's Col.; N.Y. Univ.; & with Samuel Yellin, Victor Van Lossberg, Riccardo Bertelli. *Member*: Arch. L.; Art in Trades Cl. of N.Y.; Soc. of Designer-Craftsmen. *Work*: U.S. Naval Acad.; Yale Univ.; mem. fountain, Phila., Pa.; Dept. Justice Bldg., Wash., D.C.; Cathedral St. John the Divine, N.Y. Lectures: Metalwork; Wrought

Iron; etc. *Position*: Des., Roman Bronze Corp., Corona, N.Y.; Edw. F. Caldwell & Co., N.Y.; Graff Washbourne & Dunn, N.Y.; Lighting by Fedor, N.Y., and others.

HOFER, PHILIP—*Museum Secretary, Des., W., L., T.*

Harvard Library; h. 88 Appleton St., Cambridge 38, Mass.

B. Cincinnati, Ohio, Mar. 14, 1898. *Studied*: Pomfret Sch., Conn.; Harvard Col., A.B.; Harvard Univ., A.M. *Member*: Atheneum, London; Am. Acad. A. & Sciences; Grolier Cl.; Century Assn.; Cl. of Odd Volumes, Boston; Council of Foreign Relations, N.Y. Ed. & Co-Author: "The Drawings of Fragonard," 1947; Author: "A Survey of Baroque Illustration," 1951. Contributor to Gazette des Beaux-Arts; Print Collector's Quarterly; The Colophon & New Colophon; Harvard Library Bulletin, and others. Lectures on Graphic Arts. *Positions*: Trustee: Corning Glass Mus., Parsons Sch. Des., BMFA, Boston Atheneum, Groton Sch., Boys' Cl. of Boston; Sec., Fogg A. Mus., Harvard Univ., 1949- , Rhinelander Fnd.; Advisor, Spencer Coll., N.Y. Pub. Lib., 1930-34; Asst. Dir., Morgan Lib., 1934-38; Cur., Founder, Dept. Graphic A., Harvard Lib., 1938- ; L. FA, Harvard Univ., 1938- .

HOFF, SYD—*Cartoonist*

4335 Post Ave., Miami Beach, Fla.

B. New York, N.Y., Sept. 4, 1912. Illus., "Feeling No Pain," 1944; Author, I., "Oops! Wrong Party," 1950; "Oops! Wrong Stateroom," 1953; "Okay, You Can Look Now!," 1955; "It's Fun Learning Cartooning With Hoff," 1952; "Mom, I'm Home," 1946; "Eight Little Artists," 1954; "Patty's Pet," 1955; "Danny and the Dinosaur," 1953. Creator of daily newspaper panel "Laugh It Off," King Features Syndicate. Contributor to New Yorker, Look, Esquire and other national magazines.

HOFFMAN, EDWARD FENNO, III—*Sculptor*

501 Conestoga Rd.; h. 353 Oak Terrace, Wayne, Pa.

B. Philadelphia, Pa., Oct. 20, 1916. *Studied*: PAFA; Henry Clews Mem. A. Fnd., La Napoule, France. *Member*: F., PAFA; Phila. A. All; NSS; AAPL (Pres. Pa. Chptr.); Grand Central A. Gal. *Awards*: Cresson traveling scholarship, 1948; Tiffany Fnd. grant, 1950; prizes, NAD, 1951; Phila., Pa., 1954; Woodmere A. Gal., 1955. *Work*: mem. tablet, Villanova Univ.; war mem., Pa. Hospital; Lansdowne, Pa.; Brookgreen Gardens, S.C.; St. Alban's Church, Newtown Square, Pa.; Col. of Physicians, Phila., Pa.; Trinity Episcopal Church, Swarthmore, Pa.; St. Mary's Church, Wayne, Pa.; Am. Episcopal Cathedral, Rome; La Napoule, France; Huntington Mus., W. Va.; Grand Central A. Gal. *Exhibited*: La Napoule, France, 1953-54; NAD, 1955, 1956; one-man: Phila. A. All., 1956; Bryn Mawr A. Center, 1956; Grand Central A. Gal., 1956; AAPL, 1957, 1958.

HOFFMAN, FLORICE W.—*Painter*

691A Colorado Ave., Palo Alto, Cal.

B. Scranton, Pa., Aug. 26, 1893. *Studied*: Cal. Sch. FA; ASL; Parsons Sch. Des., Paris, France. *Member*: Cal. WC Soc.; San F. Women A. *Exhibited*: Riverside Mus. I., articles for New York Times. *Position*: Instr., Ceramics, S. Palo Alto Pub. Sch., Palo Alto, Cal.*

HOFFMAN, FRANK B.—*Painter, S., I.*

Hobby Horse Rancho, Taos, N.M.

B. Chicago, Ill., Aug. 28, 1888. *Studied*: with Wellington Reynolds, Leon Gaspard, John Singer Sargeant. *Exhibited*: AIC; Harwood Gal., Taos, N.M.

HOFFMAN, FRANK V.—*Painter, L., S.*

Lakeside, Mich.; h. 313 Wisconsin St., Chicago 14, Ill.

B. New York, N.Y., Feb. 20, 1902. *Studied*: Otis AI; AIC. *Member*: Chicago A. Cl.; NSMP. *Awards*: prizes, Hoosier Salon, 1939. *Work*: Int. Des. & Reliefs, Elkhart (Ind.) Hotel; murals, Baptist Church, Chicago; St. Anthony's Church, Panama; St. Paul & Lowry Hotel, St. Paul, Minn.; Mus. Sc. & Indst., Chicago; hotels in Austin, Tex., Davenport, Iowa, Peoria, Ill.; Duquesne Univ., Pittsburgh; Mus. Sc. & Indst., Chicago. *Exhibited*: AIC, 1938-1946, 1953; Soc. Indp. A., 1937-1942; Chicago A. Cl., 1954-1956, 1957, 1958; Tavern Cl., Chicago (one-man). Lectures: The Baroque in the Americas; The Aesthetics of Mural Painting.

HOFFMAN, HARRY L.—*Painter*

Old Lyme, Conn.

B. Cressona, Pa., 1874. *Studied*: Yale Univ., A.B.; ASL; Julian Acad., Paris, France; & with DuMond, Laurens. *Member*: ANA; NAC; AWCS; New Haven Paint & Clay Cl.; Lyme AA. *Awards*: gold med., Pan-Pacific Exp., 1915; prizes, New Haven Paint & Clay Cl.; Lyme AA. *Work*: Milwaukee AI; AIC; Boston City Cl.; NGA; Oshkosh Pub. Mus.; NAC.

HOFFMAN, HARRY ZEE—

Painter, T., Comm. A., I., Cart.

700 West 33rd St., Baltimore 11, Md.

B. Baltimore, Md., Dec. 5, 1908. *Studied*: Univ. Maryland, Ph.G.; Maryland Inst.; PIASch., and with Robert Brackman, Aldro Hibbard, Bernard Meyers. *Member*: AEA; Balt. WC Soc. *Awards*: prizes, Balt. Evening Sun, 1934, 1935, 1940, 1942, 1945; Outdoor A. Festival, 1957. *Exhibited*: PAFA, 1941, 1953; Balt. WC Soc., 1939, 1940, 1942, 1949, 1957, 1958; Albany Inst. Hist. & A., 1945; Audubon A., 1945; Laguna Beach AA, 1945, 1949; Irvington A. & Mus. Assn., 1946; Maryland Inst., 1934, 1936; Mun. Mus. Balt., 1941-1945, 1948-1952; A. Un., 1946; BMA, 1936, 1937, 1939, 1940-1946, 1949-1951, 1954, 1955; Timonium Fair, 1950; Balt. A. Dir. Cl., 1952; Terry AI, 1952; Ogunquit A. Center, 1953; Peale Mus. A., 1954, 1955; Creative Gal., 1954; Wash. WC Cl., 1954; Martick Gal., Balt., 1955 (one-man); "Racing at Laurel" exh., 1956, 1957; Outdoor A. Festival, 1957.

HOFFMAN, IRWIN D.—*Portrait Painter, Lith., Et.*

54 West 74th St., New York 23, N.Y.

B. Boston, Mass., Mar. 8, 1901. *Studied*: BMFA Sch. *Member*: SAGA. *Awards*: Page traveling F., BMFA, 1924; prize, SAGA; John Taylor Arms award, 1938; Pennell purchase prize, LC, 1938-1940. *Work*: Kansas City AI; mural, Colorado Sch. of Mines, Golden, Colo. *Exhibited*: WMAA; New Sch. for Social Research; BM; PAFA; Los A. Mus. A.; Valentine Mus.; Honolulu Acad. A.; Dayton AI; Phila. SE; SAGA; Assoc. Am. A., 1939, 1945, 1952; Newhouse Gal., 1937; Ferargil Gal., 1929; Milch Gal., 1930; many one-man exhs. Ports. of prominent persons.

HOFFMAN, MALVINA—*Sculptor*

157 East 35th St., New York 16, N.Y.

B. New York, N.Y., June 15, 1887. *Studied*: painting with John Alexander, sculpture with Gutzon Borglum, Herbert Adams, N.Y., and with Auguste Rodin, Paris, France. *Member*: F., NSS; F., N.Y. Hist. Soc.; NA; Nat. Inst. A. & Let.; Nat. Assn. Women P. & S.; Arch. Lg.; Soc. Women Geographers; Hon. Memb.: Am. Women's Assn. P. & S. Gal. Assn.; Pen & Brush Cl.; NAC. *Awards*: prizes, Paris Salon, 1911; NAD, 1917, 1921; gold medal, PAFA, 1920; gold medal, NAD, 1924; gold medal, Nat. Assn. Women P. & S.; N.Y. Lg. Bus. & Prof. Women's award, 1935; selected by Career Tours Com. as one of twelve whose work contributed to human betterment, 1939; decorations: Palmes Academiques, France, 1920; Royal Order of St. Sava III, Yugoslavia, 1921; Legion of Honor, France, 1951. Hon. Degrees: Litt.D., Mount Holyoke Col., 1937; D.F.A., Univ. Rochester, 1937, Northwestern Univ., 1945; D.H.L., Smith Col.; D.F.A., Bates Col., 1955; selected as "Woman of the Year," AAUW, 1957. *Work*: NAD; Brooklyn Inst. A. & Sc.; Acad. in Rome; Harvard war mem. Chapel; Stockholm A. Mus.; Chicago Mus. Nat. Hist.; Bush House, London; Lg. of Red Cross Societies, Paris; Queen's Hall, London; CGA; Metropolitan Opera House, N.Y.; Library, Medical Center, N.Y.; Norton Gal. A.; Frick Lib., N.Y.; Hobart Col.; Springfield A. Mus.; Am. Acad. A. & Let.; Hackley A. Gal.; Hall of Fame; N.Y. Hist. Soc.; Maryhill (Wash.) Mus.; Smith Col.; IBM; Incised reliefs on facade and Eagle above entrance and Angel in the Chapel of the American Military Cemetery, Epinal, France (Vosges); incised panels facade of the Joslin Clinic, Boston, Mass.; bronze panel of St. Andrew in St. Andrew-by-the-Sea Church, Rye Beach, N.H., and in many other museums, colleges and public bldgs. throughout the U.S. and abroad. Author: "Heads and Tales," 1936; "Sculpture Inside and Out," 1939.

HOFFMAN, RUTH ERB (Mrs. Burton A.)—

Painter, S., E.

96 Cleveland Ave., Buffalo 22, N.Y.

B. Buffalo, N.Y., Apr. 13, 1902. *Studied*: Wellesley Col., B.A.; Child-Walker Sch. FA & Crafts (Grad. F., from

Wellesley), and with Arthur Lee, Agnes Abbott, Edwin Dickinson, Charles Burchfield. *Member*: The Patteran; Albright A. Gal. *Awards*: prizes, Carnegie Inst., 1941; Terry AI, 1952; Albright A. Gal., 1939, 1940, 1946; Sisti Gal., 1955. *Work*: sc., Northwestern Univ. Hall of Fame. *Exhibited*: Carnegie Inst., 1941, 1943, 1944; MMA, 1942; AIC, 1943; Riverside Mus., 1939, 1942; AFA traveling exh., 1939; Albright A. Gal., 1932-1957; Terry AI, 1952; Chautauqua, N.Y., 1955, 1957; Butler Inst. Am. A., 1956; Crane Lib., Buffalo, 1957 (one-man); Elmwood-Franklin Sch., Buffalo, 1955 (one-man).

HOFFMANN, ARNOLD—Painter, T., L.
144 East 58th St., New York 22, N.Y.; s. Boothbay Harbor, Me.

B. Odessa, Russia, Nov. 22, 1886. *Studied*: in Russia & Germany. *Member*: AWCS; All A. Am.; Audubon A.; Knickerbocker A.; P. & S. Soc. of New Jersey; F., Intl. Inst. A. & Lets.; F., Royal Soc. A., London; Nat. Soc. Painters in Casein; Staten Island Inst. A. & Sc.; New Orleans AA. *Awards*: Med., All. A. Am., 1939, prize, 1944; NGA, 1943. *Work*: Fla. Southern Col.; Palestine Mus. A.; Nat. Mus., Prague; Post-Graduate Hospital, N.Y.; Jersey City Prep. Sch.; & in museums in Paris, Odessa, Warsaw, Moscow; Univ. Palestine. *Exhibited*: AWCS; NAD; All. A. Am.; Audubon A.; ACA Gal.; Freedom House, N.Y.; NAC; Montross Gal.; Garelick Gal., Detroit; Toledo Mus. A.; AIC; BM; Binghamton (N.Y.) Mus. A.; Albany Inst. Hist. & A.

HOFFMANN, ARNOLD, JR.—
Painter, Des., I., Comm. A.
190-17C 69th Ave., Flushing 65, L.I., N.Y.

B. New York, N.Y., Jan. 16, 1915. *Studied*: NAD, with Ivan Olinsky, Leon Kroll. *Member*: All. A. Am. *Exhibited*: AWCS, 1940, 1941, 1942, 1944, 1945; All. A. Am., 1940-1942, 1944, 1945; Audubon A., 1945. *Position*: A. Dir., New York Times Sunday Magazine and Book Review sections.*

HOFFMANN, LILLY E.—Craftsman, Des., T.
Rte. #2, Concord, N.H.

B. Alsace, France, Nov. 8, 1898. *Studied*: Columbia Univ., with Florence House; and in Germany. *Member*: Lg. New Hampshire A. & Crafts; New Hampshire Weavers Gld. *Awards*: Designer-Craftsman U.S.A., 1953. *Work*: MModA.; Currier Gal. A. *Exhibited*: Boston A. Festival, 1956; Mus. Contemp. Crafts, N.Y., 1958; AFA traveling exh., 1958-59, and many exhibitions prior to these dates. *Lectures*: Weaving as a Craft; Weaving for the Home. *Position*: Instr., Weaving, Lg. N.H. A. & Crafts, 1948- ; Currier Gal. A., 1954- ; Manchester Inst. A. & Sc., 1958- .

HOFFMASTER, MAUD MILLER—
Painter, Pr. M., W., L., T., I.
R.F.D. #4, Traverse City, Mich.

B. Manistee, Mich. *Studied*: with John Carlson, Edward Timmins; Georges Bal, in Paris. *Member*: AAPL. *Awards*: Citation, Mark Twain Soc.; Beta Sigma Phi. *Work*: State Hospital, Ypsilanti, Mich.; Olivet Col.; Olivet & Ryerson Lib., Grand Rapids, Mich.; Highland Park Soc. A., Dallas, Tex.; Traverse City State Bank; Munson Hospital and Masonic Temple, Traverse City, and in private colls., U.S. and abroad. Des., FA Bldg., Nat. Music Camp, Interlochen, Mich.; A. Supv., Nat. Music Camp, 14 years. *Exhibited*: one-man: E. B. Crocker A. Gal., Sacramento, Cal., 1957. Illus. fairy tales.

HOFFNER, MRS. PELAGIE DOANE. See Doane,
Pelagie

HOFMANN, HANS—Painter, S., E.
Hans Hofmann School of Fine Arts, 52 West 8th St.; h. 145 West 14th St., New York, N.Y.*

HOGAN, JEAN (VIRGINIA)—Painter
Farmington, Conn.

B. Hartford, Conn. *Studied*: Pembroke Col., Brown Univ., A.B. *Member*: New Haven Paint & Clay Cl.; Conn. Acad. FA; Springfield A. Lg.; Hartford Soc. Women Painters. *Awards*: prizes, Springfield A. Lg., 1938, 1942; Conn.

Acad. FA, 1943. *Exhibited*: NAD; Conn. Acad. FA; Springfield A. Lg.; New Haven Paint & Clay Cl.; Ogunquit A. Center; Town & Country, Hartford, 1950 (2-man); Harbor A. Gal., Wickford, R.I. (one-man); South County AA, Kingston, R.I., 1955 (2-man); Brown Univ.; Morton Gal., N.Y., 1945 (one-man); WFNY 1939; Hartford Soc. Women Painters. *Position*: A. Supv., South Kingstown (R.I.) Elem. Schs.

HOGNER, NILS—Painter, Et., T., L., I.
35 West 8th St., New York 11, N.Y.

B. Massachusetts, July 22, 1893. *Studied*: Boston Sch. Painting; BMFA Sch.; Rhodes Acad., Copenhagen, Denmark; & with Leon Gaspard, Ivar Nyberg. *Member*: AAPL; Arch.L.; NSMP; SC. *Awards*: prizes, Mus. Northern Arizona, 1930; New Mexico A. Lg., 1933. *Work*: Pub. Sch., Oklahoma City; Oklahoma A. Center; Hickory Mus., N.C.; Whistler House, Lowell, Mass.; St. Louis Pub. Lib.; murals, Floyd Bennett Field, N.Y.; Naval YMCA, Brooklyn, N.Y.; Baptist Temple, Phila., Pa.; First Nat. Bank, Litchfield, Conn.; State St. Trust Co., Boston, Mass.; Halloran General Hospital. *Exhibited*: Albany Inst. Hist. & A.; Hartford Atheneum; Riverside Mus.; Whistler House, Lowell, Mass.; Oklahoma A. Center; Sartor A. Gal., Dallas, Tex. (one-man); Silvermine, Conn. (one-man); Mus. New Mexico, Santa Fé (one-man). I., "Farm Animals," 1945; & many other children's books.*

HOGUE, ALEXANDRE—Painter, Lith., W., T.
4052 East 23rd St., Tulsa 4, Okla.

B. Memphis, Mo., Feb. 22, 1898. *Member*: Southwestern AA; Audubon A. *Awards*: prizes, All. A., Dallas, Tex., 1930-1933; SSAL, 1932; Dallas Pr. Soc., 1937. *Work*: Philbrook A. Center, Tulsa; Gilcrease Fnd.; Musee du Jeu de Paume, Paris, France; Dallas Mus. FA; IBM; Encyclopaedia Britannica Coll.; Lib.Cong.; Houston Mus. FA; Corpus Christi A. Fnd.; murals, USPO, Houston, Tex.; Graham, Tex. *Exhibited*: Paris Salon, 1938; Carnegie Inst., 1938, 1939 (Intl. exh.), 1946; WFNY 1939; GGE, 1939; Tate Gal., London, England, 1946; MModA; Int. Color Lithography exh., 1952; SAGA, 1952; AIC; WMAA; CGA. *Position*: Tech. I., North American Aviation Corp., 1942-45; Hd. A. Dept., Univ. Tulsa, Okla., 1945- .

HOGUE, HERBERT GLENN—Educator, C.
1103 Cliff St., Ellensburg, Wash.

B. Ellensburg, Wash., Oct. 21, 1891. *Studied*: Col. of Puget Sound; Willamette Univ.; Alfred Univ.; Washington State Col., B.A. *Position*: Hd., Dept. F. & Indst. A., Instr., Pottery & Photography, Central Washington College of Edu., Ellensburg, Wash., 1935-59; Prof. Emeritus, 1959- .

HOHENBERG, MARGUERITE (Mrs.)—
Painter, Des., C., L.
102 East Oak St., Chicago 11, Ill.

B. Vienna, Austria, Aug. 16, 1883. *Studied*: Univ. Chicago; Chicago Acad. FA. *Member*: Am. Inst. Decorators. *Awards*: No. Mississippi Valley A., 1955; Guggenheim scholarship, 1943. *Work*: Mus. Non-Objective Painting, N.Y.; Illinois State Mus.; Panelit Corp., Skokie, Ill. (Albert Sperry), 1956. *Exhibited*: AIC, 1941, 1943, 1946; Mus. Non-Objective Painting, 1941-1946; Palmer House; Chicago Pub. Lib.; 1956-58: Renaissance Soc., Chicago; Illinois State Mus.; North Shore A. Lg.; New Trier H.S., Evanston; Geneva, Ill.; one-man: Roullier Gal., Chicago, 1937; Cromer & Quint Gal., Chicago, 1954; Anna Werbe Gal., Detroit, 1954; DeKalb Lib., 1955; Ball State Col., Muncie, Ind., 1955. *Lectures*: Composition; Color; Interior Design. *Position*: Dir., Marguerite Hohenberg A. Gal., Chicago, Ill., 1950- .

HOHLEN, MAY MARJORIE—Educator, P., C., Ser.
Burlington High School; h. 1511 Summer St., Burlington, Iowa

B. Burlington, Iowa, May 5, 1896. *Studied*: Univ. Colorado, B.F.A.; T. Col., Columbia Univ., M.F.A.; & with Ernest Thurn, Hans Hofmann, Vaclav Vytlacil, Robert von Neumann, Dorothy Meredith. *Member*: Friends of Art, Davenport, Iowa. *Awards*: prizes, Iowa A. Salon, 1946, 1947, 1948. *Exhibited*: Swedish-Am. Exh., Chicago, 1940, 1941; Davenport Mun. A. Gal., 1941-1945, 1946 (one-man); Iowa A. Salon, Des Moines, 1938, 1953; Des Moines A.

Center, 1954; Iowa WC Exh., 1945, 1946; Joslyn Mus. A., 1958. *Position*: Instr. A. Edu., FA Dir., Burlington Col. & H.S., Burlington, Iowa, 1922- .

HOKE, ROBERT A.—Illustrator, Portrait Painter

The Evening Star, 11th & Pennsylvania Ave., Washington, D.C.; h. 1803 Avalon Place, Hyattsville, Md.

B. Hanover, Pa., April 24, 1910. *Studied*: San Jose (Cal.) State Col.; Corcoran Sch. A. *Position*: Pres., Corcoran Alum. Assn.; A. Dir., Sunday Magazine, Washington Evening Star, Washington, D.C., 1937- .*

HOLADAY, WILLIAM H.—Educator, P., C., Gr.

Art Department, Northern State Teachers College; h. 208½ North First St., Aberdeen, S.D.

B. Wheeling, W. Va., June 30, 1907. *Studied*: Ohio State Univ., B.A.; Franklin Univ.; Omaha Univ., M.A.; Univ. Chicago; Dakota Wesleyan Univ.; Univ. Iowa. *Member*: Assoc. Omaha A. *Awards*: South Dakota State Fair, 1951-58. *Exhibited*: Little Gal., Spearfish, S.D., 1956 (one-man); Joslyn Mem. Mus., 1948; Assoc. A., Omaha, 1947; Ohio State Univ., 1945; Dakota Wesleyan Univ., 1953; Northern State T. Col., 1958. Author: "Art History of the Middle Border." Lectures: Contemporary Art; Art Education Today; Modern Painting, etc. *Positions*: Dean of Men, Dakota Wesleyan Univ., 1948; Assoc. Prof. A., Hd. A. Dept., Dakota Wesleyan Univ., 1948-58; Asst. Prof. A., Hd. A. Dept., Northern State Teachers Col., Aberdeen, S.D., 1958- .

HOLBERG, RUTH LANGLAND (Mrs.)—Writer

11 Hale St., Rockport, Mass.

B. Milwaukee, Wis., Feb. 2, 1889. *Studied*: with Alexander Mueller, F. F. Fursman, E. A. Webster. Author, juvenile books, 28th book, "John Greenleaf Whittier: Fighting Quaker," 1958.

HOLBROOK, ALFRED H.—Museum Director, P., W., L.

Georgia Museum of Art, Jackson St.; h. 120 Fortson Drive, Athens, Ga.

B. Topeka, Kans., Nov. 26, 1874. *Studied*: Holbrook Col., Lebanon, Ohio, B.S., B.A., LL.B. Gave Holbrook Collection of 350 paintings and 250 prints to the Univ. Georgia, starting the Georgia Museum of Art, 1948. Lectures widely on art topics. Assembles and arranges 20 to 30 exhibitions per year. *Position*: Dir., Georgia Museum of Art, Univ. of Georgia, Athens, Ga.

HOLBROOK, HOLLIS HOWARD—
Educator, P., Des., I., L.

College of Architecture & Fine Arts, University of Florida; mail: Rt. #2, Box 60, Gainesville, Fla.

B. Natick, Mass., Feb. 7, 1909. *Studied*: Vesper George Sch. A.; Mass. Sch. A.; Boston Univ.; Yale Univ., B.F.A.; Universidad Michoacana. *Member*: SSAL; Fla. Edu. Assn.; Fla. Fed. A.; Fla. A. Group; Southeastern College AA. *Awards*: mural comp., USPO, St. Louis, Mo.; Social Security Nat. Comp., 1941; Somerville (Mass.) USPO, 1937. *Work*: murals, Lib., Univ. Florida; St. Augustine, Fla.; USPO, Natick, Mass., Haleyville, Ala.; Biblioteca Michoacana, Mex.; Jeanerette, La.; portraits, Univ. Florida. Contributor to Design Magazine. *Position*: I., Associated Press, 1943; Indst. Des., Warren Telechron Co., 1943-44; Instr. A., 1938-41, Asst. Prof. A., 1941-43, Assoc. Prof., 1946-48, Prof. A., Univ. Florida, 1948- .

HOLBROOK, VIVIAN NICHOLAS—Painter

Bivens Arm, Gainesville, Fla.; mail, Rt. #2, Box 60, Gainesville, Fla.

B. Mt. Vernon, N.Y., Mar. 31, 1913. *Studied*: Yale Sch. FA, B.F.A. *Member*: SSAL; Soc. Four A.; Fla. Fed. A.; Sarasota AA. *Awards*: prizes, Fla. Fed. A., 1942, 1943, 1951; Fla. State Fair, 1947; Harry Rich Comp., Miami, 1957. *Exhibited*: SSAL, 1944; Fla. Fed. A., 1942, 1943, 1945, 1951; Soc. Four A.; Butler AI, 1951, 1952; Fla. A. Group; Sarasota AA; Havana, Cuba, 1955; Atlanta AA, 1958; Norton Gal. A., 1958; Fla. State Fair, 1955; one-man: Fla. Southern Col., 1948; Miami Beach A. Gal., 1950; Jacksonville A. Mus.; Univ. Florida, 1957 (2-man). Lectures: Women in Art. *Position*: A. Instr., Colby Jr. Col., 1936-38; Univ. Florida, Gainesville, Fla.

HOLDEN, JAMES ALBERT—Mural Painter

3016 Bona St., Oakland 1, Cal.

B. England. *Member*: Bohemian Cl., San F. *Work*: murals, St. Francis Hotel, San F., Cal.; USPO, Turlock, Cal.; Hills Bros., Edgewater, N.J. *Exhibited*: Oakland A. Gal.; Bay Region AA; Soc. Western A. *Position*: A. Dir., Pacific Railway Advertising Co., San Francisco, Cal.*

HOLDEN, LEPHE KINGSLEY (Mrs.)—Educator, P.

Ludlow Rd., Westport, Conn.; w. "The Tides," Key West, Fla.

B. Hadley, Mass., May 1, 1884. *Studied*: PIASch.; ASL, and with Guy Wiggins, George Elmer Browne, de Caviedes, Merida. *Member*: Conn. Watercolorists; Conn. AA; Martello A. Assoc., Key West, Fla.; Key West A. Group; Old Lyme AA. *Awards*: prizes, Essex, Conn., 1938. *Work*: Bedford Jr. H.S., Staples H.S., Westport Women's Cl., Christ Church, Holy Trinity Church, all in Westport, Conn.; Key West Pub. Lib.; Fla. AA. *Exhibited*: NAWA, 1936-1938, 1940-1946; AWS, 1936-1943; All. A. Am., 1940-1943; AFA traveling exh.; Old Lyme AA, 1938-1955; Avery Mus. A.; Argent Gal (one-man); N.Y. Studio Gld. (one-man); Key West, Fla., 1949, 1950, 1952 (one-man), 1955; Karns Gal., Key West, Fla. (one-man). *Position*: Instr., Guy Wiggins A. Sch., Essex, Conn.*

HOLDEN, R(AYMOND) J.—Illustrator, P., Comm. A.

R.F.D. 79, North Sterling, Conn.

B. Wrentham, Mass., May 2, 1901. *Studied*: R.I.Sch.Des. *Member*: Providence WC Cl. *Exhibited*: AIGA, 1935, 1942; Providence A. Cl., 1953-1955, 1956; Ford Motor Co., 1955, 1956, 1958; one-man exh.: Jones Lib., Amherst, Mass., 1939, 1941; Boston Pub. Lib., 1941; Providence Pub. Lib., 1941; State Lib., Hartford, Conn., 1942. I., "Flowering of New England," 1941; "Poems of Whittier," 1945; "The Autocrat of the Breakfast Table," 1955, and others. Contributor to Ford Times.

HOLDER, CHARLES ALBERT—Painter, T.

47 Fifth Ave., New York, N.Y.

B. Miami, Fla., June 15, 1925. *Studied*: Univ. Florida, B.F.A.; AIC; Jerry Farnsworth Sch. A. *Member*: SC; All. A. Am. *Awards*: prizes, Tiffany award, 1950; Fla. Fed. A., 1947, 1949; All-Florida College A. Forum, 1949; Greenwich Village Exh., 1953; Coral Gables AA, 1954; Harry Rich Comp., Miami, 1955; Sarasota AA, 1954, and others; Henry White Taylor Scholarship, 1949. *Work*: many portraits, 1948-58. *Exhibited*: Tiffany Fnd., 1950; Am.-British A. Gal., N.Y., 1950; Fla. Fed. A., 1946, 1947, 1949; Sarasota AA, 1954; Coral Gables AA, 1955; SC, 1954; Rich Comp., Miami, 1955; one-man: Univ. Florida, 1950; Los Angeles, Cal., 1956; Trenton, N.J., 1958.

HOLLAND, DANIEL E.—Cartoonist

Chicago Tribune, 435 North Michigan Ave., Chicago, Ill.; h. 412 Laurel Ave., Libertyville, Ill.

B. Guthrie, Ky., Feb. 2, 1918. *Studied*: Chicago Acad. A. *Awards*: Freedom Fnd., 1949-1952. *Position*: Cartoonist, Chicago Tribune and Tribune Syndicate.

HOLLAND, JANICE—Illustrator, P.

3508 Morrison St., N.W., Washington 15, D.C.

B. Washington, D.C., May 23, 1913. *Studied*: Corcoran Sch. A.; PIASch.; & with Eliot O'Hara. *Member*: Children's Bk. Gld., Wash., D.C. *Exhibited*: PAFA, 1933; Wash. WC Cl., 1935-1937; PMG, 1935, 1936; Nat. Mus., Wash., D.C., 1935, 1936; Wash. A. Cl., 1949 (one-man); CGA, 1935 (one-man); Wash., D.C. Pub. Lib., 1946 (one-man). I., "Our Country's Story," 1945; "The Blue Cat of Castle Town," 1949; Author, I., "They Built a City," 1953; "Pirates, Planters and Patriots," 1955; "Christopher Goes to the Castle," 1957; "Hello, George Washington," 1958; "The Apprentice and the Prize," 1958, and other books.

HOLLANDER, MRS. CLIFFORD. See Wingate, Arline

HOLLERBACH, SERGE—*Painter, I.*
614 West 157th St., New York 32, N.Y.

B. Pushkin, Russia, Nov. 1, 1923. *Studied*: Acad. FA, Munich, Germany; ASL, with Ernst Fiene; Am. A. Sch., with Gordon Samstag. *Member*: AWS; Knickerbocker A. *Award*: prize, Audubon A., 1958. *Exhibited*: Knickerbocker A., 1951-1958; Audubon A., 1952-1958; AWS, 1956-1958; NAD, 1956; Carnegie Inst., 1956; Wilton, Conn., 1949 (2-man); Creative Gal., N.Y., 1952 (3-man); Panoras Gal., 1957 (2-man). Contributor to Harper's Magazine, CBS Radio, N.Y. Times Magazine.

HOLLERITH, LUCIA BEVERLY—*Painter*
1617 29th St., N.W., Washington 7, D.C.; s. Mathews, Va.

B. Washington, D.C., July 1, 1891. *Studied*: PMG Sch.; Corcoran Sch. A.; & with Cameron Burnside, Henry Snell, Karl Knaths. *Member*: NAWA; SSAL; Soc. Wash. A.; Wash. A.C. *Exhibited*: NAD; SSAL; Soc. Wash. A.; Wash. A. Cl.

HOLLISTER, PAUL—*Painter*
601 East 20th St., New York 10, N.Y.

B. New York, N.Y., Sept. 2, 1918. *Studied*: Harvard Col., B.S. *Member*: AFA. *Awards*: prize, Village A. Center, 1949. *Exhibited*: Grand Central A. Gal., 1947; ACA Gal., 1949; Riverside Mus., 1951, 1953, 1954; WMAA, 1954; N.Y. City Center, 1954, 1955, 1956; New Sch. Social Research, 1954; RoKo Gal., 1954, 1955; Los A. AA, 1950; Ft. Worth AA, 1950; One-man: Gal. Apollinaire, London, England, 1951; Panoras Gal., N.Y., 1957. Author, I., "Fine Tooth Comb," 1947; Author, Ed., Illustrated Classics. Book reviews for N.Y. Times; N.Y. Post; Manchester Guardian; Reporter magazine covers. *Positions*: Ed., Doubleday & Co., 1944-47; Instr., Feature & Critical Writing, Short Story, etc., N.Y. Univ., Dept. Journalism, 1947-50.

HOLLOWAY, H. MAXSON—
Museum Director, Historian, W., L.
59 Second St., Troy, N.Y.

B. West Liberty, Iowa, Jan. 11, 1907. *Studied*: Univ. Iowa; Univ. Alabama; N.Y. Univ. *Member*: A. Assn. for State & Local Hist. *Awards*: Rockefeller Fnd. F., 1936-37. Contributor to Quarterly Bulletin of the New York Hist. Soc. *Positions*: Dir., Mus. FA. Montgomery, Ala., 1931-36; Mus. Cur., New York Hist. Soc., 1938-47; Dir., Saginaw Mus., Saginaw, Mich., 1947-49; Cur., Chicago Hist. Soc., Chicago, Ill., 1949-54; Asst. Dir., 1954-1956; Dir., Rensselaer County Hist. Soc., Troy, N.Y., 1957- .

HOLM, MILTON W.—*Painter*
30 Hathaway Rd., Rochester 17, N.Y.

B. Rochester, N.Y., Oct. 29, 1903. *Member*: All.A.Am.; Rochester AC. *Awards*: prize, NAD, 1940; Rochester A. Cl., 1956; Rochester Mem. A. Gal., 1958. *Work*: Univ. Rochester; Rochester Mem. A. Gal.; NAD. *Exhibited*: NAD, 1935, 1937, 1938, 1940, 1942-1944; All.A.Am., 1938-1955; CM (Critic's Choice), 1945; Currier Gal. A., 1940; Syracuse Mus. FA, 1941; Phila. A. All., 1940; Rochester Mem. A. Gal., 1924-1955; Rundel Gal., Rochester, N.Y., 1938-1955; Terry AI, 1952; Manchester A. Center, 1957, 1958; Syracuse State Fair, 1958. Pres., Rochester A. Cl., 1957-59.

HOLME, SIV (MUSE)—*Painter, Gr.*
202 West 19th St., New York, N.Y.

B. Skutskar, Sweden, June 27, 1914. *Studied*: The New Sch., Stockholm; Ecole des Beaux-Arts, Paris, with Othon Frieze, Andre Lhote, and others. *Work*: Institut Tessin, Paris; Musee de Tours; French State Coll.; and in private collections in U.S. and Europe; murals in private homes and restaurants. *Exhibited*: Salon d'Automne, 1937; Salon des Independents, 1937-1939; Institut Tessin, Paris, 1946 (one-man); Museum of Cognac, France, 1956 (2-man); Museum of Angoulele, France, 1956 (2-man); Mortimer Brandt Gal.; Wildenstein Gal.; 10 American Artists Exh., 1955, circulating in French museums; one-man: Bonestell Gal., 1945; Bertha Schaefer Gal., 1947-1948, 1950.*

HOLMES, (FRANK) GRAHAM (JR.)—*Painter*
Station A, Trenton, N.J.

B. Trenton, N.J., June 22, 1908. *Studied*: PAFA; & with Wayman Adams. *Awards*: Cresson traveling scholarship, PAFA, 1931. *Work*: mural, Trenton Country Cl. *Exhibited*: PAFA, 1929; NAD, 1929, 1933; Albright A. Gal., 1929; SC.*

HOLMES, RALPH—*Painter, T.*
Box 143, Twin Lakes Park, Chatsworth, Cal.

B. La Grange, Ill., Oct. 1, 1876. *Studied*: Northwestern Univ.; and in Europe. *Member*: Cal. A. Cl.; Los A. A. Cl. *Awards*: Numerous medals and awards in exhs., U.S. *Work*: murals, in Pittsburgh, New York, and California. *Positions*: In charge School of the Art Inst. Chicago, 7 yrs.; Hd. Dept. Painting & Dec., Carnegie Inst., 5 yrs.; Hd. Dept. A. & Crafts, Margaret Morrison Carnegie Sch., 1 yr.; Instr., Drawing & Painting, Otis AI, Los Angeles, 25 yrs.

HOLMGREN, (R.) JOHN—*Illustrator*
50 Morningside Drive, New York 25, N.Y.

B. St. Paul, Minn., Nov. 28, 1897. *Studied*: St. Paul AI; ASL; Columbia Univ. *Member*: SI; A. & Writers Assn.; Dutch Treat Cl. *Awards*: Columbia Univ.; N.Y. Univ. (honorary award). *Work*: Cunard Line. *Exhibited*: AWS, 1955; SI, annually. Illus. Readers Digest Books: "The Hidden Flower"; "Island Rescue"; "Digby"; illus., Souvenir Book "North Cape Cruise," Cunard Line. Contributor of illus. to Redbook; Readers Digest; Life; Vogue; Judge; Colliers; American; Cosmopolitan; Pictorial Review and other national magazines.*

HOLT, DOROTHY M. (Mrs. Dorothy Holt Manuel)—
Painter, I., T.
12 Battery St., Newport, R.I.

B. Providence, R.I., Sept. 6, 1909. *Studied*: R.I.Sch.Des. *Awards*: prizes, Hallmark, 1952. *Work*: R.I.Sch.Des.Mus.; Bristol Yacht Cl.; Bristol Mfg. Co., R.I.; Ida Lewis Yacht Cl., Newport; N.Y. Hospital; Ford Times, 1957, 1958; Preservation Soc., Newport. *Exhibited*: PAFA, 1936, 1937, 1939, 1940, 1941, 1943, 1946; Ferargil Gal.; 1939; AIC, 1938-1941, 1944; AIC traveling exh., 1939-1940, 1940-1941; San Diego FA Soc., 1941; MMA, 1942, 1943; Toledo Mus. A., 1944; Carnegie Inst., 1941-43; Soc. Four A., 1941; WMA; AGAA; Pepsi-Cola, 1946; Stuart Gal., Boston, 1946; Portland (Me.) Mus. A., 1946; R.I.Sch.Des., 1940-1946; Armour Gal., Providence, 1936, 1939, 1941, 1946; Newport AA, 1941, 1943-1945; Tilden Thurber Gal., 1941; Brown Univ., 1941; Providence AC, 1937, 1939-1946; Boston A. Festival, 1953, 1954. Contributor to Ford Times.

HOLT, JULIA SAMUEL TRAVIS—*Painter*
241 Armistead Ave., Hampton, Va.

B. Hampton, Va., May 15, 1897. *Studied*: State T. Col., Farmville, Va.; William & Mary Col.; & with Jerry Farnsworth. *Member*: Norfolk A. Corner; NAWA; SSAL; Nat. Edu. Assn.; Pen & Brush Cl.; Tidewater A.; AAPL. *Awards*: Prize, Mariner's Mus., Newport News, Va., 1945. *Exhibited*: VMFA, 1942; NAWA, 1943, 1944, 1945; Norfolk A. Corner, 1939-1941; Argent Gal., 1943 (one-man); Butler, AI, 1945; Norfolk Mus. A. & Sc., 1944 (one-man), 1947-1950; SSAL, 1944-1946; Newport News, Va., 1945-1950; Norfolk, Va., 1944-1946; Terry AI, 1952; Pen & Brush Cl., 1948, 1949.*

HOLT, J(USTIN) GORDON—*Cartoonist*
38 Golf View Rd., Wallingford, Pa.

B. Charlotte, N.C., Apr. 19, 1930. *Studied*: Lehigh Univ., B.A.; Cartoonists & Illus. Sch., N.Y. Contributor cartoons to Colliers; True; Sat. Eve. Post; Christian Science Monitor; Audio, and other national magazines.*

HOLT, NAOMI (Mrs. John Keith Custis)—
Portrait Painter
2700 Q St., Northwest, Washington 7, D.C.

B. Washington, D.C., Nov. 27, 1911. *Studied*: San Diego Acad. FA; Corcoran Sch. A.; PAFA. *Member*: Georgetown A. Group; J.F.A. Galleries Group; Corcoran Alumni Assn. *Awards*: St. Gaudens & Alexander medals 1930;

Corcoran Sch. A., 1934. *Exhibited*: Wash. A. Cl.; Illinois State Soc.; Waukegan (Ill.) A. Cl.; CGA; J.F.A. Gal., Wash., D.C.*

HOLTON, GRACE M.—*Educator, P., Des., C., W., L.*
    65 Ogden St., Providence 6, R.I.

B. Springfield, Mass. *Studied*: PIASch; Columbia Univ., B.S., A.M.; N.Y. Univ.; Univ. London. *Member*: Am. Assn. Univ. Women; Am. Assn. Univ. Prof; New Brunswick A. Center; AAPL; State Fed. Women's Cl. *Awards*: prize, AAPL, 1944; NAD, 1954. *Exhibited*: Greenwich SA; Phila. A. All.; Phila. Plastic Cl.; Montclair A. Mus.; New Brunswick A. Center; Atlantic City AA; Kresge Gal., Newark; N.Y. Soc. Craftsmen; AAPL. *Author*: "College Instruction in Art," 1943; articles in N.J. State Div. Womens Clubs; Am. Assn. Univ. Women Bulletin, 1939-1946. Lectures: History of Art; Art Appreciation. *Position*: Prof. A., New Jersey Col. for Women, Rutgers Univ., New Brunswick, N.J., 1928-52; A.T., Conn. State T. Col. Summer Sch., Yale Univ., 1926-43; Fairleigh Dickinson Col., 1952-53; Third Dist. A. Chm., State Fed. Women's Cl., N.J., 1950-53; State A. Chm., AAUW (8 years); A. Chm., New Brunswick Women's Cl., 1945-57; New Brunswick Br., AAUW, 1935-57; Publ. Chm., Jersey Chptr., DAR, 1953-56; L., Rutgers Univ. Speakers Bureau, 1945-57; Fairleigh Dickinson Col., 1952-53.

HOLTON, LEONARD T.—*Illustrator*
    129 East 82nd St., New York 28, N.Y.
Member: SI.

HOLTY, CARL ROBERT—*Painter, L., T.*
    1245 Madison Ave., New York 28, N.Y.

B. Freiburg, Germany, June 21, 1900. *Studied*: Marquette Univ.; NAD; Royal Acad., Munich; Hofmann Sch., Munich. *Member*: Abstraction Creation, Paris; Am. Abstract A. *Work*: CAM; Milwaukee AI; Univ. Illinois; Butler AI; Phillips Exeter Acad.; Hunter Gal., Chattanooga, Tenn. *Exhibited*: WMAA; Carnegie Inst.; PAFA; CGA; AIC; MMA; CAM; CM; Los A. Mus. A.; Columbus Mus. A.; J.B. Neumann Gal., 1936-1944; Karl Nierndorf Gal., 1938; Kootz Gal., 1946-1948; New Art Circle, 1951, 1952; Duveen-Graham Gal., 1956. *Position*: Instr., Univ. Georgia, 1948-50; Univ. Florida, 1952-53; Univ. California (summer), 1951; ASL, 1939, 1940, 1950, 1951. Lectures: Psychology of Art; Role of Art in Modern Society; Traditions of Modern Art, etc., at universities and colleges.*

HOLZHAUER, EMIL EUGEN—*Painter*
    P.O. Box 368, Valparaiso, Fla.

B. Schwabish Gmund, Germany, Jan. 21, 1887. *Studied*: with Robert Henri, Homer Boss, and in Germany. *Member*: SSAL; Audubon A; Georgia AA. *Awards*: prizes, AIC, 1930; North Carolina Exh., 1942; SSAL, 1946; Carnegie grant, 1946, 1949; Southeastern annual, Atlanta, 1946, 1949, 1954; Georgia AA, 1952; medal, Alabama A., 1948; Fla. State Fair, 1958. *Work*: Albany Inst. Hist. & A.; Univ. Georgia; AIC; Newark Mus.; WMAA; Oberlin Col.; Rochester Mem. A. Gal.; Syracuse Mus. FA; Denver A. Mus.; Pensacola A. Center; Los A. Mus. A.; High Mus. A. *Exhibited*: AIC, 1927-1935, 1937, 1943; Century of Progress, 1933, 1934; PAFA, 1928, 1932; CGA, 1930, 1934, 1951; Atlanta Paper Co., 1955, 1956; Birmingham Mus. A., 1954; St. Petersburg, Fla., 1955 (one-man); Pensacola A. Gal., 1955, 1958 (one-man); Carnegie Inst., 1930; BM, 1929, 1933; Albright A. Gal., 1930, 1931; WMAA, 1933, 1934; BMA, 1933; SSAL, 1944-1946; Audubon A, 1946-1955; Southeastern annual, 1946-1955, 1956, 1957; Georgia AA, 1944-1952; Mississippi A., 1946-1950, 1952. *Position*: Prof. A., Wesleyan Col., Macon, Ga., 1942- ; Hd. Dept. A., 1952-53 (Retired 1954).

HOMBURGER, FREDDY (Dr.)—*Painter, W.*
    Oak Point Rd., Trenton, Me.; h. 759 High St., Dedham, Mass.

B. St. Gallen, Switzerland, Feb. 8, 1916. *Studied*: with Raoul Dufy. *Work*: Musee des Beaux-Arts, Geneva, Switzerland; Univ. Maine; Orono, Me. *Exhibited*: Boston A. Festival, 1953; Carstairs Gal., 1953; Musee de l'Athenee, Geneva, 1953; Zurich, 1953; Galerie Paul Petrides, Paris, 1954; Galerie St. Etienne, N.Y., 1955; Doll & Richards, Boston, 1957, 1958. Contributor to medical journals. *Position*: Research Prof., Tufts Univ., 1948-1957; Pres., Dir., Bio-Research Inst., Cambridge, Mass.

HOMER, WILLIAM INNES—*Educator, Mus. Cur., W.*
    120 Prospect Ave., Princeton, N.J.; s. Ogunquit, Me.

B. Merion, Pa., Nov. 8, 1929. *Studied*: PMSchA.; Princeton Univ., B.A.; Temple Univ. (Tyler Sch.); N.Y. Univ.; Harvard Univ., M.A., and with Lester Cooke, Harmon Neill. *Member*: CAA; Soc. Arch. Hist.; Archaeological Inst. Am. *Author*: "Seurat's Port-en-Bessin"; "The Sculpture of Carl Walters"; "Catalog of American Art: Museum of Art of Ogunquit." Contributor to Art in America; The Connoisseur, and other periodicals and museum publications. *Award*: Sachs Traveling Research Fellowship, 1957-58. *Work*: N.Y. Pub. Lib.; Princeton Univ. Lib. Theatre Coll. & Graphic Arts Dept. *Positions*: Asst. Ed. & Des., Prentice-Hall Publishers, 1952-53; Teaching F., FA, Harvard Univ., 1954-55; Instr. A. & Archaeology, Princeton Univ., 1955- ; Asst. Dir. (Actg.), The Art Museum, 1956-57; Cur., Museum of Art of Ogunquit, Ogunquit, Me., 1955- .

HOOD, ETHEL P.—*Sculptor*
    65 West 56th St.; h. 15 East 61st St., New York 21, N.Y.

B. Baltimore, Md., Apr. 9, 1908. *Studied*: ASL; Julian Acad., Paris, France. *Member*: F., NSS; NAWA. *Awards*: gold medals, Catherine L. Wolfe A. Cl., 1954; Soc. Wash. A., 1939. *Work*: S., Radio City & French Bldg., Rockefeller Center, New York, N.Y.; Brookgreen Gardens, S.C., and in private colls. *Exhibited*: Soc. Wash. A., 1939-1941, 1946; WMAA, 1940; PAFA, 1937; NAD, 1940-1948; NAWA, 1944-1946; BMA, 1933, 1934, 1936, 1939, 1940, 1943-1946; Karl Freund A. Gal., 1939 (one-man); Decorator's Cl., 1945 (one-man); Argent Gal., 1945 (one-man); Hudson Valley AA.

HOOD, (THOMAS) RICHARD—*Graphic Artist, Des., E.*
    738 Pine St., Philadelphia 6, Pa.

B. Philadelphia, Pa., July 13, 1910. *Studied*: Univ. Pennsylvania; PMSch. A. *Member*: Phila. Pr. Cl.; Am. Color Pr. Soc. (Pres. 1956-). *Awards*: Western Pa. Pr. Exh., 1940; Soldiers Art, NGA, 1945; Times-Herald Exh., Wash., D.C., 1945; Phila. Pr. Cl., 1937, 1949, 1951. *Work*: Phila. Free Lib.; Pa. State Hospital; PMA; LC; Carnegie Inst.; Pa. State Col.; Carnegie Lib.; N.Y. Pub. Lib., and in private coll. *Exhibited*: in traveling and national print exhibitions since 1938. I., "Decoys" (a portfolio of Serigraphs), 1954. *Position*: Assoc. Dir., Adv. Des. Dept., Des. Coordinator, PMSch. A., Philadelphia, Pa.

HOOK, WALTER—*Educator, P.*
    Art Department, Montana State University; h. Pattee Canyon Drive, Rt. #3, Missoula, Mont.

B. Missoula, Mont., Apr. 25, 1919. *Studied*: Montana State Univ., B.A.; Univ. New Mexico, Albuquerque, M.A. *Awards*: prizes, Butler Inst. Am. A., 1958 (purchase); SAM, 1958; Bellevue (Wash.) A. & Crafts Fair, 1958; Pacific Northwest Exh., Spokane, Wash., 1958, and others. *Work*: Butler Inst. Am. A.; Bellevue Pub. Sch. System; A. & I. Col., Art Dept., Kingsville, Tex.; Missoula County H.S. *Exhibited*: Butler Inst. Am. A., 1958; Pacific Northwest Exh., 1957, 1958; Northwest WC Soc., 1956-1958; Las Vegas Nat. A. Roundup, 1957, 1958; SAM, 1956-1958; Alabama WC Soc., 1957, 1958; Springfield Mus. A., 1958; Denver A. Mus., 1958. *Positions*: Visiting Memb. Faculty, Central Washington Col. of Edu.; Univ. Oregon; Univ. New Mexico; Chm., A. Dept.; Montana State Univ., Missoula, Mont., 1957- .

HOOKHAM, MRS. ELEANOR KING SALLEY. See *King, Eleanor*

HOOPES, THOMAS TEMPLE—*Museum Curator, L.*
    City Art Museum, Forest Park; h. 48 Washington Terrace, St. Louis 12, Mo.

B. Boston, Mass., Mar. 31, 1898. *Studied*: Harvard Col., A.B.; N.Y.Univ., A.M., Ph.D.; Columbia Univ.; Univ. Berlin. *Member*: F., Royal Geographical Soc.; F., Royal Soc. A.; member, Verein fur Historische Waffenkunde; St. Louis Arms Collectors Cl.; hon. memb., Am. Soc. Arms Collectors. *Awards*: F., N.Y.Univ., 1929-1930; Guggenheim F., 1932; Carnegie Research F., 1934-1936; Ritter Kreutz, Austria, 1936. *Author*: CAM handbook, "Armor and Arms," 1954. Contributor to: Art Bulletin & bulletins of MMA, CAM; Nelson's Encyclopaedia; "Arms

& Armor," CAM, 1954. Lectures: "Masterpieces in City Art Museum"; "The Mediaeval Tournament," etc. Arranged numerous special exhibits of Arms & Armor at MMA, & of various subjects at CAM. *Position*: Asst. & Asst. Cur., MMA, 1920-27; L., FA, Univ. Chicago, 1931; Advisor in Arms & Armor, PMA, 1929- ; In charge of reinstallation of firearms coll., Austrian Nat. Mus., 1935-36; Cur., CAM, St. Louis, Mo., 1936- .

HOOVER, F. LOUIS—*Educator, Editor*
305 North University Ave., Normal, Ill.

B. Sherman, Tex., Mar. 12, 1913. *Studied*: North Texas State T. Col., B.S.; T. Col., Columbia Univ., M.A.; N.Y. Univ., Ed. D.; New Sch. for Social Research; ASL, and with Alexandre Hogue, Jean Charlot, Amadee Ozenfant. *Member*: Am. Assn. Univ. Prof.; Nat. Edu. Assn.; Western AA; Illinois Edu. Assn.; Illinois A. Edu. Assn. (Pres.). *Exhibited*: Central Ill. exh., 1946; Dallas Mus. FA. Lectures: "Art in the Elementary School"; "Children's Art," etc.. *Positions*: Ed., (Junior) Arts & Activities magazine, 1952- ; Asst. Prof. A., North Texas State T. Col., 1935-40; Cr., A.T., Eastern Illinois State T. Col., 1941-44; Prof. & Dir. A. Edu., Illinois State Normal Univ., Normal, Ill. 1944- . Author: "A Teacher's Guide for Using Arts and Activities in the Classroom," 1955.

HOOVER, IDA L.—*Educator*
701 South Broadway, Ada, Okla.

B. Fort Smith, Ark., Sept. 16, 1892. *Studied*: Converse Col.; Univ. Oklahoma, B.F.A., A.B.; T. Col., Columbia Univ., M.A., and in Europe. *Member*: AAUW; Okla. Edu. Assn. (Council); Western A. Sect. of NEA art sect. *Positions*: Survey of A. Edu. in T. Cols. of Midwest States, 1934; Chm., State Committee to write art course of study for use in Oklahoma public schools, 1937; Study for improving art instruction in rural schools, 1938; organized and implemented Oklahoma Children's Art Project; Chm., A. Edu., Oklahoma Edu. Assn., 1930; A. Chm., Oklahoma Div., AAUW, 1938-42; Southwest Regional A. Chm., AAUW, 1943-45; Chm., A. Dept., East Central State College, Ada, Okla., 1920-58. (Retired.)

HOOWIJ, JAN—*Painter*
10500 Seabury Lane, Los Angeles 24, Cal.

B. Hengelo, Netherlands, Sept. 13, 1907. *Studied*: Acad. FA, The Hague; Grande Chaumiere, Paris. *Member*: AEA; Los Angeles AA. *Awards*: Royal subsidy for Artists, Holland, 1931-34; Van Duyl prize, 1935; Ebell Salon, Los A., Cal., 1952; gold medal, Los Angeles City A. Festival, 1951. *Work*: BM; Joslyn A. Mus.; Philbrook A. Center; Honolulu Acad. A. *Exhibited*: Holland, 1939; Palais de Chaillot, Paris, 1945; Carnegie Inst., 1948, 1949; Indianapolis, Ind., 1949; Los Angeles A. Festival, 1951; Los A. Mus., A., 1954; Butler AI, 1954; de Young Mus., 1955.

HOPE, HENRY RADFORD—*Educator*
800 Sheridan Rd., Bloomington, Ind.

B. Chelsea, Mass., Dec. 15, 1905. *Studied*: Sorbonne, Paris, France; Harvard Univ., A.M., Ph.D. *Member*: CAA; AFA; Midwestern Col. A. Conference. Lectures: "Art of the 19th & 20th Centuries." *Position*: Chm., FA Dept., Indiana Univ., Bloomington, Ind., 1941- ; Member, U.S. Nat. Comm. for UNESCO; Ed., College Art Journal; Author: Cat. of Exh. of Georges Braque, MModA, 1949; Jacques Lipchitz, MModA, 1954.

HOPKINS, JAMES R.—*Educator, P.*
Mechanicsburg, Ohio

B. Irwin, Ohio, May 17, 1877. *Studied*: Columbus A. Sch.; A. Acad. Cincinnati; & in Paris, France. *Member*: ANA; Assoc. Société Nationale des Beaux-Arts. *Awards*: med., AIC, 1916; Buenos Aires, 1910; Pan-Pacific Exp., 1915; prizes, PAFA, 1908; NAD, 1920; LL.D., Ohio State Univ. *Work*: AIC; CM; Atlanta AA. *Exhibited*: Pan-Pacific Exp.; Carnegie Inst.; CGA; PAFA; NAD; AIC; Salon Société Nationale des Beaux-Arts, Paris. *Position*: Instr., A. Acad. Cincinnati, 1914-20; Prof., 1923- , Chm. Dept. FA, 1923-44, Dir., Sch. F. & App. A., 1944-47, Ohio State Univ., Columbus, Ohio.

HOPKINS, KENDAL COLES—*Painter, T.*
Birchrunville, Pa.

B. Haddonfield, N.J., Jan. 6, 1908. *Studied*: PMSch. A.; PAFA, and in Europe. *Member*: Chester County AA;

Woodmere A. Gal.; Bryn Mawr A. Center. *Work*: in private colls. *Exhibited*: PAFA; Rockland Mus. A.; Phila. Sketch Cl.; MModA; 10 one-man exhs.; also exhibited Bryn Mawr A. Center; Westchester AA; Woodmere A. Gal.; Phillips Gal., Phila., Pa., and others. *Position*: Instr. Painting, Bryn Mawr Col.; Woodmere A. Gal.; Instr., Hd. A. Dept., Baldwin Sch., Bryn Mawr, Pa., 1951-55; Dir., Instr., Birchrunville Gal., (Pa.) at present.

HOPKINS, LIN (Mr.)—*Painter, Et.*
78 South C St., Fremont, Neb.; s. 1607 South Elm St., Casper, Wyo.

B. Omaha, Neb., Mar. 5, 1886. *Member*: Casper A. Gld.; Wyoming AA; Assoc. A. Omaha. *Work*: State Capitol, Cheyenne, Wyo.; Ft. Casper (Wyo.) Mus.; Waddell Medical Clinic, Beatrice, Neb. *Exhibited*: Univ. Wyoming, 1940; Casper FA Center, 1945 (one-man); Rock Springs, Wyo., 1935 (one-man); Fremont (Neb.) Women's Cl., 1947; Morrill Hall, Lincoln, Neb., 1949.

HOPKINS, RUTH JOY (Mrs.)—*Portrait Painter*
s. 1607 South Elm St., Casper, Wyo.; h. 78 South "C" St., Fremont, Neb.

B. Fremont, Neb., Aug. 17, 1891. *Studied*: Colorado Springs FA Center; Col. FA, Morelia, Mex. *Member*: Casper A. Gld.; Wyoming AA. *Awards*: prizes, Natrona County Fair, 1953; Wyoming State Fair, 1955. *Work*: Wyoming State Capitol, Cheyenne; Wyoming Nat. Bank, Casper; Fort Casper Mus.; St. Francis Boys' Home, Salina, Kans.; Kansas State Col.; Swedish Crucible Steel Co., Detroit. *Exhibited*: Denver A. Mus., 1935 (one-man); N.Y. Mun. Exh., 1937; NAWA, 1936, 1937; Univ. Wyoming (one-man); Rock Springs, Wyo., 1935, 1936; Joslyn A. Mus., 1947; Lincoln, Neb., 1949-1951; Natrona County Fair, 1953; Wyoming State Fair, 1955.

HOPKINSON, CHARLES—*Painter*
30 Ipswich St., Boston, Mass.; s. Manchester, Mass.

B. Cambridge, Mass., July 27, 1869. *Studied*: Harvard Univ., A.B., D.A.; & with John Twachtman, Kenyon Cox, Denman Ross, Carl Cutler; Acad. Julian, and Aman-Jean, Paris, France. *Member*: NA; Nat. Inst. A. & Let.; Am. Acad. A. & Let. *Awards*: Med., Pan-Am. Exp., 1901; St. Louis Exp., 1904; PAFA, 1915; Pan-Pacific Exp., 1915; Sesqui-Centennial Exp., Phila., Pa., 1926; AIC, 1926; prize, NAD, 1943, 1951. *Work*: portraits, Harvard, Virginia, Colorado, Pennsylvania, Yale, Columbia, Brown Univ.; Dartmouth, Bryn Mawr, Oberlin, Union, Vassar Col.; St. Mark's, Exeter, Andover Sch.; MMA; BMFA; BM; WMA; AGAA; FMA; White House, Wash., D.C. *Exhibited*: nationally.

HOPPER, EDWARD—*Painter*
3 Washington Square, North, New York 3, N.Y.

B. Nyack, N.Y., July 22, 1882. *Studied*: with Kenneth Hayes Miller, Robert Henri, William Chase. *Member*: Am. Acad. A. & Let.; Nat. Inst. A. & Let. *Awards*: Hon. degree, D.F.A., AIC, 1950; Litt.D., Rutgers Univ., 1953; gold medal, PAFA, 1935; gold medal, Nat. Inst. A. & Let.; prizes, Los A. Mus. A., 1923; AIC, 1923, 1942, 1945; Chicago Soc. Et., 1923; WMA, 1935; BMA, 1931; CGA, 1937; Hallmark Comp., 1957. *Work*: Cal. State Lib.; PAFA; BM; AIC; N.Y. Pub. Lib.; MMA; MModA; WMAA; FMA; PMG; CMA; Wadsworth Atheneum; John Herron AI; AGAA; BMFA; Randolph-Macon Col.; Toledo Mus. A.; Univ. Nebraska; WMA; Victoria & Albert Mus., London; Wichita A. Mus.; Delgado Mus. A.; Walker A. Center; Montclair A. Mus.; Newark Mus. A.; Carnegie Inst.; LC; Butler AI. *Exhibited*: nationally; Retrospective exh., WMAA, BMFA, Detroit Inst. A., 1950; Venice Biennale, 1952.

HOPPER, FLOYD D.—*Painter, Lith., T.*
R.R. #5, Box 197-B, Noblesville, Ind.

B. Martin County, Ind., Nov. 1, 1909. *Studied*: John Herron A. Sch., B.F.A.; PAFA; & with Eliot O'Hara. *Member*: Indiana AC; Phila. WC Cl.; Indianapolis AA. *Awards*: prizes, Hoosier Salon, 1936, 1942; Kansas City AI; Lithograph Exh., Oklahoma City; DePauw Univ. purchase prize, 1958. *Work*: Fort Wayne A. Mus.; Okklahoma City, Okla; Muncie (Ind.) Pub. Sch.; Ball State T. Col.; Vincennes (Ind.) Pub Sch.; DePauw Univ. *Exhibited*: AIC; CM; PAFA; Kansas City AI; Grand Rapids A. Gal.; Southern

Pr.M.; Hoosier Salon; Indiana AC; Indiana Soc. Pr.M.; Ft. Wayne Woman's Cl. Cover illus. Carpenters Magazine, 1958.

HOPPER, JO N. (Mrs. Edward)—Painter

3 Washington Square, North, New York 3, N.Y.

B. New York, N.Y. *Studied*: with Robert Henri, Kenneth Hayes Miller. *Award*: Huntington Hartford Fnd. F., 1957. *Exhibited*: CGA, 1943; PAFA, 1938; GGE, 1939; AIC, 1943; BM; Weyhe Gal., 1944; Rehn Gal., 1946; CGA, 1951; NAC, 1950; Church of the Ascension, New York, 1952; MMA, 1952, 1953; WMAA, 1953; Assn. Cape Cod A., 1953; Orleans, Mass., 1955; Gulak Greenwich Gal., N.Y., 1958; U.S. State Dept. traveling exh., to Cairo, Baghdad, Calcutta, Ankara, 1958-1961.

HORCH, NETTIE S. (Mrs.)—Museum Director

Riverside Museum; h. 310 Riverside Drive, New York 25, N.Y.

B. New York, N.Y., Nov. 15, 1896. *Studied*: Hunter Col.; Columbia Univ. *Award*: Citation and Certif., from Mayor Wagner, New York City, for 20 years as Dir. of Riverside Mus. Exhibitions arranged: International Women's Exh., 1940; First Canadian Women's Exhibit, 1946; Ten Women Artists, 1953; First Comprehensive Exh. of Contemporary Puerto Rican Artists, 1957; Ein Harod-Israel Artists, 1957; Contemporary Danish Artists, 1958-59; and numerous contemporary artist's organizations and group shows. *Positions*: Dir., Co-Founder, Master Institute of United Arts, Inc., 1922- ; Dir., Riverside Museum, New York, N.Y., 1937- .

HORD, DONAL—Sculptor

3838 Kendall St., San Diego 9, Cal.

B. Prentice, Wis., Feb. 26, 1902. *Studied*: Santa Barbara Sch. A.; Univ. Mexico; PAFA; BAID. *Member*: NA; NSS; Nat. Inst. A. & Let. *Awards*: prizes, Southern Cal. A., 1931; medal, San Diego Exp., 1935, 1936; Nat. Inst. A. & Let., 1948; Guggenheim F., 1945, 1947; gold medal, AIA, 1953. *Work*: San Diego FA Soc.; SFMA; fountain, Balboa Park, San Diego; San Diego Civic Center; basrelief, State Col., San Diego; arch. bas-reliefs, Coronado, Linda Vista, Cal.; bronze mem., American Battle Cemetery, at Henri-Chapelle, Belgium, 1958. *Exhibited*: MMoA, 1942; MMA, 1942, 1951; Am.-British exh., 1944; Modern Medaljkonst, Stockholm, 1955.

HORDER, JOCELYN CLISE—Engraver, Lith.

4354 92nd St., Southeast, Mercer Island, Wash.

B. Seattle, Wash., Aug. 4, 1923. *Studied*: Univ. Washington, B.A.; Cornish Sch., with Amelio Amero. *Member*: Northwest Pr. M. *Exhibited*: LC, 1946; Phila. Pr. Cl., 1946; Northwest Pr. M., 1945, 1949, 1950.

HORDER, NELLIE P. (Mrs. A. Morley)—Painter

3237 43rd Ave., West, Seattle 99, Wash.

B. Mount Hope, Kans., Feb. 5, 1885. *Member*: AEA; Northwest WC Soc.; Palette & Brush Cl.; Women Painters of Washington. *Awards*: prizes, Western Wash. Fair, 1951, 1952. *Exhibited*: Hathaway House, 1953 (2-man); Northwest WC Soc., 1954; Woessner Gal., 1953-1955; Northwest A., 1953 (on tour Canada & U.S.) 1954; Univ. Wash., Henry Gal., 1952, 1955; Bellevue Fair, 1952-1955; Women Painters of Washington, 1954, 1955; Palette & Brush Cl., 1950-1952, 1955; Wash. Territorial Exh., 1953; AEA, 1952-1955; Seattle Press Cl., 1949; one-man: Joe Dusanne Gal., 1956.*

HORLE, EDITH LOUISA—Etcher, Eng., P., T., C.

5730 South Salina St., Syracuse 5, N.Y.

B. Syracuse, N.Y. *Studied*: Syracuse Univ., B.S.; PMSch.A.; and with Breckenridge. *Member*: Assoc. A. Syracuse; Syracuse Pr. M.; Springfield A. Lg.; Hunterdon County AA. *Awards*: prizes, Rochester Mem. A. Gal., 1945; Syracuse Pr. M., 1946, 1957, 1958; Finger Lakes Exh., 1945; Onondaga County Hist. Soc., 1947, 1951, 1952, 1958; Syracuse Mus. FA, 1946, 1955, 1957, 1958; Cayuga Mus. A., 1946. *Work*: Rochester Mem. A. Gal.; Woodcut Soc., Kansas City, Mo.; Syracuse Univ.; Onondaga Valley Acad.; Syracuse Mus. FA. *Exhibited*: Southern Pr. M., 1936-43; LC, 1943, 1945; NAD; Phila. Pr. Cl., 1934-46; Phila. A. All.; Northwest Pr. M., 1933-37; Woodcut Soc.,

1933, 1936; New Orleans AA; Buffalo Pr. Cl.; Auburn Exh., 1945; Albany Pr. Cl., 1945, 1957; Finger Lakes Exh., Rochester, 1938-46; Assoc. A. Syracuse, 1933-46; Daubers of Syracuse, 1936-58; Syracuse Pr. M., 1938-58; BMFA; Newport, R.I.; Portland, Me.; Onondaga Hist. Soc., 1956-58; Syracuse Mus. FA, 1956, 1957; Munson-Williams-Proctor Inst., 1956, 1957; BMFA, 1957; Springfield A. Lg., 1956, 1957; Newport, R.I., 1956-58; NGA, 1957; Hunterdon County A. Center, 1957; 2-man: Onondaga Valley Acad., 1956; Munday Lib., Syracuse, 1957; Sherburne (N.Y.) A. Soc., 1958; Norwich (N.Y.) Gurnsey Lib., 1958.

HORN, AXEL—Designer, P., S.

40 West 55th St., New York 19, N.Y.; h. Spring St., South Salem, N.Y.

B. New York, N.Y., Jan. 11, 1913. *Studied*: Newark Sch. FA; ASL; & with Thomas Benton, Charles Locke, David Sequieros. *Member*: A. Lg.Am.; Assoc., IDI. *Work*: murals, Bellevue Hospital, N.Y.; Nurses Home, Welfare Island, N.Y.; USPO, Whitehall, N.Y.; Yellow Springs, Ohio; produced series of promotional books for publisher; des. Antibiotic Exhibit and 4 scientific exhibits sponsored by Nat. Science Fnd. for Brussels World's Fair; des. and produced a national visual education program for High Schools, sponsored by the National Academy of Sciences. *Exhibited*: CGA; Arch.L.; WFNY 1939; ACA Gal.; traveling exh. for Am. Chemical Soc., 1946; Chicago Mus. Sc. & Indst.; traveling exh., Army Service Forces. *Position*: Hd. Dept. A., The Displayers, New York, N.Y., 1943-48; opened indst. des. office, New York, N.Y., 1948- , inc. as Fox & Horn, 1957.

HORN, MILTON—Sculptor, P., W., L.

1932 North Lincoln Ave., Chicago 14, Ill.

B. Ukraine, Russia, Sept. 1, 1906. *Studied*: BIAD, and with Henry Kitson. *Member*: S. Gld.; AEA; CAA. *Awards*: prizes, Hardwood Industry, 1953, 1955; AIA, Chicago Chptr., 1955, citation, 1957; Chicago Assn. Commerce & Indst., 1955. *Work*: s. Brookgreen Gardens, S.C.; Olivet Col.; Seward Park H.S., N.Y.; USPO, Swarthmore, Pa.; Whitinsville, Mass.; Iron River, Mich.; monument, Olivet Col.; reliefs, groups, portraits: Lib., Blythe Park Sch., Riverside, Ill.; Univ. Pa., Medical Bldg.; West Suburban Temple, River Forest, Ill.; Nat. Hdq. Bldg., Parents & Teachers, Chicago; Temple Isaiah, Forest Hills, N.Y.; South Shore Temple, Chicago; Merchandise Mart Plaza; City of Chicago; Continental Can Co., Chicago; Milwaukee County Hospital, Wauwatosa, Wis.; Univ. West Va., Medical Campus and Chapel of Univ. hospital; relief, Jewish Fed. of Metropolitan Chicago Bldg. *Exhibited*: PAFA, 1936; WFNY 1939; BM; MMA; N.Y. Mun. Exh., 1937; S. Gld., 1938-1956; Am. A. Cong., 1939; CAA traveling exh.; VMFA; PMA; AIC; Arch. Lg.; Nat. Inst. A. & Let.; Mus. FA of Houston; one-man: BM, 1932; Gld. A. Gal., 1936; Wayne Univ., 1940; Wustum Mus., 1942; Kalamazoo Inst. A., 1942, 1945; Chicago Pub. Lib. Contributor to museum bulletins and art magazines. Lectures on art and sculptural topics to universities, colleges and groups. *Position*: S. in Res., Chm. Sch. FA, Olivet Col., Olivet, Mich., 1939-1949.

HORN, WALTER W.—Educator

University of California, Berkeley, Cal.

Position: Chm. Art Dept., University of California, Berkeley, Cal.*

HORNE, LAURA TREVITTE—Painter, Des.

284 South Columbus Ave., Mt. Vernon, N.Y.

B. Dalton, Ga., June 30, 1891. *Studied*: NAD; & with George Maynard, Francis Jones, George Bridgman, Leon Kroll. *Work*: ceramic cab., Chinese Embassy, Wash., D.C.; Trinity Church, Mt. Vernon, N.Y. *Exhibited*: NAD; All. A.Am.; SSAL; AAPL; Montclair A. Mus.; Columbia Univ.; Anderson Gal.; Babcock Gal.; Atlanta AA; WMAA; NAC; N.Y. WC Cl.; Riverside Mus.; Furman Univ.; Hudson River Mus.; New Haven, Conn., and others.

HORNUNG, CLARENCE PEARSON—Designer, I., W.

220 East 46th St., New York 17, N.Y.; h. 12 Glen Rd., West Hempstead, L.I., N.Y.

B. June 12, 1899. *Studied*: Col. City of N.Y., B.S.; N.Y. Univ.; CUASch. *Member*: AIGA; IDI; Typophiles. *Exhibited*: drawings and prints of antique automobiles circulated to 60 museums and libraries in the U.S., 1951. Author: "Trade-marks," 1930; "Handbook of Design and Devices," 1932, 1946, 1952; "Lettering from A to Z," 1946, 1954; "Handbook of Early American Advertising Art," 1947, 1954, 1956; "Wheels Across America," 1959; "Pictorial Archives of American Business and Industry," 1959; "Treasury of Horse and Buggy Days," 1960. Ed., Des., Publ.: "Portraits of Antique Automobiles"; "Early American Automobiles"; "Early American Locomotives"; "Early American Carriages"; "Early American Trolley Cars"; "Early American Fire Engines" (all publ. by Autoprints). Contributor to New York Times; Modern Packaging; American Printer; Printing News; Production Yearbook and other trade publications. *Position*: Indst. Des. specializing in trade-marks, packaging and product identification. Publ. of prints and pictures under name Autoprints, and Collectors' Prints.

HORVATH, FERDINAND HUSZTI—
Illustrator, Ceramic Des., W., Cart., C.
Temecula 68, Cal.

B. Budapest, Hungary, Aug. 28, 1891. I., "Fiddler's Green"; "Red Caboose"; "The King of the Golden River"; "Three Dragons"; "The Raven"; "The Diamond Lense," and other books; Author: "Captured," 1930. Illus. for Harper's Bazaar; New York Times. Ceramic Des. for Brayton's, Laguna Beach, Cal., and others.

HORWITZ, LOUISE McMAHAN—Painter, Des.
326 Edgewood Drive, St. Louis 5, Mo.

B. Pauls Valley, Okla., July 8, 1903. *Studied*: Kidd Key Col., Sherman, Tex.; Washington Univ.; Skowhegan Sch. A., and with Arnold Blanch, Rollin Crampton. *Member*: NAWA; St. Louis A. Gld.; Texas WC Soc. *Awards*: prizes, St. Louis A. Gld., 1949-1951; NAWA, 1951; Hallmark award, 1952; CAM, 1955. *Exhibited*: Carnegie Inst., 1941; CAM, 1948-1951; St. Louis A. Gld., 1948-1952; Joslyn A. Mus., 1948, 1952; Nelson Mus. A., 1945, 1951; Audubon A., 1951-55; Creative Gal., N.Y., 1951; Boston Soc. Indp. A., 1951, 1952; Newport AA, 1951; Amsterdam, Holland, 1956; AWS, 1958; Knickerbocker A., 1958; NAWA European traveling exh., 1956-58, and others.

HOSKINS, GAYLE PORTER—Painter, I., Des.
1625 North Rodney St., Wilmington 35, Del.

B. Brazil, Ind., July 20, 1887. *Studied*: AIC; & with Howard Pyle. *Awards*: prize, Wilmington Soc. FA. *Work*: Eleutherian-Hagley Mills Fnd. Mus., Wilmington; Delaware Chamber of Commerce; portraits: E.I. DuPont de Nemours & Co., Wilmington; Wilmington Savings Fund Soc.; Wilmington Artisans' Bank, City Council and legal firms; many private commissions. *Exhibited*: Wilmington Soc. A., 1916-58; Swope Gal. A., Terre Haute, Ind.; Indiana AA; Ogunquit, Me.; Coral Gables, Fla.; Marshall-Fields, Chicago; Wanamakers, Wilmington. Illus., national magazines and numerous books.

HOSMER, FLORENCE ARMES—Painter, T., L.
Hosmer House, Sudbury, Mass.

B. Woodstock, Conn. *Studied*: Mass. Sch. A.; BMFA Sch.; and with Joseph DeCamp, Anson Kent Cross, Charles Woodbury. *Member*: Copley Soc., Boston; Cambridge AA; Intl. Inst., Boston. *Work*: International Inst. of Boston; Essex Inst., Salem, Mass.; Park St. Church, Boston. Ports. of prominent people. *Exhibited*: Copley Soc., Boston; Boston A. Cl.; BMFA; Cambridge AA; Mass. Women Painters Germanic Mus., Cambridge; Martha's Vineyard AA; one-man: Hamilton Hall, Salem, Mass.

HOSTERMAN, NAOMI S. (Mrs. R. C.)—Painter, I.
731 Churchill Dr., Charleston 4, W. Va.

B. Elkhart, Ind., Jan. 13, 1903. *Studied*: Herron AI; Scott Carbee Sch., Boston; Indiana Univ.; CM Sch. *Member*: Hoosier Salon; Indiana AA; All.A. of W. Va. *Awards*: prizes, All. A., W.Va., 1938, 1942, 1946. *Work*: First Presbyterian Church, Baptist Temple, Charleston, W.Va.; Daywood A. Gal., Lewisburg, W.Va.; Laird Mem. Hospital, Montgomery, W.Va.; Charleston Airport; Charleston Gen'l. Hospital; Kanawha Valley Hospital; Morris Harvey Col. *Exhibited*: Hoosier Salon; All.A., W.Va.; John Herron AI. I., "Greenbrier Pioneers and their Homes," 1942; "Pioneers and their Homes on Upper Kanawha; "Lewisburg Landmarks."

HOUGH, (HELEN) HALLEY (BREWSTER)—
Art Curator, T., L.
1012 Creston Rd., Berkeley 8, Cal.

B. Oakland, Cal., Oct. 10, 1894. *Studied*: Univ. California; Univ. Washington, A.B. Lectures: Asiatic and Modern Art. *Positions*: Cur., Henry Gal., Univ. Washington, Seattle, Wash., 1927-47; Librarian, California Col. A. & Crafts, Oakland, Cal., 1951-52; Asst. Cur., Oriental Art, Gump's, San Francisco, Cal., 1954- .

HOUSE, JAMES (CHARLES), JR.—
Sculptor, E., Cart.
129 Kent Rd., Springfield, Pa.

B. Benton Harbor, Mich., Jan. 19, 1902. *Studied*: Univ. Michigan; PAFA; Univ. Pennsylvania, B.Sc. in Edu. *Work*: S., WMAA; Sch. Edu., Univ. Pennsylvania; St. Clements Episcopal Church, Phila., Pa. *Exhibited*: PAFA, 1939, 1940, 1942, 1945, 1946, 1948, 1952, 1957; Dallas Mus. FA, 1936; BM, 1932; WMAA, 1934, 1936; PMA, 1933, 1940, 1950, 1955; Carnegie Inst., 1941; Phila. A. All., 1954, 1955, 1957; N.Y.Mun. Exh., 1936; MMA (AV), 1942; MModA, 1942; Detroit Inst. A., 1932, 1935, 1938-1940, 1958; Kansas City AI, 1935. Author: "Fifty Drawings," 1930. *Position*: Assoc. Prof., Sculpture & Drawing, Univ. Pennsylvania, Philadelphia, Pa., 1936- . San Diego State Col., summer, 1956.

HOUSER, JAMES COWING, JR. (JIM)—Educator, P.
Kentucky Wesleyan College; h. 3319 Placid Place, Owensboro, Ky.

B. Dade City, Fla., Nov. 12, 1928. *Studied*: Ringling Sch. A.; Fla. Southern Col., B.S.; AIC; Univ. Florida, M.F.A.; Johns Hopkins Univ. *Member*: CAA; Southeastern Col. A. Conference; Kentucky A. Assn. *Awards*: prizes, Maryland A. Exh., 1954; Louisville A. Center, 1957. *Work*: J.B. Speed Mem. Mus.; International Harvester Co.; Evansville (Ind.) Mus. A.; mural, Wesleyan Heights Methodist Church, Owensboro. *Exhibited*: ACA Gal., N.Y., 1954; Nebraska Wesleyan Univ., 1958; Jacksonville Mus. A., 1952, 1953; Maryland Artists, 1954; Tri-State Annual, Evansville, 1955-57; Louisville A. Center, 1956-58; one-man: Jacksonville, Fla., Mus., 1953; Abbey Lane Theatre, Balt., Md., 1954; Carriage House Gal., Louisville, 1955; Murray State Col., 1957; 2-man: Evansville Mus., 1957. *Position*: Prof. A., Kentucky Wesleyan Col., Owensboro, Ky., 1954- , Chm. FA Correlate, 1957- .

HOUSER, VIC(TOR) CARL—Sculptor, W., L.
3200 Durand Drive, Hollywood 28, Cal.

B. Los Angeles, Cal., Mar. 6, 1895. *Studied*: AIC; Carl Werntz Sch. FA, Chicago, and with Lorado Taft. *Member*: Cal. A. Cl.; Laguna Beach AA; Southland AA; Las Vegas A. Gld.; Professional Artists Roost (Fndr.). *Awards*: prizes, Soc. Western A., 1954; P. & S. of Los Angeles; Cal. A. Cl., 1954-58; Laguna Beach AA, 1956, 1957; Blakeman-Florence, Cal., Citation and Award, 1956; Southland AA, 1956. *Work*: 1st Award Medals (6) for Cal. A. Cl., 1958; monument to Joe Frisco, Delmar (Cal.) Race Track; Anita Metz trophy for Cal. Yacht Cl.; portraits, heraldic arms, figureheads for yachts in private colls. Lectures, demonstrations, TV and radio talks. *Exhibited*: WMA; CAM; Madonna Festival, Santa Ana and Los Angeles; Bakersfield A. Gld.; Palos Verdes AA; All-City Show, Los Angeles; Inglewood AA; Santa Barbara, and many others; one-man: Catholic Women's Cl., Los A.; Southland AA; Whittier AA; San Marino Women's Cl.; Pacific Palisades AA; Ebell Cl., Los A.; John Decker Gal.; Santa Monica AA; Gravers Soc., Univ. So. Cal., and others.

HOUSTON, RUSSELL A.—Sculptor, W., P.
4009 Saul Rd., Kensington, Md.

B. Morgantown, W. Va., Sept. 28, 1914. *Studied*: Corcoran Sch. A.; Univ. Hawaii, and with Robert Laurent. *Member*: Soc. Wash. A.; A. Gld. Wash.; Maryland S. Gld.; Wash. S. Group; Assn. Fed. Arch. *Awards*: prizes, Corcoran Sch. A., 1940, 1941; Soc. Wash. A., 1940, 1941, 1948, 1949; Assn. Fed. Arch., 1939, 1940, 1947, 1948 (4); CGA, 1947; BMA, 1947, 1948. *Work*: des. medal for WFNY 1939; American Legion medal; s., Officer's Cl., Wash., D.C.; St. Paul's Church, Wash., D.C.; Carlton Hotel, Pittsburgh, Pa.; Shoreham Hotel, Wash., D.C. *Exhibited*: PAFA, 1946; CGA, 1943 (one-man); Morgantown, W. Va., 1938 (one-man); Soc. Wash. A., 1939-1944, 1948, 1949; Assn.

Fed. Arch., 1939, 1942, 1946, 1947, 1948; U.S. Nat. Mus., 1940, 1948-1952; Honolulu Acad. A., 1945 (one-man); Wash. A. Cl., 1947-1949; Home Builder's Exp., Wash., D.C., 1948, 1949; VMFA, 1951; Playhouse, Wash., D.C. (one-man). *Position*: Sc., Arch., Mills, Petticord & Mills Assoc., Washington, D.C.

HOVANNES, JOHN—*Sculptor, T.*
110 West 54th St., New York, N.Y.

B. Smyrna, Dec. 31, 1900. *Studied*: R.I.Sch.Des.; BAID. *Member*: S.Gld.; Audubon A.; Westchester A. & Crafts Gld. *Awards*: Guggenheim F., 1940; Eugene Meyer award, 1941; Wings for Victory competition, 1942. *Work*: Newark Mus. *Exhibited*: PAFA, 1942, 1943, 1945, 1946; AIC, 1942, 1943; MMA (AV), 1942; NAD, 1943; Riverside Mus., 1943; WMAA, 1942-1946; Nebraska AA, 1945; WFNY 1939; S.Gld., annually; Robinson Gal., 1941 (one-man). *Position*: Instr., CUASch, 1945, 1946; ASL, New York, N.Y., 1945, 1946.*

HOVELL, JOSEPH—*Sculptor, T.*
130 West 57th St., New York 19, N.Y.

B. Kiev, Russia. *Studied*: CUASch., with Brewster; NAD, with Robert Aitken. *Work*: portrait busts and bas-reliefs in private collections; plaques, busts, Carnegie Hall, N.Y.; Nordacs Club; A.F. of L. Bldg., Wash., D.C.; CIO Bldg., Wash., D.C.; New Sch. for Social Research; Nathan Sachs bronze mem. plaque. *Exhibited*: NAD; Soc. Indp. A.; BM; All. A. Am.; WMAA; Carnegie Hall Gal.; Mus. Sc. & Indst.; Lotos Club, N.Y., and others.

HOVEY, WALTER READ—*Educator*
University of Pittsburgh; h. 4801 Forbes St., Pittsburgh 13, Pa.

B. Springfield, Mass., July 21, 1895. *Studied*: Yale Univ., A.B.; Harvard Univ., A.M. *Member*: CAA; Assoc. A. Pittsburgh. Contributor to: Encyclopaedia of the Arts, 1946; Art in America, Art News, Parnassus, & other magazines. Lectures: Chinese Mediaeval & Modern Art. Author: "Catalogue of the Frick Collection, N.Y., vol. 8, Potteries and Porcelains," 1955. *Position*: Hd., Dept. FA, Univ. Pittsburgh, Pa.; Specialist, U.S. Int'l. Info. Admin., Near East, Pakistan, Ceylon, 1954-55.

HOVSEPIAN, LEON—*Painter, Gr., L., T.*
96 Squantum St., Worcester 6, Mass.

B. Bloomsburg, Pa., Nov. 20, 1915. *Studied*: WMA; Yale Univ., B.F.A. *Awards*: Traveling F., Yale Univ., 1941; prize, Fitchburg A. Center, 1948. *Work*: Fitchburg A. Center; PBA; murals, Ft. Warren, Mass.; Sheraton Hotel, Worcester, Mass.; Coronado, Aurora hotels, Worcester, Mass.; Clinton, Mass.; Hickory House, Worcester, Mass.; Hotel Lenox, Dartmouth House, Boston; Norton Abrasives Co., Worcester, Mass. Altarpiece, Holy Trinity Church, Worcester, Mass.; medical drawings, Hahnemann Hospital. *Exhibited*: AIC, 1941; WMA, 1945; NGA; CGA; MMA; PAFA; Albright A. Gal.; Milwaukee AI; Fitchburg A. Center; R.I.Sch.Des. *Position*: Instr., A., WMA Sch., Worcester, Mass.; Dir., Boylston Summer A. Sch., 1948- ; Instr., Int. Des., YWCA, 1955; Dir., Triart Designers; Consultant in Des. for mural painting for Seminary of The Oblates of Mary Immaculate, Bucksport, Me.

HOWARD, ANN AMMONS—*Teacher, P., C.*
3711 Kings Highway, Jackson, Miss.

B. Pelahatchie, Miss., July 6, 1927. *Studied*: Millsaps Col., Jackson, Miss., B.A.; Univ. Mississippi; Memphis Acad. A.; Memphis State Univ., M.A.; Mississippi Southern Col., B.A. *Member*: New Orleans AA; Mississippi AA; Allison A. Colony. *Awards*: prizes, Mississippi AA, 1950; Art News Comp., 1951. *Work*: Mississippi State Col. for Women; Mary Buie Mus., Oxford, Miss. *Exhibited*: NAD, 1950; Fla. Southern Col., 1952; Mississippi AA, 1948, 1950-1952; Mississippi Junior Lg., traveling exh., 1951-52; New Orleans AA, 1951, 1952; Allisons' Wells, Miss., 1952. *Position*: Instr. A., Mary Buie Mus., Oxford, Miss., 1951-52; Lausanne Sch. & Memphis Acad. A., Memphis, Tenn., 1952-1957; Snowden Jr. H.S., Memphis, 1956-57.

HOWARD, CHARLES—*Painter*
The End Cottage, Helions Bumpstead, Essex, England

B. Montclair, N.J., Jan. 2, 1899. *Studied*: Univ. California, B.A. *Member*: San F. AA.; Soc. Mural Painters; London;

Cambridge Soc. P. & S. *Awards*: prizes, SFMA, 1940, 1942; MMA (AV), 1942; Palace Legion Honor, 1946; Pasadena AI, 1946. *Work*: SFMA; AIC; MMA; Pasadena AI; Mus. Non-Objective Painting; Art of This Century. *Exhibited*: San F. AA, annually; AIC, 1943, 1945: Critic's Choice, Cincinnati, Ohio, 1945; MMA (AV), 1942; MModA, 1942; retrospective exh., Whitechapel A. Gal., London, 1956; St. George's Gal., London, 1958.

HOWARD, HUMBERT L.—*Painter*
Fuller Bldg., 10 South 18th St.; h. 5305 Westminster Ave., Philadelphia, Pa.

B. Philadelphia, Pa., July 12, 1915. *Studied*: Univ. Pennsylvania; Howard Univ. Sch. FA. *Member*: AEA. *Work*: PAFA, and private coll. *Exhibited*: PAFA, 1950, 1951 (one-man), 1952, 1953; WFNY 1939; Temple Univ.; PM, 1954 and prior; Phila. A. All., 1952, one-man, 1958; LC; Univ. So. California; Carlen Gal.; Phila. Sketch Cl.

HOWARD, JOHN L(ANGLEY)—*Painter, I., T.*
Van Houten St., Upper Nyack, N.Y.

B. Upper Montclair, N.J., Feb. 5, 1902. *Studied*: Univ. California; Cal. Sch. A. & Crafts; ASL, with Kenneth Hayes Miller. *Member*: San F. AA; Marin SA. *Awards*: prizes, San F. AA, 1934, 1937, 1945. *Work*: mural, Coit Mem. Tower, San F., Cal. *Exhibited*: CGA, 1943; Carnegie Inst., 1941; GGE, 1939; AIC, 1945; Palace Legion Honor, 1945, 1946. *Positions*: Illustrated for Scientific American Magazine, and others; covers of scientific subjects; Instr., PIASch., Brooklyn, N.Y., 1958- .

HOWARD, LEN R.—*Craftsman*
Kent, Conn.

B. London, England, Aug. 2, 1891. *Studied*: PIASch; ASL; St. Martin's and Camberwell A. & Crafts, London, England. *Member*: Kent AA; SC; Meriden A. & Crafts. *Award*: prize, Meriden A. & Crafts. *Work*: stained glass windows for churches & schools in Torrington, New Milford, Brookfield Center, Canaan, Conn.; Memphis, Tenn.; Augusta, Ga.; Santa Maria, Cal.; Ann Arbor, Mich.; New Orleans, La.; Salina, Kans.; Nutley, N.J.; Summit, N.J.; Winsted and Bridgeport, Conn.; Stockbridge and Longmeadow, Mass.; LaGuardia Mem., Christ Church, Riverdale, N.Y., etc. Lectures on Stained Glass Techniques.

HOWARD, LORETTA (Mrs. Howell)—*Painter*
39 East 67th St.; h. 36 East 74th St., New York 21, N.Y.

B. Chicago, Ill., Nov. 1, 1904. *Studied*: Bennett Sch., Millbrook, N.Y., and with Robert Henri. *Member*: NAWA; AAPL. *Work*: AIC. *Exhibited*: WMAA, 1936; AIC; WFNY 1939; NAWA.

HOWARD, LUCILE (Mrs. Herbert Allen Roberts)—*Painter, T., L.*
51 East Maple Ave.; h. "Overstone," Moorestown, N.J.

B. Bellows Falls, Vt., May 28, 1885. *Studied*: Phila. Sch. Des. for Women; & with Elliott Daingerfield, Henry Snell. *Member*: NAWA; AWCS; AAPL; Phila. A. All.; Phila. WC Cl.; Wilmington Soc. FA. *Awards*: Shillard med., Phila., Pa. *Work*: Wilmington Soc. FA; Swarthmore Col.; Alum. Assn., Phila. Sch. Des. for Women; Thomas Jefferson H.S., Brooklyn, N.Y. *Exhibited*: PAFA; Albright A. Gal.; CGA; NAD; AIC; Phila. AC; AWCS; Phila. WC Cl.; Balt. WC Cl.; AFA; NAWA; Overstone Studio, 1950 (one-man); Phila. A. All.; Phila. Plastic Cl.; Wilmington Soc. FA. Lectures: History of Art; History of Costume.

HOWARD, RICHARD FOSTER—*Museum Director*
Birmingham Museum of Art, City Hall, Birmingham 3, Ala.

B. Plainfield, N.J., July 26, 1902. *Studied*: Harvard Col., B.S.; Harvard Grad. Sch.; Yale Univ.; Cornell Univ. *Member*: AAMus.; AFA; Southern A. Mus. Dir. Assn.; Council, Southeastern Conf.AAMus. *Awards*: Order of the White Lion of Bohemia, 1947; Stella della Solidarieta d'Italia, 1950. Lectures on Art History & Appreciation. *Positions*: Dir., Dallas Mus. FA, 1935-42; Chief, Monuments FA Archives, 1946-49; Dir., Des Moines A. Center, 1949-50; Dir., Birmingham Mus. A., 1951- .

HOWARD, ROBERT BOARDMAN—*Sculptor, P., C., T.*

521 Francisco St.; h. 2500 Leavenworth St., San Francisco 11, Cal.

B. New York, N.Y., Sept. 20, 1896. *Studied*: Cal. Sch. A. & Crafts; ASL; & with Arthur Upham Pope, Kenneth Hayes Miller. *Member*: San F. A. Comm.; San F. AA. *Awards*: Med., San F. AA, 1923; prize, 1924, 1941, 1943, 1944, 1947, 1950, 1951, 1955. *Work*: SFMA; Mills Col., Oakland, Cal.; murals, Yosemite Nat. Park; San F. Stock Exchange Bldg.; relief maps, U.S. Navy; sc., P.G. & E. Bldg., San F.; Berkeley (Cal.) Auditorium; Univ. Cal.; sculpture, IBM, San Jose, Cal. *Exhibited*: San F. AA, 1924-1955, one-man, 1956; CGA, 1937; Carnegie Inst., 1941; AIC, 1944; Palace Legion Honor, 1946; WFNY 1939; GGE, 1939; WMAA, 1948, 1950-1955; MMA, 1951; Sao Paulo, Brazil, 1951-1952, 1955. *Position*: Instr., Sculpture & Painting, Cal. Sch. FA, San Francisco, Cal., 1944-52; Mills Col., Oakland, Cal., 1945.

HOWARD, MRS. ROBERT B. *See Kent, Adaline*

HOWE, BEATRICE—*Assistant Museum Director*

Albright Art Gallery, 1285 Elmwood Ave., Buffalo 22, N.Y.*

HOWE, GERTRUDE HERRICK—*Illustrator, P.*

100 Edgars Lane, Hastings-on-Hudson 6, N.Y.

B. Canajoharie, N.Y., Aug. 6, 1902. *Studied*: Mt. Holyoke Col., B.A.; PIASch.; & with Charles Hawthorne. *Exhibited*: AIGA; Studio Gld.; Orleans, Mass., 1958; one-man: Bronxville, N.Y., 1956. I., books for leading publishers.

HOWE, OSCAR—*Painter, E.*

Art Department, State University of South Dakota, Vermillion, S.D.

B. Joe Creek, S.D., May 13, 1915. *Studied*: Dakota Wesleyan Univ.; Univ. Oklahoma, M.F.A. *Awards*: prizes, Philbrook A. Center, Tulsa, 1947, 1949-1959; Denver A. Mus., 1952, 1953, 1954; Mus. New Mexico, 1956, 1958. *Work*: murals, Mitchell (S.D.) Lib.; Mobridge Auditorium; Nebraska City, Neb.; exterior ceramic tile mural, Hinsdale, Ill.; paintings: Joslyn A. Mus.; Gallup (N.M.) A. Gal.; Mus. New Mexico; Philbrook A. Center; Denver A. Mus.; Montclair (N.J.) A. Mus. Illus., "Legends of the Mighty Sioux"; "The Little Lost Fox"; "Bringer of the Mystery Dog"; "North American Indian Costumes." Contributor to School Arts; Indians at Work; Art Education Today; Time; Oklahoma Today; "Indian Art of the United States" (d'Harnoncourt); "A Pictorial History of the American Indian" (La Farge). Work published in foreign magazines "Riding"; "Animal and Zoo Magazine" (both London); "L'Illustration" (Paris). *Exhibitions*: Philbrook A. Center; AIC; Smithsonian Inst.; Denver A. Mus.; SFMA; Stanford Univ.; Mus. of the Southwest, Los Angeles; Mus. New Mexico; MModA; one-man: Philbrook A. Center; Fort Dodge, Iowa; Mus. New Mexico, 1957; Denver A. Mus., 1958; Joslyn A. Mus., 1959. *Position*: Asst. Prof. FA, Asst. Dir., Univ. Museum, State University of South Dakota, Vermillion, S.D., 1957- .

HOWE, ROBERT MUNSON—*Educator, Eng., Et., S.*

Southwest Missouri State College, Springfield, Mo.; h. 816 Manor Rd., Independence, Mo.

Studied: Univ. Kansas City, A.B.; Peabody Col., M.A., Ed. D.; Univ. Iowa, M.F.A., grad. asst. to Mauricio Lasansky; Kansas City AI, and with Humbert Albrizio. *Member*: Am. Soc. for Aesthetics. *Awards*: medal, Independence, Mo., 1934; Carnegie scholarship, 1940. *Exhibited*: Walker A. Center and Colorado Springs FA Center joint traveling exh., 1947; AIC, 1947; Fort Hays, 1952 (one-man); Stable Gal., 1952 (one-man); Mid-Am. A., annually; CAM, 1949; Walker A. Center, 1947, 1948; SAM, 1948. *Position*: Prof. A., Southwest Missouri State Col., Springfield, Mo., 1941- ; Visiting L., Vanderbilt Univ., Nashville, Tenn.*

HOWE, THOMAS CARR—*Museum Director*

2709 Larkin St., San Francisco 9, Cal.

B. Kokomo, Ind., Aug. 12, 1904. *Studied*: Harvard Univ., A.B., A.M. *Member*: Assn. A. Mus. Dir.; Western Assn. A. Mus. Dir.; Century Assn.; Bohemian Cl., San F.; Harvard Cl., N.Y.; Author's Cl., London. Contributor to Pacific Art Review; Art News; Art Digest, and museum bulletins. Lectures, Art History; Art Appreciation. Author: "Salt Mines and Castles," 1946. Decorated by French (Chevalier, Legion of Honor) and Dutch (Officier, Order of Orange-Nassau) Governments for assisting in recovery of works of art looted by the Germans prior to and during the last war. *Positions*: Asst. Dir., 1931-39, Dir., 1939- , California Palace of the Legion of Honor, San F., Cal.; Deputy Chief, M.F.A. & A. Section, U.S.F.E.T. Hq., 1945-46; Cultural Affairs Adv., U.S. State Dept. to High Commissioner of Germany, 1950-51.

HOWE, WINIFRED EVA—*Writer, Historian*

1102 Elm Ave., West, Collingswood, N.J.

B. Norwich, Conn. *Studied*: Norwich Free Acad.; Boston Univ., A.B. *Member*: AAUW. Author: "A History of the Metropolitan Museum of Art," 1913; "A History of the Metropolitan Museum of Art, Vol. II, 1905-1941," pub. 1946; Ed., Children's Bulletin of the MMA, 1917-1935; Bulletin of the MMA, 1911-1941. *Position*: Member MMA Staff, 1910-47; Ed., MMA Publications, 1911-41; Editorial Consultant & Historian, 1941-47 (Retired).

HOWELL, CLAUDE FLYNN—*Painter, T., L.*

Carolina Apts., Wilmington, N.C.

B. Wilmington, N.C., Mar. 17, 1915. *Studied*: with Jon Corbino, Bernard Karfiol, Charles Rosen. *Member*: AEA. *Work*: IBM; High Mus. A.; North Carolina Mus. A.; Greenville A. Center. *Awards*: prizes, North Carolina State A. Soc., 1939, 1947, 1954, 1956; IBM, 1940; Carnegie Inst., 1940; Mint Mus. A., 1945; Rosenwald F., 1948; Norfolk Mus. A. & Sc., 1954; High Mus. A., 1947; N.C.-Va. Exh., 1947, 1957. *Exhibited*: IBM; WFNY 1939; Pasadena AI, 1946; SSAL, 1946, 1947; N.C. State A. Soc., 1940-1958; Atlanta, Ga., 1947-1955; Univ. Tennessee, 1951; MMA, 1952; BMA, 1954; Gibbes A. Gal., 1955; Greensboro, N.C., 1955; one-man: Charlotte, 1947, 1958; Wilmington, 1948; Raleigh, 1948; Chapel Hill, 1950, 1953; Greenville, 1955; Durham, 1950; Asheville, 1950; Salem Col., 1953, all in North Carolina; Davidson Col., N.Y., 1952; Copain, N.Y., 1950; Mercer Univ., Macon, Ga., 1948; Florence Mus. A., 1958; Converse Col., 1958; Univ. Georgia, 1958. *Position*: Instr., A. Dept., Wilmington Col., Wilmington, N.C.; Illus. "The Hatterasman," 1958.

HOWELL, DOUGLASS (MORSE)—

Craftsman, P., Et., Eng., Hist., W., L.

1099 Washington Ave., Westbury, L.I., N.Y.

B. New York, N.Y., Nov. 30, 1906. *Studied*: in France and Italy. *Member*: Am. Craftsmen's Council; Intl. Plate Printers, Die Stampers & Eng. Union; Am. Ord. Assn. *Work*: handmade papers: BMFA; BM; handpress painting, books, N.Y. Pub. Lib.; Huntington Mus., San Marino, Cal., and in private collections. *Exhibited*: America House, 1953; Country A. Gal., Westbury, 1954; one-man: Brooklyn Pub. Lib., 1947; Newport AA, 1948; Franklin Inst., Phila., 1948; Univ. Maine, 1951; Betty Parsons Gal., 1955. Lectures: Papers and the Artist: Past, Present and Future; Paper requirements of the various art mediums. Produces facsimiles of rare prints, duplicating paper, ink, and graphic process; Experimental Workshop for research in handmade papers for the Fine Arts.

HOWELL, FELICIE (Mrs. W. Findlay Downs)—*Painter*

L'Abri—The Headlands, Rockport, Mass.; also, c/o Day & Zimmerman, 1700 Sansom St., Philadelphia 3, Pa.; h. 1810 South Rittenhouse Square, Philadelphia 3, Pa.

B. Honolulu, Hawaii, Sept. 8, 1897. *Studied*: Corcoran Sch. A.; Phila. Sch. Des. for Women. *Member*: NA; AWCS; Phila. WC Cl.; Wash. WC Cl.; NAC; Phila. A. All. *Awards*: prizes, NAWA, 1916; NAD, 1921; AIC, 1921, 1927; med., Soc. Wash. A., 1921, 1922; Wash. WC Cl., 1921. *Work*: CGA; MMA; John Herron AI; AIC; Mus. City of N.Y.; Univ. Pennsylvania. *Exhibited*: NAD; AIC; CGA; PAFA; Carnegie Inst.; Phila. WC Cl.; Wash. WC Cl.; Venice, Italy; MModA; Macbeth Gal.; Grand Central Gal.; Doll & Richards, Boston; & in Europe.

HOWELL, HANNAH JOHNSON (Mrs. Henry W., Jr.)—*Art Librarian*

10 East 71st St. (21); h. 151 East 83rd St., New York 28, N.Y.

B. Oskaloosa, Iowa, June 22, 1905. *Studied*: Penn Col.; Sch. of Library Service, B.L.S. *Member*: Am. Library

Oskaloosa, Iowa; Univ. Chicago, Ph.B.; Columbia Univ. Assn.; Art Reference Round Table; Special Library Assn.; Museum Group. *Position*: Hd. Librarian, Frick Art Reference Library, New York, N.Y., 1947- .

HOWELL, JOHN S.—*Painter, T.*

Mt. Kemble Lake, Morristown, N.J.

B. Salem, Ohio, Aug. 8, 1905. *Studied*: Graphic Sketch Cl.; PAFA, with Daniel Garber. *Member*: AWS; New Jersey WC Soc.; Phila. WC Cl.; SC. *Exhibited*: AWS, 1955-1958; All. A. Am., 1954; New Jersey WC Soc.; Montclair A. Mus.; SC, regularly since 1946.

HOWELL, MARIE (W.) *(Mrs. James A.)*—
Designer, T., C.

404 Benefit St., Providence 3, R.I.

B. Milwaukee, Wis., July 30, 1931. *Studied*: Connecticut Col. for Women; R.I. Sch. Des., B.F.A. (textile des.). *Member*: Nat. Soc. for Dec. Des.; Des.-Craftsmen of R.I. *Exhibited*: Good Design Show, Chicago & N.Y., 1954; Community A. Center, Wallingford, Pa., 1953, 1954; New England Crafts, Worcester, Mass., 1955; Boston A. Festival, 1956; Pa. Gld. Craftsmen, 1958; Smithsonian Inst. traveling exh., 1955 (with James Howell); Upholstery Leather Group Des. Comp., 1957, 1958; Wichita AA, 1958; AID Des. Comp., 1957. *Position*: Instr., R.I. Sch. Des., Providence, R.I., 1955- ; Governing Bd., Des.-Craftsmen of R.I.; Instr., Haystack Mountain Sch. of Crafts, 1958. Contributor to Design (India); Upholstering magazines.

HOWEN, ELLIS ALEXANDER—*Painter, T., L.*

1824 Los Robles Drive, Bakersfield, Cal.

B. Mondovi, Wis., June 16, 1898. *Studied*: Univ. Wisconsin; AIC. *Member*: Cal. A. Cl.; Bakersfield AA. *Awards*: in local and regional exh., 1945- . *Exhibited*: San Joaquin Pioneer Mus. & Haggin Gal., Stockton, Cal., 1955; Cal. A. Cl., 1953, 1954, 1957; San Luis Obispo County Exh., 1952; Cal. State Fair, 1950. *Position*: Pres., Bakersfield AA, 1945-48; Chm., Cal. State Fair Com. from Kern County, 1950; Lecturer women's clubs, 1948-58.

HOWEN, LILLIAN HARRIS *(Mrs.)*—*Painter*

1824 Los Robles Drive, Bakersfield, Cal.

B. Pine Bluff, Ark., Mar. 3, 1907. *Studied*: Univ. California, B.A.; Univ. Alberta (Can.), with A.Y. Jackson, J.W.G. MacDonald, James Dichmont. *Member*: Cal. A. Cl.; Soc. Western A.; Bakersfield AA. *Awards*: prizes, Kern County Fair, 1945-1957; AAUW, 1958. *Exhibited*: San Joaquin Pioneer Mus. & Haggin Gal., 1955; Cal. State Fair, 1950; Glendale AA, 1949; San Luis Obispo, 1952; Laguna Beach, 1954, 1955; Bakersfield AA, 1944-1958; Cal. A. Cl., 1953-1958; deYoung Mem. Mus., 1956-1958. *Position*: Sec., 1944-47, Vice-Pres., 1948-53, Bakersfield AA; Publ. Chm., AAPL (Bakersfield Unit), 1945-48.

HOWES, ALFRED LOOMIS—*Painter, Des.*

525 Stanley Ave., Clarksburg, W.Va.

B. Danbury, Conn., Apr. 18, 1906. *Studied*: NAD; Springfield Col. *Work*: murals, John Lester Recording Laboratories; All Souls Church, Brooklyn, N.Y.; maps, Fourco Glass Co. *Exhibited*: New Jersey Gal.; one-man exh.; Argent Gal.; Milwaukee AI. *Position*: Adv. Dir., Lalon Corp.*

HOWLAND, RICHARD HUBBARD—*Educator*

National Trust for Historic Preservation, 2000 K St., Northwest (6); h. 1516 33rd St., Northwest, Washington 7, D.C.

B. Providence, R.I., Aug. 23, 1910. *Studied*: Brown Univ., A.B.; Harvard Univ., A.M.; Johns Hopkins Univ., Ph.D. Author: "Greek Lamps from the Athenian Agora," 1958; Co-Author: "The Architecture of Baltimore," 1952. *Position*: Member Managing Comm., Am. Sch. of Classical Studies, Athens, Greece; Bd. Dir., Soc. Arch. Historians; Trustee, The Peale Mus., Baltimore, Md.; Trustee, BMFA; Evergreen Fnd.; Pres., Nat. Trust for Hist. Preservation, 1956- .

HOWLETT, CAROLYN SVRLUGA—
Educator, P., Gr., C., Des., L.

336 Coonley Rd., Riverside, Ill.; School of the Art Institute, Chicago, Ill.

B. Berwyn, Ill., Jan. 13, 1914. *Studied*: AIC, B.A. in Edu., M.A.E.; Univ. Chicago; Northwestern Univ., M.A., and with Helen Gardner, Francis Chapin, Margaret Artingstall. *Member*: Chicago A. Cl.; Nat. A. Edu. Assn.; Chicago Soc. A.; Western AA; AFA; Com. on A. Edu., MModA; Illinois A. Edu. Assn.; Chicago A. Educators Assn.; Around-Chicago A. Edu. Assn. *Awards*: AIC, 1932. *Exhibited*: Pan-American Salon; Chicago Hist. Soc., 1942; AIC, 1945, 1946, 1952, 1953; Chicago Mus. Sc. & Indst., 1948, 1949; Chicago Soc. A., 1946-1948; Findlay Gal., 1949, 1950; Riverside Mus., 1947; Renaissance Soc., Chicago, 1948; AFA, 1948; Assoc. Am. A., Chicago, 1950; "Magnificent Mile A. Exh.," 1951; Chicago A. Cl., 1952-1955; Marshall Field Co., 1953. Contributor to Design, School Arts, NAEA yearbook, 1954; Junior Arts and Activities magazines; Author, chapter on drawing & painting, "Childcraft" encyclopedia; Author, I., World Book Encyclopedia. *Positions*: Tech. Consultant, Arts & Skills Program, Am. Red Cross, 1942-45; Nat. A. Edu. Assn. Council member, 1947-50; Policy & Research Comm., 1947-53; Prof. (1953-); Hd. Dept. A. Edu., 1944- , Instr., 1937- , AIC, Chicago, Ill.; Chm., Curriculum Committee, NAEA, 1957-59.

HOYER, FRANS—*Painter*

Standish Arms Hotel, 169 Columbia Heights, Brooklyn 1, N.Y.

B. Dordrecht, Netherlands. *Studied*: BM Sch.; in Holland & Switzerland; & with Brackman, Brook, Picken, H. E. Ogden Campbell. *Exhibited*: Holland House Corp. of Netherlands, 1945; Little Gal., 1945, 1949 (one-man); Brooklyn SA, 1943; N.Y.Pub.Lib., Columbia Univ. branch, 1945; All.A.Am., 1946; AAPL, 1946; Yonkers AA, 1950.

HOYT, DOROTHY (KING)—*Painter, Et., Eng.*

14 Stuyvesant Oval, New York 9, N.Y.; s. Trumansburg, N.Y.

B. East Orange, N.J., Aug. 11, 1909. *Studied*: Cornell Univ., B.S., M.A.; ASL; New Sch. Social Research. *Member*: NAWA; Print Council of Am.; New Jersey Soc. P. & S.; Brooklyn Soc. Painters. *Awards*: prizes, NAWA, 1955, medal, 1958; New Jersey Soc. P. & S., 1957. *Exhibited*: WMAA, 1952; PAFA, 1951; LC, 1957; Boston Pr. M., 1957; One-man: Macbeth Gal., 1947; John Heller Gal., 1951; Tyringham (Mass.) Gal., 1955; Andrew Dickson White Mus. A., Cornell Univ.

HOYT, EDITH—*Painter, I.*

c/o Arts Club, 2017 I St., Washington 6, D.C.

B. West Point, N.Y., Apr. 10, 1894. *Studied*: Corcoran Sch. A.; in France; and with Charles Woodbury, Henry B. Snell. *Member*: Wash. WC Cl.; Soc. Wash. A.; AEA; Newport AA. *Work*: Quebec Provincial Mus.; Quebec Hist. Mus.; Chateau Frontenac; Canadian Nat. Railways; Canada Steamships; Clarke S.S. Lines, Guatemala; Tadoussac Hotel, Canada; Little Rock AA; Robert Woods Bliss Coll., Wash., D.C. *Exhibited*: Nationally & internationally. One-man: CGA, 1936; Joslyn A. Mus., 1937; T. Col., Columbia Univ., 1942; San Diego FA Soc., 1948; Mus. New Mexico, 1948; La Jolla A. Center, 1948; Santa Barbara Mus. A., 1950; Mexican-North Am. Cultural Inst., 1954; Instituto de Bellas Artes, Mexico City, 1953-1956; Iowa Fed. Women's Cl. traveling exh., 1953-54; Monterrey Univ., Mexico, 1957; Murray Bay, Canada, 1957, 1958; George Washington Univ. Lib., 1957; Doll & Richards, Boston, 1958; City of Montreal: Ile Helene de Champlain, 1958-59.

HOYT, ROBERT TOWNSEND—*Cartoonist, Comm., W.*

1063 Oak Lane, Plainfield, N.J.

B. Newark, N.J., June 30, 1901. *Studied*: Wesleyan Univ.; Columbia Univ. *Exhibited*: Soc. Am. Cartoonists, 1944, 1945; one-man: Waldorf-Astoria Hotel, 1947. Contributor to Sat. Eve. Post; Redbook; American; This Week; Colliers; Boston Post; Richmond Dispatch.*

HOYT, WHITNEY FORD—*Painter*

Greenbush Rd., Blauvelt, N.Y.

B. Rochester, N.Y., July 7, 1910. *Studied*: Ecole des Beaux-Arts, Fontainebleau, France, and with Camille

Liausu, in Paris; N.Y.Sch. F. & App. A. *Member*: AEA; All. A. Am.; Conn. Acad. FA; A. Fellowship. *Awards*: prize, All. A. Am., 1951; George Herdle Mem. prize, 1953. *Work*: Springfield (Mass.) Mus. FA; Rochester Mem. A. Gal.; Munson-Williams-Proctor Inst. *Exhibited*: one-man: Montross Gal., N.Y., 1939, 1941; Kraushaar Gal., 1949, 1954, 1957. *Position*: Dir., N.Y. Chptr. AEA, 1958- ; Dir., A. Fellowship, 1956- .

HUBBARD, BESS BIGHAM (Mrs. Chester A.)—
 Sculptor, Lith., Eng., C.
 1815 Ave. K, Lubbock, Tex.

B. Ft. Worth, Tex., Feb. 18, 1896. *Studied*: Chicago Acad. FA, and with Boardman Robinson, Xavier Gonzalez, Alexandre Hogue, Octavio Medellin, Ernest Freed, William Zorach. *Member*: Texas FA Assn.; NAWA; Pr. M. Gld., Dallas. *Awards*: prizes, Dallas, Tex., 1944; Mus. FA, Abilene, Tex., 1949-1951; Ft. Worth AA, 1950. *Work*: Colorado Springs FA Center; Dallas Mus. FA; Texas FA Assn.; Elisabet Ney Mus. *Exhibited*: Audubon A, 1945; Laguna Beach AA, 1943; Ney Mus., 1943; Dallas Mus. FA; Northwest Pr. M.; SSAL; Texas FA Assn.; P.&S. of the Southwest; Sch. Am. Research Mus., Santa Fe, N.M.; Mus. FA of Houston; Univ. Texas, 1944, 1945; Witte Mem. Mus.; NAWA, 1952; Argent Gal., 1951; Denver Mus. A., 1948; SAGA, 1948; All. A. Am., 1950; New Burlington Gal., London, England, 1955.*

HUBBARD, EARL WADE—Painter, S., W.
 White Hollow Rd., Lime Rock, Conn.

B. Bradford, Pa., Feb. 3, 1924. *Studied*: Amherst Col., B.A.; with Marvin Jules; Smith Col. (special training). *Exhibited*: Panoras Gal., 1956 (one-man); Sharon (Conn.) A. Gal., 1958; Mystic AA, 1958; Rehn Gal., 1958; Art:USA, 1958. Author: "One Step Two Step," 1951.

HUBBARD, WHITNEY MYRON—Painter, T.
 511 First St., Greenport, N.Y.

B. Middletown, Conn., June 18, 1875. *Studied*: Wesleyan Univ., B.S.; ASL; & with Frank DuMond. *Member*: Conn. Acad. FA; New Haven Paint & Clay Cl.; Brooklyn WC Cl. *Work*: Floyd Mem. Lib., and H.S., Greenport, N.Y.; Cahoon Mem. Lib., H.S., Southold, N.Y.; H.S., Greenport, N.Y. *Exhibited*: NAD; PAFA; AWCS; Wash. WC Cl.; one-man exh.: Montclair A. Mus.; Cornell Univ.; Wesleyan Univ.; St. Petersburg AC; Scranton Mus.; Utica Pub. Lib.; High Mus. A.; Binghamton Mus.; Pratt Inst. A., Brooklyn. *Position*: Hd. A. Dept., Suffolk Conservatory of Music & Art, 1935-40; Instr., Adult Edu., Greenport (N.Y.) H.S., 1953- .

HUBER, HELEN RUTH—Teacher, W., L., P., Cr.
 R.R. 1, Box 5, Gary, Ind.

B. East Chicago, Ind., Mar. 19, 1902. *Studied*: Chicago Acad. FA; Univ. Chicago, Ph.B.; Northwestern Univ., M.A.; & with Gaston Bolande, Richard Chase. *Member*: Nat. Com. on A. Edu. *Award*: prize, No. Indiana A. Exh. *Exhibited*: Northern Indiana A., 1946, 1956; Gary, Ind., 1945; East Chicago, Ind., 1945; Hoosier Salon; Southern Exhs., 1955-1957. Contributor to: School Arts, Indiana Teachers magazines. *Position*: Instr., Pub. Sch., Gary, Ind.; A. Cr., Gary Post-Tribune; Instr., Hist. A., Indiana Univ. Ext.; Dir. Gary A. Lg.

HUBERT, HARRY—Painter, Comm. A.
 25 Deerfield Ave., Tuckahoe, N.Y.

B. New York, N.Y., 1899. *Studied*: CUASch.; ASL. *Member*: Mt. Vernon AA; Yonkers AA. *Awards*: prizes, Bronxville Women's Cl., 1953-1956; Yonkers AA, 1956, 1957; Crestwood Women's Cl., 1957; New Haven Comp., Grand Central A. Gal., 1956. One-man exh., Bronxville Women's Cl., 1956.

HUCK, ROBERT E.—Educator, P., Gr.
 Art Department, Oregon State College; h. 604 North 16th St., Corvallis, Ore.

B. Kalispell, Mont., Feb. 26, 1923. *Studied*: Univ. Montana; Colorado Col., B.A.; Univ. Colorado, M.F.A., and with Boardman Robinson, Paul Burlin, John Heliker, and others. *Member*: AAUP; Portland AA. *Awards*: Scholar-

ship, Univ. Colorado, 1950-52; Fulbright Fellowship, 1954-55; purchase awards: Joslyn Mus. A., 1950; Alabama WC Soc., 1950; Pacific Northwest Annual, Spokane, 1948; Colorado State Fair, 1950; SAM, 1956; Portland A. Mus., 1955; Taylor Mus., Colorado Springs, 1950; Butler Inst. Am. A., 1953; Bradley Univ., 1953; Univ. So. Cal., 1953; LC, 1953; Henry Gal., Univ. Wash., 1956, 1957; Univ. Profs. Print Show, Youngstown, 1956; Univ. Minnesota, 1953; Univ. Nebraska, 1955. *Work*: See purchase awards above, plus: Univ. Illinois; Pasadena A. Mus.; mural, Northern State T. Col., South Dakota. *Exhibited*: BM, 1952, 1953; Taylor Mus., Colorado Springs, 1952; Carnegie Inst., 1952; J.B. Speed Mus. A., 1952; Colo. Springs FA Center, 1951; Oakland A. Mus., 1956, 1957; CM, 1953; CAM, 1953; Altoona A. All., 1952; Wichita, 1953; SAGA, 1953; Etchers & Pr. M., N.Y., 1953; Bordighera, Italy, 1957; Henry Gal., Seattle, 1955; Spokane, Wash., 1955-1957; CGA, 1951; Alabama WC Soc., 1950; SAM, 1950-1952, 1955-57; Portland A. Mus., 1955-1957; Duveen Gal., N.Y., 1957, and many others, including one-man exhs. *Position*: Asst. Prof. A., Oregon State College, Corvallis, Ore., 1955- .

HUDSON, JACQUELINE—Lithographer, P.
 220 Sullivan St., New York 12, N.Y.; h. Monhegan Island, Me.

B. Boston, Mass. *Studied*: NAD; ASL. *Member*: NAWA; Rockport AA. *Awards*: prizes, LC, 1951; Rockport AA, 1953, 1956, 1957. *Exhibited*: SAGA; NAD; AWS; Phila. Pr. Cl.; CM; LC; Dayton AI; NAWA; Rockport AA; Gloucester Festival A.; Ogunquit A. Center; Wiscasset, Me.; PAFA; Riverside Mus. A.; NAC; Portland Mus. A.; N.Y. City Center; Knickerbocker A.; Catherine L. Wolfe A. Cl.; All. A. Am.; Rochester Mem. A. Gal.

HUDSON, KENNETH EUGENE—Educator, P.
 St. Louis School of Fine Arts, Washington University; h. 7900 Stanford St., St. Louis 24, Mo.

B. Xenia, Ohio, Dec. 28, 1903. *Studied*: Ohio Wesleyan Univ.; Academie Royale, Brussels, Belgium; Yale Univ., B.F.A.; Fontainebleau, France. *Awards*: F., Belgian-Am. Edu. Fnd., 1935. *Work*: murals, Univ. Oregon; Mun. Bldg., Columbia, Mo. *Position*: Hd., Drawing & Painting Dept., Univ. Oregon, 1927-29; Chm. Dept. A., Univ. Missouri, 1928-38; Dean, St. Louis Sch. FA, Washington Univ., St. Louis, Mo., 1938- . Pres., Nat. Assn. Schs. Design, 1953-55.

HUDSON, KENTON WARNE—Painter, Comm., Des., I.
 Burroughs, Radnor, Pa.; h. 825 Edmonds Ave., Drexel Hill, Pa.

B. Philadelphia, Pa., May 8, 1911. *Studied*: Phila. Graphic Sketch Cl.; PMSchIA, and with Earl Horter. *Member*: Phila. A. All.; Phila. WC Cl. *Awards*: prize, Cape May, 1948. *Exhibited*: PAFA, 1942-1945, 1957; Phila. A. All., 1945, 1950 (both one-man), 1958; Phila. WC Cl., 1943-1955; Phila. Pr. Cl., 1936-1939; Cape May, 1947-1949; Rehoboth (Del.) A. Lg., 1957. *Work*: mural, Plays & Players Theatre, Phila., Pa. *Position*: Tech. Illus., Burroughs, Radnor, Pa.

HUDSON, RALPH M.—
 Educator, Des., P., W., L., Comm. A.
 Department of Art, Mississippi State College for Women; h. 1413 Second Ave., South, Columbus, Miss.

B. Fields, Ohio, Dec. 18, 1907. *Studied*: Ohio State Univ., B.A., B.Sc.E., M.A. *Member*: Col. A. Assn. of Am.; Mississippi Edu. Assn.; Southeastern AA; Nat. A. Edu. Assn.; Mississippi AA; Southeastern Col. AA. *Work*: Mus. FA, Little Rock, Ark.; Univ. Arkansas. *Exhibited*: Morehead, Ky., 1931-1932, 1933-1936 (one-man); Hendrix Col., 1940-1941 (one-man); Univ. Arkansas; Little Rock Mus. FA; Kentucky A.T. traveling exh., 1931-1936; Arkansas WC Soc., 1937-1940; Grumbacher's exh., 1938; Mississippi State Col. for Women; Meridian, Miss., AA, 1946- . Contributor to Design Magazine; Arkansas Historical Quarterly; Kappa Pi Sketch Book. Member of many exhibition juries. *Positions*: Guest Cr., Allison Art Colony, 1950- ; Instr. A., Acting Hd., Dept. A., Morehead (Ky.) State T. Col., 1931-32, 1933-36; Hd. Dept. A., & Dir. A. Gal., Univ. Arkansas, Fayetteville, Ark., 1936-46; Prof. A., Hd. Dept. A., Mississippi State Col. for Women, Columbus, Miss., 1946- . Bd. Trustees, Miss. AA; Bd. Dir., Allison Art Colony.

HUDSON, SHIRLEY D. See Musgrave, Shirley D. Hudson

HUETER, JAMES W.—*Painter, S., T.*
439 Arrow Highway, Claremont, Cal.

B. San Francisco, Cal., May 15, 1925. *Studied*: Pomona Col., B.A., M.F.A.; Claremont Grad. Sch., with Henry Lee McFee, Sueo Serisawa, Millard Sheets, Albert Stewart. *Member*: Los A. AA; Cal. WC Soc.; Pomona Valley AA. *Awards*: prizes, Pasadena A. Mus., 1953; Nat. Orange Show, 1955; Los A. County Fair, 1951; Los A. Mus. A., 1955; Friday Morning Cl., 1951; Frye Mus. A., Seattle, 1957; Cal. State Fair, 1957 (purchase). *Work*: Pasadena A. Mus.; Nat. Orange Show; Scripps Col.; Los A. County Fair Assn.; Cal. State Fair Coll., and in private colls. *Exhibited*: Butler AI, 1955, 1958; Los A. County Fair, 1949, 1951, 1952; Laguna Beach, 1952, 1955; Cal. WC Soc., 1953, 1957; Arizona A. Exh., 1949; Chaffey Col., 1951, 1955; Denver A. Mus., 1954; Los A. Mus. A., 1952, 1954, 1955, 1957, 1958; Pasadena A. Mus., 1950-1954; Nat. Orange Show, 1949-1955; Cal. State Fair, 1950-1955, 1958; Newport Harbor, 1950, 1954, 1955; Palos Verdes, 1953, 1955; Frye Mus. A., 1957; one-man: Mt. San Antonio Col., 1952; First Nat. Bank, Ontario, Cal., 1954; Pasadena A. Mus., 1955; Long Beach City Col., 1957. *Position*: Instr., Mt. San Antonio Col.; Pres. Pomona Valley AA, 1955-56.

HUEY, FLORENCE GREENE (Mrs. J. W.)—*Painter*
1914 Ruxton Rd., Ruxton 4, Md.

B. Philadelphia, Pa., Aug. 13, 1872. *Studied*: PAFA; & with DeCamp, Beaux, Clements, Thouron. *Member*: Pa. Soc. Min. P. *Awards*: prize, Balt. WC Cl., 1927. *Exhibited*: Pa. Soc. Min. P.; ASMP; Chicago World's Fair; Balt. WC Cl.

HUFFER, C(ORNELIA) CUNNINGHAM—*Painter, I., T.*
80 Silver St., Dover, N.H.

B. Savannah, Ga., Dec. 2, 1903. *Studied*: CUASch.; Grand Central Sch. A.; NAD, and with Ernest Roth. *Member*: AAPL; New Hampshire AA. *Awards*: prizes, Nat. Lg. Am. Pen Women, 1932; Currier Gal. A., 1947; Ogunquit A. Center, 1947. *Work*: Univ. New Hampshire; Union Col. *Exhibited*: Wash. WC Cl., 1934; Contemporary Am. A., 1942; Nat. Lg. Am. Pen Women, 1932, 1933; SSAL, 1931-1934; Georgia AA, 1929-1935; New Hampshire AA, 1940-1942, 1955, traveling exh., 1956; Symphony Hall, Boston; New England traveling exhibition; one-man: Ga., Miss., La., Fla. I., books and sonnets. *Position*: Instr., High Mus. A., 1927-29; Univ. New Hampshire, 1945-50, Ext. Faculty 1953-56, 1958- .

HUGHES, D(AISY) MARGUERITE—*Painter*
540 South Berendo St., Los Angeles 5, Cal.; s. Provincetown, Mass.

B. Los Angeles, Cal. *Studied*: Univ. California; ASL; & with George Elmer Browne, George Bridgman. *Member*: Los A. AA; All.A.Am.; NAWA; Cal. WC Soc.; A.T.Assn. of Southern California; Provincetown AA. *Exhibited*: NAD; CGA; NAWA; All.A.Am.; Los A. Mus. A.; Babcock Gal., (one-man); Montross Gal., 1939 (one-man); Audubon A.; P. & S. Soc., New Jersey.

HULETT, CHARLES WILLARD—*Painter, T., Cart., I.*
11147 Huston St., North Hollywood, Cal.

B. Fairmount, Ind., July 25, 1903. *Studied*: with Theodore Lukits, Christian von Schneidau, Ralph Holmes, Will Foster. *Member*: P. & S. Cl. of Los A.; Cal. A. Cl.; (Hon. V. P.) Campo de Cahuenga Mem. Assn.; San Fernando Valley A. Cl. *Awards*: prizes, San Fernando A. Cl., 1946, 1947, 1948, 1949, 1951, medal, 1952. *Work*: Campo de Cahuenga Mem., Los Angeles. *Exhibited*: Palos Verdes Gal.; Clearwater A. Mus.; Raymond & Raymond Gal.; Santa Paula, Cal.; Los A. Mus. A.; Ebell Salon; Stendahl Gal., Los A.; Greek Theatre, North Hollywood; Van Nuys (Cal.) Pub. Lib.; Los A. City Hall Gal.; Hollywood Pub. Lib.

HULETT, RALPH—*Painter, Des., Cart., I.*
2400 West Alameda St., Burbank, Cal.; h. 4909 Caminito Lane, La Crescenta, Cal.

B. Kankakee, Ill., Aug. 1, 1915. *Studied*: Chouinard AI, with H. Jepson, Phil Paradise, Millard Sheets, Phil Dike

and others. *Member*: Cal. WC Soc.; AWS; Laguna AA. *Awards*: medal and prize, Oakland A. Mus., 1951; citation, AWS, 1953; prize, Santa Cruz, Cal., 1953, and other awards in local shows. *Work*: Hoover, Paramount, Toll, La Crescenta, San Fernando, H.S.; NAD. *Exhibited*: Oakland A. Mus., 1951; PAFA, 1951; AWS, 1950-1954; Cal. WC Soc., 1951-1954; Laguna Beach, 1951-1954; one-man: Los Angeles, San Francisco, Portland, Ore., New York. Contributor illus. to Ford Times; Los Angeles Times; Westways, and other publications. *Positions*: Des., Fabrics, Barth & Dryfuss, 1955; Illus., Ford Motor Co., 1948-55; Walt Disney A., 1938- .*

HULL, MARIE ATKINSON (Mrs. Emmett J.)— *Painter, T.*
825 Belhaven St., Jackson, Miss.

B. Summit, Miss. *Studied*: PAFA; ASL; Broadmoor A. Acad., and in France and Spain. *Member*: SSAL; New Orleans AA; Mississippi AA; Wash. WC Cl.; AWCS; NAWA. *Awards*: med., prize, 1951, Miss. AA; prizes, SSAL, 1926; New Orleans AA; San Antonio, Tex., 1929; Springville, Utah. *Work*: Witte Mem. Mus.; Springville (Utah) Mus.; Miss. AA; Mun. A. Gal., Jackson, Miss.; Miss. State Capitol; Governor's Mansion, Jackson, Miss.; Hinds County Court House; Memphis Court House; Delta State T. Col.; Miss. State Office Bldg.; Miss. Hall of Fame; Tulane Univ., New Orleans; Miss. Southern Col.; Port Gibson (Miss.) Pub. Lib.; Miss. State Col., Univ. Miss.; Texas State T. Col.; Meredith Col., N.C.; Blue Mountain Col.; Belhaven Col., Miss.; Brigham Young Univ.; Abilene, Tex.; Miss. State Col. for Women; Laurel (Miss.) Mus. A. *Exhibited*: AFA traveling exh., 1939-1940; AIC, 1928, 1938; WFNY 1939; GGE, 1939; Miss. AA, annually; PAFA; AWCS; SSAL, annually; CM; Davenport Mus. A.; NAWA; BMA; Wichita Mus. A.; BM; Atlanta, Ga., annually; Delgado Mus., annually; Brooks Mem. Mus.; Butler Inst. Am. A., 1957; Provincetown, Mass., 1958.

HULL, WILLIAM—*Museum Director*
Syracuse Museum of Fine Arts (3); h. 208 Lincoln Park Drive, Syracuse 3, N.Y.

B. Pomeroy, Wash., June 27, 1920. *Studied*: Washington State Col., B.A. *Position*: Dir., Syracuse Museum of Fine Arts, Syracuse, N.Y.

HULLENKREMER, ODON—*Painter, T.*
820 Canyon Rd., Santa Fe, N.M.

B. Budapest, Hungary, June 1, 1888. *Studied*: Royal Hungarian Sch. A.; Acad. Julian, Paris, and in Munich. *Awards*: Acad. Julian, 1929; State Mus., Santa Fe, 1954. *Work*: murals, Wash., D.C.; U.S.Eng.; Lib., Raton, N.M.; Capitol, Santa Fe, and others. *Exhibited*: Budapest, Hungary; Toledo, Ohio; Miami, Fla.; Denver A. Mus.; Coral Gables, Fla.; Mus. New Mexico, Santa Fe; Art:USA, 1958.

HULT, HARRY—*Painter, Des.*
410 North Michigan Ave.; h. 6 East Ohio St., Chicago, Ill.

B. Chicago, Ill. *Studied*: AIC; ASL. *Member*: SI; AEA. *Exhibited*: Galerie Creuze, Paris, 1952 (one-man); Stevens-Gross Studios, Chicago, 1953, 1955; AIC; various group shows.

HULTBERG, JOHN PHILLIP—*Painter*
27 East 67th St., New York, N.Y.

B. Berkeley, Cal., Feb. 8, 1922. *Studied*: Fresno State Col., B.A.; Cal. Sch. FA; ASL. *Awards*: Bender Grant, San Francisco, 1948; Guggenheim Fellowship, 1956; prizes, CGA, 1955; Congress for Cultural Freedom, 1955. *Work*: MMA; WMAA; Albright Gal. A.; Univ. Illinois. Fortune Magazine, 1957. *Exhibited*: CGA, 1955-1957; Carnegie Inst., 1955, 1957; WMAA, 1955-1958; one-man: New York, 1953, 1955, 1956, 1958; London, England, 1956; Paris, France, 1957; Boston, Mass., 1957; Provincetown, Mass., 1958; Wash., D.C., 1958. *Position*: Instr. A., Skowhegan Sch. A., 1958- ; BMSch. A., 1958.

HUMBER, YVONNE TWINING—*Painter, T.*
2340 West Viewmont St., Seattle 99, Wash.

B. New York, N.Y., Dec. 7, 1907. *Studied*: NAD; Tiffany Fnd.; & with Charles Hawthorne. *Member*: Women Pain⸗

ers of Wash.; AEA (Vice-Pres., 1957-58). *Awards*: prizes, SAM, 1945; Women Painters of Wash., 1945; Lg. Am. Pen Women, 1946; Stockbridge, Mass., 1935. *Work*: SAM. *Exhibited*: Palace Legion Honor, 1946; NAD, 1935; WFNY 1939; Lg. Am. Pen Women, 1946; SAM, 1944, 1945, 1957; Inst. Mod. A., Boston, 1939, 1941; Spokane, Wash., 1945, 1946; Women Painters of Wash., annually; Stockbridge, Mass., 1934-1937; Macy Gal., 1933-1936; Contemporary A. Gal., 1940; PMG, 1937; Three A. Cl., 1929, 1930, 1931 (all one-man); SFMA, 1948, 1949; Denver A. Mus.; Tacoma Mus. A., 1957; Woessner Gal., Seattle, 1956-1958; F. & N. Little Gal., Seattle, 1956-1958; Bellevue (Wash.) traveling exh. & Fair, 1956-1958, and others. *Position*: Instr., Edison Vocational Sch., Seattle, Wash., 1945- .

HUMES, RALPH HAMILTON—Sculptor
4940 Hammock Lake Drive, Miami 56, Fla.

B. Philadelphia, Pa., Dec. 25, 1902. *Studied*: PAFA, with Albert Laessle, Charles Grafly. *Member*: NSS; Conn. Acad. FA; New Haven Paint & Clay Cl.; Soc. Wash. A.; Blue Dome F. *Awards*: Cresson traveling scholarship, PAFA, 1929, 1930; prizes, NAD, 1932; 1937; New Haven Paint & Clay Cl., 1932, 1936; Soc. Wash. A., 1937; F., PAFA, 1937; Conn. Acad. FA, 1941; med., Fla. Fed. A., 1938. *Work*: Brookgreen Gardens, S.C.; fountain, Coral Gables, Fla.; figurehead, S.S. "Comanche." *Exhibited*: PAFA, 1930-1934, 1937; NAD, 1932, 1933, 1935, 1937, 1940, 1945; New Haven Paint & Clay Cl., 1933, 1934, 1937, 1939; Conn. Acad. FA, 1934, 1937, 1939, 1941.

HUMPHREY, WALTER BEACH—Illustrator, P., T.
75 White Oak St., New Rochelle, N.Y.

B. Elkhorn, Wis., Nov. 22, 1892. *Studied*: Dartmouth Col., A.B.; ASL, with Frank DuMond. *Member*: New Rochelle AA; Hudson Valley AA; NSMP. *Work*: murals, Dartmouth Col.; New Hampton Sch. *Exhibited*: New Rochelle AA, 1922-1946. I., cover des. & fiction illus. for national magazines. *Position*: Instr., Commercial A., New Rochelle H.S., New Rochelle, N.Y., 1941- ; Mun. A. Comm., New Rochelle, N.Y.

HUMPHREYS, DAVID—Painter
Dorset, Vt.

B. Morristown, N.J., July 22, 1901. *Studied*: Princeton Univ., A.B.; ASL, Woodstock, N.Y.; John Carlson Sch. A.; Grand Central Sch. A., and with Wayman Adams, George Elmer Browne, Andre Lhote, Paris. *Member*: SC; All. A. Am.; Societe Nationale des Beaux-Arts; Conn. Acad. FA. *Awards*: prizes, Newark Mus. A., 1942; Morristown, N.J., 1944; Seton Hall Univ., 1958. *Work*: Canajoharie Mus. A.; Abilene, Tex. *Exhibited*: NAD; All. A. Am.; SC; So. Vermont A.; Ward Eggleston Gal., N.Y., 1956 (one-man). *Position*: Sec., All. A. Am.; Treas., So. Vermont A.

HUMPHREYS, SALLIE THOMSON—
Designer, P., L., E.
162 North Sandusky St., Delaware, Ohio

B. Delaware, Ohio. *Studied*: Ohio Wesleyan Univ.; ASL, Wash., D.C.; AIC; Carnegie student, FMA; in Paris, and with Eliot O'Hara, Frank Wilcox, Carl Gaertner, Charles Burchfield, John Carroll; also with Paul Sample, Aaron Bohrod, Wm. Thon, Clarence Carter. *Member*: AFA; CAA; Columbus A.Lg.; Wash. WC Cl.; Ohio WC Soc.; Wash. A. Cl.; Cincinnati Women's A. Cl. *Awards*: Special Alum. award, Ohio Wesleyan Univ.; Adam Poe medal; Founders Award for distinguished service in the field of Fine Arts to Ohio Wesleyan Univ. *Work*: Ohio Wesleyan Univ. *Exhibited*: NGA (one-man); CM (one-man); CGA, 1946, 1948, 1949, 1952; Ohio WC Soc. traveling exh., 1941-1943, 1945, 1946, 1948; Cincinnati Women's A. Cl., 1941-1952; Butler AI, 1942-1945; Wash. WC Cl., 1946-1952; NCFA, 1946-1952; one-man: Mint Mus. A., 1948; Gastonia, N.C., 1948, 1953, 1954; Magunsons Gal., Columbus, Ohio, 1948; Lyon Art Hall, Ohio Wesleyan Univ., 1947, 1953, 1955, and Ohio Wesleyan Union Bldg., 1956, 1957. *Positions*: Dir. & Prof., Dept., FA, 1906-43, Emeritus, 1943- , Ohio Wesleyan Univ., Delaware, Ohio.

HUNGERLAND, HELMUT—Educator
California College of Arts & Crafts, 5212 Broadway, Oakland 18, Cal.

Position: Dean, Graduate School, California College of Arts & Crafts, Oakland, Cal.*

HUNT, (JULIAN) COURTENAY—Painter
Jacksonville Art Museum, 1550 Riverside Ave.; h. Lake Side Drive, Orange Park, Fla. (P.O. Box 247)

B. Jacksonville, Fla., Sept. 17, 1917. *Studied*: Ringling A. Sch.; Farnsworth Sch. A., Sarasota. *Member*: Fla. A. Group; Sarasota AA; St. Augustine AA; Jacksonville A. Mus. *Awards*: prizes, Fla. Southern Col. Intl., 1952; St. Augustine AA, 1958; Fla. A. Group, 1957 (for tour). *Work*: in private collections. *Exhibited*: All. A. Am., 1951, 1953, 1955, 1956; Audubon A., 1952, 1955, 1956; Sarasota AA, 1952, 1956; Fla. Southern Col., 1952; St. Augustine AA, 1951, 1958; High Mus. A., 1951, 1952, 1955; Jacksonville A. Mus., 1949-1958.

HUNT, KARI (Mrs. Douglas M.)—Sculptor, L., C.
60 Codwise Ave., New Brunswick, N.J.

B. Orange, N.J., Jan. 29, 1920. *Studied*: Cornell Univ.; Univ. Buffalo, and with Doane Powell. *Member*: N.J. Soc. Painters & Illustrators; New Brunswick A. Cl.; Princeton A. Mus.; Archaeological Inst. Am. *Exhibited*: Montclair A. Mus., 1950; Jersey City Mus. Assn., 1950; N.J. Col. tor Women, 1950, 1952; ANTA, 1952, and in numerous l'braries. *Work*: specializes in sculptured Masks of the World; owns and exhibits the late Doane Powell coll. of portrait masks, books, masks of Java, Bali, Tibet, Siam, Japan, etc. Lectures and demonstrates the art of mask making at clubs, organizations, libraries and on television. Produced mask advertisements for Remington Rand, 1954; Geritol Corp.; Worthington Corp., 1955; Affiliated with Crawford Productions Lecture Bureau, New York, N.Y.

HUNT, ROBERT JAMES—Painter, Gr., T.
Washburn University; h. 4803 West 18th Terr., Topeka, Kans.

B. Fargo, N.D., Apr. 5, 1921. *Studied*: State Univ. of Iowa, B.A., M.F.A. *Member*: Mid-West Col. AA; CAA. *Work*: State Univ. Iowa; Mid-Am. A.; Mulvane A. Mus.; Des Moines A. Center; Kansas State Coll.; Wichita A. Mus. *Awards*: purchase prize, Wichita A. Mus., 1954; Kansas State. *Exhibited*: Wichita A. Mus.; Kansas State Col.; Mid-Am. A.; Kansas Free Fair; AFA; Magnificent Mile, Chicago; Mulvane A. Center; Joslyn Mus. A.; Des Moines A. Center; Nelson Gal. A.; Kansas State Col.; St. Benedict's Gal.; Springfield (Mo.) Mus. A.; Colorado Springs FA Center. *Position*: Asst. Prof. A., Washburn Univ., Topeka, Kans., 1950- .

HUNT, STAN(LEY) (LLOYD)—Cartoonist
Long Mountain, New Milford, Conn.

B. Bridgewater, Mass., Feb. 6, 1912. *Studied*: Brown Univ., Ph.B.; Bridgewater State T. Col., B.Sc. in Edu. *Member*: Nat. Cartoonists Soc. *Work*: Cartoons in Sat. Eve. Post; This Week; New Yorker; Saturday Review; Look, and other leading national publications.

HUNTER, DARD—Craftsman
Hayden Library, Massachusetts Institute of Technology, Cambridge, Mass.; h. Mountain House, Chillicothe, Ohio

B. Steubenville, Ohio, Nov. 29, 1883. *Studied*: Ohio State Univ.; London Tech. Col., England, and in Vienna. *Member*: AIGA; All-India Paper Industries Assn.; Am. Antiquarian Soc. *Awards*: degrees, Litt. D., Lawrence Col. 1931, Ohio State Univ., 1936; L.H.D., Wooster Col., 1938, Lehigh Univ., 1946; gold medal, AIGA, 1932; gold medal, Gutenberg Mus., Mainz, Germany, 1950; Ohio State medal, 1948; Rosenbach F., Univ. Pennsylvania, 1949. *Work*: books in many libraries throughout the world. Compiled: Handmade Paper and Its Watermarks; A History and Bibliography of Marbled Papers; Bibliographie de la Papeterie (translation); Old Papermaking; Fifteenth Century Papermaking; Watermarks; and many others. Author: Papermaking, The History and Technique of an Ancient Craft; Papermaking in Siam; Chinese Ceremonial Paper; Papermaking in Indo-China; Papermaking by Hand in America; Old Papermaking in China and Japan; Papermaking in Pioneer America; "My Life With Paper," an autobiography, 1958, and many others. Established the Dard Hunter Paper Museum, MIT, 1939. Contributing Ed., The Colophon, New York, N.Y.; contributor to Encyclopaedia Britannica. Lectures to many universities and colleges. Hon. Cur., Inst. of Paper Chemistry, Appleton, Wis.; Hon. Cur., Gr. A., Harvard Univ.

HUNTER, EDMUND ROBERT—*Museum Director, L.*

Vizcaya-Dade County Art Museum, 3251 South Miami Ave., Miami 36, Fla.; h. 6900 Talavera St., Coral Gables 46, Fla.

B. Toronto, Canada, June 4, 1909. *Studied:* Ontario Col. A., Toronto; Royal Ontario Mus. Archaeology, Toronto, with Dr. C. T. Currelly; Courtauld Inst., Univ. London. *Member:* A. & Let. Cl., Toronto; AAMus.; Southern A. Mus. Dirs. Assn.; Florida A. Group (1st Pres.); Southeastern Mus. Conf.; Miami A. Lg.; Palm Beach A. Lg.; Fla. Fed. A. *Author:* "J.E.H. MacDonald, A Biography and Catalogue of His Work," 1940; "Thoreau MacDonald," 1942. *Position:* Tech. Advisor, Montreal AA, 1938-40; Dir., Norton Gal. & Sch. A., West Palm Beach, Fla., 1943-49; Dir., Atlanta AA, High Mus. A., Atlanta, Ga., 1949-54; Consulting Dir., Pensacola AA, Pensacola, Fla., 1954- ; Dir., Jacksonville Art Museum, 1955- .

HUNTER, GRAHAM—*Cartoonist, W.*

"Lindenshade," 42 Clonavor Rd., Silver Spring Park, West Orange, N.J.

B. La Grange, Ill. *Studied:* Landon Sch. of Cartooning, Cleveland, Ohio; AIC; Art Instruction, Inc., Minneapolis. *Award:* Citation, U.S. Treasury Dept., 1943. *Work:* Saturday Evening Post; American Legion Magazine; Farm Journal; This Week; Successful Farming; Maclean's (Canada); Tit-Bits (England); and through McNaught Syndicate, King Features Syndicate, Geo. M. Adams Service. Creator: "Jolly Jingles" for Chicago Sunday Tribune and McClure Syndicate; "Sycamore Center" cartoon page in Farm Ranch; "Bicep Brothers," "Motor Laffs" and "Getting the Business" in Motor magazine; "Rhubarb Ridge" feature for Curtis Pub. Co., 1951-53; full page business feature in Banking magazine; "Busy Life" cartoon page in This Day, 1951- ; "In Hometown America," "The Office Cat" and "Only Yesterday" Industrial Press syndicated features, 1954- ; editorial syndicated cartoons for Nat. Assn. Mfgrs., 1952- ; watercolor cartoon spreads in Together magazine; specialist in sales, political, automotive cartoons; magazine covers, adv. copy, etc.

HUNTER, ROBERT DOUGLAS—*Painter, I., T., L.*

30 Ipswich St., Boston, Mass.

B. Boston, Mass., Mar. 17, 1928. *Studied:* Vesper George Sch. A.; Cape Sch. A., Provincetown, Mass.; R.H.Ives Gammel Studios, Boston. *Member:* Provincetown AA; North Shore AA; Copley Soc., Boston; Cape Cod AA. *Awards:* prizes, Ogunquit A. Center, 1955; Jordan Marsh Co., 1954-1958; North Shore AA, 1957. *Work:* Boston Advertising Cl.; Maryhill (Wash.) Mus. A.; Tufts Col.; mural, St. Mary of the Harbor, Provincetown, Mass. *Exhibited:* All. A. Am., 1954, 1955; Ogunquit A. Center, 1954, 1955; Provincetown AA, 1953-1955; Academic AA, 1954; Newport AA, 1953; Boston A. Festival, 1952-1955; Jordan Marsh. 1953-1955; series of one-man exhs., West Coast, 1958. Illus., "Walk Quietly," 1954; "True Places," 1955. *Position:* Bd. Governors, Dir. A. Com., Copley Soc., Boston.

HUNTER, SAM—*Museum Curator, W., L.*

Minneapolis Institute of Arts, Minneapolis, Minn.; h. Box 129, Route 3, Wayzata, Minn.

B. Springfield, Mass., Jan. 5, 1923. *Studied:* Williams Col., A.B.; Univ. Florence, Italy; Independent research Bernard Berenson Library, Villa I Tatti, Florence, Italy. *Member:* CAA. *Awards:* Karl Weston Grad. prize, Williams Col., 1943; Hubbard Hutchinson Fellowship, Williams Col. for 3 years research and travel. Author: "Toulouse-Lautrec," 1954; "Raoul Dufy," 1955; "Henri Matisse," 1956; "Modern French Painting," 1956; "Jackson Pollock," 1956; "Picasso: Cubism to the Present," 1957; "David Smith," 1957; "Piet Mondrian," 1958; "Modern Art: A Pictorial Anthology," 1958 (contributor); "The Graphic Art of Joan Miro," 1958; "Modern American Painting and Sculpture," 1958. Contributor to: Sat. Review; New World Writing; Partisan Review; N.Y. Times Book Review; Art in America; College Art Journal. Lectures: Modern and Italian Renaissance Art. Arranged many exhs. for MMoDA. *Positions:* Assoc. A. Cr. & Ed., N.Y. Times, 1947-49; Assoc. Ed., Harry N. Abrams, Inc., 1952-53; Assoc. Ed., The Art Digest, 1953; Assoc. Cur., Dept. Painting and Sculpture, MMoDA, 1954-55; Chief Cur., Minneapolis Inst. of Arts, Minneapolis, Minn., 1958- .

HUNTER, WILBUR HARVEY, JR.—

Museum Director, E.

The Peale Museum, 225 North Holliday St. (2); h. 1823 Fairbank Rd., Baltimore 9, Md.

B. Brooklyn, N.Y., June 15, 1915. *Studied:* U.S. Naval Acad., B.S.; Univ. Denver, M.A.; Johns Hopkins Univ., grad. studies. *Member:* Soc. Arch. Hist.; AAMus.; Am. Assn. for State & Local History; CAA. Ed., "The Architecture of Baltimore," 1953. Lectures: History of Baltimore; Architecture in Baltimore; Architecture of the Chesapeake Bay Region, etc. Exhibitions arranged: Harbor: A Century of Photographs of Baltimore's Port; Joshua Johnston; Philip Tilyard; Alfred Jacob Miller; Peale's Baltimore Museum, 1814-1830; The Architecture of Baltimore: a Pictorial History, and many others. *Position:* Dir., The Peale Museum, Baltimore, Md., 1946- .*

HUNTINGTON, ANNA HYATT (Mrs. Archer M.)—

Sculptor

Bethel, Conn.

B. Cambridge, Mass., Mar. 10, 1876. *Studied:* ASL, and with Hermon MacNeil, Gutzon Borglum. *Member:* NA; NSS; Am. Acad. A. & Let.; Hispanic Soc. Am. (trustee); Bd. member, Brookgreen Gardens, S.C. *Awards:* Accademia Cultural Adriaica; Internationalia Studia Scientiarum Litterarumque; Accademia di Belle Artes di Santa Isabel de Hungaria di Seville; Accademia di Belles Arti, Perugia; Officer, Legion of Honor, France; Grand Cross Alfonso XII; hon. degree, Dr. FA, Syracuse Univ.; Pres., Brookgreen Gardens, 1956; Hon. F., Intl. Inst. A. & Lets.; 1957; Citizen of Cuba, 1958; Woman of the Americas, 1958; F., Pierpont Morgan Lib., 1958; Gold Medal, NAD, 1958. *Work:* in over 200 museums and galleries in U.S. Statues in New York City, San Francisco, San Diego, Cal., Gloucester, Mass., Newport News, Va., Brookgreen Gardens, S.C., San Marcos, Tex., etc.; Blois, France; Seville, Spain; Buenos Aires, Argentina.

HUNTINGTON, A. MONTGOMERY—

Designer, P., Mus. Publ. Rel. Dir.

Munson-Williams-Proctor Institute, 310 Genesee St.; h. 10 Taber Rd., Utica, N.Y.

B. Cambridge, Mass., May 19, 1894. *Studied:* Mass. Normal A. Sch., with DeCamp; Major; Munsell; Dallin, Mass. Inst. Tech.; Boston Univ.; Munson-Williams-Proctor Inst., with William C. Palmer, Edward Millman. *Member:* A. Dir. Cl., N.Y.; Nat. A. Dir. Cl. *Awards:* Bok award, Harvard Univ., 1926; Award of Merit, A. Dir. Cl., 1949; Business Paper Award, 1955-1957; prizes, Nat. Packaging Exh., Chicago; Syracuse Mus. FA, 1957. *Work:* Munson-Williams-Proctor Inst. *Exhibited:* A. Dir. Cl., annual exhs.; A. of Central New York, 1937-1957; Cooperstown A. Exh., 1956-1958; St. Lawrence Univ.; one-man: Colgate Univ., 1952; Munson-Williams-Proctor Inst., 1952. Lectures: Industrial Design; Advertising Design to women's clubs, colleges and university groups. *Position:* Pub. Rel. Dir., Munson-Williams-Proctor Inst., Utica, N.Y.

HUNTINGTON, ELIZABETH HAMILTON THAYER (Mrs.)—*Painter*

500 Worcester St., Wellesley Hills 82, Mass.

B. South Braintree, Mass., Oct. 9, 1878. *Studied:* Mass. Sch. A.; Thayer Acad.; & with Ernest Lee Major, Vesper George. *Member:* Wellesley SA; Gld. Boston A. *Exhibited:* AWCS; Fifteen Gal., N.Y. (one-man); Newport AA; BMFA; Doll & Richards (2 one-man); Gld. Boston A. (one-man); Concord AA; Children's A. Center. *Position:* Pres., Wellesley Soc. A.*

HUNTLEY, DAVID COLLINS—*Painter, E., C., Des.*

Art Department, Alabama College; h. Lakewood Drive, Montevallo, Ala.

B. Lenoir, N.C., Oct. 17, 1930. *Studied:* Univ. North Carolina, A.B., M.A. *Member:* Com. on A. Edu., MModA; CAA; Southeastern AA; Alabama AA; Birmingham AA; AEA; AAUP. *Awards:* A. Scholarship, Raleigh, N.C., 1951; prizes, North Carolina A., Wilmington, N.C., 1953; Tri-State Exh., Spartanburg, 1954. *Exhibited:* PAFA, 1954; Terry AI, 1952; Provincetown, 1958; Southeastern annual, 1956; Univ. Fla., 1954; Forum Gal., 1956; Creative Gal., 1955; Virginia Intermont Exh., 1954; North Carolina Annual, 1953-1955; Tri-State Annual, 1955, 1956;

Birmingham AA, 1956-1958; six one-man, regional and national. Lectures: Art Education; Contemporary Art; Art History. *Positions*: Instr., Children's Art, Univ. North Carolina; History of A., Des., etc., Limestone Col.; Gaffney, N.C.; Prof. A., A. Dept., Alabama College, Montevallo, N.C., at present.

HUNTLEY, G(EORGE) HAYDN—*Educator*
Northwestern University, Evanston, Ill.; h. 109 Fourth St., Wilmette, Ill.

B. Endicott, Wash., July 14, 1905. *Studied*: Harvard Univ., B.S., A.M., Ph.D. *Member*: CAA; Midwestern Col. A. Conference; Soc. Arch. Historians. *Award*: Fulbright F., 1950-51. Contributor to art magazines and journals. Lectures on Renaissance Art; 19th Century Art. *Positions*: Instr., 1932-36, Asst. Prof., 1936-38, Washington Univ., St. Louis, Mo.; Asst. Prof., 1938-46, Univ. Chicago, Chicago, Ill.; Assoc. Prof., Renaissance & 19th Century Art, 1946-48, Prof., 1948- , Northwestern Univ., Evanston, Ill. Ed. Bd., Art Bulletin, 1940- ; College Art Journal, Ed., 1942-44, Adv. Ed., 1944-48, regional Ed., 1952-55.*

HUNTLEY, VICTORIA HUTSON—*Lithographer, P., L.*
The Riverbank Lodge, Geneva, Ill.

B. Hasbrouck Heights, N.J., Oct. 9, 1900. *Studied*: ASL, and with John Sloan, Max Weber, William C. Palmer, Kenneth Hayes Miller. *Member*: ANA; NSMP; An Am. Group; Audubon A; Albany Pr. Cl.; SAGA; ASL. *Awards*: prizes, AIC, 1930; Phila. Pr. Cl., 1933; LC, 1945, 1949; Assoc. Am. A., 1946; Grant, Am. Acad. A. & Let., 1947; Guggenheim F., 1948; SAGA, 1950, 1951; ASL, 1950, 1951. *Work*: MMA; AIC; BMFA; PMA; CMA; WMAA; LC; BM; IBM; Univ. Fla.; Univ. Mich.; Albany Pr. Cl.; Rochester Mem. Mus.; ASL; CM; Paris, France, 1954, also touring Italy, 1955-56, 1956-57; Mus. FA of Houston; PAFA; N.Y.Pub. Lib.; Newark Pub. Lib.; Phila. Pr. Cl.; Univ. Glasgow; Italian Govt.; murals, USPO, Springville, N.Y.; Greenwich, Conn. *Exhibited*: nationally and internationally. One-man: Weyhe Gal., 1930-1932; Phila. Pr. Cl., 1932; deYoung Mus. A., 1935; Kennedy Gal., N.Y., 1942, 1949; San Diego A. Center, 1950; Am. Acad. and Nat. Inst. A. & Let., 1947; Research Studio, Maitland, Fla., 1951; Albany Pr. Cl., 1952; Miami Beach A. Center, 1952; Circulating Pr. Gal., Wash., D.C., 1954. Lectures: "Fine Prints & Graphic Art Media"; "Five Famous Painters: Dégas, Cézanne, Van Gogh, Lautrec, Gauguin," 1956-57. Demonstrations: "How to Make a Lithograph," 1957-58; "Painting Techniques," 1958.

HUNTOON, MARY (Mrs. Willis C. McEntarfer)—*Painter, S., Gr., W., L., E.*
221 Huntoon St., Topeka, Kans.

B. Topeka, Kans., Nov., 1896. *Studied*: Washburn Univ., A.B.; ASL, with Henri, Pennell; & in Paris, France. *Member*: Nat. Lg. Am. Pen Women; Prairie WC Painters. *Awards*: prize, Women Painters, Wichita, Kan., 1936; "Woman of the Year" in A. & Sc., Topeka, Kans., 1954. *Work*: Salina AA; Fed. Women's Cl., Kan.; Topeka Pub. Lib.; Topeka State House; *Exhibited*: Brooklyn SA, 1930; Salon d'Automne, 1929; N.Y. Mun. Exh., 1936; Kansas Fed.A.; Manhattan, Wichita, Hutchison, Salina, Linsborg and Topeka, Kans.; Women Painters of Am., 1936-1938; WMAA; 1942; Am. Graphic Exh., Stockholm, Sweden, 1937; Kansas City AI, 1932, 1935, 1937, 1941; Joslyn Mem. Author, monographs: "Creative Art as Therapy"; "Art Therapy." *Position*: Dir. A., Medical Rehabilitation, Winter General Hospital, Veteran's Administration, 1946- ; Dept. Medicine & Surgery Research, 1949- .

HURD, ANGELA (M.)—*Painter, T.*
860 East Second Ave., Escondido, Cal.

B. Stafford, England, July 18, 1898. *Studied*: in England, incl. Col. of Notre Dame, Liverpool; Italy; & with C. Law Watkins, Karl Knaths. *Member*: Am. Soc. for Aesthetics; San Diego A. Gld.; San Diego FA Soc.; A. Center, La Jolla; Showcase of the Arts. *Awards*: prizes, So. Cal. Exh., Del Mar, 1956; Showcase of the Arts, 1957. *Exhibited*: VMFA, 1938; Nat. Exh. S. & Crafts, Wash., D.C., 1940; Soc. Wash. A., 1940; PMG, 1932-1943; Wash. A. Lg., traveling exh., 1933, 1934; Greater Wash. Indp. A., 1935; Phila. A. All., 1940; Whyte Gal., 1944-1946; Vista A. Gld., 1948-1950; Escondido A. Gld., 1949; Terry AI, 1952; Del Mar, Cal., 1956, 1957; Showcase of the Arts, 1956-1958; San Diego FA Gal., 1957; A. Center, La Jolla, 1957; San Diego County A. Exh., 1958.

HURD, PETER—*Painter, W.*
Sentinel Ranch, San Patricio, N.M.

B. Roswell, N.M., Feb. 22, 1904. *Studied*: PAFA; & with N.C. Wyeth. *Member*: NA; Phila. Pr. Cl.; Phila. WC Soc.; AWS; Wilmington Soc. FA. *Awards*: prizes, AIC, 1937; Wilmington Soc. FA, 1941, 1945; med., PAFA, 1945; NAD, 1953. *Work*: frescoes, USPO, Big Spring, Tex.; Dallas, Tex.; Texas Tech. Col., Lubbock; Alamogordo, N.M.; La Quinta Mun.A.Gal., Albuquerque, N.M.; AIC; mural, Prudential Insurance Co. bldg., Houston, Tex.; William Rockhill Nelson Gal.; Herron AI; MMA; BM; Nat. Gal., Edinburgh, Scotland. *Exhibited*: nationally. Coll. paintings, drawings and lithographs permanently housed in new wing of Roswell (N.M.) Mus. A. I., "The Last of the Mohicans," 1926; "Great Stories of the Sea and Ships," 1933; "Habit of Empire," 1938; & others. *Position*: War Correspondent for Life Magazine & USAAF, 1942-45; A., Life Magazine, 1946- .

HURD, MRS. PETER. See Wyeth, Henriette

HURFORD, MIRIAM STORY (Mrs. A. F.)—
Painter, Comm. A., I.
Route 1, Box 18, Santa Fe, N.M.

B. Rome, N.Y., Nov. 23, 1894. *Studied*: Syracuse Univ.; Albright A. Sch.; AIC. *Exhibited*: AWS, 1957, 1958; Santa Fe open and juried shows, traveling exhs. *Work*: illus. many textbooks, 1st to 5th grades; illus., "The American Southwest," 1955.

HURST, MRS. CARLTON. See Clephane, Rosebud

HURST, EARL OLIVER—*Illustrator, W., Des.*
33 Washington Square, West, New York 11, N.Y.; s. Cape Island, Newagen, Me.

B. Buffalo, N.Y., Aug. 19, 1895. *Studied*: Albright A. Sch.; Cleveland Sch. A.; John Huntington Inst.; & in France. *Exhibited*: Silvermine Gld. A., 1955. Contributor to: national magazines with articles & illus. Author, I., "The Big Book of Space"; "The Wonder Book of Boats." Lectures: Magazine Illustration.*

HURTIG, MARTIN—*Painter, Et., Lith., E.*
Kresge Art Center, Michigan State University; h. 1647 Kensington Ave., East Lansing, Mich.

B. South Haven, Mich., Aug. 11, 1929. *Studied*: Inst. Design, Chicago, B.S., M.A.; Atelier 17, Paris, with William Hayter. *Award*: prize, Cape Cod AA, 1955. *Exhibited*: AIC, 1952 (and traveling); Cape Cod AA, 1955-1957; Portland Mus. A., 1957; Wichita AA, 1957; PAFA, 1958; Soc. Wash. Pr. M., 1958; BM, 1958; Momentum, 1954-1956; Detroit Inst. A., 1957. *Position*: Prof. A., Michigan State University, East Lansing, Mich.

HUSE, MARION (Mrs. Robert O. Barstow)—
Painter, Gr.
Pownal, Vt.; also, 352 Beacon St., Boston 16, Mass.

B. Lynn, Mass. *Studied*: New Sch. Des., Boston; Carnegie Inst. Tech., and with Charles Hawthorne. *Member*: Southern Vermont A.; Silvermine Gld. A.; Nat. Ser. Soc.; Am. Color Pr. Soc. *Awards*: prizes, Springfield A. Lg., 1925, 1936, 1941; Conn. Acad. FA, 1933; Albany Inst. Hist. & A., 1938, 1944. *Work*: Lawrence Mus. A., Williamstown, Mass.; Wood Gal. A., Montpelier, Vt.; Bennington (Vt.) Mus. Hist. & A.; BMFA; Alabama Polytechnic Inst.; AM. Assn. Univ. Women; Univ. Wisconsin; LC; U.S. State Dept.; Howard Univ.; VMFA; Victoria & Albert Mus., London, England; Nelson Gal. A.; Tel-Aviv Mus.; State T. Col., Albany, N.Y.; Munson-Williams-Proctor Inst. *Exhibited*: Paris, France, 1947; Liege, Belgium, 1948; Haarlem, Holland, 1948; Galerie de l'Odeon, Paris, 1954, and extensively in the U.S.

HUSEBY, ARLEEN MEISTER—*Painter, C.*
6531 Stefani Drive, Dallas 25, Tex.

B. Park Ridge, Ill. *Studied*: AIC; Chicago Acad. FA. *Member*: Frank Klepper A. Cl.; Fed. Dallas A.; ReVeau Bassett A. Cl. (Pres.); Frank Reaugh A. Cl. *Awards*: prizes, Dallas County Exh., 1955; Fed. Dallas A., 1955; Texas State Fair; Texas FA Soc. *Exhibited*: Dallas County Exh.; DMFA, and many local exhs.*

HUSTED-ANDERSEN, ADDA—*Craftsman, Des., T.*
887 First Ave. (22); h. 349 East 49th St., New York 17, N.Y.

B. Denmark: *Studied*: Thyra Vieth's Sch., Copenhagen; Technical State Sch., Copenhagen; Badishe Kunstgewerbe Schule, Pforzheim, Germany, and with Jean Dunand, in Paris. *Member*: Artist-Craftsmen of N.Y. *Awards*: medal, Gold & Silversmith Gld., Copenhagen. *Work*: Newark Mus. A. *Exhibited*: nationally; Brussels World's Fair, 1958. *Position*: Instr., Jewelry Making & Enameling, Craft Student's League, New York, N.Y.

HUTCHINSON, MARY E(LIZABETH)—*Painter, T., L.*
120 LaFayette Dr., Northeast, Atlanta, Ga.

B. Melrose, Mass., July 11, 1906. *Studied*: Agnes Scott Col.; NAD, and in Europe. *Member*: NAWA; N.Y. Soc. Women A.; Lg. Present-Day A.; Soc. Indp. A. *Awards*: prizes, NAWA, 1935, 1938. *Work*: High Mus. A.; Saratoga (Cal.) Mus.; Syracuse Univ.; Georgia Mus. A.; *Exhibited*: WFNY 1939; AIC; N.Y. Mun. Exh.; AFA traveling exh.; High Mus. A., 1933, 1940 (one-man); Midtown Gal., 1934, 1938 (one-man); Phila. A. All.; Riverside Mus.; BM; Am-British A. Center; Contemporary A. Gal.; ACA Gal.; Castle Gal., Atlanta, 1950 (one-man); Chappelier Gal.; Ferargil Gal. *Positions*: Instr. A., High Mus. A. Sch., Atlanta, Ga., 1946-49; A. Dir., Write-Away Adv. Co., Atlanta, Ga., 1950-51; Hd. A. Dept., Washington Seminary, Atlanta, Ga., 1951-53; Instr. A., Christ the King H.S., Atlanta, Ga., 1953- .*

HUTCHISON, JOSEPH SHIELDS—
Museum Director, E., L., P., S.
Canton Art Institute, 1717 Market Ave., North, Canton, Ohio

B. Mt. Pleasant, Pa., Oct. 15, 1912. *Studied*: Ohio State Univ., B.F.A., M.F.A.; Western Reserve Univ.; & with James Hopkins, Edward Frey. *Member*: Am. Assn. Univ. Prof. *Awards*: prize, Columbus (Ohio) A. Lg., 1937. *Work*: S., Ohio Wesleyan Univ. *Position*: Instr., Dept. FA, Ohio State Univ., Columbus, Ohio, 1935-37; Asst. Prof., Ohio Wesleyan Univ., Delaware, Ohio, 1937-40; Former Dir., Mint Mus. A., Charlotte, N.C., 1946-51; Asst. Prof. A. Hist., Queens Col., Charlotte, N.C., 1949-51; Dir., Canton AI, Canton, Ohio, 1953- ; A. Adv., Malone Col., Canton, Ohio.*

HUTH, HANS—*Museum Curator*
The Art Institute of Chicago (3); h. 5046 Woodlawn St., Chicago 15, Ill.

B. Halle, Germany, Nov. 11, 1892. *Studied*: Univs. Vienna, Berlin, Ph.D. *Member*: CAA; Nat. Trust for Historical Preservation. Author: "Künstler und Werkstatt der Spätgotik," 1923; "Abraham und David Röntgen," 1928; "Der Park von Sans Souci," 1929; "Talleyrand in America," 1942; "Europäische Lackarbeiten," 1955; "Nature and the American," 1957; "Friderizianische Möbel," 1958. Contributor to Encyclopaedia Britannica; Thieme-Becker, and many art magazines. Arranged exhs., From Colony to Nation (with Frederick A. Sweet); Religious Art, 1954. *Position*: Cur., Royal Palaces and Parks, Berlin, 1926-37; Collaborator, U.S. Nat. Park Service, 1939-44, Consultant, 1944- ; Cur., Decorative Arts, AIC; Adv. Encyclopaedia Britannica, 1944- .

HUTH, MARTA—*Painter*
5046 Woodlawn St., Chicago 15, Ill.

B. Munich, Germany, Dec. 25, 1898. *Studied*: State Sch. of Photography, Acad., Munich. *Member*: Chicago A. Cl. *Exhibited*: AWS, 1949; Cal. PLH, 1954 (one-man); Gld. Hall, Easthampton, N.Y., 1954; AIC, 1948-1953; Chicago Pub. Lib., 1955.

HUTTON, DOROTHY WACKERMAN—*Etcher, Lith., P.*
42 Rosedale Rd., Overbrook Hills, Philadelphia 31, Pa.

B. Cleveland, Ohio, Feb. 9, 1898. *Studied*: Minneapolis Sch. A.; Univ. Minnesota, and in Paris, France. *Member*: All. A., Pr. Cl., Plastic Cl., WC Cl., all of Phila., Pa. *Awards*: prizes, Phila. Plastic Cl., 1943-1945; Nat. Comp. for needlepoint des., Nat. Cathedral, Wash., D.C. *Work*: Smithsonian Inst.; Mint Mus. A.; Atwater Kent Mus., Phila. *Exhibited*: CGA, 1936; PAFA, 1937, 1958; Phila. A. All., annually; SAGA, 1946; Carnegie Inst., 1945, 1946; Phila. Pr. Cl., annually; Phila. Plastic Cl., annually; Phila. WC

Cl., 1958; Carl Schurz Mem. Fnd., 1957; Phila. Sketch Cl., 1957-58; Am. Color Pr. Soc., 1946; LC, 1944-1947, 1952; one-man: Smithsonian Inst., 1950; Phila. Women's Cl., 1951; Phila. Plastic Cl., 1951; Mint Mus. A., 1951; Miami Beach A. Center, 1952.

HUTTON, HUGH M.—*Cartoonist*
42 Rosedale Rd., Overbrook Hills, Philadelphia 31, Pa.

B. Lincoln, Neb., Dec. 11, 1897. *Studied*: Univ. Minnesota. *Member*: Phila. Sketch Cl.; Nat. Press Cl.; Nat. Cartoonist Soc.; Phila. A. All. *Awards*: prizes, Nat. Safety Council, 1951, 1954; Freedoms Fnd., 1952, 1953. *Exhibited*: Lib. Cong., 1946. Contributor to N.Y. Times. *Position*: Ed. Cart., Philadelphia Inquirer.*

HVALE, JAMES LEANDER—*Industrial Designer, P., C.*
1949 North Cicero Ave.; h. 1438 West North Shore Ave., Chicago 26, Ill.

B. Chicago, Ill. Studied: AIC; Northwestern Univ. *Member*: F., IDI. *Exhibited*: 28th Swedish-American exh. *Position*: Des. Hvale Forge, 1933-42; Indst. Des., Ekco Products Co., Chicago, Ill.; Chm., Chicago Chptr., IDI, 1953-55; Vice-Pres., Nat. IDI, 1953-55, Exec. Bd., 1953-55.

HYDE, JOSEPHINE E. (Mrs. Josephine Herron Hyde)—
Painter, C., T.
2245 Chestnut Ave., Long Beach 6, Cal.

B. Columbus, Ohio, Aug. 4, 1885. *Studied*: Stanford Univ., A.B., and with Nell Walker Warner, Edward Withers, Will Foster, and others. *Member*: Women Painters of the West; Cal. A. Cl.; Painters of the Southwest; Long Beach AA; La Jolla A. Group. *Award*: prize, Pacific Southwest Exh. *Exhibited*: Greek Theatre, Los A.; Ebell Salon; Los A. Mus. A.; Pomona (Cal.) Fair; Laguna Beach AA; Bowers Mus., Santa Ana, Cal.; La Jolla A. Group; Carlsbad, Cal.; Long Beach, Cal. *Position*: Instr., Los Angeles and Long Beach, Cal., H.S., 1923-50.*

HYKES, ETHEL JOHNT. See Johnt, Ethel

HYSLOP, ALFRED JOHN—*Educator, P.*
Carleton College; h. 310 Maple St., Northfield, Minn.

B. Castle-Douglas, Scotland, Apr. 10, 1898. *Studied*: Edinburgh Col. A., D.A., Royal Col. A., London, A.R.C.A. *Member*: Midwestern Col. A. Conference. *Work*: murals, Buckham Mem. Lib., Faribault, Minn. *Position*: Chm. A. Dept., Carleton Col., Northfield, Minn., 1923- .

HYSLOP, FRANCIS EDWIN, JR.—*Educator*
103 Sackett Bldg., University Park, Pa., h. 301 Locust Lane, State College, Pa.

B. Philadelphia, Pa., Jan. 7, 1909. *Studied*: Princeton Univ., B.A., M.A., M.F.A., and abroad. *Member*: AFA; CAA; Am. Assn. Univ. Prof.; Soc. Arch. Historians. Translator: Le Corbusier, "When the Cathedrals Were White," 1946; "New World of Space," 1948; "Baudelaire on Poe," 1952 (with introduction and notes, in collaboration with Lois Boe Hyslop); "Baudelaire: A Self-Portrait," 1957. Contributor to College Art Journal; Gazette des Beaux-Arts. *Position*: Univ. Illinois, 1942-1945; Asst. Prof. FA, Pennsylvania State Univ., 1934-42, Assoc Prof., 1946- ; Prof., 1957- .

IANNELLI, ALFONSO—*Sculptor, Des., C., L., E., P.*
257 North Northwest Highway, Park Ridge, Ill.

B. Andretta, Italy, Feb. 17, 1888. *Studied*: Newark Tech. Sch.; ASL, and with William St. John Harper, George Bridgman, Gutzon Borglum. *Member*: IDI (Chm. Edu. Com.); AEA. *Awards*: Hon. degree M.F.A., AIC, 1928; St. Gaudens prize in sculpture; IDI Certif. of Award. *Work*: sc., Midway Gardens, Adler Planetarium, Century of Progress Expo., Prudential Bldg., Chicago; St. Francis Xavier Church, Kansas City, Mo.; St. Francis de Sales H.S., Chicago; Woodbury County Court House, Sioux City; Bronson Park Fountain, Kalamazoo, Mich.; Pub. Welfare Bldg., Baton Rouge, La. *Exhibited*: AIC, 1921, 1925 (one-man), 1948-1952; NSS; Grand Central Gal.; Minneapolis, Minn. Contributor to architectural and art magazines; Western Architect, Exhibitors Herald World, Motion Picture Herald, The American City, Chicago Market News, Indst. Des. of products, electrical appliances &

furnishings for leading manufacturers. *Position*: Instr., Inst. A., Los A. A. Cl., 1911-13; Inst. Des., Chicago and Chicago Acad. FA, 1923-24; Hd. Des. Dept., Inst. Des., AIC, 1928-30.

IGLEHART, ROBERT L.—*Educator*
1025 Pomona Rd., Ann Arbor, Mich.

B. Baltimore, Md., Feb. 2, 1912. *Studied*: Maryland Inst. A.; Johns Hopkins Univ.; Columbia Univ., B.S. in Edu.; New Sch. for Social Research. *Awards*: Scholarship for European study, Md. Inst. A. *Member*: Com. on A. Edu., MModA (Vice-Chm.); John Dewey Soc.; CAA; NAEA. Author numerous articles for professional magazines. *Position*: Assoc. Ed., School Arts magazine; Instr., Sch. A., Univ. Washington, 1938-41; Chm., Dept. A. Edu., N.Y. Univ., 1946-55; Prof., Chm. Dept. A., Univ. Michigan, Ann Arbor, Mich., 1955- .

IMLER, EDGAR—*Painter, Et., Eng., W.*
134 West 23rd St., New York 11, N.Y.; s. Osterburg, Pa.

B. Pennsylvania. *Studied*: Franklin & Marshall Col., B.A.; AIC; PAFA; ASL. *Member*: SAGA; Am. Veteran's Soc. A. *Work*: Lib. Cong.; N.Y. Pub. Lib.; MMA. *Exhibited*: many national exh., including Lib. Cong.; Carnegie Inst.; MMA; AIC. Author, I., "Silent Caravan," 1953.

IMMEL, PAUL—*Educator, P., C., Des., Comm. A.*
Broadway & Pine Sts.; h. 6727 42nd St., S.W., Seattle 16, Wash.

B. Helena, Mont., Oct. 30, 1896. *Studied*: Ball Sch. Des., Minneapolis, Minn.; & with Mark Tobey, Amelio Amero. *Member*: Puget Sound Group of Northwest Painters; Northwest WC Soc. *Work*: SAM. *Exhibited*: SAM, 1936-1946; Northwest WC Soc., 1939-1946; one-man exh., SAM, 1943; Elfrstrom Gal., Salem, Ore., 1946; Graves Gal., San F., Cal. *Position*: Staff A., Seattle Post-Intelligencer, 1930-46; Instr., Burnley Sch. A. & Des., Seattle, Wash., 1946-50; Instr. Adv. A., Edison Tech. Sch., Seattle, Wash., 1950- .

IMPERATO, MRS. EDMOND. *See Milsk, Mark*

INGLE, ELIZA—*Craftsman, Gr.*
15 Merrymount Rd., Baltimore 10, Md.

B. Baltimore, Md., Apr. 27, 1885. *Studied*: Bryn Mawr Sch.; & with Gabrielle de V. Clements, Margaret E. Haydock, Eleanore Van Sweringen. *Member*: Boston Soc. A. & Crafts; Gld. Bookworkers; Rockport AA. *Work*: specializes in bookbinding; marble & other book papers, illuminations.

INGLE, THOMAS HUGHES—*Painter, T., L., Cr.*
R.R. #1, Box 369, Old Lyme, Conn.

B. Evansville, Ind., Mar. 31, 1920. *Studied*: Princeton Univ., B.A., and with Robert Lahr, Fran Soldini. *Member*: Essex AA (Pres. 1949-57); Mystic AA; Silvermine Gld. A.; Eastern AA. *Award*: prize, Norwich AA, 1954. *Work*: Evansville Pub. Mus.; Wadsworth Atheneum, Hartford, Conn. *Exhibited*: WMAA, 1956; New Talent, 1956; Conn. Contemp. A., 1951; one-man: Carlebach Gal., N.Y., 1950; Lyman Allyn Mus., 1952; Wesleyan Univ., 1953; Silvermine Gld. A., 1957, and others. Lectures: Philosophy of Art. *Positions*: Memb. Adv. Council, Lyman Allyn Mus. A., 1955- ; Instr., Young People's Art, Lyman Allyn Mus. A., New London, Conn., 1953- .

INGLIS, ANTOINETTE (Mrs. Alexander)—*Painter*
186 Commonwealth Ave., Boston 16, Mass.

B. Cortland, N.Y., Oct. 31, 1880. *Studied*: ASL. *Member*: North Shore AA; Copley Soc., Boston; St. Augustine AA. *Awards*: prize, North Shore AA, 1944. *Work*: Sheldon Swope A. Gal., Terre Haute, Ind.

INGLIS, KATE PETERS—*Craftsman*
Westminster West, Vt.

B. New York City, N.Y., May 13, 1901. *Studied*: PIASch.; Royal Sch. of Needlework, London, and with Maija Grotell. *Work*: (ceramics) PMG; Bertha Schaefer Gal.; Indiana Univ. *Exhibited*: Delphic Gal. (one-man); Ehrlich Gal.; WMA, 1955, 1956; Smithsonian Inst. traveling exh., 1955-56.

INGRAHAM, KATHERINE ELY—*Etcher*
110 Virginia Terrace, Madison 5, Wis.

B. Minneapolis, Minn., June 1, 1900. *Studied*: Univ. Wisconsin, B.S.; ASL; & with Joseph Pennell. *Awards*: prizes, Madison AA, 1944, 1946. *Work*: Lib. Cong. *Exhibited*: SAGA, 1943, 1945, 1951; Lib. Cong., 1943; Brooklyn SE, 1926, 1927; Wisconsin Salon A., 1941, 1943, 1945; Madison AA, 1943, 1944, 1946, 1951, 1952; Univ. Cl., Madison, Wis., 1938, 1940; Madison A. Gld., 1937, 1938; Wis. State Fair, 1949-1951.

INMAN, PAULINE WINCHESTER (Mrs. Robert G.)—
Engraver, I.
419 East 57th St., New York 22, N.Y.

B. Chicago, Ill., Mar. 3, 1904. *Studied*: Smith Col., A.B.; and with Allen Lewis. *Member*: SAGA (Council); Boston Pr. M.; Conn. Acad. FA. *Work*: Carnegie Inst.; LC; MMA; Pennsylvania State; Montclair A. Mus. *Exhibited*: LC, 1944-1946, 1948, 1949, 1956; NAD, 1944, 1946, 1949, 1956; Carnegie Inst., 1945, 1949; BM, 1947; PAFA, 1948; SAGA, 1948, 1950-1958; Providence A. Cl., 1953; Boston Soc. Indp. A., 1954; Boston Pr. M., 1957-58; Royal Soc. P., Et., & Engravers, London, 1954; Exchange Exh., Rome, Italy, 1954; Academic A., Springfield, 1955; Conn. Acad. FA, 1955; Boston Pr. M., 1955; Newport AA, 1957-58; Kent AA, 1957-58; Silvermine Gld. A., 1956; Montclair A. Mus., 1956; Albany Pr. Cl., 1957. Illus., "How to Know American Antiques," 1951; "New World Writing No. 2," 1952.

INTERLANDI, FRANK—*Cartoonist, P.*
1199 Temple Hills Drive, Laguna Beach, Cal.

B. Chicago, Ill., Mar. 10, 1924. *Studied*: Chicago Acad. FA; Univ. Iowa, B.A. *Work*: William Allen White Sch. Journalism, Univ. Kansas; Albert T. Reid Cartoon Coll. *Exhibited*: Los A. Mus. A., 1957; Laguna Beach Festival A., 1955, 1957, 1958. *Position*: Syndicated Cartoonist for The Register & Tribune Syndicate, 1953- .

INVERARITY, ROBERT BRUCE—*Designer, Mus. D.*
Adirondack Museum, Blue Mountain Lake, N.Y.

B. Seattle, Wash., July 5, 1909. *Studied*: Univ. Washington, B.A.; Fremont Univ., M.F.A., Ph.D., and with Kazue Yamagishi, Mark Tobey, Blanding Sloan. *Member*: F., Royal Soc. A., London; Am. Anthropological Assn.; Am. Assn. for Advancement of Science; Am. Ethnological Soc.; AAMus. *Awards*: Wenner-Gren Fnd. grant, 1951. *Work*: U.S. Naval Coll.; mural, U.S. Naval Air Station, Seattle, Wash.; mosaics, Univ. Washington; panels, Wash. State Mus., Seattle. *Exhibited*: Brooklyn Soc. Et., Chicago Soc. Et.; Nat. Gal., Canada; Cal. WC Soc.; Northwest A.; SAM; Oakland A. Mus.; Western Painters, San F.; Los A. AA; Tokyo, Japan; John Herron AI; Columbus Gal. FA; CM; Dayton AI; Temple Univ.; Detroit Inst. A.; one-man: Edward Weston Gal., Carmel, Cal.; Workshop Gal., San F.; Santa Barbara A. Gal.; Palm Springs, Cal.; Hudson Bay Co., Vancouver, B.C.; Vancouver A. Gal., and many others. Author, I., "Blockprinting and Stenciling," 1930; "The Rainbow Book," 1931; "Manual of Puppetry," 1933; "Masks and Marionettes of the Northwest Coast Indians," 1940; "Art of the Northwest Coast Indians," 1950, and others. *Position*: Bd. Trustees, Mus of Navajo Ceremonial A., Santa Fe, 1950-54; Bd. Dir., Intl. Folk A. Fnd., 1952-54; Research Asst., Yale Univ., 1951-53; Trustee, Eskimo Art, Inc., 1953- ; Dir., Mus. Intl. Folk Art, Santa Fe, New Mexico, 1949-54; Dir., Adirondack Mus., Blue Mountain Lake, N.Y., 1954- ; Dir., Adirondack Hist. Assn., 1956- .

IPCAR, DAHLOV (Mrs.)—*Painter, I., W.*
Robinhood, Me.

B. Windsor, Vt., Nov. 12, 1917. *Studied*: Oberlin Col. *Work*: murals, USPO, La Follette, Tenn.; Yukon, Okla.; painting, WMAA; Newark A. Mus.; Fairleigh Dickinson Col.; MMA. *Exhibited*: CGA, 1939, 1943; MMA, 1942; PAFA, 1940, 1942, 1958; Carnegie Inst., 1941, 1943; Pepsi-Cola, 1944; Detroit Inst. A., 1943, 1958; Boston A. Festival, 1956, 1957; Silvermine Gld. A., 1957; Art:USA, 1958; one-man: Bignou Gal., 1940; Passedoit Gal., 1943; Phila. A. All., 1944; ACA Gal., 1946; MModA, 1939; Farnsworth Mus., 1949, 1956; Wellons Gal., 1950, 1952. I., "Little Fisherman," 1945; "Just Like You"; "Good Work"; Author, I., "Animal Hide and Seek"; "One Horse Farm"; "World Full of Horses"; "Ten Big Farms"; "The Wonderful Egg"; "Brown Cow Farm."

IPPOLITO, ANGELO—*Painter*
315 East 10th St. (9); h. 111 East 10th St., New York 3, N.Y.

B. S. Arsenio, Italy, Nov. 9, 1922. *Studied*: Ozenfant Sch., FA; BMSch. A.; Instituto Meschini, Rome, Italy. *Work*: WMAA; PC; Munson-Williams-Proctor Inst.; Sarah Lawrence Col. *Exhibited*: Museo d'Arte Moderna, Rome, 1949; Galleria della Rotonda, Bergamo, 1950; Carnegie Inst., 1956-1958; WMAA, 1956-1958; Munson-Williams-Proctor Inst., 1955-1957; Inst. Contemp. A., Wash., D.C.; Columbus Gal. FA; WAC; PC; Massillon Mus. A.; Detroit Inst. A.; BM; Chicago A. Cl.; Universities of Fla., Neb., Colo., and Wesleyan Univ.; VMFA; Stable Gal., 1953-1957; Provincetown AA; Provincetown A. Festival; Boston A. Festival; Birmingham Univ., England; Columbia Univ.; Wagner Col.; Bryn Mawr Col.; Sarah Lawrence Col.; Bertha Schaefer Gal.; Tanager Gal., and others. *Positions*: Instr. Painting, Sarah Lawrence Col.; Cooper Union; Newark Sch. Fine & Indst. Art; Asst. Dir., Tanager Gal., New York, N.Y., 1952- .

IREDELL, RUSSELL—*Painter, I., S., Des.*
860 Diamond St., Laguna Beach, Cal.

B. New Brunswick, N.J., Feb. 28, 1889. *Studied*: PAFA, and with Henry McCarter, Cecilia Beaux, Daniel Garber. *Member*: Laguna Beach AA. *Awards*: Cresson traveling scholarship, PAFA. *Work*: many private portrait commissions. *Exhibited*: Laguna Beach AA, 1943-1946, and later; Festival of A., Laguna Beach; one-man: Los A., Pasadena, La Jolla, Coronado, Santa Ana, Huntington Beach, San Francisco, Palm Springs, all in Cal.; Nassau; Lake Forest, Ill., and others. Author, I., "Drawing the Figure."*

IRELAND, RICHARD WILSON (DICK)—
Painter, T., I., Gr.
1300 Mt. Royal Ave.; h. 2337 Eutaw Place, Baltimore 17, Md.

B. Marion, Ind., Mar. 31, 1925. *Studied*: Indiana Univ., B.A., M.A.; ASL; and with Anton Refrigier. *Work*: MModA. *Exhibited*: MModA, 1956; Indiana Pr. M., 1952; John Herron AI, 1948, 1951, 1953; ACA Gal., N.Y., 1949, 1950; RoKo Gal., 1955; Stable Gal., 1956; Collectors Gal., 1956, 1957; Eastside A., 1956, 1957; March Gal., 1957, 1958; Pyramid Gal., 1957; Workshop Gal., 1958, all New York City; one-man: Indiana Univ., 1952; Cherry Lane Theatre, N.Y., 1954. *Positions*: Instr. A., Maryland Inst. A., Baltimore; Indiana Univ., Bloomington.

IRVIN, SISTER MARY FRANCIS—*Painter, E., Gr.*
Seton Hill College, Greensburg, Pa.

B. Canton, Ohio, Oct. 4, 1914. *Studied*: Seton Hill Col.; Carnegie Inst., B.F.A.; AIC; Cranbrook Acad. A., M.F.A. *Member*: Assoc. A. Pittsburgh; Greensburg A. Cl.; CAA; Catholic AA; Pa. A. Edu. Assn.; Eastern AA; NAEA. *Awards*: Assoc. A. Pittsburgh; Greensburg AA, 1944, 1945, 1955, 1957. *Work*: Carnegie Inst.; St. Charles Borromeo Church, Twin Rocks, Pa.; Peabody, Central Catholic and Elizabeth Seton H.S., Pittsburgh. *Exhibited*: LC, 1944; Assoc. A. Pittsburgh, 1943-1946, 1954, 1957; Carnegie Inst., 1944, 1956; Greensburg A. Cl., 1944-1952, 1954, 1955, 1957; Pittsburgh Playhouse, 1950, 1953; Allegheny A. Lg., 1951; Westmoreland Hospital, 1956; Catholic AA, 1953. *Position*: Assoc. Prof. A., Seton Hill Col., Greensburg, Pa.

IRVIN, MELITA (McCORMACK)—*Sculptor, P.*
8121 Drexel Ave., Chicago 19, Ill.

B. Port Hope, Ontario, Canada. *Member*: Women A. Salon, Chicago; Renaissance Soc., Univ. Chicago. *Exhibited*: Women's A. Salon, 1940-1945, 1953; Renaissance Soc., 1953-1954; Chicago No-Jury Exh., 1933-1945; Illinois State Mus., 1945; AIC, 1952. Photographs of ceramic figurines: The Viennese Lady, Lady in Waiting and Her First Bow appeared in "Canadian Artists Abroad," 1953.

IRVIN, REA—*Painter, I., Cart.*
Newtown, Conn.

B. San Francisco, Cal., Aug. 26, 1881. *Studied*: Mark Hopkins AI. I., New Yorker magazine. *Position*: A. Ed., New Yorker magazine, 21 years.

IRVIN, VIRGINIA HENDRICKSON—*Miniature Painter*
619 East University Ave., Ann Arbor, Mich.

B. Chicago, Ill., Oct. 9, 1904. *Studied*: AIC, and with Elsie Dodge Pattee. *Member*: ASMP; Pa. Soc. Min. P.; NAWA. *Awards*: medal, ASMP, 1944; prizes, Cal. Soc. Min. P., 1947, 1949; Pa. Soc. Min. P., 1950; medal, NAWA, 1954, prize, 1958. *Work*: PMA. *Exhibited*: PAFA, 1934, 1935, 1938, 1942-1944, 1948-1952; CGA, 1943; ASMP, 1932, 1935, 1938, 1940, 1943-1945, 1948, 1949, 1951, 1952; MMA, 1942, 1950; Cal. Soc. Min. P., 1936, 1938, 1941, 1942, 1949; Smithsonian Inst., 1943, 1945, 1948; Detroit Soc. Women P. & S., 1945, 1946; Ann Arbor Exh.; Four Centuries of Min. P., 1950; BM; Portraits, Inc., N.Y.; ASMP and Royal Soc. Min. Painters Exh., London, England, 1958.

IRVINE, ROSALIND—*Museum Curator*
Whitney Museum of American Art, 22 West 54th St., New York 19, N.Y.*

IRVING, JOAN (JOAN IRVING BRANDT)—
Painter, C., T.
405 Goldenrod Ave., Corona del Mar, Cal.

B. Riverside, Cal., Mar. 12, 1916. *Studied*: Riverside (Cal.) Col.; A. Center Sch., Los A., Cal., and with Barse Miller. *Member*: Cal. WC Soc.; Laguna Beach AA; AWS. *Awards*: prizes, Festival of A., Laguna Beach, 1951; Cal. WC Soc., 1951; Nat. Orange Show, 1951. *Work*: MMA; Newport H.S. Coll. *Exhibited*: Cal. WC Soc., 1948-1952; Nat. Ceramic Exh., Los A. County Fair, 1952; Laguna Beach AA, 1936-1952; Los A. Mus. A., 1951; Ebell Salon, 1949. Author, I., articles for Ford Times.*

IRWIN, WILLIAM HYDE—*Painter, T.*
Brookdale, Santa Cruz County, Cal.

B. San Francisco, Cal., Oct. 14, 1903. *Studied*: Stanford Univ., A.B.; Cal. Col. A. & Crafts; Univ. California; & with Hans Hofmann. *Member*: San F. AA; Cal. WC Soc. *Work*: mural, Old Customs House, Monterey, Cal. *Exhibited*: Chicago SE, 1930; NAC, 1930; San F. AA, 1930, 1932, 1935, 1938, 1939, 1946; Palace Legion Honor, 1934; Oakland A. Gal., 1930, 1932, 1934, 1935, 1938; Santa Cruz A. Lg., 1930, 1932-1938, 1941; Cal. WC Soc., 1938; Cal. State Fair, 1935-1937, 1939; Santa Cruz Fair, 1937, 1938, 1941. *Position*: Instr., San Francisco State Col., 1950-51; Workshops, San F. Sch. Dist., in-service program, 1951-54.*

ISAACS, BETTY LEWIS—*Sculptor*
21 East 10th St., New York 3, N.Y.

B. Hobart, Tasmania, Sept. 2, 1894. *Studied*: CUASch; ASL; Alfred Univ.; and in Vienna. *Member*: NAWA; Brooklyn Soc. A. *Awards*: prizes, NAWA, 1955, 1957. *Work*: Cooper Union Mus.; commissioned for bronze, Church of St. Anselm, Tokyo, Japan. *Exhibited*: Audubon A.; Artist-Craftsmen of N.Y.; Phila. A. All.; Cooper Union; Argent Gal.; Ferargil Gal.; Nat. A. All. & Indst., N.Y.; Pasadena, Cal.; Riverside Mus.; Contemporaries Gal.; Brooklyn Soc. A.; one-man: Pasadena, Cal.; Hacker Gal., N.Y.; Univ. Louisville. *Position*: Instr. A., CUASch., and Greenwich House, N.Y.

ISAACS, WALTER—*Educator, P., W., L.*
Rt. 2, Box 2184, Bellevue, Wash.

B. Gillespie, Ill., July 15, 1886. *Studied*: Milliken Univ., B.S.F.A.; ASL; AIC; T. Col., Columbia Univ. *Member*: Am. Assn. Univ. Prof.; Pacific AA. *Work*: SAM. *Exhibited*: Paris Salon, 1922-1923; Carnegie Inst., 1946; Northwest A., annually. Contributor to: Atlantic Monthly; Magazine of Art; College Art Journal. *Position*: Prof. FA, Dir. Sch. A., Univ. Washington, Seattle, Wash.*

ISELIN, LEWIS—*Sculptor*
432 East 84th St., New York 28, N.Y.

B. New Rochelle, N.Y., June 22, 1913. *Studied*: Harvard Univ.; ASL, with Mahonri Young. *Member*: Century Assn. *Awards*: prize, NAD, 1938; Pa. State Col., 1950; Guggenheim F., 1951-52. *Work*: American Military Cemetery, Suresnes, Paris, France (mem., fig., reliefs). *Exhibited*: NAD, 1938, 1943; PAFA, 1941; MMA, 1942; WFNY, 1939; WMAA, 1951; Pa. State Col., 1950.*

ISENBURGER, ERIC—*Painter*

c/o M. Knoedler & Co., 14 East 57th St.; h. 208 Central Park South, New York 19, N.Y.

B. Frankfurt-on-Main, Germany, May 17, 1902. *Awards*: prizes, NAD, 1945, 1957; CGA, 1949 (prize and med.); med., Pepsi-Cola, 1948; prize, Carnegie Inst., 1947. *Work*: Am. Acad. A. & Let.; MModA; PAFA; John Herron AI; IBM; NAD; deYoung Mem. Mus.; Mary Washington Col. of the Univ. Virginia; Encyclopaedia Britannica; CGA. *Exhibited*: Carnegie Inst., 1943-1950; PAFA, 1943-1945, 1948, 1949, 1951, 1952; CGA, 1943, 1945, 1947, 1949, 1951; AIC, 1942, 1945; WMAA, 1944; CAM, 1945, 1951; NAD, 1942, 1945, 1948-1951; Indianapolis, Ind., 1946; CMA, 1946; MMA, 1950; Univ. Illinois, 1948, 1951; WMA, 1948-1952; Toledo Mus. A., 1948, 1951, 1952; Los A. Mus. A., 1951; Detroit Inst. A., 1951; Denver A. Mus., 1951; Minneapolis Inst. A., 1948; Columbus Gal. FA, 1948; Lincoln, Neb., 1949; Tulsa, Okla., 1951; one-man: Knoedler Gal., 1941, 1943, 1945, 1947, 1948, 1950, 1953, 1955; deYoung Mem. Mus., 1945; BMA, 1943; Springfield Mus. A., 1945; Colorado Springs FA Center, 1945; John Herron AI, 1946; Frances Taylor Gal., Los A., 1945; Assoc. Am. A., Hollywood, 1949.

ISHIKAWA, JOSEPH—*Museum Director*

Sioux City Art Center, Commerce Bldg., Sioux City, Iowa

Position: Dir., Sioux City Art Center, Sioux City, Iowa.*

IVONE, ARTHUR—*Sculptor*

6742 Siebern Ave., Cincinnati 13, Ohio

B. Naples, Italy, May 29, 1894. *Studied*: with Achille D'Orsi, Naples; E. Ferrari, Rome; C.J. Barnhorn, Cincinnati A. Acad. *Member*: Cincinnati AA. *Work*: S., Music Hall, Walnut Hills H.S., Cincinnati; Ohio State War Mem.; Springfield (Ohio) Mus.; mem., Indianapolis, Ind.; Mt. Washington Park, Cincinnati; State Archives Bldg., Montgomery, Ala.; panels, Birmingham, Ala.; mem., Silverton, Ohio; statue, Alms Park, Cincinnati.*

IVY, GREGORY DOWLER—*Educator, P.*

Woman's College of the University of North Carolina; h. Route 1, Randleman, N.C.

B. Clarksburg, Mo., May 7, 1904. *Studied*: Central Missouri State Col., B.S.; St. Louis Sch. FA, Washington Univ.; Columbia Univ., M.A.; N.Y. Univ. *Exhibited*: AIC, 1939-1942; BM, 1938-1942; MMA, 1943; Kansas City AI; High Mus. A.; Mint Mus. A., 1952; State A. Gal., Raleigh, 1952. *Member*: North Carolina Edu. Assn.; Southeastern AA; Southeastern Col. A. Conference; South Carolina A. Cl. *Member*: of numerous art juries. Author, I., "An Approach to Design" (monograph). *Positions*: Instr., Dept. A., State T. Col., Indiana, Pa., 1932-35; Prof. A., Hd. Dept. A., Woman's Col., Univ. North Carolina, Greensboro, N.C., 1935- ; Dir., Burnsville Sch. FA. of the Woman's Col., Univ. North Carolina, 1952-53; Dir. FA, Summer Session, Beaufort, N.C., 1954; Vice-Pres., Southeastern College A. Conf., 1957-58; Bd. Dir., Exec. Com., North Carolina Mus. A., 1956-58; Memb. Policy Com., CAA, 1956-58; Memb. Policy Com., NAEA, 1957-59.

JABLONSKI, JOSEPH S.—

Educator, Et., P., C.

Marshall College; h. 1659 Washington Blvd., Huntington 1, W. Va.

B. Poland, Feb. 9, 1898. *Studied*: Harvard Univ., A.B., M.A.; & with Frank von der Lancken, Fred Wagner, Arthur Pope. *Awards*: traveling F., Harvard Univ., 1923-1924; prize, Rochester Mem. A. Gal., 1928; Huntington Gal., 1954. *Work*: Rochester Athenaeum & Mechanics Inst.; Marshall Col.; Harvard Univ. *Exhibited*: PAFA, 1926, 1927; Rockport AA, 1926; Rochester C, 1925-1928; All. A. of W. Va., 1931, 1932, 1945; Marshall Col., 1933 (one-man). *Position*: Prof. A., Marshall Col., Huntington, W. Va., 1929- .

JACK, ELLA—*Educator, P.*

1817 West Fourth Ave., Stillwater, Okla.

B. Hiawatha, Kans. *Studied*: Chouinard AI; Otis AI; AIC, B.A. in Edu.; Univ. Chicago; Claremont Col., M.A., and with Millard Sheets, Edouard Vysekal. *Member*: Assn. Oklahoma A.; NAWA. *Awards*: med., prizes, Okla. A., 1930, 1954; Philbrook A. Center, 1949, 1950; Terry AI,

1952; Okla. State Fair; NAWA, 1954. *Work*: Kansas City AI; Mayo Clinic Lib. (des. clinic lib. bookplate); Philbrook A. Center. *Exhibited*: High Mus. A., 1944; NAWA, 1939-1946, 1954; Assn. Okla. A., 1929-1946, 1954; Kansas City AI; Women Painters of Am., 1939; Stillwater, Okla. (one-man). I., medical writings. *Position*: Prof. A., Emeritus, Okla. State Univ., Stillwater, Okla.

JACKSON, ANNIE H.—*Painter*

224 Rawson Rd., Brookline 46, Mass.

B. Minneapolis, Minn., Aug. 19, 1877. *Studied*: with Pape, Murphy, Woodbury, Hawthorne, O'Hara. *Member*: ASMP; Copley Soc., Boston; Pa. Soc. Min. P. *Awards*: med., Pa. Soc. Min. P., 1925; Sesqui-Centennial Exp., Phila., 1926; Boston Tercentenary, 1935. *Work*: BM; PMA.

JACKSON, BEATRICE (HUMPHREYS)—*Painter*

450 East 63rd St., New York, N.Y.; also Dorset, Vt.

B. London, England, Dec. 25, 1905. *Studied*: Smith Col.; Grand Central A. Sch.; ASL; Colorossi Acad., Paris, and with Wayman Adams, George Elmer Browne, Andre Lhote, Paris. *Member*: All. A. Am.; NAWA; Nat. Lg. Am. Pen Women; Cosmopolitan Cl.; So. Vermont A.; Pen & Brush Cl.; Conn. Acad. FA; Catherine L. Wolfe A. Cl.; Grand Central A. Gal.; Assoc. Societe des Beaux-Arts. *Awards*: prizes, Morristown AA, 1941, 1943; NAWA, 1953; Nat. Lg. Am. Pen Women, 1955, 1957; Conn. Acad. FA, 1955; All. A. Am., medal, 1955, prize, 1958; Academic A. Assn., 1956; Wolfe A. Cl., 1956; Bronxville Pub. Lib., 1956. *Exhibited*: NAD, 1941, 1955; Conn. Acad. FA, 1954-1957; NAWA, 1952-1957; All. A. Am., 1941, 1948, 1950-1958; Paris Salon, 1928 and later; Salon d'Automne, 1931; Salon des Tuileries; Knickerbocker A.; So. Vermont A., 1942-1958; Morristown AA, 1941-1943; Van Dieman-Lilienfeld Gal., 1955; Bronxville Pub. Lib., 1955, 1956; Studio Gld., 1953; Art:USA, 1958; Grand Central A. Gal., 1958 (one-man); Nat. Lg. Am. Pen Women, 1956, 1958.

JACKSON, DENNIS EMERSON—*Painter, E., W.*

144 Louis Ave., Cincinnati 20, Ohio

B. Ridgeport, Ind., Sept. 3, 1878. *Studied*: Indiana Univ., A.B., A.M., Ph.D.; Rush Medical Col., M.D. *Member*: Am. Physicians AA; Cincinnati AC; Am. Assn. Univ. Prof. *Exhibited*: Am. Physicians AA Exh., in many cities of U.S.; Cincinnati AC; Univ. Cincinnati. *Position*: Prof., Univ. Cincinnati, Ohio, 1918-48; Prof. Emeritus, 1948- .

JACKSON, ELLA F. (Mrs.)—*Painter, Gr., T.*

50 Lefferts Ave., Brooklyn 25, N.Y.

B. New York, N.Y., June 24, 1894. *Studied*: CUASch.; T. Col., Columbia Univ., and with Hans Hofmann, Gabor Peterdi. *Member*: Brooklyn Soc. A.; Provincetown AA; Cape Cod AA. *Awards*: prizes, Brooklyn Soc. A., 1950; BM Sch. Alumni, 1958. *Exhibited*: BM, 1946, 1947, 1949; AFA traveling exh., 1947; NAWA; Wichita AA, 1952; Phila. Pr. Cl.; Brooklyn Soc. A., 1945-1951, 1954, traveling exh., 1955-56; Bodley Gal., 1957 (one-man). *Position*: Instr., A. Workshop, New York, N.Y.

JACKSON, EVERETT GEE—*Educator, P., I.*

1234 Franciscan Way, San Diego 16, Cal.

B. Mexia, Tex., Oct. 8, 1900. *Studied*: Texas A. & M. Col.; AIC; San Diego State Col., A.B.; Univ. Southern California, M.A. *Member*: Am. Assn. Univ. Prof.; San Diego FA Soc. *Awards*: prizes, San F., Cal., 1928; Laguna Beach, Cal. AA, 1934; Los A. Mus. A., 1934. *Work*: Houston Mus. FA; San Diego FA Soc.; Los A. Mus. A. *Exhibited*: Houston Mus. FA; San Diego FA Soc.; Laguna Beach AA; Legion Honor, 1946. I., "Paul Bunyan," 1945; "The Ugly Duckling," 1949; "Popol Vuh," 1955; "The Conquest of Peru," 1957; "American Chimney Sweeps," 1958. *Position*: Prof. A., Chm. A. Dept., San Diego State Col., San Diego, Cal., 1930- .

JACKSON, HARLAN—*Painter*

458 West Broadway, New York 12, N.Y.

B. Cleburne, Tex., Apr. 21, 1918. *Studied*: State T. Col., Pittsburgh, Kans.; Cal. Sch. FA, San F.; Hans Hofmann Sch. A. *Member*: AEA; San F. AA. *Awards*: Rosenberg traveling Scholarship, San F. AA, 1948. *Work*: IBM. *Exhibited*: San F. AA, 1947, 1948, 1954; Oakland Mus. A., 1947; Cal. PLH, 1947; Pan-Am. Union Exh., Wash.,

D.C., 1951; one-man: A. Gld. Gal., San F., 1947; Centre d'Art, Haiti, 1950; Intl. Exh., Palais des Beaux-Arts, Haiti, 1950; Barnet Aden Gal., Wash., D.C., 1950; Panoras Gal., 1955.

JACKSON, HAZEL BRILL—*Sculptor, Eng.*
"Twin Oaks," Balmville Rd., Newburgh, N.Y.

B. Philadelphia, Pa. *Studied*: BMFASch.; in Italy; & with Bela Pratt, Charles Grafly. *Member*: Gld. Boston A.; NSS. *Awards*: med., Nat. Acad., Rome, 1930; prize, NAD, 1945, 1948. *Work*: Concord A. Mus.; Montpelier (Vt.) A. Mus.; Hotchkiss Sch., Lakeville, Conn. *Exhibited*: NAD, 1944-1948, 1950, 1953, 1955-1957; Nat. Acad., Rome, 1927-1930; Nat. Acad., Firenze, Italy, 1927-1930; Grand Central A. Gal.; Gld. Boston A.; CGA (one-man). Specializes in animal sculpture, especially horses and dogs.

JACKSON, LEE—*Painter*
22 East 66th St., New York 21, N.Y.

B. New York, N.Y., Feb. 2, 1909. *Studied*: ASL, and with William McNulty, George Luks, John Sloan. *Member*: ASL; Nat. Soc. Painters in Casein; Audubon A.; AEA; AWS. *Awards*: prizes, Nebraska AA, 1946; SC, 1950; Nat. Soc. Painters in Casein, 1955; Grumbacher, 1956; NAD, 1951; Guggenheim F., 1941. *Work*: MMA; CGA; Nebraska AA; Los A. Mus. A.; Athens Mus. A.; St. Bonaventure Col., N.Y.; Walker A. Center. *Exhibited*: PAFA, 1937, 1948-1952; NAD, 1938, 1942, 1944, 1945, 1948-1955, 1957, 1958; GGE, 1939; Carnegie Inst., 1941, 1943, 1948; WMAA, 1941, 1943-1946, 1948-1952; CGA, 1941, 1943, 1945, 1949; AIC, 1942, 1946; VMFA, 1942; Nebraska AA, 1944, 1946, 1948-1951; CAM, 1945; Los A. Mus. A., 1945; Soc. Four A., 1942; Butler AI, 1946; Univ. Illinois, 1949; Newark Mus., 1952; Toledo Mus. A., 1949; Des Moines A. Center, 1951; Dayton AI, 1951; Altoona A. All., 1950; Dallas Mus. FA, 1949; Santa Barbara Mus. A., 1949; Mus. FA of Houston, 1949; Walker A. Center, 1948; Joslyn A. Mus., 1949; Audubon A., 1948-1955; BMFA, 1955; Mus. City of New York, 1958; Art:USA, 1958; Davenport Mun. A. Gal., 1951, and others. One-man: Babcock Gal., 1941, 1943, 1948-1952, 1958; Nat. Gal., Canada, 1940; A. Gal., Toronto, 1940; Montreal AA, 1940; Inst. Mod. A., Boston, 1945.

JACKSON, VAUGHN LYLE—
Commercial Artist, Des., I., P.
Johns Hopkins University; h. 9803 Broad St., Bethesda 14, Md.

B. Raymond, Ohio, Jan. 7, 1920. *Studied*: Columbus A. Sch.; Ohio State Univ.; Corcoran Sch. A., with Richard Lahey, Edmund Archer; also with Eliot O'Hara, Hans Hofmann; American Univ. *Member*: Nat. Soc. A. Dir.; A. Dir. Cl. of Metropolitan Washington; Wash. WC Cl. (Bd. Managers); Landscape Cl. of Wash.; Am. A. Lg.; Montgomery County AA. *Awards*: prizes, Washington A. Fair, 1954; Hilltop House Exh., Harpers Ferry, W. Va., 1956; Wash. A. Cl., 1955; silver medal, Landscape Cl. of Wash., 1955. *Exhibited*: Wash. WC Cl., 1954-1958; AAPL, 1950-1952, 1957; Landscape Cl. of Wash., 1954-1958; Wilson T. Col., 1955; CGA, 1955, 1956; Am. A. Lg., 1958; A. Lg. of Northern Virginia, 1955, 1956; one-man: Washington, D.C., 1956, 1958. *Positions*: Adv. Illus.: Washington Post-Times Herald; Agricultural Chemicals magazine; Washington Evening & Sunday Star; Editor & Publisher magazine; Printers Ink; Aviation Age; Electronics magazine; Artist with: Columbus Citizen, 1938-42; S. Kann Sons, Wash., D.C., 1946-47; Kal, Ehrlich & Merrick Adv. Co., Wash., D.C., 1947-52; Asst. A. Dir. with Operations Research Office, The Johns Hopkins Univ., Bethesda, Md., 1952- ; Vice-Pres., Wash. WC Cl., 1959-60.

JACOBS, ELMER—*Illustrator, P., L., Des.*
6101 Sheridan Rd., Chicago 40, Ill.

B. Streator, Ill., May 9, 1901. *Studied*: with Moholy-Nagy, Schroeder, Gyorgy Kepes. *Member*: Soc. Typographic A.; A. Gld., Chicago; Am. A. Group: "9" Illustrators; 27 Chicago Designers. *Awards*: prizes, AIGA, 1937-1939; Direct Mail Advertising Assn., 1937-1949, also plaque, 1945; Soc. Typographic A., 1935-1937, 1945; A. Gld., Chicago, 1941; Indst. Editors Assn., Chicago, 1942-1945; Carey-Thomas aid. award. I., "Anthology of the Flame"; "Qwert Yuiop"; "House of Morrell," and others. Designed 1953 Christmas Seal. Contributor to Print magazine.

JACOBS, JAY WESLEY—*Portrait Painter*
Jupiter Island, Hobe Sound, Fla.; also 4040 Altamont Rd., Birmingham 13, Ala.

B. Carthage, Mo., Jan. 3, 1898. *Studied*: Harvard Col., A.B. *Member*: The Island Cl., Hobe Sound, Fla. *Exhibited*: Salon des Beaux-Arts, Paris, France (3 years). *Work*: portraits: Pres. Truman, in The Capitol, Wash., D.C.; Chm. Bd., du Pont Co., Wilmington, Del.; Admirals Halsey, Land, Vickery, and many others of prominent persons.

JACOBS, LEONEBEL—*Portrait Painter*
11700 National Blvd., Los Angeles, Cal.

B. Tacoma, Wash. *Member*: AWS; NAWA. Author: "Portraits of Thirty Authors." Many recent portraits of prominent persons.

JACOBS, TED SETH—*Painter, Des.*
45 West 74th St., New York 23, N.Y.

B. Newark, N.J., June 11, 1927. *Studied*: ASL. *Awards*: prizes, Kansas City AI; ASL, 1953; John F. & Anna Lee Stacey award, 1954. *Work*: ASL, and in private colls. *Exhibited*: Springfield (Mass.) Mus. A., 1952; Randolph-Macon Col., 1954; Walker A. Center; Ross A. Gal., 1946; Portraits, Inc., annually; Barzansky Gal.; Riverside Mus.; Hewitt Gal., 1958. *Position*: The Art Centre, W. & J. Sloane Co., New York, 1957- .

JACOBSON, ARTHUR R.—*Painter, Gr., E.*
Rt. 2, Cochise Rd., Scottsdale, Ariz.

B. Chicago, Ill., Jan. 10, 1924. *Studied*: AIC; Chicago Acad. FA; Univ. Wisconsin, B.S., M.S. *Awards*: prizes, New Mexico State Fair, 1954, 1955; Phoenix Annual, 1956; New Mexico Annual, 1956; Tucson, Ariz., 1958. *Work*: Hastings Col., Hastings, Neb. *Exhibited*: Denver A. Mus., 1952, 1958; Wisconsin Salon, 1950; Los A. Mus. A., 1948; Missouri Annual, 1951; Colorado Springs FA Center, 1953; Mus. New Mexico, Santa Fe, 1953-1956; Oklahoma A. Center, 1953; Arizona State Fair, 1954; Phoenix A. Center, 1954; Boston Pr. M., 1956; CGA, 1957; Phila. Pr. Cl., 1958; Butler Inst. Am. A., 1958; Terry AI, 1952; Tulsa, Okla., 1954; DMFA, 1957; Tucson, Ariz., 1958; Univ. Arizona, 1954, 1955, 1958; Stockton, Cal., 1955; one-man: Kendall Gal., San Angelo, Tex., 1952; Okla. A. & M. Col., 1954; Ruins Gal., Taos, 1954; American Gal., Los A., 1955. *Position*: A.T., Philbrook A. Center; Phoenix A. Center; Desert Sch. A.; Prof. A., Arizona State College, Tempe, Ariz., 1956- .

JACOBSON, NATHANIEL JUDAH—*Painter, T.*
1 Holden St., Brookline 46, Mass.; h. 131 Kilsyth Road, Boston 46, Mass.

B. Salem, Mass., Mar. 3, 1916. *Studied*: Mass. Sch. A.; Yale Univ. Sch. FA, B.F.A. *Work*: murals, Boston Univ.; Tufts Univ. *Exhibited*: Carnegie Inst., 1941; CM, 1943.*

JACOBSON, OSCAR BROUSSE—*Painter, E., W., L.*
Allenspark P.O., Colo.; h. 609 Chautauqua Ave., Norman, Okla.

B. Sweden, May 16, 1882. *Studied*: Bethany Col., B.P., D.F.A.; Yale Univ., B.F.A.; & in Paris, France. *Member*: CAA; AAUP. *Awards*: med., Kansas City AI, 1931; IBM, 1940; GGE, 1939. *Work*: McPherson A. Gal., Kan.; Bethany Col. A. Gal.; State Cap'ol, Oklahoma City, Okla.; Broadmoor A. Acad.; Oklahoma Hall of Fame; Univ. Oklahoma; Oklahoma A. Lg. *Exhibited*: WFNY 1939; Colorado Springs FA Center, 1940; Albuquerque, N.M., 1940; CGA; one-man exh.: Kansas City AI; Dallas Mus. FA; Mus. FA of Houston; Colorado Springs FA Center; Univ. Wisconsin; Univ. Kansas; Syracuse Univ.; Cornell Univ.; Oklahoma A. Center; Grinnell Col.; Wichita A. Mus.; Philbrook A. Center. Author: "Kiowa Indian Arts"; Co-Author, with Jeanne d'Ucel, "Les Peintres Indiens d'Amerique"; "Costumes Indiens de l'Amerique du Nord"; articles for magazines. *Position*: Research Prof., Emeritus, Univ. Oklahoma, Norman, Okla. (Retired).

JACOBSSON, EDWARD GUSTAVE—*Painter, T., Des.*
139 East 52nd St., New York 22, N.Y.; Berkshire Art Center; h. Queechy Farm, Canaan, N.Y.

B. New York, N.Y., July 29, 1907. *Studied*: NAD; ASL; Grand Central A. Sch.; AIC; Colorossi Acad., Paris, &

with Ivan Olinsky, Jean Charlot, Sigurd Skou, Boardman Robinson. *Member*: Conn. Acad. FA; Springfield A. Lg.; North Shore AA; Mid-Vermont A.; Ogunquit A. Center; Berkshire A. Center. *Awards*: prizes, Swedish Cl., Chicago, Ill., 1946, 1947; Conn. Acad. FA, 1946; North Shore AA, 1946. *Exhibited*: PAFA; Palace Legion Honor, 1946; Mint Mus., 1945, 1946; George Walter Vincent Smith Gal., 1945, 1946; Springfield Mus. FA, 1945; Morgan Mem., 1945, 1946; SC; Albany Inst. Hist. & A., 1945, 1946; Phila. Sketch Cl., 1945, 1946; Jersey City Mus., 1945; Berkshire Mus. *Position*: Founder & Dir., Berkshire A. Center, Canaan, N.Y.*

JACOBY, NED (LEVERING)—*Designer, T., P.*

816 West 5th St., Los Angeles 17, Cal.

B. Norwalk, Ohio, Oct. 1, 1918. *Studied*: Dartmouth Col., B.A.; Chouinard AI. *Member*: A. Dir. Cl., Los A. (1st V-Pres.); Nat. Soc. A. Dir.; Cal. WC Soc.; SAGA. *Awards*: Certif. of Merit, West Coast Adv. & Editorial A., 1954. *Exhibited*: West Coast Adv. & Ed. A., annually; Cal. WC Soc., 1954.*

JAMES, ALFRED EVERETT—

Painter, S., Et., Des., T., C.

110 East Magnolia Ave.; h. Meadow Brook Dr., Auburn, Ala.

B. Edgewood, R.I., Apr. 17, 1908. *Studied*: R.I. Sch. Des.; Tiffany Fnd.; Thurn Sch. Mod. A.; & with Hans Hofmann. *Member*: Scarab Cl.; Alabama A. Lg.; Photographers Assn. Am. *Awards*: prizes, West Palm Beach Army Exh., 1943; Montgomery Mus. FA, 1945, 1947, 1950; Alabama A. Lg., 1952, 1954. *Work*: Birmingham Mus. A.; murals, Providence Pub. Lib. *Exhibited*: U.S. Army Exh., West Palm Beach, Fla., 1943; High Mus. A., 1950; Montgomery Mus. FA, 1940-1943, 1945, 1947, 1950; Civic A. Gal., Greenville, S.C., 1941. *Position*: Instr. A., Alabama Polytechnic Inst., Auburn, Ala., 1937-46.

JAMES, BESS B. (Mrs. H. M.)—*Painter*

1403 North 2nd St., Monroe, La.

B. Big Spring, Tex., Jan. 12, 1897. *Studied*: Las Vegas Univ.; Southwest Texas Col.; & with Marie Hull, Roy Henderson. *Member*: SSAL; Mississippi AA; New Orleans AA; Nat. Lg. Am. Pen Women. *Awards*: prizes, Louisiana Fed. Women's Cl., 1936; Miss. AA, 1942; Lubbock, Tex., 1938. *Work*: in private collections. *Exhibited*: Chicago AC, 1943; SSAL, 1936, 1938, 1940, 1941; Miss. AA, 1937, 1939, 1942.*

JAMES, EVALYN GERTRUDE—*Painter, I., W., E.*

Road 340 West, Route 4; h. Box 61, Route 4, Brazil, Ind.

B. Chicago, Ill., May 22, 1898. *Studied*: Herron AI; Earlham Col.; Indiana Univ., A.B., A.M.; & with William Forsythe. *Member*: Hoosier Salon; Indiana AC; Western AA; AAPL. *Awards*: prizes, Indiana State Fair. *Work*: Brazil (Ind.) Court House; St. Paul's Lutheran Church and Bee Ridge Christian Church, both Brazil, Ind. *Exhibited*: Herron AI; Hoosier Salon, annually; Swope A. Gal.; Purdue Univ.; & in Terre Haute, Brazil, Ind.; Terry AI; Galerie Internationale, N.Y. Contributor to: national magazines. Lectures: "Art in Indiana"; "Art Education"; "Chemically Related Pigments for Artists."

JAMES, FRANCES K.—*Painter*

6441 Peach Ave., Van Nuys, Cal.

B. Los Angeles, Cal., May 31, 1916. *Studied*: Los A. AI, and with Christian von Schneidau, Nicholi Fechin. *Member*: Las Artistas A. Cl.; Cal. A. Cl.; San Fernando Valley A. Gld. *Awards*: prizes, Grenshaw Fair, 1948; Madonna A. Festival, Los A., 1955. *Work*: murals, Rands, Hollywood. *Exhibited*: Cal. A. Cl., 1953; Los A. City Hall, 1948, 1949; Madonna A. Festival, 1955; one-man: San Fernando; Greek Theatre, 1953; Jeane-Blenn Gal., 1953.*

JAMES, FREDERIC—*Painter, I., Des.*

3626 Warwick Blvd.; h. 644 Westover Rd., Kansas City 13, Mo.

B. Kansas City, Mo., Sept. 28, 1915. *Studied*: Univ. Michigan, Col. of Arch., B.Des.; Cranbrook Acad. A. *Member*: AWS. *Awards*: prizes, Denver A. Mus., 1950;

Nelson Gal. A., Kansas City, 1951. *Work*: Nelson Gal. A.; Denver A. Mus.; Univ. Missouri; Cranbrook Acad. A.; murals, Trinity Lutheran Church, Mission, Kans.; Overland Park State Bank, Overland Park, Kans.; Consumer's Cooperative Assn., Kansas City. *Exhibited*: AIC, 1940, 1941; BM, 1941; NAD, 1949; AWS, 1950, 1952; Boston Soc. Indp. A., 1951; MMA, 1952; Midwestern A., 1935, 1940; Mid-America Annuals, 1950-1955, 1958; Denver A. Mus., 1950; Springfield (Mass.) Mus. A., 1954; one-man: Assoc. Am. A., N.Y., 1952; Univ. Kansas, 1952; Univ. Kansas City, 1953; Nelson Gal. A., 1954; Maynard Walker Gal., N.Y., 1955. I., "Introduction to Music"; "Bright Heritage." Illus. travel articles for Kansas City Star. *Position*: Instr. Watercolor, Kansas City AI, 1947-51.

JAMES, MACGILL—*Museum Curator, W.*

"Four Winds," Westminster, Md.

B. Baltimore, Md., Aug. 2, 1897. *Studied*: Columbia Univ.; Harvard Univ. Co-Author: "Great American Paintings," 1943. *Position*: Dir., Mun. Mus., Baltimore, Md., 1933-40; Asst. Dir., NGA, Washington, D.C., 1940-1956; Cur., Biltmore House, Biltmore, N.C., 1956-57 (Retired).

JAMES, SANDRA—*Painter*

Winter Harbor, Me.

Member: AWS; Audubon A.; All. A. Am. *Work*: Florida Gulf Coast A. Center, and in private coll. *Awards*: prizes, Irvington Mus. Assn.; L.D.M. Sweat Mem. Mus., 1957.

JAMES, WILLIAM—*Painter*

95 Irving St., Cambridge, Mass.

B. Cambridge, Mass., June 17, 1882. *Studied*: Harvard Univ., A.B.; BMFA Sch. *Work*: Fenway Court, Gardner Mus., Boston; Providence A. Mus.; BMFA; Harvard Univ.; Radcliffe Col.*

JAMESON, DEMETRIOS GEORGE—*Educator, P., Gr.*

K-211, Art Department, Oregon State College; h. 735 North 28th St., Corvallis, Ore.

B. St. Louis, Mo., Nov. 22, 1919. *Studied*: Corcoran Sch. A.; Washington Univ., Sch. FA, B.F.A.; Univ. Illinois, M.F.A., and with Max Beckmann, Fred Conway, Stephen Greene. *Member*: AEA; AAUP; Portland A. Mus. Assn. *Awards*: John T. Milliken Foreign Traveling Scholarship, Washington Univ., 1949; prizes, and purchase prizes, CAM, 1947; Denver A. Mus., 1951; Portland A. Mus., 1951, 1952, 1954; SAM, 1954; Oregon State Fair, 1957 (2); Northwest A. & Crafts, Bellevue, Wash., 1957, and others. *Work*: Denver A. Mus.; Portland (Ore.) A. Mus.; SAM; Univ. Illinois. *Exhibited*: AEA exhs., Chicago, 1948-50; Butler Inst. Am. A., 1951, 1952, 1954, 1956; CAM, 1947-49; CGA, 1953; Denver A. Mus., 1951, 1953-1956; Frye Mus. A., Seattle, 1957; Joslyn A. Mus., 1949; LC, 1952-1958; Mulvane A. Mus., 1948; Oakland A. Mus., 1950, 1951, 1952; Oregon State Fair, 1956, 1957; Spokane, Wash., 1954-1957; Portland A. Mus., 1950-1958; St. Louis A. Gld., 1948, 1949; SFMA, 1951, 1952; SAM, 1951-57; Springfield (Mo.) A. Mus., 1948; Athens, Greece, 1955; Univ. Illinois, 1949; Univ. Oregon, 1950; Oregon State Col., 1950-1954, 1956, 1958; DMFA, 1954; Guggenheim Mus., N.Y., 1954; others 1957-58 include: Oregon State College Intl. Exchange Exhibit in Italy, France and England; Provincetown A. Festival; Bellevue, Wash.; Pasadena Print Festival, and many others. One-man: Willamette Univ., Salem, Ore., 1952, 1955; Portland A. Mus., 1952; Kraushaar Gal., N.Y., 1953; Oregon State Col., 1957, etc. *Position*: Asst. Prof. A., Oregon State College, Corvallis, Ore., at present.

JAMIESON, BERNICE EVELYN—

Museum Asst. Curator, Des., Eng., Ser., I., L., P.

New Jersey State Museum, State House Annex; h. 103 Grandview Ave., Yardville Heights, Trenton 10, N.J.

B. Providence, R.I., Apr. 18, 1898. *Studied*: R.I.Sch.Des., B.F.A.; Harvard Univ.; Brown Univ.; BAID; & with Steinhof, Thurn, Hibbard. *Member*: AAMus; N.J. Hist. Soc.; Early Am. Indst. Assn.; N.Y. State Hist. Assn.; Soc. Arch. Historians; N.J. Archaeological Soc.; CAA. *Awards*: prize, Pencil Points competition, 1927; N.J. State Fed. Women's Cl., 1955. *Exhibited*: AIC, 1935, 1939, 1940; Int. Exh. Pr. M., Los A., Cal., 1934-1937; NAD; textile exh., Greensboro,, N.C., 1944; Boston AC; Wash. WC Cl., 1936, 1938; Providence AC; Phila. Pr. Cl.; Phila. A. All., 1935, 1937, 1938; BM, 1933; Southern Pr.M., 1938, 1939; Wichita AA,

1936; Studio Gld., 1938; MMA, 1942; Providence Mus. A.; Univ. Minnesota, 1946; Audubon House, 1952; Acad. Natural Sc., 1952; Rahway A. Center, 1953; N.J. State Mus., 1953, 1954; Trenton Jr. Col., 1954; N.J. State Fed. Women's Cl., 1955; A. Center of the Oranges, 1955; Montclair A. Mus., 1953; one-man: Daytona Beach, 1953. Illus.: series of books for St. James Church, N.Y., 1942. Author: article on silk screen printing for the "Dictionary of the Arts," 1943; illus., "Or Forfeit Freedom." *Position*: Asst. Cur., New Jersey State Mus., Trenton, N.J., 1944- .

JAMIESON, MITCHELL—*Painter, T.*
2333 Holmes Run Drive, Falls Church, Va.

B. Kensington, Md., Oct. 27, 1915. *Studied*: Washington, D.C. and Mexico City. *Awards*: prizes, Soc. Wash. A., 1941; MModA, 1940; Marian Anderson mural comp., 1941; Guggenheim F., 1946; Bronze Star for work as Navy Combat Artist, 1946; Grant, Am. Acad. A. & Lets., 1947; CGA, 1953. *Work*: White House, Wash., D.C.; WMAA; MMA; BM; Cornell Univ.; CGA; PC; Wichita A. Mus.; SAM; Ft. Worth A. Center; Portland A. Mus.; Henry Gal., Univ. Washington, Seattle; Norton Gal. A.; WAC; murals, Interior Bldg., Wash., D.C.; Comptroller Gen. Suite, Wash., D.C.; USPO, Upper Marlboro, Laurel, Md.; Willard, Ohio. *Exhibited*: Nationally. One-man: Santa Barbara Mus. A.; SAM; Des Moines A. Center; Cal. PLH; Norton Gal. A.; Ft. Worth A. Center; CGA. *Positions*: Paintings for Life Magazine, 1957; Hd. Painting Dept., Cornish Sch., Seattle, Wash., 1949-51; Instr., Painting, Madeira Sch., Greenway, Va., 1952-55; Visiting Instr., Norton Gal. & Sch. A., 1952-53, 1956-57.

JAMISON, CELIA (Mrs. Clifford H. Sankey)— *Painter, T., C.*
302 Denton St., Denton, Tex.

B. Prosper, Tex., Jan. 17, 1920. *Studied*: Texas State Col. for Women, B.S.; Univ. Iowa, M.A.; & with Philip Guston. *Award*: prize, DMFA, 1957. *Work*: Univ. Iowa; Ft. Worth AA. *Exhibited*: Weyhe Gal., 1945; Ft. Worth AA; Mus. FA of Houston, 1945, 1946; Kansas City AI, 1942; Mus. of New Mexico, 1957; DMFA, 1957 and prior; Witte Mem. Mus., 1957; Mus. FA of Houston, 1958; Beaumont Mus. A., 1958, & in San Antonio, Austin, Tex. *Position*: Instr. A., Texas State Col. for Women, Denton, Tex., 1945-49.

JAMISON, PHILIP—*Painter, T.*
303 South High St.; h. 705 West Union St., West Chester, Pa.

B. Philadelphia, Pa., July 3, 1925. *Studied*: PMSch A. *Member*: AWS; Phila. WC Soc.; All. A. Am.; Wilmington Soc. FA; Chester County AA. *Award*: prize, Wilmington Soc. FA, 1957. *Exhibited*: AWS, 1956-1958; NAD, 1956; PAFA, 1949, 1953, 1957; All. A. Am., 1957; Wilmington Soc. FA; Phila. WC Cl.; one-man: Chester County AA, 1956; Phila. A. All., etc. *Position*: Instr., Chester County AA; Delaware night classes.

JANKOWSKI, JOSEPH P.—*Painter, E., C., L.*
The Cleveland Institute of Art (6); h. 16704 Invermere Ave., Cleveland 28, Ohio

B. Cleveland, Ohio, Jan 12, 1916. *Studied*: St. Mary's Col., Orchard Lake, Mich.; John Huntington Polytechnic Inst.; ASL; Cleveland Inst. A., B.F.A. *Member*: ASL; CAA; Polonaise A. Cl. *Awards*: Page scholarships, 1949, 1950; Ranney scholarship, 1940; prizes, Albright A. Gal., 1949; CMA, 1950, 1951; Alliance Col., 1951; Fla. Southern Col., 1952; Akron AI; Mississippi AA; Alabama AA; Wichita AA; Ohio State Fair, 1956, 1958. *Work*: CMA; Akron AI; Univ. Alabama; Cleveland Pr. Cl.; Cleveland AA; St. Mary's Col.; U.S. Air Force Coll.; Stations of the Cross, St. Mary's Church, McKeesport, Pa. *Exhibited*: CMA; Akron AI; AIC; Albright A. Gal.; Audubon A.; Delgado Mus. A.; High Mus. A.; Birmingham Mus. A.; Univ. of Alabama, Georgia, Florida, Mississippi; one-man: Women's Forum, Wichita Falls, Tex.; Univ. Alabama; Meridian, Miss.; Women's Cl., Cleveland; Notre Dame Col., Cleveland. *Position*: Assoc. Prof. A., Univ. Alabama, 1949-53; Instr., A., Notre Dame Col., 1954; Cleveland Inst. A., Cleveland, Ohio, 1953- ; Supv. Evening School, Cleveland Inst. A., 1955- .

JANNELLI, VINCENT—*Painter, T.*
189 Hunterdon St., Newark 3, N.J.

B. Andretta, Italy, Aug. 29, 1882. *Studied*: NAD; Royal Inst. FA, Naples, Italy; Columbia Univ.; Rutgers Univ. *Member*: Un. Scenic A. of Am. *Awards*: Kresge Exh., Newark, N.J., 1934, 1938; Contemporary Gal., Newark, 1936; med., AAPL, 1942. *Exhibited*: PAFA, 1935, 1936, 1938, 1939; CGA, 1937; NAD, 1936, 1940, 1941; VMFA, 1940; PBA, 1939; Newark AC, 1931-1943; Contemporary Gal., Newark, 1936, 1937; Montclair A. Mus., 1932-1942; Kresge Exh., Newark, 1934-1941; Newark Mus. A., 1957. *Position*: Instr. FA, Newark Sch. F. & Indst. A., Newark, N.J., 1922-58.

JANOWSKY, BELA—*Sculptor*
637 Madison Ave.; h. 52 West 57th St., New York 19, N.Y.

B. Budapest, Hungary, 1900. *Studied*: Ontario Col. A.; PAFA; Cleveland Sch. A.; BAID, and with Charles Grafly, Alexander Blazys. *Member*: F., PAFA; All. A. Am. *Awards*: prize, All. A. Am., 1951. *Work*: bust, Queens Univ., Kingston, Ont.; gold medal, Royal Soc. Canada; bronze reliefs, U.S. Dept. Commerce Bldg., Wash., D.C.; bronze mem., USPO, Cooperstown, N.Y.; bronze plaque, Naval Shipyard, Brooklyn, N.Y. *Exhibited*: All. A. Am., 1939, 1940, 1946-1949, 1951; AAPL, 1945, 1947; NAD, 1935, 1940, 1942; WFNY 1939; NSS.*

JANOWSKY, MRS. BELA. See Bell, Clara Louise

JANSSEN, HANS—*Educator, Mus. Cur., L.*
104 East 15th St., Yankton, S.D.

B. Wuppertal-Barmen, Germany, Dec. 11, 1896. *Studied*: Univ. Cologne; Univ. Pennsylvania; Pa. State Univ., M.A., Ph.D. *Position*: Prof., Hd. Dept. A. Hist., Cur., Yankton Col. Durand Coll., Yankton, S.D., 1942- ; Visiting Prof., Freie Univ., Berlin, Germany, 1953.

JAUSS, ANNE MARIE—*Painter, I., Des.*
590 Third Ave., New York 16, N.Y.

B. Munich, Germany, Feb. 3, 1907. *Studied*: Sch.A., Munich. *Member*: AIGA. *Work*: N.Y.Pub. Lib., and work in private colls. *Exhibited*: Salon of Mod. A., Portugal, 1942-1946; Neue Sezession, Munich; Flechtheim Gal., Berlin; Portraits, Inc., 1947 (one-man); Suffolk Mus.; 1949; Carl Schurz Fnd., 1951 (one-man); Lisbon, Portugal, 1940, 1943, 1945 (one-man). Illus., "The Stars in Our Heaven," 1948; "Fabulous Beasts," 1954; "The Stubborn Donkey," 1949; Grimm's "Fairy Tales," 1951; "Some Dogs," 1950; "The Storks of Lillegaard," 1950; "The Moon is a Crystal Ball," 1952; "In Came Horace," 1954; "Think, Mr. Platypus," 1958, and others. Author, I., "Wise and Otherwise," 1953; "Legends of Saints and Beasts," 1954; "Discovering Nature The Year Round," 1955; "The River's Journey," 1957. Contributor to American and European magazines.

JAYNE, DE WITT WHISTLER—*Illustrator*
1518 Delmont Ave., Havertown, Pa.

B. Boston, Mass., Sept. 18, 1911. *Studied*: PMSchIA; Wheaton Col., B.S.; Univ. Chicago; & with Allen Lewis. *Work*: Wheaton Col., Wheaton, Ill. I., "Deep Water Days," 1929; Periodical covers and illus., 1955-58 for: Rod & Gun; Argosy; True; Mercury. *Position*: Instr., A. Dept., Wheaton Col., Wheaton, Ill., 1936-46; Adv. I., 1946; A., A. Dir., W.L. Stensgaard, 1946-49; Freelance Illus., 1949- .

JAYNE, HORACE H. F.—*Museum Vice-Director*
Philadelphia Museum of Art, Philadelphia 30, Pa.; h. Wallingford, Pa.

B. Cape May, N.J., June 9, 1898. *Studied*: Harvard Univ., A.B.; Univ. Pennsylvania, A.M. *Position*: Cur., Oriental A., 1923-26, Chief, Div. Eastern A., 1926-40, PMA; Dir., Univ. Pennsylvania Mus., 1929-40; Vice-Dir., MMA, New York, N.Y., 1941-49; U.S. State Dept., 1949-53; Vice-Dir., Phila. Mus. A., 1955- .

JECT-KEY, DAVID WU—*Painter*
49 East 9th St., New York 3, N.Y.

B. Chung Shan, China. *Studied*: Royal Canadian Acad., Montreal; ASL; Grand Central A. Sch. *Member*: All. A.

Am.; Knickerbocker A.; SC; North Shore AA. *Awards*: prizes, SC, 1956; Knickerbocker A., 1957; All. A. Am., 1958. *Exhibited*: NAD, 1956, 1957; All. A. Am., 1954-1958; Knickerbocker A., 1953, 1955-1958; SC, 1954-1958; North Shore AA, 1958.

JECT-KEY, ELSIE—Painter
49 East 9th St., New York 3, N.Y.

B. Koege, Denmark. *Studied*: ASL, with Homer Boss, Frank DuMond, George Bridgman; NAD, with Murphy, Neilson, Olinsky; BAID. *Member*: NAWA; Knickerbocker A.; Creative A. Assoc. *Exhibited*: NAWA, 1947-1958; Argent Gal., 1947, 1948, 1949, 1952-1954; State T. Col., Indiana, Pa., 1950, 1951, 1953; Knickerbocker A., 1951, 1952, 1955; Newport AA, 1950; N.Y. City Center, 1955; Creative AA, 1948, 1950, 1951, 1953; Pen & Brush Cl., 1955; SC, 1955; All. A. Am., 1957; Art:USA, 1958; Athens and Salonika, Greece; Brussels, Belgium; Central Louisiana AA; Louisiana A. Lg.; group shows, 1957-58; State T. Col., Kutztown, Pa.; Canton AI; Massillon Mus. A.; Eastern Ky. State Col.; Decatur A. Center; Univ. Neb.; State Univ. Iowa; Stephens Col.; Cottey Col., Nevada, Mo.; State T. Col., Pittsburg, Kans.; Stephen Austin State Col., Nacodoches, Tex.; Mary Hardin-Baylor Col., Belton, Tex.

JEFFERY, CHARLES BARTLEY—Craftsman, T.
1865 Nela Ave., East Cleveland 12, Ohio

B. Paducah, Ky., July 6, 1910. *Studied*: Cleveland Sch. A.; Western Reserve Univ., B.S., M.A. *Member*: Western AA; NAEA; NEA; Ohio A. Edu. Assn.; Ohio Edu. Assn. *Awards*: prizes, Cleveland A. & Craftsmen, 1942-1955; Huntington Gal., W. Va. (purchase); Syracuse Mus. FA; Pomona, Cal. A. & Crafts Exh., 1953, 1956; Miami Nat. Ceramic, 1956, 1957; Butler Inst. Am. A., 1956; Wichita AA, 1958. *Work*: CMA; Syracuse Mus. FA; Huntington Gal.; Univ. Michigan; Wichita AA. *Exhibited*: Syracuse Mus. FA, 1937-55, 1956; Des.-Craftsmen, 1953; Smithsonian Inst., 1953-55; Univ. Indiana, 1953; Wichita A. & Crafts; Boston Soc. A. & Crafts; Cooper Union, 1954; El Paso, Tex., 1954; Sioux City A. Center, 1954; Mus. Contemp. Crafts, N.Y., 1956, 1957; Rochester Mem. A. Gal., 1956; AFA traveling Exh., 1958-59; Brussels World's Fair, 1958. *Position*: Dir. A., Shaker Heights Bd. of Edu., Shaker Heights, Ohio, 1946- .

JELINEK, HANS—Graphic A., Wood Eng., E.
16 Minetta Lane, New York 12, N.Y.

B. Vienna, Austria, Aug. 21, 1910. *Studied*: Wiener Kunstgewerbe Schule; Univ. Vienna. *Member*: ANA; Audubon A.; SAGA; Boston Pr. M.; Xylon. *Awards*: prizes, Tiffany award, 1947; AV, 1943; LC, 1945; Boston Pr. M., 1953, 1957. *Work*: N.Y.Pub. Lib.; VMFA; Munson-Williams-Proctor Inst.; LC; Alabama Inst. Tech.; MMA; Cooper Union Mus.; NAD; Dartmouth Col.; Albion Col., and others. *Exhibited*: NAD, 1942-1946; Smithsonian Inst., 1951; PAFA, 1941, 1942; SFMA, 1943-1946; SAM, 1943-1945; Albany Inst. Hist. & A.; Laguna Beach AA; Denver AA; MMA; Royal Soc. Et., Gravers, London; Zurich, Switzerland; Rome, Naples, Florence, Italy; Denver A. Mus.; Santa Barbara Mus. A.; Carnegie Inst., 1945; LC, 1945, 1946; Oakland A. Gal., 1943, 1944; Cal. Soc. Et., 1943; VMFA; Mint Mus. A. *Position*: Instr., Wood engraving & Illus., New School for Social Research; Assoc. Prof. A., City Col., New York, N.Y.

JEMNE, ELSA LAUBACH (Mrs. Magnus)—Painter, I.
212 Mt. Curve Blvd., St. Paul 5, Minn.

B. St. Paul, Minn. *Studied*: St. Paul A. Sch.; PAFA, and with Olle Nordmark. *Member*: Minn. AA; St. Paul P. & S. Soc.; AEA. *Awards*: Cresson Traveling Scholarship, PAFA (2); silver medal, St. Paul A. Sch.; gold medals, St. Paul Inst., and Minnesota State Fair, also Minneapolis Inst. A.; prizes, Minn. State Fair and other awards. *Work*: murals, Armory, Minneapolis; Intl. Inst., St. Paul; St. Cloud, Ely, Hutchinson, Minn.; Ladysmith, Wis.; mural and terrazzo floors, City Cl., St. Paul. *Exhibited*: Arch. Lg.; AIC; Wm. Rockhill Nelson Gal. A.; Univ. Texas, Austin; CGA; PAFA; Joslyn Mus. A., 1950-58; for many years at: Minneapolis Inst. A.; WAC; Minnesota State Fair; St. Paul Lib.; St. Paul Gal. A.; one-man: St. Paul Lib.; Hanley Gal.; Minn. State Fair, 1957; WAC, 1957. *Illus.* "Norwegian Farm," 1933; "Norwegian Family," 1934; "Rudi Finds a Way," 1941; "We of Frabo Stand," 1944.

JENNEWEIN, C. PAUL—Sculptor
538 Van Nest Ave., Bronx 60, N.Y.

B. Stuttgart, Germany, Dec. 2, 1890. *Studied*: ASL; **Am.** Acad. in Rome; & with Clinton Peters. *Member*: NA; Nat. Inst. A. & Let.; AIA; NSS; Century Cl.; FA Comm., New York, N.Y. *Awards*: Prix de Rome, 1916; F., Am. Acad. in Rome; prizes, Arch. L., 1912; Fairmount Park AA, 1926; Saltus award, 1949; med., Concord AA, 1926; Arch. L., 1927; PAFA, 1932, 1939; NAD, 1942. *Work*: S., MMA; BMA; BM; CGA; CM; Detroit Inst. A.; Finance Bldg., Harrisburg, Pa.; Herron AI; Dept. Justice Bldg., Wash., D.C.; Mus. FA of Houston; Hartford Atheneum; Newark Mus.; PAFA; Brookgreen Gardens, S.C.; PMA; Eastman Sch. Music, Rochester, N.Y.; mem., Wash., D.C.; Providence, R.I.; Worcester, Mass.; Boston, Mass.; Dauphin County Court House, Harrisburg, Pa.; House of Representatives, Wash., D.C.; W.Va. State Office Bldg.; British Bldg., Rockefeller Center, N.Y.; City Hall, Kansas City; George Washington Mem. Park; Admin. Bldg., Atlanta; statue of Geo. Washington, Valley Forge Tower for DAR; Am. Military Cemetery, Belgium; 2 panels, Exec. Mansion; Inaugural Medal, Harry S. Truman; Portrait Medal and Plaque of Judge Learned Hand, 1957, and others.

JENNEY, PRISCILLA BURG—Painter, E., W.
8 Willow Place, Cazenovia, N.Y.

B. Sutton, Neb., May 8, 1916. *Studied*: Syracuse Univ., B.F.A.; State Univ. Iowa, M.F.A.; & with Emil Ganso, Fletcher Martin. *Member*: NAWA; Syracuse Assoc. A.; Phila. WC Cl. *Awards*: prizes, Syracuse Assoc. A., 1943; Cayuga Mus. Hist. & A., 1944, 1945. *Work*: Children's Hospital, Iowa City, Iowa; Radio Station WSYR, Syracuse; Rochester Mem. A. Gal.; Cazenovia Jr. Col.; Syracuse Mus. FA. *Exhibited*: VMFA, 1942; PAFA, 1942; NAWA, 1942-1945; Cayuga Mus. Hist. & A.; Syracuse Assoc. A.; Utica A. Exh.; Cortland State Fair, N.Y. *Position*: Instr., Cazenovia Jr. Col., Cazenovia, N.Y.

JENNINGS, FRANCIS A.—Painter, S., T.
1019 Clinton St., Philadelphia 7, Pa.

B. Wilmington, Del., Feb. 27, 1910. *Studied*: Wilmington Acad. A.; Phila. Graphic Sketch Cl. *Member*: Group 55. *Work*: mural, Delaware Indst. Sch. for Boys. *Exhibited*: PAFA, 1939, 1942, 1943, 1954; Wilmington A. Center, 1935-1937, 1939-1943; Pyramid Cl., 1950-1952; Ellen Donovan Gal., Phila., 1951 (one-man); Beryle Lush Gal., 1953 (one-man); Phila. A. All., 1953; Dubin Gal., 1954; Traveling Art, Inc., traveling exh., 1954-55, 1955-56; Little Gal., Phila., 1955; Group 55, 1955; Dubin-Lush Gal., 1956.*

JENNINGS, RIXFORD—Painter, Adv. Des., Et., T.
374 Delaware Ave., Buffalo 2, N.Y.; h. Maple Rd., East Aurora, N.Y.

B. Troy, N.Y., Feb. 26, 1906. *Studied*: Buffalo Sch. FA; Buffalo AI. *Member*: AWS; Buffalo Soc. A.; Buffalo Pr. Cl.; Phila. WC Cl. *Awards*: bronze, silver and gold medals, Buffalo Soc. A. *Position*: Instr., Painting, Univ. Buffalo, N.Y.; Bd. Dir., Prof. A. Gld. of Buffalo, 1955- .*

JENNISON, MRS. M. W. See Kerfoot, Margaret

JENSEN, GEORGE—Painter, T., Comm. A.
628 Nicholas Ave., Toledo 9, Ohio

B. Port Clinton, Ohio, Aug. 9, 1878. *Studied*: AIC; & with John Carlson, George Elmer Browne. *Member*: Toledo AC. *Awards*: prizes, Toledo Mus. A., 1930, 1931, 1943. *Work*: Toledo Pub. Sch. *Exhibited*: Scandinavian-Am. A., 1932-1936; Columbus Gal. FA, 1935; Soc. Indp. A., 1934; Ft. Wayne A. Sch.; Toledo Mus. A., 1954 (one-man).

JENSEN, MARGARET (EDMONDS) (Mrs. Claude)—
Painter, Ser.
6307 Hampton St., Pittsburgh 6, Pa.

B. Buffalo, N.Y. *Studied*: Carnegie Inst.; Univ. Pittsburgh; Hans Hofmann Sch. FA. *Member*: NAWA; Nat. Ser. Soc. (Bd. Trustees); Provincetown AA; Abstract Group of Pittsburgh. *Awards*: prizes, Carnegie Inst. Group, 1945; VMFA, 1947 (purchase). *Work*: VMFA; Pittsburgh Pub. Schs.; Unity Center of Pittsburgh; Cultural Div., USIA. *Exhibited*: CM, 1945; Portrait of America, 1946; VMFA, 1946; CGA, 1947; PAFA, 1952; NAD, 1954; BM, 1954; N.Y.City Center, 1954; Butler AI, 1946-1949; Assoc. A.

Pittsburgh, 1940-1954; Carnegie Inst., 1940-1946; Ohio Univ., 1946, 1948; Pittsburgh WC Soc., 1945-1955; Provincetown AA, 1954-1958; AFA traveling exh., 1954-1955; Soc. Wash. Pr. M., 1957; Nat. Ser. Soc., 1951-1958; One-Thirty Gal., Pittsburgh, 1956 (one-man). *Position*: Bd. Dir., A. & Crafts Center, Pittsburgh, Pa., 1956- .

JERRY, CHERRY BARR—Painter, C., Gr., T.
2519 Northwestern Ave., Racine, Wis.

B. Denver, Colo., Feb. 19, 1909. *Studied*: Nat. Sch. F. & App. A., Wash., D.C. *Member*: Wisconsin P. & S. *Exhibited*: Albany Inst. Hist. & A.; Phila. Pr. Cl.; SFMA; Wisconsin P. & S.; Wisconsin Un.; Detroit Inst. A.; AIC, 1957; Racine Painters; Wisconsin Graphics. *Position*: Instr., Drawing, Racine Center of the Univ. Wisconsin.

JERRY, SYLVESTER—Museum Director, Lith., P.
2519 Northwestern Ave., Racine, Wis.

B. Woodville, Wis., Sept. 20, 1904. *Studied*: Layton Sch. A.; ASL. *Position*: Dir., Wustum Mus. FA, Racine, Wis., 1941- .

JESWALD, JOSEPH—Painter
Calebs Lane, Rockport, Mass.

B. Leetonia, Ohio, May 17, 1927. *Studied*: Academie Julian, Paris, France; Fernand Leger, Paris, France; Columbia Univ. *Member*: Rockport AA. *Exhibited*: Ogunquit Mus. A., 1958; Univ. Iowa, 1958; "Americans in Paris" exh., Paris, 1949; A.F.I. Gal., N.Y.; G Gal., N.Y.; one-man: A.F.I. Gal., 1951, 1952; G Gal.; Anna Herb Mus., Augusta, Ga., 1954. *Positions*: Coordinator of A. Instruction and Dir. Children's A. Program, Rockport Public Schools, Rockport, Mass.

JEWETT, ELEANOR (Mrs. Godfrey Lundberg)—
  Critic, W., L.
R.R. #2, Box 723, Travers City, Mich.

B. Chicago, Ill., Feb. 9, 1892. *Studied*: Univ. Illinois; Univ. Wisconsin, and in Italy. *Member*: Lg. Am. Pen Women; Palette & Chisel Acad. FA (Hon.); Nat. Soc. A. & Let.; Cordon Cl.; A. Cl. *Awards*: Union Lg. Cl., Chicago, Distinguished Service to Art Award, 1956; Kappa Kappa Gamma Achievement Award, 1958; AAPL medal, 1958. Author: "From the Top of My Column"; "In the Wind's Whistle." Lectures: Contemporary Art; Political and Aesthetic Art, at Women's Clubs and Art Clubs. *Position*: A.Cr., Chicago (Ill.) Tribune, 1917-1957.

JEX, GARNET W.—Painter, I., Des.
6010 20th St., North Arlington 5, Va.

B. Kent, Ohio, Oct. 19, 1895. *Studied*: Corcoran Sch. A.; George Washington Univ., A.B., M.A.; PAFA. *Member*: A. Lg. of Northern Virginia; Wash. Landscape Cl.; Wash. A. Cl.; Fed. A. & Des., Wash., D.C. *Awards*: medal, Soc. Wash. A., 1937; Landscape Cl., 1941. *Work*: Nat. Zoological Park, Wash., D.C.; murals, Smithsonian Inst.; George Washington Univ. Lib. *Exhibited*: national and regional exhs., 1922-1958. *Position*: Staff A., Nature Magazine, 1926- ; Visual Information Presentation Specialist, U.S. Pub. Health Service, 1936- , and Chief Graphic Sect., 1953- ; A. Dir., I., for numerous Federal and other publications; Instr., Graphic A., U.S. Dept. Agriculture Grad. Sch., 1956- .

JIROUCH, FRANK LOUIS—Sculptor, P., Des.
4821 Superior Ave., Cleveland 3, Ohio; h. 3905 Essex Rd., Cleveland Heights 18, Ohio.

B. Cleveland, Ohio, Mar. 3, 1878. *Studied*: Cleveland Sch. A.; PAFA; Julian Acad., Paris, France. *Member*: NSS; Cleveland City Art Committee; Cleveland Soc. A. *Awards*: PAFA; CMA. *Work*: sc., CMA; Cleveland FA Gardens; mem. tablet, Havana, Cuba; plaque, Bird Sanctuary, Cleveland; war mem., Indianapolis, Ind.; panels, USPO, Cleveland, Ohio; statues and busts, Cleveland Cathedral; St. Ann's Church; Cultural Gardens, Cleveland; Spanish War Veterans statue, Columbus, Ohio; panels, Severance Hall, Cleveland; figure, Tomalson Hall, Cleveland; Medal, Oberlin College and Pickands Mather & Co. *Exhibited*: Paris Salon; PAFA; CMA; Los A. Mus. A.; AIC; CAM; Arch. Lg.; PMA.

JOACHIM, HAROLD—Museum Curator
Art Institute of Chicago, Michigan Ave. at Adams St., Chicago 3, Ill.

Position: Cur., Prints & Drawings, Art Institute of Chicago.*

JOACHIM, PAUL LAMAR—Painter
58 East Walton Place (11); h. 1400 Lake Shore Drive, Chicago 10, Ill.

B. Washington, D.C., Apr. 3, 1912. *Studied*: Nat. A. Sch., Wash., D.C. *Award*: Irene Leach Mem. prize, Norfolk Mus. A. & Sc., 1954. *Exhibited*: Norfolk Mus. A. & Sc., 1953, 1954; Springfield (Ill.) Mus. A., 1957; CGA, 1951; NGA, 1951, 1952; Illinois State Fair, 1956, 1957; Evansville, Ind., 1958; Navy Pier, Chicago, 1957, 1958.

JOCHIMSEN, MARION—Painter, T.
895 West End Ave., New York 25, N.Y.

B. Juneau, Alaska. *Studied*: Cal. Sch. Des.; & with Frank Van Sloan. *Member*: AWCS. *Exhibited*: AWCS, 1936-1945; NAWA, 1941; New Jersey State Mus., Trenton, 1937; Albany Inst. Hist. & A., 1938; Newhouse Gal., 1935 (one-man). *Position*: Instr., City Col., N.Y., Ext. Div.*

JOFFE, BERTHA—Textile Designer
77 Parker Ave., Maplewood, N.J.

B. Leningrad, Russia, Oct. 11, 1912. *Studied*: N.Y. Phoenix Sch. Des.; Col. City of N.Y., B.S. in Edu.; T. Col., Columbia Univ., M.A.; N.Y.Univ.; ASL; & with Zorach, Winold Reiss, Malderelli. *Work*: textile des. used in leading hotels. *Exhibited*: Provincetown AA, 1940; AV, 1942; Int. Textile Exh., 1944; des., Art in Business Exh., 1942. *Position*: Free lance textile des., Mead & Montague, Inc.; Schumacher & Co.; Thortel Fireproof Fabrics, Inc.; Witcombe McGeachin & Co., etc., 1941- .

JOHANN, HELEN L.—Printmaker, T.
2219 East Menlo Blvd., Milwaukee 11, Wis.

B. West Depere, Wis., May 30, 1901. *Studied*: Milwaukee State. T. Col.; Columbia Univ., B.S. *Awards*: prizes, Milwaukee AI, 1936, 1940, 1945, 1951, 1952, 1954; Wis. State Fair, 1957. *Work*: Lib.Cong. *Exhibited*: Oakland A. Gal., 1942, 1943; PAFA, 1941, 1942; MMA (AV), 1942; LC, 1943-1946, 1951, 1952; Milwaukee AI, 1936-1945, 1951-1954; NAD, 1946; Wisconsin Salon, 1943, 1957; Wichita, 1948; Phila. Pr. Cl., 1948; Joslyn A. Mus., 1948; Buffalo Pr. Cl., 1951; Wisconsin Pr. M., 1957.

JOHANSEN, JOHN C.—Portrait Painter
15 Gramercy Park, New York 3, N.Y.

B. Copenhagen, Denmark, Nov. 25, 1876. *Studied*: AIC, and with Frank Duveneck. *Member*: NA; Nat. Inst. A. & Let.; NAC; Century Assn. *Awards*: medal, AIC; Santiago, Chile; St. Louis Exp.; Saltus medal, NAD; gold medal, PAFA. *Work*: Carnegie Inst.; CGA; AIC; Nat. Gal., Santiago, Chile; Smithsonian Inst.; Frick Col.; MMA; White House, Wash., D.C.; Dept. Justice, Navy Dept., Wash., D.C.; Dept. Agriculture; West Point Military Acad.; State House, Boston; Yale Univ.; Air Force Acad., Denver, Colo.; Cornell Univ.; Univ. Wisconsin; Univ. North Carolina; Univ. Minnesota; Wadsworth Atheneum, Hartford, Conn.

JOHN, GRACE SPAULDING—Painter, S., W.
1306 Barbee St., Houston, Tex.

B. Battle Creek, Mich. *Studied*: St. Louis Sch. FA; AIC; NAD, and with Charles Hawthorne, Emil Bisttram. *Member*: Taos Design Group. *Work*: Houston Pub. Lib.; Hist. Bldg., Austin, Tex.; Mus. of FA of Houston; Huntsville (Tex.) Lib.; Princeton Univ.; murals, City Hall and Sidney Lanier Sch., Houston, Tex.; Jack Tar Hotel, Balinese Cl., Lakewood Yacht Cl., Galveston; Roanoke Steel Corp., Pub. Lib., Roanoke, Va.; Nat. Bank Commerce, San Antonio; Nat. Bank of Lufkin, Tex. *Exhibited*: PAFA, 1923; Highland Park Mus., Dallas, 1928; Cal. PLH, 1933; World's Fair, Chicago, 1933; one-man: Mus. of FA of Houston, 1936, 1953; Oakland A. Gal., 1935; Los A. Mus. A., 1935; Town Hall, N.Y., 1944; Galveston Pub. Lib., 1951; Stables Gal., Taos, 1955-1958. Author, I., "Memo"; "Azalea."

JOHNS, ERIK—*Painter*
178 Fifth Ave., New York 10, N.Y.

B. Los Angeles, Cal., June 7, 1927. *Studied*: Los Angeles City Col., and in France and Italy. *Exhibited*: Los A. Mus. A.; N.Y. City Center; Mississippi Southern Col.; One-man: Parma Gal., N.Y., 1957.

JOHNSON, ARTHUR CLARK—*Portrait Painter*
404 Winnacunett Rd., Hampton, N.H.

B. Hyde Park, Mass., Sept. 5, 1897. *Studied*: BMFA Sch.; Corcoran Sch. A. *Member*: Springfield AA. *Work*: Illinois State Lib.; Farnsworth Mus. A.; Springfield AA; Intl. Postal Union, Berne, Switzerland (port. former Postmaster General, U.S.A., and co-founder of Postal Union, the late Montgomery Blair); many corporation portraits and others of prominent persons.

JOHNSON, AVERY F.—*Painter, I., T.*
R.F.D. #1, Dover, N.J.

B. Wheaton, Ill., Apr. 3, 1906. *Studied*: Wheaton Col., B.A.; AIC. *Member*: N.J. WC Soc.; AWS; Audubon A.; Assoc. A. of New Jersey. *Awards*: prizes, Montclair A. Mus., 1949, 1956, 1957; New Jersey WC Soc., 1958; AWS, 1951, 1953. *Work*: Newark Mus.; Montclair A. Mus.; murals, USPO, Marseilles, Ill.; Liberty, Ind.; Lake Village, Ark.; Bordentown, N.J.; North Bergen, N.J.; Catonsville, Md.; portfolio of paintings for Standard Oil Co., and Humble Oil & Refining Co. *Exhibited*: PAFA; AIC; AWS; NAD; GGE, 1939; Kansas City AI. I., books for leading publishers. *Position*: Instr., W.C., mural & illus., Newark (N.J.) Sch. F. & Indst. A.; Montclair (N.J.) A. Mus.

JOHNSON, BEN(JAMIN FRANKLIN)—*Painter*
Route 1, Box 933, Woodstock, N.Y.

B. Brooklyn, N.Y. *Studied*: PIASch.; Sch. F. & Appl. A. *Member*: Woodstock AA. *Awards*: Tiffany Fnd. Scholarships, 1930, 1933. *Exhibited*: BM, 1925, 1927; Salons of America, 1929; GRD Gal., N.Y., 1931-1933; Advanced Gal., N.Y.; Zabriskie Gal., N.Y., 1958; one-man: Zabriskie Gal., 1957; in Woodstock: Parnassus Gal.; Retrospective Exh., 1949; Polari Gal., 1955-1958; Zena Gal., 1954; also Woodstock AA, 1945-1958.

JOHNSON, BUFFIE—*Painter*
East Hampton, N.Y.

B. New York, N.Y., Feb. 20, 1912. *Studied*: ASL; Univ. California at Los Angeles, M.A. *Member*: Group Espace, Paris. *Work*: BMFA; BMA; Newark Mus. A.; WAC; MMA; CM; Layton Gal. A.; Univ. Mich.; Munson-Williams-Proctor Inst. *Exhibited*: Carnegie Inst., 1941; Realites Nouvelles, 1949, 1950, 1957; BM, 1953; WMAA, 1954; Univ. Illinois, 1955; Minneapolis Inst. A., 1951; Art of this Century, 1943; Howard Putzel Gal., 1945; Betty Parsons Gal., 1950; Stable Gal., 1954; Galerie Bing, Paris, 1956; Hanover Gal., London, 1949; Cavallino Gal., Venice, 1948; Ringling Mus. A., 1948, and in Bonn, Switzerland, Weimar, Germany, and others.

JOHNSON, DORIS MILLER (Mrs. Gardiner)—
Painter, T.
329 Hampton Rd., Piedmont 11, Cal.

B. Oakland, Cal., Dec. 8, 1909. *Studied*: Univ. California, B.A.; Cal. Col. A. & Crafts. *Member*: San F. Women A.; San F. AA. *Awards*: prizes, Colorado Springs FA Center; San F. Women A., 1938; San F. AA, 1940. *Exhibited*: AIC, 1934, 1935 (also traveling exh.); Oakland A. Gal.; San F. Women A.; San F. AA; Santa Cruz A. Lg., 1938; Sacramento State Fair, 1939; GGE, 1939; SFMA, traveling exh., 1938-1942; Univ. Texas, 1941; Fnd. Western A., 1940; Portland (Ore) A. Mus., 1936; St. Paul A. Mus., 1936; one-man exh.: Berkeley Women's City Cl., 1936; SFMA, 1938; Crocker A. Gal., 1939; Hotel Senator, Sacramento, Cal., 1937. *Position*: Bd. Dir., San F. AA, 1940-44; Dir., Children's A. Classes, Oakland A. Mus., and A. Lg. of the East Bay, 1940-52; Pres., San F. Women A., 1946-48, Bd. Dir., 1958- ; Bd., Piedmont A. & Crafts Gld., 1952-56; Bd., Junior Center of A., Oakland, 1953-55; Memb. Bd., Oakland Mus. Assn., 1955- ; Chm., Rental Gal., Oakland Mus., 1955-57; Activities Bd., SFMA, 1958- .

JOHNSON, EDVARD (ARTHUR)—*Educator, Des., P.*
Address unknown

B. Chicago, Ill., Dec. 18, 1911. *Studied*: Chicago Acad. FA; Ill. Inst. Tech., M.S.; AIC; Univ. Georgia, B.F.A.; Inst. Des., Ill. *Member*: CAA. *Awards*: prizes, NGA, 1945; Swedish Cl., Chicago, 1945; Mississippi AA, 1950; Gld. Freelance A., 1943; Rockefeller F., 1951-52. *Work*: Nat. Mus., Vexio, Sweden; Georgia Mus. A., Athens. *Positions*: A. Dir., "The Yachtsman" magazine, 1935-37; Dir. Promotion & Research, The Branham Co., Chicago, 1938-47; Des., Training Aids & Visual Information, U.S. Army, 1944-46; Instr., Asst. Prof., Univ. Georgia, Athens, Ga., 1947-51; Instr., Visual Fundamentals, Inst. Des., Ill. Inst. Tech., 1952; A.Dir., Small Homes Guide, Home Modernizing Magazines, 1953- . (In Europe at present.)

JOHNSON, EVERT A.—*Educator, P., C.*
Art Department, Westmar College; h. Lakeside Motel, Le Mars, Iowa

B. Sioux City, Iowa, Mar. 2, 1929. *Studied*: Sioux City A. Center; Morningside Col., B.A.; State Univ. Iowa, M.A. *Member*: Sioux City A. Center Assn.; A. Ed. Iowa; Sioux City A. Group (Pres.). *Awards*: 2 purchase prizes, Sioux City A. Center. *Exhibited*: Iowa May Show, 1951, 1958; Iowa WC Exh.; A. Group, 1955-1958; Area Artists, 1956, 1958; Siouxland WC Exh., 1956; one-man: Community Theatre, Sioux City, 1956; Sioux City Lib., 1957, 1958; Morningside Col., 1958; Unitarian Church, 1957; 3-man: Sioux City A. Center, 1957. *Position*: Hd. Art Dept., Westmar College, Le Mars, Iowa.

JOHNSON, FERD—*Cartoonist*
220 East 42nd St., New York, N.Y.; h. 356 Reeves Drive, Beverly Hills, Cal.

B. Spring Creek, Pa., Dec. 18, 1905. *Studied*: Chicago Acad. FA. *Member*: Nat. Cartoonists Soc.; Newspaper Comic Council, Inc. *Positions*: Creator, Comics, "Texas Slim" (now discontinued); "Lovey Dovey." Asst. to the late Frank Willard who created "Moon Mullins," 1923-58, and now producing this feature personally, 1958- ; Sport Cart., Advertising cartoons, Chicago Tribune, 1929-35; I., for Westbrook Pegler's Sports Stories, Chicago Tribune, 1929-35.

JOHNSON, GEORGE H. BEN—*Painter, Cart., I.*
730 North Third St., Richmond 19, Va.

B. Richmond, Va., Mar. 1, 1888. *Studied*: Hampton Inst.; Columbia Univ. *Member*: Craig House A. Center, Richmond, Va. *Awards*: prizes, Cross Assn., Boothbay Harbor, Me., 1936, 1937; VMFA, 1945. *Work*: Valentine Mus. A.; J. B. Speed Mem. Mus.; Va. Union Univ.; State Trooper's Gal.; Bronze Art Card Gld. (paintings reproduced); Am. Lib. Color Slides; Va. State Col.; VMFA; Second Baptist & Trinity Baptist Churches, Richmond, Va. *Exhibited*: Imperial Gal., London, England; VMFA, 1945; WMAA; Dillard Univ., New Orleans, La., 1939-1941; Tanner Gal., Chicago, 1940; Atlanta Univ., 1942-1946. *Position*: Instr. A., Veteran's Admin., Virginia Regional, 1953- .*

JOHNSON, GRACE MOTT—*Sculptor, P., W.*
Box 149, Pleasantville, N.Y.

B. New York, N.Y., July 28, 1882. *Studied*: ASL; & with Gutzon Borglum. *Awards*: NAWA, med., 1927, prizes, 1917, 1935, 1936. *Work*: WMAA; Brookgreen Gardens, S.C.; Encyclopaedia Britannica; Pub. Lib., Pleasantville, N.Y., and in private collections.

JOHNSON, IVAN EARL—*Educator, C.*
Arts Education Department, Florida State University; h. 920 West College St., Tallahassee, Fla.

B. Denton, Tex., Sept. 23, 1911. *Studied*: North Texas State Col., B.A., B.S.; Columbia Univ., M.A.; N.Y. Univ., Inst. FA; N.Y. Univ.; Inst. Middle Am. Research, Mexico, and with Henry McFee, William Zorach. *Member*: Western AA; Southeastern AA; NAEA; Nat. Com. on A. Edu.; Dallas Craft Gld., and others. Contributor to Journal of Art Education. Lectures on Art Education to universities and colleges and state art groups. *Positions*: Book Ed., Arts & Activities Magazine, 1950- ; Consultant, Instructor Magazine, 1956- ; Instr. A. Edu. and Crafts, Southwest Texas State Col., North Texas State Col., Woman's Col. of Univ. North Carolina, N.Y. Univ., Columbia Univ.,

Univ. Tulsa; Dir., Dallas Pub. Schs., 1946-52; Pres., Western AA; Vice-Pres., NAEA, etc.; Hd., Dept. Arts Edu., Florida State Univ., Tallahassee, Fla., at present.

JOHNSON, J. THEODORE—*Painter, E.*

Art Department, San Jose State College; h. 19510 Prospect Rd., Cupertino, Cal.

B. Oregon, Ill., Nov. 7, 1902. *Studied*: AIC; & with Andre L'Hote, Aristide Maillol, in Paris, France. *Awards*: Lathrop European scholarship, 1925; med. prizes, AIC, 1928, 1931; Santa Cruz, Cal.; Swedish Cl., Chicago, 1929; Chicago Galleries Assn., 1929; Guggenheim F., 1929; Minneapolis Inst. A., 1943, 1944; Minn. State Fair, 1944. *Work*: AIC; Toledo Mus. A.; Vanderpoel Coll.; IBM Coll.; Minneapolis Inst. A.; Univ. Chicago; Field Mus.; murals, Garden City, L.I., N.Y.; Oak Park Ill.; Morgan Park, Ill.; Western Illinois State T. Col. *Exhibited*: CGA, 1928, 1930, 1937; Carnegie Inst., 1929, 1930; PAFA, 1929, 1937; AIC, 1928-1930, 1932, 1940; NAD, 1936; GGE, 1939; Toronto, Canada, 1940; Nat. Gal., Canada, 1940; Montreal AA, 1941; BM, 1932; Minneapolis Inst.A., 1938-1944; SFMA, 1946; Minn. State Fair, 1941-1944; WMAA; Denison Univ., 1954 (one-man); Western A., 1955; Swedish Cl., Chicago, traveling exh., 1953. *Position*: Instr., Hd. Dept., Minneapolis Sch. A., 1938-45; Assoc. Prof., San Jose Col., San Jose, Cal., 1945- .*

JOHNSON, M. MARTIN—*Designer*

276 Wagner Rd., Northfield, Ill.

B. Rockford, Ill., Dec. 4, 1904. *Studied*: with Gyorgy Kepes. *Member*: Soc. Typographic A.; Chicago A. Gld.; "27" Chicago Designers. *Awards*: prizes, Lithographers Nat. Assn., 1952; Los A. Mus. Assn., 1948; A. Dir. Cl., N.Y., 1939; AIGA, 1937, 1938, 1940, 1944, 1952; Soc. Typographic A., 1937-1941, 1944, 1954; Direct Mail Typographic A., 1937-1941, 1944, 1954; Direct Mail Adv. Assn., 1943; Chicago A. Gld., 1943, 1945. *Exhibited*: Chicago A. Dir., 1951-1953; A. Dir. Cl., N.Y., 1938, 1939, 1952; AIGA, 1937, 1938, 1940, 1944, 1952; Chicago A. Gld., 1943, 1945, 1955; Magnificent Mile, 1953-1955; AIC, 1940-1951; Denver A. Mus., 1949; Illinois State Mus., 1940, 1951; Greek Theatre, Los A., 1946-1948; Arch. Lg., 1935. Contributor to "Art & Industry," 1954.

JOHNSON, SELINA TETZLAFF (Mrs. H. Herbert)—
Museum Director, E., I.

Bergen Community Museum, Fort Lee Rd. at Overpeck Creek, Teaneck, N.J.; h. 24 Hawthorne Terrace, Leonia, N.J.

B. New York, N.Y., Sept. 7, 1906. *Studied*: Hunter Col., A.B.; City Col. N.Y., M.S. in Ed.; N.Y. Univ. Ph.D. candidate. *Member*: AAMus.; Mus. Council of New Jersey; SAGA; Bergen County A. Gld.; N.Y. Acad. Sciences (Life); Caduceus (Hon.). *Award*: Silver Orchid, N.J. State Fed. Women's Cl. *Work*: (photography) Bergen Community Mus. Author, I., "Classification of Insects," 1932; "Adventures with Living Things," 1938; monographs: Creating a Community Museum, 1954; Developing a Community Museum, 1956; Museums for Youth in the United States (Ph.D. thesis in process). Lectures: Our Community Museum as Area Resource; Tools of the Creative Artist; Gold and Silver in Art Through the Ages, etc. Arranged exhs., "Prints and Printmakers of Bergen County," 1956; "The Art of Charles Chapman, N.A.—Three Score and Ten Years," 1957; "Paintings by People of Palisades Park," 1958. *Position*: Organizing Dir., Youth Museum of Leonia, N.J., 1950-56; Dir., Bergen Community Museum, Teaneck, N.J., 1956- .

JOHNSON, STANLEY ORDEANE—*Painter, C., T.*

V-9 Tennis Village, Grand Forks, N.D.

B. Crookston, Minn., June 11, 1919. *Studied*: Univ. North Dakota, B.S., M.A., with Paul E. Barr; Ill. Inst. Tech. *Awards*: prize, Univ. North Dakota, 1952. *Exhibited*: Bismarck, N.D.; Univ. Minnesota; Inst. Des., Ill. Inst. Tech., and in local exhibitions. *Position*: Instr. A., Univ. North Dakota, Grand Forks, N.D., 1953- .*

JOHNSON, TOM LOFTIN—*Painter, Des., E., Arch.*

Bisbee Lane, Bedford Hills, N.Y.

B. Denver, Colo., Oct. 5, 1900. *Studied*: Yale Univ., B.F.A.; Ecole des Beaux-Arts, Paris, France; & with Lucien Simon. *Awards*: Winchester F., Yale Univ., 1923; prize, Carnegie Inst., 1941. *Work*: Denver A. Mus.; murals, U.S.

Military Acad., West Point, N.Y.; Headquarters Bldg., Governors Island, N.Y.; Radio Station WOR, N.Y. *Exhibited*: Arch. Lg.; CGA; Carnegie Inst. Lectures: "Art in Merchandise."

JOHNSON, UNA E.—*Museum Curator, W.*

Brooklyn Museum, Eastern Parkway, Brooklyn 38, N.Y.

B. Dayton, Iowa. *Studied*: Univ. Chicago, A.B.; Western Reserve Univ., M.A. *Awards*: Carnegie traveling scholarship, 1939. Author: "Ambroise Vollard, Editeur," (An Appreciation and Catalogue), 1944; "Woodblock Color Prints of Louis Schanker," catalogue (BM), 1943; "Boris Margo," Cat. of his Gr. Works, 1943-47; "American Woodcuts, 1670-1950"; "The Woodcuts of Antonio Frasconi," Print, 1950-51; "Georges Rouault and His Prints" (BM), 1951, and others. Contributor to: Print Collector's Quarterly, 1941, "The Wood-Engravings by Whistler"; American Artist, 1945, "The Graphic Art of Mary Cassatt"; "New Expressions in Fine Printmaking" (BM), 1952; "Contemporary American Drawings," in magazine Perspectives No. 13, 1955; "Ten Years of American Prints, 1947-1956" (BM), 1956; "Golden Years of American Drawings" (BM), 1957. *Position*: Cur., Prints & Drawings, Brooklyn Museum, Brooklyn, N.Y.

JOHNSTON, RANDOLPH W.—*Sculptor, I., W., C.*

Man-o-War Cay, Bahamas

B. Toronto, Canada, Feb. 23, 1904. *Studied*: Ontario Col. A.; Univ. Toronto; Central Sch. A. & Crafts, London. *Member*: S. Center. *Awards*: prize, Springfield (Mass.) A. Lg.; 1937. *Work*: mem. tablets, Toronto & Montreal, Canada; reliefs, Smith Col.; mem. panels, Eagle Brook Sch.; Univ. Nebraska; Arch. or Ecclesiastical Sc. in Toronto, Montreal, Canada; Worcester, Northampton, Mass.; Houma, La., and work in private colls. *Exhibited*: Royal Canadian Acad., 1925, 1926; Nat. Gal., Ottawa, 1927; Soc. Indp. A., 1942; AV, 1942; Audubon A., 1945; Clay Cl., 1944 (one-man), 1945; Springfield A. Lg., 1937, 1938; WMAA, 1949; Smith Col., 1948-1951; Pittsfield A. Lg., 1936; George Walter Vincent Smith A. Gal., 1945 (one-man); PAFA, and others. Author, I., "The Country Craft Book," 1937; I., "The Golden Fleece of California." Contributor to: Art and Yachting magazines. Author, I., "Escapist's Notebook," 1956; Author: "The Practice of Direct Casting and the Direct Casting of Figures," 1940-41.

JOHNSTON, Mrs. S. H. See Aitken, Irene Anabel

JOHNSTON, YNEZ—*Painter, Et.*

348 N. Camden Drive, Beverly Hills, Cal.

B. Berkeley, Cal., May 12, 1920. *Studied*: Univ. California, Berkeley, B.M., M.A. *Awards*: Guggenheim F., 1952-53; Tiffany Fnd. grant, 1955; prize, MMA, 1952. *Work*: Santa Barbara Mus. A.; MMoDA; WMAA; MMA; CAM; Los A. Mus. A.; Philbrook A. Center; Univ. Michigan; Univ. Illinois; Wadsworth Atheneum; PMA. *Exhibited*: Carnegie Inst., 1955; WMAA, 1951-1955; Univ. Illinois, 1951-1954; SFMA; Los A. Mus. A., and others. *Position*: Instr., Univ. California, Berkeley, 1950, 1951; L., Colorado Springs FA Center, summers, 1954, 1955.

JOHNSTONE, B. KENNETH—*Architect, E.*

206 Richland Lane, Pittsburgh 8, Pa.

B. Chicago, Ill., Jan. 20, 1907. *Studied*: Univ. Illinois, B.S.; Yale Univ., B.F.A.; Am. Acad. in Rome, F.A.A.R. *Member*: AIA. *Awards*: prize, Rome, Italy, 1929. *Position*: Instr., 1933-45, Hd. Dept. Arch., 1938-45, Pennsylvania State College; Dir., Col. FA, Carnegie Inst. Tech., Pittsburgh, Pa., 1945-52.*

JOHNT, ETHEL (Mrs. Willis E. Hykes)—*Painter, T.*

1444 Kenmore Ave., Buffalo 23, N.Y.

B. Hamburg, N.Y., Oct. 22, 1904. *Studied*: Buffalo Sch. FA; NAD. *Member*: Patteran Soc.; Nat. Lg. Am. Pen Women; Buffalo Craftsmen; Kenmore A. Soc. *Awards*: prizes, Albright A. Gal. *Exhibited*: Carnegie Inst., 1941; AFA traveling exh., 1941-1943; Great Lakes exh.; Albright A. Gal., annually; The Patteran Soc. *Position*: A. T., Elmwood-Franklin Sch., Buffalo, N.Y.

JONAS, SCHUBERT EMERSON—

Museum Director, Hist., T., L.

Fort Lauderdale Art Center, 625 East Olas Blvd.; h. 4307 West Tradewinds, Lauderdale-by-the-Sea, Fla.

B. Houghton, Mich., Apr. 20, 1908. *Studied*: Univ. Michigan, A.B. in A. Edu., M.A.; Univ. Iowa; Wayne Univ. Lectures: Modern Art; Genesis of Modern Art, etc. to universities, museums and schools. *Position*: Dir., Fort Lauderdale Art Center, Fla.

JONES, ALLAN D., JR.—*Painter, E., L., Cr.*

44 Claremont Ave., Hampton, Va.

B. Newport News, Va., Feb. 25, 1915. *Studied*: Univ. Pennsylvania; PAFA, B.F.A.; and with Arthur Carles. *Member*: Phila. WC Cl.; F., PAFA; VMFA; NSMP. *Awards*: F., PAFA; Cresson traveling scholarships, 1938, 1939; prizes, Norfolk Mus. A., 1945, 1949, 1952; Toppan award, PAFA, 1939; Phila. WC Cl., 1949. *Work*: PMA; VFMA; PAFA; Aircraft Carrier "Ranger," 1958; Newcomb Hall, Univ. Virginia, Charlottesville, Va.; murals, USPO, Athens, Pa.; SS Pres. Monroe; Newport News Court House; Bank of Warwick; Southampton and Newmarket Cooperatives, Hampton & Newport News, Va.; Newport News Pub. Lib.; David Cooper Co., Hampton, Va. *Exhibited*: Norfolk Mus. A.; VMFA; PAFA; Nat. Cathedral, Wash., D.C.; WMA; Southeastern annual, Atlanta, Ga., 1956. Lectures: Art and Architecture. *Position*: Asst. Prof., mural dec., PAFA, Philadelphia, Pa., 1946-50; Instr., Robert Sugden Sch. A., Hampton, Va.; Official A., Hampton Roads Port of Embarkation, 1944.

JONES, AMY—*Painter, I., T., L.*

Byram Lake Rd., Mount Kisco, N.Y.

B. Buffalo, N.Y., Apr. 4, 1899. *Studied*: PIASch.; & with Peppino Mangravite, Anthony di Bona, Xavier Gonzalez. *Member*: AEA; AWS; NAWA; Balt. WC Cl.; Phila. WC Cl.; Village A. Center; Silvermine Gld. A. *Awards*: F., Buffalo SA, 1931; prizes, Balt. WC Cl., 1941, 1954, 1958; Village A. Center, 1951 (2), 1954, 1957; Women's Cl., Ossining, N.Y.; Jr. Lg. of Westchester, 1955; Saranac A. Lg., 1939-1942; NAD, 1956; Pleasantville, N.Y., 1957. *Work*: Wharton Sch. Finance, Univ. Pennsylvania, Phila., Pa.; N.Y. Hospital; Marine Hospital, Carville, La.; murals, USPO, Winsted, Conn.; Painted Post, N.Y.; Schenectady, N.Y. *Exhibited*: AIC; NAD; PAFA; AWS, annually; NAWA; Northwest Pr. M., Laguna Beach AA; Carnegie Inst.; New Haven Paint & Clay Cl; AFA traveling exh.; Portraits, Inc., traveling exh.; Mississippi AA; Balt. WC Cl.; Albright A. Gal.; Mid-Vermont A.; Soc. Wash. A.; Phila. WC Cl.; Village A. Center; North Westchester A.; Butler AI; Leicester Gal., London, 1954-1956; Brighton, England, 1954; NAC; many one-man exhs., including Venice, Italy, 1958. I., "Child's Garden of Verses," 1946; "Prance," 1950. Represented in "21 Water Color Painters"; Jacket des., "The Spider's Web," 1955. Contributor articles and paintings to Ford Publications. *Position*: Instr. A., Bedford-Rippowam Sch., 1950-54; Adult Edu., Valhalla Jr. H.S., N.Y., 1955; L., N.Y. Pub. Lib., 1953-55.

JONES, CATHERINE (Mrs. Catherine Jones Bollam)—

Writer, Cr.

112 Maple Blvd., Troutdale, Ore.

B. Madison, Minn., Mar. 20, 1899. *Studied*: Oregon State Col., B.S. *Position*: A.Cr.; Dir., Women's Activities, The Oregonian, Portland, Ore., 1934- .

JONES, DAVID TAYLOR SWATLING—

Museum Director, P., C., Gr., S.

Gertrude Herbert Art Institute, 506 Telfair St., Augusta, Ga.

B. Camden, N.J., May 13, 1926. *Studied*: Williams Col., B.A.; Yale Univ. Sch. FA. *Work*: Gertrude Herbert AI.; Westbrook Gal., Westbrook, Conn. *Exhibited*: Westbrook Gal., 1956-58. Co-author: "The Philistine Traveler," 1954. *Position*: Instr. Painting, Dir., Gertrude Herbert Art Institute, Augusta, Ga.

JONES, DORIS JARDINE (Mrs. Kenneth M.)—

Painter, Comm. A.

249 Belleville Ave., Bloomfield, N.J.

B. Jersey City, N.J., Sept. 4, 1911. *Studied*: NAD; Dwight Sch., Englewood; Parsons Sch. Des.; Monmouth Col.; Rutgers Univ.; ASL. *Member*: AAPL; Essex WC Cl.; Verona-West Essex AA; Bloomfield A. Lg.; Art Center of the Oranges. *Awards*: prizes, AAPL, 1955, 1956, 1957; Bloomfield A. Lg., 1953. *Work*: Bloomfield Civic Center; DAR, Tamassee, S.C. Coll. *Exhibited*: AAPL, 1957, 1958, 1959; N.J. Soc. P. & S.; Jersey City Mus.; Bloomfield Pub. Lib., 1953-1956; Newark Pub. Lib.; Verona-West Essex Pub. Lib. (one-man); Glen Ridge Woman's Cl. (one-man); NAC; Bloomfield Civic Center, etc. *Position*: Owner, Essex Artists Co., 1959- .

JONES, E(DWARD) P(OWIS)—*Painter, Et.*

1501 3rd Ave.; h. 925 Park Ave., New York 28, N.Y.

B. New York, N.Y., Jan. 8, 1919. *Studied*: Harvard Univ.; ASL; Academie Ranson, Paris. *Member*: AEA; Phila. Pr. Cl.; Century Assn.; Mun. A. Soc. (Dir.). *Work*: MModA; Riverside Mus. *Exhibited*: PAFA, 1946; WMAA, 1946, 1947; Audubon A., 1948; Kraushaar Gal., 1946 (one-man); 1949, 1953; Bard Col., 1948 (one-man); Phila. Pr. Cl., 1954, 1955; MModA, 1953; John Herron AI, 1958; New Gal., 1955, 1957, 1958. Contributor to Art in America. Illus. for Liturgical Arts. Lectures: The Modern Illustrated Book.

JONES, ELBERTA MOHLER—*Painter, W., L.*

1202 Arden Rd., Pasadena 5, Cal.

B. Kansas City, Mo., Mar. 16, 1896. *Studied*: AIC; Otis AI; Chouinard AI. *Member*: Cal. AC; Women Painters of the West. *Work*: Los A. Conservatory of Music; Birmingham Hospital; Los A. Athletic Cl.; Bethlehem Pacific Coast Co. (mural). *Exhibited*: Los A. Mus. A. Painted portraits of servicemen in Army & Navy hospitals, 1941-46. *Positions*: A. Representative, "Los Angeles Beautiful"; Ed., "Woman Painters News.*

JONES, ELIZABETH ORTON—*Illustrator, W., P., Gr.*

Mason, N.H.

B. Highland Park, Ill., June 25, 1910. *Studied*: Univ. Chicago; Ecole des Beaux-Arts. *Awards*: Hon. deg. M.A., Wheaton Col.; Caldecott medal, 1945; Lewis Carroll Shelf award, Univ. Wisconsin, for "Prayer for a Child," 1958. *Work*: mural, Crotched Mt. Rehabilitation Center, Greenfield, N.H.; panel, Univ. New Hampshire Lib. Author, I., "Ragman of Paris"; "Minnie the Mermaid"; "Maminka's Children"; "Twig"; "Big Susan"; "How Far Is It to Bethlehem?"; Illus., "The Peddlar's Clock"; "Small Rain"; "Prayer for Little Things"; "Secrets"; "This is the Way"; "Song of the Sun"; "Lullaby for Eggs"; "Deep River," and many more books. Contributor to The Horn Book; Nat. Parent-Teacher.

JONES, ELSIE (BROWN)—*Painter*

1100 Lake Shore Dr., Chicago, Ill.

B. Evanston, Ill., June 11, 1903. *Studied*: Northwestern Univ., B.A., M.A.; AIC, and with Francis Chapin. *Member*: AEA; Women's A. Salon; Chicago A. Cl.; Renaissance Soc. *Exhibited*: CGA, 1941; MMA, 1942; PAFA, 1942; NAD, 1942; AIC, 1938-1944, 1952, 1955; Springfield, Ill., 1952; one-man: Glencoe, Ill., Pub. Lib., 1951; Evanston A. Center, 1950; Tally-Ho Gal., Evanston. Lectures on Modern Techniques in Painting. *Position*: Instr., Painting, Park Ridge (Ill.) Sch. for Girls.

JONES, EUGENE A.—*Etcher*

47 Fifth Ave., New York 3, N.Y.

B. Brooklyn, N.Y. *Member*: SC; Brooklyn SA; Southern Pr.M. *Awards*: prizes, SAE, 1942. *Work*: Newark Mus.; Ft. Worth Mus.; Lib. Cong.; N.Y. Hist. Soc. *Exhibited*: SAE; SC; Brooklyn SA; Southern Pr.M.

JONES, FRANCES FOLLIN—

Assistant to Museum Director, Cur.

The Art Museum, Princeton University; h. 116 Alexander St., Princeton, N.J.

B. New York, N.Y., Sept. 8, 1913. *Studied*: Bryn Mawr Col., A.B., M.A., Ph.D.; Am. Sch. Classical Studies, Athens. *Member*: Archaeological Inst. Am. Contributor to American Journal of Archaeology; Hesperia; The Record of the Art Museum; "Excavations at Gözlü Kule, Tarsus," Vol. I. *Position*: Asst., Inst. for Advanced Study, 1939-46; Sec., Asst. Cur., 1943-46, Asst. to Dir., Cur., Classical Art, 1946- , A.Mus., Princeton Univ., Princeton, N.J.

JONES, GERTRUDE FISH. See Savage, Trudi

JONES, HESTER—*Museum Curator*

Museum of New Mexico, Santa Fe, N.M.

B. Wausau, Wis., Nov. 30, 1894. *Studied*: Vassar Col., B.A.; Univ. New Mexico. *Positions*: Rec. Sec., Hist. Soc. New Mexico; Cur., A., Mus. New Mexico, Santa Fe, N.M. (Retired).

JONES, JAMES POPE—*Painter*

Apt. 303, 1108 West Franklin St., Richmond, Va.

B. Crewe, Va., Feb. 23, 1890. *Member*: Richmond AA. *Awards*: prizes, Richmond Acad. Sc. & FA, 1930, 1938; VMFA, 1938, 1943, 1945. *Work*: VMFA; Richmond Acad. Sc. & FA; mural, Labor Temple, Richmond, Va. *Exhibited*: WFNY 1939; VMFA, 1938, 1939, 1945, 1946; Richmond Acad. Sc. & FA, 1930, 1938; Valentine Mus. A., 1951, 1952.

JONES, JOHN PAUL—*Etcher, P.*

702 North La Cienega Blvd., Los Angeles 46, Cal.

B. Indianola, Iowa, Nov. 18, 1924. *Studied*: Iowa State Univ., B.F.A., M.F.A. *Awards*: Tiffany Fnd., 1951. *Work*: BM; SAM; Des Moines A. Center; Dallas Mus. FA; Joslyn A. Mus.; Kansas State Col. *Exhibited*: BM, 1949-1952; Northwest Pr. M., 1950-1952; SFMA, 1949, 1950; PAFA, 1950; Univ. Minnesota, 1951; Bradley Univ., 1951, 1952; Des Moines A. Center, 1949-1951; Denver A. Mus., 1949, 1950; Springfield (Mo.) A. Mus., 1949-1952.*

JONES, JOSEPH JOHN (JOE)—*Painter, Lith.*

Blackberry Lane, Morristown, N.J.

B. St. Louis, Mo., Apr. 7, 1909. *Awards*: med., PAFA; Guggenheim F., 1937; prize, NAD, 1946. *Member*: NSMP. *Work*: PAFA; WMAA; MMA; WMA; CMA; CAM; Walker A. Center; Encyclopaedia Britannica Coll.; Lib. Cong.; Nebraska Univ.; U.S. Army; Standard Oil Co.; Pennsylvania State Col.; murals, Am. Export Lines, SS. Independence, Excalibur, Exeter, Excorda, Excambion; USPO, Seneca, Kan.; Magnolia, Ark.; Anthony, Kan.; Charleston, Mo., & others. *Exhibited*: WMAA, 1935, 1946; Carnegie Inst., 1937, 1947; CGA; PAFA; GGE, 1939; WFNY 1939; Colorado Springs FA Center; Kansas City AI; CAM; Detroit Inst. A.; Dayton AI; Assoc. Am. A., 1953, 1955. *Position*: Instr., St. Bernards Sch. for Boys, Ralston, N.J.; Peck Sch., Morristown, N.J.*

JONES, LOIS MAILOU (Mrs. Vergniaud Pierre-Noel)— *Painter, Des., E., Comm. A.*

2401 6th St., Washington 1, D.C.

B. Boston, Mass., Nov. 3, 1906. *Studied*: Boston Normal A. Sch.; BMFA Sch.; T. Col., Columbia Univ., A.B.; Howard Univ.; & in Paris and Rome. Also with Philip Hale, Jules Adler, Joseph Berges. *Member*: AWS; Wash. A. Gld.; Wash. WC Cl.; A. Dir. Cl.; Soc. Wash. A. *Awards*: F., General Edu. Bd., 1937, 1938; prizes, BMFA Sch., 1926; Nat. Mus., Wash., D.C., 1940, 1947, 1954; CGA, 1941, 1949; Atlanta Univ., 1942, 1949, 1952, 1955; Haitian Gov. Dec. & Order, 1954; Lubin award, 1958. *Work*: PMG; IBM; BM; H.S. of Practical A., Boston, Mass.; Palais National, Haiti; Atlanta Univ.; Howard Univ.; W. Va. State Col.; Rosenwald Fnd.; Retreat for Foreign Missionaries, Wash., D.C. (mural); Barnett Aden Gal.; mural, Cook Hall, Howard Univ. *Exhibited*: Paris Salon, 1938, 1939; Galerie de Paris, 1938; Galerie Charpentier, 1938; PAFA, 1934-1936, 1938, 1939; CAA traveling exh., 1934; Harmon Fnd., 1930, 1931; Texas Centennial, 1936; BMA, 1939, 1940, 1944; Inst. Mod. A., Boston, 1943; Am-British A. Center, 1944; NAD, 1942, 1944; AWCS, 1942, 1944, 1946; Albany Inst. Hist. & A., 1945; Vose Gal., 1939 (one-man); Howard Univ., 1937 (one-man); Barnett Aden Gal., 1946; PMG, 1941, 1942, 1944, 1945; Wash. A. Gld., 1929-1958; Whyte Gal., 1941-1944; Soc. Wash. A., 1938-1943, 1945, 1946; Wash. WC Cl., 1931-1936, 1939-1958; Whyte Gal., 1948 (one-man); Dupont Theatre, 1951 (one-man); Haiti, 1954 (one-man); Pan-Am. Union, 1955 (one-man); ACA Gal.; Gr. Central A. Gal.; BMA; American Univ. I., books & periodicals. *Position*: Assoc Prof., Des. & WC Painting, Howard Univ., Washington, D.C., 1930-59.

JONES, MILDRED C.—*Painter*

79 High St., Rockport, Mass.

B. Scranton, Pa., July 1, 1899. *Studied*: PMSchA.; Academies Julian, Colorossi, Grande Chaumiere, Paris, France. *Member*: All. A. Am.; Copley Soc., Boston; Rockport AA; North Shore AA. *Awards*: prizes, Rockport AA, 1949, 1953; North Shore AA, 1948. *Work*: in private colls. *Exhibited*: All. A. Am.; Copley Soc., Boston; Rockport AA; North Shore AA; Fitchburg (Mass.) Mus. A. Lectures and demonstrations portrait painting to many art organizations.

JONES, MURRAY—*Painter, E., Gr.*

Art Department, Michigan State University, East Lansing, Mich.; h. 4625 Okemos Rd., Okemos, Mich.

B. Durham, N.C., Nov. 5, 1915. *Studied*: Duke Univ.; AIC, B.F.A., M.F.A. *Awards*: prizes, Detroit Inst. A. (purchase), 1948, 1957 (2); Grand Rapids Mus., 1949; Bay Pr. M., San F., 1955; Andover, Mass., 1953. *Work*: Detroit Inst. A.; Grand Rapids Mus.; Oakland A. Mus.; Albion Col.; Abbott Laboratories; Collectors of Am. A. *Exhibited*: Univ. Illinois, 1956; WMAA, 1957; Bay Pr. M., 1955; Andover, Mass., 1953; Provincetown A. Festival, 1958; Exh. Momentum, Chicago, 1953; Mich. A. annual, 1946-1957; one-man: Duke Univ., 1946; AIC, 1946; New York City (4), and others. *Position*: Assoc. Prof. A., Michigan State Univ., East Lansing, Mich., 1946- .

JONES, NANCY (Mrs. George P. Love)—*Painter, T.*

25 Homestead Ave., West Barrington, R.I.

B. Providence, R.I., May 7, 1887. *Studied*: R.I. Sch.Des.; Fontainebleau Sch. FA; & with Charles Hawthorne, Harry Leith-Ross. *Member*: Providence WC Cl.; Alumni, R.I. Sch. Des.; Fontainebleau Sch. FA. *Work*: R.I.Sch.Des.; Hebrew Synagogue, Wash., D.C.; Mt. Pleasant H.S.; Providence A. Cl.; R.I.Sch.Des.Mus. *Exhibited*: BMA; PAFA; Providence AC; R.I.Sch.Des.; BMFA; Boston AC; Grace Horne Gal. *Position*: Instr. A., Rhode Island Sch. Des., Providence, R.I., 1912-52 (retired).

JONES, NELL CHOATE—*Painter*

296 Clermont Ave., Brooklyn 5, N.Y.

B. Hawkinsville, Ga. *Studied*: Adelphi Acad. *Member*: NAWA; Pen & Brush Cl.; SSAL; Boston A. Cl.; Brooklyn Soc. A.; Intl. Council of Women. *Work*: High Mus. A.; Ft. Worth Mus. A. *Awards*: prizes, Pen & Brush Cl., 1951, 1953; Lorillard Wolfe A. Cl., 1950, 1954; NAWA med., 1955, prize, 1958; citation, Milledgeville (Ga.) State Col. for Women, 1951. *Exhibited*: Clearwater Mus., 1946; FA Mus., Little Rock, Ark., 1946; Massillon Mus. A., 1947, 1950; Univ. Colorado, 1947; Wichita A. Mus., 1947; Illinois State Mus., 1947; Wustum Mus. A., 1947, 1949; Berkshire Mus. A., 1947; Dartmouth Col., 1947; Greenwich (N.Y.) Lib., 1947; Buck Hill Falls (Pa.) AA, 1947; Harrisburg AA, 1947; Pa. State Mus., 1947; Elisabet Ney Mus., 1948, 1951; Texas Tech. Col., 1948, 1951; Univ. Oklahoma, 1958; Nelson Gal. A., 1949, 1950; Butler AI, 1949; Springfield AA, 1949; Grinnell Col., 1949; Neville Pub. Mus., 1949; Kenosha A. Mus., 1949; Toronto, Canada, 1950; Paris, France, 1951, 1953; Amsterdam, Holland, 1950; Neville Pub. Mus., 1949; Kenosha A. Mus., 1949; Brussels and Antwerp, Ostend, Berne and Lugano, 1954-1957; Neville Pub. Mus., 1949; Kenosha A. Mus., 1949; Allegheny Col., 1949; Arnot A. Gal., 1950; Albany Inst. Hist. & A., 1950; CM, 1950; Canton AI, 1950; Richmond (Ind.) AA, 1951; Mulvane A. Mus., 1951; Brooks Mem. A. Gal., 1951; NAD; NAWA; Brooklyn Soc. A., etc. *Position*: Pres. Brooklyn Soc. A., 1949-52; NAWA, 1951-55; Memb. U.S. Com. Intl. Assn. of Plastic Arts, 1952-56; Nat. Council of Women of the U.S., 1956-59.

JONES, PAUL HALLER—*Painter, T.*

141 Crescent Ave., Leonia, N.J.

B. Champaign, Ill., May 2, 1917. *Studied*: Univ. Illinois, B.A., B.F.A., with La Force Bailey; ASL, with Corbino, Liberte; Cranbrook Acad. A., M.F.A., with Sepeshy. *Awards*: prize, Detroit Inst. A., 1946. *Work*: Grand Rapids A. Gal.; Kalamazoo Inst. A. *Exhibited*: CGA, 1956; PAFA, 1956; Michigan A., 1946, 1949, 1953; Western Mich. A., 1949-1953; one-man: Martha Jackson Gal., N.Y., 1955; Kalamazoo Inst. A., 1957; Grand Rapids A. Gal., 1957.

JONES, PRESCOTT M.—*Painter, Et., T.*
14 Mill Lane, Rockport, Mass.

B. Haverhill, Mass., Feb. 27, 1904. *Studied*: Tufts Col.; Vesper George Sch. A. *Member*: Boston WC Soc.; Boston Soc. Indp. A.; Rockport AA. *Awards*: F., Tiffany Fnd., 1934; prize, Soldiers & Sailors Exh., Boston, 1942. *Work*: BMFA; U.S. Dept. Interior, Wash., D.C.; City of Boston Coll.; Fitchburg A. Mus.; Ford Times, 1957, 1958; IBM Coll.; City of Haverhill Coll. *Exhibited*: PAFA, 1936-1938; AIC, 1935, 1937, 1938, 1940, 1941; WFNY 1939; Phila. Pr.Cl., 1935, 1936; Phila. A.All., 1935, 1937; Cal. WC Soc., 1941; AGAA, 1938-1941; Grace Horne Gal., 1930-1940; Milch Gal., 1941; Doll & Richards Gal., 1948 (one-man); Terry AI, 1952. *Position*: Instr., Painting, Vesper George Sch. A.

JONES, MRS. P. T. See Donelson, Mary Hooper

JONES, RALSTON—*Cartoonist*
King Features Syndicate, 235 East 45th St., New York, N.Y.*

JONES, (ARTHUR) SIDNEY (H.)—*Painter*
P.O. Box 227, Red Bank, N.J.

B. Montreal, Canada, Jan. 22, 1875. *Studied*: ASL. *Member*: NAC; SC. *Exhibited*: NAD; PAFA; SC; NAC.*

JONES, SUSAN ALICE—*Painter, Comm. A.*
3845 North Park Ave., Philadelphia 40, Pa.

B. Philadelphia, Pa. *Studied*: Moore Inst.; PAFA. *Awards*: prizes, med., F., & Cresson traveling scholarship, PAFA. *Member*: F., PAFA. *Exhibited*: Phila. AC; PAFA. *Position*: A.Dept., Phila. Signal Depot, Philadelphia, Pa., 1941-1947. Evart Art Service, Phila., Pa., 1951-58.

JONES, THEODORE STEPHEN—*Educator*
Center for Design Studies, Institute of Contemporary Art, 230 The Fenway, Boston 15, Mass.; h. 88 Columbine Rd., Milton 87, Mass.

B. Chicago, Ill., Aug. 22, 1910. *Studied*: Yale Univ., A.B.; Harvard Univ., A.M.; Cambridge Univ., Cambridge, England. *Member*: Am. Personnel & Guidance Assn.; Indst. Des. Edu. Assn. Author, Publ.: "Your Opportunity to Help Yourself and to Help Others," 1952; Co-author: "Lovejoy-Jones College Scholarship Guide," 1957. Contributor to Perspectives, No. 9, 1954 (co-author). Lectures Design in Industry; Opportunities for Artists and Designers, etc. *Positions*: Directed project handled by The Inst. Contemp. A., Boston, for U.S. Commissioner General's Office, Brussels World's Fair, 1958: Selection, Procurement & Shipment of Objects for Indst. Des., Interior Des., and Crafts Exh., American Pavilion. Dir., Center for Design Studies, Inst. Contemp. A., Boston, Mass., at present.

JONES, THOMAS BENEDICT—*Painter, Lith., Ser.*
2609 North Charles St., Baltimore 18, Md.

B. Philadelphia, Pa., Dec. 6, 1893. *Studied*: PAFA, and in Europe. *Awards*: prize, Cresson traveling scholarship, PAFA. *Work*: Ecclesiastical murals, New York City, Baltimore, Md. *Exhibited*: CGA; PAFA; NAD; Boston, Mass., and abroad.*

JONES, TOM DOUGLAS—*Museum Director*
International Business Machines Corp.; h. 2440 Sedgwick Ave., New York 68, N.Y.

B. Kansas City, Mo. *Studied*: Kansas City AI; T. Col., Columbia Univ.; N.Y. Univ.; Univ. Kansas; Univ. Iowa; Ecole des Beaux-Arts, and with Paul Bornet, in Paris. *Member*: Am. Soc. for Aesthetics; SC. *Awards*: grant, Nat. Acad. Sc., 1943. Contributor to American Journal of Psychology; Coronet magazine. *Positions*: Asst. Prof., Univ. Kansas, 1937-45; L., Syracuse Univ., 1948-49; Dir., IBM Gal. of Arts & Science, New York, N.Y.

JONES, THOMAS HUDSON—*Sculptor*
1415 36th St., Northwest, Washington, D.C.

B. Buffalo, N.Y., July 24, 1892. *Studied*: Albright A. Gal.; Carnegie Inst.; BMFA Sch.; Am. Acad. in Rome. *Member*: ANA; Century Assn.; F., Am. Acad. in Rome. *Awards*: Prix de Rome, 1919-1922. *Work*: Hall of Fame, N.Y.; Columbia Univ.; mem., reliefs, monuments, doors, busts,

Holyoke, Mass.; St. Matthew's Church, Wash., D.C.; Mechanics Inst., N.Y.; Am. Acad. in Rome; Houston (Tex.) Pub. Lib.; Brooklyn Pub. Lib.; Rochester, N.Y.; House of Representatives, Wash., D.C.; Pennsylvania Station, Newark, N.J.; Trinity Col., Hartford, Conn.; Amherst Col.; war mem., Port Chester, N.Y.; U.S. Treasury Dept.; Tomb of the Unknown Soldier, Arlington, Va.; des. and executed many medals including: World War II; The Freedom Medal; Women's Army Corps; Armed Forces Reserves; Nat. Defense; Selective Service; For Humane Service (German Airlift); Army of Occupation; Univ. Missouri Journalism med.; N.Y. Univ. Meritorious Service, and others. *Position*: Former instr. S., Albright A. Gal.; Columbia Univ.; Am. Acad. in Rome.

JONNIAUX, ALFRED—*Portrait Painter*
712 Bay St., San Francisco, Cal.; and 7 East 63rd St., New York 21, N.Y.; h. 1200 California St., San Francisco, Cal.

B. Brussels, Belgium. *Studied*: Academie des Beaux-Arts, Brussels, Belgium. *Awards*: Hon. D.F.A., Calvin Coolidge College of Liberal Arts, Boston, 1958. *Work*: Univ. California; Northeastern Univ.; Mass. Inst. Tech.; Pentagon, Supreme Court, Capitol, Wash., D.C.; Rockefeller Inst.; Mills College; Boston Children's Hospital; Univ. California Hospital; Stanford Univ. Hospital; Mass. General Hospital; State House, Boston; State House, Columbus, Ohio; City Hall, Baltimore, and many portraits of prominent persons in U.S., South America, and Europe. *Exhibited*: Royal Acad., Royal Soc. Portrait Painters; London; de Young Mem. Mus.; Kennedy Gal., N.Y.; Portraits, Inc., N.Y.; Vose Gal., Boston; Municipal Mus., Baltimore; Gumps Gal., San Francisco; Smithsonian Inst.; United Nations Cl., Wash., D.C., and widely in Europe.

JONSON, Raymond—*Painter, Gal. Dir.*
1909 Las Lomas Rd., Northeast, Albuquerque, N.M.

B. Chariton, Iowa, July 18, 1891. *Studied*: Portland (Ore.) A. Sch.; Chicago Acad. FA; AIC. *Awards*: prizes, AIC, 1920, 1923; Swedish Cl., Chicago, 1921; Mus. New Mexico, 1925; New Mexico State Fair, 1940, 1941, 1945; Hon. F., FA, Sch. Am. Research & Mus. New Mexico, 1956. *Work*: Chicago Mun. Coll.; Univ. Oklahoma; Milwaukee AI; Mus. New Mexico; Vanderpoel Coll.; Mus. FA of Houston; Univ. Texas; CM; Texas Tech. Col.; Oklahoma A. & M. Col.; Univ. Arkansas; Univ. Tulsa; Louisiana State Univ.; Spooner Thayer Mus. A., Lawrence, Kan.; Santa Barbara Mus. A.; CMA; retrospective group of 486 works owned by Univ. New Mexico; murals, Univ. New Mexico; Eastern New Mexico Col. *Exhibited*: AIC, 1913-1915, 1917-1923, 1943-1947; Minneapolis Inst. A.; CAM; Milwaukee AI; CM; Roerich Mus.; Norfolk Mus.; GGE, 1939; Vancouver A. Gal.; Los A. Mus. A.; Phila. A. All.; Colorado Springs FA Center; Dallas Mus. FA; Mus. New Mexico, many one-man exh. *Position*: Dir., Johnson Gal., Univ. New Mexico, Albuquerque, N.M., at present; Prof Emeritus, Univ. N.M., 1934-54.

JONYNAS, VYTAUTAS K.—*Painter, Des., Gr., T.*
182-39 Jamaica Ave., Jamaica-Hollis 23, N.Y.; h. 85-52 168th St., Jamaica 32, N.Y.

B. Alytus, Lithuania, Mar. 16, 1907. *Studied*: Nat. A. Col., Kaunas, Lithuania; Conservatoire Nat. des Arts et Metiers, and Ecole Boulle, Paris, France. *Member*: Audubon A.; SAGA; AWS. *Awards*: prizes, Phila. Pr. Cl., 1956; gold medal, Paris World's Fair, 1937; medals, Audubon A., 1957, 1958. *Work*: National Museums in Lithuania, Latvia, Estonia; Weimar and Hamburg, Germany; Antwerp, Belgium, Amsterdam City Mus.; MMA; N.Y. Pub. Lib.; PMA; LC, and others. Stained glass windows for numerous churches in U.S. *Exhibited*: Weyhe Gal., N.Y.; Univ. Maine, 1954; Alverno Col., Milwaukee, and in Europe, all one-man; also, Audubon A., 1957, 1958; MMA, 1954; BM, 1958; AWS traveling exh., 1956-58; AFA traveling exh., 1958-60; SAGA, 1953-1958, and others. Contributor illus. to Das Kunstwerk, 1947, 1950, 1957; American Artist Magazine, 1952. *Positions*: Instr., Drawing, Painting, Graphic A., in colleges and institutes, Europe, 1935-51; Catan-Rose Inst. FA, 1952-57; Fordham Univ., 1956- .

JORDAN, DOROTHY (FOOTE) (Mrs. Harold J.)—
Painter
3740 Canyon Crest Rd., Altadena, Cal.

B. London, Ontario, Canada, May 13, 1912. *Studied*: San Diego State Col.; ASL. *Member*: Pasadena Soc. A.; Cal.

WC Soc.; Pasadena A. Mus. (Trustee). *Awards*: prizes, Pasadena A. Mus., 1952, 1955 (purchase); Los A. Mus. A., 1953; Laguna Beach, 1955; Cal. WC Soc., 1954 (purchase); Palos Verdes Community AA, 1950 (purchase); Pasadena Soc. A., 1942, 1946, 1951, and others. *Work*: Pasadena A. Mus.; Long Beach Mun. A. Center; Palos Verdes Community AA; Laguna Beach, Cal. *Exhibited*: MMA, 1952; GGE, 1939; Cal. WC Soc., 1948-1955; traveling exh., Canadian and U.S. Watercolors, 1955-1957; Cal. State Fair, 1950-1954; Nat. Orange Show, 1952-1955; Los A. Mus. A., 1948, 1952, 1953, 1954; San Gabriel Valley A., 1948-1955; one-man: Pasadena A. Mus., 1946, 1951; Occidental Col., 1953; Palos Verdes AA, 1955; Cowie Gal., Los A., 1956, 1958.

JORDAN, MRS. L. B. See Schwinn, Barbara E.

JORGULESCO, JONEL—*Designer*
7 Glenwolde, Tarrytown, N.Y.; also, St. Thomas, Virgin Islands

B. Berlin, Germany, Aug. 18, 1904. *Studied*: Stage des., Berlin and Frankfurt Opera Houses. *Member*: SI; Dutch Treat Cl. Designed settings for: "Too True to be Good," N.Y. Theatre Gld.; for Metropolitan Opera: "Don Pasquale," "La Traviata," "The Secret Marriage," "Marriage of Figaro," "Daughter of the Regiment," etc., 1934-41. Contributor to "20th Century Stage Decoration"; "The Opera and Its Future in America"; "Sets and Costumes of the Modern Stage"; "A History of the Theatre"; jacket des., "The Story of the Drama." *Position*: Stage Des., Boston Repertory Theatre, 1925-28; A. Dir., Young & Rubicam, 1930-42; Des. Consultant, County Trust Co., 1945- ; A. Editor, Redbook Magazine, 1942- .*

JOSIMOVICH, GEORGE—*Painter, Des., Lith., C.*
1400 North Sedgwick St., Chicago 10, Ill.

B. Mitrovica, Srem, Yugoslavia, May 2, 1894. *Studied*: AIC, and with George Bellows. *Member*: Chicago Soc. A. *Awards*: medal, Chicago Soc. A., 1929. *Work*: Mattoon (Ill.) H.S.; Joslyn A. Mus. *Exhibited*: Carnegie Inst., 1929; Toledo Mus. A., 1930; AIC, 1934, 1936, 1939, 1941, 1942, 1944, 1949; Univ. Chicago, 1943 (one-man); Knoedler Gal., Chicago, 1932 (one-man); Galerie d'Art Contemporaine, Paris, 1927 (one-man); North Mississippi Valley A., 1949, 1951, 1953, 1955; Mandel Bros. Gal., 1950. *Position*: Des., Solar Light Mfg. Co., Chicago, Ill., 1943-46; Cory-Mitchell Mfg. Co., Chicago, Ill.

JOSLYN, FLORENCE BROWN—*Painter, Des., I.*
134½ East Park St., Oklahoma City, Okla.

B. Michigan. *Studied*: AIC; ASL; Chicago Acad. FA. *Exhibited*: Oklahoma AA; Muskogee State Fair; Tri-State Fair, Amarillo, Tex.; SSAL; Midwest AA; Spokane, Wash.; Edmond Normal Col., Okla.; Chicago Acad. FA; Delgado Mus. A.; Int. Bookplate Exh., Los A., Cal.*

JOYNER, HOWARD WARREN—*Educator, P., L., Des.*
Art Department, Arlington State College; h. 1611 West Second St., Arlington, Tex.

B. Chicago, Ill., July 12, 1900. *Studied*: Kansas City AI; Univ. Missouri, B.F.A., A.M.; Univ. California; Univ. Iowa, M.F.A.; Ecole des Beaux-Arts, Fontainebleau, France. *Member*: Assoc. A. Instr. of Texas; Ft. Worth AA (Bd. Dir.). *Awards*: Carnegie scholarship, Harvard Univ., 1933; prize, Lansing, Mich., 1930. *Exhibited*: Rockefeller Center, N.Y., 1936; Detroit Inst. A., 1931; Kansas City AI, 1934; Joslyn Mem., 1936; Texas General Exh., 1941, 1942; Ft. Worth, Tex., 1941-1943. *Position*: Prof., Hd. A. Dept., Arlington State Col., Arlington, Tex.

JUDD, DON—*Painter, Lith., T.*
326 East 85th St., New York 28, N.Y.

B. Excelsior Springs, Mo., June 3, 1928. *Studied*: ASL, with Bouche, Bosa, Barnet; Col. of William & Mary; Columbia Univ., B.S. *Awards*: prize, Montclair A. Mus., 1953. *Work*: Staten Island Inst. A. & Sciences. *Exhibited*: Phila. Pr. Cl., 1954; BM, 1954; Montclair A. Mus., 1953; N.Y. City Center, 1954-1956; Panoras Gal., 1955-1957. *Position*: Instr., Allen-Stevenson Sch., New York, N.Y.

JUDSON, SYLVIA SHAW—*Sculptor, C.*
1230 Green Bay Rd., Lake Forest, Ill.

B. Chicago, Ill., June 30, 1897. *Studied*: AIC; Grande Chaumiere, Paris, France, with Bourdelle. *Member*: NSS; ANA; Chicago A. Cl. *Awards*: prizes, AIC, 1929; Carr prize, 1947; Intl. Sculpture Show, Phila., 1949; Mun. A. Lg., 1957; Hon. Degree, D.S., Lake Forest Col., 1952; Chicago Chptr. AIA, 1956; medal, Garden Cl. of Am., 1956. *Work*: PMA; Dayton AI; Springfield Mus. A.; Davenport, Iowa. *Exhibited*: PMA; WMAA; MModA; MMA; Century of Progress, Chicago; WFNY 1939; GGE, 1939; one-man: AIC, and other midwestern mus.; Arden Gal., N.Y.; Illinois State Mus., 1948; Chicago Pub. Lib., 1955; Sculpture Center, N.Y., 1957. Author: "The Quiet Eye," 1954.

JUHRE, WILLIAM H.—*Museum Curator*
Neville Public Museum, Green Bay, Wis.
Position: Cur. of Art, Neville Public Museum, Green Bay, Wis.*

JULES, MERVIN—*Painter, Gr., I., L., E.*
50 Dryads Green, Northampton, Mass.; s. 613 Commercial St., Provincetown, Mass.

B. Baltimore, Md., Mar. 21, 1912. *Studied*: Baltimore City Col.; Maryland Inst.; ASL, with Benton. *Member*: An Am. Group; A. Lg. Am.; Boston Pr. M.; AEA; SAGA; AAUP; Springfield A. Lg.; Audubon A. *Awards*: med. and prizes, BMA, 1939-1941; prizes, MModA, 1941; LC, 1945; BM, 1946; Springfield A. Lg., 1955; Cape Cod AA, 1957; Carlisle award (purchase) Eastern States A. Exh., 1957. *Work*: MModA; MMA; BMA; BM; AIC; Smith Col.; Mt. Holyoke Col.; Tel-Aviv Mus., Israel; PMA; BMFA; LC; Portland (Ore.) A. Mus.; PC; Walker A. Center; Illinois State Mus.; Encyclopaedia Britannica; Brandeis Univ.; N.Y. Pub. Lib.; Princeton Univ.; Dartmouth Col.; Louisiana A. Comm.; Univ. Minnesota; Univ. North Carolina Woman's Col.; Abilene Christian Col.; Albion Col.; FMA; Carnegie Inst.; Springfield Mus. A. *Exhibited*: Nationally; 29 one-man exhibitions to 1958. Lectures: Understanding Modern Art. *Position*: Instr., MModA, 1943-46; Visiting A., 1945-46, Assoc. Prof. A., 1946- , Smith Col., Northampton, Mass.; L., Univ. Wisconsin (summer), 1951; Staff, George Walter Vincent Smith Mus., 1952-53; L., Univ. Ext., Mass. Dept. Edu., 1955-56; Adv. Ed., School Arts magazine.

JULIO, PAT T.—*Educator, C., Eng.*
Art Department, Western State College; h. Coronado Hall, Gunnison, Colo.

B. Youngstown, Ohio, Mar. 1, 1923. *Studied*: Wittenberg Col., B.F.A., with Ralston Thompson; Univ. New Mexico, M.A., with Raymond Jonson, Lez Haas; Ohio State Univ., with Edgar Littlefield; Texas Western Col., with Wiltz Harrison. *Member*: AAUP; CAA; Western AA; Colorado AA. *Work*: in private colls. *Exhibited*: Colorado Springs FA Center, 1951; Bradley Univ., 1951; DMFA, 1950; Community A. Gal., 1958; Colorado A. Faculty Show, 1958; Springfield AA, 1948; Columbus AA, 1955; Mus. New Mexico, 1949-1951; Denver A. Mus., 1950; Paul Shuster A. Gal., 1950-1952; Plaza A. Gal., 1949-1952. Contributor to Colorado Art Edu. Assn. Bulletin. *Position*: Asst. Prof. A., Western State College, Gunnison, Colo., 1956- .

JUNGE, CARL STEPHEN—*Designer, P., I.*
937 Ontario St., Oak Park, Ill.

B. Stockton, Cal., June 5, 1880. *Studied*: Hopkins AI; Partington Sch. Illus., San F., Cal.; & abroad. *Member*: Chicago W. Gld.; Austin, Oak Park & River Forest A. Lg.; F., Royal Soc. A., London. *Awards*: prizes, Am. Bookplate Soc., 1916, 1917, 1921, 1922, 1925; The Bookplate Assn., 1926; Hoosier Salon. *Work*: Lib. Cong.; British Mus., London; Columbia Univ.; MMA; BMFA; Toledo Mus. A.; Vanderpoel Coll. *Exhibited*: AIC; Carnegie Inst.; NAC; Toledo Mus. A.; Los A. Mus. A., etc. I.: "Bookplates"; "Ex Libris." Contributor light verse to newspapers and magazines.

JUNGWIRTH, IRENE GAYAS [Mrs. Leonard D.]—*Painter, E., L., C.*
Route 1, Box 603A, East Lansing, Mich.

B. Pennsylvania, Dec. 23, 1913. *Studied*: Marygrove Col., Detroit, A.B.; Wayne Univ. *Awards*: prizes in national and local exhs. *Work*: Detroit Inst. A. *Exhibited*: national, regional and local exhs.; one-man in Illinois and Michigan. Ecclesiastical commissions for stained glass windows, paintings and gold ornaments for churches; portraits. Lectures and writings on art and aesthetics.

JUNGWIRTH, LEONARD D.—*Sculptor, E., L.*
Route 1, Box 603A, East Lansing, Mich.

B. Detroit, Mich., Oct. 18, 1903. *Studied*: Univ. Detroit, B. Arch.; Wayne Univ., M.F.A., and in Europe. *Member*: Mich. Acad. A. Sc., & Let. *Awards*: prizes, Michigan A. Exh.; one-man exh. throughout Michigan. *Work*: Detroit Inst. A.; Kalamazoo Inst. A., and in libraries and schools; statue, campus, Michigan State Univ. Ecclesiastical commissions for churches; monuments, reliefs, memorials and portraits throughout U.S.; Dominican Republic medal and others. Lectures: Sculpture and Techniques. *Position*: Instr., Wayne Univ., 1936-40; Assoc. Prof. A., Michigan State Univ., East Lansing, Mich., 1940.

JUNKER, LEO HELMHOLZ—*Painter, Et.*
166 West 72nd St., New York 23, N.Y.

B. Chicago, Ill., Oct. 30, 1882. *Studied*: AIC; PAFA. *Exhibited*: SAGA; LC; and other national exhs. Color Consultant, Crow, Lewis & Wick, Architects.

JUNKIN, MARION MONTAGUE (Mr.)—*Painter, E.*
3819 Richland Ave., Nashville 5, Tenn.

B. Chunju, Korea, Aug. 23, 1905. *Studied*: Washington & Lee Univ., B.A.; ASL, and with Randolph Johnston, George Luks, George Bridgman, Edward McCarten. *Awards*: prizes, VMFA, 1946; Butler AI, 1946; IBM. *Work*: VMFA; IBM; murals, Hdq. Virginia State Police Dept., Richmond; McCormick Lib., Lexington, Va.; Stonewall Jackson Hospital, Lexington, Va.; Fed. Savings & Loan Assn., Memphis, Tenn. *Exhibited*: AIC; PAFA; CGA; VMFA; Carnegie Inst.; WMAA; WFNY 1939; IBM, and others. *Position*: Hd. Dept. FA, Vanderbilt Univ., Nashville, Tenn., 1941-46; Assoc. Dir., Richmond Sch. A., Richmond, Va.; Prof., Hd. Dept. FA, Washington & Lee Univ., Lexington, Va., at present.*

JUNOD, ILA M.—*Portrait Painter, I.*
8510 Navaho St., Chestnut Hill, Philadelphia 18, Pa.; h. Chanute, Kans.

Studied: Univ. Kansas, B.F.A. *Awards*: George Innes scholarship; Luella Stewart scholarship; Certif., U.S. Marine Corps, 1953; Letters of Commendation from ranking Officers of U.S.M.C. *Work*: portraits and other work: Phila. Naval Base; Navy Bldg., Wash., D.C.; Naval War Col., Newport, R.I.; USMC, Russell Hall, Quantico, Va.; War Mem. Bldg., Camp Lejeune, N.C.; Commandant's House, Wash., D.C.; Marine Corps Birthday poster, 1953; Marine Corps A Bomb poster, 1952; mem. plaque, First Methodist Church, Chanute, Kans., and in many private collections. *Position*: I., Boeing Aircraft Co., Wichita, Kans.; I., Paleontology and Zoological depts., Univ. Kansas; Asst. to Col. J. J. Capolino, USMC, Officer in Charge, Marine Corps-Navy Publ. Bureau, Philadelphia, Pa., at present.*

JURECKA, CYRIL—*Educator, S.*
163 West 11th St., Claremont, Cal.

B. Prikazy, Moravia, Czechoslovakia, July 3, 1884. *Studied*: in Czechoslovakia. *Member*: AFA; Cal. AC. *Position*: Prof. S., Pomona Col., Claremont, Cal. (Retired, 1950).*

JUSTUS, ROY BRAXTON—*Cartoonist*
425 Portland Ave., South., h. 2432 Clinton Ave., Minneapolis 4, Minn.

B. Avon, S.D., May 16, 1901. *Studied*: Morningside Col., Sioux City, Iowa. *Member*: Nat. Cartoonists Soc.; Assn. Am. Editorial Cartoonists; Nat. Press Cl., Wash., D.C. *Awards*: Nat. Headliner's Award, 1944; Freedoms Fnd., annually, 1949-56; Christopher award, 1955. *Position*: Ed. Cart., Sioux City (Iowa) Journal & Tribune, 1927-43; Ed. Cart., Minneapolis Star, Minneapolis, Minn., 1944- ; Pres. Assn. Am. Ed. Cart., 1958.

KABOTIE, FRED—*Painter, I., T., W., L.*
P.O. Box 43, Oraibi, Ariz.

B. Shungopavy, Ariz., Feb. 20, 1900. *Studied*: U.S. Indian Sch.; Alfred Univ., and with Olof Nordmark. *Awards*:

French Gov't. "Awardes Palmiques," 1954; Guggenheim F., 1945-1946; scholarship, Div. Indian Edu., 1949; Indian Council, Chicago, 1949. *Work*: Mus. New Mexico, Santa Fé; Mus. of the Am. Indian, Heye Fnd., New York, N.Y.; murals, Indian Tower, Grand Canyon, Ariz.; Indian A. & Crafts Bd.; Bright Angel Lodge, Grand Canyon, Ariz., 1958; Container Corp. of Am. *Exhibited*: GGE, 1939; MModA, 1941; Philbrook A. Center, 1946; Inter-Tribal Ceremonials, Gallup, N.M., 1946. I., "Tatay's Tales," 1925; "Five Little Katchinas," 1929; "The Rains Will Come," 1954; "Swift Eagle of the Rio Grande," 1929. *Author*: "Designs from the Ancient Mimbrenos," 1949. Lectures: History & Art of the Hopi & other Southwest Indians. *Position*: T., Arts & Crafts, Hopi H.S., Oraibi, Ariz., 1937- ; Mngr., Hopi Silvercraft Cooperative Gld.

KAEP, LOUIS J.—*Painter*
225 Fourth Ave., New York, N.Y.; h. 14 Anderson Rd., Greenwich, Conn.

B. Dubuque, Iowa, Mar. 19, 1903. *Studied*: Loras Col., Dubuque; AIC; Julian Acad., Paris, France. *Member*: ANA; Baltimore WC Cl.; All. A. Am.; AWS; Hudson Valley AA; Conn. WC Soc.; Iowa AA; Greenwich Soc. A.; Chicago Galleries Assn.; AAPL; A. & Writers Assn.; Springfield A. Lg.; SC; Soc. Royal A., London; Fairfield WC Group. *Awards*: gold medal, Hudson Valley AA, 1955; prizes, All. A. Am., 1955; Greenwich Soc. A., 1950-1957; AAPL, 1956; SC, 1958; AIA, 1958; A. Lg. of Long Island, 1958. *Work*: Loras Col.; Dubuque Pub. Lib.; Dubuque Sr. H.S.; City of Chicago Coll.; Janesville (Wis.) A. Lg.; Chicago Galleries Assn.; Amherst Col.; Soc. of N.Y. Hospital. *Exhibited*: AIC, 1927, 1928, 1930, 1932, 1940, 1943; PAFA, 1928-1934; New Westminster, Canada, 1928; Illinois Soc. FA, 1927-1931, 1934, 1936, 1937, 1939-1941; AWS, 1946-1958; Wash. WC Cl., 1948, 1950; Conn. WC Soc., 1950-1954; Audubon A., 1946, 1951, 1954; NAC, 1950-1952, 1954, 1955, 1957, 1958; SC, 1950-1958; Greenwich Soc. A., 1950-1955; All. A. Am., 1951, 1955, 1957, 1958; Butler AI, 1955; Hudson Valley AA, 1955-1958; MMA, 1952; NAD, 1956-1958; AAPL, 1956-1958; Knickerbocker A., 1957, 1958; Mississippi AA, 1958; A. Lg. of Long Island, 1958; Balt. WC Cl., 1958. *Position*: Instr., AIC, 1923-25; Chicago Acad. FA, 1932-41; V-Pres., Chicago Gld. Freelance A., 1942-43; Bd. Dir., Chicago P. & S., 1943-45; Treas., AWS, N.Y., 1953- ; Treas., Greenwich Soc. A., 1953-54; Vice-Pres., Vogue-Wright Studio, New York, N.Y.

KAESELAU, CHARLES ANTON—*Painter, T.*
Court St. Studio; h. 530 Commercial St., Provincetown, Mass.

B. Stockholm, Sweden, June 26, 1889. *Studied*: Kensington Sch. A., London; AIC, and with Charles Hawthorne, Joaquim y Sorrolla. *Member*: Provincetown AA; AEA; Boston WC Soc.; AAPL; Scandinavian-Am. Fnd. *Work*: BMFA; Provincetown Mus. A.; Louisville A. Mus.; U.S. Dept. Agriculture; PMG; Newark Mus.; mem. Wash., D.C.; murals, USPO, Concord, Mass.; Lebanon, N.H. *Exhibited*: extensively in U.S.

KAESER, WILLIAM FREDERICK—*Painter, Des.*
316 South Audubon Rd., Indianapolis 19, Ind.

B. Durlach, Germany, Oct. 31, 1908. *Studied*: John Herron AI; Indiana Univ., B.S. *Member*: Indiana AA; Indiana A. Cl.; Hoosier Salon; Brown County Gallery Assn.; The Twenty. *Awards*: Hoosier Salon, 1951, 1953; L. Strauss & Co. purchase prize, 1953; Presidential Citation for designing "Employ the Handicapped" symbol. *Work*: Culver Military Acad.; USPO, Pendleton, Ind. *Exhibited*: CGA; CM; Carnegie Inst.; PAFA; Hoosier Salon; Indiana A.; WFNY 1939, and others. Pres., The Twenty; Indiana Fed. A. Cl.

KAGANOVE, JOSHUA—*Painter, T.*
751 Bittersweet Place, Chicago 13, Ill.

B. Kiev, Russia, Aug. 22, 1892. *Studied*: CUASch.; AIC. *Awards*: prize, Am. Jewish A. Cl., 1958. *Exhibited*: AIC; Wichita A. Mus.; AFA traveling exh.; Springfield Mus. A.; MMA; Assoc. Am. A., Chicago; Old Northwest Territory Exh.; Northwestern Univ. (one-man).

KAGY, SHEFFIELD, (HAROLD)—*Painter, Gr., E., S.*
5515 Carolina Place, Northwest, Washington 16, D.C.

B. Cleveland, Ohio, Oct. 22, 1907. *Studied*: Cleveland Sch. A.; Corcoran Sch. A.; John Huntington Polytechnic Inst.,

Cleveland; & with Henry Keller, Paul Travis, Robert Laurent, Ernest Fiene, Olof Nordmark. *Member*: A.Gld. Wash.; Soc. Wash. A.; Landscape Cl., Wash., D.C.; Wash. WC Cl. *Awards*: prizes, White Sulphur Springs, W. Va., 1936; CMA, 1933, 1935; medal, Wash. Landscape Cl., 1950, 1958; Wash. WC Cl., 1958. *Work*: murals, USPO, Walterboro, S.C.; Luray, Va.; map, Presidential Yacht "Williamsburg." *Exhibited*: AIC, 1934; WMAA; PAFA; PMG; AFA; Nat. Mus., Wash., D.C.; CMA; CGA; Palm Beach A. Center; Norfolk Mus. A.; WFNY 1939; GGE, 1939. *Position*: Instr., Nat. Sch. A., Washington, D.C., 1946-1956; Dir., Instr., Graphic Arts Workshop, 1958- .

KAHAN, SOL B.—Sculptor

1717 Bryant Ave., Bronx 60, N.Y.

B. Zitomir, Russia, Dec. 23, 1886. *Studied*: Columbia Univ.; ASL, with Robert Laurent. *Exhibited*: NAD; WMAA; CAA; BM; Arch. Lg.*

KAHN, ELY JACQUES—Educator, Arch., P.

2 Park Ave.; h. 1185 Park Ave., New York 28, N.Y.

B. New York, N.Y., June 1, 1884. *Studied*: Columbia Univ., A.B., B.Arch.; Ecole des Beaux-Arts, Paris, France. *Member*: F., AIA; Arch. Lg. *Award*: Paris Salon, *Exhibited*: one-man, Bonestell Gal., 1946; Feigl Gal., 1950. Author: "Design in Art & Industry," 1936.*

KAHN, MRS. LAWRENCE R. See Beling, Helen

KAHN, MAX—Lithographer, E.

Art Institute of Chicago, Michigan Ave. at Adams St., Chicago 3, Ill.

Position: Prof. Lith., Art Institute of Chicago.*

KAHN, OLIVIA—Painter

118 East 18th St. (2); h. 144 East 36th St., New York 16, N.Y.

B. New York, N.Y., July 9, 1920. *Studied*: Fontainebleau, France; ASL; Bryn Mawr Col., B.A. *Member*: AEA; NAWA. *Awards*: prizes, NAWA, 1947, 1957. *Exhibited*: PAFA, 1947, 1951; All. A. Am., 1958; Silvermine Gld. A.; NAWA; N.Y. City Center; one-man: Wellons Gal., 1951, 1954; Feigl Gal., 1956; Juster Gal., 1959; Feingarten Gal., 1958 (4-man).

KAHN, WOLF—Painter

813 Broadway, New York 3, N.Y.

B. Stuttgart, Germany, Oct. 4, 1927. *Studied*: Hans Hofmann. Sch. FA; Univ. Chicago, B.A. *Work*: MMA; CAM; FA Center of Houston; VMFA; Brandeis Univ.; Univ. Illinois; Univ. Nebraska. *Exhibited*: WMAA, 1957; CGA, 1958; Univ. Illinois, 1956; Stable Gal., N.Y., annually; 3 one-man exhs., N.Y.

KAINEN, JACOB—Museum Curator, Et., Lith., P.

4522 49th St., Northwest, Washington 16, D.C.

B. Waterbury, Conn., Dec. 7, 1909. *Studied*: ASL; PIASch.; N.Y. Univ.; George Washington Univ.; N.Y. Sch. Indst. A., and with Kimon Nicolaides, Frank Leonard Allen. *Member*: Wash. A. Gld.; Wash. Soc. Et.; Soc. Wash. A. *Awards*: prizes, CGA, 1950, 1951, 1953, 1955. *Work*: MMA; BM; Brooklyn Pub. Lib.; Queens Col.; PMG, BMA; Carnegie Inst.; LC; CGA; Howard Univ.; East Texas State T. Col.; H. Biggs Mem. Hospital. *Exhibited*: AIC; Albright A. Gal.; Phila. Pr. Cl.; PMG; Oakland A. Gal.; Springfield Mus. A.; LC; BMA; Nat. Mus., Wash., D.C.; VMFA; Grand Central Moderns; Italian-American Exchange Print Show. Author: "George Clymer and the Columbian Press," 1950; "The Development of the Halftone Screen," 1951. *Position*: Cur., Div. Graphic A., U.S. Nat. Mus., Washington, D.C.

KAINZ, LUISE—Etcher, Eng., T., W.

208 East 15th St., New York 3, N.Y.

B. New York, N.Y., May 3, 1902. *Studied*: T. Col., Columbia Univ.; Munich Acad. F. & App. A. *Exhibited*: Weyhe Gal.; NAC; Brooklyn SE; Dudensing Gal. Co-Author: "Exploring Art." Contributor to: Design magazine. *Position*: Chm. A. Dept., Bay Ridge H.S., Brooklyn, N.Y.*

KAINZ, MARTIN—Painter, Lith.

Crane Road, R.F.D., Carmel, N.Y.

B. Dachau, Germany, May 7, 1899. *Studied*: Munich Acad. FA. *Member*: AAPL. *Exhibited*: Weyhe Gal.; Dudensing Gal.; Lilienfeld Gal.; Reading Mus. A.; Carl Schurz Fnd.; Munich, Germany (all one-man).

KAISH, LUISE—Sculptor

107 MacDougal St., New York 12, N.Y.

B. Atlanta, Ga., Sept. 8, 1925. *Studied*: Syracuse Univ., Col. FA, B.F.A., M.F.A.; in Mexico and Italy; and with Ivan Mestrovic. *Awards*: prizes, Syracuse Mus. A., 1947; Rochester Mem. A. Gal., 1951; NAWA, 1954; Emily Lowe award, 1956; grant, Louis Comfort Tiffany Fnd., 1951; Guggenheim F., 1959. *Work*: Rochester Mem. A. Gal.; figure, Syracuse Univ. Campus; AMOCO offices, New York, N.Y. *Exhibited*: MMA, 1951; PAFA, 1952; NAD, 1952; Sculpture Center, 1952; Birmingham Mus. A., 1954; NAWA, 1954, 1955; WMAA, 1955; New Burlington Gal., London, England, 1956; Audubon A., 1956, 1958; Staten Island Mus. A. & Sc., 1956; Louisville Lib., 1956; Intl. Biennial of Religious A., 1958-59; Rochester Mem. A. Gal., 1958; Univ. Iowa, 1958; one-man: Sculpture Center, 1955, 1958; Rochester Mem. A. Gal., 1955; Manhattanville Col., 1955; Syracuse Mus. A., 1947; Finger Lakes, Rochester 1951 (group).

KAJIWARA, TAKUMA—Painter

58 West 57th St., New York 19, N.Y.

B. Japan, Nov. 15, 1876. *Member*: St. Louis A. Gld.; A. & Writers Assn.; AAPL; All.A.Am.; SC; Audubon A. *Awards*: prizes, St. Louis A. Gld., 1922; Weinmar prize 1924; Mallinckrodt prize, 1926; silver med., Kansas City AI, 1926; Baldwin prize, 1928, 1932; Werner prize, 1929; All.A.Am., 1945, 1948, gold medal, 1951. *Work*: Washington Univ.; St. Louis Univ.; Stony Brook (L.I.) Sch.; Hunter Col.; Tuttle Mem., St. Louis; Johns Hopkins Univ. *Exhibited*: NAD, 1922, 1943; PAFA, 1924, 1926, 1928-1930, 1932; CAM, 1930; AFA traveling exh., 1928-1929; Toledo Mus. A., 1928; Detroit Inst. A., 1929; Kansas City AI, 1926, 1928; Springfield (Mo.) Mus. A.; All.A.Am.; Audubon A.; SC; Knickerbocker A.

KALER, GLADYS R. (Mrs.)—Craftsman, Des., P.

21 Sunset Rd., Weston 93, Mass.

B. Waltham, Mass., Dec. 30, 1889. *Studied*: Boston Normal A. Sch.; Boston Univ.; R.I.Sch.Des. *Member*: Medalist, Boston Soc. A. & Crafts; Lexington A. & Crafts; Wellesley SA; Boston Textile Gld.; Boston Weavers' Gld.; deCordova & Dana Mus. A. *Exhibited*: Jordan-Marsh, Boston; Farnsworth Mus.; handicraft exh. in Boston, Wellesley, Waltham, Lexington, Weston, Worcester, Mass., and others.

KALLEM, HENRY—Painter, Gr.

51 West 28th St., New York 1, N.Y.

B. Philadelphia, Pa., May 1, 1912. *Studied*: NAD. *Member*: Nat. Soc. Painters in Casein. *Awards*: prize, Pepsi-Cola Exh. *Exhibited*: WFNY 1939; NAD; PAFA; Audubon A.; Carnegie Inst.; CGA; John Heller Gal.

KALLMAN, KERMAH—Sculptor

161 East 88th St., New York 28, N.Y.

B. Sweden, April 11, 1905. *Studied*: with Aaron Goodelman, Saul Berman. *Member*: Audubon A.; N.Y. Soc. Women A.; NAWA. *Exhibited*: Am-British A. Center; Riverside Mus.; NAD; ACA Gal.; Bonestell Gal.; Peikin Gal.; Chappelier Gal.; Norlyst Gal.; NAC; Argent Gal.; Am. Acad. A. & Let.; Contemporary A. Gal.; DeMotte Gal.; Laurel Gal.; PAFA, 1947, 1949, 1952. *Position*: Dir., N.Y. Soc. Women A., New York, N.Y., 1943, 1950-51.*

KALLWEIT, HELMUT G.—Painter, S., Des.

215 Cozine Ave., Brooklyn 7, N.Y.; s. Shinnecock Hills, L.I., N.Y.

B. Germany, Sept. 18, 1906. *Member*: Lg. Present-Day A. *Exhibited*: Riverside Mus.; Argent Gal.; Burliuk Gal.; RoKo Gal.; Contemporary A. Gal.; ACA Gal.; Wellons Gal.; Bodley Gal.; Crespi Gal.; James Gal.; Art:USA, 1958; Parrish Mus. A.; Guild Hall, Easthampton, L.I.

KAMEN, SAMUEL—*Painter*

800 East 17th St., Brooklyn 30, N.Y.

B. Brooklyn, N.Y., June 15, 1911. *Studied*: ASL; NAD. *Member*: Brooklyn Soc. A.; Int. Soc. Color Council; AEA; AWS. *Awards*: American Artist Magazine Citation, 1954. *Exhibited*: AWS, 1942, 1944-1946, 1948-1952, 1954-1958; All. A. Am., 1943, 1944, 1950, 1957; NAD; Brooklyn Soc. A., 1943, 1945, 1957.

KAMINSKY, DORA *(Mrs. Leon Gaspard)—*
Serigrapher, P., Des., C., L.

Box 643, Taos, N.M.

B. New York, N.Y., Aug. 10, 1909. *Studied*: in Paris, Stuttgart, Munich and Vienna; ASL. *Member*: Nat. Ser. Soc.; N.Y. Soc. Craftsmen; Taos AA; Taos Moderns. *Work*: MMA; Albany Inst. Hist. & A.; Carville Marine Hospital; Moore McCormick Lines; United States Lines. *Awards*: prize, Mus. New Mexico, Santa Fe, 1955. *Exhibited*: Norlyst Gal., 1943 (one-man); Nat. Ser. Soc., 1947 (one-man); Terry AI; Denver A. Mus.; Mus. New Mexico, Santa Fe; Mus. Intl. Folk Art, Santa Fe. Lectures widely on wax resist method and serigraphy.

KAMMERER, HERBERT LEWIS—*Sculptor*

117 Edgars Lane, Hastings-on-Hudson, N.Y.

B. New York, N.Y., July 11, 1915. *Studied*: Yale Univ., B.F.A.; Am. Acad. in Rome; NAD; ASL. *Member*: F., NSS (Rec. Sec.); Am. Acad. in Rome; Century Assn. *Awards*: Widener gold medal, 1948; Fulbright award, 1949-51; Nat. Inst. A. & Lets., grant, 1952; NAD, 1953. *Work*: medals for Nat. Assn. for Prevention of Blindness; Elkins Nat. Bank; Beloit Machinery Co., and others; memorial, Gate of Heaven Cemetery, Chicago, Ill.; sc. map, Barnhart Power Dam, St. Lawrence Seaway, etc. *Exhibited*: NAD, 1942, 1952-1954; PAFA, 1941, 1947-1949, 1952; Palazzo Venezia, Rome, 1950, 1951. *Position*: Instr. S., Parsons Sch. Des., New York, N.Y., 1956- .

KAMROWSKI, GEROME—*Educator, P.*

Department of Art, University of Michigan; h. 1501 Beechwood Drive, Ann Arbor, Mich.

B. Warren, Minn., Jan. 29, 1914. *Studied*: St. Paul Sch. A.; ASL. *Member*: Ann Arbor Group. *Awards*: F., Solomon Guggenheim Fnd.; Research grant, Horace H. Rackham, 1957; prizes, Wayne Univ., 1948; Detroit Inst. A., 1949, 1954, 1955; Grand Rapids, 1958. *Work*: PC. *Exhibited*: WMAA, 1947, 1948, 1951, 1953; Univ. Illinois, 1950, 1952; AIC, 1945, 1946; Albright A. Gal., 1946; Hugo Gal., 1947; traveling exh., SFMA, CM, Denver A. Mus., SAM, Santa Barbara Mus. A.; Detroit Inst. A., 1948, 1950, 1952, 1954, 1958; GGE, 1939; Springfield, Ill.; Univ. Iowa, 1946; Ann Arbor AA, 1947-1954; Faculty Exh., Univ. Mich., 1946-1956; South Bend, 1955; Provincetown, 1958; Univ. Oklahoma, 1958; Artists Market, 1952, 1958; one-man: Hugo Gal., 1951; Betty Parsons Gal., 1948; Brandt Gal., 1946; Galerie Creuze, Paris, 1950, 1958; Saginaw Mus. A., 1954; Univ. Mich., 1952; Cranbrook Acad. A., 1947 and others. *Position*: Asst. Prof. Painting, Dept. A., Univ. Michigan, Ann Arbor, Mich., 1946- .

KAMYS, WALTER—*Painter, T.*

Cave Hill Farm, Montague, Mass.

B. Chicago, Ill., June 8, 1917. *Studied*: AIC, and with Gordon Onslow-Ford in Mexico. *Member*: Springfield A. Lg.; Berkshire AA. *Awards*: Prix de Rome, 1942; F., AIC, 1942-43; Trebilcock award, AIC, 1943; Raymond traveling F., 1943-44; prizes, Springfield A. Lg., 1953 (2); Pittsfield, Mass., 1954; Boston A. Festival, 1955; Amherst, Mass., 1957, 1958. *Work*: Yale Univ.; Wesson Mem. Hospital, Springfield, Mass.; Smith Col.; Mount Holyoke Col.; Regional Contemp. A. Coll., Fargo, N.D. *Exhibited*: Salon des Realites Nouvelles, Paris, 1951; PAFA, 1954, 1955, 1954; Silvermine Gld. A., 1954, 1955; BM, 1955; Inst. Contemp. A., Wash., D.C., 1955; MMoA, 1956; USIA, European Tour, 1956-57; AIC, 1957; Univ. Utah, 1957; Mt. Holyoke, 1957; Ball State T. Col., 1957; Carnegie Inst., 1955, 1956; Crocker Gal. A., 1956; Adelphi Col., 1957; Canton AI, 1957; Bryn Mawr Col., 1957; No. Carolina State Col., 1957; Des Moines A. Center, 1958; Randolph-Macon Col., 1955; Nebraska AA, 1955; Carnegie Inst., 1955; Butler AI, 1955; A. of U.S., Latin America, 1955, 1956; one-man: G.W.V. Smith Mus. A., 1948; Margaret Brown Gal., 1949; Mortimer Levitt Gal., 1953; Bertha Schaefer Gal., 1955, 1957; Inst. Contemp. A., Boston, 1954;

Deerfield Acad., 1956; Concordia Col., Moorhead, Minn., 1957. *Position*: Instr. Painting, G.W.V. Smith Mus. A., 1947- .

KANE, MARGARET BRASSLER—*Sculptor*

30 Strickland Road, Cos Cob, Conn.

B. East Orange, N.J., May 25, 1909. *Studied*: Syracuse Univ.; ASL; and with John Hovannes. *Member*: Sculptors Gld.; NAWA; Pen & Brush Cl.; Brooklyn Soc. A.; Greenwich A. Soc.; Silvermine Gld. A. *Awards*: prizes, NAWA, 1942, med., 1951; New Jersey State Exh., 1943; N.Y. Arch. Lg., 1944; BM. 1946, 1951; Greenwich Soc. A., 1952, 1954, 1958; Silvermine Gld. A., 1954-1956. *Work*: U.S. Maritime Commission; plaque, for "Burro" mon., Fairplay, Colo.; Limited Editions Lamp Co. *Exhibited*: Sculptors Gld., 1938-1958; NAWA, 1942-1958; Brooklyn Soc. A., 1946-1958; Pen & Brush Cl., 1950-1958; Greenwich Soc. A., 1952-1958; Silvermine Gld. A., 1954-1958; MMA, 1943; PMA, 1940, 1949; WMAA, 1938, 1939, 1940, 1945; PAFA, 1945, 1946, 1948; Audubon A., 1945; NSS, 1938, 1940, 1944; AIC, 1940; NAD, 1940; Am. Mus. Natural Hist., 1951-1954; Guggenheim Mus. Gardens, 1955; Grand Central A. Gal., 1956; Roosevelt A. Center, 1957; Argent Gal. nat. tour, 1958. Reproductions in nat. publications. Lectures: The Creative Approach to Sculpture, with color slides. *Position*: Council & jury memb., Greenwich Soc. A., 1958; memb. jury of selection and award, Am. Machine & Foundry Co., 1957.

KANE, THEODORA—*Painter, T.*

902 20th St., Northwest, Washington 6, D.C.; s. Route 15, Buckland, Prince William County, Va.

B. Boston, Mass., Apr. 8, 1906. *Studied*: N.Y. Sch. F. & App. A.; Corcoran Sch. A., and abroad. Also with Richard Lahey. *Member*: Soc. Wash. A.; Wash. A. Cl.; Wash. WC Cl. *Awards*: prizes, Nat. Lg. Am. Pen Women, 1950-1952; Wash. A. Cl., 1955; Georgetown A. Group, 1955; Harpers Ferry, W. Va., 1955. *Work*: mural, Claridge Hotel, Wash., D.C. *Exhibited*: CGA, 1939, 1951; Springfield (Mass.) Mus. A., 1957; VMFA, 1958; U.S. Nat. Mus.; PAFA, 1950; Smithsonian Inst.; Wash. A. Cl.; Pan American Union, 1952; one-man: Whyte Gal., Wash., D.C., 1950; Wash. A. Cl., 1949; Caracas, Venezuela, 1954; Chester County (Pa.) A. Center, 1954; Schneider Gal., Rome, Italy, 1956. Contributor to national magazines, and book jackets for publishers. *Position*: Instr., Port. Painting, YWCA, Washington, D.C.; Dir. A. Dept., Longfellow Sch., Bethesda, Md.; Painting Instr., Dist. of Columbia Recreational Assn., Chevy Chase, Md.; private instr. at own studio.

KANTOR, MORRIS—*Painter, T.*

42 Union Sq., New York 3, N.Y.; h. New City, N.Y.

B. Minsk, Russia, Apr. 15, 1896. *Studied*: Indp. Sch. A., with Homer Boss. *Member*: Fed. Mod. P. & S. *Awards*: med., prize, AIC, 1931; prize, CGA, 1939; med., PAFA, 1940. *Work*: WMAA; Univ. Illinois; Carnegie Inst.; WMA; MMA; MMoA; AIC; PAFA; Detroit Inst. A.; PMG; Denver A. Mus.; Univ. Nebraska; Univ. Arizona; Newark Mus.; Wilmington Soc. FA. *Exhibited*: Carnegie Inst., 1931, 1932, 1934, 1936, 1938, 1940-1945, 1950; PAFA, 1929-1946, 1947-1951; AIC, 1929-1945, 1948, 1951; CGA, 1945. *Position*: Instr. FA, CUASch, ASL, New York, N.Y., at present.

KAPLAN, JOSEPH—*Painter*

161 West 22nd St., New York 11, N.Y.

B. Minsk, Russia, Oct. 3, 1900. *Studied*: NAD; Edu. All. *Member*: AEA; Audubon A.; Nat. Soc. of Painters in Casein. *Awards*: prizes, Audubon A., 1950, 1952, 1954, 1956, 1958; gold medal, Cape Cod AA, 1952 (2), 1954-1956; Nat. Soc. Painters in Casein, medal of honor, 1955. *Work*: Mus. Western A., Moscow; Biro Bidjan Mus.; Tel-Aviv Mus.; Ain Harod Mus., Israel; Butler AI, and in many private colls. *Exhibited*: Carnegie Inst.; PAFA; NAD; CGA; Univ. Illinois; Hallmark Exh.; Audubon A.; Walker A. Center; Boston A. Festival, 1954-1957; one-man: Provincetown, Mass.; New York; Butler AI; Johnson-Humrickhouse Mem. Mus., Coshocton, Ohio; Massillon Mus. A.; Dayton AI; Univ. Nebraska.

KAPPEL, PHILIP—*Etcher, I., W., L.*

Park Lane, New Milford, Conn.

B. Hartford, Conn., Feb. 10, 1901. *Studied*: PIASch; & with Philip Little. *Member*: Chicago SE; SAGA; Conn.

Acad. FA; SC. *Awards*: prizes, Assoc. Am. A., 1946; Meriden AA, 1950, 1955; SC, 1947, 1955; SAGA, 1952; Brooklyn SE, 1926; Marblehead (Mass.) AA, 1926. *Work*: Morgan Mem., Hartford, Conn.; Lib.Cong.; Montclair A. Mus.; BM; Peabody Mus.; MMA; CGA; Nat. Mus., Wash., D.C.; Wesleyan Univ.; Toledo Mus. A.; Carnegie Inst. *Exhibited*: NAD, 1928-1946; WFNY 1939; Conn. Acad. FA; Kent AA; Meriden A. & Crafts Soc.; print exh., U.S. & abroad. I., American Etchers Series, Vol. 4, 1929; "Yankee Ballads," 1930; & other books. Illus., Yachting Magazine. Author, I., "Louisiana Gallery," 1950. Pres., Washington (Conn.) AA.

KAPPEL, R. ROSE (Mrs. Irving Gould)—
Painter, Des., I., Et., T., Lith., Comm. A.
  35-36 76th St., Jackson Heights, N.Y.

B. Hartford, Conn., Sept. 23, 1910. *Studied*: PIASch; N.Y. Univ., B.S.; Harvard Univ.; Fordham Univ.; Washington Univ. *Member*: NAWA. *Award*: prize, NAD, 1956. *Work*: Lib.Cong.; BMFA; Gloucester AA; CMA; FMA; murals, Culture & Health Sch., Brooklyn, N.Y. *Exhibited*: NAWA, 1929-1952; PAFA, 1939, 1940; BMFA, 1940; Newark Mus., 1937; N.Y. WC Cl., 1939-1941; NAD, 1943, 1945; Lib. Cong., 1943, 1944; SAGA, 1946-1952. *Position*: A. Instr., Bureau for Edu. of Physically Handicapped Children, Bd. Edu., New York, N.Y., 1940-46.

KAPUSTIN, RAZEL—Painter
  2524 Pine St., Philadelphia 7, Pa.

B. Ladizhen, Russia, Dec. 26, 1908. *Studied*: Barnes Fnd.; & with David Alfaro Siqueiros. *Member*: Phila. A. All.; Phila. Pr. Cl.; PAFA. *Work*: mural, Frederick Douglass Sch., Phila., Pa.; PMA. *Exhibited*: Albany Inst. Hist. & A., 1943-1945; Lib. Cong., 1944-1946; PAFA, 1944, 1945; Los A. Mus. A., 1945; AV, 1945; Albany Pr.Cl., 1945; Oakland A. Gal., 1943-1945; Butler AI, 1943, 1944; Mint Mus. A., 1943; Phila. A. All., 1943; PMA, 1946; Phila. Pr. Cl., 1944-1946; Dubin Gal., Phila., 1946; AIC, 1948; one-man: YMHA, Phila., 1950; Community Center, Atlantic City, N.J., 1948; Donovan Gal., Phila., 1951, 1953; Lush Gal., 1955; Panoras Gal., 1955.

KARABERI, MARIANTHE—Sculptor, P.
  2990 Newcastle Ave., Silver Spring, Md.

B. Boston, Mass. *Studied*: PAFA; Univ. Pennsylvania; Barnes Fnd.; ASL, with John Hovannes, and with Antonio Salemme, Heinz Warnecke, Pietro Lazzari. *Award*: prize, CGA, 1957. *Work*: many portrait busts of prominent persons. *Exhibited*: CGA; NAD; Mint Museum, Charlotte, N.C., 1958 (one-man), and in many group exhibitions.

KARASZ, MARISKA—Craftsman, Des., W.
  Brewster, N.Y.

B. Budapest, Hungary, 1898. *Studied*: CUASch., and with Ethel Traphagen. *Work*: State Dept., Wash., D.C.; Ball State T. Col.; CMA; Grand Rapids A. Gal.; de Cordova and Dana Mus.; Amagansett A. Gal.; Univ. Delaware; Newark Mus. A.; Montclair A. Mus.; Mus. Contemp. Crafts. *Award*: prize, Pen & Brush Cl., 1950. *Exhibited*: Columbus Gal. FA, 1951; Phila. A. All., 1951; Univ. Minnesota, 1951; Denver A. Mus.; WMAA; one-man: Bonestell Gal., 1948; America House, 1949; Bertha Schaefer Gal., 1950-1951, 1952, 1954, 1956; Des Moines A. Center, 1951; UCLA, 1951; AIC, 1951; Ball State T. Col., 1951; Iowa State Col., 1951; Ohio State Univ.; Cornell Univ.; Currier Gal. A., 1951, 1953; Univ. Michigan, 1952; deYoung Mem. Mus., 1952; in 1953; Binghampton FA Soc.; Oregon Ceramic Studios, Portland; Vancouver A. Gal.; Henry Gal., Univ. Wash.; Bennington Col.; Delaware A. Center; Taft Mus. A.; Akron AI; 1954; Eastern Ill. State Col.; Munson-Williams-Proctor Inst.; CMA; Oneonta State T. Col.; deCordova & Dana Mus.; Amagansett A. Gal.; Riverside Mus.; 1955: Butler AI; Rockport, Me.; Grand Rapids A. Gal.; Cranbrook Acad.; Mich. State Univ.; BMA, etc. Specializes in needlework compositions. Author: "See and Sew"; "Adventure in Stitches"; "How to Make Growing Clothes for Your Baby." Contributor to School Arts magazine. *Position*: Guest Needlework Ed., House Beautiful magazine, 1952-53; Instr., Summer Workshop, Miami Univ., Oxford, Ohio and in Haystack, Me. Contributor to Interiors, Esquire and Holiday magazines.

KARAWINA, ERICA (Mrs. Sidney C. Hsiao)—
Craftsman, P., Des., Gr., L.
  3529 Akaka Place, Honolulu 14, Hawaii

B. Germany, Jan. 25, 1904. *Studied*: in Europe; and in Boston with Frederick W. Allen and Charles Connick. *Member*: Boston Soc. Indp. A.; Hawaii P. & S. Lg.; Artists of Hawaii; Honolulu Pr. M. *Award*: John Poole Mem. award, 1952. *Work*: LC; MMA; BMFA; WMA; Colorado Springs FA Center; Los A. Mus. A.; AGAA; MModA; Honolulu Acad. A.; Stained glass windows (in collab. with the late Charles Connick): Cathedral of St. John the Divine, N.Y.C.; First Presbyterian Church, Chicago; Christ Church, Cincinnati; St. John's Cathedral, Denver, Colo.; Grace Cathedral, San Francisco; American Church, Paris, France and others. In process, 6 stained glass windows for Waioli Chapel, Honolulu. Commissioned to make rubbings of the bas-reliefs of Angkor Wat, Cambodia, 1956. *Exhibited*: Boston A. Cl., annually; Boston Soc. Indp. A., annually; PAFA; Honolulu Acad. A., 1950-1954; Honolulu Pr. M., 1950-1952; Pasadena A. Mus., 1954; San Diego FA Center, 1955; one-man: Grace Horne Gal., Boston, 1933; Univ. New Hampshire, 1936; Wadsworth Atheneum, 1938; Colby Col., 1938; Texas State Col., 1938; Univ. Dayton, 1938; Oklahoma A. Center, 1939; Grand Rapids A. Gal., 1940; Ferargil Gal., 1947; Charles Smith Gal., Boston, 1948; Fitchburg A. Mus., 1949; Currier Gal. A., 1949; U.S. Bureau of Fisheries, 1949; in Honolulu: Gima Gal., 1953; Beaux-Arts Gal., 1952; Oahu Interiors, 1954; and others. Contributor to Stained Glass.

KARFUNKLE, DAVID—Painter, T.
  20 East 14th St., New York 3, N.Y.

B. Austria, June 10, 1880. *Studied*: NAD, with Francis Jones, Edgar Ward; Royal Acad., Munich, Germany; & with Bourdelle, Paris, France. *Work*: Newark Mus.; CMA; murals, Grace Church, Jamaica, L.I., N.Y.; Mun. Court, New York, N.Y. *Exhibited*: Carnegie Inst.; PAFA; AIC; NAD; Boston AC; & abroad.*

KARNES, HARLEY—Cartoonist
  2325 Polk Way, Stockton, Cal.

B. Spokane, Wash., Dec. 9, 1920. *Studied*: Burnley Sch. A. & Des., Seattle; Univ. Washington; Federal Schools. Contributor cartoons to: Sat. Eve. Post; Fawcett Publications; MacFadden Publications, and other national publications.

KAROLY, ANDREW B.—Painter, Et.
  54 West 74th St., New York 23, N.Y.

B. Varanno, Hungary, May 5, 1895. *Studied*: Univ. A. & Arch., Budapest, Hungary, B.A., M.A.A. *Member*: Budapest AC; Royal Acad. A., Budapest. *Work*: Nat. Mus., Budapest; A. Mus., Helsinki, Finland; murals, Bellevue Hospital, St. Clement Church, Pennsylvania Hotel, N.Y.; Thompson Aircraft Products Co., Hotel Cleveland, Cleveland, Ohio; Manhattan Savings Bank; Soc. for Savings Bank, Cleveland; Farm Bureau Insurance Co., Columbus, Ohio; Cities Service Oil Co., N.Y., Ohio Oil Co., Findlay, Ohio; City of Pittsburgh; City of Cleveland.

KAROLY, FREDRIC—Painter
  80 West 40th St. (18); h. 111 East 48th St., New York 17, N.Y.

B. Budapest, Hungary, May 24, 1898. *Studied*: in Berlin and Munich, Germany. *Member*: Nat. Soc. for Dec. Des. *Exhibited*: WMAA, 1952, 1953; Salon des Realites Nouvelles, Paris, 1949-1955; Tokyo, Japan, 1952; Sao Paulo, Brazil, 1951; one-man: Hugo Gal.; New Gal., N.Y.; Galerie Mai, Paris; Univ. Brazil, Sao Paulo, 1951; Museu de Arte, Sao Paulo, Brazil.

KARPF, FAY B.—Writer, T., P.
  221 North Swall Dr., Beverly Hills, Cal.

B. Austria, Apr. 17, 1893. *Studied*: Chicago Normal Col., Certif.; Northwestern Univ., B.S.; Univ. Chicago, Ph.D., and with Emil Bisttram, Paul Lauritz, and others. *Member*: Cal. A. Cl.; Am. Psychological Assn.; Am. Sociological Assn.; Am. Soc. for Aesthetics. *Exhibited*: Cal. A. Cl., annually. Author: "American Social Psychology," 1932; "The Psychology and Psychotherapy of Otto Rank," 1953. Instr. A., in public schools. Engaged in the study of social and psychological factors in art history and art criticism.

KARPICK, JOHN J.—*Painter, Des., Lith.*
115 Cabrini Blvd., New York 33, N.Y.

B. Posen, Germany, Aug. 24, 1883. *Studied:* ASL of Buffalo, N.Y.; De Paul Univ., LL.B., and with Edward Duffner, U. Wilcox, Lucius Hitchcock. *Member:* AAPL; Audubon A (co-founder); Bronx A. Gld.; Knickerbocker A. (founder). *Exhibited:* NAD, 1942; Oklahoma A. Center, 1940-1942; AWS, 1931; All. A. Am., 1941; Mississippi AA, 1946; Audubon A., 1942-1945, 1948-1952; AAPL, 1944, 1945; Yonkers AA, 1934-1944; Woodmere A. Gal., 1944-1946; Bronx A. Gld., 1931, 1946-1952; Vendome Gal., 1941; Contemporary A. Gal., 1942; Knickerbocker A., 1947-1952; Albany Pr. Cl., 1949; Laguna Beach AA, 1949; LC, 1949.

KASSOY, BERNARD—*Painter, T., Cart.*
130 Gale Place, Bronx 63, N.Y.

B. New York, N.Y., Oct. 23, 1914. *Studied:* CUASch.; BMSch. A., with John Ferren, Arthur Osver, Isaac Soyer; City Col. of New York, B.S.S., M.S. in Ed.; Grad. Sch., T. Col. *Member:* AEA; A. T. Assn. *Work:* in private colls. *Exhibited:* Riverside Mus., 1946, 1951; New-Age Gal., 1947; ACA Gal., 1950-1954; Photo Lg. of N.Y., 1950; AEA, 1951; Peter Cooper Gal., 1954-1956; Little Red Sch. House, 1952, 1954, 1956; Downtown Community Sch., 1954-1957; Art:USA, 1958; one-man: SEAC Hq., Kandy, Ceylon, 1945; Bronx H.S. Science, 1951; Teachers Center Gal., N.Y., 1952; Philip Enfield Designs, N.Y., 1953; Panoras Gal., 1959; 2-man: ACA Gal., 1954. Contributor editorial cartoons to New York Teacher News (weekly), 1947- .

KASTEN, KARL—*Painter, E., Et.*
Art Department, University of California, Berkeley 5, Cal.; h. 1228 Pleasant Hill Road, Lafayette, Cal.

B. San Francisco, Cal., Mar. 5, 1916. *Studied:* Univ. California, M.A.; Univ. Iowa; Hans Hofmann Sch. FA. *Member:* San F. AA; Intl. Inst. A. & Lets.; Bay Pr. M. Soc. *Awards:* prizes, Artist Council, San F., 1939; San F. AA, 1953; Western Painters, 1954 (purchase); Nat. Print Exh., Oakland, 1955; Graphic award, Richmond A. Center, 1951, 1958, and others. *Work:* Oakland A. Mus.; Auckland City Mus.; Mills Col.; San F. AA; Univ. California; Oakland Pub. Lib.; deYoung Mem. Mus.; State of California Coll. *Exhibited:* AIC, 1946; Detroit Inst. A., 1947; San F. AA, 1938, 1939, 1948-1950, 1952, 1956, 1957; WMAA, 1952; Sao Paulo, Brazil, 1955; Univ. Illinois, 1956; LC, 1956; Colorado Springs FA Center, 1955; Northwest Pr. M., 1955, 1957, etc. *Positions:* Instr. A., Univ. Michigan, 1946-47; Prof. A., San Francisco State Col., 1947-50; Prof. A., Univ. California, Berkeley, Cal., 1950- .

KASTOR, HUGO—*Painter*
1947 Broadway; h. 1040 Fifth Ave., New York 28, N.Y.

B. Bamberg, Germany, Sept. 16, 1887. *Member:* AAPL; SC; All. A. Am.; Boston Soc. Indp. A.; Newport AA. *Exhibited:* Newport AA, 1953; AAPL, 1954, 1955; SC, 1953, 1954; Boston Soc. Indp. A., 1953; one-man: Carstairs Gal., N.Y., 1953, 1955.*

KATHE, BETTY (KATHRYN BERNSTEIN)—
Painter, Lith., L.
1 Jane St., New York 14, N.Y.; h. 652 Marlborough Rd., Brooklyn 26, N.Y.

B. London, England, Dec. 31, 1896. *Studied:* Brooklyn Col., and with Yasuo Kuniyoshi. *Member:* AEA; Am. A. Group; Provincetown AA; Brooklyn Soc. A. *Awards:* prize, Brooklyn Soc. A., 1950, 1953. *Work:* Fla. Southern Col.; UNESCO Sch., Paris, France; Am. A. Group. *Exhibited:* Morton Gal., 1941; Salpeter Gal., 1949; N.Y. Pub. Lib. circulating exh., 1951; AWS, 1946, 1947, 1949, 1950; Audubon A.; NAD; Provincetown AA; Macbeth Gal.; Assoc. Am. A.; BM; Riverside Mus.; Massillon (Ohio) Mus. A.; Salon d'Automne, Paris; Univ. Maine, 1953 (one-man); WMAA; N.Y. City Center.*

KATO, KAY—*Cartoonist, I., P., L.*
60 Chapman Place, Glen Ridge, N.J.

B. Budapest, Hungary, Dec. 11, 1916. *Studied:* A. Acad., Budapest; PAFA; and with Janos Vaszary. *Member:* Am. Soc. Magazine Cart. *Exhibited:* cart., Wartime Conservation, Am. FA Soc. Gal., 1943; Anti-Axis War Bond Exh., Treas. Dept., 1942; OWI Exh., on Absenteeism,

1943; "Cartoonist Looks at War," Boston Pub. Lib., 1945 (one-man); Vose Gal., 1945 (one-man); PAFA, 1941; Jordan Marsh, Boston, 1950; Montclair A. Mus., 1953, 1956, 1957; Bloomfield A. Lg., 1955; Glen Ridge Women's Cl., 1955 (one-man); Verona (N.J.) Pub. Lib., 1955 (one-man); Newark Pub. Lib., 1957. Contributor to Sat. Eve. Post; This Week; Nation's Business; Christian Science Monitor; Baby Talk, and others; "Best Cartoons of the Year," 1943; American Weekly. Book jacket for "The Television-Radio Audience and Religion," 1955; cover, Am. Tel. & Tel. Magazine, 1954; N.Y. Herald-Tribune "Today's Living," 1957. Lectures: The Art of Cartooning. Guest Cartoonist on NBC-TV network; Jack Paar Show, 1958; Denver, Colo., 1957; ABC-TV, 1956-58.

KATZ, A. RAYMOND—*Painter, Des., W., L.*
30 East 14th St.; h. 260 Riverside Dr., New York 25, N.Y.; s. Rt. #1, Poughquag, N.Y.

B. Kassa, Hungary, Apr. 21, 1895. *Studied:* AIC; Chicago Acad. A. *Member:* NSMP. *Awards:* prizes, Century of Progress, Chicago, 1934; Mississippi AA, 1944; Evanston AA, 1944. *Work:* Murals, frescoes, stained glass, mosaics, sculpture: Elizabeth (N.J.) YMHA; USPO, Madison, Ill.; Oak Park Temple, Ill.; Temple Beth El, Knoxville; Temple Emanuel, Chicago; Temple Emanuel, Roanoke; Beth El, Poughkeepsie, N.Y.; Anshe Emet Temple, Vaughan Army Hospital, Chicago; Stephen Wise Free Synagogue, N.Y.; Nassau Community Temple, Long Island, N.Y.; Temple Beth Miriam, Elberon; B'nai Israel, Little Rock, Ark.; The Temple, Nashville, and others. *Exhibited:* AIC, 1930, 1934-1937, 1939, 1940, 1944; PAFA, 1934; BM, 1934; CGA, 1939; Mississippi AA; Ferargil Gal., 1940; CM, 1940; Carnegie Inst., 1941; Los A. Mus. A., 1945; SFMA, 1945; NAD, 1944, 1945; Albany Inst. Hist. & A., 1945; Milwaukee AI, 1941, 1942, 1944; WMAA; Riverside Mus.; Tercentenary travel. Exh., 1955; Newark Mus. A., 1957; Mus. Contemp. Crafts, 1957; Art:USA, 1958; Marino Gal., 1958; one-man: Chicago Room, 1946; Evansville Mus. FA, 1937; Univ. Arkansas, 1941; Springfield Mus. A.; Binet Gal., 1949-1951; Jewish Mus., 1953; St. Vincent's Abbey, 1953, 1955; Mississippi State Col., 1954; Fleming Mus. A., Univ. Vt., 1955; Werbe Gal., Detroit, 1955; Rochester Inst. Tech., 1957; Univ. Kansas, 1958; Ghent, Belgium, 1956, and others. *Author:* "Black on White," portfolio brush drawings, 1933; "The Ten Commandments," portfolio in color, 1946; "A New Art for an Old Religion," 3rd ed., 1952; "Adventures in Casein," 1951; "The Festivals," 1958.

KATZ, ETHEL—*Painter, T., Lith.*
45 Grove St., New York 14, N.Y.

B. Boston, Mass., July 12, 1900. *Studied:* BMFA Sch.; Mass. Normal A. Sch.; ASL, and with Randall Davey, Howard Giles, Samuel Halpert. *Member:* N.Y.Soc. Women A.; NAWA. *Awards:* prize, NAWA, 1939, 1947, med., 1950, 1954; Brooklyn Soc. A. *Work:* Riverside Mus. *Exhibited:* BM, 1935, 1950, 1952; CAA traveling exh. 1935-1937; AFA traveling exh.; WFNY 1939; Brooklyn Soc. A., 1949-1952; NAWA traveling exh., 1942, 1943, 1949-1952; High Mus. A., 1944; NAWA, 1939-1955; N.Y. Soc. Women A., 1937-1955. *Position:* Instr., ASL, New York, N.Y., 1943- .*

KATZ, HILDA—*Painter, Gr.*
90 East 210th St., Bronx 67, N.Y.

Studied: NAD; New Sch. for Social Research. *Member:* Audubon A.; SAGA; Conn. Acad. FA; Phila. WC Cl.; Print Council of Am.; Am. Color Pr. Soc.; Boston Pr. M.; Albany Pr. Cl. *Awards:* prizes, NAWA, 1945, 1947; Mississippi AA, 1947; SAGA, 1950. *Work:* LC; BMA; FMA; Santa Barbara Mus. A.; Colorado Springs FA Center; SAGA; Pennell Coll.; AGAA; Syracuse Univ.; California State Lib.; N.Y. Pub. Lib.; Newark Pub. Lib.; Pa. State T. Col.; Springfield (Mo.) A. Mus.; Pennsylvania State Univ.; MMA; Bezalel Mus., Israel. *Exhibited:* SAGA; CGA; LC; Phila. WC Cl.; Audubon A.; Albany Pr. Cl.; NAD; Conn. Acad. FA; BM; Delgado Mus. A.; N.Y. Pub. Lib.; Boston Pub. Lib.; MMA; Cal. State Lib.; Bowdoin Univ.; Jewish Mus.; Boston Pr. M.; Intl. Women's Cl., England; Italian Fed. Women in Art, Italy; Paris, France; Venice Biennale; Ecuador; Israel; Graphic A. Exchange Exh., England; Am.-Italian Exchange Exh.; one-man: Bowdoin Univ., 1951; Cal. State Lib., 1953; Albany Pr. Cl., 1955; Univ. Maine, 1955, 1958; Massillon Mus., 1955; Jewish Mus., N.Y., 1956; Pa. State T. Col., 1956;

Springfield A. Mus., 1957; Ball State T. Col., 1957; Miami Beach A. Center, 1958; Richmond (Ind.) AA, 1959, and others.

KATZ, LEO—Painter, Gr., E., W., L.
217½ Whitehall St., Southwest, Atlanta 3, Ga.

B. Roznau, Austria, Dec. 30, 1887. *Studied*: Acad. FA, Vienna and Munich. *Member*: Atelier 17; CAA; SAGA; AEA. *Awards*: prizes, Long Beach, Cal., 1938; LC, 1946. *Work*: Bibliotheque Nationale, Paris; MMA; BM; N.Y. Pub. Lib.; LC; BMA; Howard Univ.; BMFA; Boston Pub. Lib.; MModA; Norfolk Mus. A.; NGA; Atlanta AA; Tel-Aviv Mus., Israel; murals, Johns-Manville Bldg., Century of Progress, Chicago; Wiggins Trade Sch., Los A.; Albertina Mus., Vienna, and other work abroad. *Exhibited*: Ehrich, Seligmann, Montross, Puma Gals., New York; CMA; Atlanta AA; U.S. Embassy, Paris; MMA, 1950; Los A. Mus. A.; San Diego FA Soc.; BM; Smithsonian Inst.; Govt. Exh. prints to India, Egypt, Israel, 1958; Emory Univ., 1958. Author, I., "Understanding Modern Art," 1936 (3 vols.); Chapters to Encyclopaedia of Social Sciences; Encyclopaedia of Photography; Miniature Camera Work. Lectures on Pre-Columbian and Far Eastern Art; Living American Art. *Positions*: Instr., Brooklyn Col., 1943-46; CUASch., 1938-46; Chm. A. Dept., Hampton Inst., Hampton, Va., 1946-1953; Dir., Atelier 17, N.Y., 1954-55; Prof., A.-in-Res., Spelman Col., Atlanta, Ga., 1955-57.

KATZENELLENBOGEN, ADOLF—Educator
310 Broxton Road, Baltimore 12, Md.

B. Frankfurt-am-Main, Germany, Aug. 19, 1901. *Studied*: Freiburg, Leipzig, Munich, Frankfurt Univ.; Univ. Hamburg, Ph.D. *Member*: CAA. Author: "Allegories of the Virtues and Vices in Mediaeval Art," 1939. Contributor to: Art magazines. Lectures: Mediaeval Art. *Position*: Prof. A., Johns Hopkins University, Baltimore, Md.

KATZENSTEIN, IRVING—Painter, T., W., L.
71 Asylum St., Hartford 3, Conn.

B. Hartford, Conn., June 13, 1902. *Studied*: Hartford A. Sch.; PAFA and with Arthur Carles. *Member*: Conn. Acad. FA; Conn. WC Soc. *Awards*: prizes, Conn. WC Soc.; Conn. Acad. FA; Boston A. Festival. *Work*: Wadsworth Atheneum; New Britain A. Mus. *Exhibited*: MMA; Boston A. Festival; PAFA; Conn. Acad. FA; Conn. WC Soc.; Kraushaar Gal. *Position*: Instr., Hartford Jewish Center, 1949- ; Hartford A. Lg., 1951- .

KATZMAN, HERBERT—Painter
200 West 107th St., New York 25, N.Y.

B. Chicago, Ill., Jan. 8, 1923. *Studied*: AIC. *Awards*: Grant, Nat. Inst. A. & Lets., 1957; Fulbright Fellowship, 1955; F., AIC, 1946; prizes, AIC, 1951; PAFA, 1952. *Work*: MModA; WMAA; AIC. *Exhibited*: Carnegie Inst., 1953, 1955; Venice Biennale, 1956; WMAA, 1951-1957; AIC, 1951; PAFA, 1952; MModA, 1952.

KATZMAN, LAWRENCE—Designer, Cart.
540 12th Ave. (36); h. 11 Riverside Drive, New York 23, N.Y.

B. Ogdensburg, N.Y., June 14, 1922. *Studied*: Univ. Pennsylvania, B.S.; ASL, with Reginald Marsh. *Member*: ASL; Nat. Cartoonists Soc. Author, I., "Nellie Nifty, R.N.," cartoon album, 1953; "Taking A Turn for the Nurse," 1956; "Nellie the Nurse," 1958. Contributor cartoons to: Sat. Eve. Post; Esquire and other leading national magazines and newspapers; magazines and newspapers in France, England, Belgium, Holland, etc. *Position*: Pres., Genl. Mngr., Kaz Mfg. Co., Inc., 1947- .

KAUFMAN, ENIT—Painter
404 Riverside Dr., New York 25, N.Y.

B. Rossitz, Czechoslovakia, Feb. 28, 1899. *Studied*: T. Col., Columbia Univ.; Kunstgewerbe Schule and Acad. FA, Vienna. *Member*: AEA. *Work*: N.Y. Hist. Soc.; Univ. Tennessee; Manchester (Vt.) A. Center. *Exhibited*: Vienna, Austria, 1924; Gallery Tedesco, Paris, 1937; Columbia Univ., 1939; Nat. Mus., Wash., D.C., 1944; BMA, 1945; Albany Inst. Hist. & A., 1945; deYoung Mem. Mus., 1945; SAM, 1945; Univ. Arizona, 1946; Wichita, Kans., 1946; Gibbes A. Gal., 1946; Springfield A. Mus., 1946; Dayton

AI; Montreal (Can.) AA; NAD; Lilienfeld Gal., and others. Author: "American Portraits," 1946. *Positions*: Instr., City Col., New York, N.Y.; Southern Vermont A. Center; L., Art.

KAUFMAN, JOE—Illustrator
208 Central Park, South, New York, N.Y.

B. Bridgeport, Conn., May 21, 1911. *Studied*: Laboratory Sch. Indst. Des., and with Herbert Bayer. *Member*: SI. *Work*: MModA. *Exhibited*: A. Dir. Cl., 1943-1952; SI, 1945; Fleisher A. Mem., Phila., 1950 (one-man). Illus. appeared in Fortune, American, Graphis, Charm, House Beautiful, Collier's, House & Garden and other leading national magazines.

KAUFMANN, ARTHUR—Painter, E.
414 West 121st St., New York 27, N.Y.

B. Muelheim, Germany, July 7, 1888. *Studied*: in Europe. *Member*: Muelheim-Ruhr A. Soc. (Hon.). *Award*: Audubon A. *Work*: portrait, Medical Center, N.Y.; New Sch. Social Research, N.Y.; Mus. Mod. A., Sao Paulo, Brazil; Duke Univ.; & abroad. *Exhibited*: one-man exh.: Marie Sterner Gal.; Stendahl A. Gal., Los A. Cal.; Ministry of Edu., Rio de Janeiro, Brazil; Domus Gal., Sao Paulo, Brazil, 1948; Feigl Gal., 1949 (one-man); Jewish Mus., N.Y., 1958; New Sch. Social Research, 1952; Duesseldorf, Germany, 1953 (retrospective); Muelheim, Germany, 1954, 1958 (retrospective); Tel-Aviv Mus., Israel, 1955. Contributor to: Fortune magazine.

KAUFMANN, EDGAR, JR.—Teacher, Cr., W., L., Des.
450 East 52nd St., New York 22, N.Y.

B. Pittsburgh, Pa., Apr. 9, 1910. *Studied*: painting, in New York, Vienna, Florence, London; Apprentice with Frank Lloyd Wright. *Member*: F., Royal Soc. A., London; IDI; AID; CAA; Chicago A. Cl. Contributor to: Art News; Interiors; Magazine of Art; articles in: New York Times; Living for Young Homemakers; Arts & Architecture; College Art Journal, etc.; abroad in: Horizon; Architectural Review; Architects' Yearbook and journals of the Royal Soc. A. and the Museums' Association. Author, books for MModA: "Prize Designs for Modern Furniture"; "What is Modern Design?"; "What is Modern Interior Design?"; "Taliesin Drawings" (on Frank Lloyd Wright's work); Ed., "An American Architecture" by Frank Lloyd Wright. Lectures, TV and Radio; L., N.Y. Univ. Inst. FA; Bemis L., MIT, 1956; Adv., Dept. Des. in Indst., Parson's Sch. Des., N.Y., 1955-56; Merchandise Mngr., Home Dept., Kaufmann's Dept. Stores, Pittsburgh, 1955-40; MModA, 1938-55; Dir., "Good Design," thrice-yearly exhs. sponsored by Merchandise Mart, Chicago, and MModA; Dir., Dept. Indst. Des., MModA, 1946-49; Dir., Intl. Competition for Low-Cost Furniture Design and resulting exh.; Planned and assembled exh. "Textiles and Jewelry from India," 1954-55; Dir., two exhs. of progressive des. "U.S. Consumer Wares," circulated by U.S.Govt. in Europe, 1950-1955, and many others. Member, AIC Comm. on 20th Century Painting & Sculpture; Ed. Bd., Art in America; Trustee, AFA; a Dir. of AIGA.*

KAUFFMAN, (CAMILLE) ANDRENE—Painter, S., E.
5005 West Superior St., Chicago 44, Ill.

B. Chicago, Ill., Apr. 19, 1905. *Studied*: AIC, B.F.A.; Univ. Chicago M.F.A.; & with Andre L'Hote. *Member*: Chicago A. Cl.; Renaissance Soc., Univ. Chicago; Chicago SA; Am. Assn. Univ. Prof. *Awards*: European scholarship, AIC, 1926. *Work*: murals & s., public bldgs.; murals, USPO, Ida Grove, Iowa; medal, Rockford (Ill.) Col.; mural, Science Bldg., Rockford Col.; ceramic murals & stained glass windows, Third Unitarian Church of Chicago. *Exhibited*: AIC, annually; WMAA, 1934; BM, 1934. *Position*: Instr., AIC, Chicago, Ill., 1926- ; Prof., Rockford (Ill.) Col., 1943- .

KAUFFMAN, G. FRANCIS—Cartoonist, Comm. A.
Cooper Rd., Fanwood, N.J.

B. Chicago, Ill., May 31, 1900. *Studied*: AIC; Chicago Acad. FA; Van Emburgh Sch. A., Plainfield, N.J. Contributor to national magazines; industrial posters; art for industrial publications; advertising art.

KAWA, FLORENCE KATHRYN—*Painter, T.*

508 East Pensacola St., Tallahassee, Fla.

B. Weyerhauser, Wis., Feb. 24, 1912. *Studied*: Wisconsin State T. Col., B.S.; Louisiana State Univ., M.A.; Columbia Univ.; Cranbrook Acad. A.; Minneapolis Sch. A. *Awards*: prizes, Milwaukee AI, 1938; Wisconsin Salon, 1939, 1947; Wisconsin State Fair, 1939; Nat. Polish-Am. Exh., 1940; Jackson, Miss., 1943; Louisiana Art Comm., 1949; Fla. Fed. A., 1950, 1951; Fla. A. Group, 1951; Fla. Southern Col., 1952. *Exhibited*: in addition to the above, PAFA, 1946; Contemporary A. Gal., annually; BM, 1951, 1955, 1957; Terry AI, 1953; Nebraska AA, 1952; Fla. A. Group traveling exh., 1950-1952; MMA, 1952, 1953; Univ. Florida, 1953; WMAA, 1953; Contemp. A. Gal. traveling exh., annually; U.S. Embassy, Paris, 1954-1956; Sarasota AA, 1955; Ringling Mus. A., 1955; Minneapolis Sch. A., 1955; Forum Gal., N.Y., 1955; High Mus. A.; Soc. Four A., 1955; Fla. State Fair, 1956; San Joaquin Mus., Stockton, Cal., 1953 (one-man); USIA, European traveling exh., 1957-58; USIA permanent installation in U.S. Embassies abroad, 1957; Contemp. A. Gal., N.Y., 1951, 1953 (one-man); San Joachin Mus., Stockton, Cal., 1953 (one-man). *Position*: Instr., Florida State Univ., Tallahassee, Fla., 1946- .

KAYSER, STEPHEN S.—*Educator, W., L.*

1109 Fifth Ave., New York, N.Y.

B. Karlsruhe, Germany, Dec. 23, 1900. *Studied*: Classical State Sch., Karlsruhe, Germany; Univ. Heidelberg, Ph.D. *Member*: CAA. Contributor to: Parnassus, Review of Religion, Pacific Art Review. Author: "Jewish Ceremonial Art," 1955; "The Book of Books in Art," 1956. Lectures: History of Painting; Synagogue Art & Architecture. *Position*: L., Univ. California, Berkeley, Cal., 1941-44; Prof., Hist. A., San Jose Col., San Jose, Cal., 1945- ; Cur., and Dir. of Exhibits, The Jewish Mus., New York, N.Y.

KAZ, NATHANIEL—*Sculptor, T.*

36 Grace Court, Brooklyn 1, N.Y.

B. New York, N.Y., Mar. 9, 1917. *Studied*: ASL, with George Bridgman. *Member*: S. Gld.; Woodstock Soc. A.; Brooklyn Soc. A.; Audubon A.; Arch. Lg. *Awards*: prizes, Detroit Inst. A., 1929; AV, 1943; Audubon A., 1947; Brooklyn Soc. A., 1948, 1952. *Work*: BM; Abraham Lincoln H.S.; Jr. H.S. 164, Queens, N.Y.; WMAA; MMA; USPO, Hamburg, Pa.; Vine St. Temple, Nashville; P.S. 59, Brooklyn, N.Y. *Exhibited*: AIC, 1937-1939; PMA, 1940; Univ. Gal., Lincoln, Neb., 1945; Riverside Mus., 1943; WMAA, 1938, 1942-1945; MMA; BM; MModA.; one-man: Downtown Gal., 1939; Assoc. Am. A., 1946; Grand Central Moderns, 1954. *Position*: Instr. S., ASL, New York, N.Y.

KEANE, BIL—*Cartoonist*

6748 North 58th Place, Phoenix, Ariz.

B. Philadelphia, Pa., Oct. 5, 1922. *Member*: Nat. Cartoonists Soc. *Work*: Syndicated nationally by The Register and Tribune syndicate feature: "Channel Chuckles"; adv. cartoons and others for national magazines. Weekly feature for Phila. Bulletin, "Silly Philly's Mirthquakers." *Position*: Staff A., Philadelphia Bulletin, 1946-58.

KEANE, LUCINA MABEL—*Educator, P., S., I., L.*

Art Department, Morris Harvey College; h. 2908 Noyes Ave., Charleston 4, W. Va.

B. Gros, Neb. *Studied*: Ashland (Ohio) Col.; Ohio State Univ., B.S. in Ed.; T. Col., Columbia Univ., M.A.; Pa. State Univ.; Temple Univ. *Member*: CAA; NAEA; Eastern A. Edu. Assn.; All. A. of West Virginia; NEA; West Virginia Edu. Assn. *Awards*: prizes, All. A. of West Virginia, 1936, 1939, 1955, 1957. *Exhibited*: All. A. West Virginia; Clarksburg A. Center. Lectures: Sculpture; Art Appreciation. *Positions*: Instr., A. Univ. North Dakota, 1926-29; Illinois State Normal Univ., 1930-31; Assoc. Prof. A., Morris Harvey College, Charleston, W. Va., 1936- .

KECK, SHELDON—*Conservator*

87 State St., Brooklyn, N.Y.

B. Utica, N.Y., May 30, 1910. *Studied*: Harvard Univ., A.B. *Award*: Guggenheim F., 1959. *Member*: F., Int. Inst. for Conservation of Museum Objects; Century Assn.; Rembrandt Cl.; ICOM Com. on Research Laboratories. Contributor: Technical Studies in the Fine Arts, for BM publications. *Position*: Conservator, Brooklyn Mus.; Solomon R. Guggenheim Mus.; MModA.; Joint-Ed., I.I.C. Newsletter.

KEELER, CHARLES B(UTLER)—*Etcher, P.*

34039 El Encanto, Dana Point, Cal.

B. Cedar Rapids, Iowa, Apr. 2, 1882. *Studied*: Harvard Univ.; AIC; & with Bertha E. Jaques. *Awards*: med., St. Paul Inst., 1915; Chicago SE, 1934. *Work*: St. Paul Mus.; Lib.Cong.; Smithsonian Inst.; Los A. Mus. A.; AIGA; Pub. Lib., Cedar Rapids, Iowa; NGA. *Exhibited*: Chicago SE; Pasadena Pr.M.; Brooklyn Pr. Cl.; New Haven Paint & Clay Cl.; Smithsonian Inst.; Fifty Prints of the Year, 1927; Fine Prints of the Year, London, 1929; one-man exh.: Los A., San F., Cal.; St. Paul, Minn.; in Morocco & Spain.

KEELER, KATHERINE SOUTHWICK (Mrs. R. Burton)—*Illustrator, W.*

Newtown, Conn.

B. Buxton, Me. *Studied*: Chicago Acad. FA; AIC; PAFA. *Awards*: Cresson traveling scholarship, PAFA, 1911, 1913. Author, I., "Children's Zoo," 1942; "Dog Days," 1944; "Apple Rush," 1944; Meadow Brook Farm series, 1946-49; "In the Country," 1953, and other books for children.

KEELER, LOUIS BERTRAND ROLSTON—*Painter*

35 Main St., Bethel, Conn.

B. New York, N.Y., Nov. 9, 1882. *Studied*: NAD. *Work*: New Haven Hist. Soc.; mural panels, Bridgeport Orphanage, Brooklawn, Conn.; Groton H.S., Groton, Conn.; watercolors, Soldier's Home, Rocky Hill, Conn.; Fairfield State Hosp., Newtown, Conn. *Exhibited*: NAD; PAFA; Phila. WC Cl.; AWCS; Conn. WC Soc.

KEELER, R. BURTON—*Painter, Des.*

Newtown, Conn.

B. Philadelphia, Pa., April 5, 1886. *Studied*: PMSchIA; PAFA. *Awards*: Cresson traveling scholarship, PAFA, 1911, 1912, prize, 1912. *Exhibited*: PAFA; Phila. A. Cl.; MMA; Arch. Lg.; NAC; WFNY 1939; Scarsdale AA.

KEEN, HELEN B.—*Painter*

130 West 57th St., New York 19, N.Y.

B. Tacoma, Wash., Aug. 12, 1899. *Studied*: Cal. Sch. FA; ASL., and with Mark Tobey, Robert Beverly Hale, Jon Corbino, Vaclav Vytlacil. *Member*: ASL; Phila. WC Soc. *Award*: prize, Tower Gal., Tacoma, Wash., 1945. *Work*: SAM, and in private colls. *Exhibited*: PAFA, 1957; BM, 1957; MModA traveling exh., France, 1956-58; one-man: Tower Gal., Tacoma, 1945-1951; SAM, 1945; Dusanne Gal., 1952; Artists Gal., N.Y., 1956; Pavilion Gal., Blue Hill, Me., (2-man with Vytlacil); Northwest A., 1935-45; Southwest A., Tacoma, 1935-1945.

KEENER, ANNA ELIZABETH (ANNA KEENER WILTON)—*Painter, Gr., E.*

312 Cadiz Rd., Santa Fe, N.M.

B. Flaglor, Colo., Oct. 16, 1895. *Studied*: Bethany Col., B.F.A., A.B.; AIC; Kansas City AI; Colorado State T. Col.; Univ. New Mexico, M.A.; and in Mexico City. *Member*: AAUP; AAUW; Western AA; NAEA; New Mexico A. Edu. Assn.; Santa Fe Assn. A.; Taos AA. *Awards*: Medal, Kansas City AI; prize, Mus. New Mexico, Santa Fe, 1953 (purchase); Roswell Mus. A., 1956. *Work*: San F. Pub. Lib.; Vanderpoel Coll.; Sul Ross State T. Col.; Mus. New Mexico; Oklahoma Univ., and in private colls.; mural, Court House, Gallup, N.M. *Exhibited*: Dallas Print Exh.; Avant Guard, Mus. New Mexico; all traveling exhs. of Taos AA and Mus. New Mexico; one-man: Mus. New Mexico, 1956; Springville, Utah, 1957, 1958; Tucson A. Festival, 1958; Rodeo de Santa Fe, 1958; Alcove Show, Mus. New Mexico, 1958 (one-man); Sandzen Mem. Gal., Lindsborg, Kans., 1959 (one-man). *Position*: State Rec. Sec., Delta Kappa Gamma; Com. memb., Western AA; Judge, 1955 Graphic A., Mus. New Mexico; Council, New Mexico A. Edu. Assn.; A. Consultant, Rocky Mountains Rural Life & Edu.; State FA Chm., New Mexico Fed. Women's Cl., 1956-60.

KEES, WELDON—*Painter, W., Cr.*

c/o Peridot Gallery, 820 Madison Ave., New York, N.Y.; h. 204 Western Dr., Point Richmond, Cal.

B. Beatrice, Neb., Feb. 24, 1914. *Studied*: Univ. Nebraska, A.B.; Univ. Denver, B.S. *Exhibited*: WMAA, 1949, 1950; Am. Abstract A., 1949; one-man: Peridot Gal., 1948, 1949, 1951, 1952; Cal. PLH, 1951. Author: "The Last Man," 1943; "The Fall of the Magicians," 1947. Contributor of articles to N.Y. Times, Magazine of Art, Partisan Review, The Nation. *Position*: A.Cr., The Nation, 1949, 1950.*

KEILER, MANFRED L.—*Painter, E.*

202 Morrill Hall, University of Nebraska; h. 3515 Van Doren St., Lincoln 6, Neb.

B. Berlin, Germany, 1909. *Studied*: State Acad., Weimar, Germany, B.A., M.A.; Bauhaus, Dessau, Germany; Ecole des Beaux-Arts, Paris; Acad. FA, Berlin, with Orlick. *Member*: Nebraska AA; Lincoln A. Gld.; Western AA. *Exhibited*: All.A.Am., 1944; ACA Gal., 1945; Springfield Mus. A., 1948, 1949; BMFA, 1951; Denver A. Mus., 1952; Lincoln A. Gld., 1948, 1949, 1951; Mulvane A. Mus., 1948, 1953; Walker A. Center, 1953, 1954; Joslyn Mus. A., 1949, 1951. Author, I., "Art in the Schoolroom," 1951, 2nd ed., 1955. *Position*: Assoc. Prof. A., University Nebraska, 1950- .

KEITH, D. G.—*Museum Curator*

Rhode Island School of Design, 224 Benefit St., Providence, R.I.

Position: Cur. Decorative Arts, Rhode Island School of Design Museum.*

KELEMEN, PAL—*Writer, Historian, E.*

Box 276, Norfolk, Conn.

B. Budapest, Hungary, Apr. 24, 1894. *Studied*: Univ. Budapest, Munich, Paris. *Member*: Corr. Memb. Acads. of Colombia, Guatemala; F., Royal Anthropological Inst.; Societe des Americanistes, Paris. *Awards*: Commander, Order of Merit, Ecuador, 1952. Author: "Battlefield of the Gods, Aspects of History, Exploration, and Travel of Mexico," 1937; "Medieval American Art, A Survey of pre-Columbian Art," 2 vols.; "Baroque and Rococo in Latin America," 1951. Contributor to: Encyclopaedia Britannica; World Art History (Stauffacher, Zurich), Art magazines. Lectures: pre-Columbian and Colonial Latin American Art; Art History for Americans; L., for State Dept., Inf. Service, 1956, in Portugal, Spain, Italy, Greece and Turkey; Visiting Prof., Univ. Texas, 1953; Trustee, Textile Mus., Wash., D.C.

KELLAM, JACK BURNETT—*Painter, E.*

Centre College; h. East Drive, Danville, Ky.

B. Austin, Tex., Aug. 24, 1914. *Studied*: Univ. Texas, A.B.; AIC; Columbia Univ., A.M.; State Univ. Iowa, M.F.A. *Awards*: prizes, Ky. and So. Indiana Exh., 1949; Kentucky State Fair, 1952 (purchase). *Work*: Seagram Coll.; Aetna Coll.; Ky. State Fair Coll.; mural, Centenary Methodist Church, Danville. *Position*: Prof., Centre College, Danville, Ky., 1947- .

KELLEHER, PATRICK J.—*Museum Curator, Hist.*

Nelson Gallery-Atkins Museum, 4525 Oak St., Kansas City, Mo.; h. 6017 Lockton Lane, Mission, Kans.

B. Colorado Springs, Colo., July 26, 1917. *Studied*: Colorado Col., A.B.; Princeton Univ., M.F.A., Ph.D. *Awards*: Prix de Rome, 1947-49, Am. Acad. in Rome. Author: "The Holy Crown of Hungary," 1951. Lectures: Ancient to Contemporary Art. Arranged exhs.: "The Theatre Collects," 1950; "Expressionism in American Painting," 1952; "What Is Painting?," 1953 (Albright A. Gal.); "Century of Mozart," 1956 (Nelson Gal.). *Positions*: Chief Cur. A., Los A. Mus. A., 1949; Cur. Collections, Albright A. Gal., Buffalo, 1950-54; Cur., European A., Nelson Gallery, Atkins Museum, Kansas City, Mo., 1954- .

KELLER, DEANE—*Educator, P.*

Yale University Art Gallery, New Haven, Conn.; h. 133 Armory St., Hamden 14, Conn.

B. New Haven, Conn., Dec. 14, 1901. *Studied*: Yale Univ., B.A., B.F.A., M.A.; F., Am. Acad. in Rome, and with George Bridgman, E. C. Taylor, Eugene Savage. *Member*: Portraits, Inc.; Council Am. Acad. in Rome; Grand Central A. Gal.; Conn. Acad. FA. *Awards*: prizes, New Haven Paint & Clay Cl.; Conn. Acad. FA; Prix de Rome; numerous military awards, 1944-46. *Work*: 30 portraits, Yale Univ.; many portraits in public and private coll. in U.S. and abroad; state port. Gov. Lodge, Hartford; Sen. Robt. Taft, Taft Sch., Watertown, Conn.; mural (with B. LaFarge), New Haven Pub. Lib.; 2 mural paintings, Shriver Hall, Johns Hopkins Univ.; port. of Sen. Robert Taft, Senate Reception Chamber, The Capitol, Wash., D.C. *Positions*: FA Officer, Fifth Army, in charge of returning art treasures to European museums; Prof., A., Yale Univ., New Haven, Conn., 1930- .

KELLEY, ALBERT S.—*Educator*

Adelphi College, Garden City, N.Y.

Position: Chm., Arts Division, Adelphi College, Garden City, N.Y.*

KELLNER, MARY—*Sculptor*

105 Lincoln Rd., Brooklyn 25, N.Y.; s. Stony Creek, Conn.

B. New York, N.Y., June 16, 1900. *Studied*: Ogunquit Sch. A.; Clay Cl., and with Robert Laurent; Chaim Gross. *Member*: NAWA; Brooklyn Soc. A.; A. Lg., Guilford, Conn.; AEA; Meriden A. & Crafts; Silvermine Gld. A.; N.Y. Soc. Women A.; Conn. Acad. FA; Lg. of Present Day A.; New Haven Paint & Clay Cl. *Awards*: prizes, Brooklyn Soc. A., 1949, 1951, 1955; Silvermine Gld. A., 1952. *Work*: Bezalel Mus., Israel. *Exhibited*: NAWA, 1946-1952; ACA Gal., 1948 (one-man); BM, 1945-1948, 1950, 1952; All. A. Am., 1945, 1953; Audubon A., 1947; Meriden A. & Crafts, 1949-1952; Argent Gal., 1953; N.Y. Hist. Soc.; Silvermine Gld. A., 1952; Riverside Mus., 1950, 1953; Gallery 75, 1954; BM, 1954; NAD, 1954, 1955; Brooklyn Soc. A., 1954; Burlington Gal., London, Eng., 1955. *Position*: Pres., Brooklyn Soc. A., 1952-54.*

KELLOGG, JANET REID—*Painter*

Palmetto, Fla.

B. Merrill, Wis., Jan. 19, 1894. *Studied*: AIC; Milwaukee-Downer Col., A.B.; Grande Chaumiere, Paris; & with George Pearse Ennis, George Elmer Browne. *Member*: AWCS; All.A.Am.; Florida A. Group. *Awards*: prizes, NAD, 1930; Milwaukee AI.

KELLY, ELLSWORTH—*Sculptor, P.*

3 Coenties Slip, New York 4, N.Y.

B. Newburgh, N.Y., May 31, 1923. *Studied*: BMFA Sch.; Ecole des Beaux-Arts, Paris. *Work*: WMAA. Brass sculptures and aluminum sc., lobby, Transportation Bldg., Phila., Pa.; lobby mural, Eastmore House, New York, N.Y. *Exhibited*: Am. Pavilion, Brussels World's Fair, 1958; Carnegie Inst., 1958; MMoA, 1956; WMAA, 1957; Salon de Realites Nouvelles, Paris, 1950, 1951; Betty Parsons Gal., N.Y., 1956, 1957; Galerie Mai, Paris, France, 1951, 1952, 1958.

KELLY, FRANCIS ROBERT, JR.—*Painter, Gr.*

11155 Montana Ave., Los Angeles 49, Cal.

B. St. Paul, Minn., May 1, 1927. *Studied*: A. Center Sch.; Grande Chaumiere, Paris, France; Univ. Hawaii; Univ. California at Los A., with John Paul Jones. *Member*: Los A. AA; Cal. WC Soc. *Awards*: Fulbright F., 1955-56; prizes, Los A. Mus. A., 1955; California State Fair, 1953; Nat. Veteran's Show, 1953, 1954; Douglas Aircraft Exh., 1954 (2). *Work*: Los A. Mus. A. *Exhibited*: Los A. Mus. A., 1955; Cal. State Fair, 1953, 1954; Nat. Veteran's Show, 1953, 1954; LC, 1954; Phila. Pr. Cl., 1954, 1955; Oakland A. Mus., 1955; SFMA, 1954; Santa Paula, Cal., 1953-1955; Santa Cruz, 1953; Cal. WC Soc., 1954; Newport Beach, 1955; Laguna Beach, 1955; Douglas Aircraft Exh., 1954. *Position*: I., Douglas Aircraft Co., Santa Monica, Cal.*

KELLY, GORDON RAY—*Painter, T.*

1024½ Main St., Richmond, Ind.

B. Wells County, Ind., Jan 29, 1924. *Studied*: ASL, with Kenneth Hayes Miller, Reginald Marsh. *Member*: ASL. *Awards*: prize, Indiana AA, 1946. *Work*: ASL; Trinity Church, Ossining, N.Y.; Public School System, Ossining, N.Y. *Exhibited*: Indiana AA, 1943, 1946, 1947; Hoosier Salon, 1946; Indiana State T. Col., 1946 (one-man); ASL Instructors Exh., 1949; NAC, 1953, 1954; NAD, 1953; St. George's Episcopal Church, Indianapolis, 1958; Richmond AA, 1958 (one-man). *Position*: Instr., ASL, New York, N.Y., 1949-50; Dir., A., Scarborough Sch., Scarborough, N.Y.

KELLY, JOHN MELVILLE—Craftsman, Et.

4117 Black Point St., Honolulu 15, Hawaii

B. Oakland, Cal., Nov. 2, 1877. *Studied*: Mark Hopkins Sch. A.; Partington Sch. A. *Member*: Honolulu Pr. M.; Cal. Soc. Et.; Chicago Soc. Et. *Awards*: prizes, Chicago Soc. Et.; Honolulu Pr. M. *Work*: N.Y. Pub. Lib.; NGA; FMA, and in private colls. Author, I., "Etchings and Drawings of Hawaiians," 1943; "The Hula as Seen in Hawaii," 1955.

KELLY, LEON—Painter

Harvey Cedars, N.J.

B. Perpignan, France, Oct. 21, 1901. *Studied*: PAFA; and in Europe. *Work*: MModA; MMA; WMAA; Wadsworth Atheneum; Tel-Aviv Mus., Israel; PMA; Hist. Mus. of Mexico, and others; in private colls., U.S. and abroad. *Exhibited*: European Intl. Exh., Venice, 1927; Carnegie Inst.; Cal. PLH; Louis Carre, Paris; one-man: Galerie Van Leer, Galerie Sacre de Printemps, Paris; Galeria Amici de Francia, Milan; Julian Levy Gal.; Hugo Gal.; Kipnis Gal., Westport, Conn., 1955; Edwin Hewitt Gal., 1956.

KELPE, PAUL—Painter, E., Lith.

939 Longfellow St., Northwest, Washington 11, D.C.

B. Hanover, Germany. *Studied*: Hanover, Germany; Univ. Chicago, M.A., Ph.D. *Member*: AAUP; Am. Abstract A.; CAA. *Work*: Detroit Inst. A.; Dept. Labor, Wash., D.C.; Indiana State T. Col.; Maryland State T. Col.; Univ. Illinois; Univ. Nebraska. *Exhibited*: nationally. *Position*: Prof. A., Univ. Texas, 1948-54; Howard Univ., Washington, D.C., 1957- .

KELSEY, DOROTHY STOREY—Painter

North Canton, Conn.

B. Kingston, N.Y., Aug. 30, 1893. *Studied*: Albany Sch. FA; PAFA; PIASch. *Member*: F., PAFA; AAPL. *Awards*: prizes, Albany Prof. Women's Exh.; Hartford Women Painters, 1954, 1955. *Exhibited*: Mystic, Conn., 1955; Mattatuck Hist. Soc., Waterbury, Conn., 1955; Exh. rugs and paintings on museum circuit, 1923-1926; Hartford, New Britain, Conn.; New Haven A. Festival. *Position*: Des. rugs, Vermont Hooked Rug Industry, for 10 years.

KELSEY, MURIEL CHAMBERLIN—Sculptor

167 East 69th St., New York, N.Y.; h. 1252 Fourth St., Sarasota, Fla.

B. Milford, N.H. *Studied*: Univ. New Hampshire, B.S.; Columbia Univ.; New Sch. for Social Research, and with Dorothea Denslow. *Member*: S. Center; A. Lg. of Manatee County, Fla.; Assoc. Florida Sculptors. *Awards*: prize, Sarasota Festival of Arts, 1953. *Work*: Brookgreen Gardens, S.C.; garden pieces and many small sculptures in private collections. *Exhibited*: Conn. Acad. FA; PAFA; Newark Mus. A.; Syracuse Mus. FA; Wilmington Mus. A.; Fairmount Park, Phila.; Ringling Mus. A.; Sarasota AA; Sarasota S. & Ceramic Group, 1953, 1954, 1955; Sculpture Center, N.Y., 1935-1958; Junior A. Gal., Louisville; A. Lg. Manatee County, 1956, 1957; Assoc. Fla. Sculptors, 1958; Audubon A., 1958; Searles Gal., Bradenton A. Center, 1957 (one-man).

KELSEY, PHILIP H.—Educator, Comm. A.

Swain School of Design, 19 Hawthorn St., New Bedford, Mass.; h. Prospect Road, Mattapoisett, Mass.

B. Walpole, Mass., Oct. 30, 1919. *Studied*: Swain Sch. Des.; Boston Univ., B.S. in A. Edu. *Exhibited*: Cape Cod AA, 1952; New Bedford AA, 1957, 1958. *Positions*: Instr. App. A., 1946-1953, Asst. Prof., 1953-56, Sch. of Practical A. & Lets., Sch. F. & App. A., Boston Univ.; Dir., Swain School of Design, New Bedford, Mass., 1956- .

KELSEY, RICHMOND (DICK)—Designer, P., Comm. A.

3600 Berry Drive, North Hollywood, Cal.

B. San Diego, Cal., May 3, 1905. *Studied*: Otis AI; Santa Barbara Sch. A.; Los Angeles A. Center Sch. *Member*: Cal. WC Soc.; AWS. *Awards*: bronze medal, San Diego Expo., 1935; NAD, 1956. *Work*: San Diego FA Soc.; habitat group, Smithsonian Inst.; Cal. PLH. *Exhibited*: Cal. WC Soc. Author, I., "Gismo," 1948; Illus., 8 Golden Books. *Position*: A. Instr., Santa Barbara, Cal., 1935-37; A. Dir., Walt Disney Studios, 1938-1950; A. Dir., California Artists, 1953-54; A. Dir., Marco Engineering Co., Los Angeles, Cal.

KEMPER, JOHN GARNER—Educator, P., Des., L., W.

609 West Lovell St., Kalamazoo 46, Mich.

B. Muncie, Ind., June 3, 1909. *Studied*: Ohio State Univ., B.F.A.; Chicago Acad. FA; T. Col., Columbia Univ., M.A. *Member*: Mich. Acad. Sc. A. & Let.; Western AA; NAEA; Michigan Edu. Assn. *Awards*: prizes, Fort Exh. advertising art, Minneapolis, Minn., 1941, 1951-1957; Kalamazoo Inst. A., 1943; Grand Rapids A. Gal., 1946; Ohio Valley, 1954; Religious Christmas Card Comp., Detroit Inst. A., 1955. *Exhibited*: Minneapolis, Minn., 1941, 1951-1958; Kalamazoo Inst. A., 1943-1945 (one-man, 1946), 1946, 1947, 1951, 1955, 1956; Grand Rapids A. Gal., 1946, 1947, 1956, 1957; Butler AI, 1946; Detroit Inst. A., 1944, 1946, 1955; Ohio Valley Exh., 1947-1949, 1954; Ogunquit A. Center, 1948-1953, 1958; Mich. Acad. Sc. A. & Let., 1951, 1953, 1954, 1955, 1956. Illustrated lectures: "So You Don't Like Modern Art?"; "Scandinavia." Des. book jackets, mural, etc., Western Michigan Univ.; NAEA 1954 Yearbook "Research in Art Education"; des. seal for Western Mich. Univ., 1957. *Position*: Assoc. Prof. A., Western Michigan Univ., 1942- .

KEMPSTER, RUTH—Painter

1633 Amberwood Drive, South Pasadena, Cal.

B. Chicago, Ill., Jan. 17, 1904. *Studied*: Los A. County AI; ASL; Academie des Beaux-Arts; Nat. Acad., Florence, Italy. *Member*: Pasadena Soc. A.; Women Painters of the West. *Awards*: prizes, Cal. State Fair, 1931, 1932, 1936; Pasadena Soc. A., 1936, 1940, 1944, 1951; Women Painters of the West, 1951; medal, Int. Olympic Games, exh., 1932. *Work*: Pasadena AI; murals, Huntington Mem. Hospital, Pasadena. Toured Korea as port. artist for Armed Forces, Far East Command, 1953.*

KEMPTON, ELMIRA—Painter, E.

Earlham College; h. 75 South 17th St., Richmond, Ind.

B. Richmond, Ind. *Studied*: Cincinnati A. Acad.; Cincinnati Univ.; Earlham Col., and with Wayman Adams, Eliot O'Hara, Albert Krehbiel. *Member*: NAWA; Cincinnati Woman's A. Cl.; Indiana A. Cl.; Cincinnati Mus. Assn.; Indiana Assn. of A. Edu.; The Twenty; Am. Assn. of Studies. *Exhibited*: Nationally; one-man: Argent Gal.; Dayton AI; Loring Andrews Gal.; Lieber Gal.; NAWA traveling exh., nationally & in Europe; Indiana State T. Col.; Richmond AA. *Position*: Hd. A. Dept., Asst. Prof., Earlham Col.; Instr. A. Hist. & Ceramics, and studio classes, Earlham College-Indiana Univ. Center.

KENDALL, BEATRICE—Painter, C., Des., T., L.

245 East 84th St.; h. 308 East 84th St., New York 28, N.Y.

B. New York, N.Y. *Studied*: Yale Sch. FA, B.F.A.; Univ. London. *Member*: NSMP; AID; Soc. for Japanese Studies; McDowell Assoc. *Awards*: Winchester F., Yale Univ., 1922; prize, New Haven Paint & Clay Cl. *Work*: Lyman Allyn Mus.; mural, So. New England Tel. Co. Bldg., New Haven, Conn. *Exhibited*: NAD; New Haven Paint & Clay Cl.; Ogunquit A. Center; Conn. Acad. FA; VMFA; one-man: Newport AA; Brooklyn Botanical Gardens; Studio Gld.; AWS; Hartford Town & Country Cl.; Saybrook Col., Yale Univ.; Barbizon Hotel, N.Y.; The Homestead, Hot Springs, Va.*

KENDALL, VIONA ANN (Mrs. Giles A.)—Painter, T.

6557 Costello Ave., Van Nuys, Cal.

B. Berkeley, Cal., Aug. 28, 1925. *Studied*: Occidental Col.; Lukits Acad. FA, and with T.N. Lukits, Samuel Hyde Harris, Leon Franks. *Member*: A. of the Southwest; Cal. A. Cl.; Valley A. Gld.; Burbank AA; AAPL. *Awards*: prizes, Burbank AA, 1952-1954; Cal. A. Cl., 1954, 1955; Valley A. Gld., 1956-1958; Friday Morning Cl., 1958; Cal. State Fair, 1958. *Work*: in many private collections. *Exhibited*: Duncan Vail Gal., 1953-1955; Cal. A. Cl., 1953-1958; Laguna Beach A. Gal., 1953-1958; Burbank AA, 1953-1955; Friday Morning Cl., 1954-1958; Van Nuys and

Burbank Woman's Cl., 1953; Burbank Pub. Lib., 1955; North Hollywood Woman's Cl., 1954; Greek Theatre, 1954-1958; Ebell Cl., 1955-1958; Cal. State Fair, 1957, 1958; Orange Show, 1958; AAPL, 1958 and traveling exh. Demonstrations, lectures to women's clubs, art galleries and on TV. *Position*: Pres., 1954, Dir., 1955, Burbank AA; Cor. Sec., Bd. Dir., Valley A. Gld., 1954, 1955; Bd. Gov., Hollywood AA, 1954.

KENNEDY, CLARENCE—*Educator*
    Hillyer Gallery, Smith College; h. 44 Pomeroy Terrace, Northampton, Mass.

B. Philadelphia, Pa., Sept. 4, 1892. *Studied*: Univ. Pennsylvania, B.S. in Arch., M.A.; Harvard Univ., Ph.D.; Am. Sch. for Classical Studies, Athens. *Awards*: Norton F., 1920; Guggenheim F., 1930; F., CAA, 1931. I., Ed., "Studies in the History & Criticism of Sculpture," Vol. 1-7, 1927; "Sculpture of the Dreyfus Collection," 1930. Lectures: Italian Renaissance Sculpture. *Position*: Prof. A., Smith Col., Northampton, Mass., 1924- . Carnegie Prof., Toledo Mus. A., 1938-39.

KENNEDY, DAWN S.—*Educator, L., P.*
    Montevallo, Ala.

B. Crawfordsville, Ind. *Studied*: PIASch.; Columbia Univ., B.S., M.A. *Member*: NAEA (Past Council Member); Southeastern AA (Past Pres.); Alabama A. Lg.; Alabama WC Soc. (Past Pres.); State A. Edu. Assn. (Past Pres.); Birmingham AA. Lectures: Modern Art. *Position*: Hd. A. Dept., Univ. Wyoming, 1931-34; Hd. A. Dept., Alabama College, Montevallo, Ala., 1934-1956 (retired).

KENNEDY, J(ANET) ROBSON (Mrs. W. Alfred)—
Painter
    3586 Avocado Ave., Miami 33, Fla.

B. Bridgeport, Conn., May 17, 1902. *Studied*: AIC, with Albin Polasek, John Norton; ASL, with William Zorach and others; also with Lauren Ford, Syd Solomon. *Awards*: prizes, Sarasota AA, 1955; Nat. Sacred Heart Comp., 1956; Soc. Four Arts, Palm Beach, 1957; Boca Raton, 1958. *Work*: in private colls.; ports. of prominent persons. *Exhibited*: Butler AI, 1955, 1958; Sarasota Nat. Exh., 1955, 1957; Soc. Four Arts, 1957; Sarasota Print Exh., 1956-1958; Southeastern Exh., 1955; Provincetown and Hyannis, Mass., 1955; Univ. Wisconsin, 1956, 1957; Univ. Illinois, 1956, 1957; Huber Gal., Miami Beach, 1957, 1958; Johnson Gal., Chicago, Ill., 1958; McGoughan Burr Gal., St. Louis, 1958.

KENNEDY, JOHN WILLIAM—*Painter, E., L.*
    1003 West Union St., Champaign, Ill.

B. Cincinnati, Ohio, Aug. 17, 1903. *Studied*: Cincinnati A. Acad.; Carnegie Tech., A.B.; Univ. Illinois, M.F.A. *Work*: in many public and private collections. *Exhibited*: nationally. Lectures: "Painting the Crucifixion"; "Contemporary American Painting." *Position*: Prof. A., Dept. A., Univ. Illinois, Urbana, Ill., 1926- . Conducts summer school of painting, Wellfleet, Mass.

KENNEDY, LETA M.—*Craftsman, Des., Gr., L., E.*
    5315 North East Cleveland Ave., Portland 11, Ore.

B. Pendleton, Ore., July 4, 1895. *Studied*: Portland (Ore.) Mus. A. Sch.; T. Col., Columbia Univ., B.S.; & with Hermann Rosse, Hans Hofmann, Moholy-Nagy, Dorothy Wright Liebes, and others. *Member*: Portland AA; Portland Potters Group (Sec.-Treas.); Oregon Ceramic Studio. *Awards*: prize, Northwest Pr.M., 1938. *Exhibited*: Phila. A. All., 1939; Portland Mus. A.; Northwest Pr.M., 1938, 1939; Oregon Ceramic Studio, 1946, 1956, 1958. Lectures: Ceramics; Textiles. *Position*: Instr., Design, Ceramics, Textiles, Mus. A. Sch., Portland, Ore. Juror, Northwest Ceramic Annual, 1956.

KENNEDY, RUTH WEDGWOOD—*Educator, L.*
    Hillyer Gallery, Smith College; h. 44 Pomeroy Terrace, Northampton, Mass.

B. Providence, R.I., Aug. 19, 1896. *Studied*: Radcliffe Col., B.A.; Oxford Univ. *Member*: CAA. *Awards*: Guggenheim F., 1930. Author: "Alesso Baldovinetti," 1938; "The Renaissance Painter's Garden," 1948. Contributor to: art magazines & bulletins. Lectures: Italian Renaissance Art. *Position*: L., Springfield Col., 1932-1936; L., Toledo Mus.

A., 1938-39; Prof. A., 1955- ; L., 1941- , Smith Col., Northampton, Mass.; Visiting L., Wellesley Col., 1954-55; Ed. Bd., Art Bulletin, 1954- .

KENNEDY, SYBIL—*Sculptor*
    15 Gramercy Park (3); h. 55 East 86th St., New York 28, N.Y.

B. Quebec, Canada, Aug. 13, 1899. *Studied*: Montreal A. Sch., and with Alexander Archipenko. *Member*: Sculptor's Soc. of Canada; NAWA; Audubon A.; N.Y. Soc. Women A.; Assoc., Royal Canadian Acad. (1953). *Awards*: Huntington prize, NAWA, 1941; Amelia Peabody prize, 1948. *Work*: Nat. Gal., Canada; Montreal Mus. FA. *Exhibited*: NAD, 1936, 1952; AIC, 1938; XIV Olympiad, London, 1948 (representing Canada); Maynard Walker Gal., 1938; Weyhe Gal., 1949 (both one-man); A. Gal. of Toronto, 1955.

KENNEDY, WILLIAM D.—*Painter, Et.*
    77 Nyack Ave., Lansdowne, Pa.

B. Havre de Grace, Md., Mar. 12, 1899. *Studied*: Temple Univ., and with Earl Horter. *Member*: Wallingford A. Center. *Awards*: prizes, Philadelphia Electric Co., 1955-1957. *Work*: Poor Richard Cl., Keneseth Israel, Phila. Inquirer, all Phila., Pa.

KENNON, ETHELYN M.—*Craftsman, T.*
    1028 North Clay Ave., Springfield 2, Mo.

B. Livonia, Mo., Dec. 9, 1902. *Studied*: Northeast Missouri State Col.; Southwest Missouri State Col., and with Raymond M. Kennon, Elsie Bates Freund, Munson Howe, F. G. Kieferndorf, and others. *Member*: Missouri Fed. A. & Crafts. *Exhibited*: Stephens Col., 1950-1952; People's A. Center, St. Louis, 1950-1952; Springfield A. Mus., 1952; Ozark Empire Dist. Fair, 1949-1952. *Position*: Instr., Elementary Schs., Springfield, Mo.*

KENNON, RAYMOND KENNETH—*Painter, C., Des.*
    1033½ St. Louis St.; h. 1028 North Clay Ave., Springfield, Mo.

B. Dunnegan, Mo., Feb. 28, 1903. *Awards*: prizes, Springfield (Mo.) A. Mus., 1936, 1939, 1940, 1941, 1943; Missouri State Fair, 1940. *Work*: Springfield A. Mus. *Exhibited*: Philbrook A. Center; CAM; William Rockhill Nelson Gal.; Little Rock A. Mus.; Kansas City AI; Ogunquit A. Center; Wichita A. Mus.; Joslyn A. Mus.; Fayetteville A. Center; Springfield A. Mus.; PAFA. *Position*: Founder, Instr., Ozark A. & Crafts Center, Springfield, Mo.*

KENT, ADALINE (Mrs. Robert B. Howard)—
Sculptor, P.
    523 Francisco St.; h. 2500 Leavenworth St., San Francisco 11, Cal.

B. Kentfield, Cal., Aug. 7, 1900. *Studied*: Vassar Col., A.B.; Cal. Sch. FA; Grande Chaumiere, Paris, France, and with Ralph Stackpole, Antoine Bourdelle. *Member*: San F. AA. *Awards*: prizes, SFMA, 1937; West Coast Ceramics, 1945, 1948; San F. A. Council, 1952; Lafayette sc. prize, 1955. *Work*: Stanford Univ.; Mills Col.; SFMA. *Exhibited*: WFNY 1939; San F. AA, 1935-1953; Cal. PLH, 1946, one-man, 1955; AIC, 1948; MMoA, 1951; Betty Parsons Gal., one-man: 1949, 1953; Am. Drawings, Paris, 1954; Sao Paulo, Brazil, 1955; Santa Barbara Mus. A., 1953 (one-man).*

KENT, FRANK WARD—*Painter, E., Gr., I.*
    45 Sandburg Drive, Sacramento 19, Cal.

B. Salt Lake City, Utah, Feb. 16, 1912. *Studied*: Univ. Utah; ASL; Syracuse Univ., B.F.A., M.F.A., and in Europe and Mexico. *Member*: AAUP; Assoc. A. of Syracuse; Utah A. Colony. *Awards*: prizes, Heyburn, Idaho, 1934; Univ. Utah, 1935; Syracuse Mus. FA, 1951; Rochester Mem. A. Gal., 1949. *Exhibited*: SFMA, 1934; Springville, Utah, 1934-1940; Univ. Utah, 1935-1939; All-Illinois, 1940-1942; Peoria A. Lg., 1940-1943; AIC, 1940-1942; Kansas City AI, 1940; Decatur, Ill., 1942; Syracuse Mus. FA, 1944-1955; Rochester Mem. A. Gal.; Utica, N.Y.; Pan-American Union, 1955; one-man: New Georgetown Gal., Wash., D.C., 1953; Mexican Embassy, Wash., D.C., 1954. *Position*: Prof. FA, Syracuse Univ.; Dir., Mexican Art Workshop, Taxco, Mexico, 1949-55; L., Positano A. Sch., Positano, Italy, 1956; Dir., E. B. Crocker Art Gallery, Sacramento, Cal., 1958- .

KENT, JACK (JOHN WELLINGTON)—Cartoonist
103 West Johnson St., San Antonio 4, Tex.

B. Burlington, Iowa, Mar. 10, 1920. *Member*: Nat. Cartoonists Soc. Author, I., "King Aroo," 1952. Creator, comic strip, "King Aroo," McClure Syndicate, translated into French and Swedish. *Work*: LC.

KENT, NORMAN—Engraver, P., W., L., Des.
24 West 40th St., New York 18, N.Y.; h. 437 Carroll Ave., Mamaroneck, N.Y.

B. Pittsburgh, Pa., Oct. 24, 1903. *Studied*: Rochester Inst. Tech.; ASL; and in Italy. *Member*: NA; Rochester Pr. Cl.; ASL; Prairie Pr. M.; Typophiles; A. Dir. Cl.; Century Assn.; Phila. WC Cl.; Audubon A.; AWS; SAGA. *Awards*: prizes, Univ. Rochester, 1929; Rochester Pr. Cl., 1935; Phila. Pr. Cl., 1941; LC, 1951 (purchase); AWS, 1954. *Work*: in more than 40 public collections, including: MMA; CMA; Syracuse Mus. FA; PMA; BMA; Rochester Mem. A. Gal.; Elmira Mus. A.; Milwaukee AI; Carnegie Inst.; Nat. Gal., Canada; LC; Rochester, Arlington, Haverhill and New York public libraries. *Exhibited*: nationally; one-man: Milwaukee AI; Albright A. Gal.; Rochester Mem. A. Gal.; Syracuse Mus. FA; New Britain A. Mus.; Woodmere A. Gal.; Racine, Wis.; Albany, N.Y.; and many others, in universities, colleges and libraries throughout U.S., 1927-1958, and in Rome, 1934, and Spain, 1953-54. Co-Editor (with Ernest Watson) "Watercolor Demonstrated," 1945; "The Relief Print," 1945; Author: "Drawings by American Artists," 1947; "The Book of Edward A. Wilson," 1948; "Water Color Methods," 1955; "Seascapes and Landscapes in Watercolor," 1956. Many reproductions with articles in major publications of woodcuts. Des. and illus., "The Genesee Country," and others. *Position*: Mng. Ed., American Artist Magazine, 1943-48; A. Dir., International Editions, Reader's Digest, 1948-51; A. Ed., True, 1952-55; Ed., American Artist Magazine, New York, N.Y., 1956- .

KENT, ROCKWELL—Engraver, Lith., P., I., W., L.
Au Sable Forks, N.Y.

B. Tarrytown Heights, N.Y., June 21, 1882. *Studied*: Columbia Univ.; & with William Chase, Robert Henri, Abbott Thayer. *Work*: MMA; AIC; BM; CGA; PMG, etc.; murals, USPO, Fed. Bldg., Wash., D.C.; room of House Committee on Interstate & Foreign Commerce, Wash., D.C. Author, I., "Wilderness," 1920; "Voyaging," 1924; "N By E," 1930; "Salamina," 1935; "This Is My Own," 1940; "It's Me, O Lord," 1955. I., "Candide," "Leaves of Grass," & other books. Lectures: "Art and Democracy."*

KENYON, NORMAN—Painter, I., Comm. A.
44 East 50th St., New York, N.Y.; h. Croton Lake Rd., Mt. Kisco, N.Y.

B. Holyoke, Mass., Jan. 7, 1901. *Studied*: PIASch. *Member*: SI; A. Gld.; Mystic AA; AWS. *Work*: Army Air Corps; U.S. Maritime Comm.; Wartime Shipping Administration. *Exhibited*: NAD; A. Dir. Cl.; Mystic AA; AWS. I., Cosmopolitan, Redbook, Colliers and other national magazines.*

KEPES, GYORGY—Painter, Des., E., W.
117 Walker St., Cambridge, Mass.

B. Selyp, Hungary, Oct. 4, 1906. *Studied*: Royal Acad. FA, Budapest. *Member*: F.; Am. Acad. A. & Sc. *Awards*: prizes, AIGA, 1944, 1949; A. Dir. Cl., Chicago, 1943; Univ. Illinois, 1954 (purchase). *Work*: Univ. Illinois; MMoDA; AGAA; Cranbrook Mus. A.; murals, Grad. Center, Harvard Univ.; Children's Lib., Fitchburg, Mass.; des., Arts of the United Nations, AIC, 1944; Am. Housing Exh., Paris, France, 1946. *Exhibited*: one-man: AIC, 1944; SFMA, 1952; San Diego FA Center, 1952; Royal Acad., Copenhagen, 1950; Stedelijk Mus., Amsterdam, Holland; Margaret Brown Gal., 1955; CM, 1954; Inst. Contemp. A., Boston, 1954; Mun. A. Center, Long Beach, Cal., 1954; SFMA, 1954; Syracuse Mus. FA, 1957; Mus. FA of Houston, 1958; DMFA, 1958, and in Rome, Milan, Ivrea, Firenze, Italy, 1958. Contributor to Graphis; Arts & Architecture; Cimaise; Art in America; Craft Horizon; Transformation; College Art Journal and other publications. Author: "Language of Vision," 1944; "The New Landscape," 1956. *Position*: Prof. Visual Des., Mass. Inst. Tech., 1946- .

KERCHEVILLE, CHRISTINA (Mrs.)—Painter, C., T.
1819 Roma Ave., Northeast, Albuquerque, N.M.

B. Altus, Ark., Aug. 14, 1906. *Studied*: Univ. South Dakota, B.A.; Univ. Wisconsin; Univ. New Mexico, and with Lynn Mitchell, Kenneth Adams, Lloyd Goff, Randall Davey, Frederic Taubes, Galvez Suares, Guatemala, and others. *Member*: A. Lg. of Albuquerque; Intl. Soc. A. & Lets.; San Felipe Galleries; Las Artistas. *Exhibited*: Nat. Lg. Am. Pen Women, 1952; Las Artistas, 1956-1958; Mus. New Mexico, Santa Fe; Roswell Mus. A.; Clovis A. Lg.; State Col., Las Cruces; State Fairs; galleries in Taos, Albuquerque; Mus. New Mexico traveling exh., 1954, and in 1955 annual; A. Lg. of Albuquerque; Guadalajara, Mexico, 1955, 1958 (one-man); Clovis A. Lg., 1954 (one-man); Sheldon Swope A. Gal., 1956, 1957; San Juan A. Lg., Farmington, N.M., 1957; New Mexico A. Lg., 1956-1958; Sandia Base Exh., Albuquerque, 1958, and others. Co-Dir., European Cultural Tours, sponsored by N.M. Edu. Assn. & N.M. Dept. of Edu.

**KERFOOT, MARGARET (Mrs. M. W. Jennison)—
    Educator, P.**
307 Standish Dr., Syracuse 3, N.Y.

B. Winona, Minn., July 4, 1901. *Studied*: Hamline Univ., A.B.; AIC; N.Y.Sch. FA, in Paris; Univ. Iowa, M.A., with Grant Wood. *Awards*: Carnegie scholarship, Harvard Univ., 1941. *Work*: Denver Pub. Sch. I., "Guide to Central City, Colorado," 1946. *Exhibited*: Syracuse Mus. FA, 1956, 1958; N.Y. State Fair, 1958. *Position*: Instr. A., 1937-39, Asst. Prof. A., 1939-45, Carlton Col.; Asst. Prof., Acting Chm., 1945-46, Allegheny Col., Meadville, Pa.; Asst. Prof., 1946-48, Hood Col., Frederick, Md.; Prof. A., Hd. Dept. A., Hamline Univ., St. Paul, Minn., 1948-52; L., Syracuse Univ., 1952.

KERMES, CONSTANTINE JOHN—Painter
981 Landis Valley Road, Lancaster, Pa.

B. Pittsburgh, Pa., Dec. 6, 1923. *Studied*: Carnegie Inst. Tech., B.F.A. *Work*: Everhart Mus., Scranton, Pa.; Shaker Heights Hist. Soc., Cleveland, Ohio; Shaker Mus., Old Chatham, N.Y.; 60 Paintings—Holy Cross Greek Orthodox Church, Pittsburgh, Pa. *Exhibited*: Jacques Seligmann Gal., N.Y., 1950, 1951, 1953, 1956; N.Y. State Mus., 1951; Notre Dame Univ., 1953; Des Moines A. Center, 1953; Roswell Mus., 1953; DMFA, 1953; Philbrook A. Center, Tulsa, 1953; Art:USA, 1958; A. & Crafts Center, Pittsburgh, 1954. Illus., "Shaker Cookbook," 1958.

KERNS, MAUDE IRVINE—Painter, Gr., E.
1059 Hilyard St., Eugene, Ore.

B. Portland, Ore., Aug. 1, 1876. *Studied*: Univ. Oregon, A.B.; Columbia Univ., B.S.; AIC; Cal. Sch. FA; Academie Moderne, Paris, and with Arthur Dow. *Member*: AAPL; Oregon Soc. A.; Cal. WC Cl.; Kansas City Pr. M.; Pen & Brush Cl.; NAWA. *Awards*: medal, Alaska-Yukon Expo., Seattle, Wash.; prize, Pen & Brush Cl., 1954. *Work*: Murray Oriental Mus., Eugene, Ore.; SAM; Portland A. Mus.; Solomon Guggenheim Mus. *Exhibited*: NGA; Guggenheim Mus., 1941-1952; Denver A. Mus.; Cal. WC Soc.; SAM, 1946 (one-man); Univ. Oregon; NAWA, 1955 (one-man); Pen & Brush Cl., 1954 (one-man); Wash., D.C., 1954; U.S. traveling exh., Amsterdam, Holland, 1955-56; Salon Realites Nouvelle, Paris, France, 1948-49; Albany, N.Y., 1954 and others abroad. *Position*: Assoc. Prof. A., Hd. A. Edu., Univ. Oregon, Eugene, Ore., 1921-41, Emeritus, 1947- .

KERR, JAMES WILFRID—Painter, L.
117 Dora Ave., Waldwick, N.J.

B. New York, N.Y., Aug. 7, 1897. *Studied*: N.Y. Sch. F. & App. A., with Howard Giles. *Member*: All. A. Am.; AEA; Am. Veterans Soc. A. (Pres. 1958-59); N.J. Soc. P. & S.; New Orleans AA; SC; Assoc. A. New Jersey. *Awards*: prizes, N.J. State Exh., Montclair, 1943; NAD, 1945; Plainfield AA, 1946; Irvington A. & Mus. Assn., 1948, 1949; Ridgewood AA, 1948, 1952; Am. Veteran's Soc. A., 1951, 1954, 1957. *Work*: Community Church, New York City; Fla. Southern Col.; Grand Central A. Gal.; Am. Legion Hall, Waldwick, N.J.; Midland Park (N.J.) Mun. Bldg.; Traphagen Sch., Waldwick, N.J. *Exhibited*: NAD, 1944, 1945; All. A. Am., 1944-1958; Am. Veteran's Soc. A., 1940-1958; VMFA, 1948; Ridgewood AA, 1940-1952; New Jersey P. & S., 1948-1955; Davenport Mus. A., 1948; Mus. FA of Houston, 1949;

Norfolk Mus. A., 1948; Audubon A., 1948, 1950; Delgado Mus. A., 1948, 1952; Irvington A. & Mus. Assn., 1948-1952; Carnegie Inst., 1949; SC, 1950-1952; Conn. Acad. FA, 1950; Newark Mus. A., 1951, 1952, 1958; Trenton, N.J., 1953; Art:USA, 1958. *Positions*: Treas., 1952-55, Bd. Dir., 1955-58, Jury of Selection, 1953, Jury Awards, 1955, 1958 of All. A. Am.; Exec. Com., Intl. Assn. Plastic Arts, 1953-58; Jury Selection, New Jersey P. & S., 1955; Bd. Dir., Assoc. A. of N.J., 1954; Nat. Mus. Com., AEA, 1954-58; Chm. Nat. Mus. Com., AEA, 1958 and Co-Chm. Joint Artists-Museums Com., 1958.

KERR, MRS. WILLIAM J. *See Deachman, Nelly*

KESKULLA, CAROLYN WINDELER—
Lithographer, P., T.
R.F.D. 1, Millington, N.J.

B. Farmingdale, N.J., Jan. 20, 1912. *Studied*: ASL; PIA Sch.; N.Y.Univ., B.S. in Edu. *Member*: Hunterdon County A. Center; Assoc. A. New Jersey. *Work*: in private colls. *Exhibited*: SFMA, 1942, 1943; Oklahoma Lithograph Exh., 1942; Phila. Pr. Cl., 1943; Texas FA Center, 1943; Lib. Cong., 1943; Newark Mus., 1940, 1941, 1949, 1951, 1955; Montclair A. Mus., 1939, 1940, 1946, 1950, 1954, 1955, 1956, 1957; CMA, 1942, 1943, 1945; Butler AI, 1943; Ohio Pr.M., 1941-1943; Parkersburg, W. Va., 1942-1945; Irvington Lib., 1946-1948; Newark A. Lib., 1951, 1954, 1957; Barbizon-Plaza, 1952; Princeton Pr. Cl., 1952; Farnsworth Mus., 1954, 1955, 1957; Ohio Pr. M., 1954, 1955. *Position*: Pres., Assoc. A. of New Jersey, 1957-58, Sec., 1952-57.

KESTER, LENARD—Painter, Des., Gr., I., T.
1117 North Genesee Ave., Los Angeles 46, Cal.

B. New York, N.Y., May 10, 1917. *Member*: ANA. *Awards*: prizes, Los A. Mus. A., 1943, 1955; Oakland A. Gal., 1943, 1944, 1951; Soc. Western A., 1950, 1956; NAD, 1951, 1956, gold medal, 1958; Cal. State Fair, 1951, 1957, 1958; Denver A. Mus., 1952; Tiffany Fnd. grant, 1949; Laguna Beach AA, 1957, 1958. *Work*: BM; Univ. Miami; Toledo Mus. A.; BMFA; Cal. State Fair Coll.; Denver A. Mus.; Mayo Clinic (mural). *Exhibited*: nationally, including CGA; AIC; NAD; Carnegie Inst.; Encyclopaedia Britannica, and others. One-man: de Young Mem. Mus., 1946; Vigeveno Gal., Los A., 1946, 1948, 1952; Midtown Gal., 1947, 1948; Phila. A. All., 1948; Santa Barbara Mus. A., 1952; Gump's, San F., 1952; San Diego FA Gal., 1953; Nelson Gal. A., Kansas City, 1953; Assoc. Am. A., 1953; Pasadena A. Mus., 1958; Frye Mus. A., Seattle, 1958.

KETCHAM, HENRY KING (HANK)—Cartoonist
Carmel Valley, Cal.

B. Seattle, Wash., Mar. 14, 1920. *Studied*: Univ. Washington. *Member*: Nat. Cartoonists' Soc. *Awards*: Billy De Beck award: Cartoonist of the Year, 1952; Boys' Clubs of Am. Certif. for best comic magazine, 1956. *Work*: Albert T. Reid Coll.; William Allen White Fnd., Univ. Kansas; Achenbach Fnd. for Graphic Arts. Cal. PLH. Author, Illus., "Dennis the Menace," 1952; "More Dennis the Menace," 1953; "Baby Sitter's Guide" (with Bob Harmon), 1954; "Wanted: Dennis the Menace," 1956; "Dennis the Menace: Household Hurricane," 1957; "Dennis the Menace vs. Everybody," 1955; "In This Corner: Dennis the Menace," 1958; "Dennis the Menace Rides Again," 1955. (Dennis the Menace appears in over 600 daily and Sunday newspapers in U.S. and in 42 foreign countries in 14 languages). Contributor cartoons to: San Francisco Chronicle; Wash. Post & Times-Herald; Chicago Tribune; Atlanta Journal & Constitution; Baltimore Sun; Phila. Bulletin; Spokane Spokesman-Review; Omaha World Herald, and many others.

KEVE, FLORENCE—Educator, P., C.
Evansville College; h. 1905 B East Gum St., Evansville, Ind.

B. Arlington, Iowa, June 22, 1906. *Studied*: Cornell Col., Mt. Vernon, Iowa, B.A.; Columbia Univ., M.A.; summers, AIC; Cal. Col. A. & Crafts; Univ. Iowa, and in Mexico. *Member*: Hoosier Craft Gld. (Fndr.); Midwest Col. A. Assn.; Indiana A. Educators. *Exhibited*: Tri-State Exh., Evansville; Evansville Col.; Kappa Pi regional; Cornell Col. Contributor article to Illinois Teacher. Lectures with slides on art and architecture to women's clubs, classes, faculty and church groups. *Positions*: Instr., Danville (Ill.) H.S., 1929-39; A. Supv., Whiting (Ind.) Pub. Schs., 1939-45; Instr., College of Idaho, Caldwell, Idaho, 1947-48; Prof. A., Hd. A. Dept., Evansville College, 1948- .

KEY, TED—Cartoonist, W.
Box 735, Gulph Road, Wayne, Pa.

B. Fresno, Cal., Aug. 25, 1912. *Studied*: Univ. California at Berkeley, A.B. *Member*: Nat. Cartoonists Soc.; The Players. *Work*: Drama, "The Clinic," selected for anthology "Best Broadcasts of 1939-40," written for NBC. Author, I., "Hazel," 1946; "Here's Hazel," 1949; "Many Happy Returns," 1951; "If You Like Hazel," 1952; "Hazel Rides Again," 1955; Author: "So'm I," 1954; "Fasten Your Seat Belts," 1956; "Phyllis," 1957; "All Hazel," 1958. Work appears in many anthologies. Contributor to: Sat. Eve. Post; This Week; Colliers; Look; American; Ladies Home Journal; Sports Illustrated, and other leading national magazines.

KEYES, BERNARD M.—Portrait Painter
Fenway Studios, 30 Ipswich St., Boston, Mass.; h. 411 Main St., Waltham 54, Mass.; s. Echo Lodge, Peterborough, N.H.

B. Boston, Mass., Aug. 27, 1898. *Studied*: BMFA Sch.; FMA. *Member*: ANA; Gld. Boston A.; Provincetown AA. *Awards*: Paige traveling scholarship, 1921-22; prizes, CGA, 1937; NAD, 1938. *Work*: Harvard Univ.; Brown Univ.; Tufts Col.; Mt. Holyoke Col.; Holyoke (Mass.) Pub. Lib.; Newton-Andover Theological Col.; Gordan Col.; Leslie Col., Cambridge, Mass.; Boston City Hospital; Mass. General Hospital; Nat. Shawmut Bank; Newton Nat. Bank; Quincy Savings Bank; Masonic Bldg., Boston; John Hancock Ins. Co., Boston; Cunningham Mem., Quincy, Mass.; Newton Pub. Lib.

KEYES, EMILY (Mrs. Frederick W. Evans)—
Writer, Cr.
3500 Washington Rd., West Palm Beach, Fla.

B. Quincy, Fla. *Studied*: Agnes Scott Col., B.A. *Position*: Feature Ed., Palm Beach Daily News, Palm Beach Life; Palm Beach Correspondent, Social Spectator, Palm Beach and New York. (Feature Ed. includes art activities).*

KEY-OBERG, ELLEN BURKE—Sculptor, T.
425 West 21st St., New York 11, N.Y.

B. Marion, Ala., Apr. 11, 1905. *Studied*: CUASch. *Member*: Audubon A.; AEA; S. Gld.; NAWA; Arch. Lg.; N.Y. Soc. Ceramic A. *Awards*: prizes, Audubon A., 1944; NAWA, 1949. *Work*: Univ. Wisconsin. *Exhibited*: MMA, 1942; PAFA, 1942; All. A. Am., 1941; NAD, 1943; Audubon A., 1943; New York Soc. Women A., annually; S. Gld., 1951, 1952; Phila. A. All., 1951; Syracuse Mus. FA, annually; AFA traveling exh., 1951-52; WMAA; Smithsonian Inst. *Position*: Instr., S., Chapin Sch., N.Y.; South Shore Arts Workshop; Newark Mus. Arts Workshop.

KEY-OBERG, ROLF—Ceramist, T.
59 East 3rd St., New York 3, N.Y.

B. Sweden, June 20, 1900. *Studied*: in Sweden. *Member*: N.Y. Soc. Ceramic A. *Work*: MModA; Boston Inst. Contemp. A.; R.I. Sch. Des.; Newark Mus. A.; Cooper Union Mus.; wall, Socony Mobile Oil Co. *Exhibited*: Syracuse Mus. FA, annually; "Design for Use—U.S.A." traveling exh. to Europe, MModA; regularly in ceramic exhs., 1941- . Contributor to Craft Horizons. *Position*: Instr. Ceramics, Newark Museum Arts Workshop at present.*

KEYSER, ROBERT—Painter
R.D., Frenchtown, N.J.; h. 1109 Lexington Ave., New York 21, N.Y.

B. Philadelphia, Pa., July 27, 1924. *Studied*: Univ. Pennsylvania, and with Fernand Leger in Paris, France. *Work*: Munson-Williams-Proctor Inst.; Olsen Fnd., Guilford, Conn. *Exhibited*: PAFA, 1951; WMAA, 1956; Yale Univ., 1958; 6 One-man: Paris, Philadelphia, New York City and Washington.

KHOURI, ALFRED—*Painter, L., T.*

M. Grumbacher, Inc., 460 West 34th St., New York 1, N.Y.; h. 4121 7th Ave., Brooklyn 32, N.Y.

B. New York, N.Y., Feb. 27, 1915. *Studied*: ASL; NAD; PIASch.; with Andre Lhote, Paris and with Jerry Farnsworth. *Member*: P. & S. Soc. of New Jersey; Tidewater A. *Awards*: Tiffany Fnd. Scholarship, 1937; George Roper purchase award, 1957. *Work*: Norfolk Mus. A.; Seton Hall Univ., Newark, N.J.; Virginia Beach H.S., Va. *Exhibited*: AWS, 1955, 1958; All. A. Am., 1957, 1958; Norfolk Mus. A., 1957, 1958; P. & S. Soc. of New Jersey, 1957, 1958; Gibbes A. Gal., Charleston, S.C., 1957; Irene Leach Mem. Mus., 1954, 1956; VMFA, 1955; one-man: Norfolk Mus. A.; 1957. *Position*: Color Consultant, M. Grumbacher, Inc., New York, N.Y., 1957- .

KIDD, STEVEN R.—*Painter, I., W.*

33 Orchard Lane, Elmsford, N.Y.

B. Chicago, Ill., June 27, 1911. *Studied*: AIC; ASL, and with Harvey Dunn. *Member*: SI. *Work*: Hist. Properties Section, Pentagon, Wash., D.C.; murals, Daily News, N.Y. Illus. to: Daily News; Cosmopolitan; Redbook; Liberty; Argosy; Sports; Saga; Life magazines. Lectures: History of Art. *Position*: I., Daily News, New York, N.Y., 1932- .

KIDDER, ALFRED—*Assistant Museum Director*

University of Pennsylvania Museum, 33rd & Spruce St., Philadelphia 4, Pa.

Position: Assistant Director, Univ. Pennsylvania Museum.*

KIENBUSCH, WILLIAM AUSTIN—*Painter, S.*

c/o Kraushaar Gallery, 1055 Madison Ave.; h. 44 Greenwich Ave., New York 11, N.Y.

B. New York, N.Y., Apr. 13, 1914. *Studied*: Princeton Univ., B.A. *Member*: AEA. *Awards*: prizes, MMA, 1952; BM, 1952. *Work*: MMoDA; WMAA; Toledo Mus. A.; Wichita A. Mus.; New Britain Inst.; Ft. Worth AA; Univ. Nebraska; Univ. Michigan; MMA; Munson-Williams-Proctor Inst.; Univ. Delaware; VMFA; Newark Mus. A.; Univ. Minnesota; Mus. FA of Houston; Nelson Gal. A. *Exhibited*: BM, 1953, 1955; VMFA, 1954; Walker A. Center, 1953; Carnegie Inst., 1955 (retrospective 1954); WMAA, 1955, and others. *Position*: Instr., Brooklyn Mus. Sch. A., 1948- .

KIENZLE, GEORGE VINCENT—*Commercial Artist*

1501 Broadway, New York, N.Y.; h. 700 Ocean Ave., Brooklyn 26, N.Y.

B. New York, N.Y., Dec. 12, 1904 *Studied*: ASL; Grand Central Sch. A., and with George Bridgman, Thomas Benton, Erich Pape, and others. *Member*: Brooklyn Soc. A.; Am. Newspaper Gld. *Exhibited*: Riverside Mus., 1951; Contemporary A., 1950; BM, 1953. Contributes illus. to Paramount Pictures and prominent agencies.

KIESLER, FREDERICK JOHN—*Architect, S., P., Des.*

432 Fourth Ave.; h. 56 Seventh Ave., New York 11, N.Y.

B. Vienna, Austria, Sept. 22, 1896. *Studied*: Technische Hochschule, Vienna, M.A.; Acad. FA, Vienna. *Work*: interior des., furniture construction, scenic design, Juilliard Sch. Music, Metropolitan Opera Co., opera des., Juilliard Sch., 1956. *Exhibited*: MMoDA, 1952; Sidney Janis Gal., 1954. Author: series of articles for Architectural Record; Architectural Forum, Art News, L'Architecture D'Aujourd'hui, Paris, etc. *Position*: Scenic Dir., Juilliard Sch. Music, New York, N.Y., 1934-56; Dir., Arch. Lab., Columbia Univ., 1936-42; Architect, Peggy Guggenheim and World House Gals., N.Y., 1940, 1957, respectively.

KILEY, ROBERT L.—*Painter, Gr., E.*

Art Department, University of Connecticut, Storrs, Conn.

B. Fall River, Mass., Dec. 7, 1924. *Studied*: Cleveland Sch. A.; Univ. New Mexico; Univ. Michigan, B.S., M.S. *Member*: National Ser. Soc. *Work*: William Rockhill Nelson Gal. A.; VMFA; Wisconsin Union; Mus. of New Mexico, Santa Fe; MMA, and others. *Exhibited*: nationally. Also, Serigraphes Americaine, France, 1955; Bordighera, Italy, 1956; 20th Century Am. Graphic Arts traveling exh., 1956-1958; and others. One-man: Serigraph Gal., N.Y.,

1948, 1950; Meltzer Gal., N.Y., 1955, 1958. *Position*: Prof. A., Dept. Art, Univ. Connecticut, Storrs, Conn. at present.

KILGORE, RUPERT—*Educator*

Illinois Wesleyan University, Bloomington, Ill.
Position: Dir., School of Art, Illinois Wesleyan Univ., Bloomington, Ill.*

KILIAN, AUSTIN FARLAND—*Educator, P., Des., L.*

Baylor University; h. 4017 North 27th St., Waco, Tex.

B. Minnehaha County, S.D., Sept. 19, 1920. *Studied*: Augustana Col., B.A., with Palmer Eide; South Dakota State Col.; State Univ. Iowa, M.F.A., with James Lechay, Stuart Edie, Mauricio Lasansky, Humbert Albrizio; Mexico City Col., with Jose Gutierrez; Acad. Montmartre, Paris, with Fernand Leger; Ohio State Univ., with James Grimes; Baylor Univ. *Member*: AAUP; CAA; Am. Studies Assn.; Texas FA Assn.; Dallas AA; Waco A. Forum; Sarasota AA; Birmingham AA; European Assn. for Am. Studies; New Orleans AA; Texas WC Soc. *Awards*: prizes, Texas FA Assn., 1954; D. D. Feldman Coll. Contemp. Texas A., 1955; Waco A. Forum, 1957; citation, Texas FA Assn., 1958. *Exhibited*: Terry AI, 1952; New Orleans AA, 1952, 1953, 1954, membership show, 1953, 1955, 1956; Cedar City, Utah, 1957; Texas FA Assn., 1953-1958; Texas Fed. Women's Cl., 1954 (2-man); State Univ. Iowa, 1949; Contemp. Texas A., 1955, 1958; Ohio State Univ., 1954; Waco A. Forum, 1957, 1958; Baylor Theatre, 1955 (one-man); Stephen F. Austin Col., 1957 (one-man); State Exh., Austin, Tex., 1958. Lectures: Design; Aesthetics; Art History and Modern Art. *Positions*: Instr., Photography, Univ. Idaho, 1949-50; Instr., Painting, A. Hist., Dillard Univ., New Orleans, 1950-53; Asst. Prof., Design, A. Hist., Baylor University, Waco, Tex., 1953- .

KILLAM, WALT—*Painter, Gr., T., C.*

Old Pound Rd., Westerly, R.I.

B. Providence, R.I., June 18, 1907. *Studied*: R.I.Sch. Des. *Member*: Mystic AA; Essex AA; Norwich AA. *Awards*: prizes, Norwich AA, 1951-1953; Silvermine Gld. A., 1954; Hartford, Conn., 1934; Essex AA, 1956. *Work*: Millbrook Sch.; Lyman Allyn Mus. A.; South County AA, and in private colls. *Exhibited*: Nationally and internationally; 1956-58: Boston A. Festival, 1956; Mystic AA, 1956-1958; Silvermine Gld. A., 1956, 1957; Essex AA, 1956-1958; Norwich AA, 1956-1958; de Cordova & Dana Mus., 1958; New Haven Lib., 1957, 1958; Lyman Allyn Mus., 1958. one-man: Contemp. A., 1951, 1952; Conn. Col., New London, 1955; Lyman Allyn Mus. A., 1943, 1953; Providence, R.I., 1948, 1951, 1957; Detroit Inst. A.; Kingston AA, 1957; Wesleyan Univ., 1958. *Position*: Pres., Mystic AA, 1955-56.

KILPATRICK, MARY (GRACE)—*Painter, W.*

100 West University Parkway, Baltimore 10, Md.

B. Baltimore, Md., Jan. 28, 1879. *Studied*: Bryn Mawr Col., A.B.; Maryland Inst.; & with Charles Woodbury, Bernard Karfiol. *Member*: AAPL; Balt. WC Cl.; Ogunquit AA; Mun. A. Soc., Balt.; Md. *Exhibited*: BMA, 1939, 1940, 1941, 1951, 1952, 1953-1955; Mt. Vernon A. Cl., 1951, 1952, 1953, 1955; Ogunquit A. Center, 1940-1945; Maryland Inst.

KIMAK, GEORGE—*Painter, Gr., T., L.*

Minoa Grade & High School, Minoa, N.Y.; h. 840 James St., Syracuse, N.Y.

B. Auburn, N.Y., May 14, 1921. *Studied*: AIC; Syracuse Univ., B.F.A. *Member*: N.Y. State A. T. Assn.; N.Y. State T. Assn.; AAMus. *Awards*: 4 year Scholarship, Syracuse Univ., 1942. *Exhibited*: Cayuga Mus. Hist. & A., 1939-1941; Syracuse Mus. FA, 1953-1955; Munson-Williams-Proctor Inst., 1956; Rochester Mem. A. Gal., 1956; Emily Lowe A. Gal., Syracuse Univ., 1956; Art:USA, 1958. Contributed articles on "Museum-on-Wheels" services for schools and communities to many newspapers and educational bulletins, 1952-1958. Arranged exhs.: Mestrovic Drawings for Univ. New Mexico, 1951; Print Show for State Teachers Col., New Paltz, N.Y., 1951; Exchange Exhibition with Cornell Univ., 1951; Contemporary Student Paintings for Addison Gal. Am. Art, 1951; Contemporary Student Exhibition for Wells College, Aurora, N.Y., 1952; Print Exhibition for Binghamton H.S., 1952. *Positions*: Instr. A., in many New York State grade and high schools;

Gal. Asst., Cayuga Mus. Hist. & A., 1936-40; Gal. Asst., Emily Lowe A. Center, Syracuse Univ., 1949-52; Exh. Des., N.Y. State Fair, 1952-55; Dir., 1947-54, Exec. Vice-Pres., 1954-58, Artmobile, Inc.

KIMBALL, YEFFE—Painter, Des., I., W.
11 Bank St., New York 14, N.Y.

B. Oklahoma, Mar. 30, 1914. *Studied*: ASL, with William McNulty, George Bridgman, Jon Corbino; East Central Col.; Univ. Oklahoma. *Member*: ASL; Nat. Congress Am. Indians; AEA; Arrow, Inc.; Oklahoma AA. *Work*: Portland (Ore.) A. Mus.; Encyclopaedia Britannica; Chrysler A. Mus., and in many private colls. *Exhibited*: 1942-1958: NAD; WMAA; Carnegie Inst.; Telfair Acad. A. & Sc., Savannah; Mint Mus. A.; Encyclopaedia Britannica; San Diego FA Center; VMFA; Randolph-Macon Col.; Savannah A. Mus.; Norton Gal. A.; Clearwater A. Center; Delgado Mus. A.; Am. Indian Exh., Philbrook A. Center, Tulsa; Univ. Georgia; Rollins Col.; Wesleyan Sch. FA, Macon; High Mus. A.; William Rockhill Nelson Gal. A.; Mattatuck Hist. Soc., Conn.; La Jolla AA; Birmingham A. Mus.; Toledo Mus. A.; Montclair A. Mus.; PAFA; deYoung Mem. Mus.; James Graham Gal., N.Y.; Rehn Gal.; Art:USA, 1958; Provincetown A. Festival; Chrysler A. Mus. one-man: Rehn Gal., 1946, 1949, 1952; Denver A. Mus., 1947; Pasadena AI, 1947; Crocker Gal. A., Sacramento, 1947; Davenport Mun. Gal., 1947; Joslyn Mem. Mus., 1947; Wichita AA, 1947; Delgado Mus. A., 1947; Philbrook A. Center, 1948; Mus. New Mexico, Santa Fe, 1948, 1957; Univ. New Mexico, 1948, 1957; Galerie Gireaux, Brussels, 1948; Portland (Ore.) A. Mus., 1949; State Col. of Washington, 1950; FA Gal., San Diego, 1950; Santa Barbara Mus. A., 1950; Rochester A. Center, Minn., 1951; Golden Jubilee Exh., Okla. City, 1957; Gallery 313, Wash., D.C., 1957; Dayton AI, 1958, and many others. *Position*: Member, Nat. Cong. Am. Indians; Bd. Control, ASL, New York, N.Y.; Consultant on native arts, Portland (Ore.) A. Mus., and Chrysler Mus. A., Provincetown, Mass.; trustee, Arrrow, Inc.; Advisor, Indian Art, U.S. State Dept.

KIMBERLY, CARA DRAPER—Painter
1316 New Hampshire Ave., Northwest, Washington 6, D.C.

B. St. Louis, Mo., July 19, 1876. *Studied*: Washington Univ.; BMFA; AIC; Chicago A. Acad.; & with Hawthorne, Vanderpoel, Messer, Farnsworth. *Member*: Wash. A. Lg.; Soc. Wash. A.; Wash. WC Cl.; Wash. A.C. *Award*: prize, Soc. Wash. A. *Work*: interiors, White House, Arlington House, Dumbarton House, Mt. Vernon. *Exhibited*: AIC; BMFA; Boston WC Cl.; CGA; PMG; Soc. Wash. A.; Wash. WC Cl.; CAM.*

KIMBROUGH, VERMAN—Educator
Ringling School of Art; h. 225 Wisteria St., Sarasota, Fla.

B. Rockford, Ala., Apr. 6, 1902. *Studied*: Birmingham-Southern Col., A.B.; Univ. Florida, and in France, Italy. *Position*: Pres., Ringling Sch. A., Sarasota, Fla., 1931- .

KIMMEY, ZARA B. (Mrs.)—Educator
4 Windsor Terrace, White Plains, N.Y.

B. Wilmington, Del., July 23, 1880. *Studied*: T. Training Col., Corinth, N.Y.; State T. Col., Albany, N.Y., B.Pd.; T. Col., Columbia Univ.; ASL; N.Y.Univ.; Rutgers Univ. *Member*: Eastern AA. Contributor to: State Teachers magazine. Organized N.Y. State A. T. Assn. (life memb.). *Position*: State Regents Examiner in A. & Mechanical Drawing, 1910-23; New York State Supv. Drawing, 1923-50 (Retired).

KIMURA, SUEKO M. (Mrs.)—Painter, E., Des., I., Eng.
2567-B Henry St., Honolulu 16, Hawaii

B. Hawaii, June 10, 1912. *Studied*: Univ. Hawaii, B.A.; Chouinard AI, Los A., with Rico Lebrun; Columbia Univ., with Dong Kingman; BMSch. A., with Arthur Osver; ASL, with Kuniyoshi. *Member*: Hawaii P. & S. Lg.; Honolulu Pr. M. *Awards*: prizes, Honolulu Acad. A., 1955-1957. *Work*: Honolulu Acad. A.; fresco mural, Univ. Hawaii Chemistry Bldg. *Exhibited*: Long Island, N.Y., 1956; Honolulu Acad. A., 1952-1957. Lectures: Communication in Magazine Layout.

KIMURA, WILLIAM—Painter
1025 11th Ave., Anchorage, Alaska

Exhibited: nationally in U.S. Currently in traveling exh., Smithsonian Inst.

KING, CLINTON (BLAIR)—Painter
Guadalupe No. 13, Taxco, Guerrero, Mexico; h. 1235 Astor St., Chicago, Ill.

B. Ft. Worth, Tex., Oct. 3, 1901. *Studied*: Princeton Univ. *Awards*: prizes, AIC. *Work*: Mus. New Mexico, Santa Fe; Ft. Worth A. Mus.; Petit Palais, Paris, France. *Exhibited*: AIC, 1929, 1942-1946; NAD, 1945; PAFA, 1932, 1944; CGA, 1941; Toledo Mus. A., 1929; Springfield Mus. A., 1944, 1945; Carnegie Inst., 1946; Paris, France, 1950, 1959; London, England, 1959. Casa Blanca, 1953; Lisbon, Portugal, 1953.

KING, EDWARD S.—Museum Director, E.
5403 St. Albans Way, Baltimore 12, Md.

B. Baltimore, Md., Jan. 27, 1900. *Studied*: Johns Hopkins Univ.; Princeton Univ., A.B., M.F.A.; Harvard Univ. *Member*: AAMus.; Assn. A. Mus. Dir. Contributor to: Art Builetin; Journal of the Walters Art Gallery. Lectures: Art History. *Position*: Assoc. Cur., Paintings & Far Eastern A., 1934-41, Cur., 1941- , Acting Administrator, 1945-46, Administrator, 1946-51, Dir., Walters A. Gal., Baltimore, Md.

**KING, ELEANOR (Mrs. Eleanor King Salley Hookham)
—Painter, W., L., T., Cr.**
289 Adelia St., Elmhurst, Ill.; Pensacola, Fla.

B. Marlow, Okla., Apr. 5, 1909. *Studied*: Oklahoma City Col. *Member*: Pensacola AC; Gulf Coast AA; Fla. Fed. A.; Elmhurst A. Gld.; Tallahassee AC; SSAL; All-Illinois A. Cl. *Awards*: prizes, Elmhurst A. Gld., 1952-1954; Gulf Coast AA, 1929; Pensacola AC, 1928. *Work*: Tallahassee Woman's Cl.; Pensacola AC; Capitol City Bank, Tallahassee, Fla.; Elmhurst Col.; Florida Capitol Bldg.; Senate Chamber, Supreme Court of Fla.; murals, Pensacola Beach Corp.; C.P.O. Cl., Naval Air Station, Pensacola, Fla. *Exhibited*: West Palm Beach A. Center, 1935; Montross Gal., 1939 (one-man), 1940, 1941 (one-man), 1942; Gulf Coast AA, 1929; SSAL, 1934; Fed. A. Gal., Pensacola, 1940 (one-man); Milton A. Center, 1940; Woman's Cl., Pensacola, Fla., 1946; Pensacola AC, 1946; Stevens Hotel, Chicago; All-Illinois A. Cl., 1950; Elmhurst A. Gld., 1951, 1952 (one-man); Bican Book Store, 1955 (one-man). I., "Old Pensacola Landmarks," 1932. *Position*: Pres. Elmhurst A. Gld.; Chm. Bldg. Fund, A. Gld., 1955.*

KING, FRANK O.—Cartoonist
c/o Chicago Tribune-New York News Syndicate, New York, N.Y.; h. Pine Tree Road, Winter Park, Fla.

B. Cashton, Wis., Apr. 9, 1883. *Studied*: Chicago Acad. FA; AIC. *Member*: SI; Nat. Cartoonists Soc. *Awards*: two medals, Freedom Fnd. *Exhibited*: deYoung Mus. A., San F.; Illinois State Mus., Springfield. Author, I., four "Skeezix" books, Chicago Tribune-New York Syndicate. *Position*: Staff A., Cart., Minneapolis Times, 1901-05, Chicago Examiner, 1906-09, Chicago Tribune, 1909-19; Author, I., "Gasoline Alley" since 1919, for Chicago Tribune-N.Y. News Syndicate, Inc.*

KING, MRS. HARRY—Craftsman, Des.
255 North 8th St., Batesville, Ark.

B. Powhatan, Ark., Sept. 20, 1895. *Studied*: Arkansas Col.; CM Sch. A.; Newcomb Col., Tulane Univ. *Exhibited*: Eastern States Exp., 1940; Memphis Mus. A.; Ridgefield House, Chicago, 1941, 1946; Woman's City Cl., Ft. Worth, Tex., 1942; Philbrook A. Center, 1940; Woman's City Cl., Little Rock, Ark.; Brooks Mem. A. Gal.; Dallas, Tex.; Nat. A. Week, Little Rock; Atlanta, Ga.; Quincy, Ill.; Tulsa, Okla.; Springfield, Ill.; New Orleans, La. Work featured in Life, 1940, Nat. Geographic, 1946; McCall's, 1941, & La Revue des Fermieres magazine, 1942. Lectures: The Art & History of Hooked Rugs. Author: "How to Hook Rugs," 1948. Des., Hooked Rug Patterns; Instr., Rug Hooking.

KING, HELEN A. (HATTORF)—*Painter, C., T.*

4313 Stuart Ave., Richmond 21, Va.

B. Huntington, Ind., Feb. 12, 1900. *Studied*: DePauw Univ.; Northwestern Univ., B.A.; AIC; ASL; T. Col.; Columbia Univ., M.A. *Member*: NAWA; P. & S. Soc.; Richmond AA. *Awards*: prizes, Hoosier Salon, 1930, 1932. *Work*: Huntington (Ind.) Pub. Lib. *Exhibited*: AIC, 1929, 1930, 1934, 1938; PAFA, 1931, 1932, 1938; CGA, 1930, 1937; VMFA, 1937-1951, 1957; Valentine Mus., 1949, 1952, 1954, 1956, 1958.

KING, HORACE—*Educator, Des., P., L.*

Department of Art, Denison University; h. 209 West Broadway, Granville, Ohio

B. Pittsfield, Ohio, April 27, 1906. *Studied*: Ohio State Univ., A.B., A.M.; Illinois Inst. Tech., and with Felix Payant, James R. Hopkins, Ralph Fanning, H.G.Spencer. *Member*: Am. Assn. Univ. Prof.; CAA; Midwest A. Conference; Ohio Valley Regional A. Conference. *Awards*: prize, Hess award, glassware des., Nat. Glass and China exh., Waldorf-Astoria Hotel, 1954. *Work*: mural, Admin. Bldg., E. T. Rugg Co., Newark, Ohio; glass & china exh. rooms, A.H.Heisey & Co.; Santa Fe Bldg., Dallas, Tex.; paintings, Doane Lib., Denison Univ.; St. Luke's Church, Granville, Ohio; Zanesville AI, and in private colls. Lectures: "Local Greek Revival Houses in Metropolitan Collection," and on contemporary architecture and industrial design. *Position*: Chm. Dept., Prof. A., Denison Univ., Granville, Ohio.*

KING, JANE SPEAR—*Painter*

202 East 73rd St., New York 21, N.Y.

B. La Grange, Ill., Mar. 24, 1906. *Studied*: AIC. *Work*: Ryerson Coll., Chicago; Chicago Hist. Soc. *Exhibited*: AIC, 1929, 1935, 1936. Cartoons for Collier's, Sat. Eve. Post, Look Magazine.

KING, JOSEPH WALLACE—*Painter*

Reynolda Estate; h. 1201 Arbor Road, Winston-Salem, N.C.

B. Spencer, Va., May 11, 1912. *Studied*: Corcoran Sch. A., and in Italy and France. *Member*: Lotos Cl., N.Y.; Am. Intl. Acad., N.Y.; Intl. FA Council, Paris, France. *Work*: Wake Forest Col.; Lincoln Mus., Wash., D.C.; Va. Military Inst.; Governor's Mansion, Raleigh, N.C.; Lotos Cl., N.Y., and in private collections. Mural, Community Center Bldg., Winston-Salem, N.C. *Exhibited*: CGA, 1938; Paris, France, 1957; Fra Angelico Salon, Rome, 1957; Royal Soc. British A. Exh., London, 1959; one-man: Bernheim-Jeune, Dauberville, Paris, 1958.

KING, JOHN M.—*Portrait Painter, T.*

215 Kenwood Ave., Dayton 5, Ohio

B. Richmond, Ind., July 1, 1897. *Studied*: Cincinnati A. Acad; Earlham Col. *Member*: Dayton Soc. P. & S.; Men's A. Cl., Cincinnati. *Awards*: Margaret Ball Petty prize, Chicago, 1926, 1927; Buckingham prize, 1928; Buffington prize, 1929; Indiana AA, 1936; Winterlich prize, Dayton, 1952; gold medal, PAFA, 1954. *Work*: Purdue Univ.; Phi Kappa Tau Hqtrs., Oxford, Ohio; McGuire Hall, Richmond, Ind.; Procter & Gamble, Cincinnati, Ohio; John H. Patterson H.S., Federal Court, Miami Valley Hospital, Gem City Bldg. & Loan, Rubicon House, Dayton AI, Dayton Univ., all of Dayton, Ohio; portraits in private collections. *Position*: Hd. Dept. drawing & painting, Dayton AI, 1927-59; Visiting Instr., Univ. Cincinnati, 1927-28; John Herron AI, 1935-36; Earlham Col., 1933-34; Miami Univ., 1932-33.

KING, ROY E.—*Sculptor*

2443 Pacific Heights Rd., Honolulu, Hawaii

B. Richmond, Va., Nov. 22, 1903. *Studied*: Univ. Richmond; BAID; & with Bridgman, Lawrie, Jennewein. *Member*: NSS. *Work*: S., busts, figures, panels, Col. City of N.Y.; USPO, Bloomsburg, Pa.; U.S. Military Acad., West Point, N.Y.; Honolulu, Hilo, Schofield, St. Andrew's Cathedral, all in Hawaii.*

KING, MRS. WILLIAM C. See Peacock, Jean Eleanor

KING, WILLIAM DICKEY—*Sculptor*

78 East 10th St.; h. 68 East 12th St., New York 3, N.Y.

B. Jacksonville, Fla., Feb. 25, 1925. *Studied*: Univ. Florida; CUASch.; and in Rome, Italy. *Awards*: Fulbright F., 1949; prizes, CUASch., 1948; BM, 1949; Margaret Tiffany Blake fresco award, 1951; Henry Street Settlement mural comp., 1958. *Work*: AGAA; SS "United States." *Exhibited*: PMA, 1949; WMAA, 1950, 1951, 1953-57; MModA, 1951; AGAA, 1951, 1958; Carnegie Inst., 1958; Downtown Gal., N.Y.; 1952; Alan Gal., N.Y., 1952, 1958 (one-man); Univ. Illinois, 1954, 1956; BM, 1949, 1950, 1954, 1955, 1957, 1958; Cooper Union Mus., 1949, and others. *Position*: Instr. S., BMSch.A., 1953- .

KINGHAN, CHARLES R.—*Painter, Comm., I., T.*

2 Division St.; h. 7 Lomond Place, New Rochelle, N.Y.

B. Anthony, Kans., Jan. 18, 1895. *Studied*: Chicago Acad. FA; Am. Acad. A., Chicago; AIC, and with Carl Scheffler, J. Wellington Reynolds, H. A. Oberteuffer, and others. *Member*: ANA; AWS; SC; Phila. WC Cl.; Hudson Valley AA; New Rochelle AA; All. A. Am. *Awards*: prizes, Hudson Valley AA, 1951; New Rochelle AA, 1945, 1946, 1948; Larchmont Women's Cl., 1948; New Rochelle Woman's Cl., 1951, 1953; SC, 1953, 1957; Westchester Woman's Cl., 1954; AWS, 1954, 1957; gold medal, All-Illinois Soc. A., 1933. *Work*: mural, New Rochelle YMCA. *Exhibited*: AWS, 1949-1956; All A. Am. 1949-1956; AIC, traveling exh., 1933; Frye Mus. A., Seattle, Wash., 1955. Author, I., "Rendering Techniques," 1956. Contributor to American Artist magazine.

KINGMAN, DONG—*Painter, T.*

21 West 58th St., New York, N.Y.

B. San Francisco, Cal., 1911. *Studied*: in China. *Awards*: many awards including gold medal, Audubon A.; Guggenheim F. (2); prizes, AWS; AIC. *Work*: MMA; WMAA; Am. Acad. A. & Let.; MModA; BM; deYoung Mem. Mus.; Mills Col., Oakland, Cal.; Univ. Wisconsin; Springfield (Ill.) AA; Davenport Mun. A. Gal.; San Diego FA Gal.; Univ. Nebraska; Bloomington AA; Cranbrook Acad. A.; Butler AI; Ft. Wayne Mus. A.; Oswego State Col.; U.S. State Dept.; AGAA; Wadsworth Atheneum; Evansville Pub. Mus. *Exhibited*: nationally. I., "China's Story"; "The Bamboo Gate"; covers for Fortune magazine. *Position*: Instr., watercolor painting, Columbia Univ., New York, N.Y.; Famous Artist Sch., Westport, Conn.

KINGMAN, EUGENE—*Museum Director, P., Lith.*

Joslyn Art Museum, 2218 Dodge St.; h. 312 South 56th St., Omaha 32, Neb.

B. Providence, R.I., Nov. 10, 1909. *Studied*: Yale Univ. B.A.; Yale Sch. FA, B.F.A. *Member*: AAMus.; Assn. A. Mus. Dir.; Audubon A; Providence A. Cl. *Awards*: prizes, Providence A. Cl., 1929, 1957; Delgado Mus. A., 1940; Oklahoma A., 1940; Mulvane A. Center, 1952. *Work*: LC; Philbrook A. Center; Mulvane A. Center; murals, Crompton Richmond Co., N.Y.; USPO, Hyattsville, Md.; Kemerer, Wyo.; East Providence, R.I.; Mus. Glacier Nat. Park, Montana; New York Times Bldg., N.Y. *Exhibited*: NAD, 1937-1942; San F. AA, 1937-1939; Kansas City AI, 1940; Colorado Springs FA Center, 1940, 1942; Okla. A., 1940; Dallas Pr. Soc., 1943; Providence A. Cl., 1927-1952. I., "The Rocky Mountains," 1945. *Position*: Instr., R.I.Sch. Des., 1936-39; Dir., Philbrook A. Center, 1939-42; Cartographer, OSS, 1942-45; Asst. Dir., 1946-47, Dir., 1947- , Joslyn A. Mus., Omaha, Neb.; U.S. Delegate to Conf. on Regional Museums, Schaffhausen, Switzerland, 1954; Consultant on Exhibitions, Smithsonian Inst., 1957-58; Consultant, Missouri River Powerhouse exhibits, U.S. Corps of Engineers, 1958. Contributor article "Painters of the Plains," American Heritage Magazine, 1954; Midwest Heritage Conf., Coe College, Cedar Rapids, Iowa, 1956.

KINGSLAND, JAMES—*Painter*

East Pondmeadow Road, Westbrook, Conn.

B. Woodbury, Conn., June 1, 1923. *Studied*: Hartford A. Sch., with Henrik Mayer, Paul Zimmerman, Russell Limbach and Henry Kreis. *Member*: Mystic AA; Essex AA; Clinton (Conn.) AA. *Awards*: prizes, Mystic AA, 1955; Clinton AA, 1957. *Exhibited*: Silvermine Gld. A., 1957; Essex AA; Mystic AA; Clinton AA; Conn. Acad. FA; Hartford WC Soc., all regularly; one-man: West Hartford, 1957.

KINIGSTEIN, JONAH—*Painter, Des., Comm. A.*
220 East 14th St., New York 3, N.Y.

B. New York, N.Y., June 26, 1923. *Studied*: CUASch.; Grande Chaumiere, Paris, France. *Awards*: Fulbright F., 1953-54; Nat. Inst. A. & Lets. grant; prize, Butler AI. *Work*: MMoA; WMAA; Albright A. Gal.; Brandeis Univ.; Wichita Mus. A.; William Rockhill Nelson Gal. A.; Butler AI; BM. *Exhibited*: Univ. Illinois, 1956, 1958; WMAA, 1955, 1957; MMoA.; BM; PAFA; AIC; Downtown Gal., N.Y., 1952, 1953; Alan Gal., N.Y., 1954, 1958; Nat. Inst. A. & Lets., 1957.

KINSTLER, EVERETT RAYMOND—*Portrait Painter, I.*
15 Gramercy Park, New York, N.Y.

B. New York, N.Y., Aug. 5, 1926. *Studied*: ASL, with DuMond and portraiture with Wayman Adams. *Member*: Portraits, Inc.; Grand Central A. Gal.; ASL; All. A. Am.; Hudson Valley AA; NAC; SI. *Awards*: gold medal, NAC, 1956; prize, Hudson Valley AA, 1958. *Work*: Col. Robert McCormick Estate, Cantigny, Ill.; NAC; Carnegie Mansion, Columbia Univ.; Players Cl.; Mus. of the City of New York; many portraits of prominent persons. *Exhibited*: NAC, 1947-1958; Hudson Valley AA, 1956-1958; SI, 1957; All. A. Am., 1956-1958; Nat. Soc. of Painters in Casein, 1956; Grand Central A. Gal.; Portraits, Inc., and others. Illus., "Our Federal Government," 1958; "The Story of Dan Beard," 1958; "Mystery of McClellan Creek," 1958; "Jeb and the Bank Robbers," 1958, and several hundred book jackets since 1945. Contributor to Artist Magazine; Washington Square Spring Magazine. *Positions*: Instr., Phoenix Sch. Des., 1958; Chm., Exh. Com., NAC, 1957- ; Dir., All. A. Am., 1958- .

KINZINGER, EDMUND D.—*Painter, S., C., Gr.*
134 South 6th St., Delavan, Wis.

B. Pforzheim, Germany, Dec. 31, 1888. *Studied*: Univ. Iowa, Ph.D.; Ecole Moderne, Paris, France, and in Germany. *Awards*: prizes, Ft. Worth, Tex., 1942, 1944; Texas FA Assn., 1945; Texas General, 1947. *Work*: DMFA; Mus. FA of Houston; San Antonio and Abilene, Tex. *Exhibited*: AIC; Bloomsbury Gal., London, England; Rouillier Gal., Chicago; Texas Centennial; WFNY 1939; GGE, 1939; Galerie Pierre, Paris, France (one-man). *Position*: Chm. A. Dept., Baylor Univ., Waco, Texas, 1935-1950.*

KIPP, LYMAN E., JR.—*Sculptor*
630 Saw Mill River Road, Ardsley, N.Y.; h. 147 Farragut Ave., Hastings-on-Hudson, N.Y.

B. Dobbs Ferry, N.Y., Dec. 24, 1929. *Studied*: PIASch.; Cranbrook Acad. A. *Work*: Cranbrook Mus. A. *Exhibited*: nationally. One-man: Cranbrook Acad. A., 1954; Betty Parsons Gal., 1954, 1956, 1958; Myrtle Codes Gal., Glen Coe, Ill., 1957; Arizona State Col., Tempe, 1957; Pensacola A. Center, 1958; Providence A. Cl., 1958. *Position*: Instr., Harvey Sch., Hawthorne, N.Y.; Asst. S. Instr., Cranbrook Acad. A., Bloomfield Hills, Mich.

KIPP, ORVAL—*Painter, E., Gr., I., L.*
Art Department, State Teachers College; h. 1122 Grant St., Indiana, Pa.

B. Hyndman, Pa., May 21, 1904. *Studied*: J.B. Stetson Univ.; Carnegie Inst., A.B.; T. Col., Columbia Univ., A.M.; Univ. Pittsburgh, Ph.D. *Member*: NEA; Eastern AA; AAUP; Assoc. A., Pittsburgh; AEA; Indiana AA; All. A. Johnstown; Pa. A. Edu. Assn. (Council). *Awards*: scholarships, Carnegie Inst.; prizes, Indiana AA, 1946, 1949, 1950, 1952-1957. *Work*: in the colls. of the following schs.: Latrobe H.S., Aspinwall H.S., Greensburg Pub. Schs., Indiana Pub. Schs., Uniontown H.S., all in Pennsylvania. *Exhibited*: Provincetown AA, 1936, 1937; All. A. Am., 1938; All. A. Johnstown, 1931-1957; Assoc. A. Pittsburgh, 1932-1957; Cooperative A. Exh., Indiana, Pa., 1944-1952; AFA traveling exh., 1940; Indiana AA, 1943-1952; Studio Gld., West Redding, Conn., traveling exh., 1957-1959; Kottler Gal., N.Y., 1958; Fla. Southern Col., 1952. I., Des., "Indiana Through the Camera's Eye"; "An Experimental Study of Color Perception." Lectures: "Trick or Treat in Art Education," Indianapolis, Ind., State Art Teachers, 1955. *Position*: Bd. Dir., Vice-Pres., Assoc. A. of Pittsburgh, 1955, Pres., 1957-58; Instr. A., 1936-41, Dir. & Instr. A. Dept., 1941- , State T. Col., Indiana, Pa.

KIRBY, GLO—*Painter, Lith.*
55 Hotaling Place; h. 762 De Haro St., San Francisco 7, Cal.

B. Mackenzie, Canada, July 21, 1912. *Studied*: Univ. Washington, A.B.; ASL; Cal. Sch. FA, San F. *Member*: San F. AA; AEA; San F. Soc. Women A. *Work*: mosaic mural, Presidio of San Francisco. *Exhibited*: SFMA, 1953, 1954; Richmond A. Center, 1952, 1954, 1955; Oakland A. Mus., 1954; Denver A. Mus., 1952-1954.

KIRCHNER, EVA LUCILLE (EO)—
Ceramist, S., Ser., T., L.
1435 South Cherry St., Denver 22, Colo.

B. Rich Hill, Mo., Sept. 25, 1901. *Studied*: Denver A. Acad.; Denver Univ.; Univ. Chicago; Columbia Univ.; Univ. So. California; Alfred Univ. *Member*: Colorado Soc. Ceramists; 15 Colorado A. *Awards*: purchase prize, Community A. Gal., Denver, 1957, 1958, prizes, 1957, 1958. *Exhibited*: Denver A. Mus.; Denver Community A. Gal.; Central City, Colo.; Gilpin AA. *Work*: s. panels, City and County Bldg., Denver, Colo.; garden s., St. Anne's Orphanage, Denver, and in private colls. *Position*: A.T., Peter Pan Sch., Denver, Colo.

KIRK, FRANK C.—*Painter*
38 Union Sq., New York 3, N.Y.

B. Zitomir, Russia, May 11, 1889. *Studied*: PAFA, with Hugh Breckenridge, Daniel Garber, Cecilia Beaux, Philip Hale; & in Paris. *Member*: ANA; Conn. Acad. FA; Soc. Wash. A.; AEA; Audubon A; Boston AC; All.A.Am.; Wash. AC; North Shore AA; Copley Soc., Boston; Springfield A. Lg.; Grand Central A. Gal. *Awards*: F., PAFA; Cresson traveling scholarship, PAFA; prizes, Conn. Acad. FA, 1934, 1939, 1951, 1953; Ogunquit A. Center, 1935, 1954; All.A.Am., 1943, 1945; Springfield A. Lg., 1943; North Shore AA, 1947, 1948, 1951. *Work*: Mus. Western A., Moscow, Russia; State Mus., Trenton, N.J.; Binghamton Mus. A.; Cayuga Mus. Hist. & A.; PMA; Biro-Bidjan Mus., Russia; Springville, Utah, H.S. *Exhibited*: nationally.

KIRKBRIDE, E(ARLE) R(OSSLYN)—*Etcher*
704 South Front St., Philadelphia 47, Pa.

B. Pittsburgh, Pa., Mar. 11, 1891. *Studied*: with Vanderpoel, Buehr, Clarkson. *Member*: Cliff Dwellers; Phila. Sketch Cl.; A. Dir. Cl., Chicago; Ch'cago Et. Soc.; Phila. Soc. Et. Illus.: "Sunny Sam"; stories for Red Book; covers and stories for Colliers; monthly editorial article "Sub Deb" for Ladies Home Journal; Good Housekeeping; Country Gentleman and others. Books: Our World and How We Use It; Making the Goods We Need; Marketing the Things We Use; Look and Learn; The Story of Our Country, etc. *Positions*: A. Dir., Hamilton Advertising Agency, Chicago; Klau, Van Pietersom, Dunlap Assoc., Milwaukee; Mandl Co., and others.

KIRKLAND, VANCE—*Educator*
University of Denver, 1446 Court Place, Denver, Colo.
Position: Dir., School of Art, Univ. Denver.*

KIRKPATRICK, HARRIET—*Painter*
1153 Westwood Ave., Columbus 12, Ohio

Studied: Columbus (Ohio) A. Sch.; & with Haw'horne, Carlson, Thurn, Hofmann, Rattner. *Member*: Ohio WC Soc.; Columbus A. Lg.; Clearwater A. Group. *Awards*: Columbus A. Lg., 1947, medal, 1953; prizes, Columbus A. Lg., 1922, 1931, 1936; Ohio State Fair, 1954, 1955. *Work*: Columbus Gal.FA. *Exhibited*: AWCS; N.Y. WC Cl.; Phila. A. All., 1944; Athens Univ., 1943 (one-man); Columbus Gal. FA, 1947 (one-man).

KIRKPATRICK, MARIE (Mrs. James R.)—
Industrial Designer
330 Fountain St., Northeast, Grand Rapids 3, Mich.

B. Grand Rapids, Mich., Aug. 20, 1900. *Studied*: Grand Rapids Sch. Des. *Member*: IDI; Grand Rapids Furniture Des. Assn. *Awards*: F., IDI. *Exhibited*: IDI, 1949. Lectures: History of Period Styles. *Position*: Partner, Kirkpatrick & Kirkpatrick, Grand Rapids, Mich., 1925- .

KIRSCH, DWIGHT—Art Consultant, P., E., W., L.
1701 Casady Drive, Des Moines 15, Iowa

B. Pawnee County, Neb., Jan. 28, 1899. *Studied*: Univ. Nebraska, A.B.; ASL, with Henri, Boardman Robinson, Frank DuMond, A.S. Calder, and others. *Member*: Assn. A. Mus. Dir.; AEA; Assoc. A. Omaha; AIA (Hon.); Des Moines Weavers Gld. (Hon.). *Awards*: Hon. Degree, D.F.A., Grinnell Col., 1953. *Work*: in collections including, Murdock Coll.; Wichita A. Mus.; PMA; Sioux City A. Center; Nebraska AA and several private colls. *Exhibited*: at many regional and national shows since 1916, including, AIC; Colorado Springs FA Center; MMA; Phila. A. All.; PAFA; SFMA; Walker A. Center; WMAA. Juror of Regional Exhs. and lecturer in many states. Contributor of articles to Art in America; American Magazine of Art; New York Times, etc. *Position*: Instr. A., Univ. Nebraska, 1924- ; Chm. Dept. A., 1931-47; Dir., A. Gal., Univ. Nebraska, 1936-50; Guest Instr., Joslyn A. Mus., Omaha, 1949; Dir., Des Moines A. Center, 1950-1958. Freelance artist, art consultant and lecturer, at present.

KIRSCHBAUM, ARMOND—Painter, Comm. A.
1045 N St., Anchorage, Alaska

KIRSCHENBAUM, JULES—Painter
21 East 10th St., New York 3, N.Y.

B. New York, N.Y., Mar. 25, 1930. *Studied*: BMSch.A. *Member*: AWS; Phila. A. All. *Awards*: Fulbright Fellowship, 1956; prizes, Emily Lowe Comp., 1950; NAD, 1953-1955; Butler Inst. Am. A., 1957; medal, PAFA, 1952. *Work*: WMAA; Butler Inst. Am. A.; Univ. Nebraska, and in private colls. *Exhibited*: MMA, 1952; PAFA, 1952, 1953, 1954, 1957; CGA, 1952; WMAA, 1953-1957; MModA; BM; Santa Barbara Mus. A.; Pasadena A. Mus.; FA Center of Houston; DMFA; AFA traveling exh., 1955; AIC, 1957; Butler Inst. Am. A., 1957; Spoleto, Italy, 1958; Paris, France, 1958; Univ. Illinois, 1957.

KIRSTEIN, LINCOLN EDWARD—Critic, W., L.
130 West 56th St., New York, N.Y.

B. Rochester, N.Y., May 4, 1907. *Studied*: Harvard Univ., B.S. Author: "American Mural Painters," 1932; "Gaston Lachaise," 1935; "American Battle Painting," 1944; "Cartier-Bresson," 1946 (MModA); "Dance, A Short History," 1934; "Blast at Ballet," 1938; "Ballet Alphabet," 1939; "Pedro Figari," 1946. Contributor to: art & national magazines, with critical reviews & articles on history of art. *Position*: Advisor, Dept. Latin-Am. A., MModA, New York, N.Y., 1941-43; A. Cr., New Republic, 1948-51; Dir., N.Y. City Ballet.*

KIRSTEN, RICHARD CHARLES—Painter, Gr., S.
900 North 102nd St., Seattle 33, Wash.

B. Chicago, Ill., April 16, 1920. *Studied*: AIC; Univ. Washington. *Member*: AFA; Puget Sound Group of Northwest Painters; Northwest WC Soc.; Northwest Pr. M.; AEA; Cal. WC Soc.; Creative A.Assoc. *Awards*: prizes, SAM, 1949, 1950; Music & Art Fnd., 1951; Northwest WC Soc., 1952; Seattle Boat Show exh., 1955-1957; Bellevue (Wash.) A. & Crafts exh., 1956, 1957. *Work*: SAM; LC; MMA; Tokyo Mus. Mod. A., and in private colls. *Exhibited*: SAM, 1945, 1947-1958; Western Wash. Fair, 1949-1957; Music & Art Fnd., 1949-1958; Pacific Northwest exh., Spokane, Wash., 1949-1951; Northwest Pr. M., 1950-1958; Buffalo Pr. Cl., 1951; Riverside Mus., N.Y., 1953, 1956; Morris Gal., N.Y., 1955; MModA, 1954; Oakland A. Mus., 1955; SFMA, 1954; AEA (Seattle Chptr.), 1952; LC, 1957; NGA, 1957; Rochester Mem. A. Gal., 1958; Mobile AA, 1958; Univ. Wisconsin, 1958; Portland (Ore.) A. Mus., 1958; Bucknell Univ., 1958; deYoung Mem. Mus., 1958; Butler County Hist. Soc., El Dorado, Kans., 1958; Riverside Mus., N.Y., 1958; one-man: SAM, 1943; Studio Gal., 1949, Millard Pollard Assoc., 1952, Hathaway House, 1952, 1955, Campus Gal., 1955, 1956, 1958, all in Seattle; Yoseido Gal., Tokyo, Japan, 1958. *Position*: Ed. A., Seattle Post-Intelligencer, 1948- .

KISELEWSKI, JOSEPH—Sculptor
433 East 82nd St., New York 28, N.Y.

B. Browersville, Minn., Feb. 16, 1901. *Studied*: Minneapolis Sch. A.; NAD; BAID; AM. Acad. in Rome; Acad. Julian, Paris. *Member*: NA; NSS; Arch. Lg. *Awards*: Prix de Rome, 1926-1929; Watrous gold medal; prize, Beaux-

Arts, Paris. *Work*: statue, Milwaukee, Wis.; groups, Bronx County Court House, N.Y.; fountain, Huntington Mus., S.C.; pediment, Commerce Bldg., Wash., D.C.; George Rogers Clark mem., Vincennes, Ind.; plaques, Capital Bldg., Wash., D.C.; Covington, Ky., John Peter Zanger Sch., N.Y.; reliefs, General Accounting Bldg., Wash., D.C.; panels, Loyola Seminary, Shrub Oak, N.Y.; statue, Veterans' Cemetery, Margraten, Holland.

KISH, MAURICE—Painter
70 South 3rd St., Brooklyn, N.Y.

B. Dvinsk, Latvia, Feb. 19, 1898. *Member*: All. A. Am.; Brooklyn Soc. A.; Conn. Acad. FA; North Shore AA; P. & S. Soc., New Jersey; Am. Veterans' Soc. A.; Audubon A. *Work*: Ein Harod Mus., Israel. *Awards*: prizes, All. A. Am., 1945; Conn. Acad. FA, 1945; Grand Central A. Gal., 1947; Veteran's Soc. A., 1949, 1955; P. & S. Soc., New Jersey, 1951 (medal); A. Festival, 1951; Grumbacher award, 1954; Irvington A. & Mus. Assn., 1952. *Exhibited*: NAD; CGA; PAFA; VMFA; AFA traveling exh.; WFNY 1939; All. A. Am.; Conn. Acad. FA; BM; Brooklyn Soc. A.; Ogunquit A. Center; North Shore AA; Riverside Mus.; Audubon A.; Am.-British A. Center; Edu. All.; Findlay Gal.; ACA Gal.; Macbeth Gal.; P. & S. Soc., New Jersey; Irvington A. & Mus. Assn.; Fla. Southern Col.; Terry Al; Newport AA; Delgado Mus. A.; Carnegie Inst.; Am. Veterans Soc. A.; Ein Harod Mus., Israel; Grand Central A. Gal.; Butler Inst. Am. A.; Detroit Inst. FA, etc.

KIZER, CHARLOTTE E.—Craftsman, P., T.
Westchester Workshop, County Center, White Plains, N.Y.; h. Eton Lodge, Scarsdale, N.Y.

B. Lincoln, Neb., Jan. 8, 1901. *Studied*: Univ. Nebraska, B.F.A.; T. Col., Columbia Univ., M.A.; & with Charles Martin, Adda Husted-Andersen; Rudolph Schumacher. *Member*: Artist-Craftsmen of New York (Vice-Pres., 1949-52, Pres., 1952-55); Westchester A. & Crafts Gld.; Nat. A. Edu. Assn.; Eastern AA. *Work*: Joslyn Mem. *Exhibited*: Nat. Exh. Am. A., N.Y., 1936; Syracuse Mus. FA, 1936; Contemporary Crafts Exh., Phila., Pa., 1937; N.Y. Soc. Craftsmen; Designer-Craftsmen U.S.A., 1953-1955; Westchester A. & Crafts Gld.; Kansas City AI; Joslyn Mem.; Nebraska AA; Lincoln A. Gld.; Palm Beach, Miami, Fla. *Position*: Dir., A. & Crafts, Westchester Workshop, County Center, White Plains, N.Y.; Sec., Westchester A. & Crafts Gld., 1955- .

KLAPP, FREDA LESLIE—Lecturer, W.
4328 Central Ave., San Diego 5, Cal.

B. Jamestown, N.D. *Studied*: Columbia Univ. Lectures: The Graphic Arts. Former Dir., A. Center, La Jolla, Cal.*

KLAR, WALTER HUGHES—Educator, W., P., L.
Motch Rd.-Bolton-R.F.D. 2, Manchester, Conn.

B. Westfield, Mass., Mar. 20, 1882. *Studied*: Mass. Sch. A., B.S. in Edu.; NAD. *Member*: Eastern AA (Pres., 1934); Springfield A. Lg.; Nat. Edu. Assn. *Award*: prize, Assoc. A., Pittsburgh, 1919. *Exhibited*: Assoc. A. Pittsburgh; Springfield A. Lg. (Pres., 1953); Buffalo, N.Y.; Greenfield, Mass. Co-Author: "Appreciation of Pictures," 1930; "Theory and Practice of Art Education," 1933. Contributor to: Educational magazines & journal articles on art education. Lectures: Art Education; Architecture; Painting. *Position*: Supv. Practical Arts, Greenfield, Mass., 1908-16; Hd. A. Dept., Buffalo State Normal Sch., 1916-18; Prof. F. & Indst. A., Univ. Pittsburgh, 1918-21; Assoc. Prof., Carnegie Inst. Tech., 1921-25; Supv. A. Edu., Springfield, Mass., Pub. Schs., 1934-52 (Retired).

KLASSEN, JOHN P.—Teacher, L., S., C., P.
339 South Jackson St., Bluffton, Ohio

B. Ukraine, Russia, Apr. 8, 1888. *Studied*: Switzerland; Germany; Ohio State Univ. *Member*: Columbus A. Lg.; CAA. *Awards*: prize, Columbus A. Gal., 1945. *Exhibited*: Syracuse Mus. FA, 1939; Columbus A. Gal., 1939-1955; one-man: Columbus A. Gal., 1947; Univ. Illinois, 1947; State T. Col., Oswego, N.Y., 1947; Ohio State Fair, 1950, 1951; Ohio State Univ., 1952; Decatur A. Center, 1952. Lectures: Mennonite Art; Ceramics; Woodcarving. *Position*: Assoc. Prof., Emeritus, Bluffton Col., Bluffton, Ohio (Retired).

KLEIDMAN, ROSE—Painter, Ser.

972 Manzanita St., Los Angeles 29, Cal.

B. New York, N.Y., May 27, 1910. *Studied*: Edu. All. Sch., with Moses Soyer. *Member*: Cal. WC Soc.; AEA. *Awards*: prize, Glendale AA, 1949. *Exhibited*: PAFA, 1940; Nat. Exh. Prints, 1953; Laguna Beach, 1944, 1949; Fresno A. Lg., 1949.*

KLEIN, FRANK ANTHONY—Sculptor, C.

1244 East 45th St., Brooklyn 34, N.Y.

B. Trier, Germany, June 23, 1890. *Studied*: in Germany, with Van de Velde, Grasseger, Sobry; BAID; ASL. *Member*: All.A.Am. *Work*: statues, portraits, mem., monuments: Court St., Brooklyn, N.Y.; St. Nicholas Cemetery, Passaic, N.J.; St. Catherine of Siena Church, N.Y.; Brooklyn Tech. H.S.; Richmond Hill, N.Y.; St. Stephens Church, Arlington, N.J.; Our Lady of Angels Church, Brooklyn, N.Y., also work in ceramics. *Exhibited*: Arch.L.; NSS; WMAA; BM; PAFA; N.Y.Hist. Soc. Contributor: articles & illus., newspapers & magazines.

KLEIN, I(SIDORE)—Cartoonist, P.

48-32 38th St., Long Island City, N.Y.

B. Newark, N.J., Oct. 12, 1897. *Studied*: NAD; ASL. *Member*: Screen Cart. Gld.; Nat. Cartoonists Soc. *Exhibited*: NAD, 1922-1930, 1942, 1943, 1946; BM; NAC; AIC; Newport AA, 1950. I., cartoon books and contributor to New Yorker, Colliers, Sat. Eve. Post; animated cartoons for motion pictures, 1935-54; cartoons for TV and industrial motion pictures, 1954- . Created "The Fiery Furnace," an animated painting in sound and color, 1955.

KLEIN, J. ALAN. See Alan, Jay

KLEIN, MEDARD—Painter, Gr.

54 East Delaware Place, Chicago 11, Ill.

B. Appleton, Wis., Jan. 6, 1905. *Studied*: Chicago A. Schs. *Exhibited*: AIC; Salon des Realites Nouvelles, Paris, France; Palais des Beaux-Arts, Paris; Mus. Non-Objective Painting (Solomon Guggenheim Mus.), N.Y.; Joslyn A. Mus.; SFMA; Everhart Mus. A.; Illinois State Mus.; Assoc. Am. A., Chicago; Benjamin, Finley, New Studio, Gambit galleries, Chicago; 1020 Art Center, Chicago; Oakland A. Mus.; Albany Inst. Hist. & A.; NAD; LC; Wichita AA; Phila. Pr. Cl.; PAFA; Northwest Pr. M.; Laguna Beach AA; BM; Rochester Mem. A. Gal.; Carnegie Inst.; CM; George Binet Gal.; Bookbuilders Workshop, Boston; AGAA; Olivet Col.; Univ. Washington; Lawrence Col.; Cal. PLH; Pasadena AI; Univ. Mich.; Cranbrook Acad.; AFA traveling exh.; one-man: Paul Theobold Gal., Chicago; St. Louis A. Center; Univ. Minn.; Springfield A. Mus.; Lawrence Col.; Chicago Pub. Lib.; Univ. Chicago; New Trier H.S.; Evanston H.S.; Wustum Mus. FA; Cliff Dwellers, Chicago; Iowa State T. Col.; Richardson Bros., Winnipeg, Canada, and others.

KLEINBARDT, ERNEST—Painter, L.

436 Nuber Ave., Mt. Vernon, N.Y.

B. Lodz, Poland. *Studied*: in Germany. *Member*: Munich A. Soc.; Am. A. Soc. *Awards*: med., Berlin, Leipzig, Breslau, Hanover, Nurnberg, Germany. *Work*: St. Mary's Church, St. Mark's Church, Brooklyn, N.Y.; St. Lazarus Church, Newark, N.J. *Exhibited*: abroad.*

KLEINHOLZ, FRANK—Painter, T.

19 Second Ave., Port Washington, N.Y.

B. Brooklyn, N.Y., Feb. 17, 1901. *Studied*: Fordham Univ., LL.B.; Am. A. Sch.; & with Alexander Dobkin, Yasuo Kuniyoshi, Sol Wilson. *Member*: An Am. Group; A. Lg. Am. *Awards*: AV, 1942. *Work*: MMA; PMG; BM; Newark Mus. A.; Univ. Alabama; Univ. Arizona; Tel-Aviv Mus.; Encyclopaedia Britannica Coll.; Brandeis Univ. *Exhibited*: Carnegie Inst., 1941, 1943-1946; PAFA, 1942, 1944, 1945; VMFA, 1942, 1944; WMAA, 1943, 1945; AIC, 1943; Pepsi-Cola, 1944; Univ. Nebraska, 1944; State Univ. Iowa, 1944-1946; CGA, 1945; Albright A. Gal., 1946; CAM, 1945; Springfield Mus. A., 1945; MMA (AV), 1942; PMG, 1943 (one-man); Whyte Gal., 1944 (one-man); Assoc. Am. A., 1942, 1944, 1945 (one-man); An Am. Group, 1944, 1945; Art:USA, 1958; Audubon A., 1955-1958; NAD, 1957, 1958; BM, 1944; A. Lg. Am., 1944, 1945; one-man: New York City, 1948, 1950; Detroit, Mich., 1955; Palmer House

Gal., Chicago, 1956. Lectures: Contemporary Art. *Position*: Instr., BM Sch. A., Brooklyn, N.Y., 1946. Visiting A., Hofstra Col., Hempstead, N.Y., 1952.

KLEINSCHMIDT, FLORIAN ARTHUR—Educator, L.

2324 Broadway, Lubbock, Tex.

B. Mankato, Minn., Oct. 4, 1897. *Studied*: Univ. Minnesota, B.S. in Arch.; Harvard Univ., M. in Arch.; Ecole des Beaux-Arts Americaine, Fontainebleau, France. *Member*: AIA. Lectures: Greek Art; Florentine Painting; etc. *Position*: Prof., Dept. Arch. & Allied A., Texas Tech. Col., 1928- .

KLEP, ROLF—Illustrator, Comm. A., Des.

Surf Pines, Gearhart, Ore.

B. Portland, Ore., Feb. 6, 1904. *Studied*: Univ. Oregon, B.A.; AIC; Grand Central Sch. A. *Member*: SI; Eugene Field Soc.; A. Gld.; Pacific A. Gld. Author, I., "Album of the Great," 1937; "The Children's Shakespeare," 1938; I., "Beowulf," 1941; Contributing I., "Across the Space Frontier," 1952; "Conquest of the Moon," 1953. Lecture and exhibit, Univ. Oregon, 1958. *Position*: Technical, Marine and Aeronautical illus. for national magazines and advertising agencies.

KLETT, WALTER CHARLES—Illustrator, P., Des.

434 East 52nd St., New York 22, N.Y.

B. St. Louis, Mo., April 28, 1897. *Studied*: St. Louis Sch. FA, Washington Univ. *Member*: SI; A. Gld.; A. & W. Assn.; Lotos Cl. *Exhibited*: PAFA; CAM; Kansas City AI; Ferargil Gal.; Reinhardt Gal.; Grand Central A. Gal.; MMA; SC; Lotos Cl.; AIGA; SI; one-man: Lotos Cl.; SI; PIASch.; N.Y. Sch. Des. Author: "Figure Painting." Contributor to American Artist magazine. *Position*: Instr., Port. and Figure Painting, PIASch., Brooklyn, N.Y.; Dir., Lotos Cl.; Trustee, A. Fellowship.

KLINE, EDITH L. B(OLLINGER) (Mrs.)—Painter, T.

Studio 350, 34 South 17th St., Philadelphia, Pa.; h. 228 Maypole Rd., Upper Darby, Pa.

B. Philadelphia, Pa., Nov. 8, 1903. *Studied*: PMSchIA; Moore Inst.; Univ. Pennsylvania, B.F.A.; PAFA; Ecole des Beaux-Arts, Fontainebleau, France, & with Earl Horter, John Lear. *Member*: Phila. A. All.; Phila. WC Cl.; Phila. A. T. Assn.; Nat. A. Assn. *Awards*: F., PAFA; prizes, NAC, 1941; Phila. A. T. Assn., 1944, 1954. *Exhibited*: PAFA; Ecole des Beaux-Arts; Arch. L.; NAC; Phila. A. All.; Phila. Sketch Cl.; Woodmere A. Gal.; Phila. WC Cl.; Women's Univ. Cl., Phila. (one-man); Reading Mus. A. (one-man). *Position*: A.T., Tilden Jr. H.S., Phila., Pa.

KLINE, FRANZ JOSEF—Painter

242 West 14th St., New York, N.Y.

B. Wilkes-Barre, Pa., May 23, 1910. *Studied*: Girard Col., Phila., Pa.; Boston Univ. *Award*: prize, AIC, 1957. *Work*: MModA; WMAA; Albright A. Gal.; Carnegie Inst.; Guggenheim Mus. *Exhibited*: nationally and internationally, including MModA; Wildenstein Gal., N.Y.; Sao Paulo, Brazil; Brussels World's Fair, 1958; Solomon Guggenheim Mus.

KLINE, HIBBERD VAN BUREN—Painter, I.

2 Centennial Drive, Syracuse 7, N.Y.

B. Auriesville, N.Y. *Studied*: Syracuse Univ., B.P.; ASL. Contributor to national magazines. *Position*: Hd. Dept. Illus., Col. FA, Syracuse Univ., Syracuse, N.Y. (Retired 1952).

KLINKER, ORPHA—Etcher, P., I., L.

3401 Wonder View Dr., Hollywood 28, Cal.

B. Fairfield, Iowa. *Studied*: Univ. California, Los A.; Julian Acad., Paris, France; & with Will Foster, Mildred Brooks, Edgar Payne. *Member*: SAGA; Cal. SE; Cal. AC; Laguna Beach A. Cl.; Nat. Acad. Belas Artes, Brazil & Argentina; Women Painters of the West; Am. Soc. Heraldry; Los A. AA; Nat. Soc. Sc. & A., Mexico. *Awards*: F., Andhra Research Univ., India; med., Univ. Panama; Academician, Am. Int. Acad., Wash., D.C.; Croix de Commandeur, Belgium. *Work*: Los A. City Hall; Los A. Polytechnic H.S.; Los A. AA; MMA; City Hall, Los A.; Campo de Cuhuenga, Los A., and in private colls. *Ex-*

hibited: MMA (AV), 1943; Grand Central A. Gal., 1940; NAD, 1943, 1944, 1946; PAFA, 1939; WMAA, 1944; GGE, 1939; Mexico, D.F., 1944; Lib. Cong., 1944; Laguna Beach AA, 1943-1946; Denver A. Mus., 1945; Los A. Mus. A., annually; Palace Legion Honor; Soc. of Western A., 1943-1945; Cal. SE, 1939-1956; Ebell Cl., Los A.; Oakland A. Gal., 1940-1956. I., "The City that Grew"; "Winning a Fortune"; "Enchanted Pueblo," & other books. Lectures: "The Romance of Early California"; "Historical Trees of California," and other art lectures.

KLITGAARD, GEORGINA—*Painter*
Bearsville, N.Y.

B. New York, N.Y., July 3, 1893. *Studied*: Barnard Col., A.B.; NAD. *Member*: AEA; Audubon A.; Woodstock AA. *Awards*: med., PAFA, 1930; prize, Pan-Am. Exp., 1931; Guggenheim F., 1933; Carnegie Inst.; AIC. *Work*: MMA; WMAA; Newark Mus.; Dayton AI; New Britain AI; BM; Wood Gal. A., Montpelier, Vt.; murals, USPO, Poughkeepsie, N.Y.; Goshen, N.Y.; Pelham, Ga.; painting reproduced in "Through the American Landscape." *Exhibited*: Carnegie Inst., 1929-1946; CGA, 1928-1946; AFA traveling exh.; one-man: Parnassus Gal., Woodstock, N.Y., 1955; CGA; St. Gauden's Mem. Gal.; Cincinnati, Ohio; Miami, Fla.; PAFA, annually; VMFA, annually; & in many other U.S. museums. *Position*: Instr., Durham Sch. of Painting.

KLITZKE, THEODORE E.—*Educator, C.*
College of Ceramics, Department of Design, Alfred University, Alfred, N.Y.

Position: Prof. Des., College of Ceramics, Alfred Univ.*

KLONIS, STEWART—*Painter, T., L.*
215 West 57th St., New York 19, N.Y.

B. Naugatuck, Conn., Dec. 24, 1901. *Studied*: ASL. *Member*: Century Assn.; The Players. *Work*: IBM Coll. Lectures: History of Art. *Positions*: member, A. Aid Comm., 1932-36; Bd. Control, 1934, Treas., 1935-36, Pres., 1937-45, Exec. Dir., 1946- , ASL, New York; V. Pres., 1939-41, Pres., 1941- , Am. FA Soc.; Trustee, McDowell Traveling Scholarship Fund, 1934-45; Instr., Queens Col., 1940-45; Bd. Governors, 1951-52, Chm. A. Comm., 1952, NAC, New York; Dir.-at-large, AEA, 1952; Member Arts Comm., Fulbright Awards, 1949-52; Chm., Arts Comm., Fulbright Awards, 1953-55 and 1957.

KLOSS, GENE—*Etcher, P.*
Taos, N.M.

B. Oakland, Cal., July 27, 1903. *Studied*: Univ. California, A.B.; Cal. Sch. FA. *Member*: NAD; SAGA; Pr. Cl., Albany; Phila. WC Cl.; Prairie Pr.M.; Cal. SE; F., Intl. Inst. A. & Lets.; Taos AA; Laguna Beach AA; Cal. Soc. Pr. M.; New Mexico A. Lg. *Awards*: med., PAFA, 1936; prizes, Cal. SE, 1934, 1940, 1941, 1944, 1949; Oakland A. Gal., 1939; Chicago SE, 1940, 1949, 1951, 1952, 1954, 1956; Tucson FA Assn., 1941; Phila. Pr. Cl., 1944; Lib. Cong., 1946; Meriden AA, 1947, 1951; SAGA, 1953. *Work*: Carnegie Inst.; Smithsonian Inst.; Lib. Cong.; N.Y. Pub.Lib.; PAFA; AIC; SFMA; Honolulu Acad. A.; Dallas Mus. FA; Mus. New Mexico, Santa Fé; Oklahoma Univ.; Texas Tech. Inst.; MMA; Peabody Mus. A.; Univ. Pa.; Prairie Pr. M.; & in many other col. & univ. *Exhibited*: annually; NAD; SAGA; PAFA; Lib.Cong.; Cal. SE; Chicago SE; Prairie Pr.M.; also, Carnegie Inst., 1943-1945; DMFA, 1954; SAGA European traveling exh., 1954-55; Audubon A., 1955; WFNY 1939; GGE, 1939; U.S. exh. in Paris, France, 1938; Sweden, 1937; Italy, 1938; Mus. New Mexico, Santa Fé; SFMA; Oakland A. Gal.; San Diego FA Soc.; Denver A. Mus.; Baylor Univ.; Witte Mem. Mus. Executed Presentation Print, Albany Pr. Cl., 1953, SAGA, 1954; Pr. M. Soc. of California, 1956; one-man: Botts Mem. Hall, Albuquerque, N.M., 1956, 1958; Findlay Gal., Chicago, 1957.

KLOSTER, PAULA REBECCA—
Museum Curator, E., P., W.
Arizona State College, Tempe, Ariz.; h. 8102 East Palo Verde St., Scottsdale, Ariz.

B. Hatton, N.D. *Studied*: Univ. Minnesota; Minneapolis Sch. A.; Univ. North Dakota, B.S.; Stanford Univ., M.A.; Chouinard AI; ASL; Univ. So. California, and with Dan

Lutz, Carlos Merida, Jean Charlot, Frank McIntosh. *Member*: CAA; AAMus.; NAEA; Pacific AA (Council memb. 1935-38); Ariz. A. Edu. Assn. (Pres., 1934, 1950); AAUW (A. Chm., 1956-58); Nat. Council of Women of the United States; Ariz. College Assn. *Awards*: prizes, Arizona State Fair, 1930, 1931. *Exhibited*: Phoenix FA Assn.; Tucson FA Festival; Arizona A. Gld.; Arizona State Fair; one-man: Desert Sch. A., Scottsdale, 1950; Phoenix Little Theatre, 1951; Univ. Nevada, Reno, 1958. Participates on national and state art panels; addresses national and state conventions; TV and radio. Author: "The Arizona State College Collection of American Art," 1954; compiled brochures of College Collection, 1950-1952; Co-Author: A Guide for the Improvement of the Teaching of Art in the Schools of Arizona. Contributor to American Homes magazines; Design; Bulletin of Dept. A., Nat. Edu. Assn. *Position*: A. T., Jr. H.S., Grand Forks, N.D., 1923-25; Supv. student art, State T. Col., Valley City, N.D., 1926-27; Actg. Hd., Dept. A., 1928-31, Hd., 1933-54, Arizona State Col., Tempe; Cur., American Collection, Ariz. State Col., Tempe, Ariz., 1950- ; Prof. A., 1949- .

KLOUS, ROSE (Mrs. I. P.)—*Painter, Et.*
s. 7 Marble Rd., East Gloucester, Mass.; h. 333 West 57th St., New York 19, N.Y.

B. St. Petersburg, Russia. *Studied*: T. Col., Columbia Univ.; Academie Julian, Paris. *Member*: AAPL; ASL; Lg. Present-Day A.; St. Augustine AA. *Work*: Kiev Mus., Russia. *Exhibited*: Wash. WC Cl., 1948; Columbia Univ., 1931; Riverside Mus.; BM, 1949; Am.-British A. Center; AAPL; Burliuk Gal.; New York, N.Y.; Gloucester, Mass.

KLYNN, HERBERT DAVID—
Painter, Des., Cart., Comm., I., L.
4440 Lakeside Dr., Burbank, Cal.; h. 6160 Teesdale Ave., North Hollywood, Cal.

B. Cleveland, Ohio, Nov. 11, 1917. *Studied*: Ohio State Univ.; Western Reserve Univ.; Cleveland Sch. A. *Member*: Cal. WC Soc.; Los A. AA. *Awards*: prizes, Denver Mus. A.; Cleveland Mus. A. *Exhibited*: Cal. WC Soc.; Los A. Mus. A.; Cal. PLH; Santa Barbara Mus. A.; Denver A. Mus.; CMA; Cal. State Fair; Fresno A. Lg.; Long Beach AA; Santa Paula, Cal.; Columbus Mus. A.; Dayton AI. *Position*: Exec. Production Mngr., 1949- , A. Dir., 1951-1955, Vice-Pres. in charge of TV, UPA Pictures, Inc., Burbank, Cal.

KNAPP, FRANK DE VILLO—
Industrial Illustrator, Des., P.
Cornell University Aeronautical Laboratory; h. 424 Ashland Ave., Buffalo 22, N.Y.

B. Jamestown, N.Y., Apr. 28, 1896. *Studied*: Buffalo Sch. FA; PAFA; Cornell Univ.; & with Catherine L. Holmes. *Exhibited*: Albright A. Gal., 1935-1939, 1943; Chautauqua County SA. 1941, 1942. *Contributor*: illus. to publications of Curtiss-Wright Research Lab.; Cornell Aeronautical Lab. *Position*: Indst. I., Curtiss-Wright Corp. & Research Lab., 1942-45; Cornell Aeronautical Lab., Buffalo, N.Y., 1946-1956.*

KNAPP, WALTER HOWARD—
Illustrator, Comm. A., Des., P.
Charles Corsi Advertising, Inc., 754 Ballough Rd., Daytona Beach, Fla.; Box 512, Edgewater, Fla.

B. Cleveland, Ohio, Nov. 2, 1907. *Studied*: Oberlin Col.; Cleveland Sch. A.; & with Henry Keller. *Work*: CMA. *Exhibited*: CMA, 1932-1934; Argent Gal., 1940 (one-man); Northport A. & Hist. Soc., 1948-1952; SI, 1940, 1941; Stetson Univ., 1955, 1956; Nat. A. Dir. exh., 1957.

KNATHS, (OTTO) KARL—*Painter, L., T.*
8 Commercial St., Provincetown, Mass.

B. Eau Claire, Wis., Oct. 21, 1891. *Studied*: AIC., M.F.A. *Member*: Nat. Inst. A. & Lets. *Awards*: silver medal, AIC; prizes, Carnegie Inst.; MMA, 1950; Hon. deg., AIC. *Work*: MMA; AIC; Detroit Inst. A.; PAFA; CAM; SFMA; WMAA; PMA; PMG; Albright A. Gal.; Walker A. Center; MModA. *Exhibited*: extensively in leading U.S. museums and abroad. Lectures on Art History.

KNAUBER, ALMA JORDAN—
Educator, P., Des., W., I.
9871 Lorelei Drive, Cincinnati 31, Ohio

B. Cincinnati, Ohio, Aug. 24, 1893. *Studied*: Ohio State Univ., B.S., M.A.; Cincinnati A. Acad.; Univ. Cincinnati, and with Charles Hawthorne, Gifford Beal, Emil Bisttram, William Thon. *Member*: Prof. A. & Woman's A. Cl., Cincinnati; CAA; AAUP; Nat. Home Economics Assn. *Awards*: prizes, Columbus, Ohio, 1926; Cincinnati, Ohio, 1941. *Exhibited*: one-man: Cincinnati and Columbus, Ohio. Illus., Consumer Conference booklet. Author: "Knauber Art Ability and Art Vocabulary Tests and Examiners Manuals." *Position*: Assoc. Prof. A., College of Home Economics, Univ. Cincinnati, Ohio.

KNAUTH, ARNOLD WHITMAN, II—*Painter*
12 Hale St., Rockport, Mass.

B. New York, N.Y., Oct. 18, 1918. *Studied*: Harvard Univ.; NAD; Hibbard Summer Sch. Painting; Wellfleet A. Sch., with Xavier Gonzalez. *Member*: SC; AWS; Phila. WC Soc.; Audubon A.; All. A. Am.; Gld. Boston A.; North Shore AA; Rockport AA. *Awards*: gold medal, All. A. Am., 1950; Bronze medal, NAC, 1952; prizes, North Shore AA, 1951; Rockport AA, 1950; SC, 1952-1954; All. A. Am., 1955; Academic A., 1955. *Exhibited*: NAD, 1955; John Herron AI, 1947; PAFA, 1947; St. Botolph Cl., 1946; BMFA, 1950.*

KNECHT, KARL KAE—*Cartoonist, W.*
Evansville Courier, 216 Vine St.; h. 31 Adams St., Evansville 13, Ind.

B. Iroquois, S.D., Dec. 4, 1883. *Studied*: AIC. *Member*: Am. Assn. Editorial Cartoonists. *Work*: Hoosier Salon; Evansville Mus. A. Author, I., "Surprise Puzzle Drawing Book"; & others. Contributor to: Billboard, Variety, Saw Dust Ring, & other publications. *Position*: Vice-Pres., Evansville Courier, Evansville, Ind.; Editorial Cart., Evansville Courier, 1906- ; Dean, U.S. Ed. Cart.

KNEE, GINA (Mrs. Alexander Brook)—*Painter*
c/o Willard Gallery, 23 West 56th St., New York, N.Y.; h. Sag Harbor, L.I., N.Y.

B. Marietta, Ohio, Oct. 31, 1898. *Member*: AEA. *Awards*: prizes, Cal. WC Soc., 1938; N.M. State Fair, 1939; New Orleans, La., 1947. *Work*: Denver A. Mus.; PMG; Santa Barbara Mus. A.; Buffalo FA Acad. *Exhibited*: AIC, 1940-1946, 1947; BM, 1946, 1948; Cal. PLH, 1943; Los A. Mus. A., 1941-1944; PAFA, 1948; MMA, 1953; Bucknell Univ., 1955; Pyramid Gal., Wash., D.C., 1955; BM, 1955; Gld. Hall, East Hampton, 1954; Hampton Gal., 1954; Columbus A. Gal., 1951; VMFA, 1947; Guild Hall, East Hampton, L.I., 1949, 1950; one-man: Hatfield Gal., Los A., 1942; Santa Barbara Mus. A., 1943; Cal. PLH, 1943; Willard Gal., 1941, 1943, 1949, 1955.

KNIGHT, FREDERIC (CHARLES)—*Painter, E.*
430 West 116th St., New York 27, N.Y.

B. Philadelphia, Pa., Oct. 29, 1898. *Studied*: PMSchIA, and abroad. *Member*: Woodstock AA; An Am. Group; AAUP. *Awards*: Woodstock AA, 1931. *Work*: Dartmouth Col.; Univ. Arizona; IBM; Everhart Mus., and others; murals, USPO, Johnson City, N.Y. *Exhibited*: Carnegie Inst., 1941, 1943, 1945; CGA, 1935, 1943, 1945, 1947, 1951; PAFA, 1948; PMA, 1938; WFNY 1939; GGE, 1939; WMAA, 1933, 1937, 1939; AIC, 1944; NAD, 1945, 1951; Columbia Univ., 1955-1958; one-man: Babcock Gal., 1947; Everhart Mus., 1948; Columbia Univ., 1955. *Position*: Asst. Prof. Painting, Newcomb Sch. A., 1943-46; Instr., Lehigh Univ., 1949; L., Instr., 1946- , Asst. Prof. Painting, Sch. P. & S., Columbia Univ., New York, N.Y., 1954- . In Charge of Drawing, Painting and Sculpture, Summer School, 1958- .

KNIGHT, HILARY—*Painter, I.*
334 East 51st St., New York, N.Y.*

KNIGHT, JULIA MURRAY—*Painter*
600 Knight Way, La Canada, Cal.

B. Frankfort, Ky., Jan. 14, 1889. *Studied*: T. Col., Columbia Univ. *Member*: Cal. A. Cl.; Northern Cal. A. Cl. *Exhibited*: Crocker A. Gal., Sacramento, Cal. *Position*: Instr. A., Los Angeles Polytechnic H.S.

KNIGHT, NORMAH (ALCOTT) (Mrs. B. M.)—*Painter*
121 West Buchanan St., Harlingen, Tex.

B. Dallas, Tex., July 25, 1910. *Studied*: Dallas AI; Southern Methodist Univ.; A. Instruction, Inc.; Julian Acad., Paris, and with Harry deYoung, Peter Hondstedt. *Member*: Texas FA Assn. (Dir. 20 years); Rio Grande Valley A. Lg.; A. & Craftsmen Assn. *Awards*: prizes, Texas Fed. Women's Cl. *Work*: Allen Gal., Houston; Pub. Lib., Chamber of Commerce, Nat. Bank, Reese-Wil-Mond Hotel, Flamingo Hotel, Airforce Officers Cl., all Harlingen, Tex.; murals, Holsum Baking Co., First Nat. Bank, Nehi Bottling Co., all Harlingen, Tex. Cover and article in "The Illustrator." Lectures to clubs and organizations on art subjects. *Exhibited*: Locally and in regional exhs. Also, Art:USA, 1958; A. & Craftsmen traveling exh., 1958-59.

KNIPSCHILD, ROBERT—*Painter, T.*
17C University Houses, Madison 5, Wis.

B. Freeport, Ill., Aug. 17, 1927. *Studied*: Univ. Wisconsin, B.A.; Cranbrook Acad. A., M.F.A. *Awards*: prizes, Walker A. Center, 1949; Old Northwest Territory exh., 1951; Milwaukee AI, 1949; Springfield A. Mus., 1955. *Work*: PAFA; Cranbrook Acad. Mus.; LC; BMA; PC; Illinois State Mus.; Brandeis Univ.; Univ. Wisconsin; Univ. Minnesota; Univ. Michigan. *Exhibited*: Milwaukee AI, 1949; Denver A. Mus., 1949, 1950; Walker A. Center, 1949; BM, 1950; SAM, 1950; MMA, 1950; PAFA, 1950, 1952; Downtown Gal., 1951-1954; Cranbrook Mus., 1951, 1953; PC, 1952, 1953; CGA, 1953, 1955; Carnegie Inst., 1953; MModA, 1953-1955; WMAA, 1953, 1954; BMA, 1952-1955; Alan Gal., 1953-1958 (one-man); American Univ., 1951 (one-man); BMA, 1952-1954 (one-man); Butler AI, 1954, 1955; Springfield A. Mus., 1955, 1956; Joslyn A. Mus., 1955; BMFA, 1955; Colorado Springs FA Center, 1955; Wadsworth Atheneum, 1955; Des Moines A. Center, 1955; CM, 1955; Stonebridge Gal., Tokyo, 1955. *Position*: Instr., BMA, 1951, 1952; American Univ., 1952; University of Connecticut, 1954-1956. Visiting Lecturer, Univ. of Wisconsin, Madison, Wis., at present.

KNOBBS, HARRY R.—*Etcher, P.*
419 West Grant St., Pueblo, Colo.

B. McCook, Neb., Apr. 30, 1902. *Studied*: Pueblo Acad. FA; Cape Cod Sch. A. *Member*: Provincetown AA. *Exhibited*: SAE, 1938; WFNY 1939; Buffalo Pr. Cl., 1940; Southern Pr.M., 1936-1942; Denver A. Mus.; Kansas City AI; Provincetown AA; Mus. New Mexico, Santa Fé; Soc. Liberal A., Omaha, Neb.*

KNOBLER, LOIS JEAN—*Painter*
24 Eldridge St., Manchester, Conn.

B. New York, N.Y., Feb. 2, 1929. *Studied*: Syracuse Univ., B.F.A.; Florida State Univ., M.A. *Awards*: prizes, Berkshire Mus. A., 1954; Springfield, Mass., 1956, 1957; Chambers-Storck Co. award, Norwich, Conn., 1955; Mystic AA, 1957. *Work*: Florida State Univ. *Exhibited*: AFA traveling exh., 1956-1958; Univ. Connecticut, 1958; Berkshire Mus. A., 1954-1957; Springfield Mus. A., 1955-1957; deCordova & Dana Mus., 1954; Slater Mus. A., 1955; Norwich AA, 1955-1957; Boston A. Festival, 1955-1958; New Haven A. Festival, 1958; Mystic AA, 1956, 1957; Silvermine Gld. A., 1953, 1954, 1956; Essex AA, 1956.

KNOBLER, NATHAN—*Painter, E., Lith.*
24 Eldridge St., Manchester, Conn.

B. Brooklyn, N.Y., Mar. 13, 1926. *Studied*: Syracuse Univ., B.F.A.; Florida State Univ., M.A. *Awards*: prizes, Witte Mem. Mus., San Antonio, 1945; Berkshire Mus. A., 1955; Conn. WC Soc., 1956, 1957; Norwich AA, 1957. *Work*: Florida State Univ.; Munson-Williams-Proctor Inst.; U.S. Information Service. *Exhibited*: Ball State T. Col., 1951, 1958; BM, 1958; AFA traveling exh., 1958; Boston A. Festival, 1956, 1958; Conn. WC Soc., 1952-1957; Berkshire AA, 1954-1957; Springfield A. Mus., 1955-1957; de Cordova & Dana Mus., 1956, 1957; New Haven A. Festival, 1958; Inst. Contemp. A., Boston, 1958; Norwich AA, 1956-1958. *Position*: Prof. A., Graphics, Drawing, Art Appreciation, University of Connecticut.

KNOCHE, LUCILLE (MORLEY)—*Designer, S., P.*
35 East Wacker Dr., Chicago 1, Ill.; h. R.R. 2, Woodstock, Ill.

B. Mt. Vernon, N.Y., Mar. 23, 1899. *Studied*: AIC; Ill. Inst. Tech., and in Europe. *Member*: Inter-Soc. Color

Council; Com. on A. Edu.; Fashion Group of Chicago; IDI. *Awards*: All Am. Packaging award, 1942; Bolender award, Home Fashions Lg., Chicago, 1954. Co-Editor, "Descriptive Color Names Dictionary," 1950. Contributor to Forum; Interior Design; Better Homes & Gardens; House and Garden, and other national magazines. Lectures on Color and Design. *Work*: Color planning and interiors for U.S. Gypsum Research Village; Interiors for national advertising: Pittsburgh Plate Glass Co.; Pittsburgh Paint Co.; U.S. Gypsum Co.; Nat. Oak Flooring Assn.; Bruce Oak Floors; Pabco Linoleum; Pittsburgh Paint of Canada; U.S. Gypsum periodicals; color planning and interiors for: Loebl, Schlossman & Bennett, Archs.; Highland Park H.S.; Van Straaten Chemical Co.; Securities Service Corp. Hotels; Airguide Instrument Co., and others. Interior Des. for Abbott Laboratories, N. Chicago, Ill.; West School, Highland Park; Winnetka Pub. Lib.; Lake Tower Motel, Chicago. *Position*: Fabric Stylist, Montgomery Ward, N.Y.; Color Technician, Montgomery Ward, Chicago; Butler Bros.; Sears Roebuck Co.; Dir., Owner, Lucille Knoche Assoc., Chicago, Ill.

KNOLLENBERG, MARY TARLETON—Sculptor

Parker's Point, Chester, Conn.

B. Great Neck, N.Y., June 9, 1904. *Studied*: Sch. Am. Sculpture, with Mahonri Young; Grande Chaumiere, with Bourdelle, Paris, France; Corcoran Sch. A., with Heinz Warneke. *Member*: S. Gld.; Conn. Acad. FA; Essex AA. *Awards*: Guggenheim Fellowship, 1933. *Work*: in private collections. *Exhibited*: PAFA; S. Gld.; annually with Essex AA; frequently at Conn. Acad. FA.

KNOPF, NELLIE A(UGUSTA)—Painter, T., L.

122 South River St., Eaton Rapids, Mich.

B. Chicago, Ill. *Studied*: AIC; & with Charles Woodbury. *Awards*: prizes, Broadmoor A. Acad., Colorado Springs, Colo.; Hon. degree, D.F.A., MacMurray Col. *Work*: Lafayette (Ind.) AA; MacMurray Col., Jacksonville, Ill. *Exhibited*: AIC, 1920-1922, 1925-1927, 1929, 1930, 1937; CGA, 1929, 1935; PAFA, 1925, 1927, 1929; NAD, 1926; CAM; AWCS; Balt. WC Cl.; Detroit Inst. A., 1942, 1943; Toledo Mus. A.; Illinois Acad. FA; Indiana A. Cl.; All.A.Am.; Phila. WC Cl.; John Herron AI; Conn. Acad. FA; AFA; Michigan A., annually. *Position*: Prof. A., Emeritus, MacMurray College, Jacksonville, Ill.

KNOWLTON, DANIEL GIBSON—Craftsman, Des., T.

1200 Hope St., Bristol, R.I.

B. Washington, D.C., Nov. 14, 1922. *Member*: Boston Soc. A. & Crafts; Min. P. & S. Soc., Wash., D.C.; Providence Handicraft Cl. *Exhibited*: Smithsonian Inst., 1947, 1948, 1950, 1951; CGA, 1943-1945; R.I.Sch. Des., 1950, 1952, 1954, 1955, 1956; Bristol Hist. Soc., 1952; Providence Handicraft Cl., 1949-1952, 1954, 1956-1958; Brown Univ., 1955; Min. P. & S. Soc., 1954, 1956. *Positions*: Instr., Bookbinding, Providence Handicraft Soc.; Owner, Knowlton Hand Bindery, Bristol, R.I.; Bookbinder, Brown Univ., and Ext. Div., at present.

KNOX, HELEN ESTELLE—Painter

129 Sumner Ave., Springfield 8, Mass.

B. Suffield, Conn. *Studied*: Smith Col., A.B.; Hartford A. Sch.; & with W. Lester Stevens, Harve Stein, E. F. Marsden. *Member*: AWCS; AAPL; Springfield A. Lg. *Awards*: prize, Stockbridge (Mass.) AA, 1931. *Exhibited*: AWCS, 1931-1933, 1936, 1938-1946; WFNY 1939; Am. Lib. Color Slides, 1941; Phila. WC Cl., 1934; Wash. WC Cl., 1940; Amherst Col., 1935; Mt. Holyoke Col., 1936; Am.-British A. Center, 1941; New England Women A., 1934; Boston AC, 1933-1939; New Haven Paint & Clay Cl., 1934, 1940, 1941, 1945; Westfield Atheneum, 1932; G.W.V. Smith Mus., 1933; Springfield Mus., 1938; Ogunquit AA, 1939-1941; Springfield A. Lg., 1931-1939, 1941, 1943-1946; Phillips Acad., Andover, Mass., 1931; Stockbridge AA, 1931-1938. Lectures: British Art; History of Watercolor.*

KNOX, SUSAN RICKER—Painter

c/o Bank of Manhattan Co., 31 Union Sq., New York 3, N.Y.; s. Frazier Pasture Lane, near Marginal Way, Ogunquit, Me.

B. Portsmouth, N.H. *Studied*: Drexel Inst., Phila.; CUASch; & with Howard Pyle, Douglas Volk, Clifford Grayson, and in Europe. *Member*: AAPL; Chicago Galleries Assn.; Pen & Brush Cl.; North Shore AA; Ogun-

quit AA; New Hampshire AA; Ogunquit A. Center. *Awards*: prizes, St. Louis, Mo., 1929; Mus. Northern Arizona, 1932, 1935; Ogunquit AA, 1946; North Shore AA, 1935. *Work*: Cornell Coll., Mt. Vernon, Iowa; Wesleyan Col., Macon, Ga.; Brooks Mem. A. Gal.; Kansas City Bd. of Trade; Univ. of the South; Home for Children, Cedar Rapids, Iowa; Morris H.S., New York, N.Y.; England and Mexico. *Exhibited*: All.A.Am., 1938, 1940; AIC; PAFA; one-man exh.: CGA; San Diego FA Soc., 1929; Currier Gal., 1932; State Mus., Springfield, Ill.; Kansas City AI, 1933; FA Gal., Phoenix, Arizona, 1934; Brooks Mem. A. Gal., 1933, 1943; Palacio de Bellas Artes, Mexico, D. F., 1943; Am. Mus. Natural Hist.; WFNY 1939; Layton A. Gal.; Columbus Gal. FA; Fitchburg A. Center; Mus. City of N.Y., 1953, etc. Many other one-man exhs. in col. and univ.†

KOCH, BERTHE COUCH—Painter, E., S., Gr., W., L.

408 Oak Knoll Blvd., Mankato, Minn.; s. East Gloucester, Mass.

B. Columbus, Ohio, Oct. 1, 1899. *Studied*: Columbia Univ.; Ohio State Univ., B.A., M.A., Ph.D. in Fine Arts; & with Gifford Beal, Leon Kroll, Alexander Archipenko, James Hopkins. *Member*: CAA; Midwestern Col. A. Conference; AFA. *Awards*: F., Ohio State Univ., 1928, 1929. *Work*: IBM Coll.; Passedoit Gal.; Ohio State Univ.; Syracuse Mus. FA. *Exhibited*: Extensively in U.S. Author: monograph, "Apparent Weight of Colors"; "Chemistry of Art Materials"; "Physics of Light as Applied to Art"; "Lithography"; "Psychological Principles of Vision as Applied to Art Techniques." Contributor to: Parnassus, College Art Journal. *Position*: Graduate Prof. A., Mankato State College, Mankato, Minn.

KOCH, GERD—Painter, S., Gr., T., Des.

Rt. 1, Box 60 K, Ojai, Cal.

B. Detroit, Mich., Jan. 30, 1929. *Studied*: Wayne Univ., B.F.A.; UCLA Film Workshop and Graduate Sch. *Member*: Cal. WC Soc.; Los A. AA. *Award*: Cal. WC Soc., 1956. *Work*: Long Beach Mus. A.; Pasadena Mus. A.; Grumbacher, Inc.; Coca Cola of So. California. *Exhibited*: Cal. WC Soc., 1955-1957; Nat. Orange Show, 1954, 1957, 1958; Laguna Beach A. Festival, 1955; SFMA, 1957; Los A. Mus. A., 1957; 2-man (with Irene Koch): Ojai Music Festival, 1956; NOW Gal., Los A., 1956; Santa Monica A. Gal., 1958; Pasadena A. Mus., 1958. Designed interior and exterior of "The Ash Grove" Gallery, Los Angeles, 1958; organized first exhibition of Southern Cal. Painters.

KOCH, HELEN C.—Painter

3425 Michigan Ave., Cincinnati 8, Ohio

B. Cincinnati, Ohio, Mar. 2, 1895. *Studied*: Univ. Cincinnati, B.S.; Cincinnati A. Acad., and with Henry Snell. *Member*: Woman's A. Cl., Cincinnati; Prof. A. of Cincinnati. *Awards*: prizes, CM, 1945; Woman's A. Cl., 1951, 1955. *Work*: East Vocational H.S., Central H.S., Bond Hill H.S., Cincinnati. *Exhibited*: Ohio WC Soc., 1941, 1943, 1956; Cincinnati Prof. A., 1950-1956; Woman's A. Cl., 1948-1956; one-man: Town Club, Cincinnati, 1950-1954; Loring Andrews Gal., 1944, 1946, 1948 (one-man). Contributor to School Arts magazine. *Position*: A. T., East Vocational H.S., 1940-53.

KOCH, IRENE SKIFFINGTON—Painter, Gr., T.

Rt. 1, Box 60 K, Ojai, Cal.

B. Detroit, Mich., Nov. 5, 1929. *Studied*: Wayne Univ. *Member*: Cal. WC Soc.; Los A. AA. *Award*: Cal. WC Soc., 1957. *Work*: Long Beach Mus. A.; Pasadena A. Mus. *Exhibited*: Cal. WC Soc., 1955-1957; Michigan A., 1949; Laguna Beach A. Festival, 1955; Pacific Coast Biennial, 1955; SFMA, 1957; Los A. Mus. A., 1957; Santa Barbara Mus. A., 1957; Arts of So. California, 1958; 2-man (with Gerd Koch): Ojai Music Festival, 1956; Santa Monica A. Gal., 1958; NOW Gal., Los A.; Pasadena A. Mus., 1958. *Position*: Instr., privately, Ojai and Los Angeles, Cal.

KOCH, JOHN—Painter

300 Central Park West, New York, N.Y.; h. Setauket, L.I., N.Y.

B. Toledo, Ohio, Aug. 18, 1909. *Awards*: NAD, 1952; Cal. PLH, 1952. *Work*: BM; Boston Inst. Mod. A.; Nelson Gal. A.; Springfield Mus. A.; Canajoharie A. Gal.;

Newark Mus.; Cal. PLH; NAD; MMA; Toledo Mus. A.; Joslyn A. Mus.; Des Moines A. Center; Lehigh Univ. *Exhibited*: Carnegie Inst., 1939-1946, 1955; WMAA; CGA; PAFA; AIC; Valentine Gal., N.Y., 1939, 1941, 1943, 1946; BM; New Britain Mus. A.; Bennington Mus.; Univ. Georgia; one-man: Kraushaar Gal., 1949-1951, 1954, 1958; Portraits, Inc., 1951; Syracuse Mus. FA, 1952; Suffolk County Mus., Stony Brook, L.I., 1951 (retrospective); Cowie Gal., Los A., 1951; Provo, Utah, 1951.

KOCH, LIZETTE J.—*Illustrator, Comm. A., P., T.*

1819 Southeast 9th St., Ft. Lauderdale, Fla.; s. "Flying Bridge," Ogunquit, Me.

B. Brooklyn, N.Y., Aug. 25, 1909. *Studied*: PIASch. *Member*: Nat. All. A. & Indst. *Awards*: prize, Eberhard Faber Co. Comp. *Exhibited*: Nat. All. A. & Indst.; Montclair A. Mus. Illus., children's books, American Book Co., N.Y.; illus., cover designs: Motor Boating; Yachting; Rudder, and other magazines. *Position*: A. T., Englewood and Teaneck, N.J. H.S.

KOCH, M. ROBERT—*Craftsman, E., Gr., L.*

Mankato State College; h. 408 Oak Knoll Blvd., Mankato, Minn.

B. Columbus, Ohio, Jan. 23, 1888. *Studied*: Ohio State Univ.; N.Y. School of Ceramics; and with Alexandre Archipenko, Bernard Karfiol, Robert Laurent. *Member*: Am. Ceramic Soc.; Museo di Ceramiche, Faenze, Italy. *Work*: IBM. *Exhibited*: Syracuse Mus. FA, Ceramic Exh.; Columbus Gal. FA; Passedoit Gal., N.Y.; Univ. Omaha. Contributor articles on ceramics to Ceramic Age; Ceramic Industry. Lectures: Ceramic Materials; Influence of the Arabic Ceramics on the Faiences of France, Spain and Italy. *Position*: Visiting Prof., Ceramics, Mankato State College, Mankato, Minn., 1958-59.

KOCH, ROBERT,—*Educator, W., L.*

9 Outer Road, South Norwalk, Conn.

B. New York, N.Y., Apr. 7, 1918. *Studied*: Harvard Col., A.B.; N.Y. Univ. Inst. FA, M.A.; Yale Univ., Ph.D. *Member*: Soc. Arch. Hist.; Silvermine Gld. A.; Connecticut AA. Author: Louis Comfort Tiffany (catalogue) 1957, publ. by Am. Craftsmen's Council; "New York Armories," Journal of the Soc. Arch. Hist., 1955; "Posters and the Art Nouveau," Gazette des Beaux-Arts, 1957; "Art Nouveau Bing," Gazette des Beaux-Arts, 1959. Lectures: Ancient, Medieval, Renaissance and Modern Art. *Positions*: Instr., History of Art, Queens Col., 1951-53; Yale Univ., 1953-56; Asst. Prof. A., 1956- , Chm. A. Dept., 1958- , New Haven State Teachers College, New Haven, Conn.

KOCH(MEISTER), SAMUEL—*Painter*

82-02 Rockaway Beach Blvd., Rockaway Beach 93, L.I., N.Y.

B. Warsaw, Poland, Nov. 13, 1887. *Work*: Univ. Arizona; R.I. Mus. A. *Exhibited*: BMA; CGA; Univ. Arizona; MMA; Kelekian Gal.; CAM; Cal. PLH; BM; R.I.Mus. A.; Albright A. Gal.; MModA; Ferargil Gal.; Smithsonian Inst. European Exh.; Audubon A.; one-man: Contemporary A. Gal., 1942, 1950; Bignou Gal., 1944; Niveau Gal., 1946; Salpeter Gal., 1948; Chapellier Gal., 1953; Panoras Gal., N.Y., 1957.

KOCHERTHALER, MINA—*Painter*

124 West 79th St., New York 24, N.Y.

B. Munich, Germany. *Studied*: City Col. of N.Y., with Ralph Fabri. *Member*: Nat. Soc. Painters in Casein; Audubon A. *Awards*: prize, Nat. Soc. Painters in Casein, 1958. *Exhibited*: All. A. Am., 1958; Audubon A., 1959; Nat. Soc. Painters in Casein, 1957-1959; Knickerbocker A., 1958; NAC, 1958; Nat. traveling exh., Casein Soc., 1958-59.

KOCSIS, ANN—*Painter*

327 West 76th St., New York 23, N.Y.

B. New York, N.Y., *Studied*: Art Inst. Pittsburgh; NAD. *Member*: NAWA; Creative A. Assoc.; Knickerbocker A.; Pen & Brush Cl.; AAPL; Assoc. A. Pittsburgh; NAC; Tucson FA Assn. *Awards*: scholarship, Art Inst. Pittsburgh; citation, Fla. Southern Col., 1952; Gold Key and Grumbacher award, Seton Hall Univ., 1958. *Work*: San Manuel Lib., Ariz.; Arizona-Sonora Desert Mus., Tucson;

Fla. Southern Col.; Square & Compass Crippled Children's Clinic, Tucson; American-Hungarian Mus., Elmhurst, Ill. *Exhibited*: Argent Gal.; Audubon A.; Westchester Fair; Newton Gal.; State Col., Fredonia, N.Y.; State Col., Indiana, Pa.; Swope Gal. A.; Brazil (Ind.) Pub. Lib.; Coker Col.; Mars Hill (N.C.) Col.; Guilford Col.; Mercersburg (Pa.) Acad. A. Gal.; St. Vincent's Archabbey, Latrobe, Pa.; Creative A. Gal., N.Y.; Peter Kolean Gal.; Carnegie Lib., Tucson, Ariz.; Arizona State Mus.; Burr Gal., 1955-56; Assoc. A. of Pittsburgh, 1948, 1951-1953; NAWA, 1947-1952; AAPL, 1951, 1952; one-man: Montross Gal.; Morton, Vendome, Contemporary A. Gal., N.Y.; All. A. Am.; AAPL.

KOEHLER, HENRY—*Illustrator, Des.*

219 East 49th St., New York 17, N.Y.

B. Louisville, Ky., Feb. 2, 1927. *Studied*: Yale Univ., B.A. *Member*: SI; Soc. Typographic A.; Yale Assoc. in FA. Illus. for House Beautiful; Parents magazine; True; Esquire; Good Housekeeping. *Position*: 1st Vice-Pres., SI, 1958-59.

KOEHLER, WILHELM R. W.—*Educator*

Fogg Museum of Art, Harvard University, Cambridge, Mass.; h. 223 Marsh St., Belmont 78, Mass.

B. Reval, Estonia, Dec. 17, 1884. *Studied*: Univ. Strassburg, Ph.D. *Position*: Prof. Emeritus, Dept. FA, Harvard Univ., Cambridge, Mass.

KOEPF, WERNER—*Painter*

New Haven Ave., Orange, Conn.

B. Neckarsulm, Germany, Sept. 21, 1909. *Studied*: Kunstgewerbe Schule, Stuttgart, Germany; ASL; Yale Univ. *Member*: Essex AA; New Haven Paint & Clay Cl. *Awards*: prizes, Milford A. Lg., 1951; New Haven Paint & Clay Cl., 1951, 1952; Silvermine Gld. A., 1953; Essex AA, 1953; Conn. WC Soc., 1954. *Exhibited*: Soc. Indp.A., 1935-1937; Contemporary A. Gal., 1938 (one-man); PAFA, 1938, 1939, 1941; Montclair A. Mus., 1940; AIC, 1941, 1942; Springfield Mus. A.; Conn. State Development Comm., 1951; Guilford A. Lg., 1951; Milford A. Lg., 1951; Silvermine Gld. A., 1951; New Haven Paint & Clay Cl., 1951, 1952.*

KOEPNICK, ROBERT CHARLES—*Sculptor, T.*

215 Kenilworth Ave., Dayton 5, Ohio

B. Dayton, Ohio, July 8, 1907. *Studied*: Dayton AI; Cranbrook Acad. A.; & with Carl Milles. *Member*: Dayton Soc. P. & S. *Awards*: prizes, CAA, 1931; NAD, 1940, 1941; Nat. Catholic Welfare Comp., 1942; NGA, 1945. *Work*: S., County Court House, St. Paul's Church, Parker Cooperative Sch., Roosevelt H.S., Fairview H.S., Colonel White H.S., Hickorydale Elem. Sch., all in Dayton, Ohio. St. Mary's Church, Oxford, Ohio; St. Anthony's Church, Dayton; Sacred Heart Church, Salina, Kans.; panels in schools in Dayton, Ohio; Our Lady of La Crosse (Wis.); bronze sc., St. Peter in Chains Cathedral, Cincinnati, 1956; relief panel, Convent of Carmelite Sisters, East Chicago, Ind., 1957; stone carvings, Society of Mary, St. Joseph's Chapel, Marcy, N.Y., 1957; marble sc., Franciscan House, Centerville, Ohio, 1958; bronze port. of Frank M. Tait, Tait Mfg. Co., Dayton, 1958. *Exhibited*: PAFA, 1936-1938, 1940; NAD, 1938-1940, 1941; Dance Int., 1937; AIC, 1937; Syracuse Mus. FA, 1938; CM, 1935-1937, 1939, 1940, 1955; Dayton Soc. P. & S., 1937-1945; MMA, 1951; Ohio State Univ., 1954. *Position*: Hd., Sculpture Dept., Sch. of Dayton AI, Dayton, Ohio, 1936-41, 1946- . Visiting Sculptor, Antioch Col., 1953-54; Mt. St. Joseph Col., 1951-1955.

KOERNER, DANIEL—*Painter, Cart., Comm. A., T.*

408 East 10th St., New York 9, N.Y.

B. New York, N.Y., Nov. 16, 1909. *Studied*: ASL; Edu. All. A. Sch. *Work*: MMA; Queens Col.; CAM. Contributor cartoons to: Colliers; N.Y. Times; Sat. Review; Nation's Business; Ladies Home Journal; This Week; Cosmopolitan; King Features; Better Homes & Gardens; True; Argosy, and other national magazines. Lectures: Cartooning. *Position*: Private instr., 1938-41; Cartoon Instr., Cartoonist & Illustrators Sch., 1948-52.

KOERNER, HENRY—*Painter*
1046 Murray Hill Ave., Pittsburgh 17, Pa.

B. Vienna, Austria, Aug. 28, 1915. *Studied*: Acad. App. A., Vienna, and with Victor Theodor Slama. *Award*: medal, PAFA, 1949. *Work*: WMAA; MModA; Springfield Mus. A.; Univ. Nebraska; Des Moines A. Center; AIC; MMA; Walker A. Center; Wichita Mus. A.; Delgado Mus. A. *Exhibited*: nationally, including Carnegie Inst.; CGA; PAFA; Cal.PLH; WMAA; MModA; Nat. Acad. A. & Let.; Des Moines A. Center; Midtown Gal., 1948-1952, 1956; Cal. PLH, 1955 (one-man); Berlin, Germany, 1947; numerous one-man exhibitions. I., Saroyan's "Tracy's Tiger." Contributor to College Art Journal; cover for Time magazine. *Position*: A.-in-Res., Pa. Col. for Women, Pittsburgh, Pa., 1953-54; Instr., Cal. Col. A. & Crafts (summer) 1955.*

KOFFLER, MARY MINTZ—*Painter*
55 Central Park West, Apt. 19 F, New York 23, N.Y.

B. Morristown, N.J., Apr. 7, 1906. *Studied*: ASL. *Member*: AEA. *Awards*: prizes, Hunterdon A. Center, 1955-1957; Morristown AA; PAFA purchase prize, 1958. *Work*: PAFA. *Exhibited*: PAFA, 1954, 1958; Newark A. Mus.; Montclair A. Mus.; Hunterdon A. Center; Morristown AA; Asbury Park AA; NAD, 1958.

KOGAN, BELLE—*Industrial Designer*
145 East 35th St., New York 16, N.Y.; also, North Quaker Hill, Pawling, N.Y.

B. Russia, June 26, 1902. Studied: N.Y. Univ.; R.I. Sch. Des.; ASL; Winold Reiss Studios, and in Germany. *Member*: F., IDI (Pres. N.Y. Chptr., 1945-46). *Awards*: medal, IDI, 1942. *Exhibited*: Phila. A. All., 1946 (one-man); Akron AI, 1955-56. Contributor to trade, shelter, and fashion magazines, newspapers. Designer for: Red Wing Potteries; Quaker Silver Co.; Heller Hostessware; Boonton Molding Co.; Reed & Barton; Towle Mfg. Co.; Libbey Glass Co.; Maryland Plastics Co.; Lincoln Metal Products; The Washington Co.; United States Glass Co.; Federal Glass Co. and many others. Lectured on "Color in the Home," N.Y. Univ.

KOHLER, MEL(VIN) (OTTO)—*Designer*
300 E. St.; h. 2505 Brooke Blvd., Anchorage, Alaska

B. Wilcox, Sask., Canada, Dec. 7, 1911. *Studied*: Univ. Washington, Seattle, B.F.A.; Cal. Sch. FA with Maurice Sterne; Columbia Univ., M.A. *Positions*: Instr., Hist. A., Des., Interior Des., Painting, College of Puget Sound, Tacoma, Wash., 1934-44; Cur., Henry Gallery, Univ. Washington, 1948-53.

KOHLHEPP, DOROTHY IRENE—*Painter*
2116 Lauderdale Rd., Louisville 5, Ky.

B. Boston, Mass. *Studied*: Mass. Sch. A.; New Orleans A. & Crafts; Grande Chaumiere, Julian Acad., Andre L'Hote, Paris, France. *Member*: Salon des Tuileries; Mod. Eng. & Am. Painters, France; Louisville A. Center Assn. *Awards*: prizes, Louisville A., 1944, 1945; Jeffersontown, Ky., Fair, 1954; Kentucky & Southern Indiana A., 1945, 1946, 1949; Louisville A. Cl., 1946. *Work*: Seagram Coll.; Univ. Louisville; J. B. Speed A. Mus.; Devoe & Raynolds Coll. *Exhibited*: Ky.-Indiana A.; J. B. Speed Mus. A., 1950; Interior Valley Exh., 1955; Chicago, Ill., 1955; Salon des Tuileries, Paris; VMFA; New Orleans, Louisville, 1932-1946; one-man: Louisville A. Cl., 1937, 1940, 1945, 1948, 1949; J. B. Speed A. Mus., 1938, 1948; Univ. Louisville, 1944; Anchorage, Ky., 1945; Nichols General Hospital, U.S. Army, 1947, 1949; Louisville Woman's Cl., 1947, 1950. *Position*: Pres. Bd., 1940-41, V. Pres. Bd., 1942-47, A. Center Sch. & Assn., Louisville, Ky.*

KOHLHEPP, NORMAN—*Painter, Lith.*
2116 Lauderdale Rd., Louisville 5, Ky.

B. Louisville, Ky. *Studied*: Univ. Cincinnati; Grande Chaumiere, Paris; Academie Colorossi, and with Andre L'Hote. *Awards*: prizes, Ky. & Indiana A., 1940, 1941, 1947; Louisville A. Cl., 1945, 1948; Kentucky State Fair, 1952, 1953, 1955; Va.-Intermont Exh., 1958. *Work*: J. B. Speed A. Mus.; Univ. Louisville; Seagram Coll.; Devoe & Raynolds Coll. *Exhibited*: J. B. Speed A. Mus., 1938, 1948, 1950, 1955; Louisville A. Cl., 1940, 1949; Univ. Louisville; Chicago, Ill., 1955; Interior Valley Biennial, 1958. *Position*: Treas., A. Center Assn., 1958-59.

KOHN, MISCH—*Etcher, Eng., Lith., P., E.*
Institute of Design, Illinois Institute of Technology; h. 1200 East Madison Park, Chicago 15, Ill.

B. Kokomo, Ind., Mar. 26, 1916. *Studied*: John Herron AI, B.F.A. *Awards*: prizes, Phila. Pr. Cl., 1950, 1951, 1955, 1956, 1958; AIC, 1951, 1952, 1958; John Herron AI, 1952, 1956; SAM, 1950 (purchase); BM, 1950, 1951 (purchase); NAD, 1955; Guggenheim Fellowship, 1952, renewed 1954; Pennell medal, PAFA, 1952, Eyre medal, 1949. *Exhibited*: Salon de Mai, Paris, France, 1952, 1953; PAFA, 1949, 1952, 1956; BM, 1949-1957; Phila. Pr. Cl., 1949-1958; Boston Pr. M.; Seattle Pr. Cl.; AIC; also AIC, 1949-1958; one-man: Weyhe Gal., N.Y.; Phila. A. All.; AIC; Los A. Mus. A.; William Rockhill Nelson Mus. A. *Position*: Assoc. Prof. A., Inst. of Design, Illinois Institute of Technology, Chicago, Ill.

KOLB, DELMAR M.—*Museum Curator, C., T.*
The St. Paul Gallery & School of Art, 476 Summit Ave.; h. 85 B St., St. Paul 6, Minn.

B. Chicago, Ill., Jan. 14, 1912. *Studied*: Univ. Chicago, Ph.B., J.D.; AIC; N.Y. Univ., and with Amedee Ozenfant. Lectures: Crafts, Ceramics and Textiles. Planned, organized and administered exhs.: Fiber, Clay, and Metal, 1952, 1955, 1957, a biennial national craft show; "Selections '56" and "Selections '57," selected work of Minnesota artists. *Positions*: Instr., Ceramics, N.Y. Univ. and St. Paul Gal. & Sch. A.; Instr., Textiles, N.Y. Univ. and St. Paul Gal. & Sch. A.; Instr., N.Y. Univ., 1949-50; Asst. Dir. in charge of Program, St. Paul Gal. & Sch. A., 1950-56; Cur. Edu., St. Paul Gal. & Sch. A., St. Paul, Minn., 1956- .

KOLIN, SACHA—*Painter, S.*
221 East 78th St., New York 21, N.Y.

B. Paris, France, May 11, 1911. *Studied*: Sch. App. A., Acad. FA, Vienna, and in Paris, France. *Member*: AEA; NAWA. *Awards*: prizes, Societe Nationale des Beaux-Arts, Paris, France, 1934-1936; Village A. Center; East Hampton Gld. Hall. *Exhibited*: Vienna, Austria, 1934; Paris, France, 1934-1936; WFNY 1939; Burliuk Gal.; Hampton Bays; Contemporary A.; Delgado Mus. A.; Salon des Realites Nouvelles, Paris; Easthampton Gld. Hall; Parrish Mus., L.I., N.Y.; Smithsonian Inst.; BM; and in Amsterdam, Holland; Bern, Switzerland.

KOMARNITSKY, MRS. R. S. See Olshanska, Stephanie

KONI, NICOLAUS—*Sculptor, P., C., T.*
41 East 60th St., New York 22, N.Y.

B. Transylvania, May 6, 1911. *Studied*: Acad. FA, Vienna; also in Paris, France and Florence, Italy. *Member*: NSS; Arch. L.; Navy Lg.; Quill A. Soc., Palm Beach (Co-Chm.). *Award*: Pilsudski award. *Work*: BM; Rockford (Ill.) Mus.; Annapolis Naval Acad. Mus.; Washington County Mus. FA; Birmingham Mus. A.; High Mus. A.; Bezalel Mus., Israel; monuments, mem., in Europe. *Exhibited*: U.S. and abroad.

KONRAD, ADOLF FERDINAND—*Painter, T.*
16 Central Ave., Newark 2, N.J.

B. Bremen, Germany, Feb. 21, 1915. *Studied*: Newark Sch. F. & Indst. A.; Cummington Sch. A., with Herman Maril. *Member*: Assoc. A. of New Jersey; AEA (Pres. N.J. Chptr., 1953-56). *Awards*: prizes, F. Tiffany Fnd., 1937; N.J. State Exh., Morris Plains, N.J., 1954; N.J. State Exh., Tinton Falls, N.J., 1955; Montclair A. Mus., 1955; "Artist of the Year," Jersey City Mus. and Hudson County Artists, 1956; NAD, 1956; Springfield Mus. A., 1957; P. & S. of New Jersey, 1957. *Exhibited*: Montclair A. Mus., 1953, 1955, 1957; NAD, 1953; Newark Mus. A., 1955, 1958; Springfield, Mass., 1957; Butler Inst. Am. A., 1957. *Work*: Newark Mus. A.; Newark Pub. Lib.; Ciba Pharmaceutical Co., Basle, Switzerland.

KONZAL, JOSEPH—*Sculptor*
161 West 23rd St., New York 11, N.Y.

B. Milwaukee, Wis., Nov. 5, 1905. *Studied*: BAID; ASL. *Member*: S. Gld.; Brooklyn Soc. A.; ASL; Fed. Mod. P. & S.; Am. Abstract A. *Awards*: prizes, BM, 1950; Riverside Mus., 1950, 1954; Silvermine Gld. A., 1955-1958; Brooklyn Soc. A., 1950, 1956; Audubon A., 1958.

Work: in private colls.; N.Y. Hospital for Speech Disorders; Jamaica, L.I. Mun. Office Bldg. *Exhibited*: AIC, 1938; WMAA, 1948; Audubon A., 1950, 1953; S. Gld., 1942-1952; PAFA, 1953, 1954, 1958; one-man: Contemporary A., 1950, 1952, 1955. Contributor to Ceramic Age. Lectures, Demonstrations. *Position*: Instr., S., Brooklyn Mus. A. Sch., Brooklyn, N.Y.; Assoc. Prof. S., Adelphi Col., Garden City, L.I. (summers), 1954-55; North Shore A. Center, 1955-56.

KOOTZ, SAMUEL M.—Writer, Gal. Dir.
1018 Madison Ave. (21); h. 1025 Fifth Ave., New York 28, N.Y.

B. Portsmouth, Va., Aug. 23, 1898. *Studied*: Univ. Virginia, LL.B. Author: "Modern American Painters," 1928; "New Frontiers in American Painting," 1943; "Puzzle in Paint," 1943, and other books. *Position*: Dir., Samuel M. Kootz Gal., New York, N.Y., 1945- .

KOPENHAVER, JOSEPHINE Y(OUNG)—Painter, T.
Los Angeles City College, 855 North Vermont Ave., Los Angeles 29, Cal.

B. Seattle, Wash., June 9, 1908. *Studied*: Univ. California, A.B.; Univ. Southern California, M.F.A.; Chouinard AI; & with Millard Sheets. *Member*: Cal. WC Soc.; Audubon A. *Awards*: prizes, Women Painters of the West, 1940; Cal. WC Soc., 1944. *Work*: Los Angeles City Col. *Exhibited*: Audubon A., 1945, 1947, 1948, 1950; traveling exh., Cal. WC Soc., 1938-1954; Riverside Mus., 1944, 1946; Los. A. Mus. A.; San Diego FA Soc.; Oakland A. Gal.; Santa Cruz A. Lg.; Fnd. Western A.; Los A. AA; GGE, 1939; Santa Barbara Mus. A.; Pasadena AI; SAM; Los A. City Col.; Royar's A. Gal., and other local exhs.

KOPMAN, BENJAMIN—Painter, Gr., I.
77 West 104th St., New York 25, N.Y.

B. Vitebsk, Russia, Dec. 25, 1887. *Studied*: NAD. *Member*: AEA. *Awards*: gold medal, PAFA, 1947; prize, MMA, 1945. *Work*: BM; WMAA; MModA; MMA; Carnegie Inst.; PAFA; PMA; Butler AI; WMA; Detroit Inst. A.; Acad. A. & Let.; Tel-Aviv, Ain-Harod Mus., Israel; PC; Nelson Gal. A., and in private collections. *Exhibited*: Carnegie Inst., 1942-1951; more than 20 one-man exhs., nationally. Illus., "Crime and Punishment," 1944; "Frankenstein," 1948.

KOPPE, MRS. RICHARD. See Hinkle, Catherine

KOPPE, RICHARD—Educator, P., S.
Institute of Design, Illinois Institute of Technology; h. 4144 North Clarendon Ave., Chicago 13, Ill.

Studied: St. Paul Sch. A., with Cameron Booth, LeRoy Turner, Nicoli Cikovsky; New Bauhaus, Chicago, with Lazlo Moholy-Nagy, Gyorgy Kepes, Alexander Archipenko, and others. *Awards*: prizes, AIC, 1947, 1948, 1950; San F. AA, 1948; Springfield State Fair, 1950; Chicago A., Navy Pier, Chicago, 1958; Univ. Minnesota (purchase), 1950; BM (purchase), 1951. *Work*: Smith Col. Mus.; Illinois State Mus.; Univ. Minnesota; BM; WMAA; AIC; Indiana Univ., and in many private collections; murals, Hotel Sherman, Chicago, Ill.; Medical Bldg., Chicago; sc. panel, Club Lido, South Bend, Ind. *Exhibited*: Artists Gal., N.Y.; John Heller Gal., N.Y.; many Chicago galleries; Michigan State Univ. (2-man) with Misch Kohn), 1958; Oklahoma State Univ., 1958; Art:USA, 1958; AIC, 1941-1957; Carnegie Inst., 1952; MMA, 1950, 1952; WMAA, 1951, 1953, 1954, 1956; BM, 1950, 1951; Univ. Illinois, 1948-1951; PAFA, 1951; San F. AA, 1948, 1949; Nebraska AA, 1951; Illinois State Fair, 1947, 1948, 1950; Univ. Minnesota, 1951; Denver A. Mus., 1951; Wildenstein Gal., 1949; Exhibition Momentum, Chicago, 1950, 1952, 1953; Illinois State Mus., 1949; NAD, 1947; A. & Crafts Cl., New Orleans, 1948; BM, 1957; Ravinia (Ill.) Festival A., 1957; AIC, 1957 (on tour Europe, 1957-59), 1958, and many others; one-man: (1936-58) St. Paul. Sch. A.; St. Catherine's Col.; Minnesota State Fair; Well-of-the-Sea Gal., Chicago; Palmer House, Chicago; Elman Gal., St. Louis; Cabiniss Gal., Denver; Ryan Gal., Chicago; Studio, Chicago; Gallery 4, Detroit; Cliff Dwellers, 1955; Feingarten Gal., Chicago, and many others. *Position*: Assoc. Prof., Hd. Visual Des., Institute of Design, Illinois Institute of Technology, Chicago, Ill., 1946- .

KOPPELMAN, CHAIM—Etcher, T.
20 West 16th St., New York 11, N.Y.

B. New York, N.Y., Nov. 17, 1920. *Studied*: Am. Artists Sch.; A. Col. of Western England, Bristol; Ozenfant Sch. FA. *Member*: Soc. for Aesthetic Realism; SAGA; Boston Pr. M.; Comm. on A. Edu. *Awards*: Tiffany Fnd. Grant, 1956; prize, SAGA, 1955. *Work*: Victoria & Albert Mus., London, England; MModA; LC; MMA; Dartmouth Col.; Syracuse Univ. Print comm.; Intl. Graphic A. Soc., 1958; Assoc. Am. A. Gal., 1958. *Exhibited*: WMAA, 1948, 1950; PAFA, 1950; LC, 1955-1957; BMFA, 1955-1958; BM, 1955, 1956, 1958; Phila. Pr. Cl., 1955-1958; Oakland A. Mus., 1957, 1958; Yale Univ. A. Gal.; DMFA; Santa Barbara Mus. A.; MModA; one-man: Phila. A. All., 1958; Terrain Gal., N.Y., 1956. *Positions*: Instr., Rhodes Prep Sch., N.Y., 1951- (Chm. A. Dept.); New Paltz State T. Col., 1952-58; N.Y. Univ., Dept. A. Edu., 1947-55; Brooklyn College, Brooklyn, N.Y., 1950- .

KORMENDI, ELIZABETH (Mrs. Eugene)—Painter, S.
2943 Upton St., Northwest, Washington, D.C.

B. Budapest, Hungary. *Studied*: in Europe. *Member*: Soc. FA, Budapest. *Work*: Mus., City of Budapest; Nurnberg Mus.; Immaculate Conception Church, East Chicago, Ill.; Boy's Town; Our Lady of the Lake Church, Wawasee, Ind.; murals, St. Catherine's Church, St. Louis, Mo.; Mt. Carmel, St. Louis, Mo.; 14 aluminum reliefs, St. Peter's Church, Oshkosh, Wis. *Exhibited*: one-man exh.: Milwaukee AI, 1940, 1945; Renaissance Soc., Univ. Chicago, 1941; Oak Park A. Lg., 1941; Herron AI, 1943; Norton Gal., 1944; & in Nurnberg, Germany; Venice, Italy; Barcelona, Spain; Budapest, Hungary; etc. Publ.: "The Art of Eugene and Elizabeth Kormendi."

KORMENDI, EUGENE (JENO)—Sculptor
2943 Upton St., Northwest, Washington, D.C.

B. Budapest, Hungary, Oct. 12, 1889. *Studied*: A. Acad. Budapest; & in Paris. *Member*: Soc. FA, Budapest; Soc. Four A., Palm Beach, Fla.; Audubon A. *Awards*: Soc. Four A., Palm Beach, 1945; Hoosier Salon, 1946; med., Barcelona Int. Exp. *Work*: Heeres Mus., Vienna; Budapest Mus.; mem., monuments, statues, Valparaiso, Ind.; Univ. Notre Dame; Mt. Mary Col., Milwaukee; Boys Town, Neb.; Ft. Wayne, Ind.; St. Louis, Mo.; Oshkosh, Wis.; Wash., D.C.; woodcarving, St. Peter's Church, Oshkosh, Wis.; statue, St. Peter's Church, Olney, Md.; New Rochelle, N.Y.; Pres. Truman plaque, 1949, & many works abroad. *Exhibited*: one-man exh.: Milwaukee AI, 1940, 1945; Norton Gal., 1944; Renaissance Soc., Univ. Chicago, 1941; Oak Park A. Lg., 1941; Herron AI, 1943; also, Hoosier Salon, 1946; Audubon A., 1946; AIC, 1946; & abroad.

KORN, ELIZABETH P.—Painter, E., I.
Drew University, Madison, N.J.; h. 531 Washington St., Hoboken, N.J.

B. Germany. *Studied*: Breslau Univ.; Acad. F. & App. A., Berlin; ASL; Rome, Italy; Columbia Univ., and with Emil Orlik, Berlin. *Member*: AAPL; N.J. Art Council; CAA; NAWA; AAUP; Kappa Pi (Hon.). *Awards*: prizes, Posnan Mus., Poland; Newark Mus.; N.J. State Mus.; 1949; Orange, N.J. State Exh., 1952; Grumbacher prize, Rahway, N.J., 1951. *Work*: Columbia Univ.; Newark Mus. A. *Exhibited*: NAD, 1942, 1943; AWS, 1942, 1943; Newark Mus.; Montclair A. Mus.; N.J. State Mus.; Drew Univ. (one-man); Rahway, N.J.; Theodore Kohn Gal., N.Y. (one-man); Morristown Woman's Cl.; N.J. Art Council; Rome, Italy (one-man); N.Y. City Center, 1956-1958; NAWA, 1958; I., "At Home with Children," 1943; "Skippy's Family," 1945; "Portraits of Famous Physicists," 1944; "Aladdin"; "Apple Pie for Louis." Co-author, I., "Trail Blazer to Television," 1950; "Read Up On Life," 1952 (textbook); "Nando of the Beach," 1958. Contributor to leading magazines and newspapers. *Position*: Assoc. Prof. A., L., Hd. Dept. A., Drew Univ., Madison, N.J.; Guest Lecturer, Newark Col. of Engineering.

KORTHEUER, DAYRELL—Portrait Painter, T., W.
709 Ardsley Rd., Charlotte 7, N.C.

B. New York, N.Y., July 25, 1906. *Studied*: McBurney Sch.; Rutgers Prep. Sch.; ASL, with Frank DuMond, George Bridgman, John Carroll; NAD, with Charles Hawthorne, and in Sweden. *Member*: Portraits, Inc.; North Carolina State A. Soc.; Mint Mus. A.; *Awards*: F., Tiffany Fnd., 1928; prizes, NAC, 1928; Mint Mus. A., 1941,

1942; Blowing Rock AA, 1955, gold medal, 1954. *Work*: portraits, Merchant's Assn., N.Y.; Mint Mus. A.; Emory Univ.; Queens Col., Charlotte; Univ. North Carolina; Davidson Col.; Winthrop Col., Rock Hill, S.C.; Erskine Col.; Governor's Mansion, Raleigh, N.C.; Fulton Nat. Bank, Atlanta; Presbyterian Hospital, Charlotte, and in private collections. *Exhibited*: one-man: Greenville, S.C., 1941; Mint Mus. A., 1945, 1951; Vose Gal., Boston, 1949; A. Cl., Wash., D.C., 1950; Hartford, Conn., 1950; Asheville Mus. A., 1953; Lancaster, S.C., 1954; Blowing Rock AA, 1955; Statesville, N.C., 1957; Hickory (N.C.), 1958. Contributor to Art Life with articles on Rembrandt and Velazquez. Instr., Painting, Mint Mus. A.

KOSA, EMIL J., JR.—*Painter, Lith., W., L.*

300 South Canyon View Dr., Los Angeles 49, Cal.

B. Paris, France, Nov. 28, 1903. *Studied*: Acad. FA, Prague, with Thille; California AI; Ecole des Beaux-Arts, Paris, and with Kupka, Laurens. *Member*: NA; AWS; Audubon A.; Cal. WC Soc. *Awards*: medal, Pan-Pacific Exh., 1928; prizes, AWS, 1938, 1939, 1953; Balt. WC Cl. 1939; San Diego A. Gld., 1937, 1942; Oakland A. Mus., 1938, 1942, 1950; Fnd. Western A., 1942, 1945; Los A. Mus. A., 1945; Santa Cruz, 1932, 1938, 1941, 1942, 1948; Cal. State Fair, 1934, 1938, 1949; Arizona State Fair; NAD, 1941, 1949, 1951, 1954; Acad. A. & Sc., 1952; Newport Harbor H.S.; Westwood AA, 1953; Sacramento State Fair, 1954; P. & S. Cl., 1938, 1939, 1941, 1944; Cal. A. Cl., 1938, 1940-1942, Jarvis House award, Art:USA, 1958. *Work*: NAD; Cal. State Lib.; Springfield Mus. A.; Cranbrook Acad. A.; Dover (Del.) H.S.; Wash. State Col.; Chaffey Jr. Col.; Santa Barbara Mus. A.; Los A. Mus. A., and others; murals, Lockheed Aircraft Corp. *Exhibited*: NAD; PAFA; CGA; AWS; AIC; Carnegie Inst.; VMFA; MMA; Denver A. Mus.; Toledo Mus. A.; Colorado Springs FA Center; Los A. Mus. A.; Frye Mus. A., Seattle, and many others nationally. Author: "Watercolor Methods," 1955. *Position*: Instr., Los A. Art Inst.; Chouinard AI.

KOSLOWSKY, NOTA—
Painter, Des., Eng., I., W., T., Cart.

41 Union Square West (3); h. 185 Lexington Ave., New York 16, N.Y.

B. Porozowa, Poland, Apr. 20, 1906. *Studied*: A. Sch. & T. Inst., Warsaw; NAD; ASL, with Olinsky, DuMond, Lewis. *Member*: AEA; AAPL; Rockport AA; North Shore AA. *Award*: prize, AAPL, 1955. *Work*: portraits of prominent persons in private colls. *Exhibited*: AAPL, 1952-1955; WMAA; Riverside Mus.; one-man: Israel, 1951; Norlyst Gal., 1948; Contemp. Foreign Art, N.Y., 1955; Caravan Gal., N.Y., 1957. Author, I., Ed., "Israel, Its People and Places," 1958 (portfolio of prints). Contributor cartoons and illus. to: Day; Morning Journal; Kinder Journal (USA); Davar L'Yelodim, Israel; illus. many children's books.

KOSTKA, RICHARD LOUIS—*Industrial Designer*

National Retail Furniture Assn., 666 Lake Shore Dr., Chicago 11, Ill.; h. 12490 Keystone Island Dr., North Miami, Fla.

B. Baltimore, Md., May 18, 1905. *Studied*: City Col., Balt.; Univ. Tennessee; Univ. North Carolina; Univ. Florida; Miami Univ. *Member*: IDI; Furniture Cl. Am. Author, I., "Modern Stores," 1948-52. Contributor to National Furniture Review. Wrote scripts, des. sets and directed films for Nat. Retail Furniture Assn., 1947. Lectures: Store Modernization. *Position*: Dec., Consultant, Morrison-Neese, Greensboro, N.C., 1936-39; Instr., Univ. North Carolina, 1939-40; Dir., Store Modernization, Nat. Retail Furniture Assn., Chicago, Ill., 1947- . Chm., Florida Chptr. IDI, 1958-59.

KOTIN, ALBERT—*Painter, E., L.*

90 East 10th St. (3); h. 210 East 34th St., New York 16, N.Y.

B. New York, N.Y., Aug. 7, 1907. *Studied*: ASL; NAD; BAID; in Paris; & with Charles Hawthorne. *Member*: CAA; A. Cl., N.Y. *Work*: Syracuse Mus. FA; Brooklyn Pub. Lib.; Newark Bd. Edu.; Bryant, Theodore Roosevelt H.S., New York, N.Y.; U.S. Marine Hospital; murals, USPO, Arlington, N.J.; Ada, Ohio; N.Y. Univ., and in private colls. *Exhibited*: An Am. Group, 1938; LC; PAFA; Assoc. Am. A.; Luyber Gal.; Wichita A. Mus.; Stable

Gal.; Hacker Gal., 1951 (one-man); March Gal., 1957; Tanager Gal., 1957-58; Stable Gal., 1957; Grand Central Moderns, 1958 (one-man). Lectures: "Historical Background of Modern Painting." *Position*: Instr., City Col. New York, 1947-51; Brooklyn Polytechnic Inst., Brooklyn, N.Y., 1952- .

KOVNER, SAUL. See *Saul*

KOZLOW, SIGMUND—*Painter*

Finesville, N.J.; h. 1651 Metropolitan Ave., New York 62, N.Y.

B. New York, N.Y., Dec. 7, 1913. *Studied*: NAD; Ecole des Beaux-Arts, Paris, France. *Member*: AEA; Audubon A.; Delaware Valley AA; Tiffany Fnd.; Assoc. A. of New Jersey; MacDowell A. Colony; Fontainebleau Alumni. *Awards*: Pulitzer traveling scholarship, 1936-37; Tiffany F., 1936; prizes, NAD, 1945; Munson-Williams-Proctor Inst., Utica, N.Y.; Kosciuszko F., 1947, 1948, 1950; State T. Col., Pa., 1948-49; Cambridge Springs, Pa., 1951; Terry AI, 1952; Clinton, N.J., 1956; Orange, N.J., 1958. *Work*: State T. Col., Indiana, Pa.; Univ. Georgia; AIC; Simmons Col.; Munson-Williams-Proctor Inst. *Exhibited*: AIC, 1936; CGA, 1943; Carnegie Inst., 1943-1945; PAFA, 1936, 1937, 1948; VMFA, 1938; NAD, 1934, 1945, 1950; Detroit Inst. A., 1945; Albright A. Gal., 1946; BM, 1943; GGE, 1939; State T. Col., Indiana, Pa., 1945, 1946, 1948, 1949; Audubon A., 1948-1958; AWS, 1948; Alliance Col., Pa., 1951; Butler AI, 1948-1952; Newark Mus., 1952; Trenton Mus. A., 1954, 1956, 1958; Montclair A. Mus., 1956, 1958; Phila. A. All., 1956, 1958; Everhart Mus. A., 1958; New Hope, Pa., 1948-1958.

KRAMER, HELEN KROLL—*Craftsman*

277 Park Ave., New York 17, N.Y.

B. Buffalo, N.Y., July 9, 1907. *Studied*: Traphagen A. Sch., and in Munich, Germany. *Member*: Am. Craftsmen's Council. *Work*: Cooper Union Mus.; Jewish Mus., N.Y.; Hesslein Lib. of the Phila. Textile Sch.; Mem. Lib., Lowell Technological Inst., and in museums in Israel. Tapestry, Brandeis Univ. Jewish Chapel. *Exhibited*: WFNY 1939; GGE, 1939; Univ. Minnesota A. Gal., 1951; Wisconsin Union, 1952; Rochester Mem. A. Gal., 1951; Fla. Gulf Coast A. Center, Clearwater, 1955; Des Moines A. Center, 1954; Coe College, Cedar Rapids, 1954; Dwight Mus., Mount Holyoke, 1955. Contributor to Journal of the Am. Assn. Univ. Women. Lectures: Texture, Color and Material; Textiles; History of Textures.

KRAMER, HILTON—*Critic, W., T., L.*

Arts Magazine, 116 East 59th St., New York 22, N.Y.; h. 112 Willow St., Brooklyn 1, N.Y.

B. Gloucester, Mass., Mar. 25, 1928. *Studied*: Syracuse Univ., B.A.; Columbia Univ.; New Sch. for Social Research; Harvard Univ.; Indiana Univ. Contributor to Arts Magazine; Partisan Review; Commentary; New Republic; The Progressive; Western Review; Industrial Design and other publications. Lectures: "Art Today." *Position*: Assoc. Ed., Feature Ed., Arts Digest, 1954-55; Managing Ed., Arts Magazine, 1955- .*

KRAMER, REUBEN ROBERT—*Sculptor, T.*

1201 Eutaw Place, Baltimore 17, Md.

B. Baltimore, Md., Oct. 9, 1909. *Studied*: Rinehart Sch. S.; Am. Acad. in Rome, and in London and Paris. *Member*: F., Am. Acad. in Rome; AEA; Am. Acad. in Rome Alumni Assn. *Awards*: Rinehart traveling scholarship, 1931, 1933; Prix de Rome, 1934; medal, prizes, Frederick Douglas Homes Comp., Balt., 1940; Nat. A. Week, Md., 1941; BMA, 1940, 1946, 1948, 1949, 1951, 1952, 1954; Peale Mus. A., 1949; S. Gld., 1947; Wash. S. Group, Smithsonian Inst., 1952, 1954; BMA, IBM, CGA (all purchase awards), award for sc., 1957. *Work*: Martinet Col., Balt.; USPO, St. Albans, W. Va.; relief, St. Mary's Seminary, Alexandria, Va.; BMA; IBM; CGA. *Exhibited*: BMA, 1940, 1941, 1943-1958; PMA, 1940, 1949; PAFA, 1949-1953, 1957; Am. Jewish Tercentenary Exh. traveling, 1954-55; Am. Acad. in Rome; Grand Central A. Gal.; CGA, 1951-1957; one-man: BMA, 1939, 1951; Am. Univ., Wash., D.C., 1953; Hagerstown, Md., 1955. *Position*: Dir., Eve. Sch., Balt. A. Center.

KRAMER, SHIRLEY—*Teacher, P., L., Des., C.*

10 Flower Lane, New Hyde Park, N.Y.

B. New York, N.Y., May 28, 1917. *Studied*: Brooklyn Col., B.A.; T. Col., Columbia Univ., M.A.; NAD; Craft Students Lg.; ASL. *Member*: Nat. Com. on A. Edu.; Long Island A. T. Assn.; N.Y. State A. T. Assn.; Nat. Assn. Pub. Sch. Adult Educators. *Award*: A. T. exh., 1955. *Exhibited*: N.Y. City Center, 1954; Contemp. Arts Gal., 1957; Country A. Gal., Westbury, L.I., 1957; BM; Suffolk Mus. A., 1957; A. All., 1957. Lectures on Art Education; Understanding Children's Art to museum, parent and art groups. *Position*: Hd. A. Dept., Queens Youth Center of the Arts, 1958-59.

KRAMRISCH, STELLA (Dr.)—

Museum Curator, E., Cr., L.

Philadelphia Museum of Art; mail: Box 17, Bennett Hall, University of Pennsylvania (4); h. 1720 Spruce St., Philadelphia 3, Pa.

B. Mikulov, Austria. *Studied*: Univ. Vienna, Ph.D., with J. Strzygowski, A. Dvorak. *Member*: CAA; Am. Oriental Soc.; Assn. of Asian Studies; Asia Soc.; Oriental Cl. (Phila.); Royal Soc. of India and Pakistan (London); Indian Soc. of Oriental Art (Calcutta); The Asiatic Soc. (Calcutta). Author, Ed., "The Hindu Temple," 1946; "The Art of India," 1954; "Kerala and Dravida," 1952; "Indian Sculpture," 1932; "Principles of Indian Art," 1922, and many others; numerous articles, particularly in the Journal of the Indian Society of Oriental Art, Calcutta (Ed. of the Journal, 1932-50). Contributor to Artibus Asiae; Journal of the Indian Soc. of Oriental Art; American Oriental Soc.; Bulletin of the Philadelphia Mus. Lectures: Indian Art to universities in US and Europe. *Positions*: Consultant to the government of India on the teaching of art and of art in industry; Consultant to the Exhibition of Indian Art (Royal Acad. A., London, 1947); Cur., Indian Art, Philadelphia Museum of Art, Philadelphia, Pa., at present.

KRAUS, ROBERT—*Cartoonist, I., W.*

"Eastview," Joe's Hill Rd., Danbury, Conn.

B. Milwaukee, Wis., June 21, 1925. *Studied*: Layton Sch. A., with Gerrit Sinclair; ASL, with Yasuo Kuniyoshi, Cameron Booth. *Awards*: scholarship, ASL, 1946. Author, I., "Junior, The Spoiled Cat," 1955; "All the Mice Came," 1955; "Ladybug, Ladybug," 1956. Contributor cartoons to New Yorker, Colliers, Sat. Eve. Post.*

KRAUSE, GLEN ADOLPH—*Museum Director, P., T.*

Phillips Exeter Academy, Exeter, N.H.; s. Port Sheldon Store, West Olive, Mich.

B. Chicago, Ill., Sept. 10, 1914. *Studied*: AIC; Univ. Chicago, and with Boris Anisfeld. *Member*: New Hampshire AA; Sch. A. Instr. Assn. *Awards*: scholarships, 1933-34, 1935, traveling F., 1936, prizes, 1940, 1941, all from AIC; prizes, Grand Rapids A. Gal., 1951, 1952; Currier Gal. A., 1950, 1952-1954, 1956; BMFA, 1956; Boston A. Festival, 1957. *Work*: Grand Rapids A. Gal.; AGAA; U.S. Export Lines; LC; N.Y. Pub. Lib.; Albion Col.; de Cordova & Dana Mus. A.; New Britain Mus. A.; Currier Gal. A.; Hope Col. *Exhibited*: nationally. One-man: Grand Rapids A. Gal., 1950; Mortimer Levitt Gal., 1950, 1953; Lamont A. Gal., 1954; Currier Gal. A., 1951; New Britain Mus. A., 1957; John Esther Gal., 1957, and in many schools and colleges. *Positions*: Instr. A., AIC, 1938-42; Naval Air Corps, 1943-45; Dir. A., Dir., Lamont A. Gal., Phillips Exeter Acad., Exeter, N.H., at present.

KRAUSE, LA VERNE (Mrs. L. G.)—*Painter, Gr., Des.*

2302 Southeast 47th St., Portland 15, Ore.

B. Portland, Ore., July 21, 1924. *Studied*: Univ. Oregon, B.S.; Portland A. Mus. Sch. *Member*: Portland A. Mus.; AEA (Pres. Ore. Chptr. 1954-55). *Awards*: prizes, Northwest Pr. M., (purchase), 1954. *Work*: Henry Gal., Univ. Washington. Hand printed wallpaper from woodblocks, lounge of the Selling Bldg., Portland, Ore. *Exhibited*: Wichita AA, 1954; SAM, 1947, 1955; Artists of Oregon, 1949-1956, 1958.

KREBS, COLUMBA (Mrs. Annabell Culverwell)—

Painter, W., I.

Hollywood Hotel, Hollywood, Cal.; h. 55 Glenwood Ave., East Orange, N.J.

B. Greensburg, Pa., July 13, 1902. *Studied*: Hood Col.; ASL; N.Y.Sch. F. & App. A.; NAD. *Member*: St. Peters-

burg A. Cl., Newark A. Cl. *Work*: mural panel, Textile H.S., N.Y. *Exhibited*: Hall of Art, N.Y.; Indp. A., 1932, 1933; Strauss Gal., N.Y., 1951; Bloomfield (N.J.) A. Cl.; Newark A. Cl. Author, I., "The Adventures of Skuddabud"; cartoon strip of same story in comic magazines of Brazil, Mexico, and Argentina. Contributor frontispiece, Flying Magazine. Lectures: The Mysteries of Man and the Universe, illus. with color slides. *Position*: Pres., Skuddabud Creations, 1936-40; Owner, Heated Doll Co., 1941-45; Dir., owner, Symbolart Co., 1954- .*

KREBS, ROSE K.—*Ceramic Sculptor, P.*

304 West 89th St., New York 24, N.Y.

B. Germany. *Studied*: Bauhaus, Germany; Ceramic Workshop; ASL, with William Zorach. *Member*: Ogunquit AA; Artist-Craftsmen of N.Y. *Award*: prize, Pen & Brush Cl., 1958. *Work*: ceramic vases for Mercedes-Benz showrooms, N.Y.; Cooper Union Mus. *Exhibited*: Syracuse Mus. FA, 1950-1952, 1958; N.Y. Ceramic A. Soc., 1948-1958; Mus. Natural Hist., N.Y.; Cooper Union Mus.; Sculptors Gal., 1954; Ogunquit AA, 1953-1955; Chautauqua AA, 1958. *Positions*: A. Cr., Craftsmen's Newsletter; Instr., S., Ogunquit Sch. for Painting & Sculpture, 1955 (summer).

KREDEL, FRITZ—*Illustrator, Cart.*

180 Pinehurst Ave., New York 33, N.Y.

B. Michelstadt, Germany, Feb. 2, 1900. *Studied*: in Europe, and with Rudolf Koch, Victor Hammer. *Awards*: gold medal, Paris Salon, 1938; Citations, Limited Editions Cl., 1949, 1954. *Exhibited*: Washington County Mus., Hagerstown, Md., 1957. I., The True Meaning of Christmas, 1955; All About Birds, 1955; The Complete Andersen, 1954 (Limited Ed.); Oscar Wilde: Epigrams, 1955; Prose and Poetry of England, 1955; Prose and Poetry of America, 1955; Map of "Michelstadt," 1955; Book of Books, 1956; Book of Life, 1956; Rebel's Roost, 1956; The Warden, 1956 (Limited Ed.); Tom Paine, 1957; Poems of Heinrich Heine, 1957 (Limited Ed.); All About Moths and Butterflies, 1957; Aucassin and Nicolette, 1957; The Journal and Letters of Philip Vickers Fithian, 1957; The Life of the Book, 1957; Simplicissimus, 1958; Barchester Towers, 1958 (Limited Ed.); All About the Desert, 1958; Dolls and Puppets of the XVIII Century, 1958 (Limited Ed.); and many other books prior to 1950.

KREHM, WILLIAM P.—*Painter*

327 South Burlington Ave., Los Angeles 5, Cal.

B. Kansas City, Kan., Feb. 2, 1901. *Studied*: with Dana Bartlett, William T. McDermitt, James Swinnerton. *Member*: Artists of the Southwest; Cal. AC; P. & S Cl. *Awards*: prize, P. & S. Cl., 1944. *Exhibited*: GGE, 1939; Ariz. State Fair, 1941; Palace Legion Honor, 1945; Los A. Mus. A., 1944; Cal. AC, 1944; P. & S. Cl., 1945.*

KREINDLER, DORIS BARSKY—*Painter, Et., T.*

75 Central Park, West, New York 23, N.Y.

B. Passaic, N.J., Aug. 12, 1901. *Studied*: Contemporaries Graphic A. Center; N.Y. Sch. App. Des. for Women; NAD; ASL, and with Ethel Katz, Hans Hofmann, Ivan Olinsky, Charles Hinton. *Member*: Brooklyn Soc. A.; NAWA; Nat. Soc. Painters in Casein; New Orleans AA; Provincetown AA; Knickerbocker A. *Awards*: F., Research Studios, Maitland, Fla.; Brooklyn Soc. A., 1955; AEA, 1953; Collectors Print, Contemporaries Gal., 1958. *Exhibited*: BM, annually; PAFA, 1932-1944; Columbus Gal. FA; Brooklyn Soc. A. traveling exh.; traveling exh. to Switzerland, Greece, Canada; Montross Gal.; NAWA; Butler Inst. Am. A., 1958; one-man: Seligmann Gal., 1952, 1954; Research Studios; Esther Robles Gal., Los A., 1957; Santa Monica A. Gal., 1957; Fresno A. Center; Rosequist Gal., Tucson, Ariz., 1958.

KREIS, HENRY—*Sculptor, T.*

Denison Rd., Essex, Conn.

B. Essen, Germany, July 27, 1899. *Studied*: State Sch. App. A., Munich, with Joseph Wackerle; BAID. *Member*: NA; Nat. Inst. A. & Let.; Am. Numismatic Soc.; Lynn AA; Essex AA; NSS; Arch. Lg.; Conn. Acad. FA. *Awards*: Lindsey Morris prize, 1936; AV 1942; Henry Avery prize, 1944; gold med., PAFA, 1942; gold med., NAD, 1951, 1954; silver med., Numismatic Soc., 1950. *Work*: MMA; WMAA; Wadsworth Atheneum; PAFA; Iowa State Univ.; Int. Magazine Bldg., N.Y.; Court House, Erie, Pa.; Social Security Bldg., Wash., D.C.; Dept. Justice Bldg., Wash.,

D.C.; Educational Bldg., Harrisburg, Pa.; USPO, Bronx, N.Y.; Stamford Housing Project; monument, Fairmount Park, Phila., Pa.; Mem., Va Polytechnic Inst., Blacksburg, Va.; Mem., U.S. Military Cemetery, Carthage, Tunis, North Africa; figures, St. Elizabeth Church, Van Nuys, Cal.; Loyola Seminary, Shrub Oak, N.Y.; relief, Ft. Moore Pioneer Mem., Los Angeles; Supreme Court Bldg., Brooklyn; medals, Conn. Tercentenary, 1935; WFNY med., 1939; Medal of Honor, NSS; U.S. coins: Conn. Tercentenary Half-Dollar; Bridgeport Centennial Half-Dollar; Sen. Robinson Commemorative Half-Dollar. *Exhibited*: nationally. Several one-man exhs. *Position*: Instr., S., Hartford A. Sch., 1936-1955 and Yale Univ., 1954.

KREMP, MARIE ADA—*Painter, Et., T., S., L.*
  58 West 57th St., New York 19, N.Y.

B. Reading, Pa. *Studied*: CMA Sch.; PAFA; & with Garber, Breckenridge, McCarter. *Member*: Rockport AA; F., PAFA; Catholic A. Gld. *Awards*: F., PAFA; prize, H. C. J. Acad., Sharon Hill, Pa. *Work*: PAFA; West Phila. H.S. portraits of many prominent persons. *Exhibited*: PAFA, 1944; Rockport AA, 1946; Gloucester AA, 1946; F., PAFA, 1938-1945; Barbizon Plaza, N.Y.; Ogunquit A. Center, annually. Lectures: "Art As We Live It"; "Color and Arrangement of Flowers"; "Portrait Painting."

KRENTZIN, EARL—*Craftsman, S., E.*
  Art Department, University of Wisconsin (6); h. 2020 University Ave., Madison 5, Wis.

B. Detroit, Mich., Dec. 28, 1929. *Studied*: Wayne Univ., B.F.A.; Cranbrook Acad. A., M.F.A.; Royal Col. A. (London). *Member*: Am. Craftsmen's Council; Midwest Des.-Craftsmen. *Awards*: Fulbright Fellowship, 1957-58; prizes, Mich. Artist-Craftsmen, 1954; Young Americans exh., 1956; Wisconsin Salon A., 1956; Wis. P.&S., 1957; Mich. Artist-Craftsmen, 1958. *Work*: Detroit Inst. A.; Cranbrook Mus. A. Also work in private colls. *Exhibited*: Mus. Contemp. Crafts, 1955, 1957, 1958; AFA traveling exhs.; Mich. Artists, 1950-1958; Mich. Craftsmen, 1952-1958; Detroit Inst. A.; Wisconsin Salon A., 1956-1958; Wisconsin P. & S., 1957, 1958; Wisconsin Craftsmen, 1956-1958; Midwest Des.-Craftsmen, 1956-1958. Contributor to Craft Horizons. *Positions*: Instr., A. & A. Edu., University of Wisconsin, Madison, Wis., 1956- .

KRIENSKY, MORRIS E.—*Painter*
  323 West 17th St., New York 11, N.Y.

B. Glasgow, Scotland, July 27, 1917. *Studied*: ASL; Sch. P. & S., Mexico; Professional Des. Sch.; BMFA Sch.; & with Alma O. Le Brect. *Member*: AWCS; ASL. *Work*: M. Knoedler & Co. *Exhibited*: AWCS, 1946; Inst. Inter-American Relations, Mexico, 1951; one-man exh.: Dept. Interior, Wash., D.C.; White House, Wash., D.C.; Malden (Mass.) Pub. Lib.; George Walter Vincent Smith A. Gal.; Indiana Univ.; Currier A. Gal.; AIC; Hackley A. Gal.; Wilmington Soc. FA; Dartmouth Col.; M. Knoedler & Co.

KRIZE, EMILIE MARY—*Painter, Medical I.*
  210 South Main St., Suffolk, Va.

B. Luzerne, Pa., Aug. 6, 1918. *Studied*: Maryland Inst.; PAFA; Johns Hopkins Univ.; Norfolk Div., of William & Mary Col., and with Maroger. *Member*: Maryland Inst. Alumni Assn.; Tidewater A. *Awards*: merit scholarship, traveling scholarship, medal, Maryland Inst. *Work*: Planters Nut & Chocolate Co. Cl.; Norfolk Naval Shipyard Lib.; State House, Annapolis, Md. *Exhibited*: BMA, 1941 (one-man), 1942; Norfolk Mus. A. & Sc., 1941, 1946-1949 (one-man); U.S. Dept. Interior FA Gal., 1941; Norfolk YMCA, 1949; VMFA, 1947; Women's Cl., Suffolk, Va. *Position*: I., Norfolk Navy Yard, 1942-46; Medical I., Portsmouth, Va., Naval Hospital, 1946.*

KROLL, LEON—*Painter, Lith., L.*
  15 West 67th St., New York 23, N.Y.

B. New York, N.Y., Dec. 6, 1884. *Studied*: ASL; NAD; Julian Acad., Paris; & with John Twachtman, Jean Paul Laurens. *Member*: NA; Am. Acad. A. & Let.; Nat. Inst. A. & Let. *Awards*: many national prizes; Int. prize, Carnegie Inst., 1936; Chevalier Legion of Honor, France. *Work*: MMA; WMAA; AIC; MModA; CGA; SFMA; Carnegie Inst.; Dayton AI; Columbus Gal. FA; CMA; Detroit Inst. A.; Minneapolis Inst. A.; Denver A. Mus.; San Diego FA Soc.; Clearwater (Fla.) Mus.; Norton Gal.; Los A.

Mus. A.; PAFA; Univ. Nebraska; Wilmington Soc. FA, etc.; murals, Justice Bldg., Wash., D.C.; war mem., Worcester, Mass.; Senate Chamber, Indianapolis, Ind.; Johns Hopkins Univ. auditorium; mosaic dome, U.S. Military Cemetery, Omaha Beach, France. *Exhibited*: nationally and internationally. *Position*: Pres., U.S. Com., Intl. Assn. Plastic Arts.

KROLLMANN, GUSTAV WILHELM—*Painter, T.*
  604 Summit Ave., Minneapolis 4, Minn.

B. Vienna, Austria, July 31, 1888. *Studied*: in Vienna. *Member*: Minneapolis Soc. FA. *Work*: murals and portraits, Univ. Minnesota; & in homes, theatres, hotels. *Exhibited*: Minneapolis Inst. A.

KRONBERG, LOUIS—*Painter*
  c/o Lotos Club, 5 East 66th St., New York, N.Y.

B. 1872. *Studied*: BMFA Sch.; ASL; Julian Acad., Paris, France. *Member*: NA. *Awards*: Chevalier, Legion of Honor, France, 1951; Longfellow Scholarship, Boston. *Work*: MMA; BMFA; Isabelle Stewart Gardner Mus.; Joslyn Mem.; PAFA; Société Nationale, Paris; & others.

KROTH, RICHARD—*Painter, L., T.*
  Threefold Farm, Spring Valley, N.Y.; h. 318 West 56th St., New York 19, N.Y.

B. Frankfurt-am-Main, Germany, Sept. 10, 1902. *Studied*: NAD; CUASch.; AIC; & with W.E.B. Starkweather, N. Remisoff. *Member*: Anthroposophical Soc. *Awards*: med., CUASch. *Exhibited*: CAA; PAFA, 1932; N.Y. WC Cl., 1934, 1937, 1938; Soc. Indp. A.; England and Switzerland, 1955; Wanamaker Ex., 1934; one-man exh.: N.Y., 1935, 1944, 1946. Lectures: Goethe's Color Studies; Modern Art; History of Costume; Ice Age Art, etc.*

KRUEGER, LOTHAR—*Educator*
  Art Department, University of Arkansas, Fayetteville, Ark.*

KRUGER, LOUISE—*Sculptor, Des., Gr.*
  531 Hudson St.; h. 222 East 15th St., New York 3, N.Y.

B. Los Angeles, Cal., Aug. 5, 1924. *Studied*: Scripps Col. *Member*: S. Gld. *Work*: MModA; N.Y. Pub. Lib.; Mus. Mod. A., Sao Paulo, Brazil. *Exhibited*: MModA; Carnegie Inst.; WMAA; BMA; BM; Bradley Univ.; PAFA; MMA; LC; Kunsthaus, Geneva, Switzerland, and other exhibitions in U.S., Europe and South America.

KRUSE, ALEXANDER ZERDIN—
  Painter, Et., Lith., W., Cr., L., T.
  54 Riverside Dr., New York 24, N.Y.

B. New York, N.Y., Feb. 9, 1890. *Studied*: Edu. All.; NAD; ASL, with McBride, Carlsen, Sloan, Luks, Henri. *Work*: MMA; MModA; Philbrook A. Center; BM; N.Y. Pub. Lib.; Lib. Cong.; British Mus.; Royal Albert Mus.; Nat. Gal., Canada; PMA; AGAA; State Mus., Biro-Bidjan, Mus. Mod. A., Russia; Bibliotheque Nationale, Paris; Univ. Arizona; Berry Col., Ga.; Mus. City of N.Y. *Exhibited*: AIC; 50 Prints of the Year; Phila. SE; Fine Prints of the Year; Los A. Mus. A.; Int. Exh., Sweden; SAE; WMAA; NAD; Grand Central A. Gal.; BM; Dudensing Gal.; Findlay Gal.; Weyhe Gal. I., "Two New Yorkers." Author: "How to Draw and Paint"; "A-B-C's of Pencil Drawing"; contributor to New York Post, Art Digest. *Position*: A. Cr., Brooklyn Eagle, Brooklyn, N.Y. 1938-46; Instr., Portrait & Figure Painting, Brooklyn Mus. A. Schl. & Brooklyn Col., 1946- ; Fndr., Heywood Broun Mem. Coll.; Newspaper Gld.; Lena Kruse Mem. Coll., BM, Brooklyn, N.Y.*

KUBACH, ALLEN EDWARD—*Painter, Lith., Des., T.*
  5 Sandy Hollow Road, Port Washington, N.Y.

B. Sandusky, Ohio, Mar. 12, 1921. *Studied*: Carnegie Inst. Tech., B.A.; Northwestern Univ., M.A.; Grande Chaumiere, Paris, France; ASL, with Vytlacil, Kantor, Barnet. *Member*: AAUP. *Work*: MModA. *Exhibited*: Soc. Wash. Pr. M., 1952; Phila. Pr. Cl., 1953; Butler AI, 1948; AIC, 1948, 1951, 1952; Springfield (Mo.) Mus. A., 1949; Bordelon Gal., Chicago, 1950; one-man: Northwestern Univ., 1952; Newman Brown Gal., Chicago, 1952; Contemporary A. Gal., Evanston, Ill., 1952; Panoras Gal., 1955. *Positions*: Instr. A., Kansas State Col., 1946-47; Northwestern Univ., 1948-54.

KUBACKI, RAYMOND—*Painter*
395 East Palm St., Altadena, Cal.

B. Rochester, N.Y., Jan. 16, 1917. *Studied*: Chouinard AI. *Member*: Cal. WC Soc.; Los A. AA. *Exhibited*: Cal. WC Soc., 1954; Frye Mus. A., Seattle, 1955; Los A. Mus. A., 1953; San Gabriel Valley, 1955; Newport, 1955.

KUBINYI, MRS. DORIS HALL. See *Hall, Doris*

KUBINYI, KALMAN MATYAS BELA—
Enamelist, C., Et., P., I.
337A Newbury St. (6); h. 94 Beacon St., Boston 16, Mass.; s. 203 Western Ave., Gloucester, Mass.

B. Cleveland, Ohio, July 29, 1906. *Studied*: Cleveland Inst. A., and with Alexander Von Kubinyi. *Member*: AEA; NSMP. *Awards*: prizes, CMA, 1930-1933, 1936, 1938, 1941, 1948-1952. *Work*: CMA; Cleveland Mun. Coll.; mural, Mich. State Univ. (with Doris Hall); Whiting Lane Sch. *Exhibited*: Am. A. Cong., 1936; Phila. Pr. Cl., 1942; AIC, 1938, 1939; Springfield Mus. A., 1938; WFNY 1939; CMA, 1925-1952; WMAA, 1937; Boise (Idaho) Mus., 1944; 1030 Gal., Cleveland, 1945. I., "The Goldsmith of Florence," 1929; "Sokar and The Crocodile," 1928. Author section on Aquatint Processes for Dictionary of the Arts. Contributor to American Magazine of Art, 1934, 1935. *Position*: Instr., Cranbrook Acad. A., Bloomfield Hills, Mich., 1946-50; Pres. New England Chptr, AEA, 1951-52; Dir., 1953-58; A. Dir., Bettinger Corp.

KUBLER, GEORGE—*Educator, W., L.*
406 Humphrey St., New Haven 11, Conn.

B. Los Angeles, Cal., July 26, 1912. *Studied*: Univ. Berlin & Munich; Yale Univ.; N.Y. Univ. *Member*: CAA; Am. Geographical Soc.; Am. Archaeological Assn. *Awards*: Guggenheim F., 1943-1944, 1952-1953, 1956-1957; F., Am. Council Learned Soc., 1941. Author: "Religious Architecture of New Mexico," 1940; "Mexican Architecture of the Sixteenth Century," 1948; "The Tovar Calendar," 1951; "Cuzco" (UNESCO), 1952; "Arquitechera española, 1600-1800" (Ars Hispaniae XIV, Madrid, 1957). Contributor to: Art & Archaeological publications. Lectures: American Archaeology; Mediaeval Architecture, etc. *Position*: L., Wesleyan Univ., 1942-43; L., Univ. Chicago, 1946; Univ. San Marcos, Lima, Peru; L., Univ. Mexico, 1958; Prof., Hist. A., Yale Univ., New Haven, Conn., 1947- .

KUCHARYSON, PAUL—*Etcher, Eng., C., Des., I., S.*
Inter-Collegiate Press, 615 Wyandotte Ave.; h. 2221 East 68th Terrace, Kansas City 5, Mo.

B. Utica, N.Y., July 2, 1914. *Studied*: John Huntington Inst. A.; Cleveland Sch. A. *Awards*: prizes, WFNY 1939; CMA; Dayton, Ohio; Oakland, Cal. *Position*: A., Inter-Collegiate Press, Kansas City, Mo., 1946- .*

KUEHNE, MAX—*Painter, C., Gr.*
25½ East 61st St., New York 21, N.Y.

B. New York, N.Y., Nov. 7, 1880. *Studied*: with Kenneth Hayes Miller. *Member*: SAGA; Phila. SE. *Work*: WMAA; Los A. Mus. A.; Detroit Inst. A.; Hispanic Soc.; MMA; LC; Victoria & Albert Mus., London; N.Y. Pub. Lib.

KUEKES, EDWARD D.—*Cartoonist*
Cleveland Plain Dealer, 1801 Superior Ave., Cleveland 14, Ohio; h. 6180 Columbia Road, North Olmsted, Ohio

B. Pittsburgh, Pa., Feb. 2, 1901. *Studied*: Baldwin-Wallace Col.; Cleveland Inst. A.; Chicago Acad. FA. *Awards*: C.I.T. Fnd. award, 1937; Newspaper Gld., 1947, 1958; Freedoms Fnd., 1949, and medal; 1950, 1951, 1952, 1953, 1954, 1956, 1957, 1958 and Distinguished Service award for winning the awards in 1949-1952; Nat. Safety Council, 1949; Pulitzer Prize, 1953; Resolution, 100th General Assembly State of Ohio, House of Representatives, 1953; Baldwin-Wallace Col. Alumni Merit Award, 1953; Governor's Award, State of Ohio, 1953; Silver "T" Square award, Nat. Cartoonists Soc., 1954; Ohio State Dental Assn. Award, 1954; U.S. Treasury Presidential Prayer Award, 1954; Christopher Award, 1955; Certif. of Recognition, Nat. Conf. of Christians and Jews, 1955, 1958; Eisenhower appointment "People to People" Committee, 1956; George M. Humphrey Medal, 1957; Hon. Degree, D.L.H., Baldwin-Wallace Col., 1957. Author, I., "Funny Fables," 1938; Cart., "Alice in Wonderland" for United Features Syndicate (1940). Lectures: "So You Can't Draw a Straight Line, Either," to art groups.

KUGHLER, (WILLIAM) FRANCIS VANDEVEER—*Painter*
Hotel des Artistes, 1 West 67th St., New York, N.Y.; h. 2870 Heath Ave., Kingsbridge, N.Y.

B. New York, N.Y., Sept. 20, 1901. *Studied*: NAD. *Member*: SC; NAC. *Awards*: prizes, SC, 1944; Tiffany F., 1925. *Work*: portrait, Hudson River Mus.; War Correspondents Mem., Associated Press, 1946; Univ. North Carolina; Mus. A., Oslo, Norway; Doctors Mem. Sch. Medicine, Chapel Hill, N.C.; murals, Univ. North Carolina. *Exhibited*: NAD; PAFA; SC; NAC; Chappelier Gal., N.Y., 1954 (one-man). *Position*: Pres. A. Fellowship, New York, N.Y., 1950-53.

KUH, KATHARINE (Mrs.)—*Museum Curator, W., L.*
Art Institute of Chicago; h. 2933 North Sheridan Rd., Chicago 14, Ill.

B. St. Louis, Mo., July 15, 1904. *Studied*: Vassar Col., B.A.; Univ. Chicago, M.A.; N.Y. Univ. Author: "Art Has Many Faces," 1951; "Leger," 1953. Worked on grant from Fund for Adult Education of the Ford Fnd., developing a series of discussion groups in modern art. Wrote special book "Looking At Modern Art," for the groups. *Position*: Cur. Painting and Sculpture, AIC, Chicago, Ill., to 1959 (Resigned).

KUHLMANN, EDWARD—*Writer, P.*
6 Elizabeth St., Milford, Del.

B. Woodville, Ohio, Sept. 26, 1882. *Studied*: Capital Univ., Columbus, Ohio; AIC; and with Leo Blake. Author: "Watch Yourself Go By"; "Cross Examined"; "How Do You Do"; "Choosing Our Memories"; "Marks of Distinction," and others.

KUHN, CHARLES L.—*Museum Curator*
Busch-Reisinger Museum of Germanic Culture, Harvard University, Cambridge, Mass.

Position: Cur., Busch-Reisinger Museum.*

KUHNE, HEDVIG (HARRIETT B.)—
Painter, C., S., T., E.
Browngate Studio, Hart, Mich.

B. Berlin, Germany, Apr. 8, 1891. *Studied*: AIC; Chicago Acad. FA, and with Archipenko. *Member*: AAPL. *Awards*: prize, AIC, 1942. *Exhibited*: MMA, 1942; AIC, 1942; Hackley A. Gal., 1950, 1951, 1952 (one-man); Michigan State Fair, 1954; Fremont, Mich., 1954 (one-man); Ludington, Mich., 1955 (one-man); Pleasantville, N.Y., 1958; Court House, Hart, Mich. *Position*: Dir. Browngate Summer Sch. A.

KUMM, MARGUERITE ELIZABETH—*Painter, Eng., Et.*
R.F.D. 5, Box 291, Vienna, Va.

B. Redwood Falls, Minn. *Studied*: Minneapolis Sch. A.; Corcoran A. Sch., and with Cameron Booth, Richard Lahey, Anthony Angarola. *Member*: SAGA; Phila. Plastic Cl. *Awards*: prizes, SAGA, 1943; Int. award in Dec. Des., N.Y., 1926, Boston, 1929; LC, 1951. *Work*: LC; BMFA; Valentine Mus.; VMFA; Oregon State Col.; SAGA; Wash. County Mus. FA, Hagerstown, Md.; Col. State Lib.; Witte Mem. Mus.; Pa. State Univ.; MMA; Smithsonian Inst.; Mint Mus. A.; Butler AI; murals, Lowry Hill Children's Clinic, Minneapolis, Minn. *Exhibited*: SAGA, 1938-1952; WFNY 1939; San F. AA, 1939; Northwest Pr. M., 1939; Albright A. Gal., 1940, 1943, 1951; Southern Pr. M., 1940-1942; Phila. Pr. Cl., 1942; NAD, 1942, 1944, 1949; AFA traveling exh., 1943-44; Mint Mus. A., 1943, 1944; LC, 1943-1946, 1951-1952; Venice, Italy, 1940; SAGA traveling exh., 1940, 1943; Valentine Mus., 1939, 1941, 1943, 1949, 1950; Wash. Soc. Et., 1939, 1945; PMG, 1939; Wash. WC Cl., 1940-1942; Wash. Min. Soc., 1940-1945; CGA, 1949, 1951; Phila. A. All., 1949, 1950; Am. Color Pr. Soc., 1951; Carnegie Inst., 1943, 1946, 1951; Phila. Plastic Cl., 1951; Wichita AA, 1952; one-man: VMFA,

1945; Smithsonian Inst., 1950; Mint Mus. A., 1951; Butler AI, 1952; Stanford Univ., 1952; Miami Beach A. Center, 1952; Wash. County Mus. FA, 1952; Massillon Mus., 1952; DePauw Univ., 1952; Ohio Univ., 1952; Delgado Mus. A., 1952; Cedar Rapids AA, 1952; Hood Col., 1953; Cal. State Lib., 1953; Witte Mem. Mus., 1953.

KUMMER, ERWIN GEORGE—*Painter, T., L.*

6134 North Seeley Ave., Chicago 45, Ill.

B. Chicago, Ill., Oct. 9, 1900. *Studied*: Chicago Acad. FA; AIC; & with Edward J. F. Timmons. *Member*: Palette & Chisel Acad.; All-Illinois Soc. FA; Assn. Chicago P. & S. *Awards*: prize, Evanston Women's Cl., 1944; A. Lg., Harrison, Ark., 1958; gold medal, Palette & Chisel Acad., 1956. *Work*: Neville Pub. Mus., Green Bay, Wis. *Exhibited*: AIC, 1945; Neville Pub. Mus., 1941, 1944; Assn. Chicago P. & S., 1946; Palette & Chisel Acad., 1941-1946; All-Illinois Soc. FA, 1942-1946; Evanston Women's Cl., 1944; Ill. State Fair, 1955. *Position*: Bd. Dir., Chicago P. & S.; Pres., Palette & Chisel Acad., 1956.

KUP, KARL—*Librarian, Curator, T., L., Cr.*

New York Public Library, 476 Fifth Ave.; h. 136 East 36th St., New York 16, N.Y.

B. Haarlem, Holland, May 7, 1903. *Studied*: Univ. Munich, with Wolfflin; Univ. Berlin, with Goldschmidt; Univ. Leipzig, with Rehm; in Paris, with Diehl; Lakeside Press Sch. of Printing, Chicago. *Member*: AIGA; Bibliographical Soc. Am.; Grolier Cl.; London Bibliographical Soc.; Soc. for Japanese Studies. Author: "The Council of Constance, 1414-18"; "The Girdle Book"; "Books and Printing" (with Carolyn F. Ulrich). Contributor to N.Y. Pub. Lib. Bulletin, American Artist, Library Journal, Publisher's Weekly, Antiques, and other publications. Lectures: Book Illustration; Illuminated Manuscripts; Prints. *Positions*: Contributing Ed., Publisher's Weekly, 1941- ; American Artist, 1941-49; Hd., Juvenile Dept., Oxford Univ. Press, 1928-34; Cur., Spencer Coll., 1934- , Cur., Prints, 1941- , Dir., Exhibitions, 1947-55, Chief, A. & Architecture Div., 1956- , New York Public Library, New York, N.Y.

KUPER, ROSE—*Painter*

60 Park Terrace West, New York 34, N.Y.

Studied: Hunter Col., B.A.; in France; and with Hans Hofmann, Abraham Rattner and others. *Member*: NAWA; Brooklyn Soc. A.; Manhattan Gallery Group; ASL; Creative A. Assoc.; Village A. Center. *Awards*: prizes, NAWA, 1952; Brooklyn Soc. A., 1954; Village A. Center. *Work*: San Diego FA Soc.; Philbrook A. Center; Dallas Mus. FA; Santa Barbara Mus. A.; Jewish Mus., N.Y.; Hunter Col.; Long Island Univ.; Fashion Inst. Tech.; Light House for the Blind, Israel; Ashlawn, Va. (home of James Monroe); Riverside Mus.; Design Center, N.Y. *Exhibited*: NAWA, 1940-1955; Argent Gal., 1947; Brooklyn Soc. A., 1954, 1955; BM; Birmingham Mus. A.; Helena (Mont.) Mus. A., 1954; Paris, France. *Position*: Instr., New York City Pub. Schs.; Bd. Dir., Manhattan Gal. Group, 1955; Exec. Bd., NAWA, 1951-1954.

KUPFERMAN, LAWRENCE—*Painter, E.*

Massachusetts School of Art, 370 Brookline Ave., Boston, Mass.; h. 26 Walnut St., Natick, Mass.

B. Boston, Mass., Mar. 25, 1909. *Studied*: BMFA Sch.; Mass. Sch. A., B.S. in Edu. *Member*: ANA; SAGA; Phila. WC Cl.; F., Royal Soc. A., London; CAA; AAUP; Boston Soc. WC Painters. *Awards*: prizes, AV, 1942; San F. AA, 1938; SAGA, 1939. *Work*: Mills Col., Oakland, Cal.; LC; MMA; Carnegie Inst.; BMFA; IBM; BMA; SFMA; FMA; Harvard Univ.; WMA; Boston Pub. Lib.; AGAA; MMoDA; WMAA; Wadsworth Atheneum; Univ. Michigan; BM; murals, Am. Export Lines "Independence" and "Constitution." *Exhibited*: Carnegie Inst., 1941; PAFA, 1938, 1940-1945, 1950; WMAA, 1938, 1940-1942, 1945, 1946, 1948-1952, 1953, 1956, 1957; AIC, 1938, 1948, 1957; BM, 1943, 1945, 1951, 1953, 1955; SFMA, 1938, 1939, 1941-1944, 1946; SAGA, 1937, 1939-1941, 1943, 1944; WFNY 1939; MMoDA, 1943; Walker A. Center, 1954; Butler AI; Tokyo, Japan, 1955; MMA, 1955; Nat. Acad. FA, Rome, Italy, 1955; Inst. Mod. A., Boston, 1943; Univ. Nebraska, 1948, 1956; Univ. Illinois, 1949, 1953; BMA, 1948, 1949; CAM, 1951; Brandeis Univ., 1956; BMFA, 1956, 1957; de Cordova & Dana Mus., 1956; Boston A. Festival, 1956-1958; NAD, 1958; AFA traveling exh., 1959; Strasbourg, France, 1956; one-man: Mortimer Levitt Gal., 1948, 1949, 1951, 1953; Mortimer

Brandt Gal., 1946; Phila. A. All., 1946; Boris Mirski Gal., Boston, 1944-1946; Shore Studio, Boston, 1953; Martha Jackson Gal., N.Y., 1955; Swetzoff Gal., 1956; Verna Wear Gal., 1956; Ruth White Gal., 1958; Gropper Gal., Cambridge, 1958. *Position*: Prof. Painting, Mass. Sch. A., Boston, Mass., 1941- .

KUPFERMAN, MURRAY—*Painter, C., T.*

1270 East 19th St., Brooklyn 30, N.Y.

B. Brooklyn, N.Y., Mar. 10, 1897. *Studied*: PIASch.; NAD; BAID. *Member*: Provincetown AA; Cape Cod AA. *Work*: murals, churches and theatres, and in private collections. *Exhibited*: America House; Georg Jensen Co.; Arch. Lg.; NAD; G-R-D Gal.; Marie Harriman Gal.; Ferargil Gal.; BM; Am. Mus. Natural Hist.; Midtown Gal.; N.Y. WC Cl.; Dudensing Gal.; Brooklyn Soc. A.; Riverside Mus.; Morton Gal.; Provincetown AA; Brooklyn Pub. Lib.; Lord & Taylor; John Wanamaker; W.J.Sloane Co.; Cape Cod AA; McElvey Gal., Clearwater, Fla.; All. A. Am.; Lowe Gal., Miami Univ.; Audubon A.; Silvermine Gld. A.; Eve Tucker Gal., Miami Beach; Boca Raton, Fla.; Gulf AA; Mystic AA; Woodstock AA; Normandie & Paris Theatres, N.Y.; Little Gal., N.Y. and Phila.; Crespi Gal.; Salpeter Gal.; Morris Gal., N.Y.; Shaw Gal., Provincetown, Mass. Inventor of Kuli Printing Press for schools and studios. Also of Kupferman Pre-Flight Ground Training Machine. *Position*: Instr. FA, N.Y. Bd. of Edu., 1927- ; Brooklyn Tech. H.S., since 1948.

KURTZ, BENJAMIN T(URNER)—*Sculptor, E., W., L.*

215 Woodlawn Rd., Baltimore 10, Md.

B. Baltimore, Md., Jan. 2, 1899. *Studied*: with Charles Grafly, Albert Laessle. *Member*: Phila. A. All.; Archaeological Inst. Am.; NSS; Arch. L. *Awards*: F., PAFA; Cresson traveling scholarship, PAFA, 1922; prizes, Arch. L., 1926; AIC, 1926; med., Sesqui-Centennial Exp., Phila., 1926. *Work*: Pub. Lib., Ft. Worth, Tex.; Curtis Inst. Mus., Phila.; Pub. Lib., Camden, Me.; BMA; Brookgreen Gardens, S.C.; Johns Hopkins Hospital, Balt.; Peale Mus., Balt.; NGA; s., decorations, Radio Station WBAL, Balt.; Hochild-Kohn Dept. Store, Balt.; fountain, Norton Gal., West Palm Beach, Fla.*

KURTZWORTH, H(ARRY) M(UIR)—
Art Director, P., Des., W., E., L.

810 South Lucerne Blvd., Los Angeles 5, Cal.

B. Detroit, Mich., Aug. 12, 1887. *Studied*: Detroit Acad. FA; Columbia Univ.; Pa. Sch. Indst. A., and in Europe. *Member*: AIA; Cal. A. Cl. *Awards*: A.F.D. (hon.) Andhra Univ., India, 1936; medal honor, France, 1939; Commander Cross, Grand Prix Humanitaire, Belgium, 1939. Designer, 10th Olympiad Diploma of Award. *Author*: "Genius, Talent or Mediocrity," 1924; "Industrial Art a National Asset" (U.S. Dept. Interior, 1919); "International Art," 1937. Contributor to World Book Encyclopaedia since 1945. Lectures on Industrial Design; Mural Painting; Art in Industry. *Positions*: Dir., Sch. A. & Indst., Grand Rapids, Mich., 1915-20; Assoc. Dir., Chicago Acad. FA, 1920-21, 1926-30; Dir., Kansas City AI, 1921-25; Dir., Michigan AI, 1920-26; A. Dir., Los A. Mus. A., 1930-32; Dir., Los Angeles AA, 1932-37; A. Dir., Woodbury Col., Los Angeles, Cal., 1946-53; Dir., Am. Art Soc.

KURWACZ, WILLIAM—*Craftsman*

Craft Center, 25 Sagamore Road (8); h. 10 Dean St., Worcester, Mass.

B. Shutesbury, Mass., July 29, 1919. *Studied*: Sch. for Am. Craftsmen, Alfred Univ.; Ringling Sch. A. *Member*: Mass. Assn. Handicraft Groups. *Awards*: Baron Fleming award, Wichita, Kans., 1950; Va. Highlands Exh., Abingdon, Va. *Exhibited*: Va. Highlands Exh., 1950; Mass. Crafts Exh., 1955; New England Crafts Exh., 1955; Smithsonian Inst. traveling exh., 1956-57; Sterling Silversmiths Gld. of Am., 1957; U.S. Nat. Pavilion, Brussels World's Fair, 1958. *Position*: Metalsmith, Old Sturbridge Village (Mass.), 1950-51; Instr., silversmithing and jewelry, Craft Center, Worcester, Mass., 1953- .

KUSANOBU, MURRAY—*Painter*

c/o Tyrrell, 321 East 43rd St., New York 17, N.Y.

B. Montreal, Canada, Jan. 30, 1907. *Studied*: Columbia Univ.; ASL, with William Zorach, William Von Schlegell. *Member*: Assoc. A., New Jersey; AEA. *Work*: Newark

Mus. *Exhibited*: Montclair A. Mus.; Riverside Mus.; New Jersey Gal., Newark, N.J.; WFNY 1939; Newark Mus., 1945; Rabin & Kreuger Gal.; A. of Today; ACA Gal.; Art:USA, 1958.

KUSHNER, DOROTHY BROWDY—Painter, C., T.
1210 South Fourth Ave., Arcadia, Cal.

B. Kansas City, Mo., Mar. 20, 1909. *Studied*: Kansas City T. Col., B.S.; AIC; Columbia Univ., M.A.; Kansas City AI, with Thomas Hart Benton; ASL, with Reginald Marsh. *Member*: Kansas City Soc. A.; A.T. Gld.; Cal. WC Soc.; Am. Color Print Soc.; Los Angeles AA. *Awards*: medal, Univ. Missouri, 1926; prize, Highland Park, Cal., 1951; Santa Paula, Cal., 1952, 1955; San Gabriel Mission, 1954, 1955; Pasadena A. Mus., 1955. *Work*: Pasadena A. Mus.; Camino Grove Sch., Arcadia, Cal.; Univ. Illinois; Los Angeles Unitarian Church. *Exhibited*: Kansas City AI, 1934, 1935; Women's City Cl., Kansas City, 1938; Kansas City Soc. A., 1935-1938; Los A. Mus. A., 1952, 1954, 1955; Los A. City Exh., 1951; Cal. WC Soc., 1951-1958; San Gabriel Valley Exh., 1951-1958; Los Angeles AA, 1952-1958; Cal. State Fair, 1952-1955; Oakland A. Gal., 1952; Boston Pr. M., 1954; LC, 1955; Am. Color Pr. Soc., 1956-1958; Wash. Pr. M., 1956-1958.

KUSHNER, FLORENCE TAYLOR. See Sherman, F. Taylor

KUTKA, ANNE (Mrs. David McCosh)—Painter
1870 Fairmount Blvd., Eugene, Ore.

B. Danbury, Conn. *Studied*: ASL, with Kimon Nicolaides, Kenneth Hayes Miller, Eugene Fitsch. *Member*: ASL. *Awards*: Tiffany F., 1928, 1930; Gladys Roosevelt Dick traveling scholarship, 1933. *Work*: Portland A. Mus. *Exhibited*: AIC, 1935; WFNY 1939; Denver A. Mus., 1938; AV, 1943; Am. Red Cross traveling exh., 1942; G-R-D Gal., 1931; SAM, 1936-1939, 1941, 1945; Portland (Ore.) A. Mus., 1935, 1937-1939, 1946-1951 (1948, one-man), 1953-1957; Northwest Pr. M., 1940; Contemporary A., 1938; Univ. Oregon, 1944; MMA, 1953; Willamette Univ., 1957 (one-man).

KWONG, HUI KA—Craftsman
Brooklyn Museum Art School; 136 East 26th St.; h. 240 Sullivan St., New York 12, N.Y.

B. Hong Kong, China, Aug. 16, 1922. *Studied*: Shanghai Sch. FA; Apprentice, Cheng Ho, sculptor, Hong Kong; Alfred Univ., Sch. Ceramics, B.F.A., M.F.A.; Pond Farms Sch., Guerneville, Cal. *Member*: N.Y. Soc. Ceramic A.; N.Y. Craftsmen's Soc. *Work*: Cooper Union Mus. Dec. A.; Wichita A. Gal.; Syracuse Mus. FA. *Awards*: prizes, Syracuse Mus. FA, 1954 (purchase); Wichita, Kans., 1952 (purchase); Cannes, France, Ceramic Intl., 1955. *Exhibited*: Syracuse Mus. FA, 1949-1954, 1958; Wichita Natl., 1952; Miami, Fla., 1955; Cannes, France, 1955; Bertha Schaefer Gal.; N.Y. Ceramic Soc., 1953-1955; N.Y. Craftsmen's Soc., 1955; BM, 1955; Wash. Kiln Cl., Smithsonian Inst., 1955; Mus. Contemp. Crafts, 1957; Phila. A. All., 1958 (3-man). *Position*: Instr., pottery, Brooklyn Mus. Sch. A., Brooklyn, N.Y.; Douglass Col., Rutgers Univ.

La CHANCE, GEORGES—Painter
Nashville, Ind.

B. Utica, N.Y., Oct. 13, 1888. *Studied*: St. Louis A. Sch. *Member*: Brown County A. Gld.; Hoosier Salon. *Awards*: prizes, Hoosier Salon, 1937, 1939, 1942, 1945, 1954, 1956, 1957; Ft. Wayne Women's Cl., 1954; Chicago Galleries Assn., 1955; Downs award, Chicago, 1940; Rector mem. award, Chicago, 1941; Brown County AA, 1941; Kappa Kappa Kappa prize, 1948; Honeywell prize, 1948. *Work*: Indiana Univ.; De Pauw Univ.; Alma Col.; Fed. Bank, Greenwood, Ind.; Vincennes Jr. H.S.; Old Territorial Hall, Vincennes, Ind.; murals, County Court House, Vincennes, Ind.; Toledo Scale Auditorium; Nashville House, Nashville, Ind.; Bloomington (Ind.) Limestone Co. *Exhibited*: Hoosier Salon; Brown County A. Gal.; Swope Gal.; Marshall Field Gal.; Findlay Gal.; Lafayette (Ind.) A. Gal.; Chicago Galleries. *Position*: Pres., Brown County A. Gld., 1956-57, 1957-58.

LA COM, WAYNE CARL—Painter, Des., Comm. A., T., Ser.
608 Pioneer Drive, Glendale 3, Cal.

B. Glendale, Cal., Oct. 11, 1922. *Studied*: A. Center Sch., Los A.; Chouinard AI; Jepson AI; Univ. California Ext. *Member*: Cal. WC Soc.; Glendale AA. *Awards*: prizes, Glendale AA, 1948, 1949; Intl. Flower Show A. Exh., 1951. *Work*: Fairfax, Hoover, Wilmington High Schools; Los Angeles Elementary Schs. *Exhibited*: Cal. WC Soc., 1950-1955, 1958; Newport Beach, 1949-1951; Arizona State Fair, 1947; Nat. Orange Show, 1950-1952, 1955; Los A. Mus. A., 1952, 1954; Cal. State Fair, 1951; Walnut Creek, Cal., 1951; Canadian-American traveling exh., 1955-56; Palos Verdes, 1958. *Position*: Instr., Adult Edu. classes, 1948-; Des., La Com Cards, Booklets, Brochures, etc.

LACY, MARGARET LUELLA—Educator, P., C.
Art Department, Hardin-Simmons University; h. 2426 Simmons Ave., Abilene, Tex.

B. Belton, Tex., Oct. 9, 1900. *Studied*: Hardin-Simmons Univ., B.A.; North Texas State Col., M.A.; Columbia Univ.; Parsons Sch. Des.; Univ. Colorado, and with Dong Kingman, Xavier Gonzales. *Member*: NAEA; Western AA; Texas FA Assn.; West Texas AA; AAUW; Texas AEA; Nat. Lg. Am. Pen Women. *Awards*: prizes, Abilene Morning News, 1930; Abilene Reporter News, 1931; Abilene Mus. A., 1950; State prize, Fort Worth, 1955. *Work*: Radio station KRBC, Abilene. *Exhibited*: West Texas AA; Texas FA Assn.; Abilene Mus. A.; and locally, 1939, 1945, 1956. Contributor to Texas Outlook. *Position*: Asst. Prof. A., Dir. A. Edu., Hardin-Simmons Univ., Abilene, Tex.

LAESSLE, PAUL—Painter, I.
6142 Southwest 42nd St., Miami 43, Fla.

B. Philadelphia, Pa., Dec. 21, 1908. *Studied*: PMSchIA; PAFA; Barnes Fnd., and in Europe. *Member*: Miami AA; F., PAFA; Blue Dome A. Fellowship; Fla. Fed. A. *Awards*: Cresson traveling scholarship, PAFA, 1935; prizes, Blue Dome Fellowship, Miami, 1947-1952; Coral Gables Woman's Cl., 1948, 1949; Miami A. Lg., 1948-1951; YM-YWHA, Miami Beach, 1950; Fla. Fed. A., 1950. *Work*: Phila. Pub. Lib., PAFA; Univ. Miami; many portraits. *Exhibited*: WFNY 1939; PAFA; Phila. WC Cl.; Phila. A. Cl.; Harrisburg (Pa.) State Mus.; Miami and Miami Beach, Fla.; Palm Beach A. Lg.; Soc. Four A.; Fla. Fed. A.; Havana, Cuba; Terry AI; one-man: F., PAFA; PMA; PMSchIA; Miami Beach A. Center. *Position*: Instr., Terry AI, Miami, Fla., 1951-56. Tech. Illus., Port. Painter at present.

LAFON, GERTRUDE VAN ALLEN (Mrs. A. F.)—Painter, C.
R.F.D. 2, Southbury, Conn.

B. Brooklyn, N.Y., Oct. 15, 1897. *Studied*: CUASch.; PIASch.; N.Y. Univ., B.S., M.A. in A. Edu., and with Ralph Pearson, Louis Wolchonok. *Member*: NAWA; Cape Cod AA.*

LA GAMBINA, VINCENT—Painter, T., Gr.
351 West 4th St., New York, N.Y.

B. Italy, Sept. 21, 1909. *Studied*: NAD; ASL, with Sidney Dickinson, Frank DuMond, Olinsky. *Member*: SC; Audubon A.; All. A. Am.; Grand Central A. Gal. *Awards*: prize, Village A. Center. *Work*: murals, frescoes, Evander Childs H.S., Bellevue Hospital, Technical H.S., New York, N.Y. *Exhibited*: CGA; Carnegie Inst.; Terry AI; NAD; BM; All. A. Am.; Audubon A.; Riverside Mus.; Grand Central A. Gal.; SC.*

LAGING, DUARD WALTER—Educator
208 Morrill Hall, University of Nebraska; h. 1140 South 20th St., Lincoln, Neb.

B. Spring Valley, Minn., Nov. 7, 1906. *Studied*: Univ. Minnesota, B.A., M.A.; Minneapolis AI; Univ. Iowa, and with Philip Guston. *Member*: Minnesota AA; Nebraska AA; CAA; Lincoln A. Gld.; AAMus.; Midwest Col. A. Conference. Assembled Nebraska AA Exh., 1950-52; All-Nebraska Exh.; Art for Use, 1951; Contemporary Ceramics, 1951; Sheldon Bequest; Lester Danielson Loan;

Art in the 19th Century; 20th Century Expressionism, 1952. *Position*: Asst. Prof., Michigan State Col., 1945-47; Prof., A. Hist., 1952- , University of Nebraska, Lincoln, Neb.

LAGORIO, IRENE R.—*Painter, Gr., Des., W., L.*

2409 Telegraph Ave., Berkeley, Cal.; h. 545 57th St., Oakland 9, Cal.

B. Oakland, Cal., May 2, 1921. *Studied*: Univ. California, A.B., M.A.; Columbia Univ. *Member*: San F. AA; Cal. WC Soc.; San F. Women A.; Boston Pr. M.; Nat. Ser. Soc.; Pr. Council of Am.; Am. Color Pr. Soc. *Awards*: prizes, San F. Women A., 1955; SFMA, 1953 (purchase); Cal. WC Soc., 1953. *Work*: SFMA; San F. Women A. Coll. *Exhibited*: Boston Pr. M., 1954, 1955; Newport, 1954, 1955; Sao Paulo, Brazil, 1955; WMAA, 1953; MMA, 1952; SFMA, 1943-1956; BM, 1958; Meltzer Gal., N.Y., 1958; one-man: Gump's, San F., 1958; Kramer Gal., Los A., 1958; Richmond A. Center, 1958; Valley A. Center, 1958; Louisiana A. Comm., 1958-59. Contributor to Cal. PLH catalogues and bulletins. Lectures: "Prints & Printing"; "From Durer to Dali"; "Squares and Circles," etc. Exhibitions arranged: "The Garden—Romantic and Classic"; "New Directions in Contemporary Printmaking"; "Approaches to Leisure"; "Jose Posada: Artist of the People" and others for Cal. PLH.

LA GRANGE, JACQUES (JACQUES LA GRANGE VAN HUYZEN)—*Painter, T., Gr.*

2905 Ivyside Dr., Altoona, Pa.

B. Clanwilliam, C.P., South Africa, Sept. 13, 1895. *Studied*: London Univ., B.A., and with W. A. Wyllie, Axel Gallen-Kallela. *Member*: NAC; AEA. *Work*: Peabody Mus.; Army-Navy Cl., Phila.; Czechoslovakia Pub. Coll. *Exhibited*: NAC, 1951, 1952; Newhouse Gal.; Bridgeport A. Lg., 1938, and in Capetown, South Africa; one-man: Buchanan Gal., 1929; 56th St. Gal., 1930; Babcock Gal., 1930; Roerich Mus., 1931; Wellons Gal., 1951, 1952, I., "America's Cup Races," 1935; "Clipper Ships of America and Great Britain," 1936. *Position*: Dir., Altoona (Pa.) A. All., Altoona, Pa.*

LAHEE, ARNOLD WARBURTON—*Painter, E.*

75 Central Ave., Montclair, N.J.

B. Hingham, Mass., May 7, 1888. *Studied*: Harvard Univ., A.B., M.A., Ph.D., and with Wayman Adams, Frank DuMond, Alphonse Shelton, Stephen Juharos. *Member*: AAPL; Orange A. Center; Bloomfield A. Lg.; Verona AA. *Awards*: prizes, Orange, N.J., 1957; Vanderlipp Mem. award, A. Center of the Oranges, 1957; Bloomfield A. Lg., 1957, 1958; Kresge's New Jersey Exh., and others. *Exhibited*: widely, locally and in regional exhs.; FMA; Stowe, Vt., etc.

LAHEY, RICHARD (FRANCIS)—*Painter, Gr., E., L.*

Corcoran School of Art, Washington 6, D.C.; h. R.F.D. 4, Vienna, Va.; s. Ogunquit, Me.

B. Jersey City, N.J., June 23, 1893. *Studied*: ASL; & with Henri, Bridgman. *Member*: Soc. Wash. A.; Wash. A. Gld. *Awards*: prizes, AIC, 1925; PAFA, 1929; med., Soc. Wash. A., 1940, 1944, 1946, prize, 1951; Ogunquit AA. *Work*: PAFA; Goucher Col.; BM; Detroit Inst. A.; WMAA; AGAA; Toledo Mus. A.; CGA; BMA; MMoDA; Lib. Cong.; N.Y. Pub. Lib.; ASL; U.S. Supreme Court; Newark Pub. Lib.; Elk's Cl., Wash., D.C.; mural, USPO, Brownsville, Pa. *Exhibited*: VMFA, 1943 (one-man); CGA, 1935-1945, 1949-1951, 1953, 1955, 1957; Carnegie Inst., 1943, 1944; AIC, 1945; PAFA, 1940-1946, 1950, 1951; VMFA, 1942-1946; WFNY 1939; GGE, 1939; CMA; George Washington Univ., 1951 (one-man); Goucher Col. (one-man) 1951. Lectures: "American Artists I Have Known"; "Understanding Modern Painting"; etc. *Position*: Instr., ASL, New York, N.Y., 1923-35; Principal, Corcoran Sch. A., 1935- ; Prof., Goucher Col., 1935- ; George Washington Univ., Washington, D.C., 1940- .

LAHEY, MRS. RICHARD. *See Gonzales, Carlotta*

LAISNER, GEORGE ALOIS—
     Sculptor, C., P., E., L., Gr.

1822 Duncan Lane, Pullman, Wash.

B. Czechoslovakia, May 5, 1914. *Studied*: AIC, B.A.E.; Univ. Chicago, M.A.E., and with Chapin, Polasek, Anis-

feld. *Member*: Northwest AA; Pullman AA; NAEA. *Awards*: prizes, Puyallup, Wash., 1939; Lewiston Exh., 1953; SAM, 1943, 1944; SFMA, 1943, 1948; Pacific Coast P. & S., 1939; Oakland A. Gal., 1947; Northwest WC Soc., 1947; Pacific Northwest Exh., Spokane, 1948; Western Wash. Fair, 1948; Arizona State Fair, 1950. *Work*: SAM; SFMA; Northwest Pr. M.; sc. mural, Student Union Bldg., Washington State Col., and sc., in gymnasium bldg. *Exhibited*: AIC; LC; SAM; Northwest Pr. M.; SFMA; GGE, 1939; San F. AA; Oakland A. Mus.; and others. *Position*: Instr. A., 1937-41, Prof. FA, 1942- , State Col. of Washington, Pullman, Wash.; Trustee, Wash. A. & Crafts Assn.

LAMB, ADRIAN—*Portrait Painter*

1 West 67th St., New York, N.Y.; h. New Canaan, Conn.

B. New York, N.Y., Mar. 22, 1901. *Studied*: ASL; Julien Acad., Paris, France. *Member*: All. A. Am.; ASL; SC. *Work*: portraits: Columbia Univ.; Union Col.; American Embassy, Paris; Anderson House, Wash., D.C.; Univ. North Carolina; N.Y. Univ.; Univ. Wyoming; N.Y. Law Sch.; Harvard Business Sch.; Supreme Court, Florida; War Dept., Wash., D.C.; Cosmopolitan Cl. N.Y.; Brownsville (Tex.) Mem. Center; Roosevelt Mem. Mus.; Greenwich Hospital, Conn.; St. Luke's Hospital, N.Y.; Glasgow Memb. Lib., Richmond, Va.; Catholic Univ., Wash., D.C.; U.S. Capitol Bldg.; Exec. Office, Book of the Month Cl., N.Y.; Cosmopolitan Cl., N.Y.; St. John The Divine Church, N.Y.; Varner Plantation Mus., Houston, Tex. *Exhibited*: All. A. Am., 1950, 1953-1958; New Canaan Lib., 1956; Greenwich, Conn., 1957.

LAMB, KATHARINE (Mrs. Trevors Tait)—
     Designer, P., C.

Lambs' Lane, Cresskill, N.J.

B. Alpine, N.J., June 3, 1895. *Studied*: T. Col., Columbia Univ.; NAD; ASL; CUASch. *Member*: NSMP; NAC. *Work*: stained glass windows, Newark Mus.; First Presbyterian Church, Mt. Vernon, N.Y.; Camp LeJeune, N.C.; U.S. Naval Hospital Chapel, Chelsea, Mass.; First Baptist Church, St. Peter's Church, Richmond, Va.; All Souls Chapel, Morris, N.Y.; Old Mariners Church, Detroit, Mich.; All Saints Episcopal Church, Detroit, Mich.; St. James Church, Birmingham, Mich.; Tuskegee Inst.; Ferncliff Mausoleum, N.Y.; mosaic murals, churches in Wash., D.C.; Brooklyn, N.Y.; First Presbyterian Church, Vancouver, Wash., etc.

LAMBDIN, ROBERT L.—*Painter, I., Des.*

10 Greenacre Lane, Westport, Conn.

B. Dighton, Kan., Oct. 7, 1886. *Studied*: Read Sch. A., Denver, Colo.; Kansas City AI. *Member*: A. Gld.; NSMP; Westport AA. *Work*: murals, USPO, Bridgeport, Conn.; Bridgeport Brass Co.; Black Rock Bank & Trust Co., Bridgeport, Conn.; Benj. Harris & Co., Chicago Heights, Ill.; Pub. Sch., Westport, Conn.; mural panels, Beekman Downtown Hospital, N.Y. I., many juvenile books, & for national magazines.

LAMBERT, GEORGE E., JR.—*Designer*

2 Park Square, Boston, Mass.; h. 33 Lincoln Ave., Lynnfield Centre, Mass.

B. Boston, Mass., Jan. 3, 1889. *Studied*: Eric Pape Sch. A. *Work*: BMFA. *Position*: Owner, The Lambert Studios, Boston, Mass., adv. illus.

LAMBERTON, CLARK DIVEN—*Educator*

Western Reserve University, Cleveland 6, Ohio

Studied: Dickinson Col., A.B.; Princeton Univ., M.A., Ph.D.; Am. Sch. of Classical Studies, Rome. *Member*: CAA; Archaeological Inst. Am. Contributor to: American Journal of Archaeology. *Position*: Instr., Hist. A., Western Reserve Univ., Cleveland, Ohio (Retired, 1952).

LA MENDOLA, GEORGE (George Dole)—
     Cartoonist, I., P.

823 Main St., Westbrook, Me.; h. 6 David Rd., Portland 5, Me.

B. New York, N.Y., July 24, 1920. *Studied*: NAD; PIA Sch.; ASL. *Member*: Soc. Magazine Cartoonists. Contributor cartoons to Esquire, Sat. Eve. Post, Argosy magazines and others. *Work*: "Best Cartoons of the Year," 1940-1956; "You've Got Me in Stitches."

LA MOND, STELLA LODGE—
Craftsman, Lith., Ser., E., L.
Art Department, Southern Methodist University; h. 3211 Westminster Ave., Dallas 5, Tex.

B. Morganfield, Ky., Sept. 30, 1893. *Studied*: Peabody Col., B.S.; Columbia Univ., M.A.; Cranbrook Acad. A.; Berea Col.; Instituto de Allende, Mexico, & with Alexander Hogue. *Member*: Craft Gld. of Dallas; AAUP; Texas Pr. M.; Dallas AA; Texas Des.-Craftsmen; Contemp. Handweavers of Texas; Dallas Pr. Soc. *Awards*: prizes, San Antonio Pr. Soc., 1944; Int. Textile Exh., Greensboro, N.C., 1945; State Fair of Texas, 1950, 1951, 1954, 1957; Tulsa, Okla., 1958. *Work*: Evansville (Ind.) A. Mus.; Dallas Mus. FA; Southern Methodist Univ.; Texas Tech. Col.; Corpus Christi (Tex.) Mus.; Mus. A., Greensboro, N.C.; Nebraska Wesleyan Univ.; Sam Houston Col. *Exhibited*: NAD, 1942; Int. Textile Exh., 1944, 1945; Dallas Mus. FA, annually; Texas General Exh., annually; Sam Houston Col., 1958; Dallas All. A., annually; SSAL. *Position*: Prof. A., 1936- , Dir., Sch. Des., 1945- , Southern Methodist Univ., Dallas, Tex.

LAMONT, FRANCES (Mrs.)—*Sculptor*
21 West 10th St., New York 11, N.Y.
Studied: with Solon Borglum, Mahonri Young. *Member*: NSS. *Awards*: prizes, AV, 1942; All. A. Am., 1958. *Work*: CMA; mem., New Canaan, Conn.; New Rochelle, N.Y.; MMA; Cranbrook Mus. A.; Denver A. Mus.; Colorado Springs FA Center; Ogunquit A. Mus.; Albright A. Gal. *Exhibited*: Salon des Tuileries, Paris, 1937-1939; AV, 1942; WMAA, 1941-1951; PMA, 1940-1949; PAFA, 1948; Ogunquit A. Mus., 1953-1955; All. A. Am., 1958; one-man: G.W.V. Smith Mus., 1950; Denver A. Mus., 1952; traveling exh., 1952-53; Nelson Gal. A., 1953; Albright A. Gal., 1953; Bermuda Soc. A., 1956.

LA MORE, CHET HARMON—*Painter, Gr., T.*
503 South First St., Ann Arbor, Mich.
B. Dane County, Wis., July 30, 1908. *Studied*: Colt Sch. A., Madison, Wis.; Univ. Wisconsin, B.A., M.A.; Columbia Univ. *Awards*: prizes, MMoA, 1937. *Work*: MMA; MMoA; Lib. Cong.; San Diego FA Soc.; Dallas Mus. FA; Syracuse Mus. FA; Albright A. Gal.; Dept. State, Wash., D.C.; FMA; Birmingham Mus. A.; Mich. State Col.; Mills Col., Oakland; Lowe Gal., Coral Gables; mural, Polytechnic Inst., Baltimore, Md. *Exhibited*: NAD, 1938; WMAA, 1942-1943, 1945-1946, 1948, 1950; PAFA, 1939, 1940, 1945; WFNY 1939; AIC, 1938; MMoA, 1943-1945; Palace Legion Honor, 1945; Paris, France, 1946; Carnegie Inst., 1949; Albright A. Gal., 1943-1945; one-man exh.: ACA Gal., 1941, 1942; Perls Gal., 1944; Albright A. Gal., 1943; AFA traveling exh., 1941, 1943-1944; Carlebach Gal., 1948, 1950. *Position*: Assoc. Prof. Painting, Dept. A., Univ. Michigan, 1946- .

LANDACRE, PAUL HAMBLETON—*Engraver, I., T.*
2006 El Moran St., Los Angeles 39, Cal.
B. Columbus, Ohio. *Studied*: Ohio State Univ. *Member*: Intl. Soc. Wood Engravers; NA; SAGA; Am. Soc. Wood Engravers. *Awards*: prizes, Phila. Pr. Cl., 1933, 1936, 1944; Northwest Pr. M., 1937, 1940, 1944; LC, 1943, 1946, 1953; Assoc. Am. A., 1946. *Work*: LC; N.Y. Pub. Lib.; MMoA; BMFA; PMA; Rochester Mem. A. Gal.; Mills Col.; Honolulu Acad. A.; SFMA; Columbus (Ohio) Pub. Lib.; SAM; Los A. Pub. Lib.; Univ. California; Pomona Col.; Los A. City Col.; Springfield (Mass.) Lib.; Hackley A. Gal.; San Diego FA Soc.; MMA; Victoria & Albert Mus., London; Encyclopaedia Britannica; IBM, and others. Illus. numerous books, 5 of which were included in "50 Books of the Year"; "Of the Nature of Things"; "The Great Chain of Life." Contributor: "The Relief Print." *Position*: Instr., wood engraving, Los Angeles Art Inst.

LANDAU, ROM—*Sculptor, E., W., L.*
2230 Steiner St., San Francisco, Cal.
B. England, Oct. 17, 1899. *Studied*: with George Kolbe; and in Germany, Italy. *Exhibited*: in England and the Continent. Author: "Minos the Incorruptible," 1925; "The Arabesque, The Abstract Art of Islam," 1955; Chapters on

art in "Love for a Country," 1939; "Outline of Moroccan Culture," 1957; "Arab Contribution to Civilization," 1958; "Islam and the Arabs," 1958. Lectures: The Arts of Islam, at various universities and clubs. *Position*: Prof. Islamic & North African Studies, College of the Pacific, Stockton, Cal., 1956- .

LANDECK, ARMIN—*Etcher, Eng., Lith.*
3 East 14th St., New York 3, N.Y.; h. R.D. 1, Litchfield, Conn.
B. Crandon, Wis., June 4, 1905. *Studied*: Columbia Univ. *Member*: NA; SAGA. *Awards*: prizes, Lib. Cong., 1943, 1944, 1945; SAGA, 1932; AIC, 1942; med., PAFA, 1938. *Work*: MMA; AIC; N.Y. Pub. Lib.; Toledo Mus. A.; Newark Mus.; Nebraska State Mus.; Lib. Cong.; Swedish Nat. Mus., Stockholm.

LANDERS, BERTHA—*Painter, Librarian, Et., W.*
4930 Coliseum St., Los Angeles 16, Cal.
B. Winnsboro, Tex. *Studied*: ASL, with Reginald Marsh; Colorado Springs FA Center, B.A., with Arnold Blanch, Henry Varnum Poor, Boardman Robinson and others. *Member*: Los A. AA. *Work*: Dallas Mus. FA; Univ. Texas; Corpus Christi Mus. A.; Witte Mem. Mus. *Exhibited*: Dallas All. A.; Texas General; Texas FA Assn.; Denver A. Mus.; Oakland A. Gal.; LC; NAD; Laguna Beach AA; Oklahoma A. Center; SSAL; Kennedy Gal., New York; BM; Mid-Am. A., and in national print exhibitions; one-man: Elisabet Ney Mus.; Dallas Mus. FA; Sul Ross Col.; NGA; Univ. Kansas City; Lawrence Gal.; Kansas City AI. *Position*: Dir., the Art, Music and Film Dept., Kansas City Pub. Lib., Kansas City, Mo., 1950-58; Ed. & Publ. "Bertha Landers Film Reviews," 1956- .

LANDERS, DELLA A.—*Painter, T., Gr., L.*
South Junior High School, Abilene, Tex.; h. P.O. Box 120, Ovalo, Tex.
B. Lawn, Tex. *Studied*: Hardin-Simmons Univ., B.A.; Univ. Colorado; Peabody Col.; Colorado Springs FA Center; Univ. Texas, M.A.; San Angelo Sch. Painting; East Hampton (L.I.) Sch. FA. *Member*: Texas FA Assn.; Texas WC Soc.; Creative A. Cl.; Texas A. Edu. Assn.; West Texas AA; Abilene Classroom T. Assn.; NEA; Texas State T. Assn.; AAUW. *Awards*: prizes, Abilene Mus. FA, 1948, 1950, 1952, 1953; Southern Sun Carnival, El Paso, 1951, 1952; San Angelo Texas General, 1952; West Texas AA, 1957, 1958; West Texas Fair, 1956, 1958; Creative A. Cl., Abilene, 1954, 1956, 1958. *Work*: Abilene Mus. FA.; Ovalo Baptist Church (Tex.). *Exhibited*: Texas Print, DMFA, 1947; Texas FA Assn., 1947, 1949-1954, 1957; Abilene Mus. FA, 1948-1958; Prints & Drawing Exh., DMFA, 1948-1950, 1952; Fort Worth, 1949, 1950; Texas P. & S. Exh., Dallas and San Antonio, 1950; Sun Carnival, El Paso, 1951, 1953; San Angelo General, 1952-1954; Texas WC Soc.; Witte Mem. Mus., 1952-1954; Creative A. Cl., 1954-1958; West Texas Fair, 1956-1958; West Texas AA, 1957, 1958; one-man: Abilene Mus. FA, 1954; Creative A. Cl., 1954; 2-man, San Angelo, Tex., 1957. *Position*: Instr. A., Port Arthur Pub. Sch., 1929-45; Wichita Falls Pub. Schs., 1945-47; Abilene Pub. Schs., 1948-58; Conducted summer art workshops, Hardin-Simmons Univ., 1951-52; Instr., South Junior H.S., Abilene, Tex., at present.

LANDIS, LILY—*Sculptor*
400 East 57th St., New York 22, N.Y.
B. New York, N.Y. *Studied*: ASL; with Jose de Creeft, and abroad. *Member*: Audubon A.; Arch. Lg.; AEA; S. Gld. *Work*: David Doniger Co.; Noma Electric Co., and in private collections. *Awards*: AIC; Audubon A. *Exhibited*: CGA; PAFA; AIC; NAD; WMAA; S. Gld., 1948-1955; Bonestell Gal. (one-man). Delegate, U.S. Com., IAPA, UNESCO.*

LANDMESSER, ARTHUR CHARLES. See Landy, Art

LANDON, EDWARD—*Serigrapher, S., W.*
Bondville, Vt.
B. Hartford, Conn., Mar. 13, 1911. *Studied*: Hartford A. Sch.; ASL; & in Mexico. *Member*: Boston Pr. M.; Phila. Pr. Cl.; Am. Color Pr. Soc.; Nat. Serigraph Soc. *Awards*: prizes, Springfield A. Lg., 1934, 1945; Northwest Pr. M.,

1944, 1946; Fulbright award, 1950-51; Bradley Univ., 1952; Pr. M. of So. Cal., 1952; Boston Pr. M., 1954; Nat. Ser. Soc., 1958. *Work*: Springfield Mus. FA; Smith Col.; PMA; Cornell Univ.; Wesleyan Univ.; AGAA; SFMA; Carnegie Inst.; Lib. Cong.; U.S. State Dept.; Albright A. Gal.; PAFA; Honolulu Acad. A.; Berkshire Mus.; SAM; Mt. Holyoke Col.; Florida State Col.; MMA; Phila. Pr. Cl.; Am. Assn. Univ. Women; Berkeley Bd. Edu.; murals, Trade Sch., Springfield, Mass. *Exhibited*: nationally in print exh. since 1941. Author, I., "Picture Framing," 1946; "Scandinavian Design," 1951. Lectures: Serigraphy. *Position*: Ed., Serigraph Quarterly.

LANDY, ART (ARTHUR CHARLES LANDMESSER)—
Painter, Lith., T., C., Ser.
861 North Seward St., Hollywood, Cal.; h. 5518 Bevis Ave., Van Nuys, Cal.

B. Newark, N.J., May 18, 1904. *Studied*: Fawcett Sch. A., Newark; Otis AI, and with George Biddle, Alexander Brook, F. Tolles Chamberlin, and others. *Member*: Cal. WC Soc.; AWS; Los Angeles P. & S. Soc.; Cal. A. Cl.; Laguna Beach AA; Whittier (Cal.) AA; Bellflower AA; Long Beach AA; Fullerton AA. *Awards*: prizes, P. & S. Soc., 1944, 1945; Whittier AA, 1943, 1947, 1949; Cal. State Fair, 1947; Ramona Sch. award, 1950, 1955; Gallatin Sch. purchase award, 1957. *Work*: Jersey City Pub. Lib.; Whittier AA; Los Angeles County Lib.; Pomona Col.; Gallatin Sch. *Exhibited*: Cal. WC Soc., 1941-1950, 1953; AWS, 1947, 1948; Laguna Beach AA; Walt Disney Studios, 1946-1949 (one-man); Oakland A. Gal., 1945-1947, 1949, 1950; Northwest Pr. M., 1944; Los A. Mus. A., 1945; Grand Central Gal., 1948; Oklahoma A. & M. Col., 1948; Long Beach AA, 1945-1948 (one-man); Santa Barbara Mus. A., 1949; Pasadena AI, 1947-1951; Arizona State Fair, 1945-1949; Whittier AA, 1949 (one-man); Fullerton AA, 1954.

LANE, HARRY—*Painter*
Upland Farm, State Line, Mass.

B. New York, N.Y., Dec. 26, 1891. *Studied*: in Europe. *Member*: Nat. A. Soc.; AEA; Berkshire AA. *Awards*: prizes, Berkshire AA, 1951, 1952; Berkshire A. Dir. award, 1955. *Work*: MMA; WMA; Standard Oil Co.; Berkshire Mus. A.; BMFA; murals, USPO, Port Washington, N.Y.; Oakdale, La. *Exhibited*: PAFA, 1933, 1940; DMFA, 1936; WFNY 1939; Toledo Mus. A., 1932, 1940; Berkshire Mus. A., Pittsfield, Mass., 1952-1955; All. A. Am., 1955; Albany Inst. Hist. & A., 1948, 1952-1955; one-man: T. Col., Univ. State of N.Y., 1958.

LANE, MARIAN U. M.—*Bookbinder, Illuminator*
1851 Columbia Rd., N.W., Washington, D.C.

B. England. *Studied*: with Sangorski, Sutcliffe, Clifford. *Member*: Wash. WC Cl.; Wash. AC. *Awards*: prizes, Smithsonian Inst., 1937, 1938, 1940, 1950, 1951, 1952, 1956. *Exhibited*: Wash. WC Cl., annually; CGA; Smithsonian Inst. *Position*: Instr., Bookbinding, Lettering, Illumination. Des. special cards publ. & distr. by Washington Cathedral, Wash., D.C.

LANFAIR, HAROLD EDWARD—*Designer, I., P.*
1050 Norman Place, Brentwood, Los Angeles 49, Cal.; h. 1315 Tremaine Ave., Los Angeles 19, Cal.

B. Portland, Ore., Feb. 3, 1898. *Studied*: Los A. Sch. A. & Des.; Nicholas Haz Sch.; Los Angeles County AI; John Huntington Sch., Cleveland. *Member*: Los A. AA. *Awards*: prize, CMA, 1932. *Work*: CMA. *Exhibited*: AIC, 1932, 1933, 1934, 1940; SFMA, 1941; CMA, 1932; Kneifel Gal.; Simone Gal.; Los A. AA. *Position*: Des., I., Columbia, Twentieth Century Fox, Universal, Goldwyn & other motion picture companies, 1931-45; Des. A. Dir., Chrysons, Hollywood, Cal., 1946-50.

LANG, MRS. WILL. See Sibley, Marguerite

LANGE, ERNA—*Painter, T.*
1700 East Northern Ave., Phoenix, Ariz.

B. Elizabeth, N.J., Oct. 19, 1905. *Studied*: ASL; NAD; CUASch; Julian Acad., Grande Chaumiere, Paris; & with Cecilia Beaux, Ferdinand Olivier. *Member*: AAPL; Societe Nationale des Beaux-Arts, Paris; Phoenix FA Assn.; Arizona A. Gld. *Position*: Dir., Erna Lange A. Gal., Phoenix, Ariz.

LANGE, MRS. FREDERIC G. M. See Condit, Louise

LANGE, KATHARINE GRUENER (Mrs. Oscar J.)—
Sculptor
2718 Wadsworth Rd., Shaker Heights 22, Ohio

B. Cleveland, Ohio, Nov. 26, 1903. *Studied*: Smith Col., A.B.; Cleveland Sch. A. *Awards*: prizes, CMA, 1936, 1939, 1940-1942, 1945, 1946, 1948-1950, 1952, 1953-1955, 1957. *Work*: CMA; Republic Steel Corp., Cleveland. *Exhibited*: Arch. Lg., 1938; WFNY 1939; CAM, 1935-1946; WMAA, 1940; MMA, 1942; Butler AI, 1955; CMA, 1936-1957.

LANGENBACH, CLARA EMMA—*Painter*
21 Colvin Ave., Buffalo 16, N.Y.

B. Ontario, Canada. *Studied*: Albright A. Sch.; PIASch.; ASL, Woodstock, N.Y., and with John Carlson, Walter Goltz; Frederick Mulhaupt, Ernest Fosbery, Anna Fisher. *Member*: North Shore AA; Nat. Lg. Am. Pen Women; Zonta Cl., Buffalo. *Awards*: prizes, Nat. Lg. Am. Pen Women, 1936, medal, 1942. *Exhibited*: North Shore AA; Nat. Lg. Am. Pen Women; Boston A. Cl.; Phila. A. All.; Providence A. Cl.; Buffalo Soc. A.; Genesee Group, Rochester, and others; Conservative Painters Exh., CAM, 1943; several one-man exhs. Lectures on Art. *Position*: Sec., Western N.Y. Branch, Nat. Lg. Am. Pen Women; Genesee Group, Rochester, N.Y.

LANGFORD, RUTH BETTY—*Painter, Gr., T.*
George Pepperdine College, 1121 West 79th St., Los Angeles 44, Cal.; h. Mt. Enterprise, Tex.

B. Sherman, Tex. *Studied*: Harding Col., B.A.; Colorado FA Center; Univ. Iowa, M.A., M.F.A.; & with Fletcher Martin, Emil Ganso, Philip Guston. *Awards*: prizes, Arkansas State Exh., 1946. *Work*: Hendrix Col., Ark. *Exhibited*: Ney Mus. A., 1943; Texas General, 1948; Cal. State Exh., 1949; Los A. Mus. A., 1949; Kansas City AI, 1942; Arkansas State Exh., 1942, 1946. *Position*: Hd. A. Dept., Harding Col., Searcy, Ark., 1942-46; Asst. Prof. A., George Pepperdine Col., Los Angeles, Cal., at present.*

LANGLAIS, BERNARD—*Painter*
212 West 28th St., New York, N.Y.; h. Star Route, Thomaston, Me.

B. Old Town, Me., July 23, 1924. *Studied*: Corcoran Sch. A.; BMSch. A.; Grande Chaumiere, Paris, France; Nat. Acad., Oslo, Norway, and with Richard Lahey, Henry Varnum Poor. *Awards*: Scholarship, CGA exh., to Skowhegan, Me.; grant, BM, 1952; Fulbright grant to Norway, 1954-55, 1956. *Work*: Univ. Maine; American Embassy, Oslo, Norway. *Exhibited*: BM, 1952, 1957; Wash. AA, 1950; Univ. Maine (one-man); RoKo Gal., 1955, 1957 (one-man); Area Gal., N.Y., 1957 (one-man).

LANGS, MARY METCALF—*Sculptor*
2032 Whirlpool St., Niagara Falls, N.Y.

B. Burford, Ontario, Canada, Mar. 12, 1887. *Studied*: with Bourdelle, Despiau, Gimond, in Paris, France. *Member*: AEA; The Patteran. *Awards*: prizes, Albright A. Gal., 1938, 1941, 1945, 1950. *Exhibited*: Salon de Printemps, Paris, 1929, 1931, 1932; Salon d'Automne, Paris, 1933; NAD, 1931; PAFA, 1937, 1938, 1953; Audubon A., 1953, 1955; Art:USA, 1958; Albright A. Gal., annually, 1931- .

LANGSDORF, MARTYL SCHWEIG. See Martyl

LANGTON, BERENICE (Mrs.)—*Sculptor*
1 Ascan Ave., Forest Hills, N.Y.

B. Erie County, Pa., Sept. 2, 1878. *Studied*: with Augustus Saint-Gaudens, Augustus Rodin. *Member*: NAWA; PBC. *Awards*: Barnett prize, New York, 1915; Crowninshield prize, Stockbridge, Mass., 1939; Medal, Pen & Brush Cl., 1948. *Work*: Booth Mem., N.Y.; Haas Mem., Paterson N.J.; Miller mem., Vevey, Switzerland; reliefs, Lawrence Hospital, New London, Conn.; many fountains, garden dec., small sculptures, port. busts privately owned. *Exhibited*: MMA (AV), 1942; PAFA; Walters Gal., Balt., Md.; NAD; Berkshire Mus.; Salon des Beaux-Arts, Salon des Tuileries, Paris, France; Pen & Brush Cl.*

LANIER, FANITA (McCLEAN) (Mrs. Robert)—
Illustrator, P., Des.

8057 Bowen Road, El Paso, Tex.

B. Miami, Fla., Aug. 15, 1903. *Studied*: Texas State Col.
for Women; ASL; Ecole des Beaux-Arts, Paris, France;
Texas Western Col., with Vera Wise, Robert Massey.
Member: El Paso AA. *Awards*: prizes, Seton Hall Univ.,
1957; 2 awards, White Sands Missile Range, N.M., for
Diorama, 1957, 1958. *Work*: mural maps, Fed. Bldg.,
Texas Centennial, 1936; Hotel El Rancho, Gallup, N.M.;
Fed. Reserve Bank, Dallas, Tex. *Exhibited*: Seton Hall
Univ., 1957; El Paso AA, 1958. Illus. "My Adventures
in Zuni," 1941; "Texas, Land of the Tejas," 1942;
"Vicente Silva and His 40 Bandits," 1947; Air Force
History "U.S. Army Air Forces in World War II," 1947-
52 (4 vols.) Illus. for Saturday Review. Arranged Exhs.,
El Paso Lib., 1958; Sun Carnival Show, El Paso, 1958.
Positions: Illustrator for Office of Secretary of the Air
Force, Wash., D.C., 1942-1952; White Sands Missile
Range, White Sands, N.M., 1954-57.

LANING, EDWARD—Painter, T.

30 East 14th St., New York 3, N.Y.

B. Petersburg, Ill., Apr. 26, 1906. *Studied*: Univ. Chicago;
AIC; ASL; Academia di Belle Arti, Rome. *Member*:
NA; Audubon A. *Awards*: prizes, AIC, 1945; VMFA,
1945, grant, Am. Acad. A. & Let., 1945; Guggenheim F.,
1945; Fulbright F., 1950-52. *Work*: WMAA; William
Rockhill Nelson Gal. A.; murals, N.Y. Pub. Lib.; Rich-
mond Professional Inst.; Admin. Bldg., Ellis Island, N.Y.;
Hudson Gld., N.Y.; Mayflower Hotel, Wash., D.C.;
Sheraton Hotels, Los Angeles, Cal., and Dallas, Tex.;
USPO, Rockingham, N.C.; Bowling Green, Ky. *Exhibited*:
nationally & internationally. *Position*: Hd., Painting Dept.,
Kansas City AI, 1945-50; Instr., ASL, New York, N.Y.,
1952- .

LANING, MRS. EDWARD. See Fife, Mary E.

LANKES, JULIUS J.—Engraver, I.

2414 Club Blvd., Durham, N.C.

B. Buffalo, N.Y., Aug. 31, 1884. *Studied*: ASL, Buffalo,
N.Y.; BMFA Sch. *Member*: NA; SAGA. *Work*: Lib.
Cong.; MMA; British Mus., London; BM; BMA; Newark
Pub. Lib.; Bibliotheque Nationale, Paris. *Exhibited*: one-
man exh.: CGA; Carnegie Inst.; Albright A. Gal.; BMA;
Rochester Mem. A. Gal.; Richmond Acad. FA; etc.
Author: "A Woodcut Manual," 1932. I., many books.
Contributor to: Print magazine.

LANSFORD, ALONZO—Painter, I., W., Cr., L.

Lansford Gallery, 632 St. Peter St.; h. 1418 Gov.
Nicholls St., New Orleans, La.

B. Ocala, Fla., Oct. 13, 1910. *Studied*: Univ. North Caro-
lina, B.A.; PAFA; ASL. Contributor to art magazines;
Assembled and arranged: Delgado Mus. Coll.; Contempo-
rary American Painting and Sculpture; Brussels, Belgium,
1947; Louisiana Painters—AFA traveling exh., 1950-51;
American Children's Painting, Cheltenham, England,
Geneva, Calcutta; Kress Coll. Italian Renaissance Paint-
ing, Delgado Mus. A., 1952; Five Centuries of French
Masterpieces; Paintings and Drawings by Van Gogh, etc.
Positions: Dir., Telfair Acad., Savannah, Ga., 1939-44;
Assoc. Ed., Art Digest, 1946-48; Dir., Delgado Mus. A.,
New Orleans, La., 1948-1957.

LANSING, AMBROSE—Museum Curator

Apache Junction, Ariz.

B. Cairo, Egypt, Sept. 20, 1891. *Studied*: Washington &
Jefferson Col.; Univ. Leipzig. Contributor to: Bulletin of
MMA. Lectures: Egyptian Art. *Position*: Cur., Dept.
Egyptian A., MMA, New York, N.Y., 1939-52.*

LANSING, WINIFRED JUSTINE—Sculptor

370 Central Park West, New York 29, N.Y.

B. Rochester, N.Y., Sept. 29, 1911. *Studied*: ASL; Brook-
lyn Mus. A. Center. *Member*: S. Gld.; N.Y. Soc. Ceramic
A. *Work*: Rochester Mem. A. Gal.; Rochester Pub. Lib.
Exhibited: AFA traveling exh., 1954; NAD, 1945-1955;
AIC; Syracuse AI; S. Gld., annually; one-man: Oklahoma
A. Center; Am.-British A. Gal.; Rochester Mem. A. Gal.

LANSNER, FAY GROSS—Painter, Des., Cr.

513 East 84th St., New York, N.Y.

B. Philadelphia, Pa., June 21, 1921. *Studied*: Wanamaker
Inst.; Tyler Sch. FA, Temple Univ.; ASL; with Hans
Hofmann, and in Paris, with Leger, L'Hote; Holland;
England. *Member*: A. Cl., New York. *Exhibited*: Con-
temporaries, 1952; N.Y. City Center Gal., 1953; Hansa
Gal., N.Y., 1955, one-man: 1956, 1958; and abroad.
Reviewer, Art News magazine. Illus. children's books;
Textile Des.

LANTZ, MICHAEL—Sculptor

979 Webster Ave., New Rochelle, N.Y.

B. New Rochelle, N.Y., Apr. 6, 1908. *Studied*: NAD;
BAID, and with Lee Lawrie. *Member*: NA; F., NSS;
BAID. *Awards*: prizes, medals, BAID, 1926, 1927, 1929,
1930, 1931; Nat. Comp. Fed. Trade Comm. Bldg., Wash.,
D.C., 1938; City of N.Y. Comp. for Golden Anniversary
Medal, 1948; Morris award, 1950; Bennett award, 1947;
silver medal, Int. Exh. of medals, Madrid, Spain, 1952.
Work: equestrian groups, Fed. Trade Bldg., Wash., D.C.;
U.S. Battle Monument, St. Avold, France; s. panels, Co-
lumbus Sch., New Rochelle, N.Y.; Celanese Corp. Bldg.,
Charlotte, N.C.; Spring Hill Temple, Mobile, Ala.; Court
House, Lynchburg, Va.; Dupont Plaza Hotel, Wash., D.C.;
Burlington Mills Corp.; Lone Star Cement Corp.; Sinclair
Oil Tourist Bureau, N.Y.; Howard Trust Co., Burlington,
Vt.; SS "United States"; med., Soc. Medalists; Golden
Anniversary med., N.Y.C.; Christmas Font, Steuben Glass
Corp. *Exhibited*: PAFA, 1941, 1945; Phila. A. All., 1946;
Arch. Lg., 1946; NAD.

LANZI, EMILIO—Painter, W., L.

1306 Quintero St., Los Angeles 26, Cal.

B. Berne, Switzerland. *Studied*: Swiss Acad. A., with
Plinio Colombi, Christopher Baumgartner; Julian Acad.,
Colorossi Acad., Ecole des Beaux-Arts, Paris, France.
Member: AAPL; Bohemian Cl.; Prof. A. Gld.; Cal. A.
Cl.; Soc. P. & S., and societies in Paris. *Awards*: prizes,
Acad. Julian, 1912; Hafs Acad., 1941; Cal. A. Cl., 1948;
Soc. P. & S., 1950, 1952; AAPL, 1953. *Work*: Schatford
Gal.; Baldwin Gal.; Inst. Music & A.; Ovenshire Gal.,
and in many private collections. *Exhibited*: Acad. FA,
Berne, Switzerland; Acad. Julian, Paris; Hafs Acad.,
Munich; Locarno, Switzerland; AAPL, 1953; Bohemian
Cl.; Cal. A. Cl.; Soc. P. & S.; Los A. Mus. A.; Ebell
Cl.; Friday Morning Cl.; City Hall, Los A.; and others.
Contributor to U.S. and Canadian publications. *Position*:
Mgr., Los Angeles Mun. A. Exh., 1949; Vice-Pres., P. &
S., 1952; Chm., Jury of Awards, 1953-55.

LAPORTE, PAUL M.—Educator, Pr. M., C., W., L.

1626 Elevado St., Los Angeles 26, Cal.

B. Munich, Germany, Nov. 22, 1904. *Studied*: Acad.,
Munich; Univ. Munich, Ph.D. *Member*: CAA; AEA.
Awards: F., Belgian-American Edu. Fnd.; Fulbright F.,
1954-56. Author: "Johann Michael Fischer," 1934. Contributor to Centennial Review and other magazines. *Position*: Instr., Inst. Des., Chicago, 1948; Ethel Walker Sch.,
1940-45; Olivet Col., 1945-49; Chm., Dept. A., Macalester
Col., St. Paul, Minn., 1949-1956; Prof. A., Immaculate
Heart College, Los Angeles, Cal., at present.

LARIAR, LAWRENCE—Cartoonist, I., W., Editor, S.

57 West Lena Avenue, Freeport, N.Y.

B. Brooklyn, N.Y., Dec. 25, 1908. *Studied*: N.Y. Sch. F.
& App. A.; Colorossi, Paris; ASL. *Exhibited*: MMA.
Author: "Easy Way to Cartooning," 1951; "Careers in
Cartooning," 1951; I., "Ordeal of Sergeant Smoot."
Author: "The Man with the Lumpy Nose"; "He Died
Laughing"; "The Day I Died"; "The Salesman's Treasury";
"Best Cartoons from Abroad," 1955; "Fish and Be
Damned," 1953; "You've Got Me in Stitches," 1954;
"You've Got Me and How!," 1955; "Happy Holidays,"
1956; "You've Got Me from 9 to 5," 1956; "How Green
Was My Sex Life," 1955; "You've Got Me Behind the
Wheel," 1956; "You've Got Me in the Suburbs," 1957;
"Treasury of Sport Cartoons," 1957; "Bed and Bored,"
1958, etc., and many other books. *Positions*: Pres., Am.
Soc. Magazine Cartoonists; OWI Cartoon Exhibits Staff;
Dir., Professional Sch. Cartooning; Writer, Walt Disney
Studios, 1938- ; Ed., Cartoons for Parade Magazine, 1957-
58. Contributor to leading national magazines.

LARKIN, OLIVER—*Educator, W., Cr., L.*
37 Henshaw Ave., Northampton, Mass.

B. Medford, Mass., Aug. 17, 1896. *Studied*: Harvard Col., A.B., A.M. *Member*: Am. Assn. Univ. Prof. *Awards*: Pulitzer prize in History, 1950. Contributor to Magazine of Art, Art in America, College Art Journal, and others. Author: "Art and Life in America," 1949; "Samuel F. B. Morse," 1954. *Position*: Prof. A., Smith Col., Northampton, Mass., 1924- ; Instr., Salzburg (Austria) Seminar in American Studies, 1950, 1955.

La ROCCO, ANTHONY—*Craftsman*
Craft Center, 40 Highland St.; h. 16 Institute Rd., Worcester 9, Mass.

B. Torrington, Conn., Dec. 13, 1920. *Studied*: Sch. for Am. Craftsmen, Alfred Univ.; Acad. FA, Milan, Italy. *Member*: De Cordova Craftsmen. *Awards*: Fulbright F., 1949-50; prize, St. Paul (Minn.) A. Gal., 1952. *Work*: St. Paul A. Gal. *Exhibited*: BM, 1955; St. Paul A. Gal., 1952; WMA, 1955; Smithsonian Inst. traveling exh., 1953; Eastern States Fair, Springfield, 1953; deCordova & Dana Mus., 1953; Fitchburg A. Mus., 1954; Geo. Walter Vincent Smith Mus., Springfield, 1955; Mus. Contemp. Crafts, N.Y., 1956, 1957; Mass. Crafts, Boston, 1956; Boston A. Festival, 1956, 1957; Univ. Illinois, 1957; Craft Center Instructors' Exh., WMA, 1958. *Position*: Dir., Cabinet Shop, Old Sturbridge Village, 1950-51; Instr., woodworking, cabinet making, Craft Center, Worcester, Mass., 1951- .

LARSEN, BENT FRANKLIN—*Painter, E.*
733 North, Fifth West, Provo, Utah

B. Monroe, Utah, May 10, 1882. *Studied*: Brigham Young Univ., A.B.; Univ. Chicago; AIC; Univ. Utah, M.A., and in Europe. *Member*: French Soc. Indp. A.; AWS; Utah State Instr. FA; Assoc. Utah A.; Creative A. of Utah. *Awards*: prizes, Springville, Utah, 1927 (purchase), 1955; Utah County Exh., 1927, 1930; Mississippi State Exh., 1930 (purchase); Utah State Fair, 3 purchase awards; Brigham Young Alumni Distinguished Service Award, 1953; Utah Acad. Sciences, A. & Let., 1955; Special Honor award, Utah State Inst. FA, 1957; Meritorious Service award, Utah A. Edu. Assn., 1957. *Work*: Springville AA; Utah State Coll.; Weber Col.; Brigham Young Univ. Coll.; Miss State Col.; Utah State Agri. Col. *Exhibited*: New York, Cincinnati, Cleveland, Jackson, Denver, Tucson, Salt Lake City, etc., and in Paris. Contributor to newspapers and educational magazines. Lectures: Art History and Appreciation. *Position*: Prof. Emeritus, Brigham Young Univ., Provo, Utah.

LARSEN, ERIK—*Educator, Cr., W., L.*
103 East 86th St., New York 28, N.Y.; also, 2013 New Hampshire Ave., Northwest, Washington, D.C.

B. Vienna, Austria, Oct. 10, 1911. *Studied*: Institut Sup. d'Histoire de l'Art et d'Archéologie, Brussels, Belgium; Catholic Univ., M.F.A.; Sequoia Univ., Litt. D. (Hon.) *Member*: CAA; Cor. Memb., Academie d'Aix-en-Provence, France; Cor. Academician, Real Academia de Bellas Artes, Malaga; Hon. Memb., Comité Cultural, Argentina; Hon. Academician, Accademia di Belle Arti, Perugia, Italy. Author: Peter Paul Rubens (with a complete catalog of his works in America), 1952; Frans Post, Interprete du Bresil (in print). Contributor to many art magazines in Europe. *Positions*: Dir. & Ed.-in-Chief, "Pictura," 1945-46; Research Prof. in Art, Manhattanville College of the Sacred Heart, 1947-55; Instr., City Col. of N.Y., 1955- ; L., Visiting Prof., Assoc. Prof. FA, Georgetown Univ., Washington, D.C., 1955- .

LARSSON, KARL—*Painter, S., Eng., I., T.*
Old Santa Fe Trail, Santa Fe, N.M.

B. Skovde, Sweden, Sept. 16, 1893. *Studied*: ASL. *Member*: AWS. *Work*: AIC; Mus. Intl. Folk Art, Santa Fe, N.M.; mural, Chapel, Lady of Guadalupe, Jemez Springs, N.M.; silver sculpture in churches at Tucson, Ariz.; Albuquerque, N.M.; Fort Defiance, Ariz.; Phoenix, Ariz. *Exhibited*: AWS; Gotenburg, Sweden; Mus. of New Mexico, Santa Fe. Illus., "Pedro," 1943; "The Mother Ditch," 1955.

LASANSKY, MAURICIO—*Painter, Gr.*
Art Department, State University of Iowa; h. 404 South Summit St., Iowa City, Iowa

B. Buenos Aires, Argentina, Oct. 12, 1914. *Studied*: Superior Sch. FA, Buenos Aires. *Awards*: Guggenheim F., 1943, 1945, 1953; prizes, SAM, 1944; PMA, 1945, 1946; LC, 1945, 1948, 1950; Denver A. Mus., 1946; BM, 1948; Northwest Pr. M., 1948, 1951, 1955; PAFA, 1948; Springfield Mus. A., 1948, 1951; Des Moines A. Center, 1949, 1951, 1955; Walker A. Center, 1949; Iowa State A. Salon, 1950, 1955; Phila. Pr. Cl., 1951; Bradley Univ., 1951; Instituto Nacional de Bellas Artes, First Mexican Biennial, 1958. *Work*: NGA; MModA; AIC; BM; PMA; SAM; N.Y. Pub. Lib; Rosenwald Coll.; CAM; Univ. Washington; PAFA; Springfield Mus. A.; Colorado Springs FA Center; IBM; Univ. Indiana; Univ., Minnesota, Illinois, Nebraska, Georgia, and Bradley Univ.; New Britain Mus. A.; Univ. Delaware; Des Moines A. Center; Iowa Wesleyan Univ.; Nelson Gal. A.; Oakland A. Mus. *Exhibited*: PMA, 1945, 1946; Fairfield, Conn., 1953; Brooks Mem. Gal., 1953; Mus. Mod. A., Paris, 1955; Yugoslavia, 1955; Washington Univ., St. Louis, 1955; Barcelona, Spain, 1955; SAM, 1944; LC, 1945, 1948, 1950; Denver A. Mus., 1946; one-man: Walker A. Center, 1949; Louisiana State Univ., 1952; Univ. Georgia, 1952; Tulane Univ., 1952; Univ. Kentucky, 1952; Memphis Acad. A., 1953; Univ. Arkansas, 1953; Museo de Arte Moderna, Madrid, Spain, 1954; Barcelona, 1954; Cedar Rapids AA, 1954. *Position*: Prof. A., State Univ. Iowa, Iowa City, Iowa, 1945- .

LASKER, JOSEPH LEON (JOE)—*Painter*
20 Dock Rd., South Norwalk, Conn.

B. New York, N.Y., June 26, 1919. *Studied*: CUASch.; and in Mexico. *Awards*: prizes, Hallmark award; NAD, 1949, 1950, 1955, 1958; Audubon A., 1951; Abbey Mem. Scholarship, 1946-47; Prix de Rome, 1950-51; Guggenheim F., 1954. *Work*: WMAA; PMA; Springfield (Mass.) Mus. A., BMA; Cal. PLH; Munson-Williams-Proctor Inst.; murals, Henry Street Settlement, N.Y.; USPO, Calumet, Mich., Millbury, Mass. *Exhibited*: WMAA, 1947-1956; PAFA, 1948-1950, 1952, 1953; Univ. Illinois, 1951, 1952; NAD, 1947, 1949, 1950, 1955; Des Moines A. Center, 1953; Rome, Italy, 1952; AIC, 1951, 1954; VMFA, 1948, 1950, 1954; Carnegie Inst., 1949; Los A. Mus. A., 1951; CGA, 1953; BM, 1953; Walker A. Center, 1950, 1954; Nebraska AA, 1954, 1955; Munson-Williams-Proctor Inst., 1955; John Herron AI, 1950, 1955; MMA, 1950; MModA traveling exh., 1950, and others. Contributor illus. to Esquire; Fortune; Charm magazines. *Position*: Assoc. Prof. Painting, Univ. Illinois, 1953-54; Instr., Famous Artists School, Westport, Conn., 1954- .

LASKOSKI, PEARL—*Painter*
2011 40th Place, Des Moines 10, Iowa

B. Steamboat Rock, Iowa. *Member*: NAWA; Des Moines AA. *Awards*: prizes, Iowa Art Salon, 1947, 1949, 1951; Iowa A. Comp. Exh., 1951 (purchase). *Work*: Des Moines A. Mus.; Iowa State Fed. Women's Cl., and in private collections. *Exhibited*: MModA; Argent Gal.; NAD; Manhattan Rotary Show; Stuart Gal., Boston; 4 Nat. Traveling Exhs.; Sioux City, Iowa; State Univ. Iowa City; Cornell Col.; Iowa State Col.; Joslyn Mus. A.; one-man: Argent Gal.; Tallcorn Hotel, Marshalltown, Iowa; Des Moines Lib.; Des Moines AA; Bohemian Cl., Des Moines; Des Moines A. Mus.

LASSAW, IBRAM—*Sculptor, T., W., L.*
487 Sixth Ave., New York 11, N.Y.; also R.F.D., Fireplace Rd., East Hampton, L.I., N.Y.

B. Alexandria, Egypt, May 4, 1913. *Studied*: BAID; Col. City of N.Y., and with Dorothea Denslow, Ozenfant. *Member*: Am. Abstract A.; S. Gld.; A. Cl., N.Y. *Work*: BMA; Albright A. Gal.; WMAA; MModA; Carnegie Inst.; Museu de l'Arte Moderna, Rio de Janeiro; Temple Beth El, Springfield, Mass.; Temple Beth El, Providence, R.I.; and for temples in Cleveland, Ohio and St. Paul, Minn.; St. Leonard Priory, Centerville, Ohio; Temple in Portchester, N.Y. *Exhibited*: WMAA, 1936-1952, 1954, 1955, 1957; Am. Abstract A., 1936-1955; MModA, 1951, 1953, 1956; Mus. Modern A., Paris, 1950; AFA traveling Exh., 1951; Phila. A. All.; AIC, 1951, 1954, 1955; Univ. Indiana; Univ. Nebraska; PMA; Venice Biennale, 1954; Stable Gal., 1953, 1954; PAFA, 1954; Japan, 1955; Am. Exh., Paris, France, 1955; BM, 1955; Cornell Univ.; Sao

Paulo, Brazil, 1958; Yale Univ., 1954; one-man: Mass. Inst. Tech., 1957 (retrospective); Kootz Gal., N.Y., 1951, 1952, 1954, 1958, and many others in U.S. and abroad.

LASSONDE, OMER THOMAS—Painter

269 Hanover St., Manchester, N.H.; s. Fort Acres, Boscawen, N.H.; w. Inspiration & Bay View, Carmel, Cal.

B. Concord, N.H., Aug. 9, 1903. *Studied*: Manchester Inst. A. & Sc.; PAFA; Barnes Fnd., and with Hugh Breckenridge. *Member*: New Hampshire AA; AEA; Manchester (N.H.) Inst. A. & Science; Silvermine Gld. A.; Boston Soc. Indp. A.; F., PAFA; Cape Ann Soc. Mod. A.; Rockport, Gloucester, Ogunquit AA; Societe des Artistes Francais, Paris. *Awards*: F., PAFA; Cresson traveling scholarship and numerous prizes, PAFA; prizes, New Jersey P. & S. Soc., 1949; Huckleberry Mountain, N.C., 1946; Brick Store Mus.; Currier Gal. A., 1949, 1951; Fla. Southern Col., 1952; medal, Yonkers AA, 1949. *Work*: portraits, State House, Concord, N.H.; Cathedral, Nashville, Tenn.; PAFA; Fed. Bldg. & Loan Assn., Manchester, N.H.; Rundlet H.S., Concord, N.H. *Exhibited*: Paris Salon, 1934; WFNY 1939; WMA, 1935; AGAA; Babcock Gal., 1931; Grace Horne Gal.; Brooks Mem. Mus.; New Orleans A. & Crafts; Contemporary A. Cl.; Studio Gld. Am.; Boston Inst. Contemp. A.; Hartford Atheneum; Currier Gal. A.; Ogunquit AA, 1954, 1955; Springfield A. Mus.; NAD, 1950; F., PAFA; Silvermine Gld. A., 1951-1955; Boston A. Festival, 1951, 1952, 1954; Carmel AA, 1954, 1955; Burliuk Gal., 1953 (one-man); Knickerbocker A., 1952; AEA; deCordova & Dana Mus.; New Hampshire AA, 1952; Creative A. Gal., Caravan A.; New Jersey P. & Sc. Soc., 1947-1952; Fla. Southern Col., 1952; Ruthermore Gal., San Francisco, 1957 (one-man).

LASSWELL, FRED—Cartoonist

c/o King Features Syndicate, 235 East 45th St., New York, N.Y.

Creator of "Snuffy Smith" syndicated cartoon.*

LASZLO, GEORGE—Painter, Et., Lith., L.

Raven Rock, Stockton, N.J.

B. Hungary, Mar. 12, 1896. *Studied*: Royal Tech. & Arch. Univ., Budapest; ASL, with DuMond, Wickey, Locke and Miller. *Member*: Hunterdon County A. Center. *Work*: Mus. FA, Budapest; Nat. A. Gal., Dublin, Ireland. Work also in college collections and owned privately. *Exhibited*: Carnegie Inst., 1934; SAGA, 1937 and subsequently; Audubon A., 1945; Phillips Mill Assn., 1952, 1954, 1956, 1958; one-man: Ferargil Gal., N.Y., 1937; Cheshire Gal., 1938; Newhouse Gal., 1935; BM, 1935. Lectures: Modern Printmaking; The Laszlo Method of Gelatin Printing.

LATHAM, BARBARA—Painter, Gr. I.

Ranchos de Taos, N.M.

B. Walpole, Mass., June 6, 1896. *Studied*: Norwich (Conn.) A. Sch.; ASL. *Work*: MMA; Mus. New Mexico; Dallas Mus. FA. *Exhibited*: AIC; PAFA; Denver A. Mus.; Colorado Springs FA Center; WMAA; BM; NAD; Phila. Pr. Cl.; Phila. A. All.; Lib. Cong.; one-man exh.: Weyhe Gal.; Witte Mem. Mus.; Slater Mem. Mus.; Dallas Mus. FA. I., "The Silver Dollar"; "Hurdy-Gurdy Holiday"; "Maggie"; "The Green Thumb Story"; "Honey Bee"; "Downy Woodpecker," 1953; "Monarch Butterfly," 1954; "Tree Frog," 1954; "Flying Horse Ranch," 1955; "Tales of Old-Time Texas," 1955; "I Like Caterpillars," 1958, and other juvenile books.

LATHROP, CHURCHILL PIERCE—Educator, Gal. Dir.

6 Valley Rd., Hanover, N.H.

B. New York, N.Y., Aug. 26, 1900. *Studied*: Rutgers Univ., Litt. B.; Princeton Univ., A.M. *Member*: Am. Assn. Univ. Prof.; CAA; Soc. Arch. Historians. *Awards*: Hon. degree, A.M., Dartmouth Col. Author: sections on Sculpture and the Pictorial Arts in "The Individual and the World," 1942. *Positions*: Instr. A., 1928-31, Asst. Prof., 1931-36, Prof. A., 1936-56, Chm. A. Dept., 1935-39, 1944-51, Dir., Carpenter Gal. A., 1940-59, Dartmouth Col.. Hanover, N.H.; Bldg. Com., Hopkins A. Center.

LATHROP, DOROTHY P(ULIS)—
Illustrator, W., Eng., P.

151 South Allen St., Albany 8, N.Y.

B. Albany, N.Y., Apr. 16, 1891. *Studied*: T. Col., Columbia Univ.; PAFA; ASL, and with Henry McCarter, F. Luis Mora. *Member*: NAD; NAWA; SAGA; Albany Pr. Cl.; Phila. WC Cl. *Awards*: Caldecott Award, 1938; Eyre medal; PAFA, 1941; prize, LC, 1946. *Work*: LC; Albany Inst. Hist. & A.; Albany Pr. Cl. *Exhibited*: NAD; PAFA; LC; SAGA; NAWA. Author, I., "The Little White Goat"; "The Snail Who Ran"; "The Colt from Moon Mountain"; "An Angel in the Woods"; "Let Them Live," and many other children's books. Illus., "Animals of the Bible"; "Crossings"; "Silverhorn"; "Made-to-Order Stories"; "The Little Mermaid" and others.*

LATHROP, GERTRUDE K.—Sculptor

151 South Allen St., Albany, N.Y.

B. Albany, N.Y., Dec. 24, 1896. *Studied*: ASL; Sch. Am. Sculpture, N.Y., and with Solon Borglum, Charles Grafly. *Member*: NA; Nat. Inst. A. & Let.; Hispanic Soc. Am.; Am. Numismatic Soc.; All.A.Am.; Albany Pr. Cl.; NAWA; NSS; Soc. Medalists. *Awards*: prizes, NAD, 1928, 1931, 1936; Stockbridge AA, 1937; NAWA, 1933, 1943; Am. Acad. A. & Let. grant, 1943; NSS, 1944; All.A.Am., 1950; medals, Hispanic Soc. Am., 1950; Am. Numismatic Soc., 1950. *Work*: Houston (Tex.) Pub. Lib.; Albany Pub. Lib.; N.Y. State T. Col.; Smithsonian Inst.; war mem., Memorial Grove, Albany, N.Y.; commemorative Half-Dollar Albany and New Rochelle, N.Y.; medals, Garden Cl. of Am., 1942, 1950; Brookgreen Garden, S.C., 1946; Hispanic Soc. Am., 1950; Mariners' Mus., Newport News, Va.*

LAUCK, ANTHONY (REV.)—Sculptor, E., W., L.

University of Notre Dame; h. Moreau Seminary, Notre Dame, Ind.

B. Indianapolis, Ind., Dec. 30, 1908. *Studied*: John Herron AI, D.F.A.; Corcoran Sch. A.; ASL; Columbia Univ., and with Richard Lahey, Louis Bouche, Julian Levi, Carl Milles, Ivan Mestrovic, Hugo Robus, Oronzio Maldarelli, Heinz Warneke. *Member*: Indianapolis AA; Newport AA; Audubon A.; Provincetown AA. *Awards*: prizes, Fairmount Park AA, 1949 (purchase); Indiana State Fair, 1954, 1955; Indiana AA, 1954; Ecclesiastical A. Gld., Detroit, 1955; gold medal, PAFA, 1953. *Work*: PAFA; CGA; John Herron AI; Norfolk Mus. A.; Notre Dame A. Gal., Univ. Notre Dame; South Bend AA; sculpture, Notre Dame Univ. Campus; Chicago H.S. *Exhibited*: NAD; PAFA, 1948, 1949, 1953, 1954; Audubon A., 1948-1958; Conn. Acad. FA; Provincetown AA; New Jersey P. & S., 1948-1950, 1954; Indiana AA; Indiana State Fair; South Bend AA; Hoosier Salon; Wash. A. Exh., 1948, and others. Contributor to Catholic Art Quarterly; Ave Maria; The Priest; Catholic Digest; Liturgical Arts Quarterly. Assembled exh. of Greek Art for the A. Festival, Notre Dame, 1954; Early Christian Arts Festival, 1957, and other art exhibitions. *Position*: Prof. A., Notre Dame Univ., Notre Dame, Ind., 1950- ; Chm. Jury for Natl. Comp. Drawings of the Sacred Heart, 1956.

LAUFMAN, SIDNEY—Painter, T.

58 West 57th St., New York 19, N.Y.; s. Woodstock, N.Y.

B. Cleveland, Ohio, Oct. 29, 1891. *Studied*: AIC; ASL. *Member*: NA; AEA; Woodstock AA. *Awards*: prizes, AIC, 1932, gold medal, 1941; ASL, 1950; Carnegie Inst., 1934; gold medal, PAFA, 1951; NAD, 1937, 1949, gold medal, 1953; Ranger Fund purchase, 1954; Hassam Fund purchase, 1954; prize, Butler AI, 1954. *Work*: MMA; WMAA; MModA; AIC; CMA; Toledo Mus. A.; Nelson Gal. A.; John Herron AI; Minneapolis Inst. A.; Univ. Oregon; Am. Acad. A. & Let.; Zanesville AI; Washington County Mus. FA, Hagerstown, Md.; Dudley Peter Allen Mem. Mus., Oberlin, Ohio; CAM; Butler Inst. Am. A.; Parrish Mus., Southampton, L.I.; Colorado Springs FA Center; Georgia Mus. A., Athens, Ga. *Exhibited*: nationally. *Position*: Instr., ASL, New York, N.Y., 1938-1959; Memb. Council, NAD, 1947-50; Nat. Sec., AEA, 1948-49; Pres., N.Y. Chapter, AEA, 1949-50; Chm., Woodstock A. Conf.. 1950.

LAUNE, PAUL—Illustrator, Port. P., Des., S.

130 Heights Drive, Yonkers, N.Y.

B. Milford, Neb., May 5, 1899. *Member*: SI. Author, I., "The Thirsty Pony," 1940; "Sand in My Eyes," 1956. *Exhibited*: Ft. Lauderdale, Fla., 1958.

LAURENT, JOHN LOUIS—*Painter, T., Gr.*

c/o Kraushaar Galleries, 1055 Madison Ave., New York, N.Y.

B. Brooklyn, N.Y., Nov. 27, 1921. *Studied*: Syracuse Univ., B.F.A.; Academie de la Grande Chaumiere, Paris; Indiana Univ., M.F.A., and with Walt Kuhn. *Member*: Boston Pr. M.; New Hampshire AA; Ogunquit AA. *Awards*: Hazard Traveling F., Syracuse Univ., 1948; prizes, John Herron AI, 1954; Currier Gal. A., Manchester, N.H., 1954, 1955, 1956, 1957; Sweat Mus. A., Portland, Me., 1955. *Exhibited*: PAFA, 1951, 1954; CGA, 1955; John Herron AI, 1950-1954; Sweat Mus. A., 1955; J. B. Speed Mus. A., 1954; WMAA, 1956; Currier Gal. A., 1956, 1957; Boston A. Festival, 1958; Art:USA, 1958; Provincetown A. Festival, 1958. *Position*: Instr., Des., Painting, Graphics, Va. Polytechnic Inst., 1949-53; Univ. New Hampshire, 1949- ; Ogunquit Sch. Painting & Sculpture, 1949- , (summers).

LAURENT, ROBERT—*Sculptor, E.*

Indiana University, Bloomington, Ind.; h. Cape Neddick, Me.

B. Concarneau, France, June 29, 1890. *Studied*: British Acad., Rome, Italy; & in Paris, with H. E. Field, Frank Burty. *Member*: Audubon A.; NSS; Salons of Am.; S.Gld., AEA. *Awards*: med., prize, AIC, 1924, 1938; prizes, BM, 1942; John Herron AI, 1943, 1944, 1945, 1947, 1949, 1952, 1953; J.B. Speed Mus. A., 1954; Hoosier Salon, 1945, 1946, 1947-1949, 1952, 1953; Audubon A., 1945. *Work*: WMAA; BM; AIC; Newark Mus.; Vassar Col.; Ariz. State Col.; PAFA; Univ. Nebraska; Barnes Fnd.; Brookgreen Gardens, S.C.; Hamilton Easter Field Fnd.; Fairmount Park, Phila., Pa.; Radio City Music Hall, N.Y.; Fed. Trade Bldg., Wash., D.C.; MMA; IBM Coll.; Norton Gal. A.; MModA; Indiana Univ.; USPO, Garfield, N.J. *Exhibited*: WMAA; BM; PAFA; AIC; MMA; WFNY 1939; GGE, 1939; one-man exh.: Daniel Gal.; Bourgeois Gal.; Kraushaar Gal.; Valentine Gal.; A. & Crafts Cl., New Orleans, La.; Vassar Col.; CGA; John Herron AI; Rome, Italy, 1955; Indiana Univ. Contributor to Encyclopaedia Britannica, 1946. *Position*: Prof., Indiana Univ., Bloomington, Ind., 1942- ; Dir., Ogunquit Sch. P. & S., Ogunquit, Me.; Pres. Hamilton Easter Field Fnd.; A.-in-Res., Am. Acad. in Rome, 1954-55.

LAURER, ROBERT—*Assistant Museum Director*

Museum of Contemporary Crafts, 29 West 53rd St., New York 19, N.Y.*

LAURITZ, PAUL—*Painter, T., L.*

3955 Clayton Ave., Los Angeles 27, Cal.

B. Larvik, Norway, Apr. 18, 1889. *Member*: Soc. Western A.; Cal. A. Cl. *Awards*: prizes, Cal. State Exp., 1920, 1922-1926, 1930, 1932, 1934, 1939, 1940; State Exp., Santa Ana, Cal., 1923; San Diego FA Soc., 1928; Long Beach, 1928; Pasadena AI, 1928; Pomona (Cal.) 1930; Santa Cruz, 1929, 1943, 1949, 1950; State Exp., Phoenix, Ariz., 1931, 1948; Acad. Western Painters, 1936; Cal. A. Cl., 1940, 1946, 1947, 1949, 1950, 1952, 1953 (2 gold med.), 1954 (gold medal) and 1956; Cal. PLH, 1942 (medal and prize); Los A. Mus. A., 1943, 1954; Oakland A. Gal., 1944, 1949, 1950; Friday Morning Cl., 1946, 1952, 1955; Patrons of Art, San Pedro, 1955; deYoung Mem. Mus., 1950, 1955; Long Beach, Western A., 1951; Ebell Cl., Los A., 1943, 1949, 1950, 1951, 1952, 1956; Lodi, Cal., 1956, 1957; Laguna AA, 1957; medals, SFMA, 1939; Scandinavian-Am. Painters, 1939; Soc. Western A., 1940, 1943; Cal. PLH, 1942; Oakland A. Gal., 1943, 1944, 1950; Cal. A. Cl., 1950; San Fernando AA, 1950; deYoung Mem. Mus., 1949; and many others. *Work*: Vanderpoel Coll.; Univ. Chicago; San Diego FA Gal.; Univ. California; Santa Paula Chamber of Commerce; Ebell Cl., Los A.; Hollywood Athletic Cl., and in many H.S. and private coll. *Exhibited*: nationally.

LAVALLE, JOHN—*Painter*

825 Fifth Ave., New York 21, N.Y.

B. Nahant, Mass., June 24, 1896. *Studied*: Harvard Univ., A.B.; BMFA Sch.; Julian Acad., Paris; & with Philip Hale, Jean Francis Auburtin, Paris. *Member*: Gld. Boston A.; AWS; Am. Veteran's Soc. A.; Century Assn.; Boston Soc. WC Painters; Copley Soc.; Rockport AA; SC; Providence A. Cl.; North Shore AA. *Awards*: prizes, AAPL, 1947; Providence A. Cl., 1953; medal, NAC, 1955. *Work*: BM; BMFA; U.S. Army Air Forces Coll.; British Air Ministry;

Harvard Univ.; St. Paul's Sch., Concord, N.H.; Columbia Univ. Cl.; Harvard Cl.; Parrish Mus.; Brown Univ.; Long Island Univ.; Amherst Col.; Boston Col.; Court House, Morristown, N.J.; Mass. State Coll. *Exhibited*: CGA; NAD; AWS; All.A.Am.; Am. Veteran's Soc. A.; SC; Century Assn.; PAFA; AIC; Carnegie Inst.; Albright A. Gal.; Milwaukee AI; CM, 1940; BMFA; Newport AA; Balt. WC Cl.; Boston Soc. WC Painters, 1927-1942; Rockport AA, 1927-1942. I., "Mediterranean Sweep," 1944; "Bay Window Ballads."*

LAW, PAULINE—*Painter*

Lindy's Lake, Butler, N.J.

B. Wilmington, Del., Feb. 22, 1908. *Studied*: ASL; Grand Central A. Sch., and with Carlson, Hibbard, Snell. *Member*: NAC; NAWA; Pen & Brush Cl.; New Jersey P. & S.; North Shore AA. *Awards*: prizes, Hudson Valley AA, 1955, 1957; Pen & Brush Cl. (2); Catherine L. Wolfe A. Cl. (2). *Work*: Athens (Greece) Museum A. *Exhibited*: All. A. Am.; Knickerbocker A.; NAWA; Lowell AA; Rochester Mem. A. Gal.; Binghamton Mus. A.; Pen & Brush Cl.; Amsterdam, Holland.

LAWRENCE, JACOB—*Painter, I.*

385 Decatur St., Brooklyn 33, N.Y.

B. Atlantic City, N.J., Sept. 7, 1917. *Studied*: Am. A. Sch.; Harlem A. Workshop. *Member*: AEA. *Awards*: prize, MMA, 1942; medal, AIC, 1948; grant, Am. Acad. A. & Let., 1953; Chapelbrook F., 1955; Guggenheim F., 1946; Rosenwald F., 1940-1942. *Work*: MMA; MModA; WMAA; PC; BM; BMA; VMFA; WMA; Mus. Modern A., Sao Paulo, Brazil; Alabama Polytechnic Inst.; Portland (Ore.) Mus. A. Illus., Fortune magazine; "One Way Ticket," 1948. *Exhibited*: nationally.*

LAWRENCE, JAMES A.—
Painter, T., Comm. Photographer

1504 deYoung Bldg., San Francisco 4, Cal.; h. Rock Creek Ranch, Gardnerville, Nev.

B. Burlingame, Cal., May 23, 1910. *Studied*: Univ. California; A. Center Sch., Los A.; Chouinard AI; ASL; N.Y. Sch. Modern Photography, and with Louis Rogers, Barse Miller, Stanley Reckless, Fred Archer, and others. *Member*: Cal. WC Soc.; Nevada AA; 13 Watercolorists of San F.; Cal. Alumni Assn. *Awards*: medal, Cal. State Fair, 1948; prizes, Oakland A. Mus.; Nevada State Fairs; Terry AI, 1952. *Exhibited*: GGE, 1939; AIC; Cal. WC Soc.; Cal. PLH; deYoung Mus. A.; SFMA; Oakland A. Mus.; Crocker A. Gal.; Sacramento, Cal.; San Diego FA Soc.; Santa Barbara Mus. A.; Brooks Mem. Mus.; MMA; Riverside Mus.; Soc. Western A.; one-man: Reed Gal., N.Y.; Gump's Gal., San F.; Univ. Nevada; Nevada A. Gal. Contributor photographs and watercolors to national magazines. *Position*: Adv. Editorial Photography, Landscape Painting.

LAWRENCE, MARION—*Educator, Historian*

88 Morningside Dr., New York 27, N.Y.

B. Longport, N.J., Aug. 25, 1901. *Studied*: Bryn Mawr Col., A.B.; Radcliffe Col., A.M., Ph.D.; Am. Acad. in Rome; Inst. for Advanced Study, Princeton, N.J. *Member*: CAA; Archaeological Inst. Am.; Mediaeval Acad. Am. *Awards*: Carnegie F., 1926-1927; F., Inst. for Advanced Study, 1941-1942; Fulbright award, 1949-50. Author: "The Sarcophagi of Ravenna," 1945. Contributor to: art magazines & journals. Lectures: Early Christian Art. *Position*: Instr., Asst. Prof., Assoc. Prof., Prof., Chm. FA Dept., Barnard Col., Columbia Univ., New York, N.Y., 1929- ; Pres., Mediaeval Cl. of N.Y., 1953-55; Pres. Women's Faculty Cl., Columbia Univ.

LAWRENCE, RUTH (Mrs. James C.)—
Museum Director, E., L., W., S., C.

310 Northrop Auditorium; h. 521 5th Ave., Southeast, Minneapolis 14, Minn.

B. Clarksfield, Ohio, June 9, 1890. *Studied*: Ohio State Univ.; Akron Univ.; Univ. Minnesota; Univ. Hawaii; Cranbrook Acad. A.; & in Italy. *Member*: CAA; Western AA; Am. Mus. Dir. Assn.; S. Gld.; Am. Soc. for Aesthetics. *Award*: Huntington Hartford Fnd. F., 1958. *Work*: Univ. Minnesota; Cranbrook Acad. Contributor to: art magazines & educational journals. *Position*: Instr., Cur., Gal. A., 1934-40; Dir., Univ. Gal., Asst. Prof., Univ. Minnesota, Minneapolis, 1940-1958 (Retired).

LAWRIE, LEE—*Sculptor*

Locust Lane Farm, Easton, Md.

B. Rixford, Germany, Oct. 16, 1877. *Member*: NA; Am. Numismatic Soc.; Hon. F., NSS; AAD; Nat. Inst. A. & Let.; Am. Acad. A. & Let.; Arch. Lg. (hon.); BAID (hon.); AIA (hon.); NAC (life); Century Assn.; Royal Soc. A., London. *Awards*: medals, AIA, 1921, 1927; Arch. Lg., 1931, 1954; Am. Numismatic Soc., 1937; NSS, 1951, 1954. *Work*: Harkness Mem. Tower, Yale Univ.; Nat. Acad. Sc., Wash., D.C.; Nebraska State Capitol; MMA; Los A. Pub. Lib.; Bok Carillon Tower, Fla.; Goodhue Mem., N.Y.; Cornell Univ.; City Hall, St. Paul, Minn.; RCA Bldg., N.Y.; Peace Mem., Gettysburg, Pa.; "Atlas," Rockefeller Center, N.Y.; statue, Wash., D.C. Cathedral; mem., Octagon House Garden, Wash., D.C.; portrait, U.S. Capitol; reliefs, groups, St. James U.S. War Mem. Chapel, France; mem. and reredos, St. Thomas's Church, N.Y.; St. Vincent Ferrer Church, N.Y., and in many other churches.*

LAWSON, EDWARD PITT—*Educator*

Toledo Museum of Art, Monroe St. at Scottwood Ave. (1); h. 2150 Parkwood Ave., Toledo 2, Ohio

B. Newton, Mass., Sept. 12, 1927. *Studied*: Bowdoin Col., B.A.; N.Y. Univ., Inst. FA, A.M. *Member*: CAA; Nat. Comm. on A. Edu.; Ohio A. Edu. Assn. (Vice-Pres. 1959). *Awards*: Belgian-American Summer Fellowship, 1956. *Positions*: Instr., Toledo Mus. A. Sch. Des., 1954-56; Curatorial Asst., 1956-57; Supv. A. Edu., 1957- , Toledo Mus. A., Toledo, Ohio.

LAWTON, ALICE—*Craftsman,* W.

40½ Water St., St. Augustine, Fla.

B. Boston, Mass. *Studied*: Boston Univ., A.B.; Sorbonne, Ecole des Beaux-Arts, Ecole du Louvre, Paris, France; Univ. Lausanne, Switzerland. *Member*: Boston Soc. A. & Crafts: Authors Lg. Am.; Boston Authors Cl.; St. Augustine AA. *Exhibited*: Grace Horne Gal.; Children's A. Center; Women's City Cl., Boston. Contributor to: national magazines. Author: "Goose Towne Tales." Lectures: History of Art. *Position*: A.Ed., The Boston Post, Boston, Mass., 1928-52.

LAX, DAVID—*Painter,* E., L.

106 West 3rd St., New York 12, N.Y.

B. New York, N.Y., May 16, 1910. *Studied*: Ethical Culture Sch.; & with Victor Frisch, Alexander Archipenko. *Awards*: prizes, Ethical Culture Sch., 1929; Mills grant, 1932-1940. *Work*: War Dept., Wash., D.C.; Clearwater A. Mus.; Grand Central Gal.; in Paris, France; Veteran's Admn. Bldg., N.Y. (mural); s. frieze, Brill Bldg., N.Y. Book of paintings, "Denunciation, A Series of Paintings Concerning Man's Fate." *Exhibited*: War Dept., Wash., D.C., 1945; Galerie Borghese, Paris, 1945; one-man exh.: Grand Central Gal., 1940, 1944, 1949; Mus. Sc. & Indst., Radio City, N.Y., 1945; Union Col., 1945; Filene's, Boston, 1945; Westfield Atheneum, 1945; Providence Sch. Des., 1945; High Mus. A., 1945; Clearwater A. Mus., 1945; Zanesville AI, 1945; Springfield A. Mus., 1946; Mus. New Mexico, Santa Fé, 1946; de Young Mem. Mus, 1946; Crocker A. Gal., 1946; Portland A. Mus., 1946; Assoc. Am. A., Los A. & N.Y., 1950; British Mus., London; N.Y. Pub. Lib.; Columbia, Harvard Univ.; FMA; SAM, 1946; also, Carnegie Inst. 1940; Grand Central Gal., 1939-1946; Arden Gal., 1941; CGA, 1943; Phila. A. All., 1939; Joslyn Mem., 1941. I., "A Series of Paintings of the Transportation Corps, U.S. Army, in the Battle of Europe," 1945. Contributor to: Yank magazine, newspapers & art periodicals. *Position*: Consulting A. Dir., Mills Music Corp.; Laurel Process Co., New York, N.Y.; Prof. A., Dutchess Community College; Consulting A. Dir., California Texas Oil Co., Ltd.

LAYTON, GLORIA (Mrs. Harry Gewiss)—*Painter*

1842 Watson Ave., New York 72, N.Y.

B. New York, N.Y., Jan. 5, 1914. *Member*: AAPL; Conn. Acad. FA; All. A. Am.; AEA; A. Lg. of Long Island. *Award*: prize, Conn. Acad. FA, 1956. *Exhibited*: NAD, 1954, 1958; All. A. Am., 1939-1958; NAC, 1939-1955; AAPL, 1958; Butler Inst. Am. A., 1953, 1954, 1957, 1958; Academic A., Springfield, 1957, 1958; Eastern States Exh., 1957; Conn. Acad. FA, 1956, 1958; Silvermine Gld. A., 1957, 1958; Hudson Valley AA, 1953, 1955, 1958; New Sch. Assoc., 1957; So. Vermont A. Center, 1957; Ogunquit A. Center, 1954, 1955; A. Lg. of Long Island, 1956-1958;

Audubon A., 1957; Catherine L. Wolfe A. Cl., 1958; P. & S. Soc. of New Jersey, 1954, 1955; Knickerbocker A., 1953, 1955; Seton Hall Univ., 1958. *Work*: ports. in private colls.

LAZARD, ALICE A.—*Painter*

1610 Linden Ave., Highland Park, Ill.

B. New Orleans, La., 1893. *Studied*: Newcomb Col., Tulane Univ.; AIC. *Member*: North Shore A. Lg.; AEA; Evanston A. Center, AIC. *Awards*: prizes, North Shore A. Lg., 1948-1952; Mile of A. Exh., Highland Park, 1954. *Work*: Vanderpoel Coll.; Sinai Temple, Chicago; Vance Publ. Co., Chicago. *Exhibited*: MModA; AIC; PAFA; Am. Lib. Color Slides; Springfield A. Mus.; Evanston, Ill.; Winnetka, Ill.; Highland Park Women's Cl., 1956 (one-man); Univ. Chicago, 1955; Mile of Art Exh., Highland Park, 1953, 1954; Glencoe Pub. Lib., 1955 (one-man); Evanston A. Center, 1958; New Trier H.S., 1957, 1958; Marshall Fields, 1958; New Horizons, 1957; Chicago No-Jury Exh., 1957, 1958; A. Fair, 1958; County A. Center, 1957, 1958 (both one-man); Highland Park Pub. Lib., 1958 (2-man).

LAZZARI, PIETRO—*Painter,* S., T.

3609 Albemarle St., Northwest, Washington 8, D.C.

B. Rome, Italy, May 15, 1898. *Studied*: Ornamental Sch. of Rome, M.A. *Member*: NSMP; A. Gld. of Wash.; AAUP. *Awards*: Fulbright F., 1950; prize, Ornamental Sch. Rome. *Work*: BMA; AIC; PC; Collectors of Am. A.; Howard Univ.; American Univ.; Honolulu Acad. FA; murals, Jasper, Fla.; Brevard, N.C.; Sanford, N.C. Executed murals under Section FA, U.S. Treasury Dept., 1936-42. *Exhibited*: MMA, 1942; WMAA, 1934; AIC, 1943; NAD, 1944, 1945; Contemporary A. Gal., 1939; Whyte Gal., 1943; Crosby Gal., 1945; Musee Nationale d'Art Moderne, Paris, France; Smithsonian Inst.; CGA; PAFA; BMA; Arch. Lg. *Position*: Instr., American Univ., 1943-48; Hd. A. Dept., Dunbarton Col. of the Holy Cross, 1949-50.*

LEA, TOM—*Painter,* I., W.

2401 Savannah St., El Paso, Tex.

B. El Paso, Tex., July 11, 1907. *Studied*: AIC. *Work*: Dallas Mus. FA; murals, Court House, El Paso, Tex.; El Paso Pub. Lib.; USPO, Pleasant Hill, Mo.; Odessa, Tex.; Seymour, Tex.; Wash., D.C. Author: I., "Peleliu Landing," 1945; "A Grizzly from the Coral Sea," 1944; "The Brave Bulls," 1949; "The Wonderful Country," 1952; "The King Ranch," (2 vols.), 1957. Contributor to Life Magazine, eye-witness paintings of war, accompanying text; Atlantic Monthly. *Position*: A., War Correspondent, Life Magazine, 1941-45.

LEACH, ETHEL P(ENNEWILL) B(ROWN)—

Painter, Gr.

Frederica, Del.; s. 46 Columbia Ave., Rehoboth Beach, Del.

B. Wilmington, Del. *Studied*: ASL; PAFA; & with Howard Pyle. *Member*: Wilmington Soc. FA; A. All.; Pr. Cl.; F. PAFA, Plastic Cl., all of Phila. *Awards*: prizes, Wilmington Soc. FA; Rehoboth Beach A.Lg.; Phila. Plastic Cl., 1944, silver medal, 1951. *Work*: Mississippi AA; Wilmington Soc. FA; State House, Dover, Del.; Dickinson Col.; Washington Col., Chestertown, Md.; Court House, Bellefonte, Pa., and in private colls. *Exhibited*: Wilmington Soc. FA (regularly); Cottage A. Tour, Rehoboth Beach, Del., 1954; Rehoboth A. Lg.; Phila. Plastic Cl. I., "Once Upon a Time in Delaware."

LEACH, FREDERICK DARWIN—

Educator, P., Lith., Eng., L., Cr.

School of Painting & Allied Arts, Ohio University; h. 165 East State St., Athens, Ohio

B. Arkansas City, Kans., Sept. 19, 1924. *Studied*: James Millikin Univ., B.A., Univ. Wisconsin; State Univ. Iowa, M.A., M.F.A., Ph.D. *Member*: AAUP; Midwest Col. A. Conf.; CAA. *Awards*: prizes, Old Northwest Territory Exh., Springfield; Central Illinois A.; Ohio State Fair; Exhibition 80. Lectures: Contemporary Art; Renaissance, Baroque, Classical Art; Italian Renaissance; Theory of Art. *Positions*: Instr. A., State Univ. Iowa; James Millikin Univ.; Prof. A., Ohio University, Athens, Ohio, at present.

LEACH, RICHARD—*Educator*
Art Department, Albion College, Albion, Mich.*

LEAKE, EUGENE WALTER, JR.—*Painter, T., L.*
Art Center Association, 2111 South First St.; h. 7504 Shelbyville Rd., Louisville 7, Ky.

B. Jersey City, N.J., Aug. 31, 1911. *Studied*: Yale Sch. FA; ASL. *Awards*: prizes, Virginia Intermont Col., 1950, 1952; Kentucky State Fair, 1949, 1952; BMA, 1953; CM, 1955; Interior Valley Exh., 1955. *Work*: Seagram & Son's Coll.; Univ. Louisville. *Exhibited*: Butler AI, 1952, 1953; BM, 1943; AIC, 1942; MMA, 1942; Ohio Valley Watercolor Exh., 1948, 1950, 1952; Virginia Intermont Col., 1950, 1952; PAFA, 1957; Columbia Biennial, 1957; Art: USA, 1958; Interior Valley Exh.; 1955, 1958. *Position*: Dir., Art Center Assn., Louisville, Ky., 1949- .

LEAKE, GERALD—*Painter, T.*
Island City Art School, Key West, Fla.

B. London, England, Nov. 26, 1885. *Member*: ANA; SI; NAC; Royal Soc. A., London; Lakeland FA Soc.; Key West A. & Hist. Soc. *Awards*: prizes, SC, 1923, 1926, 1927; NAD, 1934, 1937; Key West A. & Hist. Soc., 1952, 1953; Grumbacher award, 1953; medals, All. A. Am., 1929; NAD; Fla. Southern Col., 1952. *Work*: NAC. *Exhibited*: Royal Acad., England; Royal Soc. British A.; Walker Gal., Liverpool, England; NAD; All. A. Am.; NAC; SC; Conn. Acad. FA; Grand Central A. Gal.; BMFA; AIC; PAFA; CGA; Albright A. Gal.; Santa Barbara Mus. A.; Detroit Inst. A.; Knoedler Gal.; Algonquin A. Cl., Maine; one-man: Ferargil Gal.; Grand Central A. Gal. *Position*: Dir., Island City A. Sch., Key West, Fla.

LEASON, PERCY ALEXANDER—*Painter, E., L., W.*
30 Castleton Park, Staten Island 1, N.Y.

B. Kaniva, Victoria, Australia, Feb. 23, 1889. *Studied*: Nat. Gal. Sch., Melbourne, Australia; Meldrum's Sch. Painting. *Member*: F., Staten Island Inst. A. & Sc.; SC; Audubon A.; All. A. Am.; AAPL. *Awards*: prizes, Audubon A., 1945; Staten Island Inst. A. & Sc., 1946; SC; AAPL. *Work*: Melbourne and Sydney, Australia, Nat. Galleries; Staten Island Inst. *Exhibited*: NAD; All. A. Am.; Audubon A.; Staten Island Inst., annually; SC; AAPL (one-man). Author: "The Chief Factors in the Rise and Decline of Painting"; "The Dead Model Theory of Quatenary Cave Painting"; "Obvious Facts of Quatenary Cave Art"; "Some Aspects of Reality." *Positions*: Cart., Sydney (Australia) Bulletin and Melbourne Punch and Table Talk; Illus. for Collier's and Liberty magazines; Pres., Section of Art, Staten Island Inst. A. & Sc., eight years; Dir., Staten Island Sch. Painting.

LEAVITT, THOMAS WHITTLESEY—*Museum Director*
Pasadena Art Museum, 46 North Los Robles Ave.; h. 690 Westminster Drive, Pasadena, Cal.

B. Boston, Mass., Jan. 8, 1930. *Studied*: Middlebury Col., A.B.; Boston Univ., A.M.; Harvard Univ., Ph.D. *Member*: CAA; Western Assn. A. Mus. Dirs. *Award*: Bacon Traveling Fellowship, Harvard Univ., 1956. Contributor articles on Washington Allston to Art in America; Art Quarterly; Harvard Alumni News. Lectures: Nineteenth Century American Painting, and other lectures primarily on museum topics. Arranged Exhs.: "The Evolution of Watercolor Painting," (FMA, 1954); "Print Festival" (Pasadena A. Mus., 1958); "The New Renaissance in Italy" (Pasadena A. Mus. 1958), and many smaller exhibitions. *Positions*: Exec. Sec., The Fine Arts Comm. of the People-to-People Program, Wash., D.C.; Asst. to Dir., Fogg Museum of Art, 1954-56; Dir., Pasadena Art Museum, Pasadena, Cal., 1956- .

LEAYCRAFT, JULIA SEARING—*Painter, T., W., Cr., Lith.*
1172 Park Ave., New York 28, N.Y.

B. Saugerties, N.Y., Nov. 1885. *Studied*: Vassar Col., A.B.; ASL; Woodstock Sch. Landscape Painting, with Birge Harrison. *Member*: NAWA; Woodstock AA; AEA. *Exhibited*: NAWA, 1944-1946, 1948, 1950-1955; Albany Inst. Hist. & A., 1942-1944, 1947, 1948, 1951; Conn. Acad. FA, 1937; Woodstock AA, 1955; Buck Hill Falls, and in Paris, 1948; one-man: Dalton Sch., 1936; Woodstock AA, 1948, 1950; Argent Gal., 1949. A. Cr., Craftsman Magazine; Ulster County News; A.T., Slater Mus. A., Norwich, Conn.

LEBEDEV, VLADIMIR—*Painter*
325 East 56th St., New York 22, N.Y.

B. Moscow, Russia, June 17, 1911. *Studied*: Acad. A., Leningrad. *Work*: Acad. A., Leningrad; in museums of Moscow and Khazan, Russia; in private colls., Cleveland, Los Angeles and New York. *Exhibited*: in France, Holland, Belgium and Germany, 1945-1950; M. Antoville Gal., N.Y., 1956, 1958; Barzansky Gal., N.Y., 1957 (one-man).

LEBER, ROBERTA (McVEIGH)—*Craftsman, T.*
Wingarth Studios; h. Leber Rd., Blauvelt, N.Y.

B. Hoboken, N.J. *Studied*: N.Y. State Col. Ceramics, Alfred Univ., B.S.; Columbia Univ. *Member*: Artists-Craftsmen of N.Y. (Vice-Pres. 1958); Keramic Soc. N.Y. (hon. memb.); AAUW; Religious Soc. of Friends. *Exhibited*: WMA; MMA; WFNY 1939; Seligmann Gal.; Argent Gal., N.Y.; Univ. Minnesota; Staten Island Mus. A. & Sc., 1955; Syracuse Mus. FA, 1958 and prior. *Position*: Instr., Ceramics, Craft Students Lg., New York, 1939- ; A. Workshop, New York, 1938- ; Rockland Fnd., 1953- .

LE BRON WARREE CARMICHAEL (Mrs. Adolphe)—*Painter*
Hatchatoy, Rockford, Ala.

B. Elba, Ala., Jan. 23, 1910. *Studied*: Huntington Col.; Sullins Col.; ASL; Ecole des Beaux-Arts, Paris, France. *Member*: Alabama A. Lg.; Alabama WC Soc.; Mobile WC Soc. *Work*: Montgomery Mus. FA; Alabama Col.; Alabama War Mem. Mus.; mural, Sycamore, Ala., Church. *Award*: Kelly Fitzpatrick award, 1954. *Position*: A. T., Sylacawga H.S.; Dir., Dixie A. Colony.; Sec., Alabama A. Lg.

LEBRUN, RICO (FEDERICO)—*Painter, T., L.*
11632 San Vicente Blvd., Los Angeles, Cal.

B. Naples, Italy, Dec. 10, 1900. *Studied*: Beaux-Arts Acad., Naples. *Member*: AEA. *Awards*: Guggenheim F., 1936-37, 1937-38; prizes, AIC, 1947; Los A. Mus. A., 1948; Univ. Illinois, 1949; MMA, 1950; Am. Acad. A. & Let., 1952; PAFA, 1953. *Work*: Encyclopaedia Britannica Coll.; Los A. Mus. A.; MMA; Munson-Williams-Proctor Inst.; MModA; Santa Barbara Mus. A.; Univ. Illinois; Univ. Nebraska; FMA; BMFA; Columbus Gal. FA; William Rockhill Nelson Gal. A.; R.I. Sch. Des.; St. Paul Gal. & Sch. A.; Univ. Hawaii; WMAA; deYoung Mem. Mus. *Exhibited*: CAM, 1945; Los A. Mus. A., 1945, 1948-1951; Carnegie Inst., 1945, 1952, 1955; AIC, 1947, 1948, 1951; WMAA, 1948-1950, 1952; Cal. PLH, 1949, 1952; A. Gal., Toronto, 1949; CM, 1950; Venice Biennale, 1950; Scripps Col., 1949; MMA, 1950; PAFA, 1951, 1952, 1953, 1956; Univ. Illinois, 1951; Univ. Minnesota, 1951; BM, 1951; Colorado Springs FA Center, 1941, 1946, 1951; Sao Paulo, Brazil, 1953, 1955; one-man: AIC, 1955; Pomona Col., 1956; Art Gallery, Toronto, 1958; Yale Univ., 1958. *Position*: Instr., ASL, 1936-37; Chouinard AI, 1938-39; Walt Disney Studios, 1940; Newcomb A. Sch., 1942-43; Colo. Springs FA Center, 1945; Jepson AI, 1947-50; Inst. Allende, Mexico, 1953-54; Instr., Summer Schools: UCLA, 1956, 1957; Yale-Norfolk Sch., Norfolk, Conn., 1956; Visiting Prof., Yale Univ., 1958-59.

LECHAY, JAMES—*Painter, E.*
State University of Iowa; h. 1191 Hotz Ave., Iowa City, Iowa

B. New York, N.Y., July, 1907. *Studied*: Univ. Illinois. B.A. *Member*: AEA. *Awards*: prizes, PAFA, 1942; med., AIC, 1941, 1943; Iowa State Fair, 1946, 1951, 1955; Denver A. Mus., 1946; Walker A. Center, 1947; Minnesota Centennial, 1949; Des Moines A. Center, 1950, 1952, 1953; Davenport A. Center, 1950. *Work*: AIC; PAFA; Univ. Arizona; State Univ. Iowa; BM; New Britain Mus. A.; Univ. Nebraska; Illinois Wesleyan Univ.; Wichita A. Center; Philbrook A. Center; Brooks Mem. Mus.; Des Moines A. Center; Coe College; Iowa State T. Col.; Joslyn Mem. A. Mus. *Exhibited*: nationally. One-man: New York City; Toledo, Ohio; Chicago, Ill.; Springfield, Ill.; Louisville, Ky.; Wesleyan Univ., Conn.; Joslyn A. Mus.; in Iowa: Cedar Rapids, Des Moines, Iowa City, Ft. Dodge, Cedar Falls, Davenport, Mt. Pleasant and Sioux City. *Position*: Prof. A., State Univ. of Iowa, Iowa City, Iowa.

LE CLAIR, CHARLES (GEORGE)—*Painter, E., L.*

Chatham College, Pittsburgh, Pa.

B. Columbia, Mo., May 23, 1914. *Studied*: Univ. Wisconsin, B.S. in Edu.; Columbia Univ., and with Cameron Booth. *Awards*: prizes, Albright A. Gal., 1944; Assoc. A. Pittsburgh, 1947, 1948, 1951, 1952, 1954, 1955, 1956, 1957; Butler Inst. Am. A., 1956; "Pittsburgh Artist of the Year," 1957; Pittsburgh Playhouse Comp., 1950; Ford F., 1952-53. *Work*: Milwaukee Journal Coll.; Albright A. Gal.; Wisconsin Union; Madison Pub. Schs.; Tuscaloosa Pub. Sch.; Ala. Col. for Women; Hundred Friends of Pittsburgh coll.; Butler Inst. Am. A. *Exhibited*: Carnegie Inst., 1941, 1943-1945, 1947-1949; AIC, 1944, 1945; VMFA, 1944; Albright A. Gal., 1944-1946, 1955; MMA, 1950; WMAA, 1951, 1956; Butler AI, 1951, 1956; CGA, 1953; one-man: Carnegie Inst., 1954; Rochester Inst. Tech., 1958; Salpeter Gal., 1956. Author: "Integration of the Arts" in Accent on Teaching, 1954. *Position*: Hd. Dept. A., Asst. Prof., Univ. Alabama, 1935-42; Hd. A. Dept., Asst. Prof., Albion Col., 1942-43; Instr. A., Albright A. Sch., 1943-46; Hd. A. Dept., Assoc. Prof., 1946-52, Prof., 1952- , Chatham College, Pittsburgh, Pa.

LEDERER, EDNA THERESA—*Painter*

12440 Saywell Ave., Cleveland 8, Ohio

B. Cleveland, Ohio, Sept. 12, 1909. *Studied*: Cleveland Sch. A.; ASL; & with Sandor Vago, Robert Brackman. *Awards*: prizes, CMA, 1932, 1936. *Exhibited*: CMA, 1932, 1933, 1936, 1938, 1945; Butler AI; Ohio State Fair, 1936.

LEDERER, LUCY (CHRISTINE) (KEMMERER)— *Painter, Ser., L., Des.*

P.O. Box 861, Manor Hills, State College, Pa.

B. Milton, Pa. *Studied*: PIASch; Pennsylvania State Univ., B.S.; ASL, and with Pittman, Miller, Marsh. *Member*: Phila. A. All.; Central Pa. Painters; ASL; Exh. Comn., Pa. State Univ., 1955. *Work*: Pa. State Univ.; Presbyterian Church, State College, Pa.; American Legion Headquarters, Illinois (mural). *Exhibited*: Butler AI; Palm Beach, Fla. (one-man), 1955; CGA, 1935; Conn. Acad. FA, 1936; CM, 1936; NAWA, 1938; Bucknell Univ., 1937, 1951, 1952, 1956; Reading Mus., 1938; PAFA, 1937; VMFA, 1940; Pa. State Col., 1938, 1942, 1951, 1952; Phila. A. All., 1948; Grace Lutheran Church, 1958; Ligonier, Pa., 1958. Lectures: Contemporary Art.

LEDERER, WOLFGANG—*Designer, E., Comm. A., I.*

251 Kearny St. (8); h. 315 29th Ave., San Francisco 21, Cal.

B. Mannheim, Germany, Jan. 16, 1912. *Studied*: Akademie fuer Graphische Kuenste und Buchgewerbe, Leipzig, Germany; Academie Scandinave, with Othon Friesz, Paris, France; Officina Pragensis, with H. Steiner-Prag, Prague, Czechoslovakia. *Award*: 1st prize for design of emblem, Psychiatric Assn. Am., 1942. *Work*: SFMA. *Exhibited*: San F. AA, 1943; one-man: Vienna, Austria, 1937; Elder Gal., San Francisco, 1941; SFMA, 1942. Illus., "The Two Islands"; "Elements of Psychology." I., Wines and Vines; Mademoiselle magazine; I., A. Dir., The American Wine Merchant. Lectures: Design; Illustration; The Work of H. Steiner-Prag, museums and art societies. *Position*: Chm., Dept. Design, California College of Arts & Crafts, Oakland, Cal., 1945- .

LEDOUX, EVA M. B., (Sister Mary of the Divine Saviour, C.S.C.)—*Painter, T., Des.*

R.F.D. 567, 357 Island Pond Rd., Manchester, N.H.

B. Manchester, N.H., June 17, 1899. *Studied*: Univ. New Hampshire; Sch. Practical Art, Boston; Beaux-Arts, Montreal, Canada; Manchester Inst. A. & Sc., and with Philip Hicken, R. Coleman, Charles Maillard, A. Schmaltz, John Chandler, John Hatch, and others. *Member*: New Hampshire AA. *Awards*: Currier Gal. A., 1955; prizes, Manchester Inst. A. & Sc., 1942, 1945; Am. Soc. for Control of Cancer, 1942; Manchester A. Festival, 1958. *Work*: religious paintings, des. liturgical altars and cemetery memorials. *Exhibited*: Ogunquit A. Center; Dartmouth Col.; Jordan Marsh, Boston; Manchester Women's Cl., 1942 (one-man); Currier Gal. A. *Position*: Instr. A., Holy Cross A. Sch., Manchester, N.H.

LEE, ALIX. See Hastings, Alix Lee

LEE, AMY FREEMAN—*Painter, Cr., L., W., T.*

127 Canterbury Hill, San Antonio 9, Tex.; s. Ogunquit, Me.

B. San Antonio, Tex., Oct. 3, 1914. *Studied*: Univ. Texas; special work, aesthetics and criticism, Incarnate Word Col. *Member*: Nat. Soc. A. & Let.; AFA; Boston Soc. Indp. A.; New Orleans AA; San Antonio A. Lg.; Texas FA Assn.; Am. Soc. for Aesthetics; Texas A. Edu. Assn.; CAA; AEA; Assn. Internationale des Critiques d'Art, Paris, France. *Awards*: prizes, San Antonio A., 1949, 1956; Smith Col., 1950; Boston Soc. Indp. A.; Charles Rosen award, 1950; Texas FA Assn., 1950, 1958; Texas WC Soc., 1955 (purchase); Neiman-Marcus award, 1953; Grumbacher award, 1953; Hall Mem. (purchase), 1954; Rosengren award, 1953; Silvermine Gld. A., 1957; Beaumont Mus., 1957; "Artist of the Year," San Antonio, 1958; Theta Sigma Phi Headliner award, 1958, and others. *Work*: Witte Mem. Mus.; Smith Col.; Baylor Univ.; BMA lending coll.; Community Guidance Center, San Antonio; Feldman Coll., Dallas (Republic Nat. Bank). *Exhibited*: Miami Beach A. Center, 1947; New Orleans AA, 1948, 1953, 1954; Boston Soc. Indp. A., 1949-58; State T. Col., Indiana, Pa., 1949, 1951, 1952, 1954; Colorado Springs FA Center, 1950; Newport AA, 1951, 1954; Alabama WC Soc., 1952; Fla. Southern Col., 1952; Experimental Painters, New Zealand, 1948; Dayton AI, 1950, 1951; Witte Mem. Mus., 1945-1955, 1957, 1958; Texas WC Soc., 1950-1955; Texas FA Assn., 1946-1955; Beaumont Mus., 1952; Knoedler Gal., 1952; Houston Contemp. A., 1952; Texas P. & S., 1949, 1953-1955; Maine WC Soc., 1953-1955; Butler AI, 1954, 1958; McNay AI, 1955; Silvermine Gld. A., 1955; Foreign Service of U.S.A., Paris, 1956; DMFA, 1956, 1957, 1958; Feldman Exh., 1956-1958; Austin, Tex., 1956-1958; Audubon A., 1957; PAFA, 1957; Exchange Exh., Paris, France, 1956-58, and many others. Author: "Hobby Horses"; "A Critic's Note Book"; "Remember Pearl Harbor." *Position*: A. Cr., San Antonio Express, 1939-41; Staff Cr., Radio Station KONO, San Antonio, 1947-51; L., Trinity Univ., 1954-56; San Antonio AI, 1955-56, and other colleges and museums.

LEE, CUTHBERT—*Portrait Painter*

327 Charlotte St., Asheville, N.C.

B. Boston, Mass., June 26, 1891. *Studied*: Harvard Univ., A.B.; Academie Julian, Paris, France. *Member*: AAPL; Harvard Cl.; Pen & Plate Cl.; Biltmore Forest Country Cl. *Work*: Busch-Reisinger Mus., Harvard; Columbia Univ.; Columbia Cl.; Univ. North Carolina; Georgia Inst. Technology; Capitol, North Dakota; Governor's Mansion, N.C.; De le Brook Manor, Md.; Worthington Corp., N.Y.; Episcopal Cathedral, Atlanta; Federal Court of Appeals. *Exhibited*: Studio Gld.; Mint Mus. A., 1946; Jesup Lib. A. Gal., Bar Harbor, 1947; Asheville A. Mus., 1952. Author: "Contemporary American Portrait Painters," 1929; "Early American Portrait Painters," 1930.

LEE, DORIS—*Painter, Gr., I.*

Woodstock, N.Y.

B. Aledo, Ill., Feb. 1, 1905. *Studied*: Rockford Col.; Kansas City AI, with Ernest Lawson; Cal. Sch. FA, with Arnold Blanch and in Paris, France with Andre Lhote. *Member*: An Am. Group; Woodstock AA. *Awards*: prize and medal, 1935, prize, 1936, AIC; med., PAFA, 1944; Hon. deg., LL.D., Rockford Col.; D.L.T., Russell Sage Col.; prizes, Carnegie Inst., 1943; LC, 1947; A. Dir. Cl., N.Y., 1946, 1950, gold medal, 1957; WMA, 1938. *Work*: mural, USPO, Wash. D.C.; AIC; MMA; LC; PMG; Albright A. Gal.; Univ. Nebraska; Cranbrook Mus.; Encyclopaedia Britannica Coll.; PAFA; Lowe Gal., Miami; Honolulu Acad. FA; R.I.Sch. Des.; Univ. Arizona; Rockford Col.; Mt. Holyoke Mus.; Fla. Gulf Coast A. Center. *Exhibited*: nationally. Contributor to Life Magazine. I., "The Great Quillon"; "Hired Man's Elephant"; "St. John's River"; "Painting for Enjoyment"; "Mr. Benedict's Lion"; "Rodgers & Hart Songbook"; "Touch Blue," 1958. Des. curtain for "Oklahoma!" Guest Artist, Univ. Hawaii, 1957.

LEE, GEORGE JOSEPH—*Museum Curator*

Brooklyn Museum, Eastern Parkway, Brooklyn 38, N.Y.; h. 136 Fourth St., New York 12, N.Y.

B. Boston, Mass., July 14, 1919. *Studied*: Harvard Univ., A.B., A.M. *Member*: Chinese A. Soc. of Am.; Far Eastern Ceramic Group; Oriental Ceramic Group (London); Oriental Club of New York City. *Awards*: Chinese Government Cultural Fellowship, Harvard Univ., 1945-48. Contributor of articles to scholarly magazines, museum bulletins and in catalogues. Lectures Oriental subjects to museum and lay audiences. Some exhs. arranged: "The Floating World of Japan" (BM, 1950); "The Art of T'ang China" (New York, 1953); "Thank God for Tea!" (Brooklyn, 1955); major assembling and installing of Oriental material at Brooklyn Mus., since 1949. *Positions*: Staff Memb., Harvard Army Specialized Training Program (Far Eastern Language and Area Studies) and (simultaneously) Fogg Mus. A., 1942-45; Asst. Cur., Oriental A., Fogg Mus. A., 1948-49; Cur. Oriental Art, Brooklyn Museum, 1949- .

LEE, MANNING DE VILLENEUVE—Painter, I.
Boxwood Farm, Ambler, Pa.

B. Summerville, S.C., Mar. 15, 1894. *Studied*: PAFA, with Hugh Breckenridge, Daniel Garber, Philip Hale. *Member*: Phila. A. All.; F., Royal Soc. A., London. *Awards*: prize, PAFA, 1922; Cresson traveling scholarship, 1921. *Work*: U.S. Mint. Phila., Pa.; series commemorative postage stamps for Republics of Liberia and Indonesia, 1947, 1948; U.S. Naval Acad., Annapolis, Md. I., numerous books & contributor to national magazines.

LEE, MUSIER (TAINTOR) (Mrs. Lawrence Lee)—
Painter
510 Roslyn Place, Pittsburgh 32, Pa.

B. New York, N.Y., Mar. 6, 1909. *Studied*: in France and Italy; ASL. *Member*: Assoc. A. Pittsburgh. *Exhibited*: ACA Gal., 1943-1945; Riverside Mus., 1946; Assoc. A. Pittsburgh, 1951, 1954, 1957, 1958; one-man: Chatham Col., 1950; Pittsburgh Playhouse, 1951, 1958.

LEE, RENSSELAER WRIGHT—Educator, L.
120 Mercer St., Princeton, N.J.

B. Philadelphia, Pa., June 15, 1898. *Studied*: Princeton Univ., A.B., Ph.D. *Member*: Archaeological Inst. Am.; Mediaeval Acad. Am.; CAA (Pres. 1945-46); Am. Soc. for Aesthetics. Contributor to Art Bulletin; College Art Journal, etc. *Position*: Assoc. Prof. A., 1931-33, Prof. Chm. A. Dept., 1933-40, Northwestern Univ.; Prof. A., Smith Col., 1941-48; Columbia Univ., 1948-54; N.Y.Univ., 1954-55; Chm. Dept., Princeton Univ., 1955- ; Ed., The Art Bulletin, 1943, 1944; Chm. Com. Research & Publ. in FA, Am. Council of Learned Soc., 1942-44, Bd. of Dir., 1953- ; Exec. Sec., Am. Council Learned Soc. on Protection of Cultural Treasures in War Areas, 1944-45; Memb., Inst. for Advanced Study, Princeton, N.J., 1939, 1942-44, 1946-47; Adv. Council to Inst. FA, N.Y. Univ.; Visiting Comm. to Dept. FA and Fogg Mus., Harvard Univ., 1957- ; Trustee, Am. Acad. in Rome, 1958; Bd. Dir., Union Academique Internationale, 1956- .

LEE, ROBERT J.—Painter, Des., Cart., Comm. A., I., T.
Seminary Hill, Carmel, N.Y.

B. Oakland, Cal., Dec. 26, 1921. *Studied*: San Francisco Acad. A. *Member*: SI. *Awards*: prizes, Assn. A. Studios, Chicago, 1947 (5); gold medal, All. A. Am., 1958. *Work*: Springfield (Mass.) Mus. FA. *Exhibited*: Cal. PLH, 1946; NAD, 1958; All. A. Am., 1958; Provincetown A. Festival, 1958; Oakland A. Mus., 1946, 1947; AIC, 1951, 1952; N.Y. City Center, and others. One-man: San F. Acad. A.; Feingarten Gals., San F. and Chicago; Petite Gal., N.Y.; Ferargil Gal., N.Y. Illus. "Music Through the Year"; "Voices of America"; "Music Across Our Country"; "This is a Town"; "A Day in the Bleachers"; "Buffalo Bill"; "The Story of the Atom." Cart., I., for Esquire; Elks Magazine; American; N.Y. Times; San Francisco Chronicle; N.Y. Journal American; Philadelphia Bulletin, etc. *Positions*: Instr., Painting & Illustration, San Francisco Acad. A.; Pratt Inst., Brooklyn, N.Y.; Chm. Edu. Com., 1955-56.

LEE, RUTH HUDSON—Painter
6904 Strathmore St., Chevy Chase 15, Md.

B. Ellisburg, N.Y., June 9, 1885. *Studied*: Syracuse Univ., B.A., M.A., and with Hawthorne, Adams, Ennis, O'Hara. *Member*: AWS; Wash. WC Cl.; NAWA; Assoc. A. Syracuse; Nat. Lg. Am. Pen Women; Eight Syracuse Watercolorists; Balt. WC Cl. *Awards*: prizes, Syracuse Mus. FA, 1948; Nat. Lg. Am. Pen Women, 1950; Rochester Mem. A. Gal., 1948; Munson-Williams-Proctor Inst. *Work*: Syracuse Mus. FA. *Exhibited*: Phila. WC Cl.; AWS; NAWA; Balt. WC Cl.; Springfield A. Lg.; Argent Gal.;

Rochester Mem. A. Gal.; Munson-Williams-Proctor Inst.; Assoc. A. Syracuse; one-man: Binghamton A. Gal.; Albany Inst. Hist. & A.; Everhart Gal.; Auburn A. Mus.; Charleston, W. Va.; East Aurora, N.Y.; Syracuse Mus. FA. *Position*: Prof. A., Syracuse Univ., Syracuse, N.Y., 1921-51; Prof. Emeritus, 1951- .

LEE, SHERMAN EMERY—Museum Director, Cur.
Cleveland Museum of Art, 11150 East Blvd., (6); h. 2536 Norfolk Road, Cleveland 18, Ohio

B. Seattle, Wash., Apr. 19, 1918. *Studied*: Washington Univ., B.A., M.A.; Western Reserve Univ., Ph.D. *Member*: Far Eastern Assn.; Am. Oriental Soc.; CAA; AAMus.; Assn. A. Mus. Dirs. Author: "Chinese Landscape Painting," 1954; Co-author: (with Wen Fong) "Streams and Mountains Without End," 1955. *Positions*: Cur., Far Eastern Art, Detroit Inst. A., 1941-47; Hd. Dept. A. & Monuments Div., Civil Inf. & Edu. Section, Gen. Hdqs., Tokyo, Japan, 1946-48; Asst. Dir., Assoc. Dir., Seattle A. Mus., 1948-52; Cur., Oriental Art, 1952- , Asst. Dir., 1956—thru May, 1957, Assoc. Dir., 1957—thru Mar., 1958, Dir., 1958- , Cleveland Mus. A., Cleveland, Ohio.

LEECH, DOROTHY SHERMAN—Painter
1666 Hillview St., Sarasota, Fla.

B. Pittsburgh, Pa., Dec. 28, 1913. *Studied*: Carnegie Inst.; Ringling A. Sch. *Member*: Sarasota AA; Fla. Fed. A.; Fla. Artists Group; A. Lg. of Manatee County; Clearwater AA. *Work*: murals, Congregational Church, Riga, N.Y.; Wauchula (Fla.) H.S.; Methodist Church, Winter Park, Fla.; other work in Hamilton A. Gal., Ont., Canada; Hickory Mus. A., North Carolina; Montclair A. Mus., New Jersey.

LEECH, HILTON—Painter, T.
1666 Hillview St., Sarasota, Fla.

B. Bridgeport, Conn. *Studied*: Grand Central A. Sch.; ASL. *Member*: AWS; Phila. WC Cl.; SC; Florida A. Group; Sarasota AA; New Orleans AA; Wash. WC Cl. *Awards*: prizes, Atlanta, Ga.; Fla. A. Group; SC; N.Y. WC Cl.; Western N.Y. Exh.; Four Arts Cl., Fla. Fed. A.; West Palm Beach A. Lg.; Audubon A.; Knickerbocker A.; All. A. Am.; NAC. *Work*: High Mus. A.; DMFA; Hickory (N.C.) Mus. A.; Univ. Florida; John Herron AI; Guild Hall, Easthampton, L.I., N.Y.; Hamilton A. Gal., Canada; Stetson Univ.; Norton Gal. A., West Palm Beach, and in private collections; murals, Court House, Chattanooga; USPO, Bay Minette, Ala. Contributor to American Artist magazine. Established Amagansett A. 1946; Guest Instr., John Herron AI, Indianapolis, Ind., 1953.

LEEPA, ALLEN—Painter, E., W.
1023 North Capitol Ave., Lansing 6, Mich.

B. New York, N.Y., Jan. 9, 1919. *Studied*: Am. A. Sch., N.Y.; ASL; New Bauhaus, Chicago; Columbia Univ., B.S., M.A.; Sorbonne, Paris, France; Grande Chaumiere, Paris. *Member*: Com. A. Edu.; MModA; Michigan Acad. A., Sc. & Let. *Awards*: Fulbright award, 1950-51; scholarships to Am. A. Sch., New Bauhaus, Chicago; Hans Hofmann Sch. A., Columbia Univ.; prize, Michiana Exh., South Bend., Ind., 1954; Western Mich. A., 1958. *Work*: South Bend Mus. A. *Exhibited*: MModA traveling exh., 1953; PAFA, 1950, 1951; Birmingham Mus. A., 1954; Detroit Inst. A., 1945, 1946, 1948-1950, 1953-1955; Northwest Territory Exh., 1948; Madison, Wis., 1953; Grand Rapids, Mich., 1948. Author: "The Challenge of Modern Art," 1949. Contributor (book review) College Art Bulletin. Lectures: Challenge of Modern Art; Creative Problems in Art; Art & Science, etc. *Position*: Instr., Hull Sch., Chicago, 1947-48; Brooklyn A. Center, 1939-41; Brooklyn Mus., 1940; MMA, 1941; Assoc. Prof A., Michigan State Univ., Lansing, Mich., 1945- .

LEEPER, JOHN PALMER—Museum Director
McNay Art Institute, 755 Austin Highway, San Antonio, Tex.

B. Denison, Tex., Feb. 4, 1921. *Studied*: Southern Methodist Univ., B.S.; Harvard Univ., M.A. *Member*: AAMus.; Assn. A. Mus. Dirs. Contributor to Arts; National Geographic; Texas Quarterly; New Mexico Quarterly, and museum bulletins. *Positions*: Instr., Univ. So. California, 1952; Ford Fnd. Fund for Adult Edu., 1953; Trinity Univ., San Antonio, 1956-58; Asst. Dir., CGA; Dir., Pasadena A. Mus.; Dir., McNay AI, San Antonio, Tex., 1958- .

LEEPER, JOHN P.—Painter
3836 San Rafael Ave., Los Angeles 65, Cal.

B. Dandridge, Tenn., Apr. 23, 1909. *Studied*: Los A. County AI. *Member*: Cal. WC Soc. *Awards*: prizes, Cal. WC Soc., 1952, 1957 (purchase); Cal. State Fair, 1954 (purchase); Newport Harbor, 1955, 1958; Los A. Mus. A., 1956, 1958; Los A. Festival Art, 1956, 1957; San Jose State Col., 1957; Laguna Beach Festival Art, 1958. *Work*: IBM; Long Beach Mus. Coll.; Cal. State Fair Coll.; mural, Arizona State Col. *Exhibited*: Cal. WC Soc.; Los A. Mus. A.; Cal. and Canadian traveling exh., 1955; Los A. County Fair, 1953; one-man: Cowie Gal., Los A., 1949, 1952; Santa Barbara Mus. A., 1950; Landau Gal., 1954.

LEEPER, VERA—Painter, T., L.
2449 Altura Ave., Montrose, Cal.

B. Denver, Colo., Mar. 13, 1899. *Studied*: Denver Univ.; BMFA Sch.; N.Y.Univ.; & in Paris. *Member*: NSMP; Highland Park A. Gld.; Nat. Puppetry Cl. *Awards*: prizes, Wolfe A. Cl., 1920; N.Y. WC Cl., 1926; Kansas City AI, 1934; Brown Robertson competition, N.Y., 1928; NAD, 1929. *Work*: Denver A. Mus.; murals, pub. sch. in New York & New Jersey. *Exhibited*: Paris Salon; MMA; NSMP; Grand Central Gal.; Wolfe A. Cl.; Hudson Valley AA; Chappaqua A. Gld.; Los A. City Hall, 1951, 1952. *Position*: Instr., Pasadena Dept. of Recreation.

LEES, HARRY HANSON—Illustrator
43-55 Kissena Blvd., Flushing 55, L.I., N.Y.

B. McKeesport, Pa., Jan. 31, 1888. *Studied*: AIC; Cleveland Sch. A.; ASL; and with Walter Biggs, Harry Leith-Ross. *Member*: SI (Life). *Awards*: citation, War Dept., 1943; assisted Ezra Winter on murals in monument for George Rogers Clark, Vincennes, Ind. Illus., numerous juvenile subjects: history, biography, animal stories.

LEFEVRE, LAWRENCE E.—Painter
R.F.D. 1, Shore Rd., Chazy, N.Y.

B. Plattsburgh, N.Y., Dec. 9, 1904. *Studied*: Plattsburgh State T. Col.; & with Eliot O'Hara. *Awards*: prizes, Elizabethtown, N.Y., 1938; Saranac Lake, N.Y., 1941; CGA, 1942. *Work*: CAM. *Exhibited*: PAFA, 1938; AWCS, 1940, 1941; Wash. WC Cl., 1942; Plattsburgh A. Gld., 1934-1940; O'Hara Gal., 1937, 1939-1943, 1945; Saranac Lake A. Lg., 1938, 1940, 1941, 1956; Albany Inst. Hist. & A., 1939; Terry AI, 1951; St. Lawrence Univ., 1952; Wm. A. Farnsworth Mus., 1954 (one-man); Barn Gal., Plattsburgh, N.Y., 1957, 1958.

LEFF, RITA—Painter, Pr. M.
125 Amherst St., Brooklyn 35, N.Y.

B. New York, N.Y., Mar. 10, 1907. *Studied*: ASL; BMSch. A., and with George Picken, Louis Schanker, Abraham Rattner, Adja Yunkers. *Member*: Audubon A.; SAGA; Boston Pr. M.; Am. Color Pr. Soc.; NAWA; Brooklyn Soc. A.; N.Y. Soc. Women A.; Nat. Soc. Painters in Casein. *Awards*: prizes, Audubon A., 1955-58; NAWA, 1951, 1954, 1955, 1958; Brooklyn Soc. A., 1950, 1953, 1957; Brooklyn Mus. Alumni Assn., 1955-57; Boston Pr. M., 1954; SAGA, 1954; Village A. Center, 1953-1955; Creative Graphic Exh., 1958, and many exhs. prior to these dates. *Work*: MMA; LC; Univ. Maine; Pa. State Univ.; DMFA; Abraham Lincoln H.S.; ed. of 100 prints, Collectors of Am. Art, 1951, 1952, 1954, 1956; limited ed. 30 prints, Contemporary Gal., 1956. *Exhibited*: MMA; MModA; LC; WMAA; BM; Conn. Acad. FA; DMFA; BMFA; PAFA; Smithsonian Inst.; Galerie Bosc, Paris, France; Maison de Arts, Brussels, and other galleries and museums in U.S. and Canada. One-man: Abraham Lincoln H.S., 1951; Bodley Gal., 1958; Village A. Center, 1954, 1955; Univ. Maine, 1958. Illus., "Little Boy and Girl Land"; "Audacious Ann"; "A Double Story," and other children's books and book jackets. *Positions*: Jury of Scholastic Magazine Art Awards, 1958; memb. Bd., NAWA, Brooklyn Soc. A.

LEFRANC, MARGARET (Mrs. Margaret Schoonover) —Painter, Des., I., C., L., T., Gr.
3734 Matheson Ave., Coconut Grove, Miami 33, Fla.

B. New York, N.Y., Mar. 15, 1907. *Studied*: N.Y. Univ., and with Schoukaieff, Bourdelle, L'Hote, in Paris. *Member*: Nat. Lg. Am. Pen Women; AEA; Miami AA; Fla.

Graphic A. Soc. *Exhibited*: PAFA; WFNY 1939; New Mexico Soc. A.; Soc. Indp. A.; Salon des Tuileries, Salon d'Automne, Salon des Francais, Paris; Oklahoma AA, 1949-1951; Southwestern AA, 1951, 1952; Mus. New Mexico, 1956 and traveling; Graphic A. Exh.; New Mexico, 1957; Univ. Mexico Exch. Exh., 1957, and others; one-man: Philbrook A. Center, 1949, 1952; Oklahoma A. Center, 1950; Mus. New Mexico, 1949, 1951; Recorder Workshop, Miami, 1957. Contributor to Southwest Review. I., "The Valley Below," 1949; "Indians on Horseback," 1948; "Indians of the Four Corners," 1952; "Maria, The Potter of San Ildefonso," 1948, and others.

LEHMAN, HAROLD—Painter, S., T., Des.
46 West 21st St., New York 10, N.Y.

B. New York, N.Y., Oct. 2, 1913. *Studied*: Otis AI; & with Fettelson, Siqueiros. *Member*: A.Lg. Am.; Woodstock AA. *Awards*: prizes, Los A. Mus. A., 1933; Mun. A. Gal., N.Y., 1937. *Work*: Newark Mus.; MModA; murals, Rikers Island, N.Y.; USPO; Renovo, Pa. *Exhibited*: WFNY 1939; WMAA, 1940; MModA, 1943; NAD, 1943; Woodstock AA, 1942-1945; NGA, 1943; Assoc. Am. A. *Position*: Instr., YMCA, New York, N.Y., 1947-50; Des., exhs., displays, for leading companies and department stores; Dec., Storyland Village, Neptune, N.J.*

LEHMAN, IRVING G.—Painter, Eng., Des., T.
70 LaSalle St., New York 27, N.Y.

B. Russia, Jan. 1, 1900. *Studied*: CUASch.; NAD. *Member*: Am. Abstract A.; Audubon A.; Alabama WC Soc.; Brooklyn Soc. A.; Sarasota AA. *Awards*: prizes, SAGA, 1947; Alabama WC Soc., 1948; Wash. WC Cl., 1949; Terry AI, 1952. *Work*: Oxford Univ., England; Ain-Harod, Bezalel Museums, Israel; Archives et Musee d'Art Populaire Juif, Paris. *Exhibited*: Albany Inst. Hist. & A.; Alabama WC Soc.; BM; AIC; CAM; Davenport Mun. Mus.; Mobile AA; Nat. Mus., Wash., D.C.; Nebraska AA; Norfolk Mus. A.; PAFA; Riverside Mus.; SAM; South Bend AA; J.B. Speed Mus. A.; WMAA; and in Europe; one-man: ACA Gal.; Uptown Gal., 1938-1940; Salpeter Gal., 1947, 1948, 1950, 1954, 1955; Phila. A. All., Oxford Univ., 1950.

LEHMAN, LOUISE BRASELL (Mrs. John)—Painter
476 North Willett St., Memphis 12, Tenn.

B. Orwood, Miss., Oct. 15, 1901. *Studied*: Mississippi State Col. for Women; George Washington Univ.; Corcoran Sch. A.; T. Col., Columbia Univ., B.S. *Member*: New Orleans AA; *Awards*: prizes, Brooks Mem. A. Gal., 1954; Tenn. All-State A. Exh., Nashville, 1955; Memphis Acad. A. *Work*: Montgomery Mus. FA; Miss. State Col. for Women. *Exhibited*: Audubon A., 1945; VMFA, 1946; Whistler Mus.; New Orleans AA; Palette & Brush Cl.; Brooks Mem. A. Gal., 1953-1955; Sarasota AA, 1955; Nat. Mus., Wash., D.C., 1954; Atlanta-Mead Paper Co. Exh., 1958; Provincetown A. Festival, 1958; Delta A. Exh., Little Rock, 1958; Mississippi AA, 1958; Soc. Four Arts, Palm Beach, 1958; Memphis Acad. A., 1958; one-man: Mary Buie Mus., 1953; Allison's Wells A. Colony, 1953; Miss State Col. for Women, 1953. *Position*: State Dir., American A. Week, Tenn., 1944-46.

LEICH, CHESTER—Etcher, P.
1224 South Thomas St., Arlington, Va.

B. Evansville, Ind., Jan. 31, 1889. *Studied*: Columbia Univ., and in Europe. *Member*: SAGA; Soc. Wash. Pr. M. *Awards*: med., Montclair A. Mus., 1932, 1938; Paris Exp., 1937; prize, Tucson FA Assn., 1938. *Work*: LC; NCFA; Newark Pub. Lib.; Mus. New Mexico; MMA; Evansville (Ind.) Pub. Mus.; Swope A. Gal. *Exhibited*: SAGA; Chicago Soc. Et.; Indiana Soc. Pr. M.; AIC; WFNY 1939; Nat. Mus., Stockholm, Sweden; NAD; Paris Exp., 1937; Montclair A. Mus.; CGA; Wash. Soc. Pr. M.; LC; Studio Gal., Alexandria, Va.; Phila. Sketch Cl.; Geo. Washington Univ. Lib., 1958 (one-man). Demonstration exhibits of Graphic Arts owned by and circulated among museums, libraries and colleges.

LEIF, FLORENCE (Mrs. Florence Leif Peers)—Painter
72 Paine Ave., Cranston 10, R.I.

B. New York, N.Y., Mar. 17, 1913. *Studied*: R.I.Sch.Des.; & with John R. Frazier. *Member*: Provincetown AA. *Work*: Providence AC; IBM Coll. *Exhibited*: Carnegie

Inst., 1941; Nat. Exh. Am. Art, 1938; WMA; Newport AA; R.I.Sch.Des.; Provincetown AA; Boston A. Festival, 1955.*

LEIGH, MRS. WILLIAM R. See Traphagen, Ethel

LEIGHTON, CLARE—Printmaker
Woodbury, Conn.
Member: NA.*

LEIGHTON, THOMAS C.—Portrait Painter, T., L.
712 Bay St., San Francisco 9, Cal.

B. Toronto, Canada, Sept. 3, 1913. *Studied:* Ontario Col. A.; Evanston Acad. FA, Chicago, with Karl Scheffler; Russell Acad., Toronto, with John Russell, and in England. *Member:* Soc. Western A.; Niagara AA; Keith AA; Santa Cruz AA; AAPL (Nat. Dir., 1956-). *Awards:* prizes, Brittany Scholarship, Toronto, 1934; Soc. Western A., 1954, 1956; Santa Cruz Statewide Exh., 1953, 1957; Lodi (Cal.) Statewide Exh., 1952, 1953, 1954. *Work:* Wakefield A. Gal., Yorkshire, England; Cal. Hist. Soc.; portraits in many private colls. in Canada, Britain, U.S., and Denmark. *Exhibited:* Royal Canadian Acad., 1938-1942, 1948; Nat. Gal., Ottawa, 1941; Montreal A. Gal., 1940; A. Gal. of Toronto, 1938, 1939, 1942, 1948; Canadian Nat. Exh., 1939, 1940; Los A. Mus. A., 1955; Soc. Western A., de Young Mus., 1950-1957; Cal. State Fair, 1952, 1954, 1957; Oakland A. Mus., 1955, 1956; Santa Cruz, 1952-1957, and others; 28 one-man exhs., U.S. and Canada. *Positions:* Instr. A., Russell Acad., 1934, 1936; Dir. Fine Arts, Ridley Col., 1936-42; Dir. Vocational A., Niagara Falls Voc. Inst., 1938-42; Instr. A., Arts & Lets. Cl., Toronto, 1948; L. & Instr. of port. painting, figure & still-life, Art. Lg. of California, San Francisco, Cal., 1948-55.

LEIN, MALCOLM E.—Museum Director, E.
St. Paul Gallery & School of Art, 476 Summit Ave. (2); h. 857 Fairmount Ave., St. Paul 5, Minn.

B. Havre, Mont., July 19, 1913. *Studied:* Univ. Minnesota, B. Arch. *Position:* Dir., St. Paul Gal. & Sch. A., St. Paul, Minn.

LEITH-ROSS, HARRY—
Painter, Comm. A., T., W., Cr., L.
R.D. 2, Box 103, New Hope, Pa.

B. Mauritius (British Colony), Jan. 27, 1886. *Studied:* NAD with C. Y. Turner; ASL with Birge Harrison, J. F. Carlsen; Julian Acad., Paris, with Jean Paul Laurens; in England with Stanhope Forbes. *Member:* NA; SC; Conn. Acad. FA; AWS; Phila. WC Cl.; Balt. WC Cl. *Awards:* NAD, 1927, 1955 (purchases); Morse gold medal, 1955; Obrig prize, 1956; bronze medal, 1953, gold medal, 1955; NAC; prizes, SC, 1915, 1938, 1944, 1946, 1949, 1953; Conn. Acad. FA, 1921, 1943; AWS, 1937, 1941, 1953, 1956; PAFA, 1946; Balt. WC Cl., 1948, 1955, 1956. *Work:* PAFA; NAD; Phila. WC Cl.; mural, USPO, Masontown, Pa. *Exhibited:* NAD, 1915-1958; PAFA, 1916, 1922-1929, 1933, 1935, 1937, 1939, 1941, 1943, 1945-1947, 1952; CGA, 1919, 1921, 1933, 1935, 1937, 1939, 1941, 1943, 1945, 1956; Carnegie Inst., 1943-45; AIC, 1914, 1916, 1920-1927; AWS, 1936, 1938-1955; MMA, 1942; NAC, 1953, 1955. *Position:* Visiting Instr., Univ. Buffalo, 1941, Univ. Utah, 1955, Col. of So. Utah, 1955. Author: "The Landscape Painter's Manual," 1956.

LEKBERG, BARBARA (HULT)—Sculptor
Sculpture Center, 167 East 69th St.; h. 20 West 16th St., New York 11, N.Y.

B. Portland, Ore., Mar. 19, 1925. *Studied:* Univ. Iowa, B.F.A., M.A., and with Humbert Albrizio. *Member:* Soc. for Aesthetic Realism; Sculpture Center; Audubon A.; Am. Soc. for Aesthetics. *Awards:* Nat. Inst. A. & Lets., Grant, 1956; Guggenheim F., 1957, 1959. *Work:* Knoxville, Tenn., A. Center; Socony Bldg., N.Y.; Des Moines A. Center; Beldon-Stratford Hotel, Chicago, and in private colls. *Exhibited:* PAFA, 1950, 1952, 1958; Nebraska AA, 1952; SFMA, 1952; Phila. A. All., 1951; Sculpture Center, 1949-1955; Denver A. Mus.; Walker A. Center: Des Moines A. Center; WMAA, 1953, 1957; Rochester Mem. A. Gal.; Cranbrook Acad. A., 1954; Inst. A. & Lets., 1956; Sculpture Center, 1959 (one-man); Montclair A. Mus. 1956 (one-man); Sculpture Center, N.Y., 1956 (2-man).

LELLA, CARL—Painter
200 East 60th St., New York 22, N.Y.; h. Colonia, N.J.

B. Bari, Italy, Feb. 4, 1899. *Studied:* with Barry Faulkner, Augustus Vincent Tack. *Member:* Arch.L. *Work:* mural panels, Farmers Nat. Bank, Reading, Pa.; Bushwick, H.S., Thomas Jefferson H.S., Brooklyn, N.Y.; Pub. Sch. No. 148, Queens, N.Y.; Woodbridge (N.J.) H.S.; Perth Amboy (N.J.) H.S.

L'ENGLE, LUCY (B.)—Painter, C.
Truro, Mass.

B. New York, N.Y., Sept. 28, 1889. *Studied:* ASL; & in Paris. *Member:* N.Y. Soc. Women A.; St. Augustine AC; Provincetown AA. *Exhibited:* N.Y. Soc. Women A.; Provincetown AA; St. Augustine AC; Palm Beach, Fla.; Wellons Gal., 1951; Bodley Gal., N.Y., 1955; 3 one-man exhs., Wellfleet and Provincetown, Mass.

LENNEY, ANNIE (Mrs. William Shannon)—
Painter, T., L.
29 Coolidge Ave., West Caldwell, N.J.

B. Potsdam, N.Y. *Studied:* Col. St. Elizabeth, N.J., B.A.; Grand Central A. Sch.; ASL; N.Y. Univ.; St. Lawrence Univ.; Syracuse Univ., and with Hayley Lever. *Member:* All. A. Am.; Audubon A.; NAWA; Phila. WC Cl.; N.J. WC Cl. *Awards:* prizes, Newark A. Cl., 1940, 1949, 1951; Irvington A. & Mus. Assn., 1940, 1948; Kresge Exh., 1940; Spring Lake, 1946, 1948, 1950; NAWA, 1948, 1954; A. Cl. of the Oranges, 1952; Montclair A. Mus., 1952, 1953; Seton Hall Univ., 1958. *Work:* Seton Hall Univ.; College of St. Elizabeth, Convent, N.J.; Kappa Pi.; Pub. Sch., Newark, and in private colls. *Exhibited:* Newark Mus. A.; Montclair A. Mus.; State Mus., Trenton; Oakland A. Mus.; Lehigh A. Gal.; Princeton Univ.; Massillon Mus. A.; Richmond (Ind.) AA; Decatur A. Center; Joslyn Mus. A.; Mus. New Mexico, Santa Fe; Art:USA, 1958; NAD; Argent Gal.; Creative Gal.; N.Y. City Center; Riverside Mus.; Mills Col., Oakland, Cal.; Univ. Wyoming; Boise AA; Wash. State Hist. Soc.; State T. Col., Valley City, N.D.; Kansas City AI; Kenosha Pub. Mus.; one-man: Argent Gal., 1949; Creative Gal., N.Y., 1954; Ward Eggleston Gal., N.Y., 1956, 1957, 1958; Cortland Pub. Lib., 1958; Col. of St. Elizabeth, 1956; Attleboro Mus. A., 1958; Utica Pub. Lib., 1958; Charlotte (N.C.) Pub. Lib., 1958, and many scheduled for 1959; also exhibited in Athens, Salonika, Greece; Brussels, Belgium; Lisbon, Portugal; Naples, Italy; Paris, France. Contributor to art magazines.

LENSKI, LOIS (Mrs. Arthur Covey)—
Illustrator, W., P.
Green Acres, R.F.D. 2, Torrington, Conn.

B. Springfield, Ohio, Oct. 14, 1893. *Studied:* Ohio State Univ., B.Sc. in Edu.; ASL; Westminster Sch. A., London. *Awards:* Ohioana med., 1944; Newbery med., 1946; Child Study Assn. award, 1947. Author, I., "Blueberry Corners," 1940; "The Little Farm," 1942; "Strawberry Girl," 1945; "Blue Ridge Billy," 1946; "Prairie School," 1951; "We Are Thy Children" (Hymnal), 1952; "On a Summer Day," 1953; "Mama Hattie's Girl," 1953; "Corn-Farm Boy," 1954; "Songs of Mr. Small," 1954; "San Francisco Boy," 1955; "A Dog Came to School," 1955; "Flood Friday," 1956; "Houseboat Girl," 1957; "Davy and His Dog," 1957; "Little Sioux Girl," 1958, & many other juvenile books. I., numerous books.

LENSON, MICHAEL—Painter, E., L., W., Cr.
16 Enclosure, Nutley 10, N.J.

B. Russia, Feb. 21, 1903. *Studied:* NAD; Univ. London; Ecole des Beaux-Arts, Paris. *Member:* Assoc. A., New Jersey. *Awards:* Chaloner Paris prize, 1928; prizes, Montclair A. Mus., 1957; Bamberger award, 1957; New Jersey "Artist of the Year," 1958. *Work:* Newark Mus. A.; Essex Mountain Sanatorium; Newark City Hall; Mt. Hope, W. Va.; Electronic Corp., N.Y. *Exhibited:* CGA, 1938, 1950; PAFA, 1939; Carnegie Inst., 1943; Newark Mus. A., 1944-1946; Riverside Mus., 1944-1946; Albright A. Gal., 1955; DMFA, 1955; N.Y. City Center, 1955; Art:USA, 1958; Butler Inst. Am. A., 1958. Author: "Realm of Art," art column in Newark Sunday News. Lecturer: Art Techniques and Aesthetics. *Position:* Instr., Montclair A. Mus.; Formerly Dir., Newark Sch. F. & Indst. A., Newark, N.J., 1944-45, 1945-46; Instr., Rutgers Univ. Ext., Newark, N.J.

LENSSEN, HEIDI (RUTH) *(Mrs. L. Fridolf Johnson)—*
Painter, I., W., T.
106 East 17th St., New York 3, N.Y.

B. Frankfurt, Germany, Aug. 23, 1909. *Studied*: in Europe.
Member: Audubon A. *Awards*: prizes, Baden, Germany,
1929, 1931. *Work*: European museums & galleries. *Exhibited*: WFNY 1939; Audubon A., 1944, 1945; Mod. A.
Studio, N.Y., 1945; one-man exh.; Jordan Gal., 1937;
Schoneman Gal., 1940; Am. Sch. Des., 1940; Lynn Kottler
Gal., 1954. Author, I., "Art and Anatomy," 1944, second
edition, 1946; "Hands in Nature and Art," 1955. *Position*:
Instr., Adult Edu., N.Y. City Col., 1945- ; Hunter Col.,
1949-51; Jamesine Franklin Sch. Prof. A., New York,
N.Y., 1952- .

LENTELLI, LEO—*Sculptor*
Via Don Rua 37, Rome, Italy

B. Bologna, Italy, Oct. 29, 1879. *Member*: NA; Arch. L.
Awards: prize, Arch.L., 1911, 1913, 1921, 1922; San F.
AA, 1916. *Work*: S., Cathedral St. John the Divine, N.Y.;
San F. Pub. Lib.; panels, Straus Bank Bldg., N.Y.; Corning
(N.Y.) Free Acad.; Steinway Bldg., Rockefeller Center,
N.Y.; equestrian statue, Charlottesville, Va.; Cardinal Gibbons Monument, Wash., D.C.

LENZ, NORBERT—*Painter, Des., I., Comm. A.*
Free Lance Artists Pent House, Standard Bldg. (13);
h. 14221 Woodworth Rd. No. 1, Cleveland 12, Ohio

B. Norwalk, Ohio, Mar. 2, 1900. *Studied*: Cleveland Sch.
A.; John Huntington Polytechnic Inst. *Member*: Cleveland
Soc. A. *Exhibited*: PAFA, 1930-1939; AIC, 1936; Butler
AI, 1943-1952; CMA, 1930-1955; Ohio WC Exh., 1945;
AFA, 1931.*

LEONG, JAMES CHAN—*Painter*
1314 Pacific Ave., San Francisco 9, Cal.

B. San Francisco, Cal., Nov. 27, 1929. *Studied*: California
College of A. & Crafts, B.F.A., M.F.A.; San Francisco
State College, M.A. *Awards*: John Hay Whitney Fnd.
Opportunity F., 1952-53; Fulbright grant (Norway), 1956-
57; Guggenheim Fellowship, 1958-59. *Work*: murals,
Chung Mei Home for Boys, El Cerrito, Cal.; Ping Yuen
Housing Project, San Francisco; San Francisco State Col.
Exhibited: Barone Gal., N.Y., 1956; WMAA, 1955; Holst
Halvorsen Gal., Oslo, Norway, 1956; Western Assn. Mus.
Dirs. traveling exh., 1958; Mi Chou Gal., N.Y., 1958;
one-man: Barone Gal., 1954, 1956; American Gal., Los A.,
1955; Paletten Gal., Oslo, Norway, 1957; Haghfelt Gal.,
Copenhagen, 1957.

LEPPER, ROBERT LEWIS—*Painter, Des., E.*
905 Maryland Ave., Pittsburgh 32, Pa.

B. Aspinwall, Pa., Sept. 10, 1906. *Studied*: Carnegie Inst.,
B.A.; Harvard Univ. Grad. Sch. *Member*: Abstract Group
of Pittsburgh. *Awards*: AIA Producer's Council. *Work*:
KLM Royal Dutch Airlines, Pittsburgh and Washington,
D.C.; mural, USPO, Caldwell, Ohio; Grayling, Mich.;
West Virginia Univ.; windows, St. Lucy Church, Campbell, Ohio; Sch. Indst. A., Carnegie Inst. *Exhibited*: AIC,
1936; Carnegie Inst., 1941; Assoc. A. Pittsburgh; Arch.
Lg., N.Y., 1952. Des., many folders and booklets for
architectural uses of aluminum, 1945-54. Contributor to
College Art Journal; Architectural Record; Journal of
Eastern AA; Industrial Design magazine. *Position*: Prof.
Des., Carnegie Inst. Tech., Pittsburgh, Pa., 1930- .

LERMAN, LEO—*Writer, E., L., Des.*
1453 Lexington Ave., New York, N.Y.

B. New York, N.Y. Author: "Leonardo da Vinci: Artist
and Scientist"; "Michaelangelo, A Renaissance Profile."
Contributor to Vogue First Reader; High Lights of Modern Literature; Dance Annual. Contributing editor,
Mademoiselle and The Musical Courier; Feature Ed.,
Playbill; monthly column on dance in Theatre Dance
Magazine, and contributor to national magazines and
literary journals. Lectures frequently on TV and radio.
For seven seasons wrote program notes for New York
Philharmonic Symphony Saturday morning concerts. Lectured, N.Y. Univ. on the art of biography and the
writing of children's books.

LERMAN, MERRYLEN TOWNSEND. *See Merrylen*

LERNER, ABE—*Book Designer, A. Dir.*
World Publishing Co., 119 West 57th St., New York
19, N.Y.; h. 809 East 16th St., Brooklyn 30, N.Y.

B. New York, N.Y., Sept. 14, 1908. *Member*: AIGA.
Awards: Books included in "Fifty Books of the Year,"
1938, 1939, 1941, 1943, 1945, 1948, 1951, 1954; Trade
Book Clinic Monthly Selections, since 1938. *Exhibited*:
Cooper Union, 1948. Contributor of articles on typography
and book production to Publisher's Weekly and Book
Production (formerly Bookbinding and Book Production);
also articles to The Writer. Lectures: Series of lectures
on design problems and their solution, for young book
designers, AIGA. Arranged exh. of art books "Every
Home a Museum," 1951, Assoc. Am. A. Gallery, under
auspices of AIGA. Member Exec. Com., Trade Book
Clinic, AIGA, 1941-42; Chm., Trade Book Clinic, 1953-
54; Chm., Fifty Books of the Year Com., 1955. *Positions*:
Instr., Book Des. and Production, AIGA, 1941-42; Instr.,
Book Des. and Production, Columbia Univ., New York,
N.Y., 1953- ; A. Dir., Production Mgr., World Publishing
Co. of Cleveland and New York.

LESH, RICHARD D.—*Educator, P.*
Art Department, Nebraska State College; h. 505 East
10th St., Wayne, Neb.

B. Grand Island, Neb., May 3, 1927. *Studied*: Univ. Denver, B.A., M.A. *Member*: CAA; Nebraska A. Edu. Assn.;
NAEA; Omaha Assoc. A.; Midwest College AA. *Awards*:
prizes, Nat. Scholastic awards, 1943, 1944, 1945; Joslyn
Mem. Mus., 1943-1945, 1947, 1948; Omaha Assoc. A.,
1947, 1948. *Exhibited*: Nat. Scholastic Comp., 1942-1945;
Midwest A., 1952, 1954, 1958; Joslyn Mem. Mus., 1943-
1945, 1947, 1948, 1953, 1954, 1957, 1958; Denver A. Mus.,
1950; Area Artists, 1956, 1957; Sioux City A. Center, 1955-
1957. *Position*: Assoc. Prof. A., Nebraska State College,
Wayne, Neb., 1951- .

LESOVSKY, ADOLF—*Painter, Des.*
5218 Almont St., Los Angeles 32, Cal.

B. Humpolec, Czechoslovakia, June 14, 1885. *Studied*:
Humpolec College; Univ. So. California. *Member*: Los A.
Professional A. *Awards*: gold and silver medals, Pacific
Southwest Expo., 1928. *Work*: Riverside (Cal.) Gal. A.;
Elks Club, Santa Barbara; murals, Texas Centennial Expo.

LESTER, WILLIAM LEWIS—*Painter, T., Lith.*
1102 Bluebonnet St., Austin, Tex.

B. Graham, Tex., Aug. 20, 1910. *Awards*: prizes, Dallas,
Tex., 1940-1942; Witte Mem. Mus., 1941; Texas Print annual, 1941; Texas General, 1945. *Work*: Dallas Mus. FA;
Texas Tech. Col.; MMA; Houston Mus. FA; Witte Mem.
Mus.; Am. Embassy, Paris; PAFA; Am. Acad. A. & Let.
Exhibited: Rockefeller Center, N.Y., 1935; Texas Centennial, 1936; Pan-American Exp., 1937; WFNY 1939; GGE,
1939; PAFA, 1940, 1941; BM, 1941; San Diego FA Soc.,
1941; AIC, 1941, 1942; VMFA, 1946; Colorado Springs
FA Center, 1946; MMA; Passedoit Gal.; NAD. Contributor
to Life magazine. *Position*: Prof. A., Univ. Texas, Austin,
Tex., 1942- .

LE SUEUR, MAC—*Painter, L., T.*
Eden Prairie, Rt. 1, Hopkins, Minn.

B. San Antonio, Tex., Dec. 13, 1908. *Studied*: Minneapolis
Sch. A. *Member*: Minnesota AA. *Awards*: prizes, Minneapolis Inst. A.; Minn. State Fair. *Work*: Minneapolis Inst.
A.; Walker A. Center. *Exhibited*: Palace Legion Honor;
AIC; WMAA; Critics Show, 1944; WFNY 1939; Minn.
State Fair; Minneapolis Inst. A.; Walker A. Center (one-
man). Lectures: Abstract Art in Teaching; Modern Art.
Position: Dir., Walker A. Sch., 1940-50; Dean, St. Paul's
Sch. A., St. Paul, Minn.; Instr. Advanced Painting, Minneapolis Sch A.*

LEVENSON, MINNIE G. *(Mrs.)*—*Educator*
8 Hawthorne Rd., Holden, Mass.

B. Russia, Feb. 5, 1905. *Studied*: Boston Univ., B.A.;
Harvard Univ.; Columbia Univ., M.A. *Member*: Comm.
on A. Edu. *Position*: Cur., Education, Worcester A. Mus.,
Worcester, Mass., 1948- .

LEVENTHAL, ETHEL S.—*Painter, Lith.*

47 Plaza St., Brooklyn, N.Y.

B. Brooklyn, N.Y., Dec. 20, 1911. *Studied*: N.Y. Univ.; Brooklyn Mus. Sch. A.; ASL; New Sch. for Social Research. *Member*: NAWA; AEA; Woodstock AA; Kaaterskill Group; Woodstock Gld. Craftsmen. *Exhibited*: NAWA, 1947-1949, 1951, 1952, 1954; All. A. Am., 1953; AEA, 1950, 1952; Hyde Park Playhouse; Woodstock AA; NAWA traveling exh., U.S. and in Europe; Argent Gal.; RoKo Gal.; Parnassus Gal.; Square Galleries, Woodstock; Burr Gal.; BM, 1958; New Jersey Soc. P. & S., 1958; YMHA, N.Y., 1958. *Position*: Instr., Sec., Brooklyn Mus. Sch. A. Alumni.

LEVERING, ROBERT K.—*Illustrator*

c/o C.E. Cooper, Inc., 136 East 57th St.; h. 330 East 79th St., New York 21, N.Y.

B. Ypsilanti, Mich., May 22, 1919. *Studied*: Univ. Arizona, A.B.; AIC. *Member*: SI; Lambs Cl. *Work*: paintings, U.S. Air Force coll., Pentagon, Wash., D.C. Contributor illus. to McCalls; Good Housekeeping; Cosmopolitan and other leading national magazines. Dir. campaigns for national companies including Philip Morris, Pepsi Cola, etc.*

LEVI, JULIAN CLARENCE—*Painter, Arch., Et.*

11 West 42nd St. (36); h. 205 West 57th St., New York 19, N.Y.

B. New York, N.Y., Dec. 8, 1874. *Studied*: Columbia Univ., B.A.; Ecole des Beaux-Arts, Paris, France. *Member*: Nat. Inst. for Arch. Edu.; AFA; NSS; AIA; NSMP; Arch. Lg.; hon. member: Academie d'Architecture, France; Architectural Institutes of Brazil, Chile, Mexico, Argentina, Peru, Cuba, and Uruguay and of the AID, NSS, NSMP. *Awards*: Chevalier, Legion of Honor, 1921, Officier, 1939, Commandeur, 1951; Officier de l'Instruction Publique, 1927; Medal, Ministry of Pub. Health, 1937, all in France; Royal Order of the North Star, Knight, 1931, Sweden; Medal of Honor, Mexico, 1952; Medal, Historical Monuments, France, 1955; gold medal, Santiago, Chile, 1923; President's Medal, Arch. Lg., 1933; Grand Prix, Intl. Expo., Paris, 1937; Bronze Trophy, Nat. Inst. for Arch. Edu.; U.S. Delegate to various Pan-American and Intl. Congresses. *Exhibited*: Paris Salon, 1904-05; Santiago, 1923; Turin, Italy, 1926; Boston A. Cl.; BM; Sch. A. Lg. traveling exhs.; N.Y. WC Cl.; AIC; Arch. Lg.; etc.

LEVI, JULIAN (E)—*Painter, T.*

c/o Nordness Gallery, 700 Madison Ave., New York, N.Y.

B. New York, N.Y., June 20, 1900. *Studied*: PAFA; & in France. *Awards*: Cresson traveling scholarship, PAFA, 1919; F., PAFA, 1944, 1956; prizes, AIC, 1942, 1943; NAD, 1945; Pepsi-Cola, 1945; VMFA, 1946; Univ. Illinois, 1948; East Hampton, 1952; Am. Inst. A. & Lets. grant, 1955; N.Y. State Fair, 1958. *Work*: MMA; MModA; WMAA; Springfield (Mass.) Mus.; Albright A. Gal.; AIC; Toledo Mus. A.; New Britain AI; PAFA; Newark Mus.; Univ. Nebraska; Univ. Arizona; Cranbrook Acad. A.; Encyclopaedia Britannica Coll.; Walker A. Center; U.S. State Dept.; Butler Inst. Am. A.; NAD; Detroit Inst. A.; Michigan State Univ. *Exhibited*: nationally and internationally. Contributor to: Magazine of Art. *Position*: Instr., ASL, New York, N.Y., and New Sch. for Social Research.

LEVINE, JACK—*Painter*

Alan Gallery, 32 East 65th St.; h. 2 West 15th St., New York 11, N.Y.

B. Boston, Mass., Jan. 3, 1915. *Studied*: with Denman W. Ross. *Member*: Am. Acad. A. & Sciences; AEA; Nat. Inst. A. & Let. *Awards*: prize, AV, 1943; Guggenheim F., 1945; grant, Acad. A. & Sciences, 1946. *Work*: MMA; MModA; AGAA; Univ. Nebraska; Portland (Ore.) Mus. A.; Walker A. Center; Univ. Arizona; WMAA; AIC. *Exhibited*: annually: Carnegie Inst.; AIC; WMAA, etc.; Retrospective exh., Inst. Contemp. A., Boston, 1953; WMAA, 1955. Lectures: AIC and Skowhegan Sch. Painting and Sculpture.*

LEVINE, SHEPARD—*Painter, E., Lith., L.*

Oregon State College; h. 3750 Hayes St., Corvallis, Ore.

B. New York, N.Y., June 21, 1922. *Studied*: Univ. New Mexico, B.A., M.A.; Univ. Toulouse, France. *Member*:

AAUP. *Exhibited*: AGAA, 1951; BM, 1953; Henry Gal., Univ. Washington, 1954; SFMA, 1957; Portland (Ore.) A. Mus., 1954-1958; SAM, 1954-1958; Spokane A. Mus., 1954-1958; one-man; France-Etats Unis., Toulouse, 1953; Mus. New Mexico, 1952; Portland A. Mus., 1956. Lectures: "Roots of Contemporary Expression"; "The Artist's Vision," to museum and private groups. *Position*: Prof. A., Oregon State College, Corvallis, Ore.

LEVINSON, FRED (FLOYD)—*Cartoonist, Comm. A.*

25 Woodhollow Lane, Huntington, L.I., N.Y.; h. 2828 Kings Highway, Brooklyn 29, N.Y.

B. New York, N.Y., May 23, 1928. *Studied*: Syracuse Univ., B.F.A. *Member*: SI. *Exhibited*: English (1953), Italian (1954) and French (1954) exhibitions of cartoons. All New York State Exhs. Contributor of cartoons to: "Best Cartoons from True," 1954-55; "Cartoon Cavalcade," 1954; "Best Cartoons of the Year," 1954-55; "Honey, I'm Home," 1954. Cartoons for Sat. Eve. Post; Colliers; Look; True; This Week; American Weekly; American magazine; Redbook; Better Homes & Gardens; New York Post; Liberty; MacLean's, and others. *Position*: A. Dir., Wylde Productions (animations for TV).*

LEVIT, HERSCHEL—*Painter, I., E.*

220 West 93rd St., New York 25, N.Y.

B. Shenandoah, Pa., May 29, 1912. *Studied*: PAFA; Barnes Fnd. *Awards*: Cresson traveling scholarship, PAFA, 1933. *Work*: murals, Rowan Sch., Phila.; Recorder of Deeds Bldg., Wash., D.C.; USPO, Lewisville, Ohio; Jenkintown, Pa.; 33 portrait drawings of Red Seal Artists, RCA Victor, 1958. *Exhibited*: PAFA; AIC; Phila. A. All.; Springfield A. Mus.; All. A. Am.; Phila. Pr. Cl.; BM; MMA; WMAA; Carnegie Inst.; Am. Soc. Pr. M.; Grand Central A. Gal.; one-man: John Myers Gal., N.Y., 1954; RoKo Gal., N.Y., 1958. Author: Avant Garde section in "Graphic Forms," 1950. *Position*: Prof. Advanced Des., PIASch., Brooklyn, N.Y.

LEVITAN, ISRAEL—*Sculptor, T.*

59 East 9th St., New York 3, N.Y.

B. Lawrence, Mass., June 13, 1912. *Studied*: A. & Crafts Sch., Detroit; AIC; with Zadkine in Paris, France and with Ozenfant, Hofmann. *Member*: Am. Abstract A.; New Sculpture Group. *Work*: in many private collections. *Exhibited*: Paris, France, 1951; WMAA, 1952, 1953; Am. Abstract A., 1953, 1954, 1955 (and traveling show to Tokyo), 1956, 1957; PAFA, 1953; Stable Gal., 1954-1957; RoKo Gal., 1955; Tanager Gal., 1955, 1956; Artists Gal., 1955; Zabriskie Gal., 1955; Terrain Gal., 1956 (3-man); Camino Gal., 1956, 1957; Barone Gal., 1957 (2-man) and group shows; Assoc. Am. A. Gal., 1957 (5-man); James Gal., 1957; Contemporaries, 1957; Morris Gal., 1957; Hansa Gal., 1957; Pyramid Gal., 1957; Workshop Gal., 1958; Brata Gal., 1958 (all these galleries are in New York City); Ohio State Univ., 1954; Detroit Inst A., 1955; Nat. Council of Jewish Women, Orange, N.J., 1958; one-man: Artists Gal., 1952; Weyhe Gal., 1953. *Positions*: Instr., Painting & Sculpture, BM, Dept. of Edu.; Cooper Union Drawing Group; Greenwich House, etc.

LEVITT, ALFRED—*Painter, Lith., L., W.*

210 West 14th St., New York 11, N.Y.

B. Aug. 15, 1894. *Studied*: ASL, and with Hans Hofmann. *Award*: F., MacDowell Colony, 1956. *Exhibited*: Babcock Gal., 1945, 1946; Phila. A. All., 1947 (one-man); Am. Veterans Soc. A., 1943; Wildenstein Gal., 1943; ACA Gal., 1944; Manchester Community Center, 1946; Butler AI, 1946; PAFA, 1948; BM, 1947, 1951, 1953, 1955; WMAA, 1949, 1952, 1955. *Work*: Tel-Aviv Mus., Israel, and in private collections. Contributor to Jewish Forum, Arts, and others.

LEV-LANDAU—*Painter*

222 West 23rd St., New York 11, N.Y.

B. Warsaw, Poland, Apr. 17, 1896. *Studied*: Graphic Sketch Cl., Phila., Pa., and with Sol Wilson. *Member*: AEA; Audubon A.; Brooklyn Soc. A.; Painters in Casein. *Awards*: prizes, Brooklyn Soc. A., 1954; Abraham Lincoln H.S., Brooklyn, 1955 (purchase); Painters in Casein, 1955; Newspaper Gld., 1951, 1953, 1957. *Work*: Tel-Aviv and Ain-Harod Museums, Israel; Lincoln H.S., Brooklyn, and in many private colls. *Exhibited*: ACA Gal., 1943-44 (one-man); Carnegie Inst., 1945; PAFA, 1952, 1953;

CGA, 1950; NAD, 1951-1953, 1956; Dayton AI traveling exh., 1955-56; annually: Audubon A.; Brooklyn Soc. A.; Painters in Casein, etc.

LEVY, BEATRICE S.—*Painter, Gr.*
1451 Torrey Pines Road, La Jolla, Cal.

B. Chicago, Ill., Apr. 3, 1892. *Studied*: AIC; & with Charles Hawthorne, Vojtech Preissig. *Member*: Chicago SA; Chicago SE; Chicago AC; Renaissance Soc., Univ. Chicago; San Diego FA Gld.; La Jolla A. Center. *Awards*: prizes, AIC, 1923, 1930; Springfield (Ill.) Acad., 1928; Coronado AA, 1952, 1956, 1957; Del Mar, Cal., 1953; San Diego FA Gld., 1955, 1957; med., Chicago SA, 1928. *Work*: Chicago Mun. Coll.; Bibliotheque Nationale, Paris; AIC; Lib. Cong.; La Jolla A. Center; Davenport Mun. A. Gal.; Smithsonian Inst.; Vanderpoel Coll. *Exhibited*: AIC, 1917, 1919, 1922, 1923, 1928, 1929-1940, 1942-1946; Carnegie Inst., 1929; PAFA, 1923, 1924, 1929, 1931; NAD, 1945, 1946; SAE, 1938, 1940, 1944, 1945; Chicago SE, 1914-1919, 1922-1931, 1935-1945; Lib. Cong., 1945, 1946; Fifty Prints of the Year, 1932, 1933; Chicago, 1953; Davenport Mun. A. Gal., 1953; Des Moines, Iowa, 1953; Grinnell, Iowa, 1953; San Diego FA Gld., 1953-1958; Univ. New Mexico, 1957 (one-man).

LEVY, HILDA—*Painter, Ser.*
2411 Brigden Road, Pasadena 7, Cal.

B. Pinsk, Russia. *Studied*: Univ. California, Berkeley, A.B. in Soc. Economics; Jepson AI, and with Joseph Krause, Kenneth Nack, Leonard Edmondson. *Member*: Cal. WC Soc.; Bay Pr. M.; San F. AA. *Awards*: prizes, Cal. WC Soc., 1954-1957; Nat. Orange Show, 1955; New Orleans AA, 1955, 1956; Portland A. Festival, 1958, and others. *Exhibited*: Cal. WC Soc., 1953-1957; Bay Pr. M., 1955; Nat. Mus., Ottawa, Can., 1955-56; Alabama WC Soc., 1955; Los A. Mus. A.; San Gabriel Valley A., 1952-1955; Nat. Orange Show, 1955; Santa Paula, Cal., 1954, 1955; Newport Harbor, 1954; Nat. Flower Show A. Exh., 1955; Butler Inst. Am. A.; SFMA; Denver A. Mus.; Cal. PLH; Pasadena A. Mus.; Delgado Mus. A., etc.

LEWANDOWSKI, EDMUND D.—*Painter, T.*
1360 North Prospect Ave., Milwaukee, Wis.

B. Milwaukee, Wis., July 3, 1914. *Studied*: Layton Sch. A. *Member*: Wisconsin P. & S.; Polish-Am. A.; Chicago FA Cl. *Awards*: prizes, Wisconsin P. & S., 1938; Wisconsin State Fair, 1939, 1946; Univ. Wisconsin, 1939; Grand Rapids A. Gal., 1940; Milwaukee Journal, 1940; Gimbel Centennial, 1948, 1952; Polish-Am. A., 1949; Hallmark Award, 1952, 1953, 1957; Southeastern WC award, 1953; Wisconsin State Centennial, 1948; medal, Milwaukee AI, 1940. *Work*: AGAA; BM; BMFA; Grand Rapids A. Gal.; Layton A. Gal.; Milwaukee AI; Univ. Wisconsin; Beloit Col.; Marquette Univ.; St. Patrick's, Menasha, Wis.; Am. Acad. A. & Let.; Acad. FA, Warsaw, Poland; Mus. FA, Krakow, Poland; Univ. Oklahoma; Gimbel Bros. Coll.; Florida State Univ.; Hallmark Coll.; Dartmouth Coll.; MModA; Shell Oil Co.; U.S. Maritime Comm.; Allen-Bradley Co.; Flint A. Center. *Exhibited*: AIC; Carnegie Inst.; CGA; PAFA; BM; Wisconsin P. & S.; Wisconsin Salon; one-man: MModA, 1943; Layton A. Gal.; Minnesota State Fair; Fla. State Univ., 1950. Contributor covers and reproductions to Fortune magazine. *Position*: Dir., Layton Sch. A., Milwaukee, Wis.

LEWICKI, JAMES—*Illustrator, P., Des., T.*
Box 968, R.F.D. 2, Stony Hollow Road, Northport, N.Y.

B. Buffalo, N.Y., Dec. 13, 1917. *Studied*: Detroit Soc. A. & Crafts Sch.; PIASch. *Member*: Audubon A.; AWS; SI. *Awards*: prize, Am. A. Group, 1943. *Exhibited*: AWS, 1940-1952; Audubon A., 1945-1952. I., "New York from Village to Metropolis," 1939; "The United States in Literature," 1952; "Christmas Tales"; Life's "World We Live In"; paintings for Life's series on American Folklore. Illus. in Life, Collier's, N.Y. Times, Holiday, Sat. Eve. Post, and other national magazines.

LEWIS, CYRIL ARTHUR—*Painter, Des., L.*
25 Orchard Meadow Rd., East Williston, L.I., N.Y.

B. Birmingham, England, July 24, 1903. *Studied*: Birmingham Col. A. & Crafts, England. *Member*: SC; All.A.Am.; Audubon A.; A.Lg. of Nassau County. *Awards*: med.,

All.A.Am., 1943. *Work*: IBM Coll. *Exhibited*: AWCS; All.A.Am.; Audubon A.; SC. *Position*: Sec., AWS, New York, N.Y.*

LEWIS, JEANNETTE MAXFIELD (Mrs. H. C.)—*Etcher, Eng., P.*
P.O. Box 352, Pebble Beach, Cal.

B. Oakland, Cal., Apr. 19, 1896. *Studied*: Cal. Sch. FA, with Armin Hansen; and with Winold Reiss, Hans Hofmann. *Member*: SAGA; NAWA; AFA; Soc. Western A.; AAPL; Chicago Soc. Et.; Wash. WC Cl.; Pr. M. of So. Cal.; Cal. Soc. Et.; Fresno A. Lg.; Carmel AA. *Awards*: prizes, Boston Pr. M., 1954; Cal. State Fair, 1954; SAGA, 1954; Soc. Western A., 1955. *Exhibited*: SAGA, 1953-1955; NAWA, 1953-1955; Pr. M. of So. Cal., 1953-1955; Portland Soc. A. (Me.), 1953; Chicago Soc. Et., 1953, 1954; Academic A. Springfield, Mass., 1954, 1955; LC, 1955; Soc. Western A., 1954, 1955; Cal. Soc. Et., 1954; Boston Pr. M., 1954; Conn. Acad. FA, 1955; Wash. WC Cl., 1954, 1955; Phila. Sketch Cl., 1955; Santa Cruz A. Lg., 1954, 1955, and many others prior to these dates; one-man: A. Gld., Carmel, 1954; Humbolt State Col., 1955; Western Rouze Gal., Fresno, 1955; Cal. PLH, 1955; Pebble Beach Gal., 1955; deYoung Mem. Mus., 1955; Argent Gal., N.Y., 1956; Brooks Mem. A. Gal., 1957; San Joaquin Mus. A., Stockton, Cal., 1957. *Position*: Adv. Bd., Cal. Soc. Et.

LEWIS, LALLA WALKER—*Painter, Comm. A., Eng.*
202 West Jefferson St., Greenwood, Miss.

B. Greenwood, Miss., Nov. 14, 1912. *Studied*: Mississippi State Col. for Women, B.A. *Awards*: prize, SSAL, 1935; Minneapolis Inst. A., 1936. *Work*: Mississippi State Col. for Women; Delgado Mus.; Belhaven Col. & Mun. A. Gal., Jackson, Miss.; Newcomb Col., Tulane Univ.; mural, Greenwood (Miss.) Pub. Lib. *Exhibited*: Laguna Beach AA, 1945; Lib. Cong., 1944; Carnegie Inst., 1944; Phila. Pr. Cl., 1946, and others in U.S. and France.

LEWIS, MARGARET SARAH—*Teacher, P., Gr., Des., C., L.*
Board of Education, 329 South Lindberg Ave.; h. 42 West Market St., York, Pa.

B. York, Pa., Feb. 8, 1907. *Studied*: Maryland Inst.; T. Col., Columbia Univ., B.S., M.A., and with Millard Sheets, Charles J. Martin, James Chapin. *Award*: fame, York A. Club., 1956. *Member*: Pa. State Edu. Assn.; Eastern AA; York A. Cl.; NEA; NAEA; Phila. WC Cl.; Pa. Gld. Craftsmen. *Awards*: traveling scholarship, Maryland Inst., 1929. *Work*: State Edu. Bldg., Harrisburg, Pa. (on loan); York County Hist. Soc.; Ferguson Sch. and Administration Bldg., York, Pa.; murals in local buildings. Illus. for curriculum guide for Speech Correction. *Exhibited*: LC, 1943, 1944, 1946; AFA traveling exh., 1943; PAFA, 1945; York A. Cl., 1931-1958; Pa. State Univ., 1935-1937; Hagerstown, Md., 1935; Maryland Inst., 1937, 1953, faculty exh., 1957, Alumni exh., 1958; York A. Center, 1944, 1947, 1953; Allenberry Summer Theatre, 1953; and others. One-man: Maryland Inst., 1937; Martin Lib., York, Pa., 1937.

LEWIS, MARTIN—*Printmaker, P.*
439 East 89th St., New York 28, N.Y.

B. Victoria, Australia. *Member*: SAE; Chicago SE; AWCS. *Awards*: prizes, SAE, 1926, 1940; Boston AC, 1929; Chicago SE, 1929; AWCS, 1929; Phila. Pr. Cl., 1930, 1931; med., Int. Exh. Pr.M. of Southern Cal., 1934. *Work*: BMFA; MMA; CMA; WMAA; AGAA; AIC; Lib.Cong.; N.Y. Pub. Lib.; Nat. Mus., Stockholm, Sweden; Univ. Glasgow, Scotland; Chicago SE; Cleveland Pr.Cl.; SAE. *Exhibited*: Lib.Cong.; SAE; Chicago SE; Phila. Pr. Cl.; P.M. of Southern Cal.; Boston AC; WFNY 1939; AV; etc.

LEWIS, MONTY—*Painter, Des., L., E., W.*
176 C Ave.; h. 692 Margarita Ave., Coronado, Cal.

B. Cardiff, Wales, Sept. 6, 1907. *Studied*: ASL, with Kenneth Hayes Miller, Kimon Nicolaides; & in Europe. *Member*: NSMP; San Diego A. Gld.; Mural A. Gld.; Coronado AA (Founder, Pres., 1949-50, Bd. Dir., 1951-56). *Awards*: F., Tiffany Fnd., 1928; Guggenheim F., 1930. *Work*: San Diego FA Soc.; frescoes, N.Y. Sch. Women's Garment Trades. *Exhibited*: MModA, 1932, 1939, 1942;

WMAA, 1933; AGAA, 1932; AIC, 1936; PAFA, 1937; Newark Mus., 1940; CGA, 1943; San Diego FA Soc., 1942-1945; one-man exh.: mus. & gal. in New York, N.Y.; San F., Cal.; La Jolla, Cal.; Baltimore, Md.; St. Louis, Mo., etc. Lectures: Modern Mural Painting. *Position*: Founder & Dir., Coronado Sch. FA, Coronado, Cal.

LEWIS, NORMAN—*Painter*
   c/o Willard Gallery, 23 West 56th St., New York, N.Y.

B. New York, N.Y., 1909. *Studied*: Columbia Univ., and with Augusta Savage. *Work*: AGAA; Munson-Williams-Proctor Inst.; AIC, and in private colls. *Awards*: prize, Carnegie Inst., 1955. *Exhibited*: Willard Gal., 1949-1952, 1954.*

LEWIS, ROSS A.—*Cartoonist*
   333 West State St.; h. 7242 North Barnett Lane, Milwaukee 17, Wis.

B. Metamora, Mich., Nov. 9, 1902. *Studied*: Milwaukee State T. Col.; Wisconsin Sch. A.; Layton Sch. A.; ASL. *Member*: Milwaukee Press Cl.; Nat. Cartoonists Soc.; Am. Assn. Editorial Cartoonists (Exec. Com.). *Awards*: Pulitzer Prize, 1936. *Work*: Huntington A. Gal., Los A., Cal.; Milwaukee AI; Univ. Minnesota; Univ. Missouri; Kent Col.; Boston Univ.; Peabody Inst.; Columbia Univ. *Exhibited*: AIC; Milwaukee AI; Kalamazoo Inst. A.; Wustum Mus. FA; & in New Orleans, La.; Los A., Cal.; Sacramento, Cal. *Position*: Cart., Milwaukee Journal, Milwaukee, Wis., 1933- .

LEWIS, RUTH—*Painter*
   154 Lorraine Ave., Mt. Vernon, N.Y.

B. New York, N.Y., Oct. 6, 1905. *Studied*: ASL; and with Raphael Soyer, Moses Soyer, Francis Criss, Sidney Laufman. *Member*: NAWA; N.Y. Soc. Women A.; Brooklyn Soc. A. *Award*: prizes, NAWA, 1947, 1956, 1957. *Work*: Everhart Mus. A., Scranton, Pa., and in private colls. *Exhibited*: Nationally and internationally.

LEYDEN, LOUISE HANNON (Mrs. Donald W.)—
   Painter, C., Des.
   26926 Vista del Mar.; h. Capistrano Beach, Cal.

B. Fresno, Cal. *Studied*: with William Griffith, Thomas Hunt, Eleanor Colburn, and others. *Member*: Laguna Beach AA; Nat. Lg. Am. Pen Women; Women Painters of the West. *Awards*: prizes, Laguna Beach Festival A., 1939, 1958; Women Painters of the West; Las Vegas A. Lg., 1957; Nat. Lg. Am. Pen Women, 1958 (2). *Exhibited*: Las Vegas A. Lg., 1957, 1958; Ebell Cl., Los A., 1957, 1958; Laguna Beach AA, regularly; Nat. Lg. Am. Pen Women, 1957, 1958; one-man: Las Vegas A. Lg., 1958; Ebell Cl., 1958. Des. comm. lithographs and silk screen for linen.

LIAS, THOMAS R. (TOM)—*Painter, S., E., Gr.*
   303 Grant Ave., Dayton, Pa.

B. Dayton, Pa., Nov. 1, 1903. *Studied*: Carnegie Inst. Technology, B.A. in Illus.; State Univ. Iowa, M.A., M.F.A. *Awards*: prizes, Iowa Salon, 1946; Dayton AI, 1949, 1951 (purchase); Wash. WC Cl., 1950; Des Moines A. Center, 1951; Assoc. A. Pittsburgh, 1951, 1958; Nat. Veteran's Exh., Santa Monica, Cal.; 1951; AIC, 1953. *Work*: Hundred Friends of Art, Pittsburgh; Alabama Polytechnic Inst.; Davenport Mun. A. Gal.; Des Moines A. Center; Research Studio. *Exhibited*: Am. Soc. Et., 1948, 1949, 1950; Northwest Pr. M., 1947, 1949, 1950, 1951; BM, 1947, 1950; Phila. Pr. Cl., 1947; PAFA, 1950; Am. Sc. Exh., 1952; Assoc. A. Pittsburgh, 1929, 1942; AIC, 1953. *Position*: A.T., Pittsburgh Pub. Sch., 1928-42; Prof. A., Fla. State Univ., 1947-50; Dir., South Bend AA, 1951-1956; Hd. A. Dept., Redbank Valley Joint Schools, 1956- .

LIBBY, FRANCIS O.—*Painter*
   2 Drew Rd., South Portland 7, Me.

B. Portland, Me., Aug. 7, 1883. *Studied*: Princeton Univ., B.A. *Member*: SC; Portland Soc. A.; Ogunquit A. Center; Haylofters; Maine Hist. Soc.; Portland Natural Hist. Soc.; Maine WC Soc. (Pres.); Copley Soc., Boston; Soc. Colonial Wars; Portland Camera Cl.; F., Royal Photographic Soc. of Great Britain, and others. *Awards*: medal,

Boston Soc. A. & Crafts. *Work*: L.D.M. Sweat Mus. A.; Princeton Univ.; Bowdoin Col. *Exhibited*: PAFA; Pa. Soc. Miniature Painters; ASMP; BM; AIC; Balt. WC Cl.; Portland Soc. A.; Boston A. Cl.; Ogunquit A. Center; North Shore AA; SC; one-man: Portland Mus. A.; Bowdoin Col.; Brick Store Mus., Kennebunk, Me.; and in Boston, New York, Barbados, B.W.I.

LIBBY, WILLIAM CHARLES—*Painter, Pr. M., I.*
   203 Garden City Drive, Monroeville, Pa.

B. Pittsburgh, Pa., Feb. 6, 1919. *Studied*: Carnegie Inst. Technology, B.A. *Member*: SAGA. *Awards*: prizes, Assoc. A. Pittsburgh; Wichita AA; BM; Pittsburgh Playhouse; Hist. Soc. Western Pa. *Work*: Butler AI; Carnegie Inst.; LC; MMA; BM; Pa. State Univ. *Exhibited*: LC; Laguna Beach AA; John Herron AI; Carnegie Inst.; Assoc. A. Pittsburgh; Wichita AA; BM; Pittsburgh Playhouse, etc. *Position*: Pres., Assoc. A. Pittsburgh; Assoc. Prof., Carnegie Inst. Technology, Pittsburgh, Pa.*

LIBERI, DANTE—*Painter, I.*
   15 Ardis Lane, Plainview, L.I., N.Y.

B. New York, N.Y., Oct. 15, 1919. *Studied*: Abracheff Sch. A. *Member*: Brooklyn Soc. A.; Knickerbocker A.; Am. Veteran's Soc. A. *Exhibited*: BM; Audubon A; Norlyst Gal. (one-man). Contributor illus. to New Yorker magazine.

LIBERTE, L. JEAN—*Painter, T., C., L.*
   32 East 22nd St., New York 10, N.Y.

B. New York, N.Y., Mar. 20, 1896. *Studied*: CUASch; ASL; BAID; & with Arthur Crisp, David Karfunkle. *Member*: ANA; Am. Fed. P. & S.; Audubon A.; Soc. Painters in Casein. *Awards*: prize, CGA, 1945; NAD, 1947; Pepsi-Cola Comp. (purchase); Audubon A., 1947, 1948. *Work*: WMAA; MMA; Telfair Acad.; Babcock Gal.; Tel-Aviv Mus., Israel; CM; Nebraska AA; St. Bonaventure Col., N.Y.; Walker A. Center; Univ. Arizona; Univ. Georgia, and in private colls. *Exhibited*: GGE, 1939; PAFA, 1945; Nebraska AA, 1944-1946; Carnegie Inst., 1943-1946; CGA, 1945; AIC, 1944; MModA, 1943; WMAA, 1944, 1945; VMFA, 1942, 1944, 1946; Clearwater A. Mus., 1943-1945; BM, 1945; Walker A. Center, 1943; Critics Choice, N.Y., 1945; Wilmington Soc. FA, 1958; Overseas Press Cl., Europe, 1958. *Position*: Instr., ASL, New York, N.Y., 1946; Great Neck AA, 1946; Instr., North Shore Community Center A. Sch., 1955-56; Scarsdale (N.Y.) A. Center; Roslyn A. Center.

LIBERTS, LUDOLFS—*Painter, Des., E.*
   150-76 87th Road, Jamaica 32, L.I., N.Y.

B. Tirza, Latvia, Apr. 3, 1895. *Studied*: Sch. FA, Moscow, Russia. *Member*: CAA, and many art associations in Latvia. *Awards*: gold medal, Barcelona, 1929; Grand Prix and medal, Paris, 1937. *Work*: Mus. of Sevres, France; Royal Mus., Brussels; N.Y. Pub. Lib.; Nat. Gal., Stockholm; Musée des Arts Decoratifs, Paris; Musée Jeu de Paume, Paris; White House, Wash., D.C.; Okla. A. Center; Fla. Southern Col.; Mus. Malmoe, Sweden; Nat. Lib., Vienna; Theatre Mus., Cologne, Germany; Theatre Inst. & The Atheneum, Helsinki, Finland, and in many museums in Latvia. *Exhibited*: one-man exh. in France, Germany, Latvia, Sweden, Belgium, U.S.

LICHTEN, FRANCES—*Writer, Des., Et., I., Mus. Cur.*
   Pennsylvania Academy of the Fine Arts, Broad & Cherry Sts., Philadelphia 2, Pa.

B. Bellafonte, Pa., Aug. 6, 1889. *Studied*: PMSchA.; Graphic Sketch Cl., Phila. *Awards*: prize, NAC, 1946. Author, I., "Folk Art of Rural Pennsylvania," 1946; "Pennsylvania German Chests," 1948; "Decorative Art of Victoria's Era," 1950; "Folk Art Motifs of Pennsylvania," 1954. Contributor to Antiques, American Heritage magazines. Lectures: Victorian Arts and Decorations; Folk Art of Pennsylvania Dutch. *Position*: State Supv., Index of American Design in Pennsylvania, 1936-41; Research Assoc., PMA; Archivist, PAFA.

LICHTENAUER, J(OSEPH) MORTIMER—*Painter, S.*
   Westport, Conn.; and Florence, Italy

B. New York, N.Y., May 11, 1876. *Studied*: ASL; Julian Acad., Paris; & with Mowbray, Merson. *Member*: NSMP; Arch. L.; Silvermine Gld. A.; SC; A. Fellowship; AAPL;

Soc. Leonardo da Vinci, Florence, Italy. *Awards*: med., Arch. L., 1903, 1905; Paris Salon, 1937. *Work*: Smithsonian Inst.; MMA; BM; Dun & Bradstreet; Am. Acad. A. & Let.; ceiling, Shubert Theatre, N.Y.; triptychs, U.S. Army. *Exhibited*: NSMP; SC; Silvermine Gld. A.; one-man: Argent Gal., 1946; Silvermine Gld. A., 1957; Florence, Italy, 1958.

LICHTENBERG, MANES—Painter, T.
1 Burnside Ave., Lawrence, L.I., N.Y.

B. New York, N.Y., July 22, 1920. *Studied*: Academie Grande Chaumiere, Paris, France; ASL, and with Leger, Paris, France. *Member*: AWS; All. A. Am. *Awards*: prizes, Emily Lowe award, 1954; All. A. Am., 1955; NAD, 1957; Costa Brava, Spain, 1957; AWS, 1958. *Exhibited*: PAFA, 1952; Los A. Mus. A., 1955; NAD, 1958; Salon d'Automne, Paris, 1958; AWS, 1951, 1952, 1954-1956, 1958; All. A. Am., 1954, 1955, 1957, 1958; Audubon A., 1952, 1955; Berkshire Mus. A., 1955; Galerie Bernheim, Paris, 1958.

LICHTNER, MRS. RUTH GROTENRATH. See Grotenrath, Ruth

LICHTNER, SCHOMER—Painter, C., Des., Ser., T.
2626 A North Maryland Ave., Milwaukee 11, Wis.

B. Peoria, Ill., Mar. 18, 1905. *Studied*: State T. Col., Milwaukee, Wis.; AIC; ASL; Univ. Wisconsin, and with Gustave Moeller. *Awards*: prizes, Milwaukee AI, 1945, 1946. *Work*: murals, Northern Bank, Milwaukee; Walker Jr. H.S.; USPO, Sheboygan, Wis.; Hamtramck, Mich.; Hodgenville, Ky.; mosaic, Allis-Chalmers Co., Milwaukee; Aluminum and stained glass exterior screen, Masonic Hdqts., Milwaukee; Stained glass and brass panels, St. Peter's Church, Milwaukee. *Exhibited*: AIC; Wisconsin Hist. Soc.; Milwaukee City Cl.; Carnegie Inst.; NGA; Milwaukee AI; Gimbel's, Milwaukee; Wisconsin Salon; 2-man (with Ruth Lichtner) Layton Sch. A., 1953; Lawrence Col., 1954; Cardinal Stritch Col., 1954; Forrest-Syvertsen Gal., Milwaukee, 1957; Frank Ryan Gal., Chicago, 1958.

LIDOV, ARTHUR—Painter, Des., Gr., S., I.
Poughquag, N.Y.

B. Chicago, Ill., June 24, 1917. *Studied*: Univ. Chicago, A.B. *Awards*: prizes, Univ. Chicago, 1933; A. Dir. Cl., Chicago, 1946, 1957; A. Dir. Cl., N.Y., 1948; A. Dir. Cl., Detroit, 1952; AIGA, 1956. *Work*: Pub. Sch., Chicago; USPO, Chillicothe, Ill.; Monsanto Chemical Co.; Coca-Cola Co.; Wright Aeronautics; Radio Corp. Am.; Reynolds Aluminum Corp.; Lederle Pharmaceutical Co.; N.Y. Central R.R.; U.S. Playing Cards; U.S. Army; Schenley Distillers; National Distilleries; Chase National Bank, and many other leading U.S. firms. *Exhibited*: Univ. Chicago, 1933; AIC, 1933, 1934; NAD, 1946-1948; Milwaukee AI, 1945; Nat. traveling exh., Fortune magazine, 1948; A. Dir. Cl., Chicago, 1946, N.Y., 1947, 1949, 1950; Detroit, 1952. Contributor Illus. to national magazines.

LIDOW, LEZA—Painter
10162 Sunset Blvd., Los Angeles 24, Cal.

B. Kansas City, Mo., Feb. 5, 1924. *Studied*: in Europe. *Member*: AWS; Cal. WC Soc. *Awards*: prizes, Denver A. Mus., 1952 (purchase); Los A. Mus. A., 1952 (purchase); Art in Electronics Exh., San F., 1957. *Work*: in private colls., U.S. and Europe.

LIEBER, HUGH GRAY—Educator P., I., W.
Department of Fine Arts, Long Island University, 385 Flatbush Ave., Ext. (1); h. 624-A 3rd St., Brooklyn 15, N.Y.

B. Maryville, Mo., Apr. 17, 1896. *Studied*: Univ. Oklahoma, A.B.; Columbia Univ., M.A. Author: "Comedie Internationale," 1954; "Goodbye Mr. Man, Hello Mr. NEWman," 1949, 1958; "A Bouquet of Quordoodles for Elarel," 1957. Illus. for seven mathematical books by Lillian Lieber, 1940-1959. *Positions*: Prof. Mathematics, 1929- , Prof., Hd. Dept. FA, 1945- , Long Island University, Brooklyn, N.Y.; A. Consultant, Galois Inst. of Math. & A., Brooklyn, N.Y., 1932- .

LIEBERMAN, WILLIAM S.—Museum Curator
Museum of Modern Art, 11 West 53rd St., New York 19, N.Y.

B. Paris, France, Feb. 14, 1924. *Studied*: Swarthmore Col., B.A.; Harvard Univ. *Member*: Intl. Graphic Arts Soc. (juror); Adv. Bd., Pratt Contemp. Graphic A. Centre; Print Council of Am. (Dir.). Author of numerous monographs on modern artists; contributor to art magazines. Arranged 26 exhs. devoted to prints and 6 exhs. including graphic work, 1949- . Organized exhibitions for the International Program. *Position*: Cur., Abby Aldrich Rockefeller Print Room, Museum of Modern Art, New York, N.Y.

LIEBES, DOROTHY (Mrs. Relman Morin)—
Textile Designer, C., L., W., T.
305 East 63rd St. (21); h. 131 East 66th St., New York, N.Y.

B. Santa Rosa, Cal., Oct. 14, 1899. *Studied*: Cal. Sch. FA; Univ. California, A.B.; Columbia Univ. *Member*: Cosmopolitan Cl.; Am. Des. Inst.; Fashion Group (Dir.); F., Royal Soc. A. *Awards*: prizes, textiles, Lord & Taylor, N.Y.; Neiman-Marcus, Dallas, Tex.; Paris, Exp.; AID; AIA; ADI; Plastic Assn.; Am. Women's Assn., 1950; Nat. Business & Prof. Women; Arch. Lg., 1950; deg., LL.D., Mills Col., 1948. *Exhibited*: one-man textile exh., SFMA; BM; CAM; Dayton AI; CM; MIT; Portland A. Mus.; AIC; Walker A. Center; MModA; MMA; Cranbrook Museum; Taft Museum A.; deYoung Mem. Mus.; Detroit Inst. A.; Albright A. Gal.; MModA, traveling exh., Europe, 1950; Univ. Minnesota, 1951; BMFA, 1951; Univ. Illinois, 1952; Univ. Missouri, 1955; Cornell Univ., 1955; MMoodA, 1955; deYoung Mus., 1955, 1956. Contributor to leading design and art magazines. *Positions*: A. Dir., Arts & Skills Corps., Wash., D.C., 1943-46; Des., Goodall Textiles, Rosemary Sales, New York, N.Y.; United Wall Paper, Chicago, Ill.; Kenwood Mills, Rensselaer, N.Y.; Columbia Mills, Syracuse, N.Y.; Galashiels Mills, Scotland; Dobeckmun Co.; DuPont de Nemours Co.; Jantzen, Inc.; Quaker Lace Co.; Stead & Miller Co.; Bd., America House, New York, N.Y.; Bd., California Arts & Architecture; Adv. Com., Indst. Des., BM; Adv. Com., Norfolk Mus. A.; Adv. Bd., Parsons Sch. Des., New York, N.Y.*

LIEBMAN, ALINE MEYER (Mrs. Charles J.)—
Painter
Meeting House Rd., Mt. Kisco, N.Y.

B. Los Angeles, Cal. *Studied*: Barnard Col.; Columbia Col.; & with Henry Mosler, Stephan Hirsch. *Exhibited*: Walker A. Gal., 1936 (one-man); SFMA, 1937 (one-man); Bennington Col., 1937 (one-man); Portland A. Mus., 1939; Kelekian Gal., 1942; Weyhe Gal., 1943, 1947 (one-man); Art of this Century, 1943; Salons of Am., 1929, 1930, 1932, 1934, 1935.

LIEPE, WOLFGANG—Educator, Mus. Cur., W.
1509 Mulberry St., Yankton, S.D.

B. Schulzendorf, Germany, Aug. 27, 1888. *Studied*: Univ. Berlin; Univ. Paris; Univ. Halle, Ph.D. Author: "Natur und Kunst in Goethes bildnerischem Erlebnis," 1932. *Position*: Prof. Hist. A., Cur., Yankton Col. A. Coll., Yankton, S.D., 1939-1942; Prof. Emeritus, Univ. Chicago, Dept. German Literature.*

LIGGET, JANE STEWART—Sculptor
1718 Cherry St., Philadelphia 3, Pa.; h. Merion Manor Apts. J-I, Merion, Pa.

B. Atlantic City, N.J., Sept. 4, 1893. *Studied*: PAFA, with Beatrice Fenton; & in Paris, France. *Member*: NAWA; AAPL; Phila. A. All.; AFA. *Awards*: F., PAFA; Cresson traveling scholarship, PAFA, 1915. *Exhibited*: Woodmere A. Gal., 1941-1945; PAFA, 1941-1946; All. A. Am., 1943; Phila. A. All., 1942-1946; NAWA, 1942. *Position*: Instr., S., Valley Forge General Hospital, Phoenixville, Pa., 1944-45.*

LILLIE, ELLA FILLMORE (Mrs. Charles D.)—
Lithographer, P., Ser.
South American Rd., Danby, Vt.

B. Minneapolis, Minn. *Studied*: Minneapolis Sch. FA; AIC; N.Y.Sch.FA; Cincinnati A. Sch. *Member*: Indiana Soc. Pr. M.; Hoosier Salon; Albany Pr. Cl.; So. Vermont

AA; Boston Pr. M.; SAGA. *Awards*: prizes, Southern Pr. M., 1938; Hoosier Salon, 1945, 1946, 1950, 1958; John Herron AI, 1956; Northwest Pr. M., 1940; Springfield, Mo., 1941, 1942; LC, 1945; Indiana Pr. M., 1947; Boston Pr. M., 1948; SAGA, 1951. *Work*: Fleming Mus.; BMFA; LC; Dayton AI; Cal. State Lib.; SAM; Wesleyan Col. Macon, Ga.; MMA; Pa. State Univ.; Colt, Avery, Morgan Mem.; Carnegie Inst.; AIC; Toledo Mus. A.; Telfair Acad.; High Mus. A.; Brooks Mem. A. Gal.; Honolulu Inst. A.; Minneapolis AI. *Exhibited*: AIC; CGA; PAFA; Minneapolis Inst. A.; SFMA; John Herron AI; Albright A. Gal.; SAM; Conn. Acad. FA; Oklahoma A. Center; Oakland A. Gal.; Carnegie Inst.; LC; NAD; Mid-Vermont A.; Hoosier Salon; So. Vermont AA; SAGA Exchange Exh., England, 1954, and other shows, 1956-58; Cal. Pr. M.; SAGA Indiana Pr. M.; Ohio Pr. M.; Boston Pr. M.; Cal. Pr. M.; Albany Pr. Cl.; one-man: Currier Gal. A.; Bryn Mawr Col.; Western Reserve Mus.; Berkshire Mus. A.; Stockbridge (Mass.) Theatre Gal.; Tryon (N.C.) Lib.; Brooks Mem. Mus.; Wood A. Gal., Montpelier, Vt.; Albany Inst. Hist. & Art; Guanajuato, Mexico; Bronxville (N.Y.) Pub. Lib.; So. Vermont A. Center; Springfield (Vt.) A. Center.

LIMBACH, RUSSELL T.—*Lithographer, P., E., W.*
Davison Art Center, Wesleyan Univ., Middletown, Conn.; h. 271 Washington Terrace, Middletown, Conn.

B. Massillon, Ohio, Nov. 9, 1904. *Studied*: Cleveland Sch. A. *Member*: ANA; SAGA; AAUP. *Awards*: prizes, CMA, 1926-1929, 1931, 1934, 1935; med., Phila. Pr. M., 1928; prize, Lib. Cong., 1946. *Work*: CMA; AIC; BM; MMA; N.Y.Pub.Lib.; WMAA; Lib. Cong.; Yale Univ.; Wesleyan Univ.; SFMA; Herron AI; U.S. Nat. Mus.; Carnegie Inst.; Glasgow Univ.; Lyman Allyn Mus.; Massillon Mus.; Hunter Col.; Univ. Wisconsin. Author, I., "American Trees," 1942; "But Once a Year," Am. A. Group, 1941. Lectures: The Art of Lithography. *Position*: Prof. Painting, Gr. A., Wesleyan Univ., Middletown, Conn., at present.

LINDBORG, ALICE WHITTEN (Mrs.)—*Painter, W.*
The Maples, Newtown Square, Pa.

B. Wilmington, Del., Jan. 18, 1912. *Studied*: Smith Col., B.A.; PAFA; & with Arthur Carles. *Member*: Wilmington Soc. FA; Wilmington AC. *Awards*: F., PAFA; prizes, Wilmington AC, 1936, 1937; New Haven Paint & Clay Cl., 1948. *Work*: PAFA. Author: "My Trip to Europe," 1957. *Exhibited*: Wilmington Soc. FA, annually; Wilmington AC, annually; PAFA, 1939-1943; Friends Central Sch. Gal., 1940-1945, and in national exhs.

LINDBORG, Carl—*Painter, S., W., I., T.*
The Maples, Bishop Hollow Road, Newtown Square, Pa.

B. Philadelphia, Pa., Nov. 27, 1903. *Studied*: PMSch. A.; PAFA; Julian Acad., Paris, France, and with Andre Lhote. *Member*: F., PAFA; AAPL. *Awards*: F., PAFA; med., Phila. A. Cl., 1937. *Work*: Pa. Military Col.; PAFA; Friends Central Sch. Gal.; Allentown Mus., and in private colls. *Exhibited*: CGA, 1931; PAFA; WMAA; Friends Central Sch., annually; F., PAFA; PMA; Phila. A. Cl., and in national exhs. One-man: Wellons Gal., 1952; Phila. A. All.; Am.-Swedish Mus., Phila., Pa.; Warwick Gal., Phila.; Butler Inst. Am. A., 1958. Author, I., "Under Europe's Skies," 1957.

LINDENMUTH, MRS. TOD. See Warren, Elizabeth B.

LINDENMUTH, TOD—*Painter, Gr.*
46 Carrera St., St. Augustine, Fla.; s. Rockport, Mass.

B. Allentown, Pa., May 4, 1885. *Studied*: Chase Sch. A.; & with Robert Henri, Ambrose Webster, George Elmer Browne, W. H. W. Bicknell. *Member*: A. Gld., St. Augustine, Fla.; Rockport AA. *Awards*: prize, PAFA. *Work*: Newark Mus.; Pennsylvania State Col.; Allentown Mus. FA; Bibliotheque Nationale, Paris; Springfield Mus. A.; Kansas City AI; Mus. FA of Houston; N.Y.Pub.Lib.

LINDNER, RICHARD—*Painter, I., T.*
178 East 95th St., New York 28, N.Y.

B. Hamburg, Germany, Nov. 11, 1901. *Studied*: Academy Nuremburg; Academy Munich, and in Paris. *Work*: Con-

tainer Corp., Chicago, and in private collections. *Exhibited*: AIC, 1954; Walker A. Center; MModA; one-man: Betty Parsons Gallery, 1953, 1956, 1958; London, England; Paris, France and Berlin, Germany. Illus., "Tales of Hoffman," 1946; "Madame Bovary," 1944; "Continental Tales of Longfellow," 1948. Contributor illus. to Vogue, Harpers Bazaar, Fortune, Esquire, McCall, Seventeen, and other national magazines. *Position*: Instr., Pratt Institute, Brooklyn, N.Y.

LINDNEUX, ROBERT OTTOKAR—*Painter, T., L.*
Star Route 2, Box 39, Evergreen, Colo.

B. New York, N.Y., Dec. 11, 1871. *Studied*: Nat. Acad. A., Dusseldorf, Germany; Ecole des Beaux-Arts, Paris, France; Franz Stuck Acad., Munich, Germany. *Member*: Royal Soc. A., London; State Hist. Soc. of Colorado; Am. Pioneer Trail Assn. (charter memb.); Buffalo Bill Mem. Mus. Assn. (life). *Awards*: silver medal, Nat. Acad., Dusseldorf. *Work*: Buffalo Bill Mem. Mus., Cody, Wyo.; Colorado State Hist. Mus.; Frank Phillips Mus., Bartlesville, Okla.; Thomas Gilcrease Inst. Am. Hist. & A., Tulsa, Okla.; Northwestern Univ.; Univ. Oklahoma; many portraits of Indian Chiefs and western personages. Exhibited in U.S., and in London, Paris, Berlin, Vienna, Munich and Budapest.

LINDQUIST, RONALD EDWARD—*Cartoonist, Comm. A.*
537 West 53rd St.; h. 235 East 80th St., New York 21, N.Y.

B. New York, N.Y., July 17, 1929. *Studied*: Sch. Indst. A.; ASL, with Reginald Marsh. *Awards*: Scholastic art award, 1947; certif. merit, Greater New York & Westchester County A. Exh. Contributor cartoons to Year 1954; Sat. Eve. Post; Redbook; True; New Yorker; Park East and others. *Position*: A., Rahl Studios, 1949-50; J.P. Curtin Studios, 1950-54; Union Bag & Paper Co., 1954-55.*

LINDSAY, KENNETH C.—*Educator, W., L.*
Harpur College; h. 3200 East Main St., Endicott, N.Y.

B. Milwaukee, Wis., Dec. 23, 1919. *Studied*: Univ. Wisconsin, Ph.B., Ph.D., M.A. *Member*: CAA. *Awards*: Fulbright Fellowship, 1949; N.Y. State Research Fnd. grant, 1956, 1957. Author: "The Harpur Index of Masters' Thesis in Art," 1956. Contributor to Art Bulletin; College Art Journal; Journal of Aesthetics and Art; Criticism (Denmark), and others. Lectures: 19th and 20th Century Painting. *Position*: Prof. A. Hist., Harpur College, Endicott, N.Y.

LINDSAY, RUTH A(NDREWS) (Mrs. Harry W.)—*Painter*
1025 Topeka St., Pasadena 6, Cal.

B. Ada, Ohio, Nov. 23, 1888. *Studied*: ASL; PAFA; NAD; & abroad. *Member*: Pasadena SA; Women Painters of the West. *Awards*: prizes, Pasadena SA, 1938, 1945; Pasadena Mus. A., 1955; Friday Morning Cl., 1957. *Exhibited*: Los A. Mus. A.; Pasadena AI; Stanford Univ.; Laguna Beach AA; San Diego FA Soc.; La Jolla A. Center.

LINDSTROM, CHARLES WESLEY—*Museum Curator, T., L., P., Des.*
M. H. deYoung Memorial Museum, Golden Gate Park; h. 838 Arguello Blvd., San Francisco 18, Cal.

B. Tacoma, Wash., Jan. 23, 1910. *Studied*: Stanford Univ., B.A.; grad. study, Univ. California. Author, I., "What Makes Art Work?," 1941; contributor to Pacific Art Review; San Francisco Chronicle "This World." *Exhibited*: Gelber-Lilienthal Gal., San. F. Des. the installation of the Lou Henry Hoover Memorial of the Hoover Inst. and Lib., Stanford Univ., 1948. *Positions*: Cur., San Francisco Museum Art, 1935-41; Cur. & Dir. Edu., deYoung Memorial Museum, San Francisco, 1941- ; Faculty, Univ. California Ext. Div., 1947- .

LINDSTROM, GAELL—*Painter, C., E.*
Utah State University; h. 286 North 1st St. West, Logan, Utah

B. Salt Lake City, Utah, July 4, 1919. *Studied*: Univ. Utah, B.S.; California Col. of A. & Crafts, M.F.A., and with Roy Wilhelm, Gloucester, Mass. *Member*: AWS; Cal. WC Soc. *Awards*: prizes, Utah State Fair, 1952, 1953, 1954; purchase awards, Utah State Fair, 1954, Utah State AI, 1954; AWS, 1957. *Work*: Utah State Univ.; College So. Utah; State of Utah Coll. Murals, College So. Utah; Cedar City Pub. Lib. *Exhibited*: AWS, 1953, 1957; Cal. WC Soc., 1957. Arranged exhs.: Nat. Painting Exh., 1958, Nat. Ceramic Exh., 1957, 1958, both at Utah State Univ.; Maynard Dixon Exh., 1955 at College of So. Utah. *Positions*: Prof. A., Col. So. Utah, 1953-56; Utah State Univ., 1957, 1958; Utah State Inst. FA, 1957-61, Logan, Utah.

LINDSTROM, MIRIAM B. *(Mrs. Charles W.)*—
Museum Curator, E., W., L.
deYoung Memorial Museum, Golden Gate Park; h. 838 Arguello Blvd., San Francisco 18, Cal.

B. Chicago, Ill., May 19, 1914. *Studied*: N.Y. Univ.; ASL; Univ. Chicago; AIC; Univ. of Paris and School of the Louvre. *Member*: AFA; deYoung Mus. Soc. *Exhibited*: CAA; Univ. Chicago; Cite Universitaire, Paris. Author: "Children's Art," 1957. Contributor to Pacific Review; Everyday Art. Lectures: Impulse to Art; Tradition and Transition; Children's Art; Works of Art in the Museum, to museum, study, parent-teacher groups, etc. Arranged series of exhs. "Tradition and Transition"; series of children's art exhs., local and foreign; text labels in lieu of catalog for "Art of the United Nations," 1945; "Pottery 1958"; "Art of the Pacific Basin," 1958, all for the deYoung Mem. Mus. *Position*: Asst., San Francisco Museum of Art, 1937-39; Cur., Assoc. Dir. of Edu., deYoung Mem. Museum, San Francisco, Cal.

LINK, CARL—*Painter*
41 East 61st St., New York, N.Y.; s. Lake Tahoe, Kings Beach, Cal.

B. Munich, Germany, Aug. 13, 1887. *Studied*: Academy FA, Dresden and Munich, Germany. *Awards*: prizes, Royal Acad., Munich, 1913; Palm Beach A. Lg., 1941. *Exhibited*: AWS, 1946; Intl. Dance Exh., 1938; Palm Beach A. Lg., 1941, 1942. I., costumes of the world for "World Book Encyclopaedia," 1946-47. Scenic and Costume dec., "Aphrodite"; "Mecca"; "Chauve-Souris." Ports. of Oberammergau players.

LINTON, *(MRS. LINTON ROLAND)*—*Sculptor*
880 Fifth Ave., New York 21, N.Y.

B. New York, N.Y. *Studied*: Brooklyn Acad., and with Robert Laurent, Jose de Creeft. *Member*: NAWA; N.Y. Soc. Women A. (Pres.); Audubon A. *Awards*: prizes, IBM, 1947 (2); NAWA, 1947; Long Island A. Festival; medal, Audubon A. *Exhibited*: BM; NAD; Riverside Mus.; Argent Gal.; Bonestell Gal.; Grace Borgenicht Gal.; Chase Gal. *Work*: IBM, and in private collections.

LION, HENRY—*Sculptor*, P.
1137 Arapahoe St., Los Angeles, Cal.

B. Fresno, Cal., Aug. 11, 1900. *Studied*: Otis AI; & with S. MacDonald-Wright. *Awards*: prizes. Otis AI, 1923, 1940, 1941; Nat. S. Comp., 1923; Pacific Southwest Exp., 1928; Los A. County Fair, 1933, 1934, 1939; Ebell Salon, 1937, 1942; Cal. AC, 1938. *Work*: figures, fountains, Los A. City Hall; Ebell Cl., Los. A.; Fed. Bldg., Los A.; & others. *Exhibited*: Los A. County Fair; P. & S. Soc.; Pacific Southwest Exp.; GGE, 1939; one-man exh., Los A. Mus. A., 1937, 1945. Author: "Sculpture for Beginners."*

LIONNI, LEO—*Painter, Des., E., Cr.*
Hillside Rd., Greenwich, Conn.

B. Amsterdam, Holland, May 5, 1910. *Studied*: Univ. Zurich; Univ. Genoa, Ph.D. *Member*: AEA; AIGA (Pres.). *Awards*: "A. Dir. of the Year," 1955, Nat. Soc. A. Dir.; numerous awards and medals from A. Dir. Cl., and AIGA. *Work*: PMA; MMoA. *Exhibited*: MMoA, 1954; one-man: Norlyst Gal., 1947; Phila. Pr. Cl., 1948; WMA, 1958. Contributor illus. to Ladies Home Journal; Charm; Fortune; Holiday and other national magazines. *Position*: Ed., Print Magazine, 1955; A. Dir., N.W. Ayer Co., 1939-49; A. Dir., Fortune Magazine, 1949- ; Des. Dir., Olivetti Corp., 1950- .

LIPINSKY DE ORLOV, LINO SIGISMONDO—
Painter, Et., S., Conservator, Des.
120 East 82nd St., New York 28, N.Y.

B. Rome, Italy, Jan. 14, 1908. *Studied*: British Acad. A.; Royal Acad. A., Rome, and with Siegmund Lipinsky. *Member*: SAGA; Audubon A.; Chicago Soc. Et.; United Scenic A. Union; Am.-Italy Soc.; Calcografia Romana, Rome, Italy. *Awards*: medal, Rome, Italy, 1931; Officer of the Order of Merit of the Republic of Italy, 1958; Paris Salon, 1937; Budapest, Hungary, 1936; prizes, Chicago Soc. Et., 1941; SAGA, 1942; LC, 1942; Detroit Inst. A., 1943; Kosciuszko Fnd., 1948. *Work*: Severance Music Hall, Cleveland, Ohio; St. Patrick's Cathedral, N.Y.; Mus. City of New York; Boston Symphony Hall; N.Y.Pub. Lib.; LC; Detroit Inst. A.; Cranbrook Acad. A.; MMA; Vassar Col.; Fla. State Univ.; Yale Univ.; Radcliffe Music Bldg.; many churches in U.S. and abroad. *Exhibited*: Los A. Mus. A., 1927, 1928, 1932; AIC, 1934; Chicago Soc. Et.; SAGA; Grand Central A. Gal.; LC; NAD; CMA; Detroit Inst. A.; Albany Inst. Hist. & A.; Audubon A.; Carnegie Inst.; Mills Col., Oakland, Cal.; Albright A. Gal., and abroad; one-man: Avery Hall, Columbia Univ.; Cosmos Cl., Wash., D.C.; Smithsonian Inst.; Nat. Mus., Wash., D.C.; Galleria Costa, Palma di Mallorca, Spain; Vose Gal.; Symphony Hall, Boston; Jr. Lg., Boston; St. Paul's Gld.; Knoedler Gal. Co-author: "Anatomy for Artists," 1931; Author: "Pocket Anatomy in Color for Artists," 1947; "Giovanni daVerrazzano, The Discovery of New York Bay, 1524," 1958. *Positions*: Hd. Exhibits Des. Dept., Mus. City of New York; Dir., Garibaldi & Meucci Mem. Mus., Staten Island, N.Y.; A Consultant, Italian Embassy, Wash., D.C., and to Consulate General of Italy in New York; Dir., annual Winter Antiques Show, N.Y.

LIPMAN, JEAN—*Writer, Editor, L.*
Cannondale, Conn.

B. New York, N.Y., Aug. 31, 1909. *Studied*: Wellesley Col., B.A.; N.Y. Univ., M.A. Author: "American Primitive Painting," 1942; "American Folk Art," 1948; "Primitive Painters in America" (with Alice Winchester), 1950; "Rufus Porter, Yankee Wall Painter," 1950; "American Folk Decoration" (with Eve Menhudyke), 1951. Contributor to art and national magazines. *Position*: Assoc. Ed., Art in America, 1938-40, Ed., 1941-58.

LIPMAN-WULF, PETER—*Sculptor, Pr. M., T.*
766 Sixth Ave., New York 10, N.Y.

B. Berlin, Germany, Apr. 27, 1905. *Studied*: State Acad. FA, Berlin, M.A., with Ludwig Gies. *Member*: AEA; Brooklyn Soc. A.; Artist-Craftsmen of N.Y. *Award*: gold medal, Exposition Mondiale, Paris, 1937; Guggenheim Fellowship, 1949. *Work*: sc., WMAA; Isaac Delgado Mus. A.; Metropolitan Opera Assn.; Yale Univ. Lib.; drawings: Smith Col.; Southern Methodist Univ.; Detroit Inst. A.; Staten Island Mus. A. & Sc.; Evansville (Ind.) Mus. A. & Sc.; Richmond AA; Birmingham Mus. A.; Lowe Gal., Coral Gables; prints: PMA; MMA; BMA; Phila. Pr. Cl.; fountains: City of Berlin; many ports. of prominent persons. *Exhibited*: PAFA, 1951, 1953, 1954; WMAA, 1950, 1952-1956, 1958; SAGA, 1951, 1952, 1954; BM, 1951, 1954; PMA, 1949; Syracuse Mus. FA., 1947-1949, 1956, 1958; San F. AA, 1953; Phila. Pr. Cl., 1947, 1950, 1951; Carlebach Gal., 1953; Bradley Univ., 1951, 1952; CMA, 1954; Artist-Craftsmen of N.Y., 1953, 1956, 1957; Brooklyn Soc. A., 1954, 1955, 1957; Nat. Inst. A. & Lets., 1957; AEA; Silvermine Gld. A., 1958; Am. Color Pr. Soc., 1958, and abroad. One-man: New School, 1950; Delius Gal., 1950, 1952; Hudson Gld., 1957; Carl Schurz Fnd., 1958; two-man: The Contemporaries, 1953, 1955; Phila. Pr. Cl., 1956. *Positions*: Instr., N.Y. City Col., Sch. of Gen. Studies, 1948-58; Queens Col., N.Y., L., 1951-56 (intermittently), Instr., Sch. Gen Studies, 1952-58.

LIPPINCOTT, JANET—*Painter*
P.O. Box 1412, Santa Fe, N.M.

B. New York, N.Y., May 16, 1918. *Studied*: ASL; Bisttram Sch. A., Taos, N.M.; San F. A. Lg., and with Alfred Morang, John Skolle. *Member*: Taos AA; New Orleans AA. *Exhibited*: New Mexico Traveling Exhibition; Little Gal., N.Y.; New Mexico A., 1955; Delgado Mus. A.; Massillon Mus. A.; Mississippi AA; Mus. Modern A., Albuquerque (one-man); New Mexico State Mus.; Burro Alley Gal., Santa Fe, 1954 (one-man); Mus. New Mexico, Santa Fe.*

PORTRAIT OF ELIZABETH WENTWORTH

by

John Singleton Copley

Recently acquired by the Atlanta Art Association

KNOEDLER

ESTABLISHED 1846

14 EAST 57th STREET - NEW YORK

PARIS
22 rue des Capucines

LONDON
34 St. James's Street

LIPPINCOTT, J. GORDON—*Designer, W., L.*

430 Park Ave., New York 22, N.Y.; h. 1 Tompkins Rd., Scarsdale, N.Y.

B. White Plains, N.Y., Mar. 28, 1909. *Studied*: Swarthmore Col., B.S.; Columbia Univ., M.S. *Member*: ADI; IDCA; Arch.L. Lectures: Industrial Design. Author: "Design for Business." *Position*: Chm. Bd., Lippincott & Margulies, Inc., New York, N.Y.

LIPPOLD, RICHARD—*Sculptor, E., Des.*

Lattingtown Harbor, L.I., N.Y.

B. Milwaukee, Wis., May 3, 1915. *Studied*: AIC, B.F.A.; Univ. Chicago. *Awards*: prize, Intl. Sculpture Comp., Inst. Contemp. A., London, 1954; Brandeis Univ., 1958. *Work*: MModA; AGAA; Wadsworth Atheneum; Munson-Williams-Proctor Inst.; MMA; Detroit Inst. A.; Inland Steel Co., Chicago; Carnegie Fnd.; Seagram Bldg., N.Y.; Baron de Rothschild, Bordeaux, France; monument, Harvard Univ. *Exhibited*: Mus. Mod. A., Sao Paulo, Brazil, 1951; PMA, 1949; WMAA, 1947, 1951, 1954; Detroit Inst. A., 1948, 1949; CAM, 1948; Cal. PLH, 1948; Tate Gal., London, 1954; Musée d'Arte Moderne, Paris, 1955; A. Cl., Chicago, 1953; AIC, 1953; Willard Gal., 1947, 1948, 1950, 1952 (one-man); MModA, 1952; Contemp. A. Mus., Houston, Tex., 1957; Brandeis Univ., 1958. Contributor articles to art magazines. *Positions*: Instr., Layton Sch. A., Milwaukee, 1940-41; Univ. Michigan, 1941-44; Goddard Col., 1945-47; Hd. A. Dept., Trenton Jr. Col., Trenton, N.J., 1947-52; Prof., Hunter Col., 1952- .

LIPTON, SEYMOUR—*Sculptor*

1939 Grand Concourse, New York 53, N.Y.

B. New York, N.Y., Nov. 6, 1903. *Awards*: prizes, AIC, 1957; Sao Paulo, Brazil, 1957 (Purchase); Inst. A. & Lets. grant, 1958. *Work*: MModA; MMA; BM; Des Moines A. Center; Albright A. Gal.; Franklin Inst., Phila., Pa.; Toronto A. Gal.; Sao Paulo, Brazil, Mus.; WMAA; Yale Univ. Mus.; Wadsworth Atheneum; Manufacturers Trust Co.; Temple Israel, Tulsa, Okla.; Temple Beth-El, Gary, Ind.; Santa Barbara Mus. A.; Tel-Aviv Mus., Israel; Munson-Williams-Proctor Inst.; Carstairs Mus., Bahamas, West Indies. *Exhibited*: MModA; WMAA; AIC; SFMA; Yale Univ.; PAFA; PMA; WMA; Grand Rapids, Mich.; CAM; Kalamazoo A. Center; J. B. Speed Mus. A.; CMA; Dallas Mus. FA; BMA; Vassar Col.; Delande Mus., New Orleans; Univ. Iowa; Des Moines A. Center; VMFA; Stephens Col.; Louisville A. Center; Margaret Browne Gal.; Boston Inst. Contemp. A.; and in leading museums in France, Spain, Germany, Italy, England, etc.; one-man: Betty Parsons Gal., 1948, 1950, 1952, 1954; New Paltz Col., 1955; Watkins Gal., Wash., D.C., 1950; MModA, 1956; Venice, Italy, 1958. Contributor articles to art magazines. *Position*: Instr. S., New School for Social Research, New York, N.Y.

LISSIM, SIMON—*Painter, Des., E., I., L.*

55 Magnolia Dr., Dobbs Ferry, N.Y.

B. Kiev, Russia, Oct. 24, 1900. *Studied*: Sorbonne, Louvre Sch., Paris, France, and in Russia. *Member*: Salon d'Automne; Artistes Decorateurs, Paris; Audubon A.; CAA; Theatre Lib. Assn.; AAMus.; AIGA; Hon. Corr. member, Royal Soc. A., Royal Soc. Min. P., S. & Gravers, England; corr. member, Royal Acad. FA of St. George, Spain; Hon., F., Am.-Scandinavian Fnd. *Awards*: medals, Int. Exh., Paris, 1925; Barcelona, 1928; two Grande Diplomes, d'Honneur, Paris, 1937. *Work*: Musee du Jeu de Paume; Musee des Arts Decoratifs, Paris; The City of Paris; Sevres Mus.; Victoria and Albert Mus.; Stratford-on-Avon Mus., England; Albertina Mus., Nat. Lib., Vienna; Nat. Mus., Mun. Mus.; Theatre Mus., Riga, Latvia; BM; N.Y. Pub. Lib.; MMA; CMA; BMFA; FMA; VMFA; Nat. Gal. of Canada; Hyde Park Lib., and others. *Exhibited*: nationally and internationally. I., books and contributor of articles on art and art education to newspapers and art magazines. Lectures on art and design. Five monographs publ. in France, 1928, 1933; U.S., 1949, 1958; England, 1955. *Position*: Hd., A. Edu. Project, N.Y. Pub. Lib., 1942- ; Assoc. Prof. A., City College of N.Y., 1954- ; Asst. Dir., Sch. General Studies, Ext. Div., City College of N,Y., 1948- ; Chm. Nat. Selection Com. on Fulbright Awards in painting, sculpture & graphic arts, 1956.

LISZT, MARIA—*Painter*

50 East 66th St., New York, N.Y.; also, 12 Wonson St., East Gloucester, Mass.

B. Boston, Mass. *Studied*: Scott Carbee Sch. A.; BMFA Sch.; ASL; Cincinnati A. Acad. *Member*: Boston A. Cl.;

North Shore AA; NAWA; New Jersey P. & S. Soc.; Boston Soc. Indp. A. *Work*: murals, hotels and restaurants, New York, Boston, and in Florida. *Exhibited*: NAD; NAWA; North Shore AA; New Jersey P. & S. Soc.; Ogunquit A. Center; Boston A. Cl.; Cincinnati Acad. A.; West Palm Beach AA; ASL. Specializes in port. and landscape painting.

LITAKER, THOMAS FRANKLIN—*Painter, T.*

University of Hawaii, College of General Studies; h. 3913 Gail St., Honolulu 15, Hawaii

B. Concord, N.C., Apr. 26, 1906. *Studied*: Georgia Tech., B.S. Arch.; Mass. Inst. Tech., M.S.; and with John Whorf, John Frazer, Ralston Crawford, Max Ernst, Arnold Blanch, Hans Hofmann. *Member*: Hawaii P. & S. Lg.; Honolulu Pr. M. *Awards*: prizes, Honolulu A. Soc., 1942 (purchase); Honolulu A. Acad., 1950, 1953. *Work*: Honolulu A. Acad. *Exhibited*: Artists of Hawaii, 1942-1958; Honolulu Pr. M., 1942-1958. *Position*: Instr. A., University of Hawaii, College of General Studies, Honolulu, Hawaii, 1948- .

LITTLE, GERTRUDE L.—*Miniature Painter*

1660 Lyman Pl., Los Angeles 27, Cal.

B. Minneapolis, Minn. *Studied*: ASL; & with Ella Shepard Bush, S. MacDonald-Wright. *Member*: Cal. Soc. Min. P.; Pa. Soc. Min. P. *Awards*: prizes, Seattle FA Soc., 1921; Cal. Soc. Min. P., 1923, 1925, 1928; San Diego FA Soc., 1926; Pacific Southwest Exp., 1926; Los A. County Fair, 1928. *Work*: PMA. *Exhibited*: PAFA, 1924-1926; AIC, 1927; Phila. Sesqui-Centennial Exp., 1926; Century of Progress, Chicago, 1933; Cal. Pacific Int. Exp., 1935; GGE, 1939; CGA.

LITTLE, JOHN—*Painter*

Box 1871, East Hampton, N.Y.; h. Three Mile Harbor Road, East Hampton, N.Y.

B. Andalusia, Ala., Mar. 18, 1907. *Studied*: Buffalo Acad. FA; ASL, with George Grosz; Hans Hofmann Sch. FA. *Awards*: prize, San F. AA, 1948. *Work*: in many private collections. *Exhibited*: Provincetown AA; Phila. Pr. Cl.; Birmingham WC Soc.; NAC; SFMA, 1948; East Hampton, N.Y., 1953; Stable Gal., 1955; Executive House, N.Y., 1956; Signa Gal., East Hampton, N.Y., 1957; Castelli Gal., N.Y., 1957; Mus. Contemp.A., Dallas; Univ. Arkansas; Ball State T. Col.; Indiana State T. Col.; one-man: Cal. PLH, 1946-47; Betty Parsons Gal., 1948; Hannibal French House, Sag Harbor, N.Y., 1954; Bertha Schaefer Gal., N.Y., 1957, 1958; Executive House, 1958; Mills Col., N.Y., 1958.

LITTLEFIELD, EDGAR—*Craftsman, E.*

School of Fine & Applied Arts, Ohio State University, Columbus 10, Ohio; h. 6417 Linworth Rd., Worthington, Ohio

B. Nashville, Tenn., July 27, 1905. *Studied*: Ohio State Univ., B. Cer. Engr., with Arthur E. Baggs. *Member*: Columbus A. Lg. *Awards*: prizes, Syracuse Mus. FA, 1934, 1935, 1941 (purchase); nine awards, Columbus A. Lg., 1930-1955. *Work*: Columbus Gal. FA; Syracuse Mus. FA. *Exhibited*: Nat. Ceramic Exh., Syracuse Mus. FA, 1933-1940, 1946-1953; Am. Ceramic Exh., Sweden, Denmark, Finland, England, 1937; GGE, 1939; several traveling exhs.; Columbus A. Lg., 1930-1955; Ohio State Fair, 1953, 1955. Contributor to Ceramics Monthly; Journal of Am. Ceramic Soc. *Position*: Ceramic Engineer, Des., Hyalyn Porcelain, Inc., 1946-47; Asst. Prof., 1939-41, Assoc. Prof. 1941-45, Prof., 1945- , Ohio State Univ., Columbus, Ohio.*

LITTLEFIELD, WILLIAM HORACE—*Painter*

29 Depot Ave., Falmouth, Mass.

B. Roxbury, Mass., Oct. 28, 1902. *Studied*: Harvard Col., A.B. *Work*: BMFA; FMA; WMA; Smith Col.; Vassar Col.; Albright A. Gal.; Lockwood Mem. Lib., Univ. Buffalo; William Rockhill Nelson Gal.; MModA; Univ. Michigan; mural, Falmouth (Mass.) Sch. *Exhibited*: nationally, group and one-man exhibitions; annually with Provincetown and Cape Cod AA.

LITTLETON, HARVEY KLINE—*Ceramic Craftsman*

Department of Art Education, University of Wisconsin, Madison, Wis.; h. Rte. 1, Verona, Wis.

B. Corning, N.Y., June 14, 1922. *Studied*: Univ. Michigan, B. Des.; Cranbrook Acad. A., M.F.A. *Member*: Am.

CARLEBACH
ARCHAIC, PRIMITIVE AND ORIENTAL ART

REgent 7-0116

1040 MADISON AVENUE
COR. 79 ST., NEW YORK 21

Crafts Council (Trustee, 1957-58); Midwest Des.-Craftsmen (Treas. 1954-55, Chm. 1955-56); Wis. Des.-Craftsmen. *Awards*: prizes, Syracuse Mus. FA; Am. Art Clay award, 1954; AIC, 1954; Mich. A. & Crafts, 1951; Detroit Inst. A., 1954; Wis. State Fair, 1953, 1954; Wis. Des.-Craftsmen, 1951, 1954, 1958; Milwaukee AI, 1954, 1957, 1958, and others. *Work*: Detroit Inst. A.; Detroit Children's Mus.; Milwaukee AI; Arnot A. Gal., Elmira, N.Y.; Univ. Nebraska; Univ. Michigan; Univ. Illinois; Am. Art Clay Co. *Exhibited*: Syracuse Mus. FA; Wichita, Kans.; St. Paul Gal. A., 1952, 1953, 1955; Des.-Craftsmen, 1953; Intl. Expo., Cannes, France, 1955; Am. Craft Exh., 1955 and others; one-man and small groups: Toledo Mus. A., 1954; Univ. Wisconsin, 1955; Bertha Schaefer Gal., 1954, 1955; Univ. Michigan, 1951. Contributor to Craft Horizons. *Position*: Instr., Toledo Mus. A., 1949-51; Instr., 1951-54, Asst. Prof., 1954- , Univ. Wisconsin, Madison, Wis.

LIVINGSTON, SIDNEE—*Painter, Pr. M.*

14 Minetta St., New York 12, N.Y.

B. New York, N.Y., Dec. 7, 1909. *Studied*: N.Y. Univ.; NAD. *Member*: AEA; NAWA. *Work*: Altoona (Pa.) A. Center; Collectors Am. A., N.Y.; Lincoln A. Gld.; Univ. Mississippi; Princeton Univ.; Everhart Mus.; and in private collections in U.S. and Europe. *Exhibited*: Kansas City AI; Denver A. Mus.; Butler AI, 1949, 1951; PAFA, 1949, 1951, 1953-1955; Univ. Nebraska, 1948, 1950, 1953, 1954; AIC, 1948-1950; Minn. State Fair, 1947; VMFA, 1948; Ill. State. Mus., 1949; Wells Col., 1948; Stephens Col., 1949; Springfield (Mo.) Mus. A., 1948; Ohio State Univ., 1949; South Bend A. Center, 1949-1951; Davenport Mun. Gal., 1950; Cowie Gal., Los A., 1950; WMAA, 1951; CAM, 1951; Terry AI, 1952; Harcum Jr. Col., 1952; NAD, 1952; Joslyn Mus. A., 1953-1955; Audubon A., 1953; Silvermine Gld. A., 1953; NAWA, 1953-1955; NAC, 1953-1955; Little Gal., Phila., Pa., 1953-1955; Midwest Landscape Exh., 1953; Contemp. A. Gal., 1953-1955; Springfield A. Lg., 1955; SFMA, 1954; Dayton AI, 1956; LC, 1956; New School, N.Y., 1957; AWS, 1958; Jersey City Mus. A., 1958; Galerie Philadelphie, Paris, France, 1957; Am. Gal., Greece, 1958, and others; one-man: Salpeter Gal., 1947; Assoc. Am. A., Chicago, 1949; Wellons Gal., 1951-1954; Univ. Miss., 1953; Elizabeth Nelson Gal., Chicago, 1953; Everhart Mus., 1957; Univ. Miami, Coral Gables, Fla., 1958.

LLORT, MARTHA (CROCKETT de GARCIA-LLORT)— *Educator, P., Comm. A.*

Art Department, Louisiana College; h. 1129 College Drive, Pineville, La.

Studied: Univ. Alabama, B.F.A.; Memphis Acad. A.; Sorbonne, Academie de la Grande Chaumiere, Paris, France; Columbia Univ. *Member*: NAEA. *Exhibited*: Alabama AA; Mississippi AA; New Mexico AA; Am. A., in Paris. *Position*: Instr., Drawing & Painting, Lauren Rogers Mus. A., Laurel, Miss.; Prof. A., Dept. A., Louisiana College, Pineville, La.

LOBER, GEORG JOHN—*Sculptor*

33 West 67th St., New York 23, N.Y.

B. Chicago, Ill. *Studied*: NAD; BAID; Columbia Col. *Member*: NA; NSS; SC; Lotos Cl.; NAC; Century Cl. *Awards*: med., prizes, NAC; Montclair A. Mus.; All.A. Am.; NSS, 1952; Clinedinst award, 1950; Danish med. awarded by the King of Denmark, 1946; Knighted "Ridder of Dannebrog," 1950. *Work*: MMA; Hall of Fame, N.Y.; BM; Smithsonian Inst.; Museum des Medailles, Paris; Nat. Mus., Copenhagen, Denmark; mem., Niagara Falls, N.Y.; Port Chester, N.Y.; Aquia, Va.; statue, Burnham Park, Morristown, N.J.; medal for Soc. of Medalists, 1955; Hans Christian Andersen Memorial, Central Park, N.Y.; George M. Cohan Statue, Times Square, N.Y. *Exhibited*: NAD, annually; PAFA; All.A.Am.; NAC; Montclair A. Mus.; Century Cl. Contributor to: Grolier Encyclopedia. Lectures: Sculpture. *Position*: Exec. Sec., A. Comm., City of New York.

LOBINGIER, ELIZABETH MILLER (Mrs. John L.)— *Painter, W., E.*

4 Manchester Rd., Winchester, Mass.

B. Washington, D.C., April 17, 1889. *Studied*: Univ. Chicago, Ph.B.; Chicago Acad. A.; AIC. *Member*: Cape Ann Soc. Mod. A.; Copley Soc., Boston; Rockport AA; North Shore AA; Ogunquit A. Center; Winchester (Mass.) AA;

Boston Soc. Indp. A.; Boston Inst. Contemp. A. *Awards*: prizes, Assn. Georgia A.; High Mus. A.; Mint Mus. A., 1945; Boston Open exh., 1955; Rockport, AA, 1947, 1948, 1951, 1953; Ogunquit A. Center, 1951; gold medal, Jordan Marsh exh., 1957. *Work*: Mint Mus. A.; Winchester (Mass.) Pub. Lib. *Exhibited*: Assn. Georgia A., 1935-1949; SSAL, 1937-1947; Copley Soc., 1935-1959; Boston A. Cl., 1935-1942; North Shore AA, 1943-1959; Rockport AA, 1941-1959; Gloucester Soc. A., 1944-1946; Ogunquit A. Center, 1945-1959; Winchester AA, 1934-1959; Boston A. Festival, 1952, 1953; Jordan Marsh, 1946-1959; Cape Ann Soc. Mod. A., 1957-1959; Cape Ann Festival A., 1953-1959; one-man: Copley Soc., 1935, 1943, 1949; Boston City Cl., 1935; Winchester AA, 1935, 1951, 1955; Oberlin Col., 1936; Boston A. Cl., 1939; Rockport AA, 1948, 1952; Marblehead AA, 1950; Tufts Univ., 1955; Town & Country Cl., Hartford, Conn. Co-author: "How Children Learn to Draw"; Author: "Ship East, Ship West"; "Activities in Child Education." and other books. *Position*: Instr., Winchester Studio Gld., Winchester, Mass., 1935-53; Instr., BMFA, Div. Edu., 1952- .

LOCHRIE, ELIZABETH—*Painter, S., L.*

1102 West Granite St., Butte, Mont.

B. Deer Lodge, Mont., July 1, 1890. *Studied*: PIASch., B.A.; Stanford Univ., and with Winold Reiss, Dorothy Puccinelli, Victor Arnautoff, Nicholas Brewer. *Member*: AAPL; Northwest AA; AFA; Montana Hist. Soc. *Awards*: Nat. Pencil Comp., 1937; Nat. WC Comp., 1939. *Work*: murals, USPO, Burley, Idaho; St. Anthony, Idaho; Dillon, Mont.; Montana State Tuberculosis Hospital, Galen, Mont.; panel and fountain, Finlen Hotel, Butte, and many port. busts. *Exhibited*: Arthur Newton Gal., 1952 (one-man); Young Gal., Chicago; Finlay Gal., Chicago; Donaldsons, Minneapolis; Lounsbery's, Seattle; Lynch Gal., Los A. (one-man); River Oaks Garden Cl., Houston; Town Hall, N.Y.; 7 natl. exhs., 1957-58, and others including London, England. Lectures: "Art in Montana"; "Indians of the Plains"; "Indian History"; "Northwest Art," etc. State Chm. Nat. Art, 1958.

LOCKE, CHARLES WHEELER—*Painter, Gr., Cart., I.*

Old Post Rd., Garrison, N.Y.

B. Cincinnati, Ohio, Aug. 31, 1899. *Studied*: Ohio Mechanics Inst.; Cincinnati A. Acad.; ASL, with Joseph Pennell. *Member*: NA; Century Cl. *Awards*: Logan award, 1936; Tiffany F., 1920; grant, Am. Acad. A. & Let. *Work*: MMA; WMAA; Nat. Gal., London; CM; CGA; PC; N.Y. Pub. Lib. *Exhibited*: nationally. Illus. "Tale of a Tub"; "Walden"; "Capt. Stormfield's Visit to Heaven." Contributor illus. to Freeman magazine. Lectures: Lithography.*

LOCKE, LUCIE H(ARRIS) (Mrs. David R.)— *Painter, W., I., T., S., Cr.*

401 Southern St., Corpus Christi, Tex.

B. Valdosta, Ga., Feb. 22, 1904. *Studied*: Newcomb Col., Tulane Univ.; San Antonio Sch. A., and with Charles Rosen, Xavier Gonzales, Increase Robinson, Frederic Taubes, and others. *Member*: Texas WC Soc.; AFA; Corpus Christi A. Fnd.; Nat. Lg. Am. Pen Women; South Texas A. Lg.; Texas F.A. Assn. *Awards*: prizes, Corpus Christi A. Fnd., 1946, 1949, 1954, 1955. *Work*: Montgomery Mus. FA; Del Mar Col.; Corpus Christi A. Fnd.; murals, Corpus Christi Civic Center. *Exhibited*: Caller-Times Exh., 1945; Nat. Lg. Am. Pen Women, 1946-1948; San Antonio, 1933-1935, 1940; South Texas A. Lg., 1935-1958; Texas FA Assn., 1933, 1945-1958; Texas WC Soc., 1950, 1952; Corpus Christi A. Fnd., 1946-1958; Mus. New Mexico, Santa Fe, 1949; Terry AI, 1952; New Orleans AA, 1933-1943, 1945; SSAL, 1931-1945; Texas-Oklahoma General, 1941; Texas General, 1944, 1945; one-man: Houston, 1949; San Antonio, 1935, 1950; Corpus Christi, 1950; Austin, Tex., 1950. Author, I., "Naturally Yours, Texas." *Position*: Chm., Corpus Christi A. Fnd., 1946-47; Dir., Texas FA Assn., 1947-48; A. Cr., Caller-Times, 1945-58.

LOCKHART, JAMES LELAND—*Illustrator, P., W.*

980 East Walden Lane, Lake Forest, Ill.

B. Sedalia, Mo., Sept. 26, 1912. *Studied*: Univ. Arkansas; Am. Acad. A.; AIC, with Edmund Giesbert. *Member*: A. Gld. Chicago; Lake Forest A. Lg. *Awards*: medal, A. Dirs. of Chicago, 1947; prizes, A. Gld. of Chicago, 1948, 1957. *Work*: Container Corp. of America; Baseball Hall

EMILY LOWE COMPETITION

JOE AND EMILY LOWE FOUNDATION ● 969 MADISON AVE., N.Y.C. 21

of Fame Mus., Cooperstown, N.Y.; Ferry Hall Sch.; Lincoln Room, Gettysburg Mus. *Exhibited*: One-man: A. Gld. of Chicago, 1958; Ferry Hall Sch., 1958; Great Lakes Naval Base, 1958; Lake Forest Pub. Lib., 1958. Illus. for Saturday Evening Post; Colliers; Coronet; Sports Afield; American Artist; True Magazine: Lectures: Wild Life Painting; Magazine Illustration.

LOCKWOOD, DOUGLAS—*Painter, T.*
301 Arch St., Seaford, Del.

B. Flint, Mich., July 14, 1905. *Studied*: Univ. Michigan; Chicago Acad. FA; N.Y. Sch. F. & App. Des.; Pa. State Col., B.S., M. Edu. *Awards*: Taliesin F., 1945-47; Wilmington Soc. FA, 1954, 1956-1958. *Exhibited*: BM, 1949, 1955; AIC, 1949; Willard Gal., 1949 (one-man); Exh. Taliesin, 1945-1947; Columbus Gal. FA, 1950; Ellen Donovan Gal., 1954; Willard Gal., 1954 (one-man); Wilmington Soc. FA, 1954, 1955; Blue Hill, Me., 1951; Pa. State Univ., 1957 (one-man); Syracuse Univ., 1957; Paris, France, 1957; Rome, Italy, 1957. *Position*: Dir., Crafts Sch., Henry St. Settlement, New York, N.Y., 1935-43; Pa. State Col., 1943-45; Instr. A., Seaford Special Sch., Seaford, Del., 1951- .

LOCKWOOD, WARD—*Painter, E., L.*
Department of Art, University of California, Berkeley, Cal.

B. Atchison, Kans., Sept. 22, 1894. *Studied*: Univ. Kansas; PAFA; Academie Ranson, Paris. *Awards*: prizes, AIC, 1931; SFMA, 1932, 1952; Kansas City AI, 1937; Texas FA Assn., 1946; deYoung Mem. Mus., 1950; San F. Art Festival, 1950; F., PAFA; Santa Rosa, Cal., 1954; San F. AA, 1957 (purchase); Distinguished Service Citation, Univ. Kansas, 1956. *Work*: WMAA; PAFA; Denver A. Mus.; Cal.PLH; PMG; AGAA; Dallas Mus. FA; McNay A. Mus., San Antonio; Iowa State Col.; Baker Univ.; Santa Barbara Mus. A.; BMA; City of San F.; San F. AA; Kansas State College; Univ. Kansas; murals, Taos (N.M.) County Court House; Colorado Springs FA Center; USPO Dept. Bldg., Wash., D.C.; USPO, Wichita, Kans., Lexington, Ky.; Edinburg, Tex., Hamilton, Tex. *Exhibited*: PAFA; CGA; Carnegie Inst.; Cranbrook Acad.; WMAA; AIC; Weyhe Gal.; Kansas City AI; Cal. PLH; Dallas Mus. FA; BM; Nebraska AA; deYoung Mem. Mus.; SFMA; Mus. New Mex.; Venice Intl., 1937; Univ. Utah, 1955; AGAA; Colorado Springs FA Center; William Rockhill Nelson Gal. A.; MMA; Walker A. Center; Dayton AI; Univ. Illinois, and many others; one-man: Mulvane A. Mus.; Rehn Gal.; Mus. FA of Houston; Witte Mem. Mus.; CAM; Nelson Gal. A.; Wichita A. Mus.; Crocker A. Gal., Sacramento, Cal.; Univ. Texas; Luyber Gal., and others. *Position*: Visiting Prof. & Artist-in-Residence, Univ. Kansas, 1957-58 (on leave from Univ. California); Prof. A., Univ. California, Berkeley, Cal., 1949- .

LOEDERER, RICHARD A.—
Painter, Et., Des., I., Cart., Comm. A., W.
67 West 67th St.; h. 349 West 84th St., New York 24, N.Y.

B. Vienna, Austria, Mar. 26, 1894. *Studied*: Acad. FA, Vienna; Schule Reimann, Berlin; & with Winold Reiss. *Work*: murals, Somers Hotel, St. George's, Bermuda; Nat. Canadian Exp., Toronto; Des., series of 6 postage and airmail stamps (Sport Series) for African Republic of Liberia; Des., 16 stamps of the life of Theodore Roosevelt for the American Hall of Fame stamp series, for the Roosevelt Centennial, 1957; painting commissioned for the Danse-Court Bldg., Melbourne, Australia, 1958. *Exhibited*: Acad. FA, Vienna; Newport A. Center; Pan-Am. Union, Wash., D.C., 1942; Am. Commons, N.Y., 1944. Author, I., "Voodoo Fire in Haiti," 1935; "Immortal Men of Music," 1940; I., "One Lives to Tell the Tale"; "From an Ozark Holler"; "G. I. Songs." Illus., New Yorker, London Studios, Creative Art & other magazines.

LOEW, MICHAEL—*Painter, T., W.*
818 Broadway; h. 15 West 29th St., New York 1, N.Y.

B. New York, N.Y., May 8, 1907. *Studied*: ASL, with Boardman Robinson, Richard Lahey, Thomas Benton; Academie Scandinave, Paris, with Othon Friesze and Du-Fresne; Hans Hofmann Sch. FA; Atelier Leger, Paris. *Member*: Am. Abstract A.; CAA; Fed. P. & S.; *Awards*: Sadie A. May Fellowship, Baltimore, 1929; prizes, Nat.

mural Comp. for War Dept. Bldg., Wash., D.C. *Work*: PMA; BMA; murals, Hall of Pharmacy and Hall of Man, WFNY 1939; USPO, Amherst, Ohio; Belle Vernon, Pa. *Exhibited*: WMAA, 1949; MMA, 1952; WAC, 1953; traveling exh. to Europe, U.S. Com. for IAPA, 1956-57; AFA traveling exh., 1957-58; Arch. Lg., 1935; Brown Univ., 1935; Kalamazoo Inst. A., 1935; AGAA, 1935; Stable Gal., 1953-1956; Farnsworth Mus. A., 1950; Springfield (Mass.) Mus. A., 1952; Riverside Mus., 1950-1957; New School, N.Y., 1948, 1950, 1951, 1953; Portland (Ore.) A. Mus., 1957, and in France, Italy, Denmark, Germany and Japan; one-man: Artists Gal., N.Y., 1949; Rose Fried Gal., N.Y., 1953, 1955, 1957; Portland (Ore.) A. Mus., 1956. *Positions*: Visiting Artist, Museum A. Sch., Portland (Ore.) A. Mus., 1956-57; Instr., School of Visual Arts, N.Y., 1958- .

LOFTUS, JOHN—*Painter*
R.F.D. #2, Old Lyme, Conn.

B. Cumberland, Md., July 1, 1921. *Studied*: ASL; Hans Hofmann Sch. FA; Columbia Univ., M.A. *Work*: Mulvane Mus. A., Topeka, Kans. *Exhibited*: Laurel Gal., N.Y., 1949; Norwich (Conn.) AA, 1958; New Haven A. Festival, 1958; one-man: Mulvane Mus. A., 1948; Artists Gal., 1954, 1958; Record Gal., Denver, Colo., 1957; Central City, Colo., 1957. *Position*: Pub. Rel. Dir., Denver A. Mus., Denver, Colo., 1957.

LOGAN, ELIZABETH D(ULANEY) (Mrs. Loyd A. Collins)—*Illustrator, Cart., Comm. A.*
65 West 95th St., New York 25, N.Y.

B. Bowling Green, Ky., Oct. 26, 1914. *Studied*: Antioch Col.; Ohio State Univ., and with Carl Holty, Hans Hofmann. Illus., for children's books, periodicals, cook books, advertising, promotion.

LOGAN, FREDERICK M.—*Painter, E., L., W.*
2913 Waunona Way, Madison 5, Wis.

B. Racine, Wis., July 18, 1909. *Studied*: Milwaukee State T. Col., B.E.; AIC; T. Col., Columbia Univ., M.A., and with Gustave Moeller, Arthur Young, E.H. Swift, Victor D'Amico. *Member*: NAEA; Wisconsin Edu. Assn.; Wisconsin A. Edu. Assn.; AAUP; Com. on A. Edu. (Council Member); Am. Soc. for Aesthetics; Wisconsin Acad. A., Lets. & Sc. *Exhibited*: widely in Wisconsin and the Midwest. Contributor articles to: College Art Journal; Journal of Aesthetics; Review of Educational Research. Author: "Growth of Art in American Schools," 1955. *Position*: Prof., A. & A. Edu., University of Wisconsin, Madison, Wis., at present.

LOGAN, HERSCHEL C.—
Engraver, Des., I., W., Comm. A.
Mail: P.O. Box 184; h. 433 South 8th St., Salina, Kans.

B. Magnolia, Mo., Apr. 19, 1901. *Studied*: Chicago Acad. FA. *Member*: Prairie Pr.M.; Cal. Pr.M.; Salina AA *Awards*: med., prizes, Kansas City AI, 1926, 1927, 1930, 1934, 1937; Rocky Mt. Pr.M., 1934; Kansas Fed. A., 1935, 1938; Friends of A., 1935; WFNY 1939. *Work*: Lib.Cong.; Univ. Kansas; Denver A. Mus.; N.Y.Pub.Lib.; Mass. State Col. *Exhibited*: Prairie Pr.M.; Cal. Pr.M. Author, I., "Hand Cannon to Automatic," 1944; "Cartridges," 1948; "Buckskin and Satin," 1954. I., "Other Days," 1928. Contributor to: Hobbies Magazine, Muzzle Blasts, The American Rifleman, with articles on antique arms. *Position*: A. Dir., Consolidated Printing & Stationery Co., Salina, Kan.; Pres., Am. Soc. of Arms Collectors, 1955-56, 1957-58; Contrib. Editor, The American Rifleman.

LOGAN, ROBERT FULTON—*Painter, Et., E., L., Des.*
Tenants' Harbor, Me.; w. 24 Pinckney St., Boston, Mass.

B. Manitoba, Canada, Mar. 25, 1890. *Studied*: AIC; BMFA Sch. *Member*: SAGA; Chicago Soc. Et.; Mystic AA; Societe de la Gravure Originale en Noir, Paris; Salon Nationale, Paris. *Awards*: med., AIC, 1921; Logan Medal, 1937. *Work*: Luxembourg Mus., Paris; Yale Univ.; MMA; AIC; BMFA; NGA; British Mus., London; Bibliotheque Nationale, Paris; Lyman Allyn Mus.; Avery Mem., Hartford, Conn.; Am. Embassy, Paris; BM; Detroit Inst. A.; Wiggins Coll., Boston; Ann Arbor AA; Liege Mus., and others. *Exhibited*: PAFA, 1916-1928; CGA, 1916-1922;

Chicago Soc. Et., 1921-1930; SAGA, annually; Mystic AA, annually; MMA; Lyman Allyn Mus., 1956 (one-man). *Positions*: Prof. Emeritus A., Connecticut Col., New London, Conn., 1954- ; Cur., Lyman Allyn Mus., New London, Conn.; Member, Standing Comm. Artists Oil Paints, Bureau of Standards, Dept. Commerce; A. Lecturer, Newton College, 1958-59.

LOGGIE, HELEN A.—*Etcher*
2203 Utter St., Bellingham, Wash.; s. Orcas Island, Wash.

B. Bellingham, Wash. *Studied*: Smith Col.; ASL, and with John Taylor Arms, Mahonri Young. *Member*: ANA; SAGA; Cal. Pr. M.; Meriden A. & Crafts; Academic A.; Conn. Acad. FA; Cal. Soc. Et.; Northwest Pr. M.; Audubon A.; Phila. WC Cl.; Albany Pr. Cl.; Chicago Soc. Et.; Boston Soc. Indp. A. *Awards*: prizes, Albany Pr. Cl., 1953; Fla. Southern Col., 1952; NAD, 1955; Northwest Pr. M., 1939; LC, 1943; Pacific Northwest A. & Crafts Assn., 1950. *Work*: Univ. Nebraska; LC; Mus. FA of Houston; SAM; Western Wash. Col. of Edu.; Springfield Mus. A.; LC; MMA; Pa. State Univ.; Nat. Mus., Stockholm; Glasgow Univ., Scotland; British Mus., England; Lyman Allyn Mus.; PMA; IBM; Albany Inst. Hist. & A. *Exhibited*: NAD; SAGA; PAFA; Phila. Pr. Cl.; Denver A. Mus.; SAM; Cal. Soc. Et.; Southern Pr. M.; Albany Inst. Hist. & A.; Albany Pr. Cl.; San F. AA; SFMA; Carnegie Inst.; WMAA; LC; Audubon A.; Phila. WC Cl.; Laguna Beach AA; Chicago Soc. Et.; Wichita AA; Northwest Pr. M.; NAD; Fla. Southern Col.; L. D. M. Sweat Mem. Mus.; AFA travel. exh.; Am. Acad. A. & Let; Smithsonian Inst. Travel. exh.; London, England; Rochester Pr. Cl.; Colby Col.; Fairfield (Conn.) Pub. Lib.; New Britain Mus.; Academic A.; Boston Soc. Indp. A.; Conn. Acad. FA; Boston Pr. M.; Meriden A. & Crafts; Wash. WC Cl.; Henry Gal., Univ. Washington; Cal. Soc. Pr. M.; Norfolk Mus. A.; Phila. Sketch Cl.; Hunterdon County A. Center; Los A. Mus. A.; AIC; CGA; Buffalo Pr. Cl., and many others. (Exh. dates 1930-1958.)

LOHR, KATHRYN LAVINA—*Painter, T.*
911 Austin St.; h. 401 Glenwood Ave., Johnstown, Pa.

B. Johnstown, Pa., Aug. 17, 1912. *Studied*: Johnstown AI; Univ. Pittsburgh; Indiana State T. Col., B.S. in Edu.; St. Francis Col.; Pa. State Col., and with Orval Kipp, Ralph Pearson. *Member*: NAWA; AAPL; Assoc. A. Pittsburgh; All. A. Johnstown; Eastern AA; Pa. A. Edu. Assn.; Nat. A. Edu. Assn.; New Orleans AA; Asheville A. Gld. *Awards*: prizes, All. A. Johnstown, 1940, 1942-1945; Cambria County Fair, 1937; FA Cl., Johnstown, 1938; AAPL, 1949, 1950; Golden Triangle A., 1948; "Teacher of the Year" award, Pa. State Univ., 1952; gold pin, AAPL, 1949. *Work*: State T. Col., Indiana, Pa.; U.S. Veteran's Hospital, Aspinwall, Reading, Pa.; Univ. Pittsburgh; Lebanon Valley Veteran's Hospital. *Position*: Pa. Dir., Am. A. Week, 1947-56.*

LOHSE, WILLIS R.—*Designer, I.*
245 East 37th St., New York 16, N.Y.

B. Dresden, Germany, Jan. 30, 1890. *Member*: SI; AWCS; MModA. Specialty, black and white illus.*

LOMBARDO, JOSEF VINCENT—
Educator, P., W., L.
100-11 70th Ave., Forest Hills 75, N.Y.

B. New York, N.Y., Nov. 11, 1908. *Studied*: Assoc. A.; CUASch.; Royal Acad. FA, Florence, Italy; N.Y. Univ., B.F.A., B.A.; Columbia Univ., M.A., Ph.D.; Florence, Litt. D.; Villanova Univ., LL.D. *Member*: AFA; Nat. Edu. Assn.; Am. Assn. Univ. Prof.; Eastern AA; Nat. A. Edu. Assn.; Inst. Int. Edu. *Awards*: Carnegie scholarship; gold medal, Univ. medal, Univ. Florence; F., Royal Acad. FA, Florence, Italy; scholarships, Columbia Univ. Author: "Santa Maria del Fiore: Arnolfo di Cambio," 1934; "Attilio Piccirilli, Life of an American Sculptor," 1944; "Chaim Gross, Sculptor," 1949; Co-author: "Engineering Drawing," 1953, rev. ed. 1956 (Chinese ed. 1959). Lectures: Modern Art in Italy. *Positions*: Chm. A. Dept., Queens Col., 1938-42; Columbia Univ., 1946-49; N.Y.Univ., 1944; Queens Col., 1938- . Chm., Adv. Com. FA, Carlton Publ. Corp.; A. Consultant, Prang Company Publ.; Memb. Adv. Com. on Schools, Borough Pres. of Queens, N.Y.

SCHAEFFER GALLERIES

•

PAINTINGS

and

DRAWINGS

•

983 PARK AVENUE

NEW YORK 28

Tel. LEhigh 5-6410

LO MEDICO, THOMAS G.—*Sculptor*

50 East 42nd St., New York, N.Y.; also 61 Main St., Tappan, N.Y.

B. New York, N.Y., July 11, 1904. *Studied*: BAID. *Member*: F., NSS; S. Gld.; All. A. Am.; Arch. Lg.; F., Am. Numismatic Soc. *Awards*: Citation, 1948, awards, 1949, 1952; Saltus medal, Am. Numismatic Soc., 1956. *Work*: panels, groups, medals, trophies: USPO, Wilmington, N.C.; Crooksville, Ohio; WFNY 1939; Herbert Adams Mem. Award Medal, NSS; Soc. Medalists; designed, Laker Award for Laker Fnd.; Walter W. Moyer Mem.; Walter E. Otto trophy; "Hall of Fame Tablet" for Popular Mechanics; Public Service Award of Inst. of Life Insurance; 6 statues for the National Shrine of the Immaculate Conception, Wash., D.C.; Univ. Puerto Rico medal; panels, Court House, Wilmington, N.C. *Exhibited*: MMA; Mus. Natural Hist., N.Y.; WMAA; PAFA; NAD; SC; Arch. Lg., and many others.

LONERGAN, JOHN—
Lithographer, Ser., P., C., W., T.

651 East 14th St., New York 9, N.Y.

B. Troy, N.Y., Jan. 15, 1897. *Studied*: Ecole des Beaux-Arts, Paris; ASL; & with Pierre Vignon. *Member*: An Am. Group. *Awards*: prize, Am. A. Cong., 1939; Roerich Mus., 1934; Phila. Graphic Soc., 1940; Nat. Contest of Int. Workers Order, Brooklyn, N.Y., 1940. *Work*: Tucson (Ariz.) Mus.; Phillips Acad., Andover, Mass.; MMA; Princeton Univ. *Exhibited*: WMAA, 1941; Assoc. Am. A., 1941, 1942; MMA, 1942; one-man exh.; ACA Gal., 1938-1940; Ferargil Gal., 1943. Author: "Techniques and Materials of Gouache Painting," 1939. *Position*: Instr., Friends Seminary, N.Y.; Greenwich House, New York, N.Y.

LONEY, DORIS HOWARD (Mrs.)—*Painter, T.*

2134 North Alvernon Way, Tucson, Ariz.

B. Everett, Wash., Jan. 24, 1902. *Studied*: Univ. Washington, B.A.; ASL, with Robert Brackman, Yasuo Kuniyoshi; Farnsworth Sch. A.; Scripps Col. Grad. A. Dept., and with Millard Sheets, Fletcher Martin, Dong Kingman. *Member*: ASL; Pen & Brush Cl., and other local A. Assns. *Awards*: prizes, SAM, 1950; Arrow Head Show, Duluth, Minn., 1948-1950, 1958; Tri-State Fair, Superior, Wis., 1948-1950; other prizes in Tucson, Ariz. *Work*: Ports.: Wisconsin State College, Superior, Wis.; First Nat. Bank, Superior, Wis., and many portraits of prominent persons, 1945-1958. *Exhibited*: SAM, 1950; Sarasota AA, 1947-1949, 1951, 1957; Minn. State Fair, 1948; Tri-State Fair, Superior, Wis., 1948-1950; Arizona State Fair, 1952, 1953, 1958; Arrow Head Show, Duluth; Tucson FA Assn., e.c.; one-man: 7 one-man exhs. in Superior, Wis.; Duluth, Minn.; Everett, Wash.; Tucson, Ariz.

LONG, FRANK WEATHERS—*Painter, Eng., C., L.*

Berea, Ky.; and 609 South First St., Gallup, N.M.

B. Knoxville, Tenn., May 7, 1906. *Studied*: AIC; N.M. State T. Col.; PAFA; Julian Acad., Paris, France. *Member*: Southern Highlanders Handicraft Gld. *Work*: IBM Coll.; Berea Col. Coll.; murals, Univ. Kentucky; Davidson (N.C.) Col.; USPO, Berea, Morehead, Louisville, Ky.; Drumright, Okla.; Crawfordsville, Ind.; Hagerstown, Md. *Exhibited*: WFNY 1939; GGE, 1939; AFA traveling exh.; IBM traveling exh. to South America; one-man exh.: Speed Mem. Mus., 1940; Berea Col., 1938-1940; Ashland (Ky.) AA, 1939. Author, I., "Herakles: The Twelve Labors," 1931 (wood engravings). *Position*: Supv. A. & Crafts Program, for Indian A. & Crafts Bd., U.S. Dept. of Interior, Juneau, Alaska, 1951-1957; same position, at present, covering the Southwest, U.S.A.

LONG, R(OBERT) D(ICKSON)—*Painter, C., L.*

108 Ramsey Ave., Carnegie, Pa.

B. Pittsburgh, Pa., June 18, 1884. *Member*: Assoc. A. Pittsburgh; A. & Crafts Center, Pittsburgh. *Work*: Pittsburgh, Carnegie, Forest Hills, Latrobe, Greensburg H.S., and in many private coll. in Western Pa. *Exhibited*: PAFA, 1931; CM, 1931; Assoc. A. Pittsburgh, annually; Carnegie Inst., 1926- ; Terry AI, 1952.*

LONG, SCOTT—*Cartoonist*

Minneapolis Tribune; h. 4501 Dupont Ave. South, Minneapolis, Minn.

B. Evanston, Ill., Feb. 24, 1917. *Studied*: Harvard Col., A.B. *Member*: Am. Assn. Editorial Cartoonists; Nat. Cartoonists Soc. *Awards*: Page One Award, 1950-1954; Nat. Headliners Award, 1954; Freedoms Foundation Award, 1949; Christopher Award, 1953; Sigma Delta Chi national award, 1957. *Position*: Cart., Minneapolis Tribune, Minneapolis, Minn.

LONG, WALTER KINSCELLA—
Museum Director, P., S., Des., T.

Cayuga Museum of Art; h. 10 Nelson St., Auburn, N.Y.

B. Auburn, N.Y., Feb. 2, 1904. *Studied*: Syracuse Univ., B.F.A., M.F.A. *Member*: F., Royal Soc. A., London; IDI. *Awards*: F., Mus. Assn., Rochester Mus. A. & Sciences. *Work*: paintings: Syracuse Mus. FA; sc., Univ. Florida Bldgs.; WFNY 1939; church murals; portraits privately owned; City of Auburn Civic Award medal; Syracuse Univ. School of Journalism. *Exhibited*: Syracuse Mus. FA; Rochester Mem. A. Gal. Editor, Archaeological Soc. of Central N.Y. Bulletin. Lectures: Art Appreciation; World Art; History of Art, etc., to civic groups, museums, schools, study groups. Arranged exhibitions: "Homespun Art"; "Shoes Thru the Ages"; "Cayuga County Inventions," and others. *Position*: Dir., Cayuga Museum of Hist. & A., Auburn, N.Y.; Cayuga County Historian; Instr., Basic Art & Art Appreciation, Auburn Community College; Sec.-Treas., Northeast Mus. Conf., Dir., Finger Lakes AA; Dir., Instrument Research Inst.

LONGACRE, MARGARET GRUEN (Mrs. J. J., IV)—
Etcher, Lith., L.

3460 Oxford Terrace, Cincinnati 20, Ohio

B. Cincinnati, Ohio, Nov. 21, 1910. *Studied*: Univ. Cincinnati, B.A.; Cincinnati A. Acad.; & with E. T. Hurley; and in Paris, France and Lausanne, Switzerland. *Member*: New Orleans AA; Springfield A. Lg.; Ohio Pr. M.; New England Pr. Assn.; Am. Color Pr. Soc.; Wash. WC Cl.; Soc. Min. P., Gravers & S.; Woman's AC, Mus. Assn.. A. Circle, Pr. Soc., all of Cincinnati. *Awards*: prizes, Lib. Cong., 1943; Cincinnati Crafters, 1950, 1952; Cincinnati Woman's Cl., 1951, 1953, 1955, 1956; Wash. Min. P. & Gr. Soc., 1952, 1954, 1958; Pan-Am. Exh., 1949; Print of the Year, Mass., 1943; CM, 1944; CMA, 1941. *Exhibited*: NAD, 1941, 1943-1958; Ohio Pr.M., 1938-1958; Northwest Pr.M., 1941, 1942; Phila. Pr. Cl., 1941, 1942, 1944-1946; Boston Soc. Indp. A., 1941; Conn. Acad. FA, 1941-1943, 1945; Springfield A. Lg., 1941-1946; Oakland A. Gal., 1941, 1945; PAFA, 1941; SAGA, 1942-1945; New England Pr. Assn., 1941; San F. AA, 1942, 1943; CGA, 1942-1946; New Haven Paint & Clay Cl., 1942, 1944; Am. Color Pr. Soc., 1942-1944; Denver A. Mus., 1942-1944; MMA, 1942, 1943; Texas FA Assn., 1943, 1944; Lib.Cong., 1943-1958; Laguna Beach AA, 1942-1944; Mint Mus. A., 1943-1946; New Orleans AA, 1944-1958; CM, 1940-1958; Audubon A., 1945; SFMA, 1941; Balt. WC Cl., 1942; one-man exh.: Loring Andrews Gal., 1942, 1946; Town Cl. Gals., 1959, and others; private exhs.: Oxford, England, 1945, 1955; Geneva and Zurich, Switzerland, 1955; Sao Paulo, Brazil, 1956. Lectures: "The Making of Etchings and Drypoints"; "The Graphic Arts and Artists Through the Ages"; "The Symphony of Art and Music."

LONGLEY, BERNIQUE—*Painter, C.*

427 Camino Del Monte Sol, Santa Fe, N.M.

B. Moline, Ill., Sept. 27, 1923. *Studied*: AIC, and with Francis Chapin, Edouard Chassaing. *Award*: Lathrop traveling scholarship, AIC, 1945. *Work*: Mus. New Mexico, Santa Fe; and in private colls. *Exhibited*: AIC, 1948; Denver A. Mus., 1948, 1952; Mus. New Mexico, 1949-1958; one-man: Van Dieman-Lilienfeld Gal., N.Y., 1953; Denver A. Mus., 1952-1955; SFMA, 1955; Santa Fe, 1950-1958; San Francisco, 1955, 1956.

LONGLEY, EVELYN L(OUISE)—
Painter, I., Comm. A., T., L.

Bear Skin Neck, Rockport, Mass.; also, 7439 1st Way North, St. Petersburg 3, Fla.

B. Somerville, Mass., May 15, 1920. *Studied*: Child-Walker Sch. Des., Boston, Mass.; P. G. Stuart Sch., Des. Dept., and with Albert F. Jacobson, Lawrence Beall Smith, Arthur T. Lougee, Theodore Carl Muller, Arnold Geissbuhler, Joseph Hudnut. *Member*: Nat. Lg. Am. Pen Women; Rockport AA; North Shore AA; Boston Soc. Indp. A.; St. Petersburg A. Cl. (Pres. 1954-55, 1955-56);

Fla. West Coast A. Center; Creative A. Group of Tampa; Fla. Fed. A. *Awards*: prizes, Royall House, Medford, Mass., 1947, 1948, 1950, 1951; Nat. Lg. Am. Pen Women, 1954, 1956; Fla. Fed. A., 1956, 1957. *Work*: The James Wallace Longley Mem., Christ Methodist Church, St. Petersburg; World War II Mem., Edward Peterson Post #98, Am. Legion (14 ports. war dead), Rockport, Mass.; five ports. of interiors of Beauport Mus., Gloucester, Mass. *Exhibited*: Nat. Lg. Am. Pen Women, 1954, 1956; Sweat Mem. Mus., Portland, Me., 1958; Jordan Marsh, Boston, 1943, 1944, 1946; Harvard Univ., 1941; Jacksonville Mus. A., 1953; Norton Gal. A., 1956; Miami Beach A. Center, 1955; Rockport AA, 1940-1957; North Shore AA, 1943-1957, and others. One-man: Bear Skin Neck A. Gal., 1938; Rockport AA, 1946, 1948, 1951, 1954; St. Petersburg A. Cl., 1951; Eastman Mem. House, So. Berwick, Me., 1939. Illus. for Boston Herald-Traveler, Globe and Post; Holiday; Field & Stream magazines. *Positions*: Asst. A. Dir., R.H. White Co., Boston, 1941; Indst. Illus., Army-Navy Ordinance, 1942-45; A. Supv., Chapel Hill Sch., Waltham, Mass., 1945-46; Instr. own summer school, Rockport, 1936-54; A. Dir., Safety Harbor Spa, Safety Harbor, Fla., 1957-58.

LONGMAN, LESTER D.—*Educator, L., W.*

University of California, Los Angeles 24, Cal.; h. 718 Enchanted Way, Pacific Palisades, Cal.

B. Harrison, Ohio, Aug. 27, 1905. *Studied*: Oberlin Col., A.B., M.A.; Princeton Univ., M.F.A., Ph.D.; Harvard Univ. *Member*: Am. Soc. for Aesthetics; Midwestern Col. A. Conf.; CAA. *Awards*: Phi Beta Kappa, Oberlin Col.; Carnegie F., Princeton Univ., 1928-29, 1929-30; F., Am. Council of Learned Soc. for research in Europe, 1930-31; Fulbright Research F., Italy, 1952-53; Hon. L.H.D., Iowa Wesleyan Col., 1955. Author: "History and Application of Art"; "Toward General Education." Contributor to: Art Bulletin; College Art Journal; Journal of Aesthetics and Art Criticism; Art News, etc. Former Ed., Parnassus. Lectures in various universities and museums on Modern Art, Aesthetics and Art Criticisms, etc. *Position*: Hd. A. Dept., Prof. A. Hist., Univ. of Iowa, Iowa City, Iowa, 1936-1958; Chm. A. Dept., University of California, Los Angeles, Cal., 1958- .

LONGSTREET, STEPHEN—
Painter, S., T., Cr., W., L.

610 North Elm Dr., Beverly Hills, Cal.

B. New York, N.Y., Apr. 18, 1907. *Studied*: Rutgers Univ.; N.Y. Sch. F. & App. A., and with Bonnard, Tanguy. *Member*: Functionist West; Los A. AA (Bd. Dir.); Acad. Motion Picture Arts & Sciences. *Awards*: gold medal, Photoplay Magazine, 1948; Billboard-Donaldson medal, 1948; Stafford medal, London, 1946; Bowman prize, 1948. *Work*: Univ. Arizona; Studebaker Mus.; Los A. AA; UCLA; Scripps Col.; Los A. Mus. A.; Rand Mus., London; City Col., Los A.; murals, Winick Camp, Pittsfield, Mass.; Church of Christ, Phila., Pa.; Army Air Force Room, England, and other work in private colls. *Exhibited*: Functionist West, Los A.; one-man: Univ. Arizona, 1953; Robles Gal., 1945-1947, 1950, 1953-1956; UCLA; Univ. So. California; SFMA; Los A. Mus. A., and others. Author of more than 40 books including "The Pedlocks," 1951; "The World Revisited," 1953; "Man of Montmartre," 1957; "The Burning Man," 1958; "The Lion at Morning," 1956; "The Real Jazz Old and New," 1956; "The Lexicon of Jazz," 1957, many motion picture stories and plays. Illus., "Last Man Around the World"; "Nine Lives with Grandfather"; "Chico Goes to the Wars"; "Boy in the Model-T," and others. Contributor articles and cartoons to Gourmet magazine; Life; Judge; Colliers; Sat. Eve. Post; New Yorker; College Humor, etc. *Position*: Staff L., Los A. AA, 1950-56; Contributing A. Ed., Gourmet Magazine, 1940-59; A. Cr., Los Angeles Free Press, 1955-56; former Editor on Time Magazine and Saturday Review.

LOOMER, GIFFORD C.—*Painter, E., S.*

Art Department, Western Illinois University; h. 227 Western Ave., Macomb, Ill.

B. Millard, Wis., Nov. 29, 1916. *Studied*: Iowa State T. Col., B.A.; Columbia Univ., M.A.; Univ. Wisconsin, Ph.D. *Member*: NEA; NAEA; Western AA; Illinois A. Edu. Assn. *Work*: mural, lobby of Student Union, Western Illinois Univ. *Exhibited*: Faculty Exhibitions at Muncie, Ind., and Charleston, Ill. *Position*: Hd., A. Dept., Western Illinois University, Macomb, Ill.

PORTRAITS, INC.
PORTRAIT CENTER OF AMERICA
136 EAST 57th STREET, NEW YORK 22, NEW YORK

LOOMIS, KENNETH BRADLEY—*Educator, P.*

2202 Fowler Dr., Denton, Tex.

B. Steubenville, Ohio, Aug. 25, 1900. *Studied*: AIC; NAD; ASL; BAID; Univ. Toledo, Ph.B.; Univ. Iowa, M.A. *Member*: NSMP; Westchester County Hist. Soc. *Awards*: med., BAID, 1933; prizes, Butler AI, 1945; med., Toledo Mus. A., 1945; Illinois A. Exh., 1945; Texas FA Assn., 1954. *Work*: Illinois Wesleyan Univ.; murals, Peddie Sch.; Huron H.S.; Tarrytown H.S.; Univ. Georgia; Univ. Toledo; Texas State Col. for Women. *Exhibited*: Arch.L., 1930-1932; NSMP, 1936; AIC, 1945; Butler AI, 1943-1945; Kansas City AI, 1941; Toledo Mus. A., 1944, 1945; Texas General, 1948-55; Milwaukee AI, 1946; Illinois A. Exh., 1945. *Position*: Dean Col. FA, Prof., Dir. Dept. A., Texas Womans University, Denton, Tex., 1948- .

LOOMIS, LILLIAN (ANDERSON)—*Designer, P.*

International Business Machines Corp.; h. Woodstock, N.Y.

B. Peitaiho, North China, July 29, 1908. *Studied*: Mass. Sch. A., Boston, and with Alice B. Tufts, Marion Huse, Guy Wiggins, Eliot O'Hara. *Member*: Dutchess County AA; Hudson Valley AA; Woodstock Gld. Craftsmen. *Work*: Central Hudson Gas & Electric Co., Poughkeepsie, N.Y.; murals, in private homes. *Exhibited*: NAWA, 1942; Dutchess County AA, 1942 (one-man), and others; Fifteen Gal., 1941; AWS, 1941; Morton Gal., 1941; Vendome Gal., 1941; Hudson Highlands Exh., Newburgh, N.Y.; Hudson Valley AA, 1951-1954; IBM A. Cl., 1951-1955 (1954 one-man); IBM, N.Y., 1954, 1955; Oakwood Sch., Poughkeepsie, 1954 (one-man). Lectures: "How to Paint a Watercolor." *Position*: Tech. I., IBM Corp., Kingston, N.Y., 1942- ; Instr., Dept. Adult Edu., Poughkeepsie and New Paltz, N.Y.

LOPEZ, RHODA LeBLANC—*Craftsman, T., Medical I.*

2998 Geddes Ave., Ann Arbor, Mich.

B. Detroit, Mich., Mar. 16, 1912. *Studied*: Wayne Univ.; Univ. Michigan; Cranbrook Acad. A.; Claremont Col., Claremont, Cal., and special work with Maija Grotell, Cranbrook. *Member*: Ann Arbor Potters Gld.; Ann Arbor AA. *Work*: Univ. Wisconsin; Claremont Col. *Exhibited*: Cranbrook Acad. A., 1951; Scripps Col., 1955; Syracuse Mus. FA, 1949-1952; Michigan A.-Craftsmen, 1949-1958; Ceramic Exh. (with the late Carlos Lopez) 2-man: Detroit, Chicago, Claremont Col., Univ. Wisconsin, 1949-1952; Ann Arbor Potters Gld., 1955; Alumni Exh., Cranbrook Acad. A., 1954; Los A. County Fair, 1952, 1954, 1955. Contributor illus. to Medical Journals, Teaching Manuals (art as applied to medicine). *Position*: Instr., Potters Gld., 1950- ; A., Univ. Michigan Medical School, Ann Arbor, Mich., 1953- .

LOPEZ-REY, JOSE—*Educator, W., L.*

Institute of Fine Arts, 17 East 80th St.; h. 5 Peter Cooper Rd., New York 10, N.Y.

B. Madrid, Spain, May 14, 1905. *Studied*: Univ. Madrid, B.A., M.A., Ph.D.; Univ. Florence; Univ. Vienna. *Member*: CAA; corr. member, Hispanic Soc. Am. Author: "Antonio del Pollaiuolo y el fin del 'Quatrocento'," 1935; "Realismo e impresionismo en las artes figurativas espanolas del siglo XIX," 1937; "Goya y el mundo a su alrededor," 1947; "Francisco de Goya," 1950; "Goya's Caprichos: Beauty, Reason and Caricature," 1952; "A Cycle of Goya's Drawings: The Expression of Truth and Liberty," 1956; "Velazquez: A Catalogue Raisonné of the Pictures and Drawings" by A.L. Mayer, Revised Ed. with an introductory study by José López-Rey, 1959-60. Contributor to leading art magazines in U.S. and abroad, with articles on aesthetic criticism of old and 20th-century masters. *Positions*: Prof., Univ. Madrid, 1932-39; Advisor FA to Spanish Ministry of Edu., 1933-39; L., Smith Col., 1940-47; L., Inst. FA, N.Y. Univ., 1944-51; Adjunct Prof., Inst. FA, New York, N.Y., 1951-53; Assoc. Prof., 1953- .

LORAN, ERLE—*Painter, E., W.*

10 Kenilworth Court, Berkeley 7, Cal.

B. Minneapolis, Minn., Oct. 3, 1905. *Studied*: Univ. Minnesota; Minneapolis Sch. A., with Cameron Booth. *Awards*: Paris prize, Chaloner F., 1926; Minn. A. Soc., 1924; Minneapolis Inst. A., 1925, 1931; Minn. State Fair, 1924, 1945, 1946; SFMA, 1942, 1944, 1945, 1950, 1952, 1954; Cal. WC Soc., 1947; Pepsi-Cola, 1948; Cal. State Fair, 1940, 1947-1950; Oakland A. Mus., 1937, 1942, 1944, 1945,

1956 (purchase). *Work*: SFMA; Denver A. Mus.; Univ. Minnesota; U.S. Treasury Dept., Wash., D.C.; San Diego AI; Univ. Utah; Schools in Cedar City, Utah; Santa Barbara Mus. A.; IBM. *Exhibited*: MModA traveling exh., 1933; Rockefeller Center, 1935; Colorado Springs FA Center, 1938; WMAA, 1937, 1941, 1944, 1948, 1951, 1952; AIC, 1933, 1938, 1939, 1941, 1943, 1944, 1946; Toledo Mus. A., 1943; Cal. PLH, 1945, 1946, 1948, 1951, 1952; PAFA, 1940, 1945; Chicago A. Cl., 1943; SFMA, 1936-1946, 1948-1952, 1954, 1955; Oakland A. Gal., 1936-1946; Cal. WC Soc., 1941-1946; Carnegie Inst., 1941; Univ. Illinois, 1949, 1951, 1953; MMA, 1951, 1953; Pepsi-Cola, 1946, 1948, 1949; Cranbrook Acad. A.; Stanford A. Gal., 1956; one-man: Kraushaar Gal., 1931; Viviano Gal., 1952, 1954; Dalzell Hatfield Gal., 1949; SFMA, 1952, and others. Author: "Cezanne's Composition," 6th printing, 1950. Contributor to The Arts; Am. Magazine of Art; Art News and others. *Position*: Prof. A., Dept. A., Univ. California, Berkeley, Cal.

LORD, DON W.—*Painter*

649 Downing Court, Erie, Pa.

B. Erie, Pa., Jan. 13, 1929. *Studied*: Cleveland Sch. A. *Awards*: prizes, A. Cl. of Erie, 1945-1948; CMA, 1948; Butler AI, 1948, 1955, 1957; Fed. Erie A., 1954, 1955 (purchase); Montpelier Seven States Exh., 1955; N.Y. Tri-State Exh., 1955; Butler AI, 1955 (purchase); Edinboro State T. Col., 1958; Warren A. Mus., 1957; Springfield Mus. A., 1957; El Paso A., 1958; Chautauqua, N.Y., 1958. *Work*: Butler AI; Fed. Erie A.; Edinboro State T. Col.; Warren A. Mus.; Springfield Mus. A.; School Dist. of Erie, and in many private colls. *Exhibited*: PAFA, 1954, 1955, 1957, 1958; NAD, 1949; Butler AI, 1947-1958; CMA, 1948; Miss. AA, 1947; Fed. Erie A., 1951-1955; N.Y. Tri-State Exh., 1955; Ohio WC Soc., 1955; Mint Mus. A.; Canton AI; Columbus Gal. FA; Ohio Univ.; Springfield Mus. A., 1957, 1958; Indiana State T. Col., 1957; Kent State Univ.; Audubon A., 1956; DMFA; Montclair A. Mus.; Norton Gal. A.; Univ. Alabama; Columbia Mus. A. *Position*: Pres., Fed. Erie A., 1951-56.

LORENZANI, ARTHUR E.—*Sculptor*

273 McClean Ave., Staten Island 5, N.Y.

B. Carrara, Italy, Feb. 12, 1886. *Studied*: Acad. A., Carrara, Italy. *Member*: F., NSS; All. A. Am.; AAPL; Staten Island Mus. *Awards*: Rome prize, Carrara, Italy, 1905; Intl. Sculpture prize, Parma, Italy. *Work*: Modern A. Gal., Carrara, Italy; Brookgreen Gardens, S.C. *Exhibited*: NAD; BMA; CM; Albright A. Gal.; Staten Island Mus.; SC; NAC; PAFA. *Position*: Instr., S., Staten Island Mus., Staten Island, N.Y.

LORING, PAULE STETSON—

Watercolorist, Des., Cart., I.

Providence Journal; h. Pleasant St., Wickford, North Kingstown, R.I.

B. Portland, Me., Mar. 24, 1899. *Member*: South County AA; Lymington Yacht Cl., England; 50 American Artists; Am. Assn. Editorial Cartoonists; F., Royal Soc. A., London, England. *Work*: Fla. Southern Col.; many cartoons in public and private coll. Contributor to Yachting Magazine, Yankee Magazine, Saltwater Sportsman Magazine. Illus., "Never Argue with the Tape," 1954; "Three Sides to the Sea," 1956. Cartoon reproduced in the American Peoples Encyclopedia Year Book, 1958. *Position*: Ed. Cart., Providence Sunday Journal, Providence Evening Bulletin; Consulting A. Ed., "Skipper" magazine.

LORNE, NAOMI—*Painter, W., L.*

124 East 24th St., New York 10, N.Y., and 8 East 23rd St., New York, N.Y.; h. 316 Beach 146th St., Rockaway Beach, N.Y.

B. New York, N.Y. *Studied*: City Col. of N.Y.; Hunter Col., and with A. T. Hibbard, George Bridgman, Frederick J. Waugh. *Member*: Audubon A.; NAWA; N.Y. Soc. Women A.; Nat. Soc. Painters in Casein; New Jersey P. & S. Soc.; Silvermine Gld. A.; AEA; Brooklyn Soc. A. *Awards*: medal, Audubon A., 1944, prize, 1947; Silvermine Gld. A., 1956; NAWA, 1956. *Work*: Staten Island Hospital; General Steel Corp.; Am. Cyanamid Co.; Ain-Harod Mus., Israel; Maryknoll T. Col. *Exhibited*: Vendome Gal., 1940 (one-man); BM; Arch. Lg.; NAC; NAD; Argent Gal.; Carnegie Inst.; WMAA; PAFA; N.Y. Pub. Lib.; Riverside Mus.; Am. Acad. A. & Let.; Albany Inst. Hist. & A.; Dartmouth Col.; Berkshire Mus.; Massillon Mus.; Canton AI; Butler AI; Pa. State Mus.; Illinois State Mus.; Richmond AA; Univ. Oklahoma; Mus. FA, Little Rock;

Fine Paintings
of All Schools

HIRSCHL & ADLER

alleries inc.

21 East 67th Street, New York 21   LE 5-8810

D U V E E N

Established 1869

MASTERPIECES OF

PAINTINGS · SCULPTURE

PORCELAIN · FURNITURE

TAPESTRIES

DUVEEN BROTHERS, Inc.

18 East 79th Street, New York 21, N. Y.

Univ. Colorado; Nelson Gal. A.; Elisabet Ney Mus.; High Mus. A.; Mun. A. Gal., Jackson, Miss.; Brooks Mem. Gal.; Rollins Col.; Clearwater Mus. A.; Lehigh Univ.; Decatur A. Center; Binghamton (N.Y.) Mus.; Stedelijke Mus., Holland; Switzerland, Greece and Belgium, 1957-58; traveling exhs., NAWA, Painters in Casein, Brooklyn Soc. A.; Art:USA, 1958; Springfield A. Mus.; Univ. Missouri; Southwestern State Col.; Okla. Col. for Women; Beaumont A. Mus.; Mills Col.; Howard Univ., etc., one-man: Wash., D.C.; Phila., Pa.; Stamford, Conn., and extensively in Canada. *Position*: Publ. Relations Dir. for numerous art societies; Member Com. of FA, Nat. Conf. of Christians and Jews.

LORRAINE, HELEN LOUISE—*Medical Illustrator*
5212 Sylvan Rd., Richmond 25, Va.

B. Webster Groves, Mo., June 23, 1892. *Studied*: Richmond Sch. A.; Johns Hopkins Medical Sch., Dept. A. as applied to Medicine. *Member*: Assn. Medical I.; Hon. memb. Medical A. Assn. of Great Britain; Hon. memb. Johns Hopkins Assn. Medical Illustrators. *Work*: Col. of Physicians, Phila., Pa. *Exhibited*: Richmond, Va. (Hist. of Medical Illustration in Va.); Southern Surgical Assn.; AMA Exh.; Med. AA. of Great Britain, London; Medical Soc. Va.; Exh. by Modern Medicine, of medical illus. I., numerous medical, surgical publications. *Position*: Hd., Medical Illus. Dept., St. Elizabeth's Hospital, Richmond, Va., 1915-1945; Freelance, 1945- .

LOTTERHOS, HELEN JAY—*Painter, T.*
1703 St. Ann St., Jackson 2, Miss.

B. McComb, Miss. *Studied*: Millsaps Col., B.A.; AIC, and with Marie A. Hull. *Member*: Mississippi AA. *Awards*: gold medal, 1940, prizes, 1936, 1949-1951, 1953, 1956, Mississippi AA; prizes, SSAL, 1944; Mississippi Col. WC Exh., 1955, and others. *Work*: Jackson Mun. A. Gal.; Miss. State Col. for Women; Miss. Col. *Exhibited*: Mississippi AA, annually from 1932; Nat. Exh. Am. A., N.Y., 1936-1938; New Orleans AA, 1935, 1936; New Orleans A. & Crafts Cl., 1948; Caller-Times Exh., Corpus Christi, Tex., 1945-1947; Memphis, 1946-1955; Southeastern Exh., Atlanta, 1947-1949, 1951, 1952; Ogunquit A. Center, 1955; SSAL, 1935-1947, and others.

LOUDEN, ADELAIDE BOLTON—*Writer, I.*
R.D. 2, Quakertown, Pa.

B. Philadelphia, Pa. *Studied*: Mt. Holyoke Col., B.A.; PAFA, with Henry McCarter. *Member*: F., PAFA; Phila. Plastic Cl. *Exhibited*: PAFA, 1936; Lehigh Univ., 1950; Phila. A. All. Author, I., "Historic Costumes," 1936. I., juvenile books.

LOUDEN, NORMAN P.—*Designer, L.*
R.D. 2, Quakertown, Pa.

B. Quakertown, Pa., Sept. 2, 1895. *Studied*: PAFA, with Henry McCarter. *Awards*: Cresson traveling scholarship, PAFA. *Exhibited*: Phila. A. All., 1921; PAFA, 1934, 1936; Lehigh Univ., 1950. Collaborated on "Historic Costumes," 1936. Lectures: History of Art. *Position*: Tech. Illus., Philco Corp., Philadelphia, Pa.

LOUDEN, ORREN R.—*Painter, W., L.*
2441 Oxford Ave., Cardiff-by-the-Sea, Cal.

B. Trenton, Ill., Apr. 24, 1903. *Studied*: George Washington Univ., Corcoran Sch. A.; ASL; Provincetown Sch. A.; Santa Clara Univ.; & with DuMond, Bridgman, Tucker, Benton. *Member*: Springfield AA; A. Council, San Diego. *Exhibited*: Progressive A., N.Y.; Am. Salon, N.Y.; Springfield AA; Georgetown Gal., Wash., D.C.; Ferguson Gal., La Jolla, Cal.; Village Sch. A. Gal., San Diego, Cal. Contributor to: Nat. Geographic magazine; American Motorist magazine. *Position*: Dir., Village Sch. A., San Diego, Cal., 1945-46; Dir., San Diego Sch. A., La Jolla, Cal.; Dir., Village Sch. A., Cardiff-by-the-Sea, Cal., at present; Corr., North County News & Oceanside Blade Tribune.

LOURIE, HERBERT S.—*Painter, E.*
Art Department, Elmira College, Elmira, N.Y.; h. 15 Monmouth Court, Brookline, Mass.

B. Boston, Mass., Dec. 26, 1923. *Studied*: Indiana Univ.; Yale Univ., B.F.A., M.F.A. *Member*: CAA; New Hamp-

shire AA. *Award*: prize, Currier Gal. A., 1955. *Exhibited*: Dartmouth Col.; Colby Junior Col.; Fitchburg A. Mus.; Keene State T. Col.; Phillips Exeter Acad.; N.H. Hist. Soc.; Currier Gal. A.; Inst. Contemp. A., Boston; R.I. Sch. Des. Mus.; deCordova & Dana Mus.; Univ. New Hampshire; Univ. Rhode Island; Springfield Mus. A.; Berkshire Mus.; Wadsworth Atheneum; Farnsworth Mus.; Rockport Soc. A.; Brookline A. Soc.; Boston A. Festival, and others. *Positions*: Asst. Prof. A., Nasson Col., Springvale, Me., 1952-55; Visiting I., Univ. New Hampshire, 1953-54; Instr., Univ. Rhode Island, 1956-58; Asst. Prof. A., Elmira College, Elmira, N.Y. at present.

LOVE, GEORGE PATERSON—*Painter, T.*
25 Homestead Ave., West Barrington, R.I.

B. Providence, R.I., Mar. 28, 1887. *Studied*: R.I.Sch.Des.; BMFA Sch.; & with Edmund Tarbell, Frank Benson. *Member*: Providence WC Cl.; R.I.Sch.Des. Alumni Assn. *Work*: Masonic Temple, Providence, R.I. *Exhibited*: NAD, 1941; Currier Gal. A., 1942, 1943; Providence AC; Boston AC; BMFA; R.I.Sch.Des.; Attleboro Lib.

LOVE, MRS. GEORGE P. *See Jones, Nancy*

LOVELL, TOM—*Illustrator*
Old Hill Rd., Westport, Conn.

B. New York, N.Y., Feb. 5, 1909. *Studied*: Syracuse Univ., B.A. *Member*: SI; SC. *Work*: U.S. Marine Corps. *Exhibited*: SI. Illus. for Cosmopolitan; McCalls; Ladies Home Journal; True; Good Housekeeping, and other national magazines.

LOVET-LORSKI, BORIS—*Sculptor*
131 East 69th St., New York 21, N.Y.; also Rome, Italy

B. Lithuania, Dec. 25, 1894. *Studied*: Acad. A., St. Petersburg, Russia. *Member*: ANA; NSS; Lotos Cl. *Awards*: Knight of the Legion of Honor, 1948. *Work*: Luxembourg Mus., Petit Palais, Bibliotheque Nationale, Paris, France; British Mus., London; MMA; Dumbarton Oaks; San Diego FA Assn.; Los A. Mus. A.; SAM; SFMA; City Hall, Decatur, Ill.; City of Paris, France; sculpture and mosaics for Chapel of American War Mem., Manila, Philippines. *Exhibited*: one-man exh. nationally.

LOVICK, ANNIE PESCUD (Mrs. H. J.)—*Painter*
2409 Glenwood Ave.; h. 540 North Person St., Raleigh, N.C.

B. Raleigh, N.C., Aug. 5, 1882. *Studied*: with Greacen, Hilderbrandt, Mora, Brackman, Cole and others. *Member*: North Carolina State A. Soc.; Studio Gld., N.Y. *Work*: portraits, Nat. Mus.; Guilford (N.C.) Court House; altarpiece, children's room, Christ Church, New Bern, N.C. *Exhibited*: Mint Mus. A.; Winston-Salem, N.C.; Min. P. & S., Wash., D.C.; CGA; Raleigh, N.C.; G.W.V. Smith Mus., 1953; Ligoa Duncan Gal. A.; New York and Paris, 1958-59; Springfield A. Mus.; North Carolina Fed. Women's Cl., and others.

LOVINS, HENRY—*Mural Painter, Des., W., E., L., C.*
2025 North Highland Ave., Hollywood 28, Cal.

B. New York, N.Y., Mar. 12, 1883. *Studied*: Col. City of N.Y., B.S.; N.Y.Sch. F. & App. A. Also with Jean Mannheim, William M. Chase, Robert Henri, William Keith, Edgar L. Hewitt. *Member*: Cal. A. Cl.; Los A. AA; NSMP; San Diego Mus. of Man; Laguna Beach AA; Los A. Mus. A. *Work*: murals, Southwest Mus., Los A.; San Diego Mus. of Man; Mus. New Mexico, Santa Fe, and other work in galleries and private collections. *Exhibited*: nationally. Specializing in reviving the art of Toltec, Aztec and Mayan cultures applicable to modern decoration. Contributor to Art & Architecture and other magazines. *Position*: Vice-Pres., Cal. Assn. of Vocational Schs.; Fndr., Dir., Hollywood A. Center Sch., Hollywood, Cal.

LOW, JOSEPH—*Graphic Artist, Des.*
Eden Hill Rd., Newtown, Conn.

B. Coraopolis, Pa., Aug. 11, 1911. *Studied*: Univ. Illinois; ASL with George Grosz. *Member*: AIGA.

THE COMPLETE EXHIBITOR'S SERVICE

SHIPPING   PACKING   WAREHOUSING

FOR OPENINGS AND ITINERARIES

SPECIALISTS IN MOVING ART AND

SCIENTIFIC EXHIBITIONS

CO-ORDINATOR **ALL** FORMS TRANSPORTATION

LOCAL   NATIONWIDE   WORLDWIDE

MOVING VANS — STORAGE
Temperature controlled

Designers of VAN VAULTS for exhibitions

PACKING   WAREHOUSING

◆

SCHUMM TRAFFIC AGENCY, INC.
Transportation Consultants
25 Beaver Street
New York 4, N. Y.

WHitehall 4-9140   TWX NY 1-4661

LOW, SANFORD—Painter, E., Mus. Dir.

56 Lexington St., New Britain, Conn.; h. Southington, Conn.

B. Honolulu, Hawaii, Sept. 21, 1905. *Studied*: with Philip Hale, Pruett Carter, Henry Hunt Clark, Leslie Thompson. *Member*: AWS; SC; New Britain A. Lg.; Springfield A. Lg.; Conn. Acad. FA. *Awards*: prize, New Britain A. Lg., 1931, 1932; Sage-Allen award, Conn. WC Soc., 1956. *Work*: Avery Mem., Hartford, Conn.; Springfield Mus. FA; New Haven Paint & Clay Cl.; FMA; Mus. of the New Britain Inst.; murals, Hartford Fed. Savings & Loan Assn.; Phoenix State Bank & Trust Co., Hartford, Conn.; Burritt Mutual Savings Bank, New Britain, Conn., and in numerous hotels. *Position*: Hd. A. Dept., Loomis & Chaffee Schools, Windsor, Conn.; Dir., A. Mus. of the New Britain Inst., New Britain, Conn.

LOWE, EMILY (Mrs. Joe)—Painter

969 Madison Ave.; h. 785 Park Ave., New York 21, N.Y.

B. New York, N.Y., Jan. 8, 1902. *Studied*: Columbia Col.; N.Y. Univ.; Academie Julian, Paris, France; ASL; Hofstra Col.; Miami Univ., M.F.A., and with George Picken, Frank J. Reilly, Frank DuMond. *Member*: NAWA; AEA; ASL; Audubon A. (Dir.); Union des Femmes Peintres et Sculptors, Paris. *Work*: in private coll. in U.S., Canada, France. *Exhibited*: NAWA, 1952-1956; Salon d'Automne, 1949-1952; PAFA, 1953, 1954; Audubon A., 1954-1956; Exp. Mod. A., Paris, 1951; one-man: Paris, France, 1949, 1952; New York City, 1947, 1949, 1956; Syracuse Univ., 1950; Cornell Univ., 1953; Miami Univ., 1952. Sponsor of Emily Lowe Awards, a non-profit project of the Joe and Emily Lowe Fnd. Donor of Joe and Emily Lowe Art Gal., Univ. Miami; Lowe A. Center, Syracuse Univ.; art classes in Hudson Gld. Settlement House, New York, N.Y.; Forrest Settlement House, Bronx, N.Y.; art classes and "Camp on Wheels"; scholarships to France, Italy and Mexico. Memb. Adv. Council, CUASch., N.Y.; Pres., Joe and Emily Lowe Fnd.; Founder Emily Lowe Competition (annual).

LOWENFELD, VIKTOR—Educator, W., L.

Department of Art Education, Pennsylvania State University, University Park, Pa.; h. 728 Franklin St., State College, Pa.

B. Linz, Austria, Mar. 21, 1903. *Studied*: College of App. A., Vienna, M.A.; Acad. FA, Vienna; Univ. Vienna, Ed. D. *Member*: Nat. Com. on A. Edu.; Am. Soc. for Aesthetics (Bd. Memb.); NAEA (Research Bd.); Intl. Soc. of Edu. through Art; Intl. Fed. A. Edu.; Eastern AA. *Awards*: Citation, Congress of India, for outstanding educational achievement, 1934; Citation, for outstanding educational book, NEA, 1952 and by Enoch Pratt Library Research, 1957. *Author*: "Plastische Arbeiten Blinder," 1934; "The Nature of Creative Activity," 1938, London and 1939, New York rev. ed., 1952; "Your Child and His Art," 1954 (trans. into Swedish, Japanese, Hebrew, German, Spanish); "Creative and Mental Growth," 3rd rev., 1957; "Die Kunst des Kindes," 1957, and many others, 1937-57. Contributor of articles to educational journals and art magazines. *Positions*: Delegate to White House Conf., 1950 and to UNESCO, 1952; Adv. Committee to White House Conf., 1958; Prof. A. Edu., Hd. Dept. A. Edu., Pennsylvania State University, University Park, Pa., at present.

LOWRIE, AGNES POTTER—Commercial Artist, P.

20 Rawson Woods Circle, Cincinnati 20, Ohio

B. London, England, Oct. 31, 1892. *Studied*: Univ. Chicago, Ph.B.; N.Y. Sch. F. & App. A.; Minneapolis Sch. A.; AIC, and with Hawthorne, Breckenridge. *Member*: Chicago A. Cl.; Cincinnati Assn. Professional A.; Cincinnati Woman's A. Cl. *Awards*: prizes, AIC, 1929; Chicago A. Dir. Exh., 1954; medal, A. Dir. Cl., N.Y., 1955; Chicago Woman's A. Cl., 1932; CM, 1945; Cincinnati A. Dir. Exh., 1952, 1953. *Work*: paintings, Widdicomb Furniture Co., N.Y., Grand Rapids, Mich.; City of Chicago Mun. Coll.; FMA; Eli Lilly Co. Coll.; Bishop Bank, Honolulu. *Exhibited*: NAD, 1949; WMAA, 1952; one-man: Ferargil Gal., 1949; Loring Andrews Gal., Cincinnati, 1949; Hewitt Gal., N.Y., 1956.

LOXLEY, MRS. BENJAMIN RHEES. See Younglove, Ruth Ann

LOZAR, RAJKO—Museum Director

Rahr Civic Center and Public Museum; h. 610 North 8th St., Manitowoc, Wis.

B. Ljubljana, Yugoslavia, Aug. 29, 1904. *Studied*: Univ. of Ljubljana, B.A.; Univ. Vienna, M.A., Ph.D. *Member*: AAMus.; Midwest Mus. Conf.; Little Gal., Inc., Manitowoc, Wis. *Author*: "The Sculptor Franc Gorse," 1938; "Oeuvre-Catalog of the Brothers John and George Subic," 1938. Contributor to art magazines and newspapers. *Positions*: Cur., Nat. Mus., Ljubljana, Yugoslavia, 1928-40; Dir., Mus. Ethnology, Ljubljana, 1940-45; In charge of Exhibits, Dir., Rahr Civic Center and Public Mus., Manitowoc, Wis., at present.

LOZOWICK, LOUIS—Printmaker, P., W., I., L.

62 Massel Terrace, South Orange, N.J.

B. Russia, Dec. 10, 1892. *Studied*: Ohio State Univ., B.A.; NAD; & abroad. *Member*: An Am. Group; AEA; Assoc. A. New Jersey; Phila. WC Cl.; Audubon A.; Boston Pr. M. *Awards*: prizes, AIC, 1929; Phila. A. All., 1930; CMA print prize, 1930; Oakland A. Gal., 1946; Rochester Pr. Cl., 1948; BM, 1950; SAGA, 1951, 1957; Audubon A., 1954; DMFA, 1953; Creative Graphics, N.Y., 1958; Boston Pr. M. *Work*: WMAA; MMoDA; MMA; N.Y.Pub.Lib.; CMA; Lib. Cong.; PMA; CM; BMFA; Honolulu Acad. A.; Mus. FA of Houston; Los A. AA; Carnegie Inst.; Syracuse Mus. FA; Rochester Mem. A. Gal.; Newark Mus.; Victoria & Albert Mus., London; Mus. Western A., Moscow; Yale Univ.; Memphis (Tenn.) Mus.; murals, USPO, New York, N.Y. *Exhibited*: BM, 1926; Steinway Hall, 1926; MMoDA, 1943; WMAA, 1933, 1941; AIC, 1929; Carnegie Inst., 1930; CGA, 1932; WFNY 1939; MMA (AV), 1942; Pepsi-Cola, 1946; New Art Circle, 1926; Weyhe Gal., 1929, 1931, 1933, 1935; Grand Central A. Gal., 1930; Stendahl Gal., Los A., 1932; Courvoisier Gal., San F., 1932; Downtown Gal., 1929, 1930, 1931; An Am. Group, 1938-1941; PAFA, 1929; NAD, 1935; Audubon A.; SAGA; Conn. Acad. FA; Smithsonian Inst.; Am. Acad. A. & Let.; Birmingham Mus.; Montclair Mus.; Newark Mus. A.; Springfield (Mass.) A. Mus.; Tel-Aviv Mus., Israel, and in Paris; AEA. Co-Author: "Voices of October," 1930; Co-Editor, "America Today," 1936. *Author*: "Treasury of Drawings"; "Modern Russian Art"; "100 American Jewish Artists." Contributor to: Nation, Theatre Arts, New Masses, Hound and Horn, Encyclopaedia Americana, "Russian Art," etc., with articles on art & the theatre. Lectures: Evolution of Modern Art; Russian Art.

LUBAN, BORIS—Portrait Painter

Carnegie Hall, West 57th St.; h. 214 East 58th St., New York 22, N.Y.

B. Moscow, Russia, July 25, 1881. *Studied*: Royal Acad., Antwerp, Belgium; Royal Acad., Berlin, Germany; & with Leisticow, Berlin. *Work*: Harvard Univ.; Mitchell Field Airport; Columbia Univ.; Col. City of N.Y.; Erasmus Hall H.S., Brooklyn, N.Y.; Tilden H.S.; Manual Training H.S.; many portraits of prominent persons.*

LUBIN, JACK—Painter, T.

346 Livingston St.; h. 15 Butler Place, Brooklyn 38, N.Y.

B. Brooklyn, N.Y., Oct. 15, 1907. *Studied*: NAD, with Ivan Olinsky; ASL, with Mahonri Young. *Member*: NSMP. *Work*: Mint Mus. A.; CGA; murals, Statler Hotels, Dallas, Tex., Hartford, Conn., Wash., D.C.; Buffalo, N.Y., Hotel Penn, N.Y., Hotel Roosevelt, New Orleans; N.Y. Bd. Edu. P.S. #272, Brooklyn; Passaic Nat. Bank, N.J.; Church of the Little Flower, Brooklyn; mosaic mural, Morn'ngside Health Center, Harlem, N.Y.C., and others. *Exhibited*: Midtown Gal., 1933; Marquie Gal., 1949; Arch. Lg., 1956; BM, 1953, 1958; MMoDA, 1940; one-man: Mint Mus. A., Charlotte, N.C. *Position*: Instr., Inst. Des. & Constr., Brooklyn, N.Y.

LUCAS, BLANCHE WINGERT—Painter, T., W., L.

236 South 14th St., Allentown, Pa.

B. Alburtis, Pa., Mar. 7, 1888. *Studied*: Bloomsburg State T. Col.; Kutztown State T. Col.; N.Y. Univ., B.S.; Lehigh Univ., M.A.; and with Walter Baum; also with Franz Cizek, Vienna and Augustus John, London, England. *Member*: AAUW; Allentown Woman's Cl.; A.T. Gld., London; A. All.; British A. Gld. (Life). *Work*: in many private colls.; Everhart Mus. A.; Allentown Pub. Lib. and

Public Auction Sales • *September to June*

OLD MASTERS
MODERN AND OTHER PAINTINGS
DRAWINGS • PRINTS • SCULPTURES
CLASSICAL AND ORIENTAL ART

ALSO FINE FURNITURE • RUGS
TAPESTRIES AND WORKS OF ART
BIBELOTS • VALUABLE JEWELRY
RARE BOOKS AND MANUSCRIPTS
OTHER LITERARY MATERIAL

From Distinguished Sources

Monthly *Bulletin* mailed free on request

PARKE-BERNET GALLERIES • Inc

980 MADISON AVENUE • NEW YORK 21

WATSON-GUPTILL PUBLICATIONS, INC.

• publisher of the magazine AMERICAN ARTIST—largest readership and circulation (ABC) in the world among art teachers, art students, and practicing artists.

• publisher of famous technical and inspirational ART BOOKS.

• send for sample copy of AMERICAN ARTIST and latest check list of ART BOOKS.

WATSON-GUPTILL PUBLICATIONS, INC.
24 West 40th Street, New York 18, N. Y.

Hospital; New Milford, Conn. and Galax, Va. hospitals. *Exhibited*: in college galleries and art museum education galleries, nationally, 1936-1957. Specializes in Child Art with exhibitions in England, Holland, Belgium, France, Switzerland, Germany, Austria, Scotland and Italy. Lectures: Art in Our Public Schools. Contributor to School Arts magazine and to many school journals; Am. Poetry Magazine; Ladies Home Journal, and others. *Position*: A. Supv., Allentown Pub. Schs., 1917-53; Consultant, Adv., Victoria & Albert Mus., London, England, 1935-36 (Retired).

LUCE, MOLLY (Mrs. Alan Burroughs)—Painter
　Three Ways, Little Compton, R.I.

B. Pittsburgh, Pa., Dec. 18, 1896. *Studied*: Wheaton Col.; ASL, with Kenneth Hayes Miller. *Work*: MMA; WMAA. *Exhibited*: CGA, 1939, 1943, 1945; PAFA, 1938-1943; Carnegie Inst., 1939, 1943, 1945; NAD, 1943, 1945; WMAA, 1938, 1940, 1943-1945; 1950; AIC, 1930-1932; GGE, 1939.

LUCHTEMEYER, EDWARD A.—Painter, Des., Comm. A.
　320 Georgia Ave., Melrose Park, Ft. Lauderdale, Fla.

B. St. Louis, Mo., Nov. 19, 1887. *Member*: Fla. Fed. A.; Broward A. Gld.; Am. A. All. of St. Louis; West Palm Beach A. Lg.; AAPL. *Awards*: prizes, Cal. A. Cl.; Fla. Southern Col.; Palm Beach A. Lg.; Harry Rich award, Miami. *Exhibited*: Oakland A. Mus.; Kansas City, Mo.; Springfield, Mo.; Little Rock, Ark.; Norton Gal. A.; West Palm Beach A. Lg.; Fla. Southern Col.; Memphis, Tenn.; Miami Beach A. Center; Stephens Hotel, Chicago; CAM; Delgado Mus. A.; Fla. Fed. A., Circuit Exh., 1955; Ogunquit A. Center; Washington Gal., Miami Beach, 1957 (one-man); Monday Cl., Webster Groves, Mo., 1945, 1952 (one-man), and others.

LUCIONI, LUIGI—Painter, Et.
　33 West 10th St., New York 11, N.Y.; h. Manchester Depot, Vt.

B. Malnate, Italy, Nov. 4, 1900. *Studied*: CUASch; NAD. *Member*: NA; SAE. *Awards*: Tiffany med., 1929; All. med. of honor, 1929; prizes, Carnegie Inst., 1939; CGA, 1939, 1941, 1949; Lib.Cong., 1946; Nat. Print Exh., 1947. *Work*: MMA; WMAA; Carnegie Inst.; PAFA; Lib.Cong.; Toledo Mus. A.; Denver A.Mus.; SAM; BM; Victoria & Albert Mus., London. *Exhibited*: NAD; CGA; Carnegie Inst.; PAFA; AIC; Toledo Mus. A.; Herron AI; PAFA; MMA; WMAA; Audubon A., etc.

LUCK, ROBERT HENRY—Art Administrator
　The American Federation of Arts, 1083 Fifth Ave., New York 28, N.Y.

B. Tonawanda, N.Y., Oct. 31, 1921. *Studied*: Albright A. Sch.; Univ. Buffalo, B.F.A.; Harvard Univ., M.A.; Instituti Meschini, Rome, Certif. *Member*: CAA; AAMus.; Cincinnati MacDowell Soc. Contributor to The Art Quarterly; Arts Digest. Lectures: "The Art of Egypt"; "The Child and His Art"; "Flowers in Art"; "Collectors and Collecting," etc., in museum galleries, to clubs, art students, universities and colleges. Exhibitions arranged with catalogues: "David Smith, Sculpture, Drawings, Graphics," 1954, CM; "Eterna Primavera: Young Italian Painters," 1954, CM; "Recent Acquisitions #8," 1955, CM; "The Interior Valley Painting Competition," 1955, CM; "The Edwin C. Shaw Collection of Paintings," 1955. Akron. *Position*: Instr., Toledo Mus. A., 1952-54; Cur., Contemporary A. Center, CM, 1954-55; Dir., Akron AI, Akron, Ohio, 1955-56; Dir., Telfair Academy Arts & Sciences, Savannah, Ga., 1956-1957; Special Representative, The American Federation of Arts, New York, N.Y., 1958- .

LUDEKENS, FRED—Illustrator, Des.
　Belvedere, Cal.

B. Hueneme, Cal., May 13, 1900. *Member*: SI; A. Dir. Cl., N.Y. & San F. *Exhibited*: Int. Gal., N.Y. (Contemporary Am. Illustration). I., "Ghost Town"; "The Ranch Book"; Contributor to: Saturday Evening Post, This Week, Fawcett Publ. *Positions*: Co-founder, V. Pres., Faculty, Famous Artists Schools, Westport, Conn.; Sr. Vice-Pres., Assoc. Creative Dir., Foote, Cone & Belding, New York, N.Y.

LUDEROWSKI, THEODORE EDWARD—
　Educator, Indst. Des., P.
　Packaging & Product Development Institute, 1077 Celestial St., Cincinnati 2, Ohio; h. R.R. #1, Belfast-Goshen Rd., Cozzadale, Ohio

B. New York, N.Y., Jan. 10, 1911. *Studied*: Columbia Univ.; Cranbrook Acad. A. *Award*: F., Cranbrook Acad. A. for study with Eliel Saarinen; prize, Michigan A. *Member*: IDI; Contemp. AI, Cincinnati; Cincinnati A. Cl.; Mich. Soc. A., Let. & Sc. *Work*: Detroit Inst. A.; and in private colls. *Exhibited*: Michigan Inst. A.; Birmingham Mus. A.; Univ. Michigan; Silvermine Gld. A.; Detroit Inst. A.; Cincinnati A. Cl.; MMoDA; one-man: Cranbrook Acad. A. Lectures: Basic Design; Furniture; Industrial Design. Reproductions of Houses, Industrial Design, Furniture, etc., in Arts & Architecture; Interiors; Industrial Design; Better Homes & Gardens and other trade journals and publications. *Positions*: Des., Eliel and Eero Saarinen; Hd., Des. Dept., Cranbrook Acad. A., Bloomfield Hills, Mich., 1948-56; Vice-Pres., Dir. of Des., Product & Packaging Design, Inc., Cincinnati, Ohio, at present.

LUDINS, EUGENE—Painter
　Woodstock, N.Y.

B. Mariupol, Russia, Mar. 23, 1904. *Studied*: ASL. *Member*: Woodstock AA. *Awards*: Temple medal, PAFA, 1948. *Work*: WMAA; Des Moines A. Center; Univ. Iowa. *Exhibited*: Carnegie Intl., 1956; PAFA; AIC; VMFA; WMAA; MMoDA; MMA; Cal. PLH; one-man: Des Moines A. Center; Assoc. Am. A.; Passedoit Gal. (7 exhs.). *Position*: Chm., Woodstock AA, 1955-56; Assoc. Prof. Painting, State Univ. Iowa, 1948- .

LUDINS, HANNAH S. See Small, Hannah S.

LUDINS, RYAH (Miss)—
　Painter, I., W., Gr., Des., T., L.
　222 West 23rd St., New York 11, N.Y.

Studied: Columbia Univ., B.S. in Edu.; ASL; with William S. Hayter and in Paris with Andre Lhote. *Member*: AEA. *Work*: CMA; Toledo Mus. A.; MMoDA; AIGA; N.Y. Pub. Lib.; Newark Pub. Lib.; murals, J. B. Kendall Co., Wash., D.C.; Bellevue Hospital, N.Y.; USPO, Nazareth, Pa.; Cortland, N.Y.; State Mus., Michoacan, Mexico. *Exhibited*: MMoDA; WMAA; Arch. Lg.; Downtown Gal.; Willard Gal.; Cal. PLH; CGA; Albright A. Gal.; CMA; FA Gal., Chicago; DMFA; Rochester Mem. A. Gal.; Phila. A. All.; Mexico City, Mexico, and abroad. *Position*: Instr., T. Col., Columbia Univ.; Ohio Univ., Athens, Ohio; and privately, New York and Putnam Valley, N.Y. (summers).*

LUELOFF, MARJORIE KALTENBACK—Painter, Des., L.
　7055 North River Rd., Milwaukee 17, Wis.

B. Kenosha, Wis., June 26, 1906. *Studied*: AIC; Univ. Wisconsin; with Hubert Ropp, John Carroll. *Member*: Wis. P. & S. Soc. (Bd. Dir.). *Awards*: prize, Milwaukee AI, 1940. *Exhibited*: Detroit Inst. A., 1935, 1937, 1939; Milwaukee AI, 1934, 1940, 1945, 1946; Madison A. Salon, 1936-1938.*

LUFFMAN, CHARLES E.—Painter
　10 Fourth St., South Orange, N.J.

B. London, England, Mar. 24, 1909. *Studied*: Newark Sch. A.; ASL; New Sch. for Social Research, and in Kyoto, Japan. *Member*: AWS; New Jersey WC Soc.; Wash. WC Cl. *Awards*: prizes, Greenwich Village A. Center, 1949; Bell Exh., 1951, 1952. *Exhibited*: AWS, 1943, 1944, 1946, 1949; Phila. WC Cl., 1941; N.J. State Exh., 1938, 1940, 1943, 1945, 1948, 1956; New Jersey WC Soc., 1950, 1951, 1954; Audubon A., 1948, 1957; Newark Mus., 1952; State Mus., Trenton, 1953; Montclair A. Mus., 1954; Riverside Mus., 1953; Wash. WC Cl., 1954, 1956, 1957; Art Centre of the Oranges, 1956; Long Beach (Cal.), 1958.

LUGANO, INES SOMENZINI (Mrs. G.)—
　Miniature and Portrait Painter
　1646 St. Andrew St., New Orleans, La.

B. Verretto, Pavia, Italy. *Studied*: Acad. FA, Pavia, Italy, and with Romeo Borgognoni. *Member*: New Orleans AA; Pa. Soc. Min. P. *Awards*: silver medal, Nat. Exh., Milano, Italy; medal of honor, Cal. Soc. Min. P., 1935; prizes, New Orleans AA, 1939. *Work*: Tulane Univ.; Delgado Mus. A.

No. 71. Cover by Delessert · Special number: Present-day graphic art in France · Advertising art · Church art · Ceramics and small sculpture by painters · New ceramics of Picasso · Tapestry · Stage Design · Air France

No. 72. Cover by Piatti · 3rd AGI exhibition · Swiss cartoonists · Balzac portraits by Picasso · Lester Rossin Assoc., artists' agency · Photography of Heinz Hajek-Halke · Kenji Itoh · Bindings by C. Stahly · Tavant Frescoes

No. 75. Cover by Jean Lurçat · Tapestry by Lurçat · Pierre Monnerat · Vogue magazine promotion · Jack Wolfgang Beck · Robert Osborn · Los Angeles advertising art · Window sculpture of Janine Janet · Romanesque Church Portals

No. 77. Cover shows a child's painting · Teaching of painting in schools · Woodcuts of Antonio Frasconi · Swiss Posters 1957 · Swissair publicity · Herbert Matter ads for Knoll · Karel Kezer · Modern Playing Card designs

No. 79. Cover and work by Siné · Hans Fischer · Artistic textbooks · English Slate Headstones · Richard Erdoes · The Fathers of German Expressionism · Erik Nitsche · Artists' cards · Australian Bark Paintings · Paul Hogarth

No. 80. Cover and work by Ronald Searle · Italian House Organs · Coventry Cathedral Windows · The Education of the Commercial Artist · Push Pin Studios · Natural and Artistic Form · New Hungarian Poster designs · Match-Box labels

NAMES KNOWN AND UNKNOWN . . .

GRAPHIS is a name that will be known to everyone whose interest lies in the graphic and applied arts; for fifteen years it has shown the work of the leading artists of the world, as well as of those with talent and promise but as yet young and unknown. The receipt of Graphis Magazine every two months ensures a knowledge of certain aspects of traditional art, of current activities and of future trends; and some of the pleasure and inspiration to be had from the rich and varied field it covers will be suggested by the contents of the six typical issues listed above.

Each issue of GRAPHIS is about 100 pages with 200 illustrations, many in colour. It costs $15. for 6 numbers (one year); $28. for 12 numbers (two years). Orders can be placed by sending a check to: Swiss Bank Corporation ('Graphis Account'), 15 Nassau Street, New York 5. A prospectus is available from:

G R A P H I S

AMSTUTZ & HERDEG · GRAPHIS PRESS   45 NUSCHELERSTRASSE · ZURICH, SWITZERLAND

Exhibited: Century of Progress, Chicago, 1933; Smithsonian Inst., 1940, 1941; Am. Soc. Min. P., 1940-41; Grand Central A. Gal., 1941, 1942, 1943; Pa. Soc. Min. P.; Delgado Mus. A.; Indianapolis, Ind.; Birmingham, Ala.; Mus. FA of Houston, and in Italy.

LUHDE, ERNEST T.—*Museum Director*

Stamford Museum and Nature Center, Stamford, Conn.*

LUKITS, THEODORE N.—*Painter, I., E., L.*

736 South Citrus Ave., Los Angeles 36, Cal.

Studied: Washington Univ., St. Louis, with Miller, Wuerpel; AIC, with Alphonse Mucha, W. J. Reynolds, K. A. Buehr. *Member*: AAPL; A. Fellowship; Am. Inst. FA; P. & S. Cl. of Los A.; Hon. Memb., Jonathon Cl., Los A. *Awards*: prizes, AIC, 1918, traveling scholarship, 1919; Los A. Mus. A., 1937; gold med., Intl. A. Lg., 1927; gold med., P. & S. Soc., Los A., 1942; Greek Theatre, Los A.; Hon. Deg., M.F.A. & Membership: Andhra Research Univ., Vizianagram, India, 1938; L. Lit. et Artistique de France, 1939; F., Atenio Nacionale of Sc. & A., Mexico; F., Academia Hispano-Americano, Cadiz; Hors Concours, P. & S. Cl., Los A., 1950-55. *Position*: Pres., Dir., Instr., Anatomy, Color, Composition, Lukits Acad. FA, Los Angeles, Cal.

LUKOSIUS, RICHARD—*Painter*

20 Church St., Noank, Conn.

B. Waterbury, Conn., Oct. 26, 1918. *Studied*: Yale Univ. Sch. FA, B.F.A., M.F.A. *Exhibited*: Boston A. Festival, 1956, 1958; Lyman Allyn Mus. A., 1958; WMA, 1958; Lyman Allyn Mus. A., 1958 (one-man); AFA, 1956-57.

LUMPKINS, WILLIAM THOMAS—*Designer, P., C., S.*

115 East Palace St.; h. 300 East Houghton St., Santa Fé, N.M.

B. Marlow, Okla., Apr. 8, 1909. *Studied*: Univ. New Mexico; Colorado State Col.; Univ. California at Los A.; Texas Christian Univ. *Work*: murals, Native Market, Santa Fé, N.M.; designed sch., trade & indst. bldgs., in Southwest. *Exhibited*: Palace Legion Honor, 1934; Southwest Annual, 1934-1940, 1946; Chappell House, Denver, Colo., 1938; WFNY 1939; Paris Salon; Memphis, Tenn., 1945. Author, I., "Modern Pueblo Homes."*

LUND, DAVID NATHAN—*Painter*

200 Bleecker St., New York 3, N.Y.

B. New York, N.Y., Oct. 16, 1925. *Studied*: Queen's College, N.Y., B.A.; and with Vytlacil, Kuniyoshi. *Awards*: Fulbright Fellowship, 1957-58, 1958-59, to Rome, Italy. *Exhibited*: Nebraska annual, 1958; WMAA, 1958; Stable Gal., Zabriskie Gal., Tanager Gal., Camino Gal., March Gal., Grand Central Moderns Gal., all New York City.

LUNDBERG, MRS. GODFREY. See Jewett, Eleanor

LUNDEAN, LOUIS—*Illustrator, P., W., L., T.*

1 West 67th St., New York 23, N.Y.

B. Council Bluffs, Iowa, Mar. 29, 1896. *Studied*: Univ. Omaha; Missouri Univ.; & with Boardman Robinson, Naum Los, George Luks. *Work*: St. Luke's Hospital, N.Y.; pub. sch. in Scarsdale, N.Y.; Grasslands Hospital, N.Y.; BMA; N.Y. State Police Headquarters, Albany & Hawthorne, N.Y., and in private colls. *Exhibited*: Grand Central A. Gal.; Kennedy Gal.; Portraits, Inc.; Mint Mus. A.; Blowing Rock (N.C.) AA; Macbeth Gal., N.Y.; Sporting Gal., N.Y.; CAA; WMAA; Rockefeller Plaza, N.Y., 1951 (one-man); Colony Cl., Phila., Pa.; Westchester AA; Hudson Valley AA. I., "Golden Hoofs"; "Stories Boys Like Best"; & other books. Contributor to: national magazines including Town & Country, Saturday Evening Post, Sportsman, Outdoor Life, Fortune, etc.

LUNDEAN, MRS. J. LOUIS. See Daingerfield, Marjorie

LUNDGREN, ERIC (B. E. K.)—*Painter, Gr., I., T., L.*

Country Club Rd., West Palm Beach, Fla.

B. Linkoping, Sweden, May 5, 1906. *Studied*: N.Y. Sch. Des.; ASL; AIC. *Member*: A. Gld.; Palm Beach A. Lg.

Work: BMFA. Exhibited: PAFA, 1937; Phila. A. All., 1939; AIC, 1938; Marshall Field Gal., 1937, 1938 (one-man); Palm Beach A. Lg.; Hays Gal. (one-man). Contributor to: Esquire, Coronet, Professional Art Quarterly. Lectures: "Primitives & Children's Art." *Position*: Instr. A., Norton Gal. A., West Palm Beach, Fla., at present.

LUNDY, FRED RALPH—*Cartoonist*

1240 31st Ave., San Francisco 22, Cal.

B. Bottineau, N.D., Sept. 1, 1902. *Studied*: Univ. Oregon; Cal. Sch. FA; Cal. Col. A. & Crafts. *Member*: Mechanics Inst., San F. Represented in cartoon books including: New Yorker 1950-55 Album of Cartoons: "But That's Unprintable," 1955; "You've Got Me on the Hook," 1955; "Too Funny for Words," 1954, etc. Contributor cartoons to Colliers; Esquire; New Yorker; This Week; King Features Syndicate; Redbook; American; American Weekly; Ladies Home Journal; Sat. Review; Cosmopolitan; MacLeans (Canada); Woman's Home Companion, and other national magazines. Cartoons reprinted in England, France, Belgium, Australia and Mexico. *Position*: A., Oakland Tribune (7 years); A., San Francisco Examiner, 1936- .*

LUNEAU, OMER JOACHIM—*Painter, T., L.*

11 Chapel St., Concord, N.H.

B. Canada, Aug. 22, 1909. *Studied*: Newark Sch. F. & Indst. A.; N.Y. Univ., and with Leo Blake. *Member*: New Hampshire AA; Audubon A.; AAPL. *Awards*: prizes, Maine and New Hampshire exhs.; Brick Store Mus.; Morganstern Fnd., 1957; Currier Gal. A. *Exhibited*: All. A. Am.; Audubon A.; Argent Gal. (one-man), 1945; Currier Gal. A. (one-man); Dartmouth Col.; Carpenter Gal., Manchester, N.H. Lectures: Art Appreciation; Contemporary Art, and others.

LUPORI, PETER—*Sculptor, E.*

Art Department, College of St. Catherine, St. Paul 5, Minn.

B. Pittsburgh, Pa., Dec. 12, 1918. *Studied*: Carnegie Inst., B.F.A.; Univ. Minnesota, M. Ed.; and with John Rood, Johns Hopkins, Josephine Lutz Rollins. *Member*: Soc. Minnesota Sculptors; Minnesota AA; Assoc. A. Pittsburgh; AEA; St. Paul P. & S. Assn. (Vice-Pres., 1954-58); St. Paul Council A. & Sc. *Awards*: prizes, Scholastic Art Comp., Pittsburgh, 1936, 1937, 1938; Carnegie Scholarships, 1939-41; Prix de Rome sculpture comp., 1941; Assoc. A. Pittsburgh, 1942, 1943, 1948, 1949, 1952, 1954, 1955, 1957; Beaux-Arts sculpture comp., N.Y., 1942; Minnesota State Fair, 1947, 1949, 1951-1954; WAC, 1947, 1948; Minneapolis Woman's Cl., 1948; Pittsburgh A. & Crafts Center, 1950; Western Pa. Sculpture Exh., Pittsburgh, 1954; Minnesota Sculpture Group, 1955 (4). *Exhibited*: one-man: Albuquerque, N.M., 1947; Minnesota State Fair, 1948; A. & Crafts Center, Pittsburgh, 1950; College of St. Catherine, St. Paul, 1951; St. Paul Gal. & Sch. A., 1952; World Theatre A. Gal., St. Paul, 1953; Petit Salon, Minneapolis, 1953; Webb Publ. Co., St. Paul, 1954. *Work*: statues, religious sc.: Ball State T. Col.; Mt. Zion Temple, St. Paul; Abbey of Our Lady of New Melleray, Dubuque, Iowa; College of St. Thomas, St. Paul; College of St. Catherine, St. Paul; Alumnae Assn. of Col. of St. Catherine; Church of the Holy Childhood, St. Paul; and many others. Murals: Union Bldg., and Northrup Auditorium, Univ. Minnesota. *Positions*: Instr., Univ. Minn., 1946-49; Asst. Prof., College of St. Thomas, 1949-51; Instr., 1947-49, Asst. Prof., 1949-54, Assoc. Prof. A., 1954- , College of St. Catherine, St. Paul, Minn.

LUQUIENS, HUC-MAZELET—*Etcher, P., E.*

4528 Kahala Ave., Honolulu 15, Hawaii

B. Auburndale, Mass., June 30, 1881. *Studied*: Yale Univ., B.A., B.F.A.; Ecole des Beaux-Arts, Paris; & with J. F. Weir, J. H. Niemeyer, Bonnat, Merson. *Member*: Chicago SE; Cal. SE; Honolulu A. Soc.; Honolulu Pr. M. *Awards*: F., Yale A. Sch., 1904; prize, New Haven Paint & Clay Cl., 1925, 1934; Cal. SE, 1938; Honolulu Pr. M., 1933, 1939. *Work*: N.Y. Pub. Lib.; NGA; Yale Sch. FA; Honolulu Acad. A. *Exhibited*: New Haven Paint & Clay Cl., Cal. SE; Chicago SE; Prairie Pr. M.; SAE; Honolu'u Pr. M. Author: "Hawaiian Art." *Position*: Instr., A. Dept., 1924- , Chm. A. Dept., 1936- , Prof. A., 1943- , Univ. Hawaii, Honolulu, Hawaii, retired Aug. 31, 1946.

10 Good Reasons why you should be a Member of The American Federation of Arts

For a $15 Annual Membership you receive:

1. 25% discount on art books
2. Free annual subscription to ONE of three leading magazines: *Art News* OR *Arts* OR *Art in America*
3. Free annual subscription to A F A *Art Newsletter*
4. Substantial discounts on A F A publications: *The American Art Directory* and *Who's Who in American Art*
5. 15% discount on frames and certain reproductions
6. Special rates for extra subscriptions to *Art News*, *Arts* and *Art in America* and discounts on 23 other magazines related to the arts
7. 20% discount on membership in the International Graphic Arts Society
8. Special mailings of catalogs, publicity, announcements of Art events and Previews of A F A Exhibitions
9. Invitation to A F A Conventions and Meetings
10. The satisfaction of supporting the most vital and far-reaching art organization in the United States today

Members who contribute $25 or more in Annual Dues receive, in addition to all other privileges, a complimentary copy of Arts Yearbook and are invited periodically to visit important Private Art Collections.

For a $25 Chapter Membership, your organization will receive:

1. Discounts on participation fees for all A F A Traveling Exhibitions and One-Third discount on participation fee for A F A Color-Slide Lectures (Write for Extension Services Catalog for details)
2. Free annual subscription to ONE of three leading magazines: *Art News* OR *Arts* OR *Art in America*
3. Free annual subscription to A F A *Art Newsletter*
4. 25% discount on art books
5. Substantial discounts on A F A publications: *The American Art Directory* and *Who's Who in American Art*
6. 15% discount on frames and certain reproductions
7. Special Rates for extra subscriptions to *Art News, Arts and Art in America* and discounts on 23 other magazines related to the arts
8. 20% discount on membership in the International Graphic Arts Society
9. Special mailings of catalogs, publicity, announcements of Art events and Previews of A F A Exhibitions
10. Privilege of sending at least one voting delegate to annual A F A meetings and invitation to attend A F A conventions

Chapter Members using A F A services save more than the minimum $25 annual dues in discounts on traveling exhibitions and publications.

The American Federation of Arts is a 50-year-old national, non-profit organization, composed of more than 2,300 individuals. groups and institutions concerned with the development of art in America. A F A circulates exhibitions of the art of many nations and periods to art centers in the United States and Canada; imports and exports many shows for circulation at home and abroad in a program for international exchange of art; sponsors publication of reference books; plans and directs projects which can be undertaken only by a national organization devoted solely to art.

We Cordially Invite You To Join

The American Federation of Arts

1083 FIFTH AVENUE - NEW YORK 28, NEW YORK - SAcramento 2-2452

LUSH, VIVIAN—Sculptor

1922 East 14th St., Brooklyn 29, N.Y.

B. New York, N.Y., Aug. 3, 1911. *Studied*: Leonardo da Vinci A. Sch.; NAD; ASL; & with Attilio Piccirilli, Charles Keck, Robert Aitken. *Member*: NAWA; Clay Cl. *Awards*: prize, NAWA. *Work*: collaborated with Robert Garrison, Riverside Church, N.Y.; Attilio Piccirilli on panels, International & Italian Bldgs., Rockefeller Center, N.Y.; figure, Port Richmond H.S.; Unity Hospital, Brooklyn, N.Y.; Monroe, Roosevelt H.S., Bronx, N.Y.; Children's Wing, Pub. Lib., Trinidad, B.W.I. (port.).*

LUTZ, DAN—Painter, T.

794 Mt. Washington Dr., Los Angeles 65, Cal.

B. Decatur, Ill., July 7, 1906. *Studied*: AIC; Univ. Southern California, B.F.A.; & with Boris Anisfeld. *Member*: Cal. WC Soc.; AWCS; Phila. WC Cl. *Awards*: Raymond traveling scholarship, AIC, 1931; prizes, San Diego FA Soc., 1937; NAD, 1941; Cal. WC Soc., 1942; Los A. Mus. A., 1942, 1954; PAFA, 1945; Caller-Times, Corpus Christi, Tex., 1945; VMFA, 1940, 1946. *Work*: PMG; Los A. Mus. A.; Encyclopaedia Britannica Coll.; San Diego FA Soc.; Colo. Springs FA Center; Arizona State Univ.; Santa Barbara A. Mus.; Pasadena AI. *Exhibited*: CGA, 1941, 1943; VMFA, 1940, 1942, 1944, 1946; NAD, 1941, 1942; PAFA, 1940-1946; Los A. Mus. A.; AIC, 1940-1946; WMAA, 1944, and many other leading museums and galleries. *Position*: Instr., Chouinard AI, Los Angeles, Cal., 1945-46; Summer Sch. Painting, Saugatuck, Mich., 1950-52; Visiting A., San Antonio AI, 1953; Univ. Georgia, 1955.*

LUTZ, JOSEPHINE. *See Rollins, Josephine Lutz*

LUX, GLADYS MARIE—Painter, E., Ser., C.

Nebraska Wesleyan University, 50th & St. Paul Sts.; h. 5203 Garland St., Lincoln 4, Neb.

B. Chapman, Neb. *Studied*: Univ. Nebraska, B.F.A., A.B., M.A.; AIC. *Member*: Lincoln A. Gld.; Nebraska A. T. Assn.; Western AA; Nat. A. T. Assn. *Work*: Doane Col.; Peru State Col.; Nebraska Wesleyan; Lincoln A. Gld.; Pub. Sch., Kearney, Neb. *Exhibited*: Rockefeller Center, N.Y., 1936-1938; WFNY 1939; AIC, 1936; Women's Nat. Exh., Wichita, 1936-1938; LC, 1944; Kansas City AI, 1934-1938; Denver A. Mus.; Joslyn A. Mus.; Lincoln A. Gld.; Walker A. Center, 1947; Topeka, Kans., 1947, 1948; Sioux City A. Center, 1955; Cheyenne, Wyo., 1955; Capper Fnd. Exh., 1949-50; State T. Col., Peru, Neb.; Univ. Nebraska, 1952. Contributor to Western AA bulletin. *Position*: Assoc. Prof. A., Nebraska Wesleyan Univ., Lincoln, Neb., at present.

LUX, GWEN—Sculptor

342 East 69th St., New York 21, N.Y.

B. Chicago, Ill. *Studied*: Maryland Inst. A.; BMFA Sch.; in Paris, and with Ivan Mestrovic. *Member*: Arch. Lg.; S. Gld.; Audubon A.; Nat. Women P. & S. Soc. *Awards*: Guggenheim F., 1933; prizes, Detroit Inst. A., 1945, 1946; Nat. Lith. prize, 1947; NAWA, 1947; Audubon A, 1954. *Work*: S., Assoc. Am. A.; Radio City, N.Y.; McGraw-Hill Bldg., Chicago; Trustees System Service, Chicago; Univ. Arkansas; Victoria Theatre, N.Y.; Bristol (Tenn.) Hospital; SS. "United States." Texas Petroleum Cl., Dallas; Northland Shopping Center, Detroit; General Wingate Sch., Brooklyn; General Motors Research Center, Detroit; Socony Bldg., N.Y.C.; R. H. Macy-Roosevelt Field, N.Y.; P.S. 19, New York City; Aviation Trades H.S., Long Island, N.Y.; Country Day Sch., Lake Placid, N.Y. *Exhibited*: PMA, 1933; NAD, 1933; Salon d'Automne, Salon des Tuileries, Paris; Weyhe Gal., 1932; Detroit A. Market, 1942; WMAA, 1947; Audubon A., 1956; Sculptors Gld., 1957; one-man: Delphic Studio, 1932; Detroit A. Market, 1942; Assoc. Am. A., 1946. *Position*: Instr. S., A. & Crafts Soc., Detroit, Mich., 1945-48.

LYNCH, DONALD CORNELIUS—Illustrator, P., T.

North Broadway, Upper Nyack, N.Y.

B. Harrison, N.J., June 17, 1913. *Studied*: ASL, with Harvey Dunn, Alexey Brodovitch. *Member*: SI. *Awards*: prizes, MModA, 1942; 4th Annual Book Jacket Comp., 1958. Illus., "G.E. Scrapbook History," 1953; "The New American Profile," 1954; "Profile of a President," 1954; "Antique Cars," L.I. Auto Museum, 1955; "Exploring New York State," 1956; "Favorite Tales from Shakespeare," 1957; "Robin Hood," 1957; "Witness to Witchcraft," 1957;

"Man of Montmartre," 1958; "The Gold of Troy," 1959; "Marquette and Joliet," 1958; "Friar Among Savages," 1958; Indian Section of 1958 Book of Knowledge; "St. Anthony"; "It's Your Education," 1958; "Bronze Billy," 1959. Other work: Book illus., fiction, juvenile, textbooks and jackets. Contributor to Look; Harpers; N.Y. Times; Parents magazines. *Position*: Instr., Workshop School, 1949-54.

LYNCH, IRENE DEROCHE—Painter

240 West 98th St., New York 25, N.Y.

B. Mattawa, Ont., Canada, July 16, 1908. *Studied*: in Canada. *Member*: Women's A. Soc., Montreal; Indp. AA, Montreal. *Exhibited*: annually, Women's A. Soc. and Indp. AA, Montreal.

LYNCH, JAMES O'CONNOR—Critic, P., E.

240 West 98th St., New York 25, N.Y.

B. Sydney, Nova Scotia, Canada, Oct. 8, 1908. *Studied*: with Eugenio Renazzi, Allesandro Frattini, Rome, Italy; Royal Canadian Acad., with Edmond Dyonnet, Montreal. *Member*: Indp. AA., Montreal. *Work*: Maryhill Mus. A.. Maryhill, Wash.; ports. in private colls. (1938-58). *Exhibited*: annually in Canada.

LYON, ROWLAND—Painter, Gr., T., C., Cart.

3835 S St., Washington, D.C.

B. Washington, D.C., July 16, 1904. *Studied*: Corcoran Sch. A.; George Washington Univ., B.A., M.A., and with Charles Hawthorne. *Member*: A. Gld. of Washington; Washington S. Group; Washington A. Cl.; Soc. Wash. A.; Wash. WC Cl.; Landscape Cl., Wash.; Wash. Soc. Et. *Awards*: Soc. Indp. A., 1933, 1935; Fed. Women's Cl., 1934; Wash. Landscape Cl., 1937; Times Herald A. Fair, Wash., D.C., 1944; Metropolitan State A. Contest, 1944; Georgetown A. Group, 1955; medal, Soc. Wash. A., 1935; Landscape Cl., 1945, 1947; The Plains, Va., 1952; Harper's Ferry, 1955; Denton, Md., 1958. *Exhibited*: Soc. Wash. A., 1930-1946; Wash. Landscape Cl., 1935-1946; Wash. WC Cl., 1942-1946; Wash. Soc. Et., 1943-1946; Terry AI, 1952, and in Italy & Spain, 1954-55; Greece, 1957. *Position*: Staff, NCFA, Smithsonian Inst., Washington, D.C.; Instr., Dept. Agriculture Graduate Sch., 1945- .

MacAGY, DOUGLAS—Educator, W.

77 Washington Place, New York 11, N.Y.

B. Winnipeg, Canada, July 8, 1913. *Studied*: Univ. Toronto, Canada; Courtauld Inst., London, England; Univ. Pennsylvania; Barnes Fnd.; Western Reserve Univ. *Member*: CAA; AAMus. Contributor to professional journals, general periodicals. Ed. Staff, Gazette des Beaux-Arts. Author: "The Museum Looks in on TV," 1955; "Going for a Walk with a Line," 1959. *Position*: Dir., Research, Wildenstein Gal., New York, N.Y., at present.

MacAGY, JERMAYNE—Museum Director

Contemporary Arts Museum, 6945 Fannin St. (25); h. 3416 Yoakum Blvd., Houston 6, Tex.

B. Cleveland, Ohio, Feb. 14, 1914. *Studied*: Radcliffe Col., B.A.; Western Reserve Univ., Ph.D. Contributor to Art in America; Art News; Museum Bulletins and Catalogues. *Positions*: Asst. Dir.. California Palace of the Legion of Honor, San Francisco, Cal., 1941-55 (and Actg. Dir. part of this period); Dir., Contemporary Arts Museum, Houston, Tex., 1955- .

MacALISTER, PAUL (R.)—Designer, C., W., L.

1226 North Dearborn Pkway., Chicago 10, Ill.; h. Arden Shore Lane, Lake Bluff, Ill.

B. Camden, N.J., Oct. 15, 1901. *Studied*: PAFA; PMSchIA; Yale Univ.; PIASch; Ecole des Beaux-Arts, Paris, France. *Member*: F., IDI. *Work*: Interiors for leading manufacturers and industrial companies. Creator, miniature room settings for TV use, AIC, and Chicago Pub. Lib. Author, I., "Plan-a-Room"; "Display for Better Business." Producer, Dir., numerous TV programs having decorating and design themes. Award's: prize, Better Rooms contest, Chicago Tribune, 1948. Doro hy Dawes award for contribution to TV field. *Positions*: Pres., Paul MacAlister, Inc., 1926-46; Dir., Bureau Indst. Des. & Int. Dec., Montgomery Ward & Co., Chicago, 1946-48; Paul MacAlister Assoc., 1948- ; Nat. Pres., IDI, 1950-51; Chm. & Fndr., IDI Des.

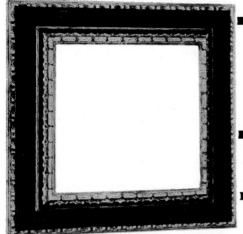

. . . creative designs in

modern & hand-carved

CUSTOM FRAMES

Galleries, Art Collectors, Artists,

Decorators and Framers from coast to coast are delighted with our

WRITE FOR
FREE ILLUS.
CATALOG

beautifully designed frames . . . each a masterpiece by itself . . .

carved and superbly finished by expert craftsmen.

the frameguild, inc.

503 EAST 72nd STREET, NEW YORK, N.Y. • REgent 7-3572

Award Comm., 1950-1955; Indst. Des. & Color Consultant, NBC Home Show, 1954-56; Des., Producer of Decorama Slide Films.

MACCOY, GUY—Painter, Ser., L.
21308 Mayan Dr., Chatsworth, Cal.

B. Valley Falls, Kan., Oct. 7, 1904. *Studied*: Kansas City AI; ASL; Broadmoor A. Acad.; & with Thomas Benton, Ernest Lawson, Jan Matulka, A. J. Kostellow. *Awards*: prizes, Laguna Beach AA, 1943; AIGA, 1944; CMA, 1946. *Work*: Encyclopaedia Britannica Col.; N.Y. Pub. Lib.; Toledo Mus. A.; Santa Barbara A. Mus.; Parkersburg FA Center; Univ. Iowa; Univ. California, Los A.; Pepperdine Col.; SFMA; Carnegie Inst.; Lib. Cong.; MMA; Newark Mus.; PMA; Honolulu Acad. A.; Univ. Minnesota; Philbrook A. Center; Univ. Oklahoma; Oklahoma A. & M. Col.; map mural, BM; murals, Brooklyn Indst. H.S. for Girls; First Nat. Bank, Lubbock, Tex.; Phillips 66 mural, Tulsa, Okla. Contributor to: Lithographers Journal. Lectures: Serigraphy. Assisted Jorn Tumbo's production of 23-minute History of Serigraphy 16 mm Color film. *Position*: Instr., Jepson AI, Los A. County AI; Co-Founder, Dir., Western Serigraph Inst.*

MacDERMOTT, STEWART SINCLAIR—Painter, Et.
Main St., Salisbury, Conn.

B. New York, N.Y., July 14, 1889. *Studied*: ASL; Conservatoire Americaine, Paris, France. *Member*: NAC; Berkshire AA; Lotos Cl. *Awards*: prize, Springfield A. Lg., 1931. *Work*: MMA. *Exhibited*: NAD; Carnegie Inst.; CGA; PAFA; AIC; Salon d'Automne, Paris, France.

MacDONALD, GENEVA A.—Graphic Artist
88A West Cedar St., Boston, Mass.

B. Natick, Mass., Aug. 28, 1902. *Studied*: Mass. Sch. A.; BMFA Sch.; Harvard Univ. *Member*: Boston Pr. M. *Awards*: Carnegie FA scholarsh'p, 1939; prize, LC, 1952. *Work*: LC. *Exhibited*: NAD; NAWA; BMFA; DeCordova & Dana Mus.; LC; Boston A. Festival, and others.*

MacDONALD, HERBERT EVANS—Painter
173 Stonehouse Rd., Glen Ridge, N.J.

B. Brooklyn, N.Y., Nov. 14, 1898. *Studied*: Wesleyan Univ., B.S.; ASL, with DuMond, Grosz, Vytlacil, Kantor and others. *Member*: New Jersey WC Soc.; ASL (life); Bloomfield A. Lg.; Essex WC Cl.; Montclair A. Mus. *Awards*: prizes, Bloomfield A. Lg.; Essex WC Cl.; New Jersey WC Soc., 1958; Verona AA, and others. *Exhibited*: AWS, 1938; All. A. Am., 1951; N.Y. City Center Gal., 1955, 1956; Montclair A. Mus., 1951-1953, 1955-1957; Newark A. Mus., 1952, 1955, 1957; AAPL; Bloomfield A. Lg.; Essex WC Cl.; Panoras Gal., 1955, 1956 (one-man); Am. Acad. A. & Let., 1958; Art:USA, 1958; New York City Center, 1957, 1958. Lectures: Abstract Art. *Position*: Instr., locally, and in private classes.

MacDONALD, KATHARINE HEILNER—Printmaker, T.
1309 Balboa Ave., Burlingame, Cal.

B. Brooklyn, N.Y., Nov. 30, 1882. *Studied*: PIASch; Fed. A. Sch., Minneapolis, Minn.; & with Arthur Dow. *Work*: San Diego FA Soc.; Fed. A. Sch., Minneapolis.*

MacDONALD, ROBERT (H.)—Designer, Comm. A., I.
1810 Cortelyou Rd., Brooklyn, N.Y.

B. Brooklyn, N.Y., July 29, 1903. *Studied*: PIASch.; ASL, with Bridgman, DuMond, Dodge, Morgan, Rockwell; Grand Central Sch. A., with Cornwell, Carter; N.Y. Univ. *Member*: SI; A. Gld., N.Y.; ASL (life). *Exhibited*: A. Gld., 1954. *Position*: 1st Vice-Pres., A. Gld., 1954-55; Pres., 1955-56; Treas., 1956-58; Consulting A. Dir., MacDonald Assoc., at present.

MacDONALD, WILLIAM ALLAN—
Assistant Museum Director, E.
The Baltimore Museum of Art, Baltimore 18, Md.; h. R.R. #5, Box 4, Westminster, Md.

B. Lorain, Ohio, July 28, 1911. *Studied*: Oberlin Col., A.B.; Johns Hopkins Univ., A.M., Ph.D. *Member*: CAA. *Positions*: Prof. His'. A., Western Maryland Col., Westminster, Md.; Asst. Dir., Baltimore Museum of Art, Baltimore, Md.

MACDONALD-WRIGHT, STANTON—
Painter, W., L.
336 Bellino Drive, Pacific Palisades, Cal.

B. Charlottesville, Va., July 8, 1890. *Studied*: Sorbonne, Grande Chaumiere, Julian Acad., Ecole des Beaux-Arts, Paris, France. *Work*: MMA; MModA; Detroit Inst. A.; BMFA; PMA; Columbus Gal. FA; Newark Mus. A.; BM; Grand Rapids A. Gal.; Denver A. Mus.; Pasadena AI; San Diego FA Soc.; Los A. Mus. A.; Univ. Chicago; Univ. Minnesota; murals, Santa Monica City Hall, H.S. and Pub. Lib. *Exhibited*: Nationally and internationally including MMA; MModA; Janis Gal.; BM; Honolulu Acad. FA; Mus. Sc., Hist. & A., Los Angeles, 1956 (retrospective); An American Place, N.Y.; Bernheim Jeune, Galerie Arnaud, Galerie Creuze, Galerie Denise Rene, all in Paris, France; Saint-Etienne Musee d'Art et d'Industrie, Saint-Etienne, France; Galerie Kasper, Lausanne, and in Milan, London, and Warsaw. Author: "Treatise on Color"; "History of Mosaics"; "Beyond Aesthetics" (in Japanese), Tokyo. Contributor to Encyclopaedia of the Arts, and to art magazines. *Position*: Prof. Oriental A. Hist., Aesthetics and Iconography, Univ. California at Los Angeles (to 1954). Also, Univ. Hawaii; Tokyo, Japan; Univ. So. California; Scripps Col., Claremont, Cal.

MacFADDEN, PRISCILLA SOPHIA—*Art Librarian*
Boston Public Library, Copley Sq.; h. 71 Pinckney St., Boston 14, Mass.

B. Haverhill, Mass., June 30, 1901. *Studied*: Boston Univ. *Member*: Am. Lib Assn.; Special Lib. Assn. *Position*: Asst. in Charge, FA Dept., 1936-40, Chief FA Dept., 1940- , Boston Pub. Lib., Boston, Mass.

MacFARLANE, JANET R.—*Museum Director, Hist., P.*
Albany Institute of History & Art, 125 Washington Ave. (10); h. Loudon House, Dutch Village, Menands, Albany 4, N.Y.

B. Rochester, N.Y., May 10, 1911. *Studied*: Skidmore Col., B.S. *Awards*: purchase prize, Munson-Williams-Proctor Inst., 1952. *Work*: Munson-Williams-Proctor Inst. *Exhibited*: Cooperstown AA, 1948-1958; Munson-Williams-Proctor Inst., 1946-1953; Soc. Four Arts, Palm Beach, 1954; Lowe Gal. A., 1954; Syracuse Mus. FA, 1951; Albany Inst. Hist. & A., 1951; Cortland County Fair. Ed., catalog "18th Century Paintings" in the Albany Institute collection (with others). Contributor to Art in America; Antiques. Lectures: American Folk Art, 18th and 19th Centuries, using outdoor museum collections. Installed Folk Art Galleries at Fenimore House, Cooperstown, N.Y. *Positions*: Cur., N.Y. State Hist. Assn. Museums (Fenimore House, Farmer's Museum), Cooperstown, N.Y., 1942-1956; Dir., Albany Inst. Hist. & Art, Albany, N.Y., 1956- .

MacGINNIS, HENRY RYAN—*Painter, T.*
Lake Morey, Fairlee, Vt.

B. Martinsville, Ind. *Studied*: Royal Acad., Munich, Germany; in Paris; & with Adams, Steele, Forsythe. *Member*: AAPL; All.A.Am.; Audubon A.; SC; Hoosier Salon; Soc. Indiana A. *Awards*: prizes, Richmond, Ind., 1929; Hoosier Salon, 1930. *Work*: State House & Masonic Temple, Trenton, N.J.; Lehigh Univ.; Univ. Georgia; Herron AI; Ball Coll.; Muncie, Ind.; Customs House, N.Y.; Rutgers Univ.; murals, Gregory Sch., Ewing Cemetery Assn., Trenton, N.J.; St. Thomas Church, Woodhaven, L.I., N.Y. *Exhibited*: AIC; Omaha Exp.; PAFA; Int. Exh., Munich; NAD; one-man: Fleming Mus.; Wood A. Gal.; Carpenter A. Gal., Dartmouth Col. *Position*: Hd. FA Dept., Sch. Indst. A., Trenton, N.J., 1906-46; retired June, 1946.

MACHETANZ, FRED—
Printmaker, P., L., W., Film Producer, I.
Palmer, Alaska

Lecturer; book illustrator (with Sara Machetanz).

MACHETANZ, SARA (Mrs. Fred)—
Printmaker, P., L., W., I.
Palmer, Alaska

Lecturer; book illustrator, etc. (with Fred Machetanz).

MACK, FRANK—*Painter*
2750 Northside Dr., Northwest 5, Atlanta, Ga.

B. Chicago, Ill. *Studied*: AIC. *Member*: Atlanta AA; Assn. Georgia A.; AAPL. *Award*: traveling scholarship, AIC. *Exhibited*: nationally. *Work*: S. panels, Cyclorama Bldg., Atlanta; portraits, Columbia Seminary, Decatur, Ga.; DeKalb County Court House, Decatur; Spring Place, Ga.; Union Theological Seminary, Richmond, Va.; Massingil Bldg., Bristol, Tenn.; also banks in Thomson, Swainsboro, Ga. and ports of prominent persons. *Position*: State Chm., Am. A. Week, AAPL.

MACKALL, (ROBERT) McGILL—*Painter, E., Des.*
2423 Pickwick Rd., Baltimore 7, Md.

B. Baltimore, Md., Apr. 15, 1889. *Studied*: Maryland Inst.; ASL; Julian Acad., Colorossi Acad., Paris; Royal Acad. A., Munich, and with Jean Paul Laurens, Richard Miller. *Member*: Mun. Art Comm., Balt., Md.; Salon d'Automne, Paris. *Work*: portraits, Constitution Hall, Wash., D.C.; City Hall, Johns Hopkins Hospital & Univ., Union Mem. Hospital, Franklin Square Hospital, Court House, Presbyterian Hospital, Loyola Coll., Md. Nat. Guard Armory, Hannah More Acad., all of Baltimore; St. Johns Coll., Annapolis; Univ. Georgia; St. Francis Hospital, Evanston, Ill.; Georgetown Univ., Wash., D.C.; mural dec., Maryland War Mem. Bldg., Fidelity-Baltimore Nat. Bank, "The Sun Papers" Bldg., Ashburton Filtration plant (Lobby), Hotel Emerson, Grand Concourse-Friendship Intl. Airport, Loyola Fed. Savings & Loan Assn., Augusta Bldg. & Loan Assn., Merchants Cl., all Balt., Md.; 2nd Nat. Bank, Towson, Md.; U.S. Naval Acad.; stained glass mem. windows, Ral Parr Mausoleum, Pikesville, Md.; Emmanuel Episcopal Church, Cumberland, Md.; Huguenot Mem. Church, Pelham Manor, N.Y.; Christ Episcopal Church, Balt.; St. Ambrose Catholic Church, Balt.; also churches in Luray, Va.; Frederick, Md.; West River, Md., and many others. *Exhibited*: nationally and internationally. *Position*: Hd. FA Dept., Maryland Inst., Baltimore, Md.

MACKAY-SMITH, JEAN ELEANOR BOWMAN. See
Bowman, Jean

MacKENDRICK, LILIAN—*Painter*
230 Central Park, South, New York 19, N.Y.

B. Brooklyn, N.Y. *Studied*: N.Y. Univ., B.S.; Col. City of N.Y.; ASL. *Member*: AEA. *Awards*: gold medal, Bordighera, Italy. *Work*: WAC; Georgia Mus. A.; Wadsworth Atheneum; Mus. FA of Houston; MMA; Brandeis Univ.; Bezalel Mus., Jerusalem; Galeria di Arti Contemporanea, Bordighera, Italy. *Exhibited*: Audubon A., 1951, 1952; Witte Mem. Mus., 1951; Fla. Gulf Coast A. Center, 1955; "Eleven Americans," touring France, 1956-57; one-man: Mortimer Levitt Gal., N.Y., 1949, 1951; Feigl Gal., N.Y., 1953, 1955; Georgia Mus. A., 1955; Hirschl & Adler Gal., N.Y., 1958; Benezit Galerie, Paris, France, 1956, 1957; USIS, Ostend, 1957, and in Italy.

MACKEY, WILLIAM ERNO—
Painter, Des., Gr., Cart., Comm., T., W.
1615 Spruce St., Philadelphia 3, Pa.

B. Philadelphia, Pa., Feb. 17, 1919. *Studied*: Graphic Sketch Cl., Phila.; PAFA; Barnes Fnd. *Member*: Phila. Pr. Cl.; A. Gld. of Phila.; Am. Mus. Natural Hist.; Contemporary A. Assn. of Phila. *Awards*: F., PAFA, prize, PAFA, 1939. *Work*: PAFA; AIC. *Exhibited*: PMA, 1955. *Position*: Instr., Hussian Sch. A.; Philographic Sch. A.; Children's Class painting & drawing, Graphic Sketch Cl.; Print Cl., all in Philadelphia, Pa.

MacLANE, JEAN—*Painter*
15 Gramercy Park, New York, N.Y.
Member: NA.*

MacLEAN, J. ARTHUR—*Writer, L., C., E., Gr.*
2310 Glenwood Ave., Toledo 10, Ohio

B. Winchester, Mass., 1879. *Studied*: Kenyon Col., M.F.A.; Harvard Univ. Ext. *Member*: Tile Cl., Toledo; Toledo A. Cl.; Toledo Fed. A.; F., Rochester Mus. A. & Sc; Torch Cl.; Toledo Craft Cl. *Exhibited*: Toledo Mus. A. Author: "Modern Japanese Prints," 1936; "East Indian

The standard guide to **museums**
art schools
art associations
in the U.S. and Canada

American Art Directory

In addition to the master lists above, you'll find:

Architectural Societies
Art Clubs
Art Commissions &
Municipal Art Societies
Art Critics
Art Magazines
Art Teachers
Ceramic Societies
University and College
Art Galleries
Design Institutes
Etching Societies
Exhibitions, circulating
Graphic Arts Clubs
and Societies
Handcraft Societies
Industrial Art Societies
Interior Decoration Institute
Libraries (with art galleries
or important collections)
Major Foreign Museums
and Art Schools
Museum Directors
National and Regional
Organizations
Numismatic Societies
Print Collections
Sculpture Guilds and
Societies
Water Color Societies

Here in one source is complete, detailed information on the important people and places in the American art world. The American Art Directory brings you the latest available data — data gathered by intensive survey and compiled by the painstaking efforts of an editor and staff skilled in the art directory field.

Museum listings include personnel, collections, activities, and publications. Art schools in the U.S. and Canada are listed with head of school or dept., degrees and courses offered, enrollment, tuition, and other details. And organizations are listed with description, names of officers, chapters, addresses, etc. (including full details on the American Federation of Arts). A convenient master index to each entry guides you to special collections, organizations, key people. Edited by Dorothy B. Gilbert, revised 1958. 411 pages. $20 net pp. Order *today* from R. R. BOWKER CO., 62 W. 45th St., N. Y. 36.

Published for the American Federation of Arts

Sculpture," 1940; "Ancient Chinese Bronzes," 1941; "Northeastern Asiatic Art," 1942. Contributor to art magazines, museum bulletins. Northwestern Ohio Archaeological Journal, and other publications. Lectures: Art & Culture of the Orient; American Art; European Art. *Position*: Past Sec.-Treas., Assn. A. Mus. Dir. of U.S. & Canada (18 yrs.); Delegate at large, Toledo Fed. A. Soc.; Cur., Oriental A., BMFA, 1906-13; CMA, 1913-20; Asst. Dir., AIC, 1920-21; A. Dir., John Herron AI, 1922-1926; Cur., Toledo Mus. A., 1926-47, Emeritus, 1947- .

MacLEARY, BONNIE—*Sculptor*
    8 Gibson Park, Washington, N.J.

B. San Antonio, Tex. *Studied*: N.Y. Sch. A.; Julian Acad., Paris; ASL; & with Frank DuMond, James Earle Fraser. *Member*: ANA; NSS; All.A.Am.; AAPL; Texas Cl. (hon.); Southern Soc. (hon.). *Awards*: prize, Women's A. & Indst. Exh., 1928, 1929. *Work*: MMA; Brooklyn Children's Mus.; Wesleyan Col., Macon, Ga.; Baylor Univ.; Witte Mem. Mus.; CGA; monuments, Univ. Puerto Rico; San Juan, Puerto Rico; San Antonio, Tex. *Exhibited*: NAD; NAC; NAWA; PAFA; SSAL; Arch.L.; All.A.Am. Lectures: "Sculpture in the Making."*

MacLELLAN, CHARLES ARCHIBALD—*Painter, T.*
    1305 Franklin St., Wilmington, Del.

B. Trenton, Ontario, Canada, June 22, 1885. *Studied*: AIC. *Member*: Wilmington Soc. FA. *Awards*: prizes, Wilmington Soc. FA, 1942; Pasadena AI, 1946. *Work*: Wilmington Soc. FA. *Exhibited*: PAFA, 1944; Pasadena AI, 1946; Wilmington Soc. FA, 1936-1946; Terry AI, 1952. *Position*: Accessions Com., Wilmington Soc. FA (25 years), Chm., 1953-58 (ret.).

MacLENNAN, EUNICE CASHION—
  Painter, Lith., T., I., W., Cr., L.
    Mail: Box 2292; h. Camino Real at 13th St., Carmel, Cal.

B. St. Louis, Mo., Apr. 28, 1890. *Studied*: St. Louis Mus. FA, Washington Univ.; PIASch.; AIC; Julian Acad., Grande Chaumiere, Paris, France. *Member*: NAWA; Cal. WC Soc.; Santa Barbara AA; Santa Barbara Pr. M.; Carmel AA. *Awards*: prizes, NAWA, 1935; Cal. State Fair, 1930, 1931; Santa Cruz, 1936; San Diego FA Gal.; silver medal, Washington Univ. *Work*: Univ. California, Santa Barbara branch; Santa Barbara Pub. Lib.; Cal. State Lib.; Monterey Pub. Lib.; Santa Barbara Mus. A., and in private colls. *Exhibited*: NAWA annually, 1930-1941; PAFA, 1939; Nat. Gal., Toronto, Canada, 1937; Los A. Mus. A., 1935, 1936, 1937, 1938, 1939; Laguna Beach AA, 1938; Santa Barbara Mus. A., 1943, 1944, 1951; Cal. PLH, 1933; SFMA, 1941; WFNY 1939; GGE, 1939; one-man: Illsley Gal., Los A., 1934; Santa Barbara Mus. A., 1943, 1944, 1951, 1954; Carmel AA, regularly; Carmel A. Gld., 1948, 1959; Beardsley AA, 1953. *Position*: Tech. A., Lockheed Aircraft, 1943-44; Hd. A. Dept., Smith Acad., St. Louis, Mo., 1909-14; Supv. A., Los A. Pub. Schs., 1914; Instr., Santa Barbara State Col., 1919-20. Contributor art reviews to "Carmel Pine Cone."

MacLEOD, ALEXANDER SAMUEL—*Lithographer, P.*
    2174 Makiki Round Top Dr., Honolulu 14, Hawaii

B. Orwell, P.E.I., Canada, April 12, 1888. *Studied*: McGill Univ.; Cal. Sch. Des. *Member*: Honolulu Pr. M.; Cal. Soc. Et.; Hawaii P. & S. *Awards*: prizes, 1930, 1949; Honolulu Pr. M., 1933, 1934, 1935, 1942, 1943, 1945, 1947; Northwest Pr. M., 1934; Assn. Honolulu A., 1941-1944; Cal. Soc. Et., 1949. *Work*: Honolulu Acad. A.; SAM; LC; NGA; Newark Pub. Lib.; Smithsonian Inst.; Univ. Hawaii; Lib. of Hawaii; Gift Print, Honolulu Pr. M., 1956; N.Y. Pub. Lib.; Stanford Univ. *Exhibited*: NAD, 1917, 1941; N.Y. WC Cl., 1917; BM, 1935; Nat. A. Gal., New South Wales, 1942; PAFA, 1930; MMA, 1942; AIC, 1931-1935; Cal. PLH, 1933; Carnegie Inst., 1941; San F. AA; Phila. Pr. Cl.; Vancouver A. Gal.; Honolulu Pr. M., Los Angeles AA. Author, I., "The Spirit of Hawaii—Before and After Pearl Harbor," 1943. *Position*: Hd. Graphic A. Dept., Adjutant General Div., U.S. Army, Pacific Ocean Areas, 1945- .

MacNICOL, ROY VINCENT—*Painter, Des., T., W., L.*
    Casa MacNicol, Zaragosa 307, Chapala-on-the-Lake, Jalisco, Mexico; also, 35 Madison Ave., New York, N.Y.

B. New York, N.Y., Nov. 27, 1889. *Member*: Baltimore WC Soc.; Lotos Cl., N.Y.; Pan-American Union. *Work*:

Randolph-Macon Woman's Col.; Univ. Havana, Cuba; Univ. Illinois; Reporter's Cl., Havana; Findlay Gal., Chicago, and in private colls. Murals, Geneve Hotel, Mexico City; Moore-McCormack SS Lines; Harmon Fnd. *Exhibited*: Arch. Lg.; NAD; Anderson Gal.; Seligmann Gal.; AIC; Dudensing Gal., N.Y.; Seville, Spain; Everglades Cl., Palm Beach; Los A. Mus. A.; Hamilton House, Shanghai, China; Marshall Field Co.; Lyceum, Havana, Cuba; Newhouse Gal.; Royal Victoria Inst., Trinidad, B.W.I.; Bridgetown, B.W.I.; Milch Gal.; Pan-American Union; Hudson Co., Detroit; Findlay Gal., Chicago; Barker Bros., Los A.; Bellas Artes, Mexico City; Aeta Gal., Stockholm, Sweden (first American one-man exh. to be presented there); Paris, France and Copenhagen, Denmark, 1956; Weil Gal., Paris; Gallery Vivienne, N.Y., 1949 (exh. televised by NBC), and many others nationally and internationally. Creator of first Good Neighbor Exhs., Mexican theme, in interest of international good will. 50 one-man exhs., opened in Wash., D.C., 1943 at Pan-American Union, sponsored by Mrs. Eleanor Roosevelt and Pres. Miguel Aleman, the Mexican Cabinet and Pan-American Union. Author: "Paint Brush Ambassador," 1957; "The Flame of Genius" (on El Greco), in press. *Position*: Assoc. Ed., American Historical Company, New York, N.Y. Contributor to Christian Science Monitor; Atlanta Journal-Times Herald; Mexico City News; Havana Post, etc. Lectures: Art and Spain.

MacNUTT, GLENN GORDON—*Painter, I.*
    129 Minot St., Dorchester 22, Mass.

B. London, Ontario, Canada, Jan. 21, 1906. *Studied*: Mass. Sch. A.; BMFA Sch. *Member*: Boston Soc. WC Painters (Vice-Pres.); Gld. Boston A.; Phila. WC Soc.; AWS. *Work*: BMFA; New Britain Mus. A.; Farnsworth Mus., Rockland, Me.; Mather Sch., Dorchester, Mass.; Harvard Univ.; Wheaton Col., and in private colls. *Awards*: prizes, American Artist magazine, 1952; Mitton award, 1942, 1955; Concord AA, 1953; Boston Soc. WC Painters, 1954; AWS, 1956. *Exhibited*: MMA; AIC; BMFA; Toledo Mus., A.; PMA; CM; Los A. Mus. A.; SAM; BM; London-Ontario; Canton AI. Contributor to American Artist magazine; Ford Times News, etc.

MacNUTT, J. SCOTT—*Portrait Painter*
    72 Vandeventer Pl., St. Louis 8, Mo.

B. Fort D.A. Russell, Wyo., Jan. 11, 1885. *Studied*: Harvard Univ., A.B.; MIT, B.S.; BMFA Sch., and with Charles H. Woodbury. *Work*: Harvard Univ.; Univ. Missouri; Washington Univ.; Union Station, St. Louis; St. Luke's Hospital, St. Louis, and in many schools and institutions.

MACOMBER, ALLISON R.—*Sculptor*
    Segreganset, Mass.

B. Taunton, Mass., July 5, 1916. *Studied*: Mass. Sch. A., and with Cyrus E. Dallin, Raymond Porter. *Member*: Utopian Cl., Providence. *Award*: Utopian Cl. Medal of Honor, 1957. *Work*: mem., tablets, busts, med., bronze doors and statues, Edith C. Baker Sch., Brookline, Mass.; Reany Mem. Lib., St. Johnsville, N.Y.; State T. Col., Lowell, Mass.; Univ. Mississippi; Notre Dame Univ.; U.S. Marine Corps; Anaconda Copper Mines; St. Mary's Cathedral, Trenton, N.J.; Buffalo Medical Soc.; Boston Gridiron Cl.; Dartmouth Col.; Moline (Ill.) Hist. Soc.; Providence Water Comm.; bronze port., Jordan Hospital, Plymouth, Mass.; Boston Univ.; sc., Mem. Stadium, Univ. Rhode Island; rotunda, Howard State Hospital, Providence, R.I.; Masonic Lodge, Rhode Island, and in Taunton, England; New Church of The Sacred Heart, Taftville, Conn.; Chenery Lib., Boston Univ. *Exhibited*: PAFA, 1938, 1939, 1948; Boston Soc. S.; Lyme AA; NSS, 1952.

MACPHERSON, MRS. J. HAVARD. See Edgerly,
  Beatrice

MacRAE, EMMA FORDYCE (Mrs. Homer Swift)—
  Painter
    888 Park Ave., New York 21, N.Y.

B. Vienna, Austria. *Studied*: ASL; N.Y. Sch. A., with Kenneth Hayes Miller. *Member*: NA; NAWA; All. A. Am.; NSMP; North Shore AA; Cosmopolitan Cl. *Awards*: prizes, Pen & Brush Cl., 1946, 1950, 1955; NAWA, 1941, 1945; All. A. Am., 1942; medal, NAC, 1930. *Work*: Wesleyan Col.; Cosmopolitan Cl.; NAD, and in private colls. *Exhibited*: Carnegie Inst.; AIC; CGA; PAFA; Joslyn Mus.

A.; Mus. FA of Houston; de Young Mus. A.; SAM; Colorado Springs FA Center; Newport AA; NAD; All. A. Am.; NAWA; one-man: Lyman Allyn Mus. A.; Berkshire Mus., Pittsfield, Mass.; Joslyn Mus. A.; Rutgers Univ.; Oxford (Miss.) Mus. A.; Nashville Mus. A.; Currier Mus. A.

Mac SPARRAN, TERRY—*Painter*
400 Shreveport Road, Barksdale Air Force Base, Louisiana

B. San Antonio, Tex., Nov. 24, 1917. *Studied*: Sophie Newcomb Col.; Univ. Texas; and in Morocco, North Africa and Italy. *Member*: Texas FA Assn.; Beaumont Mus.; Texas WC Soc.; New Orleans AA. *Awards*: prizes, New Orleans AA, 1958 (purchase); Beaumont Mus. A., 1958 (purchase); Texas WC Soc., 1956 (purchase); Louisiana State Exh., Baton Rouge, 1957; USAF Strategic Command A. Exh., 1957; Shreveport A. Cl., 1957. *Work*: Frost Bros., San Antonio; Beaumont Mus. A.; New Orleans AA; Hdqtrs., Strategic Air Command, Omaha. *Exhibited*: Provincetown A. Festival, 1958; New Orleans AA, 1956-1958; Mississippi AA, 1957; USAF A. Exh., 1957; Southeastern Annual, 1955, 1958; Beaumont Mus. A., 1956-1958; Texas WC Soc., 1956, 1957; Texas Painting & Sc. Exh., 1956; Louisiana State Exh., 1957; Texas FA Assn., 1956-1958; Assn. Georgia A., 1955; Savannah A. Cl.; Shreveport A. Cl.; Men of Art Gld., San Antonio, 1957 (one-man).

MACSOUD, NICHOLAS S.—*Painter*
1 Hanson Pl. (17); h. 131 76th St., Brooklyn 9, N.Y.

B. Zahle, Syria, Mar. 7, 1884. *Studied*: NAD. *Member*: SC; Brooklyn Soc. P. & S. *Awards*: prize, Soc. Four A., Palm Beach, Fla. *Work*: BM; Pocono Manor Inn; Hotel Dennis, Atlantic City, N.J.*

MADSEN, VIGGO HOLM—*Painter, T., Lith.*
318 South Park Ave., Lynbrook, N.Y.

B. Kaas, Denmark, Apr. 21, 1925. *Studied*: Syracuse Univ., B.F.A., M.F.A.; N.Y. State T. Col., Cortland, N.Y.; N.Y. Univ.; Columbia Univ.; Instituto de Allende, Mexico, with Jack Pinto. *Member*: N.Y. State A. T. Assn.; Eastern AA; Long Island A.T. Assn. (Vice-Pres.); Malverne AA. *Awards*: prizes, Syracuse Univ., 1951; N.Y. State A. T. Exh., 1957. *Work*: Peck Mem. Lib., Marathon, N.Y.; Doniphan Pub. Lib., Doniphan, Mo., and in private colls. Mural, Phila. Y.M.C.A. Camps, Downingtown, Pa. *Exhibited*: Silvermine Gld. A., 1956; A. Lg. of Long Island, 1956; Syracuse Mus. FA, 1950-1954; Rochester Mem. A. Gal., 1953, 1954; Heckscher Mus., Huntington, N.Y., 1956-1958; one-man: Syracuse Univ., 1951; Marathon (N.Y.) Pub. Lib., 1953-1956; Doniphan, Mo., 1956; Rockville Centre Pub. Lib., 1956-1958; Panoras Gal., N.Y., 1958; Setauket A. Gal. 1958. Contributor to N.Y. State Art Teachers Newsletter. *Positions*: Instr. A., Marathon and Rockville Centre, N.Y. Pub. Schs. and Adult Evening Classes.

MAGAFAN, ETHEL—*Painter*
Woodstock, N.Y.

B. Chicago, Ill., Oct. 10, 1916. *Studied*: Colorado Springs FA Center, and with Frank Mechau, Boardman Robinson,

Peppino Mangravite. *Awards*: Fulbright F., 1951; Tiffany scholarship, 1949; Stacey scholarship, 1947; prizes, NAD, 1951, 1956; Hallmark award, 1952; AWS, 1955; SFMA, 1950; Nat. Exh., Pomona, Cal., 1956 (purchase); Norfolk Mus. A., 1957; Ball State T. Col., 1958 (purchase). *Work*: MMA; Denver A. Mus.; WFNY 1939; Wilmington Soc. FA; Norfolk Mus. A.; Des Moines A. Center; murals, Senate Chamber, Recorder of Deeds Bldg., Social Security Bldg., all in Wash., D.C.; USPO, Auburn, Neb.; Wynne Ark.; Madill, Okla.; South Denver Branch, Colo. *Exhibited*: Denver A. Mus., 1938; Utah State A. Center, Salt Lake City; Contemp. A., N.Y., 1940; Raymond & Raymond Gal., Beverly Hills, 1944; Santa Barbara Mus. A., 1944; Scripps Col., 1945; Ganso Gal., 1950, 1953, 1954; Athens, Greece, 1952; Schenectady Mus. A., 1953; Albany Inst. Hist. & A., 1955; Carnegie Inst., 1938, 1941, 1943-1945, 1947, 1952; AIC, 1937-1941; Colorado Springs FA Center, 1938-1940, 1945; NAD, 1940, 1942, 1943, 1948, 1953, 1955-1958; MMA, 1942, 1950; PAFA, 1939, 1941, 1942, 1947-1949, 1952, 1954; CGA, 1939, 1948, 1949, 1951, 1953; SFMA, 1941, 1945, 1946, 1948; Watkins Gal., Am. Univ., 1951; Birmingham Mus. A., 1952, 1953; Wildenstein Gal., 1949, 1952, 1955; Univ. Texas, 1951; Springfield Mus. A., 1951; Butler AI, 1953, 1954, 1957, 1958; WMAA, 1952, 1957, 1958; Detroit Inst. A., 1958; Provincetown A. Festival, 1958; BM, 1958; Albany Inst. Hist. & A., 1950, 1952-1955; Munson-Williams-Proctor Inst., 1955; Brandeis Univ., 1954; Intl. Assn. Plastic Arts, 1956.

MAGRATH, EDMUND—*Portrait Painter*
420 North Walnut St., East Orange, N.J.

B. Spencer, Mass., Oct. 22, 1885. *Studied*: Ecole des Beaux-Arts, Paris, France; R.I. Sch. Des. *Member*: SC; AAPL; A. Center of the Oranges. *Award*: Citation, AAPL, 1955. *Work*: portraits, Bell Telephone Co., Prudential Ins. Co., American Ins. Co., Fireman's Ins. Co., Newark Col. of Engineering, all in Newark, N.J.; Am. Surety Co., N.Y.; N.Y. Bd. of Trade; S. B. Penick Co., N.Y.; City Hall, Library, Clifford Scott H.S., Panzer Col., General Hospital, all in East Orange, N.J.; Washington Col., Chestertown, Md.; State T. Col., Montclair, N.J.; Wright Aeronautical Co., Bethel, Conn., and others.*

MAHONEY, JAMES OWEN—*Painter, E.*
Twin Glens Rd., Ithaca, N.Y.

B. Dallas, Tex., Oct. 16, 1907. *Studied*: Southern Methodist Univ., B.A.; Yale Sch. FA, B.F.A.; Am. Acad. in Rome, F.A.A.R. *Member*: NSMP. *Awards*: Prix de Rome, 1932. *Work*: murals, Hall of State, Dallas, Tex.; Johns Hopkins Univ.; All Saints Episcopal Church, Chevy Chase, Md.; Fed. Bldg.; Communications Bldg., WFNY 1939; Adolphus Hotel, Dallas; Clinton Hotel, Ithaca, N.Y. *Exhibited*: PAFA, 1942; Grand Central A. Gal., 1935; Mace Gal., Dallas, 1946; Arch. Lg., 1936, 1938. *Position*: Prof. FA, Cornell Univ., Ithaca, N.Y., at present.

MAIRS, CLARA GARDNER—*Painter, Ser.*
377 Ramsey Hill, St. Paul 2, Minn.

B. Hastings, Minn., 1879. *Studied*: PAFA; Grande Chaumiere, Julian Acad., Paris, France, and with Daniel Garber. *Work*: PMA; La Jolla A. Center; San Diego FA Soc.; Minneapolis Inst. A.; Walker A. Center; LC; San Antonio Mus. A.; Atlanta, Ga.; Norton Gal. A., West Palm Beach, Fla.

Will Barnet
Wolfgang Behl
Alexander M. Bing
Cameron Booth
Charles Cajori
Robert Cronbach
Sue Fuller
Julio Girona
Balcomb Greene

Walter Kamys
Morris Kantor
Mariska Karasz
Joseph Konzal
Linda Lindeberg
Nicholas Marsicano
Lillyan Rhodes
Raymond Rocklin
John von Wicht

BERTHA SCHAEFER GALLERY · 32 E. 57th St., N. Y.

MAKARENKO, ZACHARY PHILIP—*Painter, S.*
18 75th St., North Bergen, N.J.

B. Starosherbynivka, Russia, Feb. 20, 1900. *Studied*: in Russia, Dusseldorf, Germany and Rome, Italy. *Member*: AAPL. *Awards*: prizes, Yorktown Fair, 1958; gold medal and prize, Burr Gal., 1958. *Work*: Russia, Germany and Italy; Burr Gal., N.Y. *Exhibited*: ACA Gal. 1952; Barbizon-Plaza Gal., 1953, 1954; New Jersey Soc. P. & S., 1955; A. Lg. of Long Island, 1956; Community A. Gal., Phila. Pa., 1956; NAC, 1957; All. A. Am., 1957; Burr Gal., 1958; Yorktown Fair, 1958.

MAKIELSKI, BRONISLAW ALEXANDER—
Painter, I., E., L.
955 Locust Ave., Charlottesville, Va.

B. South Bend, Ind., Aug. 13, 1901. *Studied*: AIC. *Member*: NSMP. *Work*: Univ. Michigan; Univ. Virginia; Altarpiece, Church of the Holy Comforter, Charlottesville, Va.; murals, Lincoln Sch., Ypsilanti, Mich.; Royal Oak (Mich.) H.S.; McDonald Sch., Dearborn, Mich.; ports., Michigan State Col.; Martha Jefferson Hospital, Charlottesville. *Exhibited*: Hoosier Salon; AIC; Detroit Inst. A., 1926-1945; New York, N.Y. *Position*: Instr., painting, Univ. Virginia, summer quarter, 1922-31; Detroit A. Acad., 1930-36; Dir., Jefferson Sch. F. & Appl. A., Charlottesville, Va., 1948- .

MAKIELSKI, LEON A.—*Portrait Painter, T.*
750 Arlington Blvd., Ann Arbor, Mich.

B. Morris Run, Pa., May 17, 1885. *Studied*: AIC; Julian Acad., Grande Chaumiere, Paris; & with Lucien Simon, Rene Menard, Henri Martin. *Member*: Scarab Cl., Detroit. *Awards*: prizes, traveling scholarship, AIC, 1908; Detroit Inst. A., 1917, 1919, 1921, 1923, 1925; Mich. State Fair, 1925; Scarab Cl., 1929. *Work*: port., Univ. Michigan; Purdue Univ.; Wayne Univ.; Univ. Virginia; murals, McDonald Sch., Dearborn, Mich.; Lincoln Sch., Ypsilanti, Mich.; Fordson H.S., Dearborn, Mich. *Exhibited*: U.S. & abroad. *Position*: Instr., drawing & painting, Univ. Michigan, 1915-28; Instr., Jewish Community Center, Detroit, Mich., 1932-52.

MALDARELLI, ORONZIO—*Sculptor, E.*
8 West 13th St., New York 11, N.Y.

B. Naples, Italy. *Studied*: CUASch.; NAD; BAID, and abroad. *Member*: S. Gld.; Nat. Inst. A. & Let. (Vice-Pres. 1952); Am. Acad. in Rome (Trustee); Guggenheim Mem. Fnd. (Memb. Adv. Com.). *Awards*: Guggenheim F., 1931, 1943; Grant, Am. Acad. A. & Let. & Nat. Inst. A. & Let., 1948; prizes, Fairmount Park Assn., Phila., Pa., 1929; PAFA, 1953; medals, AIC; gold medal, PAFA, 1951; silver medal, Arch. Lg., 1954, 1956. *Work*: CAM; Brookgreen Gardens, S.C.; AIC; MMA; WMAA; PAFA; VMFA; Munson-Williams-Proctor Inst., Utica, N.Y.; Fairmount Park Assn., Phila.; Newark Mus. A.; Ogunquit Mus. A., and many private colls.; sc., statues, panels, dec., reliefs, P.O. Dept. Bldg., Wash., D.C.; St. Patrick's Cathedral, N.Y.; Hartford (Conn.) Pub. Lib.; Central Park, N.Y. (bird bath); James Weldon Johnson Houses, N.Y.C. Housing Authority; American Export Lines; St. Bonaventure Col., N.Y.; Portland Cement Co., Allentown, Pa.; Queens Col. Lib.; Saxton's River, Vt.; Home Office Bldg., State Ins. Fund, N.Y.; Domestic Chapel, Loyola Seminary, Shrub Oak, N.Y.; USPO, Orange, Mass.; Lila Van der Smissen medal; Commemorative Bicentennial medal, Columbia Univ., and others. *Exhibited*: 3 one-man, Midtown Gal., 1933, 1935, 1948; Grand Central A. Gal., 1929, 1947; Sao Paulo, Brazil; MMA, 1951; S. Gld.; PAFA; Paul Rosenberg Gal., N.Y.; PMA; AIC; MModA., and many other major national exhibitions. *Position*: Prof. Sculpture, Columbia Univ., New York, N.Y., at present.

MALICOAT, PHILIP C.—*Painter*
320 Bradford St., Provincetown, Mass.

B. Indianapolis, Ind., Dec. 9, 1908. *Studied*: John Herron A. Sch.; & with Hawthorne, Hensche, Dickinson. *Member*: Provincetown AA. *Exhibited*: PAFA, 1933; CGA, 1935, 1937, 1939; NAD, 1936, 1938-1940, 1954; AIC, 1941; Phila. WC Cl., 1931, 1935; Inst. Mod. A., Boston, 1939; Provincetown AA, 1931-1952; Seligmann Gal., 1947 (one-man); Boston A. Festival, 1955-1957; Chrysler Mus. A., Provincetown, 1958; Wellons Gal., 1955 (one-man).

MALLARY, ROBERT WENLEY—
Painter, S., Gr., Des., E.
754 Coors Blvd., Albuquerque, N.M.; h. 3531 Meier St., Los Angeles 66, Cal.

B. Toledo, Ohio, Dec. 2, 1917. *Studied*: Laboratory Workshop, Boston, Mass., and in Mexico City, D.F. *Member*: AEA; CAA; AAUP. *Work*: BM; collaborator (with Dale Owen) mural, Beverly Hilton Hotel, Beverly Hills, Cal. *Exhibited*: Colorado Springs FA Center, 1935; Denver A. Mus., 1955; Sao Paulo, Brazil, 1955; Los A. Mus. A., 1950, 1953, 1954; one-man: SFMA, 1944; Santa Barbara Mus. A., 1952; San Diego FA Soc., 1952; Crocker A. Gal., Sacramento, Cal., 1944, 1953; Urban Gal., N.Y., 1954; Univ. New Mexico, 1956-1958; Mus. New Mexico, 1958; Highlands Univ., Las Vegas, N.M., 1958. Lectures: "New Media of the Artist-Sculptor"; "Tradition and Revolution in Contemporary Art"; "The Possibilities for Modern Art." *Position*: Instr., Cal. Sch. A., 1949-50; Hollywood A. Center Sch., 1950-54; Asst. Prof. A., Univ. New Mexico, Albuquerque, N.M., 1955- .

MALLON, GRACE ELIZABETH—*Illustrator, Des., P.*
Universal Studios, Universal City, Cal.; h. 4109 Kraft Ave., North Hollywood, Cal.

B. Elizabeth, N.J., Nov. 1, 1911. *Studied*: Newark Sch. F. & Indst. A.; Otis AI; Chouinard AI; & with Ralph Holmes, Millard Sheets; Phil Paradise. *Member*: Cal. WC Soc.; AWS; Cal. AC; Laguna Beach AA; San Diego AA; San Fernando Valley AC. *Awards*: med., book illus., 1937; prizes, Los A. Pub. Lib., 1939; Cal. AC, 1941; San Fernando Valley AC, 1945; Southern Cal. AC, 1946. *Work*: Cal. State Lib. *Exhibited*: Riverside Mus., 1944; GGE. 1939; de Young Mem. Mus., 1937; Santa Paula, Cal., 1935-1945; Cal. WC Soc., 1941-1945; Cal. AC, 1939-1946; Laguna Beach AA, 1939-1946. I., "First Foods of America," 1936; "Near Side and Far," 1937; & other books. *Position*: A. Dept., Universal Studios, Universal City, Cal., 1941-1946; Fairbanks Film Productions, 1946-50; I., Painter, Churchill-Wexler Film Productions, Hollywood, Cal., 1951-1956. Medical Illustrator, exhibitor in nat. exhs., 1958.

MALLOY, SUSAN RABINOWITZ (Mrs. E.)—*Painter*
15 Park Ave., New York 16, N.Y.

B. New York, N.Y., Feb. 28, 1924. *Studied*: Skidmore Col., B.S.; ASL; and with Morris Davidson. *Awards*: prizes, All. A. Am., 1957; Village A. Center, 1957. *Work*: Birndy Lib., Norwalk, Conn. *Exhibited*: All. A. Am., 1957; Art:USA, 1958; Silvermine Gld. A., 1953, 1955, 1957, 1958; Village A. Center; N.Y. City Center; New Canaan, Conn.

MALONE, LEE H. B.—*Museum Director, T., L.*
Museum of Fine Arts of Houston; h. 2122 Del Monte St., Houston, Tex.

B. Las Cruces, N.M., May 28, 1913. *Studied*: Univ. Sch., Cleveland, Ohio; Yale Sch. FA, B.A., and in Switzerland. *Member*: AAMus.; Assn. A. Mus. Dir.; AFA. *Awards*: W.L.Ehrich Mem. prize for research, Yale Univ., 1939. Author: "Spiritual Values in Art," 1953. Lectures: Gardens of the Renaissance; Sienese Art. Exhibitions arranged: "Art in Colonial Mexico," 1952; "The Three Brothers," 1957; "The Human Image," 1958. *Position*: Aide to Dir., Yale Univ. Gal., 1937-39; Dir., Columbus Gal. FA, Columbus, Ohio, 1946-53; Dir., Mus. FA of Houston, Houston, Tex., 1953- .

MALONE, PATRICK THOMAS—*Museum Director*
Art Center in La Jolla, 700 Prospect St.; h. 660 Prospect St., La Jolla, Cal.

B. Chicago, Ill., June 2, 1921. *Studied*: Univ. Chicago, with special work with G. Haydn Huntley, Ulrich Middeldorf, Franklin P. Johnson, Margaret Rickert, Ludwig Bachhofer; N.Y. Univ. Inst. FA, with Richard Offner; Walter Friedlaender, Jose Lopez-Rey, Erwin Panofsky, Walter W.S. Cook, and others. *Member*: AAMus.; Western Assn. A. Mus. Dirs.; Alumni Assn., N.Y. Univ. Inst. FA. *Awards*: Scholarships, Univ. Chicago; N.Y. Univ. Inst. FA. Author: Chapter on the use of films in museums. Films on Art, 1952; wrote script and served as Advisor for film on Velazquez, produced by Intl. Film Bureau, Chicago. Various book and film reviews for Film News and articles in AIC Quarterly. Co-authored article for Art News, 1955. Arranged exhibitions, catalogs: Graphic Work of the French Post-Impressionists, 1955; Great French

PORTRAIT
HEADQUARTERS
INFORMATION
UPON REQUEST

**GRAND CENTRAL
ART GALLERIES**

New Location
40 Vanderbilt Avenue
(Biltmore Hotel)
New York City

MUrray Hill 6-4737

---

catherine viviano
G A L L E R Y

Americans & Europeans

AFRO
BECKMANN
BIROLLI
BROWN (CARLYLE)
CREMONINI
DAVIE
FRANCESCONI
LANYON
MINGUZZI
MIRKO
MORLOTTI
PERLIN
ROSENTHAL
SAGE (KAY)
SMITH (JACK)

42 EAST 57   NEW YORK, N. Y.

JACQUES SELIGMANN & CO.
Inc.

5 East 57th St. • New York 22

*Old and Modern Paintings
Sculpture*

ATHENAEUM
of PHILOSOPHY & ART

COLLECTION
of Fine Paintings,
Oriental Art and
Antiques, Genuine
Old Master Violins
and Cellos, Rare
Music Library, etc.

COURSES
in Philosophy and Art
Correspondence Courses
Portraits and Paintings
to order

LEARN to THINK-PAINT-LIVE

Descriptions and Prices on Request

For information write:
1306 Quintero St., Los Angeles 26, Cal.

Paintings and Watercolors
by 19th and 20th Century

AMERICAN ARTISTS

———

Inquiries Invited

———

MILCH GALLERIES
21 E. 67TH ST., NEW YORK 21

Est. 1867

W. S.
BUDWORTH
& SON, INC.

424 W. 52 St.   •   N.Y.C.

**PACKERS and MOVERS
of WORKS of ART**

Tel. CO 5-2194

good taste
in
framing

• unlimited variety
• original antiques
• modern designs

the house of
heydenryk
141 w 54 st
new york 19

Paintings, 1956; San Diego—City Alive, 1956; Pre-Columbian Sculpture, 1956. Serves on many juries for art exhibitions; radio and TV broadcasts; lectures to civic and school groups. *Positions*: Asst. Cur., Painting & Sculpture, AIC, 1947-1955; Dir., Art Center in La Jolla, La Jolla, Cal., 1955-1959.

MALONEY, DANIEL—*Painter*
23 East 73rd St., New York 21, N.Y.

B. Pittsburgh, Pa., Aug. 8, 1922. *Studied*: Cincinnati A. Acad.; New Sch. for Social Research; ASL. *Exhibited*: WMAA, 1952; Wadsworth Atheneum, Hartford, Conn. 1952; Springfield Mus. A., 1950; Inst. Contemp. A., London, England, 1950. Illus. "The Four Continents," 1954.*

MALTEN, CHARLOTTE—*Craftsman, Des., T.*
Germonds Rd., West Nyack, N.Y.; h. 74 West 68th St., New York 23, N.Y.

B. Breslau, Jan. 12, 1912. *Studied*: Col. of Breslau; Ecole des Beaux-Arts, Paris, France; Craft Students Lg., N.Y.; N.Y. Univ. *Member*: N.Y. Soc. of Craftsmen; N.Y. Soc. Ceramic A. *Exhibited*: Mus. Natural Hist., 1949-1954; Hacker Gal., 1951; Barbizon-Plaza Hotel, N.Y., 1948-1952; AEA, 1955; Cooper Union Mus., 1955; Staten Island Mus. A. & Sc.; Rockland Fnd., West Nyack, N.Y.; Brentano, N.Y., 1957, 1958 (one-man). *Position*: Inst., Ceramics, Craft Students Lg., Art Workshop, N.Y. Gld. for the Blind, all N.Y.C.; YWCA, Brooklyn, N.Y.

MANCA, ALBINO—*Sculptor*
131 West 11th St., New York 11, N.Y.

B. Tertenia, Sardinia, Italy, Jan. 1, 1898. *Studied*: Royal Acad. FA, Rome, with Ferrari, Zanelli. *Member*: F., NSS; AAPL; All. A. Am. *Awards*: prizes, Royal Acad. FA, Rome. 1926, 1927; Animal in Art Exh., Rome, 1938; Montclair A. Mus., 1941; AAPL, 1941, 1950; All. A. Am. 1943. *Work*: Monument, Cagliari, Italy; USPO, Lyons, Ga.; many portraits, busts, medals; Nat. Mus., Sassari, Italy; Gal. Modern A., Littoria, Italy; Brookgreen Gardens, S.C., and in private colls. *Exhibited*: Nationally and internationally.*

MANCHAK, ALBERT—*Painter, T.*
711 118th St., Whiting, Ind.

B. Alton, Ill., July 14, 1925. *Studied*: Univ. Wyoming, M.A., B.S. *Member*: Am. Edu. Assn. *Exhibited*: Mus. Contemp. A., Houston, Tex., 1957; Art:USA, 1958; AIC, 1953; Colorado Springs FA Center, 1955; Denver A. Mus., 1955; Northern Indiana AA, 1953-1956. *Positions*: Instr. A., Dyer Central H.S., Dyer, Ind.; A. Supv., Lake County, Indiana.

MANCHESTER, MRS. EMILY BURLING WAITE. See Waite, Emily Burling

MANDEL, HOWARD—*Painter, S., I.*
Woodstock, N.Y.

B. Bayside, N.Y., Feb. 24, 1917. *Studied*: PIASch.; N.Y. Sculpture Center; ASL; and with Fernand Leger, Andre Lhote, Paris, France. *Awards*: Tiffany F., 1939, 1949; Hallmark Award, 1949, 1952, 1955; Fulbright F., 1951-52; grant, Nat. Inst. A. & Let., 1955; A. Dir. Cl., prize, 1955; Du Prix Arts, M.G.M., Paris, France, 1952. *Work*: Ft. Stanton Marine Hospital, N.M.; Lexington (Ky.) H.S. *Exhibited*: Salon des Jeunes Peintres, Paris, 1952; MMA, 1950, 1952; WMAA, 1948-1955; AWS, 1937-1955; PAFA; AIC; CGA; Delgado Mus. A.; Munson-Williams-Proctor Inst.; Columbia (S.C.) Mus. A.; Norton Gal. A.; High Mus. A.; NAD; one-man: Assoc. Am. A., 1949; Ganso Gal., 1951, 1953; Phila. A. All., 1955; Fairleigh Dickinson Col., Rutherford, N.J., 1955.

MANDELMAN, BEATRICE—*Painter, Ser.*
Taos, N.M.

B. Newark, N.J., Dec. 31, 1912. *Studied*: ASL; Newark Sch. F. & Indst. A. *Member*: Nat. Serigraph Soc. *Work*: MMA; MModA; Brooklyn Pub. Lib.; Mus. New Mexico; Univ. Omaha. *Exhibited*: AIC; PAFA; Phila. A. All.; WMAA; CGA; Carnegie Inst.; BMFA; MModA; MMA; Springfield Mus. A.; Riverside Mus. A.; BMA; SFMA; SAM; Mus. New Mexico, Santa Fé (one-man); ACA Gal.

(one-man); Hudson Walker Gal.; Colorado Springs FA Center; Denver A. Mus.; Dallas Mus. FA.; Mortimer Levitt Gal. (one-man); Bertha Schaefer Gal. (one-man). *Position*: Instr., Taos Valley A. Sch., Taos, N.M.

MANGRAVITE, PEPPINO—*Painter, E., W., L.*
224 East 49th St., New York 17, N.Y.; s. West Cornwall, Conn.

B. Lipari, Italy, June 28, 1896. *Studied*: Scuole Techniche, Belle Arti, Italy, and with Robert Henri; ASL; CUASch., N.Y. *Member*: Century Assn.; Columbia Faculty Cl.; NSMP. *Awards*: Guggenheim F., 1932, 1935; prizes, GGE, 1939; Woodmere Gal., Phila., Pa., 1944; Grant, Am. Inst. A. & Let., 1950; gold medal, Sesqui-Centennial Expo., Phila., 1926; Silver medal & Prize, AIC, 1942; Eyre medal, PAFA, 1950; Silver medal, Arch. Lg., 1955. *Work*: MMA; WMAA; CGA; PC; AIC; Denver A. Mus.; Cal. PLH; CM; Colorado Springs FA Center; PAFA; Carnegie Inst.; Santa Barbara Mus. A.; LC; Encyclopaedia Britannica; murals, USPO, Hempstead, L.I., N.Y.; Atlantic City, N.J.; Jackson Heights, L.I., N.Y.; mosaic murals, St. Anthony's Shrine, Boston, Mass. *Exhibited*: nationally and internationally. Contributor to art magazines with articles on art and art education. *Position*: Trustee, AFA, 1940-42; Am. Acad. in Rome, 1948-49; Assoc. Prof. Painting, Hd., Sch. Painting & Sculpture, Columbia University, New York, N.Y.

MANIATTY, STEPHEN G.—*Painter, T., C., Et., I., L.*
Main St., Old Deerfield, Mass.

B. Norwich, Conn., Sept. 5, 1910. *Studied*: Massachusetts Sch. A. *Member*: Southern Vermont AA; Rockport AA; North Shore AA; Deerfield Valley AA; Springfield Academic AA; Copley Soc., Boston; AAPL; Ogunquit AA, and others. *Awards*: prizes, North Shore AA, 1943, 1955; Deerfield Valley AA, 1945; Pittsfield Mus. A.; Academic AA, 1957, 1958. *Work*: Historical murals, Franklin County Trust Co.; ports. in private collections. *Exhibited*: Academic AA, 1955-1958; AAPL, 1958; Conn. Acad. FA. 1948-1950 and later; Ogunquit AA, 1955-1958; North Shore AA, 1957-1958; Rockport AA, 1948-1958; Springfield A. Lg., 1945-1950; Upper Hudson Valley, 1948-1950, and many others; one-man: Hartford, Conn.; Rockport AA; Deerfield Acad.; etc. Lectures: Art History; Italian and Greek Art to schools and civic organizations. *Positions*: A. Supv., Deerfield Union and Orange, Mass., Pub. Schs., 1936-45, 1950-58; Resident Artist, Deerfield Acad., 1945-50. Private teaching.

MANKOWSKI, BRUNO—*Sculptor, P., C.*
2231 Broadway; h. Sunnyside Gardens, N.Y.

B. Germany, Oct. 30, 1902. *Studied*: BAID, and in Berlin, Germany. *Member*: ANA; NSS; All. A. Am.; Audubon A.; AAPL; Arch. Lg. *Awards*: Certif. Craftsmanship, N.Y. Building Congress, 1937; prizes, New Jersey State Exh., 1945; NSS, 1953; AAPL, 1955, 1956; Syracuse Mus. FA, 1949; Medallic Art Comp., 1949; Nat. Inst. A. & Let. grant, 1950; Mus. A. & Crafts, Meriden, Conn. *Work*: Steuben Glass Co.; USPO, Chesterfield, S.C.; monument, Brooklyn, N.Y.; Loyola Seminary, Shrub Oak, N.Y.; Va. Polytechnic Inst.; plaque, Macombs Jr. H.S., N.Y.; figureheads, SS. Independence and Constitution; plaque, Medallic Art Co. Bldg.; Motion Picture Pioneers Award plaques; MMA; Michigan State Col., U.S. Capitol, Wash., D.C. *Exhibited*: Am. Acad. A. & Lets., 1949, 1950; PMA, 1949; PAFA, 1948-1954; NAD, 1948-1950, 1956, 1958; Arch. Lg., 1949, 1957; Syracuse Mus. FA, 1949, 1950, 1958; NSS, 1948-1952, 1956-1958; NAWA, 1950, 1951; Parke-Bernet Garden Exh., 1951, 1952; AAPL, 1955, 1956; All. A. Am., 1956, 1957; Meriden A. & Crafts, 1956-1958; NAC, 1957, and others. *Position*: Chm Exh. Com., NSS, 1956-1958.

MANN, MRS. FERDINAND. See Dehner, Dorothy

MANNEN, PAUL WILLIAM—*Painter, E., L.*
New Mexico College of Agriculture & Mechanic Arts, State College, N.M.

B. Topeka, Kans., June 22, 1906. *Studied*: Univ. Kansas, B.F.A.; Ohio State Univ., M.A. *Member*: MacDowell FA Soc. *Awards*: prize, Dayton AI, 1943. *Work*: Thayer A. Mus., Student Mem. Union, Pub. Sch., Pub. Lib., all in Lawrence, Kans. *Exhibited*: Kansas City AI, 1931-1934, 1936, 1941, 1942; Joslyn Mus. A., 1934, 1941; Columbus

PAUL DREY GALLERY

MASTERPIECES OF PAINTING
SCULPTURE • DRAWING
OBJECTS OF ART

11 EAST 57th STREET
NEW YORK 22, N. Y.

PLaza 3-2551   Cable: Asdrey, N. Y.

J. B. NEUMANN

ART CONSULTANT

41 EAST 57th STREET

NEW YORK 22   PLAZA 3-8205

MAYNARD WALKER
G A L L E R Y

Works of Art

117 E. 57th St., New York, N. Y.

We publish and distribute color prints, by domestic and foreign printers and publishers at discount.

We distribute original graphics by AMERICAN and MEXICAN artists.

KAETHE KOLLWITZ prints in all media.

**ARTHUR ROTHMANN
FINE ARTS**

1123 Broadway, New York 10, N. Y.

Our catalogue with 327 illustrations is available at 50 cents.

STENDAHL GALLERIES

Pre-Columbian Art
Modern French Paintings

7055-65 Hillside Ave., Los Angeles 28
11 East 68th St., New York 21

OVER 100 YEARS EXPERIENCE
AS

DEALERS IN FINE PAINTINGS

VOSE GALLERIES
OF BOSTON
INC.

559 BOYLSTON ST., BOSTON, MASS.

MIDTOWN

GALLERIES   A. D. GRUSKIN, DIR.

SINCE 1932

*Representing Distinguished
Contemporary*

AMERICAN ARTISTS

EXHIBITIONS CIRCUITED

17 EAST 57 ST.   NEW YORK

Gal. FA, 1938; Kansas Artists, 1936-1941; Prairie WC Traveling Exh., 1937-1942; Kansas Traveling Exh., 1938, 1951, 1955; Mus. New Mexico Traveling Exh., 1954-55; Dayton AI, 1942. Numerous one-man exhs. Lectures: Mexican Arts & Crafts; European Art. *Position*: Prof. A., H. A. Dept., Oklahoma Col. for Women, Chickasha, Okla., 1945-48; Prof. A. & Hist. A., Hd. & Fndr. A. Dept., New Mexico A. & M. Col., State College, N.M., 1948- .

MANNING, REG(INALD) (WEST)—
Cartoonist, W., Des.

Republic-Gazette Bldg.; h. 5724 East Cambridge St., Phoenix, Ariz.

B. Kansas City, Mo., April 8, 1905. *Member*: Arizona Press Cl.; Nat. Cartoonists Soc.; Phoenix Press Cl.; Am. Assn. Editorial Cartoonists; Phoenix FA Assn. (Trustee). *Awards*: Pulitzer prize, 1951; Nat. Airborne Assn., Ernie Pyle award, 1955; Freedom Fnd. award, 1950, 1951, 1952, 1955; Nat. Safety Council award, 1957. Author, I., "Cartoon Guide of Arizona," 1938; "What Kind of Cactus Izzat?", 1941; "From Tee to Cup," 1954. *Position*: Cart., Arizona Republic, 1926-48; Ed. Cart. McNaught Syndicate, 1948- .

MANNING, WRAY—*Painter*

Manning Studios, Inc., 1240 Huron Rd., Cleveland, Ohio; h. Sugar Hill, Chesterland, Ohio

B. London, Ohio, Sept. 13, 1896. *Studied*: Columbus Sch. FA; N.Y. Sch. F. & App. Des., and with Robert Henri, Walt Kuhn, Kenneth Hayes Miller. *Member*: Cleveland Soc. A.; AEA. *Awards*: numerous prizes, CMA. *Work*: CMA. *Exhibited*: PAFA; AIC; Carnegie Inst.; CMA; Butler AI. *Position*: Founder, Treas., Manning Studios.*

MANOIR, IRVING K.—*Painter, C., Et., L., W.*

415 Acacia Ave., Corona del Mar, Cal.

B. Chicago, Ill., Apr. 28, 1891. *Studied*: AIC; PAFA; with Hans Hofmann, St. Tropez, France, and in other European countries. *Awards*: prizes, J.B. Speed Mus. A., 1926; Laguna Beach AA, 1925. *Work*: AIC; Milwaukee AI; J.B. Speed Mus. A.; Cowie Gal., Los A.; Vanderpoel Coll.; mural, Vincennes (Ind.) H.S.; Chicago Pub. Sch. Coll. *Exhibited*: Century of Progress, Chicago, 1933, 1934; CGA; AIC (2 one-man); Pan-American Expo., Los A., 1926; Los A. Mus. A., 1926; PAFA; Carnegie Inst.; Milwaukee AI (one-man); Minn. State Fair, 1923 (one-man); J.B. Speed Mus. A.; Laguna Beach AA; Pasadena AI (one-man); Ainslie Gal., Los A.; Chicago Gal. Assn. (one-man); Marshall Field, Chicago (2 one-man); Jalisco, Mexico (one-man); Maui, Hawaii, 1958 (one-man). Lectures: "Creative Thinking"; "Visual and Kinesthetic," etc. *Position*: Assoc. Dir., Chicago Acad. FA, 1921; Assoc. with Prof. Hambidge, Yale Univ., teaching Dynamic Symmetry, 1920-21; Instr., painting, AIC; Layton Sch. A., Milwaukee, Wis.

MANSFIELD, RICHARD HARVEY (DICK)—
Cartoonist, L., T.

Washington Evening Star, Washington, D.C.; h. 2800 Cheverly Ave., Cheverly, Md.

B. Washington, D.C., Feb. 5, 1888. *Studied*: Corcoran A. Sch.; Evans Sch. Cartooning, Cleveland, Ohio. *Awards*: prizes and other awards, Washington Times Nat. Comp. for Cartoonists; American Legion for school talks on Safety; Nat. Safety Council; D.A.R. award; Kiwanis award, and other commendations and citations for safety talks in schools. Conducts cartoon show "Safety Circus" on TV. *Position*: Cart., Washington, D.C. Evening Star; Creator of Sunday feature "Those Were the Happy Days," Sunday Star, Wash., D.C., since 1926.

MANSHIP, PAUL—*Sculptor, L., T.*

15 Gramercy Park, New York 3, N.Y.; also, Lanesville, Gloucester, Mass.

B. St. Paul, Minn., Dec. 25, 1885. *Studied*: St. Paul Sch. FA; PAFA; Am. Acad. in Rome. *Member*: NA; NSS; Nat. Inst. A. & Let.; Am. Acad. A. & Let.; Nat. Comm. FA, Wash., D.C.; NAC; A. Comm. City of New York. *Awards*: F., Am. Acad. A. & Sc.; F. Am. Acad. in Rome; Legion d'Honneur, 1929; prize, NAD, 1913, 1917; med., PAFA, 1913; Pan-Pacific Exp., 1915; AIA, 1921; Am. Numismatic Soc., 1924; Phila. AA, 1925; Sesqui-Centennial Exp., Phila., 1926; Paris Salon, 1937; NSS, 1943. *Work*: groups, mem., monuments, reliefs: Cochran Mem. Park,

St. Paul, Minn.; Ft. Wayne, Ind.; MMA; Am. Acad. in Rome; Am. Cemetery, Thiaucourt, France; Am. Military Cemetery, Anzio, Italy; Brookgreen Gardens, S.C.; Zoological Park, N.Y.; Phillips Acad., Andover, Mass.; Rockefeller Center, N.Y.; League of Nations, Geneva, Switzerland; Norton Gal. A.; Univ. Florida; Coliseum, N.Y.; many port. busts & medal designs. *Exhibited*: nationally & internationally. Contributor to: Encyclopaedia Britannica, "The History of Sculpture," "Decorative Sculpture." Lectures: "Sculpture in the Making." *Position*: Pres., NSS, 1939-42; Pres., Am. Acad. A. & Let.; Pres., Century Assn., 1950-54; Chm., Smithsonian FA Comm.; Pres., Alum. Assn., Am. Acad. in Rome, 1939, 1941; Corresponding member, Inst. France, 1946; Corresponding member, Argentine Acad. FA, 1943; Nat. Acad., San Luca, Italy; Instr. S., PAFA, Philadelphia, Pa., 1943-46.

MANSO, LEO—*Painter, Des., T.*

2 West 15th St. (11); h. 460 Riverside Drive, New York 27, N.Y.

B. New York, N.Y., Apr. 15, 1914. *Studied*: NAD; New Sch. for Social Research. *Member*: AEA. *Awards*: prizes, Urbana, Ill., 1951 (purchase); Audubon A., 1952; Wesleyan Univ. A. Festival, Ill., 1954 (purchase). *Work*: WMAA; Urbana, Ill.; Wesleyan Univ.; Lichtenstein Mus., Israel. *Exhibited*: WMAA, 1948-1950, 1952, 1955; PAFA, 1947-1950, 1952, 1953; Audubon A., 1946-1952, 1954; Walker A. Center, 1952; BM, 1949; WMA, 1951; one-man: Norlyst Gal., 1947; Mortimer Levitt Gal., 1950; Babcock Gal., 1953, 1956. *Position*: Instr., Painting & Drawing, New York Univ.; Design & Drawing, Columbia Univ.; Painting, Cooper Union Sch. A., New York, N.Y.*

MANUEL, DONALDO—*Restorer, P., L.*

359 West Del Mar, Pasadena, Cal.

B. Buenos Aires, Argentina, 1898. *Studied*: Univ. Buenos Aires; Salamanca Univ., Spain. *Member*: F., Royal Soc. A., London, England. *Awards*: medal, Univ. Notre Dame. *Work*: Grumbacher Coll.; Rollins Col. *Position*: Technical restorer for museums and well-known private collections; conservation work for San Gabriel Missions on 14 paintings by an American Indian, 1791; four in San Fernando Mission, 1956.

MANUEL, MRS. DOROTHY HOLT. See Holt, Dorothy M.

MANVILLE, ELSIE—*Painter*

175 Lexington Ave., New York 16, N.Y.

B. Philadelphia, Pa., May 11, 1922. *Studied*: Stella Elkins Tyler Sch. FA, Temple Univ. *Awards*: Carol Beck Medal and Mary Smith Prize, PAFA, 1953; Tyler Sch. FA, 1948, 1950, 1956. *Work*: Lehigh Univ.; Temple Univ. *Exhibited*: PAFA, 1948, 1949, 1951, 1953; Butler Inst. Am. A., 1957; Springville H.S., Utah, 1957; Buck Hill Falls, 1957, 1958; Springfield Mus. A., 1957; DMFA, 1957; Mary Washington Col., 1956; Lehigh Univ., 1956, 1957.

MARANS, MOISSAYE (Mr.)—*Sculptor, L., T.*

252 Fulton St.; h. 200 Clinton St., Brooklyn 1, N.Y.

B. Kisinau, Roumania, 1902. *Studied*: Tech. Inst., Bucharest; Univ. Jassy, Roumania; CUASch.; NAD; PAFA; Cincinnati Acad. FA; BAID; N.Y. Univ. *Member*: F., NSS; Arch. Lg. (Vice-Pres., 1954-56); Audubon A., (Treas., 1955-56). *Awards*: prizes, PAFA; Football Coach of the year plaque comp., 1946; USPO Comp., York, Pa.; Avery award, Arch. Lg., 1957; AFA traveling exh.; silver medal, Arch. Lg., 1953. *Work*: Brooklyn Botanical Gardens; USPO, Boyertown, Pa.; Chagrin Falls, Ohio; West Baden Col., West Baden Springs, Ind.; WFNY 1939; Temple Emanu-El, Houston, Tex. *Exhibited*: NAD; All. A. Am.; Los A. Mus. A.; AFA; BM; Jewish Mus.; CGA; WFNY 1939; WMAA; PMA; PAFA; NSS; Arch. Lg.; Am.-Jewish Tercentenary; Univ. St. Louis, 1949; Univ. Minnesota, 1950; Mint Mus. A., 1950; Univ. St. Thomas, Houston, 1950; CMA, 1954; Sc. Center, N.Y., 1952, 1956; Detroit Inst. A., 1958; Audubon A., 1955-1958, and many others. Lectures: Sculpture, Brooklyn Col., Brooklyn, N.Y.

MARANTZ, IRVING—*Painter, T.*

198 Sixth Ave., New York, N.Y.

B. Elizabeth, N.J., Mar. 22, 1912. *Studied*: Newark Sch. F. & Indst. A.; ASL, and in China. *Member*: Nat. Sc·

THE

BURLINGTON MAGAZINE

Founded 1903

For more than fifty years

THE WORLD'S LEADING ART JOURNAL

THE BURLINGTON MAGAZINE is indispensable to all interested in the study and appreciation of the arts.

It deals with all forms of art from Ancient times to the present day.

Its contributors are acknowledged authorities in their separate fields.

Prospectus sent on request

Specimen Number $1.00. post free

Published Monthly 6s. (U.S.A. $1.00)
Annual Subscription £3.12.0 (U.S.A. $12.00)

THE BURLINGTON MAGAZINE
12 BEDFORD SQUARE, LONDON, W.C.I.

Painters in Casein; Cape Cod AA; AEA; Provincetown AA. *Awards*: prizes, Pepsi-Cola (one-man at Opportunity Gal.); Cape Cod AA, 1953. *Work*: Ein Harod Mus., Israel; Tel-Aviv Mus., Israel; Fla. Southern Col.; Butler Inst. Am. A.; Living Arts Fnd.; Bayonne Jewish Community Center. *Exhibited*: Butler Inst. Am. A., 1958; Newark Mus. A., 1958; N.Y. Univ., 1957; Congress for Jewish Culture, 1956-1958; Far East Exh., USIS; Audubon A., 1945, 1946, 1951; PAFA, 1947-1952; CGA, 1947, 1951; Univ. Illinois, 1948, 1950; WMAA, 1948; Carnegie Inst., 1949; VMFA, 1946; NAD, 1953; AFA traveling exh., 1955; one-man: Shore Studios, Provincetown, Mass., 1950, 1954, 1955; Babcock Gal., 1952, 1954, 1957, 1958. *Position*: Instr., Painting, Newark Sch. F. & Indst. A., 1949-52; Col. City of N.Y., 1951-52; Ballard Sch., N.Y., 1951-55; Provincetown Sch. Painting, 1951-55.

MARCEAU, HENRI—*Museum Director*
Philadelphia Museum of Art; h. 3423 Warden Dr., Philadelphia 29, Pa.

B. Richmond, Va., June 21, 1896. *Studied*: Columbia Univ., B.Arch.; F., Am. Acad. in Rome. *Member*: Am. Philosophical Soc. (1949-). Author: numerous exhibition catalogs, etc. Contributor to: art magazines in U.S. & abroad. *Position*: Cur., John G. Johnson Coll., PMA, Philadelphia, Pa., 1926- ; Asst. Dir., PMA, to 1945; Assoc. Dir., PMA, to 1955, Dir., 1955- ; member Phila. A. Comm., 1943- , Vice-Pres., 1947- ; member Advisory Com., Walters A. Gal., Baltimore, Md., 1935-39; Hon. Assoc. AIA; Hon. D.F.A., Temple Univ.

MARDER, DORIE—*Painter, Ser.*
223 West 21st St., New York 11, N.Y.

B. Poland, May 1, 1916. *Studied*: Sorbonne, Paris, France; ASL, and with Louis Schanker, Abraham Rattner, Morris Kantor and others. *Member*: Am. Color Pr. Soc.; Lg. Present-Day A.; ASL. *Exhibited*: Riverside Mus., 1946, 1953, 1955; Nat. Ser. Soc., 1949-1951; Am. Color Pr. Soc., 1949-1951; Northwest Pr. M.; SAM, 1950; Lg. Present-Day A., 1950, 1951; Sweat Mem. Mus., 1952; Pr. M. of So. Cal., 1952; Am. Color Pr. Soc. traveling exh., 1951; John Myers Fnd., 1952; Audubon A., 1954; ACA Gal., 1954, 1955; BMFA, 1954; New Sch. for Social Research, 1954, 1955; Village A. Center, 1955; Reading Pub. Mus., 1955; Washington Univ., 1955; Children's Mus., Nashville, Tenn., 1955; Milwaukee AI, 1955; Art: USA, 1958; Knickerbocker A.; Univ. Mich'gan; State T. Col., Cortland, N.Y.; Sienna Heights Col.; Memphis State Col.; New Jersey Soc. P. & S.; Hudson Gld. A.; Contemporary A. Gal.

MAREIN, EDMUND—*Designer, T.*
145 East 52nd St., New York, N.Y.; h. 355 East Shore Rd., Great Neck, N.Y.

B. Buffalo, N.Y., Jan. 30, 1907. *Studied*: Cornell Univ.; PIASch. *Member*: A. Dir. Cl. *Position*: Instr., Adv. Des., Cooper Union, New Sch. for Social Research, New York, N.Y.*

MARGO, BORIS—*Painter, Gr., E., L.*
8 East 18th St. (3); h. 966 Third Ave., New York 22, N.Y.

B. Wolotschisk, Russia, Nov. 7, 1902. *Studied*: Leningrad, Moscow, Odessa, Russia. *Awards*: prizes, Phila. Pr. Cl., 1946; BM, 1947, 1953, 1955; AIC, 1947. *Work*: MMA; WMAA; BM; PMA; BMA; CM; SFMA; Delgado Mus. A.; AIC; Joslyn Mus. A.; Sao Paulo, Brazil; U.S. Nat. Mus., Wash., D.C.; Univ. of: Maine, Mich., North Carolina, Arizona, Louisville, Minnesota; Yale Univ.; Cornell Univ.; Brown Univ.; colleges: Albion, Dartmouth, Texas Wesleyan, San Jose State; public libraries: New York City, Kansas City, Mo.; Currier Gal. A.; Research Studio, Fla.; R.I. Sch. Des.; Albright A. Gal., and in many European print collections and in private collections in the U.S. *Exhibited*: WMAA, 1946, 1950, 1952-1956; Walker A. Center, 1950; MMA, 1942, 1950, 1952; Univ. Michigan, 1950; Univ. Illinois, 1950-1952, 1954; AIC, 1950, 1951, 1954, 1956; A. Gal., N.Y., 1951; Sao Paulo, Brazil, 1951, 1952, 1954; Univ. Nebraska, 1951; Japan, 1951, 1957; Univ. Minnesota, 1951, 1954; AFA traveling exh., 1951; BM, 1951-1958; Paris, France, 1952; Carnegie Inst., 1952; Chicago, 1952; Los A. County Fair, 1953; Stable Gal., N.Y., 1953-1955; Dallas, Tex., 1953; Nat. Inst. A. & Let., 1953, 1958; Betty Parsons Gal., 1955, 1958 (one-man); Netherlands, 1953; MModA, 1954; LC, 1944, 1946, 1954;

Kraushaar Gal., 1954, 1957; Nat. Acad., Rome, 1954; Fed. Modern P. & S., 1955; Contemporaries, 1955; Barcelona, Spain, 1955; Venice, Italy, 1956; Tate Gal., London; Boston A. Festival; Bennington Col. (one-man).

MARGOLIES, ETHEL POLACHECK—*Painter, W., T., C.*
Jelliff Mill Rd., New Canaan, Conn.

B. Milwaukee, Wis., Aug. 1, 1907. *Studied*: Smith Col., A.B.; Silvermine Gld. Sch. A., with Revington Arthur, Gail Symon; and with Umberto Romano, Robert Roche. *Member*: Silvermine Gld. A.; Cape Ann Soc. Mod. A.; Smith Col. Cl.; New Haven Paint & Clay Cl.; Conn. WC Soc. *Awards*: prizes, Burndy Engineering Award, Silvermine Gld. A., 1957; Electric Regulator Corp., 1954; New Haven Paint & Clay Cl., 1955 (purchase); Springfield A. Lg., 1957 (purchase); Chautauqua AA, 1958. *Work*: Burndy Lib., Norwalk, Conn.; Springfield Mus. A.; New Haven Paint & Clay Cl. *Exhibited*: Audubon A., 1954; ACA Gal., 1955-1958; Conn. Acad. FA, 1952-1957; Springfield A. Lg., 1955-1958; New Haven Paint & Clay Cl., 1952, 1954-1958; Conn. WC Soc., 1955-1958; Meriden A. & Crafts, 1952; Cape Ann Soc. Mod. A., 1953-1955; Silvermine Gld. A., 1953-1958; Chautauqua AA, 1958; New School, 1957; Art: USA, 1958; traveling exh., Nat. Soc. Painters in Casein, 1958-59.

MARGOLIS, NATHAN—*Painter, Des., Lith., Ser.*
840 Asbury Terrace, Philadelphia 26, Pa.

B. Philadelphia, Pa., Jan. 26, 1908. *Studied*: Univ. Pennsylvania, B.S.; Harvard Univ.; Tyler Sch. FA, Temple Univ., M.F.A.; Barnes Fnd. *Member*: Phila. Pr. Cl.; Tyler Fellows; Am. Color Pr. Soc.; AEA; Phila. A. All. *Awards*: prizes, Graphic Sketch Cl., 1933; Conn. Acad. FA, 1945; Am. Color Pr. Soc., 1955; Tyler Sch. FA Alumni, 1957. *Work*: PMA. *Exhibited*: AIC, 1935; LC, 1942, 1945; Cleveland Pr. M., 1937; Conn. Acad. FA, 1945, 1946; PAFA, 1936, 1937, 1958; Woodmere A. Gal.; A. All., Pr. Cl., Sketch Cl., A. Cl., all of Philadelphia, Pa.; Cheltenham A. Center, 1952; Woodmere A. Gal., 1952; Tyler Sch. FA, 1950, 1952; Am. Color Pr. Soc., 1954 (one-man).

MARGON, LESTER—*Designer, W.*
312 West 23rd St., New York 11, N.Y.

B. New York, N.Y., Jan. 26, 1892. *Studied*: N.Y. Univ.; CUASch; New Sch. Social Research; PIASch; Columbia Univ.; Stevens Inst. *Member*: Soc. Designer-Craftsmen; Soc. Furniture Des.; AID. *Awards*: med., BAID, 1924, 1925; prize, Mechanics Inst., N.Y., 1920. Author, I., series of drawings & commentary, "Little-Known Furniture Treasures of the Old and the New Worlds"; "Furniture of Scandinavia"; "Construction of American Furniture Treasures," 1949; "Furniture—Yesterday, Today and Tomorrow," 1953; "World Furniture Treasures," 1954. Contributor to: trade magazines. Des., Modern stores and equipment.

MARGOULIES, BERTA (*Mrs. Berta Margoulies O'Hare***)—***Sculptor, T.*
206 East 30th St., New York 16, N.Y.; also, Flanders, N.J.

B. Lowitz, Poland, Sept. 7, 1907. *Studied*: Hunter Col., B.A.; ASL; Julian Acad., Ecole des Beaux-Arts, Paris, France. *Member*: NAWA; S. Gld.; AEA. *Awards*: F., Gardner Fnd., 1929; Guggenheim F., 1946; prizes, Arch. Lg., 1936; Am. Acad. A. & Let., 1944; Soc. Four A., 1947; PAFA, 1951; Montclair A. Mus., 1952, 1953. *Work*: Willamette Univ., Salem, Ore.; Des. Moines Pub. Schs.; WMAA; busts, reliefs, groups, carvings, Col. City of N.Y.; Wash., D.C.; Monticello, Ark.; USPO, Canton, N.Y.; comm. to des., Carol Lane awards, Nat. Safety Council, 1952. *Exhibited*: nationally.*

MARGULES, DeHIRSH—*Painter, L.*
567 Sixth Ave.; h. 15 Christopher St., New York, N.Y.

B. Jasse, Roumania, Aug. 7, 1899. *Studied*: privately. *Award*: Garrit Von Der Veen medal, Netherlands Govt. *Work*: Biro-Bidjan Mus., Russia; MModA; Tel-Aviv Mus., Israel; BMFA; BM; Univ. Arizona; U.S. State Dept.; WMAA; Univ. Georgia; Ball State T. Col.; Walker A. Center; Yale Univ. Lib. (The Alfred Stieglitz Correspondence, covering years 1929-40, and some later letters); Contributor to Pegasus (poems), 1957.

MARGULIES, JOSEPH—Painter, T.

27 West 67th St., New York 23, N.Y.

B. Vienna, Austria, July 7, 1896. *Studied*: NAD; ASL, and with Joseph Pennell. *Member*: AWS; SAGA; Chicago Soc. Et.; North Shore AA; SC; Audubon A.; Cape Ann Soc. Mod. A.; Provincetown Soc. A. *Awards*: F., Tiffany Fnd., 1920; prizes, NAD; A. Lg. Long Island, 1950, 1951, 1953; North Shore AA, 1954; Rockport AA, 1954; SC. *Work*: MMA; BM; SFMA; BMA; N.Y. State Capitol; N.Y. Theological Seminary; Queens Col.; Brooklyn Jewish Hospital; Yale Univ. Lib.; LC; N.Y. Pub. Lib.; Fed. Court, Brooklyn, N.Y.; Carnegie Inst.; Smithsonian Inst.; N.Y. County Bar. Assn.; Col. City, N.Y.; Midwood H.S., Brooklyn; Willkie Mem. Bldg., N.Y.; Iowa State Col.; Brooklyn Col.; Col. City of N.Y.; Tel-Aviv Mus. Israel; Brandeis Univ., and others. *Exhibited*: one-man: Smithsonian Inst.; Pan-Am. Bldg., Wash., D.C.; Stendahl Gal., Los A. Cal.; Midtown, Milch, Grand Central, Ferargil, Ainsley, Assoc. Am. A. galleries, N.Y. I., "Art of Aquatint"; "Understanding Prints." Lectures: Making of an Etching; Contributor to Arts magazine with 3 articles (series) on Portrait Watercolor, 1957. *Position*: Instr., A. Lg. of Long Island.

MARIL, HERMAN—Painter, T.

5705 Chilham Rd., Baltimore 9, Md.

B. Baltimore, Md., Oct. 13, 1908. *Studied*: Baltimore Polytechnic Inst.; Maryland Inst. *Member*: CAA; Wash. A. Gld.; AEA. *Awards*: prizes, BMA, 1935, 1939, 1940, 1946, 1951, 1952; Peale Mus., 1947, 1948, 1950, 1951; CGA, 1952, 1953, 1955. *Work*: MMA; Encyclopaedia Britannica; BMA; Bezalel Nat. Mus., Jerusalem; CGA; Amherst Col.; PMG; Howard Univ.; American Univ., Cone Coll.; murals, USPO, Alta Vista, Va.; West Scranton, Pa. *Exhibited*: CGA, 1939, 1941, 1943, 1945; PAFA, 1935, 1938, 1939, 1943; VMFA, 1940, 1942, 1944, 1946; Macbeth Gal.; Provincetown A. Festival, 1958; Boston A. Festival, 1958; Carnegie Inst., 1943-1945; AIC; WMAA; Pasadena AI; Cal. PLH; WFNY 1939; GGE, 1939; BMA, annually; Retrospective exh., Univ. Maryland, 1957; one-man: Babcock Gal., 1953, 1956, 1959; Phila. A. All., 1955. *Position*: Assoc. Prof., Dept. A., Univ. Maryland, College Park, Md., 1946- .

MARINSKY, HARRY—Sculptor, P., Des., I.

2 Crockett St., Rowayton, Conn.

B. London, England, May 8, 1909. *Studied*: R.I.Sch. Des.; PIASch. *Member*: AEA; Silvermine Gld. A. *Award*: prizes, A. Dir. Cl., 1945; Silvermine Gld. A., 1956. *Exhibited*: AIC, 1944; MModA, 1943; Madison Square Garden, N.Y., 1946 (one-man); Silvermine Gld. A., 1955 (one-man), 1956, (one-man), 1957; R.I. Mus. A., 1940-1942; Montross Gal., 1941; Am.-British A. Center, 1943-1945; Eggleston Gal., 1951, 1954 (one-man); Nat. Home Furnishing Show, 1952; WMAA, 1956; Bodley Gal., 1958 (one-man). I., "Mexico in Your Pocket," 1936; "Judy at the Zoo," 1945, and other books. Contributor to national magazines.

MARKELL, ISABELLA BANKS—Graphic Artist, P., S.

10 Gracie Square, New York 28, N.Y.

B. Superior, Wis. *Studied*: Maryland Inst.; PAFA; Ecole des Beaux-Arts, Paris, and with Farnsworth, Brackman, O'Hara. *Member*: SAGA; Pen & Brush Cl.; Phila. Pr. Cl.; All. A. Am.; AAPL; New Jersey Soc. P. & S.; Boston Soc. Pr. M.; Wolfe A. Cl.; NAWA; Royal Soc. P. & Et., London; New Haven Paint & Clay Cl., and others. *Awards*: prizes, Boston Pr. M.; Pen & Brush Cl., 1953; Providence, R.I., 1953, 1955; NAWA, 1958; Wilmington Soc. FA, 1958, and others. *Work*: N.Y. Pub. Lib.; N.Y. Hist. Soc.; Mus. City of N.Y.; Northwest Pr. M.; MMA; Phila. Pr. Cl.; N.Y. Hospital; Providence Mus. A.; Pa. State Col.; Phila. Free Lib.; Grinnell Pub. Lib.; Wilmington Soc. FA; many ports. of prominent persons. *Exhibited*: Newark Mus. A.; Northwest Pr. M.; MMA; BMA; Birmingham Mus. A.; High Mus. A.; All. A. Am.; N.Y. Hist. Soc.; AWS; SAGA; Mus. City of N.Y.; Argent Gal.; LC; Cal. PLH; Laguna Beach AA; Irvington (N.J.) A. Mus.; Toronto A. Gal.; Miami Beach, Fla.; New Jersey Soc. P. & S.; New Haven Paint & Clay Cl.; Ringling Mus. A.; NAD; Wilmington Soc. FA; Royal Soc. P. & Et.; Milwaukee AI; SFMA; SAM; Smithsonian Inst.; Riverside Mus.; Soc. Wash. Pr. M.; Springfield Mus. A.; in Amsterdam, Brussels, Antwerp, Ostend, and many others. One-man: Univ. Tulsa; Univ. South Carolina; Mint Mus.

subscribe to

the art gallery

America's Directory of Art Exhibitions

Ten issues per year
only $2. (Foreign $5.)

HOLLYCROFT •
IVORYTON • CONNECTICUT

Florence Walters Gallery

21 EAST 90th ST., NEW YORK 28

Penthouse D   Tel: LEhigh 4-7852

The American Center for Art Literature
from all corners of the world
is run by

Joyce & George Wittenborn

1018 Madison Avenue, New York 21
near The Metropolitan Museum

Write for our art bulletin.

GRUMBACHER
BRUSHES • COLORS
ARTISTS' MATERIALS
for the artist
WHO'S WHO
and knows
WHAT'S WHAT
AT YOUR FAVORITE ART SUPPLY STORE

A.; Hudson River Mus.; Bodley Gal.; Arch. Lg.; Cornell Col.; Douglas County Mus., Superior; N.Y. Pub. Lib.; Wustum A. Mus., and many more.

MARKHAM, KYRA (Mrs. David S. Gaither)—
Painter, Et., Lith., C.
Halifax, Vt.

B. Chicago, Ill., Aug. 18, 1891. *Studied*: AIC; ASL, with Alexander Abels. *Member*: AAPL; Deerfield Valley A.; Sou'hern Vt. A. *Work*: Smithsonian Inst.; Lib.Cong.; N.Y. Pub.Lib.; MMA; WMAA. *Exhibited*: NAD, 1937, 1938, 1945, 1946; PAFA, 1935.*

MARKOS, LAJOS—Portrait Painter
53 West 85th St., New York 24, N.Y.

B. Marosvasarhecy, Hungary, Sept. 28, 1917. *Studied*: Hungarian State Royal Belle Arti Acad., Budapest. *Member*: F., Royal Soc. A., London; Hudson County A. Soc. *Award*: Hungarian National Prize, 1942. *Work*: mural, Bethlehem Steel Co.; ports. of prominent persons. *Exhibited*: Budapest, 1941-1943; Rome, Italy, 1949; Milan, 1950, 1951; one-man: Venice, Italy, 1948; Old Mill Gallery, 1954; Grand Central A. Gal., N.Y.

MARKOW, JACK—Painter, Lith., Cart.
400 West 23rd St.; s. 2428 Cedar St., Manasquan Park, N.J.; h. 465 West 23rd St., New York, N.Y.

B. London, England, Jan. 23, 1905. *Studied*: ASL, with Boardman Robinson, Richard Lahey and Walter Jack Duncan. *Member*: Nat. Soc. Cartoonists. *Work*: MMA; Hunter Col.; Col. of City of N.Y.; BM; Univ. Georgia; Brooklyn and Queensboro Pub. Libs. *Exhibited*: one-man: ACA Gal., 1938; School of Visual A., N.Y., 1957; Hudson Gld. A., 1958. Cartoons in New Yorker, Saturday Evening Post, This Week, Times Book Review, Sunday Times Magazine, Holiday, Argosy, True, Sports Illustrated, Red Book, McCalls, Cosmopolitan, Saturday Review and other national publications. Author: "Drawing and Selling Cartoons." *Positions*: Instr., School of Visual Arts, New York, N.Y., 1947-1955; Cartoon Editor, Argosy Magazine, 1950-1952.

MARQUIS, GULIELMA DOROTHEA TOMLINSON—
Painter, Indust. Des.
919 40th St., Des Moines 12, Iowa

B. Fairfield, Iowa, June 16, 1900. *Studied*: Cummings Sch. A.; Parsons Col., Fairfield, Iowa. *Member*: AFA; Des Moines A. Center; Iowa Engineering Soc. *Awards*: prizes, Iowa A. Cl., 1933; others in Iowa, 1920-41. *Work*: Iowa State Col.; Fairfield (Iowa) Pub. Lib.; Congressional Bldg., Wash., D.C.; Charles City, Iowa, Woman's Cl.; Ames Woman's Cl.; murals, Hoisington, Kans.; Mt. Pleasant, Iowa. *Exhibited*: CGA, 1939; AFA traveling exh., 1938-39; Iowa A. Cl., 1931-35; Iowa A. Salon, 1931-1941; Joslyn Mus. A., 1932; Des Moines A. Center, 1932-1953. Author: "Before the Railroad," 1937. *Position*: A. Instr., Parsons Col., Fairfield, Iowa, 1944-46; Indst. Des., 1942- .

MARREN, JANET—Painter, Et., Lith.
Allende 18, San Cristobal Las Cacas, Chiapas, Mexico

B. New York, N.Y., Aug. 29, 1913. *Studied*: Metropolitan A. Sch.; Master Inst., Roerich Mus.; ASL; Fordham Univ., and with A. S. Baylinson. *Exhibited*: PAFA, 1941; NAD, 1946; 1947; U.S. Embassy, Paris, 1948; NAWA, 1949-1952 (traveling exh.); AFA traveling exh., 1951; WMAA, 1952; BM, 1953, 1955; Contemp. FA Exh., Am. Jewish Tercentenary at: Riverside Mus., Phila. A. All., DMFA, CMA, Albright A. Gal., CGA; Greiss Gal., N.Y., 1950 (3-man); RoKo Gal., 1950, 1952 (both one-man); Grand Central Moderns, 1954; other group shows 1938-1955; Audubon A., 1951; BM, 1957.

MARRON, EUGENIE MARIE—Painter, S. W.
152 West 57th St., New York 19, N.Y.; h. "Riverhead," Crescent Dr., Brielle, N.J.

B. Jersey City, N.J., Nov. 22, 1901. *Studied*: Columbia Univ., B.Sc., M.A.; & with Alexander Archipenko, Rudolph Belling, Fernand Leger. *Member*: NAWA. *Awards*: prizes, AAPL, 1944; Montclair A. Mus., 1944; Montclair AA, 1944. *Exhibited*: one-man exh.: Montross Gal.; Charles Morgan

Gal.; Lilienfeld Gal.; Montclair A. Mus. Ports. in private colls. Author, I., book of caricatures, "Caught in the Act," 1947 (3rd ed.); "Albacora," 1957.

MARSH, ANNE STEELE (Mrs. James R.)—
Painter, Gr., T., C.
Fiddler's Forge, Pittstown, N.J.

B. Nutley, N.J., Sept. 7, 1901. *Studied*: CUASch. *Member*: AEA; N.Y. Soc. Women A.; Assoc. A. New Jersey; Delaware Valley AA; SAGA; Boston Soc. Pr. M.; Hunterdon County A. Center (Dir. Exhibits). *Awards*: prize, Phila. Pr. Cl., 1952. *Work*: Newark Pub. Lib.; MMA; Collectors of Am. A.; PMA; MModA; LC; Montclair A. Mus. *Exhibited*: MMA; NAD; AIC; WFNY 1939; AWS; BM; Newark Mus. A.; PAFA; Venice, Italy; SAGA; BMFA; CGA; Phila. A. All.; Portland A. Mus.; Wichita AA; Montclair Mus. A.; Albany Inst. Hist. & A.; SAM; Conn. Acad. FA; DMFA; Smithsonian Inst.; Silvermine Gld. A.; Everhart Mus. A., Scranton, Pa.

MARSH, FRED DANA—
Mural Painter, S., Painter, Gr., T., C.
Ormond Beach, Fla.

B. Chicago, Ill., Apr. 6, 1872. *Studied*: AIC. *Member*: ANA; NSMP. *Awards*: med., Paris Exp., 1900; Pan-Am. Exp., Buffalo, 1901; St. Louis Exp., 1904. *Work*: Rochester Mem. A. Gal.; Hotel McAlpin, N.Y.; Un. Engineering Soc. Bldg., N.Y.; Detroit Country Cl.; Tomoka State Park, Fla.

MARSH, LUCILE PATTERSON—Illustrator, Gr.
83 Perry St., New York 14, N.Y.

B. Rapid City, S.D., Oct. 21, 1890. *Studied*: AIC. *Member*: A. Gld. *Awards*: Am. Traveling Scholarship, AIC, 1913. I., Gates "School Reader"; illus. covers for national magazines.*

MARSHALL, JONATHAN—
Writer, Cr., Program Associate
477 Madison Ave.; h. 433 East 51st St., New York 22, N.Y.

B. New York, N.Y., Jan. 20, 1924. *Studied*: Univ. Colorado, B.A.; Univ. North Carolina. *Award*: prize, Silvermine Gld. A. *Positions*: Formerly Editor & Publ., Arts Magazine, 1953-1958 and Arts Yearbook, 1957-58; Program Assoc., Humanities and The Arts Program, The Ford Foundation, 1958- .

MARSHALL, MacLEAN—Sculptor
R.F.D. 5, Rome, Ga.

B. New York, N.Y., May 2, 1912. *Studied*: ASL; Univ. Virginia; Child-Walker Sch. Des.; Yale Univ. Sch. FA, and with George Bridgman, Kimon Nicolaides, George Demetrios. *Member*: Assn. Ga. A. *Awards*: prize, NAC, 1935; Telfair Acad., 1941. *Work*: Telfair Acad. A.; park entrance gates, Shannon, Ga.; hospital doors, Rome, Ga.; war mem., Shannon and Lindale, Ga. *Exhibited*: NAC; NAFA; Telfair Acad. A.; Savannah Mus. A.; Grand Central A. Gal.; Gloucester, Mass.*

MARSHALL, MARGARET JANE—Painter, I., W.
2182 Woodlawn Ave., Glenside, Pa.

B. Philadelphia, Pa., July 29, 1895. *Studied*: PAFA. *Member*: F., PAFA; Phila. Plastic Cl.; Old York Road A. Gld. *Awards*: F., PAFA; Cresson traveling scholarship, PAFA, 1918. I., "Children of the Alps." Contributor to: national historical magazines. Specializes in Heraldry.

MARSICANO, NICHOLAS—Painter
12 West 12th St.; h. 53 West 11th St., New York 3, N.Y.

B. Shenandoah, Pa., Oct. 1, 1914. *Studied*: PAFA; Barnes Fnd. *Awards*: European traveling Scholarship, PAFA; (2) European traveling Scholarships, Barnes Fnd. *Member*: Artists Cl. *Exhibited*: PAFA, 1942; Stable Gal., N.Y., 1950-1955; Joslyn Mus. A., 1954; WAC, 1958; Vanguard, 1955; BM, 1950; Wagner Col., 1955; Douglass Col., Rutgers Univ.; one-man: Bertha Schaefer Gal., 1958. *Positions*: Instr., Brooklyn Mus. Sch. A., 1948-51; Univ. Michigan Summer Sch., 1951; Yale Univ. Norfolk Sch. A., 1951-53; Cooper Union Sch. A., 1947- ; Pratt Institute, 1955- .

PICTURES & PRINTS

THE
WORLD'S LARGEST COLLECTION
Old Masters • Moderns • Contemporaries

Oestreicher's catalog illustrates over 500 masterpieces and lists over 4700. Special service department for schools, colleges, libraries and institutions.

Catalog $1 in U.S.A.

"if it's in print—we have it"

Oestreicher's
Dept. AAD
1208 Sixth Avenue
New York 36, N. Y.

CHARLES E. SLATKIN

115 East 92nd Street

Near Park Avenue ——— New York 28

LEhigh 4-4222

Odilon Redon   *Ophelia*

Gouache 24 x 20

SIGMUND ROTHSCHILD

27 WEST 67TH STREET
NEW YORK 23, NEW YORK

APPRAISER

MR. ROTHSCHILD, A SENIOR MEMBER OF THE AMERICAN SOCIETY OF APPRAISERS, FELLOW OF THE VALUERS INSTITUTION OF ENGLAND, LECTURER AT NEW YORK UNIVERSITY ON APPRAISAL AND THEORIES OF VALUE, MAKES CERTIFIED APPRAISALS ACCEPTED BY INSURANCE COMPANIES AND TAX AUTHORITIES.

IN EVALUATION, THROUGH RESEARCH, HE INVENTORIES AND AIDS IN DISPOSAL OF PERSONAL PROPERTY AND IN RESTORATION OF ART OBJECTS.

HE ACTS AS CONSULTANT FOR NUMEROUS INDIVIDUALS, AND INSTITUTIONS.

TRafalgar 3-5522

KRAUSHAAR GALLERIES

20th
CENTURY
AMERICAN

PAINTINGS
SCULTPURE
WATER COLORS
DRAWINGS
PRINTS

1055 MADISON AVE.
NEW YORK 28, N. Y.
AT 80th ST.

MARSTON, CHARLES GORDON—*Painter*
4 Atlantic Ave., Rockport, Mass.

B. Brockton, Mass., June 1, 1898. *Studied*: Mass. Sch. A.; Boston Mus. Sch. A.; Grand Central A. Sch., and with Aldro Hibbard, Joseph DeCamp, Richard Andrews, Pruett Carter and others. *Member*: North Shore AA; Rockport AA; Copley Soc., Boston. *Awards*: prizes, Rockport AA, 1953, 1955, 1958; North Shore AA, 1957; Gold Medal, Mass. Sch. A. *Exhibited*: Rockport AA, group shows and one-man in 1956; North Shore AA; Copley Soc., Boston and one-man in 1957.

MARTIN, BASIL E.—*Painter*
R.D. 1, Boyertown, Pa.

B. England, Apr. 23, 1903. *Studied*: Central Sch. A., Chelsea Sch. A., London, England. *Member*: AWS. *Work*: High Mus. A., and in private coll. *Exhibited*: AWS, 1930-1936, 1948, 1950, 1951; AFA, 1932; WFNY 1939; Mickiewicz Mus., Warsaw, 1956; Reading Mus. A., 1953-1957; Woodmere A. Gal., 1958; Phila. A. All., 1955; one-man: High Mus. A., 1932; Jacksonville, Fla., 1932; Macon, Athens, Columbus, Ga., 1932; Atlanta, Ga., 1935; Van Dieman-Lilienfeld Gal., 1948; Oak Ridge, Tenn., 1951; Pa. State T. Col., 1954.

MARTIN, BEN(JAMIN) C.—*Cartoonist*
New York Herald Tribune, 230 W. 41st St.; h. 127 East 35th St., New York 16, N.Y.

B. Oakland, Cal., Nov. 28, 1913. *Studied*: Univ. California, Berkeley, A.B. *Member*: Soc. Am. Cartoonists; Newspaper Gld. Am. Author, I., "Alfred," 1938; "John Black's Body," 1939; "Mr. Smith and Mr. Schmidt," 1940. Contributor cartoons to Collier's, Sat. Eve. Post, New Yorker, Mademoiselle, This Week, Vogue, Red Book, NEA Feature Service, and others. *Position*: Asst. Ed., Judge magazine, 1936-43; Cart., NEA Feature Service, Inc., 1950-51; Syndicate Ed., New York Herald-Tribune, 1953- .

MARTIN, CHARLES E.—*Cartoonist, P., Des.*
221 Little Tor Road, New City, N.Y.

B. Chelsea, Mass., Jan. 12, 1911. *Work*: Mus. City of N.Y. *Exhibited*: BMSch. A.; Rockland Fnd; Ruth White Gal. Contributor cartoons and illus. to PM; New Yorker; Life; Time; Fortune; This Week; Harpers; Sat. Eve. Post; Sports Illustrated; Colliers; True and other national magazines.

MARTIN, CHRISTINE—*Painter*
455 East 51st St., New York 22, N.Y.

B. New York, N.Y., Aug. 15, 1895. *Studied*: T. Col., Columbia Univ.; ASL; & with Henry McFee, John Sloan, Judson Smith. *Member*: NAWA; Portraits, Inc. *Exhibited*: PAFA, 1935; NAWA, 1935-1946; Weyhe Gal., 1945, 1946; Woodstock AA; annually; Rudolph Gal., 1943-1945.

MARTIN, FLETCHER—*Painter, Lith., T., L.*
Woodstock, N.Y.

B. Palisade, Colo., Apr. 29, 1904. *Member*: AEA; CAA; AAUP; Woodstock AA. *Awards*: prizes, Los A. Mus. A., 1935, 1939; FAP, 1937; 48 States Comp., 1939; PAFA, 1947; NAD, 1949, 1954. *Work*: MMoDA; MMA; Cranbrook Acad. A.; William Rockhill Nelson Gal.; Los A. Mus. A.; LC; Denver A. Mus.; Mus. FA of Houston; SFMA; PAFA; Brandeis Univ.; State Univ. Iowa; AGAA; frescoes, North Hollywood (Cal.) H.S.; murals, Fed. Bldg., San Pedro, Cal.; USPO, La Mesa, Tex.; Kellogg, Idaho. *Exhibited*: WMAA, 1953-1955; Phila. A. All., 1955; PAFA, 1954; John Heller Gal., 1955. I., "Tales of the Gold Rush," 1944; "Mutiny on the Bounty," 1946, both Limited Editions. War A., Correspondent, Life Magazine, 1943, 1944. *Position*: Instr., Univ. Iowa, 1940; Kansas City AI, 1941-42; ASL, 1947-49; Univ. Florida, 1950-53; Mills Col., 1951; Univ. Minnesota, 1954.*

MARTIN, FRANCIS THOMAS BECKETT—*Painter*
514 Barker Bldg.; h. 3817 Dewey Ave., Apt. 6, Omaha 5. Neb.

B. Omaha, Neb., Nov. 29, 1904. *Studied*: Univ. Nebraska, A.B.; & with George Barker, J. Laurie Wallace. *Member*: AAPL; Lincoln A. Gld. *Work*: City of Fremont, Neb.; Chamber of Commerce, Omaha, Neb. *Exhibited*: Rocke-feller Center, N.Y., 1938; Kansas City AI; Omaha A. Gld.; Joslyn Mem. *Position*: Trustee, Sec., Soc. Liberal Arts, Omaha, Neb.*

MARTIN, G(AIL) W(YCOFF)—*Painter, T., Gr.*
618 Willard Ave., Newington 11, Conn.

B. Tacoma, Wash., Apr. 19, 1913. *Studied*: John Herron A. Sch., B.F.A.; State Univ. Iowa, M.F.A., with Philip Guston, Fletcher Martin, Emil Ganso; Boston Mus. A. Sch., with Karl Zerbe. *Member*: Conn. WC Soc.; Conn. Acad. FA; CAA; Springfield A. Lg.; Essex AA. *Awards*: prizes, A. Gld., St. Louis, 1943; Norwich, Conn., 1955; New England Drawing Exh., 1958; Mary Millikan European traveling scholarship, John Herron A. Sch., 1937. *Work*: LC; Wadsworth Atheneum, Hartford, Conn. Mural, USPO, Danville, Ind. *Exhibited*: AIC, 1936, 1937; Denver A. Mus., 1941, 1944; Northwest Pr. M., 1941, 1942; MMA, 1942; Color Pr. Soc., Phila., 1942; PAFA, 1942; Carnegie Inst., 1942, 1943; Conn. Acad. FA, 1947-1957; Conn. WC Soc., 1948-1956; Audubon A., 1953; Butler Inst. Am. A., 1958; Indiana A., 1939, 1941, 1951, 1957; Midwest Regional, 1941, 1942; Missouri Regional, 1941-1943; Boston A. Festival, 1955, 1956; New Haven A. Festival, 1958; New England Drawing Exh., 1958; Eastern States Exh., 1954, 1958; Silvermine Gld. A., 1954-1956; Hoosier Salon, 1949, 1951; Norwich, Conn., 1950, 1954, 1955; Essex, Conn., 1951-1955; Springfield Mus. A., 1949-1951, 1953, 1955. *Positions*: Hd. A. Dept. & Prof. A., Lindenwood Col., Missouri, 1941-43; Instr., Hartford A. Sch., Univ. Hartford, Hartford, Conn., 1947- .

MARTIN, KEITH MORROW—*Painter*
1011 North Charles St., Baltimore 1, Md.

B. Lincoln, Neb., Jan. 27, 1911. *Studied*: Univ. Nebraska; AIC. *Awards*: prizes, AIC, 1948; Denver A. Mus., 1948 (3 purchase awards); BMA, 1952, 1955; Delgado Mus. A. *Work*: Univ. Nebraska; AIC; Denver A. Mus.; BMA; Munson-Williams-Proctor Inst.; Butler Inst. Am. A.; Nebraska Univ. *Exhibited*: AIC, 1936, 1948; VMFA, 1946; Nebraska AA, 1943; Julien Levy Gal., 1936, 1937; Kuh Gal., Chicago, 1937; Vendome Gal., Paris, 1945; Blatsford Gal., London, 1945; SFMA, 1947; Joslyn Mus. A., 1947; Hugo Gal., 1949, 1951; BMA, 1953 (one-man), 1955; Norfolk Mus. A., 1954 (one-man); CGA, 1955; Obelisk Gal., Wash., D.C., 1955 (one-man); WMAA, 1955; Delgado Mus. A.; Duveen-Graham Gal., N.Y., 1956, 1958 (one-man); PAFA, 1957; BM, 1957; Columbia, S.C., 1957; Delgado Mus. A., 1957; Butler Inst. Am. A., 1957; D'Amacourt Gal., Wash., D.C., 1957 (2-man); Provincetown A. Festival, 1958. *Position*: Instr., Painting, Baltimore Mus. A., at present.

MARTIN, MARVIN B.—*Sculptor, E.*
115 Architecture Bldg., University of Illinois, Urbana, Ill.; h. 1607 Sheridan Rd., Champaign, Ill.

B. Fort Worth, Tex., July 28, 1907. *Studied*: Kansas City AI. *Member*: AAPL; Denver A. Gld. *Awards*: prizes, Missouri State Fair, 1927, 1932. *Work*: s., Fairmount Cemetery, Guldman Mem., Nat. Home for Jewish Children, Colo. Hist. Soc., Kirkland Sch. A., Rosehill Cemetery, Police Bldg., all of Denver, Colo.; H.S., A. Mus., Boulder, Colo.; U.S. Dept. Interior monument, Ignacio, Colo.; Univ. Colorado; Kent Sch. for Girls, Denver, Colo.; Benjamin Franklin Magazine gold medal des. for Univ. Ill., 1954; wood carved group, Bellflower, Ill., 1956; Juliet Bane Mem., Home Ec. Dept., Univ. Illinois. *Exhibited*: Missouri State Fair, 1927, 1933; Kansas City AI, 1933, 1935, 1938, 1939; Denver A. Mus., 1933, 1935, 1936, 1938-1941, one-man exh., 1935, 1944; CM, 1935; Univ. Colorado, 1937 (one-man); Arch.L., 1938; WFNY 1939; Univ. Illinois, one-man, 1945-1953, traveling exh., 1945; Audubon A., 1953; SFMA, 1953. *Position*: Assoc. Prof., S., Denver Univ., 1935-38; Univ. Illinois, Urbana, Ill., 1944- .

MARTIN, ROGER (H.) (JR.)—*Painter, Gr., T., I., W.*
85 Main St., Rockport, Mass.

B. Gloucester, Mass., Sept. 3, 1925. *Studied*: BMFA Sch. *Exhibited*: Boston A. Festival, 1956 and traveling (AFA); Rockport AA, 1957; Nexus Gal., Boston, 1955. Illus.: "Homes With Charac er," 1952; "American English in Action," Bks. 1-6, 1952-57; "Two Boys and a Soapbox Derby," 1958. Illus. for New Yorker Magazine; articles and illus. for Child Life Magazine. *Position*: A. Supv., Rockport, Mass., Elem. Schs.

MARTINELLI, EZIO—*Sculptor, P., Gr.*

121 West 85th St., New York 24, N.Y.

B. West Hoboken, N. J., Nov. 27, 1913. *Studied*: NAD; Barnes Fnd.; Tiffany Fnd., and in Italy. *Awards*: Guggenheim Fellowship, 1958. *Work*: WMAA; PMA; Univ. Wisconsin; Univ. Illinois; Rogers Mem., Memphis, Tenn. *Exhibited*: Art of This Century, 1942, 1943; American Drawings & Watercolors in France, 1954; AIC, 1952; USIS, Europe and Asia, 1956, 1957; Carnegie Inst., 1958; oneman: Willard Gal., N.Y., 1946, 1947, 1952, 1955-1958; Phila. A. All., 1953. *Position*: Assoc. Prof., Sarah Lawrence Col., 1947- ; Instr., Parsons Sch. Des., New York, N.Y., 1953- .

MARTINET, MARJORIE D.—*Painter, T.*

4102 Ridgewood Ave., Baltimore 15, Md.

B. Baltimore, Md., Nov. 3, 1886. *Studied*: Maryland Inst.; Rinehart Sch. S.; PAFA; & with Cecelia Beaux, William Chase. *Member*: Phila. A. All.; NAWA, AFA. *Awards*: F., PAFA; Cresson traveling scholarship, PAFA, 1909. *Exhibited*: Peabody Inst.; PAFA; Phila. Plastic Cl.; Phila. AC; BMA, 1930 (one-man); Newman Gal., Phila., 1936; McClees Gal., Phila., 1946. *Position*: Dir. Martinet Sch. A., Baltimore, Md., at present.

MARTINO, ANTONIO P.—*Painter*

16 South Broad St., Philadelphia 2, Pa.

B. Philadelphia, Pa., Apr. 13, 1902. *Studied*: PMSchIA; Spring Garden AI; Phila. Sketch Cl.; LaFrance Inst. *Member*: NA; AWS; Phila. WC Cl. *Awards*: prizes, NAD, 1926, 1927, 1937, 1943; VMFA, 1938; PMSchIA, 1939; IBM, 1940; Woodmere A. Gal., 1942, 1957; SC, 1943-1945, 1956-1958; New Haven Paint & Clay Cl., 1943; Indiana State T. Col., 1944; DaVinci All., 1944, 1947; AWS, 1945, 1946, 1953; Audubon A., 1946; SC, 1953; Springville, Utah, AA, 1953; Hickory Mus., 1954; Wayne A. Center, 1957; Warren (Pa.) A. Gal., 1957; Delaware A. Center, 1957; Chester (Pa.) AA, 1958 (2); Chautauqua AA, 1958; Phila. A. All., 1955; medals, Phila. Sketch Cl., 1926; Phila. Sesqui-centennial, 1926; PAFA, 1938; DaVinci All., 1942, 1952, 1957; NAC, 1958; Cape May, N.J., 1950; Terry AI, 1952, and others. *Work*: Wanamaker Coll.; PMA; Reading Mus. A.; PAFA; IBM; Woodmere A. Gal.; Phila. WC Cl.; Allentown Mus.; NAD; Springville (Utah) H.S.; Friends Central Sch.; Warren (Pa.) A. Gal.; Kutztown State T. Col.; Everhart Mus.; Randolph-Macon Women's Col. *Exhibited*: Carnegie Inst.; PAFA; NAD; CGA; AIC; WMAA; WFNY 1939; Detroit Inst. A.; VMFA; Macbeth Gal.; Colorado Springs FA Center; GGE, 1939; MMA.

MARTINO, GIOVANNI—*Painter*

Suite 1334, Commercial Trust Bldg., 16 South Broad St., Philadelphia 2, Pa.; h. 1512 Crest Rd., Penn Wynne, Pa.

B. Philadelphia, Pa., May 1, 1908. *Studied*: Spring Garden Inst.; La France AI; Phila. Sketch Cl. *Member*: NA.

Awards: prizes, Phila. A. All., 1934; VMFA, 1940; DaVinci All., 1940, 1944, med., 1939; NAD, 1941, 1942; Woodmere A. Gal., 1941; PAFA, 1942; Sweat Mem. Mus., 1946; State T. Col., Pa., 1946; Pepsi-Cola, 1946; SC, 1956; AWS, 1958; Medal, Phila. Sketch Cl., 1957; Gold Medal, All. A. Am., 1957. *Exhibited*: PAFA; CGA; WMAA; AIC; GGE, 1939; Carnegie Inst.; NAD; VMFA; & other galleries & museums.

MARTINSEN, IVAR RICHARD—*Educator, P.*

Art Department, Northern Wyoming Community College; h. 132 West Colorado St., Sheridan, Wyo.

B. Butte, Montana, Dec. 9, 1922. *Studied*: Montana State Col.; Univ. Wyoming. *Member*: Western Edu. Assn.; Sheridan A. Gld. *Awards*: prize, Wyoming-Nebraska Exh., 1958. *Exhibited*: Sheridan and Laramie, Wyo., traveling exh. Wyoming A. *Position*: Asst. Prof., A. Dept., Northern Wyoming Community College, Sheridan, Wyo.

MARTYL (MARTYL SCHWEIG LANGSDORF)—*Painter, Lith.*

R.R. 1, Meacham Rd., Roselle, Ill.

B. St. Louis, Mo., Mar. 16, 1918. *Studied*: Washington Univ., A.B.; Colorado Springs FA Center, with Arnold Blanch, Boardman Robinson. *Member*: AEA; Renaissance Soc., Univ. Chicago. *Awards*: prizes, Kansas City AI 1940; CAM, 1941, 1943; AIC, 1945, 1950, 1957; Los A. Mus. A., 1945. *Work*: Recorder of Deeds Bldg., Wash., D.C.; PAFA; Univ. Arizona; CAM; AIC; Wash. Univ.; Ill. State Mus.; Ill. Athletic Assn.; New Trier H.S.; Oliver Morton Sch., Indiana; murals, USPO, Russell, Kan.; Sainte Genevieve, Mo. *Exhibited*: Carnegie Inst., 1940-1945; PAFA, 1944, 1952; CAM, 1941-1944, 1946; VMFA, 1946; AIC, 1944-1946, 1948-1952; CGA, 1941; WMAA, 1945, 1946; Milwaukee AI, 1946; Univ. Illinois, 1951, 1953, 1955; AIC, 1952-1956; Univ. Wisconsin, 1952, 1953; (22 one-man to 1958). I., "How to Paint a Gouache," 1946. *Position*: A. Ed. The Bulletin of the Atomic Scientists.

MARX, ROBERT ERNST—*Painter, Gr.*

Department of Art Education, University of Wisconsin, Madison, Wis.; h. Route 1, McFarland, Wis.

B. Northeim, Germany, Dec. 10, 1925. *Studied*: Univ. Illinois, B.F.A., M.F.A., and with Abraham Rattner, Lee Chesney. *Work*: MModA; PMA; N.Y. Pub. Lib.; MMA; DMFA; Bradley Univ.; Detroit Inst. A.; Intl. Graphic A. Soc. *Exhibited*: BM, 1951, 1953-1955; MMA, 1952; Northwest Pr. M., 1953-1955; DMFA, 1953; MModA, 1953; Bradley Univ., 1952, 1954, 1955; Phila. Pr. Cl., 1951, 1953-1955; Walker A. Center, 1954; Flint Inst. A., 1954; Univ. Illinois, 1954; Dallas Pr. Soc., 1954; Victoria & Albert Mus., London, 1954; Washington Univ., 1955. *Position*: Instr., Drawing & Design, Univ. Wisconsin, at present.*

ONE OF THE MOST COMPREHENSIVE COLLECTIONS IN THE U.S.A.

GAUGUIN
Head of a Tahitian Woman
WATERCOLOR

GRAPHIC ART
WATERCOLORS - DRAWINGS

BRAQUE · CHAGALL · MATISSE
MIRO · KLEE · NOLDE · PICASSO
KIRCHNER · CORINTH · MUNCH
SCHMIDT-ROTTLUFF · HECKEL
MÜLLER · GAUGUIN

CATALOGUE AVAILABLE $1

NEW ART CENTER Gallery
1193 LEXINGTON AVENUE   NEW YORK 28, N.Y.

MARYAN, HAZEL SINAIKO—*Painter, S., T.*
330 West Diversey Parkway, Chicago 14, Ill.

B. Madison, Wis., May 15, 1905. *Studied*: Univ. Wisconsin, B.S.; AIC, and with E. Chassaing, A. Polasek, E. Simone. *Member*: Chicago A. Cl.; AEA. *Work*: in private colls. *Exhibited*: AIC, 1930-1932, 1937-1941; Wis. Salon, 1932-1945; Chicago No-Jury Exh., 1933, 1934; AEA, 1952. *Position*: Former Instr., Western Mich. Col.; Hull House, Chicago; Chicago Bd. Edu.

MARZOLO, LEO AURELIO—*Painter*
1012 North Dearborn St., Chicago 10, Ill.; h. Mignin Dr., Route 1, Warrenville, Ill.

B. Martinez, Cal., Feb. 22, 1887. *Member*: Chicago Galleries Assn.; Assn. P. & S.; Palette & Chisel Acad. A. *Awards*: med., Palette & Chisel Acad. A., 1941; Municipal A. Lg., 1958. *Work*: State Mus., Springfield, Ill. *Position*: Restorer of Paintings, AIC, Chicago, Ill., 1928-1956.

MASER, EDWARD ANDREW—*Museum Director, E.*
Museum of Art, University of Kansas; h. 1700 Vermont St., Lawrence, Kans.

B. Detroit, Mich., Dec. 23, 1923. *Studied*: Univ. Michigan; Univ. Chicago, M.A., Ph.D. *Member*: CAA; AAUP; Renaissance Soc. Am. Author (with Lando Bartoli) "The Museum of the Manufactory of Florentine Mosaic," 1954. Ed., The Register of the Museum of Art of the University of Kansas. Contributor articles to Connoisseur magazine; Univ. Chicago Grad. Library Quarterly. Exhibitions arranged: "18th Century German and Austrian Art in American Collections" (series of 3); "Austrian Rococo Drawings from the Vienna Academy," 1956; "Disguises of Harlequin by G.D. Ferretti," 1957; "Fontinalia—the Art of the Fountain," 1957; "John Steuart Curry," 1957; "Thomas Hart Benton," 1958; "Grant Wood," 1959. *Positions*: Asst. to Dir., Univ. Chicago Exchange Project at Frankfurt, Germany, 1949-50; Dir., Museum of Art, University of Kansas, Lawrence, Kans., at present.

MASON, ALICE F. (Mrs. Michael L.)—
Painter, Et., Lith., L., T.
9 East Ontario St., Tree Studio H, Chicago 11, Ill.

B. Chicago, Ill., Jan. 16, 1895. *Studied*: Northwestern Univ., B.S.; AIC, B.F.A., M.F.A. *Member*: Chicago Soc. A.; Chicago A. Cl.; AEA; Renaissance Soc.; Conn. Acad. FA. *Awards*: prizes, New Britain Mus., 1953; Phila. Pr. Cl., 1957; PAFA, 1956; Ill. State Mus., 1956; Ill. State Fair, 1957; Mun. A. Lg., 1957. *Work*: MMA; LC; CM; New Britain Mus. *Exhibited*: MMA, 1942; PAFA, 1938, 1939, 1953, 1956; CGA, 1941; AIC, 1937-1940, 1943, 1946, 1948, 1949, 1951, 1952, 1955; CM, 1950, 1952, 1954, 1956; Chicago Soc. A., 1949; Phila. Pr. Cl., 1951, 1954, 1957; Buffalo Pr. Cl., 1951; SAGA, 1952-1955; New Britain Mus., 1952; LC, 1952, 1956, 1957; Conn. Acad. FA, 1954-1957; Soc. Wash. Pr. M., 1958; Hunterdon County A. Center, 1958; Illinois State Mus., 1957, 1958. *Position*: Pres., Chicago Soc. A., 1954-55, 1955-56, 1957-58, 1958-59; Instr. Summer Sch. Painting, Saugatuck, Mich., 1954- .

MASON, ALICE TRUMBULL—*Painter, Gr.*
149 East 119th St. (35); h. 334 West 85th St., New York 24, N.Y.

B. Litchfield, Conn., Nov. 16, 1904. *Member*: Am. Abstract A.; Fed. Mod. P. & S.; SAGA; 14 Painter-Pr. M. *Awards*: prizes, Phila. Pr. Cl., 1946; SAGA, 1947; Silvermine Gld. A., 1952. *Work*: PMA; MMoDA; N.Y. Pub. Lib.; Berkshire Mus. A.; LC; BM; Solomon Guggenheim Mus. A. *Exhibited*: Pinacotheca Gal., 1948; Mus. Living A., 1942; Salon de Mai, Paris, 1952; Royal Pr. M., London, 1953; Kraushaar Gal., 1954; Solomon Guggenheim Mus. A., 1954, 1955; Mid-Western A. Conf., Indiana, 1954; CGA, 1955; WMAA, 1951, 1953, 1955; BM, 1955; one-man traveling exh., 1951-52, and others. *Position*: Instr., PAL Center, Bronx, N.Y., 1954-55.*

MASON, DORIS BELLE EATON (Mrs. Edward F.)—
Sculptor, L., T., C.
32 Olive Court, Iowa City, Iowa

B. Green River, Wyo., June 29, 1896. *Studied*: Univ. Idaho; Univ. Iowa; Univ. Southern California, B.S., M.A. *Awards*: prizes, Iowa State Fair, 1937, 1938. *Work*: Spokane AA; Mt. Home (Idaho) Congregational Church. *Exhibited*: PAFA, 1941, 1942; Mun. A. Exh., N.Y., 1936,
1937; Iowa Univ., 1938 (one-man); Joslyn Mus. A., 1943, 1944; Denver A. Mus.; Davenport Mun. A. Gal., 1938 (one-man); Walker A. Center; Des Moines A. Center, annually. Lectures: "Sculpture Inside and Out"; Ceramics, etc. Delivered 4000 demonstration-lectures on sculpture and pottery in H.S. and Colleges, 1948-58. L. and Demonstrator for Am. Assn. of Colleges, 1948-55.

MASON, ELIZABETH BREWER—*Educator, P., L.*
Art Department, Harding College; h. 1309 East Market St., Searcy, Ark.

B. Chattanooga, Tenn., Sept. 13, 1912. *Studied*: Abilene Christian Col., B.S.; Memphis Acad. A.; George Peabody Col., M.A.; Texas Tech. Col., and with Mario Medina, Eliot O'Hara, Frederic Taubes, and others, and in Mexico. *Member*: AEA; AFA; NAEA; CAA. *Exhibited*: West Texas Mus., 1938, 1940; Arkansas State Exh., 1948, 1950, 1951, 1952, 1954; Galeana Instituto Cultural de Jalisco, 1954; Universidad Autonoma de Guadalajara, 1954. Lectures: Your Child in Art; Art Education; Renaissance and Modern Art. *Position*: Prof. A., Harding College, Searcy, Ark., 1947- .

MASON, ELLA MAY—*Painter, E.*
566 Lawrence Road, Jackson 6, Miss.

B. Brookhaven, Miss., Oct. 22, 1912. *Studied*: AIC, B.F.A., M.F.A., and with Louis Ritman, Edmund Giesbert, Elmer Forsberg. *Member*: CAA; Mississippi AA; New Orleans AA. *Awards*: prizes, Mississippi AA, 1943, 1945. *Work*: Mississippi AA. *Exhibited*: SSAL, 1941-1945; Mississippi AA, 1945-1951; Caller Times Exh., Corpus Christi, Tex., 1945-1947; Memphis, Tenn., 1945-1947; Atlanta, Ga., 1947, 1948; Jackson, Miss., Nat. WC Show, 1944, 1945, 1947, 1951; New Orleans AA, 1947, 1948. *Positions*: Hd. A. Dept., Bellhaven Col., Jackson, Miss., 1938-1947; Instr., Richmond Professional Inst., Col. William & Mary, 1948-51; Hd. A. Dept., Gulf Park Col., Gulfport, Miss., 1951-52; Co-owner, Mullins-Mason Shoppe, Jackson, Miss., and des.-producer of silk screen products under name of Mason Productions, 1952-1958.

MASON, J(OHN) ALDEN—*Former Museum Curator, W.*
University Museum, 33rd & Spruce Sts., Philadelphia 4, Pa.; h. 725 Conestoga Rd., Berwyn, Pa.

B. Philadelphia, Pa., Jan. 14, 1885. *Studied*: Univ. Pennsylvania, A.B.; Univ. California, Ph.D. *Member*: Am. Anthropological Assn.; Soc. Am. Archaeology; Am. Assn. Advancement Sc.; New Jersey Archaeological Soc.; Am. Ethnological Assn. Contributor to: scientific journals. Author: "The Ancient Civilization of Peru," 1957. *Position*: Asst. Cur., Field Mus. Natural Hist., Chicago, 1917-24; Asst. Cur., Am. Mus. Natural Hist., N.Y., 1924-25; Cur. Am. Section, University Mus., Univ. Pennsylvania, Philadelphia, Pa., 1926-1955, Cur. Emeritus, 1955- ; Editor & Field Advisor, New World Archaeological Fnd., 1958- .

MASON, JOHN RUSSELL—*Curator & Librarian*
George Washington University Library, 2023 G St., Northwest, Washington 6, D.C.*

MASON, MICHAEL L. (MIKE)—*Painter, Lith.*
9 East Ontario St., Chicago 11, Ill.

B. Rossville, Ill., Apr. 23, 1895. *Studied*: Northwestern Univ., B.S., M.A.; & with F. F. Fursman, A. H. Krehbiel, Edgar Rupprecht. *Member*: Chicago SA. *Exhibited*: PAFA, 1938, 1940; GGE, 1939; AIC, 1936, 1938-1940, 1943; All-Illinois Soc. FA, 1937, 1938; SAGA, 1948, 1952, 1956; Lith. Exh., 1950, 1952, 1954, 1956; Cal. Pr. M., 1951; CM, 1954; Phila. Pr. Cl., 1953, 1956, 1957; BM, 1958; Cromer & Quint Gal., Chicago, 1957 (one-man).

MASON, ROY MARTELL—*Painter, I.*
Box 438, Woodchuck Hollow, Batavia, N.Y.

B. Gilbert Mills, N.Y., Mar. 15, 1886. *Member*: NA; AWS; SC; All. A. Am.; Audubon A.; Phila. WC Cl.; Buffalo Soc. A.; Rochester A. Cl.; Cornell Univ. Lab. of Ornithology; F., Rochester Mus. A. & Sc.; Baltimore WC Soc. *Awards*: prizes, SC, 1930, 1931; NAD, 1930; Rochester Mem. A. Gal., 1931; AWS, 1931, 1940, 1956; Watson Blair prize, Chicago, 1941; AIC, 1941; Pennell medal, Phila. WC Cl., 1941; Albright A. Gal., 1941, gold medal, 1943; gold medal, All. A. Am., 1952; gold medal, Audubon A., 1945; North Shore AA, 1956; N.Y., New Haven &

Hartford Railroad Contest, 1956; Chautauqua AA, 1958. *Work*: Reading Mus. A.; AIC; Currier Gal. A.; Illinois State Mus.; Abilene Mus. A.; Parrish A. Mus., L.I., N.Y.; Univ. Iowa; Hickory Mus. A., N.C.; Haggin A. Gal.; Dartmouth Col.; Colonial Williamsburgh; MMA; Toledo Mus. A. Art contributor to Readers Digest, True magazines.

MASON, WILLIAM N.—Assistant Museum Director

Isabella Stewart Gardner Museum, 280 The Fenway, Boston 15, Mass.*

MASSARD, JACK (KLETT)—Critic

Los Angeles Examiner, 1111 South Broadway, Los Angeles 54, Cal.; h. 2006 Manning St., Burbank, Cal.

B. Chicago, Ill., Jan. 24, 1919. *Studied*: Loyola Univ., Los A., B.S.; Univ. Cal. at Los A. *Member*: Greater Los Angeles Press Cl. (Pres., 1956). *Award*: Haynes Fnd. Fellowship Award of Merit in Journalism, 1958. *Position*: Feature A. Writer, A. Ed., Los Angeles Examiner.

MASSIN, EUGENE MAX—Painter, T.

3029 Grand Ave., Coconut Grove, Fla.; h. 12201 Southwest 62nd Ave., Miami, Fla.

B. Galveston, Tex., Apr. 10, 1920. *Studied*: AIC, B.F.A.; Univ. Chicago; Escuela Univ. de Bellas Artes, Mexico, M.F.A. *Member*: AEA; South Carolina A. Group. *Awards*: James Nelson F., AIC, 1948; prizes, Wisconsin Salon, 1950; Beloit Col., 1950; AIC; South Carolina A. Group, 1951, 1952. *Work*: Univ. Wisconsin; Beloit Col.; Gibbes A. Gal.; mural, Mexican Colonial Bldg. (in collaboration with David Siqueiros). *Exhibited*: Chicago Veteran's Exh., 1947; Univ. Wisconsin, 1950; Beloit Col., 1950; Southeastern annual, 1951; Gibbes A. Gal., 1951-1952; Ringling Mus. A.; MMA; WMAA, 1955. *Position*: Instr., Univ. South Carolina, 1953; Asst. Prof., Univ. Miami, Coral Gables, Fla., 1953- ; Pres., Fla. Chptr. AEA, 1957-58.

MAST, GERALD—Painter, E.

University of Michigan Extension Center; h. 361 Lakeside Dr., Southeast, Grand Rapids 61, Mich.

B. Topeka, Ind., July 28, 1908. *Studied*: John Herron AI; Detroit Sch. A. & Crafts, and with John Carroll. *Member*: Grand Rapids AA; John Herron AA; Friends of Am. A. *Award*: prize, Western Michigan A., 1957. *Work*: Detroit Inst. A.; Grand Rapids A. Gal.; murals, Clare (Mich.) H.S.; Morton House, Butterworth Hospital, Bronkema Center, Grand Rapids. *Exhibited*: Rhode Island A., 1948; Indiana A., 1948-1952; Michigan A., 1948-1956. *Position*: Instr., mural painting, Rhode Island Sch. Des., 1939-48; Asst. Prof., drawing & painting, Col. Arch. & Des., Univ. Michigan, in residence, Grand Rapids, Mich.

MATHESON, DONALD ROY—
Printmaker, P., E., (former) Mus. Dir.

Art Department, University of Massachusetts; h. 46 Sunset Ave., Amherst, Mass.

B. Honolulu, Hawaii, Jan. 30, 1914. *Studied*: U.S. Military Acad., West Point, B.S.; Univ. Michigan, A.M.; Ecole du Louvre, Paris, France. *Member*: CAA; Michigan Acad.

Sc., A. & Let., Print Council of Am. *Awards*: prizes, Lias award, South Bend, Ind., 1955; Graphic Arts award, Jackson, Mich., 1955; Michigan WC Soc., Detroit Inst. A., 1955; Scarab Cl. award, 1957. *Work*: Detroit Inst. A.; CM; LC; South Bend A. Center; Univ. Oklahoma. *Exhibited*: LC, 1955-1957; CM, 1956, 1958; SAGA, 1956; Boston Pr. M., 1955, 1957, 1958; Am. Color Pr. Soc., 1958; Northwest Pr. M., 1956; Detroit Inst. A., 1954, 1955, 1957; Western New York A., 1954, and others. *Positions*: Dir., West Point Mus., 1952-53; Instr. A. & Dir. Mus., Univ. Oklahoma, 1956-57; Prof. A., Univ. Massachusetts, Amherst, Mass., 1958- .

MATHIEU, MRS. DORA. See Dora

MATSON, ELINA—Craftsman

8750 Old Ocean View Road, Norfolk 3, Va.

B. Finland, Dec. 12, 1892. *Studied*: Norfolk Mus. (weaving); Penland Sch. of Handicrafts, Penland, N.C. *Member*: Tidewater Weavers Gld.; Pen & Brush Cl. *Awards*: Norfolk Mus. A., 1954; Certif. of Distinction, VMFA, 1955; Chesapeake Craftsmen Exh., purchase award, 1956; Pen & Brush Cl., 1956, 1958. *Work*: hand-woven stoles, Norfolk Mus. A., and VMFA. *Exhibited*: Delgado Mus. A., 1953; Pen & Brush Cl.; Women's Intl. Exh., N.Y., 1956, 1957; VMFA, 1955, 1957; Chesapeake Craftsmen, Norfolk Mus. A., 1954, 1956.

MATSON, GRETA—Painter, Lith., T.

4121 7th Ave., Brooklyn 3, N.Y.; h. 8750 Old Ocean View Rd., Norfolk, Va.

B. Claremont, Va., June 7, 1915. *Studied*: Grand Central Sch. A., and with Jerry Farnsworth. *Member*: NAWA; Pen & Brush Cl.; Brooklyn Soc. A.; Tidewater A.; New Jersey P. & S. Soc.; AWS; AEA; All.A.Am.; Audubon A. *Awards*: prizes, NAD, 1943, 1945; SSAL, 1945, 1946; Virginia A., 1943, 1945, 1955; NAWA, 1943, 1952, 1953, 1955-1958; State T. Col., Indiana, Pa., 1945, 1949, 1950; Norfolk Mus. A., 1943, 1948, 1954; AWS, 1949, 1955; Alabama WC Soc., 1950, 1951; Mississippi AA, 1951; Pen & Brush Cl., 1948, 1951, 1952, 1954, 1956, 1958; Conn. Acad. FA, 1952, 1953; New Orleans AA, 1949, 1952; Butler AI; 1948; New Jersey A., 1948, 1951; VMFA, 1957; New Jersey Soc. P. & S., 1957. *Work*: VMFA; Norfolk Mus. A.; State T. Col., Indiana, Pa.; New Britain AI; Texas Tech. Col.; William and Mary Col.; Texas Col. A. & Indst.; Mary Calcott Sch., Norfolk, Va.; Fla. Southern Col.; Longwood Col., Farmville, Va.; Little Rock Mus. FA; Seton Hall Univ. *Exhibited*: AIC, 1942, 1943, 1946; Carnegie Inst., 1941, 1944, 1945; NAD, 1941, 1943-1945, 1956, 1957; Pepsi-Cola, 1945; Albany Inst. Hist. & A., 1940, 1945; Butler AI, 1943-1945, 1957; VMFA, 1939, 1941-1946, 1957; SAGA, 1954; Am. Color Pr. Soc., 1954; Audubon A., 1955, 1956, 1956-1958; AWS, 1954, 1957; All.A.Am., 1953-1955, 1956-1958; one-man: Norfolk Mus. A., 1952, 1955; Pen & Brush Cl., 1955.

MATTEI, ANTONIO—Painter, C., L.

Box 204, Ogunquit, Me.

B. New York, N.Y., Jan. 9, 1900. *Studied*: CUA Sch; NAD; ASL. *Member*: AAPL; Ogunquit AA (Pres.). *Work*: N.Y. Univ.; Albright A. Gal.; MModA; Minne-

16mm Films

Over 250 films available for sale and rental, including ANSEL ADAMS —Photographer; BLINKITY BLANK; CUBISM; DESIGN; ENAMELING ART; FIDDLE DE DEE; FINGER PAINTING OF WU TSAI YEN; IMPRESSIONISM; MOSAIC EXPERIMENTS; NEIGHBORS; OPEN WINDOW; WORKING WITH WATER COLOR.

Write Dept. WW 3 for copies of latest edition of *Films for the Study and Enjoyment of Art.*

International Film Bureau Inc.

57 E. JACKSON BLVD.   CHICAGO 4, ILLINOIS

apolis Inst. A.; Detroit Inst. A.; Navy Base, Portsmouth, N.H. *Awards*: prize, Butler AI. *Exhibited*: 4 one-man exh., N.Y.; GGE, 1939; PAFA, 1941-1943; Carnegie Inst., 1941; CGA, 1935, 1939; Springfield Mus. A.; VMFA; Albright A. Gal.; N.Y. Univ.; Butler AI; MModA; Detroit Inst. A.; Minneapolis Inst. A.; Laurel Gal., 1948. Lectures: Totem Carving in Alaska; Modern Art. *Position*: A. Dir., T., Madison Square Boys Cl., N.Y.; Instr., Ogunquit, Me., Adult Classes, 1947- .*

MATTERN, KARL—*Painter, E., L., Gr.*

College of Fine Arts, Drake University (11); h. 659 33rd St., Des Moines 12, Iowa

B. Durkheim, Germany, Mar. 22, 1892. *Studied*: AIC; ASL, with George Bellows. *Member*: AAUP; AEA. *Awards*: gold medals, Kansas City AI, 1928, 1932, 1934; prizes, GGE, 1939; Denver A. Mus., 1943; AIC, 1946; Joslyn Mus. A., 1947; State T. Col., Pittsburg, Kans., 1949; Iowa WC Exh., 1949, 1951; Mid-America A., 1950; Iowa State Fair, 1955; Des Moines A. Center, 1957, 1958. *Work*: IBM; AIC; Wichita Mus. A.; Wichita AA; Nebraska AA; State T. Col., Pittsburg, Kans.; BM; Univ. Kansas; Sioux City A. Center; Baker Univ.; Kansas State Col.; Lawrence (Kans.) Pub. Schs.; Mid-America Coll.; Methodist Hospital, Des Moines, Iowa; Joslyn Mem. Mus. *Exhibited*: MMA, 1953; VMFA, 1954; PAFA, 1954, 1957; Wichita AA, 1953-1958; CGA, 1955; Joslyn Mus. A., 1954, 1956, 1957, 1958; WAC, 1956; Colorado Springs FA Center, 1956; Mulvane, 1957; Des Moines A. Center, 1956-1958; Ft. Worth A. Center, 1958; Topeka, Kans., 1955; one-man: Des Moines A. Center, 1948, 1951, 1954; Joslyn Mus. A., 1955; Nelson Gal., 1947. *Position*: Prof. Drawing & Painting, Drake Univ., Des Moines, Iowa.

MATTHEW, JOHN BRITTON—*Educator, P., L.*

1550 12th Ave., Sacramento 18, Cal.

B. Berkeley, Cal., Sept. 16, 1896. *Studied*: Univ. California, A.B.; AIC, and with Hans Hofmann, Leon Kroll, Henry McFee. *Member*: Cal. Mus. Assn. (Pres., 1957-). *Work*: murals, Ft. Ord, Cal.; St. Ann's Church, Columbia, Cal. *Exhibited*: Cal. State Fair; Crocker A. Gal.; Laguna Beach AA. *Position*: Dir., Crocker A. Gal., Sacramento, Cal., 1950; Instr. S., Sacramento Col., 1926- ; Organized and sponsored A. Students Lg., 1927-1948, which produced Art Ball, to create scholarships for worthy art students. Proceeds continuing to supply scholarships each year; Instr. TV College Art Course "Great Eras in Art," 1957.

MATTHEWS, LESTER NATHAN—
Sculptor, P., C., Des., Gr.

1766½ West 35th St., Los Angeles 18, Cal.

B. Pittsburgh, Pa., Aug. 8, 1911. *Studied*: Cal. Col. A. & Crafts; & with Sargent Johnson, M. Beckford Young, Worth Ryder. *Member*: San F. AA. *Awards*: prize, San F. AA, 1939; Am.Acad. in Rome, 1942. *Work*: S., Stockton (Cal.) Jr. Col.; Peter Burnett H.S., San Jose, Cal.; Salinas (Cal.) Jr. Col.; Ft. Ord, Cal. *Exhibited*: AIC; Oakland A. Gal.; SFMA; GGE, 1939; Sacramento A. Center; Los A. Mus. A., 1946-1948.

MATTHEWS, LOU (Mrs. Anna Lou Matthews Bedore) —*Painter, T.*

4906 46th Ave., North, St. Petersburg 4, Fla.

B. Chicago, Ill., June 26, 1882. *Studied*: AIC; Grande Chaumiere, Paris; London Sch. A.; & with Lorado Taft, Lucien Simon, Frank Brangwyn. *Member*: Chicago P. & S.; St. Petersburg A. Cl.; Green Bay A. Colony. *Awards*: prizes, AIC, 1926, 1930, 1933; South Side Community A. Center, 1925. *Work*: Rosenwald Coll.; Mun.A.Lg., Chicago; Green Bay A. Mus.; Neville Pub. Mus., West High Lib., Green Bay, Wis.; Chicago Mun. Coll.; Walter Scott Pub. Sch., Chicago. *Exhibited*: PAFA, 1930; AIC, 1944; Green Bay A. Colony; St. Petersburg A. Cl., 1955; Fla. Fed. A., 1955. *Position*: Supv. A., Pub. Sch., Indianapolis, Ind.*

MATTISON, DONALD MAGNUS—*Painter, E.*

110 East 16th St.; h. 3845 Woodstock Dr., Indianapolis 8, Ind.

B. Beloit, Wis., Apr. 24, 1905. *Studied*: Yale Sch. FA, B.F.A.; Am. Acad. in Rome, F.A.A.R. *Member*: Am. Acad. in Rome Alum.; CAA; Mid-West Col. A. Conference; Indiana A. Cl.; Grand Central A. Gal. *Awards*: Prix

de Rome; prizes, Delgado Mus. A.; John Herron AI; Hoosier Salon; Indiana A. Cl.; Tri-State Print Exh.; L. S. Ayers Anniversary Exh.; Piedmont Festival. *Work*: John Herron AI; AIC; Riley Mem. Hospital; ports., N.Y. Stock Exchange; Episcopal Diocese of Western New York; American Fletcher Bank, Indianapolis; mural, Standard Life Bldg., Indianapolis. Monograph on artists' work in "Twenty Painters." *Exhibited*: GGE, 1939; Rockefeller Center, 1939; MMA, 1950; PAFA, 1954, 1957; AIC; CGA; VMFA; Delgado Mus. A.; NAD; John Herron AI; Hoosier Salon; Indiana A. Cl.; CM, and others. *Position*: Dir., John Herron A. Sch., Indianapolis, Ind., 1933- .

MATTSON, HENRY (ELIS)—*Painter*

c/o Frank K. M. Rehn Gallery, 683 Fifth Ave., New York 22, N.Y.; h. Woodstock, N.Y.

B. Gothenburg, Sweden, Aug. 7, 1887. *Member*: NA. *Awards*: prizes, AIC, 1931; WMA, 1933; CGA, 1935, 1943; Carnegie Inst., 1935; Ft. Dodge award, 1940; med., PAFA, 1945, 1950; SC, 1946; Guggenheim F., 1935. *Work*: MMA; WMAA; Carnegie Inst.; PAFA; Newark Mus.; Cranbrook Acad.; CAM; CGA; Wichita A. Mus.; WMA; BM; CMA; Toledo Mus. A.; CM; Santa Barbara Mus. A.; Kansas City AI; Detroit Inst. A.; Ft. Dodge Mus. A.; & others; murals, USPO, Portland, Me. *Exhibited*: nationally & internationally.

MATULKA, JAN—*Painter, Lith.*

439 East 89th St., New York 28, N.Y.

B. Czechoslovakia, Nov. 7, 1890. *Studied*: NAD; & in Paris, France. *Work*: WMAA; N.Y.Pub.Lib., PAFA; SFMA; Detroit Inst. A.; Yale Univ. A. Gal., and in private colls. U.S. and Europe. *Exhibited*: Carnegie Inst., 1944; WMAA, 1944; ACA Gal., 1944; etc. Resided in Paris, 1951-55, with exhs. there.

MAULDIN, BILL—*Cartoonist*

St. Louis Post-Dispatch, St. Louis, Mo.*

MAUNSBACH, GEORGE ERIC—*Painter, S., T.*

939 Eighth Ave.; h. 58 West 57th St., New York 19, N.Y.

B. Helsingborg, Sweden, Jan. 5, 1890. *Studied*: Stockholm Acad., with Anders Zorn; Royal Acad., with Sargent; BMFA Sch., with Pape. *Member*: AAPL; Scandinavian-Am. A.; Am. Veterans Soc. A. *Work*: port. Columbia Univ.; Univ. Cl., N.Y.; Nat. Women's Rep. Cl.; Supreme Court, Louisville; Supreme Court, Elizabethtown, N.Y.; Court of Appeals, Albany, N.Y.; Governor's Island, N.Y.; White House, Wash., D.C.; Wilbraham Acad. (Mass.); County Court House, Easton, Pa.; Maywood Col., Scranton, Pa.; World War Coll., Wash., D.C.; Am. Soc. Composers, Authors & Publ., N.Y.; Lincoln & Benjamin Franklin Hotels, N.Y.; Court House, Easton, Pa.; Ft. Dix, N.J.; Symphony Hall, Detroit; Lib.Cong.; Cavalry Armory, Brooklyn, N.Y.; Ft. Jay; Ft. Slocum; Camp Upton; Lawrence Univ.; Supreme Court, Louisville, N.Y.; Swedish-Am. Hospital, Rockford, Ill.; Supreme Court, Schenectady, N.Y.; etc. *Exhibited*: BM; AIC; NAD; PAFA; Paris Salon; Newport AA; etc. Lectures: "The Art of Portrait Painting."

MAURER, SASCHA—*Painter*

Gaylordsville, Conn.

B. Munich, Germany, Apr. 18, 1897. *Studied*: Sch. App. A., Acad. FA, Munich, Germany. *Member*: Washington AA; Audubon A.; AAPL; SC; AWS; Kent AA; Academic AA; Hudson Valley AA; Berkshire AA; All. A. Am.; Conn. WC Soc. *Awards*: prizes, Great Barrington (Mass.) AA, 1950, 1954, 1956-1958; Silvermine Gld. A., 1954; New Britain A. Mus., 1957 (purchase); Washington AA, 1956; Berkshire AA, 1956; Hudson Valley AA, 1957; SC, 1958. *Exhibited*: Audubon A., annually; AWS, annually; Conn. WC Soc., annually; NAC, 1951; Silvermine Gld. A., 1951, 1954, 1957; Grand Central A. Gal., 1951, 1958 (both one-man); Springfield Academic A., 1955, 1956; Berkshire AA, 1954, 1955, 1957 (one-man); Kent AA, 1954; Washington AA, 1954, 1955-1958; Tyringham (Mass.) A. Gal., 1955 (one-man); Great Barrington AA, 1954, 1956-1958; New Jersey Soc. P. & S., 1958; New Britain A. Mus., 1957; Dartmouth Col., 1957 (one-man); PAFA, 1957; Southern Vermont A., 1957; Portland (Me.) Mus. A., 1958; SC, 1958; Hudson Valley AA, 1957; Berkshire A. Mus., 1956. Contributor to Ford Times, 1953-58.

MAURICE, ALFRED PAUL—*Educator, Des., Gr.*

The Maryland Institute, 1300 West Mount Royal Ave. (17); h. 700 West University Parkway, Baltimore 10, Md.

B. Nashua, N.H., Mar. 11, 1921. *Studied:* Univ. New Hampshire; Michigan State Univ., B.A., M.A. *Member:* CAA; Nat. Assn. Schs. Des.; AAUP; Com. on A. Edu.; NAEA. *Work:* murals, Hudson (N.H.) Jr. H.S.; Community Chest Bldg., New Hampshire. *Exhibited:* BM; Phila. Pr. Cl.; Washington WC Cl.; Laguna Beach AA. *Positions:* Instr., Gr. A., Macalester Col., St. Paul, Minn.; Lettering & Layout, Michigan State Univ.; Gr. A., Des., State Univ. T. Col., New Paltz, N.Y., and Actg. Chm. A. Dept., 1955; Exec. Dir., The Maryland Institute, Baltimore, Md., 1957- .

MAURICE, E(LEANORE) INGERSOLL (Mrs. Raymond H.)—*Painter, T.*

215 South Mountain Ave., Montclair, N.J.

B. East Orange, N.J., Sept. 5, 1901. *Studied:* Beards Sch., East Orange, N.J.; ASL, with Frank DuMond, Allen Tucker; Montclair A. Mus. Sch., with Avery Johnson, Estelle Armstrong. *Member:* ASL (life); AWS; Phila. WC Cl.; Pen & Brush Cl.; All. A. Am.; Knickerbocker A.; AAPL; New Jersey WC Soc.; Essex WC Soc. *Awards:* prizes, AAPL, prize and medal, 1950, 1955, 1956 (gold medal); NAC, bronze medal, 1957; Knickerbocker A., bronze medal, 1958; Seton Hall Univ., bronze medal, 1956; Parrish Mus., Southampton, L.I., 1951; Gld. Hall, East-hampton, L.I., 1951-1953, 1955; Newark A. Cl., 1951; Hudson Valley AA, 1952, 1953, 1957, 1958; A. Center of the Oranges, 1952-1954, 1958; West Essex and Verona AA, 1953; Montclair A. Mus.; Essex WC Exh., 1955; New Jersey WC Soc., 1955; Audubon A. 1957; Pen & Brush Cl., 1958; All. A. Am., 1950, 1958; Butler AI, 1955; AAPL, gold medal, and prize. *Work:* Montclair A. Mus.; Bloomfield Pub. Lib.; Mt. Hebron Sch., Montclair; West Essex-Verona Gram. Sch. *Exhibited:* PAFA, 1949, 1952, 1953; AWS traveling exh., 1955, 1958; AWS, 1949-1955; Butler AI; 1953, 1955; All. A. Am., 1949-1955; Audubon A., 1950, 1952-1955; NAWA; Terry AI; AAPL; NAC; Montclair A. Mus.; 1947-1955; Trenton Mus. A.; Newark Mus. A.; New Jersey WC Soc.; Parrish Mus.; Gld. Hall, and many other local and regional exhs. Lectures with demonstrations of methods. *Position:* Instr. A., A. Center of the Oranges, 1954, 1956, 1957.

MAUZEY, MERRITT—*Lithographer, W., P., I., L.*

3424 Stanford St., Dallas 5, Tex.

B. Clifton, Tex., Nov. 16, 1898. *Member:* Dallas Pr. Soc.; Texas FA Assn.; Dallas AA; AAPL; Conn. Acad. FA; Texas A. T. Assn.; SAGA; Audubon A.; Cal. Soc. Et. *Awards:* Guggenheim F., 1946; prizes, Dallas Mus. FA; Beaumont, Tex., 1952; Dallas All. A.; Texas FA Assn.; Arizona State Fair, 1946, 1947; SSAL, 1947; LC, 1947; SAGA, 1948, 1956. *Work:* lithographs, AIC; CGA; LC; PMA; PAFA; MMA; Witte Mem. Mus.; Elisabet Ney Mus.; Mus. FA of Houston; Fondren Lib., Dallas; Dallas Mus FA; N.Y.Pub.Lib.; New Britain Mus. A.; Brooks Mem. Mus.; Cal. State Lib.; Pa. State Univ., and in private colls. *Exhibited:* WFNY 1939; WMAA; MMA; NAD, 1939-1956; PAFA, 1939-1956; Conn. Acad. FA, 1939-1956; AIC, 1939; LC; Assoc. Am. A.; BM; Audubon A.; Albany Inst. Hist. & A.; Denver A. Mus.; SFMA; Oakland A.

Gal.; Carnegie Inst.; Rochester Mem. A. Gal., and many others. One-man: Delphic Studios. Lectures: Lithography. Prints included in "The Artist in America"; Southwest Review of Literature; "The Land of Beginning Again"; Author, I., "Cotton Farm Boy," 1954; "Texas Ranch Boy," 1955; "Oilfield Boy," 1956; "Rice Boy," 1958.

MAUZY, WAYNE L.—*Museum Director*

Museum of New Mexico, Santa Fe, N.M.*

MAWICKE, TRAN—*Illustrator, P.*

60 Summit Ave., Bronxville, N.Y.

B. Chicago, Ill., Sept. 20, 1911. *Studied:* AIC; Am. Acad. A. *Member:* SI; AWS; Balt. WC Cl.; A. & Writers Soc. *Work:* Schenectady Mus. A.; General Electric Laboratories; U.S. Air Force Historical Fnd. *Exhibited:* AWS, 1953-1955; Balt. WC Cl., 1953, 1954; West Chester AA, 1954, 1955; SC, 1953-1955; Frye Mus. A., Seattle, 1954; SI, 1953-1955; Santa Monica, Cal., 1954; one-man: New York City, 1958. *Position:* Chm., Joint Ethics, SI, 1954-1959; Instr., Bronxville Adult Sch., 1956-58.

MAXON, JOHN—*Museum Director*

Art Institute of Chicago, Chicago, Ill.

Studied: Univ. Michigan, B. Des.; Harvard Univ., Ph.D. *Member:* AAMus. Dirs.; AAMus.; CAA. *Position:* Dir., Mus. A., Rhode Island School of Design, Providence, R.I. to 1959; Dir. of Fine Arts, Art Institute of Chicago, 1959- .

MAXWELL, JOHN (RAYMOND)—*Painter*

3701 North Broad St., Philadelphia 40, Pa.; h. Creek Road, Hartsville, Pa.

B. Rochester, N.Y., Nov. 3, 1909. *Studied:* Univ. Rochester, and with Alling Clements, Carl W. Peters, Antonio Martino, W. Lester Stevens, Jonas Lie. *Member:* AWS; Phila. WC Cl.; Phila. A. All.; Woodmere A. Gal.; AEA. *Awards:* prizes, Indiana State T. Col., 1947, 1948; Woodmere A. Gal., 1954, 1956; Audubon A., 1951; AWS, 1952, 1957; Butler Inst. Am. A., 1957; silver medal, DaVinci All., 1953, gold medal, 1952, bronze medal, 1956; gold medal, Phila. Sketch Cl., 1951, 1956; Dana medal, PAFA, 1957. *Work:* Butler Inst. Am. A.; Lehigh Univ. *Exhibited:* AIC, 1944; Butler Inst. Am. A., 1957, 1958; PAFA, 1944, 1946-1949, 1952, 1953, 1957; CGA, 1945, 1951; NAD, 1945, 1946, 1948, 1949, 1954-1957; Woodmere A. Gal., 1950, 1952, 1954, 1956-1958; DaVinci All., 1951-1955, 1957, 1958; Nat. Soc. Painters in Casein, 1955; Phila. A. Festival, 1955; Norfolk Acad. A., 1957; Phila. WC Cl., 1952-1954, 1955, 1956, 1958; SC, 1954; VMFA, 1946; Toledo Mus. A., 1946; Indiana State T. Col., 1947-1950; AWS, 1947, 1952, 1957, 1958; Washington WC Cl., 1947, 1948, 1950, 1952, 1956; Audubon A., 1948, 1949, 1951; Phila. Sketch Cl., 1948, 1949, 1951, 1952, 1954-1958; AWS touring exh., 1951-1958, and many other exhs.

MAY, ELIZABETH M.—*Painter, C., Ser.*

608 Altara Ave., Coral Gables, Fla.

B. Chicago, Ill., Feb. 23, 1913. *Studied:* Univ. Illinois, A.B.; Am. Acad. A., Chicago. *Member:* Blue Dome Art

NEW YORK - PHOENIX SCHOOL OF DESIGN

A non-profit institution of higher education. Occupies its own building with beautiful library. Specialists in training students for art careers since 1892. Faculty of outstanding artists. All courses include Economics, English, History of Art and American History.

Carefully planned and proven 3 and 4 year courses in

ADVERTISING DESIGN, including Editorial Layout; MAGAZINE AND BOOK ILLUSTRATION; FINE ARTS, including Portraiture, Figure and Mural Painting; FASHION ILLUSTRATION, including Fashion Layout; TEXTILE DESIGN, including Flower Drawing and Painting.

Day, Evening and Saturday Morning Classes for beginners and advanced students. Exhibition of student work always on view. Successful Placements. Distinguished Alumni.

Fall, Midyear and Summer Semesters — Request Catalog W.

160 LEXINGTON AVENUE, at 30th Street, NEW YORK 16, NEW YORK • MU 5-2973

Fellowship; Miami AA; Miami A. Lg.; Miami WC Soc.; Fla. Fed. A.; AEA. *Awards*: prizes, Miami Boat Show, 1949; Poinciana Exh., 1948-1956; Blue Dome, 1950, 1955; Miami A. Lg., 1952; Wilfred Beattie awards, 1952-1954. *Exhibited*: Cuba, 1954; Lowe Gal. A., 1953; Miami AA traveling exhs.; Norton Gal. A.; St. Petersburg and Pensacola, Fla.; Lyceum & Tennis Club, Havana, Cuba, 1956; one-man: Miami Beach A. Center, 1947, 1948, 1950, 1952, 1956; ceramic tile exh., Village Corner, Miami, 1958.

MAY, JOHN—*Craftsman*
Route 4, Box 866, Sarasota, Fla.

B. Duxbury, Mass., Feb. 27, 1908. *Studied*: Boston Arch. Center. *Exhibited*: Des.-Craftsmen, 1953; Fiber, Clay & Metal Exh., 1953; Boston A. Festival, 1955; Stuttgart, Germany, 1953; Illinois, 1955; Wichita AA, 1954; Soc. Four A., Palm Beach, 1954; New Orleans, La., 1954; one-man: Sarasota AA, 1953; Farnsworth Mus., Rockland, Me., 1955.*

MAYEN, PAUL—*Designer*
235 East 58th St., New York 22, N.Y.; h. 336 Third Ave., New York 10, N.Y.

B. La Linea, Spain, May 31, 1918. *Studied*: CUASch.; ASL, Columbia Univ.; New Sch. for Social Research. *Awards*: A. Dir. Cl., N.Y. *Work*: MModA. *Exhibited*: BM; MModA; Nelson Gal. A.; Annual of Adv. Art. Contributor to Industrial Design; Interiors; Progressive Architecture; Art News Annual; Arts & Architecture; Architectural Forum magazines. Lectures: "Use of Symbols in Advertising Design"; "Is Decoration Good Design?"; "Structure & Form." *Position*: A. Dir., "Through Decorators Only," trade publication; Asst. A. Dir., F.W. Dodge-Sweet's Catalog; Des. Consultant to various industrial organizations; Book des. for leading publishers, ads, booklets, etc.; Instr., Adv. Des., CUASch.; Adv. Des., Parsons Sch., New York, N.Y.; A. Dir. for Agfa, Inc., Orradio and North American Philips Co.; Des. Ecclesiastical objects for Saarinen Chapel, MIT; Des., traveling show for USIA "Craftsmanship in a Changing World."

MAYER, MRS. BENA FRANK. See Frank, Bena Virginia

MAYER, FRED A.—*Illustrator*
195-06 Woodhull Ave., Hollis 23, L.I., N.Y.

B. Ober-Ingelheim, Germany, Apr. 4, 1904. *Studied*: Berlin A. Col., with Lucian Bernhard. I., "Nana," 1936; "Sonnets from the Portuguese," 1938. Contributor: illus. in silhouette to Stage Pictorial magazines, and N.Y. newspapers. Des., book jackets, posters & packages.*

MAYER, GRACE M.—*Former Museum Curator, W.*
Museum of Modern Art, 11 West 53rd St.; h. 40 East 78th St., New York 21, N.Y.

B. New York, N.Y. Contributor to: Bulletin of the Mus. City of N.Y. Arranged many exh. including "Currier & Ives and the New York 'Scene,'" 1938; "Philip Hone's New York," 1940; "New York Between Two Wars," 1944; "Stranger in Manhattan," 1950; "Charles Dana Gibson's New York," 1950; "Currier & Ives Printmakers to the American People," the Harry Peters Coll., 1957-58; "Once Upon a City" Photographs by Byron, 1958; Served as Asst. to Edward Steichen—"70 Photographers Look at New York," MModA, 1957-58, and others. Author: "Once Upon a City," New York from 1890 to 1910 as photographed by Byron and described by Grace Mayer with foreword by Steichen, 1958. *Position*: Cur., N.Y. Iconography, Mus. City of New York, 1931-1959; Special Asst. to Dir. Dept. of Photography, Mus. Modern Art, New York, N.Y., 1959- .

MAYER, HENRIK MARTIN—*Painter, Lith., L., E.*
Hartford Art School, 25 Atheneum Sq., North, Hartford 3, Conn.; h. Essex, Conn.

B. Nashua, N.H., Dec. 24, 1908. *Studied*: Manchester Inst. A. & Sc.; Yale Univ. Sch. FA, B.F.A. *Member*: Indiana A. Cl.; Phila. WC Cl.; Audubon A. *Awards*: Winchester F., European study, 1931; prizes, NAD, 1938, 1941; Springfield A.Lg., 1940; Conn. Acad. FA, 1940; Herron AI, 1937, 1942, 1943, 1945. *Work*: Indiana Univ.; Indiana State T. Col.; Herron AI; murals, Women's Cosmopolitan Cl., N.Y.; U.S. Marine Hospital, Louisville, Ky.;

USPO, Lafayette, Ind.; Aurora, Ind. *Exhibited*: AIC, 1937; Toledo Mus. A., 1938, 1945; NAD, 1938, 1941, 1943-1945; GGE, 1939; CGA, 1940, 1943, 1946; PAFA, 1941, 1942, 1944, 1945; Carnegie Inst., 1938, 1939, 1945; Toronto (Canada) Mus., 1940; Montreal (Canada) Mus., 1940; CAM, 1939, 1940; CM, 1941; Butler AI, 1945; Herron AI, 1934-1946. Lectures: Pictorial Analysis and Painting Techniques. *Position*: Asst. Dir., Instr. Painting, Herron AI, Indianapolis, Ind., 1933-46; Dir. Instr. Painting, Hartford A. Sch. Wadsworth Atheneum, Hartford, Conn., 1946.*

MAYER, LOUIS—*Sculptor, P., T., Cr., W., L.*
Fishkill, N.Y.; w. Box 384, Carmel, Cal.

B. Milwaukee, Wis., Nov. 26, 1869. *Studied*: in Europe. *Member*: All. A. Am. *Awards*: med., Pan-Pacific Expo., 1915; St. Paul AI. *Work*: McKinley Birthplace Mem.; Hist. Soc. Iowa; Hist. Soc. Wisconsin; Milwaukee AI; busts of Dr. Albert Schweitzer in Medical Center, Univ. Wisconsin and the Carl Cherry Fnd., Carmel, Cal.; relief plaque of Dr. Schweitzer and Walt Whitman bust in Milwaukee Pub. Lib. *Exhibited*: NAD; PAFA; Copley Soc., Boston; AIC; Milwaukee AI; CGA; Carnegie Inst.

MAYER, PETER BELA—*Painter*
320 Fifth Ave., New York 1, N.Y.; h. 27 Summit Rd., Port Washington, N.Y.

B. Loeche, Hungary, Aug. 5, 1888. *Studied*: NAD. *Member*: SC; AAPL; All.A.Am. *Awards*: prizes, SC, 1958 and prior; AAPL. *Exhibited*: CGA; PAFA; NAD; SC; All. A.Am.; AIC; Venice, Italy.

MAYER, RALPH—*Painter, W., T., L.*
240 E. 20th St., New York 3, N.Y.

B. New York, N.Y., Aug. 11, 1895. *Studied*: Rensselaer Polytechnic Inst.; ASL. *Member*: AEA; F., Am. Inst. Chemists; F., Intl. Inst. for Conservation. *Awards*: Guggenheim F., 1952-53. Author: "The Artist's Handbook of Materials and Techniques," 1941; rev., enl., 1957; "The Painter's Craft," 1948. Contributor to Technical Studies in the Field of Fine Arts; Creative Art; College Art Journal; Encyclopaedia Britannica, and other publications. *Positions*: Instr., Columbia Univ. Sch. Painting & Sculpture; Author monthly page in Arts magazine, 1949-1958.

MAYERS, MYRON—*Painter*
34 West 28th St., New York 1, N.Y.

B. Odessa, Russia, May 1, 1887. *Member*: AEA; Brooklyn Soc. A.; Lg. Present-Day A. *Award*: prize, Screen Publicists, 1946. *Exhibited*: Riverside Mus., 1945-1947, 1955; BM, 1948-1952; AEA; one-man: RoKo Gal., 1949; Bodley Gal., 1956.

MAYHEW, EDGAR DE NOAILLES—*Educator, Mus. C., L., W.*
613 Williams St., New London, Conn.

B. Newark, N.J., Oct. 1, 1913. *Studied*: Amherst Col., B.A.; Yale Univ., M.A.; Johns Hopkins Univ., Ph.D. *Member*: CAA; Conn. Antiquarian & Landmark Soc.; Soc. for Preservation of New England Antiquities. *Awards*: Carnegie F. to Johns Hopkins Univ., 1939-1941. Author: "English Baroque," 1943. Lectures: Renaissance, Gothic & Modern Art. *Position*: Instr. FA, Johns Hopkins Univ., 1941-42; Instr. FA, Wellesley Col., 1944-45; Asst. Prof. FA, Connecticut Col., New London, Conn., 1945- ; Cur., Lyman Allyn Mus., New London, Conn., 1950- .

MAYHEW, RICHARD—*Painter, I.*
716 Jefferson St., Brooklyn 21, N.Y.

B. Amityville, N.Y., Apr. 3, 1924. *Studied*: BMSch. A.; with Edwin Dickinson, Reuben Tam. *Awards*: prize, BM, 1957; John Hay Whitney F., 1958. *Exhibited*: NAD, 1955; BM, 1956-1958; New York City Center, 1955-1958; Morris Gal., 1957; Riverside Mus., 1957; Art:USA, 1958; Washington Irving Gal., N.Y., 1958. Illus. for Harper's Magazine; The Reporter Magazine.

MAYNARD, RICHARD FIELD—*Painter, S., W.*
South Crossway, Old Greenwich, Conn.

B. Chicago, Ill., Apr. 23, 1875. *Studied*: Cornell Univ.; Harvard Univ.; ASL; N.Y.Sch.A.; & with William Chase,

Irving Wiles, Joseph De Camp. *Member*: N.Y. Soc. Painters; All.A.Am.; A. Soc., Old Greenwich; Authors Lg. Am.; AWCS. *Exhibited*: N.Y. WC Cl.; NAD; AWCS; NAC; Phila. WC Cl.; CGA; AIC. Contributor: short stories to national magazines.

MAYOR, ALPHEUS HYATT—*Museum Curator, W., L.*
  Metropolitan Museum of Art; h. 51 East 97th St., New York 29, N.Y.
B. Annisquam, Mass., June 28, 1901. *Studied*: Princeton Univ., A.B.; Oxford Univ., B.Litt. *Member*: Grolier Cl. Author: "Life in America," 1939; "The Bibiena Family," 1945; "Baroque and Romantic Stage Design," 1950; "Giovanni Battista Piranesi," 1952. Contributor to: MMA Bulletin, & other publications. Lectures: Renaissance & Modern Art. *Position*: Dept. Prints, MMA, New York, N.Y., 1932- , Cur. Prints at present; Pres., Hispanic Soc. Am.; Corresponding Memb., Academia de San Fernando, Madrid; Trustee, Instituto de Valencia de Don Juan, Madrid.

MAYS, MAXWELL—*Illustrator, W., P., Des.*
  Woodlot Farm, Coventry Center, R.I.
B. Providence, R.I., Aug. 13, 1918. *Studied*: R.I.Sch. Des.; Parsons Sch. Des.; ASL. *Member*: SI; Providence A. Cl.; Providence WC Cl. Illus., "Life Among the Savages," 1953. Author: I., Colliers; Cosmopolitan; Ford Times; Lincoln Mercury Times.

MAYS, PAUL (KIRTLAND)—*Painter*
  Rte. 3, Box 108, Carmel, Cal.
B. Cheswick, Pa., Oct. 4, 1887. *Studied*: Carnegie Inst.; ASL; Grande Chaumiere, Paris; in England, and with Charles Hawthorne. *Member*: NSMP; Carmel AA. *Work*: murals, St. Francis Hotel, San F.; USPO, Norristown, Pa.; work also in private collections. *Exhibited*: CGA; WMAA; Cal. PLH; Grand Central A. Gal.; PAFA; PMA; Carmel AA; A. Gld of Am.; Stendahl Gal., Los A.; Cornwall, England; Allen Mem. Mus., Oberlin, Ohio; Arch. Lg.; Barcelona and Mallorca, Spain; Provincetown, Mass.; Am. A. Gld.; Westport (Conn.) A. Center.

THE PRATT-CONTEMPORARIES GRAPHIC ART CENTRE
AN EXTENSION OF PRATT INSTITUTE
FRITZ EICHENBERG—DIRECTOR

AFTERNOON AND EVENING CLASSES
11 MONTHS A YEAR

**LITHOGRAPHY
ETCHING ENGRAVING
WOODCUT**

CONTINUOUS REGISTRATION
PROFESSIONAL PRINTING FOR ARTISTS

1343 THIRD AVENUE   (77th ST.)
TEL. UN 1-9180   NEW YORK 21

THE SCHOOL OF FINE ARTS
WASHINGTON UNIVERSITY, ST. LOUIS

Four-year programs leading to the Bachelor of Fine Arts Degree in Painting, Sculpture, Illustration, Advertising Design, Dress Design and Teacher Education. Students may reside on campus and share in University activities. For catalog, address KENNETH E. HUDSON, Dean.

THE ART INSTITUTE OF CHICAGO

Professional School

Fine Arts, Painting, Sculpture, Advertising Arts, Lettering, Layout. Pictorial Composition. Industrial Design. Interior Decoration. Color. Ceramics; Flat Pattern Design for Rugs, Textiles, Wallpaper. Dress Design, Dress Construction, Weaving, Crafts. Teachers' Training. Accredited. Degrees, Diplomas. Distinguished Faculty. Send for Catalog. Box 247.

**MICHIGAN AVE. at ADAMS
CHICAGO 3   ILLINOIS**

THE PENNSYLVANIA ACADEMY OF THE FINE ARTS

**PAINTING

SCULPTURE

MURAL**

For catalog write:
Broad & Cherry, Phila. 2, Pa.

MAZESKI, WALTER ADOLPH—
Designer, P., I., Cart., L.

Kling Studios, 601 North Fairbanks St., Chicago 5, Ill.; h. 7704 West Diversey St., Elmwood Park 35, Ill.

B. Globe, Ariz., July 28, 1909. *Studied*: AIC; Inst. Des., Chicago, and with Charles Schroeder, Francis Chapin, and others. *Member*: Am. A. Assn.; A. Gld., Chicago. *Awards*: prizes, Milwaukee AI, 1942; Polish A. Cl., 1929-1933, 1936, 1937, 1940, 1942, 1951; Kostrubala award for sc., 1954. *Work*: Polish Nat. All. Archives Mus.; Kosciuszko Fnd. *Exhibited*: Chicago World Fair, 1933; AIC, 1937-1946, 1948; Polish A. Cl., 1933, 1945-1955; Milwaukee AI, 1940.

McAFEE, ILA (Mrs. Ila McAfee Turner)—Painter, I.
Taos, N.M.

B. Gunnison, Colo., Oct. 21, 1900. *Studied*: Western State Col., Gunnison, Colo., A.B.; ASL; NAD. *Member*: Laguna Beach AA (life); Taos AA. *Work*: murals, USPO, Cordel, Edmond, Okla.; Gunnison, Colo.; Clifton, Tex.; Greeley (Colo.) Pub. Lib.; paintings, Thomas Gilcrease Fnd., Tulsa; State Agricultural Col., Logan, Utah; Pub. Sch., Cedar City, Utah; Amarillo (Tex.) H.S.; Koshare Mus., La Junta, Colo.; Cedar City Pub. Lib.; Baylor Univ. *Awards*: prizes, New Mexico State Fair, 1943, 1950. *Exhibited*: Utah, New Mexico, Colorado, Texas, Oklahoma, I., covers and center spread "How to Draw Horses," 1952; "All the Year 'Round with the Furry Folk," juvenile book. Specializes in paintings & ports. of animals. Des., textile for Howard & Schaffer, New York, N.Y.

McANDREW, JOHN—
Museum Director, E., Hist., W., L.

Jewett Arts Center, Wellesley College; h. 107 Dover Rd., Wellesley 82, Mass.

B. New York, N.Y., May 4, 1904. *Studied*: Harvard Col., B.S.; Harvard Univ. Grad. Sch. Arch., M. Arch. *Member*: Am. Archaeological Soc.; CAA; Soc. Arch. Historians; Assn. A. Mus. Dirs. Ed., several catalogues of exhs., MModA. Contributor to Art Bulletin; Art News; Art in America; Arts; San Carlos (Mexico); Goya (Spain); Das Werk (Switzerland). Lectures: Architecture; Modern Art; Mexican Art, in museums, universities and colleges, U.S., Latin America and India. Arranged about 20 exhs. of modern architecture and industrial art, MModA; 40 exhs. of various kinds, Farnsworth Museum, Wellesley College. *Position*: Prof., Hist. Art & Arch., Vassar, Wellesley, MIT, Univ. So. California, Universidad Nacional de Mexico, Instituto Nacional de Antropologia e Historia de Mexico. Cur., Arch., MModA, N.Y., 1936-40; L., (Cultural Exchange Program) U.S. Dept. State, Latin America, 1953, India, 1956; Dir., Art Mus., Wellesley College, Wellesley, Mass., at present.

McARDLE, JIM—Illustrator, Cart.
1356 Madison Ave., New York 28, N.Y.

B. New York, N.Y., Nov. 22, 1899. *Studied*: Fordham Univ. *Member*: SI; A. & Writers Soc.; Nat. Cartoonists Soc. I., for "Davy Crockett-frontiersman," syndicated by Columbia Features (newspapers), at present.*

McBEY, JAMES—Painter, Et.
6417 Wissahickon Ave., Philadelphia 19, Pa.; also, 284 Old Mountain Rd., Tangier, Morocco

B. Newburgh, Aberdeenshire, Scotland, Dec. 23, 1883. *Awards*: Hon. Degree, LL.D., Aberdeen Univ. Official artist for Egyptian Expeditionary Force, 1917-18. *Work*: British Mus., Imperial War Mus., London, and in the Print Dept., Boston Pub. Lib.

McBRIDE, HENRY—Critic, W.
2 Peter Cooper Road, New York 10, N.Y.

Author: "Matisse"; "Some French Moderns"; "John Marin," 1936; "George Bellows," for Nat. Gal. A., Wash., D.C., and others. *Award*: AFA critics' award, 1954; Chevalier, Legion d'Honneur, French Govt., 1958. *Positions*: Instr., A. Dept., Edu. Alliance, New York, N.Y.; Dir., Sch. Int. A., Trenton, N.J. (5 yrs.); A. Cr., New York Sun (37 yrs.); A. Cr., The Dial; Ed., Creative Art; Contributing Ed., Art News, at present. Also contributor of essays to Town & Country, View, Cahiers d'Art, Paris, L'Age Nouveau, Paris, Vanity Fair, The Arts (WMAA), and other magazines.

McBRIDE, JAMES J.—Painter, Comm. A., I.
536 Russell Ave., Fort Wayne, Ind.

B. Fort Wayne, Ind., May 19, 1923. *Studied*: Fort Wayne A. Sch.; PAFA, with Franklin Watkins, Francis Speight. *Member*: Indiana A. Cl. *Awards*: prizes, Hoosier Salon, 1955, 1956, 1958 (2); Ft. Wayne A. Sch., 1954, 1957; Van Wert, Ohio, 1957; Northern Indiana A., 1953; Chicago Tribune Exh., 1954. *Work*: Univ. Indiana; Tri Kappa Coll.; murals, restaurants and churches in Indiana and work in private colls. *Exhibited*: PAFA, 1949; Chicago Tribune, 1953; Hoosier Salon, 1949, 1955-1958; Michiana, South Bend, 1958; Tri Kappa, 1950-1958; Indiana A., 1957; Hammond, Ind., 1955-1957. Illus. for Broadcasting & Telecasting magazine, and other publications. *Position*: A. Dir., WKJG Television, Fort Wayne, Ind.

McBRIDE, WALTER H.—Museum Director, T., C., P.
2738 Elmwood Dr., Southeast, Grand Rapids 6, Mich.

B. Waterloo, Ind., Apr. 20, 1905. *Studied*: Harvard Univ.; Herron A. Sch., B.A.E.; Indiana Univ. *Member*: Midwest Mus. Dir.; Am. Assn. Mus. Dir. *Position*: Instr. Des., John Herron A. Sch., Indianapolis, Ind., 1929; Dir., Ft. Wayne A. Sch. & Mus., Ft. Wayne, Ind., 1933-54; Dir., Grand Rapids A. Gal., 1954- . Pres., Midwest Mus. Assn., 1958-59.

McCALL, ROBERT THEADOR—
Painter, Des., Comm. A., I.

252 East 48th St., New York, N.Y.; also, 102 Seven Bridges Rd., Chappaqua, N.Y.

B. Columbus, Ohio, Dec. 23, 1919. *Studied*: Columbus Sch. FA. *Member*: SI; Aviation Writers Assn. *Awards*: scholarship, Columbus Sch. FA. *Work*: U.S. Air Force Hist. Coll., Pentagon, Wash., D.C. (made during tour of Arctic bases). *Exhibited*: Westchester AA, 1954, 1955. Illus., covers, Popular Science magazine; adv. illus., for leading publications including Life, Time, Sat. Eve. Post, Colliers, etc. Series of paintings illus. "The Day of Infamy," for Life magazine; U.S. Air Force painting assignment 1957, to document the world-wide activities of the Air Force. Campaigns for Ford, Buick, Goodyear, Sperry, Douglas Aircraft, United Aircraft and others.

McCALL, VIRGINIA ARMITAGE—
Painter, Med. I., Gr., W., L.

30 Hannum Dr., Ardmore, Pa.

B. Philadelphia, Pa. *Studied*: PAFA. *Awards*: Cresson traveling scholarship, PAFA, 1931, prize, 1932; medal, Phila. A. Cl., 1940; Phila. Gimbel Award, 1946; Distinguished Daughter of Pa. award, 1954. *Work*: PAFA; PMA; WMAA; Univ. Pennsylvania; Armed Forces Medical Mus., Wash., D.C. *Exhibited*: nationally and internationally; one-man Chester County AA, 1958. Lectures: "The Artist Helps the Plastic Surgeons, WW II."

McCALLUM, CORRIE (Mrs. William Halsey)—
Painter, I., T., C.

38 State St., Charleston, S.C.

B. Sumter, S.C., Mar. 14, 1914. *Studied*: Univ. South Carolina; BMFA Sch., with Karl Zerbe. *Member*: Gld. South Carolina A. *Awards*: prizes, Carolina AA, 1945; South Carolina Annual, 1955; Gld. South Carolina A., 1953, 1954. *Work*: Gibbes A. Gal., and in private collections. *Exhibited*: Telfair Acad. A.; VMFA, 1947; BMFA, 1951; High Mus. A., 1948, 1949, 1951, 1955, 1957; Norfolk Mus. A., 1954, 1958; one-man: Gibbes Gal. A., 1947-1952; Columbia Mus. A., 1954; Florence (S.C.) Mus., 1954; Winston-Salem Mus. A., 1954; Mint Mus. A., 1955; Clemson Col., 1955; Davidson Col., 1954; Augusta Mus. A., 1955. Illus., "Dutch Fork Farm Boy," 1952. *Position*: Instr., A., Telfair Acad. A., 1942-43; Gibbes Gal. A., Charleston, S.C., 1946-53; Instr. A., Charleston A. Sch., 1953- . Artist-in-Residence, Castle Hill Art Center, Charleston, 1956.

McCAUSLAND, ELIZABETH—Writer, Cr., L., T.
50 Commerce St., New York 14, N.Y.

B. Wichita, Kans., Apr. 16, 1899. *Studied*: Smith Col., A.B., A.M. *Member*: Authors Gld.; Am. Section, Intl. Assn. A. Critics; Soc. Arch. Historians. *Awards*: Alumnae F., Smith Col., 1921; Guggenheim F., 1943-1944. Author: "The Knight of Curtesy," 1922; "Changing New York," 1939; "Kathe Kollwitz," (portfolio with essay), 1941;

"Picasso" (brochure), 1944; "Life and Work of Edward Lamson Henry, N.A., 1841-1919," 1945; "George Inness, 1825-1894," 1946; "Charles W. Hawthorne," 1947; "A. H. Maurer," 1949; "Art Professions in the United States," 1950; "Careers in the Arts," 1950; "American Professional," 1950; "A. H. Maurer," 1951; "Marsden Hartley," 1952; "Roots of American Art," 1953; "Marsden Hartley," in prep.; "Why Can't America Afford Art?", 1946; "Bibliography of American Art," 1946. Photo-editor, Carl Sandburg's "Poems of the Midwest," 1946; editor, "Work for Artists." 1947. Organized exh., Berkshire Mus.; Springfield Mus. FA; N.Y. State Mus.; George Walter Vincent Smith Mus.; Walker A. Center; WMAA, and others. Special consultant for "American Processional," Wash., D.C., 1950. *Positions*: Staff, Springfield (Mass.) Republican, 1923-35, N.Y. Art Correspondent, 1936-46; Instr., Sarah Lawrence Col., 1942-44; New Sch. for Social Research, New York, N.Y.; 1946; L., Am. A., Barnard Col., 1956-57.

McCHRISTY, QUENTIN L.—Painter, Des., T., Gr., I.
    1205 North Western St.; h. 1216 Northwest 14th St., Oklahoma City 6, Okla.

B. Cushing, Okla., Jan. 24, 1921. *Studied*: Oklahoma State Univ., B.A., with Doel Reed; Cincinnati A. Acad., with Heldwhig, Crawford. *Member*: Oklahoma AA. *Awards*: prizes, Philbrook A. Center, 1947, 1948 (purchase); Joslyn Mus. A., 1950 (purchase); Oklahoma AA, 1948. *Work*: Philbrook A. Center; Joslyn Mus. A.; Morrill Hall Gal., Stillwater, Okla.; murals, Ft. Worth Children's Museum; Wesley Fnd.; Methodist Church, Stillwater, Okla.; designed decorations of glassware for Bartlett Collins, manufacturers of domestic and export tableware. *Exhibited*: Colorado Springs FA Center, 1951; New Orleans A. & Crafts Exh., 1948; SAGA, 1951; Ball State T. Col., 1958; Butler Inst. Am. A., 1958; Boston Soc. Indp. A., 1958; DMFA, 1947, 1948, 1950; Mulvane A. Mus., 1948; Joslyn Mus. A., 1948; Philbrook A. Center, 1947, 1948; Oklahoma AA, 1948; Mid-America A., 1950; Denver Mus. A., 1951; A. Gld., St. Louis, 1954; Cincinnati A. Acad.; one-man: Morrill Hall Gal., Stillwater, 1948; Collins Gal., Ft. Worth, 1950; Phillips Univ., Enid, 1951.

McCLEAN, FANITA LANIER (Mrs. Robert). See Lanier, Fanita

McCLELLAN, DOUGLAS EUGENE—Painter, T., L.
    5062 Rosewood Court, Montclair, Cal.

B. Pasadena, Cal., Oct. 10, 1921. *Studied*: A. Center Sch., Los A.; Colorado Springs FA Center, with Boardman Robinson, Jean Charlot; Claremont Graduate Sch., Cal., M.F.A. *Member*: Cal. WC Soc.; Los A. AA. *Awards*: Los A. Mus. A., 1950, 1953 (purchase); Nat. Orange Show, 1954. *Work*: Los A. Mus. A.; Pasadena A. Mus.; Los A. County Fair Coll. *Exhibited*: MMA, 1950; LC, 1948; CGA, 1953; PAFA, 1953; SFMA, 1949, 1952; Carnegie Inst., 1955, 1957; AFA, 1955; Los A. Mus. A., 1949, 1950, 1952, 1954, 1955; Los A. County Fair, 1949, 1953; West Coast Biennial, 1955; WMAA, 1957; one-man: Landau Gal., 1953, 1955, 1957; Pasadena A. Mus., 1954; Riverside, Cal., 1955. *Position*: Chm., Creative Arts Div., Chaffey Col., Ontario, Cal., 1950- .

McCLELLAND, AMY WOLLER (Mrs. Preston H.)—Educator
    300 Aderno Way, Pacific Palisades, Cal.

B. Chicago, Ill., July 18, 1902. *Studied*: Univ. Chicago, Ph.B., A.M.; N.Y. Univ., with Riefstahl, Salmony, Cook, Goldwater. *Member*: AFA; CAA; Southwest Mus. Am. Indian. Contributor to: Encyclopedia of the Arts, 1946. Lectures: American Arts; Decorative Arts. *Position*: Instr., 1927-29, Asst. Prof., 1929-31, Chm. & Assoc. Prof., 1931-40, Hd., Grad. Studies in FA, 1940-44, Univ. Southern Cal., Los Angeles, Cal.; Exec. Bd., Mus. Assn. of Los A. Mus. A., 1953-1958.

McCLOSKEY, EUNICE LonCOSKE—Painter, W., L.
    403 Oak St., Ridgway, Pa.

B. Ridgway, Pa., May 25, 1906. *Studied*: Columbia Univ. *Member*: Nat. Lg. Am. Pen Women; Pittsburgh Plan for Art; Assoc. A. of Pittsburgh; Pa. Fed. Women's Cl. *Awards*: prizes, Carnegie Inst. (Assoc. A.), 1950, Posner award, 1953; Nat. Lg. Am. Pen Women, Kansas City, 1947, Wash., D.C., 1954; Aimee Jackson Short prize, Edwin Forrest Gal., Phila., 1953; "Woman of the Year"

established 1890

situated in the west wing of the Brooklyn Museum, the Art School offers professional training in fine arts.

Full time study — days, part time — day and evening. No entrance requirements. Max Beckmann Competitive Scholarships for advanced study awarded through college art departments and professional schools. Summer courses — day and evening — full and part time. Courses leading to B.F.A. & M.F.A. in conjunction with Long Island University.

Augustus Peck, Supervisor

BROOKLYN MUSEUM
art school

CRANBROOK
ACADEMY OF ART
BLOOMFIELD HILLS   MICHIGAN

Degree courses offered in Architecture, Painting, Sculpture, Design, Ceramics, Weaving, Metalwork.
Catalog on request.

PRATT
INSTITUTE

THE ART SCHOOL: B.S. in Art Teacher Education; B.F.A. in Advertising Design, Graphic Arts & Illustration, and Interior Design; Bachelor of Industrial Design. M.S. in Art Education and Master of Industrial Design. Director of Admissions, The Art School, Pratt Institute, Brooklyn 5, N. Y.

award, 1958. *Work*: in private colls. *Exhibited*: Nat. Lg. Am. Pen Women, 1947-1954; Carnegie Inst., 1948-1958; one-man: Chautauqua, N.Y., 1957; Forrest Gal., Phila., 1951, 1953; Creative A. Gal., N.Y., 1953; Pittsburgh Plan for Art, 1958. Author, I., "Coal Dust and Crystals," 1939; "Strange Alchemy," 1940; "The Heart Knows This," 1944; "This is the Hour," 1948; "The Golden Hill," 1952; "These Rugged Hills," 1954; "This is My Art," 3 vols., 1956, 1957, 1959. Contributor to Ladies' Home Journal; McCalls; Good Housekeeping; Farm Journal; Household; Canadian Home Journal; Chatelaine; Woman (England); and reprints in magazines in South Africa, Australia, New Zealand. *Positions*: Nat. Poetry Ed., 1950-54, Asst. State Chm. Art, 1956-60, County Chm. Poetry, 1950-60, Nat. Lg. Am. Pen Women; Dir., Pittsburgh Assoc. A.; County Chm. Art, Pa. Fed. Womens Cl., 1954-56.

McCLOSKEY, MARTHA LINWOOD—*Painter*

134 East Main St., East Palestine, Ohio

B. Rogers, Ohio, Jan. 10, 1899. *Studied*: Wooster Col., B.A.; Cambridge Univ., England. *Member*: Mahoning SA. *Awards*: prizes, Butler AI, 1943, 1946; Parkersburg, W. Va., 1945; Mahoning SA, 1945. *Work*: Butler AI.*

McCLOSKEY, ROBERT—*Illustrator*, W.

Viking Press, 18 East 48th St., New York, N.Y.; h. Scott Islands, Cape Rosier, Me.

B. Hamilton, Ohio, Sept. 15, 1914. *Studied*: Vesper George Sch. A.; NAD, and with Jerry Farnsworth. *Member*: Am. Acad. in Rome. *Awards*: Scholastic Magazine award, 1932; Tiffany Fnd., 1935, 1936; Prix de Rome, 1939; Caldecott award, 1942, 1958 (for "Time of Wonder"). *Work*: bas reliefs, City Bldg., Hamilton, Ohio. Author, I., "One Morning in Maine," 1953; "Lentil," 1939; "Make Way for Ducklings," 1941; "Homer Price," 1943; "Blueberries for Sal," 1948; "Centerburg Tales," 1951; "Time of Wonder," 1957.

McCLOY, WILLIAM ASHBY—
  Educator, P., Et., Mus. Cur.

Connecticut College; h. 3 Winchester Rd., New London, Conn.

B. Baltimore, Md., Jan. 2, 1913. *Studied*: Iowa State Univ., B.A., M.A., M.F.A., Ph.D.; Yale Sch. FA. *Member*: Soc. Canadian Painters-Etchers & Gravers. *Work*: Winnipeg A. Gal.; LC; Walker A. Center; Carnegie Inst.; Joslyn Mus. A. *Exhibited*: PAFA, 1936, 1938, 1948; AIC, 1936, 1938, 1940; WMAA, 1938, 1940; Carnegie Inst., 1941; NAD, 1942; Audubon A., 1947; Canadian National, 1951, 1953; Toronto A. Gal., 1954; Boston A. Festival, 1955, and others. *Position*: Dir., Sch. A., Univ. Manitoba, 1950-54; Chm. Dept. A., Connecticut Col., 1954- ; Cur., Lyman Allyn Mus., 1954- .

McCLUNG, FLORENCE—*Painter, Lith., C., E., L.*

4508 Lorraine St., Dallas 5, Tex.

B. St. Louis, Mo., July 12, 1896. *Studied*: Southern Methodist Univ., B.A., B.S. in Edu.; Texas State Col. for Women; Colorado Col.; Taos, N.M., & with Adolph Dehn, Alexandre Hogue, Frank Reaugh, Richard Howard, Frank Klepper. *Member*: SSAL; NAWA; Texas FA Assn.; Dallas AA.; Texas Pr. M.; Dallas Pr. Soc. *Awards*: prizes, Dallas All. A., 1942, 1943, 1944, 1946; NAWA, 1945; Pepsi-Cola, 1942. *Work*: MMA; Dallas Mus. FA; LC; Mint Mus. A.; High Mus. A.; Delgado Mus.; Birmingham (Ala.) Lib.; Univ. Kansas; Univ. Texas. *Exhibited*: PAFA, 1937; NAWA, 1937-1946; WFNY 1939; Kansas City AI; Dallas Mus. FA; 1936; Pan-Am. Exp., Dallas, Tex., 1937; Texas-Oklahoma General Exh., 1941, 1952; SSAL; Texas FA Assn., circuit; Dallas All. A.; NAWA, 1941-1946; SFMA, 1942-1944; NAD, 1943, 1944, 1946; MMA, 1943; Lib.Cong., 1943, 1944; numerous one-man exhs., Texas, Louisiana, Alabama; London, England, 1946. Lectures: Printmaking; Batiks; Serigraphs. *Position*: Instr., drawing, painting, batik, art history, Trinity Univ., Waxahachie, Tex., 1928-42.

McCLURE, THOMAS F.—*Sculptor, E.*

3361 North Maple Road, Ann Arbor, Mich.

B. Pawnee City, Neb., Apr. 17, 1920. *Studied*: Univ. Nebraska, B.F.A.; Wash. State Col., Pullman, Wash.; Cranbrook Acad. A., M.F.A. *Awards*: prizes, SAM, 1942, 1953; Syracuse Mus. FA, 1948, 1949, 1950; Tulsa Mus. A., 1949;

Detroit Inst. A., 1950, 1951, 1953, 1954, 1955; Kirk of the Hills, Bloomfield Hills, Mich., 1954, 1955. *Exhibited*: Oakland Mus. A.; Albright A. Gal.; Wichita AA; MMA; AIC; Los Angeles; PMA; PAFA, 1958; Syracuse Mus. FA, 1958. *Work*: SAM; Univ. Nebraska; Cranbrook Acad. A.; Syracuse Mus. FA; Ford Motor Co.; Eastland Shopping Center, Detroit, 1957; DeWaters A. Mus., Flint, Mich., 1958. *Position*: Assoc. Prof., Dept. A., Univ. Michigan, Ann Arbor, Mich., 1953- .

McCLUSKEY, GRACE DICKOVER—*Painter, T.*

2394 Sherwood Rd., San Marino, Cal.

B. Long Beach, Cal., Dec. 25, 1891. *Studied*: Stanford Univ.; Santa Barbara State Col.; Donaldson Sch. Des.; in Japan, and with Conrad Buff, Orrin White. *Member*: Women Painters of the West. *Awards*: prize, Hollywood, Cal., 1950. *Exhibited*: Greek Theatre, Hollywood; Woman's Cl., Hollywood; Pasadena AI; San Gabriel Valley Exh.; City Hall, Los A.; Long Beach Civic A. Gal.; Laguna Beach A. Gal.; Palm Desert, Cal.; San Gabriel Woman's Cl.; San Gabriel Recreation Center; Barnsdall Gal., Hollywood; Security First Nat. Bank, San Marino.

McCOMAS, MRS. FRANCIS. See Frances, Gene

McCOMB, MARIE LOUISE—*Painter*

1496 Alabama Dr., Winter Park, Fla.

B. Louisville, Ky. *Studied*: PAFA; & with Daniel Garber, Henry McCarter. *Awards*: Cresson traveling scholarship, PAFA, 1912. *Exhibited*: PAFA; F. PAFA; N.Y. WC Cl.; Morse Gal. A., Winter Park, Fla.; Woman's Cl., Winter Park, Fla., 1948-1952; Research Gal., Maitland, Fla., 1946 (one-man); Center St. Gal., Winter Park, 1948.

McCONAHA, LAWRENCE—*Painter*

724½ Main St.; h. 405 Pearl St., Richmond, Ind.

B. Centerville, Ind., Aug. 8, 1894. *Studied*: with George Baker, Guy Wiggins. *Member*: Springfield AA; SC; Hoosier Salon; Springfield A. Lg.; Conn. Acad. FA; Wash. WC Cl.; Indiana A. Cl.; Richmond AA (Pres. 1954); AAPL. *Awards*: prizes, Earlham Col., 1927; Hoosier Salon, 1929, 1930, 1931; Richmond AA, 1929, 1930, 1931, 1933, 1934, 1936, 1939, 1944, 1947, 1949, 1950, 1953 (purchase, 1954), 1957; Indiana State Fair, 1938, 1939, 1942, 1944, 1946-1948; John Herron AI, 1932, 1936, 1937; Indiana A. Cl., 1936; Conn. Acad. FA, 1934. *Work*: Richmond AA; Pub.Lib., Tipton, Ind.

McCONNELL, JAMES HOUSTON—
  Lithographer, Ser., P.

1713 West 105th St., Chicago 43, Ill.

B. Chicago, Ill., Oct. 19, 1914. *Studied*: Denison Univ., A.B.; State Univ. Iowa, M.A., M.F.A.; & with Grant Wood, Jean Charlot, Fletcher Martin, Emil Ganso. *Member*: Nat. Serigraphy Soc.; Am. Color Pr. Soc. *Awards*: prizes, Am. Color Pr. Soc., 1942; CAM, 1942; Springfield (Mo.) Mus. A., 1942; Zanesville, Ohio, 1945. *Work*: Denison Univ.; State Univ. Iowa; CAM. *Exhibited*: Kansas City AI, 1941, 1942; Northwest Pr. M., 1942-1946; WMAA, 1941; Un. Seaman's Service traveling exh., 1943, 1944; NAD, 1946; Lib. Cong., 1946; Laguna Beach AA, 1946.*

McCORMACK, HELEN GARDNER—*Museum Director*

Carolina Art Association, Gibbes Art Gallery; h. 8 Bull St., Charleston, S.C.

B. Charleston, S.C., Mar. 17, 1903. *Studied*: College of Charleston, A.B.; Brooklyn Museum, (Interne). *Member*: AAMus.; Carolina AA; Gld. of South Carolina A.; Assoc., Intl. Inst. for Conservation of Mus. Objects; Southeastern Mus. Conf.; Southern A. Mus. Dirs. Assn. Contributor to Antiques magazine. *Positions*: Dir., The Valentine Museum, Richmond, Va., 1930-40; Cur. Collections, Carolina Art Assn., 1946-47; Cur. Collections, The Charleston Mus., 1947-53; Dir., Gibbes Art Gal., Carolina AA, Charleston, S.C., 1954- .

McCORMICK, DAN(IEL) S., JR.—*Cartoonist*

504 Liberty Ave., Jersey City 7, N.J.

B. Jersey City, N.J., Aug. 22, 1921. *Studied*: ASL. Contributor cartoons to: Sat. Eve. Post; Colliers; American; New Yorker; American Legion; Cosmopolitan; True; Argosy; Am. Weekly; Journal-American; Wall St. Journal; McNaught Syndicate; Sports Illustrated; Ladies Home Journal.

McCORMICK, KATHARINE H.—*Painter, Gr.*

300 West Upsal St., Philadelphia 19, Pa.

B. Philadelphia, Pa. *Studied*: PAFA, with Henry McCarter, Fred Wagner, Ralph Pearson. *Member*: Am. Color Pr. Soc. (Treas.); Phila. Plastic Cl.; F., PAFA. *Awards*: prizes, Phila. Plastic Cl., Woodmere A. Gal. *Work*: PMA; Atwater Kent Mus., Phila.; Woodmere A. Gal. *Exhibited*: NAD; PAFA; Phila. Pr. Cl.; Phila. A. All; Am. Color Pr. Soc.; Phila. Sketch Cl.; Phila. Plastic Cl.; BM; Temple Univ.; F., PAFA, annually; Woodmere A. Gal.; Free Lib., Phila., 1954, 1955; New Britain Mus., 1953; Meriden A. & Crafts, 1953; Phila. Acad. Music, 1954, 1955.

McCOSH, DAVID (JOHN)—*Painter, E.*

1870 Fairmount Blvd., Eugene, Ore.

B. Cedar Rapids, Iowa, July 11, 1903. *Studied*: Coe Col.; AIC. *Member*: AWS; AAUP. *Awards*: traveling scholarship, AIC, 1928; Tiffany Fnd. F., 1930. *Work*: Cedar Rapids AA; Portland A. Mus.; SAM; WMAA; IBM; Eastern Oregon Col.; murals, USPO, Kelso, Wash.; Beresford, S.D.; Dept. Interior, Wash., D.C. *Exhibited*: Carnegie Inst., 1936; CM; AIC, 1929-1938; BM, 1937; GGE, 1939; WFNY 1939; Denver A. Mus., 1940, 1955; Colorado Springs FA Center, 1935-1938, 1945, 1955; Portland A. Mus., 1952 (one-man), 1953-1957; MMA; SAM; 1951 (one-man), 1953-1955; SFMA, 1954, 1955; AWS, 1954, 1955; Spokane AA, 1957; Henry Gal., Seattle, 1958; one-man: Oregon State Col., 1953; Montana State Col., 1953, 1954; Montana State Mus., 1954; Willamette Univ., 1956; San Jose State Col., 1957; Univ. Oregon A. Mus., 1958. *Position*: Prof. A., Univ. Oregon, Eugene, Ore.; Guest Artist, Montana State Col., 1953 (summer).

McCOSH, MRS. DAVID. See *Kutka, Anne*

McCOUCH, GORDON MALLET—*Painter, Gr.*

8315 St. Martin's Lane, Philadelphia 18, Pa.; h. Porto-di-Ronco, Ticino, Switzerland

B. Philadelphia, Pa., Sept. 24, 1885. *Studied*: Chestnut Hill Acad.; Pyle Sch. A.; Royal Acad. A., Munich. *Work*: Kunst Mus., Berne, Switzerland; Zurich Mus. coll. *Exhibited*: CGA; Carnegie Inst.; Toronto, Canada; Paris Salon; A. Center, N.Y.; Phila. A. All.; Delgado Mus. A.; Ferargil Gal.; Montross Gal., and in Germany, Italy, Switzerland, etc.*

McCOY, DOROTHY H. (Mrs. Lawrence R.)—*Painter*

Manchester, Vt.

B. Worcester, Mass., Mar. 22, 1890. *Studied*: Bradford Acad., Haverhill, Mass., and with Jerry Farnsworth.

Member: NAWA; Nat. Lg. Am. Pen Women; Pen & Brush Cl.; Copley Soc., Boston; Southern Vermont A. *Awards*: prizes, WMA, 1952; Berkshire A. Mus., A. 1952; Clearwater, Fla., 1949. *Work*: Bennington Mus. Hist. & A., and in many private collections. *Exhibited*: Albany Inst. Hist. & A., 1953; Berkshire Mus. A., 1953; Boston Soc. Indp. A., 1953, 1954; Cracker Barrel Bazaar, Newbury, Vt., 1953-1955; Mid-Vermont AA, 1953, 1955; NAWA, 1955, traveling exh. to Europe, 1958; Pen & Brush Cl., 1953-1955; Southern Vermont A., 1952-1955; WMA, 1952, 1954; Union Col., 1954; Union Trust Co., N.Y., 1955; SC, 1955; one-man: Bronxville Pub. Lib., 1955; So. Vermont A., 1954, 1955; Pen & Brush Cl., 1956.

McCOY, JOHN W. (II)—*Painter, T.*

R.F.D., Chadds Ford, Pa.

B. Pinole, Cal., May 11, 1910. *Studied*: Cornell Univ. B.F.A.; Am. Sch., Fontainebleau, France. *Member*: NA; Audubon A.; AWCS; Wilmington Soc. FA. *Awards*: prizes; AWS, 1946, 1947, 1955; Audubon A., 1948; NAD, 1951; Phila. WC Cl., 1949, 1955; Balt. WC Cl., 1948; Delaware A. Center, 1940, 1941. *Work*: Delaware A. Center; Farnsworth Mus.; PAFA; Tel-Aviv Mus., Israel; murals, Metropolitan Life Insurance Bldg., N.Y.; Nemours Bldg., Wilmington, Del. *Exhibited*: Carnegie Inst., 1941, 1946; PAFA, 1940, 1946; BM, 1945; AIC, 1944; and many others nationally; one-man exh.: New York, N.Y., 1941, 1945, 1946; Boston, Mass., 1940; Utica, N.Y., 1942; Retrospective exh., Farnsworth Mus., 1955; Manchester, N.H., 1945; Wilmington, Del., 1940. *Position*: Dir., Wilmington, Del., Soc. FA, 1945-46; Instr. Painting, PAFA, Philadelphia, Pa., 1946.*

McCOY, LAWRENCE R.—*Painter*

Manchester, Vt.

B. Lakeland, Minn., Apr. 17, 1888. *Studied*: Univ. Minnesota; Univ. North Dakota; WMA Sch., and in France and Italy. *Member*: AAPL; Academic A.; Am. Veterans Soc. A.; Copley Soc., Boston; NAC; SC; Southern Vermont A. *Awards*: prizes, Academic A., 1952; Conn. Acad. FA, 1951; Essex, 1950; Rutland, Vt., 1951; St. Augustine, Fla., 1950; Sarasota, Fla., 1948; Clearwater, Fla., 1948; Citation, Univ. North Dakota, 1957. *Work*: Albany Inst. Hist. & A.; Middlebury (Vt.) Col.; Berkshire A. Mus.; Washington County Mus. FA; Fitchburg A. Mus.; Robert Hull Fleming Mus.; Bates Col., Lewiston, Me.; Wesleyan Col., Macon, Ga.; WMA; Mead Mus., Amherst; DMFA; Phoenix FA Assn.; Carnegie Inst.; Lawrence Mus., Williamstown; Bennington Mus. A.; Springfield Mus. FA; Wadsworth Atheneum, and in many private collections. *Exhibited*: NAD, 1945; All. A. Am., 1949, 1950, 1955; Conn. Acad. FA, 1945, 1946, 1951, 1955; NAC, 1951-1953; SC, 1951-1953; Springfield A. Lg., 1951-1953; WMA, 1950, 1952, 1954; many exhs. nationally, 1956-59; one-man: Albany Inst. Hist. & A., 1952, 1956; Washington County Mus. FA, 1953; Berkshire Mus., 1954; Fitchburg Mus. A., 1955; Bronxville Pub. Lib., 1955; Fleming Mus., 1956; Cayuga Mus., 1957; Everhart Mus., 1957; Phoenix, Ariz., 1958; and many other local and regional exhibitions.

CLEVELAND institute of art

PROFESSIONAL TRAINING

Painting	Fashion
Sculpture	Ceramics
Graphics	Weaving
Industrial Design	Textile Design
Interior Design	Silversmithing
Advertising	Enameling
Illustration	Teacher Training

DIPLOMAS · DEGREES · SCHOLARSHIPS · CATALOG ON REQUEST

Write: Director of Admissions, 11141 E. Boulevard, Cleveland 6, O.

McCOY, WIRTH VAUGHAN—*Painter, E., L.*
Spokane Art Center, West 507 7th Ave.; h. East 235 9th Ave., Spokane, Wash.

B. Duluth, Minn., Dec. 16, 1913. *Studied*: Univ. Minnesota, B.A.; State Univ. Iowa, M.F.A.; California Sch. FA; Grande Chaumiere, Paris, France. *Member*: AAUP; Spokane City Art Bd.; All. A. of Spokane; Washington AA. *Awards*: prizes, Arrowhead Intl., Duluth, 1946; Duluth AI, 1946, 1947. *Work*: Univ. Iowa; Spokane A. Center; Univ. Minnesota; City of Spokane; City of Duluth; mural, Duluth Zoological Gardens; set des. for plays and ballets. *Exhibited*: SFMA, 1956; Oregon Artists, 1949, 1950, 1953; A. of the Pacific Northwest, 1954-1957; Northwest A. traveling exh., 1954-55; SAM, 1949, 1954-1957; Portland (Ore.) A. Mus., 1949-1953; Western Wash. A., 1955, 1956; Henry Gal., Univ. Washington, 1954; Univ. Colorado; Univ. Iowa; Washington State Col.; Oregon State Col.; Yakima and Tacoma, Wash., and others. *Positions*: Asst. Prof. A., Oregon State Col., Corvallis, Ore., 1948-53; Assoc. Prof. A., Washington State Col., 1953-58; Res. Artist & Dir., Spokane Art Center, 1953- ; Pres., City A. Bd., 1956-57.

McCRADY, JOHN—*Painter, I., Lith., T.*
3921 Palmyra St., New Orleans, La.

B. Canton, Miss., 1911. *Studied*: Univ. Mississippi; Univ. Pennsylvania; New Orleans A. Sch.; ASL. *Awards*: prizes, New Orleans A. & Crafts Cl., 1938; Louisiana A. Comm., 1939, 1940; Blanche S. Benjamin prize, 1941; New Orleans AA, 1946; SSAL, 1946; Delgado Mus. A., 1948; Guggenheim F., 1939. *Work*: U.S. Treasury Dept.; Time magazine; Life magazine; Abbott Laboratories; CAM; High Mus. A.; SFMA; Newark Mus. A.; Delgado Mus. A.; Swope Gal. A.; IBM; USPO, Amory, Miss.; Grand Hotel, Point Clear, Ala.; Rabouin Sch., New Orleans; Delmonico's Restaurant, New Orleans. Co-author, "Mardi Gras Day"; Illus. "The Lower Mississippi."*

McCREADY, CAROLIN (Mrs. G. W.)—*Painter, T.*
Apt. 306, 5604 Fifth Ave., Pittsburgh 32, Pa.

B. Oil City, Pa., Oct. 26, 1907. *Studied*: Carnegie Inst., with Alexander Kostellow, Lazlo Gabor, Hans Hofmann. *Member*: Assoc. A. Pittsburgh. *Awards*: Assoc. A. Pittsburgh Exh. at Carnegie Inst., prizes, 1935, 1937, 1942, 1943, 1949; Pittsburgh Playhouse, 1955. *Exhibited*: CGA, 1937, 1939; MMA, 1942; AIC, 1943; CM, 1945; VMFA, 1946; Carnegie Inst., 1943-1945, 1949, 1951; Assoc. A. Pittsburgh, 1935-1955; Butler AI, 1953-1955. *Position*: Instr. Des., Carnegie Inst., Pittsburgh, Pa., 1946- .*

McCREADY, MRS. THOMAS L., JR. *See Tudor, Tasha*

McCULLOUGH, JOSEPH WARREN—*Educator, P., L.*
Cleveland Institute of Art, 11141 East Boulevard; h. 2223 Delaware Drive, Cleveland 6, Ohio

B. Pittsburgh, Pa., July 6, 1922. *Studied*: Cleveland Inst., A.; Yale Univ., B.F.A., M.F.A., with Lewis York and Josef Albers. *Member*: CAA; Assoc. A. Pittsburgh. *Awards*: prizes, Assoc. A. Pittsburgh, 1954, 1956; Ohio Univ., 1954 (purchase); Cleveland May Show, 1955, 1957, 1958; Canton AI, 1955. *Work*: CMA; other work in private collections throughout U.S. *Exhibited*: CGA, 1955; Butler Inst. Am. A., 1955; Wichita AA, 1953; Assoc. A. Pittsburgh, 1947-1958; Cleveland May Show, 1947, 1948, 1953-1958; Silvermine Gld A., 1950-1952; Springfield, Mass., 1954; Oberlin Col., 1955; Ohio WC Soc., 1956; Audubon A., 1956; Univ. Illinois, 1957½; Art Schools, USA, 1958. Author: Chapter "Art In Cleveland Architecture," AIA Handbook to Cleveland Architecture, 1958. *Positions*: Instr., San Jose State Col., 1948-49; Instr., Yale Univ., 1949-51; Asst. Dir., 1952-55, Dir., 1955- , Cleveland Inst. A.; Cleveland, Ohio. Adv. Bd., Cleveland Museum of Art; Sec., Cleveland AA.

McCULLOUGH, LUCERNE (Mrs. C. E. Robert)—*Painter, T.*
Indian Hill, Silvermine, Conn.

B. Abilene, Tex., Dec. 6, 1916. *Studied*: Tulane Univ., B.F.A.; ASL. *Member*: Silvermine Gld. A., (Bd. Managers). *Awards*: Scholarship, ASL; prizes, A. Dir. Cl., 1944; Direct Mail Advertising Assn., 1944, 1945; Silvermine Gld. A., 1954, 1956. *Work*: MModA; San Angelo Mus. A.; NAD; murals, USPO, Booneville, N.Y.; Thomas-

ton, Conn., and work in private colls. U.S. and abroad. *Exhibited*: Conn. Acad. FA; Springfield A. Lg.; Audubon A; Silvermine Gld. A.; Delgado Mus. A.; Eastern States Exh.; Art:USA, 1958; one-man: Westport, Conn., 1954, 1955; Wellons Gal., N.Y., 1953; Silvermine Gld. A., 1953, 1958; Kipnis Gal., N.Y., 1955.

McCULLOUGH, SUZANNE (Mrs. T. M. Plowden)—*Painter*
Cranbury Rd., Westport, Conn.

B. Abilene, Tex., Dec. 6, 1916. *Studied*: Newcomb Col.; Tulane Univ., B. Des.; ASL. *Member*: Silvermine Gld. A. *Awards*: Scholarship, ASL; prizes, A. Dir. Cl., 1944; Direct Mail Advertising Assn., 1944, 1945; New England Exh., 1955. *Work*: MModA; murals, USPO, Booneville, N.Y.; Thomaston, Conn. *Exhibited*: Conn. Acad. FA; Springfield A. Lg.; Audubon A.; Silvermine Gld. A.; Bathhurst and Sydney, Australia; one-man: New York, N.Y., 1953; Westport, Conn., 1954, 1955; Silvermine Gld. A., 1956; Sydney, Australia, 1958.

McCURRY, CHARLES RAY—*Painter, I.*
62 Park Lane, Long Hill, Conn.

B. Catawba, N.C., Apr. 21, 1924. *Studied*: Ringling Sch. A., and with Loren Wilford, Ben Stahl. *Member*: Fla. A. Group; Florida Fed. A.; Sarasota AA; A. Lg. of Manatee County; Longboat Key A. Center; AWS. *Awards*: prizes, Manatee A. Lg., 1954 (2); De Soto Mus. A., 1954; Ringling Mus. A., 1954; Longboat Key A. Center, 1955; AWS, 1958. *Work*: De Soto Mus.; murals in private clubs and homes; magazine and book illustrations. *Exhibited*: Sarasota AA, 1953, 1954; Fla. A. Group, 1954; Ringling Mus. A., 1953, 1954; Fla. Fed. A., 1953-1955; Fla. A. Group, 1955; AWS, 1957, 1958; New Haven A. Festival, 1958.

McDONALD, MRS. DOROTHY EISNER. *See Eisner, Dorothy*

McDOWELL, HELEN (Mrs. E. R.)—*Painter*
Oak Hill, Franklin, N.C.

B. Cleveland, Ohio, Apr. 13, 1909. *Studied*: Collins A. Sch., Tampa, Fla.; Tampa Univ.; N.Y. Sch. Int. Dec., and with Asa Cassidy, James Lorne Eno. *Member*: Tampa AI; Atlanta AA. *Awards*: prize, Tampa AI, 1951. *Exhibited*: Fla. Southern Col., 1952; Terry AI, 1952; Franklin, N.C., 1958 and prior; Atlanta, Ga., 1956.

McENTARFER, MRS. WILLIS C. *See Huntoon, Mary*

McENTEE, DOROTHY LAYNG—*Educator, I., P., Des.*
8 Montague Terr., Brooklyn, N.Y.

B. Brooklyn, N.Y., Sept. 21, 1902. *Studied*: PIASch.; PAFA. *Member*: AWS; Phila. WC Cl. *Awards*: F., PAFA. *Work*: BM. I.; "Knuckles Down," 1943; "No School Friday," 1945; "Nine Tales of Coyote"; "Pirate Island," 1955; "Nine Tales of Raven." *Position*: Instr. A., Prospect Heights H.S., Brooklyn, N.Y.

McGARVEY, ELSIE SIRATZ (Mrs. James P.)—*Museum Curator, T.*
Philadelphia Museum of Art, Parkway at Fairmount Ave., Philadelphia 30, Pa.; h. 2030 Old Welsh Road, Abington, Pa.

B. Bethlehem, Pa., May 25, 1912. *Studied*: Graphic Sketch Cl., Phila.; PMSch. A. *Member*: Fashion Group; AAUP; Phila. A. All. Lectures: History of Costume at fashion shows, schools, colleges, and women's organizations. Arranged exhs.: Costume and Accessory collections for exhibitions in 18th, 19th and 20th Century Rooms of the Museum's Fashion Wing; Phila. Acad. Music Centennial Jubilee, with mannikins costumed in 1857 garments and accessories in foyer display, etc. *Positions*: Instr., Beaver College, Jenkintown, Pa.; Cur. Costumes, Philadelphia Museum of Art, at present.

McGEE, WINSTON EUGENE—*Educator, P.*
Art Department, Lake Erie College; h. 348 Mentor Ave., Painesville, Ohio

B. Salem, Ill., Sept. 4, 1924. *Studied*: Univ. Missouri, B.J.; Univ. Wisconsin, and in France. *Member*: AAUP; AFA.

Awards: Fulbright award, 1949-50; prizes, Baldwin Mus., 1954; Cleveland Journalism Show, 1956. *Work*: mural, Student Commons Bldg., Lake Erie College. *Exhibited*: "American Artists in Europe" traveling exh., 1950; Fulbright Exh., 1951; Butler Inst. Am. A., 1955; Duveen-Graham Fulbright Exh., 1956; Barone Gal., N.Y., 1959 (one-man); Springfield Mus. A., 1948; Erie May Show, 1955, and others. *Position*: Hd. A. Dept., Lake Erie College, Painesville, Ohio, 1951- .

McGOUGH, CHARLES E.—Educator, Ser., P., Des.
East Texas State College, Commerce, Tex.; h. 1406 Glendale St., Greenville, Tex.

B. Elmhurst, Ill., Aug. 2, 1927. *Studied*: Southwestern Univ.; Hardin-Simmons Univ.; Ray Vogue A. Sch.; AIC; Univ. Tulsa, B.A., M.A. *Member*: Nat. Ser. Soc. *Awards*: prizes, Oklahoma Annual, 1950; Texas Annual, Houston, 1952. *Work*: Philbrook A. Center; DMFA; murals, Goodfellow Air Base; Southern Hills Country Cl., Tulsa; 3-dimen. displays for IBM; Dix Oil Co.; and others. *Exhibited*: Nat. Ser. Annual, 1958; SAM, 1949-1952; Tulsa, Okla., 1948-1953, 1956; Oklahoma Annual, 1949-1952; Texas Annual, 1952-1954; DMFA, 1952-1956; Southwest Print, 1957, 1958. *Position*: Hd. A. Dept., East Texas State College, Commerce, Tex., 1956- .

McILLHENNY, HENRY P.—Museum Curator
Philadelphia Museum of Art, Parkway at Fairmount Ave., Philadelphia 30, Pa.

Position: Cur., Decorative Art, Philadelphia Museum of Art.*

McINTYRE, FLORENCE M.—Educator, W., L.
707 Adams Ave., Memphis, Tenn.

B. Memphis, Tenn., Aug. 7, 1878. *Studied*: AIC; & with William Chase, A. M. Archambault, Lorado Taft, & others. *Member*: NAWA; Memphis AA; AAPL. Author: "Art and Life." *Position*: Sec., Memphis A, 1914- ; Dir., Memphis AA Free A. Sch., Memphis, Tenn., at present.

McINTYRE, OLIVER FRANKLYN—Painter, Cart., I.
c/o Miami Daily News, 600 Biscayne Blvd., Miami 30, Fla.; h. 1235 Castile Ave., Coral Gables, Fla.

B. Dayton, Ohio, July 21, 1901. *Studied*: Am. Acad. A., Chicago; & with Richard Miller, Denman Fink, Julius Katzieff. *Member*: Provincetown AA; Blue Dome F. *Exhibited*: Miami Beach Pub. Lib.; Miami & Palm Beach, Fla. I., Miami Daily News, & magazines. *Position*: A. Dir., Miami Daily News, Fla.*

McKEAN, HUGH FERGUSON—Painter, L., E.
Rollins College; h. 231 North Interlachen Ave., Winter Park, Fla.

B. Beaver Falls, Pa., July 28, 1908. *Studied*: PAFA; ASL; Ecole des Beaux-Arts, Fontainebleau, France; Rollins Col., B.A.; Williams Col., M.A.; Harvard Univ. *Member*: Fla. Fed. A.; SSAL; AEA; New Hampshire AA; Orlando AA; AFA; CAA; Palm Beach A. Lg.; Fla. A. Group; Tiffany Fnd.; McDowell Colony. *Awards*: prizes, Fla. Fed. A., 1931, 1949; Cervantes medal, Spanish Inst.; Decoration of Honor, Rollins Col. *Work*: Toledo Mus. A.; Univ. Virginia. *Exhibited*: Soc. Four A., 1948; All. A. Am., 1949; Atlanta, Ga.; 1949. *Positions*: Dir., Morse Gal. A., Rollins Col.; Pres., Fla. Fed. A., 1951-52; Acting Pres., 1951-52, Pres., 1952- , Rollins Col., Winter Park, Fla.

McKEAN, JEANNETTE. See Genius, Jeannette

McKEAN, ROBERT—Industrial Designer
108 East 37th St., New York 16, N.Y.; h. 35 Sagamore Rd., Bronxville, N.Y.

B. Troy, Pa., Jan. 12, 1905. *Studied*: PAFA; Pa. State Univ., B.S. in Arch.; N.Y. Univ. *Member*: IDI. Designer of products (electronic, furniture, fabrics, etc.); Packages; Interiors. *Position*: Exec. Com., N.Y. Chapter, Nat. Bd. Trustees, IDI; Dir. Des., Assoc., L. G. Sherburne Assoc., New York, N.Y.

McKEE, KATHERINE LOUISE (Mrs. Frank Kelsey)—
Painter, S., Gr., Des., Comm. A., C.
1698 LaLoma Ave., Berkeley 9, Cal.

Studied: T. Col., Columbia Univ., B.S., A.M.; Cleveland Sch. A.; Escuela de Pintura y Escultura, Mexico City. *Awards*: prizes, CMA, 1934, 1937, 1938-1941, 1946-1948; Am. FA Gal., N.Y., 1931; Butler AI, 1943. *Work*: CMA; Cleveland Mun. Coll. *Exhibited*: NAWA, 1931-1933, 1944; Cal. PLH, 1940; WFNY 1939; Weatherspoon Gal., North Carolina, 1944, 1948; Syracuse Mus. FA, 1947, 1948; A. Center, N.Y., 1930; Phila. A. All., 1947, 1949; Butler AI, 1939, 1943, 1945, 1946, 1948; Wichita AA, 1946-1948; Cleveland Col., 1936 (one-man); N.Y. Soc. Ceramic A., 1945; CMA traveling exh., 1940, 1941, 1948; Kearney Mem. Exh., Milwaukee, 1946; Ohio Valley Exh., 1946; Contemp. Arts, 1957 (one-man).

McKELVEY, HELEN F. (Mrs.)—Museum Director
Art Center, 209 Ninth St., West, Bradenton, Fla.; h. Palmetto, Fla.

B. Berea, Ky., Jan. 9, 1879. *Studied*: Oberlin Col., A.B.; Columbia Univ., A.B., B.S. *Member*: Florida A. Group; Ringling Mus. A.; A. Lg. of Manatee County, Bradenton. *Position*: Dir., Art League of Manatee County, Art Center, Bradenton, Fla.

McKIE, ROY—Cartoonist, Comm. A.
Phillips Chapel Rd., New Hope, Pa.; also, Castino, Me.

B. Medford, Mass., Oct. 8, 1921. *Studied*: Vesper George Sch. A.; Tiffany Fnd. *Awards*: numerous awards in A. Dir. Cl. exhs. in New York and Phila. *Exhibited*: A. Dir. Cl., N.Y. and Phila. Author, I., "The Dog," 1954. Cartoonist for many leading magazines. *Position*: Freelance for Bruce Anderson Assoc., Boston, Mass., 1943-47; N.W. Ayer & Son, Phila., Pa., 1947-51; Freelance, 1951- .

McKIM, WILLIAM WIND—Lithographer, P., T.
Kansas City Art Institute, 4415 Warwick Blvd., Kansas City 2, Mo.; h. 8704 East 32nd St., Kansas City 29, Mo.

B. Independence, Mo., May 13, 1916. *Studied*: Kansas City AI, with Benton, de Martelly. *Member*: Mid-Am. A. *Awards*: prizes, N.Y. State Fair, 1938; Kansas City AI, 1938-1941; Missouri annual, 1946, 1947; William Rockhill Nelson Gal., A., 1948; Kansas City AI, 1946-1952; AIC; Denver A. Mus.; Assoc. Am. A., 1940, 1941; Mid-Am. A., 1950, 1952; Tupperware Fnd. Exh., 1956. *Position*: Instr., Lith., Drawing, Kansas City AI, Kansas City, Mo., 1948- ; Chm. Fnd. Dept., Kansas City AI.

McKININ, LAWRENCE—Educator, P., C., Des.
Department of Art, University of Missouri; h. 1 Ingleside Drive, Columbia, Mo.

B. Yukon, Pa., Aug. 24, 1917. *Studied*: Wayne Univ., B.S.; Soc. A. & Crafts, Detroit; Cranbrook Acad. A., M.F.A.; Sch. for Am. Craftsmen; Handy & Harman Silversmithing Workshop. *Member*: Midwestern College AA; Missouri College AA. *Awards*: prizes, Stephens Col. All-Missouri Salon, 1949; Mid-America Annual, 1950 (purchase); Springfield (Mo.) Mus. A., 1950 (purchase). *Work*: Mid-America AA; Springfield Mus. A. *Exhibited*: Univ. Illinois, 1951; Decorative A. Exh., Wichita, 1950, 1952; Am. Jewelry & Related Objects exh., 1955 (circulated by Smithsonian Inst.); Michigan A., 1938, 1947; Michigan A.-Craftsmen, 1948; CAM, 1949, 1951, 1954; Springfield Mus. A., 1950; Mid-America annual, 1950, 1951; Midwest Des. Exh., 1951; one-man: Univ. Missouri, Christian Col. *Positions*: Instr. A., Detroit Pub. Schs., 1941-42, 1946; A. Dir., Archaeology Magazine, 1954-55; Instr., 1948-50, Asst. Prof., 1950-54, Assoc. Prof., & Chm. Dept. A., University of Missouri, Columbia, Mo., 1955- .

McKINNEY, ROLAND JOSEPH—
Educator, Former Mus. D., W., L.
Address unknown

B. Niagara Falls, N.Y., Nov. 4, 1898. *Studied*: Niagara Univ.; & abroad. *Work*: mural, First Presbyterian Church, Davenport, Iowa. Author: "Thomas Eakins," 1942; "English and American Painting," Grolier Encyclopaedia, 1946; "Famous Old Masters," 1951; "Degas," 1951. Lectures: Appreciation of Painting. *Position*: Dir., Davenport Mun. A. Gal., 1925-27; Dir., High Mus. A., Atlanta, Ga., 1928-

29; Dir., BMA, Balt., Md., 1929-38; Dir., Am. Section Painting, GGE, 1939; Dir., Los A. Mus. A., 1939-46; member Visiting Com., Arts & Archaeology, Princeton Univ.; Com. for a New York State A. Program; UNESCO A. Advisory Com.; Dir., Pepsi-Cola A. Competitions, 1946-48.*

McKNIGHT, ROBERT J.—*Sculptor, Indust. Des., P.*
648 East High St.; h. 1577 McKinley Ave., Springfield, Ohio

B. Bayside, L.I., N.Y., Feb. 26, 1905. *Studied*: Yale Col., Ph.B.; Yale Sch. FA, B.F.A., and with H. Bouchard, Paris; Carl Milles. *Awards*: Lake Forest Scholarship, 1930; Prix de Rome, 1932; gold medal, Electronic Magazine (for indst. des.), 1952. *Work*: Brookgreen Gardens, S.C. *Exhibited*: PMA; Carnegie Inst.; Grand Central A. Gal.; Robinson Gal., N.Y.; Brooks Mem. A. Gal., Springfield AA, 1946-1952. Lectures: History of Art; Design. *Positions*: Dir., Memphis Acad. A., 1936-41; Instr. Des., Southwestern Univ., 1941-42; Army Aviation Engineers, 1942-45; Instr. S., Ceramics, Int. Dec., Wittenberg Col., Springfield, Ohio, 1948-51; Product des. and development; portraits; new type development for outdoor sculpture.*

McLANATHAN, RICHARD BARTON KENNEDY—
Museum Director
Munson-Williams-Proctor Institute, 310 Genesee St.; h. 1400 Genesee St., Utica 4, N.Y.

B. Metheun, Mass., Mar. 12, 1916. *Studied*: The Choate Sch.; Harvard Univ., A.B., Ph.D.; Harvard Grad. Sch. *Member*: Am. Studies Assn.; Societe Poussin; AAMus.; Soc. Arch. Historians, and others. *Awards*: Soc. of Fellows, Harvard; Prix de Rome, 1948; Senior F., Am. Acad. in Rome, 1948-49. Author: "Great Americans," 1956; "Martin J. Heade, 1819-1904," 1955-56; "Ship Models," 1957; "Queen Tomyris and the Head of Cyrus," 1956; "American Marine Painting," 1955-56; Co-author: "The M. and M. Karolik Collection of American Painting, 1815-1865," 1949; Editor: "Catalogue of Greek Coins" by Agnes Baldwin Brett, 1955, and others. Contributor to Encyclopaedia Britannica; Art News; Journal of the Society of Architectural Historians; BMFA Arts Bulletins; Arte Veneta, etc. Decorative Arts Editor for next edition of Webster's unabridged International Dictionary. Installed various collections at Museum of Fine Arts, Boston. *Positions*: Asst. Cur., Dept. Paintings, 1946-48, Asst. Cur., Decorative Arts, 1949-54, Assoc. Cur., Decorative Arts, 1954-57, Boston Museum of Fine Arts; Trustee, Boston A. Festival, 1952-57; Sec., BMFA, 1952-56, Ed. Publications, 1952-57; Dir., Community A. Program, Munson-Williams-Proctor Inst., Utica, N.Y., 1957- .

McLARTY, WILLIAM JAMES (JACK)—
Painter, T., Lith.
1427 Northwest 23rd St., Portland 10, Ore.

B. Seattle, Wash., Apr. 24, 1919. *Studied*: Mus. A. Sch., Portland, Ore.; Am. A. Sch., N.Y., and with Anton Refregier, Joseph Solman. *Member*: AEA; Portland AA. *Awards*: prizes, Northwest Pr. M., 1949 (purchase); Portland A. Mus., 1953 (purchase); MModA, 1954. *Work*: murals, Collins-View Sch., Laurelhurst Sch., Portland, Ore. *Exhibited*: Northwest Pr. M., 1943, 1945, 1949; SFMA, 1943, 1945; Pasadena AI, 1946; Indianapolis Pr. M., 1946; All-Oregon A., 1942, 1944, 1946, 1953; one-man: Portland A. Mus., 1945, 1948-1950; Kharouba Gal., 1951-1953; Pacific Univ., 1953; Eugene A. Center, 1954. *Position*: Instr. A., Portland A. Mus., Portland, Ore.*

McLEAN, MRS. DONALD J. See *Porter, Doris*

McLELLAN, RALPH—*Painter, T.*
Lime Rock, Conn.

B. San Marcos, Tex., Aug. 27, 1884. *Studied*: BMFA Sch.; ASL; & with Hale, Benson, Mora. *Awards*: prizes, Conn. Acad. FA, 1917; NAD, 1919; SSAL, 1928, 1930, 1934. *Work*: Reading (Pa.) Mus.; T. Col., San Marcos, Tex.; Sam Houston State T. Col., Huntsville, Tex.; Furness Jr. H.S., Phila., Pa.

McMILLAN, ROBERT W(ARDROP)—*Educator, P.*
Art Department, Southern Illinois University; h. 810 West Walnut St., Carbondale, Ill.

B. Belleville, Ill., Jan. 22, 1915. *Studied*: Southern Illinois Univ., B. Ed.; Columbia Univ., M.A., with Maldarelli;

Washington Univ., St. Louis, with Max Beckmann; State Univ. Iowa, Ph.D., with Lester Longman. *Member*: Midwestern College A. Conf.; CAA. *Work*: State Univ. Iowa; Columbia Univ. *Exhibited*: A. Gld., St. Louis, 1938, 1939, 1941, 1942; BM, 1940; Carbondale, Ill., 1941; Joslyn Mus. A., 1943; CAM and Nelson Gal. A., 1946; Washington Univ., 1948; Univ. Indiana, 1949; Faculty Exh., Carbondale, 1953; College A. Conf., Kansas City AI, 1953; CM, 1955. *Position*: Prof. A., Art Dept., 1950- , Actg. Chm., A. Dept., 1953- , Southern Illinois University, Carbondale, Ill.

McMILLEN, JACK—*Painter, Des., T.*
480 Lexington Ave., New York 17, N.Y.; h. 145 Hendrie Ave., Riverside, Conn.

B. Jericho, Tex., Sept. 21, 1910. *Studied*: Univ. Kentucky; Univ. Illinois; Minneapolis Sch. A.; Univ. Missouri, B.F.A.; ASL. *Awards*: prizes, Missouri State Fair, 1935; Ed. & Publ., Newspaper Promotion Comp., 1949, 1953, 1954. *Work*: murals, Walter Reed Hospital, Wash., D.C.; Presbyterian Church, Kirksville, Mo.; USPO, College Park, Ga.; Tuscumbia, Ala. *Exhibited*: WFNY 1939; Playhouse A. Gal., N.Y.; N.Y. Soc. FA; Albright A. Gal.; Georgetown Gal., Wash., D.C.

McMULLEN, E. ORMOND—*Painter, I., Gr.*
78 Kirtland St., Grand Rapids 7, Mich.

B. Evart, Mich., Feb. 29, 1880. *Studied*: AIC; NAD; ASL; Grand Central A. Sch. *Member*: AWS (life); SC; Michigan WC Cl. *Awards*: prizes, Springfield A. Lg., 1948; Cooperstown AA, 1949; Silvermine Gld. A., 1950, 1952. *Exhibited*: PAFA, 1936, 1938-1945, 1946-1949; CGA, 1938-1940, 1942, 1943, 1945; AWS, 1938-1943, 1946-1950; Springfield Mus. A., 1944-1951; Hartford Atheneum, 1944, 1945; Soc. Four A., 1941; BMA, 1942; WFNY 1939; Jackson, Miss., 1942; AFA traveling exh., 1940; Albany Inst. Hist. & A., 1947-1951; Cooperstown, N.Y., 1949, 1950; Newport, R.I., 1950; Hudson Valley AA, 1950; St. Botolph's Cl., Boston, 1947; Mich. WC Soc., 1950, 1953; Scarab Cl., 1955; Univ. Michigan, 1955; Milford, Conn., 1955; Silvermine Gld. A., 1948-1953.

McNAB, ALLAN—*Museum Director, Eng., W.*
The Art Institute of Chicago, Michigan Ave. at Adams St., Chicago 3, Ill.

B. England, May 27, 1901. *Studied*: Royal Col. A., London; Ecole des Beaux-Arts, Paris. *Member*: Royal Geographical Soc., Chelsea A. Cl., London; Arch. Lg., N.Y. *Exhibited*: Royal Acad. London; Royal Scottish Acad.; Royal Soc. P. & Et.; New English A. Cl.; AIC, and in Liverpool, Leeds, Manchester, England; Glasgow, Scotland. *Work*: British Mus.; and in galleries of Australia, Italy, France, Holland. *Positions*: A. Dir., UFA, 1928-30; Des. Dir., Norman Bel Geddes, 1938-45; A. Dir., Life Magazine, 1945-50; Dir., Lowe Gallery, 1950-55; Dir., Soc. Four A., Palm Beach, Fla., 1955-56; Adv. to Nat. Mus., Havana, Cuba, 1955- ; Chm., Southern A. Mus. Dir. Assn., 1953-54; Asst. Dir., 1956-57, Assoc. Dir., 1957-59, Dir., Administration, 1959- , The Art Institute of Chicago, Chicago, Ill.

McNEAR, EVERETT C.—*Painter, Des.*
230 East Ohio St., Chicago 11, Ill.; h. 1017 Ridge Court, Evanston, Ill.

B. Minneapolis, Minn., Sept. 30, 1904. *Studied*: Minneapolis Sch. A., with Cameron Booth; also with Edmund Kinzinger, Louis Marcoussis. *Member*: Chicago A. Cl.; 27 Designers. *Awards*: prizes, AIC, 1948; Minnesota Centennial, 1950; A. Gld., 1951, 1955; Soc. Typographic A., 1949-1952; medal, A. Dir. Cl., Chicago, 1950, 1955; New York, 1951. *Exhibited*: AIC, 1935, 1936, 1939, 1940, 1942, 1945, 1947-1952, 1954, 1955; PAFA, 1949; one-man: SFMA, 1946; Crocker A. Gal., Sacramento, 1946; Rouillier Gal., 1944; Wustum Mus. FA, 1945; St. Paul Gal. A., 1943; Walker A. Center, 1948; Dickens Gal., 1950, I., "Many a Green Isle," 1941; "Young Eye Seeing," 1956. Chm. Exh. Com., Chicago A. Cl., 1953- .

McNETT, ELIZABETH VARDELL (Mrs. W. B.)—
Painter, Medical I., T., Gr.
1020 W. Perkins Road, Memphis 17, Tenn.

B. Newbern, N.C., Nov. 17, 1896. *Studied*: Flora Macdonald Col., A.B.; ASL; NAD; PAFA; Univ. Pennsylvania, B.F.A., M.F.A.; Johns Hopkins Univ. Medical Sch.,

Dept. Medical Art. *Awards*: Scholarship to PAFA from Univ. Pa. *Work*: murals, College of Pharmacy, Phila., Pa.; Lankenau Hospital, Phila., Pa.; Inst. of Cancer Research, Phila., Pa. A. All.; Montgomery County AA; one-man: Allied A., Durham, 1956; Fleischer Mus. Sch., Phila., Pa., 1953. Illus. many medical books. Contributor illus. to medical journals. Lectures: Medical Illustration. *Positions*: Instr. A., Andrew Col., Cuthbert, Ga.; Fleischer Mus. Sch., Phila., Pa.; Medical Artist, Lankenau Hospital, Phila., Pa., 18 years.

McNETT, WILLIAM BROWN—Illustrator, Lith., P.
Memphis Air Force Depot, Memphis, Tenn.; h. 1020 W. Perkins Road, Memphis 17, Tenn.

B. Omaha, Neb., Nov. 8, 1896. *Studied*; Johns Hopkins Medical Sch.; PAFA; with Roy Nuse, Daniel Garber, Max Brodel, Francis Speight. *Member*: Assn. Medical Illustrators; Am. Color Print Soc.; F., PAFA; Durham A. Gld. (Vice-Pres., 1954-55, Pres., 1955-56). *Award*: prize, Phila. WC Soc., 1940. *Work*: Flora Macdonald Col.; Davidson Col.; LC; Shoemaker Jr. H.S., Phila., Pa. *Exhibited*: Phila. A. All.; Phila. Pr. Cl.; Phila. WC Soc.; Wanamaker, Phila.; Montgomery County AA; North Carolina State Exh., 1958. Author, I., Chapter in "Medical Writing," Fishbein, 2nd ed., 1948; Illus. 25 major medical text books, 1928-54; A. Editor, Blakiston's Medical Dictionary, 1949, Morris' "Human Anatomy," 11th ed., 1953; American Red Cross First Aid Textbook, 1945, etc. Contributor to Science Counsellor, 1950. Lectures: Anatomy for Artists. *Positions*: Founder-Dir., Dept. Medical Art, Temple Medical Sch., Phila., Pa., 1932-36; A. Ed., Blakiston Co., 1944-52; Chief, Arts Section-Medical, V.A. Hosp., Durham, N.C.; Visual Information Specialist, Memphis Air Force Depot, at present.

McNULTY, MRS. AGNES TAIT. See Tait, Agnes

McNULTY, WILLIAM CHARLES—
Painter, Et., E., Comm. A., I.
1 West 64th St., New York, N.Y.; also Rockport, Mass.

B. Ogden, Utah, Mar. 28, 1884. *Work*: AGAA; Mus. City of New York; Canajoharie Mus.; MMA; BMFA; WMAA; N.Y. Pub. Lib.; LC; Detroit Inst. A.; Newark Mus. A.; N.Y. Historical Soc. *Exhibited*: AIC; MMA; WMAA; BMFA; Kraushaar Gal.; Carnegie Inst.; Retrospective Exh., ASL, 1951, and in many other national museums. *Position*: Instr., ASL since 1931.

McNULTY, MRS. WILLIAM CHARLES. See Gellman, Beatrice

McVEIGH, BLANCHE—Etcher
607½ Throckmorton St.; h. 3724 West Fourth St., Fort Worth 7, Tex.

B. St. Charles, Mo. *Studied*: St. Louis Sch. FA; AIC; PAFA; ASL; & with Daniel Garber, Doel Reed. *Member*: Cal. Pr. Soc.; SAE; Chicago SE; Dallas Pr. Cl.; SSAL; Prairie Pr. M. *Awards*: prizes, Dallas Pr. Cl., 1942, 1944, 1947, 1948, 1950; Conn. Acad. FA, 1941; SSAL, 1945; Texas General Exh., 1944, 1945; Texas FA Assn., 1946; 100 Prints, Chicago, 1936, 1938; Ft. Worth AA, 1948, 1950, 1952; SAE, 1940, 1942, 1944, 1946; LC, 1947. *Work*: Mus. FA of Houston; Ft. Worth AA; Oklahoma A. & M. Col.; Dallas Mus. FA; CM; Carnegie Inst.; Lib. Cong.; Univ. Texas. *Exhibited*: AV, 1942; Buffalo Pr. Cl., 1938, 1939; Cal. Pr. Soc., 1940-1944; Conn. Acad. FA, 1937-1946; Chicago SE, 1938-1945; Denver A. Mus., 1943, 1945; WFNY 1939; Northwest Pr. M., 1940-1942; NAD, 1943, 1944; Oakland A. Gal., 1938-1945; Phila. Pr. Cl., 1936-1945; Princeton Univ.; PAFA, 1941, 1942; SAE, 1940-1945; Lib. Cong., 1943-1946; Carnegie Inst.; 1945; SSAL; Dallas Pr. Cl., 1941-1945; Texas General Exh., 1942-1945; Texas FA Assn., 1938; MMA, 1955, etc.

McVEY, LEZA S. (Mrs.)—Ceramic Sculptor
Pepper Ridge Rd., Cleveland 24, Ohio

B. Cleveland, Ohio, May 1, 1907. *Studied*: Cleveland Sch. A.; Colorado FA Center; Cranbrook Acad. A. *Awards*: prizes, Syracuse Mus. FA, 1950, 1951; Michigan A. & Crafts, 1951; CMA, 1953-1958; Butler Inst. Am. A., 1958. *Work*: Syracuse Mus. FA; CMA; General Motors, Detroit, Mich.; Butler Inst. Am. A. *Exhibited*: Detroit Inst. A.,

1947-1952; Syracuse Mus. FA, and Nat. Circuit, 1945-1948, 1958; Wichita, Kans., 1947-1954; Smithsonian Inst., 1951-1958; Scripps Col.; University galleries: Minneapolis, Wisconsin, Nebraska, Illinois, Syracuse; Pomona, Cal., 1954; PAFA, 1954; Intl. Craftsman Exh., 1953; AFA traveling exh., 1954; BM, 1953, 1954; Butler Inst. Am. A., 1953-1958; Des.-Craftsman, 1954, 1955; CMA, 1951-1958; Akron AI; Art Colony, Cleveland, 1955; De Waters A. Center, Flint, Mich. Contributor to House Beautiful; Ceramic Monthly; Everyday Art Quarterly; Work reproduced in museum catalogues on awards; and in Domus; Craft Horizons. *Position*: Instr., museums in San Antonio and Houston, Tex., 1954; Cranbrook Acad. A., 1954; Akron AI, 1955.

McVEY, WILLIAM M.—Sculptor, T.
Pepper Ridge Rd., Cleveland 24, Ohio

B. Boston, Mass., July 12, 1905. *Studied*: WMA; Cleveland Inst. A.; Academie Colorossi, Academie de la Grande Chaumiere, Paris, France; Academie Scandinave, with Despiau, Marcel Gimond. *Member*: Am. Soc. for Aesthetics. *Awards*: prizes, Los Angeles County Fair, 1941; Syracuse Mus. FA, 1951, 1952, 1956; Wichita Des. National, 1951; Mich. Acad. Sc., A. & Let., 1951; Detroit Inst. A., 1952; numerous prizes Cleveland May Shows, Houston A. Exhs., Texas and Oklahoma Generals. *Work*: CMA; Univ. Mus., Pomona, Cal.; Syracuse Mus. FA; Harvard Univ. Lib.; Wichita AA; Mus. FA of Houston; Rice Inst.; Texas Southern Univ.; Cranbrook Mus. A.; panels, Christ Lutheran Church, Minneapolis (with Eeliel and Eero Saarinen); reliefs, and doors, San Jacinto Monument, Texas; Fed. Trade Comm., Wash., D.C.; Texas Mem. Mus., Austin; Lakeview Terrace Housing Project, Cleveland; capitals, Christ Church, Cranbrook; figures, Fairmount Presbyterian Chapel, Cleveland Heights, Ohio; Abercrombie Laboratory, Rice Inst., Houston; statue, Wade Park, Cleveland; Medusa Cement Nat. Hq., Cleveland; Masonic Temple, Houston; Eastland Shopping Center, Detroit (with Victor Gruen); Berry Monument, Cleveland Mun. Airport; monuments, Texarkana, Tex., Ozona, Tex.; Founders Mem., Brookside Sch., Bloomfield Hills, Mich.; 34 ceramic tiles, Hanzen Col., Rice Inst., and many others. Other work in private collections. *Position*: Hd., Sculpture Dept., Cranbrook Acad., 1947-54; Sculpture Dept., Cleveland Inst. A., Cleveland, Ohio, 1954- .

McVICKER, J. JAY—Painter, S., Gr., E.
Oklahoma State University; h. Route 2, Stillwater, Okla.

B. Vici, Okla., Oct. 18, 1911. *Studied*: Okla. State Univ., B.A., M.A. *Member*: Audubon A.; Phila. WC Cl.; AWS; SAGA; Nat. Ser. Soc.; Cal. Soc. Et. *Awards*: prizes, Delgado Mus. A., 1953, 1958; Joslyn Mem. Mus., 1954; Philbrook A. Center, 1955, 1958; Audubon A., 1954, 1956; DMFA, 1956; Springfield (Mo.) Mus., 1956; Assn. Okla. A., 1956; Cal. Soc. Et., 1956; Wichita AA, 1957; Nat. Ser. Soc., 1958. *Work*: MMA; DMFA; Philbrook A. Center; LC; Delgado Mus. A.; Joslyn Mem. Mus.; SAM. *Exhibited*: Denver A. Mus.; DMFA; Nelson Gal. A.; Mulvane A. Mus.; Delgado Mus. A.; Meltzer Gal., N.Y.; Burr Gal., N.Y.; Univ. Panama; Mus. New Mexico; BM; Colorado Springs FA Center. *Position*: Assoc. Prof. A., Okla. State Univ., Stillwater, Okla.

McWHINNIE, HAROLD JAMES—Printmaker, T.
333 West North Ave. (10); h. 318 West Concord Place, Chicago 14, Ill.

B. Chicago, Ill., July 15, 1929. *Studied*: AIC, B.A.E.; Univ. Oregon; Univ. Chicago, M.F.A. *Member*: CAA; Renaissance Soc.; Univ. Chicago; Phila. Pr. Cl.; Boston Pr. M.; NAEA; Western AA. *Award*: Huntington Hartford F., 1956. *Work*: Lowe Gal. A., Coral Gables, Fla. *Exhibited*: LC, 1955, 1956; Phila. Pr. Cl., 1954-1958; Boston Pr. M., 1954, 1958; PAFA, 1954; Portland (Ore.) A. Mus., 1955; Portland, Me., 1957; Denver A. Mus., 1953; Chicago No-Jury, 1957, 1958; Renaissance Soc., 1953-1958; AIC, 1952, 1958. *Position*: Dir., Print Exhs., Chicago Gallery and traveling exh. service to colleges and museums. Instr., A., Art Dept., Univ. of Chicago, Chicago, Ill., at present.

MEAD, RODERICK—Etcher, Eng., P., T.
The Heights, Carlsbad, N.M.

B. South Orange, N.J., June 25, 1900. *Studied*: Yale Sch. FA; Grand Central A. Sch.; ASL, and with George Luks,

William S. Hayter, George Ennis. *Member*: Audubon A.; AWS; SAGA; Societe des Sur Independents de Paris. *Awards*: medal, Societe des Beaux-Arts, Lorraine, France; prizes, Northwest Pr. M., 1945, 1946; LC, 1946; DMFA, 1950, 1952; Texas Western Col., 1951. *Work*: MMA; LC; Carnegie Inst.; SAM; Princeton Univ.; Royal Lib., Brussels, Belgium; Bibliotheque Nationale, Paris; MModA; Victoria & Albert Mus., London; Tel-Aviv Mus., Israel; N.Y. Pub. Lib.; Univ. Delaware; DMFA; Texas Western Univ.; Roswell Mus.; Mus. New Mexico, Santa Fe; Cal. State Lib. *Exhibited*: AWS; PAFA; AIC; SAGA; NAD; Carnegie Inst.; Mus. New Mexico; New Mexico State Fair; Salon de Mai, Salon des Sur Independents, Petit Palais, Paris, France; Soc. Wood Engravers, Manchester; Museums of The Hague; Rome; Goteborg, Sweden, and many other museums of the U.S. and South America; one-man: George Binet Gal.; Bonestell Gal.; universities of Maine, Arkansas, New Mexico and Oregon; Columbus Gal. FA; Louisville A. Center; Cal. PLH, etc.*

MEADOR, JOSHUA LAWRENCE—*Painter*
600 South Oak Knoll Ave., Pasadena, Cal.

B. Greenwood, Miss., Mar. 12, 1911. *Studied*: AIC, B.A. *Awards*: numerous medals and prizes, 1945-1956; purchase award, Los A. All-City Exh., 1957. *Exhibited*: Los A. Mus. A., 1948, 1949, 1951, 1954; Laguna Beach AA, 1951; Cal. PLH, 1952; Nat. Orange Show, 1953; NAD, 1955; deYoung Mus. A., 1949; Greek Theatre, Los A., 1948, 1953; Santa Paula, Cal., 1950, 1954; Walnut Creek Festival, 1951; Sierra Madre Lib., 1955; Pasadena A. Mus., 1954; Mus. New Mexico, Santa Fe, 1948; White's A. Gal., Montrose, Cal.; Lane Gal., Westwood Village, Cal. *Position*: A., Animator, Walt Disney Studios, Los Angeles, Cal.

MEANS, ELLIOTT—*Painter, I., S.*
178 Second Ave., New York 3, N.Y.

B. Stamford, Tex., Mar. 10, 1904. *Studied*: BMFA Sch. *Member*: SI; A. Gld. *Work*: S., reliefs: Government Printing Bldg., Wash., D.C.; Welfare Island, N.Y.; USPO, Suffern, N.Y.; Dexter, Me. *Exhibited*: NAD, 1933, 1935-1937, 1940, 1941, 1944; Grand Central A. Gal., 1958. I., "The Children's Story Bible," Grolier Soc.; "Comanche of the Seventh," and other books; national magazines.

MECKLEM, MRS. MARIANNE APPEL. See *Appel, Marianne*

MEDARY, AMIE HAMPTON—*Painter, W., L., Des.*
Little Compton Commons, R.I.

B. Groton, Conn., July 24, 1903. *Studied*: BMFA Sch.; PAFA; & with A. Margaretta Archambault. *Member*: Fla. Fed. A.; St. Petersburg A. Cl. *Exhibited*: Pa. Soc. Min. P.; ASMP, 1925-43; Little Compton, R.I.; Boston, Mass.; Wash., D.C.; St. Petersburg, Fla. *Lectures*: History of Costume; Advertising Design.*

MEDELLIN, OCTAVIO—*Sculptor*
Dallas Museum of Fine Arts; h. 715 South Barnett Ave., Dallas 11, Tex.

B. Mexico, May 21, 1907. *Work*: DMFA; Nieman-Marcus Co.; Paxton Lumber Co., Kansas City; San Antonio Tech. H.S.; Police Admin. Bldg., Houston, Tex.; Stewart Bldg., Dallas; St. Andrews Episcopal Church, Grand Prairie, Tex.; St. Henry's Catholic Church, Freeport, Tex.; Lutheran Church, Austin; Temple Emanu-El, Dallas; Mercantile Nat. Bank, Dallas; St. Bernard's Catholic Church, Dallas. *Exhibited*: MModA; WFNY 1939; SSAL; Texas General; NAD; Coronado Cuarto Centennial, New Mexico. Illus.: "The Spanish World," 1933. *Position*: Instr., S., Witte Mem. Mus.; North Texas State, Denton; Southern Methodist Univ., Dallas; at present, DMFA, Dallas, Tex.

MEEKER, DEAN JACKSON—*Printmaker, Muralist*
309 Parkway, Glen Oak Hills, Madison, Wis.

B. Orchard, Colo., May 18, 1920. *Studied*: AIC, B.F.A., M.F.A.; Northwestern Univ.; Univ. Wisconsin. *Award*: Medal Honor, Milwaukee AI, 1952, 1956; Guggenheim Fellowship, 1958. *Work*: BMFA; SAM; SFMA; DMFA; Denver A. Mus.; Milwaukee AI; Beloit Col.; Wis. State T. Col.; Phila. Pr. Cl.; Univ. Oklahoma; Wisconsin Union; Gimbel Coll. *Exhibited*: BMFA, 1954-1956; PAFA, 1946-

1953; BM, 1951-1955; LC, 1952, 1954, 1955; SAM, 1953-1955; SFMA, 1952-1954; Walker A. Center, 1952-1954; Exh. Momentum, Chicago, 1952-1954; MMA, 1953; MModA, 1955; AIC, 1952; Mun. Mus., The Hague, 1954; one-man: AIC; Milwaukee AI; Connecticut Col.; Univ. Missouri; Lawrence Col. *Position*: Assoc. Prof., A. Edu. Dept., Univ. Wisconsin, Madison, Wis., 1946- .

MEGARGEE, LAWRENCE A.—*Animal Illustrator*
16 Garden Pl., Brooklyn 1, N.Y.

B. Philadelphia, Pa., July 10, 1900. *Studied*: PAFA; NAD; ASL; PIASch; CUASch; Grand Central A. Sch. *Work*: Grand Central A. Gal.; Cross Roads of Sport; Ackerman Gal.; Harlow Gal., all in New York, N.Y. I., The Spur, Town & Country; Country Life; The Sportsman magazines.*

MEGREW, ALDEN FRICK—*Educator, Hist.*
Department of Fine Arts, Theatre 201, University of Colorado; h. 505 Baseline Road, Boulder, Colo.

B. Plainfield, N.J., Aug. 30, 1908. *Studied*: Harvard Univ., B.S., M.A. *Member*: CAA; Colo. Edu. Assn. (Council, 1947-); Midwestern Col. A. Conf. (Sec., VP, Pres.); Southwestern Col. A. Conf. (pres. twice). Author: "Outline of Northern Renaissance Art," 1947; "Outline of Medieval Art," 1947. Contributor to College Art Journal. Lectures on Art History to conferences and public audiences. *Positions*: Instr., Lawrence College, Appleton, Wis., 1934-40; Univ. Iowa, 1940-47; Prof. A., Hd. Dept. Fine Arts, University of Colorado, Boulder, Colo., 1947- .

MEIERE, HILDRETH—*Mural Painter*
131 East 66th St., New York 21, N.Y.

B. New York, N.Y. *Studied*: ASL; Cal. Sch. FA; BAID; & with Miller, DuMond, Bridgman. *Member*: ANA; NSMP; Arch. L.; Mun. A. Soc.; Soc. Designer-Craftsmen; N.Y. A. Comm. *Awards*: med., Arch. L., 1928. *Work*: Nebraska State Capitol; Nat. Acad. Sc., Wash., D.C.; mosaics, St. Bartholomew Church, N.Y.; Temple Emanu-El, Catholic Cathedral, St. Louis, Mo.; Irving Trust Co.; stained glass windows, St. Bartholomew's Church, N.Y.; cabin lounge dec., "SS United States." *Exhibited*: Arch. L.; NSMP, annually. *Lectures*: Mosaics—Old and New; travelogues with color slides and motion pictures.*

MEIERHANS, JOSEPH—*Painter*
R.D. #1, Perkasie, Pa.

B. Aargau, Switzerland, Feb. 22, 1890. *Studied*: ASL. *Member*: Am. Abstract A.; Lansdale A. Lg.; Lehigh A. All. *Award*: Albert Rue Bailley medal, Lansdale, Pa. *Exhibited*: WMAA, 1952; PAFA, 1954; Am. Abstract A., 1946-1957; AFA traveling exh., 1952-53; Am. Abstract A. traveling exh., 1948-49; European tour, 1950-1952; Tokyo, 1956; one-man: Artists Gal., N.Y., 1944, 1948, 1952, 1955, 1958; Allentown (Pa.), 1957.

MEIGS, JOHN (LIGGETT)—*Painter*
San Patricio, N.M.

B. Chicago, Ill., May 10, 1916. *Studied*: Redlands Univ.; Paris, France. *Member*: Texas WC Soc.; AEA. *Awards*: prizes, Texas WC Soc., 1955; Roswell Mus., 1955; Cattlemen's Assn., 1953, 1954; El Paso, Tex., 1952, 1953. *Work*: Texas Tech. Col.; Roswell Mus.; Feldman Col.; Ball State Mus., Muncie, Ind.; Snyder (Tex.) H.S.; Malco Oil Co., Roswell, N.M.; Reese Elementary Sch., Lubbock; murals, North Jr. H.S., Abilene, Tex.; Nickson Hotel, Roswell, and in private homes. *Exhibited*: Walker A. Center, 1954; Mus. New Mexico, Santa Fe, 1953-1955 and traveling exhs.; AWS, 1953; Texas WC Soc., 1955; Roswell Mus., 1953-1955; Texas Western Col., 1952, 1953; Cattleman's Assn., 1953, 1954; Hackley A. Gal., 1954; one-man: Mus. New Mexico, 1953; Texas Tech. Col., 1953; Southwest Oil Men's Assn., 1953; Snyder AA, 1954; Grand Central A. Gal., 1954; Plainview AA, 1954; Hackley A. Gal. (3-man), 1954; Ball State Mus., 1954; Little Gal., Santa Fe, 1954; Abilene AA, 1955; Dayton AI, 1955; Honolulu Acad. A., 1958; Currier Gal. A., 1958, and others. Contributor to Ford Times, Humble Way.

MEIGS, WALTER—*Painter, E.*
University of Connecticut, Storrs, Conn.

B. New York, N.Y., Sept. 21, 1918. *Studied*: Syracuse Univ., B.F.A.; Fontainebleau, France; State Univ. Iowa,

M.F.A. *Awards*: prizes, Mid-America A., 1951; L. E. Smith award, 1951; Springfield A. Mus., 1951, 1954, 1955; Denver A. Mus., 1952; BMA, 1955; Converse Gal., Norwich, Conn., 1954-1958; Boston A. Festival, 1954-1956; Birmingham Mus. A., 1954; Providence A. Mus., 1954; Berkshire A. Festival, 1956, 1957; Mystic AA, 1955, 1958; Butler Inst. Am. A., 1957. *Work*: Munson-Williams-Proctor Inst.; Pa. State Univ.; Birmingham Mus. A.; Denver A. Mus.; Amherst College; Springfield (Mo.) Mus. A.; Cultural Div., U.S.I.S.; Wadsworth Atheneum; Butler Inst. Am. A.; Fort Worth A. Center. *Exhibited*: nationally. One-man: Alan Gal., N.Y., 1954; Wesleyan Univ., Middletown, Conn., 1956; Lyman Allyn Mus. A., 1956; Mirski Gal., N.Y., 1957; Nordness Gal., N.Y., 1958. *Position*: Hd. A. Dept., Connecticut College, Storrs, Conn.

MEISS, MILLARD—Educator, W.
Institute for Advanced Study, Princeton, N.J.

B. Cincinnati, Ohio, Mar. 25, 1904. *Studied*: Princeton Univ., A.B.; Harvard Univ.; N.Y. Univ., M.A., Ph.D. *Member*: CAA; Mediaeval Acad. Am. Author: "Painting in Florence and Siena after the Black Death," 1951; "Andrea Mantegna as Illuminator," 1957. Contributor articles on Mediaeval & Renaissance Painting to Art Bulletin, Art in America, Burlington Magazine, & other art publications. *Position*: Prof. History of Art, Institute for Advanced Study, Princeton, N.J. Ed. Bd., Art Bulletin.

MEISSNER, LEO—Engraver, P.
Monhegan, Me.

B. Detroit, Mich., June 28, 1895. *Studied*: Detroit Sch. FA, with John P. Wicker; ASL. *Member*: ANA; Albany Pr. Cl.; SAGA; Audubon A.; Prairie Pr. M.; Boston Pr. M.; AAPL; Pr. Council Am.; Cal. Soc. Et.; Mich. Acad. Sc., A. & Let. *Awards*: prizes, Southern Pr. M., 1937, 1938; Wichita, Kan., 1937; Detroit Inst. A., 1943, 1945; LC, 1931-1956; NAD, 1953. *Work*: Lib. Cong.; Currier Gal. A.; PMG; PMA; Arnot A. Gal., Elmira, N.Y.; Detroit Inst. A.; Joslyn Mem.; City Lib. Assn., Springfield, Mass.; MMA; Brooklyn Inst. A.; Pa. State Univ.; Syracuse Univ.; N.Y. Pub. Lib.; IBM; Univ. Maine. *Exhibited*: 50 Prints of the Year, 1927-1929, 1933; AIC; CMA; Lib. Cong.; AV, 1943; AFA traveling exh.; Carnegie Inst., 1941, 1944, 1945; Int. Pr. Exh., Warsaw, Poland; Smithsonian Inst.; Los A. Mus. A.; NAD; Southern Pr. M.; Prairie Pr. M.; Northwest Pr. M.; Detroit Inst. A.; PAFA; SAGA traveling exh., England, 1954-55; Swope A. Gal.; Farnsworth A. Mus.; Portland (Me.) Mus. A.; deYoung Mem. Mus.; Wash. Pr. M.

MELCARTH, EDWARD—Painter, T., I., L.
109 West 90th St., New York 24, N.Y.

B. Louisville, Ky., Jan. 31, 1914. *Studied*: Harvard Col.; with Karl Zerbe, Cambridge, Mass.; Academie Ranson, Atelier 17, Paris, France. *Member*: NSMP; Arch. Lg. *Awards*: Am. Inst. A. & Let. grant; prizes, AIC; Bordighera, Italy; Kentucky-Indiana annual, 1957. *Work*: Wadsworth Atheneum; BMFA; Detroit Inst. A.; Seagram Co.; IBM; Univ. Louisville; Bradford, England; Bordighera, Italy. Other work: ceiling, Lunt Fontanne Theatre, 1958; Time Life, 1958; lobby & auditorium, Rooftop Theatre, N.Y., 1957; IBM, 1958; two folios, Fortune Magazine; Folio "The Lamp," Esso, 1951, etc. *Exhibited*: WMAA; CGA; PAFA; AIC; AFA traveling exh.; Contemp. A., Boston; Univ. Wisconsin; J. B. Speed Mus. A.; Los A. Mus. A.; Univ. Illinois; Sarasota, Fla., and others. Illus. for Fortune, Harper's, Life, The Lamp, Town & Country, etc. Instr., Painting & Drawing, Univ. Louisville, Parsons Sch. Des., Columbia Univ., Univ. Washington.

MELCHER, BETSY FLAGG—Miniature Painter
170 East 78th St., New York 21, N.Y.

B. New York, N.Y., Apr. 8, 1900. *Studied*: with Alfred Hoen, Cecilia Beaux, Mabel R. Welch. *Member*: ASMP. *Awards*: med., prizes, PAFA, 1933, 1937, 1944, 1945; Boardman mem. prize, N.Y., 1942; Howell Tracey Fisher prize, N.Y., 1942, 1943; Cooperstown, 1954; NAWA, 1951, 1957. *Work*: PAFA. *Exhibited*: CGA, 1937, 1943; ASMP, 1930-1946; PAFA, 1931-1946; NAWA, 1951; Royal Soc. Min. P., London, 1958; one-man: Passedoit Gal., N.Y., 1958.

MELCHERT, ERNEST ALBERT—
Etcher, Eng., Ser., L., P.
1200 Harrison St., Hollywood, Fla.

B. Chicago, Ill., Mar. 11, 1890. *Studied*: AIC; Chicago Acad. FA, and with Vanderpoel, Wellington Reynolds, Joseph Pennell. *Member*: Chicago Soc. Et. (Pres., 1939-); SAGA; Phila. Pr. Cl.; SC. *Work*: Smithsonian Inst.; LC; Beloit Col.; Knox Col. *Exhibited*: NAD; SC; SAGA; Phila. Pr. Cl.; South Bend A. Lg.; Brooklyn Soc. Et.; Chicago Soc. Et.; AIC. Lectures: Graphic Arts. Pres., Chicago Soc. Et., 1939-1959.

MELICOV, DINA—Sculptor
939 8th Ave., New York, N.Y.

B. Russia, Jan. 12, 1905. *Studied*: Iranian Inst.; Columbia Univ. *Member*: NAWA; S. Gld. *Awards*: European traveling scholarship, Ed. All. A. Sch., N.Y.; prize, NAWA. *Work*: USPO, Northumberland, Pa. *Exhibited*: WFNY 1939; PAFA, 1946; WMAA; BM; NAD; Argent Gal.; ACA Gal.; S. Gld.

MELIK, SOSS EFREM—Painter
The Chelsea Hotel, 222 West 23rd St., New York, N.Y.

B. Baku, Russia, Aug. 2, 1914. *Studied*: NAD, and with Feodor Zakharov. *Member*: AAPL. *Awards*: prizes, NAD, 1933, 1940; AAPL, 1954-1956. *Work*: ports., paintings: Intl. House, N.Y.; Columbia Univ.; The Customs House, N.Y., Am. Acad. A. & Let., N.Y.; The White House, Wash., D.C. Many portraits of prominent persons in public and private colls.

MELLEN, MARGARET RIGGS—Painter
P.O. Box 3513, Cleveland Heights 18, Ohio

B. Cleveland Heights, Ohio, July 1, 1927. *Studied*: Cleveland Inst. A., B.F.A.; Western Reserve Grd. Sch., and with Louis Bosa, Carl Gaertner, Jack Levine. *Member*: Ohio WC Soc.; Cleveland Inst. A. *Awards*: prizes, CMA, 1951; Cleveland Jr. Chamber of Commerce, 1949, 1951; Ohio WC Soc., 1950; Mary A. Burnham award, 1945. *Exhibited*: NAD, 1952; Springfield A. Lg., 1952; Butler AI, 1949, 1950, 1952; Boston Soc. Indp. A., 1949; CMA, 1947, 1950-1952; Cleveland Chamber of Commerce, 1949-1952; Ohio WC Soc., 1951, 1952; Canton, Ohio, 1951; Vice-Pres., 1952-1954, Pres., 1955-1957, Ohio WC Soc. Research on Painting Techniques of Old Masters, 1957, 1958.

MELLON, ELEANOR M.—Sculptor
15 Gramercy Park; h. 2 East 70th St., New York 21, N.Y.

B. Narberth, Pa., Aug. 18, 1894. *Studied*: ASL, with Robert Aiken; also with A. A. Weinmann, Charles Grafly, Harriet Frishmuth, Victor Salvatore. *Member*: ANA; NSS; Arch. Lg.; North Shore A. *Awards*: prizes, NAD, 1927; N.Y. Jr. Lg., 1942; med., Soc. Wash. A., 1931; AAPL, 1945. *Exhibited*: NSS, 1921, 1929, 1943; PAFA; NAD; AIC; All. A. Am.; NAWA; Soc. Wash. A.; AAPL; North Shore A; MMA; N.Y. Jr. Lg. *Position*: Memb. Council, NSS; Sec., NSS, 1936-40, 1945; Bd. Dir., Arch. Lg.; 2nd V-Pres., Municipal A. Soc., 1942-44.*

MELTZER, ANNA E(LKAN)—Painter, T.
58 West 57th St.; h. Lake Mahopac, N.Y.

B. New York, N.Y., Aug. 6, 1896. *Studied*: CUASch.; ASL, and with Alexander Brook. *Member*: Audubon A.; F., Royal Soc. A., London, England; AAPL. *Awards*: medal, Audubon A., 1942; citation, Fla. Southern Col. *Work*: BM; Pittsfield (Mass.) Mus. A.; Joslyn Mem. Mus.; Cal. PLH; Fla. Southern Col. *Exhibited*: Audubon A., 1942, 1944, 1945; NAWA, 1944-1946; All. A. Am., 1944; Pasadena AI; Erie (Pa.) Pub. Mus.; Cortland, N.Y., Gal. & Lib.; French & Co.; Fla. Southern Col.; Marie Sterner Gal.; one-man: Rockford AA; Massillon Mus. A.; Bloomington AA; Evansville Mus.; Plainfield AA; Rundle Gal., Rochester; Cayuga Mus. Hist. & A.; Univ. Florida; Vendome Gal.; Newhouse Gal.; Francis Taylor Gal., Los A.; Chase Gal., N.Y., 1958. *Position*: Instr., City Col. Sch. of General Studies, Ext. Div., New York, N.Y.; Dir., Anna Meltzer Sch. A., New York, N.Y.

MELTZER, ARTHUR—*Painter, C., L.*
1521 Welsh Rd., Huntingdon Valley, Pa.

B. Minneapolis, Minn., July 31, 1893. *Studied*: Minneapolis Sch. FA; PAFA; & with Robert Koehler, Joseph Pearson, Daniel Garber. *Member*: Woodmere AA; Phila. A. All.; F., PAFA. *Awards*: F., PAFA, 1925; Cresson traveling scholarship, PAFA; prizes, Woodmere Gal. A., 1949, 1951; prize, Conn. Acad. FA, 1931. *Work*: PAFA; Storrs Col., Conn.; Illinois Athletic Cl., Chicago; Columbus Gal. FA; Phila. A. All.; Moore Inst. A. Sc. & Indst.; Carlisle A. Mus., Pa.; Woodmere A. Gal. *Exhibited*: PAFA, 1921-1946; AIC; CGA; Woodmere A. Gal.; F., PAFA. *Lectures*: Artistic Anatomy. *Position*: Instr., Drawing & Painting, L., Anatomy, 1925- , Hd. Dept. FA, 1925-49, Moore Inst., Philadelphia, Pa.

MELTZER, MRS. ARTHUR. *See van Roekens, Paulette*

MELTZER, DORIS—*Printmaker, P., A. Dir.*
Meltzer Gallery, 38 West 57th St., New York 19, N.Y.

B. Ellenville, N.Y., Jan. 1, 1908. *Studied*: N.Y. Univ., B.S.; ASL, and in Europe. *Member*: AAMus; Print Council AM.; Nat. Ser. Soc. (Vice-Pres., Dir., 1943-). As printmaker has exhibited in Nat. Print shows 1940-50. Founded Nat. Ser. Soc., 1940, traveling exhibition service, school and gallery. Introduced Scandinavian graphic art to U.S. in series of exhibitions from 1951. Arranged exhibitions of prints and paintings for travel under auspices of U.S. Embassy, Cultural Div., Paris, 1952- . Prepared 4 educational exhibitions on American serigraphy for foreign travel, 1950. Founded the Meltzer Gallery, 1954. Prepared exhibitions for travel under sponsorship of USIA for the Overseas Program, including "American Serigraphs and How They Are Made," 1955, 1956; "Fifty Years of American Graphic Art," 1957-58 and supervised the publishing of 300 exhibitions of reproductions of 40 American paintings for "20th Century Highlights of American Painting" for the USIA, 1958.

MELVILLE, GREVIS WHITAKER—*Painter, Lith.*
U.S. Coastal Rt. 1; h. Vine St., Damariscotta, Me.

B. Damariscotta, Me., Dec. 23, 1904. *Studied*: Yale Univ. Sch. FA; ASL. *Member*: ASL (life); MModA. *Awards*: Scholarships, Yale Univ.; ASL. *Work*: Farnsworth Lib. & Mus., Rockland, Me.; Pierson Col., Yale Univ.; Damariscotta Information Bureau. *Exhibited*: PAFA, 1950; SFMA; Portland Soc. A., 1946, 1955; BM; LC; Boston Festival A.; Maine Coast A.; Ogunquit A. Center; SC; Boothbay Harbor Soc. A., 1952; Bowdoin Col., 1939 (one-man); Smith Col., 1940 (one-man); Farnsworth Mus., 1948-1950, 1954; Damariscotta A., 1941-1948, and others. Illus. "Windswept," 1941. Contributor to: N.Y. Times; N.Y. Herald-Tribune; Christian Science Monitor; Portland Sunday Telegram; Down East magazine. Lectures: Contemporary Painting and Sculpture. *Position*: Res. A., Hackley Sch., Tarrytown, N.Y., 1941-42; Dir., Damariscotta Region Improvement & Hist. Soc., and Dir., Information Bureau, 1935- .

MELVILLE, MARGUERITE LOUISE—*Painter*
34 Norman Rd., Upper Montclair, N.J.

B. Upper Montclair, N.J., May 8, 1912. *Studied*: Pembroke Col., Brown Univ., A.B.; R.I. Sch. Des.; ASL, and with Frederick Sisson, Kimon Nicolaides, Jose deCreeft, Victor Candell, Charles Seide. *Member*: ASL (life). *Award*: medal, AAPL, 1937. *Exhibited*: Montclair A. Mus.; Newark Mus.; A. Center of the Oranges.

MENCONI, RALPH JOSEPH—*Sculptor*
154 West 55th St., New York 19, N.Y.; h. Old School Lane, Pleasantville 1, N.Y.

B. Union City, N.J., June 17, 1915. *Studied*: Yale Univ., B.F.A.; Hamilton Col.; NAD; Tiffany Fnd. *Member*: NSS; Century Assn.; Mun. A. Soc. (Dir.). *Awards*: Speyer award, NAD, 1941; Tiffany Fnd. grant, 1947; Nat. Jefferson Expansion Mem. (in collaboration with Caleb Hornbostel), 1947; Jefferson Comp., 1948. *Work*: Brookgreen Gardens, S.C.; Bambergers, N.J.; St. Rose of Lima, Short Hills, N.J.; St. Joseph's Catholic Church, Camden, N.J.; Speer Mem. Lib., Princeton, N.J.; Herkimer County Office Bldg.; AFL-CIO Bldg., Wash., D.C.; medals, plaques, Nat. Book Award; N.Y. Univ. Law Center;

Kenyon Col.; Lebanon Steel Co.; Reader's Digest; Diamonds USA, Puerto Rico; Bryn Mawr Col.; Pittsburgh Bicentennial Medal; Michigan State; General Electric; Buckley Sch.; Grenfell Assoc., and many portrait commissions. *Exhibited*: NAD; NSS; Medallic Art Co., 1950; Int. Comp., Imperial Palace, Addis Ababa; Int. Comp. Hertzl Mem., Israel, 1951; Govt. of Portugal, Int'l. Comp.

MENDELOWITZ, DANIEL MARCUS—*Painter, E., W.*
Stanford University; h. 1285 Forest Ave., Palo Alto, Cal.

B. Linton, N.D., Jan. 28, 1905. *Studied*: Stanford Univ., A.B., M.A.; ASL; Cal. Sch. FA. *Member*: Pacific AA. *Awards*: prize, Santa Cruz A. Lg., 1945; Santa Clara County Fair, 1955. *Work*: mural, USPO, Oxnard, Cal. *Exhibited*: CGA, 1941; AWS, 1944-1946; San F. AA, 1946, 1954; Santa Cruz A. Lg., 1935-1946; Mississippi AA, 1945; Santa Clara County Fair, 1955; deYoung Mem. Mus., 1955; one-man: Gump's, San F., 1944; Courvoisier Gal., San F., 1940; Thos. Welton Stanford Gal., 1953-1958; Kendall Mem. Gal., San Angelo, Tex., 1954; Maxwell Gal., San F., 1955. Author: "Challenge of Education," 1937; "Education in War Time and After," 1943; "Children Are Artists," 1953. Contributor to Design magazine, with articles on Art Education. *Position*: Asst. Prof. A., San Jose State Col., San Jose, Cal., 1927-34; Instr., Asst. Prof., Assoc. Prof., Stanford Univ., Stanford, Cal., 1934-46; Prof., 1949- .

MENDENHALL, EMMA—*Painter*
2538 Hackberry St., Cincinnati, Ohio

B. Cincinnati, Ohio. *Studied*: Cincinnati A. Acad.; Julian Acad., Paris, France. *Member*: AWS; Cincinnati Woman's Cl.; Prof A., Cincinnati; 3 Arts Cl.; MacDowell Cl. *Awards*: prizes, NAC; Wash. WC Cl.; CM; Ohio WC Soc.; Woman's Cl., Cincinnati. *Work*: Kirby, Bond Hill, Hughes H.S., Cincinnati, and abroad. *Exhibited*: CM; PAFA; Phila. WC Cl.; Wash. WC Cl.; AIC; Ohio WC Soc.; NAC; Butler AI; Boston WC Cl.; AWS.

MENIHAN, JOHN C.—*Painter, Lith., Ser., T., L., Des.*
208 Alpine Dr., Rochester 18, N.Y.

B. Rochester, N.Y., Feb. 14, 1908. *Studied*: Univ. Pennsylvania, B.S. *Member*: Rochester A. Cl.; Rochester Pr. Cl.; AWS; NAD; SAGA. *Awards*: Lillian Fairchild award, Rochester, 1940; Marion S. Gould award, Rochester, 1946. *Work*: LC; Carnegie Inst.; Nazareth Col., Pittsford, N.Y.; ports., St. John Fisher Col., Rochester; St. Louis Catholic Church, Pittsford; St. Thomas Catholic Church, Rochester; Rochester Mem. A. Gal.; Rochester Pr. Cl.; des. interiors for B. Formon's "Young World," Rochester; des. & printed 1954 Presentation Print, Rochester Pr. Cl.; des. chapel, St. John the Evangelist Convent, Rochester, N.Y.; Illus., Des., "The New St. Basil Hymnal." *Exhibited*: LC, 1952; Finger Lakes Exh., 1952. Illus., "Faculty for Cooking," 1950. *Position*: Assoc. Prof., Drawing & Painting, Univ. Rochester, N.Y.

MENKEN, MARIE—*Painter, C.*
252 Fulton St.; h. 62 Montague St., Brooklyn 1, N.Y.

B. Brooklyn, N.Y., May 25, 1917. *Studied*: N.Y. Sch. F. & Indst. A.; ASL, and with Joseph Hafner, Carl Link, Kenneth Hayes Miller, K. M. Ballantyne. *Awards*: Yaddo Fnd. scholarship, 1949, 1950. *Work*: in numerous private coll.; made 3 abstract films 16 mm. (1952-55), "Visual Variations on Noguchi"; "Hurry! Hurry!"; "Glimpse of a Garden," for Gryphon Productions (all shown at Intl. Experimental Film Festival, Brussels World's Fair, 1958); created sets for Willard Maas' film poems "Image in the Snow" and "Narcissus." Completed art films: "Arabesque for Kenneth Anger" (based on Alhambra, Granada, Spain), 1958; "Dwightiana" (based on work of artist Dwight Ripley), 1958; "Bon-Sai, Bon Seki, Bon Kei" (based on Japanese miniature gardens), 1959 (Gryphon Productions). *Exhibited*: BM, 1951; BMA, 1951; DeMotte Gal., 1940; Mus. Non-Objective Painting, 1939-1941; BMFA, 1939; Inst. Mod. A., 1940; one-man: Tibor de Nagy Gal., N.Y., 1951; Betty Parsons Gal., 1949, 1951.

MENKES, SIGMUND—*Painter*
5075 Fieldstone Road, Riverdale 71, N.Y.

B. Lwow, Poland, May 7, 1896. *Studied*: in Europe. *Member*: Fed. Mod. P. & S. *Awards*: prize and medal, 1947, prize, CGA, 1941; med., PAFA, 1945; award, Nat. Inst. A. & Let., 1955; Art:USA, 1958. *Work*: MMA; Wichita AA; Cranbrook Acad. A.; Encyclopaedia Britannica Coll.; PAFA; WMAA; BM; St. Claire (N.J.) Mus.; Walker A. Center; Emily Lowe Mus. A., Miami; Davenport Mun. Gal.; Nat. Inst. A. & Let.; Abbott Laboratories Coll.; Musee du Jeu de Paume, Paris, France; Nat. Mus. Warsaw, Poland; Nat. Mus., Belgrade, Yugoslavia; Nat. Mus., Athens, Greece; Tel-Aviv, Palestine. *Exhibited*: Carnegie Inst.; AIC; CGA; PAFA; Univ. Nebraska; CMA; Am. Univ., Wash., D.C.; State Univ. Iowa; Cranbrook Acad. A.; MMA; WMAA; one-man exh.: Cornelius Sullivan Gal., N.Y.; Durand-Ruel Gal.; Assoc. Am. A., 1936-1944. *Position*: Instr., ASL, New York, N.Y.

MEREDITH, DOROTHY L(AVERNE)—Painter, C., E.
2932 North 69th St., Milwaukee 10, Wis.

B. Milwaukee, Wis., Nov. 17, 1906. *Studied*: Layton Sch. A.; Milwaukee State T. Col., B.A.; Cranbrook Acad. A., M.F.A.; & with Zoltan Sepeshy, Robert von Neumann, Myron Nutting. *Member*: Wis. P. & S.; Wis. A. Fed.; Wis. WC Soc. (Treas.); Midwest Des.-Craftsmen; Wis. Designer-Craftsmen. *Awards*: prizes, Milwaukee AI; Wisconsin State Fair; Wisconsin Designer-Craftsmen; Crafts State Fair; Milwaukee AI, 1958. *Work*: Cranbrook Acad. A.; Milwaukee AI; Nat. Soldiers Home, Wood, Wis.; Bay View H.S., South Division H.S., Milwaukee, Wis. *Exhibited*: AIC; Milwaukee AI, 1927-1955; Madison Salon; Midwest Des.-Craftsmen, and traveling exh., 1956-1958; Layton Sch. A.; Charles Allis Lib. Contributor to "Handweaver." *Position*: Assoc. Prof. A., Univ. Wisconsin, Milwaukee, Wis.; Chm., Midwest Des.-Craftsmen, 1957-58; One of 6 Nat. Craftsmen Trustees, Am. Craftsmen's Council.

MERIDETH, JOHN GRAY—Painter, Comm. A., T.
1028½ North Western Ave., Los Angeles 29, Cal.

B. Moberly, Mo., Nov. 2, 1922. *Studied*: Glendale Col.; Univ. California at Los Angeles, B.A., M.A. *Member*: Cal. WC Soc. *Work*: murals, Redwood (Cal.) Cafe. *Exhibited*: Glendale AA, 1942; Glendale Nat. WC Exh., 1945; Palos Verdes, 1951; Cal. State Fair, 1952; Cal. WC Soc., 1954; Nat. Orange Show, 1958. *Position*: Instr., Los A. City Col., 1949-51, 1951-56 (evening division).

MERKEL, WALTER M.—Critic, W., L., P., I.
1764 Temple Terr., South, St. Petersburg, Fla.

B. Berwick, Pa., May 9, 1886. *Studied*: ASL. *Member*: Worcester Gld. A. & Craftsmen; Southbridge (Mass.) AA (hon.). *Exhibited*: WMA; Worcester Telegram, Evening Gazette annual exh. Lectures: "Art and the Newspaper"; "Monuments in Havana, Cuba" (illus.); "The Color of Florida" (illus.); "Nassau" (illus.).

MERMIN, MILDRED SHIRE (Mrs.)—Painter
1185 Park Ave., New York 28, N.Y.

B. New York, N.Y., Feb. 25, 1907. *Studied*: ASL; NAD. *Member*: AEA; NAWA; MacDowell Cl.; ASL. *Award*: Am. Artist Magazine Medal of Honor, NAWA, 1957. *Exhibited*: 1953-55; Audubon A.; N.Y. City Center; Madison Square Garden, N.Y., 1957; Provincetown AA, 1958; Springfield Mus. A., 1958; NAWA, 1956-1958; Salpeter Gal., 1956 (one-man), and others prior to 1953.

MERRICK, JAMES KIRK—Painter, T., I., W., L.
Philadelphia Museum School of Art, 320 South Broad St.; h. 2107 Spruce St., Philadelphia 3, Pa.; s. Provincetown, Mass.

B. Philadelphia, Pa., Oct. 8, 1905. *Studied*: PMSchIA; & with Thornton Oakley, Henry Hensche. *Member*: Phila. A. All.; Phila. WC Cl.; Woodmere AA; SC. *Awards*: prizes, Phila. A. All., 1936; Cape May AA, 1945; SC, 1950; European traveling scholarship, PMSchA., 1931; gold medal, PM Sch. A. Alumni, 1953; medal, Phila. WC Cl., 1955. *Work*: Phila. A. All.; Phila. WC Cl. (Pres.); PMA; Cape May Col.; Phila. Pub. Sch. *Exhibited*: PAFA, 1935-1945; Phila. WC Cl., 1935-1945; AIC, 1940; State Mus., Trenton, N.J.; SC; Herron AI; NAD; Audubon A.; Woodmere AA; Lawrence Col.; Harcum Col.; State Mus., Harrisburg, Pa.; Phila. A. All. Author, I., "Brian"; I., "These Were Actors." *Position*: Instr. A., PMSchIA, Phila., Pa., 1930- ; Sec-Treas., Phila. WC Cl., 1938-1953; Sec., Bd. Dir., Phila. A. All., 1938- ; Pres., Alumni Assn., PMSch. IA., 1941-1953.

MERRICK, RICHARD L.—Painter, Gr., E.
4235 Lennox Dr., Coconut Grove, Fla.

B. Coconut Grove, Fla., Nov. 28, 1903. *Studied*: ASL, with Henri, Sloan, Luks, Pennell. *Member*: New Orleans AA; Miami AA; Palm Beach A. Lg.; Fla. A. Group. *Awards*: prizes, Norton Gal. A., 1948-1952; Lowe Gal. A., 1952; Grand Central A. Gal., 1948, and others. *Work*: LC; USPO, Miami, Fla.; Lowe Gal. A. *Exhibited*: MModA; VMFA; Lowe Gal. A.; Norton Gal. A. *Position*: Instr., 1935-44, Prof. A., 1944- , Univ. Miami, Fla.

MERRILL, HIRAM CAMPBELL—Painter, Eng.
1800 Massachusetts Ave., Cambridge 40, Mass.

B. Boston, Mass., Oct. 25, 1866. *Studied*: ASL, with Douglas Volk, Frank DuMond, Herbert Adams. *Member*: AWCS; Cambridge AA; Boston Pr. M. *Awards*: med., Pan-Am. Exp., Buffalo, N.Y., 1901; St. Louis Exp., 1904. *Work*: BMFA; Carnegie Inst.; Boston Pub. Lib. *Exhibited*: AFA; AIC; Lib. Cong.; N.Y. WC Cl.; AWCS; Phila. WC Cl.; Wash. WC Cl.; Balt. WC Cl.*

MERRILL, WALTER McINTOSH—
Museum Director, E., L., P.
Essex Institute; h. 13 Washington Square, Salem, Mass.

B. Evanston, Ill., May 26, 1915. *Studied*: Northwestern Univ., B.S.L.; Harvard Univ., A.M., Ph.D.; AIC, with Paul Weighardt; privately with Cyril Gardner. *Member*: AAMus.; Am. Assn. for State & Local Hist.; various historical societies. *Awards*: Post-doctoral F., Am. Council of Learned Societies, 1951-53. *Exhibited*: Old Northwest Territory Exh., Springfield, Ill., 1949 and other exhs. in Midwest and East. Author: "From Statesman to Philosopher," 1949; Ed., "Behold Me Once More," 1954. Contributor book reviews to scholarly journals. Lectures: American Furniture; various lectures on William Lloyd Garrison. *Position*: Instr., Asst. Prof., Amherst, Swarthmore, Northwestern and Bowdoin Colleges, 1942-1951; F., AM. Council Learned Soc., 1951-53; Bowdoin Col., 1953-54; Dir. Essex Inst., Salem, Mass., 1954- .*

MERRITT, FRANCIS SUMNER—
Painter, T., Lith., Des., L., W.
Haystack Mountain School of Crafts, Liberty, Me.; h. Searsmont, Me.

B. Danvers, Mass., Apr. 8, 1913. *Studied*: Vesper George Sch. A.; Mass. Sch. A.; BMFA Sch. A.; Yale Univ. *Member*: AEA. *Awards*: prize, Flint Inst. A., 1947. *Work*: murals, Waldo County Gen. Hosp., Belfast, Me.; Knox County Gen. Hosp., Rockland, Me. *Exhibited*: CGA, 1941; Carnegie Inst., 1941; AFA traveling exh., 1942; Detroit Inst. A., 1947-1951; Butler AI, 1949, 1950; Stuart Gal., Boston, 1946; Vose Gal., 1935, 1937 (one-man); Portland Mus. A., 1953; Saginaw (Mich.) Mus. A. 1956 (one-man). *Position*: Dir., Flint Inst. A., Flint, Mich., 1947-51; Dir., Dept. A., Bradford Jr. Col., Bradford, Mass., 1953-57; Des. 1957 Crafts Exh., Arch. Lg., N.Y.; Des., Portland A. Festival, 1957, 1958; Panel Moderator, 2nd Annual Conf., Am. Craftsmen's Council, Lake Geneva, Wis.

MERRYLEN (Merrylen Townsend Lerman)—Cartoonist
21 Hempstead Ave., Rockville Centre, L.I., N.Y.

B. Chicago, Ill., Sept. 23, 1916. *Studied*: Cincinnati Acad. A.; N.Y. Sch. Des. for Women; ASL. *Awards*: O.W.I. citations. Contributor cartoons to Sat. Eve. Post; This Week; Ladies Home Journal; Woman's Home Companion, and other national magazines.

MERTEN, JOHN WILLIAM (JACK)—
Craftsman, Des., P., W.
3420 Grace Ave., Cincinnati 8, Ohio

B. Cincinnati, Ohio, Aug. 28, 1898. *Studied*: Harvard Col., B.A., M.A.; Cincinnati A. Sch.; Univ. Cincinnati; Sorbonne, Paris, & with W. E. Hentschel, Reginald Grooms, Harold Nash. *Member*: Ceramic Gld., Cincinnati; Cincinnati Crafters Soc. *Work*: CM. *Exhibited*: Syracuse Mus. FA; Butler AI, 1946; CM; Cincinnati Crafters; Ceramic Gld.; Akron AI, 1953. *Position*: Trustee, Cincinnati Ceramic Gld., 1953-55; Cincinnati Music-Drama Gld., 1953-56. Author: Centennial History of Strobridge Lithographing Co. for Hist. & Philosophical Soc. of Ohio Bulletin.*

MERYMAN, RICHARD S.—*Painter,* **T.**
Dublin, N.H.

B. Boston, Mass., Apr. 4, 1882. *Studied*: BMFA Sch.; & with Tarbell, Benson, Thayer. *Member*: Gld. Boston A.; Century Assn.; SC. *Awards*: med., Pan-Pacific Exp., 1915; Sesqui-Centennial Exp., Phila., Pa., 1926. *Work*: Wash. (D.C.) Pub. Lib.; Army & Navy Cl. Wash., D.C.; Madison (Wis.) Hist. Soc.; Phillips Acad., Andover, Mass.; Groton (Mass.) Sch.; U.S. Navy; Mercersburg Acad. *Exhibited*: Gld. Boston A.; CGA; PAFA; etc. *Position*: Principal, Corcoran Sch., 14 Years; Instr., PAFA, 2 years.

MESIBOV, HAROLD ALLAN—*Painter*
2400 Spruce St., Philadelphia 3, Pa.

B. Philadelphia, Pa., Feb. 18, 1928. *Studied*: PMSch. A.; Phila. Sketch Cl.; Tyler Sch. FA; Barnes Fnd. *Member*: AEA. *Exhibited*: PAFA, 1949-1951; Pyramid Cl., 1957; Phila. A. All., 1953, 1955, 1956; Harcum College, 1957; one-man: Panoras Gal., N.Y., 1955, 1957.

MESIBOV, HUGH—*Painter,* **T., Ser., C.**
500 Third Ave., New York 16, N.Y.

B. Philadelphia, Pa., Dec. 29, 1916. *Studied*: Phila. Graphic Sketch Cl.; PAFA; Barnes Fnd. *Member*: F., PAFA. *Awards*: prizes, PAFA, 1952; Hallmark Award, 1952; Phila. Pr. Cl., 1941, 1946; F., PAFA, 1958. *Work*: PMA; Free Lib., Phila.; Carnegie Inst.; Univ. Wyoming; MMA; Barnes Fnd.; PAFA; mural, USPO, Hubbard, Ohio. *Exhibited*: PAFA, 1943, 1952-1955, 1957; U.S. Nat. Mus., 1938; WFNY 1939; State Mus., Harrisburg, Pa.; Carnegie Inst., 1939; Phila. A. All., 1940, 1941, 1945; BM, 1951, 1953-1955; LC, 1951; AFA traveling exh., 1951, 1954; Soc. Wash. Pr. M., 1951, 1952; Chinese Gal., N.Y.; Nat. Ser. Soc., 1953-1955; WMAA, 1956, 1957; Mint Mus. A., 1956; New Sch. Assoc., 1957; one-man: Elizabeth Nelson Gal., Chicago, 1952; Morris Gal., N.Y., 1954; Bookshop Gal., Aspen, Colo., 1951-1953; Pied Piper Gal., Aspen, Colo., 1954; Chinese Gal., N.Y., 1947; Artists Gal., N.Y., 1956, 1958; Sunken Meadow Gal., N.Y., 1958. *Position*: Instr., Lenox Hill Neighborhood Assn., New York, N.Y.; Wiltwyck Sch., Esopus, N.Y.

MESS, EVELYNNE B. (*Mrs. George Jo***)—**
Etcher, Lith., **P., I., T.**
6237 Central Ave., Indianapolis 20, Ind.

B. Indianapolis, Ind., Jan. 8, 1903. *Studied*: John Herron AI; Butler Univ.; AIC; Ecole des Beaux-Arts, Fontainebleau, France, and with Andre Strauss, Despujols. *Member*: Am. Color Pr. Soc.; Nat. Soc. A. & Let.; Cal. Soc. Et.; Indiana A. Cl.; Indiana Soc. Pr. M.; Brown County AA; Indiana Fed. A. Cl. *Awards*: prizes, Ind. State Fair, 1930, 1950, 1951; Indiana A. Cl., 1949, 1951, 1955, 1957; Ind. Fed. A. Cl., 1942; Hoosier Salon, 1947, 1948, 1950, 1953, 1958; Nat. Soc. A. & Let., 1948; Indiana A., 1949, 1955; Cal. Soc. Et.; Holcomb prize, John Herron AI, 1958. *Work*: John Herron AI; LC. *Exhibited*: SAGA, 1931, 1933-1935; Los A. Mus. A., 1934, 1936; PAFA, 1934; Phila. Soc. Et., 1935; Phila. A. All., 1936; Am. Color Pr. Soc., 1945, 1946; Phila. Pr. Cl., 1946; Hoosier Salon, 1934, 1942, 1943, 1945-1948, 1950; Indiana Soc. Pr. M., 1934-1938, 1940, 1944-1946; Herron AI, 1928, 1929, 1932-1934, 1945, 1947, 1948, 1950, 1957, 1958; Brown County AA, 1943-1946; SAM. I., "Old Fauntleroy Home," 1939. *Position*: Instr. A., John Herron AI, 1957.

MESS, GEORGE JO—*Etcher, Lith.,* **P., Des., L., T.**
6237 Central Ave., Indianapolis 20, Ind.

B. Cincinnati, Ohio, June 30, 1898. *Studied*: John Herron AI; Butler Univ.; Columbia Univ.; Inst. Mod. Des., Chicago, and in France. *Member*: SAGA; Chicago Soc. Et.; Indiana Soc. Et.; Ohio Soc. Et.; Wash. WC Cl.; Indiana A. Cl.; Brown County AA. *Awards*: prizes, Hoosier Salon, 1936, 1938, 1941, 1943-1946, 1949, 1952, 1954-1958; Indiana A. Cl., 1944, 1945, 1948, 1951, 1955, 1956; Indiana Soc. Pr. M., 1948, 1950; Herron AI, 1952, 1954; Chicago Soc. Et., 1952, 1956; Indiana State Fair, 1952, 1954, 1956, 1958. *Work*: LC; Herron AI; Grand Rapids A. Gal.; CMA; MMA; Dayton AI. *Exhibited*: SAGA, 1935-1937, 1939-1946, 1949-1958; NAD, 1936-1938, 1940, 1942-1946; MMA, 1943, 1952, 1955; PAFA, 1940, 1943-1945; Herron AI, 1941-1948, 1950, 1951, 1953, 1955-1958; Hoosier Salon, 1936-1958; Indiana Soc. Pr. M., 1936-1946, 1948, 1950; Ohio Pr. M., 1940-1958; Indiana A. Cl., 1944, 1945, 1948, 1951; Chicago Soc. Et., 1940-1958; LC, 1943-1950,

1952-1958; Intl. A. Exp., Paris; 100 American Prints, Rome Nat. Mus., Stockholm, and many others. I., "Hoosie City," 1943; "Living in Indiana," 1946. Lectures: How to Make an Etching. *Positions*: Instr., Indiana Univ., Indianapolis, 1948- ; Instr., John Herron AI, Indianapolis, Ind., summer, 1955-1956.

MESS, GORDON BENJAMIN—*Painter,* **Des., T., L.**
151 East Maryland St.; h. 5525 Allisonville Rd., Indianapolis 20, Ind.

B. Cincinnati, Ohio, Sept. 28, 1900. *Studied*: John Herron AI; Fontainebleau Sch. FA, France; and with Anthony Thieme, Emile Gruppe, Wayman Adams. *Member*: Indiana A. Cl.; Brown County A. Gld.; The Twenty Group; Indiana Fed. A. Cl.; Hoosier Gal Assn.; Alumni Assn. of Fontainebleau. *Awards*: prizes, Hoosier Salon, 1931, 1942, 1943, 1951 (2), 1952-1954, 1958; Richmond AA, 1931; Indiana State Fair, 1931; Indiana A. Cl., 1938, 1941; Ball State T. Col., 1952; Indiana Univ., 1953, 1954. *Work*: Richmond A. Gal.; Indianapolis and Valparaiso Pub. Schs. *Exhibited*: PAFA; Herron AI; CM; Hoosier Salon; Richmond A. Gal.; Ball State T. Col.; Indiana Univ.; North Dakota Col.; Dayton AI; Louisville, Ky.; Terry AI, and many other exhs. including one-man. *Position*: Dir., Instr., Circle A. Acad., Indianapolis, Ind.

MESSER, THOMAS M.—
Museum Director, **Cr., W., L., Hist.**
Institute of Contemporary Arts, 230 The Fenway, Boston 15, Mass.; h. 342 Beacon St., Boston 15, Mass.

B. Bratislava, Czechoslovakia, Feb. 9, 1920. *Studied*: Thiel Col., Greenville, Pa.; Boston Univ., B.A.; Sorbonne, Paris, France; Harvard Univ., M.A.; FMA. *Member*: AAMus.; F., Belgian-American Edu. Soc., 1953. Contributor to museum bulletins, catalogs, professional journals; Art in America. Completed survey and published report on Puerto Rican cultural projects upon invitation of Economic Development Administration in San Juan, P.R., 1954. Co-author: "Nipponism," Inst. Contemp. A. publ. *Positions*: Dir., Roswell Mus., Roswell, N.M., 1949-52; Asst. Dir., in charge of National Exhibitions Program, 1952-53, Dir. Exhibitions, 1953-55, Dir., 1955-56, American Federation of Arts, New York, N.Y.; Dir., Inst. Contemp. A., Boston, Mass., 1956- ; Dir., FA, Boston A. Festival, 1957- .

MESSERSMITH, FRED LAWRENCE—*Educator,* **P.**
Art Department, West Virginia Wesleyan College; h. 58 Boggess St., Buckhannon, W. Va.

B. Sharon, Pa., Apr. 3, 1924. *Studied*: Ohio Wesleyan Univ., M.A., B.F.A.; Ohio State Univ. *Member*: AWS; Ohio WC Soc.; All. A. W. Va.; CAA; AFA. *Awards*: prizes, All. A. W. Va., 1958; Clarksburg A. Center, 1954, 1958; Oglebay Inst., 1956, 1957; Ohio WC Soc., 1955; Butler Inst. Am. A., 1956, 1957; AWS, 1958. *Work*: Daywood A. Gal., Lewisburg, W. Va.; Ohio Univ. Mus. *Exhibited*: AWS, 1955, 1958 (traveling); Columbus A. Lg.; All. A. Am., 1957; Butler Inst. Am. A., 1951, 1952; "Religion and Man" exh., Washington (D.C.) Cathedral, 1957; Ohio WC Soc., 1954, 1955, 1956; State Regional, Bristol, Va., 1950-1954; Ohio Drawing exh., 1951-1953; Ohio Valley, 1951, 1954; Clarksburg, 1954-1958; All. A., Charleston, 1952-1958; one-man: Baker Univ., Baldwin, Kans., 1957; Chancellor Hotel, Parkersburg, 1957; Clarksburg A. Center, 1957; Laskin Gal., Charleston, 1957; Chatham Col., Pittsburgh, 1958; Barzansky Gal., N.Y., 1957. Contributor illus. to La Revue Moderne, Paris; Motive. Lectures: Landmarks in American Painting. *Position*: Assoc. Prof. A., West Virginia Wesleyan College, Buckhannon, W. Va., 1949- .

MESSICK, BENJAMIN NEWTON (BEN)—
Painter, Lith., **T., L.**
133 St. Joseph Ave., Long Beach 3, Cal.

B. Strafford, Mo., Jan. 9, 1901. *Studied*: Chouinard AI, and with F. Tolles Chamberlin, Clarence Hinkle, Pruett Carter. *Member*: Long Beach AA (Hon.); Laguna Beach AA; Cal. A. Cl.; F., Royal Soc. A., London, England; AFA. *Awards*: prizes, Los A. County Fair, 1925; PAFA, 1927; Fla. Southern Col., 1952; Seton Hall Univ., 1958. *Work*: Los A. Mus. A.; SFMA; U.S. Nat. Mus.; Smithsonian Inst.; Strafford (Mo.) Consolidated Schools; Springfield Mus. A.; Fla. Southern Col.; KWTO radio station, Springfield, Mo.; murals, Wiggins Trade

Sch., Cal. State Bldg., Hall of Records, all in Los A. *Exhibited:* Albany Inst. Hist. & A., 1943; LC, 1945; MMA, 1942; Carnegie Inst., 1941; NAD, 1945; Stendahl Gal., 1938-1940; Los A. Mus. A., 1943; Phila. Pr. Cl., 1943; Long Beach, 1955; SAGA, 1947; City of Los A., 1947; Grumbacher traveling exh., 1952, 1954, 1955; Fla. Southern Col., 1952; Cal. A. Cl., 1952; San Diego, Cal., 1952; Grand Central A. Gal., 1958; one-man: Los A. Mus. A., 1935; Chouinard AI, 1941; SFMA, 1942; Springfield Mus. A., 1943, 1948; Santa Barbara Mus. A., 1945, 1948; U.S. Nat. Mus., 1944; Nelson Gal. A., 1945; Pasadena AI, 1946; deYoung Mem. Mus., 1947; La Jolla A. Center, 1947; Palos Verde Gal., 1947; Long Beach AA, 1948, 1950; Drury Col., 1948; San Diego Sch. FA, La Jolla, 1948, 1951; San Diego FA Gal., 1950; South Pasadena A. Gal., 1950; Crocker A. Gal., 1950, 1957; Illinois State Mus., 1951; Decatur A. Center, 1951; Davenport Mun. A. Gal., 1951; Peoria A. Center, 1952; New Mexico A. Lg., 1952; Laguna Beach, 1952; Fresno A. Center, 1957; Long Beach Mus. A., 1957; San Pedro AA, 1958; Norton Gal. A., 1953; Glendale AA, 1953; Orange County AA, 1954; Palos Verde A. Gal., 1954, 1958 (3-man). *Position:* Pres., Long Beach Cultural A. Assn.; Instr. FA, Messick Studios, Long Beach, Cal. Lectures widely in California; 5 State lecture tour and demonstrations, 1956.

MESSICK, MRS. BEN. *See Hay, Velma*

MESTROVIC, IVAN—*Sculptor*
Notre Dame University, Notre Dame, Ind.; h. 214 East Pokagon St., South Bend 17, Ind.

B. Vrpolje, Croatia, Yugoslavia, Aug. 15, 1883. *Member:* Nat. Inst. A. & Let.; NSS; Inst. A. & Science in Belgium, Scotland, Austria, Germany, Roumania, Czechoslovakia, Yugoslavia. *Awards:* Hon. Ph.D., Wesleyan Univ., Ohio and Ill.; Syracuse Univ.; Colgate Univ.; Notre Dame Univ., 1955; Marquette Univ., 1955; D. Let., Columbia Univ., 1956; Legion of Honor, Paris, France, 1940; medals, Am. Acad. A. & Let.; Assumption Col., Windsor, Ont., Canada; Arch. Lg., 1955. *Work:* Tate Gal., London; Edinburgh, Scotland; BM; AIC; Rochester, N.Y.; Detroit, Mich.; Colgate Univ.; Syracuse Mus. FA; Buffalo, N.Y.; Victoria & Albert Mus., London; Musee des Beaux-Arts, Brussels; Leeds (Eng.) A. Gal.; Birmingham (Eng.) A. Gal.; CAM; Los A. Mus. A.; Museo, Montevideo; War Mus., Montreal; Mus. A., Toronto; Madrid, Barcelona, Spain; Belgrade, Rome, Florence, and in many churches abroad; monuments in: Miami and St. Augustine, Fla.; Honolulu; St. Louis, Mo.; Rochester, Minn.; Winnetka, Ill.; St. Anthony's Col., Oxford, Eng.; and in Yugoslavia. *Exhibited:* one-man (since 1947): Pittsfield, Mass.; Colgate Univ.; Syracuse Univ.; Buffalo, N.Y.; Dayton, Ohio; Washington, D.C.; Toronto, Ottawa and Montreal, Canada; Notre Dame, Ind.; Roswell Mus., N.M.; Mus. FA of Houston; DMFA; El Paso and Lubbock, Tex.; Am. Acad. A. & Lets; MMA, 1947, and others. Author: "Dennoch Will Ich Hoffen," 1945; "The Life of Christ" (10 reproductions, 1949). *Position:* Prof. S. Notre Dame Univ., Ind.

METCALF, ROBERT MARION—
Stained Glass Designer, P., E., L.
Springfield Pike, Yellow Springs, Ohio

B. Springfield, Ohio, Dec. 23, 1902. *Studied:* Columbus (Ohio) A. Sch.; Wittenberg Col.; PAFA. *Award:* Cresson traveling scholarship, PAFA, 1924. *Work:* Dayton AI (coll. 10,000 color slides of European stained glass); stained glass windows; St. James Chapel, Cathedral of St. John the Divine, N.Y.; St. Paul's Sch., Concord, N.H., etc. Lectures: Stained Glass. *Position:* Prof., Chm., Creative A. Dept., Antioch Col., Yellow Springs, Ohio, 1945- .

METZ, FRANK R.—*Painter*
760 West End Ave., New York 25, N.Y.; also, Mt. Pleasant, N.J.

B. Philadelphia, Pa., July 3, 1925. *Studied:* PMSch. A., with Martinelli; ASL, with Will Barnet, Nahum Tschacbasov; New School, with Camilo Egas. *Work:* Olsen Fnd.; Rosenwald Coll. *Exhibited:* PAFA, 1947, 1948, 1953, 1954; MMA, 1952; Washington Univ., St. Louis, 1958; Little International traveling exh., 1957; Ellen Donovan Gal., Phila., 1952; Parma Gal., N.Y., 1955-1958; Phila. Pr. Cl., 1947, 1948, 1952; one-man: Parma Gal., 1955, 1958.

METZL, ERVINE—*Illustrator, Cart., Des., T., W.*
20 Park Ave.; h. 135 East 39th St., New York 16, N.Y.

B. Chicago, Ill., May 28, 1899. *Studied:* AIC. *Member:* SI; P.O. Stamp Advisory Com. *Work:* Morgan Lib., N.Y.; Kensington Mus., London, England. Contributor to art magazines. I., books for Limited Editions Club. *Position:* Instr., Pratt Institute; Columbia Univ.

MEURER, ALBERT JOHN THEODORE (A. J. TED)—
Graphic Designer, I., P., L.
P.O. Box 282, St. Augustine, Fla.

B. Louisville, Ky., Oct. 7, 1887. *Studied:* PAFA; Corcoran Sch. A. *Member:* Wash. AC; Landscape Cl. Wash. *Awards:* prizes, Landscape Cl. Wash., 1938, 1939; Soc. Indp. A., 1933. *Work:* Lightner Mus., St. Augustine, Fla. *Exhibited:* Soc. Wash. A.; Wash. AC; Landscape Cl. Wash.; Soc. Indp. A., 1933-1946. Author, I., "Silhouettes" (Colonial Sketches). Contributor to: government & private publications. Lectures: Shrines of George Washington.

MEWHINNEY, ELLA K.—*Painter*
Holland, Tex.

B. Nelsonville, Tex., June 21, 1891. *Studied:* Texas Presbyterian Col., B.S.; ASL; Broadmoor A. Acad.; & with Bridgman, Davey, Reid. *Member:* Texas FA Assn. (Trustee). *Awards:* prizes, SSAL, 1928, 1931; Davis competition, San Antonio, Tex., 1929. *Work:* Witte Mem. Mus. *Exhibited:* SSAL; Texas FA Assn.; Texas Centennial. Lectures on Art.

MEYER, ALVIN (WILLIAM) (CARL)—*Sculptor*
Green Garden Studio, Monee, Ill.

B. Bartlett, Ill., Dec. 31, 1892. *Studied:* Maryland Inst.; PAFA; Am. Acad. in Rome. *Awards:* Cresson traveling scholarship, PAFA; Rhinehart F., Peabody Inst.; Prix de Rome. *Work:* Peabody Inst., Maryland Inst., Balt.; Chicago Daily News Bldg.; Chicago Bd. of Trade; Ohio State Office Bldg., Columbus; Archives Bldg., Springfield, Ill.; Natural Hist. Bldg., Urbana, Ill.

MEYER, FREDERICK H.—*Educator, Des.*
1635 East 22nd St., Oakland 6, Cal.

B. Hamelin, Germany, Nov. 6, 1872. *Studied:* Royal A. Sch., Berlin, A.B.; PMSchIA; Columbia Univ.; Univ. Cincinnati. *Member:* Faculty Cl., Univ. California. *Awards:* med., Pan-Pacific Exp., 1915; hon. deg., D.F.A., Cal. Col. A. & Crafts, 1954. *Exhibited:* St. Louis Exp., 1903, 1904; Pan-Pacific Exp., 1915; GGE, 1939. Contributor to School Arts magazine; Sierra Educational News. Lectures: Contemporary & Historic Architecture & Interior Design. *Position:* Founder, Pres., Cal. Col. A. & Crafts, Oakland, Cal., 1907-44, Pres. Emeritus, 1944- .

MEYER, FRED(ERICK) ROBERT—*Painter, T., S.*
Rochester Institute of Technology, 65 Plymouth Ave., South, Rochester, N.Y.; h. 17 Church St., Scottsville, N.Y.

B. Oshkosh, Wis., Dec. 20, 1922. *Studied:* Wisconsin State T. Col.; Univ. Wisconsin; Harvard Grad. Sch.; Cranbrook Acad. A., B.F.A., M.F.A. *Awards:* F., Ford Fnd., 1955; Rochester Finger Lakes Exh., 1954; Rochester, 1958. *Work:* Cranbrook Acad. Mus.; Munson-Williams-Proctor Inst. *Exhibited:* BM, 1952; AIC, 1949, 1951; WMAA, 1953; PAFA, 1952; Detroit Inst. A., 1952; Phila. A. All.; Walker A. Center; Univ. Nebraska; Syracuse Mus. FA, 1957; Rochester Finger Lakes, 1957, 1958; N.Y. State Fair, 1958; one-man: Midtown Gal., 1947, 1948. Contributor to Craft Horizons with article, "A Definition of Design"; Illus., Time magazine cover, Christmas 1950. *Position:* Instr., Kansas City AI, 1946-47; Sch. for American Craftsmen of the Rochester Inst. Technology, Rochester, N.Y., 1949-1958; Dept. A. & Des., Rochester Institute of Technology, 1958- .

MEYER, HERBERT—*Painter*
Dorset, Vt.

B. New York, N.Y., Mar. 6, 1882. *Studied:* ASL, with Twachtman, Mowbray, DuMond. *Member:* NA; SC; Southern Vermont A. *Work:* AGAA; WMAA; MMA; Wood A. Gal., Montpelier, Vt.; Fleming Mus. A., Burlington, Vt.; Ft. Worth Mus. A.; Canajoharie Mus.; NAD.*

MEYER, WILLIAM C.—*Painter*

575 North Vine St., Hazleton, Pa.

B. Freeland, Pa., Oct. 14, 1903. *Studied*: Syracuse Univ., B.F.A.; PAFA; Univ. Pennsylvania, M.A. in Edu. *Member*: AWCS; Central Inst. A. & Des., London, England. *Awards*: F., PAFA. *Exhibited*: PAFA, 1938, 1939; Wanamaker Exh., Phila., Pa., 1934; Boyer Gal., Phila., Pa., 1934; AWCS, 1939; Roerich Gal., Phila., Pa., 1939 (one-man); AFA traveling exh., 1941; Peter Jones Gal., London, England, 1944.*

MEYEROWITZ, WILLIAM—*Etcher, P.*

54 West 74th St., New York 23, N.Y.

B. Russia. *Studied*: NAD; & with F. C. Jones, Douglas Volk. *Member*: ANA; Audubon A.; SAE; Am. Color Pr. Soc.; Soc. Indp. A.; Gloucester SA; North Shore AA; Cape Ann Soc. Mod. A.; All. A. Am. *Awards*: prizes, Audubon A., 1958; Seton Hall Univ., 1958; North Shore AA, 1932, 1939, 1957; Am. Contemporary A. of New England, 1944; Currier Gal. A., 1942; Lib. Cong., 1943, 1944; Audubon A., 1955. *Work*: PMG; BM; U.S. Nat. Mus.; BMFA; Concord Mus. A.; Bibliotheque Nationale, Paris; Harvard Univ. Law Sch.; N.Y. Pub. Lib.; MMoDA; Brandeis Univ.; Jewish Mus., N.Y.; Tel-Aviv Mus., Israel; Cooper Union; State House, Albany; Fitchburg Mus. A.; Bezalel Mus., Jerusalem; Yale Univ.; Col. City of N.Y.; Univ. Pennsylvania; J. B. Speed Mem. Mus.; Boston Univ.; Herron AI; Univ. Kentucky; Harvard Cl.; MMA; Albany Inst. Hist. & A.; Lib. Cong.; Currier Gal. A.; mural, USPO, Clinton, Conn.; etc. *Exhibited*: CGA, 1935, 1941, 1945; PAFA, 1935, 1936, 1940; WMA, 1935, 1937, 1939, 1945; AIC, 1935, 1936, 1940; WMAA, 1936; Toledo Mus. A.; NAD; MMA; Carnegie Inst.; Dayton AI; Am. Acad. A. & Let.; BMFA; BMA; etc. Contributor to: The Menorah Journal.

MEYEROWITZ, MRS. WILLIAM. See Bernstein, Theresa F.

MEYERS, ROBERT WILLIAM—*Illustrator*

P.O. Box 328, Lamington Road, Bedminster, N.J.

B. New York, N.Y., June 17, 1919. *Studied*: NAD, with Ivan Olinsky; Grand Central A. Sch.; Traphagen Sch. Fashion. *Member*: SI. *Awards*: prize, A. Dir. Cl., Chicago, for one of "100 Best Posters for 1955." *Exhibited*: one-man: SI, 1955-56. Illus., "Prince of the Range," 1949; "The Winning Dive," 1950; "The Base Stealer," 1951; "The Mysterious Caboose," 1950; "The Haunted Hut," 1950; "Jockie," 1951, and other children's books. Contributor illus. to: Sat. Eve. Post; True; Argosy; Readers Digest.

MICHELSON, LEO—*Painter, I., E.*

58 West 57th St., New York 19, N.Y.

B. Riga, Latvia, May 12, 1887. *Studied*: Academie of FA, Petrograd; Academie Julian, Paris. *Member*: AEA; CAA. *Awards*: Knight of the French Legion of Honor; Latvian Order "Pour le Merite." *Work*: Musee de l'Arte Moderne, Paris; Tel-Aviv Mus., Israel; Trondheim, Norway. *Exhibited*: Carnegie Inst. Illus., "Fox Fables"; "Alsacien Medieval," and others. *Position*: Instr., Drawing, City Col., Adult Edu., New York, N.Y.

MICHENER, EDWARD C.—*Painter, I., Des.*

1007 North Front St.; Harrisburg, Pa.; h. 333 North 25th St., Camp Hill, Pa.

B. Duncannon, Pa., Oct. 25, 1913. *Studied*: PMSchIA; & with Thornton Oakley, Henry C. Pitz. *Member*: Harrisburg AA. *Awards*: prizes, Harrisburg AA, 1934, 1936, 1939, 1945, 1955. *Work*: Pennsylvania State Col. *Exhibited*: PAFA, 1936-1938; Harrisburg AA, 1934-1955; Cumberland Valley A., 1942, 1943, 1945.*

MICHNICK, DAVID—*Sculptor*

78 St. Marks Place, New York 3, N.Y.

B. Russia, Oct. 4, 1893. *Studied*: AIC; BAID. *Member*: S. Gld. *Work*: Queensboro Hall, N.Y.; Washington H.S.; Adm. Farragut H.S., Bronx, N.Y., and in private collections. *Exhibited*: GGE, 1939; WFNY 1939; MMA; S. Gld., annually; NAD; PAFA, and others.

MIDDELDORF, ULRICH ALEXANDER—*Educator, Mus. Cur., W., L.*

1410 East 56th St., Chicago 37, Ill.

B. Stassfurt, Germany, June 23, 1901. *Studied*: Univ. Berlin, Ph.D.; Univ. Giessen; Univ. Munich. *Member*: CAA; Medieval Acad. Am.; AAMus; Midwestern A. Conference; Soc. for Contemporary A., Chicago; Am. Soc. for Aesthetics; Renaissance Soc., Univ. Chicago. *Awards*: F., Kunsthistorisches Inst., Florence, Italy, 1925-1926. Co-Author: "Medals and Plaquettes from the Sigmund Morgenroth Collection," AIC, 1944; Author: "Raphael's Drawings," 1945. Lectures: History of Art. *Position*: Ed. Bd., Art in America; Ed. Bd., The Art Bulletin; Asst. Prof., 1935-38, Assoc. Prof., 1938-41, Prof., 1941- , Univ. Chicago; Hon. Cur. S., AIC, Chicago, Ill., 1941- .*

MIDDLETON, SAMUEL M.—*Painter, C.*

704 Sixth Ave., New York 10, N.Y.

B. New York, N.Y., Apr. 2, 1927. *Awards*: Scholarship, Instituto de Allende, Mexico, 1956; Scholarship from Koinonia Fnd., Balt., Md., 1957. *Work*: Sunken Meadow Fnd., L.I., N.Y. *Exhibited*: WMAA, 1958; CGA, 1958; Univ. Illinois, 1959; Provincetown A. Festival, 1958; Art: USA, 1958; Contemporary A. Gal., N.Y., 1958; Indp A., Gal., 1958; N.Y. City Center, 1955; Artists Gal., N.Y., 1958; N.Y. Pub. Lib., 1957; Morris Gal., N.Y., 1947, 1955; Marino Gal., 1956-1958; Sunken Meadow Fnd., 1958.

MIDENER, WALTER—*Sculptor, C., T.*

245 East Kirby St., Detroit 2, Mich.; h. 80 Moss Ave., Highland Park 3, Mich.

B. Germany, Oct. 11, 1912. *Studied*: Berlin Acad. F. & App. A.; Wayne Univ., M.A. *Member*: Michigan Sculpture Soc. *Awards*: prizes, Tiffany grant, 1940; Honolulu, T.H., 1943; Detroit Inst. A., 1950, 1952, 1954, 1955. *Work*: Detroit Inst. A.; WMAA; House of Living Judaism, N.Y.; Suburban Temple, Cleveland. *Exhibited*: PAFA, 1948, 1951, 1953, 1958; PMA, 1949; WMAA, 1950, 1951, 1953, 1955, 1956; MMA, 1951; MMoDA, 1950; John Herron AI, 1951; Detroit Inst. A., 1946-1958; Cranbrook Acad. A., 1950, 1953. *Position*: Instr., A. Sch., Soc. A. & Crafts, Detroit, Mich., 1946- ; Visiting Instr., Cleveland Inst. A., 1955 (summer).

MIELZINER, JO—*Stage Designer*

1 West 72nd St., New York 23, N.Y.

B. Paris, France. *Studied*: ASL; NAD; PAFA. *Member*: Scenic A. Un. *Awards*: 2 Cresson traveling scholarships, PAFA; hon. deg., D.F.A., Fordham Univ.; awards for set designs, 5 Donaldson awards; 3 Antoinette Perry awards. *Work*: Stage settings: 2 operas, Metropolitan Opera Assn.; Tudor's Ballet "Pillar of Fire," Ballet Theatre; over 225 musical and dramatic productions, New York, N.Y., 1924-1958. Commissioned by U.S. State Dept. to design setting for United Nations Conference, San Francisco, Cal., 1945. *Exhibited*: MMoDA; Mus. City of N.Y. Contributor to Theatre Arts magazine, New York Times. Lectures: Theatre Design.

MIKELL, MINNIE (ROBERTSON) (Mrs. Alexander B.)—*Painter, Comm. A., Des., T.*

71 East Bay, Charleston 1, S.C.

B. Charleston, S.C. *Studied*: with Alfred Hutty, Ambrose Webster, Edmund Kinzinger, Frank S. Herring, Edward Shorter. *Member*: Carolina AA; Gld. South Carolina A.; NAC; Charleston A. Gld. *Exhibited*: 1953-55: NAC; Carolina AA; Gld. South Carolina A.*

MILCINOVIC, DESHA A.—*Painter, Ser., Des., Lith., T.*

132 West 58th St., New York 19, N.Y.

B. Zagreb, Yugoslavia, Mar. 3, 1914. *Studied*: in Europe; & with Ivan Mestrovic. *Member*: AAPL; Greenwich SA. *Work*: Greenwich (Conn.) Lib.; Witte Mem. Mus., San Antonio, Tex. *Exhibited*: AAPL, 1940-1942; A. Dir. Cl., traveling exh., 1930-1936; Arden Gal., 1943; Dance International, N.Y., 1940; Witte Mem. Mus., 1944 (one-man); Kansas City, Mo.; Oakland A. Gal., 1943; Dallas Mus. FA, 1944; Lib. Cong., 1946; Morgan Lib., New Haven, Conn., 1946; Greenwich, Conn., 1946. I., "Adventures in Monochrome."

MILES, JEANNE PATTERSON—*Painter*
333 West 18th St., New York 11, N.Y.

B. Baltimore, Md. *Studied*: George Washington Univ., B.A.; Phillips Mem. Gal., Wash., D.C.; Grande Chaumiere, Paris; Atelier Marcel Gromaire, Paris; N.Y. Univ. *Member*: Abstract A. of Am.; NSMP. *Awards*: Traveling scholarship, 1937-1939. *Work*: mural (100 portraits) Ramon's, Wash., D.C.; Kentile Co., N.Y. and Phila., Pa.; Santa Barbara Mus. *Exhibited*: Salon des Independents, Paris, 1938; MMA, 1942; Walker A. Gal., 1952; Los Angeles State Fair, 1953; CGA, 1955; Stable Gal., N.Y., 1953-1955; Intl. Drawing Exh., Greece, 1954; Religious Art Exh., Columbia Univ. Seminary, 1954-1955; Betty Parsons Gal., N.Y., 1956 and 3 one-man exhs.; Yale Univ., 1957; Am. Abstract A., 1958; N.Y. Coliseum, 1958. Art reviewer, Pictures on Exhibit, 1955. Lectures: Contemporary Art; Early Moderns, etc. *Position*: Instr., Moravian Col., Pa.; Asst. Prof. A., Oberlin Col., Oberlin, Ohio; Private Sch., New York, N.Y.

MILHOUS, KATHERINE—*Author, Artist, Des.*
1534 Pine St., Philadelphia 2, Pa.

B. Philadelphia, Pa., Nov. 27, 1894. *Studied*: PMSchIA; PAFA; & with Thornton Oakley, Walter Hancock, Charles Grafly. *Member*: AIGA; PBC; Phila. WC Cl. *Awards*: Cresson traveling scholarship, PAFA; Caldecott award, 1950 ("The Egg Tree"); Stewardson award in sculpture; book design selected by AIGA. *Exhibited*: PAFA; Phila. A. All.; Phila. Plastic Cl.; WFNY 1939. Author, I., Des., "Snow Over Bethlehem," 1945; "The First Christmas Crib," 1944; "Herodia, The Lovely Puppet," 1942; "Lovina," 1940; "Patrick and the Golden Slippers," 1951; "Appolonia's Valentine," 1954; "With Bells On," 1955, & others. Contributor to: The Horn Book. *Position*: Book Des., Juvenile Books, Charles Scribner's Sons, 1944-46.

MILLBOURN, M(ELVILLE) VAUGHN—
Designer, T., I., Comm. A.
28 East Jackson Blvd.; h. 5311 Glenwood Ave., Chicago, Ill.

B. Charlotte, Mich., Sept. 8, 1893. *Studied*: AIC. *Member*: A. Gld. Chicago; 27 Chicago Des.; The Woodcut Soc. *Exhibited*: Northwest Pr. M., 1942, 1943; Phila. Pr. Cl., 1943, 1944; Wichita AA; Chicago A. Gld.; Soc. Typographic A., annually. *Position*: Instr., Lettering & Advertising Layout, Chicago Acad. FA, Chicago, Ill., 1928- . Botanical illus. for Encyclopaedia Britannica.*

MILLER, BARSE—*Painter, E.*
190 Bayview Rd., Plandome Manor, L.I., N.Y.

B. New York, N.Y., Jan. 24, 1904. *Studied*: NAD; PAFA; and with Henry Snell, Hugh Breckenridge. *Member*: NA; Audubon A.; Cal. WC Soc.; AWS; F., PAFA. *Awards*: F., PAFA; Cresson traveling scholarships, PAFA, 1922, 1923, medal, 1936; medal, prize, Cal. A. Cl., 1929; prizes, Los A. Mus. A., 1932; Cal. WC Soc., 1933, 1935; Phila. WC Cl., 1938; Guggenheim F., 1946; AWS, 1950, 1954, 1956; NAD, 1955. *Work*: San Diego FA Soc.; PAFA; Wood A. Gal., Montpelier, Vt.; Hackley A. Gal.; Los A. Mus. A.; Denver A. Mus.; AIC; Butler AI; PMA; BM; MMA; Glasgow Mus., Scotland; Nat. Gal., Melbourne, Australia; U.S. War Dept.; Hyde Park Mem. Lib. *Exhibited*: nationally. I., "Ballads of Eldorado," 1940. Series of feature articles, Life and Fortune magazines. *Position*: Assoc. Prof., Dept. A., Queens Col., Flushing, L.I., N.Y.

MILLER, BENJAMIN—*Printmaker*
131 East Third St., Cincinnati 2, Ohio

B. Cincinnati, Ohio, July 24, 1877. *Studied*: MIT, B.S.; Cincinnati A. Sch., with Frank Duveneck. *Member*: Cincinnati Professional A. *Awards*: prize, Tri-State Print Exh., 1945. *Work*: CM; Minneapolis Inst. A.; Bibliotheque Nationale, Paris, France. *Exhibited*: Chinese Pr. Cl., 1932; AIC, 1930; Phila. A. All.; Nat. Exh., Contemp. Prints, Sweden, 1937; Nat. Exh. Lith. and Woodcuts, N.Y., 1937; NAD, 1942; AFA, 1929; Victoria and Albert Mus.; Bibliotheque Nationale, Paris, 1928; CM; CMA, 1929; Carnegie Inst.; Norton Gal. A.*

MILLER, DONNA (Mrs. Ernest W.)—*Lithographer, P.*
4075 North Downer Ave., Milwaukee 11, Wis.

B. Macon, Mich., July 15, 1885. *Studied*: with Robert von Neumann, Gerrit Sinclair, Emily Groom. *Member*: Milwaukee Pr. M.; Wis. P. & S.; NAWA. *Awards*: prizes, Milwaukee AI, 1937, 1940, 1943, 1946, 1955; Wis. State Fair, 1941-1944. *Exhibited*: N.Y. WC Cl., 1937, 1939; PAFA, 1936; Phila. A. All., 1937; Grand Rapids A. Gal., 1940; NAD, 1943; Albany Inst. Hist. & A., 1943; Lib. Cong., 1945; Milwaukee AI, 1936, 1937, 1939, 1940, 1943-1946, 1949-1955; Renaissance Soc., Univ. Chicago, 1943; Detroit Inst. A., 1936, 1937; Madison, Wis., 1936, 1942, 1943, 1945, 1949, 1952; Denver A. Mus., 1947-1949; SAM, 1947.

MILLER, DOROTHY CANNING—*Museum Curator, W.*
Museum of Modern Art, 11 West 53rd St., New York 19, N.Y.

B. Hopedale, Mass. *Studied*: Smith Col., B.A.; N.Y. Univ. Ed., "Charles Sheeler," 1939; "Romantic Painting in America," 1943; "12 Americans," 1942; "14 Americans," 1946; "15 Americans," 1952; "Americans," 1956; "The New American Painting," 1958, & others. Co-Author: "Masters of Popular Painting," 1938. Arranged many exhibitions, MModA, 1936-58. *Position*: Asst. to Dir., 1934, Asst. & Assoc. Cur., Painting & Sculpture, 1935-43, Cur., Painting & Sculpture, MModA, New York, N.Y., 1943-47; Cur. of the Mus. Collections, 1947- .

MILLER, DOROTHY ELIZABETH (Mrs. Joseph A. Goethe)—*Painter*
706 Grove Acre, Pacific Grove, Cal.

B. Ambridge, Pa., Mar. 3, 1927. *Studied*: Finch Warshaw Sch. A.; Santa Monica City Col., AA; Univ. Cal. at Los Angeles. *Member*: AWS; Pasadena A. Mus. *Awards*: prizes, SFMA, 1958; Monterey County, 1958. *Exhibited*: Cal. WC Soc., 1952, 1953; Pacific Coast Biennial, 1955; Santa Paula, 1954, 1955, 1956; Flower Show A. Exh., 1954; Aquiana Annual, 1955; Orange County Exh., 1957; Los A. Mus. A., 1957; Oakland A. Mus., 1957; SFMA, 1958; Monterey County Exh., 1958.

MILLER, ELIZABETH SLAUGHTER—*Painter, T.*
Art Department, Drake University; h. 1238 29th St., Des Moines 11, Iowa

B. Lincoln, Neb., Apr. 24, 1929. *Studied*: Univ. Nebraska, B.F.A., with Rudy Pozzatti, Walter Meigs, Kady Faulkner; Des Moines A. Center, with Louis Bouche; Univ. Colorado, with Carl Morris. *Awards*: prizes, Lincoln A. Gld., 1951; Iowa State Fair, 1956; Des Moines A. Center, 1956, 1958; Des Moines Womens Cl., 1958; Sioux City A. Center, 1958; Mulvane A. Mus., Topeka, 1958. *Work*: Lincoln A. Gld.; Lutheran Life of Christ Coll., Des Moines A. Center; Mulvane A. Mus. *Exhibited*: Norfolk Mus. A., 1951; Wichita AA, 1953; Terry AI, 1952; Exh. Western Art, 1952; Nelson Gal. A., 1951, 1952, 1954, 1958; Joslyn Mem. Mus., 1952, 1954, 1956; Friends of Art, Manhattan, Kans., 1952, 1954, 1958; Des Moines A. Center (Iowa Artists), 1955-1958; Mulvane Mus. A., 1956-1958; Springfield, Mo., 1957; Iowa May Show, Sioux City A. Center, 1952-1954; Iowa State Fair, 1952-1958. *Positions*: Dir. A., Washington Community Center, Waterloo, Iowa, 1953-55; Edu. Co-ordinator, Des Moines A. Center, 1955-56; Instr. A., Art Dept., Drake Univ., Des Moines, Iowa, 1956- .

MILLER, EVYLENA NUNN (Mrs.)—*Painter, I., L., T.*
13141 Sandhurst Place, Santa Ana, Cal.

B. Mayfield, Kan., July 4, 1888. *Studied*: Pomona Col., A.B.; Univ. California; ASL; & abroad. *Member*: NAWA; Laguna Beach AA; Women Painters of the West (Pres. Emeritus, 1946-); A. of the Southwest; Los A. AA.; Fnd. Western A. *Awards*: prizes, Cal. State Fair, 1925; Woman's Cl., Hollywood, Cal., 1930; Festival All. A., 1934; Los A. Mus. A., 1937; Laguna Beach AA, 1953; Death Valley Exh., 1954. *Work*: Smithsonian Inst.; Pomona Col.; Women's Christian Col., Tokyo & Kobe, Japan; Chinese YMCA, San F., Cal.; First Presbyterian Church, Santa Ana, Cal.; Bowers Mem. Mus., Santa Ana, Cal. *Exhibited*: NGA, 1928; Biltmore Salon; Ainslie Gal.; Kievitz Gal.; De Vannes Gal.; Los A. Mus. A.; San Diego FA Soc.; Bowers Mem. Mus.; Palace Legion Honor; Wichita AA; Ebell Cl., Los A.; Long Beach Mun. A. Gal. I., Pomona Col. publications; "Travel Tree"; "Granite and Sagebrush," 1954. Lectures: Art and Travel. *Position*: Dir., Sec., Bowers Mem. Fnd., Santa Ana, Cal.

MILLER, MRS. GUSTAV A. See Gabriele, Gabrielle

MILLER, IRIS ANDREWS—Portrait Painter
184 Vendome Rd., Grosse Pointe Farms 36, Mich.

B. Ada, Ohio, Mar. 28, 1881. *Studied*: with Chase, Henri, Breckenridge. *Member*: AFA; Detroit Soc. Women Painters; Grosse Pointe AA. *Awards*: prizes, Detroit Inst. A., 1923; med., Scarab Cl., 1929. *Work*: Detroit Inst. A.; San Diego FA Soc.; Univ. Michigan; Wayne County Court Bldg., Detroit; Law Club, Ann Arbor; Kenton (Ohio) Pub. Lib.; Topeka Church House; Ann Arbor Hospital; Detroit City Bldg.; Kenton Hospital; Mich. Mutual Ins. Bldg., Detroit.*

MILLER, I(SABELLE) LAZARUS—Painter, C., E.
6238 North 11th St., Philadelphia 41, Pa.

B. Philadelphia, Pa., Nov. 27, 1907. *Studied*: PMSchIA; Graphic Sketch Cl.; & with Earl Horter. *Member*: Phila. Pr. Cl.; Phila. A. All.; AAPL; SAGA. *Work*: Atwater Kent Mus. *Exhibited*: PAFA, 1931, 1936, 1942; 100 Prints, 1942; NAD, 1936, 1943, 1944; AIC, 1938; Conn. Acad. FA, 1940; Grand Rapids A. Gal., 1940; AFA traveling exh., 1943-1945; SAGA, 1940-1945; Northwest Pr.M., 1943; Lib. Cong., 1943; Denver A. Mus.; Buffalo Pr. Cl., 1940, 1943; Phila. A. All., annually; Phila. Pr. Cl.

MILLER, JANE (BEACHY)—Illustrator, W.
775 Park Ave., New York, N.Y.

B. Cumberland, Md., Nov. 17, 1906. *Studied*: Md. Inst. FA & Design, and in France. Covers for This Week; Ladies Home Journal; illus. for national magazines. *Award*: gold medal, A. Dir. Cl., 1938. Author, I., "Mogo Mouse," 1932; "Lulu," 1941; "The Ill-Tempered Tiger," 1957; Illus., "A Dog of His Own," 1941; "Thirty-Three Bunn Street," 1952; "Susie and the Ballet Family," 1955, and others.*

MILLER, MRS. J. RUSSELL. See Barton, Loren

MILLER, LEON GORDON—Designer, P., Gr.
1220 Huron Road; h. 14701 South Woodland, Shaker Heights 20, Ohio

B. New York, N.Y., Aug. 3, 1917. *Studied*: New Jersey State T. Col., B.S.; ASL; Newark Sch. F. & Indst. A., C.F.A.; Fawcett A. Sch., and with Bernard Gussow. *Member*: IDI; AEA. *Awards*: prizes, CMA, 1947, 1948, 1950, 1954. *Work*: LC. *Exhibited*: St. Botolph Cl., Boston, 1947; Old Northwest Territory Exh., 1949, 1954; Audubon A, 1947; PAFA, 1949, 1952; LC, 1941, 1943; SAM, 1946, 1949; CMA, 1947-1955; CMA traveling exh., 1948, 1949, 1952-1955; Oakland A. Gal., 1948; Arch. Lg., 1955, gold medal exh., 1956, 1958; Akron AI, 1954, 1955; Hartford Atheneum, 1954; Butler AI, 1947, 1948, 1950, 1954; Jewish Mus., N.Y., 1958; one-man: Norlyst Gal., 1948; Ten-Thirty Gal., Cleveland, 1947; Art Colony, 1955; Cleveland Community Centers, 1955; Cleveland Women's Cl., 1949. *Positions*: Chief Des., Office of Chief of Ordnance, Phila. and Newark, 1941-43; Owner, Indst. Des. Studio, Cleveland, Ohio, 1948- ; Nat. Treas. & Bd. Trustees, IDI; Bd. Trustees, Inter-Society Color Council.

MILLER, MARIE CLARK—Painter, I., W., L.
654 Kenneth Rd., Glendale 2, Cal.

B. Springville, Utah, June 27, 1894. *Studied*: Brigham Young Univ., B.A.; Univ. Utah; Univ. Chicago; Columbia Univ.; AIC; Univ. Cal. at Los Angeles. *Member*: Cal. A. Cl.; AAPL; Nat. Lg. Am. Pen Women. *Awards*: prizes, Utah State Fair; Midland Empire State Fair, Bozeman, Mont.; Iowa State Fair; numerous awards, Glendale AA, 1945-52; Greek Theatre, Los A., 1952-1954; Cal. A. Cl., 1954, 1955; Dixie Col., 1949, 1955 (purchase); Nat. Lecture award, Wash., D.C., 1956; Nat. Lg. Am. Pen Women, 1958; Springville, Utah, 1956. *Work*: Brigham Young Univ.; Dixie Col., St. George, Utah. *Exhibited*: AAPL, 1952-1955; Nat. Lg. Am. Pen Women, 1950, 1952; Greek Theatre annually; Friday Morning Cl., Los A.; Ebell Cl.; Glendale Lib.; Pacific Coast Cl., Long Beach; Women's Univ. Cl.; Los A. City Hall; Springville, Utah; AAPL; Santa Paula, Cal.; de Saisset A. Gal., Santa Clara; Santa Cruz A. Lg.; Carmel Valley Inn; Los A. Pub. Lib.; one-man: Ames, Iowa; Des Moines Pub. Lib.; Salt Lake City A. Center; Stendahl Gal., Los A.; Joslyn Mus A.; Tuesday Cl., Glendale; Pacific Cl., Long Beach; Verdugo Lib.; Inglewood Womens Cl., and others. Author, I., "Holidays in Verse," 1948; "Christmas Blooms," 1949; "Panorama," 1957.

MILLER, MARION E.—Educator
414 14th St.; h. 6301 West 26th Ave., Denver 15, Colo.

B. Pennsylvania. *Studied*: T. Col., Columbia Univ., B.S., M.A.; Alfred Univ., and with Charles Binns, William Zorach. *Member*: Nat. Edu. Assn.; Western AA; Council Assoc., Nat. Com. on A. Edu.; Nat. A. Edu. Assn. Contributor to Nat. Edu. Assn. Bulletin; The Arts Cooperative Report for White House Conference; Design; Junior Arts & Activities, etc. Lectures: Art Education; Travel in Europe and the Mediterranean. *Positions*: Edu. Staff, MMA, 1928-36; Dir. A. Edu., Denver Pub. Sch., 1937- ; Pres. A. Dept., Nat. Edu. Assn., 1943-45; Advisory Comm. on Art Films, for Motion Picture Comm. of Am. Council on Edu.; Adv. Art Panel for Compton's Pictured Encyclopaedia; Edu. Advisor, Denver Art Museum, Denver, Colo.

MILLER, MARSHALL DAWSON (MARK)—Illustrator
168 Concord Ave., Hartsdale, N.Y.

B. Eldorado, Okla., Jan. 2, 1919. *Studied*: Univ. Oklahoma; Chouinard AI, and with Pruett Carter. *Member*: SI. Contributor illus. to: McCalls, Good Housekeeping, Red Book, Cosmopolitan, and other national magazines.

MILLER, MARTHA (WEINBERG)—Painter, C., T.
3 White Pine Lane, Great Neck, N.Y.

B. New York, N.Y., Feb. 18, 1924. *Studied*: Tyler Sch. FA, Temple Univ., B.S., B.F.A.; Hans Hofmann Sch. FA; Universal Sch. Handcrafts; Blumenaw Weaving Workshop. *Member*: NAWA; York State Craftsmen; Women's Nat. Inst. *Work*: Staten Island Mus. A. & Sciences. *Exhibited*: Provincetown A. Festival, 1958; Art:USA, 1958; York State Craftsmen, 1956; NAWA, 1958; Panoras Gal., 1958 (one-man); Washburn FA Center, San Carlos, Cal., 1955; Golde Gal., Great Neck, 1957 (one-man).

MILLER, MILDRED BUNTING—Painter, T., W., L.
Rt. 4, Box 601M, Valley Center, Cal.

B. Philadelphia, Pa., June 21, 1892. *Studied*: PAFA; ASL. *Member*: La Jolla A. Center. *Awards*: F., PAFA; Cresson traveling scholarship, PAFA, 1914, 1915, Mary Smith prize, 1920, 1931; San Diego A. Gld., 1947, 1949; Chester County AA, 1935; Vista, Cal., 1952; San Diego A. Gld., 1952, 1955; Carlsbad-Oceanside A. Lg., 1954, 1955, 1956, 1958; medal, Phila. Plastic Cl., 1937; San Diego County Fair, 1957; San Diego AI, 1958. *Work*: PAFA; F., PAFA; Mississippi AA; Chester County Hist. Soc.; Heyburn (Idaho) H.S.; Kemper Military Sch., Booneville, Mo. *Exhibited*: CGA; NAD; PAFA; BMA; AIC; Detroit Inst. A.; BM; PMG; San Diego FA Gal.; La Jolla A. Center; one-man: Three A. Cl., Wash., D.C.; Friends of Art, Balt.; Lynchburg Col. *Positions*: Instr., Country School of PAFA, 1928-34; Instr., Adult Edu., Escondido and Oceanside, Cal., at present.

MILLER, RALPH R(ILLMAN)—
Assistant Museum Director, P., Des.
Museum of the City of New York, 103rd St. & Fifth Ave., New York, N.Y.; h. 52 Biltmore Ave., Yonkers, N.Y.

B. Wayne, Pa., Dec. 12, 1915. *Studied*: Univ. Washington; Columbia Univ., B.S., and with A. Archipenko. *Member*: Mamaroneck A. Gld.; Westchester A. & Crafts Gld.; AAMus; Northeast Conf. AAMus. (Bd. memb.); Museums Council of New York City. *Award*: prize, Rye Women's Cl., 1958. *Exhibited*: Art:USA, 1958; New School, 1957; Westchester A. & Crafts Gld., 1957; Westchester Womens Cl., 1957; Hudson River Mus.; Village A. Center, and others. Lectures: Traditions of the American Home (Am. Dutch Dec. Arts). Designed installations at the Mus. of the City of New York including: "300 Years of New York Furniture"; "Currier & Ives" (Harry T. Peters Coll.); "The Artist in New York"; "New York Street Scenes" (1852), and others. *Position*: Adv. Bd., Stamford Mus. A. & Nature Center; Asst. Dir., Museum of the City of New York.

MILLER, REEVA (ANNA) (Mrs.)—Painter, C.
217 South Carmelina Ave., Los Angeles 49, Cal.

B. Hollywood, Cal., Nov. 23, 1912. *Studied*: Santa Monica City Col.; Univ. Cal. at Los Angeles. *Member*: Santa Monica AA; California AA; Westwood AA. *Awards*: prizes, Santa Monica AA, 1945, 1946. *Work*: Beth Sholom

Temple, Santa Monica; dome, Al Jolson Memorial, Los A.; stained glass windows; Beth Sholom Temple, Santa Monica; Maarev Temple, Encino, Cal.; Temple Sinai, Oakland, Cal. Des. & decorated religious arks in Temples in Santa Monica, Inglewood, Long Beach and Burbank, Cal., and Camp Schrader, Colo. *Exhibited*: Santa Monica AA; Westwood AA; Los A. AA; California AA. Illus., "Holy Mountain," 1953. *Position*: A. & Crafts Dir., Camp Saratoga, 1953-1958.

MILLET, CLARENCE—*Painter, Et.*
628 Toulouse St.; h. 1231 North Galvez St., New Orleans 19, La.

B. Hahnville, La., Mar. 25, 1897. *Studied*: ASL, with George Bridgman. *Member*: ANA; New Orleans AA; New Orleans A. Lg. *Awards*: med., Miss. AA, 1927; prizes, SSAL, 1928; Benjamin prize, Birmingham, Ala., 1945; La. State Exh., Shreveport, 1939; New Orleans AA, 1941, 1942, med., 1946; La. A. Comm., Baton Rouge, 1946. *Work*: Univ. Southern California; A. Fnd., Corpus Christi, Tex.; Springville (Utah) AA; La. State Gal.; City Hall, New Orleans; La. Polytechnic Inst., Ruston, La. *Exhibited*: NAD, 1943, 1945; WFNY 1939; PAFA, 1927, 1928; AIC, 1929; SAE, 1941; Nat. Exh. Am. A., N.Y., 1937; New Orleans A. Lg., 1925-1946; New Orleans AA, 1925-1946; SSAL, 1922-1946; Miss. AA, 1922-1946; one-man exh.: Currier Gal. A.; Mus. FA of Houston; Delgado Mus. A.; La. A. Comm. Gal.; Mun. A. Gal., Jackson, Miss.; State Exh. Bldg., Shreveport, La.

MILLIGAN, GLADYS—*Painter, W., Hist.*
3400 Dent Place, Northwest, Washington 7, D.C.

Studied: Western Col. for Women, Oxford, Ohio; Westminster Col., New Wilmington, Pa.; PIASch.; Fontainebleau, France, and with George Luks, Andre Lhote (Paris). *Member*: Soc. Wash. A.; Wash. WC Cl.; Wash. A. Cl. *Work*: PC. *Exhibited*: NAWA; one-man: George Washington Univ.; Wash. A. Cl. Contributor to School Arts magazine. *Position*: Instr., Painting & Hist. A., National Cathedral Sch., Washington, D.C., 1931-55.

MILLIKEN, WILLIAM MATHEWSON—
Former Museum Director
Cleveland Museum of Art; h. Wade Park Manor, Cleveland 6, Ohio

B. Stamford, Conn., Sept. 28, 1889. *Studied*: Princeton Univ., A.B., M.F.A.; Western Reserve Univ., D. Humanities; Yale Univ., D.F.A.; Oberlin Col., D.F.A.; Kenyon Col., D.H.L. *Member*: AAMus. (Pres. 1953-57); Am. Ceramic Soc.; Assn. A. Mus. Dir. (Pres. 1946-49); Cleveland Soc. A.; Century Assn.; Archaeological Inst. Am.; CAA; Mediaeval Acad. Am.; Mid-west Mus. Conf.; Royal Soc. A., London; Renaissance Soc. Am. *Awards*: Commander's Cross, Hungarian Order of Meria, 1937; The Cavalierato of the Crown of Italy, 1938; New Sweden Tercentenary medal, 1939; Cross of Chevalier of the Legion of Honor, 1950, Officer, 1955; Ehrenmitglied, Germanisches Nat. Mus., Nuremberg, 1953; Commander of the Civil Order of Alfonso X el Sabio, 1954; Civil Order of Alphonse X, the Wise, Spanish Govt., 1956. Contributor to art magazines and museum bulletins. *Position*: Am. Com. on Renaissance Studies; 1st Vice-Pres., Academie Internationale de la Ceramique, 1957-58; Vice-Pres., International Council of Museums, 1956-58; U.S. Nat. Com. for UNESCO, and Memb. Exec. Comm., 1957-58; Chm., Nat. Com. of ICOM (Vice-Pres.); Consultative Com.; Art Quarterly; Adv. Com., Cleveland Inst. A.; Cur. Dec. A., 1919-1958; Cur. Painting, 1925-30, Dir., 1930-1958, Dir. Emeritus, 1958- , Cleveland Mus. A., Cleveland, Ohio.

MILLIS, CHARLOTTE (MELISSA)—*Sculptor*
829 Laurel Ave., St. Paul, Minn.

B. Palo Alto, Cal., Dec. 23, 1906. *Studied*: Univ. Chicago, Ph.B.; AIC, B.F.A.; Carnegie A. Inst.; Univ. Oregon; Inst. Des., Ill. Inst. Tech., M.S. in A. Edu. *Member*: Soc. Minn. Sculptors; St. Paul Soc. P. & S.; Minnesota AA; AEA; CAA. *Awards*: prizes, Minneapolis Inst. A., 1935, 1936, 1941, 1944; Minn. State Fair, 1942; Walker A. Center, 1944. *Work*: IBM Coll.; Church of the Redeemer, Chicago, Ill. *Exhibited*: AIC, 1935, 1946-1950; WFNY 1939; Oakland A. Gal., 1942; Minneapolis Inst. A., 1935-1937, 1939, 1941, 1942, 1944; St. Paul Gal., 1941-1945, 1956-1958; Univ. Minnesota, 1958; Syracuse

Mus. FA, 1950; Minn. State Fair, 1939, 1942, 1944, 1958. *Position*: Hd. A. Dept., Summit Sch., St. Paul, Minn., 1935-45; A. Instr., Macalester Col., St. Paul, Minn., 1944-45; Asst. Prof., George Williams Col., Chicago, Ill., 1950-55; Visiting L., 1956-57, Asst. Prof., College of St. Catherine, St. Paul, Minn., 1957- .

MILLMAN, EDWARD—*Painter, E., L.*
Woodstock, N.Y.

B. Chicago, Ill., Jan. 1, 1907. *Studied*: AIC, with Leon Kroll, and in Mexico. *Member*: CAA; Woodstock AA; AAUP. *Awards*: Guggenheim F., 1945; prizes, Times Herald A. Fair, Wash., D.C., 1945; Ohio Univ., 1952. *Work*: AIC; MModA; CAM; PAFA; Washington Univ., St. Louis; BM; Butler AI; Clearwater A. Center; IBM; Chrysler War Coll.; Gimbels, Pa.; U.S.Navy; Abbot Laboratories; WMAA; Jewish Mus., N.Y.; and in many private colls.; murals, frescoes, USPO, Moline, Ill.; Decatur, Ill.; St. Louis, Mo. (in collaboration); Chicago City Hall; Lucy Flower Sch., Chicago. *Exhibited*: one-man: AIC, 1942, 1956; Downtown Gal., 1942; Assoc. Am. A., 1948; Univ. Kansas City, 1949; Louisiana State Univ., 1949; Florida State Univ., 1949; Clearwater A. Center, 1950; Indiana Univ., 1951; Univ. Arkansas, 1953; Philbrook Mus. A., 1953; Alan Gal., N.Y., 1954, 1956; Cornell Univ., 1954; Layton Sch. A., 1955; Rensselaer Poly. Inst., 1958; Albright A. Gal., 1955; Munson-Williams-Proctor Inst., 1956. Author: "A Compilation of Technical Procedures and Materials for Fresco Painting," 1940; "Use of the Object in Painting" (chapter in "Art of the Artist"), 1951. Lectures on mural painting in universities and colleges throughout the U.S. *Position*: Visiting A., Clearwater, Fla., A. Center, 1950-51; Indiana Univ., 1951-52; Washington Univ., St. Louis, 1952; Univ. Arkansas, 1953; Cornell Univ., 1954; Layton Sch. A., 1955; Albright A. Gal., 1955; Munson-Williams-Proctor Inst., Utica, 1955-56; Visiting Prof. A., Sch. Arch., Rensselaer Polytechnic Inst., Troy, N.Y., 1956- ; ASL, Woodstock, N.Y., summers, 1950-54 and many others.

MILLS, GEORGE THOMPSON—*Museum Curator*
Taylor Museum, Colorado Springs Fine Arts Center; h. 15 Penrose Blvd., Colorado Springs, Colo.

B. East Cleveland, Ohio, May 8, 1919. *Studied*: Dartmouth Col., B.A.; Harvard Univ., M.A., Ph.D. *Member*: AA Mus.; Am. Soc. for Aesthetics; Am. Anthropological Assn. (Fellow); Am. Assn. for Advancement of Science; Soc. for App. Anthropology. Author: "Navaho Art and Culture." Contributor of articles to College Art Journal; American Anthropologist; Brand Book; dealing with the educational role of the art museums and with the relations of art and culture. Exhibitions arranged: Saints and Kachinas, 1953; Penitentes of New Mexico and Colorado (in collaboration with Richard Grove), 1955. *Position*: Cur., Taylor Museum, Asst. Dir., Colorado Springs Fine Arts Center, Colorado Springs, Colo.

MILLS, HUGH LAUREN—*Painter, Et., Lith.*
14 Honeyman Place, Berkeley Heights, N.J.

B. Omaha, Neb. *Studied*: Univ. Nebraska; ASL, and with J. E. McBurney. *Work*: BMA; MMA; Los A. Mus. A.; N.Y. State Hist. Soc. *Exhibited*: NAD, 1928, 1929; NAC, 1927-1930; Phila. A. All., 1938; Bonestell Gal., 1937; SAGA; Charles Morgan Gal., 1938-1941 (one-man, 1938); Roerich Mus.; Tricker Gal.; ASL, 1950, 1951; CGA, 1941; ACA Gal.

MILLS, LOREN STURDEVANT (STURDY)—
Sculptor, Des., C.
2517 North 50th St., Lincoln 4, Neb.

B. Atkinson, Neb., Jan. 8, 1915. *Studied*: Minneapolis Sch. A.; Kansas City AI; Univ. Nebraska. *Member*: Lincoln A. Gld. *Award*: purchase prize, Minneapolis Soc. FA, 1955. *Exhibited*: Syracuse Mus. FA, 1940; Minneapolis Inst. A.; 1935, 1955; St. Paul A., 1935; Kansas City AI, 1938-1940; Nelson Gal. A., 1941; Missouri State Fair, 1938-1941; Philbrook A. Center, 1940; Nebraska A. Mus., 1946; Lincoln A. Gld., 1946; Joslyn A. Mus., 1950, 1955. *Position*: Instr. S. & Ceramics, Kansas City AI, Kansas City, Mo., 1938-40. Medical displays for Col. of Dentistry, Div. of Cancer Fnd., Univ. Nebraska, on permanent exhibition.

MILLS, PAUL CHADBOURNE—*Museum Director*

Oakland Art Museum, 1000 Fallon St.; h. 15 Bonita Ave., Piedmont, Cal.

B. Seattle, Wash., Sept. 24, 1924. *Studied*: Reed Col., Portland, Ore.; Univ. Washington, A.B. *Member*: AAMus.; Western Mus. Conf.; Western Assn. A. Mus. Dir. Author: "Early Paintings of California"; "Contemporary Bay Area Figurative Painting." Contributor to Art in America. *Position*: Former Vice-Pres., Western Assn. A. Mus. Dir. and of Western Mus. Conf.; Dir., Oakland A. Mus., Oakland, Cal.

MILLSAPS, DANIEL WEBSTER, III—
Painter, Des., Gr., I., T.

Rm. 504 Star Bldg.; h. 2618 K St., Northwest, Washington 7, D.C.

B. Darlington, S.C., June 30, 1919. *Studied*: Univ. South Carolina, A.B.; ASL, and with Heyward, Rembert, Marshall, and others. *Member*: ASL. *Awards*: Anthony B. Hampton award, Univ. South Carolina, 1940; VMFA, 1947; 50 Books of the Year, AIGA, 1948. *Work*: N.Y. Pub. Lib.; LC; VMFA; Univ. South Carolina. *Exhibited*: AIGA, 1948; Terry AI, 1952; WMAA, 1950, 1951; CGA, 1952; Delgado Mus. A., 1947, 1948; VMFA, 1947; Gibbes A. Gal., 1941; Mus. Non-Objective Painting, 1948; Ferargil Gal., 1952; Circulating, 1955; Dupont, 1955; Am-Korean Fnd., 1955-56; Columbia Mus. A., (10 yr. retrospective); Univ. Colorado, 1958; Trans-Lux & Plaza Gals. Author, I., "Sounds Pretty," 1948. *Position*: Des., Harper & Bros., 1947-49; Dir., AEA Bureau, 1949-52; A. Editor, U.S. Air Forces, 1952-55; Instr., Randall Sch., Hartford, Conn., 1950-52; A. Dir., Johnston Agency, Wash., D.C., 1955-1957; Pres., Allied Business Consultants, Washington, D.C., 1957- .

MILOVICH, TANASKO—*Painter, C., Des., T.*

4739 Westminster Place, St. Louis 8, Mo.

B. Fojnica, Yugoslavia, Jan. 27, 1900. *Studied*: St. Louis Sch. FA, Washington Univ., and in Paris, with Jean Marchand. *Member*: St. Louis A. Gld.; St. Louis Soc. Indp. A.; St. Louis Group 15; St. Louis A. Comm. (1950-53). *Awards*: prizes, St. Louis A. Gld., 1926, 1927, 1929, 1932, 1933, 1941-1943, 1945, 1946, 1947, 1949, 1950, 1953; St. Louis Soc. Indp. A., 1939, 1942; CAM, 1942; Denver A. Mus., 1945. *Work*: CAM; Honolulu Acad. A.; City Lib., St. Louis; stained glass window, Ethical Soc., St. Louis; batiks, Stix, Baer & Fuller, St. Louis; Aeolian Co. of Missouri. *Exhibited*: Critic's Choice, CM, 1945; Paris Salon, 1928, 1929; Salon d'Automne, 1928; Denver A. Mus., 1945, 1946; Cal. PLH, 1946; Joslyn Mus. A., 1947; Detroit Inst. A., 1949; one-man: Wanamaker's, Phila., 1930; Newhouse Gal., St. Louis, 1931; Wis. Soc. App. A., Milwaukee, 1936; SAM, 1936; Kansas City AI, 1939; Joslyn Mus. A., 1940; St. Louis A. Gld., 1943, 1949; Honolulu Acad. A., 1949; Eastern Ill. State Col., 1953, and others. *Position*: Instr., Batik, 1933-34, Instr., Drawing & Painting, 1944-56, St. Louis Sch. FA, St. Louis, Mo.*

MILSK, MARK (Mrs. Edmond Imperato)—*Etcher, Lith.*

628 Montgomery St., San Francisco 11, Cal.

B. St. Paul, Minn., Nov. 15, 1899. *Member*: Cal. SE. *Awards*: prizes, Syracuse, Ind., 1944; Cal. SE, 1942, 1943, 1945. *Work*: SFMA; State Lib., Sacramento, Cal.; Achenbach Fnd., Cal. PLH; and in Jerusalem. *Exhibited*: Venice, Italy, 1940; MMA (AV), 1942; Gumps, San F., Cal., 1941 (one-man); Crocker A. Gal., Sacramento, Cal., 1941; de Young Mem. Mus., 1940.

MINER, DOROTHY—*Museum Curator, L., W.*

Walters Art Gallery, 600 North Charles St.; h. 207 West Lanvale St., Baltimore 17, Md.

B. New York, N.Y., Nov. 4, 1904. *Studied*: Barnard Col., A.B.; Columbia Univ.; N.Y. Univ.; Univ. London. *Member*: CAA (Bd. Dir.); Mediaeval Acad. Am. (Council); Renaissance Soc. Am.; Bibliographical Soc. Am. (Chm. Southern Regional Council); Balt. Bibliophiles (Pres. 1955); Evergreen House Fnd. (V-Pres., Trustee). *Awards*: Int. F., Barnard Col., 1926-27; Carnegie FA F., 1928-29, Carnegie European F., 1929-30, President's F., 1930-31, Columbia Univ.; Rosenbach F., Univ. Pa.; Goucher Col., LL.D., 1957. Ed., Journal, monographs, and periodicals, of the Walters A. Gal.; Organized exh.: "Medieval Arts of Islam," 1953; "Living in the Past," 1953; "Medieval Parade," 1954-55, all at Walters A. Gal. Co-author:

"Proverbes en Rimes," 1937; Author: "Illuminated Books of the Middle Ages and Renaissance," 1949; Ed., "Studies in Art and Literature for Belle da Costa Green," 1952; "History of Bookbinding, 525-1950 A.D.," 1958. Contributor of articles and reviews to leading art and museum publications. Lectures: Mediaeval Art. *Positions*: Instr., Barnard Col., 1931-32; Johns Hopkins Univ., 1947, 1951; Librarian & Keeper of Manuscripts, Walters Art Gal., Baltimore, Md., 1934- .

MINEWSKI, ALEX—*Painter*

128 East 16th St.; h. 52 Irving Place, New York 3, N.Y.

B. Detroit, Mich., Dec. 13, 1917. *Studied*: ASL; Colorado Springs FA Center; Grande Chaumiere, Paris; Hans Hofmann Sch. FA. *Awards*: prizes, Ball State T. Col., 1956 (purchase); Michigan A., 1938 (purchase). *Exhibited*: Audubon A., 1947, 1948; PAFA, 1949; Butler Inst. Am. A., 1957; Columbia Mus. A., 1957; NAD; Michigan A., 1937-1939, 1945-1947; Nat. Soc. Painters in Casein, 1955, 1956; One-man: Detroit, 1946; Contemp. A. Gal., 1947; Washington Irving Gal., 1957.

MINK, DAVID D. C. (DAVE)—*Comm. A., I., P.*

2305 Brown Ave., Evanston, Ill.

B. East Liverpool, Ohio, Oct. 12, 1913. *Studied*: Chicago Acad. FA, and with Henry Keller, Jerry Farnsworth. *Member*: Chicago A. Gld. *Awards*: prizes, CMA, 1938, 1939; Butler AI, 1940; medal, Chicago A. Dir. Cl., 1942-1946. *Work*: CMA; Butler AI. *Exhibited*: Assoc. Am. A., Chicago, 1946 (one-man). I., "Tom Sawyer," 1948; produced, "Pictorial Chart of Romantic Florida," 1951; covers for Popular Mechanics, Coronet, and other magazines. Illus. for national magazines.*

MINNA, (WILHELMINA FRANCES ALLEN)—
Designer, C., T.

Franklin Square House, 11 East Newton St., Boston 18, Mass.

B. Franklin, N.H., May 2, 1898. *Studied*: BMFA Sch., with Henry Hunt Clark, George J. Hunt. *Exhibited*: Boston, Mass.; Falmouth, Mass.; Philadelphia, Pa.; Andover, Mass.; Hamilton, Mass.; and others. Instr. in many USO Camps and adult evening schools. *Position*: Des., C. H. Wallbank & Co., Brookline, Mass., 1944-48; Instr., Jewelry & Crafts, Franklin Square House, Boston, Mass., 1948- ; Instr., Jewelry, Boston Centre for Adult Education.

MINTON, HERMAN. See *Mitnitzky, Herman*

MINTY, JOHN R.—*Painter, C.*

Raytheon Manufacturing Co., Waltham, Mass.; h. 339 North Road, Bedford, Mass.

B. Detroit, Mich., Dec. 18, 1921. *Studied*: Grey's Sch. A., Aberdeen, Scotland; New Orleans A. & Crafts Assn.; and with William Hayter. *Exhibited*: PAFA, 1954; New Orleans AA, 1954, 1955; Paul Schuster Gal., Cambridge, 1954, 1955; deCordova & Dana Mus., 1955. *Position*: Instr., Drawing & Painting, deCordova & Dana Mus. A., Lincoln, Mass.

MINTZ, HARRY—*Painter, T., L.*

59 West North Ave., Chicago 10, Ill.

B. Ostrowiec, Poland, Sept. 27, 1909. *Studied*: Warsaw Acad. FA, Poland; AIC. *Member*: North Shore A. Lg.; AEA. *Awards*: prizes, AIC, 1937, 1939, 1945, 1946, 1949, 1952, 1954; Springfield, Ill., 1948; Evanston Woman's Cl., 1948, 1949, 1953; Am.-Jewish A. Cl., Chicago, 1948; Magnificent Mile Exh., Chicago, 1956; medal, Cal. PLH, 1946; Univ. Chicago, 1953. *Work*: AIC; Hackley A. Gal.; Warsaw Acad. FA; Tel-Aviv Mus., Israel. *Exhibited*: AIC, 1932-58; WMAA; PAFA; CGA; Carnegie Inst.; Cal. PLH; CM; Milwaukee AI; VMFA; Univ. Illinois; Springfield, Ill.; State Univ. Iowa; Soc. Liberal A., Omaha; Denver A. Mus.; SAM; Kalamazoo AI; Kansas City AI; Lehigh Univ.; Minnesota State Fair; Currier Gal. A.; Arnot A. Gal.; Davenport Mun. A. Gal.; Sarasota AA; Minneapolis Inst. A.; CAM; Columbus Gal. FA; Rochester Mem. A. Gal.; Los A. Mus. A., and many others; one-man: John Heller Gal., N.Y.; AIC; Los A., Cal.; Palmer House Gal., Chicago, 1952, 1953; Cliff Dwellers, Chicago, 1954; Stevens Gross Gal., Chicago, 1951, and others. *Position*: Instr.,

Evanston (Ill.) A. Center; Instr., AIC, Chicago, Ill., at present; Visiting Prof., Washington Univ., St. Louis, Mo., 1954-55.

MIRSKY, SAMUEL—*Portrait Painter*
20 West 77th St., New York 24, N.Y.

B. Russia, Dec. 24, 1883. *Studied*: London, England. *Member*: All. A. Am. *Awards*: medals, England and Scotland. *Work*: Princeton Univ. Lib.; Johns Hopkins Univ. Lib.

MISUNAS, EVERETT P.—*Educator, Eng., Des.*
2105 Crescent Ave., Waukegan, Ill.

B. De Kalb, Ill., Apr. 14, 1916. *Studied*: Northern Illinois State Univ., B. Ed.; Am. Acad. A.; Univ. Chicago, M.A.; AIC. *Member*: Illinois A. Educators Assn.; Chicago A. Edu. *Exhibited*: SAGA, 1953; Illinois State Fair, 1954; Libertyville A. Cl.; Lake County A. Lg.; and others. *Position*: Chm. A. Dept., Waukegan Township H.S.

MITCHELL, ALFRED R.—*Painter, T.*
1506—31st St., San Diego 2, Cal.

B. York, Pa., June 18, 1888. *Studied*: San Diego Acad. A., with Maurice Braun; PAFA. *Member*: La Jolla AA; Chula Vista A. Gld.; San Diego A. Gld.; Laguna Beach AA; Men's AI, San Diego. *Awards*: Cresson traveling scholarship, PAFA, 1920; med., Pan-Pacific Exp., 1915; prizes, San Diego A. Gld., 1926, 1927, 1931, 1937, 1958; Buck Hill AA, 1939; Laguna Beach AA, 1940; Chula Vista A. Gld., 1945, 1946; San Diego County Fair, 1950, 1951; Fiesta del Pacifico, 1956; La Jolla A. Center, 1956. *Work*: Univ. Oregon Medical Sch.; Van Nuys H.S.; San Diego Pub. Lib.; Reading Mus.; San Diego FA Soc.; Univ. Cl., San Diego; YMCA & YWCA, San Diego; San Diego Mus. Man; Evening H.S.; Blanden Mem. Gal., Ft. Dodge, Iowa; Ohio Wesleyan Univ.; Hahnemann Medical Col., Phila., Pa.; Univ. West Virginia. *Exhibited*: PAFA, 1920, 1927; Wilmington, Del., 1920; GGE, 1939; California-Pacific Exp., 1935, 1936; Laguna Beach AA; San Diego FA Soc.; La Jolla, Cal.

MITCHELL, BRUCE HANDISIDE—*Painter, E., L.*
R.D. 1, Milton, Pa.

B. Tayport, Scotland, Jan. 27, 1908. *Studied*: ASL, with Harry Wickey, Thomas Benton, George Grosz, and others. *Member*: AEA. *Awards*: Tiffany F., 1930, 1933; Yaddo F., 1935, 1940; Guggenheim F., 1941-42. *Work*: MMA; WMAA; PMG; Univ. Arizona; Nelson Gal. A.; Delgado Mus. A.; LC; mural, USPO, Columbia, Pa.; Lever Bldg. Coll.; U.S. Steel Co.; LC. *Exhibited*: WFNY 1939; GGE, 1939; Carnegie Inst., 1943-1945; WMAA, 1932-1946; MMA; AIC, 1934-1940; BM; one-man: Rehn Gal., 1940, 1942, 1954; Michigan State Col.; Bucknell Univ.; Syracuse Univ.; Kansas City AI; Delgado Mus. A. Contributor section, "The Story of the Arizona Plan," for symposium "Work for Artists," 1947; Chapter in "Gouache Painting"; Chapter on Mixed Media, in "Watercolor, Gouache, and Casein Painting." *Positions*: A. Advisor, Univ. Arizona Gal. Mod. Am. Painting, 1941-43; A., War Correspondent, U.S. Engineers and Life magazine, 1943-45; A. in Res., Bucknell Univ., 1947; Visiting A., Michigan State Col., 1948, New Orleans A. Acad., 1950, Kansas City AI, 1948-51; A. Advisor, Susquehanna Univ., 1951; Visiting A., Norton Sch. A., 1955-56.*

MITCHELL, G(EORGE) B(ERTRAND)—
Painter, W., L., I.
58 The Terrace, Rutherford, N.J.; also, Masons Island, Mystic, Conn.

B. East Bridgewater, Mass., Apr. 18, 1872. *Studied*: Cowles A. Sch., Boston; Julian Acad., Ecole des Beaux-Arts, Paris, France. *Member*: AWS; SC; Mystic AA; AAPL; Marine Hist. Assn. (Hon. Pres.); Rutherford AA. *Work*: Agricultural Dept., State of Conn.; Marine Hist. Assn., Mystic, Conn. *Exhibited*: Paris Salon; AWS; SC, 1917- ; Mystic AA, 1930- .

MITCHELL, GLEN—*Painter, I., T.*
142 East 18th St., New York 3, N.Y.

B. New Richmond, Ind., June 9, 1894. *Studied*: Chicago Acad. FA; AIC; Univ. Illinois; Grande Chaumiere, Paris, France. *Awards*: Guggenheim F., 1926-1927, 1928; CGA, 1936; Minneapolis Salon, 1937; Hoosier Salon, 1939.

Work: murals, theatres in Minneapolis and Red Wing, Minn. *Exhibited*: MModA; WMAA; PAFA; NAD; AIC; William Rockhill Nelson Gal.; SFMA; Oakland A. Gal. *Lectures*: Painting; Composition. Contributor to American Artist magazine. *Position*: Hd., Painting Dept., Minneapolis Sch. A., Minneapolis, Minn., 1929-1941; Instr., Parsons Sch. Des., New York, N.Y., 1949-54.*

MITCHELL, HENRY (WEBER)—*Sculptor*
Level Road, Arcola, Pa.

B. Canton, Ohio, Aug. 27, 1915. *Studied*: Princeton Univ., A.B.; Tyler Sch. FA, Temple Univ., M.F.A.; Academia di Brera, Milan, Italy, with Marino Marini. *Member*: AEA; Phila. A. All.; Plays & Players, Phila. *Awards*: Fulbright F., 1950-51. *Work*: fountain, PMA; sculpture in three Phila. park playgrounds. *Exhibited*: PMA, 1955; Munson-Williams-Proctor Inst., 1956; Rochester Mem. A. Gal., 1956; one-man: Florence, Italy, 1952; Canton AI, 1952; Kraushaar Gal., N.Y., 1953; Baltimore, 1953; Phila. A. All., 1954; Bryn Mawr A. Center, 1955. *Position*: Instr., Des., S., PMA, Philadelphia, Pa.

MITCHELL, LAURA M. D. (Mrs. Arthur A. Tennyson)
—*Miniature Painter, W.*
1428 South Marengo Ave., P.O. Box 2085, Alhambra, Cal.

B. Halifax, N.S., Canada, Jan. 12, 1883. *Studied*: ASL, with Lucia Fairchild Fuller, Kenyon Cox, George Bridgman. *Member*: Pasadena Writer's Cl.; Cal. Soc. Min. P. (Founder). *Awards*: med., Pan-Pacific Exp., 1915, 1916; prize, Cal. Soc. Min. P., 1923, 1929; med., Pacific Southwest Exp., 1928. *Work*: reproductions, Cal. State Lib.; Los A. Pub. Lib. *Exhibited*: ASMP; Pa. Soc. Min. P.; Royal Soc. Min. P., London, England, 1929, 1937; Century of Progress, Chicago, 1933; CGA, 1935; P. & S. of Southern California; Cal. AC; San Diego FA Soc.; Los A. Mus. A.; Pasadena AI; Southwest Mus., Los A., Cal. Contributor to: art magazines & newspapers.

MITCHELL, SUE (LAVINIA)—*Painter*
Copperhill, Tenn.

B. Copperhill, Tenn., Mar. 2, 1923. *Studied*: Agnes Scott Col., B.A.; Hans Hofmann Sch. FA. *Awards*: Louisville Pub. Lib., 1955. *Exhibited*: Carnegie Inst., 1955; Peridot Gal., N.Y.; Kootz Gal., N.Y.; BM; Univ. Nebraska, 1956-1958.

MITCHELL, WALLACE (MacMAHON)—*Painter, T.*
Cranbrook Academy of Art, Bloomfield Hills, Mich.

B. Detroit, Mich., Oct. 9, 1911. *Studied*: Northwestern Univ., B.A.; Cranbrook Acad. A., with Zoltan Sepeshy; Columbia Univ., M.A. *Awards*: Old Northwest Territory Exh.; prize, Detroit Inst. A., 1945. *Work*: Cranbrook Acad. A. Mus.; Detroit Inst. A. *Exhibited*: AIC, 1938-1941; Detroit Inst. A., annually; Albright A. Gal., 1939; Univ. Nebraska; Bertha Schaefer Gal., 1950, 1958 (one-man); Old Northwest Territory Exh. *Position*: Registrar, 1944- , Hd. of Galleries, 1955- , Cranbrook Acad A., Bloomfield Hills, Mich.

MITNITZKY, HERMAN—*Painter*
216 East 45th St., New York 17, N.Y.; h. 3737 Cypress Ave., Brooklyn 24, N.Y.

B. Kiev, Russia, Nov. 17, 1894. *Member*: Brooklyn Soc. A.; Collectors of Am. Art. *Exhibited*: All. A. Am.; AWS; Audubon A.; Galerie St. Etienne; Contemp. A. Gal., N.Y.; Brooklyn Pub. Lib. (one-man); traveling exh., 1956-57.

MITTLEMAN, ANN—*Painter*
710 Park Ave., New York 21, N.Y.

B. New York, N.Y. *Studied*: N.Y. Univ., and with Philip Evergood, Robert Laurent, Tschacbasov. *Member*: AEA; NAWA; Brooklyn Soc. A. *Work*: Everhart Mus. A.; SAM; Zanesville, Ohio; Smith Col.; Jewish Mus.; Hickory, N.C.; N.Y. Univ. Mus.; Richmond (Ind.) AA; Evansville (Ind.); Florence (S.C.) Mus. A.; Delgado Mus. A.; Lowe Gal. A., Coral Gables; Birmingham Mus. A. *Exhibited*: ACA Gal.; N.Y. City Center; Berlin Acad. FA, Germany; WMAA; Riverside Mus.; Creative Gal.; Panoras Gal.; Rockland A. Fnd.; NAWA; Bodley Gal., 1958.

MOCHARNIUK, NICHOLAS (NIMO)—
Sculptor, C., Des.
318 Canal St. (13); h. 192 Sixth Ave., New York 12, N.Y.

B. Philadelphia, Pa., May 11, 1917. *Studied*: Girard Col., Phila., Pa. *Awards*: prize, Springfield Mus. A., 1945. *Work*: Springfield (Mo.) Mus. A. Specializes in modern jewelry and lamps of sculptured woods. *Exhibited*: Marquie Gal., 1943-1946 (all one-man); All. A. Am., 1945; Audubon A., 1945; Lg. Present-Day A., 1946; America House, N.Y.

MOCK, GLADYS—*Painter, Eng.*
24 Washington Sq., New York 11, N.Y.

B. New York, N.Y. *Studied*: ASL, and with Kenneth Hayes Miller. *Member*: SAGA; NAWA; Audubon A.; Pen & Brush Cl. *Awards*: prizes, NAWA, 1946, medal, 1954; Pen & Brush Cl., 1946, 1955; Champlain Valley Exh.; 1951; medal, NAWA, 1951. *Work*: PAFA; Todd Mus., Kalamazoo, Mich.; LC; Kansas State Col., Hays, Kans.; MMA; Smithsonian Inst. *Exhibited*: CGA; LC; PAFA; AIC; Carnegie Inst.; NAD; SAGA; NAWA; WFNY 1939; Venice, Italy. *Position*: Bd. Dir., (1955-57) Delegate to U.S. Com. of Intl. Assn. Plastic A., 1956, Audubon A.; Council Memb., SAGA, 1955-56; Exh. Consultant, NAWA, 1955-56.

MOCK, VERN—*Designer, Comm., P., T., W., L., I.*
1105 Brookstown Ave., Winston-Salem, N.C.

B. Basin, Wyo., May 25, 1913. *Studied*: Univ. Colorado, B.F.A.; A. Center, Los Angeles; Workshop Sch., N.Y. *Member*: A. Gld.; Assoc. A. Winston-Salem; AAPL. *Exhibited*: Grumbacher Exh., 1935; La. A. Festival, 1936; A. I. Friedman Gal., 1954 (one-man); A. Gld., 1954; Assoc. A. Winston-Salem, 1956-1958; Winston-Salem Pub. Lib., 1958; Dixie Classic Fair, 1956, 1957; North Carolina Women's Cl., 1956, 1957; Roaring Gap, N.C., 1956, 1957. *Positions*: W. D. Teague Co., 1942-45; A. Dir., "Information Please," TV program, 1952; A. Dir., Vern Mock Assoc., 1945-55; Rapid Art Service, 1954-55; Michael Newmark Agcy., 1955; Instr., Cartoonists & Illus. Sch., N.Y., 1950-54; Des. Dir., Western Electric Co., at present.

MODEL, ELISABETH—*Sculptor, Gr.*
340 West 72nd St., New York 23, N.Y.

B. Bayreuth, Bavaria, May 6, 1903. *Studied*: Munich, Germany; Acad. of Amsterdam, Holland, and in Paris with Kogan. *Member*: NAWA (Chm.); Fed. Modern P. & S. (Cor. Sec.); Brooklyn Soc. A. *Awards*: medal of honor, 1950, prizes, 1951, 1952; NAWA, Brooklyn Soc. A., 1953, 1954. *Work*: CGA; Hartford Atheneum; Jewish Mus., N.Y.; Rijksprenten Kabinet, Amsterdam, Holland, and in many private colls. *Exhibited*: PAFA, 1950, 1951, 1953; Burlington Gal., London; and others; one-man exhs., Amsterdam, Holland; New York; Wash., D.C.; Wilmington, Del.; Katonah, N.Y., and Rome, Italy, 1957.

MODJESKA, MARYLKA (Mrs. Sidney Pattison)—
Painter, Et.
1144 East Linden St., Tucson 11, Ariz.

B. Chicago, Ill., Jan. 22, 1893. *Studied*: AIC; ASL, with Eliot O'Hara, George Bridgman; Julian Acad., Paris, and with George Senseney, George Degorce, Jerry Farnsworth. *Member*: Tucson FA Assn.; Palette & Brush Cl. *Work*: AIC.

MOFFETT, MRS. DOROTHY GREGORY. See Gregory, Dorothy Lake

MOFFETT, ROSS E.—*Painter*
Provincetown, Mass.

B. Clearfield, Iowa, Feb. 18, 1888. *Studied*: AIC; & with Charles Hawthorne. *Member*: NA; Audubon A.; Mass. Archaeological Soc.; Soc. Am. Archaeology. *Awards*: med., AIC, 1918, 1927; prize, NAD, 1921, 1951. *Work*: PAFA; J. B. Speed Mem. Mus.; CGA; WMAA; Univ. Nebraska; Miami Univ.; murals, USPO, Holyoke, Mass.; Eisenhower Mus., Abilene, Kans.; Somerville, Mass.; Revere, Mass. *Exhibited*: CGA; PAFA; AIC; NAD; Carnegie Inst.; Detroit Inst. A.; Albright A. Gal.; WMA; Springfield Mus. A.; Minneapolis Inst. A.; CAM; VMFA; Dayton AI; Louisville, Ky.; CMA; etc.

MOHN, SIGVARD M.—*Painter, Et.*
298 Fire Island Ave., Babylon, L.I., N.Y.

B. Northfield, Minn., May 29, 1891. *Studied*: St. Paul Inst. Sch. A.; PAFA; Grand Central Sch. A.; Julian Acad., Paris. *Member*: SC.

MOIR, ROBERT—*Sculptor, P., T.*
400 East 93rd St., New York 28, N.Y.

B. Chicago, Ill., Jan. 7, 1917. *Studied*: AIC; Columbia Univ.; N.Y. Univ.; ASL. *Member*: New Sculpture Group; S. Gld. *Work*: Honolulu Acad. A.; WMAA; Rittenhouse Savoy, Phila., Pa. *Exhibited*: AIC, 1940, 1941, 1948; WMAA, 1951-1955, 1956; MMA, 1951, 1952; Sculpture Center, N.Y., 1951 (one-man), 1954; Hacker Gal., 1953; John Heller Gal., 1954, 1955; Manhattanville Col. of the Sacred Heart, Purchase, N.Y., 1955 (one-man); Parma Gal., 1956 (one-man).

MOLIND, A.—*Painter*
4836 Roosevelt Blvd., Philadelphia 24, Pa.

B. Norfolk, Va., Apr. 1, 1898. *Studied*: Spring Garden Inst.; PMSchIA. *Exhibited*: PAFA, 1942; Phila. Sketch Cl. *Work*: in private colls.

MOLLER, HANS—*Painter, Des., Lith., T.*
150 East 49th St., New York 17, N.Y.

B. Wuppertal-Barmen, Germany, Mar. 20, 1905. *Studied*: in Germany. *Awards*: medals, awards, certif. of merit, A. Dir. Cl., N.Y., 1944, 1955, A. Dir. Cl., Chicago, 1951, A. Dir. Cl., Phila., Pa., 1954. *Work*: PAFA; PC; Walker A. Center; Univ. Georgia; Soc. Four Arts, Palm Beach; WMAA; MModA; BM; Detroit Inst. A.; N.Y. Pub. Lib.; Tapestry des. for Temple Israel, Tulsa, Okla.; Temple Beth-El, Gary, Ind., & others. *Exhibited*: PAFA, 1944, 1946-1952; AIC, 1943-1946; VMFA, 1946, 1948; CGA, 1949, 1951; BM, 1947, 1951; CM, 1952; MMA, 1950; Univ. Illinois, 1949, 1950, 1952; Albright A. Gal., 1952; WMAA, 1946-1952, and in France, Germany, Japan; Provincetown A. Festival, 1958; one-man: Borgenicht Gal., N.Y., 1951, 1953, 1954, 1956; Bonestell Gal., 1942, 1943; Chicago A. Cl., 1945; Univ. Michigan, 1945; Kleeman Gal., 1945, 1947-1950; Pen & Palette Cl., St. Louis, 1949; Macon, Ga., 1949; Atlanta, Ga., 1950; Fine Arts Assoc., 1957; retrospective exh., Leetes Island, Conn., 1955; retrospective exh. to universities, colleges and museums, U.S. and Canada. *Position*: Instr., Graphic Des., Painting, CUASch., New York, N.Y., 1944-1956.

MOLLER, OLAF—*Painter, C., Des.*
Rupert, Idaho

B. Copenhagen, Denmark, May 21, 1903. *Studied*: PAFA; & with Daniel Garber, Arthur B. Carles, N.C. Wyeth, & others. *Member*: Rockport AA; North Shore AA. *Awards*: prizes, PAFA, 1925, 1926; Tiffany Fnd. Scholarship, 1927; Springville, Utah, 1933; Heyburn, Idaho, 1934, 1937. *Work*: Augustana Col., Rock Island, Ill.; Univ. Idaho; Boise A. Mus.; Carnegie Lib., Boise, Idaho; H.S., Twin Falls, Idaho; Burley (Idaho) H.S.; Art & Travel Cl., Pocatello; Cedar City (Utah) H.S.; Columbian Cl., Boise; IBM. *Exhibited*: WFNY 1939.

MOLLISON, KAY (Mrs. Harry Ballinger)—*Painter*
Ballinger Studio, R.F.D., New Hartford, Conn.; s. Rockport, Mass.

B. Ottumwa, Iowa, June 6, 1896. *Studied*: Smith Col., A.B.; Corcoran Sch. A., and with Wayman Adams. *Member*: NAWA; Conn. Acad. FA; Springfield Academic A.; Rockport AA; North Shore AA. *Awards*: prizes, Hartford Women Painters, 1952, 1954, 1955; North Shore AA, 1952; Meriden A. & Crafts, 1954, 1957; Springfield Academic A., 1956; Conn. Acad. FA, 1957; Rockport AA, 1953, 1958; New Haven Paint & Clay Cl., 1958 (purchase).

MOLZAHN, JOHANNES—*Painter, Des., E., W., L.*
528 East 85th St., New York 28, N.Y.

B. Duisburg, Germany, May 21, 1892. *Work*: museums in Weimar, Essen, Breslau, Darmstadt, Duisburg, Germany; Yale Univ. *Exhibited*: Societe Anonyme, traveling exh., 1925-1927; MModA, 1931; traveling exh., "Abstract & Surrealist Art in America," 1944; WMAA, 1945; one-man traveling exh., "40 Years of Work," Germany, 1956-1958.

Position: Prof. A., Univ., Washington, Seattle, Wash., 1938-41; Inst. Des., Chicago, Ill., 1943-44; New Sch. for Social Research, New York, N.Y., 1947-54.

MOMMER, (PETER) PAUL—*Painter*
103 East 17th St., New York 3, N.Y.; h. 24-58 27th St., Astoria, L.I., N.Y.

B. Bonnevoi, Luxembourg, Feb. 21, 1899. *Member*: Fed. Mod. P. & S.; Audubon A. *Awards*: prizes, Audubon A., 1951, medal, 1952; medal, NAC, 1953. *Work*: MMA; Walker A. Center; Univ. Minnesota; BM; Munich State Mus., Germany. *Exhibited*: Carnegie Inst., 1942-1944; MModA; WMAA, 1934, 1936, 1938; CGA, 1937; AIC, 1937; GGE, 1939; MMA, 1950; BM, 1952, 1957; retrospective exh., NAC, 1951; AFA traveling exh., 1955, 1956; Riverside Mus., 1955; traveling exh., Europe, 1956-57, USIS. Author: "As I See It," 1938. *Position*: Pres., Fed. Mod. P. & S., 1952; V-Pres., Audubon A., New York, N.Y., 1952, 1957.

MONAGHAN, EILEEN (Mrs. Frederic Whitaker)—*Painter*
Murray St., Norwalk, Conn.

B. Holyoke, Mass. *Studied*: Mass. Sch. A. *Member*: ANA; AWS; All. A. Am.; Conn. WC Soc.; Hudson Valley AA; Providence WC Cl.; Phila. WC Cl.; New Haven Paint & Clay Cl. *Awards*: AWS, 1958; NAD, 1958; New Haven Paint & Clay Cl., 1958; All. A. Am., 1947, 1949, 1955; Providence WC Cl., 1955; Silvermine Gld. A., 1957; Hudson Valley AA, 1954; Wolfe A. Cl., 1954; Bridgeport A. Lg.; Westchester Fed. Womens Cl. *Work*: Hispanic Soc. Mus.; Atlanta A. Mus., and in private colls. *Exhibited*: AWS traveling exhs., 1955-1958; nationally in watercolor exhs.

MONAGHAN, GERTRUDE—*Mural Painter, Arch. Des.*
Buck Hill Falls, Pa.; s. Nantucket, Mass.

B. West Chester, Pa. *Studied*: Phila. Sch. Des.; PAFA. *Member*: Nantucket AA; MacDowell Assn. *Awards*: Cresson scholarship, Thouron prize, PAFA. *Work*: murals, Jacob Reed's, Phila., Pa. *Exhibited*: LC; PAFA; Nantucket AA; Phila. A. Cl.; Phila. Plastic Cl.; Phila. Pr. Cl.; Buck Hill Falls, Pa.

MONAGHAN, KEITH—*Educator, P.*
Art Department, Washington State College; h. 1501 Lower Drive, Pullman, Wash.

B. San Rafael, Cal., May 15, 1921. *Studied*: Univ. California, Berkeley, B.A., M.A. *Member*: San F. AA; Washington AA. *Awards*: prizes, San F. AA, 1948; SAM, 1950; Spokane Coliseum, 1954; Seattle Music & A. Fnd., 1954, 1957; Puget Sound Group, 1956; Frye Mus. A., 1956; Bellevue (Wash.) A. & Crafts, 1956, 1958; Spokane A. Center, 1957; Woessner Gal., 1958. *Exhibited*: San F. AA., 1946-1948, 1950, 1953; deYoung Mem. Mus.; Cal. PLH; Cal. State Fair; SAM; Henry Gal., Seattle; Woessner Gal., Seattle; Bellevue A. & Crafts Fair; Spokane Coliseum; Spokane A. Center; Vancouver A. Gal.; Oakland A. Mus.; Frye Mus., Seattle; and in many universities and colleges. *Position*: Chm. A. Dept., Washington State College, Pullman, Wash., 1951- .

MONGAN, AGNES—*Museum Curator, W., Cr., L.*
Fogg Museum of Art, Harvard University; h. 37 Kirkland St., Cambridge 38, Mass.

B. Somerville, Mass., Jan 21, 1905. *Studied*: Bryn Mawr Col., A.B.; Smith Col., A.M. *Awards*: hon. degree, L.H.D., Smith Col., 1941; Officier d'Academie (France), 1949; deg., Litt. D., Wheaton Col., 1954. Co-author (with Paul Sachs): "Drawings in the Fogg Museum of Art," 3 vols., 1940; Ed., Georgiana Goddard King's "Heart of Spain," 1941; "One Hundred Master Drawings" (in collaboration), 1949; Catalogue of the Frick Collection, French Paintings, 1950. Contributor of articles to American, English and French art periodicals; U.S. Nat. Comm. for UNESCO, 1954-57. *Position*: Cur., Drawings and Asst. Dir., FMA, Harvard Univ., Cambridge, Mass.

MONGAN, ELIZABETH—*Museum Curator*
National Gallery of Art, Smithsonian Institution, Washington, D.C.

Position: Cur., Graphic Arts.*

MONHOFF, FREDERICK—*Etcher, Lith., L., T., Arch.*
108 West 20th St., Rm. 410, Los Angeles, Cal.; h. 530 East Marigold St., Altadena, Cal.

B. New York, N.Y., Nov. 23, 1897. *Studied*: Univ. California, M.A. *Member*: Cal. Pr. M.; AIA; Chicago SE. *Awards*: med., San F., Cal., 1934. *Work*: BM; Lib. Cong.; deYoung Mem. Mus.; Los A. Mus. A. *Position*: Instr., Design, Otis AI, Los Angeles, Cal., 1926-50; Des. Arch., Los A. Arch. Div. Lecturer, Univ. Cal., Los A., Ext. Div., 1942- .*

MONTAGUE, RUTH DuBARRY (Mrs. Roland Pierson Prickett)—*Writer, L., T., P.*
Prickett-Montague Studio of Painting, Monterey, Mass.

B. Paris, France, Sept. 14, 1916. *Studied*: Ecole des Beaux-Arts, Paris; Univ. Nevada, M.F.A.; Lumis A. Acad., with Harriet Randall Lumis; PAFA. *Member*: Springfield A. Gld.; Reno (Nev.) Mus. A. Gld. *Exhibited*: Nationally and internationally. *Work*: in many private colls. *Positions*: Ed., "The Happy Painter," national art bulletin; contributor syndicated articles on art for weekly newspapers; contributor to New Yorker magazine; Health Culture; Nature magazine and others; Author publ. monographs on various phases of oil painting; co-author, 5 Home Study Courses in oil painting; lectures: Interpretive Oil Painting to women's clubs; Dir., Co-Instr., Prickett-Montague Studio of Painting, Monterey, Mass.

MONTANA, BOB—*Cartoonist*
Archie Publications, Inc., 241 Church St., New York, N.Y.

Creator, syndicated comic strip, "Archie."

MONTANA, PIETRO—*Sculptor, P., T.*
58 West 57th St., New York 19, N.Y.

B. Alcamo, Italy, June 29, 1890. *Studied*: with Brewster. *Member*: NSS; All. A. Am.; Audubon A.; AAPL. *Awards*: medal, NAD, 1931; prizes, All. A. Am., 1938, 1942, 1949; Hudson Valley A, 1945, 1950, 1951, 1953; AAPL, 1947, 1955. *Work*: s., mem., monuments, Brooklyn, N.Y.; East Providence, R.I.; Alliance, Ohio; St. John's Cemetery, N.Y.; Brookgreen Gardens, S.C.; Radio City, N.Y.; Fordham Univ.; Am. Numismatic Soc.; Mayaguez, Puerto Rico; Ft. Worth, Tex.; Blessed Eymard Seminary, Hyde Park, N.Y.; St. Anthony's Shrine, Boston; Starr Commonwealth Mus., Albion, Mich., and in Sweden, Italy, and others. *Position*: Instr., Fordham Univ., 1947-52.*

MONTGOMERY, CHARLES FRANKLIN—
Museum Director
The Henry Francis duPont Winterthur Museum; h. Winterthur, Del.

B. Austin Township, Ill., Apr. 14, 1910. *Studied*: Harvard Univ., A.B. *Member*: AAMus. (Council); Walpole Soc.; Assn. A. Mus. Dirs.; Northeast Museums Conf. (Pres.). *Awards*: M.A. degree, Univ. Delaware, 1954. Contributor articles to Antiques magazine. Lectures: various phases of American decorative arts, at Williamsburg Antiques Forum; AIC; BMFA; N.Y. Hist. Assn.; Cooperstown, N.Y.; Columbus Gal. FA; Missouri Hist. Soc.; Maryland Hist. Soc.; BM, and others. *Position*: Consultative Com. of The Art Quarterly; Dir., The Henry Francis duPont Winterthur Mus., Winterthur, Del., 1949- .

MONTGOMERY, CLAUDE—*Painter*
2144 South Norfolk Terr., Tulsa, Okla.; s. Sargent Rd., Peaks Island, Me.

B. Portland, Me., Jan. 25, 1912. *Studied*: Portland Sch. A. with Alexander Bower; NAD, with Leon Kroll, Gifford Beal; PIASch. *Member*: Portland Soc. A.; Southwestern AA. *Awards*: prize, Portland Mus. A., 1934; Montreal, Canada, 1952; medal, NAD, 1936; Paris Salon, 1937. *Work*: L.D.M. Sweat Mem. Mus.; Colgate Univ.; Mem. Hospital, Milford, Del.; Univ. Tulsa; Oklahoma City Hall of Fame. *Exhibited*: Radio City, N.Y., 1935; NAD, 1937, 1938; Paris Salon, 1937; SAGA, 1934, 1935; AWS, 1942; Portland Soc. A., 1933-1939, 1941-1945; Taxco A. Soc., Mexico, 1951; one-man: White Plains (N.Y.) A. Center, 1942; Scarsdale Woman's Cl., 1942; Philbrook A. Center, 1948; Okla. City A. Center, 1949; Junior Lg. Gal., Tulsa, 1949; Portland A. Mus., 1948, 1951; Bellas Artes, Palma, Mallorca, Spain, 1955. Author, I., "Mallorca Sketchbook," 1955.

MONTGOMERY, LORAN A. D. (Mr.)—Painter, T.
413 Church Rd., Philadelphia 11, Pa.

B. Mason City, Ill., Nov. 25, 1904. *Studied*: Chouinard AI, with Clarence Hinkle; PAFA; Barnes Fnd.; & in Paris, France. *Member*: F., PAFA. *Awards*: F., PAFA; prize, Germantown A. Lg., 1938; Cheltenham (Pa.) A. Center, 1949, 1950; gold medal, Da Vinci All., 1950. *Work*: F., PAFA; Allentown Mus.; Temple Univ.; Bartram, Radnor H.S., Pa.; Jefferson Hospital, Phila.; Carlisle (Pa.) Court House. *Exhibited*: Carnegie Inst., 1941; WFNY 1939; CGA, 1936; Phila. A. All., traveling exh., 1934, 1953; PMA, 1935, 1938, 1953; Phila. A. All., 1953; PAFA, 1940, 1948, 1950, 1953; Carlen Gal.; Woodmere A. Gal., 1941-1958; Phila. AC; Da Vinci All., 1950-1958; Gimbels, Phila., 1953; State Mus., Harrisburg, Pa. *Position*: Pres., Cheltenham Twp. A. Center, 1958.

MONTOYA, GERONIMA CRUZ (PO-TSU-NU)— Painter, T.
U.S. Indian School, Santa Fé, N.M.

B. San Juan Pueblo, N.M., Sept. 22, 1915. *Studied*: Santa Fé Indian Sch.; Claremont Col.; Col. St. Joseph, Albuquerque, B.S. in Edu.; & with Dorothy Dunn, Kenneth Chapman, Alfredo Martinez. *Member*: New Mexico Edu. Assn. *Awards*: purchase prize, deYoung Mus. A., 1954. *Work*: deYoung Mus. A. *Exhibited*: Mus. New Mexico, Santa Fé; Indian A. Exh., 1954, 1955; Mus. New Mexico traveling exh. of Indiana paintings. Lectures: Indian Design; Indian Painting. *Position*: Instr., Painting, Santa Fé Indian Sch., Santa Fé, N.M., 1935- .

MOORE, BENSON BOND—Painter, Et., T.
2019 Monroe St., N.E., Washington 18, D.C.

B. Washington, D.C., Aug. 13, 1882. *Studied*: Corcoran Sch. A. *Member*: Soc. Wash. A.; Wash. WC Cl.; Wash. Landscape Cl.; AAPL; SSAL; Balt. WC Cl.; New Haven Paint & Clay Cl.; Wash. SE; Wash. Soc. Min. P. S. & G.; Royal Soc. P. G. & S., London, England. *Work*: Lib. Cong.; White House, Wash., D.C.; Bibliotheque Nationale, Paris; N.Y. Pub. Lib.; Univ. Georgia; Smithsonian Inst.; Mus. FA of Houston; Phila. A. All.; Wash. AC; Los A. Mus. A.

MOORE, BRUCE—Painter, Des., T.
790 Lexington Ave.; h. 43 East 61st St., New York 21, N.Y.

B. Los Angeles, Cal., Oct. 6, 1889. *Studied*: Garvanza Sch. A. (affil. with Univ. So. Cal.); ASL; Grand Central A. Sch. *Member*: AAPL; NAC. *Award*: prize, Elizabethtown, N.Y. *Work*: Rochester Mem. A. Gal.

MOORE, CONSTANCE—Former Museum Director
2006 Park Dr., Wilmington 6, Del.

B. Wilmington, Del., Dec. 29, 1893. *Member*: AFA; Wilmington Soc. FA; AAMus. *Position*: Cur., Wilmington Soc. FA, 1931-1938; Dir., Delaware A. Center, Wilmington, Del., 1938-1957 (retired); Bd. of Dir., 1957- .

MOORE, E. BRUCE—Sculptor
1210 St. Matthews Court, Washington 6, D.C.

B. Bern, Kan., Aug. 5, 1905. *Studied*: PAFA, with Albert Laessle, Charles Grafly. *Member*: NA; Nat. Inst. A. & Lets.; NSS; F. Am. Numismatic Soc. *Awards*: Cresson traveling scholarship, PAFA, 1925, 1926; med., PAFA, 1929; Guggenheim F., 1929-1930, 1930-1931; prizes, NAD, 1935, 1937; Meriden A. & Crafts Assn., 1940; M. R. Cromwell F., 1937-1940; Grant, Nat. Inst. A. & Let., 1943; medal, Am. Numismatic Soc., 1952. *Work*: WMAA; Wichita A. Mus.; PAFA; Brookgreen Gardens, S.C.; Wichita AC; Steuben Glass Co.; Smithsonian Inst.; Am. Acad. in Rome; Wichita (Kan.) H.S.; ports. and animal sc. in private colls. *Exhibited*: Am. Acad. in Rome, 1938, 1939; NSS; PAFA, 1929, 1930, 1940; NAD, 1935, 1937; WMAA, 1942; Meriden A. & Crafts, 1940, 1942; Nat. Inst. A. & Let., 1943; VMFA, 1958.

MOORE, FRANK M.—Painter
P.O. Box 1313, Carmel, Cal.

B. Taunton, England, Nov. 24, 1877. *Studied*: Royal Inst., Liverpool, England; Liverpool A. Sch. *Member*: SC; Carmel AA. *Awards*: prize, med., Palace Legion Honor, 1944.

Exhibited: Carmel AA, 1945, 1946. *Work*: Honolulu Acad. A.; Auckland (N.Z.) Mus. A.; USMC Headquarters, San F., Cal.; murals, Picture Bridge, Pasadena, Cal. *Exhibited*: NAD; PAFA; CGA; N.Y. WC Cl.; Pan-Pacific Exp., 1915; Pasadena SA; Santa Cruz, Cal., 1944; Soc. for Sanity in Art, 1941-1945; Cal. SA; Cal. State Fair.

MOORE, GERTRUDE HERDLE—Museum Director, E.
Rochester Memorial Art Gallery, 490 University Ave. (7); h. 2331 Westfall Rd., Rochester 18, N.Y.

Studied: Univ. Rochester, B.A., M.A. *Member*: Assn. Mus. Dir. *Position*: Dir., Rochester Memorial A. Gal., Rochester, N.Y.

MOORE, LORAINE (ELIZABETH)—Etcher, P.
3136 North West 25th St., Oklahoma City, Okla.

B. Oklahoma City, Okla. *Studied*: Oklahoma City Univ.; Oklahoma A. & M. Col., and with Doel Reed, Marion Hartwell, Xavier Gonzalez. *Member*: NAWA; Okla. AA. *Awards*: medal, Tulsa, Okla.; prizes, 100 Best Prints of the Year, 1941; Okla. AA, 1941, 1942, 1950, 1952, 1953-1955; Southwestern Print Exh., 1948, 1951, 1953; Assn. Okla. A., 1941, 1942, 1948, 1954, 1955; Cal. Soc. Et., 1947; Northwest Pr. M., 1944. *Exhibited*: SAGA, 1938, 1940, 1941, 1945, 1951, 1952; Northwest Pr. M., 1941, 1942, 1945, 1946, 1948, 1950, 1951; NAD, 1945, 1946; LC, 1945, 1946, 1950, 1952; NAWA, 1946; Albany Pr. Cl., 1945, 1946; Kansas City AI, 1945, 1946; Tulsa AA, 1945, 1946; Okla. AA, 1940-1942, 1944-1952; Audubon A., 1952; A. of Missouri Valley, 1951; Denver A. Mus., 1951; Southwestern Exh. Prints & Drawings; Assn. of Okla. A.; Buffalo Pr. Cl.; Mid-Am. A.*

MOORE, MARTHA E. (Mrs. Louis A. Burnett)— Painter, T.
322 West 72nd St., New York 23, N.Y.

B. Bayonne, N.J. *Studied*: ASL. *Member*: ASL (life); NAWA; Catherine L. Wolfe A. Cl.; AAPL. *Awards*: prizes, ASL, 1943, scholarships, 1943-45; A. Lg. of Long Island, 1950; Wolfe A. Cl., 1951; Barbizon Plaza Gal., 1951, 1952; 8th St. Gal., 1951; AAPL, 1948; All. A. Am., 1951; Knickerbocker A., 1955. *Work*: Paintings, ports., St. Vincent's Hospital, N.Y.; Merchant Marine Military Acad., King's Point, N.Y.; Passionist Monastery, West Springfield, Mass.; and in private colls. in U.S., Canada and South America. *Exhibited*: Audubon A., 1946; All. A. Am., 1946, 1951; AWS, 1949, 1950; NAWA, 1950, 1951, 1954; New Jersey P. & S. Soc., 1950; New Jersey WC Soc., 1950; A. Lg. of Long Island, 1950; Newton A. Gal., N.Y., 1948; Butler A. Gal., N.Y., 1953-1955; Portraits, Inc., 1948-1955; Grand Central A. Gal., 1949-1955; USA, 1958; BM, 1958, and in museums and galleries throughout U.S. *Position*: Owner, Dir., Burnett Gal., New York, N.Y.; Chm. Pub. Rel., All. A. Am.

MOOSE, PHILIP ANTHONY—Painter, E.
323 West 'E' St., Newton, N.C.

B. Newton, N.C., Jan. 16, 1921. *Studied*: NAD; Columbia Univ.; Skowhegan Sch. A.; Acad. FA, Munich, Germany. *Member*: AWS; Gld. Charlotte A. *Awards*: Pulitzer prize, 1948; Tiffany award, 1949; Fulbright award, 1953. *Work*: Colchester Mus., England; Atlanta Mus. A.; Norfolk Mus. A.; Mint Mus. A.; North Carolina State Mus., Raleigh; Taos Coll., N.M. *Exhibited*: MMA, 1952; CGA, 1953; Southeastern annuals, 1950-1955; East-West Gal., San F., 1955; Ferargil Gal., 1950; one-man: Duke Univ., 1955; Univ. North Carolina, 1951; North Carolina State Gal., 1950. Illus., "History of Catawba County," 1954. *Position*: Assoc. Prof. FA, Davidson (N.C.) Col., 1951-53; Prof. FA, Queens College, Charlotte, N.C., 1955-58.

MOOTY, MARY ELIZABETH—Educator
626 West Call St., Tallahassee, Fla.

B. Cottonwood, Ala., Mar. 9, 1913. *Studied*: Florida State Col. for Women, B.A.; T. Col., Columbia Univ., M.A.; Inst. Des., Chicago, Ill. *Member*: CAA; AFA; Fla. Edu. Assn. Lectures: Art Education; Art in Daily Living. *Position*: Instr. A., 1937-46; Assoc. Prof. A. Edu. & Constructive Des., Acting Hd. Dept., 1946-52, Fla. State Univ., Tallahassee, Fla.*

MORAN, EDWARD—*Etcher, P.*

Main St., East Hampton, L.I., N.Y.

B. New York, N.Y., Apr. 14, 1901. *Work*: Lib. Cong. *Exhibited*: SAE, 1944; Lib. Cong., 1942, 1944; Albright A. Gal., 1943; Guild Hall, East Hampton, L.I., N.Y., 1932, 1933, 1943-1946. *Position*: A. Dir., Guild Hall, East Hampton, L.I., N.Y.*

MORANG, DOROTHY (ALDEN CLARK)—
Painter, Mus. Cur., C., Cr., W.

526 Canyon Rd., Santa Fe, N.M.

B. Bridgton, Me., Nov. 24, 1906. *Studied*: with Alfred Morang, Raymond Jonson, Emil Bisttram. *Member*: AFA; Santa Fe Assn. of the Arts (Pres.); Santa Fe Women A. Exhibiting Group. *Awards*: prizes, New Mexico State Fair, 1949; Mus. New Mexico, 1953, 1956; Nat. Lg. Am. Pen Women, 1953 (2). *Work*: Mus. New Mexico; Canyon (Tex.) Mus. *Exhibited*: Guggenheim Mus. A., 1944, 1945; Sweat Mus. A., 1933, 1934; Mus. New Mexico, 1937-1955 (one-man and groups); Univ. New Mexico, 1945; New Mexico State Fair, 1943-1952, 1958; La Galeria de los Artesanos, Las Vegas, N.M., 1950; Rector Gal., Roswell, N.M., 1950; A. All. Gal., Boston, 1958; N.M. All. for the Arts, 1951; Santa Fe Women A. Exhibiting Group in Okla., Cal., N.M., Texas; one-man: Jonson Gal., Albuquerque, 1956; Morris Harvey Col., Charleston, W. Va., 1957; West Texas A. Gld., 1957; New Mexico Inst. Mining & Tech., 1957; Eastern N.M. Univ., 1957; Roswell Mus., 1958. *Position*: Acting Cur. A., 1945, Hd. Dept. War Records, 1946-48, Sec. FA, 1948-55, Cur. Traveling Exhibitions, 1955- , Mus. of New Mexico, Santa Fe, N.M.; Santa Fe Chm., 1952, State Dir., 1953, 1954, American Art Week; Jury, Gallup Intertribal Indian Ceremonial Exh., 1956; Jury, Santa Fe Woman's Cl., 1958.

MORDVINOFF, NICOLAS—*Illustrator, P., W.*

Route 1, Hampton, N.J.

B. St. Petersburg, Russia, Sept. 27, 1911. *Studied*: Univ. Paris, and with Fernand Leger, Amedee Ozenfant. *Awards*: Caldecott award, 1952; Herald Tribune award, 1954; AIGA Certif. Excellence, 1955-57. *Work*: N.Y. Pub. Lib.; MMA. *Exhibited*: Paris, France; New Zealand; Hawaii; San Francisco, Los Angeles, Washington and many other U.S. cities; one-man: Tahiti, 1936, 1940, 1950; Phila. A. All., 1952; Luyber Gal., N.Y., 1949; N.Y. Pub. Lib., 1952. Contributor illus. to Harper's Magazine; Atlantic Monthly. Author, I., Des.; "Bear's Land," 1955; "Coral Island," 1957; Illus., Des.: "Just So Stories," 1952; "Alphonse, That Bearded One," 1954; "Daniel Boone's Echo," 1958; "Evangeline," 1959, and many others. Books by Will and Nicolas: "The Two Reds," 1950; "Finders Keepers," 1951 (Caldecott award); "The Magic Feather Duster," 1958; "Four Leaf Clover," 1959, and many more.

MORENON, ERNEST E.—*Sculptor, T.*

30 Ipswich St., Boston, Mass.; h. 284 Franklin St., Newton 58, Mass.

B. Marseille, France, Jan. 30, 1904. *Studied*: Ecole Nationale des Beaux-Arts, Paris, and in Italy, Belgium, England. *Member*: Arch. Lg.; Audubon A.; Indp. A., Boston; New England Contemp. Sculptors Assn.; NSS. *Awards*: Institute of France, 1929, 1930, 1932, second Prix de Rome, 1933; Medal, Salon Artistes Francais, 1932; traveling scholarship, French Govt.; 1929; Medal, Exposition Internationale, Paris, 1937; Silver Medal, 1954, Gold Medal, 1955, Arch. Lg. *Work*: S., main gate World's Fair, Paris, 1937; Carney Hospital, Boston, 1952; Nazareth Sch., Boston, 1953; church, Holyoke, Mass.; 1954; Cathedral of Baltimore, Md., 1958. *Exhibited*: PAFA, 1951; Arch Lg., 1954, 1955; Soc. Indp. A., Boston, 1949-1951, 1953, 1954, 1956; New England Sculpture (Boston, 1951, Andover, 1952, Worcester, 1954, Exeter, 1955); Boston A. Festival, 1952; Audubon A., 1954; NSS, 1958, and others. *Position*: Instr., S., Des., Cambridge Sch. Des., 1947-52; S., BMFA Sch., Boston, Mass., 1950- .

MORGAN, ARTHUR C.—*Sculptor, E., W., L.*

657 Jordan St., Shreveport, La.

B. Riverton Plantation, Ascension Parish, La., Aug. 3, 1904. *Studied*: BAID; & with Gutzon Borglum, Mario Korbel, Edward McCarten, & others. *Member*: NAC. *Awards*: medals, Inst. of Camera Art, 1938; Centenary Col., 1946. *Work*: S., Centenary Col., St. Mark's Church,

Shreveport, La.; U.S. Capitol (bronze figure of Chief Justice Edward D. White); USPO & Court House, Alexandria, La.; Terrebonne Parish Court House, Houma, La.; Southwestern Inst. A.; ports. in bronze, terra cotta and marble, dec. bronzes and garden sculpture in many private colls. *Exhibited*: Louisiana State Univ., 1927; Southwestern Inst. A., 1938; La. State Exh., 1940, 1950; Philbrook A. Center, 1952; Centennial Mus., Corpus Christi, Tex., 1957, (one-man exh.). Contributor of: art reviews to newspapers. *Position*: Dir., A. Dept., Centenary Col., Shreveport, La., 1928-33; Dir., Southwestern Inst. A., Shreveport, La., 1933- .

MORGAN, CHARLES HILL—*Educator, Mus. Dir.*

317 South Pleasant St., Amherst, Mass.

B. Worcester, Mass., Sept. 19, 1902. *Studied*: Harvard Univ., A.B., A.M., Ph.D. Author: Corinth, Vol. XI, The Byzantine Pottery, 1942. Contributor to: American Journal of Archaeology; Art in America; Hesperia. *Position*: Dir., Am. Sch. Classical Studies, Athens, Greece, 1936-38; Prof. FA, Dir., A. Mus., Amherst Col., Amherst, Mass., 1938- .

MORGAN, FRANCES MALLORY—*Sculptor*

Sunset Lane, Rye, N.Y.

B. Memphis, Tenn. *Studied*: Grand Central A. Sch.; PAFA; NAD, with Archipenko, Hovannes. *Member*: NAWA; Audubon A.; S. Gld. *Awards*: prizes, NAC, 1933, 1934; NAWA, 1941, 1944, 1946. *Work*: IBM; Brooks Mem. Mus., and in private colls. *Exhibited*: Albright A. Gal.; WFNY 1939; WMAA; CGA; Am.-British A. Center; Arch. Lg.; Riverside Mus.; PMA; PAFA; MMA; Montclair A. Mus.; NAWA, 1934-1958; Audubon A., 1945-1958; S. Gld., 1939-1958; Studio Gld. Traveling Exh., 1951-1955; Providence A. Cl., 1958.

MORGAN, GLADYS B. (Mrs. Arthur C.)—
Painter, L., T.

657 Jordan St., Shreveport 39, La.

B. Houma, La., Mar. 24, 1899. *Studied*: Randolph-Macon Col. for Women, A.B.; Columbia Univ.; & with Arthur C. Morgan, Will H. Stevens. *Member*: Shreveport WC Soc.; Louisiana A.; Shreveport A. Cl.; Univ. Woman's Cl. *Work*: Excelsior Hotel, Jefferson, Tex.; Gilmer Hospital, Shreveport, La., and in private colls. *Exhibited*: Mus. FA, Montgomery, Ala.; Old Capitol Mus., Baton Rouge, La.; Delgado Mus. A.; one-man: Lake Charles, La.; Houma, La.; Shreveport Mus. A.; Woman's Dept. Cl., Shreveport; Barksdale Air Force Base, Bossier City, La., and others. *Position*: Instr. A. & Hist. A., Centenary Col., 1928-33; Southwestern Inst. A., Shreveport, La., 1934- . Instr., Ext. Class, Barksdale Air Force Base. Lectures: "The Arts of Mexico."

MORGAN, HELEN BOSART (Mrs. J. W.)—*Sculptor, T.*

845 East High St., Springfield, Ohio

B. Springfield, Ohio, Oct. 17, 1902. *Studied*: AIC; Wittenberg Col., A.B.; Dayton AI. *Member*: NAWA; Dayton Soc. P. & S.; Springfield AA; Dayton AI. *Awards*: prizes, Springfield County Fair, 1951; Dayton AI, 1945, 1946, 1948; Springfield A. Exh., 1946-1948, 1952, 1954; Clark County Fair, 1951; Ohio State Fair, 1952. *Exhibited*: NAD, 1945; All. A. Am., 1944, 1945; NAWA, 1944, 1946, 1948, 1955; Miami Valley A., 1943, 1946; Butler AI, 1946, 1948, 1955; Springfield AA, 1946, 1948-1958; Wichita AA, 1948; Syracuse Mus. FA, 1948; CM, 1948, 1951, 1956, 1957; Ohio State Fair, 1957; Dayton AI, 1948, 1952-1958; one-man: Newman Brown Gal., Chicago, 1953.

MORGAN, LUCY CALISTA—*Craftsman, T., W.*

Penland, N.C.

B. Franklin, N.C., Sept. 20, 1889. *Studied*: Central T. Col., Mt. Pleasant, Mich.; Univ. Chicago; & with Edward F. Worst. *Member*: Southern Highland Handicraft Gld.; Bus. & Prof. Women's Cl., Spruce Pine, N.C. Contributor to: The Weaver: Practical Weaving Suggestions magazines. *Awards*: hon. deg., Dr. Humanities, Central Mich. Col. of Edu., 1952; D.H.L., Woman's Col., Univ. North Carolina, 1955; Co-author (with Le Gette Blythe) "Gift From The Hills," 1958. *Position*: Dir., Penland Weavers & Potters, 1936-46; Founder & Dir., Penland Sch. Handicrafts, Penland, N.C., 1929- .

MORGENTHALER, CHARLES ALBERT—
Illustrator, P., Des., C., T.
5950 De Giverville Ave., St. Louis, Mo.

B. Hallsville, Mo., June 18, 1893. *Studied*: St. Louis Sch.
FA; AIC, with Fred Carpenter, Elmer Forsberg, Jessie
Lacey, and others. *Member*: AAPL; Indp. A., St. Louis;
St. Louis A. Lg.; Am. A. All.; A. Dir. Cl., St. Louis.
Awards: prizes, Indp. A., St. Louis, 1944; Sedalia Fair,
1945. *Work*: ports., Cochran Veterans Hospital, St. Louis;
Supreme Court Bldg., Jefferson City; Pine Lawn (Mo.)
Bank; Crystal City H.S.; Ruggerie's Restaurant; Osteo-
pathic Hospital, Jefferson City; paintings, Bell Telephone
Co., St. Louis; Purina Mills; murals, Osage House Restau-
rant, De Soto Hotel, Bilgere Chevrolet Co., Town Hall,
Paul Brown Bldg., Keil Auditorium, St. Louis; Missouri
Pacific R.R., Kansas City and St. Louis; Fed. Savings &
Loan Assn., East St. Louis; Hall of the Presidents, Gettys-
burg, Pa., and others. *Exhibited*: Kansas City AI; St. Louis
A. Gld.; St. Louis A. Lg.; Indp. A., St. Louis; CAM,
1945-1955, 1958; Terry AI, 1952; Laguna Beach, Cal.,
1952; Springfield Mus. A., 1955; AAPL, 1956, 1957; SI,
1958; AIC, 1955, 1957, and others. *Position*: Member, St.
Louis Art Commission, 1953-55, 1955-1961.

MORLEY, GRACE L. McCANN—*Museum Director*
Solomon R. Guggenheim Museum, 7 East 72nd St.,
New York, N.Y.

B. Berkeley, Cal., Nov. 3, 1900. *Studied*: Univ. California,
A.B., M.A.; Univ. Paris, Docteur de l'Universite; & in
Grenoble, France. *Member*: CAA; AFA; AAMus; Am.
Assn. A. Mus. Dir.; Western Assn. A. Mus. Dir.; Western
Mus. Conference; Nat. Comm. for UNESCO, 1950- ;
Visual Arts Panel of Comm., 1949-51; Museums Panel and
A. Edu. Panels, 1951- . *Awards*: hon. degree, LL.D., Mills
Col., Oakland, Cal., 1937; LL.D., Univ. California at
Los Angeles, 1958. *Author*: "Le sentiment de la Nature en
France dans la première mortié du 17e siecle," Paris, 1926.
Contributor to: professional periodicals, encyclopaedias,
museum publications. Lectures: Latin American Art: Con-
temporary Art; etc. *Position*: Instr., French & A., Goucher
Col., Baltimore, Md., 1927-30; Cur., CM, 1930-33; Dir.,
SFMA, San Francisco, Cal., 1935-1958; Dir., Pacific House,
GGE, 1939; Consultant, A. Com., Office Inter-Am. Affairs,
1941-43; Advisor, Museums, UNESCO, 1946; Hd., Mu-
seums, UNESCO, 1947-49; Ed. Bd., "Museum." Asst. Dir.,
Solomon R. Guggenheim Museum, New York, N.Y., 1959- .

MORLEY, MARY CECILIA—*Painter, T.*
421 Stone St., Watertown, N.Y.

B. Watertown, N.Y., Dec. 14, 1900. *Studied*: St. Law-
rence Univ., Canton, N.Y., B.S., M.A.; Maryland Inst.;
Syracuse Univ.; N.Y. Univ. *Member*: Saranac A. Lg.;
Indp. A. Group; N.Y. State A.T. Assn.; AAPL; Eastern
AA. *Exhibited*: Acad. All. A., 1940-1943; All. A. Am.,
1941, 1943; Audubon A., 1944; Indp. A. Group, 1944,
1949, 1951; Saranac A. Lg., 1940, 1942-1944; Ogunquit A.
Center, 1952; St. Lawrence Valley Exh., 1952; Watertown
Pub. Lib., 1944 (one-man). Contributor to School Arts
magazine; Illus. for State P.T.A. pamphlets and Bd. of
Edu. publications. *Position*: Instr. A., South Jr. H.S.,
Watertown, N.Y., at present; State Sec., N.Y. State A. T.
Assn.

MORPURGO, VILNA JORGEN—*Painter, S., T., W.*
8715 37th Ave., Jackson Heights, L.I., N.Y.

B. Oslo, Norway, June 10, 1900. *Studied*: Maison Wat-
teau, Paris; sculpture with Karl Eldh in Sweden. *Member*:
AEA. *Work*: Gal. Mod. A., Stockholm; in Royal collec-
tions in Sweden, Belgium, Italy. *Exhibited*: NAD, 1947;
Helena (Mont.) Mus. A., 1955; Montross Gal.; Argent
Gal.; Riverside Mus.; RoKo Gal.; Jorgen Gal.; Norheim
Gal. Foreign Correspondent and Critic for magazines in
Sweden.*

MORRIS, ALICE—*Painter, Lith.*
26 Prescott Court, San Francisco 11, Cal.

B. Lowell, Mass. *Studied*: Emory Univ.; Chicago Univ.;
Univ. Denver; N.Y. Univ.; Ecole du Louvre, Paris, France;
Univ. So. Cal.; Cal. Sch. FA; Univ. California; Cal. Col.
A. & Crafts, and with Maurice Sterne. *Member*: Cal. WC
Soc.; AWS. *Exhibited*: Art in Nat. Defense traveling exh.,
1942-46; Riverside Mus., 1940; SFMA, 1940-1942; Los A.
Mus. A.; San Diego FA Soc.; Santa Barbara Mus. A.,
1940-1942. Fndr., Outdoor Junior A. Exh., held annually,
1942- .

MORRIS, CARL—*Painter*
919 Northwest Skyline Blvd., Portland 1, Ore.

B. Yorba Linda, Cal., 1911. *Studied*: AIC; and in Vienna,
and Paris. *Awards*: Inst. Intl. Edu. F., 1935-36; prizes,
SFMA, 1946; SAM, 1946; Denver A. Mus., 1946 (pur-
chase); Pepsi Cola, 1948; Phelan Award, Cal., 1950; Stan-
ford A. Gal., 1956 (purchase); Univ. Illinois, 1957 (pur-
chase). *Work*: SAM; Portland A. Mus.; SFMA; Denver
A. Mus.; Univ. Colorado; Univ. Oregon; Reed Col., Port-
land, Ore.; Walker A. Center; Guggenheim Mus.; Arte
Moderna, Sao Paulo, Brazil; Munson-Williams-Proctor Inst.;
Cal. PLH; Mills Col.; Stanford Univ.; Univ. Illinois;
WMAA; Colorado Springs FA Center; Nat. Inst. A. &
Lets.; Toronto A. Gal.; Santa Barbara Mus. A.; MMA;
Wichita A. Mus.; Portland State Col., and others; mural,
USPO, Eugene, Ore. *Exhibited*: WMAA, 1947, 1948, 1950,
1955, 1956, 1957; MMA, 1952; AIC, 1942, 1947; CGA;
Albright A. Gal., 1947, 1948; WFNY 1939; GGE, 1939;
AGAA, 1947, 1948; Albany Inst. Hist. & A., 1947, 1948;
BMA, 1947, 1948; Munson-Williams-Proctor Inst., 1947,
1948; SFMA, 1944, 1946, 1953, 1954; Colo. Springs FA
Center, annually since 1945; Denver A. Mus., 1945-1958;
Portland A. Mus., annually; SAM, annually; Guggenheim
Mus. A., 1954; Univ. Denver, 1954; Sao Paulo, Brazil,
1955; Carnegie Inst., 1955; SFMA, 1955; Rio de Janeiro,
1955; PAFA, 1957, 1958; Nat. Inst. A. & Lets., 1957, and
others, 1956-1958; one-man: SAM, 1940; Portland A. Mus.,
1946, 1952, 1955; Cal. PLH, 1946; Reed Col., 1950;
Kraushaar Gal., N.Y., 1953, 1956, 1958; Pepsi-Cola, 1948;
Rotunda Gal., San F., 1954; City of Paris, San F., 1954;
Zivile Gal., Los A., 1955; Mills Col., 1956; Otto Seligman
Gal., 1957, and many colleges and edu. centers.

MORRIS, DUDLEY (HENRY) (JR.)—
Painter, Lith., I., W., T.
23 Armour Rd., Princeton, N.J.

B. New York, N.Y., Apr. 26, 1912. *Studied*: Andover
Acad.; Yale Univ., A.B.; ASL, with Harry Wickey,
Alexander Brook, Charles Locke. *Member*: Century Assn.
Work: WMAA; AGAA; Presbyterian Hospital, N.Y.; New
York Hospital; Firestone Lib., Princeton Univ.; Wood-
bridge Hall, Yale Univ., 1958. *Exhibited*: nationally and
internationally. One-man: AGAA, 1935; WAC, 1936,
Princeton Univ., 1942; Little Gal., Princeton, 1956. Author,
I., juvenile books. *Position*: Chm. A. Dept., Lawrence-
ville Sch. (N.J.), 1936-43, 1946- ; Chm., Indp. Schs. A.
T. Assn.; Chm., A. Com., Secondary Edu. Bd.

MORRIS, GEORGE FORD—*Painter, W., S., I., Gr.*
Fordacre, Shrewsbury, N.J.

B. St. Joseph, Mo. *Studied*: AIC; Julian Acad., Paris,
France. *Member*: Am. Animal Artists' Assn. (Pres.); F.,
Royal Acad. A., London. *Exhibited*: Poulsen Gal., Pasa-
dena, Cal. Specializes in painting famous horses, their
owners and riders. Author, I., "Portraitures of Horses";
Illus., "George Ford Morris Animals," published for 3
consecutive years and bound in Christmas issues of "The
American Horseman." Illus. for The Horseman; Breeder's
Gazette; Western Horseman; American Field; American
Horseman; National Horseman; Arabian Horse News;
Thoroughbred Record: Thoroughbred of California and
other publications; also contributor illus. to: Century;
Scribners; and The Spur magazines.

MORRIS, GEORGE L. K.—*Painter, S., W., L., T.*
1 Sutton Place, South, New York 22, N.Y.

B. New York, N.Y., Nov. 14, 1906. *Studied*: Yale Univ.,
B.A.; ASL; Academie Moderne, Paris, France. *Member*:
Am. Abstract A.; Fed. Mod. P. & S. *Work*: Univ. Illinois;
Univ. Georgia; Darmstadt, Germany; PMA; WMAA;
Berkshire Mus.; Yale Sch. FA; PC; MMA; PAFA; Wichita
Mus. A. *Exhibited*: WMAA, 1938-1946; PAFA, 1945, 1946;
Carnegie Inst., 1944-1958; Am. Abstract A., 1936-1958;
Fed. Mod. P. & S., 1941-1958; VMFA, 1946; Berkshire
Mus., 1935, 1938, 1945. Contributor to Partisan Review,
with articles on abstract art. Lectured on American Art
in Paris, London, Vienna, Rome, Milan, Athens, Istambul,
1952. *Position*: U.S. Painting Delegate to 1952, UNESCO
Conference, Venice, Italy.

MORRIS, HILDA (Mrs. Carl)—*Sculptor*
919 Northwest Skyline Blvd., Portland 1, Ore.

B. New York, N.Y., June 1, 1911. *Studied*: ASL; CUASch.
Work: Munson-Williams-Proctor Inst.; SAM; Portland

(Ore.) A. Mus.; SFMA; Walter Chrysler Coll., and in other private colls. *Exhibited*: SAM, annually; Portland A. Mus., annually; Denver A. Mus., annually; SFMA, annually; one-man and group: SFMA, 1943; Henry Gal., Univ. Washington; Univ. Oregon, 1948; Reed Col.; Portland A. Mus., 1946, 1955; MMA, 1951; BM, 1953; Sao Paulo, Brazil, 1955; Rio de Janeiro, 1955; SFMA, 1955; "New Talent," 1957; AFA traveling exh., 1958.

MORRIS, KYLE RANDOLPH—*Painter*

243 East 17th St., New York 3, N.Y.

B. Des Moines, Iowa, Jan. 17, 1918. *Studied*: Northwestern Univ., B.A., M.A.; AIC; Cranbrook Acad. A., M.F.A. *Awards*: prizes, WAC, 1948 (purchase); SFMA, 1953 (purchase). *Exhibited*: WAC, 1948; WMAA, annually; Guggenheim Mus., 1954; AIC, 1954; Univ. Illinois, 1954, 1956; Univ. Nebraska, 1954, 1956; CGA, 1956, 1958; Minneapolis Inst. A., 1957; Worcester Mus. A., 1958; Brussels World's Fair, 1958; N.Y.-Rome Fnd., Rome, Italy, 1958; VMFA, 1958; one-man: Pepsi Cola A. Gal., N.Y., 1947; WAC, 1952; Des Moines A. Center, 1955; 3-man, Tanager Gal., N.Y., 1952. *Positions*: Instr., A. Hist. & P., Stephens Col., Columbia, Mo., 1940-41; Asst. Prof. A., Univ. Texas, Austin, 1941-46; Assoc. Prof. Painting, Univ. Minnesota, 1947-51; Assoc. Prof., Painting, Univ. California, Berkeley, 1952-54; L., A. Hist., CUASch., New York, N.Y., 1958. Ed., "Contemporary Slides," 1954-58; Delegate to UNESCO meetings, United Nations, 1952.

MORRIS, PATRICIA M.—*Painter*

135 West Ellis Ave., Inglewood 1, Cal.

B. Ashtabula Harbor, Ohio, May 8, 1927. *Studied*: Scripps Col., with Millard Sheets; Los Angeles County AI. *Member*: Cal. WC Soc. *Awards*: prizes, Denver A. Mus., 1954; Los A. Mus. A., 1952, 1955; Motion Picture A. Dir. award, 1952, 1955; Cole of California award, 1953. *Exhibited*: Cal-Canadian Watercolor Exh., 1955-56; BM, 1952; Denver A. Mus., 1953-1955; LC, 1952; Los A. Mus. A., 1952-1954; Cal. State Fair, 1951-1954; Nat. Orange Show, 1952-1954; Cal. WC Soc., 1951-1955.*

MORRISON, GEORGE—*Painter*

146 West 23rd St., New York 11, N.Y.

B. Grand Marais, Minn., Sept. 30, 1919. *Studied*: Minneapolis Sch. A.; ASL, and with Morris Kantor. *Member*: AEA; Grand Central Moderns. *Awards*: Vanderlip traveling scholarship, 1943; Fulbright F., 1952; prizes, Walker A. Center, 1951; Critic's Show, N.Y., 1946. *Work*: Minneapolis Inst. A.; Walker A. Center, and in many private colls. *Exhibited*: PAFA, 1946, 1947, 1949; CGA, 1947, 1950; WMAA, 1947, 1948, 1950; New Orleans A. & Crafts, 1947; Los A. Mus. A., 1950; Nebraska AA, 1952; Critic's Show, N.Y., 1946; Mus. FA of Houston, 1947; Walker A. Center, 1947, 1951; Twin Cities exh., Minneapolis, 1941, 1942; Minnesota State Fair, 1942, 1943; Duluth, 1947; one-man: Grand Central A. Gal., 1948, 1950; Riverside Mus., 1947, 1949, 1951.*

MORRISON, MARK—*Sculptor*

8 West 13th St., New York 11, N.Y.

B. King Fisher, Okla., Jan. 1, 1900. *Studied*: Univ. Missouri; ASL, and with John Flanagan, Jose deCreeft, William Zorach. *Member*: S. Gld.; Audubon A. *Awards*: prize, NAD, 1950; Arch. Lg., 1957. *Work*: Arizona State College. *Exhibited*: MMA, 1942, 1951; NAD, 1949, 1950; PAFA, 1949, 1950; Fairmount Park, Phila., 1949; WMAA, 1949, 1950; Nebraska FA Assn., 1946; Newark Mus., 1944; Wilmington Soc. FA, 1946; Boston A. Festival, 1955; Audubon A., 1947-1954; S. Gld., 1950-1955; New Britain, Conn., 1947.

MORRISON, MONTE B.—*Painter, E., Gr., L.*

Art Department, Wesleyan College; h. 1215 Hardeman St. #2, Macon, Ga.

B. Spokane, Wash., Jan. 4, 1928. *Studied*: Whitman Col., A.B.; Univ. Oregon, M.F.A.; Ruskin Sch. A., Ashmolean Mus., Oxford, England. *Member*: Portland (Ore.) AA. *Award*: Pennell Scholarship, Univ. Oregon, 1955. *Work*: Univ. Oregon Mus. *Exhibited*: Oregon Artists, 1953-1958; Oregon Artists print shows, 1954, 1955. *Position*: Asst. Prof. A., Wesleyan College, Macon, Ga., at present.

MORSE, JENNIE GREENE [Mrs. Henry W.]—*Educator, Des., P., C.*

Fashion Institute of Technology, 225 West 24th St., New York 11, N.Y.; h. 1327 Shore Parkway, Brooklyn 14, N.Y.

B. New York, N.Y., Mar. 19, 1908. *Studied*: N.Y. Sch. App. Des. for Women. *Member*: Am. Un. Dec. Artists & Craftsmen; Am. Assn. Jr. Col.; School A. Lg.; AAUP. *Awards*: Sch. A. Lg. scholarships, 1925-26, 1926-27; Design awards: Loren O. Thompson; Witcombe McGeachin Co.; Susquehanna Silk Mills; Schwarzenbach, Huber Co. *Exhibited*: MMA, 1931; Am. Mus. Natural Hist.; Grand Central A. Gal. *Positions*: Instr., Textile Des., N.Y. Evening Sch. Indst. A., 1929-43; Instr., H.S., New York, N.Y., 1938-45; Fashion Inst. Tech., New York, N.Y., 1945-54; Chm., Textile Des. Dept., Fashion Inst. Technology, Div. of Advanced Studies; Co-ordinator of Exec. Training Seminar in Fabric Styling, Converting & Merchandising for the Textile Industry, 1955-58.

MORSE, JOHN D.—*Writer, Editor, T.*

448 Riverside Drive, New York 27, N.Y.

B. Gifford, Ill., Sept. 26, 1906. *Studied*: Univ. Illinois, A.B., M.A.; Wayne Univ.; N.Y. Univ. *Member*: Am. Soc. for Aesthetics. Author: "Wartime Guide to American Collections of the Metropolitan Museum of Art," 1942; "The Artist and the Museum," 1947; "Old Masters in America," 1955. Contributor to: Adventures in Reading, 3rd series, 1947; Magazine of Art; museum bulletins; fiction & non-fiction in Esquire, London Evening Standard, & other magazines. Lectures: General Art History and Interpretation with emphasis on modern art. *Positions*: Asst. Ed., Am. Boy Magazine, 1928-29, 1930-31; Instr., Univ. Illinois, 1934-35; Mus. Instr., Detroit Inst. A., 1935-41; Managing Ed., The Art Quarterly, 1938-41; Assoc. in Radio, MMA, New York, N.Y., 1941-42; Ed., Magazine of Art, 1942-47; A. Ed., '47, the Magazine of the Year, 1947-48; Dir. Publ., ASL, New York, N.Y., 1948-50; Assoc. Ed., American Artist magazine, 1951-53; Conductor, American Artist magazine European Tours, 1950-52; Exec. Dir., Amateur Artists Assn. Am., 1951-53; Exec. Sec., Kent Sch., Instr., A. Hist., 1954-1956. Freelance writing, at present.

MORSE, SADIE MAY—*Educator, Des., C., P.*

286 Ocean Ave., Marblehead Neck, Mass.

B. Lexington, Mass., May 5, 1873. *Studied*: Mass. Sch. A., B.S.E.; MIT; Harvard Univ., and abroad. Lectures: Design & Color in Craft Work. *Positions*: Supv. A., Pub. Schs., Newburyport, Mass.; Troy, N.Y., Trenton, N.J.; Occupational Therapist (Reg. O.T.), Government Hospitals 8 years.

MORSON, LIDIA [Mrs. Nicolai Abracheff]—*Painter, T.*

410 West 110th St., New York 25, N.Y.

B. Ekaterinoslav, Russia, Apr. 21, 1909. *Studied*: Emerson Col., and with Nicolai Abracheff. *Exhibited*: Contemporary A. Gal., 1949-1952. *Position*: Instr., Abracheff Sch. A., New York, N.Y., 1945- .

MORTELLITO, MRS. JANE WASEY. See Wasey, Jane

MORTON, RICHARD H.—*Educator, Des., Gr., P.*

Art Department, Vocational Institute, Southern Illinois University, Carbondale, Ill.; h. R.F.D. #2, Carterville, Ill.

B. Dallas, Tex., Aug. 8, 1921. *Studied*: PIASch.; Oklahoma City Univ., B.A.; Univ. Tulsa, M.A., and with Louis Freund. *Member*: CAA; Director's AI; NEA. *Award*: prize, PIASch., 1941. *Work*: Univ. Tulsa. Des., permanent exh. "The Story of Geology," Hall of Science, Intl. Petroleum Exh., Tulsa, 1953; mural, First Nat. Bank Bldg., Oklahoma City. *Exhibited*: Assn. Oklahoma A., 1948-1950; Philbrook A. Center, 1948-1952. Contributor illus. to "G.I. Sketch Book." Lectures: Technical Visual Aids. *Positions*: Private Instr., Oklahoma City, 1947-51; Instr., Painting, Philbrook A. Center, Tulsa, 1952-53; Adv. A. Dir., Brown-Dunkin, Tulsa, 1953-55; TV A. Dir., Tulsa Broadcasting Co., 1955; Co-ordinator, Comm. A. Dept., Vocational Inst., Southern Illinois Univ., Carbondale, Ill., 1955- .

MOSCA, AUGUST—*Painter*

P.O. Box 1721, Shelter Island, N.Y.

B. Naples, Italy, Aug. 23, 1909. *Studied*: Yale Sch. FA. *Member*: AEA. *Work*: Abbott Laboratories; Parrish Mus., Southampton, N.Y. *Awards*: medal, Cal. PLH, 1946; Newspaper Gld., 1951, 1957. *Exhibited*: NAD, 1943; Mint Mus. A., 1946; 44th St. Gal.; Mississippi AA, 1946; Passedoit Gal., 1954; Provincetown A. Festival, 1958; one-man: Harry Salpeter Gal., N.Y., 1957; Guild Hall, East-hampton, N.Y.

MOSCON, HANNAH—*Painter*

240 East 18th St., Brooklyn 26, N.Y.

B. New York, N.Y. *Studied*: ASL; BMSch. A. *Member*: Brooklyn Soc. A.; NAWA; Knickerbocker A.; Lg. Present Day A.; AEA. *Awards*: prizes, BM, 1947; NAWA, 1947, 1949, 1950 (medal), 1951. *Exhibited*: AWS, 1948-1952; Audubon A., 1948, 1949, 1951; NAWA, 1945-1955; MMA, 1952; PAFA, 1952; BM, biennially; one-man: Contemporary A. Gal.; Barbizon-Plaza Hotel; Mandel Bros., Chicago, 1953.*

MOSE, CARL C.—*Sculptor, L.*

4527 Olive St.; h. 4502 Maryland Ave., St. Louis 8, Mo.

B. Copenhagen, Denmark, Feb. 17, 1903. *Studied*: AIC; ASL; BAID; & with Lorado Taft. *Member*: NSS; Nat. Soc. A. & Let. *Awards*: prizes, Minneapolis Inst. A.; St. Louis A. Gld., 1947, 1949, 1952; med., Soc. Wash. A.; winner, Nat. Comp. for Arch. S., Salina, Kan. *Work*: CGA; S., figures, monuments, mem., tablets: Old Crossing State Park, Minn.; Ft. Sumter, N.C.; U.S. Air Force Acad., Colorado Springs, Colo.; Ralston-Purina Exp. Farm, Gray Summit, Mo.; 4-H Youth Center, Bethesda, Md.; Meridian Hill Park, Wash., D.C.; Potomac Electric Power Co., Wash., D.C.; Chapel and Cloister, Sisters of 3rd Order of St. Francis, Rochester, Minn.; St. Mary of the Plains, Dodge City, Kans.; Jewish Tercentenary Mem., St. Louis, Mo.; Pershing Mem., State Capitol, Jefferson City, Mo.; Annunziata Church, St. Louis, Mo.; Washington Cathedral; City Hall, Granite City, Ill.; Deaconess Hospital, St. Louis, Mo.; Dept. Agricultural Bldg., Wash., D.C.; USPO, Maplewood, Mo.; USPO & Court House, Salina, Kan. *Exhibited*: AIC, 1918-1938; NAD; Royal Acad., Copenhagen, Denmark; Amsterdam, Holland; one-man exh.; CGA; Minneapolis Inst. A.; Soc. Wash.A.; Chicago Galleries Assn.; PMG; St. Louis A. Gld.; Mus. FA of Houston.

MOSELSIO, HERTA—*Ceramist, S., T.*

Bennington College; h. Old Bennington, Vt.

B. Berlin, Germany. *Studied*: in Europe. *Member*: N.Y. Soc. Ceramic A. *Work*: Bennington Hist. Mus. & A. Gal. *Exhibited*: Arch. Lg.; Fleming A. Gal., Burlington, Vt.; Albany Inst. Hist. & A.; WMAA; America House, N.Y.; Syracuse Mus. FA.; Bennington Mus.; Southern Vermont A., and others. Educational motion pictures in cooperation with Harmon Fnd. *Position*: Instr., ceramics, Bennington Col., 1933- .

MOSELSIO, SIMON—*Sculptor, P., T., Gr.*

Bennington College, Bennington, Vt.; h. Old Bennington, Vt.

B. Russia. *Studied*: Kunstgewerbe Schule; Royal Acad. FA, Berlin, Germany. *Member*: NSS; *Awards*: med., Paris Int. Exp. *Work*: S., WMAA; Univ. Georgia; IBM; Bennington Hist. Mus.; Weyhe Gal.; Edu. films, Harmon Fnd. *Exhibited*: WFNY 1939; WMAA, 1934, 1935, 1939, 1940-1943, 1945, 1946, 1950; AIC; PAFA; Weyhe Gal (one-man); Fleming Mus. A.; Salons of Am., 1925, 1926; N.Y. A. Center, 1926 (one-man); BM, 1930; Research Inst. Theatre, Saratoga Springs, N.Y.; LC, 1949; PMA, 1940; WMA, 1943, 1951; Buchholz Gal., 1941, 1943, 1945; Albany Inst. Hist. & A.; Springfield Mus. A., etc. *Position*: Instr. S. & A., Bennington Col., Bennington, Vt., 1933- ; Dir. Corp. of Yaddo.

MOSER, ARTUS MONROE—*Painter, W., E.*

Avalon Studio, Buckeye Cove, Swannanoa, N.C.

B. Hickory, N.C., Sept. 14, 1894. *Studied*: Univ. North Carolina, A.B., M.A.; Univ. Wisconsin; AIC; Grand Central A. Sch.; PAFA. *Member*: Asheville (N.C.) A. Gld.; Black Mountain AC; North Carolina SA. *Work*: Asheville (N.C.) Mus. A.; Swannanoa Community Cl.; Black Mountain Cl. House. *Position*: Instr. A., Lincoln Mem. Univ., Harrogate, Tenn., 1930-43; Instr. A., Asheville-Biltmore Col., Asheville, N.C., 1946-52. Lecturer on art to clubs and community organizations; writer on art and folklore; Organizer, Mngr., Art Placement Service of Western N.C., 1955-1958; L., Appalachian State T. Col., Boone, N.C., 1957-58.

MOSER, FRANK (H.)—*Painter, Cart., I., T.*

37 Hollywood Dr., Hastings-on-Hudson 6, N.Y.

B. Kansas, May 27, 1886. *Studied*: Cumming Sch. A., Des Moines, Iowa; ASL; NAD. *Member*: SC; Yonkers AA; Hudson Valley AA; AWS. *Awards*: prize, SC, 1944. *Work*: New Britain (Conn.) A. Mus. *Exhibited*: All.A.Am., 1944; SC, 1940-1946; Yonkers AA, 1940-1946; Hudson Valley AA, 1940-1946.

MOSER, JULON (MODJESKA)—*Painter*

376 Artemisia Ave., Ventura, Cal.

B. Schenectady, N.Y., Jan. 1, 1900. *Studied*: Chouinard AI; Univ. California; Scripps Col., and with Frank Taylor Bowers, Millard Sheets, Glenn Wessels, and others. *Member*: Cal. WC Soc.; Women Painters of the West (Pres., 1957-58, 1958-59); Santa Barbara AA. *Awards*: prizes, Greek Theatre, Los A., 1951, 1955; Pasadena AI, 1951; Women Painters of the West, 1938, 1940, 1942, 1944; Laguna Beach, 1953; Wilshire Ebell Cl. *Work*: Clearwater Mus. A. *Exhibited*: Pasadena AI; Los A. Mus. A.; Laguna Beach, Cal.; Cal. WC Soc.; Women Painters of the West; Oakland A. Gal., 1949-1951; Orange County Fair, 1951.

MOSES, ANNA MARY ROBERTSON *(Grandma Moses)* —*Painter*

Galerie St. Etienne, 46 West 57th St., New York 19, N.Y.; h. Eagle Bridge, N.Y.

B. Greenwich, N.Y., Sept. 7, 1860. *Awards*: prizes, Syracuse Mus. FA, 1941; A. Dir. Cl., 1947; Women's Nat. Press Cl., award presented by Pres. Harry S. Truman, 1949; Hon. Doctorate, Russell Sage Col., 1949; Hon. Doctorate, Moore Inst. A., Phila., Pa., 1951; bronze med., SI, 1955. *Work*: MMA; PMG; The White House, Wash., D.C.; Russell Sage Col., Troy, N.Y.; Rochester Mem. A. Gal.; Austrian State Gal., Vienna; Mus. A., Providence, R.I.; Syracuse Mus. FA; Pasadena AI; William Rockhill Nelson Gal. A.; Nat. A. Gal., Sydney, Australia; Queensland Nat. A. Gal., Brisbane, Australia; Musee Nationale d'Art Moderne, Paris, France. *Exhibited*: nationally and internationally, including one-man: Galerie St. Etienne, 1940, and subsequently; Syracuse Mus. FA, 1941, 1952; Currier Gal. A., 1945; St. Paul Gal. & A. Sch., 1946; BMA, 1948; PMG, 1949; Nelson Gal. A., 1951; Joslyn A. Mus., 1951; Des Moines A. Center, 1951; Denver A. Mus., 1951; Mus. FA of Houston, 1952; Delgado Mus. A., 1952; de Young Mem. Mus., 1952; Birmingham A. Mus., 1952; Fla. Gulf Coast A. Center, 1952, 1956; Lyman Allyn Mus., 1953; Brooks Mem. Mus., 1948, 1951, 1953; Buffalo Hist. Soc., 1954; SAM, 1955; Oakland A. Mus., 1955; San Diego FA Soc., 1955, and others; one-man in Europe: Vienna, Austria, 1950; Munich, Germany, 1950; Salzburg, Austria, 1950; Berne, Switzerland, 1950; The Hague, Holland, 1950; Am. Embassy, Paris, 1950; Bremen, Germany, 1955; Stuttgart, Germany, 1955; Cologne, Germany, 1956; Hamburg, Germany, 1956; London, England, 1956; Oslo, Norway, 1956; Stockholm, Sweden, 1956; Aberdeen, Glasgow, Edinburgh, Scotland, 1957 (sponsored by British Arts Council), and many others. Articles on Grandma Moses and her work have appeared in all leading magazines and newspapers in U.S. and abroad. Art film, "Grandma Moses" produced in 1950. Author: "My Life's History," 1952, German ed., Frankfurt, 1957; Dutch ed., Utrecht, 1958.

MOSHIER, ELIZABETH ALICE—*Educator, Des., P., C.*

Skidmore College, Saratoga Springs, N.Y.; h. 8 Watson Pl., Utica, N.Y.

B. Utica, N.Y., Dec. 24, 1901. *Studied*: Skidmore Col., B.S.; Columbia Univ., M.A.; Andre L'Hote Studio, Paris; Kunstgewerbe Schule, Vienna; & with Moholy-Nagy, Josef Albers, and with Mirko, in Rome, Italy. *Member*: CAA; Am. Assn. Univ. Prof.; Am. Assn. Univ. Women. *Exhibited*: Albany Inst. Hist. & A.; Syracuse Mus. FA; Rochester Mem. A. Gal.; Skidmore Col. Lectures: Modern Painting; Contemporary Design. *Position*: Instr. A., 1925- , Prof. A., 1941- , Skidmore Col., Saratoga Springs, N.Y.

MOSIER, MARTHA HINKLE—*Painter, T.*
490 West Washington St., Martinsville, Ind.

B. Martinsville, Ind., May 19, 1915. *Studied*: Indiana Univ.; AIC, and with Adolph R. Schulz. *Member*: Hoosier Salon; Brown County A. Gal. Assn. *Awards*: prizes, Indiana State Fair, 1945-1950; Hoosier Salon, 1952; Swope Gal. A., Terre Haute, 1957; Martinsville, Ind., 1958. *Work*: Indiana Univ.; Brown County A. Gal.; DePauw Univ. (loan). *Exhibited*: DePauw Univ., 1956, 1957; Hoosier Salon, 1952-1958; Swope A. Gal., 1957, 1958; Chesterton FA Soc., 1957; Indiana State Fair, 1945-1950; Brown County A. Gal., 1953-1958.

MOSKOWITZ, IRA—*Etcher, Lith., P.*
c/o Kennedy & Co., 785 Fifth Ave., New York 22, N.Y.

B. Poland, Mar. 15, 1912. *Studied*: ASL. *Member*: SAGA. *Awards*: prizes, "America in the War" exh., 1943; Lib. Cong., 1945; Guggenheim F., 1943. *Work*: MMA; Mus. New Mexico; Natural Hist. Mus., New York and Cincinnati; Philbrook A. Center; WMAA; BM; N.Y.Pub.Lib.; Albany Inst. Hist. & A.; Mus. FA of Houston; Carnegie Inst.; Lib.Cong.; Mus. Navajo Ceremonial A., Santa Fé, N.M. *Exhibited*: MMA, 1941; AIC; NAD, 1946; Carnegie Inst., 1946; Lib.Cong., 1943, 1945, 1946; Los A. Mus A., 1945; Albany Inst. Hist. & A.; Phila. Pr. Cl.; Laguna Beach AA; Springfield (Mo.) Mus. A.; Mus. FA of Houston (one-man); San Antonio Mus. A. (one-man); Natural Hist. Mus., N.Y. (one-man). Author: "Pattern and Ceremonials of the Indians of the Southwest," 1949.*

MOSKOWITZ, SHIRLEY (Mrs. Shirley Edith Moskowitz Gruber)—*Painter, T., L.*
627 Wayland Road, Plymouth Meeting, Pa.

B. Houston, Tex., Aug. 4, 1920. *Studied*: Mus. Sch. A., Houston; Rice Inst., B.A.; Oberlin Col., M.A.; Morris Davidson Sch. A. *Member*: Phila. WC Cl.; AEA; Norristown A. Lg. *Awards*: prizes, Mus. FA of Houston, 1945; Norristown A. Lg., 1958. *Work*: Allen Mem. Mus., Oberlin Col. *Exhibited*: Texas General; Mus. FA of Houston; Texas FA Assn.; Akron AI; Temple Univ., 1948, 1956 (one-man); PAFA, 1957, 1958 and prior; Phila. A. All., 1953, 1956, 1958 and prior; Phila. WC Cl., 1954, 1956, 1958; Cheltenham A. Center, 1955, 1957; Woodmere A. Gal., 1957, 1958; Detroit Inst. A., 1958; Wolpert A. Gal., Springhouse, Pa., 1957 (one-man). Lectures on art to colleges and women's clubs. *Positions*: Instr., Hist. A., Univ. Texas, 1943; A.T., Houston Col. for Negroes, 1944-45; L., Pub. Sch., Houston; A. Dir., Oberlin (Ohio) Pub. Schs., 1947-48.

MOSLEY, ZACK T.—*Illustrator, Cart.*
Riverside Drive, Stuart, Fla.

B. Hickory, Okla., Dec. 12, 1906. *Studied*: Chicago Acad. FA; AIC. *Member*: Nat. Cartoonists Soc.; Royal Soc. A., London. Creator of "Smilin' Jack," comic strip syndicated by Chicago Tribune-New York News syndicate.

MOSMAN, WARREN T.—*Sculptor, T.*
E 505 First National Bank Bldg., St. Paul, Minn.; h. 476½ Summit Ave., St. Paul 2, Minn.

B. Bridgeport, Conn., July 18, 1908. *Studied*: Yale Sch. FA, B.F.A.; Am. Acad. in Rome, F.A.A.R. *Member*: NSS; AIA. *Position*: A. Consultant, Ellerbe & Co., Architects & Engineers, St. Paul, Minn.*

MOSS, JOEL (Dr.)—*Painter, C., S., E.*
Kansas State College; h. 408 West 4th St., Hays, Kan.

B. Murray, Ky., June 2, 1912. *Studied*: Kansas State Col., B.S.; George Peabody Col., M.A.; Univ. Southern California; Columbia Univ., Ed. D., and with Glen Lukens, Saul Baizermann, Charles Martin. *Member*: Central States Craftsmen's Gld.; AAUP; NAEA. *Awards*: prize, Des-Craftsmen, 1955, 1958; Air Capital, 1958. *Exhibited*: Denver A. Mus., 1952-1954; Nat. Dec. A. Exh., Wichita, 1948-1954; Kansas Painters, 1949-1953; Ward Eggleston Gal., N.Y., 1951 (one-man); Nelson Gal., 1952-1955; Wash. WC Soc., 1954; Des-Craftsmen, 1955, 1958; Joslyn Mem. Mus., 1958; Delgado Mus. A., 1958; SFMA, 1957, 1958. Contributor to Journal of National Art Education. *Position*: Prof. A., Hd. Dept. A., Kansas State Col., Hays, Kans., 1946- .

MOTHERWELL, ROBERT—*Painter, T.*
c/o Sidney Janis Gallery, 15 East 57th St.; h. 173 East 94th St., New York 28, N.Y.

B. Aberdeen, Wash., Jan. 24, 1915. *Studied*: Stanford Univ., A.B.; Harvard Univ.; Columbia Univ.; Grenoble Univ., France. *Work*: MModA; Mus. Mod. A., Rio de Janeiro; Nat. Mus., Tel-Aviv, Israel; BMA; FMA; Smith Col. Mus.; MMA; WMAA; Univ. Nebraska; Univ. Minnesota; Norton Gal. A.; Art of This Century, Venice; Galerie Jeanne Bucher, Paris; Kootz Gal., N.Y.; Yale Univ.; Albright A. Gal.; Bennington Col. Mus.; mural, Temple B'nai Israel, Millburn, N.J. *Exhibited*: nationally and internationally including: Carnegie Inst.; WMAA; MModA; Mus. Mod. A., Paris; Mus. Mod. A., Madrid; Tate Gal., London; A. Mus., Basel, Switzerland; Nat. Mus., West Berlin; Venice Biennale; AIC; Toronto Gal. A.; Mus. Mod. A., Mexico City; SFMA; Sao Paulo, Brazil; Nat. Mus., Vienna; Amsterdam, Holland, and many others. One-man: Art of This Century, 1944; Kootz Gal., 1946, 1947, 1949, 1951, 1952; SFMA, 1946; Chicago FA Cl., 1946; MModA, 1947; Sidney Janis Gal., 1957, 1959; Bennington Col., 1959. Editor, "The Documents of Modern Art," Wittenborn & Co., 1944-1952.

MOTLEY, ARCHIBALD, JOHN, JR.—*Painter*
350 West 60th St.; h. 3518 Wentworth Ave., Chicago 9, Ill.

B. New Orleans, La., Oct. 7, 1891. *Studied*: AIC; in France; & with Karl Buehr, Albert Krehbiel. *Member*: A. Lg. Chicago. *Awards*: med., prize, AIC, 1925; Newark Mus., 1927; Harmon Fnd., N.Y., 1928; Guggenheim F., 1929. *Work*: USPO, Wood River, Ill.; murals, Nichols Sch., Evanston, Ill.; Doolittle Sch., Chicago. *Exhibited*: WMAA; Grand Central A. Gal.; Newark Mus.; BMA; WFNY 1939; AIC, 1933, 1934; Am.-Scandinavian Fnd.; one-man exh.: New A., N.Y.; Atlanta Univ.; Chicago Woman's Cl.; Chicago Pub. Lib., 1954.*

MOTTS, ALICIA SUNDT—*Painter, W., L.*
1735 West 6th St., Los Angeles 17, Cal.

B. Oslo, Norway. *Studied*: Mayville Col.; AIC, and with Gerald Brockhurst, Henry Keller. *Member*: NAWA; Composers, Authors & Artists of Am.; Woman's A. Cl., Cleveland. *Awards*: prizes, Butler AI, 1940; NAD, 1945. *Work*: murals, Sch. of Nursing, Easton, Pa.; Franklin Square Medical Lib., Balt.; Sch. of Nursing, Frederick, Md.; Youth Room, Brooklyn Y.M.C.A. *Exhibited*: CMA, 1929-1943, traveling exh., 1939-1943; AIC, 1936; CGA, 1937; Ogunquit A. Center, 1937; Madonna Festival, Los A., 1953, 1956; San F., A. Festival, 1954; NAD, 1944, 1945; Butler AI, 1938, 1940, 1941; NAWA, 1945, 1950, 1951; Riverside Mus., 1948; one-man: Gage Gal., Cleveland, 1935; Columbia Univ., 1944; Easton, Pa., 1944; Glide Gal., San F., 1953; Newcomb-Macklin Gal., N.Y., 1949. *Position*: Nat. A. Chm., Composers, Authors & Artists of Am., 1944-48; Pres., N.Y. Chptr., 1952-53; Cal. State Pres., 1953-59. Represented in "Cosmic Art," book on religious art.

MOULD, RUTH GREENE (Mrs.)—*Painter, C., T.*
Bristol, Vt.

B. Morrisville, Vt., May 22, 1894. *Studied*: St. Paul AI; ASL, with DuMond, Bishop, Soyer. *Member*: AAPL; Mid-Vermont A.; Lg. Am. Pen Women; Northern Vermont A. *Awards*: med., St. Paul AI. *Work*: Bennington (Vt.) Mus.; Fleming Mus. A. Burlington, Vt. *Exhibited*: NAWA, 1938-1940; AWCS, 1938; Fleming Mus. A., annually; Mid-Vermont A.; Ogunquit A. Center, 1946; CM, 1940; Nat. Lg. Am. Pen Women, 1958; Northern Vermont, Burlington, Vt., Lyndon T. Col., Lyndon, Vt., 1958. Author: "Refinishing and Decorating Furniture," 1953. *Position*: Instr., Adult Edu., Keeseville, N.Y., 1952-55.

MOULTON, MARY ELISABETH—*Lecturer, T.*
3845 McGee St.; h. 1872 East 76th St., Kansas City, Mo.

B. Chicago, Ill., May 11, 1906. *Studied*: Albion Col., A.B.; Univ. Chicago, M.A.; Parsons Sch. Des., Paris; AIC; Univ. Minnesota; Univ. Kansas City. *Member*: Missouri A. Edu. Assn.; Mid-Am. A.; AAPL; Am. Assn. Univ. Women; Ozark AA; Am. Fed. T. (Nat. V-Pres.). Lectures: Guatemalan Handcrafts; Old Houses of Missouri, etc. *Positions*: Instr., Starrett School, Chicago, 1931-32; Albion Col., Albion, Mich., 1932-35; Kansas City Jr. Col., Kansas City, Mo., 1935- .*

MOUNT, (PAULINE) WARD—*Painter, S., E., L.*

74 Sherman Place, Jersey City, N.J.

B. Batavia, N.Y. *Studied*: ASL; N.Y. Univ., and with Kenneth Hayes Miller, Albert P. Lucas, Joseph P. Pollia, Fiske Kimball, and others. *Member*: P. & S. Soc., New Jersey; AEA; AAPL; Palm Beach A. Lg.; Royal Soc. A., London, England; New Orleans AA. *Awards*: F., Royal Soc. A., London; prizes, Jersey City Mus., 1941; P. & S. Soc., New Jersey, 1943, 1951; Montclair A. Mus., 1945; New Jersey A., 1945; Asbury Park Soc. FA, 1946; Kearney Mus., 1947; Art Fair, N.Y., 1950. *Work*: LC; The White House, Wash., D.C.; Jersey City Mus.; Carlebach Gal.; designed silver bell of Am. for Am. Bell Assn., 1950; bronze Medal of Honor for P. & S. Soc., New Jersey; work also in Italy, Ireland, Holland, Germany, Switzerland, Sweden and France. *Exhibited*: NAD, 1944; PAFA, 1949; NSS, 1945-1948; Audubon A., 1942-1944; Trenton State Mus., 1950; Smithsonian Inst., 1951; All. A. Am., 1939-1947; WFNY 1939; Jersey City Mus., 1941-1951; Hudson River Mus., 1946; AAPL, 1941-1945, 1947, 1949; New Jersey A., 1945; N.Y. Soc. Painters, 1940-1943; Montclair A. Mus., 1944, 1945; Asbury Park FA Assn., 1941, 1942, 1946-1949; Acad. All. A., 1938-1940; VMFA, 1940; New Orleans AA, 1947; Plainfield AA, 1947; Los A. Mus. A., 1945; New Jersey, 1941-1951; New Jersey State Mus., 1940; P. & S. of New Jersey, 1941-1951; N.Y. Hist. Mus., 1942-1947; N.Y. Pub. Lib., 1939; Am-British A. Center, 1942; Carlebach Gal.; Art Center of the Oranges, 1941, 1942; Hebrew Assn., Phila., 1950; NAC, 1954; Riverside Mus., 1953, and others. *Positions*: Founder, Former Pres., P. & S. Soc., New Jersey (12 years); Founder, Former Dir. A., Jersey City Medical Center; Dir., Ward Mount A. Classes, Jersey City, N.J.

MOUNTFORT, JULIA ANN—*Painter, I., W.*

Bristol Rd., Damariscotta, Me.

B. Barford, P.Q., Canada, Jan. 14, 1888. *Studied*: Fox A. Sch.; AIC; Chicago Acad. FA; & with Sargent, Townsley. *Member*: Chicago SA; SSAL; South Shore A.; All-Illinois Soc. A.; Lg. Am. Pen Women.*

MOY, SEONG—*Painter, Gr., T., L.*

507 West 59th St., New York 19, N.Y.

B. Canton, China, Oct. 20, 1921. *Studied*: St. Paul Sch. A.; Hans Hofmann Sch. A.; ASL; Atelier 17, N.Y. *Member*: ASL; AFA; AEA; CAA; Fed. Mod. P. & S. *Awards*: John Hay Whitney Fnd. grant, 1950-51; Guggenheim F., 1955-56. *Work*: MMoA; BM; MMA; PAFA; N.Y. Pub. Lib.; Smithsonian Inst.; BM; WMA; Univ. Minnesota; Univ. Indiana; Smith Col., and others; "Print of the Month," The Contemporaries, N.Y., 1955. *Exhibited*: BM, 1947-1955; MMA, 1942; Phila. Pr. Cl., 1947-1954; MMA, 1950; WMAA, 1950; Univ. Illinois, 1951, 1953, 1954; Carnegie Inst., 1952, 1955; 17 one-man exhs. since 1943. Lectures: Modern Art; Oriental Art; Graphic Art. *Position*: Instr., Gr. A., Univ. Minnesota, 1951; Indiana Univ., 1952-53; Smith Col., 1954-55; Univ. Arkansas, 1955; Vassar Col., 1955; Columbia Univ., 1957; Pratt-Contemporaries Graphic Art Center and CUASch., at present; Dir., Seong Moy Sch. Painting & Gr. A., Provincetown, Mass. (summers), 1954- .

MOYER, ROY—*Painter, Asst. Dir. A. Fed., T.*

American Federation of Arts, 1083 Fifth Ave. (28); h. 201 West 85th St., New York 24, N.Y.

B. Allentown, Pa., Aug. 20, 1921. *Studied*: Columbia Col., B.A.; Columbia Univ., M.A. *Work*: in private colls., U.S. and Europe. *Exhibited*: Univ. Illinois, 1959; one-man: Contemporaries, N.Y., 1958, 1959. Assisted Yugoslavian Government in selection of AFA traveling exhibition, "New Painting from Yugoslavia," 1958; selected AFA traveling exhs.: "Art and the Objet Trouve," 1959 and "Wood Sculpture and Woodcuts," 1959. *Positions*: Instr., English and Art, Salonica, Greece, 1948-51; L., A. Hist., Univ. Toronto, Canada, 1953-55; Asst. Dir., American Federation of Arts, New York, N.Y., at present.

MOYNIHAN, (HELEN) S.—*Painter*

4206 North Wilson Dr., Milwaukee 11, Wis.

B. Marcus, Iowa, Apr. 13, 1902. *Studied*: Chicago Acad. FA, and with H. R. Fischer, Robert Von Neumann. *Member*: Wisconsin P. & S. A. *Awards*: prizes, Milwaukee AI, 1944; Wisconsin State Fair, 1943, 1944, 1947; Minnesota Centennial, 1949. *Work*: Minn. Centennial Coll.; Jesuit

Seminary, Florissant, Mo., and in private coll. *Exhibited*: AIC, 1943, 1944, 1950; Univ. Wisconsin, 1940 1941, 1943-1945; Wisconsin State Fair, 1939-44, 1947, 1949-1956; Wisconsin P. & S., 1940, 1941, 1943-1946, 1956; Layton A. Gal., 1950; Milwaukee AI, 1951, 1954; Dayton AI; Minnesota Hist. Soc.; Woman's Exchange, Milwaukee (one-man); Ill. State Fair, 1953, 1955-1957; Milwaukee Athletic Cl., 1957.

MOZLEY, LOREN NORMAN—*Painter, Gr., L., W.*

2102 Scenic Dr., Austin, Tex.

B. Brookport, Ill., Oct. 2, 1905. *Studied*: Univ. New Mexico, and in France. *Awards*: prizes, Texas General, 1942; San Antonio A. Lg., 1945; Cokesbury prize, Dallas, 1943. *Exhibited*: Annually in Texas A. Exhs., Dallas, Houston, San Antonio, etc. Contributor to Liturgical Arts Quarterly, 1955. *Position*: Instr., Univ. Southern California, summers, 1953-54; Assoc. Prof., Univ. Texas, Austin, Tex.*

MUELKE, ROBERT—*Designer, E., L., S., C., Comm. A.*

186 Broadway, Milford, Conn.

B. Buffalo, N.Y., April 3, 1921. *Studied*: PIASch; A. Inst., Buffalo. *Member*: IDI. *Exhibited*: Albright A. Gal., 1942. Des., Arch., Product, Advertising and Package. *Positions*: Indst. & Arch. Des., 1943-46, with Raymond Loewy, General Electric, Barnes & Reinecke, and others. Own design practice, 1945- . Instr., Indst. Des.; Univ. Bridgeport, Conn., 1953; s., Wonder Workshop, Bridgeport, 1953-55; Planning Dir., Autorama, Hartford, Conn., 1951- .

MUELLER, GEORGE LUDWIG—*Painter*

9 Summit St., East Orange, N.J.

B. Newark, N.J., Mar. 13, 1929. *Studied*: CUASch. *Awards*: prize, DMFA, 1955; Guggenheim Fellowship, 1956. *Work*: Guggenheim Mus. A.; WMAA; AIC; Newark Mus. A. *Exhibited*: DMFA, 1954, 1955; WMAA, 1954, 1955, 1957; Guggenheim Mus. A., 1955; Carnegie Inst., 1955; Univ. Illinois, 1955; Venice Biennale, 1956; Rome, Italy, 1958; Brussels World's Fair, 1958; WMA, 1958; one-man: Artists Gal., N.Y., 1951; Borgenicht Gal., N.Y., 1955.

MUELLER, HENRIETTE W. (Mrs.)—
**   *Painter, Des., Gr., T.***

1309 Steele St., Laramie, Wyo.

B. Pittsburgh, Pa., April 13, 1915. *Studied*: Northwestern Univ.; AIC; B.F.A.; ASL; Univ. Wyoming, M.A., and with Will Barnet, Ilya Bolotowsky, John Opper, George McNeil, and others. *Member*: Am. Color Pr. Soc.; AEA; Lincoln A. Gld.; Nebraska AA; Mid-Am. A.; Nat. Ser. Soc. *Awards*: Mary Griffiths Marshall Mem. F., Alpha Chi Omega, 1952; Tri-State Exh., 1958; Cummington F., 1954. *Work*: N.Y. Pub. Lib.; Joslyn A. Mus.; Henry Gal., Univ. Washington; Nelson Gal. A.; Woman's Col., Univ. North Carolina. *Exhibited*: Anchorage, Alaska, 1952; SAGA, 1950; MMA, 1950; BM, 1950-1952; LC, 1950; Northwest Pr. M., 1950-1952; Bradley Univ., 1951, 1952; Univ. So. California, 1952; Am. Color Pr. Soc., 1951, 1952, 1955; John Herron AI, 1952; Denver A. Mus., 1950-1952, 1958; Colorado Springs FA Center, 1951; Joslyn A. Mus., 1951, 1952; Nelson Gal. A., 1950, 1951; Nebraska All-State, 1957; Meltzer Gal., 1953-1955; Western A., 1953-1955; Phila. A. All., 1955; Creative Gal., N.Y., 1954; The Contemporaries, 1953-1955; AFA traveling exh., 1952, 1954. *Positions*: Instr., J. Sterling Morton H.S., Chicago, 1937-38; Colby Jr. Col., New London, N.H., 1938-40; Univ. Wyoming, Laramie, Wyo., 1948-58; Univ. Nebraska, 1957-58.

MUENCH, JOHN—*Painter, Gr., T.*

97 Spring St., Portland, Me.

B. Medford, Mass., Oct. 15, 1914. *Studied*: ASL, and in France. *Member*: Phila. WC Cl.; SAGA. *Awards*: prizes, LC, 1951, 1954; BM, 1947; SAGA, 1953, 1955; Boston Pr. M., 1953; DMFA, 1954; Univ. So. Cal., 1954; Audubon A., 1956; Portland Soc. A., 1957; Tiffany F., 1948, 1954; med., Phila. WC Cl., 1954. *Work*: Princeton Univ.; BM; N.Y. Pub. Lib.; Univ. Maine; Bowdoin Col.; LC; DMFA; Univ. So. Cal.; FMA; MModA; MMA; Bibliotheque Nationale, Paris; Smith Col.; Jerusalem. *Exhibited*: LC, 1945, 1948, 1949, 1951-1954, 1955, 1956; Carnegie Inst., 1945, 1948; NAD, 1946, 1949; Northwest

Pr. M., 1946; BM, 1947, 1950; SAGA, 1947, 1950-1952; Boston Pr. M., 1948-1952; Audubon A., 1947, 1948, 1956; PAFA, 1949, 1950; Contemp. Am. Gr. A., France, 1950-1951, 1952; Phila. Pr. Cl., 1947; Albany Pr. Cl., 1949-1951; Buffalo Pr. Cl., 1951; Springfield A. Lg., 1951-1952; Conn. Acad. FA, 1950, 1952; Soc. Canadian P., Et. & Eng., 1951, 1952; MMA, 1952; PAFA, 1953-1955; Univ. So. Cal.; DMFA; Bradley Univ.; CM, 1954, 1956; BM; Hartford Atheneum, and others. *Position*: Dir., Portland (Me.) Sch. F. & App. A.; Lith., The Contemporaries, New York, N.Y.; Instr., Famous Artists Course, Westport, Conn.

MUIR, EMILY—*Painter*
Stonington, Me.

B. Chicago, Ill., 1904. *Studied*: Vassar Col.; ASL, with Richard Lahey, John Carroll, George Bridgman, Leo Lentelli. *Work*: BM; Univ. Maine; U.S. Govt., and in private colls. Art work for: Moore-McCormack Lines; American Caribbean Lines; American Scantic Lines; French Line; Pan-American Airways; Finnish Travel Bureau; Swedish Travel Bureau; Trinidad Chamber of Commerce; Aluminum Corp. Am.; Aluminum Corp., Canada. *Exhibited*: NGA; CGA; BM; Phila. WC Cl.; PAFA; NAD; N.Y. WC Cl.; Soc. Indp. A., Boston, traveling exh.; Springfield A. Mus.; Portland A. Festival; Maine Artists; Maine A. Gal.; many joint exhibitions with William Muir in colleges and universities in North and South Carolina, New York, West Virginia, Ohio, Pennsylvania, New Jersey, etc. One-man: Farnsworth Mus. A.; Univ. Maine; Bowdoin Col.; Scranton Univ.; Montross Gal., N.Y.; Norlyst Gal., N.Y., and others. Lecture tours for Assn. Am. Colleges; Memb. Nat. Comm. FA, 1955; Author: "Small Potatoes."

MUIR, WILLIAM (HORACE)—*Sculptor, L., P.*
Stonington, Me.

B. Hunter, N.D., May 18, 1902. *Studied*: Minneapolis Sch. A., with Charles S. Wells; ASL, with Lentelli. *Member*: Portland Soc. A. *Awards* prize, Portland Summer A. Festival, 1957. *Work*: sc., Bowdoin Col. A. Mus.; Univ. Fredonia, N.Y.; drawings: Univ. Maine; Farnsworth Mus. A., and in private colls. *Exhibited*: NAD; BM; N.Y. WC Soc.; PAFA; WMAA, 1952; Conn. Acad. FA, 1953; Detroit Inst. A., 1958; Waltham, Mass., 1956; VMFA, 1957; N.Y. Pub. Sch. Exh., 1953-1958; Sculpture Center, 1952-1956; one-man: America House, 1948; Sculpture Center, 1951, 1953, 1955; Dartmouth Col., 1952; Bowdoin Col., 1952; Univ. Maine, 1954; Farnsworth Mus. A., 1951, and others. Lecture tours for Assn. Am. Colleges, 1952- .

MULFORD, LAURA LENORE—*Painter, E.*
548 Third Ave., Southeast, Valley City, N.D.; s. Peaceful Valley, Colo.

B. Stuart, Neb., Oct. 24, 1894. *Studied*: Park Col., Parkville, Mo., A.B.; Univ. Nebraska; Univ. Chicago; Columbia Univ., M.A.; Colorado Springs FA Center. *Member*: NAEA; Nat. Edu. Assn.; Western AA; Am. Assn. Univ. Women. *Exhibited*: Fargo FA Cl., 1939; Bismarck FA Cl., 1945-1955. Contributor to: Educational magazines. *Position*: A.Dir., State T. Col., Valley City, N.D., 1938-55.*

MULL, JANE ADDAMS—*Historian*
32 East 51st St., New York 22, N.Y.

B. Minneapolis, Minn., July 23, 1915. *Studied*: Wellesley Col., B.A., M.A.; & in Paris, France. *Member*: CAA. *Position*: Index of Christian Art, Princeton Univ., 1938-43; Am. Council of Learned Soc., Com. on Protection of Cultural Treasures in War Areas, 1943-44; Research Asst., Am. Comm. for Protection & Salvage of Artistic & Historic Monuments in War Areas, 1944-45, 1945-46; Asst. Ed., The Art Bulletin, 1944; A. Research, Fortune Magazine, 1946- .*

MULLEN, BUELL (Mrs. J. Bernard)—*Painter, C.*
222 Central Park South, New York 19, N.Y.; also Lake Forest, Ill.

B. Chicago, Ill., Sept. 10, 1901. *Studied*: Tyler Sch. A.; British Acad. A., London; Rome, Italy, with Petrucci, Lipinsky; Cicquier, Belgium. *Member*: NSMP; Arch. Lg.; F., Royal Soc. A., London. *Work*: murals on stainless steel: LC (first mural to be made on stainless steel); U.S. Naval Research Lab.; Ministry of Pub. Works, Rio

de Janeiro; Ministry of War, Buenos Aires; Great Lakes Naval Station; Dun & Bradstreet; Metals Research Lab., Niagara; Electronic Tower, I. T. & T. Co.; Int. Expo., Milan; General Motors Styling Admin., Detroit; U.S. Steel panels for private car; Nat. Carbon Lab.; Searle Lab.; Inland Steel, Indiana Harbor; first ceiling mural on stainless steel, North Adams (Mass.) Hospital; Sorg Paper Co., Middletown, Ohio; Gardner Board & Carton Co., Middletown; Allegheny Ludlum Steel Lab.; John Woodman Higgins Armory, Worcester, Mass.; room of stainless steel mural treatment, Republic Steel Co.; wall, Physics Auditorium, Case Inst. Tech.; Am. Soc. Chemists, Wash., D.C. Many ports. on metal of prominent army, musical, theatrical and national figures. *Exhibited*: Paris Salon; Rome, Italy; Ill. Soc. FA; Smithsonian Inst.; Dayton AI; Knoedler Gal.; Ferargil Gal.; Findlay Gal. (one-man).

MULLER, HELEN CHANCE (Mrs. Eugene)—*Painter*
71 Merbrook Bend, Merion, Pa.

B. Philadelphia, Pa., Jan. 19, 1891. *Studied*: with Florence Cannon, Earl Horter, Eleanor Copeland. *Member*: Plastic Cl., WC Soc., both of Phila., Pa.; Bryn Mawr A. Center; AWCS; Woodmere AA. *Exhibited*: Wash. WC Cl., 1933, 1934, 1936; PAFA, 1934, 1938, 1944; Wilmington Soc. FA, 1935; N.Y. WC Cl., 1934, 1936; AWCS, 1933, 1936, 1938, 1939, 1941, 1946.

MULLER-MUNK, PETER—*Designer*
725 Liberty Ave. (22); h. 1209 Wightman St., Pittsburgh 17, Pa.

B. Berlin, Germany, June 25, 1904. *Studied*: Univ. Berlin, B.A.; Acad. F. & App. A., Berlin, and with W. Raemisch. *Member*: F., Am. Soc. Indst. Des.; Intl. Council of Soc. of Indst. Des. (Pres.). *Work*: Detroit Inst. A.; Newark Mus. *Exhibited*: MModA; Paris Salon; GGE, 1939; Assoc. A., Pittsburgh; Phila. A. All.; Detroit Inst. A.; Newark Mus.; CMA; Triennale di Milano, 1951, 1954, 1957. Contributor to numerous magazines. *Position*: Assoc. Prof., Indst. Des., Carnegie Inst., 1935-45; Managing Partner, Peter Muller-Munk Assoc., Pittsburgh, Pa., 1945- .

MULLER-URI, HILDEGARDE (PETRONELLA) (BERNHARDINA)—*Painter, T.*
64 Dolphin Drive, St. Augustine, Fla.

B. New York, N.Y., July 5, 1894. *Studied*: Breckenridge A. Sch.; ASL; & with DuMond, Olinsky, Adams, Lewis, & others. *Member*: Fla. Fed. A.; St. Augustine A. Assn. *Awards*: numerous awards in nat. and intl. exhs. *Work*: Bowery Savings Bank, N.Y.; & in Ghent, Belgium. *Exhibited*: Gloucester SA; North Shore AA; Ogunquit A. Center; SSAL; Fla. Fed. A.; Soc. Four A., Palm Beach, Fla.; Palm Beach A. Center. *Position*: Dir., Galleon A. Sch., St. Augustine, Fla.

MULLICAN, LEE—*Painter, S., E.*
370 Mesa Road, Santa Monica, Cal.

B. Chickasha, Okla., Dec. 2, 1919. *Studied*: Abilene Christian Col.; Univ. Oklahoma; Kansas City AI; Cal. Sch. FA. *Work*: Santa Barbara Mus. A.; SFMA; San F. Mun. Coll.; Denver A. Mus.; Colorado Springs FA Center; PC; Detroit Inst. A.; MModA. *Exhibited*: CGA, 1948, 1957; MMA, 1951; AIC, 1951, 1954; Los A. Mus. A., 1951; Chaffey Col., Ontario, Cal., 1952; Long Beach Mun. A. Center, 1952, 1956; Cal. PLH, 1948, 1952; Carnegie Inst., 1952; Los A. County Fair, 1953; Univ. Illinois, 1953, 1955, 1957; Stanford Univ. A. Gal., 1950-1955; WMAA, 1952, 1956; Nebraska AA, 1953; Denver A. Mus., 1950, 1955-1957; Alan A. Gal., N.Y., 1957; Sao Paulo, Brazil, 1955; MModA, 1957; Santa Barbara Mus. A., 1957; one-man: SFMA, 1949; Swetzoff Gal., Boston, 1949; Willard Gal., N.Y., 1950, 1952, 1953; Philbrook A. Center, 1951; Oklahoma City A. Center, 1951; Oklahoma Col. for Women, 1952; Univ. Oklahoma, 1952; Gump's Gal., San F., 1952; Paul Kantor Gal., Los A., 1952, 1954, 1956; Rabow Gal., San F., 1955; Santa Barbara Mus. A., 1958; 3-man: SFMA and Stanford Univ., 1951, and others.

MULLIN, WILLARD—*Cartoonist*
27 Colonial Drive, Plandome Manor, N.Y.

Position: sport, editorial cartoonist, World-Telegram & Sun, New York, N.Y. *Awards*: many, including Nat. Cartoonists Soc., 1955, 1958; Helms Fnd.; The Silurians, and art groups from all sections of the country. Author: "A Hand in Sports," 1958.*

MULLINEUX, MARY—*Printmaker, P., T.*

4244 Terrace, Philadelphia 44, Pa.

B. Philadelphia, Pa. *Studied*: PAFA, with Breckenridge, Chase, Pearson. *Member*: Phila. Pr. Cl. *Awards*: F., PAFA. *Exhibited*: Phila. Pr. Cl., traveling exh. to leading museums in U.S. Lectures: Color Block Prints. *Position*: Hon. Pres., Am. Color Print Soc., Philadelphia, Pa.*

MULLINS, BERT RUEBIN—*Painter*

"Wood Betony," Disputanta, Ky.

B. Disputanta, Ky., Apr. 29, 1901. *Studied*: Berea (Ky.) Col.; & with F. W. Long, C. B. Clough, Richard Miller. *Member*: Louisville A. Center. *Work*: Eastern Col., Richmond, Ky.; Audubon Mem. Mus., Henderson, Ky.; Berea Col.; church murals in Kentucky & Ohio; murals, Court House, Madisonville, Ky.; USPO, Campbellsville, Ky.; Morganfield, Ky.; Renfro Valley Enterprises, Ky.; Southern Highland Gld., N.Y.; Mt. Vernon (Ky.) H.S.; London (Ky.) Baptist Church; Art and Literary Cl., Richmond, Ky.; Berea Concrete & Block Co.; ports.: Berea Col.; Cumberland Production Credit Assn., Somerset, Ky.; Magard Drug Co., Mt. Vernon, Ky. *Exhibited*: J. B. Speed Mem. Mus., 1937; Kentucky & Southern Indiana Exh., 1946; Union Col., Barboursville, Ky. (one-man); Berea Col. (one-man).

MUNDT, ERNEST KARL—*Sculptor, W., L., E.*

750 Columbus Ave., San Francisco 11, Cal.

B. Germany, Oct. 30, 1905. *Studied*: in Berlin, Grad. in Arch. *Member*: CAA. *Work*: SFMA; steel sculpture, Westmoor H.S., Daly City, Cal. *Exhibited*: WMAA, 1951; MMA, 1950; Detroit Inst. A., 1944; Nierendorf Gal., 1945, 1946; SFMA, 1946; Cal. PLH, 1949. Author, I., "A Primer of Visual Art," 1950; "Art, Form, and Society," 1952; "Birth of a Cook," 1956. Contributor to Arts & Architecture, College Art Journal, Art Quarterly magazines. *Position*: Asst. Prof., Univ. Michigan, 1941-44; Instr., Brooklyn Col., 1945-46; Cal. Sch. FA, 1947-50; Dir., Cal. Sch. FA, San Francisco, Cal., 1950-55; Asst. Prof. A., San F. State Col., 1955- .

MUNDY, ETHEL FRANCES—*Sculptor*

608 Ackerman Ave., Syracuse 10, N.Y.

B. Syracuse, N.Y. *Studied*: ASL; Fontainebleau Sch. A., France; & with Amy Sacker. *Member*: NAWA; Royal Soc. Min. P., London; Soc. Fontainebleau A. *Work*: Syracuse Mus. FA; Frick Gal., N.Y.; J. B. Speed Mem. Mus.; Louisville (Ky.) Mus. A. *Exhibited*: NAWA; Carnegie Inst.; CGA; Phila. WC Cl.; Assoc. A. Syracuse; Royal Soc. Min. P., London; Syracuse Mus. FA; Cayuga Mus. Hist. & A.; BM; Montclair A. Mus.; Denver A. Mus.; J. B. Speed Mem. Mus.; Louisville Mus. A.*

MUNIAK, HELEN—*Painter*

148-07 North Hempstead Turnpike, Flushing, L.I., N.Y.

B. Poland, Nov. 15, 1910. *Studied*: with Simon Lissim. *Member*: A. Lg., Long Island; CAA; Sustaining Assoc. Memb., AWS. *Awards*: Fla. Southern Col., 1952. *Exhibited*: Fla. Southern Col., 1952; N.Y. Pub. Lib.; one-man: Barzansky Gal.; Crespi Gal., N.Y., 1957. *Position*: Instr., A. Edu. Project, N.Y. Pub. Lib., and Ext. Div. City Col. of New York, School of General Studies.

MUNRO, THOMAS—*Museum Curator, E., W., L.*

2244 Harcourt Dr., Cleveland 6, Ohio

B. Omaha, Neb., 1897. *Studied*: Amherst Col.; Columbia Univ., A.B., A.M., Ph.D.; Hon. L.H.D., Coe College. *Member*: Am. Soc. for Aesthetics (Pres. 1942-44); AFA; CAA; F., Am. Acad. of A. & Sc.; Royal Soc. A., London; F., Am. Assn. for Advancement of Science; Chevalier, Legion of Honor, France. Author: "Primitive Negro Sculpture," 1926; "Scientific Method in Aesthetics," 1928; "Great Pictures of Europe," 1930; "The Arts and Their Interrelations," 1949; "Toward Science in Aesthetics," 1956; "Art Education: Its Philosophy and Psychology," 1956. Ed., "Art in American Life and Education," 1941. *Positions*: Cur. Edu., CMA, 1931- ; Prof. A., Western Reserve Univ., Cleveland, Ohio, 1931- ; Ed., Journal of Aesthetics and Art Criticism, 1945- ; Bd. Dir., CAA, 1956- .

MURCH, WALTER TANDY—*Painter, I.*

468 Riverside Dr., New York 27, N.Y.

B. Toronto, Canada, Aug. 17, 1907. *Studied*: Ontario Col. A.; ASL, and with Arshile Gorky. *Awards*: prize, Univ. Illinois, 1952. *Work*: BM; PAFA; AGAA; Barnes Fnd.; Lane Fnd., Leominster, Mass.; Munson-Williams-Proctor Inst.; Wadsworth Atheneum; IBM; MMA; WMAA; Carnegie Inst.; Toledo Mus. A.; Joslyn A. Mus.; Univ. Illinois, and in private collections. *Exhibited*: WMAA, 1950-1952, 1955, 1956; Inst. Contemp. A., London, England, 1950; Toronto A. Gal., 1949; Detroit Inst. A., 1952; CGA, 1945, 1951, 1955; BM, 1952; Univ. Illinois, 1951, 1952; CAM, 1951; AFA traveling exh., Japan, 1952; AIC, 1945, 1949-1952; Toledo Mus. A., 1951; PAFA, 1945, 1946; 1948-1952, 1954; MModA, 1952; MMA, 1953; AGAA, 1954; AIC, 1954; Fortune, 1955; Stained Glass Exh., AFA and Stained Glass Assn., 1953-55; 12 years at Betty Parsons Gal.; Venice Biennale, 1956; Contemp. A. Mus., Houston, 1958; U.S. Intl. Assn. Plastic Arts traveling exh., 1955-1957 (Europe); one-man: Betty Parsons Gal., 1949, 1951, 1954, 1955, 1957. I., "Men and Machines," 1930; "Stars in Their Courses," 1932. *Position*: Instr., Drawing & Painting, Pratt Inst., Brooklyn, N.Y., 1952- .

MURDOCH, FLORENCE—*Graphic A., C., P., T., W.*

3304 North Sterling Way, Cincinnati 9, Ohio

B. Lakewood, N.Y., June 14, 1887. *Studied*: Cincinnati A. Acad.; ASL; Ohio Wesleyan Univ.; Univ. Cincinnati, with Novotny, John Carlson, Sallie Humphreys and others. *Member*: Cincinnati Women's A. Cl. Specializing in restoration of art objects, and in an original series of enlarged crayon drawings of native flowers, "Magniflora Americana." These are exhibited annually in Cincinnati Woman's A. Cl., and in 16 one-man exhs., including, N.Y. Botanical Gardens, 1942; Ohio State Mus., 1945; Kingwood Center, Mansfield, Ohio, 1954; Missouri Botanical Gardens, 1955; Mus. Science, Boston, 1956. *Award*: Ohioana Lib. Comp. for drawings for historical calendar, 1957. Contributor to American Magazine of Art, with article and illus., 1932; 3 pages color, "Magniflora Americana," Sunday Pictorial Enquirer, Cincinnati. *Position*: Instr., Oakhurst Collegiate Sch., Cincinnati; Organizer-Dir., Junior A. Clubs, Cincinnati; Crafts, Camp Boulder Point, Inlet, N.Y.

MURPHEY, MIMI—*Sculptor, C.*

2913 Santa Cruz Ave., Albuquerque, N.M.

B. Dallas, Tex., Jan. 13, 1912. *Studied*: Southern Methodist Univ.; Dallas AI; ASL. *Member*: Sculpture Center, N.Y.; SSAL; A. Lg. of New Mexico. *Awards*: prizes, Texas State Fair, 1933, 1947; AAPL, 1937; New Mexico State Fair, 1944, 1948, 1949; SSAL, 1944-1946; Fiesta Exh., Santa Fe, 1957 (purchase); All-Albuquerque A., 1951. *Work*: Mus. of New Mexico, Santa Fe. *Exhibited*: Texas All. A., 1931-1933; BM, 1935; Texas A. Lg., 1935; New Jersey State Mus., 1937, 1938; SSAL, 1944-1946; Wichita AA, 1948; Mus. New Mexico, 1948-1949; Contemp. Crafts of New Mexico traveling exh., 1948-49; New Mexico A., traveling exh., 1951-52; Texas P. & S., 1950-1951; Denver A. Mus., 1952.

MURPHY, ALICE HAROLD—*Painter, Et., Lith., T.*

Hotel Chelsea, 222 West 23rd St., New York 11, N.Y.

B. Springfield, Mass. *Studied*: Parsons Sch. Des.; ASL; NAD; Grande Chaumiere, Paris, and with Charles Hawthorne, Vaclav Vytlacil. *Member*: ANA; SAGA; Boston Pr. M.; Audubon A. *Awards*: prizes, NAWA, 1946; Springfield Mus. A., 1943; Wichita AA, 1939; 100 Best Prints of the Year, 1936, 1942, 1947; NAD, 1951. *Work*: LC; Phila. A. All.; Williams Col.; N.Y. Pub. Lib.; MMA; Springfield Mus. A.; ASL; Univ. Maine. *Exhibited*: WMAA, 1933; BM, 1933, 1935; PAFA, 1928, 1935, 1948, 1950; Phila. WC Cl., 1934, 1935; AWS, 1934, 1936; CAA, 1934, 1936; AIC, 1937; Conn. Acad. FA, 1926, 1928; Phila. A. All., 1938, 1939, 1942, 1949; NAD, 1927, 1929, 1942-1944, 1946, 1948, 1949, 1951; Northwest Pr. M., 1938, 1939, 1943, 1945, 1948; Phila. Pr. Cl., 1939, 1940, 1942, 1944-1946, 1950; Buffalo Pr. Cl., 1938, 1943; Denver A. Mus., 1943; Rochester Pr. Cl., 1948; NAWA, 1948; SAGA, 1948; Wichita AA, 1948-1950, and many others. *Positions*: Instr., NAD Sch. A., 1925-39; Montclair (N.J.) A. Mus. Sch., 1944-45; ASL, New York, N.Y., 1945- .

MURPHY, MRS. CECIL T. *See Buller, Cecil*

MURPHY, CHRISTOPHER, JR.—
Painter, Et., Lith., Des., T.
11 East Perry St., Savannah, Ga.

B. Savannah, Ga., Dec. 28, 1902. *Studied*: ASL & with DuMond, Bridgman, Pennell, & others. *Member*: Savannah AC. *Awards*: prizes, SSAL, 1927, 1931. *Work*: mural, Richard Arnold Sch., Savannah, Ga. Contributor to: magazines & newspapers. Publ. book of Etchings, "Savannah," 1947. *Position*: Instr., Armstrong Col. & Telfair Acad. A., Savannah, Ga.*

MURPHY, GLADYS WILKINS (Mrs. Herbert A.)—
Painter, C., Des., Pr. M.
Bearskin Neck, Rockport, Mass.; h. The Old Mill, 19 King St., Rockport, Mass.

B. Providence, R.I., Apr. 15, 1907. *Studied*: R.I. Sch., Des. *Member*: Providence AC; Providence WC Cl.; Copley Soc., Boston; Rockport AA; North Shore AA. *Exhibited*: AWCS; N.Y. WC Cl., 1937, 1940, 1942, 1948; SAE, 1937; NAD, 1937-1943; Jordan Marsh, 1948-1950; Lib. Cong., 1943; Phila. Pr. Cl., 1937-1942; Phila. A. All., 1935; Cal. Pr. M., 1935-1940; 50 Prints of the Year, 1933, 1934; Boston AC, 1935; Northwest Pr.M.; Wichita AA, 1937-1939; Southern Pr.M., 1936-1942; Brown Univ., 1934, 1937, 1938; Copley Soc., Boston; R.I.Sch. Des.; Rockport AA. annually; Providence AC, annually; Providence WC Cl., annually; Newport AA, 1935-1941; South Country AA, 1933-1938; North Shore AA, annually. *Position*: Instr., A., Rhode Island Sch. Des., 1928-1946; Dir., A. Gal. & Craft Studio, Rockport, Mass., 1946- .

MURPHY, HARRY (DANIELS)—Cartoonist, L.
7766 Ludington Pl., La Jolla, Cal.

B. Eureka, Cal., Oct. 9, 1880. *Work*: Huntington Lib., San Marino, Cal. *Position*: Cart., numerous newspapers, 1898-1940.

MURPHY, HERBERT A.—Painter, C., Des.
Bearskin Neck; h. 19 King St., Rockport, Mass.

B. Fall River, Mass., June 13, 1911. *Studied*: R.I. Sch. Des. *Member*: Rockport AA (Chm. A. & Exhibitions & on jury); North Shore AA; Providence A. Cl.; Providence WC Cl.; Mass. State Assn. Arch. *Exhibited*: Rockport AA; North Shore AA; Providence A. Cl.; Providence WC Cl.; Jordan-Marsh Exh.; Copley Soc., Boston; R.I. Sch. Des.; Newport AA; Gloucester A. Festival annually. *Position*: Co-Dir., A. Gal. & Craft Studio, Rockport, Mass.; Reg. Architect, private practice, 1941- .

MURRAY, ALBERT K.—Portrait Painter
33 West 67th St., New York 23, N.Y.

B. Emporia, Kan., Dec. 29, 1906. *Studied*: Cornell Univ.; Syracuse Univ.; abroad; & with Wayman Adams. *Member*: Newport AA; Soc. Four A., Palm Beach, Fla. *Work*: Syracuse Univ.; Illinois; Princeton Univ.; Univ. Cl., N.Y.; Mem. Hospital, N.Y.; IBM; U.S. Govt., Defense Dept.; NGA; La Fayette Col.; U.S. Naval Acad., Annapolis, Md.; Union Cl., N.Y. *Exhibited*: war paintings, Nat. Gal., London, England; Salon de la Marine, Paris, France; in Melbourne, Sydney, Australia; Carnegie Inst.; WMA; VMFA; CGA; PMA; U.S. Naval Acad.; NAD, 1941; NGA; MMA.

MURRAY, ALEXANDER—Painter, I.
69 Broad St., Red Bank, N.J.

B. Kingston, Pa., July 20, 1888. *Studied*: PAFA; ASL; Columbia Univ., B.S. in A. Edu.; & with Cecilia Beaux, William Chase, & others. *Member*: AAPL. Author, I., "How to Draw," 1930; "How to Draw and Paint," 1946. Contributor to: American Boy, Saturday Evening Post, School Arts magazines. *Position*: Dir., Murray A. Schs., Wilkes-Barre, Scranton, Pa.

MURRAY, FLORETTA—Educator, P., S.
Art Department, Winona State College; h. 501 Harriet St., Winona, Minn.

B. Minnesota. *Studied*: Winona State Col., B. Ed.; Univ. Minnesota, M.A., plus work toward Ph.D.; Minneapolis Sch. A.; Univ. Chicago, and in France, Belgium and Italy. *Member*: AAUP; NAEA; Nat. Lg. Am. Pen Women; Minnesota Sculpture Assn.; CAA; Minnesota Edu. Assn. *Awards*: prizes, Minn. State Fair, 1938; Women's Week Expo., 1942; Indp. A., N.Y., 1947; WAC, 1941, 1945; St. Paul A. Gal., 1956. *Work*: Winona County Hist. Soc. (mural). *Exhibited*: Indp. A. Assn., N.Y., 1947, 1948; Nat. Lg. Am. Pen Women, 1956; Indiana (Pa.) Univ.; Minnesota State Fair; WAC; Minneapolis Sch. A.; Univ. Chicago; Univ. Minnesota; one-man: Winona Pub. Lib., 1954, 1958; Rochester A. Center, 1957, 1958; Univ. Minn. A. Gal., 1958. Lectures: Modern Painting; Medieval Painting; American Colonial Painters, etc. *Position*: Prof. A., Hd. A. Dept., Winona State College, Winona, Minn., 1942- .

MURRAY, HAROLD PAUL—Painter, T.
592 Oxford St., Westbury, N.Y.

B. New York, N.Y., Dec. 28, 1900. *Studied*: ASL; PAFA; & with Frank DuMond. *Member*: Nassau County A. Lg. *Exhibited*: NAD, 1931; Brooklyn Soc. Min. P., 1929; ASMP, 1930; WFNY 1939; AWCS, 1926; NAC, 1932; Nassau County A. Lg., 1936-1944.

MURRAY, MARIAN—
Writer, Former Mus. Pub. Relations
1618 Waldemere St., Sarasota, Fla.

B. Quincy, Mass. *Studied*: Wellesley Col., B.A.; Grad. study in art, England, France. Contributor to various magazines; coloring books for children, "Sarasota the Circus City," 1942; "Here Comes the Circus," 1954; "Children of the Big Top," 1958; "Circus!" (an adult history of the circus from 2500 B.C. to the present time), 1956. *Positions*: A. Cr., Hartford Times, 1929-47, Book Cr., 1935-47; Pub. Relations Dir., Ringling Museums, Sarasota, Fla., 1948-1958. Freelance at present.

MURRAY, MARTIN J.—Painter, T.
Black Point Farm, Portsmouth, R.I.; P.O. Box 6, Middletown, R.I.

B. Newport, R.I., Apr. 30, 1908. *Studied*: R.I. Sch. Des.; John Frazier Sch. Painting, Provincetown, Mass. *Member*: CAA; Phila. WC Cl.; AEA. *Work*: Brown Univ.; R.I. Pub. Sch.; murals, New England Steamship Co., Newport, R.I. *Exhibited*: PAFA, annually; Newport AA, annually; Butler AI, 1946; R.I. Sch. Des., annually; AIC; Fleming Mus. A.; Providence A. Cl.

MURTON, CLARENCE C.—
Commercial Artist, L., E., P.
Post-Intelligencer, 6th & Wall Sts.; h. 2122 Shelby St., Seattle 2, Wash.

B. McMinnville, Ore., Feb. 17, 1901. *Studied*: Univ. Washington, B.A. *Member*: Puget Sound Group of Northwest Painters. *Position*: Art Mngr., Seattle Post-Intelligencer; Instr., L., Adv. Production and Layout, Printing Processes, Univ. Washington, Seattle, Wash., 1942- .

MUSGRAVE, ARTHUR FRANKLYN—Painter
Truro, Cape Cod, Mass.

B. Brighton, England, July 24, 1876. *Studied*: in England with Stanhope Forbes. *Member*: Provincetown AA. *Exhibited*: Royal Acad., London, England; PAFA; CGA; PMG; Stuart Gal., Boston, Mass.; Mus. FA, N. Mexico.*

MUSGRAVE, SHIRLEY D. HUDSON—Painter, Gr., T.
1736 Brook St., Lawrence, Kans.

B. Lexington, Ky., Nov. 28, 1935. *Studied*: Mississippi State Col. for Women; Colorado Springs FA Center Sch.; Allison A. Colony, Way, Miss.; Univ. Kansas. *Member*: Alabama WC Soc.; Mississippi AA; Allison A. Colony. *Awards*: Scholarships, Mississippi AA, 1956-57; Colorado Springs FA Center Sch., 1956; Grad. Scholarship in FA, Univ. Kansas, 1957-58; prizes, Arkansas Artists, 1956; Allison A. Colony, 1957; Delta Phi Delta, Univ. Kansas, 1958. *Exhibited*: Allison A. Colony, 1956, 1957; Alabama

WC Soc., 1955, 1956; Mississippi AA, 1956; Norfolk Mus.
A. & Sciences, 1956, and circuit exh.; Little Rock Mus.
FA, 1956, 1957; Univ. Kansas, 1958; Kansas Free Fair,
Topeka, 1958; one-man: Mun. Gal., Jackson, Miss., 1957.
Position: Instr., Linwood H.S., Linwood, Kansas.

MUSICK, ARCHIE L.—*Painter, Lith., T., W.*
10 Studio Place, Colorado Springs, Colo.

B. Kirksville, Mo., Jan. 19, 1902. *Studied*: Northeast Mis-
souri State T. Col., B.Sc.; & with Thomas Hart Benton, S.
MacDonald-Wright, Boardman Robinson. *Work*: murals,
Cheyenne Sch., Colo. Springs; Mun. Auditorium, FA
Center, Colorado Springs, Colo.; USPO, Red Cloud,
Neb.; Manitou Springs, Colo. *Exhibited*: AIC, 1940;
Carnegie Inst., 1941; PAFA, 1941, 1951; CGA, 1951; Los
A. Mus. A., 1945; Santa Barbara Mus. A., 1945; Cleveland,
1955. Author, I., "Oil Painting for Beginners," 1930;
"Jigger Flies First," 1957 (juvenile). *Position*: A. Dir.,
Cheyenne Mountain Sch., Colorado Springs, Colo.

MUSSELMAN, DARWIN B.—*Painter, E., Comm. A.*
944 West Indianapolis Ave., Fresno 5, Cal.

B. Selma, Cal., Feb. 16, 1916. *Studied*: Fresno State Col.,
A.B.; Cal. Col. A. & Crafts, M.F.A.; Univ. California,
M.A.; Mills Col., and with Lyonel Feininger, Yasuo Kuniyoshi. *Member*: Cal. WC Soc.; AWS; San F. AA. *Awards*:
prizes, San Joaquin Valley A. Comp., 1947; Fresno A.
Lg., 1947; Oakland A. Mus., 1948; Cal. State Fair, 1949-
1952, 1955; No. Cal. A., 1954, 1955, 1956; Western A.,
1954; Fresno Fair, 1955, 1956. *Exhibited*: San F. AA,
1943, 1947, 1948, 1950, 1956, 1958; Oakland A. Gal.,
1944, 1948, 1950, 1954; Cal., PLH, 1948; Los A. Mus. A.,
1949; Cal. WC Soc., 1947-1949, 1951, 1954; Denver A.
Mus., 1950, 1954; SAM, 1951; Haggin A. Gal., Stockton,
1957 (one-man); Butler Inst. Am. A., 1956; Fresno A.
Center, 1955, 1958. *Position*: Asst. Prof. A., Fresno State
Col., 1953- .

MYER, JOHN WALDEN—*Museum Director*
1165 Fifth Ave., New York 29, N.Y.

B. London, England, Sept. 18, 1901. *Studied*: Harvard
Univ., B.S. *Member*: AAMus.; Assn. A. Mus. Dir.; AFA;
Grolier Cl.; Century Assn.; Museums Council of New
York City; Soc. Arch. Historians. Contributor to Bulletin
of the Museum of the City of New York. Lectures:
"Various Aspects of New York City History"; "Eighteenth
Century New York Architecture." *Positions*: Research
Asst., 1929-31, Asst. Dir., 1931-42, 1946-51, Dir., 1951-
1958 (retired), Museum of the City of New York. Trustee,
Soc. for Preservation of Long Island Antiquities; Sec., Hist.
Landmark Soc., N.Y.

MYERS, DENYS PETER—*Museum Director*
Des Moines Art Center, Greenwood Park, Des Moines
15, Iowa

B. Boston, Mass., Apr. 23, 1916. *Studied*: Harvard Col.,
B.S., Harvard Univ. (candidate for Ph.D); Columbia
Univ., M.A. *Member*: CAA; Soc. Arch. Hist.; AAMus.;
Steamship Hist. Soc. Am. Contributor to Soc. Architec-
tural Historians Journal. Lectures: Historical & Critical
Lectures on Mediaeval, Baroque, Romantic and Contem-
porary subjects. Exhibitions arranged: Zanesville Sesquicen-
tennial Exh., 1947; Adorations of the Magi, 1948; The
Grand Manner (Baroque Exh.), 1949; Romanticism (archi-
tectural section selected, arranged and catalogued for the
Columbus Gal. FA.). *Positions*: Dir., Art Inst. of Zanes-
ville, Ohio, 1947-55; Dir., Philbrook A. Center, Tulsa,
Okla, 1955-1958; Dir., Des Moines A. Center, Des Moines,
Iowa, 1958- .

MYERS, ETHEL (Mrs. Jerome)—*Sculptor, L., T.*
Studio 614, Carnegie Hall, West 57th St., New York
19, N.Y.; h. Orleans, Cape Cod, Mass.

B. Brooklyn, N.Y., Aug. 23, 1881. *Studied*: Hunter Col.;
Columbia Univ.; & with William Chase, Robert Henri,
Kenneth Hayes Miller. *Exhibited*: NAD; CGA; PAFA;
AIC; WMAA; BM; etc. Contributor to: magazines &
newspapers. *Position*: A. Dir., Christodora House, N.Y.

MYERS, JOHN—*Painter*
30 Rockefeller Plaza; h. 880 Fifth Ave., New York,
N.Y.

B. London, England, Sept. 1, 1900. *Member*: AEA; Palm
Beach A. Lg.; AAPL. Author, I., "Nellie Bly," 1950.

Position: Dir., Gen. Mngr., Am. Flange & Mfg. Co.,
1935- ; Pres., John Myers Fnd. & Gallery 21, N.Y.;
Member, Am. Arbitration Bd.; Patent Com., NAM; Lay
Com., Bellevue Hospital; Chm., Bd. Trustees, Symphony
Fnd. Am. Contributor of art scholarships for New Sch.
for Social Research, N.Y.*

MYERS, MALCOLM HAYNIE—*Painter, Et., Eng.*
2506 Grand Ave., South, Minneapolis, Minn.

B. Chillicothe, Mo., June 19, 1917. *Studied*: Univ. Wichita,
B.A.; Univ. Iowa, M.A., M.F.A. *Awards*: Guggenheim F.,
1950, 1951, 1953-54; prizes, SAM, 1958; WAC, 1958.
Work: LC; Walker A. Center; CAM; SAM; Bibliotheque
Nationale, Paris; Minneapolis Inst. A.; MMod.A. *Ex-
hibited*: Salon de Mai, Paris, 1951; Am. Embassy, Paris,
1951; all nat. print shows since 1946; Contemp. Am.
Gravure, Paris, 1951; MMA, 1952; Northwest Pr.M., 1946;
Phila. Pr. Cl., 1949; LC, 1945; PAFA, 1949; Bordighera,
Italy, 1956; Minneapolis Inst. A., 1958; SAM, 1958; Kansas
City AI, 1958; Univ. Illinois, 1958; one-man: Walker A.
Center, 1949, 1953, 1958; Univ. Minnesota, 1953; Harriet
Hanley Gal., 1952 (Minneapolis); High Acre Gal., Min-
neapolis, 1952; Minneapolis Inst. A., 1958. *Position*: Instr.,
Pr.M., Univ. Iowa, 1946-48; Assoc. Prof., Hd. Print Dept.,
Univ. Minnesota, Minneapolis, Minn., 1948- ; Instr., Paint-
ing, Walker Art Center, 1958.

MYERS, (CHARLES) STOWE—
Industrial Designer, E., L.
1903 Central St.; h. 2210 Hartzell St., Evanston, Ill.

B. Altoona, Pa., Dec. 7, 1906. *Studied*: Univ. Pennsylvania, B.A. in Arch. *Member*: Am. Soc. Indst. Des.;
AWCS. *Awards*: Naval Ordnance Award, 1945. *Work*:
Assoc. Des., Eastman Kodak Bldg., WFNY 1939. *Exhibited*: AWCS, annually; product designs, 1957 Triennial,
Milan; U.S. Pavilion, Brussels World's Fair, 1958, and
other Intl. Trade Fairs since 1956. *Positions*: Indst. Des.,
Walter Dorwin Teague, New York & Los Angeles, Cal.,
1934- , Partner, 1945-48; Design Projects Dir., Raymond
Loewy Assoc., 1950-54; Independent Consultant Des.,
1954- ; L., Inst. Des., Ill. Inst. Tech., 1955- .

MYERS, WILLARD—*Etcher, I., W.*
The Cambridge, Alden Park, Germantown, Philadelphia
44, Pa.

B. Philadelphia, Pa., Oct. 17, 1887. *Studied*: PMSch. IA.
Member: Phila. Sketch Cl.; AIGA; Phila. Pr. Cl.; PMA;
PAFA. *Exhibited*: SAGA, 1944; Phila. Pr. Cl., 1944, 1946,
1951; Phila. Sketch Cl., 1943-1958. Author, I., "The Un-
believable City," 1926; "Sketch Club Portfolio," 1945-49;
"Library Notes," 1952-54.

MYLONAS, GEORGE EMMANUEL—*Educator, W., L.*
Washington University, St. Louis 5, Mo.; h. 550 Bedford St., University City 5, Mo.

B. Smyrna, Dec. 9, 1898. *Studied*: International Col.,
Smyrna, B.A.; Univ. Athens, Ph.D.; Johns Hopkins Univ.,
Ph.D. *Awards*: Greek Govt. dec., 1955 for Archaeological
discoveries. *Member*: CAA; Archaeological Inst. Am.
(Pres.); Archaeological Inst. Greece; Inst. for Advanced
Study. Author: "The New Stone Age in Greece," 1927;
"Prehistoric Eleusis," 1934; "The Balkan States," 1946;
"Mycenae, Capital City of Agamemnon," 1956, & other
books. Contributor to: Archaeological journals. Lectures:
Ancient Greek History of Art; Greek Archaeology, etc.
Position: Instr., Univ. Chicago, 1929; Assoc. Prof., 1931-
33, Prof., 1939-40, Univ. Illinois; Asst. Prof., 1933-35,
Assoc. Prof., 1935-36, Prof., Hd. Dept. A. & Archaeology,
1936- , Washington Univ., St. Louis, Mo., and Prof.
Archaeology, Univ. Athens, Greece, since 1954.

MYRHL, SARAH—*Painter*
939 8th Ave., Studio #308 (19); h. 537 West 121st
St., New York 27, N.Y.

B. New York, N.Y., Sept. 16, 1912. *Studied*: Hunter Col.,
B.A.; New School for Social Research; Columbia Univ.;
ASL, with Kuniyoshi, Brook, Zorach. *Member*: ASL (life).
Awards: Metropolitan scholarship from ASL. *Work*: in
private colls. U.S. and Japan; mural (with James Brooks),
La Guardia Sea Plane Base, N.Y. *Exhibited*: Salons of
America; ACA Gal.; Riverside Mus., N.Y.

NAGEL, CHARLES—*Museum Director*, L.
City Art Museum of St. Louis, Forest Park, St. Louis 5, Mo.; h. 27 Windermere Place, St. Louis 12, Mo.

B. St. Louis, Mo., Mar. 24, 1899. *Studied*: Yale Univ., B.A., B.F.A., M.F.A.; Ecole des Beaux-Arts, Fontainebleau, France. *Member*: AIA; Assn. A. Mus. Dir.; AAMus. (Vice-Pres.). *Awards*: prize, BAID, 1936. *Position*: Cur. Dec. A., Asst. Prof. Hist A., Yale Univ., 1930-36; Acting Dir., 1942-45, Assoc. Dir., 1946, CAM, St. Louis, Mo.; Dir., BM, Brooklyn, N.Y., 1946-55; Dir., CAM, St. Louis, Mo., 1955- ; Adv. Com. on the Arts, U.S. Dept. State.

NAGEL, STINA (*Mrs. Leon Hill*)—*Painter*
2 Bank St., New York 14, N.Y.

B. Ann Arbor, Mich., Jan. 25, 1918. *Studied*: Univ. Mich., Sch. Des.; ASL, and with Jose de Creeft, Victor Candell, Charles Seide. *Member*: AEA; Audubon A. *Award*: Jane Higbee award, Univ. Mich., 1939. *Work*: in private colls. *Exhibited*: Oakland A. Mus., 1948; Audubon A., 1948, 1951, 1953-1958; All. A. Am., 1949; Newport AA, 1948; NAWA, 1949; Butler AI, 1955; RoKo Gal., 1953; Contemporary A. Gal., 1947; AEA, 1952; Tribune A. Gal., 1948; one-man: Mint Mus. A.; Davidson Col., Davidson, N.C.

NAGELVOORT, BETTY (*Mrs. Betty Nagelvoort Flint*)— *Designer*, C., Eng.
1601 East 25th St., Signal Hill 6, Cal.

B. Ann Arbor, Mich., Dec. 10, 1909. *Studied*: Univ. Washington, B.F.A.; A. Center Sch., Los A., Cal.; & with Helen Rhodes, Walter Isaacs. *Awards*: prizes, Pomona (Cal.) Fair; Los A. Mus. A., 1940, 1941. *Exhibited*: 50 Color Prints of the Year, 1933; GGE, 1939; Northwest Pr.M.; Prairie Pr.M.; Cal. WC Soc.; Pomona Fair, 1932-38; Los A. Mus. A., 1940, 1941.*

NAGLER, EDITH (KROGER)—*Painter*, I., T., W.
Alderbrook Rd., Riverdale, New York 71, N.Y.; h. Stone House, Huntington, Mass.

B. New York, N.Y., June 18, 1890. *Studied*: NAD; ASL; & with Douglas Volk, Robert Henri, Frank DuMond. *Member*: AWCS; AAPL; Springfield A. Lg. *Awards*: prizes, Springfield, Mass., 1934; Stockbridge, Mass., 1932; Bronx A. Gld. *Work*: Wadsworth Atheneum, Hartford, Conn.; Springfield Mus. A.; Highland Park Mus., Dallas, Tex.; Federal Court House, Boston; and in private colls. *Exhibited*: CGA; AIC; NAD; AWCS, 1932-1946; PAFA; Springfield Mus. A.; BMA; New Haven Paint & Clay Cl.; Bronx A. Gld.; Midtown Gal.; Eastern States Exh., 1957, 1958; Grand Central A. Gal., 1957, 1958.

NAGLER, FRED—*Painter*, S.
c/o Midtown Galleries, 17 East 57th St., New York 22, N.Y.

B. Springfield, Mass., Feb. 27, 1891. *Studied*: ASL; & with William Stock, Robert Henri, Frank DuMond. *Awards*: med., prize, VMFA; CGA, 1941; Springfield Mus. FA; NAD; Hallmark award; Grant, Am. Acad. A. & Lets. *Work*: deYoung Mem. Mus.; Lutheran Church, Reading, Pa.; Capehart Coll.; Springfield Mus. A.; AGAA; Temple Univ.; Dwight Chapel, Yale Univ.; Hallmark Coll. *Exhibited*: CGA; AIC; Albright A. Gal.; Detroit Inst. A.; PAFA; deYoung Mem. Mus.; Dallas Mus. FA; NAD; WMAA; Carnegie Inst.; CMA; Butler Inst. Am. A.; LC; John Herron AI; Los A. Mus. A.; Univ. Nebraska; Univ. Iowa, and others.

NALBANDIAN, KARNIG—*Painter*, Et.
15 Woodbine St., Providence, R.I.

B. Providence, R.I., May 18, 1916. *Work*: Carnegie Inst.; LC; BM; AGAA; R.I.Sch.Des.; Princeton Mus. Hist. Art. *Exhibited*: NAD; PAFA; Albany Inst. Hist. & A.; WMAA; Providence A. Cl.; Armour Gal.; A. Center; one-man: Arthur Newton Gal., 1946-1950; Chapellier Gal., 1952, and others.

NASH, ANNE TAYLOR (*Mrs. E. S.*)—*Portrait Painter*
329 East 48th St., Savannah, Ga.

B. Pittsboro, N.C., Jan. 29, 1884. *Studied*: Sch. FA, Fontainebleau, France; PAFA; Inst. San Miguel, Mexico; Winthrop Col., Rock Hill, S.C., and with Robert Brackman, Wayman Adams. *Member*: Carolina AA; Savannah

A. Cl.; Telfair Acad.; SSAL; Savannah A. Cl. *Awards*: prize, Telfair Acad., 1951. *Work*: Roper Hospital, Hibernian Soc., St. Andrews Soc., all in Charleston, S.C.; Colonial Dames House, Health Center, both in Savannah; N.Y. Infirmary.

NASH, HAROLD SIEGRIST—
Educator, C., Des., W., L.
3976 Clifton Ave., Cincinnati 20, Ohio

B. Buffalo, N.Y., Nov. 8, 1894. *Studied*: N.Y. State Col. Ceramics, Alfred, N.Y., B.S. *Member*: Am. Assn. Univ. Prof.; Am. Ceramic Soc. *Awards*: med., Alfred, N.Y., 1940. *Work*: CM; IBM Coll. *Exhibited*: Syracuse Mus. FA; CM; Taft Mus. A., 1954 (one-man). Contributor to: Bulletins of Am. Ceramic Soc.; Design magazine. Lectures: Ceramics. TV programs on ceramics and jewelry. *Position*: Prof. Ceramics, Univ. Cincinnati, Ohio, 1927- .

NASH, JAMES HARLEY (JIM)—
Industrial Designer, Comm. A.
527 Madison Ave., New York 22, N.Y.; also, St. Thomas 7, Virgin Islands

B. Cincinnati, Ohio, July 29, 1892. *Studied*: Cincinnati A. Acad.; ASL. *Member*: IDI; Package Des. Council (Fndr. & Fellow); U.S. Trademark Assn. *Awards*: Nat. trade mark "Made in U.S.A.," Detroit Bd. of Commerce and Detroit Adcraft Comp. awards, 1937-1941; Folding Paper Box Assn. of Cl., 1921; Wolf award, 1936, 1940; All Am. Package Am., 1951; Certif. of Award, Economic Cooperation Admin. for Tech. assistance to Marshall Plan countries, 1951. Des. many famous trademarks including Socony Flying Red Horse, the Owl for Red Owl Stores, the Rooster for Colonial Stores, and others. Contributor to trade papers and design magazines. Lecturer on trademark and package design. *Position*: Des., Consultant, Reynolds Metal Co.; Pres. and Chm. Bd., Jim Nash Assoc., Inc., New York, N.Y.

NASH, KATHERINE (*Mrs. Robert C.*)—
Sculptor, T., Gal. Dir., C., L.
Christmas Lake, Route 3, Excelsior, Minn.

B. Minneapolis, Minn., May 20, 1910. *Studied*: Univ. Minnesota, B.S.; Minneapolis Sch. A.; Walker A. Center. *Member*: Minnesota S. Group; AEA (Midwest Reg. Dir.); S. Gld.; Midwest Mus. Assn. *Awards*: prizes, Nat. Delta Phi Delta Comp., 1932; Minn. State Fair, 1941, 1942, 1944; Minneapolis Inst. A., 1944; Swedish-Am., Exh., 1948; Lincoln A. Gld., 1950; Nebraska State Fair, 1951, 1952; Joslyn A. Mus., 1954; Nebraska AA, 1955; Walker A. Center, 1951; Sioux City, 1952. *Work*: Univ. Medical Bldg., Omaha; Buffalo (Minn.) Court House; Walker A. Center; Lincoln A. Gld.; Nebraska AA; Kansas State Col.; Concordia Col.; Minneapolis Pub. Lib.; Joslyn A. Mus.; Omaha Assoc. A. *Exhibited*: Minneapolis Inst. A.; Minn. State Fair; Walker A. Center; St. Paul Gal.; Lincoln A. Gld.; Joslyn A. Mus.; Nebraska AA; Springfield A. Mus.; Denver A. Mus.; Sioux City, Iowa; SFMA; Kansas City AI; St. Louis; Univ. Manitoba, Canada; Rochester A. Center; Des Moines A. Center; S. Center, N.Y.; WMAA; Cranbrook Acad.; Brussels World's Fair; London, England, and others; one-man: Univ. Manitoba; Sioux City A. Center; WAC; Gump's Gal., San F. *Position*: A. Dir., Univ. Gal., Univ. of Minnesota.

NASH, RAY—*Writer*, E., L.
Dartmouth College, Hanover, N.H.

B. Milwaukie, Ore., Feb. 27, 1905. *Studied*: Univ. Oregon, B.A.; Harvard Univ., M.A. *Member*: CAA; Am. Antiquarian Soc.; Bibliographical Soc. Am.; AIGA (Hon. life memb.). *Awards*: F., Belgian-Am. Edu. Fnd.; Hon. Degree, A.M., Dartmouth Col.; gold med., AIGA, 1956; Artt D., New England Col. *Author*: "Calligraphy and Printing in the Sixteenth Century," 1940; "Early American Writing Books and Masters," 1943; "Durer's 1511 Drawings of a Press and Printer," 1947; "Checklist of American Writing Manuals and Copybooks to 1850," 1950; "Printing as an Art," 1955; "American Writing Masters and Copybooks," 1958. Ed., "Renaissance News"; Ed., "Printing and Graphic Arts." *Position*: Prof., Hist. Gr. A., Printing Advisor, Dartmouth Col., Hanover, N.H., 1937- ; Advisor, Musee Plantin-Moretus, Antwerp, 1953; Visiting L., Univ. Oregon; Amherst Col.; Antwerp Intl. Congress on Printing and Humanism; Colonial Soc. Mass., and others.

NASON, GERTRUDE—*Painter*

461 Ave. of the Americas, New York 11, N.Y.; s. Lyme, Conn.

B. Everett, Mass. *Studied*: Mass. Sch. A., with Joseph De Camp; BMFA Sch., with Edmund Tarbell. *Member*: NAWA; Creative A. Assoc.; N.Y. Soc. Women A.; PBC; Lyme AA. *Awards*: prizes, NAWA, 1939, 1945; PBC, 1932, 1935, 1938, 1941, 1945, 1948, 1950, 1952, 1956. *Work*: BMFA. *Exhibited*: CGA, 1925, 1933, 1935, 1937; PAFA, 1925, 1932, 1934; NAD, 1933, 1935; CAM, 1934; Dayton AI, 1946; AFA traveling exh., 1933; Lyme A. Gal.; Lyman Allyn Mus., 1945; Copley Soc., Boston, 1945; Riverside Mus., 1942, 1944, 1946, 1951, 1953, 1956; Am.-British A. Center, 1943; All.A.Am., 1942; BMFA, 1951.

NASON, THOMAS W.—*Engraver, Et., I.*

Lyme, Conn.

B. Dracut, Mass., Jan. 7, 1889. *Studied*: Tufts Col., M.A. (hon. degree). *Member*: NA; Nat. Inst. A. & Let.; SAE; SC; F.; Am. Acad. A. & Sciences; Lyme AA. *Awards*: prizes, Phila. Pr. Cl., 1929, 1930; AIC, 1930; City of Warsaw, Poland, 1933; Lib.Cong., 1943, 1945; SAE, 1935, 1938, 1945, 1950, 1951; Woodcut Soc., Kansas City, Mo., 1937; Albany Pr. Cl., 1946. *Work*: N.Y.Pub.Lib.; BM; WMAA; AIC; CMA; AGAA; Smithsonian Inst.; BMFA; Boston Pub. Lib.; Victoria & Albert Mus., London, England; Bibliotheque Nationale, Paris, France.

NATZLER, GERTRUDE—*Ceramic Craftsman*

7837 Woodrow Wilson Dr., Los Angeles 46, Cal.

B. Vienna, Austria, July 7, 1908. *Awards*: med., Paris Salon, 1937; prizes, Syracuse Mus. FA, 1939-1941, 1946, 1956; Cal. State Fair, 1948, 1949, 1952, 1954, 1955, 1956 (2), 1957; Los Angeles County Fair, 1948, 1949, 1951. *Work*: MModA; Syracuse Mus. FA; San Diego FA Soc.; BMA; CM; PMA; Santa Barbara Mus. A.; SAM; Los A. Mus. A.; AIC; Walker A. Center; Detroit Inst. A.; Univ. Minnesota; Univ. Oregon; Cranbrook Acad. A.; Newark Mus.; Slater Mem. Mus.; Dallas Mus. FA; Portland A. Mus.; Univ. Wisconsin; MMA; SFMA; Joslyn A. Mus.; Univ. Nebraska; Springfield A. Mus.; UCLA; Cal. State Fair Coll.; Arizona State Col.; Mus. FA of Houston, and in Italy. *Exhibited*: Paris Salon, 1937; Syracuse Mus. FA, 1939-1941, 1946; GGE, 1939; one-man: SFMA; Los A. Mus. A.; San Diego FA Soc.; Santa Barbara Mus. A.; AIC.

NATZLER, OTTO—*Ceramic Craftsman*

7837 Woodrow Wilson Dr., Los Angeles 46, Cal.

B. Vienna, Austria, Jan. 31, 1908. *Awards*: med., Paris Salon, 1937; prizes, Syracuse Mus. FA, 1939-1941, 1946, 1956; Cal. State Fair, 1948, 1949, 1952, 1954, 1955, 1956 (2), 1957; Los Angeles County Fair, 1948, 1949, 1951. *Work*: MModA; Syracuse Mus. FA; San Diego FA Soc.; BMA; CM; PMA; Santa Barbara Mus. A.; SAM; Los A. Mus. A.; AIC; Walker A. Center; Detroit Inst. A.; Univ. Minnesota; Univ. Oregon; Cranbrook Acad. A.; Newark Mus.; Slater Mem. Mus.; Dallas Mus. FA; Portland A. Mus.; Univ. Wisconsin; MMA; SFMA; Joslyn A. Mus.; Univ. Nebraska; Springfield A. Mus.; UCLA; Cal. State Fair Coll.; Arizona State Col.; Mus. FA of Houston, and in Italy. *Exhibited*: Paris Salon, 1937; Syracuse Mus. FA, 1939-1941, 1946; GGE, 1939; one-man: SFMA; Los A. Mus. A.; San Diego FA Soc.; Santa Barbara Mus. A.; AIC.

NAUMER, HELMUTH—*Painter*

Rancho de San Sebastian; h. P.O. Box 1302, Santa Fé, N.M.

B. Reutlingen, Germany, Sept. 1, 1907. *Studied*: in Germany; Frank Wiggins Sch. A., and with Franz Weegman, Josef Reichelt. *Work*: Mus. New Mexico, Santa Fé; Governor's Mansion, Santa Fé; Univ. New Mexico; Univ. Wyoming; Bandelier & White Sands nat. monuments, New Mexico, and in many private colls. U.S., Canada, Mexico and Europe. *Exhibited*: Springfield, Utah, 1941, 1946; Mus. New Mexico, Santa Fé, annually, with one-man exh., 1945, 1946-1955; other one-man exhs., New York, Philadelphia and Los Angeles.

NAY, MARY SPENCER *(Mrs. Lou Block)—*
Painter, Gr., T.

2111 South First St.; h. 10 Keller Court, Louisville 8, Ky.

B. Crestwood, Ky., May 13, 1913. *Studied*: Louisville A. Center Assn. Sch.; Univ. Louisville, A.B.; Cincinnati A.

Acad., with Maebelle Stamper; ASL, with Kuniyoshi, Barnet, Grosz; Intl. Sch. A., Mexico, with Merida, Zalce. *Member*: Louisville A. Center Assn.; Louisville A. Cl.; Western AA; Kentucky Edu. Assn. *Awards*: prizes, Aetna Oil purchase award, 1945, 1950; Evansville Tri-State Exh.; Ohio Valley Exh., Athens, 1954 (purchase), 1955; Kentucky State Fair, 1954; Woman's Cl., 1955; medal, IBM, 1940. *Work*: Univ. Louisville; Evansville Pub. Mus.; J.B. Speed A. Mus.; Univ. Athens (Ohio), and in private colls. Mural, Children's Room, Louisville Pub. Lib. *Exhibited*: Intl. Color Litho. Exh., Cincinnati, 1950, 1952, 1954; AIC, 1950, 1954; MMA, 1942; WFNY 1939; Minneapolis Print Exh., 1951; Ohio Valley Exhs., 1942-1955; Evansville, 1951-1955; W. Va. Regional, 1947-1954; Va. Intermont, 1946-1952; Ky.-So. Indiana Exhs., 1928-1955; Ky. State Fair, 1948-1955; Contemp. A. Soc., Cincinnati, 1955; Louisville Woman's Cl., annually; Louisville A. Cl., annually. *Position*: Instr., Louisville A. Center Sch., 1935-56; Dir., 1944-49; Instr., Adult Edu., Univ. Louisville, 1936-56.*

NAYLOR, ALICE *(Mrs. James K.)—Painter, Lith., T.*

Incarnate Word College; h. 125 Magnolia Dr., San Antonio 2, Tex.

B. Columbus, Tex. *Studied*: Witte Mem. Mus. Sch. A.; San Antonio AI, and with Charles Rosen, Etienne Ret, Andrew Dasburg, Xavier Gonzalez, Dan Lutz. *Member*: San Antonio A. Lg.; Palette & Chisel Cl.; San Antonio Pr. M.; Texas FA Assn. (Trustee); Nat. Soc. A. & Let.; River A. Group; Texas WC Soc.; Beaumont A. Lg.; Contemp. A. Group; San Antonio Craft Gld.; Texas A. Educators Assn. *Exhibited*: CM, 1945; Mus. New Mexico, 1945; Texas FA Assn.; LC, 1943; Austin, Tex., 1942; Texas WC Exh., 1950-1955; Beaumont A. Mus.; Corpus Christi A. Mus.; Romano Gal., Mexico City (4-man), 1950; Escuela Nationale, Mexico City (4-man), 1950; Sul Ross Col.; A. & M. Col., Bryan, Tex.; Designs for Living Gal., San Antonio; Laguna Gloria Mus., Austin; Elisabet Ney Mus., Austin; Texas Fed. Women's Cl., Austin (one-man); Incarnate Word Col. (one-man); Southwest Texas State T. Col. (one-man); and others. *Awards*: River A. Group, 1953-1956; Texas WC Soc., 1953, 1958; Texas A. Mart, Austin, 1955; "Woman of the Year," 1953, San Antonio; Texas FA Assn., 1957; Columbus (Tex.) A. Fair, 1957-58; Beaumont A. Mus., 1958.

NEAFIE, EDITH S.—*Painter, T.*

3335 81st St., Jackson Heights 72, N.Y.

B. Brooklyn, N.Y., Apr. 29, 1884. *Studied*: PIASch.; Grand Central Sch. A.; N.Y. State Normal, & with Anna Fisher, Lester Stevens. *Member*: AAPL; NAWA; Pen & Brush Cl. *Awards*: Wolfe AC, 1932. *Exhibited*: NAWA, 1932, 1933, 1936-1938, 1942, 1946; AWCS; PBC, 1937-1941, 1944-1946.*

NEAL, GRACE PRUDEN *(Mrs. Jesse H.)—*
Sculptor, P.

245 Citrus Ave., Dunedin, Fla.

B. St. Paul, Minn., May 11, 1876. *Studied*: St. Paul A. Sch.; AIC; ASL; Grand Chaumiere, Paris; & with Knute Akerberg, Injalbert. *Awards*: prize, Minn. State A. Soc., 1903-1905. *Work*: bronze relief, Corcoran Mem. Park, St. Paul, Minn.; bronze group, Thirty Club, London, England. *Exhibited*: NAD, 1919-1923, 1927; PAFA, 1914-1917, 1920, 1922, 1924, 1927, 1929, 1930, 1945, 1946; Carnegie Inst., 1917; AIC, 1916, 1917, 1919, 1921, 1927; Arch.L., 1920, 1921, 1923; CGA, 1945, 1946; Smithsonian Inst., 1946; Phila. Plastic Cl.; Rochester Mem. A. Gal.; All.A.Am.; Putnam County AA; Newport AA; Albright A. Gal.; Conn. Acad. FA; Minn. State A. Soc.; Indianapolis AA; Fla. Gulf Coast A. Center, 1954; Fla. Int. Exh.; one-man: Tampa AI, 1951; Clearwater A. Group, 1952; A. Cl., St. Petersburg, 1955-56.

NEAL, REGINALD H.—*Educator, Lith., P., L.*

Art Department, Southern Illinois University, Carbondale, Ill.

B. Leicester, England, May 20, 1909. *Studied*: Bradley Polytechnic Inst., B.Sc.; Univ. Chicago, M.A.; Yale Univ. Sch. FA. *Member*: CAA; Southeastern Col. AA. *Work*: Davenport Mun. A. Gal.; LC; MModA; Queen's Col, Kingston, Canada; Brigham Young Univ.; Brooks Mem. Gal.; Decatur A. Center. *Exhibited*: AIC, 1935, 1951; PAFA, 1936, 1938, 1940; MMA, 1952; State Univ. Iowa, 1947, 1948; CM, 1954; Contemporaries Gal., 1953; BM,

1950; Brooks Mem. Gal., 1949, 1951, 1953, 1955; one-man: Salpeter Gal., N.Y., 1953; Assoc. Am. A., 1950. Lectures: tours for Assn. Am. Colleges, 1953, 1954; Lecture-Demonstrations on Lithography; Film: "Color Lithography—An Art Medium," produced 1954; Univ. Miss., with demonstration and narration. *Position*: Chm., Dept. A., University of Mississippi, University, Miss.; A. Dept., Southern Illinois Univ., Carbondale, Ill., at present.

NEALE, MRS. SIDNEE—*Illustrator, Comm. A.*
   385 Madison Ave. (17); h. 121 Madison Ave., New York 16, N.Y.

B. Baltimore, Md., May 16, 1910. *Member*: SI.*

NEBEL, BERTHOLD—*Sculptor*
   Roseville Road, Westport, Conn.

B. Basel, Switzerland, Apr. 1, 1889. *Studied*: Mechanics Inst., N.Y.; ASL, with James E. Fraser; Am. Acad. in Rome. *Member*: NA; NSS. *Awards*: Prix di Rome, 1914-17; War Memorial comp., Richmond, Va. *Work*: bas-reliefs, statues, bronze doors, plaques: Hispanic Mus., N.Y.; Hall of Fame; Capitol Bldg., Wash., D.C.; Mus. American Indian, N.Y.; Geographical Soc. Bldg.; Brookgreen Gardens, S.C.; Hartford (Conn.) Capitol Bldg.; Chamber of Commerce, Pittsburgh; Congressional medals, for U.S. Bureau of Mines, and others. *Exhibited*: Arch. Lg., and in Rome, Italy.

NEDWILL, ROSE—*Painter, Et., I., T.*
   100 Artists Rd., Santa Fe, N.M.

B. New York, N.Y. *Studied*: ASL, with George Bridgman, Harvey Dunn, George Pearse Ennis. *Member*: AAPL; Santa Fe Assn. for the Arts; Nat. Lg. Am. Pen Women. *Exhibited*: Mus. New Mexico; regularly in clubs, banks, hotels, etc., Santa Fe; one-man exhs. locally.

NEHER, FRED—*Cartoonist*
   P.O. Box 708, Boulder, Colo.

B. Nappanee, Ind., Sept. 29, 1903. *Studied*: Chicago Acad. FA. *Member*: SI; A. & Writers Soc.; Nat. Cartoonists Soc.; Denver Press Cl. Creator cartoon "Life's Like That," for Bell Syndicate, 1934- . Instr., Cartooning, Univ. Colorado.

NEIDIGH, PANSY MILLS (Mrs.)—*Painter, C., T., L.*
   127 North 10th St.; h. 323 North 9th St., Richmond, Ind.

B. New Ross, Ind., Apr. 1, 1907. *Studied*: Central Normal Col., A.B.; John Herron A. Sch., B.S.; Columbia Univ., M.A. *Member*: NAC. *Awards*: prizes, Indiana State Exh.; Butler AI. *Exhibited*: NAC; Columbia Univ. Lib.; Hoosier Salon; Butler AI; Richmond AA. Contributor to: Design, School Arts magazines. *Position*: A.Dir., Supv., Pub.Sch., Richmond, Ind., 1938-55; Instr. A., Iowa State T. Col., Cedar Falls, Iowa, 1945-46; Instr., Leesburg (Fla.) H.S., at present.

NEILSON, KATHARINE B(ISHOP)—*Educator, L., W.*
   225 Benefit St., Providence 3, R.I.

B. New York, N.Y., Apr. 8, 1902. *Studied*: Bryn Mawr Col., A.B.; Radcliffe Col., A.M., Ph.D. *Member*: Am. Assn. Univ. Prof.; Am. Assn. Univ. Women; AFA; CAA; Archaeological Assn. Am. Author: "Filippino Lippi: A Critical Study," 1938. Contributor of articles and book reviews to art periodicals. *Positions*: Instr., Asst. Prof. A., Assoc. Prof. A., Wheaton Col., 1933-43; Cur. Edu., Albright A. Gal., Buffalo, N.Y.; 1943-49; Acting Dir. Edu. & Public Relations, Mus. A., R.I. Sch. Des.; Providence, R.I., 1949-52; Dir. Edu. & Ed., Museum Publications, Mus. A., R.I. Sch. Des., 1952-55.*

NEILSON, RAYMOND P(ERRY) R(ODGERS)—*Painter*
   131 East 66th St., New York 21, N.Y.

B. New York, N.Y., Dec. 5, 1881. *Studied*: ASL, with George Bridgman, George Bellows, Luis Mora, Frank DuMond; Ecole des Beaux-Arts, Julian Acad., Colorossi Acad., Grande Chaumiere, Paris, with Lucien Simon, Jean Paul Laurens, Naudin, Caro Delvai; BMFA Sch.; and with Richard Miller, William M. Chase. *Member*: NA; Century Assn.; SC; All. A. Am.; Audubon A.; AAPL; Conn. Acad. FA. *Awards*: Medal, Paris Salon, 1914; Pan-

Pacific Expo., 1915; All. A. Am., 1949; prizes, Currier Gal. A., 1941; NAD, 1941; East Hampton Gld., 1942; All. A. Am., 1942; New Haven Paint & Clay Cl., 1943; SC, 1944-45; Conn. Acad. FA, 1944-1949; Ogunquit A. Center, 1947, 1948, 1952; Academic A., 1953. *Work*: Luxembourg Mus., Paris; N.Y. Chamber Commerce; N.Y. Clearing House; N.Y. County Lawyers Assn.; Practicing Law Inst.; Cornell-N.Y. Medical Center; St. Luke's Hospital; Roosevelt Hospital; F. D. Roosevelt Lib., Hyde Park, N.Y.; Am. Col. of Surgeons, Chicago; Nat. War Col., Wash., D.C.; U.S. Naval Acad.; U.S. Military Acad., West Point; Amherst Col.; Lafayette Col.; Univ. Louisville; Cornell Univ.; Yale Univ.; U.S.S. Forrestal; Oglebay Inst., Wheeling, W. Va.; Princeton Univ. *Exhibited*: NAD, 1916- ; Pan-Pacific Expo., 1915; Albright A. Gal., 1921, 1922; AIC; Carnegie Inst.; PAFA; CGA; WFNY 1939; Currier Gal. A.; New Haven Paint & Clay Cl.; Century Assn.; Ogunquit A. Center; All. A. Am.; Grand Central A. Gal.; Portraits, Inc.; Conn. Acad. FA; SC; Old Lyme A. Gal.; Academic A., Springfield, Mass. *Position*: Instr., ASL, 1926-27; NAD, 1928-38; Council, Rec. Sec., NAD, 1937-46; Council, All. A. Am.

NELKE, DORA K. (Mrs.)—*Painter*
   8108 Washington Lane, Wyncote, Pa.

B. New York, N.Y., July 22, 1889. *Member*: Phila. A. All.; Phila. Plastic Cl.; Woodmere A. Gal. *Awards*: gold medal, Phila. Plastic Cl., 1946. *Exhibited*: Phila. Plastic Cl.; Phila. A. All.; PMA; Woodmere A. Gal.*

NELMS, MRS. R. J. See Collison, Marjory

NELSON, CARL GUSTAF—*Painter, Gr., T.*
   41 Rutland St., Boston 18, Mass.

B. Horby, Sweden, Jan. 5, 1898. *Studied*: Chicago Acad. FA; ASL, with Kimon Nicolaides. *Member*: AEA (N.E. Chptr. Pres., 1954; V-Pres., 1955); Soc. Indp. A., Boston. *Awards*: prizes, Jordan Marsh Co., 1953; Natick A. Festival, 1957, 1958; Cambridge AA, 1952-1958. *Work*: Binghamton (N.Y.) Mus.; Dept. Labor Bldg., Wash., D.C.; WMA; AGAA; Walker A. Center; Boston YWCA; Fitchburg A. Mus. *Exhibited*: Carnegie Inst., 1935-1938; WMAA, 1934, 1936, 1938; AIC, 1936; PAFA, 1935; Toledo Mus. A., 1936; AFA traveling exh., 1937; Am. A. Cong.; WFNY 1939; Colorado Springs FA Center, 1935, 1938; Georgia Tech., 1950; Univ. Illinois, 1950; WMA, 1947, 1949; Inst. Contemp. A., Boston, 1949; New England P. & S. traveling exh., 1949; Soc. Indp. A., traveling exh., 1949; deCordova and Dana Mus., 1951-1952, 1953; Cambridge AA, 1950, 1951, 1953, 1954; Boston YWCA 1953; Denver A. Mus., 1953; Boston A. Festival, 1953, 1955; one-man: Macbeth Gal., 1931, 1933; Brockton Lib., 1954-1958; Boris Mirski Gal., 1946-1953; Iowa traveling exh., 1940; Fitchburg A. Mus., 1957; MIT Faculty Cl., 1958. *Positions*: Instr. A., YWCA Work Shop, Boston, Mass., 1946- ; Cambridge Sch. Des., 1948-52; Cummington Sch. A., 1949-52.

NELSON D. EARLE—*Industrial Designer, P., Gr.*
   41 Mt. Laurel Rd., Moorestown, N.J.

B. Poughkeepsie, N.Y., Sept. 21, 1902. *Studied*: PMSchIA, and with Thornton Oakley, J.R. Sinnock, Herbert Pullinger. Contributor to national magazines. At present specializing in industrial design for products, industry, housing and public buildings, also photography of architecture and industry.

NELSON, GEORGE LAURENCE—*Painter, Lith.*
   Kent, Conn.

B. New Rochelle, N.Y., Sept. 26, 1887. *Studied*: NAD; ASL; Julian Acad., Paris, with J. P. Laurens. *Member*: NA; Kent AA (Pres.); Grand Central Gal.; AWS; NAC; AllA.Am.; SC; Conn. Acad. FA. *Awards*: med., NAD, 1921; NAC, 1939; prizes, Conn. Acad. FA, 1926, 1935; Meriden (Conn.) A. & Crafts Soc., 1945. *Work*: portraits, NAD; NAC; Am. Acad. A. & Let.; N.Y. Hospital; Mt. Sinai Hospital, N.Y.; N.Y. Acad. Medicine; Univ. Buffalo; New Britain A. Mus.; Bennington (Vt.) Hist. Soc.; Peace Palace, Geneva, Switzerland; "Cochran House," Fairfield State Hospital, Newtown, Conn.; Canterbury Sch., New Milford, Conn.; Canajoharie A. Gal.; lithographs, MMA; N.Y. Pub. Lib.; Carnegie Inst.; mural, Pub. Sch., Bronx, N.Y. *Exhibited*: Los A. Mus. A.; Toledo Mus. A.; Albright A. Gal.; Rochester Mem. A. Gal.;

Montclair A. Mus.; AIC; John Herron AI; Texas State Fair; Detroit Inst. A.; Maryland Inst.; Retrospective Exh., "Fifty Years of Painting," New Britain A. Mus., 1958. Lectures: Portrait Painting; Still Life and Flowers. *Position*: Instr., Drawing & Painting, CUASch, 1915-23; Instr., Drawing, NAD, New York, N.Y., 1915-41.

NELSON, HANS PETER—
  Industrial Designer, E., I., C.
  Wayne University, Detroit 2, Mich.; h. 532 North York Blvd., Dearborn 7, Mich.

B. Chicago, Ill. *Studied*: Illinois Inst. Technology, B. Sc.; Northwestern Univ.; Wayne Univ., M.A. *Member*: Am. Soc. for Engineering Edu.; Dearborn AI; Eng. Soc. Detroit. *Exhibited*: BM, 1945; Benedict A. Gal., Chicago, 1950; Pickwick A. Gal., Park Ridge, 1951; Detroit Inst. A., 1953-1955; Kirk-in-the-Hills, Bloomfield Hills, Mich., 1953, 1954; Dearborn Hist. Mus., 1956, 1957; Dearborn AI, 1956, 1957; Ecclesiastical A. Gld. of Detroit, J. L. Hudson Co. A. Gal., 1957; Detroit Pub. Lib., 1957. Des. publ.: "Modern Plastics," "Plastics," "Armour Research Bulletin." Contributor to Industrial Finishing magazine, "Design of the Little Chef," 1947; Author: articles, "Tomorrow's Toy Designers Go To School" and "Designs of the Future," Toys and Novelties magazine, 1949, 1950. Author: "A Guide to Technical Illustration," Machine Design magazine, 1958. *Position*: Indst. Des., Bureau of Des., Montgomery Ward & Co., Chicago, and Westclox Co., Peru, Ill.; Instr., Illinois Inst. Tech., 1949-51; Asst. Prof., Wayne Univ., Detroit, Mich., 1952- .

NELSON, LEONARD L.—Painter, T., Gr., S.
  1720 Sansom St., Philadelphia 3, Pa.

B. Camden, N.J., Mar. 5, 1912. *Studied*: PAFA; Barnes Fnd.; PMSchIA. *Member*: Phila. Pr. Cl. *Awards*: Cresson traveling scholarship, PAFA, 1939, 1956; Bryn Mawr, 1956; prize, Nat. Woodblock Exh., 1948. *Work*: PMA; Walker A. Center. *Exhibited*: PAFA, 1943, 1946, 1949-1958; Phila. Pr. Cl., 1946 (one-man); Brandt Gal., 1944, 1945; Phila. A. All., 1944, 1958 (one-man); PMA, 1946; BM, 1946, 1950-1952; MModA, 1950-1952; Binet Gal., 1950; one-man: Moore Inst. A., 1948; Dubin Gal., Phila., 1949-1952; Peridot Gal., New York, 1949; Hugo Gal., 1954; Dubin Gal., Phila., 1955. *Position*: Prof. A., Moore Inst. A., Sc. & Indst., Philadelphia, Pa.

NELSON, LUCRETIA—Educator, P.
  Department of Decorative Art, University of California, Berkeley, Cal.; h. 1641 Grand View Dr., Berkeley 5, Cal.

B. Nashua, N.H., Feb. 19, 1912. *Studied*: Univ. California, A.B., M.A.). *Member*: San F. AA. *Awards*: Taliesin F., 1934-1935; European scholarship, Univ. California, 1936-1937; prize, San F. Soc. Women A., 1944. *Exhibited*: PAFA, 1938; SAM, 1947 (one-man); deYoung Mem. Mus.; San F. AA. I., "Textiles of the Guatemala Highlands," 1945. *Position*: Instr. Design, 1938-42, Asst. Prof. Design, 1942-46, Assoc. Prof. Des., 1946-52; Prof. Des., 1956- , Univ. California, Berkeley, Cal.*

NELSON, RALPH L.—Painter
  Guild's Hollow Rd., Bethlehem, Conn.

B. Coal City, Ill., Feb. 1, 1885. *Studied*: Des Moines Sch. A.; Cleveland Sch. A.; ASL; Corcoran Sch. A., and with Dean Cornwell, Harvey Dunn, Walter Biggs. *Member*: A. & Writers of Conn. *Work*: Conn. Pub. Schs. (murals). *Exhibited*: New York; Wash., D.C.; Wilton, Waterbury, Bridgeport, Hartford and Bethlehem, Conn.; Washington AA; Kent AA. I., "Paddles," 1942; "Destination Tokio," 1943. *Position*: I., Bethlehem Greeting Cards; Hallmark Greeting Cards.

NELSON, RICHARD L.—Educator, P., L.
  Department of Art, University of California; h. 752 Campus Way, Davis, Cal.

B. Georgetown, Tex., Feb. 27, 1901. *Studied*: AIC; Stevens Inst. Tech., Univ. California, Berkeley, B.A., M.A.; Ecole des Beaux-Arts, Paris. *Member*: Pacific AA; CAA; Am. Soc. for Aesthetics; Western A. Dirs. Assn. *Awards*: prizes, San F. AA, 1950; SFMA, 1953; Crocker Mus. A., Sacramento, 1953. *Exhibited*: nationally, including SFMA, 1950, 1951, 1953, 1954; Oakland A. Mus., 1954; deYoung Mem. Mus., 1956, 1958; California State Fair, 1953, 1955-

1957, and in Canada. Lectures: Contemporary Art & Aesthetics. *Positions*: Prof. A., Washington State College, 1948-52; Prof. A., Chm., A. Dept., Univ. of California, Davis, Cal., at present.

NELSON, WILLIS WILMOT—Painter
  2204 10th Ave., North, Grand Forks, N.D.

B. Minot, N.D., Jan. 22, 1930. *Studied*: Minot State T. Col., B.S.; Univ. North Dakota, M.A. *Awards*: prizes, first North Dakota annual, 1957 (purchase); Bowman AA, 1956. *Work*: Bismarck Jr. Col.; Minot State T. Col.; Univ. North Dakota. *Exhibited*: WAC, 1958; Bismarck AA, 1956, 1957; one-man: North Dakota Agricultural Col.; Univ. North Dakota, 1956; 2-man: Minot Quota Cl., 1957; 3-man: Univ. North Dakota, 1958.

NEPOTE, ALEXANDER—Painter, E., L.
  410 Taylor Blvd., Millbrae, Cal.

B. Valley Home, Cal., Nov. 6, 1913. *Studied*: Cal. Col. A. & Crafts, B.A. in A. Edu.; Mills Col.; Univ. California, M.A. *Member*: Cal. WC Soc.; San F. AA; Peninsula AA. *Awards*: Phelan Award, San F., 1941-42; Cal. WC Soc., 1955 (purchase); Oakland A. Mus., 1955 (purchase); prizes, Oakland A. Mus., 1947, 1948; San Mateo County Fair, 1954-1957; San F. A. Festival, 1951-1953; SFMA, 1953; Pasadena A. Mus., 1957 (purchase); Cal. State Fair, 1957, 1958; Peninsula A. Festival, 1958; Cal. PLH, 1958; silver medal, Oakland A. Mus., 1957. *Work*: SFMA; Oakland A. Mus.; Los A. Mus. A.; Pasadena A. Mus.; Cal. PLH; Mills Col.; Univ. Michigan; San F. Mun. Coll. *Exhibited*: United Nations Conf. Exh., 1945; Grand Central A. Gal., N.Y., 1948; Cal. PLH, 1947, 1948, 1952; Univ. Illinois, 1951, 1952; WMA, 1951; AFA traveling exhs., 1958-1959; MMA, 1952; Sao Paulo, Brazil, 1955; SFMA, 1955; Provincetown, Mass., 1958; Art:USA, 1958; West Coast Museums, 1957 and AFA traveling exh. *Position*: Prof. A., Dean of Faculty, Cal. Col. A. & Crafts, Oakland, 1945-1950; Assoc. Prof. A., Coordinator of Grad. A., San F. State Col., San Francisco, Cal., 1950- .

NESBITT, ALEXANDER JOHN—
  Designer, E., W., L.
  Rhode Island School of Design; h. 142 Prospect St., Providence 6, R.I.

B. Paterson, N.J., Nov. 14, 1901. *Studied*: ASL; CUA Sch, with Harry Wickey, and abroad. *Member*: Type Dir. Cl. of New York; Friends of Cooper Union. *Work*: St. John's Church, Stamford, Conn.; Houghton Lib., Harvard Univ.; Cooper Union Mus.; mem. tablets, book and catalog des., lettering, etc. *Exhibited*: NAD; Houghton Lib., Harvard Univ.; Bookbuilders, Boston; Cooper Union Mus.; A. I. Friedman Gal., N.Y., 1955. Author, I., "The History and Technique of Lettering," 1950, 2nd ed., 1957. Contributor to Direct Advertising; Graphis; Intl. Assn. Printing House Craftsmen's "Printing Progress"; The Concise Encyclopedia of American Antiques. Lectures on Lettering and Direct Advertising Design. *Position*: Tech. A. Dir., Jordanoff Aviation Corp., 1942; Prod. Mngr., A. Dir., Technographic Publ., 1943-44; Instr., Lettering and Typography, Cooper Union; Instr., Dir., Adv. Des., N.Y. Univ.; Instr. and L., New York-Phoenix Sch., New York, N.Y., 1950-57; Assoc. Prof., Lettering & Typography, Rhode Island Sch. Des., Providence, R.I., 1957.

NESBITT, JACKSON LEE—Painter, Et., I.
  2859 Ridgemore Road, Northwest, Atlanta 18, Ga.

B. McAlester, Okla., June 16, 1913. *Studied*: Univ. Oklahoma; Kansas City AI. *Awards*: SAGA, 1946; Kansas City AI, 1937, 1941; Lib. Cong., 1943, 1946; Philbrook A. Center, 1940. *Work*: Univ. Alabama; Univ. Missouri; Corpus Christi A. Mus.; Denver A. Mus.; Lib. Cong.; Philbrook A. Center. *Exhibited*: AIC, 1937; PAFA, 1941; Lib. Cong., 1943, 1946; Kansas City AI, 1937-1941; CAM, 1941; Philbrook A. Center, 1940.

NESS, (ALBERT) KENNETH—Painter, E., Des.
  Ackland Art Center, University North Carolina; h. Farrington Mill Rd., Chapel Hill, N.C.

B. St. Ignace, Mich., June 21, 1903. *Studied*: Univ. Detroit; Detroit Sch. App. A.; Wicker Sch. FA; AIC. *Member*: North Carolina Chptr. AIA (hon.). *Awards*: prizes, traveling scholarship, 1932, prize, 1934, AIC; prize, North Carolina AA, 1953. *Exhibited*: Johnson Gal., Chicago (one-man); WMAA, 1933; AIC, 1934-1940; GGE,

1939; Evanston A. Center, 1940; San Diego FA Soc., 1938; Cal. PLH, 1938; SAM, 1938; Dayton AI; Flint Inst. A., 1938; Grand Rapids A. Gal., 1938; Person Hall, Univ. N.C., 1941 (one-man); Butler AI; Va. Intermont; High Mus. A., 1951; North Carolina AA, 1952, 1953; Atlanta, Ga., 1952; PAFA; Univ. Florida; Birmingham Mus. A.; Lowe Gal. A., Miami; Soc. Four Arts, Palm Beach; Georgia Mus. A., Athens; Norton Gal. A.; Witherspoon A. Gal., Greensboro; Beloit, Wis., 1954; Duke Univ. (one-man); AGAA; AFA traveling exh., 1955; CMA; Florence (S.C.) Mus. *Position*: Resident A., Prof. A., Univ. North Carolina, Chapel Hill, N.C., 1941- ; Actg. Chm., Dept. A., 1957, 1958; Dir., Person Hall A. Gal., 1957, 1958.

NETTER, FRANK H.—*Medical Illustrator*
East Norwich, L.I., N.Y.

B. New York, N.Y., Apr. 28, 1906. *Studied*: Col. City of N.Y., B.S.; N.Y. Univ. Medical Col., M.D.; NAD; ASL. *Member*: SI; SC; AMA; A. Gld.; N.Y. Med. Medicine (F.). *Work*: Anatomical illus., medical paintings: Field Mus., Chicago; Ciba Series; Armour & Co.; Army Medical Mus., Wash., D.C.; Banting Inst., Toronto, Canada. *Exhibited*: A. Gld., 1936. I., medical books and illus. for Colliers, Sat. Eve. Post, Esquire and other magazines.

NEUFELD, PAULA—*Painter, T.*
418 East 9th St., Studio Bldg. 303, Kansas City 6, Mo.

B. Berlin, Germany. *Studied*: Art Inst., Berlin; Berlin Acad. A., and with von Koenig, Eugene Spiro, Willy Jaekel; Colo. Springs FA Center. *Award*: F., Huntington Hartford Fnd., 1957. *Work*: Bernheimer Mem., Kansas City, Mo.; Temple B'nai Jehudah, Kansas City; Mannheim Mus., Germany; Jewish Mus., Berlin; ports., Jackson County Circuit Court; and in Germany; murals, ports. in many private colls. U.S. and abroad. *Exhibited*: AIC; Kansas City AI; William Rockhill Nelson Gal.; CAM; Breslau; London, England; one-man: Broadmoor Hotel, Colorado Springs; Denver A. Mus.; Kansas City Pub. Lib.; Woman's City Cl., Kansas City; Berlin, Stuttgart, Mannheim, Germany; AIC; Jewish Center, Kansas City.

NEUFELD, WOLDEMAR—*Painter, Eng., T.*
New Preston, Conn.; w. 1700 York Ave., New York 28, N.Y.

B. Waldheim, Russia, Nov. 10, 1909. *Studied*: Cleveland Sch. A.; Western Reserve Univ., B.S. in A. Edu. *Member*: AEA; Silvermine Gld. A. *Awards*: prizes, Am. Color Pr. Soc., 1946; CMA, 1937-1944; 50 Prints of America. *Work*: CMA; N.Y. Pub. Lib.; MMA; New Britain Mus. A.; LC. *Exhibited*: AWS; Audubon A.; SAGA; All. A. Am.; Kent AA; Silvermine Gld. A.; Conn. Acad. FA; Eastern States Exh., Springfield, Mass.; Art:USA, 1958. One-man: New Britain AI, 1958; Silvermine Gld. A., 1957. *Position*: Instr., Millbrook Sch., Millbrook, N.Y.; private instr., s. New Preston, Conn., w., New York, N.Y.

NEUHAUS, EUGEN—*Painter, W., L., E.*
20 Camino Sobrante, Orinda, Cal.

B. Wuppertal, Germany, Aug. 18, 1879. *Studied*: Royal A. Sch., Kassel, Germany; Kgl. Kunstgewerbemuseum, Berlin. *Member*: San F. AA; Am. Soc. for Aesthetics. *Awards*: hon. degree, Ph.D., Univ. Marburg, 1932. *Exhibited*: AIC, 1920-1925; PAFA, 1921, 1922; San F. AA, annually; Cal. PLH, 1928, 1930 (one-man). *Author*: "History and Ideals of American Art"; 1931; "World of Art," 1934; translator, Max Doerner's "Materials of the Artist"; "William Keith"; "The Art of Treasure Island," etc. *Position*: Prof. A., Univ. California, Berkeley, Cal., 1907-49, Emeritus since 1949.

NEUMAN, DOROTHY B. (Mrs. E. A.)—*Librarian*
13th & Olive Sts.; h. 5932 A Etzel Ave., St. Louis 12, Mo.

B. Springfield, Mo. *Studied*: Washington Univ. St. Louis; St. Louis Univ.; St. Louis Lib. Sch. *Member*: Am. Lib. Assn.; Missouri Lib. Assn. *Position*: Chief, A. Dept., St. Louis (Mo.) Pub. Lib., 1929- .

NEUMAN, VINCENT HOWARD—*Comm. A., Des., P.*
1228 Garland Ave., Green Bay, Wis.

B. West Allis, Wis., Mar. 19, 1916. *Studied*: Layton Sch. A., and with Gerhard H. Baker, Gerrit Sinclair, Emily

Groom. *Member*: Wisconsin P. & S. *Awards*: prizes, Wis. P. & S., 1943; Madison AA, 1943. *Exhibited*: AIC, 1944; Wis. P. & S., 1940-1946; Madison AA, 1941-1945; Findlay Gal., Chicago, 1944, 1945, 1951, 1952. *Positions*: Indst. Des., Milwaukee Handicraft Project, 1940; Adv. A., Badger Carton Co., 1942-46; Clarvan-Meyer Display Co., Milwaukee, 1946-48; Meyer Display Co., 1948-51; Creative Art Service, Milwaukee, Wis., 1951-52; Advertising Creations, Madison, Wis., 1952-1958; Williams Adv. Des., Green Bay, Wis., 1958- .

NEUMARK, ANNE—*Painter*
255 West 19th St., New York 11, N.Y.

B. Boston, Mass., May 3, 1906. *Studied*: Mass. Sch. A.; Designer's A. Sch., Boston, Mass. *Work*: Edgar Allan Poe Shrine, Richmond, Va. *Exhibited*: Boston AC; Gloucester SA.

NEUMEYER, ALFRED—*Educator, Mus. Dir., W.*
Mills College, Oakland 13, Cal.

B. Munich, Germany, Jan. 7, 1901. *Studied*: Univ. Munich; Univ. Berlin, Ph.D. *Member*: Western Mus. Dir. Assn.; Am. Soc. for Aesthetics; Ford F., 1952, 1953-54. *Award*: Guggenheim F., 1958. *Author*: "Durer," 1929; "Josef Scharl," 1945; "Cezanne Drawings," 1958. Contributor to: Art Bulletin, College Art Journal, Journal of Aesthetics; Books Abroad; Art Quarterly, & other publications, with articles on contemporary & historical art. *Position*: Prof. A. Hist., 1935- , Dir. A. Gal., 1937, Mills Col., Oakland, Cal.; Guest L., Harvard Univ., 1938, 1948; Free Univ. of Berlin, 1952, 1953-54; Univ. Heidelberg, 1958. Chm., Section on Art, 2nd Conference on Humanities, Stanford Univ., Palo Alto, Cal., 1943; Vice-Pres., Renaissance Conference Northern California, 1957-58.

NEUWIRTH, MORRIS—*Designer, Comm. A., P.*
30 Church St., New York, N.Y.; h. 830 Bronx River Rd., Bronxville 8, N.Y.

B. New York, N.Y., May 18, 1912. *Studied*: NAD, with Leon Kroll. *Work*: MMA. *Exhibited*: MMA; NAD; ACA Gal. *Position*: Des., book jackets; illus. for New Yorker, N.Y. Times; A. Dir., Ed. Layout, "The Woman," Everybody's Digest, American Builder, 1948- .

NEVELL, THOMAS G.—*Industrial Designer, W.*
101 Park Ave., New York 17, N.Y.; h. Leeward Lane, Riverside, Conn.

B. London, England, Sept. 16, 1910. *Studied*: N.Y.Univ., Col. of FA; Columbia Univ. *Member*: Am. Soc. Indst. Des.; Assoc., Am. Soc. Mechanical Engineers; IDI. *Awards*: Modern Plastic award, 1939; Electrical Manufacturing award, 1940; IDI award, 1951 (all in collaboration with George Cushing). Contributor of articles on Industrial Design to leading trade magazines. *Position*: Partner, Cushing & Nevell, New York, N.Y., 1933- .

NEVELSON, LOUISE—*Sculptor*
29 Spring St., New York, N.Y.

B. Kiev, Russia. *Studied*: U.S., Europe and Central America. *Member*: Fed. Mod. P. & S. (1st V-Pres.); AEA (Exec. Bd.); ASL; NAWA; Sculpture Center; S. Gld. (Exec. Bd.); All. A. Am. *Work*: Mus. FA of Houston; Farnsworth Mus., Rockland, Me.; Brandeis Univ.; Birmingham Mus. A.; WMAA; MMoDA; N.Y. Univ.; Queens Col.; Carnegie Inst.; Riverside Mus.; Univ. Nebraska; BM, and others. *Exhibited*: U.S.; England; Japan; France.

NEW, GEORGE (EDWARD)—*Painter, Et., E., L., W.*
726 North Milwaukee St., Milwaukee 2, Wis.

B. Fountain Hill, Bethlehem, Pa., Nov. 27, 1894. *Studied*: Univ. Paris, Ph.D.; Ecole des Beaux-Arts, Paris; Am. Acad. in Rome; & with John Singer Sargent, George de Forest Brush, Joseph Pennell. *Member*: Societe des Beaux-Arts. *Awards*: hon. degrees, LL.D., St. Andrews Univ., 1935; L.H.D., Mount Mary Col., 1937; med., Paris Salon, 1937; prizes, Wis. Salon A., 1943; Milwaukee AI, 1942, 1944; Marquette Univ., 1957. *Work*: Marquette Univ.; Stout Inst.; Mount Mary Col.; MMA; Lib. Cong.; Milwaukee AI; Kenosha Mus. A.; Bibliotheque Nationale, Paris; Victoria & Albert Mus., London, England; many portraits of prominent persons. *Exhibited*: SAGA, 1943-

1955; Lib. Cong., 1943, 1945; Wis. Salon A.; Milwaukee AI, annually; Albright A. Gal., 1951; New Britain Mus. A., 1951. Lectures: Etchers & Etchings. *Position*: Prof., L., Art, Mount Mary Col., 1937-42; Instr., Graphic A., Univ. Wisconsin, 1941-42; L., Art, Marquette Univ., Milwaukee, Wis., 1942- . Dir., Veterans Bd. of Directors, Milwaukee County War Memorial Center, Inc.

NEWBERRY, CLARE TURLAY—*Writer, I.*
1330 Cerro Gordo Rd., Santa Fe, N.M.

B. Enterprise, Ore., Apr. 10, 1903. *Studied*: Univ. Oregon; Portland (Ore.) Mus. A. Sch.; San F. Sch. FA; Grande Chaumiere, Paris. Author, I., "Herbert the Lion," 1931; "Mittens," 1936; "Babette," 1937; "April's Kittens," 1940; "Marshmallow," 1942; "Pandora," 1944; "The Kittens' A B C," 1946; "Smudge," 1948; "T-Bone the Baby Sitter," 1950; "Percy, Polly, and Pete," 1952; "Ice Cream for Two," 1953; "Widget," 1958, & other animal stories for children.

NEWBERRY, JOHN S.—*Museum Curator*
Detroit Institute of Arts, Detroit 2, Mich.; h. Lonehill Farm, Route 2, Romeo, Mich.

B. Detroit, Mich., Jan. 16, 1910. *Studied*: Harvard Univ., A.B.; Univ. London. *Member*: Grolier Cl., N.Y.; Scarab Cl., Detroit. Contributor to: Art News; Print Collector's Quarterly; Bulletin of the Detroit Institute of Arts. *Position*: Hon. Cur., Detroit Inst. A., 1935-40; Cur., Alger House Mus., Grosse Pointe Farms, Mich., 1940-45; Asst. to Dir., 1945-46, Cur. Graphic A., 1946- , Detroit Inst. A., Detroit, Mich.

NEWCOMB, REXFORD—*Writer, E., L.*
415 East 20th St., Santa Ana, Cal.

B. Independence, Kan., Apr. 24, 1886. *Studied*: Univ. Kansas; Univ. Illinois, B.S. Arch., M. Arch.; Univ. Southern California, M.A. *Member*: F., AIA; Am. Soc. Arch. Hist. Author: many articles on Architecture, Art, Ceramics, in technical magazines, & numerous books on architecture & historic houses. *Position*: Prof., Hist. Arch., 1918- , Dean, Col. F. & App. A., 1931- , Univ. Illinois, Urbana, Ill.; Dir., Bureau Community Planning, Univ. Illinois, 1934-54; Emeritus, 1954.

NEWCOMBE, WARREN—*Painter, Lith.*
M.G.M. Studio, Culver City, Cal.; h. 2177 Mandeville Canyon Rd., Los Angeles 24, Cal.

B. Waltham, Mass., Apr. 28, 1894. *Studied*: Mass. Normal A. Sch., Boston; & with Joseph De Camp. *Member*: Charter member, Motion Picture A. & Sc. *Awards*: Acad. Motion Picture A. & Sc., for special effects on picture, "Thirty Seconds Over Tokyo," 1944. *Work*: Wood A. Gal., Montpelier, Vt.; Los Angeles Museum Art; MMA; BMFA; PMA. *Exhibited*: one-man exh.: A. Center, N.Y., 1922; Wilshire Gal., Los A. 1929; Stendahl Gal., Los A., 1931; Pasadena AI, 1932; SFMA, 1933; Univ. California at Los A., 1936, etc. Also at Los A. Pub. Lib., 1938; Fnd. Western A., 1935-1945; Mus. FA of Houston; San Antonio, Dallas, Ft. Worth, Tex.; CGA, 1931, 1935, 1937; SFMA, 1931, 1938, 1940; CM, 1931; San Diego FA Soc., 1931, 1934; Soc. Indp. A., 1933, 1934; Los A. AA, 1934, 1941, 1944; Colorado Springs FA Center, 1935-1939; Denver A. Mus., 1935; PAFA, 1936, 1937; John Herron AI, 1936; Crocker A. Gal., 1938; Currier Gal. A., 1939; Faulkner Mem. A. Gal., Santa Barbara, Cal., 1938, 1939, 1940; GGE, 1939; Los A. Mus. A., 1933, 1934, 1938, 1942, 1943, 1945; Oakland A. Gal., 1943; Weyhe Gal., 1933-1935; etc. Contributor to: art & national magazines & newspapers.*

NEWHALL, ADELAIDE—*Painter*
43 Alexander Ave., Upper Montclair, N.J.

B. Worcester, Mass., Jan. 22, 1884. *Studied*: Smith Col., A.B.; Syracuse Univ.; Montclair A. Mus., with Estelle Armstrong, Douglas Prizer, Avery Johnson; and with Dwight Tryon, Charles Hawthorne, Jerry Farnsworth. *Member*: Cape Cod AA; AAPL; Montclair AA; A. Center of the Oranges; Provincetown AA. *Awards*: prize, Kresge Exh., Montclair, 1939; A. Center of the Oranges, 1953; Bloomfield (N.J.) A. Lg. *Work*: in private colls. *Exhibited*: Montclair A. Mus., 1926-1953; Newark A. Cl.; Ridgewood AA; 1953-55; Trenton State Mus.; NAC; Provincetown AA; Cape Cod AA; Nieta Cole Gal., Orleans, Mass.; Terry AI; Spring Lake, N.J.; Paper Mill Playhouse, Milburn, N.J.; Art Center of the Oranges, 1958; Crespi Gal., 1958; Newark Mus. A., and others; one-man: Verona (N.J.) Pub. Lib.; Montclair Women's Cl., 1957 and in East Orange, Glen Ridge, Caldwell, N.J., and Brewster, Mass.

NEWHALL, BEAUMONT—*Museum Director*
George Eastman House, 900 East Ave.; h. 7 Rundel Park, Rochester 7, N.Y.

B. Lynn, Mass., June 22, 1908. *Studied*: Harvard Univ., A.B., A.M.; Institut d'Art et d'Archeologie, Univ. Paris; Courtauld Inst. A., Univ. London, England. *Member*: F., Royal Photographic Soc. of Great Britain; F., Photographic Soc. Am.; Professional Photographers Assn. (Hon. Master of Photography); Corr. Memb., Deutsche Gesellschaft fuer Photographie. *Award*: Guggenheim F., 1947. Author: "The History of Photography," MModA, 1949; "On Photography: A Source-Book of Photo-History in Facsimile," 1956; (with Nancy Newhall) "Masters of Photography," 1958. Contributor to national magazines and encyclopedias. Lectures frequently on the history of photography at museums and universities. *Positions*: Asst., PMA, 1931-32; Asst., MMA, 1932-33; Libn., 1935-42, Cur. Photography, 1940-42, 1945, 46, MModA; Cur., George Eastman House, Rochester, N.Y., 1948-58, Dir., 1958- . Instr., Hist. of Photography, Univ. Rochester, 1954-56; Rochester Inst. Tech., 1957- ; History of Motion Pictures: Salzburg Seminar in American Studies, Salzburg, Austria, 1958, 1959.

NEWMAN, BARNETT—*Painter*
100 Front St.; 685 West End Ave., New York 25, N.Y.

B. New York, N.Y., Jan. 29, 1905. *Studied*: Col. City of N.Y., B.A.; Cornell Univ.; ASL, with John Sloan, William von Schlegell. *Work*: The Miller Co., Meriden, Conn., and in private collections. *Exhibited*: AIC, 1947; Walker A. Center, 1950; Carnegie Inst., 1958; one-man: Betty Parsons Gal., 1950, 1951; Minneapolis Inst. A., 1957; European Tour, Intl. Council, MModA, 1958-59; Retrospective Exh., Bennington Col., Vermont, 1958. Contributor to the Tiger's Eye.

NEWMAN, ELIAS—*Painter, L., T., W.*
201 West 16th St., New York 11, N.Y.; s. 2 Rowe Ave., Rockport, Mass.

B. Stashow, Poland, Feb. 12, 1903. *Studied*: NAD; Edu. All. A. Sch.; Grande Chaumiere, Paris. *Member*: AEA (Nat. Sec. 1953, Dir. 1955); Cape Ann Soc. Mod. A. (Pres. 1955, 1958); Audubon A.; Nat. Soc. Painters in Casein; Rockport AA. *Work*: BMA; BM; Butler AI; Haifa Mus., Israel; Brandeis Univ.; BMFA; Jewish Mus., N.Y.; SFMA; Denver A. Mus.; John Herron AI; Tel-Aviv Mus., Israel; Norfolk Mus. A.; Univ. Nebraska; Jewish Theological Seminary, N.Y. *Exhibited*: Los A. Mus. A., 1944; Rockport AA, 1953-1955; NAD, 1950, 1953; Audubon A., 1945, 1954; Am-British A. Center, 1944, 1945; Assoc. Am. A., 1944; Norfolk Mus. A. & Sc.; Dayton AI; Birmingham Mus. A.; Rochester Mem. A. Gal.; AWS; Butler Inst. Am. A.; Art:USA, 1958; Cape Ann A. Festival; Nat. Soc. Painters in Casein; one-man: Montross Gal., 1932; A. Center, N.Y., 1935; BMA, 1934, 1940; Maryland Inst. A., 1932, 1935, 1938; Tel-Aviv Mus., 1939, 1949; Maxwell Gal., San F., 1945; Modernage Gal., 1945; Phila. A. All., 1946; Babcock Gal., 1947, 1949, 1951, 1953; Doll & Richards, Boston, 1948, 1950; Jewish Mus., 1949; Werbe Gal., Detroit, 1956. *Position*: Dir., AEA, N.Y. Chapter, 1951-52, Cor. Sec., 1952-53, Nat. Sec., 1953, Dir., 1954, 1955, Exec. Dir., 1957-58; Ed., AEA, "Improvisations," 1950-52, Bulletin, "News," 1957-58; "Directory of Open Exhibitions," 1957-58, etc. Chm., Cape Ann Soc. Mod. A., 1955.

NEWMAN, GEORGE W.—*Painter, Med. I., Gr.*
907 Strand St.; h. 3915 Broadway, Galveston, Tex.

B. Galveston, Tex., May 22, 1909. *Studied*: AIC; Texas A. & M. Col. *Member*: Galveston A. Lg.; Assoc. Medical Illustrators. *Awards*: prizes, Galveston A. Lg.; SSAL. *Exhibited*: Texas FA Assn.; Mus. FA of Houston; Galveston A. Lg. Contributor to medical journals and bulletins. Illus., "Introduction to Parasitology"; "Morris Anatomy," (Section on Digestive System); "Heart and Arteries"; "Angiocardiography." *Position*: Dir., Dept. Medical Illus., Univ. Texas Medical Branch, Galveston, Tex.

NEWMAN, IRENE HODES—*Painter*
124 West 85th St., New York 24, N.Y.

B. Cameron, Mo. *Member*: Audubon A.; Baltimore WC Cl.; AAPL; NAC. *Exhibited*: CGA, 1939; AWS, 1939, 1941, 1942; Morton Gal., 1939, 1940; All. A. Am., 1939-1942; BMA, 1939, 1940, 1948-1952; AIC, 1940, 1941, 1949; Kansas City AI, 1940; BM, 1941; San Diego FA Soc., 1941; MMA, 1942; Audubon A., 1944, 1948, 1950-1955; Springfield Mus. A., 1945; AAPL, 1945; Milch Gal., 1948-1955; Toledo Mus. A., 1950; PAFA, 1950; NGA, 1955; Grand Central A. Gal., 1955.

NEWMAN, JOSEPH—*Painter*
1 West 67th St., New York 23, N.Y.

B. New York, N.Y., Sept. 4, 1890. *Studied*: PIASch; Adelphi Col.; & in Paris, France. *Member*: SC; AWCS; Rockport AA. *Awards*: med., Adelphi Col.; F., Tiffany Fnd.; prizes, P. & S. Soc.; Rockport AA, 1949; SC, 1945. *Work*: BM; Newark Mus.; Tiffany Fnd. *Exhibited*: nationally.

NEWMAN, RALPH ALBERT—*Cartoonist, W.*
189 Old Kings Highway South, Darien, Conn.

B. Newberry, Mich., June 27, 1914. *Studied*: Albion Col., A.B. *Awards*: Fairfield County (Conn.) art exhibitions, 1956-58. Contributor cartoons to New Yorker, Colliers, This Week, True and many others. Gagman to many cartoonists; contributor greeting card ideas, verse, design to Norcross, Barker, Citation and other card companies. *Position*: Cart., Stars and Stripes, 1944-46; Research, Terrytoons, 1948-54; Animated cartoon gagman and plotter, Terrytoons, 1955-56. Author of over 1000 short scripts for comic books, animated cartoons.

NEWTON, EARLE WILLIAMS—
Museum Director, Hist., E.
Pennsylvania State Museum, Harrisburg, Pa.; h. Willowbrook, R.D. #3, Mechanicsburg, Pa.

B. Cortland, N.Y., Apr. 10, 1917. *Studied*: Amherst Col., A.B.; Columbia Univ., A.M. *Member*: AAMus.; Northeast Mus. Assn. (Vice-Pres.); New England Mus. Conf.; Soc. Am. Historians; Am. Assn. for State & Local History (Sec. 1946-53). *Awards*: 3 awards of merit, AIGA, 1950-1952; Nat. award, Am. Assn. for State & Local History, 1949. Author: "Vermont: History of the Green Mountain State," 1949; Ed., "American Wall Painting" (Nina F. Little), 1953. Contributor to American Heritage; Vermont Life; Vermont Quarterly. Lectures: Historic Restorations and Museums. Arranged exhs.: English and American 18th Century Porcelains, Pa. State Mus., 1958; Jacob Eicholtz, Pennsylvania Painter, 1959. *Positions*: Ed. Bd., Art in America, 1953-56; Ed., American Heritage, 1949-54; Ed., Vermont Life, 1946-50; Senior Research F., Univ. London, 1955-56; Dir., Old Sturbridge Village, 1950-54; Dir., Bureau of Museums, Commonwealth of Pennsylvania, 1956- .

NEWTON, EDITH—*Lithographer, P., W.*
Mallett's Lane, New Milford, Conn.

B. Saginaw, Mich., June 7, 1878. *Awards*: prizes, Northwest Pr.M.; Lib. Cong., 1946. *Member*: SAGA. *Work*: WMAA; MMA; Newark Lib.; SAM; Lib.Cong.; Boston Pub. Lib.; PMA.

NEWTON, FRANCIS JOHN—*Museum Curator*
Portland Art Museum, Southwest Park at Madison St.; h. 1831 Southwest Park St., Portland 1, Ore.

B. Butte, Montana, Dec. 27, 1912. *Studied*: Univ. Idaho, B.A., M.A.; Univ. Iowa, Ph.D. *Member*: CAA; AAMus. *Positions*: Cur. Asst., WMA, Worcester, Mass., 1951-53; Cur. of the Museum, Portland Art Museum, Portland, Ore., 1953- .

NEWTON, HELEN F.—*Painter, W., T.*
Seymour Rd., Woodbridge, New Haven 15, Conn.

B. Woodbridge, Conn., Mar. 17, 1878. *Studied*: Santa Barbara State Col.; Mount Holyoke Col., B.A.; & with Harry Leith-Ross, Charles Hawthorne. *Member*: Conn. Acad. FA; Bridgeport A. Lg.; New Haven Paint & Clay Cl.; Brush & Palette Cl.; Meriden A. & Crafts Assn.; Copley Soc., Boston. *Awards*: prizes, Bridgeport A. Lg., 1941, 1944; State Fed. Women's Cl., 1942. *Work*: New Haven

Paint & Clay Cl.; City Hall, Norwich, Conn. *Exhibited*: New Haven Paint & Clay Cl., 1923-1939, 1942-1952, 1953, 1955; Conn. Acad. FA, 1924-1928, 1931, 1932, 1937, 1938, 1941, 1942, 1944-1948, 1951; SAM, 1929; Laguna Beach AA, 1929, 1930, 1934, 1935; Santa Cruz A. Lg., 1930, 1935, 1936; Los A. Mus. A.; Pasadena AI; Stockbridge, Mass., 1931; Santa Barbara Mus. A., 1934-1936; Williams Col., 1932; Mount Holyoke Col., 1937, 1952; Springfield Mus. A., 1945; Bridgeport, Conn., 1942, 1944-1946, 1952; Meriden, Conn., 1941-1949, 1952, 1954, 1955; Hartford, 1955; New Britain, 1954; Milford, 1953; one-man: Converse A. Gal., 1931; New Haven Pub. Lib.; 1931; Mt. Holyoke Col., 1937; Hartford, West Haven, Bridgeport, Conn.; Palo Alto, Cal.

NEWTON, MARION CLEEVER WHITESIDE—
Painter, I., Des.
1212 Fifth Ave., New York 29, N.Y.

B. Boston, Mass., Mar. 23, 1902. *Studied*: Radcliffe Col.; Parsons Sch.Des.; in Paris; & with Ivan Olinsky, Lydia Field Emmet, George Bridgman. *Work*: MMA; Mus. City of N.Y. Creator of "Story Book Quilts" exhibited at Lilienfeld Gal., N.Y.; Detroit Inst. A.; and other exhs. in New Jersey, Conn., Maryland, Pa., Mass. They are in the collections of MMA; Mus. of City of New York; Baseball Hall of Fame, Cooperstown, N.Y.; U.S. Lines; Ladies Home Journal; Good Housekeeping, McCalls, etc. *Exhibited*: Salon des Artistes Francais, Paris; N.Y. WC Cl.; New Haven Paint & Clay Cl.; Phila. WC Cl.; Balt. WC Cl.; NAC.

NICHOLS, ALICE WELTY—
Educator, P., Gal. Dir., Des.
Art Department, Ball State Teachers College; h. 402 North Calvert St., Muncie, Ind.

B. St. Joseph, Mo., June 15, 1906. *Studied*: Texas State Col. for Women; Univ. Texas, B.A., M.A.; Columbia Univ., Ed. D. *Member*: NAEA; Western AA; Indiana A. Edu. Assn.; CAA. *Exhibited*: Texas, Colorado, Indiana. Author: "Let's Make Something." Contributor to School Arts; State Art Publications; The Palette; Western Arts Journal. Ed., The Palette. *Positions*: Prof., A. Edu., West Texas State T. Col.; Univ. Texas; Des. & Crafts, Univ. Denver; Prof. A., Hd. Art Dept., Dir., Ball State Gallery, Ball State T. Col., Muncie, Ind., at present.

NICHOLS, DALE (WILLIAM)—
Painter, Des., Lith., I., W., L., E.
3143 East Speedway, Tucson, Ariz.

B. David City, Neb., July 13, 1904. *Studied*: Chicago Acad. FA; AIC; & with Joseph Binder. *Member*: Soc. Typographic A.; Tucson Archaeological Soc. *Awards*: prizes, AIC, 1935, 1939. *Work*: MMA; AIC; Joslyn Mem.; Nebraska AA; Univ. Arizona; Boys Town, Neb.; Mural, USPO, Morris, Ill. *Exhibited*: AIC, 1936, 1938, 1939; Carnegie Inst., 1937, 1946; Denver A. Mus., 1943; Century of Progress, Chicago, 1934; WFNY 1939; GGE, 1939; Dallas Mus. FA, 1936. Author: "A Philosophy of Esthetics," 1938; I., "Two Years Before the Mast," 1941; "A World History," 1940. Contributor to: national magazines. *Position*: Carnegie Visiting Prof., A., in Residence, Univ. Illinois, 1939-40; A. Ed., Encyclopaedia Britannica Publications, 1945- ; A. Chm., Tucson Regional Plan, 1943-45.*

NICHOLS, EDITH L.—*Painter, W., C., T.*
160 Columbia Heights, Brooklyn 2, N.Y.

B. Brooklyn, N.Y. *Studied*: PIASch; T. Col., Columbia Univ., M.A., & with Henry B. Snell, Anna Fisher, Charles Martin. *Member*: NAWA; Brooklyn SA; AAPL; Eastern AA; Nat. A. Edu. Assn.; Nat. Assn. Women in Administration. *Exhibited*: Brooklyn SA, 1929-1940; NAWA, 1938-1940; Catherine Lorillard Wolfe Cl., 1936-1938. Contributor to: School Arts magazine, with articles on art education.*

NICHOLS, HOBART—*Painter*
41 Sunnybrook Rd., Bronxville, N.Y.

B. Washington, D.C., May 1, 1869. *Studied*: Julian Acad., Paris, with Castellucho; & with Howard Helmick. *Member*: NA; AWCS; Soc. Wash. A.; Wash. WC Cl.; SC; NAC; All.A.Am.; Century Cl.; Conn. Acad. FA; North Shore AA; Nat. Inst. A. & Let. *Awards*: prizes, Wash. WC Cl., 1901, 1904, 1906; Soc. Wash. A., 1902; SC, 1913, 1915,

1924, 1927, 1939; F., PAFA; med., NAC, 1915, 1920; prizes, NAD, 1923, 1925, 1928, 1934; SAE, 1936; Century Cl., 1938. *Work*: NGA; Am. Mus. Natural Hist., N.Y.; CGA; MMA; New Zealand A. Mus. *Position*: Pres., NAD, New York, N.Y., 1939-49; Pres. Emeritus, 1949- .

NICHOLS, JEANNETTIE D.—*Painter, E., Des.*
955, Ogden Dunes, Gary, Ind.

B. Holland, Mich., July 27, 1906. *Studied*: AIC, B.A.E.; Univ. Chicago; Inst. Des., Ill. Inst. Tech., and with Frances Chapin, Peppino Mangravite. *Member*: NEA; Gary A. Lg. (Pres. 1957-58); Chicago A. Edu. Assn. (Pres. & Bd. Memb.); Western AA; A. Educators Assn., Chicago; Chicago T. Union; AEA. *Awards*: prizes, Chesterton, Ind. 1954, 1955; Gary A. Lg., 1955; Gary Ceramic Exh., 1955; South Bend A. Center, 1956 (3). *Exhibited*: PAFA; AIC; AEA, Chicago; Mandel's, Chicago; Assoc. Am. A., Chicago; Indiana State Fair, 1954; Michiana Exh., South Bend, 1955; one-man: Cottage Studios, Chicago, 1953; Gary Hotel, 1957. Lectures: Composition; Landscape Painting; Techniques of Painting, Gary A. Lg. *Position*: Hd. A. Dept., Washington H.S., Chicago, 1957- .

NICHOLS, RAYMOND D.—*Educator, P.*
Louisiana College, Pineville, La.

B. Clifton Forge, Va., Dec. 28, 1918. *Studied*: William & Mary Col., B.F.A.; Columbia Univ., M.A. *Position*: Hd. A. Dept., Louisiana Col., Pineville, La.*

NICHOLSON, DOUGLAS CORNWALL—*Painter, I.*
50 Alamo Ave., Berkeley 7, Cal.

B. Omaha, Neb., Sept. 8, 1907. *Studied*: Univ. California, A.B., and with Hans Hofmann. *Member*: Assoc., IDI. *Work*: PBA; mural, USPO, Camas, Wash. I., "Report on Strategic Bombing of Oil Industry in Japan," U.S. War Dept., 1946. *Positions*: Des., Dobeckmun Co., Div. of Dow Chemical Co., Berkeley, Cal.; I., Schlage Lock Co. and Safeway Stores, San F., Cal., 1948-56.

NICHOLSON, EDWARD—*Portrait Painter, T.*
R.R. 6. Peoria 8, Ill. (Spring Bay)

B. Lincoln, Ill., June 13, 1901. *Studied*: Chicago Acad. FA; Grand Central Sch. A., and with Wayman Adams. *Member*: Hoosier Salon; Laguna Beach AA; Santa Barbara AA; Indiana A. Cl. *Awards*: gold medal, Illinois Soc. FA, 1940; Hoosier Salon, 1941-1956; Laguna Beach AA, 1949, 1950, 1951, 1954; Santa Barbara AA, 1951; prizes, Peoria AI, 1932; Hoosier Salon, 1944-46, 1949-1953, 1957; Indiana A. Cl., 1954. *Work*: Indiana State T. Col.; Ebell Cl., Long Beach, Cal.; Long Beach H.S.; Peoria Pub. Lib.; Bradley Univ.; Tri Kappa Coll. *Exhibited*: Ill. Soc. FA, 1939, 1940, 1944; Oakland A. Mus., 1938, 1939, 1945; Faulkner Mem. Mus., Santa Barbara, 1935, 1936, 1952, 1953; Santa Barbara Mus. A., 1948; Smithsonian Inst., 1949; John Herron AI, 1950; All. A. Am., 1950; Hoosier Salon, 1941-1958; Laguna Beach AA, 1949-1955; Indiana A. Cl., 1954-1958; Ill. State Fair, 1956, and others. *Position*: Port. Painter to the Exec. Furniture Gld. of Am.; Instr. A., Des., Bradley Univ., Peoria, Ill., 1946-47.

NICKERSON, RUTH *(Jennie Ruth Greacen)*—*Sculptor*
106 Woodcrest Ave., White Plains, N.Y.

B. Appleton, Wis., Nov. 23, 1905. *Studied*: NAD; BAID. *Member*: ANA; F., NSS; Scarsdale AA; Westchester A. & Crafts Gld.; Audubon A.; White Plains Civic A. Comm. *Awards*: medal, NAD, 1933; NAC, 1933; Hudson Valley AA, 1953; Westchester A. & Crafts Gld., 1955; AAPL, 1937; Montclair A. Mus., 1939; prize, NAWA, 1946; Guggenheim F., 1946. *Work*: Newark Mus.; Cedar Rapids AA; S., USPO, New Brunswick, N.J.; mural, USPO, Leaksville, N.C.; s. group, Children's Lib., Brooklyn, N.Y. *Exhibited*: NAD, 1932-1933, 1937; 1945 1949, 1951, 1952; PAFA, 1934, 1949; Soc. Indp. A., 1935; All. A. Am., 1934; WMAA, 1936; Montclair A. Mus.; Roerich Mus.; BM; MMA; Audubon A., 1948, 1949, 1951, 1952; Westchester A. & Crafts Gld., 1948-1952; Hudson Valley AA, 1948, 1951; one-man: White Plains Pub. Lib.; NAWA, 1949. *Positions*: Instr., S., Westchester Workshop, 1948-50; Hackley Boys Sch., Tarrytown, N.Y., 1952; Dir., Audubon A., 1953 & 1955; s. Jury, Audubon A., 1955; NSS Com., 1953-55.*

NICKFORD, JUAN—*Sculptor*
167 East 69th St., New York 21, N.Y.; h. 910 Sheridan Ave., Bronx 51, N.Y.

B. Havana, Cuba, Aug. 8, 1925. *Studied*: San Alejandro A. Sch., Havana; Univ. Havana Sch. Arch. *Member*: Sc. Center, New York City. *Awards*: prizes, Audubon A., 1955; Arch. Lg., 1955. *Work*: Outdoor, mural, wall, group sculpture: Malibu Beach, Cal.; Trade Show Bldg., N.Y.; Socony Mobil Bldg., N.Y.; Merchandise Mart, Chicago; S.S. Santa Rosa; Ambassador Town House, Phila., Pa.; and in private colls. *Exhibited*: WMAA, 1950, 1951, 1953, 1955-1958; PAFA, 1949-1951, 1953, 1958; Audubon A., 1955, 1956; NAD, 1949; de Cordova & Dana Mus., 1951, 1958; VMFA, 1950, 1956; Nebraska AA, 1950, 1953, 1955; Iowa State Univ., 1949; MMA, 1951; Fairmount Park, Phila., 1949; Sculpture Center, 1947-1958; WMA; Rochester Mem. A. Gal.; Wash. A. Cl.; SFMA; Univ. Arkansas; Los A. County Fair; Phila. A. All.; N.Y. Bd. Edu. traveling exh.; WAC. *Position*: Instr., S., Sculpture Center, New York, N.Y., 1953- .

NICKSON, LIA *(Mrs. J. Richard)*—*Painter, Ser., T.*
Box 671, Roswell, N.M.

B. Durham, N.C., Feb. 18, 1924. *Studied*: Albion Col.; Univ. North Carolina, A.B.; ASL, with Louis Bouche; Jepson AI, Los A., with Rico LeBrun; Grande Chaumiere, Paris, France. *Member*: AEA. *Award*: prize, Mus. New Mexico, 1958 (purchase). *Work*: Roswell Mus., N.M.; Mus. New Mexico. *Exhibited*: North Carolina A., 1952; Mus. New Mexico, Santa Fe, 1955; Mus. New Mexico traveling exh., 1955; Roswell Mus. A., 1955, one-man, 1958. Illus., "First Love," 1951. *Position*: Instr., Painting & Drawing, Univ. New Mexico Ext., Roswell Mus. A., New Mexico.

NICODEMUS, CHESTER R.—*Sculptor, C., T.*
447 Clinton Heights Ave., Columbus 2, Ohio

B. Barberton, Ohio, Aug. 17, 1901. *Studied*: Pennsylvania State Col.; Cleveland Sch. A.; Univ. Dayton; Ohio State Univ. *Member*: NSS; Columbus A. Lg. *Award*: Ohio State Fair. *Work*: tablet, Wilbur Wright H.S., Dayton, Ohio; Columbus Gal. FA. *Exhibited*: Syracuse Mus. FA; Columbus A. Lg.; Butler AI; Ohio State Fair. *Position*: Instr. S., Dayton AI, 1925-30; Instr., S. & Pottery, Columbus A. Sch., Columbus, Ohio, 1930-43.*

NICODEMUS, MRS. JOAN BAIN. See *Bain, Joan*

NICOLOSI, JOSEPH—*Sculptor, L.*
414 Saint Pierre Rd., Los Angeles 24, Cal.

B. Italy, Aug. 4, 1893. *Studied*: BAID, with Solon Borglum. *Member*: F., NSS; Arch. Lg.; Am. Veterans Soc. A.; A. Gld., California. *Work*: statues, busts, memorials, bas-reliefs, monuments: Brookgreen Gardens, S.C.; Univ. Chicago; Caracas, Venezuela; Guatemala Nat. Palace; Mellon Bank, Pittsburgh, Pa.; City and County Bldg., Denver; Peabody Auditorium, Daytona Beach, Fla.; St. Mary Parochial Sch., Manhasset, N.Y.; USPO, Mercersburgh, Pa.; Finch Jr. Col.; Harlem Settlement House, N.Y.; Bowers Mus., Santa Ana, Cal.; Elmont Hospital, Cal.; San Fernando Jr. Seminary; Parklawn Mem. Park, Md.; Saint Kevins Irish Church, Los A.; Los A. Mem. Coliseum; Stanford Univ.; Cedars of Lebanon Hospital, Los A.; Virgin St. Mary's Church, Whittier, Cal. *Exhibited*: many museums and galleries in U.S. and abroad. Lectures: Art; Sculpture; Philosophy.

NIESE, HENRY ERNST—*Painter, T.*
Hackettstown, N.J.

B. Jersey City, N.J., Oct. 11, 1924. *Studied*: Cooper Union; Columbia Univ. Sch. P. & S., B.F.A.; Academie Grande Chaumiere, Paris. *Member*: AEA; Assoc. A. of New Jersey. *Awards*: Pulitzer traveling scholarship, 1954; Emily Lowe award, 1954; CGA, 1955; Grant, Nat. Inst. A. & Lets., 1958. *Work*: CGA; Columbia Univ., and in private colls. *Exhibited*: New Jersey P. & S., 1952, 1954, 1955; NAD, 1954; Audubon A., 1954; Passedoit Gal., 1953-1955; Canada A. Circuit, 1955-56; CGA, 1955, 1957; Butler AI, 1955-1956; Montclair A. Mus., 1947-1949, 1951, 1953, 1955; Newark Mus. A., 1952-1958; WMAA, 1958; Ogunquit A. Center, 1958; Univ. Nebraska, 1958; MModA, 1956; Toledo Mus. A., 1957; Stanford Univ., 1958; Delgado Mus. A., 1958; one-man: 'G' Gal., 1957, 1959;

Everhart Mus. A., 1958. *Position*: Instr., BMSch A., Brooklyn, N.Y., 1951-54; Children's Art, Newark Mus. A.; painting, Summit (N.J.) AA; Morris County AA.

NIETO, GRACE A.—*Painter, C., S.*
717 Schumacher Dr., Los Angeles 48, Cal.

B. Los Angeles, Cal., Dec. 29, 1899. *Studied*: Otis AI, with Lukits; and with Vysekel, Will Foster, Ralph Holmes, Sam Harris, and others. *Member*: Cal. A. Cl.; Desert A. Cl.; Ebell Cl., Los A. *Exhibited*: Cal. A. Cl.; City Hall, Los A.; Greek Theatre, Los A. *Position*: Co-Chm. A., Van Nuys Women's Cl.; A. Chm., Progressive Women's Cl., Gardena, Cal.

NILES, ROSAMOND—*Painter, Et.*
Library Lane, Old Lyme, Conn.

B. Portsmouth, N.H., Nov. 5, 1881. *Studied*: ASL; & with DuMond, Bridgman, Pennell; in Paris, with Andre L'Hote. *Member*: NAC. *Work*: Witte Mem. Mus.; Randolph Aviation Field; Woodberry Forest Sch., Chatham Sch., Va.; Radcliffe Hicks Mem. Sch., Tolland, Conn.*

NIMMO, LOUISE EVERETT—*Painter, C.*
Ojala, Rte. #4, Ojai, Cal.

B. Des Moines, Iowa, Apr. 9, 1899. *Studied*: Grinnell Col.; Otis AI; Chouinard AI; Immaculate Heart Col., mosaic workshop; Fontainebleau Sch. A., Julian Acad., Paris, France. *Member*: Women Painters of the West; Ojai A. Center. *Awards*: med., Pacific-Southwest Exp., 1928; prizes, Laguna Beach AA, 1923; Cal. State Fair, 1936; Cal. A. Cl., 1951; Pasadena AI, 1950. *Work*: Opportunity Sch., Des Moines, Iowa; Beverly Hills Women's Cl.; St. Andrews Episcopal Church, Ojai, Cal. *Exhibited*: Pacific-Southwest Exp., 1928; GGE, 1939; Los A. Mus. A.; Cal. AC; Women Painters of the West; Laguna Beach AA, 1923-1946.

NISBET, MARY JACQUETTA—
Designer, C., P., I., S., T.
668 Lexington Ave., New York 22, N.Y.

B. Kuala Pilah, Fed. Malay States, Sept. 30, 1928. *Studied*: Edinburgh Univ., Certif. Hist. FA; Edinburgh Col. A., Scotland, D.A. *Member*: Greenwich House Potters; Nat. Soc. Dec. Des.; A. Cooperative Service. *Awards*: Scholarship, Edinburgh Col., 1949; prizes, Greenwich House Potters, 1952, 1955. *Exhibited*: Syracuse Mus. FA; N.Y. Soc. Ceramic A., 1954; Greenwich House Potters, 1952-1955. Illus., "Tie-Dyeing"; "Tee Dee Loom"; "Rhythm: Activities and Instruments," Arts Cooperative Service. *Position*: Instr., Crafts, Brearley Sch., New York, N.Y., 1955.*

NISBET, ROBERT H.—*Painter, Et., T., Eng., L.*
South Kent, Conn.

B. Providence, R.I., Aug. 25, 1879. *Studied*: R.I. Sch. Des.; ASL; in Europe, and with Henry Snell, Frank DuMond. *Member*: NA; All. A. Am.; Conn. Acad. FA; NAC; Lotos Cl.; ASL; Audubon A.; Wash. AA (Hon.); SC; Providence A. Cl.; SAGA; A. Fund Soc.; A. Fellowship; Kent AA (Emeritus); Arch. Lg. (Emeritus); Phila. Soc. Et.; AWS. *Awards*: med., Pan-Pacific Expo., 1915; prizes, Conn. Acad. FA; Conn. Soc. A.; NAD; Cal. Pr. M.; NAC; Talcott prize, SAGA; Great Barrington, Mass. *Work*: R.I.Sch. Des.; R.I. Hospital; Telfair Acad. A.; Butler AI; Conn. State Agricultural Col.; R.I. State Col.; NAC; Lotos Cl.; Sherman (Conn.) Lib.; MMA; N.Y. Pub. Lib.; BM; Milwaukee AI; Detroit Inst. A.; Univ. Nebraska; Oberlin Col.; A. Council, N.Y.; Yale Univ.; Bibliotheque Nationale, Paris; NGA; LC; Montclair A. Mus.; Howard Univ.; Univ. Connecticut; Stockbridge (Mass.) Pub. Lib.; Wesleyan Univ., Macon, Ga.; Litchfield Hist. Soc.; Pa. State Univ.; Springfield Mus. A.; Hamilton A. Gal., Canada. *Exhibited*: nationally. Lectures: Print Making.

NISWONGER, ILSE (Mrs.)—*Sculptor, C.*
Westport, Conn.

B. Metz, France, Jan. 26, 1900. *Studied*: ASL, and with Alexander Archipenko, Hans Hofmann, Rudolph Belling. *Work*: Liturgical Sculpture in churches in Westport, Fairfield, New Haven, New Canaan, West Hartford, Norwalk, Bolton, Conn.; Harrisburg, Pittsburgh, Pa.; Brooklyn, N.Y.; Glendora, Cal.; Moncton, Canada; Baraboo, Wis.; Don Bosco Sch., Paterson, N.J., and others.

NITSCHE, ERIK, *Designer, I.*
R.F.D. 1, Ridgefield, Conn.

B. Lausanne, Switzerland, July 8, 1908. *Studied*: Switzerland; Munich, Germany with Prof. Ehmke; Paris, France, with Maximilien Vox. *Exhibited*: A. Dir. Cl., 1949; AIGA, 1951-1955, 1958; Nat. Ex. Adv. & Editorial Art, 1937-1959; Intl. Poster Exh., Paris, 1949; MMoA, 1947-1951; Assoc. Am. A., 1950; Akron AI, 1950; Intl. Exh. Typography, London, England, 1952; Tokyo, 1957; Stockholm, 1957; Crawford Hall, London, 1958; Cologne, 1958; SI, 1959, and others. *Awards*: Direct Mail Adv. Assn., 1948; gold medal, A. Dir. Cl., 1949, prizes, 1957, 1958; AIGA, 1951-1959. Covers, illus., photographs, art dir. for Vanity Fair; Today; Arts & Decorations; Harper's Bazaar; Vogue; House & Garden; House Beautiful; Town & Country; Life; Fortune; Woman's Home Companion; U.S. Camera, and other national magazines from 1935-48; Magazine A. Dir. for: Air Tech.; Air News; Home & Food; Advertising campaigns, Direct Mail, Promotion, Industrial Design, etc., for many leading retail stores, film companies, RCA Victor, Decca Records, airlines and many others. Articles published, work shown or reviewed in A. Dir. Annuals; Graphis; Publimondial; American Printer; Fortune and other magazines.

NIX, FRANCES (NIMMO) GREENE—
Museum Director, P.
Montgomery Museum of Fine Arts; h. 426 South Goldthwaite St., Montgomery 4, Ala.

B. Montgomery, Ala., June 25, 1907. *Studied*: with Anne Goldthwaite, Kelly Fitzpatrick, Wayman Adams. *Member*: Nat. Soc. A. & Lets.; Alabama A. Lg.; Press & Authors Assn. *Awards*: prizes, Press & Authors, 1955; Alabama A. Lg., 1957. *Work*: Montgomery Mus. FA; Calhoun County (Ala.) Court House; Judicial Bldg., Montgomery. *Exhibited*: Assn. Georgia A.; Alabama A. Lg., 1947-1957. Contributor to Montgomery Advertiser-Journal. *Position*: Dir., Montgomery Museum of FA, Montgomery, Ala.

NOBACK, GUSTAVE JOSEPH—*Sculptor, E., L.*
15 Gramercy Park, New York 3, N.Y.; h. 70-05 Groton St., Forest Hills, N.Y.

B. New York, N.Y., May 29, 1890. *Studied*: Cornell Univ., B.S.; Univ. Minnesota, M.A., Ph.D.; & with W.C. Baker, Heinz Warneke, Wheeler Williams. *Member*: NAC; AAPL. *Work*: N.Y. Univ.; China Inst. Am. *Exhibited*: Arch. L., 1938; PAFA, 1940, 1942, 1946; NAD, 1945, 1946; All.A.Am., 1941-1945; Clay Cl., 1934, 1935; Asbury Park Soc. FA, 1939, 1940; Montclair A. Mus., 1945; NAC, 1944-1946; Minneapolis S. Exh., 1945. Lectures: Human Anatomy in Art. *Position*: Prof. Anatomy, N.Y.Univ., New York, N.Y., 1924-45.*

NOBLE, JOHN ALEXANDER—*Marine Painter, Lith.*
270 Richmond Terrace, Staten Island 1, N.Y.

B. Paris, France, Mar. 17, 1913. *Studied*: Friends Seminary; Univ. Grenoble, France; NAD. *Member*: ANA; Audubon A.; SAGA. *Awards*: gold medal, Audubon A., 1956. *Work*: LC; Carnegie Inst.; MMA; Mariner's Mus.; PMA; New Britain Mus. A.; Penobscot Mus. A.; presentation print, SAGA, 1952; print comms., for Shipbuilding, Stevedoring, Tugboat and Industrial firms. *Exhibited*: nationally. One-man print exh., Staten Island Mus. A. & Sc., 1952.*

NOBLE, MAMIE JONES (Mrs. J. V.)—
Painter, C., W., L., T.
208 North 30th St., Corsicana, Tex.

B. Ellis County, Tex. *Studied*: AIC; & with Rose Crosman, George Oberteuffer, Cyril Kay-Scott, & others. *Member*: SSAL; Dallas AA; Texas FA Assn. *Awards*: prizes, Miss. State Fair, 1929, 1931; Fed. Women's Cl., Corsicana, Tex., 1937. *Work*: Pub. Sch., Corsicana, Tex.; murals, First Baptist Church, Itasca, Tex.; Mem. Church, Emmanuel Church, Corsicana, Tex. *Exhibited*: Ft. Worth AC; Texas Centennial Exh.; Junior Col., Goodman, Tex.; Texas Women's Col., Ft. Worth. Contributor to: Texas State Teachers magazine, "The Outlook." *Position*: Regional Dir., Texas FA Assn., Austin, Tex., 1935-45; Chm. A. Dept., Women's Cl., Corsicana, Tex.; Chm. A. Dept., Navarro County Fair.*

NOBLE, VERRILL RUTH—*Writer, Des., L.*

18 Brattle St.; h. 5 Craigie Circle, Cambridge 38, Mass.

B. Portland, Me. *Studied*: Wellesley Col., B.A.; Columbia Univ. Sch. Lib. Service, B.S. *Member*: AAMus.; Inst. Contemp. A., Boston; BMFA. Ed., "Famous Paintings in American Galleries"; "Bibliography of W.A. Dwiggins" in selective checklist of Press Books, 1947; Co-author, Preliminary Memoranda for Conference on International Cultural, Educational and Scientific Exchanges, Chicago Am. Lib. Assn., 1947; *Author*: "Dwiggins, Master of Arts," Publishers' Weekly, 1947; "Maine Profile," 1954; "A Guide to Distinctive Dining," 1957; "A Guide to New England Dining," 1957; the following calendars published annually: Cat; Dog; Animal; Historic American Landmarks; Maine; Massachusetts; Cape Cod. *Lectures*: Historic American Landmarks and other subjects. *Positions*: A. Libn., FMA, Harvard Univ., 1940-42; Libn., R.I. Sch. Des., Providence, 1942-46; Pres., Ed.-in-Chief, Berkshire Publ. Co., 1950- .

NOE, SYDNEY PHILIP—*Museum Curator, W.*

American Numismatic Society, Broadway at 156th St., New York 32, N.Y.; h. 5 Bishop Pl., New Brunswick, N.J.

B. Woodbridge, N.J., Apr. 4, 1885. *Studied*: Rutgers Univ., B. Sc., A.M.; Am. Sch. Classical Studies, Athens, Greece. *Awards*: medal, Am. Numismatic Soc.; Royal Numismatic Soc. *Position*: Chief Cur., Emeritus, Am. Numismatic Soc., New York, N.Y.

NOFZIGER, ED(WARD) (C.)—*Cartoonist, I., W.*

805 Temple Hills Dr., Laguna Beach, Cal.

B. Porterville, Cal., June 14, 1913. *Studied*: Univ. California, Los A., B.E. *Author*: I., "Shorty," 1941; "Two Trees," 1944; "Spunky," 1946; illus., "How to Attract the Wombat," 1949. *Exhibited*: Laguna Beach Festival A. Nationally syndicated by Chicago Sun-Times: "Animal Antics"; Writer and story sketch for TV series "Ruff and Reddy," and "Huckleberry Hound."

NORDFELDT, MRS. B. J. O. See *Abbott, Emily*

NORDGREN, OKE GUSTAF—*Painter*

461 Livingston St., Elmira, N.Y.

B. Stockholm, Sweden, Feb. 22, 1907. *Studied*: Corcoran Sch. A.; Webster Sch. A., Provincetown, Mass.; Stetson Univ.; & with Richard Lahey. *Awards*: prizes, Swedish-Am. Exh., Chicago, 1939, 1940; Pepsi-Cola, 1945; Soc. Wash. A., 1941, med. 1942, prize, 1944; F., Tiffany Fnd., 1937-1939, 1941; Arnot A. Gal., purchase prize; medal, Hofstra Col., 1950; Nassau County A. Lg., 1950, 1952, gold med., 1953-55. *Work*: Univ. Maine: Stetson Univ., Deland, Fla. *Exhibited*: VMFA, 1940; PAFA, 1941, 1942; Phila. A. All., 1940; NAD, 1941, 1943; CGA, 1943, 1945, 1951; Carnegie Inst., 1941; Pepsi-Cola traveling exh., 1945, 1946; Soc. Wash. A., 1933-1945; PMG, 1939-1943; A. Gld. Wash., 1943-1945; Nat. Mus., Wash., D.C., 1939-1941; one-man: Hofstra Col., 1950; Univ. Maine, 1950; Stetson Univ., 1955.

NORDHAUSEN, AUGUST HENRY—*Painter, T., L.*

Hotel des Artistes, 1 West 67th St., New York 23, N.Y.

B. Hoboken, N.J., Jan. 25, 1901. *Studied*: N.Y. Sch. F. & App. A.; Royal Acad., Kunstgewerbe Schule, Munich, Germany. *Member*: AWS; Audubon A.; SC; All. A. Am.; A. Fellowship, Inc.; Sch. A. Lg. *Awards*: prizes, Lempert Mem. prize, 1949; Kriendler Mem. prize, 1950; Audubon A., 1949; SC, 1948, 1950, 1952; Am. Veterans Soc. A., 1950; F., McDowell Colony; F., Tiffany Fnd.; F., Trask Fnd. *Work*: CMA; New Britain A. Mus.; Ga. Tech. Univ., Atlanta; Syracuse Univ.; Long Island Univ.; C.W. Post Col.; Denver A. Mus. *Exhibited*: AIC; PAFA; CGA; NAD; All. A. Am.; AGAA; Audubon A.; SC, and others. *Positions*: V.-Pres., SC, 1950; A. Fellowship, 1951; Trustee, School Art League, New York, N.Y., 1950.

NORDMARK, OLOF E. (OLLE)—*Painter, Gr., W., T.*

Cold Spring, N.Y.

B. Dalecaslia, Sweden, May 21, 1890. *Studied*: Tech. Sch., Altins A. Sch., Stockholm, Sweden, and in Italy. *Member*:

AEA. *Work*: murals, Court House, Stockholm; First Swedish Baptist Church, N.Y.; Church of God, N.Y.; Cathedral of Learning, Pittsburgh, Pa.; Am.-Swedish Hist. Mus., Phila., Pa.; paintings, Carl Milles Mus., Stockholm, and in private colls., U.S., Sweden and Finland. *Exhibited*: Delphic Studio, N.Y. (one-man); Three Arts Gal., N.Y.; Swedish Modern Exh., DMFA. *Author*: "Fresco Painting," 1947. *Positions*: Instr., Fresco Painting, U.S. Indian Service, 1938-43; Tech. Supv., Frescoes, Dept. of Justice, Lincoln Station P.O., Wash., D.C., Hightstown, N.J., Secco murals, Custom House, New York City.

NORLING, ERNEST RALPH—*Painter, I., W., C.*

4832 52nd Ave., South, Seattle 8, Wash.

B. Pasco, Wash., Sept. 26, 1892. *Studied*: Whitman Col., B.S.; Chicago Acad. FA; AIC; Tiffany Fnd. *Member*: Puget Sound Group Painters. *Work*: SAM; St. James Cathedral, Seattle; White House, Wash., D.C.; murals, Alaska Bldg., Seattle; Student Union Bldg., Univ. Washington; Bremerton Navy Yard Lib. *Exhibited*: CGA, 1935; SAM; Smithsonian traveling exh., 1958. *Author*: "Pencil Magic," 1935; "Perspective Made Easy," 1939; "Perspective Drawing"; I., children's books. Article on Perspective for Encyclopaedia Britannica.

NORLING, JO(SEPHINE) (STEARNS)—*Writer*

4832 52nd Ave., South, Seattle 18, Wash.

B. Kalamo, Mich., July 22, 1895. *Studied*: Univ. Washington, B.S.; Central Col. of Edu., Washington. *Member*: Nat. Lg. Am. Pen Women; Northwest Acad. A.; Seattle Free Lances. *Awards*: Theta Sigma Phi Matrix award; Nat. Lg. Am. Pen Women (Seattle Branch) award for achievement in letters. *Author*: "Pogo" series for children including Pogo's Fishing Trip, 1942, Sky Ride, 1943, Mining Trip, 1945, Farm Adventure, 1948, Sea Trip, 1950, Truck Ride, 1954, Oil Well, 1955, and others; "First Book of Water," 1952.

NORMAN-WILCOX, GREGOR—
Museum Curator, W., L.

Los Angeles County Museum, Los Angeles 7, Cal.; h. 1261 San Pasqual St., Pasadena, Cal.

B. Cleveland, Ohio, Sept. 9, 1905. *Studied*: Cleveland Sch. A. *Author*: weekly "Antiques" feature, Sunday Magazine of the Los Angeles Times. *Position*: Cur., Decorative Arts, Los Angeles County Mus. Los Angeles, Cal., 1932- .

NORMENT, JOHN MURRAY—*Cartoonist*

300 West 10th St., New York 14, N.Y.

B. Lebanon, Tenn., Nov. 28, 1911. *Studied*: AIC; Chicago Acad. FA. *Member*: Nat. Cartoonists Soc. *Exhibited*: MMA Cartoon Exh., 1953; Coronation Exh. of Am. Cartoons, London, England; Brussels World's Fair, 1958. *Author*: I., "Laugh Time," 1958. Contributor cartoons to: Sat. Eve. Post; American; King Features; McNaught Syndicate, and others. Columnist, Writer's Digest; Ed., "Raining Cats and Dogs," 1958.

NORRIS, BEN—*Painter, E., Et., Des.*

100 Poloke Place, Honolulu 14, Hawaii

B. Redlands, Cal., Sept. 6, 1910. *Studied*: Pomona Col., B.A.; Harvard Univ. (FMA); Sorbonne, Paris, and with S. Macdonald-Wright, Jean Charlot, Max Ernst, Josef Albers. *Member*: Cal. WC Soc.; Phila. WC Cl.; Hawaii P. & S.; Honolulu Pr. M. *Awards*: prizes, Honolulu Acad. A., 1938, 1941, 1944, 1948, 1950, 1952; Honolulu Pr. M., 1943, and others. *Work*: LC; N.Y. Pub. Lib.; Honolulu Acad. A.; murals, Officer's Cl., Pearl Harbor; Kaneohe Naval Air Station, Oahu; Bishop Bank, Kapiolani Branch, Honolulu. *Exhibited*: Cal. WC Soc., 1935-41, 1947-1949; AIC, 1938-1941; Phila. WC Cl., 1938-1940, 1941, 1949; WFNY 1939; AWS, 1936, 1938, 1939; one-man: Honolulu Acad. A., 1936, 1938, 1940, 1942, 1944; Cal. PLH, 1945; Crocker A. Gal.; 1946; Santa Barbara Mus. A., 1946; SAM, 1946; Pomona Col., 1935, 1946; Passedoit Gal., 1952; Gima and Beaux Arts Galleries, Honolulu, 1952; The Gallery, Honolulu, 1956 (one-man). *Position*: Instr., A., 1937-52, Prof. A., 1952- , Chm. A. Dept., 1946-1955, Prof. A., 1955- , Univ. Hawaii, Honolulu 14, T.H. Fulbright Lecturer (Prof. Western Art), Tokyo Univ. of Edu., Tokyo, Japan, 1955-56. Arch. Des. Collaboration and Art Supv., on major Honolulu buildings.

NORRIS, S. WALTER—*Painter, W.*

1716 Chestnut St.; h. 135 South 18th St., Philadelphia 3, Pa.

B. Philadelphia, Pa., Jan. 12, 1868. *Studied*: Univ. Pennsylvania; PMSchIA; PAFA; & in Paris. *Awards*: med., PAFA, 1930, 1933; F., PAFA. *Exhibited*: PAFA, annually; Phila. AC, annually; NAD; CAM; WMAA; AIC; GGE, 1939; CGA; PMA; Toledo Mus. A.; BM; Phila. A. All.; SAM; Decatur AI; etc. Contributor to: national magazines.

NORRIS, VERA (PEARL)—*Painter*

17 South Cordova St., Alhambra, Cal.

B. Nevada, Iowa, Apr. 19, 1905. *Studied*: with Jennie Crawford, Trudy Hanscomb. *Member*: Women Painters of the West. *Award*: prize, Friday Morning Cl., Los A., 1951. *Exhibited*: Women Painters of the West, 1949, 1950; Ebell Cl., 1950, 1951; Bowers Mem. Mus., Santa Ana, Cal. 1951; Hollywood Woman's Cl., 1951; Friday Morning Cl., 1950, 1951; Hollywood Pub. Lib., 1950; Recreation Center, 1950; Los. A. Univ. Cl., 1952.*

NORTON, ANN—*Sculptor*

253 Barcelona Rd., West Palm Beach, Fla.

Studied: NAD; ASL; CUASch; & with Charles Keck, Leon Kroll, John Hovannes, Charles Rudy, & others. *Awards*: Carnegie F., for European study, 1932, 1935; prizes, Soc. Four A., Palm Beach, Fla., 1944, 1945; Lowe Gal., 1952; Norton Gal., 1943-1945. *Exhibited*: MModA, 1930; NSS, 1940, 1941; Soc. Four A., 1943-1945, 1948, 1950-1952; Norton Gal., 1943-1946, 1948-1951; Seligmann Gal.; Clay Cl., N.Y.; Lowe Gal., 1952; Nat. Gal., Havana, Cuba; Mus. FA, Houston; Worth A. Gal., Palm Beach, Fla.

NORTON, ELIZABETH—*Sculptor, Gr.*

353 Lowell Ave., Palo Alto, Cal.

B. Chicago, Ill., Dec. 16, 1887. *Studied*: AIC; ASL; NAD. *Work*: Detroit Athletic Cl.; Stanford Univ.; Cal. State Lib.; All Saints Church, Palo Alto; MMA; AIC; LC; Smithsonian Inst.; Hackley A. Gal.; FMA; Am. Mus. Natural Hist.; bas-reliefs, Menlo Sch. T. Col., Menlo Park, Cal.; San Mateo County Lib., Redwood City, Cal. *Exhibited*: GGE, 1939; Cal. Min. Pr. Soc., 1941; NAD, 1942; Am. Color Pr. Soc., 1944; Wichita AA, 1946; Prairie Pr. M., annually; Palo Alto A. Cl., annually; one-man: Cal. State Lib., 1942; Stanford Univ., 1950.

NORTON, PAUL F.—*Educator, Hist.*

Department of Art, University of Massachusetts, Amherst, Mass.

B. Newton, Mass., Jan. 23, 1917. *Studied*: Oberlin Col., A.B.; Princeton Univ., M.F.A., Ph.D. *Member*: Soc. Arch. Historians; CAA; Mediaeval Acad. of Am.; Soc. Arch. Bibliographers; Societe francaise d'archeologie. *Awards*: Am. Council of Learned Societies Fellowship, 1951-52; Fulbright Fellowship, 1953-54. Author two chapters, "Nassau Hall," Princeton, 1956. Contributor to Journal of Soc. of Arch. Historians; Art Bulletin. *Positions*: Ed., Bd. Dirs., Journal of the Society of Architectural Historians; Prof. A. History, Pennsylvania State Univ., 1947-58; Prof. A. Hist., Chm., Dept. Art, University of Massachusetts, Amherst, Mass., 1958- .

NOTARO, ANTHONY—*Sculptor*

19 Pinecrest Terrace, Wayne, N.J.

B. Italy, Jan. 10, 1915. *Studied*: Rinehart Sch. Sculpture, Maryland Inst., Balto.; and with Harry Lewis Raul, Hans Schuler, Herbert Adams, William Simpson, Malvina Hoffman. *Member*: NSS. *Awards*: Rinehart Sch. S., scholarship, 1935, prize, 1939; prizes, NAD, 1956; Tiffany Fnd., 1957, and regional awards. *Work*: statue, St. Agnes Catholic Church, Paterson, N.J.; Sarah Josepha Hale Award Medal, 1957; Anniversary Medallion, Geiger Engineering & Mfg. Co., 1957; port. reliefs, medals and architectural sculpture. *Exhibited*: NAD; NSS; Providence A. Cl.; All. A. Am.; Audubon A.; New Haven Paint & Clay Cl.; Conn. Acad. FA; Newark Mus. A.; Montclair A. Mus.; Greenwich Soc. A.

NOVAK, LOUIS—*Printmaker, P., T.*

84 Edward Rd., Watertown 72, Mass.

B. Zilina, Czechoslovakia, Oct. 13, 1903. *Studied*: Mass. Sch. A., B. Sc. in Edu.; BMFA Sch. *Member*: Cambridge AA; Prairie Pr. M.; Watertown (Mass.) AA. *Work*: prints: BMFA; Princeton Pr. Cl.; Reading Public Mus.; New Orleans AA; Delgado Mus. A. *Exhibited*: LC, 1943, 1946; NAD, 1943; Jordan Marsh, Boston, 1946; Cambridge AA, 1952. *Position*: Instr., Arch. & Eng. Drawing, Wentworth Inst., Boston, Mass., at present.

NOVOTNY, ELMER LADISLAW—*Painter, E.*

Twin Lakes, Kent, Ohio

B. Cleveland, Ohio, July 27, 1909. *Studied*: Cleveland Sch. A.; Univ. London; Yale Univ.; Western Reserve Univ., A.B.; Kent Univ., M.A. *Member*: Cleveland SA; Akron SA. *Awards*: prizes, CMA, 1930, 1937, 1938; Canton AI, 1944, 1945, 1946; Butler Inst. Am. A., 1958 (purchase); Akron AI, 1958 (purchase). *Work*: CMA; Cleveland Mun. Coll.; Coshocton Mus.; Butler Inst. Am. A.; Akron AI. *Exhibited*: Carnegie Inst., 1941; Milwaukee AI, 1945; Butler AI, 1940-1950; Akron AI, 1946; CMA, 1929-1945. *Position*: Instr., Portrait Painting, Cleveland Sch. A., 1944-1952; Asst. Prof., 1938-40, Assoc. Prof., 1941-43, Prof. A., 1944- , Chm., Sch. A., Kent State Univ., Kent, Ohio.

NOWAK, LEO—*Portrait Painter, Cart., Comm. A., I.*

4316 Van Nuys Blvd., Sherman Oaks, Cal.

B. Elizabeth, N.J., Dec. 24, 1907. *Studied*: John Huntington AI; Cleveland Sch. A.; Darvas Sch. Des., and with Frank Wilcox, Henry J. Keller. *Member*: Cal. A. Cl. *Awards*: prizes, CMA, 1937; Laguna Beach A. Festival, 1952; Griffith Park Theatre, Los A., 1955; Cleveland Telenews A. Gal., 1943; New York, N.Y., 1940. *Work*: mural, N.Y. Central R.R. Engineer's Bldg., Cleveland; Hunters Tavern, Cleveland. *Exhibited*: CMA, 1929-1943 (traveling exh., 1940); Laguna Beach, 1951, 1952; Cleveland, Ohio. Illus. "Trampo the Sailor," 1929; "Uncle Wiggly," 1929. Contributor cartoons and illus. to Superman magazine; NEA Newspaper Service. *Position*: Comm. A., Cleveland, Ohio, 1928-43; Los Angeles, Cal., 1946- .

NOYES, BERTHA—*Painter*

614—19th St., Northwest, Washington 6, D.C.

B. Washington, D.C. *Studied*: Corcoran Sch. A.; and with Charles Hawthorne, Jerry Farnsworth. *Member*: Soc. Wash. A.; Wash. WC Cl.; NAWA; Newport AA; Providence A. Cl.; Wash. A. Cl.; Soc. Women Geographers. *Exhibited*: one-man: CGA; R.I. Sch. Des.; Newport AA; Wesleyan Univ., Delaware, Ohio; Currier Gal. A.; George Washington Univ.; Mus. A. & Sc., Rochester, N.Y.

NUDERSCHER, FRANK BERNARD—*Painter, Des.*

406 Market St., St. Louis 2, Mo.; h. 7408 Parkdale Ave., Clayton 5, Mo.

B. St. Louis, Mo., July 19, 1880. *Member*: NSMP; A. Gld., Indp A., 2 x 4 Soc., all of St. Louis, Mo. *Awards*: prizes, CAM, 1945, 1946; Chamber of Commerce, A. Gld., A. Lg., all of St. Louis; Missouri State Fair; Missouri State purchase prize. *Work*: Capitol, Governor's Mansion, Women's Cl., Jefferson City, Mo.; CAM; Little Rock A. Mus.; Farmington (Mo.) Lib.; H.S., University City, Clayton, Maplewood, Point Lookout, Mo.; State T. Col., Maryville, Mo.; murals, St. Louis Zoological Gardens; many banks, hospitals, etc.*

NUGENT, A(RTHUR) W(ILLIAM)—*Cartoonist, I., W.*

12 Tuxedo Parkway, Newark, N.J.

B. Wallingford, Conn., Feb. 20, 1891. *Studied*: Fawcett A. Sch., Newark, N.J.; SI A. Sch., N.Y. *Member*: SI. Author, I., numerous children's puzzle & game books; Author, Cart., Publ., "Circus of Fun Comics." Creator, "Funland," a puzzle page feature syndicated by The Associated Newspapers in U.S. and abroad. *Position*: Puzzle Cart., Assoc. Newspapers, 1932- .

NUHFER, OLIVE HARRIETT—*Painter, S., T., L.*

50 Hathaway Court, Pittsburgh 35, Pa.

B. Pittsburgh, Pa., Aug. 16, 1911. *Studied*: Univ. Oklahoma, B.F.A.; Carnegie Inst. *Member*: Assoc. A. Pittsburgh. *Work*: murals, USPO, Westerville, Ohio; altar mural, St. John's Church, Norman, Okla.; paintings, Mellon Jr. H.S., Beltzhoover H.S., Penn Jr. H.S., Pittsburgh. *Exhibited*: Assoc. A. Pittsburgh, 1958 and prior;

one-man: William Penn Playhouse, Pittsburgh, 1956-1958. *Position*: Instr., A. & Crafts Center, Pittsburgh, Pa., 1954; P. & S., YWCA, Pittsburgh.

NUHN, MARJORIE ANN—*Painter*

607 Tremont St., Cedar Falls, Iowa

B. Cedar Falls, Iowa, Oct. 31, 1898. *Studied*: Chicago Acad. A.; AIC, and with Grant Wood, Adrian Dornbush, and others. *Member*: Cedar Falls AA. *Awards*: prizes, Sioux City A. Center, 1945; Cedar Falls A. Gal., 1944, 1945. *Work*: Purdue Col. *Exhibited*: Des Moines A. Center, 1948, 1953; Cedar Falls, Iowa, 1948-1952, 1955; Terry AI, 1952.

NUNES, GORDON—*Painter, E.*

University of California; h. 3229 Cabrillo Blvd., Los Angeles 66, Cal.

B. Porterville, Cal., Aug. 1, 1914. *Studied*: Univ. California at Los Angeles. *Member*: Cal. WC Soc. *Exhibited*: MMA, 1953, 1954; Los A. Mus. A.; Cal. WC Soc. *Position*: Prof. A., Univ. California, Los Angeles, Cal.

NUNGESTER, MILDRED. See Wolfe, Mildred

NUNN, FREDERIC—*Painter*

Cape May Court House, R.F.D., N.J.

B. Philadelphia, Pa., Aug. 18, 1879. *Studied*: PAFA; & with Cecilia Beaux, Charles Grafly, Hugh Breckenridge, & others. *Member*: AAPL; F. PAFA; Phila. A. All.; Phila. WC Cl.; Cape May (N.J.) County A. Lg. *Awards*: F., PAFA; prizes, F. PAFA, 1936; Cape May A. Lg., 1944. *Work*: PMA; Los A. Mus. A.; Reading (Pa.) Mus. A.; F. PAFA; City Hall, Cape May, N.J.; Cape May Court House Lib. *Exhibited*: PAFA; CGA; NAD; Carnegie Inst.; one-man: Phila. A. All.; Temple Univ.; Harcum Col. *Position*: A. Dir., Cape May annual summer art exhibition, 1939-58.

NUSBAUM, ESTHER COMMONS—*Painter, T.*

145 South 20th St., Richmond, Ind.

B. Richmond, Ind., Jan. 12, 1907. *Studied*: Univ. Wisconsin. *Member*: NAWA; The Twenty; Indiana A. Cl.; Richmond A. Cl.; Richmond AA. *Awards*: Hoosier Salon, 1934; Indiana State Fair, 1947, 1948, 1952, 1957, 1958; Richmond AA, 1947, 1949, 1953, 1957; L. S. Ayers award, Indianapolis, 1956, 1958; AAUW, 1956; Va. Highlands Festival, 1958. *Work*: Richmond AA; Richmond Y.W.C.A. *Exhibited*: NAWA, 1952, 1953, 1955, 1957, 1958; NAWA traveling exhs., Amsterdam, 1956, Brussels, 1956, Bern, 1957; John Herron AI, 1948, 1949, 1951, 1957, 1958; Va. Highlands Festival, 1958; Dayton AI, 1956; Hoosier Salon, 1953; Indiana AA, annually; Richmond AA, annually.

NUSE, OLIVER—*Painter, T.*

504 Harvey St., Philadelphia 44, Pa.

B. Oberlin, Ohio, Jan. 20, 1914. *Studied*: PAFA; Univ. Pennsylvania, B.F.A., M.F.A. *Member*: Phila. WC Cl.; Phila. A. All.; Phila. A. T. Assn.; F., PAFA; AEA. *Awards*: prizes, Woodmere A. Gal., 1945; F., PAFA; Phila. Sketch Cl., 1951; Phila. A. T. Assn., 1950, 1952. *Work*: Samuel Fleisher Mem.; Woodmere A. Gal.; F., PAFA. *Exhibited*: BMA; PAFA; F., PAFA; Phila. Sketch Cl.; Woodmere A. Gal.; Friends Central Sch.; Butler AI; Phila. A. All.; PMA; Cheltenham A. Center. *Position*: Instr., A. & Crafts, 1941-44, Dir. A., 1945- , William Penn Charter Sch., Philadelphia, Pa.; Instr., Painting, Samuel Fleisher Art Memorial.*

NUSE, ROY CLEVELAND—*Painter, W., L., T.*

Rushland, Pa.

B. Springfield, Ohio, Feb. 23, 1885. *Studied*: Cincinnati Acad. A.; Oberlin Col.; PAFA; & with Frank Duveneck. *Awards*: prize, med., Phila. Sketch Cl., 1921; med., F. PAFA, 1941; Cresson traveling scholarship, PAFA. *Work*: Jefferson Medical Col., Hahnemann Medical Col., Phila., Pa.; PAFA. *Exhibited*: Carnegie Inst.; NAD; CGA; AIC; CM; Toledo Mus. A.; PAFA, annually; F., PAFA; Phila. Sketch Cl.; Phila. AC. *Position*: Instr. A., 1925- , Coordinated Programs Dir., 1933-54, PAFA, Philadelphia, Pa.

NUTTING, MYRON C.—*Painter, Gr., T., Cr.*

1012 North Clark St., Los Angeles 46, Cal.

B. Panaca, Nev., Oct. 18, 1890. *Studied*: Univ. Paris, France; BMFA Sch.; ASL; Julian Acad., Paris, and with Maurice Denis, Andre Lhote. *Member*: Cal. WC Soc.; AWS; Texas WC Soc.; San Antonio A. Lg.; Texas FA Assn. *Work*: murals, Mus. Natural Hist., Milwaukee, Wis.; Beaver Dam (Wis.) H.S.; and in France. *Exhibited*: PAFA; AIC; Los A. Mus. A.; San Diego FA Soc.; SFMA; Societe des Artistes Francaise, Salon d'Automne, Salon des Tuileries, Paris, France; Texas FA Soc.; San Antonio A. Lg. *Position*: Instr., Layton Sch. A., Milwaukee, Chouinard AI, Los A., Los A. Art Center Sch., San Antonio AI, Texas.

NYME, JOSEPH—*Painter, C.*

79 East Canton St., Boston 18, Mass.

B. Cleveland, Ohio, Apr. 10, 1908. *Studied*: Cleveland Sch. A.; BMFA Sch., and with Henry Keller, Frank Wilcox, Karl Zerbe. *Member*: A. Gld. *Awards*: prizes, Spokane, Wash., 1944; Butler AI, 1940. *Exhibited*: CM, 1940; Carnegie Inst.; Butler AI, and in other national and regional exhibitions.*

OAKLEY, VIOLET—*Painter, S., Des., I., W., L.*

Lower Cogslea, St. George's Rd., Philadelphia 19, Pa.

B. Jersey City, N.J. *Studied*: ASL; PAFA; Drexel Inst.; in Paris, and with Howard Pyle. *Member*: NA; F., Intl. Inst. A. & Lets.; Phila. A. All.; AIA (hon.); Phila. WC Cl.; F., PAFA (Vice-Pres.); Woodmere A. Gal. *Awards*: LL.D., Drexel Inst., 1948; D. Litt., Delaware Col., Newark, Del.; gold and silver medal, St. Louis Expo., 1904; gold medal, PAFA, 1905; gold medal, San F. Expo., 1915; gold medal, Arch. Lg., 1916; Pennell med., PAFA, 1932; gold med., Springside Sch., Phila., 1932; Emily Taylor med., Pa. Soc. Min. P., 1941; special award and citation, PAFA, 1955; prizes, PAFA, 1922, 1940, 1948; Woodmere A. Gal., 1947. *Work*: State Capitol, Harrisburg, Pa.; murals in Governor's Room, Senate Chamber, Supreme Court; mural, mosaic altarpiece, All Angel's Church, N.Y.; other mural paintings, stained glass windows, portraits, panels: Chestnut Hill Acad. Lib.; House of Apostolic Delegate, Wash., D.C.; Cuyahoga County Court House, Cleveland, Ohio; Vassar Col.; United Nations Lib., Geneva, Switzerland; Samuel Fleisher Mem., Phila.; 25 altarpieces, U.S. Army and Navy; First Presbyterian Church, Germantown, Pa.; Moral Re-Armament Hdqs., London, England; Sarah Lawrence Col.; Bryn Mawr Col., and many others. *Exhibited*: Nationally and internationally. Author, I., "The Holy Experiment," 1922; "Law Triumphant," 1932; "Dramatic Outline of Life of Samuel F. B. Morse," 1939; "Life of Jane Addams," 1955, and other books. S., Phila. Medal of Award; Medal of Honor, for Phila. WC Cl.

O'BRIEN, NELL POMEROY [Mrs. John A.]— *Painter, S., L.*

4124 Walmsley Ave., New Orleans 25, La.

B. New Orleans, La. *Studied*: Tulane Univ.; ASL; New Orleans A. & Crafts Sch.; Fontainebleau Sch. FA; Paris, France, and with Wayman Adams. N.Y. *Member*: New Orleans AA (Bd.). *Awards*: prizes, Delgado Mus. A., 1934, 1936, 1940, 1944-1946. *Work*: Browning Lib., Waco, Tex.; La. State Mus.; New Orleans Assn. of Commerce, Court House and Library; Loyola Univ.; Beaumont (Tex.) A. Cl.; Woman's Cl., Beaumont. *Exhibited*: nationally. One-man: Delgado Mus. A.; La. State Mus.; Lake Charles, La.; Beaumont, Galveston, Houston, Tex.; Birmingham, Ala. *Position*: Officer, 1939-1949, Bd. Memb., 1950-1959, New Orleans AA; Instr. A., New Orleans Jr. AA, 1943-1947.

O'CALLAHAN, KEVIN B.—*Designer, Gr., C.*

112 Winspear Ave., Buffalo 1, N.Y.

B. Buffalo, N.Y., Feb. 14, 1902. *Studied*: Cornell Univ.; Carnegie Inst. *Member*: Buffalo Pr. Cl. *Work*: Lib. Cong.; Albright A. Gal.; Farnsworth Mus., Rockland, Me. *Exhibited*: NAD, 1936-1938, 1941, 1942, 1944, 1946; PAFA, 1936, 1938, 1940, 1941, 1943; Phila. Pr. Cl., 1937, 1938, 1940-1944; SAE, 1937, 1940, 1942; Northwest Pr. M., 1942-1944; Denver A. Mus., 1941, 1942; SFMA, 1941-1943; Lib. Cong., 1943, 1944; Laguna Beach, Cal., 1943-1945; Albright A. Gal., 1934, 1935, 1937-1941, 1943-1946. Lectures: Prints & Printmaking. *Position*: Instr., Eng. Sch., Univ. Buffalo, Buffalo, N.Y.*

OCHTMAN, DOROTHY (Mrs. W. A. Del Mar)—
Painter

Stanwich Lane, Greenwich, Conn.

B. Riverside, Conn., May 8, 1892. *Studied*: Smith Col., A.B.; Bryn Mawr Col.; NAD, and abroad. *Member*: ANA; Audubon A.; Hudson Valley AA; Grand Central A. Gal.; Greenwich Soc. A.; All. A. Am.; NAWA. *Awards*: prizes, NAD, 1921, 1924; Greenwich Soc. A., 1930, 1945, 1947, 1951, 1953-1957; Fontainebleau Alum. Assn., 1937; NAWA, 1941, medal, 1952; Guggenheim F., 1927. *Exhibited*: NAD; NAWA; Audubon A.; All. A. Am.; Greenwich Soc. A.; Hudson Valley AA; Silvermine Gld. A.; Conn. Acad. FA; NAC; Montclair A. Mus.; CGA; PAFA; Currier Gal. A.; Toledo Mus. A.; one-man: Grand Central Gal., 1931, 1946; Pasadena AI, 1931; Greenwich Lib., 1941, 1953.

O'CONNOR, HENRY M.—*Painter, Et.*

47 Fifth Ave., New York 3, N.Y.; s. 480 Staffa St., Allenhurst, N.J.

B. Brookline, Mass., Mar. 5, 1892. *Studied*: Mass. Normal A. Sch.; BMFA Sch.; Julian Acad., Paris; & with Joseph De Camp, Frank Benson, Abbott H. Thayer. *Member*: SAGA; SC (Pres.); A. Fellowship. *Awards*: med., Sesqui-Centennial Exp., Phila., 1926. *Work*: Mass. State Capitol; Medical Center, Jersey City, N.J.; Harvard Univ.; Newark Mus. *Exhibited*: NAD, 1927. I., "Book of the Gloucester Fishermen"; "Navy Men."

O'CONNOR, JOHN GERARD—
Painter, Lith., Mus. Dir., Des.

Gallup Museum of Indian Arts & Crafts; h. 710½ East Logan St., Gallup, N.M.

B. Wallasey, Cheshire, England, Feb. 20, 1922. *Studied*: Highlands Univ., Las Vegas, N.M.; Univ. New Mexico. *Award*: prize, New Mexico State Fair, 1950. *Work*: Univ. New Mexico and in private colls. *Exhibited*: N.Y. City Center, 1958; Sun Carnival, 1952; Santa Fe Fiesta; New Mexico State Fair, 1950; Wichita A. & Crafts Exh., 1951; Kappa Pi annual, San Antonio, 1951; one-man: Mus. New Mexico, 1955; Jonson Gal., Univ. New Mexico, 1956. *Positions*: A. Ed. & Illus., Intertribal Indian Ceremonial Magazine, 1956-58; Dir., Gallup Mus. Indian A. & Crafts, Gallup, N.M., 1956- .

ODORFER, ADOLF—*Craftsman, E.*

Fresno State College; h. 4715 North Thorne St., Fresno, Cal.

B. Vienna, Austria, Dec. 6, 1902. *Studied*: in Austria and Germany. *Awards*: prizes for ceramics, Syracuse Mus. FA (several); SFMA (2). *Work*: Syracuse Mus. FA. *Exhibited*: Syracuse Mus. FA Ceramic exhs., 1937-1943, 1945, 1947-1958; Cranbrook Acad. A., 1948, 1950, 1953; Scripps Col., 1949; Los A. County Fair; Denver A. Mus., and others. *Position*: Assoc. Prof. A., Ceramics, Fresno State College, Fresno, Cal., 1948- .

OEHLER, HELEN GAPEN (Mrs. Arnold J.)—
Painter, L., T.

"Blithe Hill," 630 West Blithedale, Mill Valley, Cal.

B. Ottawa, Ill., May 30, 1893. *Studied*: AIC; & with George Elmer Browne. *Member*: All.A.Am.; AWCS; AAPL; NAWA; Audubon A.; Lg. Am. Pen Women; New Jersey WC Soc.; P. & S. Soc. New Jersey; Ridgewood AA. *Exhibited*: NAD, 1941, 1943; Salon d'Automne, 1938; Salon des Artistes Francaise, 1939; AFA traveling exh.; WFNY 1939; Pepsi-Cola, 1945; Dayton AI; Newark Mus.; Audubon A., 1953-1955; All.A.Am., 1953-1955; State Fed. Women's Cl.; Mill Valley (Cal.) Outdoor Exh., 1954 (one-man); New Jersey State Mus.; Montclair A. Mus. *Positions*: Nat. Dir. Am. A. Week, 1949-50; Nat. Sec., AAPL, 1950-52; Trustee, A. Council of New Jersey, 1945-52; Hon. Sec., Art Council of New Jersey, 1952- ; Rep., Outdoor A. Cl. for Civic Improvement, Mill Valley, Cal.; Com. local A. Festival, Am. A. Week.

OENSLAGER, DONALD (MITCHELL)—*Scenic Designer*

Times Bldg., 1475 Broadway; h. 825 Fifth Ave., New York, N.Y.

B. Harrisburg, Pa., Mar. 7, 1902. *Studied*: Harvard Univ. *Member*: Century Assn.; Harvard Cl.; United Scenic A.; Neighborhood Playhouse School for Theatre (Pres.). *Awards*: Sachs FA traveling F.; hon. deg., D.F.A., Col-

orado Col., 1953; Hon. Phi Beta Kappa, Harvard Univ., 1954. Des. over 185 Broadway productions, 1925-1952. *Exhibited*: Nat. Lib., Vienna; MModA; Phillips Acad.; Ohio State Univ. Theatre; Conn. Exh. of Am. Scene Designers; Norton Gal. A., West Palm Beach; Mus. City of N.Y.; Marie Sterner Gal.; Am.-British A. Center; BM; Pratt Inst.; FMA; PMSchIA; Detroit Inst. A., 1956; AFA traveling exh., 1957-58. Author: "Scenery, Then and Now," 1938; "Theatre of Bali," 1941; Ed., "Handbook on Scene Painting," 1952. Contributor to newspapers and theatrical magazines. Lectures: The Theatre; "Stage Design." *Position*: Prof. Stage Design, Yale Univ. Sch. FA, New Haven, Conn.; Bd. Dirs., Parsons Sch. Des., MacDowell Assn., ANTA; Neighborhood Playhouse Sch. of the Theatre; Brooklyn Acad. A. & Sc.; Pratt Inst.; Mun. A. Soc.; American Theatre Wing.

OFFIN, CHARLES Z.—*Critic, Et.*

30 East 60th St. (22); h. 907 Fifth Ave., New York 21, N.Y.

B. New York, N.Y., Feb. 5, 1899. *Studied*: Col. City of N.Y.; NAD; ASL; Ecole des Beaux-Arts, Fontainebleau, France. *Work*: etchings, MMA; N.Y.Pub.Lib. *Exhibited*: one-man exh.: Paris, Barcelona, New York. *Position*: Instr., Col. City of New York, 1932-35; A. Cr., Brooklyn Eagle, 1933-36; Ed., Pub., "Pictures on Exhibit," 1937- ; Dir., Charles Z. Offin A. Fund.

OFFNER, RICHARD—*Educator*

17 East 80th St.; h. 229 East 79th St., New York 21, N.Y.

B. Vienna, Austria, June 30, 1889. *Studied*: Harvard Univ.; Am. Acad. in Rome; Univ. Vienna, Ph.D. *Awards*: F., Am. Acad. in Rome; Sachs F., Harvard Univ. *Author*: "Studies in Florentine Painting," 1927; "Works of Bernardo Daddi," 1930; "A Corpus of Florentine Painting," Sec. III, Vols. I-IV, 1930-1934, Vol. V, 1946; & other works. Contributor to: art magazines. *Position*: Prof., Emeritus, Hist. FA, N.Y. Univ., Inst. FA, New York, N.Y., 1923- .*

OGG, OSCAR—*Designer, W., L., T., Cr.*

345 Hudson St., New York 14, N.Y.; h. Westover Rd., Stamford, Conn.

B. Richmond, Va., Dec. 13, 1908. *Studied*: Univ. Illinois, B.S. in Arch.; Colorado Springs FA Center. *Member*: Grolier Cl.; Typophiles; AIGA; Soc. Typographic A., Chicago. *Author*, I.: "An Alphabet Source Book," 1940; "Lettering as a Book Art," 1946; "The 26 Letters," 1948. Contributor to Encyclopaedia Americana; Art of the Book; Books and Printers; American Artist; Three Italian Writing Masters, 1953; Sixty-three Drawings by Warren Chappell, 1955. Lectures on Calligraphy. *Position*: V.Pres. & A. Dir., Book-of-the-Month Club, New York, N.Y., at present.

O'GORMAN, JACQUI (Mrs. Jacquelen Ann Page)—
Painter

3413 Rosendahl St., San Diego 10, Cal.

B. St. Louis, Mo., May 8, 1930. *Studied*: Immaculate Heart Col., Los A., B.A. *Member*: Cal. WC Soc. *Exhibited*: Cal. WC Soc., 1953, 1954, and traveling exh., 1954; BMA, 1953; New Britain Mus. A., 1953; So. Cal. Pr. M., 1953; Immaculate Heart Col., traveling exhs., 1953-1954; Nat. Orange Show, 1953; Los A. Mus. A., 1953, 1954; San Diego FA Soc., 1953, 1955. *Position*: Instr., A. & Crafts, San Bernardino (Cal.), City Schools, 1953-55.*

O'HANLON, RICHARD EMMETT—*Sculptor, L.*

616 Throckmorton Ave., Mill Valley, Cal.

B. Long Beach, Cal., Oct. 7, 1906. *Studied*: Cal. Col. A. & Crafts; Cal. Sch. FA. *Member*: San F. AA; Marin Soc. A. *Awards*: prizes, Cal. Sch. FA, 1933; San F. AA, 1940; Bender Grant, San F., Cal., 1941; prize, Marin Soc. A., 1946. *Work*: S., Univ. California; SFMA; USPO, Salinas, Cal.; WMAA; AGAA; WMA; Walker A. Center; BMA; Smith Col.; Univ. Cal. at Davis, Cal., and in many private colls. *Exhibited*: nationally; one-man: Willard Gal., 1953; Rochester Mem. A. Gal. *Position*: Asst. Prof. Sculpture, Col. of Arch., Univ. California, Berkeley, Cal., 1950- .

O'HARA, DOROTHEA WARREN—*Potter, P., W.*

Apple Tree Lane, Darien, Conn.

B. Malta Bend, Mo. *Studied*: Munich, Germany; Royal Col. A., London, England; Columbia Univ., and with Lewis Day, C. F. Binns. *Member*: NAC; Pen & Brush Cl.; Keramic Soc. & Des. Gld., N.Y. *Awards*: med., Pan-Pacific Expo., 1915. *Work*: MMA; Cranbrook Acad. A.; Syracuse Mus. FA; William Rockhill Nelson Gal. A.; Mary Atkins Mus., Kansas City; Stamford (Conn.) Mus. A.; Bennington Mus. A. *Exhibited*: Paris Salon; MMA; Harlow Gal.; Grand Central A. Gal.; NAC; Pen & Brush Cl.; and in London, Stockholm, Tokyo.

O'HARA, ELIOT—*Painter, Gr., W., L., T.*

2025 O St., Washington 6, D.C.

B. Waltham, Mass., June 14, 1890. *Studied*: In U.S. and Europe. *Member*: NA; AWS; Wash. WC Cl., Gld. and Landscape Cl.; Laguna Beach AA; Alameda AA; St. Augustine AA. *Awards*: Guggenheim F., 1928; prizes, AWS, 1931; Ogunquit AA; New Haven Paint & Clay Cl.; Phila. WC Cl., 1938; Wash. Landscape Cl., 1946, 1950; Soc. Four A., 1945, 1947; Laguna Beach AA, 1949, 1953-1955; Alabama WC Soc., 1950; Wash. WC Cl., 1952; Soc. Western A., 1953. *Work*: Fitzgerald Mus., Brookline, Mass.; Mappin Gal., Sheffield, England; Guggenheim Mem. Fnd.; Hispanic Soc., N.Y.; BM; A. Gal., La Paz, Bolivia; The White House, Wash., D.C.; LC; Telfair Acad. A.; Choate Sch., Wallingford; Carolina AA; San Diego FA Soc.; Phila. WC Cl.; John Herron AI; Montana State Col.; Indiana Univ.; U.S. State Dept.; Joslyn A. Mus.; CAM; Toledo Mus. A.; Brooks Mem. A. Gal.; Encyclopaedia Britannica; NAD; IBM; BMFA; Norton Gal. A., and many other major colls. *Exhibited*: nationally. Over 500 one-man exhs. Author: "Making Watercolor Behave," 1932; "Making the Brush Behave," 1935; "Watercolor Fares Forth," 1938; "Art Teacher's Primer," 1939; "Watercolor at Large," 1946; "Portraits in the Making," 1948; "Watercolor Portraiture" (with Walker & Short), 1948, 1949; "Watercolor Painting in the United States" (with Shirley P. O'Hara) 1949 (in "Old Water-Colour Society's Club Volume," Pub. London). Maker of 14 films on art. *Position*: Dir., Eliot O'Hara Water Color Sch., Washington, D.C.

O'HARA, (JAMES) FREDERICK—
Graphic Artist, P., E., L.

Route 2, Box 558, Albuquerque, N.M.

B. Ottawa, Canada, Aug. 16, 1904. *Studied*: Mass. Sch. A.; BMFA Sch. *Awards*: prizes, Paige traveling scholarship, BMFA Sch., 1929-31; Tucson, Ariz., 1940; N.M. Print Exh., 1950, 1951, 1953, 1955, 1956; Phila. Pr. Cl., 1956; DMFA, 1956; Rodeo Show, Santa Fe, 1958. *Work*: Springfield Mus. A.; State Collection, Rabat, Morocco; NGA; DMFA; BMA; Santa Barbara Mus. A.; Denver A. Mus.; Mus. New Mexico; LC; CGA; SFMA; MMA; CM; Immaculate Heart Col., Los A.; Four commissions for editions for Intl. Graphic Arts Soc., N.Y. *Exhibited*: PAFA, 1940, 1941; Denver A. Mus., 1945, 1955; AFA traveling exh., 1951; BM, 1951; Phila. Pr. Cl., 1951, 1956; SAM, 1952, 1956; Kennedy Gal.; Gal. Chalette; Landau Gal., Los A.; CM, 1958; USIS, European exh., 1957-58; Pr. Council of Am., 1956-57; Stadtmuseum, Karlsruhe, Germany, 1956 (one-man); DMFA, 1956; one-man: Santa Barbara Mus. A., 1953, 1955; Coronado Sch. FA, 1955; Highlands Univ., Las Vegas, N.M., 1955; Univ. New Mexico, 1955; Yoseido Gal., Tokyo, 1956; Galeria Escondido, Taos, 1957; N.M. Highlands Univ., 1958. I., New Mexico Quarterly, 1951 (15 lithos.). *Position*: Asst. Ed., "Prints in the Desert," Art and Literary quarterly; Visiting Prof. A., 1949-50, 1958, Instr., 1954, Univ. New Mexico; Instr., Coronado Sch. FA, 1953; Memb. Art Adv. Com., Mus. New Mexico A. Gal., 1954-56.

O'HARE, MRS. BERTA MARGOULIES.
See Margoulies, Berta

OJA, ALEXANDER—*Painter, Lith., T.*

301 Lafond Ave., St. Paul 3, Minn.

B. Buhl, Minn., Feb. 26, 1903. *Studied*: St. Paul Sch. A. *Member*: Minnesota AA; St. Paul Assn. P. & S.; AAMus. *Awards*: prizes, Minn. State Fair, 1932, 1941. *Work*: PMA. *Exhibited*: WMAA, 1942. *Position*: Des. Exhibits, St. Paul Science Mus., 1942- ; Instr. A., St. Paul Center, 1938-48; Instr. A., St. Paul Gal. & Sch. A., St. Paul, Minn., 1942-51.

O'KEEFFE, GEORGIA—*Painter*

Abiquiu, N.M.

B. Sun Prairie, Wis., Nov. 15, 1887. *Studied*: AIC; ASL; Univ. Virginia; Columbia Univ. *Member*: Nat. Inst. A. & Let. *Awards*: Hon. degrees, D.F.A., William & Mary Col.; Litt. D., Univ. Wisconsin. *Work*: MMA; MModA; WMAA; BM; AIC; PMG; Detroit Inst. A.; Springfield Mus. A.; CMA; BMFA; PMA; Newark Mus.; John Herron AI, and many others. *Exhibited*: nationally. Paintings first exhibited by Alfred Stieglitz at "291" in 1916-17; yearly exh. 1926-1946, 1950, Intimate Gal., and An American Place. Retrospective one-man exh., BM, 1927; AIC, 1943; MModA., 1946.*

O'KEEFFE, NEIL—*Illustrator, Comm. A.*

440 East 79th St., New York 21, N.Y.

B. Creston, Iowa, Apr. 19, 1893. *Studied*: Washington Univ.; ASL; AIC, and with Robert Henri, George Bellows. *Member*: SI; New Rochelle AA; A. & Writers Assn., N.Y. *Awards*: medal, A. Dir. Cl., Detroit, Mich., 1925; citation, Detroit Hist. Mus., 1953; Freedom Fnd. award, 1950. *Work*: Lib. of Sons of the Revolution, N.Y. *Exhibited*: SI, 1922-1927; New Rochelle AA, 1925-1927, 1950. I., children's books; Creator comic strip, "Dick's Adventures." Contributor to national magazines. *Position*: A. Dir., American Weekly, New York, N.Y., 1945.

OKERBLOOM, CHARLES I., JR.—*Painter, Gr., E.*

Art Department, University of Arkansas; h. 370 Arkansas Ave., Fayetteville, Ark.

B. Harrisburg, Pa., Aug. 13, 1908. *Studied*: Ohio State Univ., B.A.; State Univ. Iowa, M.A. *Work*: Delgado Mus. A.; Columbus Gal. FA; Philbrook A. Center; DMFA; State Univ. Iowa; Springfield (Mo.) Mus. A. *Exhibited*: nationally and regionally. *Positions*: Instr. A., State Univ. Iowa, 1933-42; Univ. Arkansas, Fayetteville, Ark., 1953- .

OLCOTT, LILLIA MORWICK—
Painter, W., E., Des., L.

24 Owego St., Cortland, N.Y.

B. Syracuse, N.Y., June 18, 1879. *Studied*: Syracuse Univ.; N.Y. Univ., B.A., M.A. *Member*: Lg. Am. Pen Women. *Exhibited*: Cortland (N.Y.) Pub. Lib.; Finger Lakes Exh.; Newport Richey, Fla. (one-man); Cortland County Exh. (one-man). Author: several art syllabi, N.Y. State Edu. Dept. Lectures: Decoration of Textiles; American Indian A. & Crafts. *Position*: Specialist in A., N.Y. State Edu. Dept.; Hd. Dept. A., N.Y. State T. Col., Cortland, N.Y. (Retired).

OLD, BERT(RAND) (E.)—*Painter, T.*

502 North Everett St., Stillwater, Minn.

B. St. Paul, Minn., July 10, 1904. *Studied*: Minneapolis Inst. A.; St. Paul Sch. A.; & with Cameron Booth. *Awards*: prize, Minn. State Fair, 1934. *Work*: Univ. Minnesota. *Exhibited*: AIC, 1942; Minn. State Fair, 1944; Minneapolis Inst. A., 1946, & others; Walker A. Center, 1946 (one-man). *Position*: Adv. Production Dept., Andersen Corp., Bayport, Minn.

OLDFIELD, OTIS WILLIAM—*Painter, C., Des., Lith., T.*

968 Union St., San Francisco 11, Cal.

B. Sacramento, Cal., July 3, 1890. *Studied*: Best A. Sch., San F., Cal.; Julian Acad., Paris, France. *Member*: San F. AA. *Awards*: med., prizes, San F. AA, 1925, 1935, 1939; prizes, Springville, Utah; Fnd. Western A., 1934; San F. AA, 1947; Cal. State Fair, 1933. *Work*: BM; SFMA; Palace Legion Honor; murals, Coit Tower, San F., Cal.; windows, San F. Stock Exchange Cl. *Exhibited*: Salon des Independents, Salon d'Automne, Paris, 1912-1924; one-man exh.: San F., Los A., Sacramento, Cal.; Oklahoma; Texas; etc. *Position*: A. Instr., Cal. Sch. FA, San Francisco, Cal., 1925-42; Asst. Prof. Painting & Drawing, Cal. Col. A. & Crafts, Oakland, Cal., 1946-52. Artists Council, San F. AA.*

OLDS, ELIZABETH—*Painter, I., W., L.*

53 East 11th St., New York 3, N.Y.

B. Minneapolis, Minn., Dec. 10, 1897. *Studied*: Univ. Minnesota; Minneapolis Sch. A.; ASL, and with George Luks. *Awards*: Guggenheim F., 1926-27; prizes, Phila. Pr. Cl., 1937; Phila. A. All., 1938; PM competition, "Artist as Reporter," 1940; MModA, 1941; BMA, 1953; medal, Kansas City AI, 1934. *Work*: MMA; MModA; BM; PMA; N.Y. Pub. Lib.; LC; BMA; SAM; SFMA; Glasgow Univ. *Exhibited*: one-man: ACA Gal., 1937-1941, 1950, 1952, 1955. Author, I., "The Big Fire," 1945, Jr. Literary Gld. selection; "Riding the Rails," 1948; "Feather Mountain," 1951; "Deep Treasure," 1958, Junior Literary Guild selection. Illus. to national magazines. Lectures: Origin and Growth of Silk Screen Process; History and Technique of Serigraphy, etc.

OLDS, MARION (Mrs. Reginald B.)—Painter
14720 La Cuarta, Whittier, Cal.
Studied: Univ. Southern California; Otis AI. *Member*: Women Painters of the West; Los Angeles AA. *Awards*: prizes, Denver A. Mus., 1941. *Work*: Chaffey Col., Ontario, Cal. *Exhibited*: Denver A. Mus.; SFMA; Los A. Mus. A., 1935-1952; Santa Barbara Mus. A.; CGA; Pasadena AI, and others.*

OLDS, SARA WHITNEY (Mrs. Robert Zoeller)—
Portrait Painter, T.
Harbor Rd., Route 1, Mount Sinai, L.I., N.Y.
B. Springfield, Ohio, Jan 16, 1899. *Studied*: Carnegie Inst.; Art Inst., Pittsburgh, and with Guiseppi Trotta. *Member*: Art Lg., Long Island. *Awards*: prizes, Mineola Fair, 1944, 1945; Springfield AA, bronze medal, 1952-1954; Art Lg., Long Island, 1945, 1946, 1949, 1950; Stony Brook Mus. A., 1950; Springfield, Ohio, 1951; St. James, Long Island, 1951. *Work*: portraits, Medical Lib., U.S. Army, Wash., D.C.; Warder Pub. Lib., Springfield, Ohio; Station Hospital, Mitchell Field, L.I.; Parrish Mus., and in private coll. *Exhibited*: Art Lg., L.I.; Stony Brook Mus. A.; Old Town A. & Crafts; Springfield AA; one-man: Springfield, Ohio, 1951; New York City, 1951; Cutchogue, L.I., 1952. Specializes in children's portraits. *Position*: Hd. A. Dept., Hewlett Sch. for Girls, East Islip, N.Y.

OLEY, MOSES—Painter, Gr.
108 West 90th St., New York 24, N.Y.
B. Lodz, Poland, May 1, 1896. *Studied*: Grande Chaumiere, Paris; NAD; & in Germany. *Work*: Wood Gal. A., Montpelier, Vt.; Ein-Harod Mus., Israel; Oklahoma Univ.; U.S. Treasury Dept., Wash., D.C.; Oneonta Hospital, N.Y. *Exhibited*: CGA, 1935, 1937; PAFA, 1934, 1935, 1938, 1942; AIC, 1935, 1938, 1940; VMFA, 1938, 1940; Toledo Mus. A., 1936; NAD, 1938, 1940; WMAA, 1938; Phila. A. All., 1937-1939; Oklahoma A. Center, 1939-1941; Am. A. Cong., 1937-1941; GGE, 1939; San F. AA, 1946; ACA Gal., 1934-1946; Minneapolis Inst. A., 1935; Iowa State Univ.; William Rockhill Nelson Gal. A., 1935; Flint Inst. A., 1937; Grand Rapids A. Gal., 1937; Dayton AI, 1937; NAC, 1937; Jewish Mus., N.Y., 1949.

OLINSKY, IVAN G.—Painter, T.
27 West 67th St., New York 23, N.Y.
B. Russia, 1878. *Studied*: NAD; and abroad. *Member*: NA; A. Fund; NSMP; AWS; SC; NAC; All. A. Am.; Lotos Cl.; AFA. *Awards*: prizes, NAD, 1914, 1929, 1931, 1940, 1952, 1953, 1955; SC, 1919, 1936, 1937, 1939; Lyme AA, 1922, 1926, 1930, 1937; NAC, 1931, 1935; gold medal, All. A. Am., 1935; medal, Montclair A. Mus., 1935; Lotos Cl., 1941; De Camp prize, Boston, 1942. *Work*: Joslyn Mus. A.; DMFA; Detroit Inst. A.; Butler AI; Norfolk Mus. A.; Montclair A. Mus.; Everhart Mus., Scranton, Pa.; Beach Mem. Coll., Agricultural Col., Storrs, Conn.; NAD; Lotos Cl.; Century Assn.; NAC; Court House, Brooklyn, N.Y., Dayton AI; Minneapolis Inst. A. *Exhibited*: nationally.

OLIVER, ELISABETH PAXTON (Mrs. Herbert D.)—
Painter
"Fancy Hill," Tryon, N.C.
B. Rockridge County, Va., Jan 28, 1894. *Studied*: Maryland Inst.; in Europe; & with George Elmer Browne. *Member*: NAWA; AAPL; SSAL; Georgia AA; Studio Cl., Atlanta. *Awards*: Lowenstein prize; Atlanta Newspaper Assn. award; Atlanta AA. *Work*: High Mus. A.; Corpus Christi (Tex.) Mus. *Exhibited*: NAWA, 1935-1955; SSAL, 1925-1946; Georgia AA, 1925-1955; High Mus. A., 1925-1955; Salon des Artistes Francaise, Paris; Newhouse Gal. (one-man); Robert Vose Gal.; Atlanta AA; Argent Gal.

OLIVER, FREDERICK W.—Painter
30 Ipswich St., Boston, Mass.; h. 8 Granite St., Rockport, Mass.
B. New York, N.Y., Sept. 4, 1876. *Member*: Rockport AA; Copley Soc., Boston. *Exhibited*: Jordan Marsh, 1945; Rockport AA; etc.

OLIVER, JANE—Painter, Comm. A., I.
Hanzl & Hanzl, Inc., 420 Lexington Ave., New York, N.Y.; h. 20 Park Ave., Maplewood, N.J.
B. West Haven, Conn., Mar. 21, 1921. *Studied*: Franklyn Sch. Prof. A. *Member*: Audubon A.; AWS; NAWA; New Jersey WC Soc.; Essex WC Soc. *Awards*: prizes, Audubon A., 1945, 1953; AWS, 1950; NAWA, 1951, medal, 1952; medal, N.J. WC Soc., 1954. *Work*: Newark Mus.; Abilene (Tex.) Mus. A.; Upsala Col. Mus., East Orange, N.J. *Exhibited*: AWS, 1944-1952; Audubon A., 1945-1952; NAWA, 1949-1952; New Jersey A., 1952; Montclair Mus. A., 1942-1952. Contributor of cover series, "American Scenes," This Week magazine, 1954.

OLMES, MILDRED YOUNG (Mrs. Hugh H.)—
Painter, Ser., C.
1424 24th St., Northeast, Canton 4, Ohio
B. Oil City, Pa., Feb. 12, 1906. *Studied*: Carnegie Inst., A.B.; Tyler Sch. FA, Phila., Pa.; Royal Univ. for Foreigners, Perugia, Italy; private study in Paris, France. *Member*: NSMP; Canton AI. *Awards*: Canton AI, 1944, 1948, 1953; Chester County AA, 1951; Ohio Drawing Exh., 1951; Ohio Valley Exh., 1951; Massillon Mus. A., 1949. *Work*: Massillon Mus. A.; Canton AI; Canton Chamber of Commerce Bldg.; murals, YMCA, West Chester, Pa.; Aultman Hospital, Canton; Toledo Airport; pub. schs., Canton, Massillon, Ohio; Pittsburgh, Pa.; murals, portraits and paintings in private colls. Ohio, New York, Ill., Cal., Ind., etc. *Exhibited*: Paris Salon, 1931; AIC, 1932, 1936; Univ. Alabama; Mississippi AA; Akron AI, 1949, 1950, 1952; Ohio WC Exh., 1950; Ohio Drawing Exh., 1950-1952; Butler AI, 1936-1951; Massillon Mus. A., 1949-1954; CGA, 1951; Canton AI, 1943-1955; Chester County AA, 1943-1952; Ohio Valley Exh., 1951, 1952; North Canton Little Gal., 1952, 1955; Ohio State Fair, 1952.

OLMSTED, ANNA WETHERILL—
Museum Director, W., L., Cr.
407 James St.; h. 832 James St., Syracuse 3, N.Y.
B. Syracuse, N.Y. *Studied*: Syracuse Univ., Col. FA. *Member*: AAMus.; Zonta Int.; Nat. Lg. Am. Pen Women; Professional Women's Lg. Contributor to Journal of Aesthetics, Encyclopaedia of the Arts; Nelson's Encyclopaedia, etc. Lectures: "Contemporary American Ceramics." Founded and organized Ceramic National, 1932. Assembled first exh. Contemporary Ceramics for foreign museum exhibitions, 1937. *Positions*: U.S. Delegate to Int. A. Congress, in Paris, 1937; A. Cr., Syracuse Post Standard, 1928-44; Asst. Dir., 1930, Dir., 1931-1957, Dir. Emeritus, Cur. Dec. Arts, 1957- , Syracuse Mus. FA; A. Cr., Syracuse Herald American, 1945- . Organized first Intl. Ceramic Exh., 1958.

OLSEN, CHRIS E.—
Painter, C., S., Mus. Preparator, L.
Hillside Ave., West Nyack, N.Y.
B. Copenhagen, Denmark, Apr. 8, 1880. *Studied*: Allen's A. Sch., Perth Amboy, N.J.; Mechanics Inst., and with Peter Eggers. *Member*: Scandinavian-Am. *Awards*: prize, Mechanics Inst. *Work*: American Mus. Natural Hist. Hall of Ocean Life; Boston Mus. Science, Science Hall, and in many other museums and colleges in the U.S. *Exhibited*: NAD; High Mus. A.; Scandinavian-Am.; Am. Mus. Natural Hist.; Staten Island Mus. A. & Sc., Arnot A. Gal. Arranged numerous marine exh. in museums. Specializes in undersea painting. Contributor to scientific entomological publications. *Position*: A., Modeler, Am. Mus. Natural Hist., New York, N.Y., 1916-52 (Retired).

OLSEN, EARLE—Painter
247 West 15th St., New York 11, N.Y.
B. Chicago, Ill., Dec. 26, 1926. *Studied*: AIC, B.F.A. *Work*: WMAA. *Exhibited*: WMAA, 1956; Univ. Nebraska, 1957; Illinois Wesleyan Univ., 1957; Washington Univ., St. Louis, 1957; R.I. Sch. Des., 1956; one-man: Bodley Gal., 1955; Borgenicht Gal., 1958.

OLSEN, HARRY EMIL—Painter, I.
200 East 56th St., New York 22, N.Y.; h. 190-17 103rd Ave., Hollis, L.I., N.Y.

B. Brooklyn, N.Y., Sept. 20, 1892. *Studied*: Adelphi Col. *Member*: SC; AWS; All. A. Am.; Phila. WC Cl.; Audubon A. *Awards*: prizes, AWS, 1932; SC, 1937; All. A. Am., 1941; WFNY 1939; PAFA, 1939-1946; Albany Inst. Hist. & A., 1940; Barbizon Plaza, N.Y., 1945. *Exhibited*: AWS, 1932, 1949; SC, 1932, 1950; All. A. Am., 1933-1951; N.Y. State Fair, 1951; Albany Inst. Hist. & A., 1940 (one-man); Barbizon Plaza, 1945 (one-man). *Position*: A. Dept., SARRA Studios, New York, N.Y., at present.*

OLSEN, HERB(ERT) (VINCENT)—Painter, W., L.
Bayberry Lane, Westport, Conn.

B. Chicago, Ill., July 12, 1905. *Studied*: AIC; Am. Acad. A., Chicago. *Member*: ANA; AWS; Phila. WC Soc.; SC; Royal Soc. A., London; Balt. WC Soc.; Conn. WC Soc.; All. A. Am.; SC; Silvermine Gld. A. *Awards*: prizes, NAD, 1949, 1953; AWS, 1951; Hudson Valley AA, 1951, gold medal, 1953; SC, 1951, 1957; silver medal, Swedish-Am. A., 1951, gold medal, 1953; NAC, 1951; New England Exh., 1953; All. A. Am., 1953; Conn. WC Soc., 1954; New Haven R.R. Exh., 1956; Audubon A., 1957; Balt. WC Cl., 1957; AIA, 1957. *Work*: Notre Dame Univ.; Lafayette Mus. A.; Grand Central A. Gal.; Kennedy Gal.; Chicago Gal. Assn.; Doll & Richards, Boston. *Exhibited*: AIC; NAD; Conn. Contemporaries and others. Over 20 one-man exhs. Contributor of illus. to Collier's, American, Outdoor Life and other national magazines. Author: "Water Color Made Easy," 1955.

OLSHAN, BERNARD—Painter, Des.
630 West 135th St., New York 31, N.Y.

B. New York, N.Y., Jan. 31, 1921. *Studied*: Am. A. Sch., and with Fred Peloso, Joseph Solman, Amedee Ozenfant; N.Y. Univ.; Academie Grande Chaumiere, Paris, France. *Member*: AEA. *Work*: in private colls. *Awards*: Emily Lowe award, 1950. *Exhibited*: DMFA; Mortimer Brandt Gal.; RoKo Gal.; WMAA; ACA Gal.; A.F.I. Gal.; Syracuse Univ.; Univ. Miami; Hofstra Col.; Audubon A.; Nat. Soc. Painters in Casein; Art:USA, 1958; 2-man: Ward Eggleston Gal., 1958, one-man: 1952, 1954; 3-man: Westside Gal., 1959. *Position*: Designer, Advertising, Olshan & Michelson, New York, N.Y.

OLSHANSKA, STEPHANIE (Mrs. Stephanie Olshanska-Komarnitsky)—Painter, E., L.
1800 Beaver Grade Rd., Coraopolis, Pa.

B. Galicia, Mar. 23, 1900. *Studied*: Vienna, Austria; ASL; Columbia Univ., B.S., M.A.; Washington Univ.; Cranbrook Acad. A., and with George Elmer Browne. *Member*: AAPL; Montclair AA; AAUW; Am. Lib. Color Slides; Assoc. A. Pittsburgh. *Work*: Cliffside Park Woman's Cl., and in private colls. *Awards*: New Jersey Gal., Newark, 1936. *Exhibited*: Montclair A. Mus.; Newark Mus. A.; NAD; New Jersey Gal.; Provincetown AA; AFA traveling exh., 1939-40; NAC, 1939; Montclair Woman's Cl., 1940; Detroit Inst. A., 1942; Sewickley Acad., Pa., 1950; Allegheny A. Lg.; Terry AI, 1952; A. & Crafts Exh., Moon Township, Pa., 1952-1954; Pittsburgh Airport, 1957; Pittsburgh Playhouse, 1957 (one-man). *Position*: Prof. A., Centenary Col., 1931-35; Instr. A., Sewickley Acad., Pa., 1948-50. Organized Verona-West Essex (N.J.) AA, 1939; Western Pa. Assn., 1958.

OLSON, HENRY (W.)—Painter, E.
3600 Albemarle St., Northwest, Washington 8, D.C.

B. Canton, Ohio, Oct. 19, 1902. *Studied*: Columbus Sch. A.; Corcoran Sch. A.; Otterbein Col., Westerville, Ohio, A.B., B.S.; Ohio State Univ., M.A., Ph.D. *Member*: AAUP; Wash. Landscape Cl., Soc. A., WC Cl., A. Cl. *Awards*: med., Wash. Landscape Cl., 1941, 1944, 1949; prizes, Wash. A. Cl., 1944-1947; Soc. Wash. A., 1947; Outdoor A. Fair, 1954. *Work*: Dunbarton Col., Wash., D.C.; murals, Wilson T. Col. *Exhibited*: Univ. Florence, Italy, 1945 (one-man); Wilson T. Col. (one-man); Soc. Wash. A.; Wash. Landscape Cl.; Wash. WC Cl.; Times-Herald Fair, Beaumont, Tex.; Central Lib., Wash., D.C. (one-man); Wash. A. Cl.; York (Pa.) A. Gal., 1955; Rockport AA, 1957; Harpers Ferry, W. Va., 1958; one-man: Wash. A. Cl., 1958; Wash. WC Cl., 1956-1958; Wash. Landscape Cl., 1956-1958; Soc. Wash. A., 1956-1958. *Position*: Prof., District of Columbia T. Col., Washington, D.C., 1937- ; Chm., Wash. Outdoor A. Fair, 1954; Jury of Selection, Wash. WC Cl., 1950-54.

O'MEARA, MAE (Mary M. Golden O'Meara)—Painter, T., S., L.
40-17 149th Place, Flushing 54, N.Y.

B. Weehawken, N.J. *Studied*: BM Sch.A., with Konzal; and with Guiseppi Trotta, Ben Wilson. *Member*: AAPL; AWS; Catherine L. Wolfe A. Cl.; New Jersey P. & S. Soc.; Com. on A. Edu., MModA; Catholic A. Soc.; Easthampton Gld. Hall AA. *Awards*: prizes, Smithsonian Inst., 1950, 1951; Douglaston A. Lg., 1947, 1948. *Work*: portraits in private colls. *Exhibited*: Smithsonian Inst., 1950; AAPL, 1952-1955; NAC, 1951; Knickerbocker A., 1955; Creative A., 1951; New Jersey Soc. P. & S., 1949, 1950, 1954, 1955; Wolfe A. Cl., 1952-1955; Butler AI, 1954; Kottler Gal., 1952; Gal. "21," 1955; Douglaston A. Lg., 1941-1949; 8th St. Gal., 1953, 1954; Crespi Gal., 1953; Stony Brook Mus. A., 1951, 1952; Hudson Valley AA, 1950-1952. *Position*: Dir., N.Y. State Chap., AAPL; Chm., Am. A. Week, Queens & Long Island, 1947-58; Com. Queens Botanical Garden Soc. A. Festival, 1948-58; Fndr., Dir., Flushing A. Center; Pres., A. Lg. of Long Island, 1949-51.

O'NEAL, FRANK E.—Cartoonist
Carmel Valley, Cal.

B. Springfield, Mo., May 9, 1921. *Studied*: Jefferson Machamer Sch. A. *Member*: Carmel AA. Contributor cartoons to Sat. Eve. Post; Colliers; Redbook; Better Homes & Gardens; Cosmopolitan; Look; Esquire and other national magazines; King Features Syndicate, etc. Syndicated comic strip "Short Ribs," syndicated by NEA Service.

O'NEAL, WILLIAM BAINTER—Educator, Mus. C., W.
Fayerweather Hall, University of Virginia; h. 714 Rugby Rd., Charlottesville, Va.

B. Zanesville, Ohio, Aug. 21, 1907. *Studied*: Carnegie Inst., B. Arch.; PAFA; Ohio State Univ. *Member*: Va. Chptr. AIA; Soc. Arch. Historians. *Position*: Assoc. Prof., Sch. Arch., Cur., Univ. Va. Mus. FA, Univ. Virginia, Charlottesville, Va.*

O'NEIL, JOHN—Painter, E.
University of Oklahoma, Norman, Okla.

B. Kansas City, Mo., June 16, 1915. *Studied*: Univ. Oklahoma, B.F.A., M.F.A.; Colorado Springs FA Center; Univ. Florence, Italy. *Work*: SAM; Joslyn A. Mus.; Laguna Beach AA; Dallas Mus. FA; Kansas State Col.; Philbrook A. Center; Denver A. Mus. *Exhibited*: Abstract & Surrealist A., Chicago, 1947; Color Lith. Exh., Cincinnati, 1950; Carnegie Inst., 1941; Colorado Springs FA Center, 1939, 1940, 1946-1950; Denver A. Mus., 1940, 1946-1950, 1955; Kansas City AI, 1953; Assn. Okla. A., 1953; AFA, 1954; Southwest Artists, Santa Fe, 1957. *Position*: Dir. A. Sch., Oklahoma, Norman, Okla.

ONETO, JOSEPH A.—Painter
2029 Filbert St., San Francisco 23, Cal.

B. San Francisco, Cal., May 27, 1911. *Member*: AAPL; San F. AA; Marin Soc. A. *Awards*: prizes, Cal. State Fair, 1948, 1950; San F. Art Festival, 1951; Marin Soc. A., 1949, 1950; San F. AA, 1952. *Work*: Cal. State Agriculture Comm.; Crocker A. Gal. *Exhibited*: Carnegie Inst., 1952; PAFA, 1950, 1951, 1953; AIC, 1951; Cal. PLH, 1949, 1951, 1952, 1955 (one-man); AFA traveling exh., 1952; Terry AI, 1952; Cal. State Fair, 1948-1951, 1954; Denver A. Mus., 1948-1951, 1953, 1954, 1955; Butler AI, 1953, 1954, 1955; Arizona State Fair, 1948; Santa Cruz A. Lg., 1948, 1949; San F. AA, 1948, 1953; Colorado Springs FA Center, 1955; San F. Art Festival, 1948-1951.*

ONTON, SOPHIE W(ALL) (Mrs.)—Painter, Comm., T.
235 Old Post Road, Nixon, N.J.

B. New York, N.Y., May 8, 1907. *Studied*: Parsons Sch. Des.; Traphagen Sch. Fashion; Indst. Sch. A., and with Howard Giles. *Member*: New Brunswick A. Center. *Award*: prize, Traphagen Sch. Fashion. *Work*: Am. Appliance Corp., Miami, Fla.; Insular, San Juan, Puerto Rico; Hall of Art, Miami. *Exhibited*: Fed. A. Lg. of Florida; Miami A. Lg.; Women's Cl., Miami; Raritan A. Exh., Arnold Constable, N.Y., 1957-58; New Brunswick A. Center, 1956-1958; Crespi Gal., 1958; Burr Gal., 1958. *Position*: Instr. A., Edison Township Sch. System, N.J., 1954-1956.

OPDYCKE, LEONARD—*Educator*
Department of Fine Arts, Harvard University, Cambridge, Mass.
Position: Chm., Fine Arts Dept., Harvard Univ.*

OPPENHEIM, S. EDMUND—*Portrait Painter*
40 West 57th St.; h. 64 West 9th St., New York 11, N.Y.
Studied: NAD; ASL. *Member*: SC; All. A. Am.; Grand Central A. Gal.; AAPL; Hudson Valley AA; A. Fellowship. *Awards*: prizes, All. A. Am., 1950; Hudson Valley AA, 1957; AAPL, 1956; SC. *Exhibited*: NAD; Grand Central A. Gal. (one-man); Audubon A.; All. A. Am.; Hudson Valley AA; AAPL; Mus. of the City of New York; Provincetown AA; Chrysler Mus. A. *Work*: The White House, Wash., D.C.; West Point Military Acad.; NAD; Grand Central A. Gal.; Oxford Paper Co.; Sylvania Electric Co.; Otis Elevator Co.; Fed. Bank & Trust Co., and others.

OPPENHEIMER, SELMA L.—*Painter*
3506 Bancroft Rd., Baltimore 15, Md.
B. Baltimore, Md., Jan. 13, 1898. *Studied*: Goucher Col., A.B.; Maryland Inst. *Member*: AEA (Pres. Md. Chptr., 1953-1955); Balt. WC Soc.; A. Un., Balt.; AFA; NAWA; Nat. Lg. Am. Pen Women. *Awards*: med., Maryland Inst., 1933; BMA, 1935, 1938; NAWA, 1952; Maryland Fed. Women's Cl., 1952. *Work*: Pub. Schs., Balt., Md. *Exhibited*: PAFA; VMFA; AIC; CGA; MModA; NAWA; PC; NAD; BMA; Rockefeller Center, N.Y.; Friends of Art, Balt.; Peale Mus. A., Balt.; Hagerstown, Md.; Western Maryland Col., Westminster; Goucher Col.; Southern States Exh., 1947; Midtown Gal.; Phila. A. All., 1940; PC; Contemp. Gal., Atlantic City, 1955; Smithsonian Inst., 1957, 1958; one-man: BMA, 1941; Hilltop Sch. A., 1954. *Position*: Memb. A. Com., BMA, 1953-55.

ORB, OVAN (JOHN CARBONE)—
    Sculptor, P., L., T., C.
Sunset Rd., Blauvelt, N.Y.; also, 122 East 11th St., New York 3, N.Y.
B. Cranston, R.I., Mar. 2, 1911. *Studied*: R.I. Sch. Des.; BAID; & with Leo Lentelli, Edward McCartan, Ossip Zadkine. *Member*: R.I. Abstract A.; Providence AC; A. & W. Un., Rhode Island. *Awards*: prize, R.I. Sch. Des., 1928; R.I. Col. Edu., 1941. *Work*: S., Technical H.S. Lib., Providence, R.I.; Roger Williams Park, Jamestown, R.I.; R.I. Sch. Des. *Exhibited*: Providence AC, 1937-1941; R.I. Sch. Des., 1927-1943; Brown Univ., 1941; R.I. Col. Edu., 1940; Contemporary A. Gal., 1944; Guggenheim Mus. A., 1953; New Sch. Social Research, 1954; Open Circle A. Gal., Los A., 1957. Lectures: Sculpture.

ORFUSS, ELSIE—*Painter, Des.*
55 East 10th St. (3); h. 7 Cooper Road, New York 10, N.Y.
B. Harrisburg, Pa., Oct. 4, 1913. *Studied*: Grand Central Sch. A.; Hans Hofmann Sch. FA; ASL; and in Europe. *Member*: NAWA; AEA; Provincetown AA; ASL. *Award*: bronze medal, NAWA, 1956. *Exhibited*: NAWA, 1956-1958; N.Y. City Center, 1954; Argent Gal., N.Y., 1957. *Work*: Chrysler Coll.

ORLING, ANNE—*Painter*
69 Shelter Lane, Roslyn Heights, L.I., N.Y.
B. New York, N.Y. *Studied*: with Paul Wood, Morris Davidson, Larry Rivers. *Member*: A. All. of Am. *Exhibited*: N.Y. City Center, 1954-1958; Contemp. A. Gal., 1956, 1957; Suffolk Mus. A., Stony Brook, N.Y., 1957; Country A. Gal., Westbury, N.Y., 1957.

ORNSTEIN, JACOB ARTHUR—*Painter, W., L., E.*
141-55 72nd Crescent, Flushing 67, L.I., N.Y.
B. Brooklyn, N.Y., June 7, 1907. *Studied*: Parsons Sch. Des.; N.Y. Univ., B.S., M.A.; & with Morris Davidson. *Member*: A.T. Gld.; AEA. *Exhibited*: All. A. Am., 1939; San Diego FA Soc., 1941; AWCS, 1942; Mississippi AA, 1942, 1943; Denver A. Mus., 1942; Elisabet Ney Mus., 1943; Newport AA, 1944; BM, 1941; Brooklyn SA, 1942. Author, I., "Lettering for Fun," 1939; "Paintbrush Fun for Home Decoration," 1944. *Position*: Instr., 1935-46, Hd. A. Dept., 1946-1954, Andrew Jackson H.S., St. Albans,

L.I., N.Y.; Pres. A. Chm. Assn., Bd. Edu., New York, N.Y., 1948-50; Feature writer for "High Points," Bd. Edu., New York, N.Y., 1950-58; Panel Member, Nat. A. Edu. Assn., 1951; Principal, East Elmhurst Jr. H.S., New York, N.Y., 1954- ; Nat. Com. on A. Edu.; Chm., A. Section, N.Y. Soc. for Experimental Study of Edu.; Assoc. Ed., "Intercom," Bd. of Edu., N.Y., 1957- .

ORR, ELEANOR MASON—*Miniature Painter*
112 Homer St., Newton Centre, Mass.
B. Newton Centre, Mass., Aug. 15, 1902. *Studied*: BMFA Sch.; & with Annie Hurlburt Jackson. *Member*: Alumni Assn., Sch. Mus. FA.; Women's Com., BMFA. *Work*: many portraits of servicemen at Marine Hospital, Brighton, Mass.; Union Service Cl., Boston; Cushing General Hospital, Framingham, Mass.; 500 portraits, including newspaper series for Waltham Tribune, 1946. *Exhibited*: PAFA, 1925, 1926, 1932, 1941; ASMP, 1926, 1935; Brooklyn Soc. Min. P., 1926, 1938; Grace Horne Gal., 1926; Newton Centre Woman's Cl., 1925-1928, 1932, 1934-1936; Newtonville Lib., 1943 (one-man); Alumni Assn., BMFA Sch., 1954.

ORR, ELLIOT—*Painter*
733 Main St., Chatham, Mass.
B. Flushing, N.Y., June 26, 1904. *Studied*: Grand Central A. Sch. with George Ennis, Charles Hawthorne, George Luks, and others. *Member*: Cape Cod AA; Provincetown AA. *Awards*: prizes, BMA, 1930; Cape Cod AA, 1948. *Work*: BM; PMG; Spokane A. Mus.; WMAA; BMFA; Detroit Inst. A. *Exhibited*: MMA, 1950; Carnegie Inst.; PAFA; WMAA; Boston A. Festival; Chrysler Mus. A.; Univ. Illinois; VMFA; MModA; CGA; AIC, and other national exhs. One-man: Contemporary A., 1931; Balzac Gal., 1932; Macbeth Gal., 1936; Kleeman Gal., 1941, 1942; Babcock Gal., 1948; Mellon Gal., Phila., 1934; Rochester Mem. A. Gal., 1937; Cape Cod AA, 1955; Country A. Gal., Westbury, N.Y., 1956.

ORR, FORREST (WALKER)—
    Painter, I., Comm., Des., C.
Boardman St., Norfolk, Mass.
B. Harpswell, Me., May 5, 1895. *Studied*: Portland (Me.) Mus. Sch. A.; ASL, with George Bridgman, Frank DuMond, Harvey Dunn. *Member*: Gld. Boston A.; Boston Soc. WC Painters; Maine WC Soc.; AWS. *Awards*: prize, North Shore AA, 1945; AWS, 1948; NAD, 1956 (purchase). *Work*: BMFA; Farnsworth Mus. A., Rockland, Me. *Exhibited*: Boston Soc. WC Painters, annually; AWS, annually; NAD; North Shore AA; Gld. Boston A.; Maryhill Mus., Maryhill, Wash.; Maine WC Soc.; Portland A. Festival; Bates Col.; Boston A. Festival, 1953-1955; Portland, Me., 1955. I., juvenile books, fiction. Contributor to national magazines.

ORTLIP, AIMEE E. (Mrs. H. W.)—*Painter, E.*
Houghton College, Houghton, N.Y.
B. Philadelphia, Pa., Apr. 21, 1888. *Studied*: PAFA. *Member*: CAA. *Award*: Cresson traveling scholarship, PAFA, 1909. *Exhibited*: NAD; Montclair A. Mus.; All. A. Am. *Position*: Assoc. Prof. A., Houghton Col., Houghton, N.Y.

ORTLIP, H. WILLARD—*Painter, E.*
Houghton College, Houghton, N.Y.
B. Norristown, Pa., Mar. 28, 1886. *Studied*: PAFA, and with William Chase, Henry McCarter, Sargent Kendall, Cecilia Beaux. *Member*: All. A. Am.; NSMP. *Awards*: Cresson traveling scholarships, 1908, 1909; prizes, PAFA; medal, Montclair A. Mus., 1936. *Work*: church murals, Buffalo, Johnson City, N.Y.; Camden, N.J.; Chester, Pa.; murals, First Nat. Bank, Huntington, L.I.; Asbury Theological Seminary, Wilmore, Ky.; Wesleyan Methodist Church, Akron, Ohio; Wesleyan Church, Florence, N.J.; portraits: Chamber of Commerce, Pub. Lib., York, Pa.; Woman's Cl., Hackensack, N.J.; Fuller Seminary, Pasadena, Cal.; Country Club, York, Pa. *Exhibited*: All. A. Am.; WFNY 1939; SC; Rundel Mem. Gal., Rochester, N.Y.; David A. Howe Pub. Lib., Wellsville, N.Y. *Position*: Assoc. Prof., Emeritus, Port. Painting, Houghton Col., Houghton, N.Y.

ORTMAYER, CONSTANCE—Sculptor, E.

773 Antonette Ave., Winter Park, Fla.

B. New York, N.Y., July 19, 1902. *Studied*: Royal Acad. FA, Vienna, Austria; Master Sch., Vienna, Austria. *Member*: NSS; Fla. Fed. A.; Fla. A. Group. *Awards*: prizes, NAD, 1935; WMAA, 1940; Fla. Fed. A., 1948; Dec. of Honor, Rollins Col., 1947. *Work*: Brookgreen Gardens, S.C.; Am. Numismatic Soc., N.Y.; S., reliefs, USPO, Arcadia, Fla.; Scottsboro, Ala. *Exhibited*: PAFA, 1934, 1935; WMAA, 1940; Arch. Lg., 1937; BM, 1933; WFNY 1939; Fla. Fed. A., Orlando, Daytona Beach, Jacksonville, Sarasota, Bradenton, Fla.; Winter Haven, Palm Beach, Miami, Fla.; Morse Gal. A., Winter Park. *Position*: Prof. S., Rollins Col., Winter Park, Fla., 1937- .

OSBORNE, LUE—Painter, Eng.

45 Tieman Place, New York 27, N.Y.

B. Belleville, Ill. *Studied*: AIC, and with Robert Henri. *Member*: Audubon A.; AEA. *Exhibited*: CGA; BM; Balzac Gal.; Morton Gal.; Contemporary A. Gal.; Audubon A.; Weyhe Gal.; WMAA; Ferargil Gal.; Geneva, Ill.; City Lib., Batavia, Ill.; Regional A. Gal., N.Y.

OSBORNE, ROBERT LEE—Painter, T.

Central High School; h. 5001 Warren Dr., Evansville, Ind.

B. Chandler, Ind., June 24, 1928. *Studied*: Indiana Univ., B.S., with Pickens, Marx, Engel, Ballinger and Hope; Univ. Iowa, with Lechay, Hecksher. *Member*: AEA; Evansville State T. Assn.; NEA. *Awards*: Gold Key award, Evansville, Ind., 1946; Indiana Univ., 1952. *Exhibited*: CM, 1955; John Herron AI, 1955; Tri-State Exh., 1950-1955; Evansville Col., 1955 (one-man). I., "Organization of Aquatic Clubs," 1955. *Position*: Instr., Evansville Pub. Schs., and Evansville Col., Indiana.*

OSBORNE, ROLAND DONOVAN—Painter

102 Lowry Drive, West Milton, Ohio

B. Richmond, Ind., Sept. 8, 1904. *Member*: Indiana A. Cl.; Brown County Gallery Assn. *Awards*: prizes, John Herron AI, 1948; Hoosier Salon, 1950; Indiana A. Cl., 1951-1954, 1957. *Work*: DePauw Univ.; Richmond AA; Tri-Kappa Coll.; Indiana Univ.; Soldier's and Sailor's Mem. Coll., Knightstown. *Exhibited*: NGA, 1949; CM, 1947, 1948; Dayton AI, 1956, 1957; Hoosier Salon, 1949-1957; John Herron AI, 1947-1956; Indiana A. Cl., 1949-1957.

OSHIVER, HARRY J.—Painter, Des., Typographer

802 Chestnut St.; h. 6903 Ardleigh St., Philadelphia, Pa.

B. Moscow, Russia, Feb. 14, 1888. *Studied*: Spring Garden Inst., with Franz Lesshaft; PMSchIA; PAFA, with Hugh Breckenridge, Henry McCarter, Daniel Garber. *Member*: F., PAFA; Phila. Gr. A. Forum; Phila. Printing Industries. *Awards*: Cresson traveling scholarships, PAFA, 1924, 1925; John Frederick Lewis award, PMSchIA; Direct Mail Adv. awards, 1928, 1929; medal, Phila. Sketch Cl., 1930. *Work*: Franklin Inst., Phila., Pa.; Jewish Mus., N.Y.*

OSTENDORF, SISTER CAMILLE—

Teacher, P., Des., Gr., C.

Providence High School, 119 South Central Park Blvd., Chicago 24, Ill.

B. Vincennes, Ind., Jan. 19, 1901. *Studied*: St. Mary-of-the-Woods Col., B.A.; Northwestern Univ., M.A.; AIC; Am. Acad. A., Chicago; & with Oscar Gross. *Member*: Indianapolis AA; Hoosier Salon; Indiana A. Cl. *Exhibited*: Hoosier Salon, 1935, 1940; John Herron AI, 1934, 1935, 1942; Indiana A. Cl., 1935-1939; First Archdiocesan Religious Art Exh., Wash., D.C., 1958. *Position*: A. Instr., Providence H.S., Chicago, Ill.

OSTROWSKY, ABBO—Painter, Et., T.

95-28 67th Ave., Forest Hills, L.I., N.Y.

B. Elisabetgrad, Russia, Oct. 23, 1889. *Studied*: NAD; Col. City of N.Y.; & in Russia. *Member*: SAE; A. Lg. Am. *Awards*: prize, SAE, 1937. *Work*: Lib. Cong.; Bibliotheque Nationale, Paris; Mus. Western A., Moscow; Lincoln Univ.; Bezalel Mus.; Israel; Am. Fed. Labor, Wash., D.C.; MMA; Tel-Aviv Mus., Israel. *Exhibited*: NAD; PAFA; AIC; Los A. AA; Mus. Western A., Moscow;

SAE; Phila. Pr. Cl.; Phila. A. All.; BMA, 1931 (one-man); U.S. Nat. Mus., 1931 (one-man); Victoria & Albert Mus., London; Oslo Mus., Norway. *Position*: Fndr., Educational Alliance Art Sch., 1914-55, Dir. Emeritus, since 1955.

OSVER, ARTHUR—Painter

50 Victory Blvd., Staten Island 1, N.Y.

B. Chicago, Ill., July 26, 1912. *Studied*: Northwestern Univ.; AIC, and with Boris Anisfeld. *Member*: AEA; Audubon A. *Awards*: Raymond traveling F., 1936; medal, PAFA, 1946; VMFA, 1944; prizes, Pepsi-Cola, 1944; Audubon A.; Critic's Show, N.Y., 1946; Guggenheim F., 1949-51; Prix de Rome, 1952, 1953. *Work*: MModA; Pepsi-Cola Coll.; WMAA; Davenport Mun. A. Gal.; Peabody Mus., Salem, Mass.; PAFA; MMA; PMA; Toledo Mus. A.; Mus. FA of Houston; Walker A. Center; Colorado Springs FA Center; Montclair A. Mus.; CAM; Delgado Mus. A.; Sarah Lawrence Col.; Univ. Cincinnati; Geo. Washington Univ.; Univ. Georgia; Univ. Syracuse; Univ. Illinois; Univ. Nebraska; Univ. Michigan; IBM; Mus. Mod. A., Rio de Janeiro. *Exhibited*: AIC, 1938, 1939, 1942, 1943, 1945; PAFA, 1940, 1944, 1946; GGE, 1939; Carnegie Inst., 1944-1946; VMFA, 1944, 1946; WMAA, 1944, 1945; Grand Central A. Gal., 1947; one-man: Fairweather-Garnett Gal., Evanston, 1954; Univ. Chattanooga, 1948; Univ. Syracuse, 1949; Fairweather-Hardin Gal., Chicago, 1955; Grand Central Moderns, 1949, 1951, 1957; Univ. Hamline (Minn.), 1950; Univ. Florida, 1952. *Position*: Instr. Painting, BM A. Sch., 1949-51; Columbia Univ., 1952; Univ. Florida, 1954-55; Visiting Critic in Painting, Yale Univ., 1956-57; Painter-in-Res., Am. Acad. in Rome, 1957-58; Instr., Painting, CUASch., New York, N.Y., at present.

OSVER, MRS. ARTHUR. See Betsberg, Ernestine

OTIS, GEORGE DEMONT—Painter, Et., L.

Otis Studio, 907 Sir Francis Drake Blvd., Kentfield, Cal.

B. Memphis, Tenn., Sept. 21, 1879. *Studied*: AIC; Chicago Acad. FA; CUASch; ASL; & with John Carlson. *Member*: Chicago SA; Palette & Chisel Cl., Chicago; Soc. for Sanity in Art. *Work*: AIC; Hackley A. Gal.; & other galleries & museums in U.S. & abroad. Series of watercolors of Indians of Ariz., New Mexico and Mexico. Lectures on these at schools and clubs.

OTT, PETERPAUL—Sculptor, C., Gr., L., T.

390 Hauser St., Los Angeles, Cal.

B. Pilsen, Czechoslovakia, June 4, 1895. *Studied*: in Dresden, Germany; Emmerson Univ., Los A., Cal.; CUASch; & with Archipenko. *Member*: Laguna Beach AA. *Awards*: prizes, small sculpture comp., N.Y., 1930, 1931; Chicago A. Group, 1932; Evanston, Ill., 1934-1936, 1938; AIC, 1934; Laguna Beach AA, 1943, 1944; & numerous awards in Germany. *Work*: S., decorations, portrait busts, reliefs; Greater New York Savings Bank, Brooklyn, N.Y.; Massillon (Ohio) Mus.; Lane Tech. H.S. Lib., Chicago; U.S. Govt.; USPO, Oak Park, Chicago, Plano, Ill.; & many works abroad. *Exhibited*: Arch. L., 1928-1930; Soc. Indp. A. 1929; Boston Arch. Cl., 1929; Ferargil Gal., 1929; Montclair A. Mus., 1929; NAD, 1929, 1930; NAC, 1929; Palace Legion Honor, 1929; CAA traveling exh., 1930 PAFA, 1931-1933; AIC, 1931-1940; Evanston (Ill.) Acad. FA, 1932 (one-man), 1933-1940; Chicago SA, 1935-1937, 1939, 1940; PMA, 1940; Carnegie Inst., 1940; Laguna Beach AA, 1941-1946; & many others.*

OUDIN, DOROTHY SAVAGE—Painter

Cooperstown, N.Y.

B. Baltimore, Md., July 19, 1898. *Studied*: PAFA; & with Garber, Carles, Hawthorne, Adams. *Member*: Cooperstown AA. *Awards*: F., PAFA; med., 1932, prize, 1924, Balt., Md. *Exhibited*: NAD; AIC; PAFA; Phila. AC; BMA; Balt. Charcoal Cl.; Maryland Inst.; one-man exh.: Wash. AC; Schenectady Studio Cl.; Norfolk A. Corner; F., PAFA.*

OZENFANT, AMEDEE J.—Painter, W., E., L.

Palais de Provence, Cannes, France

B. Saint Quentin, France, April 15, 1886. *Studied*: in France. *Member*: Fed. Mod. P. & S. *Awards*: Legion d'Honneur, France, 1922. *Work*: MMA; AIC; SFMA; Mus. Art Moderne, Paris; Providence, R.I.; Moscow, Russia; Phila., Pa.; San Francisco, Cal.; Wash., D.C.; Stockholm, Sweden; Chicago, Ill.; New York, N.Y.; Minneapolis, Minn. *Exhibited*: Carnegie Inst.; WFNY 1939; and in museums throughout the U.S. Contributor to L'Encyclopedie Francaise, 1935; L'Encyclopedie Photographique de L'Art, 1936; and others. Ed., "L'Esprit Nouveau." Author: "Apres le Cubisne"; "Foundations of Modern Art"; "Peinture Moderne"; "Leben und Gestaltung"; "Journey Through Life." *Positions*: L., French Inst., Univ. Paris, 1936-38; Prof. A., Univ. Washington, 1938-39; L., New Sch. for Social Research, N.Y., 1938-39; Univ. Michigan, 1940; Yale Univ., 1938-41; CUASch., 1939-40; Harvard Univ., 1941; Hd., Ozenfant Sch. FA, New York, N.Y. 1939-1955; Atelier Ozenfant, Cannes, France.

OZIER, KEN(NETH) (H).—
Painter, Et., Lith., Des., W.
Institute for American Universities, 21 Rue Gaston-de-Saporta, Aix-en-Provence, France

B. Cincinnati, Ohio, Feb. 12, 1905. *Studied*: Univ. Cincinnati; Cincinnati A. Acad.; PAFA; George Washington Univ.; & with Leon Kroll, Barse Miller, & others. *Member*: Cincinnati Professional A.; Cincinnati AC. *Awards*: F., PAFA; prize, Wash., D.C. Open-Air Show, 1944. *Work*: murals, Woodward H.S., Union Central Annex Bldg., Pub. Lib., Univ. Cincinnati, all of Cincinnati, Ohio; etching, Old Kentucky Home Mus., Bardstown, Ky. *Exhibited*: Los A. Mus. A., 1936; Northwest Pr. M., 1941; Southern Pr. M., 1935, 1941; AIC, 1939, 1940; Ohio Pr. M., 1935, 1941; Ohio WC Soc., 1935-1939; PAFA, 1940; F., PAFA, 1931-1940; Wash. WC Cl., 1942, 1943; PMG, 1942; CM, 1938-1941, 1954; Wash., D.C. Open-Air A. Exh., 1944. I., "Primitive & Pioneer Sports," 1937; "The Biology and Chemotherapy of Infections with Plasmodium Cynomolgi." Creator of "Anatomical Mannikin" for use in Cincinnati Pub. Schs. *Position*: Fndr., Dir., Instr., Children's Sketch Cl., Cincinnati, Ohio; Pres., Cincinnati Prof. A., 1950-52.*

OZMUN, PAULINE GRAFF (Mrs. Donald Charles)—
Painter
Land of Oz Farm, Mt. Prospect, Ill.

B. Evanston, Ill., Mar. 20, 1902. *Studied*: Northwestern Univ.; AIC; & with Andre L'Hote, Hans Hofmann. *Exhibited*: AIC, 1935-1946; Chouinard AI, Los A., 1956 (one-man); Montana State Mus., Helena, 1957 (one-man).

PACE, MARGARET (Mrs. David)—Painter, C., T.
208 Morningside Dr., San Antonio 9, Tex.

B. San Antonio, Tex., Dec. 9, 1919. *Studied*: Newcomb Col., B.F.A., and with Will Stevens, Etienne Ret, Xavier Gonzalez. *Member*: San Antonio A. Lg.; Texas FA Assn.; River A. Group; Texas WC Soc.; Contemporary A. Group; San Antonio Craft Gld. *Awards*: Charles Rosen award, 1947; Henry Steinbomer award. Texas WC Soc., 1949; Emma Freeman award, 1951; Texas Craft Exh., 1957; Texas FA, 1958. *Work*: in private colls. *Exhibited*: Winston-Salem, N.C., 1945; Texas FA Assn., 1947, traveling exh., 1954-1958; SFMA, 1948; Texas A. & M. Col., 1949; Texas WC Soc., 1950-1958; Miami Beach, 1950; Witte Mem. Mus., 1952 (one-man). *Position*: Instr., San Antonio AI.

PACHNER, WILLIAM—Painter, Lith., T.
Woodstock, N.Y.; Clearwater, Fla.

B. Brtnice, Czechoslovakia, Apr. 7, 1915. *Studied*: Kunstgewerbe Schule, Vienna, Austria. *Member*: AEA; Woodstock AA. *Awards*: prize, Nat. Inst. A. & Let.; Atlanta AA, 1958; New Orleans AA, 1958; Fla. State Fair, 1958; Sarasota AA, 1958 (purchase). *Work*: Milwaukee AI; Ain-Harod Mus., Israel; Florida Gulf Coast A. Center; Chrysler Coll. *Exhibited*: Carnegie Inst., 1948; WMAA, 1948-1951, 1958; CGA, 1949, 1951; Am. Acad. A. & Let., 1949; PAFA, 1950; Univ. Colorado, 1951; Springfield Mus. A., 1951; Witte Mem. Mus.; Albany Inst. Hist. & A.; Assoc. Am. A., 1949; Weyhe Gal., 1948; Ganso Gal., 1951, 1955 (one-man); Sarasota AA, 1953 (one-man), 1958; AFA traveling exh.; Provincetown A. Festival, 1958; Art:USA, 1958; Ringling Mus. A., 1955. Contributed article to "The Art of the Artists," 1951. Illus. to leading national magazines. *Position*: Dir., own art school, Clearwater, Fla.

PACKARD, EMMY LOU—Painter, C., Gr., I.
69 Water St., San Francisco, Cal.

B. Imperial Valley, Cal., 1914. *Studied*: Univ. California, Berkeley; Cal. Sch. FA., and in Europe. *Member*: San F. AA; San F. Women A. *Awards*: prizes, San F. Women A., 1942, 1955, 1956; Gump award, 1947; Cal. State Fair, 1948; San Francisco A. Commission, 1951, 1953, 1954; Oakland A. Festival, 1958. *Work*: prints, Princess Kaiulani Hotel, Honolulu; mosaic mural, Hillcrest Elem. Sch., San Francisco; mural panels, SS "Mariposa"; woodcuts, SS "Mariposa" and SS "Monterey"; wood figures with mosaic, SS "Lurline"; Inlaid linoleum back-bar for SS "Matsonia"; other work, Rotunda Gal., San F.; AGAA; Achenbach Fnd., San F. *Exhibited*: Stendahl Gal., Los A., 1941; Rotunda Gal., San F., 1946; Raymond & Raymond Gal., 1946; AGAA, 1947; 3-man, SFMA, 1942; Cal. State Fair, 1948; San F. Women A., 1942, 1955, 1956; Oakland A. Festival, 1958; one-man: SFMA, 1942; Raymond & Raymond Gal., 1942, 1945.

PACKER, CLAIR LANGE (Mr.)—
Painter, Comm. A., Des., Cart., I.
3307 East 5th Place, Tulsa 12, Okla.

B. Geuda Springs, Kans., Aug. 27, 1901. *Studied*: Univ. New Mexico, and with Millard Sheets, Barse Miller, Kenneth Adams, Victor Higgins, O. E. Berninghaus, and others. *Member*: Tulsa A. Gld. *Exhibited*: Witte Mem. Mus.; Philbrook A. Center; Dallas Mus. FA; Terry AI; Mus. FA of Houston; Elisabet Ney Mus. A. *Position*: A., Tulsa World, Tulsa, Okla.

PACKMAN, FRANK G.—Painter, T., Des., I., L.
12 East Hancock St., Detroit 1, Mich.; h. 10755 Kingston Rd., Huntington Woods, Mich.

B. England, June 5, 1896. *Studied*: Detroit Sch. FA; & with Paul Honore. *Member*: Scarab Cl., Detroit; Michigan Soc. A., Sc. & Let. *Exhibited*: Scarab Cl., Detroit; Detroit Inst. A.; Univ. Michigan. Lectures: Color. *Position*: Asst. Dir., Instr., Illus. & Layout, Meinzinger A. Sch., Detroit, Mich.

PADDOCK, JO(SEPHINE)—Painter, T., L., W.
20 East 68th St., Apt. 11A, New York 21, N.Y.

B. New York, N.Y., Apr. 18, 1885. *Studied*: ASL, and with Robert Henri, Kenyon Cox, William M. Chase, John Alexander; Barnard Col., A.B. *Member*: AWS; All. A. Am.; Conn. Acad. FA; New Haven Paint & Clay Cl.; Grand Central A. Gal.; North Shore AA; AAPL; Easthampton Gld. Hall; Springfield A. Lg. *Awards*: prizes, BM, 1935; New Haven Paint & Clay Cl., 1935; Conn. Acad. FA, 1937; AWS, 1946; Kappa Kappa Gamma. *Work*: portraits, paintings, Barnard Col. Cl., N.Y.; Wesleyan Col.; Colgate Univ.; Dayton AI; Berkshire Mus. A.; Newport A. Mus.; Shelton Col., N.J. *Exhibited*: PAFA; NAD; AIC; Conn. Acad. FA; AWS; BM; All. A. Am.; New Haven Paint & Clay Cl.; Paris Salon, 1951; Royal Inst., London, England, 1950; Berkshire Mus. A., 1955 (one-man); AAPL; Audubon A.; Conn. Acad. FA; Guild Hall, Easthampton; North Shore AA.

PADDOCK, ROBERT ROWE—Theatrical Designer
Mavis Glen, Greenwich, Conn.

B. Mansfield, Ohio, Aug. 12, 1914. *Studied*: Cleveland Sch. A.; Western Reserve Univ., B.S. *Award*: for best live commercial, "Pillsbury's Xmas Show," 1957. Des. for theatrical productions: Ballet "Pinocchio," 1939; "Robin Hood," 1940; "Burlesque," 1946; "Alice in Wonderland," 1947; Tech. Dir., "Winged Victory"; Reading Bi-Centennial, 1949; J. L. Hudson's Fashionscope, 1948-1950; "Macbeth," Met. Opera, 1959. *Exhibited*: CGA; Butler AI; CMA. *Position*: Instr., Television Workshop, 1950; Television Des., CBS-TV, New York, N.Y., 1951-57; Pres., United Scenic A., 1953-58; Bd. of Governors, Television Acad., 1955-58.

PAEFF, BASHKA (Mrs. Bashka Paeff Waxman)—
Sculptor, L.
21 Foster St., Cambridge, Mass.

B. Minsk, Russia, Aug. 12, 1893. *Studied*: Mass. Normal A. Sch.; BMFA Sch., with Bela Pratt, and in Paris. *Member*: Gld. Boston A. *Awards*: medal, Tercentenary Exp., Boston, 1933. *Work*: mem., monuments, statues, portraits,

State House, Boston, Kittery, Me., Westbrook, Me., Ravina, Ill., Waverly, Mass., Birmingham, Ala.; MIT; BMFA; Harvard Univ.; Rockefeller Inst., N.Y.; Univ. Buenos Aires; BMFA, and others. *Exhibited*: Boston Gld. A. (one-man).

PAGE, ADDISON FRANKLIN—Museum Curator, T.
The Detroit Institute of Arts, 5200 Woodward Ave.; h. 650 Merrick Ave., Detroit 2, Mich.

B. Princeton, Ky., Oct. 9, 1911. *Studied*: Wayne State Univ., B.F.A., M.A.; Belgian A. Seminar. *Member*: Scarab Cl.; Michigan WC Soc. Author: "Modern Sculpture," 1950 (museum handbook); "Diego Rivera's Detroit Frescoes," 1956 (museum handbook). Lectures: Understanding Modern Art; Collecting Modern Art; Impressionism to Cubism, etc. Exhs. arranged: The Winston Collection, 1957; Pa. Academy-Detroit Inst. Arts Exh. of American Painting and Sculpture, 1958; Michigan Artists Exhibition, 1958; Michigan Artist-Craftsmen Exhibition, 1958. *Positions*: Asst. Cur. Edu., 1954-57; Cur. Contemp. A., 1957- , Detroit Institute of Arts, Detroit, Mich.

PAGE, ELIZABETH AMIE—Painter, Lith., Des.
1730 Delancey Pl., Philadelphia 3, Pa.

B. Brookline, Mass., Feb. 27, 1908. *Studied*: ASL; BMFA Sch.; & with Alexander Brook. *Member*: Phila. A. All.; ASL. *Awards*: prize, Phila. Pr. Cl., 1943. *Exhibited*: PAFA, 1938, 1939, 1943; NAD, 1943; Lib. Cong., 1943, 1944; Northwest Pr. M., 1944; Boston Indp. Exh., 1938; Phila. A. All., 1943 (one-man), 1954-1958; Butler AI, 1939, 1940, 1944.

PAGE, MRS. JACQUELEN ANN. See O'Gorman, Jacqui

PAGET-FREDERICKS, J. ROUS-MARTEN—
Illustrator, W., Des., L., E.
2503 Hilgard Ave., Berkeley 9, Cal.

B. San Francisco, Cal., Dec. 22, 1906. *Studied*: Univ. California; in Europe; & with Leon Bakst, John Singer Sargent. *Member*: Los A. Mus. Assn.; Am. Soc. P. & S. *Awards*: Berlin, Germany, 1936; Stanford Univ., 1935. *Work*: Mills Col., Oakland, Cal.; Univ. California; coll. in London, Paris, Rome, Venice. *Exhibited*: special mem. exh. of Pavlova Coll., San F., 1951, for Sadler's Wells Ballet. AIC; N.Y. Pub. Lib.; in Europe & South America. Author, I., "Green Pipes," 1929; "Anna Pavlova," published in Paris; "The Paisley Unicorn"; & other books. I., "Selected Poems of Edna St. Vincent Millay," 1929; "The Macaroni Tree"; "Sandra and the Right Prince," 1951; "Gift of Merimond," 1952; Author, I., "I Shall Always Love the West," 1952 (memories of Pavlova in California), etc. Lectures: "The Russian Ballet"; "La Loie Fuller, Fortuny & Bakst." *Position*: Instr., Color & Design, Cal. Col. A. & Crafts; Asst. Dir., San F. A. Center.*

PAGON, KATHARINE D.—Painter
1431 Bolton St., Baltimore 17, Md.

B. Philadelphia, Pa., Dec. 25, 1892. *Studied*: PAFA; Barnes Fnd.; Columbia Univ.; Johns Hopkins Univ.; Maryland Inst., with Hugh Breckenridge. *Member*: NAWA; Mun. A., Balt. *Awards*: 4 study scholarships and 2 Cresson Traveling scholarships, PAFA. *Exhibited*: BMA; PAFA; NAD; CGA; PC; Kenneth Taylor Gal.; Sweat Mem. Mus.; and many others. *Position*: Instr., A. & Skills, Marine Hospital; Instr. A., Bryn Mawr Sch. for Girls, Balt., Homewood Sch., Balt., and BMFA.

PAIER, EDWARD THEODORE—Painter, T., L.
Paier School of Art, 6 Prospect Court, Hamden 11, Conn.; h. 90 Smith St., West Haven 16, Conn.

B. Hamden, Conn., Mar. 15, 1918. *Studied*: Yale Univ. Sch. FA, B.F.A. and Dept. Edu.; Columbia Univ. T. Col. *Work*: portraits in private colls. *Position*: Dir., Paier School of Art, Hamden, Conn., 1946- .

PALANCHIAN, MRS. ENID BELL. See Bell, Enid

PALANSKY, ABRAHAM—Painter, S.
1012 South Plymouth St., Los Angeles, Cal.

B. Lodz, Poland, July 1, 1890. *Studied*: AIC. *Member*: Los A. WC Soc.; No-Jury Soc., Chicago. *Awards*: prizes, AIC, 1941, 1945; Pasadena AI, 1952. *Exhibited*: Nat. A. Week, Chicago, 1940; AIC, 1940-1945, 1941; Illinois State Mus., 1940; No-Jury Soc., 1941, 1942; Los A. Mus. A., 1944 (one-man), 1943, 1945, 1948, 1949, 1952; Oakland A. Gal., 1944; SFMA, 1944; Riverside (Cal.) Mus., 1946, 1948; Madonna Festival, Los A., 1949; Chicago Bd. Jewish Edu., 1950; Pasadena AI, 1947-1950; Greek Theatre, Los A., 1946, 1947, 1948, 1951.*

PALMER, ARTHUR W.—Painter, Et., T.
545 Sutter St., San Francisco, Cal.; h. Redwood Dr., Woodacre, Cal.

B. Chicago, Ill., Nov. 27, 1913. *Studied*: Chouinard AI, and with F. Tolles Chamberlin. *Member*: Marin Soc. A.; Soc. Western A.; Bohemian Cl., San F. *Awards*: prize, Los A. AA, 1934. *Work*: portraits, Stanford Lane Hospital, Univ. Cal. Medical Sch., Univ. Cal. Dental Col., Shriner's Hospital for Crippled Children, all in San Francisco; Evanston (Ill.) Hospital; Tulane Univ.; Bohemian Cl., and in private colls. *Exhibited*: PAFA, 1933, 1935, 1936; Mississippi AA, 1944; AWS, 1944; Oakland A. Gal., 1944; Los A. County Fair, 1933; San Diego FA Soc., 1934; Los A. Mus. A., 1935; Pasadena Soc. A., 1935, 1938; Portland (Ore.) A. Mus., 1944; Terry AI, 1952; Bohemian Cl., 1952-1958; Marin Art & Garden Show, 1955-1958; deYoung Mem. Mus., 1956. *Positions*: Supv. Effects Animator, Walt Disney Studios, 1935-41; Inst., Portrait Painting at present; Instr., Cal. Col. A. & Crafts, 1952, 1953.

PALMER, JESSIE (Mrs. Carl E.)—Painter, S., T.
3505 Dartmouth St., Dallas 5, Tex.

B. Lawrence, Tex., Oct. 19, 1882. *Studied*: Dallas Tech. Col.; Broadmoor A. Acad.; & with John Carlson. *Member*: SSAL; Texas FA Assn.; Amarillo AA. *Awards*: med., Dallas Woman's Forum, 1924; prize, Texas-Oklahoma Fair, 1926, 1927. *Work*: Travis Sch., Dallas, Tex.; Dallas Woman's Forum. *Exhibited*: SSAL, 1928, 1934, 1944, 1945; Texas FA Assn., 1930-1940; Elisabet Ney Mus., 1935 (one-man); Texas State Fair, 1934; Frank Reaugh A. Exh., 1925-1946; Dallas AA, 1940. *Position*: Sec., Frank Keaugh AC, Dallas, Tex., 1944-46. (Retired.)*

PALMER, LUCIE MACKAY—Painter, L.
3693 Lindell Blvd., St. Louis 8, Mo.

B. St. Louis, Mo., May 23, 1913. *Studied*: BMFA Sch.; St. Louis Sch. FA, Washington Univ.; ASL, with Raphael Soyer, J. N. Newell, Robert Brackman. *Member*: NAWA; St. Louis A. Gld. *Awards*: prize, NAWA, 1944. *Exhibited*: NAWA, 1944-1946; Am. Mus. Natural Hist., 1943 (one-man), 1958-59 (one-man); Boston Mus. Natural Hist., 1942; St. Louis A. Gld., 1934-1946. Specializes in under water painting. Lectures: "Painting Above and Below the Sea."

PALMER, MILDRED TRUMBULL—Bookbinder
988 Memorial Drive, Cambridge 38, Mass.

B. Cambridge, Mass., Feb. 11, 1890. *Studied*: in Paris, France. *Member*: Boston Soc. A. & Crafts. Lectures: Bookbinding.

PALMER, WILLIAM C.—Painter, L., E.
Munson-Williams-Proctor Institute School of Art, 310 Genesee St., Utica 4, N.Y.; h. Butternut Hill, Clinton, N.Y.

B. Des Moines, Iowa, Jan. 20, 1906. *Studied*: ASL; Ecole des Beaux-Arts, Fontainebleau, France. *Member*: AEA; Audubon Soc. *Awards*: med., Paris Salon, 1937; Audubon A., 1947; prize, NAD, 1946; grant, Am. Acad. A. & Let., 1953. *Work*: WMAA; AGAA; Des Moines A. Center; Munson-Williams-Proctor Inst.; MMA; Cranbrook Acad. A.; Encyclopedia Britannica Coll.; Am. Acad. A. & Let.; Rochester Mem. A. Gal.; murals, PO Dept. Bldg., Wash., D.C.; First Nat. City Bank, N.Y.; Queens General Hospital, Jamaica, L.I., N.Y.; Homestead Savings & Loan Assn., Utica, N.Y., 1957. *Exhibited*: CGA; VMFA; Carnegie Inst.; BM; AIC; Toledo Mus. A.; WMAA; MModA;

Kansas City AI; etc. Contributor to: American Artist magazine. *Position*: Dir., Munson-Williams-Proctor Inst. Sch. A., Utica, N.Y., 1941- .

PANCHAK, WILLIAM (WASYL)—*Painter*
Fleischmann, N.Y.; h. 131 Riverside Drive, New York 24, N.Y.

B. Czernica, Ukraine, Aug. 19, 1893. *Studied*: Carnegie Inst.; PAFA; NAD; ASL. *Member*: Woodstock AA; AAPL. *Work*: Newark Mus. A.; Skene Mem. Lib., Fleischmann, N.Y.; churches in Pittsburgh, Pa.; McKeesport, Pa.; Rome, N.Y.; Bridgeport, Conn.; New York City, and in many private colls. *Exhibited*: Indp. A., N.Y.; Salons of America; NAD; Indp. A., Buffalo; one-man: Newark Mus. A.; Burr Gal., N.Y.

PANCOAST, MORRIS HALL—*Painter, I., Cart.*
20 Palmer St., Cambridge 38, Mass.

B. Salem, N.J., Apr. 27, 1877. *Studied*: with Jean Paul Laurens, in Paris; PAFA, with Thomas Anshutz. *Member*: SC; Phila. Sketch Cl. *Awards*: med., F., PAFA, 1924. *Work*: PAFA; Reading (Pa.) Mus.; Williamsport (Pa.) Lib.; Speed Mem. Mus.; Mus. FA of Houston; Milwaukee AI. *Exhibited*: PAFA; CGA; NAD; Baltimore Charcoal Cl.; GGE, 1939; Gloucester SA; Rockport AA.

PANDOLFINI, JOSEPH PAUL—*Painter, C., I., T.*
203 Bleecker St., New York 12, N.Y.

B. Italy, June 6, 1908. *Studied*: Royal Acad FA, Italy. *Work*: Univ. Minnesota. *Exhibited*: Musee du Jeu de Paume, Paris, 1938; MModA, 1938; AIC, 1939; WMAA, 1940; NAD, 1950.

PAPASHVILY, GEORGE—*Sculptor*
Ertoba Farm, Bucks County, Quakertown, Pa.

B. Kobiankari, Georgia (now USSR), Aug. 23, 1898. *Member*: Phila. A. All.; Lehigh A. All.; AEA. *Exhibited*: PAFA, 1952-1954, 1958; All. A. Am., 1953, 1954; Audubon A., 1952, 1955-1958; Phila. A. All., 1952; Lehigh Univ., 1953, 1954; Detroit Inst. A., 1958; one-man: Phila. A. All., 1953; Allentown Mus. A., 1951; Lehigh Univ., 1957; Washington Irving Gal., N.Y., 1958. *Awards*: prizes, All. A. Am., 1953; Phila. A. All., 1952; Audubon A., 1958. Author (in collaboration with Helen Waite Papashvily): "Anything Can Happen," 1945; "Yes and No Stories," 1946; "Thanks to Noah," 1950; "Dogs and People," 1954.

PAPSDORF, FREDERICK—*Painter, Et.*
Northeastern YMCA, 10100 Harper St. (13); h. 12783 Jane St., Detroit 5, Mich.

B. Dover, Ohio, June 10, 1887. *Studied*: Detroit Inst. A. *Member*: Progressive A. Cl., Detroit. *Work*: CAM; PAFA; MModA; Detroit Inst. A.; Detroit Artists Market, and in private collections. *Position*: Instr., Northeastern YMCA, Detroit, Mich.

PARADISE, PHIL—*Painter, Lith., Ser., T., L.*
P.O. Box 416, Cambria, Cal.

B. Ontario, Ore., Aug. 26, 1905. *Studied*: Chouinard AI. *Member*: AWS; ANA; Cal. WC Soc.; Phila. WC Cl. *Awards*: prizes, GGE, 1939; Phila. WC Cl., 1943; Cal. State Fair, 1949; Los A. County Fair Assn., 1952; merit award, AV, 1943; San Diego FA Soc., 1940; Pepsi-Cola, 1945; med., PAFA, 1941. *Work*: Cornell Univ.; San Diego FA Soc.; Univ. California; Marine Hospital, Carville, La.; PAFA; Kansas State Univ.; Los A. County Fair. *Exhibited*: Carnegie Inst., 1943-1945; CGA, 1942, 1944; AIC; PAFA; NAD; WMAA; SFMA; Los A. Mus. A.; San Diego FA Soc.; Denver A. Mus. I., Fortune, & other national magazines. *Position*: Dir., FA Dept., Chouinard AI, Los A., Cal., 1936-40; Production Des., Motion Picture Studios, 1944-45; Dir. Painting, Gerry Peirce Sch., Tucson, Ariz., 1952-53; L., Scripps Col., 1955-56; Claremont Col., 1956; Dir., Phil Paradise Summer A. Sch., Cambria, Cal., 1957- .

PARAMINO, JOHN F.—*Sculptor, W.*
108 Edmunds Rds., Wellesley Hills 82, Mass.

B. Boston, Mass., Dec. 25, 1888. *Studied*: BMFA Sch. *Member*: Gld. Boston A.; Copley Soc., Boston. *Awards*: med., Mass. Horticultural Soc., 1929. *Work*: S., bas-reliefs, mem., monuments, busts: State House, Boston,

Mass.; World War II Mem., Four Freedoms Mem., Boston; A. Platt Andrew Mem., Gloucester, Mass.; Plymouth, Mass.; Hall of Fame, N.Y.; Boston Commons; Cambridge, Mass.; Boston Univ. Law Sch.; Harvard Univ.; Nantucket Island, Mass.; U.S. Army; New Suffolk County Court House, Boston; Northampton, Mass.; Wellesley Col.; etc. Author: "Sculpture As A Medium of Expression," 1945.*

PARAVICINI, LIZETTE—*Painter, C., T.*
5810 Ashland Ave., Philadelphia 43, Pa.

B. Philadelphia, Pa., Oct. 30, 1889. *Studied*: Univ. Pennsylvania, A.B., A.M.; PAFA; & with Frank Linton, Earl Horter, Arthur Carles. *Member*: A. All., Plastic Cl., WC Cl., A.T. Assn., all of Phila., Pa.; Woodmere AA. *Exhibited*: PAFA; Phila. WC Cl.; F., PAFA; Phila. Plastic Cl.; Woodmere A. Gal.; DaVinci All.; Phila. A. All. (one-man); also one-man exhs. at Women's Cl., Ardmore, Swarthmore and Philadelphia, Pa. *Position*: T., Kensington H.S., Philadelphia, Pa., 1921-55 (Retired).

PARCELL, MALCOLM STEPHENS—*Painter*
11 North Main St., Washington, Pa.

B. Claysville, Pa., Jan. 1, 1896. *Studied*: Carnegie Inst.; Washington & Jefferson Col., D.A. *Awards*: prizes, Assoc. A., 1918; med., NAD, 1919; AIC, 1924; Int. A. Exh., Pittsburgh; Carnegie Inst., 1953. *Work*: Butler AI; Carnegie Inst.; Univ. Pittsburgh; Foster Mem., Pittsburgh; Pa. State Univ.; Univ. Chicago; Northwestern Univ. *Exhibited*: nationally. Contributor to International Studio; Harpers; Vanity Fair; Art and Archaeology; International Blue Book.*

PARIS, DOROTHY—*Painter*
88 Seventh Ave., New York 14, N.Y.

B. Boston, Mass. *Studied*: Grande Chaumiere, Paris; Univ. Hawaii; Honolulu Acad. A.; ASL. *Member*: Brooklyn Soc. A.; NAWA. *Awards*: prizes, Honolulu Acad. A., 1946; NAWA, 1953; Fla. Intl. Exh., 1952; Jersey City Mus. A., 1956. *Work*: Univ. Miami; Evansville Mus. A.; Richmond (Ind.) Mus. A.; Birmingham Mus. A.; and in private colls. *Exhibited*: one-man: Galerie Zak, Paris, 1950; Van Dieman-Lilienfeld Gal., 1951; Barzansky Gal., N.Y., 1954. *Position*: Instr., Ceramic Workshop & Sch. FA, N.Y., 1938-40; Organized first ceramic Co-operative for Puerto Rican Govt., 1937.

**PARISH, BETTY WALDO (Mrs. Richard Comyn Eames)
—*Painter, Pr., M.***
2 West 15th St.; h. 19 West 12th St., New York 11, N.Y.

B. Cologne, Germany, Dec. 6, 1910. *Studied*: Chicago Acad. FA; ASL; Julian Acad., Paris; New Sch. for Social Research. *Member*: SAGA; NAWA; Pen & Brush Cl.; All. A. Am.; Audubon A.; Phila. WC Cl.; ASL (life); Chicago Soc. Et. *Awards*: prizes, NAWA, 1939, 1946, 1957; U.S. Treasury Dept.; SAGA, 1943; Washington Square A. Show, 1949; LC, 1949, 1952; Pen & Brush Cl., 1954, 1956, 1957. *Work*: MMA; SAM; LC; AIC; Treasury Dept., Wash., D.C.; Collectors of Am. A.; N.Y. Pub. Lib.; Montgomery Mus. A.; Birmingham Pub. Lib.; Col. FA, Syracuse Univ.; Pa. State Univ.; N.Y. Historical Soc.; Mus. of the City of N.Y.; British Mus., London; Royal Mus., Brussels. *Exhibited*: LC, NAD; PAFA; NAWA; WFNY 1939; SAGA; AIC; Argent Gal.; Albany Inst. Hist. & A.; Carnegie Inst.; Cal. Soc. Et.; London Exchange Exh., SAGA; Audubon A.; Greece, Holland, Switzerland, 1956-58; Pulitzer Gal., N.Y., 1959 (one-man); traveling exhs. of graphic art, and many others.

PARK, A. E.—(Betty)—*Painter, T.*
1023 12th Ave., Anchorage, Alaska

Exhibited: several exhs., Northwest Annual, SAM.

PARK, DAVID—*Painter, T.*
1629 La Vereda Rd., Berkeley 9, Cal.

B. Boston, Mass., Mar. 17, 1911. *Member*: San F. AA. *Awards*: prizes, San F. AA, 1935, 1951, 1953, 1955, 1957; Oakland A. Mus., 1957 (gold medal). *Work*: SFMA. *Exhibited*: San F. AA; AIC; Cal. PLH; Univ. Illinois; Mass. Inst. Tech., 1953; Richmond A. Center, 1955; Sao Paulo, Brazil, 1955; Minneapolis Inst. A., 1957; Art:USA, 1958; Richmond, Va., 1958. *Position*: Hd. A. Dept.,

Winsor Sch., Boston, Mass., 1936-41; Instr., Painting, Cal. Sch. FA, San Francisco, 1944- ; Asst. Prof. A., Univ. California, Berkeley, Cal., 1955- ; Bd. Dir., San F. AA.

PARK, (HAZEL A.) HANES—*Painter, C.*

3574 East 7th St., Los Angeles 23, Cal.

B. Waukee, Iowa, Sept. 28, 1887. *Studied*: Otis AI; Cummings A. Sch., Des Moines, and with Paul Lauritz, Ralph Holmes, F. Tolles Chamberlin, Eduard Vysekal, John H. Rich, E. Roscoe Shrader. *Member*: Cal. A. Cl.; Southland AA; A. of the Southwest; Whittier AA; Women Painters of the West; San Gabriel A. Gld.; San Fernando Valley Prof. A. Gld.; Southern Cal. Hand Weavers. *Awards*: prizes, Whittier AA, 1942, 1943; San Fernando Valley A. Gld., 1948; Cal. A. Cl., 1952; Ebell Cl., 1955; Greek Theatre, Los A., 1953. *Exhibited*: Descanso Gardens, La Canada, Cal., 1957, 1958; Cal. A. Cl., 1958; one-man: Drusdale Gal., Van Nuys, Cal., 1946; Signal Oil Bldg. lobby, Los A., 1946; Long Beach, Cal., 1953.

PARK, MADELEINE F.—*Sculptor*

87 Bedford Rd., Katonah, N.Y.

B. Mt. Kisco, N.Y., July 19, 1891. *Studied*: ASL; & with A. Phimister Proctor, Naum Los, Lawrence T. Stevens, & others. *Member*: NSS; NAWA; PBC; Soc. Medallists; AFA; Putnam County AA; Westchester A. & Crafts; N.Y. Zoological Soc.; All. A. Am.; Hudson Valley AA. *Awards*: prizes, Am. Women's Assn., 1933, 1940; PBC, 1938; Hudson Valley AA, 1944. *Work*: specializes in wild & domestic animal sculpture. *Exhibited*: Paris Salon; NAD; Arch. L.; PAFA; AIC; SFMA; WMAA; MMA; N.Y. Zoological Soc.; one-man exh.: Brooks Mem. A. Gal.; Buie Mus., Oxford, Miss.; Mississippi AA; Univ. Florida; Converse Col.; Mint Mus.; J.B. Speed Mem. Mus.; Buffalo Mus. Sc.; Rochester Mem. A. Gal.; Erie A. Mus.; Utica Pub. Lib.; Cortland Free Lib.; Arnot A. Gal.; Illinois State Mus.; Wichita Mus. A.; Wustum Mus. FA; Kansas City State T. Col.; Univ. Wichita; Oklahoma A. Center; Massillon Mus. Lectures: "Experiences of a Sculptor."*

PARK, ROSEMARY—*Museum Director*

Lyman Allyn Museum, 100 Mohegan Ave., New London, Conn.

Position: Dir., Lyman Allyn Museum.*

PARKE, JESSIE BURNS—*Painter*

83 Robbins Rd., Arlington 74, Mass.

B. Paterson, N.J., Dec. 2, 1889. *Studied*: N.Y. Sch. App. Des. for Women; BMFA Sch., and with Philip Hale, William James, Frederick L. Bosley. *Member*: Pa. Soc. Min. Painters; Assoc., Min. Painters, Sculptors & Gravers, Wash., D.C. *Awards*: Paige traveling scholarship, BMFA Sch., 1921; medal, Pa. Soc. Min. P., 1945; Elizabeth Muhlhofer award, 1953. *Work*: portraits, miniatures, Northwestern Univ.; South Boston H.S.; PMA; Boston College H.S. *Exhibited*: PAFA; Albright A. Gal.; Pa. Soc. Min. P., annually; Ogunquit A. Center; Paris Salon; Soc. Indp. A.; Fed. Women's Cl., Mass.; P. S. & Gravers, Wash., D.C., 1953-1955.

PARKE, NATHANIEL ROSS—*Painter, T., Des.*

77 Van Buren Ave., West Hartford 7, Conn.

B. Williamsport, Pa., Oct. 20, 1904. *Studied*: Trinity Col.; Yale Sch. FA, B.F.A. *Member*: New Haven Paint & Clay Cl.; Assn. Conn. A.; West Hartford A. Lg. (hon.). *Awards*: med., prize, BAID, 1927; Fla. Southern Col., 1952; Mansfield (Conn.) Fair, 1956; Glastonbury (Conn.), 1957. *Work*: West Hartford (Conn.) Trust Co.; West Hartford A. Lg.; official bookplate, D.A.R.; restoration of dec., Congregational Church, Grafton, Vt. *Exhibited*: All. A. Am., 1936; New Haven Paint & Clay Cl., 1929; Williamsport A. Lg., 1929; Pa. State Col., 1936; Hartford Women's Cl., 1931; West Hartford A. Lg., 1935-1956; Conn. Acad. FA, 1936; Indp. A. Connecticut, 1938. *Position*: A.T., Conn. Gen. Life Insurance Co., 1954, 1956; Phoenix Mutual Life Insurance Co., 1956; Instr., Adult Edu., William Hall H.S., West Hartford, Conn., 1951- .

PARKER, ALFRED—*Illustrator*

P.O. Box 227, Carmel Valley, Cal.

B. St. Louis, Mo., Oct. 16, 1906. *Studied*: St. Louis Sch. FA. *Member*: SI; Westport A. (Pres. 1950); A. Gld.;

St. Louis Ad Cl. (hon.); San F. Ad Cl. *Awards*: N.Y. A. Dir. Cl.; Phila. A. Dir. Cl.; Citation Washington Univ., St. Louis. Lectures and exhibitions in major cities of U.S. and Canada. Contributor illus. to: Ladies Home Journal; Good Housekeeping; Town & Country; McCalls; Cosmopolitan, and other leading national magazines. Creator of Mother and Daughter covers for Ladies Home Journal. Fndr.-Memb., Famous Artists Schools, Westport, Conn.

PARKER, GLADYS—*Cartoonist*

1351 North Havenhurst, Hollywood, Cal.

B. Tonawanda, N.Y. *Member*: SI; Nat. Cartoonists Soc. Creator of syndicated cartoon "Mopsey."*

PARKER, HELEN MARY—*Lecturer*

531 North Ave., Lake Bluff, Ill.

B. Chicago, Ill. *Studied*: Univ. Chicago, Ph.B.; Ecole du Louvre, Sorbonne, Paris. *Award*: Citation, Univ. Chicago, 1952. Author: "Arno Art Studies," 1930; "Art Quiz," 1939; "The Christmas Story in the Art Institute Collections," 1949. Lectures: History of Art; Collections & Exhibitions of the Art Institute of Chicago. *Position*: Asst. Mus. Instr., 1914-26, Hd. Dept. Edu., 1926-53, AIC, Chicago, Ill. (Retired).

PARKER, JOHN CLAY—*Painter*

3708 Louisiana Ave. Parkway, New Orleans 25, La.

B. McComb, Miss., Feb. 1, 1907. *Member*: New Orleans AA. *Work*: portraits, Masonic Temple, Wash., D.C.; Medical Sch., Tulane Univ.; Univ. Mississippi Lib.; Medical Sch., Univ. Alabama; Louisiana Supreme Court, New Orleans; College of Surgeons Hdqtrs., Chicago, Ill.; Alton Ochsner Hospital, New Orleans; Eye, Ear, Nose & Throat Hospital, New Orleans; Mary Buck Health Center, New Orleans. *Exhibited*: Mississippi AA; New Orleans AA.*

PARKER, MARGERY (SHALE)—*Painter, T.*

1020 West Flora St., Stockton 3, Cal.

B. Sauk County, Wis., Mar. 31, 1921. *Studied*: Univ. Wisconsin, B.S.; BMSch. A., with Reuben Tam, Yonia Fain, Louis Grebenak; also with Irving Marantz. *Exhibited*: N.Y. City Center, 1955, 1956; Brooklyn Soc. A., 1956; one-man: Panoras Gal., 1956.

PARKER, ROY D.—*Painter*

88 Highland Ave., Middletown, N.Y.

B. Raymond, Iowa, Feb. 23, 1882. *Member*: Middletown A. Group. *Awards*: prizes, Orange County Fair. *Work*: Private coll. of D.D. Eisenhower, and others. *Exhibited*: one-man: Panoras Gal., N.Y.; Everhart Mus., Scranton, Pa.; Berkshire Mus. A., Pittsfield, Mass., 1958, and in local and regional exhs.

PARKER, VIOLA WOLFE. See *Wolfe-Parker, Viola*

PARKHURST, CHARLES PERCY—
Museum Director, E., Hist.

Allen Memorial Art Museum, Oberlin College; Oberlin, Ohio

B. Columbus, Ohio, Jan. 23, 1913. *Studied*: Williams Col., B.A.; Oberlin Col., M.A.; Princeton Univ., M.F.A. *Member*: CAA; Archaeological Soc. of Am.; Soc. for Aesthetics & A. Criticism; Intl. Inst. for Conservation (Fellow); Intermuseum Conservation Assn. (Trustee). *Awards*: Jacobus F., Princeton Univ., 1940-41; Ford Fnd. F., 1952-53; Fulbright F., 1956-57; Chevalier, Legion of Honor, France, 1947. *Work*: NGA; Albright A. Gal.; Princeton Univ. Mus.; Allen A. Mus. Ed., Allen A. Mus. Bulletin; Author: "Light and Color," brochure, 1955; "Good Design is Your Business," Albright A. Gal., and Contributor to scholarly publications. *Positions*: Prof., A. & Arch. Hist., Princeton Univ.; Prof., Arch. Hist., Introd. to Art, Color, Dir., Allen Mem. A. Mus., Oberlin College, Oberlin, Ohio, 1949- .

PARKS, JAMES DALLAS—*Painter, Lith., E.*

Lincoln University; h. 923 East Dunklin St., Jefferson City, Mo.

B. St. Louis, Mo., Aug. 25, 1907. *Studied*: Bradley Univ., B.S.; AIC; State Univ. Iowa, M.A., and with Jean Charlot,

Philip Guston. *Member*: CAA. *Work*: Atlanta Univ.; Springfield Mus. A.; Lincoln Univ.; State Univ. Iowa; Howard Univ.; Carver Sch., Kansas City, Mo.; mural, Lincoln Univ. *Exhibited*: CAM, 1946, 1947; Atlanta Univ., 1942, 1944, 1946, 1950, 1951; William Rockhill Nelson Gal. A., 1951; Springfield Mus. A., 1946, 1947. Contributor to Design Magazine, Everyday Art. *Position*: Hd. A. Dept., Lincoln Univ., Jefferson City, Mo., 1927- .

PARKS, ROBERT OWENS—*Museum Director*
Smith College Museum, Tryon Art Gallery, Northampton, Mass.*

PARRISH, JOSEPH LEE—*Cartoonist*
976 Private Road, Winnetka, Ill.
B. Summertown, Tenn., Sept. 15, 1905. *Member*: Assn. Am. Editorial Cart. Cartoonist, Chicago Daily News.

PARRISH, MAXFIELD—*Painter, I.*
Box 63, Windsor, Vt.
B. Philadelphia, Pa., July 25, 1870. *Studied*: Haverford Col.; PAFA; & with Howard Pyle. *Member*: NA; Phila. WC Cl. (hon.).

PARROTT, ALLEN—*Museum Curator*
Museum of International Folk Art, Museum of New Mexico, Santa Fe, N.M.
Position: Cur., Mus. International Folk Art.*

PARSONS, MRS. AUDREY BULLER. See *Buller, Audrey*

PARSONS, CLAUDE P.—*Painter, L.*
1265 North Kenmore Ave., Los Angeles 29, Cal.
B. New York, N.Y., Mar. 23, 1895. *Studied*: with Will Foster, William J. Harrison, Sam Hyde Harris. *Member*: P. & S. Cl., Los Angeles; A. of the Southwest; Valley A. Gld.; Laguna Beach AA. *Awards*: prizes, P. & S. Cl., Greek Theatre, Los A., 1951, 1953, 1955; A. of the Southwest, 1951, 1952, 1954; Valley A. Gld., 1953; Laguna Beach AA; Friday Morning Cl., 1951, 1953. *Work*: Friday Morning Cl.; California Bank, Hollywood. *Exhibited*: many local and regional exhs. Lectures: "Color in Oil Painting"; "Painting in Europe"; "Art Appreciation," etc.*

PARSONS, ERNESTINE—*Painter*
825 North Weber St., Colorado Springs, Colo.
B. Booneville, Mo., Sept. 20, 1884. *Studied*: Colorado Col., A.B.; Columbia Univ., A.M.; Broadmoor A. Acad.; ASL; Colorado Springs FA Center, and with Randall Davey, Paul Burlin, and others. *Member*: Colorado Springs A. Gld.; Colorado Springs FA Center (Bd. Trustees). *Awards*: prizes, Broadmoor A. Acad., 1927; Colorado State Fair, 1945. *Work*: Colorado Springs H.S. *Exhibited*: Carnegie Inst., 1928; Albright A. Gal., 1927, 1930; Denver A. Mus., 1933, 1942, 1951; Pueblo, Colo., 1953; Jewish Center, Denver, 1953; Wooster Col. (one-man); Colorado Springs FA Center, 1944, 1945, 1948-1955; Central City, Colo., 1951, 1952, 1956-1958; Ogunquit A. Center, 1952; Miami, Fla., 1951; Canon City, Colo., 1956-1958; Rocky Ford, Colo., 1956, 1958; one-man: Colorado Springs FA Center, 1952, 1956, 1958; Canon City, Colo., 1953; St. Francis Hospital, Colo. Springs, 1954; Overton Gal., Colorado Springs, 1956-1958.

PARSONS, KITTY (Mrs. Richard H. Recchia)—
Painter, W.
Hardscrabble, Rockport, Mass.
B. Stratford, Conn. *Studied*: PIASch.; T. Col., Columbia Univ.; Boston Univ.; Univ. Chicago; & with Richard H. Recchia. *Member*: NAWA; Rockport AA; Nat. Lg. Am. Pen Women; North Shore AA; Copley Soc., Boston; Boston Soc. Indp. A.; N.Y. Writers Gld. *Awards*: prize, Nat. Lg. Am. Pen Women, 1955, 1956. *Work*: Rockport H.S. *Exhibited*: NAWA, 1941, 1944; CGA, 1941; Portland SA, 1942, 1944; Soc. Indp. A.; Audubon A.; Springfield A. Lg.; Mint Mus. A.; Alabama WC Soc.; Newport AA, 1944, 1945; Rockport AA; North Shore AA; Conn. Acad. FA; J. B. Speed Mem. Mus.; Palm Beach A. Lg.; one-man exh.: Doll & Richards, Boston; Berkshire A. Mus.; Argent Gal.; Bennington Mus.; Whistler House, Lowell, Mass.;

Winchester (Mass.) AA; Nashville Mus. A.; Milwaukee Pub. Lib.; Bowdoin Col. Author: "Ancestral Timber," 1957; several books of poetry; contributor to magazines & newspapers. *Position*: Bd. member, Rockport AA, 1940-55; Bd. Maine Writers' Conf., 1957-58.

PARSONS, LLOYD HOLMAN—*Painter, Des.*
West Road, Little Compton, R.I.
B. Montreal, Canada, Feb. 2, 1893. *Studied*: McGill Univ., B. Arch; ASL, with Kenneth Hayes Miller. *Member*: Providence A. Cl. *Work*: WMAA. *Exhibited*: CGA; AIC; NAD; PAFA; Carnegie Inst.; WMAA.

PARSONS, WALTER EDWARD—*Painter*
East Commercial St., Wellfleet, Mass.
B. Troy, Pa., Nov. 11, 1890. *Studied*: Yale Univ.; Carnegie Inst.; NAD; ASL, and with Charles Hawthorne, Hans Hofmann, Jerry Farnsworth. *Member*: SC. *Exhibited*: SC, 1955; Provincetown AA, 1953-1955; Cape Cod AA, 1953-1955; VMFA.*

PARTCH, VIRGIL FRANKLIN (VIP)—*Cartoonist*
Box 35 A, Capistrano Beach, Cal.
B. St. Paul Island, Alaska, Oct. 17, 1916. *Studied*: Chouinard AI, Los Angeles. Author: "It's Hot in Here"; "Water on the Brain"; Author, I., "Bottle Fatigue"; "Here We Go Again"; "Wild, Wild Women"; "Man the Beast"; "Deadgame Sportsman"; "Hanging Way Over"; "VIP Throws a Party." Contributor cartoons to Look, True magazines.

PARTEE, McCULLOUGH—*Sculptor, I., T., Des.*
318 Murfreesboro Rd.; h. 408 Fairfax Ave., Nashville 12, Tenn.
B. Nashville, Tenn., Feb. 19, 1900. *Studied*: Chicago Acad. FA; AIC; ASL; NAD; Grand Central Sch. A., and with Hawthorne, Dunn, Carter and others. *Member*: Nat. Soc. A. Dir. I., national magazines. *Work*: port. plaques, Tenn. Agricultural Hall of Fame, Nashville, Greenville, and Univ. Tennessee. *Position*: A. Dir., Farm & Ranch and Southern Agriculturalist, 1935- , Nashville, Tenn.

PARTON, NIKE—*Painter, T., S.*
209 Ninth St., West, Bradenton, Fla.; h. 7728 Westmoreland Dr., Sarasota, Fla.
B. New York, N.Y., June 23, 1922. *Studied*: ASL, with George Grosz; Jay Connaway Sch. A.; Ringling Sch. A. *Member*: Fla. A. Group; A. Lg. Manatee County; Sarasota AA; Assoc. Fla. Sculptors. *Awards*: prizes, Sarasota AA, 1953; A. Lg. Manatee County, 1954, 1957, 1958; Longboat Key A. Center; Fla. A. Group, 1956, 1957. *Work*: A. Lg. Manatee County; Univ. Fla., Gainesville; Stetson Univ. *Exhibited*: Sarasota AA, 1953-1958; PAFA, 1947; Fla. A. Group, 1955, 1956, 1958; Ft. Lauderdale, 1955; Southern Vt. A., 1947-1950; Boston A. Festival, 1953; A. Lg. Manatee County, 1952-1958; Ogunquit A. Center, 1951-1955; Sculptors & Ceramists Group, 1952, 1953; Assoc. Sculptors, 1957, 1958; Fla. Fed. A., 1957, 1958; one-man: Sarasota AA, 1953; A. Lg. Manatee County, 1953, 1956-1958; Tampa AI, 1957, 1958. *Position*: Instr., Manatee A. Lg., 1955-59.

PARTRIDGE, CHARLOTTE RUSSELL—*Educator, L., Cr.*
Route 2, Box 315, Thiensville, Wis.
B. Minneapolis, Minn. *Studied*: Northern Illinois T. Col.; Emma M. Church Sch. A.; AIC; ASL; & abroad. *Member*: CAA; AFA; AAMus; Wis. P. & S.; Wis. Designer-Craftsmen. *Awards*: Oberlander F., 1936; Carnegie Grant, 1940. Lectures: Art in Contemporary Life; Enjoyment of Modern Art; How to Look at Paintings; Art Education. *Position*: Prof. A., Dir. A. Dept., Milwaukee-Downer Col., 1914-22; Wisconsin Dir., FAP, 1935-39; Fndr., Dir., Layton Sch. A., 1920-54, Dir., Layton A. Gal., Milwaukee, Wis., 1921-53, Dir., Emeritus, 1954- .

PARTRIDGE, ROI—*Etcher, E.*
Mills College P.O. (13); h. 6558 Simson St., Oakland 5, Cal.
B. Centralia, Wash., Oct. 14, 1888. *Studied*: NAD. *Member*: NA. *Awards*: med., NAD, 1910; gold med., Cal. Soc. Pr. M., 1929; AIC, 1921; prizes, Brooklyn, N.Y., 1921;

San F., Cal., 1921; Los A., Cal., 1922, 1925, med., 1929; Lib. Cong., 1943; New York, 1947. *Work*: Lib. Cong.; Cal. State Lib.; WMA; N.Y. Pub. Lib.; Walker Gal.; Crocker A. Gal.; Hackley A. Gal., Muskegon, Mich.; Mills Col. A. Gal.; Springfield (Mass.) Mus. A.; Liverpool, England; Toronto A. Gal.; deYoung Mem. Mus.; SFMA; AIC; MModA; Los A. Mus. A.; Honolulu Acad. A.; San Diego FA Soc.; Wells Col., N.Y.; BM; Carnegie Inst.; NGA; etc. *Position*: Instr. A., Prof. A., Mills Col., Oakland, Cal., 1921-46. (Retired).

PASCAL, DAVID—*Cartoonist*
Long Meadow Lane, Bethel, Conn.

B. New York, N.Y., Aug. 16, 1918. *Member*: Nat. Cartoonists Soc. *Awards*: prizes, United Seamen's Service, 1943, 1944. *Exhibited*: MMA, Cartoon Exh., 1951; Grand Central A. Gal.; CGA, and other galleries and museums. Illus., "The Sale Begins When the Customer Says No," 1953; Best Cartoons of 1947-1958; many cartoon anthologies. Contributor of Cartoons to Punch; Sat. Eve. Post; Sports Illustrated; New Yorker and other national magazines. *Position*: Former Instr., Sch. Visual Arts, New York, N.Y. Toured Far East Military Installations, Auspices of U.S. Army, 1958.

PASCAL, THEO—*Painter, C., Des., I., Pub. Rel.*
c/o Pisarro Studios, 146 East 46th St.; h. 522 East 83rd St., New York, N.Y.

B. Dallas, Tex., Sept. 1, 1915. *Studied*: ASL, and with Howard Trafton. *Awards*: Scholarship, Drake Univ. Sch. Journalism. *Exhibited*: one-man: Worth Ave. Gal. A., Palm Beach, 1945; Carstairs Gal., N.Y., 1946, 1947. I., "Johnny Groundhog's Shadow," 1947. Contributor to McCalls magazine. *Position*: Home Ed., Charm Magazine, 1946-50; J. Walter Thompson Agency, 1952-57; Product Merchandising Mgr., Good Housekeeping Magazine, 1958-59; Dir., Pub. Rel., American Federation of Arts, New York, N.Y., 1958- .

PASTERNACKI, VETOLD HENRY—*Painter*
4000 Overlea Court, Bloomfield Hills, Mich.

B. Detroit, Mich., May 31, 1896. *Studied*: John P. Wicker A. Sch., Detroit; Acad. Moderne, Paris. *Member*: Scarab Cl. Detroit. *Awards*: prizes, Detroit, Mich.; 1932; Detroit Inst. A., 1943; med., Scarab Cl., 1935. *Work*: Wayne Univ.; Scarab Cl. *Exhibited*: Salon d'Automne, Paris, 1929; AIC, 1938; Pepsi-Cola, 1946; Detroit Inst. A., 1930-1945; AFA traveling exh., 1956-58.

PATERSON, MRS. ZAMA VANESSA HELDER.
See Helder, Z. Vanessa

PATRICK, RANSOM R.—*Educator, P., Hist.*
Department Aesthetics, Art & Music, Duke University, 6605 College Station; h. 116 Pinecrest Rd., Durham, N.C.

B. Santa Barbara, Cal., July 28, 1906. *Studied*: Univ. Washington, B.A.; Princeton Univ., M.F.A. *Member*: CAA; Am. Soc. for Aesthetics; AAUP. *Work*: mural, U.S. Naval Air Base, Sand Point, Wash. *Exhibited*: SAM, 1930-1942. Contributor to Art Bulletin. *Positions*: Prof., A. Hist., Aesthetics & Criticism, Oberlin College, Univ. Minnesota, Western Reserve Univ., Duke University; Dir., Div. A. & Arch., Western Reserve Univ., 1949-54; Chm., Dept. Aesthetics, Art & Music, Duke Univ., Durham, N.C., 1954- .

PATTEE, ELSIE DODGE—*Painter, I., T., W., L.*
Old Lyme, Conn.

B. Chelsea, Mass., Sept. 4, 1876. *Studied*: Julian Acad., Paris. *Member*: ASMP; Mystic AA; Old Lyme AA; Brooklyn Soc. Min. P. *Awards*: med., Pan-Pacific Exp., 1915; Brooklyn Soc. Min. P., 1935, 1939; prizes, Cal. Soc. Min. P., 1927; ASMP, 1930, 1936. *Work*: MMA; BM; PMA; PAFA. I., juvenile publications.

PATTERSON, AMBROSE—*Painter, E.*
3927 Belvoir Pl., Seattle 5, Wash.

B. Daylesford, Victoria, Australia, June 29, 1877. *Studied*: with Lucien Simon, Andre L'Hote, Maxime Maufra, in Paris. *Work*: Sydney, Adelaide, Canberra, Australia; Hono-

lulu, T.H.; Seattle, Wash.; mural, USPO, Mt. Vernon, Wash. *Position*: Prof. Emeritus, Painting, Univ. Washington, Seattle, Wash.

PATTERSON, CHARLES ALLEN—*Painter*
405 East 92nd St., New York 28, N.Y.

B. Littleton, N.C., Sept. 5, 1922. *Studied*: ASL, with Reginald Marsh, Julien Levi, Morris Kantor. *Exhibited*: Hewitt Gal., 1953-1958; one-man: Paris, France, 1951.

PATTERSON, GEORGE W. PATRICK—
Museum Director, P.
Woolaroc Museum; h. 912 Osage St., Bartlesville, Okla.

B. Centralia, Ill., Dec. 29, 1914. *Studied*: Univ. Oklahoma, B.F.A., and with Paul Laune, O. McDowell. *Work*: Ecclesiastical art; many portraits. Author, I., "Kemoha," 1948. *Lectures*: Art History; Western Art; Prehistoric Art. Assembled, arranged, catalogued museum collection, 55,000 items, Western Art, American Indian Artifacts. *Position*: Dir., Woolaroc Museum, Bartlesville, Okla., 1939- .

PATTERSON, HOWARD ASHMAN—
Painter, Lith., Des., T.
14½ Vandevender Ave., Princeton, N.J.

B. Philadelphia, Pa., Sept. 13, 1891. *Studied*: PMSchIA; PAFA, with Henry McCarter. *Member*: Am. Veterans Soc. A. *Work*: Luxembourg Mus., Paris; F. PAFA. *Exhibited*: PAFA; NAD; AIC; F. PAFA; Carnegie Inst.; Palace Legion Honor; CM.

PATTERSON, MARION L(OIS)—*Educator, P., L.*
300 North Sixth St.; h. Route 1, Vincennes, Ind.

B. Knox County, Ind., Nov. 3, 1909. *Studied*: Indiana State T. Col., B.S.; Syracuse Univ., M.F.A. *Member*: Indiana State T. Assn.; NEA; Hoosier Salon; NAWA; Indiana A. Cl.; Vincennes T. Assn.; Western AA; Nat. A. Edu. Assn.; Indiana A. Edu. Assn.; Indianapolis AA; Am. Assn. Univ. Women; Vincennes T. Fed. *Awards*: prizes, Hoosier Salon, 1942, 1948; Wabash Valley A., 1948, 1950. *Exhibited*: AWS, 1941; NAWA, 1943-1945, 1949, 1950, 1951; Swope A. Gal., 1948-1951; Indiana A. Cl., 1948; Hoosier Salon, 1942-1958; Hoosier A. Gal., 1942; Indiana A., 1942, 1944, 1945, 1951; Hoosier Salon traveling exh., 1946; Syracuse Univ., 1942 (one-man); Vincennes Fortnightly Cl., 1946 (one-man); Ogunquit A. Center, 1954; Nelson Wilson Mem. Exh., Evansville, 1955; Wabash Valley A., 1947, 1948, 1950, 1951. *Position*: Hd. A. Dept., Vincennes City Sch., Vincennes, Ind., 1936- ; Faculty, A. Dept., Vincennes Univ.; Adult Edu., Indiana Univ., 1951- ; Western AA and NAEA Membership Chm. for State of Indiana, 1952-53, 1953-54; Memb. Adv. Bd., So. Indiana Reg. Scholastic A. Exh., 1955-56; A. Cr., T., Indiana State T. Col., 1957-58.

PATTERSON, PATTY (Mrs. Frank Grass)—
Painter, C., T., L., W.
2506 Northwest 66th St., Oklahoma City, Okla.

B. Oklahoma City, Okla., Jan 16, 1909. *Studied*: Univ. Oklahoma, B.F.A.; Ecole des Beaux-Arts, Fontainebleau, France; Taos Sch. A.; ASL; Okla. State Univ., & with Emil Bisttram. *Member*: Okla. AA; Okla. A. Lg. *Awards*: med., McDowell Cl., 1940, 1944; Okla. A. Lg., 1942. *Exhibited*: Fontainebleau, France; Arch. L.; Okla. Hist. Soc.; YWCA, Okla. City (one-man); MIT; Okla. AA, 1932-1958; Tulsa AA. Lectures: Art Trends to Clubs and Art Organizations. *Position*: A. Instr., Oklahoma City Schs. and Oklahoma City Univ., Okla., 1934- ; Vice-Pres., Sec., Okla. AA.

PATTERSON, VIOLA—*Painter*
3927 Belvoir Place, Seattle 5, Wash.

B. Seattle, Wash., May 20, 1898. *Studied*: Univ. Washington, B.A., M.F.A.; in Paris with Andre Lhote, and with Alexander Archipenko, Amedee Ozenfant. *Awards*: SAM, 1932, 1946; Northwest WC Exh., 1952, 1954; Artists of the Seattle Region, 1955. *Work*: SAM. *Exhibited*: Oakland A. Mus., 1953; Henry A. Gal., Univ. Wash., 1953 (one-man); Col. of Puget Sound, 1954 (one-man); SAM, 1953-1955, 1957 (one-man); Univ. Washington, Sch. A. Faculty Exh., 1953-1956; Zoe Dusanne Gal., 1954. 1958 (both one-man); A. of Seattle Region, 1953-1955; Woessner Gal., 1955. *Position*: Assoc. Prof. A., Univ. Washington, Seattle, Wash.; Bd. Memb., Seattle Chptr., AEA, 1955-56.

PATTISON, ABBOTT—*Sculptor, P.*
526 Aldine Ave., Chicago 13, Ill.; h. 334 Woodland Ave., Winnetka, Ill.

B. Chicago, Ill., May 15, 1916. *Studied*: Yale Col., B.A.; Yale Sch. FA, B.F.A. *Member*: Chicago A. Cl. *Awards*: Scholarships, Yale Univ. and Yale Col., 1937-38, traveling F., 1939; prizes, AIC, 1942, 1946, 1950, 1953; MMA; 1020 A. Center, Chicago, 1955. *Work*: sc., South Side Filtration Plant, Chicago; Nat. Bar. Assn. Hdqs., Chicago; Chicago Branch Lib.; Louis Solomon Bldg., Chicago; AIC; Holbrook Mus., Georgia. *Exhibited*: AIC, 1949, 1953, 1957; WMAA, 1953, 1956, 1957; MMA, 1951, 1952, and others including Chicago Area exhs. since 1942; one-man: Boidelon Gal. and AIC, 1946; Contemp. Gal., Chicago, 1950; Feingarten Gal., 1952, 1957; Elgin Acad. A., and Finn Gal., Winnetka, 1953; Holbrook Mus., Univ. Georgia, 1954; Hill Gal., Wellfleet, Mass., 1954; Todes Gal., Winnetka, 1954; Sculpture Center, N.Y., 1956. *Positions*: Instr., AIC, 1946-52; Sculptor-in-Res., Univ. Georgia, 1954; Instr., Skowhegan Sch. A., 1955-56.

PATTISON, MRS. SIDNEY. See Modjeska, Marylka

PATTY, WILLIAM A.—*Painter, T., L.*
259 Arch St., Laguna Beach, Cal.

B. Hartford, Conn., Mar. 17, 1889. *Studied*: Conn. Lg. of A. Students; NAD; Julian Acad., Paris, France. *Work*: murals, Trinidad, B.W.I.; St. Petersburg, Fla.; Los Angeles, Cal.; Miami, Fla.; Phoenix, Ariz. Other work in private collections, U.S. and abroad. *Exhibited*: NAD; CGA; PAFA; BM; Conn. Acad. FA; Wilmington Soc. FA; Witte Mem. Mus., San Antonio, Tex.; Exhs. of block prints and painting, 1957-58.

PAUL, BERNARD H.—*Craftsman*
414 Hawthorne Rd., Linthicum Heights, Md.

B. Baltimore, Md., Apr. 22, 1907. *Studied*: Maryland Inst. *Awards*: prizes, Maryland Inst., 1929, 1933, 1937. *Position*: Instr., Puppetry, Maryland Inst., Baltimore, Md., 1929-47. Dir. television program, "Paul's Puppets," WBAL-TV, Baltimore, Md., 1948-1957; WMAR-TV, 1957-58. Puppets used by U.S. Dept. Health, Edu. & Welfare for series of motion pictures for Social Security TV spots. Miniature model sets for Hutzler's Dept. Store's 100th Anniversary, 1958; marionettes for opera with Peabody Conservatory of Music, 1957; Christmas Shows, Colonial Williamsburg, 1956-57.

PAULLIN, ETHEL PARSONS (Mrs. Telford)—*Painter, Eng., Indst. Des.*
54 West 74th St., New York 23, N.Y.

B. Chardon, Ohio. *Studied*: BMFA Sch. *Member*: NSMP. *Work*: St. Bartholomew's Church, Church of St. Vincent Ferrer, N.Y.; St. Stephen's Church, Stevens Point, Wis.; Fed. Bldg., Albany, N.Y.; Mutual Casualty Ins. Bldg., Stevens Point, Wis.; Christ Church, West Haven, Conn.; Trinity Church, Ft. Wayne, Ind.; St. Paul's Episcopal Church, Brooklyn, N.Y.; Church of the Epiphany, Roslyn, L.I., N.Y.; Brooke General Hospital Chapel, U.S. Army, San Antonio, Tex.; stained glass windows: Dana Chapel, Madison Ave. Presbyterian Church, N.Y. 30 religious triptychs for U.S. Armed Forces.

PAULIN, RICHARD CALKINS—*Museum Director, T.*
Harry & Della Burpee Art Gallery, 737 North Main St.; h. 2211 Lawndale Ave., Rockford, Ill.

B. Chicago, Ill., Oct. 25, 1928. *Studied*: DePauw Univ., B.A.; Univ. Denver, M.A. *Member*: Rockford AA; NEA; Illinois A. Edu. Assn. Assembled exhs., "Director's Choice: Collector's Showcase," 1958; "Men and Metal," 1959. *Positions*: Instr. A. & Crafts, Roosevelt Jr. H.S., Rockford, Ill.; Basic & Intermediate A. Courses, Rockford AA; Dir., Harry and Della Burpee Art Gallery, Rockford, Ill., at present.

PAVAL, PHILIP—*Painter, S., C., L., Des.*
15022 Ventura Blvd., Sherman Oaks, Cal.; h. 2244 Stanley Hills Dr., Hollywood 46, Cal.

B. Nykobing Falster, Denmark, Apr. 20, 1899. *Studied*: Borger Sch.; Tech. Sch. Des., Denmark. *Member*: Cal. A. Cl. (Pres.); P. & S. Cl.; Los A. Mus. A.; Scandinavian-Am. AA; Sociedade Brasileira de Belas Artes, Brazil; and honorary member of many art societies and organizations in South America and abroad. *Awards*: many honorary degrees and decorations from France, Sweden, Belgium, Italy, British India and the U.S.; prizes, Los A. Mus. A., 1935, 1936, med., 1942; Cal. State Fair, 1935-1940, 1955, 1957; Hollywood Riviera Gal., 1936; Wichita, Kans., 1946; Ebell Cl., Los A., 1950; gold medals, State Expo., 1941; Cal. A. Cl., 1953, and others. *Work*: MMA; Los A. Mus. A.; Philbrook A. Center; Wichita AA; Newark Mus.; Pasadena AI; Devi Palace, Vizianagaram, So. India; Presidential Palace, Quito, Ecuador; Le Grand Palace, Paris, France; Buckingham Palace, London; Mus. Am. Comedy, Fla.; Rosenborg Castle, Denmark; St. Martin of Tours, Brentwood, Cal.; Lutheran Church, Los A.; Mataro Mus., Spain; Nat. Mus., Iceland; Nat. Mus., Copenhagen, Denmark; Nat. Mus., Oslo, Norway; Masonic Lodge, Hollywood and San Francisco, and many others; work also in numerous private colls. *Exhibited*: leading galleries and museums, nationally and internationally.

PAXSON, ETHEL (Mrs. Clement E.)—*Painter, T., W., L.*
2400 Sedgwick Ave., New York 68, N.Y.

B. Meriden, Conn., Mar. 23, 1885. *Studied*: Corcoran Sch. A.; PAFA; & with Cecilia Beaux, Hugh Breckenridge, William Chase, & others. *Member*: NAWA; New Haven Paint & Clay Cl.; AAPL; Meriden A. & Crafts Assn.; A. Lg. Nassau County. *Awards*: prize, Meriden A. & Crafts Assn. *Work*: Am. Embassy, Rio de Janeiro, Brazil. *Exhibited*: NAD; NAWA; All. A. Am.; AWCS, 1945, 1946; New Haven Paint & Clay Cl., annually. Contributor & I., Brazilian-American, Rio de Janeiro, Brazil. Writer, L., on Fine Arts; Exh. Sec., AWS, 5 yrs.; private classes in fine arts.

PAYANT, FELIX—*Writer, L., E.*
926 Montezuma Ave., Las Vegas, N.M.

B.Faribault, Minn., Apr. 10, 1891. *Studied*: Univ. Minnesota; PIASch; Columbia Univ., B.S. Author: "Our Changing Art Education," 1935; "Design Technics"; "Create Something." Lectures: "Design and People." *Position*: Prof. A., Ohio State Univ.; Visiting Prof., Syracuse Univ.; Ed., Design magazine, 1920-49; Assoc. Prof., A. Dept., New Mexico Highlands Univ., to 1958 (retired). Conducts art study courses in Mexico each summer.

PAYNE, ELSIE PALMER (Mrs. Edgar A.)—*Painter, T., L.*
1269 Ozeta Terr., Los Angeles 46, Cal.

B. San Antonio, Tex., Sept. 9, 1884. *Studied*: Best's A. Sch., San F., Cal.; Chicago Acad. FA. *Member*: Laguna Beach AA (Fndr. member); Women Painters of the West (Fndr. member); Cal. A. Cl.; Cal. WC Soc.; A. of the Southwest; Nat. Soc. A. & Lets. *Awards*: prizes, Los A. Mus., 1942, 1944; Cal. A. Cl., 1943; Ebell Cl., 1943; Greek Theatre, Los A., 1948, 1949; Pasadena AI, 1950; Laguna Beach AA, 1951; Laguna Beach A. Festival, 1952. *Work*: Pub. Sch. in Laguna Beach, Los A., Cal.; bronze plaque, entrance to Laguna Beach A. Gal. *Exhibited*: Paris, France; NAWA; NAD; Cal. WC Soc.; Riverside Mus.; Los A. Mus. A.; Laguna Beach AA; Ebell Cl., Los A.; Pasadena AI. Publ., Distr., "Composition of Outdoor Painting," by Edgar A. Payne.

PAYNE, GEORGE KIMPTON—*Designer, P., Gr., S., C., I.*
Woodward & Lothrop, 11th & G Sts., Washington 13, D.C.; h. 2230 North Roosevelt St., Arlington 5, Va.

B. Springville, N.Y., May 23, 1911. *Studied*: ASL, with George Bridgman, Allen Lewis, Thomas Benton. Contributor to: New Yorker magazine. *Award*: Intl. Silk Assn., 1958. *Position*: Scientific A., Nat. Zoo Park, Wash., D.C., 1936; Advertising A., 1937-43; USNR Terrain Map Model Maker, 1943-45; Mgr., Displays, Des., Woodward & Lothrop, Washington, D.C., 1950- .

PAYOR, EUGENE—*Painter, Des., I., Comm. A.*
147 West 87th St., New York 24, N.Y.

B. New York, N.Y., July 28, 1909. *Studied*: Univ. California; ASL, with John Steuart Curry, Jean Charlot, Raphael Soyer. *Awards*: prizes, A. Dir. Cl., N.Y.; Lithographers Nat. Assn.; Southampton Mus. A. *Exhibited*: All. A. Am.; WMAA; Salons of Am.; VMFA; SFMA; Univ. Georgia, 1944 (one-man). *Position*: Prof. A., Univ. Georgia, Athens, Ga., 1943-45.*

PEABODY, AMELIA—*Sculptor*
Dedham St., Dover, Mass.; h. 120 Commonwealth Ave., Boston 16, Mass.

B. Marblehead Neck, Mass., July 3, 1890. *Studied*: BMFA Sch., and with Charles Grafly; Archipenko Sch. A. *Member*: Copley Soc., Boston; North Shore AA; Gld. Boston A.; NSS; NAWA; AAPL; New England Sculptors' Assn. *Award*: Medalist, A. & Crafts Soc., Boston, 1950. *Work*: BMFA; portraits, medals, garden and architectural sculpture, in bronze, stone, and pottery. *Exhibited*: PAFA; WFNY 1939; AIC; Boston S. Soc.; Gld. Boston A. (one-man); PMA; N.E. Assn. for Contemp. S., 1951; BMFA, 1950, 1951; NAD, 1952; Festival of Boston, 1952. *Position*: Chm. A. & Skills Corps, Am. Red Cross, 1944-58; Vice-Pres., A. & Crafts Soc., Boston; Trustee, Inst. Contemp. A., Boston; Bd., Soc. Indp. A., Mus. Science.

PEACOCK, CLAUDE—
Illustrator, Comm. A., P., T., Cart.
3103 Goode St.; h. 418 East Delano St., Montgomery, Ala.

B. Selma, Ala., July 18, 1912. *Studied*: Huntingdon Col., Montgomery, Ala. *Member*: Alabama A. Lg. *Awards*: prizes, Army Art Comp., Jefferson Barracks, Mo., 1942; Alabama A. Lg., 1946. *Work*: Archives & History Dept., State of Alabama; WMAA; Montgomery Mus. FA; murals, Napier Field Army Air Base, Dothan, Ala. *Exhibited*: Army A. Exh., Atlanta, Gal., 1945. I., covers for American Druggist, Outdoorsman magazines; color work for Life magazine. *Position*: Wild Life Artist for Dept. of Conservation, State of Alabama.*

PEACOCK, JEAN ELEANOR (Mrs. Lewis M. Knebel)—
Painter, Gr., T.
3315 South Wakefield St., Apt. A-1, Arlington 6, Va.

B. Norfolk, Va. *Studied*: Longwood Col., Va., B.S.; Columbia Univ., M.A.; ASL, and with Arthur Young, Harry Wickey, Edwin Ziegfeld and others. *Member*: NAWA; Va. Edu. Assn.; NAEA; Eastern AA; NEA. *Exhibited*: NAWA; VMFA; Irene Leach Mem. Mus., and others. *Position*: Former Supv. A., Fredericksburg, Va.; Instr., summers, Radford Col., William & Mary Col., Wilson T. Col.; A.T., Hd. A. Dept., George Washington H.S., Alexandria, Va.; A.T., Elementary Schs., Alexandria, Va., at present.

PEARCE, HELEN S. (Mrs. Thomas M.)—
Painter, Des., I., T.
1712 Sigma Chi Rd., Northeast, Albuquerque, N.M.

B. Reading, Pa., Feb. 17, 1895. *Studied*: Phila. Sch. Des. for Women (now Moore Inst. A., S. & Indst.); Univ. New Mexico, with Raymond Jonson, Kenneth Adams, Randall Davey; Pasadena City Col., with Kenneth Nack; also with George Bridgman, Henry B. Snell, Leopold Seyffert, Lucile Howard. *Awards*: prizes, New Mexico State Fair, 1942-1945, 1957; Nat. Mus., Wash., D.C., 1950, 1952; Albuquerque A., 1953-1955. *Exhibited*: Nat. Lg. Am. Pen Women, 1950, 1952; Terry AI, 1952; Roswell Mus. A., 1953; P. & S. of the Southwest, 1943-1954; New Mexico A., 1955; Mus. New Mexico traveling exh., 1948-1950; New Mexico State Fair, 1942-1954; Jonson Gal., 1942-1955; All-Albuquerque A., 1950-1955; 3 one-man exhs., Mus. New Mexico, 1943, 1946, 1951. Illus., "Southwesterners Write," 1946. Work reproduced in Art Digest and School Arts magazines.

PEARLSTEIN, PHILIP—*Painter*
181 Ave. A, New York 9 N.Y.

B. Pittsburgh, Pa., May 24, 1924. *Studied*: Carnegie Inst., B.F.A.; N.Y. Univ., Inst. FA, M.A. *Work*: in private colls. *Exhibited*: Carnegie Inst., 1955; WMAA, 1955;

Univ. Nebraska, 1956; Walker A. Center, 1956; other group and one-man exhs., in Pittsburgh, Pa., New York, N.Y. Contributor to Arts magazine.*

PEARMAN, KATHARINE K.—*Painter, L., T.*
920 King St., Rockford, Ill.

B. Beloit, Wis., Feb. 11, 1893. *Studied*: with Hugh Breckenridge, Grant Wood, Francis Chapin. *Member*: Chicago SA; Rockford AA; Contemp. A. Group; Chicago AC. *Awards*: prizes, Rockford AA, 1927, 1930, 1931, 1934, 1935, 1937, 1939, 1942, 1943; AIC, 1951; Wis. Salon, 1942, 1943. *Work*: Burpee A. Gal., Rockford, Ill.; Wisconsin Un.; Abbott Laboratories Coll.; mural, St. Paul's Chapel, Camp Grant, Ill. *Exhibited*: NAD, 1944; Grand Rapids, Mich., 1940; PAFA, 1941; CGA, 1941; Carnegie Inst., 1941, 1943; Rockford AA, 1927-1946; AIC, 1929, 1932, 1935, 1940-1943, 1945; Chicago A. Cl., 1952; Burpee A. Gal., 1949, 1951; Wis. Salon A., 1939, 1940, 1942-1945; Milwaukee, Wis., 1946. Lectures: Contemporary Painting. *Position*: Instr. A., Rockford Col., Rockford, Ill., 1943-45.

PEARSON, ANTON—*Craftsman, P., S.*
510 South Main St., Lindsborg, Kan.

B. Lund, Sweden, May 23, 1892. *Studied*: Bethany Col.; Lindsborg, Kans., and with Birger Sandzen. *Member*: Smoky Hill AA. Contributor to: Kansas Magazine. Lectures: Woodcarving & Hobbies.

PEARSON, EDWIN—*Sculptor, P., C., Des., T.*
East Park Road, Hyde Park, N.Y.

B. Yuma County, Colo., Dec. 20, 1889. *Studied*: Royal Acad. A., Munich, Germany; AIC with Harry Wolcott. *Award*: prize, Swedish-Am. A. *Work*: S., Nat. Mus., Wash., D.C.; Federal Hall, N.Y.; Petersburg (Va.) Mus.; Grand Canyon Nat. Park Mus.; Nat. Mus., Munich; State Lib., Weimar, Germany. *Exhibited*: PAFA; NAD; Arch. Lg.; Swedish-Am. A.; one-man: Milwaukee AI; AIC. *Position*: Mus. Exh. Des. Specialist & S., Nat. Park Service, Washington, D.C., 1950-1957.

PEARSON, MARGUERITE S.—*Painter, T.*
47 Marmion Way. Rockport, Mass.

B. Philadelphia, Pa. *Studied*: BMFA Sch., with William James, F. A. Bosley; also with A. T. Hibbard, Harry Leith-Ross. *Member*: Gld. Boston A.; All. A. Am.; North Shore AA; Rockport AA; AAPL. *Awards*: prizes, North Shore AA; Springville (Utah) AA; New Haven Paint & Clay Cl.; All. A. Am.; Ogunquit A. Center; Academic A., Springfield (Mass.) A. Mus.; Rockport AA. *Work*: Springville A. Gal.; New Haven Pub. Lib.; Beach Mem. A. Gal., Storrs, Conn.; Monson (Mass.) State Hospital; Gardiner (Mass.) H.S.; Boston Music Sch.; Brigham Young Univ.; Mechanics Bldg., Boston; Episcopal Diocesan House, Boston; Trade Sch. for Girls, and Wilson, Brooks, and Burke Sch., Boston; Grimmins and Chandler Sch., Somerville, Mass.; Somerville, Medford and Gloucester City Halls; Case Inst. Tech., Cleveland, Ohio; Brooks Sch., Andover, Mass.; Draper Sch., Draper, Utah; Salem (Mass.) Court House; Bruckner Mus., Albion, Mich. *Exhibited*: NAD; PAFA; CGA; All. A. Am.; Portraits, Inc.; Jordan Marsh Gal., Boston; North Shore AA; Rockport AA.

PEASE, LUCIUS CURTIS—*Cartoonist*
105 Durand Road, Maplewood, N.J.*

PEASE, MARION DIETZ—*Educator, C.*
Art Department, Skidmore College; h. 38 Circular St., Saratoga Springs, N.Y.

B. Huntington, Mass., Aug. 6, 1894. *Studied*: PIASch.; Columbia Univ., T. Col., B.S., M.A.; special courses, Harvard Univ.; Univ. California, with Millard Sheets and Glen Lukens; Chicago Sch. Des., with Moholy-Nagy; Cranbrook Acad. A., with Marianne Strengel. *Member*: CAA; N.Y. State Craftsmen. *Exhibited*: Skidmore Col. Faculty Exhs.; Albany Inst. Hist. & A.; Schenectady Mus. A.; N.Y. State Craftsmen. *Positions*: Hd. A. Dept., Oklahoma College for Women, 1921-25; Chm., A. Dept., Skidmore College, Saratoga Springs, N.Y., 1926- .

PEAT, WILBUR DAVID—*Museum Director, W., L.*
North Pennsylvania & 16th Sts.; h. 5473 North Capitol Ave., Indianapolis 8, Ind.

B. Chengtu, China, Nov. 8, 1898. *Studied*: Ohio Wesleyan Univ.; Cleveland Sch. A.; NAD; ASL; Univ. Chicago. *Member*: AAMus.; Indiana Hist. Soc.; Midwest Mus. Conference; Indiana AC. *Awards*: hon. degrees, L.H.D., Hanover (Ind.) Col., 1944; LL.D., Indiana Central Col., Indianapolis, 1956. *Author*: "Portraits and Painters of the Governors of Indiana" (Ind. Hist. Soc.), 1944; "Pioneer Painters of Indiana" (Art Assoc. Indianapolis), 1954. Contributor to: Bulletins of the Indianapolis AA; Indiana Magazine of History; Art Quarterly. Lectures: Pioneer Painters of Indiana; etc. *Position*: Dir., Akron, (Ohio) AI, 1924-29; Dir. Mus., John Herron AI, Indianapolis, Ind., 1929- .

PECK, AUGUSTUS—*Educator*
Brooklyn Museum Art School, Eastern Parkway, Brooklyn, N.Y.

Position: Supv., Brooklyn Museum Art School.*

PECK, CLARA ELSENE—*Illustrator, P., Et.*
519 Steinwehr Ave., R.D. #2, Gettysburg, Pa.

B. Allegan, Mich., Apr. 18, 1883. *Studied*: Minneapolis Sch. FA; PAFA, with William Chase. *Member*: AWS; A. Gld.; SI; Women P. & S. Soc. *Exhibited*: AWS traveling exh.; MMA European traveling exh., 1956-57; Washington County Mus. A., Hagerstown, Md., 1958; one-man: Gettysburg Col.; York (Pa.) A. Center; New Canaan, Conn., 1958. I., in national magazines; covers, text books and children's books, 1906-1940.

PECK, GLENNA, (HUGHES)—*Painter, Des.*
50 Lake Howell Rd., Winter Park, Fla.

B. Huntsburg, Ohio. *Studied*: N.Y. Sch. F. & App. A.; Syracuse Univ., B.F.A. *Member*: Texas FA Assn.; Orlando AA; Sarasota AA. *Awards*: prizes, A. All., N.Y., 1931; Thibaut prize, 1932; United Piece Dyeworks prize, 1932; Assoc. A. Syracuse, 1940. *Exhibited*: Assoc. A. Syracuse, annually; Finger Lakes Exh., 1939; Syracuse Mus. FA, 1934; Bradenton (Fla.) AA, 1941; Orlando AA, 1958; one-man: Austin, Tex., 1950; Vienna, Va., 1954.

PECK, JAMES EDWARD—*Painter, Des., I.*
1917 North Broadway, Seattle 2, Wash.

B. Pittsburgh, Pa., Nov. 7, 1907. *Studied*: Cleveland Sch. A.; John Huntington Polytechnic Inst., and with Henry G. Keller, Rolf Stoll, Carl Gaertner. *Member*: AWS; AEA; Puget Sound Group of Northwest Painters; Seattle A. Dir. Soc. *Awards*: prizes, CMA, 1939, 1941, 1945; Guggenheim F., 1942, 1945. *Work*: CMA; Dayton AI; Carville (La.) Mem. Hospital; Cleveland AA; City of Cleveland Coll.; Am. Acad. A. & Let.; SAM; enamels: Butler AI. *Exhibited*: PAFA; AWS; AIC; CMA; Dayton AI; Cleveland Sch. A.; Cincinnati Mod. A. Soc.; Little A. Center, Dayton; Butler AI, 1953-55; Anchorage, Alaska; SAM; Henry Gal., Univ. Washington; Univ. Gal., Univ. Minnesota; Frye Mus. A., Seattle; one-man: Henry Gal.; AWS; Spokane, Wash.; Frederick A. Nelson, Seattle; Klamath Falls, Ore.; Portland, Ore.; Manchester-Pierce Gal., Bellevue, Wash. Contributor to Ford Times; Lincoln-Mercury Times; American Artist magazine. *Position*: Dir. A. Dept., Cornish Sch., Seattle, 1946-52; Asst. A. Dir., Miller, Mackay, Hoeck & Hartung Adv. Agcy., Seattle, Wash., at present. Vice-Pres., 1954, Pres., 1955, Puget Sound Group Painters; Vice-Pres., Seattle A. Dir. Soc., 1955.

PECK, VERNA JOHNSTON (Mrs. W. C.)—*Painter, T.*
910 Home Ave., Kansas City 22, Mo.

B. Hutchinson, Kans., Feb. 23, 1889. *Studied*: Southwestern Col.; Wichita Univ.; Kansas City AI, B.F.A.; Independence, Mo., B.F.A., M.A., and with Grace Raymond, Clayton Henri Staples, Thomas Hart Benton, and others. *Member*: Mid-Am. A.; Community A. Assn., Independence, Mo. *Awards*: prizes, Kansas State Fair, 1940, 1942; Kansas Artists, 1942; State Fair, Sedalia, Mo., 1955. *Work*: Mid-Am. A. Gal. *Exhibited*: State Fair, Independence, Mo., Sedalia, Mo.*

PEERS, MRS. FLORENCE LEIF. See *Leif, Florence*

PEERS, GORDON FRANKLIN—*Painter, T.*
Rhode Island School of Design, Providence, R.I.; h. 72 Paine Ave., Cranston 10, R.I.

B. Easton, Pa., Mar. 17, 1909. *Studied*: R.I. Sch. Des.; ASL; BAID; & with John R. Frazier. *Awards*: prize, Boston A. Festival, 1955; Newport AA, 1958. *Work*: R.I. Sch. Des. *Exhibited*: Carnegie Inst., 1942, 1943; VMFA, 1940; WFNY 1939; GGE, 1939; Nat. Exh. Am. A., N.Y., 1936, 1938; Pepsi-Cola, 1946; Mus., R.I. Sch. Des.; Newport AA; WMA, 1958; Boston AC; Provincetown AA, 1958; Dept. Interior, Wash., D.C.; Univ. Illinois; Rockford (Ill.) AA; Boston A. Festival, 1958. *Position*: Hd., Dept. Painting, R.I. Sch. Des., Providence, R.I., 1934-36, 1938- .

PEET, MARGOT (MARGUERITE MUNGER PEET)—
Painter
6624 Wenonga Rd., Kansas City, Mo.

B. Kansas City, Mo., June 8, 1903. *Studied*: Kansas City AI; Colorado A. Acad., and with Randall Davey, Thomas Hart Benton. *Member*: Mid-Am. A. *Exhibited*: CGA, 1940; Milwaukee AI, 1939; Midwest Exh., 1926, 1934, 1939; Mid-Am. A., 1950, 1953.*

PEETS, ORVILLE HOUGHTON—*Painter, Gr.*
Indian River Hundred, R.D., Millsboro, Del.; s. Woodstock, N.Y.

B. Cleveland, Ohio, Aug. 13, 1884. *Studied*: Julian Acad., Ecole des Beaux-Arts, Paris, France. *Member*: Wilmington Soc. FA; Rehoboth (Del.) A. Lg. *Awards*: med., Int. Pr. M. Exh., Los A., Cal., 1931; prizes, CMA, 1932; Wilmington Soc. FA, 1942-1944; BMA, 1953. *Work*: Musee du Jeu de Paume, Paris; Hispanic Mus., N.Y.; Delaware A. Center; State House, Dover, Del.; N.Y. Pub. Lib.; Lib. Cong.; Cal. State Lib.; Los A. Mus. A.; PMA; CMA; Wilmington Soc. FA; BMA. Made 1954 Presentation Print for Pr. M. of Cal.

PEIRCE, GERRY—*Painter, Et., I., W., T., L.*
857 South Swan Rd.; h. 4756 Calle Jabell, Tucson, Ariz.

B. Jamestown, N.Y., June 3, 1900. *Studied*: Cleveland Inst. A.; ASL. *Member*: SAGA; Chicago Soc. Et.; AWS; Cal. Pr. M. *Work*: Joslyn A. Mus.; IBM; BMFA; CMA; MMA; LC; J. B. Speed A. Mus.; FMA; Ariz. State Mus.; Denver A. Mus. *Exhibited*: SAGA, 1935-1945. I., "Plants of Sun and Sand," 1939. *Position*: Dir., Instr., Gerry Peirce School, Tucson, Ariz.

PEIRCE, WALDO—*Painter, I., W.*
Searsport, Me.

B. Bangor, Me., Dec. 17, 1884. *Studied*: Phillips Acad.; Harvard Univ., A.B., and in Paris, France. *Awards*: prizes, Pomona, Cal., 1939; Pepsi-Cola, 1944; Carnegie Inst., 1944. *Work*: MMA; WMAA; AGAA; PAFA; BM; Farnsworth Mus. A.; Encyclopaedia Britannica; Pepsi-Cola Co.; The Upjohn Co.; Univ. Arizona; State House, Augusta, Me.; Bangor (Me.) Pub. Lib.; Troy, N.Y.; Peabody, Mass. *Exhibited*: nationally. I., "The Magic Bed Knob," 1943; "The Children's Hour," 1944.*

PELIKAN ALFRED GEORGE—*Educator, W., L., P., C.*
School Administration Bldg., 1111 North 10th St.; h. 7845 North Links Circle, Milwaukee 17, Wis.

B. Breslau, Germany, Mar. 5, 1893. *Studied*: Carnegie Inst., B.A.; Columbia Univ., M.A.; ASL; & in England. *Member*: Wis. P. & S. (hon.); Wis. Designer-Craftsman (hon.); Seven A. Soc. (hon.); A. Dir. Cl. (hon.). *Awards*: F., Royal Soc. A., London; Milwaukee Journal prize, 1931, 1957; Helen F. Mears prize, 1936. *Exhibited*: Wisconsin P. & S., 1958. *Author*: "The Art of the Child," 1931; "Fun With Figure Drawing," 1947. *Co-Author*: "Simple Metalwork," 1940. Contributor to: School Arts, Design, Education, & other magazines. *Position*: Dir., Milwaukee AI, 1926-41; Dir. A. Edu., Milwaukee (Wis.) Pub. Sch., 1925- ; Ext. L., Univ. Wisconsin; Exh. Com., Milwaukee AI.

PELL, MRS. HERBERT. See *Bigelow, Olive*

PELLEW, JOHN C.—*Painter*

Murray St., R.F.D. 4, Westport, Conn.

B. Penzance, England, Apr. 9, 1903. *Member*: NA; AWS; All. A. Am.; SC. *Awards*: prizes, AWS, 1951; SC, 1950, 1951; medal, All. A. Am., 1951. *Work*: MMA; BM; Newark Mus.; Unio Cultural, Sao Paulo, Brazil; Georgia Mus. A., Athens; mural, Pub. Sch. No. 122, Queens, N.Y. *Exhibited*: CGA, 1935, 1936; Carnegie Inst., 1943-1946; PAFA, 1936-1938; BM, 1935, 1939, 1943; NAD, 1937, 1942, 1944; AIC, 1938, 1939, 1943; MModA, 1943; one-man: New York, N.Y., 1934, 1938, 1944, 1948.

PELS, ALBERT—*Painter, T.*

171 West 71st St., New York 23, N.Y.

B. Cincinnati, Ohio, May 7, 1910. *Studied*: Univ. Cincinnati; Cincinnati A. Acad.; ASL; BAID; & with Benton, Palmer, Brook & others. *Member*: NSMP; Soc. Indp. A.; AEA; Audubon A. *Awards*: med., BAID, 1936; prize, Parkersburg, W. Va., 1942. *Work*: CM; Massillon Mus. A.; PMA; murals, Wilmington (Del.) Court House; Norfolk Naval Base; Anniston, Ala., Army Base; S.S. Monroe; USPO, Normal, Ill.; assisted with murals, USPO, Wash., D.C.; Queens General Hospital. *Exhibited*: WMAA, 1938, 1939, 1942, 1944; Carnegie Inst., 1941-1945; NAD, 1938, 1940-1942, 1945; PAFA, 1937, 1943, 1944; CM, 1932-1938, 1940, 1941, 1942 (one-man); Rochester Mem. A. Gal.; William Rockhill Nelson Gal.; Dayton AI; Riverside Mus.; Butler AI; Conn. Acad. FA; Massillon Mus. A.; Parkersburg FA Center; one-man: Macbeth, Babcock, Laurel Gal., Chase Gal., etc. Illus. juvenile books. *Position*: Dir., Albert Pels Sch. A., New York, N.Y., Br.: 1026 Park Ave., N.Y.

PELTON, AGNES—*Painter*

Box 64, E St., Cathedral City, Cal.

B. Stuttgart, Germany, Aug. 22, 1881. *Studied*: PIASch; in Rome; & with Arthur Dow, W. L. Lathrop. *Member*: NAWA; AAPL; Riverside (Cal.) AA. *Work*: San Diego FA Soc.; Santa Barbara Mus. A. *Exhibited*: NAWA, annually until 1932; Armory Exh., N.Y., 1913; Terry AI, 1952; PAFA, 1930; Knoedler Gal., 1917; Mus. New Mexico, Santa Fé, 1933; BM, 1931; one-man exh.: Montross Gal., 1929; Argent Gal., 1931; San Diego FA Center, 1934; SFMA, 1943; Santa Barbara Mus. A., 1943; Crocker A. Gal., Sacramento, Cal.; Pomona Col.; Laguna Beach AA, 1947; Palm Springs (Cal.), 1950, 1955; El Mirador Hotel, Palm Springs, 1954; Laguna Beach AA, 1947; Desert A. Center, 1951-1955; Univ. Redlands, 1951.

PEN, RUDOLPH T.—*Painter, Lith., T.*

55 West Schiller St., Chicago 10, Ill.

B. Chicago, Ill., Jan. 1, 1918. *Studied*: AIC, B.F.A. *Awards*: traveling scholarship, AIC, 1943; prizes, NAD, 1945; PAFA (purchase); Illinois State Fair. *Exhibited*: NAD; LC; Carnegie Inst., annually, 1943-1955; AIC, annually, 1943-1955; PMA; Illinois State Fair; Milwaukee AI; AWS; PAFA; one-man: Carroll Carstairs Gal., N.Y.; Mexico City; Marshall Fields Gal.; Palmer House Gal.; Benjamin Franklin Lib., Chicago; Frank Oehlschlaeger Gal., Chicago.*

PENDLETON, CONSTANCE—*Painter, T.*

Bryn Athyn, Pa.

B. Philadelphia, Pa. *Studied*: Columbia Univ., B.S., M.A.; in Europe; & with Arthur Carles, Hugh Breckenridge, Arthur Dow. *Member*: Phila. A. T. Assn.; Eastern AA. *Exhibited*: A. All., Plastic Cl., Sketch Cl., all of Phila., Pa.; Argent Gal. *Position*: Hd. A. Dept., Kensington H.S., Philadelphia, Pa. Retired, 1952.

PENFIELD, FLORENCE BENTZ (Mrs.)—*Painter, T.*

606 Brighton Ave., Reading, Pa.

B. Buffalo, N.Y., Jan. 15, 1895. *Studied*: Univ. Buffalo, Ph.C., B.S., M.S.; Buffalo Sch. FA; PAFA, and with Florence Bach, Roy Nuse, Daniel Garber, and others. *Member*: F., PAFA; Buffalo Soc. A.; Woodmere A. Gal.; AAPL; AEA. *Awards*: prize, Albright A. Gal., 1941; F., PAFA. *Work*: Reading (Pa.) Pub. Mus. *Exhibited*: Albright A. Gal.; Parkersburg FA Center; Reading Pub. Mus.; Miami, Fla., 1952; Buffalo Soc. A.; Reading A. Gal.; traveling exh., Pa., Md., Va., Ga. Teaching, private studio.

PENNEY, JAMES—*Painter*

101 Campus Road, Clinton, N.Y.

B. St. Joseph, Mo., Sept. 6, 1910. *Studied*: Univ. Kansas, B.F.A., with Albert Bloch, Karl Mattern and Raymond Eastwood; ASL, with Charles Locke, John Sloan and George Grosz. *Member*: Audubon A.; CAA; ASL. *Awards*: prizes, Paintings of the Year, 1948; West N.Y. Pr. M., 1950; Cooperstown, N.Y., 1958; Munson-Williams-Proctor Inst., 1955, 1957 (purchase); Kansas State, 1950, 1954 (purchase); medal, Kansas City AI, 1931. *Work*: Springfield Mus. A.; Munson-Williams-Proctor Inst.; Univ. Nebraska; Kansas State Col.; New Britain Inst.; Nelson Gal. A.; Clearwater Mus. A.; Phillips Acad.; Wichita A. Mus.; Nat. Soc. A. & Let.; Ft. Worth A. Center; Des Moines A. Center; Utica Col.; Hamilton Col.; murals, Flushing (L.I.) H.S.; USPO, Union, Palmyra, Mo. *Exhibited*: CGA, 1937, 1941, 1947, 1949, 1951, 1953; AIC, 1939, 1943, 1954; BM, 1947, 1949, 1951; Carnegie Inst., 1942, 1943, 1952; MMA, 1942; Toledo Mus. A., 1950; WMAA, 1941, 1942, 1951, 1955, 1958; PC; Los A Mus. A.; SFMA; CAM, 1958; Provincetown A. Festival, 1958; Audubon A., 1957, 1958; Munson-Williams-Proctor Inst., 1957, 1958; Univ. Nebraska, 1957, 1958; Audubon A., 1950-1955; PAFA, 1950, 1952-1954; Walker A. Center, 1949, 1954; Des Moines A. Center, 1949-1951, 1953-1958; Cal. PLH, 1952, and many others; one-man: Kraushaar Gal., 1950, 1954, 1957; Utica Col., 1957; Colgate Univ., 1951, 1954; Union Col., 1955; Wells Col., 1953; Kansas State Col., 1955; Wichita A. Mus., 1955; Vassar Col., 1955. *Position*: Instr. A., Hunter Col., 1941-42; Bennington Col., 1946-47; F., in art, Hamilton Col., 1948-1955; Instr., Munson-Williams-Proctor Inst., 1948-55; Visiting A., Kansas State Col., 1955; Asst. Prof. A., Vassar Col., 1955-56; Hamilton Col., 1956- .

PENNY, AUBREY J(OHN) R(OBERT)—*Painter*

1551 Cahuenga Blvd., Los Angeles 28, Cal.; h. 12216 Montana Ave., West Los Angeles 49, Cal.

B. London, England, July 30, 1917. *Studied*: London Univ.; Univ. California at Los A., A.B., M.A. *Member*: Victoria Inst.; Contemp. A. Soc.; Inst. Contemp. A. Soc., London; Cal. WC Soc.; Am. Soc. for Aesthetics. *Award*: Cal. WC Soc., 1955. *Exhibited*: Cal. WC Soc., 1953-1956; Nat. Orange Show, 1953; Los A. Mus. A., 1954-1957; AWS, 1957, 1958; CGA, 1957; Santa Barbara Mus. A., 1955.

PENNY, CARLTON P.—*Painter*

50 East 42nd St.; h. 1060 Park Ave., New York 28, N.Y.

B. Metuchin, N.J. *Studied*: Columbia Univ.; Univ. Rochester; ASL; N.Y. Univ. *Member*: SC; Nat. Pastel Soc.; AAPL; Arch. Lg.; Audubon A. (Co-founder); Mun. A. Soc.; Nat. Soc. Painters in Casein. *Exhibited*: NAD; Harvard Univ.; NAC; Arch. Lg.; Whistler Mus.; Am. Acad. A. & Let. *Positions*: Dir., AAPL; Town Hall Cl.; Chm., Town Hall Cl. A. Com.; Pres., Nat. Soc. Painters in Casein; Member-Delegate, FA Fed., New York, N.Y.*

PEOPLES, AUGUSTA H. (Mrs. R. E.)—*Painter, T.*

3325 West Coulter St., Philadelphia 29, Pa.

B. Philadelphia, Pa., Apr. 2, 1896. *Studied*: Phila. Sch. Des. for Women; Spring Garden Inst.; PAFA. *Member*: Phila. A. All.; AAPL; Phila. Plastic Cl. *Work*: Moore Inst., Phila. *Exhibited*: PAFA, 1933-1935; CGA, 1935-1937, 1939; Phila. A. All., 1945 (one-man); Phila. Plastic Cl.; Phila. Sketch Cl.; Woodmere A. Gal.; Newman's Gal.; Bala Cynwyd Women's Cl., 1946 (one-man); Delaware County A. Group, 1955; Women's City Cl., Phila., 1957 (one-man); Cape May AA, 1955-1958.

PEPI, VINCENT—*Designer, P.*

299 Madison Ave., New York 17, N.Y.; h. 103 Lagoon Blvd., Massapequa, N.Y.

B. Boston, Mass., June 25, 1926. *Studied*: Workshop Sch. Comm. A.; CUASch.; Pratt Inst.; Meschini Inst., Rome, and with Pericle Fazzini, Rome, Italy. *Awards*: Assn. Univ. Evening Col., 1952, 1954, 1958. *Work*: Mural, U.S. Naval Training Station, Sampson, N.Y. *Positions*: A., Sterling Adv. Agcy.; Asst. A. Dir., Batten, Barton, Durstine & Osborne, New York, N.Y.; A. Dir., Office of Publ. & Printing, A. Dir., N.Y. Univ. Press; Freelance A. Dir. & Des., at present.

PEPPER, STEPHEN COBURN—*Educator, W., L., Cr.*

2718 Buena Vista St., Berkeley, Cal.

B. Newark, N.J., Apr. 29, 1891. *Studied:* Harvard Univ., A.B., M.A., Ph.D.; Colby Col., L.H.D. *Member:* Am. Soc. for Aesthetics; CAA; Am. Philosophical Assn.; Am. Acad. A. & Sc. Author: "Aesthetic Quality," 1938; "World Hypotheses," 1942; "The Basis of Criticism in the Arts," 1945; "Principles of Art Appreciation," 1949; "The Work of Art," 1955; "The Sources of Value," 1958, & others. Contributor to: Journal of Philosophy, Philosophical Review, College Art Journal, Parnassus magazines. *Position:* Instr., 1919-20, Asst. Prof., 1923-27, Assoc. Prof., 1927-30, Prof., 1930- , Asst. Dean, Let. & Sc., 1939-47, Chm. A. Dept., 1938-51, Chm., Philosophical Dept., 1952-1958, Emeritus, 1958- , Univ. California, Berkeley, Cal.

PEREIRA, I. RICE—*Painter, T., L.*

121 West 15th St., New York 11, N.Y.

B. Boston, Mass., Aug. 5, 1907. *Studied:* Academie Moderne, Paris; ASL, and with Richard Lahey, Jan Matulka. *Member:* AEA. *Awards:* prize, Pepsi-Cola, 1946. *Work:* MMoDA; MMA; Newark Mus.; Univ. Arizona; Howard Univ.; Mus. Non-Objective Painting; WMAA; Wadsworth Atheneum; Toledo Mus. A.; SFMA; AIC; BMA; AGAA; DMFA; Detroit Inst. A.; Vassar Col.; Delgado Mus. A.; Walker A. Center; PMG; Smith Col.; Ball State T. Col.; Butler Inst. Am. A.; CM; Mus. A., Phoenix, Ariz.; Houghton Lib., Harvard Univ. (orig. mss. of "The Lapis"); Am. Assn. Univ. Women; Miller Coll., Meriden, Conn.; Dutch Ministry of Information, The Hague; Munson-Williams-Proctor Inst., and in private colls. *Exhibited:* CGA; Carnegie Inst.; PAFA; AIC; and others; Musee d'Art Moderne, Paris; Tate Gal. A., Inst. Contemp. A., both in London; Brussels, Berlin, Antwerp, Vienna and other European cities; Sao Paulo, Brazil; one-man: Barnett Aden Gal., Wash., D.C.; ACA Gal., 1949; Phillips Acad., 1949; Santa Barbara Mus. A., 1950; deYoung Mem. Mus., 1950; Memphis Acad. A., 1951; Univ. Syracuse, 1951; BMA, 1951; Ball State T. Col., 1951; Durlacher Bros., 1951, 1953, 1954; PC, 1952; Dayton AI, 1952; WMAA, retrospective, 1953; Des Moines A. Center, 1953; SFMA, 1953; DMFA, 1953; Vassar Col., 1953; Adele Lawson Gal., 1954; Hofstra Col., 1954; Univ. Michigan, 1954; Phila. A. All., 1955; CGA, 1956; Wellons Gal., N.Y., 1956. Contributor to the Palette; Mysindia; Western AA Bulletin. Author: "Light and New Reality"; "The Transformation of Nothing and the Paradox of Space"; "The Nature of Space"; "The Lapis."

PERHAM, ROY GATES—*Painter, L.*

269 Raymond St., Hasbrouck Heights, N.J.

B. Paterson, N.J., Apr. 18, 1916. *Studied:* Grand Central A. Sch., and with Frank DuMond, Frank J. Reilly. *Member:* Ridgewood AA; Bergen County A. Gld.; Rutherford AA; Hackensack A. Cl.; Portraits, Inc.; SC. *Awards:* Ridgewood AA, 1940, 1950; Rutherford AA, 1951; Bergen County A. Gld., 1953; Rutherford Trust Co., 1952. *Work:* Univ. South Carolina; murals, First Reformed Church, Hasbrouck Heights, N.J.; Lutheran Church, East Orange, N.J.; Rutherford (N.J.) Baptist Church; Madison Ave. Presbyterian Church, Paterson, N.J.; port., Diocesan Col. Magill Univ., Montreal, Canada. *Exhibited:* All. A. Am., 1946; Newcomb-Macklin Gal., 1948, 1950 (one-man); Montclair Mus. A., 1940, 1943; Ridgewood AA, 1940-1947; Bergen County A. Gld., 1946-1952; Art Center of the Oranges, 1952.

PERI, EVE—*Textile Designer, C.*

78 Irving Pl., New York 3, N.Y.; h. 161 West Penn St., Philadelphia 44, Pa.

B. Bangor, Me., Sept. 25, 1898. *Member:* Home Fashion League. *Awards:* AID, 1952 (2 awards). *Work:* AGAA; Container Corp. Am.; Swedish Airlines, and numerous private commissions. *Exhibited:* Toledo Mus. A., 1938; Arch. Lg., 1940; AGAA, 1948; Friends Lib. Germantown, Pa., 1952; one-man: Phila. A. All., 1949; Hacker A. Gal., 1950; Everhart Mus., 1951.*

PERINI, MAXINE WALKER—*Painter, L., T.*

1141 Elmwood Dr., Abilene, Tex.

B. Houston, Tex., Nov. 6, 1911. *Studied:* Wellesley Col.; AIC; & with Boris Anisfeld. *Exhibited:* AIC, 1936, 1937, 1941; Texas Centennial Exh., Dallas, Tex.; Corpus Christi, Tex.

PERKINS, EDNA—*Painter*

Kennebunk Beach, Me.

B. Jersey City, N.J., June 29, 1907. *Studied:* ASL, with Kenneth Hayes Miller. *Member:* NAWA; Maine WC Soc.; N.Y. Soc. Women A.; Assoc. A. New Jersey. *Awards:* certificate of award, Montclair A. Mus., 1944. *Exhibited:* PAFA; WFNY 1939.

PERKINS, G. HOLMES—*Educator*

University of Pennsylvania, Philadelphia, Pa.

Position: Dean, Sch. FA, University of Pennsylvania.*

PERKINS, HARLEY—*Painter*

Fenway Studios, 30 Ipswich St., Boston, Mass.

B. Bakersfield, Vt., Apr. 28, 1883. *Studied:* Brigham Acad.; Mass. Sch. A.; BMFA Sch. *Work:* BMFA; WMAA; mural, Ala. State Bldg., Montgomery, Ala. *Exhibited:* AIC; BM; Doll & Richards, Boston; one-man: Rehn Gal.; Montross Gal., and others. Contributor to: The Arts; Pictures on Exhibit; Radio Art Commentator. *Position:* A. Ed., Boston Transcript, 1922-28; Dir. Exh., Boston A. Cl., 1923-28; Mass. State Dir., FAP, 1936-39; Tech. Adv., Nat. A. Program, Wash., D.C., 1940-41; Pres., Boston Soc. Indp. A., 1940-54.

PERKINS, STELLA MARY (Mrs. J. V.)—*Painter, W., L.*

14 North Chicago Ave., Freeport, Ill.

B. Winslow, Ill., May 12, 1896. *Studied:* Rockford Col.; Univ. Wisconsin; & with Marques Reitzel, Frederic Taubes, Briggs Dyer. *Member:* Burpee AA. *Awards:* prizes, Burpee A. Gal., Rockford, Ill., 1935, 1940, 1941, 1953, 1954, 1957. *Work:* Freeport Pub. Lib.; Freeport Hist. Mus. *Exhibited:* AIC traveling exh., 1938; Burpee A. Gal.; Freeport Pub. Lib.; Freeport Hist. Mus.; Springfield Mus., 1950-1955; Decatur, Ill., 1955; Art:USA, 1958; Rockford AA. Contributor to: American Home. Lectures on "Color."

PERLIN, BERNARD—*Painter, I.*

365 West 22nd St., New York 11, N.Y.

B. Richmond, Va., Nov. 21, 1918. *Studied:* NAD; ASL, and in Poland. Awards: Kosciuszko Fnd. Scholarship, 1938; Chaloner Fnd. award, 1948; Fulbright F., 1950; Guggenheim F., 1954-55, 1959. *Work:* MMoDA; Tate Gal., London; Springfield (Mass.) Mus. A.; Cal. PLH; VMFA; USPO, South Orange, N.J.; U.S.S. "Pres. Hayes." *Exhibited:* Carnegie Inst., 1948-50 and later; WMAA, from 1947; ICA Gal., London, 1951; Brussels World's Fair, 1958; Univ. Illinois, 1950 and later, and others nationally. Contributor illus. to Life, Fortune magazines.

PERLMUTTER, JACK—*Lithographer, P., T.*

3826 Halley Terr., Southeast, Washington 20, D.C.

B. New York, N.Y., Jan. 23, 1920. *Member:* SAGA; A. Gld. Wash. *Awards:* prizes, Butler Inst. Am. A.; 1956; LC, 1950, 1951, 1956, 1957; CGA, 1951, 1952, 1955, 1956; Phila. Pr. Cl., 1954; Bradley Univ., 1953; BM, 1958; CM, 1958; Turkish Govt., 1958; BMFA, 1957. *Work:* PC; CGA; Smithsonian Inst.; MMA; Pa. State Univ.; PMA; LC; Carnegie Inst.; Bradley Univ.; N.Y. Univ.; Watkins Gal.; CAM; BM; CM; Turkish Govt. *Exhibited:* CGA, 1949, 1956; Butler AI 1945, 1957; PAFA, 1952; BM, 1952, 1953, 1956, 1958; Phila. Pr. Cl., 1950, 1952, 1956; LC, 1950, 1951, 1954, 1956, 1957; CM, 1952, 1954, 1956, 1958; AFA European Traveling exh. 1952-1954, 1956-1958; U.S. 1956-1958; U.S. Foreign Service Traveling exh. Europe, 1954-1956; International Triennial, Grenchen, Switzerland, 1958; Youngstown, Ohio, 1956; Silvermine Gld. A. 1956, 1958; Amer. Color Print Soc. 1949, 1952, 1953, 1955, 1956; SAGA, 1950-1956; Boston Pr. M. 1954, 1956, 1958; Audubon A. 1948, 1950, 1953; BMA, 1955, 1957, 1958; Oakland A. Mus., 1953; Univ. Maine, 1956; PC; Smithsonian Inst.; CGA, annually; 13 one-man Wash., D.C. since 1945; CGA, 1956. *Position:* Instr., Dir. Gal., District T. Col., Wash., D.C.

PERRET, FERDINAND—
Art Historian, P., Des., Gr., I., W., L.

524 Tigertail Rd., Los Angeles 49, Cal.

B. Illzach, France, Nov. 1, 1888. *Studied:* Ecole des Beaux-Arts, Paris, France with Jules Perret; Folkwang Mus., Germany, with Rohlfe and Weiss; London Sch. A.,

London, England, with C. P. Townley; Stickney Mem. Sch. FA, Pasadena, Cal., with Jean Mannheim and Guy Rose; and with William Chase. *Member*: William Keith AA, Berkeley, Cal.; Cal. A. Cl.; Los A. P. & S. Cl.; A. of the Southwest; Laguna Beach AA; Santa Monica AA. *Awards*: prize, Stickney Mem., Pasadena, 1917; medal, Int. Aero A. Exh., Los A., 1937; Los A. P. & S. Cl., 1949. *Exhibited*: Cal. Int. Exp., San Diego, 1935-36. Founder and Donor of the "Perret Art Reference Library," NCFA, Wash., D.C. Lectures: The Arts and Crafts of the American Indian. Dir. and Founder, Ferdinand Perret Hispano-American Art Reference Library, Los Angeles, Cal., 1947, with all collected material for public use. Author and Donor of the Perret Encyclopedia of Spanish Colonial Art (15 vols.) to the Museum of the Santa Barbara Hist. Soc., 1958.

PERRIN, C(HARLES) ROBERT—
Painter, Des., Cart., I., L.
44 Bromfield St., Boston 8, Mass.; h. 61 Warren St., West Medford, Mass.

B. Medford, Mass., July 13, 1915. *Studied*: Sch. Practical A. *Member*: AWS; Boston Soc. WC Painters; Rockport AA; Copley Soc.; A. Assoc. of Nantucket; North Shore AA; Boston Soc. Indp.; A. Dir. Cl., Boston. *Awards*: prizes, Boston Soc. Indp. A., 1952; Rockport AA, 1953, 1954; North Shore AA, 1954; Boston Soc. WC Painters, 1955; Grand Central A. Gal., 1956. *Work*: Ford Motor Co.; Currier Gal. A.; Russell Large Fnd. Illus. "Dixie Dishes," 1941. Contributor to Ford Times, Christian Science Monitor.

PERROT, PAUL N.—*Assistant Museum Director*
The Corning Museum of Glass; h. 10 West 2nd St., Corning, N.Y.

B. Paris, France, July 28, 1926. *Studied*: Ecole du Louvre, Paris; N.Y. Univ. Inst. FA. *Member*: CAA; AAMus.; Special Lib. Assn.; Soc. Glass Technology. Author: "Three Great Centuries of Venetian Glass," 1958 (catalogue and introd.). Contributor to Antiques magazine. Lectures: History and Aesthetics of Glass; Liturgical Art; Medieval Art. Arranged exhs.: "Leonardo da Vinci, Artist and Inventor"; "Contemporary American Glass"; "Venite Adoremus"; "Art for Your Christmas"; "Three Great Centuries of Venetian Glass." *Positions*: Asst., The Cloisters, Metropolitan Mus. Art.; Asst. Dir., The Corning Museum of Glass, Corning, N.Y., at present.

PERRY, BART—*Painter, T.*
133 Seventh Ave., New York 11, N.Y.

B. Boston, Mass., Sept. 29, 1906. *Studied*: Harvard Univ.; N.Y. Univ. (grad. work); Cal. Sch. FA. *Member*: Woodstock AA; AEA. *Award*: prize, San F. AA., 1953. *Exhibited*: San F. AA; Woodstock AA, 1958; one-man: SFMA, 1946; Labaudt Gal., San F., 1954; Camino Gal., N.Y., 1957. *Position*: Instr., A. Hist., Univ. Pittsburgh, 1933-34; Hist. 19th & 20th Century Painting, Mills College, 1948.

PERRY, KENNETH F.—*Educator*
Colorado State College, Greeley, Colo.
Position: Chm., Art Dept., Colorado State College.*

PERRY, RAYMOND—*Painter, I., Des., L.*
145 East 34th St., New York 16, N.Y.

B. Sterling, Ill., 1876. *Studied*: AIC. *Member*: SC. *Work*: windows, St. Andrew's Church, Pittsburgh, Pa.; Mem. Lib., Hanover, Pa.; portraits, 7th Regiment Armory, Fraunces Tavern, N.Y.; Press Cl., Baltimore, Md.; Poe Cottage, Phila., Pa.

PERSHING, LOUISE—*Painter, L.*
New Hope, Pa.

B. Pittsburgh, Pa. *Studied*: PAFA; Carnegie Inst.; Univ. Pittsburgh; and with Hans Hofmann. *Member*: Pittsburgh WC Soc.; Assoc. A. Pittsburgh. *Awards*: prizes, Assoc. A. Pittsburgh, 1931, 1932, 1940, 1941, 1943, 1946, 1947, 1949, 1950; PAFA, 1950; NAWA, 1936; Wichita Mus., 1936; Indiana State T. Col., 1944. *Work*: Pittsburgh Pub. Schs.; Pa. State Col.; Indiana State T. Col.; murals, Dormont (Pa.) Pub. Sch.; Shadyside Hospital, Pittsburgh. *Exhibited*: CM, 1936-1940; CGA, 1939; Carnegie Inst., 1932-1950;

GGE, 1939; PAFA, 1934, 1936, 1950; VMFA, 1942; NAD, 1934; AIC, 1934-1938, 1942; WMAA, 1950; Springfield Mus. A., 1944, 1945; Butler Inst. Am. A., 1936-1950; John Herron AI, 1949; Sao Paulo, Brazil, 1948; one-man: Argent Gal., 1937; Carnegie Inst., 1942; Chautauqua, N.Y., 1943; Contemp. A. Gal., N.Y., 1943, 1947, 1950; Cleveland One Thirty Gal., 1949; Chatham Col., 1950; Univ. Ohio, 1953. *Position*: Dir., New Hope (Pa.) Progressive Gal., 1953-55; Des., Mark Cross, N.Y., 1954-56.

PERSONS, SIMMONS—*Painter*
c/o Robert Donaldson, 232 East 64th St., New York 21, N.Y.

B. Norfolk, Va., Dec. 5, 1906. *Studied*: ASL, with Frank DuMond, George Bridgman, Kimon Nicolaides. *Award*: F., Huntington Hartford Fnd., 1952. *Work*: WMAA. *Exhibited*: AIC, 1943, 1944; WMAA, 1938, 1939, 1941, 1945, 1946, 1949, 1951, 1953; PAFA, 1945; VMFA, 1941; Rehn Gal., 1950, 1955 (one-man). *Position*: Instr. Drawing, Hunter Col., New York, N.Y., 1950-54.*

PESCHERET, LEON RENE—*Etcher, C., Des., I., W., L.*
519 Main St., Whitewater, Wis.

B. Chiswick, England, Mar. 15, 1892. *Studied*: AIC; Royal Col. of Engraving, Kensington, England. *Member*: Chicago Soc. Et.; Pr. M. Soc. of Cal.; Am. Color Pr. Soc.; Soc. Am. Pr. M.; Palette & Chisel Cl., Chicago; Print Council of Am.; Cal. Soc. Et. *Awards*: Lila Mae Chapman award, 1936, 1937. *Work*: British Mus.; LC; Cabinet du Roi, Brussels; N.Y. Pub. Lib.; AIC; presentation prints for. Am. Color Pr. Soc., 1943; Buck Hills AA, 1947; Chicago Soc. Et., 1956; Pr. M. Soc. of Cal., 1958. *Exhibited*: Buck Hills AA, 1948, 1949; Chicago Galleries Assn., 1951. Author, I.; "Principle and Practice of Interior Decorating"; "An Introduction to Color Etching." I., "The Spirit of Vienna," 1935; "Chicago Welcomes You," 1933. Contributor of color etchings to American Artist and Arizona Highways magazines.*

PETERDI, GABOR—*Painter, Et., Eng., L., T.*
108 Highland Ave., Rowayton, Conn.

B. Budapest, Hungary, Sept. 17, 1915. *Studied*: Hungarian Acad., Budapest; Julian Acad., Paris; Academie Scandinavian, Paris, and others. *Awards*: Prix de Rome, 1930; gold med., for mural with Lurcat, Paris, 1937; BM, 1950, 1952; Am. Color Pr. Soc., 1951; New England Annual, 1953-1957; Oakland Mus. A., 1957; gold medal, PAFA, 1957. *Work*: MMoDA; MMA; N.Y. Pub. Lib.; BM; Smithsonian Inst.; AIC; Cranbrook Acad. A.; PMA; Sao Paulo, Brazil; Clearwater Mus. A.; Univ. Indiana; Vassar Col.; Brown Univ.; Univ. Michigan; Northwestern Univ.; Univ. Oklahoma; Illinois Wesleyan; Currier Gal. A.; Smith Col.; Achenbach Fnd., San F.; Abilene Christian Col.; Berea Col.; Dartmouth Col.; Michigan State Univ.; New Jersey State Univ.; Oregon State Col.; Texas Wesleyan; Honolulu Acad. FA; Mus. of Budapest; Mus. of Prague; Mus. of Rome; Brooks Mem. Mus.; Univ. Nebraska; Brandeis Univ.; Univ. Georgia; Yale Univ.; Albion Col.; Princeton Univ.; Firestone Lib., Princeton; WMAA; R.I. Sch. Des.; PAFA; Minneapolis Inst. A.; BMFA; Oakland A. Mus.; Beloit Col.; Columbia (S.C.) Mus. A.; Univ. Illinois. *Exhibited*: nationally. One-man: Ernst Mus., Budapest, 1930, 1934; Rome, 1930; Galerie Jean Bucher, Paris, 1936; Julian Levy Gal., N.Y., 1939; Norlyst Gal., 1943, 1944; Laurel Gal., 1948-1950; Phila. A. All., 1950, 1955; Smithsonian Inst., 1951; Silvermine Gld. A., 1952; Fla. Gulf Coast A. Center, 1953; Borgenicht Gal., 1952, 1953, 1955, 1957; N.Y. Pub. Lib., 1956; Kanegis Gal., Boston, 1956-57; St. George's Gal., London, 1958. *Position*: Instr., BM Sch. A., 1949-53; Hunter Col. and Yale Univ., at present.

PETERS, CARL W.—*Painter*
Jefferson Ave., Fairport, N.Y.

B. Rochester, N.Y., Nov. 14, 1897. *Studied*: with Charles Rosen, John F. Carlsen, Harry Leith-Ross. *Awards*: prizes, Univ. Rochester, 1924; NAD, 1925, 1926, 1928, 1932; Rochester A. Cl., 1927, 1928; North Shore AA, 1931; Rockport AA, 1951, 1955; Rochester Me. A. Gal., 1932; medal, Rochester A. Cl., 1925. *Work*: murals, Genesee Valley Trust Co., Rochester; Acad. Medicine, Univ. Rochester; Fairport Pub. Lib.; Madison, West and Charlotte H.S., Rochester. *Exhibited*: NAD; CGA; PAFA; Milwaukee AI; AIC; North Shore AA; Rockport AA; Springfield Mus. A.; Rochester Mem. A. Gal.; Albright A. Gal.; Syracuse Mus. FA; Fort Worth (Tex.) Mus. A.

PETERS, ERIC A.—*Painter, Gr., Cart., Comm. A., L.*
46 West 73rd St.; h. 102 West 75th St., New York 23, N.Y.

B. Vienna, Austria, May 12, 1909. *Studied*: with Prof. Schmutzer, Vienna, Austria; Acad. A., and with Profs. Orlik, Balushek, Steinhard, all Berlin, Germany; Acad. A., Naples, Italy. *Awards*: USO, 1942. *Work*: Gr. A. Col., Albertina Mus., and State Lib. of Austria, Vienna. *Exhibited*: MMA, 1943; one-man in Vienna and Berlin. Illus., "Matadore der Politik," 1932. Contributor cartoons to Sat. Eve. Post; Colliers and other magazines. Cartoonist for newspapers in Berlin, Vienna and Naples.

PETERS, FRANCIS CHARLES—*Painter*
2029 M. St., Northwest; h. 3749 Jocelyn St., Northwest, Washington, D.C.

B. Dunkirk, N.Y., Dec. 16, 1902. *Studied*: Albright A. Sch., Buffalo; ASL. *Member*: AAPL (Adv. Bd.); Am. A. Lg., Wash. D.C. (Pres.). *Awards*: prizes, AAPL, 1955, 1956; Wash. Landscape Cl., 1957; Wash. A. Cl., 1957. *Exhibited*: AAPL, 1956-1958; CGA, 1956; Metropolitan Exh., 1954-1957; Wash. A. Cl., 1952-1958.

PETERSEN, EUGEN H.—
Educator, P., Des., Comm. A., I., L.
345 Park Ave., Manhasset, N.Y.

B. Bluefields, Nicaragua, Feb. 16, 1892. *Studied*: PIASch.; N.Y. Univ., B.A.; & with John Carlson, George Elmer Browne, George Bridgman. *Exhibited*: MMA; PMA; NAD; BM; SC. Lectures: Perspective & Free Hand Drawing. *Position*: Prof. A., PIASch., Brooklyn, N.Y., 1921-.

PETERSHAM, MAUD FULLER—*Illustrator, W.*
Woodstock, N.Y.

B. Kingston, N.Y., Aug. 5, 1889. *Studied*: Vassar Col.; N.Y.Sch.F.&App.A. *Awards*: Caldecott med., 1946. *Work*: children's books in libraries. Author, I., children's books, text books.

PETERSHAM, MISKA—*Illustrator, W.*
Woodstock, N.Y.

B. Torokszentmiklos, Hungary, Sept. 20, 1888. *Studied*: Royal Acad., Budapest, Hungary. *Awards*: Caldecott med., 1946. *Work*: children's books in libraries. Author, I., children's books, text books.

PETERSON, DANIEL (ROY)—*Craftsman*
1453 St. James Court, Louisville 8, Ky.

B. Campbellsville, Ky., June 4, 1909. *Studied*: Cranbrook Acad. A.; Univ. Indiana; Univ. Louisville. *Member*: Kentucky A. Edu. Assn.; Midwest Des-Craftsmen; Louisville A. Center Assn. *Awards*: prizes, Louisville A. Center, 1949, 1951, 1955. *Exhibited*: Am. Jewelry Exh., 1955; Phila. A. All., 1950, 1951; Cranbrook Alumni Ex., 1954; Louisville A. Center, 1948-1958; 2-man exh. (with Nelle Peterson) A. Center Gal., 1953, 1957.

PETERSON, GARLAND BURRUSS. See Burruss, Garland

PETERSON, JANE—*Painter*
1007 Fifth Ave., New York 28, N.Y.

B. Elgin, Ill. *Studied*: PIASch.; & with Sorolla, Brangwyn, Andre L'Hote. *Member*: AWCS; NAWA; Audubon A.; PBC; Wash. WC Cl.; Phila. WC Cl.; N.Y. Soc. Painters; AFA; All.A.Am.; A.Lg.Am.; Miami A. Lg.; Soc. Four A., Palm Beach, Fla. *Awards*: prizes, Girls AC, Paris, France, 1915; Conn. Acad. FA, 1916; NAWA, 1919, 1927; Fla. SA, 1938; Wash. WC Cl., 1940; Gloucester Soc. A., 1955; AAPL, 1955. *Work*: BM; Grand Rapids AA; Boise City (Iowa) A. Coll.; Sears A. Gal., Elgin, Ill.; Syracuse Mus. FA; Richmond (Ind.) A. Mus.; Frances Shimer Col.; Soc. Four A., Palm Beach, Fla.; Wesleyan Col., Macon, Ga.; Wichita A. Mus. *Exhibited*: CGA; NAD; PAFA; All.A.Am.; NAWA; Phila. WC Cl.; AIC; AWCS; N.Y. Soc. Painters; Wash. WC Cl.; Conn. Acad. FA; Soc. Four A.; Buffalo Mus. Sc.; Cayuga Mus. Hist. & A.; Chautauqua Women's Cl.; Binghamton Mus. A.; Arnot A. Gal.; Montclair A. Mus.; Rutgers Univ.; Audubon A.; Gloucester Soc. A.; Princeton Univ.; Everhart Mus.; Mint Mus. A.; High Mus. A.; Chattanooga AA;

Brooks Mem. A. Gal.; J. B. Speed Mem. Mus.; Butler AI; Ball State T. Col., etc.; one-man exh.; Kenosha Hist. & A. Mus.; Oshkosh Pub. Mus.; Wustum Mus.; Syracuse Mus. FA; Davenport Mun. A. Gal.; Springfield A. Mus.; Philbrook A. Center; Thayer Mus.; Wichita AA; Joslyn Mem.; Crocker A. Gal., Sacramento, Cal.; Haggin Mem. Gal., Stockton, Cal.; Santa Barbara Mus. A.; San Jose State Col.; etc. Author: "Flower Painting."

PETERSON, NELLE FREEMAN—*Teacher, C.*
1453 St. James Court, Louisville 8, Ky.

B. LaGrange, Ky., Sept. 13, 1903. *Studied*: Univ. Louisville, B.A., M.A.; Cranbrook Acad. A.; Univ. Indiana. *Member*: A. Cl. of Louisville; Midwest Des-Craftsmen; CAA; Western AA; Ky. Edu. Assn.; Ky. A. Edu. Assn.; A. Center of Louisville. *Exhibited*: Am. Jewelry Exh., 1955; Univ. Nebraska, 1952; Cranbrook Alumni Exh., 1954; A. Center, Louisville, 1948-1955; 2-man (with Daniel Peterson) A. Center Gal., 1953. Lectures: Color in Weaving; Kentucky Crafts. *Position*: Instr., Crafts, A. Center Assn. and Univ. Louisville, Ky.

PETRINA, CHARLOTTE KENNEDY (CARLOTTA)—
Painter, I., Gr., T.
Anacapri St., Capri, Naples, Italy.

B. Kingston, N.Y., Sept. 6, 1901. *Studied*: ASL; CUASch. *Member*: ASL. *Awards*: Guggenheim F., 1933, 1934. *Work*: N.Y. Pub. Lib. *Exhibited*: Salon d'Automne, Salon des Artistes Francais, Paris; AIC; PAFA; Phila. Pr. Cl.; BM; WMAA; Dudensing Gal.; AIGA; Capri, Italy, 1950; one-man: Galleria "La Finestra," Rome, 1952; Crespi Gal., N.Y., 1957. Illus. (Limited Ed. Cl.) "South Wind"; "Paradise Lost"; "The Aeneid"; "Henry VI."

PETROFF, GILMER—*Painter, Des., E.*
5318 Pine Straw Rd., Columbia, S.C.

B. Saranac Lake, N.Y., Mar. 20, 1913. *Studied*: Yale Sch. FA; Univ. Wisconsin, and with Richard E. Miller. *Member*: Carolina AA. *Awards*: prizes, Mint Mus. A., 1946; Alabama WC Soc., 1946; High Mus. A., 1947; Carolina AA, 1951; Sears Roebuck, 1954; Girls H.S., Atlanta, Ga., 1947. *Work*: High Mus. A.; Columbia (S.C.) Mus. A.; Staten Island Hist. Soc.; Saranac Lake AA; murals, Colonial Bldg. & Loan Assn., Staten Island, N.Y.; Clemson House, Clemson Col.; State Highway Bldg., Columbia; Tapps Dept. Store, Columbia, S.C. *Exhibited*: AWS; PAFA; Atlanta AA; Greenville (S.C.) A. Lg.; High Mus. A.; Columbia Mus. A.; Saranac Lake AA. *Position*: Assoc. Prof. Arch., Clemson Col., South Carolina, 1946-50; Bd. Trustees, Columbia Mus. A.; Instr., Richland County A. Sch.; Pres., Gld. South Carolina A., 1956.

PEZZATI, PIETRO—*Portrait Painter*
Fenway Studios 430, 30 Ipswich St., Boston 15, Mass.; h. 67 School St., Manchester, Mass.

B. Boston, Mass., Sept. 18, 1902. *Studied*: Child-Walker Sch. A.; in Europe and privately; also with Charles Hopkinson. *Work*: Harvard Univ.; Harvard Cl., Boston; Mass. General Hospital; Court Houses in Boston, Worcester, Fitchburg, Mass.; Univ. Pennsylvania; Mississippi AA; FMA; Mun. A. Gal., Jackson, Miss.; Phillips Acad., Andover, Mass.; Lawrence (Mass.) Gen. Hospital, and in private colls. *Exhibited*: CGA; PAFA; WFNY 1939; NGA; Jordan Marsh Gal., Boston; Boston A. Festival; one-man: Vose Gal., Margaret Brown Gal., Copley Soc., Child Gal., all in Boston; Mississippi AA, Jackson; 2-man (with Chas. Hopkinson) Fitchburg A. Mus.

PFEIFFER, FRITZ—*Painter, T.*
Provincetown, Mass.

B. Gettysburg, Pa., June 3, 1889. *Studied*: PAFA, and with Robert Henri, Hugh Breckenridge, William M. Chase. *Member*: Provincetown AA (Hon. V. Pres., 1938-56); AEA. *Work*: Springfield Mus. A. *Exhibited*: PAFA; AIC; one-man: Detroit Inst. A., 1946; Newhouse Gal.; Harvard Univ., 1940; Michigan State Normal Col., 1941; Gordon Beer Gal., Detroit, 1940, 1942, 1944; Boris Mirski Gal., Boston, 1944; Adams Gal., Buffalo; Hall of Fame, Miami, 1952; Wellons Gal., N.Y., 1955. *Position*: Instr., Albright A. Gal., Buffalo, N.Y., 1944-49.

PFEIFFER, HEINRICH (HARRY R.)—*Painter*

18 Aviles St., St. Augustine, Fla.; s. 244 Commercial St., Provincetown, Mass.

B. Hanover, Pa., Oct. 19, 1874. *Studied*: ASL, with John Carlson; PAFA, with Hugh Breckenridge, Henry Mc-Carter. *Exhibited*: CGA; PAFA; AIC.*

PFEIFFER, HOPE VOORHEES (Mrs. Fritz)—
Painter, T.

Provincetown, Mass.

B. Coldwater, Mich., Jan. 28, 1891. *Studied*: Adrian Col.; Detroit Sch. Des.; & with Fritz Pfeiffer, Blanche Lazzell. *Member*: Provincetown AA. *Exhibited*: Detroit Inst. A., 1946; Los A. Mus. A., 1932; PAFA, 1941; SAM, 1932; Wichita A. Mus., 1931; Mich. State Normal Col., 1941 (one-man); Adrian Col., Detroit, 1940 (one-man); Buffalo, N.Y., 1945 (one-man); Wellons Gal., N.Y., 1955 (one-man). *Positions*: A. Instr., Grosse Pointe Country Day Sch., 1920-42; Elmwood Franklin Sch., Buffalo, N.Y., 1943-49.

PFLAGER, DOROTHY HOLLOWAY (Mrs. Henry B.)—
Painter

The Frontenac, Apt. 11-F, 40 North Kingshighway, St. Louis 8, Mo.

B. Los Angeles, Cal., Nov. 26, 1900. *Studied*: Wellesley Col., B.A.; Washington Univ., M.A. *Member*: St. Louis A. Gld.; St. Louis Studio Group; AEA; NAWA; Cincinnati Woman's A. Cl.; MacDowell Soc.; Friends of the City Art Mus. *Awards*: prize, BMA, 1942. *Exhibited*: Loring Andrews Gal., Cincinnati, 1945; CAM, 1945, 1946; St. Louis A. Gld., 1946; 1957 (one-man); St. Louis, Mo., 1944 (one-man); 8th St. Gal., N.Y., 1951 (one-man).

PHELAN, LINN LOVEJOY—*Craftsman, Des., T.*

Alfred-Almond Central School, Almond, N.Y.

B. Rochester, N.Y., Aug. 25, 1906. *Studied*: Rochester Inst. Tech.; Ohio State Univ., B.F.A.; Alfred Univ., M.S. in Edu. *Award*: prize, A. & Crafts Festival, Abingdon, Va., 1950. *Work*: Cranbrook Acad. A.; Dartmouth Col. *Exhibited*: Phila. A. All., 1937-1958; Syracuse Mus. FA, 1932-1956; Rochester Mem. A. Gal., 1929-1958. Contributor to magazines. *Positions*: Owner, "Linwood Pottery," Almond, N.Y.; Ceramic Instr., Sch. for Am. Craftsmen, Alfred, N.Y., 1944-50; A. Supv., Alfred-Almond Central Sch., Almond, N.Y., 1950- ; Trustee, Vice-Pres., "Artmobile, Inc.," 1954-58. Chm., York State Craftsmen Fair, 1957-59, Ithaca, N.Y.; 2nd V.P., New York State A.T. Assn., 1958.

PHELPS, EDITH CATLIN—*Painter*

225 Miramar Ave., Santa Barbara, Cal.

B. New York, N.Y., Apr. 16, 1875. *Studied*: Julian Acad., Paris; & with Charles Hawthorne. *Awards*: Prizes, San Diego FA Soc., 1938; Sacramento State Fair, 1938, 1941; Conn. Acad. FA; Madonna Festival, Los A., 1951, 1956. *Work*: New York (N.Y.) Court House; Wilshire Presbyterian Church. *Exhibited*: PAFA; CGA; AIC; GGE 1939; Los A. Mus. A.; San Diego FA Soc.; Sacramento State Fair; Oakland A. Gal.; Santa Cruz A. Lg.; Santa Barbara Mus. A., 1945 (one-man).

PHILBRICK, ALLEN ERSKINE—*Painter, Et., Eng., E.*

982 Elm St., Winnetka, Ill.

B. Utica, N.Y., Nov. 19, 1879. *Studied*: AIC; Julian Acad., Ecole des Beaux-Arts, Paris, France. *Member*: Chicago SE. *Awards*: prize, AIC, 1922; Chicago Soc. Etchers, 1953. *Work*: murals, Juvenile Court, Chicago, Ill.; People's Trust & Savings Bank, Cedar Rapids, Iowa; portrait, Iowa State Hist. Mus. *Exhibited*: NAD, 1942-1946; Lib. Cong., 1942-1946; 1946; AIC.

PHILBRICK, MARGARET ELDER (Mrs.)—*Etcher, P.*

323 Dover Rd., Westwood, Mass.

B. Northampton, Mass., July 4, 1914. *Studied*: Mass. Sch. A. *Member*: SAGA; Chicago Soc. Et.; Boston Pr.M.; Boston Soc. A. & Crafts; Boston Soc. W. C. Painters; Pr. M. Soc. Cal. *Awards*: co-winner, Southern Pr. M. Presentation Print award, 1939; LC, 1948 (purchase); SAGA, 1953; New Britain A. Mus., 1953 (purchase); Presentation Print award, Boston Pr. M., 1954; Springfield

Mus. A. *Work*: LC; Bezalel Mus., Jerusalem; AGAA; FMA; Amherst Col.; MMA; New Britain A. Mus.; Univ. Maine. *Exhibited*: SAGA, annually; Chicago Soc. Et., annually; NAD; Northwest Pr. M.; Albany Pr. Cl.; Buffalo Pr. Cl.; LC; Carnegie Inst.; BM; BMFA; and in American Exhs. in Italy, Israel, England; U.S. State Dept. traveling exh. Far East.

PHILBRICK, OTIS—*Painter, Lith., E.*

Massachusetts School of Art, Brookline Ave., Boston, Mass.; h. 323 Dover Rd., Westwood, Mass.

B. Mattapan, Mass., Oct. 21, 1888. *Studied*: Mass. Sch. A. *Member*: Boston Soc. WC Painters; SAGA; Boston Pr. M.; Copley Soc.; Boston Soc. WC Painters. *Awards*: Boston Pr. M., 1949 (purchase); Presentation Print award, Boston Pr. M., 1951. *Work*: Boston Pub. Lib.; LC; Bezalel Mus., Jerusalem; Amherst Col.; FMA; Dartmouth Col.; AGAA; Univ. Maine. *Exhibited*: Nat. Mus., Wash., D.C.; NAD; Albany Pr. Cl.; Buffalo Pr. Cl.; LC; Carnegie Inst.; Boston Soc. WC Painters, annually; American Exhs. in France, Israel, Italy, England; U.S. State Dept. traveling exh. Far East. *Position*: Prof. A., Mass. Sch. A., Boston, Mass.; Pres., Boston Pr. M.

PHILIPP, ROBERT—*Painter*

200 West 57th St., New York 19, N.Y.

B. New York, N.Y., Feb. 2, 1895. *Studied*: ASL, with DuMond, Bridgman; NAD, with Volk, Maynard. *Member*: NA; Lotos Cl. *Awards*: prizes, NAD, 1922, 1947, 1951; Carnegie Inst., 1937; Laguna Beach AA; medal, prize, AIC, 1936; CGA, 1939; IBM, 1939; bronze medal, All.A.Am. 1958. *Work*: WMAA; BM; Mus. FA of Houston; CGA; Norton Gal. A.; High Mus. A.; IBM; Davenport Mun. A. Gal.; Encyclopaedia Britannica; Dallas Mus.; Univ. Arizona; Joslyn A. Mus. *Exhibited*: nationally. *Positions*: Instr., High Mus. A., 1946; Visiting Prof., Univ. Illinois, 1940; Instr., ASL, NAD, New York, N.Y., at present.*

PHILLIPS, ANN COLE (Mrs. Phillips W. Phillips)—
Painter

152 West 57th St.; h. 895 Park Ave., New York 21, N.Y.

B. New York, N.Y., Mar. 12, 1911. *Studied*: NAD; ASL; in France, Italy and Spain, and with Jose Clemente Orozco. *Member*: Silvermine Gld. A.; Brooklyn Soc. A.; N.Y. Soc. Women A. (Bd. Dir.); NAWA (Bd. Dir.); AEA (Bd. Dir.). *Awards*: Karasink award, 1947; NAD, 1955; Lehman award, 1956. *Work*: Union Col., Schenectady, N.Y.; Georgia Mus. A., Athens; Columbia (S.C.) Mus. A.; Washington County Mus., Hagerstown, Md.; High Mus. A., Atlanta. *Exhibited*: PAFA, 1946, 1956; WMAA, 1950; NAD, annually since 1945; Riverside Mus. A., annually since 1945; Union Col., 1957; Canton AI; Massillon Mus. A.; Georgia Mus. A.; Columbia, S.C.; Univ. Nebraska; N.Y. Univ.; in Berne and Lugarno, Switzerland; Argent Gal., N.Y.; Paris, France; one-man: Vendome Gal., 1946; Schaefer Gal., 1952; Galerie Andre Weil, Paris, 1957; Chase Gal., N.Y., 1958.

PHILLIPS, BLANCHE (HOWARD)—*Sculptor*

Van Houten St., Upper Nyack, N.Y.

B. Mt. Union, Pa., Feb. 26, 1908. *Studied*: CUASch.; ASL; Stienhofs Inst. Des.; Cal. Sch. FA, and with Zadkine, Hofmann. *Member*: S. Gld.; New Sculpture Group; N.Y. Soc. Women A. *Work*: WMAA. *Exhibited*: SFMA, 1942, 1943, 1945-1947, 1949; Oakland A. Mus., 1946, 1948; Los A. Mus. A., 1949; WMAA, 1952, 1957; BMFA, 1958; Mus. FA of Houston, 1958; Riverside Mus., 1958; Art:USA, 1958; one-man: SFMA, 1943, 1949; Crocker A. Gal., Sacramento, Cal., 1949; RoKo Gal., N.Y., 1955, 1957; and in Mexico, 1951.

PHILLIPS, CLAIRE DOONER—*Painter, Et.*

P.O. Box 1099; h. 416 Perry St., Prescott, Ariz.

B. Los Angeles, Cal., Jan. 31, 1887. *Studied*: Stanford Univ., A.B.; T. Col., Columbia Univ., with Arthur Dow. *Work*: Prescott (Ariz.) Pub. Sch., Arizona Fed. Women's Cl. *Awards*: prizes, Yavapai County Fair; Arizona State Fair.

PHILLIPS, DOROTHY SKLAR. See Sklar, Dorothy

PHILLIPS, DUNCAN—*Museum Director, W., L., Cr., P.*

1600 21st St.; h. 2101 Foxhall Rd., Washington 7, D.C.

B. Pittsburgh, Pa., June 26, 1886. *Studied:* Yale Univ., B.A. *Member:* AFA; Hon. F., Berkeley Col., Yale Univ.; AAMus. *Awards:* hon. degree, M.A., Yale Univ.; D.H.L., Kenyon Col., 1951; D. Let., Am. Univ., 1955; officer, Legion of Honor, 1948. *Work:* PC. Author: "Collection in the Making," 1926; "The Artist Sees Differently," 1931; "The Leadership of Giorgione," 1937; Co-Author: "Daumier," 1923. Ed. & Contributor to: PMG publications & catalog introductions to exhibitions of Graves, Tomlin, Knaths, Dove, and other painters. Contributor essays to Kenyon Review, Art, Art News and other magazines. *Position:* Dir., PC, Washington, D.C.; Trustee & Member, Acquisitions Com., NGA, Wash., D.C.; Chm., Com. for Modern American Paintings, Tate Gal., London, England, 1946.

PHILLIPS, JOHN GOLDSMITH—*Museum Curator*

Metropolitan Museum of Art, Fifth Ave., at 82nd St.; h. 53 East 96th St., New York 28, N.Y.

B. Glens Falls, N.Y., Jan. 22, 1907. *Studied:* Harvard Univ., A.B. *Award:* Guggenheim Fellowship, 1957. Author: "Early Florentine Designers and Engravers," 1955; "China-Trade Porcelain," 1956. Lectures on various aspects of European Art, including New Installations at the Metropolitan Museum. *Position:* Cur., Renaissance and Post-Renaissance Art, Metropolitan Museum of Art, New York, N.Y.

PHILLIPS, MARGARET McDONALD—
Painter, T., W., L.

34 East 38th St., New York 16, N.Y.

B. New York, N.Y. *Studied:* Hunter Col., B.A.; Grand Central Sch. A.; Wayman Adams Sch. of Portraiture, and with Eric Pape, Frank Schwartz, Edmund Graecen. *Member:* F., Royal Soc. A., London; The Fifty American Artists, Inc. (Fndr., Pres.); Palm Beach A. Lg.; A. Gld.; AAPL; Nat. Lg. Am. Pen Women. *Awards:* Citation, Fla. Southern Col.; PAFA scholarship; Grand Central Sch. A. scholarship; Nancy Ashton award, Hunter Col. *Work:* Fla. Southern Col.; Muskingum Col., New Concord, Ohio; Fifth Avenue Presbyterian Church, N.Y.; Home for the Aged and Infirm, N.Y.; Eastern Star of N.Y. State. and in private colls. *Exhibited:* Fla. Southern Col., 1952; Fifty Am. A., 1954-1955, 1957; Ogunquit A. Center, 1954, 1955; Grand Central A. Gal., 1954; Virgin Isles A. Center, 1950; traveling exh. to Mint Mus. A., Columbus Gal. FA, Hickory Mus. A., Asheville Mus. A., Oklahoma A. Center, and others; one-man: Metropolitan Gal., 1945; Arthur Newton Gal., 1954; Pelham Manor Cl., 1955; Schneider-Gabriel Gal., 1944. Contributor to art magazines. Lectures: "Portrait Painting Today"; "Aesthetic Enjoyment"; "Judging an Art Exhibition," Portraiture, etc. Talks on Contemporary and Modern Art, WABC & WNEW-TV.

PHILLIPS, MARJORIE—*Associate Museum Director, P.*

2101 Foxhall Rd., Northwest, Washington, D.C.

B. Bourbon, Ind., Oct. 25, 1894. *Studied:* ASL, with Boardman Robinson, Kenneth Hayes Miller. *Awards:* prize, CGA, 1955. *Work:* BMFA; PC; Yale Univ. Mus.; WMAA; CGA. *Exhibited:* CGA, 1925-1945, 1955; Carnegie Inst., 1934-1946; AIC, 1931, 1940, 1941; WMA; MModA, 1933; PAFA, 1944, 1945, 1953; WFNY 1939; GGE 1939; Tate Gal., London, England, 1946; Denver A. Mus., 1941; PC, 1941; Butler AI, 1953; Franz Bader Gal., Wash., D.C.; one-man: Durlacher Bros., 1956; Kraushaar Gal., 1941; Durand-Ruel Gal., 1941; Santa Barbara Mus. A., 1945; CGA, 1955, 1956; PC, 1958. Arranged many exhs. for PC, 1937- . *Position:* Assoc. Dir., PC, Washington, D.C., 1922- .

PHILLIPS, MEL(VILLE) (A.)—*Painter, T., Comm., I.*

110 West 54th St., New York 19, N.Y.; h. 1 Second St., Lynbrook, L.I., N.Y.

B. New York, N.Y., Jan. 1, 1893. *Studied:* NAD, and with George Maynard, Ivan Olinsky. *Member:* SI. *Awards:* NAD; Motion Picture award for Poster, 1938. *Work:* NAD; many portraits of prominent persons. Contributor illus. to Coronet; American Legion; Womans Home Companion and others. Advertising illus. to many national magazines.

PHILPOT, S. H.—*Painter, T., I.*

1822 North Charles St., Baltimore 1, Md.

Studied: Maryland Inst.; ASL; PIASch; & with Henry Roben, George Bridgman, Frederick Goudy, Anna Fisher, Jacques Maroger. *Work:* Fed. Land Bank, Baltimore, Md. *Exhibited:* Maryland Inst.; BMA; CGA; Ogunquit A. Center; Hagerstown, Md. *Position:* Freelance A. Dir.

PHOENIX, LAUROS MONROE—*Painter, E., Des., L.*

160 Lexington Ave., New York 16, N.Y.; h. 14 Alden Place, Bronxville, N.Y.

B. Chicago, Ill., Feb. 23, 1885. *Studied:* AIC; & with John Vanderpoel, Thomas Wood Stevens, Louis W. Wilson, & others. *Member:* NSMP; New Rochelle AA; Alpha Delta Sigma; Quill Cl. *Work:* murals, St. Paul Hotel and Lowry Doctors' Bldg., St. Paul, Minn.; Donaldson Bldg., Elks Cl., Minneapolis, Minn. *Position:* Pres., Dir., Instr., N.Y.-Phoenix Sch. Des., New York, N.Y., Adjunct Prof., N.Y. Univ. (Emeritus).

PICKEN, GEORGE—*Painter, Et., Lith., T., L.*

61 East End Ave., New York 28, N.Y.

B. New York, N.Y., Oct. 26, 1898. *Studied:* ASL; & abroad. *Awards:* prizes, CGA, 1943. *Work:* CGA; Lowe A. Center, Syracuse Univ.; Lowe A. Ga'., Miami Univ.; Hudson River Mus.; WMAA; Newark Mus.; N.Y. Pub. Lib.; Dartmouth Col.; IBM Col.; Univ. Arizona; Staten Island Mus. Hist. & Art; Inland Steel Corp., Chicago; murals, USPO, Edward, N.Y.; Hudson Falls, N.Y.; Chardon, Ohio. *Exhibited:* Herron AI, 1944, 1945; CGA, 1941, 1943, 1945; WMA, 1943; AIC, 1941-1945; MMA, 1943; PAFA, 1944-1946; WMAA, 1942-1946; BM, 1944-1946; Carnegie Inst., 1944-1946; Iowa State Univ., 1946; VMFA, 1942, 1944, 1946; Berkshire Mus.; one-man: Marie Harriman Gal., Frank Rehn Gal.; Cowie Gal., Los A., 1949. Contributor to: Magazine of Art; ASL Bulletin. *Position:* Instr. A., CUASch; Asst. Prof. Painting, Departmental Rep., Sch. Painting & Sc., Columbia Univ., New York, N.Y.

PICKERING, ERNEST—*Educator*

College of Applied Arts, University of Cincinnati, Cincinnati, Ohio

Position: Dean, College of Applied Art, University of Cincinnati.*

PICKERING, S(IMEON) HORACE—
Painter, I., L., Comm. A., Hist.

320 Schaeffer St., Brooklyn 27, N.Y.

B. Salt Lake City, Utah, Oct. 18, 1894. *Studied:* AIC; Grand Central A. Sch.; & with Wayman Adams, Dean Cornwell. *Member:* Nat. Parks Assn.; AAPL; Am. Mus. Natural Hist.; Am. Veterans Soc. A. *Work:* Nat. Park Service. *Exhibited:* Soc. Indp. A., 1927-1946; Am. Veterans Soc. A., annually; AIC; Greenwich Village A. Center; New York, N.Y., 1955; Jersey City, N.J., 1956. Contributor: maps & illus. to Nat. Park Service periodicals. *Position:* Color Photographer, Nat. Parks Service; Tour Leader Supv., Statue of Liberty, New York, N.Y.

PICKFORD, ROLLIN, JR.—*Painter, Des., I.*

1839 Van Ness (21); h. 930 Sierra Madre, Fresno 4, Cal.

B. Fresno, Cal., May 23, 1912. *Studied:* Fresno State Col.; Stanford Univ., A.B., and with Louis Rogers. *Member:* Cal. WC Soc.; Carmel AA; Laguna Beach AA; A. Lg., Fresno. *Awards:* prizes, A. Lg. Fresno, 1946-1950, 1952-1958; Santa Cruz, 1947, 1949, 1952, 1958; Festival of Art, Laguna Beach, 1947, 1957; San Joaquin Valley, 1947; Laguna Beach AA, 1948, 1949, 1953; Soc. Western A., 1950; Mississippi AA, 1951; Monterey Fair, 1952, 1953; Stockton, Cal., 1952, 1953, 1954, 1956, 1957; No. Cal. A., 1954, 1956; Cal. State Fair, 1955; Rotunda Gal., San F., 1955. *Exhibited:* Cal. WC Soc., 1946-1950, 1952; San F. AA, 1946, 1952; Terry AI, 1952; Soc. Western A., 1949, 1950, 1952; Santa Cruz A. Lg., 1946, 1947, 1949, 1950, 1952, 1956-1958; Oakland A. Gal., 1946, 1948, 1950; Cal. State Fair, 1949, 1950, 1956, 1957; Monterey County Fair, 1952; Stockton, Cal., 1952, 1956, 1957; Fresno A. Lg., 1956-1958; San Luis Obispo AA, 1957; No. Cal. A., 1956, 1957; All-Cal. A., 1956, 1957; New Orleans AA, 1957; Rotunda Gal., San F., 1956. Contributor to Ford Times, Lincoln-Mercury Times, with illus.

PICKHARDT, CARL E., JR.—*Painter, Et., Lith., T., L.*
Forest St., Sherborn, Mass.

B. Westwood, Mass., May 28, 1908. *Studied*: Harvard Univ., B.A. *Awards*: prizes, NAD, 1942; Boston Soc. Indp. A., 1950. *Work*: BMFA; BM; LC; N.Y. Pub. Lib.; AGAA; PMA; FMA; WMA; DeCordova Mus.; Wadsworth Atheneum. *Exhibited*: Illinois Exh., 1951; BM, 1952; New Britain Inst., 1952; Phila. Pr. Cl., 1952; Int. Color Lith. Exh., 1952; Carnegie Inst., 1953; Intl. Exh., Japan, 1952; France, 1957. *Position*: Instr. A., Worcester Mus. Sch., 1953-54; Fitchburg (Mass.) A. Mus., 1951- .

PIERCE, DANNY—*Painter, Et., Eng.*
330 Summit Ave., Kent, Wash.

B. Woodlake, Cal., Sept. 10, 1920. *Studied*: Am. A. Sch.; BM Sch. A.; Chouinard AI. *Member*: Soc. Indp. A., Boston; Conn. Acad. FA; AEA; Am. Color Pr. Soc. *Awards*: prizes, BM, 1952 (purchase); Bradley Univ., 1952; LC, 1952, 1953, 1958 (purchase); Univ. So. California, 1952; SAM, 1952; Henry Gal., 1955. *Work*: BM; N.Y. Pub. Lib.; LC; MModA; Clearwater Mus. A.; Bradley Univ.; Univ. So. California; Princeton Univ.; SAM; Sweat Mem. Mus.; Nat. Mus., Stockholm, Sweden. *Exhibited*: Los A. Mus. A.; Oakland A. Mus.; BMFA; Springfield A. Mus.; SAM; Portland (Ore.) A. Mus.; BM; Munson-Williams-Proctor Inst.; LC; CGA; Carnegie Inst.; Erie Pub. Mus.; Milwaukee AI; Butler AI; New Britain Mus. A.; Avery Mem.; Univ. Maine; Clearwater Mus. A.; Bradley Univ.; Univ. Mississippi; Creative Gal. (one-man); Contemporaries (one-man); Univ. So. Cal.; DMFA; Denver A. Mus.; MModA; Sanford-Tiel Mem. Mus., Cherokee, Iowa; PAFA; Nat. Mus., Stockholm; Sao Paulo, Brazil; Barcelona, Spain, and others. *Positions*: Instr. A., Burnley Sch. of Prof. A., Seattle, Wash.; Faculty, Seattle Univ.

PIEROTTI, JOHN—*Cartoonist*
New York Post, 75 West St., New York, N.Y.; h. 100 Bay 26th St., Brooklyn 14, N.Y.

B. New York, N.Y., July 26, 1911. *Studied*: ASL; Mechanics AI; CUASch. *Member*: Baseball Writers of Am.; Tennis Writers of Am.; A. Writers Soc.; Nat. Cartoonists Soc. *Awards*: prize, Best Editorial Cartoon, Los A. Press Assn., 1955; Page One Award, 1955. *Exhibited*: MMA, 1947, 1951. *Positions*: Sport Cart., Washington Post, 1933-34; King Features, 1938; Sports Ed. & Cart., United Features, 1937-39; Cart., PM, 1940-50; Sports Ed., Cart., McClure Syndicate, 1950-51; Sports Cart., New York Post, 1951- ; Treas., Nat. Cart. Soc., 1948-57, Pres., 1957-59.

PIERRE-NOEL, MRS. VERGNIAUD.
See Jones, Lois Mailou.

PIKE, JOHN—*Painter, I.*
Woodstock, N.Y.

B. Boston, Mass., June 30, 1911. *Studied*: with Charles Hawthorne, Richard Miller. *Member*: NA; AWS; SI; SC; Woodstock AA; Phila. WC Cl. *Awards*: prizes, AWS; NAD; SC, and others. *Work*: paintings for U.S. Air Force Hist. Fnd.—France, Germany, Greenland, Ecuador, Columbia, Panama, etc. *Exhibited*: nationally, and 18 one-man exhs. Contributor illus. and covers to Colliers; Readers Digest; Life; Fortune; True magazine; advertisements for: Lederle Laboratories; Alcoa; Standard Oil; Falstaff; Goodyear; Hamilton Propeller, etc. *Position*: Instr., ASL, summer school.*

PILLIN, POLIA—*Painter, C.*
6151 Barrows Drive, Los Angeles 48, Cal.

B. Poland, Sept. 1, 1909. *Studied*: Hull House, Chicago; Jewish People's Inst., Chicago. *Member*: So. California Des. Assn. *Awards*: prizes, Los A. County AI, 1949 (ceramics); Syracuse Mus. FA, 1950; Cal. State Fair, 1951. *Work*: ceramics: DMFA; Long Beach Mun. A. Gal.; Syracuse Mus. FA; Los A. AI. *Exhibited*: AIC, 1947, 1948; SFMA, 1948; Wichita AA, 1947-1949, 1951; Denver A. Mus., 1952; Oakland A. Mus., 1950; Los A. Mus. A., 1948, 1950, 1952; Landau Gal., 1952; The Willow, N.Y., 1948-1956. Contributor to Arts & Architecture; The Arts; American Artist magazines.

PINE, GERI (Mrs. Geraldine Pine Werner)—*Painter*
215 East 11th St., New York 3, N.Y.

B. New York, N.Y., Mar. 17, 1914. *Studied*: ASL, with John Sloan. *Work*: Queens (N.Y.) Pub. Lib. *Exhibited*: WMAA, 1943; ACA Gal., 1936, 1940, 1941, 1949 (all one-man); Bonestell Gal., 1945; BM, 1938; Artisans Gal., 1954 (one-man); La Tausca Pearls Exh., 1947.

PINEDA, MARIANNA (PACKARD TOVISH)—*Sculptor*
164 Rawson Road, Brookline 46, Mass.

B. Evanston, Ill., May 10, 1925. *Studied*: Cranbrook Acad. A.; Bennington Col.; Univ. Cal., Berkeley; Columbia Univ.; Zadkine Sch. S., Paris, France. *Member*: S. Gld.; AEA. *Awards*: prizes, Albright A. Gal., 1948; WAC, 1951 (purchase); San F. AA, 1955; AIC, 1957; Portland, Me., 1957; Providence A. Cl., 1958; Boston A. Festival, 1957. *Work*: WAC; BMFA; Williams Col.; Dartmouth Col.; Wadsworth Atheneum; AGAA; Munson-Williams-Proctor Inst. *Exhibited*: BM, 1947; MMA, 1957; WMAA, 1953, 1954, 1957; AIC, 1957; Albright A. Gal., Buffalo, 1948; WAC, 1951-1953; Minneapolis Inst. A., 1955; Denver A. Mus., 1956; Boston A. Festival, 1957, 1958; San F. AA, 1955; Univ. Illinois; Portland (Me.) Mus. A., 1957; Providence A. Cl., 1958; United Nations Exh., San F., 1955; Galerie 8, Paris, France, 1951; Currier Gal. A., 1954; de Cordova & Dana Mus., Lincoln, Mass., 1954; Colorado Springs FA Center, 1953.

PINKNEY, HELEN LOUISE—*Museum Curator, Librarian*
Dayton Art Institute, Forest & Riverview Aves.; h. 37 Stoddard Ave., Dayton 5, Ohio

B. Decatur, Ill. *Studied*: Dayton AI Sch. *Exhibited*: Dayton AI Alum. Assn., annually. *Position*: Librarian, Registrar of Collections, 1936-45, Cur., Librarian, 1945- , Dayton AI, Dayton, Ohio.

PINTNER, DORA—*Painter, C., Des.*
45 Coolidge Hill Rd., Cambridge 38, Mass.

B. Great Britain. *Studied*: Glasgow Col. A., Scotland; Radcliffe Col., A.A.; Boston Univ., M.A. *Member*: Watertown (Mass.) AA; Copley Soc., Boston; Cambridge AA; Pa. Soc. Min. P. *Work*: stained glass windows, Angell Mem. Hospital, Boston; Nat. Mus. *Exhibited*: AIC; Nat. Mus., Wash., D.C., 1943, 1952; CGA, 1944-1946; Copley Soc., 1937-1958; Cal. Soc. Min. P., 1937, 1938, 1941; Chicago Soc. Min. P., 1938, 1940, 1942; Contemp. New England A., 1942-1946; Cambridge AA, 1944-1958; Pittsfield Mus. A., 1951. Lectures on Stained Glass.

PINTO, JAMES—*Painter*
Beneficencia #6 Bis, San Miguel de Allende, Gto., Mexico

B. Yugoslavia, Apr. 23, 1907. *Studied*: Univ. Zagreb, Yugoslavia; Chouinard AI, Los Angeles. *Member*: Los A. AA. *Awards*: prizes, Nat. Veterans' Exh., Santa Monica, 1947; Univ. Mexico, 1948; Fresno A. Lg., 1949; Leon, Gto., Mexico, 1950; Fargo, N.D., 1957. *Work*: Witte Mem. Mus.; American Life Ins. Co. *Exhibited*: AIC, 1955; MMA, 1952; Denver A. Mus., 1956; Santa Monica, 1947; Los A. Mus. A., 1952, 1956; Santa Barbara Mus. A., 1952; de Young Mem. Mus. San F., 1952; Los A. AA, 1953; Pasadena AA, 1950; Mexico City, 1948, 1949, 1951, 1956; San Jose, 1957. *Position*: Hd. Dept. Painting, Instr. Painting and Mural Painting, Instituto de Allende, Mexico, 1951- .

PITTMAN, HOBSON—*Painter, L.*
560 New Gulph Rd., Bryn Mawr, Pa.

B. Tarboro, N.C., Jan. 14, 1900. *Studied*: Rouse A. Sch., Tarboro, N.C.; Pa. State Col.; Carnegie Inst.; Columbia Univ., and abroad. *Member*: NA; Phila. WC Cl.; Phila. A. All.; AEA. *Awards*: prizes, PAFA, 1943; Cal. PLH, 1947; CGA, 1947; Carnegie Inst., 1949; Butler AI, 1950; medal, PAFA, 1944; gold med., NAD, 1953; Guggenheim F., 1955; prize & purchase, Butler AI, 1955. *Work*: MMA; PAFA; WMAA; BM; PMG; VMFA; Nebraska AA; Butler AI; CMA; Carnegie Inst.; Brooks Mem. A. Gal.; AGAA; PMA; Nat. Inst. A. & Let.; Cranbrook Acad. A.; PMA; Herron AI; Santa Barbara Mus. A.; Wilmington Soc. FA; IBM; Pa. State Univ.; Encyclopaedia Britannica; Toledo Mus. A.; Montclair A. Mus.; Abbott Laboratories. *Exhibited*: nationally, with many one-man exh., also in Paris, London, Cairo, Venice and other European art centers.

Lectures: "American Painting Today," "Portrait and Figure Painting Today"; "International Contemporary Painting"; "Chardin and Picasso." Lectures given 1956-58: PAFA, Univ. Virginia, Mary Washington Col., Univ. Richmond, Randolph-Macon Col., and William & Mary Col. *Positions*: Instr., Painting, Pa. State Univ.; PAFA; PMA.

PITTMAN, KITTY BUTNER (Mrs. James T.)—
Painter, T., S.
Sherman Square Studios, 160 West 73rd St., Apt. 13-H, New York 23, N.Y.

B. Philadelphia, Pa., Dec. 20, 1914. *Studied*: Oglethorpe Univ.; & with Fritz Zimmer, Robert Dean, Maurice Seiglar. *Member*: NAWA; Atlanta A. Exhibitors. *Work*: port., The Memminger Mem. Study, All Saints Church, Atlanta, Ga. *Exhibited*: SSAL, 1935-1940; Assoc. Georgia A., 1933-1936, 1938, 1940; Atlanta Studio Cl., 1932-1940; Atlanta AA, 1936, 1938; Atlanta A. Exhibitors, 1940-1942; Chicago North Shore A. Lg., 1937; NAWA.

PITZ, HENRY C.—Illustrator, E., W., P.
320 South Broad St., Philadelphia, Pa.; h. Plymouth Meeting, Pa.

B. Philadelphia, Pa., June 16, 1895. *Studied*: PMSchIA; Spring Garden Inst., Phila. *Member*: ANA; AWCS; Phila. A. All. (V.Pres.); Phila. Sketch Cl.; Phila. Pr. Cl.; Audubon A.; A.Lg. Am. *Awards*: med., Los A. Mus. A., 1932; PAFA, 1933, 1951, gold medal, 1956; PMSchIA, 1934; Phila. A. All., 1941; Paris Salon, 1934; prize, Phila. Pr. Cl., 1937; AWS, 1952; NAD, 1953, 1957; Butler AI, 1953; SC, 1951; gold med., Phila. Sketch Cl., 1955; Woodmere A. Gal., 1952; Silver Star Cluster, Phila. Mus. Col. A., 1956; SI. *Work*: Los A. Mus. A.; Lib. Cong.; Nat. Acad. A. & Let.; CMA; PAFA; Harcum Col.; Univ. Maine; N.Y.Pub.Lib.; PMA; Denver A. Mus.; Allentown Mus.; etc.; mural, Franklin Inst., Phila. *Exhibited*: Dayton AI; Univ. Maine; Rochester Inst.; Cayuga Mus. A.; NAD; AIC; Los A. Mus. A.; Stockholm, Sweden; PAFA, 1930-1946; PMA; AWCS, 1933-1937, 1944; BM; BMA; Wilmington Soc. FA; Paris Salon, 1934; WFNY 1939; etc. Author: "Early American Costumes," 1930; "The Practice of Illustration," 1946; "Treasury of American Book Illustration," 1947; "Pen, Brush and Ink," 1948; "Drawing Trees," 1956; "Pen Drawing Techniques," 1957. I., many books, and illus. for Colliers, Readers Digest, Gourmet and other magazines. Contributor to: national magazines. Position: Dir. Dept. Illus., PMSchIA, Philadelphia, Pa., 1934-52; Instr. A., PAFA summer session, 1938-45; visiting L., Univ. Pennsylvania, 1941; Assoc. Ed., American Artist magazine.

PITZ, MOLLY WOOD (Mrs. Henry C.)—Painter, T.
Plymouth Meeting, Pa.

B. Ambler, Pa., May 12, 1913. *Studied*: PMSchIA. *Member*: Phila. A. All.; Phila. WC Cl.; Bryn Mawr A. Center A.T. Workshop; Allen Lane A. Center; PMSch. A. Alumni Assn. *Work*: Pa. State Univ., and in private colls. *Exhibited*: Phila. WC Cl., 1935-1945; Woodmere A. Gal., 1943-1946, 1948-1952; Plymouth Meeting Friends Sch., 1948-1952; William Jeanes Mem. Lib., 1948-1952, 1953-1955.

PIZZITOLA, VINCENT—Painter, T.
8 West 13th St., New York 11, N.Y.

B. Alcamo, Italy, Nov. 9, 1890. *Studied*: Acad. of Rome, with Spinetti; and with Cellini, Ferrari, Atanasia. *Member*: Soc. Indp. A.; NAC. *Awards*: prize and medal, Acad. of Rome. *Work*: paintings and murals in private colls. *Exhibited*: Soc. Indp. A.; Montross Gal. (one-man); All. A. Am.; Burr Gal. (2-man). *Position*: Instr., City Island Sch. A., New York, N.Y.

PLATT, ELEANOR—Portrait Sculptor
Hotel Wales, 92nd St. & Madison Ave., New York 28, N.Y.

B. Woodbridge, N.J., May 6, 1910. *Studied*: ASL. *Member*: NAD; NSS. *Awards*: Chaloner scholarship, 1939-1941; Grant, Am. Acad. A. & Let., 1944; Guggenheim F., 1945. *Work*: BMFA; MMA; portraits, N.Y. Bar Assn.; Hebrew Univ., Jerusalem; Carnegie Corp.; Harvard Univ. Law Sch. Lib.; Mus. of the City of New York; Supreme Court Bldg.; MMA. Executed medals to be awarded for merit: Manley O. Hudson, James Ewing, George Wharton Pepper, Reginald Heber Smith.

PLATT, MARY CHENEY—Painter, Des., T.
100 East End Ave.; h. 169 East 78th St., New York 21, N.Y.

B. New York, N.Y., May 12, 1893. *Studied*: Parsons Sch. Des.; ASL; NAD; & with George Bridgman, Arthur Crisp, Charles Hawthorne. *Member*: NAWA. *Work*: murals, Russell Sage Fnd.; Spanish House, Columbia Univ. *Exhibited*: NAWA, 1934-1945, 1946; Montclair A. Mus., 1932; Contemporary A., 1933; Mun. A. Com. Exh., 1936; Montclair Women's Cl., 1954 (one-man). *Position*: Hd. A. Dept., Chapin Sch., New York, N.Y., 1935- .

PLAUT, JAMES S.—Former Museum Director
225 Brattle St., Cambridge 38, Mass.

B. Cincinnati, Ohio, Feb. 1, 1912. *Studied*: Harvard Col., A.B.; Harvard Univ., A.M. *Awards*: Legion of Merit (U.S.); Legion d'Honneur, Paris (Chevalier); Royal Order of St. Olav, Norway. Industrial Des. Consultant to: Corning Glass Works; Steuben Glass; Cheney Brothers; Elgin Watch Co.; Congoleum-Nairn; Shenango Pottery; Castleton China; Reynolds Metals and others, 1947- ; Adv. to State of Israel in indust. des. matters, 1951; Organized six international art exhs. Author: "Steuben Glass," 1949; "Oskar Kokoschka," 1950; Ed., of approx. 20 books published by Inst. of Contemp. A., Boston. Frequent contributor to Atlantic Monthly; Saturday Review and art periodicals. *Positions*: Asst., Dept. FA, Harvard, 1934-35; Asst. to Cur. Paintings, BMFA, 1935-39; Dir., Inst. Mod A., Boston, 1939; after World War II duty resumed Dir., Inst. of Contemp. A., Boston, 1946-56 (Dec.); Dir. Emeritus, Trustee, 1956- ; Deputy United States Commissioner General, Brussels World's Fair, 1958.

PLAVCAN, CATHARINE BURNS (Mrs. Joseph M.)—
Critic, T., P., L.
232 Gridley Ave., Erie, Pa.

B. Springfield, Ill. *Studied*: Col. William & Mary; PAFA; Mercyhurst Col., B.A. *Member*: A. Cl. of Erie; Fed. Erie A. *Awards*: prizes, A. Cl. of Erie, 1931, 1936, 1948; Fed. Erie A., 1952. *Work*: mural asst., Press Cl., Treacy Sch., St. Vincent Hospital, all Erie, Pa.; church decorations, Lorain, Ohio, Meadville and DuBois, Pa. *Exhibited*: Indiana, Pa., 1943; Butler AI, 1943; Ohio Valley Exh., Athens, Ohio, 1944; Fed. Erie A., 1950-1955. Lectures: Children's Art. *Position*: A. Instr., Erie Day Sch., 1937-42; Erie Pub. Schs., 1946- ; A. Cr., Erie Dispatch, 1937-1957; Erie Sunday Times-News, 1957- ; Sec., Fed. Erie A.

PLAVCAN, JOSEPH MICHAEL—Painter, T., L.
232 Gridley Ave., Erie, Pa.

B. Braddock, Pa., July 19, 1908. *Studied*: PAFA; Univ. Pittsburgh. *Member*: Am. Fed. T.; Am. Watercolor Assn.; Erie A. Cl.; Fed. Erie A. *Awards*: Cresson Traveling Scholarship, PAFA, 1929; med., Soc. Wash. A., 1929; prizes, CGA, 1931; Parkersburg FA Center, 1944; Erie A. Cl.; F., PAFA; Butler AI, 1944. *Work*: murals, Press Cl., Treacy Sch., St. Vincent's Hospital, Erie, Pa.; Church of Nativity, Lorain, Ohio; St. Agatha's, Meadville, Pa.; DuBois, Pa. *Exhibited*: PAFA, 1928-1930, 1932-1936, 1941, 1951, 1952; Carnegie Inst., 1930; CGA, 1931, 1933, 1951; AIC, 1931, 1935, 1936; NAD, 1943, 1944, 1950, 1952; Pepsi-Cola, 1946; Indiana, Pa., 1943, 1944; Butler AI, 1938, 1939, 1942-1945, 1949, 1951; Ohio Valley Exh., 1943-1954; Parkersburg FA Center, 1943, 1944; Erie, Pa., 1928-1955; Edinboro, Pa., Slippery Rock, Pa., 1955 (one-man); Thiel Col., 1958 (one-man). *Position*: T., Dir. A., Erie Tech. H.S., Erie, Pa., 1932- ; Erie Veteran's Sch., 1946- .

PLEADWELL, AMY MARGARET—Painter
82 Chestnut St., Boston, Mass.

B. Taunton, Mass. *Studied*: Mass. Sch. A.; Grande Chaumiere, Ecole Moderne, Paris. *Member*: NAWA; Copley Soc., Boston; Boston Soc. Contemp. A. *Exhibited*: numerous water color exh.*

PLEIMLING, WINNIFRED (Mrs. Harold O.)—Painter
1213 East 54th St., Chicago 15, Ill.

B. Jackson, Mich. *Studied*: AIC. *Member*: Women A. Salon, Chicago (Pres. & Founder); Assn. Chicago P. & S.; AIC Alumni Assn. (Vice-Pres.); Chicago A. Cl. *Award*: prize, Chicago A. Cl. *Work*: in private colls.

PLEISSNER, OGDEN—*Painter*

33 West 67th St.; h. 35 East 9th St., New York 3, N.Y.

B. Brooklyn, N.Y., Apr. 29, 1905. *Studied*: ASL. *Member*: SC; NA; All. A. Am.; AWS; Balt. WC Soc.; Phila. WC Soc.; So. Vermont AA; Conn. Acad. FA; NAC; Century Assn.; ASL. *Awards*: prizes, All. A. Am., 1951; NAC, 1952 (medal); NAD, 1952; Concord AA (medal), 1950; Conn. Acad. FA, 1950; Balt. WC Cl., 1949. *Work*: BM; Davenport Mun. A. Gal.; Lyman Allyn Mus. A.; Univ. Georgia; Philbrook A. Center; Univ. Maine; Colby Col.; IBM; U.S. War Dept.; MIT; New Hampshire State Lib.; Syracuse Mus. FA; Chrysler Coll. War Art; Univ. Vermont; WMA; Springville (Utah) H.S.; NAD; MMA; PMA; W.R. Conner Fnd.; Amherst Col.; CM; New Britain A. Mus.; Wash. County Mus. A.; Los A. Mus. A.; WMA; Minneapolis Inst. A.; Toledo Mus. A. *Exhibited*: AWS; All. A. Am.; NAD; Conn. Acad. FA; Balt. WC Cl.; Phila. WC Cl.; WMAA; MMA; PAFA; ASL; Concord AA; Maine WC Soc.; New Britain Inst.; Southern Vermont A.; and many others.*

PLOWDEN, MRS. T. M. See McCullough, Suzanne

PLIMPTON, RUSSELL—*Museum Director*

Society of the Four Arts; h. 10 Four Arts Plaza, Palm Beach, Fla.

B. Hollis, N.Y., Aug. 26, 1891. *Studied*: Princeton Univ. *Member*: Assn. A. Mus. Dirs.; AAMus.; AFA; Southern A. Mus. Dir. Assn., and others. Contributor to Bulletin of the Minneapolis AI. Lectures: Painting; Decorative Arts, Radio and TV, Minneapolis. Increased collections and arranged many exhibitions at Minneapolis AI. *Positions*: Asst. Cur., Dept. Dec. A., Metropolitan Museum of Art, N.Y., 7 years; Dir., Minneapolis AI, 35 years; Dir., Society of the Four Arts, Palm Beach, Fla., 1956- .

PLUNGUIAN, GINA—*Painter, S., T., L.*

115 East Park Place, Newark, Del.

Studied: Ecole des Beaux-Arts, Montreal, Canada; Dayton AI. *Member*: AEA; NAWA; Assoc. A., New Jersey; CAA; Council of Del. A. *Awards*: prizes, Hunter Gal., 1954, 1955; Delaware A. Center, 1958. *Work*: Kirkman Vocational H.S., Chattanooga; Tel-Aviv Mus., Israel; Southern Missionary Col., Tenn.; portraits in many private colls. *Exhibited*: PAFA; Butler AI; All. A. Am.; WMAA; Lighthouse A. Exh., N.Y.; Newark Mus. A.; Montclair A. Mus.; New Jersey WC Soc.; New Jersey State Mus., Trenton; Columbus Gal. FA; Dayton AI; Hunter Gal., Chattanooga; one-man: Princeton Group A. (2); Princeton Present Day Cl.; New Brunswick A. Center; Oglethorpe Univ., Georgia; Argent Gal., N.Y.; Univ. Delaware, 1958; Lincoln Univ., 1959; Octorara (Pa.) AA, 1957. Lectures on art to clubs, teacher's organizations, college and art groups. *Position*: Instr., Delaware A. Center, Wilmington, Del.

PNEUMAN, MILDRED YOUNG (Mrs. Fred A.)— *Painter, Gr.*

1129 11th St., Boulder, Colo.

B. Oskaloosa, Iowa, Sept. 15, 1899. *Studied*: Univ. Colorado, B.A., M.F.A. *Member*: Boulder A. Gld.; AAPL. *Work*: P.E.O. Mem. Lib., Mt. Pleasant, Iowa. *Exhibited*: Phila. Color Pr. Soc., 1945; Hoosier Salon, 1928-1935; Denver A. Mus., 1944; Univ. Colorado; Central City A. Gal.; Boulder A. Gld. traveling exh., 1954-1958; Brewster Gal., Boulder, 1954 (one-man); Colorado Chautauqua Assn., 1957 (one-man).

POHL, HUGO DAVID—*Painter, Et., T.*

Box 286, Route 8, San Antonio 1, Tex.

B. Detroit, Mich., Mar. 11, 1878. *Studied*: Detroit Inst. A.; ASL; Julian Acad., Paris; & in Germany, Holland, Spain, Italy. *Work*: San Antonio (Tex.) Auditorium; murals, Int. Harvester Co., Chicago; Union Pacific R.R. *Exhibited*: NAD; Scarab Cl., Detroit; Palette & Chisel Cl., Chicago.

POHL, LAVERA ANN (Mrs. William)—*Painter, W., L.*

Twin Gables Apartments, 36 Riverside Ave., Red Bank, N.J.

B. Port Washington, Wis., Jan. 20, 1901. *Studied*: Univ. Bonn, Ph.D., Univ. Cologne, Germany; Wis. Sch. FA;

Milwaukee State T. Col.; Milwaukee AI. *Member*: Wis. P. & S.; Wis. Designer-Craftsmen; CAA; AFA; Am. Assn. Univ. Women; NAWA. *Awards*: prize, Wis. P. & S., 1942; Marquette Univ. Matrix Award, 1953; Senior Lg. Service Cl. of America Award, 1954. *Work*: des. Women's Army Corps med.; murals, Milwaukee Univ. *Exhibited*: NAWA, 1944, 1945; Milwaukee AI, 1946; Wis. P. & S., 1918-1946; Beloit Coll., 1940, 1942, 1946; Col. Women's Cl., Milwaukee, 1940, 1946 (one-man); Argent Gal.; 1945; Barbizon Plaza Gal., 1946. Author: "American Painting," 1938. Contributor to: newspapers & college year books. Lectures on art topics; art advisor. *Position*: Dir., Milwaukee AI, Milwaukee, Wis., 1950-55; Dir., Layton A. Gal., 1953-55.

POHL, LOUIS G.—*Painter, Lith., T.*

3921 Gail St., Honolulu 15, Hawaii

B. Cincinnati, Ohio, Sept. 14, 1915. *Studied*: Cincinnati A. Acad. *Member*: Hawaii P. & S. Lg.; Honolulu Pr. M. *Awards*: prizes, Honolulu Acad. A., 1947, 1949, 1956, 1957; Watamull Fnd. purchase awards, 1950, 1952; McInerny Fnd. Grant, 1954-1955. *Work*: CM; Honolulu Acad. A. *Exhibited*: Annual exh. American Art, 1938, 1940, 1941; Butler Inst. Am. A., 1939, 1944; Riverside Mus., N.Y.; Art of Cincinnati, 1940-1942; one-man: CM; Honolulu Acad. A., and many galleries in Cincinnati and Honolulu. Cartoonist: "School Daze," daily cartoon, Honolulu Advertiser. *Position*: Instr., Univ. Hawaii, 1953-56; Honolulu Sch. A.; Honolulu Acad. A.

POHL, MRS. MINETTE. See Teichmueller, M.

POIDIMANI, GINO—*Sculptor, T.*

51 via Margutta, Rome, Italy.

B. Rosolini, Italy, Jan. 2, 1910. *Studied*: Royal Sch. A., Siracuse, Italy; Royal Liceo Artistico of Rome; Royal Acad. FA, Rome. *Member*: Int. Artistic Assn., Rome; Artistic & Cultural Cl., Siracuse, Italy; NSS; All. A. Am. *Awards*: Gov. scholarship to Royal Acad. FA, Rome; gold medal, for sculpture, Tripoli, 1929. *Work*: statues, bas-reliefs, Cathedral of Messina, Rome; St. Joseph's Catholic Church, Rosolini, Italy; Monumental Cemetery, Milan, and others; numerous portrait busts in private coll. *Exhibited*: Florence, 1942; San Remo prize exh., 1937, 1939, 1940; Venice Biennale, 1941; Rome, 1947 (one-man); Audubon A., 1947, 1950-1952; PAFA, 1948; Fairmount Park, Phila., 1949; NSS, 1951, 1952; Argent Gal., 1951; All. A. Am., 1951.*

POLAND, REGINALD— *Museum Director, W., L., T., Cr.*

High Museum of Art, 1280 Peachtree St., Northeast, Atlanta 9, Ga.

B. Providence, R.I., Sept. 28, 1893. *Studied*: Brown Univ., B.A., D.F.A. (hon.); Princeton Univ., A.M.; Harvard Univ., A.M. *Member*: AAMus.; Assn. A. Mus. Dir., and of Western Assn. A. Mus. Dir. (hon.); San Diego FA Soc. (hon.); Atlanta WC Cl. (hon.); AAPL (Vice-Pres. Atlanta Chptr.). *Awards*: F., Am. Acad. in Rome, 1916; Traveling F., Carl Schurz Fnd., 1936; Royal Order of Spain, 1931; gold medal, Intl. Expo., San Diego, 1935. Guest of West German Republic, Mus. Dirs. Group, summer 1958. Contributor to art magazines. Lectures: Spanish Art; French Decorative Art. *Position*: Dir., Denver AA, 1919-21; Edu. Dir., Detroit Inst. A., 1921-26; Dir., San Diego FA Soc., 1926-50; Dir., Norton Gal. & Sch. A., West Palm Beach, Fla., 1952-54; Dir., Museums, Atlanta, Ga., AA, 1954- .

POLASEK, ALBIN—*Sculptor*

633 Osceola Ave., Winter Park, Fla.

B. Frenstat, Czechoslovakia, Feb. 14, 1879. *Studied*: Am. Acad. in Rome; PAFA; & with Charles Grafly. *Member*: NA; NSS; Arch.L.; Assn. Chicago P. & S.; Bohemian A. Cl.; AFA. *Awards*: Prix de Rome, 1910; med., prize, PAFA, 1914, 1925; Pan-Pacific Exp., 1915; AIC, 1917, 1922; med., Milwaukee AI, 1917; Chicago SA, 1922; Assn. Chicago P. & S., 1933; prize, Chicago Galleries Assn., 1937. *Work*: MMA; PAFA; AIC; Detroit Inst. A.; Ball State T. Col., Muncie, Ind.; mem., Springfield, Ill.; Hartford, Conn.; Chicago, Ill.; Vincennes, Ind.; St. Cecelia's Cathedral, Omaha, Neb.; Masaryk Mem., Chicago.

POLKINGHORN, GEORGE—*Painter*

5200 Encino Ave., Encino, Cal.

B. Leadville, Colo., Oct. 11, 1898. *Studied*: Univ. California, A.B.; Otis AI. *Member*: Cal. A. Cl.; Cal. WC Soc.; Laguna Beach AA. *Award*: prize, Cal. A. Cl., 1952, and gold medal. *Exhibited*: Cal. WC Soc.; Laguna Beach AA; San Diego FA Center; Los A. Mus. A.; Santa Cruz A. Lg.; Cal. A. Cl.; AWS.*

POLLACK, REGINALD MURRAY—*Painter, S., Gr.*

2 Pass. Dantzig, XV; h. 11 Impasse Ronsin, Paris, France

B. Middle Village, L.I., N.Y., July 29, 1924. *Studied*: with Moses Soyer, Boardman Robinson, Wallace Harrison. *Awards*: Maurice Fromke scholarship, Spain, 1951; Prix Neumann, Paris, 1952; medal, Salon Othon Friesz, 1954; prize, Museé d'Art Moderne, 1958. *Work*: Tel-Aviv Mus., Haifa Mus., Ein Harod Mus., Israel; Mint Mus. A.; Govt. of France Coll. *Exhibited*: Salon de Mai, 1949, 1951, Salon d'Automne, 1949, 1950, 1953, 1954, Gal. Presses Litteraires de France, 1951, Salon de Jeune, 1952, 1953, 1954, Gal. St. Placide, 1952 (one-man), Salon des Independants, 1955-1958, Gal. Vincy, 1955, Gal. Cazenov, Gal. de Seine, all in Paris, France; Joslyn A. Mus., 1951; Peridot Gal., N.Y., 1949-1952, 1953 (one-man), 1955, 1956, 1957 (one-man); WMAA, 1953, 1955, 1956, 1958; Underwood Corp., Bridgeport, Conn., 1955; VMFA, 1954; Univ. Nebraska, 1957; Illinois Wesleyan Univ., 1958.

POLLAK, MAX—*Etcher, P.*

104 Bulkley Ave., Sausalito, Cal.

B. Prague, Czechoslovakia, Feb. 27, 1886. *Studied*: in Vienna. *Member*: Chicago SE; Cal. SE. *Awards*: prizes, Chicago SE, 1942; Cal. SE, 1944, 1945. *Work*: MMA; N.Y.Pub.Lib.; deYoung Mem. Mus.; Cal. State Lib.; LC; SFMA; British Mus., London; Albertina Mus., Vienna; A.Mus., Prague; Mus. der Stadt Wien. I., "My City," 1929.

POLLAK, THERESA—*Educator, P., L.*

901 West Franklin St.; h. 1102 West Grace St., Richmond 20, Va.

B. Richmond, Va., Aug. 13, 1899. *Studied*: Westhampton Col., Univ. Richmond, B.S.; ASL; FMA, Harvard Univ.; Hans Hofmann Sch. FA. *Member*: ASL; Richmond AA; VMFA; Valentine Mus. *Awards*: F., Tiffany Fnd., 1932; Carnegie F., 1933; prizes, Studio Cl., N.Y.; 1926; Richmond A., 1931, 1938, 1957; VMFA, 1939. *Work*: VMFA; Richmond Professional Inst.; Univ. Virginia; Mary Baldwin Col. *Exhibited*: CGA, 1930; WMAA, 1932; BMFA, 1933; Rockefeller Center, N.Y., 1936, 1938; Oakland A. Gal., 1941-1943; Richmond Woman's Cl., 1928-1930; Richmond Acad. A., 1931-1938; VMFA, 1938-1955; Va.-Intermont Exh., 1944; one-man exh.: VMFA, 1940; Westhampton Col., 1940; Univ. Virginia, 1940; Randolph-Macon Col. for Women, 1940; Farmville State T. Col., 1941; Richmond, Va., 1958. *Position*: Prof. A. of Richmond Professional Inst., Col. William & Mary, Richmond, Va., 1928- .

POLLET, JOSEPH—*Painter, Gr., W., L., T.*

3 Washington Sq., New York 3, N.Y.

B. Albbruck, Switzerland, Oct. 17, 1897. *Studied*: in Europe; ASL; & with John Sloan, Robert Henri. *Member*: Soc. Indp. A.; Woodstock AA. *Awards*: Guggenheim F., 1929. *Work*: Newark Mus.; WMAA; Los A. Mus. A.; Dartmouth Col.; N.Y. Univ. *Exhibited*: CGA, 1926-1936; PAFA, 1926-1944; MMoDA, 1930; Carnegie Inst., 1929-1945; AIC, 1929-1936; N.Y. Mun. Exh., 1933; VMFA; Newark Mus., 1944; WFNY 1939; WMAA, 1923-1946; numerous one-man exh., N.Y., 1923- . Contributor to: art magazines. *Position*: Dir., Sawkill Sch. A., Woodstock, N.Y., 1937-42; Instr. A., N.Y. Univ., 1946-47.*

POLLOCK, CHARLES CECIL—*Painter, T.*

Box 173, Okemos, Mich.

B. Denver, Colo., Dec. 25, 1902. *Studied*: Otis AI; ASL. *Work*: murals, Mun. Water Plant, Lansing, Mich.; Mich. State Col., East Lansing. *Exhibited*: AIC, 1937, 1942; SAE, 1937; SFMA, 1939; WFNY 1939; Colorado Springs FA Center, 1937, 1938; PAFA, 1941; Detroit Inst. A., 1939, 1940, 1945. *Position*: Asst. Prof., Graphic Design, Painting, Lettering, Etching, Michigan State Univ., East Lansing, Mich., 1942- .

POLONY, ELEMER—*Painter, T.*

96 Fifth Ave., New York 11, N.Y.

B. Zomba, Hungary, May 11, 1911. *Studied*: Royal Acad. FA, Budapest, with Gyula Rudnay; Acad. FA, Rome, Italy; and with Aba-Novak. *Member*: Arch. Lg.; NSMP. *Awards*: Gold medal, Budapest, 1938; Grand Prix and traveling scholarship, Budapest, 1939; Ministry of Edu. traveling F., 1941; F., Rome, 1946; prize, Henry Street Settlement mural comp., 1958. *Work*: Univ. Kansas City, and in Hungary, Czechoslovakia. Fresco and mosaics, churches in Europe; murals, Univ. Kansas City. *Exhibited*: in Budapest, 1939-1943; Intl. Exh. Sacred Art, Vatican, 1950; Intl. Exh., Rome, Italy, 1949; William Rockhill Nelson Gal. A., Kansas City, 1953; CMA, 1955, 1957; one-man: Budapest, 1939, 1941-1943; Czechoslovakia, 1948; Rome, Italy, 1949; Florence, Italy, 1950; Kansas City AI, 1952; Arch. Lg., 1957.

POLOS, THEODORE C.—*Painter, Lith., T.*

5398 Bryant Ave., Oakland 11, Cal.

B. Mytelene, Greece, Feb., 1902. *Studied*: Cal. Col. A. & Crafts; Cal. Sch. FA; & with Xavier Martinez, Constance Macky. *Member*: San F. AA. *Awards*: prizes, San F. AA, 1937, 1938; SFMA, 1939; Rosenberg F., 1940; med., Richmond, Va., 1942. *Work*: SFMA; VMFA; Mills Col.; Crocker A. Gal. *Exhibited*: MModA, 1943; Carnegie Inst., 1943, 1944; AIC, 1943, 1945; CGA; VMFA, 1942; Fnd. Western A.; SFMA; Palace Legion Honor; Crocker A. Gal.; WFNY 1939; GGE, 1939. *Position*: Instr., Acad. Advertising A., San Francisco, Cal.; Cal. Col. A. & Crafts, Oakland, Cal.; Cal. Sch. FA, San Francisco, Cal.

POLVOGT, CARL WILLIAM, JR. (BILL)—*Cartoonist, Comm. A., Des.*

2611 Pasadena Place, Dallas, Tex.

B. Dallas, Tex., Mar. 31, 1929. *Studied*: Southern Methodist Univ., Dallas; Univ. Texas, Austin, B.S. *Member*: Nat. Professional Adv. Fraternity. Contributor cartoons to Sports Illustrated; Sat. Eve. Post and other national magazines. *Position*: A. Dir., Tech. Publications, Chance Vought Aircraft Co., 1951-54; A. Dir., Chas. B. Russell & Assoc., Dallas, Tex., 1954- .*

POMEROY, ELSIE LOWER—*Painter, I., T.*

33 Elm Ave., Mill Valley, Cal.

B. New Castle, Pa. *Studied*: Corcoran Sch. A.; & with Phil Dike, Millard Sheets, Eliot O'Hara. *Member*: Cal. WC Soc.; San F. AA; Wash. WC Cl.; San F. Women A.; Marin Soc. A. *Awards*: prizes, A.Lg., Wash., D.C., 1935; Marin Soc. A., 1948; Butler AI, 1942; Riverside (Cal.) FA Gld., 1946; Mill Valley, Cal., 1957. *Work*: Los A. AA; Butler AI; San F. Mun. Coll.; Carville, La.; Riverside (Cal.) H.S. *Exhibited*: AIC, 1938, 1939; GGE, 1939; AWCS, 1942; NGA, 1941; Chicago AC, 1943; Cal. WC Soc.; Butler AI; Wash. WC Cl.; San F. Women A., 1955. I., botanical illus. for U.S. Dept. Agriculture. Contributing A, SFMA rental library; Instr., Adult Edu., Tamalpais H.S. *Position*: Instr. A., Y.W.C.A., San Francisco, Cal.

POMFRET, JOHN—*Art Library Director*

Henry E. Huntington Library & Art Gallery, San Marino, Gal.*

POMMER, MILDRED NEWELL—*Painter, Gr., Des., C., T.*

2961 Clay St., San Francisco 15, Cal.

B. Sibley, Iowa, May 29, 1893. *Studied*: Otis AI; Chouinard AI; Cal. Sch. FA, and with Beniamino Bufano. *Member*: San F. AA; Contemp. Handweavers of Cal. *Awards*: prizes, San F. AA, 1939; SFMA, 1943. *Work*: SFMA; Cal. Hist. Soc.; Cal. PLH. *Exhibited*: San F. AA, annually; deYoung Mem. Mus., 1952; San F. A. Festival, annually.

PONCE DE LEON, MICHAEL—*Printmaker, P., T.*

30 East 14th St., New York 3, N.Y.

B. Miami, Fla., July 4, 1922. *Studied*: NAD; PAFA; Univ. Mexico City; ASL, with Booth, Vytlacil, Barnet; BM Sch. A., with Ferren, Shahn, Peterdi. *Awards*: prizes, Bradley Univ., 1954 (purchase); DMFA, 1954 (purchase); SAGA, 1954; Tiffany F., 1953, 1955; Phila. Pr. Cl., 1958; Fulbright F., 1956-57. *Work*: DMFA; BM; Bradley Univ.;

MModA; CM; Sarasota AA; Palacio de Bellas Artes, Mexico; Stockholm Mus. A.; Nat. Mus., Oslo; PMA; LC; N.Y. Pub. Lib. Edition of 200 prints made for Book Find Club, 1955; 350 Christmas Cards for Contemporary Gal., 1955; 40 prints for BM, 1954; IGAS, 1958. *Exhibited*: MMA; MModA; BM; LC; PAFA; DMFA; BMFA; CM; SAM; Univ. So. California; Portland A. Mus.; Phila. Pr. Cl.; SAGA; New York City Center; Contemporary Gal.; Audubon A.; Mexico City, 1958; Grenchen, Switzerland, 1958; Bradley Univ.; Denver A. Mus.; AIC; Oslo, Norway; Stockholm; NAD; BMFA; Univ. Illinois; Bodley Gal., 1958, and many others; oneman: Mexico City. Contributor cartoons and illus. to Sat. Eve. Post; New Yorker; American Legion and other national magazines.

PONSEN, TUNIS—*Painter, T.*
    5809 Harper Ave., Chicago 37, Ill.

B. The Netherlands, Feb. 19, 1891. *Studied*: AIC, and abroad. *Member*: Chicago P. & S.; Chicago Soc. A.; Chicago Gal. Assn.; Renaissance Soc., Univ. Chicago. *Awards*: prizes, AIC; Ill. Soc. A., 1954. *Work*: Hackley A. Gal.; Flint Inst. A.; City of Chicago Coll.; Chicago Pub. Schs. *Exhibited*: AIC, 1927, 1929, 1930-1935; Toledo Mus. A.; PAFA; Chicago P. & S.; Chicago Soc. A.; Chicago Gal. Assn., 1950-1955 (one-man).*

PONT, CHARLES E.—*Printmaker, P., I., L., C., W.*
    Wilton, Conn.

B. St. Julien, France, Jan. 6, 1898. *Studied*: Shelton Col.; PIASch; CUASch; ASL. *Member*: AWCS; Soc. Typophiles; Southern Pr. M. *Awards*: prize, Southern Pr.M., 1941; SAE, 1937; AAPL, 1957. *Work*: Lib. Cong.; MMA; Syracuse Mus. FA; N.Y.Pub.Lib.; Newark Pub.Lib.; Peabody Mus.; Appalachian Mus., Mt. Airy, Ga. *Exhibited*: NAD, 1933-1940; MMA, 1941; AIC, 1936, 1937; PAFA, 1932, 1940; Warsaw, Poland, 1935; Phila. Pr. Cl., 1932, 1939; Phila. A. All., 1930, 1931; Lib. Cong., 1943; SFMA; WFNY 1939; Southern Pr.M.; Conn. Acad. FA; AWCS; CMA; etc. Author, I., Des., "Tabernacle Alphabet," 1946; "The World's Collision," 1956. I., many books. Contributor to: magazines & newspapers. Lectures: Art and Theology. *Position*: A. Dir., Magazine Digest, 1951-52; Asst. A. Dir., Grosset & Dunlap, 1954- .

POOLE, EARL L(INCOLN)—
    Former Museum Director, I., Gr., S., P., E.
    509 Sunset Rd., West Reading, Pa.

B. Haddonfield, N.J., Oct. 30, 1891. *Studied*: PMSchIA; PAFA; Univ. Pennsylvania. *Member*: Reading T. Assn.; Pa. State Edu. Assn.; Nat. Edu. Assn.; AAMus. *Awards*: F., PAFA; Hon. degree, Sc. D., Franklin and Marshall Col., 1948. *Work*: Univ. Michigan; s., Reading Mus. Park, Reading, Pa. *Exhibited*: PAFA; Univ. Michigan; Lib. Cong.; Los A. Mus. A.; Harrisburg (Pa.) AA; CAM; Am. Mus. Natural Hist. I., "Birds of Virginia," 1913; "Mammals of Eastern North America," 1943; & other books. Lectures: Symbolism in Art. *Position*: Dir. A. Edu., Reading Sch. District, 1916-39; Asst. Dir., 1926-39, Dir., 1939-55, Reading (Pa.) Pub. Mus.*

POOLE, LYNN D. (Mr.)—*Educator*
    112 West University Parkway, Baltimore 10, Md.

B. Eagle Grove, Iowa, Aug. 11, 1910. *Studied*: Western Reserve Univ., A.B., M.A. *Member*: NEA; Am. Soc. for Aesthetics; Eastern AA; CAA; Am. Pub. Relations Assn.; Pub. Relations Soc. of Am.; Nat. Assn. Edu. Broadcasters; Am. College Pub. Relations Assn. (Pres., 1956-57). *Awards*: 19 national awards for educational television, including George Foster Peabody award, 1950, 1952. Contributor to America, School Arts, Eastern Arts Bulletin and others, with articles on Art Education and Public Relations. *Position*: Dir. Edu. Activities, Walters A. Gal., Balt., Md., 1938-42; Dir., Pub. Relations, Johns Hopkins Univ., Baltimore, Md., 1946- .*

POOR, HENRY VARNUM—*Painter, C., S., E., W.*
    c/o Frank K. M. Rehn Gallery, 683 Fifth Ave., New York 22, N.Y.; h. South Mountain Rd., New City, N.Y.

B. Chapman, Kan., Sept. 30, 1888. *Studied*: Stanford Univ., A.B.; Slade Sch., London; Julian Acad., Paris; & with Walter Sickert. *Work*: MMA; WMAA; PMG; Nat. Inst. A. & Let.; SFMA; CMA; AGAA; BM; Newark

Mus.; PMA; Kansas City AI; Los A. Mus. A.; Dallas Mus. FA; WMA; frescoes, Dept. Justice, Interior Bldg., Wash., D.C.; Pa. State Univ.; ceramic mural, Mt. Sinai Hospital; ceramic mural, exterior H.S., Flushing, N.Y. *Exhibited*: nationally. Author, I., "Artist Sees Alaska," 1945; "A Book of Pottery," 1958; I., Jack London's "Call of the Wild" (Limited Editions Cl.). *Position*: Prof. A., Columbia Univ., New York, N.Y., at present; Pres., Skowhegan Sch. P. & S., Skowhegan, Me.

POPE, ANNEMARIE H. (Mrs. John A.)—
    Chief, Traveling Exhibition Service
    Smithsonian Institution (25); h. 2425 California St., Northwest, Washington 8, D.C.

B. Dortmund, Germany. *Studied*: Univ. Munich; Univ. Heidelberg, Ph.D.; Sorbonne, Paris, France; Radcliffe Col. *Member*: AAMus.; CAA. Arranged exhibition: "Master Drawings," GGE, 1939. *Award*: Order of Merit, Fed. Republic of Germany, 1956; Royal Swedish Order of the Polar Star, 1957. *Positions*: Asst. Dir., Portland (Ore.) A. Mus., 1942-43; Asst. Dir. in charge of Traveling Exhs., AFA, 1947-51; Chief, Traveling Exh. Service, Smithsonian Inst., Washington, D.C., 1951- .

POPE, JOHN ALEXANDER—*Assistant Museum Director*
    Freer Gallery of Art, Washington 25, D.C.

B. Detroit, Mich., Aug. 4, 1906. *Studied*: Yale Col., A.B.; Harvard Univ., A.M., Ph.D.; Courtauld Inst., Univ. London. *Member*: Am. Oriental Soc.; Oriental Ceramic Soc., London; Assn. for Asian Studies; The Asia Soc.; The Japan Soc.; Far Eastern Ceramic Group (Pres.). Compiler: A Descriptive and Illustrative Catalogue of Chinese Bronzes, 1946. Author: Fourteenth Century Blue and White: A group of Chinese porcelains in the Topkapu Sarayi Müzesi, Istanbul, Freer Gal. A. Occasional Papers, vol. 2, no. 1, 1952; Chinese Porcelains from the Ardebil Shrine, xvi, 171 pp., 144 plates, Freer Gal. A., 1956. Contributor to Harvard Journal of Asiatic Studies; Archives of the Chinese Art Society of America; Oriental Art (Oxford); Transactions of the Oriental Ceramic Society. *Positions*: L., Chinese A., Columbia Univ., 1941-43; Assoc. in Research, 1943-46, Asst. Dir., 1946- , Freer Gal. A., Washington, D.C.; Pres., Far Eastern Ceramic Group.

POPINSKY, ARNOLD DAVE—*Sculptor, E., Gr.*
    Art Department, Beloit College; h. 719½ Church St., Beloit, Wis.

B. New York, N.Y., Aug. 21, 1930. *Studied*: N.Y. State Univ., Col. for T., B.S.; Albright A. Sch.; Univ. Wisconsin, M.S. *Position*: Prof. S., Beloit College, Beloit, Wis., at present.

PORTER, BEATA BEACH. See Beach, Beata

PORTER, DORIS (Mrs. Donald J. McLean)—
    Painter, L., T.
    2406 Vinewood Blvd., Ann Arbor, Mich.

B. Portsmouth, Va. *Studied*: PAFA; Wayne Univ., M.A.; Univ. Michigan, M.A. *Member*: Norfolk A. Corner; Detroit Soc. Women Painters; Portrait Assn., Detroit; Grosse Pointe A.; Ann Arbor AA; Mich. WC Soc.; Ann Arbor Women Painters (Pres.); Palette and Brush Cl., Detroit. *Awards*: prizes, Grosse Pointe A., 1950; Detroit Soc. Women Painters, 1947, 1949. *Work*: Toledo Mus. A.; PAFA; Univ. Michigan; Cranbrook Acad. A.; St. Mary's Hall, Burlington, N.J.; Ford Sch., Highland Park, Mich.; Mich. State Normal Col., Ypsilanti; Dearborn Hist. Soc. *Exhibited*: CGA, 1939; NAD, 1934; PAFA, 1934; VMFA, 1934; Norfolk, Va., annually; Detroit Inst. A., 1939, 1941, 1943, 1946, 1948, 1953, 1955, 1956; Terry AI, 1952; VMFA, 1952; Flint Mus. A., 1950 (one-man); Mich. WC Soc., 1952; Scarab Cl., 1950; Univ. Michigan; Grosse Pointe A., annually; Palette & Brush Cl., 1951, 1952. *Positions*: A. Instr., Michigan State Normal Col., 1939-41; Univ. Michigan, Ann Arbor, Mich., 1945; Art Inst., Wayne, Mich.

PORTER, ELMER JOHNSON—*Craftsman, P., E., L.*
    Art Department, Indiana State Teachers College; h. Clifton House, Route 4, Box 464, Terre Haute, Ind.

B. Richmond, Ind., May 5, 1907. *Studied*: AIC, B.A.E.; Ohio State Univ., M.A.; Earlham Col.; Univ. Cincinnati;

Univ. Colorado; Butler Univ., and in Guatemala. *Member*: Western AA; Am. Soc. Bookplate Collectors & Des.; Com. A. Edu.; Nat. A. Edu. Assn.; CAA; Pen & Brush Cl.; Indiana A. Edu. Assn. (Sec.-Treas.). *Awards*: prizes, Indianapolis AA, 1929; Hoosier Salon, 1939. *Work*: Richmond (Ind.) H.S. Coll.; Earlham Col.; Indiana State T. Col. *Exhibited*: Hoosier Salon; Columbus A. Lg.; Richmond, Ind.; Cincinnati, Ohio; Chicago, Ill.; New York, N.Y. *Position*: Chm. A. Dept., Dir. College A. Gal., Indiana State T. Col., Terre Haute, Ind.

PORTER, JAMES A.—*Painter, W., E.*

1201 Girard St., Northwest, Washington 9, D.C.

B. Baltimore, Md., Dec. 22, 1905. *Studied*: Howard Univ., B.S.; ASL; N.Y. Univ., M.A., and in Paris, France. *Member*: CAA; Belgian-American Art Seminar. *Work*: Howard Univ. Gal. A.; Lincoln Univ., Jefferson City, Mo.; Harmon Fnd., N.Y.; IBM. I., "Playsongs of the Deep South"; "Talking Animals"; Author: "Robert S. Duncanson, Midwestern Romantic-Realist," 1951. Contributor to Art in America. *Position*: Prof. A., Howard Univ., Washington, D.C.*

PORTER, JAMES TANK—*Sculptor*

4990 Porter Hill Rd., La Mesa, Cal.

B. Tientsin, China, Oct. 17, 1883. *Studied*: Pomona Col., B.A.; ASL; & with George Bridgman, Robert Aitken, Gutzon Borglum. *Member*: San Diego A. Gld.; Contemporary A. San Diego. *Awards*: prize, San Diego FA Soc., 1924. *Work*: Beloit Col.; San Diego FA Soc.; Yale Univ. A. Gal.; San Diego Mus. Natural Hist.; Am. Legion Hall, La Mesa. *Exhibited*: NAD; PAFA; San Diego FA Soc., 1923-1941; GGE, 1939.

PORTER, L(AURA) SCHAEFER (Mrs.)—*Painter, E.*

Fort Edward, N.Y.

B. Fort Edward, N.Y., Oct. 16, 1891. *Studied*: N.Y. Sch. A.; ASL; Skidmore Col., and with Robert Henri, William M. Chase, Kenneth Hayes Miller, Wayman Adams, and others. *Member*: ASL; Southeastern AA; Georgia A.; AAPL; Phila. A. & Crafts Gld.; Assn. Syracuse A. *Work*: Pittsburgh Lib.; Brenau Col., Gainesville, Ga.; Simmons Col. Chapel; Walter Reed Hospital, Wash., D.C.; Fort Edward A. Center; Labor Union offices, Fort Edward; Kappa Pi Coll. *Exhibited*: N.Y. WC Cl.; Phila. A. & Crafts Gld.; MMA; Glens Falls Lib., 1953 (one-man); Ogunquit A. Center, 1953; Town Hall, N.Y.; Mill A. Colony, Elizabethtown, N.J., 1953; Fort Edward (N.Y.) A. Center, 1953-1955; Syracuse Mus. FA, 1954, 1955; Syracuse Univ., 1954; numerous State Fairs. *Position*: Prof. A., Fort Edwards, N.Y.

PORTER, PRISCILLA MANNING—
Craftsman, T., W., L.

People's Art Center, Museum of Modern Art, 21 West 53rd St. (19); h. 31½ East 65th St., New York 21, N.Y.

B. Baltimore, Md., Feb. 1, 1917. *Studied*: Bennington Col., B.A.; Greenwich House Pottery, N.Y.; Alfred Univ. (summer). *Member*: Artist-Craftsmen of N.Y. *Work*: Intl. Pottery Mus., Faenza, Italy; mosaic triptychs, Emmanuel Church, Balt., Md.; First Unitarian Church, Balt., Md. *Exhibited*: Syracuse Mus. FA, 1953; N.Y. Soc. Ceramic A., 1947-1955; N.Y. Soc. Craftsmen, 1954, 1955. Contributor articles on ceramics to Ceramics Monthly; American Girl (Girl Scout official magazine). Lectures: Ceramics. *Position*: Instr., Pottery & Ceramics, People's Art Center, MModA, New York, N.Y., 1953- .

PORTER, VERNON CARROLL—*Director, P., Des.*

1083 Fifth Ave., New York 28, N.Y.; h. Tompkins Corners, Putnam Valley 1, Putnam County, N.Y.

B. Cleveland, Ohio, Aug. 6, 1896. *Studied*: ASL; Grand Central Sch. A.; Mechanics Inst.; Brooklyn Polytechnic Inst. *Member*: Am. FA Soc. *Position*: Dir., NAD, 1950- , NAD Sch. FA, 1950- , New York, N.Y.

PORTER, MRS. VERNON. See *Beach, Beata*

PORTMANN, FRIEDA (BERTHA) (ANNE)—
Painter, T., Gr., C., Des., W., L., S.

1203 James St., Seattle 4, Wash.

B. Tacoma, Wash. *Studied*: Univ. Washington; Oregon State Col., B.S.; AIC; Univ. Chicago; Cal. Sch. FA; Univ. So. California. *Member*: Northwest Pr. M.; Boston Pr. M.; Wash. (D.C.) Pr. M.; San F. AA; AEA. *Awards*: prizes, Women Painters of Wash., 1940, 1943, 1946; Puyallup (Wash.) Fair, 1946, 1952. *Work*: Cal. Col. A. & Crafts; St. Joseph's Sch., Seattle. *Exhibited*: Northwest Pr. M., 1936-1954; NAWA, 1936-1939; SAM, 1937-1954; Puyallup Fair, 1946-1954; BM; Wichita AA; Portland (Me.) Mus. A.; Albright A. Gal.; Albany Inst. Hist. & A.; BMFA; Phila. Pr. Cl.; Arch. Inst., Wash., D.C.; Oakland A. Gal.; Bradley Univ.; Henry A. Gal., Seattle; Syracuse Mus. FA; Denver A. Mus.; Arizona State Fair.*

PORTNER, LESLIE JUDD (Mrs.)—*Art Critic, W.*

Washington Post, 1515 L St., Northwest; h. 2401 Calvert St., Northwest, Washington 8, D.C.

B. New York, N.Y. *Studied*: PAFA, with Henry McCarter. *Member*: Women's Nat. Press Cl. *Awards*: Cresson traveling F., PAFA, 1936; Nat. Art Critics award, CAA, 1954, 1955. Contributor to Washington Post; Christian Science Monitor; USIA; Pan American Union Bulletin. *Positions*: Sec. to Dir., MMoA, New York, 1939-43; Specialist, Exhibits Br., U.S. Office of Education, Wash., D.C., 1943-44; Specialist, Visual Arts Div., Pan American Union, 1944-45; Art Critic, Washington Post, Wash., D.C., 1951- .

POSEY, LESLIE THOMAS—*Sculptor, C., T., L.*

401 North Tuttle Ave., Sarasota, Fla.

B. Harshaw, Wis., Jan. 20, 1900. *Studied*: Wis. Sch. F. & App. A.; PAFA; AIC. *Member*: Indianapolis Arch. Assn.; Bradenton A. Center; Wisconsin P. & S.; Fla. Sculptors & Ceramists. *Awards*: med., prize, Milwaukee AI, 1923; prizes, Hoosier Salon, 1930; Fla. Fed. A., 1945; Creative Arts, 1957; med., Indiana Arch. Assn., 1928. *Work*: mem., arch. des., monuments, Walker A. Center; Brightwood Park, Indianapolis; Wildwood Park, Wis.; Oneco, Fla.; Univ. Georgia, Athens, Ga. *Exhibited*: Nationally and internationally. Lectures: Sculpture-Old and New; Sculpture & Architecture. *Position*: Dir., Instr., Posey Sch. Sculpture, Sarasota, Fla., 1953-55; Hd. S. & Ceramics, Bradenton (Fla.) A. Center; Pres., Fla. Sculptors & Ceramists.

POST, GEORGE (BOOTH)—*Painter, E.*

327 Cumberland St., San Francisco 14, Cal.

B. Oakland, Cal., Sept. 29, 1906. *Studied*: Cal. Sch. FA. *Member*: AWS; San F. AA; Cal. WC Soc.; Intl. Inst. A. & Lets. *Awards*: prizes, Cal. WC Soc., 1953; San F. A. Comm., 1954; Mother Lode Exh., 1955, 1958; Oakland A. Gal., 1936, 1947; Cal. WC Soc., 1947; Los A. Mus. A., 1945; SFMA, 1936; Jack London Sq. A. Festival, 1957; Richmond A. Center, 1958. *Work*: SFMA; SAM; Cal. PLH; San Diego FA Soc.; MMA; VMFA; Wharton Sch., Univ. Pennsylvania; Mills Col.; Univ. Oklahoma; Santa Barbara Mus. A.; Texas Tech. *Exhibited*: MMA; SFMA; deYoung Mem. Mus.; SAM; San Diego FA Gal.; Oakland A. Gal.; Riverside Mus., N.Y.; PMG; Santa Barbara Mus. A.; Gump's Gal., San F.; WMA; CMA; AIC; Cal. PLH; Mills Col.; Henry Gal., Seattle; San Diego FA Center; Denver A. Mus.; Colorado Springs FA, and others. Contributor illus., to Fortune, California Arts & Architecture, Art Digest magazines. *Positions*: Instr., Stanford Univ., 1940; San Jose Col., 1951-52; Prof., Painting, Cal. Col. A. & Crafts, Oakland, Cal., 1947- .

POTTERVELD, BURTON LEE—
Designer, P., E., Gr., W.

4132 North Farwell Ave., Milwaukee, Wis.

B. Dubuque, Iowa, Mar. 15, 1908. *Studied*: Layton Sch. A.; Univ. Dubuque; Univ. Wisconsin; Univ. Iowa. Contributor writings to Standard Edu. Soc., Chicago. *Exhibited*: National and local exhs. *Position*: Assoc. Prof., Univ. Wisconsin, Milwaukee, Wis.

POUCHER, ELIZABETH MORRIS—*Sculptor, Lith.*

8 Beech Tree Lane, Bronxville 8, N.Y.

B. Yonkers, N.Y. *Studied*: Vassar Col., A.B.; FA Grd. Study, N.Y. Univ., Columbia Univ.; ASL, and with Alexander Archipenko. In Paris, France: La Grande Chaumiere, Ecole Animalier, and with Andre L'Hote. *Member:* All. A. Am.; Pen & Brush ,Cl.; Hudson Valley AA. *Awards:* Gold medal, Hudson Valley AA, 1958; Medal of Honor, Pen & Brush Cl., 1954; prizes, Bronxville A. Project, 1953, 1957; Westchester Fed. Women's Cl., 1955, 1956; Hudson Valley AA, 1958. *Exhibited:* All. A. Am., 1953, 1955, 1956, 1958; Bronxville A. Project, 1953-1958; Hudson Valley AA, 1954-1958; NAD, 1956; Pen & Brush Cl., 1953-1958.

POUGIALIS, CONSTANTINE—*Painter, E.*

1402 North Northpark Ave., Chicago 10, Ill.

B. Corinth, Greece, Nov. 29, 1894. *Studied:* AIC, and with George Bellows, Wellington Reynolds, Leopold Seyffert; also in Greece, France and Italy. *Awards:* prizes and medals, AIC, 1925, 1931, 1935, 1936, 1950; Union Lg. Cl., Chicago, 1955. *Work:* AIC; Univ. Minnesota; John Vanderpoel A. Gal., Chicago; Chicago Sun-Times; and in private colls. *Exhibited:* AIC; MModA; Frank Rehn Gal., N.Y.; WMAA; CGA; Carnegie Inst.; PAFA; Chicago Artists Exh., France, 1957-58; Los A. Mus. A.; Toledo Mus. A.; DMFA; Mun. A. Gal., Jackson, Miss.; Albright A. Gal., Buffalo; CM; one-man: AIC; Robinson's Gal., Chicago; Rehn Gal., N.Y.; Marshall Fields Gal., Chicago; Stevens-Gross Gal., Chicago. *Positions:* Prof. A., AIC, Chicago, Ill., 1938- ; Trustee, MModA, New York, N.Y.

POUSETTE-DART, NATHANIEL—
Painter, Des., Et., T., W., L..

111 Madison Ave., Valhalla, N.Y.; s. Nantucket, Mass.

B. St. Paul, Minn., Apr. 7, 1886. *Studied:* St. Paul Sch. A.; ASL; PAFA, and with Robert Henri; Chase Sch. A. *Member:* F., PAFA; Fed. Mod. P. & S.; A. Dir. Cl. (life); Nat. A. Dir. Cl.; Westchester A. & Crafts Gld.; Am. Soc. for Aesthetics; Div. on Aesthetics, Am. Psychological Assn. *Awards:* 2 Cresson Traveling Scholarships, PAFA, 1911, 1912; Certif. Merit, A. Dir. Cl.; prizes, Minn. State A. Soc., 1914, 1915; Westchester A. & Crafts Gld., 1953; A. Dir. Exh., 1954; F., PAFA. *Exhibited:* nationally. Author: "Ernst Haskell, His Life and Work"; series of six books "Distinguished American Artists Series, 1924-30"; "American Painting Today, 1950-1956," 1956; "Art Directing"; "The Techniques of Visual Communication and Selling," 1956. Contributor to Art News; American Artist, and other art magazines. L., PIASch., Columbia Univ., and many lectures on television.

POWELL, LESLIE J.—*Painter*

60 Morton St., New York 14, N.Y.

B., Fort Sill, Okla., Mar. 16, 1906. *Studied:* Univ. Oklahoma; Chicago Acad. FA; ASL; N.Y. Univ.; Columbia Univ., B.F.A., M.A. *Member:* NSMP. *Work:* Univ. Arizona; BM; Newark Mus. A.; Columbia Univ.; Lehigh Univ.; Univ. Oklahoma; BM; Matthews Mus. Theatre Arts; Cooper Union Mus. for Dec. A. *Exhibited:* New Orleans A. & Crafts, 1926, 1931, 1945; Delgado Mus. A., 1927; Morgan Gal., N.Y., 1939, 1940; Lehigh Univ., 1943; Carlebach Gal., N.Y., 1948; Monmouth (Ill.) Col., 1949; Norlyst Gal., 1949; Third St. Gal., Los A., 1950; Avery Lib., Columbia Univ., 1950; Mercersburg (Pa.) A. Gal., 1951; one-man: Esther Gentle Gal., 1955; Gal. "21," 1955; Barzansky Gal., 1956; Philbrook A. Center, 1957; Oklahoma A. Center, 1958; Bodley Gal., N.Y., 1958; Laguna Gloria A. Center, Austin, Tex., 1958; Galleria Mexico, Santa Fe, 1958; 5-man: Donnell Lib. Center, N.Y., 1958.

POWELL, VIOLET (LOUISE) (Mrs. Willard B., Sr.)—
Painter

9330 Southwest 63rd Court, Miami 43, Fla.

B. Philadelphia, Pa., July 8, 1902. *Studied:* PIASch.; ASL, and with James Lunnon. *Member:* Blue Dome A. Fellowship; Miami A. Lg.; Coral Gables A. Cl.; Palm Beach A. Lg.; AAPL; Coral Gables Woman's Cl. *Awards:* prizes, A. & Writers, Miami, 1948, 1951, 1952; Poinciana Festival, Miami, 1948; Miami A. Lg., 1949; AAPL, 1950. *Exhibited:* PIASch.; ASL; Miami A. Lg., 1947-1951; Poinciana Festival, 1948; A. & Writers, 1948-1952; AAPL, 1950, 1951; Blue Dome, 1951; Miami Beach A. Center; Miami Springs Woman's Cl.; Coral Gables Woman's Cl.; one-man: Musicians Cl. of Am., Colony Theatre, both in Maimi.*

POWERS, MARY (SWIFT)—*Painter*

455 East 51st St., New York 22, N.Y.

B. Leeds, Mass., Sept. 7, 1885. *Studied:* Framingham (Mass.) Normal Sch. *Member:* Southern Vermont A. *Work:* Williams Col.; Wood Gal. A., Montpelier, Vt.; WMAA; AGAA. *Exhibited:* NAD; AWCS; AIC; Syracuse Mus. FA; Macbeth Gal.; Marie Sterner Gal. (one-man).

POZZATTI, RUDY O.—*Painter, Gr., I., E.*

Art Department, Indiana University, Bloomington, Ind.; h. Silverton, Colo.

B. Telluride, Colo., Jan. 14, 1925. *Studied:* Univ. Colorado, B.F.A., M.F.A., and with Emilio Amero,` Max Beckmann, Ben Shahn. *Member:* CAA. *Awards:* prizes, Urbana, Ill., 1949; Nebraska State Fair, 1950; Fulbright award, 1952-53; F., Yale-Norfolk Summer Sch., 1955; purchase awards: 1952-55, Bradley Univ.; CAM; Joslyn A. Mus.; Mulvane A. Center; Phila. Pr. Cl.; Univ. Illinois; Youngstown Col.; SAM; Sioux City A. Center; Texas Western Col.; Oakland A. Mus.; prizes, Boston Pr. M., 1958; Soc. Wash. Pr. M., 1958; LC, 1958; John Herron AI, 1958. *Work:* in the above colls., and Munson-Williams-Proctor Inst.; Univ. Puerto Rico; LC; FMA; CMA; MMA; Achenbach Fnd., San F.; BMA; SFMA; N.Y. Pub. Lib.; BMFA; Univ. Nebraska; Univ. Maine; PAFA; BM; Herron AI; Indiana Univ. *Exhibited:* nationally, including the following one-man exhs.: Phila. A. All.; AIC, 1954; Martha Jackson Gal., N.Y., 1954; Concordia Col., 1955; CMA, 1955; Weyhe Gal., 1957; Carleton Col., 1957; Smithsonian Inst., 1956; traveling exh., Art Schools, U.S.A., 1955. *Position:* Asst. Prof. A., Indiana Univ., Bloomington, Ind., 1956- .

PRASSE, LEONA E.—*Museum Assoc. Curator*

Cleveland Museum of Art, Cleveland 6, Ohio; h. 1541 Arthur Ave., Lakewood 7, Ohio

B. Cleveland, Ohio. *Studied:* Flora Mather Col., Western Reserve Univ., B.S., B.A.; Cleveland Inst. A. *Award:* Guggenheim F., 1956. Contributor to CMA Bulletin, with numerous articles on prints and drawings. Assembled exhibitions and compiled catalogues of: Sesquicentennial Exhibition of the The Art of Lithography, 1948; The Work of Lyonel Feininger, 1951; Work of Antonio Frasconi, 1952; Drawings of Charles E. Burchfield, 1953; Prints and Drawings by Walter R. Rogalski, 1954; Work of Rudy Pozzatti, 1955; Recent Work of Peter Takal, 1958. *Position:* Asst., 1925, Asst. Cur., 1926-30; Assoc. Cur., 1930- Dept. Prints & Drawings, CMA, Cleveland, Ohio; Sec., Print Club of Cleveland, 1947- .

PRATT, ANN SPENCER. See Spencer, Ann Hunt

PRATT, DUDLEY—*Sculptor*

Box 238, Croton Falls, N.Y.

B. Paris, France, June 14, 1897. *Studied:* Yale Univ., B.A.H.C.; BMFA Sch.; Grande Chaumiere, Paris, and with E. A. Bourdelle, Charles Grafly. *Member:* AEA. *Work:* SAM; IBM Coll.; arch. s., Civic Auditorium, Henry A. Gal., Doctor's Hospital, Univ. Washington Medical Sch., World War II Mem., all in Seattle, Wash.; Womens' Gymnasium, Social Science Bldg., Univ. Washington; Hoquiam (Wash.) City Hall; Bellingham City Hall; Washington State College Lib., etc. *Exhibited:* SAM; Oakland A. Gal.; WFNY 1939; Sculpture Center, N.Y., 1957-58; PAFA; Detroit Inst. A., 1958. Lectures: History of Sculpture.

PRATT, ELIZABETH (SOUTHWICK)
(Mrs. R. Winthrop)—*Painter, Lith.*

Argent Gallery, 67 East 59th St. (22); h. 41 Fifth Ave., New York 3, N.Y.

B. New York, N.Y. *Studied:* Mass. Sch. A.; Cleveland Sch. Des., and in Paris, London, Florence and Rome. *Member:* Washington Square Assn. (Bd.); NAWA (Pres.); Pen & Brush Cl. (1st V. Pres.); Engineering Woman's Cl. (Bd). *Award:* medal, NAWA, 1957. *Work:* many portraits in U.S. and abroad. *Exhibited:* NAWA, 1947-1956; Pen & Brush Cl., 1945-1956. Lectures on Art for women's clubs, museums and art groups.

PRATT, FRANCES (Mrs. Bumpel Usu)—Painter
33 West 12th St., New York 11, N.Y.

B. Glen Ridge, N.J., May 25, 1913. *Studied*: N.Y.Sch. App. Des. for Women; ASL, with Richard Lahey, Hans Hofmann. *Awards*: prizes, NAWA, 1946, 1950, 1955; Audubon A., 1952. *Work*: VMFA; BM. *Exhibited*: Layton Gal. A., 1941; Denver A. Mus., 1942; Mun. A. Gal., Jackson, Miss., 1943, 1946; AGAA, 1945; Mint Mus. A., 1946; Marquie Gal., 1943 (one-man); Am.-British A. Center, 1945 (one-man); Laurel Gal., 1946 (one-man); BM, 1947, 1949; CGA, 1949. Author: "Encaustic, Materials and Methods." *Position*: Inst. Painting, YWCA, Central Branch, New York, N.Y.; Parsons Sch. Des., 1948-51; Mexican Art Workshop, 1950-51; Dir., Frances Pratt Gal. A., New York, N.Y.

PRATT, INGA—Painter, Comm. A., I.
110 Portland Road, Highlands, N.J.

B. Brookings, S.D., Dec. 8, 1906. *Studied*: Acad. Colorossi, Paris; ASL. *Member*: ASL; SI. *Award*: Direct Mail Adv. Assn., 1946. *Exhibited*: Lotos Cl., 1953. Contributor illus. to Harpers magazine. Freelance for various advertising agencies at present.

PRATT, KATHARINE—Craftsman
45 School St., Dedham, Mass.

B. Boston, Mass., Aug. 3, 1891. *Studied*: BMFA Sch.; & with George C. Gebelein. *Member*: Boston Soc. A. & Crafts (Master Craftsman & Medalist). *Exhibited*: BMFA; Paris Salon, 1937. *Position*: Instr., Silversmithing, Boston Sch. Occupational Therapy, 1943- .

PREHN, HANS ERNST—Sculptor, P., C.
158 West 10th St., New York 14, N.Y.

B. Philadelphia, Pa., Nov. 17, 1895. *Studied*: Acad. FA, Budapest; CUASch.; BAID. *Member*: Artist-Craftsmen of N.Y. *Awards*: prizes, CUASch., 1927, 1931, bronze medal, 1933. *Work*: paintings, Marble Collegiate Church, N.Y.; bas-relief panel, USPO, Bishopville, S.C.; work also in church in Csepa, Hungary. *Exhibited*: Medallic A. Soc., 1950; Arch. Lg.; SC (NSS exh.), 1951, 1952, 1954; N.Y. Soc. of Craftsmen, 1953-1957.

PRENDERGAST, JAMES DONALD—
Painter, E., L., Lith., W.
College of Architecture & Design, University of Michigan; h. 1039 Martin Place, Ann Arbor, Mich.

B. Chicago, Ill., Oct. 17, 1907. *Studied*: AIC; Univ. Chicago, B.F.A.; Univ. California, Los A.; & with Boris Anisfeld, Edward Weston. *Member*: San F. AA; Audubon A.; CAA; Am. Assn.Univ.Prof. *Awards*: John Quincy Adams traveling Fellowship, 1931-1932. *Work*: Univ. Arizona. *Exhibited*: WFNY 1939; GGE, 1939; MMA; Univ. Arizona, 1943; SFMA, 1939-1941; 1943; PAFA, 1939, 1942; AIC, 1933, 1935, 1942; BMA, 1939; CGA, 1941; VMFA, 1942; BMA, 1939; CGA, 1941; VMFA, 1942; Audubon A., 1945; La Tausca Pearls Exh., 1946; San Diego FA Soc., 1940; Los A. Mus. A., 1938-1940; Central American traveling exh.; Louisiana A., 1941; Detroit Inst. A., 1944, 1945. *Position*: Visiting Instr., Univ. Southern California, 1937-40; Instr., New Orleans A. & Crafts Sch., 1940-42; Asst. Prof., Univ. Arizona, 1942-44; Asst. Prof., Dept. Drawing & Painting, Col. Arch. & Des., Univ. Michigan, Ann Arbor, Mich., 1944-48; Assoc. Prof., 1948- .

PRESCOTT, PRESTON L.—Sculptor, T.
Alba Rd.; h. Rt. 1, Box 2013, Ben Lomond, Santa Cruz County, Cal.

B. Ocheydan, Iowa, Aug. 10, 1898. *Studied*: Minneapolis Inst. A.; Otis AI; ASL; & with Gutzon Borglum, David Edstrom. *Member*: Cal. AC; Laguna Beach AA. *Awards*: prizes, Cal. AC, 1935, 1936; Laguna Beach AA, 1936; Los A. Chamber of Commerce, 1927-1929. *Work*: s. port., Cal. State Bldg., Los A.; mem., Arcadia, Cal., and in many private colls. *Exhibited*: MMA, 1942; Carmel Lib., 1950, 1952; deYoung Mem. Mus., 1953; Los Gatos AA, 1954, 1955; Santa Cruz A. Lg., 1955; de Saisset A. Gal., Univ. of Santa Clara, 1956, 1957 (one-man); Marin A. & Garden Show, 1958; Montalvo AA, 1958. *Position*: Pres., Dir., Bridge Mt. Fnd., Ben Lomond, Cal.

PRESCOTT, WILLIAM LINZEE—Painter
Tuxedo Park, Tuxedo, N.Y.

B. New York, N.Y., July 31, 1917. *Studied*: Chouinard Sch. A., Los Angeles. *Member*: NSMP; Portraits, Inc. *Work*: murals, N.Y. Hospital; Metropolitan Life Ins. Co., and in private homes and restaurants. *Exhibited*: NSMP, Arch. Lg., 1956; Madrid, Spain, 1958 (one-man).

PRESSER, JOSEF—Painter, E., L.
30 East 14th St., New York 3, N.Y.

B. Lublin, Poland, Apr. 18, 1911. *Studied*: BMFA Sch.; & in Europe. *Member*: Woodstock AA. *Awards*: prizes, New Haven Paint & Clay Cl., 1939; Toledo AA, 1944. *Work*: Royal Mus., Florence, Italy; MMA; Newark Mus.; PMA; AGAA; Syracuse Mus. FA; WMAA; Smith Col.; murals, Bristol, Pa.; USPO, Southern Pines, N.C. *Exhibited*: Carnegie Inst., 1941-1946; AIC, 1938-1946; PAFA, 1937-1946; Contemporary A.; Assoc. Am. A.; Weyhe Gal.; Nierndorf Gal.; MModA. I., jacket des., "Soul of the Sea," 1945. *Position*: Instr., L., Painting, CUASch., New York, N.Y.; Instr., Painting, North Shore A. Center, Roslyn, L.I., N.Y.*

PRESSOIR, ESTHER—Painter, C., I.
122 West 21st St., New York 11, N.Y.

B. Philadelphia, Pa. *Studied*: R.I.Sch.Des. (Grad.); ASL. *Member*: AEA; American Craftsmen's Cooperative Council; Cal. WC Soc. *Work*: PAFA; Los A. Mus. A. *Exhibited*: AIC; PAFA; Los A. Mus. A.; WFNY 1939; CAA; Rockefeller Center, N.Y. (one-man). Contributor to: Fiction Parade, New Yorker, Tomorrow magazines. *Position*: Instr., Crafts, Hospitals and Art Centers.

PRESTINI, JAMES—Designer, S., C., E.
College of Architecture, University of California; h. 2324 Blake St., Berkeley 4, Cal.

B. Waterford, Conn., Jan. 13, 1908. *Studied*: Yale Univ.; BAID; and in Sweden and Italy. *Awards*: prizes, MModA, Intl. Comp. Low-Cost Furniture Des.; Los Angeles County Fair, Contemp. Crafts; 10th Triennale, Italy, Diploma d'Onore; deYoung Mem. Mus., Des.-Craftsmen of the West award. *Work*: MModA; CMA; SAM; WAC; Mus. Contemp. Crafts; Dept. of State Coll. of U.S.A. design for India; Albright A. Gal.; Northwestern Univ.; Wayne Univ.; Univ. Minnesota; Ball State T. Col.; Russell Sage Fnd. *Exhibited*: Brussels World's Fair; Milan Trade Fair; 10th Triennale, Italy; Guatemala Nat. Fair; Haiti Peace Festival; AIC; Smithsonian Inst.; WMA; Detroit Inst. A.; DMFA; SFMA; Denver A. Mus.; BMA; Inst. Contemp. A.; Portland (Ore.) A. Mus.; Akron AI; CAM; Newark Mus. A.; Toledo Mus. A.; Dayton AI, etc. Author: "The Place of Scientific Research in Design"; "Research in Low-Cost Seating for Homes"; "Survey of Construction Materials Demonstration & Training Center." *Positions*: Instr., Lake Forest Acad.; Mills College; Black Mountain College; Texas State T. College; Univ. California; Research Des., Armour Research Fnd.; Des. Research Consultant, Midwest Research Inst.; Survey of Italian furniture industry for Knoll International; Survey construction materials in Latin America for Dept. of State.

PRESTON, HARRIET (BROWN)—Painter, T., Cr.
The Headlands, Norwood Ave., Rockport, Mass.

B. Hackensack, N.J., Mar. 13, 1892. *Studied*: Trenton Normal College; N.Y. Univ.; Columbia Col.; Parsons Sch. Des., and with Harvey Dunn. *Member*: Bergen County A. Gld.; New Jersey Soc. P. & S.; Rockport AA; North Shore AA; AAPL. *Awards*: prizes, N.J. Women's Cl., 1950, 1951; A. Council of New Jersey, 1951; Bergen County A. Gld., 1953, 1954; Pascack Valley Regional, 1955; gold certif., N.J. Soc. P. & S., 1955. *Work*: Tenafly (N.J.) H.S.; Rockport (Mass.) H.S. *Exhibited*: New Jersey Soc. P. & S., 1950-1958; All. A. Am., 1951, 1953, 1955, 1956; AWS, 1951; AAPL, 1953-1956; NAC, 1952, 1953; Knickerbocker A., 1957; Academic A., 1956-1958; Bergen County A., 1943-1958; Rockport AA, 1949-1958; North Shore AA, 1949-1958; N.J. WC Soc., 1951; Trenton Mus., 1951, 1954, 1956; Montclair A. Mus., 1952, 1953, 1955, 1956; Wolfe A. Cl., 1954, 1955; Silvermine Gld. A., 1954; A. Center of the Oranges, 1955, 1956.

PRESTON, H. MALCOLM—Painter, E.
Hofstra College, Hempstead, N.Y.; h. 306 Ridge Rd., Douglaston, N.Y.

B. West New York, N.J., May 25, 1918. *Studied*: Univ. Wisconsin, B.S.; Columbia Univ., M.A., Ph.D. *Member*:

AAUP; CAA; Nat. A. Edu. Assn.; N.Y. State A. T. Assn.; AEA; Eastern AA; AFA. *Awards*: Emily Lowe award, 1950; Joe and Emily Lowe Fnd. Edu. Research awards, 1951; Ford Fnd. (Art Curriculum Study), 1958; prize, Utica, N.Y., 1957. *Work*: Dayton AI; Univ. Miami; Lowe Coll. *Exhibited*: one-man: Ward Eggleston Gal.; 1951, 1952, 1954; Assoc. Am. A.; New-Age Gal.; Wisconsin Salon of Art, 1938-1940; San Diego WC Exh., 1939; 3-man, Roosevelt Field A. Center, 1957; Art:USA, 1958; Hansa Gal., 1958; Shore Studio Gal., Provincetown, 1957, 1958. *Position*: Prof., Chm. Dept. FA, Hofstra Col., Hempstead, N.Y., 1949- ; developed and conducted TV series "The Arts Around Us," 1955-56.

PRESTOPINO, GREGORIO—*Painter, T.*
Roosevelt, N.J.

B. New York, N.Y., June 21, 1907. *Studied*: NAD. *Awards*: prize, Pepsi-Cola, 1946, 1947; Temple med., PAFA, 1946. *Work*: WMAA; MModA; Hawaii, T.H.; Univ. Oklahoma; Univ. Nebraska; Univ. Illinois; Walker A. Center; Rochester Mem. A. Gal.; U.S. State Dept.; PC; IBM; Univ. Alabama; AIC; Martha Washington Univ.; AGAA; Butler Inst. Am. A. *Exhibited*: WMAA; AIC; WFNY 1939; CAM; GGE, 1939; PAFA; Albright A. Gal.; Pepsi-Cola; MModA; Rochester Mem. A. Gal.; CGA; Smith Col.; Phillips Acad.; Univ. Iowa; Univ. Minnesota; Santa Barbara Mus. A.; Witte Mem. Mus.; CAM; Venice, Italy; U.S. State Dept. Exh., Paris, France, (all exhs. 1936-58). 8 one-man exhs., New York City, 1943-1957. *Position*: Instr. Painting, New Sch. for Social Research, New York, N.Y., 1949- .

PRETSCH, JOHN EDWARD—*Cartoonist, Comm. A., P.*
Philadelphia Evening Bulletin, 30th & Market Sts. (1); h. 4337 H. St., Philadelphia, Pa.

B. Philadelphia, Pa., Apr. 14, 1925. Illus. "Five Years, Five Countries, Five Campaigns with the 141st Infantry Regiment," 1945. Contributor cartoons to Colliers; Sat. Eve. Post; Phila. Evening Bulletin. *Position*: Sunday Supplement A., 6 years, News A., 2 years, Promotional Layout A., at present, Phila. Evening Bulletin, Philadelphia, Pa.*

PREU, JOHN D.—*Teacher, C., P.*
469 Main St., Newington 11, Conn.; also, Fells Lane, Pochet, East Orleans, Cape Cod, Mass.

B. Hartford, Conn., July 23, 1913. *Studied*: PIASch; N.Y. Univ.; Dixon Sch. Metalcraft; Hartford A. Sch. *Member*: Conn. Acad. FA; New Haven Paint & Clay Cl.; Conn. WC Soc.; Meriden A. & Crafts; West Hartford A. Lg. *Work*: Biro-Bidjan Mus., Russia; Berkshire Mus.; Pittsfield A. Lg., 1949-1952; Avery Mem., 1949; N.Y. WC Cl., 1934-1940; AWCS, 1935-1940; All.A.Am., 1935; Conn. Acad. FA, 1936-1946; Conn. WC Soc.; AIC; Wadsworth Atheneum Jewelry exh., 1955; Osterville Fair, Cape Cod, 1955; Springfield A. Lg., 1936-1939; CAA traveling exh., 1935; New Haven Paint & Clay Cl.; Glastonbury Lib. (one-man). *Position*: A. Instr., Weaver H.S., Hartford, Conn., 1937-46; Chm.A.Dept., 1949- ; Instr., metal & jewelry, West Hartford (Conn.) A. Lg., 1937-46; Dir., Soc. Conn. Craftsmen, 1949- ; Instr., jewelry and enameling classes for Hartford YWCA, Conn. General Ins. Co., and Newington, Conn. Adult Classes; A. Com., Newington Lib. A. Exhs.

PREUSS, ROGER EMIL—*Painter, I., Des., W.*
2224 Grand Ave.; h. 2222 Grand Ave., Minneapolis 5, Minn.

B. Waterville, Minn., Jan. 29, 1922. *Studied*: Mankato Commercial Col.; Minneapolis Sch. A., with Edmund M. Kopietz. *Member*: Minnesota AA; Outdoor Writer's Assn. of America; Soc. A. & A. Dirs.; Natural Hist. Soc. *Awards*: prizes, Federal Duck Stamp Des. award, U.S. Dept. of Interior, 1949; Des., Waterfowl decoys, Nat. Sportsman's Show, N.Y., 1951; Minnesota Outdoor Art Award, 1955; gold award, Minneapolis, 1957; Centennial Award, Minneapolis, 1958 (for contributions to the field of conservation education through paintings). *Work*: Demarest Mem. Mus.; St. Paul FA Gal.; Anglesey Coll., and work in many business and private colls. in U.S. and Canada. *Exhibited*: Omaha Biennial of Bird Painting, Joslyn Mem. Mus., 1948; Nat. Wildlife A. Exh., Milwaukee, 1949, 1951-1954; North American Wildlife Exh., 1952; Waterfowl A. Exh., 1953, 1958; Minnesota Centennial Exh., 1949; Fed. Author's Exh., Minneapolis, 1951; Minn. Hist. Soc., 1952; St. Paul Carnival Annual,

1955-1958; Minnesota AA, 1955-1957; Golden Rule Annual, St. Paul, 1958; American-Swedish Inst., Minneapolis, 1958; one-man: Northwest Sportsman's Show, Minneapolis, 1947; Kerr Gal., Beverly Hills, Cal., 1947; Beard Gal., Minneapolis, 1951; La Miracle Cl., 1955; Bjorkman's Petit Salon, Minneapolis, 1956; St. Paul FA Gal., 1958. Compiler, I., "Outdoor Horizons," 1957; I., "Wing Shooting, Trap & Skeet," 1955; Illus. for "Christmas Echoes," 1955; "Hunting Adventures," 1958. Author, I., "Roger Preuss Wildlife Calendar" (Annual). Contributor illus. to: Sports Afield; Minneapolis Star & Tribune; St. Paul Pioneer Press; Sports & Recreation, and others.

PREUSSER, ROBERT ORMEROD—*Painter, T., L.*
20 Highland Ave., Cambridge 39, Mass.

B. Houston, Tex., Nov. 13, 1919. *Studied*: Chicago Inst. Des., with Moholy-Nagy, Gyorgy Kepes, Robert J. Wolff; Los A. A. Center, and with McNeill Davidson. *Awards*: prizes, Texas State Fair, 1946; San Antonio A. Lg., 1948; Mus. FA of Houston, 1940, 1949, 1951; Texas WC Exh., 1950; Contemp. AA, 1952. *Work*: Mus. FA of Houston; Contemp. A. Mus., Houston; Witte Mem. Mus.; Texas Christian Univ. *Exhibited*: Carnegie Inst., 1941; AIC, 1942, 1947, 1951; VMFA, 1946; Mus. FA of Houston, 1935-1955; Kansas City AI, 1936; Southeast Texas Exh., 1937-1939; Texas General, 1940-1952, 1953, 1955; Denver Mus. A., 1954; Pepsi-Cola, 1946; WMAA, 1946, 1947; Colorado Springs FA Center, 1948; Exchange Exh., New Zealand, 1948; Mus. FA of Houston, 1948 (one-man); Mus. New Mexico, 1951, 1952; San Antonio, 1951, 1952; Downtown Gal., N.Y., 1954; Mirski Gal., Boston, 1955 (one-man). *Position*: Instr. Visual Arts., Sch. Arch. Planning, Mass. Inst. Technology; Instr., Drawing, Grad. Sch. Des., Harvard Col., Cambridge, Mass.*

PREZZI, WILMA MARIA—*Painter, S., T.*
1 West 67th St., New York 23, N.Y.

B. Long Island City, N.Y., Sept. 2, 1915. *Studied*: New York State Edu. Dept.; Metropolitan A. Sch.; ASL. *Member*: Life F., Am. Intl. Acad.; Life F., Intl. Inst. A. & Lets.; Arch. Lg.; Intl. FA Council. *Awards*: F. grant, Intl. FA Council, 1949, gold medal, 1954; Hon. degree, Doctor of Humanities, Philathea Col., Canada; Dame d'Honneur, Ordre de Lion des Ardennes, de Luxembourg, Paris, 1955; Dama Commendatrice Orden Militar de S.S. Salvador y Santa Brigida de Svecia, Spain, 1955; Membre d'Honneur, Les Violetti Picards et Normands, Paris, France, 1957; Membre d'Honneur, Club des Intellectuels, Français, Paris, 1957; Croix de Commandeur, Ligue Universelle de Bien Public, Paris; Hon. Ph.D., St. Andre's Ecumenical Univ., London, England, 1957; Byzantine Gold Medal, Biblioteca Partenopea, Naples, Italy, 1956; Medaille D'Or au Merite, Institut Nord Africain D'Etudes Metapsychiques, Tunis, North Africa, 1957; Medaille d'Argent, Prix Thorlet de L'Academie Français, Arts-Sciences-Lettres, Paris, 1958; Medaille d'Argent, Switzerland; Palma Academica, Argentina; Gran Premio de Honor, Sociedad Gente de Arte del Sur, Buenos Aires; Benediction Scroll, Pope Pius XII, 1957. *Work*: S., murals, paintings: Rickshaw Restaurant, Boston; Mus. Religious A., Utrecht, Netherlands; St. Gregory's Seminary, Cincinnati; Fla. State Univ., Olin Downs Music Lib.; Elmhurst Col., Illinois; N.Y. Univ. Music Lib.; Xavier Univ., Albers Hall; Hermitage Fnd., Norfolk, Va.; many sculptured portraits of prominent persons; 25 are in Wisconsin Hall of Fame, Milwaukee and 9 in Baseball Hall of Fame, Cooperstown, N.Y., executed by Prezzi-Kilenyi Assoc. *Exhibited*: nationally, group and one-man exhs.

PRIBBLE, EASTON—*Painter, L.*
207 Vine St., Lawrenceburg, Ind.

B. Falmouth, Ky., July 31, 1917. *Studied*: Univ. Cincinnati. *Work*: WMAA. *Exhibited*: AIC, 1948; WMAA, 1949, 1954, 1955; CM, 1941, 1943, 1947; Walker A. Center, 1953; Univ. Nebraska, 1954, 1955, 1957, 1958; Brandeis Univ., 1954; BMA, 1955; Alan Gal., N.Y., 1955 (one-man), 1956, 1957; Munson-Williams-Proctor Inst., 1957 (one-man), 1958; Ill. Wesleyan Univ., 1956; Des Moines A. Center, 1957. *Position*: A.-in-Res., Munson-Williams-Proctor Inst., Utica, N.Y., 1957-58, 1958-59.

PRICE, ALICE HENDEE (Mrs. Chester B.)—*Painter*
66 Palmer Ave., Bronxville 8, N.Y.

B. Arcadia, Iowa, Sept. 30, 1889. *Studied*: Kansas City AI; NAD; N.Y.Sch. F. & App. A., and with Wayman

Adams, Jerry Farnsworth. *Member:* Hudson Valley AA; Pen & Brush Cl. *Awards:* scholarship, N.Y.Sch. F. & App. A.; prizes, Hudson Valley AA, 1946; Westchester County A. Project, 1949, 1954, 1955; Crestwood, 1952; Pen & Brush Cl., 1955. *Work:* NAD; murals, triptych, Chapel, Christ Church, Bronxville. *Exhibited:* WFNY 1939; Arch. Lg.; Pen & Brush Cl.; NAC; Hudson Valley AA; Westchester County A. Project; Bronxville Women's Cl., 1956 (one-man).

PRICE, CHESTER B.—*Illustrator, Et.*
   101 Park Ave., New York 17, N.Y.; h. 66 Palmer Ave., Bronxville 8, N.Y.

B. Kansas City, Mo., June 11, 1885. *Studied:* ASL; Washington Univ., St. Louis, Mo.; Royal Col. A., London, England; & with Malcolm Osborne, Robert Austin. *Member:* AIA; Arch. L.; SAGA; Chicago Soc. Et. *Awards:* prize, Arch. L., 1928. *Work:* N.Y.Pub.Lib.; Nat. Mus., Wash., D.C.; Univ. Nebraska. *Exhibited:* Arch. L., 1915-1937; NAD; SAGA; WFNY 1939; Chicago SE. I., 14th Ed., Encyclopaedia Britannica, article on architecture. Illus. for national magazines. Lectures: Architectural Illustration. *Position:* Assoc. in Arch., Columbia Univ., New York, N.Y., 1942-44; Pres., Arch.Lg., 1949-50.*

PRICE, EDITH BALLINGER—*Illustrator, P., W.*
   16 Battery St., Newport, R.I.

B. New Brunswick, N.J., Apr. 26, 1897. *Studied:* BMFA Sch.; NAD; ASL, with Alexander James. *Exhibited:* Newport AA; South County AA. Author, I., numerous books of fiction.

PRICE, FREDERIC NEWLIN—*Museum Director, W., L.*
   New Hope, Pa.; h. 19 East 55th St., New York 22, N.Y.

B. Philadelphia, Pa., Jan. 25, 1884. *Studied:* Swarthmore Col. *Member:* SC. Author: "Arthur B. Davies," 1930; "Albert P. Ryder," 1932; "Horatio Walker"; "Ernest Lawson"; & other books. Contributor to: International Studio magazine. Lectures: Benjamin West. *Position:* Dir., Benjamin West Mus., Swarthmore, Pa., at present; Dir., Ferargil Gal., New York, N.Y.

PRICE, GARRETT—*Illustrator*
   393 Kings Highway, Westport, Conn.
Member: SI.*

PRICE, GEORGE—*Cartoonist*
   81 Westervelt Ave., Tenafly, N.J.
Contributor cartoons to New Yorker Magazine.*

PRICE, HELEN F.—*Painter, W., L.*
   510 Edgehill Dr., Johnstown, Pa.

B. Johnstown, Pa., Nov. 9, 1893. *Member:* All. A. Johnstown; NAWA; Assoc. A. Pittsburgh. *Awards:* prizes, All. A. Johnstown, 1940, 1942, 1944, 1948, 1950. *Work:* Pub. Sch., Somerset, Pa.; Lutheran Col., Gettysburg, Pa.; Bethlehem Steel Gen. Offices; Somerset Bank; Johnstown Bank; Univ. Pittsburgh. *Exhibited:* All.A.Am., 1936, 1937, 1939; Assoc. A. Pittsburgh, annually; All. A. Johnstown, annually; Western Pa. Hist. Soc., 1940 (one-man); Butler AI, 1945-1947; NAWA; Argent Gal.; Univ. Pittsburgh; 4 one-man exhs., Mountain Playhouse, Jennertown, Pa.

PRICE, IRENE—*Portrait Painter*
   Blowing Rock, N.C.

B. Savannah, Ga., Nov. 28, 1900. *Studied:* Duke Univ., A.B.; Corcoran Sch. A.; & with Charles Hawthorne, Robert Brackman. *Member:* SSAL; AAPL; N.C. State A. Soc. *Work:* Duke Univ.; Virginia Military Inst.; many portraits. *Exhibited:* SSAL; Piedmont Festival A., 1944.

PRICE, JOHN M.—*Cartoonist, A. Dir., Des.*
   N. W. Ayer & Son, Washington Sq., Philadelphia, Pa.; h. 2100 Walnut St., Philadelphia, Pa.

B. Plymouth Meeting, Pa., Feb. 5, 1918. *Studied:* Pa. State Univ., B.A. *Exhibited:* Phila. WC Soc., 1940; Greenwich Soc. A., 1949-1952; Ferargil Gal., 1952. Author, I., Ed., "Don't Get Polite With Me!", 1952. (A collection of Price cartoons reprinted from Sat. Eve. Post, New Yorker

and other publications). Contributor Cartoons to Sat. Eve. Post; Esquire; New Yorker; American; Ladies Home Journal; King Features Syndicate; Marshall Field Syndicate and many others. Work represented in Art Directors' Annual, 1957. *Position:* Television A. Dir., N.W. Ayer & Son, New York, N.Y., 1954- .

PRICE, M. ELIZABETH—*Painter, L., T.*
   New Hope, Bucks County, Pa.

B. Martinsburg, W. Va. *Studied:* PMSchIA; PAFA, and with William L. Lathrop. *Member:* F., PAFA. *Exhibited:* CGA; Carnegie Inst.; NAD; PAFA; Grand Central A. Gal.; Ferargil Gal.; Phillips Mill, New Hope, Pa. *Work:* in many private collections.

PRICE, MARGARET EVANS—*Illustrator, W., P.*
   East Aurora, N.Y.

B. Chicago, Ill., Mar. 20, 1888. *Studied:* Mass. Normal A. Sch.; & with Joseph De Camp, Vesper George. *Work:* N.Y. Hist. Soc.; N.Y. Hist. Mus.; Bermuda AA; Bermuda Cathedral. Portraits in U.S., Scotland and England. *Exhibited:* Boston AC; Albright A. Gal.; Grand Central A. Gal., 1953-1956; Bermuda AA, 1956, 1957; numerous exh. of book illus. Author, I., "Legends of the Seven Seas"; "Down Comes the Wilderness"; "Mirage," 1955; "Myths and Enchantment Tales," 1954-1958, etc. I., "Bounty of Earth"; "West Indian Play Days"; & other books. Contributor to: Woman's Home Companion, Nature, Child Life magazines.

PRICE, ROSALIE PETTUS [Mrs. William A.]—*Painter*
   300 Windsor Dr., Birmingham 9, Ala.

B. Birmingham, Ala. *Studied:* Birmingham-Southern Col., A.B., and with Hannah Elliott, A. L. Bairnsfather, Wayman Adams. *Member:* Cal. WC Soc.; Alabama WC Soc.; Mobile WC Soc.; New Orleans AA; Birmingham AA. *Awards:* prizes, Birmingham AA, 1944, 1945, 1950; Alabama WC Soc., 1948; New Orleans AA, 1948; Pen & Brush Cl., 1950. *Exhibited:* Phila. WC & Print Exh., 1948; Cal. WC Soc., 1945-1948, 1954; Riverside Mus., 1946, 1948; Cal. WC Soc. traveling exh., 1947, 1948; Alabama WC Soc., 1948, 1949; AWS, 1947; Mobile WC Soc., 1948; New Orleans AA, 1947, 1948; Mississippi AA, 1947; Newport AA, 1946; High Mus. A., 1947-1949; SSAL, 1936, 1943, 1946; Long Beach AA, 1944, 1945; Birmingham AA, 1934, 1935, 1944, 1945, 1947, 1950, 1951; Pen & Brush Cl., 1949, 1950.

PRICKETT, ROLAND PIERSON—*Painter, W., T., I.*
   Prickett-Montague Studio of Painting, Monterey, Mass.

B. Springfield, Mass., May 31, 1896. *Studied:* Cornell Univ., B.S.; Lumis A. Acad., with Harriet Randall Lumis; PAFA. *Member:* SC; Springfield A. Gld. *Awards:* prize, BMFA, 1926. *Work:* Conn. Acad. FA; Travelers Ins. Co.; Jamaica, B.W.I. Railways; Mexican Nat. Railways; U.S. Army Air Force Tactical Color Research, 1943. Color Indexing, 1948; Lincoln Mem. Lib., Brimfield, Mass; Parrish A. Mus. *Exhibited:* Springfield A. Lg., 1945, 1946; Springfield A. Gld., 1945, 1946; Royal Inst., Jamaica, B.W.I., 1943, 1944; Westfield (Mass.) Atheneum; San Juan, Puerto Rico, 1951; Ogunquit A. Center, 1958; one-man: Hotel Grant, San Diego, 1940; Witherle Mem., Castine, Me., 1954; Hotel Floridian, Miami Beach, 1955; Bar Harbor, Me., 1956; Juneau, Alaska, 1957. *Position:* Originator, Instr., 5 Home Study Courses via airmail; Prickett Simplified Palette of Colors; leader of nationwide Happy Painters Guild for Skillful Art; writer of "Paint and Be Happy" column of instructions and art comments for American weekly newspapers; author of published monographs on various phases of oil painting.

PRICKETT, MRS. ROLAND PIERSON.
   See Montague, Ruth Du Barry

PRIDE, JOY—*Painter, C., Des., T., L.*
   23 East 9th St., New York 3, N.Y.

B. Lexington, Ky. *Studied:* Univ. Kentucky, A.B., M.A.; Julian Acad., Paris; ASL; Barnes Fnd.; N.Y. Univ.; and with Stuart Davis. *Member:* NAWA; Pen & Brush Cl.; AAUW. *Work:* Senate Office Bldg., Wash., D.C. *Exhibited:* CAA; CGA; NAWA, 1943-1955; Pen & Brush Cl., 1947-1954; J.B.Speed A. Mus., 1929-1933; Univ. Kentucky, 1932 (one-man); Circle Gal., Hollywood, Cal., 1943. *Position*: A.T., Barmore Sch., New York, N.Y., 1950-53; A. Ed., Am. Book Co., 1953-55; Radio Scripts, Voice of America, CBS, WQXR, 1948-52; Assoc. A. Ed., The Macmillan Co., New York, N.Y., 1955- .

PRIEBE, KARL—*Painter, T., L.*
c/o Perls Galleries, 32 East 58th St., New York 22, N.Y.; h. 3140 South Wollmer Road, Milwaukee 19, Wis.

B. Milwaukee, Wis., July 1, 1914. *Studied*: Layton Sch. A.; AIC. *Awards*: prizes, Milwaukee AI, 1943-1945. *Work*: Layton Gal. A.; Milwaukee AI; Encyclopaedia Britannica Coll.; VMFA; Barnes Fnd.; IBM Coll.; Detroit Inst. A.; Fisk Univ.; Marquette Univ.; Reader's Digest Coll.; & others. *Exhibited*: nationally and in Paris, France, 1951; one-man exh.: Perls Gal., 1943, 1944, 1946; Hammer Gal., N.Y., 1956; Univ. Wisconsin, 1958. *Position*: Asst. in Ethnology, Milwaukee Pub. Mus., 1938-42; Dir., Kalamazoo AI, Kalamazoo, Mich., 1944; Instr., Painting, Layton Sch. A., Milwaukee, Wis.

PRIES, LIONEL H.—*Educator, P., Et., L.*
University of Washington; h. 3132 West Laurelhurst Dr., Seattle 5, Wash.

B. San Francisco, Cal., June 2, 1897. *Studied*: Univ. California, A.B.; Univ. Pennsylvania, M.Arch.; & with Paul Cret, Dawson, Gumaer. *Awards*: prizes, Am. Acad. in Rome, 1921; LeBrun traveling F., 1922. *Work*: mem., Univ. California. *Exhibited*: Arch.L., 1921; Palace Legion Honor; SAM; Univ. Washington. Lectures: Ornament; Architecture; Textiles. *Position*: Dir., SAM, Seattle, Wash., 1929-30; Assoc. Prof. Arch., Univ. Washington, Seattle, Wash., 1928- .*

PRIEST, ALAN—*Museum Curator*
Metropolitan Museum of Art, Fifth Ave. and 82nd St., New York 28, N.Y.

B. Fitchburg, Mass., Jan. 31, 1898. *Studied*: Harvard Univ., B.A. *Awards*: Carnegie F., China, 1925; Sachs F., China, 1926-1927. Author: "Chinese Sculpture in the Metropolitan Museum of Art," 1943; "Costumes from the Forbidden City" (monograph), 1945; "Aspects of Chinese Painting," 1954; various other monographs & catalogs. Contributor to: Bulletin of the MMA. Lectures: Oriental Art. *Position*: Asst., Instr., Harvard Univ., 1922-23; Cur., Far Eastern A., MMA, New York, N.Y., 1928- .

PRIEST, HARTWELL WYSE—*Etcher, Lith., P.*
R.F.D. #5, Bellair, Charlottesville, Va.

B. Brantford, Ontario, Canada, Jan. 1, 1901. *Studied*: Smith Col., A.B.; with Maurice Sievan, Joe Jones, Hans Hofmann and with Andre Lhote in Paris, France. *Member*: NAWA; Pen & Brush Cl.; Conn. Acad. FA; New Orleans AA; Palm Beach A. Lg.; Springfield A. Lg.; AAPL; SAGA. *Awards*: Pen & Brush Cl., 1954; Palm Beach A. Lg., 1953; Wash. WC Cl., 1955; medal, NAWA, 1953; Albany Inst. Hist. & A., 1955. *Work*: LC; Newark Pub. Lib.; Univ. Maine; Albany Inst. Hist. & A.; murals, Children's Ward, University Hospital, Charlottesville, W. Va. *Exhibited*: Chicago Soc. Et., 1930, 1931; Brooklyn Soc. Et., 1931; Intl. Pr. M. Soc. of Cal., 1933; Phila. WC Cl., 1931; Carnegie Inst., 1945; NAWA, 1940-1955; LC, 1944, 1947, 1952, 1955; SAGA, 1932, 1934. 1944, 1947, 1951, 1952, 1954, 1955; New Orleans AA, 1954, 1955; Conn. Acad. FA, 1954, 1955; Albany Pr. Cl., 1953-1955; Audubon A., 1954; Knickerbocker A., 1954, 1955; Phila. Pr. Cl., 1947, 1955; Pen & Brush Cl., 1942-1955; Springfield A. Lg., 1954, 1955; Creative Gal., 1954; Summit (N.J.) AA, 1935-1952; New Jersey A., Newark, 1952; Albemarle AA, 1953-1955; one-man: The Print Corner, Hingham, Mass., 1931; Col. of Idaho, 1941; Univ. Maine, 1950; Summit AA, 1951; Morristown, N.J., 1951; Argent Gal., 1955. Lectures: "Making an Etching"; "Lithography," to women's clubs and art groups.*

PRINS, BENJAMIN KIMBERLY—*Illustrator*
Wilton, Conn.

B. Leiden, Holland, Jan. 20, 1904. *Studied*: N.Y. Sch. F. & App. A.; PIASch.; ASL. *Member*: Westport AA; Wilton Hist. Soc. *Awards*: gold medal, A. Dir. Cl., N.Y. *Work*: Hist. and photographs of work included in "Illustrating for the Saturday Evening Post," 1951. Contributor covers and illus. to Sat. Eve. Post; illus. for McCalls, Good Housekeeping; Woman's Home Companion, Nations Business, and other national magazines.

PRIOR, HARRIS KING—*Art Administrator, E.*
American Federation of Arts, 1083 Fifth Ave. (28); h. 440 East 79th St., New York 21, N.Y.

B. Hazardville, Conn., Mar. 10, 1911. *Studied*: Trinity Col., Hartford, Conn., B.S., M.A.; Harvard Univ.; Yale Univ.; Univ. Paris; Univ. Brussels; N.Y. Univ., Inst. FA. *Award*: Hon. degree, D.F.A., Cal. Col. A. & Crafts, Oakland, Cal., 1959. *Member*: AAMus.; CAA; Am. Studies Assn. Contributor to Italian Encyclopaedia; Oregon Hist. Quarterly; ASL Quarterly. Lectures: Early Art of the American West; Contemporary Painters of the Pacific Northwest. Arranged exhs.: Ten Painters of the Pacific Northwest, 1947; Utica Looks Ahead (City Planning), 1949; Formal Organization in Modern Painting, 1953; What is Industrial Design?, 1954; Italy Rediscovered, 1955; The Figure in Contemporary Sculpture, 1956. *Positions*: Asst. Instr., English & FA, Trinity Col., 1932-36; Hd. Sch. FA, Olivet Col., Mich., 1937-39; Dir., Community A. Program, Munson-Williams-Proctor Inst., Utica, N.Y., 1947-1956; Dir., American Federation of Arts, New York, 1956 (Dec.)- .

PRITCHARD, THEODORE JAN—*Designer, E.*
804 Apple Lane, Moscow, Idaho

B. Thief River Falls, Minn., May 28, 1902. *Studied*: Univ. Minnesota, B.A.; Harvard Univ., M.Arch. *Member*: AIA. *Position*: Prof., Hd. A. Dept., Univ. Idaho, Moscow, Idaho, at present.*

PROCTOR, CHARLES—*Museum Curator*
Thomas Gilcrease Institute of American History & Art, 2400 West Newton St., Tulsa, Okla.

Position: Cur., Gilcrease Institute of American History & Art.*

PROHASKA, RAY—*Illustrator, P.*
Amagansett, N.Y.

B. Mulo Dalmata, Yugoslavia, Feb. 5, 1901. *Studied*: Cal. Sch. FA. *Member*: SI; A. & Writers; Audubon A.; Nat. Soc. Painters in Casein. *Awards*: prizes, Hallmark Award, 1949; Audubon A., 1954, medal, 1956; Nat. Soc. Painters in Casein, 1956; Parrish Mus.; 1949; Gld. Hall, East Hampton, N.Y., 1956. *Exhibited*: Audubon A.; Terry AI; WMAA; PAFA; Univ. Illinois; NAD; Hallmark Comp.; Nat. Soc. Painters in Casein; Gld. Hall, East Hampton; Parrish Mus.; A. Dir. Cl.; one-man: SI, 1948; Mortimer Levitt, 1952. Illustrator for books, advertising and magazines.

PROSS, LESTER FRED—*Educator, P.*
Berea College, Art Department; h. 21 Prospect St., Berea, Ky.

B. Bristol, Conn., Aug. 14, 1924. *Studied*: Oberlin Col., B.A., M.A., and with Ben Shahn, Jack Levin, Sidney Simon, Henry Varnum Poor. *Award*: Haskell Traveling F., Oberlin Col., 1957-58. *Member*: AAUP; Ky. A. Edu. Assn. *Work*: Allen Mem. Mus., Oberlin Col.; Seagram Coll. of Kentucky Art. *Exhibited*: Ohio Valley, 1949; Ky-Indiana, 1951; Va. Intermont Southeastern Exh., 1948, 1949; Central Kentucky Exh., 1949-1953; one-man: Louisville, 1951, and Univ. Kentucky, 1954. Illus. "Mountain Life and Work." *Position*: Co-Chm., Assoc. Prof.A., A. Dept., Berea Col., 1950- . Fulbright Lecturer, Dept. FA, Univ. of the Panjab, Lahore, Pakistan, 1957-58.

PROSSER, MARGARET (Mrs. Margaret Prosser Allen) —*Educator, P.*
119 Briar Lane, Newark, Del.

B. Vancouver, B.C., Jan. 26, 1913. *Studied*: Univ. Washington, B.A., M.F.A., and with Alexander Archipenko, Amedee Ozenfant. *Member*: AAUP; Comm. on A. Edu., MModA. *Award*: prize, Wilmington Soc. FA, 1949. *Work*: Wilmington Soc. FA. *Exhibited*: Wilmington Soc. FA, 1942-1945, 1947-1949, 1951, 1953-1958; Univ. Delaware, 1946 (one-man); Northwest Exh., 1938, 1941, 1943, 1945, 1947, 1948; Weyhe Gal., 1947; Rehoboth A. Gal., 1952. *Position*: Instr. A., 1942-48, Asst. Prof. A., 1949- , Univ. Delaware, Newark, Del.

PRUNIER, ARTHUR WILLIAM—
Painter, T., Des., Comm. A.
Nuestro Rancho, Vista, Cal.

B. Lynn, Mass., Jan. 31, 1905. *Studied*: Mass. Normal A. Sch.; Washington State T. Col.; ASL of Los A.; San Diego Sch. A. & Crafts, and with S. MacDonald-Wright; Everett Jackson, Nicolas Brigante. *Member*: Vista A. Gld. (Fndr.); Carlsbad-Oceanside A. Lg. *Awards*: prizes, Carlsbad-Oceanside A. Lg., 1952, 1954, 1957; Vista A. Gld., 1952, 1954, 1955; San Diego County Fair, 1952. *Work*: murals, Hayward Hotel, Los A.; Sunkist Bldg., Los A.; Coast Grinding Co., Los A., and numerous cafes and private homes. *Exhibited*: Oceanside, Cal., 1945; Vista A. Gld., 1946-1957; Coronado AA, 1951; A.T. Exh., Los A., 1952; Oceanside-Carlsbad, 1952-1957; Escondido, Cal., 1957; San Diego County Fair, 1952-1955; one-man: Contemp. Gal., Hollywood; Carlsbad Hotel, 1948, 1953; San Diego Sch. A. & Crafts, 1952; Palomar Col., 1957, 1958; Santa Fe, 1958.

PUCCINELLI, RAYMOND—*Sculptor, P., E., L.*
126 Divisadero St., San Francisco 17, Cal.; also, 68 State St., Brooklyn 2, N.Y.

B. San Francisco, Cal., May 5, 1904. *Studied*: Univ. California; Schaeffer Sch. Des., San F., and abroad. *Member*: NSS. *Awards*: prizes, medal, Oakland A. Gal., 1938, 1941, 1942; Los A. Mus. A., 1939; San F. AA, 1938; Sacramento, Cal., 1949. *Work*: S., wood carvings, etc., Mills Col.; Univ. Cal.; SFMA; IBM; Salinas (Cal.) Jr. Col.; House of Theology, Centerville, Ohio; San F. Stock Exchange; Corpus Christi Church, Piedmont, Cal. *Exhibited*: WMAA, 1940, 1948, 1949; PAFA, 1942, 1952; CM, 1941; NSS; Arch. Lg.; WFNY 1939; SFMA, 1936-1946; Los A. Mus. A., 1939; San Diego Exp., 1935; Portland A. Mus., 1939; CGA, 1942; Grand Central A. Gal., 1946, 1947; BM, 1954; Nat. Inst. A. & Let., 1953, 1955; Pomona, Cal., 1952; Fairmount Park, Phila., 1949; one-man: Cal. PLH, 1946; Mills Col., 1945; Univ. California, 1945; deYoung Mem. Mus., 1944; Santa Barbara Mus. A., 1954; Oakland A. Gal., 1938-1942; Scripps Col., 1941; Crocker A. Gal., 1941; SFMA; Bucknell Univ., 1954; Coeval Gal., N.Y., 1954; Phila. A. All.; Schneider Gal., Rome, Italy, 1957; Pater Gal., Milan, Italy, 1958. *Positions*: L., Univ. California, Berkeley, Cal., 1942-47; Instr. S., Mills Col., Oakland, Cal., 1938-47; A. in Residence, Univ. North Carolina, 1948-49; Instr., Queens Col., Flushing, N.Y., 1948-51; U.S. Dept. State Cultural Representative in Latin America, 1956; Dean Rinehart Sch. of Sculpture, Baltimore, Md., 1958- .

PUGH, MABEL—*Educator, P., Gr., I., W., L.*
Peace College, Raleigh, N.C.

B. Morrisville, N.C. *Studied*: ASL; PAFA; Columbia Univ.; North Carolina State Col., and with Hawthorne, Adams, Martin. *Member*: CAA; N.C. State A. Soc. *Awards*: F., PAFA; Cresson traveling scholarship, PAFA, 1919; prizes, N.C. State Fair, 1922; Southern Pr. M.; Mint Mus. A.; medal, Phila. Plastic Cl., 1926. *Work*: LC; Waynesville Court House; Peace Col. Lib.; portraits Franklin Community Center; Dir. Room, Insurance Bldg., Raleigh; White Mem. Presbyterian Church, Raleigh; John Marshall House, Richmond; Chatham Hospital; Cary H.S.; Agricultural Com. Room, House of Representatives, Wash., D.C.; Marine & Fisheries Committee Room, House of Representatives, Wash., D.C.; Warren County Mem. Lib.; Queens Col., Charlotte, N.C. *Exhibited*: Nationally and Internationally. Author, I., "Little Carolina Bluebonnet", 1933; Illus. for leading publishers. *Position*: Hd. A., Dept., Peace Col., Raleigh, N.C., 1936- .

PULLINGER, HERBERT—*Printmaker, P., I., T.*
1430 South Penn Square; h. 5301 Knox St., Philadelphia 44, Pa.

B. Philadelphia, Pa., Aug. 5, 1878. *Studied*: PMSchIA; Drexel Inst.; PAFA. *Member*: Phila. Pr. Cl.; Phila. Sketch Cl.; Phila. WC Cl. *Awards*: F., PAFA; med., PAFA, 1925; Sesqui-Centennial Exp., Phila., 1926. *Work*: N.Y.Pub.Lib.; Luxembourg Mus., Paris; Springfield (Mass.) Lib.; PAFA; Phila. Pub. Lib.; PMA; CMA; Newark Mus. Author, I., "Washington, the Nation's Capitol," 1921; "Old Germantown." Illus. for national magazines. *Position*: Instr., Graphic A., PMSchA., Philadelphia, Pa., at present.

PUMA, FERNANDO—*Painter, W., Cr., E.*
Address unknown

B. New York, N.Y., Feb. 14, 1919. *Studied*: N.Y. Univ.; Columbia Univ. *Work*: PMG; Detroit Inst. A.; Randolph-

Macon Col. *Exhibited*: Albany Inst. Hist. & A., 1943, 1944; Detroit Inst. A., 1944; Critics Show, N.Y., 1945; PMG; Adelphi Col.; Randolph-Macon Col.; Minneapolis Inst. A.; Univ. Illinois, 1952; one-man: New York City; SFMA; Santa Barbara Mus. A.; in Paris, France, 1949; Gallery D, 1939-1947; Art Review radio program, 1942-43. Author: "Modern Art Looks Ahead," 1947; "Love This Horizontal World," 1949; "7 Arts," 1953, 3rd ed., 1955.*

PURDUE, CHRIS(TINE) M.—*Craftsman, S., T.*
44 North Lake Drive, Hamden, New Haven 14, Conn.

B. New Haven, Conn., Nov. 10, 1902. *Studied*: Greenwich House, N.Y.; ASL; Univ. Pa.; Whitney A. Sch., New Haven; Alfred Univ. (summer); Worcester (Mass.) Craft Center; Silvermine Gld. in France, Italy and England, and with Paul Manship. *Member*: New Haven Paint & Clay Cl.; N.Y. Soc. Ceramic A.; Silvermine Gld. A.; Soc. Conn. Craftsmen. *Awards*: prizes, Silvermine Gld. A., 1954; New England Exh., 1955; Essex AA. *Exhibited*: New Haven Paint & Clay Cl., 1951, 1952, 1955; Whitney A. Sch., 1950, 1951; Silvermine Gld. A., 1954, 1955, 1958; N.Y. Soc. Ceramic A., 1953, 1954; Essex AA, 1952. Contributor to Ceramic Monthly.

PURDY, MAUD H.—*Illustrator, P.*
Pomona Country Club, Spring Valley, N.Y.

B. Philadelphia, Pa., Nov. 29, 1873. *Studied*: PIASch.; Adelphi Col. *Exhibited*: PAFA, and in New York, N.Y. I., "Fundamentals of Botany"; "Families of Dicotyledons"; "Illustrated Guide to Trees and Shrubs"; "All About African Violets." *Position*: I., Brooklyn Botanical Gardens (retired).

PURSER, MARY MAY—*Painter, Des., E., I., C.*
2210 Northwest Second Ave., Gainesville, Fla.

B. Chicago, Ill., Dec. 9, 1913. *Studied*: AIC; Louisiana Col.; Univ. Mississippi, A.B.; Univ. Florida, M.F.A., and study abroad. *Member*: Southeastern AA; Fla. A.T. Assn.; NAEA. *Awards*: prizes, Fla. Fed. A., 1952, 1955; Fla. State Fair, 1958 (purchase). *Work*: murals, USPO, Clarksville, Ark. Illus. for "Supervision for Better Schools" (2nd ed.). *Exhibited*: AIC; New Orleans AA, 1942; Delgado Mus. A. (one-man); Mississippi AA (one-man); Soc. Four Arts, 1955; Birmingham Mus. A., 1955; Fla. State Fair, 1958. *Positions*: A.T., AIC; Louisiana Col.; Univ. Chattanooga; A. Supv., Gainesville, Fla., 1955-57; Asst. Prof. A., San Fernando Valley State Col., Los Angeles, Cal., 1958-59.

PURSER, STUART R.—*Painter, E.*
2210 Northwest 2nd Ave., Gainesville, Fla.

B. Stamps, Ark., Feb. 7, 1907. *Studied*: Louisiana Col., A.B.; AIC, B.F.A., M.F.A.; & abroad. *Awards*: prizes, New Orleans AA; Mississippi AA, 1942. *Work*: murals, USPO, Leland, Miss.; Gretna, Ferriday, La.; Carrollton, Ala. *Exhibited*: PAFA, 1946; AIC, 1936, 1938; WFNY 1939. *Position*: Hd. Dept. A., Louisiana Col., Pineville, La., 1935-45; Univ. Chattanooga, Tenn., 1946-49; Hd. Dept. A., Univ. Mississippi, Oxford, Miss., 1949-51; Hd. Dept. A., Univ. Florida, 1951-56; Prof. A., Univ. Florida, 1956-58; Visiting Prof. A., San Fernando Valley State Col., Los Angeles, Cal., 1958-59.

PURVES, AUSTIN—*Mural Painter, S., C., E.*
R.F.D. 1, Litchfield, Conn.

B. Chestnut Hill, Pa., Dec. 31, 1900. *Studied*: PAFA; Julian Acad., Am. Conservatory, Fontainebleau, France. *Member*: Arch.L.; NSMP; Century Assn. *Work*: reredos, St. Paul's Church, Duluth, Minn.; Grace Church, Honesdale, Pa.; mem., Wash., D.C.; fresco, St. Michael's Church, Torresdale, Pa.; s., map, des., S.S. America; S.S. Santa Rosa; Colgate Univ. Lib.; St. Stephen's Church, Armonk, N.Y.; other work, Firestone Mem. Lib., Princeton Univ.; Am. Battle Monuments Comm.; S.S. United States; Fed. Reserve Bank of Boston; Providence Hospital, Wash., D.C.; mural, Children's Chapel, Trinity Church, Ft. Wayne, Ind. *Position*: Chm. Adv. Council, CUASch., New York, N.Y.; Trustee, Darrow Sch., New Lebanon, N.Y.; Trustee, Hartford A. Sch., Univ. of Hartford, Conn.

PUTNAM, BRENDA—*Sculptor, W., T.*
42 Sharp Hill Road, Wilton, Conn.

B. Minneapolis, Minn. *Studied*: BMFA; Corcoran Sch. A.; ASL, with James Earle Fraser, and with Charles Grafly and Archipenko; in Florence, Italy with Libero Andreotti. *Member*: Nat. Inst. A. & Let.; NA; NSS; NAC. *Awards*: Barnett prize, NAD, 1922; gold medal, PAFA, 1923; prize, NAWA, 1923; Avery prize, Arch. Lg., 1924; gold medal, NAD, 1935, and others. Comp. for Congressional Medal, presented to Fleet Admiral King, 1947. *Work*: Folger Shakespeare Lib., Wash., D.C.; Acad. A. & Let.; Hall of Fame, N.Y. Univ.; Detroit Inst. A.; DMFA; Brookgreen Garden, S.C.; Lynchburg, Va.; South Orange, N.J.; mural reliefs: USPO, Caldwell, N.J.; St. Cloud, Minn.; marble fig., Norton Gal. A.; 3 plaques, House of Representatives, Wash., D.C.; many garden figures, portraits of children, etc.; bust of Susan B. Anthony for Hall of Fame, 1952. Author: "The Sculptor's Way," 1939; "Animal X-rays," 1947.

PUTNAM, MARION WALTON. See *Walton, Marion*

PUTNAM, WALLACE B.—Painter, W., I.
Baptist Church Road, Yorktown Heights, N.Y.

B. West Newton, Mass., 1899. *Studied*: BMFA Sch. *Member*: Fed. Modern P. & S. *Work*: Yale Univ.; MModA. *Exhibited*: BM; MModA; Bignou Gal., 1945 (one-man); Chinese Gal., 1948; Passedoit Gal., 1951, 1953, 1954. Author, I., "Manhattan Manners."*

PUZINAS, PAUL—Painter, E.
301 West 57th St., New York 19, N.Y.

B. Riga, Latvia, Aug. 3, 1907. *Studied*: A. Acad., Latvia, M.A.; and in Belgium. *Member*: A. Lg. of Long Island; AAPL; All. A. Am., and many art organizations in California. *Awards*: prizes, Lithuania Nat. award, 1938 and others; Greek Theatre, Los Angeles, 1950; Madonna Festival, Los Angeles, 1951; Intl Flower Show A. Exh., 1951; Am. Traditional A. Exh., Los A., 1955; AAPL, Grand Nat. award, 1956; Emily Lowe Fnd., N.Y., 1957; Lockman award, N.Y., 1957; Huntington award, 1958; A. Lg. of Long Island, 1958, and others. *Work*: Nat. Mus., Kaunas and in Vilnius, Lithuania; State A. Mus., Riga, Latvia; mural, Paneveszy Cathedral, Lithuania. *Exhibited*: Art: USA, 1958; Audubon A.; All. A. Am., 1957; Butler Inst. Am. A., 1958; All-City A. Exh., Los A., 1950-1952; Intl. Flower Show A. Exh., 1951; Am. Traditional A. Exh., Los A., 1955; A. Lg. of Long Island, 1956, 1958; AAPL, 1957; Hudson Valley AA, 1958.

PYE, FRED—Painter, T.
5400 Kugler Mill Road, Cincinnati 36, Ohio

B. Hebden Bridge, Yorkshire, England, Dec. 1, 1882. *Member*: SC; Cincinnati Men's AC; Cincinnati Professional A. *Work*: Luxembourg Mus., Paris; Mus. A., Edmonton, Canada. *Exhibited*: CM.

PYLE, MARGERY KATHLEEN—Painter
110 West 30th St., Wilmington 218, Del.

B. Wilmington, Del., July 6, 1903. *Studied*: PAFA; Univ. Delaware. *Member*: Wilmington Soc. FA; Rehoboth (Del.) A. Lg. *Awards*: prizes, Wilmington AC, 1934. *Exhibited*: Rehoboth A. Lg., 1939, 1947 (one-man); F. PAFA, 1936; Wilmington Soc. FA, annually.*

PYTLAK, LEONARD—Serigrapher, Lith., P., T.
221 East 59th St., New York 22, N.Y.

B. Newark, N.J., Mar. 3, 1910. *Studied*: Newark Sch. F. & Indst. A.; ASL. *Member*: A.Lg.Am.; Nat. Serigraph Soc.; Audubon A.; Phila. Color Pr. Soc. *Awards*: Guggenheim F., 1941; prizes, MMA, 1942; AV, 1943; Phila. Pr. Cl.; Phila. Color Pr. Soc.; NAD, 1946; Lib.Cong., 1946; SAM. *Work*: MMA; BM; Carnegie Inst.; Denver A. Mus.; SAM; BMFA; N.Y.Pub.Lib.; PMA; Newark Lib.; MModA; Contemporary A.; Nat. Serigraph Soc. *Exhibited*: Lib.Cong., 1944-1946. Lectures: Silkscreen Process.*

QUAN, MUN S.—Painter
5020 Quan Drive, Jacksonville 5, Fla.

B. Canton, China, July 14, 1917. *Studied*: Canton Acad. A., China, and with Ko-Kim Fu, Canton; Nicholas Volpe, Jacksonville, Fla. *Member*: Sarasota AA; New Orleans AA; Fla. Fed. A.; Fla. A. Group. *Awards*: prizes, Canton, China, 1948; Governor's award, Macao, 1949; Fla. Fed.

A., 1952, 1953; Jacksonville A. Mus., 1951-1958; St. Augustine AA, 1951, 1953-1956. *Work*: Jacksonville A. Mus.; Univ. Florida. *Exhibited*: Fla. Fed. A.; Fla. A. Group; Delgado Mus. A.; Sarasota AA; one-man: Jacksonville A. Mus., 1952, 1953, 1956, 1957; Jacksonville Univ., 1957; Daytona AA, 1953; Univ. Florida, 1958. *Position*: Instr., Watercolor, Jacksonville A. Mus., Florida.

QUANCHI, LEO—Painter
Ridge Rd., R.D. #1, Upper Saddle River, N.J.

B. New York, N.Y., Sept. 23, 1892. *Studied*: Col. City of N.Y.; NAD; ASL; Parsons Sch. Des. *Member*: Audubon A.; Assoc. A., New Jersey; AEA. *Awards*: prizes, Montclair A. Mus., 1944; Newark Mus. A., 1952; PAFA, 1953. *Work*: WMAA; Newark Mus. A.; PAFA. *Exhibited*: NAD, annually; Pepsi-Cola, 1944, 1946; Montclair A. Mus., annually; WMAA, 1954; Newark Mus. A., 1952, 1958; CGA, 1951, 1957; Univ. Illinois, 1951; Birmingham Mus. A., 1954; Butler Inst. Am. A., 1958; Columbia Univ., 1958; Columbia, S.C., 1958; one-man: New York, N.Y., 1923, 1940, 1947, 1949, 1950; St. Louis, Mo., 1949; Silvermine Gld. A., 1951; Univ. Florida, 1953; Salpeter Gal., 1952, 1958.

QUANDT, RUSSELL JEROME—Museum Art Restorer
Corcoran Gallery of Art, 510 17th St., Northwest, Washington 6, D.C.; h. 3433 34th St., Northwest, Washington 8, D.C.

B. New London, Conn., Sept. 18, 1919. *Studied*: Yale Col. *Member*: F.; Intl. Inst. for the Conservation of Museum Objects. Restoration commissions for Phillips Gal., J.B. Speed A. Mus.; Colonial Williamsburg, and others. *Position*: Restorer, Corcoran Gal. A., 1950- ; Conservator, Abby Aldrich Rockefeller Folk Art Coll., Williamsburg, Va., 1954- .

QUASTLER, GERTRUDE (Mrs. Henry)—Printmaker, P.
R.R. #1, Brookhaven, N.Y.

B. Vienna, Austria, Feb. 10, 1909. *Studied*: Columbia Univ.; Univ. Illinois; Chicago Inst. Des. *Member*: Boston Pr. M.; Print Council of Am. *Work*: MModA; Farnsworth Mus. A.; AIC; BMFA; FMA; Boston Pub. Lib.; Phila. Free Lib.; R.I. Sch. Des.; Univ. of Delaware, Maryland and Nebraska. *Exhibited*: 1949-55: PAFA; BM; LC; Audubon A.; Univ. Nebraska; Springfield, Ill.; Denver A. Mus.; Univ. Indiana; one-man: Chicago, 1950, 1952, 1953; Decatur, 1955; Boston, 1955; Philadelphia, 1953; Stonybrook, N.Y., 1958.

QUATTROCCHI, EDMONDO—Sculptor
P.O. Box 214, Long Island City, N.Y.

B. Sulmona, Italy. *Studied*: CUASch.; ASL; in Paris, and with Philip Martiny, D. C. French, C. C. Rumsey, F. MacMonnies. *Member*: NA; All. A. Am.; NSS; AAPL; Intl. Inst. A. & Lets. *Awards*: Chevalier, Legion d'Honneur, France; prizes, NSS; All. A. Am.; AAPL, 1958. *Work*: bronze tablet, Clock Tower Square and statue, Roslyn, L.I., N.Y.; statue, Pelham Bay Park, N.Y.; Port. busts, N.Y. Pub. Lib.; Council on Foreign Relations, N.Y.; N.Y.Univ. Hall of Fame, and others. Also many bas-reliefs and medals. In France, monument (des. by Mac Monnies) commemorating the Battle of the Marne, gift from America to France. *Exhibited*: Salon des Artistes Francais, Paris; Bossuet Mus., Meaux, France; Sheldon Swope Mus. A., Terre Haute, Ind.; MMA; NSS; NAD; IBM.

QUEST, CHARLES F.—Painter, Gr., E.
Washington University School of Fine Arts (5); h. 12331 Harflo Lane, Town and Country, St. Louis 22, Mo.

B. Troy, N.Y., June 6, 1904. *Studied*: Washington Univ. Sch. FA; and in Europe. *Member*: SAGA; Am. Color Pr. Soc.; Phila. Pr. Cl. *Awards*: prizes, St. Louis A. Gld., 1923, 1925, 1927, 1929, 1930-1933, 1948-1952; CAM, 1932, 1942, 1944, 1947, 1948, 1950, 1951; Kansas City AI, 1932; Springfield Mus. A., 1945, 1947; Phila. Pr. Cl., 1946, 1947, 1950; Joslyn A. Mus., 1948; BMFA, 1949; Bradley Univ., 1951; LC, 1952. *Work*: MMA; MModA; LC; CAM; Springfield A. Mus.; Joslyn A. Mus.; PMA; U.S. War Dept.; AIC; Univ. Michigan; Univ. Wisconsin; Mills Col.; Munson-Williams-Proctor Inst.; Washington Univ.; Beloit Col.; BM; FMA; Toledo Mus. A.; Smithsonian Inst.; N.Y.

Pub. Lib.; Bibliotheque Nationale, Paris; Victoria & Albert Mus., London; British Mus., London; Nat. Mus., Stockholm; Nat. Mus., Jerusalem; murals, Carpenter Lib.; St. Michael, St. George Episcopal Church, Trinity Church, Herzog Sch., all St. Louis; St. Mary's Church, Helena, Ark. *Exhibited*: nationally and internationally; since 1953: Vienna, Austria; Sao Paulo, Brazil; Univ. Puerto Rico; St. Thomas, Virgin Islands; Middle East. *Position*: Assoc. Prof. Drawing, Washington Univ. Sch. FA, St. Louis, Mo., 1945- .

QUEST, DOROTHY (JOHNSON) (Mrs. Charles F.)— Portrait Painter, E., L.
12331 Harflo Lane, Town and Country, St. Louis 22, Mo.

B. St. Louis, Mo., Feb. 28, 1909. *Studied*: Washington Univ. Sch. FA; Columbia Univ., and in Europe. *Member*: St. Louis A. Gld. *Work*: Collaborated with Charles F. Quest in painting murals, Carpenter Lib., St. Michael, St. George Episcopal Church, Trinity Church, Herzog Sch., all St. Louis; St. Mary's Church, Helena, Ark. Many portrait commissions, 1931-55. *Exhibited*: CAM, 1932, 1934, 1938-1940; St. Louis A. Gld., 1935, 1938, 1940; 7 one-man: 1933, 1939, 1940, 1943, 1945, 1951, 1955. Lectures: Still Life Painting; Portraiture. *Positions*: A. Instr., Community Sch., Clayton, Mo., 1936-38; Sacred Heart Acad., St. Louis, 1939-41; Maryville Col., St. Louis, 1944-45. Painting portraits in studio, 1945- .

QUILLIN, ELLEN S. (Mrs.)—Museum Director
Witte Memorial Museum, Brackenridge Park, San Antonio, Tex.*

QUINCY, EDMUND—Painter
4 Charles River Square, Boston 14, Mass.

B. Biarritz, France, May 15, 1903. *Studied*: Harvard Col.; and with Albert Herter, Georges Degorce, George Noyes. *Member*: Newport AA. *Awards*: prizes, PAFA, 1937; Syracuse AA, 1940. *Work*: Musee de Grenoble, France; Univ. Arizona; PAFA. *Exhibited*: Salon d'Automne, 1928, 1929, 1935, 1936, 1951-1953; Salon des Tuileries, 1938; PAFA, 1932, 1937, 1943, 1945; CGA, 1937, 1945; AIC, 1937, 1943; Carnegie Inst., 1941-1945; WMA, 1936; Newport AA, 1941-1945; Ogunquit A. Center, 1941; N.Y. State Exh., 1941; Ars Sacra, Naples, 1951; Bordighera, 1952; Venice, 1950; Turin, 1951; Galerie Lucy Krogh, Paris, 1955; Galerie Marcel Bernheim, Paris, 1955; one-man: Boston Atheneum, 1955; Galeria La Bussola, Turin, 1951; Galerie Marseille, Paris, 1953; Galerie de l'Institut, Paris, 1955.*

QUINN, NOEL—Painter, Des., E., I., Gr.
3946 San Rafael Ave., Los Angeles 65, Cal.

B. Pawtucket, R.I., Des. 25, 1915. *Studied*: R.I.Sch. Des.; N.Y. Sch. F. & App. A.; Ecole des Beaux-Arts, Paris, France. *Member*: Cal. WC Soc.; Nat. Soc. A. Dir.; Intl. Inst. A. & Lets.; AWS; SI; Soc. Motion Picture Illustrators. *Awards*: prizes, Parsons F., R.I. Sch. Des., 1936; Cal. State Fair, 1949, 1954; deYoung Mem. Mus., 1949; Cal. WC Soc., 1951; Hallmark, 1952; AWS, 1954; Los A. Mus. A., 1954, 1957; Santa Cruz, 1955; Wash. WC Cl., 1956; Butler Inst. Am. A., 1958; Laguna Beach AA, 1958. *Work*: Cal. State Agricultural Soc.; Cole Coll.; Hollywood Turf Cl.; Air Force Acad., Colorado; Butler Inst. Am. A., and in numerous private colls. in U.S. and abroad. *Exhibited*: nationally and internationally. *Position*: Instr., Watercolor Painting, Los Angeles County AI, Los Angeles, Cal.

QUINN, ROBERT HAYES— Illustrator, Gr., W., Comm. A.
R.F.D. 2, Pig St., Mechanicville, N.Y.

B. Waterford, N.Y., Nov. 1, 1902. *Studied*: Syracuse Univ.; PIASch. *Exhibited*: Cooperstown, N.Y., 1953, 1954; Schenectady Mus. A., 1953; Kennedy Gal., N.Y., 1953. Contributor to Yankee; Trails Magazine; Rural New Yorker; New England Homestead; Comm. A. for various publications. Cover A., Trails magazine, 1933- . *Position*: Member Young Adult Council, YMCA; Bd. Dir., Sec., Mechanicville YMCA; Instr., Adult Edu. Classes, Mechanicville H.S.

QUINTANILLA, LUIS—Painter, Gr., L.
26 West 8th St., New York 11, N.Y.

B. Santander, Spain, June 13, 1895. *Studied*: in Spain. *Work*: Mus. Mod. A., Madrid; Mus. Mod. A., Barcelona; Musee d'Art Decoratif, Paris; MModA; MMA; AIC; Princeton Univ.; BM; Univ. Kansas City, Mo.; Spanish Consulate, Hendaye, France. *Exhibited*: WFNY 1939; one-man exh.: Pierre Matisse Gal., 1934; MModA, 1938; All. A. Am., 1939; New Sch. Social Research, 1940; Knoedler Gal., 1944; de Young Mem. Mus., 1944. I., "All the Brave," 1939; "Franco's Black Spain," 1945; "Gulliver's Travels," 1947; "Three Exemplary Novels," 1950, and other books.*

QUIRK, FRANCIS J.—Painter, E., L., Cr.
Peterspen, Macadam Rd., Rte. 23, Bethlehem, Pa.; s. Peterspen North, Box 1685, Ocean Park, Me.

B. Pawtucket, R.I., June 3, 1907. *Studied*: R.I.Sch. Des.; Univ. Pennsylvania, and in Provincetown, Mass.; Woodstock, N.Y., and in Europe. *Member*: Phila. A. All.; Phila. WC Cl.; Bethlehem Palette Cl.; Lehigh A. All. *Awards*: prizes, R.I.Sch. Des.; Providence A. Cl.; Kinney Shores; Ocean Park; Phila. WC Cl.; Woodmere A. Gal. *Exhibited*: PAFA; CGA; Buffalo, N.Y.; Portland, Me.; Providence, Newport, R.I.; Bethlehem Palette Cl.; Lehigh A. All.; Exchange Cl. *Positions*: Hd. A. Dept., Montgomery Sch., 1930-35, 1938-45; Instr., A. Ogontz Jr. Col., Ogontz Sch., Pa., 1935-46, Hd. Dept. A., Ogontz, 1946-50; Assoc. Prof., Hd. Dept. FA, Lehigh Univ., Bethlehem, Pa., 1950- , Prof., 1953- ; Cur. & Dir., Lehigh Univ. Permanent A. Coll., and A. Gal., 1950- . Conducts biweekly radio program; Memb., Comm. on Architecture for public bldgs., Bethlehem, Pa.

QUIRT, WALTER—Painter, E.
University of Minnesota, Minneapolis, Minn.

B. Iron River, Mich., Nov. 24, 1902. *Work*: MModA.; Walker A. Center; WMAA; Newark Mus.; Wadsworth Atheneum; Univ. Minnesota; Univ. Iowa. *Exhibited*: one-man: New York, N.Y. *Position*: Assoc. Prof., Dept., A., Univ. Minnesota, Minneapolis, Minn.

QUISTGAARD, HAROLD IVAR de REHLING—Painter
General Delivery, Miami, Fla.

B. New York, N.Y., Aug. 13, 1914. *Studied*: Ecole de l'Etat, Acad. Colorossi, Grande Chaumiere, Paris, France; NAD; Leonardo da Vinci A. Sch., N.Y.; Colorado Springs FA Center, with Boardman Robinson; ASL; New Orleans A. Acad. *Member*: Pirate's Alley A. Group, Chartres St. AA, Assoc. A. Gal., Delgado Mus. AI, all in New Orleans, La. *Awards*: prizes, Louisiana State Fair, 1952; Pirate's Alley Exh., 1953. *Work*: Bourbon House; Assoc. A. Studio, both New Orleans; murals, Officer's Cl., Christmas Island; Newport, L.I., N.Y. and work in private colls. *Exhibited*: Ecole de l'Etat, Paris, 1931; Ecole des Arts Decoratifs, Paris, 1932; Savannah AI, 1936; U.S. Nat. Exh., 1937; Schofield Barracks, Oahu, Hawaii, 1940; Christmas Island, 1943; ASL, 1945; Assoc. A., New Orleans, 1951; Louisiana State Fair, 1952; Pirate's Alley, New Orleans, 1953; Delgado Mus. A., 1954.*

QUISTGAARD, JOHANN WALDEMAR de REHLING— Painter
70 West 55th St., New York 19, N.Y.

B. Orsholtgaard, Denmark, Feb. 9, 1877. *Studied*: in Denmark. *Member*: Chicago A. Cl.; N.Y. Genealogical & Biographical Soc.; AEA; AFA. *Awards*: Knighthood of Danneborg, Denmark, 1919; Chevalier French Legion of Honor, 1926; Distinguished award, A. Dir. Cl., 1944. *Work*: Mus. of the Kings of Denmark, Copenhagen; Christiansborg Castle and King's private Coll. at Amalienborg Castle, Denmark; St. John's Cathedral, Denver; Washington Univ., St. Louis; N.Y. Genealogical & Biographical Soc., N.Y.; U.S. Dept. Agriculture and Treasury; Brookings Fnd., Wash., D.C.; many portraits of prominent persons. *Exhibited*: St. Louis World Fair, 1904; Arthur Tooth & Son Gal., N.Y., 1906; Guildhall A. Gal., London, 1907; French Miniature Soc., 1907, Royal Acad., London, 1908; Walker A. Gal., Liverpool, 1908, 1924; Salon des Artistes Francais, 1907-1909, 1924-1926; Royal Acad., Copenhagen, 1910; ASMP, 1912; Int. Exh. Miniatures, Ghent, Belgium, 1913; Reinhardt Gal., 1914; John Levy Gal., 1921; Durand-Ruel, Paris, 1925; Durand-Ruel, N.Y., 1927; Union League, N.Y., 1929; Decorator's A.

Gal., 1935-1937; Woman's Cl., Charlotte, N.C., 1935;
Colorado Springs FA Center, 1938; Denver A. Mus., 1938;
Roullier Gal., Chicago, 1942; Woman's Cl., Rockford,
Ill., 1942, Chicago A. Cl., 1943-1946; Arthur Newton Gal.,
N.Y., 1944; Flint, Mich., 1947; Newcomb-Macklin Gal.,
N.Y., 1949.*

RABUT, PAUL—*Illustrator, Des., P.*

110 West 54th St., New York, N.Y.; h. Easton Rd.,
Westport, Conn.

B. New York, N.Y., Apr. 6, 1914. *Studied*: Col. City
of N.Y.; NAD; ASL, and with Jules Gottlieb, Harvey
Dunn, Lewis Daniel. *Member*: SI; Westport A. *Awards*:
medal, NAD, 1932; A. Dir. Cl., 1942, 1943, 1946, 1951.
Work: U.S. Army Medical Mus., Wash., D.C. *Exhibited*:
AIC, 1943; MMA, 1942; PAFA, 1941; A. Dir. Cl., 1942-
1953; SI, 1941-1956; NAD, 1950; State Dept. traveling
exhibition to Europe and South America, of adv. art,
1952-1953. Lectures on Illustration: "An Artist Looks at
Photography"; "Primitive Arts of Africa, Northwest Coast
and South Seas." Illus. for leading national magazines.
Author, I., "Paul Rabut Visits the Tall Timber," True
Magazine, 1949, "My Life as a Head Hunter," 1953,
Argosy magazine.*

RACHOTES, MATENE (Mrs. Jo Cain)— *Painter, T., Lith.*

University of Rhode Island; h. 1315 Kingstown Rd.,
Kingston, R.I.

B. Boston, Mass., June 13, 1905. *Studied*: Mass. Normal
A. Sch.; BMFA Sch.; Child Walker Sch. FA; Harvard
Univ. *Member*: Contemporary A. Group; South County
A. *Awards*: Harvard Univ. F.; Tiffany Fnd. F. *Exhibited*:
PMA; CGA; AIC; Providence Mus. A.; South County AA.
Position: Instr. A., Mary Wheeler Sch., Providence,
R.I. & Asst. Prof. A., Co-Dir., Summer Art Workshop,
Univ. Rhode Island, Kingston, R.I., at present.

RACKLEY, MILDRED (Mrs. Mildred Rackley Simon)— *Serigrapher, P., C.*

4141 Los Arabis Rd., Lafayette, Cal.

B. Carlsbad, N.M., Oct. 13, 1906. *Studied*: Univ. Texas;
New Mexico Normal Univ., A.B.; Kunstgewerbe Schule,
Hamburg, Germany, and with Walter Ufer, George
Grosz. *Member*: Nat. Ser. Soc. *Awards*: prizes, Diablo A.
Festival, 1958; Concord, Cal., 1958. *Work*: MMA; PMA;
Springfield A. Mus.; Princeton Pr. Cl. *Exhibited*: Spring-
field A. Lg., 1944-1946, 1948; Denver A. Mus.; Newport
AA, 1945, 1946, 1948; Laguna Beach AA, 1946; SAM;
Mint Mus. A., 1946; MMoGA, 1940; Nat. Ser. Soc., 1948-
1952; Oakland A. Gal.; Gump's, San F.; AIC; Mus. New
Mexico; Audubon A., 1948; Phila. Pr. Cl., 1948; LC,
1948; Carnegie Inst., 1948; Northwest Pr. M., 1949.
Position: Vice-Pres., Valley A. Center, 1957-58, Instr.,
Mosaic, Silk Screen, Valley A. Center, Lafayette, Cal.,
1956-1958.

RACZ, ANDRE—*Painter, Gr., E., W., L.*

501 West 121st St., New York 27, N.Y.

B. Cluj, Rumania, Nov. 21, 1916. *Studied*: Univ. Buchar-
est. *Awards*: Guggenheim F., 1956; Fulbright Research F.,
Univ. Chile, 1957. *Member*: SAGA; AAUP. *Work*:
MMoGA; BM; N.Y. Pub. Lib.; LC; NGA; Rosenwald
Coll.; State Dept., Wash., D.C.; Hartford Catholic Lib.;
Univ. Minnesota; Univ. St. Louis; Univ. Tennessee; Mus.
of Cordoba, Argentina; SFMA; Tulsa, Okla.; Bibliotheque
Nationale, Paris; Mus. Salzburg; Univ. Chile; Columbia
Univ.; Smith Col.; Smithsonian Inst. *Exhibited*: MMoGA,
1944-1946, 1948, 1949, 1951; WMAA; BM; N.Y. Pub.
Lib.; LC; Carnegie Inst.; SAM; SFMA; and in London,
Paris, Rome, Zurich, Hawaii, Warsaw, Barcelona, Oslo,
Capetown, and others; one-man: New York, N.Y., 1942-
1944, 1946, 1948, 1949, 1951; Univ. Tennessee, 1948;
Univ. Iowa, 1948; Green Lake, Wis., 1951; AFA travel-
ing exh. (one-man) 1948-1951; Rio de Janeiro, 1946;
Buenos Aires, 1949; Santiago de Chile, 1947-1950, 1952;
one-man: New York, N.Y., 1942-1944, 1946, 1948, 1949,
1951, 1953, 1956, 1957; retrospective, N.Y. Pub. Lib., 1955;
Museo de Bellas Artes, Santiago, Vina del Mar, Chile,
1957; Valparaiso, 1957; Bordighera, Italy, 1957; Mexico
City, 1958; Religious Art, Salzburg, 1958. Author, I.,
books of engravings, "The Flowering Rock," 1943; "The
Battle of the Starfish," 1944; "The Reign of Claws," 1945;
"The XII Prophets," 1947; "Via Crucis," 1948; "Mother

and Child," 1949; "Voz de Luna," 1952; "Sal de Dunas,"
1953; "Canciones Negras," 1953; "Salmos y Piedras,"
1955. I., "Poemas de las Madres," 1950. *Position*: Instr.,
Sch. Painting & Sculpture, Columbia Univ.,New York,
N.Y., 1951-55, Asst. Prof., 1956- .

RADULOVIC, SAVO—*Painter, C., Gr., T., L.*

25 West 88th St., New York 24, N.Y.

B. Yugoslavia, Jan. 27, 1911. *Studied*: St. Louis Sch. FA,
Washington Univ.; FMA, Harvard Univ.; Academie de
Belle Arte, Rome, Italy. *Awards*: Carnegie F. to Fogg
Mus. A., Harvard Univ., 1937; purchase prize, CAM, 1941;
Fulbright F., Rome, Italy, 1949-50. *Work*: CAM; Univ.
Arizona; Hist. Section, War Dept., Pentagon, Wash., D.C.;
in private colls. U.S.A. and abroad. *Exhibited*: NAD;
WMAA; CAM; Wildenstein Gal., N.Y.; PMA; Washing-
ton Irving Gal., N.Y.; Park Ave. Gal., Mt. Kisco, N.Y.,
and in museums throughout U.S.; Rome, Italy.

RAFFEL ALVIN R.—*Painter, T.*

6720 Mad River Rd., Dayton 49, Ohio

B. Dayton, Ohio, Dec. 25, 1905. *Studied*: Chicago Acad.
FA; AIC. *Member*: Dayton Soc. P. & S. *Work*: Dayton
AI. *Exhibited*: Pepsi-Cola, 1945; Carnegie Inst., 1946,
1947, 1948; Dayton AI, 1933, 1935-1943; 1945; Magnificent
Mile Exh., Chicago, 1955; Provincetown A. Festival, 1958.
Position: Instr., Dayton AI, Dayton, Ohio.

RAGAN, LESLIE—*Painter, I.*

952 Sand Dunes Road, Pebble Beach, Cal.

B. Woodbine, Iowa, Nov. 29, 1897. *Studied*: Cumming
Sch. A.; AIC; Chicago Acad. FA. *Member*: A.Gld.; Car-
mel AA; SC; A. Fellowship. *Awards*: certificate of merit,
Phila. A. All., 1940; AIC, 1940. *Exhibited*: AIC; NAD;
All.A.Am.; Boston AC; SC; SI; Carmel AA.

RAHJA, VIRGINIA HELGA— *Educator, P., S., C., Gal., Dir.*

111 East 6th St.; h. 894 St. Clair Ave., St. Paul,
Minn.

B. Aurora, Minn., Apr. 21, 1921. *Studied*: Hamline Univ.,
B.A., and grad. work with Lowell Bobleter. *Member*:
Minnesota Edu. Assn. *Awards*: various awards in local
and national exhs. *Work*: paintings and ceramics in private colls. *Exhibited*: WAC; Univ. Minnesota; Minneapolis Inst. A.; St. Paul Gallery; Minnesota State Fair;
Hamline Univ., all annually since 1941. One-man exhs.
locally. *Positions*: Asst. Prof. A., 1941-48, Prof. A.,
1948- , Hamline University, St. Paul, Minn.; Dir., Hamline Univ. Galleries, 1941-48; Asst. Supt., Minn. State
Fair, 1942-48; Dir., Assoc. Arts Gal. and Dir. FA, Sch.
of the Assoc. Arts, 1948- .

RAHMING, NORRIS—*Painter, E., Et., L.*

Box 66, Gambier, Ohio

B. New York, N.Y., May 1, 1886. *Studied*: NAD; ASL;
N.Y.Sch.A.; & with Emil Carlsen, William Chase, Robert
Henri. *Member*: CAA; Cleveland SA; Columbus A. Lg.
Awards: prize, CMA, 1927. *Work*: CMA; Newark Mus.;
City of Cleveland Coll.; Cleveland YMCA; Senate Office
Bldg., Wash., D.C.; Am. Embassy, Paris, France; murals,
USPO, Gambier, Ohio; Rocky River (Ohio) Pub. Lib.
Exhibited: CGA; PAFA; CAM; Great Lakes Exh., 1937;
CMA, 1925-1937; Columbus A. Lg., 1938, 1939. *Position*:
Dir., Dept. A., Kenyon Col., Gambier, Ohio, 1936-1952
(retired); Study and Research, Mexico and the Southwest,
1953- .*

RAINE, EARL THOMAS—*Painter*

Route 3, Box 169, Thiensville, Wis.

B. Penns Grove, N.J., Aug. 9, 1911. *Studied*: Marquette
Univ.; Univ. Arizona; Layton Sch. A. *Member*: Wis. P. &
S. *Work*: Layton A. Gal. *Exhibited*: Grand Rapids A.
Gal., 1940; PAFA, 1940, 1941, 1946; AIC, 1936, 1938-
1940, 1948, 1952; Denver A. Mus., 1936-1938, 1949; CM,
1940, 1941; Wis. P. & S., 1935-1942, 1946, 1949-1953,
1957; Layton A. Gal., 1936, 1938, 1940, 1946 (one-man),
1949; Univ. Wisconsin, 1935-1940; Milwaukee AI, 1949;
Minn. Centennial, 1949; Wisconsin Centennial, 1948;
Gimbel's Wis. Centennial, 1948; Ozaukee County Exh.,
1948-1958. *Position*: Chm., Ozaukee County A. Com.,
1949-56, 1958.

RAINEY, FROELICH—Museum Director, E., W., L.
University of Pennsylvania Museum, 33rd & Spruce Sts., Philadelphia, Pa.; h. Valley Forge, Pa.

B. Black River Falls, Wis., June 18, 1907. Contributor to American Antiquity; American Anthropologist; Applied Anthropology. *Positions*: Prof. Anthropology, 1935-42; Consultant, State Dept., 1948-52; Dir., Univ. Pennsylvania Museum, Philadelphia, Pa., 1948- .

RAINEY, ROBERT E. L. (ren)—Painter, Ser., Des., T.
3550 Orion Rd., North Canton, Ohio

B. Jackson, Miss., Dec. 25, 1914. *Studied*: Univ. Chicago; AIC, M.F.A.; & with Francis Chapin, Boris Anisfeld. *Member*: Am. Soc. for Aesthetics. *Awards*: prizes, Northwest Pr.M., 1945; Canton AI, 1946. *Work*: SAM. *Exhibited*: AIC, 1938, 1940, 1942, 1944, 1946; Providence AC, 1945; Massillon Mus., 1945; Canton AI, 1946 (oneman). *Position*: Dir., Little A. Gal. of the North Canton Lib., North Canton, Ohio.

RAKEMAN, CARL—Painter, I.
8813 Kensington Parkway, Chevy Chase, Md.

B. Washington, D.C., Apr. 27, 1878. *Studied*: in Europe. *Awards*: med., Sesqui-Centennial Exp., Phila., 1926. *Work*: U.S. Capitol Bldg., Wash., D.C.; Hayes Mem., Fremont, Ohio; U.S. Dept. Commerce; Kenyon Col., Gambier, Ohio; U.S. Soldiers Home, Tenn.; State House, Columbus, Ohio; murals, U.S. Court House, Dallas, Tex. *Exhibited*: CGA; Soc. Wash. A.; GGE, 1939. Contributor to Highways of History.

RALSTON, J(AMES) K(ENNETH)—Painter, I.
2102 Grand Ave., Billings, Mont.

B. Choteau, Mont., Mar. 31, 1896. *Studied*: AIC. *Work*: murals, Wonderland Mus., Hart-Albin Co., Northern Hotel, Covert Ins. Co., MacIntyre Motors, Lazy KT Motel, all in Billings, Mont.; Waite Ins. Co., Bozeman; Empire Savings & Loan Co., Livingston; Airport Terminal, Billings; Noble Hotel, Billings (painting); paintings in private colls. *Exhibited*: Western Gal., and Montana State Hist. Mus., Helena, Mont., 1954-1955. Illus., "Good Men and Salty Cusses."

RAMBO, JAMES I.—Museum Curator
California Palace of the Legion of Honor, San Francisco, Cal.*

RAMSDELL, M. LOUISE (LEE)—Painter
1 Main St., Housatonic, Mass.

B. Housatonic, Mass. *Studied*: Univ. California; Smith Col., B.A.; ASL; Grand Central Sch. A.; in Vienna; and with Wayman Adams, George Luks, Jerry Farnsworth, and others. *Member*: All. A. Am.; NAWA; Pen & Brush Cl.; NAC; Berkshire AA. *Awards*: prizes, St. Petersburg A. Cl., 1936, 1937; Pen & Brush Cl., 1951, 1954; Albany Inst. Hist. & A., 1955; Academic A., Springfield, 1954. *Exhibited*: Grand Central Sch. A., 1930; Ringling Sch. A., 1931; St. Petersburg A. Cl., 1936, 1937; Berkshire Mus. A., 1942 (one-man); Pen & Brush Cl., 1941, 1943, 1944 (one-man), 1951, 1954; New Jersey P. & S., 1948; Albany Inst. Hist. & A., 1955; Academic A., 1954; NAD; NAWA; All. A. Am.; Portraits, Inc.; NAC; Pittsfield A. Lg., and others. *Position*: Bd. Dir., Berkshire AA, 1953- .

RAND, PAUL—Designer, P., W., I., T., Cr.
Goodhill Rd., R.F.D. 2, Westport, Conn.

B. New York, N.Y., Aug. 15, 1914. *Studied*: PIASch.; Parsons Sch. Des.; ASL. *Member*: F., Royal Soc. A., London; A. Dir. Cl.; Swedish Soc. Indst. Des.; AIGA. *Awards*: prizes, AIGA, 1938; medal, A. Dir. Cl., 1945, 1952, 1953; included in selection "50 Books of the Year"; Sch. A. Lg., medals and scholarship; Direct Mail Advertising award; Soc. Typographic A.; One of the 10 Best Houses of 1953, MModA and Merchandise Mart; Best Fabric, "Good Design" Exh., 1954; 1 of 10 Best A. Dir., A. Dir. Cl. poll. *Work*: N.Y. Pub. Lib.; MModA. *Exhibited*: AIGA, 1938, 1942; A. Dir. Cl., 1936-1955; Musee de l'Art Moderna, Paris, 1955; Louvre Mus., Paris, 1955. Author, I., "Thoughts on Design"; "Typography in the United States"; "Black in the Visual Arts"; "The Trademark as an Illustrative Device"; "The Poster"; Illus.,

"I Know a Lot of Things," children's book, 1956; "Sparkle and Spin." *Positions*: A. Dir., Esquire magazine (N.Y. Office), 1937-41; Instr., Pratt Inst., Brooklyn, N.Y., 1946; CUASch., New York, N.Y., 1942; N.Y. Des. Laboratory, 1941; Yale Univ., 1956; Adv. Bd., Cambridge Sch. Des. Book des. for leading publishers.

RANDALL BYRON—Painter, Eng., T.
67 Water St., San Francisco 11, Cal.

B. Tacoma, Wash., Oct. 23, 1918. *Member*: San F. A. Gld.; San F. AA; Council All. A. Los A.; AEA; Marin County Soc. A. *Work*: SFMA; PMG; mural, YM-WHA, Montreal, Canada. *Exhibited*: BMA, 1939; SFMA, 1946, 1950, 1951; John Herron AI, 1946; AIC, 1949; London, England, 1952; Los A., Cal., 1948; Toronto, Canada, 1948; one-man: Univ. Oregon, 1942; Los A. City Col., 1942; ACG Gal., Los A., 1945; Raymond & Raymond, San F., 1943, 1945; Little Gal., Los A., 1944; SAM, 1941; Whyte Gal., 1939; Three Arts Gal., Poughkeepsie, N.Y., 1956; one-man sponsored by City of Montreal, 1956.

RANDALL, ELEANOR ELIZABETH—Painter, E.
175 Dartmouth St., Boston 16, Mass.

B. Holyoke, Mass. *Studied*: Wheaton Col., A.B.; BMFA Sch.; Boston Univ., M.A. *Member*: CAA; Rockport AA; North Shore AA. *Position*: Asst. Prof. A., Wheaton Col., Norton, Mass., 1926-42; Senior Instr., Div. Edu., BMFA, Boston, Mass., at present.

RANDALL, RUTH HUNIE (Mrs.)—Educator, C., W.
College of Fine Arts, Syracuse University, Syracuse 10, N.Y.; h. 104 Hillcrest Rd., Syracuse 3, N.Y.

B. Dayton, Ohio, Sept. 30, 1896. *Studied*: Cleveland Sch. A.; Syracuse Univ., B.F.A., M.F.A.; in Vienna; & with Ruth Reeves; one year's research on Ceramics, in the Orient, 1957. *Member*: Syracuse Ceramic Gld.; Lg. Am. Pen Women. *Awards*: prizes, Nat. Ceramic Exh., Assoc. A. Syracuse, 1945; Syracuse Mus. FA, 1939. *Work*: IBM Coll.; Syracuse Mus. FA; San Antonio Mus. A.; Butler AI. *Exhibited*: Syracuse Mus. FA, 1932-1942; Cranbrook Acad. A., 1946; WFNY 1939; GGE, 1939; Paris Salon, 1937; MMA; Phila. A. All., 1936, 1942-1945; Finger Lakes Exh., Rochester, Utica, N.Y., Youngstown, Ohio, Kansas City, Mo.; Western Texas; ceramic exh., Scandinavian countries. Contributor to Craft Horizons & Design magazines. Author: "Ceramic Sculpture." Lectures: Ceramic Sculpture. *Position*: Prof., Syracuse Univ., Syracuse, N.Y., at present.

RANDALL, THEODORE A.—Craftsman, E., S.
State University of New York, College of Ceramics at Alfred University, Alfred, N.Y.

B. Indianapolis, Ind., Oct. 18, 1914. *Studied*: Yale Univ., B.F.A.; State Univ. of N.Y. Col. of Ceramics, M.F.A. *Member*: Am. Ceramic Soc.; Acad. Intl. Ceramics; CAA. *Awards*: prizes, Syracuse Mus. FA; Wichita; Finger Lakes, N.Y.; Albright A. Gal.; Pomona, Cal.; Smithsonian Inst.; York State Craftsmen. *Work*: pottery, Syracuse Mus. FA; Wichita; Pomona. S., St. Stephens Church, Albany, N.Y. Contributor to Journal and Bulletin of the Am. Ceramic Soc.; Ceramic Age; Ceramic Industry; Ceramics Monthly. Lectures: Motives and Meaning in Art; Ceramics Today, etc. *Position*: Acting Chm., Dept. Des., Prof., Des., Pottery, Sculpture, College of Ceramics, Alfred Univ., Alfred, N.Y.

RANDOLPH, GLADYS CONRAD (Mrs. Paul H.)— Painter, W.
630 Northeast 55th St., Miami 37, Fla.

B. Whitestone, L.I., N.Y. *Studied*: N.Y.Sch. F. & App. A.; Terry AI; Portland (Ore.) A. Mus.; Univ. Pennsylvania; N.Y. Univ., and with Hobson Pittman, Revington Arthur. *Member*: Fla. Fed. A.; Miami WC Soc.; AEA; Fla. A. Group; Miami AA; Miami A. Lg. (Exec. Chm.); Blue Dome Fellowship; Nat. Lg. Am. Pen Women (A. Chm.). *Awards*: prizes, Miami A. Lg.; Blue Dome; Fla. Fed. A.; AAPL; Terry AI; Nat. Lg. Am. Pen Women. *Exhibited*: Terry AI, 1952; Fla. Southern Col., 1952; Ringling Mus. A.; Tampa State Fair; Lg. Am. Pen Women, 1950; Norton Gal. A., 1952; Soc. Four A., 1951; Miami A. Lg.; Blue Dome; AAPL; Poinciana Festival; Miami Women's Cl., and other local and regional exhibitions; group traveling exhs. of Fla. Fed. A.; Fla. A.

Group; Miami AA.; one-man: Research Center, Maitland, Fla. (2); Miami Beach A. Center. Also exh. in
Havana, Cuba. Contributor of articles to The Minerolo-
gist, Portland Oregonian, Oregon Journal, American Boy,
and other publications and newspapers.

RANDOLPH, JOHN W.—*Educator, P., Lith.*
   Art Department, Phillips University; h. 2110 East
Broadway, Enid, Okla.
   B. Ada, Okla., July 3, 1920. *Studied*: Univ. Oklahoma,
B.F.A., M.F.A. *Position*: Hd., A. Dept., Phillips Univ.,
Enid, Okla.

RANKIN, MARY KIRK (Mrs. W. H.)—*Painter*
   2510 Cumberland Rd., San Marino 9, Cal.
   B. El Paso, Tex., Sept. 3, 1897. *Studied*: Chouinard AI,
and with Loren Barton, James Couper Wright. *Member*:
Women Painters of the West; Pasadena Soc. A.; Laguna
Beach AA; Nat. Soc. A. & Let.; A. of the Southwest;
Nat. Lg. Am. Pen Women. *Awards*: prizes, Hollywood
Lib.; Women Painters of the West, 1952. *Exhibited*:
Pasadena AI, 1949-1952; Greek Theatre, Los A., 1948-
1951; Laguna Beach AA, 1947-1951; Ebell Cl., Los A.,
1948-1951, and others.*

RANNELLS, EDWARD WARDER—*Writer, E., L., P.*
   1251 Eldermere Rd., Lexington, Ky.
   B. Osceola, Mo., Nov. 12, 1892. *Studied*: Ohio State
Univ., A.B.; FMA, Harvard Univ.; Univ. Chicago, M.A.
Member: AFA; CAA; Nat. Edu. Assn.; Mid-Western
Col. A. Conference. *Exhibited*: Columbus, Ohio; Louis-
ville, Lexington, Ky. Contributor to: College Art Journal,
Design, School Review, Gazette des Beaux-Arts, Journal
of Aesthetics, with articles on art education & art criti-
cism. *Position*: Assoc. Dean, AIC, 1926-29; Prof., Hd.
Dept. A., Univ. Kentucky, Lexington, Ky., 1929-51, Prof.
A., 1951- .*

RANNELLS, WILL—*Illustrator*
   4345 Central College Road, Westerville, Ohio; h. 216
East Lane Ave., Columbus 1, Ohio
   B. Caldwell, Ohio, July 21, 1892. *Studied*: Cincinnati A.
Acad. *Exhibited*: Phila. WC Cl.; AWCS. I., "Dog Stars,"
1916; "Waif, the Story of Spe," 1937; "Animals Baby
Knows," 1938; "Farmyard Play Book," 1940; "Jack, Jock
and Funny," 1938; "Timmy," 1941; Author, I., "Animal
Picture Story Book," 1938; I., "Just a Mutt," 1947.
Illus. for Life, Judge, McCall's, Country Gentleman mag-
azines. *Position*: Assoc. Prof. FA, Ohio State Univ.,
Columbus, Ohio.

RANNEY, GLEN ALLISON—*Painter, T.*
   3919 Vincent Ave., South, Minneapolis 10, Minn.
   B. Hustler, Wis., Sept. 4, 1896. *Studied*: Minneapolis Sch.
A.; ASL; & with Richard Lahey, Cameron Booth, George
Luks. *Awards*: prizes, Minn. State Fair, 1936, 1939, 1943,
1944, 1946, 1949; Minneapolis Inst. A., 1935, 1937, 1943;
Kansas City AI, 1938; Minneapolis Women's Cl., 1936-
1957. *Work*: Minneapolis Inst. A.; Cape May (N.J.)
Court House; Univ. Minnesota; U.S. Marine Hospital,
Carville, La. *Exhibited*: CM, 1937, 1938; PAFA, 1937,
1938, 1941; CGA, 1939; AIC, 1925, 1937, 1938; Kansas
City AI, 1938-1940; Davenport, Iowa, 1940; Minneapolis
Inst. A., 1923, 1936-1946; Minn. State Fair, 1923, 1936-
1944; Minneapolis Women's Cl., 1935-1957; St. Paul A.
Gal., 1940-1946; No. 10 Gal., N.Y., 1941, 1942 (one-
man); Kilbride-Bradley Gal., Minneapolis, 1957 (one-man).

RANNIT, ALEKSIS—*Educator, Hist., Cr., W.*
   New York Public Library, 5th Ave. at 42nd St.,
New York, N.Y.; h. 87-25 169th St., Jamaica 32, N.Y.
   B. Kallaste, Estonia, Oct. 14, 1914. *Studied*: Univ. Tartu,
Estonia, Diploma in A. Hist.; Columbia Univ., M.S.
Member: Intl. Assn. A. Critics; Intl. Congresses A. Hist.;
Intl. Pen Clubs, London (Exec. Com.); Assn. German A.
Hist.; Assn. German Writers; Lithuanian Writers' Assn.;
Estonian Literary Soc. (Pres.) *Awards*: Olsen Fnd. F.,
for research and writing on Coptic art and symbolism,
1955. Author: monographs, "Eduard Wiiralt," 1943, 1946
(2); "V. K. Jonynas," 1947; "M. K. Ciurlionis," 1949
(UNESCO publ.). Contributor to Brockhaus Encyclo-
paedia; Schweizer Lexicon; Benezit; Das Kunstwerk (American Corr.); La Biennale di Venezia; Les Arts Plastique

and others. *Position*: Chief Cur. Prints and Rare Books,
Lithuanian Nat. Lib., Kaunas, Lithuania, 1941-44; Prof.
A. Hist., Ecole Superieure des Arts et Metiers, Freiburg,
Germany, 1946-50; Scientific Sec., Div. FA, French High
Comm. in Germany, 1950-53; A. Reference Libn. & Cata-
loger of Prints, Art & Arch. Div., New York Public
Library at present.

RANSON, NANCY SUSSMAN (Mrs.)—*Painter, Ser.*
   1299 Ocean Ave., Brooklyn 30, N.Y.
   B. New York, N.Y., Sept. 13, 1905. *Studied*: PIASch.;
ASL, and with Laurent, Charlot, Brackman, Brook.
Member: NAWA; Brooklyn Soc. A.; AEA; Nat. Ser. Soc.;
Am. Color Pr. Soc.; N.Y. Soc. Women A.; Audubon A.;
Nat. Soc. Painters in Casein. *Awards*: prizes, Critic's
Choice Exh., 1947; NAWA, 1952, 1953, 1958, medal,
1956; Nat. Ser. Soc., 1953; Grumbacher award in Casein,
1954; Print chosen for Am. Color Pr. Soc. presentation,
1955, prize, 1955; Brooklyn Soc. A., 1955; Audubon A.,
1958. *Work*: Brandeis Univ.; Mexican Govt. Tourist Comm.;
Key West A. & Hist. Soc.; Reading Pub. Mus.; Free Lib.,
Phila.; Mus. of the City of N.Y.; Nat. A. Gal., Sydney,
Australia. *Exhibited*: AWS, 1940, 1942, 1943, 1951;
NAWA, 1943-1958; Brooklyn Soc. A., 1941-1958; A. for
Victory, 1944; Critic's Choice, 1947; Prize Winners Show,
1947; Butler AI, 1950; BM, 1950, 1954, 1956; Ferargil
Gal., 1947; Paris, 1949; Switzerland, 1958; Audubon A.,
1950-1958; NAWA traveling exh., 1949, 1951-1953;
WMAA, 1951; Mobile WC Soc., 1951; Nat. Ser. Soc.,
1951-1955; Portland Soc. A., 1952, 1954; Bradley Univ.,
1952, 1954; Northwest Pr. M., 1952; N.Y. Soc. Women
A., 1952-1958; Am. Color Pr. Soc., 1954, 1955, 1956, 1958;
Nat. Soc. Painters in Casein, 1955; Boston Pr. M., 1955;
Nat. Exh. Contemp. A., 1956; PAFA, 1957; one-man:
Binet Gal., 1948, 1950; Brooklyn Pub. Lib., 1951; Mexi-
can Govt. Tourist Comm., Radio City, 1952.

RAPOZA, FRANCISCO—*Painter, T., L.*
   17 Thatcher St., South Dartmouth, Mass.
   B. New Bedford, Mass., May 21, 1911. *Studied*: Boston
Univ.; New Bedford Textile Inst., B.S.; Swain Sch. Des.,
and with Harry Neyland. *Member*: Providence A. Cl.; New
Bedford AA; Nat. Congress P.T.A.; Eastern AA; Dart-
mouth T. Assn. *Awards*: New Bedford Centennial prize,
1947; New Bedford AA, 1954. *Work*: Old Dartmouth
Hist. Soc.; Crapo Gal., New Bedford; murals, New
Bedford Mun. Airport; Bass River Bank, Hyannis, Mass.
Exhibited: Boston, Mass., 1948; New Bedford AA, 1952-
1955; New Bedford A. Group, 1948-1952. Lectures: Art
Appreciation; Color Theory: Impressionism to Present Day
Art, etc. *Position*: A. Instr., Swain Sch. Des., New Bed-
ford, Mass., 1943-55; also part-time, Tabor Acad., Marion,
Mass., 1948-52; Instr. A., Dartmouth H.S., Dartmouth,
Mass., 1955- .

RASCHEN, CARL MARTIN—*Painter, I., Et., T.*
   100 Scio St., Rochester 4, N.Y.
   B. Dec. 17, 1882. *Studied*: Rochester Atheneum; and with
Gilbert Gaul. *Member*: Rochester A. Cl.; Brush & Pencil
Cl. *Work*: Univ. Rochester, and in Europe. I., magazines,
newspapers, books.

RASKIN, JOSEPH—*Painter, Et.*
   59 West 71st St., New York 23, N.Y.
   B. Nogaisk, Russia, Apr. 14, 1897. *Studied*: NAD. *Mem-
ber*: Woodstock AA; Audubon A.; AEA. *Awards*: Euro-
pean scholarship, NAD, 1921; F., Tiffany Fnd., 1921.
Work: Dept. Labor Bldg., Wash., D.C.; Dartmouth Col.
Lib.; Harvard Law Sch. Lib.; Ain-Harod Mus., Israel.
Exhibited: Assoc. Am. A., 1945; Tricker Gal., 1939;
Schneider-Gabriel Gal., 1941; Steinway Hall, 1942; CGA;
Carnegie Inst.; PAFA; Miami Beach A. Center, 1956
(one-man); VMFA; NAD; SAGA; Schervee Gal., Boston,
1927; Hebraica Gal., N.Y., 1958 (one-man). Author:
"Portfolio of Etchings of Harvard University"; Co-illus.,
"Home-Made Zoo," 1952.

RASKIN, MILTON W.—*Painter*
   517 North California St., Burbank, Cal.
   B. Boston, Mass., Jan. 27, 1916. *Studied*: BMFA Sch.;
Sch. of Practical A., Boston, with Philip Martin, W.
Lester Stevens, John Whorf, Harold Rotenberg and others;
privately in Los Angeles with Leon Franks, Nicolai
Fechin, G. Thompson Pritchard and Will Foster. *Mem-*

ber: Cal. A. Cl.; San Fernando Valley A. Cl.; San Fernando Valley Prof. A. Gld. *Awards*: prizes, Greek Theatre, Los A., 1953; San Fernando Valley A. Cl., 1953; San Fernando Prof. A. Gld., 1953.

RASKIN, SAUL—Etcher, Lith., P., I., W., L.
5 West 16th St., New York 11, N.Y.

B. Nogaisk, Russia, Aug. 15, 1878. *Member*: AWCS; SAE; Audubon A. *Awards*: prizes, AIC; Phila. Pr. Cl.; SAE. *Work*: MMA; BM; AIC; Pittsfield Mus. A.; CAM; VMFA; N.Y. Pub.Lib.; Lib.Cong.; Mus. FA of Houston; Brooks Mem. A. Gal.; etc. I., "The Genesis"; "The Book of Psalms"; "The Hagadah"; & other books.

RASKO, MAXIMILIAN AUREL REINITZ—
Portrait Painter, T., L.
33 West 67th St., New York 23, N.Y.

B. Budapest, Hungary, June 13, 1883. *Studied*: Royal Acad., Munich, Germany; Dresden Acad. Des. & Painting; Julian Acad., Paris, France; Acad. FA, Vienna; Acad. FA, Rome, Italy. *Awards*: prizes, Budapest, 1903; Int. Exp., Bordeaux, France, 1927; Civil Order of Merit, Bulgaria; Little Cross of Portugal; Cross from Ordinis Sanctae Maria de Bethlehem, 1951; Commendatorem Gratia, 1952; Senior Citizenship Ctf., from Gov. Harriman, New York State, 1958. *Work*: Nat. Democratic Cl.; U.S. Treasury Dept., Wash., D.C.; The Vatican, Rome, Italy; Phillips Exeter Acad., Exeter, N.H.; U.S. Stamp printed, 1958, from port. of Louis Kossuth, liberator. *Exhibited*: Audubon A.; in Budapest, Munich, Paris and other European exhs. I., "The Mysteries of the Rosary."

RASMUSEN, HENRY N.—Painter, W., E.
198 Lovell Ave., Mill Valley, Cal.

B. Salt Lake City, Utah, Apr. 20, 1909. *Studied*: AIC; Am. Acad. A., Chicago. *Member*: San F. AA; AEA. *Awards*: prizes, Utah State Fair, 1939, 1943, 1948; Utah State Inst. FA, 1944; IBM, 1939; Texas FA Assn.; San F. AA, 1952, 1956. *Work*: Utah State Fair Assn.; Utah State Inst. FA; Brigham Young Univ.; Denver A. Mus.; SFMA; IBM; murals, Utah State Capitol Bldg. (in collaboration). *Exhibited*: WFNY 1939; AIC, 1939, 1940; CGA, 1940; MMoDA, 1940; Am. A. Cong., 1939; Utah State A. Center, 1939, 1941; Denver A. Mus., 1940, 1947; Portland A. Mus.; San Diego FA Soc.; Oakland A. Gal.; Texas Western Col.; deYoung Mem. Mus.; Cal. PLH; Albright A. Gal.; Vancouver (B.C.) A. Gal.; Wash. State Col.; Dallas Mus. FA; Mus. FA of Houston, and others. One-man: Witte Mem. Mus.; Ft. Worth AA; Texas FA Assn.; Corpus Christi AA; Texas State T. Col.; N.Y. Pub. Lib.; Santa Barbara Mus. A.; Denver A. Mus.; SFMA. Author: "Art Structure," 1950; "The Painters Craft" (chapter in The Book of Knowledge"), 1952. *Positions*: Instr., Univ. Texas; FA Center of Houston; Utah State A. Center; Albright A. Sch., Buffalo, N.Y.

RATH, FREDERICK L., Jr.—
Historian, Mus. Dir., L., W.
New York State Historical Association; h. 103 Pioneer St., Cooperstown, N.Y.

B. New York, N.Y., May 19, 1913. *Studied*: Dartmouth Col., B.A.; Harvard Univ., M.A. (Am. Hist.). *Member*: Am. Hist. Assn.; Am. Assn. for State & Local Hist.; Soc. Arch. Historians; AAMus. Ed., "FDR's Hyde Park" (with Lili Rethi). Lectures: New Trends in Historic Preservation, etc. *Position*: Historian, Nat. Park Service, 1937-42, 1946-48; Exec. Sec., Nat. Council for Historic Sites & Bldgs., 1948-50; Dir., Nat. Trust for Historic Preservation, 1950-56; Vice-Dir., New York State Hist. Assn., Cooperstown, N.Y., 1956- .

RATHBONE, AUGUSTA PAYNE—Painter, Et., I.
2908 Broderick St., San Francisco 23, Cal.

B. Berkeley, Cal., Dec. 30, 1897. *Studied*: Univ. California, B.A.; Grande Chaumiere, Paris, France, and with Claudio Castelucho, Lucien Simon. *Member*: AAPL; Cal. Soc. Et.; San F. Women A. *Awards*: prizes, Cal. Soc. Et., 1947(purchase); San F. A. Festival, 1951. *Work*: de Young Mem. Mus.; Cal. State Lib.; BM. *Exhibited*: BM, 1933; Cal. Soc. Et., 1950, 1953; San F. A. Festival, 1951; deYoung Mem. Mus., 1954; Cal. State Lib., 1952; Raymond & Raymond Gal.; Cal. PLH, 1958; SFMA, and others. Illus., "French Riviera Villages."

RATHBONE, PERRY TOWNSEND—Museum Director
Boston Museum of Fine Arts, Huntington Ave., Boston 15, Mass.; h. 151 Coolidge Hill, Cambridge 38, Mass.

B. Germantown, Pa., July 3, 1911. *Studied*: Harvard Col., A.B.; Harvard Univ. *Member*: AAMus.; AAMus. Council; Royal Soc. A., London. *Awards*: Hon. Phi Beta Kappa, Harvard Chptr., 1958; Hon. D.F.A., Washington Univ., St. Louis, Mo., 1958. Author: "Charles Wimar: Painter of the Indian Frontier," 1946; "Max Beckmann," 1948; "Mississippi Panorama," 1949; "Westward the Way," 1954. Contributor to art magazines and museum bulletins. *Positions*: Cur., Detroit Inst. A., 1936-40; Sec., Dir., Masterpieces of Art, WFNY 1939; Dir., CAM, St. Louis, Mo., 1940-55; Dir., Boston Mus. FA, Boston, Mass., 1955- .

RATHBONE, RICHARD ADAMS—Painter, E., L., W.
440 Humphrey St., New Haven 11, Conn.

B. Parkersburg, W. Va., 1902. *Studied*: Yale Sch. FA, B.F.A.; N.Y. Sch. F. & App. A., Paris, France. *Member*: New Haven Paint & Clay Cl. *Work*: Yale Univ. A. Gal. Lectures: History of Painting, Sculpture, Ornament. Author: "Introduction to Functional Design," 1950. *Position*: Asst. Prof., Drawing & Painting, Yale Univ. Sch. FA, New Haven, Conn., at present.

RATHBUN, SEWARD HUME—Painter, T., W.
1622 Massachusetts Ave., N.W., Washington 6, D.C.

B. Washington, D.C., Jan. 18, 1886. *Studied*: Harvard Col., A.B.; Harvard Univ., M.A. *Member*: Wash. WC Cl.; AWCS; AIA. *Exhibited*: AWCS; Wash., D.C. (one-man); Stanford Univ. (one-man). Author: "A Background to Architecture," 1926. Contributor to: Encyclopaedia of Social Sciences. (Retired).

RATKAI, GEORGE—Painter, I., Lith.
350 West 57th St., New York 19, N.Y.

B. Budapest, Hungary, Dec. 24, 1907. *Member*: A. Lg. Am.; AEA; Provincetown AA; Audubon A.; Nat. Soc. Painters in Casein. *Awards*: prize, Art of Democratic Living, 1951; gold medal, Audubon A., 1953, memorial medal, 1956. *Work*: Tel-Aviv Mus., Israel; Abbott Lab. Coll.; Univ. Illinois; Butler Inst. Am. A.; Univ. Nebraska. *Exhibited*: Pepsi-Cola, 1945, 1946; Springfield Mus. A.; Hungarian A. in Am.; PAFA; Carnegie Inst.; Illinois Wesleyan Univ., 1955-1958; Univ. Illinois, 1950-1957; WMAA, 1949, 1950, 1952-1956, 1958; Nebraska AA; Toledo Mus. A.; NAD; CGA; Audubon A., 1955-1958 and prior; MMA; WMA, 1951, 1956; Des Moines A. Center, 1951, 1956; BM, 1951, 1956; MMoDA, 1956; Provincetown AA, 1956-1958; Davenport Mus. A., 1957; Altoona AA, 1957; Mint Mus. A., 1957; AWS, 1956; Rochester Mem. A. Gal., 1957; Columbus Ga. FA, 1956, 1957; one-man: Assoc. Am. A., 1947; Babcock Gal., N.Y., 1950, 1954, 1956, 1959.

RATKAI, HELEN—Painter
350 West 57th St., New York 19, N.Y.

B. New York, N.Y., July 5, 1914. *Studied*: ASL, with Yasuo Kuniyoshi. *Member*: A.Lg.Am. *Work*: Abbott Laboratories (Booklets). *Exhibited*: PAFA, 1942; SFMA, 1942; AV, 1942; MMoDA, 1942; AIC, 1943; "Tomorrow's Masterpieces" Exh., 1943; Wildenstein Gal., 1941, 1942; Marquie Gal., 1943; Peiken Gal., 1944; Assoc. Am. A., 1943-1945; New-Age Gal., 1945, 1946; N.Y.Pub.Lib., 1944; Pepsi-Cola, 1946; Salpeter Gal., 1949, 1950; New Sch. for Social Research, 1953; WMAA, 1951; Provincetown AA, annually.

RATTNER, ABRAHAM—Painter
8 West 13th St., New York 11, N.Y.

B. Poughkeepsie, N.Y., July 8, 1895. *Studied*: Corcoran Sch. A.; PAFA; Ecole des Beaux-Arts, Julian Acad., Grande Chaumiere, Paris, France. *Awards*: Cresson traveling scholarship, PAFA, 1919; medal, PAFA, 1945; prizes, Pepsi-Cola, 1946; La Tausca Pearls Comp., 1947; Univ. Illinois, 1948. *Work*: U.S. State Dept.; MMoDA; WMAA; PAFA; Albright A. Gal.; AIC; BMA; Ft. Worth AA; Encyclopaedia Britannica; Pepsi-Cola Co.; Clearwater A. Mus.; PMG; MMA; PMA; CAM; Univ. Illinois; Des Moines A. Center; French Govt. *Exhibited*: nationally and extensively abroad; one-man: Vassar Col., 1948; Univ. Illinois, 1952. A.-in-Residence, Am. Acad. in Rome, 1951.*

RATZKA, ARTHUR L.—*Portrait Painter*
330 East 79th St., New York 21, N.Y.

B. Andrejova, Hungary, Sept. 24, 1869. *Studied*: Acad. FA, Vienna and Munich. *Member*: All. A. Am.; AAPL. *Awards*: prizes, NAD, 1930; AAPL, 1948. *Exhibited*: NAD, 1930, 1931; All. A. Am., 1932-1951; AAPL, annually. Contributor for articles on pastel and portrait painting to "Werkstatt der Kunst."

RAUL, HARRY LEWIS—
Sculptor, Former Mus. Administrator, L., Des.
Museum of the United States, Department of the Interior; h. 2115 Huidekoper Pl., N.W., Washington 7, D.C.

B. Easton, Pa. *Studied*: N.Y.Sch.A.; ASL; PAFA; Lafayette Col., & with William Chase, Frank DuMond, Charles Grafly, & others. *Member*: AAPL; AAMus; Min. P. S. & Gr. Soc., Wash., D.C.; A. Center of the Oranges. *Awards*: F., Royal SA, London, England; prize, A. Center of the Oranges, 1930; med., Montclair A. Mus., 1931; med., U.S. Dept. Interior, 1949. *Work*: s., mem., statues, reliefs: International Mus., Asbury Park, N.J.; Montclair A. Mus.; U.S. Nat. Mus., Wash., D.C.; Lafayette Col., Easton, Pa.; West Chester, Pa.; Lincoln Trust Co. Bldg., Scranton, Pa.; Englewood, N.J.; Orange, N.J.; Yonkers, N.Y.; Jersey City, N.J.; Morristown, N.J.; Berea Col., Ky.; Univ. of the South, Sewanee, Tenn.; Richmond, Va.; bronze port. tablet of Philip Murray in Blantyre, Scotland; Allan Haywood port. tablet, Yorkshire, England; B.B. Burgunder port. tablet, Wash., D.C. *Exhibited*: NAD; Arch.L.; CGA; Pan-Pacific Exp., 1915; PAFA; Hispanic Soc., N.Y.; BMA; Montclair A. Mus.; Newark Mus.; Ferargil Gal.; Newark AC. Lectures: "The Technique of Sculpture." *Position*: Administrator, Mus. of the U.S., Dept. of the Interior, Washington, D.C., 1938-1958 (Retired).

RAVESON, SHERMAN HAROLD—
Painter, Des., Typographer, A. Dir.
832 Lake Shore Drive, Delray Beach, Fla.

B. New Haven, Conn., June 11, 1907. *Studied*: Cumberland Univ., A.B., L.L.B.; ASL; and with Vincent Mundo. *Member*: AWS; Phila. WC Cl. *Awards*: medal, A. Dir. Cl., 1934, 1939; Nat. Advertising award, 1941; Certif. of Award, Best Nat. Adv. of 1949-50; prize, AWS, 1950; NAC, medal of honor, 1951. *Work*: Nat. Mus. of Racing, Saratoga Springs, N.Y.; Sporting Gal., New York City. *Exhibited*: CGA, 1935-1939; PAFA, 1935-1939; NAD, 1935, 1937, 1939; Toledo Mus. A., 1938; Phila. WC Cl.; All. A. Am.; AWS, 1934-1958; Carnegie Inst., 1936; Iowa State Fair, 1936; Wash. State Fair, 1936; AIC, 1935, 1936, 1938-1940; WFNY 1939; one-man: Assoc. Am. A., 1941; Grand Central A. Gal., 1955, 1956; Carriage House Studios, Phila., 1956; others, 1956-58 in the following club houses: Hialeah, Churchill Downs, Monmouth Park, Saratoga Raceway, Seagate. *Positions*: A. Ed., Vanity Fair magazine, 1929-34; A. Dir., Life magazine, 1935; Esquire magazine, 1936; Pettingell & Fenton, 1937-41; Consultant A. Dir., 1945-51; V. Pres. & A. Dir., Sterling Adv. Agcy., New York, N.Y., 1951-55.

RAWLS, JAMES—*Illustrator, P., Comm. A.*
7945 18th Ave., Hyattsville, Md.

B. Molino, Tenn., Sept. 8, 1894. *Studied*: Watkins Inst.; ASL; Clinton Peters Portrait Painting Sch., N.Y. *Member*: SI; A. Dir. Cl.; Nat. Soc. A. Dir.; Wash. Film Council; Soc. Fed. A. & Des.; Nat. Press Cl. *Position*: A. Dir., Dir. Pub. Relations, Creative Arts Studio, Washington, D.C.*

RAWSKI, CONRAD HENRY—
Fine Arts Librarian, L., T., W.
Fine Arts Department, Cleveland Public Library; h. 325 Superior Ave., Cleveland 14, Ohio

B. Vienna, Austria, May 25, 1914. *Studied*: Univ. Vienna, Ph.D.; Western Reserve Univ., Sch. Lib. Sc., M.A. in L.S.; Harvard Univ.; Cornell Univ. (Visiting Fellow). *Member*: Am. Soc. for Aesthetics; Mediaeval Acad. of Am.; Am. Lib. Assn.; Ohio Lib. Assn.; Am. Musicological Soc. *Awards*: Ford F., 1952-53. Contributor criticisms, articles and reviews to publications on art, music and medieval aesthetics. Lectures: The Gothic Cathedral; Education Through Art; History of the Book; Book Selection and Reference in Fine Arts. *Positions*: Prof., Ithaca Col-

lege, 1940-56; L., Schenectady Mus., 1946-48; Hd. FA Dept., Cleveland Public Lib., 1957- ; L., History of the Book, Sch. of Lib. Sci., Western Reserve Univ., Cleveland, 1957- .

RAY, ROBERT DONALD—*Painter, Gr.*
Box 1538, Taos, N.M.

B. Denver, Colo., Oct. 2, 1924. *Studied*: Drake Univ., Des Moines, Iowa; Univ. So. California, B.F.A.; Mexico City College, M.A. *Awards*: prize, DMFA, 1955; purchase prizes, BM, 1956; Mus. of New Mexico, 1956; Columbia Mus. A. (S.C.), 1957. *Work*: Joslyn Mem. Mus.; Mus. of New Mexico; Roswell Mus.; Columbia Mus. A.; Colorado Springs FA Center; BM; BMA. *Exhibited*: Conn. Acad. FA, 1954; LC, 1955; BM, 1956; Phila. Pr. Cl., 1956; Univ. Illinois, 1957, 1959; Colorado Springs FA Center, 1957, 1958; Columbia Mus. A., 1957; AFA traveling exh., 1956; Denver A. Mus., 1954-1957; Univ. Nebraska, 1957; Provincetown AA, 1958; Joslyn Mem. Mus., 1954; DMFA, 1956; Mus. of New Mexico, 1956-1958; Jonson Gal., Univ. N.M., 1956; Nelson Gal. A., Kansas City, 1957, 1958; Colorado Springs FA Center, 1955, 1957; Highlands Univ., Las Vegas, N.M., 1957; Tucson A. Festival, 1958; one-man: Roswell Mus., 1957; Mus. of New Mexico A. Gal., 1959.

RAY, RUTH (Mrs. John Reginald Graham)—
Painter, Comm. A.
291 Mansfield Ave., Darien, Conn.

B. New York, N.Y., Nov. 8, 1919. *Studied*: ASL, and with Jon Corbino, Morris Kantor, George Bridgman, and others. *Member*: ASL; Audubon A.; All. A. Am.; NAWA; Silvermine Gld. A. *Awards*: NAWA, 1945, 1952, 1953; La Tausca Comp., 1946; NAD, 1948; Springfield Mus. A., 1946; Conn. Contemp. Exh., 1951; Silvermine Gld. A., 1953; Conn. Acad. FA, 1953; Alice Collins Durham award, 1954, 1955. *Work*: Springfield Mus. A. *Exhibited*: Carnegie Inst., 1946-1949; NAD, 1948, 1950, 1952-1955; Pepsi-Cola, 1945; Terry AI, 1952; NAWA, 1945-1952; All. A. Am., 1949-1955; Audubon A., 1949-1955; Contemp. A., Conn., 1951, 1952; Silvermine Gld. A., 1950, 1951, 1953-1955; WMAA, 1949; Slater Mus. A., 1955; Argent Gal., 1956; one-man: Norlyst Gal., 1944; Ferargil Gal., 1947, 1949; Raymond & Raymond, 1947; Stamford Mus., 1950; Silvermine Gld. A., 1952; Darien (Conn.) Lib., 1958; Grand Central A. Gal., 1958; East River Savings Bank, N.Y., 1958. Illus., "Doctors of the Mind", "Blood, Oil and Sand," 1952. Contributor illus. to Abbott Laboratories "What's New?"; Lederle "Bulletin"; "Seventeen"; book jackets for leading publishers; Xmas cards for Am. A. Group. Radio and TV programs for Am. A. Group, 1955. *Positions*: Conn. State Dir. Am. A. Week; 1st Vice-Pres., NAWA.

RAY, S(ILVEY) J(ACKSON)—*Cartoonist*
The Kansas City Star, Kansas City, Mo.; h. Gashland, Mo.

B. Marceline, Mo., Mar. 15, 1891. *Studied*: ASL. *Awards*: Citation, U.S. Treasury Dept., 1942; Christopher Medal award, 1954; Freedoms Foundation awards, 1951, 1954. *Work*: Huntington Library, San Marino, Cal.

RAYMOND, EUGENIA—*Art Librarian, E.*
Seattle Public Library, Seattle 4, Wash.; h. 5529 25th Ave., Northeast, Seattle 5, Wash.

B. Toledo, Ohio. *Studied*: Mt. Holyoke Col., B.A.; Lib. Sch., N.Y.Pub.Lib. *Member*: Washington AA; Lib. Assn.; Pacific Northwest Lib. Assn.; Pacific AA. Contributor to: Bulletin of CM, with articles on early and contemporary book illustration. *Position*: Librarian, CM, 1930-37; Reference Asst., AIC, 1938-39; A. Librarian, Seattle Pub. Lib., Seattle, Wash., 1940- .

RAYMOND, FLORA ANDERSEN—*Painter, L.*
6816 North Ridge Road, Chicago 45, Ill.

B. Pewaukee Lake, Wis. *Studied*: AIC; Hyde Park Peoples Col., and with Edmond Giesbert, Frederick Grant, and others. *Member*: Lg. Am. Pen Women; All-Illinois AA; North Shore AA. *Awards*: prizes, Parent-Teacher Assn., Springfield, Ill., 1933 (2); Fed. Women's Cl., 1938; Highland Park, Ill., 1938; Lg. Am. Pen Women, 1948-1950, 1953. *Work*: University California at Los A. *Exhibited*: AIC, 1938, 1942; Evanston Women's Cl.; Hilton, Drake,

Bismarck and Swiss Chalet hotels, Chicago; one-man: Women's Cl., Chicago, 1938; Hyde Park Hotel, 1940; Normal Park Lib., 1939.

RAYMOND, GRACE RUSSELL—*Painter, L., T.*

923 Mansfield St., Winfield, Kan.

B. Mount Vernon, Ohio, May 1, 1876. *Studied*: Southwestern Col., Ph.B., D.F.A.; AIC; Corcoran Sch. A.; PAFA; Heatherleys Sch. FA, London, England, and with Henry Snell, George Elmer Browne, Guy Wiggins, Mrs. Gertrude Massey, & others. *Member*: AFA; Wash. WC Cl. Lectures: "Giotto's Influence Today"; "Japanese Influence in Western Painting." *Work*: Winfield (Kans.) H.S. Art Gallery; Newton Mem. Hospital; Douglass (Kans.) Pub. Lib. *Position*: Instr., Drawing & Painting, L., Art History & Appreciation, Southwestern Col., Winfield, Kan., 1930-45. Private classes at present.

RAYMOND, L(EONE) EVELYN—*Sculptor, L., T.*

3116 Hennepin Ave., South, Minneapolis, Minn.

B. Duluth, Minn., Mar. 20, 1908. *Studied*: Minneapolis Sch. A.; & with Charles S. Wells. *Member*: Minnesota AA; Minnesota S. Group. *Awards*: prizes, Minn. State Fair, 1941, 1943, 1944; Minneapolis Inst. A., 1944; Walker A. Center, 1944, 1945. *Work*: bas-relief, International Falls (Minn.) Stadium; wood carvings, Sebeka (Minn.) H.S.; Farmer's Exchange Bldg., St. Paul; Hall of Statuary, Wash., D.C., for the State of Minnesota; marble sc., Lutheran Church of Good Shepherd, Minneapolis; relief, Church of St. Joseph, Hopkins, Minn.; interior of St. George's Episcopal Church, including sconces, font, etc., and two Crucifixes, St. Louis Park, Minn. *Exhibited*: annually at local & regional exh. Contributor to: School Arts magazine. *Position*: Dir., Evelyn Raymond Clay Cl., Minneapolis, Minn.; Hd. S. Dept., Walker Art Center, 1940-51.

RAYNER, ADA (Mrs. Rayner Henschel)—*Painter*

Beach Highway, Provincetown, Mass.

B. London, England, Feb. 9, 1901. *Studied*: ASL; Cape Sch. A.; & with Henry Henschel. *Member*: Provincetown AA. *Exhibited*: Provincetown AA; Chrysler Mus. A., Provincetown; Ft. Wayne Mus. A.

RAYNESS, VELMA WALLACE—*Painter, I.*

3018 Oakland St., Ames, Iowa

B. Davenport, Iowa, Oct. 31, 1896. *Studied*: Cumming Sch. A. *Member*: Iowa A. Gld. *Awards*: prizes, Des Moines Women's Cl., 1919; Iowa State Fair, 1935. *Work*: Collegiate Presbyterian Church, Ames, Iowa; St. John's Methodist Church, Van Buren, Ark.; U.S. Govt.; port., Botany Hall, Iowa State College, Ames, Iowa. *Exhibited*: CGA, 1934; Joslyn Mem., 1939, 1946; Iowa Fed. Women's Cl.; Univ. Iowa; Cornell Col.; Mt. Vernon; Davenport Mus. A.; Sioux City A. Center; Des Moines A. Center; Iowa A. Gld.; CGA, and others. I., "The Corn is Ripe," 1944. Author: "Campus Sketches of Iowa State College," 1949.

REA, GARDNER—*Cartoonist*

Meadow Lane, Brookhaven, N.Y.

B. Ironton, Ohio, Aug. 12, 1892. *Studied*: Ohio State Univ., A.B.; Columbus A. Sch., and with Albert Fauley, Malcolm Fraser. *Member*: Am. Acad. Political Science. *Exhibited*: nationally and internationally. Author: "The Gentleman Says It's Pixies"; "Gardner Rea's Side Show." Contributor to Judge; New Yorker; Sat. Eve. Post; Colliers; Look and other national magazines.

REA, JAMES EDWARD—*Painter, S., Des., L., T., I.*

615 Courtland Dr., San Bernardino, Cal.

B. Forsyth, Mont., Jan. 14, 1910. *Studied*: St. Paul Sch. A.; Am. Acad. A., Chicago; Univ. Minnesota, B.S.; Univ. Redlands; Claremont Col. *Awards*: prizes, Minn. State Fair, 1933, 1934; San Bernardino, Cal., 1957. *Work*: Custer State Park Mus., S.D.; Hotel Lenox, Duluth, Minn.; murals, Holy Rosary Church, Arrowhead Motel, both San Bernardino. *Exhibited*: Grumbacher Exh., 1935; Minn. State Fair; Minneapolis Inst. A., 1932-1942; Nat. Orange Show. Lectures: History of Art. *Position*: Instr. FA, San Bernardino Polytech. H.S., 1946- .

REA, PAULINE DE VOL—*Painter, Des., T.*

3901 Goldfinch St., San Diego 3, Cal.

B. Chicago, Ill., Oct. 7, 1893. *Studied*: Chicago Acad. FA; & with Rudolph Schaeffer, Cyril Kay-Scott, & others. *Member*: San Diego A. Gld.; La Jolla A. Center. *Awards*: prize, San Diego FA Soc., 1941. *Work*: San Diego FA Soc. *Exhibited*: AIC, 1918; Los A., Cal.; La Jolla A. Center; Laguna Beach AA; Cedar City, Utah. *Position*: Dir., San Diego Acad. FA, 1929-41; Dir., La Jolla A. Center Children's Class, 1941-1958; Dir., Inst., Casa Manana, La Jolla, Cal., at present.

READ, RALPH (MINER)—*Painter*

Pond Meadow Road, Killingsworth P.O., Higganum, Conn.

B. New Haven, Conn., Feb. 10, 1890. *Studied*: Yale Univ., Ph.B.; Columbia Univ.; with Guy Wiggins, and in Paris. *Member*: Lyme AA; Essex AA; Studio Gld., West Redding, Conn. *Exhibited*: Hudson River Mus., Yonkers, N.Y., 1957; in museums and other exhs. in Oswego, Cortland, Rochester, N.Y.; Brockton, Amherst, Mass.; Portland, Me.; Florence, S.C.; Kansas City, Mo., Waterloo, Iowa; Peoria, Ill.; Easton, Pa.; Morgantown, W. Va.; Milwaukee, Wis. (1951-1958); Lyme AA, annually; Essex AA, annually; New Haven, Conn., 1958.

READIO, WILFRED A.—*Painter, Lith., E.*

204 Gladstone Rd., Pittsburgh 17, Pa.

B. Northampton, Mass., Nov. 27, 1895. *Studied*: Carnegie Inst. Tech., B.A. *Member*: Assoc. A. Pittsburgh. *Awards*: prizes, Assoc. A. Pittsburgh, 1921, 1940; Rocky Mountain Pr. M., 1935. *Work*: Pittsburgh Pub. Sch.; Latrobe (Pa.) H.S.; Carnegie Inst.; Pennsylvania State Col. *Exhibited*: SFMA, 1955; Cleveland Pr. Cl., 1935; Cal. Pr. M., 1935, 1936; Phila. Pr. Cl., 1934-1945, 1951, 1953, 1957; Buffalo Pr. Cl., 1938-1943; AIC, 1934, 1935, 1937, 1940; Wichita AA, 1934-1938; Laguna Beach AA, 1945, 1946, 1951-1955; Lib.Cong., 1944, 1945-1952, 1957, 1958; SAGA, 1950, 1951; Assoc. A. Pittsburgh, annually since 1921. *Position*: Chm., Dept. Painting & Des., 1929-39, Hd. Dept., 1939-55, Prof., 1955- , Carnegie Inst. Tech., Pittsburgh, Pa.

REARDON, M(ARY) A.—*Painter, Et., Lith., I.*

30 Ipswich St., Boston 15, Mass.; h. 74 Greenleaf St., Quincy 69, Mass.

B. Quincy, Mass., July 19, 1912. *Studied*: Radcliffe Col., A.B.; Yale Sch. FA, B.F.A., and in Mexico. *Member*: North Shore AA; Liturgical A. Soc.; AEA; NSMP. *Work*: St. Theresa's, Watertown, Mass.; Good Shepherd Convent, N.Y.; murals, Radcliffe Col.; Cardinal Spellman H.S., Brockton, Mass.; Boston Col.; St. Francis Xavier Chapel, Boston; St. Peter & St. Paul Church, Boston, Mass.; altar painting, St. John's Seminary, Boston; Maryknoll & Brookline Chapel, Boston; ports., Children's Medical Center, Boston; Boston State T. Col.; triptych, U.S.S. Wasp. *Exhibited*: Northwest Pr. M., 1940; Inst. Mod. A., Boston; Univ. Illinois; Radcliffe Col.; Cambridge AA; BMFA; North Shore AA; Quincy, Mass. (one-man); St. Thomas Univ., Houston, Tex.; Eastern State Exh., Springfield. I., "Snow Treasure," 1942; "They Came from Scotland," 1944; "Bird in Hand," 1945; "Giant Mountain," 1955; "Young Brave Algonquin," 1955; Co-author, "Pope Pius XII, Rock of Peace." *Position*: Instr., Painting, Emmanuel Col., Boston, Mass.; BMFA.

REBAJES, FRANCISCO—*Craftsman, Des., T.*

377 Fifth Ave.; h. 498 Hempstead Ave., Malverne, N.Y.

B. Puerto Plata, Dominican Republic, Feb. 6, 1907. *Studied*: in Dominican Republic & Spain. *Member*: Soc. Designer-Craftsmen; F., Royal Soc. A., London. *Awards*: med., Paris Salon, 1937. *Work*: WMAA. *Exhibited*: MMA, 1937; BM, 1938. *Position*: Pres., Copper Craftsmen, Inc., New York, N.Y.; Pres., Rebajes, Fifth Ave., New York, N.Y.*

REBAY, HILLA (HILDEGARD REBAY von EHRENWIESEN)—*Painter, W., L.*

Franton Court, Greens Farms, Conn.

B. Strasbourg, Alsace, May 31, 1890. *Studied*: Academies in Duesseldorf, Paris, Munich. *Work*: in Museums in N.Y., France, Italy, Switzerland, Germany. *Exhibited*:

Salon des Independentes, Paris, 1913; Acad. Julian, 1912; Freie Secession, Berlin, 1918; Secessions, Munich, 1914; WMA, 1928; Salon des Tuileries, Salon d'Automne, Salon Nouvelles Realities, Paris, France, since 1929; Cal. PLH; Bernheim Jeune, Carpentier, Wildenstein galleries, Paris; Marie Sterner, Wildenstein galleries, N.Y. Author: "Wassily Kandinsky"; "Kandinsky Memorial"; "Moholy-Nagy Memorial." Contributor to Southern Literary Digest, Carnegie Inst. Magazine, New Age, Realities, and other publications. *Position*: Dir., Mus. Non-Objective Painting, Solomon R. Guggenheim Fnd., New York, N.Y., 1937-52; Trustee, Dir. Emeritus, 1952- , Solomon R. Guggenheim Mus.

REBECK, STEVEN AUGUSTUS—*Sculptor*

1028 Roanoke Rd., Cleveland Heights, Ohio

B. Cleveland, Ohio, May 25, 1891. *Studied*: Cleveland Sch. A.; & with Karl Bitter, Carl Heber. *Member*: NSS; Cleveland SA. *Awards*: prizes, CMA, 1922, 1923. *Work*: CMA; mem., Alliance, Ohio; Civil Court House, St. Louis, Mo. Specializes in medals.

RECCA, GEORGE—*Painter, Comm. A.*

15 East 26th St., New York 10, N.Y.; h. 92-05 Whitney Ave., Elmhurst, L.I., N.Y.

B. Palermo, Italy, Aug. 15, 1899. *Studied*: PIA Sch. *Member*: AWCS; SC; All. A. Am.; Audubon A.; Grand Central A. Gal. *Awards*: prize, Ogunquit A. Center, 1938; All. A. Am., 1941-1943. *Exhibited*: NAD, 1935, 1940, 1942; PAFA, 1940, 1941, 1944.

RECCHIA, RICHARD H(ENRY)—*Sculptor*

Hardscrabble, Rockport, Mass.

B. Quincy, Mass. *Studied*: BMFA Sch.; & abroad. *Member*: NA; Rockport AA; NSS. *Awards*: prizes, BMFA Sch.; NSS, 1939; med., Pan-Pacific Exp., 1915; Int. Exp., Bologna, Italy, 1931; NAD, 1944. *Work*: Harvard Univ.; Brown Univ.; Purdue Univ.; Boston State House; Somerville Pub. Lib.; Malden H.S.; Red Cross Mus., Wash., D.C.; Buffalo Mus. A. & Sc.; J. B. Speed Mem. Mus.; Boston Psychoanalytical Inst.; Brookgreen Gardens, S.C.; mem., Northeaston, Mass.; equestrian statue, Manchester, N.H.; bas-reliefs on BMFA. *Exhibited*: AIC; NAD, annually; NSS, 1939-1946; CGA, 1928; BMFA; many one-man exh.

RECCHIA, MRS. RICHARD H. See *Parsons, Kitty*

RECKENDORF, J. ANGELIKA—*Craftsman, E.*

Pembroke State College, Pembroke, N.C.

B. Freiburg, Germany, Aug. 12, 1893. *Studied*: Cranbrook Acad. A.; Carnegie Inst.; Univ. North Carolina, M.A.; in Europe, with Hans Ehmke, Heinrich Wolfflin, & others. *Member*: CAA; Southeastern A.; Southeastern A. Edu. Assn.; N.C. State A. Soc. *Exhibited*: North Carolina A., 1940, 1944; Wichita AA, 1952, 1954; Greensboro Textile Exh., 1950, 1954; & in Europe. Contributor to: "High School Journal," with articles on Art Education in the Public Schools. *Position*: Hd. Dept. A., Pembroke Col., Pembroke, N.C., 1942- ; Instr., Crafts Workshop, Univ. North Carolina, Chapel Hill, N.C., 1943-44.

REDDEN, ALVIE EDWARD—*Educator, P.*

Art Department, Mesa College; h. 2350 Orchard Ave., Grand Junction, Colo.

B. Hamilton, Tex., July 22, 1915. *Studied*: West Texas State Univ., B.S.; Univ. Colorado, M.F.A.; grad. study, Ohio State Univ., Columbia Univ.; and with Grant Reynard. *Member*: Mesa County FA Center (Trustee); NAEA; Colo. A. Edu. Assn.; Pacific AA. *Positions*: Prin., Samnorwood Elem. Schs., 1940-42, 1945; A. T., West Texas State College, 1946; A. Dir., Mesa College, Grand Junction, Colo., 1947- ; Non-resident A. Instr., Univ. Colorado, 1949- .

REDEIN, ALEX—*Painter, T.*

108 East 81st St., New York 28, N.Y.; s. Ocean Beach, Fire Island, N.Y.

B. Bridgeport, Conn., Jan. 21, 1912. *Studied*: Yale Univ. Sch. FA; ASL, and in Mexico City. *Member*: AEA. *Work*: Butler AI; Albany Inst Hist. & A.; Phila. A. All.;

Ain Harod Mus., Israel, and in private colls. *Exhibited*: PAFA, 1949; NAD, 1950; AWS, 1950; Butler AI, 1955, 1958; Farnsworth Mus., 1950; Phila. A. All., 1951, 1958; CMA, 1956; Minn. State Fair, 1949; Pinacotheca Gal., 1944 (one-man); 10 one-man, John Heller Gal., N.Y.

REDER, BERNARD—*Sculptor, Et., Eng., Lith.*

41 West 72nd St., New York, N.Y.; (temp.)—53 via del Campuccio, Florence, Italy

B. Czernowitz, Roumania, June 29, 1897. *Studied*: Acad. FA, Prague, with Sturza. *Work*: MModA; PMA; Tel-Aviv Mus., Israel; BMA; FMA; N.Y. Pub. Lib.; NGA; AIC; MMA; Museu d'Arte Moderna, Sao Paulo, Brazil, and in many private colls. *Exhibited*: PAFA, 1949; PMA, 1949; MModA, 1951, 1953, and prior; BM; NGA; WMAA; Weyhe Gal., N.Y.; Phila. A. All.; Phila. Pr. Cl.; Borgenicht Gal., N.Y.; Wildenstein Gal., Paris; Tel-Aviv Mus.; Dominion Gal., Montreal, 1953; Univ. Illinois, 1953; European traveling exh., MModA, 1955; Galleria d'Arte Moderna L'Indiano, Florence, Italy, 1956, 1957.

REDFIELD, EDWARD W. —*Painter*

Center Bride R.D., New Hope, Pa.

B. Bridgeville, Del., Dec. 18, 1869. *Studied*: PAFA; & with Bouguereau, Robert-Fleury in Paris. *Member*: NA; Phila. AC. *Awards*: F., PAFA; med., prize, PAFA, 1903, 1905, 1907, 1912, 1920; prize, NAD, 1904, 1918, 1919, 1927; med., St. Louis Exp., 1904; Carnegie Inst., 1905, 1914; CGA, 1907, 1908; med., Paris Salon, 1909; AIC, 1909, 1913; prize, Springfield AA, 1930; Newport AA, 1933; & others. *Work*: Luxembourg Mus., Paris; CGA; CM; Carnegie Inst.; BMFA; PAFA; Detroit Inst. A.; AIC; Minneapolis Inst. A.; R.I.Sch.Des.; MMA; NGA; Butler AI; Kansas City AI; CAM; PMA; etc.

REDKA, EUGENIA—*Painter, T., Gr., Des.*

High School of Music and Art, 135th St. & Convent Ave., New York, N.Y.; h. 4828 Osgood St., Bronx 70, N.Y.

B. New York, N.Y. *Studied*: Hunter Col., B.A.; T. Col., Columbia Univ., M.A. *Awards*: prize, Hunter Col.; 2 awards for photography from Popular Photography Intl. Photo Comp.; prizes for photos, World Telegram & Sun, Travel, Flower Grower magazines. *Work*: photographs in Popular Photography Las Americas; Travel; The Priest; Pictures and other publications. *Exhibited*: Lib.Cong.; Phila. WC Cl.; Wash. WC Cl.; MMA; Northwest Pr.M.; 8th St. Gal.; Bradley Univ. *Position*: Instr. A., T. Col., Columbia Univ., New York, N.Y.

REDNICK, HERMEN—*Painter, Lith.*

P.O. Box 173, Taos, N.M.

B. Philadelphia, Pa., Mar. 9, 1902. *Studied*: NAD. *Exhibited*: NAD; CGA; PAFA; Albright A. Gal.; one-man: Morton Gal., N.Y., 1936-1938; Francis Webb Gal., Los A., 1942; Ojai (Cal.) Gal., 1946; Mus. New Mexico, 1950, 1953, 1955.

REECE, DORA—*Painter*

1540 North 55th St., Philadelphia 31, Pa.

B. Philipsburg, Pa. *Studied*: Phila. Sch. Des.; PAFA, and in Europe. *Member*: Pa. Soc. Min. P.; F., PAFA. *Awards*: prizes, Phila. Sch. Des.; Rittenhouse Flower Market, Phila. *Work*: PMA; Mem. Lib., Philipsburg, Pa.

REED, DOEL—*Etcher, P., E., L.*

109 West 7th St.; h. 1820 Arrowhead Place, Stillwater, Okla.

B. Logansport, Ind., May 21, 1894. *Studied*: Cincinnati A. Acad., and in France and Mexico. *Member*: NA; SAGA; Chicago Soc. Et.; Phila. WC Cl.; Audubon A.; Indiana Pr. M.; SSAL; Cal. WC Soc.; Albany Pr. Cl.; Boston Pr. M. *Awards*: prizes, Phila. Pr. Cl., 1940; Chicago Soc. Et., 1938, 1949; Currier Gal. A., 1942; Northwest Pr. M., 1942, 1944; Tulsa AA, 1935; Philbrook A. Center, 1944, 1946, 1947, 1948, 1957; LC, 1944, 1949; Laguna Beach AA, 1944, 1947; SSAL, 1944; Oakland A. Gal., 1945, 1947; Wichita AA, 1946, 1952, 1958; Assoc. Am. A., 1947; Conn. Acad. FA, 1947, 1953; Dayton AI, 1947, 1949; Carnegie Inst., 1948; Joslyn A. Mus., 1948, 1952; Dallas Mus. FA, 1948, 1949; John Herron AI, 1949, 1952, 1958; Okla. A. Center, 1949, 1951; Delgado Mus.

A., 1949, 1951; Indiana Soc. Pr. M., 1950; Mid-Am. A., 1950; SAGA, 1950, 1957; Audubon A., 1950; medal, 1951, 1954; Boston Pr. M., 1953; Ohio State Univ., 1954; Kansas State Col., 1952; Assoc. Okla. A., 1957 (2); Contemp. A., Pomona, Cal., 1956. *Work*: PMA; LC; Carnegie Inst.; SAM; Honolulu Acad. A.; N.Y. Pub. Lib.; Philbrook A. Center; Mus. FA of Houston; Univ. Montana; Joslyn A. Mus.; Kansas State Col.; Ohio State Univ.; MMA; Delgado Mus. A.; Zanesville AI; Nelson Gal. A., Kansas City; Butler AI; DMFA; Dayton AI; Cal. State Lib., and many others; murals, Okla. State Office Bldg. *Exhibited*: nationally and internationally. *Position*: Prof. A., Chm. A. Dept., Oklahoma State Univ., Stillwater, Okla., 1924- .

REED, FLORENCE (Mrs. Holway)—Painter, Gr., T., L.
62 East Main St., Hyannis, Mass.

B. Belmont, Mass., June 2, 1915. *Studied*: Mass. Sch. A.; ASL; Mass. General Hospital Medical Arts Course. *Member*: Cape Cod AA. *Work*: Acton (Mass.) Pub. Lib.; Mass. General Hospital. *Exhibited*: Boston A. Cl., 1938, 1939; Jordan Marsh Gal., 1938, 1943; Chatham, Mass., 1938, 1939; Vose Gal., 1941; Marblehead, Mass., 1941; Hyannis, Mass.; Barnstable Fair, 1954; one-man: Staten Island, N.Y., 1940; South Yarmouth, Mass., 1941, 1956.*

REED, ROBERT K.—Painter
Sunken Garden Art Colony, Brackenridge Park; h. 802 East Grayson St., San Antonio 8, Tex.

B. Cadillac, Mich., Sept. 5, 1906. *Studied*: Univ. Texas, & with Frederick Taubes, Xavier Gonzales, Jacob Getlar Smith, Minna Citron. *Member*: Texas WC Soc.; Texas FA Assn.; Craft Gld. of San Antonio. *Awards*: prizes, San Antonio A., 1947; Texas FA Assn., 1950; River A. Group, 1951, 1955; Texas WC Soc., 1950, 1954. *Exhibited*: San Antonio A., 1946-1955; Texas FA Assn., 1947-1955; Texas WC Soc., 1949-1955. *Work*: Witte Mem. Mus., and in private colls.

REED, (TRUMAN) GERVAIS—
Assistant Museum Director, T.
Henry Art Gallery, University of Washington, Seattle 5, Wash.; h. 5264 148th St., Southeast, Bellevue, Wash.

B. Wichita, Kans., May 2, 1926. *Studied*: Yale Univ., B.A. *Member*: Western Assn. A. Mus.; Wash. A. & Crafts Assn.; Archaeological Inst. Am.; Seattle All. A. *Positions*: Ed. Asst., Magazine of Art, N.Y., 1949-50; Actg. Dir., Film Center, Univ. Washington, 1950-52; Supt., A. Dept., Western Washington Fair, 1952-57; Asst. Dir., Henry Gallery, University of Washington, Seattle, Wash., 1952- .

REEDER, FLORA MacLEAN (Mrs. Harold L.)—
Painter, T.
2474 Brentwood Rd., Columbus 9, Ohio

B. Saginaw, Mich. *Studied*: Ohio State Univ., B.A., B.Sc. in FA; Univ. Kansas; Columbus A. Sch.; San F. Sch. A., and with Charles Hawthorne, Maurice Sterne, John Carroll, William Thon. *Awards*: prizes, Ohio State Fair; Columbus A. Lg. 1956, and prior; Ohio State Journal; Columbus Gal. FA, 1954, 1955; Ohio WC Soc.; Ohio Valley Exh., 1955. *Work*: Columbus Gal. FA. *Exhibited*: Columbus A. Lg., 1956, 1957, and prior.

REEP, EDWARD—Painter, T., Lith.
3856 Reklaw Dr., Studio City, Cal.

B. Brooklyn, N.Y., May 10, 1918. *Studied*: A. Center Sch., Los. A., & with Willard Nash, Emil Bisttram, Stanley Reckless. *Member*: Cal. WC Soc.; San Diego A. Gld.; Los A. Mus. Assn. *Awards*: prizes, Life magazine Comp., 1942; Carmel AA, 1942; Am. Contemp. Gal., 1946; San Diego, Cal., 1946, 1950; Los A. County Fair, 1948; Coronado Int. Exh., 1949; Los A. Mus. A., 1950, 1952; Carlsbad-Oceanside Exh., 1950; Cal. Int. Flower Show, 1951; Gardena, Cal., 1952; Guggenheim F., 1945-46; Cal. WC Soc., 1955. *Work*: Life magazine war painting coll.; New Mexico Marine Hospital; A. Group Am.; U.S. War Dept.; World-wide painting Commission by Life magazine, 1956; Cole of California Coll.; State of California Coll.; Los A. Mus. A.; Gardena (Cal.) H.S. *Exhibited*: WMAA, 1946-1948; NAD; Los A. Mus. A.; NGA; Los A .AA; Mod. Inst., Los A.; CGA; PAFA; SFMA; CAM; Oakland A. Gal.; BMA; VMFA; Pa. State Mus.; Syracuse Mus. FA;

Dayton AI; Newark Mus.; Slater Mem. Mus.; Decatur AI; Cedar Falls AA; Rockford AA; Zanesville AI; Brooks Mem. Mus.; Currier Gal. A.; LC; and others. One-man: Italy, 1944; Cowie Gal., Los A., 1949; Bisttram Sch. A., 1950; Coronado Sch. FA, 1950; Fresno State Col., 1951; San Diego Mus. A., 1951; Pasadena Mus. A., 1955 (one-man). *Positions*: Instr., Drawing & Painting, A. Center Sch., Los Angeles, 1947-50; Bisttram Sch. A., 1950-51; Chouinard AI, Los Angeles, 1950- . Pres., Cal. WC Soc., 1956-57.

REESE, DAVID MOSLEY—Museum Director, P., T.
Telfair Academy of Arts & Sciences, 121 Barnard St.; h. 58-A Lamara Apts., Savannah, Ga.

B. Newnan, Ga., Oct. 9, 1915. *Studied*: Atlanta AI; ASL; Florida State Univ. *Member*: Am. Assn. Mus. Dirs.; Southeastern Mus. Dirs. Assn.; Macdowell Fellowship. *Awards*: Southeastern Annual, Atlanta, 1954; Assn. Georgia A., 1955; Carnegie Grant, 1952. *Work*: Atlanta AA Gal.; Columbus (Ga.) Mus. A. & Crafts; Ford Motor Co., Dearborn, Mich.; mural, Union Bag-Camp Paper Corp., Savannah, Ga. *Exhibited*: Southeastern Annual, 1946-1950, 1952, 1953, 1955, 1956; Am. Assn. Mus. Exh., 1958; Assn. Georgia A., 1955-1957. Arranged exh., "Masterpieces in Georgia Collections" for Telfair Acad. A. & Sciences, 1958. *Position*: Dir., Telfair Acad. A. & Sciences, Savannah, Ga.

REEVES, RUTH—Designer, C., P., W., L., T.
434 Lafayette St., New York 3, N.Y.

B. Redlands, Cal. *Studied*: PIASch; San F. Sch. Des.; ASL; in Paris, with Fernand Leger. *Member*: A.Lg.Am.; AEA; NAWA (Com. on A. Edu.); Needle & Bobbin Cl. *Awards*: Gardner Grant, 1931; Carnegie traveling F., 1934-1935; Guggenheim F., 1940-1942. *Work*: textile des., wall coverings, Radio City Music Hall, N.Y.; hangings, Children's Room, Mt. Vernon (N.Y.) Pub. Lib.; murals, St. Albans (N.Y.) H.S.; textiles, Victoria & Albert Mus., London, England. *Exhibited*: Am.Des. Gal., 1929; BM, 1931; Minneapolis Inst. A.; MMA, 1929, 1931; BMFA, 1930, 1931; PMA, 1930; AIC, 1930; CAM, 1930; Carnegie Inst., 1930; Dayton AI, 1930; CM, 1930; BMA, 1930; Toledo Mus. A., 1931; CMA, 1931; Arch.L., 1931; State T. Col., Farmville, Va.; Univ. Chicago; Phila. A. All.; AGAA; Kansas City AI; Denver A. Mus.; U.S. State Dept. traveling exh., 1952. I., "Daphnis and Chloe." Limited Editions Cl., 1934. Contributor to University brochures, art bulletins & magazines. *Position*: First Supt., Index of American Design, Wash., D.C.; Instr., Textile Design, CUASch, New York, N.Y.; L., Sch. Painting & Sculpture, Columbia Univ., 1952- ; A.T., Children's Workshop classes, AEA, New York, N.Y., 1952-53; Instr., Cleveland Inst. A., 1954 (summer); L., Colby Col., Detroit Inst. A., Cleveland Inst. A., 1955.*

REFREGIER, ANTON—Painter
Woodstock, N.Y.

B. Moscow, Russia, 1905. *Studied*: R.I. Sch. Des.; in France, & with Hans Hoffman, Munich. *Member*: AEA; NSMP. *Award*: Hallmark Comp., 1953. *Work*: MModA.; WMAA; MMA; Walker A. Center; Univ. Arizona; Encyclopaedia Britannica, and many others; murals, USPO, San F., Cal.; Plainfield, N.J.; SS "Independence"; SS "Constitution"; Phoenix Insurance Co., Hartford, Conn.; Mayo Clinic, Rochester, Minn.; Covington Fabrics, N.Y.; Hillcrest Jewish Center, L.I., N.Y.; ceramic and tile mural, Tokeneke Sch., Darien, Conn.; Dec. in several public rooms, Sheraton Hotel, Phila.; mosaic wall, Hotel Americana, Fla.; over 50 supermarkets throughout New England and Long Island for First National chain; ceramic tile mural, P.S. 146, for N.Y. Bd. Edu. *Exhibited*: ACA Gal. (one-man) 1955, 1958, & in leading national exhibitions. Contributor to Fortune, What's New, & other magazines. Author: "Natural Figure Drawing." Artist-Correspondent, Fortune magazine, at UNO Conference, San F., Cal. Visiting Instr., Univ. Arkansas; Cleveland Sch. FA (summer session).

REGENSTEINER, ELSE F.—Textile Designer, C., T., L.
reg/wick Studio, 8340 Ingleside Ave.; h. 6009 South Woodlawn Ave., Chicago 37, Ill.

B. Munich, Germany, Apr. 21, 1906. *Studied*: Univ. Munich; Inst. Des., Chicago, & with Moholy-Nagy, Marli Ehrman, Annie and Joseph Albers. *Member*: IDI; Midwest Designer-Craftsmen. *Awards*: prize, Int. Textile Exh., Univ.

North Carolina, 1946; Citation, AID, 1947, 1948, 1951. *Work*: Many commissions for textiles for architects and interior decorators, 1946-52; des. for industry, 1953- . *Exhibited*: Int. Textile Exh., Greensboro, N.C., 1946-1948; Inst. Contemp. A., Boston; traveling exhibition AID, 1947, 1948, 1951; Walker A. Center; Des Moines A. Center; Western AA, 1950; Ohio State Univ., 1950; St. Paul Gal. 1950; AIC, 1948; Chicago Pub. Lib., 1951; MModA; traveling exhs., Am. Designer-Craftsmen and Midwest Designer-Craftsmen; Merchandise Mart., Chicago; Renaissance Soc., Univ. Chicago, 1948, 1950-1952; Mus. Compt. Crafts, N.Y., 1956, 1958; Ravina A. Festival, 1957, 1958; "Design Derby," 1957. Lectures on Textile Design; Hand Weaving. *Positions*: Instr., Inst. Des., Chicago, 1942-46; Hull House, Chicago, 1942-46; Asst. Prof., AIC, Chicago, Ill., 1945-1957, Prof. 1957- .

REGESTER, CHARLOTTE—*Painter, S., C., Des., T.*
3 Mill Lane, Rockport, Mass.

B. Baltimore, Md. *Studied*: Albright A. Sch.; ASL; Columbia Univ.; Greenwich House. *Member*: Cape Ann Gld. Craftsmen; NAWA; Pen & Brush Cl.; N.Y. Ceramic Soc. *Award*: Pen & Brush Cl., 1939. *Exhibited*: 1954-1958: Cape Ann A. Festival; Pen & Brush Cl.; ceramics, Cape Ann Gld. Craftsmen; Rockport AA. *Positions*: Hd. A. Dept., Todhunter Sch., N.Y., 1927-39; A. Dept., Dalton Sch., N.Y., 1939-45; Westchester Workshop of A. & Crafts, White Plains, N.Y., 1945-52; Ceramics, City Col. N.Y., 1951-52; Studio Workshop for Painting & Ceramics, Rockport, Mass., 1952- .

REHBERGER, GUSTAV—*Painter, Des., Comm. A., I.*
1206 Carnegie Hall, New York 19, N.Y.

B. Riedlingsdorf, Austria, Oct. 20, 1910. *Studied*: AIC. *Member*: Audubon A.; SI; MModA. *Awards*: prizes, Audubon A., 1948; A. Dir. Cl., 1954, 1955; Soc. Typographic A., Chicago, 1938. *Exhibited*: SI, 1957 (one-man).

REIBEL, BERTRAM—*Wood Engraver, Gr., S.*
1127 Hardscrabble Road, Chappaqua, N.Y.

B. New York, N.Y., June 14, 1901. *Studied*: AIC, & with Alexander Archipenko. *Member*: AEA; Am-Jewish A. Cl.; Springfield AA; Village A. Center. *Exhibited*: NAD; Int. Pr. M.; PAFA; MMA; CM; Oakland A. Gal.; Northwest Pr.M.; AIC; Kansas City AI; Detroit Inst. A.; Southern Pr. M.; Buffalo Pr. Cl.; Denver A. Mus.; Phila. Pr. Cl.; SFMA; LC; Conn. Acad. FA; Los A. Mus. A.; Rochester Pr. Cl., Wichita AA.

REIBER, CORA SARAH (Mrs. Charles F. Rothweiler)
Painter, Des.
1035 West 8th St., Plainfield, N.J.

B. New York, N.Y. *Studied*: N.Y.Sch.App.Des. for Women; ASL; & with Charles Jeltrup, Alphonse Mucha. *Work*: mural, Wadsworth Ave. Baptist Church, New York, N.Y. Lectures: Perspective. *Position*: Des., Wallpaper & Fabrics for leading manufacturers; Instr., N.Y. Sch. Des. for Women, & Traphagen Sch., New York, N.Y. (retired).

REIBER, R(ICHARD) H.—*Painter, Et., S., Des., L., T.*
1200 Murryhill Ave., Pittsburgh 17, Pa.

B. Crafton, Pa., Oct. 2, 1912. *Studied*: Cornell Univ.; & with Kenneth Washburn, Olaf Brauner, Walter Stone. *Member*: Pittsburgh AA; Pittsburgh Arch. Cl.; Pittsburgh Pr. Cl. Lectures: "Process of Etching."*

REICH, JEAN HEYL—*Ceramic Craftsman*
Tryon, N.C.

B. Columbus, Ohio. *Studied*: Cincinnati A. Acad.; Univ. Cincinnati; & with Harold S. Nash, H. H. Wessel, James Hopkins. *Member*: Woman's AC, Crafters, Ceramic Gld., Cincinnati Professional A., all of Cincinnati. *Work*: IBM Coll. *Exhibited*: Syracuse Mus. FA, 1939-1941, traveling exh., 1939-1941; Woman's AC, Cincinnati, 1939-1945; Nat. A. Week, Wash., D.C., 1940; CM, 1939-1942; NAC, 1940; Cincinnati Crafters, 1941; Ceramic Gld., 1943; CM, 1944 (one-man); Dayton AI, 1945 (one-man). *Position*: Instr., Ceramics, CM, Cincinnati, Ohio, 1949-57; Instr. Ceramics, Jean and Fred Reich Studio, Tryon, N.C.

REICHERT, OSCAR ALFRED—*Painter, Des., Arch.*
519 Penn St.; h. 725 Penn St., Reading, Pa.

B. Germany. *Studied*: Frankfurt AI & Sch. Des.; Offenbach Inst. Tech.; Dusseldorf Acad. FA, Germany. *Member*: Knickerbocker A.; Am. Veteran's A. Soc. *Awards*: Nat. German Comp., Mem. Monument, City of Beckum, 1927; Olympic Comp. Arch. Sec. (U.S. Team), Berlin, 1936 (medal); Regional A. Comp., 1940; Jersey City Mus. A., 1955. *Work*: Reading Mus. A. *Exhibited*: Knickerbocker A., 1949-1952, 1954; Am. Veteran's Soc. A., 1949-1955; AWS, 1950; Audubon A., 1950; Acad. in Rome, 1950; Reading Mus. A., 1930-1957; Berks County Arch. Soc., Reading Mus., 1958, and others nationally and internationally. Contributor to Sports Afield; La Revue Modern, Paris; Vanity Fair; Reading Times. *Position*: Arch. & A. Adv., Hist. Section of City of Friedberg and Budingen, 1923, 1924; Arch., Des., A. Adv., Hist. Section, City of Pirmasens, 1925; Studio Prof., Emil Fahrenkamp, Arch., Des., Dusseldorf, 1927-28; Textiles, Wyomissing, Pa., Arch., Des., 1931- .

REID, AURELIA WHEELER—*Painter, C., S.*
3444 Farnsworth Ave., Los Angeles 32, Cal.

B. Beeckman, Dutchess County, N.Y. *Studied*: CUASch.; T. Col., Columbia Univ.; Winthrop Col., S.C.; Univ. California at Los A.; Los A. County AI. *Member*: Pa. Soc. Min. P.; Cal. Soc. Min. P.; Am. Assn. Univ. Women; San Pedro AA; San Pedro A. Patrons. *Awards*: prizes, San Pedro Fair; San Pedro AA. *Work*: S., Los A. State Bldg.; miniature, PMA. *Exhibited*: Terry AI; Smithsonian Inst.; Madonna Festival, Los A.; Greek Theatre, Los A.; PAFA; San Pedro Fair; El Sereno, Cal.; one-man: Cabrillo Hall, San Pedro.

REIDER, DAVID H.—*Designer, E., Photog.*
2837 Pittsfield Blvd., Ann Arbor, Mich.

B. Portsmouth, Ohio, Apr. 6, 1916. *Studied*: Univ. Buffalo; Cleveland Sch. A. *Member*: AAUP; Com. on A. Edu., MModA. *Work*: Milwaukee AI. *Exhibited*: (photography) Milwaukee AI; Albion Col.; Univ. Michigan; Saarbrucken, Germany; AFA exh., 1959-61. Photographs reproduced in numerous architectural and industrial publications. *Position*: L., Des., Buffalo State T. Col., 1942; Instr. Des., Univ. Buffalo, 1942-46; Hd. Dept. Des., Albright A. Sch., 1942-47; Asst. Prof. Des., 1947-54, Assoc. Prof. Des., 1955- , Univ. Michigan, Ann Arbor, Mich.

REIF, RUBIN—*Painter, Gr., Des., Comm. A., E.*
Art Department, University of Arkansas; h. 416 Gunter St., Fayetteville, Ark.

B. Warsaw, Poland, Aug. 10, 1910. *Studied*: CUASch.; ASL; Hans Hofmann Sch. FA; Acad. FA, Florence, Italy. *Awards*: purchase prizes, ASL, 1947; Ohio Univ., 1948; prize, Ohio State Fair, 1952. *Work*: Ohio Univ.; ASL; Cooper Union Coll.; Arkansas Indst. Development Comm., and work in many private colls. *Exhibited*: BM, 1947; AFA traveling exh., 1948-49; Phila. Pr. Cl., 1947; PAFA, 1949; Akron AI, 1950, 1951; Butler Inst. Am. A., 1952, 1953; Bradley Univ., 1953, 1955, 1957; Kansas City AI, 1953; Seligmann Gal., N.Y.; J.B. Speed Mus. A.; Beloit Col.; Ohio State Univ.; Illinois Wesleyan Univ.; Columbus A. Gal.; The Jewish Center, Columbus, Ohio; CM, and others. *Position*: Assoc. Prof. A., Art Dept., University of Arkansas, Fayetteville, Ark.

REIFF, ROBERT FRANK—*Painter, E.*
625 5th Ave., St. Cloud, Minn.

B. Rochester, N.Y., Jan. 23, 1918. *Studied*: Columbia Univ., M.A.; Univ. Rochester, A.B.; Colorado Springs FA Center, and with Boardman Robinson, Adolf Dehn. *Awards*: Belgian-Am. Edu. Fnd. traveling scholarship, 1952; prizes, Rochester Mem. A. Gal., 1941, 1945, 1958; Albright A. Gal., 1956. *Work*: Pasadena AI; Rochester Mem. A. Gal.; SFMA. *Exhibited*: Rochester Mem. A. Gal., 1936-1952; Albright A. Gal., 1952; WAC, 1957; N.Y. City Center, 1957, 1958; N.Y. State Fair, Syracuse, 1958; Berkshire AA, 1958; one-man: deYoung Mem. Mus., 1944; Santa Barbara Mus. A., 1944; Pasadena AI, 1944; Rochester Mem. A. Gal., 1945; Univ. Virginia; Arena A. Gal., Rochester, 1955; Allen A. Mus., Oberlin Col., 1952. *Positions*: Instr. A., Muhlenburg Col., Allentown, Pa., 1947-49; Oberlin Col., Oberlin, Ohio, 1950- . (on leave, 1952-53); Asst. Prof., Univ. Chicago, 1954-55; State T. Col., St. Cloud, Minn., 1955-1957.

REILLY, FRANK JOSEPH—Painter, T., L., W., I.
33 West 67th St., New York 23, N.Y.; also, Glasco Turnpike, Woodstock, N.Y.

B. New York, N.Y., Aug. 21, 1906. *Studied*: ASL. *Member*: ANA; NSMP; SC; Century Assn.; All. A. Am.; Inter-Color Soc.; SI. *Award*: AAPL. *Work*: murals, in New York City schools, Bronx H.S. of Science; Johnson City, Tenn. Has made 12 full color, sound motion pictures on Artists. Lectures on many phases of art to art schools, museums and clubs; 14 yearly lectures at ASL. Contributor to American Artist; Art News and other publications. *Exhibited*: NAD; AAPL; All. A. Am.; SI; Liberty Hall, Phila., Pa. *Positions*: Instr., Grand Central Sch. A.; Moore Inst. A.; Pratt Inst.; Art Associates; Instr., Drawing & Painting, ASL; Vice-Pres., ASL. Author: Weekly art column for Newhouse Syndicate.

REILLY, MILDRED A.—Painter
118 East 59th St.; h. 3524 78th St., Jackson Heights, L.I., N.Y.

B. Milwaukee, Wis., Nov. 8, 1902. *Studied*: Milwaukee A. Sch.; Layton Sch. A.; ASL, with Robert Brackman, Robert Philipp, Howard Trafton. *Member*: NAWA. *Awards*: prizes, North Shore Hospital Benefit, Levittown, N.Y., 1951. *Work*: many portraits in private colls. *Exhibited*: Levittown, N.Y., 1951; Contemporary A. Gal., 1952; NAWA, 1954. *Position*: Freelance Fashion Illus. for leading stores and fashion magazines; Instr., Layton Sch. A., Milwaukee, Wis., 1945-48.

REIMER, CORNELIA (Mrs. E. K.)—P., T.
184 West Montecito Ave., Sierra Madre, Cal.

B. San Jacinto, Cal., Dec. 20, 1894. *Studied*: Pomona Col.; Univ. California, A.B., M.A.; Univ. Panama, with Cedeno; Pasadena Sch. FA, with Ejnar Hansen, Frode Dann, Orrin White. *Member*: Canal Zone A. Lg.; Nat. Lg. Am. Pen Women; Pasadena AA. *Awards*: prizes, Nat. Lg. Am. Pen Women, 1949 (Canal Zone Br.); 1957 (Pasadena Br.). *Exhibited*: Nat. Lg. Am. Pen Women, 1949, 1952, 1957; Las Vegas, Nevada, 1957, 1958; one-man: Tivoli Gal., Canal Zone, 1950, 1951; Altadena (Cal.) Lib., 1954; Sierra Madre, Cal., 1953-58; Pasadena A. Fair, 1957, 1958; San Gabriel, Cal., 1958.

REIN, HARRY—Painter, Ser., Des., C.
1797 Denison St., Pomona, Cal.

B. New York, N.Y. *Member*: Western Ser. Inst., Los A. *Work*: murals, Greenpoint Hospital, Brooklyn, N.Y.; Westwood Hills Christian Church, Westwood, Cal.; First Christian Church, Whittier, Cal.; Pasadena Child Guidance Clinic; Hollywood-Beverly Christian Church, Los A. *Exhibited*: MMA, 1935; New Haven Paint & Clay Cl., 1936; MModA, 1939; WFNY 1939; Jepson AI, 1950; Pomona Col., 1951. *Position*: Dir., Western Serigraph Inst., Los Angeles, Cal., 1951.

REINDEL, EDNA—Painter
804 Harvard St., Santa Monica, Cal.

B. Detroit, Mich., Feb. 19, 1900. *Studied*: PIASch. *Awards*: medal, A. Dir. Cl., 1935; F., Tiffany Fnd., 1926, 1932; prize, Beverly Hills A. Festival, 1939. *Work*: MMA; DMFA; WMAA; Ball State T. Col.; Canajoharie A. Gal.; Life magazine coll.; New Britain AI; Labor Bldg., Wash. D.C.; murals, Fairfield Court, Stamford, Conn.; Governor's House, St. Croix, Virgin Islands; USPO, Swainsboro, Ga. *Exhibited*: WMAA, 1937, 1938, 1940, 1949; Carnegie Inst., 1937, 1938, 1944-1946, 1947-1949; AIC, 1934, 1935, 1945, 1948; Macbeth Gal., 1934, 1937, 1940, 1949; Stendhal Gal., Los A., 1939, 1940; Francis Taylor Gal., Beverly Hills, 1941, 1942, 1945; Los A. Mus. A., 1940; Dallas, Tex.; Balt., Md.; Vigaveno Gal., Los A., 1953.*

REINDORF, SAMUEL—Painter, Eng., Lith., I.
342 Madison Ave., New York 17, N.Y.; h. Bayberry Lane, Westport, Conn.

B. Warsaw, Poland, Sept. 1, 1914. *Studied*: Am. A. Sch., N.Y.; & with Nahum Tschacbasov, Sol Wilson, Sol Baiserman. *Member*: A.Lg.Am. *Work*: Toronto A. Gal. *Exhibited*: WFNY 1939; Toronto A. Gal., 1935, 1937-1939; Riverside Mus., 1945. I., "The Land of the Whip," 1939; "I Came Out Alive," 1941.

REINHARDT, AD F.—Painter, E., L.
732 Broadway, New York 3, N.Y.

B. Buffalo, N.Y., Dec. 24, 1913. *Studied*: Columbia Univ. B.A.; Inst. FA, and abroad. *Work*: Mus. Living A.; PMA; WMAA; Toledo Mus. A; Yale Univ. *Exhibited*: extensively in the U.S.; one-man: BM, 1946; Columbia Univ., 1943; Betty Parsons Gal., 1946-1956. Contributor to Art News; College Art Journal; Arts & Architecture; Art D'Aujourd'hui. Co-Editor, "Modern Artists in America," 1952. *Position*: Assoc. Prof. A., Brooklyn Col., N.Y., 1947- ; Visiting Prof. A., Cal. Sch. FA, 1950; Univ. Wyoming, 1951; Yale Univ., 1952-53; N.Y.U., 1955.

REINHARDT, SIEGFRIED GERHARD—Painter, Des., T., L.
635 Craig Woods Drive, Kirkwood 22, Mo.

B. Eydkuhnen, Germany, July 31, 1925. *Studied*: Washington Univ., St. Louis, A.B. *Member*: St. Louis A. Gld. *Awards*: Scholarship, John Herron AI, 1943; prizes, 20th Century Book Cl. award, 1945; St. Louis A. Gld., 1951, 1953, 1954, 1955, 1957, 1958; CAM, 1951, 1953, 1955, 1956; Rand McNally Comp., 1952; Cincinnati Contemp. A. Center, 1958. *Work*: Abbott Laboratories; Am. Acad. A. & Lets.; CAM; Concordia T. Col.; Southern Illinois Univ.; Beloit Col.; WMAA; Cincinnati Contemp. A. Center; R.I. Sch. Des.; Nelson Gal. A., Kansas City. Murals, Rand McNally, Skokie, Ill.; Edison Bros. Shoe Co., St. Louis; Medical Bldg., Teamsters Local 88; Nooter Corp., St. Louis. *Exhibited*: Hugo Gal., N.Y., 1945; Washington Univ., 1950 (5-man); Inst. Contemp. A., Boston, 1958; USIS traveling exh. Europe, 1959; CAM, 1943-1945, 1947-1949; 1951, 1953-1958; AIC, 1954, 1956; MMA, 1950; Los A. Mus. A., 1951, 1955; WMAA, 1951-1955; WAC, 1954; DMFA, 1954; Beloit Col., 1954; AFA traveling exh., stained glass; Cincinnati A. Center, 1955, 1958; PAFA, 1958; Schweig Gal., St. Louis, 1955; Art: USA, 1958; N.Y. City Center, 1955; Hewitt Gal., N.Y., 1957, 1958; Kansas State Col., 1958. One-man: Eleanor Smith Gal., St. Louis, 1942, 1943, 1947; St. Louis A. Gld., 1951; Southern Illinois Univ., 1951, 1952; A. Mart, Clayton, Mo., 1953; Stevens-Gross Gal., Chicago, 1952; Texas Western Univ., 1954; T. Col., Bloomington, Ill., 1954; Schweig Gal., St. Louis, 1956; Hewitt Gal., 1957; St. Louis A. Gld., 1958, and others. Lectures to private groups and on TV and radio. Painted "Man of Sorrows" on 7 half-hour weekly TV shows, 1955, 1957, 1958. Work reproduced in leading art publications. *Positions*: Des., executor of stained glass windows for Emil Frei, Inc., 1948- ; Instr., painting & drawing, Washington University, St. Louis, Mo., 1955- .

REINMAN, PAUL—Painter, I., Cart., Comm. A.
1768 Stuart St., Brooklyn 29, N.Y.

B. Germany, Sept. 2, 1910. *Member*: Nat. Cartoonists Soc.; New Jersey P. & S. *Work*: Illus. Harwyn's Picture Encyclopedia, 1958. *Exhibited*: Nechemia Glezer Gal., N.Y., 1957; Viennese A. Gal., N.Y., 1957.

REINSEL, WALTER—Designer, P., Et.
2218 Rittenhouse Sq., Philadelphia 3, Pa.

B. Reading, Pa., Aug. 11, 1905. *Studied*: PAFA, & with Andre L'Hote, in Paris; also with Arthur B. Carles. *Member*: Phila. Pr. Cl.; Phila. A. All.; Phila. WC Cl. *Awards*: F., PAFA (3); several medals for layout design and typography; medal, Phila. Sketch Cl., 1952. *Work*: IBM; Reading Mus. A.; PMA; Capehart Coll.; Container Corp. Coll. *Exhibited*: PAFA, 1939-1955; Reading Mus. A., 1945; Phila. A. All. (3 one-man); Dubin Gal., Phila., 1951 (one-man); PAFA, 1948 (one-man); Audubon A., 1953, 1954, 1955; Butler AI, 1954-1958. *Position*: Assoc. A. Dir., N. W. Ayer & Son, Philadelphia, Pa.

REISMAN, PHILIP—Painter, I., Et., T.
1033 3rd Ave., New York 21, N.Y.

B. Warsaw, Poland, July 18, 1904. *Studied*: ASL, with George Bridgman, Wallace Morgan, Harry Wickey. *Member*: An Am. Group; A. Lg. Am.; AEA. *Awards*: prizes, Pepsi-Cola, 1944; Mickiewicz Centenary Comp., 1956; NAD, 1956 (gold medal). *Work*: MMA; Wadsworth Atheneum; N.Y. Lib.; MModA; Bibliotheque Nationale, Paris; mural, Bellevue Hospital, N.Y. *Exhibited*: PAFA; Pepsi-Cola; MModA; nat. print exhs.; 17 one-man exhs., including ACA Gal., 1953, 1955, 1957. I., "Anna Karenina," 1940; "Crime and Punishment," 1945. Contributor to national magazines. *Position*: Instr., Workshop Sch., New York, N.Y.; South Shore Arts Workshop, Rockville Center, N.Y., and privately.

REISS, HENRIETTE—*Painter, Des., L., T., W.*
10 Fifth Ave., New York 1, N.Y.

B. Liverpool, England, May 5, 1890. *Studied*: in Switzerland, Germany, England, & with Schildknecht in Germany. *Member*: AEA. *Exhibited*: MMA; WMAA; AIC; BMFA; BM; CMA; AFA; Am. Mus. Natural Hist.; Newark Mus.; PMA; CAM; Carnegie Inst.; Dayton AI; CM; BMA; Am. Des. Gal.; Rochester Mem. Gal.; MModA; one-man: Toledo Mus. A.; CMA; Univ. Nebraska; Univ. Kentucky; Univ. Delaware; Hackley A. Gal.; Fashion and Indst. Exh.; (music paintings) 58th St. Music Lib., N.Y., 1956-1959; extensively in Europe. Contributor to national magazines. Lectures: Design correlating music with art, to art organizations, universities and art groups U.S. and abroad. *Positions*: Taught special classes in design for supervisors, public & H.S. teachers of Bd. Edu., New York, N.Y.; Instr., Fashion Inst. Tech., (Br. State Univ.), Textile Des. Dept., New York, N.Y., at present.

REISS, LEE (Mrs. Manuel)—*Painter*
75-30 Vleigh Place, Flushing 67, N.Y.

B. New York, N.Y., July 4, 1907. *Studied*: CUASch.; A. All. Sch.; ASL; Am. A. Sch.; Queens Col., with Robert Philipp, Raphael Soyer, Ivan Olinsky. *Member*: AAPL; Long Island A. Lg. *Awards*: prize, AAPL, 1956. *Work*: in private colls. *Exhibited*: AAPL, 1956, 1957; Long Island A. Lg., 1955-1957. *Position*: Instr., Painting & Composition, Community Centre, Kew Gardens and Port Jervis, N.Y.

REISS, LIONEL S.—*Painter, Lith., I., Et., Des.*
206 East 59th St.; h. 370 Central Park West, New York 25, N.Y.

B. Austria, Jan. 29, 1894. *Member*: AWS; Audubon A. *Awards*: prizes, "Artists as Reporter" Comp.; MModA, 1940; Am. A. Group; Assoc. Am. A., 1943. *Work*: BM; Jewish Mus., N.Y.; Jewish Theological Seminary, N.Y.; Sinai Center, Chicago; Tel-Aviv Mus., Israel; Bezalel Mus.; Columbia Univ., and others. *Exhibited*: AIC; BM; Carnegie Inst.; CM; Los A. Mus. A.; WMAA; PAFA; AWS; NAD, etc. One-man: Midtown Gal., 1939; Assoc. Am. A. Gal., 1946. Author: "My Models Were Jews," 1938; "New Lights and Old Shadows," 1954.

REITER, FREDA LEIBOVITZ (Mrs.)—*Painter, Gr., I.*
3404 Federal St., Camden, N.J.

B. Philadelphia, Pa., Sept. 21, 1919. *Studied*: Moore Inst. Des.; PAFA; Barnes Fnd.; San Carlos Acad., Mexico, D.F. *Member*: AEA; Nat.Lg. Prof. Women A.; Phila. Pr. Cl. *Awards*: prizes, Graphic Sketch Cl., 1938, 1940. *Work*: Lib.Cong.; Carnegie Inst.; drawings, Phila. Inquirer. *Exhibited*: PAFA, 1936, 1938, 1941, 1942, 1954; NAD, 1941, 1944-1946, 1957, 1958; Carnegie Inst., 1943; MMA, 1943, 1949; Carlen Gal., 1942 (one-man); Phila. Pr. Cl., 1944 (one-man); Phila. YW-YMHA, 1954. Lectures: Mexican Art. I., numerous books.

REITZEL, MARQUES E.—*Painter, E., Gr., L.*
P.O. Box 186, Pescadero, Cal.

B. Fulton, Ind., Mar. 13, 1896. *Studied*: AIC, B.F.A.; Ohio State Univ., M.A., Ph.D.; Cleveland Col., Western Reserve Univ.; & with Bellows, Kroll, Hopkins, & others. *Member*: Press and Union Lg. Cl., San F.; Commonwealth Cl., San F.; Chicago SA; Pacific AA; Western Col. AA; Soc. Western A.; Indiana Soc. of Chicago. *Awards*: med. & prize, AIC, 1927, 1928; Hoosier Salon, 1929; med., Century of Progress, 1934; Chicago Galleries Assn., 1937, 1943; San Jose A. Lg., 1940, 1941; med., Century of Progress Exh., 1934. *Exhibited*: Carnegie Inst., 1929; CGA, 1929; PAFA, 1928, 1929, 1931; AIC, 1927-1929, 1931, 1934; CMA, 1931; Hoosier Salon, 1928-1931, 1940, 1942, 1944, 1945; All-California Exh., 1940, 1941, 1944; Oakland A. Gal., 1941-1943; Century of Progress, Chicago, 1934; GGE 1939. *Position*: Prof. A., San Jose State Col., San Jose, Cal., Emeritus, 1956- ; Pres., Actg. Dir., Pescadero Summer Sch. A.

REMBSKI, STANISLAV—*Painter, W., T., L.*
1404 Park Ave., Baltimore 17, Md.; s. Deer Isle, Me.

B. Sochaczew, Poland, Oct. 8, 1896. *Studied*: Technological Inst., Ecole des Beaux-Arts, Warsaw, Poland; Royal

Acad. A., Berlin, Germany. *Member*: Charcoal Cl., Balt.; NSMP; AAPL. *Work*: Univ. Cl., Balt.; Cathedral Church of the Incarnation, Balt.; Univ. Maryland Medical Sch.; NAD; Univ. North Carolina; murals, St. Bernard Sch., Gladstone, N.J.; port., Columbia Univ.; Kent Sch., Conn.; Adelphi Col.; Brooklyn Polytechnic Inst.; NAD; St. John's Hospital, Brooklyn, N.Y.; Mus. Osage Indian, Pawhuska, Okla.; Johns Hopkins Univ.; Goucher Col.; Loyola Col.; Bd. Edu., Balt.; State House, Annapolis, Md.; Woodrow Wilson Shrine, Wash., D.C.; Naval War Col., Newport, R.I.; Acad. Sciences, N.Y.; Wake Forest (N.C.) Col.; Meredith Col., N.C. *Exhibited*: one-man: Dudensing Gal.; Carnegie Hall Gal.; Newton Gal.; Chambers Gal.; BMA; Maryland Inst. A. Lectures: "Art for Life's Sake"; "Greatness in Art"; "Michelangelo"; "The Individual, Freedom, and Art"; "Mysticism in Art," and others, to universities, clubs and groups.

REMLINGER, JOSEPH J.—*Painter*
1026 Quinton Ave., Trenton 9, N.J.

B. Trenton, N.J., Aug. 29, 1909. *Studied*: Trenton Sch. Indst. A.; PAFA. *Member*: F., PAFA; Morrisville-Trenton A. Group; PAFA. *Awards*: prizes, Trenton A. Lg., 1929, 1931, 1935; PAFA, 1933; Plainfield A. Group, 1938; Westfield, N.J., 1939; Shore & River A. Group, 1941. *Exhibited*: Asbury Park Soc. FA, 1938; South Jersey Soc. A., 1936; Montclair A. Mus., 1937-1940; Kresge Gal., 1938-1941; PAFA, 1941, 1948; AIC, 1941; Univ. Iowa, 1941; Joslyn A. Mus., 1941; Denver A. Mus., 1941; New Jersey State Mus., 1939, 1945, 1950, 1954; Morrisville-Trenton A. Group, 1949-1955; F., PAFA, 1952.

REMSEN, HELEN Q.—*Sculptor, T.*
Pine Needle Rd., Siesta Key, Sarasota, Fla.

B. Algona, Iowa, Mar. 9, 1897. *Studied*: Univ. Iowa; Northwestern Univ., B.A.; Grand Central Sch. A., and with Georg Lober, John Hovannes. *Awards*: prizes, Soc. Four A., Palm Beach, Fla., 1942; Norton Gal. A., 1944; DMFA, 1944; Fla. Fed. A., 1941, 1942, 1944; Nat. Sculpture Exh., Sarasota, 1953; Smithsonian Inst., 1954; New Orleans AA, 1955, 1957. *Exhibited*: NAD, 1936; PAFA, 1937; All. A. Am.; Soc. Four A., 1942-1945; Norton Gal. A., 1944; Fla. Fed. A., 1939, 1941-1945; Berkshire Sc. Group, 1954; New Orleans AA, 1954, 1955, 1956, 1957; Washington Sc., 1954; Silvermine Gld. A., 1955; All. A. Am., 1955; Sarasota AA, 1957, 1958; Fla. Sculptors, 1958; Manatee A. Center, 1958 (one-man). *Work*: fountains: Jungle Gardens, Sarasota; St. Boniface Church, Sarasota, and in private homes.

RENIER, JOSEPH EMILE—*Sculptor*
145 East 22nd St., New York 10, N.Y.

B. Union City, N.J., Aug. 19, 1887. *Studied*: ASL; Am. Acad. in Rome, F.A.A.R.; in Paris and Brussels. *Member*: NA; NSS; Medallic A. Soc.; Arch. Lg.; NAC. *Awards*: prizes, Garden Cl. Am., 1928, 1929; Nat. Comp. for medal depicting 50th anniversary of the Medallic Art Co., 1949. *Work*: Brookgreen Gardens, S.C.; Mattatuck Mus., Waterbury, Conn.; med. for Medallic A. Soc.; des., Omar Bradley medal, awarded by Veterans of Foreign Wars; Merit Award medal; Al Jolson medal, both awarded by the Veterans of Foreign Wars; Young Mem. medal, Monarch Life Ins. Co., 1951; Ross Mem. medal, for Am. Tuberculosis Assn., 1952; triptych, Citizens Com. for the Army and Navy, 1945; bronze war mem. plaque, P.S. no. 45, Ozone Park, N.Y., 1947; s., State of Texas Bldg., Dallas, Tex.; Postal Administration Bldg., Wash. D.C.; s. panels, entrance to Domestic Relations Court, Brooklyn, N.Y.; medals, S.S. "United States"; submarine "Nautilus," 1954; Pangborn Bros.; 75th Anniversary medal for Am. Soc. Mech. Engineers, 1955; Nat. Heart Assn. award medal, 1958; Seley Fnd. medal, 1958; Daniel C. Gainey tablet, 1958; Charles E. Howard mem. medal, 1956; mem. plaques of Charles Henry and May Hanford MacNider, 1955; Arthur T. Galt, 1956; Robt. H. Gore & M. A. Hortt Mem. tablet, 1956; numerous portraits, reliefs and statuettes. *Exhibited*: PAFA; Newark Mus.; NAD; Arch. Lg.; NSS; Montclair A. Mus.; New Haven Paint & Clay Cl.

RENNIE, HELEN SEWELL—*Painter, Des.*
3073 Canal St., Northwest, Washington 7, D.C.

B. Cambridge, Md. *Studied*: Corcoran Sch. A.; NAD. *Member*: AWS; Soc. Wash. A. *Awards*: prizes, Soc. Wash. A., 1948; BMA, 1958. *Work*: PC; mural, Roosevelt H.S., Wash. D.C. *Exhibited*: MModA., 1946, 1956; CGA, 1953, 1954; BMA, 1954; one-man: Franz Bader Gal., Wash. D.C., 1954, 1958; Dupont Theatre, Wash. D.C., 1956.

RENSIE, FLORINE (Mrs. William J. Eisner)—Painter
180 West 58th St., New York 19, N.Y.

B. Philadelphia, Pa., Oct. 9, 1883. *Studied*: ASL, with Alexander Brook, Sidney Laufman. *Member*: NAWA. *Award*: Terry AI, 1952. *Exhibited*: PAFA, 1937; CGA, 1941; VMFA, 1942; "Masterpieces of Tomorrow" Exh.; NAWA; Woodstock, N.Y. (one-man); Woodstock AA; N.Y. City Center Gal.*

RET, ETIENNE (Mr.)—Painter, W., L.
Slade House, 1621 North Martel Ave., Hollywood, Cal.

B. Bourbonnais, France, Jan. 6, 1900. *Studied*: Ecole des Arts Decoratifs, Paris; & with Maurice Denis, Georges Desvallieres. *Work*: de Young Mem. Mus.; Santa Barbara Mus. A.; Pasadena AI; San Diego FA Soc.; Witte Mem. Mus.; State Mus., France; Encyclopaedia Britannica Coll. *Exhibited*: nationally. Author: "Blindman's Bluff," 1929.*

RETHI, LILI—Industrial Artist, I., Lith.
102 West 85th St., New York 24, N.Y.

B. Vienna, Austria, Nov. 19, 1894. *Studied*: Vienna Acad., with Otto Friedrich. *Work*: Sperry Gyroscope Co.; Turner Construction Co.; Spencer, White & Prentis; Merritt, Chapman & Scott; Lever Bros.; Walsh Construction Co., all of N.Y.; S.C. Bliss Co., Canton, Ohio; Eastern Stainless Steel Corp., Balt., Md.; Cities Service Co.; Surveyor, Nenninger & Chenevert, Montreal, Canada; Moran Towing & Transportation, N.Y.; Am. Soc. Mech. Engineers, and others. *Exhibited*: one-man: Arch. Lg.; Am. Soc. Civil Eng.; MMA; also in Austria, Germany, Denmark, Sweden, etc. I., "U.S. Naval Dry Dock Construction," 1941, 1943; "Builders for Battle," 1946; "Tanker Construction," 1946; "The White House Reconstruction," 1950; illus. for Encyclopaedia Americana, N.Y. and Chicago; Illus., "Favorite Tales of Long Ago," 1955; "Big Bridge to Brooklyn," 1956; "Witchcraft in Salem," 1956. Contributor of drawings to New York Times Magazine on construction of U.N. Building; Brooklyn Bridge; The White House, etc. Permanent Exh., Wallace Clark Center, N.Y. Univ. Autobiography over Radio Salzburg in series "Culture & Science," 1955; Illus.: "St. Thomas More"; "St. Philip," 1957; "St. Elizabeth," 1958; "Pasteur," 1958; "Mere Marie of New France," 1958; "Panama Canal," 1958; "Italy," 1958; "West Germany," 1958, and others.

REVA—Painter, Comm. A., I., Des.
16 West 10th St., New York 11, N.Y.

B. Coney Island, N.Y., Oct. 15, 1925. *Studied*: ASL, with Robert Hale. *Award*: Carnegie Scholarship, (ASL), 1942. *Exhibited*: Colorado Univ., 1958; Carnegie Inst., 1958; CGA, 1958; Salzburg Biennale, 1958; U.S.S traveling exh., Europe, 1958-59. *Position*: Adv. Illus. & Des., 1944- .

REVOR, SISTER MARY REMY—Educator, Des., C.
Mount Mary College, Milwaukee 10, Wis.

B. Chippewa Falls, Wis., Sept. 17, 1914. *Studied*: Mount Mary Col., B.A.; AIC, B.F.A., M.F.A.; John Herron AI. *Member*: CAA. *Awards*: prizes, Fleischman Nat. Comp. (carpet des.), Detroit, 1951; Wisconsin Des.-Craftsmen (textile des.), 1953, 1956; Wisconsin State Fair, 1955-1957. *Exhibited*: St. Paul A. Gal., 1957; Univ. Illinois, 1957; Wustum Mus. A., Racine; Alverno Col., Milwaukee; Milwaukee-Downer Col.; AIC; Midwest Des.-Craftsmen. *Position*: Prof. Des., Mount Mary College, Milwaukee, Wis.

REWALD, JOHN—Writer
67 Park Ave., New York 16, N.Y.

B. Berlin, Germany, May 12, 1912. *Studied*: Univ. Hamburg; Univ. Frankfort-on-Main; Sorbonne, Paris, Ph.D. *Awards*: prizes, Academie Française, 1941; Knight, Legion of Honor, 1954. Author: "Cezanne," 1948; "Gauguin," 1938; "Maillol," 1939; "Georges Seurat," 1943; "The History of Impressionism," 1946; "Bonnard," 1948; "Post-Impressionism—From Van Gogh to Gauguin," 1956. Ed., Cezanne's "Lettres," 1941; Gauguin's "Letters to Vollard and Fontainas," 1943; Pissarro's "Letters to His Son Lucien," 1943; Degas' "Works in Sculpture," 1944, 1958; "The Woodcuts of Maillol," 1943, 1951; "Renoir Drawings," 1946; "Cezanne, Carnets de Dessins," 1951; "Gauguin Drawings," 1958. Contributor to art magazines. Lectures on The Revolution of Impressionism; Aristide Maillol, etc.

REY, H(ANS) A(UGUSTO)—
Illustrator, W., Lith., Cart., L., Comm. A.
82 Washington Pl., New York 11, N.Y.

B. Hamburg, Germany, Sept. 16, 1898. *Studied*: Univ. Munich; Univ. Hamburg. *Member*: AIGA. *Awards*: "Curious George" chosen by AIGA, 1941, as one of 24 best Picture Books published in U.S. between 1937 and 1941; "Look for the Letters" and "Park Book" chosen as one of 58 best Picture Books, 1943 to 1945, by "1946 Books by Offset Lithography Exhibit," New York, 1946. Author, I., "Curious George," 1941; "Cecily G." 1942; "Pretzel" (with Margret Rey), 1944; "Look for the Letters," 1945; & numerous others, mainly for children. I., "Park Book," 1944; "Spotty," 1945; "Curious George Takes a Job," 1947; "Billy's Picture," 1948; "The Stars—A New Way to See Them," 1952; "Curious George Rides a Bike," 1952; "Find the Constellations," 1954; "See the Circus," 1956; "Curious George Gets a Medal," 1957; "Curious George Flies a Kite," (with Margret Rey), 1958.

REYNAL, JEANNE (SILLS)—Craftsman
240 West 11th St.; h. 140 West 11th St., New York 14, N.Y.

B. White Plains, N.Y., Apr. 1, 1903. *Award*: purchase prize, SFMA, 1944. *Work*: WMAA; MModA; SFMA; Mural, Fund for Adult Edu., White Plains, N.Y. *Exhibited*: MModA; WMAA; SFMA; BMA; Galerie Numero, Mills Col. of Edu., 1957.

REYNARD, GRANT (TYSON)—Painter, Et., Lith., L.
312 Christie Heights, Leonia, N.J.

B. Grand Island, Neb., Oct. 20, 1887. *Studied*: AIC; Chicago Acad. A.; & with Harvey Dunn, Harry Wickey, Mahonri Young. *Member*: ANA; AWCS; SAGA; Audubon A.; Assoc. A. of New Jersey; Cal. Pr. M.; AAPL; All. A. Am.; Am. A. Group; Prairie Pr.M. *Awards*: prizes, SC; Lib.Cong., 1944; Hon. deg., L.H.D., Baldwin-Wallace Col., 1955. *Work*: Montclair A. Mus.; Norton Gal. A.; Newark Mus.; FMA; Univ. Tulsa; MMA; N.Y. Pub.Lib.; Lib.Cong.; AGAA; de Young Mem. Mus.; Univ. Nebraska; N.J. State Mus., Trenton; panels, Calvary Episcopal Church, N.Y.; mural, First Baptist Church, Hackensack, N.J. *Exhibited*: WFNY 1939; AGAA (one-man); Lib.Cong.; Joslyn Mem.; Univ. Nebraska; Univ. Tulsa; AIC; PAFA; NAD; one-man exh.: Kennedy & Co.; Clayton Gal.; Grand Central A. Gal.; Assoc. Am. A.; McDowell Cl.; Bucknell Univ.; 1946; Montclair A. Mus., 1958. I., "Rattling Home for Christmas," 1941 (Am. A. Group). Contributor to: Scribner's, & other national magazines. *Position*: Pres., Montclair A. Mus., Montclair, N.J.; Council, AWS, 1958-60.

REYNERSON, JUNE—Educator
2520 North 7th St., Terre Haute, Ind.

B. Mound City, Kan., Feb. 21, 1891. *Studied*: Indiana State Normal Sch.; PIASch; Indiana State T. Col., B.S.; Columbia Univ., M.A.; & with Robert Henri, Joseph Pennell. *Member*: AAPL; PBC. Lectures: "Contemporary Trends in Painting"; "Architecture of Today and Yesterday." *Position*: Prof. Emeritus A., Indiana State T. Col., Terre Haute, Ind.*

REYNOLDS, CHARLES H(ENRY)—Painter
Kit Carson St., Box 1395; h. Brooks St., Taos, N.M.

B. Kiowa, Okla., Oct. 1, 1902. *Studied*: AIC, and with John Eliot Jenkins. *Member*: Taos AA. *Work*: Koshare Mus., La Junta, Colo.; Gilcrease Fnd., Tulsa; Southwestern Univ., Georgetown, Tex. *Exhibited*: Conn. Acad. FA, 1940; Tulsa AA, 1936-1946; Oakland A. Mus., 1943, 1948; El Paso AA, 1948; Mus. New Mexico, 1947-1953; Oklahoma AA, 1949; Harwood Lib. & A. Mus., Taos, 1947-1952; Springville H.S., 1951, 1952; Terry AI, 1952; Louisiana State Mus., 1952; one-man: Philbrook Mus. A., 1943-1950; Raton AA, 1949; San Angelo AA, 1949; Oklahoma A. Center, 1949; Phillips Univ., Enid. Okla., 1949; Tulsa A. Gld., 1950; Amarillo Col., 1950; Oklahoma City Univ., 1951; Phoenix FA Assn., 1952; Tri-State Fair, Amarillo, Tex., 1953, 1955; Texas FA Assn., 1954; Manhattan (Kans.) Pub. Lib., 1955; Mus. New Mexico; Louisiana State Mus.; Laguna Gloria Mus., and many others.

REYNOLDS, DOUGLAS WOLCOTT—Painter, E.
Kent State University; h. 1577 South Boulevard, Twin Lakes, Kent, Ohio

B. Columbus, Ga., June 14, 1913. *Studied*: Columbia Univ., M.F.A., F.A. in Edu.; North Carolina State Col.,

Sch. Des.; Ringling Sch. A.; Univ. Miami; Yale Univ., B.F.A. *Member*: N.C. State A. Soc.; Am. Soc. for Aesthetics; N.C. Edu. Assn. *Awards*: F., Yale Univ., 1941-42; Beaux-Arts Comp., 1940; Southern F. Fund grant, 1955. *Work*: Southwestern Univ., and in private colls. *Exhibited*: North Carolina State Col. Union; Columbia A. Gal.; Rome, Italy, 1941; Fla. Fed. A., 1934-1936; Fla. State Expo., 1930; New Haven, Conn., 1941, 1942 (one-man); North Carolina, 1947-1955; New York City, 1949 (one-man); Virginia, 1952. Lectures: Oriental Art and Philosophy; "On Bringing Criticism of Southern Sung Painting Up to Date," (Col. A. Conf., Cleveland), 1958 (publ. in Journal of Aesthetics, 1959). *Position*: Hd. A. Dept., Southwestern Univ., Georgetown, Tex., 1943-46; Hd., A. Dept., Meredith Col., Raleigh, N.C., 1946-1957; Kent State Univ., School of Art, Kent, Ohio, 1957- .

REYNOLDS, GORDON L.—*Educator, L., C., P.*
364 Brookline Ave., Boston 15, Mass.; h. 87 Winslow Rd., Waban 68, Mass.

B. Lynn, Mass., Sept. 6, 1907. *Studied*: Mass. Sch. A., B.S. in Edu.; Harvard Univ.; Columbia Univ.; Univ. Montana; Boston Univ. *Member*: Nat. A. Edu. Assn.; Eastern AA; Am. Soc. for Aesthetics; AFA. *Awards*: Carnegie award, Harvard Univ.; Honor award, Mass. Sch. A. Ed., 1949 Year Book, Eastern AA, "Art in General Education." *Positions*: Exec. Bd., Nat. Assn. Sch. Design; Adv. Council, A. Dept., Pub. Sch., City of Boston; Instr., State T. Col., Bridgewater, Mass., 1932-38; Pres., Mass. Sch. A., Boston, Mass., 1939- ; State Dir. A. Edu. for Massachusetts, 1939- .*

REYNOLDS, HARRY REUBEN—*Painter, C., E.*
519 North 6th East, Logan, Utah

B. Centerburg, Ohio, Jan. 29, 1898. *Studied*: AIC; Iowa State Univ., and with Birger Sandzen, B.J.O. Nordfeldt, Grant Wood and others. *Awards*: med., AIC, 1923. *Work*: Bethany Col., Lindsborg, Kans.; Utah State Fair Coll.; Ogden Pub. Schs.; Branch Agricultural Col., Cedar City, Utah; Logan H.S.; Utah State Agricultural Col. *Exhibited*: SFMA, 1931; Oakland A. Mus., 1929, 1932; Utah State Fair; Salt Lake City A. Center (one-man); photographs and paintings, Univ. Utah Lib., 1954-55 and Cache County Lib., Logan, Utah, 1954-55. *Position*: Instr., Asst. Prof., Assoc. Prof. A., Utah State Agricultural Col., Logan, Utah, 1923- ; Chm. A. Com., Exec. Com. FA, Utah State Centennial Comm., 1946-47, Production Chm., Utah State Centennial Theatrical Production of Cache County, Utah, 1955-56; Instr. A., Art Barn, Salt Lake City, Utah, 1952; Bd. Dirs., Utah State Fair Assn., 1958, Dir. of Music & FA.

REYNOLDS, JOSEPH G., JR.—*Designer, C., L., W.*
1 Washington St., Boston 14, Mass.; h. 296 Payson Rd., Belmont 78, Mass.

B. Wickford, R.I., Apr. 9, 1886. *Studied*: R.I. Sch. Des., and abroad. *Member*: Mediaeval Acad. Am.; Nat. Inst. Social Sc.; Providence A. Cl.; AFA; Boston Soc. A. & Crafts. *Awards*: medals, Boston Soc. A. & Crafts, 1929; Boston Tercentenary Exh., 1930; Paris Int. Exp., 1937; AIA, 1950. *Work*: stained glass windows, Washington Cathedral; Cathedral of St. John the Divine, N.Y.; Riverside and St. Bartholomew churches, N.Y.; Princeton Univ. Chapel; American Church in Paris; Am. Mem. Cemetery Chapel, Belleau, France; churches in Pittsburgh, Glens Falls, N.Y.; Providence, Newport, Pawtucket, Westerly and Narragansett, R.I.; Philadelphia, Lancaster, Mercersburg, Pa.; Litchfield, Conn.; Laconia, Franklin, Dover, N.H.; Wellesley Col. Chapel; Colorado Col. Chapel, and many others. Contributor to Cathedral Age, American Architect. Lectures on Stained Glass at art museums, clubs and societies, universities, colleges.

REYNOLDS, RALPH WILLIAM—*Educator, P.*
363 South Third St., Indiana, Pa.

B. Albany, Wis., Nov. 10, 1905. *Studied*: AIC; Beloit Col., B.A.; State Univ. Iowa, M.A., and with Grant Wood, Jean Charlot, Eliot O'Hara, Charles Burchfield, William Thon, Clarence Carter. *Member*: Assoc. A. Pittsburgh; Pittsburgh WC Soc.; All. A. Johnstown; NEA; Pa. State Edu. Assn.; AAUP. *Exhibited*: Oklahoma A. Center, 1939; Phila. A. All., 1939; Am. Color Pr. Soc., 1942; Iowa State Fair, 1939, 1940; Kansas City AI, 1940; Butler AI, 1941, 1942; Assoc. A. Pittsburgh, 1942-1955; Athens, Ohio, 1945, 1946; Parkersburgh FA Center 1945, 1946;

P. & S. Soc., New Jersey, 1947; All A. Johnstown, 1953-1955. *Awards*: prizes, Cornell Col., 1940; Assoc. A. Pittsburgh, 1943; Pittsburgh WC Soc., 1951, 1952, 1955. *Position*: Asst. Prof., Hd. A. Dept., Univ. South Dakota, 1940-41; Assoc. Prof., State T. Col., Indiana, Pa., 1941- .*

REYNOLDS, RICHARD (HENRY)—*Educator, P., Des., S., W., L., Cr.*
Department of Art, College of the Pacific; h. 626 North Central Ave., Stockton 4, Cal.

B. New York, N.Y., May 16, 1913. *Studied*: Santa Barbara Community A. Sch.; San Bernardino Valley Col., A.A.; Univ. California, A.B.; UCLA; Mills Col.; College of the Pacific, M.A. *Member*: CAA; NAEA; Pacific AA; San F. AA; Western Col. AA; Stockton A. Lg.; AAUP. *Awards*: prizes, Stockton A. Festival, 1951; bronze medal, Oakland A. Mus., 1952; Crocker A. Gal., Sacramento, 1952, 1953; San Joaquin Pioneer Mus., 1953; Nat. Magazine Cover Comp., 1957. *Work*: Helms Hall of Athletic Fame, Los Angeles; wall sc., lounge, Women's Dormitory, Col. of the Pacific; garden and other sc. in private colls. *Exhibited*: Oakland A. Mus., 1948, 1950-1953, 1955-1957; SFMA, 1948, 1949, 1951; Nebraska Wesleyan Univ., 1958; Stockton A. Annual, 1951-1958; Walnut Creek A. Festival, 1952; Crocker A. Gal., 1952, 1953, 1957; Cal. State Fair, 1952, 1955-1957; Mother Lode AA, 1953, 1955-1958; No. California Arts, 1956; Jack London Square A. Festival, Oakland, 1957; Auburn A. Festival, 1957; Santa Cruz, 1958. Contributor to Arts & Architecture magazine; College Art Journal. Lectures: Modern Art; Abstraction; Today's Sculpture, etc., to clubs, church groups, civic organizations, television. *Positions*: Instr. A., Asst. Chm., Div. A. & Lets., Stockton College, 1939-48; Prof. A., Chm. Dept. A., College of the Pacific, Stockton, Cal., 1948- .

RHODEN, JOHN W.—*Sculptor*
285 Eighth Ave., New York 1, N.Y.

B. Birmingham, Ala., Mar. 13, 1918. *Studied*: Columbia Univ. *Awards*: Rosenwald award, 1947-48; Tiffany Fnd. award, 1950; Fulbright Fellowship, 1951-52; Prix de Rome, 1953-54; prizes, Columbia Univ., 1948-1950; New Jersey P. & S., 1950. *Work*: Carl Milles Mus., Stockholm, Sweden; Wilmington Soc. FA; Columbia Univ.; s., Sheraton Hotel, Phila., Pa., and in private colls. *Exhibited*: MMA, 1950; Audubon A., annually; PAFA; NAD; Nat. Acad. A. & Lets.; Camino Gal., Rome, Italy; Fairweather-Hardin Gal., Chicago, 1955; Saidenberg Gal., N.Y., 1955; Schneider Gal., Rome, 1954 (one-man); traveling exh. sponsored by U.S. State Dept., (one-man) to Iceland, Ireland, Finland, Norway, Italy, Germany, etc., 1955-56; traveling exh., U.S. State Dept., to Russia, Poland, India, Siam, Cambodia, etc., 1958-59.

RHODES, DANIEL—*Educator, C.*
College of Ceramics, Alfred University, Alfred, N.Y.
Position: Prof., College of Ceramics, Alfred, N.Y.*

RHODES, LILLYAN (MRS. DANIEL)—*Sculptor*
Alfred, N.Y.

B. Des Moines, Iowa, May 15, 1915. *Studied*: Univ. Iowa; AIC; Alfred Univ. *Awards*: prizes, Western New York A., 1957; Syracuse Mus. FA, 1958.

RIBAK, LOUIS—*Painter, T.*
Taos, N.M.

B. Russia, Dec. 3, 1903. *Studied*: PAFA, with Daniel Garber; ASL, with John Sloan; Edu. All. A. Sch., N.Y. *Member*: AEA. *Work*: WMAA; Univ. Arizona; Newark Mus.; BM; mural; USPO, Albemarle, N.C. *Exhibited*: CGA; PAFA; AIC; WFNY 1939; GGE, 1939; WMAA; WMA; Walker A. Center; VMFA; MMA; Springfield Mus. FA; BM; Newark Mus.; numerous traveling exh. *Position*: Dir., Instr., Taos Valley A. Sch., Taos, N.M.*

RICCI, JERRI—*Painter*
12 Hale St., Rockport, Mass.

B. Perth Amboy, N.J. *Studied*: N.Y. Sch. App. Des. for Women; ASL, with Scott Williams, George Bridgman, Mahonri Young, and others. *Member*: AWS; All. A. Am.; ANA; Phila. WC Cl.; Audubon A.; Rockport AA; North Shore AA; Gld. Boston A. *Awards*: gold medal, All. A. Am., 1942; prizes, Rockport AA, 1943, 1946; All. A. Am.,

1948; AWS, 1948; North Shore AA, 1949; Charles Stuart Mem. prize, 1953; NAD, 1954; Herbert Pratt purchase prize, 1950; Butler AI; gold med., Audubon A., 1955; bronze med., Concord AA, 1953; silver med., Catherine L. Wolfe A. Cl. *Work:* Fairleigh Dickinson Col.; Parrish Mus., Southampton, N.Y.; Am. Acad. A. & Let.; Clark Univ.; Butler AI; Ranger Fund. *Exhibited:* Toledo Mus. A.; PAFA; AIC; Dayton AI; AGAA; Am. Acad. A. & Let.; one-man: Milch Gal., 1947, 1951, 1953, 1955.*

RICCI, ULYSSES ANTHONY—*Sculptor*

1947 Broadway; h. 420 Riverside Dr., New York 25, N.Y.

B. New York, N.Y., May 2, 1888. *Studied:* CUASch; ASL; & with James Earle Fraser. *Member:* ANA; Am. Numismatic Soc.; NSS; All. A. Am.; SC. *Awards:* prize, med., Rome, Italy, 1926; prizes, SC; All. A. Am. *Work:* medals, Am. Numismatic Soc.; s., Plattsburg, N.Y.; Bowery Savings Bank; Rundel Mem. Lib.; Rochester Univ.; Arlington Mem.; Am. Pharmaceutical Bldg., Wash., D.C.; LeMoyne Univ., Syracuse, N.Y.; Anabel Mem., Cornell Univ.; Dept. Commerce Bldg., Wash., D.C.; & others. *Exhibited:* PAFA; MMA (AV), 1942; NAD; All. A. Am.; Arch. L.; SC.

RICE, HAROLD R.—*Educator, Cr., W., Gr., L.*

Moore Institute of Art, Science & Industry, Broad & Master Sts., Philadelphia 21, Pa.; h. 1210 West Wynnewood Rd., Wynnewood, Pa.

B. Salineville, Ohio, May 22, 1912. *Studied:* Univ. Cincinnati, B.S. in Edu., M.S. in Edu.; Columbia Univ., Ed. D. *Member:* MModA; PAFA; Franklin Inn Cl.; Phila. A. All.; Nat. Assn. Sch. Des.; Eastern AA; AFA; Nat. A. Edu. Assn.; Nat. Edu. Assn.; Am. Assn. Univ. Prof. *Awards:* Dow Scholar, Columbia Univ., 1943-44. *Exhibited:* CM; Montgomery Mus. FA; Birmingham Pub. Lib.; Univ. Cincinnati; Univ. Alabama. Contributing Ed., Junior Arts & Activities, 1937-46; compiled and published Encyclopaedia of Silk Magic, Vol. 1, 1948, Vol. 2, 1952. *Positions:* A. Supv., Wyoming, Ohio, Pub. Sch., 1934-42; Cr., T., Univ. Cincinnati, 1942-43; Assoc. Prof. A., Acting Hd. Dept. A., Univ. Alabama, 1944, Prof. A., Hd. Dept., 1945-46; Dean, Moore Inst. A., Sc. & Indst., Philadelphia, Pa., 1946- , Pres., 1951- . Adv. A. Ed., The Book of Knowledge, The Children's Encyclopaedia, Grolier Soc., 1951- ; General Chm., Arts & Skills Corps, Am. Red Cross, Alabama, 1944-46; Nat. Jury Col. A. Scholarships, Scholastic Awards, Pittsburgh, Pa., 1949; Sec., 1949-55, Pres., 1955-1957, Nat. Assn. Sch. Des.; Vice-Pres., 1956-58, Pres., 1958-60, Eastern AA; Dir., 1947- , Phila. A. All.; Dir., 1953-54, 1958- , Harcum Jr. College; Dir., 1958- . Wynnewood Civic Assn.

RICE, NORMAN LEWIS—*Educator, Gr., P.*

Carnegie College of Fine Arts, Pittsburgh 13, Pa.

B. Aurora, Ill., July 22, 1905. *Studied:* Univ. Illinois, B.A.; AIC. *Member:* Cliff Dwellers, Chicago. *Position:* Assoc. Dean, Dean, AIC, 1930-42; Dir., Sch. A., Col. FA, Syracuse Univ., Syracuse, N.Y., 1946-54; Pres., Nat. Assn. Schs. of Des., 1957- ; Pres., Pittsburgh Plan for Art, 1958- ; Dean, Col. FA, Carnegie Inst. Tech., Pittsburgh, Pa., 1954- .

RICE, WILLIAM SELTZER—
Etcher, T., P., Des., I., W., L.

2083 Rosedale Ave., Oakland 1, Cal.

B. Manheim, Pa., June 23, 1873. *Studied:* PMSchIA; Drexel Inst.; Col. A. & Crafts, Oakland, Cal., B.F.A.; & with Howard Pyle. *Member:* Cal. SE; Cal. Soc. Pr. M.; Prairie Pr. M. *Awards:* prizes, PMSchIA, 1904; Cal. SE, 1943, 1945. *Work:* Cal. State Lib. *Exhibited:* Lib. Cong., Phila. Pr. Cl., 1943, 1944, 1946; Cal. SE, annually since 1912. *Author:* "Block Printing in the School"; "Block Prints—How to Make Them." *Contributor to:* School Arts, Design magazines; Christian Science Monitor. *Lectures:* Block Print Making. *Position:* Hd. Dept. A., Fremont H.S., 1914-30; Castlemont H.S., Oakland, Cal., 1930-40; Instr., Univ. California Extension Dept., 1932-43.

RICH, DANIEL CATTON—*Museum Director, W., L.*

Worcester Art Museum; h. 3 Tuckerman St., Worcester 9, Mass.

B. South Bend, Ind., Apr. 16, 1904. *Studied:* Univ. Chicago, Ph.B.; Harvard Univ. *Member:* Intl. Council of Museums; Am. Soc. for Aesthetics; AID; Hon. Memb., Chicago Chptr., AIA; Assn. A. Mus. Dirs.; Am. Assn. Mus. *Awards:* Chevalier, Officier Legion d'Honneur; Officer of the Order of Orange Nassau; Knight of the Merit. *Author:* "Seurat and The Evolution of 'La Grande Jatte,' " 1935; Charles H. and Mary F. S. Worcester Collection Catalogue, 1938; "Degas," 1951. *Contributor to* Art News; Atlantic Monthly; College Art Journal. *Lectures:* Degas; The Two Tiepolos; all phases of Painting and Sculpture especially in 17th, 18th and 19th century painting. *Arranged exhs:* The Two Tiepolos; Henri Rousseau, 1946; Toulouse-Lautrec, 1931; Rembrandt and His Circle, 1935; Hogarth, Constable & Turner, 1946; The Art of Fr. Goya, 1941; Chauncey McCormick Memorial Exhibition, 1955; Georges Seurat, 1958, and others. *Positions:* Ed., "Bulletin," 1927-32, Asst. Cur. Painting & Sculpture, 1929-31, Assoc. Cur., 1931-38, Cur., 1938- , Dir. FA, 1938-43, Dir., 1943-58, Art Institute of Chicago; Trustee, 1955-58, Hon. Gov. Life Memb., Art Institute of Chicago; Dir., Worcester Art Museum, Worcester, Mass., 1958- .

RICH, FRANCES—*Sculptor*

4385 Marina Dr., Santa Barbara, Cal.

B. Spokane, Wash., Jan. 8, 1910. *Studied:* Smith Col., B.A.; BMFA Sch.; Cranbrook Acad. A.; Claremont Col.; Columbia Univ., and with Malvina Hoffman, Carl Milles, Alexander Jacovleff. *Member:* Arch. Lg.; NSS; Cosmopolitan Cl.; Botolph Group, Boston; Liturgical A. Soc. *Work:* Army-Navy Nurse mem., Arlington Nat. Cemetery; Purdue Univ.; Wayside Chapel of St. Francis, Grace Cathedral, San F.; Mt. Angel Abbey, St. Benedict, Ore.; Hall of Fame, Ponca City, Okla.; Oklahoma A. & M. Col.; Smith Col.; St. Peters Church, Redwood City, Cal.; Univ. Cal., Berkeley; Madonna House, Combermere, Ont., Canada; Carl Milles Mus. Garden, Stockholm; Univ. Oklahoma; sc. medals, Dr. Jonas Salk; Florence Corliss Lamont; many port. busts in private colls. *Exhibited:* Am. Acad. Des., N.Y., 1936; Cranbrook Acad. A., 1938, 1939; Santa Barbara Mus. A., 1941, 1942, 1952 (one-man); Greek Theatre, Los A., 1946-1952; Nat. Mus. Mod. A., Rome, Italy, 1952; deYoung Mem. Mus., 1952; Madonna Festival, Bel Air and Santa Barbara, Cal., 1954; Margaret Brown Gal., Boston, 1954; Merrill Coll. Religious Art, Wash., D.C. and Alexandria, Va., 1954, 1955; Denver A. Mus., 1955; Am. Baptist Assembly, Green Lake, Wis., 1955; Print Room Gal., Tucson, 1956; Nat. Decorators' Show, San F., 1956; Grace Cathedral, San F., 1957; one-man: Cal. PLH, 1955; Laguna Blanca Sch., Santa Barbara, 1955; A. Center, Phoenix, 1955.

RICHARD, BETTI—*Sculptor*

Durham Road, Larchmont, N.Y.

B. New York, N.Y., Mar. 16, 1916. *Studied:* ASL with Mahonri Young, Paul Manship. *Member:* All. A. Am.; NSS; Arch. Lg.; Mun. A. Soc.; Audubon A. *Awards:* prizes, NAD, 1947; med., Pen & Brush Cl., 1951; gold medal, All. A. Am., 1956. *Work:* doors, Oscar Smith Mausoleum; Church of the Immaculate Conception, N.Y.; Pieta, Skouras Mem., N.Y.; three bronze panels, Bellingrath Gardens, Mobile, Ala.; monument to race horse "Omaha" at Ak-Sar-Ben Track, Omaha; fig., Austrian Legation, Tokyo; fig. Sacred Heart Rectory, Roslindale, Mass.; statue, St. Francis of Assisi Church, N.Y.; House of Theology, Centerville, Ohio, and numerous port. busts in private colls. *Exhibited:* NAD, 1944-1956; PAFA, 1949; All. A. Am.; Audubon A.; PMA, 1949; Arch. Lg.; Pen & Brush Cl.; Vienna, Austria, 1954, 1955.

RICHARDS, GLENORA—*Miniature Painter*

Gerrish Lane, New Canaan, Conn.

B. New London, Ohio, Feb. 18, 1909. *Studied:* Cleveland Sch. A. *Member:* ASMP; NAWA. *Awards:* medal, ASMP, 1947; Pa. Soc. Min. P., 1947; medal, NAWA, 1953; Wash. Min. P. & S. Soc., 1956, 1957. *Work:* PMA. *Exhibited:* ASMP, 1947-1956; NAWA, 1953-1956.

RICHARDS, JEANNE HERRON—*Etcher, Eng., Lith.*

3506 Cameron Mills Rd., Alexandria, Va.

B. Aurora, Ill., Apr. 8, 1923. *Studied:* Univ. Illinois; Colorado Springs FA Center; Iowa State Univ., B.A., and with William S. Hayter, Mauricio Lasansky. *Member:* Pr. Council of Am.; CAA. *Awards:* Fulbright F., 1954-55; prizes, Des Moines A. Center, 1953; Univ. So. Cal., 1954; Bradley Univ., 1954; Nelson Gal. A., 1954. *Work:* SAGA; Des Moines A. Center. *Exhibited:* SAM, 1946; Denver A.

Mus., 1946; SAGA, 1947, 1950, 1951, 1957; LC, 1948, 1957, 1958; J. B. Speed A. Mus., 1950; Flint Inst. A., 1950; Syracuse Mus. FA, 1950; BM, 1951, 1953, 1954; Bradley Univ., 1952, 1954; Joslyn A. Mus., 1952; SFMA, 1952; Wash. A. Cl., 1948 (one-man); Des Moines A. Center, 1952, 1953; Phila. Pr. Cl., 1949; MMA, 1952; SAM, 1953, 1955; DMFA, 1953, 1954; Univ. So. Cal., 1953, 1954; LC, 1954; Youngstown Col., 1954; Springfield A. Mus., 1955; Oakland A. Mus., 1955; Paris, France, 1955; Soc. Boston Pr. M., 1956, 1957; Bay Pr. M., 1956, 1957; Wash. Pr. M., 1957, 1958; Univ. Kansas, 1958; CGA, 1957; 3-man: Studio Gal., Alexandria, Va., 1957; State Univ. Iowa, 1957; Nelson Gal. Art, 1958. *Position*: Instr., Prints & Drawing, University of Nebraska, Lincoln, Neb., 1957- .

RICHARDS, KARL FREDERICK—*Educator, P., W.*
Art Department, Texas Christian University; h. 1303 West Presidio St., Fort Worth 3, Tex.

B. Youngstown, Ohio, June 14, 1920. *Studied*: Cleveland Inst. A.; Western Reserve Univ., B.S. in Edu.; State Univ. Iowa, M.A.; Ohio State Univ., Ph.D. *Member*: Cleveland Soc. A.; AFA; AAUP. *Awards*: prizes, Ohio Valley Exh., 1948; Toledo Area Exh., 1953; Butler Inst. Am. A., 1953, 1954; A. Festival, Pinellas Park, Fla., 1956. *Exhibited*: Indiana (Pa.) State T. Col., 1954; Creative Gal., N.Y., 1954; Contemp. A. Gal., N.Y., 1954; Palm Beach, Fla., 1955; Massillon A. Mus., 1953, 1955; Sarasota, Fla., 1955; Florida State Fair ,1956; Ohio Valley Exh., Athens, Ohio, 1948; Butler Inst. Am. A., 1944, 1949, 1953, 1954; Canton AI, 1950, 1952, 1953, 1955; Louisville, Ky., 1950, and numerous local exhs.; one-man: Pinellas Park, Fla. *Positions*: Instr. A., Bowling Green State University, Bowling Green, Ohio, 1947-56; Assoc. Prof. A., Chm., A. Dept., Texas Christian University, Fort Worth, Tex., 1956- .

RICHARDS, WILLIAM COOLIDGE—*Painter*
400 East 59th St., New York, N.Y.; h. Ocean Springs, Miss.

B. Columbus, Miss., Mar. 23, 1914. *Studied*: Univ. Virginia; Tulane Univ., B.A.; Cincinnati A. Acad.; ASL, with Brook, Kuniyoshi, Laurent and Zorach. *Exhibited*: Galerie Raspail, France, 1948; Little Studio, 1952, 1955 (one-man); Jackson (Miss.) A. Mus.; Mobile AA, 1957; Telfair Acad., Savannah, 1957.

**RICHARDSON, CONSTANCE (COLEMAN) (*Mrs. E. P.)*
—*Painter***
734 Glynn Court, Detroit 2, Mich.

B. Indianapolis, Ind., Jan. 18, 1905. *Studied*: Vassar Col.; PAFA. *Work*: John Herron AI; Detroit Inst. A.; PAFA; Saginaw Mus. A.; Grand Rapids A. Mus.; New Britain Inst. *Exhibited*: AIC, 1940, 1941, 1945; Carnegie Inst., 1941, 1943-1945; CGA, 1945, 1951; WMAA, 1944, 1945; PAFA, 1944, 1945, 1958; deYoung Mem. Mus., 1943, 1947; CM, 1945; Detroit Inst. A., 1945-1957; Cal. PLH, 1948; Montclair A. Mus., 1951; MMA, 1951; Utica, N.Y., 1951; Macbeth Gal., 1950; Wildenstein Gal., 1955; Butler Inst. Am. A., 1958; USIS traveling exh., Latin America, 1956-57; USIS traveling exh., Greece, Israel, Turkey, 1958-59.

RICHARDSON, E(DGAR) P(RESTON)—
Museum Director, W., L.
5200 Woodward Ave.; h. 734 Glynn Court, Detroit 2, Mich.

B. Glens Falls, N.Y., Dec. 2, 1902. *Studied*: Univ. Pennsylvania; Williams Col., A.B.; PAFA. Author: "The Way of Western Art," 1939; "American Romantic Painting," 1944; "Washington Allston," 1948; "Painting in America—The Story of 450 Years," 1956. Exhibition catalogues: for USIS exh. in Israel "Nine Generations of American Painting," 1958; for exh. in South America, "Collection Fleischman," 1957. Pamphlet: "The Adoration with Two Angels by Andrea del Verrocchio and Leonardo da Vinci," 1957. *Position*: Dir., Detroit Institute of Arts, Detroit, Mich.; Ed., The Art Quarterly; Dir., Archives of American Art.

RICHARDSON, GERARD—*Painter, Des.*
1534 North 22nd St., Arlington 9, Va.

B. New York, N.Y., 1910. *Studied*: Ecole des Beaux-Arts, Paris. *Work*: Specialist in nautical paintings, sportscar

and air activities, historical and combat paintings. Artwork reproduced in magazines in Italy, France and England. Covers for Motor Boating magazine and paintings for Socony (Small Craft Div.) in New York. Art work and murals: Perpetual & Federal Guardian Bldgs., illus. Navy League activities, Wash., D.C. Private patrons include household names in Finance, Sports and the Professions, U.S. and abroad. Served as Official Artist, International Naval Review, 1957 making official gift paintings for visiting Allied Navies. Cited for "Creating International Goodwill." Created Navy's mural contribution to the new Armed Forces Staff College auditorium, Norfolk, Va. Des. official State parade floats for Presidential Inauguration 1957, Derby Festival, Louisville, Ky., "500" parade, Indianapolis, and many others. *Exhibited*: Europe; Truxton-Decatur Mus., and Pentagon, Wash., D.C., USN's nationwide Operation "Palette."

**RICHARDSON, GRETCHEN (*Mrs. Ronald Freelander)*
—*Sculptor***
631 Park Ave., New York 21, N.Y.

B. Detroit, Mich., Nov. 14, 1910. *Studied*: Wellesley Col., B.A.; ASL with William Zorach; Acad. Julian, Paris, France. *Member*: NAWA; AEA. *Awards*: prizes, NAWA, 1952, 1955. *Exhibited*: PAFA, 1953; NAD, 1948, 1950; Audubon A., 1948-1958; NAWA, 1950-1958; Pen & Brush Cl., 1950, 1952; Women's Intl. A. Cl., London, 1955.

RICHERT, CHARLES H.—*Painter, T.*
10 Linden St., Arlington 74, Mass.

B. Boston, Mass., July 7, 1880. *Studied*: Mass. Normal A. Sch.; & with Joseph De Camp, Ernest L. Major. *Member*: Boston Soc. WC Painters. *Awards*: med., BAID, 1919, 1920. *Exhibited*: PAFA; NAD; AIC; BMFA.

RICHEY, OAKLEY E.—*Painter, E., L., P.*
Arsenal Technical Schools, 1500 East Michigan St.; h. 3738 Colorado Ave., Indianapolis 18, Ind.

B. Hancock County, Ind., Mar. 24, 1902. *Studied*: John Herron AI, M.A.E.; Grand Central Sch. A.; ASL, and with DuMond, Purves, Pogany. *Member*: Nat. Edu. Assn.; Indiana State T. Assn.; Indianapolis Fed. Pub. Sch. T.; Indianapolis AA; Richmond AA. *Awards*: prizes, Hoosier Salon, 1948, 1950, 1953; Indiana State Fair, 1950. *Work*: Richmond (Ind.) AA; murals, Connersville (Ind.) H.S.; West Lafayette (Ind.) Pub. Sch.; Pittsburgh (Kans.) Pub. Lib. *Positions*: Instr., John Herron A. Sch., 1924-35; Instr. A., 1935- , Hd. A. Dept., 1942-48, 1952- , Arsenal Technical Schools, Indianapolis, Ind.; I., Indiana Univ. Ext., Indianapolis, Ind., 1932- .

RICHMAN, ROBERT M.—*Museum Director, W., Cr., E.*
Institute of Contemporary Arts; h. 3102 R St., Northwest, Washington 7, D.C.

B. Connersville, Ind., Dec. 22, 1919. *Studied*: Western Michigan Univ., A.B. (English), A.B. (Hist.); Univ. Michigan, A.M. *Member*: Am. Assn. Mus. Dirs.; AAMus.; CAA; AEA. *Awards*: Hopwood awards, 1942-1944. Ed., "The Arts at Mid-Century," 1954; publ., "The Potter's Portfolio," 1950; Author: "Nature in the Modern Arts." Contributor to New Republic; Kenyon Review; Casa Bella; Encounter; and other magazines. Lectures: on The Philosophy of Modern Art, at the Nat. Gal. A.; Library of Congress, etc. Arranged over 70 exhs. of recent work by contemporary artists from Europe, Asia and The Americas. *Positions*: Literary & Art Ed., The New Republic magazine, 1951-54; Actg. Dir., the Washington Festival of Arts, 1958; Trustee, Inst. Contemp. A.; ANTA; Exec. Comm., Washington A. Festival; Exec. Bd., President's Fine Arts Committee (People-to-People); Fndr., Dir., The Institute of Contemporary Arts, Washington, D.C., 1947- .

RICHMOND, AGNES M.—*Painter*
211 Green Ave., Brooklyn 38, N.Y.

B. Alton, Ill. *Studied*: St. Louis Sch. FA; ASL. *Member*: All. A. Am.; Fifty Am. A.; NAWA; AAPL. *Awards*: prizes, NAWA, 1911, 1922, 1933; New Rochelle, N.Y., 1932; All. A. Am., 1947, 1952, 1953. *Work*: San Diego FA Soc.; Hickory (N.C.) Mus. A. *Exhibited*: CGA; PAFA; Carnegie Inst.; NAD; Phila. WC Cl.; Toronto, Montreal, Canada; NAWA; AAPL; All. A. Am.

RICHMOND, EVELYN K.—*Painter*

1600 Garden St., Santa Barbara, Cal.

B. Boston, Mass., Jan. 29, 1872. *Studied*: with Henry B. Snell. *Member*: NAWA; Providence WC Cl.; Santa Barbara A. Lg.; Cal. WC Soc.

RICHMOND, GAYLORD D.—*Painter, Des., C., T.*

32619 Whispering Palms Trail, Palm Springs, Cal.

B. Milan, Mo., Mar. 23, 1903. *Studied*: Otis AI; Yale Univ., B.F.A., M.F.A.; & with E. Roscoe Shrader. *Member*: Cal. AC; New Haven Paint & Clay Cl.; Conn. Acad. FA. *Awards*: prizes, New Haven Paint & Clay Cl., 1931, 1938. *Position*: Dir., Richmond Gal., Palm Springs, Cal.; Pres., Desert A. Center.

RICHTER, GISELA MARIE AUGUSTA—
Museum Curator, W., L., C.

American Academy, Rome, Italy

B. London, England, Aug. 15, 1882. *Studied*: Girton Col., Cambridge; British Sch. Archaeology, Athens, Greece; Trinity Col. Dublin, Litt. D.; Cambridge Univ., England, Litt. D. *Member*: F., Am. Numismatic Soc.; Archaeological Inst. Am.; Int. Fed. Univ. Women; Pont. Accademia Romana; Am. Acad. in Rome; Hellenic & Roman Soc.; London; Hon. F., Somerville Col., Oxford; Hon. F., Girton Col., Cambridge; hon. degrees, L.H.D., Smith Col., 1935; D.F.A., Rochester Univ., 1940; Univ. of Oxford, 1952; award, Am. Assn. Univ. Women, 1944. Author: "Animals in Greek Sculpture," 1930; "Handbook of the Etruscan Collection," 1940; "Kouroi," 1942; "Attic Red-figures Vases, A Survey," 1946; "Archaic Greek Art," 1949; "Sculpture and Sculptors of the Greeks," 1950; "Three Critical Periods in Greek Sculpture," 1951; "Ancient Italy," 1955; "Introduction to Greek Art," 1959; & many other handbooks, catalogs, etc., on collections of the MMA. Contributor to: Archaeological & museum journals and bulletins. Lectures: Greek, Roman and Etruscan Art & Archaeology, 1000 B.C.-300 A.D. *Positions*: Asst., Classical Dept., 1906-10, Asst. Cur., 1910-22, Assoc. Cur., 1922-25; Cur., 1925-48, Hon. Cur., 1948- , MMA, New York, N.Y.; Assoc. Ed., Am. Journal of Archaeology; Pres., N.Y. Soc. of the Archaeological Inst. Am., 1941-46; L., Yale Univ., 1938, Bryn Mawr Col., 1941, Oberlin Col., 1943; Dumbarton Oaks, 1949; Univ. Michigan, 1952; Am. Acad. in Rome, 1952; Somerville Col., Oxford, 1954; Roman Soc., London, 1957; Visiting L., Columbia Univ.

RICHTER, JULIUS—*Painter, Eng., L., Et.*

2556 Main St., Buffalo 14, N.Y.

B. Allegheny, Pa., Dec. 19, 1876. *Studied*: with Volney A. Richardson, Mildred C. Green, Emile Gruppe. *Member*: Buffalo SA; Buffalo Pr. Cl.; Am. Physicians AA. *Awards*: "Print of the Year," 1950; medal, Buffalo Soc. A., 1945. *Exhibited*: Am. Physicians Exh., annually; Buffalo SA, annually; Albright A. Gal., 1946. *Position*: L., Anatomy in Art, Albright A. Sch., Buffalo, N.Y., 1924-1934.

RICHTER, LOUISE C. (Mrs. William F.)—*Designer, E.*

School of Fine Arts, Washington Univ., St. Louis 5, Mo.; h. Route 1, West, Box 52, Washington, Mo.

B. Akron, Ohio, Dec. 4, 1918. *Studied*: Carnegie Inst., B.F.A. *Work*: Univ. West Virginia; Granite City Steel Co., Granite City, Ill.; designed Univ. medallion, Washington Univ., St. Louis, Mo. *Position*: Instr. Des., Washington Univ. Sch. FA, St. Louis, Mo., 1941- ; Consultant Des., Wrought Iron Range Co., St. Louis, Mo., 1944- ; Master Plastic Molding Corp., St. Louis, Mo., 1945- .*

RICKEY, GEORGE WARREN—*Sculptor, P., E.*

Newcomb College, Tulane Univ.; h. 2808 Calhoun St., New Orleans, La.

B. South Bend, Ind., June 6, 1907. *Studied*: Trinity Col., Glenamond, Scotland; Balliol Col., Oxford, B.A., M.A.; Ruskin Sch. Drawing; Academie Lhote, Paris; N.Y. Univ.; Univ. Iowa; Inst. Des., Chicago. *Member*: CAA; Mid-West AA; AAUP; Southeastern AA. *Awards*: prizes, Denver A. Gld., 1947; Delgado Mus. A., 1947; Evansville, Ind., 1954; Louisville A. Center; J. B. Speed Mus. A. *Work*: Allentown Mus. A. (Pa.); Grand Rapids A. Gal.; murals, Olivet Col., Mich.; Knox Col.; sc., BMA. *Exhibited*: Kraushaar Gal., 1951-1955; Margaret Brown Gal., Boston, 1953-1955; MMA, 1951; PAFA, 1952, 1954;

WMAA, 1952, 1953; John Herron AI, 1952-1954; Tri-State Exh., Evansville, 1952, 1953; Ogunquit Mus. A., 1954; Louisville A. Center, 1952, 1954; Joslyn Mus. A., 1955; Univ. Nebraska, 1955; Univ. Minnesota, 1955; one-man: John Herron AI, 1953; Kraushaar Gal., 1955, 1959; Delgado Mus. A., 1956. Author, chapter, "Kinetic Sculpture" in "Art and Artist," 1956; illus. "The Beggar & Other Stories," 1949. Contributor to College Art Journal; Denver Post & Rocky Mountain News; Assn. Am. Colleges Bulletin; Art Education Today; Les Temps Modernes, and others. *Position*: Hd. A. Dept., Olivet Col., 1937-39; Kalamazoo Col., 1939-40; Kalamazoo Inst. A., 1939-40; Knox Col., 1940-41; Muhlenberg Col., 1941-48; Univ. Indiana, 1949-55; Tulane Univ., New Orleans, La., 1955- ; Trustee Delgado Mus. A.

RICKLY, JESSIE BEARD—*Painter, Gr., L., Cart.*

471 Foote Ave., Webster Groves 19, Mo.

B. Leeper, Mo., Oct. 5, 1895. *Studied*: St. Louis Sch. FA; Harvard Univ., and with Charles Hawthorne. *Member*: Missourians; St. Louis A. Gld. *Awards*: Carnegie scholarship to Harvard Univ., 1940; prizes, St. Louis A. Gld., 1927, 1945; medal, Kansas City AI, 1934. *Work*: Flynn Park Sch. & Jr. H.S., University City, Mo.; Executive Mansion, Jefferson City, Mo.; Butler County Court House; Hodgens Sch., Maplewood; University City Sr. H.S. *Exhibited*: CAM, 1928, 1939; SSAL, 1933, 1934; Kansas City AI, 1929, 1940; Carroll Knight Gal., St. Louis, 1948; Joslyn A. Mus., 1949; Monticello Col., Godfrey, Ill., 1952; State Col., Cape Girardeau, Mo., 1950; Henry George Sch., N.Y., 1951; St. Louis A. Gld., 1957. *Positions*: Instr., Washington Univ. Sch. A., 1951.

RIDABOCK, RAY(MOND) (BUDD)—*Painter, T.*

South Lane, Redding Ridge, Conn.

B. Stamford, Conn., Feb. 16, 1904. *Studied*: Williams Col., and with Amy Jones, Anthony di Bona, Peppino Mangravite, Xavier Gonzalez. *Member*: AWS; AEA; SC; Silvermine Gld. A.; Alabama WC Soc.; Conn. WC Soc.; Nat. Soc. Painters in Casein; New Jersey P. & S. Soc. *Awards*: New Jersey P. & S. Soc., 1949, 1950, 1954, 1955, 1956, 1958; Ross A. Gal., 1949; Knickerbocker A., 1952, 1954, 1958; Munson-Williams-Proctor Inst., 1954; Springfield A. Lg., 1954, 1955; State T. Col., Indiana, Pa., 1954; Wilmington Soc. FA, 1954, 1956; Caravan Gal., 1955; Albany Inst. Hist. & A., 1955; Village A. Center, 1955; New Haven Paint & Clay Cl., 1956, 1958; Silvermine Gld. A., 1956, 1957; Wash. WC Cl., 1956; New Orleans AA, 1957; Audubon A., medal, 1958. *Work*: New Britain A. Mus.; N.Y. Hospital; Ross A. Gal.; Williams Col.; Munson-Williams-Proctor Inst.; State T. Col., Indiana, Pa.; Delaware A. Center; Dr. Lawrason Brown Mem. Coll., Saranac Lake, N.Y.; New Haven Paint & Clay Cl. *Exhibited*: AWS, 1953, 1954; PAFA, 1953; All. A. Am., 1953; Audubon A., 1954, 1955; NAC, 1954; Wash. WC Cl., 1947, 1954, 1955; Berlin, Germany, 1954; BMA, 1955; Norton Gal. A., 1950; All New England Exh., 1953-1955; Dayton AI, 1950; Nat. Soc. Painters in Casein, 1955; one-man: Lawrence A. Mus., Williams Col., 1947; St. Lawrence Univ., 1951, 1953; Silvermine Gld. A., 1955; Danbury State T. Col., 1957; Kipnis Gal., Westport, 1956, 1957, and others. *Position*: Instr., Silvermine Gld. A., 1958- ; Danbury State T. Col., 1957- .

RIDGELY, FRANCES SUMMERS (Mrs. J. A.)—
Museum Curator, W., L., P.

1037 Woodland Ave., Springfield, Ill.

B. Curran, Ill., Aug. 22, 1892. *Studied*: Syracuse Univ.; AIC. *Member*: Springfield AA; Nat. Lg. Am. Pen Women; (State Art Chm.). *Exhibited*: Springfield AA; Illinois State Mus. Contributor to Child Life Magazine; The Living Museum. Painter of backgrounds for habitat groups. *Position*: Cur. A. Illinois State Mus., Springfield, Ill., 1941- .

RIDGEWAY, FRANK EDWARD, JR.—*Cartoonist*

114 Island Circle, Sarasota, Fla.

B. Danbury, Conn., Apr. 7, 1930. *Studied*: ASL; Cartoonists & Illustrators Sch., N.Y. *Work*: comic strip "Mr. Abernathy" for King Features Syndicate. *Position*: Instr., Cartooning, Famous Artist Schools, Westport, Conn.

RIEGGER, HAL—*Craftsman, E., S.*

Route 1, Box 193-A, Mill Valley, Cal.

B. Ithaca, N.Y., July 21, 1913. *Studied*: N.Y. State Ceramic Col., Alfred Univ., B.S.; Ohio State Univ., M.A. *Member*: San F. Potters Assn.; Fla. Craftsmen Assn. *Awards*: prizes, Syracuse Mus. FA, 1939, 1949; West Coast Ceramic Annual, 1948; San F. Potters Assn., 1956; Cal. State Fair, 1956. *Work*: Syracuse Mus. FA; MMA; MModA. *Exhibited*: GGE, 1939; Syracuse Mus. FA; WFNY 1939; WMAA; Phila. A. All.; European traveling exh. ceramics; AFA traveling exh. "California Crafts"; 2-man (with Jack Larsen) Phila. A. All.; Oregon Ceramic Studios, Portland; Richmond (Cal.) A. Center, 1958 (one-man). Contributor to Ceramic Industry; Ceramics Monthly. *Position*: Prof. Ceramics & Sculpture, Florida Gulf Coast A. Center, Clearwater, Fla.

RIEKER, ALBERT GEORGE—*Sculptor*

628 Toulouse St.; h. 541 St. Ann St., New Orleans 16, La.

B. Stuttgart, Germany, Oct. 18, 1889. *Studied*: Univ. Munich; Royal Acad. FA, Munich; Royal Acad. FA, Stuttgart. *Member*: New Orleans A. Lg.; SSAL; New Orleans AA. *Awards*: prize, Stuttgart, 1910; Nuremberg, 1911; St. Wurtemberg, Stuttgart, 1921; New Orleans AA, 1934, 1940, 1941; SSAL, 1938; La. State Exh., 1939. *Work*: monuments, mem., figures: Vicksburg (Miss.) Nat. Park; State Capitol, Baton Rouge, La.; Courthouse, Pascagoula, Miss.; State Col. Lib., Starkville, Miss.; St. Augustine Seminary, St. Louis, Miss.; Jackson, Miss.; stone tablets, First Baptist Church; crucifix, Lutheran Church, sc., Civic Center, all New Orleans, La.; many port. busts and medals. *Exhibited*: AIC, 1929; PAFA, 1929, 1930, 1937; New Orleans A. Lg.; SSAL; La. State Exh.; New Orleans AA.

RIESENBERG, SIDNEY—*Painter, I., T.*

25 Amherst Drive, Hastings-on-Hudson, N.Y.

B. Chicago, Ill., Dec. 12, 1885. *Studied*: AIC. *Member*: All.A.Am.; SC; Yonkers AA; Rockport AA. *Awards*: prizes, Yonkers AA, 1930; Westchester A. Gld., 1940, 1951; Rockport AA. *Work*: Hudson River Mus.; Vanderpoel Coll.; Central Nat. Bank, Yonkers, N.Y. *Exhibited*: NAD, 1930, 1931, 1933, 1938, 1940, 1941; All.A.Am., 1936, 1938-1945; WFNY 1939; N.Y. WC Cl., 1940, 1941; Montclair A. Mus.; Hudson Valley AA; New Rochelle AA; Rockport AA; Currier Gal. A. I., "With Whip and Spur," 1927; "Pioneers All," 1929. Contributor: illus. to national magazines. *Position*: Instr., Westchester Workshop, White Plains, N.Y.

RIFFLE, ELBA LOUISA (Mrs. Elba Riffle Vernon)—*Illustrator, Comm. A., P.*

Greasy Creek Rd., Nashville, Ind.; h. 136 East New York St., Indianapolis 4, Ind.

B. Winamac, Ind., Jan. 3, 1905. *Studied*: John Herron AI; Indiana Univ.; Purdue Univ.; & with Myra Richards, Forsythe. *Member*: Hoosier Salon; Indiana AC. *Awards*: prizes, Northern Indiana A., 1931; Midwestern Exh., Wichita, Kan., 1932; Hoosier Salon, 1934; Ind. State Fair, 1930-1932, 1934, 1935, 1938. *Work*: Christian Church, H.S., Pub. Lib., Winamac, Ind.; Pub. Lib., Tipton, Ind.; Indiana Univ.; Woman's Cl. House, Clay City, Ind. Illus., "Cats Magazine"; "Our Dumb Animals Magazine"; "One Hundred Years of Service" (Hist. of YMCA in Indianapolis).*

RIGGS, ROBERT—*Printmaker*

51 West Walnut Lane, Germantown, Philadelphia, Pa.

B. Decatur, Ill., Feb. 5, 1896. *Member*: NA; Phila. WC Cl. *Awards*: med., Phila. WC Cl., 1932; PAFA, 1934; prizes, Phila. Pr. Cl., 1938; N.Y. A. Dir. Cl. medal, six times. *Work*: Phila. WC Cl.; AIC; BM; WMAA; N.Y. Pub. Lib.; Dallas Mus. FA; LC; MMA; Nat. Mus., Copenhagen, Denmark.*

RILEY, BILL—*Cartoonist, I.*

1947 Broadway; h. 551 West 149th St., New York 31, N.Y.

B. Charleston, S.C., Oct. 1, 1921. *Studied*: Cartoonist & Illustrators Sch., with Burne Hogarth. Contributor cartoons to New Yorker; Sat. Review; Reporter, and others. *Position*: A. Dir., Cartoonist Workshop, New York, N.Y.*

RILEY, KEN(NETH)—*Illustrator*

R.F.D. #4, Danbury, Conn.

Studied: Kansas City AI; ASL. *Member*: SI; Westport A. *Work*: War paintings, U.S. Coast Guard. Illus., "The Eustace Diamonds," 1951; "The Greatest Story Ever Told," 1950. Contributor illus. to Sat. Eve. Post; Nat. Geographic; Cosmopolitan; Readers Digest; McCalls; Womans Home Companion; True; Redbook; Esquire; Coronet.*

RINES, FRANK M.—*Painter, T.*

18 Pond St., Jamaica Plain 30, Mass.

B. Dover, N.H., June 3, 1892. *Studied*: Eric Pape Sch. A., Boston; Mass. Sch. A. *Member*: Wash. WC Cl.; North Shore AA; Copley Soc., Boston. *Exhibited*: Wash. WC Cl.; North Shore AA, 1938-1958; Copley Soc., 1946, 1955, 1958; Jordan Marsh Gal., 1932-1958; North Shore AA; Logan Airport, Phila.; Lunquist A. Center. Author, I., "Drawing in Lead Pencil," 1929; "Pencil Drawing," 1939; "Tree Drawing," 1946. *Position*: A. Instr., Boston (Mass.) Univ., 1939-1946; Instr., Boston Center of Adult Edu., 1937- ; Mass. Univ. Extension, 1937-1947; Boston Y.M.C.A., 1947-1958.

RIPLEY, A(IDEN) LASSELL—*Painter, Et.*

52 Follen Rd., Lexington, Mass.

B. Wakefield, Mass., Dec. 31, 1896. *Studied*: Fenway Sch. Illus.; BMFA Sch. *Member*: ANA; AAPL; Audubon A.; All. A. Am.; NSMP; Gld. Boston A.; AWCS; Boston Soc. WC Painters. *Awards*: prizes, med., AIC, 1928, 1936; med., Boston Tercentenary Exh., 1930; AWCS, 1945, 1947, 1952; prizes, Boston AC, 1929; N.Y. WC Cl., 1933; Am. Artist Magazine, 1952; NAD, 1953; AWS, 1954; AAPL, med., 1954, prize, 1955; Boston WC Soc., 1954, 1955; Boston A. Festival, 1955; All. A. Am., 1957; Concord AA, prize and med., 1955; Jordan Marsh, 1955, award & medal, 1958. *Work*: AIC; BMFA; Davenport Mun. A. Gal.; murals, Winchester (Mass.) Pub. Lib.; USPO, Lexington, Mass. *Exhibited*: PAFA, 1928, 1930, 1936, 1937, 1939, 1945; AWCS, 1939-1958; AIC, 1927-1932, 1934-1945; NAD; MMA (AV), 1942; Balt. WC Cl., 1940-1942; Toledo Mus. A., 1938; N.J. State Mus., Trenton; WFNY 1939; AGAA, 1939; WMA, 1940; BMFA, 1938; Gld. Boston A., 1942; Currier Gal. A.; Boston Soc. WC Painters; Grand Central Gal., 1949 (one-man). Author: Chapter in "Water Color Methods," 1955.

RISING, DOROTHY MILNE—*Painter, T., L., W.*

5033 17th Ave., Northeast, Seattle 5, Wash.

B. Tacoma, Wash., Sept. 13, 1895. *Studied*: PIASch.; Cleveland Sch. A.; Univ. Washington, B.A., M.F.A. *Member*: Women Painters of Washington; Nat. Lg. Am. Pen Women; Northwest WC Soc.; Washington A.; NAEA; AEA. *Awards*: prizes, Nat. Lg. Am. Pen Women, 1946, 1948, 1950, 1951, 1955, 1956, 1957 (Seattle and San Jose, Cal.); Women Painters of Wash., 1948, 1954, 1956, 1957; Woessner Gal., Seattle, 1955; Spokane, Wash., 1948; Henry Gal., 1951; Northwest WC Soc., 1957. *Work*: City of Spokane Coll. *Exhibited*: Massillon Mus., 1953-1955; Ohio WC Soc., 1954-55 traveling exh.; Springfield Mus. FA, 1953-1955; Oakland A. Mus., 1954, 1957; SAM, 1940-1957; Lucien Labaudt Gal., 1948 (one-man); Univ. Washington, 1955; Port Angeles, Wash., 1955 (one-man); Wash., D.C., 1956; Grand Central A. Gal., 1957; Tacoma, Wash., 1957; Frye Mus., Seattle, 1957, 1958; Woessner Gal., Seattle, 1957, 1958; Bellevue (Wash.) traveling exh., 1956, 1957; 4 one-man exhs., Seattle, 1957, 1958.

RISLEY, JOHN—*Sculptor, Des., E.*

Davison Art Center, Wesleyan University; h. 77 Pearl St., Middletown, Conn.

B. Brookline, Mass., Sept. 20, 1919. *Studied*: Malvern Col., England, B.L.A.; Amherst Col., B.A.; R.I.Sch. Des., B.F.A., with Valdimar Raemisch; Cranbrook Acad. A., M.F.A., with William McVey. *Member*: Silvermine Gld. A.; New England Sculptors Assn. *Awards*: prizes, Syracuse Mus. FA, 1954; BM, 1953; Mystic AA, 1955; Manila, P.I., 1953; R.I. Artists, 1948; Norwich AA, 1958; Meriden AA, 1958; Silvermine Gld. A., 1958; Portland A. Festival, 1958. *Work*: sculpture in private collections; furniture and wood products in national production. *Exhibited*: Syracuse Mus. FA, 1950, 1951, 1954; Wichita AA, 1950, 1958; Delgado Mus. A., 1951; Boston A. Festival, 1953-1958; U.S. Des.-Craftsmen, BM, 1953; Manila, P.I., 1952; Sweat Mem. Mus., 1954; BMFA, 1951; Detroit

Inst. A., 1951; Brooks Mem. Mus., 1952; Univ. Miss., 1952; Alabama Polytechnic Inst., 1952; Univ. Fla., 1952; Cornell Univ., 1953; Tacoma A. Lg., 1953; Haggin Gal., Sacramento, 1953; Montana State Col., 1953; Univ. Minnesota, 1953; North Dakota Agricultural Col., 1953; AIC, 1953; SFMA, 1953; Silvermine Gld. A., 1954, 1955, 1957, 1958; Mystic AA, 1955, 1957; Rochester Mem. A. Gal., 1955; Fleming Mus. A., 1955; CM, 1955; Ohio State Univ., 1955; Toledo Mus. A., 1955; Oregon Ceramic Studios, 1955; Cranbrook Acad. A., 1951; Univ. Conn., 1955; Slater Mem. Mus., 1955; Norwich AA, 1956, 1958; NAD; Univ. Rhode Island, 1956; J. B. Speed A. Mus., 1956; Jacksonville A. Mus., 1957; Fla. Gulf Coast A. Center, 1957; Conn. Acad. FA, 1957; New Britain A. Mus., 1957; Mus. Contemp. Craft, 1957; Springfield A. Lg., 1957; Brookfield Craft Center, 1957; St. Paul Gal. A., 1958; Meriden, Conn., 1958; Portland A. Festival, 1958, and others. *Position*: Instr. S., Cranbrook Acad. A.; Philippine Islands under ECA; Asst. Prof. S., Des., Wesleyan Univ., Middletown, Conn., at present.

RISLEY, MARY KRING—Craftsman, T.
   77 Pearl St., Middletown, Conn.

B. Detroit, Mich., July 4, 1926. *Studied*: Univ. Michigan, B. Des.; Cranbrook Acad. A., M.F.A., with Maija Grotell. *Member*: Soc. Connecticut Craftsmen (Bd. Dir.). *Awards*: prizes, Cranbrook Acad. A., 1951; Wadsworth Atheneum, 1955; Craft Fair, Hartford, 1951. *Exhibited*: Wichita Ceramic Exh., 1949-1952, 1954, 1955; Syracuse Mus. FA, 1949-1954 and traveling exhs.; Des.-Craftsmen, U.S.A., 1953 and traveling exh.; Los A. County Fair, 1949; Walker A. Center, 1951-1954; Detroit Inst. A., 1948-1952; Cranbrook Acad. Alumni, 1953; Sweat Mem. Mus., 1954; New Britain Mus. A., 1955; WMA, 1955; Slater Mus. A., Hartford, 1955. Author: United Nations Report on Ceramics in the Philippines. Lectures on Ceramics to museums, art groups, church groups, etc. *Position*: Instr., Ceramics, Ox Bow Summer Sch., Saugatuck, Mich.; Toledo Mus. A.; Potter's Gld., Ann Arbor; U.N. Technician in Ceramics, Manila, P.I.; Haystack Summer Sch. of Crafts, Liberty, Me.*

RIST, LOUIS G. (LUIGI)—Printmaker
   R.D. 2, Nottingham, Pa.

B. Newark, N.J., Jan. 26, 1888. *Studied*: Newark Technical Sch., with Sigrid Skou; Grand Central A. Sch. *Member*: Am. Color Pr. Soc.; Southwest Pr. M.; Albany Pr. Cl.; Prairie Pr. M.; Assoc. A., New Jersey (Treas.). *Awards*: prizes, Am. Color Pr. Soc., 1941, 1943, 1944, 1949; Northeast Pr. M., 1946; Montclair A. Mus., 1941, 1948; Laguna Beach AA, 1947; Wichita AA, 1950; LC, 1951; New Britain Inst., 1951; Newark Mus., 1952; Wichita AA, 1955. *Work*: N.Y. Pub. Lib.; MMA; CM; Newark Lib.; Springfield A. Mus.; BMFA; LC; New Britain Inst.; Trinity Univ., Texas; Newark Mus.; Presentation Print for Rochester Pr. Cl., 1955. *Exhibited*: LC; Phila. Pr. Cl.; Phila. A. All.; Am. Color Pr. Soc.; Laguna Beach AA; Northwest Pr. M.; Buck Hill AA; Princeton Pr. Cl.; Albany Pr. Cl.; Wichita AA; SFMA; PAFA; BM; Montclair A. Mus.; Buffalo Pr. Cl.; Carnegie Inst.; Int. Colour Woodcut Exh., Victoria & Albert Mus., London, 1954-55; PAFA; Assoc. A. New Jersey, and others. One-man: Princeton Pr. Cl.; Raban & Krueger Gal.; Newark Pub. Lib.; Univ. Richmond (Va.); Kent State Univ. (Ohio); Univ. Maine; Albany Pr. Cl.; Martin Lib., York, Pa.; Nottingham (Pa.) Inn.

RITCHIE, ANDREW C.—Museum Director, L., W.
   Yale University Art Gallery, 1111 Chapel St., New Haven, Conn.

B. Bellshill, Scotland, Sept. 18, 1907. *Studied*: Univ. Pittsburgh, B.A., M.A.; Univ. London, Ph.D. *Member*: CAA; Assn. A. Mus. Dir. *Awards*: Foreign Study F., Univ. Pittsburgh, 1933-35. Author: "English Painters, Hogarth to Constable," 1942; "Aristide Maillol" (Ed.), 1945; "British Contemporary Painters." 1946; Catalogs of Painting and Sculpture. (Ed.), Albright A. Gal., 1949; "Charles Demuth," 1950; "Franklin Watkins," 1950; "Abstract Painting and Sculpture in America," 1951; "Sculpture of the 20th Century," 1953; "Edouard Vuillard," 1954; "The New Decade: 22 European Painters and Sculptors" (Ed.), 1955. Contributor to art publications with articles and book reviews on English and French art. Lectures on British Art; French and Spanish Post-Renaissance Painting; Modern Art. *Positions*: L., Research Asst. Frick Coll., N.Y., 1935-42; Visiting L., N.Y. Univ., 1936-40; Dir.,

Albright A. Gal., Buffalo, N.Y., 1942-49; Dir., Dept. Painting & Sculpture, MModA, New York, N.Y., 1949-1957; Dir., Yale University Art Gallery, New Haven, Conn., 1957- .

RITER, CARL FREDERICK—Painter, E.
   1301 East Albion Place, Milwaukee 2, Wis.

B. Carroll, Iowa, May 28, 1915. *Studied*: Univ. Wisconsin; N.Y. Univ. Inst. FA; Univ. South Dakota; Ohio State Univ.; Univ. Iowa. *Position*: Prof. A., Chm. Dept. A., & FA Div., Milwaukee-Downer Col., Milwaukee, Wis.

RITMAN, LOUIS—Painter, E.
   19 East Pearson St., Chicago, Ill.

B. Russia, Jan. 6, 1889. *Studied*: AIC; Ecole des Beaux-Arts, Paris. *Member*: NA; Assoc. Nationale Beaux-Arts, Paris. *Awards*: medal, Pan-Pacific Exp., 1915; prizes, AIC, 1930, 1932, 1940, 1941; NAD, 1951. *Work*: Chicago Mun. A. Lg.; Des Moines A. Center; PAFA. *Position*: Prof. A., AIC, Chicago, Ill., 1930- .*

RITMAN, MAURICE—Painter, W., L., T.
   5509 West Hirsch St., Chicago 51, Ill.

B. Chicago, Ill., Oct. 11, 1906. *Studied*: AIC. *Member*: Chicago SA; Am. A. Cong. *Awards*: prizes, AIC, 1938, 1944.

RITTENBERG, HENRY R.—Painter, T.
   222 Central Park South, New York 19, N.Y.

B. Libau, Latvia, Oct. 2, 1879. *Studied*: PAFA; Bavarian Acad., Munich (scholarship); & with William Chase. *Member*: NA; BAID (hon.); P. & S. Assn.; AAPL; N.Y. Soc. Painters; Audubon A.; A. Fellowship. *Awards*: F., PAFA; Cresson traveling scholarship, PAFA, 1904; prizes, NAD, 1920, 1926; AIC, 1925; NAC, 1938. *Work*: N.Y. Hist. Soc.; Columbia Univ.; Butler AI; Dept. Justice, Wash., D.C.; State Capitol, Harrisburg, Pa.; Univ. Pennsylvania; Fed. Court, Phila.; Phila. Bar Assn.; Univ. Panama; Panama Republic; Jefferson Medical Col.; Univ. Virginia; N.Y. Chamber of Commerce; N.Y. Acad. Medicine; Franklin Marshall Col.; Skidmore Col. Taught Life class, BAID; Port., Still Life, ASL; NAD; Rutgers Univ.; Phila. Free Lib.; Am. Acad. A. & Lets.; Hall of Am. Artists, N.Y. Univ. *Exhibited*: nationally and internationally.

RITTER, CHRIS—Painter
   Ogunquit, Me.

B. Iola, Kans., Dec. 9, 1908. *Studied*: Univ. Kansas, B.A.; ASL; Columbia Univ.; BMSch. A. *Awards*: prizes, Denver A. Mus., 1938; Nat. Army A. Exh., 1945; Phila. Pr. Cl., 1948; Mississippi AA, 1947; BM, 1949. *Work*: BM; WMA; N.Y. Pub. Lib.; LC; Everhart Mus. A. *Exhibited*: MMA; BM; PAFA; CGA; AIC; Kansas City AI; Oakland A. Mus.; Mississippi AA; CM; one-man: Uptown Gal., 1939, 1942; Marquie Gal., 1943; Am.-British Gal., 1945, Laurel Gal., 1948, 1950, all in N.Y.; Phila. A. All., 1948. *Position*: Dir., Laurel Gal., New York, N.Y., 1946-51; Instr. A., Hunter Col., 1939-41; Cornell Univ., 1947; Ballard Sch., 1947-53; Midland (Tex.) A. Center, 1954; Pres., Ogunquit AA, 1957-59.

RITZ, MADELINE GATEKA—Educator
   1029 Circle Drive, Brookings, S.D.

B. Chickasha, Okla, July 14, 1903. *Studied*: Oklahoma Col. for Women, A.B.; Columbia Univ., M.A.; AIC; Pa. State Univ., Ed. D.; Univ. Iowa; Ohio State Univ.; Univ. Chicago; Univ. Wisconsin. *Member*: Am. Assn. Univ. Women; S.D. State Edu. Assn. *Exhibited*: Oklahoma AA; Midwest A. *Position*: Hd., Dept. A., South Dakota State Col., Brookings, S.D.

RIU, VICTOR—Sculptor
   201 East State St., Coopersburg, Pa.

B. Italy, July 18, 1887. *Studied*: in Italy. *Member*: Lehigh A. All. *Award*: prize, PAFA, 1958. *Work*: PAFA; Lehigh Univ. *Exhibited*: Phila. A. Festival, 1955; PAFA, 1958; Detroit Inst. A., 1958; Cheltenham A. Cl.; New Hope Workshop; Phila. A. All., 1957, 1958; Lehigh Univ., 1955 (one-man).

RIVERS, CORNELIA McINTIRE—*Painter, T.*
Wymberley, Isle of Hope, Savannah, Ga.

B. Savannah, Ga., Nov. 25, 1912. *Studied*: Vassar Col., A.B.; Univ. Georgia; ASL; Am. A. Sch., and with Robert Brackman. *Member*: Am. Portrait A.; Georgia AA; Savannah A. Cl.; St. Augustine AA. *Awards*: Univ. Georgia, 1935; Savannah A. Cl., 1942; ASL, 1946; Manchester, Vt., 1947. *Work*: Woodville H.S., Savannah; Ericson Mem. Hall, Savannah. *Exhibited*: Portraits, Inc., 1949, 1951; Audubon A., 1949; Hallmark Awards, 1950; Am. Portrait A., 1950; Terry AI, 1952; Creative Gal., 1952; Savannah A. Cl., 1935; Manchester, Vt., 1947; Southeastern exh., 1952; St. Augustine AA, 1952; one-man: Quantico, Va., 1947; Telfair Acad., 1947.*

ROBB, DAVID M.—*Educator*
University of Pennsylvania, Philadelphia 4, Pa.; h. 506 Narberth Ave., Merion Station, Pa.

B. Tak Hing Chau, South China, Sept. 19, 1903. *Studied*: Oberlin Col., A.B., A.M.; Princeton Univ., M.F.A., Ph.D. *Member*: CAA; Archaeological Inst. Am.; Soc. Arch. Historians. *Awards*: Guggenheim F., 1956-1957; Fulbright Research F., 1956-1957. Co-Author: "Art in the Western World," 1935, revised 1942, 1953; Author: "Harper History of Painting," 1951, rev., 1955. Contributor to: Art Bulletin, Encyclopaedia Americana, Art Journal, Archaeological Journal. Lectures: Mediaeval, Modern, American Art. *Position*: Assoc. Prof. FA, Univ. Minnesota, 1935-39; Prof. A. Hist., 1939- , Chm. Dept. FA, 1946-1955, Univ. Pennsylvania, Philadelphia, Pa.

ROBBINS, FRANK—*Cartoonist, P., I.*
285 Central Park West, New York 24, N.Y.

B. Boston, Mass., Sept. 9, 1917. *Studied*: BMFA Sch.; NAD. *Member*: Nat. Cartoonists Soc. *Awards*: prize, NAD, 1936. *Work*: port., Polyclinic Hospital, N.Y. *Exhibited*: NAD, 1936, 1937; Roerich Mus., 1945; WMAA, 1956; CGA, 1957, 1958; Toledo Mus. A., 1957, 1958; NAD, 1957, 1958; Audubon A., 1957, 1958. Author, I., "Scorchy Smith" comic strip, 1939-44; "Johnny Hazard" comic strip, Kings Features Syndicate, at present. Contributor to: Life, Look, Cosmopolitan, & other national magazines.

ROBBINS, HULDA D(ORNBLATT)—*Serigrapher, P., T.*
300 East 89th St., New York 28, N.Y.

B. Atlanta, Ga., Oct. 19, 1910. *Studied*: PMSchIA; Barnes Fnd.; Prussian Acad., Berlin. *Member*: Nat. Ser. Soc.; Am. Color Pr. Soc.; Phila. Pr. Cl. *Awards*: Scholarship, Barnes Fnd., 1939; prizes, MModA, 1941; Pepsi-Cola, 1945; Nat. Ser. Soc., 1947-1949, 1954. *Work*: Lehigh Univ.; Am. Assn. Univ. Women; Smithsonian Inst.; A. Mus., Ontario, Canada; Princeton Pr. Cl.; N.Y. Sch. Int. Dec.; Purchase Sch., N.Y.; Highview Sch., Oakville, Tenn.; U.S. Army; MMA. *Exhibited*: Oakland A. Gal., 1939, 1940; Northwest Pr. M., 1941; LC, 1948; BM, 1948; Indiana Pr., 1948; Carnegie Inst., 1948; Wichita A. Mus., 1949; Lehigh Univ., 1933; Little Gal., Wash., D.C., 1939; MModA, 1940; Serigraph Gal., 1947 (one-man); Nat. Ser. Soc., 1940-1952; France, 1956-57; Italy, 1957. *Position*: Instr. Ser., Nat. Ser. Soc., New York, N.Y.

ROBERT, MRS. C. E. *See McCullough, Lucerne*

ROBERTS, COLETTE (JACQUELINE)—
Art Critic, L., P., Gal. Dir.
Grand Central Moderns, 1018 Madison Ave. (21); h. 154 East 28th St., New York 16, N.Y.

B. Paris, France, Sept. 16, 1910. *Studied*: Sorbonne, B.A.; Academie Ranson, with Roger Bissiere; Ecole du Louvre; Institut d'Art et Archeologie, with Henri Focillon. *Exhibited*: in France. Author: "Mark Tobey," 1958-59. Contributor art editorials to France-Amerique. Lectures: The Road to Modern Art. Directed and organized a "Meet the Artist" program for N.Y. Univ. Arranged Intl. Print Exh., Argent Gal., 1947; One World benefit exh., UNICEF; various exchange exhs. with Paris, France, under the sponsorship of French Embassy, N.Y., and American Embassy, Paris. *Position*: Dir., Grand Central Moderns Gallery, N.Y.

ROBERTS, DWIGHT V.—*Portrait Painter*
329 Westport Rd.; h. 104 East 68th Terr., Kansas City 5, Mo.

B. Kansas City, Mo., Apr. 29, 1908. *Studied*: Kansas City AI; ASL, with Frank Reilly, and in Europe. *Member*: Kansas City AI Alum.; Mid-Am. A. *Work*: portraits, Nat. Bank of Am., Salina, Kans.; First Baptist Church, Tulsa, Okla.; Town House Hotel, Kansas City, Kans.; Planters State Bank, Salina, Kans.; Kehilath Israel Synagogue, Kansas City. *Exhibited*: Midwestern Exh., 1941; one-man: Woman's City Cl., Kansas City, 1951; Junior Lg., Houston, 1952.*

ROBERTS, GILROY—*Engraver, S.*
U.S. Mint, Philadelphia, Pa.; h. 144 Summit Ave., Upper Darby, Pa.

B. Philadelphia, Pa., Mar. 11, 1905. *Studied*: Corcoran Sch. A., and with John R. Sinnock, Paul Remy, Eugene Weis, Heinz Warnecke. *Member*: NSS. *Awards*: gold medal, Madrid Exh. of Medals, 1951. *Work*: medals, Drexel Inst., 1936; Brandeis Lawyer's Soc., 1948; Einstein award medal, 1950; Schaefer Brewing Co. Achievement Award, 1951; Am. Medical Assn., Dr. Hektoen Medal, 1952; placques: Dr. Albert Hardt Mem., 1950; Lewis N. Cassett Fnd., 1950; Theodore Roosevelt H.S., 1952; State Seals: Valley Forge Patriots Mem., 1952; Congressional medals; ports. of prominent persons. Work from 1955-1958: medals, des. and modeled ports. for Congressional and Presidential gold medals honoring Irving Berlin, Dr. Jonas Salk, Winston Churchill, Enrico Fermi, Veterans of the Civil War; coins: ports. of Pres. Marti, Cuba, Pres. Duvalier, Haiti; plaques and medals, Helen Keller; Gen. David Sarnoff; Pres. Riley and Haag, Todd Shipyards; and others. *Exhibited*: PAFA, 1930, 1934, 1945, 1946; Int. Exh. of coins and medals, Paris, France, 1949, Madrid, Spain, 1951. *Position*: Banknote Engraver, Bureau of Engraving & Printing, Wash., D.C., 1938-44; Chief Sculptor, Engraver, U.S. Mint, Philadelphia, Pa., 1936- .

ROBERTS, MRS. HERBERT ALLEN. *See Howard, Lucile*

ROBERTS, MORTON—*Painter, I., T.*
81 Highfield Road, Harrison, N.Y.

B. Worcester, Mass., Jan. 7, 1927. *Studied*: Yale Univ. Sch. FA, B.F.A. *Member*: NA; AWS; All. A. Am.; Copley Soc., Boston. *Awards*: Abbey F., NAD, 1950; prizes, Yale Univ., 1947; State of Mass., 1953; Pinanski prize, 1952; NAD, 1954-1957; AWS, 1953, 1955, silver medal, 1956; citation and medal, American Artist magazine, 1955. *Work*: NAD; Yale Univ.; Parrish Mus., Southampton, and in private colls. *Exhibited*: Milch Gal.; Butler Inst. Am. A.; NAD, 1954-58; Audubon A.; Boston A. Festival; AWS; All. A. Am.; Parrish Mus.; Phila. A. All., 1956 (one-man); Childs Gal., Boston, 1955 (one-man). Commissioned paintings for Readers Digest; Life magazine; Sports Illustrated, and others. Work reproduced in 1957 ed. Encyclopedia Britannica. Traveling group shows, 1951. *Position*: Instr., PIASch., Brooklyn, N.Y., 1951-1955.

ROBERTSON, PAUL CHANDLER—*Painter, Des.*
1022 Park Ave., New York 28, N.Y.

B. St. Paul, Minn., Mar. 9, 1902. *Studied*: Univ. California; Cal. Sch. F. & App. A.; N.Y. Sch. F. & App. A.; & abroad. *Member*: NSMP; A.I.D.; Arch. Lg. *Awards*: prizes, House Beautiful Cover Comp., 1933; Office Emergency Management, 1942. *Work*: murals, Aluminum Corp.; Grace Lines; Claridge Hotel, Atlantic City; Dempsey Hotel, Macon, Ga.; Bowery Savings Bank; Farrell Lines; Atlantic Rayon Co.; Cities Service Oil Co.; Sulgrave Cl., Wash. D.C.; Alpha Cement Co., Easton, Pa.; Watertown Fed. Savings & Loan Co.; Lord & Taylor, James McCreery, W. & J. Sloane, R. H. Macy, N.Y.; & in numerous hotels. *Exhibited*: Anderson Gal.; Gal. Mus. French A., 1932; Kimball, Hubbard & Powell, 1933; Putnam County AA, 1936; Parsons Sch. Des., 1937; Decorators Cl., 1937-1939; Decorator's War Relief Exh., 1941; Arch.L., 1946, 1956; N.Y. Coliseum, 1958; Design Center, N.Y., 1958; Office Emergency Management traveling exh., 1942. Contributor to: House Beautiful, House & Garden, New Yorker, & other national magazines. Lectures: Mural Painting as a Profession, Fed. FA, New York, N.Y.

ROBERTSON, PERSIS W. *(Mrs.)—Lithographer*
331—28th St., Des Moines, Iowa

B. Des Moines, Iowa, May 10, 1896. *Studied:* Wells Col., B.A.; Columbia Univ. *Member:* Audubon A. *Awards:* prize, Kansas City AI, 1940. *Exhibited:* AIC, 1935, 1937, 1939; Northwest Pr. M., 1937, 1939, 1940; Phila. Pr. Cl., 1936, 1937, 1939, 1940; Phila. A. All., 1936, 1939; Wash. WC Cls., 1939, 1940; Phila. WC Cl., 1940; Buffalo Pr. Cl., 1938, 1940, 1951; Boston Soc. Indp. A., 1941; Southern Pr. M., 1938; Oakland A. Gal., 1938, 1939, 1941; Okla. A. Center, 1940, 1941; Lib. Cong., 1945, 1950; Audubon A., 1945, 1951; Joslyn Mem., 1936, 1938, 1940, 1941; Silver Springs (Md.), 1955; Kansas City AI, 1936-1941; Wichita, Kan., 1938-1940; one-man exh.: Ferargil Gal., 1939; Hanley Gal., Minneapolis, 1939; Denver A. Mus., 1939; William Rockhill Nelson Gal., 1940; Iowa A., 1950, 1951; Des Moines A. Center, 1951 (one-man); Hanley Gal., Minneapolis; Old Town A. & Crafts, Southold, L.I.; Smithsonian Inst., 1955. Lectures: Lithography.

ROBIN, FANNY—Painter
2132 Spruce St., Philadelphia 3, Pa.

B. Philadelphia, Pa., June 28, 1888. *Studied:* Moore Inst. Des.; PAFA; & with Breckenridge, Snell, Horter. *Member:* Woodmere A. Gal.; PAFA; Plastic Cl., A. All., A.T. Assn., all of Phila., Pa. *Awards:* prize, DaVinci All., 1942; med., Phila. Plastic Cl., 1943, gold medal, 1955. *Exhibited:* PAFA, 1936, 1939; Phila. A. All., 1943 (one-man).*

ROBINS, SEYMOUR—Illustrator, P.
24 West 45th St., New York 36, N.Y.*

ROBINSON, ADAH MATILDA—Painter, Des., L., E.
The Aurora, San Antonio 6, Tex.

B. Richmond, Ind., July 13, 1882. *Studied:* Earlham Col.; AIC; & with Charles Hawthorne, George Elmer Browne, John Carlson. *Member:* San Antonio A. Lg.; Southwestern AA; Prairie Pr. M. (hon.); CAA. *Awards:* hon. degree, D.A., Univ. Tulsa, 1936. *Work:* Oklahoma City A. Lg.; Philbrook A. Center; designed interior, First Church of Christ Scientist, Tulsa, Okla.; Second Church of Christ Scientist, Tulsa; Boston Ave. Methodist Church, Tulsa. Lectures: Historical & Modern Art Periods. *Position:* Chm., Dept. A., Tulsa Univ., Tulsa, Okla., 1927-45; Trinity Univ., San Antonio, Tex., 1945- .

ROBINSON, FREDERICK BRUCE—
Museum Director, E., L.
49 Chestnut St., Springfield 5, Mass.; h. 135 Forest Glen Rd., Longmeadow 6, Mass.

B. Boston, Mass., Dec. 23, 1907. *Studied:* Harvard Univ., B.S. Contributor to: museum bulletins, art magazines & newspapers. Lectures: "Art & Architecture of 17th and 18th Century America"; "General Art History & Criticism." *Position:* Asst. to Dir., FMA, Harvard Univ., 1931-37; Asst. to Dir., BMFA, 1937-40; Dir., Springfield Mus. FA, Springfield, Mass., 1940- .

ROBINSON, IRENE BOWEN *(Mrs.)—Illustrator, P.*
132 North Almont Dr., Los Angeles 48, Cal.

B. South Bend, Wash. *Studied:* Drury Col., A.B.; Univ. Chicago; Broadmoor A. Acad. *Member:* Cal. WC Soc. *Awards:* prizes, San Diego FA Soc., 1927; Cal. AC, 1931; Los A. Mus. A., 1936; Ebell Salon, 1934, 1942, 1945, 1951; Glendale AA, 1945. *Work:* Pasadena AI. *Exhibited:* Los A. Mus. A., 1930-1945, 1950. I., "At the Zoo," 1940; "Picture Book of Animal Babies," 1946; "The Forest and the People," 1946, "Land in California," 1948, "The Malibu," 1958, and other books.

ROBINSON, (VIRGINIA) ISABEL—
Educator, P., C., Gr.
2500 Fifth Ave., Canyon, Tex.

B. Eagle Ranch, Adair County, Mo. *Studied:* Cranbrook Acad. A.; Chouinard AI; Kirksville (Mo.) State T. Col.; Univ. Missouri, B.S.; Columbia Univ., M.A.; Otis AI; & with Millard Sheets. *Member:* Texas State T. Assn.; Assoc. A. Instr., Texas. *Awards:* prize, Tex. Fed. Women's Cl., Abilene, Tex., 1946; Contemp. Hand Weavers of Texas, 1955. *Exhibited:* SSAL; All. A. & Indst., N.Y.; Texas Centennial Exh., Dallas, 1936; Dallas Mus. FA; Ft. Worth, Austin, San Antonio, Houston, Tex.; Michigan State Col., 1937 (one-man); Tex. Fed. Women's Cl., 1946; College Lib., Canyon, Tex., 1958 (one-man). Lectures: "Early and Contemporary Art & Artists of Texas." *Position:* Instr. A., Ohio Univ., Athens, Ohio, 1924-25; Hd. Dept. A., Assoc. Prof., West Texas State Col., Canyon, Tex., 1927-58.

ROBINSON, MARY TURLAY—Painter, L.
171 West 12th St., New York 11, N.Y.

B. Massachusetts, Sept. 7, 1888. *Studied:* Vassar Col., A.B.; ASL; Am. Sch. FA, Fontainebleau, France; & with DuMond, Luks, Beaudoin, Despujols. *Member:* AFA; AEA. *Awards:* Officer of French Acad., France, 1933; prize, Am. Woman's Assn., 1937. *Work:* CAD. *Exhibited:* NAWA, 1929-1936; Am. Woman's Assn., 1932-1938; Anderson Gal., 1930 (one-man); Nantucket AA, 1933-1945; Bignou Gal., 1941, 1942; Binet Gal., 1950 (one-man); Hartford Atheneum; Salon d'Automne, 1926; Les Independents, Paris, France, 1926. *Position:* French-American Liaison Officer, Fontainebleau Am. Sch. FA, 1928-32; Com. on Int. Cultural Relations, AEA, 1951- . Lectures (on grant from Intl. Edu. Services, Dept. of State) in Switzerland, Belgium, France, Algeria and Yugoslavia, 1954. Talks on current exhs. and discussion groups for laymen. Exec. Com., Nantucket AA, 1957- .

ROBINSON, MAUDE—Craftsman
175 East 71st St., New York 21, N.Y.; s. Sharon, Conn.

B. Corning, N.Y., Nov. 20, 1880. *Studied:* ASL; Newcomb Col., Tulane Univ.; N.Y. State Ceramic Sch.; & with Charles Binns, Arthur Dow, John Twachtman, & others. *Member:* N.Y. Keramic Soc. (hon.). *Exhibited:* MMA; AIC; Sharon, Conn. Author: "Technique of Terra Cotta Sculpture," 13th Ed., Encyclopaedia Britannica; chapter on "Pottery" in "Careers for Women"; "Pottery and Porcelain" in the World Book Encyclopaedia. Lectures: Technique of Pottery. Des. and executed medal for Millbrook (N.Y.) Garden Club, 1954-55. *Position:* Dir., Greenwich House Pottery, New York, N.Y., 1911-41; Consultant in Ceramic Technique, MMA, New York, N.Y.; Dir., Owner, Maude Robinson Pottery, N.Y., 1917-56.

ROBINSON, RUTH M.—Painter, Des., T.
2528 Garrett Rd., Drexel Park, Pa.

B. Philadelphia, Pa., Jan. 15, 1910. *Studied:* Moore Inst. A., Sc. & Indst., B.S. in A.Edu.; PAFA; & with Earl Horter, Umberto Romano. *Member:* A. All., Plastic Cl., WC Cl., all of Phila., Pa., Bryn Mawr A. Center. *Awards:* F., PAFA; prizes, Moore Inst. Des., 1930; Phila. Plastic Cl., 1932; Cape May A. Lg., 1940; med., Phila. Plastic Cl., 1941. *Work:* Marine Hospital, Carville, La.; Ft. Knox, Ky.; Carnegie Corp. *Exhibited:* Phila. WC Cl., 1930-1946; PAFA, 1940; GGE 1939; AIC, 1936, 1937; Grand Central A. Gal.; Contemporary A. Gal.; Phila. A. All.; Mortimer Levitt Gal.; numerous one-man exh., Phila., N.Y. *Position:* Instr., Occupational Therapy, A., Pub. Schs.

ROBINSON, VIRGINIA C(AROLYN)—Painter, Hist., I.
1484 College Station, Columbus, Miss.

B. Maryville, Mo. *Studied:* William Woods Col., A.A.; Northwest Missouri State Col., A.B.; Columbia Univ., B.S. in L.S. *Member:* Am. Lib. Assn.; AAUW; Long Beach (Cal.) AA; New Orleans AA; Miss. Lib. Assn.; Miss. AA; Miss. Hist. Assn.; Miss. Edu. Assn.; Laguna Beach AA; Nat. Audubon Soc.; Palette & Brush Cl. *Awards:* Kappa Pi (hon.), 1955. *Exhibited:* Mun. A. Gal., Jackson, Miss., 1950, 1951; Brooks Mem. A. Gal., 1955, 1957; AAUW exh., Maryville, Mo., 1953-1955; Delgado Mus. A., 1957; One-man: Miss. State Col. for Women, 1955; Delta AA, Greenwood, Miss., 1955; Meridan AA, 1955; Lauren Rogers Mem. Mus., Laurel, Miss., 1956; Youth Center, Starkville, Miss., 1955; Allison's Wells, Way, Miss., 1957; Miss. Hist. Soc., 1958; Wm. Carey Col., 1958; Clarksdale, Miss.; Pub. Lib., 1956; Mary Buie Mus., Oxford, Miss., 1956. *Work:* Miss. Dept. Archives & Hist., Jackson, Miss.; Miss. State Col. for Women; Blue Ridge Assembly, Black Mountain, N.C.; U.S.S. Everett Larson, Illus., "Somebody Might Come," 1958. *Position:* Asst. Catalog Dept., Kansas City Pub. Lib., 1926-27; Circ. Dept., Grinnell Col. Lib., 1928-29; Assoc. Librarian & Cataloger, Miss. State Col. for Women, Columbus, Miss., 1929- .

ROBISON, ANN(A) DOROTHY—*Painter, Et., T.*
2312 Ronda Vista Dr., Los Angeles 27, Cal.

B. Palmyra, Ill. *Studied*: Univ. California at Los A., B.A.; Otis AI; & with John Hubbard Rich, Paul Clemens, & others. *Exhibited*: Lib. Cong., 1944; San Gabriel A. Gld., 1942; Fnd. Western A., 1932-1944; Palace Legion Honor, 1933; Women's Univ. Cl., Los A., 1955 (one-man). *Position*: A.T., 1931- , Chm. Dept. A., 1944- , Franklin H.S., Los Angeles, Cal.

ROBUS, HUGO—*Sculptor, T.*
37 East 4th St., New York 3, N.Y.

B. Cleveland, Ohio, May 10, 1885. *Studied*: Cleveland Sch. A.; NAD; Grande Chaumiere, Paris, France, with Bourdelle. *Member*: S. Gld.; Shilling Fund Jury. *Awards*: prize, AV, 1942; Shilling Fund, 1946; Widener gold medal, 1950; Alfred Steel Mem. prize, 1953; citation and grant, Nat. Inst. A. & Lets., 1957. *Work*: MMA; MMoA; WMAA; IBM; Munson-Williams-Proctor Inst.; CMA. *Exhibited*: MMA; PAFA, annually; WFNY 1939; MMoA; S. Gld., annually; WMAA, annually.

ROCHE, LEO JOSEPH—*Cartoonist*
Buffalo Courier-Express (5); h. 269 Sanders Road, Buffalo 23, N.Y.

B. Ithaca, N.Y., Feb. 20, 1888. *Studied*: Syracuse Univ. Sch. FA. Illus., Cart., for Saturday Evening Post, and other national magazines. *Awards*: Nat. Safety Council; Disabled Veterans Soc. *Work*: LC; Henry Huntington Mus. A.; F. D. Roosevelt and Harry S. Truman libraries, and others. *Position*: Ed. Cart., Buffalo Courier-Express, Buffalo, N.Y., 1934- .

ROCHE, M. PAUL—*Painter, Et., Lith., S., L.*
723 Evesham Ave., Baltimore 12, Md.

B. Cork, Ireland, Jan. 22, 1888. *Studied*: St. John's Col.; PIASch.; NAD, with Charles Hawthorne. *Awards*: prizes, NAD; Brooklyn SE; NAC; AIC. *Work*: BM; CMA; Lib. Cong.; Cal. State Lib.; N.Y. Pub. Lib.; murals, Washington Col., Chestertown, Md.; Enoch Pratt Lib., Catholic Cathedral, St. Joseph's Church, all of Balt., Md. *Exhibited*: NAD. Lectures: American Mural Painting.*

ROCK, JOHN HENRY—*Educator, P., Lith.*
Art Department, Oregon State College; h. 947 North 11th St., Corvallis, Ore.

B. Tillamook, Ore., Nov. 27, 1919. *Studied*: Oregon State Col., B.S., with Gordon Gilkey; Cal. Col. A. & Crafts, M.F.A., with Leon Goldin, Nathan Oliveira. *Member*: Portland AA. *Awards*: prizes, Portland A. Mus., 1955 (purchase), 1956; Univ. Washington, 1955 (purchase); Oregon State Fair, 1957, 1958. *Work*: Portland A. Mus.; Henry Gal., Univ. Washington; U.S. Information Agency. *Exhibited*: print and lith. exhs., BM, 1956; Bordighera, Italy, 1957; SAM, 1956, 1957; Wichita, Kans., 1958; CM, 1958; New Canaan, Conn., 1958; Oakland A. Mus., 1956, 1958; Portland A. Mus., 1951, 1952, 1955, 1956; Denver A. Mus., 1953; Northwest Pr. M., Seattle, 1951, 1955, 1957; DMFA, 1958; Northwest A., 1958. *Position*: Prof. Drawing, Painting, A. Hist., Midwestern Texas Univ.; Prof. Drawing, Graphics, Oregon State College, Corvallis, Ore., at present.

ROCKWELL FREDERICK (F.)—*Painter, S.*
Box 724, Augusta, Me.

B. Brooklyn, N.Y., Jan. 12, 1917. *Studied*: Columbia Univ.; NAD; Tiffany Fnd.; & with Oronzio Malderelli, Arnold Blanch, George Grosz, William Zorach, & others. *Member*: Audubon A. *Award*: F., Tiffany Fnd., 1948. *Work*: U.S. Marine Hospital, Carville, La. *Exhibited*: WFNY 1939; AWCS, 1939, 1942, 1943; AIC, 1940, 1943, 1944; PAFA, 1943, 1946; NGA, 1941; WMAA, 1941; Portland Mus. A., 1944, 1956; Ogunquit A. Center, 1945, 1957, 1958; Audubon A., 1945, 1949-1952; MMA, 1952; Farnsworth Mus., 1949; Morton Gal., 1941 (one-man), 1943; Univ. Maine, 1956 (one-man); NSS, 1956, 1957; Five Islands annual, 1957; Art: USA, 1958; Wiscasset, Me., 1958.

ROCKWELL, NORMAN—*Illustrator*
Stockbridge, Mass.

B. New York, N.Y., Feb. 3, 1894. *Studied*: ASL. *Member*: SI. Contributor to: Saturday Evening Post.

RODDY, EDITH JEANNETTE—*Painter, Et.*
930 South Orange Ave., Sarasota, Fla.

B. Meadville, Pa. *Studied*: BMFA Sch.; in Europe; & with Charles Hawthorne, George Pearse Ennis, & others. *Member*: NAWA; Fla. Fed. A.; Sarasota AA; Clearwater AA. *Awards*: med., Fla. Fed. A., 1938; prize, Clearwater AA, 1946; citation, Sarasota Fed. A. *Work*: Syracuse Mus. FA. *Exhibited*: Florida AA; Sarasota AA; Clearwater AA; Palm Beach A. Lg.; Gulf Coast Group. Contributor to: School Arts League, Design, & other magazines; covers for Literary Digest. Lectures: Art History & Art Appreciation.*

RODERICK, JOHN M.—*Painter*
2147 Logan St., Harrisburg, Pa.; also, 5346 Lena St., Philadelphia 44, Pa.

B. Wilmington, Del., Nov. 13, 1877. *Member*: Wilmington Soc. FA. *Work*: PAFA; Wilmington Soc. FA; mural decorations in churches in Cambridge, Md.; Easton, Md.; Wilmington, Del.; Pendleton, Ore.; Collegeville, Pa.; Riverton, N.J.; Harrisburg and Philadelphia, Pa.

ROECKER, JULIA (Mrs.)—*Museum Director*
Saginaw Museum, 1126 North Michigan Ave., Saginaw, Mich.*

ROEDER, NORBERT—*Museum Director*
Kenosha Public Museum, Civic Center, Kenosha, Wis.*

ROESCH, KURT (FERDINAND)—
**　*Painter, Et., Eng., T., I.***
Todd Road, Katonah, N.Y.

B. Berlin, Germany, Sept. 22, 1905. *Studied*: Acad. A., Berlin, with Karl Hofer. *Member*: New Hampshire AA. *Work*: MMA; MMoA; Univ. Minnesota; Univ. Nebraska; Albright A. Gal.; VMFA; Ft. Worth Mus. A. *Exhibited*: Carnegie Inst., 1941-1945, 1952, 1958; AIC; VMFA; traveling exh., German Fed. Republic, 1951; one-man: Curt Valentin Gal., 1949, 1953; Currier Gal. A., 1955; Kassel, Germany, 1955; Rose Fried Gal., 1958, and in major national exhibitions, 1948-1958. *Position*: Instr., A. Dept., Sarah Lawrence College, Bronxville, N.Y.

ROGALSKI, WALTER—*Printmaker, C., T.*
Pratt-Contemporaries, 1343 Third Ave., New York 21, N.Y.; h. 15 Cross St., Locust Valley, L.I., N.Y.

B. Glen Cove, N.Y., Apr. 10, 1923. *Studied*: BMSch. A., with Gonzales, Osver, Seide, Peterdi. *Awards*: prize, BM, 1954; purchase awards: BM, 1952; SAM, 1952; DMFA, 1953. *Work*: MMoA; BM; CMA; FMA; SAM; New Britain Inst.; Yale Univ.; N.Y. Pub. Lib. *Exhibited*: Univ. Minnesota, 1950; BM, 1951, 1952, 1954; LC, 1951; MMoA, 1952; SAM, 1952; DMFA, 1953; Phila. Pr. Cl., 1958; Korman Gal., 1955 (one-man); Riverside Mus., 1959. Lectures on Etching, Engraving. *Positions*: Instr., Et., Eng., Enameling, BMSch. A.; Graphic Art, PIASch. and Pratt-Contemporaries, New York.

ROGERS, CHARLES B.—*Painter, Et., Lith., T., C.*
Huntington Hartford Foundation, 2300 Rustic Canyon Road, Pacific Palisades, Cal.

B. Great Bend, Kans., Jan. 27, 1911. *Studied*: NAD; Bethany Col., B.F.A.; Tiffany Fnd.; Cal. Col. A. & Crafts, M.F.A.; Jay Connaway Sch. A. *Member*: SAGA; Chicago Soc. Et.; Cal. Soc. Et.; Carmel AA; Cal. Soc. Pr. M.; Prairie WC Painters; Los A. AA; P. & S. Cl., Los. A. *Awards*: prizes, LC, 1943; Kansas State Fair (many); Kansas City AI, 1939; Smoky Hill, 1940; Bethany Col., 1941, 1943; Santa Paula, Cal., 1956; Tri-Club, Los A., 1958; numerous awards, Nat. Vet. Exhs.; F., Tiffany Fnd., 1937, 1940; Hartford Foundation F. (2). *Work*: Thayer Mus., Univ. Kansas; LC; Hutchinson (Kans.) Jr. Col.; MMA; LC; mural, USPO, Council Grove, Kans. *Exhibited*: Audubon A.; NAD; Los A. Mus. A.; Phila. Pr. Cl.; New Orleans A; Oakland A. Mus.; SAGA; Wash. WC Cl.; Wichita AA; Kansas City AI; Northwest Pr. M.; Alabama AA; CM; one-man: Smithsonian Inst.; Cayuga Mus. A.; AIC; Rochester Inst. Tech.; de Young Mem. Mus.; Mus. New Mexico; Thayer Mus. A.; Bethany Col.; Univ. Oklahoma; Mexico City; J. W. Robinson's, Los A., and others. *Position*: Asst. Dir., Huntington Hartford Foundation, Pacific Palisades, Cal.

ROGERS GERTRUDE [Mrs. Roy W.]—Painter
7834 Ternes St., Dearborn, Mich.

B. Ionia County, Mich., Sept. 4, 1896. *Member*: Friends of Art. *Awards*: prizes, Grand Rapids A. Gal., 1950, 1955; Erie (Pa.) A. Gal., 1952; Huntington Gal., W. Va., 1953. *Exhibited*: European tour of Am. Primitive Paintings; Smithsonian tour of Am. Primitive Painters; Western A. Mus. Director's tour; Des Moines A. Center; Galerie St. Etienne, N.Y., 1952; one-man: Am-British A. Gal., 1950, 1952; Grand Rapids A. Gal., 1951; Erie Pub. Mus., 1952; Erie A. Gal., 1952.*

ROGERS, JOHN—Painter, I., T., L.
502 Ridge Rd., Elmont, L.I., N.Y.

B. Brooklyn, N.Y., Dec. 9, 1906. *Studied*: ASL. *Member*: AWS; Brooklyn Soc. A.; SC; Am. A. Group; Balt. WC Cl.; Nassau A. Lg.; A. Lg. of Long Island. *Awards*: medal, AWS, 1944; prizes, Brooklyn Soc. A., 1950; SC, 1956. *Work*: Industrial, marine and railroad colls. *Exhibited*: AWS, 1939-1955; Brooklyn Soc. A., 1939-1955; St. Botolph Cl., Boston, 1947; SC, 1950, 1956; NAC, 1952; Grand Central A. Gal., 1954; Bohne Gal., 1955; Academic A., 1955. Contributor to art magazines and newspapers. Lectures.

ROGERS, MARGARET ESTHER—Painter, T.
234 Alhambra Ave., Santa Cruz, Cal.

B. Birmingham, England, May 1, 1872. *Studied*: with F. L. Heath, L. P. Latimer, Alexander Bower. *Member*: Santa Cruz A. Lg.; Soc. Western A.; Salinas FA Assn. *Awards*: prizes, Cal. State Fair, 1938, 1939, 1941; Santa Cruz County Exh.; Watsonville, Cal., annually. *Exhibited*: New York, N.Y., Chicago, Ill., Portland, Ore., Boise, Idaho, and in many cities of California.

ROGERS, MEYRIC REYNOLD—
  Museum Curator, E., W., L.
1078 Chapel St., New Haven, Conn.

B. Birmingham, England, Jan. 8, 1893. *Studied*: Harvard Univ., A.B., M. Arch. *Member*: AA Mus.; CAA. *Awards*: Legion of Honor, 1948; Star of Italy, 1952. *Author*: "Carl Milles, Sculptor," 1940; "American Interior Design," 1947; "Handbook, Italy at Work," 1950. *Co-Author*: "Handbook to the Pierpont Morgan Wing," MMA, 1923; "Handbook to the Lucy Maud Buckingham Medieval Collection," 1945. Contributor to: Encyclopaedia Britannica with article on Am. Interior Dec. & Am. Furniture, 1956; museum bulletins & art periodicals. *Position*: Asst., Asst. Cur., Decorative A. Dept., MMA, 1917-23; Prof. A., Smith Col., 1923-26; Assoc. Prof. FA, Harvard Univ., 1927; Dir., BMA, 1928-29; Dir., CAM, 1929-39; Cur. Decorative A. & Instit. A., AIC, Chicago, Ill., 1939-1959 (leave 1958-59); Organizing Sec., "Italy at Work" Exh., 1950; L., Am. Art, Yale Univ., 1956; Trustee, Am. Craftsmen's Edu. Council, N.Y.; Cur. Garvan and related Collections, Yale Univ. A. Gal., New Haven, Conn., 1958- .

ROGERS, MILLARD BUXTON—
  Associate Museum Director, Hist.
Seattle Art Museum, Volunteer Park; h. 1615 Peach Court, Seattle 2, Wash.

B. Danville, Ill., Sept. 1, 1912. *Studied*: AIC, M.F.A.; Univ. Chicago, M.A. *Member*: Am. Archaeological Soc.; CAA; Oriental Ceramic Soc.; Far Eastern Assn.; Siam Soc. *Awards*: F., AIC, 1955; F., Univ. Chicago, 1938-1940; Rockefeller Grant, travel and study in the Orient, 1948-1949. Contributor of articles to Artibus Asiae; reviews to Journal of Asiatic Studies; Far Eastern Ceramic Bulletin, and others. Lectures: Art of the Far East; Islamic Art; Medieval Art; Contemporary Art, at museums, universities, cultural organizations, scholarly societies, etc. Arranged several permanent exhibitions, Field Museum, Chicago; regularly, Seattle Art Museum. *Positions*: Instr., Humanities, Univ. Chicago, 1940-43; Hd. A. Dept., Univ. So. California, 1946-47 and Visiting L., 1947; Asst. Prof., Stanford Univ., 1947-50, Visiting L., 1952; L. in Art History, Univ. Washington, 1952- ; Asst. in Anthropology, Field Mus. Nat. Hist., Chicago, 1941-43; Assoc. Dir., Seattle Art Museum, Seattle, Wash., 1952- .

ROGERS, ROBERT STOCKTON—Painter, T., L.
1262 Peachtree St., Northeast (9); h. 3197 Paces Ferry Place, Northwest, Atlanta 5, Ga.

B. Burton, Kans., Dec. 16, 1896. *Studied*: Fairmount Conservatory, Wichita (grad.); AIC; Am. Acad. A., Chicago,

and with A. Oberteuffer. *Member*: A. Dir. Cl. of Atlanta; Assn. Georgia A.; Atlanta WC Cl. *Awards*: Atlanta A. Dir. Cl., 1954-1956; Atlanta WC Cl., 1955; Carnegie grants, 1947, 1949. *Work*: Univ. Georgia; Brown Univ., Providence, R.I.; IBM; Atlanta AA; Rich's, Inc., Atlanta. *Exhibited*: VMFA; MModA; PAFA; Rockefeller Center, N.Y.; Atlanta AA; BMFA; Vose Gal., Boston; Mint Mus. A.; Dayton AI; Tupper Ware Nat. traveling exh., 1956; Birmingham, Ala., 1954; Southeastern annual, Atlanta; Painting of the Year, Atlanta, 1956-58; Audubon A., 1958; Knickerbocker A., 1958; one-man: Shreveport A. Gal.; Gertrude Herbert Mus. A., Augusta; Brenau Col.; Mint Mus. A.; Stevens-Gross Gal., Chicago. *Position*: Dir., Atlanta Art Inst., 1942-52; Instr., Atlanta Art Inst., 1929- .

ROGOWAY, ALFRED—Painter
Ranchos de Taos, N.M.

B. Portland, Ore., Apr. 4, 1905. *Studied*: Univ. So. California at Los A.; Univ. California, Berkeley; Univ. Mexico; Cal. Sch. FA, San F.; Cal. Col. A. & Crafts; Mills Col., with Leger, Feininger. *Work*: Mus. New Mexico, Santa Fe.; Galerie le Mage, Vence, France; Galerie Grimaldi, Cannes, France. *Exhibited*: nationally and internationally, 1925-1956.

ROHDE, MRS. W. ALLEN. See *Carothers, Sarah Pace*

ROHRBACH, CHARLES—
  Commercial Artist, Des., P., C.
425 Franklin St., Buffalo 2, N.Y.; h. 432 Linden Ave,. East Aurora, N.Y.

B. Berne, Switzerland. *Member*: Buffalo Soc. A.; Aurora A. Cl. *Work*: Buffalo Mus. Science; WBEN-TV Reception Room. Cover illus., Buffalo Courier-Express Pictorial Magazine; illus., textbooks for N.Y. State Edu. Dept., Bureau of Vocational Training. *Exhibited*: local and regional exhs.*

ROIR, IRVING—Cartoonist
2095 Cruger Ave., New York 62, N.Y.

B. Austria, Dec. 26, 1907. *Studied*: CUASch.; NAD; ASL; with William McNulty, George Bridgman. *Member*: Nat. Cartoonists Soc. Contributor cartoons to King Features; Chicago Tribune; N.Y. News Syndicate; Esquire; Sat. Eve. Post; Colliers; American and other national magazines.

ROJANKOVSKY, FEODOR STEPANOVICH—Illustrator
17 McIntyre St., Bronxville, N.Y.

B. Mitava, Russia, Dec. 24, 1891. *Studied*: Acad. FA, Moscow. *Award*: Caldecott Award, 1956 for illus. in "Frog Went A-Courtin'." I., 'Daniel Boone"; "Jacques Cartier"; "Tall Mother Goose"; "Treasure Trove of the Sun"; "Frog Went A-Courtin'," and many other children's books.

ROLAND, JAY—Painter
1270 Sixth Ave.; h. 880 Fifth Ave., New York, N.Y.

B. New York, N.Y., Sept. 28, 1904. *Studied*: NAD; ASL; Grand Central A. Sch. *Member*: AWCS; Audubon A.; Phila. WC Cl.; Brooklyn SA; Arch. L. *Awards*: prizes, BM, 1944; Brooklyn SA, 1944; Audubon A., 1945. *Work*: BM. *Exhibited*: N.Y. WC Cl., 1934-1937; AWCS, 1933-1946; AIC, 1935, 1941, 1946; BM, 1943; CA, 1933, 1934, 1936; MMA (AV), 1942; Phila. WC Cl., 1940-1946; Audubon A., 1944, 1945; Brooklyn SA, 1941-1946; Am.-British A. Center, 1942-1944; Wash. WC Cl., 1942, 1943; NAD, 1943; one-man exh.: Marie Sterner Gal., 1941; Campbell-Ewald Co. Gal., 1941.*

ROLAND, MRS. JAY.See *Linton*

ROLLER, SAMUEL K.—Painter, E.
416 Main St.; mail: Box 265, Lynchburg, Va.; h. Madison Heights, Va.

B. New Market, Va. *Studied*: CGA; N.Y. Sch. A.; Chicago Acad. A.; Univ. Virginia, and with Robert Henri, George Ennis, and others. *Member*: AAPL; Cooperstown AA; Lynchburg A. Cl.; Lynchburg A. Center. *Work*: N.Y. Hist. Soc.; Am. A. Group; Hickory Grove Inn, Cooperstown, N.Y. *Exhibited*: VMFA, 1942-1944; Norfolk Mus. A.,

1944-1953; Lynchburg A. Cl., 1941-1958; Lynchburg A. Center, 1954-1958; Cooperstown AA, 1953-1955; Norton Gal. A., Palm Beach, Fla., 1942; one-man: Morton Gal., N.Y., 1935, 1936, 1939, 1940; Lynchburg Woman's Cl., 1942; Huckleberry Mountain Workshop, 1950; Lake Charles, La., 1950; DeRidder, La., 1950; Argent Gal., N.Y., 1939, 1940; Lynchburg A. Center, 1950, 1956. Contributor covers to Richmond Times Dispatch Magazine. *Position*: Instr., Cooperstown, N.Y., 1951 - (summers); Univ. Virginia Ext., Dan River, Va., 1957- .

ROLLINS, CARL PURINGTON—*Book Designer,* **C.**
   146 Armory St., Hamden (P.O. New Haven), Conn.

B. West Newbury, Mass., Jan. 7, 1880. *Studied*: Harvard Univ. *Member*: AIGA; Columbiad Cl. of Conn.; Grolier Cl. (hon.); Century Assn.; Club of Odd Volumes, Boston (hon.); Double Crown Cl., London. *Awards*: Hon. deg., M.A., L.H.D., Yale Univ.; gold medal, AIGA, 1941. *Exhibited*: "Fifty Books of the Year," annually; Dartmouth Col., 1946; retrospective exhs., Yale Univ., 1948, Grolier Cl., 1948. Des. books for Grolier Cl., MMA, Limited Editions Cl., Yale Univ., Yale Univ. Press. Contributor to: Saturday Review; Dolphin; Print; and other trade publications. Lectures: History and Practice of Printing. *Position*: Des., Yale Univ. Press. 1918-48 (retired); Printer, Yale Univ., New Haven, Conn., 1920-48, Emeritus, 1948- .

ROLLINS, HELEN JORDAN *(Mrs.)*—***Painter,* C., I.**
   2443 Laughlin Ave., La Crescenta, Cal.

B. Hayward, Cal., Mar. 4, 1893. *Studied*: Los A. Sch. A. & Des., and with J. E. McBurney, J. Francis Smith, Theodore Lukits. *Work*: Southwest Mus., Los A., Cal.; Pub. Sch., Los A.; mural, Edu. Bldg., San Diego, Cal. Authority on early California-Spanish historical subjects. *Position*: Chm. Hist. & Landmarks Com., Los Compadrinos de San Gabriel Club.

ROLLINS, JOSEPHINE LUTZ—*Painter,* **E.**
   University of Minnesota, Minneapolis, Minn.; h. 621 5th St., Southeast, Minneapolis 14, Minn.

B. Sherburne, Minn., July 21, 1896. *Studied*: Cornell Col., Mt. Vernon, Iowa; Univ. Minnesota B.A., M.A.; Corcoran Sch. A.; Minneapolis Sch. A.; & with Hans Hofmann, Cameron Booth, Edmund Kinsinger. *Member*: Minn. Assn. A. *Awards*: (2) purchase prizes, WAC. *Work*: Univ. Minnesota; Virginia (Minn.) Lib.; Owatonna (Minn.) Lib.; Crosby-Tronton H.S., Minn.; mural, University H.S., Minneapolis, Minn. *Exhibited*: AWCS, 1936, 1946; All. A. Am., 1946; Newport AA, 1946; Sacramento, Cal., 1941; Minneapolis Inst. A., annually; Minn. State Fair, annually; Oakland A. Gal.; one-man traveling exh., 1958; Monterey, Cal., 1958; St. Paul Gal., 1956. *Position*: Assoc. Prof., Painting, Drawing, Univ. Minnesota, Minneapolis, Minn., at present.

ROLLINS, WARREN ELIPHALET—*Painter,* **T.**
   Paradise Valley, Ariz.; h. 18 Midvale Rd., Roland Park, Baltimore 10, Md.

B. Carson City, Nev., Aug. 8, 1861. *Studied*: Cal. Sch. Des. *Awards*: med., Cal. Sch. Des. *Work*: Santa Fé Railroad; triptychs, Bishops' Lodge, Santa Fé, N.M.; Tower Bldg., Balt., Md.; murals, USPO, Gallup, N.M.; Harvey House, Gallup, N.M.; Mus. New Mexico, Santa Fé; hotel, Arrowhead Springs, Cal.; Nat. Bank, Phoenix, Ariz.; Huntington Gal., Los A. *Exhibited*: Mus. New Mexico, Santa Fé; Am. A. Assn., Los A.; Maryland Inst.; Barbizon Plaza, N.Y.; Gunnison, Colo.; Delmonico's, New York, N.Y., Sheraton Belvedere Hotel, Balt., Md., 1947 (one-man.)

ROLLO, J(OSEPH)—*Painter*
   11 Charles St., New York 14, N.Y.

B. Ragusa, Italy, Feb. 27, 1904. *Studied*: AIC; ASL; & with Leon Kroll, John Carroll, George Luks. *Work*: WMAA; CAA. *Exhibited*: CGA, 1939; Carnegie Inst., 1929, 1931, 1936; AIC, 1930, 1934, 1936-1938; Detroit Inst. A., 1951, 1952; Toledo Mus. A., 1951; Terry AI, 1952.

ROMANO, CLARE (ROSS)—*Lithographer,* **Eng., P.**
   110 Davison Place, Englewood, N.J.

B. Palisade, N.J., Aug. 24, 1922. *Studied*: CUASch.; Ecole des Beaux-Arts, Fontainebleau, France; Instituto

Statale d'Arte, Florence, Italy. *Member*: SAGA. *Awards*: Fulbright F., 1958-59; Tiffany F., 1952; prizes, BM, 1951; LC, 1951; SAGA, 1952. *Work*: BM; MMA; N.Y. Pub. Lib.; LC; Rochester Mem. A. Gal.; Pa. State Univ. *Exhibited*: MModA, 1953; BM, 1951-1953, 1956-1958; MMA, 1953; LC, 1951, 1952, 1955; Phila. Pr. Cl., 1956, 1958; Santa Monica City Col., 1957; Carnegie Inst.; PAFA; SAGA; CM; Arts Council traveling exh. Europe; SAM; Bradley Univ.; Newark Mus. A., and others. Illus., "Manhattan Island," 1957; "The God Around Us," 1958; "A Way of Knowing," 1958.

ROMANO, EMANUEL GLICEN—*Painter,* **I., T.**
   163 East 74th St., New York 21, N.Y.

B. Rome, Italy, Sept. 23, 1901. *Studied*: in Switzerland; and with Enrico Glicenstein. *Member*: A. Lg. Am. *Work*: FMA; New London Mus.; Detroit Inst. A.; Musee de La Ville de Paris; Musee Nationaux de France; mural, Klondike Bldg., Welfare Island, N.Y. *Exhibited*: PAFA, 1945; AIC, 1940; WMAA; Ft. Worth AA; Contemporaries, N.Y.; Kagan & Dreyfus, N.Y.; one-man: Passedoit Gal.; Feigl Gal.; Macon (Ga.) AA; Kleeman Gal.; Katia Granoff Galerie, Paris. Lectures: Mural Painting in Ancient and Modern Times.

ROMANO, UMBERTO—*Painter,* **Lith., S., T., L.**
   162 East 83rd St., New York 28, N.Y.; s. Gallery-on-the-Moors, East Gloucester, Mass.

B. Salerno, Italy, Feb. 26, 1906. *Studied*: NAD, and in Italy. *Member*: ANA. *Awards*: prizes, Conn. Acad. FA; North Shore AA; AIC; Pulitzer Prize; Springfield A. Lg.; NAD; medals, Tiffany Fnd.; Suydam silver medal; Crown-inshield award. *Work*: FMA; WMA; Springfield Mus. FA; AGAA; BMA; Mt. Holyoke Col.; Tel-Aviv Mus., Israel; Univ. Georgia; PAFA, and in many private colls. in U.S. and abroad. *Exhibited*: nationally. One-man: Rehn Gal., 1928 and subsequently; Paris, France, 1948; Assoc. Am. A., 1942, 1944, 1946, 1950; WMA, 1933; Kleemann Gal., 1934; Springfield Mus. FA, 1943; Assoc. Am. A., Chicago, 1947; Chicago, Ill., 1955; Rochester, N.Y., 1955; Castle Hill Fnd. (Mass.) 1955. I., Dante's "Divine Comedy," 1946. *Position*: Hd., WMA Sch. A., Worcester, Mass., 1934-40; Hd., Romano Sch. A., Gloucester, Mass., 1933- ; New York City, 1954- .*

ROMANS, CHARLES JOHN—*Painter,* **T., C.**
   1033 New York Ave., Cape May, N.J.

B. New York, N.Y., Mar. 4, 1893. *Studied*: State T. Col., Buffalo, N.Y.; N.Y. Univ.; NAD, and with George Elmer Browne, X.J. Barile. *Member*: Provincetown AA; Gotham Painters; Hudson Valley AA; All. A. Am.; Audubon A.; P. & S. Soc. New Jersey; SC; Nat. Assn. Painters in Casein. *Awards*: New Jersey P. & S. Soc., 1944, 1950; Jersey City Mus. A., 1948, 1952; Asbury Park FA Assn., 1948; Newark A. Cl., 1949; A. Council of New Jersey, 1950, 1951; Hudson A. of New Jersey, 1953; Rahway A. Center, 1953; Hudson Valley AA, 1954. *Exhibited*: AWS, 1939; NAD, 1941; Montclair A. Mus., 1937-1950; All. A. Am., 1938-1958; Audubon A., 1944; Jersey City Mus., 1944-1957; Asbury Park FA Asn., 1946-1950; NAC, 1950-1952; Hudson Valley AA, 1952-1954; Riverside Mus., 1954, 1955; Polish-American A. Exh., 1948-1950; AFA traveling exh., 1939, 1940. *Position*: Instr., FA Workshop.

ROMANS, MRS. CHARLES J. See Gilmore, Ethel

RONAY, STEPHEN R.—*Painter,* **Comm. A., I.**
   50 Rockefeller Plaza, New York 20, N.Y.; h. 12 Hillside Ave., Port Washington, L.I., N.Y.

B. Hungary, Feb. 27, 1900. *Studied*: Royal Acad. Des., Budapest; Vienna, Austria; NAD. *Exhibited*: Assoc. Am. A.; Contemporary A. Gal.; Macbeth Gal.; MModA; CGA; Van Dieman-Lilienfeld Gal., 1951 (one-man); GGE 1939; CM; NAD; Audubon A. Contributor drawings and cartoons to Hearst Publications; Vanity Fair; New Yorker; Sat. Eve. Post; Cosmopolitan; Colliers and other national magazines.

RONDELL, LESTER—*Designer,* **P.**
   3 East 14th St.; h. 23 East 11th St., New York 3, N.Y.

B. New York, N.Y., Feb. 8, 1907. *Studied*: N.Y. Sch. F. & App. A.; ASL, with Kimon Nicolaides. *Member*: A.

Dir. Cl.; SI. *Awards*: med., Sch. A. Lg., 1925; prizes, U.S. Treasury Dept., 1943, 1944; Pepsi-Cola, 1946. *Exhibited*: PAFA, 1941; Carnegie Inst., 1945. Lectures: Design & Layout in Advertising.*

RONEY, HAROLD ARTHUR—*Painter, T.*
Address unknown

B. Sullivan, Ill., Nov. 7, 1899. *Studied*: Chicago Acad. A.; AIC; & with Harry Leith-Ross, John Folinsbee, & others. *Member*: SSAL; Texas FA Assn. *Awards*: prize, South Bend, Ind., 1923. *Work*: Sullivan (Ill.) Pub. Lib.; Witte Mem. Mus.; Austin (Tex.) Pub. Lib.; South Bend (Ind.) Pub. Sch.; Southwest Texas State T. Col. *Exhibited*: SSAL, 1929-1932, 1945; Conn. Acad. FA, 1937; Texas FA Assn., 1929-1933, 1944, 1952; San Antonio, Tex., 1944, 1945; New Orleans AA, 1928, 1929, 1931; New Hope, Pa., 1935, 1936; San Angelo, Tex., 1952; Beaumont, Tex., 1952; one-man exh.; Phila., Pa.; San Antonio, Austin, Tex.; etc.*

RONNEBECK, LOUISE EMERSON—*Painter, L., T.*
Beck's-hill, Harrington Sound, Bermuda

B. Philadelphia, Pa., Aug. 25, 1901. *Studied*: Barnard Col.; ASL; Am. Sch., Fontainebleau, France; & with Kenneth Hayes Miller, George Bridgman. *Member*: AEA; Denver A. Gld.; NSMP. *Work*: frescoes, County Hospital, Greeley, Colo.; Morrey Jr. H.S., Speer Hospital, Sloanes Lake Cl. House, murals, Church Holy Redeemer, Children's Hospital, Denver A. Mus., Albany Hotel, all of Denver, Colo.; Bermuda H.S. for Girls; Bermuda Dept. of Agriculture; USPO, Worland, Wyo.; Grand Junction, Colo.; dec. partition in children's branch of Denver A. Mus. *Exhibited*: Los A. Mus. A.; SFMA; Colorado Springs FA Center; Denver A. Mus.; Joslyn Mem.; Am. A. Exh., New York, N.Y.; Bermuda Soc. A., 1956-1958. *Position*: Instr. A., Denver Univ., Denver, Colo., 1946-47; Prof. Drawing & Painting, 1947-51. A. T. Bermuda H.S. for Girls, 1955-58.

ROOD, HENRY, JR.—*Painter, I., T.*
214 North Cedar St., Greensboro, N.C.

B. Pleasantville, N.Y., Feb. 20, 1902. *Studied*: ASL; N.Y. Univ., and with John Carlson, Frank DuMond. *Member*: North Carolina State A. Soc. *Work*: North Carolina State Capitol Bldg., Governor's Mansion, State Welfare Bldg., State Col., all Raleigh; Wake Forest Col.; Univ. North Carolina; Pharmacy Bldg., Chapel Hill; Guilford Col.; High Point Col.; Woman's Col. of Univ. North Carolina; Greensboro Col.; Guilford County Courthouse; Mint Mus. A.; Davidson Col.; North Carolina State Hospital, Morganton; Medical Col. of Virginia, Richmond; South Carolina State Sch. for the Blind, Spartanburg; Dartmouth Col., Hanover, N.H.*

ROOD, JOHN—*Sculptor, P., W., L., E.*
1650 Dupont Ave., South, Minneapolis 5, Minn.

B. Athens, Ohio, Feb. 2, 1902. *Studied*: Ohio Univ. *Member*: Minnesota AA; Soc. Minn. Sculptors; AEA. *Awards*: Minneapolis Inst. A.; Minnesota State Fair; WAC; SFMA, and others. *Work*: Cranbrook Acad. A.; Ohio Univ.; St. Mark's Cathedral, Minneapolis; Our Lady of Grace Church, Edina, Minn.: Mt. Zion Lutheran Church, Minneapolis; Hamline Univ.; Wellesley Col.; Austin Jr. H.S., Austin, Minn.; Minneapolis Athletic Cl.; Nat. Hdqtrs., AAUW, Wash., D.C.; AGAA. *Exhibited*: nationally; 15 one-man exhs., New York; and in Milan and Rome, Italy, 1956; Mexico City, 1958. *Author*: "Wood Sculpture," 1940; "Sculpture in Wood," 1950; Chapter on Sculpture, Book of Knowledge, 1952. *Position*: Prof. A., University of Minnesota, Minneapolis, Minn., at present.

ROOK, EDWARD F.—*Painter*
Rt. 1, Old Lyme, Conn.

B. New York, N.Y., 1870. *Studied*: with Jean Paul Laurens, Benjamin Constant, Paris, France. *Member*: NA; Lotos Cl., N.Y. *Awards*: Temple gold medal, PAFA, 1898; bronze medal, Buffalo Expo., 1901; two silver medals, St. Louis Expo., 1904; bronze medal, Carnegie Inst., 1910; silver medal, Intl. FA Expo., Buenos Aires, 1910; gold medal, Panama Expo., 1915; bronze medal and prize, CGA, 1920; Lyme AA, 1929. *Work*: PAFA; PMA; CM; Boston A. Cl.; Portland Mus. A.; CGA; Lotos Cl., N.Y.

ROPP, HUBERT—*Painter, E.*
Art Institute of Chicago; h. 727 Ravine Ave., Lake Bluff, Ill.

B. Pekin, Ill., Apr. 15, 1894. *Studied*: AIC, and in Vienna and Paris. *Member*: Chicago A. Cl.; Chicago Soc. A. *Awards*: citation, AIGA. *Exhibited*: AIC; Carnegie Inst.; Boyer Gal., Phila., Pa.; Nat. Gal. Toronto, Canada; GGE 1939; Chicago A. Cl. *Position*: Instr. A., Nat. Acad. A., Chicago, 1924-27, Dean, 1927-31; Instr., 1938-44, Dean, 1944- , Art Inst. of Chicago, Ill.

RORIMER, JAMES J.—
Museum Director & Curator, W., L.
Metropolitan Museum of Art, Fifth Ave. at 82nd St. (28); h. 1000 Park Ave., New York 28, N.Y.

B. Cleveland, Ohio, Sept. 7, 1905. *Studied*: Harvard Univ., B.A.; in Europe. *Member*: AAMus.; AFA; F., Am. Geographical Soc.; AID (Hon.); Archaeological Inst. Am.; Art & Antique Dealers Lg. (Hon.); Assn. A. Mus. Dirs.; Cleveland Inst. A. (Adviser); CAA; France-America Soc.; French Inst. in the U.S.; Intl. Inst. of Conservation; Medieval Acad. Am. (Councillor, 1955, Exec. Com., 1957-58); Mus. Council of New York City (Chm. 1950-51); Nat. Council U.S. Art; Swedish Royal Acad. Let., Hist. & Antiquities (Foreign Corres. Memb.); Ex-officio Trustee, Mus. City of N.Y.; NSS (Hon.); F., Morgan Lib.; N.Y. Hist. Soc. (Assoc. Life Memb.); Intl. Center Romanesque Art (Hon. Chm.); F., Am. Acad. A. & Lets.; Arch. Lg. (Hon.), and many others. *Awards*: Chevalier French Legion of Honor. Author: "The Cloisters—The Building and the Collection of Medieval Art," 1938; "Ultra Violet Rays and Their Use in the Examination of Works of Art," 1931; "Unicorn Tapestries," 1945; "Medieval Jewelry," 1944; "Survival, The Salvage and Protection of Art in War," 1950; "The Nine Heroes Tapestries at the Cloisters," 1953, and other books. Contributor to Creative Art, Art Bulletin, MMA Studies, and others. *Position*: Asst., Dept. Dec. A., 1927-29, Asst. Cur., 1929-32, Assoc. Cur., 1932-34, Cur., Medieval Art & The Cloisters, 1938-49, Dir., The Cloisters, 1949-1955; Dir., MMA, New York, N.Y., 1955- . Monuments, Fine Arts & Archives Officer, Normandy, Paris, and Western Military Dist., World War II.

ROSE, CARL—*Illustrator*
Rowayton, Conn.
Member: SI.*

ROSE, DOROTHY—*Painter*
312 East 21st St., Brooklyn 26, N.Y.

B. Brooklyn, N.Y. *Studied*: BAID; New Sch. for Social Research; ASL. *Member*: AEA; ASL. *Work*: Staten Island Mus. Hist. & A., and in private colls. *Exhibited*: N.Y. City Center, 1956-58; Panoras Gal., N.Y., 1955-1957 (all one-man); Village A. Center, 1957, 1958; Silvermine Gld. A., 1956.

ROSE, HERMAN—*Painter, T.*
55 Morton St., New York 14, N.Y.

B. Brooklyn, N.Y., Nov. 6, 1909. *Studied*: NAD. *Member*: AEA. *Award*: F., Yaddo Fnd., 1955. *Work*: MModA. *Exhibited*: PAFA, 1952; MModA, 1948, 1952; WMAA, 1948, 1949, 1953, 1955; ACA Gal., 1955 (one-man). *Position*: Instr., New Sch. for Social Research, New York, N.Y., 1954-55.*

ROSE, IVER—*Painter*
15 West 67th St., New York, N.Y.

B. Chicago, Ill., Apr. 17, 1899. *Studied*: Hull House, Chicago; AIC; Cincinnati Acad. A. *Member*: Audubon A.; All. A. Am.; Rockport AA. *Awards*: prizes, Audubon A., 1950, 1953; Rockport AA, 1944, 1955. *Work*: Chicago Pub. Libraries; Walker A. Center; Cranbrook Acad. A.; AGAA; Univ. Georgia; Des Moines A. Center; Phila. A. All.; San Diego FA Gal.; Witte Mem. Mus.; Am. Acad. A. & Let.; Birmingham Mus. A.; Hassam Fund; Mus. of the New Britain Inst.; Parrish Mus., Southampton, L.I.; San Angelo A. Lg.; Encyclopaedia Britannica; NAD; Springfield (Mass.) Mus. A. *Exhibited*: MMA; Carnegie Inst.; AIC; PAFA; CGA; Clearwater Mus. A.; BMA; Univ. Nebraska; Springfield A. Mus.; CMA; AFA traveling exh.; Montclair A. Mus.; VMFA; DePauw Univ.; Nelson Gal. A.; Kansas City AI; Dayton AI; Joslyn A.

Mus.; Univ. Illinois; NAD; Audubon A.; All. A. Am.; Milch Gal., 1949-1952; MModA traveling exh., 1954-55; one-man: Kleeman Gal.; Schneider-Gabriel Gal.; Kraushaar Gal., 1938, 1940, 1942, 1945, 1947, 1949.

ROSE, RUTH STARR—*Painter, Lith., Ser., L., T.*

"High Design," 733 Latham St., Alexandria, Va.

B. Eau Claire, Wis. *Studied*: Vassar Col., A.B. *Member*: NAWA; N.Y. Soc. Women A.; AEA; Phila. Pr. Cl.; Washington Pr. M.; Nat. Ser. Soc. *Awards*: prizes, NAWA, 1937, 1944; State of New Jersey, 1944; Washington Pr. M., 1951; Norfolk Mus. A. & Sc., 1950; CGA, 1951; Va. Pr. M., 1957; Wash. Area Pr. M., 1957; A. Fair, Alexandria & Wash., 1957; Religious A. Fair, 1958. *Work*: LC; MMA; Vassar Col.; PMA; Wells Col.; Williams Col.; Milliken Col.; Norfolk Mus. A. & Sc. *Exhibited*: NAD, 1945, 1946; Nat. Color Pr. Soc., 1945-1950; LC, 1945, 1946, 1950; Carnegie Inst., 1950; Phila. Pr. Cl., 1944, 1945; Northwest Pr. M., 1949; NAWA, 1944, 1945, 1949, 1950, 1951; CM, 1954; one-man: Rehoboth A. Lg.; Farnsworth Mus. A., Rockland, Me. Lecturer to schools, and professional organizations.

ROSE, WILLIAM F.—*Illustrator*

478 Kent Court, Oceanside, N.Y.

B. Pittsburgh, Pa., Sept. 16, 1909. *Studied*: Univ. Pittsburgh; Carnegie Inst., B.A. *Member*: SI. *Exhibited*: SI, 1945, 1946. Contributor to: Collier's, Today's Woman, This Week magazines.*

ROSEBERG, CARL ANDERSON—*Sculptor, Eng., E.*

College of William and Mary, Williamsburg, Va.

B. Vinton, Iowa, Sept. 26, 1916. *Studied*: Iowa State Univ., B.F.A., M.F.A., with Humbert Albrizio, Lasansky; Cranbrook Acad. A., with William McVey, Maija Grotell. *Member*: Audubon A.; CAA. *Awards*: prizes, Springfield, Mo.; Walker A. Center; Huckleberry Mountain A. Center; VMFA, 1955, 1957; Virginia A. *Work*: monuments, Rockingham County, Harrisonburg, Va. *Exhibited*: PAFA, 1948; Syracuse Mus. FA, 1948; Audubon A., 1948, 1950-1956, 1957, 1958; Ball State T. Col., Muncie, Ind., 1955; Walker A. Center, 1946, 1947; Springfield Mus. A.; Denver A. Mus., 1947; Wash. Sculptors Group, 1952; VMFA, 1948, 1951, 1953, 1955, 1957; Univ. Iowa, 1957; Jamestown Festival, 1957. *Position*: Instr., Asst. Prof. FA, College of William and Mary, Williamsburg, Va., 1947-1957; Assoc. Prof., 1957- .

ROSEN, ESTHER YOVITS—*Painter*

243 Cherry Lane, Teaneck, N.J.

B. Schenectady, N.Y., June 3, 1916. *Studied*: with Samuel Brecher. *Member*: NAWA; Bergen County A. Gld. *Awards*: prize, Bergen County A. Gld., 1956. *Work*: Collectors of Am. A. *Exhibited*: Audubon A., 1951; NAWA, 1948-1951; Rutherford, N.J., 1952. *Position*: Hd. A. Dept., and Children and Adult Classes, Teaneck (N.J.) Community Center, 1952- .

ROSEN, HY(MAN) (JOSEPH)—*Cartoonist*

Times-Union Sheridan Ave.; h. 33 Verplank St., Albany, N.Y.

B. Albany, N.Y., Feb. 10, 1923. *Studied*: AIC; ASL. *Member*: Nat. Cartoonists Soc. *Awards*: prizes, Nat. Physicians Comm., 1948; Disabled Am. Veterans, 1949; Freedom Fnd., 1950, 1952-1954, 1955. *Work*: LC; work used by Voice of America. *Exhibited*: MMA, Cartoonists Exh., 1951; London cartoon exh., 1958. Contributor cartoons to Hearst papers. *Position*: Ed. Cart., Times-Union, Albany, N.Y., 1945- .

ROSENBAUER, WALLACE—*Educator, S., Mus., Cur.*

Miry Brook Rd., Danbury, Conn.

B. Chambersburg, Pa., June 12, 1900. *Studied*: Washington Univ., St. Louis, Mo., and with Alexander Archipenko. *Member*: AID. *Awards*: medal, Kansas City AI, 1925-1927, 1929; prizes, 1927, 1935, 1936, 1939, 1940; CAM, 1929; AAPL, 1954. *Work*: Nelson Gal. A.; Springfield A. Mus.; St. Peter's Church, Kansas City; Tower of the Ascension, Kansas City; Cavalry Lutheran Church, Kansas City; war mem., Concordia, Kans.; Raytown Elem. Sch., Raytown, Mo. *Exhibited*: CAM; WMAA; Kansas City AI; WFNY 1939; one-man: New York City; Stamford Mus.

A. *Position*: Asst. Dir. and Cur. Visual A., Stamford Mus. & Nature Center; Instr. A. Appreciation & Drawing, Stamford Branch, Univ. Connecticut, at present, L., Instr., Parsons Sch. Des., New York, N.Y., 1950-53; Dir. Kansas City AI, 1940-49.

ROSENBERG, JAKOB—*Museum Curator, E.*

Fogg Museum of Art, Harvard University, Cambridge, Mass.; h. 19 Bellevue Rd., Arlington 74, Mass.

B. Berlin, Germany, Sept. 5, 1893. *Studied*: Univ. Munich, Ph.D.; Bern, Zurich, Frankfort. *Member*: CAA; F., Am. Acad. A. & Sc.; Hon. F., Pierpont Morgan Lib. *Awards*: Hon. degree, A.M., Harvard Univ., 1942. *Author*: "Drawings of Martin Schongauer," 1922; "Jacob van Ruisdael," 1928; "Lucas Cranach," 1932; "Rembrandt," 1948. Contributor to: The Art Quarterly; Magazine of Art; FMA Bulletin, with articles on Graphic Arts and Baroque painting. *Position*: Resident F., L., Harvard Univ., 1937-39; Cur. Prints, Prof. FA, FMA, Cambridge, Mass., 1939- .

ROSENBERG, LOUIS CONRAD—*Etcher, I., Arch.*

West Way Rd., Greens Farms, Conn.

B. Portland, Ore., May 6, 1890. *Studied*: MIT; Royal Col. A., London, England. *Member*: NA; F., Royal Soc. Painters, Etchers & Engravers, London; AIA. *Awards*: med., Cal. Pr. M., 1924; AIA, 1948; Chicago SE, 1925, 1927; prizes, AIC, 1932; Brooklyn SE, 1926; SAE, 1932, 1938; Albany Pr. Cl., 1946. *Work*: Smithsonian Inst.; Lib. Cong.; N.Y. Pub. Lib.; Boston Pub. Lib.; BMFA; Albany Inst. Hist. & A.; British Mus., Victoria & Albert Mus., London; Univ. Nebraska; Honolulu Acad. A.; CMA; Montana State Col.; Slater Mem. Mus., Norwich, Conn.; AGAA; Howard Univ.; Acad. A., Stockholm; Peabody Mus., Cambridge; Royal Insurance Co., N.Y.; Cleveland Terminal Co.; Cincinnati Terminal Co. *Exhibited*: NAD, 1930-1958; SAE, 1932-1941; AIC, 1932; Albany Inst. Hist. & A., 1945; Albany Pr. Cl., 1945; Wichita AA, 1946; Am.-British Goodwill Exh., London, 1945; etc. *Author*: "Davanzati Palace," 1922; I., "Bridges of France," 1924; "Middle East War Projects of Johnson-Drake & Piper," 1943, & other books. Contributor to: print magazines.

ROSENBERG, SAMUEL—*Painter, E.*

Carnegie Institute, Fine Arts College; h. 2721 Mt. Royal Rd., Pittsburgh 17, Pa.

B. Philadelphia, Pa., June 28, 1896. *Studied*: Carnegie Inst., B.A. *Member*: Assoc. A. Pittsburgh: Abstract Group; CAA; AAUP; A. Comm. City of Pittsburgh. *Awards*: prizes, Carnegie Inst., 1945, 1954; Assoc. A. Pittsburgh, 1917, 1920, 1921, 1930, 1936, 1946, 1948; Pittsburgh Soc. A., 1928, 1929; Butler AI, 1939, 1943, 1947; Indiana State T. Col., 1946; Pepsi-Cola, 1947, 1948; Grensfelder prize, 1953, 1955; "Man of the Year in Art," Pittsburgh Jr. Chamber Commerce and A. & Crafts Center; prize and silver medal, Ligonier Valley A. Lg. *Work*: Carnegie Inst.; Encyclopaedia Britannica; Butler AI; Somerset County Sch.; Pittsburgh Bd. Edu.; Slippery Rock (Pa.) State T. Col.; Pa. State Univ.; Indiana State T. Col. *Exhibited*: Carnegie Inst.; WMAA; John Herron AI; Univ. Illinois; Butler AI; AIC; Walker A. Center; Milwaukee AI; Minneapolis Inst. A.; CAM; Toledo Mus. A.; Springfield Mus. FA; VMFA; one-man: Bucknell Univ.; Univ. Tennessee; Butler AI; Cheltenham A. Center; BMFA Sch.; Pittsburgh Playhouse; Jewish Community Center, Cleveland; Indiana (Pa.) State T. Col.; Pittsburgh A. & Crafts Center; Carnegie Inst., 1922-1937, 1956; Weirton Community Center, 1957; Hewlett Gal., Carnegie Inst., 1958. *Position*: Prof., Drawing & Painting, Carnegie Inst., Pittsburgh, Pa.

ROSENBLATT, ALICE—*Craftsman, P., Des., T.*

Tuckahoe 7, N.Y.

B. New York, N.Y. *Studied*: T. Col., Columbia Univ., B.S.; Columbia Univ., M.A.; Grand Central Sch. A., and with Henry B. Snell, George Bridgman, and others. *Member*: Eastern AA; Westchester A. & Crafts Gld.; Yonkers AA; Mt. Vernon AA (Bd. Dir.). *Awards*: prize, White Plains County Center, 1949 Yonkers AA; Villager cover contest, 1952. *Work*: mural, Jr. H.S. No. 55, N.Y.; leather tooled and illuminated volumes, James Monroe H.S., Theodore Roosevelt H.S., N.Y. *Exhibited*: PAFA; Barbizon Plaza, N.Y.; Hudson River Mus., 1949; Westchester A. & Crafts Gld., 1948-1955; Hudson Valley AA, 1951, 1952, 1955; Fla. Southern Col., 1952. *Position*: Instr., A., Theodore Roosevelt H.S., New York, N.Y.*

ROSENDALE, HARRIET—*Painter*

Bayberry Lane, Westport, Conn.

B. Buffalo, N.Y. *Studied*: N.Y. Sch. F. & App. A.; ASL with Frank DuMond, Jon Corbino. *Member*: NAWA; Conn. Acad. FA; New Haven Paint & Clay Cl.; Silvermine Gld. A.; Springfield A. Lg. *Awards*: prizes, NAWA, 1953; New England Regional, 1957. *Exhibited*: NAWA, 1950-1958; Conn. Acad. FA, 1954-1958; New Haven Paint & Clay Cl., 1954-1958; Hartford Atheneum; Massillon Mus. A.; Univ. Bridgeport, 1957 (one-man); Springfield A. Lg., 1955.

ROSENFELD, EDWARD—*Painter*

913 Tyson St., Baltimore 1, Md.

B. Baltimore, Md., July 22, 1906. *Member*: Balt. A. Un.; Balt. A. Gld.; Wash. A. Gld.; AEA. *Awards*: prizes, FMA, 1943, 1945, 1947; Peale Mus., 1943. *Work*: PMG; BMA; Babcock Gal.; San Diego FA Soc.; Am. Univ., Wash., D.C.; Washington County Mus. FA, Hagerstown, Md. *Exhibited*: BMA; Little Gal., Wash., D.C.; CGA; WFNY 1939; GGE, 193; Babcock Gal.; Whyte Gal.; Carnegie Inst.; PMG; Boyer Gal., Phila. and N.Y.*

ROSENHOUSE, IRWIN JACOB—
Lithographer, Des., I., P.

132 West 15th St., New York 11, N.Y.

B. Chicago, Ill., Mar. 1, 1924. *Studied*: Los A. City Col.; CUASch. *Member*: AEA; Print Council of Am. *Awards*: Huntington Hartford F., 1954; Tiffany Fnd. F., 1955. *Work*: Cooper Union Mus.; N.Y. Pub. Lib.; Everhart Mus., Scranton, Pa. *Exhibited*: BM, 1949, 1958; Phila. Pr. Cl., 1951, 1956, 1957; Sweat Mem. Mus., 1952; PAFA, 1953, 1954, 1957; LC, 1954, 1955; Boston Pr. M., 1955; DMFA, 1954; Newport AA, 1954; CM, 1954, 1956; Audubon A., 1956; MModA, 1953, 1956; Howard Univ., 1956; SFMA, 1957; Soc. Wash. Pr. M., 1958; Everhart Mus., 1958 (one-man). *Positions*: Des., MModA, 1953-55; Harcourt Brace, Inc., 1956-57; Freelance at present.

ROSENMEIER, ISADOR—*Painter*

Straits Road, Chester, Conn.

B. Schwein, Germany, May 16, 1896. *Studied*: Nurnberg A. Sch., M.A. *Member*: Silvermine Gld. A.; Essex AA; Springfield A. Lg. *Award*: prize, New England Regional Exh., 1955. *Exhibited*: Silvermine Gld. A.; Essex AA; Springfield A. Lg.; New England Regional.

ROSENSON, OLGA—*Painter, Et.*

41 Eastern Parkway, Brooklyn 38, N.Y.

B. Brooklyn, N.Y. *Studied*: Packer Collegiate Inst.; ASL, with George Luks, Vincent DuMond, Joseph Pennell; BMSch. *Member*: NAWA; Brooklyn Soc. A. *Exhibited*: BM; NAD; Argent Gal.; Riverside Mus.; NAC; Brooklyn Lib.; traveling exhs. U.S. and abroad.

ROSENTHAL, ABRAHAM—*Painter*

Rockport, Mass.; h. 54 West 74th St., New York, N.Y.

B. Russia, Dec. 21, 1886. *Studied*: ASL; CUASch. *Member*: Rockport AA. Work reproduced in Christian Science Monitor, 1950. Lectures with demonstrations.

ROSENTHAL, BERNARD—*Sculptor*

22223 West Carbon Mesa Rd., Malibu, Cal.

B. Highland Park, Ill., 1914. *Studied*: Univ. Michigan, B.A.; Cranbrook Acad. A., with Carl Milles. *Member*: S. Gld.; Audubon A.; Fed. Abstract P. & S. *Awards*: prizes, SFMA, 1950; Los A. Mus. A., 1950, 1957; Los A. City Exh., 1950, 1951; So. Cal. Chapter, AIA; UCLA, 1951; PAFA, 1954; Audubon A., 1953. *Work*: S., Los A. Mus. A.; Illinois State Mus.; Univ. Arizona; Milwaukee A. Center; Arizona State Col.; deCordova & Dana Mus.; Long Beach Mus. A.; Architectural commissions: Robinson's, Beverly Hills; General Petroleum Bldg., Los A.; 1000 Lake Shore Dr., Chicago; Police Bldg., Los A.; Beverly-Hilton, Beverly Hills; Temple Emanuel, Beverly Hills, and others. *Exhibited*: MMA; AIC; PAFA; Arch. Lg.; PMA; SMFA; S. Gld.; AFA traveling exh.; Los A. Mus. A.; Audubon A.; WMAA; Univ. Nebraska; Yale Univ.; Univ. Illinois; Sao Paulo, Brazil; WAC; Inst. Contemp. A., Boston; Brussels World's Fair, 1958; one-man:

SFMA, 1951; Western Mus. Assn. traveling exh., 1951; Santa Barbara Mus. A., 1952; Catherine Viviano Gal., N.Y., 1953, 1958; Carnegie Inst., 1959; Long Beach, 1952, 1958, and others. *Position*: Instr., UCLA, Los Angeles, Cal., 1952-53.

ROSENTHAL, DORIS—*Painter, Lith., Des., T.*

c/o Midtown Galleries, 17 East 57th St., New York 22, N.Y.; h. St. Tomas 2, Oaxaca, Oax., Mexico

B. Riverside, Cal. *Studied*: T. Col., Los A., Cal.; Columbia Univ.; ASL with George Bellows, John Sloan. *Awards*: Guggenheim F., 1932, 1936; prize, Northwest Pr. M.; NAD, 1952; Am. Acad. A. & Let., grant, 1952. *Work*: MMA; AGAA; MModA; Colorado Springs FA Center; Rochester Mem. A. Gal.; Toledo Mus. A.; Univ. Arizona; Lib. Cong.; San Diego FA Gal.; Davenport Mun. A. Gal.; Cranbrook Acad. A.; Encyclopaedia Britannica. Compiler, A., "Pertaining to Man—Birds, Animals, Trees, Boats," a series of Primitive Art Designs. *Exhibited*: Mus. Mod. A., Paris, 1938; PAFA; WMA; VMFA; R.I. Sch. Des.; Dallas Mus. FA; GGE, 1939; AIC; Latin America traveling exh.; MMA; Dayton AI. One-man: BMA; Slater Mem. Mus.

ROSENTHAL, GERTRUDE—*Museum Curator, E.*

2202 North Charles St., Baltimore 18, Md.

B. Mayen, Germany, May 19, 1906. *Studied*: Sorbonne, Paris; Univ. Cologne, Ph.D. *Member*: CAA. *Awards*: Traveling F., Inst. FA, Univ. Cologne, 1930. Author: "French Sculpture in the Beginning of the 18th Century," 1933. Contributor to: Journal of the Walters A. Gal., Vol. V-VIII; Journal of Aesthetics; BMA "News," with articles on paintings & sculptures and their attribution. Lectures: History of Art of Europe and U.S.A. *Position*: A. Librarian, Goucher Col., 1940-45; Dir. Research, BMA, Baltimore, Md., 1945-48; General Cur., BMA, 1948-1957; Chief Cur., 1957- ; Grad. Teaching, Johns Hopkins Univ., Art Dept.

ROSIN, HARRY—*Sculptor, T.*

New Hope, Pa.

B. Philadelphia, Pa., Dec. 21, 1897. *Studied*: PMSchIA; PAFA; & in Paris, France. *Awards*: Cresson traveling scholarship, 1926, med., 1939, 1940, prize, 1941, PAFA; Grant, Am. Acad. A. & Let., 1946; med., PMA, 1951; prize, Audubon A., 1956. *Work*: PAFA; PMA; Papeete, Tahiti; Deerfield, Mass.; mem., Fairmount Park, Phila.; bronze statue, Connie Mack, City of Phila. *Exhibited*: World's Fair, Chicago, 1934; Texas Centennial, 1936; GGE, 1939; WFNY 1939; AIC, 1934-1946; WMAA; PAFA, 1933-1946, 1958; Detroit Inst. A., 1958; Carnegie Inst.; Mod. Am. A., Paris, 1932; Salon de L'Oueure Unique, Paris, 1932; MMA, 1951. *Position*: Instr., S. and Drawing, PAFA, Philadelphia, Pa., 1939- .

ROSS, ALEX—*Illustrator, P.*

Chestnut Hill Rd., Wilton, Conn.

B. Dunfermline, Scotland, Oct. 28, 1909. *Studied*: Carnegie Inst., with Robert Lepper. *Member*: SI; AWS; Silvermine Gld. A.; Fairfield WC Group; Westport AA; St. Paul Gld. A. *Awards*: prize, New England Regional Exh., 1957; Hon. deg. M.A., Boston Col., 1953. *Work*: U.S. Air Force Acad., Colorado Springs, Colo., and in private colls. *Exhibited*: Contemp. Am. Illustration, 1946; one-man exhs. in Detroit, Pittsburgh, New York, Los Angeles and various group shows. Covers for Good Housekeeping magazine, 1942-1954. Contributor to Sat. Eve. Post; Ladies Home Journal; Cosmopolitan; McCalls magazines. Lectures: colleges, art clubs and organizations on Art of Illustration. *Position*: Dir., Seminar, Creative Painting, Creative Art Workshop, Catholic Univ., 1954.

ROSS, ALVIN—*Painter*

127 West 20th St., New York 11, N.Y.

B. Vineland, N.J., Jan 12, 1920. *Studied*: Tyler Sch. FA, Temple Univ., B.F.A., B.S. in Ed.; Barnes Fnd., and in Florence, Italy. *Exhibited*: NAD, 1958; Charles Fourth Gal., N.Y., 1947, 1948; Davis Gal., 1953; Hewitt Gal., 1958.

ROSS, BARBARA ELLIS *(Mrs. Robert T.)—Painter*
  Pioneer Oaks, R.R. 1, Lincoln 2, Neb.

B. Deadwood, S.D., Jan. 29, 1909. *Studied*: Univ. Nebraska. *Member*: Art Assn. Rental Gal. *Awards*: med., IBM. *Exhibited*: WFNY 1939; SFMA, 1944; NAWA, 1945; Pasadena AI, 1946; IBM; Carnegie Inst.; Lincoln, Neb.; Omaha, Neb.; Wichita, Kan.

ROSS, DAVID P., JR.—*Museum Director, P., S.*
  3831 Michigan Ave.; h. 5400 Michigan Ave., Chicago 15, Ill.

B. St. Louis, Mo., Feb. 21, 1908. *Studied*: AIC; Univ. Kansas; & with Bert Ray. *Work*: Howard Univ.; Douglas Pub. Sch., Chicago. *Exhibited*: South Side Community A. Center, 1939, 1941; Barnett Aden Gal., 1940; AIC, 1941; Atlanta Univ., 1958. Lectures: "Influence of Contemporary Art." *Position*: Exh. Dir., South Side Community A. Center, 1939-42; Dir., 1957- ; South Side Community A. Center, Chicago, Ill.; Instr. Int. Dec., Dunbar Vocational Sch., Chicago, 1951-52.

ROSS, JOHN—*Engraver, Lith., T.*
  110 Davison Place, Englewood, N.J.

B. New York, N.Y., Sept. 25, 1921. *Studied*: CUASch.; Ecole des Beaux-Arts, Fontainebleau, France; Columbia Univ.; and in Florence, Italy. *Member*: SAGA; Phila. Pr. Cl. *Awards*: Tiffany F., 1954; purchase prizes, DMFA, 1954; New Britain Mus.; Bradley Univ., 1953; Albany Pr. Cl., 1952; Wichita Pr. Cl.; SAGA. *Work*: MMA; LC; DMFA; New Britain Mus. A.; Albany Pr. Cl.; N.Y. Univ. *Exhibited*: MModA, 1953; BM, 1951, 1953, 1955; Albright A. Gal., 1952; Carnegie Inst.; LC, 1951, 1955, 1958 and traveling exh. to Germany, 1959; Swedish A. Council, 1954; BMFA; MMA, 1955; So. Cal. Pr. Cl.; PMA; DMFA; Oakland A. Mus.; Phila. Pr. Cl., and others. Illus. (with Clare Romano)"Manhattan Island," 1957; "The God Around Us," 1958; "A Way of Knowing," 1958. *Position*: Instr., New Sch. for Social Research, New York, N.Y., 1957-58.

ROSS, KENNETH—*Museum Director, Cr., L.*
  Municipal Art Commission, Room 351, City Hall, Los Angeles, Cal.

B. El Paso, Tex., Aug. 1, 1910. *Studied*: A. Center, Los A.; Nat. Acad., Florence, Italy; Grande Chaumiere, Paris, and with Duncan Grant, London; Othen Frieze, Paris. *Positions*: Cr., Pasadena Star News; Los A. Daily News, 1940-49; L., Univ. So. California, A. Dept.; Dir., Pasadena AI; Modern AI, Beverly Hills; General Mngr., Municipal Art, Los Angeles, Cal., at present.

ROSS, LOUIS—*Mural Painter, C.*
  15 Vanderbilt Ave.; h. 123 East 57th St., New York 22, N.Y.

B. New York, N.Y., July 21, 1901. *Studied*: NAD; ASL, with Kenneth Hayes Miller, Boardman Robinson. *Member*: NSMP; Arch. Lg.; Soc. Designer-Craftsmen. *Work*: murals, Bellevue Hospital, N.Y.; Manhattan Center; Am.-South African Steamship Lines; Pennsylvania Railroad; Moore-McCormack Lines; United States Lines; Panama Lines; Northwest Airlines; Fordham Univ. Lib.; Valley Hospital, Ridgewood, N.J.; St. Luke's Episcopal Church, Evanston, Ill.; Stanvac Oil Co., N.Y.; Nat. Lead Co., N.Y.; Pfizer Intl., N.Y.; Travelers Ins. Co., Hartford; Matson Lines; Chicago Western R.R.; Nestle Co., White Plains, N.Y.; triptychs, Army & Navy Chapels; embellishments: Loyola Seminary; St. Anthony's Church, Boston; Temple Keneseth Israel, Allentown, Pa.; Central Synagogue, Rockville Centre; Temple Beth Sholom, Miami Beach; Temple Emanu-l, Lynbrook, L.I.; Temple Adas Israel, Passaic, N.J.; mural panels, Northern Pacific Railroad; Canadian Pacific Railroad diners, etc. *Exhibited*: NSMP, 1956; Arch. Lg., 1941, 1950. *Positions*: Treas., NSMP, New York, N.Y.

ROSS, MARVIN CHAUNCEY—*Museum Curator, W.*
  Address unknown

B. Moriches, N.Y., Nov. 21, 1904. *Studied*: Harvard Univ., A.B., M.A.; N.Y. Univ. *Member*: CAA; AAMus; Am. Oriental Soc.; Medieval Acad. Am.; Archaeological Inst. Am.; Hispanic Soc. Am. (corresponding member). Contributor to: Art magazines, museum bulletins & journals.

Position: Cur., BM, 1934; Cur., Medieval A., Walters A. Gal., Baltimore, Md.; Former Chief Cur. A., Los A. Mus. A., Los Angeles, Cal.*

ROSSER, ALVIN RAYMON—*Painter, T.*
  145 Florence Ave., Irvington, N.J.

B. Port Clinton, Ohio, July 5, 1928. *Studied*: Ohio Univ., B.F.A., M.F.A.; Hans Hofmann Sch. FA. *Member*: Bethlehem Palette Cl.; Lehigh Valley A. All. *Work*: Ohio Univ.; Chagrin Falls AI; Lehigh Univ. *Exhibited*: Ward Eggleston Gal., 1953, 1954; RoKo Gal., 1954, 1955; CMA, 1955; Lehigh Univ., 1956; N.Y. City Center Gal., 1958, 1959; one-man: Ohio Univ., 1953. *Position*: Visual Presentation A., Mutual Broadcasting System, 1954; A.T., Chagrin Falls, Ohio, Pub. Schs., 1955; Instr., FA, Lehigh Univ., Bethlehem, Pa., 1955-1957.

ROSSI, JOSEPH—*Painter, Des., T., L.*
  45 Lockwood Dr., Clifton, N.J.

B. Paterson,N.J., Mar. 8, 1919. *Studied*: Newark Sch. F. & Indst. A.; post-grad., Columbia Univ., and with John Grabach, Harvey Dunn. *Member*: AWS; SC; All. A. Am.; New Jersey WC Soc. *Awards*: prizes, Montclair A. Mus., 1946, 1948; SC, 1950; All. A. Am., 1953; Winsor Newton award, 1954; New Jersey WC Soc., 1955; Arthur Hill Mem. prize, 1951; Ernest Townsend purchase prize, 1952; Ellerhusen award, 1952, and others. *Work*: SC, and in private colls. *Exhibited*: NAD; AWS; Audubon A.; All. A. Am.; SC; NAC; Newark Mus. A.; Montclair A. Mus.; Trenton Mus. A.; and other galleries and museums. *Position*: Instr., Newark Sch. F. & Indst. A., Newark, N.J.

ROST, MILES ERNEST—*Painter*
  2037 Grandview, Carlsbad, Cal.

B. New York, N.Y., Oct. 21, 1891. *Member*: Carlsbad-Oceanside A. Lg. (Chm. A. Com., 1955); Escondido A. Gld. (Hon.); Desert A. Center, Palm Springs. *Work*: in museums, libraries, schools and universities. *Exhibited*: World's Fair, Chicago; and in Los Angeles, San Diego, La Jolla, Oceanside, Carlsbad, Palm Springs, and other local and regional galleries and museums. Illus., "My Attainment of the Pole"; "Candles of Christmas." Contributor illus. to scientific journals and Desert magazines. Lectures: "Pen Etchings"; "American Food and Game Fish."

ROSTAND, MICHEL—*Painter*
  67-25 Dartmouth St., Apt. 7 B, Forest Hills, N.Y.; also, 4050 St. Catherine Road, Montreal, Canada

B. Sadagor, Roumania, Aug. 9, 1895. *Studied*: Univ. Vienna, LL.D. *Member*: Assn. Fed. Art Libre, Paris. *Work*: Buckingham Palace, London; White House, Wash., D.C.; City of Granby, Canada. *Exhibited*: Mus. FA, Paris, 1948, 1949; Assn. Art Libre, Paris, 1948; Sweden, 1950; Mus. FA, Montreal, 1953; Ottawa, 1953; Museum of Granby, 1956; Quebec, 1957; Montreal, 1958, and others abroad.

ROSTON, ARNOLD—*Designer, P., E., W.*
  Station Road, Great Neck, L.I., N.Y.

B. Racine, Wis. *Member*: A. Dir. Cl. *Awards*: gold medal, A. Dir. Cl., 1954; prizes, Nat. Exh. Advertising A., 1941-1957; MModA, 1941, 1942; AIGA, 1949, 1951-1955; Adv. & Printing Trade Assn., 1940-1956. *Work*: MModA. *Exhibited*: PAFA; Contemp. A. Gal.; Mun. A. Exh., N.Y.; Montclair A. Mus.; A. Dir. Cl., 1940-1957. Contributor to American Printer, Graphis, Art Directors' Annual and other trade magazines. *Positions*: A. Dir., Assoc. Creative Dir., Mutual Broadcasting System, RKO Teleradio Pictures, 1942-56; N.Y. Times Promotion Dept., 1935-42; Visual Information Specialist, U.S. Govt., 1942-43; A. Dir., Adv. Des., Cooper Union, N.Y., 1945- ; BMSchA., Brooklyn, N.Y., 1951; Pratt Inst., Brooklyn, 1951, 1954-55; Chm., 36th Annual Nat. Exh. Adv. Art & Des.; Des., 29th Art Directors Annual; Group Hd., A. Dir., Grey Advertising Agency, N.Y., 1956- .

ROSZAK, THEODORE J.—*Sculptor, Des., P., L., W.*
  1 St. Lukes Pl., New York 14, N.Y.

B. Poland, May 1, 1907. *Studied*: AIC; NAD; Columbia Univ. *Awards*: F., AIC, 1928, 1929, prize, 1934; WMAA, 1934; medals, World's Fair, Poznan, Poland, 1930; AIC,

1948, 1951; PAFA, 1956; prize, Sao Paulo, Brazil, 1951. *Work*: WMAA; AIC; MIT Chapel, Cambridge, Mass.; Smith Col.; MModA.; Norton Gal. A.; Mus. Mod. A., Sao Paulo, Brazil. *Exhibited*: AIC, 1929-1931, 1933, 1934, 1938, 1941, 1947, 1948, 1951; WMAA, 1932-1938, 1941-1945, 1946-1952, retrospective, 1956; Minneapolis Inst. A., 1932-1937; AGAA, 1932; Cal. PLH, 1932; Honolulu Acad. A., 1933; PAFA, 1936; Columbus Gal. FA, 1937; Roerich Mus., 1934, 1935; A. Gld., 1936; Julien Levy Gal., 1941; MMA, 1946, 1950, 1952, 1953; Antwerp, Belgium, 1950; PMA, 1949; WAC, 1957; Los A. Mus. A., 1957; SFMA, 1957; SAM, 1957; Brussels World's Fair, 1958; one-man: Matisse Gal., 1950, 1952. *Position*: Intl. Architectural Sculpture Comm., 1957; L., "The New Sculpture," MModA; "In Pursuit of an Image," AIC (publ. by AIC, 1955).

ROTAN, WALTER—*Sculptor*
45 Christopher St., New York 14, N.Y.

B. Baltimore, Md., Mar. 29, 1912. *Studied*: Maryland Inst.; PAFA; & with Albert Laessle. *Member*: NSS. *Awards*: F., PAFA; Cresson traveling scholarship, 1933, prize, 1946, PAFA; Tiffany Fnd. F., 1938; prizes, NAD, 1936, 1942, 1944, 1945; All. A. Am., 1956. *Work*: PAFA; Brookgreen Gardens, S.C. *Exhibited*: NAD, 1936-1940, 1942-1945, 1947; PAFA, 1935-1938, 1940-1946, 1947, 1948, 1951; AIC, 1936, 1938; PMA, 1940, 1949; Carnegie Inst., 1941; Chicago AC, 1943; MMA, 1943; WFNY 1939; CM, 1938; WMAA, 1940; Audubon A., 1945; Phila. A. All., 1946; Conn. Acad. FA, 1938; Arch. L.; Springfield A. Lg.; NAC; NSS, 1950, 1952; New Haven Paint & Clay Cl.; Milch Gal.; Andre Seligmann Gal.; Arden Gal.; Ferargil Gal. *Position*: Hd. A. Dept., Taft Sch., Watertown, Conn., 1938-1953.

ROTENBERG, HAROLD—*Painter, T.*
Rockport, Mass.; h. 557 Boylston St., Boston, Mass.

B. Attleboro, Mass., July 12, 1905. *Studied*: BMFA Sch., and abroad. *Member*: Mus. Contemp. A., Boston; Cape Ann Soc. Mod. A.; East Gloucester Soc. A.; North Shore AA; Rockport AA. *Exhibited*: Beaux-Arts Gal., Paris, France; San Diego FA Soc.; Cowie Gal., Los A.; Babcock Gal.; Vose Gal., Boston; PMA; CGA; BMFA. *Work*: BMFA; San Diego FA Gal.; Knesset Israel, and in many private colls., U.S., Paris, Rome and Israel.

ROTH, BEN—*Cartoonist*
8 Longview Drive, Scarsdale, N.Y.

B. Seletyn, Roumania, Oct. 28, 1909. *Studied*: ASL, with Kimon Nicolaides, George Bridgman, William McNulty. *Member*: Nat. Cartoonists Soc. Ed., "Best Cartoons From Abroad," 1955-1958. *Award*: "Prefect Cup," Intl. Cartoon Exh., Bordighera, Italy, 1958. Contributor cartoons to Sat. Eve. Post; Colliers; Look; American; Ladies Home Journal; This Week; True, and other national magazines. *Position*: Cartoon Ed., Argosy Magazine, 1948; Owner, Ben Roth Cartoon Agency, syndicating in foreign countries the cartoons of 450 American cartoonists.

ROTH, JAMES BUFORD—*Painter, Conservator*
William Rockhill Nelson Gallery of Art, Kansas City 2, Mo.; h. 425 West 70th St., Kansas City, Mo.

B. California, Mo., May 11, 1910. *Studied*: Kansas City AI; Harvard Univ. *Member*: F., Intl. Inst. for Conservation of Mus. Objects. *Awards*: medal, 1932, prize, 1937, Kansas City AI; prize, CAA, 1933. *Work*: Altarpiece, Grace and Holy Trinity Cathedral, Chapel, Rockhurst Col., both in Kansas City, Mo. Lectures on Method and Processes, Materials and Techniques of Painting. Author: "Discovery and Separation of Two Layers of Ancient Chinese Wall Painting," Artibus Asiae. *Position*: Resident Conservator, William Rockhill Nelson Gallery of Art, Kansas City, Mo., 1935- .

ROTHBORT, SAMUEL—*Painter, S., W., L.*
823 Avenue S, Brooklyn 23, N.Y.

B. Wolkovisk, Russia, Nov. 25, 1882. Author: "Out of Wood and Stone." Dir., Rothbort Home Museum of Direct Art, Brooklyn, N.Y., exhibiting work in paint, wood, glass, etc., by Samuel and Lawrence Rothbort. Illus. lecture, "The Vanished Life of the Ghettos."

ROTHKO, MARK—*Painter, W., L.*
102 West 54th St., New York, N.Y.

B. Sept. 25, 1903. *Studied*: Yale Col.; ASL. *Member*: Fed. Mod. P. & S. *Work*: Art of this Century; WMAA. *Exhibited*: WMAA, 1946; PAFA, 1940; one-man exh.: J. B. Neumann Gal., 1930; Art of this Century, 1945; Mortimer Brandt Gal., 1946; SFMA, 1946.*

ROTHMAN, HENRY L.—*Painter, Des., Et., Lith.*
6927 North 19th St., Philadelphia 26, Pa.

B. Philadelphia, Pa., Feb. 18, 1918. *Studied*: Barnes Fnd.; Graphic Sketch Cl., Phila.; PAFA; & with Henry McCarter, George Harding, James Chapin. *Member*: F., PAFA. *Awards*: F., PAFA; Cresson traveling scholarship, PAFA, 1938; prize, Graphic Sketch Cl., 1933. *Work*: PAFA; mural, Pine Camp, N.Y. *Exhibited*: PAFA, 1938, 1939, 1941 (one-man).*

ROTHMAN, JOSEPH—*Painter*
195 Willoughby Ave., Brooklyn 5, N.Y.

B. Brooklyn, N.Y., May 30, 1905. *Studied*: Corcoran Sch. A.; ASL; N.Y. Univ., and with Fletcher Martin, Morris Davidson. *Member*: Albany A. Group; Berkshire AA. *Awards*: Mrs. Frederick Beinecke award, Great Barrington, Mass., 1955. *Exhibited*: Albany Inst. Hist. & Art, 1948-1955; Munson-Williams-Proctor Inst., 1955, 1957; Berkshire Mus. A., Pittsfield, Mass., 1954, 1956; Great Barrington, Mass., 1955, 1956; Cooperstown, N.Y., 1956; N.Y. State Civil Service Employees Exh., Albany Inst. Hist. & A., 1951, 1952; Schenectady Mus. A., 1950, 1951, 1954, 1955; BM, 1958; Argent Gal., 1951; State T. Col., Albany, 1954, and others; one-man: Albany Inst. Hist. & A., 1953, 1956; State T. Col., Albany, 1954; Brooklyn Arts Gal., 1958; L., State T. Col., and Milne H.S., Albany, N.Y., 1956.

ROTHSCHILD, LINCOLN—*Sculptor, P., W., E., L.*
63 Livingston Ave., Dobbs Ferry, N.Y.

B. New York, N.Y., Aug. 9, 1902. *Studied*: Columbia Univ., A.B., A.M.; ASL, with Kenneth Hayes Miller. *Work*: WMAA. *Awards*: prize, Village A. Center, 1948. Author: "Sculpture Through the Ages," 1942. Contributor to Journal of Philosophy, Parnassus, Sat. Review of Lit., World Book Encyclopaedia, Collier's Encyclopaedia. *Positions*: Instr., FA Dept., Columbia Univ., 1925-35; Dir., N.Y. Unit of American Design, 1938-40; Asst. Prof., Chm. A. Dept., Adelphi Col., Garden City, N.Y., 1946-50; L., ASL, 1948-51; Exec. Dir., AEA, New York, N.Y., 1951-1957.

ROTHSTEIN, ELIZABETH L.—*Painter, T., Des., L.*
No. 12 Dutch Village, Albany 4, N.Y.

B. New York, N.Y., Sept. 3, 1907. *Studied*: PAFA; ASL; Parsons Sch. Des.; N.Y. Univ.; New Sch. for Social Research; BMSch. A. *Member*: Albany A. Group. *Awards*: prizes, First Civil Service A. Exh. *Work*: Pub. Bldgs.; Public Service Comm., Albany, and in private colls. *Exhibited*: A. of the Upper Hudson, 1943-1952; Albany A. Group, 1946-1952; Munson-Williams-Proctor Inst., 1951; one-man: Albany Inst. Hist. & A., 1947, 1952.

ROTHSTEIN, IRMA—*Sculptor*
27 West 15th St., New York 11, N.Y.

B. Rostov, Russia. *Studied*: Vienna, Austria, and with Anton Hanak. *Member*: NAWA; Springfield A. Lg.; Arch. Lg. *Awards*: prizes, Mint Mus. A., 1946; AAPL, 1946; New Jersey P. & S. Soc., 1948; Springfield A. Lg., 1951, 1958; NAWA, 1954. *Work*: Newark Mus. A.; Syracuse Mus. FA; G. W. V. Smith Mus., Springfield, Mass. *Exhibited*: MMA, 1942; Syracuse Mus. FA, 1948-1952, 1954; PAFA, 1954; one-man: A. Gal., 1940, 1943; New Sch. for Social Research, 1942; Bonestell Gal., 1940, 1946; Galerie St. Etienne, 1954, 1956.

ROTHWEILER, MRS. CHARLES F.
See Reiber, Cora Sarah

ROTIER, PETER—*Painter, Des., T.*
2701 South Shore Dr., Milwaukee, Wis.

B. Baldwin, Wis., Nov. 5, 1887. *Studied*: ASL of Milwaukee; Milwaukee Normal A. Sch.; Chicago Acad. A.; ASL,

N.Y.; & with Henri, DuMond. *Member*: AWCS; Wis. P. & S. *Awards*: prizes, Milwaukee AI, 1930, 1932, 1934; Milwaukee Journal, 1939; med., Wis. State Fair, 1942. *Work*: Milwaukee AI. *Exhibited*: AWCS, annually; Kansas City AI; AIC; Milwaukee AI.

ROUSSEAU, ANGELINE MARIE—*Painter*
     36905 Ann Arbor Trail, Livonia, Mich.

B. Detroit, Mich., Aug. 16, 1912. *Studied*: Marygrove Col., Detroit, B.A. *Member*: AAPL. *Work*: Am. Lib. Color Slides. *Exhibited*: PAFA, 1937; AFA traveling exh.; Detroit Inst. A., 1933; AIC, 1936; Phila. A. All., 1939.

ROUSSEAU, THEODORE, JR.—*Museum Curator*
     Metropolitan Museum of Art, Fifth Ave. at 82nd St.; h. 4 East 78th St., New York 21, N.Y.

B. Freeport, L.I., N.Y., Oct. 8, 1912. *Studied*: Harvard Univ., B.A., M.A.; Eton Col., Windsor. *Member*: Century Assn.; Grolier Cl. *Awards*: Harvard Traveling F., 1938-1939; Legion of Merit; Legion of Honor, France; Order of Orange-Nassau. Contributor to MMA and other museum Bulletins; Art News; Revue de Paris. Lectures on Painting, at universities and museums. Author: "Paul Cezanne," 1953; "Titian," 1955; "The Metropolitan Museum," 1957. Arranged Van Gogh Exhibition, MMA, AIC, 1949-50; Cezanne Exhibition, MMA, AIC, 1952; Vienna Art Treasures, 1950; Dutch Painting: The Golden Age, MMA, Toledo Mus. A., Art Gal. of Toronto, 1954-55. *Positions*: Asst. Cur., Paintings, Nat. Gal. A., Wash., D.C., 1940-41; U.S. Navy, 1941-46; Assoc. Cur., Paintings, 1947, Cur., 1948- , MMA, New York, N.Y.

ROVELSTAD, TRYGVE—*Sculptor*
     535 Ryerson Ave., Elgin, Ill.

B. Elgin, Ill. *Studied*: AIC; Univ. Washington, and with Lorado Taft. *Work*: Designed and was in charge of completing the American Roll of Honor, World War II and which is placed in the American Chapel of St. Paul's Cathedral, London, England. Des. and executed U.S. Elgin Commemorative Half Dollar; U.S. Army of Occupation of Germany Medal; Legion of Merit; Bronze Star; sc. life size port. of Sen. William Barr, placed in the Capitol, Springfield, Ill.; dedication plaque of Gov. Stratton in Illinois State Office Bldg.; eleven bronze portrait medallions of Gov. Stratton for new State bldgs.; and other works. *Positions*: Sculptor, U.S. War Dept., Shrivenham, England, 1945-46; Des.-Sculptor for business firms and studios; Heraldic Artist, Medalist, O.Q.M., Wash., D.C.; A.-Lith., Coast & Geodetic Survey, Map Div., Wash., D.C.; Des.-Modeler, Haegar Potteries, Dundee, Ill., and others.

ROWAN, FRANCES—*Painter*, Gr., T.
     210 Pine St., Freeport, L.I., N.Y .

B. Ossining, N.Y., Dec. 17, 1908. *Studied*: Randolph-Macon Woman's Col.; CUASch. *Member*: Nat. Lg. Am. Pen Women; Nassau A. Lg.; Malverne A. *Awards*: prizes, Nassau A. Lg., 1951, 1952, 1958; Malverne A., 1954; gold medal, Hofstra Col., 1957; gold medal, Malverne A., 1952. *Exhibited*: Audubon A., 1958; BM, 1958; AFA traveling exh., 1958; Nat. Lg. Am. Pen Women, 1954, 1956; Country A. Gal., 1955-1958; Hofstra Col., 1950, 1951, 1954-1957; Panoras Gal., N.Y., 1958 (2-man). *Position*: Instr., Country A. Gal., Westbury, N.Y., 1955-

ROWE, CORINNE—*Painter*, Cart., I.
     106 Cabrini Blvd., New York, N.Y.

B. Marion, Wis., Nov. 5, 1894. *Studied*: Detroit Sch. FA. *Member*: AEA. *Work*: LC, and in colls in U.S. and abroad. *Exhibited*: CGA, 1928; Detroit Inst. A., 1926-1942; Michigan Acad. A. & Let., 1930; NAWA, 1932, 1933; Detroit A. Market; Wadsworth Atheneum, 1932; WMAA, 1951; Riverside Mus., 1952; BMA, 1934 (one-man). Illus. "The Christmas Dates," 1945. Contributor cartoons and illus. to Sat. Eve. Post; Mademoiselle; Detroit Free Press.*

ROWE, GUY (GIRO)—*Painter*, Des., I., L.
     40 West 64th St., New York 23, N.Y.

B. Salt Lake City, Utah, July 20, 1894. *Studied*: Detroit Sch. FA. *Member*: Royal Soc. A., London. *Award*: Christopher award, 1951. *Work*: LC; San Angelo (Tex.) A.

Mus. *Exhibited*: Detroit Inst. A.; Time magazine traveling exh., 1944-1956; BMA; Assoc. Am. A.; Wayne Univ.; Georgetown A. Gal.; one-man: NAC; Pasadena AI; Peoria Pub. Lib.; N.Y. Pub. Lib.; Univ. Illinois; Allentown Mus. A.; Grand Forks (N.D.) Lib.; Southern Methodist Univ., Dallas; Univ. Texas; Houston Pub. Lib.; Marshall Fields, Chicago, and others. I., Time magazine covers; I., "In Our Image."

ROWELL, SAMUEL TORRIGROSSA—
Painter, Cart., T.
     Waverly Place; h. 42 Glenmore Circle, Melbourne, Fla.

B. Kansas City, Mo., Feb. 24, 1924. *Studied*: Clemson Col.; Kansas City AI, B.A.; Skowhegan Sch. Painting. *Member*: Greenville (S.C.) A. Lg.; Mid-America AA; Melbourne (Fla.) AA; Fla. Fed. A. *Awards*: prizes, Missouri State Fair, 1952 (3), 1954; Melbourne AA, 1954, 1957. *Work*: William Allen White Coll., Univ. Kansas; Melbourne Pub. Lib.; Westminster Col., Fulton, Mo.; People's Bank, Warrensburg, Mo.; and in many private colls. *Exhibited*: Missouri State Fair, 1949, 1950, 1952, 1953, 1954; Joslyn Mem. Mus., 1949; Springfield Mus. A., 1948; Nelson Gal. A., Kansas City, 1952; Melbourne AA, 1954-1957; Vero Beach AA, 1955; Fla. Fed. A., 1957; one-man: Bahama Beach Cl., 1955. Contributor cartoons to The Star-Journal, Warrensburg, Mo.; The Daily Times, Melbourne, Fla. *Position*: Asst. Prof., Kansas City AI, 1948; Instr., Melbourne AA, Melbourne, Fla., 1957-58.

ROWLAND, BENJAMIN, JR.—*Educator*, W., P., L.
     154 Brattle St., Cambridge 38, Mass.

B. Overbrook, Pa., Dec. 2, 1904. *Studied*: Harvard Col., B.S.; Harvard Univ., Ph.D. *Member*: CAA; Am. Archaeological Assn.; Boston Soc. WC Painters; Chinese A. Soc. (Ed.). *Exhibited*: WMAA, 1949, 1950; New Hampshire AA, 1951; PAFA, 1953; Boston A. Festival, 1954, 1956, 1957; one-man: Doll & Richards, Boston, 1949, 1950, 1952, 1954; BMA, 1949; Detroit Inst. A., 1952; Cal. PLH, 1953. *Work*: BMFA; FMA; Detroit Inst. A.; CAM. Author: "Jaume Huguet," 1932; "Wall-Paintings of India, Central Asia and Ceylon," 1938; Ed., Translator: "The Wall-Paintings of Horyuji," 1944; Author: "Harvard Outline and Reading Lists for Oriental Art," 1952; "Art and Architecture of India," 1953; "Art in East and West," 1955. Contributor to art publications. Lectures, "Indian Images in Chinese Art," etc. *Position*: Instr., 1930-35, Asst. Prof., 1935-40, Assoc. Prof., 1940-50, Prof., 1950- , Harvard Univ., Cambridge, Mass.

ROWLAND, DAVID LINCOLN—*Industrial Designer*
     49 West 55th St., New York 19, N.Y.

B. Los Angeles, Cal., Feb. 12, 1924. *Studied*: Principia Col., Elsah, Ill., B.S.; Cranbrook Acad. A., M.F.A. in Indst. Des., and with Moholy-Nagy at Mills Col. (summer sessions). *Awards*: prize, Illuminating Eng. Soc., 1951; Chair Des. award, Nat. Cotton Batting Inst., 1958; office des., for Nametra Travel Agcy., New York, N.Y.

ROWLAND, EARL—*Museum Director*, L., E., P.
     1221 West Flora St., Stockton 24, Cal.

B. Trinidad, Colo. *Studied*: AIC; Sch. Illus., Los A., Cal. *Awards*: prizes, Women's Cl., Phoenix, Ariz., 1923; purchase prize, Inglewood (Cal.) H.S. *Work*: San Diego FA Soc.; Bd. Edu., Pub. Lib., Los A., Cal. Author: "The Instruction of Children in Museums." Lectures: "Rembrandt"; "The Paintings in the Huntington Galleries." *Exhibited*: LC. *Position*: Dir., Pioneer Mus. & Haggin A. Gal., Stockton, Cal., 1927- .

ROWLAND, ELDEN—*Painter*, T.
     5453 Avenida del Mare, Sarasota, Fla.

B. Cincinnati, Ohio, May 31, 1915. *Studied*: Cincinnati A. Acad.; Central Acad. Comm. A., Cincinnati; Farnsworth Sch. A.; San Antonio AI, and with Robert Brackman. *Member*: Cape Cod AA; Provincetown AA; Sarasota AA; Bradenton AA; Florida A. Group (Circuit Dir.); New Orleans AA; Richmond (Ind.) AA. *Award*: Richard Milton award, Boston, 1951. *Work*: Monsanto Chemical Co., Springfield, Mass.; McQuire Hall A. Mus., Richmond, Ind. *Exhibited*: Soc. Four A.; Palm Beach, 1955; Sarasota AA, 1948-1955; All. A. Am., 1947; Phoenix, Ariz., 1949; New Orleans AA, 1946-1949; Newport, R.I., 1949;

Youngstown, Ohio, 1949; Southeastern Exh., Atlanta, 1950; All New England Exh., Boston, 1951-1954; Fla. A. Group, traveling exhs.; Provincetown AA, 1946-1955; Boston A. Festival, 1955, and others. *Position*: Dir., Rowland Traveling Exhibitions Service.

ROWLAND, MRS. HERRON—*Museum Director*
Mary Buie Museum, 510 University Ave.; h. 618 University Ave., Oxford, Miss.

B. Ft. Smith, Ark., Apr. 30, 1891. *Studied*: Ward Seminary, Nashville, Tenn.; Deshler Inst., Tuscumbia, Ala. *Position*: Dir., Mary Buie Mus., Oxford, Miss.

ROX, HENRY—*Sculptor, E., I., Comm. A.*
102 College St., South Hadley, Mass.

B. Berlin, Germany, Mar. 18, 1899. *Studied*: Univ. Berlin; Julian Acad., Paris, France. *Member*: ANA; NSS; CAA; Springfield A. Lg. *Awards*: prizes, Springfield A. Lg., 1941, 1943, 1945, 1947, 1949, 1953, 1955; Syracuse Mus. FA, 1948, 1950; Wichita AA, 1949; Arch. Lg., 1949, 1954, 1955; Silvermine Gld. A., 1950, 1952; A. Dir. Cl., Chicago, 1950, 1957; Audubon A., 1951, medal, 1954; Boston A. Festival, 1953, medal, 1956; Guggenheim F., 1954; NAD, 1952 (medal). *Work*: Springfield Mus. FA; Mt. Holyoke Col.; Los A. Mus. A.; Smith Col.; Merchandise Mart, Chicago; AGAA; John Herron AI; Dartmouth Col.; Syracuse Mus. FA; Faenza, Italy; Liturgical A. Soc. *Exhibited*: PAFA; WMAA; PMA; Nat. Inst. A. & Let.; Syracuse Mus. FA; Yale Univ.; A. Dir. Cl.; AGAA; Wadsworth Atheneum; MMA; Smith Col.; Inst. Contemp. A., Boston; WMA; Boston A. Festival; Univ. Wisconsin; Denver A. Mus.; Detroit Inst. A.; Oregon Ceramic Studio, Portland; Portland (Me.) A. Festival, and in Europe; one-man: Concord State Lib., 1945; A. Headquarters Gal., N.Y., 1945; Springfield Mus. FA, 1945; Kleeman Gal., 1946; deYoung Mem. Mus., 1947; WMA, 1948; Univ. New Hampshire, 1950; Dartmouth Col., 1950; Fitchburg A. Mus., 1953. Author numerous children's books. *Positions*: Prof. A., Mount Holyoke Col.; Instr. S., Worcester A. Mus., Worcester, Mass., 1946-52.

ROYSHER, HUDSON (BRISBINE)—
Craftsman, Des., E., L.
1784 South Santa Anita Ave., Arcadia, Cal.

B. Cleveland, Ohio, Nov. 21, 1911. *Studied*: Cleveland Inst. A.; Western Reserve Univ., B.S.; Univ. So. California, M.F.A. *Member*: Am. Soc. Indst. Des.; Am. Craftsmen's Council; CAA; Pacific AA; NAEA; So. California Des.-Craftsmen (Chm., 1958-59). *Awards*: prizes, CMA, 1933, 1934, 1936, 1940, 1946; Wichita AA, 1949. *Work*: All Saints' Episcopal Church, Beverly Hills, Cal.; Assumption Roman Catholic Church, Pasadena; Assumption Roman Catholic Church, Ventura; St. Peter's Episcopal Church, San Pedro; Holy Innocent's Catholic Church, Long Beach; St. Paul's Episcopal Church, Cleveland Heights, Ohio; St. Brigid's Church, Los A.; Univ. So. California; Immaculate Heart Retreat Chapel, Montecito; Syracuse Univ.; Los A. State Col.; and in churches in Oakland, Apple Valley, Long Beach, La Crescenta, and Pasadena, Cal.; Claremont (Cal.) Community Church. *Exhibited*: America House, N.Y., 1950; Eleven So. Californians, 1952; deYoung Mem. Mus., 1952; Cal. State Fair, 1950-1952; Des.-Craftsmen of the West, 1957; So. Cal. Des.-Craftsmen, 1958; Los A. County Fair, 1952; State Dept. traveling exh., 1950-1952; Univ. Illinois, 1953; Smithsonian Inst. traveling exh., 1953-1955; Denver A. Mus., 1955. Contributor to Craft Horizons; American Artist; Design; College Art Journal; Progressive Architecture. *Position*: Instr., Indst. Des., Univ. Illinois, 1937-39; Asst. Prof. Indst. Des., Univ. So. California, 1939-42; Des., Gump's, San F., 1944-45; Dir., Indst. Des., Chouinard AI, 1945-50; Prof. A., Los A. State Col. App. A. & Sc., 1950- .

RUBEN, RICHARD—*Painter, T., Ser.*
604 Frontenac Ave., Los Angeles 65, Cal.

B. Los Angeles, Cal., Nov. 29, 1924. *Studied*: Chouinard AI. *Member*: Cal. WC Soc. *Awards*: prizes, Bradley Univ., 1952; SFMA, 1953-1955; Pasadena A. Mus., 1953-1955; BM, 1953, 1954; Los A. Mus. A., 1957; Cal. WC Soc., 1953-1957; Oakland A. Mus., 1956; Stanford Univ., 1958; Univ. So. Cal., 1954; Tiffany Grant, 1954. *Work*: Pasadena A. Mus.; Los A. Mus. A.; BM; Bradley Univ.; Stanford Univ.; North Carolina Mus. A.; Univ. So. Cal.; Oakland A. Mus. *Exhibited*: Carnegie Inst., 1955; Sao

Paulo, 1955; BM, 1953-1955; Guggenheim Mus., 1954; Univ. Illinois, 1952, 1956; CGA, 1953; PAFA, 1954; SFMA, 1953-1955; Bradley Univ., 1952, 1953; DMFA, 1953; Northwest Pr. M., 1954, 1955; Santa Barbara Mus. A., 1955, 1958; Los A. Mus. A., 1948, 1953, 1955, 1957; Cal. WC Soc., 1953-1957; Pasadena A. Mus., 1951-1957; Downtown Gal., N.Y., 1955; Colorado Springs FA Center, 1958; Stanford Univ., 1958; one-man: Grand Central Moderns, N.Y., 1958. *Position*: Instr., Chouinard AI, Los Angeles, 1954- ; Dept. A., Pomona Col., 1958-59.

RUBENSTEIN, LEWIS W.—*Painter, E., Gr.*
Art Department, Vassar College; h. 153 College Ave., Poughkeepsie, N.Y.

B. Buffalo, N.Y., Dec. 5, 1908. *Studied*: Harvard Col., A.B., and in France, Italy, Mexico, Japan. *Member*: SAGA. *Awards*: Traveling F., Harvard Univ., 1931-33; Fulbright F., 1957-58; prizes, SAGA, 1952, 1954; Am. A. Group. *Work*: FMA; MMA; Pa. State Univ.; Vassar Col.; AGAA; R.I. Sch. Des. Mus.; murals. FMA; Busch-Reisinger Mus.; Buffalo Jewish Center. *Exhibited*: WMAA, 1941; CGA, 1942, 1944; NAD, 1946, 1952; MModA, 1934; Albright A. Gal., 1941, 1946; FMA, 1932, 1936, 1937; AGAA, 1935; Vassar Col., 1940, 1945, 1952; LC, 1952-1955; Munson-Williams-Proctor Inst., 1951; Berkshire Mus., 1955; Busch-Reisinger Mus., 1955; AWS, 1955; Birmingham Mus. A., 1954; SAGA, 1952-1955; CMA, 1954; International House, Tokyo, 1958. Produced film "Time Painting," 1956. *Position*: Prof. A., Vassar Col., Poughkeepsie, N.Y.

RUBINS, DAVID KRESZ—*Sculptor, Lith., T.*
3923 La Salle Court, Indianapolis 5, Ind.

B. Sept. 5, 1902. Studied: Dartmouth Col.; BAID; Ecole des Beaux-Arts, Julian Acad., Paris; & with James E. Fraser. *Awards*: F., Am. Acad. in Rome, 1928; grant, Nat. Inst. A. & Let., 1954; prize Arch.L., 1932. *Work*: Minneapolis Inst. A.; John Herron AI; Indiana Univ.; Archives Bldg., Wash., D.C. (in collaboration). *Exhibited*: Arch.L., 1932; NAD, 1932; Indiana A., 1936, 1938, 1940, 1942, 1944, 1946. Author: "The Human Figure—An Anatomy for Artists," 1953. *Position*: Instr. S., Anatomy, Drawing, John Herron A. Sch., Indianapolis, Ind., at present.

RUDD, TRACY PORTER—*Designer, C., I.*
9 Harcourt St.; h. 11 Queensberry St., Boston 15, Mass.

B. Meran, Austria. *Studied*: Norwich A. Sch.; ASL; NAD. I., "The Beggars Vision," 1921; "The Ring of Love," 1923. *Position*: Des., Draughtsman, Charles J. Connick Associates, Boston, Mass., at present.

RUDY, CHARLES—*Sculptor, E.*
R.D., Ottsville, Pa.

B. York, Pa., Nov. 14, 1904. *Studied*: PAFA. *Member*: ANA (Elect); NSS; AFA; Pa. State A. Comm. *Awards*: Cresson traveling scholarship, PAFA, 1927-28, prize, 1947; Guggenheim F., 1942; prizes, Am. Acad. A. & Let., 1944; Woodmere A. Gal. *Work*: Brookgreen Gardens (S.C.); Michigan State Col.; PAFA; Univ. Virginia; Sun Oil Co.; Univ. Pennsylvania; USPO, Bronx, N.Y.; war mem.; Virginia Polytechnic Inst.; Audubon Shrine, Montgomery County, Pa.; fig., Republic Steel Co., Cleveland; Edgar Allan Poe statue for Capital Grounds, Richmond, Va.; medal of Soc. of Medalists, 1958. *Exhibited*: PAFA, 1930, 1946, 1948, 1954, 1956, 1957; WMAA, 1935, 1941-1946; Carnegie Inst., 1938; AIC, 1932, 1943; NAD, 1942, 1952-1955; AFA traveling exh.; Trenton, N.J.; MMA, 1951; S. Gld., 1952; PMA, 1950; NAD, 1956-1958; NSS traveling exh., 1958. *Position*: Instr., PAFA, Philadelphia, Pa., 1956- .

RUELLAN, ANDREE—*Painter, Lith., Et.*
c/o Kraushaar Gallery, 1055 Madison Ave., New York 22, N.Y.; h. Woodstock, N.Y.

B. New York, N.Y., Apr. 6, 1905. *Studied*: ASL; in Europe, and with Maurice Sterne, Charles Dufresne, and others. *Member*: Woodstock AA; Phila. WC Cl.; SAGA; ASL. *Awards*: prizes, WMA, 1938; N.Y. State Fair, 1951; Ball State T. Col., 1958; Am. Acad. A. & Let. Grant, 1945; Guggenheim F., 1950; medal, PAFA, 1945, 1950; Pepsi-Cola, 1948. *Work*: MMA; FMA; Nelson Gal. A.; PMG; Springfield Mus. FA; Zanesville AI; Encyclopaedia

Britannica; IBM; PMA; Pa. State Col.; Staten Island Mus.; Univ. Nebraska; LC; WMAA; Norton Gal. A.; Univ. Georgia; New Britain Mus.; murals, USPO, Emporia, Va.; Lawrenceville, Ga. *Exhibited*: AIC, 1937, 1938, 1940, 1941, 1943; Carnegie Inst., 1930, 1938-1940, 1943-1945, 1948-1950; CGA, 1939, 1941, 1943; CM, 1937, 1938, 1940; PAFA, 1934, 1935, 1939-1944, 1948-1953, 1957, 1958; VMFA, 1943; CAM, 1938, 1939, 1941, 1946; Detroit Inst. A., 1943, 1958; WMAA, 1934, 1937, 1938, 1940, 1942-1945, 1949, 1951-1954, 1956; MMA, 1943; Univ. Nebraska, 1938, 1939, 1941, 1958; BM; NAD, 1948-1952, 1956-1958; Univ. Illinois; Los A. County Fair, 1953; Century Cl., 1953; Witte Mem. Mus., 1954; Southern Circuit, 1953-54; Am. Acad. A. & Let., 1953 and traveling exh.; Phila. AA, 1956; IBM, 1957; So. Vermont A., 1957-58; Springville, Utah, 1957, 1958; Des Moines A. Center, 1958; Butler Inst. Am. A., 1958; Norfolk Mus. A., 1957; Ball State T. Col., 1958, and others; one-man: Phila. A. All., 1954; Kraushaar Gal., 1956; Staten Island Mus., 1958, and others.

RUMMLER, ALEXANDER J.—*Painter*
　　63 Maple Tree Ave., Glenbrook, Conn.

B. Dubuque, Iowa, July 25, 1867. *Studied*: ASL; Julian Acad., Paris; & with Jean Paul Laurens. *Member*: AAPL; SC. *Work*: murals, H.S., St. John's Lodge, Norwalk, Conn. *Exhibited*: WFNY 1939.†

RUNGIUS, CARL—*Painter, Et.*
　　27 West 67th St., New York 23, N.Y.

B. Berlin, Germany, Aug. 18, 1869. *Member*: NA; NAC; SC; Century Assn. *Awards*: prizes, NAD, 1924, 1926, med., 1929; prizes, SC; CGA. *Work*: N.Y. Zoological Soc. *Exhibited*: NAD, 1898-1943; PAFA, 1901-1934; AIC; CAM; CGA; Carnegie Inst.; etc. Specializes in Big Game Painting.

RUNQUIST, ARTHUR—*Painter, Et., Lith., T.*
　　Rt. 1, Box 174, Nehalem, Ore.

B. South Bend, Wash., Oct. 27, 1891. *Studied*: Univ. Oregon, B.S.; ASL; Portland A. Mus. Sch. *Member*: Oregon A. Gld. *Work*: Portland A. Mus.; murals, Univ. Oregon Lib.; H.S., Pendleton, Ore. *Exhibited*: WFNY 1939; GGE 1939; Portland A. Mus.; SAM.

RUPPRECHT, GEORGE—*Illustrator, Des.*
　　572 Madison Ave., New York 22, N.Y.; h. 8615 75th St., Woodhaven 21, L.I., N.Y.

B. Brooklyn, N.Y., Nov. 19, 1901. *Studied*: PIASch. *Member*: SI; A. Gld. *Position*: A. Ed., Hearst Magazines.

RUSH, OLIVE—*Painter*
　　630 Canyon Rd., Santa Fé, N.M.

B. Fairmount, Ind., 1873. *Studied*: Corcoran Sch. A.; ASL. *Awards*: prizes, John Herron AI; Hoosier Salon; Denver A. Mus.; Nebraska AA; Wilmington Soc. FA. *Work*: WMA; BM; PMG; John Herron AI; Mus. New Mexico; FA Center of Houston; Wilmington Soc. FA; Witte Mem. Mus.; murals, La Fonda Hotel & Pub. Lib., Santa Fé, N.M.; A. & M. Col. of New Mexico; USPO, Florence, Colo.; Pawhuska, Okla. *Exhibited*: CGA; AIC; Carnegie Inst.; Mus. New Mexico, Santa Fé; Nebraska AA; MMA; BMFA, etc.

RUSK, WILLIAM SENER—*Educator*
　　Aurora, N.Y.

B. Baltimore, Md., Sept. 29, 1892. *Studied*: Princeton Univ., A.B.; Johns Hopkins Univ., A.M., Ph.D.; & abroad. *Member*: Am. Assn. Univ Prof.; CAA; Am. Soc. for Aesthetics; Am. Soc. Arch. Hist. Author: "William Henry Rinehart, Sculptor," 1939. Contributor to Thieme-Becker Allegemeines Kunstlerlexikon; Dictionary of American Biography; Dictionary of the Arts; etc. Articles on Art History, Architecture, Education, for journals & magazines. *Position*: Instr., Prof. FA, Wells Col., Aurora, N.Y., at present.

RUSSELL, BRUCE ALEXANDER—*Cartoonist*
　　Los Angeles Times, 202 West 1st St.; h. 3814 Lorado Way, Los Angeles 43, Cal.; s. 2934 Hermosa Ave., Hermosa Beach, Cal.

B. Los Angeles, Cal., Aug. 4, 1903. *Studied*: Univ. California, Los A.; Fed. Sch. Cart.; & with C. L. Bartholomew,

W. L. Evans. *Member*: President's People-to-People Com.; Nat. Cartoonists Soc.; Am. Assn. Editorial Cartoonists. *Awards*: Pulitzer prize, 1946; Freedom Fnd., 1950-1958; Sigma Delta Chi, 1946, 1947, 1950, 1951; Headliners cartoon award, 1948; U.C.L.A., 1951; U.S. Treasury Dept., 1958; Christopher Award, 1953. *Work*: FBI Coll.; Huntington Lib., San Marino, Cal.; Nat. Press Cl. Created comic strip "Rollo Rollingstone," Assoc. Press Feature Service, 1931-33. *Position*: Sports Cart., Los A. Evening Herald, 1925-27; Staff Cart., 1927-34, Ed. Cart., 1934- , Los Angeles (Cal.) Times.

RUSSELL, C. D.—*Illustrator*
　　c/o King Features Syndicate, 245 West 45th St., New York 19, N.Y.
Member: SI.*

RUSSELL, FRANK (JOHN)—*Painter, C., Comm. A.*
　　48-24 65th St., Woodside 77, N.Y.

B. Philadelphia, Pa., Apr. 25, 1921. *Studied*: ASL. *Member*: AEA; Spiral Group. *Exhibited*: BM; PMA, 1952, 1954; Univ. Illinois, 1953; Sunken Meadow A. Center, 1958; Great Neck, L.I., 1957; Artists Gal., N.Y., 1952, 1955; Contemp. A. Gal., 1946; Brown Univ., 1954; Dallas Collectors Club; Riverside Mus., 1956, 1958; Contemp. A. Collectors; Univ. Maine, 1957. Illus. for Living for Young Home Makers; House & Gardens; Homes Guide; N.Y. Times; N.Y. Post; Herald-Tribune, etc.

RUSSELL, GERTRUDE BARRER. See Barrer, Gertrude

RUSSELL, MARK—*Painter, Des., I.*
　　The Gables, 5807 North High St., Worthington, Ohio

B. Springfield, Ohio, Sept. 9, 1880. *Work*: Last Judgment Window, Little Church Around the Corner, N.Y.; Le Veque Lincoln Tower Peace mural, Columbus, Ohio. I., "Perennial Flowers"; "Plant Welfare."

RUSSIN, ROBERT I.—*Sculptor, P., C., E.*
　　Art Department, University of Wyoming, Laramie, Wyo.

B. New York, N.Y., Aug. 26, 1914. *Studied*: BAID; Col. of City of N.Y. *Member*: S. Gld.; AIA (Assoc.); AAUP. *Awards*: prizes, Arizona FA Fair, 1947, 1949; Wyoming State Fair, 1950; Ford Fnd. F., 1953-54; Research F., Univ. Wyoming, 1954. *Work*: S., USPO, Evanston, Ill., Conshohocken, Pa.; bronze monument, campus Univ. Wyoming; s. mural, Wyo. Highway Bldg., Cheyenne; Bas-relief, Wyo. Northern Community Col., Sheridan; marble bust, Am. Studies Bldg., Univ. Wyo.; Hd. F. D. Roosevelt, Roosevelt Univ., Chicago, Ill.; mural, Park Hotel, Rock Springs, Wyo. *Exhibited*: Assoc. Am. A.; MMA; WMAA; Main St. Gal., Chicago; Am. Mus. Natural Hist.; AIC; Denver A. Mus.; Joslyn A. Mus.; Schneider Gal., Rome; Univ. Nebraska; Wellons Gal., N.Y., 1955 (one-man); Nelson Gal. A.; Kansas City AI; PAFA; Colorado Springs FA Center; NAD; New Orleans A. & Crafts; Arch. Lg.; Fairmount Park, Phila.; Phila. A. All.; WFNY 1939; Oakland A. Gal.; Syracuse Mus. FA, and others. Contributor to College Art Journal. *Position*: Prof. A., Univ. Wyoming, Laramie, Wyo.

RUSSO, MRS. ELEANOR PLATT. See Platt, Eleanor

RUSSO, MRS. SALLY HALEY. See Haley, Sally

RUST, EDWIN C.—*Sculptor, E.*
　　3725 Waynoka Ave., Memphis 11, Tenn.

B. Hammonton, Cal., Dec. 5, 1910. *Studied*: Cornell Univ.; Yale Univ., B.F.A., and with Archipenko, Milles. *Member*: NSS. *Work*: Col. William and Mary; St. Regis Hotel, N.Y.; U.S. Court House, Wash., D.C.; Baptist Mem. Hospital, Univ. Tenn. Medical Sch., Memphis State Univ., Memphis. *Exhibited*: WMAA, 1940; Carnegie Inst., 1940; MMA, 1942; VMFA, 1938; PMA, 1940, 1949; Brooks Mem. Mus., 1950, 1952. *Positions*: Assoc. Prof. S., 1936-43, Hd. FA Dept., 1939-43, College of William and Mary, Williamsburg, Va.; Dir., Memphis Acad. A., 1949- .

RUTLAND, EMILY (Mrs.)—Painter

Route 2, Box 46, Robstown, Tex.

B. Travis County, Tex., July 5, 1894. *Studied*: with Xavier Gonzales, Frederick Taubes, Jacob Getlar Smith. *Member*: South Texas A. Lg.; Texas FA Assn.; Texas WC Soc.; A. Fnd., Corpus Christi (Hon.). *Awards*: prizes, South Tex. A. Lg., 1953-1958; Texas WC Soc., 1953, 1955; A. Fnd., 1953, 1954, 1956, 1958; Kingsville, Tex., 1955. *Work*: Witte Mem. Mus., San Antonio; DMFA; Texas Tech. Col., Lubbock; Delmar Col., Corpus Christi; Corpus Christi Mus. A. *Exhibited*: Miami Beach, 1953; one-man: Corpus Christi Mus. A., 1953; A. & I. Col., Kingsville, Tex., 1954, 1957; Goliad, Tex., 1958; Alice, Tex., 1955.

RUTT, ANNA HONG—Writer, L., P., E.

851 Delgado Drive, Baton Rouge 8, La.

B. Monona County, Iowa, Feb. 21, 1889. *Studied*: Otis AI; Iowa State T. Col.; Cal. Sch. FA; Univ. California, Los A.; Univ. Washington, B.F.A.; Columbia Univ., M.S. *Member*: Nat. Lg. Am. Pen Women; AAUW; Nat. Council State Garden Clubs. *Awards*: prizes, Los A. Mus. A., 1926; Painters of the Northwest, 1925; Nat. Council State Garden Clubs, 1951; Nat. Lg. Am. Pen Women, 1958. *Exhibited*: AIC; Lousiana A. Comm.; Nat. Lg. Am. Pen Women. Author: "The Art of Flower and Foliage Arrangement," 1958. Lectures on Am. Flower Arrangement, U.S. and abroad. *Positions*: State Chm. of the Arts, AAUW, 1958; State Historian, Accredited Judges Council, 1958.

RUVOLO, FELIX—Painter, E.

2019 Hearst St., Berkeley, Cal.

B. New York, N.Y., Apr. 28, 1912. *Studied*: AIC, and in Sicily. *Awards*: prizes, AIC, 1942, 1946, 1947; Cal. PLH, medal, 1946; SFMA, 1942, 1945, 1946, 1949, 1950, 1953, 1955, 1958; VMFA, 1944; Milwaukee AI, 1946; Grand Central A. Gal., 1946; Pepsi-Cola, 1947, 1948; Univ. Illinois, 1949; Philbrook A. Center, 1951; San F. A. Festival, 1951; Richmond (Cal.) A. Center, 1956, 1957; Jack London Square Exh., 1956. *Work*: AIC; Univ. Illinois; Denver A. Mus.; Dennison Col.; Mills Col.; SFMA; Des Moines A. Center; Philbrook A. Center; Univ. Wisconsin; Univ. Michigan. *Exhibited*: Universities of Illinois, Wisconsin, Michigan, Minnesota, Ohio, Kansas, Nebraska, Iowa, Oklahoma, Colorado, Indiana, Southern Illinois, Utah; Cornell Univ.; colleges: Mills, Adelphi, Smith, Carleton, Skidmore, North Dakota Agricultural, MacMurray, Eastern Illinois State; WMAA; VMFA; Carnegie Inst.; PAFA; CGA; AIC; SFMA; BM; MMoDA; MMA; NAD; PC; PMFA; Galerie Creuze, Paris, 1957; Sao Paulo, Brazil, 1955; Vancouver (B.C.) A. Gal., 1958; AFA traveling exh., 1958, and many others. One-man: Viviano Gal., 1950, 1951, 1954; Grand Central Moderns, 1949; deYoung Mem. Mus., 1948 ,1957; Poindexter Gal., N.Y., 1958; Mills Col., 1948; Durand Ruel Gal., 1947; Rockford (Ill.) Mus., 1942. *Position*: Assoc. Prof. A., Univ. California, Berkeley, Cal., 1950- .

RYAN, SALLY—Sculptor, P.

2 West 67th St., New York 23, N.Y.; h. Redding, Conn.

B. New York, N.Y., July 13, 1916. *Member*: NSS. *Exhibited*: Paris Salon, 1934, 1935; Royal Acad., London, 1935; Royal Scottish Acad., 1935, 1936; Toronto A. Gal., 1933; Montreal A. Gal., 1933; WMAA; WFNY 1939; CM; AIC; PMA, 1950; Delgado Mus.; Hartford Atheneum; SFMA; PMA, 1940; Independents, N.Y.; one-man exh.: Cooling Gal., London, 1937; Marie Sterner Gal., 1937; Montreal AA, 1937, 1941; Wildenstein Gal., 1944; Am-British A. Center, 1950.*

RYDER, WORTH—Painter, E., L.

2772 Hilgard Ave., Berkeley 9, Cal.

B. Kirkwood, Ill., Nov. 10, 1884. *Studied*: Royal Acad., Bavarian State Acad., Hofmann Sch., all in Munich, Germany; Univ. California; ASL. *Member*: San F. AA; Univ. California A. Cl. & Faculty Cl. *Work*: SFMA; Cal. Acad. Sc.; Piedmont (Cal.) H.S. *Exhibited*: San F. AA annually. Contributor to Art Education Today. *Position*: Prof. A., Univ. California, Berkeley, Cal., 1926-55; Prof. A. Emeritus, 1955- .*

RYERSON, MARGERY AUSTEN—Painter, Et., Lith., W.

58 West 57th St., New York 19, N.Y.

B. Morristown, N.J., Sept. 15, 1886. *Studied*: Vassar Col., A.B.; Columbia Univ.; ASL, with Bridgman, Henri, Hawthorne. *Member*: ANA; All.A.Am. (Vice-Pres., 1952-53); Audubon A. (Cor. Sec., 1958-59); AWS; SAGA; New Jersey WC Soc. *Awards*: prize, SAGA; med., Montclair A. Mus.; Hudson Valley AA, 1952, 1956, 1957, 1958; medal, NAC, 1957. *Work*: BM; Bibliotheque Nationale, Paris; CMA; William Rockhill Nelson Gal.; IBM; Smithsonian Inst.; Lib.Cong.; Honolulu Acad. A.; N.Y. Pub.Lib.; Montclair A. Mus.; MMA; Uffizi Gal., Florence, Italy. *Exhibited*: NAD; PAFA; CGA; AIC; CAM; Phila. WC Cl.; Wash. WC Cl.; BM; AWCS; Chicago WC Cl.; New Jersey WC Cl.; Audubon A.; SAGA; WMAA; Chicago SE; Phila. SE; Southern Pr.M.; Cal. Pr.M.; Phila. Pr. Cl.; All.A.Am.; NAC; etc. Ed., Henri's "The Art Spirit," 1924; "Hawthorne on Painting"; I., "Winkie Boo."

SAALBURG, ALLEN RUSSELL—Painter, Des., Comm. A., I., Ser.

Frenchtown, N.J.

B. Rochelle, Ill., June 25, 1899. *Studied*: ASL, with John Sloan, Kenneth Hayes Miller, Mahonri Young. *Work*: WMAA; PMA; murals, Pennsylvania Railroad; commissions for U.S. Steamship Lines; N.Y. Park Dept.; stores, restaurants and private homes. *Exhibited*: one-man: Bernheim Jeune, Paris; Kraushaar Gal., N.Y.

SAARINEN, LILY—Sculptor

224 Brattle St., Cambridge, Mass.

Studied: with Heinz Warneke, Albert Stewart, Brenda Putnam, Maija Grotell. *Awards*: prizes, NAWA, 1937, 1947; Wash., D.C. A. Fair, 1943; Detroit Inst. A., 1954. *Work*: sc., bas-reliefs, fountains, USPO, Carlisle, Ky.; Bloomfield, Ind.; Crow Island Sch., Winnetka, Ill.; Tofanetti Restaurant, Chicago; Jefferson Nat. Expansion Mem., St. Louis, Mo.; Detroit Federal Reserve Bank; J. L., Hudson's Northland Shopping Center; IBM Coll.; many commissions for private homes and gardens. *Exhibited*: WFNY 1939; Midtown Gal., 1943 (one-man); Cranbrook Acad. A., 1946; MMA; BMA; AIC; Detroit Inst. A.; Boston A. Festival, 1955; other museums and traveling exhs. Contributor to Architectural Forum; Arts & Architecture; Interiors; Child Life, and other leading magazines. Author: "Who Am I?" "Who Helps Who?", 1946.*

SABATINI, RAPHAEL—Painter, S., E., Gr., L.

7318 Oak Lane Rd., Melrose Park 26, Pa.

B. Philadelphia, Pa., Nov. 26, 1898. *Studied*: PAFA; in Europe with Leger, Bourdelle; and with Charles Grafly. *Member*: AAUP; F., PAFA; Phila. Pr. Cl. *Awards*: Two Cresson European scholarships, PAFA, 1918, 1919; silver medal, Da Vinci All., 1952; prizes, F. PAFA, 1951, 1958; PAFA, 1954; Phila. A. All., 1957. *Work*: PAFA; PMA; Allentown (Pa.) Mus. A.; arch. sc., FA Bldg., Sesquicentennial, Phila., Pa.; N.W. Ayer Bldg.; Mother Mary Drexal Chapel, Langhorne, Pa. *Exhibited*: PAFA, 1918-1920, 1924-1930, 1949-1954, 1956, 1958; GGE 1939; Intl. Sc. Exh., Phila., 1932, 1940, 1949; Phila. Pr. Cl., 1949-1954, 1956, 1957; Phila. A. All., 1956, 1958; AIC, 1957; Columbia (S.C.) A. Mus., 1957 (one-man). Lectures on Fine Arts to groups and in galleries. Author: "Manual for Sculpture Processes." *Position*: Prof. FA, Temple Univ., 1936-1958.

SABINE, JULIA—Art Librarian

Newark Public Library, 5 Washington St.; h. 371 Lake St., Newark 4, N.J.

B. Chicago, Ill., Feb. 4, 1905. *Studied*: Cornell Univ., B.A.; Yale Univ.; Institut d'Art et d'Archeologie, Paris; Univ. Chicago, Ph.D. Contributor to professional, art and historical publications. *Position*: Supv. Art & Music Librarian, Newark Pub. Library, Newark, N.J.

SACHS, PAUL JOSEPH—Educator, W., L., Cr.

987 Memorial Drive, Cambridge 38, Mass.

B. New York, N.Y., Nov. 24, 1878. *Studied*: Harvard Univ., A.B. *Member*: Archaeological Inst. Am.; AAMus.; Am. Philosophical Soc.; Century Assn.; Am. Assn. Mus. Dir.; AFA; Am. Acad. A. & Sc.; Am. Com. for Protection & Salvage of Artistic & Hist. Monuments in War Areas. *Awards*: hon. degrees, LL.D., Univ. Pittsburgh;

D.A., Harvard Univ.; D.A., Colgate Univ.; Princeton Univ.; D.H.L., Yale Univ. Author: "Focillon Memorial Volume of Gazette des Beaux-Arts"; Co-Author: "Drawings in the Fogg Museum," 1941; "Great Drawings," 1951; "Modern Prints and Drawings," 1954. Lectures: 18th Century French Art. *Positions*: Assoc. Dir., Emeritus, FMA, 1915-44; L., Wellesley Col., 1916-17; Asst. Prof. FA, 1917-22, Assoc. Prof. FA, 1922-27, Prof. FA, 1927-49, Harvard Univ., Cambridge, Mass.; Exchange Prof. to France, 1932-33; Administrative Com., Dumbarton Oaks Research Lib.; Trustee, BMFA; MMoDA; Wellesley Col.; Smith Col., Radcliffe Col. (Retired.).

SAFFORD, RUTH PERKINS—*Painter*

2821 Dumbarton Ave., Washington 7, D.C.

B. Boston, Mass. *Studied*: Mass. Sch. A., B.S.; & with Henry B. Snell. *Member*: Gld. Boston A.; AWCS; Grand Central A. Gal.; Wash. WC Cl.; Wash. AC. *Work*: portraits, Lee Mansion, Marblehead, Mass.; Arlington, Va.; U.S. Naval Acad., Annapolis, Md.; paintings of interiors of Roosevelt home, Hyde Park; Nat. Gal. A., Wash., D.C.; Nat. Headquarters, AIA, Octagon House. *Exhibited*: Critics Choice, Cincinnati; New England Contemporary A.; AWCS; CGA; etc.

SAGE, KAY (TANGUY)—*Painter*

Woodbury, Conn.

B. Albany, N.Y., June 25, 1898. *Awards*: prizes, AIC, 1945; CGA, 1951; Conn. Development Comm., 1951. *Work*: AIC; Cal. PLH; WMAA; Wesleyan Univ., Conn.; MMA; MMoDA; Walker A. Center. *Exhibited*: WMAA, 1946-1955; Carnegie Inst., 1946-1950; AIC, 1945-1947, 1951; Toledo Mus. A., 1947-1949; Cal. PLH, 1949, 1950; Univ. Illinois, 1949, 1951; John Herron AI, 1947, 1948, 1951; Los A. Mus. A., 1951; BM, 1951; Wadsworth Atheneum, 1954 (with Yves Tanguy); Detroit Inst. A., 1952; one-man: Milan, Italy, 1936; Matisse Gal., 1940; SFMA, 1941; Julien Levy Gal., 1944, 1947; Viviano Gal., 1950, 1952, 1958, and abroad. Author, I., "Piove in Giardino," 1937; "The More I Wonder," 1957 (verse); "Demain, Monsieur Silber," 1957 (verse, French).

SAHLIN, CARL FOLKE—*Painter, Comm. A., I.*

6400 Snapper Creek Dr., Miami, Fla.

B. Stockholm, Sweden, Apr. 30, 1885. *Studied*: ASL. *Member*: NAC; AWS; Miami A. Lg.; Blue Dome F.; CGA. *Awards*: prizes, Blue Dome Fellowship, 1950, 1951; Miami A. Lg.; 1943; gold medal, Fla. WC Soc., 1943. *Work*: Swedish Hist. Mus., Stockholm; Musee Art Chinois, Montreal, Canada; Hickory (N.C.) Mus. A. *Exhibited*: AWS, 1943-1956; NAC; CGA; Blue Dome F.; Miami A. Lg., 1942-1956; one-man: CGA; NGA; Swedish Hist. Mus.; Lowe Gal.; Coral Gables, Fla., etc. Illus., "This New World."*

SAINT, LAWRENCE—*Painter, W., L., C.*

2539 Huntington Pike, Huntingdon Valley, Pa.

B. Sharpsburg, Pa., Jan. 29, 1885. *Studied*: PAFA, and with William Chase, Cecelia Beaux. *Awards*: Cresson traveling scholarship, PAFA, 1908. *Work*: Stained glass drawings, Victoria & Albert Mus., London; Carnegie Inst.; N.Y.Pub. Lib.; Free Lib., Phila.; glass formulas drawings, Corning Mus. of Glass; CM; MMA; stained glass windows, Washington Cathedral (D.C.) including North Trancept Rose; St. Paul's Episcopal Church, Willimantic, Conn.; murals, Church of the Open Door, Phila., Pa.; Kemble Park Church, Phila. Pa.; Bob Jones Univ., Greenville, S.C.; Christ Church, Bethlehem, Pa.; Bethel Chapel, Huntingdon Valley, Pa. I., "A Knight of the Cross," 1914; "Stained Glass of the Middle Ages in England and France," 1913 (recently reprinted, 4th ed.). Lectures on stained glass in museums, colleges and art societies.

ST. JOHN, BRUCE—*Museum Director*

Delaware Art Center; h. 1021 Trenton Place, Wilmington 6, Del.

B. Brooklyn, N.Y., Jan. 10, 1916. *Studied*: Middlebury Col., A.B.; Columbia Univ., T. Col.; N.Y. Univ. *Member*: AAMus.; Southern A. Mus. Dirs. Assn. (Hon.). Lectures: American Portrait Painting to 1850; American Still Life Painting; American Landscape Painting; to museum audiences, art organizations, etc. *Positions*: Dir., Mint Mus. A., Charlotte, N.C., to 1955; Asst. Dir. (Nov. 1, 1957), Dir., Delaware Art Center, Wilmington, Del., 1957- .

SAINZ, FRANCISCO—*Painter, C., Des., Gr., L.*

70 West 95th St., New York 25, N.Y.

B. Santander, Spain, May 8, 1923. *Studied*: Acad. FA, Madrid, and with F. Sainz de la Maza, Barcelona. *Exhibited*: Knickerbocker A., 1956; Panoras Gal., 1956 (one-man); Huebsch Gal., Woodstock, 1957; Saranac Lake, 1957. Des., I., "Antique French Paperweights," 1955. Lectures: Wrought Iron; Spanish Art.

SAKIER, GEORGE—*Designer, P., W.*

340 East 71st St., New York 21, N.Y.

B. New York, N.Y., Dec. 23, 1898. *Studied*: Columbia Univ.; PIASch. *Member*: F., Am. Soc. Indst. Des. *Exhibited*: MMA; MMoDA; Gld. Hall, East Hampton, N.Y.; Phila. A. All. (one-man); PMA; WMA; GGE 1939; WFNY 1939; Paris Salon. Contributor to many technical and trade publications.

SALA, JEANNE—*Painter, T.*

1305 Franklin St.; h. 1403 Shallcross Ave., Wilmington 6, Del.

B. Milan, Italy, July 3, 1899. *Studied*: Wilmington A. Center; Barnes Fnd.; PAFA, and in Europe. *Member*: Nat. Lg. Am. Pen Women; Phila. A. All.; Phila. Plastic Cl.; Rehoboth A. Lg.; Wilmington A. Center; Wilmington Studio Group. *Exhibited*: Wilmington A. Center, 1941-1952; F., PAFA, 1943-1946, 1952; Studio Group, 1940-1952; Woodmere A. Gal.; Phila. Plastic Cl., 1946; Rehoboth A. Lg., 1944, 1951; NCFA, 1952. *Position*: Instr., Painting, privately.

SALEMME, ANTONIO—*Sculptor, P., T., L.*

237 East 81st St., New York 28, N.Y.

B. Gaeta, Italy, Nov. 2, 1892. *Member*: BAID (Hon.) *Awards*: Guggenheim F., 1932, 1936; Guild Hall, East Hampton, N.Y. *Work*: MMA; Newark Mus.; Syracuse Mus. FA; port., C.I.T. Bldg., N.Y.; N.Y. Hospital. *Exhibited*: PAFA; AIC; WMAA; MMA; Salon d'Automne, Paris; Salon des Tuileries, Paris; traveling exh. to leading museums; five one-man exhs., New York City; Pietrantonio Gal.; Guild Hall, East Hampton, N.Y.; Art: USA, 1958.

SALEMME, MARTHA—*Painter*

237 East 81st St., New York 28, N.Y.

B. Geneva, Ill., Aug. 30, 1912. *Studied*: with Antonio Salemme. *Work*: N.Y. Hospital. *Exhibited*: Van Diemen-Lilienfeld Gal., 1948 (one-man), 1949 (2-man); Burr Gal., 1957, 1958; Guild Hall, East Hampton, N.Y., 1958.

SALERNO, CHARLES—*Sculptor, T.*

269 Little Clove Road, Staten Island 1, N.Y.

B. New York, N.Y., Aug. 21, 1916. *Studied*: ASL, with Nicolaides; N.Y. State Univ., T. Col.; and in Mexico; Grande Chaumiere, Paris, with Zadkine. *Member*: S. Gld.; Audubon A. *Awards*: Tiffany F., and grant, 1948; Macdowell F., 1948, 1949. *Work*: sculpture, Wadsworth Atheneum; R.I. Mus. A.; High Mus. A., Atlanta; SAM; Arizona State Col., Tempe; Albion Col., Mich. *Exhibited*: Brussels World's Fair, 1958; Fairmount Park, Phila., 1949; WMAA, 1952; PAFA, 1950, 1953, 1954; Audubon A., 1955, 1956; traveling exh., MMoDA, 1950-1952, 1955; AFA traveling exh., 1953; one-man: Weyhe Gal., 1946, 1947, 1949, 1951, 1958; Mexico City, 1950; Fort Worth AA, 1950; S. Gld., 1947, 1951, 1952, 1954, 1955. *Position*: Instr., S., Ceramics, Washington Irving H.S., N.Y., 1946- ; Guest Instr., Adelphi Col., Garden City, N.Y., 1957.

SALKO, SAMUEL—*Painter*

1117 Walnut St., P.O. Box 203, Philadelphia 5, Pa.

B. Russia, Feb. 11, 1888. *Studied*: Art Schs., Russia; PAFA. *Member*: F., PAFA. *Awards*: scholarship, PAFA; prizes, Huckleberry A. Colony; F., Macdowell A. Colony; prize, Gilcrease Inst. Am. Hist. & A. *Work*: U.S. War Dept.; Phila. Sketch Cl.; Jefferson Medical Col., Phila.; Univ. Pa. Sch. Medicine; Butler Inst. Am. A.; Temples in Merion, Pa.; Boston, Mass., and in private colls. *Exhibited*: 1935-1958: AWS; PAFA; Phila. Sketch Cl.; Butler Inst. Am. A.; PMA; Balt. WC Cl.; Mint Mus. A.; Oakland A. Mus.; Providence WC Cl.; Ohio Univ.; Conn. Acad. FA; New Jersey Soc. P. & S.; Irvington A. & Mus. Assn.; Parkersburg FA Center; Woodmere A. Gal.; Phila.

A. All.; F., PAFA; CGA; Phila. Free Lib.; Gilcrease Inst. Am. Hist. & A.; Jersey City Mus. A.; Hudson River Mus.; Sears Acad. FA, Elgin Ill.; Cal. WC Soc.; Crocker A. Gal., Sacramento; Mint Mus. A.; Providence A. Cl.; Newport AA; Portland (Me.) AA; Montgomery WC Soc., and many others; one-man: (N.J.) Pub. Lib., 1944; Cushing Mem., Newport, 1945; Butler Inst. Am. A., 1947, 1952; Phila. Sketch Cl., 1952; Snellenburgs, Phila., 1952; Ardmore (Pa.) Women's Cl., 1953; Wanamakers, Phila., 1954; Gimbel, Phila., 1954; Temple Univ., Sullivan Lib., 1957; Germantown Saving Fund Soc., Phila., 1957, and others.

SALMI, HAZEL GOWAN—*Art Center Director*
Richmond Art Center, Civic Center; h. 411 Western Drive, Richmond, Cal.

B. Rockport, Cal., Nov. 30, 1893. *Studied*: Cal. Sch. FA; Cal. Col. A. & Crafts; Rudolph Schaefer Sch. Des.; Univ. California. *Member*: Western Assn. A. Mus. Dirs.; AA Mus.; Western Mus. Conference. *Position*: Founder, Richmond A. Center, 1936; Dir., 1936- , Richmond, Cal.

SALO, GEORGE K.—*Craftsman*
Sutton, N.H.

B. Chicago, Ill., Mar. 4, 1915. *Studied*: AIC, with Elmer Forsberg; Whitney Sch. A., New Haven, Conn. *Awards*: Des-Craftsmen exh., 1953; Wichita, Kans., 1955. *Exhibited*: BM, 1953; Wichita AA, 1955; WMA, 1955; Huntington Gal., 1955; AFA traveling exh., 1950, 1953-1955. *Position*: Instr., Lg. of New Hampshire A. & Crafts; Sample Maker & Des., Napier Silver Co., Meriden, Conn., 1946-48.*

SALTER, GEORGE—*Book Designer, T.*
40 East 10th St., New York 3, N.Y.

B. Bremen, Germany, Oct. 5, 1897. *Studied*: Municipal Sch. A. & Crafts, Berlin. *Member*: AIGA; Corres. Member, Bund Deutscher Buchkuenstler; A. Gld.; Book Jacket Des. Gld.; Grolier Cl.; Soc. for Italic Handwriting, London. *Exhibited*: Fifty Books of the Year, 1937-1950; Book Jacket Des. Gld., 1948-1952. *Author*: "Book Jacket in U.S.A." *Position*: Instr., Jacket Des., Columbia Univ., 1936; Book Des., N.Y. Univ., 1950, 1951; Lettering, Calligraphy, Illus., CUASch., New York, N.Y., 1937- ; A. Dir., Mercury Publications, 1939-1958.

SALTER, STEFAN—*Book Designer, T.*
Cove Ridge Lane, Old Greenwich, Conn.

B. Berlin, Germany, Sept. 28, 1907. *Studied*: in England & Germany. *Awards*: prizes, AIGA, "50 Books of the Year." *Exhibited*: AIGA, 1945. Contributor to: Book Binding & Book Production Magazine; Book Parade; Publisher's Weekly. *Position*: A. Dir., American Book-Stratford Press, 1937-43; H. Wolff Book Manufacturing Co., 1943-47; freelance, 1947- .

SALTONSTALL, ELIZABETH—*Lithographer, P.*
231 Chestnut Hill Rd., Chestnut Hill 67, Mass.

B. Chestnut Hill, Mass., July 26, 1900. *Studied*: BMFA Sch.; & with Andre L'Hote, in Paris; Stow Wengenroth, Frank Swift Chase. *Member*: Pen & Brush Cl.; Springfield A. Lg.; Audubon A.; Boston Pr. M.; Prairie Pr. M.; NAWA; Nantucket AA. *Work*: BMFA; Boston Pub. Lib.; Lib.Cong.; Yale Univ. *Exhibited*: Lib.Cong., 1944-1946; NAD, 1944, 1946; NAWA, 1940-1946; Jordan Marsh Inst. Mod. A., Boston, 1943-1945; Northwest Pr.M., 1945, 1946; BM, 1948; Carnegie Inst., 1951; Laguna Beach AA, 1945, 1946. *Position*: Instr. A., Milton Acad., Milton, Mass., 1928- .

SALTZMAN, WILLIAM—*Painter, Mus. Dir., T., L.*
Rochester Art Center; h. 422 7th Ave., Southwest, Rochester, Minn.

B. Minneapolis, Minn., July 9, 1916. *Studied*: Univ. Minnesota, B.S. *Member*: Minnesota AA. *Awards*: prizes, Minneapolis Inst. A., 1936; Minn. State Fair, 1937, 1940; Walker A. Center, 1949, 1951. *Exhibited*: Cal. PLH, 1946; Minn. State Fair, 1936-1941, 1946-1958; Minneapolis Inst. A., 1936-1941; St. Paul Gal. A., 1946, 1954, 1957; Minneapolis Women's Cl., 1953-1955; Walker A. Center, 1941 (one-man), 1949, 1951-1958; St. Olaf Col., 1952; Univ. Minnesota, 1939 (one-man); SFMA, 1948; Colorado Springs FA Center, 1948; Joslyn A. Mus., 1949, 1951, 1958;

WMAA, 1951; CGA, 1950; Walker A. Center traveling exh., 1950-1952; Chicago, Ill., 1952; Carnegie Inst., 1952; AIC, 1947; one-man: Rochester A. Center, 1948-1958; Kilbride-Bradley A. Gal., Minneapolis; Univ. Nebraska, 1950; Stephens Col., 1950; Carlton Col., 1951; Dayton AI, 1952. *Work*: Walker A. Center; St. Olaf Col.; St. Paul Women's Cl.; Joslyn Mus. A.; Sioux City A. Center; Ft. Hays (Kans.) Mus.; Dayton Co., Minneapolis; mural, Mayo Clinic; First Universalist Church, Rochester; Northwest Nat. Bank, mosaics, Northwest Nat.-Bank Bldg., Rochester, Minn.; 10 stained glass windows, Temple of Aaron, St. Paul. *Positions*: Asst. Dir., Univ. Minnesota A. Gal., 1946-48; Res. A., Dir., Rochester A. Center, Rochester, Minn., 1948- .

SALVATORE, VICTOR—*Sculptor*
22 East 17th St., New York 3, N.Y.; h. Springfield Centre, N.Y.

B. Tivoli, Italy, July 7, 1884. *Studied*: CUASch.; ASL; and with A. Phimister Proctor, Gutzon Borglum, Solon Borglum, Karl Bitter, Charles Niehouse. *Member*: ANA; NSS; All. A. Am.; Cooperstown AA; Century Assn. *Awards*: medal, St. Louis Expo.; 1904; Pan-Pacific Expo., 1915; prize, NAD, 1919. *Work*: MMA; BM; Portland (Ore.) Mus. A.; Cooperstown Baseball Mus.; N.Y. Hist. Soc.; Cooperstown Hall of Fame, and in many private collections. *Exhibited*: St. Louis Expo.; Pan-Pacific Expo.; MMA; NAD; PAFA; AIC; Concord Mus. A.; NSS; Portland (Ore.) Mus. A.; MacDowell Cl.; Grand Central A. Gal.*

SAMERJAN, GEORGE E.—*Designer, P., T., L., S.*
80 West 40th St., New York 18, N.Y.; h. 289 Davenport Ave., New Rochelle, N.Y.

B. Boston, Mass., May 12, 1915. *Studied*: Otis AI; Chouinard AI; & with Alexander Brook, Willard Nash. *Member*: Cal. WC Soc.; A.Dir. Cl., Los A. *Awards*: prizes, AWS, 1952; Fla. Southern Col., 1952; A. Dir. Cl., 1950, 1952, 1956; A. Dir. Cl., Phila. Pa., 1951; Westchester A. & Crafts Gld., 1952; AIGA, 1941; Los A. Advertising Cl., 1940; A. Fiesta, San Diego, 1938; Cal. WC Soc., 1943; Santa Cruz A. Lg., 1942; med., Oakland A. Gal., 1940. *Work*: San Diego FA Soc.; Hospital, Lexington, Ky.; Am. Red Cross; N.Y. Hospital; Fla. Southern Col.; Cole of California; murals, USPO, Maywood, Calexico, Culver City, Cal. *Exhibited*: NAD, 1941; VMFA, 1940, 1942, 1943; PAFA, 1938-1940, 1943; AWCS, 1941, 1942; Cal. WC Soc., 1938-1942; Denver A. Mus., 1941, 1942; San F. AA, 1940-1942; San Diego FA Soc., 1938-1942; Los A. Mus. A., 1939, 1941, 1942; New Haven Paint & Clay Cl., 1941; Wash. WC Cl.; CGA; Riverside Mus.; CGA; Oakland A. Gal.; Los A. County Fair, 1938, 1939, 1941; Cal. State Fair, 1939-1941; Santa Paula, Cal., 1942-1945; Santa Barbara A. Mus.; Laguna Beach AA; Grand Central A. Gal.; SAM; Los A. AA; Santa Cruz A. Lg.; Cal. Inst. Tech.; Assoc. Am. A.; SFMA; A. Dir. Cl.; All. A. Am.; Portland Mus.; Audubon A.; Fla. Southern Col.; Silvermine Gld. A., and many others; Liege, Belgium; Paris, France.*

SAMPLE, PAUL—*Painter*
Dartmouth College, Hanover, N.H.; h. Norwich, Vt.

B. Louisville, Ky., Sept. 14, 1896. *Studied*: Dartmouth Col., B.S.; Otis AI; & with Jonas Lie, F. Tolles Chamberlin. *Member*: NA; AWCS; Cal. AC. *Awards*: prizes, Los A. Mus. A., 1930, 1936; Cal. AC, 1930, 1931; NAD, 1931, med., 1932; Pasadena AI, 1932; NAD, 1947; med., PAFA, 1936. *Work*: MMA; BMA; AIC; Springfield Mus. A.; Fnd. Western A., Los A., Cal.; White House, Wash.D.C.; San Diego FA Soc.; AGAA; Butler AI; PAFA; Joslyn Mem.; Brooks Mem. A. Gal.; Univ. Nebraska; Swarthmore Col.; Williams Col.; Univ. Minnesota; Univ. Southern California; High Mus. A.; Montclair A. Mus.; Encyclopaedia Britannica; Providence (R.I.); Currier Gal. A.; New Britain Mus. A.; Dartmouth Col.; Univ. Iceland; Ft. Worth A. Center; Allegheny Col.; Hallmark Coll.; Utah State Col.; Sheldon Swope A. Gal.; Parrish Mus., Long Island, N.Y. *Position*: Assoc. Prof. Painting, Univ. Southern California, 1926-36; War A.-Correspondent, Life Magazine, 1942-45; A. in Residence, Dartmouth Col., Hanover, N.H., 1938- .

SAMSTAG, GORDON—*Painter, I., T., L.*
111 Fenimore Road, Mamaroneck, N.Y.

B. New York, N.Y., June 21, 1906. *Studied*: NAD. *Member*: ANA; AWS; Audubon A.; Mamaroneck A. Gld.

Awards: prizes, NAD, 1936; PAFA, 1936; All.A.Am., 1936; Conn. Acad. FA; Pulitzer traveling scholarship, 1928. *Work*: Toledo Mus. A.; Santa Barbara A. Mus.; murals, USPO, Scarsdale, N.Y.; Reedsville, N.C. *Exhibited*: Carnegie Inst.; CGA; PAFA; NAD; All.A.Am.; one-man: Montross Gal.; Milch Gal., N.Y.; Gimbels, Phila., Pa., etc. *Position*: Dir., American A. Sch., New York, N.Y.

SAMUELS, BETTY ESMAN. See Esman, Betty

SAMUELSON, FRED B.—*Painter, T.*
   Apartado Postal 70, San Miguel de Allende, Mexico; h. Box 27, Estes Park, Colo.

B. Harvey, Ill., Nov. 29, 1925. *Studied*: Knox Col.; AIC, B.F.A., M.F.A.; Univ. Chicago. *Member*: Cal. WC Soc.; ASL. *Awards*: prizes, Denver A. Mus., 1954; Cheyenne Tri-State Exh., 1955. *Exhibited*: Denver A. Mus., 1953-1958; Mulvane A. Center, Topeka, Kans., 1955; Cheyenne, 1955; Atkins Mus., Kansas City, 1956; Mus. New Mexico, 1957; Elisabet-Ney Mus., 1957; Beaumont A. Mus., 1957; Joslyn A. Mus., 1958. *Position*: Instr., Instituto Allende, San Miguel de Allende, Mexico.

SANBORN, HERBERT J.—*Lithographer, L.*
   R.F.D. Box 144 W, Alexandria, Va.

B. Worcester, Mass., Oct. 28, 1907. *Studied*: NAD; T. Col., Columbia Univ.; Univ. Chicago. *Awards*: Pultizer traveling F., 1929; prize, W.Va. Artists, Parkersburg, 1940. *Member*: AIGA. *Exhibited*: Arch.L., 1931; Davenport Mun. A. Gal., 1933; Joslyn Mem., 1934; Parkersburg FA Center, 1940; Wickford (R.I.) AA, 1929; VMFA. I., Ed., "Hill Towns of Spain," ten lithographs, 1930. *Lectures*: American Art; The Art of the Book in the 20th Century. Contributor to American Artist; Publisher's Weekly; Library Journal. Author (brochure): "Modern Art Influences in Printing Design." *Positions*: Dir., Davenport Mun. A. Gal., 1933-35; Dir. Mus. Oglebay Inst., Wheeling, W. Va., 1936-42; Exhibits Officer, U.S. Library of Congress, Washington, D.C., 1946- .

SANDERS, ADAM A.—*Sculptor, W., T., P.*
   107 St. Felix St., Brooklyn 17, N.Y.

B. Sweden, June 15, 1889. *Studied*: CUASch.; BAID. *Member*: AFA. *Work*: Lincoln Mem. Coll., Wash., D.C.; Lib. of Friends of Music, N.Y.; Col. of City N.Y.; Brooklyn Col.; Tel-Aviv Mus., Israel; Am. Lib. Color Slides; des., Schubert medal. *Exhibited*: NSS; NAC. Author: "The Theory of Altoform," 1945; "Cosmogony," 1950; "Man and Immortality," 1956.

SANDERS, ANDREW—*Painter, T.*
   5019 Commonwealth Drive, Sarasota, Fla.

B. Erie, Pa., Dec. 22, 1918. *Studied*: PMSchA. *Awards*: prizes, Sarasota AA, 1951-1955; Maitland (Fla.) Research Studio, 1951; Milner award, 1951; Ringling Mus. A., 1954. *Exhibited*: PAFA, 1941; Sarasota Nat. Exhs., 1951-1956; Mississippi Nat., 1952-1955; Butler Inst. Am. A., 1953-1955; Mus. FA of Houston, 1956; Nat. Mus., Havana, Cuba, 1956; Sarasota AA annuals, 1950-1956; Southeastern Exh., 1951-1953; Soc. Four Arts, 1952-1954; Ringling Mus. A., 1955; Delgado Mus. A., 1954, 1955. *Lectures*: Modern Art. *Positions*: Instr. A., Ringling Sch. A.; A.; Dir., Sarasota A. Festival, 1953; Exh. Chm., Sarasota AA; 1953, 1954; Faculty Adv., Libn., 1955.

SANDERSON, RAYMOND PHILLIPS—*Sculptor*
   8002 East Palos Verde, Scottsdale, Ariz.

B. Bowling Green, Mo., July 9, 1908. *Studied*: AIC; Kansas City AI, and with Raoul Josset. *Award*: City of Phoenix purchase prize, 1954. *Work*: Miners mon., Bisbee, Ariz.; carvings, U.S. Maritime Comm.; Hotel Westward Ho; Hotel Adams, Phoenix; Valley Nat. Banks in Winslow, Casa Grande, Chandler, Mesa and Phoenix, Ariz.; war mem., Univ. Arizona, Tucson; bust, Duncan (Ariz.) Chamber of Commerce; sc., Arizona State Col. Coll. of Am. Art.; 1956-58: small sculpture for private colls. *Position*: Instr., S., Arizona State Col., Tempe, Ariz., 1947-54.

SANDFORD, FRANK LESLIE—*Painter, Des.*
   2445 Monterey Road, San Marino, Cal.

B. Oakland, Cal., Oct. 27, 1891. *Studied*: A. Center Sch., Los A., with Al King; J. Francis Smith A. Acad. *Member*: Cal. Color Soc.; Cal. A. Cl. (Pres., 1956); P. & S. Cl. *Awards*: prize, Cal. A. Cl., 1958; P. & S. Cl., Los A., 1940, 1941; prize, 1955, medal, 1953, Cal. A. Cl. *Exhibited*: P. & S. Cl.; Cal. A. Cl., and other local and regional exhs. *Position*: Hd. A. Dept., Martin Scenic Studios, 1920-26; Scenic A. Dept., Lowe's Inc., (MGM) 1926-45, Asst. Hd. Dept., 1934-42, Hd., 1942-45.

SANDGREN, ERNEST NELSON—*Educator, P., Lith.*
   Art Department, Oregon State College; h. 421 North 11th St., Corvallis, Ore.

B. Dauphin, Man., Canada, Dec. 17, 1917. *Studied*: Univ. Oregon, B.A., M.F.A.; Univ. Michoacan, Mexico; Chicago Inst. Des. *Member*: Portland A. Mus.; Oregon A. All. *Awards*: prizes, SAM, 1955; Portland A. Mus., 1952, 1956 (purchase); Northwest Painting, Exh., Spokane, Wash., 1957; deYoung Mem. Mus., 1958. *Work*: Portland A. Mus.; Am. Embassy Coll.; Victoria & Albert Mus., London. Murals in Eugene, Corvallis and Portland, Ore. *Exhibited*: Denver A. Mus., 1954, 1958; Santa Barbara Mus. A., 1955, 1957, and nat. tour; BM, 1958 and nat. tour; Am. Cultural Center, Paris; Victoria & Albert Mus., London; Turin and Bordighera, Italy; Johannesburg, Africa. Creator (with William Lesher) 25 min., full color art film, "A Search for Visual Relationships," for educational use. *Positions*: Instr. A., Univ. Oregon, Eugene, Ore., 1947; Assoc. Prof. A., Oregon State College, Corvallis, Ore., 1948- .

SANDONA, MATTEO— *Portrait Painter*
   471 Buena Vista Ave., San Francisco, Cal.

B. Schio, Italy, Apr. 15, 1883. *Studied*: Acad. FA, Verona, Italy. *Member*: Soc. Western A. *Awards*: prizes, Cal. State Fair, 1926; Chicago Galleries Assn., 1926; Santa Cruz A. Lg., 1932; Soc. Western A., 1954; med., Lewis & Clark Exp., 1905; Cal. State Fair, 1917. *Work*: NGA; Palace Legion Honor; Mills Col.; Salt Lake City, H.S.; Springville (Utah) H.S.; Univ. California; Peninsula Hospital, San Mateo, Cal.; Women's City Cl., San F., Cal.; portraits of several governors; plaque, Veterans War Mem., San F.; ports. in private colls. *Exhibited*: NAD; Sesqui-Centennial Exp., Phila., Pa., 1926; PAFA, 1926; AIC, 1927.

SANDZEN, MARGARET (Mrs. Charles Pelham Greenough, III)—*Painter, L., T.*
   123 East State St., Lindsborg, Kan.

B. Lindsborg, Kan., June 16, 1909. *Studied*: Bethany Col., A.B.; Columbia Univ., M.A.; ASL; Paris, France, with Edouard Lèon; & with Birger Sandzen, George Bridgman, Frank DuMond. *Member*: NAWA. *Awards*: prizes, Kansas State Fair, 1940; Rockefeller F., 1939-1940, 1940-1941. *Exhibited*: NAWA, 1941; Kansas City AI; & in Stockholm, Sweden. Contributor to: Kansas magazine. *Lectures*: Swedish Arts & Crafts; The Life and Art of Birger Sandzen; The Life and Art of Edvard Munch. *Position*: Instr. A., Bethany Col., Lindsborg, Kan., 1934-37, 1942-46; Sec., Kansas State Fed. A., 1956-58.

SANFORD, ISOBEL BURGESS—*Painter, Des., Eng.*
   1407-A Sanchez Ave., Burlingame, Cal.

B. Edmonton, Alberta, Canada, Dec. 22, 1911. *Studied*: Cal. Sch. FA; ASL, with Morris Kantor; Parsons Sch. Des. *Member*: San F. AA; Peninsula AA. *Exhibited*: NAD, 1946; Los A. Mus. A., 1945; AV War Posters Exh., 1942; Gump's, San F., 1954; San F. AA, 1935, 1936, 1940, 1941, 1944, 1954, 1955, 1956, 1958; Des., Int. Des. Dept., Gump's, San Francisco, Cal., 1947- .

SANFORD, MARION—*Sculptor, I.*
   Wells Hill Rd., Lakeville, Conn.

B. Guelph, Ontario, Canada, Feb. 9, 1904. *Studied*: PIASch; ASL; & with Brenda Putnam. *Member*: ANA; NSS; All.A.Am.; Arch.L.; AAPL. *Awards*: Guggenheim F., 1941-1943; med., NAD, 1943; All.A.Am., 1945; prizes, AAPL, 1945; PBC, 1946; NAD, 1947; Meriden, Conn., 1949; Springfield (Mass.) Mus. A., 1957. *Work*: PAFA; CGA; Brookgreen Gardens, S.C.; Warren (Pa.) Pub. Lib.; Haynes Coll., Boston; Norton Hall, Chautauqua,

N.Y.; Warren General Hospital, Pa.; Cosmopolitan Cl., N.Y.; Trinity Mem. Church, Warren, Pa.; St. Mary's Chapel, Faribault, Minn.; mural, USPO, Winder, Ga. *Exhibited*: WFNY 1939; WMAA, 1940; PAFA, 1943-1946; NAD, 1938-1946; All.A.Am., 1944, 1945; NAWA; Audubon A., 1945; Newport AA, 1940; Fairmount Park, Phila., 1949. I., "The Sculptor's Way," 1942.

SANGER, WILLIAM—Painter, Gr.
70 West 11th St., New York 11, N.Y.

B. France, Mar. 10, 1888. *Studied*: CUASch, B.S.; ASL. *Work*: Hispanic Mus.; WMAA; Newark Mus.; BM; VMFA; MMA.*

SANKEY, MRS. CLIFFORD H. See Jamison, Celia

SANKOWSKY, ITZHAK—Painter, Eng., T.
217 Upland Rd., Merion, Pa.

B. Roumania, Mar. 9, 1908. *Studied*: Univ. Pennsylvania, M.A., and in Italy. *Member*: Phila. A. All.; AEA; Phila. WC Cl.; Phila. Pr. Cl. *Award*: prize, YMHA, 1950. *Work*: PMA; Tel-Aviv Mus., Israel; medallions for stained glass windows, Har Zion Temple, Phila., Pa.; candelabra, Phila. Psychiatric Hospital; other work in private colls. *Exhibited*: Wash. WC Cl., 1941, 1950, 1952; AIC, 1941; PAFA, 1951; Woodmere A. Gal., 1940, 1941, 1950, 1952; BM, 1954; SAGA, 1955; one-man: Phila. A. All., 1947, 1952, 1958; A. & Crafts Center, Pittsburgh; Lush Gal., Phila., Pa., 1953. *Position*: Instr., PMASch. A., and Allens Lane A. Center, at present.

SANSONE, LEONARD—Designer, Cart.
7315 Southwest 61st St., Miami 43, Fla.

B. Norwood, Mass., May 4, 1917. *Studied*: Mass Sch. A. *Member*: Nat. Cartoonist Soc.; A. Dir. Cl., Miami. *Awards*: A. Dir. Exh., Miami, 1953-1957. *Exhibited*: MMA, 1950. Author: "The Wolf," 1945; I., "Semi-Private," 1943; "The Chain of Command," 1945; "Private Purkey's Private Peace," 1945; Creator, "Willie," daily comic strip for United Features Syndicate, 1945-1956.

SANTO, PASQUALE (PATSY)—Painter
224 Dewey St., Bennington, Vt.

B. Corsano, Italy, Dec. 25, 1893. *Awards*: prizes, Berkshire Mus., 1954; Portsmouth AA, 1954. *Work*: MMoA; Canajoharie Mus.; WMAA; Univ. Arizona; Carnegie Inst. *Exhibited*: Carnegie Inst., 1943-1945; PAFA, 1944; CGA, 1943, 1945; CAM, 1945; Stendahl Gal., Los A., Cal., 1941; AGAA, 1943; Toledo Mus. A., 1943; Marie Harriman Gal., 1940-1942; Macbeth Gal., 1944; MMoA, 1939, 1943; MMA, 1943; Albany Inst. Hist. & A., 1942, 1945; Pittsfield A. Lg., 1943; Williams Col., 1941; Bennington, Vt.; St. Etienne Gal., 1952; European traveling exh., sponsored by Smithsonian Inst. & U.S. Information Agcy., 1954-55; Bennington Col., 1955; Tyringham (Mass.) Gal., 1955.

SAPP, KITT GEORGE (Mr.)—Painter
9626 Linwood St., Kansas City, Mo.

B. Independence, Mo., Nov. 20, 1887. *Member*: AEA; Kansas City AI Alum. *Studied*: Kansas City AI; Univ. Kansas City; Colorado Springs FA Center. *Awards*: prizes, Sedalia State Fair, 1939; Springfield, Mo., 1940; Joslyn Mem., 1945. *Work*: murals, Kansas City Stock Exchange. *Exhibited*: Kansas City AI; Downtown Gal., 1951.*

SARDEAU, HELENE (Mrs. George Biddle)—Sculptor
Mount Airy Rd., Croton-on-Hudson, N.Y.

B. Antwerp, Belgium, July 7, 1899. *Studied*: ASL; N.Y. Sch. Am. S. *Member*: S. Gld. *Awards*: prize, Arch.L., 1934. *Work*: reliefs, Croton-on-Hudson H.S.; USPO, Greenfield, Mass.; Fairmount Park, Phila., Pa.; Nat. Lib., Rio de Janeiro; Supreme Court, Mexico City; WMAA; PAFA; PMA; Tel Aviv Mus., Israel. *Exhibited*: Salon d'Automne, Paris, 1928; PMA, 1934; Arch.L., 1934, 1941; GGE, 1939; WFNY 1939; AIC, 1941; MMoA, 1940; AFA, 1940; PAFA, 1946; MMA, 1940; BM, 1940; Carnegie Inst., 1941; one-man exh.: Arden Gal., 1923; NAC; Ehrich Gal., 1930; Rome, Italy, 1932; Julian Levy Gal., 1934; Santa Barbara Mus. A., 1943; Assoc. Am. A., 1944; Carlen Gal., 1946.*

SARFF, WALTER—Painter, Des., I., Comm. Photog.
13 West 46th St., New York 36, N.Y.

B. Pekin, Ill., Oct. 29, 1905. *Studied*: Chicago Acad. A.; ASL; Grand Central Sch. A.; Sch. Mod. Photography, and with Hubert Ropp, Adolph Fassbender. *Member*: Woodstock AA; AEA; ASL; Am. Soc. Magazine Photographers; Photographic Soc. Am.; Village Camera Cl. *Awards*: prizes, Woodstock A. 1931; WMA, 1937. *Exhibited*: San Diego Expo., 1935; U.S. Nat. Mus.; CGA; Grand Central A. Gal.; WMA; Natural Hist. Bldg., Wash., D.C.; Denver A. Mus.; Bard Col.; Pekin Pub. Lib.; Springfield Mus. A.; SFMA; SAM; Montclair A. Mus.; Portland (Ore.) Mus. A.; Albany Inst. Hist. & A.; Woodstock AA; Sawkill Gal., Woodstock; Assoc. Am. A., and others.

SARGENT, MARY F. (Mrs. William Dunlap)—Etcher, C.
Orchard Lane, Westport, Conn.

B. Somerset, Pa., July 4, 1875. *Studied*: Pa. Col. for Women; ASL; T. Col., Columbia Univ.; in Paris, London; & with William P. Robbins, Paul Bornet, St. Gaudens, Wickey, & others. *Member*: PBC; Conn. Acad. FA; NAWA; Silvermine Gld. A. *Awards*: med., Pa. Col. for Women. *Work*: MMA; Lib. Cong.; BM; Brooks Mem. A. Gal.; G. W. V. Smith A. Mus. *Exhibited*: SAE, 1942-1944; Lib. Cong., 1944; NAD, 1943; NAWA, 1942, 1943; Silvermine Gld. A., 1940-1943; Conn. Acad. FA, 1940-1942, 1946; New England Pr. Assn., 1941; Soc. Liberal A., Omaha, Neb., 1944; Morton Gal., 1939 (one-man); Studio Gld., 1940; PBC, 1944-1946. I., House Beautiful magazine. Lectures: History & Appreciation of Etching.*

SARKISIAN, SARKIS—Educator, P.
The Society of Arts & Crafts, 245 East Kirby St.; h. 91 Atkinson Ave., Detroit 2, Mich.

B. Smyrna, Turkey, May 15, 1909. *Studied*: John P. Wicker A. Sch.; Soc. A. & Crafts, Detroit. *Member*: Mich. Acad. A. & Science. *Awards*: prizes, Michigan A., 1931, 1935, 1937-1942, 1945, 1947-1950, 1952, 1954, 1957; GGE, 1939; Old Northwest Territory Exh., 1950; Butler AI, 1951, 1955. *Work*: Detroit Inst. A.; Univ. Michigan; Butler AI; Ford Admin. Bldg.; Church of the Incarnation, Detroit; St. Mary's Episcopal Church, Detroit; Flint (Mich.) Armory, and in private collections. *Exhibited*: Butler AI 1953, 1955; Michigan A.; CGA, 1954; Grand Rapids AI, 1954; South Bend AA, 1955; Cal. PLH; AIC; Cincinnati AI; Toledo Mus. A.; PAFA; Carnegie Inst., and numerous exhs., New York. *Position*: Hd. Dept. Painting, Dir., Soc. A. & Crafts, Detroit, Mich., 1947- .

SARNOFF, ARTHUR—Illustrator, Comm. A.
44 Deepdale Drive, Great Neck, L.I., N.Y.

B. Pittsburgh, Pa., Dec. 30, 1912. *Studied*: Grand Central Sch. A.; N.Y. Sch. Indst. A., and with Harvey Dunn. *Member*: SI. *Awards*: prize, Outdoor Poster award, 1957. *Exhibited*: SI. Illus. for national magazines and national advertisers.

SARRE, CARMEN G.—Painter, L., T.
1206 Webster St., New Orleans 18, La.

B. Antwerp, Ohio. *Studied*: Agnes Scott Col.; Univ. Michigan, A.B.; N.Y. Sch. Des. for Women; PM Sch. A. *Member*: New Orleans AA; New Orleans A. Gld. *Exhibited*: Wash. WC Cl.; Chevy Chase Women's Cl.; New Orleans AA; New Orleans A. Gld. Lectures: Decorative Art. *Position*: Dir., Young People's Painting Class, Delgado Mus. A.; Hd. Sch. for Ecclesiastical Embroidery at Trinity Church, New Orleans, La.

SASLOW, HERBERT—Painter
568 Thurnau Drive, River Vale, Westwood, N.J.

B. Waterbury, Conn., Apr. 1, 1920. *Studied*: NAD; ASL. *Member*: ASL. *Awards*: Suydam medal, NAD, 1940; purchase award, Am. Acad. A. & Let., 1955. *Work*: Massillon Mus. A.; Newark Mus. A.; Crocker A. Gal., Sacramento, Cal.; Am. Acad. A. & Let.; De Beers Diamond Coll. *Exhibited*: MMA, 1942; Univ. Illinois, 1955, 1957; WMAA, 1955; Univ. Nebraska, 1956; Mint Mus. A.; BM; PAFA, 1958; CGA, 1957; Babcock Gal., 1955, 1958 (both one-man). Contributor illus. to Cosmopolitan; Redbook; Field & Stream; Good Housekeeping magazines.

SATO, TADASHI—*Painter*

410 West 110th St., New York 25, N.Y.

B. Maui, Hawaii, Feb. 6, 1923. *Studied*: Honolulu Sch. A.; BMSch.A.; PIASch.; and with Ralston Crawford, Stuart Davis. *Awards*: John Hay Whitney Fnd. F., 1954; Honolulu Community Fnd. scholarship, 1955; Albert Kapp award, Conn., 1958. *Work*: Guggenheim Mus. A.; Albright A. Gal.; Honolulu Acad. A. *Exhibited*: CM, 1953; Univ. Alabama, 1953; Nebraska Annual, 1954; Guggenheim Mus., 1954; DMFA, 1954; Honolulu Acad. A., 1954, 1955; SFMA, 1957; Silvermine Gld. A., 1958; VMFA, 1958; WMA, 1958; Rome, Italy, 1958; one-man: Gallery 75, N.Y., 1955; Willard Gal., 1958; Honolulu Acad. A., 1952.

SATTERTHWAITE, LINTON—*Museum Curator*

University of Pennsylvania Museum, 33rd & Spruce Sts., Philadelphia 4, Pa.

Position: Cur. American Section, Univ. Pennsylvania Museum.*

SAUER, LEROY D.—*Designer, Comm., A., C., L.*

506 Volusia Ave., Dayton 9, Ohio

B. Dayton, Ohio, Feb. 17, 1894. *Studied*: Cincinnati Acad. A.; Cleveland Sch. A.; Western Reserve Univ.; & with Henry Keller, Frank Wilcox, Ernest Peixotto, & others. *Member*: Dayton SE; Ohio Pr.M.; Florida AA. *Awards*: prizes, Florida AA, 1940; Lib.Cong., 1943. *Work*: Lib. Cong.; Dayton AI; galleries in Canada. *Exhibited*: Dayton SE, 1921-1945; Ohio Pr. M., 1928-1945; NAD, 1943, 1944; Lib. Cong., 1943; Tri-State Exh., 1944, 1945. Lectures: Making of Prints, Demonstrations.

SAUER MARGARITA—*Painter*

1731 Connecticut Ave., N.W.; h. 5649 Western Ave., Northwest, Washington 15, D.C.

B. New York, N.Y., June 20, 1925. *Studied*: Corcoran Sch. A., and with Eliot O'Hara, Andrea Zerega, Peggy Bacon, Richard Lahey. *Member*: NAWA. *Awards*: prizes, Zerega Group, 1948; Fla. Southern Col., 1952. *Exhibited*: United Nations Cl., 1948; Wash. WC Cl., 1949, 1950; Soc. Wash. A., 1948; CGA, 1949, 1951; Ward Eggleston Gal., 1952 (one-man); Grand Central Gal., 1952; Fla. Southern Col., 1952; one-man: Georgetown Gal., 1953; Venables Gal., 1955.*

SAUL (SAUL KOVNER)—*Etcher, Lith., P.*

1113 North Myers St., Burbank, Cal.

B. Russia, Jan. 13, 1904. *Studied*: NAD; & with Ivan Olinsky, Charles Hawthorne, William Auerbach-Levy. *Member*: SAGA; AEA; Los A. AA. *Awards*: med., PAFA, 1942. *Work*: MMA; Montpelier (Vt.) Mus. A.; Lib. Cong.; Brooklyn Col.; State T. Col., Indiana, Pa.; East New York H.S.; Princeton Univ. *Exhibited*: Morton Gal., 1943; Chabot A. Gal., Los A., 1949 (one-man); Bullock's, Pasadena, 1950 (one-man); Glendale Pub. Lib., 1950 (one-man).

SAULNIER, JAMES PHILIPPE—
Portrait Painter, Des., I., Comm. A.

295 West Wyoming Ave., Melrose 76, Mass.

B. South Hamilton, Mass., Oct. 8, 1898. *Studied*: Mass. Normal A. Sch., with Ernest Major, Richard Andrew, Wilbur Hamilton; Harvard Univ. *Member*: Gld. Boston A. *Awards*: gold medal, Jordan Marsh, Boston, 1942, 1943; *Work*: Toledo Mus. A. *Exhibited*: Gld. Boston A.; North Shore AA; East Gloucester AA; Grace Horne Gal.; Nashua (N.H.) Lib.; Jordan Marsh; New England Contemp. A. Exh.; AWS; AIC.

SAUNDERS, ALBERT FREDERIC—*Designer, W., L.*

Oneida, Ltd., Sherrill, N.Y.; h. 106 Rugby Rd., Syracuse 6, N.Y.

B. Brooklyn, N.Y., Nov. 21, 1877. *Studied*: Adelphi Col.; PIASch. *Member*: Assoc. A. Syracuse. *Exhibited*: Syracuse Mus. FA, 1939-1942, 1945, 1946. Contributor to: jewelers' pamphlets & magazines. Lectures: Silverware Design. *Position*: Chief Des., George W. Shiebler Co., 1904-07; A. Dir., Benedict Mfg. Co., East Syracuse, N.Y., 1907-50; Oneida, Ltd., 1950- ; Iroquois China Co., Syracuse, N.Y., 1955-56.; Stetson China Co., Lincoln, Ill., 1958.

SAUNDERS, AULUS WARD—*Educator, P.*

165 East Third St., Oswego, N.Y.

B. Perry, Mo., Sept. 22, 1904. *Studied*: Westminster Col., Fulton, Mo., A.B.; Washington Univ., M.A.; State Univ. Iowa, Ph.D.; St. Louis Sch. FA; N.Y. Univ, and with Charles Cagle, and others. *Member*: Eastern AA; Nat. Edu. Assn. *Awards*: prizes, Finger Lakes Exh., 1946; Syracuse Mus. FA, 1947; Oneida Community Plate Co., 1947. *Exhibited*: Munson-Williams-Proctor Inst., 1955; Author: "The Stability of Artistic Aptitude." Lectures: "The Meaning of Modern Art"; "Structure and Emotion in Painting"; "The Psychology of Child Art." *Position*: Research Assoc. in A. Psych., State Univ. of Iowa, 1932-34; Prof. A. & Chm. Dept. A., State Univ. New York, T. Col., at Oswego, 1937- .

SAUNDERS, GUY HOWARD—*Painter, Des.*

Ringling School of Art; h. 1191 27th St., Sarasota, Fla.

B. Anita, Iowa, Dec. 18, 1901. *Studied*: Chicago Acad. FA. *Member*: Fla. A. Group; Sarasota AA; Manatee A. Lg.; Contemp. A. Group, Pinellas, Fla.; Tampa Realistic A. *Award*: Contemp. A. Gal., Pinellas Park, 1957. *Exhibited*: one-man: Sarasota AA; Mint Mus. A.; Gertrude Herbert Mus., Augusta; St. Petersburg AA; Contemp. Gal., Pinellas; Pasadena AI; Tampa Realistic Gal.; Tampa AI; Hartman A. Gal., Sarasota.

SAUNDERS, JOHN ALLEN—*Cartoonist, W., L.*

717 Security Bldg.; h. 4108 River Rd., Toledo, Ohio

B. Lebanon, Ind., Mar. 24, 1899. *Studied*: Wabash Col., A.B., M.A.; Univ. Chicago; Chicago Acad. FA. *Member*: Tile Cl., Torch Cl.; Nat. Cartoonist Soc.; Newspaper Comics Council (Past Chm.). *Work*: Author, I., "Steve Roper"; "Mary Worth"; "Kerry Drake," widely syndicated comic strips. Contributor to Coronet, Colliers and many popular fiction magazines. Lectures: "Comics are Serious Business"; "The Philosophy of Humor." *Position*: Continuity Editor, Publishers Syndicate, 1940- .

SAUNDERSON, LAURA HOWLAND DUDLEY (Mrs. Henry H.)—*Museum Curator, W., L.*

24 Avon Hill St., Cambridge 40, Mass.

B. Cambridge, Mass., Aug. 16, 1872. *Studied*: Radcliffe Col., A.B., A.M. *Member*: AA Mus. Contributor to Print Collectors Quarterly; FMA Notes; Harvard Library Notes. Lectures: History of Engraving. Arranged & catalogued collections of prints, History of Book Illustration, and many loan exhibitions of prints & early illustrated books, FMA. *Position*: Keeper of Prints, 1897-1939, Keeper of Prints Emerita, 1939- , FMA, Harvard Univ., Cambridge, Mass.

SAUTER, WILLARD J.—
Educator, P., Des., Comm. A., L.

Mohawk Valley Technical Institute, Box 525, Utica, N.Y.; h. Deansboro Rd., Clinton, N.Y.

B. Buffalo, N.Y., July 23, 1912. *Studied*: Albright A. Gal. Sch. FA; Buffalo State T. Col.; International Sch. A. *Member*: Buffalo Soc. A.; Syracuse Assoc. A.; Utica A. Cl.; Munson-Williams-Proctor Inst. *Awards*: silver medal, Buffalo Soc. A., 1943, 1947, Patrons prize and gold medal, 1956; prizes, Roy Mason F., 1948; Albright A. Gal., 1944; Utica A. Cl.; Buffalo Soc. A., 1946, 1952; Munson-Williams-Proctor Inst.; Norman Hadley prize, Buffalo, 1952; Sherburne A. Soc., 1958; special gold ctf., N.Y. State Dept. Commerce, 1958. *Work*: Mohawk Valley Tech. Inst.; Munson-Williams-Proctor Inst.; YMCA, Buffalo; Gloria Dei Lutheran Church, Detroit; Zion Evangelical Church, Utica. *Exhibited*: Artists of Central N.Y.; Munson-Williams-Proctor Inst.; Utica A. Cl.; Syracuse A.; A. of the Upper Hudson; Buffalo Soc. A.; Clinton A. Exh.; Old Forge Exh.; N.Y. State Fair; one-man: Utica, N.Y. Lectures: "Color and You"; "Window Display from Idea to Sale," etc. *Position*: Instr., State Univ. Inst. and Mohawk Valley Tech. Inst., Utica, N.Y.

SAVAGE, EUGENE FRANCIS—*Painter, T., S.*

Woodbury, Conn.

B. Covington, Ind., 1883. *Studied*: CGA; AIC; Am. Acad. in Rome. *Member*: NA; NSMP; Century Assn. *Awards*: F., Am. Acad. in Rome, 1912-15; med., Arch. Lg., 1921;

AIC, 1922-1924; prizes, NAD, 1922, 1924; AIC, 1925; Grand Central Gal., 1926. *Work*: AIC; CAM; Los A. Mus. A.; Providence Mus. A.; fountain, Grand Army Plaza, Brooklyn; Nebraska State Mus.; Herron AI; Oshkosh Pub. Mus.; murals, Yale Univ.; Columbia Univ.; USPO, Wash., D.C.; mosaics, Tabernacle facade, Honolulu U.S. Military Mem., Epinal, France; murals, WFNY 1939; Elks Nat. Mem., Chicago; Covington (Ind.) Court House; Texas State Centennial Mem., Dallas; work reproduced in Encyclopaedia Britannica. *Position*: Appointed to Nat. Comm. FA, by Pres. Hoover, reappointed by Pres. Roosevelt; William Leffingwell Prof. FA, Emeritus, Yale Univ.

SAVAGE, WHITNEY LEE—*Painter, Des.*
Orchard Terrace, Piermont, N.Y.

B. Charleston, W. Va., Dec. 17, 1928. *Studied*: Univ. West Virginia; PIASch.; ASL; New Sch. Social Research. *Awards*: prizes, Village A. Center, 1950; Athens, Ohio, 1949; Armed Forces Painting, 1951; Silvermine Gld. A., 1957. *Work*: Columbia (S.C.) Mus. FA; mural, Armed Forces Center, Mannheim, Germany. *Exhibited*: Silvermine Gld. A., 1957; Butler Inst. Am. A., 1956, 1957; Tri-State Annual, Athens, Ohio, 1949; Village A. Center, 1949, 1950, 1957; RoKo Gal., N.Y., 1950, 1951; Chase Gal., N.Y., 1957 (one-man).

SAVAGE-JONES, JAMES—*Sculptor, P., C.*
605 East Pine St., Clearwater, Fla.

B. Kelty, Scotland, Aug. 22, 1913. *Member*: Sculpture Center, N.Y.; Fla. Fed. A. *Work*: Fla. Gulf Coast A. Center; fountain, Clearwater, Fla. *Exhibited*: PAFA, 1938; Arch. Lg., 1936; Conn. Acad. FA, 1937; BM, 1936; Clearwater A. Mus., 1947; Fla. Gulf Coast A. Center, 1948, 1949; Fla. Fed. A., 1948, 1949; Gainesville Assn. FA, 1948; St. Petersburg A. Cl., 1950.

SAVAGE-JONES, TRUDI (Mrs. James)—*Portrait Sculptor, T.*
605 East Pine St., Clearwater, Fla.

B. Roselle Park, N.J., Sept. 28, 1908. *Studied*: Grand Central Sch.A.; PAFA; Clay Cl., N.Y. *Member*: Fla. Fed. A.; Clay Cl.; Fla. Gulf Coast Group; Clearwater AA. *Awards*: prize, PAFA, 1930. *Work*: in private collections. *Exhibited*: NAD; Montclair Mus. A.; Clearwater A. Mus.; Fla. Fed. A.; Fla. Gulf Coast A. Center; Gainesville Assn. FA; St. Petersburg A. Cl. *Position*: Instr., Port S., Gulf Coast A. Center, 1956-57.

SAVIOUR, SISTER MARY DIVINE.
See *Ledoux, Eva M. B.*

SAVITZ, FRIEDA—*Painter*
2 West 15th St., New York 11, N.Y.

B. New York, N.Y., Dec. 3, 1932. *Studied*: Univ. Wisconsin; Columbia Univ.; N.Y. Univ., B.S., M.A.; CUASch., and with Hans Hofmann and abroad. *Exhibited*: Nat. Mus., Wash., D.C.; BM; Montclair A. Mus.; Newark Mus. A.; RoKo Gal.; G. Gal.; Louisiana State Capitol; Fleischman Gal.; N.Y. City Center; one-man: Greenwich (Conn.) Theatre, 1957; Actor's Playhouse, N.Y., 1957; N.Y. Univ., 1958, and others. *Position*: Instr., Newark Mus., Bd. of Edu., Newark, N.J.; Walt Whitman Sch. and Greenwich House, New York, N.Y.

SAWYER, ALAN R.—*Museum Curator, L.*
The Art Institute of Chicago, Chicago 3, Ill.; h. 18433 Martin Ave., Homewood, Ill.

B. Wakefield, Mass., June 18, 1919. *Studied*: Bates Col., Lewiston, Me., B.S.; BMFA Sch.; Boston Univ.; Harvard Univ., M.A. Author: "Handbook of the Nathan Cummings Collection of Ancient Peruvian Art," 1954; "Catalogue of the Mr. and Mrs. Raymond Wielgus Collection of African Art," 1957; "Animal Sculpture in Pre-Columbian Art," 1957, all AIC. Co-author (with Dr. Leon Goldman) "Medicine in Ancient Peruvian Art," Journal of the History of Medicine and Allied Sciences, 1958. Group discussion leader, "Looking at Modern Art," Ford Fnd.-AIC, 1955-57. Installed exhs. AIC, Designer-Craftsmen USA '54; Design in Scandinavia, 1956, and installation of all primitive art material in Art Institute collections since 1952; Co-ordinator of Midwest Designer-

Craftsmen '57 exh. *Positions*: Dir., Park Forest A. Center, Ill., 1956; Memb. Univ. Pennsylvania Archaeological Expedition to Bolivia, 1955; Asst. to the Cur., Dec. A., 1952- ; Asst. Cur., Dec. A., 1954- ; Assoc. Cur. in charge Primitive Arts, 1956- ; Cur. Primitive Arts, 1958- , Art Institute of Chicago, Chicago, Ill.

SAWYER, CHARLES HENRY—*Educator, Mus. Dir.*
University of Michigan; h. 2 Highland Lane, Ann Arbor, Mich.

B. Andover, Mass., Oct. 20, 1906. *Studied*: Yale Univ., A.B.; Harvard Univ. Graduate Sch. *Member*: AFA; AA Mus.; Assn. A. Mus. Dir.; CAA; Am. Antiquarian Soc.; Am. Acad. A. & Let.; Century Assn. Author: "Art Education in English Public Schools," 1937. Contributor to: various art magazines. *Position*: A. Com., AGAA, Andover, Mass., 1940-; A. Com., Amherst Col., 1941- ; Mass. A. Comm., 1943-45; Asst. Sec., Am. Comm. for Protection & Salvage of Artistic & Historical Monuments in War Areas, 1945; Dir., WMA, Worcester, Mass., 1940-1947; Dean, Sch. Arch. & Des., Prof. Hist. A., Yale Univ. Sch. Arch. & Des., New Haven, Conn., 1947-1957; Dir. Mus. A., Prof. FA, Univ. of Michigan, Ann Arbor, Mich., 1957- .

SAWYER, DANTAN WINSLOW—*Painter, Arch. Des.*
Box 325, South Hamilton, Mass.

B. Clinton, Mass., Aug. 10, 1910. *Studied*: Dartmouth Col., A.B.; in France, and with Jose Clement Orozco, Bernard Karfiol. *Member*: Castle Hill A. Center, Ipswich, Mass. (Exec. Com.). *Work*: Wheaton Col.; Dartmouth Col. *Exhibited*: WMA; Carnegie Inst.; Inst. Mod. A.; MMA; R.I. Sch. Des.; AGAA; Passedoit Gal., N.Y.; Kreitzer Gal., Chicago; Silvermine Gld. A.; Marblehead AA; Topsfield (Mass.) Pub. Lib., and others. Lectures: Modern Painting.

SAWYER, EDMUND J.—*Painter, I., W., L., Des., C.*
Kirkland, Wash.

B. Detroit, Mich., Mar. 1, 1880. *Member*: Northwest Bird & Mammal Soc. (corresponding member); Agassiz Assn. (hon.). *Work*: N.Y. State Mus.; Albright A. Gal.; Yellowstone Park Mus.; murals, USPO, Dennison, Ohio. *Exhibited*: Cornell Univ. Author, I., "Land Birds of Northern New York," 1925; "Game Birds and Others of the Northwest," 1945; I., "American Natural History"; & other bird books. Contributor to: Nature, Bird-Lore, Field & Stream, & other magazines.

SAWYER, ESTHER (HOYT) (Mrs. Ansley W.)—*Painter, Gr.*
770 West Ferry St., Buffalo 22, N.Y.

B. Buffalo, N.Y. *Studied*: Albright A. Sch.; ASL, and with Charles Hawthorne, Edwin Dickinson, Nicholas Vasilieff. *Member*: The Patteran (Bd. Dir.); Nantucket AA; A. Collectors' A. Assn. (Pres.). *Exhibited*: Albright A. Gal.; Buffalo Mus. Science; Patteran Soc.; Kenneth Taylor Gal., Nantucket.*

SAWYER, HELEN (Mrs. Helen Sawyer Farnsworth)—*Painter, Lith., T., W.*
s. North Truro, Mass.; w. 3482 Flamingo, Sarasota, Fla.

B. Washington, D.C. *Studied*: NAD, and with Charles Hawthorne. *Member*: NA; NAC; Florida A. Group (Pres. 1953-55); Sarasota AA. *Awards*: prizes, Hudson Valley A. Inst., 1935, 1936; Fine Prints of the Year, 1937; Ringling Mus. A. Circus Exh., 1950, 1951; Fla. Fed. A., 1956, 1957. *Work*: LC; Toledo Mus. A.; WMAA; John Herron AI; PAFA; Vanderpoel Coll.; Miami Univ., Oxford, Ohio; IBM; Chesapeake & Ohio Coll.; Nat. City Bank, N.Y.; High Mus. A., Atlanta, and others. *Exhibited*: Carnegie Inst.; CGA; PAFA; GGE, 1939; MMA; NAD; Audubon A.; PMA; Univ. Illinois; Montclair A. Mus.; New Britain Inst.; one-man: Milch Gal.; Univ. Illinois; Sarasota Mus., 1952. *Position*: Instr., Farnsworth Sch. A., Sarasota, Fla.

SAWYER, WELLS M.—*Painter*
47 Fifth Ave., New York 3, N.Y.; w. Sarasota, Fla.
B. Iowa, Jan. 31, 1863. *Studied*: With John O. Anderson, Howard Helmick, John Vanderpoel; Corcoran Sch. A.;

ASL. *Member*: Chicago Soc. A.; Soc. Wash. A. (Hon.); Yonkers AA (Hon. Pres.); AWS; All. A. Am.; AFA; SC (Hon.); Sarasota AA; Fla. A. Group; former Pres., Wash., D.C., ASL. *Work*: CGA; Mus. City of N.Y.; Hudson River Mus.; LC; Thos. J. Watson Coll.; IBM Coll.; U.S. Dept. State. *Exhibited*: CGA; AIC; Soc. Wash. A.; NAD; All. A. Am.; AWS; Yonkers AA; Babcock, Ferargil, Milch galleries, N.Y. One-man: CGA; Nat. Gal. Mod. A., Madrid, Spain, 1928; Salon Belles Artes, Amigos del Pais, Malaga, 1934; (old) U.S. Nat. Gal. A., 1931; Southern Art Project, Univ. Georgia and other universities, colleges and galleries in the State of Georgia; AFA traveling exh., 1939-1941; Salon of the Univ. Cl., Mexico City (paintings executed in Mexico, 1936-41); Ringling Mus. A., 1950 (paintings executed in Spain); Sarasota AA, 1955 (paintings from Spain, Mexico, Morocco, India and the U.S.).

SAXE, CAROLYN N.—Painter, T., L., Des.
   60 Centre Ave., Lynbrook, N.Y.

B. West Hurley, N.Y., Aug. 14, 1904. *Studied*: Univ. Buffalo; Parsons Sch. Des.; T. Col., Columbia Univ., B.S.; & with Charles J. Martin. *Member*: Woodstock AA; AEA; NAWA. *Exhibited*: PAFA; Phila. A. All.; N.Y. WC Cl.; Argent Gal.; NAWA; AWS; Gloucester A. Festival, 1956. *Lectures*: Art and the Child. *Position*: Supv., A., Pub. Sch., Lynbrook, N.Y., 1930-46.

SAXON, CHARLES D.—Cartoonist
   32 Weed St., New Canaan, Conn.

B. New York, N.Y., Nov. 13, 1920. *Studied*: Columbia Univ., B.A. Contributor cartoons to New Yorker magazine and other major publications. *Author*: "Don't Worry About Poopsie," 1958; I., "Minty's Magic Garden," 1954; "Little Doe Who Wore Earmuffs," 1957; "What Makes You Tick?", 1958; "Gabriel Wrinkles," 1959. Work in humor anthologies, 1957, 1958; cartoons for This Week; Woman's Day; McCalls; Sat. Eve. Post, and others. *Positions*: Cartoon Ed., This Week, 1948-49; Ed., Dell Publ. Co., 1950-55.

SCALELLA, JULES—Painter, Des., T.
   933 Wellington Rd., Elkins Park, Pa.

B. Philadelphia, Pa., Mar. 31, 1895. *Studied*: PMSchIA; Spring Garden Inst.; Phila. Graphic Sketch Cl. *Member*: Phila. Sketch Cl.; A. Dir. Cl., Phila.; DaVinci All.; Phila. A. All. *Awards*: med., DaVinci All., 1943; Snellenburg Exh., 1955. *Exhibited*: PAFA, 1926-1928, 1930, 1932, 1939, 1940, 1950; CAM, 1926, 1927; AIC, 1926; NAD, 1928; Phila. AC, 1927, 1928; Montclair A. Mus., 1931; Woodmere A. Gal., 1941-1955; Delaware County AA, 1929-1932; Graphic Sketch Cl., Phila., 1929, 1931, 1932, 1944, 1945.*

SCANES, ERNEST WILLIAM—Painter, Des.
   281 McKinley St., Grosse Pointe Farms 36, Mich.

B. Lorain, Ohio, Nov. 6, 1904. *Studied*: Cranbrook Acad. A.; and with John P. Wicker. *Member*: Michigan WC Soc.; Scarab Cl., Detroit; Mich. Acad. Science, A. & Let.; Detroit Mus. A. Founders Soc. *Awards*: prizes, Detroit Inst. A., 1936, 1937, 1941, 1957; Milwaukee AI, 1944; WFNY 1939; Michigan A., 1949; Scarab Cl., 1955, 1958, medal, 1950, 1951. *Exhibited*: AIC, 1938, 1941; Albright A. Gal.; Detroit Inst. A., 1936-1945; Butler AI, 1942; Milwaukee AI, 1944, 1945; Scarab Cl., 1950, 1951, 1955. *Position*: A. Dir., Dept. Public Relations, 1945- , A. Dir., Engineering Journal, 1953- , General Motors Corp., Detroit, Mich.

SCARPITTA, NADJA—Sculptor, L., W., T., P.
   2684 North Beachwood St., Hollywood 28, Cal.

B. Kovel, Poland, Mar. 5, 1900. *Studied*: ASL, and in Munich, Germany, Rome, Italy. *Work*: sculpture, portraits in private colls. Lectures for television and clubs.

SCARAVAGLIONE, CONCETTA—Sculptor, T.
   441 West 21st St., New York, N.Y.

B. New York, N.Y., July 9, 1900. *Studied*: NAD; ASL. *Member*: NSS; S. Gld.; An. Am. Group. *Awards*: Prix de Rome, 1947-50; Medal, PAFA; Am. Acad. A. & Let. grant. *Work*: WMAA; Roerich Mus.; PAFA; Arizona State Col.; U.S. Federal Trade Commerce Bldg., Wash.,

D.C.; WFNY 1939. *Exhibited*: WMAA; MModA; BM; AIC; Fairmount Park, Phila.; CGA; Carnegie Inst.; PAFA; GGE, 1939; MMA. *Position*: Instr., N.Y. Univ., Masters Inst., Sarah Lawrence Col.; Vassar Col., at present.*

SCHABBEHAR, ANN (BRENNAN)—
   Illustrator, Comm. A., T.
   74 Cayuga St., Seneca Falls, N.Y.

B. Dobbs Ferry, N.Y., June 12, 1916. *Studied*: PIASch.; Am. Sch. Des. Contributor illus. to Vogue; House & Gardens; American Home; Good Housekeeping; Seventeen; Mademoiselle and other leading magazines; fashion illus. for Saks Fifth Ave.; Bonwit Teller, N.Y.; national cosmetic ads; Victrola Record album covers, etc. *Position*: Instr., Fashion Illus., ASL, New York, N.Y.*

SCHAEFER, JOSEPHINE M.—Painter, T.
   767 North Water St.; h. 1961 North Summit Ave., Milwaukee 2, Wis.

B. Milwaukee, Wis., May 12, 1910. *Studied*: Layton Sch. A.; AIC; in Europe, South America, and with Louis Ritman. *Member*: Chicago AC; Wis. P. & S. *Awards*: prizes, Wis. P. & S., 1945. *Exhibited*: AIC, 1935-1937, 1939-1941, 1943, 1944, 1946, 1949, 1950; Grand Rapids A. Gal., 1940; Wis. P. & S., 1936, 1939-1941, 1944-1946; Minneapolis Inst. A., 1942; Columbus A. Gal., 1942; Illinois State Mus., 1935-1937, 1940; Rochester Mem. A. Gal., 1940, 1941; Kansas City AI, 1940; WMA, 1945; AGAA, 1945; CMA, 1945; Gimbel Wisconsin Exh., 1949; Wis. P. & S., 1947, 1949, 1950, 1952; Springfield (Mo.) A. Mus., 1945; Walker A. Center, 1945; Portland (Ore.) A. Mus., 1945; Kalamazoo Inst. A.; Layton A. Gal. (one-man); Milwaukee AI (one-man), and group, 1953. *Position*: Instr., Layton Sch. A., Milwaukee, Wis., at present.

SCHAEFER, MATHILDE (Mrs. Mathilde Schaefer Davis)—Sculptor
   Route 2, Box 347, Scottsdale, Ariz.

B. New York, N.Y., Mar. 20, 1909. *Studied*: with Raoul Josset, Walter Lemcke. *Work*: S., IBM; Mus. Northern Arizona; Katherine Legge Mem., Hinsdale, Ill. *Exhibited*: AIC, 1938; WFNY 1939; SFMA, 1938-1940; Denver A. Mus., 1938, 1939; one-man: Santa Barbara Mus. A., 1942; Mus. Northern Arizona, 1943; Univ. New Mexico, 1940; Dallas Mus. FA, 1947. *Position*: Instr., pottery & sculpture, Desert Sch. A., Scottsdale, Ariz., 1950-57.

SCHAEFER, ROCKWELL B.—Painter L., T., Lith., W.
   1501 Broadway, New York 18, N.Y.

B. New York, N.Y., Dec. 26, 1907. *Studied*: Columbia Univ.; ASL; BAID, and with Frank Mechau. *Member*: NAC; A. & Writers; Am. Poetry Lg.; Town Hall A. Cl.; Nat. Soc. Painters in Casein; Springfield A. Lg.; Sarasota AA; Academic A.; Audubon A.; Am. Veterans Soc. A.; SC; Westchester A. & Crafts Gld.; Irvington A. & Mus. Assn.; Meriden A. & Crafts; Alabama WC Soc.; Wash. WC Soc.; Conn. WC Soc. *Awards*: prizes, Pa. State T. Col., 1950-1952; New London Naval Base, 1948; Nat. Soc. Painters in Casein, 1953; AAPL, 1956; Westchester A. Gld., 1957. *Work*: Scranton Mus. A.; PMA; U.S. Navy Dept., Wash., D.C. *Exhibited*: All. A. Am., 1938, 1939, 1941, 1943; Audubon A., 1943-1951; AWS, 1942-1945; Am. Veterans Soc. A., 1941-1945; Vendome Gal., 1937, 1942; BM, 1941, 1945; Norwegian-Am. Relief Exh., 1940; Conn. WC Soc., 1949, 1951; New Jersey Painters Gld., 1948, 1951; Butler AI, 1950, 1951; Naval Personnel Exh., Wash., D.C.; Alabama WC Soc., 1952; Life magazine Exh., 1949; exh. in all membership exhs., 1953-1957; Hotel New Yorker, 1958; Critics' traveling exh., 1958.

SCHAEFER, HENRI-BELLA (Mrs. H. Bella De Vitis)—Painter, T.
   111 Bank St., New York 14, N.Y.

B. New York, N.Y. *Studied*: Columbia Univ. Ext.; Grande Chaumiere, All. Francaise, and with William A. MacKay; Andre Lhote, Paris. *Member*: NAWA; AEA. *Work*: Fla. Southern Col., and in private colls. *Exhibited*: A. Gal., N.Y., 1941, 1942, 1948-1950, 1953-1958; NAC, 1946-1951; NAWA, 1948, 1950, 1951; Bar Harbor, 1950, 1951; AEA, 1951; WMAA, 1951; Fla. Southern Col., 1952; North Side Center for Child Development, N.Y.,1954-1957; Art:USA, 1958; Butler Inst. Am. A.,

1958; AFA, 1955, 1956; Salon d'Automne, 1938, Salon des Tuileries, Paris, 1939; one-man: A. Gal., 1941, 1949, 1951, 1953. *Position*: Welfare Com., 1950-55, Nat. Welfare Com., 1953-55, Equity Fund Com., 1954-55, Dir., N.Y. Chapter, 1954, Bd. Dir., 1954-55, Nat. Dir., Chm., summer activities com., AEA.

SCHAEFFER, MEAD—*Illustrator*
   1 West 67th St., New York, N.Y.

B. Freedom Plains, N.Y., July 15, 1898. *Studied*: PIASch., and with Dean Cornwell. *Member*: SI. *Awards*: gold medal, PAFA, 1944; Am. Red Cross, 1944; SC. Contributor illus. to Sat. Eve. Post; Ladies Home Journal; Country Gentleman; Holiday; American; Cosmopolitan; Good Housekeeping; McCalls; Redbook; Harpers; Scribners; True and other magazines; I., 16 Classics (Melville, Dumas, etc.). Permanent exhs. in libraries and public bldgs., in the U.S. A., War Correspondent for Sat. Eve. Post, 1942-1944. War Paintings exhibited widely in U.S.*

SCHAEFFLER, LIZBETH—*Sculptor, P., T., Comm. A.*
   78 Irving Pl., New Rochelle, N.Y.; s. Harbor View #1, Commercial Wharf, Nantucket, Mass.

B. Sommerville, Mass., Oct. 27, 1907. *Studied*: PIASch.; NAD; ASL; Clay Cl., N.Y., and with Mahonri Young. *Member*: Nantucket AA; New Rochelle AA. *Awards*: prize, New Rochelle AA. *Work*: mem., Church of the Highlands, White Plains, N.Y. *Exhibited*: NSS, 1936-1938, 1957, 1958; Clay Cl.; N.Y. Soc. Ceramic A.; New Rochelle AA; Nantucket AA (one-man). *Position*: Sec.-Treas., Nantucket AA; Dir., Kenneth Taylor Gal., Nantucket, Mass.

SCHAFER, ALICE PAULINE—*Etcher, Eng.*
   33 Hawthorne Ave., Albany 3, N.Y.

B. Albany, N.Y., Feb. 11, 1899. *Studied*: Albany Sch. FA. *Member*: Albany Pr. Cl.; SAGA; Chicago Soc. Et.; Pen & Brush Cl.; Cooperstown AA; NAWA. *Work*: MMA; Albany Pr. Cl.; SAGA; Nat. Commercial Bank & Trust Co., Albany. *Exhibited*: Albany Pr. Cl., 1945-1958; SAGA, 1947-1958; Chicago Soc. Et., 1950-1958; NAD, 1949; Buffalo Pr. Cl., 1940, 1951; LC, 1949; Cooperstown 1949-1948; NAWA, 1951-1958; Pen & Brush Cl., 1957, 1958; London, England, 1954; Holland, 1956; Switzerland, 1957. *Position*: Registrar, Albany Inst. Hist. & A., Albany, N.Y.

SCHAINEN, HERMAN JACK—*Sculptor, Des.*
   200 East 41st St., New York 17, N.Y.; h. Carroll Road, Mt. Freedom, N.J.

B. New York, N.Y., Apr. 25, 1934. *Studied*: Pratt Inst., Sch. of Arch., B. Arch. Co-Designed and executed sculpture for lobby of Lorillard Bldg., N.Y.C.

SCHALDACH, WILLIAM J(OSEPH)—*Etcher, P., W.*
   Sasabe, Ariz.

B. Elkhart, Ind., Feb. 15, 1896. *Studied*: ASL; & with Harry Wickey. *Member*: SC; Indiana Soc. Pr. M.; F., Instituto Interamericano; life F., Am. Mus. Natural Hist. *Work*: SAGA; Vanderpoel Coll.; N.Y. Pub. Lib.; MMA; Pa. State Univ.; Dartmouth Col.; Lib. Cong.; SC. *Exhibited*: NAD, 1935-1944; PAFA, 1941; SAGA, 1928-1947; Chicago SE, 1929, 1930; SC; WFNY 1939; MMA (AV); Phila. Pr. Cl., 1930-1936; Indiana Soc. Pr. M., 1938-1946; Southern Pr.M., 1939, 1940; Currier Gal. A., 1939, 1940; John Herron AI, 1946, 1952; Dartmouth Col., 1942, 1946. Author: "Carl Rungius, Big Game Painter," 1945; "Fish by Schaldach," 1937; "Currents and Eddies," 1944; I., "Coverts and Casts," 1943; "Upland Gunning," 1946. Contributor to: Esquire, Natural History, Print Collectors Quarterly, & other magazines.

SCHANKER, LOUIS—*Pr. M., E., P., S.*
   126 West 23rd St., New York, N.Y.

B. New York, N.Y., July 20, 1903. *Studied*: ASL; CUASch., and abroad. *Member*: Fed. Mod. P. & S. *Awards*: F., Yaddo Fnd., Saratoga Springs, 1958; prizes, BM, 1947; Wash. Pr. Cl., 1949; Univ. Illinois, 1958. *Work*: BM; MMA; PMA; CM; WMAA; AIC; PMG; CMA; Toledo Mus. A.; MModA; Detroit Inst. A.; Univ. Michigan; Univ. Wisconsin; Wesleyan Col.; N.Y. Pub. Lib.; Walker A. Center; Rosenwald Coll. *Exhibited*:

VMFA; WMAA, 1935, 1936, 1940, 1941, 1942, 1951, 1958; Passedoit Gal., 1937; Am. Abstract A., 1937-1941; Bennington Col., 1938; BM, 1938, 1951, 1955; Guggenheim Mus., 1954; SFMA, 1938, 1942; Phila. A. All., 1938, 1939; WFNY 1939; SAGA, 1937-1939; Berkshire Mus., 1939; Willard Gal., 1940; GGE, 1939; Valentine Mus. A., 1940; LC, 1944; Inst. Mod. A., 1944; N.Y. Pub. Lib., 1944; MModA, 1944; Victoria & Albert Mus., London, 1954; Rome, Italy, 1958; Univ. Illinois, 1950, 1954, and many others; one-man: Contemp. A., 1933; New Sch. for Social Research, 1934, 1938, 1942; A. Gal., 1939, 1941, 1942; BM, 1943; Munson-Williams-Proctor Inst., 1942; Univ. Michigan, 1943; Willard Gal., 1944-1948, 1950; Kleeman Gal., 1944; Bloomington A. Gal., 1944; Univ. Wisconsin, 1944; PMG, 1946; Grace Borgenicht Gal., 1952, 1953, 1955, 1957; N.Y. Pub. Lib., 1955; Sculpture Center, 1952, and others. Author: "Line-Form-Color," 1944. *Position*: Teacher, New Sch. for Social Research, New York, N.Y., 1946- ; Assoc. Prof. A., Bard Col., Annandale-on-Hudson, N.Y., 1949- .

SCHANTZ-HANSEN, LAURENTZA—*Educator, L.*
   1005 Sixth St., West Lafayette, Ind.

B. Neenah, Wis., July 31, 1888. *Studied*: Univ. Chicago, Ph.B.; Columbia Univ., M.A.; & with Albert Heckman. *Member*: Mid-Western Col. A. Conference; Am. Assn. Univ. Prof.; Am. Assn. Univ. Women. Contributor to: Better Homes in American Bulletin No. 6 & No. 7. Lectures: American Contemporary Artists; etc. *Position*: Hd., Dept. App. Des., Purdue Univ., West Lafayette, Ind., 1930-56; Prof. Emeritus, 1957- . (Retired.)

SCHAPIRO, CECIL—*Painter, T.*
   36 West 84th St., New York 24, N.Y.

B. New York, N.Y. *Studied*: Hunter Col., A.B.; T. Col., Columbia Univ., A.M.; ASL; Alfred Univ. *Member*: Phila. WC Cl.; AEA; NAWA. *Exhibited*: N.Y. Soc. Ceramic A., 1923-1930; Morton Gal., 1936-1941; AEA, 1951; AWS; All. A. Am.; Phila. A. All., 1952-1955; Phila. WC Cl.; NAWA, 1954, 1955; AFA traveling exh., 1939-40; Art:USA, 1958. *Position*: Instr. FA, New York City Schs.

SCHAPIRO, MEYER—*Educator*
   279 Fourth St., New York 14, N.Y.

B. Shavly, Lithuania, Sept. 23, 1904. *Studied*: Columbia Univ., A.B., M.A., Ph.D. *Award*: Guggenheim F., 1939, 1942; F., Am. Acad. A. & Sciences. Author of books and articles on mediaeval and modern art. *Positions*: L., Dept. FA & Archaeology, 1928-36, Asst. Prof., Assoc. Prof., 1946-52, Prof., 1952- , Columbia Univ.; L., New Sch. for Social Research, N.Y., 1938, 1940-1953; Warburg Inst., London Univ., 1947; Bd. Ed., Journal of the History of Ideas, 1957.

SCHARFF, CONSTANCE (KRAMER)—*Painter, Pr. M.*
   115 Jaffrey St., Brooklyn 35, N.Y.

B. New York, N.Y. *Studied*: With George Pickens, Louis Schanker, Adja Yunkers. *Member*: Audubon A.; Brooklyn Soc. A.; NAWA; AEA; Nat. Soc. Painters in Casein. *Awards*: prizes, NAWA, 1951, 1958; Brooklyn Soc. A., 1954; Village A. Center, 1954, 1955; gold medal, Audubon A., 1955. *Work*: Collectors of Am. A. (full ed. of 100 prints purchased, 1956). *Exhibited*: BM, 1948, 1952, 1954; LC, 1954, 1955; Audubon A., 1951, 1952, 1955; SAGA, 1954; NAWA, 1950-1956; traveling print exh., Amsterdam, Holland, 1956; Contemporaries, 1955; Contemp. A., 1950-1955; N.Y. City Center, 1954, 1955; traveling exhs. U.S., Europe and Canada; Contemp. A. of U.S., 1956; Smithsonian Inst., 1957, 1958; Conn. Acad. FA, 1958. Lectures: Print-making (on television). *Position*: Corr. Sec., 1953- , Chm. traveling WC Exh., 1954-56, Exec. Bd., 1953-58, Brooklyn Soc. A.

SCHARY, SAUL—*Painter, I., Des., Gr.*
   56 West 10th St., New York 11, N.Y.; also, New Milford, Conn.

B. Newark, N.J., Nov. 3, 1904. *Studied*: ASL; PAFA, and in Paris, France. *Member*: AEA; F., PAFA; CAA; Royal Soc. A., London. *Work*: PAFA; CMA. *Exhibited*: WMAA, 1932, 1936, 1940, 1942-1945; AIC, 1942; Carnegie Inst., 1943, 1944; PAFA; Cal. PLH; one-man: Daniel, John Becker, Milch, Perls, Luyber, Salpeter galleries, all New York, N.Y.; All. A. Am. Gal., Los Angeles; Phila. A. All. I., "Alice in Wonderland," 1930.

SCHATZ, ZAHARA—Designer, P., C.
200 East 20th St., New York 3, N.Y.

B. Jerusalem, Israel, July 20, 1916. *Studied*: Ecole Nationale Superieur des Artes Decoratifs; Academie de la Grande Chaumiere, Paris, France. *Member*: Am. Abstract A.; San F. AA. *Awards*: prize, Bezalel Mus., Jerusalem, 1952. *Work*: Phillips Acad., Andover, Mass.; Munson-Williams-Proctor Inst.; Bezalel Mus.; mural, Warrick House, Atlantic City, N.J. *Exhibited*: Am. Abstract A., 1951, 1952; Phillips Acad., 1949; Detroit Inst. A., 1949; Walker A. Center, 1948-1949; Akron AI, 1947; San F. AA, 1945-1947; Mus. Non-Objective Painting, 1947-1952; Columbus Mus. FA, 1951; Cooper Union, 1950; Yale Univ., 1950; one-man: Mus. New Mexico, 1939; SFMA, 1944; Pinacotheca, 1947; Phila. A. All., 1949; Bertha Schaefer Gal., 1951.*

SCHAUER, MARTHA K.—Teacher, P., L.
Stivers High School, 1313 East 5th St.; h. 356 Kenilworth Ave., Dayton 5, Ohio

B. Troy, Ohio, Feb. 13, 1889. *Studied*: PIASch; Wittenberg Col., Springfield, Ohio, B.F.A.; Univ. Dayton, M.A. *Member*: Ohio WC Soc.; Dayton Soc. Painters. *Work*: Dayton AI. *Exhibited*: Ohio WC Soc.; Dayton AI, annually. *Position*: A. Instr., Asst. Principal, Stivers H.S., Dayton, Ohio, 1912-1956. Dir., Sat. Morning Sch. for Children, Dayton AI, 1926-1957.

SCHAUFFLER, MARGARET REYNOLDS—Painter, E., C.
Allen Memorial Art Building; h. 100 South Cedar St., Oberlin, Ohio

B. Cleveland, Ohio, June 4, 1896. *Studied*: Oberlin Col., B.A.; Cleveland Sch. A.; Western Reserve Univ., M.A.; & with Breckenridge, Forrest, Warshawsky. *Member*: AAUP; CAA. *Exhibited*: CMA, 1922, 1937, 1940; Allen Mem. A. Mus., Oberlin Col.; 1925, 1931, 1934, 1937, 1943, 1945, 1947, 1949, 1951, 1955, 1956, 1958; Wichita AA, 1952; Ogunquit A. Center, 1956-1958. *Position*: Instr., Asst. Prof. FA, Oberlin Col., Oberlin, Ohio, 1923- .

SCHEFFEL, HERBERT H.—Painter, Comm. A.
25 Mahar Ave., Clifton, N.J.

B. Clifton, N.J. *Studied*: Newark Sch. F. & Indst. A.; New Sch. for Social Research; Cape Sch. of Painting, and with Wang Chi-Yuan. *Member*: AWS; Audubon A.; Boston Soc. Indp. A.; Rockport AA. *Work*: Berkshire Mus.; Montclair A. Mus.; Carpenter Gal., Dartmouth Col.; Interstate Payment Corp. *Exhibited*: New York, California, Massachusetts, New Jersey, Wash., D.C. Numerous one-man exhibitions.

SCHEFFLER, RUDOLF—Painter
Valley Cottage, Rockland County, N.Y.

B. Zwickau, Germany, Dec. 5, 1884. *Studied*: Royal Acad., Dresden, and in Paris, France, Italy, Holland. *Member*: NSMP. *Awards*: Prix de Rome gold medal. *Work*: Springfield (Ill.) Hospital; New State Office Bldg., Columbus, Ohio; murals in European galleries; mosaics and murals: churches in N.Y., Conn., Wash., Mont., Wis., Ill., La., Cal., Ky., Ohio, Mo., and many others; mosaic, Seminary of St. Francis, Milwaukee; triptych for Bishop of Houston, Tex.; mosaic reredos for church in Minster, Ohio. Hist. murals, Liederkranz Bldg., New York, N.Y.

SCHEIER, EDWIN—Ceramist, E., S., P.
University of New Hampshire; h. 63 Mill Road, Durham, N.H.

B. New York, N.Y., Nov. 11, 1910. *Studied*: ASL; Columbia Univ. *Member*: Am. Ceramic Soc.; Am. Assn. Univ. Prof. *Awards*: prize, Syracuse Mus. F.A.; BM, 1953; medal, Intl. Exh. ceramics, Cannes, France, 1955. *Work*: Walker A. Center: CM; AIC; MMoDA; Syracuse Mus. FA; Phila. A. All.; Mus. R.I. Sch. Des.; Detroit Inst. A.; MMA; Exeter Acad.; Fitchburg A. Mus.; Currier Gal. A.; Stuttgart, Germany; Tokyo Mus.; Royal Ontario Mus.; Intl. Mus. of Ceramics, Florence, Italy; Rochester Mem. A. Gal.; Newark Mus.; VMFA; AGAA; Univ. Kansas; Univ. Nebraska; Univ. Minnesota; Univ. Illinois and Wisconsin. *Exhibited*: WMA; BMA; CM; Syracuse Mus. FA; Phila. A. All.; one-man: Detroit Inst. A.; Toledo Mus. A.; Milwaukee AI; Dartmouth Col.;

Univ. Puerto Rico; Univ. Minnesota; Univ. New Hampshire; Currier Gal. A. *Position*: Assoc. Prof. A., Univ. New Hampshire, Durham, N.H.

SCHEIER, MARY—Ceramist, Des., C., E., P.
63 Mill Road, Durham, N.H.

B. Salem, Va., May 9, 1910. *Studied*: ASL; Parsons Sch. Des. *Awards*: prizes, Syracuse Mus. FA, 1940 and subsequently. *Work*: AIC; Syracuse Mus. FA; CM; MMoDA; Univ. New Hampshire; Walker A. Center; Detroit Inst. A.; Rochester Mem. A. Gal.; Newark Mus.; VMFA; Currier Gal. A.; Fitchburg A. Mus.; Tokyo Mus., Japan; Royal Ontario Mus.; Univ. Illinois; AGAA; Univ. of Kansas, Nebraska, Minnesota, Wisconsin. *Exhibited*: Syracuse Mus. FA; WMA; BMA; CM; Phila. A. All.; Mus. R.I. Sch. Des.; Currier Gal. A.; Univ. New Hampshire; VMFA; one-man: Detroit Inst. A.; Toledo Mus. A.; Milwaukee AI; Dartmouth Col.; Univ. Puerto Rico; Univ. Minnesota; Univ. New Hampshire; Currier Gal. A. (one-man in collaboration with Edwin Scheier).

SCHEIN, EUGENE—Painter, T.
441 Washington Ave.; h. 1070 Stillwater Drive, Miami Beach 41, Fla.

B. Austria. *Studied*: Hunter Col., B.A.; Columbia Univ., M.A.; Univ. New Mexico; Nat. Univ., Mexico. *Member*: AEA; AAUP; NAWA. *Work*: Carville Mus. A.; Lowe Gal. of A.; Norton Gal. A. *Exhibited*: BM; NGA; CM; PAFA, 1950; Riverside Mus., 1951; Wash. WC Cl., 1957; one-man: Midtown Gal., N.Y., 1937, 1941; Argent Gal., 1940; Salpeter Gal., 1950; Huber Gal., Miami, 1959; Havana, Cuba, 1956; Mexico City, D.F., 1956; Kaufmann Gal., N.Y.; Uptown Gal., N.Y.

SCHEIRER, GEORGE A.—Hand Bookbinder
5506 Sonoma Rd., Bethesda 14, Md.

B. Elmira, N.Y., June 14, 1895. *Studied*: with Marian Lane. *Member*: Wash. Soc. Min. P. S. & Gr. *Award*: prize, Smithsonian Inst., 1957. *Exhibited*: CGA, 1936; Wash. AC, 1946; Phila. A. All., 1937; Wash. Soc. A. & Crafts, 1929; Pub. Lib., Wash., D.C., 1934; Soc. Min. P. S. & Gr., 1937-1954; Gibbes A. Gal., 1954; Bethesda (Md.) Pub. Lib., 1955; Smithsonian Inst., 1957, 1958. *Position*: Instr., Bookbinding, "Woodnook Bindery," Bethesda, Md., 1950- .

SCHELL, SUSAN GERTRUDE—Painter, T.
320 South Broad St.; h. 54 West Tulpehocken Ave., Philadelphia 44, Pa.

Studied: State T. Col., West Chester, Pa.; PAFA. *Member*: NAWA; Phila. A. All. *Awards*: prizes, NAWA, 1936, 1940. *Work*: New Britain Mus.; State T. Col., Pa. *Position*: Instr. A., Advisor, PMSchA, Philadelphia, Pa. 1930-56.*

SCHELLIN, ROBERT—Painter, C., E.
335 North Bartlett Ave., Milwaukee 11, Wis.

B. Akron, Ohio, July 28, 1910. *Studied*: Milwaukee State T. Col., B.E.; Columbia Univ.; Univ. Wisconsin, M.S., and with Hans Hofmann. *Member*: Wis. P. & S.; Wis. A. Edu. Assn.; Midwest Des.-Craftsmen; Wis. Des.-Craftsmen. *Awards*: prizes, Wis. State Fair, 1943, 1944, 1954, 1956, 1957; Madison AA, 1945; Milwaukee AI, 1947, 1949, 1950 (2), 1952 (2), 1953, 1957; Wis. Des.-Craftsmen, 1952, 1957; medal, AIC, 1933. *Work*: Milwaukee AI; Whitefish Bay (Wis.) Pub. Sch.; Milwaukee State T. Col.; Univ. Wisconsin. *Exhibited*: AIC, 1944; AGAA, 1945; CMA, 1945; WAC, 1946; Milwaukee AI, 1939, 1956-1958; Newark Mus., 1945; Portland A. Mus., 1946; Kalamazoo AI, 1946; Wis. P. & S., 1930-1946; Wis. State Fair, 1956-1958; Midwest Des.-Craftsmen, 1956, 1957 and others. *Position*: Instr. A., Milwaukee State T. Col., 1945- ; Chm., Dept. A. & A. Edu., Univ. Wisconsin, Milwaukee, Wis.

SCHENCK, EDGAR C.—Museum Director
Brooklyn Museum, Eastern Parkway (38); h. 161 Henry St., Brooklyn 1, N.Y.

B. Hot Springs, N.C., Dec. 6, 1909. *Studied*: Princeton Univ., A.B., M.F.A. *Member*: AAMus.; CAA; AFA; Assn. A. Mus. Dir.; Mus. Council, New York, N.Y. Author: "Expressionism in American Painting," 1952; "Painter's

Painter," 1953; "What *Is* Painting?" 1953. Contributor to Am. Journal of Archaeology; Art Bulletin; College Art Journal; Bulletin of the Albright Art Gallery; Annual Bulletin, Honolulu Academy of Arts. Lectures: Oriental, Polynesian, Western Painting, to museums, clubs and universities. Exhibitions arranged: Moore and Rodin, 1948; Pompaiana, 1949; Eugene Speicher, 1950; Expressionism in American Painting, 1952; Fifty Paintings, 1905-1913 and others. *Position*: Dir., Honolulu Acad. A., 1934-1947; Dir., Smith Col. Mus., 1947-49; Dir., Albright A. Gal., 1949-55; Dir., Brooklyn Mus., 1955- .

SCHENCK, MARIE (PFEIFER) (Mrs. Frank)—
Art Director, S.
Miami Beach Art Center, 2100 Collins Ave.; h. 731 Northeast 81st St., Miami 38, Fla.

B. Columbus, Ohio. *Studied*: Cleveland Sch. A.; Columbus Sch. A., and with Hugo Robus, John Hussey, Bruce Wilder Saville, Alys Roysher Young, and others. *Member*: Am. Soc. for Aesthetics; Miami A. Lg. *Award*: Miami Woman's Cl., medal, 1957. *Exhibited*: Columbus A. Lg.; Miami A. Lg.; Sarasota AA. *Positions*: Instr., S., Columbus A. Sch.; A. Instr., Coburn Private Sch., Miami Beach; A. Dir., City of Miami Beach A. Center, 1942- .

SCHEU, LEONARD—Painter, E.
309 Agate St., Laguna Beach, Cal.

B. San Francisco, Cal., Feb. 19, 1904. *Studied*: Cal. Sch. FA; ASL. *Member*: Cal. WC Soc.; AEA; Los A. AA; Pr. Council of Am.; Nat. Soc. Painters in Casein; Laguna Beach AA. *Exhibited*: N.Y. WC Cl., 1936; Laguna Beach AA, 1935-1946, 1948-1955, 1958 (one-man); GGE, 1939; BM, 1941; Oakland A. Gal., 1938, 1945, 1946, 1951; Santa Cruz A. Lg., 1935, 1938; Fnd. Western A., 1936, 1938, 1939; San Diego FA Soc., 1938; Cal. State Fair, 1938, 1940, 1941; San Diego A. Gld., 1938, 1939; Bowers Mem. Mus., 1939; Aquarelle Painters of Southern Cal., 1939; Santa Paula, Cal., 1941, 1942; Cal. WC Soc., 1943; Riverside Mus., 1946; Walnut Creek (Cal.), 1950; Orange County Fair, 1951; Newport Harbor Exh., 1952; Los A. Mus. A., 1948, 1952; Nat. Orange Show, 1952-1955; Orange County AA, 1955; Nat. Soc. Painters in Casein, 1955; Los A. AA, 1954, 1955; Oakland A. Mus., 1953; Ford Motor Co., 1955; Sonora, Cal., 1955; deYoung Mem. Mus., 1957; Crocker A. Gal., Sacramento (one-man); Mus. New Mexico (one-man). Contributor to Ford Times; Lincoln-Mercury Times.

SCHEUCH, HARRY WILLIAM—Painter
219 Race St., Pittsburgh 18, Pa.

B. Elizabeth, N.J., Apr. 5, 1906. *Studied*: Carnegie Inst.; Univ. Pittsburgh. *Member*: Assoc. A. Pittsburgh. *Awards*: prizes, Butler AI, 1942; Assoc. A. Pittsburgh, 1946-1948, 1951, 1952; medal, Pepsi-Cola, 1947, 1948. *Work*: Butler AI; Pa. State Univ.; Pittsburgh Pub. Schs.; Labor Bldg., Wash., D.C., and in private colls. *Exhibited*: AIC, 1937, 1938; Carnegie Inst.; WMAA, 1948; Butler AI, 1955, and other national exhs. *Position*: Instr., Irene Kaufmann Settlement and privately.*

SCHILDKNECHT, EDMUND G.—Painter, Et., T.
Redoubt Hill, Eastport, Me.

B. Chicago, Ill., July 9, 1899. *Studied*: Wisconsin Sch. A.; PAFA; Julian Acad., Grande Chaumiere, Paris, France. *Member*: Indiana AC. *Awards*: prizes, John Herron AI, 1932, 1933, 1939; Hoosier Salon, 1943, 1944, 1946; Indiana A. Cl., 1952-1955. *Work*: John Herron AI; Univ. Indiana; Arsenal Tech. H.S., Crispus Attucks H.S., Indianapolis. *Exhibited*: CGA, 1930; AIC, 1928, 1929, 1931, 1934-1936; PAFA, 1930-1932, 1935, 1944; SAGA, 1937, 1938, 1943; CM, 1931-1934; Kansas City AI, 1935, 1936; John Herron AI, 1924-1946, 1951-1956; Magnificent Mile, Chicago, 1955; Indiana A. Cl., 1950-1956. *Position*: Instr., Arsenal Technical Schools, Indianapolis, Ind., 1924-57.

SCHINNELLER, JAMES ARTHUR—Educator
204 Bordner Dr., Madison, Wis.

B. Pittsburgh, Pa., Jan. 27, 1925. *Studied*: Edinboro (Pa.) State T. Col., B.S. in A. Edu.; Univ. Iowa, M.A. in A. Edu., M.F.A. *Member*: Wisconsin A. Edu. Assn.; NAEA. Contributor to Journal of Education by Film and Radio. Lectures: Why We Have Art in the Schools. *Position*: Panel Memb., NAEA, "Art and the Community," Cleve-

land, 1955; Cr., T., A. Ed., Western Illinois State Col., 1950-52; Instr., Univ. Iowa, 1952-54, Actg. Hd. Dept. A., Univ. Iowa, 1952-53; Instr., A. Edu. Dept., Univ. Wisconsin, Madison, Wis., 1954- .*

SCHIWETZ, EDWARD M.—Designer, P., L.
455 Caroline St.; h. 3106 Albans Rd., Houston 5, Texas

B. Cuero, Tex., Aug. 24, 1898. *Studied*: Texas A. & M. Col., B.S. in Arch.; ASL. *Member*: Cal. WC Soc.; Texas WC Soc. *Awards*: prizes, SSAL, 1936; New Orleans A. Soc., 1936; Philbrook A. Center; Mus. FA of Houston, 1933; Witte Mem. Mus., 1944; Ft. Worth AA, 1948; San Antonio Conservation Soc.; AWS, 1954; Hughes Tool Co., 1950. *Work*: Dallas Mus. FA; Mus. FA of Houston; Ft. Worth AA; indst. paintings for Standard Oil Co.; Union Oil Co.; Humble Oil & Refining Co.; Dow Chemical Co.; Monsanto Chemical Co. *Exhibited*: AIC, 1931, 1943, 1945; AWS, 1930, 1952, 1954; Phila. WC Soc., 1930; Grand Rapids A. Gal., 1940; Colorado Springs FA Center, 1947; Arch. Lg.; Cal. PLH; LC; Knoedler Gal.; and others; one-man: Mus. FA of Houston; Witte Mem. Mus.; Dallas Mus. FA; Austin, Tex.; Corpus Christi, Tex. Contributor illus. to Architectural Record, Architectural Forum, Pictorial Review, and other leading magazines. *Position*: A. Consultant, McCann Erickson Co., Houston, Tex.*

SCHLAG, FELIX OSCAR—Sculptor
107 West Exchange St., Owosso, Mich.

B. Frankfort-on-Main, Germany, Sept. 4, 1891. *Studied*: Acad. A., Munich, Germany. *Work*: Champaign (Ill.) Jr. H.S.; Bloom Township H.S., Chicago Heights, Ill.; USPO, White Hall, Ill.; des. Jefferson nickel, U.S. Mint, Wash., D.C. *Exhibited*: AIC; Detroit, Mich.; New York, N.Y.; & abroad.

SCHLAGETER, ROBERT—Museum Director
Mint Museum of Art, 501 Hempstead Place, Charlotte 7, N.C.*

SCHLAIKJER, JES WILHELM—Portrait Painter, I., T.
4526 Verplanck Pl., Washington 16, D.C.

B. New York, N.Y., Sept. 22, 1897. *Studied*: Ecole des Beaux-Arts, France; AIC; & with Forsberg, Cornwell, Dunn. *Member*: NA. *Awards*: prizes, NAD, 1926, 1928. *Work*: NAD; U.S. War Dept.; U.S. Naval Acad., Annapolis, Md.; Dept. of State; Am. Red Cross; Nelson Gal. A., Kansas City; Univ. Indiana; Walter Reed Hospital, Wash., D.C.; Marine Corps Sch., Quantico, Va.; Federal Reserve Bank, Kansas City; Georgetown Univ.; U.S. Public Health Service, Wash., D.C. *Exhibited*: nationally. Contributor to: national magazines. *Position*: Official A., 1942-44, A. Consultant, 1945- , U.S. War Dept., Washington, D.C.

SCHLAPP, CHARLES W. L.—Painter, Lith., T.
Art Academy of Cincinnati, Eden Park, Cincinnati 6, Ohio; h. 8412 St. Clair Ave., Rossmoyne, Ohio

B. Cincinnati, Ohio, Des. 20, 1895. *Studied*: Cincinnati A. Acad. *Member*: Cincinnati AC; Cincinnati Professional A. *Work*: Knox Presbyterian Church, Medical Col., Mabley & Carew Co., all of Cincinnati; Hayes Building Works, Du Quoin, Ill.; Hale Hospital, Wilmington, Ohio. *Exhibited*: Cincinnati AC; Cincinnati Professional A. *Position*: Instr. A., Cincinnati A. Acad., Cincinnati, Ohio, 1921- ; Sec.-Treas.; Cincinnati A. Cl., 1926- .

SCHLATER, KATHARINE—Painter, I., Lith., Des., L.
1000 Caminos Rancheros, Santa Fé, N.M.

Studied: PMSchIA; & with Hugh Breckenridge, Ralph M. Pearson. *Member*: Phila. A. All.; Phila. Pr. Cl.; AAPL. *Work*: Fabric des. for Celanese Corp.; Murals in private homes. *Exhibited*: nationally. Several one-man exhs.

SCHLAZER, MICHAEL—Painter, I., T.
2853 Southwest 23rd St., Miami, Fla.

B. Poland, Aug. 25, 1910. *Work*: Bd. Edu., N.Y.; Mus. Non-Objective Painting; P.S. No. 94, N.Y.; Ft. Hamilton H.S. Illus. "Flying Health." *Award*: prize, Intl. Boat Show, 1957. *Exhibited*: BM; MMoA; Mus. Non-Objective

Painting, 1946, 1947; Contemporary A. Gal.; New Sch. Social Research; Exh. Am. A., N.Y., 1938; Univ. Miami, 1955; FA Lg. of Carolinas; BM. Lectures: Children's Art.

SCHLEETER, HOWARD BEHLING—Painter, C., E., L.

1469 Canyon Road, Santa Fe, N.M.

B. Buffalo, N.Y., May 16, 1903. *Member:* A. Lg. of New Mexico. *Awards:* purchase prize, Mus. New Mexico, Santa Fe, 1951, 1955; purchase, New Mexico Highlands Univ., 1957. *Work:* Encyclopaedia Britannica; Research Studio, Maitland, Fla.; A. Lg of N.M.; Mus. of New Mexico, Santa Fe; murals, A. & M. Col., New Mexico. *Exhibited:* Phila. A. All., 1945 (one-man); deYoung Mem. Mus., 1946; Kansas City AI, 1936-1938; Cedar City (N.M.), 1941-1946; AIC, 1947; Vienna, Austria, 1952; Guggenheim Mus., 1954; Karlsruhe Mus., Germany, 1955; Stanford Univ., 1955 (one-man); New Mexico Highlands Univ., 1957; Colo. Springs FA Center, 1958; Swope A. Gal., and other group and one-man exhs. in the U.S. *Position:* Instr., Univ. New Mexico, 1950-51, 1954.

SCHLEMOWITZ, ABRAM—Sculptor

139 West 22nd St., New York 11, N.Y.

B. New York, N.Y., July 19, 1910. *Studied:* BAID; NAD; ASL; Design Laboratory. *Member:* S. Gld.; Am. Abstract A.; New Sculpture Group. *Exhibited:* Woodstock AA; Riverside Mus.; RoKo, Collectors', Camino, Terrain, March, Brata and Stable galleries, N.Y. *Position:* Instr. S., YMHA; Lighthouse for the Blind; Children's Div., Bellevue Hospital, all New York City.

SCHLICHER, KARL THEODORE—Educator, P., W.

Art Department, Stephen F. Austin State College; h. 315 East California St., Nacogdoches, Tex.

B. Terre Haute, Ind., May 14, 1905. *Studied:* Univ. Wisconsin, B.S., M.S.; Colt Sch. A.; AIC; Univ. Chicago; Ohio State Univ., Ph.D., and with Reynolds, Giesbert, Coats, Hopkins, Grimes, and others. *Member:* CAA; Texas FA Assn.; Texas A. Edu. Assn. (Pres. 1956-58); Texas State T. Assn.; Royal Soc. A., London; Western AA; NAEA. *Work:* portraits in private colls. *Exhibited:* Contemp. A. of the Southwest, 1956; Lufkin A. Lg.; Nacogdoches Fair; Stephen F. Austin State Col. Faculty Exhs. Contributor to Texas Outlook; Western Arts Assn. Research Bulletin; Texas Trends in Art Education (Ed. & Publ., 1951-56). *Position:* Prof. A., Stephen F. Austin State College, Nacogdoches, Tex.

SCHMECKEBIER, LAURENCE E.—
Educator, L., Cr., W., S.

Syracuse University, School of Art (10); h. 227 Scottholm Terrace, Syracuse 3, N.Y.

B. Chicago Heights, Ill., Mar. 1, 1906. *Studied:* Univ. Wisconsin, B.A.; Univ. Marburg, Germany; Sorbonne, Paris, France; Univ. Munich, Germany, Ph.D., and with Max Doerner, Hans Hofmann. *Member:* CAA; Soc. Architectural Historians; Cleveland Soc. A. Author: "A Handbook of Italian Renaissance Painting," 1938; "Modern Mexican Art," 1939; "Appreciation of Art" (U.S. Armed Forces Institute), 1945; "John Steuart Curry's Pageant of America," 1943; "Art in Red Wing," 1946. Contributor to Art magazines and journals. *Exhibited:* Cleveland Inst. A.; CMA; Syracuse Mus. FA; Munson-Williams-Proctor Inst.; Rochester Mem. A. Gal.; Corning Glass Center. *Awards:* Cleveland, 1949-1951; George L. Herdle award, Rochester, 1955; N.Y. State Fair, 1958. *Position:* Asst. Prof. A. Hist., Univ. Wisconsin, 1931-38; Prof., Chm. Dept. FA, Univ. Minnesota, 1938-46; Dir., Cleveland Inst. A., 1946-54; Prof. A. Hist., Dir., Sch. A., Syracuse Univ., Syracuse, N.Y., 1954- ; Ed., College Art Journal, 1949-53; Adv. A. Ed., Encyclopaedia Americana, 1952- . Bd. Trustees, Everson Mus. A., 1956- .

SCHMEIDLER, BLANCHE J.—Painter, Gr ., Des.

Studio 409, 2 West 15th St., New York, N.Y.; h. 35-35 75th St., Jackson Heights 72, N.Y.

B. New York, N.Y., Nov. 1, 1915. *Studied:* Hunter Col.; Columbia Univ., B.A.; Samuel Brecher A. Sch.; ASL, with Harry Sternberg, Vytlacil. *Member:* NAWA; Silvermine Gld.; AEA; Cosmopolitan A.; N.Y. Soc. Women A.; Nat. Soc. Painters in Casin; Brooklyn Soc. A. *Award:* prizes, NAWA; Jersey City Mus. A., 1958. *Work:* in private collections. *Exhibited:* Amsterdam, Holland; ACA

Gal.; Assoc. Am. A. Gal.; Argent Gal.; NAD; Audubon A.; NAC; WMAA; Riverside Mus.; Queens Soc. FA, all of N.Y.; Silvermine Gld.; Albany Inst. Hist. & A.; Ball State T. Col.; Stratford Col., Danville, Va.; Univ. South Carolina; Herbert Inst. A., Augusta; Beaumont (Tex.) AI; Stephen Austin State Col.; Oklahoma A. & M. Col., Stillwater; Jersey City Mus.; South Bend AA; Oklahoma A. Center; Columbus Mus. A.; Massillon Mus. A.; Swope Gal. A.; Univ. New Mexico; Univ. Texas; Everhart Mus. A.; Georgia Mus. A.; Wesleyan Col.; Univ. South Carolina, and others. One-man: Feigl Gal., N.Y., 1957.

SCHMID, ELSA—Painter, C.

10 Newberry Place, Rye, N.Y.

B. Stuttgart, Germany, Mar. 22, 1897. *Studied:* ASL. *Work:* BMA; Newark Mus. A.; FMA; MModA; mosaic fresco, Yale Univ. Chapel; mosaics, Church of St. Brigid, Peapack, N.J.; mosaic floor, U.S. Cemetery, Carthage, Africa. *Exhibited:* Nationally.

SCHMIDT, AL(WIN) (E.)—Illustrator

Putnam Park Rd., Bethel, Conn.

B. Des Peres, Mo., June 27, 1900. *Studied:* St. Louis Sch. FA; & with Fred Carpenter. *Member:* SI; Westport A. *Exhibited:* Am. A. Exh., 1933, 1934; CAM, 1922; Mayfair A. Salon, St. Louis, 1933; St. Louis A. Gld., 1933, 1934; CM, 1933; Terry AI, 1952; SI, 1944, 1945. Illus., for children's books.*

SCHMIDT, STEPHEN—Museum Director

House of Refuge Museum, Box 1297, Stuart, Fla.; h. Orange Ave., Rio Jensen, Fla.

B. New York, N.Y., Dec. 11, 1925. *Studied:* Univ. New Mexico, B.A. *Position:* Dir., House of Refuge, Stuart, Fla.

SCHMITT, CARL—Painter, W., T.

Silvermine, Wilton, Conn.

B. Warren, Ohio, May 6, 1889. *Studied:* NAD, with Emil Carlsen; in Italy; & with Solon Borglum. *Work:* Brady Mem. Chapel, Wernersville, Pa.; Oxford Univ., England; Pittsburgh Athletic Cl.; Mamaroneck (N.Y.) Theater. *Exhibited:* Carnegie Inst., annually; & other major exh. throughout U.S. Contributor to: national magazines.

SCHMITZ, CARL LUDWIG—Sculptor, T.

246 West 80th St.; h. 501 East 84th St., New York 28, N.Y.

B. Metz, France, Sept. 4, 1900. *Studied:* in Europe; BAID, and with Maxim Dasio, Joseph Wackerle, and others. *Member:* NA; NSS (Council, 1957-60); Arch. Lg.; Audubon A.; All. A. Am. *Awards:* prizes, Syracuse Mus. FA, 1939; NSS, 1934, 1940; Our Lady of Victory Comp., 1945; All. A. Am., 1951; Meriden, Conn., 1952; medal, Paris, France, 1937; PAFA, medal, 1940; Guggenheim F., 1944; Am. Acad. A. & Let. grant, 1947. *Work:* Syracuse Mus. FA; IBM; N.Y. Mun. Coll.; Justice Bldg., USPO Dept. Bldg., Federal Trade Comm. Bldg., all in Wash., D.C.; Federal Bldg., Covington, Ky.; USPO, York, Pa.; Des., Delaware Tercentenary half-dollar and medal for City Planning; Bar Assn. medal; Electrochemical Soc. medal; other work, Parkchester, N.Y.; Michigan State Col.; reliefs, Loyola Seminary, Shrub Oaks, N.Y.; statues, Ciudad Trujillo, D.R.; House of Theology, Centerville, Ohio; reliefs, Pieta, Sorrowful Mother Shrine, Chicago, Ill. *Exhibited:* PAFA, 1934-1952, 1957, 1958; WMAA, 1936, 1938-1942, 1944; AIC, 1936-1940; Syracuse Mus. FA, 1938-1941, 1946-1958; CGA, 1936, 1939; SFMA, 1935, 1936, 1941; NAD, 1934, 1935, 1942, 1944, 1948-1951, 1952, 1957; Arch. Lg., 1936, 1942, 1944, 1949, 1950-1955; NSS, 1934, 1939-1941, 1943, 1944, 1946-1955, 1956, 1957; All. A. Am., 1951, 1956-1958; Audubon A., 1945, 1950, 1951, 1957, 1958. *Position:* Inst. S., Michigan State Col., 1947; Art Workshop, New York, N.Y., 1948- .

SCHNABEL, DAY—Sculptor

151 Ave. B., New York, N.Y.

B. Vienna, Austria, Mar. 1, 1905. *Studied:* Acad. A., Vienna, and in Paris with Malfray, Maillol and Zadkine. *Exhibited:* one-man: Betty Parsons Gal., 1946, 1947, 1952, 1957; WMAA, 1949-1953, 1957, 1958, and abroad. *Work:* WMAA; BM; Carnegie Inst.; WAC.

SCHNAKENBERG, HENRY—*Painter*

Taunton District, Newtown, Conn.

B. New Brighton, N.Y., Sept. 14, 1892. *Studied*: Staten Island Acad. *Member*: Nat Inst. A. & Let. *Awards*: hon. degree, D.F.A., Univ. Vermont. *Work*: MMA; WMAA; BM; Montclair A. Mus.; PAFA; Savannah (Ga.) Gal.; AGAA; Springfield, Mass.) Mus.; Newark Mus.; New Britain A. Mus.; Wichita A. Gal.; Princeton Univ. A. Mus.; Wadsworth Atheneum; Fleming Mus.; Wood Mus., Montpelier, Vt.; Dartmouth Col. Gal.; Canajoharie (N.Y.) A. Gal.; AIC; Univ. Nebraska; Minneapolis Inst. A.; Palace Legion Honor; Dallas Mus. FA; murals, USPO, Amsterdam, N.Y.; Fort Lee, N.J. *Exhibited*: nationally.*

SCHNEIDER, ELSBETH—*Painter, E., Eng.*

238 Hazel St., Chico, Cal.

B. Chicago, Ill., Dec. 28, 1904. *Studied*: Univ. California, B.A., M.A. *Member*: Lg. Am. Pen Women; Cal. Soc. Et. *Awards*: prize, Lg. Am. Pen Women, 1937. *Exhibited*: Oakland A. Gal., 1940, 1941, 1943-1953; Laguna Beach AA, 1944; Cal. SE, 1945, 1946, 1949; San F. AA, 1937. *Position*: Assoc. Prof. A., Chico State Col., Chico, Cal., 1926- .

SCHNIER, JACQUES—*Educator, S., W.*

Art Department, University of California, Berkeley, Cal.; h. 1637 Taylor St., San Francisco 11, Cal.

B. Roumania, Dec. 25, 1898. *Studied*: Stanford Univ., A.B.; Univ. California, M.A.; Cal. Sch. FA. *Member*: F., NSS; San F. AA; Am. Soc. for Aesthetics; Faculty Cl., Univ. Cal. *Awards*: prizes, San F. AA, 1928; SAM, 1928; Oakland A. Mus., 1936, medal, 1940, 1948; Los A. Mus. A., 1934. *Work*: SFMA; Cal. Hist. Soc.; SS "Lurline"; Congressional Cl., Wash., D.C.; Mills College; Univ. California; Berkeley H.S.; Ann Bremer Mem. Lib., San F.; designed U.S. half-dollar commemorating San F.-Oakland Bay Bridge. Author: "Sculpture in Modern America," 1948. Contributor of articles on Psychoanalysis and Art to Journal of Aesthetics & Art Criticism; College Art Journal; Intl. Journal of Psychoanalysis; American Imago; Psychoanalytical Review; Yearbook of Psychoanalysis, Samiksa, India. Lectures: Psychoanalysis of Art Expression; Function and Origin of Form; The Blazing Sun of Van Gogh, etc. *Position*: L., 1936-38, Instr., 1938-42, Asst. Prof., Dept. Arch., 1942-48, Assoc. Prof., 1948-53, Prof., 1953- , Univ. California, Berkeley, Cal.

SCHNITTMAN, SACHA S.—*Sculptor, W., L., E.*

46 Vandeventer Pl., St. Louis 8, Mo.

B. New York, N.Y., Sept. 1, 1913. *Studied*: CUASch; NAD; BAID; Columbia Univ.; & with Attilio Piccirilli, Robert Aitken, Olympio Brindesi, & others. *Member*: NSS; Soc. Indp. A.; Russian S. Soc. *Awards*: prizes, Soc. Indp. A., 1942; CAM, 1942; Jr. Lg. Missouri Exh., 1942; Kansas City AI, 1942; Pan-Am. Arch. Soc., 1933; Fraser med., 1937. *Work*: busts, mem., monuments: Pan-Am. Soc.; Am. Mus. Natural Hist.; Dayton AI; Moscow State Univ., Russia; Mem. Plaza, St. Louis, Mo.; Dorsa Bldg., St. Louis, Mo.; others in Wash., D.C., New York, N.Y., Virginia, etc. *Exhibited*: All.A.Am., 1935, 1936; William Rockhill Nelson Gal., 1942; Soc. Indp. A., 1942-1944; St. Louis A. Gld., 1942; WMAA, 1943; Chicago AC, 1943; Kansas City AI, 1942; CAM, 1942; Indp. A., St. Louis, 1941-1945; SAM, 1942. Author, I., "Anatomy and Dissection for Artists," 1939; "Plastic Histology," 1940. Contributor to: Architectural magazines, with articles on arch. sculpture.*

SCHNITZLER, MAX—*Painter*

Hopewell Junction, N.Y.

B. Bukowsko, Poland, May 12, 1903. *Studied*: in Paris, with Leger, Ozenfant, L'Hote. *Work*: Collectors of Am. A. *Exhibited*: WMAA; CM; Denver A. Mus.; SAM; SFMA; Albright A. Gal.; Springfield Mus. A.; Wildenstein Gal.; Stable Gal.; Albany Inst. Hist. & A.; Poindexter Gal., N.Y., 1957; one-man: T. Col., Columbia Univ.; Zborowski Gal.; Contemp. A. Gal.; Pinacotheca, etc.

SCHOCH, PEARL—*Painter*

82 Buell Lane, East Hampton, N.Y.

B. New York, N.Y., July 3, 1894. *Studied*: PIASch.; N.Y. Univ.; Columbia Univ., and with Anna Fischer, Morris Davidson, Charles J. Martin. *Member*: NAWA;

Brooklyn Soc. A.; Pen & Brush Cl. *Award*: prize, Pen and Brush Cl., 1952. *Exhibited*: AWS; BM; NAWA; Pen & Brush Cl.; and traveling watercolor exhs. in U.S., and Canada.

SCHOENER, ALLON THEODORE—*Museum Curator*

Contemporary Arts Center, Cincinnati Art Museum (6); h. 433 Collins Ave., Cincinnati 2, Ohio

B. Cleveland, Ohio, Jan 1, 1926. *Studied*: Yale Col., B.A.; Yale Univ., M.A.; Courtauld Inst. A., Univ. London. *Member*: AAMus.; Intl. Des. Conf., Aspen, Colo. Contributor to Museum; Quarterly of Screen, Radio and Television. Arranged Swiss Graphic Designers exhibition, circulating from 1957 to present; "An American Viewpoint in 20th Century American Painting," 1957. *Positions*: Asst. Cur., San Francisco Mus. A., 1950-55; Cur., The Contemporary Arts Center, Cincinnati A. Mus., 1955- .

SCHOENER, JASON—*Painter, C., S., E.*

5667 Ocean View Dr., Oakland 18, Cal.

B. Cleveland, Ohio, May 17, 1919. *Studied*: Cleveland Inst. A.; Western Reserve Univ., B.S. in A. Edu.; ASL, with Morris Kantor; T. Col., Columbia Univ., M.A. *Member*: San F. AA; AEA; CAA; Maine WC Soc.; ASL. *Awards*: prizes, Syracuse Mus. FA, 1953; CMA, 1947; Ohio WC Soc., 1951; Brick Store Mus., Kennebunk, Me., 1953, 1958; Richmond (Cal.) A. Center, 1957; San F. Festival of A., 1956; Cal. State Fair, 1958; CMA, 1956. *Work*: CMA; Munson-Williams-Proctor Inst.; Cal. PLH; WAC; Bowdoin Col. *Exhibited*: PAFA, 1940-1942 ,1950-1953; Butler AI, 1940, 1941, 1947, 1948, 1950-1953, 1958; Audubon A., 1947; Syracuse Mus. FA, 1951-1953; Wichita AA, 1951, 1952; San F. AA, 1951, 1955-1957; Munson-Williams-Proctor Inst., 1950-1953; CMA, 1938-1943, 1948-1958; Ohio WC Soc., 1949-1953; Oakland A. Mus., 1953; Western Painters, 1954; Cal. PLH, 1958 (one-man); CGA, 1957; Univ. Nebraska, 1958; Art:USA, 1958; Colo. Springs FA, 1957; Univ. Maine, 1958 (one-man); Bowdoin Col., 1958; Humboldt State Col., 1956 (one-man). *Positions*: Instr., Munson-Williams-Proctor Inst., Utica, N.Y., 1949-53; Assoc. Prof., 1953- , Chm. Dept. FA, 1955- , Dir. Pub. Relations & Special Services, 1953-55, Dir., Evening Col., California Col. A. & Crafts, Oakland, Cal., 1955- .

SCHOOLEY, ELMER WAYNE—*Lithographer, P., E.*

Montezuma, N.M.

B. Lawrence, Kans., Feb. 20, 1916. *Studied*: Univ. Colorado, B.F.A.; Univ. Iowa, M.A. *Awards*: prizes, BM; Wichita AA; DMFA; SAGA; Mus. New Mexico. *Exhibited*: Denver A. Mus.; Kansas City AI; SAM; Los A. Mus. A.; New Britain Mus. A.; LC; Carnegie Inst.; Rochester Mem. A. Gal. *Work*: Mus. New Mexico; DMFA; Wichita AA; BM; LC; Roswell (N.M.) Mus.; MMA. *Position*: Hd. Dept. A. & Crafts, New Mexico Highlands Univ., Las Vegas, N.M.

SCHOOLEY, GERTRUDE ROGERS. See *DuJardin, Gussie*

SCHOOLFIELD, GARCIE M.—*Painter, C., Ser.*

120 Gatewood Dr., San Antonio 9, Tex.

B. Knox, Ind., Apr. 15, 1915. *Studied*: Ringling Sch. A.; AIC, B.A.E.; Univ. Chicago; Texas State Col. for Women. *Member*: Texas FA Assn.; Texas WC Soc.; San Antonio A. Lg.; Contemp. Weavers of Texas; San Antonio Craft Gld. *Exhibited*: Intl. Textile Exh., 1947, 1948; Texas State Ceramic & Textile exh., 1952; Texas Crafts, 1955; San Antonio A. Exh., 1953-1955; Texas FA Assn., 1953-1955; Contemp. Weavers, 1954, 1955.*

SCHOONOVER, MRS. MARGARET. See *Lefranc, Margaret*

SCHOR, RHEA IRESS—*Painter, S., W.*

6810-52 Drive, Maspeth 78, N.Y.

B. New York, N.Y., Oct. 5, 1906. *Studied*: Samuel Brecher Sch. A.; Lonzar Sch. Sculpture; Sculpture Center. *Member*: NAWA; Cosmopolitan A.; Nat. Lg. Am. Pen Women; Sculpture Center; ASL. *Awards*: prizes, Queens FA Soc., 1950, 1952; Huntington Hartford F., 1958.

Work: Columbia Univ.; Barnard Col.; Dayton AI. *Exhibited*: NAWA, 1946, 1947, 1951, 1953, 1954; Tomorrows Masterpieces Exh., 1944; MMA, 1938; AEA, 1948; Riverside Mus., 1952-1954; Contemp. A. Gal.; Barzansky Gal., 1956 (one-man), and others. Author: "To Understand," 1948; "Revelations to the Young Girl," 1954; "A String of Pearls," 1956.

SCHRACK, JOSEPH EARL—*Painter, T., Des., I., L.*
   148 West Juniper St., San Diego 1, Cal.

B. Pottstown, Pa., Feb. 26, 1890. *Studied*: AIC; ASL; John Herron AI, and with Hans Hofmann, George Inness, Jr. *Member*: Audubon A.; Men's AI, San Diego; La Jolla A. Center; La Jolla AA; San Diego FA Soc. *Awards*: prizes, AIC, 1913; Carlsbad AA, 1954. *Work*: murals, First Federal Savings Bank, San Diego; First Nat. Bank, El Cajon, Cal.; La Jolla A. Center; San Diego FA Soc.; Men's AI; Carlsbad AA. *Exhibited*: All. A. Am.; Audubon A., and others. Lectures: History and Theory of Classical and Modern Art. *Position*: Instr., San Diego FA Gal. On leave of absence for 2-year tour and art study in Europe, North Africa, 1956-58.

SCHRADER, GUSTAVE—*Painter*
   Woodstock, N.Y.

B. Elmhurst, L.I., N.Y., May 15, 1900. *Studied*: Woodstock Sch. Painting. *Member*: Woodstock AA. *Exhibited*: VMFA; CGA; Albany Inst. Hist. & A.; Woodstock AA; Key West A. & Hist. Soc.; Key West A. Group; Fla. Southern College.

SCHRAG, KARL—*Painter, Gr., T., L., I.*
   127 East 95th St., New York 28, N.Y.

B. Karlsruhe, Germany, Dec. 7, 1912. *Studied*: Ecole des Beaux-Arts, Grande Chaumiere, Paris, France; ASL, with Lucien Simon, Harry Sternberg, Stanley W. Hayter. *Member*: ASL; SAGA; Atelier 17; AEA. *Awards*: prizes, SAGA, 1954; Phila. Pr. Cl., 1954; Am. Color Pr. Soc., 1957. *Work*: LC; NGA; U.S. Nat. Mus.; MModA; BM; PMA; N.Y. Pub. Lib.; CMA; MMA; Wadsworth Atheneum; Joslyn Mem. Mus.; Los A. Mus. A.; Dartmouth Col.; Providence Mus. A. *Exhibited*: WFNY 1939; N.Y. Pub. Lib., 1945; WMAA, 1943, 1955-1957; SFMA, 1941-1945, 1946; Soc. Indp. A., 1940-1944; LC, 1944, 1945, 1947, 1948, 1958; Carnegie Inst., 1944-1947; "50 American Prints," "Modern Art in America," traveling exhs.; Contemp. A., 1940-1943; Willard Gal., 1945; Phila. A. All., 1942-1944; Phila. Pr. Cl., 1942, 1946-1958; Leicester Gal., London, 1947; Petit Palais, Paris, 1949; Am. Embassy, Paris, 1951; Musée Nat. d'Art Moderne, Paris, 1954; SAGA, 1953-1955; BM, 1955, 1956, 1958; Lugano, Switzerland, 1952; AIC, 1948; Instituto de Bellas Arts, Mexico, 1958; one-man: U.S. Nat. Mus., 1945; Phila. A. All., 1952; Wagner Col., 1955; Univ. Alabama, 1949; Univ. Maine, 1952; Kraushaar Gal., 1947, 1950, 1952, 1954, 1956, 1959, and in Karlsruhe, Baden-Baden, Germany, 1958. I., "The Suicide Club," 1941, Limited Edition. *Position*: Instr., Gr. A., CUASch., New York, N.Y., 1954-58; L., A. Dept., Columbia Univ., 1958.

SCHRECKENGOST, DON—*Sculptor, P., C., E.*
   2617 St. Clair Ave., East Liverpool, Ohio

B. Sebring, Ohio, Sept. 23, 1911. *Studied*: Cleveland Sch. A., and in Stockholm, Sweden; Mexico. *Member*: F., Am. Ceramic Soc.; U.S. Potters Assn.; Ceramic Edu. Council (Mem. Com.); Inter-Soc. Color Council. *Awards*: prizes, Albright A. Gal., 1938; Rochester Mem. A. Gal., 1940; SAGA, 1941; Syracuse Mus. FA, 1941, 1954; bronze med., Alfred Univ., 1946. *Work*: in museums and private colls. *Exhibited*: nationally and internationally. *Position*: Modeler, Gem Clay Forming Co., Sebring, Ohio, 1934-35; A. Dir., Salem China Co., Salem, Ohio, 1934-35; Prof. Indst. Ceramic Des., N.Y. Col. Ceramics, Alfred Univ., 1935-45; Adult classes, St. Bonaventure Col., 1943-44; A. Dir., Dubois Press, Rochester, N.Y., 1942-43; Des. Consultant, Tuvache Perfume Co., N.Y., 1942-45; Des., S., Albert Victor Bleininger medal; Planned and designed United Potters Assn. Exh., Nat. Home Furnishings Show, N.Y., 1953.*

SCHRECKENGOST, VIKTOR—*Sculptor, Des., C., P., E.*
   2265 Stillman Rd., Cleveland Heights 18, Ohio

B. Sebring, Ohio, June 26, 1906. *Studied*: Cleveland Sch. A.;Kunstgewerbe Schule, Vienna, and with Michael Pow-

olny. *Member*: Cleveland Soc. A.; Am. Ceramic Soc.; F., Intl. Inst. A. & Lets.; Arch. Lg.; U.S. Potters Assn.; IDI; AWS; Am. Soc. Indst. Des.; Ohio WC Soc. *Awards*: prizes, CMA, 1931, 1932, 1934, 1936-1943, 1946-1955; Award of Merit, Phila., 1940; Syracuse Mus. FA, 1938, 1947, 1948, 1950, 1951, 1954; IBM, 1954; AWS, 1955; Butler AI, 1949; medal, Alfred Univ., 1939; gold medal, AIA, 1958. *Work*: MMA; WMAA; Syracuse Mus. FA; Albright A. Gal.; CMA; IBM; Brooks Mem. A. Gal.; Butler AI; Dartmouth Col.; Slater Mem. Mus.; Cleveland Zoo; Lakewood (Ohio) H.S.; Cleveland Airport; Texas Tech. Col.; Walker A. Center. *Exhibited*: nationally in leading museum and galleries, 1931-1952; many traveling exhibitions in U.S. and abroad. *Position*: Hd., Dept. Indst. Des., Cleveland Inst. A., Cleveland, Ohio; A. Dir. & Des., Murray Ohio Mfg. Co., Nashville, Tenn.; Salem (Ohio) China Co.; Consultant, Indst. Des., Harris-Intertype Corp., Cleveland, Dayton, Westerly, R.I.; Holophane Co., Newark, Ohio.

SCHREIBER, GEORGES—*Painter, Lith., Des.*
   1 Union Square; h. 8 West 13th St., New York 11, N.Y.

B. Brussels, Belgium, Apr. 25, 1904. *Studied*: Acad. FA, Berlin and Dusseldorf, Germany. *Awards*: prizes, AIC, 1932; MModA, 1939; medal, A. Dir. Cl., 1943. *Work*: MIT; Philbrook A. Center; Maryland Inst.; Lehigh Univ.; Rutgers Univ.; WMA; Univ. Maryland; Conn. State T. Col.; Syracuse Mus. FA; Smith Col.; Mint Mus. A.; Springfield (Mass.) Mus. A.; MMA; BM; WMAA; Swope A. Gal.; Davenport Mun. A. Gal.; Mus. City of N.Y.; White House Lib., Wash., D.C.; Toledo Mus. A.; LC; Encyclopaedia Britannica; U.S. Navy Dept. *Exhibited*: nationally in leading museums and galleries. Author, I., Ed., "Portraits and Self Portraits," 1936; Author, I., "Bombino the Clown," 1947; I., "Light of Tern Rock," 1952; "Professor Bull's Umbrella," 1954; "Ride on the Wind," 1956; "That Jud!," 1957; "Bombino's Return" (Author, I.), 1959.

SCHREIBER, ISABEL—*Painter*
   415 North 9th St., Atchison, Kan.

B. Atchison, Kan., Aug. 17, 1902. *Studied*: Kansas Univ., B.P. *Member*: Am. Assn. Univ. Women; Kansas State Fed. A.; Prairie WC Painters. *Work*: Kansas State Col.; mural backgrounds for bird exhibits in Dyche Mus., Lawrence, Kan.; murals, Atchison Pub. Sch. *Exhibited*: PAFA; Kansas City AI; Young Gal., Chicago.

SCHROEDER, ERIC—*Museum Curator, P.*
   9 Follen St., Cambridge 38, Mass.

B. Sale, Cheshire, England, Nov. 20, 1904. *Studied*: Corpus Christi Col., Oxford Univ., B.A.; Harvard Univ. Graduate Sch. *Work*: BMFA; FMA. *Exhibited*: Margaret Brown Gal., Boston, 1949; Today's A. Gal., Boston, 1945. Author: "Iranian Book Painting," 1940; "Persian Miniatures in the Fogg Museum," 1942; "Muhammad's People," 1955; Co-Author: "Iranian & Islamic Art," 1941. Contributor to: Collier's Encyclopaedia; Book of Knowledge; Survey of Persian Art, Encyclopaedia of the Arts, Ars Islamica, Parnassus, & other art publications. *Position*: Keeper of Islamic Art, FMA, Harvard Univ., Cambridge, Mass., 1938- .

SCHROM, ARCHIE MARK—*Designer, Gr.*
   461 East Ohio St., Chicago 11, Ill.; h. 1315 Greenwood St., Wilmette, Ill.

B. Santa Cruz, Cal., Mar. 27, 1911. *Studied*: AIC. *Member*: Chicago Assn. Commerce & Indst.; Soc. Photographic Illus.; Assn. Color Research; Gld. Freelance A.; A. Dir. Cl., Chicago; Soc. Typographic A. *Awards*: prizes, Soc. Typographic A., 1946, 1952, 1954, 1957 (2); medal, A. Dir. Cl., Chicago, 1942; Package Des. Council, 1953; Nat. Offset-Litho. Comp., 1953; Certif. Merit, Curtis Paper Co., 1958. *Exhibited*: AIC.

SCHROYER, ROBERT McCLELLAND—*Designer, I., T.*
   62 East 90th St., New York 28, N.Y .

B. Oakland, Cal., Aug. 13, 1907. *Studied*: Carnegie Inst.; Parsons Sch. Des., and in Europe. *Member*: SI; AID; Parsons Sch. Des. Alumni Assn. *Awards*: scholarship (3) Parsons Sch. Des.; scholarship, House & Garden; Upholstery Leather Group Des. Comp.; Nat. Award for Adv. A. for Burdine's, Miami, Fla. Contributor illus. to

House & Garden, House Beautiful, Good Housekeeping, Woman's Home Companion, Interior Design, and other national magazines. *Position*: Des., Delineator Magazine, 1931-35 and subsequently; Freelance Des.-Illus., for advertising and publications specializing in interior architecture, design and decoration; Asst. Instr., Stage Des., Parsons Sch. Des.; Instr., Interior Arch. & Dec., Parsons Schs., France & Italy.

SCHUCKER, CHARLES—*Painter, T.*
33 Middagh St., Brooklyn 1, N.Y .

B. Gap, Pa., Jan. 9, 1914. *Studied*: Maryland Inst. *Member*: Yaddo Fnd. *Awards*: Walters traveling scholarship, Maryland Inst., 1936; Guggenheim F., 1953. *Work*: New Britain Mus.; BM; WMAA; Am. Acad. A. & Let.; mural, Balt. City Col., Balt., Md. *Exhibited*: nationally. One-man: Macbeth Gal., 1946, 1949, 1953; Passedoit Gal., 1955, 1958. *Position*: Instr., PIASch., Brooklyn, N.Y., 1956- .

SCHUENEMANN, MARY B.—*Painter, T.*
6900 North 19th St., Philadelphia 26, Pa.

B. Philadelphia, Pa., Sept. 5, 1898. *Studied*: Univ. Pennsylvania, B.S. in Edu.; PMSchIA; Tyler Sch. A.; with John Lear; & with Earl Horter, Ernest Thurn. *Member*: A. All., Plastic Cl., WC Cl., Woodmere Gal., all of Phila.; Phila. A. T. Assn.; Eastern AA. *Awards*: med., Plastic Cl., 1945, 1946, 1952, 1953, prize, 1954, 1955; A. T. Assn., 1950 (Placque). *Work*: Phila. Pub. Sch. *Exhibited*: PAFA, 1942-1944; Phila. A. All., 1940, 1943, 1957 (all one-man exhs.); PMA. *Position*: A. T., Pub. Sch., Philadelphia, Pa.

SCHULEIN, JULIUS W.—*Painter, T.*
41 West 83rd St., New York 24, N.Y.

B. Munich, Germany, May 28, 1881. *Studied*: in Munich, Germany and Paris, France. *Member*: Munich Acad. FA (Hon.). *Exhibited*: Salon d'Automne, Salon des Tuileries, Paris; WMAA; Carnegie Inst.; Univ. Illinois; one-man: Knoedler Gal.; Delius Gal.; Schoneman Gal., 1955.

SCHULEIN, MRS. JULIUS W. See Carvallo, Suzanne

SCHULLER, GRETE—*Sculptor*
Sculpture Center, 167 East 69th St.; h. 116 East 83rd St., New York 28, N.Y.

B. Vienna, Austria. *Studied*: ASL, and with William Zorach. *Member*: NAWA; Arch. Lg. *Awards*: prizes, NAWA. *Exhibited*: NAWA; NAD; NSS; Sculpture Center, 1952-1955, 1958 (one-man); Des Moines A. Center; Audubon A.; PAFA, 1952-1954; Am. Acad. A. & Let., 1955.

SCHULTE, ANTOINETTE—*Painter*
146 BD Montparnasse, Paris XIV, France; h. 26 East 63rd St., New York 21, N.Y.

B. New York, N.Y. *Studied*: ASL, with George Bridgman, Homer Boss; Fontainebleau Sch. FA, Paris; and with Lopez Mezquita. *Member*: Audubon A. *Awards*: prize, Salons of Am., 1931. *Work*: Benjamin West Mus.; BM; CGA; CM; Newark Mus.; Montclair A. Mus.; MMA; French Govt. Coll.; Aix-en-Provence, France. *Exhibited*: Salon des Tuileries, Salon d'Automne, Paris; PAFA; CGA; Toronto, Canada; WMAA; Audubon A.; NAD; one-man: Brussels, Belgium, 1955; Galerie Andre Weil, Paris, 1956; Galerie Charpentier, Paris, 1950. Exhibited extensively in U.S.*

SCHULTHEISS, CARL MAX—*Etcher, Eng., I., P.*
84-44 Beverly Rd., Kew Gardens 15, N.Y.

B. Nuremberg, Germany, Aug. 4, 1885. *Studied*: in Germany. *Member*: NA; SAGA (Hon. Pres.); Audubon A. *Awards*: prizes, Talcott prize, 1940; Lib. Cong., 1943, 1944, 1945; John Taylor Arms prize, 1943, 1944; Wichita, Kan., 1946; Laguna Beach AA, 1946; NAD, 1947, 1952, 1955; SAGA, 1957; Nat. Inst. A. & Let. grant, 1953; medals, Phila., 1947; Audubon A., 1946, 1952. *Work*: Lib. Cong.; N.Y. Pub. Lib. *Exhibited*: Carnegie Inst., 1914, 1944, 1945; AIC, 1938; NAD, 1940-1946; CGA, 1946 (one-man); SAGA, annually.

SCHULTZ, HAROLD A.,—*Painter, L., E.*
118 Architecture Bldg., University of Illinois; h. 2017 Burlison Dr., Urbana, Ill.

B. Grafton, Wis., Jan 6, 1907. *Studied*: Layton Sch. A.; Northwestern Univ., B.S., M.A. *Member*: AAUP; Illinois A. Edu. Assn.; Nat. A. Edu. Assn.; Western AA.; Intl. Soc. for Edu. Through Art (UNESCO). *Exhibited*: AIC, 1928-1942; Chicago SA, 1931-1942; BM, 1931; Ferargil Gal., 1940. Lectures: American Art Today. Author: (with J. Harlan Shores) "Art in the Elementary School," 1948. *Position*: Hd. A. Dept., Francis W. Parker Sch., Chicago, 1932-40; Prof., A. Edu., Univ. Illinois, Urbana, Ill., 1940- .

SCHULZ, CHARLES MONROE—*Cartoonist*
2162 Coffee Lane, Sebastopol, Cal.

B. Minneapolis, Minn., Nov. 26, 1922. *Awards*: Outstanding Cartoonist of the Year, Nat Cartoonists Soc., 1955; Outstanding Humorist of the Year, Yale Univ., 1957. Author, I., "Peanuts," 1953; "More Peanuts," 1954; "Good Grief, More Peanuts," 1955; "Good Ol' Charlie Brown," 1957; "Snoopy," 1958; "The Weekend Peanuts," 1959. Illus., "Kids Say the Darndest Things" (Art Linkletter). Cartoons reproduced in 400 newspapers, U.S. and abroad.

SCHULZE, FRANZ—*Painter, Des., E., Cr.*
Department of Art, Lake Forest College; h. #1 College Campus, Lake Forest, Ill.

B. Uniontown, Pa., Jan. 30, 1927. *Studied*: Northwestern Univ.; Univ. Chicago, Ph.B.; AIC, B.F.A., M.F.A.; Akademie der bildenden Kunste, Munich, Germany, grad. research. *Member*: AAUP; CAA. *Work*: AIC. *Exhibited*: AIC; BM; CM; Univ. Minnesota; Univ. Illinois; Northwestern Univ.; Purdue Univ.; Lake Forest Col.; Allan Frumkin Gal., Chicago; Galerie 17, Munich. One-man: Galerie 17, Munich. *Positions*: Instr., Dept. A., Purdue Univ., 1950-52; Lecturer in Humanities, Univ. Chicago, 1952-53; Chm. Dept. A., 1952- , A.-in-Res., 1958- , Lake Forest College; Chicago Critic, Art News, 1958- .

SCHUS, ADOLPH—*Cartoonist*
Penfield Ave., Harmon, N.Y.

B. New York, N.Y., June 15, 1908. *Studied*: N.Y. Sch. F. & App. A. *Member*: Am. Soc. Magazine Cart. Contributor to: various magazines.*

SCHUSTER, CARL—*Writer*
R.F.D. Box 416, Woodstock, N.Y.

B. Milwaukee, Wis., Nov. 9, 1904. *Studied*: Harvard Col., A.B.; Harvard Univ., A.M.; Univ. Vienna, Ph.D. *Awards*: Harvard-Yenching F., 1929-1932; Guggenheim F., 1937-1939; Fulbright F., 1950-1951; Bollingen F., 1952-1953. Contributor of articles on design-traditions among primitive peoples to Anthropos, Far Eastern Quarterly, Communications of the Royal Tropical Institute (Amsterdam), Mankind (Sydney, Australia), Sudan Notes and Records (Khartum), Papers of 29th International Congress of Americanists, Anales del Museo de Historia Natural de Montevideo, Revista do Museu Paulista, Paul Rivet Memorial Volume, Artibus Asiae, and other publications.

SCHUTZ, ANTON—*Etcher, Editor*
95 East Putnam Ave., Greenwich, Conn.; h. 4 Heathcote Rd., Scarsdale, N.Y.

B. Berndorf, Germany, Apr. 19, 1894. *Studied*: Univ. Munich, M.E.; Royal Acad. A., Munich; ASL. *Member*: SAGA; Chicago Soc. Et.; AFA. *Exhibited*: in the U.S. and abroad. Author: "New York in Etchings," 1939 (book of 24 etchings); "Fine Art Reproductions of Old and Modern Masters," 1951. Publ., Co-Editor, UNESCO World Art Series: India, Egypt, Australia, 1954; Yugoslavia, Norway, 1955; Italy, Iran, Spain, Ceylon, Japan, 1956; U.S.S.R., Czechoslovakia, 1957; Turkey, Greece, Bulgaria, Israel, 1958.

SCHWABACHER, ETHEL K.—*Painter, W.*
1192 Park Ave., New York 28, N.Y.

B. New York, N.Y., May 20, 1903. *Studied*: in Europe and with Max Weber, Arshile Gorky. *Work*: WMAA; Rockefeller Inst. *Exhibited*: PAFA, 1953; CGA, 1959; WMAA touring exh., 1958-59; PC; Los A. Mus. A.;

SFMA; WAC; CAM; Riverside Mus.; WMAA annuals, 1948-1958; one-man: Passedoit Gal., 1935, 1947; Betty Parsons Gal., 1953, 1956, 1957. Author: "Arshile Gorky," 1957; Foreword to catalogue Arshile Gorky Memorial Show, WMAA, 1951.

SCHWACHA, GEORGE—*Painter, T., L.*
R.F.D. 1, Hanover, N.J.; also, 273 Glenwood Ave., Bloomfield, N.J.

B. Newark, N.J., Oct. 2, 1908. *Studied*: with Arthur W. Woelfle, John Grabach. *Member*: AWCS; Audubon A. (Pres., 1958-59); Phila. WC Cl. *Awards*: prizes, Mun. A. Exh., Irvington, N.J., 1936; New Jersey Gal., 1937, 1939, 1940, 1942; A. Center of the Oranges, 1937; AAPL, 1939; New Haven Paint & Clay Cl., 1939, 1944; Asbury Park Soc. FA, 1940, 1942; Newark AC, 1942; Mint Mus. A., 1943, 1946; Springfield A. Lg., 1943; AWCS, 1944; Denver A. Mus., 1944; Alabama WC Soc., 1944, 1951, medal, 1954, prize, 1955; New Jersey P.&S. Soc., 1945; All. A. Am., 1945; Meriden A. & Crafts, 1952; Fla. Southern Col., 1952; Wash. WC Cl., 1946, 1955; Audubon A., 1953; Conn. Acad. FA, 1946; med., State A. Exh., Montclair, N.J., 1937; gold medal, Nat. Soc. Painters in Casein, 1956. *Work*: Albany Inst. Hist. & A.; Mint Mus. A.; AWCS; Elisabet Ney Mus.; Laguna Beach, Cal.; New Haven Paint & Clay Cl.; Montgomery Mus. FA; Montclair A. Mus.; Fla. Southern Col.; Newark Mus.; Women's Cl., Perth Amboy, Bloomfield, N.J.; Butler AI; Delgado Mus. A. *Exhibited*: CM; CGA; Currier Gal. A.; Denver A. Mus.; Elgin Acad. A.; Delgado Mus. A.; Mint Mus. A.; NAD; NAC; Newark Mus.; New Jersey State Mus., Trenton; PAFA; VMFA; AIC; etc.

SCHWANKOVSKY, FREDERICK JOHN—
Painter, T., W., L.
571 Graceland Drive, Laguna Beach, Cal.; s. Meadow Lakes via Auberry, Cal.

B. Detroit, Mich., Jan. 21, 1885. *Studied*: PAFA; ASL. *Member*: Laguna Beach AA (life); Southwest AA (Hon. Pres.); Central Cal. AA; Soc. Western A. (Founding Past-Pres.). *Awards*: prizes, Soc. Western A., 1955 (2). *Work*: Mission Beach (Cal.) A. Gal.; Manual Arts H.S., Los A.

SCHWARM, WESLEY, A.—*Painter*
17 North Chatsworth Ave., Larchmont, N.Y.

B. Lafayette, Ind. *Studied*: PIASch.; & with Robert Henri. *Work*: Jefferson, Ford, & Washington Sch., Lafayette, Ind. *Exhibited*: Indiana A.; MacDowell Cl.; N.Y. Mun. Exh., 1938, 1939; Town Hall Cl., N.Y.; Westchester A.

SCHWARTZ, ALVIN HOWARD—*Painter, Des.*
Westinghouse Electronics Division, Baltimore 3, Md.; h. 623 Greenwood Rd., Pikesville 8, Md.

B. Baltimore, Md., Oct. 13, 1916. *Studied*: NAD; Maryland Inst.; N.Y. Univ. *Member*: Maryland A. Un.; Maryland WC Cl. *Awards*: prizes, Maryland A. Un., 1948-1950; BMA, 1952. *Work*: BMA; City of Balt., Sch. Bd. Coll.; Sinai Hospital, Balt.; Jewish Edu. All., Balt.; murals, adv. des., Lord Baltimore Hotel; American Oil Co., and numerous restaurants. *Position*: Des., Illus., Glen L. Martin Co., 1955-1958; Presentation Des. & A., Westinghouse Electric Corp., Electronics Div., Baltimore, Md., 1958- .

SCHWARTZ, MANFRED—*Painter, T., L.*
22 East 8th St., New York 3, N.Y.

B. Lodz, Poland, Nov. 11, 1909. *Studied*: ASL; NAD. *Member*: Fed. Mod. P. & S. *Work*: Univ. Minnesota; N.Y. Pub. Lib.; MMA; BM; WMAA; Newark Mus.; PMA. *Exhibited*: 1942-1955: Carnegie Inst.; WMAA; MMA; VMFA; PAFA; AIC; BM; Wildenstein Gal.; Durand-Ruel Gal.; Butler AI; BMA; Cal. PLH; Inst. Contemp. A., Boston; Nelson Gal. A.; Walker A. Center; Portland (Ore.) Mus. A.; CAM; Denver A. Mus.; CM; High Mus. A.; Norton Gal. A.; Delgado Mus. A.; one-man: FA Assoc., 1953, 1955.*

SCHWARTZ, MARJORIE WATSON (Mrs. Merrill)—
Painter, C., T.
1260 Vinton Ave., Memphis 4, Tenn.

B. Trenton, Tenn., Jan. 4, 1905. *Studied*: State T. Col., Memphis, Tenn.; Newcomb Col., Tulane Univ., B.Des.

Member: Memphis Gld. Handloom Weavers; AAPL. *Exhibited*: San Diego FA Soc., 1943; New Haven Paint & Clay Cl., 1946; Mississippi AA, 1946; Va.-Intermont Exh., 1946; Brooks Mem. A. Gal. (one-man); Gld. Handloom Weavers, 1954, 1955; traveling exh., 1954.*

SCHWARTZ, MARVIN DAVID—*Museum Curator*
Brooklyn Museum, Eastern Parkway, Brooklyn 38, N.Y.

B. New York, N.Y., Feb. 15, 1926. *Studied*: City Col., N.Y., B.S.; N.Y. Univ. Inst. FA; Univ. Delaware, M.A. *Member*: CAA; Soc. Arch. Hist.; Soc. for Preservation of New England Antiquities. *Awards*: Belgian-American Edu. Fnd., 1949; Winterthur Mus. Fellowship, 1952-54. Contributor articles on American furniture to Encyclopedia of American Antiques, 1958. Also articles to Apollo Magazine; New York News & Views. Lectures: American Decorative Arts and Architecture (1640-1900) to museums, historical societies, women's clubs, etc. Arranged exhibition "Country Style," American furniture, ceramics, silver, pewter, 1955. *Positions*: Instr., Art Appreciation, City Col., N.Y. (evening sessions); Junior Cur., Detroit Inst. A., 1950-51; Cur., American Decorative Arts, Brooklyn Museum, Brooklyn, N.Y., at present.

SCHWARTZ, WILLIAM SAMUEL—*Painter, Lith.*
102 East Hubbard St., Chicago, Ill.

B. Smorgon, Russia, Feb. 23, 1896. *Studied*: Vilna A. Sch., Russia; AIC. *Awards*: prizes, Detroit, Mich., 1925, 1926; AIC, 1927, 1928, 1930, 1945, and later; Oklahoma A. Center, 1939, 1942; Corpus Christi, Tex., 1945; Monticello Col., Godfrey, Ill., 1939. *Work*: AIC; Encyclopaedia Britannica; Detroit Inst. A.; LC; U.S. Dept. Labor; Phila. A. All.; Dallas Mus. FA; Madison AA; Tel-Aviv Mus., Israel; Biro-Bidjan Mus., Russia; Oshkosh Mus. A.; Montclair A. Mus.; Standard Oil Co.; SFMA; PAFA; Joslyn A. Mus.; Santa Barbara Mus. A.; Henry Gal., Seattle; Denver A. Mus.; Ain-Harod Mus.; Israel; Univs., Illinois, Nebraska, Wyoming, Minnesota, Missouri, Chicago; Am. People's Encyclopaedia; State T. Col., DeKalb; State Normal Univ., Carbondale; Monticello Col.; Beloit Col.; Bradley Univ.; libraries of Davenport, Iowa, Glencoe, Ill., Cincinnati, Ohio, Chicago, Ill.; Musée d'Art Juif, Paris; Des Moines A. Center; Little Gallery, Cedar Rapids; Chicago Pub. Schs. Coll.; Chicago Normal College. *Exhibited*: nationally and internationally, since 1918.

SCHWARTZ, FELIX CONRAD—*Painter, E., W., L.*
Department of Fine Arts, Wesleyan College, Macon, Ga.; (studio) 1009 Gray St., Stillwater, Okla.

B. New York, N. Y., Apr. 13, 1906. *Studied*: Corcoran Sch. A.; George Washington Univ., B.A., M.A.; Columbia Univ., Ph.D.; & in Europe. *Member*: CAA; Western A.; Soc. Wash. A.; Oklahoma AA; Enid (Okla.) A. Lg.; NAEA; AAUP; Southeastern AA; Midwestern AA; Eastern AA. *Awards*: Teaching F., George Washington Univ., 1926-1927; Research F., Editorship, Columbia Univ., 1939-1941. *Work*: George Washington Univ. *Exhibited*: CGA, 1927-1935; PAFA, 1924-1934; Carnegie Inst., 1930-1934; Walker A. Center, 1934-1939; Univ. Minnesota; Univ. Georgia; Phillips Univ.; Tricker Gal., N.Y., 1939 (one-man); Soc. Wash. A.; SSAL; Minnesota A.; Virginia A.; Enid A. Lg.; Okla. AA; etc. Contributor to: educational & art magazines. *Position*: Hd. A. Dept., Mary Washington Col., 1932-34; Prof. A., Dir. Sch. A., Phillips Univ., Enid, Okla., 1944-48; Visiting Prof. A., Northwestern, Louisiana, 1959- ; Prof. & Chm., Dept. Fine Arts, Wesleyan College, Macon, Georgia, 1957- .

SCHWARTZ, HEINRICH—*Museum Curator, W., L.*
Wesleyan University, Davison Art Center, Middletown, Conn.

B. Prague, Czechoslovakia, Nov. 9, 1894. *Studied*: Univ. Vienna, Ph.D.; Wesleyan Univ., M.A. *Member*: CAA; AFA. Author: "Amicis," Yearbook of the Austrian State Gallery, 1927; "D. O. Hill, Master of Photography," 1931; "Carl Schindler," monograph (in cooperation with F. M. Haberditzl), 1931; "Salzburg und das Salzkammergut," 1936, 1958 (3rd ed.), and other books. Contributor of scientific articles to European and American magazines. Lectures on Painting and Graphic Arts. *Positions*: Asst., Albertina, Vienna, 1921-23; Cur., Austrian State Gallery, Vienna, 1923-38; Research Asst., Albright A. Gal., 1941-42; Cur., Paintings, Drawings & Prints, Mus. A., Rhode Island Sch. Des., Providence, R.I., 1943-53; Visiting Prof.

& Cur. of Collections, Davison Art Center, Wesleyan Univ., Middletown, Conn., 1954-1956; Prof., 1956- ; Visiting L., Wellesley Col., 1952; Mt. Holyoke, 1954, Yale Univ., 1958.

SCHWARZ, MYRTLE COOPER—Educator, C., W.
Oklahoma State University; h. 1009 Gray St., Stillwater, Okla.

B. Vanzant, Ky., Dec. 10, 1900. *Studied*: Western Kentucky State Col., A.B.; Univ. Kentucky; Univ. Virginia; Col. of William & Mary; Columbia Univ., M.A., Ed. D. *Member*: NEA; Oklahoma Edu. Assn.; NAEA; Western A. Edu. Assn.; Nat. Assn. of Curriculum Development; Nat. Assn. of Student Teaching; Assn. of Childhood Edu. International. *Exhibited*: Oklahoma AA, 1954-1957; Enid A. Lg., 1944-1947; Philbrook A. Center, 1944-1957; VMFA, 1931-1943. Contributor to Virginia Journal of Education; Kentucky Magazine. *Position*: Prof. A., Dir. A. Edu., Oklahoma State Univ., Stillwater, Okla., at present.

SCHWARZ, WILLIAM TEFFT—Painter, I.
Fairfield Farm, Arlington, Vt.

B. Syracuse, N.Y., July 27, 1888. *Studied*: Syracuse Univ.; & abroad. *Work*: Onondaga County Savings Bank, Syracuse, N.Y.; Fulton Nat. Bank, Lancaster, Pa.; Conastoga Inn, Bryn Mawr, Pa.; Shriner's Hospital, Phila., Pa.; State House, Montpelier, Vt.; Shriner's Hospital, Phila., Pa.; hotels in Atlantic City, N.J.; Phila., Pa.; Utica, N.Y.; Syracuse, N.Y.; WFNY 1939; Masonic Temple, Phila., Pa., and Arlington, Vt. I., Saturday Evening Post.

SCHWARZBURG, NATHANIEL—Painter, L., T.
4121—42nd St., Long Island City 4, N.Y.

B. New York, N.Y., Nov. 18, 1896. *Studied*: Col. City of N.Y.; ASL; & with George Bridgman, Sigurd Skou. *Member*: A.Lg.Am. *Exhibited*: Midtown Gal., 1934; Contemporary A., 1937; ACA Gal., 1941, 1946; Am. A. Cong., 1938, 1941; Vanderbilt Gal., 1944; Riverside Mus., 1945. Lectures: Modern Contemporary Art. *Position*: Instr., Bryant Adult Center.

SCHWEBEL, CELIA—Painter
Baldwin Rd., Yorktown Heights, N.Y.

B. New York, N.Y., Feb. 14, 1903. *Studied*: ASL, with Kenneth Hayes Miller. *Member*: ASL; AEA. *Exhibited*: CAA; Whitney Cl.; Marie Harriman Gal.; NAWA; Woodstock Gal.; Roerich Mus., 1956; Dartmouth Col., 1957; Bernheim Gal., Paris, France, 1958; one-man: Assoc. Am. A.; The Hotchkiss Sch., 1949; N.Y. State Mus., 1950; Hudson River Mus., 1951; Nat. Audubon Soc., 1951; Hunter Col., 1951; Roerich Mus., 1952, 1954; N.Y. Pub. Lib., 1952 (2 traveling exh.); Berkshire Mus., 1954; Caravan Gal., 1954.

SCHWEIG, AIMEE (Mrs. Martin)—Painter, T.
5314 Waterman Ave., St. Louis 12, Mo.

B. St. Louis, Mo. *Studied*: St. Louis Sch. FA, Washington Univ., and with Charles Hawthorne, Henry Hensche. *Member*: NAWA; St. Louis A. Gld.; AEA; A. Gld., 1942, 1946, 1955. *Work*: CAM. *Exhibited*: MMA, 1942; CAM; CGA; Denver A. Mus.; Kansas City AI; Springfield, Mo.; Springfield, Ill.; Mid-Am. A.; Renaissance Soc., Univ. Chicago; Colorado Springs FA Center; NAWA; St. Louis A. Gld. *Position*: Hd. Painting Dept., Upper School of Mary Inst., Clayton, Mo.

SCHWEITZER, GERTRUDE—Painter
Hillside, N.J.

B. New York, N.Y., 1911. *Studied*: PIASch.; NAD; Julian Acad., Paris, France. *Member*: NA; AWS; Wash. WC Cl.; New Jersey WC Soc. *Awards*: prizes, Phila. WC Cl., 1936; Norton Gal. A., 1946, 1947; Montclair A. Mus., 1947, 1952; Soc. Four Arts, 1947, 1948, 1950, 1951; Miami, Fla., 1951; AAPL, 1953, 1956, 1957; medals, AAPL, 1937; AWS, 1933. *Work*: BM; Canajoharie Gal. A.; Toledo Mus. A.; Atlanta AA; Norton Gal. A.; Hackley A. Gal.; Davenport Mun. A. Mus.; High Mus. A.; Witte Mem. Mus.; Mus. Mod. A., Paris, France; Mus. of Albi, France; Montclair A. Mus., and many private colls U.S., and abroad. *Exhibited*: nationally. One-man: U.S.; Milan, Rome, Venice, Italy; Paris, France.

SCHWIEDER, ARTHUR—Painter, T.
80 West 40th St., New York 18, N.Y.

B. Bolivar, Mo., Dec. 2, 1884. *Studied*: Drury Col., Springfield, Mo.; AIC. *Member*: AEA. *Exhibited*: Rehn Gal., 1955; Carnegie Inst., 1945, 1948; PAFA, 1945. *Position*: Dir., Instr., Schwieder Art Classes, New York, N.Y.

SCHWINN, BARBARA E. (Mrs. F. B. Jordan)—Painter
1 West 67th St., New York, N.Y.; also, Sterling Forest, Tuxedo, N.Y.

B. Jersey City, N.J., Oct. 20, 1907. *Studied*: Parsons Sch. Des.; Grand Central A. Sch.; ASL, with Frank DuMond, Luigi Lucioni, and others; Grand Chaumiere, Julian Acad., Paris, France. *Member*: SI. *Awards*: prizes, Gld. Hall, East Hampton, N.Y.; A. Dir. Cl. *Work*: Contributor to Ladies Homes Journal; Good Housekeeping; Colliers; Cosmopolitan; McCalls; Sat. Eve. Post, and French, British, Belgian, Danish, Swedish magazines and other publications. *Exhibited*: SI (2 one-man exhs.); Barry Stephens Gal. (one-man); NAD, 1955; Royal Acad., England, 1956. Lectures: Illustration; Portrait Painting. *Position*: Instr., Illus., Parsons Sch. Des., New York, N.Y. 1952-54; Advisory Council, Art Instruction, Inc., 1956-58.

SCOLAMIERO, PETER—Painter, S., I., T.
14 Central Ave., Newark 2, N.J.; h. 520 East 12th St., New York 9, N.Y.

B. Newark, N.J., Aug. 12, 1916. *Studied*: Newark Sch. F. & Indst. A., and with Louis Schanker. *Awards*: BM, 1950. *Work*: BM; Newark Pub. Lib.; murals, Camp Kilmer, N.J. *Exhibited*: AFA traveling exh., 1950; Exchange Exh. to Germany, 1952; Phila. Pr. Cl., 1950, 1951; BM, 1950-1952; Hacker Gal., 1951; Peridot Gal., 1950; Univ. Arkansas, 1950; Rabin & Krueger Gal., Newark, 1951 (one-man); Newark Mus., 1952; MMA, 1952; 3-man exh., Morris Plains, N.J., 1953.*

SCOTT, BENTON—Painter, T.
11305 Valley Spring Lane, North Hollywood, Cal.

B. Los Angeles, Cal., June 25, 1907. *Studied*: in Europe, and with Will Foster. *Member*: Cal. A. Cl.; P. & S. Cl., Los A.; Soc. Western A. *Awards*: prizes, Los A. Mus. A., 1943; Cal. A. Cl., 1946, 1950; Cal. State Fair, 1941; Pepsi-Cola, 1949; Soc. Western A., 1951, 1953. *Exhibited*: Los A. Mus. A., 1940, 1942-1947; Cal. State Fair, 1941, 1947, 1950; Cal. PLH, 1946; Santa Barbara Mus. A., 1944; Carnegie Inst., 1949; NAD, 1949, and in Paris, France, 1949, 1950; deYoung Mem. Mus., 1951, 1953, I., "With a Feather on My Nose." *Position*: Instr., FA, Los Angeles County AI, 1952-55.

SCOTT, BERTHA—Portrait Painter, W.
402 Shelby St., Frankfort, Ky.

B. Frankfort, Ky., Mar. 25, 1884. *Studied*: Wellesley Col., and with Anson Kent Cross, Andrene Kauffman, Gerrit A. Beneker. *Member*: Louisville AC; Louisville AA; SSAL. *Work*: many portraits privately owned. Work also, Kentucky Capitol and in historical shrines and pub. schs.

SCOTT, CATHERINE—Painter
744 South Cedar St., Ottawa, Kan.

B. Ottawa, Kan., Dec. 17, 1900. *Studied*: AIC. *Exhibited*: Kansas City AI; Joslyn Mem.

SCOTT, C(HARLOTTE)) T. (Mrs. Hugh B.)—Painter
1746 National Rd., Wheeling, W. Va.

B. East Liverpool, Ohio, Aug. 19, 1891. *Studied*: with Virginia B. Evans. *Member*: AAPL; Wheeling A. Cl.; Grand Central A. Gal. *Award*: prize, Oglebay Mansion Mus. A. Festival, 1950. *Work*: Oglebay Mansion Mus. *Exhibited*: WFNY 1939; Parkersburg FA Center, 1941; Clarkesburg, V. Va., 1943; Intermont Col., 1946, 1950; Oglebay Mus., 1946, 1948, 1950, 1951, 1956-1958; Terry AI, 1952; Ogunquit A. Center, 1952, 1954-1958.

SCOTT, CLYDE EUGENE—Painter
10425 Ilona Ave., West Los Angeles 64, Cal.

B. Bedford, Iowa, Jan. 24, 1884. *Studied*: Boston A. Sch.; & with Richard Andrews, Edward Kingsbury, E. Felton

Brown. *Member*: Cal. AC; P. & S. Cl., Los A., Cal.; A. of Southwest; Soc. Western A.; Laguna Beach AA; Santa Monica AA. *Awards*: prizes, Gardena (Cal.) H.S., 1939; Laguna Beach AA, 1939, 1956; Cal. AC, 1940; P. & S. Cl., 1942, 1945, 1948-1952; Ebell Salon, 1944, 1958; Santa Monica, 1957; Santa Paula, 1956; Greek Theatre, Los A.; Chaffey Jr. Col., 1944. *Work*: Haggin Mem. Gal., Stockton, Cal.; Chaffey Jr. Col.; Santa Monica Mun. Coll.; Clearwater H.S., Gardena H.S., Cal. *Exhibited*: Pan-Pacific Exp., 1915; GGE, 1939; Los A. Mus. A.; Haggin Mem. Gal.; Stanford Univ.; Pomona Col.; Santa Cruz A. Lg.; Oakland A. Gal.; San Gabriel A. Gal.; Laguna Beach AA; Cal. AC; Univ. So. California; deYoung Mem. Mus.; Santa Monica AA; A. of Southwest; Soc. Western A.; Westwood AA; P. & S. Cl., Los A.; Arizona State Fair; Cedar City, Utah; Los A. Pub. Lib.; Santa Monica Pub. Lib.; Palace Legion Honor; Glendale AA; San Juan Capistrano; Chaffey Jr. Col.; etc. *Position*: A., Special Visual Effects, 1933-1950, 20th Century Fox Film Corp., Beverly Hills, Cal. (Retired).

SCOTT, DAVID WINFIELD—*Painter*

Scripps College; h. 561 Baughman Drive, Claremont, Cal.

B. Fall River, Mass., July 10, 1916. *Studied*: Univ. California; Harvard Col., A.B.; ASL, with John Sloan and others; Claremont Grad. Sch., M.A., M.F.A. *Awards*: Tiffany Fnd. F., 1937, 1938; Del Amo Fnd. grant, study in Spain, 1951, 1957; Danforth Teacher F., 1955-56. *Exhibited*: AWS, 1938; Phila. WC Cl., 1939, 1941; Cal. WC Soc., 1940, 1945-1954; Los A. Mus. A., 1949, 1950; San Gabriel Valley, 1948, 1949; MMA, 1953. Lectures on Mexican and Spanish Art. *Positions*: Instr., A. Dept., Riverside Col., 1940-1942; L., Asst. Prof. A., Assoc. Prof. A., Scripps Col., and Claremont Graduate Sch., Claremont, Cal., 1946- ; Chm., A. Faculty, Scripps Col., 1956- .

SCOTT, DOROTHY CARNINE (Mrs. Ewing C.)—
Painter, Pr. M., L.

741 Livingston Ave., Syracuse 10, N.Y.

B. Hannaford, N.D., Jan. 30, 1903. *Studied*: Colorado Col., A.B.; Univ. Chicago, M.A.; Colorado Springs FA Center; Syracuse Univ., B.S., & with Robinson, Snell, Lockwood, Montague Charman, & others. *Member*: Syracuse Pr. M.; Assoc. A. Syracuse. *Awards*: prizes, Virginia A. Exh., 1939; Lynchburg Civic A. Lg., 1937; Print of the Year, Syracuse Pr. M., 1958. *Work*: Sweet Briar Col.; Beth-el Hospital, Colorado Springs, Colo.; VMFA; John Wyatt Jr. Sch., Lynchburg, Va. *Exhibited*: CGA, 1937; Wichita, Kan., 1939; Lynchburg AC, 1932-1946; Lynchburg Civic A. Lg., 1933-1940; VMFA, 1932-1945; Richmond Acad. A. & Sc., 1938-1940; Colorado Springs FA Center, 1934; Wash. WC Cl., 1934; SSAL, 1936-1939; Va.-Intermont Col., 1944-1946; Assoc. A. Syracuse, 1946-1955; Munson-Williams-Proctor Inst., 1949; Syracuse Mus. FA, 1954, 1955; one-man exh.: Sweet Briar Col., 1938, 1944; Lynchburg A. Gal., 1938; Rio de Janeiro, 1942; VMFA, 1944; etc.

SCOTT, GERALDINE ARMSTRONG—*Painter, L., T.*

Walnut Manor, Kokomo, Ind.

B. Elkhart, Ind., Oct. 1, 1900. *Studied*: Northwestern Univ.; N.Y. Sch. F. & App. A.; Parsons Sch. Des., N.Y. and Paris; Indiana Univ. Center, Kokomo. *Member*: Kokomo AA; Indiana A. Cl. *Work*: Butler Univ.; Carnegie Lib., Kokomo; Carnegie Lib., Tipton, Ind.; Indiana Fed. Cl.; Northwestern Univ. *Exhibited*: Hoosier Salon; Indiana A. Cl. *Position*: Lecturer in FA, Instr. A., Indiana Univ. Kokomo A. Center, 1945-1957.

SCOTT, HENRY (EDWARDS) JR.—
Painter, Des., L., E., Mus. Cur., W.

University of Kansas City, Fine Arts Department; w. 1625 East 76th St., Kansas City 5, Mo.; s. South Rd., Chilmark, Mass.

B. Cambridge, Mass., Aug. 22, 1900. *Studied*: Harvard Univ., B.A., M.A.; ASL; in Italy with Edward Forbes; in New York with George Bridgman. *Member*: CAA; Mid-Am. A. *Awards*: Sachs F., 1925, Bacon A. Scholarship, 1926-28, Harvard Univ.; prize, Rochester A., 1928. *Work*: FMA; Univ. Kansas Medical Center; Univ. Kansas City Law Sch.; Amherst Col.; Univ. Kansas City Playhouse. *Exhibited*: Rochester A., 1928; Pittsburgh A., 1930-1934; Amherst Col., 1941; Springfield, Mass., 1942;

Martha's Vineyard, 1947, 1952, 1955; Mid-Am. A., 1950-1954. Author: "Historical Outline of the Fine Arts," 1936. *Positions*: L., Asst. Div. FA, Harvard Univ. and Radcliffe Col., 1923-26; Instr. A., Asst. to Dir., Mem. A. Gal., Univ. Rochester, 1928-29; Asst. Prof. A., Univ. Pittsburgh, 1929-34; Assoc. Prof. A., & Cur., Amherst Col., 1935-43; Assoc. Prof., Chm. A. Dept., Univ. Kansas City, Kansas City, Mo., 1947- .

SCOTT, JAMES P(OWELL)—*Painter, E., Lith. I.*

College of Fine Arts, University of Arizona, Tucson, Ariz.

B. Lexington, Ky., Apr. 22, 1909. *Studied*: AIC; & with Anisfeld, Ritman, Chapin. *Member*: Tucson Palette & Brush Cl.; Am. Assn. Univ. Prof. *Awards*: prizes, Chicago Mun. A. Lg., 1930; Tucson FA Assn., 1938, 1951; Arizona State Fair, 1953. *Work*: Little Rock (Ark.) A. Mus. *Exhibited*: AIC, 1930, 1931; Tucson FA Assn., 1936-1955; Oakland A. Mus., 1953; NAD, 1946. I., "Dusty Desert Tales," 1941. *Position*: Prof. A., Univ. Arizona, Tucson, Ariz., at present.

SCOTT, JONATHAN—*Painter, T.*

790 Pinehurst Drive, Pasadena, Cal.

B. Bath, England, Oct. 30, 1914. *Studied*: Heatherly Sch. A., London; Heymann Schule, Munich; Academie de Belli Arti, Florence. *Member*: Pasadena Soc. A.; Cal. WC Soc.; Los A. AA (bd. memb.). *Awards*: prizes, Cal. WC Soc., 1955; Pasadena Soc. A., 1942-1944, 1947, 1948, 1952, 1956; A. of So. Cal., Laguna Beach, 1958. *Work*: Pasadena A. Mus.; Cal. AA; ports. in private colls. *Exhibited*: Cal. WC Soc., 1954-1957; Los A. Mus. A., 1940, 1948, 1949; Sacramento State Fair, 1949, 1950; Los A. County Fair, 1939, 1940, 1950; Laguna Beach, 1955-1957; Santa Barbara A. Mus., 1955 (one-man); Butler Inst. Am. A., 1956; Frye Mus., Seattle, 1958. *Position*: Instr., Drawing & Painting, Pasadena Sch. FA.

SCOTT, STELLA BRADFORD (Mrs. Roger M.)—
Painter, Lith.

59 Beechmont St., Worcester 9, Mass.

B. Providence, R.I., Aug. 21, 1920. *Studied*: R.I. Sch. Des., B.F.A.; Colorado Springs FA Center. *Member*: Providence A. Cl. *Awards*: prize, R.I. Sch. Des., 1941. *Exhibited*: NAD, 1942; LC, 1942, 1946; Rhode Island A. Cl., 1941, 1942, 1946; Contemp. A., 1941, 1946; Providence A. Cl., 1947-1951, 1953, 1954; WMA, 1949, 1951, 1952, 1953; Lowell A. Gal., Worcester, Mass., 1950. One-man: Providence A. Cl., 1946; Corycia Gal., Hancock, N.H., 1948.

SCRUGGS-CARRUTH, MARGARET ANN (Mrs.)—
Etcher, T., I., W., L., C.

3715 Turtle Creek Blvd., Dallas 19, Tex.

B. Dallas, Tex. *Studied*: Bryn Mawr Col.; Southern Methodist Univ., B.A., M.A.; & with Frank Reaugh, Ralph Pearson. *Member*: Texas FA Assn.; Dallas AA; SSAL; AFA; AAPL; Soc. Medalists; Southern Pr. M.; Dallas Pr. Soc.; Prairie Pr. M.; Cal. Pr. M.; & others. *Awards*: Garden Center Flower exhs., Dallas, 1951-1955, 1958 (and des. their bookplate, 1958); prize, Dallas All. A., 1932. *Work*: Elisabet Ney Mus.; CGA; Am. Embassy, Bucharest, Roumania; Nat. Soc. DAR; Tex. Fed. Garden Cl. Illus., co-author, "Gardening in the South and West" (new ed., 1959); "French Period" and "Victorian Period" Flower Arrangements." Contributor to House & Gardens; Better Homes & Gardens; Horticultural magazines and others. Heraldic artist, handmade lineage books, Coats of Arms, Lineage Trees, etc. *Exhibited*: WFNY 1939. Lectures: Etching.

SCULL, NINA WOLOSHUKOVA—*Painter, L., T.*

1927 Chestnut St., Philadelphia, Pa.; s. Cape May, N.J.

B. St. Petersburg, Russia, Oct. 28, 1902. *Studied*: ASL; Corcoran Sch. A.; Columbia Univ.; & with Wayman Adams, George Elmer Browne. *Member*: F. PAFA; New Jersey P. & S. Soc.; Phila. Plastic Cl.; Da Vinci A. All.; AFA; All. A. Am.; Provincetown AA; Phila. A. All.; Somerset AA; New Jersey A. & P.; Nat. Soc. Mod. A.; Assoc. A. Pittsburgh. *Work*: 100 Friends of Art, Pittsburgh; Imperial Gal., Phila.; Pittsburgh Pub. Schs.; and in private colls. *Exhibited*: NAD, 1939-1944; Carnegie

Inst., 1936-1946; AFA traveling exh., 1939; Ogunquit A. Center, 1940; PAFA, 1942-1945; MMA (AV), 1942; Montclair A. Mus., 1942; Provincetown AA, 1940-1944; Phila. Sketch Cl., 1945; MMA; Da Vinci All., 1943-1945; Haverford Col., 1942; Norfolk Mus. A. & Sc., 1939; Pa. State T. Col., 1938, 1939; Assoc. A. Pittsburgh, 1939; 100 Cl., Phila., 1955 (one-man); Newman Gal., Phila., 1939; All. A. Johnstown; Glassboro (N.J.) State T. Col.; Brooks Mem. Mus.; Phila. A. All., and others. Contributor to: newspapers & magazines. *Position*: Owner, Dir., Instr., Inperial A. Sch., Philadelphia, Pa., at present.*

SEARCY, ELISABETH—*Painter, Et., T., W., L.*
1934 Vinton Ave., Memphis 4, Tenn.

B. Memphis, Tenn. *Member*: CAA. *Work*: MMA; Mus. City of N.Y.; LC; Mus. A., Helena, Ark.; PC; Brooks Mem. A. Gal. *Exhibited*: Arch. Lg.; Delgado Mus. A.; Brooks Mem. A. Gal.; Sulgrave Cl., Wash., D.C., 1941, (one-man); numerous exhs. in N.Y. galleries. Lectures: History and Romance of Etching.*

SEARLES, STEPHEN—*Sculptor, T.*
126 Massachusetts Ave., Boston 15, Mass.

B. New York, N.Y., June 10, 1914. *Studied*: ASL; Grand Central Sch. A.; Corcoran Sch. A.; Fontainebleau, France. *Member*: Copley Soc.; NSS; New England S. Soc.; AAPL; Am. Veterans Soc. A. *Work*: Biarritz, France; Army Medical Mus., Wash., D.C.; religious sculpture for New England churches; many portrait busts; statue, "Our Lady of Good Voyage," Gloucester, Mass. *Exhibited*: CGA; Grand Central A. Gal.; Montclair A. Mus., 1938-1952; Ogunquit A. Center; All. A. Am.; Copley Soc., Boston. *Position*: Former Instr., Newark Sch. F. & Indst. A., Newark, N.J.; Am. Univ., Biarritz, France; Boston Center for Adult Edu.

SEATON WALTER WALLACE—*Illustrator*
Woodstock, N.Y.

B. San Francisco, Cal., Mar. 22, 1895. *Studied*: Cal. Inst. Des., San F.; Univ. California; ASL. *Member*: SI. I., Cosmopolitan, Saturday Evening Post, Ladies Home Journal, Collier's magazines.*

SEAVER, ESTHER ISABEL (Mrs. R. H. Burno)—
Educator, Dir.
415 Aldine Ave., Chicago 13, Ill.

B. Beloit, Wis., Dec. 16, 1903. *Studied*: Beloit Col., A.B.; Radcliffe Col., A.M., Ph.D.; & with A. K. Porter, Paul Sachs, & others. *Member*: AFA; CAA; Am. Assn. Univ. Prof.; Am. Inst. Archaeology. Ed., "Patron and Artist: Pre-Renaissance and Modern," symposium, 1936. Lectures: Scandinavian Art; Modern Painting. Wrote museum catalogues: "Thomas Cole (1801-1848): One Hundred Years Later," Wadsworth Atheneum and WMAA, 1948; "The Life of Christ," Wadsworth Atheneum, 1948; "City by the River and the Sea: Five Centuries of Skylines," Dayton AI, 1951; "Flight, Fantasy, Faith and Fact," Dayton AI, 1953. Contributor to art publications. *Position*: Hd. Dept. A., 1930-46, Prof. A., 1935-46, Wheaton Col., Wheaton, Ill.; Edu. Dir., Wadsworth Atheneum, Hartford, Conn., 1946-50; Dir. Dayton AI, Dayton, Ohio, 1950-56.

SECKAR, ALVENA V(AJDA)—*Painter, W.*
333 Pompton Ave., Pompton Lakes, N.J.

B. McMechen, W. Va., Mar. 1, 1916. *Studied*: PMSchIA; N.Y. Univ., B.A., M.A., and with Walter Emerson Baum, Sol Wilson, Phil Reisman. *Member*: Nat. Lg. Am. Pen Women. *Award*: Herald Tribune Book Festival; prize, Montclair A. Mus., 1957. *Exhibited*: Irvington A. Mus., 1949; Phila. Y.M.H.A.; Montclair A. Mus., 1955; Hackensack A. Cl.; Newark A. Cl.; one-man: Allentown (Pa.) A. Mus., 1950; Pittsburgh A. Cl., 1947; Cohn Gal., 1944; Barzansky Gal., 1952, and abroad. *Author*: "Zuska of the Burning Hills"; "Trapped in the Old Mine," 1953; "Misko of the Moving Hills," 1956.

SECKLER, DOROTHY GEES—*Critic, T., L.*
64 Sagamore Rd., Bronxville 8, N.Y.

B. Baltimore, Md., July 9, 1910. *Studied*: T. Col., Columbia Univ., B.S. in A. Edu.; Maryland Inst. A.; N.Y. Univ. and in Europe. *Award*: Traveling scholarship, Md. Inst A., 1931; AFA award for art criticism, 1954. *Work*:

MModA. Co-author: "The Questioning Public," MModA Bulletin, 1949; "Figure Drawing Comes to Life," 1957; Modern Art Section of "Famous Artist's Course," 1953. Contributor of numerous articles to Art News including Artist Paints a Picture, and Can Painting Be Taught? series. Also reviews on exhibitions and monographs. Lectures on Modern Art. Contributor art features to "MD," medical news magazine. *Positions*: Instr., N.Y. Univ. (part time), 1947-52; L., MModA., 1945-49; Assoc. Ed., Art News and Art News Annual, New York, N.Y., 1950-55; Gallery Ed., Art in America, Cannondale, Conn., 1955; L., Instr., City Col. of New York, 1957.

SEELY, W(ALTER) FREDRICK—*Painter, Cr.*
8226 Sunset Blvd., Los Angeles 46, Cal.

B. Monkton, Canada, Dec. 7, 1886. *Studied*: Otis Sch. Painting, and with J. W. Smith. *Member*: P. & S. Cl., Los A.; Cal. A. Cl. (Pres. 1957-58); A. of the Southwest. *Awards*: medal, Los A. Mus. A., 1942, and numerous prizes. *Work*: ports. in private colls. *Exhibited*: nationally.†

SEEMAN, JAMES—*Painter, Des., Ser.*
134-12 Atlantiv Ave., Richmond Hill 19, N.Y.; h. 17 Norfolk Rd., Great Neck, N.Y.

B. Austria, Aug 11, 1914. *Studied*: Pratt Inst. A.; and in Vienna. *Member*: NSMP; IDI; AID; Arch. Lg.; Nat. Soc. Int. Des.; Am. Des. Inst. *Award*: Allenan award, 1954. *Work*: murals, Eden Roc Hotel, Miami Beach; Bulova Watch Co.; Belmont Plaza Hotel, N.Y.; Progressive Cl., Atlanta; The Texas Co.; Metropolitan Indst. Bank; sc.; Americana Hotel, Miami Beach. *Position*: Pres., Seeman Studios, Murals, Inc., Richmond Hill, N.Y., and James Seeman Designs, New York, N.Y.; Pres., Murals, Inc., and Art for Architecture, New York, N.Y.

SEGEL, (JACOB) YONNY—*Craftsman, T., Des., S.*
9 Stuyvesant Oval, New York 9, N.Y.

B. New York, N.Y., Feb. 14, 1912. *Studied*: Edu. All. A. Sch.; BAID; City Col. of N.Y., M.S. in Edu.; N.Y. Univ., Post-Grad. in Edu. *Exhibited*: MMA, 1942; Univ. Nebraska, 1944; New Sch. for Social Research, 1940; AFA traveling exh., 1953-56; Am. Mus. Natural Hist., 1950; American House, 1952; Florence (S.C.) Mus., 1955; St. Paul A. Gal., 1952; Brussels World's Fair, 1958 (jewelry). *Position*: Instr., New School for Social Research, New York, N.Y.

SEGY, LADISLAS—*Painter, W., L., T., Cr.*
708 Lexington Ave.; h. 35 West 90th St., New York, N.Y.

B. Budapest, Hungary, Feb. 10, 1904. *Studied*: College de France. *Member*: F., Royal Anthropological Inst. of England and Ireland; Int. African Inst., London; Royal African Soc., London; Societe des Africainistes, Paris; N.Y. Acad. Science; Intl. Soc. for Normal & Abnormal Ethnopsychology, Paris; Am. Soc. for Aesthetics. *Awards*: Hon. deg., Litt.D., Central State Col., Wilberforce, Ohio. *Work*: PMG; BM; N.Y. Pub. Lib. *Exhibited*: Wildenstein Gal., 1943; Pepsi-Cola, 1945; Finley Gal., 1937; Newhouse Gal., 1938; Decorator's Cl., 1938; Acad. All. A., 1939; Seligmann Gal., 1942, 1943; Am-British A. Center, 1942-1944; A. Assoc., 1942; Niveau Gal., 1943; Marquie Gal., 1943; Peikin Gal., 1944; N.Y. Pub. Lib., 1944; A. Lg. Am., 1944; one-man: A. Headquarters, N.Y., 1944; Raymond & Raymond, 1941; Acquavella Gal., 1941, 1951; Am-British A. Center, 1943; Marquie Gal., 1944; Niveau Gal., 1945; N.Y. Pub. Lib., 1944; Assoc. Am. A., Hollywood, 1950. Lectures on African Art to museum, college and art audiences in U.S. and abroad. *Author*: "African Sculpture Speaks," 1952; "African Art Studies," Vol. 1, 1956; "African Sculpture," 1958; "Buma-African Sculpture Speaks"—a short moving picture. Contributor of articles and essays on African art, art appreciation and French Modern Art to art magazines, anthropological magazines, museum bulletins U.S. and abroad. Contributor, African Art to Encyclopaedia Britannica. *Position*: Expert and Consultant on African Art and Dir., Segy Gal., New York, N.Y.

SEIBEL, FRED(ERICK) O(TTO)—*Cartoonist*
104 North 4th St.; h. 40 Willway Ave., Richmond, Va.

B. Durhamville, N.Y., Oct. 8, 1886. *Studied*: ASL. *Work*: Huntington Lib., San Marino, Cal.; Alderman Lib., Univ. Virginia. *Exhibited*: VMFA, 1944 (one-man exh. of 200 cartoon originals).

SEIDE, CHARLES—*Painter, T., L., W.*

252 Fulton St.; h. 1 Centre Dr., Great Neck, N.Y.

B. Brooklyn, N.Y., May 14, 1915. *Studied*: NAD. *Member*: AEA; Brooklyn Soc. A. *Awards*: Elliott and Suydam medals; Hallgarten award; Tiffany Fnd., F.; prizes, Pepsi-Cola, 1946, 1948; Brooklyn Soc. A., 1950, 1956. *Work*: FMA, and private colls. *Exhibited*: Pepsi-Cola, 1946, 1948; PAFA, 1952; Brooklyn Soc. A., 1949-1958; NAD; WMAA; Luyber Gal.; Assoc. Am. A.; Contemp. A. Gal.; ACA Gal.; Norlyst Gal.; Laurel Gal; Artists Gal., 1956 (one-man), and others. Contributor to art and art materials magazines. *Position*: Instr., Brooklyn Mus. Sch. A., 1946- ; Cooper Union, 1950- ; Dir., Seide Workshops; Brooklyn and Great Neck, N.Y.; Tech. Dir., Museum Artists Materials Co.

SEIDENBERG, (JACOB) JEAN—*Painter, S., Des., T.*

618 Short St., New Orleans 18, La.

B. New York, N.Y., Feb. 14, 1930. *Studied*: BMSch. A., with John Bindrum; Syracuse Univ., Col. of FA. *Awards*: Scholarship, Syracuse Univ.; prizes, Louisiana State A. Comm. (2); New Orleans AA, 1953, 1954. *Work*: mosaic mural, Motel de Ville; Saratoga Bldg.; sculpture, Simon-Diaz Clinic, all in New Orleans. *Exhibited*: Riverside Mus., N.Y., 1958; Orleans Gal. Group; Pensacola A. Center, 1959; Delgado Mus. A., 1955 (one-man); New Orleans AA, 1951, 1953, 1954, 1956, 1958; La. State A. Comm., 1951-1954, 1958.

SEIDLER, DORIS—*Painter, Et., Eng.*

30 Irving Place, New York, N.Y.; h. 14 Stoner Ave., Great Neck, N.Y.

B. London, England, Nov. 26, 1912. *Studied*: with Stanley W. Hayter. *Member*: Phila. Pr. Cl.; NAWA. *Awards*: medal and prize, NAWA; Wash. WC Cl.; Chicago Soc. Et. *Work*: PMA; SAM; LC; Hofstra Col., N.Y. *Exhibited*: PAFA, 1953; BM, 1953, 1958; LC, 1953, 1956; Toronto, Canada; Inst. Contemp. A., London; Nat. group shows for paintings and prints; New York City group shows, 1952-1958; Ruth White Gal., N.Y.; Portland Mus. A., 1956; NAD, 1956; Wash. Pr. M., 1956, 1957; one-man: England (3); Holland (3), including Tilbury Acad. FA, 1958.

SEIPP ALICE—*Illustrator, Comm. A., W., P.*

38 Gramercy Park, New York 10, N.Y.

B. New York, N.Y. *Studied*: CUASch; ASL. *Member*: PBC; AWCS; NAWA. *Exhibited*: NAWA; AWCS, PAFA; NAC; CGA; Balt. WC Cl. Author, I., textbooks, on costume design, for Woman's Inst. Domestic A. & Sc., 1940.

SEITZ, WILLIAM CHAPIN—*Painter, W., E., L.*

McCormick Hall, Princeton University; h. 1073 Kington Rd., Princeton, N.J.

B. Buffalo, N.Y., June 19, 1914. *Studied*: Albright A. Sch.; Univ. Buffalo, B.F.A.; Princeton Univ., M.F.A., Ph.D. *Member*: CAA; Soc for Aesthetics; AAUP. *Awards*: Proctor F., Princeton Univ., 1951-1952; Advanced Grad. F., Nat. Council of Learned Soc., 1952-53; Fulbright F., 1957-58. *Work*: Princeton Univ. *Exhibited*: BM, 1949; WMAA, 1949; Albright A. Gal., 1935, 1936, 1940-1949; Allen Mem. A. Mus., Oberlin Col., 1951; CMA; Milwaukee A; Columbus Gal. FA; Univ. Illinois; MMoMA; Princeton Univ.; one-man: Arista Gal., N.Y., 1938; Willard Gal., 1949, 1951, 1953; Princeton Univ. Mus., 1949, 1951. Contributor to Princeton Museum Record; Brooklyn Mus. Bulletins; Allen Mem. Mus. Bulletin; College Art Journal, "Claude Monet's Men of Nature," 1957, Exh. cat., Minneapolis Inst. A. *Position*: Instr. A. Hist., Univ. Buffalo, 1946-47, Asst. Prof., 1947-56, on leave, 1956-59; Cr. in Residence, Princeton Univ., 1952-53; Asst. Prof. & Bicentennial Preceptor, Princeton Univ., 1956-58.

SEKULA, SONIA—*Painter*

c/o Hans Heimat, St. Moritz, Switzerland

B. Lucerne, Switzerland, Apr. 8, 1918. *Studied*: ASL, and with Morris Kantor, Kurt Roesch; also study in Italy. *Work*: SFMA; BM, and in private coll. *Exhibited*: BM; Santa Barbara Mus. A.; Nebraska AA, 1949; Mus. New Mexico, 1951; Univ. Illinois, 1952; Paris, France, 1948; Sao Paulo, Brazil, 1948; one-man: Betty Parsons Gal., 1948, 1949, 1951, 1952.*

SELETZ, EMIL—*Sculptor*

405 North Bedford Dr., Beverly Hills, Cal.; h. 2515 North Commonwealth, Los Angeles 27, Cal.

B. Chicago, Ill., Feb. 12, 1909. *Studied*: Univ. Chicago, B.S.; Temple Medical Sch., Phila., Pa., M.D.; studied sc., with Jo Davidson and George Grey Barnard. *Member*: Cal. P. & S. Cl.; A. of the Southwest; Cal. A. Cl.; F. Am. Col. of Surgeons. *Awards*: prizes, Cal. P. & S., 1950, 1952; A. of the Southwest, 1951, 1953, 1955. *Work*: specializes in sc. port. busts of prominent doctors: Johns Hopkins Hospital; Cedars of Lebanon Hospital; Los Angeles General Hospital; Univ. California, San F.; Inst. Neurosurgery, Panama. Many bronze busts in private collections. *Exhibited*: Greek Theatre, Los A.; Los A. Mus. A.; Cal. PLH. Lectures: What is Art?; A Doctor Looks at Sculpture. *Position*: Bd. Dir., A. of the Southwest and Authors Cl., 1955; Asst. Prof., Neurosurgery, Univ. Southern California, School of Medicine, 1950- .

SELEY, JASON—*Sculptor, E.*

232 East 84th St., New York 28, N.Y.

B. Newark, N.J., May 20, 1919. *Studied*: Cornell Univ., B.A.; ASL; Ecole des Beaux-Arts, Paris. *Member*: CAA; ASL; New Sculpture Group. *Awards*: Fulbright F., 1949-50; U.S. State Dept. & U.S. Office of Edu. grant for work in Haiti, 1947-48, 1948-49. *Work*: Newark Mus.; Centre d'Art, Port-au-Prince, Haiti; Episcopal Church, Port-au-Prince. Statues for Haitian Govt., Crucifixion, Cathedral St. Trinite; wall relief, Vulcan Materials Co., Birmingham, Ala., 1957. *Exhibited*: Fairmount Park, Phila., 1949; WMAA, 1952, 1953; Audubon A., 1951, 1957, 1958; Art:USA, 1958, and others. Contributor to "Americas," magazine of the Pan-American Union. Lectures: Haitian Art. *Position*: Prof., S., Ceramics, A. Hist., Hofstra College, Hempstead, N.Y., 1953- .

SELIGER, CHARLES—*Painter, Des., T.*

Commercial Decal, Inc.; h. 171 Pearsall Dr., Mt. Vernon, N.Y.

B. New York, N.Y., June 3, 1926. *Work*: MMoMA; WMAA; Newark Mus. A.; Tel-Aviv Mus., Israel; Mun. A. Mus., The Hague; Iowa State Univ.; Wellesley Col.; USIS Coll.; Vancouver (B.C.) A. Gal.; SAM; BMA; Vassar Col., and in private colls. *Exhibited*: WMAA, 1949-1958; AIC, 1948; MMoMA, 1951; Japan, 1955; Venice, 1948; Carnegie Inst., 1955; one-man: A. Center Sch., Los A., 1949; deYoung Mem. Mus., 1949; Cal. PLH, 1952; Willard Gal., 1952, 1953, 1955; Paris, 1950; Italy and Holland, and others. One-man: Willard Gal., 1956, 1958; Otto Seligmann Gal., Seattle, Wash., 1956-1958. *Position*: A., Decal, Inc., Mt. Vernon, N.Y.; Instr., Mt. Vernon A. Center, 1954- ; Des., for the china industry.

SELIGMANN, KURT—*Painter, Gr., E., W., L.*

80 West 40th St., New York 18, N.Y.

B. Basel, Switzerland, July 20, 1900. *Studied*: Ecole des Beaux-Arts; Geneva, Switzerland; Italy and France. *Work*: Albright A. Gal.; Smith Col.; Univ. Illinois; MMA; MMoMA; WMAA; N.Y. Pub. Lib.; BM; AIC; PAFA; Coll. des Musees Nationaux de France; Kundstkredit, Basel, Switzerland; Coll. de la Manufacture d'Aubusson, France; Palacio Bellas Artes, Mexico City; Bibliotheque Nationale, Paris; Mus. Mod. A., Lodz, Poland. *Exhibited*: GGE, 1939; Carnegie Inst.; Canadian Nat. Exh., 1939; WFNY 1939; PAFA, and other leading museums; one-man: Paris, London, Milan, Rome, Tokyo, Mexico City, Hollywood, Minneapolis, New York City, and many others. I., "Vagabondages Heraldiques," 1934; "Hommes et Metiers," 1935; "Oedipus," 1944, and others; "The History of Magic," 1948, 1950, 1952, 1954, English ed., 1958, French ed., 1957, German ed., 1958. Contributor to American and European art magazines. Stage des. for modern and ballet dancers.

SELINGER, ARMAND—*Painter*

1737 California St., Carlsbad, Cal.

B. Riverside, Cal., Jan. 13, 1918. *Studied*: San Diego State Col., B.A. M.A.; Claremont Grad. Sch. *Member*: Laguna Beach AA; Carlsbad AA. *Work*: murals, Oceanside Lodge of Elks Cl.; Acapulco Gardens; Royal Palms Inn. *Exhibited*: Laguna Beach, La Jolla A. Center and Carlsbad Gal., annually. *Position*: Hd., A. Dept., Oceanside-Carlsbad Col., 1945-50; Prin., Oceanside-Carlsbad H.S. at present.

SELLA, ALVIN CONRAD—*Painter, E.*
Department of Art, Sullins College, Bristol, Va.

B. Union City, N.J., Aug. 30, 1919. *Studied*: Yale Sch. A.; ASL, with Brackman; Bridgman; Columbia Univ., Dept. A., with Machau; Syracuse Univ., Col. FA; Univ. New Mexico; and in Mexico, D.F. *Member*: ASL; AAUP; CAA. *Work*: painting, Bristol Iron & Steel Co. *Exhibited*: CGA, 1951, 1957; Toledo Mus. A., 1958; Birmingham Mus. A., 1956; Memphis Mus. A., 1955; Virginia Intermont Col., 1949, 1955, 1957; East Tennessee State Col., 1958; Contemp. A. Gal., N.Y., 1945 (one-man), 1947, 1949; Palacio de Bellas Artes, Mexico City, 1946, (one-man). *Position*: Hd., Dept. A., Sullins College, Bristol, Va., 1948- .

SELLECK, MARGARET—*Painter, I., L.*
607 9th St., Wilmette, Ill.

B. Salt Lake City, Utah, Aug. 28, 1892. *Studied*: AIC; Univ. Wisconsin; Western Univ., & with Dudley Crafts Watson, Rudolph Weisenborn, Oskar Gross. *Member*: AEA; Nat. Lg. Pen Women; Northwest A. Lg.; All-Illinois Soc. FA. *Awards*: med., All-Illinois Soc. FA, 1934. *Exhibited*: PAFA, 1941; CM, 1936; one-man exh.: Allerton Gal., Chicago; Stevens Hotel, Chicago; Layton Gal. A., Milwaukee, Wis.; Union, Univ. Wisconsin; Beloit Col.; Oshkosh A. Mus.; Contemp. A. Gal., Evanston, Ill. I., school textbooks. Lectures: "Historic Wisconsin"; "Drama of Chicago"; "Old Northwest Territory," etc.*

SELZ, PETER H.—*Museum Curator, E., Hist., W.*
Museum of Modern Art, 11 West 53rd St., (19); h. 333 Central Park West, New York 25, N.Y.

B. Munich, Germany, Mar. 27, 1919. *Studied*: Univ. Chicago, M.A., Ph.D.; Univ. Paris. *Member*: CAA; Soc. Arch. Hist. *Awards*: Fulbright award, Univ. Paris, 1949-50; Univ. Chicago F., 1946-49; Belgian-American Edu. Fnd. F., 1953; Pomona Col., Trustee F., 1957. *Author*: "German Expressionist Painting," 1957; "Understanding Modern Art," 1955. Contributor to Art Bulletin; Art News; College Art Journal; Arts; Arts & Architecture; School Arts; Penrose Annual and other publications; article "Painting" and others in Encyclopaedia Britannica. Exhs. arranged at Pomona College: Toulouse-Lautrec; Greene & Greene; Leon Golub; Primitive Art of Haiti; Rico Lebrun; California Drawings; The Art of Greece and Rome; German Expressionist Painting; Buckminster Fuller; Modern Religious Art; The Stieglitz Circle, and others. *Positions*: Asst. Prof. A. Hist., Inst. Des., Univ. of Chicago, 1953-54; Hd., A. Edu. Program, Inst. Des., Illinois Inst. of Tech., 1953-55; Chm. A. Dept., & Dir. A. Gal., Pomona College, Claremont, Cal., 1955-58; Cur., Painting & Sculpture Exhs., Museum of Modern Art, New York, N.Y., 1958- .

SENNHAUSER, JOHN—*Painter, T.*
35-26 79th St., Jackson Heights 72, N.Y.

B. Rorschach, Switzerland, Dec. 10, 1907. *Studied*: in Italy; CUASch. *Member*: Am. Abstract A.; Spiral Group; Assoc. Memb., Intl. Inst. A. & Let., Zurich; Fed. Mod. P. & S. *Awards*: prizes, WMAA, 1951; Philbrook A. Center, 1951. *Work*: Guggenheim Fnd.; WMAA; Philbrook A. Center; Munson-Williams-Proctor Inst. *Exhibited*: NAD, 1935; PAFA, 1936-1953; Albright A. Gal., 1940; AIC, 1947, 1952, 1953; WMAA, 1948-1955; BM, 1943, 1949, 1951, 1953; Philbrook A. Center, 1951; Guggenheim Mus., 1942-1944; WMA, 1951; CGA, 1953; Univ. Illinois, 1953; Walker A. Center, 1953; Springfield Mus. A., 1952; AFA traveling exh., 1947-1949, 1952, 1954, 1955; Western Assn. A. Dir. traveling exh., 1947-1949, 1955, 1956; Brown Univ., 1954; Univ. Maine, 1955; CAM, 1956; one-man: N.Y., 1936, 1939, 1942, 1947, 1950, 1952, 1956, and many other exhs. nationally, and in Europe and Canada. *Position*: Hd. A. Dept., C. R. Gracie & Sons, New York, N.Y.

SENTOVIC, JOHN M.—*Illustrator, Comm. A.*
2676 Ridgeview Drive, San Diego 5, Cal.

B. Lead, S.D., Dec. 16, 1924. *Studied*: La Jolla Sch. A. & Crafts; Los A. A. Center Sch. *Member*: Tech. Publishing Soc. *Work*: Book illustrations; silk screen brochures. Cart., Illus., Copley Press. *Awards*: prizes, Tech. Pub. Soc. Exh. (3). Contributor to Life Magazine; Missile & Rockets Magazine. *Position*: Special Asst. to Dr. Krafft Ehrike, Convair Astronautics, Space Illustrations.

SEPESHY, ZOLTAN—*Painter, T.*
1 Academy Rd., Bloomfield Hills, Mich.; s. Second Hill Rd., Bridgewater, Conn.

B. Kassa, Hungary, Feb. 24, 1898. *Studied*: Acad. FA & A. Instr., Budapest, Hungary, M.F.A.; & in Vienna, Paris. *Member*: NA; AAPL; Nat. Inst. A. & Lets. *Awards*: prizes, Carnegie Inst., 1947; Detroit Inst. A., 1925, 1930, 1936, 1938, 1940, 1945, 1953, 1955; The Patteran, 1939; IBM, 1940; Pepsi-Cola Comp., 1945; Am. Acad. A. & Let., 1946; med., PAFA, 1946; NAD, 1952; Tupperware F., 1957. *Work*: MMA; Sheldon Swope A. Gal.; Tupperware Mus., Orlando, Fla.; Detroit Inst. A.; AIC; Toledo Mus. A.; Albright A. Gal.; Swope A. Gal.; Wichita A. Mus.; San Diego FA Soc.; CAM; Butler AI; Milwaukee AI; Lincoln Mus. A.; Nelson Gal. A.; Univ. Michigan; PAFA; Akron AI; Dallas Mus. FA; Davenport Mun. A. Gal.; Walker A. Center; Howard Univ.; High Mus. A.; Grand Rapids A. Gal.; Flint Inst. A.; Univ. Arizona; Encyclopaedia Britannica Coll.; IBM Coll.; Cranbrook Acad. A. Mus.; McGregor Pub. Lib., Highland Park, Mich.; U.S. State Dept.; Tel-Aviv Mus., Israel; Santa Barbara Mus. A.; Telfair Acad.; VMFA; murals, General Motors Bldg., Detroit; Fordson H.S., Dearborn, Mich.; USPO, Lincoln Park, Mich.; Nashville, Ind.; Rackham Fnd., Detroit. *Exhibited*: nationally and internationally. *Author*, I., "Tempera," 1946. Contributor to: art magazines; illus., Fortune magazine. *Position*: Resident Instr., Painting & Drawing, Cranbrook Acad. A., Bloomfield Hills, Mich., 1932- .

SEREDY, KATE—*Writer, I.*
Montgomery, N.Y.

B. Budapest, Hungary. *Studied*: Budapest Acad. A. *Awards*: Newbery medal, 1937. *Author*, I., "The Good Master"; "Listening"; "The White Stag"; "A Tree for Peter"; "Singing Tree"; "The Open Gate"; "Gypsy," "The Chestry Oak," 1935-51; "Philomena," 1955; "The Tenement Tree," 1959.

SERGEANT, EDGAR—*Painter*
160 Satterthwaite Ave., Nutley 10, N.J.

B. New York, N.Y., Nov. 25, 1878. *Studied*: Columbia Univ.; ASL; Grand Central A. Sch.; & with Frank DuMond, Gifford Beal, and others. *Member*: SC. *Awards*: prizes, NAD; All.A.Am.; Montclair A. Mus. *Exhibited*: Newark Mus.; All.A.Am.; Montclair A. Mus.; NAD.

SERGER, FREDERICK B.—*Painter*
130 West 57th St., New York 19, N.Y.; also, Woodstock, N.Y.

B. Ivancice, Czechoslovakia, Aug. 25, 1889. *Studied*: Acad. A., Munich, Germany, and in Paris and Vienna. *Member*: Woodstock AA; AEA; A. Lg. Am. *Awards*: prizes, Delgado Mus. A., 1948; Norton Gal. A., 1950; G. W. V. Smith Mus. A., 1950, and many honorable mentions. *Work*: Mus. City of Paris; Art Collectors & A. Assn., Buffalo, N.Y.; Butler AI; SFMA. *Exhibited*: Carnegie Inst.; NAD; Santa Barbara Mus. A.; Springfield AA; Conn. Acad. FA; PAFA; CGA; Butler AI; Toledo Mus. A.; Univ. Illinois, and others; one-man: Paris, France; deYoung Mem. Mus.; Mus. of New Mexico; Springfield (Mo.) Mus. A.; Butler Inst. Am. A.

SERISAWA, SUEO—*Painter, T.*
10469 Santa Monica Blvd., Los Angeles 25, Cal.; h. 3950 San Rafael Ave., Los Angeles, Cal.

B. Yokohama, Japan, Apr. 10, 1910. *Studied*: Otis AI, and with George Barker. *Awards*: prizes, Cal. State Fair, 1940, 1949; Hallmark Exh., 1949; medals, PAFA, 1947; Pepsi-Cola, 1948. *Work*: San Diego FA Assn.; Santa Barbara Mus. A.; Pasadena AI; Univ. Arizona; Cal. State Fair Coll.; Los A. Mus. A.; MMA. *Exhibited*: AIC; Los A. Mus. A.; San Diego FA Soc.; Denver A. Mus.; SFMA; Univ. Illinois; Univ. Nebraska; La Tausca Exh.; Carnegie Inst.; Walker A. Center; Hallmark awards; Int. traveling exh. to Tokyo, Japan; Sao Paulo, Brazil; CGA; AFA traveling exh.; WMAA, 1958; Stanford Univ. *Position*: Instr., Painting, Scripps Col., Claremont, Cal., 1949; Kann Inst. A., Beverly Hills, Cal., 1947-51.

SERRA, DANIEL (DANIEL SERRA BADUE)—
**   *Painter, E., W., Gr.***
27 #905 Vedado, Havana, Cuba

B. Santiago de Cuba, Sept. 8, 1914. *Studied*: NAD; ASL; Columbia Univ.; & in Spain. *Awards*: prizes, John Wanamaker Comp., 1928; Guggenheim F., 1939, 1940; PAFA, 1941; gold medal, Univ. Tampa, 1951; Havana, Cuba, 1954. *Work*: Palacio de Bellas Artes, Havana; Museo Municipal, Santiago, Cuba. *Exhibited*: AIC, 1938; All. A. Am., 1938; WFNY 1939; GGE, 1939; Univ. Michigan, 1939; WMAA, 1940; CAM, 1941; Toledo Mus. A., 1941; PAFA, 1941; Carnegie Inst., 1941; & in Spain & Cuba. *Position*: Prof., Escuela Prov. de Artes Plásticas and Escuela Profesional de Periodismo, Santiago de Cuba, at present.

SERTH, ARTHUR (ARTHUR M. SERTICH-SERTH)—
  Painter, C.
  4402 Auburn Dr., Royal Oak, Mich.

B. Podlapac, Croatia, Yugoslavia, Apr. 16, 1898. *Studied*: Univ. Michigan; in Europe, & with John P. Wicker, William Pascoe, & others. *Member*: Scarab Cl., Detroit. *Awards*: prizes, Detroit Inst. A., 1926; Mich. State Fair, 1927, 1928, 1931, 1939. *Work*: murals in many churches in Detroit, Mich.; Chicago, Ill.; & abroad; Mus. Sc. & Indst., Chicago; Dioramas, General Motors Parade of Progress; background for stage, General Motors Motorama; transportation murals (2) and diorama, General Motors; mural, Croatian Home Bldg., Detroit, Mich. *Exhibited*: Detroit Inst. A., 1922-1946; Scarab Cl., numerous one-man & group exhs. in Detroit; WFNY 1939; Saugatuck, Mich., 1957 (one-man); Chicago World's Fair; Mus. Sc. & Indst., Chicago, 1957; Brussels World's Fair, 1958. *Position*: Ed., Asst. Supv., Aeronautical Charts, Army Map Service, 1942-45; A., H.B. Stubbs Co., 1947-56.

SERWAZI, ALBERT B.—*Painter, Des., I.*
  Ladies Home Journal, Independence Square, Phila-delphia 5, Pa.; h. Gradyville Rd., Newtown Square, Pa.

B. Philadelphia, Pa., Aug. 20, 1905. *Studied*: PMSch. Indst. A.; PAFA. *Member*: PAFA; A. Dir. Cl. *Awards*: prizes, A. Dir. Cl., Phila., 1948; Award of Merit, Magazine Advertising Art, N.Y. 1950; J. Henry Scheidt Mem. prize, PAFA; medals, Phila. Sketch Cl.; DaVinci A. All. *Work*: PAFA; Friend's Central Sch.; WMAA; Los A. Mus. A.; Allentown A. Mus. *Exhibited*: MMA, 1943; GGE, 1939; Butler AI; NAD; AIC; Carnegie Inst.; CAM; Toledo Mus. A.; CGA; VMFA; Contemp. A. Gal.; Phila. A. All., 1957 (one-man) and prior; Phila. A. Cl.; PAFA, 1933-1952; Phila. Sketch Cl. *Position*: A. Dir., Lewis & Gilman, 1943-48; Chief A. Dir., Neal D. Ivey Co., 1949-51, Philadelphia, Pa.; Adv. Dept., Dupont Co., 1951-52; A. Dir., McKee & Albright, Philadelphia, Pa., 1952-53; Ladies Home Journal, 1953- .

SESSLER, ALFRED—*Painter, E., Gr., L.*
  740 Langdon St., Madison, Wis.

B. Milwaukee, Wis., Jan. 14, 1909. *Studied*: Layton Sch. A., B.S. in A. Edu.; Univ. Wisconsin, M.S. *Member*: Madison AA. *Awards*: prizes, Univ. Wisconsin, 1934, 1935, 1943, 1944, 1946, 1950, 1951, 1953; Milwaukee AI, 1935, 1937, 1939, 1942, 1945, 1946, 1950-1952, 1955; Wisconsin State Fair, 1938, 1940-1944, 1946-1955; Madison A. Exh., 1946, 1948, 1949, 1953; SAGA, 1955; Wichita AA, 1953; Gimbel, 1949-1953; LC, 1949, 1951, 1955; Milwaukee Pr. M., 1951, 1952, 1955. *Work*: Milwaukee AI; Univ. Wisconsin; murals, USPO, Lowell, Mich.; Moriss, Minn.; work also in colls. of Gimbels, Milwaukee; LC; Lawrence Col., Appleton, Wis.; Beloit Col.; Wichita AA. *Exhibited*: Wis. P. & S., 1947, 1950-1952, 1955; Walker A. Center, 1947, 1949, 1951; Wis. State Fair, 1947-1955; Wis. Salon, 1947, 1949, 1951-1953, 1955; Milwaukee Pr. M., 1947, 1951, 1952; PAFA, 1949, 1950, 1953, 1954; LC, 1949, 1951, 1952, 1954, 1955; SAGA, 1950, 1952-1955; MMA, 1950; New Britain Mus., 1952, 1953; SFMA, 1952; Univ. So. Cal., 1953; Springfield, Ill., 1953; Univ. Illinois, 1953; Soc. Wash. Pr. M., 1953; BM, 1955; Denver A. Mus., 1954, 1955; Walker A. Center, 1954 and many others throughout the U.S. *Position*: Asst. Prof., 1949, Assoc. Prof., 1951- , Univ. Wisconsin, Madison, Wis.*

SESSLER, STANLEY SASCHA—
  Painter, E., Et., L.
  1126 Manchester Drive, South Bend 15, Ind.
B. St. Petersburg, Russia, Mar. 28, 1905. *Studied*: Courtauld Inst. A., Univ. London; Mass. Sch. A. *Member*: F., Royal Soc. A., London; F., Intl. Inst. A. & Let., Germany; AAUP; Midwestern Col. A. Conference;

Catholic AA. *Awards*: prizes, Hoosier Salon, 1938-41; South Bend, Ind., 1942; Northern Ind. A. Salon, 1952, 1953, 1955, 1958; Michiana Exh., 1950. *Work*: Univ. Galleries, Univ. Notre Dame; St. James Cathedral, South Bend; Moreau Seminary, Notre Dame, Ind.; altar piece, St. Mary's Church, Floyd's Knobs, Ind.; mural, Buchanan (Mich.) Pub. Lib. *Exhibited*: Hoosier Salon, 1929-1942, 1949-1951; Indiana A. Cl., 1939-1942; Northern Ind. A., 1929-1946, 1949, 1952, 1953, 1955; Ogunquit A. Center; Palm Beach A. Center; Michiana Exh., 1950, 1952; South Bend AA, 1950 (one-man); South Bend Women's Cl., 1951 (one-man); Lansing, Mich., 1958; Champaign, Ill., 1952. Illus. books for Ave Maria Press, Notre Dame, Ind., 1948-53. *Position*: Dir. Dept. A., 1937-55, Prof. A., 1928- , Univ. Notre Dame, Ind.

SETTERBERG, CARL—*Painter, I.*
  45 Tudor City Place, New York 17, N.Y.

B. Las Animas, Colo., Aug. 16, 1897. *Studied*: AIC. *Member*: AWS; Nat. Soc. Painters in Casein; SI; F., Intl. Inst. A. & Lets. *Work*: permanent exh., at Air Force Acad., Colo., and McChord Air Force Base, Tacoma, Wash. *Awards*: prizes, NAD (purchase); AWS; Arcier and Clinedinst awards. *Exhibited*: AWS; NAD; NAC; Soc. Painters in Casein; SI; SC. Contributor to national magazines.

SETTLEMYRE, JULIUS LEE, JR.—
  Painter, L., T., Mus. Dir.
  Children's Nature Museum, Rock Hill, S.C.; h. Mc-Connells, S.C.

B. Hickory, N.C., Jan. 1, 1916. *Studied*: George Washington Univ.; Corcoran Sch. A.; in Paris; & with Richard Lahey, Catherine Critcher. *Member*: Gaston A. Lg.; AAMus.; Southeastern Assn. Mus. *Award*: D.A.R., 1955. *Work*: mural, Shakespeare Auditorium, Shelby, N.C.; Snyder Mem., Charlotte, N.C.; Winnesboro Mem. Bldg., Montreat, N.C.; Court House, Shelby, N.C.; Univ. North Carolina; ports., Baptist Hospital, Columbia, S.C.; Court House, York, S.C.; Medical Col., Charleston, S.C. *Exhibited*: Sorbonne Sch. FA, Paris, 1940; CGA, 1937, 1939; Mint Mus. A., 1940, 1943, 1946; Chapel Hill, N.C., 1943; MMA, 1942. Lectures: Early American Art; Natural History; Indians of the Region; Non-objective and Abstract Art. *Position*: Dir., Children's Nature Mus., Rock Hill, S.C.*

SEVERANCE, JULIA GRIDLEY—*Sculptor, Et.*
  3120 Udal St., San Diego 6, Cal.

B. Oberlin, Ohio, Jan. 11, 1877. *Studied*: AIC; Cleveland Sch. A.; ASL; Oberlin Col. *Member*: San Diego A. Gld. *Work*: Oberlin Col.; Lib. Cong.; St. Mary's Sch., Knoxville, Ill.; Allen Mem. Mus., Oberlin, Ohio; San Diego FA Gal.

SEVERINO, D. ALEXANDER—*Educator, L., P.*
  College of Education, Ohio State University, Columbus 10, Ohio; h. 6215 Olentangy River Road, Worthington, Ohio.

B. Boston, Mass., Sept. 14, 1914. *Studied*: Mass. Sch. A., B.S.; Boston Univ., Ed. M.; Harvard Univ., Ed. D. *Member*: NAEA; Nat. Com. on A. Edu., AFA; Western AA; Am. Assn. Col. for T. Preparation; NEA. *Awards*: F., AIA. *Position*: Instr., R.I. Col. of Edu., 1938-42, Asst. Prof., 1942-43; Asst. Dean, R.I. Sch. Des., 1946-47; Prof., Chm., Bradford Durfee Tech. Inst., 1947-52; Assoc. Prof., Univ. Wisconsin, 1952-55; Prof., Dir. Sch. F. & App. A., Ohio State Univ., Columbus, Ohio, 1955-1958; Prof. FA, Assoc. Dean, College of Edu., Ohio State Univ., 1958- .

SEVIN, WHITNEY—*Educator, P., S.*
  Art Department, Franklin College; h. 290 South Forsythe St., Franklin, Ind.

B. Birmingham, Mich., Oct. 9, 1931. *Studied*: Kalamazoo Col.; Cranbrook Acad. A., B.F.A., M.F.A. *Member*: AEA; CAA. *Awards*: prizes, Kalamazoo AA, 1952; Army Photographic Comp., 1956; South Bend AA, 1957 (purchase). *Work*: Cranbrook Acad. A.; South Bend AA; Cranbrook Sch. Galleries. *Exhibited*: Butler Inst. Am. A., 1957, 1958; Ball State T. Col., 1957, 1958; Provincetown A. Festival, 1958; Columbia Mus. A., 1957; Exh. Momentum, Chicago, 1952, 1953; Michigan A., 1953-1957; Michiana Regional, 1957. *Position*: Prof. A., Art Dept., Franklin College, Franklin, Ind.

SEWELL, AMOS—Illustrator
Sturges Highway, Westport, Conn.

B. San Francisco, Cal., June 7, 1901. *Studied*: Cal. Sch. FA; ASL; Grand Central Sch. A., and with Guy Pene du Bois, Harvey Dunn, Julian Levy. *Member*: SI. *Work*: SI. *Exhibited*: Annual exh. American Illustration; SC; Cambridge (Mass.) Sch. Des.; SI, annually; traveling exh. of illustrations for Sat. Eve. Post. I., for national magazines.

SEWELL, JACK VINCENT—Museum Curator
The Art Institute of Chicago (3); h. 1350 Lake Shore Drive, Chicago 10, Ill.

B. Dearborn, Mo., June 11, 1923. *Studied*: Univ. Chicago, M.A.; Harvard Univ. *Member*: Far Eastern Ceramic Group; Japan-American Soc. of Chicago (Dir. & Vice-Pres.); The Cliff Dwellers, Chicago. Contributor to Archaeology, AIC Quarterly. Lectures: Indian and Far Eastern Art; The Arts of China; Strength in Delicacy—A Study of Archaic Chinese Bronzes; Sculpture of Gandharan. In charge of complete reinstallation of Oriental Collections in Art Institute, 1958. *Position*: Cur., Oriental Art, The Art Institute of Chicago.

SEXTON, FREDERICK LESTER—Painter, T., L.
14 Kenter Pl., New Haven 15, Conn.

B. Cheshire, Conn., Sept. 13, 1889. *Studied*: Yale Sch. FA, B.F.A.; & with Sergeant Kendell, Edwin Taylor. *Member*: SC; Lyme AA; New Haven Paint & Clay Cl.; Meriden A. & Crafts Cl.; Conn. Acad. FA. *Awards*: Winchester traveling F., Yale Univ., 1915; prizes, New Haven Paint & Clay Cl.; Meriden A. & Crafts Cl., 1941; Conn. Acad. FA, 1927, 1938; Carney prize, Hartford, Conn., 1944. *Work*: Hospital, Hopkins Sch., City Hall, all New Haven; St. Margaret's Sch., Waterbury; Conn. Univ., Storrs, Conn.; St. John's Mem. Chapel, Waterbury. *Exhibited*: NAD; SC; Lyme AA; Meriden A. & Crafts Cl.; Lyman Allyn Mus.; Bridgeport AA; New Haven Paint & Clay Cl.; East Hampton (L.I.) AA.*

SEYFFERT, RICHARD L.—Painter
15 Gramercy Park, New York 3, N.Y.; h. St. John's Place, New Canaan, Conn.

B. Philadelphia, Pa., Aug. 11, 1915. *Studied*: NAD; in Switzerland, and with Leon Kroll, Gifford Beal. *Member*: All. A. Am.; Nat. Soc. Painters in Casein; NAC; AAPL; Knickerbocker A. *Awards*: prize, NAD, 1936; AAPL, 1958. *Exhibited*: AIC, 1942, 1943; NAC, 1959; AAPL, 1958.

SEYLER, DAVID WOODS—Sculptor, P., I., Des., E
2809 Woodsdale Blvd., Lincoln 2, Neb.

B. Dayton, Ky., July 31, 1917. *Studied*: Cincinnati A. Acad.; AIC, B.F.A.; Univ. Chicago; Univ. Wisconsin, M.S., and with Francis Chapin, Paul Burlin, W. Colescott, Edmund Giesbert, and others. *Awards*: prizes, Syracuse Mus. FA, 1938; Trebilcock prize, 1938; Thomas C. Woods grant, 1959-60. *Work*: Univ. Chicago; Syracuse Mus. FA; CM; murals, Philippine Island Base, U.S. Navy; Great Lakes Naval Station. *Exhibited*: nationally and internationally. One-man: AIC, 1944; Loring Andrew Gal., Cincinnati, 1943; Univ. Chicago, 1940; Miller & Paines Gal., N.Y. Des. & Illus., "Food Becomes You"; "Young Man with Screwdriver." *Position*: Des., S., Rookwood Pottery, 1936-39; Pres., Dir., Kenton Hills Porcelains, Erlanger, Ky., 1939-45; A. Dir., S. Belvedere Pottery, Lake Geneva, Wis., 1945-49; Asst. Prof., A. Dept., Univ. Nebraska, 1949- .

SEYMOUR, CHARLES, JR.—
Educator, Mus. Cur., Historian, L.
Yale University, New Haven, Conn.

B. New Haven, Conn., Feb. 26, 1912. *Studied*: King's Col., Cambridge Univ.; Yale Col., B.A.; Univ. Paris; Yale Univ., Ph.D., and with Henri Focillon. *Award*: Guggenheim F., 1954-55. Author: "Notre Dame of Noyon in the 12th Century," 1939; "Masterpieces of Sculpture in the National Gallery of Art, Washington, D.C." 1949; "Tradition and Experiment in Modern Sculpture," 1949. Contributor to Gazette des Beaux-Arts, Parnassus, Art Bulletin. Lectures: Renaissance Sculpture; 19th Century Sculpture, etc. *Positions*: Inst., Hist. A., Yale Univ., 1938-39; Cur. S., 1939-42, Asst. Chief Cur., 1946-49, NGA, Washington,

D.C.; L., Am. Univ., Washington, D.C., 1942; L., Johns Hopkins Univ., Assoc. Prof. Hist. A. and Cur. Renaissance A., 1949-54; Prof. Hist. A., 1954- , Chm., Hist. & A. Dept., 1956-59, Yale University, New Haven, Conn.; Dir., CAA, 1940-42, 1958- ; Visiting L., Univ. Colorado, 1958 (summer session).

SEYMOUR, MAY DAVENPORT—Museum Curator
Museum of the City of New York, 1220 Fifth Ave. (29); h. 24 East 93rd St., New York 28, N.Y.

B. Boston, Mass., Dec. 5, 1883. *Member*: AAMus.; Actors' Fund of Am.; Episcopal Actors Gld. Arranged all exhs. held in Theatre Gallery of the Museum of the City of New York, including, Alfred Lunt's Toy Theatres; Gertrude Lawrence and Ruth Draper Memorials; James and Eugene O'Neill; The Pageant of the Opera; The Art of the Negro in Dance, Music and Drama, and others. *Position*: Cur., Theatre and Music Coll. of the Museum of the City of New York, 1926- .

SEYMOUR, RALPH FLETCHER—
Etcher, Des., I., W., P.
410 South Michigan Ave.; h. 152 West Schiller St., Chicago 5, Ill.

Studied: Cincinnati Acad. A., and in Paris, France. *Member*: Caxton Cl.; Cliff Dwellers; Chicago Hist. Soc. *Awards*: hon. deg., D.F.A., Knox Col., Galesburg, Ill.; prizes (for etchings) Hoosier Salon; Chicago Soc. Et.; Phila. Pr. Cl. *Work*: AIC; Sorbonne, Paris; AFA; Knox Col.; Newberry Lib., Chicago; NGA; Bibliotheque Nationale, Paris; series of murals, LaSalle Hotel, Chicago; mural, Custer Hotel, Galesburg, Ill.; painting of Lincoln-Douglas Debate for Knox College, Galesburg, Ill. I., Des., bookplates. Author, I., "Across the Gulf"; "Some Went This Way"; "Our Midwest."

SHACKELFORD, KATHARINE BUZZELL—Painter, T., C.
4528 El Camino Corto, La Canada, Cal.

B. Fort Benton, Mont. *Studied*: Montana State Col.; Univ. California, B.E., and with Nicolai Fechin. *Member*: Glendale AA (Exec. Bd.); A.T. Assn.; NEA; AEA; Women Painters of the West; Verdugo Hills AA; Los A. AA. *Awards*: prizes, Glendale AA, 1953-1955; Women Painters of the West, 1954. *Exhibited*: Los A. AA; Glendale City Hall; Los A. City Hall; Madonna Festival; Pasadena AI; Sao Paulo, Brazil; Great Falls (Mont.) Pub. Lib., and others. Lectures: Approach to Portraiture; Art and Religion.

SHACKELFORD, SHELBY—Painter, E., W., I., Gr.
300 Northfield Pl., Baltimore 10, Md.

B. Halifax, Va., Sept. 27, 1899. *Studied*: Maryland Inst.; in Paris; & with Marguerite & William Zorach; Othen Frieze, Fernand Leger. *Member*: AEA. *Awards*: purchase prizes, BMA, 1952, 1956. *Work*: N.Y. Pub. Lib.; BMA. *Exhibited*: Graphic Exh., N.Y., 1936; 50 Prints of the Year, 1930-1932; BMA, 1944-1946, 1955; Peale Mus. A., 1954, 1955; one-man: BMA, 1957; Western Md. College, 1958; Jefferson Place Gal., Wash., D.C., 1958. Author, I., "Now for Creatures," 1934; "Electric Eel Calling," 1941; I., "Time, Space and Atoms," 1932. *Position*: A. Advisor, Friends Sch., Baltimore, Md., 1945-46; A. T., BMA, Baltimore, Md., 1946; Hd. A. Dept., St. Timothy's Sch., Stevenson, Md., 1946- . Instr., Adult Edu., BMA, 1954- .

SHAFER, BURR—Cartoonist, L., W., Hist.
421 North Sycamore St.; h. 901 Spurgeon St., Santa Ana, Cal.

B. Fostoria, Ohio, Oct. 24, 1899. *Studied*: Occidental Col. Author, I., cartoon books: "Through History with J. Wesley Smith," 1951 (cartoon character feature "Through History with J. Wesley Smith" has appeared weekly in Sat. Review since 1945); "Through More History with J. Wesley Smith," 1953; "Louder and Funnier," 1954. Contributor cartoons to Sat. Review; Sat. Eve. Post; Christian Science Monitor; New York Times; and other major magazines. L., "Through History with J. Wesley Smith," for Columbia Lecture Bureau, N.Y.

SHAFER, ELIZABETH DODDS (Mrs. Ver! R.)—Painter
1915 Broad St., New Castle, Ind.

B. Cairo, Ill., Feb. 12, 1913. *Studied*: Butler Univ., A.B., and with Wayman Adams, Jerry Farnsworth. *Member*:

Indiana A. Cl. *Awards*: prizes, Indiana State Fair, 1949, 1952, 1954, 1957; Hoosier Salon, 1951, 1955, 1956; Indiana A. Cl., 1953, 1954, 1955, 1957; Michiana Regional, 1956. *Work*: in private colls. *Exhibited*: Hoosier Salon; Indiana A. Cl.; John Herron AI; Indiana State Fair; Old Northwest Territory Exh., Springfield; Nat. Exh. Am. A., New York, N.Y.; Michiana Regional.

SHAFFER, OWEN VERNON—*Museum Director, E., P.*
 Wright Art Center, Beloit College; h. 1141 Brewster Ave., Beloit, Wis.

B. Princeton, Ill., Jan. 26, 1928. *Studied*: Beloit Col., B.A.; Michigan State Univ., M.A. *Member*: AFA; AAMus.; Midwest Mus. Conf.; CAA. *Work*: City of Beloit. Arranged, designed and installed over 30 exhibitions for the Art Center, Beloit College; Designed and constructed exhibition of American Indian objects for the USIS for Overseas Exh. *Position*: Dir., Wright Art Center, Beloit College, Beloit, Wis.

SHAHN, BEN—*Painter, I., Ser., L.*
 Roosevelt, N.J.

B. Kovno, Lithuania, Sept. 12, 1898. *Studied*: N.Y. Univ.; City Col. of N.Y.; NAD; ASL; and in Paris. *Member*: AEA; Nat. Inst. A. & Let. *Awards*: Pennell medal, PAFA, 1939, 1953; A. Dir. medal, 1950; Charles Eliot Norton Prof. of Poetry, Harvard Univ., 1956-57; medal, AIGA, 1958.*Work*: MMA; MMoA; WMAA; AIC; SFMA; CAM; Joslyn A. Mus.; Wadsworth Atheneum; AGAA; Smith Col., and many other major museums and collections; Social Security Bldg., Wash., D.C.; USPO, Bronx, N.Y., and Jamaica, L.I., N.Y.; fresco, Hightstown (N.J.) Sch. *Exhibited*: all national exhibitions and also one-man retrospective exh., MMoA, 1947; one-man Venice, 1954 & in England. Contributor illus. to Fortune, Harpers, Town and Country, New Republic, Portfolio, and other leading, national magazines.*

SHALKOP, ROBERT L.—*Museum Director*
 Everhart Museum, Scranton 10, Pa.

B. Milford, Conn., July 30, 1922. *Studied*: Maryville (Tenn.) Col.; Univ. Chicago, M.A.; Sorbonne, Univ. Paris. *Member*: AAMus.; Am. Anthropological Assn.; Royal Anthropological Inst. of Great Britain and Ireland; Soc. for Am. Archaeology. Arranged exhs., among others, The George May Collection, 1957; "Collectors' Choice"; Regional Art Exhibition, 1958. *Positions*: Dir., Rahr Civic Center, Manitowoc, Wis., 1953-56; Dir., Everhart Museum, Scranton, Pa., at present.

SHALLENBERGER, MARTIN—*Painter, L.*
 Harrods Creek, Ky.; s. Eferding, Upper Austria

B. San Francisco, Cal., Sept. 22, 1912. *Studied*: Corcoran Sch. A.; ASL; NAD; U.S. Naval Acad., B.S.; Univ. Vienna, M.A. *Member*: AWS; NSMP. *Work*: murals, Supermarket, Stewart's Dry Goods Store, Commonwealth Bldg., Southside Baptist Church, all Louisville, and in private homes. *Exhibited*: Joslyn Mem. Mus.; Louisville, Ky.; Ferargil Gal.; Minneapolis, Minn.; and in France and Germany; one-man: Vienna, 1937; Budapest, 1936; Greenwich, Conn., 1939; Hanley Gal., Minneapolis, 1938; Joslyn Mem. Mus., 1939; Louisville A. Center, 1940; Louisville River Road Gal., 1942; Galerie Jeanne Castel, Paris, 1946; Ferargil Gal., 1946; Cal. PLH, 1947; San Diego FA Soc., 1948; Ruth Dicken Gal., Chicago, 1952; Louisville A. Center, 1953.

SHANE, FREDERICK E.—*Painter, Lith., E.*
 T-8, Dept. of Art, University of Missouri; h. 305 South Garth St., Columbia, Mo.

B. Kansas City, Mo., Feb. 2, 1906. *Studied*: Broadmoor A. Acad.; Kansas City AI, and with Randall Davey. *Awards*: prizes, CAM, 1942, 1943; Springfield Mus. A.; Davenport Mun. A. Gal., and others. *Work*: Scruggs-Vandervoort-Barney; CAM; William Rockhill Nelson Gal. A.; Palestinian Nat. A. Mus., Israel; Denver A. Mus.; Springfield (Mo.) Mus. A.; IBM; Abbott Laboratories; USPO, Eldon, Mo. *Exhibited*: AIC, CGA; PAFA; WFNY 1939; WMAA; Pepsi-Cola, 1945; Kansas City AI; Denver A. Mus.; CAM; Assoc. Am. A.; Los A. Mus. A.; Davenport Mun. A. Gal.; Joslyn A. Mus.; one-man: GRD Gal., N.Y.; Assoc. Am. A.; Kansas City AI; Vanguard Gal., St. Louis; Denver A. Mus.; Stendahl Gal., Los A.; Michi-

gan State Col.; Univ. Missouri (retrospective), 1951. *Position*: Prof. A., Chm., A. Dept., Univ. Missouri, Columbia, Mo.

SHANES, HARRY B.—*Painter, C.*
 Crafts Center, Salisbury, Vt.

B. Philadelphia, Pa., June 27, 1902. *Studied*: PAFA; Temple Univ.; Univ. Pennsylvania. *Member*: So. Vermont AA. *Exhibited*: PAFA.*

SHANES, MRS. HELEN BERRY. See *Berry, Helen Murrin*

SHANKS, BRUCE (McKINLEY)—*Editorial Cartoonist*
 Buffalo Evening News (5); h. 408 Ashland Ave., Buffalo 22, N.Y.

B. Buffalo, N.Y., Jan. 29, 1908. *Awards*: Freedoms Fnd. awards, 1952-1955, 1957; Pulitzer Prize for 1957 editorial cartoon. *Work*: Cartoons on permanent exh., Dept. Justice and Supreme Court Offices, Washington, D.C. *Exhibited*: Cartoon exhs., in schools, banks, colleges, etc. Cartoons reproduced in New York Times, Herald-Tribune, and other newspapers.

SHANNON, AILEEN PHILLIPS (Mrs. Edmund G.)—*Painter*
 1042 South Alameda Blvd., Las Cruces, N.M.

B. Gillsburg, Miss., Mar. 12, 1888. *Studied*: PAFA; Chicago Acad. FA, and with Pemberton Ginther, William M. Chase, Wayman Adams; Julian Acad., Paris; Art Instruction Inc., Minneapolis. *Member*: NAWA; Miss. AA; F., PAFA. *Work*: Miss. AA; Rock Springs (Wyo.) AA; New Mexico State Col.; Brannigan Mem. Lib., Las Cruces, N.M. *Exhibited*: Soc. Wash. A.; CGA; Grand Central A. Gal.; PAFA; Miss. AA; Delgado Mus. A.; El Paso, Tex.; DMFA; Santa Fe, N.M.; Albuquerque, N.M.; Parkersburg FA Center; Va. Intermont Col.; one-man: Jackson, Miss.; Santa Fé, N.M.; Alamogordo, Tularosa, Hobbs, N.M.

SHANNON, HOWARD J.—*Illustrator, W., P.*
 88-60 162nd St., Jamaica 32, L.I., N.Y.

B. Jamaica, L.I., N.Y., May 20, 1876. *Studied*: PIASch; & with Herbert Adams, Frank DuMond. *Work*: Queensboro Pub. Lib., Jamaica Branch. *Exhibited*: BM, 1935; PIASch; Queensboro Lib.; Jamaica, Far Rockaway, L.I., N.Y. Author, I., "The Book of the Seashore," 1935; Nature & Natural Science articles for Journal of Am. Mus. Natural Hist., Scientific Monthly, Nature, Harpers, American Forests, & other magazines.

SHANNON, MRS. WILLIAM. See *Lenney, Annie*

SHAPIRO, DANIEL—*Painter, Gr., E., Des.*
 Bennington College, Bennington, Vt.

B. New York, N.Y., Apr. 8, 1920. *Studied*: CUASch.; Columbia Univ. *Member*: AEA. *Work*: Graphic Des., record albums and magazine covers. *Exhibited*: nationally and internationally. One-man: Peter Cooper Gal., 1952. *Position*: A. Faculty, Bennington College, Bennington, Vt., 1947- .*

SHAPIRO, FRANK D.—*Painter*
 190-17B 69th Ave., Fresh Meadows, N.Y.

B. New York, N.Y., July 28, 1914. *Studied*: NAD; Col. City of N.Y., M.A. *Work*: mural, USPO, Washington, N.J. *Exhibited*: CGA, 1939; Syracuse Mus. FA, 1941; Detroit Inst. A.; etc. *Position*: Chm., A. Dept., Fashion, Inst. Tech., New York, N.Y.

SHAPLEY, FERN RUSK (Mrs. John)—*Museum Curator, W.*
 National Gallery of Art, Constitution Ave. at 6th St., Northwest (25); h. 326 A St., Southeast, Washington, 3, D.C.

B. Mahomet, Ill., Sept. 20, 1890. *Studied*: Univ. Missouri, A.B., A.M., Ph.D.; Bryn Mawr Col. *Awards*: F., in Archaeology, Bryn Mawr Col.; European Fellowship Grant,

1915; Resident F., Univ. Missouri, 1915-16. Author: "George Caleb Bingham, The Missouri Artist," 1917; "European Paintings from the Gulbenkian Collection," 1950; Co-author: "Comparisons in Art," 1957. Contributor articles to Gazette des Beaux-Arts; Art Quarterly; Art in America; American Journal of Archaeology, etc. *Positions*: Asst. in A. & Archaeology, 1916-17, Asst. Prof. A., 1925, Univ. Missouri; Research Asst., 1943-47, Cur., Paintings, 1957-56, Asst. Chief Cur., 1956- , National Gallery of Art, Washington, D.C.

SHARP, HAROLD—*Cartoonist*
50 East 191st St., New York 68, N.Y.

B. New York, N.Y., Mar. 2, 1920. *Studied*: NAD; Columbia Univ. Regular contributor to national magazines and newspapers. Feature panel in Journal of the American Medical Association.

SHARP, HILL—*Painter, Lith., T.*
3725 Riverside Ave., Muncie, Ind.

B. Pendleton County, Ky., Feb. 22, 1907. *Studied*: Ball State T. Col.; John Herron AI; in Europe; & with George Luks, George Pearse Ennis, Wayman Adams. *Member*: AEA; Indiana A.Cl.; Indiana Pr.M. *Awards*: prizes, Muncie AA, 1928, 1929, European scholarship, 1932; Hoosier Salon, 1934, 1936, 1938, 1939, 1941, 1943; Indiana A., 1939; Southern Pr.M., 1940; Indiana Pr.M., 1946; Indiana A.Cl., 1942, 1946. *Work*: Am. Church in Paris; Univ. Wisconsin; Univ. Cl., Madison, Wis.; Court House, Baraboo, Wis.; Indiana Univ.; Ft. Wayne A. Mus.; Ball State T. Col. *Exhibited*: VMFA, 1939; All.A.Am., 1939; Phila. Pr.Cl., 1939; Southern Pr.M., 1940; Hoosier Salon, 1929-1946; Indiana A., 1929-1946; Indiana A.Cl., 1940-1946; Indiana Pr.M., 1945, 1946.*

SHARP, MARION LEALE (Mrs. James R.)—*Painter*
1160 Fifth Ave., New York 29, N.Y.

B. New York, N.Y. *Studied*: ASL; and with Lucia Fairchild Fuller. *Member*: Nat. Lg. Am. Pen Women; Balt. WC Cl.; MMA. *Awards*: prizes, NCFA, 1946, 1952; Nat. Lg. Am. Pen Women, 1938. *Exhibited*: PAFA; Pa. Soc. Min. P.; BMA; Nat. Lg. Am. Pen Women; BM; Los A. Mus.; All. A. Am.; Grand Central A. Gal.; Soc. Min. P., New York; Detroit A. & Crafts Cl.; Chicago Soc. Min. P.; Governor's Exh., Nassau, Bahamas; Newport AA (one-man); Paris Salon, France.

SHARP, WILLIAM—*Painter, Et., Lith., I.*
66-20 108th St., Forest Hills 75, N.Y.

B. Lemberg, Austria, June 13, 1900. *Studied*: Acad. FA and Indst., Lemberg; Acad. FA, Crakow, and in Germany. *Member*: SAGA. *Awards*: prizes, LC; SAGA, and others. *Work*: LC; Carnegie Inst.; N.Y. Pub. Lib.; MMA, and other museums. *Exhibited*: LC; WMAA; MMA; Carnegie Inst. Contributor illustrations, cartoons to Life magazine; N.Y. Times magazine; Esquire; Coronet; N.Y. Post; and illus. for books.

SHATALOW, VLADIMIR—*Painter*
1920 Sansom St.; h. 2104 Poplar St., Philadelphia 30, Pa.

B. Bielgorod, Russia, June 20, 1917. *Studied*: A. Sch., Kharkow; Kiev AI, with Prof. Sharonow and Showkunenko. *Member*: Augsburg (Germany) AA. *Work*: Kiev AI; Hist. Mus., Dniepropetrovsk, Russia; Ministry of Edu., Czechoslovakia, and in private colls. in U.S. and Europe.*

SHAW, ALICE HARMON (Mrs. Donald B. Kirkpatrick)
Painter, Et.
Mitchell Rd., Cape Elizabeth, Me.; h. 31 Ocean View Ave., South Portland, Me.

B. Portland, Me., July 11, 1913. *Studied*: Sch. F. & Applied A., Portland, Me.; & with Alexander Bower. *Member*: Portland SA; Portland WC Cl.; Maine WC Soc. *Work*: Farnsworth Mus., Rockland, Me. *Exhibited*: Farnsworth Gal., Rockland, Me.; Los A. Mus. A., 1937; San Diego FA Soc., 1941; Denver A. Mus., 1941; AWCS, 1939, 1941; NAWA, 1939, 1941-1944; Portland SA, 1934-1955; Currier Gal. A., 1939, 1942; Portland WC Cl., 1942-1949; Hayloft AC, Portland, 1935-1949; Brick Store Mus., Kennebunk, Me., 1941, 1942, 1946-1958; Laing Gal., Portland, Me., 1955, 1958 (one-man); Maine WC Soc., 1949-1958.

SHAW, CHARLES GREEN—*Painter, I., W., Des.*
340 East 57th St., New York 22, N.Y.

B. New York, N.Y., May 1, 1892. *Studied*: Yale Univ., Ph.B.; Columbia Univ. *Member*: Am. Abstract A.; AEA; Century Assn.; Fed. Mod. P. & S.; Nantucket AA. *Award*: Nantucket AA, 1958. *Work*: PMA; BMA; Guggenheim Mus.; WMAA; Detroit Inst. A.; BM; CMA; Lawrence Mus.; Nantucket Fnd.; MModA; MMA; SFMA; BMFA; Newark Mus.; Cal. PLH; Dayton AI; CM; Yale Univ. Gal. FA; Berkshire Mus. *Exhibited*: AIC, 1943; MModA, 1951, 1957; Paris, France, 1950; Rome, Italy; Tokyo, Japan, 1954; Walker A. Center, 1954; Joslyn A. Mus., 1955; traveling exh., Europe, Intl. Assn. of Plastic A., 1956-57; Carnegie Inst., 1945; WMAA, 1946, 1957; Chicago AC, 1938; SFMA, 1938; SAM, 1938; Am. Abstract A., 1937-1958; Fed. Mod. P. & S., 1942-1958; Inst. Mod. A., Boston, 1945; one-man exh.: Valentine Gal., 1934, 1938; Gal. Living Art, N.Y., 1938; Art of Tomorrow Mus., 1940; Passedoit Gal., 1945, 1946, 1950, 1951, 1954, 1956, 1957, 1958; Nantucket AA, 1953-1958; BM, 1957; other exhs.: AFA traveling exh., 1955-56; Galerie Pierre, Paris, 1936; Mayor Gal., London, 1936; Berkshire Mus., 1940; Am-British A. Center, 1949 (one-man); 8 x 8 Exh., PMA, 1945; Riverside Mus., 1957, 1958. Author: "New York—Oddly Enough," 1938; "The Giant of Central Park," 1940; & other books. I., "The Milk that Jack Drank," "Black and White," 1944; "It Looked Like Spilt Milk," 1945. Contributor to: national magazines, newspapers, poetry magazines and anthologies.

SHAW, ELSA V. (Mrs. Glenn M.)—*Painter, C., Des*
Hickory Lane, Moreland Hills Village, Chagrin Falls, R.D. 4, Ohio

B. Cleveland, Ohio, Jan. 28, 1891. *Studied*: Cleveland Sch. A.; & with Henry Keller, Charles Hawthorne. *Member*: Cleveland Women's AC. *Awards*: prizes, CMA, 1923, 1927, 1929, 1932, 1934, 1937, 1944, 1945, 1955; Dayton AI, 1934. *Work*: murals, Severance Hall, Cleveland, Ohio; S.S. President Polk. *Exhibited*: CMA; Ohio WC Soc.*

SHAW, GLENN MOORE—*Painter, Des., T.*
175 Hickory Lane, Moreland Hills Village, Chagrin Falls, R.D. 4, Ohio

B. Olmsted Falls, Ohio, Feb. 6, 1891. *Studied*: Cleveland Inst. A.; & with Henry Keller, Charles Hawthorne. *Member*: Cleveland SA; Ohio WC Soc.; FA Com., Cleveland City Planning Comm. *Awards*: prizes, CMA, 1926, 1928, 1952. *Work*: CMA; murals, Central Nat. Bank, Cleveland, Ohio; Lincoln Nat. Bank, Ft. Wayne, Ind.; Old Nat. Bank, Lima, Ohio; Fed. Reserve Bank, Pittsburgh, Pa.; Statler Hotels, Cleveland, Ohio; Buffalo, N.Y.; Case Inst. Tech. Observatory; Shaker Savings Assn.; Rocky River war mem.; S.S. America; USPO, Canton, Warren, Perrysburg, Ohio; Wells Col., Aurora, N.Y. *Exhibited*: CMA, 1921-1954; Ohio WC Soc., 1928-1952; CMA traveling exh. *Position*: Pres., Cleveland SA, 1937-38, 1938-39; Pres., Ohio WC Soc., 1939, 1940; Instr., Cleveland Inst. A., Cleveland, Ohio (Retired 1957).

SHAW, HARRY HUTCHISON—*Painter, E., L.*
122 Edgewood Terrace, Lafayette, La.

B. Savannah, Ohio, Oct. 4, 1897. *Studied*: Univ. Michigan; Stanford Univ.; Univ. Mexico; PAFA; Ohio State Univ., B.F.A., M.A.; Cleveland Sch. A.; & with Hawthorne, Moffett, Garber, & others. *Member*: New Orleans AA. *Work*: Research Studio, Maitland, Fla.; Massillon Mus.; Canton AI; Southwestern La. Inst.; Akron YWCA; Akron Pub. Lib.; mural, Univ. Michigan; Lafayette (La.) Pub. Lib. *Exhibited*: PAFA, 1926; Phila. WC Cl., 1925; Phila. AC, 1926; Fla. Southern Col.; High Mus. A.; New Orleans AA; Contemp. A., N.Y.; Soc. Indp. A., 1926; Butler AI; Columbus Gal. FA; CM; Massillon Mus.; etc. I., "Quest," 1934 (a book of block prints). *Position*: Assoc. Prof., Southwestern Louisiana Inst., Lafayette, La., 1942-1958.

SHAW, MRS. HARRY HUTCHISON. See Allen, Margo

SHAW, LOIS HOGUE (Mrs. Elmer E.)—*Painter*
309 West Texas St., Sweetwater, Tex.

B. Merkel, Tex., Aug. 6, 1897. *Studied*: AIC; Baylor Col.; ASL, and with John Sloan and others. *Awards*: Texas FA Assn. (several); West Texas AA; Ft. Worth. *Work*: murals, Sweetwater H.S. *Exhibited*: group and one-man exhibitions regularly. *Position*: Instr. A., McMurry Col., Abilene; Baylor Col., Belton, Tex., and in public schools.

SHAW, WILFRED B.—*Painter, Et., I., W., Historian*
2026 Hill St., Ann Arbor, Mich.

B. Adrian, Mich., Jan. 10, 1881. *Studied:* Univ. Michigan, A.B.; Frank Holme Sch. Illus., Chicago. *Member:* Ann Arbor AA. *Exhibited:* Detroit, New York, Ann Arbor, Toronto, Chicago, Wash., D.C.; one-man exh., Hackley A. Gal.; Ann Arbor, Mich.; Detroit, Mich. Author, I., "Short History of Univ. Michigan," 1937; I., Michigan Alum. Quarterly Review; "Ballads and Songs of Southern Michigan"; "Fortress Islands of the Pacific"; "Short Account of the Copts," and others. Contributor to: International Studio, Craftsman, Scribner's, & other magazines.

SHAYN, JOHN—*Painter, Des., W., L.*
10 West 58th St. (19); h. 54 West 46th St., New York 36, N.Y.

B. Boston, Mass., Jan. 15, 1901. *Studied:* Boston Univ.; BMFA Sch.; Mass. Normal; ASL. *Member:* AEA. *Awards:* prize, N.Y. Building Congress for Des., 1927. *Exhibited:* PAFA, 1952; AWS, 1945-1947; Audubon A., 1947; All. A. Am., 1943. Lectures: Wax Color.

SHEA, AILEEN ORTLIP (Mrs. Alton J.)—*Painter, T.*
211 West State St., Wellsville, N.Y.

B. Philadelphia, Pa., Aug. 5, 1911. *Studied:* NAD; Sorbonne, Paris, France. *Awards:* Pulitzer traveling scholarship, 1935. *Exhibited:* Rochester-Finger Lakes Exh., 1946; David A. Howe Mem. Lib., Wellsville, N.Y., 1955. *Position:* Instr., A., Public Schools, Wellsville, N.Y.

SHEAR, FERA WEBBER—*Painter, L.*
600 Woodmont Ave., Berkeley 8, Cal.

B. Eustace, Fla., Mar. 20, 1893. *Studied:* Cornell Univ., B.E.; N.Y. Univ.; Cal. Col. A. & Crafts; Cal. Sch. FA. *Member:* Soc. Western A.; All Arts Cl., Berkeley. *Awards:* prizes, Cal. State Fair, 1934, 1936, 1937; GGE, 1939. *Exhibited:* Springville, Utah, 1935-1942, 1946; Oakland A. Mus., 1934-1940, 1948; Gump's, San F., 1934; Mission Inn, Riverside, Cal., 1933-1935; All Arts Cl., Berkeley, 1934-1940, 1951, 1954; Cal. PLH, 1939, 1940, 1942, 1945, 1947; Berkeley Woman's City Cl., 1934; Cal. State Fair, 1933-1938; Bay Region AA, 1935-1938; Soc. Western A., 1939-1942, 1945; GGE, 1939, and others. Many lectures on historic homes and buildings of California, accompanied by exhibition, to women's clubs, art groups and civic organizations.

SHECTER, PEARL S.—*Craftsman, S., P., T.*
1385 Lexington Ave., New York 28, N.Y.

B. New York, N.Y., Dec. 17, 1909. *Studied:* Hans Hofman Sch. A.; Columbia Univ., M.F.A.; New Bauhaus Sch. Des., Ill.; and with Adda Andersen, Ilse von Drage. *Member:* Intl. Soc. of Edu. through Art. *Award:* Carnegie grant, 1938. *Work:* sc., metal, jewelry, Miami Univ., Oxford, Ohio; sc., Mus. of Natural Hist., N.Y. *Exhibited:* Mus. Contemp. Crafts, N.Y.; DMFA, 1958; Huntington Gal., Huntington, W. Va.; 1956; WAC, 1955; VMFA, 1955; Camino Gal., N.Y., 1958; one-man: Mus. Nat. Hist.; Contemporaries Gal., 1956; IFA Gal., Wash., D.C., 1957. Author: "Designed by You in Silver," 1954. Contributor to Art Today magazine. L., N.Y. Univ., 1958- .

SHEELER, CHARLES—*Painter*
Dows Lane, Irvington-on-Hudson, N.Y.

B. Philadelphia, Pa., July 16, 1883. *Studied:* PMSchIA; PAFA; & with William Chase. *Awards:* Harris prize, med., 1945; Hallmark award, 1957. *Work:* BMFA; FMA; Columbus Gal. FA; WMA; Springfield Mus. A.; AIC; PAFA; MModA; Newark Mus.; Santa Barbara Mus. A.; Univ. Nebraska; WMAA; Detroit Inst. A.; Palace Legion Honor; PMG; CMA; and many others. *Exhibited:* nationally; retrospective exh., UCLA, 1954, and subsequently on circuit; one-man: Downtown Gal., 1958. *Position:* A. in Residence, Phillips Acad., Andover, Mass., 1946; Currier Gal. A., Manchester, N.H., 1948.

SHEETS, MILLARD OWEN—*Painter, T., Des., I., L.*
Claremont, Cal.

B. Pomona, Cal., June, 1907. *Studied:* Chouinard AI. *Member:* NA; Cal. WC Soc.; AWS; Soc. Motion Picture A. Dirs. *Awards:* prizes, AIC, 1938; Cal. State Fair, 1930, 1932, 1933, 1938; Santa Cruz A. Lg., 1931, 1933; Los A.

Mus. A., 1932, 1945; P. & S. Cl., 1932; Los A. County Fair, 1928, 1930; Arizona State Fair, 1928-1930; San Antonio, Tex., 1929; Cal. WC Soc., 1927. *Work:* MMA; AIC; Los A. Mus. A.; White House, Wash., D.C.; WMAA; BM; SFMA; Dayton AI; CMA; SAM; R.I. Sch. Des.; Witte Mem. Mus.; Mus. FA of Houston; Wood Mem. Gal.; Albany Inst. Hist. & A.; Ft. Worth Mus. A.; San Diego FA Soc.; Hackley A. Gal.; deYoung Mem. Mus.; Univ. Oklahoma; N.Y. Pub. Lib.; Los A. Pub. Lib.; numerous sch. & col.; Des., Home Savings & Loan Bldg., Nat. Am. Insurance Bldg., Los A., 1956. Murals, Pomona First Federal Savings & Loan; Interior & exterior of Our Lady of the Assumption Church, Ventura, Cal.; Altar mural, Precious Blood Church, Los A.; annual calendar, United Airlines. *Exhibited:* AIC; WFNY 1939; Denver A. Mus.; Faulkner Mem. Gal.; Currier Gal. A.; BMFA; CGA; VMFA; Sao Paulo, Brazil, 1955; WMAA; Carnegie Inst.; CAM; Oakland A. Gal.; Albright A. Gal.; Kansas City AI; Nebraska AA, etc.; one-man exh.: Delgado Mus. A.; Brooks Mem. A. Gal.; Springfield A. Mus.; Rochester Mem. A. Gal.; High Mus. A.; Honolulu Acad. A.; Milch Gal.; Dalzell Hatfield Gal., Los A.; & many others. I., "Sketches Abroad." *Position:* Hd. A. Dept., Scripps Col., Claremont, Cal., 1932-35; A., Life magazine, Burma-India front; Balch L., Scripps Col.; Hd., Los Angeles County AI, Los Angeles, Cal., 1953- ; Prof. A., Scripps Col., 1938- .

SHEETS, NAN (Mrs. Fred C.)—*Museum Director, Cr., P., L.*
Plaza Circle, Fair Park, Box 3967; h. 401 Northwest 18th St., Oklahoma City 3, Okla.

B. Albany, Ill., Dec. 9, 1889. *Studied:* Valparaiso (Ind.) Univ.; & with John Carlson, Robert Reid, Birger Sandzen, Hugh Breckenridge, & others. *Member:* Oklahoma A. Lg.; F., Royal Soc. A., London; Assn. Oklahoma A. *Awards:* prizes, Broadmoor A. Acad., 1924; Kansas City AI, 1924; SSAL, 1929; elected to Oklahoma Hall of Fame for contribution to cultural life of the State. *Work:* Kansas City AI; Fla. Southern Col.; Springfield (Ill.) Mus. A.; Oklahoma Univ.; Vanderpool Coll.; Dallas Mus. FA. Contributor: art column, Daily Oklahoman. *Position:* Dir., Oklahoma A. Center, Oklahoma City, Okla., 1935- .

SHEFFIELD, CLINTON A.—*Educator*
State Teachers College, Dickinson, N.D.
Position: Dir. Art Dept.*

SHELTON, ALPHONSE JOSEPH—*Painter*
Wiscasset, Me.

B. Liverpool, England, Feb. 11, 1905. *Studied:* BMFA Sch. *Member:* Gld. Boston A.; Grand Central A. Gal. *Awards:* med., Soc. for Sanity in Art, 1941. *Work:* Farnsworth Mus. A., Rockland, Me.; Bowdoin Col.; Sheldon Swope A. Mus., Terre Haute, Ind. *Position:* Chm., Maine Art Commission.

SHEPARD, GILBERT C.—*Painter*
9422 80th St., Ozone Park 16, N.Y.

B. New York, N.Y., July 10, 1884. *Studied:* NAD. *Member:* A. Lg. of Long Island (Pres., 1958); St. Luke's A. Gld. *Awards:* N.Y. State Fair, 1940, 1942, 1956; A. Lg. of Long Island, 1948, 1952, 1955-1957; St. Luke's A. Gld., 1952, 1956, 1957, 1958. *Work:* A. Lg. of Long Island, and in private colls. *Exhibited:* Queens A. Festival, 1950-1957; A. Lg. of Long Island, 1948-1958; Washington Square, N.Y., 1949-1952; Flushing, L.I., 1949-1951; St. Luke's A. Gld., 1953-1958; N.Y. State Fair, 1940, 1942, 1946; N.Y.C. Golden Jubilee, 1948; group shows, 1953-1955.

SHEPHERD, DOROTHY G. (Payer)—*Museum Curator*
Cleveland Museum of Art, Cleveland 6, Ohio; h. Giles Road, Moreland Hills (Chagrin Falls P.O.), Ohio

B. Wellend, Ont., Canada, Aug. 15, 1916. *Studied:* Univ. Michigan, A.B., M.A.; N.Y. Univ., Inst. FA. *Member:* CAA; Archaeological Soc. Am.; Am. Research Center in Egypt; Centre Intl. des études des Textiles Anciens, Middle East Institute; Am. Soc. for Aesthetics. Contributor to Ars Orientalis; Bulletin of the Cleveland Museum of Art. Lectures: Islamic Art and Architecture; Art & Architecture of Spain; Islamic and Medieval Textiles. *Positions:*

Monuments Officer, Monuments and Fine Arts Section, SHAEF (Berlin), 1945-47; Cur. Textiles, Cleveland Museum of Art, Cleveland, Ohio, at present.

SHEPHERD, J. CLINTON—*Painter, S., L.*
262 Sunrise Ave., Palm Beach, Fla.

B. Des Moines, Iowa, Sept. 11, 1888. *Studied:* Univ. Missouri; Kansas City Sch. FA; AIC; BAID; & with Walter Ufer, Harvey Dunn. *Member:* Palm Beach A. Lg.; Soc. Four A. *Awards:* prize, Miami A. Lg., 1940; Palm Beach A. Lg., 1941. *Work:* John Herron AI; mem., Westport, Conn. *Exhibited:* NAD; PAFA; Norton Gal.; Silvermine Gld. A. Lectures: History of Art; Art Appreciation.

SHEPLER, DWIGHT (CLARK)—*Painter, I., W., S.*
95 Dudley Rd., Newton Center 59, Mass.

B. Everett, Mass., Aug. 11, 1905. *Studied:* BMFA Sch.; Williams Col., B.A. *Member:* St. Botolph Cl., Boston; Gld. Boston A.; Boston Soc. WC Painters. *Work:* U.S. Navy; Lawrence A. Mus., Williams Col., Williamstown, Mass.; Dartmouth, England, Mus.; murals, U.S. Naval Acad., Annapolis, Md.; port., U.S. Naval War Col., Newport, R.I.; NAD; mon., Ellsmore Island, for Arctic Inst. North America; habitat backgrounds, Boston Mus. Sc. *Exhibited:* PAFA, 1936; AIC, 1940; CGA, 1943; Carnegie Inst., 1944; BMFA, 1943, 1951, 1952, 1957, 1958; NAD, 1956; Minneapolis Inst. A., 1943; NGA, 1943-1945; Joslyn A. Mus., 1955; Salon de la Marine, Paris, 1945; MMA, 1945, 1949; Montclair A. Mus., 1941 (one-man); Philbrook A. Center, 1942; one-man exh., Boston, New York, Chicago, etc. I., "Many a Watchful Night," 1944; "The Navy at War," 1943; Life's Picture History World War II, 1950, & other books. Contributor to: Sportsman, Country Life, Pageant, Life, Ford Times, & other national magazines.

SHERIDAN, JOSEPH MARSH—
Painter, Gr., S., I., L., E.
P.O. Box 174, New Wilmington, Pa.

B. Quincy, Ill., Mar. 11, 1897. *Studied:* Beloit Col., B.A.; ASL; AIC; Univ. California, M.A.; & with Norton, Hofmann, Archipenko. *Member:* San F. AA; San Diego A. Gld.; A. Cong. *Awards:* prize, Minneapolis Inst. A., 1931. *Work:* SFMA; Berkeley (Cal.) Pub. Lib.; Oakland Pub. Lib.; Univ. California; Beloit Col.; Univ. Minnesota; AF of L Bldg., San F., Cal.; Univ. Arizona; Mills Col.; Westminster Col., Pa.; Oakland (Cal.) H.S.; Piedmont (Cal.) H.S. *Exhibited:* Minneapolis Inst. A., 1930; European & Am. Abstractions Exh., 1933; Oakland A. Gal., 1932-1945; SFMA, 1932-1945; AIC, 1931, 1933; many one-man exh. in U.S. *Position:* Instr., A., Univ. Minnesota, 1928-30; Asst. Prof. A., Univ. Arizona, 1944-45; Acting Hd., Dept. A., Westminster Col., New Wilmington, Pa., 1945-46.*

SHERIDAN, MARK—*Designer, P.*
Ridgeland, S.C.

B. Atlanta, Ga., May 23, 1884. *Studied:* Georgia Sch. Tech.; PAFA. *Member:* NAC; Georgia AA; Savannah AC. *Work:* Telfair Acad. A. & Sc., Savannah, Ga. *Exhibited:* NAC, 1940, 1945; Georgia AA; Savannah AC.*

SHERMAN, EFFIM H.—*Painter, Gr., T., I.*
315 East 9th St., New York 3, N.Y.

B. Roumania. *Studied:* CUASch; NAD, and with Emil Carlsen, Douglas Volk, and others. *Member:* SAGA; Wash. WC Cl.; Conn. Acad. FA. *Awards:* prizes, SAGA, 1943; Carnegie Inst., 1950; Audubon A., 1954; Albany Pr. Cl., 1957. *Work:* MMA; BM; PMA; AGAA; Carnegie Inst.; Pa. State Univ.; and in many H.S., New York. *Exhibited:* NAD, 1938-1946; PAFA, 1937, 1938, 1950; AIC, 1939; Los A. Mus. A., 1938; SFMA, 1942, 1944, 1946, 1953; SAM, 1937-1946; SAGA, 1937-1946, 1948-1957; Phila. Pr. Cl., 1950, 1952, 1954; Albany Inst. Hist. & A., 1943-1945, 1957; CGA, 1940; Portland Soc. A., 1952; Conn. Acad. FA, 1948-1958; Smithsonian Inst., 1952, 1956-1958; Audubon A., 1948-1952, 1956, 1957; Chicago Soc. Et., 1952-1956; Newport AA, 1948-1958; LC, 1948-1951; Carnegie Inst., 1948, 1950; Laguna Beach AA; Albany Soc. Et.; Buffalo Pr. Cl.; MMA, 1952, 1955; Portland Mus. A., 1953-1955; Albany Pr. Cl., 1955, 1957; Wash. WC Cl., 1954, 1955, and others.

SHERMAN, F. TAYLOR (FLORENCE TAYLOR KUSHNER)—*Painter*
22 Anthony Arcade, Coconut Grove, Fla.; h. 2224 South West 16th Ave., Miami 35, Fla.

B. Boston, Mass., Sept. 20, 1911. *Studied:* BMFA Sch.; & with Philip Hale, Florence Spaulding, Bernard Keyes. *Member:* Miami A. Lg.; Blue Dome F.; Fla. Fed. A. (Dir.); Copley Soc., Boston. *Awards:* prizes, Fla. Fed. A., 1937; Miami A. Lg., 1941, 1942, 1944; AAPL, 1941, 1943, 1944. *Exhibited:* Sarasota, Fla., 1936, 1937; Blue Dome F., 1941, 1945; Miami Beach A. Gal., 1941; Miami A. Lg., 1940-1942; Fla. Fed. A., 1937, 1938, 1940-1946; Univ. Nebraska, 1938. *Lectures:* Early History of Portrait Painting.*

SHERMAN, JAMES RUSSELL—*Painter, Lith., I.*
317 West 56th St., New York 19, N.Y.; s. Box 751, Lamar, Colo.

B. Maxwell, Iowa. *Studied:* Kansas City AI; ASL. *Work:* Philbrook A. Center; Logan County A. Mus., Colo.; murals, USPO, Loveland, Colo.; U.S. Army. *Exhibited:* WFNY 1939; Lib. Cong., 1943, 1945, 1946; AIC, 1939, 1940; PAFA, 1942; Carnegie Inst., 1943; Denver A. Mus., 1940, 1942; Philbrook A. Center, 1945 (one-man); 8th St. Gal., 1938 (one-man). I., "So You Think It's New," 1939; "City Government," 1941; & other books. Contributor to: national magazines & newspapers. *Position:* A. Ed., Nat. Ice Skating Guide, 1943, 1944, 1946-52.*

SHERMAN, JESSIE (GORDAN)—*Painter, Des.*
27 West Cedar St., Boston 8, Mass.

B. Lenox, Mass. *Studied:* with Vesper George, William B. Hazelton, Umberto Romano. *Member:* NAWA; Boston Soc. Indp. A. *Exhibited:* Inst. Mod. A., Boston, 1941, 1944; NAWA, 1945; Jordan Marsh Gal., annually; Boston Soc. Indp. A., annually. *Position:* Dir., Boston Soc. Indp. A.

SHERMAN, JOHN K(URTZ)—*Critic*
2502 West 22nd St., Minneapolis 5, Minn.

B. Sioux City, Iowa, Apr. 19, 1898. *Studied:* Univ. Minnesota. *Position:* A. Ed. & Cr., Music & Drama Cr., Minneapolis (Minn.) Star & Tribune, at present.

SHERMAN, WINNIE BORNE (Mrs. Lee D.)—
Painter, L., T.
96 Fifth Ave.; h. 176 East 77th St., New York 21, N.Y.

B. New York, N.Y. Nov. 10, 1902. *Studied:* T. Col., Columbia Univ.; CUASch., B.F.A.; NAD; ASL. *Member:* ASL; AWS; AAPL; All. A. Am.; Catherine L. Wolfe A. Cl.; NAC; F., Royal Soc. A., London; Westchester A. & Crafts; New Rochelle AA. *Awards:* prizes, American Artist magazine, 1953; New Rochelle AA; Westchester County Fed. Women's Cl., 1954; Westchester A. & Crafts, 1954; Fla. Southern Col., 1952; New Rochelle Women's Cl., 1954, 1957, and others. *Work:* Seton Hall Univ. Lib.; Grand Central A. Gal.; Grumbacher Coll.; IBM. *Exhibited:* AWS, 1933; Grand Central Gal., 1955; AAPL, 1954-1958; NAC, 1955-1959; Fifty American Artists, Newton Gal., 1955-1958 and SC, 1955-1958; Hudson Valley AA, 1953-1955; New Rochelle AA, 1945-1957; Mt. Vernon AA, 1953-1957; Westchester A. & Crafts Gld., 1945-1958; Burr Gal., 1957-1959; Vendome Gal., 1941, 1942; Ligoa Duncan Gal., 1958; one-man: Westchester County Center, 1951; New Rochelle Pub. Lib., 1953; Arch. Lg., N.Y., 1954; Burr Gal., 1957. Lectures: Watercolor Techniques. "Poems in Paint" demonstrations, to women's clubs, TV, art clubs, etc.

SHERMUND, BARBARA—
Cartoonist, I., Gr., P., Comm. A.
115 East 37th St., New York 16, N.Y.; also, 901 Ocean Ave., Seabright, N.J.

B. San Francisco, Cal. *Studied:* Cal. Sch. FA; ALS. *Member:* SI; Nat. Cartoonists Soc. Contributor to King Features Syndicate, Esquire, New Yorker, and others.

SHERRY, WILLIAM GRANT—*Painter, T.*
Spear St., Rockport, Me.

B. Amagansett, L.I., N.Y., Dec. 7, 1914. *Studied:* Academie Julian, Paris, France, with Pierre Jerome; The

Heatherly Sch. A., London, England, with Ian McNab. *Awards*: prizes, Laguna Beach Festival A.; purchase prize, Springfield Mus. A. *Work*: Springfield Mus. A., Springfield, Mass. *Exhibited*: Laguna Beach Festival A., 1949, 1950, 1951; Portland (Me.) A. Mus., 1953-1958; Boston A. Festival, 1956; Art:USA, 1958; Silvermine Gld. A., 1957; Delgado Mus. A., 1958; Colby Col., 1956; Farnsworth Mus. A., 1956-1957; Univ. Maine, 1956-1958; oneman: Univ. Maine, 1958; Maine A. Gal., Wiscasset, 1958; Ringling Mus. A., Sarasota, 1949; Portland (Me.) Mus. A., 1959. *Position*: Instr., Painting, A. Dir., Florida Gulf Coast A. Center, Clearwater, Fla.

SHIBLEY, GERTRUDE—*Painter*
    92 Christopher St., New York 14, N.Y.

B. New York, N.Y., Dec. 10, 1916. *Studied*: Brooklyn Col., B.A., with Francis Criss; Hans Hofmann Sch. FA. *Member*: Spiral Group (Sec.) *Awards*: prize, Village A. Center, 1949. *Exhibited*: WFNY 1939; Springfield Mus. A.; Riverside Mus.; Contemp. A.; Art:USA, 1958; oneman: Panoras Gal., 1954, 1958; Copain Gal., 1953. *Position*: Instr., Community Center of East Side, 1938-42; Ruth Ettinger Sch., 1954-55; Beach Brook Sch., 1955-56.

SHIFF, E. MADELINE (Mrs. Madeline Shiff Wiltz)—
    Painter, C.
    Woodstock, N.Y.

B. Denver, Colo. *Studied*: Adelphi Col., B.A.; ASL. *Member*: Woodstock AA. *Awards*: prize, Charlotte R. Smith Mem. award, Baltimore, Md., 1923. *Work*: WMAA. *Exhibited*: Rudolph Gal., Woodstock; Coral Gables, Fla.

SHIMIN, SEMYON—*Painter, I.*
    32 East 10th St., New York 3, N.Y.

B. Astrakhan, Russia, Nov. 1, 1902. *Studied*: CUASch., and with George Luks. *Member*: AEA. *Work*: murals, Dept. Justice, Wash., D.C.; USPO, Tonawanda, N.Y.; Chrysler A. Mus. *Award*: purchase prize, Provincetown A. Festival. *Exhibited*: WMAA; CGA; AIC; Nat. Mus., Ottawa, Canada; U.S. Exh., Guatemala, 1941; BM; NGA; Provincetown A. Festival. Illus. for children's books.

SHIMON, PAUL—*Painter, C.*
    340 Cherry St., New York, N.Y.

B. New York, N.Y., Nov. 11, 1922. *Studied*: ASL, and with Jean Liberte. *Awards*: Shiva scholarship, 1948; Emily Lowe award, 1954. *Exhibited*: Audubon A., 1951, 1956; Soc. Painters in Casein, 1956; Alabama WC Soc., 1948, 1951; one-man: RoKo Gal., 1946; Tribune, 1950, 1952; Panoras Gal., 1955 (group); N.Y. City A. Center, 1954-1956.*

SHIPLEY, JAMES R.—*Educator, Des.*
    University of Illinois, Urbana, Ill.; h. 1409 West Healey St., Champaign, Ill.

B. Marion, Ohio, Dec. 26, 1910. *Studied*: Cleveland Sch. A.; Western Reserve Univ., B.S.; Univ. Southern California; Inst. Des., Chicago; Univ. Illinois, A.M. *Member*: Am. Soc. Indst. Des.; CAA; Indst. Des. Edu. Assn.; IDI; Midwest Col. A. Conf. Lectures: "What is a Designer?"; "The Modern Movement." *Positions*: Des., General Motors Corp., Styling Section, 1936-39; Prof. Indst. Des., 1939- , Actg. Chm., Dept. A., 1955-56, Hd. Dept. A., 1956- , University of Illinois; Edu. Comm., Am. Soc. Indst. Des., 1957-58; Vice-Pres., Indst. Des. Edu. Assn., 1957-58; Chm., Program Comm., Midwest Col. A. Conf., 1958; Memb., Visual Arts Comm., Festival of the Americas, Chicago, 1959. Contributor articles to professional journals. Design Consultant to many Illinois firms.

SHIRLEY, ALFARETTA DONKERSLOAT—
    Craftsman, S., T.
    Parsonage Hill Rd., Short Hills, N.J.

B. New Jersey, Aug. 2, 1891. *Studied*: Parsons Sch. Des.; Columbia Univ., B.S., M.A.; Alfred Univ., with Charles F. Binns. *Member*: CAA; Nat. Assn. A. Edu.; Am. Assn. Univ. Women; Artist-Craftsmen of N.Y.; Millburn-Short Hills A. Center; Nat. Edu. Assn.; New Jersey Edu. Assn.; Newark AC. *Exhibited*: Syracuse Mus. FA; Arch. L.; Montclair A. Mus.; Newark Mus.; N.Y. Ceramic Soc. traveling exh.; Rutgers Univ.; Millburn-Short Hills A.

Center. *Position*: Instr., Ceramics, Newark Sch. F. & Indst. A., 1921-34; Instr., A. & A. Hist., Barringer H.S., Newark, N.J., 1935-56; Parsonage Hills Studio, 1956- .

SHIVELY, PAUL—*Painter*
    230 East 48th St., New York 17, N.Y.
Member: AWS.*

SHOEMAKER, MRS. EDNA COOKE. See Cooke, Edna

SHOEMAKER, VAUGHN—*Cartoonist*
    Box V, Ocean View & Scenic Dr., Carmel, Cal.

B. Chicago, Ill., Aug. 11, 1902. *Studied*: Chicago Acad. FA. *Member*: Nat. Cartoonists Soc.; Nat. Press Cl. *Awards*: Pulitzer prize, 1938, 1947; Freedoms Fnd., 1949-1953, 1957; National Headliners award, 1942; National Safety Council grand award, 1945, 1949; Hon. degree, D. Litt., Wheaton Col., Wheaton, Ill. *Exhibited*: O'Brien Gal., Chicago, 1935, 1936; Marshall Field, 1938; perm. cart. coll., Huntington Lib., San Marino, Cal. Author, I., 6 cartoon books; first telecasting of cartoon, Chicago, 1930; TV shows "Over Shoemaker's Shoulder," WBKB, NBC, ABC, 1949, 1950. *Position*: Instr., Chicago Acad. FA, 1927-42; Cart., 1922- , Chief Cart., 1925-50, Chicago (Ill.) Daily News; Editorial Cart., N.Y. Herald Tribune & Syndicate, 1956.

SHOENFELT, JOSEPH FRANKLIN—*Painter, C., E.*
    State Teachers College, Oswego, N.Y.

B. Everett, Pa., Nov. 17, 1918. *Studied*: State T. Col., Indiana, Pa., B.S. in A. Edu.; T. Col., Columbia Univ., M.A.; Grad. study, Syracuse Univ., and Sch. for Am. Craftsmen, Rochester, N.Y.; Univ. Guanajuato, Mexico, M.F.A. *Member*: AFA; NAEA; CAA; Syracuse Univ. A. Faculty. *Work*: mural, State T. Col., Indiana, Pa. *Exhibited*: Harrisburg AA, 1941; All. A. Johnstown; Finger Lakes Exh., 1953; N.Y. State Fair, 1953, 1954; San Miguel de Allende, Mexico, 1958. *Position*: Assoc. Prof. A., State T. Col., Oswego, N.Y.; Guest Instr., San Miguel de Allende, 1958.

SHOESMITH, MARK—*Sculptor*
    1324 Alaska Ave., Alamogordo, N.M.

B. Payette, Ida., Aug. 11, 1912. *Studied*: Univ. Oregon, B.A., and grad. study in sculpture with Oliver Barrett; Master Inst. of United Artists, with Louis Slobodkin; T. Col., Columbia Univ., M.A., and with Maldarelli, Archipenko. *Work*: Hyde Park Mus., and in private colls.; busts, plaques, statues, Oregon State Sch. for the Blind; Ripley Odditorium; Albertina Kerr Nursery Home, Portland, Ore.; Presidential Palace, Buenos Aires, Argentina; Royal Canadian Golf Assn., Toronto. *Exhibited*: Nat. Exh., N.Y., 1938; Arch. Lg., 1941; Mus. New Mexico, Santa Fé, 1954, 1955. *Position*: A.T., N.Y. Inst. for the Blind, 1938-44; Mngr. Dept. for Blind, Goodwill Industries, Dayton, Ohio, 1944-48; Mngr., New Mexico Industries for the Blind, Div. New Mexico Sch. for Visually Handicapped, 1948- .*

SHOKLER, HARRY—*Printmaker, P., L., W., T.*
    Londonderry, Vt.

B. Cincinnati, Ohio, Apr. 25, 1896. *Member*: Grand Central A. Gal.; Nat. Serigraph Soc.; So. Vermont A. *Awards*: Friburg traveling scholarship, 1927. *Work*: MMA; Syracuse Mus. FA; PMA; Newark Mus.; Dayton AI; Carnegie Inst.; Munson-Williams-Proctor Inst.; Cincinnati Pub. Lib.; Princeton Pr. Cl.; Lib. Cong. *Exhibited*: NAD, 1943-1946; Lib. Cong., 1944, 1945; SFMA, 1945; Northwest Pr. M., 1944, 1945; etc. Author: "Artists Manual for Silkscreen Printmaking," 1946. Lectures: Serigraphy.

SHONNARD, EUGENIE F.—*Sculptor, C.*
    226 Hickox St.; (mail) P.O. Box 1249, Santa Fé, N.M.

B. Yonkers, N.Y., Apr. 29, 1886. *Studied*: ASL; & with Emile Bourdelle, Auguste Rodin, Paris, France. *Member*: Taos AA; NSS; Salon d'Automne, Salon Nationale des Beaux-Arts, Paris. *Awards*: prizes, New Mexico State Fair, 1940, 1941. *Work*: Tingley Hospital for Crippled Children, Hot Springs, N.M.; Luxembourg Mus., Paris; MMA; CMA; Colorado Springs FA Center; Brookgreen Gardens, S.C.; Catholic Seminary, Santa Fé; Supreme

Court, Santa Fé; Presbyterian Hospital, Albuquerque; Mus. New Mexico, Santa Fé; Sandia Sch., Albuquerque, N.M.; Statue, St. Francis, Denver, Colo.; St. Andrews Episcopal Church, Las Cruces, N.M.; IBM Coll. *Exhibited*: Mus. New Mexico, 1953, 1954, 1956-1958; retrospective, 1954; New Mexico A., 1956-1958; Arch. L.; WFNY 1939; WMAA, 1940; one-man exh., Paris, France, 1926.

SHOOK, JANET (Mrs. Phil)—Painter, T., C.
510 Carleton St., San Antonio, Tex.

B. Austin, Tex., July 9, 1912. *Studied*: Incarnate Word Col., and with Hugo Pohl, Dan Lutz, Alice Naylor, and others. *Member*: Texas WC Soc. *Awards*: prizes, Texas FA Festival, Austin, 1953; Texas WC Soc., 1954; San Angelo Mus. A., 1954. *Exhibited*: Audubon A.; Texas General, 1946-1948, 1950; Texas WC Soc., 1952, 1954; San Antonio A. Lg.; San Angelo Mus. A.; one-man: Frost Bros., San Antonio, 1955; Witte Mus. A.; La Villeta, San Antonio; Elisabet Ney Mus.; and others. Founder, Julian Onderdonk Mem. Fund (purchase prize fund for Texas artists).*

SHOPEN, KENNETH—Painter
2052 North Orleans St., Chicago 14, Ill.

B. Elgin, Ill., Sept. 11, 1902. *Studied*: Univ. Illinois, B.A.; AIC. *Member*: CAA; AAUP; Am. Soc. for Aesthetics. *Work*: Norton Gal. A.; Dartmouth Col.; Toledo Mus. A.; Chicago Pub. Lib. *Exhibited*: CGA; PAFA; AIC; Carnegie Inst.; VMFA, and others. *Positions*: Instr. A., AIC, 1932-45; Biarritz Am. Univ., France, 1945-46; Assoc. Prof. A., Univ. Illinois, Chicago Div., 1946- ; A. Cr., Chicago Daily News, 1953-1956.

SHORE, LILLI ANN KILLEN—Craftsman, E.
Henry Street Settlement (2); h. 375 Riverside Drive, New York 25, N.Y.

B. Detroit, Mich., July 22, 1924. *Position*: Hd. A. Dept., Henry Street Settlement, New York, N.Y.

SHORTER, EDWARD SWIFT—
Museum Director, P., E., Cr., W., L.
Columbus Museum of Fine Arts, 1251 Wynnton Rd.; h. Folly Hill, River Rd., Columbus, Ga.

B. Columbus, Ga., July 2, 1902. *Studied*: Mercer Univ., A.B.; Corcoran Sch. A.; Fontainebleau, France, and with Wayman Adams, Hugh Breckenridge, and with Andre L'Hote, in Paris. *Member*: AAPL; Soc. Wash. A.; AEA; SAGA; NAC; SC; Studio Gld.; All. A. Am.; SSAL; Assn. Ga. A.; Columbus AA. *Awards*: prizes, Assn. Georgia A., 1934; Soc. Wash. A., 1938; Atlanta, Ga., 1947; Studio Gld., 1940. *Work*: Montgomery Mus. FA; High Mus. A.; Georgia Mus. A., Athens; Kansas State Mus., Hays, Kans.; Mercer Univ.; Baylor Univ.; Southern Baptist Seminary, Louisville; Washington Mem. Lib., Macon, Ga.; Wesleyan Col., Macon, Ga.; Fed. Housing Project, Columbus, Ga.; First Baptist Church, Columbus. *Exhibited*: PAFA; CGA; WFNY 1939; SSAL; SFMA; Southeastern AA, 1954; Soc. Wash. A.; Assoc. Georgia A., annually, and others. *Positions*: Instr. Painting, Burnsville, N.C.; Acting Dir., Columbus Mus. A. & Crafts, Columbus, Ga., 1953-55; Dir. 1955- ; Pres., Assn. Georgia A., 1955-57; Columbus AA.*

SHOTWELL, HELEN HARVEY—
Painter, Pictorial Photog.
Woodstock, N.Y.; also, 257 West 86th St., New York, N.Y.

B. New York, N.Y., Apr. 21, 1908. *Studied*: painting, with Henry Lee McFee; photography with Flora Pitt Conrey. *Member*: NAWA; Woodstock AA. *Work*: IBM; Fitchburg A. Mus.; Albert Schweitzer Fnd.; China Inst., N.Y. *Exhibited*: Dayton AI; Montclair A. Mus.; High Mus. A.; Carnegie Inst.; PAFA; CGA; SFMA; WFNY 1939; one-man: Argent Gal.; Fitchburg A. Center; Carolina AA; photographs shown in international salons, New Zealand, Iceland, India, Spain, South America, U.S.

SHOUDY, THEODORE—Painter, T.
Wells, N.Y.; w. 9 Chester St., Mt. Vernon, N.Y.

B. Brooklyn, N.Y., Mar. 23, 1881. *Studied*: Adelphi Col.; ASL, and with William Chase, Jane Peterson. *Member*: Academic A., Springfield; SC; New Orleans AA; AEA; Mt. Vernon AA; Hudson Valley AA; AAPL; Yonkers

AA. *Awards*: prizes, Mt. Vernon AA, 1947; Westchester Women's Cl., 1948; Hudson Valley AA, 1953, 1956; Yonkers AA, 1958. *Work*: Mt. Vernon A. Center; Vanolyn Gal., Fleetwood, N.Y.; Hall of Art; Little Studio, N.Y. *Exhibited*: SC, 1933-1950, 1956-1958; All. A. Am., 1952; Hudson Valley AA, 1946-1958. One-man: Barbizon Gal., 1957; Bronxville, 1958.

SHOULBERG, HARRY—Painter, Ser.
567 Ave. of the Americas; h. 1915 Walton Ave., New York 53, N.Y.

B. Philadelphia, Pa., Oct. 25, 1903. *Studied*: Col. of the City N.Y.; Am. A. Sch., and with Sol Wilson, Carl Holty, G. Glintenkamp. *Member*: AEA; An Am. Group; Nat. Soc. Painters in Casein; Silvermine Gld. A.; New Jersey Soc. P. & S.; Audubon A. *Awards*: prizes, Am. Color Pr. Soc.; Bronx, N.Y.; Nat. Ser. Soc.; Parrish Mus.; Gld. Hall, Easthampton, 1953, 1955; New Jersey Soc. P. & S., 1956; Silvermine Gld. A., 1957; Emily Lowe award, 1957. *Work*: MMA; BMA; Milwaukee Inst. A.; SFMA; Carnegie Inst.; Univ. Wisconsin; Univ. Oregon; State Dept.; Ball State T. Col.; Marshall Col.; U.S. Army; Denver Pub. Sch.; Brooks Mem. A. Gal.; Denver A. Mus.; Univ. State of N.Y.; Tel-Aviv Mus., Israel; Ain-Harod Mus., Israel. *Exhibited*: LC; SAM; Bradley Univ.; NAD; Art:USA, 1958; Audubon A. 1958; New Jersey Soc. P. & S., 1958; "Prize Prints of the 20th Century"; one-man: Modern Age, N.Y., 1945; Nat. Ser. Soc., 1947; Webb Gal., Los A., 1947; Univ. Denver, 1948; Teacher's Center Gal., 1951; Salpeter Gal., 1951; Hudson Gld., N.Y., 1955.

SHOUSE, HELEN BIGONEY (Mrs.)—
Craftsman, P., Des., E.
P.O. Box 444, Hillandale Farm, Appomatox, Va.

B. Rockville Centre, N.Y., Aug. 26, 1911. *Studied*: PIASch; N.Y. Univ., B.S. in Edu.; T. Col., Columbia Univ., M.A. *Member*: N.Y. Soc. Craftsmen. *Exhibited*: N.Y. Soc. Craftsmen, 1946. Lectures: Ceramic Art. *Position*: Asst. Prof., Indst. A., Richmond Professional Inst., Col. William & Mary, Richmond, Va., 1945-47. Lectures on design and color; flower arrangement, to women's clubs, garden clubs.

SHOVER, EDNA MANN—Painter, Des., I., W., T.
1468 North New Jersey St., Indianapolis 2, Ind.

B. Indianapolis, Ind. *Studied*: PMSchIA. *Member*: Indianapolis AA. *Awards*: med., Alum. Assn., PMSchIA, Phila. Author, I., "Art in Costume Design."

SHRYOCK, BURNETT HENRY, SR.—Painter, E., Des.
1218 Carter St., Carbondale, Ill.

B. Carbondale, Ill., Feb. 4, 1904. *Studied*: Univ. Illinois, A.B.; Am. Acad. A., Chicago; AIC; T. Col., Columbia Univ., M.A. *Member*: NEA; NAEA; AAUP. *Awards*: prizes, CM, 1943; Alabama WC Exh., 1944; La Tausca Pearls Comp., 1946. *Work*: CAM; Southern Illinois Univ. *Exhibited*: AIC, 1936, 1938, 1944, 1946; Alabama WC Exh., 1944; Denver A. Mus., 1944, 1945; La Tausca Pearls Comp., 1946; Kansas City AI, 1945; one-man exh.: William Rockhill Nelson Gal., 1946; Jackson, Miss., 1944; CAM, 1943-1945; New Orleans A. & Crafts, 1948. *Position*: Asst. Prof. A., 1935-42, Chm. A. Dept., 1942-44, Southern Illinois Univ.; Assoc. Prof. A., Chm. A. Dept., 1944- , Univ. Kansas City, Mo.; Chm., Prof. A., 1950- , Dean, Sch. FA. & Prof. A., 1955- , Southern Illinois Univ.

SHUCK, KENNETH MENAUGH—
Museum Director, P.
Springfield Art Museum, 1111 East Brookside Drive; h. 938 Elm St., Springfield, Mo.

B. Harrodsburg, Ky., May 21, 1921. *Studied*: Ohio State Univ., B.S. in FA, M.A. in FA; Univ. Chile, Santiago, Chile. *Member*: Midwest Mus. Conference; Missouri State Archaeological Soc.; Missouri Hist. Soc. *Awards*: Pan-American Travel Grant, 1950. *Exhibited*: Denver A. Mus., 1952. Lectures: Painting of Chile, to colleges and art organizations. *Position*: Dir., Springfield A. Mus., Springfield, Mo., 1951- .

SHUFF, LILY (Mrs. Martin M. Shir)—Painter, Eng.
652 Eastern Parkway, Brooklyn 13, N.Y.

B. New York, N.Y. *Studied*: Hunter Col., A.B.; ASL; Brooklyn Acad. FA; Farnsworth Sch. A.; and with Jon

Corbino. *Member*: Brooklyn Soc. A.; AEA; N.Y. Soc. Women A.; NAWA; AAPL; Provincetown AA; Nat. Soc. Painters in Casein; Silvermine Gld. A.; Conn. Acad. FA; New Jersey Soc. P. & S.; Soc. Wash. Pr. M. *Awards*: prizes, Brooklyn Soc. A., 1953, 1957; New Jersey Soc. P. & S., 1956; Caravan Gal., 1958; NAWA, 1958; Conn. Acad. FA, 1956. *Work*: Pakistan Consulate, N.Y.; Lane Col., N.Y.; James Fennimore Cooper H.S.; Georgia Mus. FA; Yale Univ.; Mueller Coll., Paris, France. *Exhibited*: Independents, 1941; Vendome Gal.; NAC; BM, 1943-1958; LC, 1955; Conn. Acad. FA, 1954; Audubon A.; RoKo Gal.; NAD; LC traveling exh., 1954-55; AFA traveling exh.; Brooklyn Soc. A., 1943-1958; NAWA, 1942-1958; N.Y. Soc. Women A., 1944-1958; A. Lg. Am., 1944; Long Island A. Festival, 1946; Hofstra Col., 1945; Argent Gal., 1944; Van Dieman-Lilienfeld Gal., 1948, 1952; Riverside Mus.; Provincetown A. Festival, 1958; Art:USA, 1958; traveling print shows, U.S. and abroad, 1954-1958; one-man: Argent Gal., 1947, 1956; Van Dieman-Lilienfeld Gal., 1948, 1952; Paris, 1951; AEA, 1951; WMAA, 1951; Laurel Gal.; DeMotte Gal.; Lotos Cl.; BM. *Positions*: Rec. Sec., Nat. Soc. Painters in Casein, 1957-58; Chm. Memb. Jury, NAWA, 1956-58; Bd. Gov., NAWA, 1958; Bd. Gov., N.Y. Soc. Women A., 1956-58.

SHULER, CLYDE—Designer, E.
1717 Sansom St., Philadelphia, Pa.; h. Robin Hill, Rosetree Rd., Media, Pa.

B. Pottstown, Pa., July 3, 1892. *Studied*: PMSch A.; BAID, and with Paul Phillipi Cret. *Member*: Phila. A. A.; F.IDI; Phila. Sketch Cl. *Exhibited*: Arch. & Indst. Des., Phila. Sketch Cl.; PMSch. A.; Phila. A. All. *Work*: Arch. Des., offices, homes, stores, etc. Lectures: Industrial Design. *Positions*: Int. Des., John Wanamaker, 1914-15; Price & McLanahan, 1915-18; McLanahan & Bencker, 1918-21; Des. in Chief, Ralph Bencker, 1921-29; Clyde Shuler Assoc., 1929- ; William Heyl Thompson, 1953.*

SHULKIN, ANATOL—Painter, Gr., L., T.
80 West 40th St., New York 18, N.Y.

B. Russia, Apr. 1901. *Studied*: NAD; ASL; Columbia Univ.; BAID; and with Charles Curran, George Bellows, and others. *Member*: NSMP; AEA. *Awards*: Chaloner scholarship, NAD, 1921; mural comp., Sect. FA, Wash., D.C., 1935, 1937, 1938, 1940. *Work*: MMA; WMAA; murals, Barbizon-Plaza Hotel, N.Y.; USPO, Canajoharie, N.Y., and in private homes. *Exhibited*: Carnegie Inst.; PAFA; NAD; CGA; CM; VMFA; WMAA; MMA; AIC; R.I. Mus. A., and others. *Position*: Instr., CUASch., N.Y., 1932-36; Newark Sch. Fine & Indst. A., Newark, N.J., 1944-45.*

SHULTZ, GEORGE LEONARD—Portrait Painter, L.
1618 South Cheyenne St., Tulsa 19, Okla.

B. St. Louis, Mo., Feb. 16, 1895. *Studied*: St. Louis Sch. FA; in France; & with Robert Bringhurst, Richard Miller. *Work*: many portraits for private coll. & business firms including, Am. Legion Headquarters, Indianapolis; City Hall, St. Louis; Nat. Real Estate Exchange, Chicago. *Exhibited*: St. Louis A. Gld.; Soc. Indp. A.; Am. A. All.; CAM; Joslyn A. Mus.; Philbrook A. Center. Lectures to Service Clubs and church groups.

SHULZ, ADOLPH ROBERT—Painter
Nashville, Ind.

B. Delavan, Wis., June 12, 1869. *Studied*: AIC; ASL; Julian Acad., Paris; & in Germany. *Member*: Brown County Galleries Assn.; Chicago Galleries Assn. *Awards*: prizes, AIC, 1900, 1904, 1908; Med., Milwaukee AI, 1918; prize, Brown County Galleries Assn., 1937.

SHULZ, ALBERTA REHM—Painter
Nashville, Ind.

B. Indianapolis, Ind., July 6, 1892. *Studied*: Butler Univ.; Univ. Texas; Indiana Univ.; Herron AI; Ringling Sch. A.; & with Adolph Shulz, C. Curry Bohm. *Member*: Brown County Galleries Assn.; Hoosier Salon; Sarasota AA (hon.). *Exhibited*: Hoosier Salon; Brown County Galleries Assn.; Swope A. Gal.; & other exh. in Indiana & Florida.*

SHUMATE, JESSAMINE W.—Painter, Ser.
708 Mulberry St., Martinsville, Va.

B. Martinsville, Va. *Studied*: Univ. North Carolina Woman's Col.; Univ. Virginia; ASL. *Member*: AFA;

VMFA; Roanoke AA; Lynchburg AA. *Awards*: prizes, VMFA; Assn. Univ. Women, Roanoke, Va., 1956; Va. Highlands Festival, 1956. *Work*: VMFA; Univ. North Carolina Woman's Col. *Exhibited*: Norfolk Mus. A.; Roanoke AA; Lynchburg AA; VMFA; Springfield Mus. A., 1957.

SHUSTER, WILL—Painter, Gr., S.
550 Camino del Monte Sol., Santa Fé, N.M.

B. Philadelphia, Pa., Nov. 26, 1893. *Studied*: with J. William Server, John Sloan. *Member*: Santa Fé P. & S.; Los Cinco Pintores; AAPL. *Awards*: prizes, N.M. State Fair; Grand Junction, Colo. *Work*: Mus. New Mexico, Santa Fé; Newark Mus.; BM; N.Y. Pub. Lib.; s., Spanish Am. Normal Sch., El Rio, N.M.; Carlsbad Caverns Nat. Park. *Exhibited*: Sesqui-Centennial Exp., Phila., 1926; WFNY 1939; GGE, 1939; Mus. New Mexico, Santa Fé, 1946 (one-man); numerous traveling exh.; Santa Fé Fiesta; Santa Fé Rodeo Assn.*

SHUTE, BEN E.—Painter, T., Comm. A.
1262 Peachtree St.; h. 2879 Normandy Dr., Northwest, Atlanta, Ga.

B. Altoona, Wis., July 13, 1905. *Studied*: AIC; Chicago Acad. FA. *Member*: Assn. Georgia A.; Nat. Soc. Painters in Casein. *Awards*: Carnegie Grant, 1948, 1950. *Work*: Atlanta AA, and in many private colls. *Exhibited*: Pasadena AI, 1946; Assoc. Am. A., 1945; AIC, 1929; Cal. PLH; Assn. Georgia A.; Argent Gal., N.Y., 1949; Butler Inst. Am. A., 1957; Atlanta Mead Paper Co. exh., 1958; Atlanta AA, 1958; Telfair Acad. A., 1958 (one-man). Lectures Contemporary American Painting. *Position*: Instr., 1928-43, Hd., FA Dept., 1943- , Atlanta AI, Atlanta, Ga.; Chm., 9-State Southeastern Annual Exh.

SHUTE, NELL CHOATE—Painter
2879 Normandy Drive, Northwest, Atlanta, Ga.

B. Athens, Ga., Oct., 1900. *Studied*: Hollins Col.; Atlanta AI; Parsons Sch. F. & App. A.; and Fontainebleau, France. *Member*: Assn. Georgia A.; NAWA. *Awards*: prizes, High Mus. A. *Exhibited*: NAWA; Southeastern AA, 1945-1955, 1958; Assn. Georgia A.; AFA traveling exh., 1956; High Mus. A.; Atlanta Paper Co. exh., 1958, and others.

SIBLEY, CHARLES KENNETH—Painter, E.
Norfolk, Va.

B. Huntington, W. Va., Dec. 20, 1921. *Studied*: Ohio State Univ., B.A.; AIC; Columbia Univ., M.A.; State Univ. Iowa, M.F.A. *Awards*: Tiffany F., 1951; NAD; Texas AA, 1954. *Work*: MMA; Rochester Mem. Mus.; North Carolina State Gal.; Norfolk Mus. A.; Ohio Valley States Coll.; Winston-Salem Coll.; Va. State Mus.; Laguna Gloria Mus., Austin, Tex.; Iowa State Univ. *Exhibited*: MMA, 1950; WMAA, 1953; PAFA, 1954; NAD, 1951, 1953, 1954; CGA, 1951, 1953; Carnegie Inst.; Cal. PLH, 1953; High Mus. A., 1954; one-man: Univ. Ohio, 1951; Norfolk Mus. A., 1955. *Position*: Instr., Duke Univ., 1949; Texas State Univ., 1952-54; Hd. Dept. A., College of William & Mary, Norfolk Div., 1956- .

SIBLEY, MARGUERITE (Mrs. Will Lang)—Sculptor
2401 Oxford St., Rockford, Ill.

B. Butler, Ind. *Studied*: Minneapolis Sch. A.; Grande Chaumiere, Paris, France; Rockford Col.; & with Marques Reitzel, Stephen Beams & others. *Member*: Rockford AA; Winnebago County Hist. Soc. *Work*: Burpee A. Gal., Rockford, Ill.; Chicago Temple, Chicago, Ill.; Emanuel Episcopal Church, Rockford, Ill. *Exhibited*: CGA, 1938, 1939, 1941-1944, 1946; Burpee A. Gal., 1931, 1933-1936, 1938, 1941-1946; Beloit Col., 1940; Rockford Col., 1934, 1940; Burpee A. Gal., 1941, 1951 (both one-man); Belle Keith Gal., Rockford, 1932, 1940; Smithsonian Inst., 1947-1951; Rockford AA, 1952-1958; Rockford Woman's Cl., 1958.

SICARD, LOUIS G.—Painter
4525 Finley Drive, Shreveport, La.

B. New Orleans, La., Aug. 7, 1897. *Studied*: with Luis Granier, Ellsworth Woodward. *Member*: Coppini Acad. FA; Shreveport A. Cl. (Pres.); New Orleans AA (Adv. Bd.); Intl. Soc. A. & Lets.; A. & Writers Gld. *Awards*:

prizes, Shreveport A. Cl., 1949, 1957; Holiday in Dixie A. Exh., Shreveport, 1956; Shreveport Regional, 1942. *Work*: murals, Southwestern Electric Power Co., Selber Bros., B & B System, Inc., all of Shreveport. *Exhibited*: Shreveport A. Cl.; Louisiana A. Comm.; New Orleans AA; Caller-Times, Corpus Christi, Tex.; Coppini Acad. FA; 3-man: Mus. FA of Houston.

SICKMAN, JESSALEE B(ANE)—*Painter, T.*

808 17th St., Northwest; h. 3639 Jennifer St., Northwest, Washington 15, D.C.

B. Denver, Colo., Aug. 17, 1905. *Studied*: Univ. Colorado, B.A.; Goucher Col.; Corcoran Sch. A. *Member*: Soc. Wash. A. *Awards*: prize, Corcoran Sch. A., 1941; Barney prize, Wash., D.C., 1945. *Work*: CGA, and in private colls. *Exhibited*: Soc. Wash. A.; Corcoran Alum. Exh.; Wash. (D.C.) Pub. Lib. (one-man); CGA (4-man). I., Forum magazine. *Position*: Instr., Corcoran Sch. A., Washington, D.C., at present.

SICKMAN, LAURENCE C. S.—*Museum Director, L.*

901 East 47th St., Kansas City 10, Mo.

B. Denver, Colo., Aug. 27, 1907. *Studied*: Harvard Univ., A.B. *Member*: Chinese A. Soc. of Am.; Assn. for Asian Studies; Am. Oriental Soc.; Japan Soc.; Far Eastern Ceramic Group. *Awards*: Harvard-Yenching F., China, 1930-34; Fogg A. Mus., Research F. & Lecturer, 1937-39. Contributor to Revue des Arts Asiatiques, Gazette des Beaux-Arts and other art publications. Author (with Soper) "The Art and Architecture of China," London, 1956; Editor, The University Prints, Oriental Art, Series O, "Early Chinese Arts," Section II, 1938. Lectures: on Chinese Painting, Sculpture and Ceramics. *Positions*: Bd. Gov., Ed. "Archives," Chinese Art Soc. of America, 1948- ; Memb. Comm. on Far Eastern Studies, Am. Council of Learned Societies, 1948-53; Bd. Gov., Far Eastern Assn., 1951-53; Cur. Oriental Art, 1935-45, Vice-Dir., 1946-53, Dir., 1953- , Nelson Gallery of Art, Kansas City, Mo.

SIDER, DENO—*Painter, S., C., T.*

1706 North McCadden St.; h. 1784 Las Palmas St., Los Angeles 28, Cal.

B. Norwich, Conn., Mar. 2, 1926. *Studied*: Norwich Acad., and with Leon Franks. *Member*: Cal. A. Cl.; Valley A. Gld.; Hollywood AA; Burbank AA; San Fernando Valley A. Cl. *Awards*: Perkins medal of Conn.; Cranbrook Inst. A. scholarship, 1943; BMFA scholarship, 1943; Professional A. Sch., N.Y. scholarship, 1943; John and Anna Stacey scholarship, 1955, 1956; prizes, Burbank AA, 1954-1958; San Fernando Valley A. Cl., 1954-1958. *Exhibited*: Burbank AA, 1954, 1955; Cal. A. Cl., 1953-1955; San Fernando Valley A. Cl., 1954, 1955; Burbank A. Cl.; Cal. AA; Valley A. Gld.; and others.

SIDERIS, ALEXANDER—*Painter*

118 East 59th St.; h. Hudson View Gardens, New York 33, N.Y.

B. Skopelos, Greece, Feb. 21, 1895. *Studied*: ASL; Julian Acad., Paris, France; & with George Bridgman, Pierre Laurence. *Member*: AAPL (Vice-Pres. N.Y. Chptr., 1956-58). *Awards*: gold medal, Knickerbocker A.; prize, AAPL, 1953. *Work*: Amarillo Mus.; Amarillo Col. (Tex.); Greek Church, Phila., Pa.; Church of the Annunciation, Pensacola, Fla.; murals for churches in Salt Lake City, Utah and Newport News, Va. *Exhibited*: NAD, 1938; All. A. Am., 1940-1944, 1957; WFNY 1939; Soc. Indp. A.; Oakland A. Gal.; Argent Gal., 1935 (one-man); NAC, 1955; Knickerbocker A.; AAPL, 1953; Barbizon Gal., 1954; Vendome Gal., Delphic Studio, 1939 (one-man); Arthur Newton Gal., 1946, 1947, 1949, 1950, 1953, & in Paris, France; Athens, Greece.

SIEBERNS, CAROLINE LENORE (Mrs. Gerald R. Bradbury)—*Painter, Des.*

4712—39th St., San Diego 16, Cal.

B. Spring Valley, Wis., Jan. 14, 1911. *Studied*: Minneapolis Sch. A.; Columbia Univ.; & with B. J. O. Nordfeldt, Dong Kingman, & others. *Member*: San Diego A. Gld.; Spanish Village A. Center. *Awards*: prizes, San Diego FA Soc., 1940, 1941; Spanish Village A. Center, 1958. *Work*: Acad. of the Holy Angels, Minneapolis, Minn.; mural, Hotel Bella Vista, Cuernavaca, Mexico;

mural dec., Pres. Aleman's Rancho Florido. *Exhibited*: San F. AA, 1940; AWCS, 1941; Minneapolis Inst. A., 1935-1937; San Diego A. Gld., 1940-1942, 1945, 1946, 1953; Spanish Village A. Center, 1954-1958; Denver A. Mus., 1945. *Position*: Sec., Spanish Village A. Center, San Diego, Cal., 1952-54.

SIEDSCHLAG, LYDIA—*Educator, Des.*

304 Sprague St., Kalamazoo, Mich.

B. Flint, Mich., Feb. 12, 1891. *Studied*: AIC, B.A.E.; T. Col., Columbia Univ., A.M.; Mills Col.; & with Archipenko. *Member*: Mich. Acad. A. Sc. & Let. *Work*: designed furniture & decorated residence halls & bldgs., Western Michigan Univ. *Position*: Hd. A. Dept., Western Michigan Univ., Kalamazoo, Mich., 1924- ; A. Consultant, Univ. Bldg. Project.

SIEGEL, ADRIAN—*Painter, Photog.*

1907 Pine St., Philadelphia 3, Pa.; h. R.F.D., Bearsville, N.Y.

B. New York, N.Y., July 17, 1898. *Member*: Phila. A. All.; Woodstock AA. *Exhibited*: CGA; PAFA; Friends' Exh., Phila.; Phila. A. All.; photographs exhibited: MMoMA; George Eastman House, Rochester, N.Y.; Grand Central Station, N.Y.; PMA; Newark Mus. A.

SIEGEL, LEO DINK—*Illustrator, Cart.*

64 West 56th St., New York 19, N.Y.

B. Birmingham, Ala., June 30, 1910. *Studied*: Univ. Alabama; NAD. *Member*: SI. I., Saturday Evening Post, Cosmopolitan, Good Housekeeping, Esquire, & other national magazines.

SIEGRIST, LUNDY—*Painter, Gr., T.*

5203 Miles Ave., Oakland 9, Cal.

B. Oakland, Cal., Apr. 14, 1925. *Studied*: Cal. Col. A. & Crafts. *Member*: AEA; San F. AA. *Awards*: prizes, SFMA, 1949; Albert Bender Grant, San F., 1952; Cal. State Fair, 1949, 1951; Oakland A. Gal., 1952, medal, 1954; San F. AA, 1953, 1954; Santa Barbara Mus. A., 1955; Cal. PLH, 1952; Terry AI, 1952; Jack London Square Exh., Oakland, 1956, 1958; Richmond (Cal.) A. Center, 1956; deYoung Mem. Mus., 1957; San F.A. Festival, 1957; Valley A. Center, Lafayette, Cal., 1958. *Work*: Cal. PLH; Phelan Coll.; Terry AI; Cal. State Agricultural Soc.; SFMA; Santa Barbara Mus. A.; San F. A. Comm.; Denver A. Mus.; Valley A. Center; LC; Oakland Pub. Lib. *Exhibited*: PAFA, 1949, 1950; Univ. Illinois, 1952, 1953, 1955; Audubon A., 1950; Terry AI, 1952; Ft. Worth Mus., 1952; Cal. PLH, 1951, 1952; SFMA, 1950-1952; Oakland A. Gal., 1948-1952; Cal. State Fair, 1947-1952; Denver A. Mus., 1950, 1953-1955; Los A. Mus. A., 1949; Colo. Springs FA Center, 1953; DMFA, 1954, 1955; Carnegie Inst., 1955; Sao Paulo, Brazil, 1955; Stanford Univ., 1956; Cal. Painting traveling exh., 1956; AFA traveling exh., 1956, 1957, 1958; Cal. Drawings traveling exh., 1957; WMAA, 1957; Brussels World's Fair, 1958; VMFA, 1958; Flint AI, 1958; Bolles Gal., San F., 1958; Provincetown A. Festival, 1958; Vancouver (B.C.) A. Gal., 1958. *Position*: Instr., Acad. A., San Francisco; Jr. Center of A. & Science, Oakland, Cal.

SIEVAN, MAURICE—*Painter, T.*

76-47 171st St., Flushing, L.I., N.Y.

B. Ukraine, Russia, Dec. 7, 1898. *Studied*: NAD; & with Leon Kroll, Charles Hawthorne. *Member*: CAA; AEA; Woodstock AA; Fed. Mod. P. & S.; Provincetown AA. *Awards*: prize, Queens Botanical Gardens Soc., 1949; Audubon A., 1946. *Work*: Univ. Arizona; Univ. Georgia; Fla. Southern Col.; BM. *Exhibited*: Salon d'Automne, Paris, 1931; CGA, 1945; PAFA, 1944, 1946, 1949; Carnegie Inst., 1943-1945; AIC, 1941; BM, 1941, 1953; MMA (AV), 1942; VMFA, 1944; MMoMA, 1943, 1956; WMAA, 1943; NAD, 1926, 1938, 1942-1945; AWCS, 1941; Minn. State Fair, 1943; deYoung Mem. Mus., 1943; G. W. V. Smith A. Mus., 1944; Tomorrow's Masterpieces traveling exh., 1943-1944; Wadsworth Atheneum, 1944; Inst. Mod. A., Boston, 1945; Bucknell Univ., 1940; Riverside Mus., 1943; Wildenstein Gal., 1942-1946; Midtown Gal., 1933-1934; Contemporary A., 1939, 1944; Audubon A., 1952, 1953; Jewish Mus., 1948, 1956; Woodstock AA, 1951, 1956; Rudolph Gal., 1951, 1956, 1957, 1958; Dayton AI, 1955, 1956; Farnsworth Mus., 1950; AFA traveling exh., 1953-54, 1955-56; Dayton AI, 1949; Nelson Gal. A., 1947;

Rochester Mem. Gal., 1946; ACA Gal., 1938, 1946; Gal. Mod. A., 1944; Babcock Gal., 1943, 1944; Mortimer Brandt Gal., 1944-1946; Provincetown AA, 1957, 1958; Art:USA, 1958; one-man exh.: Contemporary A., 1939, 1941; Brandt Gal., 1945; Summit (N.J.) AA, 1945, 1952; Passedoit Gal., 1955, 1957; Mint Mus. A., 1955; Salpeter Gal., 1948, 1949, 1951. *Position*: Instr., Queens Col., Flushing, N.Y.

SIEVERS, FREDERICK WILLIAM—*Sculptor, C.*

1208 West 43rd St., Richmond 25, Va.

B. Fort Wayne, Ind., Oct. 26, 1872. *Studied*: Royal Acad. FA, Rome, Italy; Julian Acad., Paris, France. *Awards*: prizes, Royal Acad. FA, Rome. *Work*: monuments, mem., statues; Abingdon, Va.; Gettysburg, Pa.; Richmond, Va.; Vicksburg, Miss.; State Capitol, Va.; Hall of Fame, N.Y.; Leesburg, Va.; Elmira, N.Y.; State Capitol, Nashville, Tenn. *Exhibited*: NSS; VMFA.

SIGISMUND, VIOLET—*Painter, Lith.*

1 Sheridan Square, New York 14, N.Y.

B. New York, N.Y. *Studied*: ASL. *Member*: AEA; ASL; Woodstock AA; Knickerbocker A. *Awards*: Knickerbocker A., 1952; Village A. Center. *Exhibited*: PAFA, 1940; Telfair Acad. A., 1939; Audubon A., 1947, 1948, 1952; Knickerbocker A., 1952, 1953, 1955; All. A. Am., 1942, 1948; NAD, 1952; Woodstock, N.Y., 1943-1955; Lenox Gal., 1952; ACA Gal., 1947 (one-man) 1953, 1954; Village A. Center.*

SILER, ELMER WAYNE—*Painter, Gr., A. Hist.*

P.O. Box 37, Bloomington, Ill.

B. Brule, Neb., Feb. 9, 1910. *Studied*: (A. Hist.) with Dimitri Tselos, Lorenz Eitner, H. Harvard Arnason; (art) with Kyle Morris, Malcolm H. Myers, Walter Quirt, Syd Fossum, and others; and in France and Ireland; Univ. Illinois, A.B.; Univ. Minnesota, M.A. *Member*: Des Moines A. Center. *Awards*: prize, Des Moines A. Center. *Exhibited*: WAC; Minneapolis Inst. A.; St. Paul Sch. A. Gal.; Univ. Minnesota.

SILINS, JANIS (MR.)—
Educator, Gal. Dir., P., W., L., Hist.

Rollins College; h. El Cortez Apts., East Morse Blvd., Winter Park, Fla.

B. Riga, Latvia, June 1, 1896. *Studied*: Univ. Moscow; Moscow Acad. A.; Univ. Riga, Ph.D.; Univ. Marburg; Univ. Stockholm. *Member*: Assn. A., Soc. of Historians, both Riga; Prof. Union of A., Munich; Soc. A. Historians, Univ. Munich; Hon. Memb., Baltic Inst., Bonn; Orlando AA; Southeastern Mus. Conf. *Award*: State award in A. Hist., Riga. *Exhibited*: widely in Europe and in Winter Park and Orlando, Fla. *Author*: monographs: Rudolfs Perle, 1928; Karlis Zale, 1942; Ludolfs Liberts, 1943; other writings, "Latvian Landscape Painting," 1936; "Essays on Art," 1942; "Gailis, a Latvian Landscape Painter," 1948. Contributor to many European publications with articles and papers on art and art philosophy. Lectures on Art History. Arranged and catalogued exhs., Rollins Col., "The Arts of Norway," 1957; 8th Annual Fla. A. Group, 1957; Memorial Exh. of Paintings by Leonard Dyer; and many more in U.S. and Europe. *Position*: Asst. Prof. A., 1956- , Dir., Morse Gal. Art, 1956- , Rollins College, Winter Park, Fla. (Other teaching positions in Latvia and Germany, 1933-51.)

SILKOTCH, MARY ELLEN—*Painter, T.*

Hazelwood Pl. (Arbor), Dunellen, N.J.

B. New York, N.Y., Sept. 12, 1911. *Studied*: Van Emburgh Sch. A., Plainfield, N.J., and with Jonas Lie, Sigismund Ivanowski. *Member*: AEA; NAWA; AAPL; Plainfield AA; Westfield AA. *Awards*: prizes, Plainfield AA, 1950 (2), 1952, 1955-1958; AAPL, 1951; East Orange, N.J., 1952. *Exhibited*: Plainfield AA, 1948-1958; Paper Mill Playhouse, 1948; AAPL, 1948-1951; Montclair A. Mus., 1950; Irvington Mus. & A. Assn., 1948-1952 (1951, one-man); Raritan Valley AA, 1950-1952; Barrett A. Gal., Plainfield, N.J., 1949 (one-man); Swains, Plainfield, 1951, 1953, 1955, 1956 (one-man). *Positions*: Instr., Van Emburgh Sch., Plainfield, N.J., 1944- ; Instr., A., Adult Edu., Dunellen, N.J., 1948-57; Bound Brook Adult Edu., 1950-57; North Plainfield, 1951-54; Pres., Plainfield AA, 1952- .

SILLS, JEANNE REYNAL. See Reynal, Jeanne

SILSBY, CLIFFORD—*Painter, Et.*

14243 Greenleaf St., Sherman Oaks, Cal.

B. New Haven, Conn. *Studied*: Julian Acad., Ecole des Beaux-Arts, Paris; & with Lucien Simon, Jules Pages, J. Francis Smith, & others. *Work*: Los A. Mus. A.; Victoria & Albert Mus., London. *Exhibited*: Paris Salon, 1923; Cal. Pr. M., 1929, 1930, 1936; GGE, 1939; Los A. Mus. A., 1940-1945, one-man, 1936; Los A. P. & S., 1929, 1935-1937, 1943; Oakland A. Gal., 1935, 1944; San Diego FA Soc., 1940; Santa Cruz A. Lg., 1936; Santa Paula, Cal., 1941-1943. *Positions*: Special Effects A., Motion Pictures, Hollywood & New York, 1918- .*

SILVAN, RITA—*Painter, T., L.*

73 White Beeches Drive, Dumont, N.J.

B. Minneapolis, Minn., Mar. 21, 1928. *Studied*: Univ. Minnesota, B.A.; N.Y. Univ. Grad. Sch., and with Paul Burlin, Ralston Crawford, Cameron Booth. *Member*: AEA. *Awards*: prizes, Minnesota State Fair, 1948, 1949 (3). *Exhibited*: N.Y. City Center, 1958; Newark Mus., 1958; Minneapolis Inst. A., 1950; Minnesota State Fair, 1948-1950; one-man: Harriet Hanley Gal., Minneapolis, 1951. *Position*: Instr., A., Art Center, Englewood, N.J.; Y.W.C.A., Ridgewood, N.J.; Research Asst., Dept. Photography, MMoMA, New York, 1953.

SILVERCRUYS, SUZANNE (Mrs. Suzanne Silvercruys Stevenson)—*Sculptor, W., L.*

1 West 67th St., New York 23, N.Y.; h. "Shorehaven," East Norwalk, Conn.

B. Maeseyck, Belgium. *Studied*: Yale Sch. FA, B.F.A.; & in Belgium, England. *Awards*: Hon. degree, L.H.D., Temple Univ., 1942; Rome Alum. prize, 1928; BAID, 1927; decoration, Order of Leopold; Officer d'Academie de France; Coronation med.; Queen Elizabeth med.; & others. *Work*: busts, plaques, mem., Louvain Lib.; McGill Univ., Canada; Yale Sch. Medicine; Reconstruction Hospital, N.Y.; First Lutheran Church, New Haven, Conn.; Duell award for N.Y. Press Photographers Assn.; Rumford (R.I.) Mem.; Government House, Ottawa, Can.; MMA; Amelia Earhart Trophy for Zonta Cl.; Queen Astrid Mem., Brussels; war mem., Shawinigan Falls, Canada; gold medal, presented by Young Democrats to Jas. Farley; many portrait busts of prominent persons. *Exhibited*: CGA; BAID; Salon de Printemps, 1931. *Author*: "Suzanne of Belgium"; "A Primer of Sculpture," 1942.

SILVERMAN, MILES (M.)—*Painter, Gr., I., E.*

5421 30th Place, Northwest, Washington 15, D.C.

B. Flint, Mich., Sept. 26, 1910. *Studied*: Notre Dame; Univ. Michigan; Univ. Toledo; AIC. *Member*: Ohio WC Soc.; AEA; Palette Cl., Toledo; Toledo Fed. A. Soc. (Pres. 1951-52). *Awards*: prizes, Toledo Mus. A., 1941, 1944-1948, 1950, 1952; Toledo Fed. A. Soc., 1950; Butler AI, 1948. *Work*: Geneva Col., Beaver Falls, Pa.; Toledo Mus. A. *Exhibited*: Ohio Valley Exh., 1948, 1949; Commerce Nat. Bank, Toledo, 1950; Illinois State Fair; Montgomery County (Ill.), 1949, 1950; Wash. WC Soc., 1949, 1952, 1953; Wash. Area A., CGA, 1954. I., "Jerry Goes to Camp." *Position*: Instr., Toledo Pub. Schs., 1947-52; Toledo Mus. A., 1948-52; Supv. Publ. Prod., Erco Div., ACF Industries, Riverdale, Md.; A. Dir., Interstate Electronic Corp., Wash., D.C., 1958- .

SIMA. See Cohen, Esther Sima

SIMKHOVITCH, HELENA—*Sculptor*

48 West 10th St., New York 11, N.Y.

B. New York, N.Y. *Studied*: in Paris, France. *Member*: Fed. Mod. P. & S.; S. Gld.; AEA. *Awards*: Palmes Academiques: Officier de l'Instruction Publique, Paris, 1955. *Work*: WMAA; Wadsworth Atheneum, and in private colls. *Exhibited*: WMAA, 1953, 1955, 1956, 1957; PAFA, 1953, 1954; AFA traveling exh., 1952; MMoMA traveling exh., 1955, 1956; Fed. Mod. P. & S., 1947, 1952-1956; S. Gld., 1952-1958; Petit Palais, Paris, 1950; Musee d'Anvers, Belgium, 1950. Founder, "New York Six" (Paris) and "Sculpture in a Garden" (biennial exh., N.Y., 1954, 1956, 1958). Lectures: "American Sculpture," auspices U.S. Dept. of State, in Europe. *Positions*: Dir. at large, Chm., Intl. Cultural Relations Comm., AEA, 1954-58; Nat. Sec., AEA, 1957, 1958; Exec. Bd., S. Gld., 1958; U.S. Delegate, Intl. Assn. of Plastic Arts, Venice, 1954, Dubrovnik, 1957; Memb. U.S. Nat. Comm. for UNESCO, 1958.

SIMMONS, CORDRAY—*Painter, Gr., T.*

45 Tieman Place, Apt. 3A, New York 27, N.Y.

B. Jersey City, N.J. *Studied*: ASL. *Member*: Audubon A.; AEA. *Work*: MMA. *Exhibited*: AIC, 1935, 1943; AFA traveling exh., 1931; PAFA, 1935; Univ. Indiana, 1940; BM, 1930; WMAA, 1944; CGA, 1934; Utica A. Soc.; Feragil Gal.; Morton Gal.; Rehn Gal.; Kennedy & Co.; All. A. Am.; MMA, 1942; Grant Gal.; Macy Gal.; Weyhe Gal.; Audubon A., 1944-1955; Geneva, Ill., 1955; Batavia (Ill.) Pub. Lib.; and others.

SIMMS, THEODORE FREELAND—
Industrial Designer, Gr., P., C.

16419 Third Ave., S.W., Seattle 66, Wash.

B. Arvada, Colo., Jan. 14, 1912. *Studied*: Univ. Southern California, B.Arch.; Chappell House, Denver, Colo.; & with Dan Lutz, Clayton Baldwin, & others. *Member*: Southern Cal. WC Soc.; Scarab Cl. *Work*: Central City Opera House Assn., Denver, Colo. *Exhibited*: Denver A. Mus., 1934, 1937; Chappell House, Denver, 1934 (one-man): Southern Cal. WC Soc., 1939. Lectures: Architecture.*

SIMON, ELLEN R.—*Craftsman, Lith., I., Des.*

419 West 119th St., New York 27, N.Y.

B. Toronto, Canada, Apr. 15, 1916. *Studied*: Ontario Col. A.; ASL; New Sch. Social Research and with Joep Nicolas, Yvonne Williams. *Member*: Canadian Soc. Gr. A. *Work*: Albertina Coll., Vienna; N.Y. Pub. Lib.; BM; Nat. Gal. of Canada; A. Gal. of Toronto; stained glass medallions, Detroit Pub. Lib. Stained glass windows in many churches and synagogues in Canada including Windsor, Ont.; Toronto, Winnipeg, York Mills, Montreal, Newtonbrook, etc.; Temple Emanuel, Tuscaloosa; Sidney Hillman Mem. window, and others. *Exhibited*: Pasadena AI, 1945 (one-man); Nat. Gal. of Canada; PMA; Albany Pr. Cl.; Mississippi AA; Smithsonian Inst.; N.Y. Pub. Lib.; Picture Loan Soc., Toronto; Hart House, Toronto Univ.; Wash. Kiln Cl.; Carnegie Lib., Pittsburgh; Mus. Contemp. Crafts, N.Y.; DMFA, and others. Author, I., "The Critter Book," 1940; "Inga of Porcupine Mine," 1942; "Americans All," 1944; "Music for Early Childhood," 1952.

SIMON, GRANT MILES—*Painter, Arch., Lith., L.*

2214 St. James St., Philadelphia 3, Pa.

B. Philadelphia, Pa., Oct. 2, 1887. *Studied*: PMSchIA; Univ. Pennsylvania, B.S., M.S.; PAFA; Ecole des Beaux-Arts, Paris. *Member*: F. AIA; AWCS; Nat. Inst. Arch. Edu. (Hon.). *Awards*: Cope prize, 1907; Stewardson scholarship, 1910; Brooke prize, 1911. *Work*: Easton (Pa.) Court House; PAFA; BM; Atwater Kent Mus., Phila.; Pa. Hist. Soc.; LC. *Exhibited*: AWCS, 1943-1955; NAD, 1945, 1946; Lib.Cong., 1941-1943; Ferargil Gal., 1938. Contributor to: "Historic Philadelphia." Co-author, "Historic Germantown," 1955. Author: "The Beginnings of Philadelphia," 1957. Lectures: Theory of Design.

SIMON, HOWARD—*Portrait Painter, I., Gr.*

27 West 67th St., New York 23, N.Y.; s. Stanfordville, N.Y.

B. New York, N.Y., July 22, 1903. *Studied*: NAD; Julian Acad., Paris, France. *Member*: AIGA; Cal. Soc. Et.; Dutchess County AA. *Award*: prize, Long Island A. Lg., 1955. *Work*: MMA; BMA; N.Y. Pub. Lib.; Brooks Mem. A. Gal.; Mus. Col.; Little Rock Mus. A. *Exhibited*: 50 Prints of the Year; 50 Books of the Year; Victoria & Albert Mus., London; Int. Pr. M., Los A.; one-man: Smithsonian Inst.; A. Center, N.Y.; Bonestell Gal. I., Limited Editions Club, "Lyrics of Francois Villon"; Dickens' "Christmas Stories"; Mark Twain's "The Prince and the Pauper"; "Rabelais," etc. Author: "500 Years of Art in Illustration"; "A Primer of Drawing," 1954. *Position*: Instr., Port. & Figure Painting, Drawing, N.Y. Univ., Div. General Edu., New York, N.Y., 1947- . L., Instr., Sch. for Visual Arts, New York, N.Y., 1954- .

SIMON, MRS. MILDRED RACKLEY. See Rackley, Mildred

SIMON, SIDNEY—*Painter, T., S.*

South Mountain Rd., New City, N.Y.

B. Pittsburgh, Pa., May 21, 1917. *Studied*: Univ. Pennsylvania, B.F.A.; PAFA; Barnes Fnd., and with George Harding. *Awards*: Cresson traveling F., PAFA, 1940; Abbey F., 1940; prize, Carnegie Inst., 1941, 1945. *Member*: AEA; CAA. *Work*: U.S. War Dept., Wash., D.C.; Am. Embassy, Paris, France; MMA; Temple Beth Abraham, Tarrytown, N.Y. *Exhibited*: NGA; MMA, 1945, 1950; Assoc. A. Pittsburgh, 1936-1941, 1945; PAFA, 1946-1952; CGA, 1948, 1950; WMAA, 1950; one-man: PAFA, 1946; Queensland Nat. A. Gal., Brisbane, 1944-45; Nat. Gal. Victoria, Melbourne; Nat. Gal. South Australia, Adelaide; Tokyo, Japan, 1953; Nat. Gal. of New South Wales, Sydney, Australia; Niveau Gal., N.Y., 1949; Grand Central Moderns, 1950, one-man, 1953. *Position*: Instr., Painting, CUASch., 1946-47; Brooklyn Mus. Sch., 1948-55; Skowhegan Sch. Painting & Sculpture, 1946-58.

SIMONI, JOHN PETER—
Educator, P., C., S., W., L., Gal. Dir.

Art Department, University of Wichita; h. 1816 Harvard St., Wichita 14, Kans.

B. Denver, Colo., Apr. 12, 1911. *Studied*: Colorado State Col. of Edu., B.A., M.A.; Nat. Univ. Mexico; Kansas City AI, with Thomas Hart Benton; Colorado Univ., with Max Beckmann; Ohio State Univ., Ph.D.; Mass. Inst. Tech.; and in Trentino, Italy. *Member*: AAUP; Am. Soc. for Aesthetics; CAA; Kansas Fed. A.; Kansas A. Edu. Assn.; Midwest Col. A. Assn. *Awards*: The Trentino prize, Italy, 1928; Carter prize, Denver, Colo., 1931. *Work*: Colorado Friends of Art Coll.; reliefs, sc., murals, Southwest-Citizens Fed. Savings & Loan Assn., Wichita; Kansas State Bank, Newton; Fine Arts Center Theatre, Univ. Wichita; painting, Mathewson Intermediate Sch., Wichita; St. Paul Methodist Church, Wichita. *Exhibited*: Mulvane Mus. A.; Wichita A. Mus.; Colorado State Col. Contributor book reviews to College Art Journal; Art Critic, weekly column for Wichita Eagle. Lectures: Art Education Today; Italian Renaissance; Art in Religion, etc. Organized and directed the Elsie Allen Art Gallery, Baker Univ. and assembled the Allen Collection of paintings; arranged and catalogued the Bloomfield Collection of paintings for Univ. Wichita, 1956. *Positions*: Hd. Dept. A. & Gal. Dir., Baker Univ., 1937-55; Chm., Dept. A. & Dir., of the university galleries, University of Wichita, 1957- .

SIMONSON, LEE—*Designer, W., L.*

411 East 50th St., New York 22, N.Y.

B. New York, N.Y., June 26, 1888. *Studied*: Harvard Univ., B.A. *Work*: N.Y. Pub. Lib.; settings for numerous stage productions including "Heartbreak House," "Back to Methusaleh," "Amphytrion 38," Wagner's "Ring of the Nibelungen." *Exhibited*: Int. Exh. Theatre A.; MModA, 1933; MMA, 1945; FMA, 1950; WMA, 1940; WFNY 1939. Author: "The Stage is Set," 1932; "Part of a Lifetime," 1943; "The Art of Scenic Design," 1950, & others. Contributor to: architectural, art & theatre magazines. Lectures: History of Stage Settings; History of Costume. Contributor to Encyclopaedia Britannica, "Modern Theatre Design." *Position*: Consultant, Costume Exh., MMA, 1944, 1945; Consultant, Theatre, Univ. Wisconsin, Univ. Indiana, Hunter Col.

SIMONSON, MARION—*Painter*

Lively, Va.

B. New York, N.Y., Mar. 9, 1913. *Studied*: Phoenix AI; ASL; Grand Central A. Sch.; Farnsworth Sch. A., and with Jay Connaway. *Member*: ASL; NAWA; Rappahannock A. Lg. *Awards*: medal, NAD, 1941, 1942; Hudson Valley AA, prize, 1954. *Work*: Am. Univ., Cairo, Egypt; Domestic Relations Court, Birmingham, Ala.; Hunter Col. H.S.; Denville Mem. Lib., Denville, N.J.; Baptist Foreign Mission Bd., Richmond, Va., and ports. in private colls. *Exhibited*: Hudson Valley AA, 1953, 1954; Westchester A. & Crafts Gld., 1942, 1947, 1952, 1953; NAWA, 1953, 1954; Portraits, Inc., 1952-1955.

SIMONT, MARC—*Illustrator, W.*

West Cornwall, Conn.

B. Paris, France, Nov. 23, 1915. *Studied*: Academie Julian, Academie Ranson, and with Andre L'hote, Paris, France; NAD. *Awards*: Tiffany Fnd. F., 1937; Caldecott Award, 1956. Contributor illus. to: Woman's Day; Sports Illustrated; Newsweek; N.Y. Times; N.Y. Herald Tribune. Author, I., "Polly's Oats," 1951; "The Lovely Summer," 1952; "Mimi," 1954; "The Plumber out of the Sea," 1955; "Opera Souffle," 1951; Illustrator: "The First Story," 1947; "The First Christmas," 1948; "The Happy Day," 1949; "The Big World and the Little House," 1950; "Fish Head," 1954; "A Tree is Nice," 1956; "American Folklore and Legend," 1958; "The 13 Clocks," 1950; "The Wonderful O," 1958; "Mr. Robbins Rides Again," 1958.

SIMPSON, HERBERT WILLIAM—*Designer*

214 Sycamore St. (5); h. 106 South Alvord Blvd., Evansville 14, Ind.

B. Evansville, Ind., Dec. 27, 1904. *Member*: Soc. Typographic A., Chicago; Cliff Dwellers; Soc. for Italic Handwriting, England. *Awards*: "Best of Industry" Design awards, Direct Mail Adv. Assn., 1947-1950; Certif., AIGA, 1952, 1953.

SIMPSON, MAXWELL STEWART—*Painter*

Old Raritan Rd., Scotch Plains, N.J.

B. Elizabeth, N.J., Sept. 11, 1896. *Studied*: NAD; ASL, and abroad. *Member*: Audubon A. *Awards*: prize, Montclair A. Mus., 1943; medal, NAC, 1951; Terry AI, 1952; NAD, 1953; Art Center of the Oranges, 1955, 1958; Plainfield AA, 1956; NAC, 1957. *Work*: Newark Mus.; NGA; N.Y. Pub. Lib.; Briarcliff Sch.; Newark Pub. Lib. *Exhibited*: NAD, 1945, 1948, 1949; Los A. Mus. A., 1945; Carnegie Inst., 1941, 1943; NGA, 1940; CGA, 1939; WFNY 1939; WMAA, 1934; GGE, 1939; Montclair A. Mus., 1943, 1944; Riverside Mus., 1944; Newark Mus., 1943, 1952; NAC, 1951; MMA, 1942; BMA, 1934; Pepsi-Cola, 1947; Terry AI, 1952; PAFA; AIC; Albright A. Gal.; Rochester Mem. A. Gal.; BMFA; MMA; Nat. Univ. Mexico; one-man: Dudensing Gal., 1930, 1932; Artists Gal., 1941. I., "Aucassin and Nicolete," (50 Books of the Year), 1936.

SIMPSON, MERTON D.—*Painter*

445 East 78th St., New York 21, N.Y.

B. Charleston, S.C., Sept. 20, 1928. *Studied*: N.Y. Univ.; CUASch., and with William Halsey. *Awards*: prizes, Red Cross Exchange Exhibit, France, Japan, 1950; Oakland A. Mus., 1952; Atlanta Univ., 1950, 1951, 1956; Intercultural Cl., 1951; South Carolina Cultural Fund F., 1951; Gibbes A. Gal., 1956. *Work*: Atlanta Univ.; Howard Univ.; Gibbes A. Gal.; Scott Field Mus., Chicago. *Exhibited*: Atlanta Univ.; Contemp. A. Gal., N.Y.; Bertha Schaefer Gal., N.Y.; Intercultural Cl., N.Y.; Oakland A. Mus.; Gibbes A. Gal.; MMA; Univ. Michigan; Guggenheim Mus., N.Y., and others; one-man: Kuhar Gal., Charleston; Aden Gal., Wash., D.C.; Barone Gal., N.Y.

SIMPSON-MIDDLEMAN (Roslynn Middleman)— *Painter, T.*

1230 East Front St., Plainfield, N.J.

B. Philadelphia, Pa., Aug. 22, 1929. *Studied*: New Jersey Col. for Women; Newark Sch. F. & Indst. A., and with W. Benda, R. Nakian, B. Gussow, and others. *Work*: WMAA; Newark Mus. A.; MMA. *Exhibited*: CGA, 1955, 1956; WMAA, 1951, 1955; Newark Mus. A., 1952, 1954, 1955; Univ. Nebraska, 1956; BMFA, 1955; Mem. Union Gal., Madison, Wis.; St. Paul Gal. A.; DMFA, 1956; Toledo Mus. A., 1956; Boeing Airplane, Seattle, 1957; Nat. Aeronautical Inst., 1958; Schenectady Mus. A., 1956; one-man: Rose Fried Gal., 1951; John Heller Gal., 1955, 1957.

SIMS, AGNES—*Painter, S.*

600 Canyon Road, Santa Fe, N.M.

B. Rosemont, Pa., Oct. 14, 1910. *Studied*: Phila. Sch. Des. for Women; PAFA. *Member*: Hon. Assoc., Archaeology, School of American Research. *Awards*: Am. Philosophical Soc. grant, 1949 (for research and recording of Southwest Indian Petroglyphs); Neosho grant, 1952. *Work*: Mus. New Mexico; Colorado Springs FA Center; Denver A. Mus. Arranged exhibition of reproductions of Southwest Indian petroglyphs, BM, 1953, and Musee de L'Homme,

Paris, 1954. *Exhibited*: one-man: Mus. New Mexico; Colorado Springs FA Center; Santa Barbara Mus. A.; Wash. A. Cl.; Phila. A. All.; Viviano Gal., N.Y.; Boissevain Gal., N.Y.; WAC. Author, I., "San Cristobal Petroglyphs," 1950.

SIMS, FLORENCE—*Miniature Painter*

2 Salem Rd., North Haven, Conn.

B. Birmingham, Ala., Dec. 26, 1891. *Studied*: Yale Univ., B.F.A. *Member*: New Haven Paint & Clay Cl.; Pa. Soc. Min. P. *Awards*: prize, Pa. Soc. Min. P., 1951. *Exhibited*: PAFA, 1933-1936, 1938, 1941, 1943, 1945; Smithsonian Inst., 1944, 1945; ASMP, 1933, 1935-1938, 1941; Cal. Soc. Min. P., 1936, 1941.

SINCLAIR, ELLEN CHISHOLM—*Painter, Gr.*

6701 Franklin St., Sylvania, Ohio

B. Philadelphia, Pa., Sept. 6, 1907. *Studied*: PAFA; Colorassi Acad., Paris, France; Barnes Fnd. *Member*: AEA. *Awards*: Cresson traveling scholarship, 1930, 1931; prizes, PAFA, 1932; Indianapolis AA, 1938; Toledo Mus. A., 1953; Downtown Exh., Toledo, 1955. *Work*: PAFA; Toledo Fed. A. Coll. *Exhibited*: PAFA, 1932, 1953; DMFA, 1953; CGA, 1936; VMFA, 1937, Nat. Ser. Soc., 1955; one-man: Boyer Gal., Phila., 1936; Toledo Mus. A., 1940, 1954; Town Gal., Toledo, 1953; Carriage House Studios, Phila., 1956.

SINGER, BURR (Mrs. Burr Lee Friedman)— *Painter, Lith.*

2143 Panorama Terr., Los Angeles 39, Cal.

B. St. Louis, Mo. *Studied*: St. Louis Sch. FA; AIC; ASL, and with Waltar Ufer. *Member*: Cal WC Soc. (Vice-Pres., 1958); AEA; Los A. AA; Council All. A. *Awards*: prize, Marineland Exh., 1955; Los A. County Fair, 1951, 1953. *Work*: Warren Flynn Sch., Clayton Mo.; LC; Beverly-Fairfax Jewish Community Center, Los A.; Child Guidance Clinic, Los A. *Exhibited*: WFNY 1939; GGE, 1939; Denver A. Mus., 1943-1946; Audubon A., 1945; Pepsi-Cola, 1944; Los A. Mus. A., 1940-1945, 1952, 1954, 1955; Cal. WC Soc., 1940-1945, 1953-1958; Fnd. Western A., 1943-1945; Santa Barbara Mus. A., 1952; Greek Theatre, Los A., 1951; LC, 1948, 1950; Phila. Pr. Cl., 1952; Gump's San F., 1952; Cal. State Fair, 1949-1951, 1953; Oakland A. Mus., 1954; Maryhill (Wash.) Mus., 1951; Intl. Color Lithog., 1954; one-man: Chabot Gal., Los A., 1949; Esther Robles Gal., Los A., 1957; Cafe Galeria, Los A., 1958; Comara Gal., Los A., 1958.

SINGER, CLYDE J.—*Painter, T.*

524 Wick Ave.; h. 210 Forest Park Dr., Youngstown 12, Ohio

B. Malvern, Ohio, Oct. 20, 1908. *Studied*: Columbus A. Sch.; ASL, with John Steuart Curry, Kenneth Hayes Miller, Alexander Brook; Research Studio, Maitland, Fla. *Member*: Columbus A. Lg. *Awards*: prizes, NAD, 1938; Butler AI, 1938, 1942, 1948, 1953; Portland (Ore.) A. Mus., 1939; Columbus A. Lg., 1937-1939, 1946, 1951; Canton AI, 1949; medal, AIC, 1935; Ohio State Fair, 1955, 1958; Gilcrease Inst. Am. Hist. & Art, 1958. *Work*: PAFA; Vanderpoel Coll.; Canton AI; Massillon Mus.; Columbus Gal. FA; Butler AI; Wadsworth Atheneum; Research Studio; IBM; Canton Repository; Fla. Southern Col.; Columbus Pub. Sch.; Akron AI; Gilcrease Inst.; mural, USPO, New Concord, Ohio. *Exhibited*: PAFA, 1935, 1936-1939, 1941, 1949, 1950; CM, 1935-1940; AIC, 1935-1938; NAD, 1936, 1938, 1953, 1955, 1958; WFNY 1939; GGE, 1939; Carnegie Inst., 1936-1939, 1946-1948; WMAA, 1936, 1940; CGA, 1937, 1939; VMFA, 1940, 1942; Butler AI, 1937-1958; Columbus A. Lg., 1936-1939, 1941, 1947-1955; All. A. Am., 1957; Denver A. Mus.; Oakland A. Gal.; Milwaukee AI; John Herron AI; Los A. Mus. A.; New Haven Paint & Clay Club; Conn. Acad. FA; SFMA; Colorado Springs FA Center; Dallas Mus. FA; Montclair A. Mus.; BMA; Cal. PLH, and many others. *Position*: Asst. Dir., Butler AI, Youngstown, Ohio; A. Cr., Youngstown Vindicator.

SINGER, GEORGE FREDERIC—*Painter, Comm. A.*

205 South Vann Ave., Evansville 14, Ind.

B. Evansville, Ind., Oct. 11, 1927. *Studied*: AIC; John Herron AI, B.F.A.; Indiana Univ., and with Jack Tworkov, Harry Engle. *Awards*: prizes, Tri-State Exh., 1949, 1954;

Ky-So. Indiana Exh., 1954. *Work*: Evansville Pub. Mus.; Kentucky Wesleyan Col., *Exhibited*: Audubon A., 1950; Indiana A., 1951, 1957; Butler AI, 1950; Tri-State Exh., 1949-1957; Ky-So. Indiana Exh., 1950, 1953, 1954. *Position*: Staff A., Evansville Printing Corp., 1947-50 (summers); Des., Swanson-Nunn Signs, 1953-54; Instr. A., Columbus (Ind.) Jr. H.S., 1956- .

SINGER, WILLIAM EARL—*Painter, W., L., T.*
12897 San Vicente Blvd., "Brentwood," West Los Angeles 49, Cal.

B. Chicago, Ill., July 10, 1910. *Studied*: Univ. Chicago; AIC; in Paris; & with Charles Wilimovsky, John Norton. *Member*: Chicago SA; Cal. WC Soc.; Beaux-Arts Soc., Paris, France. *Awards*: prizes, A. Fair, Chicago, 1933; Davis award, Chicago, 1932; Beaux-Arts Soc., Paris, 1934; Rosenfield award, Chicago, 1940; Denver A. Mus., 1938; Havana, Cuba, 1946; Nat. Sch., 1949; Santa Cruz, 1948. *Work*: Grand Rapids A. Gal.; Illinois State Mus.; Scopus Col., Melbourne, Australia; Presidential Palace, Colombia; Israeli Govt.; Am. Embassy, Paris; Cook County Hospital, Chicago; Court House, Foley, Ala.; Joslyn A. Mus.; Newark Mus.; Univ. Minnesota; AIC; Lib. Cong.; Univ. Illinois; U.S. Govt.; Libertyville (Ill.) Court House; Biro-Bidjan Mus., Russia; Osaka Mus., Japan; St. Mary's Col., Winnipeg, Canada; Chanute Field Air Base; Bernheim Gal., Paris; Mexico City; Am. Fnd., Mexico City; Thomas Mann Mem., Zurich; Buenos Aires, Argentina; Israel Legation, Copenhagen, etc. *Exhibited*: AIC, 1932-1941; WFNY 1939; GGE, 1939; Great Lakes traveling exh., 1939; Denver A. Mus., 1938, 1939; Albright A. Gal., 1939; Toronto (Canada) A. Mus., 1938-1939; AIC, 1940 (one-man); traveling exh., European capitols, 1951, 1956-57; South America, 1953. Contributor to: "New Horizons in American Art," MModA; "American Art Today," Nat. A. Soc. Lectures: Contemporary Painting & the Old Masters. Author; I., "Paintings of Israel." Color consultant, Chicago World's Fair & Brussels International.

SINSABAUGH, ARTHUR R.—*Teacher, Photog.*
403 West Blackhawk St., Chicago 10, Ill.

B. Irvington, N.J., Oct. 31, 1924. *Studied*: Inst. Des., Chicago, B.A., with Moholy-Nagy, Harry Callahan. *Member*: Soc. Typographic A.; AAUP; Soc. Photographic Engineers. *Work*: MModA. *Exhibited*: George Eastman House, Rochester, N.Y., 1957; WAC, 1949; Chicago A. Cl., 1952; MModA, 1950, 1958; AFA traveling exh., 1957, 1958; Momentum Exh., Chicago, 1948, 1950, 1952-1954, 1956. Contributor illus. to: Chicago A. Dir. Bulletin; Photography (London); Architectural Review; Western AA Bulletin. Lectures: "The Approach to Photography as a Creative Medium." *Positions*: Instr., Photography, Inst. Des., Chicago, 1949-52; Illinois Inst. Technology, 1952- . Consulting Graphic Des. Dir., 1958.

SINZ, WALTER A.—*Sculptor, T., L.*
12210 Euclid Ave., Cleveland 6, Ohio; h. 3585 Raymont Blvd., University Heights 18, Ohio

B. Cleveland, Ohio, July 13, 1881. *Studied*: Cleveland Sch. A.; Julian Acad., Paris; & with Paul Landowski. *Member*: Cleveland SA; NSS. *Awards*: prizes, CMA, 1938, 1941, 1943, 1948-1950. *Work*: CMA; Case Inst. Tech.; Mount Union Col., Alliance, Ohio; medal for Metallurgical Soc., Detroit; Nat. Air Race Trophies; medal for Case Inst. Tech., 1953, port. busts of prominent persons. *Exhibited*: WMAA, 1941; PAFA, 1935; Jewish Mus., N.Y., 1953; Ohio State Fair, 1953; Syracuse Mus. FA, 1954; Butler AI, 1954; CMA, annually; Cleveland Soc. A., 1958 (one-man). Contributor to Ceramic Monthly; Arts magazine. Lectures: Sculpture. *Position*: Instr. S., Cleveland Sch. A., Cleveland, Ohio, 1912- .

SIPLE, ELLA SIMONS (Mrs. Walter H.)—
Writer, L., Mus. Cur., E., C.
9 Ash St., Cambridge 38, Mass.

B. Virden, Ill., Jan. 8, 1889. *Studied*: Wellesley Col., B.A.; & in Europe. *Member*: CAA; AAMus. Contributor to: Burlington magazine, news of Art in America; WMA Bulletins; etc., with articles on art, with special emphasis on tapestries. Lectures: Appreciation of the Arts; Art History. *Positions*: Hd. Edu Dept., 1918-23, Cur. Decorative A., 1923-29, WMA; L., CM, 1935-39; Special Editor for Tapestries, Historical Fabrics & Costumes, Webster's New International Dictionary, 1927-31; L., Mass. Dept. Edu. Div. Univ. Ext., 1921-29, 1951-1955.

SIPORIN, MITCHELL—*Painter, E.*
300 Franklin St., Newton 58, Mass.

B. New York, N.Y., May 5, 1910. *Studied*: AIC; Crane Col., Chicago; Am. Acad. in Rome. *Member*: AFA; AEA; Brandeis Univ. Creative A. Comm. *Awards*: medal, PAFA, 1946; AIC, 1947; Guggenheim F., 1946; prizes, AIC, 1942, 1947; Prix de Rome, 1949; Hallmark award, 1950; Nat. Inst. A. & Lets., 1955. *Work*: AIC; MMA; WMAA; MModA; Wichita Mus. A.; Smith Col.; Univ. New Mexico; Encyclopaedia Britannica; Univ. Georgia; AGAA; Alabama Polytechnic Inst.; Univ. Arizona; Brandeis Univ.; Cranbrook Acad. A.; FMA; Univ. Iowa; Newark Mus. A.; N.Y. Pub. Lib.; frescoes, USPO, St. Louis, Mo.; Decatur, Ill. *Exhibited*: WMAA, 1956-1958; AFA traveling exh., 1956-58; AIC; one-man: Downtown Gal., 1938-1942, 1947-1957; MModA, 1942; de Cordoba Mus., 1954. *Positions*: Hd. Dept. Painting, BMFA Summer Sch., 1949; Instr., Drawing, Columbia Univ., New York, N.Y., 1951; Assoc. Prof. FA, A.-in-Res., 1951-58, Chm. FA Dept., 1956-58, Brandeis University.

SIRUGO, SALVATORE—*Painter*
536 East 13th St., New York 9, N.Y.

B. Pozzallo, Italy, Aug. 18, 1920. *Studied*: ASL, with A. Blanch, P. Guston, V. Vytlacil, M. Kantor; Brooklyn Mus. Sch. A., with J. Ferren, G. Peterdi. *Member*: AEA; ASL; Brooklyn Mus. Sch. Alumni. *Awards*: Emily Lowe award, 1951; Brooklyn Mus. Sch. A. Scholarship, 1952; Woodstock Fnd., 1952. *Exhibited*: WMAA, 1952; PAFA, 1953; Art:USA, 1958; Provincetown A. Festival, 1958; Woodstock AA; Newman Gal., Phila.; Argent, Eggleston, Peridot, Laurel, Borgenicht, Camino Gals., N.Y.; Trinity Col.; Univ. Miami; Rutgers Univ., NAD, and others.

SISSON, FREDERICK R.—*Painter, Cr., T.*
Box 424, Falmouth, Mass.

B. Providence, R.I., Sept. 5, 1893. *Studied*: R.I.Sch.Des.; BMFA Sch.; Grande Chaumiere, Paris; & with Abbott Thayer. *Member*: Providence A.Cl. *Work*: R.I.Sch.Des.; Brown Univ.; L.D.M. Sweat Mem. Mus.; mural, Houston, Tex. *Exhibited*: MMA (AV); L.D.M. Sweat Mem. Mus., 1946; Providence A.Cl., 1955; Brown Univ. Contemporary A., Providence; R.I.Sch.Des.; R.I. State Col.; Attleboro (Mass.) Mus., all in 1946; Texas A. & M. Col., 1954; Univ. Houston, 1954; One-man: Providence A. Cl., 1951; Van Dieman-Lilienfeld Gal., 1952; Cape Cod AA, 1952.*

SISSON, LAURENCE PHILIP—*Painter*
Bay St., Boothbay Harbor, Me.

B. Boston, Mass., Apr. 27, 1928. *Studied*: WMA Sch.; Yale Summer Sch. *Member*: AWS; Boston WC Soc.; New Jersey P. & S. Soc. *Awards*: prizes, Fitchburg Mus. A., 1948; Yale Summer Sch., 1949; Hallmark award, 1949; All. A. Am., 1955; Boston Outdoor Show, 1950; Boston A. Festival, 1956; Portland A. Festival (purchase), 1957; bronze medal, New Jersey P. & S., 1951. *Work*: BMFA; Berkshire Mus. A.; Bowdoin Col.; Hickory Mus. A.; Columbia (N.C.) Mus. A.; New Britain Mus., and in private colls. *Exhibited*: Illinois Festival, 1951; CGA, 1952; NAD, 1951, 1953, 1954; All. A. Am., 1955; AFA traveling exh.; one-man: Clark Univ., Worcester, Mass.; CM; Bradford Jr. Col.; Portland (Me.) Mus. A. Contributor cover to Fortune magazine, 1951. *Position*: A. in residence, Publick House, Sturbridge, Mass., 1950; Guest Instr., CM, 1953; Dir., Portland Sch. F. & App. A., 1955.

SITTON, JOHN MELZA—*Painter, Gr., Des., W., L., E.*
34-25 Crescent St., Long Island City 6, N.Y.

B. Forsyth, Ga., Jan. 9, 1907. *Studied*: Yale Univ., B.F.A.; ASL; NAD; Am. Acad. in Rome; & with Eugene Savage, Ivan Olinsky, & others. *Member*: All.A.Am.; NSMP; N.Y. Mun. A. Soc.; Audubon A.; Century Assn.; SC; Newcomen Soc. of Am.; Nat. Indst. Adv. Assn.; Charcoal Cl., Balt. Md. *Awards*: Prix de Rome, 1929; prize, High Mus. A., 1946; Suydam med. *Work*: Yale Univ. A. Gal.; AGAA; Mint Mus. A.; IBM Coll.; Bendix Radio Coll.; Texas Tech. Col., Lubbock, Tex.; Fed. Reserve Bank, Atlanta, Ga.; Riverside Mem. Chapel, N.Y.; USPO, Clifton, N.J. *Exhibited*: NAD, 1932; WMAA, 1937; Pepsi-Cola, 1943; SSAL, 1943-1946; All.A.Am., 1944; Audubon A., 1945; Mint Mus. A., 1943; Dayton AI, 1946; Century Assn. 1945; SC, 1943; Laguna Beach AA, 1943; one-man exh.: High Mus. A., 1942; Dayton AI, 1933; Grand Central A. Gal., 1945, 1946; Telfair Acad., 1943; Clearwater A. Mus.,

Watson Publ. Co., 1955- .

SIVARD, ROBERT PAUL—Painter, Des., Lith.
United States Information Agency (25); h. 3013 Dumbarton St., Northwest, Washington, D.C.
B. New York, N.Y., Dec. 7, 1914. *Studied*: PIASch.; 1943; Cornell Univ., 1944; BMA; Montana State Univ. Contributor to American Artist; Printer's Ink; Modern Railroads and business publications. *Positions*: Asst. Prof. FA, Cornell Univ., Ithaca, N.Y., 1941-44; A. Supv., Bendix Radio, 1944-46, Dir., Adv., 1946-49; Eastern Mngr., Modern Railroads Publ. Co., 1949-54; Vice-Pres., Eastern Mngr., NAD; New Sch. for Social Research; Academie Julian, Paris, France. *Awards*: prizes, Dept. of State Comp., 1957; CGA, 1956; NAD, 1958. *Work*: murals, Oregon State Capitol; GGE, 1939; WFNY 1939. *Exhibited*: Musee d'Arte Moderne, Paris, 1953; Galerie Charpentier, Paris, 1954; CGA, 1956, 1957; Carnegie Inst., 1957; one-man: Galerie Craven, Paris, 1953; U.S. Embassy, Paris, 1954; Midtown Gal., N.Y., 1955, 1958. *Positions*: A. Dir., Fawcett Publ., 1940-42, 1946-48; Dir., Intl. Refugee Organization, Geneva, Switzerland, 1948-49; Dir., Visual Information, U.S. Embassy, Paris, 1951-54; Dir., Exhibits Div., U.S. Information Agency, Wash., D.C., 1958- ; Postmaster General's Public Stamp Advisory Com., 1957-58; Special Projects Com., AFA, 1958.

SIVYER, HENRIETTA R.—Educator
University of Tennessee, Knoxville 16, Tenn.
Position: Hd., Dept. Art.*

SIZER, THEODORE—Educator, C., W.
Yale University, New Haven, Conn.; h. Sperry Rd., Bethany, New Haven 15, Conn.
B. New York, N.Y., Mar. 19, 1892. *Studied*: Harvard Univ., B.S.; & with Denman W. Ross. *Awards*: Hon. degree, M.A., Yale Univ., 1931; Order of the Crown of Italy, 1945; Guggenheim F., 1947. Contributor to: various art and history periodicals & to the Dictionary of American Biography. Author: "Works of Col. John Trumbull, Artist of the American Revolution," 1950; "The Autobiography of Col. John Trumbull," 1953 (ed.); "The Recollections of John Ferguson Weir," 1957 (ed.). *Position*: Assoc. Prof., Hist. A., 1927-31, Prof., 1931-1957. Dir. A. Gal., to 1947, Prof. A., 1947-1957, Prof. Emeritus, 1957- , Yale Univ., New Haven, Conn.

SKEELE, ANNA KATHARINE—Painter, T.
314 South Mentor Ave., Pasadena, Cal.
B. Wellington, Ohio. *Studied*: ASL; Acad. FA, Florence, Italy; & with Andre L'Hote in Paris, France. *Member*: Laguna Beach AA; Cal. WC Soc.; Council All. A., Los A. *Awards*: prizes, Madonna Festival, Los A., 1952; San Diego FA Soc., 1930, 1933; Sacramento State Fair, 1930; Pomona County Fair, 1930; Los A. Mus. A. *Work*: San Diego FA Soc.; Los A. Mus. A.; mural, Torrance (Cal.) H.S. *Exhibited*: Palace Legion Honor, 1946; Doheny Lib., Univ. Southern California. *Position*: Instr., Drawing and Painting, Pasadena Sch. FA, Pasadena, Cal.*

SKEGGS, DAVID POTTER—Designer, P., C., Gr., L.
Garth Andrew Company; h. 1854 Orchard Drive, Bath, Ohio
B. Youngstown, Ohio, Feb. 5, 1924. *Studied*: Denison Univ., A.B.; Iowa State Univ., M.A., and with Hans Hofmann. *Member*: Nat. Ser. Soc.; Com. on A. Edu., MModA; Midwest Mus. Assn.; Experimentalists. *Work*: Akron AI; Smith Col.; Youngstown Col.; Indiana State T. Col.; Butler AI; Dayton AI; Des Moines A. Center; Joslyn Mus. A.; Nebraska State T. Col.; Sioux City A. Center; U.S. Embassies, abroad; and private colls. *Exhibited*: Canton AI; Akron AI; Butler AI; CMA; Toledo Mus. A.; Dayton AI; CM; Columbus Gal. FA; Indiana State T. Col.; AIC; Detroit Inst. A.; South Bend AA; Denison Univ.; Kenyon Col.; Massillon Mus. A.; Terry AI; BMFA; Syracuse Mus. FA; Ohio State Univ.; Newark Mus. A.; Bradley Univ.; BM; LC; Phila. Pr. Cl.; Serigraph Gal., N.Y.; SAM; Newport AA; Wadsworth Atheneum; Los A. Mus. A.; Colorado Springs FA Center; J.B. Speed Mus. A.; Columbia Gal. FA; Smith Col., Ohio, Iowa State Fairs, and many others. *Position*: Asst. Prof. A., 1948-52, Hd. Dept. A., 1952-54, Youngstown Col.; Dir., Sioux City A. Center, Sioux City, Iowa, 1954-1957; Des., Garth Andrew Co., Bath, Ohio, 1957- .

SKELLY, GLADYS GERTRUDE—Craftsman
3355 Oak Hill St., St. Louis 16, Mo.
B. Mexico, Mo., Feb. 13, 1901. *Studied*: St. Louis Sch. FA. *Member*: Artist-Craftsmen of N.Y.; Boston Soc. A. & Crafts. *Exhibited*: SAM, 1941; deYoung Mem. Mus., 1941; Philbrook A. Center, 1941; CAM, 1940-1943, 1950, 1951; Mus. FA of Houston, 1941; Davenport A. Gal., 1951; Allen Mus., Oberlin, Ohio, 1942; Oshkosh Mus. A., 1942; Brooks Mem. A. Gal., 1942; America House, 1952; Phila. A. All., 1950; Wichita, Kans., 1950, 1952; Mid-Am. A., 1952; St. Louis Women A., 1952; Delgado Mus. A., 1953; Brentano, N.Y., 1958.

SKELTON, PHILLIS HEPLER—Painter
505 South College Ave., Claremont, Cal.
B. Pittsburgh, Pa., Dec. 31, 1898. *Studied*: Univ. So. California, A.B.; Scripps Grad. Col., and with Eliot O'Hara, Phil Dike, Millard Sheets, Dong Kingman. *Member*: Cal. WC Soc.; Pasadena Soc. A.; Laguna Beach A. Gal. *Awards*: AWS, 1954; Cal. WC Soc. *Work*: Pasadena A. Mus., and in private colls. *Exhibited*: Butler AI, 1954; AWS, 1953; Cal. WC Soc., 1952-1954; Nat. Orange Show, 1953; Intl. Flower Show, 1955; San Gabriel Valley, 1953-1955; Palos Verdes, 1955; Pasadena Soc. A., 1954, 1955; Denver A. Mus., 1954; Cal. WC Soc. traveling exhs.; All-California A. Exh., 1955; one-man: Pasadena A. Mus., 1954; Laguna Beach A. Gal., 1954; Twenty-Nine Palms, Cal., 1953. *Position*: Instr. Children's Classes, Scripps Col., Claremont, 1958-59.

SKEMP, ROBERT OLIVER—Painter, Comm. A., I.
184 East 72nd St., New York, N.Y.; h. Sylvan Rd., North, Westport, Conn.
B. Scottdale, Pa., Aug. 22, 1910. *Studied*: ASL, with Benton, Bridgman, DuMond; Grand Central A. Sch., with Ballinger, Carter; George Luks Sch. A. *Member*: SI. *Awards*: prizes, Outdoor Adv. A., 1952, 1953, 1954; 100 Best Posters, 1937-1954. *Work*: Chicago Sch. Bd. *Exhibited*: A. Dir. Cl., Chicago, 1936-1954; A. Dir. Cl., N.Y.; Portraits, Inc., 1955; White Plains City Center; Grand Central A. Gal.; Art:USA, 1958; Bridgeport Pub. Lib., 1955, 1956, 1957. Contributor illus. to Sat. Eve. Post; Colliers; St. Nicholas; Liberty; Sports Afield.

SKILES, CHARLES—Cartoonist
126 Cedar St., Daytona Beach, Fla.
B. Pekin, Ind., Dec. 29, 1911. Contributor to: Sat. Eve. Post; Colliers; True; Look; American; Cosmopolitan; American Legion; Town Journal; Phila. Inquirer; King Features Syndicate; McNaught Syndicate; Better Homes & Gardens. Draws "Josephine" panel for General Features Corp.

SKILTON, JOHN DAVIS, JR.—
Writer, Former Mus. Cur.
3282 Congress St., Fairfield, Conn.
B. Cheshire, Conn., Feb. 28, 1909. *Studied*: Yale Univ., A.B., A.M.; Univ. Paris; N.Y. Univ. *Member*: Cercle de l'Union Interalliee, Paris, France. *Awards*: La Medaille de la Reconnaissance Francaise; Rockefeller F., 1935-36; Legion d'Honneur, 1957; Order of Merit First Class, German Govt., 1958. *Work*: AIC; NGA. Author: "Defense de l'Art Europeen," 1948; "Wurzburg," 1945; "Aus Dem Tagebuch Eines Amerikanischen Kunstschutzoffiziers," 1952. *Positions*: Research Asst., Am. Nat. Com. Engraving, 1940; Cur., Marcella Sembrich Mem., Lake George, 1941; Sr. Mus. Aide, NGA, 1942-43; Asst. to Dir., Detroit Inst. A., 1946-47; Parke-Bernet Gal., N.Y., 1949-53; Monuments Special Officer, World War II; Dir., Collectors of American Art, Inc.

SKINAS, JOHN CONSTANTINE—Painter
4 Mercer St.; h. 682 Bergen Ave., Jersey City, N.J.
B. Passaic, N.J., July 13, 1924. *Studied*: Newark Sch. F. & Indst. A.; ASL. *Member*: ASL. *Awards*: prizes, Village A. Center, 1954; Guggenheim Mus., 1954; Midwestern A. Conference, Bloomington, Ind., 1954. *Exhibited*: Solomon Guggenheim Mus., 1954; Midwestern A. Conference, 1954; DMFA, 1955; Guggenheim Mus. traveling exh., 1955-56; Athens, Greece, 1955; Village A. Center, 1954.

SKINNER, FRANCES JOHNSON—*Painter, T.*

3379 Tampa Dr., Houston 21, Tex.

B. Dallas, Tex. *Studied*: BMFA Sch.; Chouinard AI; & with Everett Spruce. *Member*: Texas FA Assn.; NAWA. *Awards*: prizes, Dallas Mus. FA, 1940, 1941; Mus. FA of Houston, 1943; Texas FA Assn., 1943, 1948; Texas General, 1947; NAWA, 1945, 1949. *Work*: Dallas Mus. FA; Dallas Pub. Sch. Coll.; Mus. FA of Houston; Texas FA Assn., and in private colls. *Exhibited*: PAFA, 1938; Nat. Exh. Am. A., N.Y., 1938; Kansas City AI; Texas Centennial; SFMA; Denver A. Mus.; New Zealand-Wesleyan Col. Exchange Exh.; NAD; Argent Gal., N.Y.; one-man: Sartor Gal., Dallas; Dallas Little Theatre; Texas FA Assn.; Junior League, Houston. *Position*: Instr. A., Mus. FA of Houston, Tex., at present.

SKINNER, ORIN ENSIGN—*Designer, L., W., C.*

9 Harcourt St., Boston 16, Mass.; h. 37 Walden St., Newtonville 60, Mass.

B. Sweden Valley, Pa., Nov. 5, 1892. *Studied*: with Herman J. Butler, Frank von der Lancken. *Member*: Boston Soc. A. & Crafts (Master Craftsman); Mediaeval Acad. Am.; Newcomen Soc., England. *Work*: stained glass windows, Cathedral St. John the Divine, St. Patrick's Cathedral, N.Y.; St. John's Cathedral, Albuquerque, N.M.; Princeton Univ. Chapel; Browning Mem. Lib., Baylor Univ., Waco, Tex.; St. John the Evangelist Cathedral, Spokane; St. John's Cathedral, Denver; Chapel, U.S. Naval Acad.; Chapel, U.S. Submarine Base, New London, Conn.; Grace Cathedral, San F.; Heinz Mem. Chapel, Univ. Pittsburgh; Daniel L. Marsh Chapel, Boston Univ. Contributor to art, architectural, religious magazines, with articles on Stained Glass. Series of lectures on Mediaeval Crafts, MM. *Position*: Pres., Treas.; Charles J. Connick Assoc.; Ed., Mngr., "Stained Glass," official publication of Stained Glass Assn. Am., 1932-49; Pres., Stained Glass Assn. Am., 1948-50.

**SKLAR, DOROTHY (Mrs. Dorothy Sklar Phillips)—
*Painter, T., Des.***

6612 Colgate Ave., Los Angeles, Cal.

B. New York, N.Y. *Studied*: Univ. California at Los A., B.E. *Member*: NAWA; New Orleans AA; Cal. WC Soc.; Laguna Beach AA; AEA; Alabama WC Soc.; Women Painters of the West; Westwood AA; Nat. Soc. Painters in Casein. *Awards*: prizes, Ala. WC Soc., 1944-1946; New Orleans AA, 1946, 1950, 1951; Laguna Beach AA, 1945-1947, 1952, 1954, 1957; Cal. A. Cl., 1949, 1951, 1953, 1954; Madonna Festival, 1955; Westwood AA, 1953, 1957; Santa Monica, 1946; NAWA, 1957; Women Painters of the West, 1958 (3). *Exhibited*: Cal. PLH, 1945; Alabama WC Soc., 1944-1956; Delgado Mus. A., 1944-1954, 1957; Gloucester, Mass., 1944-1946; NAWA, 1946-1948, 1957; Portland A. Lg., 1944-1947, 1953; Denver A. Mus., 1945, 1946, 1950, 1951; Oakland A. Mus., 1945, 1950; Laguna Beach AA, 1944-1958; Santa Cruz A. Lg., 1944, 1946; Santa Paula Chamber of Commerce, 1944-1949; Arizona State Fair, 1946, 1949; Greek Theatre, Los A., 1949-1951; Cal. State Fair, 1949, 1950, 1954-1957; Audubon A., 1947, 1958; PAFA, 1953, 1954; Butler Inst. Am. A., 1955, 1958; Nat. Orange Show, 1953, 1958; Los A. Mus. A., 1954, 1955; AWS, 1958; Art:USA, 1958; Frye Mus. A., Seattle, 1957, 1958; Knickerbocker A., 1956, 1958; Little Gal., Los A., 1956-1958; Madonna Festival, 1954-1957; Tupperware, 1957, and many more; one-man: Oklahoma Baptist Univ.; Cortland (N.Y.) Lib.; Rutgers Univ.; DeKalb (Ill.) Pub. Lib.; Massillon Mus. A.; Univ. Tennessee; Chabot Gal., Los A.; Laguna Beach AA, 1958 (2-man).

SKLAR, GEORGE—*Animal Painter, E., L., Des.*

2554 Bond Ave., Drexel Hill, Pa.

B. Philadelphia, Pa., Aug. 24, 1905. *Studied*: PIASch.; BAID, with Landowski, Paris; Yale Sch. FA, B.F.A., M.F.A. *Member*: Traveling Arts, Inc., Phila.; Phila. Zoological Soc.; Phila. Pr. Cl.; Phila. WC Cl. *Awards*: European scholarship, Phila., 1927; Tiffany Fnd. F., 1929; prize, Ecole des Beaux Arts, Paris, 1932; F., Yale Sch. FA, 1933. *Work*: PMA, and in private colls.; drawings for Phila. Zoo; Am. Mathematical Soc. *Exhibited*: PAFA; Phila. A. All.; PMA; Woodmere A. Gal.; Rochester Mem. A. Gal.; Lafayette AA (Ind.); Butler AI; Stephens Col., Columbia, Mo.; Weyhe Gal.; Moore Inst. A. & Sc. (one-man); Am. Mus. Nat. Hist. (one-man); Phila. Pub. Lib.; Univ. Pa. Sch. FA; Fellowship House, Univ. Pa.; Phila. Plastic Cl.; Audubon A.; Laurel Gal., N.Y.; Florence

(S.C.) Mus. A.; Canton AI. *Position*: Instr., Yale Sch. FA, 1935-37; New Jersey Col., Rutgers Univ., 1937-41; Parsons Sch. Des., 1945-50; Prof., Moore Inst. A., Phila., Pa., 1945- ; L., Fine Arts.

SKOLLE, JOHN—*Painter, T., I., L.*

Box 4374, Coronado Station, Santa Fé, N.M.

B. Plauen, Germany, Feb. 7, 1903. *Studied*: Acad. FA, Leipzig, Germany. *Awards*: prize, Denver A. Mus., 1930; Medal, Cal. PLH, 1946. *Work*: Denver A. Mus.; DMFA; Roswell Mus. A. *Exhibited*: MMoDA, 1942; Cal. PLH, 1946; Colorado Springs FA Center; Carnegie Inst.; one-man: Bonestell Gal.; Mus. New Mexico, Santa Fé; Univ. New Mexico; SAM; Santa Barbara A. Mus. I., Holiday Magazine. Contributor articles to Hudson Review; Southwest Review; Landscape, magazines. Author: "Azalai," 1956. Illus., "Maya," 1958. *Position*: Hd. A. Dept., Brownmoor Sch. for Girls, Phoenix, Ariz., 1945-51.

SLACK, ERLE B.—*Cartoonist, I.*

World-Tribune; h. 102 East King St., Tulsa, Okla.

B. Nashville, Tenn., Feb. 22, 1892. *Studied*: with Carey Orr, Sykes, McCrutcheon. *Member*: Nat. Cartoonist Soc.; Int. Typographical Un. *Awards*: Freedom Fnd. medal, Valley Forge, Pa. *Work*: Archives of the State of Oklahoma; LC; Univ. Oklahoma; des. and created the Seal of Tulsa. Drawings of Will Rogers in Claremore Roundup Club Bldg., Claremore, Okla. Many drawings of prominent persons. *Position*: Cart., World-Tribune, Tulsa, Okla.*

SLOAN, ROBERT SMULLYAN—*Painter*

1412 Arlington St., Mamaroneck, N.Y.

B. New York, N.Y., Dec. 5, 1915. *Studied*: Col. City of N.Y., A.B.; N.Y. Univ.; Ecole des Beaux Arts, Paris. *Member*: Mamaroneck A. Gld. (Pres.). *Awards*: Nat. Soldier Exh., 1945. *Work*: U.S. Treasury Dept.; IBM; Bradford Col.; Am. Flange Co.; Triangle Publ., and in private colls. *Exhibited*: U.S. Nat. Mus.; ASL; BM; Carnegie Inst.; CGA; AWS, 1957; Portraits, Inc. ,1958, and others. One-man: Leger Gal., White Plains, N.Y., 1955. Contributor to Time, Life, Coronet and other publications with reproductions of work.

SLOANE, E. K.—*Museum Director*

Hermitage Foundation, 7637 North Shore Road, Norfolk, Va.*

SLOANE, ERIC—*Illustrator, W., P., L.*

"Weather Hill," New Milford, Conn.

B. New York, N.Y., Feb. 27, 1910. *Studied*: ASL; N.Y. Sch. F. & Appl. A.; Yale Univ. Sch. FA. *Work*: Des. and executed Willett's Memorial, Am. Mus. Natural History; murals, International Silver Co., Meriden, Conn.; Morton Salt Co., Chicago; Wings Club, N.Y., and many others. Author, I., "Skies and the Artist"; "Our Vanishing Landscape"; "American Yesterday"; "Seasons of America's Past"; "Book of Storms"; "Clouds, Air and Winds"; "Eric Sloane's Weather Book," and others. Contributor to: Look; Life; American Heritage; New Yorker; Field & Stream; Popular Science; American Artist; Popular Mechanics and other publications.

SLOANE, JOSEPH CURTIS—*Educator, Hist., Mus. Dir.*

Department of Art, University of North Carolina; h. Morgan Creek Road, Chapel Hill, N.C.

B. Pottstown, Pa., Oct. 8, 1909. *Studied*: Princeton Univ., A.B., M.F.A., Ph.D. *Member*: CAA (Sec., 1954-56, Pres. 1956-58, Vice-Pres. 1958-). *Awards*: Hodder Fellow, Princeton Univ., 1948-49; Fulbright Research grant, France, 1952-53. Author: "French Painting Between the Past and the Present," 1951. Contributor to: Art Bulletin; Art Quarterly; Journal of Aesthetics; Art Criticism, etc. Lectures: 19th Century French Painting. *Position*: Prof. A., Chm., Dept. of A., & Dir., Ackland Art Center, University of North Carolina, Chapel Hill, N.C.

SLOBODKIN, LOUIS—*Sculptor, W., I., L., T.*

333 Fourth Ave.; h. 150 West 80th St., New York 24, N.Y.

B. Albany, N.Y., Feb. 19, 1903. *Studied*: BAID. *Member*: An Am. Group; S. Gld.; AIGA; AEA (Bd. Nat. Dirs.).

Awards: Caldecott med., 1943. *Work*: Madison Square P.O., N.Y.; mem. tower, Phila., Pa.; Interior Bldg., Wash., D.C. *Exhibited*: WMAA, 1935-1944; PAFA, 1941-1945; WFNY 1939; AIC, 1939-1943; MMA, 1942; S. Gld., traveling exh.; An Am. Group, 1939-1946; AIGA, 50 Best Books Exh., 1944; MMA Illus. Exh., 1944; AV Good-Will Tour, Europe; AFA traveling exh., 20 Best Children's Books, 1944. Author: "Magic Michael," 1944; "Sculpture Principles and Practice," 1949; "Clear the Track," 1945; "First Book of Drawing," 1958, & other books. I., "Rufus M," 1943; "Many Moons," 1943; "Tom Sawyer," 1946; "Robin Hood," 1946; & many others. Contributor to: Magazine of Art, Horn Book. Lectures: Contemporary Sculpture; Designing & Illustrating Children's Books. *Position*: Hd. S. Dept., Master Inst., New York, N.Y., 1934-37; Hd. S. Div., New York City Art Project, 1941-42; Pres., An Am. Group, 1945-46; Bd. Dir., S. Gld., 1940-45.

SLOBODKINA, ESPHYR—*Painter, I., W., Des., C.*
20 West Terrace Rd., Great Neck, N.Y.; h. 108 East 60th St., New York 22, N.Y.

B. Tcheliabinsk, Russia, Sept. 22, 1914. *Studied*: NAD; & abroad. *Member*: Am. Abstract A.; Fed. Mod. P. & S. *Work*: WMAA; CGA; PMA. *Exhibited*: WMAA; John Heller Gal.; Fed. Mod. P. & S.; Am. Abstract A. Author, I., "Caps for Sale"; "Sleepy ABC"; "The Wonderful Feast"; "Little Dog Lost," & other books.*

SLONIMSKY, MRS. NICOLAS. See Adlow, Dorothy

SLUSSER, JEAN PAUL—*Museum Director, P., W., E.*
1223 Pontiac St., Ann Arbor, Mich.

B. Wauseon, Ohio, Dec. 15, 1886. *Studied*: Univ. Michigan, A.B., A.M.; Univ. Munich; BMFA Sch.; ASL, and with Hofmann, McFee, Shahn, and others. *Member*: Am. Assn. Univ. Prof.; AEA; CAA; AAMus. *Awards*: prizes, Detroit Inst. A., 1924, 1931, 1937, 1945; Michigan WC Soc., 1951; Old Northwest Territory Exh., 1951. *Work*: IBM; Detroit Inst. A.; Ann Arbor AA; Univ. Michigan; Illinois State Mus.; murals, USPO, Blissfield, Mich. *Exhibited*: CGA, 1934; AIC; WMAA; BM; Detroit Inst. A., 1926-1952; Ann Arbor AA, 1926-1952; Michigan WC Soc., 1946-1952; Old Northwest Territory Exh., 1951, 1952. Author: text, "Bernard Karfiol," Am. A. Series, 1931. *Position*: Acting Chm., 1926-54, Prof., 1945-56, Dir., Mus. A., 1947-56, Emeritus, 1957- , Univ. Michigan, Ann Arbor, Mich.

SMALL, AMY GANS—*Sculptor*
317 West 89th St., New York 24, N.Y.; also, Woodstock, N.Y.

B. New York, N.Y., Apr. 22, 1915. *Studied*: Hartford A. Sch.; ASL; Nat. Park Col., and with Seymour Lipton. *Member*: AEA; Westchester A. & Crafts Gld.; Woodstock AA. *Work*: in private colls. *Exhibited*: The Contemporaries Gal.; Riverside Mus.; AEA; Barone Gal.; RoKo Gal.; Rudolf Gal., Woodstock; Woodstock AA; Kramer Gal. (one-man), 1958, and others.

SMALL, HANNAH (LUDINS)—*Sculptor*
Woodstock, N.Y.

B. New York, N.Y., Jan. 9, 1908. *Studied*: ASL. *Awards*: prize, AIC, 1940. *Work*: Univ. Nebraska, and in private coll. *Exhibited*: Fairmount Park, Phila., Pa.; AIC; WMAA; Woodstock AA; Rudolph Gal., Woodstock; Des Moines A. Center, 1951. One-man: Passedoit Gal., 1942, 1950.

SMALLEY, JANET—*Illustrator*
830 Rundale Ave., Yeadon, Pa.

B. Philadelphia, Pa., May 16, 1893. *Studied*: PAFA. *Awards*: Cresson traveling scholarship, PAFA, 1915; F., PAFA. Illus.: "Silver Yankee," 1953; "House Next Door," 1954; "Farm Girl," 1955; "Let's Play a Story," 1957; "Gift from the Mikado," 1958. Contributor to Jack and Jill, Children's Hour, magazines.

SMILEY, HELEN A.—*Craftsman, T., W.*
6445 Greene St., Philadelphia 19, Pa.

B. Philadelphia, Pa., July 8, 1900. *Studied*: Temple Univ., B.S.; Columbia Univ., M.A.; PMSchIA. *Member*: Phila. A. All.; Pa. Soc. Craftsmen. *Awards*: prize, Phila. A. All., 1941. *Exhibited*: Phila. A. All., 1953.

SMILEY, RALPH J.—*Portrait Painter*
1759 Orchid Ave., Hollywood 28, Cal.

B. New York, N.Y., July 24, 1916. *Studied*: ASL; NAD; with George Bridgman, Frank DuMond, Robert Brackman, Dean Cornwell and others. *Member*: Los A. AA; Los A. P. & S. Cl.; Cal. A. Cl.; ASL. *Awards*: prizes, Cal. A. Cl., 1955; Los A. P. & S. Cl., 1958. *Work*: ports. in private colls. *Exhibited*: Los A. AA; Cal. A. Cl.; Audubon A.; NAD; ASL; Los A. P. & S. Cl.

SMITH, ALBERT DELMONT—*Painter*
222 Central Park South, New York 19, N.Y.; h. School Lane, Huntington, L.I., N.Y.

B. New York, N.Y., Feb. 14, 1886. *Studied*: ASL; & with Frank DuMond, William Chase. *Member*: All. A. Am. *Awards*: med., All. A. Am., 1940, 1946. *Work*: Toledo Mus. A.; CAM; Detroit Inst. A.; Gallop A. Center; East Hampton, L.I., N.Y.; N.Y. Hist. Soc. Author: Pamphlets, "Shepard Alonzo Mount," 1945; "Robert Feke," 1946.*

SMITH, ANDRE—*Painter, Arch., Et., S., W.*
Maitland, Fla.

B. Hong Kong, China, 1880. *Studied*: Cornell Univ., B.S. in Arch., M.S. in Arch. Founder & Dir., The Research Studio, Maitland, Fla., an art center for the development of modern art.

SMITH, (ROBIN) ARTINE—*Painter, Comm. A.*
6270 Richmond Ave., Dallas 14, Tex.

B. Warren, Ark., July 18, 1903. *Studied*: AIC; Northwestern Univ.; in Vienna, Austria, and with Hubert Ropp, Eliot O'Hara. *Member*: Dallas AA; Texas FA Assn.; NAWA; Texas WC Soc. *Awards*: prizes, All. A., Dallas, 1943, 1944, 1948, 1953; Texas FA Assn., 1945; Texas WC Soc., 1950, 1951; DMFA, 1953; Dallas County Exh., 1955. *Work*: Dallas Mus. FA. Exhibited: AWS, 1945, 1948, 1952; AWS, Chicago, 1948, 1952; NAWA, 1945, 1946, 1948; All. A., Dallas, 1943-1946, 1948-1950, 1952; Texas General Exh., 1943-1946, 1948, 1949; Texas FA Assn. 1945, 1946, 1948, 1949, 1951; Terry AI, 1952; Texas WC Soc., 1950-1952, 1957; one-man: Austin, Tex., 1948; San Antonio, Tex., 1951; Dallas, Tex., 1951.

SMITH, BARBARA BALDWIN. See Baldwin, Barbara

SMITH, BISSELL PHELPS—*Painter, T., Gr., I., W., L.*
114 Coleman Road, Wethersfield 9, Conn.

B. Westbrook, Conn., July 10, 1892. *Studied*: Syracuse Univ.; Yale Univ., Sch. FA, and with Arthur J. E. Powell, Glenn Newall, Harry Waltman, Stanley Woodward, Emile Gruppe. *Member*: Academic Artists Assn.; AFA; Am. A. Group; AAPL; A. & Writers of Conn.; Berkshire AA; Conn. Acad. FA; Dutchess County AA; Hudson Valley AA; Kent AA; Meriden A. & Crafts Assn.; New Britain A. Lg.; SC; South Windsor A. Lg.; Torrington Artists; Lyme AA; Rockport AA; Berkshire Mus.; Wadsworth Atheneum and others. *Awards*: prizes, A. & Writers of Conn., 1954; Washington AA, 1955; Grumbacher Award of Merit, 1959; South Glastonbury AA, 1955, 1956, 1957, 1958, 1959. *Work*: oils: Roosevelt Memorial Lib.; Welles-Turner Memorial; Wethersfield and Wallingford (Conn.) Libs.; Syracuse Univ.; Choate School; Loomis School, and in private colls. *Exhibited*: Kent AA, 1939-1958; Ogunquit A. Center; Conn. Acad. FA, 1942-1958; Meriden A. & Crafts, 1956-1958; Terry AI, 1952; Cape Ann A. Festival, 1956-1958; A. & Writers of Conn., 1955, 1956; Washington AA, 1954-1957; Torrington AA, 1955-1958; Pawling Mission, 1938, 1939; Albany Inst. Hist. & A., 1956; Berkshire AA, 1955-1958; Rockport AA, 1954, 1955; one-man: Welles-Turner Memorial; Wethersfield Lib.; West Hartford A. Lg. Author, A. Ed., "Veeder's Digest," monthly industrial magazine, Veeder-Root, Inc., 1948- . Conducts oil painting demonstrations and lectures.

SMITH, CHARLES (WILLIAM)—*Painter, Gr., E.*
211 Fourth St., Northeast, Charlottesville, Va.

B. Lofton, Va., June 22, 1893. *Studied*: Univ. Virginia; Corcoran Sch. A.; Yale Univ. *Work*: FMA; MMoA; Hollins Col.; Portland (Ore.) A. Mus.; Valentine Mus.; Mus. Non-Objective Painting; Yale Univ.; N.Y. Pub. Lib.; Detroit Inst. A.; Williams Col.; Springfield (Mass.) Mus.; BMA; Newcomb Col.; Rosenwald Coll., and others. *Exhibited*: nationally and internationally. One-man: Willard Gal., N.Y.; AIC; BMFA; VMFA MModA; Ferargil Gal.; Phila. A. All.; Detroit Inst. A.; Montclair A. Mus.; Univ. of Kansas, Chicago, Virginia; Newcomb Col.; Yale Univ.; Bennington Col.; Hollins Col.; High Mus. A.; SFMA, and many others. Author: "Linoleum Block Printing," 1925; "Old Virginia in Block Prints," 1929; "Old Charleston," 1933; "Abstractions by Charles Smith," 1939; "The University of Virginia" (32 woodcuts), 1937; "Experiments in Relief Printmaking," 1954. *Position*: Prof. A., Chm. A. Div., Univ. Virginia, Charlottesville, Va.

SMITH, DAVID—*Sculptor, Eng.*
Terminal Iron Works, Bolton Landing, N.Y.

B. Decatur, Ind., 1906. *Awards*: Guggenheim F., 1950-51, 1951-52. *Work*: Detroit Inst. A.; WMAA; MModA; CAM; Walker A. Center; Univ. Michigan; AIC; Univ. Minnesota; Brandeis Univ.; CM; Carnegie Coll., Pittsburgh; Munson-Williams-Proctor Inst., and in private colls. *Exhibited*: Nationally and internationally. Retrospective shows: Buchholz Gal., 1946; Willard Gal., 1946; Walker A. Center, 1950; SFMA, 1954; MModA, 1957; Venice Biennale, 1958; more than 40 one-man exhs., 1938-1958. *Position*: Visiting Prof., Sarah Lawrence Col.; Univ. Arkansas; Univ. Indiana; Univ. Mississippi, etc. Delegate to Intl. Congress Plastic Arts, Venice, 1954.

SMITH, DOROTHY ALDEN—*Book Designer, I.*
Walnut & Juniper Sts.; h. 608 Weadley Road, Strafford, Wayne, Pa.

B. Atlantic City, N.J., June 1, 1918. *Studied*: N.Y. Sch. F. & App. A.; Sch. Professional A., N.Y. *Member*: Phila. A. All.; PAFA; MModA; PMA. *Awards*: prizes, 50 Best Books of the Year, 1945, 1946; Phila. Book Exh., 1946-1955 (Book Show Chm., 1953); A. Dir. Cl., Phila., 1948-1955, silver medal, 1957. *Position*: Asst. Adv. Dir., Theodore Pressers Co., Phila., Pa., 1940-41; A. Dir., Des., The Westminster Press, Philadelphia, Pa., 1944- ; Juror, Phila. Book Exh., 1956; Cur., King of Prussia Hist. Soc., 1958.

SMITH, DOROTHY OLDACH—*Teacher, P., W., L.*
1121 University Terr., Linden, N.J.

B. Philadelphia, Pa., Nov. 8, 1906. *Studied*: Univ. Pennsylvania, B.S.; Moore Inst., Phila.; N.Y. Univ., M.A.; & with Yarnall Abbott, Stanley Woodward. *Member*: AAPL; Eastern AA; New Jersey A. Edu. Assn.; Nat. Edu. Assn. *Exhibited*: Assoc. Am. A., N.Y.; Linden (N.J.) Nat. A. Week Exh. Author: "Monographs on Contemporary Artists." Lectures: Masterpieces of Art (Renaissance to Early 20th Century). *Position*: Hd. A. Dept., Linden H.S., Linden, N.J., at present.

SMITH, EMILY GUTHRIE (Mrs. Tolbert C.)—
Painter, T.
408 Crestwood Dr., Ft. Worth, Tex.

B. Ft. Worth, Tex., July 8, 1909. *Studied*: Texas State Col. for Women; Oklahoma Univ.; ASL, with Robert Brackman. *Member*: Texas FA Assn.; Ft. Worth AA (Sec. A. Memb. Group). *Awards*: prizes, West Texas annual, 1953; Ft. Worth AA, 1955, 1957. *Work*: DMFA; Ft. Worth Mus. A.; Lubbock Mus. A.; Lone Star Gas Co.; murals, Eagle Mountain Marine Base; Ridgelea Country Club; Radio Station KFJZ; Western Hills Hotel; Kent Motor Co.; Panther Oil Co.; mosaic, All Saints Hospital, Ft. Worth. *Exhibited*: Knickerbocker A.; Mississippi AA; Dallas, Tex., 1957; AWS, 1946; Corpus Christi, Tex., 1945; Texas General; Texas FA Assn.; Ft. Worth AA, 1953-1958; 6 One-man exhs., Texas, 1953-1958. *Position*: Instr., A., Ft. Worth A. Mus.

SMITH, EUNICE HATFIELD—*Portrait Painter*
62 Woodland Ave., Poughkeepsie, N.Y.

B. Mamaroneck, N.Y., June 6, 1911. *Studied*: Syracuse Univ., B.F.A.; ASL. *Member*: Am. Assn. Univ. Women; Dutchess County AA. *Work*: many portraits, U.S. & abroad. *Exhibited*: Dutchess County AA.

SMITH, FRANK VINING—*Marine Painter, W.*
64 High St., Hingham 9, Mass.

B. Whitman, Mass., Aug. 25, 1879. *Studied*: BMFA Sch.; & with Frank Benson, Edmund Tarbell. *Awards*: med.,

Jordan Marsh, Boston, 1939, 1942, 1945, 1946. *Work*: Mariners' Mus., Newport News, Va.; murals for steamship companies. *Exhibited*: one-man exh. in leading galleries since 1922. Contributor to: Yachting, Field & Stream, Outdoors magazines.

SMITH, GORDON MACKINTOSH—*Museum Director*
Albright Art Gallery (22); h. 35 Irving Pl., Buffalo 22, N.Y.

B. Reading, Pa., June 21, 1906. *Studied*: Williams Col., A.B.; Harvard Univ. Grad. Sch. A. & Sc.; travel and study in Europe. *Member*: Assn. A. Mus. Dirs.; AFA; CAA; AAMus. Contributor to Art News. Numerous lectures to art organizations and in museums. *Position*: Asst. Regional Dir., WPA, 1936-42; Chief, Plans & Intelligence Div., Camouflage Br., Ft. Belvoir, Va., 1942-44; Projects Specialist, Office Strategic Services, Wash., D.C., 1944-46; Dir., Currier Gallery A., Manchester, N.H., 1946-55; Dir., Albright A. Gal., Buffalo, N.Y., 1955- .

SMITH, HARRY KNOX—*Painter, C., Gr.*
601 West 115th St., New York 25, N.Y.
B. Philadelphia, Pa., Apr. 24, 1879. *Studied*: PAFA. *Work*: stained glass windows in many public buildings and churches; paintings in private collections.

SMITH, HELEN LEONA—*Painter, C.*
R.F.D. 5, Frederick, Md.

B. Frederick, Md., Jan. 21, 1894. *Studied*: Md. Inst. A. & Des. *Member*: Frederick A. Cl. *Work*: Masonic Temple, Frederick, Md.; Unionville Church, Burkettsville, Md.; Methodist Church, Libertytown, Md.; portraits, Univ. Virginia Masonic Temple, Frederick and Balt., Md.; Hood Col.; Maryland State Sch. for the Deaf; Frederick Mem. Hospital; Univ. Maryland; First Baptist Church, Frederick, Md. *Exhibited*: Frederick County A. Exh.

SMITH, HELEN M. (Mrs.)—*Educator, P., Des.*
Art Department, Maryville College, 1900 Meramec St. (18); h. 11415 Clayton Road, St. Louis 22, Mo.

B. Canton, Ohio, Oct. 19, 1917. *Studied*: Univ. Melbourne, Australia; Washington Univ., St. Louis, B.F.A., M.A. *Member*: St. Louis A. Gld.; Archaeological Soc. Am. *Award*: Ruth Kelso Renfrow A. Cl., St. Louis, 1955. *Exhibited*: St. Louis A. Gld., 1952-1955; Annual Missouri Exh., 1954; Religious Art Exh., Ladue, Mo., 1954, 1956; Ars Sacra Exh., 1955, 1956; Collector's Choice, 1955; St. Louis Metropolitan Church Federation, 1956; one-man: Clayton, Mo., 1954. Illus., "Aghios Kosmos," 1959. *Position*: Instr. A., Villa Duchesne, 1953-56; Hd., A. Dept., Maryville College, St. Louis, Mo., 1958- .

SMITH, HOWARD E.—*Painter*
904 Sylvania St., West Chester, Pa.

B. New Hampshire, Apr. 27, 1885. *Studied*: ASL with George Bridgman; BMFASch., with E.C. Tarbell; and with Howard Pyle; also in France, Spain and Italy. *Member*: ANA; BMFA; AWS; Chester County AA. *Awards*: prizes, NAD, 1908, 1930; Wanamaker prize, Phila., 1909; AIC; Wilmington Soc. A.; medal, San Francisco Expo., 1915; gold medal, NAD, 1920. *Work*: PAFA; de Cordova & Dana Mus.; Univ. Nebraska; Brown Univ.; State House, Boston; State House, Sacramento, Cal.; U.S. Treasury Dept.; Crocker A. Gal., Sacramento; Diocesan House, San Francisco. *Exhibited*: NAD; CGA; PAFA; AIC; LC; Chester County AA; Woodmere A. Gal.; Carmel AA; Soc. Western A.; Sacramento State Exh. Illus., "Children's Longfellow."

SMITH, HOWARD ROSS—*Museum Curator*
970 Greenwich St., San Francisco 11, Cal.

B. Los Angeles, Cal., Aug. 21, 1910. *Studied*: Univ. California, M.A.; Cal. Col. A. & Crafts, and with Eugen Neuhaus. *Position*: Hd. Dept. A., Univ. Maine, Orono, Me., 1942-49; Cur., Cal. PLH, San Francisco, Cal., 1951-55; Asst. Dir., Cal. PLH, San F., 1955- .

SMITH, IRWIN ELWOOD—*Painter*
2202 Butler St., Leesburg, Fla.

B. Labette, Kan., Feb. 14, 1893. *Studied*: Chicago Acad. FA; Washburn Univ. *Member*: Kans. Fed. A.; Fla Fed.

A.; Leesburg AA (Treas.); Topeka A. Gld. *Awards*: prizes, Kansas Fair, 1934, 1936; Kansas A. Exh., Topeka, 1945. *Work*: Kansas Fed. Women's Cl.; Highland Park Jr. H.S., Boswell Jr. H.S., Crane Jr. H.S., Topeka, Kan.; Stephenson Sch., Winfield, Kan.; Nat. Hdqtrs. Gal., Nat. Assn. Ret. Civil Employees, Wash., D.C. *Exhibited*: Kansas City AI; Joslyn Mem.; Kansas Fair; Topeka A. Gld.; Prairie WC Traveling Exh.; Kansas State Col.; Eustis (Fla.) AA; Leesburg AA; Ocala AA; Bushnell (Fla.) Women's Cl. (one-man); Wildwood (Fla.) Women's Cl., (one-man).

SMITH, JEROME IRVING—*Museum Curator, W.*
Henry Ford Museum, Dearborn, Mich.

B. New York, N.Y., Nov. 24, 1907. *Studied*: Columbia Univ. *Member*: AAMus.; Special Lib. Assn.; N.Y. Lib. Cl. Author: article on New York City in the Encyclopedia Americana. Contributor to: Country Life, Antiques, Town & Country, Art in America, & other magazines. *Position*: Cur. Lib., Dir. Publicity, Ed. Bulletin, Mus. City of N.Y., 1933-51; Des. permanent gallery showing "History of Fires and Fire Fighting," Mus. City of N.Y.; Dir., Seattle Mus. Hist. & Indst., 1951; Henry Ford Mus., Dearborn, Mich., 1952- .

SMITH, JOHN BERTIE—*Painter, E., W.*
Art Department, Hardin-Simmons University; h. 1825 Sandefer Ave., Abilene, Tex.

B. Lamesa, Tex., June 5, 1908. *Studied*: Baylor Univ., A.B.; Univ. Chicago, A.M.; AIC; Columbia Univ., Ed. D., and with Josef Bakos, Peppino Mangravite. *Member*: CAA; Midwestern Col. A. Conference (Pres. 1954); Missouri Col. A. Conference (Pres. 1952-54); Southeastern AA; AAUP; AEA; Mid-Am. A.; Nat. A. Edu. Assn.; Texas FA Assn. *Awards*: scholarship, Univ. Chicago, 1931; Dow scholarship, Columbia Univ., 1936. *Work*: Denver A. Mus.; Univ. Wyoming; Athens (Tex.) Pub. Lib. *Exhibited*: Denver A. Mus., 1938, 1939, 1941, 1943, 1945; Colorado Springs FA Center, 1945; AIC, 1931; Mulvane A. Center, 1954; Texas FA Assn. traveling exh., 1958; Texas WC Soc., 1955; one-man: Univ. Colorado, 1945; Mobile A. Gal., 1957; Abilene A. Mus., 1957; Wichita Falls A. Gal., 1958. Contributor to Design, School Review and other publications. *Position*: Dean, Kansas City AI, Kansas City, Mo., 1949-54; Hd. Dept. A., Chm. Humanities Div., Hardin-Simmons Univ., Abilene, Tex., 1954- .

SMITH, JUDSON—*Painter, T., L.*
Woodstock, N.Y.

B. Grand Haven, Mich., July 14, 1880. *Studied*: with John La Farge, John Twachtman. *Awards*: medal, Detroit Inst. A., 1926; prize, AIC, 1933; VMFA, 1944. *Exhibited*: nationally. One-man: Woodstock AA, 1949; Phila. A. All., 1950; Durand Ruel Gal., 1948; Hacker Gal., 1950; Stephens Col., Columbia, Mo., 1951; Retrospective exh., Woodstock AA, 1953-54; N.Y. State Univ., New Paltz, N.Y. *Position*: Prof. A., Univ. Texas, Austin, Tex., 1945; Dir., Woodstock Sch. Painting, Woodstock, N.Y., at present.*

SMITH, LAWRENCE BEALL—
Painter, I., Lith., Comm. A.
Cross River, N.Y.

B. Washington, D.C. *Studied*: Univ. Chicago; AIC, and with Thurn, Hopkinson, Zimmerman. *Work*: John Herron AI; Harvard Univ.; AGAA; Swope A. Gal.; Univ. Minnesota; Mus. City of N.Y.; Brandeis Univ.; MIT; Philbrook A. Center; Washington County Mus. A.; Reading Mus. A.; Honolulu Acad. FA; Fitchburg A. Center. Illus. "Robin Hood"; "Mad Anthony Wayne"; "The Black Arrow"; "Caine Mutiny."*

SMITH, LEON P.—*Painter, L., E.*
82 West 12th St., New York 11, N.Y.

B. Chickasha, Okla., May 20, 1906. *Studied*: East Central State Col., Ada, Okla., A.B.; T. Col., Columbia Univ., M.A. *Member*: Nat. Edu. Assn.; Am. Council Learned Soc. *Awards*: Guggenheim F., 1944. *Work*: Indiana Mus. Mod. A.; Univ. Arizona; Univ. Georgia. *Exhibited*: BM, 1942-1944; AIC, 1943; WMAA, 1946; SFMA, 1944; Telfair Acad. A., 1941; MMA, 1943; Riverside Mus., 1954; Segna Gal., East Hampton, N.Y.; Yale Univ. A. Gal., 1956; one-man exh.: New York, 1941, 1943, 1946; Mills Col.,

N.Y., 1955; Betty Parsons Gal., 1958. Lectures: History of Modern Art. *Position*: Instr., Rollins Col., 1949-51; Hd. A. Dept., Mills Col. of Edu., New York, N.Y., 1952-58.

SMITH, (DAVID) LOEFFLER—*Educator, P., L.*
Art Department, Chatham College (32); h. 5655 Forbes St., Pittsburgh 17, Pa.

B. New York, N.Y., May 1, 1928. *Studied*: Bard Col., B.A.; Cranbrook Acad. A., and with Hans Hofmann, Raphael Soyer. *Exhibited*: group shows in New York, Boston, Pittsburgh. Series of lectures on American Art, European Art for educational television programs. *Position*: Prof. A., Chatham College, Pittsburgh, Pa.

SMITH, MARIE VAUGHAN—*Educator, P., C., L., W.*
Oak St., South Pasadena, Cal.

B. Tacoma, Wash., Dec. 28, 1892. *Studied*: Cal. Col. A. & Crafts; Portland (Ore.) Mus. A. Sch.; Univ. Chicago; Univ. Oregon, B.S.; UCLA; Chouinard AI, and with Millard Sheets, Walter Sargent, Joseph Binder, and others. *Member*: Women Painters of the West; Pasadena Soc. A.; Cal. WC Soc.; So. Cal. A.T. Assn. *Awards*: prizes, Women Painters of the West, 1946, 1950. *Exhibited*: Los A. Mus. A.; Hollywood, Cal.; Pasadena AI; Washington State Fair; Cal. State Fair; So. Cal. A.T. Assn.; Cal. WC Soc. *Positions*: Dir. A., Alhambra, Cal. (20 years); Supv. A., Vancouver, Wash. (8 years); Duluth, Minn.; Dodge City, Kans. Ed., Women Painters of the West News, 1948-51.*

SMITH, MINNA WALKER—*Painter*
531 Edgewood Ave., New Haven, Conn.

B. New Haven, Conn., Mar. 29, 1883. *Studied*: Yale Sch. FA. *Member*: AWS; Conn. WC Soc.; Academic AA, Springfield; Meriden A. & Crafts; New Haven Paint & Clay Cl. *Awards*: prizes, Ogunquit A. Center, 1932; New Haven Paint & Clay Cl. *Work*: Wesleyan Col., A. Mus., Macon, Ga.

SMITH, MIRIAM TINDALL—*Painter, C.*
2115 Delancy Pl., Philadelphia 3, Pa.

B. Norwood, Pa. *Studied*: PMSchA; & with Arthur Carles. *Awards*: med., PMSchIA, 1933; Phila. Sketch Cl., 1940. *Work*: murals, Lutheran Church, Norwood, Pa.; N.Y. Central & Santa Fé railways; Children's Ward, Univ. Pennsylvania Hospital. *Exhibited*: AIC, 1934-1936; William Rockhill Nelson Gal., 1936; Minneapolis Inst. A., 1936; Dayton AI, 1936; PMA, 1935; PAFA, 1931, 1937; Woodmere A. Gal., 1941; Phila. A. All.; Frankford Hist. Soc.; one-man: Warwick Gal., 1937; Blood Gal., 1955; Allentown A. Mus., 1955.*

SMITH, OLIVER—*Craftsman, P.*
Studio: Bryn Athyn, Pa.; s. Pigeon Cove, Mass.; h. 406 Inness Drive, Tarpon Springs, Fla.

B. Lynn, Mass., Oct. 1, 1896. *Studied*: R.I. Sch. Des.; with Charles Hawthorne, and in London, England. *Member*: Phila. WC Cl.; SC; Clearwater AA; Sarasota AA; Rockport AA; Washington AA. *Awards*: Tampa Fair; Pinellas County Fair. *Work*: Univ. Florida; Gainesville Pub. Lib.; Tarpon Springs, and in many private colls. Stained glass windows, Temple Emanu-El, New York; Princeton Univ. Chapel; Mellon Cathedral, Pittsburgh, and in many churches over a 35-year period.

SMITH, MRS. OLIVER. See *Banta, E. Zabriskie*

SMITH, PAUL—*Designer, I., W.*
247 Park Ave., New York, N.Y.; h. 78 Battin Rd., Fair Haven, N.J.

B. Worthington, Minn., Jan. 18, 1907. *Studied*: Univ. Minnesota. *Member*: SI; A. Dir. Cl. *Awards*: medal, A. Dir. Cl., N.Y., 1934, 1935, 1942, 1945, 1948, 1952; A. Dir. Cl., Chicago, 1930-1933, 1945, 1947, 1948; Advertising Arts, 1942. *Exhibited*: MModA, 1952. *Position*: Pres., Calkins & Holden, New York, N.Y., 1957- . Editor, "Creativity," 1958.

SMITH, PAUL K(AUVAR)—*Painter*
1039 Stuart St., Denver 4, Colo.

B. Cape Girardeau, Mo., Feb. 27, 1893. *Studied*: St. Louis Sch. FA; Denver A. Acad. *Member*: 15 Colorado A.; Denver A. Gld.; Denver A. Mus.; Community A. Gal. *Awards*: purchase awards: Heyburn, Idaho, 1940, 1951; Gilpin County AA, 1950; Denver A. Mus., 1951; Colo. State Fair, 1952; Denver Metropolitan Exh., 1956; prizes, Canyon City, Colo., 1958; Gilpin County AA, 1958; Colo. State Fair, 1958; Denver A. Gld., 1937, 1946, 1954. *Exhibited*: Joslyn A. Mus., 1939-1958; Denver A. Mus., 1923-1956; Denver Metropolitan Exh., 1956-1957; 15 Colo. A., 1949-1958; Mulvane A. Center, Topeka, 1956; Community A. Gal., Denver, 1957; Denver A. Gld., 1934-1958; Gilpin County AA, 1949-1958, and others. One-man: Denver A. Mus.; Pueblo, Colo.; Loretto Heights Col., 1958; Sak's Gal., Denver, 1958; Bauer's Cherry Creek Center, 1958, Denver.

SMITH, R(OBERT) HARMER—*Painter, Arch. Delineator*
231 Wilkinson Ave., Jersey City 5, N.J.

B. Jersey City, N.J., July 27, 1906. *Studied*: PIASch.; Yale Univ., B.F.A.; & with Ernest Watson. *Member*: SC; Jersey City Mus. Assn. (Trustee). *Exhibited*: AWCS; Arch. L.; Jersey City Mus. Assn. Contributor to: American Artist, Architectural Record, Pencil Points magazines.

SMITH, RUSSELL TRAIN—*Educator, Des., L.*
465 Huntington Ave., Boston 15, Mass.; h. 107 Upland Rd., Brookline 46, Mass.

B. Concord, Mass., Mar. 14, 1905. *Studied*: Harvard Univ., A.B., M.Arch. *Member*: Wash. WC Cl. Lectures: Design; Art History. *Position*: Hd. A. Dept., Univ. North Carolina, 1936-40; Hd., BMFA Sch., Boston, Mass., 1940- ; Prof. A., Tufts Col., Medford, Mass., 1943- .*

SMITH, SAM—*Painter, E., C., Des., I.*
Art Department, University of New Mexico; h. 213 Utah St., Northeast, Albuquerque, N.M.

B. Thorndale, Tex., Feb. 11, 1918. *Member*: AAUP. *Work*: Albuquerque Pub. Lib.; Abilene Mus. A.; Encyclopaedia Britannica. *Exhibited*: White House, Pentagon, Nat. Mus., all of Wash., D.C.; Mus. New Mexico; Santa Fe and Taos, N.M.; Biltmore Gal., Los Angeles; Abilene, Ft. Worth and San Antonio, Tex.; CGA, 1949 (one-man); and in England; Nat. Mus., Mexico, D.F. Illus., "Cowboy's Christmas Tree," 1957; "Life of Frank Grouard," 1958; "George Gurry, an Autobiography," 1958. *Position*: Prof. A., University of New Mexico, 1956- .

SMITH, SIBLEY—*Painter*
Wakefield, R.I.

B. New York, N.Y., June 26, 1908. *Studied*: Harvard Univ.; Yale Univ. Sch. Arch. *Awards*: Pioneer Valley AA, 1953; Mystic AA, 1957; South County (R.I.) AA, 1957; Essex AA, 1958. *Work*: Providence (R.I.) Mus. A.; Rochester Mem. A. Gal. *Exhibited*: FAP, Wash., D.C., 1942; Inst. Mod. A., Boston, 1945; Providence Mus. A., 1943-1946; Tilden-Thurber Gal., Providence, 1942; Willard Gal., N.Y., 1945, 1948, 1950 (one-man), 1955; Pinacotheca; Soc. Four A., Palm Beach, Fla.; Boston AC; Margaret Brown Gal., 1949, 1950; WMAA, 1948, 1950; U.S. State Dept. traveling exh. Europe, 1954; BM, 1955.

SMITH, MRS. STOWELL Le CAIN. See Fisher, Stowell Le Cain

SMITH, VERNON B.—*Painter, C.*
Orleans, Mass.

B. Cortland, N.Y., Aug. 9, 1894. *Studied*: with Howard Giles, R. Sloan Bredin. *Member*: Cape Cod AA; Provincetown AA; Eastern AA; Mass. A. Edu. Assn. *Work*: BMFA; Springfield Mus. A.; New Britain Mus.; Dartmouth Col. Mus. *Exhibited*: nationally, including one-man exhs., in New York and Boston, 1949-1953.

SMITH, WALT ALLEN—*Sculptor, Des., L., T.*
656 North Occidental Blvd., Los Angeles 26, Cal.

B. Wellington, Kans., Mar. 1, 1910. *Studied*: Los A. County AI. *Member*: Cal. A. Cl.; Los A. County AI Alumni Assn. (Pres. 1953-58). *Award*: gold medal, Cal.

A. Cl., 1955. *Work*: Cole Co.; Electronic Eng. of California; memorial for the Hungarian Revolution of 1957 commissioned by Baron & Baroness Von Braun de Bellatini, 1957. Work also in private colls. *Exhibited*: Nat. Orange Show, 1948, 1950; Cal. Intl., 1950, 1956; Cal. Centennial, 1949; Palm Springs, 1955, 1956; Greek Theatre, Los A., 1949, 1950; Los Angeles A. Festival, 1949-1951, 1956-1958; Bowers Mem. Mus., 1956-1958; Wilshire Ebell, 1957; Cunningham Mem. Gal., Bakersfield, 1957; Los A. Mus. A., 1957, 1958; Descanso Gardens, 1957, 1958; Duncan Vail Gal., 1956-1958; Palos Verdes Lib., 1956, 1957; Florentine Gal., Pacific Palisades, 1956, 1957; Whittier Gal., 1956, 1957; Pacific Coast Cl., Long Beach, 1958; Madonna Festival, 1956, 1957; Gal. A. Cl., 1955, 1956, 1958; Glendale Lib., 1957, and many others. Lectures with demonstrations on Sculpture and Jewelry Design.

SMITH, WILLIAM ARTHUR—*Painter, Lith., I., L.*
Windy Bush Road, Pineville, Pa.

B. Toledo, Ohio, Apr. 19, 1918. *Studied*: Univ. Toledo, and with Theodore J. Keane; Ecole des Beaux Arts, Grande Chaumiere, Paris, France. *Member*: NA; AWS (Bd. Dir., 1954-55); Phila. WC Cl.; Cal. WC Soc., Audubon A.; SI; Toledo Tile Cl. *Awards*: medal, AWS, 1948, 1952, prize, 1954; NAD, 1949, 1951; Cal. WC Soc., 1948; Obrig prize, 1953; Butler AI, 1953; Ranger Fund, 1951; prize & gold medal for "Watercolor of the Year," 1957; Dorne purchase prize, 1958; Pennell Mem. purchase, 1956; SAGA; Hon. deg., M.A., Toledo Univ., 1954. *Work*: Chrysler Corp.; Fla. Southern Col. MMA; LC; Los A. Mus. A. *Exhibited*: MMoA, 1953, 1954; MMA, 1952, 1953; LC, 1953, 1954; DMFA, 1953, 1954; PAFA, 1954; AWS, 1953-1955; NAD, 1953, 1954; Audubon A., 1954, 1956; Phila. WC Cl., 1953; CAM, 1953; one-man: Phila., Pa., 1953; Italy, Greece, Turkey, India, Japan and others, all 1954; Singapore, Manila, 1955. U.S. Delegate to Intl. Conference Plastic Arts, Venice, 1954. Lectures: American Art, Univ. Santo Tomas, Manila, 1955; Univ. Philippines, 1955; Acad. FA, Athens, Greece, 1954. Rec. Sec., NAD, 1953-55; Pres., 1956-57, Hon. Pres., 1957- , AWS; Memb., Cultural Delegation of P. & S. to the U.S.S.R., 1958.

SMITH, WUANITA—*Painter, Gr., I., W.*
260 South 21st St., Philadelphia 3, Pa.

B. Philadelphia, Pa., Jan. 1, 1866. *Studied*: Phila. Sch. Des. for Women; PAFA; ASL, and in Paris, France. *Member*: Am. Color Pr. Soc. (Founder); Phila. Pr. Cl.; F. PAFA; Phila. Plastic Cl. (hon.); Woodmere A. Gal.; New Haven Paint & Clay Cl.; Bridgeport AA. *Awards*: F., PAFA; prizes, Phila. Pr. Cl.; New Haven Paint & Clay Cl.; Irvington (N.J.) AA. *Work*: PAFA; LC; Phila. Plastic Cl.; Phila. Sch. Des. for Women; PMA; Oklahoma A. Center; Scranton Mus. A. & Sc. *Exhibited*: Wilmington AA, 1952; Woodmere A. Gal., 1954. *Position*: Treas., Am. Color Pr. Soc., 1940-51.

SMOLEN, FRANCIS (FRANK)—*Painter, I., Des., S., C., T.*
396 Logan Ave., Sharon, Pa.

B. Manor, Pa., Jan. 8, 1900. *Studied*: Fed. Sch., Inc.; Carnegie Inst.; & with Bicknell, Readio, Ashe, & others. *Awards*: prizes, Sharon AA, 1935, 1939, 1943. *Work*: Buhl Girls Cl., Sharon, Pa., and in private colls. *Exhibited*: Devoe & Raynolds Exh., 1940; Assoc. A. Pittsburgh, 1928, 1931-1934; Butler AI, 1935, 1936, 1938, 1941, 1943; Sharon AA, 1938-1942, 1945; Albright A. Gal., 1949; Alliance Col., Cambridge Springs, Pa., 1951; Watercolor traveling exh., 1952.*

SMONGESKI, JOSEPH L.—*Book Designer, P., Lith., Ser., T.*
285 Columbus Ave., Boston, Mass.; h. 42 Brook St., Wollaston, Mass.

B. Two Rivers, Wis., Feb. 6, 1914. *Studied*: Univ. Chicago; Univ. Wisconsin; AIC, and with Louis Ritman. *Member*: Book Builders Cl., Boston. *Exhibited*: AIC, 1939; Madison Salon, 1938-1940; Contemp. A. Gal., 1942; Chappellier Gal., 1953; one-man: Elmira (N.Y.) A. Gal., 1945; Tardif Gal., Belmont, Mass., 1949; Cornell Col., 1950; Publick House, Sturbridge, Mass., 1951; BMFA, 1950; Milton, Mass., 1953; Quincy, Mass., 1953, 1956. Des. & illus., "Cocina Criolla," Spanish Cookbook. *Position*: Instr., Painting, Adult Classes, Milton H.S.

SMUL, ETHEL LUBELL—Painter, Lith., T., L.
155 West 20th St., New York 11, N.Y.

B. New York, N.Y., Sept. 11, 1897. *Studied*: Hunter Col.; ASL, and with Brackman, Olinsky, Robinson, and others. *Member*: NAWA; N.Y. Soc. Women A.; Brooklyn Soc. Mod. A.; AEA; ASL (life). *Exhibited*: NAD, 1936, 1952, 1954; Argent Gal., 1934-1952; LC, 1948, 1949; Carnegie Inst., 1949; Rotary Shows, U.S. and Canada, 1946, 1948-1958; Italy, 1946; France, 1949; Everhart Mus. A.; CM, 1952-1954; Riverside Mus., 1949, 1952, 1955, 1957. Lectures: Arts and Crafts. *Position*: Instr. A., Jr. H.S., New York City; Treas., N.Y. Soc. Women A., 1952, 1953, 1956-1958.

SMULLYAN, ROBERT SLOAN. See Sloan, Robert S.

SMYTH, CRAIG HUGH—Educator
Institute of Fine Arts, New York University, 17 East 80th St., New York 21, N.Y.; h. 84 Hillside Ave., Cresskill, N.J.

B. New York, N.Y., July 28, 1915. *Studied*: Princeton Univ., A.B., M.F.A., Ph.D. *Member*: CAA. *Awards*: Fulbright F., 1949-50; ACLS grant, 1958. Contributor to Art Bulletin. *Position*: Sr. Mus. Aide, NGA, 1941-42; Dir., Central Art Collection Point, Munich, Germany, 1945-46; Research Asst., L., Frick Collection, N.Y., 1946-49; Asst. Prof., 1950-53, Assoc. Prof., 1953- 1957, Prof., 1957- ; Hd. Grad. Dept. FA, Inst. FA, New York Univ., 1953- ; A. Dir., CAA, 1953-1957, Sec., 1956.

SMYTH, EDMUND R.—Designer, P.
2805 North Buena Vista St., Burbank, Cal.

B. Toronto, Canada, Nov. 6, 1902. *Studied*: AIC; Chicago Acad. FA; Grande Chaumiere, Paris, France; Rome, Italy; Munich, Germany. *Member*: Tech. Illus. Management Assn. (Treas., 1958). *Exhibited*: Charney Gal., 1934; Allerton Gal., 1935; Davis Gal., 1935, 1936, all in Chicago; All-Illinois Soc. FA, 1936; Chicago Jubilee Exh., 1937.

SMYTHE, WILLARD GRAYSON—
Painter, T., Des., W., I.
5036 North Parkside, Chicago 30, Ill.

B. Bellefontaine, Ohio, Feb. 12, 1906. *Studied*: AIC. *Member*: 27 Chicago Des.; AAUP. *Awards*: prize, Chicago Soc. Typographic A., 1931; Award of Excellence, AIGA, 1937, 1952; Certif. Award, Chicago and Midwest Book Clinic, 1950-51, 1954, 1955. *Work*: mem. plaque, Santa Fé Railroad; advertising des., Abbott Laboratories, Monsanto Chemical Co., Searle Laboratories, & others. *Exhibited*: AIC, 1934, 1936, 1938, 1939, 1942, 1945, 1946, 1947, 1955; Nat. Advertising A. & Illus. Exh., 1940; AIGA, 1935, 1937, 1938, 1952; Great Lakes Exh., 1939; Northern Mississippi Valley A., 1943; Soc. Typographic A., 1929-1944; A.Dir. Cl., Chicago, 1936, 1939, 1940, 1943, 1944, 1948; A.Dir.Cl., N.Y., 1938; Toledo, Ohio, 1948; Palmer House Gal., 1949-50, 1953; Magnificent Mile Exh., Chicago, 1951, 1952; Chicago Pub. Lib., 1954, and others. Contributor to: Printing Art, Design & Color magazines. *Position*: Instr. Adv. Des., AIC, Chicago, Ill., 1928- ; A.Ed., Printing Art Quarterly, 1938-41; A.Ed., Quarrie Corp., World Book Encyclopedia, 1943-46; Exec. A.Dir., Consolidated Book Publishers, Chicago, Ill., 1946- ; Memb. Gilbert Letterhead Award panel, Gilbert Paper Co., Menasha, Wis.; Memb. Jury for Golden Reel Film Festival, Film Council of Am., 1958.

SNELL, CARROLL C(LIFFORD)—Designer, I., L.
96 Bank St., New York 14, N.Y.

B. Medina, N.Y., Aug. 15, 1893. Illus. for leading publishers; posters, displays, des., for Theatre Guild, R. H. Macy & Co., Lord & Taylor, etc. Lectures: Chromatics. Originator of Snell System of Color Harmony (Retired).

SNIFFEN, HAROLD S.—Assistant Museum Director
Mariners Museum, Newport News, Va.*

SNODGRASS, JEANNE OWEN (Mrs. Charles T.)—
Museum Curator, Comm. A., L.
Philbrook Art Center, 2727 South Rockford Road (14); h. 119 East 34th St., Tulsa, Okla.

B. Muskogee, Okla., Sept. 12, 1927. *Studied*: Art Instruction; Northeastern State Col.; Oklahoma Univ. Lectures: American Indian Painting: It's History and It's Artists.

Assisted with and arranged many exhibitions for Philbrook Art Center including: Good Design, 1956; The American Indian's Contribution to Our Civilization, 1956; Tulsa Collects Indian Art, 1958; The American Indian Painting Exhibition (Annual); Oklahoma Artists Annual, as well as other exhibitions of sculpture, ceramics, and artifacts associated with the American Indian. *Position*: Asst. to the Director, Cur., American Indian Art, Cur., Exhibitions, Philbrook Art Center, Tulsa, Oklahoma.

SNOW, MARY RUTH (Mrs. Philip J. Corr)—Painter
4856 Loughboro Road, Northwest, Washington 16, D.C.

B. Logan, Utah, Mar. 6, 1908. *Studied*: Univ. Utah, B.A.; Corcoran Sch. A.; ASL; Otis AI; and in Paris, France. *Member*: Soc. Wash. A., Wash. A. Cl.; NAWA; Wash. A. Gld.; Wash. WC Cl. *Awards*: prizes, Soc. Wash. A., 1952; Wash. A. Cl., 1952. *Exhibited*: CGA; Soc. Wash. A.; Wash. A. Cl.; VMFA; Whyte Gal., 1951; MMA; Wash. WC Cl.; PC; Georgetown Gal.; Wash. A. Gld.; American Univ., Wash., D.C.; Norfolk Mus. A. & Sc.; NCFA; Los A. Mus. A.; NAD; NAWA, and in Germany. Oneman: Wash. A. Cl., 1945; Chequire House, Alexandria, 1950; Silver Springs (Md.), A. Center, 1950; Alexandria Pub. Lib., 1945, 1950. *Position*: Pres., Soc. Wash. A., Washington, D.C., 1951-1953; Advisor, Bd. Edu., Arlington County, 1951-52; Pres. Wash. A. Gld., 1958-59.

SNOWDEN, CHESTER DIXON—Painter, I., T., W.
1310 Truxillo St., Houston 4, Tex.

B. Elgin, Tex., Oct. 8, 1900. *Studied*: Univ. Texas; CUASch; ASL, and with Boardman Robinson, Walter J. Duncan, Harry Sternberg. *Member*: SSAL. *Awards*: prizes, Mus. FA of Houston, 1938, 1946, 1954, 1955; A. Lg. of Houston, 1953, 1955; Beaumont Mus. A., 1958. *Exhibited*: CGA, 1939; Southwest Texas Exh., 1946 and prior; Mus. FA of Houston, annually; Texas General; Laguna Gloria Mus., Austin, Tex.; Elisabet Ney Mus., Austin; Junior Lg., Houston, 1952 (one-man). I., "Shafts of Gold," 1938; "Children of Hawaii," 1939; "Ape of Heaven"; "Half Dark Moon"; "Wildwood Friends," and other books. Author: "Pioneer Texas" (a play).

SNOWDEN, GEORGE HOLBURN—Sculptor, T., L.
2248 Broadway, New York, N.Y.

B. Yonkers, N.Y., Dec. 17, 1901. *Studied*: Yale Sch. FA, B.F.A.; Grande Chaumiere, Paris; Am. Sch., Athens. *Member*: NA; F., NSS; Am. Acad. in Rome; Yale Cl.; Books & Authors Assn.; P. & S. Assn. *Awards*: medal, NAD; prizes, New Haven Paint & Clay Cl.; Am. Acad. in Rome; FA Fed., N.Y. *Work*: panels, figures, monuments, memorials, Springfield Mus. A.; Saratoga Springs, N.Y.; Bronx County Courthouse, N.Y.; State Capitol Grounds, Hartford, Conn.; USPO, Washington, D.C., and others; ecclesiastical work: Church of Our Lady of Refuge, Long Beach; Mt. Carmel Chapel, Los A.; Sacred Heart H.S., Loretto H.S., Los A.; St. Timothy's Church, West Los A.; St. Therese Church, Alhambra, Cal.; St. Francis Church, Cataiina, Cal.; Father Juniper Serra statue, San F.; St. Sebastian Church, Santa Paula, Cal.; and others. *Exhibited*: AIC; Grand Central A. Gal.; Madonna Festival, etc.*

SNOWDEN, WILLIAM ETSEL, JR.—
Designer, I., Gr., W.
1428 West Peachtree St., Northwest; h. 1270 Brookhaven Terr., Atlanta, Ga.

B. Elberton, Ga., May 29, 1904. *Studied*: Georgia Sch. Tech.; Maryland Inst.; Fed. Sch., Inc. *Member*: SSAL; Direct Mail Advertising Assn.; Augusta AC; Assn. Georgia A.; Atlanta Cl. of Printing House Craftsmen; AIGA. *Awards*: Direct Mail Assoc., 1940; prizes, Augusta AC, 1936; Printing House Craftsmen, 1945. *Work*: historical maps & brochures; Elbert County (Ga.) War Mem., Aiken, S.C.; Augusta, Ga.; Atlanta, Ga. *Exhibited*: Maryland Inst.; Assn. Georgia A., 1934-1936, 1938; AIGA, 1945; Augusta AC, 1936, 1937, 1938; Atlanta AA. Contributor to: trade publications. *Position*: Pres., Snowden & Steward Advertising, Atlanta, Ga.

SNYDER, CORYDON GRANGER—
Illustrator, Comm. A., P., T., W., L.
1935 South Michigan Ave.; h. 520 North Paulina St., Chicago 22, Ill.

B. Atchison, Kan., Feb. 24, 1879. *Studied*: AIC; Minneapolis Inst. A.; Toronto AI. *Work*: Historical Soc., St.

Paul, Minn. *Exhibited*: Palette & Chisel Acad., 1931 (one-man); Ill. State Fair, 1955; Central YMCA A. Cl., Chicago. Author, I., "Fashion Illustration," 1916; "Pen and Ink Technique," 1920; "Art and Human Genetics," 1952. *Position*: Instr., Fed. Schs., Minneapolis, 1916-18; Meyer Both Comm. A. Sch., 1920-30; Krompier Sch. Des., Chicago, 1940-43; Advertising Illustrator, Meyer Both Co., Chicago, Ill., at present.

SNYDER, JEROME—*Painter, Des., I.*
92 Jane St., New York, N.Y.

B. New York, N.Y., Apr. 20, 1916. *Awards*: prizes, AIGA, 1953, 1954; A. Dir. Cl., 1954, 1955. *Work*: Container Corp.; murals, USPO, Fenton, Mich.; Social Security Bldg., Wash., D.C. *Exhibited*: A. Dir. Cl., 1949-1955; Danish Des. Circle; MMA; AIC; MModA; and other museum and art organization exhs. Contributor to Charm, Mademoiselle, Harper's Bazaar, Graphis, and other publications. *Position*: A. Dir., Sports Illustrated.*

SNYDER, SEYMOUR—*Illustrator, Des., Comm. A.*
11 East 44th St.; h. 315 East 68th St., New York 21, N.Y.

B. Newark, N.J., Aug. 11, 1897. *Studied*: Fawcett Sch. Indst. A., Newark, N.J.; ASL; Grand Central Sch. A. Illus. & covers for House & Garden, American Home, McCall's, & other magazines. Nat. advertising illus. for Westinghouse, General Electric, Nat. Lead Co., Johns-Manville, Dupont, and many others.

SOBLE, JOHN JACOB—*Painter, T.*
Bushkill, Pa.; h. 1505 Grand Concourse, New York 52, N.Y.

B. Russia, Jan. 14, 1893. *Studied*: NAD. *Member*: AEA; Lehigh A. All.; All.A.Am. (Pres., 1957-58). *Awards*: prizes, All.A.Am., 1957; Academic AA, Springfield, Mass., 1958. *Work*: Toledo Mus. A. *Exhibited*: NAD, 1925, 1929, 1932, 1936, 1938; PAFA, 1936, 1937; Toledo Mus. A., 1936, 1937; Audubon A., 1950; Terry AI, 1952; All.A. Am., 1951; GGE, 1939; AIC, 1936; Carnegie Inst., 1941; CGA, 1937; VMFA, 1938; Pepsi-Cola, 1945; Ain-Harod Mus., Israel. *Position*: A. Dir., Tamiment (Pa.) A. Gal.

SOBY, JAMES THRALL—*Writer, Cr.*
Brushy Ridge Rd., New Canaan, Conn.

B. Hartford, Conn., Dec. 14, 1906. *Studied*: Williams Col. Author: "After Picasso," 1935; "The Early Chirico," 1941; "Salvador Dali," 1941; "Tchelitchew," 1942; "Romantic Painting in America" (with Dorothy C. Miller), 1943; "Georges Rouault," 1945; "The Prints of Paul Klee," 1945; "Ben Shahn," 1947; "Contemporary Painters," 1948; "Twentieth Century Italian Art" (with Alfred H. Barr, Jr.), 1949; "Modigliani," 1951; "Giorgio de Chirico," 1955; "Yves Tanguy," 1955; "Balthus," 1956; "Modern Art and the New Past," 1957; "Ben Shahn, His Graphic Art," 1957; "Juan Gris," 1958; "Joan Miro," 1959. Contributor of articles and criticisms to leading art publications. *Positions*: Asst. Dir., 1943, Dir., Painting & Sculpture, 1943-45, Trustee, 1943- , Chm. Committee on the Museum Collections, at present, MModA., New York, N.Y.; A. Cr., Saturday Review of Literature, 1946- ; Acting Ed., 1950-51, Chm. Editorial Bd., 1951-52, Magazine of Art.

SOCHA, JOHN MARTIN—*Painter, T.*
5747 Auto Club Road, Minneapolis 20, Minn.

B. St. Paul, Minn., Mar. 3, 1913. *Studied*: Minneapolis Sch. A.; Univ. Minnesota; & with Glenn Mitchell, Robert Brackman. *Member*: Minnesota AA; Minn. Edu. Assn.; Minneapolis Soc. FA; Walker A. Center; Western AA. *Awards*: prizes, Minnesota State Fair, 1940, 1941; Minneapolis Woman's Cl., 1942; Walker A. Center, 1949; Minneapolis Inst. A., 1942. *Work*: Univ. Nebraska; Minneapolis Inst. A.; Minneapolis Woman's Cl.; Walker A. Center; Dayton Co.; Univ. Minnesota; Am. Red Cross, Wash., D.C.; murals, Winona (Minn.) State T. Col.; Univ. Minnesota; Fed. Reserve Bank, Minneapolis; St. Luke's Cathedral, St. Paul, Minn.; New Ulm H.S.; St. James Episcopal Church, Minneapolis Chapel, Ft. Snelling, Minn. *Exhibited*: Minneapolis Inst. A., 1938-1944, 1946; AIC, 1941, 1942; MMA, 1941, 1942; WMAA, 1942; NGA, 1940, 1942; Guatemala City, 1940; Mexico City, 1942; Minnesota State Fair, 1938-1942; Walker A. Center, 1938, 1940; Davenport Mun. A. Gal., 1941; St. Paul A.

Gal., 1939-1942; Minneapolis Woman's Cl., 1938-1942; Denver A. Mus.; Univ. Wisconsin; one-man: Fed. Courts Bldg., Hamline Univ., St. Catherine's Col., Pub. Lib., St. Paul Park H.S., all in St. Paul; Guy Mayer Gal., N.Y.; Mankato State Col., 1957. *Position*: Instr., Marshall H.S., Minneapolis, Minn., 1951- .

SOCHOR, BOZENA (Miss)—*Painter*
26 Nutt Ave., Uniontown, Pa.

B. Sonov, Czechoslovakia, Sept. 5, 1901. *Studied*: Pennsylvania State Col.; Carnegie Inst. *Member*: Uniontown (Pa.) AC; Assoc. A. Pittsburgh; All. A. Johnstown. *Exhibited*: Carnegie Inst., 1945; Butler AI, 1944; Parkersburg FA Center, 1943-1946; Ohio Univ., 1945; Uniontown (Pa.) AC, 1941-1958; Uniontown (Pa.) Pub. Lib., 1952 (one-man); All. A. Johnstown, 1948-1958.

SODERBERG, YNGVE EDWARD—*Painter, Et., T., W., Comm. A.*
51 Clift St., Mystic, Conn.

B. Chicago, Ill., Dec. 21, 1896. *Studied*: AIC; ASL. *Member*: Mystic AA; SAGA. *Awards*: prize, SAGA, 1945. *Work*: AIC; Lib. Cong.; Smithsonian Inst.; Lyman Allyn Mus. *Exhibited*: Grand Central A. Gal.; Kennedy Gal., N.Y.; one-man: Grand Central A. Gal., 1949, 1954; Am.-Swedish Mus., Phila., 1954; Lyman Allyn Mus., 1955; Old Mystic A. Center, 1958. Author: "Drawing Boats and Ships," 1958. *Position*: Instr., A., New London H.S., New London, Conn.

SOGLOW, OTTO—*Cartoonist*
330 West 72nd St., New York 23, N.Y.

B. New York, N.Y., Dec. 23, 1900. *Studied*: ASL, with John Sloan. *Member*: SI; Cartoonist Soc. Author, I., "Pretty Pictures"; "Everything's Rosey"; "Wasn't the Depression Terrible"; "The Little King." I., many books. Contributor to: New Yorker, Colliers, Life magazines; syndicated in many newspapers by King Features Syndicate.

SOHNER, THEODORE—*Painter, L.*
2114 Fremont Ave., South, Minneapolis 5, Minn.

B. St. Paul, Minn., Mar. 18, 1906. *Studied*: St. Paul Sch. A.; Minneapolis Sch. A., and with Andre LHote, in Paris; Michele Garinei in Florence, Italy. *Member*: Minnesota AA. *Awards*: prizes, Minneapolis Inst. A., 1943, 1944, 1945, 1951; Minnesota State Fair, 1932, 1933, 1944, 1946; Minneapolis Woman's Cl., 1946-1949. *Work*: Minnesota State Capitol; St. Olaf Col.; Minneapolis Inst. A.; Univ. Minnesota; Univ. Illinois; South Dakota State Capitol; Kenyon Col.; House of Temple, Wash., D.C.; St. Mary's Hall; St. James Military Sch.; Breck Sch.; mural, Scottish Rite Temple, Minneapolis. *Exhibited*: Minn. State Fair; Minn. Centennial, 1949, 1950; Minneapolis Inst. A., 1949-1951; Minneapolis Woman's Cl., 1948-1952; Swedish Inst. A., 1952; Joslyn A. Mus., 1952; Minn. Artists, St. Paul, 1958.

SOKOLE, MIRON—*Painter, T., W., L., Gr.*
250 West 22nd St., New York 11, N.Y.; s. Maverick Road, Woodstock, N.Y.

B. Odessa, Russia, Nov. 20, 1901. *Studied*: CUASch; NAD. *Member*: AEA; Audubon A. *Awards*: prize, medal, NAD. *Work*: IBM; Upjohn Co.; U.S. State Dept.; Univ. Minnesota; Tel-Aviv Mus. *Exhibited*: CGA, 1941, 1943, 1958; AIC, 1931, 1932, 1935, 1940-1944; WMAA, 1939, 1943, 1945, 1946, 1948, 1953, 1954; BM, 1939, 1943; DMFA; Detroit Inst. A.; Rochester Mem. A. Gal.; Dayton AI, 1953; Albany Inst. Hist. & A.; Minneapolis Inst. A.; CM, 1958; Albright A. Gal.; PAFA, 1940-1942, 1952; Springfield Mus. A.; BMA; Columbus Gal. FA, 1951, 1953, 1957; Carnegie Inst., 1943-1945, 1949; VMFA, 1944; MMA, 1942, 1944, 1945; WAC, 1944; Birmingham Mus., 1952, 1953; Audubon A., 1952; Univ. Nebraska, 1954, 1956; Miami Beach A. Center, 1953; John Herron AI, 1954; Des Moines A. Center, 1956; Memphis Mus. A., 1956; Butler Inst. Am. A., 1957; Montreal, Canada, 1954; Springfield Mus. A., 1956; Univs. of Iowa, Alabama, North Carolina, Illinois, and others; one-man: Midtown Gal., 1934, 1935, 1937, 1939, 1944, 1951, 1956; Kansas City AI, 1947; Nelson Gal. A., 1948, etc. Many traveling exhs.

SOLMAN, JOSEPH—*Painter, T., W., L.*
156 2nd Ave., New York, N.Y.

B. Russia, Jan. 25, 1909. *Studied*: NAD; Columbia Univ. *Member*: Fed. Mod. P. & S. *Work*: PC; WMAA. *Exhibited*: PAFA, 1951, 1952; CGA, 1943, 1945, 1951, 1955; Carnegie Inst., 1943, 1945; PMG, retrospective exh., 1949; ACA Gal.; New Art Circle; WMAA, 1955.*

SOLOMON ALAN ROBERT—*Museum Director, E.*
White Art Museum, Cornell University; h. 110 Triphammer Rd., Ithaca, N.Y.

B. Quincy, Mass., Aug. 13, 1920. *Studied*: Harvard Univ. *Position*: Instr., A. Hist., Col. A. & Sciences, Cornell Univ.; Dir., Andrew Dickson White Mus. A., Cornell Univ., Ithaca, N.Y.*

SOLOMON, MITZI. *See Cunliffe, Mitzi Solomon*

SOLOMON, SYD—*Painter, T., Lith.*
1216 First St.; h. 2428 Portland St., Sarasota, Fla.

B. Uniontown, Pa., July 12, 1917. *Studied*: AIC; Ecole des Beaux Arts, Paris, France. *Member*: AWS; AEA; Fla. A. Group; Alabama WC Soc.; Mississippi WC Soc. *Awards*: prizes, Sarasota AA, 1951-1954, 1958; Fla. Intl. purchase, 1952; Lowe Gal. A., 1952; Hallmark, 1952; High Mus. A., 1953, 1956, 1957, purchase 1958; Jackson, Miss., 1954; Birmingham Mus. A., 1954; Fla. Fed. A., 1951, 1955-1957; All Fla. Annual, 1953; Clearwater Mus. A., 1953, 1954, 1955; Atlanta, Ga., 1958; Butler Inst. Am. A., 1957; Audubon A., 1957; Soc. Four Arts, 1956, 1957; New Orleans AA, 1958; Fla. A. Group, 1956, 1958; gold medal, Nat. Soc. Painters in Casein, 1957, and others. *Work*: Fla. Southern Col.; Clearwater A. Mus.; High Mus. A.; Birmingham Mus. A.; Mississippi AA; Fla. Fed. A.; BMA; Delgado Mus. A.; Mead Atlanta Paper Co.; Sarasota AA; Ga. Tech. Univ., and others. *Exhibited*: 1951-58: AWS; MMA; BMA; Audubon A.; Butler Inst. Am. A.; Birmingham Mus. A.; DMFA; AFA traveling exhs.; Univ. Fla.; New Orleans AA; Alabama WC Soc.; Fla. Southern Col.; Lowe Gal. A.; Soc. Four A.; High Mus. A.; Sarasota AA; Inst. Contemp. A., Boston; Munson-Williams-Proctor Inst.; Carnegie Inst.; Colo. Springs FA Center; Mus. FA of Houston; etc. One-man: Sarasota AA; Tampa AA; Clearwater, Fla.; Lowe Gal.; Stetson Univ.; Univ. Fla.; Assoc. Am. A.; traveling exh. to Jerusalem, Haifa, Tel-Aviv; Ringling Mus. A.; Barry Col., Miami; AAA Gal., N.Y., and others. *Positions*: Instr., Painting, Pittsburgh AI, 1947; Ringling Mus. Sch. A., 1951, 1953-56, 1958; Directing Faculty, Famous Artists Course, 1953- ; Dir., Instr., Sarasota Sch. A., 1951- .

SOLOWEY, BEN—*Painter, S.*
Bedminster, Pa.

B. Warsaw, Poland, Aug. 29, 1900. *Member*: AWS; Phila. WC Cl.; AEA. *Awards*: medal, Phila. WC Cl.; F. PAFA medal, 1953. *Exhibited*: nationally. *Position*: Instr., New Hope (Pa.) FA Workshop; Instr., PMSch.A.

SOMMER, A. EVELYN—*Painter, Gr., T., Des., W., L.*
Box 3, Waverly Station, Baltimore 18, Md.

B. Jersey City, N.J. *Studied*: Maryland Inst.; Johns Hopkins Univ., B.S.; T. Col., Columbia Univ., M.A.; Woodstock, N.Y.; Provincetown, Mass., and with Albert Heckman, Emil Ganso, and others. *Member*: AEA; Nat. A. Edu. Assn.; Eastern AA; CAA; Nat. Edu. Assn. *Exhibited*: BMA; Chesapeake Cl., Balt., Md. *Positions*: Instr., Maryland Inst. Day School, 1927-29; Balt. Pub. Sch., 1931- ; Eastern H.S., 1942- ; Instr., Painting, in art curriculum under Carnegie Grant, Eastern H.S., Baltimore, Md., 1942- .

SOMMERBURG, MIRIAM—*Sculptor, C., Gr., P.*
1825 First Ave., New York 28, N.Y.

B. Hamburg, Germany, Oct. 10, 1910. *Studied*: with Friedrich Adler, Richard Luksch, in Germany. *Member*: NAWA; Am. Color Pr. Soc.; AEA; Audubon A.; Brooklyn Soc. A.; Creative A. Assoc. *Awards*: Fla. Southern Col., 1952; Village A. Center, 1948, 1949, 1950, 1951, 1957; Creative A. Gal., 1950; New Jersey P. & S., 1955; silver medal, Knickerbocker A., 1954. *Work*: Fla. Southern Col., Springfield (Mo.) A. Mus.; MMA. *Exhibited*: Fla. Southern Col., 1952; NAWA, 1952-1958; BM, 1951,

1954; Audubon A., 1948, 1950, 1952-1958; New Orleans AA, 1947, 1949, 1950-1952, 1954, 1955; SAGA, 1947, 1948, 1951; All. A. Am., 1949; Cal. Soc. Et., 1946; Syracuse Mus. FA, 1945; WMAA, 1951, 1954; Riverside Mus., 1947, 1948, 1953-1958; PAFA, 1954; BMFA, 1951-1954; Amsterdam, Holland, 1956; Belgium, 1956; Baton Rouge, La., 1957, 1958; Contemporaries, 1956, 1957; Young Am. A., 1955; Silvermine Gld. A., 1958; Jewish Tercentenary traveling exh., 1955; Berlin, Germany, 1954; Burlington Gal., London, 1955; one-man: Village A. Center, 1950, 1958; Creative A. Gal., 1951; Salpeter Gal., 1953; Kaufman Gal., 1954; Carl Schurz Fnd., 1955.

SONED, WARREN—*Painter, Des., S., T., L.*
208 Biscayne St., Miami Beach, Fla.; h. 16200 Northeast 10th Ave., North Miami Beach, Fla.

B. Berlin, Germany, Sept. 15, 1911. *Studied*: FA Acad., Dusseldorf, Germany; Ecole des Beaux-Arts, Grande Chaumiere, Paris, France; Univ. Miami, B.A. *Member*: Mural A. Gld.; Soc. Indp. A.; "Lead & Ink" (hon.), Nat. Journalistic Fraternity, Univ. Miami; Fla. A. T. Assn. *Awards*: prize, Nat. Army Exh., 1945; prize and silver medal, A. Dir. Cl., Miami, 1953; Best Trade Magazine adv., 1953. *Work*: Des., Covers of Univ. Miami Yearbook, 1949-51 (won All-Am. Intercollegiate award for Des.); bas-reliefs, Broad Causeway, Bay Harbor, Fla.; murals, USPO, Hapeville, Ga.; N.Y. Telephone Bldg.; Pildes Optical Co., N.Y.; Barbizon Sch. Fashion Modeling, N.Y.; Walter Reed Hospital, Wash., D.C.; Tides Hotel, Miami Beach; Biscayne Osteopathic Hospital, Miami; North Miami Beach Clinic; Bible Baptist Church, North Miami; Bayfront Clinic, Miami; Veteran's Admin., N.Y.; glass murals, interiors, exteriors, sculptures, etc., in many clubs, restaurants, homes, in U.S. and abroad. *Exhibited*: Soc. Indp. A.; Army A. Exh., 1945; Lowe Gal., Univ. Miami, 1949-1953. *Position*: Fndr., Dir., Artists Anonymous, Miami Beach A. Sch., 1952- ; Instr., A. Dept., Univ. Miami; Instr., A. Consultant, Dade County Schs., 1957-58.

SONNENBERG, JACK—*Printmaker, P.*
128 East 16th St.; h. 110 East 16th St., New York, N.Y.

B. Toronto, Canada, Dec. 28, 1925. *Studied*: Ontario Col. A.; Sch. for Art Studies, N.Y., with Lewis Daniel, Ernest Fiene, Sol Wilson; Washington Univ. Sch. FA, St. Louis, with Fred Conway, Paul Burlin and Fred Becker. *Awards*: prizes, Peoria A. Center, 1955; Bradley Univ., 1956, purchase; Springfield Mus. FA, 1957. *Work*: Bradley Univ.; 100 graphics for Intercontinental Hotels. *Exhibited*: BM, 1953, 1954, 1956, 1958; BMFA, 1955; Springfield Mus. FA, 1956, 1957; Pomona, Cal., 1956; PAFA, 1957; Butler Inst. Am. A., 1958; Provincetown A. Festival, 1958; CAM, 1951.

SOPHER, AARON—*Painter, Cart., I., P.*
718 North Charles St. (1); 4300 Penhurst Ave., Baltimore 15, Md.

B. Baltimore, Md., Dec. 16, 1905. *Studied*: Baltimore Polytechnic Inst.; Maryland Inst. *Member*: AEA. *Awards*: prizes, BMA, 1943, 1946; Balt. Evening Sun., 1931, 1933, 1943, 1945; CGA, 1953. *Work*: PMG; BM; Dumbarton Oaks Coll.; BMA; Edward Bruce Mem. Coll.; Cone Coll., Balt.; Nelson Gutman Coll., Balt., and others. *Exhibited*: NAD, 1945, 1946; WMAA, 1942; Lib. Cong., 1943, 1945; BM, 1941; Carnegie Inst., 1943; AIC, 1938, 1940, 1942; Albany Inst. Hist. & A., 1943, 1945; BMA, 1940-1946. I., "Rivers of the Eastern Shore," 1944; portfolio 45 drawings, "Maryland Institutions," 1949; "Princess Mary of Maryland," 1956; "People, People," 1956 (poems); "Aaron Sopher's Baltimore," (TV program). Included in "6 Maryland Artists," 1955. Contributor to: Baltimore Sun papers; Harpers; Johns Hopkins magazine; New Yorker; Wall Street Journal, & other publications.

SOPHIR, MRS. JACK J. *See Young, Dorothy O.*

SORBY, J. RICHARD—*Painter E., Des.*
2020 South York St., Denver 10, Colo.

B. Duluth, Minn., Dec. 21, 1911. *Studied*: Univ. Minnesota; Colorado State Col. Edu., A.B., M.A.; AIC; Mexico City Col.; U.C.L.A.; Univ. Colorado. *Member*: 15 Colorado A. *Awards*: prizes, Nelson Gal. A., 1955; Denver A. Mus., 1954; Central City, Colo., 1955; Joslyn Mem.

Mus., 1956. *Work*: Marine Hospital, Carville, La.; Utah State Agricultural Col.; Brigham Young Univ.; Rural Electrification Admin.; Nelson Gal. A.; Denver A. Mus.; Central City, Colo. *Exhibited*: NGA, 1941; Denver A. Mus., 1937, 1938, 1940, 1941, 1946, 1948-1955; Nelson Gal. A., 1950, 1955; Joslyn A. Mus., 1941-1943, 1945, 1954, 1956; PAFA, 1941; Kansas City AI, 1941; Salt Lake City, 1954; Cedar City, Utah, 1948, 1956; one-man: Denver A. Mus., 1948, 1954. *Position*: Assoc. Prof. A., Univ. Denver, Colo.

SORENSEN, JOHN HJELMHOF—*Cartoonist*
6504 Beacon St., Little Rock, Ark.

B. Copenhagen, Denmark, Nov. 22, 1923. *Studied*: in Copenhagen, Denmark; Famous Artists Course, Westport, Conn. *Member*: Nat. Cartoonists Soc. *Awards*: prize, Arkansas Mus. FA, 1955; Outdoor Advertising Assn. of Am., 1956, 1957. Contributor to Sat. Eve. Post; True; American Weekly; King Features Syndicate; Esquire; Cosmopolitan; Sat. Review, and other national magazines. Cartoons published in Denmark, England, France, Italy, Switzerland, etc.

SORGMAN, MAYO—*Teacher, P., Des., L.*
811 Shippan Ave., Stamford, Conn.

B. Brockton, Mass., Mar. 29, 1912. *Studied*: Mass. Sch. A., B.S.; N.Y. Univ., M.A.; Parsons Sch. Des.; Taos Valley A. Sch.; Kansas City AI. *Member*: Silvermine Gld. A., Conn. WC Soc.; Rockport AA; Eastern AA; Nat. Edu. Assn.; Conn. T. Assn. *Award*: Silvermine Gld. A., 1955; Emily Lowe award, 1956. *Exhibited*: Audubon A.; CAM, 1944; Nelson Gal. A., 1944; Conn. WC Soc., 1941-1945, 1956, 1958; Rockport AA; Springfield A. Lg.; NGA; Grand Central A. Gal., 1949; Wadsworth Atheneum; Dartmouth Col.; Riverside Mus.; New Britain A. Mus.; Silvermine Gld. A.; AWS, 1958; Cape Ann Mod. A., 1957; Audubon A.; Rockport AA; one-man: Silvermine Gld. A.; Eleanor Smith Gal., St. Louis; Stamford Mus.; Rockport AA, 1955. *Position*: Hd. A. Dept., Stamford (Conn.) H.S.; Chm., Cultural Comm., Cape Ann Soc. Mod. A.; Dir., Conn. AA.

SORIA, MARTIN SEBASTIAN—
Educator, W., L., Mus. Consultant
Art Department, Michigan State University, East Lansing, Mich.

B. Berlin, Germany, July 3, 1911. *Studied*: Univ. Madrid, B.A.; Univ. Zurich; Harvard Univ., M.A., Ph.D., with Chandler Post, J. Rosenberg, B. Rowland. *Member*: CAA; Renaissance Soc. Am.; Am. Soc. for Aesthetics. *Awards*: Rich scholarship, Harvard Univ., 1940; Bacon traveling F., Harvard Univ., 1941; Latin American travel grant, Am. Council Learned Soc., 1942; Bollingen F., 1950, 1955, 1956; Guggenheim F., 1950; Am. Philosophical Soc. grant, 1951, 1955. Author: "The Paintings of Zurbaran," 1953, 2nd ed., 1954; "Agustin Esteve y Goya," 1957; "La pintura del siglo XVI en Sudamerica," 1956; "The Arts and Architecture of Spain, Portugal and their Dominions 1500-1800" (with G. Kubler), 1959; numerous articles in Art Bulletin, Art Quarterly, Art in America, Gazette des Beaux Arts, Burlington Magazine, and others. Lectures on Spanish and Latin American Art, especially painting from Greco to Goya; Baroque Art, Graphic Art. Consultant to American and European museums and to the Intl. Council Mus. for Conservation of Art Objects. *Position*: Instr., Princeton Univ., 1944-46; Mich. State Univ., A. Dept., 1948- ; Visiting Prof., Columbia Univ., summer, 1951.

SORIANO, ESTEBAN—
Painter, C., Des., Cart., Comm. A., I.
157 West 22nd St., New York 11, N.Y.; h. 41-15 46th St., Long Island City 4, N.Y.

B. San Juan, Puerto Rico, Mar. 11, 1900. *Exhibited*: BMA, 1945; CM, 1946; Mus. Natural Hist. (Animals in Art). Illus., "Three Times I Bow," 1942; "Illiterary Digest"; "Almanac for New Yorkers," 1937, 1938, 1939. Contributor cartoons to New York Tribune, New York World, New York Times, New York Herald-Tribune, Sat. Review, Colliers, Sat. Eve. Post, Panama American, etc.*

SOTTER, ALICE BENNETT (Mrs. George W.)—
Craftsman, P., Des.
Holicong, Pa.

B. Pittsburgh, Pa. *Studied*: Pittsburgh Sch. Des. for Women; Carnegie Inst. *Member*: Woodmere A. Gal. Ex-

hibited: Pittsburgh and Phila., Pa.; Phillips Mill, New Hope, Pa., 1957. *Work*: stained glass windows, Father Coakley Mem. Chapel, Sacred Heart Church, Pittsburgh, Pa. *Position*: Collaborator with the late George W. Sotter in stained glass and decorative work.

SOUDER, BERT(HA) KLANDRUD—*Painter*
1547 Coles Ave., Mountainside, N.J.

B. La Crosse, Wis., Mar. 20, 1914. *Studied*: with Frank LaVanco, Gerald Foster, Joachim Loeber, Maxwell Simpson. *Member*: Westfield AA (Pres.); AAPL; Am. Veterans Soc. A.; Hunterdon County A. Center. *Awards*: prizes, Rahway A. Center, 1954; Westfield AA, 1955; Am. Veterans Soc. A., 1957; St. John's Exh., Elizabeth, N.J., 1958; AAPL, 1958; Patrons award, South Orange A. Gal., 1958. *Exhibited*: NAD, 1956; Silvermine Gld. A., 1957; Art:USA, 1958; Springfield Mus. A., 1957, 1958; Montclair A. Mus., 1955, 1957, 1958; Newark Mus., 1955, 1958; Hunterdon County A. Center, 1954-1958; A. Center of the Oranges, 1956-1958; Am. Veterans Soc. A., 1956, 1957.

SOUTHWORTH, HELEN McCORKLE (Mrs.)—*Painter*
617 West Mt. Airy Ave., Philadelphia 19, Pa.

B. Detroit, Mich. *Studied*: with Justin Pardi, Guy Wiggins. *Member*: AAPL; Woodmere A. Gal.; AEA; NAWA; Bryn Mawr A. Center; Phila. A. All.; Phila. Plastic Cl. *Awards*: medals, Phila. Plastic Cl., 1949, 1951, 1955, 1957, prize, 1953; prize, Fla. Southern Col., 1952. *Work*: Allentown (Pa.) Mus. A.; Woodmere A. Gal. *Exhibited*: Phila. Plastic Cl., 1944-1946, 1949, 1951, 1958; Woodmere A. Gal., 1942-1946, 1948-1952, 1958; Phila. A. All., 1944; Phila. Sketch Cl., 1940, 1944, 1945; DaVinci All., 1940, 1943, 1944, 1949-1952, 1958; Ogunquit A. Center, 1946, 1949, 1950, 1952; Bryn Mawr A. Center, 1946 (one-man); Fla. Southern Col., 1952; Women's City Cl., Phila., 1947 (one-man); Temple Univ., 1949; Vernon House, Phila., 1954 (one-man); PMA; AAPL.

SOWERS, MIRIAM (R.) (Mrs.)—*Painter*
3020 Glenwood Drive, Northwest, Albuquerque, N.M.

B. Bluffton, Ohio, Oct. 4, 1922. *Studied*: Univ. Miami; AIC. *Member*: New Mexico A. Lg. *Awards*: prizes, Toledo Mus. A., 1952; New Mexico A. Lg., 1954. *Work*: Nat. Mus., Israel; Findlay (Ohio) Col.; Lovelace Clinic, Albuquerque; many colls. and ports. of prominent persons. *Exhibited*: Akron AI, 1951; Massillon Mus. A., 1951; Ohio State Fair, 1951, 1952; Toledo Mus. A., 1951, 1952; Canton AI, 1952; Dayton AI, 1952; Butler Inst. Am. A., 1952; Montpelier Tri-State, Ohio, 1952; Mus. New Mexico, 1954-1958; New Mexico State Fair, 1954-1958; Albuquerque Mod. Mus., 1954; Albuquerque Workshop, 1954, 1955; Botts Mem., 1954, 1955; Sheldon Swope Gal., 1957; Roswell, N.M., 1957; El Paso Sun Carnival, 1957; Tucson Fiesta, 1958; Summerhouse Theatre, 1958; one-man: Old Albuquerque Mus., 1954; Casa de los Huertas, 1954; Galeria de Arte, 1955; Sowers Studio, 1955-1958; Griegos Lib., 1956; Mus. New Mexico, 1957-58; Unitarian Church, 1958. Contributor fashion illus. to Albuquerque Journal & Tribune.

SOWINSKI, JAN—*Sculptor, P.*
30-31 37th St., Long Island City 3, N.Y.

B. Opatow, Poland, Oct. 2, 1885. *Studied*: BAID; & in Poland. *Member*: Modelers & Sculptors of Am. & Canada. *Awards*: prizes, BAID. *Work*: theatre & church interiors; murals, St. Stephen's Church, Paterson, N.J.; Trinity Church, Utica, N.Y.; & others; many medallions, medals, and trophies.*

SOYER, ISAAC—*Painter, Lith.*
2 Columbus Circle; h. 122 East 61st St., New York 21, N.Y.

B. Russia, 1907. *Studied*: CUASch.; Edu. All. A. Sch., N.Y., and in Paris, France, Madrid, Spain. *Awards*: prizes, Albright A. Gal., 1944; Audubon A., 1945. *Work*: WMAA; DMFA; Albright A. Gal.; State T. Col., Buffalo, N.Y.; Tel-Aviv Mus., Israel. *Exhibited*: WMAA; CGA; AIC; Milwaukee AI; CM; VMFA; Audubon A.; Akron AI; Cal. PLH; Soc. Four A.; WAC; MMoDA; PAFA, and others; one-man: Midtown Gal., N.Y.; Phila. A. All.; William Rockhill Nelson Gal. A.

SOYER, MOSES—Painter, T.
50 West 9th St.; h. 356 West 21st St., New York 11, N.Y.

B. Russia, Dec. 25, 1899. *Studied*: CUASch; NAD; BAID; & abroad. *Member*: An Am. Group. *Work*: MMA; Newark Mus.; Swope A. Gal.; PMG; Toledo Mus. A.; WMAA; Nat. Inst. A. & Let.; mural, USPO, Phila., Pa. *Exhibited*: nationally.*

SOYER, RAPHAEL—Painter, Gr., E.
1947 Broadway; h. 410 Central Park, West, New York 25, N.Y.

B. Russia, Dec. 25, 1899. *Studied*: CUASch; NAD; ASL; with Guy Pene du Bois. *Member*: Am. Soc. P. S. & Gr.; Nat. Inst. A. & Lets. *Awards*: Temple gold medal, 1943; bronze medal, CGA, 1943; gold medal, NAD, 1957; gold medal, Nat. Inst. A. & Lets., 1957; prize, AIC, 1940. *Work*: WMAA; PMG; MMA; BMA; N.Y. Pub. Lib.; AGAA; Columbus Gal. FA; CGA; Buffalo AA; BM, etc.; mural, Kingsessing Postal Station, Phila., Pa. *Positions*: Instr., ASL; Am. A. Sch.; at present, New School for Social Research, N.Y.

SOZIO, ARMANDO—Painter, T., Eng.
R.D. #2, Blairstown, N.J.; h. 664 Varsity Rd., South Orange, N.J.

B. Salerno, Italy, Oct. 16, 1897. *Studied*: Faucett Sch. F. & Indst. A.; NAD; N.Y. Univ. *Member*: Eastern AA; Elizabeth T. Assn.; N.J. High School T. Assn.; AAPL; All. A. Am.; New Jersey WC Soc.; A. Centre of the Oranges; South Orange A. Gal.; Maplewood A. Gal. *Awards*: prizes, silver med., 1918-1921, bronze medal, 1917, 1922, NAD; gold med., All. A. Am., 1955, prize, 1957; prize, A. Center of the Oranges, 1955, 1956; Washington, N.J., 1949; New Jersey Soc. P. & S., 1958; prize and silver med., Seton Hall Univ., 1956, 1958; AAPL, 1957; New Jersey WC Soc., 1958. *Exhibited*: All. A. Am., 1946, 1953, 1955; NAC, 1954, 1955; AWS, 1955; Montclair A. Mus., 1949, 1950, 1952, 1955; Tinton Falls, N.J.; AAPL, 1955; A. Center of the Oranges, 1955; Newark, N.J., 1937; Washington, N.J., 1949. *Position*: A. T., Jefferson H.S., Elizabeth, N.J., 1931-1956; Instr., Newark Sch. F. & Indst. A., Newark, N.J., at present.

SPAGNA, VINCENT—Painter
47 East 9th St., New York 3, N.Y.

B. Sicily, Italy, Oct. 24, 1898. *Studied*: Conn. Lg. A. Students, Hartford, Conn. *Awards*: prizes, Pepsi-Cola, 1944; La Tausca Pearls Comp. *Work*: AGAA; Pepsi-Cola Coll.; IBM Coll. *Exhibited*: CGA; PAFA; MMA; Carnegie Inst.

SPAMPINATO, CLEMENTE—Sculptor
270 6th Ave., New York 14, N.Y.

B. Italy, Jan. 10, 1912. *Studied*: Royal Sch. of the Medal, Royal FA Acad., Rome. *Member*: NSS. *Awards*: prizes, AAPL, 1951; Nat. prize, Rome, 1940, 1941; U.S. Naval Acad. Comp. for monument, 1956. *Work*: statues, monuments, Navy Stadium, Italicum Forum, Rome; figures, Walsh Coll., New York City; sc., New York City Bd. Edu. *Exhibited*: Nat. Exh., sport sculpture, Rome, 1940, 1948; AAPL, 1947, 1951; All. A. Am., 1948; NSS, 1952; Grand Central Palace, N.Y., 1952; Int. Triennial, Naples, Italy, 1952; NSS, 1958.

SPARKS, JOSEPH—Painter, Lith., L.
8724 Smart St., Detroit 10, Mich.

B. Jersey City, N.J., Dec. 23, 1896. *Studied*: with Percy Ives, Paul Honore, Leon Kroll, & others. *Member*: Scarab Cl., Detroit; Michigan Acad. Sc. A. & Let. *Work*: St. Michael's Church, Detroit; Detroit Inst. A.; Detroit Hist. Lib.; Lib. Cong.; murals, Winterhalter Sch., Detroit; Ft. Wayne, Mich.; Maple Sch. Lib., Dearborn, Mich. Author, Ed., Illus., Portfolios of prints & designs. *Exhibited*: Detroit Inst. A., annually; Lib. Cong., 1945; Ferargil Gal.; J. L. Hudson Co.; Univ. Michigan; CAA traveling exh., 1932; Mexico City, 1932; Rochester Mem. A. Gal., 1935; Detroit A. Market, 1937. I., "Letters to a Pagan"; "The Pine Tree of Michigan."

SPARLING, JOHN EDMOND JACK)—
Illustrator, Cart., P., S.
98 South Bergen Pl., Freeport, N.Y.

B. Winnipeg, Canada, June 21, 1916. *Studied*: A. & Crafts Cl., New Orleans, La.; Corcoran Sch. A. *Member*: SI; Cartoonists Soc., N.Y. *Awards*: Treasury Dept. Citations, 1944, 1945. *Work*: Hyde Park Coll. Created, wrote & produced "Hap Hopper, Washington Correspondent," United Features Syndicate, 1939-43; "Claire Voyant," Chicago Sun & PM newspaper Syndicate, 1943-46. *Position*: Editorial Cart, New Orleans Item-Tribune, 1935-37; Washington Herald, 1937-39.*

SPAULDING, WARREN (DAN)—Painter, E.
6806 Pershing Ave., University City 5, Mo.

B. Boston, Mass., Oct. 7, 1916. *Studied*: Mass. Sch. A.; Yale Univ. Sch. FA, B.F.A., M.F.A. *Member*: St. Louis A. Gld. *Awards*: Alice Kimball English F. for foreign travel, Yale Univ., 1949; prizes, U.S. Section FA comp., 1940; St. Louis A. Gld., 1951, 1954, purchase, 1958; Joslyn A. Mus., purchase, 1958. *Work*: Marine Hospital, Carville, La.; St. Louis A. Gld.; Joslyn A. Mus., and in private colls. *Exhibitions*: 1953-58: CAM; PAFA; Springfield A. Mus.; A. of the Missouri Valley, Topeka; Am. Graphic A. & Drawing annual, Wichita; Kansas State Col.; Joslyn A. Mus. *Position*: Asst. Prof. in Composition, Sch. FA, Washington Univ., St. Louis, Mo.

SPEAR, ARTHUR P.—Painter
59 Wyman St., Waban 68, Mass.

B. Washington, D.C., Sept. 23, 1879. *Studied*: George Washington Univ.; ASL; Julian Acad., Paris. *Member*: ANA; Gld. Boston A.; St. Botolph's Cl. *Awards*: med., Pan-Am. Exp., 1915; prize, NAD, 1922.

SPEAR, LLOYD—Educator
Bethany College, Lindsborg, Kans.
Position: Dean, College of Fine Arts.*

SPEARS, ETHEL—Painter, Lith., Ser., I., T.
221 East Superior St.; h. 9700 South Winchester Ave., Chicago 43, Ill.

B. Chicago, Ill., Oct. 5, 1903. *Studied*: AIC; & with Alexander Archipenko. *Member*: NSMP; Chicago SA. *Awards*: prizes, AIC; Rogers Park Woman's Cl., Chicago. *Exhibited*: AIC, 1946, 1951, & prior; Chicago SA; San Diego FA Soc., 1944; La Jolla A. Center, 1944; New Trier H.S., Winnetka, Ill., 1945; Chicago Col. Cl., 1946; 750 Gal., 1952; Palmer House, Chicago, 1952; Oak Park Woman's Cl., 1945; Chicago Woman's Cl., 1945; etc. Demonstrations of silk screen printing. *Position*: Instr., Drawing, Design, Silk Screen Printing, Enameling, AIC, Chicago, Ill., 1944-52.*

SPEED, ROSALIE—Painter, Des., Comm. A.
4434 Vandelia St., Dallas 19, Tex.

B. Dallas, Tex., Nov. 27, 1908. *Studied*: Aunspaugh A. Sch., Dallas, Tex.; Southern Methodist Univ.; Texas State Col. for Women, Denton, Tex. *Awards*: prizes, Dallas Mus. FA, 1935, 1940, 1943. *Work*: Dallas Mus. FA. *Exhibited*: Texas Centennial, 1936; SSAL, 1936; Art of the Americas, 1937; San F., Cal., 1938; Kansas City AI, 1938; Texas FA Assn., 1943-1946; Dallas All. A., 1935, 1940, 1943, 1946, 1949, 1950.

SPEICHER EUGENE—Painter
165 East 60th St., New York 22, N.Y.

B. Buffalo, N.Y., Apr. 5, 1883. *Studied*: Albright A. Gal. Sch.; ASL; abroad; & with Chase, DuMond, Henri. *Member*: NA; NAC; Boston AC; Nat. Inst. A. & Let. *Awards*: prizes, NAD, 1911, 1914, 1915; SC, 1913; Pan-Pacific Exp., 1915; CGA, 1928, 1935; VMFA, 1938; med., PAFA, 1920, 1921, 1938; Carnegie Inst., 1922; AIC, 1926. *Work*: MMA; Albright A. Gal., CMA; CGA; Detroit Inst. A.; MModA; WMAA; PMG; FMA; Carnegie Inst.; Toledo Mus. A.; Munson-Williams-Proctor Inst.; Newark Mus. A.; Delgado Mus. A., and in private colls.

SPEIGHT, FRANCIS—*Painter, T.*

Almshouse Road, Doylestown, Pa.

B. Windsor, N.C., Sept. 11, 1896. *Studied*: Corcoran Sch. A.; PAFA. *Member*: NA; Century Assn. *Awards*: Nat. Inst. A. & Let. grant, 1953; prizes, NAD, 1953, 1955, 1958. *Work*: MMA; BMFA; Toronto Gal. A.; PAFA; Rochester Mem. A. Gal.; Norton Gal. A.; Butler AI, and others. *Position*: Instr., PAFA, Philadelphia, Pa., 1925- .

SPELLMAN, COREEN MARY—
Lithographer, P., Des., I., T., L.

203 Third St., Denton, Tex.

B. Forney, Tex., Mar. 17, 1909. *Studied*: Texas State Col. for Women, B.S.; Columbia Univ., M.A.; ASL; Univ. Iowa, M.F.A.; & with Charles Martin. *Member*: Pr.M. Gld. *Awards*: prizes, West Texas A. Exh., 1940, 1942, 1945, 1946; Univ. Iowa, 1942; Texas Pr. Exh., 1942, 1943, 1945; Texas FA Assn., 1943, 1945; Texas General Exh., 1943; SSAL, 1944; DMFA, 1951. *Exhibited*: 50 Prints of the Year, 1932; Am. A. Cong., 1936; Nat. Exh. Am. A., N.Y., 1937; WFNY 1939; Phila. A. All., 1939; WMAA, 1941; SAE, 1943; AFA traveling exh., 1944-1945; Assoc. Am. A., 1946; Denver A. Mus., 1944-1946; Texas Pr. Exh., 1941-1945; Kansas City AI, 1936, 1937, 1942; Pr.M. Gld., 1940-1955; Texas General Exh., 1940-1950; Texas FA Assn., 1932, 1933, 1940, 1943-1950; DMFA, 1953; Texas Centennial, 1936; Texas State Fair, 1938, 1939; West Texas A. Exh., 1940-1946. I., "Dona Perfecta," 1940; "El Mundo Espanol," 1942; "A Wedding in the Chapel"; & others. Des. brick mural, Texas State Col. for Women, 1955; pictorial map of campus, 1947. Represented in "Prize Prints of 20th Century"; "12 From Texas," 1951. *Position*: Assoc. Prof. A., Texas State T. Col., Denton, Tex., at present.*

SPENCER, ANN HUNT (Mrs. Ann Spencer Pratt)—
Painter, T.

8 Grove St., New York 14, N.Y.

Studied: NAD; Sarah Lawrence Col., & with Jerry Farnsworth. *Awards*: prize, NAC, 1937; traveling scholarship, Kosciuszko Fnd., 1937; U.S. Govt. mural, Southington, Conn. *Work*: ports. (12) lobby, No. 2 Fifth Ave., N.Y.; work also in private colls. *Exhibited*: CGA, 1941; NAD, 1939, 1940; Berkshire Mus.

SPENCER, BERTHA AUGUSTA—
Craftsman, Et., E., W., L.

Kansas State Teachers College, Pittsburgh, Kan.; h. R.R. 4, Edbert Pl., Carthage, Mo.

B. Paxton, Ill. *Studied*: Stout Inst., Menomonie, Wis.; Handicraft Gld., Minneapolis, Minn.; Kansas State T. Col., B.S.; Columbia Univ., A.M.; & in Europe. *Member*: Nat. Edu. Assn.; Nat. A. Edu. Assn.; Western AA; Kansas Fed. A.; Kansas State A. T. Assn. (hon. life memb.); Ozark A. Gld. *Awards*: Nat. Block Print prize, Minneapolis, Minn. *Exhibited*: ceramics & metalcraft in many cities. *Position*: Assoc. Prof. A., 1921-42, Acting Hd. A. Dept., 1943-46, Hd., 1946- , Dir., A. Div., 1947-52 (Retired), Kansas State T. Col., Pittsburg, Kan.; Nat. Sec.-Treas., Kappa Pi, 1946- .

SPENCER, EDNA ISBESTER—*Sculptor, P., T., Comm. A.*

3450 Northwest 79th St., Miami 47, Fla.

B. St. John, N.B., Canada, Nov. 12, 1883. *Studied*: BMFA Sch.; ASL; & with Bela Pratt, Robert Aitken. *Member*: Miami A. Lg. *Awards*: prizes, Concord AA; Miami A. Lg., 1940. *Work*: numerous portrait busts. *Exhibited*: Paris Salon, 1926; PAFA; Miami A. Lg.; Medallic Art Co., 1952.

SPENCER, ELEANOR PATTERSON—*Educator*

Goucher College, Baltimore 4, Md.

B. Northampton, Mass., Jan. 29, 1895. *Studied*: Smith Col., B.A., M.A.; Radcliffe Col., Ph.D.; Ecole du Louvre, Sorbonne, Paris, France. *Member*: AFA; CAA; Am. Assn. Univ. Prof.; Am. Soc. Arch. Historians. *Awards*: Sachs F., Harvard Univ., 1928-1929, 1929-1930. Contributor to: Magazine of Art; Gazette des Beaux-Arts. *Position*: Chm. Dept. A., Goucher College, Baltimore, Md., 1930- .

SPENCER, HENRY CECIL—*Educator, P., I., W.*

10824 South Washtenaw Ave., Chicago 43, Ill.

B. Magnum, Okla., Mar. 3, 1903. *Studied*: Baylor Univ., A.B.; Texas Agricultural & Mechanical Col., B.S. in Arch., M.S. *Member*: Soc. for the Promotion of Engineering Edu.; Am. Inst. Draftsmen. *Work*: Baylor Univ., Waco, Tex. Author: "Technical Drawing," 1940; "The Blueprint Language," 1946; & others. Contributor to: Journal of Engineering Drawing. *Position*: Instr. to Prof., Hd. Dept. of Engineering Drawing, Texas A. & M. Col., College Station, Tex., 1930-40; Chm., Prof. Technical Drawing, Technical Illus., Illinois Inst. Technology, Chicago, Ill., 1941- .*

SPENCER, HOWARD BONNELL—*Painter, T.*

R.D. #5, West Chester, Pa.

B. Plainfeld, N.J. *Studied*: with Frank DuMond, George Elmer Browne, Albert Lucas, Walt Kuhn. *Awards*: prizes, All. A. Am., 1949, 1951; AAPL, 1951-1953. *Work*: Wesleyan Col., Macon, Ga.; Oregon State AAPL Chptr.; City Hall, N.Y., and in private colls. *Exhibited*: NAD; All. A. Am.; Ogunquit A. Center; Provincetown AA; Town Hall, N.Y.; NAC; Buck Hills Falls, Pa., and others. *Position*: Pres., All. A. Am., 1946-48; Dir., SC, 1948-51; Dir., AAPL; Hudson Valley AA; Vice-Pres., Nat. Soc. Painters in Casein, Nat. Pastel Soc., FA Fed., N.Y.

SPENCER, HUGH—*Illustrator, L.*

Pratt St., Chester, Conn.

B. St. Cloud, Minn., July 19, 1887. *Studied*: Chicago Sch. App. & Normal A.; ASL; N.Y. Evening Sch. Indst. A.; & with Charles Chapman, Arthur Covey. *Member*: Soc. Conn. Craftsmen; Meriden A. & Crafts; Meriden Nature Cl.; Conn. Botanical Soc. I., Nature & Science Readers & Textbooks (drawings & photographs). Illustrated Nature Lectures. Contributor to Natural History and Nature magazines.

SPENCER, JEAN—*Painter*

890 Park Ave., New York, N.Y.; h. 101 Sutton Manor, New Rochelle, N.Y.

B. Oak Park, Ill. *Studied*: Wellesley Col.; AIC; Grand Central Sch. A., and with Wayman Adams. *Member*: NAWA; Audubon A.; Portraits, Inc.; Grand Central A. Gal.; Martha's Vineyard AA; All. A. Am.; Audubon A. *Awards*: medal, Grand Central Sch. A.; prizes, Pen & Brush Cl.; NAWA. *Work*: portraits, pub. bldgs., Charlottesville, Va.; Sioux Falls ,S.D.; Trenton, N.J.; Court House, High Point, N.C.; N.Y. Pub. Lib.; Osteopathic Clinic, N.Y.; House Office Bldg., Wash., D.C.; Fla. Southern Col. Work in private colls. *Exhibited*: NAD; All. A. Am.; NAWA; All-Illinois Soc. Painters; NAC; Studio Gld.; Pen & Brush Cl.; Audubon A.; one-man: B. T. Batsford, Ltd., N.Y.; Marshall Field & Co., Chicago; Wilton, Conn.; Creative A. Gal., Charlottesville, Va.; Martha's Vineyard AA; IFA Gal., Wash., D.C. Author: "Fine and Industrial Arts."

SPENCER, LEONTINE G.—*Painter, T.*

100 Lefferts Ave., Brooklyn 25, N.Y.

B. New York, N.Y. *Studied*: Hunter Col.; ASL; T. Col., Columbia Univ.; Grand Central Sch. A.; & with Frank DuMond, George Pearse Ennis, Arthur Woelfle. *Member*: ASL; AWCS; Catherine L. Wolfe A. Cl.; AAPL. *Exhibited*: NAD, 1934; All. A. Am., 1933, 1934, 1936, 1937, 1940-1942; AWCS, 1932, 1934; Rockefeller Center, N.Y., 1934; BM, 1939, 1940, 1943; Brooklyn P. & S., 1934, 1936; NAC, 1954, 1955, 1956, 1957; 8th St. Gal., 1954; Butler Gal., 1954-1957; Wolfe A. Cl., 1956-1958; AAPL, 1956, 1957; Crespi Gal., 1956.

SPENCER, MARGARET FULTON (Mrs. Robert)—
Painter

Las Lomas, Route 9, Box 984, Tucson, Ariz.

B. Philadelphia, Pa., Sept. 1882. *Studied*: Bryn Mawr Col.; MIT; N.Y. Sch. Des.; in Paris, France, and with Birge Harrison. *Member*: AIA. *Exhibited*: Paris Salons; Rome, Italy; AIC; PMA; Carnegie Inst.; BMA; Memphis Acad. A.; Santa Barbara Mus. A.; Tucson FA Assn., 1956-1958; Rosequist Gal., regularly, and others.

SPENCER, MARION DICKINSON (Mrs. Ivar D.)—
Painter, E.
1317 Knollwood Ave., Kalamazoo 73, Mich.

B. Grand Rapids, Mich., July 18, 1909. *Studied*: Western
Michigan Univ., B.A.; Colorado State Col., M.A. *Member*:
Michigan Acad. A., Sc. & Let.; Am. Assn. Univ. Women;
Michigan A. Edu. Assn.; Nat. Edu. Assn. *Awards*: prizes,
Kalamazoo Inst. A., 1937; Grand Rapids A. Gal., 1942.
Exhibited: Kalamazoo Inst. A.; Grand Rapids A. Gal.;
Barnsdall A. Center, Los A., 1948; Kalamazoo Clothesline
Exh., 1953. *Positions*: Instr., A., Kalamazoo Pub. Sch.,
1932-44; Dir., Kalamazoo Inst. A., 1944-47; Librarian,
Chouinard AI, Los A., 1947; Asst. to Dir., Mod. Inst. A.,
Beverly Hills, Cal., 1948; Instr. A. Edu., Western Michi-
gan Col., 1950; Consultant, Instr. A., Kalamazoo City
Schs., 1952- ; Instr., Vicksburg Elem. Sch., 1954-57; Chm.
A. Section, Kalamazoo Region, Mich. Secondary Schs.,
Col. Agreement Assn., 1954; Hd. East Campus Branch,
Audio-Visual Center, Western Mich. Univ., 1957- .

SPENCER, MARY JONES—Painter, Des., L.
634 East Garcia St., Santa Fé, N.M.

B. Terre Haute, Ind., Jan. 14, 1900. *Studied*: Indiana State
T. Col.; AIC; Chicago Acad. FA. *Member*: A. All. New
Mexico; Assn. Chicago P. & S.; Chicago Soc. A. *Awards*:
prize, Hoosier Salon, 1940. *Work*: Mason City (Iowa)
Pub. Lib.; Pub. Sch., Chicago, Ill. *Exhibited*: NAWA,
1937, 1938; Conn. Acad. FA, 1939; Hoosier Salon, 1934-
1940; AIC, 1936, 1939; South Carolina A., 1943, 1944;
A. Gal., Santa Fé; Springfield, Ill.; State Mus., Santa Fé.
Lectures: Color. *Position*: Artist, L., Navajo Ceremonial
A. Mus.; Display Designer, Palace of the Governor's Mus.,
Santa Fé.

SPICER-SIMSON, THEODORE—Sculptor
3803 Little Ave., Miami 33, Fla.

B. Havre, France, June 25, 1871. *Studied*: Academie
Julian, Ecole des Beaux-Arts, Paris. *Member*: ANA; F.,
NSS; F., Numismatic Mus. *Awards*: medals, Int. Exh.,
Belgium, 1913; Int. Exp., San Francisco, 1915; NSS, 1955;
N.Y. Numismatic Soc., 1956. *Work*: MMA; Victoria &
Albert Mus.; Nat. Portrait Gal., London; Numismatic
Mus., N.Y.; Pub. Lib., Paris, and many others in U.S.
and abroad. Designed medals of award for Nat. Acad. Sc.;
Guggenheim Aeronautical; Electrical Research, Princeton
Univ., and others. Numerous busts and statues in England,
France, India and U.S. Lectures: Portraits and Medals.
Ports. of prominent persons in private colls.

SPIDELL, ENID JEAN—Painter, E.
Pratt Institute, 215 Ryerson St., Brooklyn, N.Y.; h.
50 Jackson St., New Rochelle, N.Y.

B. Hampton, N.B., Canada, June 5, 1905. *Studied*: Par-
sons Sch. Des.; N.Y. Univ., B.S. in A. Edu.; T. Col.,
Columbia Univ., M.A.; & with George Pearse Ennis.
Member: AWS; Int. Soc. Color Council; AAPL; New
Rochelle AA. *Awards*: prize, AV-Am. A. Group design
competition, 1943. *Exhibited*: in member organizations;
one-man: New Rochelle Pub. Lib., 1956. *Position*: Assoc.
Prof. A., Hd. Dept.-Related Arts, Pratt Inst., Brooklyn,
N.Y., at present; Dir., New Rochelle AA, 1956- .

SPIEGEL, DORIS—Etcher, Eng., I., W.
163 West 23rd St., New York 11, N.Y.; h. 150 Rock-
wood Pl., Englewood, N.J.

B. New York, N.Y., June 8, 1907. *Studied*: in Paris; &
with Clinton Balmer. *Awards*: Guggenheim F., 1930. *Exhibited*: NAD, 1939; AIC, 1935; SAE, 1936; Lib. Cong.,
1945. Author, I., "Danny and Company 92," 1945; &
other books. Contributor: illus. to New Yorker magazine.*

SPIEGEL, DOROTHY A.—Painter
3029 Sutherland Ave., Indianapolis 5, Ind.

B. Shelbyville, Ind., Dec. 8, 1904. *Studied*: Indiana Univ.;
John Herron AI, B.A.E.; Butler Univ.; & with Eliot
O'Hara, Emil Bisttram & others. *Awards*: prizes, Hoosier
Salon, 1936; Indiana State Fair, 1941; prize, med., Goose
Rocks Beach, Me., 1938. *Exhibited*: Indiana Fed. A. Cl.,
traveling exh.

SPIERER, WILLIAM McK.—Designer, T., P., L.
100 Park Ave., New York, N.Y.; h. 367 Abbey Rd.,
Manhasset, N.Y.

B. New York, N.Y., Jan. 2, 1913. *Studied*: ASL; NAD;
Syracuse Univ., B.F.A., and with DuMond, Boss, Bridg-
man. *Member*: AWS; A. Dir. Cl.; Nat. Soc. A. Dir.
Awards: several for advertising designs. *Exhibited*: AWS;
NAD; PAFA. Lectures on Advertising Art. *Position*: A.
Dir., Sales Prom. Mngr., Ethyl Corp., New York, N.Y.

SPIRO, EUGENE—Painter, Et., Lith., T., I.
15 West 67th St., New York 23, N.Y.

B. Breslau, Germany, Apr. 18, 1874. *Studied*: A. Acad.,
Breslau, Munich, Germany; & with Frans von Stuck. *Mem-
ber*: SC. *Awards*: Officer d'Academie des Beaux-Arts
Francaise, Paris; Herman Wick Mem. award, SC, 1958.
Work: Archdiocese, Detroit, Mich.; Mus. City of N.Y.;
German Embassy, Wash., D.C.; Carnegie Inst.; Musee du
Jeu de Paume, Paris; & in numerous museums in Ger-
many. *Exhibited*: MMoA, 1942; one-man exh.: St.
Etienne Gal., N.Y., 1943, 1945, 1947, 1949, 1950, 1952,
1954. I., "In Konzert," 1922 (lithographs of famous musi-
cians); "Antique Frescoes," 1922.

SPIVAK, MAX—Painter, C., Des.
175 Madison Ave., New York 16, N.Y.

B. Bregnun, Poland, May 20, 1906. *Studied*: Col. City of
N.Y.; ASL; Grande Chaumiere, Paris. *Member*: Am. Ab-
stract A.; NSMP. *Award*: Silver med., Arch. Lg., 1956.
Work: BMA; Newark Mus.; mosaic murals, SS "Consti-
tution"; SS "Independence"; Statler Hotel, Los A.;
Calderone Theatre, Hempstead; Gen. Wingate H.S., Brook-
lyn; Cerebral Palsy Sch., N.Y.; Warner-Lambert, Morris
Plains, N.J.; Johnson & Johnson, New Brunswick, N.J.;
Jr. H.S. 189, Queens, N.Y.; Textile Center, New York,
N.Y. *Exhibited*: WFNY 1939; GGE, 1939; MMoA, 1936,
1950; Mortimer Levitt Gal., 1948-1950 (one-man); WMAA,
1948, 1949.

SPOHN, CLAY (EDGAR)—Painter, T.
Taos, N.M.

B. San Francisco, Cal., Nov. 24, 1898. *Studied*: Mark
Hopkins Inst. A., San Francisco; Berkeley Sch. A. &
Crafts; Univ. California; ASL; Acad. Moderne, Paris,
France. *Member*: San F. AA; Taos AA. *Awards*: prizes,
San F. AA, 1939, 1945; Albert Bender Grant, San F.,
Cal., 1944-1945. *Exhibited*: Palace Legion Honor, 1945,
1946; San F. AA, 1929, 1939; Am. Abstract A., 1949;
Colorado Springs FA Center, 1951; Denver A. Mus., 1952;
Taos AA; Blue Door and Ruins Gal., Taos; Inter-
mountain region traveling exh.; Los Alamos Gal.; Univ.
Illinois, 1953. SFMA, 1942 (one-man), 1946; one-man:
Rotunda Gal., San F., 1946; Taos, N.M., 1952. *Position*:
Instr., Drawing & Painting, Cal. Sch. FA, San Francisco,
Cal., 1945-50; Visiting L., Dept. A., Mount Holyoke Col-
lege, South Hadley, Mass., 1957-58.

SPONGBERG, GRACE—Painter, C., Gr.
1367 North Clark St., Chicago 10, Ill.

B. Chicago, Ill., Apr. 25, 1906. *Studied*: AIC. *Member*:
Chicago Soc. A.; Am. Color Pr. Soc. *Work*: Bennett Sch.,
Byford Sch., Horace Mann Sch., all in Chicago; Mus.
Vaxco, Sweden. *Exhibited*: CM; PAFA; AIC; Joslyn A.
Mus.; Chicago Soc. A.; Riverside Mus.; Evanston A. Cen-
ter; Laguna Beach AA; Oakland A. Gal.; Miami Beach
A. Center; Springfield Mus. FA; Grand Rapids, Mich.;
LC; Am. Color Pr. Soc.; Hull House, Chicago; SAM.

SPRAGUE, ROBERT BURKITT—
Painter, Des., T., Comm. A., W., L., Cr.
Sprague Art School, 1101 9th St., North (1); h. 2827
13th St., North, St. Petersburg 4, Fla.

B. Dayton, Ohio, June 12, 1904. *Studied*: Antioch Col.,
B.A.; Dayton AI; Roerich Mus., N.Y.; Taos Sch. A., and
with Guy Wiggins, Emil Bisttram, Carl Holty. *Member*:
Fla. A. Group; Fla. Fed. A.; St. Petersburg A. Lg.
Awards: prizes, Dayton, Ohio, 1934; Fla. State Fair, 1952,
1953; Fla. Gulf Coast Group; citation of merit, Fla.
Southern Col., 1952; Clearwater, Fla., 1953. *Work*:
Coshocton, Ohio, Pub. Lib.; Dept. Justice Bldg., Wash.,
D.C.; Clearwater A. Group; murals, Jackson Sch., Dayton;
Courthouse, Roswell, N.M.; Trailside Mus., Cincinnati;
and in private colls. *Exhibited*: CM; PAFA; Riverside

Mus.; AIC; Conn. Acad. FA; Denver A. Mus.; Nelson Gal. A.; Oklahoma City A. Center; Mus. New Mexico, Santa Fé; Ferargil Gal.; Hoosier Salon; Southeastern Annual, 1956; Delgado Mus. A., 1958; CAA; Soc. Four Arts, 1956; Ringling Mus. A.; High Mus.; Atlanta; Grand Central A. Gal.; Fla. Fed. A. traveling exhs.; Fla. A. Group. and others. One-man: Denver A. Mus.; Nelson Gal. A.; Dayton AI; Richmond AI; Tampa AI; Stetson Univ.; Oklahoma A. Center; Winter Haven, Fla. Contributor to St. Petersburg Times. *Position*: Dir., Roswell (N.M.) Mus. A., 1935-36; Dir., Sprague A. Sch., St. Petersburg, Fla., at present.

SPRINCHORN, CARL—*Painter*

c/o Babcock Gallery, 805 Madison Ave.; h. Pioneer Acres, Beaver Dam Road, Selkirk, N.Y.

B. Broby, Sweden, May 13, 1887. *Studied*: N.Y. Sch. A.; and with Robert Henri. *Member*: AEA. *Work*: PC; FMA; MMA; High Mus. A.; Springfield (Mass.) Mus. A.; Univ. Maine; PMA; City of N.Y.; BM; New Britain Mus.; Providence Mus. A.; Am-Swedish Hist. Soc., Phila., Pa., and others. *Exhibited*: nationally. One-man: WMA; Chicago A. Cl.; and the following galleries: George Hellman, Knoedler, Marie Sterner, Frank Rehn, Ainslie's, Macbeth, and others.

SPRINGER, EVA—*Painter, Gr.*

1002 Pecos Trail, Santa Fé, N.M.

B. Cimarron, N.M. *Studied*: Highlands Univ., Las Vegas, N.M., B.A.; Columbia Univ.; Julian Acad., Grande Chaumiere, Paris; ASL. *Member*: Brooklyn Soc. Min. P.; Pa. Soc. Min. P.; ASL; Wash. Soc. Min P. *Awards*: med., prize, Julian Acad., Paris. *Work*: Mus. New Mexico, Santa Fé; Pa. Soc. Min. P.; PMA. *Exhibited*: Grand Central A. Gal.; NCFA; Wash. WC Cl.; Pa. Soc. Min. P.; PAFA; NAC; BM; ASMP; Wash. Soc. Min. P. S. & Gr.; Mus. New Mexico, Santa Fé, 1953, 1955 (one-man); Albuquerque, N.M.; NAD; CGA; N.M. Artists, Mus. N.M., 1953-1955; State Fair, Albuquerque, 1955, 1956, 1958, and in Paris, London, Rome, Florence.

SPRINGWEILER, ERWIN FREDERICK—*Sculptor, C.*

21 Springs Drive, Wyandanch, L.I., N.Y.

B. Pforzheim, Germany, Jan. 10, 1896. *Studied*: Aircraft Sch., Pforzheim; Acad. FA, Munich; asst. to Paul Manship, Herbert Hazeltine. *Member*: NSS; ANA; Intl. Inst. A. & Let.; Conn. Acad. FA; McDowell Colony. *Awards*: prizes, NSS, 1937; NAD, 1938, 1949; Arch. Lg.; 1949; Medal of Honor, NAC, 1956. *Work*: Congressional gold medals of George M. Cohan and General W. L. Mitchell; statues, Washington Zoo and Detroit, Mich.; Brookgreen Gardens; reliefs, Washington Zoo, USPO, Chester, Pa., Manchester, Ga. *Exhibited*: NAD; PAFA; AIC; and other major exhibitions.

SPRUANCE, BENTON MURDOCH—*Lithographer, P., E.*

45 West Walnut Lane, Philadelphia 44, Pa.

B. Philadelphia, Pa., June 25, 1904. *Studied*: Univ. Pennsylvania Sch. FA; PAFA. *Member*: NAD; SAGA; Phila. Pr. Cl.; Phila. A. All. *Awards*: Cresson traveling scholarship; Guggenheim F., 1950. *Work*: Carnegie Inst.; NGA; PMA; PAFA; N.Y.Pub.Lib.; LC, and in major museums in the U.S.; mural, Municipal Court Bldg., Phila., Pa. *Exhibited*: all national print shows; Carnegie Inst., 1950; PAFA, and others. *Position*: Prof. FA, Beaver Col., Jenkintown, Pa.; Dir., Graphic Art, PMSch.A., Philadelphia, Pa.; Memb. Phila. A. Comm.; Pennell Purchase Fund Comm., LC, Wash., D.C.

SPRUCE, EVERETT FRANKLIN—*Painter, E.*

Department of Art, University of Texas; h. 15 Peak Rd., Austin, Tex.

B. Faulkner County, Ark., Dec. 25, 1908. *Studied*: Dallas AI, & with Olin H. Travis. *Awards*: prizes, Dallas Mus. FA, 1955; D.D. Feldman Comp., Dallas, 1955; Texas FA Assn., 1942; SFMA, 1940; Texas General Exh., 1945; WMA, 1945; Pepsi-Cola, 1946; La Tausca Exh., 1947; Am. Exh., Brussels, 1950. *Work*: U.S. State Dept.; Mus. FA of Houston; Dallas Mus. FA; PMG; Witte Mem. Mus.; MModA; North Texas State T. Col.; Nelson Gal. A.; PAFA; Newark Mus.; MMA; Cal. PLH; Illinois Wesleyan Univ.; Univ. Nebraska; Des Moines A. Center; Colorado Springs FA Center; Mus. FA, Rio de Janeiro; N.Y.Pub. Lib.; Delgado Mus. A. *Exhibited*: CGA, 1939, 1941, 1943,

1945, 1951; MModA, 1942; CM, 1944; Carnegie Inst., 1948, 1949, 1951; Dallas Mus. FA, 1932-1935, 1938-1940; Texas General, 1939-1945; Pepsi-Cola, 1946; Univ. Illinois, 1948, 1950, 1951, 1952; La Tausca Pearls, 1947; Brussels, Belgium, 1950; Bordighera, Italy, 1955; one-man: Hudson Walker Gal., 1939; Levitt Gal., 1945, 1947, 1949, 1953; Dallas Mus. FA, 1933; Witte Mem. Mus., 1943. *Position*: Instr., A., 1940-45, Asst. Prof., 1945-52, Prof., 1952- , Univ. Texas, Austin, Tex.*

SPURGEON, SARAH (EDNA M.)—*Educator, P.*

802 "C" St.; h. 204 East 9th St., Ellensburg, Wash.

B. Harlan, Iowa, Oct. 30, 1903. *Studied*: State Univ. Iowa, M.A.; Harvard Univ.; Grand Central Sch. A.; & with Grant Wood, Paul Sachs, & others. *Member*: Nat. Edu. Assn.; Am. Assn. Univ. Prof.; Wash. Edu. Assn.; Women Painters of Wash. *Awards*: Carnegie F., 1929-1930; prizes, State Univ. Iowa, 1931; Iowa A. Salon, 1930, 1931. *Work*: Iowa Mem. Un., Iowa City; mural, Univ. Experimental Sch., Iowa City, Iowa; SAM; Ginkgo Mus., Vantage, Wash.; Henry Gal., Univ. Washington. *Exhibited*: Kansas City AI; Joslyn Mem.; Cal SE; Des Moines A. Salon; SAM; Gumps, San F., Cal. One-man: Campus Music & Gal., Seattle, 1956-1958. Contributor to: Design, Childhood Education magazines. *Position*: Assoc. Prof., Central Washington Col., Ellensburg, Wash., 1939-42, 1944- .

SQUAREY, GERRY—*Painter, T., L.*

39 Hopkins St.; h. 64 Garden St., Hartford 5, Conn.; s. Waquoit, Cape Cod, Mass.

B. Sydney, Canada, Sept. 15, 1905. *Studied*: Mass. Sch. A., B.S. in Edu.; Hyannis T. Col., M.E.; Boston Univ.; Connecticut Univ.; Hillyer Col. *Member*: NAWA; Hartford Soc. Women P.; Conn. WC Soc.; Cape Cod AA; Provincetown AA; Conn. AA; Eastern AA; Conn. Edu. Assn. *Awards*: prizes, Hartford Soc. Women P., 1950, 1953, 1954; Conn. WC Soc., 1953, purchase, 1958; NAWA, 1953; Cape Cod AA, 1955. *Exhibited*: NAD; Argent Gal.; Wadsworth Atheneum; Springfield Mus. FA; Yale Univ.; Lyman Allyn Mus. A.; Farnsworth Mus.; Slater Mus. A.; New Britain Mus. A.; Portland Mus. A.; Silvermine Gld. A.; Cape Cod AA; Provincetown AA; Boston A. Festival, 1957; New Britain T. Col., 1958; one-man, Cape Cod AA, 1959. *Position*: Asst. Prof. Painting, Chm., A. Dept., Hartford Pub. H.S.

SQUIER, DONALD GORDON—*Painter, Comm. A.*

Epping Road, Exeter, N.H.

B. Amherst, Mass., Oct. 17, 1895. *Studied*: BMFA Sch.; in France, Germany, Italy; & with Tarbell, Hale, & others. *Member*: Copley Soc. *Work*: many portraits of prominent persons. *Exhibited*: NAD; CGA; PAFA; Whistler House, Lowell, Mass.; one-man exh.: Boston AC, 1935; Copley Soc., Boston, 1934, 1953; No. 10 Gal., 1936.

SQUIER, JACK—*Educator, S.*

Art Department, Cornell University; h. 120 Eastwood Terr., Ithaca, N.Y.

B. Ithaca, N.Y., Feb. 27, 1927. *Studied*: Indiana Univ., B.S.; Cornell Univ., M.F.A.; Oberlin Col. *Work*: Cornell Univ.; WMAA, and in private colls. *Exhibited*: Indiana Univ., 1950; Ogunquit A. Center, 1950-1952; Cornell Univ., 1951, 1952; John Herron AI, 1950; Downtown Gal., N.Y., 1952, 1953; Alan Gal., N.Y., 1953-1958, 2-man, 1954, 3-man, 1955; Univ. Minnesota, 1955; MModA, 1955-1958; Mus. FA of Houston, 1956; Perls Gal., Los A., 1956; Margaret Brown Gal., Boston, 1956; Tanager Gal., N.Y., 1956; Stable Gal., N.Y., 1956, 1957; WMAA, 1957, 1958; AIC, 1957; AFA traveling exh.; Phillips Acad., 1957; Time & Life Bldg., N.Y., 1957; one-man: Cornell Univ., 1952; Alan Gal., 1956. *Position*: Asst. Prof. A., Cornell Univ., Ithaca, N.Y., at present.

STACEY, DOROTHY HOWE-LAYMAN—
**   *Painter, Des., W., Comm. A.***

1800 Keo St.; h. 705 Clinton Ave., Des Moines 13, Iowa

B. Des Moines, Iowa, Sept. 30, 1904. *Studied*: Des Moines Univ., B.A.; Cumming Sch. A. *Member*: Iowa A. Gld.; Soc. for Sanity in Art; Composers, Authors & Artists Am. (Nat. Exec. Sec.). *Awards*: prizes, Des Moines Lib. scholarship, 1925; Iowa A. Salon, 1929-1933, 1935, medal, 1929; prize, Des Moines Women's Cl., 1930. *Exhibited*:

Grand Central A. Gal.; Univ. Idaho; Denver A. Mus.; Col. A. Cl., Santa Maria, Cal.; Iowa A. Gld., 1928-1959; Univ. Iowa, 1928-1959; Cedar Rapids, Iowa; Cornell Col.; Blandon Mem. Gal., Ft. Dodge, Iowa; Iowa State Col., 1950-1959; Sioux City A. Center, 1951, 1952, 1955, 1959; Des Moines A. Center, 1948-1959; CMA, 1957. *Position:* Mngr., Assoc. Des., Lynn Stacy Co., Des Moines, Iowa, 1951- .

STACEY, LYNN (NELSON)—
Painter, Des., I., Comm. A.
1800 Keo St.; h. 705 Clinton Ave., Des Moines 13, Iowa

B. Washington, D.C., May 24, 1903. *Studied:* Univ. Iowa, B.A.; Cumming Sch. A.; NAD, with Frances Jones, Raymond Neilson. *Member:* Des Moines Press & Radio Cl.; AFA; A. Dir. & Artists Assn. Am.; AAPL; Iowa A. Gld.; Soc. for Sanity in Art; Composers, Authors & Artists Am. (Nat. Pres., 1951-54, Dir., 1954-57); Am. Advertisers & Illus. *Awards:* prizes, Des Moines Women's Cl., 1928, 1955, 1956; medal, Iowa A. Salon, 1927-1928, 1930, 1931; CMA, 1957 (2). *Work:* Univ. Iowa; CGA; Nat. Bank, Dallas, Tex.; Iowa State Col.; Des Moines Women's Cl.; pub. bldgs., Wash., D.C. *Exhibited:* NAD, 1931; N.J.Sch. Indst. A., 1936; Michigan State Col., 1936; CGA, 1934; Duluth A. Center, 1936; Illinois State T. Col., 1936; Univ. North Dakota, 1936; Iowa A. Gld., 1928-1955; Iowa State Col., 1948-1955; Sioux City A. Center, 1951, 1955; Des Moines A. Center, 1948-1955, & others. Contributor illus., covers to Wallace Farmer, Iowa Homestead; des. for Shaeffer Pen Co.; N.W.Bell Telephone Co.; General Motors; Ford Motor Co., and others. *Position:* A.Dir., Freeman Decorating Co., 1927-1955; 1st V.-Pres., Freeman Contractors, 1940- ; Partner, Freeman-Stacy, Des Moines, Iowa, 1941-51; Owner, Lynn Stacey Co., Des Moines, Iowa, 1951- .

STACKEL, ALIE (Ann Liebman)—Sculptor, P., T.
748 Saratoga Ave., Brooklyn 12, N.Y.

B. New York, N.Y., Sept. 28, 1909. *Exhibited:* NAD; N.Y. Univ.; with Prof. Feldman & with Joseph Boston, Carnegie Hall Studios. *Member:* Brooklyn Soc. A. *Award:* Sculpture House. *Work:* Edu. A. Sch., Port Hope, Ontario, Canada. *Exhibited:* BM, 1946, 1947; Riverside Mus., 1950, 1952, 1957; NSS, 1951; New Sch. for Social Research, 1940; Rockefeller Center, 1940; Hofstra Col., 1946; Abraham & Straus, Brooklyn, 1949, 1951, 1953; Medallic Art Exh., 1949-1950; Hotel New Yorker, 1956; NAC, 1958. *Position:* Instr., S., New York Lg. of Girls Clubs, 1950.

STAEHLE, ALBERT—Illustrator, Des.
28 Fairview Ave., Mt. Pocono, Pa.

B. Munich, Germany, Aug. 19, 1899. *Studied:* ASL; Wicker Sch. FA, Detroit; in Germany; & with Charles Hawthorne. *Member:* SI. *Awards:* prizes, A.Dir.Cl., N.Y., 1943; A.Dir.Cl., Phila., 1942; Kerwin Fulton med., 1938-1940. *Exhibited:* Outdoor Advertising Exh., Chicago, 1937-1942, 1946. Originated "Smoky" the Bear and "Butch" covers for American Weekly magazine. Designed "Butch" ceramics for Goebel Co., creators of Hummel figurines.

STAHL, BEN(JAMIN) (ALBERT)—
Painter, I., L., T., Lith.
Siesta Key, Sarasota, Fla.

B. Chicago, Ill., Sept. 7, 1910. *Member:* Westport A.; SI; Sarasota AA; A. & W. Gld. *Awards:* prizes, Chicago Gld. Freelance A., 1937; Chicago Fed. Advertising Cl., 1939, 1941; A. Dir. Cl., Chicago, 1943, 1944, 1947, 1948; A. Dir. Cl., New York, 1947, 1952; Chicago Fed. Advertising Cl., 1939-1941; medals, A. Dir. Cl., Chicago, 1943; NAD, 1949. *Exhibited:* AIC, and in many other national exhibitions. Lectures: Illustration and Methods. *Position:* Member, Founding Faculty, Famous Artists Schs., Westport, Conn.; Chm. Com. for Sarasota A. Fnd.*

STAHL, LOUISE ZIMMERMAN (Mrs. Charles H.)—
Painter, T., I., L.
Moore Institute of Arts, Broad & Master Sts. (4); h. 2930 Fanshawe St., Philadelphia 49, Pa.

B. Philadelphia, Pa., Jan. 16, 1920. *Studied:* Moore Inst. A., B.F.A.; PMSch.A.; PAFA with Millard Sheets, Henry Pitz, Daniel Garber, and others. *Exhibited:* PAFA, 1943; Moore Inst. A., 1946-1958; Phila. A. All. Contributor

illus., Sat. Eve. Post. Lectures: History of Color Theory; How and Why We See Color, etc. Des., currency for foreign governments, E.A. Wright Co.

STALLMAN, EMMA S.—Craftsman
927 West Main St., Norristown, Pa.

B. Chestnut Hill, Philidelphia, Pa., Nov. 6, 1888. *Studied:* Moore Inst. A. & Sc.; R.I.Sch. Des. *Member:* Phila. Plastic Cl.; Pa. Gld. Craftsmen. *Work:* Mus. Northern Arizona, Flagstaff, Ariz. *Exhibited:* Phila. A. All.; Pa. Gld. Craftsmen; Phila. Plastic Cl.; Hershey Park (Pa.) Mus., 1951.

STAMATY, STANLEY—Cartoonist, Comm. A., I.
P.O. Box 75, Elberon, N.J.

B. Dayton, Ohio, May 21, 1916. *Studied:* Cincinnati A. Acad. *Member:* Nat. Cartoonists Soc. Contributor to Esquire; True; Sat. Eve. Post. Illus. textbook "Thought and Expression," Macmillan Co.

STAMBAUGH, DEAN—Painter, T.
St. Albans School, Washington 16, D.C.

B. Galeton, Pa., June 30, 1911. *Studied:* Edinboro (Pa.) State T. Col., B.S. in A. Edu.; Pa. State Col., M. in Edu.; & with Hobson Pittman. *Work:* Pa. State Univ. *Exhibited:* PAFA, 1940, 1944; Carnegie Inst., 1941; CGA, 1943, 1945; Butler AI, 1945, & prior; NAD, 1935; BMA. *Position:* Instr. A., St. Albans Sch. for Boys, Washington, D.C., at present.*

STAMOS, THEODOROS—Painter, T., I., Des.
East Marion, L.I., N.Y.

B. New York, N.Y., Dec. 31, 1922. *Studied:* Am. A. Sch., with Simon Kennedy. *Member:* A. Lg. Am. *Award:* F. grant, Nat. Inst. A. & Lets., 1956; Tiffany F., 1951. *Work:* MModA; MMA; WMAA; AGAA; PMG; Albright A. Gal.; BMA; Univ. Nebraska; Univ. Iowa; Cal.PLH; Wadsworth Atheneum; Tel-Aviv Mus.; Walker A. Center; Mus. Mod. A., Rio de Janeiro; Munson-Williams-Proctor Inst. *Exhibited:* Carnegie Inst., 1945, 1947, 1950, 1958; WMAA, 1946-1951, 1955; PAFA, 1947, 1948, 1950, 1951; Univ. Illinois, 1950; Univ. Iowa, 1947, 1948; Univ. Nebraska, 1950; Colorado Springs FA Center, 1948; Cal. PLH, 1949, 1950; MModA, 1949, 1951, 1955, and European traveling exh.; Walker A. Center, 1948; AIC, 1947; Soc. Four A., 1950; MMA, 1950; Betty Parsons Gal., 1947-1951; Venice Biennale, 1949; CGA, 1958-59, retrospective exh., 1958; numerous one-man exhibitions. Illus. book of poems, 1950. *Position:* Instr., Black Mountain Col., 1950; Cummington (Mass.) Sch. A., 1952, 1953; ASL, 1958 (winter).

STAMPER, WILLSON Y.—
Educator, P., Des., A. Sch. Dir.
Honolulu Academy of Arts, 900 South Beretania St., Honolulu, Hawaii

B. Brooklyn, N.Y., Jan. 5, 1912. *Studied:* ASL; Cincinnati A. Acad. *Member:* Hawaii P. & S. Assn. *Awards:* prizes, scholarship, ASL, 1933-36; CM, 1942; Honolulu Acad. A., 1947, 1948 (3), 1952, 1956; "Artist of Hawaii," 1949; Watumull Fnd. purchase prize, 1946, 1949. *Work:* CM; MModA; Honolulu Acad. A. *Exhibited:* CM, N.Y.; Willard Gal., N.Y.; CM, group and one-man exhs.; SFMA; Weyhe Gal., N.Y.; Butler Inst. Am. A.; Columbus Gal. FA; Riverside Mus.; Cincinnati Mod. A. Soc.; Ohio Graphic A. Soc., traveling exh.; Honolulu Acad. A., group and one-man exhs.; Dayton AI; CMA; Taft Mus. A.; Carnegie Inst. *Positions:* Instr., Tech. Adv., Honolulu Acad. Arts; Fndr., Dir., Honolulu Acad. A. Sch., Honolulu, Hawaii, 1946- .

STAN, WALT(ER) (P.)—Illustrator, Des., Cart., P.
112 Waverly Rd., Fairfax, Wilmington, Del.

B. Wilmington, Del., Sept. 9, 1917. *Studied:* PMSchIA, B.A.; & with Robert Riggs. *Member:* Am. A. Assn.; Phila. Graphic Sketch Cl.; Advertising Assn.; Phila. WC Cl. *Awards:* prizes, Delaware A. Center; PMSchIA. *Work:* mural, New Castle Army Air Base, Del.; Du Pont Co.; Children's ward, Delaware Hospital, Wilmington. *Exhibited:* PAFA, 1939, 1958; Pepsi-Cola, 1944; Delaware A. Center, 1941, 1942, 1944, 1945; Phila. A. All., 1958. I., for manufacturers appearing in national magazines. Lectures: Production Illustrations.

STANFIELD, MRS. MARION BAAR. See *Baar, Marion*

STANKIEWICZ, RICHARD (PETER)—*Sculptor*

647 Broadway, New York 12, N.Y.

B. Philadelphia, Pa., 1922. *Studied*: Hans Hofmann Sch. FA; and with Fernand Leger, Ossip Zadkine in Paris, France. *Exhibited*: PAFA, 1954; WMAA, 1956; Stable Gal., 1954, 1955; Univ. Minnesota, 1955; Denver Children's Mus., 1955; Hacker Gal., N.Y., 1953; Hansa Gal., 1953, 1955, 1956, 1957, 1958; Frumkin Gal., Chicago, 1955, 1957; Tanager Gal., N.Y., 1955, 1957; Martha Jackson Gal., N.Y., 1956, 1957; Camino Gal., N.Y., 1956, 1957; Silvermine Gld. A., 1957; James Gal., N.Y., 1957, 1958; WMAA, 1957; Riverside Mus., 1957, 1958; Mus. FA of Houston, 1957; Brata Gal., N.Y., 1958; Rutgers Univ., 1958; MModA, 1958; Carnegie Inst., 1958, and others; one-man: Hansa Gal., 1953- 1958; Frumkin Gal., 1958. *Work*: WMAA; MModA., and in private colls.

STANTON, ELIZABETH CADY (Mrs. William Harold Blake)—*Painter, L., T.*

54 Morningside Dr., New York 25, N.Y.

B. New York, N.Y., Dec. 31, 1894. *Studied*: ASL; Tiffany Fnd., & with Cecilia Beaux, F. Luis Mora. *Member*: NAWA; Tiffany Fnd.; Women's Faculty Cl., Columbia Univ. *Awards*: medals, Columbia Univ., 1954; NAWA, 1957. *Exhibited*: NAD; PAFA; NAWA; AWS; Tiffany Fnd.; Newport AA; Women's Faculty Cl.; & in London, England.

STANTON, GIDEON TOWNSEND—*Painter*

1314 Jackson Ave., New Orleans 13, La.

B. Morris, Minn., July 14, 1885. *Studied*: Rugby Acad., New Orleans; Balt. Charcoal Cl., & with S. Edwin Whiteman. *Member*: New Orleans AA; St. Augustine AA; Assoc., MMA. *Awards*: prizes, New Orleans AA, 1925; medal, 1912; New Orleans A. Lg., 1937, 1947. *Work*: Louisiana State Univ., & in private coll. *Exhibited*: Soc. Indp. A., Balt.; Atlanta, Ga.; Ogunquit A. Center, & others.

STAPLES, CLAYTON HENRI—*Painter, L., E.*

Cuchara, La Veta, Colo.

B. Osceola, Wis., Feb. 4, 1892. *Studied*: AIC, and abroad. *Member*: AWS. *Work*: in many private colls. *Position*: Former Dir. A., Univ. Wichita, Kans.; Dir., Cuchara Summer Sch. A., La Veta, Colo., at present.

STAPP, RAY V.—*Educator, C., P., S., Comm. A.*

Edinboro State Teachers College; h. 222 Erie St., Edinboro, Pa.

B. Norton, Kans., July 10, 1913. *Studied*: Bethany Col., B.F.A., with Birger Sandzen; Kansas City AI, with Thomas Hart Benton; ASL, with DuMond, Reilly, Trafton; T. Col., Columbia Univ., M.A., & Pa. State Univ. *Member*: NAEA; Eastern AA; Pa. A. Edu. Assn.; CAA. *Work*: Mem. painting, Farmer's Co-op, Dodge City, Kans. *Exhibited*: Wichita Dec. Art & Ceramic Exh., 1957; Kansas State Fed. A. traveling exh., 1949-1956; Kansas Des.-Craftsmen Exh., Lawrence, Kans., 1955. Contributor to Arts & Activities. *Positions*: Instr. A. & A. Edu., Bethany Col., Lindsborg, Kans., 1949-55; Asst. Prof. & Hd. A. Dept., 1955-56; Asst. Prof., Edinboro College, Edinboro, Pa., 1957- .

STARIN ARTHUR N(EWMAN)—*Painter*

Box 135, Royal Oak St., Talbot County, Md.

B. Falls Church, Va. *Studied*: PIASch.; ASL; George Washington Univ., & with C. C. Rosencranz, Eliot O'Hara. *Member*: Acad. A., Easton, Md. Council); New Jersey Soc. Arch. *Work*: Fla. Southern Col, and in private colls. *Exhibited*: All. A. Am., 1933-1952; Fla. Southern Col., 1952; traveling exh., Casein Paintings, 1952; AIC; Ferargil Gal.; Vendome Gal.; Wash. WC Cl.; CGA; Newark Mus.; Newark A. Cl.; New Jersey Gal., Newark; Paper Mill Playhouse; A. Center of the Oranges, 1952; Eastern (Md.) A. Festival, 1957, 1958; Morris County AA, 1948-1955, Contributor to architectural magazines.

STARK, FORREST F.—*Portrait Painter, S., T.*

222 Wawonaissa Trail, Ft. Wayne 6, Ind.

B. Milwaukee, Wis., May 29, 1903. *Studied*: Milwaukee State T. Col.; Mills Col.; PAFA; & with Leon Kroll, Charles Grafly, George Harding. *Member*: Indiana AC. *Awards*: Cresson traveling scholarship, PAFA, 1927; prizes, Hoosier Salon, 1932, 1952; Milwaukee AI, 1933; Thieme award, Ft. Wayne A. Sch., 1954, 1957. *Work*: Ft. Wayne A. Mus.; John Herron AI. *Exhibited*: PAFA, 1938; Indiana A., annually; Ft. Wayne A. Mus., annually. *Position*: Instr. A., Ft. Wayne A. Sch. & Mus., Ft. Wayne, Ind.

STARK, MELVILLE F.—*Painter, E., L.*

Zionsville, Pa.

B. Honesdale, Pa., Sept. 29, 1904. *Studied*: East Stroudsburg (Pa.) State T. Col., B.S.; Univ. Pennsylvania, M.S.; Syracuse Univ.; & with Walter E. Baum. *Work*: Reading A. Mus.; Allentown A. Mus. *Exhibited*: PAFA; NAD; Phila. Sketch Cl.; Woodmere A. Gal.; Phila. A. All.; Reading A. Mus.; Scranton A. Mus.; Lehigh Univ.; Univ. Pennsylvania; Allentown A. Mus. *Position*: Instr., Cedar Crest Col.; Muhlenberg Col.; Dir., Allentown A. Mus.; Baum A. Sch.

STARKEY, JO-ANITA (Mrs. Lee D.)—*Painter, C., Des.*

607 North Detroit St., Los Angeles 36, Cal.

B. Gresham, Neb., Sept. 20, 1895. *Studied*: with Loren Barton, Orrin White, Marion K. Wachtel, & others. *Member*: Women Painters of the West. *Awards*: prizes, Hollywood, Cal., 1948; Ebell Cl., Los A., 1949, 1950; Pasadena AI, 1950; Greek Theatre, Los A., 1950. *Exhibited*: Hollywood Women's Cl.; Pasadena Pub. Lib.; Laguna Beach AA; Santa Monica Women's Cl.; Los A. Mem. Lib.; Ebell Cl.; Bowers Mus. A.; Santa Ana, Cal.; Greek Theatre, Los A.; Pasadena AI, & others.

STARKS, ELLIOTT ROLAND—*Educator, A. Dir.*

Wisconsin Union, University of Wisconsin (10); h. 3509 Gregory St., Madison 5, Wis.

B. Madison, Wis., Feb. 24, 1922. *Studied*: Univ. Wisconsin, B.A., M.S. in A. Edu. *Positions*: Instr., Social Ed., Adv. and Dir., Wisconsin Union Gallery, University of Wisconsin.

STARKWEATHER, WILLIAM (EDWARD) (BLOOMFIELD)—*Painter, W., L., T.*

26 Garden Place, Brooklyn 1, N.Y.

B. Edinburgh, Scotland, May 16, 1879. *Studied*: ASL; in Paris; & with Sorolla, in Madrid, Spain. *Member*: All.A. Am.; AWCS; Hispanic Soc. Am.; Phila. WC Cl.; New Haven Paint & Clay Cl. *Awards*: prizes, WC Exh., N.Y., 1925; Balt., Md., 1926; PAFA, 1929; med., PAFA, 1925. *Work*: MMA; BM; San Diego FA Soc.; Univ. Pennsylvania; Randolph-Macon Col. for Women; Instituto de Valencia de Don Juan, Madrid, Spain; Hickory Mus. A.; murals, Endless Caverns, New Market, Va. *Exhibited*: Salon des Artistes Francais, Paris, 1912-1926; NAD; PAFA; All.A.Am., 1926-1946; AWCS, 1915-1946; Mus.A., New Market, Va. (permanent exh.). Author: "Drawings and Paintings by Francisco Goya in the Collection of Hispanic Society of America." Contributor to: Mentor magazine; article on Goya to New Century Cyclopaedia of Names, 1955. Lectures: Spanish Painting. *Position*: Instr. Drawing & Painting, Hunter Col., New York, N.Y., 1936-46.

STARR, LORRAINE WEBSTER (Mrs. William)—*Painter, I., L., T.*

Bozman, Talbot County, Md.

B. Old Holderness, N.H., June 24, 1887. *Studied*: Vassar Col.; B.A.; BMFA Sch.; ASL; Am. Sch. Min. P., & with Mabel Welch, Elsie Dodge Pattee, William Paxton, Philip Hale, Lewis Pilcher, & others. *Member*: Pa. Soc. Min. P.; Balt. WC Cl. *Work*: PMA. *Exhibited*: PAFA; ASMP; Wash. WC Cl.; Balt. WC Cl.; BMA; Carnegie Inst.; Detroit Inst. A.; CAM; Cal. Soc. Min. P.; NCFA. Lectures: History of Architecture, Painting & Sculpture.

STARR, MAXWELL B.—*Painter, S., T.*

54 West 74th St., New York 23, N.Y.

B. Odessa, Russia, Feb. 6, 1901. *Studied*: NAD; BAID; N.Y. Univ. *Member*: Arch. Lg.; NSMP; All. A. Am.; Tiffany A. Gld.; Rockport AA; Audubon A.; AEA; North Shore A. *Awards*: prizes, NAD, 1919, 1921-1924, med., 1920; Tiffany Fnd. F., 1923-1924; Intl. Mural Comp., 1925; Chaloner prize, 1922-1924; medal, BAID, 1922-1924; NAD, 1923. *Work*: Am. Mus. Numismatics; murals, U.S. Customs Office, N.Y.; Brooklyn Tech. H.S.; USPO, Siler City, N.C.; Rockdale, Tex.; Amarillo, Tex.; St. Louis, Mo.; Social Security Bldg., Wash., D.C. *Exhibited*: NAD; PAFA; All. A. Am.; AIC; WMAA; MModA; BMFA; WFNY 1939. *Position*: Founder, Dir., Maxwell Starr Sch. A., New York City and East Gloucester, Mass.*

STARR, POLLY THAYER. See *Thayer, Polly*

STAVENITZ, ALEXANDER RAOUL—
Etcher, Lith., Des., T.

5 Outer Rd., P.O. Box 336, South Norwalk, Conn.

B. Kiev, Russia, May 31, 1901. *Studied*: St. Louis Sch. FA, Washington Univ., B. Arch.; ASL. *Awards*: Guggenheim F., 1931; numerous awards in "Fifty Prints of the Year," "Fine Prints of the Year." *Work*: N.Y.Pub. Lib.; WMAA; Wesleyan Col. Lectures: Design and the Arts. *Positions*: Instr., Indst. Des., Pratt Inst., Brooklyn, N.Y., 1945-47; Instr., Arch. Des., Inst. Des. & Construction, Brooklyn, N.Y., 1947- ; Assoc. Prof. A., City Col. of N.Y., 1950; Instr., People's A. Center, MModA, 1954- ; Com. on A.Edu., MModA. *Member*: Rudolph Assoc., New York, N.Y., 1946- .

STEA, CESARE—*Sculptor, P., T.*

222 Lafayette Ave., Chatham, N.J.

B. Bari, Italy, Aug. 17, 1893. *Studied*: NAD; CUASch.; BAID; Grande Chaumiere, Paris, with Anton Bourdelle, & with Hermon MacNeil, Sterling Calder, & others. *Member*: NSS; S.Gld. *Awards*: prizes, NAD, 1926; Montclair A. Mus., 1933; Am. Veterans' A.Soc., 1952. *Work*: WMAA; Brooklyn Col.; Evander Childs H.S., N.Y.; Queensbridge Housing Project; Bowery Bay Disposal Bldg., N.Y.; U.S. Military Acad., West Point, N.Y.; USPO, Necomertoun, Ohio; Wyomissing, Pa. *Exhibited*: Palace Legion Honor; Hispanic Mus.; WFNY 1939; PAFA, 1944; BM, 1941; MMA, 1942, 1951; WMAA, 1943.

STEADMAN, L. ALICE TUTTLE (Mrs. Harold)—
Sculptor, P., T.

115 Cherokee Rd., Charlotte 7, N.C.

B. Stokes County, N.C., Mar. 10, 1907. *Studied*: Meredith Col., Raleigh; PAFA; and with Hugh Breckenridge, Oberteuffer, Eliot O'Hara, Naum Los, and others. *Member*: Gld. Charlotte A.; North Carolina State A. Soc. *Awards*: Margaret Graham silver cup, 1935; Raleigh Studio Cl. gold medal, 1936; Ethel Parker silver cup, 1937; Blowing Rock, N.C., 1957, 1958; Mint Mus. A., 1958. *Work*: port. sculpture in private colls.; many bas-relief and port. commissions; statues, Police Club; Boy Scout "Camp Steere." *Position*: Instr. A., Mint Mus. Sch. A., Charlotte, N.C., 1936- . Queens Col., 1953-54.

STEADMAN, WILLIAM E., JR.—
Museum Director, E., P., L.

Museum of Fine Arts; h. 34 Edgehill St., Little Rock, Ark.

B. Pigeon, Mich., Jan. 31, 1921. *Studied*: Michigan State Univ., B.A.; Univ. Arizona, B.F.A.; Yale Univ., B.F.A., M.F.A. *Member*: AAMus.; Ohio WC Soc. *Exhibited*: one-man: Roswell, N.M.; Grand Central A. Gal., 1955; New Britain Inst., 1956. Contributor "The Sully Portraits at West Point," to Antiques Magazine. Lectures: Italian Renaissance; Post Impressionism; Contemporary Art. Arranged exhs.: Southwestern Artifacts; Early Spanish Art, at Roswell Mus., N.M.; The Thomas Sully Portrait Collection; The George Catlin Collection; Early American Prints of West Point by Archibald Robertson; The Rindisbacher Watercolors at West Point; Military Prints of the 18th and 19th Centuries, at West Point. *Positions*: Instr., A. Hist. & Appreciation, Connecticut State Teachers College, New Britain, Conn.; Univ. New Mexico, Roswell, N.M.; West Point, N.Y.; Cur., FA, United States Military Academy, West Point, N.Y., 1953-57; Dir., Museum of Fine Arts, Little Rock, Ark., 1957- .

STEARNS, JOHN BARKER—*Educator*

Department of Art, Dartmouth College; h. 3 Downing Road, Hanover, N.H.

B. Norway, Me., Feb. 13, 1894. *Studied*: Dartmouth Col., A.B.; Princeton Univ., M.A., Ph.D. *Member*: Am. Philological Assn.; Archaeological Inst. Am.; Am. Classical Lg.; Classical Assn. of New England. *Author*: "Studies of the Dream as a Technical Device," 1927; "The Assyrian Reliefs at Dartmouth," 1953; "Byzantine Coins in the Dartmouth Collection," 1954. Contributor to Classical Weekly; Classical Philology; Classical Journal. *Positions*: Instr., Hist. Ancient Art, Classical Civilization, Alfred Univ., 1920-21, Princeton Univ., 1922-24, Yale Univ., 1925-28; Prof., 1928- , Chm., Department of Art, 1954- , Dartmouth College, Hanover, N.H.

STEBBINS, ROLAND STEWART—*Painter, E., L.*

Old Plow Inn Studio, 3402 Monroe St., Madison, Wis.

B. Boston, Mass., 1883. *Studied*: Royal A. Acad., Munich, Germany; Grande Chaumiere, Paris; PAFA; & with Charles Chapman, Hugh Breckenridge, Charles Hawthorne, Joseph de Camp. *Member*: Boston AC; Copley Soc., Boston; North Shore AA, Madison AA; AFA; Wis. P. & S. *Awards*: prizes, Madison AA, 1942, 1944, 1945; Wis. State Fair, 1944. *Work*: Univ. Wisconsin; City Lib., Madison, Wis.; murals, Medical Sch., Madison, Wis. Ports., Medical Sch., Law Sch., Pine Bluff Observatory, all Madison, Wis. *Exhibited*: Miami, Fla.; NAD, 1945; North Shore Gal., Gloucester, Mass., annually; Boston AC; Copley Soc., Boston; Madison AA, 1944-1946; Madison Salon, 1944-1946; Boca Raton, Fla., 1954, 1955; Milwaukee P. S., 1945, 1946; Grace Horne Gal., 1928 (one-man); Paris, France, 1928 (one-man). I., Christian Endeavor World. Lectures: Techniques of Painting. *Position*: Prof., A. Emeritus, Univ. Wisconsin, Madison, Wis.

STECHOW, WOLFGANG—*Educator*

260 Oak St., Oberlin, Ohio

B. Kiel, Germany, June 5, 1896. *Studied*: Univ. Göttingen, Germany, Ph. D. *Member*: CAA; Archaeological Inst. Am.; Am. Soc. for Aesthetics. *Author*: "Apollo und Daphne," 1932; "Salomon van Ruysdael," 1938; various museum & exhibition catalogs. Contributor to: Art in America, Art Quarterly, Art Bulletin, Gazette des Beaux-Arts, & other art magazines. Lectures: Renaissance and Baroque Art; Iconography; Aesthetics. *Positions*: Acting Asst. Prof., 1936, Assoc. Prof., 1937-40, Univ. Wisconsin; Prof. Hist. A., Oberlin Col., Oberlin, Ohio, 1940- ; Ed-in-Chief, Art Bulletin, 1950-52. Memb. Com. on Visual Arts, Harvard Univ., 1954-56; Adv. Council, Dept. of Germanic Languages & Literatures, Princeton Univ.

STECK, ALDEN L.—*Painter, T.*

106 Fifth St., Calumet, Mich.; h. 409 Kearsarge St., Laurium, Mich.

B. Calumet, Mich., Nov. 15, 1904. *Awards*: prize, Soumi Col., 1956. *Exhibited*: Grand Rapids A. Gal., 1942; AIC, 1938; CM; Kansas City AI, 1938, 1939; SFMA, 1938, 1940; Oakland A. Gal., 1938, 1941, 1944; AWCS, 1944; Acad. All. A., 1940; NAD, 1944; Mississippi AA, 1943; Springfield A. Mus., 1945; Detroit Inst. A., 1941, 1945; Soumi Col., 1956, 1957.

STECKEL, EDWIN M.—*Museum Director*

Oglebay Institute, Wheeling, W. Va.*

STEED, ROBERT—*Painter, T., Des.*

230 East 15th St., New York 3, N.Y.

B. Elizabeth, N.J., May 13, 1903. *Studied*: NAD, with Hawthorne, Olinsky, Curran; ASL; Cape Cod Sch. A.; Buffalo State T. Col.; N.Y. Univ., M.A. in A. Edu. *Award*: N.Y. State Exh., 1931. *Work*: Fiske Univ., and in private colls. *Exhibited*: PAFA, 1947; Barone Gal., 1954, 1957; Buck Hill Falls, Pa., 1957; one-man under auspices of U.N. Ambassador of India, 1958. *Position*: Instr. A., N.Y. Bd. Edu.; Columbia Univ. Res. in Contemp. India Proj. (in India, 1949-51, in New York, 1952-54); Book & Magazine Des., 1926-32.

STEEL, MRS. RHYS CAPARN. See *Caparn, Rhys*

STEELE, MARIAN WILLIAMS (Mrs. Chauncey D., Jr.)
—Painter

16 Chauncey St.; h. Hotel Continental, Cambridge 38, Mass.; s. Brier Neck, Gloucester, Mass.

B. Trenton, N.J., Jan. 4, 1916. *Studied*: PAFA; Trenton Sch. Indst. A.; Barnes Fnd. *Member*: Gld. Boston A.; Academic A.; Cambridge AA; AAPL; Cal. AA; Laguna Beach AA; Rockport AA; North Shore AA. *Awards*: Cresson traveling scholarship, PAFA, 1936; prizes, PAFA, 1933-1937; AAPL, 1938, 1939; Laguna Beach AA, 1934; Santa Paula, Cal., 1944; North Shore AA; Long Beach AA, 1944; Busch-Reisinger Mus., Harvard Univ., 1958. *Work*: port., N.J. State Hospital; Leahy Clinic, Boston; Boston Skating Cl. *Exhibited*: Los A. Mus. A., 1944; F. PAFA, 1935-1937, 1939, 1943; AAPL, 1938-1941; Rockport AA, 1942, 1953-1955; Newark Mus., 1938; Long Beach AA, 1944; Santa Paula, Cal., 1944; Laguna Beach AA, 1933-1935; Jordan-Marsh, Boston, 1942, 1953-1955; Gld. Boston A., 1953-1955 (one-man); North Shore AA, 1953-1955; Academic A., 1954-1956; Cambridge AA, 1953-1956.

STEENE, WILLIAM—Portrait Painter

Gulf Hills, Ocean Springs, Miss.

B. Syracuse, N.Y., Aug. 18, 1888. *Studied*: ASL; NAD; Fontainebleau Sch. A., Acad. Colarossi, Acad. Julian, Ecole des Beaux-Arts, all Paris, France. *Awards*: medals, BAID; Mississippi AA. *Member*: NSMP; AFA; Grand Central A. Gal.; Conn. Acad. FA; A. Fund of Am.; Lotos Cl.; SC. *Exhibited*: Arch. Lg.; NAD; Macbeth Gal.; Milch Gal.; Grand Central A. Gal.; All. A. Am.; Conn. Acad. FA; BM; Southern State AA; PAFA; Lyme AA. *Work*: many portraits of prominent national, business, educational and professional persons; panels, murals, State of Louisiana; Martha Washington Seminary; Raleigh Hist. Soc.; City Hall, Galveston; State House, Tahlequah, Okla.; Washington County Court House, Fayetteville, Ark.; Presbyterian Church, New Rochelle, N.Y., and others.

STEERE, LORA WOODHEAD—Sculptor

2814 Glendover Ave., Hollywood 27, Cal.

B. Los Angeles, Cal., May 13, 1888. *Studied*: Univ. Southern California; BMFA Sch., with Bela Pratt; Stanford Univ., A.B.; George Washington Univ., M.A.; Cal. Sch. FA; in Berlin, with Herr Torff; & with Ralph Stackpole. *Work*: Los A. Mus. A.; Univ. Southern California; Lincoln Mem. Univ., Cumberland Gap, Tenn.; Jordan H.S., Los A., Cal.; Forest Lawn, Los A.; Albert Wilson Hall, Los A.; Stanford Univ. Scientific drawings for Smithsonian Inst.; porcelain port. of children; port. busts, Idyllwild Sch. Music & A. *Exhibited*: AIC; PAFA; SFMA; Los A. Mus. A.; Mission Gal., Riverside, Cal., 1933 (one-man). *Position*: Instr. Ceramics, S., Los A. High Schools, Los Angeles, Cal.; Idyllwild Sch. Music & Art, Idyllwild, Cal.

STEG, J(AMES) L(OUIS)—Educator, Pr. M.

Art Department, Newcomb College, Tulane University (18); h. 64 Davis Blvd., New Orleans 21, La.

B. Alexandria, Va., Feb. 6, 1922. *Studied*: Rochester Inst. Tech.; State Univ. of Iowa, B.F.A., M.F.A., with Mauricio Lasansky. *Awards*: prizes, Phila. Pr. Cl., 1950; purchase prizes: BM, 1948, 1952; DMFA, 1953, 1958; LC, 1948; SAM, 1949; Univ. Minnesota, 1950; Delgado Mus. A., 1952, 1953, 1955. *Work*: LC; BM; SAM; FMA; MModA; DMFA; Carnegie Inst.; N.Y. Pub. Lib.; PMA; CMA; Munson-Williams-Proctor Inst.; Delgado Mus. A.; Univs. of: Minn., Neb., Del.; Albion Col.; Princeton Pr. Cl.; Bezalel Mus., Israel; Mus. Mod. A., Sao Paulo, Brazil; Davenport Mus. *Exhibited*: nationally and abroad; one-man: Weyhe Gal., 1945; Phila. A. All., 1957; Munson-Williams-Proctor Inst., 1951; Davenport Mus. A., 1958. *Position*: Assoc. Prof. A., Tulane University, New Orleans, La.

STEGALL, IRMA MATTHEWS (Mrs. Charles W.)—
Painter, L.

Ware's Ferry Rd., Montgomery 7, Ala.

B. Llano, Tex., Jan. 5, 1888. *Studied*: North Texas State T. Col.; Dallas AI; & with Martha Elliott, Olin Travis, & others. *Member*: Ala. A. Lg.; AAPL; Texas FA Assn.; Ala. WC Soc.; SSAL; Am. Assn. Univ. Women. *Awards*: Alabama A. Lg., 1932, 1947. *Exhibited*: Texas FA Assn.; SSAL; Ala. A. Lg.; Ala. WC Soc.; Birmingham A. Lg.; one-man exh.: Woman's Cl., Montgomery, Ala.; Mont-gomery Mus. FA; Carnegie Lib., Montgomery. Contributor to: Montgomery Advertiser, on current art exhibits. *Positions*: A.Dir., Am. Assn. Univ. Women, Montgomery Branch, 1944-45, 1945-46; Woman's Cl., 1944-45, 1945-59; Bd. Member, Montgomery Mus. FA, 1945-46, 1954-56.

STEGNER, NICHOLAS—Painter, C.

332 Grove St., Honesdale, Pa.; 15 Gramercy Pk., New York, N.Y.

B. Honesdale, Pa., Sept. 16, 1882. *Member*: AAPL. *Work*: "The White Deer Inn," Hawley, Pa. *Exhibited*: Studio Gld., 1939; Hallmark Exh., 1949, 1952; Hawley Lake, Pa., 1958. Decorator of china, glass, and furniture.

STEIG, WILLIAM—Cartoonist, S.

R.D.#2, Cream Ridge, N.J.

B. New York, N.Y., Nov. 14, 1907. *Studied*: Col. City of N.Y.; NAD. *Work*: sculpture, Smith Col.; R.I. Mus. A.; painting, BM. *Exhibited*: Downtown Gal., and in various group exhibitions. Author, I., Books of Drawings: "The Lonely Ones"; "About People"; "All Embarrassed"; "Till Death Do Us Part"; "Persistent Faces"; "Small Fry"; "The Agony in the Kindergarten"; "The Rejected Lovers"; "Dreams of Glory." Illus., "Listen Little Man." Contributor to the New Yorker and other leading magazines.

STEIN, HARVE—Illustrator, P., E., Gr., L.

Noank, Conn.

B. Chicago, Ill., Apr. 23, 1904. *Studied*: AIC; Julian Acad., Paris, and with Harvey Dunn. *Member*: SI (Hon. Life); AWS; Audubon A.; A. Fellowship. *Awards*: prizes, Cert., Chicago Book Clinic, 1952; Audubon A., 1955; Providence WC Cl., 1956; New Haven P. & Clay Cl., 1957. *Work*: U.S. State Dept.; Univ. Minnesota; Brown Univ.; Public Archives, Toronto, Canada; Montclair A. Mus.; N.Y. Pub. Lib. *Exhibited*: National watercolor exhs. throughout U.S. Illustrator of many books. Contributor to national magazines. Author article "The Illustrator Explains," American Artist magazine, 1958. *Positions*: Assoc. Prof. FA, Hd. Dept. Illustration, Rhode Island Sch. Des., 1944-59; Instr., Painting, Connecticut College, 1946, 1947, 1951; New London A. Students Lg., 1948-1959; Mitchell Col., New London, Conn., summer session, 1955-56.

STEINBERG, ISADOR N.—Designer, I., Cart., T.

57 West 69th St., New York 23, N.Y.

B. Odessa, Russia, June 14, 1900. *Studied*: Sch. Des. & Liberal A.; ASL; N.Y. Univ.; Grande Chaumiere, Paris, and with John Sloan, Max Weber. *Awards*: Scholarship, Sch. Des. & Liberal A.; AIGA, 1941; Fifty Books of the Year, 1939. *Exhibited*: Newark A. Cl., 1935; AIGA Fifty Books of the Year and Textbook Exh., 1939, and others including 1958. Illus., technical and scientific books including Einstein's "Evolution of Physics"; Mayer's "Artist's Materials and Techniques"; "Tools of War"; "Military Roentgenology"; Columbia Viking Encyclopaedia, 1953; Dictionary of Antiques and Decorative Arts, 1957; "Exploring Science," 1958, and others. Wrote, des., executed U.S. Army courses in Botany, Surveying, Lettering, Mechanical Drawing, etc. *Positions*: L., Sch. Des.; Consultant on book production & illustration to Pentagon, 1943; former Instr., Adv. Des., Columbia Univ., Extension; Owner, York Studios, New York, N.Y.

STEINBERG, NATHANIEL P.—Etcher, P., I.

415 Aldine Ave., Chicago 13, Ill.

B. Jerusalem, Palestine, Feb. 15, 1893. *Studied*: AIC; also with Walcott, Bellows, Sterba. *Member*: Palette and Chisel Acad., Chicago; Wash. WC Cl.; Chicago Soc. Et. *Awards*: prizes, Indiana Soc. Et., 1947; SAGA, 1950; Chicago Soc. Et., 1935, 1949. Print chosen by SAGA for Paris Salon, 1937; Palette & Chisel Cl., gold medal, 1953; Chicago A. Gld., 1955; Bruce Parsons award, Union Lg. Cl., Chicago, 1957. *Work*: Fed. Court, Chicago; Smithsonian Inst.; Herzl H.S., Chicago. *Exhibited*: in many museums and galleries in U.S.

STEINBERG, SAUL—Painter, Cart., Des.

179 East 71st St., New York, N.Y.

B. Roumania, June 15, 1914. *Studied*: R. Politecnico, Milan, Italy. *Work*: MModA; MMA; FMA; Detroit Inst.

A.; Victoria & Albert Mus., London; murals, Plaza Hotel, Cincinnati; four Am. Export Lines ships. *Exhibited*: MModA, 1946; Betty Parsons Gal., 1952; Sidney Janis Gal., 1952; Inst. Contemp. A., London, 1952; AIC, 1949; Obelisco, Rome, 1951; one-man: Galerie Mai, Paris, 1953; Kunstmuseum, Basel, 1954; Stedeljik Mus., Amsterdam, 1953; Museo de Arte, Sao Paulo, Brazil, 1952; Galerie Blanche, Stockholm, 1953; Hanover, 1954; AFA, 1953-55. Author: "All in Line," 1945; "The Art of Living," 1949; "The Passport," 1954. Contributor to national magazines.*

STEINBOMER, DOROTHY H. (Mrs. Henry)—
Designer, C., L.
800 Burr Road, San Antonio 9, Tex.

B. Bayonne, N.J., May 27, 1912. *Studied*: Our Lady of the Lake Col., B.A., and with Harding Black; Etienne Ret; Michael Frary; Dan Lutz; Fletcher Martin. *Member*: Stained Glass Assn. of Am.; AFA; Am. Craftsmen's Council; Craft Gld. of San Antonio; Texas FA Assn.; FA Adv. Council, Univ. Texas; San Antonio A. Lg. (Pres. 1956-58). *Work*: stained glass windows: Jefferson Methodist Chapel, Redeemer Lutheran Church, Northwood Presbyterian Church, Aldersgate Methodist Church, all in San Antonio; St. John Lutheran Church, Temple, Tex.; fused glass hanging Cross, First Presbyterian Church, Midland, Texas. *Exhibited*: Texas FA Assn., 1957 (2-man); Southwest Tex. State College, 1956; A. & M. Col., 1959; Witte Mem. Mus., 1957; numerous studio shows in Southwest of stained glass.

STEINFELS, MELVILLE P.—Painter, Des., I., E.
322 Talcott Pl., Park Ridge, Ill.

B. Salt Lake City, Utah, Nov. 3, 1910. *Studied*: AIC; Chicago Sch. Des. *Member*: Catholic AA. *Work*: frescoes, Our Lady of Lourdes Church, Indianapolis; Church of the Epiphany, Chicago; Loyola Univ.; ceramic tile murals, Univ. Detroit H.S.; Newman Cl., Ann Arbor; St. Mary Magdalen Church, Melvindale, Mich.; Mosaic murals, Chapel of Siena Heights Col., Adrian ,Mich.; Mary, Seat of Wisdom Church, Park Ridge, Ill.; Holy Ghost Fathers Seminary, Ann Arbor, Mich.; St. Michael's Church, Pontiac, Mich.; paintings, in churches in Memphis, Tenn., Lincoln Park, Mich., Plymouth, Mich., Detroit, Mich., Marysville, Mich. I., "Power." *Position*: A. in Residence, Siena Heights Col., Adrian, Mich., 1945-50.

STEINITZ, KATE TRAUMAN—Art Librarian, P., W., L.
Elmer Belt Library of Vinciana; h. 631½ Bonnie Brae, Los Angeles 57, Cal.

B. Beuthen, Germany, Aug. 2, 1893. *Studied*: in Berlin with Kollwitz, Lovis Corinth; Univ. Paris, Grand Chaumiere, Sorbonne; Tech. Hochschule, Hanover, Germany. *Member*: Am. Soc. for Aesthetics; Los A. County Mus. Assn.; Special Libraries Assn. Mus. Group; Archaeological Inst. Am. *Award*: State Dept., Specialists' Div., travel grant to Europe, 1956. *Works*: Hanover, Germany, Mus.; Societe Anonyme, Yale Univ. *Exhibited*: Berlin, Hanover, Germany; N.Y. Pub. Lib.; WFNY 1939. Contributor to art magazines in the U.S. and abroad. Author: "Leonardo da Vinci's Manuscripts," 1948; "Leonardo da Vinci's Trattato della pittura," Research Monography, 1956. Lectures: Leonardo da Vinci; Modern Art, etc. Arranged exhibitions of rare books and exhibitions of da Vinciana, Univ. Southern Cal., Redlands Univ., Los A. Mus. A., Cal State Exhibitions, UCLA, Los A. Pub. Lib., 1945- . *Position*: Librarian, The Elmer Belt Library of Vinciana, Los Angeles, Cal.; Instr., Italian Renaissance, Pomona College, Claremont, Col., 1958-59.

STEINKE, BETTINA (BLAIR)—Painter, Comm. A.
1623 South Main St., Tulsa, Okla.

B. Biddeford, Me., June 25, 1913. *Studied*: CUASch., with Alpheaus Cole; Phoenix AI, with Gordon Stevenson, Thomas Fogarty. *Member*: SI; Press Cl. *Awards*: prize, New Rochelle AA; medal, CUASch. *Work*: Baldwin Piano Co.; Circus Saints & Sinners Coll.; The Press Box, N.Y.; Pratt & Whitney Co.; United Fruit Co.; Standard Oil Co. of New Jersey; Philbrook A. Center; NBC, and many others including work in private colls. *Exhibited*: Richardson Bros., Winnipeg, Can., 1953-54; SI, 1950; A. Center, Curacao, N.W.I., 1947; Oklahoma City A. Center, 1953; Philbrook A. Center, 1952; Tucson, Ariz., 1951; Reynolds Gal., Taos, N.M., 1955; New Rochelle AA, 1940, etc. Illus., "NBC Symphony Orchestra," 1939 (98

portraits); other books of portraits, 1946, 1948; "The Last War Trail," 1954. Contributor illus. to Standard Oil Co.'s "The Lamp"; Readers Digest, and for other magazines.*

STENBERY, ALGOT—Painter, I., T.
51 East 9th St., New York 3, N.Y.

B. Cambridge, Mass., Apr. 24, 1902. *Studied*: Hartford A. Sch.; BMFA Sch.; ASL; & with Kimon Nicolaides, Frederick Bosley, Albertus Jones. *Member*: An Am. Group; Audubon A. *Work*: MMA; murals, Harlem Housing Project; USPO, Wayne, Mich. *Exhibited*: PAFA, 1939; WFNY 1939; WMAA, 1945; Walker A. Gal., 1937 (one-man). Illus., "The Giant"; "Far Country"; "Bridges at Toko-Ri"; "Little Britches"; "The Sojourner"; "Time to Remember"; "Seven Steeples"; also numerous juveniles.

STENVALL, JOHN F.—
Painter, C., T., W., Comm. A., Gr., Cart.
1159 North State St., Chicago 10, Ill.

B. Rawlins, Wyo., Sept. 25, 1907. *Studied*: Univ. Nebraska, B.F.A.; AIC; Stanford Univ., M.A. *Member*: CAA; Illinois A. Edu. Assn.; Around Chicago A. Edu. (Pres. 1954); NAEA; Midwest Des. Lg. *Awards*: prize, AIC, 1936. *Exhibited*: MModA, 1936, 1941; WFNY 1939; Wichita A. Mus., 1934; Phila. Soc. Et., 1934; Univ. Minnesota, 1938; Phila. WC Cl., 1938; Rockefeller Center, 1936; BM, 1937; Musee du Jeu de Paume, Paris, 1938; CM, 1939; AIC, 1934-1938, 1940, 1941, 1946; Chicago Soc. A., 1934-1941; Swedish-Am. Exh., 1939, 1955; Chicago Graphic Group, 1937, 1938; one-man: Leonard Linn Gal., 1953; Oldschlager Gal., 1955-56; Nelson Gal., 1953, all Chicago. Ed., Illinois A. Edu. Assn. Yearbook, 1954. Contributor to School Arts magazine; Arts & Activities magazine. *Position*: Instr., New Trier H.S., Winnetka, Ill.; Pres., Illinois A. Edu. Assn., 1957-58; Ed., Western AA magazine, 1956-58; Ed. Bd., NAE.

STEPHENS, RICHARD—
Painter, Cart., L., T., Comm. A.
431 Sutter St., San Francisco, Cal.; h. 23 De Sabla Rd., San Mateo, Cal.

B. Oakland, Cal., Dec. 3, 1892. *Studied*: Univ. California; Scripps Col.; Cal. Col. A. & Crafts; Cal. Sch. FA; Andre L'Hote, Julian Acad., Paris, France. *Member*: Cal. WC Soc.; A. & A. Dir. Cl.; San F. Advertising Cl. *Awards*: prizes, San Mateo Fair, 1954. *Work*: Scripps Col. *Exhibited*: Drawing Exh., San F., 1940; Oakland A. Gal., 1930-1940, 1945, 1949; Santa Cruz, Cal., 1940, 1948, 1949; Cal. WC Soc., 1950, 1952; Scripps Col., 1951; Gump's Gal., San F., 1935; Raymond & Raymond, 1933; City of Paris, San F., 1948-1952, 1955; Richmond, Cal., 1953. I., "Glen Warner's Book for Boys," 1932; "Live English." Contributor cartoons to Sunset, College Humor, American Artist, Western Advertising, Judge magazines. *Position*: Founder, Instr., Acad. Advertising Art, San Francisco, Cal.

STEPHENS, THOMAS EDGAR—Painter
15 Gramercy Park, New York 3, N.Y.

B. Cardiff, South Wales. *Studied*: Cardiff Univ. Sch. FA; Heatherly Sch., London; Acad. Julian, Paris. *Member*: SC; NAC; Univ. Cl., Wash., D.C.; Savage Cl., London. *Work*: White House, Wash., D.C.; NGA; U.S. Supreme Court; U.S. Treasury Dept.; U.S. Senate; Pentagon, Wash., D.C.; Walter Reed Hospital; West Point Military Acad.; U.S. Naval Acad.; N.Y. Genealogical Soc.; Eisenhower Mus., Abilene, Kans.; Legion of Honor Gal., Paris; U.S. Embassy, London; IBM; Cornell Univ.; Columbia Univ.; Harvard Univ.; Ft. Benning Inf. Sch.; Harry Truman Lib., and others.

STEPPAT, LEO LUDWIG—Sculptor, E.
Department of Art Education, University Wisconsin; h. 1105 Rutledge St., Madison, Wis.

B. Vienna, Austria, July 10, 1910. *Studied*: Acad. FA, Vienna, M.F.A. *Member*: CAA; Com. on A. Edu., MModA. *Awards*: prizes, Wisconsin Salon, 1955-57; WAC, 1958; Milwaukee A. Center, 1956-1958; John Herron AI, 1951, 1952; War Dept., Pub. Bldg. Admin., Wash., D.C., 1941; medal, Vienna, Austria, 1930, 1932. *Work*: WMAA; Smithsonian Inst.; Museo Nacional, Mexico City; Guggenheim Mus.; Milwaukee AI, and in private colls. *Exhibited*:

Illinois P. & S. exh., 1955; WMAA, 1954, 1955, 1958; WAC, 1958; Milwaukee A. Center, 1956-1958; PAFA, 1954; AFA traveling exh., 1954-55; Nat Ecclesiastical exh., N.Y., 1950; Forum Gal., N.Y., 1955; Wisconsin Salon, 1955-1957; Kootz Gal., 1954 (one-man); Indiana A. John Herron AI, 1950-1952; Springfield, Ill., 1951; BMA, 1947; CGA, 1942, 1944, 1945, 1947; one-man: Whyte Gal., Wash., D.C., 1944; Secession Gal., Vienna, 1936; Kunstlerhaus, Vienna, 1933, and others. Contributor to College Art Journal. *Positions*: Instr., Am. Univ., Wash., D.C., 1947-49; Asst. Prof., Indiana Univ., 1949-52; Assoc. Prof., Univ. Mississippi, 1952-54; Dir., Forum Gal., N.Y., 1955; Assoc. Prof., Univ. Wisconsin, Madison, Wis., 1955- .

STERBA, ANTONIN—*Painter, Et., T.*
4 East Ohio St., Chicago 11, Ill.

B. Hermanec, Czechoslovakia, Feb. 11, 1875. *Studied*: AIC; Julian Acad., Paris, France. *Member*: Assn. Chicago P. & S.; Chicago Galleries Assn.; Chicago Soc. Et.; Bohemian A. Cl. *Awards*: medal, Bohemian A. Cl., 1923; Assn. Chicago P. & S., 1943; prize, Mun. A. Lg., 1938. *Work*: portraits, Northwestern Univ.; DePauw Univ.; Baylor Univ. *Exhibited*: CGA; PAFA; AIC; Chicago Galleries Assn., annually; one-man: Pasadena, Cal.; Chicago, Ill.; Nashville, Tenn.; Shreveport, La.; Little Rock, Ark.; San Antonio, Tex.; Beloit Col.; Elgin Acad. A.

STERCHI, EDA—*Painter*
South Fair St., Olney, Ill.; also, 4601 East Cholla St., Phoenix, Ariz.

B. Olney, Ill. *Studied*: AIC; Grande Chaumiere, Paris, France. *Awards*: French decoration, "Palmes Academique"; Tunisian decoration. "Nichan Iftikhar." *Exhibited*: one-man: AIC; Santa Barbara Mus. A.; Mus. New Mexico; Boston, Mass.; New York, N.Y.; Paris, France; Tunisia.

STERINBACH, NATALIE—*Painter*
108-35 66th Road, Forest Hills 75, N.Y.

B. New York, N.Y., Dec. 25, 1910. *Studied*: ASL, with Morris Kantor, Sam Adler, Camilo Egas, and others. *Member*: NAWA; Lg. Present Day A.; AEA; Brooklyn Soc. A. *Award*: prize, Village A. Center. *Exhibited*: NAWA, 1954, 1956, 1958; Contemp. A. Gal., 1955-1958; Lg. Present Day A., 1956, 1957; N.Y. City Center, 1956; Village A. Festival, 1958; one-man: Panoras Gal., 1957.

STERN, ALFRED CHARLES—*Sculptor*
200 East 41st St., New York 17, N.Y.; h. 48-51 190th St., Flushing 65, N.Y.

B. New York, N.Y., Mar. 6, 1936. *Studied*: PIASch., B. Arch. *Work*: Co-designer "Noon City," lobby Lorillard Bldg., N.Y.

STERN, CAROLINE (Mrs.)—*Painter*
815 Park Ave., New York 21, N.Y.

B. Germany, June 17, 1894. *Studied*: Julian Acad., Paris, France. *Member*: AWS. *Exhibited*: AWS.*

STERN, LUCIA—*Painter, S., C., L.*
3332 North Shepard Ave., Milwaukee 11, Wis.

B. Milwaukee, Wis., Dec. 20, 1900. *Member*: Wis. P. & S. Soc.; Springfield A. Lg.; Wisconsin Des. Craftsmen. *Awards*: prizes, Milwaukee AI, 1945, 1946. *Work*: Smith Col. Mus.; Milwaukee AI; Mus. Non-Objective Painting, N.Y. *Exhibited*: Mus. Non-Objective Painting, 1944-1952; Springfield A. Lg.; 1945-1951; Salon de Realites Nouvelles, Paris, France, 1948, 1951, 1952; one-man: Detroit Inst. A., 1945; Milwaukee AI, 1942. Lectures: History of Art.

STERNBERG, HARRY—*Painter, Gr., T., L., Des.*
30 East 14th St., New York 3, N.Y.; h. 9 St. James Pl., Glen Cove, L.I., N.Y.

B. New York, N.Y., July 19, 1904. *Studied*: ASL; & with Harry Wickey. *Member*: AEA. *Awards*: Guggenheim F., 1936; Fifty Prints of the Year, 1930; Fine Prints of the Year, 1932-1934; 100 Prints of the year Year, 1938; prize, Phila. Pr. Cl., 1942; Assoc.Am.A., 1946, 1947; Audubon A., 1955. *Work*: MModA; MMA; WMAA; N.Y. Pub. Lib.; Lib. Cong.; FMA; PMA; CMA; Univ. Minnesota

(complete coll. of Sternberg's prints); Victoria & Albert Mus., London, England; Bibliotheque Nationale, Paris, France; murals, USPO, Chicago, Ill.; Chester, Pa.; Sellersville, Pa. *Exhibited*: nationally. One-man: ACA Gal., 1956, 1958; Univ. Minnesota, 1957; Gorelick Gal., Detroit, 1958; Brigham Young Univ., 1958; Idyllwild Sch. A., 1958. Author, I., "Silk Screen Color Printing," 1945; "Modern Methods and Materials of Etching," 1949; "Composition," 1958; "Modern Drawing," 1958. *Position*: Instr., Graphic A., painting, ASL. Summer Instr., Idyllwild (Cal.) School of Art, 1957, 1958; L. & Workshop, Brigham Young Univ., Provo, Utah, 1958.

STERNE, DAHLI—*Painter*
344 West 72nd St., New York 23, N.Y.

B. Stettin, Germany, 1901. *Studied*: Kaiserin Auguste Victoria Acad., B.A.; and in the U.S. with Albert Pels, Ludolf Liberts, Josef Silhavy. *Member*: 50 Am. Artists; All. A. Am., AAPL; Wolfe A. Cl.; Hon. Memb., Kappa Pi; F., Royal Soc. A., London, England. *Awards*: prizes, Grumbacher award, 1952; AAPL, 1955; citation, Okla. AA, 1954; citation, Seton Hall Univ.; gold medal, Ogunquit A. Center, 1957. *Work*: Oklahoma City A. Center; Fla. Southern Col.; Seton Hall Univ. *Exhibited*: NAC, 1953-1958; All. A. Am., 1955; 50 Am. Artists, 1955-1958; Grace Pickett traveling exh.; Grumbacher traveling exh.; one-man: New York City. Contributor illus. to Today's Art magazine.

STERNE, HEDDA—*Painter*
179 East 71st St., New York 21, N.Y.

B. Bucharest, Roumania, Aug. 4, 1916. *Studied*: abroad. *Work*: Univ. Illinois; MMA; MModA; Univ. Nebraska; WMAA; Carnegie Inst. *Exhibited*: PAFA, 1947-1952; Carnegie Inst.; MMA; WMAA; AIC; MModA; Santa Barbara Mus. A.; Los A. Mus. A.; Albright A. Gal.; VMFA; SFMA; Vassar Col.; Saidenberg Gal.; Chicago A. Cl.; Univ. Nebraska; Soc. Contemp. A.; WMA; MModA traveling exh.; Univ. Illinois, and others. Numerous one-man shows, including Sao Paulo, Brazil, 1953; Rome, Italy; San Francisco, Cal., and Betty Parsons Gal., regularly.

STERNER, HAROLD—*Painter, W.*
340 East 63rd St., New York 21, N.Y.

B. Paris, France, Oct. 29, 1895. *Studied*: St. George's Sch., Newport, R.I.; MIT, B.S. *Member*: AEA; BAID. *Work*: BMFA. *Exhibited*: PAFA, 1943, 1944; CGA, 1943, 1944; AIC, 1943; WMAA, 1944, 1945; MMA (AV), 1944; CAM, 1944; Carnegie Inst., 1946, 1948; one-man: Knoedler Gal., 1955; British-Am. A. Center, 1951.

STERNFELD, EDITH A.—*Painter, E.*
Brande Apartments, Grinnell, Iowa

Studied: Northwestern Univ., B.A.; AIC, B.A.E.; Univ. Iowa, M.A.; Cranbrook Acad. A.; Claremont Grad. Sch., and with Eliot O'Hara, Grant Wood, Jean Charlot, Rex Brandt. *Member*: CAA; Am. Assn. Univ. Women. *Awards*: prizes, All-Iowa Exh., 1937; Joslyn Mem., 1937, 1940; Iowa WC Exh., 1945, 1953; Chicago Tribune Comp., 1953; numerous prizes in regional exh. *Exhibited*: AIC; Wis. P. & S.; AWCS; Phila. WC Cl.; Balt. WC Cl.; Cal. WC Soc.; Wash. WC Cl.; Kansas City AI; Joslyn Mem.; WFNY 1939; Iowa WC Exh., since 1945; Des Moines, Iowa; Denver A. Mus.; Mid-Am. A.; Springfield (Mo.) A. Mus.; several one-man exh. Lectures: Painting. *Position*: Prof. A., Chm. Dept. A., 1930- , Chm. Div. FA, 1944-46, 1951-53, Grinnell Col., Grinnell, Iowa.

STERRETT, CLIFF—*Cartoonist*
Brassie Lane, Bronxville, N.Y.

B. Fergus Falls, Minn., Dec. 12, 1883. *Studied*: Chase Sch. A. *Member*: SI. I., "Polly and Her Pals," King Features Syndicate.*

STETSON, KATHARINE BEECHER (Mrs. Katharine Beecher Stetson Chamberlin)—*Sculptor, P.*
223 South Catalina Ave., Pasadena 5, Cal.

B. Providence, R.I., Mar. 23, 1885. *Studied*: in Europe; PAFA, with Kendall, Anshutz, Poore. *Member*: Pasadena SA. *Awards*: med., Los A. Mus. A., 1925; prizes, Los A. County Fair, 1927; Pasadena SA, 1940. *Exhibited*:

PAFA, 1912, 1914, 1915, 1916, 1919, 1926; NAD, 1914-1916, 1919, 1925; Arch L., 1915, 1917; AIC, 1915-1917, 1926; Los A. Mus. A., 1921-1926; Pasadena SA, 1924-1951.

STEVENS, BERNICE A.—*Craftsman, T.*
908 Washington Ave., Evansville 13, Ind.

B. Evansville, Ind. *Studied*: Evansville Col., B.S.; Univ. Tennessee, M.S. in crafts; Gatlinburg Craft Sch.; Ringling Sch. A.; Saugatuck Sch. Painting. *Member*: Hoosier Craft Gld. *Awards*: Delta Kappa Gamma Fellowship, 1955; Ford F., 1955-56. *Exhibited*: Huntington, W. Va., Nat. Jewelry Exh., 1955, and Rochester, N.Y., 1956, circulated by Smithsonian Inst.; Southern Highlands Fair, 1948-1950; Evansville Tri-State Exhs., 1940-1956; Hoosier Craft Gld., 1950-1956; Louisville, Ky., 1955; John Herron AI, 1955; Ft. Wayne traveling exh., 1955. Contributor to School Arts magazine. *Position*: Instr. A. & Crafts, Evansville Pub. Schs., 1927-55; Jewelry, Evansville Col., 1947-55; Jewelry, Cherokee, N.C., summer, 1954-1957. Presently conducting craft survey of the Southern Highlands for Southern Appalachian Studios, sponsored by Ford Fnd.

STEVENS, DWIGHT ELTON—*Designer, P., E.*
151 South Willis St., Stillwater, Okla.

B. Sharon, Okla., May 1, 1904. *Studied*: Oklahoma A. & M. Col., B.S. in Arch.; Cincinnati A. Acad. *Member*: SSAL; AIA; Cal. WC Soc. *Awards*: prizes in arch. des., national and regional comp.; CM, 1925; Okla. Chapter, AIA, 1954. *Exhibited*: Denver A. Mus., 1943; Oakland A. Gal., 1943; AWS, 1946, 1948; SSAL, 1946; Oklahoma A., 1944-1946; CM, 1929; Philbrook A. Center, 1943-1948; Cal. WC Soc., 1946, 1948; PMA, 1947; Dallas Mus. FA, 1947; Delgado Mus. A., 1948; Okla. A. & M. Col. (one-man). *Position*: Prof. Arch. Des., Dept. Arch., Oklahoma State Univ., Stillwater, Okla.

STEVENS, EDWARD JOHN, JR.—*Painter, Et.*
621 Palisade Ave., Jersey City 7, N.J.

B. Jersey City, N.J., Feb. 4, 1923. *Studied*: State T. Col., Newark, B.S.; T. Col., Columbia Univ., M.A. *Member*: AEA; Audubon A.; Phila. WC Cl. *Work*: WMAA; Newark Mus.; Smith Col.; Detroit Inst. A.; SAM; Univ. Washington; Honolulu Acad. A.; Princeton Pr. Cl.; Chappell Mem. A. Gal., Univ. Omaha; Pa. State Univ.; BMFA; Montclair A. Mus.; Am. Univ.; Phila. Pr. Cl.; BMA; Univ. Alabama; Univ. Delaware; LC. *Exhibited*: Pasadena AI, 1946; BM, 1945, 1946; WMAA; PAFA; SFMA; AGAA; Amherst Col.; Bryn Mawr Col.; Munson-Williams-Proctor Inst.; Soc. Four A.; Phila. A. All.; one-man: Mills Col., 1951; BMA, 1948; Weyhe Gal., 1944-1959. *Position*: Instr., Newark Sch. F. & Indst. A., 1947- .

STEVENS, KELLY HAYGOOD—*Painter, C., T.*
507 East 10th St., Austin 1, Tex.

B. Mexia, Tex., Mar. 30, 1896. *Studied*: Gallaudet Col., Wash., D.C., B.A.; Corcoran Sch. A.; Trenton (N.J.) Sch. Indst. A.; N.Y. Sch. F. & App. A.; Louisiana State Univ., M.A.; & with Messer, Adams, & others. *Member*: Louisiana T. Assn. *Exhibited*: Dallas Mus. FA; Roerich Mus.; State A. Gal., Shreveport, La.; SSAL; Texas FA Assn.; & in Madrid, Brussels, Paris.

STEVENS, LAWRENCE TENNEY—
Sculptor, Gr., P., L., T.
519 West 8th St., Tempe, Ariz.

B. Brighton, Mass., July 16, 1896. *Studied*: BMFA Sch.; Am. Acad. in Rome; & with Charles Grafly, Bela Pratt. *Member*: NSS; Alumni, Am. Acad. in Rome; Alumni BMFA Sch.; Grand Central A. Gal. *Awards*: Prix de Rome, 1922. *Work*: Univ. Pennsylvania; Brookgreen Gardens, S.C.; BM; Perry Clinic, Tulsa; Woodward, Okla.; Central H.S., Chamber of Commerce, both Tulsa; Will Rogers Mem., Claremore, Okla.; Woodmen Accident & Life Co., Lincoln, Neb.; Security Bldg., Valley Nat. Bank, Phoenix; Security-First Nat. Bank, Palm Springs; Valley Bank, Prescott and Phoenix, Ariz.; Fairgrounds, Dallas, Tex.; Pomona, Cal.; Scripps Col., Claremont, Cal. *Exhibited*: PAFA, 1929; Arch.L., 1926; NAD, 1927, 1928; BMFA, 1926, 1931; Grand Central A. Gal.; Boston AC; Philbrook A. Center, 1944, 1946. Lectures: Sculpture.

STEVENS, MAY—*Painter*
152-16 Melbourne Ave., Flushing 67, N.Y.

B. Boston, Mass., June 9, 1924. *Studied*: Mass. Sch. A., B.F.A.; ASL; Julian Acad., Paris; Queens Col.; City Col. of N.Y.; Hunter Col. *Awards*: prize, Silvermine Gld. A., 1958. *Exhibited*: N.Y. City Center, 1957, 1958; Art:USA, 1958; Salon d'Automne, Paris, 1951; Salon de Femmes Peintres, Paris, 1951; BM; Silvermine Gld. A., 1956, 1958; one-man: Galerie Huit, Paris, 1951; Galerie Moderne, N.Y., 1955.

STEVENS, MILDRED LAPSON—
Painter, T., L., W., Ser., Des.
848 Ridgeside Drive, Monrovia, Cal.

B. New York, N.Y., Jan. 4, 1923. *Studied*: BMSch.A.; ASL; Am. Sch. Des., N.Y.; Jepson AI, Los A. *Member*: Conn. WC Soc.; Los A. AA; Pasadena AA; Soc. Western A.; Los A. A.T. Assn.; Nat. A.T. Assn.; AEA. *Awards*: gold medal, City-wide Exh., Rockefeller Center, 1935; scholarships, ASL, BMSch.A., Am. Sch. Des.; prizes, Gregor Beaux-Arts, Hartford; Wadsworth Atheneum; Los A. County Fair, 1951 (2), and others. *Exhibited*: Conn. WC Soc., 1945-1947, 1952; San Gabriel Valley A., Pasadena Mus. A., 1958; BM; MMA; Gregor Beaux-Arts, 1946 (one-man); Long Beach A. Gal., 1953; Pasadena Mus. A., 1954, 1958; Santa Barbara Mus. A., 1954; Oakland A. Mus., 1954; deYoung Mem. Mus., 1954; San Diego FA Gal., 1954; Monrovia Pub. Lib., 1957, 1958; Mid-Valley A. Lg., 1958 (one-man); Pasadena Pub. Lib., 1958; Los A. AA, 1958; Los A. Arboretum, 1958, etc. Contributor to Popular Science; Life magazine (original des. for new toys). *Position*: A.T., Pasadena City College, Los Angeles, Cal.

STEVENS, STANFORD—*Painter, W., T.*
Manuel Mateos 5, Tequisquiapan, Qro., Mexico

B. St. Albans, Vt., Oct. 5, 1897. *Studied*: Harvard Univ., A.B.; Acad. Julian, Paris; ASL. *Member*: AWS. *Work*: Wood A. Gal., Montpelier, Vt.; Rockland (Me.) A. Gal.; IBM; Ford Coll. Author: "Plants of Sun and Sand." *Exhibited*: nationally and internationally.

STEVENS, VERA *(Mrs. Vera Stevens Anderson)*—
Painter, T.
62 Albemarle Rd., Waltham 54, Mass.

B. Hustontown, Pa., Aug. 5, 1895. *Studied*: PMSchIA; & with George Elmer Browne. *Member*: NAWA; Conn. Acad. FA; Provincetown AA. *Exhibited*: Paris Salon, 1929; Conn. Acad. FA; Springfield A. Lg.; New Haven Paint & Clay Cl.; NAD; NAWA; PAFA. *Position*: Instr., Shore Country Day Sch., Beverly, Mass.

STEVENS, W. LESTER—*Painter*
Cricket Hill, Conway, Mass.

B. Rockport, Mass., June 16, 1888. *Studied*: BMFA Sch.; & with Parker S. Perkins. *Member*: NA; AWCS; Rockport AA; Springfield (Mass.) A. Lg.; Gld. Boston A.; Phila. WC Cl.; N.Y. WC Cl.; New Haven Paint & Clay Cl.; North Shore AA; Boston WC Cl. *Awards*: prizes, Wash. Landscape Cl., 1939; Mass. Fed. Women's Cl., 1930-1933; Meriden, Conn., 1938-1942; Springville, Utah, 1931, 1941; Wash. WC Cl., 1942; Wash. A. Cl., 1941; Rockport AA, 1953, 1956, 1957; North Shore AA, 1953; Ogunquit, Me., 1952-1954, 1956; Gloucester, Mass., 1958; CGA, 1921; Conn. Acad. FA, 1924; NAD, 1927; AWCS, 1928; New Haven Paint & Clay Cl., 1929, 1933, 1942; Springfield A. Lg., 1932, 1953-1955; med., Quincy A. Lg., 1932. *Work*: Canton AI; Hickory Mus. A.; Asheville Mus. A.; Rochester Mem. A. Gal.; Springfield Mus. FA; Boston AC; Birmingham (Ala.) Pub. Lib.; Gloucester (Mass.) H.S.; Rockport (Mass.) H.S.; Tewksburg (Mass.) State Sanitorium; Mint Mus. A.; USPO, Dedham, Rockport, Mass.

STEVENSON, AMY LEANOR—*Painter, C., Des., T.*
220 Sullivan St., New York 12, N.Y.

B. St. Sylvestre, Que., Canada. *Studied*: CUASch.; NAD; ASL, and with Hawthorne, Savage, Brackman. *Member*: A. All. Am.; Gotham Painters; Catherine L. Wolfe A. Cl.; AAPL; NAC. *Awards*: Tiffany Fnd. F., 1923; prizes, A. All. Am., 1928. *Exhibited*: Arch. Lg.; Soc. Indp. A.; AWS; WMA, 1953, 1954; Salons of Am.; Tiffany Fnd.; Anderson Gal.; Barbizon-Plaza Gal.; Catherine L. Wolfe

A. Cl., 1953, 1954; NAC, 1954, 1955; Calgary (Can.) All. A. Centre, 1956 (one-man); NAD, 1956; Village A. Center, 1958. Des., rugs, for Capitol Palace, Manila, P.I.; Veterans Mem. Civic Center, Detroit, Mich.; Des., Persian Rug Mfg. Co.

STEVENSON, BEULAH—*Painter, Lith.*
252 Fulton St. (1); h. 99 Lafayette Ave., Brooklyn 17, N.Y.

B. Brooklyn, N.Y. *Studied*: ASL, with John Sloan, and with Hans Hofmann, Provincetown, Mass. *Member*: NAWA; Fed. Mod. P. & S.; Creative AA; N.Y. Soc. Women A.; SAGA; Phila. Pr. Cl.; Brooklyn Soc. A.; Provincetown AA. *Awards*: BM; Brooklyn Soc. A.; NAWA. *Work*: N.Y. Pub. Lib. *Exhibited*: PAFA; Phila. Pr. Cl.; AIC; BM; Riverside Mus.; CM; Portland Mus. A., and many other museums and galleries in U.S. and abroad including Paris and London. One-man: Mus. New Mexico, Santa Fé; 9 one-man in New York City.

STEVENSON, BRANSON GRAVES—
Graphic Artist, C., P., L.
301 Barber Lydiard Bldg.; h. 715 Fourth Ave., North, Great Falls, Mont.

B. Franklin County, Ga., Apr. 5, 1901. *Studied*: A. Sch.; Instituto Nacional, Panama; & with Roberto Luiz. *Member*: SAGA; Great Falls AA. *Work*: Montana Hist. Soc.; State Capitol, Helena, Mont.; mural, Army Air Base, Great Falls, Mont. *Exhibited*: Henry Gal., Univ. Wash.; Portland Ceramic Studios; Spokane, Wash.; traveling exh., Germany; Univ. Montana, 1958; Montana State Fair, 1953-1958. Lectures: Graphic Arts Processes. Contributor articles on Ceramic pottery, processes and glazes, to Craft Horizons and Ceramic Age magazines. *Position*: Chm., Dept. FA, Montana State Fair, Great Falls, Mont., 1942- . Advisory Counsel to Bd. Dir., Montana Inst. of the Arts, Vice-Pres., 1954-55; One of Fndrs., Dir., Sec., The Archie Bray Fnd., Helena Mont.; One of the Fndrs., Dir., Chm. Exhs., C. M. Russell Gallery, Great Falls, Mont.

STEVENSON, EDNA BRADLEY—*Painter, E., L.*
1419 North West 24th St., Oklahoma City 6, Okla.

B. Hebron, Neb., Feb. 8, 1887. *Studied*: AIC; Univ. Cal. at Los A.; Univ. Illinois; Julian Acad., Paris; Oklahoma City Univ., B.F.A.; & with Emil Bisttram, Snow Froelich, & others. *Member*: Okla. State AA; NEA; NAEA; Okla. Edu. Assn. *Exhibited*: Philbrook A. Center; Assn. Okla. A.; Okla. State AA; one-man exh.: Okla. A. Center; Okla. City Univ., 1958; Okla. Medical Research Fnd., 1958; Okla. State Fair; Santa Fé, N.M.; Harwood Gal., Taos, N.M. *Position*: Hd. A. Dept., Classen H.S., 1921-43; Dir. A., Oklahoma City Univ., Oklahoma City, Okla., 1943-1958 (Retired).

STEVENSON, ELAINE LOUISE—*Craftsman, E.*
911 West South St., Kalamazoo, Mich.

B. Port Huron, Mich., Apr. 13, 1891. *Studied*: Western Michigan Univ.; AIC, B.A.E.; Ohio State Univ., M.A.; Cranbrook Acad. A.; Columbus Sch. A.; & with Emma M. Church. *Exhibited*: Kansas City AI; Norton Gal., West Palm Beach, Fla.; & in Michigan, Ohio. *Position*: Asst. Prof., A. Edu., FA, Western Michigan Univ., Kalamazoo, Mich., 1917- .

STEVENSON, FLORENCE EZZELL (Mrs. Earle D.)—
Painter, L., Des.
9411 Longwood Dr., Chicago 20, Ill.

B. Russellville, Ala. *Studied*: Athens Col.; Tuscaloosa Conservatory of A. & Music; AIC; Chicago Acad. FA. *Member*: AAPL; SSAL; All-Illinois Soc. FA; No-Jury Soc. A.; South Side AA; Mun. A. Lg., Chicago; Nat. Lg. Am. Pen Women; Chicago A. Cl.; Ridge AA, Chicago; The Cordon. *Awards*: medals, All-Illinois Soc. FA, 1936; prizes, South Side AA, 1939; Ill. Fed. Women's Cl., 1940; Nat. Lg. Am. Pen Women, 1945-1957; Cordon Cl., 1950; AIC. *Work*: Rosenwald Coll.; Hanover Col., Indiana; Vanderpoel Coll.; Mun. Bldg., Russellville, Ala.; Morgan Park H.S., Chicago; Sutherland Sch., Gage Park Sch., Chicago; Midlothian (Ill.) Sch. *Exhibited*: AIC; The Parthenon, Nashville, Tenn.; one-man: Birmingham Pub. Lib.; The Cordon, Chicago; Drake, Congress hotels, Chicago; Smithsonian Inst., 1948, 1954; Brooks Mem. Mus.; Ridge AA; Vanderpoel A. Gal.; Birmingham A. Cl.;

Chicago A. Cl., and others. Paintings on covers of La ReVue Moderne, Paris; Christian Science Monitor; Art World; Literary Digest, and others.

STEVENSON, GORDON—*Portrait Painter*
48 Gramercy Park, New York 10, N.Y.; s. R.F.D. Parksville, Sullivan County, N.Y.

B. Chicago, Ill., Feb. 28, 1892. *Studied*: AIC; and in Madrid, Spain with Sorolla. *Member*: Am. Veteran's Soc. A.; Century Assn. *Awards*: John Quincy Adams traveling scholarship, 1911-12. *Work*: BM; Rutgers Univ.; Harvard Univ.; Col. of City N.Y.; Rockefeller Inst., and in many private colls. *Exhibited*: AIC; NAD; European traveling exh. American Portraits; one-man exhs., throughout eastern U.S.

STEVENSON, RUTH ROLSTON (Mrs. Bruce)—
Painter, T., Et.
41 Union Square; h. 26 West 9th St., New York 11, N.Y.

B. Brooklyn, N.Y., May 27, 1897. *Studied*: PIASch.; ASL, with John Sloan. *Member*: NAC; Pen & Brush Cl.; NAWA; AWS. *Awards*: prizes, Small Paintings Exh., 1928; Pen & Brush Cl., 1951, 1954; SC, 1955. *Work*: in private colls. *Exhibited*: NAC, 1923, 1931, 1953, 1955; NAWA, 1949-1956; AWS, 1954, 1955; Holland, 1956.*

STEVENSON, SUZANNE SILVERCRUYS. see *Silver-*
cruys, Suzanne

STEWART, ALBERT T.—*Sculptor*
4215 Via Padova, Claremont, Cal.

B. Kensington, England, Apr. 9, 1900. *Studied*: BAID; ASL, and with Paul Manship. *Member*: NSS; Am. Mus. Natural Hist.; NA. *Awards*: silver medal, BAID, 1923; gold medal, NAD, 1927; gold medal, PAFA, 1928; prizes, NAD, 1931, citation, 1955; Arch. Lg., 1932; Los A. County Fair, Pomona, 1940, 1949; Chaffey AA, 1951; Pasadena AI, 1948. *Work*: MMA; FMA; Allentown Mus. A.; tablets, panels, figures, doors, fountains, etc.: Seamen's Mem., N.Y.; Buffalo (N.Y.) City Hall; St. Paul City Hall and Court House; St. Bartholomew's Church, N.Y.; Am. Battle Monument, Thiacourt, France; Cosmopolitan Cl.; Kansas City Mun. Auditorium; Labor Bldg., Wash., D.C.; Amherst and Williams Colleges; County Court House, Mineola, N.Y.; White House, Wash., D.C.; County Court House, Los A.; Fort Moore Mem., Los A.; Mercantile Bank, Dallas, Tex.; U.S. Mint, San F.; Cal. Inst. Tech.; Scripps Col.; Community Church, Claremont, Cal., and many other churches throughout California; USPO, Albany, N.Y.

STEWART, DAVID—*Painter, T.*
Grafton, Vt.; w. 268 East 241st St., New York 70, N.Y.

B. Glasgow, Scotland, Nov. 27, 1879. *Studied*: ASL; N.Y. Univ. B.S. in Edu.; & with H. Siddons Mowbray, Frank DuMond, & others. *Member*: SC; AAPL; Gotham Painters; Yonkers AA. *Exhibited*: AWCS; All. A. Am.; Bronx A. Gld.; Yonkers AA; NAC, 1942; Gotham Painters; Audubon A.*

STEWART, ESTHER L.—*Painter, T., L.*
Route 3, Colorado Springs, Colo.

B. Moorestown, N.J., Dec. 13, 1895. *Studied*: Swarthmore Col.; PMSchIA; PAFA; Corcoran Sch. A. *Member*: Soc. Wash. A.; Colo. Springs A. Gld. *Work*: murals, numerous hotels & dept. stores; Fairfax County (Va.) Court House; Arabian Embassy; Quantico Marine Cl. *Exhibited*: CGA; PMG; Whyte Gal.; Wash. Pub. Lib.; Colorado Springs, Canon City, Rocky Ford, Colo. *Position*: A. Chm., Va. Cooperative Edu. Assn., 1944-46; Trustee, Va. A. All., VMFA, Richmond, Va., 1945, 1946; Trustee, Colorado Springs FA Center, 1956- .

STEWART, ETHELYN COSBY—*Painter, C., Gr.*
302 East 30th St., New York, N.Y.

B. Arlington, N.J., Jan. 19, 1900. *Studied*: CUASch. *Work*: PAFA; Smithsonian Inst. *Exhibited*: NAD; PAFA.

STEWART, GRACE BLISS (Mrs.)—Painter

50 West 45th St., New York 36, N.Y.

B. Atchison, Kans., Apr. 18, 1895. *Studied*: ASL, and with Charles Hawthorne. *Member*: NAWA; Pen & Brush Cl.; New Hampshire AA. *Awards*: prizes, Pen & Brush Cl. (several); Laconia, N.H. *Exhibited*: Toronto, Canada, 1937; Pen & Brush Cl.; Palm Beach AA; NAWA, annually; New Hampshire AA; Paris, France; Amsterdam, Holland; one-man traveling exh. to U.S. museums for 4 years; 5 one-man exhs., New York City. Author: "The Good Fairy," 1930, and other books.*

STEWART, JARVIS ANTHONY—Educator, P.

Lyon Art Hall, Ohio Wesleyan University; h. 61 Westgate Drive, Delaware, Ohio

B. Maryville, Mo., Dec. 28, 1914. *Studied*: Phillips Univ., Enid, Okla., B.F.A.; San Miguel Allende, Mexico; Ohio State Univ., M.A., Ph.D. *Member*: Am. Studies Assn.; Columbus A. Lg. *Work*: Columbus Gal. FA. *Exhibited*: Art:USA, 1958; Northwest Missouri AA; Oklahoma AA; Oklahoma State Fair; Ohio State Fair; Columbus A. Lg., 1945-1957; Exh. Momentum, Chicago; Interior Valley Exh., 1955; one-man exhs. *Position*: Prof. A., Chm., Dept. FA, Ohio Wesleyan University, Delaware, Ohio, 1953- .

STEWART, LeCONTE—Painter, Gr., E., L.

University of Utah, Salt Lake City, Utah; h. 172 West 1st South, Kaysville, Utah

B. Glenwood, Utah, Apr. 15, 1891. *Studied*: Univ. Utah; ASL; PAFA; & with Edwin Evans, Frank DuMond, George Bridgman, & others. *Member*: Assoc. Utah A. *Awards*: prizes, Utah State Fair, 1915, 1937; Utah AI, 1916; Art Barn, Utah State prize, 1938. *Work*: Utah State Coll.; Springville (Utah) H.S.; Ogden City Coll.; Univ. Utah; Utah Agricultural Col.; Kaysville City Coll.; Springville, Utah; Ricks Col., Rexburg, Idaho; Heyburn (Idaho) Pub. Sch. Coll.; murals, Hotel Ben Lomond, Ogden; L.D.S. Temples, Canada, Hawaii, Arizona; Denver State House. *Exhibited*: Painters of the West, 1928; Colorado Graphic AC, 1938-1940; Springville, Utah, 1940; Utah AI, 1941; Assoc. Utah A., 1945; Ogden Palette Cl., 1945, 1955; Salt Lake City, 1955 (one-man); Heyburn, Idaho, 1946; Boulder (Colo.) Women's Cl., 1946. Lectures: Graphic Arts; Mural Painting. *Position*: Hd. Dept. A., Prof. A., Univ. Utah, Salt Lake City, Utah, 1938-1956.

STEWART, MARIE H.—Painter, Des., C., T., W.

R. R. #1, Oxford, Ohio

B. Eaton, Ohio, Aug. 20, 1887. *Studied*: PIASch.; John Herron AI; Butler Univ., B.F.A., M.S. *Member*: Indiana State T. Soc.; NEA; NAEA; AAUW; Indianapolis AA; Indiana A. Cl. *Awards*: Lincoln tablet des., 1907; prizes, Hoosier Salon, 1942. *Exhibited*: PIASch.; Indiana A., 1936-1951; John Herron AI, 1957; CM, 1957; Oxford A. Cl., 1952-1957; Hoosier Salon; and others. Contributor to Design Magazine; School Arts Magazine. Author: Legal Status of Indiana Teachers; co-author radio script "Art Adventures." *Position*: Supv. A., Indianapolis Pub. Schs., 1918-43; Asst. Dir. A., in charge of A. Edu., Indianapolis, Ind., 1943-52 (retired).

STILES, JOSEPH E(DWIN)—Educator, P., Lith.

Art Department, Kansas Wesleyan University; h. 508 West Iron Ave., Salina, Kans.

B. Spring Hill, Kans., Oct. 14, 1931. *Studied*: Univ. Kansas, B.F.A., M.A.; Univ. New Mexico; ASL, with Louis Bouche, Will Barnet. *Member*: AAUP. *Award*: prize, Kansas Painters, 1953. *Exhibited*: Balt. WC Cl., 1953; CM, 1954; Terry AI, 1952; Kansas Painters, 1953, 1954; Missouri Valley, 1953; Friends of Art Biennial, 1958; Nelson Gal. A., 1958; one-man: Oklahoma A. Center, 1953; Baker Univ., 1958. *Position*: Asst. Prof. A., Hd. A. Dept., Kansas Wesleyan University, Salina, Kans.

STEWART, MARION LOUISE—Painter

94 Olean St., East Aurora, N.Y.

B. Buffalo, N.Y. *Studied*: Radcliffe Col., A.B.; Ecole des Beaux-Arts, Fontainebleau, France; Columbia Univ.; ASL. *Member*: The Patteran. *Awards*: prize, Albright A. Gal., 1938. *Exhibited*: WFNY 193; Carnegie Inst., 1941.*

STILLMAN, ARY—Painter

66 Avenue de Chatillon, Paris 14e, France

B. Russia, Feb. 13, 1891. *Studied*: AIC; NAD; ASL, and with Andre Lhote, Paris, France. *Member*: Fed. Mod. P. & S. *Work*: New Britain (Conn.) Mus. A.; Mus. FA of Houston; Sioux City A. Center. *Exhibited*: Salon des Beaux-Arts, Paris, 1926, 1927, 1933; Salon d'Automne, 1928; Salon des Tuileries, 1930, 1933; PAFA, 1929, 1934, 1937, 1946, 1949; Carnegie Inst., 1943, 1945; WMAA, 1948-1952; BM, 1949, 1951, 1953; CAM, 1929 (one-man); CGA, 1949; AIC, 1929, 1934, 1947, 1952; Cal. PLH, 1937; deYoung Mem. Mus., 1947; VMFA, 1951; Nelson Gal. A., Kansas City, 1947; Wadsworth Atheneum, 1944; Inst. Mod. A., Boston, 1945 and many others.*

STILWELL, WILBER MOORE—
Educator, P., Des., Gr., L., I., W.

University of South Dakota, Vermillion, S.D.

B. Covington, Ind., Feb. 2, 1908. *Studied*: Kansas City AI; Kansas State T. Col., B.S. in Edu.; State Univ. Iowa, M.A. *Member*: Am. Assn. Univ. Prof.; South Dakota Edu. Assn. *Awards*: med., Kansas City AI, 1933, 1936; prizes, Oklahoma A. Exh., Tulsa, 1940; Kansas A. Exh., Topeka, 1941. *Exhibited*: PAFA, 1934; Kansas City AI, 1933, 1936, 1939; Topeka, Kan., 1939-1941; Missouri A., 1938; Tulsa, Okla., 1940. Lectures: Contemporary Art. Co-author, articles for art education and education magazines. *Position*: Hd. A. Dept., Prof. A., Univ. South Dakota, Vermillion, S.D., 1941- . Fndr., Dir., South Dakota Annual H.S. Art Comp.

STIMPSON, HELEN TOWNSEND—Painter

294 Collins St., Hartford 5, Conn.

B. Brooklyn, N.Y., May 30, 1886. *Studied*: NAD; CUASch.; & with Emil Carlsen, Charles Hawthorne. *Member*: Springfield Academic A.; Conn. Acad. FA; Rockport AA; Hartford Soc. Women Painters; New Haven Paint & Clay Cl.; North Shore AA. *Awards*: prizes, Hartford Soc. Women Painters, 1940; New Haven Paint & Clay Cl., 1941. *Exhibited*: Conn. Acad. FA, 1923-1956; New Haven Paint & Clay Cl., 1925-1956; Hartford Soc. Women Painters, 1928-1956.*

STINSON, HARRY (EDWARD)—Sculptor, E.

Hunter College, 695 Park Ave.; h. 446 East 66th St., New York 21, N.Y.

B. Wayland, Iowa, Jan. 3, 1898. *Studied*: Univ. Iowa, B.A., M.F.A.; Cumming Sch. A.; NAD; ASL. *Member*: AAUP; Audubon A.; Sculpture Center; CAA. *Awards*: prizes, Kansas City AI, 1935. *Work*: mem., statues, Lake View, Council Bluffs, Iowa City, Iowa. *Exhibited*: PAFA, 1930, 1931, 1948; Kansas City AI, 1935; Nebraska AA, 1942; Sculpture Center, 1944-1946, 1948-1958; Grand Central Palace, 1950; Bennington Col., 1949, 1956; Nebraska AA, 1950; Des Moines A. Center, 1953, 1956, 1958; Audubon A., 1954-1958; NAD, 1929, 1955; Staten Island Mus., 1955, 1956; Wash. A. Cl., 1954; Phila. A. All., 1952. *Position*: Prof., Hunter Col., New York, N.Y.

STIRLING, DAVE—Painter

Estes Park, Colo.

B. Corydon, Iowa, Jan. 24, 1889. *Studied*: Chicago Acad. FA; Cumming A. Sch. *Award*: Hon. deg., D.F.A., Kansas Wesleyan Univ., 1954. *Exhibited*: one-man exh. in "Studio in the Woods," Rocky Mountain Nat. Park, 1922-1956. *Position*: Resident Landscape Painter, Rocky Mountain National Park, Colo.; How Deg Doctor of Aesthetics, Sterling Col., Sterling, Kans., 1957.

STITES, RAYMOND SOMERS—
Educator, Historian, W., L.

11212 Kenilworth Ave., Garrett Park, Md.

B. Passaic, N.J., June 19, 1899. *Studied*: Brown Univ., A.M.; R.I. Sch. Des.; & in Vienna, Austria. *Member*: CAA; Am. Archaeological Soc.; Ohio Valley AA. *Exhibited*: MMA; Denver Archaeological Mus.; Dayton AI; Am. Mus. Natural Hist. Author: "The Arts and Man," 1940. Contributor to: Art magazines. Lectures: Leonardo da Vinci. *Position*: Chm., Dept. A. & Aesthetics, Antioch Col., Yellow Springs, Ohio, 1930-48; Cur. in charge of Edu., Nat. Gal. Art, Washington, D.C., 1948- ; Dir., Culture Films, Inc.

STODDARD, ALICE KENT (PEARSON)—*Painter*

8235 Seminole St., Philadelphia 18, Pa.

B. Watertown, Conn. *Studied*: Phila. Sch. Des. for Women; PAFA. *Member*: ANA; F., PAFA. *Awards*: Cresson Scholarship; Clark prize and Isadore Medal, NAD, 1917, 1928; gold medal, Phila. A. Cl.; prize, PAFA. *Work*: PAFA; Reading, Pa.; Dallas, Tex.; ports., Supreme and Federal Court Judges, Pa. *Exhibited*: CGA; PAFA, 1912-1957; NAD; Albright A. Gal.; BM; Wilmington A. Cl.; PM; Phila. A. All.; Woodmere A. Gal., Phila.; Newport, R.I.; Conn. Acad. FA; and others.

STODDARD, DONNA MELISSA—*Educator*, W., L., P.

Florida Southern College; h. 925 East Lexington St., Lakeland, Fla.

B. St. Petersburg, Fla., July 1, 1916. *Studied*: Fla. Southern Col., B.S.; Pittsburgh AI; Pennsylvania State Col., M.A.; N.Y. Sch. Int. Des. *Member*: Am. Assn. Univ. Women; Fla. Fed. A.; Southeastern AA; Nat. AA; CAA; Southeastern Col. AA. *Awards*: prizes, AAPL, 1951; Am. Culture Award, 1952; Fla. Southern Col., 1942. *Work*: Directed the Fla. Int. A. Exh., 1952; Organized and installed permanent Contemporary art collection of Fla. Southern Col.; contributor to Design magazine; arranges exhibitions for Fla. Southern Col., and other organizations. *Position*: Dir. A., Fla. Southern Col., Lakeland, Fla.

STODDARD, MUSETTE OSLER—*Painter*, C., T., L.

Skyline Cabin, Nashville, Ind.

B. Carson, Iowa. *Studied*: AIC; & with Ralph Johonnot, Charles Hawthorne, & others. *Member*: Brown County A. Gld.; Indiana AC; Indiana Weaver's Gld.; Hoosier Salon. *Awards*: med., Pan-Pacific Exp., 1915.*

STOESSEL, OSKAR—*Etcher*, P., T.

Carnegie Hall, West 57th St., New York 19, N.Y.

B. Neonkirchen, Austria, Jan. 17, 1879. *Studied*: in Europe. *Member*: AAPL; CAA. *Awards*: several prizes & med., Austria. *Work*: MMA; British Mus.; & in Germany, Austria, Roumania. *Exhibited*: CGA (one-man); Harlow Gal. (one-man). Contributor to: Print Collector's Quarterly, London; & other art publications in Europe. Folio of etchings of many prominent persons.

STOFFA, MICHAEL—*Painter*, T., Cr., L.

36 Prospect St., Westfield, N.J.; h. 168 Plainfield Ave., Metuchen, N.J.

B. Hlinne, Czechoslovakia, Dec. 18, 1923. *Studied*: Newark Sch. F. & Indst. A.; PAFA, with Walter Stuempfig, Hobson Pittman; ASL, with Robert Philipp. *Member*: New Brunswick A. Center; New Brunswick Work Shop Group; Rahway A. Center; Cranford Creative A. Group. *Awards*: Scholarship, Newark Sch. F. & Indst. A.; prizes, Plainfield AA, 1950; New Brunswick A. Center, 1957, 1958. *Exhibited*: ASL, 1957; Old Mill AA, 1957, 1958; PAFA, 1951; Rahway A. Center, 1958; Cranford AA, 1958; Westfield AA, 1958; New Brunswick AA, 1956-1958; Asbury Park, N.J., 1958; Burr Gal., 1958; Crespi Gal., N.Y., 1958.

STOLL, JOHN (THEODOR) (EDWARD)—*Etcher*, P., S.

Box 382, San Anselmo, Cal.

B. Goettingen, Germany. *Studied*: Acad. FA, Dresden, Germany; Cal. Sch. FA. *Member*: San F. AA; Cal. SE (Pres. 1948-54). *Awards*: prize, Cal. SE, 1924, 1936, 1948, 1950. *Work*: Palace Legion Honor; SFMA; Mills Col.; Oakland A. Gal.; Cal. Historical Soc.; Buckingham Palace, London; Marine Mus., San F.; Achenbach Fnd., San F.; Ain Harod and Tel-Aviv Mus., Jerusalem; mem. mural & sculpture, Sailors Union of the Pacific. *Exhibited*: Int. Pr. M., Los A., 1930-1953; Cal. SE; AIC; CAM; CMA; Honolulu Acad. A.; SAM; Boise, Idaho, 1938, 1942; Stanford Univ.; SFMA, 1941, 1942; Univ. Nevada, 1943; LC, 1949; Carnegie Inst., 1949; Palacio des Bellas Artes, Mexico City; & in Madrid, Spain; Rome, Italy; Caracas, Venezuela, 1954. Lectures: Etching.*

STOLL, ROLF—*Portrait Painter*

120 Bryn Mawr Drive, Lake Worth, Fla.

B. Heidelberg, Germany, Nov. 11, 1892. *Studied*: Acad. FA, Karlsruhe; Acad. FA, Stuttgart, Germany. *Member*:

Cleveland Pr. Cl. *Awards*: prizes, CMA, 1925, 1926, 1933, 1934, 1937, 1938, 1940-1944; Butler AI, 1942, 1943. *Work*: CMA; Columbus Gal. FA; Univ. Nebraska; Army Medical Lib., Wash., D.C.; Western Reserve Univ.; Mun. Coll., Case Sch. App. Sc., Fed. Reserve Bank, Bd. Edu. Bldg., all in Cleveland, Ohio; U.S. Supreme Court; Ohio Supreme Court; NAD; Duke Univ.; Rutgers Univ.; Univ. Akron; mural, USPO, East Palestine, Ohio. *Exhibited*: PAFA, 1933, 1937; Carnegie Inst., 1941; GGE, 1939; WFNY 1939; AIC, 1940; CM, 1943; CMA, 1925-1954; Butler AI, 1932, 1934-1937, 1942-1944. Lectures: History of Art. *Position*: Hd., Dept. Portrait Painting, Cleveland Inst. A., 1928-1937.

STOLOFF, CAROLYN—*Painter*

Studio 404, 2 West 15th St., New York, N.Y.

B. New York, N.Y., 1927. *Studied*: Univ. Illinois; Columbia Univ., B.S.; with Xavier Gonzalez, Eric Isenburger, and abroad. *Exhibited*: PAFA; Laurel Gal.; Audubon A.; NAD; Argent Gal.; Contemp. A. Gal.; Ross Gal.; Westchester Gld. A. & Crafts; Arthur Brown Gal.; WMAA; ACA Gal.; New Jersey Soc. P. & S.; Long Island A.Lg.; N.Y. City Center.*

STOLOFF, IRMA (Mrs. Charles I.)—*Sculptor*

46 East 91st St., New York 28, N.Y.

B. New York, N.Y. *Studied*: ASL, and with Alexander Archipenko. *Member*: NAWA; AEA; ASL. *Award*: NAWA, 1953. *Exhibited*: Salons of Am., 1931; Woodstock Gal., 1934; Argent Gal., 1947, 1958; NAWA, 1947-1956; NAD, 1950, 1953; New Jersey Soc. P. & S., 1955; Art: USA, 1958; Silvermine Gld A., 1957; and in Paris, France. Work reproduced in many art publications in Mexico, Paris, Rome, and Buenos Aires; Sculpture Jury, NAWA, 1952-54, 1955-57.

STOLTENBERG, HANS JOHN—*Painter*, T.

2570 Pilgrim Rd., Brookfield, Wis.

B. Flensburg, Germany (now Denmark), Apr. 8, 1879. *Studied*: Milwaukee AI. *Awards*: prizes, Milwaukee Journal Comp., 1918; Milwaukee AI, 1920, 1940. *Work*: Oshkosh Mus.; Madison Hist. Mus.; Milwaukee AI; Whitewater State T. Col.; Kenosha Hist. Mus.; Carroll Col.; Country Day Sch., Milwaukee; Vanderpoel Coll., and in many private colls.

STONE, ALLEN—*Painter*, T., L.

50-16 41st St., Long Island City 4, N.Y.

B. New York, N.Y., Feb. 19, 1910. *Studied*: NAD, with Sidney Dickinson, Leon Kroll, Raymond Neilson, Ivan Olinsky; ASL, with Maxwell Starr. *Member*: ASL; Am. Veterans Soc. A. *Awards*: prizes, Army Regional Exh., Fla., 1946; Citation, Fla. Southern Col., 1953; Am. Veterans Soc. A., 1957. *Work*: Grumbacher Coll.; Fla. Southern Col.; Burke Fnd.; Beth David Hospital, N.Y.; Seton Hall Univ., and in private colls. *Exhibited*: CAA traveling exh.; Laguna Beach A. Center; Soc. Indp. A.; Minnesota State Fair; Minneapolis, Minn.; All. A. Acad., N.Y.; Tallahassee, Fla.; Grand Central A. Gal.; Lynn Kottler Gal.; Mun. Gal., N.Y.; Insel Gal., N.Y., 1958; N.Y. City Center. Compiled books on Art Techniques of Famous Present Day Illustrators, 1951; contributor illus. to many national magazines. Lectures and demonstrations, New York and New Jersey. *Position*: Instr., Caton Rose Inst. FA, Long Island; Sch. Adv. A., Newark, N.J.

STONE, (RUTH) ANDRESS—*Painter*, C., Gr., W.

4400 Wildwood Dr., Shreveport, La.

B. St. Louis, Mo., Nov. 8, 1914. *Studied*: Univ. Missouri, B.F.A.; AIC; Kansas City AI, and with Charles Schroeder, John McCrady, Ross Braught, and others. *Member*: Shreveport A. Cl.; Louisiana A., Inc.; Allison Wells A. Colony. *Awards*: prizes, Missouri State Fair, 1946, 1948-1951; Mississippi AA, 1947, 1948; Louisiana State Fair, 1955-1957; "Holiday in Dixie" exh., 1955; Regional A. Exh., 1955. *Exhibited*: Little Rock, Ark.; Allisons Wells, Miss.; New Orleans, 1955; Shreveport Regional, 1954-1957; Baton Rouge, 1957, 1958; Joslyn A. Mus.; Nelson Gal. A.; La. State Fair, 1955-1957; one-man: Tulsa, Okla., 1955; Philbrook A. Center; and others. Author: "Enameling on Copper," 1952; A.T., Southfield School, Shreveport, La., 1956-58.

STONE, BEATRICE (Mrs. J. C.)—Sculptor
630 Park Ave., New York 21, N.Y.

B. New York, N.Y., Dec. 10, 1900. *Studied*: Smith Col.; in Paris, France, and with Heinz Warneke, Jacques Loutchansky (Paris). *Member*: NSS; All. A. Am.; NAWA; N.Y. Soc. Women A.; N.Y. Ceramic Soc.; Scarsdale AA. *Awards*: prizes, Huntington award, 1943; Scarsdale AA; Westchester A. & Crafts Assn. *Work*: Ethical Culture Soc.; Hudson Gld.; Aluminum Corp of Am., and in private colls. *Exhibits*: PAFA, 1938, 1942, 1949, 1950, 1951, 1953; AIC, 1944; PMA, 1949; NAD, 1940; Audubon A., 1950-1958; Arch. Lg.; Scarsdale AA, 1948-1955; Phila. A. All., 1946; WMAA, 1949, and others. One-man: Van Dieman-Lilienfeld Gal., 1952; San Diego FA Soc., 1953; deYoung Mus. A., San F., 1953; Atlanta AA, 1958; St. Louis A. Mart, 1958.

STONE, FERN CUNNINGHAM (Mrs. Ernest)—
Painter, T., L., C.
16054 Northfield Ave., Pacific Palisades, Cal.

B. Defiance, Ohio, Aug. 4, 1889. *Studied*: Defiance Col.; Van Emburg Sch. A., Plainfield, N.J.; Fontainebleau Sch. FA, France and with John Carlson, George Elmer Browne. *Member*: NAWA; Toledo AA; Nat. A. Fnd., Hollywood; Nat. Lg. Am. Pen Women; Miami AA; Sarasota AA; St. Petersburg AA; Santa Monica AA; AAPL; Nat. FA Fnd., Hollywood; Fontainebleau Alumni Assn.; Pacific Palisades AA. *Work*: Bryan Pub. Lib.; Defiance H.S. *Awards*: prizes, Pacific Palisades AA. *Exhibited*: Cleveland, Ohio; Argent Gal.; Butler AI; Toledo Mus. A.; Greeneville (S.C.) A. Mus.; Studio Gld.; Pa.-Ohio traveling exh.; Florida A. Center; N.Y. Mun. Exh.; Miami Women's Cl.; Sarasota A. Gal.; Tampa Univ.; Palladium, Hollywood; AAPL; Pacific Palisades A. Center, and others. *Position*: Pres., Santa Monica Chptr., Nat. Lg. Am. Pen Women; Nat. A. Chm., Nat. Soc. A. & Lets., Santa Monica; Dir., Nat. FA Fnd., Hollywood; and others.

STONE, HELEN—Illustrator, Des., P.
819 Madison Ave., New York 21, N.Y.

B. Englewood, N.J., Oct. 31, 1903. *Studied*: N.Y. Sch. I. & App. A.; & in Paris, France. *Exhibited*: Delphic Studios, N.Y., 1932 (one-man); Fed. A. Exh., N.Y., 1944. I., "Horse Who Lived Upstairs," 1944; "Plain Princess," 1945; "Bundle Book"; "The Most Wonderful Doll in the World"; "A Tree for Me"; "Little Ballet Dancer"; "Cats and People," and many others. Contributor to: Horn Book. Lectures: Book Printing.*

STONE, IVA GOLDHAMER—Painter, T.
3360 Kenmore Rd., Shaker Heights 22, Ohio

B. Cleveland, Ohio, July 2, 1917. *Studied*: Cleveland Sch. A. *Position*: Instr., Advertising Layout, Cleveland Sch. A., Cleveland, Ohio.*

STONE, LOUIS K.—Painter
Coon Path, Lambertville, N.J.

B. Findlay, Ohio, July 22, 1902. *Studied*: Cincinnati A. Acad.; PAFA; ASL; & with Hans Hofmann, Munich; Andre L'Hote, Paris. *Work*: mural panels, Fla. State Col. for Women, Tallahassee, Fla. *Exhibited*: WFNY 1939; Am. A. Cong., 1937, 1938; Newark Mus.; Phila. A. All.; Woodstock, N.Y.; Jacksonville, Fla.; Princeton, N.J.; New Hope, Pa.; State Mus., Trenton, N.J., 1958, & traveling exh.

STONE, MAYSIE—Sculptor
2 East 23rd St.; h. 414 West 118th St., New York 27, N.Y.

B. New York, N.Y. *Studied*: Cornell Univ.; Univ. Wisconsin, B.A.; PAFA; & with Charles Grafly, Albert Laessle. *Exhibited*: PAFA; NAD; Arch. L.; Salon de Printemps, Paris; Smithsonian Inst.; AEA.

STONE, SEYMOUR MILLAIS—Painter
39 West 67th St., Apt. 1204, New York 23, N.Y.

B. Poland, June 11, 1877. *Studied*: Julian Acad., Paris; Royal Acad., Munich; AIC; ASL; & with John Singer Sargent, Anders Zorn, & others. *Member*: Royal Soc. A., London; AAPL. *Awards*: Knight Commander of Merit of Constantinian Order of St. George, 1921. *Work*: port.,

Peekskill Military Acad., N.Y.; Peekskill Lib.; Rollins Col.; Ft. Worth Cl.; Brown Univ.; Univ. Virginia; Smithsonian Inst.; State House, Montgomery, Ala.; Army & Navy Cl., N.Y.; U.S. Military Acad., West Point, N.Y.; Texas Mem. Mus., Austin; White House, Wash., D.C.; & many more. *Exhibited*: CGA; AIC; Guild Hall, London, England; N.Y. Hist. Soc.; A. & M. Col., Charlottesville, Va.

STONE, STANFORD BYRON—Painter, Des., I.
81 State St., Brooklyn 1, N.Y.

B. Denver, Colo., Mar. 17, 1906. *Studied*: Col. City of N.Y.; ASL. *Member*: NAC; Brooklyn SA; New Rochelle AA; A. Lg. Nassau: All.A.Am. *Exhibited*: PAFA, 1932; NAD, 1934, 1935; Montross Gal., 1941 (one-man); Community Gal., 1939 (one-man); All.A.Am., 1932-1936, 1938, 1939, 1941, 1943, 1944; Huntington Mus., 1941 (one-man); Neville Pub. Mus., 1942; Kenosha A. Mus., 1942. I., children's books. Lectures: Figure Drawing. *Position*: Indst. A. Adv. Dir., freelance agency, and indst. manufacturers.

STONE, WILLIAM ELLSWORTH—Painter
815 North Walnut Ave., Alliance, Ohio

B. Limaville, Ohio, Jan. 20, 1895. *Studied*: Youngstown Col.; & with Charles Murphy, Louis Evans, Clyde Singer, & others. *Awards*: prizes, Stark Co., Canton, Ohio, 1928; Butler AI, 1941, 1944-1946, 1956; Midland, Pa., 1958; All. A. Center, 1955; Canton AI, 1943. *Work*: Butler AI. *Exhibited*: AWCS, 1939; Butler AI, 1947-1952, 1957 (one-man); Parkersburg FA Center; Canton AI; Massillon, Ohio; Athens, Ohio; Akron AI, 1948; Phila. A. All., 1957.

STONEBARGER, VIRGINIA—Teacher, P.
Route #1, Hartland, Wis.

B. Ann Arbor, Mich., Mar. 9, 1926. *Studied*: Antioch Col.; Colorado Springs FA Center; ASL; Hans Hofmann; N.Y. Univ. *Awards*: Scholarship, Colo. Springs FA Center; ASL; Hans Hofmann; N.Y. Univ.; prize, Watertown, Wis., 1958. *Exhibited*: Univ. Minnesota, 1954; Art:USA, 1958; ACA Gal., 1951, 1952; Urban Gal. Group, 1953; one-man: Panoras Gal., N.Y., 1958; Watertown, Wis., 1958. *Position*: A. T., University Lake School, Hartland, Wis.

STONIER, LUCILLE HOLDERNESS (Mrs. Harold)—
Painter, C., Comm. A.
200 North Griffing Blvd., Asheville, N.C.

B. Uvalde, Tex., Apr. 24, 1890. *Studied*: Col. of Pacific, Stockton, Cal.; Chouinard AI; Parsons Sch. Des.; & with Eliot O'Hara, Lester W. Stevens, S. Peter Wagner. *Member*: Lg. Am. Pen Women; Asheville (N.C.) A. Gld.; Black Mountain AC; Palm Beach A. Lg.; SSAL. *Awards*: prizes, Palm Beach A. Lg., 1938, 1944; Fla. State Fed., 1944; Lg. Am. Pen Women, 1941, 1955; First Nat. Bank Exh., Asheville, 1955. *Work*: Norton Gal., West Palm Beach, Fla.; Veteran's Hospital, Otean, N.C. *Exhibited*: Lg. Am. Pen Women, 1945, 1946; Norton Gal., 1942 (one-man); West Palm Beach A. Lg., 1938, 1942, 1943, 1945, 1946; Asheville A. Gld., 1936, 1940 (one-man); Orlando, Fla., 1952 (one-man); Little A. Gal., 1954 and Victorian Gal., 1955 (one-man), Asheville; Southeastern States Exh.; Manor Hotel Gal.; and others.

STORM, LA RUE—Painter, Et., Lith.
3737 Justison Road, Coconut Grove, Miami, Fla.

B. Pittsburgh, Pa., Oct. 23, 1908. *Studied*: Univ. Miami, Coral Gables, Fla.; ASL, Woodstock, N.Y., and in France. *Member*: Miami AA; Florida A. Group; AEA. *Award*: gold medal, Univ. Miami, 1955. *Exhibited*: Detroit Inst. A., 1952, 1957; Southeastern Annual, Atlanta, 1950, 1953, 1958; Mayo Gal., Wellfleet, Mass., 1954; Nat. Mus., Havana, Cuba, 1956; Lyceum Cl., Havana, 1956; Ringling Mus. A., 1955; Soc. Four Arts, 1955-1957; CGA, 1957; Toledo Mus. A., 1957; Norton Gal. A.; Lowe Gal. A.; Sarasota AA; Fla. State Fair, 1958; Art:USA, 1958; Butler Inst. Am. A., 1958.

STORY, ALA—Former Museum Director
Pine Hill, Great Barrington, Mass.

B. Hruscha, Austria, Apr. 25, 1907. *Studied*: Lycee Weiner Neustadt, Austria; Acad. FA, Vienna; Univ. Vienna;

Pitman's Col., London. *Member*: Cosmopolitan Cl. *Positions*: Mngr., Wertheim Gal., London, 1932-34; Co-Dir., Partner, Redfern Gal., London, 1934-37; Co-Partner, Dir., Storran Gal., London, 1937-39; Founder, Pres., Am.-British A. Center, N.Y., 1940-51; Co-Partner, Vice-Pres., Falcon Films, Inc., N.Y.; Dir., Santa Barbara Mus. A., Santa Barbara, Cal., 1952-57.

STOTESBURY, HELEN. *See Coe, Helen Stotesbury*

STOUT, GEORGE LESLIE—*Museum Director*
Isabella Stewart Gardner Museum; h. 163 Worthington St., Boston, Mass.

B. Winterset, Iowa, Oct. 5, 1897. *Studied*: Grinnell Col.; Univ. Iowa, A.B.; Harvard Univ., A.M.; & abroad. *Awards*: Carnegie F., Harvard Univ., 1926-1929. Co-Author: "Painting Materials, A Short Encyclopaedia," 1942; Author: "The Care of Pictures," 1948; Ed., "Color and Light in Painting." Contributor to: Technical Studies in the Field of the Fine Arts; Magazine of Art; Mouseion; with articles on conservation, methods of examination, & treatment of works of art. *Position*: Fellow for Technical Research, FMA, & L. on Design, Harvard Univ., 1929-33; Hd. Dept. Conservation, FMA, & L. on FA, Harvard Univ., Cambridge, Mass., 1934-47; F., Am. Acad. A. & Sciences; F., Int. Inst. for Conservation of Museum Objects; Member, ICOM Comm. for the Care of Paintings, 1948-1954; Dir., WMA, Worcester, Mass., 1947-1954; Dir., Isabella Stewart Gardner Mus., Boston 15, Mass., 1955- .

STRAIN, OMA (Miss)—*Educator, P.*
759 West 21st St., San Pedro, Cal.

B. Crawfordsville, Iowa. *Studied*: State Univ., Iowa, B.A., M.A., and with Grant Wood, Alexander Archipenko. *Member*: Nat. Edu. Assn.; Pacific AA. *Exhibited*: CM; Cincinnati Women's A. Cl.; Oakland A. Gal.; Santa Cruz A. Lg.; Haggin Mem. Gal., Stockton, Cal.; Pomona, Cal. (one-man). Contributor to Design, School Arts magazines. *Positions*: Hd. A. Dept., Drake Univ., Des Moines, Iowa, 1930-36; Chm. A. Dept., Norwood (Ohio) H.S., 1939-44; Asst. Prof. A. Edu., San Jose State Col., 1944-46; A. Supv., Stockton, Cal., 1946-48; Instr., Sr. H.S., Los Angeles City Schools, 1948- .

STRATER, HENRY—*Painter, Mus. Dir.*
Shore Rd., Ogunquit, Me.

B. Louisville, Ky., Jan. 21, 1896. *Studied*: Princeton Univ.; ASL; PAFA; Julian Acad., Paris; Royal Acad., Madrid, and with Charles Grafly. *Member*: Palm Beach A. Lg.; Ogunquit AA; Louisville AA; Portland Soc. A.; F., PAFA; Soc. Four Arts. *Awards*: prize, GGE, 1939. *Work*: J. B. Speed A. Mus.; Univ. Indiana; IBM; Univ. Louisville; Portland Mus. A.; PMA; Bowdoin Col. Mus.; Ogunquit Mus. A.; Farnsworth Mus. A. *Exhibited*: Salon d'Automne, Paris; Whitney Studio Cl.; NAD; J. B. Speed A. Mus.; WMAA; Kansas City AI; PAFA; CGA; Norton Gal. A.; Soc. Four Arts; one-man: Montross Gal., 1931, 1933, 1934, 1936, 1939; Louisville, Ky., 1938; Van Horn Gal., Boston, 1939; Portland Mus. A., 1939, 1952; Laurel Gal., 1952; Univ. Indiana, 1952; Princeton Univ., 1952; Walker A. Center, 1938, 1952; Louisville A. Cl.; Univ. Maine, 1952. *Work*: Mus. A., 1952. I., "Sixteen Cantos"; "In Our Time"; "Conquistador"; "Portfolio of 25 Drawings by Henry Strater," 1958. *Position*: Dir., Trustee, Mus. A. of Ogunquit, Me., 1953- .

STRATTON, ALZA (Mrs. Alza Stratton Hentschel)—
Painter, Des., T., Comm. A.
Burlington, Ky.

B. Lexington, Ky., July 2, 1911. *Studied*: Univ. Kentucky, A.B.; NAD; Cincinnati A. Acad., and with W. E. Hentschel. *Member*: Prof. A. of Cincinnati; Cincinnati Woman's A. Cl. *Awards*: prizes, Cincinnati Crafters, 1954; Woman's A. Cl., 1950. *Work*: IBM; mural, Western and Southern Life Ins. Bldg., Cincinnati (in collaboration with W. E. Hentschel). *Exhibited*: nationally. *Position*: Instr., Des., Drawing & Painting, Cincinnati A. Acad., Cincinnati, Ohio, to 1948; Asst. to W. E. Hentschel, mural painting, 1948- .

STRATTON, GRACE HALL—*Craftsman, Des.*
10 Museum Rd., Boston 15, Mass.

B. Cambridge, Mass., Aug. 7, 1877. *Studied*: BMFA Sch. *Member*: Boston Soc. A. & Crafts. *Position*: Instr., Boston Sch. Occupational Therapy, Boston, Mass., 1936-46; Des. embroideries and restorer of antique textiles.

STRAUS, MRS. GUSTAV. *See Bloch, Julia*

STRAUSS, CHARLES EARL—*Cartoonist, Comm. A., T.*
"The Pink House," Frenchtown, N.J.

B. Jeffersonville, Ind., Apr. 7, 1911. *Studied*: Oberlin Col., A.B.; Chicago Acad. FA; ASL, with Rudolph Weisenborn; Grande Chaumiere, Paris, France. Contributor cartoons to Sat. Eve. Post; Boys Life; N.Y. Journal American, N.Y. Times, and others. *Position*: Instr., Grand Central Sch. A.; Frenchtown, N.J., Pub. Schs.; N.Y. Sch. Visual Arts.

STRAWBRIDGE, EDWARD R(ICHIE)—*Painter*
58 Peninsula Rd., Belvedere, Cal.

B. Germantown, Pa., Nov. 22, 1903. *Studied*: PMSchIA; PAFA; Cape Cod Sch. A. *Member*: Marin Soc. A.; Phila. A. All.; AWS; Phila. Sketch Cl.; Phila. WC Cl. *Work*: Ford Motor Co., Milpitas, Cal.; Phila. WC Cl.; Univ. Pennsylvania; Germantown Friend's Sch., Phila.; Haverford Col.; Strawbridge & Clothier, Phila., Pa., and in private colls. *Exhibited*: PAFA; NAD; N.Y. WC Cl.; AWS; Newport AA; Provincetown AA; Ogunquit A. Center; All. A. Am., Phila. A. All.; Cal. PLH; McClees Gal., Phila.; Germantown A. Lg.; Woodmere A. Gal.; Benjamin West Soc.; State Mus., Trenton; John Herron AI; NAC; Wilmington Soc. FA; SC; Phila. Sketch Cl.; Ferargil Gal.; Marin Soc. A., and many others.

STREETT, TYLDEN WESTCOTT—*Sculptor*
2½ East Eager St.; h. 712 Park Ave., Baltimore 1, Md.

B. Baltimore, Md., Nov. 28, 1922. *Studied*: Johns Hopkins Univ.; St. John's Col.; Maryland Inst. FA, B.F.A., M.F.A., and with Sidney Waugh, Cecil Howard. *Member*: NSS. *Awards*: Rinehart Traveling F., 1953, 1954; Louis Comfort Tiffany Fnd., 1956. *Work*: Kirk-in-the-Hills, Bloomfield, Mich.; many portrait busts of prominent persons.

STRAWN, MEL(VIN) (NICHOLAS)—
Painter, S., Des., Gr., T., Ser.
5380 Shafter Ave., Oakland 9, Cal.

B. Boise, Idaho, Aug. 5, 1929. *Studied*: Chouinard AI; Los A. County AI; Jepson AI; Cal. Col. A. & Crafts, B.F.A., M.F.A., and with Rico Lebrun, Richard Haines, Leon Goldin and others. *Member*: San F. AA; Nat. Ser. Soc.; Bay Pr. M. Soc. (Co-Dir.). *Exhibited*: Nat. Ser. Soc., 1954, 1955; SFMA, 1954; Am. Color Pr. Soc., 1955; Ball State T. Col., 1955; LC, 1955; Bay Pr. M. Soc., 1955; Oakland A. Mus., 1951, 1952, 1954; Richmond A. Center, 1953, 1955; Cal. State Fair, 1952, 1954; Am. Painters Exh., France, 1954-55; one-man: Boise A. Gal., 1950; Labaudt Gal., San F., 1951; Cal. PLH, 1952; Texas Western Col., 1953; Gray Shop, Oakland, 1953; Gump's, San F., 1954; Redding Jr. Col., 1955, etc. Lectures: History of Serigraphy.*

STRINGER, MARY EVELYN—*Educator, P.*
Art Department, Mississippi State College for Women; h. Faculty Club, Columbus, Miss.

B. Huntsville, Mo., July 31, 1921. *Studied*: Univ. Missouri, A.B.; Univ. North Carolina, M.A., and with Julio De Diego, Clemens Sommer. *Member*: Mississippi AA; CAA; AAUW. *Awards*: prizes, Meridian, Miss., 1951; Fulbright F., 1955-56; Jackson, Miss., 1951. *Exhibited*: Jackson, Miss., 1949-1956; Atlanta, Ga., 1949, 1950; New Orleans AA, 1951; 2-man exh., Allison Wells, Miss., 1952, 1954, 1958; one-man, Meridian, Miss., 1955; Norfolk, Va., 1954; Ft. Dodge, Iowa, 1957. *Position*: Assoc. Prof. A., Mississippi State Col. for Women, Columbus, Miss., 1947- .

STROBEL, OSCAR A.—*Painter, Lith., I.*
Route 2, Box 147, Scottsdale, Ariz.

B. Cincinnati, Ohio, May 29, 1891. *Studied*: with Duveneck, Rabes, Henri, Herrman, and in Munich and Berlin,

Germany. *Awards*: prize, Texas Exp., 1930. *Work*: Austin Cl., Security Trust Bank, Austin, Tex.; German Embassy, Wash., D.C.; Valley Bank & Trust Co., Phoenix, Ariz.; murals, Westward Ho Hotel, Phoenix, Ariz.; San Marcos Hotel, Chandler, Ariz.; Greyhound Bus Depots, Phoenix, Flagstaff, Ariz.; San Diego, Cal.; Reno, Nev. *Position*: A., Brown & Bigelow Calendars.

STROMSTED, ALF JORGEN—*Painter, T.*
   22 Sherman Ave., Summit, N.J.

B. Loedingen, Norway, July 14, 1898. *Studied*: Norwegian Inst. Tech., E.E., and with Rudolf Jacobi. *Member*: Soc. Naval Arch. & Marine Engineers; Assoc. A. New Jersey. *Awards*: prizes, A. of Today, Newark, 1944; PAFA; NAC, 1953; State Exh., East Orange, N.J. *Work*: PAFA. *Exhibited*: CGA, 1939, 1941; Carnegie Inst., 1944-1946; Portland (Ore.) Mus. A.; BM; Albright A. Gal.; Museo Nationale, Rio de Janeiro; Sao Paulo, Brazil; Audubon A.; Springfield Mus. FA; Newark Mus.; Montclair A. Mus.; in Norway, and in traveling exhs. to various colleges. *Position*: Instr., Summit AA, New Jersey.*

STROUD, CLARA—*Painter, C., Des., W.*
   Herbertsville, N.J.

B. New Orleans, La. *Studied*: PIASch., and with Ralph Johonnet, Jay Hambridge, Hilton Leech, and others. *Member*: AAPL; AWS; NAWA. *Awards*: prizes, AAPL, 1939, 1952; Montclair A. Mus., 1953; Barmark award, 1954. *Position*: Bd. Member, AAPL, N.J.

STRUPPECK, JULIUS—*Sculptor, E., W.*
   Newcomb Art School, New Orleans 18, La.

B. Grangeville, La., May 20, 1915. *Studied*: Univ. Oklahoma, B.F.A.; Louisiana State Univ., M.A. *Awards*: prizes, New Orleans AA, 1953. *Work*: Univ. Oklahoma; Lowe Gal. A., Miami; Bertha Schaefer Gal.; Marine Hospital, New Orleans, La.; Court House, New Iberia, La.; USPO, Many, La. *Exhibited*: AFA traveling exh., 1941; Bertha Schaefer Gal., 1953; WMAA, 1954; Arch. Lg., 1954. *Author*: "The Creation of Sculpture"; Contributor to Design magazine. *Position*: Prof. S., Newcomb Col., Tulane Univ., New Orleans, La., at present.

STUART, KENNETH JAMES—*Illustrator*
   Saturday Evening Post, Philadelphia 5, Pa.; h. Bethel Rd., Lansdale, R.D., 2, Pa.

B. Milwaukee, Wis., Sept. 21, 1905. *Studied*: PAFA, and in Paris, France. *Position*: A. Editor, Saturday Evening Post, Philadelphia, Pa., 1944- .

STUBBS, STANLEY A.—*Museum Curator*
   Museum of New Mexico, Santa Fe, N.M.
Position: Cur., Collections.*

STUEMPFIG, WALTER—*Painter*
   Gwynedd Valley, Pa.
Member: NA.*

STULTS, ELWIN MARTIN, JR. (LARRY)—*Painter, Des.*
   Cabbage Key, Boca Grande, Fla.

B. Orwell, Ohio, July 19, 1899. *Studied*: AIC; Carnegie Inst., B.A.; & with Charles Hawthorne, Edmund Giesbert, Francis Chapin. *Member*: Fla. A. Group. *Exhibited*: North Shore AA; Evanston (Ill.) A. Center; Massillon Mus. A.; Sarasota AA; Fla. A. Group.

STURGES, LILLIAN—*Illustrator, P., W.*
   2956 Belrose Ave., Pittsburgh 16, Pa.

B. Wilkes-Barre, Pa. *Studied*: PMSchIA; PAFA; Carnegie Inst., B.A. *Member*: Author's Cl.; Assoc. A. Pittsburgh; Pittsburgh WC Soc. *Exhibited*: Carnegie Inst.; Hist. Soc. Western Pa. I., "Treasury of Myths"; "Bible A-B-C"; *Author*: "Money for Cats." Color covers for the Junior Magazine of the United Presbyterian Church, 1956- .

STURTEVANT, EDITH LOUISE—*Painter, E.*
   107 McCartney St., Easton, Pa.

B. Utica, N.Y., Dec. 23, 1888. *Studied*: PAFA; Carnegie Inst.; N.Y. Univ., B.S. in Edu. *Member*: Phila. Plastic Cl.; Nat. Edu. Assn. *Awards*: F., PAFA; Cresson traveling scholarship, prize, PAFA. *Work*: PAFA; Easton Woman's Cl. *Exhibited*: CGA; PAFA; BMA; AIC; Phila. Plastic Cl.; Phila. AC. *Position*: A. Supv., Easton Sch. District, Easton, Pa., 1922- .

STURTEVANT, LOUISA CLARK—*Designer, P., T.*
   Second Beach Rd., Newport, R.I.

B. Paris, France, Feb. 2, 1870. *Studied*: BMFA Sch.; & with Jacques Blanche, Paris, France. *Member*: AAPL; Newport AA. *Awards*: med., Pan-Pacific Exp., 1915. *Exhibited*: PAFA; Pan-Pacific Exp. Des., stained glass, textiles.*

STURTEVANT, WALLIS HALL (PETER LADD)—
   Painter, I.
   99 St. James Ave., Springfield, Mass.

B. Greenfield, Mass., Apr. 22, 1897. *Studied*: ASL; Mass. State T. Col.; Univ. Louisville, and with Wilson, Randall, Winter. I., "Old Times in the Colonies"; "Days of the Leader"; *Author*, I., "The Story of Hansel and Gretel and The Gingerbread Castle."

STUTTMAN, JOY LANE—*Painter, Et., T.*
   831 Madison Ave., New York, N.Y.

B. Chicago, Ill., July 2, 1929. *Studied*: Univ. Chicago, B.Ph.; Mills Col., Oakland, Cal., B.A., and with Tschacbasov, Hans Hofmann. *Member*: NAWA; Woodstock AA; Com. on A. Edu. *Exhibited*: NAWA; N.Y. City Center; Washington Univ., St. Louis, Mo.; Sun Gal., Provincetown, Mass.; one-man: John Heller Gal., N.Y.; Caricature Coffee Shop, N.Y. *Position*: Instr., Children's Classes, Contemporaries Workshop, N.Y.*

SUBA, SUSANNE—*Illustrator, Des.*
   210 East 63rd St., New York 21, N.Y.

B. Budapest, Hungary. *Studied*: PIASch. *Awards*: A. Dir. Cl., Chicago and New York; BM; 50 Best Books of the Year. *Work*: BM; Mus. City of N.Y. *Exhibited*: one-man: AIC. Illus., "Rocket in My Pocket"; "Dancing Star"; "There's No Place Like Paris"; "Roly-Poly Snowman"; "My Aunt Lucienne"; "Sonny-Boy Sim"; "Gabriel and the Creatures," and many other books. Contributor spot designs, covers to New Yorker magazine. Promotional books for: Steinway; Castleton China; Seabury Press.

SUDLOW, ROBERT NEWTON—*Painter, E.*
   University of Kansas, Department of Painting, Lawrence, Kans.

B. Holton, Kans., Feb. 25, 1920. *Studied*: California Col. A. & Crafts; Univ. Kansas, B.F.A.; Univ. California; Andre L'Hote, Grande Chaumiere, Paris, France. *Member*: Kansas Fed. A. *Awards*: prizes, CAM, 1946; Joslyn A. Mus., 1947; Topeka A. Gld., 1947, 1951, 1955-1957; Mulvane A. Mus., 1948; Kansas State Col.; Huntington Hartford F., 1957; Elizabeth Watkins F., 1958. *Work*: CAM; Joslyn A. Mus.; Mulvane A. Mus.; St. Benedict's, Atchison, Kans.; Kansas State Col. *Exhibited*: PAFA, Kansas State Col.; Kansas State T. Col., Springfield Mus. A.; Univ. California; Ariz. State T. Col.; CAM; Joslyn A. Mus.; Wichita; Colorado Springs FA Center; William Rockhill Nelson Gal. A.; Mulvane A. Mus. *Position*: Asst. Prof., Univ. Kansas, Lawrence, Kans., 1946- .

SUGIMOTO, HENRY—*Painter, Gr., I., T.*
   948 Columbus Ave., New York 25, N.Y.

B. Los Angeles, Cal. *Studied*: Cal. Sch. FA; Cal. Col. A. & Crafts, B.F.A. *Member*: San F. AA; Cal. WC Soc.; Print Council of Am.; Fnd. Western A. *Awards*: prizes, San F. Lg. A., 1936; Fnd. Western A., 1937; Arkansas State Exh., 1946; med., GGE, 1939; AIGA, 1957 (purchase). *Work*: Palace Legion Honor; Hendrix Col., Ark.; Univ. Arkansas; Cal. Col. A. & Crafts; & in France. *Exhibited*: Salon d'Automne, Paris, 1931; Cal.-Pacific Exp., 1935; GGE, 1939; San F. AA; Los A. AA; Fnd. Western A.; Cornell Univ., 1950 (one-man); LC, 1950, 1955; PAFA, 1953; Tokyo, Japan, 1953; BMFA, 1957; AIC,

1957; Memphis Acad. A., 1957; Univ. Minnesota, 1957; AIGA, 1957. Illus., "Songs from the Land of Dawn"; "New Friends for Susan"; Toshio and Tama."

SULLIVAN, MAX WILLIAM—*Museum Director, E.*

Portland Art Museum, S.W. Park & Madison St., (5); h. 1785 Southwest Montgomery Drive, Portland 1, Ore.

B. Fremont, Mich., Sept. 27, 1909. *Studied*: Western State T. Col., A.B.; Harvard Univ., A.M. *Member*: AIA; CAA; Assoc., John Carter Brown Lib.; AAMus.; Harvard Cl. *Award*: Hon. deg., LL.D., Providence Col., 1950. *Positions*: Instr., Cranbrook Acad., 1933-35; Instr., A. & Crafts, Middlesex Sch., Concord, Mass., 1935-38; Hd. A. Dept., Groton (Mass.) Sch., 1938-42; Consultant on A. Edu., Harvard Sch. of Edu., 1940-42; Dir. Exh. of New England Handicrafts, WMA, 1942-43; Consultant, MMA, 1943-44; Dir. Edu., R.I. Sch. Des., 1944-45, Dean of Sch., 1945-47, Pres. of Corp., 1947-55; Dir., Portland Art Mus., Portland Art Assn., and Mus. A. Sch., Portland, Ore., 1956-; Sec., Bd. Trustees, 1957- .

SUMAN, LAWRENCE—*Painter, C.*

332 Sturtevant Dr., Sierra Madre, Cal.

B. New York, N.Y., Jan. 30, 1902. *Studied*: Syracuse Univ.; Corcoran Sch. A.; & with Edmund Tarbell, Richard Munsell. *Member*: Cal. A. Potters Assn. *Exhibited*: Laguna Beach AA; 1942; Los A. Mus. A., 1941. *Position*: Des., Walt Disney Productions, 1942-43; Owner; A. L. Suman Properties, Sierra Madre, Cal.*

SUMM, HELMUT—*Painter, Gr., E., L.*

University of Wisconsin; h. 6183 North Lake Dr., Milwaukee 17, Wis.

B. Hamburg, Germany, Mar. 10, 1908. *Studied*: Univ. Wisconsin, B.S.; Marquette Univ., M.E.; & with Umberto Romano, Carl Peters, William H. Varnum. *Member*: Wis. P. & S.; Wis. Pr.M.; Wis. WC Soc. *Awards*: prizes, Milwaukee AI, 1945, 1946; Gimbel award, 1951; Wis. State Fair, 1951; De Pere (Wis.) A. Festival, 1955; Milwaukee Journal, 1950, 1954; Wis. P. & S., 1958; Meta-Mold Corp. purchase, 1957; Wis. Woman's Cl., 1958, purchase. *Work*: Milwaukee AI; Gimbel Coll.; Murals, St. John's Lutheran Sch., Milwaukee; Home for the Aged, Wauwatosa, Wis. *Exhibited*: John Herron AI, 1946; Lib.Cong., 1944, 1945; Phila. Pr. Cl., 1945, 1946; Kearney Mem. Exh., 1946; Wis. Pr.M., 1943-1946, 1953-1957; Wis. P. & S., annually; Wis. Salon, 1941, 1943, 1949-57; AIC, 1950, 1952; Wis. State Fair, 1948-1957; DePere A. Festival, 1955; Milwaukee Athletic Cl.; Wis. WC Cl., 1956-1958; Milwaukee Jewish Center, 1958; One-man: St. Norberts, DePere, Wis., 1957; Milwaukee-Downer Seminary, 1958. *Position*: Assoc. Prof. A. Edu., Univ. Wisconsin, Milwaukee, Wis.

SUMMER, (EMILY) EUGENIA—*Painter, T.*

Mississippi State College for Women, Columbus, Miss.; h. 208 North Main St., Yazoo City, Miss.

B. Newton, Miss., June 13, 1923. *Studied*: Miss. State Col. for Women, B.S.; Columbia Univ., M.A., and with Edwin Ziegfeld, Hugo Robus, Dong Kingman. *Member*: AAUW; Southeastern AA; Miss. AA; Alabama WC Soc.; New Orleans AA; Memphis Biennial Assn.; Allisons A. Colony; AAUP. *Awards*: Elected to "Hall of Fame," Miss. State Col. for Women, 1945; prize, Miss. AA. *Exhibited*: Miss. AA, 1947, 1949, 1951, 1956; New Orleans AA, 1952, 1953, 1955; Atlanta AA, 1951, 1952; Memphis Biennial, 1955; Allisons A. Colony, 1955, 1956, 1958; Atlanta AA, 1952; Brooks Mem. Gal., 1957. *Position*: Asst. Prof. A., Miss. State Col. for Women, Columbus, Miss., 1949- .

SUMMERFORD, BEN L.—*Museum Director*

Watkins Memorial Gallery, American University, Massachusetts & Nebraska Aves., Washington 16, D.C.*

SUMMERS, DUDLEY GLOYNE—*Illustrator, P.*

Woodstock, N.Y.

B. Birmingham, England, Oct. 12, 1892. *Studied*: ASL; Garden Sch. A., Boston. *Member*: SI; SC.

SUMMY, KATHERINE STRONG—*Painter, T.*

1673 Columbia Rd., Washington 9, D.C.; s. East Gloucester, Mass.

B. Washington, D.C., Apr. 19, 1888. *Studied*: George Washington Univ., B.A.; T. Col., Columbia Univ., B.S., M.A.; & with Ernest Thurn, Hans Hofmann, & others. *Member*: Wash. AC; Wash. WC Cl. *Exhibited*: Soc. Wash. A., 1933-1941; Wash. WC Cl., 1938-1952; Wash. A. Cl.; NGA. *Position*: Instr. A., Coolidge H.S., Washington, D.C., 1916-54 (Retired). Sec., Wash. WC Cl., 1953-57; Wash. Arts Admission Bd., 1956-58.

SUNDERLAND, ELIZABETH READ—*Educator*

College Station, Duke University, Durham, N.C.

B. Ann Arbor, Mich., June 12, 1910. *Studied*: Univ. Michigan, A.B.; Univ. Munich, Germany; Radcliffe Col., A.M., Ph.D. *Member*: Societe des Amis des Arts de Charlieu (hon.); Mediaeval Acad. Am.; CAA; AAUP; Am. Soc. of the French Legion of Honor; Société Française d'Archéologie; Académie de Mâcon; Am. Assn. Arch. Historians. Contributor to: Art Bulletin; Speculum; College Art Journal; Journal of the Soc. Arch. Hist.; Journal of the Arch. Inst. of Japan; Parnassus; South Atlantic Quarterly, & other publications. *Awards*: Guggenheim F., 1952-53; Chevalier de la Legion d'Honneur, 1954; Citoyenne d'Honneur de la Ville de Charlieu, France, 1952, and others. *Position*: Instr. FA, Duke Univ., 1939-42; Asst Prof. FA, Wheaton Col., Wheaton, Ill., 1942-43; Asst. Prof. FA, Duke Univ., Durham, N.C., 1943-1951, Assoc. Prof., 1951- .

SUNDIN, ADELAIDE ALTHIN TOOMBS (Mrs. Olof G.) —*Ceramic Sculptor, C., L., T.*

47 Alpine St., Boston, Mass.; also, Lantmatarcatan 9-D, Hudiksvall, Sweden

B. Boston, Mass., May 8, 1915. *Studied*: Mass. Sch. A.; MIT, B.S. in Edu., and with Cyrus Dallin, Raymond Porter. *Awards*: medal, Mass. Sch. A., 1936. *Work*: portraits in porcelain, Boston, New York City, Baltimore, Washington, D.C., St. Louis, Los Angeles, Wilmington, and in Sweden. *Exhibited*: PAFA, 1941; NAD, 1942; CGA, 1942; Copley Soc., Boston, 1941; Boston A. Cl., 1942; Soc. Min. S., P. & Gravers, Wash., D.C.; Boston A. Festival; one-man: Doll and Richards, Boston, 1949; Veerhof Gal., Wash., D.C., 1952; Hudiksvall Mus., Sweden; Gåvle Mus., Gåvle, Sweden; Artisans Shop, Balt., 1952. Lectures: Ceramics. Specializes in porcelain ports. of children.

SUOZZI, CON(STANTIN) N.—*Cartoonist*

2132 78th St., Jackson Heights 70, N.Y.

B. New York, N.Y., Aug. 24, 1916. Contributor cartoons to Esquire; Sat. Eve. Post; Look; True; Wall St. Journal; Saturday Review; This Week; American Weekly; Parade; New Yorker, and others.

SURENDORF, CHARLES—*Engraver, P., T.*

Columbia, Cal.

B. Richmond, Ind., Nov. 9, 1906. *Studied*: AIC; ASL; Ohio State Univ.; Mills Col. *Member*: Cal. SE; San F. AA; Northwest Pr.M.; Mother Lode AA; Richmond AA; New Orleans AA; Indiana Soc. Pr.M. *Awards*: prizes, John Herron AI, 1935, 1938; SFMA, 1937; SAM, 1938, 1945; Cal. SE, 1938, 1941, 1942, 1944, 1945, 1950-1954; GGE, 1939; Phila. Pr. Cl., 1941, 1942; Tri-State Exh., Indianapolis, Ind., 1945, 1946; Indiana A., 1929-1931, 1933, 1934, 1940; Hoosier Salon, 1930, 1948, 1952; SAGA, 1950; Cal. State Lib., 1951, 1952, 1954, and others. *Work*: SFMA; Mills Col.; Lib. Cong.; Wichita A. Mus.; Richmond (Ind.) A. Mus. *Exhibited*: CGA, 1933; PAFA, 1937; CM, 1933, 1935, 1936; SFMA, 1936-1946; AV, 1942; deYoung Mem. Mus.. 1946; Los A. Mus. A., 1936; AIC, 1938, 1940; NAD, 1941, 1946; Albany Inst. Hist. & A., 1945; Phila. Pr. Cl., 1940-1942, 1946; Northwest Pr.M., 1938, 1941, 1942, 1944-1946; John Herron AI, 1946; Wichita A. Mus., 1935-1938, 1941; Phila. A. All., 1938; Delgado Mus. A., 1949; New Orleans AA, 1949; LC, 1949; Indiana Pr. M., 1949, 1951; SAGA, 1940; Cal. State Lib., 1951, 1952, 1954. I., "Mr. Pimney," 1945. *Position*: Dir., Mother Lode A. Sch. & Gal., Columbia, Cal.*

SUSSMAN, MARGARET—Craftsman, P., S.

15 Gramercy Park; h. 119 East 19th St., New York 3, N.Y.

B. New York, N.Y., Apr. 4, 1912. *Studied*: Smith Col., B.A.; Grand Central A. Sch.; ASL; & with William Mc-Nulty, George Bridgman, Will Barnet, Harry Sternberg. *Member*: Artist-Craftsmen of N.Y.; NAC; Pen & Brush Cl. *Awards*: prizes, NAC, 1940, 1945. *Exhibited*: NAD, 1943; Audubon A., 1945; All.A.Am., 1943, 1944; Phila. Pr. Cl., 1944; Veterans Exh., ASL, 1944; N.Y. Soc. Crafts-men, 1954, 1955; Staten Island Mus. A., 1954, 1955; NAC, 1940, 1946; Contemporary A. Gal., 1943. *Position*: Silver-smith and Jeweler; Instr., Craft Students Lg., Y.W.C.A., New York, N.Y.

SUSSMAN, RICHARD N.—Painter, Gr., Des.

422 South 18th St., Richmond, Cal.

B. Minneapolis, Minn., June 25, 1908. *Studied*: Minneapolis Sch. A.; ASL. *Work*: MMA; stained glass windows for churches in many cities of U.S. *Exhibited*: PAFA, 1941; BM, 1940; MMA (AV), 1942; AIC, 1943; Palace Legion Honor, 1946, 1948; deYoung Mem. Mus., 1944; SFMA, 1949; Cal. State Fair, 1951.*

SUTTON, GEORGE MIKSCH—

Painter, I., W., L., Mus. Cur.

University of Oklahoma, Norman, Okla.

B. Lincoln, Neb., May 16, 1898. *Studied*: Bethany Col., B.S.; Cornell Univ., Ph.D. *Member*: Wilson Ornithologists' Soc.; Artic Inst. of North America; Cooper Ornithological Soc.; Am. Geographical Soc.; British Ornithologists' Union; Am. Ornithologists' Union; New Zealand Ornitho-logical Soc. I., "Birds of Florida"; "Birds of Western Pennsylvania"; "Guide to Bird Finding"; "The Golden Plover and Other Birds"; "American Bird Biographies"; "Georgia Birds"; "The Seashore Book" (in part); I., the bird section of World Book Encyclopaedia; Author, I., "Birds in the Wilderness"; "Eskimo Year"; "Mexican Birds"; and many others. Series of life-size drawings of Mexican birds, reproduced by Fnd. for Neotropical Re-search. *Position*: Prof. Zoology, Univ. Oklahoma, Norman, Okla.

SUTTON, RACHEL McCLELLAND (Mrs. W. S.)—

Painter

Fifth & Wilkins Aves., Pittsburgh 32, Pa.

B. Pittsburgh, Pa., May 19, 1887. *Studied*: Carnegie Inst.; Chatham Col.; Woodstock Summer Sch. A.; ASL. *Mem-ber*: Assoc. A. Pittsburgh; Pittsburgh WC Soc. *Awards*: prizes, Pittsburgh Soc. A., 1932; Garden Cl., 1943; Pitts-burgh WC Soc., 1954. *Work*: Pittsburgh Pub. Schs. *Ex-hibited*: Carnegie Inst., 1935-1946; Assoc. A. Pittsburgh, 1919-1958; Butler AI; Indiana, Pa., 1945; Pittsburgh WC Soc., 1945-1958; A. & Crafts Center, Pittsburgh.

SUTTON, RUTH HAVILAND—Portrait Painter, Lith.

Commercial Wharf, Nantucket, Mass.

B. Springfield, Mass., Sept. 10, 1898. *Studied*: PMSchIA; Grand Central A. Sch.; & with Jerry Farnsworth, Henry B. Snell, & others. *Member*: Nantucket AA. *Awards*: prizes, Springfield A. Lg., 1926; Assoc. Jr. Lg., Boston, 1930; Conn. Acad. FA, 1931. *Work*: Aston Col., Springfield, Mass.; Springfield Mus. FA; Lib.Cong.; Northampton (Mass.) Pub. Lib.; Carnegie Inst.; New Britain Inst. (Conn.); Taylor Gal., Nantucket; N.Y.Pub.Lib.; Boston Pub. Lib.; Mus. Natural Hist., Springfield, Mass. *Exhib-ited*: NAWA, 1928, 1929, 1945, 1946; Lib.Cong., 1945, 1946; Carnegie Inst., 1945; NAD, 1927, 1945, 1946; Conn. Acad. FA, 1928-1946; Northwest Pr.M., 1944-1956; Spring-field A. Gld., 1928-1940; Springfield A. Lg., 1928-1935.

SUZUKI, SAKARI—Painter, Des., T.

900 Windsor Ave., Chicago 40, Ill.

B. Iwateken, Japan. *Studied*: Cal. Sch. FA. *Awards*: prize, Am. A. Cong., 1936; Terry AI, 1952. *Member*: United Scenic A. Am. *Work*: High Mus. A., Atlanta, Ga.; murals, Willard Parker Hospital, N.Y. *Exhibited*: CGA, 1934; Berkshire Mus.; ACA Gal., 1936 (one-man); CAA Exh.; New Jersey Col. for Women, 1945; Artists Gal. N.Y., 1948, 1951 (one-man); Ogunquit A. Center, 1950, 1951; U.S. Dept. Army, 1951, PAFA, 1952; Mandel Bros., 1955 (one-man).

SVENDSEN, CHARLES C.—Painter

555 Elberon Ave., Cincinnati 5, Ohio

B. Cincinnati, Ohio, Dec. 7, 1871. *Studied*: Cincinnati A. Acad.; Julian Acad., Paris, France. *Awards*: med., St. Louis Exp. *Work*: Vanderpoel Coll.; mural, St. Xavier Church, Cincinnati, Ohio. *Exhibited*: Detroit Inst. A.; CAM; AIC; PAFA; Soc. Am. A.; & in Palestine & Egypt. *Position*: Commissioner FA. for Holland and Belgium, The Tennessee Centennial and Int. Exp.

SVET, M(IRIAM) (Mrs. Dore Schary)—Painter

33 East 79th St., New York, N.Y.

B. Newark, N.J., Apr. 15, 1912. *Studied*: Faucett A. Sch.; with Carl Von Schleusing, Newark; NAD; ASL, with George Bridgman, Frank V. Dumond. *Member*: AFA; Los A. AA. *Work*: Los Angeles City Hall; Brandeis Univ.; Fairleigh Dickinson Col., Teaneck, N.J. Ports. in private colls. *Exhibited*: One-man: Assoc. Am. A., 1951, 1956; Vigeveno Gal., Westwood, Cal., 1954; Los A. AA (twice yearly); Hammer Gal., N.Y., 1959.

SVOBODA, VINCENT A.—Painter, Cart.

204 Columbia Heights, Brooklyn 2, N.Y.

B. Prague, Czechoslovakia, Aug. 27, 1877. *Studied*: NAD. *Member*: SC; All.A.Am.; Cartoonists Cl. *Awards*: prizes, NAD; SC, 1935, 1937. *Position*: Editorial Cart., Brooklyn Eagle, Brooklyn, N.Y., 1940-52 (Retired).

SWAIN, JERRE (Mrs. Saint E.)—Painter, T.

4717 Redstart St., Houston 35, Tex.

B. Yoakum, Tex., May 21, 1913. *Studied*: Mary Hardin-Baylor Col., Belton, Tex.; Univ. Colorado; Mus. FA of Houston; & with Emil Bisttram, Max Beckmann. *Member*: Texas FA Assn.; Houston A.Lg.; Taos AA; Assoc. A. Houston. *Work*: St. James Episcopal Church, Houston, Tex. *Exhibited*: Assoc. A. Gal., Houston (one-man); Mus. FA of Houston; Elisabet Ney Mus. A.; Little Theatre & Jr. Lg. of Houston, Tex.; Blue Door A. Gal., Taos, N.M.; Edinburgh, Scotland (one-man); Shamrock Hotel, Houston, and others.

SWALLOW, W(ILLIAM) W(ELDON)—Sculptor, P., T.

R.D. 3, Allentown, Pa.

B. Clark's Green, Pa., Sept. 30, 1912. *Studied*: PMSchIA; Univ. Pennsylvania. *Member*: Audubon A.; Phila. WC Cl.; Lehigh Valley A. All. *Awards*: prizes, PMSchIA, 1935; AV, 1942; Syracuse Mus. FA, 1941, 1946, 1949, 1952; NSS, 1946; Audubon A., 1945; hon. degree, D.F.A. in A., Muhlenberg Col., 1948; Woodmere A. Gal., 1951-1953, 1957, 1958; Citation, Cedar Crest Col., 1954. *Work*: Syra-cuse Mus. FA; Scranton Mus.; A; MMA; Allentown A. Mus.; IBM Coll. *Exhibited*: PAFA, 1941-1945; NAD, 1943-1945; Audubon A., 1945; Syracuse Mus. FA, 1940, 1941; Wichita AA, 1946; Lackawanna County AA, 1940-1945; Lehigh Valley AA, 1940-1946; Lehigh Univ., 1940-1946. *Position*: Hd. A. Dept., Parkland Sch., Allentown, Pa.

SWAN, MARSHALL W. S.—Educator

U.S. Information Service, Oslo, Norway

B. Brockton, Mass., Nov. 10, 1917. *Studied*: Harvard Univ., A.B., A.M., Ph.D. *Member*: Soc. for Advancement of Scandinavian Studies. Contributor to: publications of the Bibliographical Soc. of Am., Journal of English Literary History, & other publications; Ed., two vols. of Scandi-navian Studies; Lectures on American Painting. *Position*: Asst. Prof., Tufts Col., Medford, Mass., 1942-46; Cur., Dir., Am. Swedish Hist. Mus., Philadelphia, Pa., 1946-49; Public Affairs Officer, American Embassy, The Hague, Holland, 1951-55; U.S. Information Service, Milan, Italy, 1955-57. Cultural Attache, American Embassy, Rome, Italy, 1957-58; Public Affairs Officer, American Embassy, Oslo, Norway, 1958- .

SWAN, WALTER BUCKINGHAM—Painter, W., L.

4340 Shirley St., Omaha 5, Neb.

B. Boston, Mass., July 13, 1871. *Studied*: Lowell Sch. Des.; BMFA with Sargent, Colcord, Kingsbury; Creighton Univ., Omaha, Neb. *Exhibited*: U.S. Nat. Mus., Wash. D.C., 1942, 1943 (75 watercolors sponsored by Mexican Ambassador. Exhibited in many cities of the U.S. under auspices of Pan-American Union).

SWANN, JAMES—*Etcher, Comm. A.*

400 Webster Ave., Chicago 14, Ill.

B. Merkel, Tex., July 31, 1905. *Studied:* Sul Ross State T. Col., Alpine, Tex. *Member:* SAGA; Cal. Pr. M.; Prairie Pr.M. *Awards:* prizes, Chicago SE, 1940; Cal. Pr.M., 1943; SSAL, 1936; med., Paris Salon, 1937; Shope prize, N.Y., 1953. *Work:* Smithsonian Inst.; AIC; N.Y.Pub.Lib.; Los A. Mus. A.; MMA; Dallas Mus. FA; Illinois State Lib.; Newark Mus. *Exhibited:* SAE; Cal. SE; NAD; Carnegie Inst.; Lib.Cong.; & other major print exh. Contributor to: American Artist magazine; Chicago Tribune; etc. Lectures: Print Collecting; Etching Process. *Position:* Sec.-Treas., Chicago Soc. Et., Chicago, Ill., 1937-46; Sec.-Treas., Prairie Pr.M., 1946- .

SWANN, SAMUEL DONOVAN (DON)—*Engraver*

4201 Linkwood Rd., Baltimore 10, Md.

B. Fernandina, Fla., Feb. 22, 1889. *Studied:* St. Johns Col., Annapolis, Md. *Member:* Etchcrafters A. Gld. (Dir.); SAE. *Work:* MMA; J. P. Morgan Lib.; BMA; VFMA; Lib. Cong.; Enoch Pratt Lib., Balt., Md.; Princeton Univ. Lib.; U.S. Naval Acad., Annapolis, Md.; Sweet Briar Col., Va.; Randolph-Macon Col., Lynchburg, Va. Co-Author, I.: "Colonial and Historic Homes of Maryland" (100 Etchings), 1938. Lectures & demonstrations on Etchings and Their Making.*

SWANSON, BENNET A.—*Painter, Lith., T.*

265 Pleasant St., St. Paul 2, Minn.

B. Winthrop, Minn., Apr. 26, 1900. *Studied:* St. Paul Inst. A.; ASL; & with Andre L'Hote, Paris, France. *Work:* Univ. Minnesota; Walker A. Center; Minneapolis Inst. A.; Nat. Red Cross, Wash., D.C.; mural, Field House, Ft. Snelling, Minn.; numerous hospitals, schools, pub. bldgs., throughout U.S. *Exhibited:* AIC, 1942; Paris Salon, 1927; Milwaukee, Wis., 1944.

SWANSON, GEORGE ALAN—*Painter, I.*

36 Orchard St., Bloomfield, N.J.

B. Hoboken, N.J., Dec. 27, 1908. *Studied:* Newark Sch. F. & Indst. A.; & with Will Barnet, Julia Hamlin Duncan. *Member:* Assoc. A. New Jersey; N.Y. Zoological Soc. *Work:* Newark Mus.; Dance Archives, MModA (on loan). *Exhibited:* Montclair A. Mus., 1938, 1939; Artists of Today, 1942, 1944; Newark Mus., 1944; Riverside Mus., 1945; Caracas, Venezuela, 1942, 1945. Author, I., "Weird Dwellers of the Deep" (Popular Science magazine), 1944; "Jungle Studio" (Animal Kingdom magazine), 1946. *Position:* Staff A., Dept. Tropical Research, N.Y. Zoological Soc., 1934-46; Staff A. on several scientific expeditions into the Pacific, Mexico, West Indies, etc.; Freelance des., wallpaper and fabrics; part-time A. Des., Norcross, Inc.*

SWANTEES, ETHEL LUCILE—*Painter, Et., Lith., T.*

Westover School, Middlebury, Conn.

B. Madison, Wis., Nov. 2, 1896. *Studied:* ASL; & with John Sloan, Harry Wickey. *Exhibited:* CGA, 1937; Dallas Mus. FA; MMA (AV), 1942; NAD, 1939, 1945; Mattatuck Mus., 1946; one-man exh.: Mattatuck Mus., 1943; Modernage Gal., 1945. *Position:* Instr. A., Westover Sch. Middlebury, Conn., 1942- .

SWARZ, SAHL—*Sculptor, P., T.*

167 East 69th St., New York 21, N.Y.

B. New York, N.Y., May 4, 1912. *Studied:* ASL, and with Dorothea Denslow. *Member:* Sculpture Center. *Awards:* Am. Acad. A. & Lets. grant, 1955; Guggenheim F., 1955, 1958. *Work:* Brookgreen Gardens, S.C.; Norfolk Mus. A. & Sc.; WMAA; USPO, Linden, N.J.; equestrian statue, Buffalo, N.Y. *Exhibited:* nationally since 1934. Oneman: Sculpture Center, 1954, 1957. *Position:* Assoc. Dir., Sculpture Center, New York, N.Y., 1938- .

SWARZENSKI, HANNS—*Educator, Mus. Cur., W.*

102 Raymond St., Cambridge, Mass.

B. Charlottenburg, Germany, Aug. 30, 1903. *Studied:* Univ. Freiburg, Munich, Berlin; Univ. Bonn, Ph.D.; Harvard Univ.; & in Italy. *Member:* Mediaeval Acad. Am. Author: "The Berthold Missal," Pierpont Morgan Lib., N.Y., 1943; Ed., F. Saxl's "English Sculptures of the XII Century," 1954; "Monuments of Romanesque Art," 1955; "European Masters of the 20th Century," 1957; "Masterpieces of Primitive Art; 1958. Contributor to: Art Bulletin, Gazette des Beaux-Arts, etc. Lectures: Romanesque Art; Illuminated Manuscripts. *Position:* Research Asst., Princeton Univ., Princeton, N.J., 1936-50; Acting Cur., Sculpture, NGA, Washington, D.C., 1943-46; Research F., BMFA, Boston, Mass., 1948- ; Part-time L., Warburg Inst., London Univ., 1950-56; Cur. Dec. Arts, Boston Museum of Fine Arts, 1957- .

SWAY, ALBERT—*Painter, Gr., I.*

445 East 68th St., New York 21, N.Y.

B. Cincinnati, Ohio, Aug. 6, 1913. *Studied:* Cincinnati A. Acad.; ASL. *Member:* SAGA. *Awards:* prize, CM, 1939. *Work:* MMA; Carnegie Inst.; N.Y. Hospital; Pa. State Univ. *Exhibited:* AIC, 1936-1938; CGA, 1939; PAFA, 1936; GGE, 1939; Paris Salon, 1937; Stockholm, Sweden, 1937-38; WFNY 1939; LC, 1943-1945; Albright A. Gal., 1951; SAGA, 1951-1957; Butler AI, 1940; NAD, 1944; Royal Soc. P., Et., Engravers, London, England, 1954; one-man: Closson A. Gal., Cincinnati, 1937; Delphic Studios, 1938; Wellons Gal., 1950, 1951.

SWEENEY, JAMES JOHNSON—*Museum Director, W.*

Solomon R. Guggenheim Museum; h. 120 East End Ave., New York 28, N.Y.

B. Brooklyn, N.Y., May 30, 1900. *Studied:* Georgetown Univ., Wash., D.C., A.B.; Jesus Col., Cambridge, England; Sorbonne, Paris, France; Univ. Sienna, Italy. *Awards:* Hon. D.F.A., Grinnell Col., 1957; Chevalier Legion d'Honneur, 1955. *Member:* F., Royal Soc. Antiquaries of Ireland (Dublin); Societe Europeene de la Culture; Fed. Internationale du Film d'Art, Paris (Hon. Pres.); Century Assn.; Grolier Cl.; AAMus., and others. Dir. Exhs.: "African Negro Art," MModA, 1935; "Joan Miro," 1941; "Alexander Calder," 1943; "Picasso," Art Gallery of Toronto, 1949; "Alfred Stieglitz," 1947; Dir. and commentary, film "Henry Moore," 1948; "Adventures of ——," 1957; Dir., Va. Biennial Exh., 1950; Installation U.S. Pavillon Bienale, Venice, Italy, 1952; memb. Jury II, Bienale Sao Paolo, 1954; Carnegie Intl. Jury, 1958; "Message on the Plastic Arts," Brussels World's Fair, 1958. Author, co-author or Ed.: "Antoni Gaudi" (with Jose Luis Sert), 1959; "Mondrian-van Doesberg Letters," 1959; "African Folk Tales and Sculpture" (with Paul Radin), 1952; "Alexander Calder," 1951; "Burri," 1955. *Positions:* L., Salzburg, 1948-49; Dir., Dept. Painting & Sculpture, MModA, 1945-46; Dir., Burlington Magazine, London, 1952- ; Adv. Ed., Partisan Review, 1948- ; Contrib. Cr., New Republic, 1952-53; Exh. Dir., Musee d'Art Moderne, Paris, and Tate Gal., London, 1952; Res. Scholar, Univ. Georgia, 1950-51; memb., W.B. Yeats Mem. Comm., Dublin; memb. Adv. Comm., Arts Center Program, Columbia Univ.; art edu. dept., N.Y. Univ.; Bennington Col. Dir., Solomon R. Guggenheim Museum, New York, N.Y., 1952- .

SWEENY, BARBARA—*Associate Museum Curator*

Johnson Collection, Parkway & 25th St., Philadelphia 30, Pa.; h. 314 Hathaway Lane, Wynnewood, Pa.

B. Philadelphia, Pa., Apr. 10, 1904. *Studied:* Wellesley Col., B.A. Compiled catalogue of the Johnson Collection, 1941; Book of Illustrations of the Johnson Collection, 1953. *Position:* Asst. to the Curator, 1931-54, Assoc. Cur., 1954- , Johnson Collection, Philadelphia, Pa.

SWEET, FREDERICK ARNOLD—*Museum Curator, W.*

1365 East 56th St., Chicago 37, Ill.

B. Sargentville, Me., June 20, 1903. *Studied:* Harvard Univ., B.A., M.A. *Member:* Chicago AC. Author: "The Hudson River School and the Early American Landscape Tradition," 1945; "Early American Room," 1936; Ed., "George Bellows," 1946. Author: "From Colony to Nation, An Exhibition of American Painting, Silver and Architecture, from 1650 to the War of 1812" (in collaboration with Hans Huth), 1949; "Sargent, Whistler and Mary Cassatt," 1954. Contributor to: The Art Quarterly, BM Bulletin, AIC Bulletin, Art News, Antiques, & other art publications. *Position:* Cur., Renaissance A., BM, 1932-36; Dir., Portland (Ore.) A. Mus., 1936-39; Assoc. Cur., Painting & Sculpture, 1939-52, Cur. Am. Painting & Sculpture, 1952- , AIC, Chicago, Ill.

SWENEY, FREDRIC—Illustrator, Comm. A., W., T.
2019 Chippewa Place, Sarasota, Fla.

B. Holidaysburg, Pa., June 5, 1912. *Studied*: Cleveland Sch. A. *Member*: Sarasota AA; Manatee A. Lg. *Awards*: prize, Cleveland Mus. Natural Hist., 1939 (bird show); Kendall Scholarship, Cleveland Sch. A. *Exhibited*: Sarasota AA; Manatee A. Lg.; St. Petersburg AA. Author, I., "Technique of Painting and Drawing Wildlife," 1959. Author, Illus., to Sports Afield; Nature Magazine; Outdoors Magazine; Outdoors Man Magazine. *Positions*: Adv. A., Cleveland Press, 8 years; Wildlife Calendar Artist, Brown & Bigelow, 10 years; Instr., Ringling Sch. A., Sarasota, Fla., at present.

**SWENGEL, FAYE (Mrs. Faye Swengel Badura)—
Painter**
North Main St., New Hope, Pa.

B. Johnstown, Pa., Oct. 28, 1904. *Studied*: PAFA; Barnes Fnd.; & with Daniel Garber, Arthur B. Carles. *Member*: F., PAFA. *Awards*: F., PAFA; Cresson traveling scholarship, PAFA, 1925; prizes, med., PAFA, 1937, 1940, 1942, 1946. *Work*: PAFA. *Exhibited*: CGA, 1932-1940; CM; PAFA, 1940-1956; NAD; VMFA; MMA, 1943; AIC, 1943; Phila. A. All., 1953; Pyramid Cl., Phila., 1956. Craftsman-restorer of antique paintings.

SWENSON, HOWARD WILLIAM—Sculptor, Des., Gr.
Box 256A, West State Rd.; h. 1822 Charles St., Rockford, Ill.

B. Rockford, Ill., June 30, 1901. *Studied*: Corcoran Sch. A. *Member*: Rockford AA; Potters Gld. Greater Chicago. *Work*: Lib. Cong.; Masonic Cathedral, Rockford, Ill., and in private colls. *Exhibited*: Soc. Wash. A.; CGA; Phila. Pr. Cl.; Rockport AA. *Position*: Dir., Garden Fair Gallery, Rockford, Ill.

SWENSON, VALERIE—Painter
Allaben, N.Y.

B. Kansas City, Mo., Apr. 11, 1907. *Studied*: Kansas City AI; Univ. Kansas, B.F.A. *Member*: AWS; Woodstock Gld. A. & Craftsmen. *Exhibited*: Woodstock Gld. A. & Craftsmen; exhs., in Chicago, Philadelphia and New York; one-man: Am. Mus. Natural Hist.; Argent Gal., N.Y.; Albany Inst. Hist. & A. Author, I. Author, I., "A Child's Book of Trees," 1953; "A Child's Book of Reptiles and Amphibians," 1954; "A Child's Book of Stones and Minerals," 1955, and illustrations for many nature books.

SWIFT, DICK—Printmaker, P., E.
1400 Randall Court, Los Angeles 65, Cal.

B. Long Beach, Cal., Nov. 29, 1918. *Studied*: Los. A. City Col., B.A.; Claremont Grad. Sch., M.F.A.; Los A. County AI; Chouinard AI; ASL, and with Henry McFee, Will Barnet, Jon Corbino and others. *Member*: CAA; Los A. AA; Boston Soc. A.; Boston Pr. M.; Print Council of Am.; Am. Color Print Soc. *Awards*: prizes, Ebell Cl., Los A., 1941; Long Beach AA, 1942, 1943; BMFA, 1956; Boston Univ., 1958; Scripps Col., 1958; purchase awards: LC, 1956; Los A. City Exh., 1957; Hunterdon County A. Center, 1957; Boston Soc. A., 1957; Tiffany F., 1957. *Work*: LC; Lamont A. Gal.; Hunterdon A. Center; Pasadena A. Mus. *Exhibited*: AIC; Minneapolis Inst. A.; Rochester Mem. A. Gal.; Carnegie Inst.; CM; Dayton AI; CAM; NAD; SAM; Los A. Mus. A.; Contemp. A. Gal., 1945 (one-man); Occidental Col.; Los A. AA; LC; exhs. 1956: BMFA; Youngstown Univ., and traveling; Butler Inst. Am. A.; Columbia Mus. A.; Univ. Redlands (one-man); SAM; NAD; Portland Mus. A., and traveling; Wichita AA; Am. Color Pr. Soc. (2 traveling exhs.); 1957: Phila. Pr. Cl.; Smithsonian Inst.; Hunterdon County A. Center; 1958: Boston Univ.; Silvermine Gld. A.; Pasadena A. Mus.; BMFA; Scripps Col.; Lang A. Gal. (one-man); Pasadena A. Mus. (3-man), and in many universities and colleges. *Position*: Asst. Prof. A., Long Beach State College, Long Beach, Cal., 1958- .

SWIFT, FLORENCE ALSTIN—Painter, C., Des.
100 Stone Wall Rd., Berkeley 5, Cal.

B. San Francisco, Cal., Sept. 30, 1890. *Studied*: Hans Hofmann Sch. A. *Member*: Am. Abstract A.; San F. AA; San F. Soc. Women A. *Awards*: medal, San F. AA; prizes, San F. Soc. Women A., 1950, 1951; Cal. State Fair. *Work*: Univ. California; Mills Col.; SFMA. *Exhibited*: SFMA (one-man); GGE, 1939; All. A. Am.*

SWIFT, MRS. HOMER. See MacRae, Emma Fordyce

SWIGGETT, JEAN (Mr.)—Educator, P., Ser., Des., C.
9275 Briarcrest Dr., La Mesa, Cal.

B. Franklin, Ind., Jan. 6, 1910. *Studied*: Chouinard AI; Claremont Grad. Sch.; San Diego State Col., A.B.; Univ. Southern California, M.F.A. *Member*: San Diego A. Gld.; La Jolla A. Center; San Diego AA. *Awards*: San Diego A. Gld., 1950-1957. *Work*: San Diego FA Soc.; La Jolla A. Center; murals, SS. Pres. Adams; SS. Pres. Jackson; USPO, Franklin, Ind.; Ridpath Hotel, Spokane, Wash.; San Diego County Hospital. *Awards*: prizes, Hoosier Salon, 1950; San Diego A. Gld., 1950, 1951; Cal. State Fair, 1951; Los A. County Fair, 1951. *Exhibited*: GGE, 1939; Los A. Mus. A., 1935-1941, 1946, 1950; SAM, 1941; San Diego FA Soc., 1937-1939, 1948-1958; SFMA, 1936, 1938; Denver A. Mus., 1951, 1952; John Herron AI, 1948-1954, 1957; Hoosier Salon, 1948-1952; Ariz. State Fair, 1950; Cal. State Fair, 1951, 1952; Albright A. Gal., 1951; La Jolla A. Center, 1956, 1957; Scripps Col., 1958; Bradley Univ., 1952. I., "California Today," 1937. Des., Art Show, So. California Expo., 1958. *Positions*: Instr., A., Univ. So. California, 1940-41; Wash. State Col., 1941-42; Prof., San Diego State Col., San Diego, Cal., 1946- .

SWINNERTON, EDNA HUESTIS (Mrs. Radcliffe Swinnerton)—Miniature Painter
333 East 68th St., New York 21, N.Y.

B. Troy, N.Y., Nov. 26, 1882. *Studied*: Emma Willard A. Sch.; Cornell Univ.; ASL. *Member*: Pa. Soc. Min. P.; Am. Soc. Min. P. *Award*: medal, Pa. Soc. Min. P., 1951. *Work*: many portrait commissions; permanent coll. PMA. *Exhibited*: Pan-Pacific Exp., 1915; Chicago World's Fair, 1933; ASMP; Pa. Soc. Min. P., from 1906 to present time.

SWISHER, AMY MARGARET—Craftsman, Et., E.
103 Griswold St., Delaware, Ohio

B. Groveport, Ohio, Aug. 14, 1881. *Studied*: Ohio Wesleyan Univ., B.L.; T. Col., Columbia Univ., B.S., M.A.; and with Hans Hofmann, Albert Heckman, Elsa Ulbricht. *Member*: Weavers Group of Delaware. *Award*: Carnegie F., to Harvard Univ. *Exhibited*: Ohio Union, Ohio Univ.; Delaware County Fair. *Position*: Hd., Dept. A. Edu., 1920-49, Prof. A. Edu. Emeritus, Miami Univ., Oxford, Ohio, 1949- .

SWOPE, EMMA LUDWIG—Craftsman, Des., T.
625 Summit St., Fallbrook, Cal.

B. Spillville, Iowa, Mar. 17, 1891. *Studied*: AIC; Washington State Col., Pullman, Wash., B.A.; Columbia Univ., M.A.; & with Ralph Pearson. *Member*: N.Y. Soc. Craftsmen. *Awards*: prizes, N.Y. Soc. Craftsmen, 1941. *Position*: A. T., George Jr. Republic, Freeville, N.Y.; George Washington Sch., Elmira, N.Y. (retired 1954).

SYKES, (WILLIAM) MALTBY—Painter, Gr., E., L.
Art Department, Alabama Polytechnic Institute; h. 116 Toomer St., Auburn, Ala.

B. Aberdeen, Miss., Dec. 13, 1911. *Studied*: with John Sloan, Wayman Adams, Diego Rivera, Fernand Leger, Stanley Hayter, André L'Hote. *Member*: NAEA; Phila. Pr. Cl.; Am. Color Print Soc.; Ala. WC Soc.; Birmingham A. Cl.; SAGA; Am. Assn. Univ. Prof. *Awards*: prizes, Ala. A. Lg., 1944, 1945; New Orleans AA, 1937, 1945, 1948, 1949; Ala. State Fair, 1939, 1941, 1958; Birmingham A. Cl., 1941, 1942, 1948, 1949, 1956; Mint Mus. A., 1945; Ala. WC Soc., 1941, 1943; AIGA, 1949; Mid-South Exh., 1957. *Work*: Ala. State Capitol Bldg.; Ala. Dept. Archives & Hist.; Montgomery Mus. FA; Univ. Alabama; Section Hist. Properties, Wash., D.C.; MMA; Ala. Col.; Ala. Polytechnic Inst.; Okla. A. & M. Col.; BMA; Birmingham Mus. A.; BM; CM; PMA; Stedelijk Mus., Amsterdam. *Exhibited*: Albany Inst. Hist. & A., 1948, 1949, 1951; AFA, 1950, 1951; AIGA, 1949; Bradley Univ., 1952; BM, 1949-1952; Carnegie Inst., 1945, 1946; Chicago Soc. Et., 1952; CM, 1952; Delgado Mus. A., 1945-1950; Laguna Beach AA, 1948; LC, 1945, 1948-1951; Mint Mus. A., 1944, 1945; NAD, 1946, 1949; PAFA, 1937, 1950; Phila. Pr. Cl., 1945; SAM, 1945, 1946, 1949, 1950, 1952; SAGA, 1951, 1952, 1956; L.D.M. Sweat Mem. Mus., 1952; Wichita AA, 1948-1950; Phila. WC Cl., 1952; Wash. WC Cl.; AWS; Salon d'Automne, 1951; BM, 1951, 1952; Intl. Color lithog., exh., 1952-1954, 1956; MMA, 1952;

Curator's Choice, 1956; Am. Color Print Soc., 1958, and others. *Position*: Assoc. Prof. A., Alabama Polytechnic Inst., Auburn, Ala., 1942, 1943, 1946- . Sec., Nat. Assn. Schs. of Design.

SYLVESTER, E. W.—*Museum Director*
Mariner's Museum, Newport News, Va.*

SYLVESTER, LUCILLE—*Painter, W., I., L., E.*
200 West 20th St., New York 11, N.Y.

Studied: ASL; Julian Acad., Paris, France. *Member*: AAPL; Audubon A.; NAWA; Knickerbocker A.; Catherine L. Wolfe A. Cl. *Award*: medal, Knickerbocker A., 1952; Wolfe A. Cl., 1957. *Exhibited*: NAD; NAWA; Audubon A.; All. A. Am.; Argent Gal.; ASL; NAC; AEA; Barbizon Hotel, 1955 (one-man); New Jersey P. & S., 1955; Butler Gal., 1955; Churchill Gal., 1957 (one-man); Hudson Gld. Gal., 1958 (2-man). Contributor to national magazines. Author, I., juvenile books. Exec. Bd., Knickerbocker A., 1957-58.

SYMON, GAIL—*Painter, T.*
New Canaan, Conn.

B. Boston, Mass. *Studied*: NAD; ASL; Grand Central A. Sch.; Otis AI. *Member*: Audubon A.; Conn. Acad. FA; Silvermine Gld. A.; New Haven Paint & Clay Cl. *Awards*: prizes, Silvermine Gld. A., 1945; New Haven Paint & Clay Cl., 1951; Conn. Acad. FA, 1953. *Exhibited*: Argent Gal.; Montross Gal.; Salpeter Gal.; Babcock Gal.; Macbeth Gal., all in New York City; Riverside Mus.; three one-man exhs., New York City. *Position*: Dir., Vice-Pres., Silvermine Gld. Sch. A., New Canaan, Conn., 1950- .

SZABO, LASZLO—*Portrait Painter, T., L.*
795 Elmwood Ave.; h. 103 Lancaster Ave., Buffalo 22, N.Y.

B. Budapest, Hungary, Aug. 18, 1895. *Studied*: Royal Acad. A., Budapest; Ecole des Beaux-Arts, Paris, France; ASL. *Member*: Pan Arts Soc.; Buffalo Soc. A.; Rationalists A. Cl. (V.P.); Gld. All. A.; Genesee Group; Batavia Soc. A.; Daubers Cl; FA Lg. *Awards*: prizes, Buffalo Soc. A., 1938, 1943, 1946, 1947, 1950, 1951-1954; Gld. All. A., 1939, 1940, 1944, 1949, 1950, 1952; Pan Arts Soc., gold medal, 1955; Rembrandt prize, 1956; Diestel & MacDonald prizes, 1957; FA Lg., silver medal, 1958. *Work*: Erie County Hall, Buffalo, N.Y.; Niagara Sanatorium, Lockport, N.Y.; Buffalo Consistory, Riverside H.S., Liberty Bank, all of Buffalo; Swope A. Gal.; N.Y. State Hist. Assn., Ticonderoga, N.Y. *Exhibited*: Buffalo Soc. A., annually; Gld. All. A.; Albright A. Gal., Rundall Gal., Rochester; Rationalists A. Cl., traveling exhs. in Rochester, Albany, Binghampton, Auburn, N.Y.; Batavia Soc. A.; Genesee Group; PAFA; Ogunquit A. Center; Sheldon Swope A. Gal.; one-man: Town Cl., Kowalski Gal., Twentieth Century Cl., Pub. Lib., Shea's Buffalo Theatre, all in Buffalo, N.Y.

SZANTO, LOUIS P.—*Painter, Et.*
54 West 74th St., New York 23, N.Y.

B. Vacz, Hungary, Oct. 8, 1889. *Studied*: Acad. A., Budapest, Hungary. *Member*: Royal Acad. Soc.; A. Cl., Budapest. *Work*: Hungarian Mus. A.; murals, Bellevue Hospital, N.Y.; St. Clement Pope Church, Poughkeepsie, N.Y.; Soc. for Savings Bank, Cleveland, Ohio; Manhattan Savings Bank, N.Y.; Farm Bureau, Columbus, Ohio; Thompson Products Co., Cleveland; Ohio Oil Co., Findlay, Ohio; Cities Service Co., N.Y.; Pittsburgh Fnd., and many ports. in private colls. Illus. "Imitation of Christ"; series of illus. for "Break-through in Science," 1958.

TABARY, CELINE MARIE—*Painter, Des., T.*
1220 Quincy St., Northeast, Washington 17, D.C.; h. #504, 200 Massachusetts Ave., Northwest, Washington 1, D.C.

B. Vermelles, France, July 29, 1908. *Studied*: in France. *Member*: Wash. Soc. A.; Societe des Artistes Lillois; A. Gld., Wash.; Washington WC Cl.; CGA. *Awards*: prizes, U.S. Nat. Mus., 1951 and prior; Wash. Soc. A., 1957. *Work*: Barnet Aden Gal.; PC; Palais National, Haiti. *Exhibited*: Paris, 1938, 1939; Am-British A. Center, 1944; Inst. Mod. A., Boston, 1944, 1947, 1948, 1950; NAD, 1945, 1948, 1950, 1952; PC, 1940, 1945, 1946-1950; Wash. Pub. Lib., 1946, 1954; Whyte Gal. A., 1941-1944, 1947,

1948, 1950, 1951; Barnet Aden Gal., 1943-1946; Howard Univ., 1941, 1942; U.S. Nat. Mus., 1940, 1944, 1954, 1956-1958; CGA, 1940, 1944, 1945-1950, 1956-1958; Wash. WC Cl., 1947-1952, 1954; BMA, 1952; Dupont A. Gal., 1950 (one-man); Playhouse Theatre, 1956, 1957; Pyramid Cl., Phila., 1957; Art Mart, 1956-1958; Watkins Gal., Wash., D.C., 1958; Art Mart, Georgetown, 1957 (one-man). Numerous exhs. in France. *Position*: Instr. A., Howard Univ., Wash., D.C., 1945-50; Morgan State Col., Balt., Md., 1954-55.

TABOR, ROBERT BYRON—*Painter*
200 South Water St., Olathe, Kans.

B. Independence, Iowa, Feb. 12, 1882. *Member*: Ozark A. Gld.; NSMP. *Work*: White House, Wash., D.C.; Lane Ins. Co.; Independence (Iowa) Pub. Lib.; murals, hotels in Des Moines, Independence, Estherville, Iowa; USPO, Independence. *Exhibited*: Nat. Exh. Am. A., N.Y., 1936; MModA, 1934; CGA, 1934; AFA; Colo. Springs FA Center, 1940, 1941; Ogunquit A. Center, 1951; Joslyn A. Mus., 1953, 1954; Waterloo (Iowa) AA, 1954 (one-man); Innes Gal., Wichita, 1955 (one-man); Kansas City AA, 1957; Cedar Rapids, 1957 (one-man); Independence, Iowa, 1958 (one-man).

TAGGART, GEORGE HENRY—*Portrait Painter*
11 Hillside Ave., Port Washington, L.I., N.Y.

B. Watertown, N.Y., Mar. 12, 1865. *Studied*: Julian Acad., Paris, France. *Work*: Palace of Governor, City of Mexico; Brigham Young Univ.; State Capitol, Salt Lake City, Utah; City Hall, Watertown, N.Y.; Tusculum Col., Greenville, Tenn.; Welch Mem. Lib., Baltimore, Md.*

TAGGART, RICHARD (T.)—*Painter, Des., W.*
P.O. Box 335, 2346 North El Molino Ave., Altadena, Cal.

B. Indianapolis, Ind., May 11, 1904. *Studied*: with Paul Hadley, Jean Mannheim, Alson Clark. *Member*: Pasadena SA; P. & S. Cl., Los A., Cal.; Cal. AC; Carmel A.; Laguna Beach AA. *Work*: Pomona Col., Claremont, Cal.; Huntington Hospital, Pasadena. *Exhibited*: GGE, 1939; Pasadena SA; Cal. AC; Carmel AA; Laguna Beach AA; John Herron AI; Purdue Univ.; Univ. Southern California; one-man exh.: Stanford Univ.; Pomona Col.; Nicholson's Gal., Pasadena, Col.; Stendahl Gal., Los A., Cal. *Position*: Visiting A., Instr. A., Pomona Col., 1940-41; Special I., Mt. Wilson Observatory, 1944; A. Dir., Exec. Producer, "Inspiration for Christmas," 16mm. color film, Esto Publ. Co., 1955; "Speaking of Sculpture," 1957; "Mildred Brooks Makes an Etching," 1958 (both films for Esto Publ. Co.); A. Dir., W., Producer, 16mm. films, Argonaut Productions, Altadena, Cal., 1954- .

TAIT, MRS. TREVORS. See Lamb, Katharine

TAIT, AGNES (Mrs. Agnes Tait McNulty)—*Painter, Lith., I.*
332 Otero St., Santa Fé, N.M.

B. New York, N.Y., June 14, 1897. *Studied*: NAD. *Work*: N.Y. Pub. Lib.; MMA; Lib. Cong.; murals, Bellevue Hospital, N.Y.; USPO, Laurinsburg, N.C. *Exhibited*: nationally. I., "Peter & Penny of the Island," 1941; "Heide."

TAKAL, PETER—*Painter, Gr.*
27 West 58th St., New York 19, N.Y.; s. Saylorsburg, Pa.

B. Bucharest, Roumania, Dec. 8, 1905. *Studied*: in Berlin; art in Paris. *Member*: AEA; Am. Color Pr. Soc.; Brooklyn Soc. A.; Boston Pr. M. *Awards*: New Haven Paint & Clay Cl., 1953; Knickerbocker A., 1955, 1958; Boston Pr. M.: 1956; Brooklyn Soc. A., 1957, 1958; Phila. Pr. Cl., 1958; Ball State T. Col., 1958. *Work*: MMA; WMAA; MModA; BM; deYoung Mem. Mus.; N.Y. Pub. Lib.; PMA; Crocker A. Gal., Sacramento; BMA; Achenbach Graphic Coll.; AGAA; DMFA; LC; John Herron AI; CMA; Mills Col., Oakland; Univ. Maine; Morgan Lib.; NGA; SFMA; Los A. Mus. A.; CAM, and others; also in European museums and collections. *Exhibited*: SFMA, 1943, 1958; PAFA, 1953; Norfolk Mus. A.; WMAA, 1955-1958; BM, 1954-1958; LC, 1955, 1957-1959; CAM, 1956; Univ. Utah, 1957; Phila. Pr. Cl., 1956-1958; Phila. A. All., 1957; Sweat Mus. A., 1956, 1958; Smithsonian Inst.,

1956, 1958; Silvermine Gld. A., 1956, 1958; Ball State T. Col., 1958; AWS, 1958; Des Moines A. Center, 1958; Dayton AI, 1958; AFA traveling Exhs., 1955-1958; Oakland A. Mus., 1955, 1958; Pr. Council Am., 1959; Contemporaries, 1959; SAM, 1959; Ringling Mus. A., 1959, and many others; 23 one-man exhs., 1932-1959; one-man traveling exh. throughout U.S., 1957-58; one-man traveling exh., Smithsonian Inst., 1959-60.

TALBOT, GRACE HELEN—*Sculptor*
Woodbury Rd., Syosset, L.I., N.Y.

B. North Billerica, Mass., Sept. 3, 1901. *Studied*: with Harriet W. Frishmuth. *Member*: NSS; NAWA. *Awards*: prize, Arch. L., 1922; med., NAWA, 1925.

TALBOT, JAROLD D.—*Painter, C., Mus. Dir.*
125 North Pine St., Decatur, Ill.

B. Solano, N.M., Aug. 28, 1907. *Studied*: Drake Univ.; Cumming Sch. A.; Tiffany Fnd., and with Ivan Olinsky. *Member*: CAA. *Awards*: numerous prizes in Iowa exhibitions; grand award and 1st prize, Jacksonville, 1958. *Exhibited*: NAD; Audubon A; Old Northwest Territory Exh.; CM, 1958, and others. *Position*: Prof. A., Millikin Univ.; Dir., Decatur A. Center; Decatur, Ill.

TALBOT, SOPHIA DAVIS—*Painter*
Ridge Crest Farm, R.F.D. 2, Melrose, Iowa

B. Boone County, Iowa, Apr. 13, 1888. *Studied*: Iowa State Univ.; Cumming Sch. A. *Member*: Nat. Lg. Am. Pen Women; Mattoon Writers' Cl.; AFA. *Awards*: prizes, Wawasee A. Gal., 1942; Swope A. Gal., 1947, 1948, 1950, 1951, 1953, 1956; Nat. Lg. Am. Pen Women, 1950, 1952. *Work*: Hawthorne, Lincoln Schs., Mattoon, Ill.; Admin. Bldg. & Booth Mem. Lib., Eastern Ill. State Col.; Lowell Sch., Mattoon, Ill.; Lincoln Sch., Brookfield, Ill.; mural, Nat. Bank of Mattoon. *Exhibited*: Women Painters of Am., Wichita, 1938; Denver A. Mus., 1941; Wawasee A. Gal., 1942, 1943; All-Illinois Soc. FA, 1939-1941; Central Illinois A., 1943, 1944; Eastern Ill. State T. Col., 1949 (with Fred Conway); Swope A. Gal., 1947, 1948, 1950, 1951, 1953; Ogunquit A. Center, 1950, 1951; Nat. Lg. Am. Pen Women, 1950-1952, 1957; Magnificent Mile Exh., Chicago, 1951; Wurlitzer Gal., Chicago, 1955; Ill. State Fair, 1955; one-man: Drake Hotel, Chicago, 1942; Eastern Ill. State T. Col., 1942; Mattoon, Ill., 1942. *Position*: Instr. Drawing, State Univ. Iowa, 1914-17; privately, 1927-51.

TALBOT, WILLIAM—*Sculptor*
Washington, Conn.

B. Boston, Mass., Jan. 10, 1918. *Studied*: PAFA, and with George Demetrios. *Member*: Arch. Lg.; S. Gld. *Awards*: Prix de Rome, 1941; Penrose award, Conn. Acad. FA, 1950. *Work*: WMAA; memorial, Bryn Mawr; fountain, Fitchburg Mass., A. Pub. Lib. *Exhibited*: PAFA, 1940, 1949; NAD, 1941; Int. Sculpture Exh., 1949; WMAA, 1950-1951; S. Gld., 1952; Sculpture Center, N.Y., 1950-1952.*

TALCOTT, DUDLEY VAILL—*Sculptor, I., W., P.*
Old Mountain Rd., Farmington, Conn.

B. Hartford, Conn., June 9, 1899. *Work*: panels, figures, etc., WFNY 1939; Hartford Nat. Bank & Trust Co., New London, Conn. branch; des., wrote & illus. brochure for Helio Aircraft Corp., Norwood, Mass., 1954, 1955. *Exhibited*: AIC, 1940; Valentine Dudensing Gal., 1927; MModA, 1930; WMAA, 1937; Grace Horne Gal., Boston; Phillips Acad., Andover, Mass. Author, I., "Noravind," 1929; "Report of the Company," 1936*

TAM, REUBEN—*Painter, T.*
549 West 123rd St., New York, N.Y.; s. Mohegan, Me.

B. Kapaa, Kauai, Hawaii, Jan. 17, 1916. *Studied*: Univ. Hawaii, Ed. B.; Cal. Sch. FA; Columbia Univ.; New Sch. for Social Research. *Member*: Fed. Mod. P. & S. *Awards*: prizes, GGE, 1939; Honolulu Acad. FA, 1939, 1941; Honolulu Pr. M., 1940; BM, 1952; Guggenheim F., 1948. *Work*: MModA; MMA; BM; IBM; Honolulu Acad. FA; Wichita A. Mus.; Massillon Mus. A.; N.Y. Pub. Lib.; Ft. Worth AA; Univ. Nebraska; Univ. Georgia; Los A. Pub. Lib.; Butler AI; Am. Acad. A. & Let.; Albright A. Gal.; DMFA; Munson-Williams-Proctor Inst.; Newark

Mus. A.; Encyclopaedia Britannica; Des Moines A. Center; WMAA. *Exhibited*: VMFA; Carnegie Inst.; PAFA; Los A. Mus. A.; Albright A. Gal.; WFNY 1939; GGE, 1939; BM; MModA; WMAA; Univ. Illinois; MMA; Walker A. Center; AIC; CGA; Boston A. Festival; U.S. State Dept. European Exh.; MModA traveling exh.; AFA traveling exh. One-man: Cal. PLH, 1940; Crocker A. Gal., 1941; Honolulu Acad. FA, 1941; Downtown Gal., 1945, 1946, 1949, 1952; Alan Gal., 1955, 1957; Phila. A. All., 1954. *Position*: Instr., Painting, Brooklyn Mus. Sch. A., Brooklyn, N.Y.

TANGUY, KAY. See Sage, Kay

TASEV, ATANAS—*Painter*
5415 Connecticut Ave., Washington, D.C.

B. Sofia, Bulgaria, Mar. 4, 1897. *Studied*: A. Acad., Prague, and in Sofia, Bulgaria. *Work*: Nat. Mus., Sofia; Dept. Edu., Prague; PMG. *Exhibited*: CGA, and extensively in Europe.

TASKEY, HARRY LeROY—*Painter, Et., Lith., I.*
R.D. 1, Milford, N.J.

B. Rockford, Ind., June 12, 1892. *Studied*: ASL; Grande Chaumiere, Paris; Hiram (Ohio) Col. *Member*: Am. Veterans Soc. A.; Audubon A. *Work*: MMA; N.Y. Pub. Lib.; Syracuse Mus. FA; Mus. City of N.Y.; John Herron AI; Wilmington Soc. FA; New Britain A. Mus. *Exhibited*: BM; AIC; NAD; Texas Centennial Exp., 1936; PAFA; Syracuse Mus. FA; CGA; Phila. A. All.; LC; Am. Pr. M.; WMAA; CM; SAGA, 1949-1951.*

TATE, SALLY—*Portrait Painter, I.*
3 Thomas Rd., Westport, Conn.

B. Sewickley, Pa., June 6, 1908. *Studied*: Vesper George Sch. A.; Parsons Sch. Des.; & with Bernard Keyes, Heinrich Moore, Jose Pillon. *Member*: Pen & Brush Cl. *Exhibited*: children's illus., Springfield Lib.; Lucien Labault Gal., San F. Author, I., "The Furry Bear"; "The Wooly Lamb"; & other children's stories; I., textbooks. Lectures: Children's Illustrations.*

TATSCHL, JOHN—*Craftsman, S., E., Gr.*
Art Department, University of New Mexico; h. 3502 12th St., Northwest, Albuquerque, N.M.

B. Vienna, Austria, June 30, 1906. *Studied*: T. Col., Vienna; Acad. App. A., Acad. FA, Master Sch. Sculpture, Vienna. *Awards*: Research Grants, Univ. New Mexico, 1950, 1953. *Work*: Mus. New Mexico, Santa Fé; mural, USPO, Vivian, La.; monument, Campus, Univ. New Mexico; wood sculpture, Lib., Univ. New Mexico; stained glass windows, St. Michael Church, First Methodist Church, Albuquerque. *Exhibited*: Nat. Sculpture Comp., N.Y., 1939; regularly in Southwest Exhs., 1946-1956. Lectures: Hebrew and Greek Culture; Taraskan Sculpture; Art Education Aims, etc. *Position*: Asst. Prof., Park Col., Mo., 1943-46; Prof. A., Univ. New Mexico, Albuquerque, N.M., 1946- .

TATTI, BENEDICT—*Sculptor, T., P.*
117 East 39th St., New York 16, N.Y.

B. New York, N.Y., May 1, 1917. *Studied*: ASL; and with Louis Slobodkin, William Zorach. *Member*: Brooklyn Soc. A. *Awards*: prizes, Brooklyn Soc. A., 1944; NGA, 1945. *Exhibited*: MMA, 1942; NGA, 1945; Brooklyn Soc. A., 1943-1947, 1951; Tribune A. Gal., 1946 (one-man); Audubon A., 1947; PAFA, 1950, 1954; Arch. Lg., 1950; Hans Hofmann Sch. A., 1949, 1950. *Position*: Raymond Loewy Assoc., 1951- .

TAUBES, FREDERIC—*Painter, Et., Lith., W., L., E., Cr.*
Haverstraw, N.Y.

B. Lwow, Poland, Apr. 15, 1900. *Studied*: Munich A. Acad., with F. von Stuck, M. Doerner; Bauhaus, Weimar, with J. Itten. *Member*: F., Royal Soc. A., London. *Work*: SFMA; William Rockhill Nelson Gal.; MMA; San Diego FA Soc.; Santa Barbara Mus.A.; deYoung Mem. Mus.; High Mus. A.; etc. *Exhibited*: Carnegie Inst., 1936-1946; CGA, 1936-1946; PAFA, 1935-1944; VMFA, 1938-1946; AIC, 1935-1946; 25 one-man exhs. in New York City. Author: "The Technique of Oil Painting," 1941; "You

Don't Know Know What You Like," 1952; "Anatomy of Genius," 1949; "Quickest Way to Paint Well," 1951; "The Mastery of Oil Painting"; "Modern Art Sweet and Sour"; "Pictorial Anatomy of the Human Body"; Collected essays: "The Art and Technique of Portrait Painting," and other books. Contributing Ed., to: American Artist magazine, with "Taubes' Page"; Former Contributing Ed., Encyclopaedia Britannica; Yearbooks. *Positions:* Carnegie Visiting Prof. A., A. in Residence, Univ. Illinois, 1940-41; Visiting Prof., Mills Col., Oakland, Cal., 1938; Univ. Hawaii, 1939; CUASch, 1943; Univ. Wisconsin, 1945, and many other universities in Canada and England, 1947-51. Formulator of Taubes Varnishes and Copal Painting Media.

TAUCH, WALDINE—*Sculptor, P., T.*
115 Melrose Place, San Antonio 12, Tex.

B. Schulenberg, Tex., Jan. 28, 1892. *Studied:* with Pompeo Coppini. *Member:* NSS; Nat. Soc. A. & Let.; Coppini Acad. FA; San Antonio A. Lg.; San Antonio River A. Group; San Antonio Conservation Soc.; San Antonio Woman's Cl. (hon.). *Awards:* Hon. deg., D.F.A., Howard Payne Col., Brownwood, Tex. *Work:* Witte Mem. Mus.; Wesleyan Col., Macon, Ga.; monument, City Hall Square, San Antonio; Canton, Tex.; Gonzales, Tex.; Bedford, Ind.; Richmond, Ky.; fountain, Pelham Manor, New York, N.Y.; relief, Children's Reading Room, Jersey City Lib.; portrait relief, Howard Payne Col., Brownwood, Tex.; monument, Buckner Boys' Ranch, Burnet, Tex.; fountain group, Kocurek Estate, San Antonio; Baylor Univ. Lib. *Position:* Assoc. Prof. S., Trinity Univ., San Antonio, Tex., 1942-45.

TAYLOR, BERTHA FANNING—
Painter, L., Mus. Cur., W., T., Cr.
Woman's Club, 524 Fairfax Ave., Norfolk 7, Va.

B. New York, N.Y., July 30, 1883. *Studied:* CUASch; Sorbonne, Univ. de Montpelier, Ecole du Louvre, Paris, France; & with Maurice Denis, Georges Desvalliers. *Member:* CAA; Am. Soc. for Aesthetics; PBC; AEA; AAPL; AWS; *Awards:* med., Paris Salon, 1937; PBC, 1942. *Exhibited:* Societe National des Beaux-Arts, Salon d'Automne, Salon des Tuileries, Salon des Artistes Independants, Musee du Jeu de Paume, Paris, France; Ferargil Gal., 1940; Garden City Community Cl., 1941 (one-man); Harlow Gal., 1944; Sharon, Conn., 1941 (one-man); PBC, 1942, 1944, 1945. *Work:* triptych: Chapel Benmoreel Protestant Church, Norfolk, Va.; many portrait commissions. Lectures: French School from Gallo-Roman period to 20th Century. *Position:* L., Louvre Mus., Paris, 1930-39; A.Cr., New York Herald-Tribune's Paris Edition, 1930-32, 1932-39; Cur., The Hermitage Fnd. Mus., Norfolk, Va., 1945-49; Instr., Adult Classes, Norfolk Mus. A. & Sciences; A.Cr., Norfolk Virginian-Pilot.

TAYLOR, CORA BLISS—*Painter, L., T.*
Saugatuck, Mich.

B. Cincinnati, Ohio, Apr. 14, 1895. *Studied:* AIC; ASL, & with Leopold Seyffert, Leon Kroll, Charles Hawthorne, & others. *Member:* Mich. Acad. A. *Awards:* prizes, AIC, 1925, 1930; Detroit Inst. A., 1955. *Work:* Chicago Pub. Sch. *Exhibited:* Detroit Inst. A.; AIC; Minneapolis Inst. A.

TAYLOR, EDGAR—*Painter, T.*
1615 La Vereda Rd., Berkeley 9, Cal.

B. Grass Valley, Cal., July 15, 1904. *Studied:* Univ. California, B.A., M.A. *Member:* San F. AA. *Awards:* Taussig traveling F., Univ. California, 1932; prizes, Texas FA Assn., 1942, 1944; SFMA, 1945, 1946. *Work:* SFMA. *Exhibited:* San F. AA, 1936-1939, 1943-1946; AIC; Los A. Mus. A., 1945, 1948, 1949; AFA traveling exh., 1940, 1948; Carnegie Inst., traveling exh., 1940; GGE, 1939; deYoung Mem. Mus., 1950; Texas General Exh., 1941-1943. *Position:* Instr., Univ. California, Berkeley, Cal., 1945-46; Univ. So. California, 1951-52.*

TAYLOR, GRACE MARTIN—*Painter, Gr., E., L.*
Morris Harvey College (4); h. 1900 McClung St., Charleston 1, W. Va.

B. Morgantown, W. Va. *Studied:* Univ. W. Va., A.B., M.A.; PAFA; Carnegie Inst.; AIC; Emil Bisttram Sch. A.; Hans Hofmann Sch. FA; Ohio Univ., and with Fritz Pfeiffer, Blanche Lazzell, William and Natalie Grauer, and

others. *Member:* Am. Color Pr. Soc.; Tri-State AA (Fndr., Bd. Dir.); Creative AA of W. Va. (Fndr., Bd. Trustees); Assn. Higher Edu., W. Va. *Awards:* prizes, 50 Best Color Prints, 1933; West Virginia AA, 1942, 1945, 1947-1949, 1953-1957; Va. Intermont Col., 1948; Tri-State Creative AA, 1953-1955; Huntington Gal., 1955; Hallmark award, 1953. *Exhibited:* Oakland A. Mus.; Smithsonian Inst.; CGA; MMA; Phila. Pr. Cl.; BM; SFMA; Los A. Mus. A.; NAD; Mint Mus. A.; Provincetown AA; Soc. Four A.; Wash. WC Cl.; AFA traveling exh.; William & Mary Col.; Ohio Valley WC Exh.; one-man: Ohio Univ.; W. Va. Univ. Author: section in "Preparation and Use of Visual Aids," 1950. *Position:* Hd. A. Dept., Mason Col. Music & FA, 1934-56; Admin. Asst., 1950-53, Dean, 1953-55, Pres., 1955-56, Faculty, 1956- , Morris Harvey College, Charleston, W. Va.

TAYLOR, JOHN C. E.—*Painter, E.*
Trinity College, Hartford, Conn.; h. 30 Four Mile Rd., West Hartford 7, Conn.

B. New Haven, Conn., Oct. 22, 1902. *Studied:* Yale Univ., B.A., M.A.; Julian Acad., Paris; & with Walter Griffin. *Member:* FA Comm., City of Hartford; Rockport AA; North Shore AA; Conn. Acad. FA; SC. *Awards:* Cooper prize, Hartford, Conn., 1935; New Orleans, 1946; Rockport AA, 1955. *Work:* New Britain (Conn.) A. Mus. *Exhibited:* CGA 1935, 1939; Pepsi-Cola, 1946; AV, 1942; Gloucester, Mass.; Hartford, Conn.; Palm Beach, Fla.; San F., Cal.; Charlotte, N.C.; Boston, Mass.; etc. *Position:* Hd. FA Dept., 1945- , Assoc. Prof., 1952- , Prof., 1956- , Trinity Col., Hartford, Conn.

TAYLOR, JOHN (WILLIAMS)—*Painter, Pr. M.*
Shady, Woodstock Twp., Ulster County, N.Y.

B. Baltimore, Md., Oct. 12, 1897. *Studied:* ASL, and with Boardman Robinson; also with J. Francis Smith, S. Mac Donald-Wright; also study abroad. *Member:* NA; CAA; Woodstock AA. *Awards:* prizes, Am. Acad. A. & Let., 1948; Paintings of the Year, 1948; BMA, 1939; medals, AWS, 1949; VMFA, 1946; Guggenheim F., 1954. *Work:* mural, USPO, Richfield Springs, N.Y.; other work: VMFA; New Britain Inst.; WMAA; MMA; Canajoharie A. Gal.; Hackley A. Gal.; NAD; ASL; Currier Gal. A.; John Herron AI; Morse Gal. A., Rollins Col. *Exhibited:* Carnegie Inst., 1941-1950; PAFA, 1948, 1949, 1951, 1952, 1954; VMFA, 1948; Univ. Illinois, 1948, 1949; WMAA, 1943-1946, 1951, 1954, 1955; AWS, 1949; John Herron AI, 1945, 1946, 1953-1955; NAD, 1945, 1949, 1951, 1952, 1954, 1955, 1957; one-man: Macbeth Gal., 1938, 1944, 1950; Milch Gal., 1955; Am. Acad. A. & Let., 1948. *Position:* Instr., John Herron AI, Indianapolis, Ind., 1950, 1954, 1957; ASL, Woodstock, N.Y., 1948-51, 1954; Visiting Instr., Pa. State Univ., 1957; Mich. State Univ., 1958; Assoc. Prof. Painting, Tulane Univ., 1958-59.

TAYLOR, KATRINA V. H. See Van Hook, Katrina

TAYLOR, PRENTISS—*Painter, Lith., T., L., I., W.*
J 718 Arlington Towers, Arlington 9, Va.

B. Washington, D.C., Dec. 13, 1907. *Studied:* ASL, and with Charles Hawthorne, Charles Locke, and others. *Member:* ANA; A. Gld. Wash.; Soc. Wash. Pr. M. (Pres.); Albany Pr. Cl.; Boston Pr. M.; SAGA; Wash. WC Cl. *Awards:* prizes, Greater Wash. Indp. Exh., 1935; VMFA, 1943; LC, 1943; Am. A. Group, 1953; NAD, 1954; Boston Pr.M., 1954; VMFA, 1955; CGA. *Work:* BMFA; AGAG; Wadsworth Atheneum; N.Y. Pub. Lib.; MMA; WMAA; PMA; BMA; PMG; LC; Univ. Virginia; VMFA; Norfolk Mus. A. & Sc.; Gibbes A. Gal.; SAM. *Exhibited:* WMAA, 1945; VMFA, 1943; Irene Ieach Mem., 1945, 1946, 1949-1952; AIC, 1933 and subsequently; PAFA; Phila. Pr. Cl.; CGA, 1949, 1951; Phila. A. All.; LC; A. Gld. Wash.; Rochester Mem. A. Gal.; Carnegie Inst., 1946-1949; Atlanta, Ga., 1957, 1958; Butler Inst. Am. A., 1957. I., "Scottsboro Limited"; "The Negro Mother." Lectures: Invention and History of Lithography; Art as Psychotherapy; Pissarro; Degas; Cezanne; Characteristics of Current American Prints. *Position:* Art Therapist, St. Elizabeths Hospital, Washington, D.C., 1943-54; L., Painting, American Univ., Wash., D.C., 1955- .

TAYLOR, RALPH—*Painter, T., Gr.*
2028 Chestnut St., Philadelphia 3, Pa.

B. Jan. 18, 1897. *Studied:* Phila. Graphic Sketch Cl.; PAFA; with Henry McCarter, and abroad. *Member:* Phila.

A. All.; F., PAFA; Phila. Pr. Cl.; Phila. WC Cl.; Wood-
mere A. Gal. *Awards*: bronze medal, Phila. A. Week;
Cresson traveling scholarship, PAFA, 1922; gold medal,
Cape May, N.J., 1949; prizes, PAFA, 1952; F., PAFA,
1954; Da Vinci All., 1955. *Work*: PAFA; F., PAFA,
LaFrance Alliance; Graphic Sketch Cl., and in private
colls. *Exhibited*: CGA; NAD; PAFA; Rochester Mem. A.
Gal.; All. A. Am.; Phila. A. All.; PMA; Woodmere A.
Gal.; Graphic Sketch Cl.; State T. Col., Indiana, Pa.;
Butler Inst. Am. A.; Phila. Pr. Cl.; and others.

TAYLOR, RICHARD LIPPINCOTT DENISON—
Cartoonist, P.
Otis Rd., Blandford, Mass.

B. Fort William, Ontario, Canada, Sept. 18, 1902. *Studied*:
Ontario Col. A., Canada; Los A. Sch. A. & Des.; Central
Tech. Sch., Toronto, and privately. *Work*: New Yorker
magazine originals in many private colls., U.S. and
abroad. Watercolor drawings: MMoA; BMFA; Albright
A. Gal.; Wichita Mus. A.; Univ. Nebraska, and private
colls. *Exhibited*: BM, 1941; AIC, 1941; BMFA, 1941;
MMA, 1942; WMAA, 1943; Carnegie Inst., 1946; 2-man
(Steig) Flint Inst. A., 1943; one-man: Walker Gal.,
N.Y., 1940; Butler AI, 1940; Albright A. Gal., 1941;
AGAA, 1941; Hudson Gal., Detroit, 1951; Rouillier Gal.,
Chicago, 1941; Valentine Gal., N.Y., 1941, and others.
Author, I., "Introduction to Cartooning," 1947; "By the
Dawn's Ugly Light," 1953; "The Better Taylors" (coll.
cartoons), 1944. I., "Sir Galahad & Other Rimes," 1936;
"I Didn't Know It Was Loaded," 1948; "One for the
Road," 1949; "Fractured French," 1950; "Compound
Fractured French," 1951; "Never Say Diet," 1954, and
many other books. Contributor illus., cartoons, to New
Yorker magazine; Sat. Eve. Post; Colliers; Esquire;
American; Town & Country; Mademoiselle; Life; McCalls,
and others.*

TAYLOR, ROSEMARY—Craftsman
721 Marshall Place, Plainfield, N.J.

B. Joseph, Ore. *Studied*: Cleveland Inst. A.; N.Y. Univ.
Member: Artist-Craftsmen of N.Y.; New Jersey Des.-
Craftsmen; Plainfield AA; Rahway A. Center. *Award*:
Plainfield AA, 1956-1958. *Exhibited*: Rahway A. Center,
1955 (one-man); New Jersey Des.-Craftsmen, regularly;
Newark Mus. A.; Mus. Nat. Hist.; annually in Craftsmen's
Groups; Montclair A. Mus.; Syracuse Mus. FA; Newark
Pub. Lib. Demonstrations of techniques of ceramics. *Posi-
tion*: Instr., Rahway A. Center, Rahway Adult Edu.;
privately.

TAYLOR, RUTH P.—Painter, Gr., E.
161 Emerson Place, Brooklyn 5, N.Y.

B. Winsted, Conn., Mar. 21, 1900. *Studied*: PIASch.;
ASL, and with Jane Freeman, George Bridgman, Kimon
Nicolaides. *Member*: NAWA; Brooklyn Soc. A.; Pen &
Brush Cl. *Award*: prize, Riverside Mus., 1956. *Exhibited*:
NAWA, 1935-1958, and traveling exhs.; N.Y. WC Cl.,
1936; AWS, 1937, 1951; LC, 1944; BM, 1941-1946, 1952;
Argent Gal., 1937-1958; Newark A. Sch., 1938-1945; Brook-
lyn Soc. A., 1948-1958, and traveling exhs.; Pen & Brush
Cl., 1951-1958, and others. *Position*: Instr., Newark A.
Sch., Newark, N.J., 1926-45; Asst. Prof., PIASch., Brook-
lyn, N.Y., 1925-56, Assoc. Prof., 1956- ; 1st Vice-Pres.,
1956-58, Rec. Sec., 1958-59, Brooklyn Soc. A.; Chm.,
Watercolor Jury, 1957-59, NAWA.

TAYSON, WAYNE PENDLETON—Sculptor, E.
Kidder Hall, Oregon State College; h. 1765 Alta Vista
St., Corvallis, Ore.

B. Afton, Wyo., Oct. 10, 1925. *Studied*: Univ. Wyoming;
Columbia Univ.; Univ. Utah, B.F.A.; Ecole des Beaux-
Arts, Paris; T. Col., Columbia Univ., M.A.; Cranbrook
Acad. A. *Member*: AAUP; Portland (Ore.) AA. *Award*:
purchase prize, Portland A. Mus., 1956. *Work*: Portland
A. Mus.; ports. in private colls.; architectural sculpture,
Medical-Dental Center and Masonic Temple, both Cor-
vallis. *Exhibited*: Detroit Inst. A., 1950; Portland A. Mus.,
1953-1958; SAM, 1954-1957; Denver A. Mus., 1953-1956;
San F. AA, 1954-1957; Northwest Sculpture, 1955-1957.
Positions: Prof. S., Univ. Oregon, 1951-52; Oregon State
College, Corvallis, Ore., 1953- .

TEAGUE, DONALD—Painter
P.O. Box 745, Carmel, Cal.

B. Brooklyn, N.Y., Nov. 27, 1897. *Studied*: ASL, and in
London, England. *Member*: NA; Audubon A.; AWS; SC.
Awards: prizes, New Rochelle AA, 1935; SC, 1936; Isador
Prize, 1939; AWS, 1939, 1944, 1954, 1955; NAD, 1932,
1947, 1949, 1952; Cal. State Fair, 1952; Soc. Western
A., 1952-1954; gold medal, AWS, 1953; Medal of Honor,
American Artist magazine, 1957; prize, Cal. Statewide
Exh., 1954, 1955. *Work*: VMFA; Frye Mus. A., Seattle;
Cal. State Fair Coll.; U.S. Air Force, Colorado Springs,
Colo. *Exhibited*: MMA; NAD; BM; AIC; Toledo Mus.
A.; Conn. Acad. FA, and in Southern and Midwestern
museums. Contributor to Sat. Eve. Post; McCalls; Colliers;
Woman's Home Companion and other national magazines.

TEAGUE, WALTER DORWIN—Industrial Designer
444 Madison Ave., New York 22, N.Y.

B. Decatur, Ind., Dec. 18, 1883. *Studied*: ASL. *Member*:
Am. Soc. Indst. Des. (F. & Past Pres.); AIGA (Past
Pres.); Royal Des. for Industry, Great Britain (Hon.).
Lecturer on Design, Harvard Univ.; N.Y. Univ.; Univ.
Wisconsin; MIT; McGill Univ.; Am. Univ., Beirut, etc.
Author: "Design This Day"; "Land of Plenty" "Flour
for Man's Bread" (with Dr. John Storck); "You Can't
Ignore Murder" (with Ruth Mills Teague). Des. Counsel
for: Eastman Kodak Co.; Boeing Airplane Co.; A. B. Dick
Co.; E. I. Du Pont de Nemours Co.; Scripto, Inc.; Ritter,
Inc.; Polaroid Corp.; Servel, Inc.; Barcalo Mfg. Co., and
others. *Position*: Senior Partner, Walter Dorwin Teague
Assoc., New York, N.Y.*

TEDFORD, ELSIE MAE (Mrs. Donald S.)—Painter
P.O. Box 1091, Española, N.M.

B. Abington, Mass., Nov. 1, 1901. *Studied*: ASL; Tiffany
Fnd., and with Hayley Lever. *Awards*: prize, State Rodeo
Show, 1955. *Work*: IBM. *Exhibited*: NAD, 1931, 1933;
G-R-D Gal., 1933, 1934; Studio Gld.; Albion Col.; New
Mexico State Mus., 1949, 1953-1958; El Paso Pub. Lib.,
1950; Southwestern Carnival, 1950-1951; P. & S. of New
Mexico, 1949-1951.

TEE-VAN, HELEN DAMROSCH—Painter, I., Des.
120 East 75th St., New York 21, N.Y.

B. New York, N.Y., May 26, 1893. *Studied*: N.Y. Sch.
Display; & with George de Forest Brush, Jonas Lie. *Member*: Soc. Women Geographers. *Work*: murals & museum
displays: Berkshire Mus.; Bronx Zoo, N.Y. *Exhibited*:
NAD, 1917; CAM, 1917; CM, 1917; Los A. Mus. A.,
1926; Am. Mus. Natural Hist., N.Y., 1925; PAFA, 1923;
Gibbes Mem. A. Gal., 1935; Buffalo Mus. Sc., 1935; Berkshire Mus., 1936; Ainslie Gal., 1927; Warren Cox Gal.,
1931; Argent Gal., 1941. I., various scientific & juvenile
books, including, "Reluctant Farmer," 1950; "Mosquitoes
in the Big Ditch," 1952; "Reptiles Round the World,"
1957. Contributor to: Forum, Animal Kingdom, Story
Parade, & other publications. *Position*: A., N.Y. Zoological Soc. Expeditions, Tropical Research Dept., 1922, 1924,
1925, 1927, 1929-1933, 1946.

TEICHMAN, SABINA—Painter
27 East 22nd St.; h. 11 East 93rd St., New York 28,
N.Y.

B. New York, N.Y., Nov. 8, 1905. *Studied*: Columbia
Univ., A.B., M.A. *Member*: AEA; NAWA; Provincetown
AA; Cape Cod AA. *Awards*: medal, Westchester Women's
Cl., 1946. *Work*: Carnegie Inst.; Brandeis Univ.; G.W.V.
Smith Mus. A.; Tel-Aviv Mus., Israel; SFMA; WMAA;
Butler Inst. Am. A.; Mus. of the Univ. of Puerto Rico;
Living Arts Fnd. Coll., N.Y. *Exhibited*: AWS, 1934-1940;
NAWA, 1938-1954; N.Y. WC Soc., 1934-1936; Audubon
A., 1950, 1952, 1953; New Sch. for Social Research, 1952;
Cape Cod AA, 1953-1955; Provincetown AA, 1949-1955;
WMAA, 1956, and Collector's exh., 1958; one-man: Sal-
peter Gal., 1947, 1949, 1952, 1954; Shore Gal., Boston,
1955; ACA Gal., 1957.

TEICHMULLER, M. (Mrs. Minette T. Pohl)—Painter
Box 286, Route 8, San Antonio 1, Tex.

B. La Grange, Tex., Jan. 26, 1872. *Studied*: Sam Houston
Normal Sch.; San Antonio Acad. A. *Work*: White House,
Wash., D.C.; mural, USPO, Smithville, Tex., and ports.
in private colls.

TELLER, JANE (SIMON)—*Sculptor*

Route 263, Lahaska, Pa.

B. Rochester, N.Y., July 5, 1911. *Studied*: Skidmore Col.; Barnard Col., B.A., and with Aaron Goodelman. *Exhibited*: PMA, 1955; MModA, 1959; Friends Exh., Phila., 1955, 1956, 1958; Phillips Mill, New Hope, Pa., 1949-1951, 1953; Edward Callanan Gal., New Hope, 1956; Bertha Schaefer Gal., 1957; Parma Gal., N.Y., 1957.

TELLING, ELISABETH—*Painter, L.*

Clapboard Hill Rd., Guilford, Conn.

B. Milwaukee, Wis., July 14, 1882. *Studied*: Smith Col., B.L.; in Munich, with Herr Heymann; & with W. P. Henderson, George Senseney, Hamilton E. Field. *Member*: Soc. Women Geographers. *Work*: AIC; Los A. Mus. A. *Exhibited*: one-man exh.: AIC, 1922, 1937; Milwaukee AI, 1923, 1924; Marie Sterner Gal., 1933 ,1937; Rouillier Gal., Chicago, 1933; Courvoisier Gal., San F., Cal., 1936; Gibbes A. Gal., 1937; CGA, 1937; Northwestern Univ. Lib., 1937; Univ. Michigan, 1937; Quito, Ecuador, 1954; Chicago Nat. Hist. Mus., 1957.

TEMES, MORT(IMER) (ROBERT)—
Cartoonist. Comm. A.

10 Sycamore Dr., Hazlet, N.J.

B. Jersey City, N.J., Apr. 15, 1928. *Studied*: ASL, with William McNulty, Robert Hale, and others; N.Y. Univ., B.A. *Member*: Nat. Cartoonists Soc.; ASL; N.Y. Univ. Alumni. *Exhibited*: in cartoonists' exhibitions. *Work*: in many anthologies. Contributor cartoons to: Sat. Eve. Post; Look; True; American Weekly; Sports Illustrated; Ladies Home Journal; American Legion; King Features Syndicate; Playboy; Pictorial Review and other national magazines.

TENGGREN, GUSTAF ADOLF—
Illustrator, P., Des., Lith.

Dogfish Head, West Southport, Me.

B. Magra Socken, Sweden, Nov. 3, 1896. *Studied*: in Sweden. *Awards*: Herald-Tribune award, 1946. *Exhibited*: Am.-Swedish Hist. Mus., Phila., Pa., 1945 (Nordfeldt & Tenggren); Am.-Swedish Inst., Minneapolis, 1950 (one-man); Akron AI, 1952; Boothbay Harbor, Me., 1948 (one-man), 1949-1952; WMA; Oklahoma A. Center; AWS; Wash. WC Cl.; Phila. A. All.; Los A. County Fair; Maine A. Gal., Wiscasset, Me., 1957. *Work*: I., "The Tenggren Mother Goose"; "The Tenggren Tell It Again"; "Stories from the Great Metropolitan Operas"; "Sing for Christmas"; "Sing for America"; "Tenggren's Cowboys and Indians"; "Pirates, Ships and Sailors"; "Tenggren's Night Before Christmas," "Tenggren's Arabian Nights," 1957, and others.

TENNANT, ALLIE VICTORIA—*Sculptor*

5315 Live Oak St., Dallas 6, Tex.

B. St. Louis, Mo. *Studied*: ASL, with George Bridgman, Edward McCartan. *Member*: F., NSS; Dallas AA (Dir.). *Awards*: prizes, Dallas AA, 1936; SSAL, 1932, 1933, 1936. *Work*: State of Texas Bldg., Dallas; Brookgreen Gardens, S.C.; Hockaday Sch.; Southwest Medical Col., Aquarium, Mus. FA, Womans Cl., all of Dallas, Tex.; mem., Corsicana, Bonham, Tex.; mural, USPO, Electra, Tex. *Exhibited*: PAFA, 1935; AIC, 1935; Kansas City AI, 1935; Texas Centennial, 1936; Arch.L., 1938; WFNY 1939; Nat. Exh. Am. A., N.Y., 1939; WMAA, 1940; NSS, 1940; Carnegie Inst., 1941.

TENNYSON, MRS. ARTHUR A. See Mitchell, Laura M.D.

TERENZIO, ANTHONY—*Painter, E.*

University of Connecticut, Storrs, Conn.; h. 27 Russell St., Manchester, Conn.

B. Settefrati, Italy, Feb. 10, 1923. *Studied*: PIASch., B.F.A.; Columbia Univ., M.A.; Am. A. Sch., with Raphael Soyer and Jack Levine. *Awards*: prizes, Emily Lowe Comp., 1950; Conn. Artists, Norwich, Conn., 1957. *Work*: Syracuse Univ. *Exhibited*: Terry AI, 1952; Butler Inst. Am. A., 1957; Boston A. Festival, 1958; BM, 1950; Ward Eggleston Gal., 1950, 1958; Springfield A. Lg., 1956; Norwich AA, 1956-1958; Berkshire A. Mus., 1957, 1958;

one-man: Creative A. Gal., N.Y., 1950, 1952; Eggleston Gal., 1958. *Positions*: Prof., Des., Fla. State Univ., 1950-51; Brooklyn College, 1951-52; Univ. Connecticut, 1955- .

TERKEN, JOHN RAYMOND—*Sculptor, T., L.*

1947 Broadway, New York 23, N.Y.; h. 386 Chambers Ave., East Meadow, N.Y.

B. Rochester, N.Y., Jan. 11, 1912. *Studied*: BAID; N.Y. Sch. F. & Indst. A.; Columbia Univ., and abroad. *Member*: NSS; AAPL. *Award*: Tiffany F., 1947; NSS, 1958. *Work*: Roswell Mus. A., N.M.; ASPCA Headquarters Bldg.; S.S. "United States"; Saratoga Racing Mus.; Central Presbyterian Church, New York City; Thomas Edison H.S., Queens; Pub. Sch. #11, Brooklyn. *Exhibited*: NSS, annually; NAD; New Jersey P. & S., 1948; Syracuse Mus. FA, 1950; Am. A. Week, 1957; Meriden A. & Crafts, 1948-1953, 1957. *Position*: Instr. S. and Drawing, East Meadow Adult Edu. Courses.

TERRELL, ALLEN TOWNSEND—*Sculptor, P., Ser.*

42 Stuyvesant St., New York 3, N.Y.

B. Riverhead, N.Y., Nov. 2, 1897. *Studied*: Columbia Univ.; ASL; Julian Acad., Ecole des Beaux-Arts, Paris, France; & with Charles Despiau. *Member*: NAC; AWCS; Mun. A. Soc.; Fontainebleau Assn. *Awards*: prizes, Ernest Piexotta award, N.Y., 1941; Village A. Center, 1943, 1949, 1954; IBM, 1945; Nat. Ser. Soc., 1950. *Work*: York Cl., N.Y.; IBM Coll.; murals, S.S. America; Aluminum Corp. Am., Garwood, N.J.; modeled Vermilve med., Franklin Inst., Phila. *Exhibited*: Salon d'Automne, 1931; NAD, 1932-1934, 1937; PAFA, 1933, 1934, 1936; AWCS, 1942-1951; WMAA, 1954; Grosfeld House, N.Y., 1957; one-man exh.: Decorators' Cl., N.Y., 1939; Stendahl Gal., 1944; Pasadena AI, 1944; Mildred Irby Gal., N.Y., 1953; Village A. Center, 1943, 1955, 1956, 1958. Author: "Drawings for Sculpture."

TERRY, DUNCAN NILES—*Craftsman, Des.*

1213 Lancaster Ave., Rosemont, Pa.; h. 752 Brooke Rd., St. Davids, Pa.

B. Bath, Me., Nov. 6, 1909. *Studied*: BMFA Sch.; Central Sch. A. & Crafts, London, England; Acad. Moderne, Paris, France; & with Henry Hunt Clark, Fernand Leger. *Member*: Phila. A. All.; Stained Glass Assn. Am. *Awards*: Traveling Scholarship, BMFA Sch., 1931-1932. *Work*: glass murals, panels, etc., Hotels in Baltimore, Philadelphia; also Bryn Mawr Col.; Beck's Restaurant, Phila., Pa.; Good Shepherd Home, Allentown, Pa.; Lutheran Deaconess Chapel, Gladwyne, Pa.; Church Good Shepherd, Rosemont, Pa.; Glass Blowers Union Bldg., Phila., Pa.; Ludington Mem. Lib., Bryn Mawr, Pa.; Lind (Wash.) Methodist Church; Jefferson Hospital Chapel, Phila.; St. Andrews-in-the-Field, Somerton, Pa.; News-Journal Bldg., Wilmington, Del.; Warminster Chapel, Richmond, Va.; Good Shepherd Lutheran Church, Phila.; St. Michael's Monastery, Oyama, Japan; Riverside Church, N.Y. *Exhibited*: one-man exh.: Dartmouth Col.; Gibbes Mem. A. Gal.; Tricker Gal., N.Y.; Woodmere A. Gal.; Phila. A. All.; & in London; traveling exh. South America, sponsored by U.S. Information Services.

TERRY, HILDA (D'ALESSIO) (Mrs. Gregory)—
Cartoonist

8 Henderson Place, New York 28, N.Y.

B. Newburyport, Mass., June 25, 1914. *Studied*: NAD; ASL. *Member*: Nat. Cartoonists Soc. Creator of "Teena," King Features Syndicate.

TERRY, MARION (E.)—*Painter, E.*

844 27th Ave., North, St. Petersburg, Fla.

B. Evansville, Ind., June 4, 1911. *Studied*: Albright A. Sch.; Buffalo AI; Univ. Buffalo; Cape Sch. A., Provincetown, Mass.; Univ. Florida, and with Xavier Gonzalez. *Member*: Florida A. Group; Fla. Fed. A.; Pen and Brush Cl.; Village A. Center, N.Y. *Awards*: prizes, Fla. Fed. A., 1938; Sarasota Nat. Exh., 1951; Fla. Southern Col., 1951; Intl. Exh., Havana, Cuba, 1954; Fla. State Fair, Tampa, 1956. *Work*: New York Hospital Coll.; Living War Memorial (476 portraits of every Dade County serviceman who lost his life in World War II). *Exhibited*: Sarasota, 1951; Terry AI, 1952; Fla. Southern Col., 1952; MMA, 1952; Village A. Center, N.Y.; Creative A. Gal.; Soc. Four A., Palm Beach; Buffalo AI; Fla. A. Group;

Fla. Fed. A.; Norton Gal. A.; Blue Dome; Lowe Gal. A., Miami; Provincetown AA; Cape Cod AA; Southeastern Annual; Ford Motor Co. traveling exhs., 1955, 1957-58; Fort Worth, Tex., 1958; one-man: Ferargil Gal., N.Y., 1950, 1952; Buffalo, N.Y.; St. Louis, Mo.; Decatur, Ill.; Cleveland, Ohio; 7 one-man, Florida. *Position*: Instr., Craft Village, St. Petersburg, Fla.

THACHER, JOHN SEYMOUR—*Museum Director*
1703 Northwest 32nd St.; h. 1735 32nd St., Northwest, Washington 7, D.C.

B. New York, N.Y., Sept. 5, 1904. *Studied*: Yale Univ., B.A.; Univ. London, Ph.D. *Member*: Century Assn.; Assoc. Intl. Inst. for Conservation of Museum Objects; F., Pierpont Morgan Lib.; Grolier Cl. Author: "Paintings of Francisco de Herrara, the Elder," Art Bulletin, '37. *Position*: Asst. to Dir., 1936, Asst. Dir., 1940- , FMA, Cambridge, Mass.; Exec. Officer, 1940-45, Acting Dir., 1945-46, Dir., 1946- , The Dumbarton Oaks Research Library & Coll., Trustees for Harvard Univ.; Trustee, Assoc. in FA, Yale Univ., 1953- ; Treas., Byzantine Inst., Inc., Washington, D.C.; Pres., Mary Ann Payne Robertson Fnd.

THAL, SAM(UEL)—*Etcher, S., P., L.*
354 Marlborough St., Boston 15, Mass.

B. New York, N.Y., May 4, 1903. *Studied*: ASL; NAD; Beaux-Arts Acad.; BMFA Sch. *Member*: SAE; Boston Arch. Cl. *Awards*: prizes, Conn. Acad. FA, 1943; SAE, 1941-1943; Lib. Cong., 1945; NAD. *Work*: BMFA; Lib. Cong.; Bibliotheque Nationale, Paris; Boston Pub. Lib.; Marblehead AA; Tufts Medical Col.; Conn. Acad. FA; MMA; Pa. State Univ.; Rogers Bros. Shoe Co., Boston; Carnegie Inst.; arch. s., panels, Cincinnati Bell Telephone Bldg.; Harvard Medical Sch.; Rindge Technical Sch., Cambridge, Mass.; East Boston Airport; Harvard Univ. Dormitory; s., B'nai Israel, Rockville, Conn. *Exhibited*: annual one-man exh.; Doll & Richards, Boston; Rockport AA; Inst. Mod. A., Boston; SAE; Lib. Cong.; U.S. Nat. Mus. Author, I., "The Okinpochee Bird Family." *Position*: Instr., The Garland School, Boston, Mass.

THALINGER, E. OSCAR—*Painter, E.*
Baxter Rd., R.R. #1, Manchester, Mo.

B. Alsace-Lorraine, Mar. 20, 1885. *Studied*: St. Louis Sch. FA, Washington Univ., and in Munich, Germany. *Member*: Group 15; St. Louis County AA; Gateway AA; AEA. *Position*: Registrar, CAM, 1914-52 (retired); Instr., People's A. Center, St. Louis, Mo.

THARSILLA, SISTER M.—*Educator, P.*
Our Lady of the Lake College, San Antonio, Tex.

B. Westphalia, Tex., Apr. 19, 1912. *Studied*: Our Lady of the Lake Col., B.A.; Columbia Univ., M.A.; AIC; N.Y. Univ.; Texas Univ., and with Constantine Pougialis, Robert Lifendahl, Buckley MacGurrin. *Member*: CAA; Catholic AA; Western AA; Texas A. Edu. Assn.; Nat. A. Edu. Assn.; Texas WC Soc. *Exhibited*: Witte Mem. Mus., 1943, 1944, 1950; Texas General, 1945-1946; Texas WC Soc., 1950. *Position*: Asst. Prof. A., Hd. Dept. A., Our Lady of the Lake Col., San Antonio, Tex.

THAYER, POLLY (Mrs. Polly Thayer Starr)—*Painter*
198 Beacon St., Boston, Mass.

B. Boston, Mass., Nov. 8, 1904. *Studied*: BMFA Sch.; ASL, with Harry Wickey. *Awards*: prizes, NAD, 1929; med., Boston Tercentenary Exh. *Work*: PAFA; BMFA; AGAA; Springfield A. Mus. *Exhibited*: New York, N.Y., 1941; Phila., Pa., 1942, 1956 (one-man); Boston, Mass., 1950, 1955 (one-man); Boston A. Festival, 1957.

THECLA, JULIA—*Painter, Des., Gr., S.*
67 East Oak St., Chicago 11, Ill.

B. Illinois. *Studied*: AIC, and with Elmer Forsberg. *Work*: AIC; Newark Mus. *Awards*: prizes, Chicago Newspaper Gld.; Illinois State Fair; Fla. Southern Col.; AIC. *Exhibited*: MModA; Art of This Century; AIC; SFMA; Carnegie Inst.; MMA.

THEIS, GLADYS HULING—*Sculptor*
615 North Spruce St., Albuquerque, N.M.

B. Bartlesville, Okla., Aug. 24, 1903. *Studied*: Oklahoma A. & M. Col.; Cincinnati A. Sch.; Corcoran Sch. A.; in Paris; & with Miller, Malfrey, Despiau. *Awards*: prize, Soc. Wash. A., 1931; Nat. Lg. Am. Pen Women, 1950, 1952; Albuquerque, N.M., 1951. *Work*: CM; Tulsa H.S., Tulsa Univ., Boston Ave. Church, all in Tulsa, Okla.; Oklahoma A. & M. Col.; Univ. Mexico; 25 portraits, Daufelser Sch. of Music. *Exhibited*: Soc. Wash. A., 1931, 1932; New Mexico A. Lg., 1937, 1950-1954; Albuquerque, N.M., 1937 (one-man); State Mus., N.M., 1940-1954; Albuquerque, 1950-1954.

THEMAL, JOACHIM H(ANS)—*Painter, T.*
71 East 2nd St., New York 3, N.Y.; h. Cottage School, Pleasantville, N.Y.

B. Koeslin, Germany, May 10, 1911. *Studied*: in Dresden with Ernst Wagner; and in Berlin. *Member*: AEA. *Awards*: Hallmark award, 1952; Huntington Hartford F., 1956; Yaddo F., 1958. *Work*: Mus. Mod. A., Seattle; Univ. Kentucky; Zanesville AI; Grand Rapids A. Gal.; Richmond AA; Florence (S.C.) Mus. A.; Mills Col., Oakland; Univ. Georgia; Fleming Mus., Univ. Vermont; Evansville Mus. A.; Wagner Lutheran Col., Staten Island; Delgado Mus. A.; Univ. Delaware. *Exhibited*: AWS, 1958 and in many national shows. *Positions*: Instr. A. and Art Therapist, Cottage School, Pleasantville, N.Y., at present.

THIEL, RICHARD G.—*Craftsman, S., T.*
1606 Virginia St., Sioux City, Iowa

B. Madison, Wis., June 27, 1932. *Studied*: Univ. Wisconsin, B.S., M.S. *Member*: Am. Craftsmens Council; Midwest Des.-Craftsmen; Wisconsin Des.-Craftsmen. *Awards*: prizes, Wis. Des.-Craftsmen, 1954, 1956, 1958; Area Show, Sioux City, 1957, 1958; Iowa May Show, 1958. *Exhibited*: Young Americans, 1956; Fiber-Clay-Metal, 1958; Midwest Des.-Craftsmen, 1957; Wis. Des.-Craftsmen, 1954-1958; Sioux City, 1957, 1958; Six States Exh., 1958. *Position*: Instr. A., Sioux City Pub. Schs.

THIESSEN (CHARLES) LEONARD—*Designer, P., Gr., S., L., T.*
3042 Stone Ave., Omaha 11, Neb.

B. Omaha, Neb., May 3, 1902. *Studied*: Univ. Nebraska; Sch. Royal Acad., Stockholm, Sweden; Heatherley's Sch., London. *Member*: AEA. *Work*: Nebraska AA; A. Gld., Lincoln, Neb.; Univ. Omaha; Joslyn A. Mus.; Univ. Nebraska; Kansas Wesleyan Univ., Salina; Alfred East Mem. Gal., Kettering, England; murals, Lincoln Municipal Auditorium, Stewart Theatre, St. Matthews Church, all Lincoln, Neb.; Paxton Hotel, St. John's Episcopal Church, First Covenant Church, all in Omaha; Lodge, Grand Teton Nat. Park, Wyoming; Dundee Presbyterian Church, Omaha; Clarkson Mem. Hospital, Omaha. Lectures: History of Art. *Position*: Instr., Painting, Joslyn A. Mus., Omaha, Neb., 1951- .

THOBURN, JEAN—*Painter, T., W., I.*
8 Robin Rd., Pittsburgh 17, Pa.

B. Calcutta, India, Nov. 27, 1887. *Studied*: Goucher Col., B.A.; T. Col., Columbia Univ.; N.Y. Sch. F. & App. A.; & with Arthur Dow, Barse Miller, Millard Sheets, Dong Kingman, Eliot O'Hara, and others. *Member*: Pittsburgh WC Soc.; Assoc. A. Pittsburgh. *Awards*: prize, Assoc. A. Pittsburgh, 1944; Pittsburgh WC Soc., 1953. *Work*: One Hundred Friends of Art, Pittsburgh, Pa. *Exhibited*: PAFA, 1937, 1939; Assoc. A. Pittsburgh, 1926, 1936-1952; Pittsburgh WC Soc., 1945; Women's Cl., Chautauqua, N.Y., 1951; Pittsburgh A. & Crafts Center, 1952 (one-man). I., children's stories including "Away in a Manger," 1942; Author, I., "Downey-True Story of an Irish Setter," 1957. *Position*: Instr. FA, Peabody H.S., Pittsburgh, Pa., 1911-53; Instr., WC, Pittsburgh A. & Crafts Center, at present.

THOELE, LILLIAN (CAROLINE) (ANNE)—*Painter, I., Comm. A., Des.*
4025 Shreve St., St. Louis 15, Mo.

B. St. Louis, Mo., Aug. 12, 1894. *Studied*: PAFA; St. Louis Sch. FA. *Member*: St. Louis Advertising Cl.; Am. Fed. Advertising; Indp. A. Soc.; Am. A. All.; Women Painters of St. Louis; A. Dir. Cl. (Nat.). *Awards*: St.

Louis Indp. A. Soc.; Indp. A.; Am. A. All. _Work_: murals, Am. Youth Fnd. Camps, Shelby, Mich., New Ossipee, N.H.; Gundlack Pub. Sch., St. James Church, German General Orphans Home, Crippled Children's Home, all of St. Louis, Mo.; Monsanto Co.; Antimite Co., Southwestern Tel. Co., St. Louis. _Exhibited_: CAM; St. Louis A. Gld.; Missouri State Fair; St. Louis Pub. Lib.; Terry AI, 1952; Indp. A. Soc.; Am. A. All.; Kirkwood, Mo.; Sheraton Hotel; Boatmen's Bank Bldg.; Am. Slide Co. traveling exh., 1957 (6 slides of paintings). I., text books and children's stories.

THOM, ROBERT ALAN—_Illustrator_, P.

6160 West Surrey Rd., Birmingham, Mich.

B. Grand Rapids, Mich., Mar. 4, 1915. _Studied_: Columbus (Ohio) Inst. FA; and with Robert Brackman. _Member_: Scarab Cl., Detroit; SI; Sarasota AA. _Work_: Parke, Davis Co.; Bohn Aluminum & Brass Corp.; Univ. Mich., College of Pharmacy; Univ. Wis., Col. of Pharmacy; Phila. Col. of Pharmacy; U.S. Pharmacopoeia Hdqtrs., N.Y. _Exhibited_: Vancouver (B.C.) A. Gal., 1955; Smithsonian Inst., 1955; Oklahoma City A. Center, 1957; Columbus Mus. A., 1957; Georgia Mus. A., Athens; Morehead Planetarium, Univ. North Carolina; Columbia (S.C.) Mus. A., 1958; Sheldon Swope Gal. A., 1958; Lehigh Univ., 1958; Washington County Mus. FA, Hagerstown, Md., 1958 (all one-man).

THOMAS, ALLAN—_Designer, I., Eng._, P.

527 North Michigan Ave., Stevens Point, Wis.

B. Jackson, Mich., Feb. 15, 1902. _Studied_: PAFA; abroad. _Member_: NSMP. _Awards_: Cresson traveling scholarship, PAFA, 1925, 1927, prize, 1926; med., Phila. WC Cl., 1929. _Work_: PAFA; murals, Upjohn Sch., Kalamazoo, Mich.; St. John's Church, Radio Station WIBM, Jackson H.S., all of Jackson, Mich.; 1st Nat. Bank, Stevens Point, Wis.; Hotel Mead, Wisconsin Rapids; USPO, Crystal Falls, Clare, Mich.; Wabasha, Minn. _Exhibited_: Phila. WC Cl., 1926-1930, 1932; AIC, 1929, 1930, 1933; Detroit Inst. A., 1934-1936; Arch. L., 1939; A. Dir. Cl., N.Y. and Chicago; FAP, Wash., D.C., 1937-1941. I., national magazines and leading publishers.

THOMAS, BYRON—_Painter, Lith._

Woodstock, Vt.

B. Baltimore, Md., July 28, 1902. _Studied_: ASL. _Awards_: prize, AIC, 1937; Carnegie Inst., 1943. _Work_: MModA; Herron AI; AIC; PAFA; Springfield A. Mus.; IBM Coll. _Exhibited_: PAFA, 1941-1943, 1945; Carnegie Inst., 1943-1945; AIC, 1942-1944; MMA, 1943; one-man: N.Y., 1940, 1944, 1956. Contributor of: Illus. to Life Magazine. _Position_: Instr. Painting, CUASch., 1931-50.

THOMAS, ED(WARD) B.—

Educational Dir., E., L., Ser., P.

Seattle Art Museum, Volunteer Park; h. 2235 Crescent Drive, Seattle 2, Wash.

B. Cosmopolis, Wash., Nov. 30, 1920. _Studied_: Columbia Univ.; N.Y. Univ.; Univ. Washington, B.A., M.F.A. _Member_: AEA; Pacific AA; Washington AA; NAEA; Nat. Com. on A. Edu.; AAMus.; Northwest Pr. M. _Awards_: prize, for School Telecasts, 1956, Am. Exh. of Edu. Radio-TV programs, Ohio Univ., and other TV awards. _Exhibited_: Nat. Ser. Soc., 1952; SFMA, 1951; SAM, 1951, 1954; regional exhs. since 1950. _Author_: Guide to Life's Illuminations Exhibit, Time, Inc., 1958. Lectures weekly TV art programs, Seattle, since 1951; recorded TV series for school use: "Man's Story"; "Treasure Trips"; "Our Neighbors"; "The Japanese"; Electronic tour of "Masterpieces of Korean Art," SAM, 1958. _Position_: Instr., A. Hist., Cornish Sch., Seattle, 1952- ; Cur. Edu., 1951-54, Edu. Dir., 1954- , Seattle Art Museum, Seattle, Wash.

THOMAS, EMMA WARFIELD—_Painter, T., W._

3409 Hamilton St., Philadelphia 4, Pa.

B. Philadelphia, Pa. _Studied_: PAFA. _Member_: Phila. A. All.; Phila. Plastic Cl.; F. PAFA. _Work_: F. PAFA. Author, Ed., "Fragments—A Journal for Artists."

THOMAS, ESTELLE L.—_Painter_

512 North Euclid Ave., Pittsburgh 6, Pa.

B. New York, N.Y. _Studied_: Pittsburgh Sch. Des. for Women; Univ. Pittsburgh; Carnegie Inst.; Parsons Sch.

Des.; & with Charles Hawthorne, John Sloan, & others. _Member_: Assoc. A. Pittsburgh; Pittsburgh WC Soc. _Exhibited_: PAFA, 1934; Assoc. A. Pittsburgh, 1910-1946, 1954; Jenner A. Gal., 1953-1955; Carnegie Inst., 1954, 1955; Pittsburgh WC Soc., 1945, 1954; Pittsburgh A. & Crafts Center.

THOMAS, GEORGE R.—_Educator, Ser., L._

University of New Hampshire; h. 17 Bagdad Rd., Durham, N.H.

B. Portsmouth, Va., Dec. 8, 1906. _Studied_: Univ. North Carolina; Carnegie Inst., B.Arch.; Columbia Univ. _Member_: AIA; New Hampshire Soc. Arch.; New Hampshire AA; Council, N.H. Lg. A. & Crafts. _Position_: Hd. Dept. A., Dir. A. Gal., Univ. New Hampshire, Durham, N.H., at present.

THOMAS, HOWARD—_Educator, P., Eng., Lith._

Art Department, University Georgia; h. 264 Florida Ave., Athens, Ga.

B. Mt. Pleasant, Ohio, Mar. 30, 1899. _Studied_: AIC; Univ. So. Cal.; Univ. Chicago. _Member_: Wisconsin P. & S.; Assn. Georgia A.; Southeastern AA; CAA. _Awards_: prizes, Wisconsin Salon, 1938, 1941; Assn. Georgia A., 1945, 1946, 1950, 1951; Southeastern AA, 1946, 1949, 1954, 1956; Va. Intermont, 1954; Soc. Four A., 1955, 1957; medal, Milwaukee AI, 1936, 1956. _Work_: Milwaukee AI; Atlanta AI; Telfair Acad.; Columbus Mus. A.; Georgia Mus. A.; 3 American Embassies. _Exhibited_: AIC, 1935-1942; Wisconsin P. & S., 1924-1942; Phila. WC Cl., 1938, 1939, 1941, 1946, 1947; Wisconsin Salon, 1934-1939, 1941; Southeastern AA, 1946-1957; MMA, 1950, 1952; BM, 1953, 1955; Duveen-Graham Gal., 1955, 1957. _Position_: Hd. A. Dept., Woman's Col., Univ. N.C., 1943; Hd. Dept. A., Agnes Scott Col., 1943-45; Prof. A., Univ. Georgia, Athens, Ga., 1945- ; Visiting L., Assn. Am. Colleges, 1948- ; Art Specialist, State Dept., lecturing Far East, 1957.

THOMAS, HOWARD ORMSBY—_Painter, Gr., Des., C._

1844 Wesley Ave., Evanston, Ill.

B. Chicago, Ill., Sept. 30, 1908. _Studied_: AIC. _Member_: Chicago A. Cl. _Work_: St. Cletus Church, La Grange, Ill.; Nichols Sch., Evanston. _Exhibited_: PAFA, 1941; ASMP, 1942; Elgin Acad. A., 1941; AIC, 1940-1942; Springfield Mus. A., 1940, 1941; Marshall Field, Chicago, 1949, 1950, 1955, 1956; Evanston A. Center, 1952-1957; Evanston Women's Cl., 1952, 1955; Chicago A. Cl., 1955, 1956, 1957.

THOMAS, MRS. IRVIN C. See Finley, Mary L.

THOMAS, MARY (ALICE) LEATH—_Painter, E._

264 Florida Ave., Athens, Ga.

B. Hazelhurst, Ga., Feb. 25, 1905. _Studied_: Georgia State Col. for Women, B.S.; Duke Univ., M. Edu.; Woman's Col., Univ. North Carolina. _Member_: Assn. Georgia A.; SSAL; Southeastern AA; Nat. A. Edu. Assn. _Awards_: prizes, North Carolina A. Exh., 1941, 1942, 1947; SSAL, 1942, 1946; Assn. Georgia A., 1948-1950, 1952. _Work_: U.S. State Dept. purchase for U.S. Embassies abroad (2); Univ. Georgia; VMFA; Atlanta AI; North Carolina A. Soc.; Telfair Acad.; Gibbes A. Gal. _Exhibited_: PAFA, 1941; Mint Mus. A., 1942, 1943; ACA Gal., N.Y., 1943; North Carolina A., 1940-1944; Piedmont Festival, Winston-Salem, N.C., 1943; SSAL, 1941-1943; Assn. Georgia A., 1945-1955; MMA, 1952; BM, 1953, 1955; LC, 1952; Gibbes A. Gal., 1958; Norfolk Mus. A., 1958; Atlanta Paper Co., 1958; Univ. Georgia, 1957 (2-man); Weyhe Gal., N.Y. _Positions_: Asst. Prof. A., Woman's Col., Univ. North Carolina, 1938-44; Prof. A., Stephens Col., Columbia, Mo., 1944-45; Assoc. Prof. A., Univ. Georgia, Athens, Ga., 1945-51; A. Supv., Athens, Ga. City Schs., 1949-1956.

THOMASITA, SISTER MARY, O.S.F.—

Painter, C., S., Des., E., L.

Studio San Damiano; h. 3195 South Superior St., Milwaukee 7, Wis.

B. Milwaukee, Wis., Feb. 23, 1912. _Studied_: Milwaukee State T. Col., B.E.; AIC, B.F.A., M.F.A. _Member_: Wisconsin P. & S.; Western AA; Catholic AA; Liturgical Arts Soc.; CAA; Milwaukee AI; Wisconsin A. Edu. Assn. _Award_: prize, Wisconsin P. & S., 1950. _Work_: sculpture in private collections; wood mosaic panels, Marquette Univ. Mem. Lib.; panels, St. Cyprian's Convent, River Grove, Ill. *Exhibited*: AIC, 1944-1947; Milwaukee AI, 1950, 1952, 1953, 1956; and in New York, Dayton, Seattle, Dallas, Portland, Madison and many other cities. Contributor to: Journal of Arts & Letters; Arts & Activities; Liturgical Arts magazine. Lectures: Contemporary Art; Contemporary Religious Art, etc. *Positions*: Exh. Com., Milwaukee A. Center, 1949- ; Bd. Dirs., Children's A. Program, Milwaukee A. Center, 1955- ; Adv., Arts & Activities Magazine, 1955- .

THOMPSON, ALAN—Painter, I., Des.
64 Halsey Dr., Old Greenwich, Conn.

B. South Shields, England, June 9, 1908. *Studied*: Carnegie Inst.; Pittsburgh AI; & with Alexander Kostellow, Clarence Carter. *Member*: Assoc. A. Pittsburgh. *Awards*: prizes, Butler AI 1940; Assoc. A. Pittsburgh, 1941; Hallmark, 1949; All. A. Am., 1952. *Work*: Pittsburgh Faculty Cl.; Pittsburgh Pub. Sch.; mural, USPO, Pittsburgh, Pa. *Exhibited*: Carnegie Inst., 1941; Assoc. A. Pittsburgh, 1939-1941; Butler AI, 1939, 1940; Parkersburg FA Center, 1940. *Position*: Des., A. Dir., Young & Rubicam, New York, N.Y.*

THOMPSON, BEN—Cartoonist
Naugatuck, Conn.

B. Central City, Neb., Apr. 20, 1906. *Studied*: Univ. Washington Sch. FA; AIC. *Member*: Nat. Cartoonists Soc. Contributor cartoons to: Sat. Eve. Post; Look; Redbook; Better Homes & Gardens; True, and other leading national magazines; newspapers: King Features Syndicate; McNaught Syndicate. *Position*: Staff Cart., Seattle Post Intelligencer, Seattle Times, Bellingham Herald, N.Y. Journal-American: magazine, newspaper and advertising cartoons at present.

THOMPSON, (JAMES) BRADBURY—Designer
575 Madison Ave., New York 22, N.Y.; h. Jones Park, Riverside, Conn.

B. Topeka, Kans., Mar. 25, 1911. *Studied*: Washburn Univ., A.B. *Member*: A. Dir. Cl.; SI; AIGA; Alliance Graphique International: Westport AA; Nat. Soc. A. Dir. *Awards*: prizes, Nat. Soc. A. Dir., 1950; A. Dir. Cl. medal, 1945, 1947, 1950 (2), 1955, prize, 1946, 1953-1955; AIGA, 1948-1955. *Exhibited*: Intl. Exh. Gr. A., Paris, France, 1955; Exh. Adv. & Editorial A., N.Y., 1943-1955; MModA, 1955. Designer: "Painting Toward Architecture," 1948; "Photo-Graphic," 1949; "Abstract Painting," 1951; "Annual of Advertising Art," 1943, 1954; "Graphic Arts Production Yearbook," 1948, 1950; "The Fiction Factory," 1955; "Art News Annual," 1945-1955. Des., Mademoiselle; Art News; Art News Annual; Graphic Arts Production Yearbook; Westvaco Inspirations; Graphis, etc. *Position*: A. Dir., Rogers, Kellogg, Stillson, Inc., 1938-41; A. Dir., Office War Information, 1942-45; A. Dir., Mademoiselle, 1945- ; A. Dir., Living for Young Homemakers, 1947-49; Des. Dir., Art News Annual, 1945- ; Publications A. Dir., Street & Smith Publ., New York, N.Y.; Visiting Critic, Yale Univ., Sch. Art & Architecture, 1956- ; Bd. Governors, Phila. Mus. Sch. A., 1956- .

THOMPSON, DOROTHY BURR (Mrs.)—
Archaeologist, W., L.
Cherry Valley Rd., Princeton, N.J.

B. Delhi, N.Y., Aug. 19, 1900. *Studied*: Bryn Mawr Col. Ph.D.; Amer. Sch. Classical Studies, Athens; Radcliffe Col. *Member*: Archeol. Inst. Amer.; Classical Assn. of Canada. *Awards*: Bryn Mawr European fellowships, 1923, '25. Author: "Terracottas from Myrina in the Museum of Fine Arts, Boston," 1934; "Swans and Amber," 1949 (trans. of Greek lyrics). Contributor: Amer. Journal of Archeol.; Hesperia. Lectures: Greek art, Roman private life, modern Greece, etc. *Position*: Staff of Agora excavations, Athens, 1931- .

THOMPSON, ERNEST THORNE—Etcher, Lith., P., E.
25 Prospect St., New Rochelle, N.Y.

B. St. John, N.B., Canada, Nov. 8, 1897. *Studied*: Mass. Sch. A.; BMFA Sch. *Member*: Chicago SE; SC; AWS; Hudson Valley AA; Maine WC Soc.; New Rochelle AA; SI. *Awards*: prizes, McCutcheon award, Chicago, 1927; Fifty Prints of the Year, 1928; New Rochelle, N.Y., 1937,

1940, 1946; 100 Prints of the Year, 1940; Lesch Medal of Honor, 1958. *Work*: Bibliotheque Nationale, Paris; N.Y. Pub. Lib.; U.S. Nat. Mus.; Univ. Notre Dame, South Bend, Ind.; McHenry, Ill. *Exhibited*: nationally in graphic arts exh., 1927-1946; WC exhs., 1947, 1955; Bibliotheque Nationale, Paris; Victoria & Albert Mus., London, 1928. *Position*: Prof. A., Col. New Rochelle, N.Y., 1929- .

THOMPSON, F(LOYD) LESLIE—
Etcher, P., Des., Comm. A., T., L.
225 North Wabash Ave., Chicago, Ill.; h. 735 Park Blvd., Glen Ellyn, Ill.

B. Chicago, Ill., June 26, 1889. *Studied*: with George Sensensy, Bertha Jacques, DeForest Shook, Anthony Buchta. *Member*: Austin, Oak Park & River Forest A. Lg.; Cliff Dwellers; Cal. Soc. Pr. M.; Am. Color Print Soc.; Chicago Soc. Et. *Awards*: prizes, Chicago Soc. Et., 1948, 1955; Chas. Muller prize, 1939; Georgia, 1940; Nat. A. Annual, 1945; Graphic prize, 1954. Lectures: Color Aquatint Etching and Printing. *Position*: Sec., Chicago Soc. Et., 1946- .

THOMPSON, F. RAYMOND (RAY THOMPSON)—
Cartoonist, Comm. A.
116 Greenwood Ave., Wyncote, Pa.

B. Philadelphia, Pa., July 9, 1905. *Studied*: Temple Univ.; PAFA; Stella Elkins Tyler Sch. *Member*: Old York Road A. Gld. *Exhibited*: Old York Road A. Gld. Contributor cartoons to national magazines and trade journals. I., newspaper comics: "Somebody's Stenog"; "Myra North, Special Nurse"; "Homer, The Ghost." Illus. for many adv. campaigns.

THOMPSON, GEORGETTE R.—Painter, Des., I., C., T.
4416 Perrier St., New Orleans 15, La.

B. New Orleans, La., Sept. 13, 1905. *Studied*: Newcomb Col., Tulane Univ., B. Des.; Chicago Acad. FA; ASL; & with Will Stevens, Ruth Van Sickle Ford, & others. *Member*: New Orleans AA. *Awards*: prizes, New Orleans AA, 1933; SSAL, 1930. *Work*: New Orleans Assn. Commerce. *Exhibited*: Soc. Indp. A., 1939; Chicago No-Jury Soc., 1928; New Orleans AA, 1927-1946; SSAL, 1927-1940.*

THOMPSON, HELEN LATHROP (Mrs. Laurance M.)—
Painter
Vineyard Haven, Mass.

B. Wilkes-Barre, Pa., Apr. 24, 1889. *Studied*: Wilkes-Barre Inst.; Vassar Col., A.B.; Corcoran Sch. A.; Wayman Adams Sch. A.; Famous Artists Sch. *Awards*: prize, A. Week, Alexandria, Va., 1944. *Exhibited*: one-man exh.: Woman's Univ. Cl., Phila., 1939; Alexandria, Va.; Binghamton, N.Y., Wash., D.C.

THOMPSON, KENNETH W.—Illustrator, P.
20 West 11th St., New York 11, N.Y.

B. New York, N.Y., Apr. 26, 1907. *Studied*: with Eric Pape, H. Ballinger, George Pearse Ennis, Wayman Adams. *Member*: Nantucket AA; AWS; SI; A. Gld. *Awards*: prizes, A. Dir., Cl., N.Y., 1947; medals, 1947, 1950, 1957; A. Dir. Cl., Chicago, 1947, 1951, 1953-1958, medal, 1955. *Exhibited*: AWS, 1936-1945, 1947-1950. Contributor to Life, Colliers, American, Look, and other national magazines.

THOMPSON, LESLIE P.—Painter, T.
140 Pleasant St., Newton Centre 59, Mass.

B. Medford, Mass., Mar. 2, 1880. *Studied*: Mass. Normal A. Sch.; BMFA Sch.; & with E. L. Major, E. C. Tarbell. *Member*: NA; Gld. Boston A.; St. Botolph Cl. *Awards*: med., St. Louis Exp., 1904; Pan-Pacific Exp., 1915; PAFA, 1919; Sesqui-Centennial Exp., Phila., 1926; prizes, NAD, 1911; Newport AA, 1914; PAFA, 1927; Boston AC, 1928. *Exhibited*: nationally.

THOMPSON, MARY TYSON. See Tyson, Mary

THOMPSON, LEWIS EUGENE—*Painter, E., Cr., W., L.*
16 North Jefferson St. (2); h. 4713 Byesville Blvd., Dayton 3, Ohio

B. Hillsdale, Mich., May 21, 1894. *Studied:* Hillsdale Col.; Univ. Michigan; in Europe and Canada. *Member:* North Shore A. Gld.; Inst. Aeronautical Sc.; Dayton Wright Air Mail Soc.; Am. Air Mail Soc.; Aviation Comm., Dayton. *Awards:* prizes, Chicago, 1939; Dayton, 1950, and others. *Work:* State of Michigan coll.; U.S. Govt.; Republic of France; State of North Carolina; U.S. Post Office Dept.; Pentagon, Wash., D.C.; Mun. Airport, Decatur; Lib., Air Force Sch. of Tech., Dayton; religious paintings & ports., Emmanuel Catholic Church, Mt. Enon Baptist Church, Allen Methodist Church, all in Dayton; St. John's Methodist Church, St. Johns, Ohio. *Exhibited:* Chicago, 1939; No-jury exh., Chicago, 1941, 1942; McGuire Gal., Richmond, Ind., 1956; Barn Colony Studio, Decatur, 1956; U.S. Air Force Mus., Dayton. Author: "American Aviation History." *Position:* Instr. A., So. Michigan, 1922-36; Chief, Dept. A., Aircraft Laboratories, Wright-Patterson Field, Dayton, Ohio 1942-47; private & public instr., 1924- .

THOMPSON, RALSTON—*Painter, E.*
Wittenberg College; h. 254 Circle Dr., Springfield, Ohio

B. Ironton, Ohio, Mar. 28, 1904. *Studied:* Wittenberg Col., A.B.; Dayton AI; Chicago Acad. FA; Ohio State Univ., M.F.A.; Columbia Univ. *Member:* Ohio WC Soc.; Phila. WC Soc. *Awards:* 41 prizes and other awards, 1941-1956. *Work:* Butler AI; Dayton AI; Ohio Univ.; CM; Procter and Gamble; Federated Stores; Wittenberg Col.; Columbus Gal. FA; Canton AI. *Exhibited:* Nationally and internationally, and one-man exhs., since 1941; Columbus Gal. FA, 1957. *Position:* Instr., Ohio State Univ., 1935-41; Dir., Dept. FA, 1941- , Assoc. Prof., 1945-47, Prof., 1947- , Wittenberg Col., Springfield, Ohio.

THOMPSON, SUSIE WASS—*Watercolorist*
Cape Split, Addison, Me.

B. Addison, Me., July 15, 1892. *Work:* Walker A. Mus., Brunswick, Me.; Library, Northeast Harbor, Me. *Exhibited:* one-man: Stanford Univ., Research Inst., 1957; Bowdoin College, 1957; Northeast Harbor (Me.) Library, 1958, and private exhibitions.

THOMPSON, ADELE UNDERWOOD (Mrs.)—*Painter, T., Cr.*
245 Kosar St., Corpus Christi, Tex.

B. Grosbeck, Tex., Apr. 28, 1882. *Studied:* AIC; Newcomb Col., Tulane Univ., and with Ellen A. Holmes, Xavier Gonzalez, and others. *Member:* SSAL; Nat. Lg. Am. Pen Women; Texas FA Assn.; Corpus Christi A. Fnd.; South Texas A. Lg. *Awards:* prizes, Corpus Christi A. Fnd., 1945, 1946, 1948; Kingsville, Tex., Fair, 1947, 1949; WC exh., 1954; Casein exh., 1954. *Exhibited:* NGA, 1946; Nat. Lg. Am. Pen Women; Nat. Mus., Wash., D.C.; Caller-Times Exh.; SSAL; Texas FA Assn.; Corpus Christi A. Fnd.; one-man: Corpus Christi Mus., 1953; Ballinger (Tex.) Lib.; Texas FA Assn., 1953; Kingsville Col., 1954; Corpus Christi Little Theatre, 1954.*

THON, WILLIAM—*Painter*
Port Clyde, Me.

B. New York, N.Y., Aug. 8, 1906. *Member:* ANA; SC; Brooklyn Soc. A. *Awards:* prizes, BM, 1942, 1945; NAD, 1944, 1951, 1954, 1955; SC, 1942; F., Am. Acad. in Rome, 1947; Dana medal, 1950; Am. Acad. A. & Let. grant, 1951; PAFA, 1952; Audubon A, 1953; Hallmark, 1955; Hon. D.F.A., 1957, medal, 1956, Bates College. *Work:* Bloomington (Ill.) AA; Swope A. Gal.; Farnsworth Mus.; Encyclopaedia Britannica; Toledo Mus. A.; MMA; Butler Inst. Am. A.; Munson-Williams-Proctor Inst. A.; Rochester Mem. A. Gal.; WMAA; BM; John Herron AI; High Mus. A.; Davenport Mun. Gal.; Wilmington Soc. FA; Cal. PLH; Univ. Michigan. *Exhibited:* CGA; PAFA; VMFA; AIC; WMAA; Kansas City AI; Albright A. Gal.; NAD; Toledo Mus. A.; Cal. PLH; Univ. Michigan. *Position:* Instr., Atlanta AA; John Herron AI; Norton Gal. A.; A-in-Residence, Am. Acad. in Rome.

THORNDIKE, CHARLES JESSE (CHUCK)—*Cartoonist, Comm. A., I., W., L., T.*
46 Northwest 105th St., Miami Shores, Fla.

B. Seattle, Wash., Jan. 10, 1897. *Studied:* Seattle A. Sch.; Univ. Washington; Cal. Sch. FA. Author, I., "Secrets of Cartooning," 1937; "Art of Cartooning," 1938; "Business of Cartooning," 1938; "Drawing for Money," 1940; "Seeing America," 1946; "Arts and Crafts for Children," 1942; "Susie and Sam in Rock City," 1948; "Oddities of Nature," 1950; "New Secrets of Cartooning," 1955. Contributor of "Oddities of Nature" and "World of Tomorrow," Curtis Syndicate, Miami Herald and other newspapers. Lectures: History of Cartooning. *Positions:* A. Dir., Animated Cartoon Adv. Agcy., San Francisco; A. Dir., General Motors Acceptance Corp., N.Y.; U.S. Navy (Civil Service), Wash., D.C.; Commentator "Cartoon Club of the Air," (radio), N.Y.

THORNE, ANNA LOUISE—*Painter*
506 Lagrange St., Toledo 4, Ohio

B. Toledo, Ohio, Dec. 21, 1866. *Studied:* AIC; Chicago Acad. FA; ASL; in Paris, France, with Delacluse; and with William Chase, Naum Los and others. *Member:* Ohio Women A.; Detroit Women P. & S.; Toledo Women A. Soc. *Awards:* prizes, Toledo Mus. A.; Scarab Cl., Detroit, and others. *Work:* Toledo Zoo; murals, Toledo Pub. Lib., and in children's dept. *Exhibited:* Salon de Francais, Paris; PMA; N.Y. Miniature Soc.; one-man: Detroit, Mich.; Toledo Mus. A.

THORNE, THOMAS—*Painter, E., L.*
Belmede, Williamsburg, Va.

B. Lewiston, Me., Oct. 5, 1909. *Studied:* Portland (Me.) Sch. F. & App. A.; Yale Sch. FA, B.F.A.; ASL, with Reginald Marsh. *Member:* Virginia A. All.; F., Intl. Inst. A. & Let. *Work:* Hobart Col., Geneva, N.Y.; murals, H.S., General Hospital, Portland, Me.; James Blair H.S., Williamsburg, Va. *Exhibited:* PAFA, 1930; N.Y. WC Cl., 1937; VMFA, 1945, 1954; Boston Soc. Indp. A., 1935-1938. Lectures: Modern Painting. Contributor to Antiques magazine. *Position:* Chm. Dept. FA, William & Mary Col., Williamsburg, Va., 1943- ; State A. Com., Jamestown Celebration, 1957.

THORPE, DOROTHY CARPENTER—*Craftsman, Des.*
902 Thompson St.; h. 814 Portola St., Glendale 6, Cal.

B. Salt Lake City, Utah, Jan. 5, 1901. *Studied:* L.D.S. Univ., Salt Lake City, Utah; Univ. Utah. *Work:* Carnegie Inst. *Exhibited:* glassware, Mus. Mod. A., Wash., D.C.; Los A. Mus. A., 1955; traveling exh., State Dept., 1956; NGA, 1956; Marshall Field, Chicago; Dallas, Houston and San Antonio, Tex.; Seattle, Wash., & with leading firms in U.S.

THORPE, EVERETT CLARK—*Painter, Des., E., I., L.*
Utah State University; h. 1445 Maple Dr., Logan, Utah

B. Providence Cache, Utah, Aug. 22, 1907. *Studied:* Utah State Univ., B.S. in Edu., M.F.A.; and with Ralph M. Pearson, Alvin Gittens, Karl Zerbe, George Grosz, Hans Hofmann. *Member:* Am. Assn. Univ. Prof.; CAA; Utah A., Sciences & Let.; Utah State Inst. FA; Provincetown AA; NSMP. *Awards:* prizes, Utah State Inst. FA, 1946; Terry AI, 1952; Utah State Fair, 1951, 1958; Intermountain Mural Comp., 1956-1958. *Work:* Utah State Inst. FA; Logan City Schs. Coll.; Cache County & Tremontan Sch. Coll.; Utah State Capitol; L.D.S. Temple, Bancroft, Idaho, Salt Lake Temple; USPO, Provo, Utah; State Capitol; Utah Hotel; Zion Bank; Dixie Col., and in private colls.; Utah State Col. *Exhibited:* CGA; Denver A. Mus.; Utah State Inst. FA; Utah A. Center; Univ. Utah; Terry AI; Cedar City, Utah; Colo. Springs FA Center; SAM; Los A. Mus. A.; Idaho Col.; Art:USA, 1958; Provincetown, Mass. Illus. "A Trip Through Yellowstone Park." *Position:* Prof. A., Utah State Univ., Logan, Utah, 1944- ; A., Deseret News.

THORWARD, CLARA—*Painter, C., Et., T.*
58 West 58th St., New York 19, N.Y.; h. 27 Walnut Court, South Orange, N.J.

B. South Bend, Ind. *Studied:* AIC; Cleveland Sch. A.; ASL; & with Hans Hofmann, Henry G. Keller. *Awards:*

prizes, CMA, 1925, 1926; A. Lg. of Northern Indiana, 1932; Nat. Lg. Am. Pen Women, 1950. *Exhibited*: CMA, 1926; Montclair A. Mus., 1939; Ringling Mus. A., Sarasota, Fla., 1939; Hoosier Salon; one-man exh.: A. Lg. of Northern Indiana, 1938; Morton Gal., N.Y., 1940; Plaza Hotel, N.Y., 1940; Witte Mem. Mus., 1944; Palace FA, Mexico City, D.F., 1946; Acad. FA, Guatemala; Int. Cl., San Salvador; Okla. A. Center.*

THRASH, DOX—*Painter, Et., Lith., W., L. Des., S.*
2340 West Columbia Ave., Philadelphia 21, Pa.

B. Griffin, Ga., Mar. 22, 1892. *Studied*: AIC; Phila. Graphic Sketch Cl.; & with H. M. Norton, Earl Horter. *Member*: Phila. Pr. Cl. *Work*: Lib.Cong.; BMA; Lincoln Univ.; FA; Bryn Mawr Col.; West Chester (Pa.) Mus. FA; N.Y.Pub.Lib.; U.S. Govt. *Exhibited*: WFNY 1939; PMA; Phila. A. All., 1942 (one-man); Smithsonian Inst., 1948 (one-man). Contributor to: Art Digest. Lectures: Modern Art Appreciation.*

THURLOW, HELEN—*Painter, I.*
10 Gramercy Park, New York 3, N.Y.

B. Lancaster, Pa. *Member*: SI; A. Gld. *Awards*: 2 Cresson traveling scholarships, F., prize, PAFA. *Work*: Lancaster (Pa.) Pub. Lib.; Muhlenberg Col., Allentown, Pa.*

THURMAN, SUE (Mrs.)—*Museum Director*
Delgado Museum of Art, New Orleans, La.

Position: Dir., Isaac Delgado Museum of Art, New Orleans, La.*

THURMOND, ETHEL DORA—*Painter, T.*
1707 North Liberty St., Victoria, Tex.

B. Victoria, Tex., Jan. 15, 1905. *Studied*: Univ. Texas; Sul Ross State T. Col., Alpine, Tex., B.S., M.A.; Univ. Colorado; & with Xavier Gonzales, Paul Ninas, & others. *Work*: mural, H.S., Victoria, Tex.; Victoria (Tex.) Col. *Exhibited*: SSAL, 1938, 1939; Caller-Times Exh., Corpus Christi, Tex., 1944, 1945; Texas FA Assn. traveling exh., 1935; Southeast Texas Exh., 1937-1939; Texas General Exh., 1940, 1945; Texas-Oklahoma Exh., 1941. *Position*: Instr., Victoria Col., Victoria, Tex.

THURSTON, GERALD (EDWIN)—*Industrial Des.*
346 Claremont Ave., Jersey City, N.J.; h. 440 Lincoln Ave., East, Cranford, N.J.

B. Delaware, Ohio, July 24, 1914. *Studied*: AIC, and with Helen Gardner. *Member*: IDI; Illuminating Engineering Soc. *Exhibited*: IDI, 1951, 1952; AID, 1950, 1951; MMoDA, 1950-1952; Chicago, Ill., 1950-1952; traveling exhibition in Europe. *Position*: Des., New Metal Crafts, Chicago; Des., Lightolier, Inc., New York, N.Y.*

THURSTON, JANE (McDUFFIE)—*Painter, Et.*
550 West California St., Pasadena 2, Cal.

B. Ripon, Wis., Jan. 9, 1887. *Studied*: AIC; in Europe. *Member*: Pasadena Soc.A.; Cal. WC Soc. *Awards*: prize, Women Painters of the West, 1922. *Work*: Pasadena AI. *Exhibited*: Los A. Mus. A., 1945, 1946; Cal. WC Soc., 1946; Pasadena SA, 1946, 1955; Los A. Tower Gal., 1955; Pomona (Cal.) Col., 1946; San Gabriel Valley Exh., 1949, 1951. Publ. "Enjoy Your Museum," series of booklets; Producer of Esto Programs "Madonna of the Renaissance" (by permission of NGA), filmstrip, 1954; "Inspiration for Christmas," 16 mm film, 1955 (author of continuity); Produced by Jane Thurston, Released by Esto: filmstrip, "Say Hello to Modern Art," 1957; films: "Speaking of Sculpture," 1957; "The Art of Etching," 1958.

THWAITES, CHARLES WINSTANLEY—*Painter*
2909 West Greenfield Ave., Milwaukee 15, Wis.; also, Taos, N.M.

B. Milwaukee, Wis., Mar. 12, 1904. *Studied*: Univ. Wisconsin; Layton Sch. A. *Awards*: prize, 48 States Comp., 1939; prizes, med., Palace Legion Honor, 1946; Milwaukee AI, 1933, 1936, 1939, 1941, 1943, 1944. *Work*: Univ. Wisconsin; Univ. Mexico; Marquette Univ.; Milwaukee Fed. Court; Milwaukee County Court; murals, USPO, Greenville, Mich.; Plymouth, Chilton, Wis.; Windom, Minn. *Exhibited*: Carnegie Inst., 1941, 1945; CGA, 1939, 1941; VMFA, 1946; MMA (AV), 1942; AIC, 1930-1932, 1936,

1937, 1940-1942, 1945, 1951, 1952, 1953; PAFA, 1936, 1938; Pepsi-Cola, 1946; SFMA, 1946; Contemporary A. Gal., 1944 (one-man); Milwaukee, Wis., 1944; Kearney Mem. Exh., 1946; Milwaukee AI, 1927-1946; Univ. Wisconsin, 1936-1938, 1945; Walker A. Center, 1952; Harwood Gal., Taos, N.M., 1953-1955; Mus. New Mexico, Santa Fé, 1955, 1956; Nelson Gal. A., 1956; New Mexico Highlands Univ., 1957; Taos Moderns, 1957, 1958; one-man: Mus. New Mexico, Santa Fé, 1957; Stables Gal., Taos, 1957, 1958.

TIBBS, THOMAS S.—*Museum Director*
Museum of Contemporary Crafts, 29 West 53rd St. (22); h. 141 East 55th St., New York, N.Y.

B. Indianapolis, Ind., Aug. 30, 1917. *Studied*: Univ. Rochester, A.B., M.F.A.; Columbia Univ. *Member*: CAA; Mus. Council of New York City; Am. Assn. Mus.; Southeastern Mus. Conference. Lectures: General Art History; The Artist, Craftsman in Our Society; Museum Education, etc. Exhibitions arranged: Exhibition 80, 1953; Craftsmanship in a Changing World, 1956; Furniture by Craftsmen, 1957; Contemporary Wall Hangings, 1957; The Patron Church, 1958; Louis Comfort Tiffany Retrospective, 1958; Young Americans Competition, 1958; Finnish Rug Designs & Contemporary Crafts from Museum Collections, 1958. Contributor to Encyclopaedia Britannica; author of numerous exhibition catalogs and contributor to museum catalogs. Lectures for many colleges, universities, museums, art organizations, etc. *Position*: Assoc. Dir. Edu.; Rochester Mem. A. Gal., 1947-52; Dir., Huntington Galleries, Huntington, W. Va., 1952-56; Dir., Mus. Contemp. Crafts, New York, N.Y., 1956- .

TIFFANY, MARGUERITE BRISTOL—*Painter, E., C., L.*
330 East 33rd St., Paterson 4, N.J.

B. Syracuse, N.Y. *Studied*: Syracuse Univ., B.S.; T. Col., Columbia Univ., M.A.; Parsons Sch. Des.; and with Emile Walters, William Zorach. *Member*: NEA; NAEA; Nat. Lg. Am. Pen Women; Am. Assn. Univ. Profs.; CAA; Assoc. Handweavers; Sch. A. Lg., N.Y.; New Jersey Edu. Assn.; Eastern AA; New Jersey AA; AAPL, etc. *Exhibited*: Montclair A. Mus., 1933-1935, 1937; Paterson AA, annually; Englewood AA; America House, N.Y., 1941, 1942; AAPL, annually; Spring Lake, N.J.; Ridgewood AA, 1951-1954; Fair Lawn (N.J.) AA, 1954, 1955; Ogunquit A. Center, 1954, 1955, 1956. Author: "Industrial Arts Cooperative Service" (pamphlet), 1935. Contributor to educational publications. Publ. Dir., for art exhs.; Metropolitan Opera Gld. A. Exhs.; New Jersey Chm. for Opera Gld. art contests. Lectures on art and travel. *Position*: Past Pres., Montclair A. Mus. A. T. Assn.; Pres., during organization of New Jersey A. Edu. Assn.; V-Pres., Sec., Paterson AA; Council Memb., Eastern AA, 6 years; Assoc. Prof., State T. Col., Paterson, N.J., 1927-1956; Fairleigh Dickinson Univ., Teaneck, N.J., 1956- .

TILLINGHAST, ARCHIE CHAPMAN—*Painter, Des., T.*
Wequetequock, Conn.; R.F.D. 2, Westerly, R.I.

B. Stonington, Conn., June 8, 1909. *Studied*: Newark Sch. F. & Indst. A. *Exhibited*: Lyman Allyn Mus. A.; Montclair A. Mus.; Newark Mus.; MMoDA; Mystic (Conn.) AC.

TILLOTSON, ALEXANDER—*Painter, Mus. Dir., E.*
Mulvane Art Museum, Washburn Municipal University; h. 3401 Huntoon St., Topeka, Kan.

B. Waupan, Wis., July 9, 1897. *Studied*: Milwaukee Sch. F. & App. A.; ASL; Milwaukee State T. Col., B.A.; Columbia Univ., M.A.; & with Kenneth Hayes Miller, Maurice Sterne, Andrew Dasburg, Max Weber. *Member*: Great Plains Mus. Assn.; Kansas State Fed. A.; Am. Assn. Univ. Prof.; CAA. *Awards*: med., prize, Milwaukee AI, 1926, 1940; Kansas State Fair, 1955; Topeka A. Gld., 1955. *Work*: Milwaukee AI; Mulvane A. Center. *Exhibited*: PAFA, 1932, 1933, 1935, 1936; CGA, 1933, 1935; Exh. Am. A., N.Y., 1936; AIC, 1936, 1940; WFNY 1939; Milwaukee AI, 1926-1938; Univ. Minnesota, 1938; Univ. Chicago, 1940; Springfield (Mo.) Mus. A., 1946; Kansas State Col., 1952-1954; William Rockhill Nelson Gal. A., 1955. *Position*: Hd. A. Dept., Milwaukee Secondary Sch., 1926-43; Instr. A., 1932-37; Dir., Junior Sch., 1937-45, Layton Sch. A., Milwaukee, Wis.; Prof. A., Hd. A. Dept., Dir., Mulvane A. Mus., Washburn Mun. Univ., Topeka, Kans., 1945- .

TILTON, JOHN KENT—

Museum Director, C., W., L., Hist.

Scalamandre Museum of Textiles, 57 East 57th St. (22); h. 6 East 37th St., New York 16, N.Y.

B. Jersey City, N.J., June 22, 1895. *Studied:* Columbia Univ.; PIASch. *Member:* AAMus.; Assoc., AID; Benefit Memb., Philadelphia Textile Inst. *Exhibited:* AID Home Furnishings Shows. Author: ten brochures upon silk, woven & printed textiles and the periods of textile design. Contributor to American Fabrics; American Collector; Interiors; Art in America magazines. Lectures: The Decorative Periods of Textile Design and Their History. *Positions:* Custodian, Wallpaper, Cooper Union; Dir., Scalamandre Museum of Textiles, New York, N.Y., at present.

TIMMINS, HARRY L.—*Illustrator, T.*

Markham Bldg., Hollywood 28, Cal.; h. 4615 Petit St., Encino, Cal.

B. Wilsonville, Neb., Nov. 20, 1887. *Studied:* AIC. *Member:* SI. I., "The Chicago" (Rivers of America Series), 1942. Contributor of: illus. to Collier's, This Week, MacLean's, Toronto Star, & others. Publicity for motion picture studios, 1953-55.*

TIMMINS, WILLIAM F.—*Illustrator, Des.*

Noroton, Conn.

B. Chicago, Ill., May 23, 1915. *Studied:* Am. Acad. A., Chicago; Grand Central A. Sch.; ASL, with George Bridgman. *Member:* SI; Westport AA. Illus., "Robin Hood and His Merry Men," 1956; "Cowboys," 1958. Contributor illus. to: Boy Scouts of America (publications and posters); National ads in newspapers, magazines and direct mail.

TINDALL, ROBERT ELTON—*Painter, T., C.*

115 West White Oak Ave.; h. 315 North Liberty St., Independence, Mo.

B. Kansas City, Mo., Oct. 11, 1913. *Studied:* Kansas City AI, B.F.A.; Univ. Kansas City, B.A., M.A., and with Thomas Hart Benton, Edward Lanning, Burnett Shryock, and others. *Member:* A. Gld., Inc.; Community AA. *Award:* Vanderslice scholarship, 1938. *Work:* St. Benedict's Col., Atchison, Kans. *Exhibited:* Carnegie Inst., 1941; Denver A. Mus., 1940, 1942; Assoc. Am. A., 1942; CAM, 1941, 1944, 1945; William Rockhill Nelson Gal. A., 1942, 1944, 1946, 1951; Evansville (Ind.) Pub. Mus., 1944 (one-man); Denison Univ., 1944 (one-man); Woman's City Cl., Kansas City, 1958 (one-man); FA Gal., Independence, Mo., 1958 (one-man). *Position:* Pres., A. Gld., Inc.; Treas., Exh. Chm., Community AA of Independence, Mo.

TINGLER, CHESTER J.—*Painter*

P.O. Box 247, Marathon, Fla.

B. Buffalo, N.Y., June 13, 1886. *Studied:* ASL, Buffalo; ASL, N.Y. *Member:* Fla. A. Group. *Awards:* prizes, Century of Progress, Chicago, 1933; Soc. Four A., and others. *Work:* mural, Miami H.S.; USPO, Sylvester, Ga. *Exhibited:* Ferargil Gal.; Norton Gal. A., West Palm Beach; Soc. Four A.; Washington A. Gal., Miami Beach; Worth Ave. Gal., Palm Beach; Terry AI.

TINKELMAN, MURRAY HERBERT—*Painter*

5316 15th Ave., Brooklyn 19, N.Y.

B. Brooklyn, N.Y., Apr. 2, 1933. *Studied:* CUASch.; Brooklyn Mus. A. Sch. *Awards:* Max Beckmann scholarship, BMSchA, 1955-56; prizes, N.Y. City Center, 1958; BMSchA. Alumni Exh., 1958. *Exhibited:* Nat. Soc. Painters in Casein, 1956; N.Y. City Center, 1956; 2-man: Panoras Gal., 1956, 1957, 3-man, 1958, one-man, 1956; Davida Gal., 1958 (one-man); Art:USA, 1958; BM, 1958. Contributor illus. to: Every Woman's magazine; Parents magazine; Seventeen; Productionwise, and others. *Position:* A. Dir., Inkweed Studios, 2 years; Staff A., Am. A. Group.

TINTNER, MRS. LEONTINE CAMPRUBI. See *Camprubi, Leontine*

TIPPIT, JACK D.—*Cartoonist, Comm. A.*

2610 Canton Ave., Lubbock, Tex.

B. Stamford, Tex., Oct. 19, 1923. *Studied:* Texas Tech. Col.; Syracuse Univ., B.F.A. Contributor cartoons to: Sat. Eve. Post; Look; American Weekly; Sports Illustrated; American Legion; King Features Syndicate.

TISHLER, HAROLD—*Designer-Craftsman*

85-04 37th Ave.; h. 71-20 34th Ave., Jackson Heights 72, L.I., N.Y.

B. Odessa, Russia. *Studied:* Kunstgewerbe Schule, Vienna, Austria, and with Michael Powolny, Joseph Hoffmann. *Awards:* gold and silver medals, Int. Exp., Paris, France, 1937. *Exhibited:* MMA; BM; Roerich Mus.; Syracuse Mus. FA; VMFA; Phila. A. All.

TOBEY, MARK—*Painter*

c/o Willard Gallery, 23 West 56th St., New York, N.Y.

B. Centerville, Wis., 1890. *Studied:* with Henry S. Hubbell; Kenneth Hayes Miller. *Member:* Nat. Inst. A. & Let. *Work:* SFMA. *Award:* Grand Intl. prize, Municipality of Venice. *Exhibited:* Beaux Arts Gal., London; BM; Cal. PLH; AIC; Colorado Springs FA Center; Detroit Inst. A.; Durand-Ruel Gal.; Univ. Illinois; Iowa State Univ.; MMA; Munson-Williams-Proctor Inst.; MModA; Pasadena AI; Venice Biennale, 1958; Western Washington Fair; WMAA; and many others. One-man: Chicago A. Cl., 1940, 1946; Contemp. A., N.Y., 1931; Detroit Inst. A., 1946; M. Knoedler Gal., 1917; Portland A. Mus., 1945; SFMA, 1945; SAM, 1935, 1942; Willard Gal., 1944, 1945, 1947, 1949, 1950, 1951, 1953, 1954, 1957; WMAA (retrospective), 1951; Berne, Switzerland, 1954; Paris, France, 1954; London, England, 1954.

TOBIAS, ABRAHAM JOEL—*Painter, S., Lith., W., L.*

98-11 65th Ave., Rego Park, L.I., N.Y.

B. Rochester, N.Y., Nov. 21, 1913. *Studied:* CUASch.; ASL; Rutgers Univ. *Member:* Arch.Lg.; NSMP; AEA. *Award:* Arch. Lg., 1952. *Work:* BM; Los A. Mus. A.; Howard Univ. Gal. A.; N.Y.Pub.Lib.; Rochester Pub. Lib.; murals, Midwood H.S., N.Y.; James Madison H.S., N.Y.; Adelphi Col.; Howard Univ. Lib.; USPO, Clarendon, Ark.; Beth Israel Hospital, N.Y.; Long Island Jewish Hospital; Domestic Relations Court, Brooklyn; Polytechnic Inst., Brooklyn. *Exhibited:* MModA, 1939; BM, 1937-1939; SFMA, 1941; ACA Gal., 1936; Delphic Studios, 1935-1937; Adelphi Col.; Arch. Lg.; N.Y. Mun. A.; one-man exh.: New Sch. Social Research; Everhart Mus., 1939; Howard Univ., 1938; Delphic Studios, N.Y. Lectures: Mural Painting. Contributor article "Mural Painting" to American Artist magazine, 1957. *Position:* A.Dir., U.S. Army Air Forces, Intelligence Div., 1944; Strategic Services, 1945; Metropolitan Opera Gld., 1946; Instr., Howard Univ., Washington, D.C., 1943-46; A. in Residence, Adelphi Col., Garden City, L.I., 1947- .

TODD, FRANCES CARROLL—*Painter*

3254 Prospect Ave., Northwest, Washington 7, D.C.

B. New York, N.Y. *Studied:* Corcoran Sch. A.; Breckenridge Sch. A., with Hugh Breckenridge; Grand Central Sch. A. *Member:* Georgetown A. Group; Soc. Wash. A.; Albemarle AA, Charlottesville, Va.; Wash. A. Cl. *Exhibited:* CGA; Soc. Wash. A., 1953; AAPL, 1953-1956; Wash. A. Cl., annually; Collectors Corner, Georgetown, Wash., D.C., 1955.

TOFEL, JENNINGS—*Painter, I., W.*

485 Central Park West, New York 25, N.Y.

B. Poland, Oct. 18, 1891. *Studied:* Col. City of N.Y. *Work:* WMAA; Brandeis Univ.; Butler AI; Tel-Aviv Mus., Israel. *Exhibited:* numerous one-man exhibitions in U.S. and abroad. Author: "B. Kopman" (monograph); essay on "Stieglitz" in "America and Alfred Stieglitz."

TOLEGIAN, MANUEL J.—*Painter, W., I., Des.*

3960 Glenridge Dr., Sherman Oaks, Cal.

B. Fresno, Cal., Oct. 18, 1911. *Studied:* ASL. *Work:* Univ. Arizona; Palace Legion Honor; Crocker A. Gal.; PMG; Chapel, St. Lazaro Island, Italy; Mardikian Coll., Beirut, Lebanon; Pub. Lib., Chico, Cal. *Exhibited:* CGA, 1939,

1941, 1943; PAFA, 1938; WMAA, 1937, 1940, 1941; Carnegie Inst., 1939; GGE, 1939; WFNY 1939; AIC, 1938, 1943; SFMA, 1941; one-man exh.: Ferargil Gal., 1936-1939; Palace Legion Honor; Crocker A. Gal.; San Diego FA Soc.; Assoc. Am. A., 1941. I., "The Dove Brings Peace," 1944; "Dinner at Omar Khayyam's," 1944. Author: "Perception and the Language of Painting."

TOLFORD, IRINA POROSHINA (Mrs.)—Painter
80 Charles St., Boston 14, Mass.

B. Verni, Russia, May 15, 1905. *Studied*: with McNulty, Corbino. *Member*: Rockport AA. *Awards*: prizes, Rockport AA, 1954, 1955. *Work*: Ohio AI traveling coll.; Women & Children's Hospital, Boston. *Exhibited*: Rockport AA, 1939-1958.

TOLFORD, JOSHUA—Painter, I.
80 Charles St., Boston, Mass.

B. Thorp, Wis., May 12, 1909. *Studied*: Layton Sch. A.; BMFA Sch.; and with Anthony Thieme. *Member*: Rockport AA. *Exhibited*: Rockport AA, 1938-1958. Illus., "Uncle Andy's Island," 1950; "Henry Ford," 1951; "Whirligig House," 1951; "Storm Along," 1952; "Texas Trail Drive," 1953; "On Your Own Two Feet," 1955; "Who Rides By?" 1955; "Bud Plays Football," 1957; and many other books. Textbooks: "Arrivals and Departures," 1957; "High Trails," 1958; "Widening Views," 1958.

TOLMAN, NELLY McKENZIE (Mrs.)—Miniature Painter
3451 Mt. Pleasant St., N.W., Washington 10, D.C.

B. Salisbury, N.C. *Studied*: Corcoran Sch. A.; Wash. Soc. Min. P.S. & Gr. *Awards*: prizes, AAPL, 1940, 1947; Wash. Soc. Min. P.S. & Gr., 1946. *Work*: NCFA; PMA.

TOLPO, CARL—Painter, S.
Reickman Drive, R.R. 2, Box 436, Barrington, Ill.

B. Ludington, Mich., Dec. 22, 1901. *Studied*: Augustana Col.; Univ. Chicago; AIC, and with Frank O. Salisbury, London, England; and with Gutzon Borglum. *Member*: AAPL. *Awards*: prizes, Chicago Nat. Portrait Comp., 1952; Illinois Abraham Lincoln Mem. Comm., 1955. *Work*: ports., Augustana Col.; Augustana Hospital, Chicago; Swedish-Am. Hist. Mus., Phila., Pa.; Mun. Court, City of Chicago; Inst. of Medicine; John Marshall Law Sch., Chicago; Univ. Illinois Medical Sch.; mural, Pioneer Room, Lagrange (Ill.) YMCA; ports in private colls.; sculpture, Saddle & Sirloin Cl., Chicago; Lincoln bronze bust, Lincoln Room, Ill. State Hist. Mus.; Springfield; Lincoln busts, Alfred W. Stern Coll., LC; Lincoln monument, Barrington, Ill. *Exhibited*: 5 one-man exhs., 1938-1944.

TOMLINSON, FLORENCE K. (Mrs. E. B.)—
Painter, Eng., I., T.
703 Glenway, Madison 5, Wis.

B. Austin, Ill. *Studied*: Colt Sch. A., Madison, Wis.; Univ. Wisconsin, and with Oscar Hagen, Frederic Taubes, and others. *Member*: Wis. P. & S.; Nat. Lg. Am. Pen Women; Madison A. Gld.; Madison AA. *Awards*: prizes, Madison A. Gld., 1944-1948; Wis. State Fair, 1938, 1942-1944; Madison, Wis., 1941, 1942. *Work*: Milwaukee AI; mural, Midland Cooperative, Minneapolis, Minn. *Exhibited*: LC, 1944, 1945, 1948-49, 1952; Milwaukee AI; Laguna Beach AA, 1945; NAD, 1942, 1943, 1948; Albright A. Gal., 1943; Northwest Pr. M., 1946; Madison A. Salon, 1940-1943, 1945, 1955, 1956; Joslyn A. Mus., 1948; Layton A. Gal., 1948; Madison, Wis., 1949-1952, 1953, 1955; Rochester Mem. A. Gal., 1953; SAGA, 1953; Bradley Univ., 1952; Madison AA, 1953, 1955, 1958 (one-man); Madison Bank & Trust Co., 1954 (one-man). *Position*: Pres., Madison A. Gld., 1945-46, 1946-47; Pres., Madison Chptr., Nat. Lg. Am. Pen Woman, 1952-1954, State A. Chm., 1955; Instr. A., Madison Vocational and Adult Sch., 1942- .

TOMPKINS, ALAN—Painter, T., I., L., Des.
157 Kenyon St., Hartford 5, Conn.

B. New Rochelle, N.Y., Oct. 29, 1907. *Studied*: Columbia Col., B.A.; Yale Univ., B.F.A. *Awards*: Winchester traveling scholarship, 1933-34. *Work*: murals, USPO, Martinsville, North Manchester and Indianapolis, Ind.; Boone, N.C.; General Electric Co., Bridgeport, Conn.; Columbia Univ. Cl., N.Y.; Central Baptist Church, Hartford, Conn.

Exhibited: Local and regional exhs. Illus., "Wedding Journey"; "In the Hands of the Senecas"; also several anthologies. *Position*: Instr., Drawing & Des., L., John Herron AI, 1934-38; CUASch., N.Y., 1938-43; Columbia Univ., 1946-51; Asst. Dir., Hartford A. Sch., Hartford, Conn., 1951-1957; Dir., 1957- .

TOMPKINS, FLORENCE (LUSK)—Painter, T.
866 North Chester Ave., Pasadena 6, Cal.

B. Washington, D.C., Sept. 3, 1883. *Studied*: Corcoran Sch. A., and with Conrad Buff, Ejnar Hansen and others. *Member*: Women Painters of the West; A. of the Southwest; Nat. Soc. A. & Let.; Laguna Beach AA; Glendale AA; Los A. A. Lg.; Pasadena Soc. A.; Pasadena FA Cl.; Pasadena AA. *Awards*: prizes, Los A. Friday Morning Cl., 1941, 1942, 1946, 1947, 1949, 1951, 1952; Cal. A. Cl., 1941; Ebell Cl., Los A., 1942-1944, 1951; Glendale AA, 1947; Bowers Mus., Santa Ana, 1947; Greek Theatre, Los A., 1948, 1949; A. of the Southwest, 1952. *Exhibited*: one-man: Pasadena, Altadena, La Jolla, Los Angeles, Whittier, San Gabriel, Glendale, all in California, 1934-1953, and many others.*

TONEY, ANTHONY—
Painter, Gr., I., Comm. A., T., W., L.
547 Riverside Dr., New York 27, N.Y.

B. Gloversville, N.Y., June 28, 1913. *Studied*: Syracuse Univ., B.F.A.; T. Col., Columbia Univ., M.A., Ed. D.; Ecole des Beaux-Arts, Grande Chaumiere, Paris, France. *Member*: AEA; CAA; Audubon A.; NEA; NSMP. *Awards*: Hiram Gee F., Syracuse Univ., 1934; prizes, AEA, 1952, 1953; Univ. Illinois, 1950; Audubon A., 1954; T. Col. Alumni F., 1953; Ohio Wesleyan, 1953; Emily Lowe award, 1955; prize, Mickewiecz Comp., 1956; Staten Island Mus. purchase, 1957. *Work*: WMAA; Staten Island Mus.; Univ. Illinois; Norton Gal. A.; mural, Gloversville (N.Y.) H.S.; Ohio Wesleyan Univ. *Exhibited*: Mortimer Brandt Gal.; CGA; AIC; MModA; Mortimer Levitt Gal.; Syracuse Mus. FA; NAD, 1946-1948, 1950-1954; Univ. Iowa; Univ. Illinois, 1948, 1950-1952, 1955; WMAA, 1948, 1949-1953, 1955; AFA traveling exh., 1949, 1956; Carnegie Inst., 1949; PAFA, 1950-1954; Salpeter Gal., 1950; Univ. Nebraska, 1950, 1952; ACA Gal., 1951, one-man: 1954, 1955, 1957; BM, 1951; Des Moines A. Center, 1951; AIC, 1951; Roswell Mus. A., 1956; Kansas City AI, 1956; Univ. New Mexico, 1956; Martick Gal., Balt. Md., 1955 (one-man); A. Gal., N.Y., 1948; Berkshire Mus. A., 1957; Tyringham Gal. (Mass.), 1958; Staten Island Mus. Hist. & A., 1958; Univ. So. Illinois, 1959. *Position*: Nat. Dir., AEA, 1952-56, 1958-59, Sec. N.Y. Chap., 1958-59, N.Y. Delegate, 1958-59; Instr., Hofstra Col., 1953-55; New Sch. for Social Research, 1953- ; Bd. Memb., Audubon A., 1958-59. Author: "Creative Learning in Higher Education."

TONKIN, JOHN CARTER—Craftsman
5 Highland Ave., Dover, N.H.

B. Mullicahill, N.J., Nov. 11, 1879. *Work*: Univ. New Hampshire. *Position*: Instr., Emeritus, Univ. New Hampshire, Durham, N.H.

TOOKER, GEORGE—Painter
77 State St., Brooklyn 1, N.Y.

B. Brooklyn, N.Y., Aug. 5, 1920. *Studied*: Phillips Acad., Andover, Mass.; Harvard Univ., A.B.; ASL, with Reginald Marsh, Kenneth Hayes Miller, Harry Sternberg. *Work*: WMAA; MMA; Walker A. Center; AIC. *Exhibited*: WMAA, 1947-1958; MMA, 1950, 1952; AIC, 1951; PAFA, 1952; CGA, 1951; Venice Biennale, 1956; Inst. Contemp. A., London, 1950; Carnegie Inst., 1958; Spoleto (Italy) A. Festival, 1958.

TORAN, ALFONSO T.—Painter
680 Lexington Ave., New York 22, N.Y.; h. 1608 Washington St., Hollywood, Fla.

B. Naples, Italy, May 17, 1896. *Studied*: in Italy. *Work*: murals, Hotels Delmonico, Pierre, New Yorker, Waldorf-Astoria, N.Y.; Texaco Co.; Chrysler Bldg.; etc. *Exhibited*: WMAA. *Position*: Dir., Creative Studios of Art & Decoration, New York, N.Y., 1935- .

TORBERT, MEG (Mrs. Donald R.)—
Museum Curator, Des.
Walker Art Center, 1710 Lyndale Ave., South (3);
h. 2116 Irving Ave., South, Minneapolis 5, Minn.

B. Faribault, Minn., Sept. 30, 1912. *Studied*: Univ. Minnesota, B.S.; Univ. Iowa, M.A. *Member*: AAMus.; AID. *Award*: Carnegie F., 1937. *Work*: Interiors for Mayo Memorial Medical Center, Minneapolis, Minn. Ed., contributor to Design Quarterly. Arranged Design exhibitions, WAC, 1950- ; Cur. Des., Walker Art Center, Minneapolis, Minn., 1950- .

TORREY, FRED M.—*Sculptor*
6127 Greenwood Ave., Chicago, Ill.

B. Fairmont, W. Va., July 29, 1884. *Studied*: AIC. *Member*: Chicago Soc. P. & S. *Award*: gold medal, Assn. Chicago P. & S., 1950. *Work*: S., dec., Paradise Theatre, Chicago; Haines County Court House, Jackson, Miss.; Haish Mem. Lib., DeKalb, Ill.; Norton Mem. Hall, Chautauqua, N.Y.; La. State Medical Sch., New Orleans; panels, State Capitol, Baton Rouge, La.; Science Bldg., Eastern Illinois State T. Col.; doors, McGregor Pub. Lib., Highland Park, Mich.; medals, Univ. Chicago, Brown Univ.; Northwestern Univ.; port. reliefs, and statues: Wesley Hospital, Chicago; Winchester, Ill.; Lincoln's Tomb, Springfield, Ill.; busts, Swedish Hall of Fame, Phila., Pa.; Univ. Chicago; tablet, Creche Home, Omaha, Neb.; fountain, Bester Mem. Plaza, Chautauqua, N.Y.; Lincoln and Jefferson H.S., Bloomington; Munn mem., Topeka; Harris mem., Sterling Colo.; medal for Am. Life Convention, Chicago, and others.*

TORREY, MABEL LANDRUM—*Sculptor, L.*
6127 Greenwood Ave., Chicago 37, Ill.

B. Sterling, Colo., June 23, 1886. *Studied*: State T. Col., Greeley, Colo.; AIC. *Member*: Chicago Soc. P. & S.; Chicago Galleries Assn. *Awards*: prize, Chicago Galleries Assn. *Work*: statues, reliefs, mem., Washington Park, Denver, Colo.; Omaha Children's Lib.; Proctor Hospital, Cincinnati, Ohio; Univ. Chicago Nursery Sch.; State Normal Col., Greeley, Colo.; Univ. Chicago; Decatur, Ill.; Crane Sch., Cincinnati; many portraits of children. *Exhibited*: AIC; Chicago Galleries Assn., etc. Lectures to art clubs and organizations.*

TOVISH, HAROLD—*Sculptor*
164 Rawson Road, Brookline 46, Mass.

B. New York, N.Y., July 31, 1921. *Studied*: Columbia Univ.; Zadkine Sch. Sculpture; Grande Chaumiere, Paris. *Member*: S. Gld.; AEA. *Awards*: prizes, WAC, purchase, 1951; Minneapolis Inst. A., 1953, 1954; Boston A. Festival, 1957, 1958; Boston Inst. Contemp. A., 1958. *Work*: sc., Minneapolis Inst. A.; WAC; WMAA; AGAA; Univ. Minnesota; drawings: Guggenheim Mus.; Minneapolis Inst. A.; WAC. *Exhibited*: MMA, 1943; WMAA, 1952-1954; 1957; AIC, 1954; San F. AA, 1952; Toledo Mus. A., 1948; Boston A. Festival, 1957, 1958; Venice Biennale, 1956; WAC, 1951, 1953, 1955; Denver Mus. A., 1952, 1953. *Positions*: Asst. Prof. Sculpture, New York State Col. of Ceramics, 1947-49; Univ. Minnesota, 1951-54; Instr., S., BMFA Sch., Boston, Mass., 1957- .

TOVISH, MARIANNA PACKARD. See Pineda, Marianna

TOWNSEND, ARMINE (Mrs. Edward H.)—*Painter*
742 17th St., Northeast, Massillon, Ohio

B. Brooklyn, N.Y., June 26, 1898. *Studied*: Buffalo AI, and with Althea Hill Platt, William B. Rowe. *Awards*: prizes, Greenwich Soc. A., 1948, 1950. *Exhibited*: Albright A. Gal., 1945; Buffalo AI, 1944; Greenwich Soc. A., 1946-1950; Canton AI, 1952-1958; Massillon Mus., 1952-1957 (1957 one-man). (Chm. A. Exh. Com., 1955-1958); Akron AI, 1957; Little Gal., North Canton, Ohio, 1958 (one-man).

TOWNSEND, ETHEL HORE (Mrs. John)—*Painter*
63 Hillside Ave., Glen Ridge, N.J.

B. Staten Island, N.Y., Sept. 26, 1876. *Studied*: Metropolitan Mus. Sch. A.; ASL. *Member*: N.Y. WC Cl.; AWS; Woman's A. Cl. of New York. *Award*: prize, N.Y. WC Cl.

TOWNSEND, MARVIN—Cartoonist, Comm. A.
631 West 88th St., Kansas City 14, Mo.

B. Kansas City, Mo., July 2, 1915. *Studied*: Kansas City AI; Col. of Commerce A. Sch. *Member*: Cartoonists Gld. of Am. Illus., "Henry's Wonderful Model T"; cartoons for advertising promotion series for local and national firms, including Falstaff Brewing Corp.; Westinghouse Electric Co., etc. Contributor cartoons to: national and trade magazines in the U.S. and Canada. Creator of comic strips "Hermalink"; "Cylinder Head"; "Quacker"; "Jane & Joey"; "Julie & Jack"; "Sanitary Sam"; "Meg & Greg"; "Jasper Tweed"; "Sam Hill," The Salesman; and industrial safety strip, "Bert" for the Nat. Safety Council, and others. Specializes in cartoon strips for children in various age groups; illus. for humorous articles; commercial art and layout.

TRACY, LOIS BARTLETT—*Painter*
Wise, Va.; also, Englewood, Fla.

B. Jackson, Mich. *Studied*: Michigan State Univ., A.B., M.A.; Rollins Col., A.B.; Ringling Sch. A., and with Ernest Lawson, Hilton Leech, Hans Hofmann. *Member*: NAWA; AEA; Pen & Brush Cl.; New Hampshire A.; Cape Ann Soc. Mod. A.; Ogunquit AA; Fla. A. Gld.; Sarasota A; AEA. *Awards*: prizes, Fla. Fed. A., 1933-1936; Sarasota AA, 1937, 1938; Clearwater Mus. A., 1946; State of Fla., 1935; WFNY 1939 (medal); Am. Assn. Univ. Women, 1948; New Hampshire AA, 1948; Pen & Brush Cl., 1948, 1950; Fla. A. Group, 1954; NAWA, 1950, 1957; Winston-Salem Gal., 1958; Norfolk Mus. A., purchase 1956; Atlanta Mus. A., 1956; Va. Intermont Exh., 1955, 1956. *Exhibited*: AFA traveling exh., 1937, 1938, 1943-1946; SSAL, 1935, 1936; Great Lakes Exh.; Exh. Am. A., Rockefeller Center, 1938; A. Gld.; New Hampshire AA; Swope Gal. A.; Columbus Mus. FA; High Mus. A.; Butler AI; George Walter Vincent Smith A. Mus.; Lyman Allyn Mus.; Rochester Mem. A. Gal.; Syracuse Mus. FA; J. B. Speed Mem. Mus.; Mt. Holyoke Col.; Amsterdam, Holland, 1955; VMFA traveling exh., 1952-55; Colgate Univ.; Canajoharie A. Gal.; Portland Mus. A.; Wadsworth Atheneum; Currier Gal. A.; All. A. Am.; Audubon A.; NAWA (and traveling exh., 1952-54); Pen & Brush Cl.; Argent Gal.; one-man: Studio Gld., N.Y., 1936; Norlyst Gal., 1945, 1947; Cape Ann Soc. Mod. A., 1948; Charles Smith Gal., Boston, 1949; Center St. Gal., Winter Park, Fla., 1949; Research Studio, Maitland, Fla., 1951; Barter Theatre, 1951; Sarasota AA, 1951; Burliuk Gal., 1951 (one-man), 1952; Telfair Acad.; Worcester A. Center, Appleton; Wustum Mus. A.; Southwest Va. Mus.; VMFA, 1957 (one-man); King Col., 1958 (one-man); Pen & Brush Cl., 1957 (one-man), and in colleges and universities.

TRAHER, WILLIAM HENRY—*Painter, I., L.*
2331 Niagara St., Denver 7, Colo.

B. Rock Springs, Wyo., Apr. 6, 1908. *Studied*: Yale Univ.; NAD. *Work*: Wyoming design, Container Corp. State Series; reviews and reproductions, N.Y. Times; Christian Science Monitor; Annual of Advertising Art; Gebrauchs Graphik, etc. Rear projection backgrounds, Barter Theatre, "The Virginian." *Position*: Chief, Background A., Denver Mus. Natural Hist.; Bd. Trustees, Denver A. Mus., Denver, Colo.

TRAPHAGEN, ETHEL (Mrs. William R. Leigh)—
Designer, T., I., W., L.
1680 Broadway; h. 200 West 57th St., New York 19, N.Y.

B. New York, N.Y., Oct. 10, 1882. *Studied*: CUASch; NAD; ASL; N.Y.Sch. F. & App. A.; & in Paris, France. *Member*: Am. Woman's Assn.; Nat. All. A. & Indst. *Awards*: prize, N.Y. Times Comp., 1913; med. CUASch; Merite Libanais, Lebanese Gov't, 1941. Author: "Costume Design and Illustration," 1918; "Fashion Work as a Career," Book of Knowledge Annual, 1942. Contributor to: Professional Arts Quarterly, North American Review, & other publications. Lectures: Costume Design & Illustration. *Position*: Pub. & Ed., "Fashion Digest" magazine; T., L., Costume Des. & Illus., CUASch; Brooklyn T. Assn.; N.Y. Univ.; etc. Extensive coll. regional costumes and library of 16,000 vols. Founder, Dir., Traphagen Sch. Fashion, New York, N.Y., at present.

TRAUERMAN, MARGY ANN—*Painter, T., Comm. A.*
998 Second Ave., New York 22, N.Y.

B. Sioux Falls, S. Dak. *Studied*: Los Angeles City Col., A.B.; State Univ. Iowa, B.F.A.; Am. Acad. A., Chicago;

ASL, and with Jacob Getlar Smith. *Member*: AWS; NAWA. *Awards*: prizes, Texas Annual, 1951; NAWA. *Exhibited*: PAFA, 1953; AWS, 1943, 1957, 1958, and traveling exh., 1957; All. A. Am., 1954-1956; Audubon A., 1958; NAWA, 1956, 1957; NAD, 1956; Knickerbocker A., 1956, 1957; Nat. Soc. Painters in Casein, 1956; Texas Annual, 1951.

TRAVER, MARION GRAY—*Painter*
205 West 57th St., New York 19, N.Y.

B. Elmhurst, L.I., N.Y., June 3, 1892. *Member*: All.A. Am.; NAWA; PBC; Catherine Lorillard Wolfe AC. *Awards*: prizes, NAD, 1931; NAWA, 1930, 1934, 1938-1941; All.A.Am., 1942; War Workers Jury prize, 1943; Wolfe AC, 1926-1928, 1944; Hoffman prize, 1945; med., Exp. Women's A. & Indst., 1928. *Exhibited*: NAD, 1930-1932, 1935, 1936; CGA, 1933; NAWA, 1925-1946; All.A. Am., 1929-1946; Int. AC, London, 1931; BM; Montclair A. Mus.; Milwaukee AI; Dayton AI; Grand Rapids A. Mus.; WFNY 1939; AFA traveling exh.; Staten Island Inst. A. & Sc.; Columbia Univ.; Union Lg. Cl., N.Y.; Argent Gal.

TRAVIS, KATHRYNE HAIL—*Painter, T.*
2410½ Mahon St., Dallas 1, Tex.; s. P.O. Box 873, Ruidoso, N.M.

B. Ozark, Ark., Feb. 6, 1894. *Studied*: Galloway Col., AIC; Cincinnati Acad. FA; Ohio Mechanics Inst.; Chicago Acad. FA. *Member*: Kathryne Hail Travis A. Cl., Dallas (Hon.). *Work*: in many private colls. *Exhibited*: one-man: Los Angeles; Seattle, Wash.; Arkansas; Oklahoma; DMFA; Texas State Fair. Co-Founder, Co-Dir., Dallas AI (later absorbed by Dallas Mus. FA); Dir., Fndr., Gallery of Art & Summer School of Painting (in Ruidoso, N.M.).

TRAVIS, OLIN HERMAN—*Painter, Lith., L., E.*
8343 Santa Clara Dr., Dallas 18, Tex.

B. Dallas, Tex., Nov. 15, 1888. *Studied*: AIC; & with Clarkson, Norton, Walcott, Sorolla. *Awards*: prizes, SSAL, 1930, 1932. *Work*: Dallas Mus. FA; Elisabet Ney Mus.; Highland Park Mus.; Hall of State, Dallas, Tex.; Love Field Airport, Tex. *Exhibited*: Rockefeller Center, N.Y.; GGE, 1939; Texas Centennial; DMFA, 1953; numerous one-man exh.; Chicago, San Antonio, Denver, Dallas, etc. Lectures: Landscape, Portrait Painting. *Position*: Founder, Dir., Dallas AI, Dallas, Tex.; Dir., San Antonio (Tex.) AI, 1944-45; Instr., Painting, Austin Col., Sherman, Tex., 1951- ; Painter of backgrounds for Dallas Mus. Natural Hist.; Pres., Dallas Soc. for General Semantics.

TRAVIS, PAUL BOUGH—*Painter, Et., Lith., T., L.*
11414 Juniper St., Cleveland, Ohio; h. 3045 Lincoln Blvd., Cleveland Heights 18, Ohio

B. Wellsville, Ohio, Jan. 2, 1891. *Studied*: Cleveland Sch. A. *Member*: Am. Soc. for Aesthetics. *Awards*: prizes, CMA, 1921, 1930, 1931, 1938, 1939, 1940, 1952, 1955-1958; Butler AI, 1940; Ohio WC Soc., 1955, 1956. *Member*: Archaeological Inst. Am. *Work*: CMA; Rochester Mem. A. Gal.; Springfield (Mass.) Mus. A.; Butler AI; Ohio WC Soc.; BM; Cleveland Mus. Natural Hist.; Univ. Utah; N.Y.Pub.Lib.; Akron AI. *Exhibited*: BM, 1931, 1935; MMoDA; AIC, 1931, 1932, 1938; GGE, 1939; PAFA, 1930, 1932, 1934; Carnegie Inst., 1931, 1932; CGA, 1930, 1932; Pasadena AI, 1946; Butler AI, 1936-1958; CMA, 1920-1958; Butler Inst. Am. A., 1950. *Position*: Instr. drawing & painting, Western Reserve Univ., Cleveland, Ohio, 1956- . Treas., Archaeological Inst. Am., 1950-56.

TREADWELL, GRACE A.(Mrs. Abbot)—*Painter, L., T.*
45 East 9th St., New York 3, N.Y.

B. West Chop, Mass., July 13, 1893. *Studied*: BMFA Sch.; ASL; Grande Chaumiere, Paris, France. *Member*: Pen & Brush Cl.; NAWA; Mississippi AA; AEA. *Awards*: prizes, Pen & Brush Cl. (8); Miss. AA. *Work*: Albright A. Gal.; murals, St. Luke's Church, Smethport, Pa.; Madonna, St. Mark's Church, St. George's Episcopal Church, N.Y., and Father Flannigan's Boys Town, Nebraska. *Exhibited*: BM; High Mus. A.; NAWA; All. A. Am.; Knickerbocker A.; 4 one-man exhs., N.Y. *Position*: Bd. Dir., NAWA.

TREADWELL, HELEN—*Painter, Des.*
33 West 67th St., New York 23, N.Y.

B. Chihuahua, Mexico, July 27, 1902. *Studied*: Vassar Col.; Sorbonne, Paris, France. *Member*: AID; NSMP; Arch. Lg. *Awards*: special award, mural paintings in Mun. Bldgs., Chile. *Work*: Hotel mural decorations include; Hotel New Yorker, N.Y.; Hotel Utah, Salt Lake City; Hotel Tourraine, Boston; Hotel Southern, Baltimore; Cipango Club, Dallas; Roslyn Country Club, Long Island, N.Y.; Burlington Railway coach panels; S.S. Uruguay; Chase Manhattan Bank, San Juan, Puerto Rico; Brooklyn Savings & Loan Bank, Bensonhurst, L.I.; Sun & Surf Cl., Atlantic Beach, L.I.; Guggenheim Dental Clinic for Children, N.Y.; indst. murals: Okonite Cable Co., Passaic, N.J.; Standard Vacuum Oil Co., Harrison, N.J. *Exhibited*: one-man: Arthur Newton Gal., 1934; Rockefeller Center, N.Y.; Arch. Lg., 1946, 1949, 1950, 1956; Crespi Gal., 1959.*

TREBILCOCK, AMAYLIA C. See Castaldo, Amaylia

TREBILCOCK, PAUL— *Painter*
44 West 77th St., New York 24, N.Y.

B. Chicago, Ill., Feb. 13, 1902. *Studied*: Univ. Illinois; AIC; & in Europe. *Member*: ANA; Chicago AC; Century Assn.; Chelsea AC, London, England. *Awards*: prizes, ASL, Chicago, 1923; AIC, 1925, 1926, 1928, 1937, med., 1929; Chicago Galleries Assn., 1926; NAD, 1931; Newport AA, 1931. *Work*: AIC; Albright A. Gal.; Cranbrook Mus.; The Pentagon, Wash., D.C.; IBM; Universities of: Rochester, Wisconsin, Harvard, Yale, Princeton, Columbia, Johns Hopkins; many portraits of prominent persons. Contributor to: American Artist magazine.

TREES, CLYDE C.
325 East 45th St.; h. 415 East 52nd St., New York, N.Y.

B. Center, Ind., Mar. 27, 1885. *Member*: A. Fellowship; Subscriber memb., NAD; life memb., Treas. & Memb. Council, NSS; Arch. Lg.; SC; Municipal A. Soc. *Awards*: Medal of Honor, NSS, 1958. *Positions*: Pres., Medallic Art Co., N.Y.; Treas., NSS; Memb., Finance Com., A. Fellowship; Member, Commission of Fine Arts of the City of New York, 1959- .

TREFETHEN, JESSIE BRYAN—*Painter, E., Et., L.*
Peak's Island, Portland, Me.

B. Portland, Me. *Studied*: Mt. Holyoke Col., B.A.; PAFA; in Europe; & with Emil Carlsen, Daniel Garber, Henry McCarter, Joseph Pearson, & others. *Awards*: Cresson traveling scholarship, PAFA, 1915. *Work*: Allen A. Mus., Oberlin, Ohio. *Exhibited*: F. PAFA, annually; PAFA; L.D.M. Sweat Mem. Mus.; Oberlin Col., 1949; Upsula Col., 1949; Bowdoin Col., 1950; Farnsworth Mus., 1950; one-man exh.: Allen A. Mus., Oberlin Col., 1941, 1942, 1944, 1945. Lectures: French Painting & Sculpture, etc. *Position*: Hd. A. Dept. Knox Sch., Cooperstown, N.Y., 1923-26; Asst. Prof. FA, 1926-44, Assoc. Prof. FA, 1944-47, Emeritus, 1947- , Oberlin Col., Oberlin, Ohio.

TREFONIDES, STEVEN—*Painter, Photog.*
277 Dartmouth St., Boston 16, Mass.

B. New Bedford, Mass., Sept. 26, 1926. *Studied*: Swain Sch. Des.; Vesper George Sch. A., Boston; BMFA Sch., with Karl Zerbe, David Aronson. *Awards*: Tiffany Fnd., 1952; Portland (Me.) A. Festival, Grand Prize, 1958. *Work*: paintings: Wadsworth Atheneum; Portland A. Mus.; New Britain A. Mus.; deCordova & Dana Mus.; Brandeis Univ.; Exeter Acad.; Deerfield Academy; photographs: MMoDA. Contributor to New York Times; Art in America magazine. *Positions*: Instr., Vesper George Sch. A., 1955-57; Brookline (Mass.) Adult Program, 1948- .

TREIMAN, JOYCE WAHL—*Painter*
844 Hibbard Rd., Winnetka, Ill.

B. Evanston, Ill., May 29, 1922. *Studied*: Stephens Col., A.A.; State Univ. Iowa, B.F.A. *Member*: AEA; North Shore A. Lg.; Chicago A. Cl. *Awards*: prizes, Denver A. Mus., 1948; Illinois State Mus., 1948; AIC, 1949-1951, 1953; Tupperware A. Fund F., 1955-1956; Magnificent Mile Exh., Chicago, 1953; Tiffany Fnd. F., 1947-48. *Work*: AIC; Illinois State Mus.; Denver A. Mus.; State Univ.

Iowa. *Exhibited*: VMFA, 1948; AIC, 1948-1954; Denver A. Mus., 1948, 1949, 1955; Springfield Mus. A., 1948, 1949; Miss. Valley Exh., 1949; Univ. Illinois, 1950-1952; MMA, 1950; WMAA, 1950, 1951; WMA, 1951; Springfield (Mass.) Mus., 1951; Watkins Gal., Wash., D.C., 1951; Los A. Mus. A., 1951; Cornell Univ., 1951; Milwaukee AI, 1951; AFA traveling exh., 1951-52, 1954, 1955; Detroit Inst. A., 1952; Chicago A. Cl., 1952; SFMA, 1951; John Herron AI, 1953; Univ. Wisconsin, 1953, 1954; Landan Gal., 1954; LC, 1954; Carnegie Inst., 1955; Dallas Mus. FA, 1951, 1954; Univ. Texas, 1951; one-man: AIC, 1947; Winnetka, Ill., 1949; Fairweather-Garnett Gal., Evanston, 1950; Edwin Hewitt Gal., N.Y., 1950; Palmer House, Chicago, 1952; Elizabeth Nelson Gal., Chicago, 1953; Feingarten Gal., 1955.*

TREVITTS, JOSEPH—Painter, T.
   397 River St., Manistee, Mich.

B. Ashland, Pa., Apr. 8, 1890. *Studied*: PAFA; and in Paris, France. *Member*: Michigan Acad. Sc., A. & Let. *Awards*: F., PAFA; Cresson traveling scholarship, PAFA, 1913. *Work*: Reading (Pa.) Pub. Mus.; Pub. Sch., Pub. Lib., Masonic Temple, Mission Covenant Church, all in Manistee, Mich.; Hotel Chippewa, Manistee; Michigan Lg. of Women's Cl., Detroit, Mich. *Exhibited*: PAFA; NAD; CGA; Univ. Michigan; Hackley A. Gal.; Newcomb Macklin Gal., Chicago; Ryerson Lib., Grand Rapids, Mich.; Willard Pub. Lib., Battle Creek, Mich.; Terry AI; Manistee Pub. Lib.

TRIBBLE, DAGMAR HAGGSTROM—Painter
   15 Gramercy Park, New York 3, N.Y.; h. 12 Battle Road, Princeton, N.J.

B. New York, N.Y., Feb. 19, 1910. *Studied*: Parsons Sch. Des. (N.Y. and Paris); ASL; Farnsworth Summer Sch. *Member*: AWS; NAWA; NAC. *Awards*: prizes, NAWA, 1955 and prior; New Jersey Soc. Women's Cl., 1950; Essex WC Cl., 1954; Women's Cl. of Orange, 1954; Rutgers Univ. *Exhibited*: AWS, 1952; Montclair A. Mus., 1951; NAWA, 1952-1956; NAC, 1951-1957; Essex WC Cl., 1954, 1955; Women's Cl. of Orange, 1954, 1955; one-man: Women's Cl. of Orange, 1951; Wellfleet A. Center, 1955.

TRICCA, M(ARCO) A.—Painter, S.
   337 East 10th St., New York 9, N.Y.

B. Italy, Mar. 12, 1880. *Awards*: Shilling award, 1944, 1948. *Work*: AIC; WMAA; Wadsworth Atheneum. *Exhibited*: CGA, 1935; AIC, 1935-1938; PAFA, 1933-1937; Mortimer Brandt Gal., 1944; BM; one-man exh.: Whitney Studio Cl.; WMAA; Contemporary A., 1940; Graham & Sons Gal., 1957.

TRIFON, HARRIETTE—Painter, T.
   84 Laurel Hill Drive, Valley Stream, N.Y.

B. Philadelphia, Pa., Dec. 4, 1916. *Studied*: with Aaron Berkman, Nahum Tschacbasov, Chaim Gross. *Awards*: prizes, Birmingham Mus. A., 1954; Long Island A., 1953, 1956 (2); Malverne A., 1954; Nassau A. Lg., 1958. *Work*: Birmingham Mus. A.; Staten Island Mus. A. & Sc. *Exhibited*: Birmingham Mus. A., 1954, 1956; All. A. Am.; ACA Gal.; Five Towns Music & A. Fnd.; Long Island A. Lg.; N.Y. City Center, 1953-1958; Panoras Gal., 1955, 1957 (one-man); Hofstra Col., 1956 (one-man). *Position*: A.T., Woodmere-Hewlett Pub. Sch., Adult Edu. Program.

TRIMM, ADON—Painter
   36 Grant St., Jamestown, N.Y.

B. Grand Valley, Pa., Feb. 20, 1897. *Member*: Soc. for Sanity in Art, Chicago, Ill. *Award*: prize, Chautauqua Soc. A., 1955. *Work*: Capitol Bldg., Albany, N.Y. *Exhibited*: Albright A. Gal., 1933, 1934; Soc. for Sanity in Art, Chicago, 1941; Chautauquqa, N.Y., 1940-1942 (one-man); Jamestown, N.Y., 1941, 1942; Erie (Pa.) Pub. Mus., 1951 (one-man); Rochester Inst. Tech., 1952 (one-man); Terry AI, 1952; Ogunquit A. Center; Canton (Ohio) AI, 1955. *Position*: Dir., Chautauqua County Soc. A., Jamestown, N.Y.

TRIMM, GEORGE LEE—Painter, I.
   9 Channing Lane, Camillus, N.Y.

B. Jamestown, N.Y., June 30, 1912. *Studied*: Syracuse Univ., B.F.A. *Member*: NSMP. *Work*: St. Lawrence Univ.;

Ohio State Univ.; U.S. War Dept., Wash., D.C.; Engineer Corps, Wash., D.C.; murals, Ft. Belvoir, Va.; Waldes Kohinoor, Inc., Long Island City, N.Y.; Le Moyne Univ.; Brighton Town Hall, Rochester, N.Y.; Syracuse, N.Y., war memorial; St. Joseph Hospital, Syracuse. *Exhibited*: one-man exh.: Syracuse, N.Y., 1946, Army paintings. *Position*: Hd. A. Dept., 6th Army Univ., Osaka & Kyoto, Japan, 1945.

TRIMM, H. WAYNE—Illustrator
   Sketch Book Farm, Chatham, N.Y.

B. Albany, N.Y., Aug. 16, 1922. *Studied*: Cornell Univ.; Syracuse Univ.; Augustana Col., A.B.; Kansas State Col.; State Col. of Forestry, B.S. *Member*: Am. Ornithologists Union; Columbia County A. & Crafts. *Work*: dioramas, Springfield Mus. A.; CMA. *Exhibited*: American Bird Artists traveling exh., sponsored by Audubon A., 1948; Joslyn Mus. A.; Buffalo Mus. Science, 1950; San Jose State Col., 1951; Erie Mus., 1952; Albany State Col., 1956. Illus., "The Mammals of California and Its Coastal Waters," 1954; "Manual of Museum Techniques," 1948. Contributor illus. to Audubon Magazine; New York State Conservationist. Lectures: Conservation, and Wildlife Painting. *Position*: Conservation Educator, N.Y. State Conservation Dept., Conservation Edu. Div., 1953- .

TRIMM, LEE S.—Painter
   165 Strong Ave., Syracuse 10, N.Y.

B. Ft. Larned, Kan., Apr. 15, 1879. *Studied*: with De Forest Carr. *Member*: Soc. for Sanity in Art, Chicago, Ill.; Jamestown Sketch Cl. (Founder). *Work*: portraits, Syracuse Univ.; Gettysburg Acad.; Puerto Rico Missionary Col.; & in many libraries. *Exhibited*: Soc. for Sanity in Art, Chicago, 1941; Utica Lib., 1938-1940 (one-man); Daytona Beach, Fla., 1941; Assoc. A. Syracuse, 1937; Jamestown, N.Y.

TRIPLETT, FRED J.—Museum Director
   Huntington Galleries, Park Hills; h. 1028 8th St., Huntington, W. Va.

B. Vallejo, Cal., Apr. 17, 1921. *Studied*: San Jose State Col., A.B.; Stanford Univ., M.A. *Member*: AAMus. *Positions*: Instr. Des., Univ. Minnesota, Duluth Branch, 1948-57; Dir., Huntington Galleries, Huntington, W. Va., 1957- .

TRIPLETT, MARGARET L.—Educator, P.
   Norwich Art School, Norwich, Conn.; h. 1 Prunier Court, Norwich, Conn.

B. Vermillion, S.D., Dec. 30, 1905. *Studied*: State Univ. Iowa, B.A.; BMFA Sch.; Yale Univ., M.A.; & with Grant Wood. *Member*: Eastern AA; Nat. Edu. Assn.; Conn. State T. Assn.; Conn. A. Assn.; Conn. WC Soc.; Mystic AA; Nat. Com. on A. Edu.; NAEA; Norwich AA. *Exhibited*: AWCS, 1940; CM, 1940; New Haven Paint & Clay Cl., 1939; Portland Mus. A., 1939; Iowa A. Salon, 1932-1934, 1938; Joslyn Mem., 1933; Conn. Acad. FA, 1937, 1938; Conn. WC Soc., 1939, 1940, 1949-1951, 1954, 1955, 1957, 1958; Mystic AA, 1948-1958; de Cordova & Dana Mus., 1953; Slater Mus. A., 1953-1958; one-man: New Britain YWCA, 1953; Audio Workshop, West Hartford, 1955; Eastern Conn. A., 1948-1952; Lyman Allyn Mus., 1958. *Position*: Instr., A., 1929-43, Dir., 1943- , The Norwich A. Sch., Norwich, Conn.; Pres. Conn. AA, 1954-56; Trustee, Hartford A. Sch., 1956-59.

TRISSEL, LAWRENCE E.—Painter, Des., I., Comm. A.
   R.R. #1, Carmel, Ind.

B. Anderson, Ind., Jan. 27, 1917. *Studied*: John Herron AI, B.F.A.; & with Eliot O'Hara, Francis Chapin, Max Kahn. *Awards*: med., BAID, 1938; prizes, Indiana AC, 1941, 1944, 1951; Ohio Valley Exh., 1944; Ind. State Fair, 1941, 1950; Hoosier Salon, 1946. *Work*: U.S. Govt.; Ball State T. Col. *Exhibited*: CM, 1940; Carnegie Inst., 1941; Oakland A. Gal., 1940, 1944; Exhibition Momentum, 1953, 1954; Indiana A., 1953, 1954; PAFA, 1941; VMFA, 1946; Butler AI, 1944; 1444 Gallery, 1958. *Position*: A. Dir., A. Sidener & Van Riper Advertising Agency, 1944-45; Keeling & Co., Indianapolis, Ind., 1945-48; Mark Gross Assoc., 1940-50, Adv. Mgr., 1951-53; Adv. A., Caldwell, Larkin & Sidener-Van Riper, Inc., 1953-

TRIVIGNO, PAT—Painter, E., L.
Tulane University; h. 435 Glendale Blvd., New Orleans, La.

B. New York, N.Y., Mar. 13, 1922. *Studied:* Tyler Sch. A., Temple Univ.; Univ. Iowa; N.Y. Univ.; Columbia Univ., B.A., M.A. *Member:* CAA; Southeastern Col. AA; MacDowell Colony Assn.; New Orleans AA. *Awards:* prizes, Delgado Mus. A., 1951, 1954, 1957; Am. Acad. A. & Let., 1950, 1951; Carnegie Univ. grant, 1957-58. *Work:* Miami, Fla.; Delgado Mus. A. *Exhibited:* WMAA, 1950; Young Painters, USA, 1951; Univ. Illinois, 1950; PAFA, 1952; Univ. Nebraska, 1951; Des Moines A. Center, 1951; Cal. PLH, 1952; Cranbrook Mus. A., 1953; Dayton AI, 1951, 1952; Toledo Mus. A., 1952; Denver A. Mus., 1955, 1957; Birmingham Mus. A., 1952; VMFA, 1952; DMFA, 1954, 1956; Univ. Florida, 1952; Atlanta, Ga., 1952; Norfolk Mus. A., 1954; Delgado Mus. A., 1951, 1953, 1954; Luyber Gal., N.Y., 1950 (one-man); Mus. FA of Houston. *Position:* Assoc. Prof. A., Tulane Univ., New Orleans, La.

TROCHE, E. GUNTER—Museum Director
Achenbach Foundation for Graphic Arts, California Palace of the Legion of Honor; h. 2242 Steiner St., San Francisco 15, Cal.

B. Stettin, Germany, Sept. 26, 1909. *Studied:* Univ. Vienna; Univ. Munich, Ph.D. *Member:* Renaissance Soc. Am.; Deutscher Verein fuer Kunstwissenschaft; Roxburghe Cl. of San Francisco. Author: "Italian Painting in the 14th and 15th Centuries," 1935; "Painting in the Netherlands, 15th and 16th Centuries," 1936; many museum catalogs and numerous articles and book reviews in professional magazines. Arranged exhs., "The Printmaker, 1450-1950," 1957; "German Expressionists," 1958, and many other exhibitions. *Positions:* Asst. Cur., State Museums, Berlin, 1932-36; Cur., Municipal Museum, Breslau, 1936-38; Cur., 1938-45, Dir., 1945-51, Germanic National Museum, Nuremberg, Germany; Dir., Achenbach Foundation for Graphic Arts, California Palace of the Legion of Honor, San Francisco, Cal., at present.

TROMMER, MARIE—Writer, Cr., P., T.
99 Bay 29th St., Apt. C-3, Brooklyn 14, N.Y.

B. Kremenchug, Russia. *Studied:* CUASch, and with Douglas Volk, Wayman Adams. *Member:* Cooper Union Alumni Assn. *Work:* Corona Mundi, N.Y.; N.Y. Hist. Soc.; Mus. City of N.Y.; N.Y. Pub. Lib.; LC; Long Island Hist. Soc.; Mus. Natural Hist., N.Y.; Theodore Roosevelt House, N.Y.; BM Lib.; and others; books in hand-made covers, Brooklyn Pub. Lib.; Cooper Union Sch. & Mus. *Exhibited:* Soc. Indp. A.; All. A. Am.; Salons of Am.; Brooklyn Soc. A.; Brooklyn WC Cl.; Brooklyn Heights Exh., 1955. Author, I., "America in My Russian Childhood," 1941, and other books. Contributor to N.Y. World Telegram & Sun, 1955-1957; Idea Exchange, 1957-58.

TROTH, CELESTE HECKSCHER—Painter
7906 Lincoln Dr., Philadelphia 18, Pa.

B. Ambler, Pa., July 19, 1888. *Studied:* PAFA; and with C. Ricciardi; & in Rome, with Sigda Pozza. *Member:* Phila. A. All. *Work:* Protestant Episcopal Cathedral, Roxborough, Pa.; Acad. Music, Phila., Pa.; Woodmere A. Gal., Chestnut Hill, Pa. *Exhibited:* F. PAFA; Woodmere A. Gal.; Warwick Gal., A. All.; Cosmopolitan Cl., Nat. Lg. Am. Pen Women, all in Phila.; Douthitt Gal., N.Y., 1941 (one-man); McClees Gal., Phila., Pa.

TROWBRIDGE, GAIL—Painter, Lith., T.
14 South Munn Ave., East Orange, N.J.

B. Marseilles, Ill., Nov. 6, 1900. *Studied:* Columbia Univ., B.S., M.A. *Member:* Com. A. Edu.; Assoc. A. New Jersey. *Awards:* prizes, NAWA, 1940; Argent Gal., 1945. *Work:* Newark Mus. *Exhibited:* Women's Int. AC, England, 1946; NAWA, 1938-1946; Newark Mus.; N.Y. Society Women A., 1945, 1946; Montclair A. Mus.; Assoc. A. New Jersey, 1958; Hunterdon County A. Center; Riverside Mus., 1944; one-man exh.: Wash. AC, 1945; Artists of Today, Newark, N.J., 1946. Lectures: Children's Art Work. *Position:* Supv. A. Edu., Elementary Sch., Millburn, N.J., 1930-59.

TROWBRIDGE, MRS. V. S. See Funsch, Edyth

TRUAX, SARAH E.—Painter
3620 Fairmount Ave., San Diego 5, Cal.

B. Marble Rock, Iowa. *Studied:* AIC; & with Howard Pyle, Alphonse Mucha, Joaquin Sorolla. *Member:* San Diego A. Gld.; La Jolla AA; Baltimore WC Cl.; Women Painters of the West; Cal. Soc. Min. P. *Awards:* med., Pan-Pacific Exp., 1915; Los A. County Fair, 1928; Cal. State Fair, 1936. *Work:* San Diego FA Soc.; Women's Cl., Lidgerwood, N.D.; First Unitarian Church, San Diego, Cal. *Exhibited:* GGE, 1939; Cal.-Pacific Int. Exp., 1935; PAFA, 1927- 1930, 1932; Brooks Mem. A. Gal.; Detroit Soc. A. & Crafts, 1928, 1929; Los A. Soc. Min. P.; Grand Central A. Gal., 1930; Oklahoma Col. for Women; Ft. Worth Mus. A.; Witte Mem. Mus.; Pacific Southwest Exh., Long Beach, Cal.; BMA; San Diego FA Soc., 1926-1939, 1945, 1946; Sacramento (Cal.) State Fair, 1930-1936; Phoenix (Ariz.) State Fair, 1932; Pa. Soc. Min. P.; Am. Soc. Min. P.; La Jolla AA; etc.*

TRUE, VIRGINIA—Educator, P.
3M 12 Martha Van Rensselaer Hall, Cornell University; h. 521 Wyckoff Rd., Ithaca, N.Y.

B. St. Louis, Mo. *Studied:* John Herron AI, B.A.E.; Cornell Univ., M.F.A. *Member:* NAWA. *Awards:* prizes, Denver A. Mus., 1932, 1933; Kansas City AI, 1935; Rochester Mem. A. Gal., 1939. *Work:* Univ. Colorado; State Col. Agriculture, Ft. Collins, Colo.; Cornell Univ. *Exhibited:* AWCS; NAWA, Carnegie Inst.; Denver A. Mus.; Kansas City AI; Rochester Mem. A. Gal.; Cornell Univ. *Position:* Instr. A. John Herron AI, 1926-28; Univ. Colorado, 1929-36; Prof. A., Cornell Univ., Ithaca, N.Y., 1936- ; Hd. Dept. Housing & Des., 1945- .

TRUEWORTHY, JAY—Painter
1931 Garfias Dr., Pasadena 7, Cal.

B. Lowell, Mass., Jan. 29, 1891. *Studied:* with Vesper George, Boston; Mabel Welch, N.Y.; Ejnar Hansen, Robert Frame, California. *Member:* Laguna Beach AA. *Awards:* prizes, Los A. Mus. A., 1935; Cal. Soc. Min. P., 1940; Ebell Cl., 1944. *Exhibited:* PAFA, 1939-1941; Grand Central A. Gal.; N.Y. Pub. Lib.; BM; Smithsonian Inst.; Concord, Durham, N.H.; Pasadena A. Mus., Dartmouth, N.H.; Los A. Mus. A.; Laguna Beach AA, and others.*

TRUITT, UNA B. (Mrs. J. J.)—Painter, W., L., T.
2203 Brentwood St., Houston 19, Tex.

B. Joaquin, Tex., Sept. 17, 1896. *Studied:* Houston Univ., A.B., M.A. *Member:* Assoc. A. Houston. *Exhibited:* Local & State exh., 1932-1946. *Position:* Supv. A. Houston City Sch., 1925-38; Supv. A. for Crippled Children, Houston, Tex., 1928-46.*

TRUMP, RACHEL BULLEY (Mrs. Charles C.)— Portrait Painter
503 Baird Rd., Merion, Pa.

B. Canton, Ohio, May 3, 1890. *Studied:* Syracuse Univ. B.P. *Member:* Phila. Plastic Cl.; Woodmere A. Gal. *Awards:* med., Phila. Plastic Cl., 1938; Woodmere A. Gal., 1943. *Work:* Circuit Court, Richmond, Va.; Haverford (Pa.) Sch.; Haverford Friends Sch.; Woman's Medical Col., Phila. *Exhibited:* NAWA; Phila. A. All.; Phila. Plastic Cl.; Woodmere A. Gal. Lectures, demonstrations of portrait painting for art groups and clubs.

TRUNK, HERMAN, JR.—Painter
135 Essex St., Brooklyn 8, N.Y.

B. New York, N.Y., Oct. 31, 1899. *Studied:* CUASch.; ASL. *Member:* Delaware AA. *Work:* WMAA; Nicaragua Seminary Coll.

TSCHACBASOV, NAHUM—Painter
222 West 23rd St., New York 11, N.Y.

B. Baku, Russia, Aug. 30, 1899. *Studied:* Lewis Inst.; Armour Inst. Tech., and in Paris. *Member:* An Am. Group. *Award:* prize, Pepsi-Cola, 1947. *Work:* MMA; State Dept., Wash., D.C.; WMAA; Dallas Mus. FA; Univ. Illinois; Brandeis Univ.; Univ. Georgia; Univ. Alabama; Univ. Nebraska; BM; Tel-Aviv Mus., Israel; PMA; Butler AI; PAFA; Smith Col.; Jewish Mus. *Exhibited:* Carnegie Inst.; AIC; PAFA; CGA; MMoA; WMAA; VMFA; Walker A. Center; MMA; Berkshire Mus.; Rochester Mem. Gal.;

Riverside Mus.; Univ. Indiana; Univ. Illinois; Univ. Iowa; and in Europe; one-man: Galerie Zak, Paris, 1934; Gallery Secession, 1935; ACA Gal., 1936, 1938, 1940, 1942, 1946; Univ. Texas, 1946; New Orleans A. & Crafts; Vigeveno Gal., Los A.; 1030 Gal., Cleveland, Ohio; Perls Gal., 1947-48; John Heller Gal., N.Y., 1951, 1953; Colorado Springs FA Center, 1946; SFMA, 1946; Nelson Gal. A., 1950; Walker A. Center, 1951; Kansas State Col.; Ohio Univ.; Indiana State T. Col.; Univs. of Missouri, Nebraska, Colorado, Florida, North Carolina; Pa. Col. for Women; Allegheny Col.; Jewish Mus., and many others throughout the U.S. Contributor to Art Students League Quarterly; Numero.*

TSCHAEGLE, ROBERT—
Lecturer, W., Mus. Cur., S., Cr.
525 Buckingham Dr., Indianapolis 8, Ind.
B. Indianapolis, Ind., Jan. 17, 1904. *Studied*: AIC; Univ. Chicago, Ph.B., A.M.; Univ. London; & with Lorado Taft. *Member*: CAA. *Exhibited*: AIC; Hoosier Salon; John Herron AI; NAD. Contributor to: Herron AI Bulletins. *Position*: Instr., Hist. A., Univ. Missouri, 1935-36; Asst. Cur., John Herron A. Mus., Indianapolis, Ind., 1937-41; Master, Park Sch., Indianapolis, Ind.

TSCHAMBER, HELLMUTH GEORGE—
Painter, T., Comm. A.
157-24 Baisley Blvd., Jamaica 34, N.Y.
B. Heidelberg, Germany, July 9, 1902. *Studied*: Brooklyn Mus. Sch. A., and in Germany. *Member*: SC; AAPL; All. A. Am.; Long Island A. Lg.; Hudson Valley AA. *Awards*: prizes, AAPL, 1947; gold medal, All. A. Am., 1955; many regional awards. *Work*: Univ. Florida; Hempstead H.S.; East Williston Pub. Lib.; City Hall, New York City. *Exhibited*: AWS, 1949, 1951; All. A. Am., 1953-1955; regularly in local and regional exhs. Contributor to Architectural magazines and newspapers.

TSELOS, DIMITRI THEODORE—Educator, L.
1494 Branston St., St. Paul 8, Minn.
B. Tripolis, Greece, Oct. 21, 1901. *Studied*: AIC; Univ. Chicago, Ph.B., M.A.; Princeton Univ., M.A., M.F.A., Ph.D.; N.Y. Univ.; & abroad. *Member*: CAA; Am. Soc. Arch. Historians; Archaeological Inst. Am. *Awards*: Carnegie F., Princeton Univ., 1928-1929, 1930-1931; FA F., N.Y. Univ., 1929-1930; Fulbright F., Greece, 1955-56. Contributor to: Am. Journal Archaeology, Art Bulletin, Magazine of Art, & other publications. Author: "Sources of Utrecht Psalter Illustrations." *Position*: Instr., Asst. & Assoc. Prof., N.Y. Univ., New York, N.Y., 1931-49; Prof., Univ. Minnesota, 1949. Summer & Collateral Lectureships: Univ. Southern California, Swarthmore Col., Columbia Univ., Vassar Col., Yale Univ., Walker A. Center, etc., 1937-46.

TSENG YU-ho, BETTY (ECKE)—Painter, T.
3460 Kaohinani Drive, Honolulu 17, Hawaii
B. Peking, China, Nov. 27, 1923. *Studied*: Fu Jen Univ., Peking, B.A.; post-grad. at universities in Peking and Hawaii. *Member*: Honolulu P. & S. *Awards*: Rockefeller Scholarship, 1953; Watamull Fnd. purchase award, 1957; prize, Stanford Univ., 1958. *Work*: Honolulu Acad. A.; AIC; Inst. Oriental Studies, Rome; murals, Catholic Church, Island of Kaui, Hawaii; cemetery, Manoa, Honolulu; stage des., Juilliard Sch. Music, N.Y.; St. John's Col., Annapolis, Md. *Exhibited*: Stanford Univ., 1958; SFMA, 1957; AFA traveling exh.; Smithsonian traveling exh., 1952-1954; and in Peking, Shanghai, London, Zurich, Paris, Rome, Hong Kong, San Francisco, Honolulu, Pasadena, Chicago, and others. Contributor "Seven Junipers of Wen Cheng-ming" (Chinese Art Soc., 1954); "Hsueh Wu and Her Orchids" (Arts Asiatiques); Note on "T'ang Yin" (Oriental Art, 1956). Lectures: Chinese Painting; Some Contemporary Elements in Chinese Pictorial Art; Some Formal Developments in Chinese Painting. *Positions*: Instr., Chinese Painting, Consultant in Chinese Painting, Honolulu Acad. A., Honolulu, Hawaii.

TUBIS, SEYMOUR—Painter, Gr., T.
573 Grand St., D 1404, New York 2, N.Y.
B. Philadelphia, Pa., Sept. 20, 1919. *Studied*: Temple Univ.; PMSch.A.; ASL; Hans Hofmann Sch. A.; Grande Chaumiere, Paris, France; Instituto d'Arte, Florence,

Italy. *Member*: ASL; SAGA; Manhattan Gallery Group. *Awards*: SAGA, 1948; Joe and Emily Lowe award, 1950, 1953, 1955; Newspaper Gld. of N.Y., 1953. *Work*: Lowe Fnd.; SAGA; MMA; ASL; LC; Pa. State Univ.; mural, U.S. Army Signal Corps, Camp Crowder, Mo. *Exhibited*: Northwest Pr. M., 1948, 1949; LC, 1948, 1949; Phila. Pr. Cl., 1948, 1949, 1952; Carnegie Inst., 1948; SAGA, 1948, 1951; Wichita AA, 1948; BM, 1949; PAFA, 1950; Lowe Fnd., 1951, 1952, 1953, 1955 (last two one-man); MMA, 1953, 1955; Riverside Mus., 1956, 1958; Lincoln H.S., N.Y., 1957 (one-man); Art:USA, 1958; N.Y. Pub. Lib., 1958; Royal Soc. P. Et., & Engravers, London, 1954; ASL, 1950. *Position*: A., New York World-Telegram & Sun, New York, N.Y.

TUCKER, CHARLES CLEMENT—Portrait Painter
3621 Arborway Dr., Charlotte 7, N.C.
B. Greenville, S.C., Sept. 13, 1913. *Studied*: ASL, with Frank DuMond, George Bridgman, Ivan Olinsky. *Member*: NAC; ASL; Atelier Cl., N.Y.; Gld. Charlotte A.; AAPL; FA Lg. of the Carolinas. *Work*: Hickory Mus. A.; Winthrop Col., Rock Hill, S.C.; Crossmore Sch., Crossmore, N.C.; Dept. Labor, Raleigh; Presbyterian Synod Home, Montreat, N.C.; Comm. Room of Foreign Affairs, Nat. Capitol, Wash., D.C.; People's Nat. Bank, Rock Hill, S.C.; Bon Marche, Asheville, N.C.; Episcopal Church, Monroe, N.C.; murals, Officer's Cl., Ft. Meade, Md.; Merchants Assn., Charlotte, N.C. *Exhibited*: one-man: Miami Beach A. Center, 1948; Mint Mus. A., 1948, 1950-1952; Little A. Gal., Asheville, N.C., 1952; Civic A. Gal., Greenville, S.C., 1940; Asheville A. Mus., 1953; St. Petersburg Fed. A. Gal.; Miami Fed. A. Gal.; Jacksonville Fed. A. Gal.; Hickory A. Mus., 1952; Group exhs.; MMA; NAC.

TUCKER, PERI (Mrs. Joseph A.)—Writer, Comm. A.
929 Mandalay Ave., Clearwater Beach, Fla.
B. Kashau, Austria-Hungary, July 25, 1911. *Studied*: Columbus Sch. A.; and with Roy E. Wilhelm, Earl C. Van Swearingen. *Exhibited*: Ohio WC Soc.; Canton, Ohio; Akron, Ohio; Massillon, Ohio. I., "Big Times Coloring Book"; "The Quiz Kids" and other books for children. Contributor to St. Petersburg Times with exhibition reviews, features stories on art and artists, etc., 1942- .

TUCKERMAN, LILIA (McCAULEY) (Mrs. Wolcott)—
Painter
"Arroyo del Paredon," Carpinteria, Cal.
B. Minneapolis, Minn., July 15, 1882. *Studied*: Corcoran Sch. A.; & with Charles Woodbury. *Member*: NAWA; NAC; Soc. Wash. A.; Santa Barbara A.; Cal. AC; San Diego A. Gld. *Work*: mural, St. Paul Church, triptych, Trinity Episcopal Church, Santa Barbara, Cal.; backgrounds for animal groups, Santa Barbara Mus. Natural Hist. *Exhibited*: NAD, 1930; Women's Int. Exh., London, 1931; NAWA, 1931, 1933, 1935, 1937-1939, 1941; NAC, 1928, 1929, 1931, 1933-1937, 1940, 1945, 1948-1958; Soc. Wash. A., 1923-1926, 1928, 1929, 1931, 1934-1937; Ogunquit, Me., 1933-1935, 1937-1940, 1945, 1948-1953, 1956-1958; Santa Barbara Mus. A., 1944, 1949, 1951, 1952, 1953; Argent Gal., 1938 (one-man); San Diego A. Gld., 1954; Santa Paula, Cal., 1954; Bar Harbor, Me., 1956 (one-man).

TUDOR, TASHA (Mrs. Thomas L. McCready, Jr.)—
Illustrator, W., Des., Comm. A.
P. O. Route 1, Contoocook, N.H.; h. Webster, N.H.
B. Boston, Mass., Aug. 28, 1915. *Studied*: BMFA Sch. I.; "Pumpkin Moonshine," 1938; "Alexander the Gander," 1939; Author, I., "Snow Before Christmas," 1942; "The White Goose," 1943; "Mother Goose," 1944; "Thistly B," 1949; "The Doll's Christmas," 1950; "Amanda the Bear,' 1951; "Edgar Allan Crow," 1953; "A is for Annabelle," 1954; and many others. Creator of the Tasha Tudor Christmas Cards. Co-Owner, Ginger & Pickles Store-Doll Museum, Contoocook, N.H. *Exhibited*: Currier Gal. A., 1955. Contributor to Horn Book; Parents Magazine; Life magazine.

TUKE, GLADYS—Sculptor, C., T.
Box 57, Westward Ho!, White Sulphur Springs, W. Va.
B. Linwood, W. Va., Nov. 19, 1899. *Studied*: Corcoran Sch. A.; PAFA, and with Albert Laessle, Maxwell Miller, Charles Tennant. *Member*: Southern Highland Handicraft

Gld. *Awards*: F., PAFA; prize, Woodmere A. Gal. *Exhibited*: PAFA, 1936-1951. *Position*: Instr., S. & Ceramics, S. & P. Art Colony, Greenbrier Hotel and Ashford General Hospital, both in White Sulphur Springs, W. Va. Demonstrations of sculpture for clubs and organizations.

TULK, ALFRED JAMES—*Mural Painter, P.*
    Webb's Hill Rd., Stamford, Conn.

B. London, England, Oct. 3, 1899. *Studied*: Oberlin Col.; Yale Univ., B.F.A.; NAD; ASL. *Member*: NSMP; Arch. Lg. *Awards*: medal, BAID, 1922. *Work*: murals, Donaghey Bldg., Little Rock, Ark.; St. Mary's Hospital, Brooklyn; Hotel Commodore, N.Y.; Cove Theatre, Glen Cove, N.Y.; St. Elizabeth's Sch., N.Y.; Culver Military Acad., Culver, Ind.; Good Samaritan Hospital, Suffern, N.Y.; S.S. "Argentina"; St. Peter's Church, Marquette, Mich.; St. Gertrude's Church, Chicago, Ill.; Salvation Army Hospital, Flushing, N.Y.; St. Ignatius Loyola, Chicago; Lutheran Church, York, Pa.; Franciscan Monastery, New Canaan, Conn., and many others; mosaics, State Capitol, Harrisburg, Pa.; SS. Peter and Paul Catholic Church, Indianapolis; St. Joseph's Church, Dunkirk and Richmond Hill, N.Y.; Mary Immaculate Seminary, Northampton, Pa.; Jr. H.S., New York City; stained glass, churches in Corpus Christi and Houston, Tex.; Col. of West Africa, Liberia; Univ., Detroit; ports., N.Y. Pub. Lib.

TUNIS, EDWIN—*Writer, I., P., Des.*
    R.F.D. 1, Reistertown, Md.

B. Cold Spring Harbor, N.Y., Dec. 8, 1897. *Studied*: Maryland Inst., and with C. Y. Turner, Joseph Lauber, Hugh Breckenridge. *Member*: Pen Cl. *Awards*: gold medal, Boys' Cl. of Am., 1956; Edison Fnd. award (for "Colonial Living"), 1957. *Work*: murals, McCormick & Co., Balt.; Title Guarantee Co., City Hospital, both of Baltimore. Author, I., "Oars, Sails and Steam," 1952; "Weapons," 1954; "Wheels," 1955; "Colonial Living," 1957.

TURMAN, WILLIAM T.—*Painter, E.*
    Taft, Cal.

B.Graysville, Ind., June 19, 1867. *Studied*: Union Christian Col., Merom, Ind.; AIC; Chicago Acad. FA; PAFA, and with J. Francis Smith, A. F. Brooks, A. Sterba, and others. *Member*: Indiana A. Cl.; Brown County Gal. Assn. *Awards*: prizes, Hoosier Salon, 1932; Indiana State Fair; Indiana A. *Work*: Indiana State T. Col.; Pub. Schs. in Columbia City, Terre Haute, Jasonville, Harrison Twp., in Indiana; Swope A. Gal.; Turman Township H.S.; Terre Haute Pub. Schs., and many others. *Exhibited*: Hoosier Salon, 1921-1952, 1955; Indiana A. Cl., 1939-1945; Swope A. Gal.; Indiana State T. Col. Author: "New Outlook Writing System." *Position*: Prof. A., Hd. A. Dept., Indiana State T. Col., 40 years; Pres. Bd. Managers, Sheldon Swope A. Gal., Terre Haute, Ind., 1941-1957.

TURNBULL, GRACE HILL—*Sculptor, P., W.*
    2233 Chancery Rd., Baltimore 18, Md.

B. Baltimore, Md. *Studied*: Maryland Inst.; ASL; PAFA. *Member*: NAWA; NSS. *Awards*: prizes, Paris, France, 1914; Huntington prize, 1932, 1944; BMA, 1939, 1944, 1945, 1947; NAWA, 1946; MMA, 1942; Gimbel award, Phila., 1932; Phi Beta Kappa, Southwestern Univ., 1956. *Work*: MMA; BMA; CGA; monument, Eastern H.S., Balt. *Exhibited*: NSS, 1908, 1916, 1943, 1948, 1950, 1951; NAWA, 1931-1936, 1941, 1942, 1944, 1946, 1947, 1950; PAFA, 1908, 1909, 1912, 1913, 1915, 1916, 1920, 1921, 1933-1935, 1942, 1946, 1948, 1950; CGA, 1908, 1909, 1917, 1920, 1941, 1948; AIC, 1912, 1914, 1916, 1920, 1936, 1941; MMA, 1942; NAD; Arch. Lg., 1921, 1933, 1937, 1951; Texas Centennial, 1936; WFNY, 1939; BMA, 1926, 1929, 1930, 1931, 1933, 1938, 1940-1949, 1951-1952; Maryland Inst., 1920, 1932, 1938-1940, 1945; PMA; one-man: BMA; CGA. Author: "Tongues of Fire," 1929; "The Essence of Plotinus," 1934; "Fruit of the Vine," 1950; "Chips From My Chisel," 1953; "The Uncovered Well," 1954.

TURNBULL, MURRAY—*Educator*
    University of Hawaii, Honolulu 14, T.H.

Position: Chm., Art Department, University of Hawaii.*

TURNER, HAMLIN—*Painter*
    193 Atlantic Ave., Marblehead, Mass.

B. Boston, Mass., Nov. 6, 1914. *Studied*: Harvard Col. *Member*: Marblehead AA; Marblehead A. Gld. (Bd. Gov.). *Exhibited*: Boston A. Festival, 1953, 1954; deCordova & Dana Mus., 1954; Lamont Gal., Exeter, N.H., 1953; Brookline Pub. Lib., 1953; Long Wharf Studios, Boston, 1954, 1955; Neptune Gal., Marblehead, 1955; King Hooper Gal., Marblehead, 1951-1958; Music Theatre Gal., Beverly, Mass., 1956-1958; Marblehead A. Gld., 1958; Jordan-Marsh, Boston, 1958.

TURNER, HERBERT B.—*Painter, S.*
    606 Zuni Drive, Del Mar, Cal.

B. Mt. Vernon, N.Y., Mar. 20, 1926. *Studied*: U.S. Military Acad., B.S.; ASL; NAD; Am. A. Sch. *Member*: San Diego A. Gld.; A. Center of La Jolla; San Diego AI. *Awards*: John and Anna Stacey Scholarship, 1955-1957; prizes, Vista A. Gld., 1955, 1956; Carlsbad-Oceanside A. Lg., 1955 (3), 1956, 1957; San Diego A. Gld., 1955; San Diego AI, 1956, 1958; Rancho Santa Fe Exh., 1956, 1958; San Diego County Fair, 1958. *Exhibited*: A. Center of La Jolla, 1954-1958; San Diego FA Gal., 1954-1958; Vista A. Gld., 1957, 1958; San Diego County Fair, 1954-1956, 1958; Oceanside A. Lg., 1954-1958.

TURNER, ILA McAFEE. See McAfee, Ila

TURNER, JANET ELIZABETH—*Painter, Gr., E., L.*
    Stephen F. Austin State College; h. 1210 Raguet St., Nacogdoches, Tex.

B. Kansas City, Mo., Apr. 7, 1914. *Studied*s Stanford Univ., B.A.; Kansas City AI; Claremont Col., M.F.A.; T. Col., Columbia Univ. *Member*: NAD; P. & S. Soc., New Jersey; Cal. WC Soc.; Texas WC Soc.; NAWA; Audubon A.; Am. Color Pr. Soc.; SAGA; Pen & Brush Cl.; Boston Pr. M.; Nat. Ser. Soc. (Pres.); NAEA; AAUW; Springfield A. Lg.; Texas FA Soc.; CAA; Texas State T. Assn. *Awards*: Guggenheim F., 1953; prizes, Texas FA Assn., 1948-1954; Dallas Mus. FA, 1948, 1949, 1951; Southwest Pr. Exh., 1949-1951; Wichita AA, 1950, 1953; NAWA, 1950-1952; Northwest Pr. M., 1952; Fla. Southern Col., 1952; SAGA, 1952; Boston Pr. M., 1953; Texas WC Soc., 1953; Springfield A. Lg., 1955, 1957; Tupperware F., 1956, and others. *Work*: Scripps Col.; Texas FA Assn.; Smith Col.; Dallas Mus. FA; Witte Mem. Mus.; Lyman Allyn Mus.; Princeton Pr. Cl.; LC; Wichita AA; Santa Barbara Col.; SFMA; SAM; New Britain Mus.; Boston Pub. Lib.; LC; PMA; CMA; Yale Univ.; Fitchburg A. Center, etc. *Exhibited*: nationally, 1941-1958; one-man: Tokyo, Japan; Jerusalem; group exh.: London, Amsterdam, Rome, etc. Several USIA exhs. abroad. Illus., "The Yazoo," (river series). *Position*: Asst. Prof. A., Stephen F. Austin State Col., 1947- .

TURNER, JEAN (LEAVITT) (Mrs. Leroy C.)—*Painter, I., S., T., L.*
    Kemper Campbell Ranch, Victorville, Cal.

B. New York, N.Y., Mar. 5, 1895. *Studied*: PIASch.; CUASch.; & with Ethel Traphagen. *Member*: AAPL; Lg. Am. Pen Women. *Exhibited*: Palace Region Honor, 1938-1939; AAPL, 1940-1946; Lg. Am. Pen Women, 1940, 1941; Laguna Beach, 1953 & various So. Cal. exhs. I., Progress Books (1-2-3 grade), 1926. Lectures: The Importance of Art in Our Everyday Life; Training the Art Student for the Professional Field.*

TURNER, MATILDA HUTCHINSON—*Miniature Painter*
    3606 Powelton Ave., Philadelphia 4, Pa.

B. Jerseyville, Ill., Mar. 2, 1869. *Studied*: Marietta (Ohio) Col.; PAFA, and with William Chase, Cecilia Beaux, Margaretta Archambault, Sargent Kendall. *Member*: PAFA (life); F. PAFA (life); Pa. Soc. Min. P.; Phila. Plastic Cl. *Awards*: F., PAFA. *Work*: PMA. *Exhibited*: PAFA, 1925-1933, 1935, 1937, 1939, 1940, 1942, 1944, 1945; BM; ASMP; Balt. WC Cl.; Century of Progress, Chicago, 1933; Cal. Soc. Min. P., 1937, 1944, 1948-1952; Smithsonian Inst., 1944, 1945; also in Indianapolis, SFMA, Memphis, Charleston, Richmond, Washington, etc. Author: "The Christmas Boy and Other Children's Stories," 1955.

TURNER, RAYMOND—*Sculptor*
137 West 28th St.; h. 51 Seventh Ave., South, New York 14, N.Y.

B. Milwaukee, Wis., May 25, 1903. *Studied*: Milwaukee AI; Wisconsin Normal Sch.; Layton Sch. A.; CUASch.; BAID. *Awards*: prize, Detroit Inst. A., 1927; Guggenheim F., 1928. *Exhibited*: NAD, 1932, 1933, 1935; PAFA, 1936, 1940; WFNY, 1939; Salon d'Automne, Paris, 1928; NSS, 1949, 1950; Medallic Art Co., 1950; Argent Gal., 1951.

TURNER, ROBERT C.—*Ceramic Craftsman*
East Valley Road, Alfred Station, N.Y.

B. Port Washington, N.Y., July 22, 1913. *Studied*: Swarthmore Col., A.B.; PAFA; Alfred Univ., M.F.A. *Member*: York State Craftsmen; Am. Craftsmen's Council. *Awards*: prizes, Wichita Mus. A., 1949, 1955; Syracuse Mus. FA, 1951, 1954; Finger Lakes Exh., 1957, 1958; silver medal, Cannes, France, 1955. *Work*: WAC; Syracuse Mus. FA; St. Paul Gal. A.; Univ. Illinois; Utah State Univ.; Los A. County Fair Assn. *Exhibited*: Los A. County Fair, 1951, 1952; Syracuse Mus. FA, 1947-1949, 1951, 1954, 1956, 1958; Wichita Mus. A., 1948, 1949, 1951; Univ. Illinois, 1952; Univ. Wisconsin, 1952; Kiln Cl., Wash., D.C., 1951, 1952; St. Paul Gal. A., 1955, 1957; Memphis Acad. FA, 1957; Utah State Univ., 1957; Scripps Col., 1951, 1957; Maryland Inst. FA, 1958; Mus. Contemporary Crafts, N.Y., 1956-1958; Brussels World's Fair, 1958; Rochester Mem. A. Gal., 1954 (one-man); Finger Lakes Exh., Rochester, 1957, 1958. *Positions*: Instr., Black Mountain Col., 1949-51; Univ. Wisconsin (summer), 1957; Ceramics, Univ. of New York, State Col. of Ceramics, Dept. Des., Alfred Univ., 1958- .

TURNEY, WINTHROP DUTHIE—*Painter*
211 Greene Ave., Brooklyn 38, N.Y.

B. New York, N.Y., Dec. 8, 1884. *Studied*: ASL; and with George De Forrest Brush, Frank DuMond, Louis Loeb. *Member*: All. A. Am.; AAPL; 50 American Artists; A. Fellowship. *Awards*: prizes, All. A. Am., 1944, 1947; AAPL, 1952-1954. *Work*: BM; Des Moines A. Center; Hickory (N.C.) Mus. A. *Exhibited*: PAFA; AWS; NAD; Newark Mus.; Milwaukee AI; WMAA; MModA.

TUROFF, MURIEL P. (Mrs.)——*Craftsman, P., S.*
5450 Netherland Ave., Riverdale 71, N.Y.

B. Odessa, Russia, Mar. 24, 1904. *Studied*: NAD; ASL; Am. A. Sch.; PIASch. *Member*: N.Y. Soc. Ceramic A.; N.Y. Soc. Craftsmen. *Work*: ceramic ports. in private colls. *Exhibited*: Syracuse Mus. FA, 1946; AAUW traveling exh., 1946-47; N.Y. Soc. Ceramic A., 1948-1955; N.Y. Soc. Craftsmen, 1948-1955; Cooper Union, 1956; Jewish Mus., N.Y., 1957, 1958. Author, I., "How to Make Pottery and Other Ceramic Ware," 1949. *Position*: Instr., Henry Hudson Day Camp, 1943; Riverdale Neighborhood House, 1942-45; Kingsbridge Veteran's Hospital, 1944-45; Pres., N.Y. Soc. Craftsmen, 1956-57; Fnd. Memb., Artist-Craftsmen of New York.

TURZAK, CHARLES—*Painter, Eng., Cart., I., Des.*
7059 North Olcott Ave., Chicago 31, Ill.

B. Streator, Ill., Aug. 20, 1899. *Studied*: AIC. *Awards*: prize, AIC, 1940. *Work*: Lib. Cong.; murals, USPO, Chicago, Ill.; Lemont, Ill. I., Publisher, "Abraham Lincoln—Biography in Woodcuts," 1933; "Benjamin Franklin—Biography in Woodcuts," 1935. *Position*: A. Dir., Today's Health Magazine, 1942- .*

TUTHILL, MRS. ALBERT GEDNEY. See Van Dyke, Ella

TUTHILL, CORINNE—*Painter, C., E.*
501 North Poplar St., Florence, Ala.

B. Laurenceburg, Ind., Oct. 11, 1892. *Studied*: Columbia Univ., B.S., M.A. *Awards*: Carnegie scholarship, Harvard Univ., 1942. *Exhibited*: Provincetown, Mass.; Wash., D.C.; Morton Gal.; SSAL. *Position*: Hd. A. Dept., State T. Col., Florence, Ala., 1933- .

TUTTLE, HELEN NORRIS—*Painter, E.*
105 County Line Rd., Bryn Mawr, Pa.

B. Croton-on-Hudson, N.Y., Sept. 26, 1906. *Studied*: Bryn Mawr Col., A.B.; Univ. Pennsylvania, M.S. in Edu.; &

with Thomas Benton, Edward Forbes, Josef Albers. *Member*: Phila. A. All.; AAPL. *Exhibited*: PAFA, 1932, 1935, 1936, 1954, 1955; Phila. AC, 1937; Bryn Mawr A. Center, 1938, 1944 (one-man); Phila. A. All., 1939, 1956; Haverford Col., 1940. *Position*: Instr., Des., Hist. & Appreciation of Art, Rosemont Col., Rosemont, Pa., 1947- .

TWARDOWICZ, STANLEY—*Painter, T.*
48 Ocean Ave., Northport, L.I., N.Y.

B. Detroit, Mich., July 8, 1917. *Studied*: Summer Sch. Painting, Saugatuck, Mich.; Skowhegan Sch. Painting & Sculpture, Maine. *Award*: Guggenheim F., 1956-57. *Work*: Columbus Gal. FA; Ball State T. Col., Muncie, Ind.; MModA; Newark Mus. A. *Exhibited*: WMAA, 1954-1956, 1958; Guggenheim Mus., 1954; AIC, 1954, 1957; Carnegie Inst., 1955; one-man: Contemporary A. Gal., N.Y., 1949, 1951, 1953, 1956; Peridot Gal., N.Y., 1958.

TWIGGS, RUSSELL GOULD—*Painter, Ser.*
424 South Aiken Ave., Pittsburgh 6, Pa.

B. Sandusky, Ohio, Apr. 29, 1898. *Studied*: Carnegie Inst. *Member*: Assoc. A. Pittsburgh; Abstract Group, Pittsburgh. *Awards*: prizes, Assoc. A. Pittsburgh, 1942, 1947, 1949, 1953, 1957, 1958; Heinz Comp., Pittsburgh, 1955; CM, 1955; Pittsburgh Playhouse, 1955; Nat. Ser. Soc., 1951. *Work*: MIT; AAUW; Univ. Wisconsin; Carnegie Inst.; Pa. State Coll.; Rochester Mem. A. Gal.; Tennessee Wesleyan Col.; Allegheny Col. *Exhibited*: Carnegie Inst., 1942-1945, 1958; PAFA, 1946-1948, 1950; AIC, 1937, 1946, 1947, 1957; Assoc. A. Pittsburgh, annually; Abstract Group, annually; A. & Crafts Center, Pittsburgh, annually; Butler Inst. Am. A., 1953-1955; Colorado Springs FA Center, 1954; Nat. Ser. Soc., 1950-1952; CGA, 1957; Minneapolis Inst. A., 1950; LC, 1952; BM, 1952, 1957; Univ. W. Va., 1952; CM, 1955; MModA, 1956; Univ. Utah, 1957; Am. Acad. A. & Lets., 1958; AFA traveling exh., 1957; one-man: Vassar Col., 1938; Pittsburgh Playhouse, 1950; Grand Central Moderns, N.Y., 1955, 1957, 1958; Allegheny Col., 1957.

TWORKOV, JACK—*Painter, T.*
234 East 23rd St., New York 10, N.Y.

B. Biala, Poland, Aug. 15, 1900. *Studied*: Columbia Univ.; NAD; ASL. *Work*: Marine Hospital, Carville, La.; MModA; MMA; Santa Barbara Mus. A.; Wadsworth Atheneum; Watkins Gal., American Univ.; BMA; New Paltz State T. Col.; WAC; WMAA; Newark Mus. A. *Exhibited*: nationally; Sidney Janis Gal.; Galerie de France, Paris, 1952; MModA European Traveling exh., 1958; one-man: Egan Gal., 1947, 1949, 1952, 1954; BMA, 1948; Stable Gal., 1957; WAC, 1957. *Position*: Instr., Pratt Inst., 1955- .

TYNG, GRISWOLD—*Painter, I., Des., E., L.*
1011 Centre St., Jamaica Plain 30, Mass.

B. Dorchester, Mass., Aug. 13, 1883. *Studied*: Mass. Sch. A., and with Joseph deCamp, Howard Pyle and others. Official A., U.S. Army, World Wars I and II. Illus. & Researcher for Boston City Planning Board; Public Relations and Design Service; Graphic A. Consultant.

TYSON, MARY (Mrs. Mary Thompson)—*Painter*
20 West 11th St., New York 11, N.Y.

B. Sewanee, Tenn., Nov. 2, 1909. *Studied*: Grand Central Sch. A.; & with George Pearse Ennis, Howard Hildebrandt, Wayman Adams, & others. *Member*: AWCS. *Work*: Nantucket AA; Nantucket Fnd. *Exhibited*: Balt. WC Cl., 1930; AGAA, 1935; BM, 1935, 1937; Phila. WC Cl., 1934, 1936; AWCS, 1936-1940, 1943, 1944; Montross Gal.; Contemporary A.; Morton Gal.; Harlow Gal.; Nantucket AA, 1952-1958.

TYTELL, LOUIS—*Painter, Gr.*
628 East 20th St., New York 9, N.Y.

Studied: Col. of City N.Y., B.S.S.; T. Col., Columbia Univ., M.A.; NAD. *Member*: AEA; Brooklyn Soc. A. *Awards*: prize, Gr. Des., 1951; New Sch., 1954; N.Y. City Center, 1954; Brooklyn Soc. A., 1954. *Work*: LC; Carville (La.) Marine Hospital. *Exhibited*: NGA; Detroit Inst. A.; WMAA; Carnegie Inst.; MModA, 1943; Walker A. Center, 1944; Pepsi-Cola, 1945; PAFA, 1949; Bradley

Univ., 1951, 1952; SAGA, 1951, 1952, 1953, 1954; BM, 1951, 1952, 1954; New Britain Mus. A., 1952; LC, 1952, 1954; AFA traveling exh., 1952; NAD, 1956. *Position*: Chm. A. Dept., Morris H.S., New York, N.Y.

UBALDI, MARIO CARMELO—*Sculptor, Des.*
     157 South Craig Pl., Lombard, Ill.

B. Monarch, Wyo., July 16, 1912. *Studied*: Indst. Mus. A., Rome, Italy; AIC. *Member*: Renaissance Soc., Univ. Chicago. *Awards*: medal, 1943, prizes, 1944, AIC. *Work*: Pasteur Sch., Chicago; Chicago Commons Settlement House. *Exhibited*: AIC, 1953; WFNY 1939; CGA; Univ. Chicago; Marc Gal., New Orleans, La.; Palmer House, Chicago, 1952 (one-man); Midwest traveling exh., 1953; Univ. Chicago, 1953; A. Center, Chicago, 1954, 1956; Marshall Field Gal., Chicago, 1958.

UHLER, MRS. A. LENOX. See *Abbott, Anne Fuller*

UHLER, RUTH PERSHING—*Painter, E., L.*
     Museum of Fine Arts of Houston, Main & Montrose St.; h. 915 Hawthorne St., Houston, Tex.

B. Pennsylvania. *Studied*: Phila. Sch. Des. for Women; & with Jean Charlot. *Member*: Houston A. Lg.; Texas FA Assn.; MModA.; Contemp. AA, Houston. *Work*: Mus. FA of Houston; mural, Houston Pub. Lib. Lectures: American Painting; American Design. *Position*: Cur. Edu., Mus. FA of Houston; Registrar, Instr., Des. & Composition, Mus. Sch. A., Houston, Tex.

ULBRICHT, ELSA EMILIE—
     Educator, C., Des., Lith., P., L.
     915 North 28th St., Milwaukee 8, Wis.

B. Milwaukee, Wis., Mar. 18, 1885. *Studied*: Wis. Sch. A.; PIASch; Milwaukee State T. Col.; & with Alexander Mueller, Francis Chapin, & others. *Member*: Wis. P. & S.; Wis. Designer-Craftsmen; Nat. Edu. Assn.; Midwest Des.-Craftsmen; Am. Craftsmen's Council. *Award*: prizes, Wis. Union, Madison, Wis.; Milwaukee AI. *Work*: Univ. Minnesota; Milwaukee AI. *Exhibited*: Wis. Union; Wis. P. & S.; Wis. Designer-Craftsmen; Milwaukee AI.; Am. Craftsmens Conf., Ravina Park, Ill. I., pamphlets on various crafts. Contributor to: Design magazine. Lectures: Crafts. *Position*: Formerly Prof. A., Supv. A. Edu., Wisconsin State Col., Milwaukee, Wis., 1911-55; Dir., Emeritus, Summer Sch. Painting, Saugatuck, Mich., 1947-58.

ULLRICH, B. (Mrs. B. Ullrich Prendergast)—
     Painter, Lith.
     5550 South Dorchester Ave., Apt. 1402, Chicago 37, Ill.

B. Evanston, Ill. *Studied*: Northwestern Univ., B.A.; AIC, B.F.A.; Univ. Chicago, M.A. *Member*: AEA; Renaissance Soc., Univ. Chicago. *Work*: Univ. Arizona; Chicago Pub. Lib.; AEA Midwest Color Slide Coll. *Exhibited*: MMA, 1943; Carnegie Inst., 1941, 1943, 1944; GGE 1939; WFNY 1939; AIC, 1937-1939, 1950; PAFA, 1938, 1939; SFMA, 1939-1941; CGA, 1939; SAM, 1940; Portland A. Mus., 1939; BMA, 1939; Denver A. Mus., 1940; Central America traveling exh., 1941; U.S. Govt. traveling exh., 1940-1941; Riverside Mus., 1940; San Diego FA Soc., 1940; Cal. WC Soc., 1938-1940; AEA, 1953-1955; Renaissance Soc., 1953-1958; Chicago Artists, 1958; Detroit Inst. A., 1940, 1944; one-man: SFMA, 1940; G Place Gal., Wash., D.C., 1944. *Position*: Dir., AEA, Chicago Chptr., 1956-58.

ULM, JOHN LOUIS (DINK)—*Illustrator, Cart.*
     2221 Monongahela Blvd., Park Forest, McKeesport, Pa.

B. McKeesport, Pa., Sept. 18, 1907. *Studied*: Am. Sch. A. *Awards*: prizes, WFNY 1939; "PT" Boat insignia, U.S. Navy. *Work*: Huntington Lib., San Marino, Cal. *Position*: Art Dir., Daily News, McKeesport, Pa., 22 yrs.

ULMAN, ELINOR—*Teacher, P.*
     1275 New Hampshire Ave., Northwest Washington 6, D.C.

B. Baltimore, Md., Feb. 21, 1910. *Studied*: Iowa State Col., Ames, Iowa, B.S. in Landscape Arch.; Wellesley Col., B.A. *Work*: BMA. I., U.S. Dept. Agriculture, 1946. Author: "Art Therapy at an Outpatient Clinic," Psychiatry magazine, 1953. *Position*: Instr. A., Dir., Recreation Program, Dept. Pub. Health, D.C., 1953-55; A. Therapist, General Hospital, Wash., D.C., 1955- ; Faculty, Washington Sch. of Psychiatry, 1957- .

ULREICH, EDUARD BUK—*Painter, S., Des.*
     1527 Pine St., San Francisco 9, Cal.

Studied: Kansas City AI; PAFA. *Awards*: prizes, A. Dir. Cl., 1927, 1929, medal, 1932; Nat. Comp., World's Fair, Chicago. *Work*: interiors, des., Edgewater Beach Hotel, Chicago; Methodist Temple, Chicago; Victor Red Seal Records; Dudensing Gal., N.Y.; murals, Ilg Ventilating Co., Chicago; Radio City Music Hall; Woodside, L.I. Pub. Lib.; Barricini Candy Co., N.Y.; Lesser Gal., 1954, San Francisco; USPO, Columbia, Mo.; Tallahassee, Fla.; Concord, N.C. *Exhibited*: AIC; PAFA; WMAA; Lesser Gal., San Francisco, 1955; Galerie du Quartier, 1958, etc.; one-man: Anderson Gal., N.Y., 1923; AIC, 1925; Dudensing Gal., N.Y., 1927, 1929; Dudensing Gal., Chicago, 1930; Hug Gal., Kansas City, 1924, 1926; Phila. A. All., 1939; Bonestell Gal., 1941; Gump's Gal., San Francisco, 1943; Assoc. Am. A., 1953; Crespi Gal., N.Y., 1955, and in Europe.

UMLAUF, CHARLES—*Sculptor*
     Department of Art, University of Texas; h. 506 Barton Blvd., Austin 4, Tex.

B. South Haven, Mich., July 17, 1911. *Studied*: AIC; Chicago Sch. Sculpture. *Member*: Texas Assn. Col. T.; Texas FA Assn.; Texas WC Soc. *Awards*: Scholarship, AIC; Guggenheim F., 1949; prizes, AIC, 1937, 1938, 1943; Oakland A. Mus., 1941; Texas Annual, 1942-1944, 1946-1949, 1951-1953; Texas FA Assn., 1948-1950, 1952, 1954, 1957; Syracuse Mus. FA, 1948; Univ. Illinois, 1957; Lubbock, Tex., 1957. *Work*: Witte Mem. Mus.; McNay Mus. A.; DMFA; Mus. FA of Houston; Ft. Worth A. Center; MMA; Santa Barbara Mus. A.; Wichita Mus. A.; Ft. Worth Children's Mus.; IBM; Liturgical A. Soc.; Univ. Illinois; Des Moines A. Center, and in private colls. Bas-reliefs: USPO, Morton, Ill.; Paulding, Ohio; Baptist Student Center, Univ. Tex.; Christian Church, Austin; fountain groups: Cook County Hospital, Lane Tech. H.S., both Chicago; crucifix, Shrine of St. Anthony, San Antonio; St. Mark's Church, Burlington, Vt.; Susan B. Allen Mem. Hospital, Eldorado, Kans.; Stonebridge Priory, Lake Bluff, Ill., and others. Liturgical A. Soc.; Merchandise Mart, Chicago. *Exhibited*: AIC, 1936-1941, 1943, 1955; Oakland A. Mus., 1941, 1946, 1949; SFMA, 1941, 1946, 1957; PAFA, 1946-1948, 1950, 1951, 1954; WMAA, 1946-1948, 1950, 1951, 1953, 1956; Denver A. Mus., 1948-1950, 1952, 1955, 1956; Syracuse Mus. FA, 1948-1950, 1958; Kansas State Col., 1958; Univ. Illinois, 1953, 1957; Intl. Religious Biennale, Salzburg, 1958 and touring 1958-59; Columbus Gal. FA, 1949; Dayton AI, 1950; Munson-Williams-Proctor Inst., 1951; Nat. Soc. A. & Lets., 1950, 1954, 1955; Newark Mus., 1956; AFA traveling exhs., 1957, 1958; Ft. Worth A. Center, 1957, 1958; DMFA, 1958; 16 one-man exhs. Other exhs. prior to above dates. *Position*: Prof. A., Univ. Texas, Austin, Tex.

UNDERWOOD, ELISABETH KENDALL—*Sculptor, P.*
     South Salem, N.Y.; w. 2459 P St., Northwest, Washington 7, D.C.

B. Gerrish Island, Me., Sept. 22, 1896. *Studied*: Yale Sch. FA. *Member*: Cosmopolitan Cl.; Wash. A. Cl. *Exhibited*: AWS; NAD; New Haven Paint & Clay Cl.; Playhouse Gal., Ridgefield, Conn.; Cosmopolitan Cl.; Wash. A. Cl.

UNTHANK, ALICE GERTRUDE—*Painter, C., T., L.*
     Androy Hotel, 1213 Tower Ave., Superior, Wis.

B. Wayne County, Ind. *Studied*: Earlham Col.; T. Col., Columbia Univ.; Univ. Nebraska, A.B.; Univ. Chicago, M.A.; in Paris; & with Pedro de Lemos, J. E. Bundy, Martha Walter, & others. *Awards*: prizes, Arrowhead Exh., Duluth, Minn., 1928; Am. Lib. Color Slides, 1940. *Work*: Carroll Col., Waukesha, Wis.; Wis. State Col. *Exhibited*: Hoosier Salon; Indiana traveling exh., 1929-1930; Terry AI, 1952; Nat. A. Week, Superior, Wis., 1940, 1941; one-man: Douglas County Hist. Mus., Superior, Wis., 1945; Duluth, Minn.; Frankfort and West Lafayette, Ind. Contributor to: School Arts, Design, magazines; Wis. Journal of Education; Dryard Press, England. *Position*: A. Instr., Training Dept., Superior (Wis.) State T. Col., 1923-49, Emeritus, 1949- ; Nat. Edu. Assn., A.*

UNWIN, NORA SPICER—Engraver, I., W.

24 Cottage St., Wellesley 81, Mass.

B. Surbiton, Surrey, England, Feb. 22, 1907. *Studied*: Royal Col. A., Kingston Sch. A., London. *Member*: ANA; Royal Soc. P., Et. & Engravers, London; SAGA; Boston Pr. M.; Albany Pr. Cl. *Awards*: SAGA, 1951; Boston Soc. Indp. A., 1952; NAWA, 1953; New Hampshire AA, 1952. *Work*: British Mus.; LC; Boston Pub. Lib.; N.Y. Pub. Lib.; Ft. Worth A. Mus.; Cal. State Lib.; MMA; Fitchburg A. Mus.; Lawrence Mus., Williams Col. Wood engravings for English and American publishers, including, among others, "Footnotes on Nature"; "Joseph"; "The Christmas Story." *Exhibited*: Royal Acad., Royal Soc. P., Et. & Engravers, London, 1931-1952; Bibliotheque Nationale, Paris, 1951; Salon de Mai, Paris, 1952; LC, 1950-1952; Phila. Pr. Cl., 1950, 1951; MMA; NAD; WMA; Buffalo Pr. Cl., 1951; SAGA, 1951, 1952; NAWA, 1952; Boston Pr. M.; Boston Soc. Indp. A.; one-man: Currier Gal. A.; Boston Pr. M., 1954; Fitchburg A. Mus., 1955; Albany Pr. Cl., 1955; Boston Atheneum; Univ. New Hampshire; Holman's Print Shop, Boston. Author, I., "Round the Year"; "Lucy and the Little Red House"; "Doughnuts for Lin"; "Proud Pumpkin"; "Poquito," 1959. Numerous children's books illus. for American and English publishers.

UPHAM, MRS. ELSIE DOREY. See Dorey

UPJOHN, EVERARD MILLER—Educator, W., L.

Columbia University, West 116th St.; h. 29 Claremont Ave., New York 27, N.Y.

B. Scranton, Pa., Nov. 6, 1903. *Studied*: Harvard Univ., B.A., M.Arch. *Member*: Athenaeum, N.Y.; CAA; Soc. Arch. Historians. Author: "Richard Upjohn, Architect and Churchman," 1939; "History of World Art," rev. ed. (with Paul S. Wingert & J. G. Mahler), 1958. Contributor to Art Bulletin, Encyclopaedia Americana, Encyclopaedia Britannica. Advisor on Art & Architecture, Grolier Encyclopedia. Lectures: The Gothic Revival. *Position*: Asst. Prof. FA, Univ. Minnesota, 1929-35; Prof. FA, Columbia Univ., New York, N.Y., at present.

UPTEGROVE, SISTER M. IRENA—
Educator, Des., P., I., S.

Saint Paul's Priory, 301 Summit Ave., St. Paul 2, Minn.

B. Melrose, Minn., Feb. 13, 1898. *Studied*: Univ. Minnesota; Col. of St. Benedict, B.A.; Univ. Michigan, M.A.; Minneapolis Inst. A.; AIC. *Member*: Western AA; Catholic AA. *Work*: Archbishop Murray Mem. H.S., St. Paul, Minn. (2 murals); Col. of St. Benedict, St. Joseph, Minn.; Mercy Hospital, Battle Creek, Mich.; St. Paul's Priory. *Exhibited*: Catholic AA; Univ. Minnesota; Xavier Univ., 1957; Nat. Liturgical Cong., 1958; traveling exh., 1956-58. I., "The Man Who Made the Secret Doors," 1946; & other books. *Position*: Prof. A., Col. of St. Benedict, St. Joseph, Minn., to 1948; Instr. Hist. A., Mount St. Scholastica, Atchison, Kans.; Supv. A., Visitation H.S., and Our Lady of Peace H.S., St. Paul, 1955; Faculty, St. Paul's Priory, St. Paul, Minn., 1956- .

URBAN, ALBERT—Painter, S., Ser., T.

149 Bleecker St. (12); h. 16 West 10th St., New York 11, N.Y.

B. Frankfurt, Germany, July 22, 1909. *Studied*: Kunst Schule, Frankfurt, with Max Beckmann, Willi Baumeister. *Awards*: prizes, Frankfurt, Germany, 1931; LC, 1945. *Work*: MMA; BMFA; AGAA; BM; NGA. *Exhibited*: Phila. Pr. Cl., 1942; Phila. A. All., 1946; Swarthmore Col., 1942; Carnegie Inst., 1945-1958; NGA, 1947; LC, 1945; de Young Mem. Mus., 1945 (one-man); AIC, 1944; Univ. Illinois, 1950-1958; Albright A. Gal., 1948; WMAA, 1944-1947; NAD, 1944-1947; N.Y. Pub. Lib., 1945; WAC, 1947; CGA, 1944-1947, 1957, 1958; PAFA, 1945-1947; Univ. Colorado, 1956-1958. *Position*: Hd., Urban Prints, New York, N.Y.

URNER, JOSEPH (WALKER)—Sculptor, P., Et.

215 East Second St.; 110 West Patrick St.; h. 36 East Second St., Frederick, Md.

B. Frederick, Md., Jan. 16, 1898. *Studied*: Baltimore Polytechnic Inst.; Maryland Inst.; & with Ettore Cadorin, Dwight Williams. *Member*: SSAL. *Awards*: prize, Cumberland Valley A., 1939. *Work*: Alabama mon., Gettysburg, Pa.; Taney monument, Frederick, Md.; Cedar Lawn Mem.; presentation port., Gen. A. A. Vandergrift, USMC; Gov. Johnson monument and Amon Burgee monument, both Frederick, Md. *Exhibited*: Cumberland Valley A., annually.*

USUI, MRS. BUMPEI. See Pratt, Frances

UTPATEL, FRANK ALBERT BERNHARDT—Engraver

Mazomanie, Wis.

B. Waukegan, Ill., Mar. 4, 1905. *Studied*: Milwaukee AI; AIC; & with John Steuart Curry. *Awards*: prizes, Milwaukee AI, 1939, 1940; Wis. State Fair, 1940, 1941; Wis. Salon, 1940; Madison A. Exh., 1940, 1941; SAM, 1941. *Work*: Milwaukee AI; Univ. Wisconsin: Layton A. Gal. *Exhibited*: CMA, 1935; Am. A. Gal., 1939; AIC, 1940; Milwaukee AI, 1939; Wis. State Fair, 1940-1941; Layton A. Gal., 1940; Meuer's A. Gal., 1940; Wis. Mem. Un., 1938-1941; Madison A. Exh., 1940, 1941; NAD, 1941, 1945; SAM, 1941, 1942; Conn. Acad. FA, 1941; PAFA, 1941, 1945; WMAA, 1942, 1943; Lib. Cong., 1944, 1956; Carnegie Inst., 1944; Laguna Beach AA, 1944. I., "Village Day," 1946; "Lives Around Us," 1942; & other books. Contributor: wood engravings, American Mercury, Tomorrow, Outdoors, & other publications.*

VACCARO, PAT(RICK) (FRANK)—Serigrapher, T.

3208 Wendover Circle, Youngstown 11, Ohio

B. New Rochelle, N.Y., Jan. 15, 1920. *Studied*: Ohio State Univ.; Youngstown Univ., B.S. in A. Edu. *Member*: Nat. Print Council; Boston Pr. M.; Am. Color Pr. Soc.; Nat. Ser. Soc.; Ohio Pr. M.; Soc. Indp. A., Boston. *Awards*: prizes, Butler Inst. Am. A., 1954, 1955; BMFA, 1954; Canton AI, 1957; purchase awards: USIS (3). *Work*: Butler Inst. Am. A.; Farnsworth Mus. A.; USIS, for embassies abroad; Canton AI; and in private colls. *Exhibited*: Intl. Ser. Soc., 1954, 1955; Northwest Pr. M., 1954; Wash. WC Cl., 1954-1956; Soc. Indp. A., Boston, 1953, 1954, 1956-1958; MModA, 1954; New Orleans AA, 1954, 1955; Exchange Exh., Italy, 1954-1957; Boston Pub. Lib., 1956; Butler Inst. Am. A., 1947, 1956-1958; BMFA; Smithsonian Inst.; Nat. Ser. Gal.; Ohio Pr. M., 1956-1958; Phila. Pr. Cl.; Sioux City A. Center, 1956; Am. Color Pr. Soc., 1957, 1958; Intl. Ser. Soc., 1956-1958; Gropper A. Gal., Mass., 1956-1958; Ball State T. Col., 1956, 1957, and others. "5 Ohio Artists" traveling exh., 1956-57.

VAGIS, POLYGNOTOS—Sculptor

104 Evergreen Ave., Bethpage, L.I., N.Y.

B. Thasos, Greece, Jan. 14, 1894. *Studied*: CUASch.; BAID. *Member*: AEA; Fed. Mod. P. & S. *Awards*: WMAA grant; Shilling prize, 1945; Levittown A. Festival, 1951; Nat. Inst. A. & Lets. grant, 1957; gold medal, Audubon A., 1955. *Work*: BM; WMAA; MMA; MMod.A.; ASL; Toledo Mus.; Tel-Aviv Mus., Israel; mem. monument, Bethpage, L.I., N.Y.; and in private colls. *Exhibited*: Chicago World Fair, 1934; Rockefeller Center, 1934; CGA, 1934, 1937; Mus. Mod. A. Gal., Wash., D.C., 1938; WFNY 1939; Carnegie Inst., 1940, 1941; BMFA, 1944; Wadsworth Atheneum, 1945; BM, 1932, 1938; S. Gld., 1938-1942; PMA, 1940; MMA, 1942, 1952; Buchholz Gal., 1945; Wildenstein Gal., 1946; deYoung Mem. Mus., 1947; Rochester Mem. A. Gal., 1947; St. Paul Gal. A., 1947; Nelson Gal. A., 1947; Mus. FA Houston, 1947; MModA, 1951; WMAA, 1950, 1952; one-man: P. & S. Gal., 1932; Kraushaar Gal., 1934; Valentine Gal., 1938; Hugo Gal., 1946; Iolas Gal., 1955.

VAIL, ROBERT WILLIAM GLENROIE—
Museum Director, E., Cr., W., L.

170 Central Park West (24); h. 270 Riverside Dr., New York 25, N.Y.

B. Victor, N.Y., Mar. 26, 1890. *Studied*: Cornell Univ., B.A.; Lib. Sch., N.Y. Pub. Lib.; Columbia Univ; Univ. Minnesota. *Award*: Hon. degree, Litt. D., Dickinson Col., 1951; L.H.D., Clark Univ., 1953. Author: "The Voice of the Old Frontier"; "Knickerbocker Birthday: A Sesquicentennial History of the New York Historical Society," 1954; "The Case of the Stuyvesant Portraits," 1958; many monographs. Ed., Sabin's Dictionary of Books on America. *Position*: Librarian, N.Y. State Lib., 1940-44; Dir., N.Y. Hist. Soc., 1944- ; Assoc. in Hist., Columbia Univ., New York, N.Y.; Rosenbach lectures in Bibliography, Univ. Pennsylvania.

VALENTINE, FRANCIS B.—
Painter, T., Comm. A., L., I.
96 Valley View Ave., Hamburg, N.Y.

B. Buffalo, N.Y., Sept. 20, 1897. *Studied:* Albright A. Sch.; Yale Sch. FA, B.F.A., and with Daniel Garber. *Member:* The Patteran; Buffalo Soc. A.; Albright A. Gal.; Prof. A. Gld., Buffalo. *Awards:* prizes, Albright A. Gal., 1945, 1954, silver medal, 1955; Hamburg Fair, 1955-1958 (3); Erie County Fair, 1958; silver medal, Buffalo Soc. A. *Work:* IBM; YMCA, Buffalo; Charlotte Ave. Sch., Hamburg, N.Y.; Hamburg Pub. Lib. *Exhibited:* Hotel Statler, Buffalo; Buffalo Soc. A.; Hamburg Fair; Albright A. Gal.; The Patteran; Grand Central A. Gal.; Yale Cl.; one-man: Hamburg, N.Y., 1953.

VAN BUREN, RAEBURN—*Illustrator, Cart., L.*
21 Clover Dr., Great Neck, N.Y.

B. Pueblo, Colo., Jan. 12, 1891. *Studied:* ASL. *Member:* Cartoonist Soc.; SI (Hon.); A. & W. Soc. *Exhibited:* SI. I., "Stag at Eve"; "Star of the North." *Contributor of:* illus. to Saturday Evening Post, New Yorker, Life, Esquire, & other magazines. Syndicated comic strip, "Abbie an' Slats." "Cartoonist of the Year," B'nai B'rith, Phila., Pa., 1958. Lectures: Comic Strip Art.

VANCE, MAE H.—*Painter, Des., I.*
3702 Northampton St., N.W., Washington, D.C.

B. Ohio. *Studied:* Cleveland Sch. A.; Corcoran Sch. A. *Member:* Lg. Am. Pen Women. *Work:* F. D. Roosevelt Coll.; White House, Wash., D.C. *Exhibited:* Indp. A., Wash., D.C.; Lg. Am. Pen Women. Pictorial Illus., Birthplaces of Presidents of US.

VAN CLEVE, HELEN (Mrs. Eric)—*Painter, S., W.*
1170 Galloway St., Pacific Palisades, Cal.

B. Milwaukee, Wis., June 5, 1891. *Studied:* Univ. California; BMFA Sch.; Grande Chaumiere, Paris, and with Bela Pratt, E. Withrow, Eliot O'Hara, Oscar Van Young, Rex Brandt, Frederic Taubes. *Member:* Western A.; Pacific Palisades AA; *Award:* prize, Wisconsin State Fair. *Work:* Cal. PLH; San Diego Pub. Lib. *Exhibited:* Santa Barbara Mus. A., 1940, 1944, 1945; Cal. PLH, 1940-1945; Laguna Beach AA, 1944; San Diego FA Soc., 1932; Montclair A. Mus., 1934; Kennebunk Village, 1934; Gump's, San F.; Rockefeller Center, 1934; Oakland A. Gal., 1948; Westwood Village AA, 1949-1952; deYoung Mem. Mus., 1949-51; Springville, Utah, 1951, 1952; Pacific Palisades AA, annually; Santa Cruz, Cal.; Santa Paula, Cal.

VAN CLEVE, KATE—*Craftsman, T., Des.*
14 Marshall St., Brookline 46, Mass.

B. Chicago, Ill., Mar. 24, 1881. *Studied:* Michigan Normal Col., M. Edu.; PIASch. *Member:* Weavers Gld., Boston; Boston Soc. A. & Crafts. *Exhibited:* de Cordova and Dana Mus., 1952; WMA, 1952; Fitchburg A. Mus., 1954; Pittsfield Mus. A., 1954; G. W. V. Smith A. Mus., 1955; Boston Soc. A. & Crafts, 1955; WMA, 1955. *Author:* "Handloom Weaving for Amateurs," 1937; *Co-Author:* "Garden Studio Notebook of Handloom Weaving," 1932; "The Weaver's Quarterly," 1932-1943. *Contributor to* "Handweaver & Craftsman," magazine. Lectures: Weaving. *Position:* Instr. Weaving, Boston Sch. Occupational Therapy, Boston, Mass.; Garden Studio, Brookline, Mass. Memb.; Craftsmen's Adv. Comm.; Dean of Textile Gld., Soc. A. & Crafts; Md. Dirs., Mass. Assn. of Handicraft Groups.

van de VELDE, ALFRED E. R.—*Painter*
1250 Hoover St., Carlsbad, Cal.

B. Bruges, Belgium, July 13, 1892. *Studied:* Royal Acad., Bruges; Inst. A., Antwerp, Belgium. *Member:* SC; Long Island A. Lg.; La Jolla AA; Laguna Beach AA; Desert A. Center; Carlsbad A. Lg.; San Diego FA Soc. *Awards:* prizes, Springville, Utah, 1931; Nassau A. Lg.; 1945; Carlsbad A. Lg., 1953, 1954; So. California Expo., San Diego, 1954. *Work:* Mus. Ostend, Belgium; Currier Gal. A., Manchester, N.H. *Exhibited:* All. A. Am., 1938; Intl. Expo., Brussels, 1912; Antwerp, Belgium, 1912; Conn. Acad. FA, 1931; Springville, Utah, 1931; Balzac Gal., N.Y., 1930; Barbizon-Plaza, 1940; SC; Boston, Mass.; Rockport, Mass.; Springfield, Mass.; Laguna Beach A. Center; La Jolla AA; Carlsbad A. Lg.; Nat. Orange Show, 1953; one-man: Ostend, Belgium, 1929; Albany Inst. Hist. & A., 1930; Currier Gal. A.; Cayuga Mus. Hist. & A.,

1943; Rochester, N.Y., 1944; Bowers Mem. Mus., Santa Ana, Cal., 1950; Long Beach, Cal., 1952; Cortlandt, N.Y., Pub. Lib., 1944; Ithaca Mus. A., 1943; Binghampton Mus. A., 1944; Laguna Beach AA, 1954; La Jolla AA, 1954; Federal Savings Bank, San Diego, 1954; Los Angeles, 1958; Palomar College, 1957.

VANDENBERGH, LOUISE. See *Altson, Louise*

VAN DER POEL, PRISCILLA PAINE (Mrs.)—
Educator, P., Cart., L.
Hillyer Art Gallery; h. 58 Paradise Road, Northampton, Mass.

B. Brooklyn, N.Y., Apr. 9, 1907. *Studied:* Smith Col., A.B., A.M.; ASL; in Italy; & with Frank DuMond, George Bridgman, Sherrill Whiton, & others. *Member:* CAA, *Exhibited:* Studio Cl., Tryon Mus., Northampton, Mass., 1936-1945. Lectures: Modern Art, etc. *Position:* Instr. A., 1935-39, Asst. Prof. A., 1939-45, Assoc. Prof. A., 1945- , Chm. Dept. A., 1954- , Smith Col., Northampton, Mass.; Pres., Faculty Arts Council, 1958- .

VAN DERPOOL, JAMES GROTE—*Educator*
Avery Hall, Columbia University (27); h. 570 Park Ave., New York 21, N.Y.

B. New York, N.Y., July 21, 1903. *Studied:* MIT, B. Arch; Am. Acad. in Rome (Research); Atelier Gromort of Ecole des Beaux-Arts (Research) Paris; Harvard Univ., M.F.A. *Member:* AIA; Soc. Arch. Historians (Nat. Pres., 1955-57); Royal Soc. A., London, England (Hon. life); Nat. Trust for Historic Preservation; Am. Scenic & Historic Preservation Soc. (Trustee); CAA; Renaissance Seminar; Century Assn.; Grolier Cl.; St. Nicholas Soc., N.Y. (Historian); Holland Soc.; Cliff Dwellers, Chicago, etc. *Awards:* Phi Beta Kappa (Hon.); Life F., Royal Soc. A., London. *Author:* "History of Avery Library," 1954; "History of Historic St. Lukes, Smithfield, Va." *Contributor of* many articles to art and architectural publications; articles to Encyclopaedia Britannica and Collier's Encyclopaedia. Lectures on Renaissance Architecture and American Architectural subjects. *Positions:* Arch. Ed., Columbia Encyclopaedia (2nd edition); Advisory Bd., Funk & Wagnalls Encyclopaedia; Assoc. Prof., Hist. Arch., Univ. Illinois, 1933-39; Hd. A. Dept., Prof. Hist. A., Univ. Illinois, 1939-46; Prof. Arch. and Hd. of Avery Memorial Architectural Library, Columbia Univ., New York, N.Y., 1946- . Bd. Dirs., Am. Mus. of Immigration.

VANDER VELDE, HENRY (F.)—*Painter, E.*
32841 Salt Creek Road, South Laguna, Cal.

B. Grand Rapids, Mich., Jan. 23, 1913. *Studied:* Univ. Michigan; NAD. *Member:* Laguna Beach AA; Laguna Festival A. Assn.; Soc. Western A. *Awards:* prizes, Nat. Art Roundup, Las Vegas, Nev., 1958; Nat. Orange Show, 1958. *Work:* in private colls. *Exhibited:* Las Vegas, 1958; Nat. Orange Show, 1958; Laguna Festival A., 1951-1958; La Jolla A. Center bi-monthly, 1951-1958; Ferguson Gal., La Jolla. *Position:* Asst. Prof. A., Long Beach State College, Long Beach, Cal., 1959.

VAN DYKE, ELLA (TUTHILL)—*Painter, E., L.*
206 North Monroe Ave., Wenonah, N.J.

B. Schenectady, N.Y., Feb. 9, 1910. *Studied:* Skidmore Col., B.S.; T. Col., Columbia Univ., M.A.; Ecole des Beaux-Arts, Fontainebleau, France. *Exhibited:* PAFA, 1934; AIC, 1935; NAWA, 1935, 1943, 1944, 1945; Detroit Inst. A., 1936; Albany Inst. Hist. & A., 1936, 1944-1946, 1949, 1952; Schenectady Mus., 1945-1950, 1952; High Mus. A., 1944; Cooperstown, N.Y., 1949-1951; one-man: Argent Gal., 1942; Skidmore Col., 1943; Univ. Connecticut, 1943; Mortimer Levitt Gal., 1951; Union Col., 1951. *Positions:* Instr. A., Central State T. Col., Mt. Pleasant, Mich., 1934-36; Hd. Dept. A., Albion (Mich.) Col., 1936-39; Asst. Prof. A., Univ. Connecticut, 1939-43; Des., General Electric Co., Schenectady, N.Y., 1943-45; A. T., Schonowe Sch., Schenectady, N.Y., 1948-53.

van GENT, COCK—*Painter*
Box 107, Gates Mills, Ohio

B. The Hague, Holland, Apr. 18, 1925. *Studied:* A. Acad., The Hague. *Award:* Catherwood Fnd. grant, 1952. *Work:* SAM; PMA; BMFA; Butler Inst. Am. A.; AGAA; CMA; DMFA; Univ. Michigan; Slater Mem. Mus.; Rosenwald

Coll.; Wadsworth Atheneum, and in Holland. *Exhibited*: SAM, 1947; SFMA, 1947; Vigeveno Gal., Los Angeles, 1948; The Hague, 1948; Weyhe Gal., N.Y., 1950; Slater Mem. Mus., 1951; Kunstzaal de Plaats, Holland, 1952; Boston, 1953; NCFA, 1957; Butler Inst. Am. A., 1957; 1020 A. Cl., Chicago, 1957; Philbrook A. Mus., 1958; Mills Col., 1958; Graham Gal., N.Y., 1958; Rosicrucian Egyptian Mus., 1958; Colorado Springs FA Center, 1958, and others. CMA exh. sponsored by Catherwood Fnd. and circulated by Smithsonian Inst., 1957-59.

VAN HOESEN, BETH (ADAMS) (Mrs. Mark)—
Printmaker
161 Divisadero St., San Francisco 17, Cal.

B. Boise, Idaho, June 27, 1926. *Studied*: Stanford Univ., B.A.; Fontainebleau, Julian Acad., and Grand Chaumiere, Paris; Cal. Sch. FA; San Francisco State Col. *Member*: San F. Women A.; San F. AA; Bay Printmakers Soc.; Cal. Soc. Et. *Awards*: prizes, Cal. State Fair, 1951 (purchase); San F. Women A., 1956. *Work*: Achenbach Fnd. for Graphic A. *Exhibited*: LC, 1956, 1957; San F. AA, 1957, 1958; Bay Pr. M., 1958; Cal. State Fair, 1951, 1952, 1954, 1958; San Diego State Fair, 1958; San F. Women A., 1951-1958; Cal. Soc. Et., 1956, 1958; one-man: Labaudt Gal., San F., 1952; Gump's Gal., 1954; Stanford Univ., 1957.

VAN HOOK, KATRINA (Mrs. Katrina Van Hook Taylor)
—Teacher, L.
American Embassy, Addis Ababa, Ethiopia

B. New York, N.Y., May 26, 1912. *Studied*: Smith Col., B.A.; Radcliffe Col., M.A.; Univ. Paris. Contributor to: Magazine of Art, Gazette des Beaux-Arts, College Art Journal. Lectures: History of Renaissance and Modern Art. *Position*: Instr., Hist. A., Smith Col., 1938-40; Mus. Aide, 1941-43, Supv. Edu., 1943-45, NGA, Wash., D.C.; A.Cr., Washington Post, Washington, D.C., 1945-46.*

VAN HOOK, NELL—Painter, S., C.
154 Pearsall Drive, Mt. Vernon, N.Y.

B. Richmond, Va. *Studied*: Hamilton Col.; ASL; NAD, and privately. *Member*: AAPL; Catherine Lorillard Wolfe A. Cl.; Gld. Hall, Easthampton. *Awards*: prizes, East Gloucester AA; Wolfe A. Cl. (2); AAPL, gold medal, 1958, prize, 1957; Westchester Exh., 1957; prize and medal, Atlanta AA. *Work*: ports. in many private colls. *Exhibited*: AAPL; Nat. Lg. Am. Pen Women; Wolfe A. Cl.; Mt. Vernon AA; and others. Covers and illus. for "Geese Fly High"; "Color on the Wing."

VAN HOUSEN, BETH—Painter, Des.
1212 H St., Anchorage, Alaska

VAN LEYDEN, ERNST OSCAR MAURITZ—Painter, S.
411 South Barrington Ave., Los Angeles 49, Cal.

B. Rotterdam, Holland, May 16, 1892. *Awards*: med., Exp. in Brussels, Paris, Amsterdam, The Hague; prizes, Venice, Italy, 1921; Los A. Mus. A. *Work*: Tate Gal., London; & in museums throughout Europe. *Exhibited*: VMFA, 1946; Pepsi-Cola, 1946; Los A. Mus. A.; Santa Barbara Mus. A.; San Diego FA Soc.; Syracuse Mus. FA; SFMA; & extensively in Europe. Creator special glass-tile technique for murals.*

VAN LEYDEN, KARIN ELIZABETH—Painter, Des., I.
411 South Barrington Ave., Los Angeles 49, Cal.

B. Charlottenburg, Germany, July 23, 1906. *Member*: Royal Soc. Mural P., Great Britain. *Work*: in many museums throughout Europe. *Exhibited*: Marie Sterner Gal., 1938; Nierendorf Gal., 1940; Bonestell Gal., 1946; Syracuse Mus. FA, 1941; San Diego FA Soc.; Santa Barbara Mus. A.; Los A. Mus. A.; SFMA & extensively in Europe, including, Paris, France, 1950; Vallauris, France, 1951.*

VAN LOAN, DOROTHY (LEFFINGWELL)—Painter, Lith.
Hull's Cove, Me.; h. 4523 Locust St., Philadelphia 39, Pa.

B. Lockport, N.Y. *Studied*: PMSchIA; PAFA; Phila. Graphic Sketch Cl. *Member*: PAFA. *Awards*: Cresson traveling scholarship, PAFA, 1927-1928; 1929; F., PAFA; prizes, Phila. Pr. Cl., 1944; F.PAFA, 1944; PAFA, 1927,

1928, 1935, 1945; med., Phila. Sketch Cl., 1935; Phila. A. All., 1936. *Work*: An American Place, N.Y.; PMA; Am. Color Slide Soc.; PAFA. *Exhibited*: Phila. Pr. Cl., 1941-1946; MMA, 1942; Marie Sterner Gal., 1937; Phila. A. All., 1945 (one-man); NAD, 1943, 1945; PAFA, 1932, 1933, 1935, 1940-1945, 1956, 1957; Carnegie Inst., 1941-1942, 1945-1946; Ragan Gal., Phila., 1941-1943; Phila. Graphic Sketch Cl., 1944, 1945; PMA, 1946; F. PAFA, 1927-1946, 1957, 1958; Woodmere A. Gal., 1941-1945.

VANN, LOLI (Mrs. Oscar Van Young)—Painter
1304 Maltman Ave., Los Angeles 26, Cal.

B. Chicago, Ill., Jan. 7, 1913. *Studied*: AIC, and with Sam Ostrowsky. *Awards*: prizes, Los A. Mus. A., 1944; Chaffey Col., 1948; Madonna Festival, Los A., 1953. *Exhibited*: AIC; Carnegie Inst.; Cal. PLH; SFMA; Santa Barbara Mus. A.; Denver A. Mus.; Chaffey Col.; Oakland A. Mus.; Los A. Mus. A.; Fnd. Western A.; Los A. AA; Pasadena AI; Laguna Beach AA; La Jolla A. Center; MMA; SAM; Los A. County Fair; Cal. State Fair; Palos Verdes, Cal.; Santa Monica Pub. Lib.; CGA; Nat. Orange Show; Scripps Col.; Cowie Gal., Los A., 1958 (one-man).

VAN ROEKENS, PAULETTE (Mrs. Arthur Meltzer)—
Painter, T.
1521 Old Welsh Rd., Huntingdon Valley, Pa.

B. Chateau Thierry, France, Jan. 1, 1896. *Studied*: PAFA; Moore Inst.; & with Samuel Murray, Henry B. Snell, Charles Grafly, & others. *Awards*: med., Phila. Plastic Cl., 1920; Phila. Sketch Cl., 1923; prizes, PAFA, 1928; Woodmere A. Gal., 1946. *Work*: PAFA; Phila. Graphic Sketch Cl.; F. PAFA; Pa. State Col.; Reading Mus. A.; Woodmere A. Cal. *Exhibited*: PAFA, 1918, 1920-1930, 1937, 1939; Carnegie Inst., 1922-1924; AIC, 1921, 1923, 1925, 1927-1930; CGA, 1921, 1923, 1926, 1933, 1937, 1939, 1943; Montclair A. Mus.; Mint Mus. A.; Woodmere A. Gal.; Phila. AC; Columbus Gal. FA, 1930; Mystic AA; Boston AC; Newport AA; one-man: Phila. A. All.; Delaware Bookshop, New Hope, Pa. *Position*: Prof., Painting & Drawing, Moore Inst. A., Philadelphia, Pa.

VAN ROSEN, ROBERT E.—Industrial Designer, P., L.
18 West 56th St. (19); h. 205 East 69th St., New York 21, N.Y.

B. Kiev, Russia, Feb. 6, 1904. *Studied*: Mun. Sch. FA, Chisinau, Roumania; Master Inst. Un. A., New York. *Member*: Package Des. Council; Soc. Am. Military Engineers. *Awards*: Grand award and others, Packaging Expo., Chicago, 1952; Eng. Constr. prize, 1953. *Work*: Queens Col.; Univ. Minnesota; des., theatrical productions, Provincetown Playhouse, Yiddish Art Theatre, N.Y. Lectures: Art and Theatre; Stagecraft, for CAA in MMA, MModA, BM. Editor, Scenic Artists Almanac, publ. by United Scenic A. *Positions*: Cur., Roerich Mus., 1926-28; A. Dir., IBM Corp. (Think magazine), 1940-42; Chief, Experimental Dept., J. Makowsky Corp., N.Y., 1943-48; Chief Des., Gardner Board & Carton Co., Middletown, Ohio, 1950-52; Des. Engineer, Robert Gair Co., New London, Conn., 1952-53; Indst. Des., Packaging Consultant, 1953- . Pres., R. E. Van Rosen Corp., New York, N.Y.

VAN SCIVER, PEARL AIMAN—Painter, T.
Glen Oaks, West Thomas Rd., Chestnut Hill, Philadelphia 18, Pa.

B. Philadelphia, Pa. *Studied*: Moore Inst.; PAFA, and with Leopold Seyffert, Violet Oakley, Paula Balano, Eliot O'Hara, Henry B. Snell, Lazar Raditz. *Member*: Phila. Plastic Cl.; Nat. Lg. Am. Pen Women; NAWA; Woodmere A .Gal. (Vice-Pres.). *Awards*: medal, Chestnut Hill, Pa.; Springside Annual; 1 silver, 2 gold medals, Phila. Plastic Cl.; Cape May County Court House; PAFA. *Work*: Allentown Mus.; Rochester Mem. A. Gal.; Ogontz Jr. Col.; Univ. Pennsylvania; Woodmere A. Gal.; Cape May County Court House, N.J. *Exhibited*: NAD; PAFA; CGA; Allentown Mus.; Cape May County Court House, N.J.; Woodmere A. Gal.; Rochester Mem. A. Gal., and others. *Position*: Vice-Pres., Woodmere A. Gal (10 years); Bd. Dir., Moore Inst. A., Philadelphia, Pa.*

VAN SOELEN, THEODORE—Painter, Lith., W.
P.O. Box 1117, Tesuque Valley, Santa Fé, N.M.

B. St. Paul, Minn., Feb. 15, 1890. *Studied*: St. Paul AI; PAFA. *Member*: NA. *Awards*: prizes, NAD, 1927, 1930; F.PAFA, 1931; N.M. State Fair, 1944, 1945; med., Sesqui-centennial Exp., Phila., Pa., 1926. *Work*: PAFA; NAD; Everhart Mus., Scranton, Pa.; IBM; Mus. New Mexico, Santa Fé; Pub. Sch., Phila., Pa.; LC; Denver, Colo.; murals, Grant County Court House, Silver City, N.M.; USPO, Portales, N.M.; Waureka, Okla.; Livingston, Tex. *Exhibited*: Carnegie Inst.; PAFA; MMA; MModA; SFMA; Los A. Mus. A.; San Diego FA Soc.; CGA; AIC; etc. Contributor to: Field & Stream magazine.

VAN VEEN, STUYVESANT—*Painter, Gr., I., W., L., E.*

Art Department, City College of New York; h. 131 East 19th St., New York 3, N.Y.; s. Whiteoak Hollow Farm, Georgetown, Ohio

B. New York, N.Y., Sept. 12, 1910. *Studied*: City Col. of N.Y.; PAFA; NAD; ASL; N.Y. Sch. Indst. A.; Columbia Univ., and with Daniel Garber, Thomas Benton, and others. *Member*: NSMP; AEA; McDowell Alum. Assn.; Nat. Com. on A. Edu.; Nat. Soc. Painters in Casein; Adv. Bd., City Center A. Gal., N.Y. *Awards*: prizes, McDowell Cl., 1936; Ohio Valley Exh., Athens, Ohio, 1945, 1946; Wright Field Army A., 1945; State Army A. Exh., 1945. *Work*: Walker A. Center; N.J. State Mus.; Ohio Univ.; N.J. State Mus.; MMA; Frick Coll., and in private colls.; murals, panels, etc.; USPO, Pittsburgh, Pa.; Fordham Hospital; Labor Dept. Bldg., Wash., D.C.; Queens Pub. Lib.; Seagram Corp.; Juvenile & Domestic Relations Court, Phila., Pa.; Wright-Patterson Air Base, Dayton, Ohio; Lincoln Nat. Bank, Cincinnati; P.S. #8, Bronx, N.Y., and others. *Exhibited*: Carnegie Inst.; AIC; MModA; WMAA; CGA; PAFA; BMFA; BM; CAM; Minneapolis Inst. A.; Syracuse Mus. FA; NGA; BMA, all from 1929 to present. Illus. "Garibaldi," 1957. *Position*: Instr., Supv., Cincinnati A. Acad., 1946-49; Faculty, A. Dept., City Col. of N.Y., 1949- . Pres., N.Y. Chaptr., AEA; Bd. Dirs., Nat. Soc. Painters in Casein.

VAN WINCKEL, DOROTHY D. *(Mrs. E. T.)—* *Educator, Lith., Eng.*

Art Department, Mary Washington College of the University of Virginia; h. 1316 Brent St., Fredericksburg, Va.

B. Chattanooga, Tenn. *Studied*: Univ. Tennessee, B.S. in Ed.; Peabody Col., M.A.; PAFA; Harvard Univ. (summer); ASL; Saugatuck (Mich.) Sch. of Painting. *Member*: NAWA; AAUW; VMFA. *Awards*: Carnegie A. Scholarship to Harvard, 1938; prizes, Phila. Pr. Cl., 1948 (purchase); NAWA, 1949; Certif. of Merit, Bibliographical Soc. of the Univ. Va., 1951. *Exhibited*: Phila. Pr. Cl., 1948; NAWA, 1948, 1949, 1955 and traveling exh. to Paris, 1948; LC, 1949; SAGA, 1950; VMFA, 1945, 1947, 1951, 1955 (3-man); Wash. WC Cl., 1948, 1949, 1950, 1951; Norfolk Mus. A. & Sciences, 1948; Albany Pr. Cl.; several one-man at Mary Washington Col. *Position*: Assoc. Prof. A., Chm., Dept. Art, Mary Washington College of the Univ. of Virginia, Fredericksburg, Va.

VAN WOLF, HENRY—*Sculptor*

14101 Chandler Blvd., Van Nuys, Cal.

B. Regensburg, Bavaria, Apr. 14, 1898. *Studied*: in Europe. *Member*: P. & S. Cl., Los. A.; Los A. AA. *Awards*: prizes, Cal. A. Cl., 1948, 1950; P. & S. Cl., 1948-1955; Prof. A. Gld., 1949; Ebell Cl., 1949; Los A. City A. Exh., 1950; A. of the Southwest, 1950, 1951, 1953, 1954; Cal. Int. Flower Show A. Exh., 1951. *Work*: USPO, Fairport, N.Y.; Red Hook Housing Project, N.Y.; Wall Mem., Hollywood; Inglewood Cemetery, Inglewood, Cal.; Cal. A. Cl. Medal; Prof. A. Gld. Medal; Beethoven Mem., La Crescenta Park, Glendale, Cal.; war mem. for German-American Lg. of Los Angeles; bronze statue of Ben Hogan, Golf Writers' Assn. of Am.; mem. port., Los A. Cal.; bronze mem. bust, Einstein Mem. Fnd.; bronze doors, Episcopal Church, Encino, Cal.; bronze Madonna, St. Timothy Church, West Los Angeles; Lincoln bust, Van Nuys H.S., and many others. *Exhibited*: in Europe, 1921-28; BM, 1932; All. A. Am., 1936, 1937; Arch. Lg., 1937; Springfield Mus. A., 1938; Cal. A. Cl., 1944-1952; P. & S. Cl., 1948-1952; A. of the Southwest, 1950, 1951; Los A. A. Exh., 1947-1950, and others.

VAN YOUNG, OSCAR—*Painter, T., L., Lith.*

1304 Maltman Ave., Los Angeles 26, Cal.

B. Vienna, Austria, Apr. 15, 1906. *Studied*: Acad. FA, Odessa, Russia; Los Angeles State Col., B.A., and with Todros Geller, Emil Armin. *Member*: AWS; F.; Intl. Inst. A. & Lets.; Cal. WC Soc.; Los A. AA. *Awards*: prizes,

AIC, 1942; Cal. WC Soc., 1943; Lewis Award of Merit, 1945; Chaffey Col., 1946; Walnut Creek (Cal.) Festival, 1951; Cal. State Fair. *Work*: Los A. Mus. A.; Chaffey Col., Ontario, Cal.; Santa Barbara Mus. A.; Frye Mus. A., Seattle; Los A. City Hall. *Exhibited*: AIC, 1937, 1946; GGE, 1939; Pepsi-Cola, 1945, 1946; NAD; VMFA; Cal. PLH, 1946; Oakland A. Gal., 1943, 1945; San F. AA, 1941, 1942, 1944, 1945; Santa Barbara Mus. A., 1944; Denver A. Mus., 1943, 1945; San Diego FA Soc., 1945; Los A. Mus. A., 1941-1955; Cal. State Fair; Los A. County Fair; Cal. WC Soc., 1953-1958; Nat. Orange Show, 1958; Scripps Col., 1958; Los A. County AI, 1958; one-man: Vigeveno Gal., 1942; Los A. Mus. A., 1942; SFMA, 1943; Pasadena AI, 1945, 1951; Santa Barbara Mus. A., 1946; Cowie Gal., Los A., 1953, 1957.

VAN YOUNG, MRS. OSCAR. See *Vann, Loli*

VARGA, MARGIT—*Writer, P.*

Brewster, N.Y.

B. New York, N.Y., May 5, 1908. *Studied*: ASL, with Boardman Robinson, Robert Laurent. *Work*: Springfield (Mass.) Mus. FA; MMA; Univ. Arizona; IBM Coll.; PAFA. *Exhibited*: R.I.Sch.Des.; Nebraska AA; GGE 1939; Cranbrook Acad. A., 1940; Dallas Mus. FA; AIC; Central Illinois Exp., 1939; CGA; VMFA; WMAA; 1951; Univ. Illinois, 1951; Carnegie Inst.; Pepsi-Cola. Author: "Waldo Peirce," 1941; "Carol Brant," 1945; Co-Author: "Modern American Painting," 1939; Ed., "America's Arts & Skills" (book). Contributor to: Magazine of Art; Studio Publications; Life magazine. *Position*: Asst. A. Dir., Life magazine, New York, N.Y., 1936- .

VARGISH, ANDREW—*Painter, Indst. Des., E., L.*

Poultney, Vt.

B. St. Tomas, Austria-Hungary, Oct. 11, 1905. *Studied*: Univ. Chicago, B.A.; T. Col., Columbia Univ., M.A. *Member*: SAGA; Chicago Soc. Et. *Awards*: prizes, SAGA, 1929; NAC, 1930. *Work*: LC; N.Y. Pub. Lib.; NGA. *Exhibited*: Chicago Soc. Et.; SAGA, annually; So. Vermont A.; one-man: Univ. Maine. *Position*: Dir., Dept. A., Green Mountain Jr. Col., Poultney, Vt., 1937- .*

VARIAN, DOROTHY—*Painter*

Studio 154, Carnegie Hall, New York 19, N.Y.; h. Bearsville, N.Y.

B. New York, N.Y., Apr. 26, 1895. *Studied*: CUASch.; ASL, and in Paris, France. *Member*: Woodstock AA; Audubon A. *Awards*: prize, William Fox Comp., N.Y. *Work*: WMAA; Newark Mus.; PMG; Dartmouth Col.; Fiske Univ.; Ogunquit Mus. A. *Exhibited*: Carnegie Inst., 1931, 1937, 1939, 1940, 1942-1945; CGA, 1935, 1937, 1939, 1941, 1943; PAFA, 1940, 1942-1945; VMFA, 1938, 1940; AIC, 1941; CAM, 1938, 1945; WMAA, 1933-1935, 1937-1941, 1948-1950, 1954; WMA, 1938; NAD, 1945; Pepsi-Cola, 1944; Woodstock AA, annually; BM, 1953; Yale Univ., 1955; La Tausca traveling exh., 1948; one-man: Durand-Ruel Gal., Paris, France, 1922; London, England, 1938. Nine one-man exhs. to 1953.

VASSOS, JOHN—*Painter, Des.*

54 West 55th St., New York, N.Y.; h. Comstock Hill, Norwalk, Conn.

B. Greece, Oct. 23, 1898. *Studied*: Robert Col., Constantinople; Fenway A. Sch., Boston; BMFA Sch.; ASL; N.Y. Sch. Des. *Member*: Silvermine Gld. A. (Pres.); IDI; Phila. A. All. *Awards*: prizes, Silvermine Gld. A., 1950; Electrical Manufacturing award, 1941; AIGA, 1927; 50 Best Books of the Year (des. & typography), 1951; medal, American Packaging. *Work*: Athens (Greece) Mus.; Athens Pub. Lib.; murals, Radio-TV Station, Phila., Pa.; Condado Beach Hotel, Puerto Rico; United Artists Theatre, Los A.; Skouras Theatres, N.Y.; Des., U.S. Trade Fair pavilions at Karachi, Pakistan and New Delhi, India; re-designed Rivoli Theatre, N.Y.; Des., electronics bldg., Dominican Republic, U.S. Trade Fair. *Exhibited*: A. Center, N.Y., 1928; N.Y. Pub. Lib., 1930; Toledo Pub. Lib., 1931; New Sch. for Social Research, 1934; Riverside Mus., 1937; Montross Gal., 1938; Warwick Gal., Phila., 1941; Silvermine Gld. A., 1950-1952. I., Oscar Wilde's Trilogy; Grey's Elegy; "Kubla Khan." Author, I., "Phobia," 1934. Contributor to art and design magazines.*

VAUGHAN, DANA PRESCOTT—*Educator*

Cooper Union Art School, Cooper Square, New York, N.Y.

B. Middleboro, Mass., June 20, 1898. *Studied*: Mass. Sch. A.; PMSchIA; Harvard Univ.; Brown Univ.; Univ. Upsala, Sweden. *Member*: New Hampshire Antiquarian Soc.; Eastern AA. Ed., Eastern Arts Yearbook, 1945, 1946. *Award*: D.F.A., Moore Inst. A., Science & Industry, Phila., Pa. Co-Author: "Art Professions in the United States," 1950. *Positions*: Memb. Corporation of Proctor Acad., Andover, N.H.; Bd. Dir., N.Y. Sch. for the Deaf; Hd. Jr. Sch., 1928-42, Dean, 1928-42, R.I.Sch. Des.; Dir., Sch. Indst. A., Trenton, N.J., 1942-45; Dean, CUASch., New York, N.Y., 1945- ; Bd. Trustees, Inst. of Trend Research, Hopkinton, N.H.; Chm. Com. on Accreditation, Nat. Assn. Schs. of Design.

VAUGHAN, LESTER HOWARD—*Craftsman*

26 Pleasant St., Raynham, Mass.

B. Taunton, Mass., Nov. 6, 1889. *Member*: Boston Soc. A. & Crafts. *Awards*: med., Boston Soc. A. & Crafts; prize, AIC.

VAUGHT, LARKEN—*Painter*

322½ South Newlin Ave., Whittier, Cal.

B. Centerville, Iowa, Dec. 3, 1904. *Studied*: Los A. AI, and with Anna Hills, Dorothy Dowiatt, Frederic Schwankowsky. *Member*: Laguna Beach AA; Whittier A. *Awards*: prizes, Whittier AA, 1945, 1949, 1952, 1954; Laguna Beach AA, 1938. *Exhibited*: Little Gallery, Taos, N.M., 1957.

VELSEY, SETH M.—*Sculptor, P., T., Des.*

1220 Xenia Ave., Yellow Springs, Ohio

B. Logansport, Ind., Sept. 26, 1903. *Studied*: Univ. Illinois; AIC; & with Albin Polasek, Lorado Taft. *Awards*: prizes, Hoosier Salon, 1928; Indiana A., 1931; Hickox prize; 1934; med., Paris Salon, 1937. *Work*: Dayton AI; Wright Field, Dayton, Ohio; St. Peter's Church, Chillicothe, Ohio; USPO, Pomeroy, Ohio; St. Peter & Paul's Church, Reading, Ohio; St. Francis fountain, Yellow Springs, Ohio. Murals, Rike-Kumler Co., Dayton, Ohio.

VERHAEREN, CAROLUS (CONSTANTINUS)—*Painter*

1111 Torrey Pines Rd., La Jolla, Cal.

B. Antwerp, Belgium, June 18, 1908. *Studied*: with George DeVore in Canada. *Member*: Soc. Western A.; Laguna Beach AA; La Jolla A. Center. *Awards*: prizes, Indp. A., Phoenix, Ariz., 1948; Carlsbad-Oceanside Exh., 1950; Soc. Western A., 1952, 1955. *Work*: many ports. of prominent persons in private colls. *Exhibited*: Wales Gal., Tucson, Ariz., 1950 (one-man); Detroit Inst. A.; deYoung Mem. Mus., 1952; Oakland A. Mus.; Chihuahua and Monterrey, Mexico (one-man).*

VERHELST, WILBERT—*Museum Curator, S., P., T.*

405 Ingalls St., Denver 15, Colo.

B. Sheboygan, Wis., June 19, 1923. *Studied*: Univ. Denver, B.F.A., M.A. *Award*: Art Faculty award, Univ. Denver, 1949. *Work*: Sioux City A. Center; Denver A. Mus.; sculpture, Lakeside Shopping Center, Lakeside, Colo., and in private colls. *Exhibited*: San F. AA, 1953, 1957; Mississippi AA, 1950; Sarasota AA, 1956; AGAA, 1949; Utah State Univ., 1957; Denver A. Mus., 1949, 1950, 1952-1956; Joslyn Mem. Mus., 1950, 1958; Nelson Gal. A., 1950, 1957; Mus. New Mexico, 1957; WAC, 1958; Des Moines A. Center, 1958, and others. Author: "Creative Projects," 1955. Contributor to School Arts magazine. *Positions*: A.T., 1948-52; Asst. Cur. Edu., 1952-55, Assoc. Cur., 1955-57, Denver A. Mus.; Dir., Sioux City A. Center, 1957-58; Assoc. Cur. Edu., Denver A. Museum, Denver, Colo., at present.

VERMES, MADELAINE—*Craftsman*

109-19 72nd Ave., Forest Hills 75, N.Y.

B. Hungary, Sept. 15, 1915. *Studied*: Alfred Univ.; Craft Students Lg.; Greenwich House Potters. *Member*: Artist-Craftsmen of N.Y.; Nat. Lg. of Am. Pen Women; York State Craftsmen. *Work*: Cooper Union Mus.; Museo International delle Ceramiche, Faenza, Italy. *Exhibited*: Syracuse Mus. FA; Mus. Natural Hist., 1956; Cooper Union Mus., 1955-1957; Barbizon-Plaza Gal., 1954; AEA 1955; Willow Gal., 1955 (one-man); Miami Nat. Ceramic exh.,

1956; Artist-Craftsmen of N.Y., 1957; The Coliseum, N.Y., 1957; A. Lg. of Long Island, 1958; Brentano's, N.Y., 1957 (one-man).

VERNER, ELIZABETH O'NEILL—*Etcher, P., W., L.*

38 Tradd St., Charleston 1, S.C.

B. Charleston, S.C., Dec. 21, 1883. *Studied*: PAFA; Central Sch. A., London, England. *Member*: F., Castle Hill A. Colony, Ipswich, Mass. *Work*: MMA; LC; BMFA; Mt. Vernon Assn.; Princeton Univ.; West Point Military Acad.; Univ. South Carolina; City of Charleston Coll.; Honolulu Acad. A. *Exhibited*: Carolina AA, 1956; Brevard (N.C.) Lib.; many nat. etching exhs. Author: "Prints and Impressions of Charleston," 1939, "Other Places," 1944; "Mellowed by Time," 1941; "South Carolina University," 1955.

VERNON, MRS. ELBA RIFFLE. See *Riffle, Elba Louisa*

VERRECCHIA, ALFEO—*Lithographer, P., Des.*

10 Howland Ave., Warwick, R.I.

B. Providence, R.I., June 16, 1911. *Studied*: R.I. Sch. Des.; Provincetown Sch. A.; & with John Frazier. *Member*: Contemporary A., Providence, R.I. *Awards*: prizes, Providence AC; Lib. Cong., 1943. *Work*: Lib. Cong. *Exhibited*: AFA traveling exh.; NAD, 1943; MMA (AV). *Position*: Pres., Gem-Craft, Inc., Cranston, R.I.*

VERSEN, KURT—*Designer*

4 Slocum Ave., Englewood, N.J.; h. 44 Hillside Ave., Tenafly, N.J.

B. Sweden, Apr. 21, 1901. *Studied*: in Germany. *Member*: IDI; Arch. Lg. *Awards*: citations, MMoDA, 1941; Tokyo Indst. Des. Exh., 1950; MMoDA, Good Des. Exh., 1951; medals, Century of Progress, 1933; Paris Int. Exp., 1937; AID, 1948. *Work*: MMoDA; State Dept. traveling exh. *Exhibited*: Century of Progress, 1933; Paris, France, 1937; MMoDA, 1933, 1937, 1941, 1947, 1951; Indst. A., Good Des., Buffalo, Providence, Indianapolis, 1948. Lectures: Lighting, Color, Design.

VERTES, MARCEL—*Painter, I.*

140 West 57th St., New York 19, N.Y.; also, 78 Rue de la Faisanderie, Paris, France

B. Ujpest, Hungary, Aug. 10, 1895. *Studied*: in Hungary and Paris, France. *Member*: A. Lg. Am.; Scenic A. *Awards*: Officer, Legion of Honor, 1955; Two "Oscars" Academy Awards for designing film "Moulin Rouge," 1954. *Work*: MMoDA; Musee des Artes Moderne, Paris; Musee Carnavalet, Paris; Luxembourg, Mus. A., Paris; murals, Dallas, Tex.; Plaza Hotel, Waldorf-Astoria and Carlyle Hotel, New York; Ballets: "La Belle Helene," Paris Opera, 1955; Scenes: Ringling Bros.-Barnum & Bailey Circus entire show, 1956; Author, I., "The Stronger Sex"; "Art and Fashion"; "Instants et Visages de Paris"; Limited Editions: "Parallelement," Paris, 1954; "Ombre de Mon Amour," Paris, 1956; "Daphnis et Chloe," Paris, 1954; "Eloge de Vertes," Paris, 1953: Art Documents Issue "Vertes," Lausanne, 1956. *Exhibited*: "As They Were" (portraits of celebrities as they were as children) in leading museums in U.S., under the sponsorship of AFA traveling exhibition service.

VIBBERTS, EUNICE WALKER (Mrs. Gerald)—*Painter*

7 Sound View Terr., Greenwich, Conn.

B. New Albany, Ind. *Studied*: PIASch.; ASL; Beaux-Arts, Fontainebleau, France. *Member*: NAWA; Greenwich SA; Scarsdale AA; Westchester A. & Crafts Gld.; Louisville AA. *Awards*: prizes, Scarsdale AA, 1941, 1943; Greenwich SA, 1945, 1946, 1952, 1954; Baekland prize, 1943. *Exhibited*: CGA; NAWA, 1925-1927, 1929-1932, 1934, 1936-1938, 1940-1944, 1946, 1947, 1950; Scarsdale AA, 1929-1945; Greenwich SA, 1943, 1944-1950, 1952-1958.

VICENTE, ESTEBAN—*Painter*

88 East 10th St.; h. 138 Second Ave., New York, N.Y.

B. Segovia, Spain, Jan. 20, 1906. *Studied*: Escuela de Bellas Artes de San Fernando, Madrid, B.A. *Work*: BMA. *Exhibited*: WMAA, 1950, 1955, 1956; Nebraska AA, 1951; Carnegie Inst., 1952, 1955; Cal. PLH, 1953; Sidney Janis Gal., 1951-52; Galerie de France, Paris, 1952; Univ. Illinois, 1952; Egan Gal., N.Y., 1955 (one-man). Visiting Prof. A., Univ. Cal., Berkeley, 1954-55.*

VICKERS, ROBERT—*Educator*
Ohio Wesleyan University, Delaware, Ohio
Position: Dir., Department of Fine Arts, Ohio Wesleyan University, Delaware, Ohio*

VICKREY, ROBERT REMSEN—*Painter*
c/o Midtown Galleries, 17 East 57th St., New York, N.Y.
B. New York, N.Y., Aug. 20, 1926. *Studied*: Yale Univ., B.A.; ASL; Yale Sch. FA, B.F.A., and with Kenneth Hayes Miller, Reginald Marsh. *Member*: AWS; Audubon A. *Awards*: Edwin Austin Abbey Mural Fellowship, 1949, and prize; American Artist magazine citation, Audubon A., 1956; AWS, 1956; NAD, 1958; Fla. Southern Col., 1952; Hallmark award, 1955. *Work*: WMAA; Museu de Arte Moderna, Rio de Janeiro; Fla. Southern Col.; Parrish A. Mus., Southampton; Delgado Mus. A.; DMFA; Sara Roby Fnd.; Munson-Williams-Proctor Inst.; NAD; Atlanta Univ.; Atlanta AA. Time magazine covers; book jackets. *Exhibited*: WMAA, 1951, 1956-1958; CGA, 1950; Audubon A., 1949-1952, 1956, 1957; AWS, 1952, 1956; NAD, 1949-1951, 1956-1958; Fla. Southern Col., 1952; MMA, 1952; Santa Barbara Mus. A., 1956; CMA, 1956; Butler Inst. Am. A., 1956, 1958; Mus. FA of Houston, 1956; Springfield Mus. A., 1956; AIC, 1956, 1957; DMFA, 1956; Memphis Mus. A., 1956; Univ. Nebraska, 1956; Denver A. Mus., 1957; Columbus (Ohio) Gal. FA, 1957; PAFA, 1952, 1957; Columbia (S.C.) Mus., 1957; Grand Rapids A. Gal., 1957; Ft. Worth, 1957; Des Moines A. Center, 1958.

VIDAR, FREDE—*Painter, E.*
1460 Pear St., Ann Arbor, Mich.
B. Denmark, June 6, 1911. *Studied*: Royal Acad., Denmark; Cal. Sch. FA; Ecole des Beaux-Arts, Julian Acad., Paris, France; Acad. FA, Munich, Germany. *Member*: Am. Acad. in Rome (Assoc.); San F. A.; NSMP; Assoc. A. New Jersey; AEA. *Awards*: Chaloner F., 1935, 1936, 1937; Guggenheim F., 1946; Special Faculty Grant of the Rackham Sch. Grad. Studies for studies of Byzantine structural forms and studies of life and culture of the Holy Mountain of Athos, 1957- . *Work*: MModA; Nat. Mus. Copenhagen; Palace Legion Honor; Newark Mus.; Pasadena AI; reproduction of war paintings for the Gen. MacArthur mem., Life Magazine, 1955. *Exhibited*: one-man: Assoc.Am.A., 1949; Rackham Gal., Ann Arbor, Mich., 1955; Univ. Michigan, 1959. *Positions*: Army Combat A., 1942-46; Documentary A., Life Magazine, 1946, 1947; Abbott Laboratories, 1947, 1950; Instr., Washington Univ., St. Louis, 1950-51; Life Magazine War Correspondent, Korea, 1950-51; Assoc. Prof. A., Dept. A., Univ. Michigan, 1953- .

VIERTHALER, ARTHUR A.—*Craftsman, E.*
University of Wisconsin, Department of Art Education, Madison, Wis.; h. Rt. #1, Waunakee, Wis.
B. Milwaukee, Wis., Sept. 15, 1916. *Studied*: Milwaukee State T. Col., B.S.; Univ. Wisconsin, M.S. *Awards*: prizes, Wisconsin State Fair, 1950-1952; Wisconsin Des-Craftsmen, 1950; Madison AA. *Work*: many jewelry commissions, religious articles, etc. *Exhibited*: Wichita Dec. A., 1949-1954; Des-Craftsmen traveling exhs., 1954-1955; Huntington Gal., 1955; Smithsonian Inst., traveling exh., 1955-1956; St. Paul Gal. A., 1955; Midwestern Des., 1953; Milwaukee Des., 1948-1954; Wisconsin State Fair, 1949-1955; Madison AA, 1948-1950. Contributor to Midwestern Designer Craftsmen. Lectures: "Pre-Historic Design"; "Contemporary Design"; "Natural Phenomena of Design Elements in Minerals"; "Gemstones," etc. *Position*: A.T., Madison Pub. Schs.; Instr., Dept. Edu., Univ. Wisconsin, Madison, Wis.*

VIESULAS, ROMAS—*Painter, Et., Lith.*
1285 Dean St., Brooklyn 16, N.Y.
B. Lithuania, Sept. 11, 1918. *Studied*: Univ. Vilnius, Lithuania; Ecole des Arts et Metiers, Germany; Ecole des Beaux-Arts, Paris. *Member*: SAGA; Phila. Pr. Cl. *Awards*: prizes, Conn. Acad. FA, and numerous hon. mentions. *Work*: LC; N.Y. Pub. Lib.; Phila. Pr. Cl.; Sloniker Coll. Religious Prints, Cincinnati. Murals, Holy Cross Church, Chicago, Ill. *Exhibited*: MModA, 1956; LC, 1954, 1955; Phila. Pr. Cl., 1953-1956; Boston Pr. M., 1955; PMA, 1955; AIC, 1952; Portland Mus. A., 1953, 1954; Audubon A., 1956; Bradley Univ., 1954; Albany Pr. Cl., 1953; SAGA, 1955, 1956; G.W.V. Smith Mus. A., 1953, 1954;

CM, 1954; Nat. Philatelic Mus., Phila., 1954; Paris, France, 1950; one-man: Institut Francais de Fribourg, Germany, 1951; N.Y. Pub. Lib., 1956; Matrix Gal., N.Y., 1954; 2-man: Phila. Pr. Cl., 1956; Panoras Gal., 1955.

VINCENT, ANDREW McDUFFIE—*Painter, E.*
1062 East 21st St., Eugene, Ore.
B. Hutchinson, Kan., May 14, 1898. *Studied*: AIC. *Member*: Am. Assn. Univ. Prof. *Awards*: prize, AIC. *Work*: SAM; Portland (Ore.) A. Mus.; murals, USPO, Toppenish, Wash;. Salem, Ore. *Exhibited*: GGE, 1939; SAM; Portland A. Mus.; San F., Cal.; Mills Col.; Denver, Colo.; Chicago, Ill.; Eugene, Ore.; Henry Gal., Univ. Washington, 1957, etc. *Position*: Hd. Dept. A., Univ. Oregon, Eugene, Ore., at present.

VINSON, CHARLES NICHOLAS—*Painter*
2302 North Locust St., Wilmington 2, Del.
B. Wilmington, Del., Nov. 19, 1927. *Studied*: PAFA; in Mexico, and with Hobson Pittman, Franklin Watkins, Walter Stuempfig. *Member*: Wash. Soc. FA; PAFA. *Awards*: prizes, PAFA, 1951; Pa. State T. Col., 1951; Delaware A. Center, 1951; Cresson traveling scholarship, PAFA, 1952. *Work*: Wash. Soc. FA. *Exhibited*: PAFA, 1952; NAD, 1952; Pa. State T. Col., 1951; Mexico City, 1948; Delaware A. Center, 1950, 1951.*

VITACCO, ALICE (L. ALICE WILSON)—
Painter, I., Des.
Old Sow Rd., Easton, Conn.
B. Mineola, L.I., N.Y., Nov. 30, 1909. *Studied*: N.Y. Sch. App. Des. for Women; Univ. Mexico; & with Winold Reiss, Kimon Nicolaides, Lucien Bernhard. *Awards*: prize, Lexington Gal., N.Y., 1939; Wolfe Mem. prize, 1931; De Forest mem. prize, NAWA, 1936. I., "Mexican Popular Arts," 1939.*

VITERBO, DARIO—*Sculptor, Gr., P.*
62 West 11th St., New York 11, N.Y.
B. Florence, Italy, Jan. 25, 1890. *Studied*: Florentine Acad., with degree. *Member*: S. Gld.; Salon d'Automne and Salon des Tuileries, Paris. *Awards*: prize, Intl. Exh. Dec. A., Paris; gold medal, Intl. Exh., Paris; silver medal, Venice; silver medal, Intl. Exh. Books, Rome, 1953. *Work*: Petit Palais, Jeu de Paume Mus., Paris; Uffizi Mus., Florence; Mus. Mod. A., Milan; MMA; Univ. Arkansas, and in many private colls. U.S. and abroad. *Exhibited*: Wildenstein Gal., N.Y. (one-man); S. Gld., Paris (several one-man); and in other galleries of Europe. Illus., Il Libro di Tobia with ten bronze plates, now in the collection of the N.Y. Pub. Lib.

VITOUSEK, JUANITA JUDY—*Painter*
4623 Kahala Ave., Honolulu, Hawaii
B. Portland, Ore., May 22, 1892. *Studied*: Univ. California; & with Millard Sheets. *Member*: AWCS; Assn. Honolulu A.; Honolulu P. & S. *Awards*: prize, Honolulu A. Soc., 1934; Honolulu Acad. A., 1937. *Work*: SAM; Honolulu Acad. A. *Exhibited*: PAFA; Riverside Mus.; Cal. WC Soc.; Assn. Honolulu A.; Honolulu Acad. A.*

VIVIANO, EMMANUEL GERALD—*Sculptor, T.*
North Ave., Westport, Conn.
B. Chicago, Ill., Oct. 18, 1907. *Studied*: AIC. *Work*: BMA; Chicago Zoological Gardens; fountain, Illinois Medical Unit, Chicago; wall ceramics, Aurora, Ill.; Oak Park, Ill. *Exhibited*: AIC, 1935-1942; WFNY 1939; GGE 1939; PAFA; Hartford Atheneum; Detroit Inst. A. *Position*: Instr., S. and Mosaic, Indiana Univ.; Columbia Univ.*

VIVIKA. See Heino, Vivika

VODICKA, RUTH—*Sculptor*
745 Sixth Ave. (10); h. 33 East 22nd St., New York, N.Y.
B. New York, N.Y., Nov. 23, 1921. *Studied*: City Col., N.Y.; Sculpture Center with O'Connor Barrett; ASL. *Member*: AEA; NAWA; S.Gld.; Audubon A. *Awards*: prizes, NAWA, 1954, 1957; NAD, 1955; Audubon A., 1957; Silvermine Gld. A., 1957, 1958. *Exhibited*: Sculp-

ture Center, N.Y., 1949-1953; Phila. A. All., 1951, 1952; de Cordova & Dana Mus., 1951; SFMA, 1952; Texas traveling exh., 1952; WMAA, 1952-1956; NAD, 1952, 1955; PAFA, 1953, 1954, 1958; Audubon A., 1954-1958; Arch. Lg., 1954; NAWA, 1954, 1955; Am. Jewish traveling exh., 1954, 1955; AIC, 1954; Burlington Gal., London, England, 1955; S. Gld., 1955-1958; AFA traveling exh., 1957-58; Detroit Inst. A., 1958; Riverside Mus., 1958; Detroit Inst. A., 1958; one-man: Assoc. Am. A., 1956; Sunken Meadow Gal., Long Island, 1957. Art Film: "Demonstration of Steel Welding" for SFMA, 1952; "Sculptress Works With Blowtorch," 1956 (Voice of America newsreel). *Positions*: Instr. S., Queens Youth Center, Bayside, L.I., N.Y., 1953-56; Nat. Dir. at-large, AEA, 1957-58.

VOGEL, DONALD—Printmaker, T.
2830 Grand Concourse, New York 58, N.Y.

B. Poland, Dec. 24, 1902. *Studied*: Parsons Sch. Des.; Columbia Univ., B.S., M.A. *Member*: SAGA. *Awards*: prizes, AV, 1943; Northwest Pr. M., 1943, 1946; Munson-Williams-Proctor Inst., 1943; LC, 1950. *Work*: SAM; Pa. State Univ.; MMA; Munson-Williams-Proctor Inst.; SAGA; LC. *Exhibited*: SAGA, 1948-1952; NAD, 1948, 1949; Carnegie Inst., 1948; LC, 1948, 1951; Northwest Pr. M., 1948, 1949; PAFA, 1949; J. B. Speed Mem. Mus., 1950; Flint Inst. A., 1950; Wichita AA, 1950; BM, 1950; AFA traveling exh., 1950; Royal Soc. P., Et. & Engravers, 1954. Contributor to Print Collector's Quarterly; Le Revue Moderne; American Prize Prints of 20th Century, and others. *Position*: Instr., FA, Sch. Indst. A., New York, N.Y.

VOGEL, VALENTINE—Painter, T.
5179 Cabanne Ave., St. Louis, Mo.; h. Cedar Hill, Mo.

B. St. Louis, Mo., Apr. 19, 1906. *Studied*: Washington Univ.; NAD; Grande Chaumiere, Paris, France; Am. Acad. in Rome. *Member*: St. Louis Soc. Indp. A.; Lg. Am. Pen Women; AEA; St. Louis Woman's Advertising Cl.; St. Louis A. Lg.; St. Louis A. All. *Awards*: med., St. Louis A. Gld., 1929, prize, 1930; med., Kansas City AI, 1930; St. Louis Post-Dispatch prize, 1931; St. Louis Little Theatre prize, 1931; YMHA prize, 1944. *Work*: murals, Crunden Lib., Clayton, Mo.; Belvue Sch., University City, Mo.; Pub. Lib., Sikstone, Mo.*

VOGELGESANG, SHEPARD—Designer
Up-on-the-Mountain, Whitefield, N.H.

B. San Francisco, Cal., Feb. 9, 1901. *Studied*: MIT, B.S. in Arch.; Staats Kunstgewerbe Schule, Vienna; & with Josef Hofmann. *Member*: Chicago AC; BAID; AIA. *Award*: traveling scholarship, MIT, 1926. Contributor to: Architectural Record, Architectural Forum, Good Furnishing, Magazine of Art, & other publications. *Position*: Des. & Supv., interior color & mural projects, Century of Progress, 1933; Asst. Dir. Decorative A., Chief Des., Com. FA, GGE 1939; Asst. Dir. & Des. Exhibits, WFNY 1939.

VOGNILD, TED (Mrs.)—Painter
1906 Lincoln Park West, Chicago 14, Ill.

B. Nov. 23, 1881. *Studied*: in Paris, France; AIC; & with Johansen, Snell, Hawthorne. *Awards*: med., All-Illinois Soc. FA, 1937.

VOIGTLANDER, KATHERINE—Painter
Apartado 2975, Mexico City, Mexico

B. Camden, N.J., Apr. 19, 1917. *Studied*: Univ. Pennsylvania, B.F.A.; Kansas City AI; PAFA; Univ. Kansas City, B.A.; & with Thomas Benton, George Harding, Francis Speight, & others. *Awards*: F., PAFA; Cresson traveling scholarship, PAFA, 1938; prizes, Woman Painters, Wichita, Kan., 1936; Cumberland Valley Exh., Hagerstown, Md., 1944; PAFA, 1940. *Exhibited*: Kansas City AI, 1931, 1936; Denver, Colo., 1939; Phila. AC, 1938; Women Painters of Am., 1936; Cumberland Valley Exh., 1944-1946. Illus., primers and story books, Linguistic Text Series, for Summer Inst. of Linguistics, Mexican Branch. Illus., "2,000 Tongues to Go," 1959.

VOLKMAR, LEON—Ceramist, P.
433 Poplar St., Laguna Beach, Cal.

B. Paris, France, Feb. 25, 1879. *Studied*: NAD. *Member*: N.Y. Ceramic Soc. (Hon. Pres.); Greenwich (Conn.) SA.

Awards: med., AIC; Paris Salon, 1937. *Work*: AIC; Detroit Inst. A.; Cranbrook Acad. A.; BMFA; BM; Newark Mus.; MMA. *Exhibited*: AIC, 1953. Lectures: Ceramics. (Retired 1951).

VOLOVICH, IAKOV—Painter, T.
170 Steuben St., Brooklyn 5, N.Y.

B. Kursk, Russia, Feb. 18, 1910. *Studied*: NAD; BAID; ASL; Hans Hofmann Sch. FA, and in Amsterdam, Holland. *Awards*: prize, All. A. Am., 1955. *Work*: murals, St. George Hotel, Brooklyn, N.Y.; Aviation Bldg., Boise, Idaho; Army Air Base, Charleston, S.C.; port., Univ. Chicago, and in private colls. *Exhibited*: Critic's Show. 1946; Pepsi-Cola, 1946; Audubon A., 1946, 1947; All. A. Am., 1948, 1955; Abstract A., 1949.*

VON ALLESCH, MARIANNA—Craftsman, Des., T.
50 West 13th St., New York 11, N.Y.

B. Ingolstadt, Germany. *Studied*: in Europe, with A. Niemayer, Bruno Paul. *Awards*: med., Government Acad., Berlin, Germany. *Work*: MMA; Detroit Inst. A.; Los A. Mus. A. *Exhibited*: WFNY 1939; GGE 1939; Syracuse Mus. FA; traveling exh.; extensively in Europe. Lectures: Glass; Interior Decoration. Des. glassware for Kensington Crystal Co.; Owner, glass and ceramic shop, New York, N.Y. Specializes in ceramic murals.

VON AUW, EMILIE—Painter, S., C., Des., W., L.
2913 Santa Cruz Ave., Southeast, Albuquerque, N.M.

B. Flushing, L.I., Sept. 1, 1901. *Studied*: in Germany; N.Y. Sch. F. & App. A.; Columbia Univ., B.A., M.A.; Univ. New Mexico, B.F.A.; Grande Chaumiere, Paris; Ecole des Beaux-Arts, Fontainebleau, France; Acad. A., Florence, Italy, etc. *Member*: New Mexico A. Lg.; Corrales AA; Nat. Soc. A. & Lets. *Award*: prizes, New Mexico State Fair. *Exhibited*: NGA; Terry AI; Albuquerque New Mexico A. Lg.; State Fair; Plaza Gal.; Ramage Gal.; Albuquerque A.; Jonson Gal.; Botts Mem. Hall; Fez Club Gal.; Mus. New Mexico traveling exhs. *Positions*: Prof. A., Univ. New Mexico, 1940-45; Dir., Studio Workshop, Albuquerque, N.M.; Bd. Memb., New Mexico A. Lg.; State Fair Mus. FA; Adv. Bd., Special Edu. Center.

VON DER LANCKEN, GIULIA—Painter, T.
80 Greenridge Ave., White Plains, N.Y.

B. Florence, Italy. *Studied*: Royal Acad. FA, Florence, Italy with Rivalta, Caloshi, Fattori, Burchi; in Venice with Hopkinson Smith. *Awards*: Diplome of Honor, Acad. FA, Florence, Italy; prizes, Oklahoma State Art Exhibit; Tulsa AA. *Exhibited*: Florence, Italy; Rochester A. Cl.; Chautauqua AA; Oklahoma City A. Center; Philbrook A. Center; Delgado Mus. A.; NAD; Washington WC Cl.; N.Y. WC Cl.; Westchester A. & Crafts; Hudson Valley AA; one-man: Tulsa A. Gld.; Philbrook A. Center. Author: "Music as a Stimulus to Creative Art."

VON EHRENWIESEN, HILDEGARD REBAY. See Rebay, Hilla

VON ERDBERG, JOAN PRENTICE—Museum Curator
Princess Farm, R.D. 1, Trenton, N.J.

B. Princeton, N.J., Mar. 3, 1908. *Studied*: Bryn Mawr Col.; Radcliffe Col.; FMA Sch. Contributor to Burlington, Antiques, American Collector magazines. Author: Catalogue of the Italian Maiolica in the Cluny Museum, Paris, 1949; Catalogue of the Italian Maiolica in the Walters Art Gallery, 1952 (with Marvin C. Ross). *Position*: Asst., 1939-42, Asst. Cur., Decorative A., 1942-43, Assoc. Cur., 1943-46, Cur., Ceramics & Metalwork, 1946-47, PMA, Philadelphia, Pa.; Chargée de Mission, Départment des Objets d'Art, Musée du Louvre, Paris, 1947-49.

VON ERFFA, HELMUT—Educator, P., W., L.
Rutgers University, Department of Art, New Brunswick, N.J.; h. R.R. 24 Hoes Lane, New Brunswick, N.J.

B. Lueneburg, Germany, Mar. 1, 1900. *Studied*: Harvard Univ.; Princeton Univ.; & in Germany, with J. Itten, Paul Klee. *Member*: CAA; Am. Arch. Soc. *Work*: Wadsworth Atheneum. *Exhibited*: Chicago, 1927, 1928; Bryn

Mawr Col., 1936; Swarthmore Women's Cl., 1945; Wadsworth Atheneum, 1930; PMA, 1946; New Jersey Col. for Women, 1949; Douglass Col., 1955; FMA. Contributor to FMA Bulletin, College Art Journal, Ars Islamica, Art Quarterly; Article: "Benjamin West," Artists in America, 1955; "Benjamin West" in Guide to Chapel of Royal Naval College, Greenwich. Lectures: The Bauhaus; Origins of Modern Art; Goya; etc. *Position*: Prof. Hist. A., Harvard Univ., 1930-32; Bryn Mawr Col., 1935-36; Northwestern Univ., 1938-43; Swarthmore Col., 1943-46; Rutgers Univ., New Brunswick, N.J., 1946- .

von FUEHRER, OTTMAR F.—*Painter, I., L.*
  Carnegie Institute, 4400 Forbes St.; h. 5306 Westminster Place, Pittsburgh, Pa.

B. Austria, Apr. 19, 1900. *Studied*: Acad. App. A., Vienna; Univ. Vienna; Carnegie Inst. Technology. *Member*: Assoc. A. Pittsburgh; Pittsburgh WC Soc. *Awards*: prize, Pittsburgh WC Soc. *Work*: murals, Carnegie Inst.; many backgrounds for dioramas; landscapes and ports, in private colls. *Exhibited*: Assoc. A. Pittsburgh, annually; Pittsburgh WC Soc., annually. Contributor to Carnegie Magazine, and to European publications. Lectures in U.S. and abroad. *Position*: Staff A., Natural Hist. Mus., Vienna, Austria; Florida State Mus., Gainesville, Fla.; Chief Staff A., Carnegie Inst. Mus., Pittsburgh, Pa., at present.

VON GROSCHWITZ, GUSTAVE—
  Museum Curator, T., L.
  2356 Park Ave., Cincinnati 6, Ohio

B. New York, N.Y., Apr. 16, 1906. *Studied*: Columbia Univ., A.B.; N.Y. Univ., M.A. *Member*: SAGA (hon.); Grolier Cl.; Cincinnati A. Cl. *Awards*: F., CAA, 1945-46. Contributor to leading art magazines. Lectures on Fine Arts, Masterpieces of Printmaking. *Position*: Senior Cur. and Cur. Prints, Cincinnati A. Mus., Cincinnati, Ohio.

VON JOST, ALEXANDER—*Painter, Et.*
  1712 Grove Ave., Richmond 20, Va.

B. Laurence, Mass., June 24, 1888. *Studied*: Johns Hopkins Univ.; Maryland Inst. *Awards*: prizes, South Carolina State Fair, 1927; Richmond Acad. A. & Sc., 1933. *Work*: Hanover County Court House, Va.; Confederate Mus., Richmond, Va.; Supreme Court, William & Mary Col., Williamsburg, Va.; Richard Cimbal Lib., Phila., Pa.; Blues Armory, Richmond, Va.; Univ. Virginia; Univ. Richmond; Va. Military Inst., Lexington, Va.

VON LEHMDEN, RALPH—*Painter, Des.*
  228 North La Salle St. (1); h. 10601 South Hale St., Chicago 43, Ill.

B. Cleveland, Ohio, Sept. 17, 1908. *Studied*: Cleveland Sch. A.; Northwestern Univ.; Western Reserve Univ. *Member*: Chicago AC; SI; SC. *Awards*: prize, AIC, 1940, 1941, 1956; medal, A. Dir. Cl., N.Y., 1949; NAD, 1942. *Work*: paintings of the Arctic for Sec. of the Air Force, 1957. *Exhibited*: AIC, 1940, 1952-1955; NAD, 1953, 1954. CMA; Butler AI, and others.

VON MANIKOWSKI, BOLES—*Painter, Des., S.*
  211 East Pulteney St., Corning, N.Y.

B. Kempen, Germany, Sept. 11, 1892. *Studied*: ASL; in Germany; & with Lars Hofstrup, Sascha Moldovan, Frederick Carder, Ernfred Anderson. *Exhibited*: Soc. Indp. A., 1936; Cayuga Mus. Hist. & A., 1940, 1941; Blue Ridge, N.C., 1942.*

VON MEYER, MICHAEL—*Sculptor, T.*
  1350 A Filbert St., San Francisco 9, Cal.

B. Russia, June 10, 1894. *Studied*: Cal. Sch. FA, San F., Cal. *Member*: San F. AA. *Awards*: med., San F., AA, 1934; prize, Women's AA, 1926. *Work*: SFMA; Palace Legion Honor; Daily Californian newspaper bldg., Salinas, Cal.; Univ. California Hospital; San F. City Hall; House Office Bldg., Wash., D.C.; USPO, Santa Clara, Cal.; GGE 1939; San F. Beach Chalet; Catholic Russian Center, San F.; Russian Orthodox Holy Trinity Cathedral, San F.; Greek Mem. Park, San Mateo, Cal.; Russian Center, Serbian Cemetery, both San F.; St. Innocent Eastern Orthodox Church, Encino, Cal.; St. Theresa Church, Fresno, Cal. *Exhibited*: Oakland A. Gal.; CGA, 1936; WMAA, 1936; Cal. AA; Palace Legion Honor; de Young Mem.

Mus.; SFMA; Crocker Gal. A., Stockton. Contributor to: Asia, Art News, Pencil Points, Am. A. Group, Univ. Cal. Press, & other publications.

VON NEUMANN, ROBERT—*Painter, Gr., L., T.*
  Wisconsin State College; h. 1050 West River View Dr., Milwaukee 9, Wis.

B. Rostock, Germany, Sept. 10, 1888. *Studied*: Kunstgewerbe Schule, Rostock, Germany; Royal Acad., Berlin, M.A.; & with Hans Hofmann. *Member*: ANA; SAE; Chicago SE; Wis. P. & S.; Milwaukee Pr. M. *Awards*: prizes, Milwaukee Journal, 1933; Madison AA, 1934; AIC, 1936; Palm Beach, Fla., 1937; Milwaukee AI, 1938; SAE, 1942; Lib. Cong., 1943; PAFA, 1944; Herron AI; med., Milwaukee AI, 1941. *Work*: Univ. Wisconsin; Milwaukee AI; AIGA; Lib. Cong.; & in Berlin, Germany. *Exhibited*: PAFA; NAD; CGA; WFNY 1939; GGE 1939; AIC; Carnegie Inst.; Minneapolis Inst. A.; Milwaukee AI; Madison Salon; etc. Contributor to: art magazines. *Position*: Prof. A., Wisconsin State Col., Milwaukee, Wis.*

von RIEGEN, WILLIAM—*Cartoonist, I., P., T.*
  230 Grant Ave., Dumont, N.J.

B. New York, N.Y., Dec. 11, 1908. *Studied*: ASL, with George Bridgman. *Member*: SI; ASL; Nat. Cartoonists Soc. *Exhibited*: MMA; SI; Louvre, Paris, France, and in many traveling exhs. of cartoons throughout U.S. Illus., "Professional Cartooning," 1950; "Ever Since Adam and Eve," 1955. Contributor cartoons and illustrations to Sat. Eve. Post; Look; Readers' Digest; Esquire; New Yorker; True; Argosy; Reader's Digest Humor Book; Cartoons, "Twenty-Five Years of Cartooning," Sat. Eve. Post; Esquire's "Cartoon Album"; and other national magazines. *Position*: Instr., ASL, part-time; PIASch.

VON RUEMELIN, ADOLPH GUSTAV WOLTER. See Wolter, Adolph G.

VON SCHMIDT, HAROLD—*Illustrator, P., L.*
  Deadman's Brook, Westport, Conn.

B. Alameda, Cal., May 19, 1893. *Studied*: Cal. Col. A. & Crafts; Grand Central A. Sch.; & with Worth Ryder, Maynard Dixon, Harvey Dunn. *Member*: SI; A. Gld. *Work*: Cal. State Capitol, Sacramento; Montana Hist. Soc.; U.S. Military Acad., West Point, N.Y.; Baseball Hall of Fame, Cooperstown, N.Y.; Air Force Acad., Denver. *Exhibited*: SI; Westport A. Group. I., "Death Comes to the Archbishop"; "December Night"; "Homespun," & other books. Contributor to national magazines. *Position*: A., Correspondent, King Features Syndicate, 1945; Founding & Faculty member, Famous Artists Sch.; Pres., SI, 1938-41; Pres., Westport AA, 1950-51.*

VON SCHNEIDAU, CHRISTIAN—*Painter, S., W., L.*
  920½ South St. Andrews Place, Los Angeles, Cal.; also, Emerald Bay, Laguna Beach, Cal.

B. Smaland, Sweden, Mar. 24, 1893. *Studied*: Acad. FA, Sweden; AIC, and with J. Wellington Reynolds, Charles Hawthorne, Richard Miller and others. *Member*: P. & S. Cl., Los A.; Cal. A. Cl.; Scandinavian-Am. A. Soc.; Laguna Beach AA; Cal. WC Soc.; Los A. AA; Fairbanks (Alaska) A. Gld.; Indp. A. Lg., Chicago. *Awards*: prizes, AIC, 1912-1916; Minnesota State Fair, 1915; Swedish-Am. Exh., Chicago, 1917; Provincetown, Mass., 1920; Southwest Mus., 1921; Pomona State Fair, 1925, 1927; Morton Mem. Hall, Phila., 1928; Creative Arts Cl., Los A., 1931; Los A. Mus. A., 1939; Scandinavian Am. A. Soc., 1940, 1941, 1943, 1945; Soc. Western A., 1947; Swedish-Am. A. Portrait Comp., 1951; P. & S. Cl., Los A., 1945, 1947, 1950-1952; Gardena H.S., 1951; Friday Morning Cl., 1951, 1952; medals, Cal. State Fair, 1919, 1920; Scandinavian-Am. A. Soc., 1939, 1940; GGE 1939. *Work*: portraits, murals, in numerous theatres, churches, hotels and clubs throughout the U.S. and abroad. *Exhibited*: nationally. Also in Fairbanks, Anchorage, Kotzebue and Juneau, Alaska. *Position*: Dir., Von Schneidau Sch. A., Los Angeles, Cal., and Palm Springs, Cal.; Prof. A., Business Men's AI, Los Angeles.

VON WICHT, JOHN—*Painter, Gr., Des.*
  55 Middagh St., Brooklyn 1, N.Y.

B. Malente-Holstein, Germany, Feb. 3, 1888. *Studied*: Darmstadt-Bauhaus Sch.; Berlin Acad., Germany. *Member*:

Fed. Mod. P. & S.; Audubon A.; Am. Abstract A.; Brooklyn Soc. A.; Inst. Intl. des Arts et Lettres. *Awards*: prizes, Brooklyn Soc. A., 1945, 1948, 1950, 1952-1954, 1957; North Shore AA, 1951; Audubon A., 1952-1955, medal, 1958; BM, 1950, 1955, 1958; Phila. Pr. Cl., 1953 (purchase), 1954; SAGA, 1954; Riverside Mus., 1958; Boston A. Festival, 1958. *Work*: Nat. Mus., Stockholm; Musee Nationale d'Art Moderne, Paris; MMA; WMAA; LC; Riverside Mus.; PMA; Inst. Contemp. A., Boston; BM; Kansas State Col.; John Herron AI; CM; de Cordova & Dana Mus.; Univ. Illinois; Bradley Univ., and many others. Murals, mosaics, stained glass: in many cities of U.S. and Canada. *Exhibited*: nationally and internationally. One-man: Artists Gal., N.Y., 1944; Univ. Cal. at Los A., 1947; Mercer (Ga.) Univ.; Kleemann Gal., 1946, 1947; Passedoit Gal., N.Y., 1950-1952, 1954, 1956, 1957; John Herron AI, 1953; Carl Schurz Mem. Fnd., 1954, and others. *Positions*: Instr., Painting, ASL, 1951, 1952 (summers); color lithography, John Herron AI, Indianapolis, Ind., 1953.

von WIEGAND, CHARMION (Mrs. Joseph Freeman)— *Painter, W.*
301 East 38th St., New York 16, N.Y.

B. Chicago, Ill., Mar. 4, 1899. *Studied*: Barnard Col.; Columbia Univ.; N.Y. Univ. *Member*: Am. Abstract A. (Pres. 1952-53); Le Salon des Realites Nouvelles, Paris. *Exhibited*: MMA, 1951; WMAA, 1955; CGA, 1955, and in Paris, Rome, Copenhagen, Munich, Tokyo, Bochiem, Germany. One-man: Rose Fried Gal., 1947; Saidenberg Gal., 1952; John Heller Gal., 1956; Massillon Mus. A.; Akron AI; Dusanne Gal., Seattle, Wash., 1955. Contributor to Journal of Aesthetics; Yale Review; Encyclopaedia of Arts, and others.*

VORIS, MARK—Educator, P., Des., Eng., L.
2626 East Lee St., Tucson, Ariz.

B. Franklin, Ind., Sept. 20, 1907. *Studied*: Franklin Col.; AIC; Instituto Allende, Mexico; Univ. Arizona, and with Paul Dougherty. *Member*: Palette & Brush Cl.; Tucson FA Assn.; Ariz. Edu. Assn.; Ariz. A. Edu. Assn. *Awards*: prize, Arizona State Fair. *Exhibited*: Rockefeller Center, N.Y., 1938; Stanford Univ.; de Young Mem. Mus. Lectures on Development and Methods of Type Design & Casting. *Position*: Assoc. Prof., A. Dept., Col. FA, Univ. Arizona, Tucson, Ariz.

VORIS, MILLIE ROESGEN—Painter, W., L., T.
727 Lafayette Ave., Columbus, Ind.

B. Dudley Town, Ind., Aug. 23, 1859. *Studied*: with A. Berger, T. C. Steele, Jacob Cox, William Chase, & others. *Member*: Nat. Soc. A. & Let.; Chicago AC; Chicago AA; AFA; Palette Cl., Chicago. *Awards*: prize, Chicago World's Fair; Woman's Dept. Cl., 1948; Marshall Field, Chicago; O'Brien Galleries, Chicago; PMA; John Herron AI; Hoosier Salon; Fla. A. Cl., Miami, and many others. *Work*: Berlin A. Mus. *Exhibited*: Hoosier Salon; Chicago World's Fair; Pettis Gal., Indianapolis, Ind.; John Herron AI; Indiana AA; Block Auditorium, 1950; etc. Author: "Newspaper Jimmy."

VOTER, THOMAS W.—Museum Director
Hudson River Museum at Yonkers, Yonkers, N.Y.*

VOUTE, KATHLEEN—Painter, Des., I.
41 South Fullerton Ave., Montclair, N.J.

B. Montclair, N.J. *Studied*: Grand Central Sch. A.; George Pearse Ennis Sch. A. *Member*: AWS; New Jersey WC Soc. *Awards*: medals, Montclair A. Mus., 1932; AAPL, 1931, 1939. *Exhibited*: Riverside Mus., 1951; State Mus., Trenton, N.J., 1951; Montclair A. Mus., 1930-1941, 1951; AWS, 1928-1936, 1939, 1940; New Jersey WC Soc., 1939-1942, 1951-1957. I., "In Bible Days"; "Caroline"; "Whole World Singing"; "Zuska"; "Starboy"; "Hidden Garden"; "World Upside Down"; "A Wish for Lutie"; "Sod House Adventure"; "Coon Holler," and other books for children.

VUKOVIC, MARKO—Painter
Woodstock, N.Y.

B. Liska, Yugoslavia, Apr. 7, 1892. *Member*: AEA; Woodstock Gld. of A. & Crafts. *Awards*: prize, Woodstock AA, 1945; Twilight Park AA, 1954. *Work*: Willard Parker Hospital, East Harlem Youth Center, N.Y.; Newark Bd.

Edu.; State T. Col., New Paltz, N.Y.; Franklyn K. Lane H.S. Brooklyn; Wood A. Gal.; Biggs Mem. H.S.; Saugerties (N.Y.) Savings Bank. *Exhibited*: Newark Mus.; WMAA; PAFA; Syracuse Mus. FA; Albany Inst. Hist & A.; Rochester Mem. A. Gal.; Cornell Univ.; NAD.

WAAGE, FREDERICK O.—Educator
Goldwin Smith Hall, Cornell Univ.; h. 103 Comstock Rd., Ithaca, N.Y.

B. Philadelphia, Pa., Oct. 7, 1906. *Studied*: Univ. Pennsylvania, B.A.; Princeton Univ., M.A., M.F.A., Ph.D. *Member*: CAA; Archaeological Inst. Am. Author: Numismatic Notes and Monographs, No. 70, N.Y.; "Antioch on the Orontes," Vol. IV, Pt. 2, Princeton. Contributor to: American Journal Archaeology, Antiquity, Hesperia magazines. *Position*: Instr. Archaeology, 1935-38, Asst. Prof. Hist A. & Archaeology, 1938-41, Assoc. Prof. 1941-45, Prof., 1945- , Chm., Dept. FA, 1942- , Cornell Univ., Ithaca, N.Y. Visiting Lecturer in Art, Elmira College, Elmira, N.Y., 1952- .

WAANO-GANO, JOE—Painter, Des., I., W., L.
8926 Holly Place, Los Angeles 46, Cal.

B. Salt Lake City, Utah, Mar. 3, 1906. *Studied*: Univ. So. California; Los A. Acad. FA; Lukits Acad. FA; Hanson Puthuff Sch. FA. *Member*: AAPL; Soc. P. & S.; A. of the Southwest; Valley Prof. A. Gld.; Laguna Beach AA; Southwest AA; Cal. A. Cl. *Awards*: prizes, Kern County Fair, 1929; Gardena H.S., 1946; Hermosa, Cal., 1953; Soc. P. & S., Greek Theatre, Los A., 1953, 1954, 1956, 1958; A. of the Southwest, 1953, 1954, med., 1955, 1958; Friday Morning Cl., 1954-1957; medals, Chicago, 1933; Indian Center, Los A., 1953-1956; Madonna Festival, Los A., 1952; med., Cal. A. Cl., 1958; special award, Intl. Flower Show, 1957. *Work*: Gardena H. S.; murals, Los A. General Hospital; Sherman Indian Inst., Riverside, Cal.; Western Airlines Offices, San F.; Rapid City, S.D. *Exhibited*: Nationally and internationally. One-man: Los A. Mus. A., 1940; Los A. City Col., 1941; Southwest Mus., Los A., 1943, 1946, 1951, 1955; Havenstrite FA Gal., 1945, 1953, 1958; La Casa, Beverly Hills, 1948; Walt Disney Studio Gal., Burbank, 1951; Woman's Cl. of Hollywood, 1952, 1956; Glendale Lib., 1952; Bowers Mem. Mus., 1943; Mt. San Antonio Col., 1953; Tuesday Cl., Glendale, 1954, 1957; Univ. Cl., Los. A., 1954; Mt. View Gal., Altadena, 1955; Intl. Flower Show, 1957. Lectures: Art of the American Indian; Mural and 3D Painting. Author: "Southwestern Indian Art"; four "How Come" books for children; "Swift Eagle" (all illustrated). Des., Indian Council Fire Honor Award, presented annually since 1933 to "Greatest Living American Indian." *Position*: Bd. Dir., Soc. P. & S.; Dir., Art Section, Cal. Intl. Flower Show, Inglewood, Cal.

WADE, CLAIRE E. (Mrs.)—Painter, T.
7924 211th St., Oakland Gardens 64, N.Y.

B. Ossining, N.Y., Jan. 18, 1899. *Studied*: N.Y. Univ., B.S. in Edu.; & with Jerry Farnsworth, Umberto Romano. *Member*: NAWA. *Awards*: prizes, A. Lg. of Long Island, 1949; Farnsworth Sch. A., Sarasota, Fla. *Exhibited*: NAWA, 1943-1946; AWCS, 1943; Brooklyn SA, 1945-1946; Sarasota SA, 1942; Knickerbocker A., 1953, 1954; All. A. Am. 1943, 1944, 1950.*

WADE, JEAN ELIZABETH (Mrs. Emil J. Frey)— *Painter, I.*
61 Pinewood Trail, Trumbull 58, Conn.

B. Bridgeport, Conn., Mar. 17, 1910. *Studied*: Yale Univ., B.F.A. *Member*: Nat. Lg. Am. Pen Women. *Awards*: prizes, CAA, 1931; Bridgeport A. Lg., 1945, 1955; Nat. Lg. Am. Pen Women, 1953-1955; Contemp. A. & Crafts, 1953; Silvermine Gld. A., 1955; Mystic AA, 1955. *Exhibited*: Audubon A., 1945; NAWA, 1945, 1946; New Haven Paint & Clay Cl., 1945, 1948; Bridgeport A. Lg., 1945, 1946; Silvermine Gld. A., 1945, 1946, 1956; Nat. Lg. Am. Pen Women, 1950, 1952-1955; Chautauqua Exh., 1958; 2-man: Little Studio, N.Y., 1956.

WADE, ROBERT—Painter, T.
18 Allen St., Bradford (Haverhill), Mass.

B. Haverhill, Mass., Oct. 30, 1882. *Studied*: Eric Pape Sch. A., and in Europe. *Work*: alter panels. St. Mary of Redford, Detroit, Mich.; St. James Church, Woonsocket, R.I.; murals, Boston Univ. Sch. Theology; Shove Mem. Chapel, Colorado College, Colorado Springs; Emanuel

Church, Newport, R.I.; Lincoln Sch., La Junta, Colo.; des. for memorial window at Bradford Jr. College. *Exhibited*: nationally. *Position*: Hd. A. Dept., Pueblo Jr. Col., Pueblo, Colo., 1937-38; Dir. A., Hd. A. Dept., Bradford Jr. Col., Bradford, Mass. 1939-53.

WADSWORTH, CHARLES E.—*Painter*
27 Gibson St., Cambridge, Mass.

B. Ridgewood, N.J., Mar. 3, 1917. *Studied*: ASL. *Member*: AEA; Cambridge AA. *Awards*: prize, Jordan-Marsh Co., Boston, 1951; Boston A. Festival, 1953; Cambridge AA, 1955. *Work*: Federal Hospital, Carville, La.; WMA; Munson-Williams-Proctor Inst.; Am. Inst. A. & Let. (presented to Allentown AA). *Exhibited*: deCordova and Dana Mus., Lincoln Mass., 1951; Butler AI, 1951; NGA, 1941; CMA; Detroit Inst. A.; WMAA, 1955; PAFA, 1951; Boston Soc. Indp. A.; BMFA; Farnsworth Mus.; Currier Gal. A.; Berkshire Mus.; Fitchburg A. Center; Wadsworth Atheneum; CGA, 1955.

WADSWORTH, FRANCES L(AUGHLIN) (Mrs. R. H.)—*Sculptor*
"Mulgrave," Day St., Granby 1, Conn.

B. Buffalo, N.Y., June 11, 1909. *Studied*: Albright A. Sch.; in Italy and France and with Gutzon Borglum, Charles Tefft, John Effl, Antoinette Hollister. *Member*: Nat. Lg. Am. Pen Women (New England Regional A. Chm.); Conn. Acad. FA; Hartford A. Cl. (Pres.). *Awards*: prizes, Nat. Lg. Am. Pen Women, 1956, 1958. *Work*: sc. portraits, Univ. Virginia; Kingswood Sch., Hartford; American Sch. for the Deaf, West Hartford; garden sc., Inst. of Living, Hartford; St. Catherine's Sch., Richmond, Va.; monuments, Thomas Hooker Monument, Hartford; Gallaudet Monument; mural, Institute of Living. *Exhibited*: Nat. Lg. Am. Pen Women, 1956, 1958; Conn. Acad. FA, 1930, 1931, 1932, 1956, 1957, 1958; Hartford Soc. Women Painters, 1930, 1931, 1932, 1956-1958. Demonstrations and lectures on sculpture techniques. *Position*: Instr., S., Drawing, Painting, The Institute of Living, Hartford, Conn., 1930-1958.

WAGNER, S. PETER—*Painter, Et., T.*
1120 Rockville Pike, Rockville, Md.

B. Rockville, Md., May 19, 1878. *Studied*: ASL; Corcoran Sch. A.; Grande Chaumiere, Paris; & with Paul Pascall. *Member*: Soc. Wash. A.; SSAL; Landscape Cl., Wash.; Wash. WC Cl.; AWCS; Sc; Soc. Four A., Palm Beach, Fla.; St. Petersburg AC; Balt. WC Cl. *Awards*: prizes, Fla. Fed. A., 1928, 1931, 1932; med., Landscape Cl., Wash., D.C., 1943, 1945.*

WAHL, BERNHARD O.—*Painter*
4005 Seventh Ave., Brooklyn 32, N.Y.

B. Lardal, Norway, Nov. 8, 1888. *Studied*: Acad. A., Oslo, Norway. *Member*: Norwegian A. & Crafts Cl., Brooklyn, N.Y. (Co-founder, Pres.); Brooklyn Soc. A.; New Jersey P. & S. Soc. *Exhibited*: BM, 1943-1951; Riverside Mus., 1947, 1949-1950; Vendome Gal., 1942; Staten Island Inst. A. & Sc., 1942, 1947; Jersey City Mus., 1947; Pan-American Gal., N.Y., 1945; Argent Gal., 1948; Hofstra Col., 1945; Long Island A. Festival, 1946, and others.

WAHL, THEODORE—*Lithographer*
R.D. #1, Milford, N.J.

B. Dillon, Kansas. *Studied*: Univ. Kansas; Kansas City AI; and with Bolton Brown. *Member*: Delaware Valley AA; Hunterdon County A. Center. *Awards*: medal, Midwestern A. Exh., 1933. *Work*: Brooklyn Pub. Lib.; Hunter Col.; Univ. Louisiana; Univ. Wisconsin; N.Y. Pub. Lib.; Smithsonian Inst.; Princeton Pr. Cl.; Newark Mus. A. *Exhibited*: CM, 1950-1952; Midwestern A. Ex., 1932-1936; Grant Studio, 1937-1939; Contemp. A., 1938; Indiana Mus. Mod. A., 1940; New Hope, Pa., 1949-1956; Delaware Valley AA, 1946-1958; Newark A. Fair, 1940; SAGA, 1953; Hunterdon A. Center, 1953-1958. *Position*: Instr., Riegel Ridge, Milford, N.J., 1947-57.

WAHLERT, ERNST HENRY—*Sculptor, P., T.*
2408 Fairmount St., Dallas, Tex.; h. 1800 Linden Drive, Denton, Tex.

B. St. Louis, Mo., Feb. 11, 1920. *Studied*: Va. Military Inst., B.A.; Southern Methodist Univ., M.A.; Temple

Univ., M.F.A., and with Boris Blai, Raphael Sabatini, Raoul Josset, and others. *Work*: mural, President's Hall, Tyler Sch. FA, Phila., Pa.; ports. in private colls. *Exhibited*: Tyler Sch. FA Alumni exhs.; N.Y. Coliseum, 1956. Author, I., instruction manual, "Technique of Making Rubber Molds of Sculptural Works," 1953-54. *Position*: Instr., A. Edu., Grand Prairie, Tex., Pub. Schs. (4 yrs.); Dallas Pub. Schs. (2 yrs.); North Texas State College, (3 yrs.)

WAITE, EMILY BURLING (Mrs. Emily Burling Waite Manchester)—*Painter, Et., L.*

B. Worcester, Mass., July 12, 1887. *Studied*: WMASch.; ASL; BMFA Sch.; & with F. Luis Mora, Frank DuMond, Philip Hale, & others. *Member*: North Shore AA; NAWA; SAGA; Gld. Boston A; Am. Veterans Soc. A.; AAPL; Worcester Gld. A. & Craftsmen; SAGA; Chicago SE; Boston Soc. A. & Crafts; Lg. Am. Pen Women. *Awards*: traveling scholarship, BMFA Sch.; award of merit, Am. Veteran's Soc. A., 1955; silver medal, Pan-Pacific Exp., 1915; prizes, Lg. Am. Pen Women. *Work*: Clark Univ., Worcester, Mass.; Tufts Col., Medford, Mass.; BMFA; Smithsonian Inst.; MMA; FMA; Episcopal Theological Sch., Cambridge, Mass. *Exhibited*: CGA; PAFA; NAD; SAGA; 1946; Chicago SE, 1945; Worcester County A., 1945; North Shore AA, 1946, 1955, 1958; Newport AA, 1946, 1955; Boston Soc. A. & Crafts; AAPL, 1958; Worcester Gld. A. & Craftsmen, 1958; one-man: Gld. Boston A., 1955, 1957, 1958; SAGA, 1955, 1958; Chicago, Ill., 1955, NAWA. Lectures: Mechanics of Etching; History of Etching.

WAKEFIELD, RUTH CRAVATH. See Cravath, Ruth

WALCOTT, ANABEL H. (Mrs. H. M.)—*Painter*
720 Adella Ave., Coronado, Cal.

B. Franklin County, Ohio. *Studied*: ASL; Chase Sch. A.; & in France, Holland. *Awards*: prize, NAD. *Exhibited*: PAFA; AIC; NAD; Paris Salon; St. Louis Exp.

WALD, SYLVIA—*Painter, Ser.*
405 East 54th St., New York 22, N.Y.

B. Philadelphia, Pa., Oct. 30, 1914. *Studied*: Moore Inst. A. *Member*: AEA; Nat. Ser. Soc.; AFA. *Awards*: prizes, MMoDA, 1941; LC, 1944; NAWA, 1949; Serigraph Gal., 1948, 1949, 1950; BM, 1951, 1954 (purchase). *Work*: Howard Univ.; Allen R. Hite Mus.; J. B. Speed Mem. Mus.; Ball State T. Col.; Assn. Univ. Women; N.Y. Pub. Lib.; MMA; Princeton Univ.; Univ. Nebraska; Munson-Williams-Proctor Inst.; Nat. Gallery, Canada; Univ. Iowa; U.S. State Dept.; PMA; MMoDA; BM; U.S. Army; LC. *Exhibited*: Carnegie Inst., 1941; WMAA, 1941, 1950, 1955; PMA, 1941; AIC, 1941; PMG, 1942; MMA, 1942, 1953; PAFA, 1949; MMoDA, 1941; BM, 1949-1952, 1958; LC, 1952; Univ. Chile, 1950; Smithsonian Inst., 1954; Univ. So. California, 1953, 1954; Japan, Germany, Austria, 1950-51; Norway, 1951; Israel, 1949; Salzburg, 1952; The Hague and Amsterdam, Holland; Switzerland, 1953; France, 1954; Italy, 1955; Sao Paulo Brazil, 1954; MMA European traveling exh., 1955-56; Univ. Illinois, 1958; Mexico City, 1958; "American Prints Today," European traveling exh., 1957-58; one-man: ACA Gal., 1939; Univ. Louisville, 1945; Kent State Col., 1954; Serigraph Gal., 1946, 1951; Allen Hite Mus., 1948; Grand Central Moderns, 1957, and numerous traveling exhibitions.

WALDREN, WILLIAM—*Painter, C.*
SA Torrenterra, Deya, Mallorca, Spain

B. New York, N.Y., Feb. 5, 1924. *Studied*: ASL; Acad. Julian, Paris, France, and in Spain. *Member*: ASL. *Awards*: purchase award, Bordighera, Italy, 1955; Audubon A., 1956. *Work*: Mus. A. Bordighera, Italy. *Exhibited*: MMA, 1952; Italy, 1953, 1955; Sarasota AA, 1952; Audubon A., 1955; Staten Island Inst. A. & Sc., 1955; Am. Painters in France, 1953; one-man: Galerie Craven, Paris, France.*

WALDRON, JAMES M. K.—*Museum Curator, P., T.*
Reading Museum and Art Gallery, 500 Museum Road, Reading, Pa.; h. 23 South 7th Ave., West Reading, Pa.

B. Hazleton, Pa., Sept. 3, 1909. *Studied*: Kutztown State T. Col., B.S; Tyler Sch FA, Temple Univ., M.F.A.

Member: Eastern AA; NAA; NEA; Pa. State Edu. Assn.
Work: Reading Mus. & A. Gal.; mural, Baptist Church,
Reading. *Exhibited*: Berks A. All., 1948, 1957 (both one-
man); Kutztown State T. Col.; Reading Mus. & A. Gal.
A. Ed., of the Pa. Art Education Bulletins, 1955, Harris-
burg; Illus. for the Berks County Historical Review.
Lectures: History of Painting. Arranged 31 regional, an-
nual exhibitions for Reading Museum and Berks County.
Positions: A. T. & Supv., West Reading School Dist.,
22 yrs.; part-time instr., Kutztown State T. Col., 8 yrs.;
Cur. Fine Arts, Reading Museum & Art Gallery, Reading,
Pa., at present.

WALKER, GENE ALDEN—*Painter*
   20 East 65th St., New York 21, N.Y.; h. Liberty St.,
   Warren, Pa.

Studied: PIASch.; NAD, and with Charles Hawthorne,
Jerry Farnsworth. *Member*: NAC; NAWA; Pen & Brush
Cl.; Audubon A.; All.A.Am. *Awards*: prizes, NAWA,
1943, 1946; NAD, 1943; Bridgeport, Conn., 1942, 1945;
Butler AI, 1948, 1949; Pen & Brush Cl., 1949, 1953; All.
A. Am., 1946; John Herron AI, 1950, 1951; medal, All.
A. Am., 1944. *Work*: Montgomery Mus. FA; NAD. *Ex-
hibited*: NAD; All. A. Am.; Pen & Brush Cl.; Phila. WC
Cl.; NAC; NAWA; Carnegie Inst.; Butler AI; I., "Range
Plant Handbook" (U.S. Dept. Agriculture), 1937.

WALKER, HUDSON D.—*Art Specialist*
   18 East 48th St., New York 17, N.Y.; h. 40 Deepdene
   Rd., Forest Hills 75, N.Y.

B. Minneapolis, Minn., June 17, 1907. *Studied*: Univ.
Minnesota; FMA, Harvard Univ. *Positions*: Dir., Marsden
Hartley Exh. MModA, 1944; Selected Annual Exh. Con-
temporary American Paintings, Walker A. Center, 1943,
1944, 1946; Pres., AFA, 1945-48, Trustee, 1944- ; Chm.
Exec. Com., Comm. for a N.Y. State Art Program, 1946;
Treas., Artist's Com., Nat. Council of Am-Soviet Friend-
ship, 1944-47; Member, U.S. Nat. Comm. for UNESCO,
1946-48; Exec. Dir., Artist's Equity, N.Y., 1947-51; Exec.
Dir., Artist's Equity Fund, 1951- . Treas. & Trustee, Print
Council of America; Pres., IGAS; Trustee & V.Pres.,
Chrysler A. Mus., Provincetown, Mass.; Chm., AFA 50th
Anniversary Development Committee; V.Pres., Friends of
the Whitney Mus. Am. A.; V.Pres., Municipal Art Soc.,
N.Y.C.

WALKER, JAMES ADAMS—*Teacher, P., W.*
   Public Schools and Mott Foundation, Flint, Mich.;
   h. Route #1, Box 420, Richland, Mich.

B. Connersville, Ind., Jan. 24, 1925. *Studied*: Western
Mich. Univ., B.S.; Columbia Univ., M.A.; Arch. Sch.,
Univ Mich.; East Carolina Col. *Member*: AEA; Mich.
WC Soc.; Mich. Edu. Assn.; Flint Inst. A. *Awards*:
prizes, Piedmont Festival, Winston-Salem, N.C., 1950; Va.-
N.C. Exh., 1952; North Carolina State A. Soc., 1954;
North Carolina A. Exh., 1954, 1955; Flint Inst. A., 1958.
Exhibited: Va-N.C. Artists, 1950-1953; Huckleberry Moun-
tain, 1950; North Carolina Artists, 1950-1952, 1954; South-
eastern AA, 1951, 1952; Mich. WC Soc., 1952; Wash.
WC Cl., 1953, 1954, 1956; Creative Gal., N.Y., 1953;
Kalamazoo Inst. A., 1954; Caravan Gal., N.Y., 1956; "30
North Carolina Artists," Clinton Court Gal., N.Y., 1956;
Scarab Cl., Detroit, 1957; Flint Inst. A., 1957, 1958; one-
man: State A. Gal., Raleigh; Norfolk Mus. A., 1958.
Green Gal.; Peace Col., Raleigh; Belhaven, N.C. Contributor
to North Carolina Education; School Arts magazine;
Raleigh News & Observer. *Positions*: Cr., T., East Carolina Col., A. Consultant, Greenville, N.C., Pub. Schs.,
1949-55; T., Northern H.S., Adult A. Edu., Mott Foundation, Flint, Mich., 1956- .

WALKER, JOHN—*Museum Director*
   National Gallery of Art, Constitution Ave. at 6th St.;
   h. 2806 N. St., Northwest, Washington, D.C.

B. Pittsburgh, Pa., Dec. 24, 1906. *Studied*: Harvard Univ.,
A.B.; Tufts Univ. *Awards*: John Harvard Fellow, Harvard
Univ., 1930-1931; Hon. D.F.A., Tufts Univ., 1958. Co-
Author: "Great American Paintings from Smibert to
Bellows," 1943; "Masterpieces of Painting from the Na-
tional Gallery of Art," 1944; "Great Paintings from the
National Gallery of Art," 1952; Author: "Paintings from
America," 1951 (Spanish, 1954); "Bellini and Titian at
Farrara," 1956. Contributor to Gazette des Beaux-Arts,
National Geographic magazines. *Positions*: Assoc. in charge,
Dept. FA, Am. Acad. in Rome, 1935-39; Trustee, Am.

Acad. in Rome; AFA; Trustee, Nat. Trust; Trustee, the
Andrew Mellon Educational & Charitable Trust; Visiting
Com. of Dumbarton Oaks; Adv. Council for Col. Liberal
Arts, Univ. Notre Dame; Accessions Com. of the Nat.
Trust for Hist. Preservation; Art Com., of New York
Hospital; Chief Cur., 1939-56, Dir., 1956- , National
Gallery of Art, Washington, D.C.

WALKER, MARIAN (BLAKESLEE)—
   Craftsman, P., Des., L.
   5829 McGee St., Kansas City 2, Mo.

B. Rock Island, Ill., Jan. 29, 1898. *Studied*: Kansas City
AI; Chicago Acad. FA; AIC, and with Wilomovsky, An-
garola, Rosenbauer, Kopietz, Robinson, and others. *Mem-
ber*: Mid-Am. A.; Kansas City AI Alum. *Awards*: prizes,
Kansas City AI, 1925; Missouri State Fair, 1930; Topeka,
Kans., 1936. *Work*: Scarritt Sch., Kansas City; numerous
murals in private homes. Specializes in Tole ware. *Ex-
hibited*: Midwestern A. Exh., 1926-1936; Kansas City Soc.
A., 1926-1936; Mid-Am. A., 1951; All-Am. Women's Exh.,
Topeka, 1936. Contributor of articles on Tole ware to
House Beautiful, House & Gardens, and other national
magazines. Lectures on Decorative Art; Color & Design;
Tole. *Position*: Pres., Marian Walker, Inc., Kansas City,
Mo., 1941- .

WALKER, MORT—*Cartoonist*
   Greenwich, Conn.

B. Eldorado, Kans., Sept. 3, 1923. *Studied*: Missouri Univ.,
A.B.; Washington Univ., St. Louis. *Member*: Nat. Cartoonists Soc.; A. & Writers Assn. *Exhibited*: MMA, 1951.
Awards: Billy De Beck award, Nat Cartoonists Soc.,
1953; Banshee award, 1955 as "Outstanding Cartoonist of
the Year." I., many cartoons in book collections, text
and humor anthologies. Creator, I., "Beetle Bailey"; 'Hi
and Lois," King Features Syndicate.

WALKER, ROBERT MILLER—*Educator*
   212 Elm Ave., Swarthmore, Pa.

B. Flushing, N.Y., Dec. 10, 1908. *Studied*: Princeton
Univ., B.A., M.F.A.; Harvard Univ., Ph.D. *Member*:
CAA; Soc. Arch. Historians (Treas.); Phila. Pr. Cl. (Vice-
Pres); Am. Archaeological Soc.; Print Council of Am. (Bd.
Dirs.). Contributor to Art Bulletin. *Position*: Instr., Wil-
liams Col., Williamstown, Mass., 1936-38; Prof. FA, Chm.,
FA Dept., Swarthmore Col., Pa., 1941- .

WALKER, SYBIL (Mrs. A. S.)—*Painter*
   920 5th Ave., New York 21, N.Y.

B. New York, N.Y., 1882. *Member*: NAWA. *Work*: BM;
Parrish Mus., Southampton, N.Y.; Tate Gal., London.
England. *Exhibited*: Detroit Inst. A.; AIC; St. Louis
World's Fair; Marie Sterner Gal.; Knoedler Gal.; Parrish
Mus., Southampton, L.I., N.Y.; AFA traveling exh.*

WALKEY, FREDERICK P.—*Museum Director*
   De Cordova Museum, Sandy Pond Road; h. South
   Great Road, Lincoln, Mass.

B. Belmont, Mass., May 29, 1922. *Studied*: Duke Univ.;
BMFA Sch. A.; Tufts Col., B.S. in Ed. *Member*: AAMus.
Position: Exec. Dir., De Cordova Museum, Lincoln, Mass.

WALKINSHAW, JEANIE WALTER (Mrs. Robert)—
   Painter, I.
   936 12th Ave., North, Seattle 2, Wash.

B. Baltimore, Md. *Studied*: with Edwin Whiteman, Rene
Menard, Lucien Simon, Paris; Robert Henri, N.Y. *Mem-
ber*: Portraits', Inc.; Women Painters of Wash.; Nat. Lg.
Am. Pen Women. *Work*: Temple of Justice, Olympia,
Wash.; Univ. Washington, Seattle; Seattle Hist. Soc.;
Diocesan House, St. Mark's Cathedral, Seattle; Children's
Orthopedic Hospital, Seattle. I., "On Puget Sound," 1929.

WALKOWITZ, ABRAHAM—*Painter, Gr., I.*
   1469 53rd St., Brooklyn 19, N.Y.

B. Tumen, Russia, Mar. 28, 1880. *Studied*: NAD; Julian
Acad., Paris, France. *Work*: BM; MMA; AGAA; PMA;
Kalamazoo Inst. A.; Lib. Cong.; N.Y. Pub. Lib.; WMAA;
BMFA; Newark Mus.; Columbus Gal. FA; PMG; MModA;
etc. *Exhibited*: nationally. Author: "Isadora Duncan";
"From the Objective to the Non-Objective," 1945. *Posi-
tion*: Dir., V.Pres., Soc. Indp. A., New York, N.Y.

WALLACE, DAVID HAROLD—Historian, Mus. Cur.
Independence National Historical Park, 420 Chestnut
St. (6); h. 5351 Wingohocking Terr., Philadelphia
44, Pa.

B. Baltimore, Md., Dec. 24, 1926. *Studied*: Lebanon
Valley Col., B.A.; Columbia Univ., M.A.; and additional
grad. study at Edinburgh Univ., and Columbia Univ.
Member: Soc. American Historians; Am. Assn. for State
& Local History. Co-author (with George C. Groce):
The New York Historical Society's "Dictionary of Ar-
tists in America, 1564-1860," 1957. *Positions*: Asst. Editor,
New York Hist. Soc., 1952-56; Museum Curator, Inde-
pendence National Historical Park, in charge of Inde-
pendence Hall Collection of Historical Portraits by Peale,
Sharples, and others, 1958- .

**WALLACE, LUCY (Mrs. Lucy Wallace de Lagerberg)
—Painter, C., Des., T.**
Wading River, L.I., N.Y.

B. Montclair, N.J. *Studied*: N.Y. Sch. F. & App. A.;
ASL; & with Kenneth Hayes Miller, John R. Koopman.
Member: Boston Soc. A. & Crafts. *Awards*: prize, New
Haven Paint & Clay Cl., 1923. *Exhibited*: CGA; CAM;
AWCS; Montclair A. Mus.; Phila. WC Cl.; Paris Salon;
Gld. Hall, Easthampton, N.Y.; Suffolk Mus., Stoney
Brook, L.I.; Parrish Mus. A., 1957, 1958.

WALLEEN, HANS AXEL—Painter, I.
William Esty Co., 100 East 42nd St., New York,
N.Y.; h. Lower Shad Road, Pound Ridge, N.Y.

B. Malmo, Sweden, Feb. 15, 1902. *Studied*: PIASch.
Member: AWS; SC; SI; Silvermine Gld. A. *Exhibited*:
AWS, 1951-1958; SC, annually; Swedish-American Exhs.,
Chicago; Silvermine Gld. A. Illus., Junior Literary Guild
edition of "Nuvat, the Brave"; "All American." *Position*:
Adv. A., William Esty Co., New York, N.Y., 1943- .

WALLING, ANNA M.—Craftsman, P., Des., T., L.
17 Robert St., Middletown, N.Y.

B. Warwick, N.Y. *Studied*: New York, N.Y.; and in
England, France and Germany. *Work*: Escutcheons, Dutch
Reform Church, New Paltz, N.Y.; and in Mexico; Holly-
wood; Kansas City, Mo.; Australia and in many states
of the U.S. *Exhibited*: MMA; Am. Mus. Natural Hist.;
Newark Mus. A.; Syracuse, N.Y., and many others.*

WALMSLEY, ELIZABETH (Mrs.)—Educator, Lith., Ser.
Art Department, Southern Methodist University; h.
5525 Edlen Road, Dallas 20, Tex.

B. Barberton, Ohio. *Studied*: Washington Univ., B. Arch.;
Texas Women's Univ., M.A.; Bethany Col.; St. Louis
Sch. FA; Colorado Springs FA Center. *Member*: Assoc.
Women in Arch.; Texas Pr. M.; Craft Gld. of Dallas;
AAUP. *Awards*: prizes, Texas FA Soc.; Dallas Pr. Soc.;
Southwestern Print Annual. *Exhibited*: in Southwestern
Print Exhs. Lectures: Contemporary Art; Modern In-
teriors. *Position*: Prof., Elem. Des., Int. Des., Hist. of
Art, Southern Methodist Univ.; Chm. Dept. A., 1956- ,
Dallas, Tex.

WALSER, FLOYD N.—Etcher, P.
76 Lake Ave., Framingham, Mass.

B. Winchester, Tex., Jan. 29, 1888. *Studied*: BMFA Sch.;
& with Plowman. *Member*: Southern Pr.M. *Exhibited*:
SAGA; CMA; Southern Pr.M. traveling exh.

WALSH, NOEMI M.—Craftsman, T.
1931 Bellevue Ave., Richmond Heights 17, Mo.

B. St. Louis, Mo., July 3, 1896. *Studied*: Washington
Univ., St. Louis, Mo. *Work*: various commissions in
jewelry & silversmithing, including Chancellor's medallion,
Washington Univ.; pins, Alton Mem. Hospital, Alton,
Ill. *Exhibited*: St. Louis A. Gld.; Wichita, Kans.; Noonan-
Kocian Gal.; CAM; Des-Craftsmen, 1953. *Position*: Instr.
Jewelry & Silversmithing, Washington Univ., St. Louis,
Mo., 1928-58; Univ. Col., St. Louis, Mo., 1942-58.

WALTER, VALERIE HARRISSE—Sculptor
202 East 31st St., Baltimore 18, Md.

B. Baltimore, Md. *Studied*: with Ephraim Keyser, Augustus Lukeman. *Awards*: prize, CGA, 1934. *Work*: CGA;

Unitarian Church, Baltimore; Baltimore Zoo; Aeronautical Ministry, Rome, Italy. *Exhibited*: NSS; NAD; Paris
Salon; CGA; BMA; PAFA; Detroit Inst. A.; SFMA.

WALTER, WILLIAM F.—Painter, T.
3027 Newark St., Northwest, Washington 8, D.C.

B. Washington, D.C., Jan. 2, 1904. *Studied*: Corcoran
Sch. A.; and with Charles Hawthorne, W. Lester Stevens,
Richard Meryman. *Member*: Soc. Wash. A.; Landscape
Cl., Wash., D.C.; Wash. A. Cl.; Am. Polar Soc. *Awards*:
prizes, Landscape Cl., 1939, 1941, 1953, 1955, 1957; U.S.
Nat. Mus., 1939, 1954. *Exhibited*: one-man: New York
City; Harvard Univ.; Univ. Iowa; Wash. A. Cl., and in
museums of the East and South. *Work*: Arctic paintings
for the U.S. Navy, 1946. *Position*: Instr., Abbott Sch. A.,
Wash., D.C., 1951-54.

**WALTERS, DORIS LAWRENCE (Mrs.)—
Painter, Comm. A.**
48 Vesta Circle, Melbourne, Fla.

B. Sandersville, Ga., Nov. 20, 1920. *Studied*: Washington
Sch. A. *Member*: Melbourne AA; Fla. Fed. A. *Awards*:
Melbourne AA, 1954 (purchase), 1955. Contributor to
Melbourne, Fla. Daily Times.*

WALTERS, EMILE—Painter, T.
Lythend Farm, R.F.D. 2, Poughkeepsie, N.Y.

B. Winnipeg, Canada, Jan. 31, 1893. *Studied*: AIC; PAFA;
Tiffany Fnd. *Member*: Tiffany Fnd. AC *Awards*: prizes,
AIC, 1918, 1919; NAD, 1923; decoration, Order of the
Falcon, King Christian, Denmark, 1939. *Work*: Smith-
sonian Inst.; Phila. AC; 100 Friends of Art, Pittsburgh,
Pa.; Mus. FA of Houston; Heckscher Mus. FA; Mus.
A., Saskatoon, Canada; FMA; Glasgow (Scotland) A.
Gal.; Grainger Mus., Melbourne, Australia; Mus. of
Rouen, France; BM; SAM; Vanderpoel Coll.; Winnipeg
(Can.) Mus. FA; Luxembourg Mus., Paris; Mun. Gal.
Mod. A., Dublin, Ireland; Nat. Mus., Helsinki, Finland;
Mus. of Iceland, Reykjavik; Pomona Col., Claremont,
Cal.; Palace Legion Honor; Newark Mus.; Los A. Mus.
A.; Fleming Mus.; Mus. New Mexico, Santa Fe; Spring-
field (Ill.) Mus. A.; SAM; Springville, Utah; NCFA;
Theodore Roosevelt Assn.; United Nations Coll.; FMA;
Univ. Mus., Bangkok, Thailand. *Exhibited*: nationally &
internationally.*

WALTON, EDWARD AUSTIN—Educator, Des., P.
Moore Institute of Art, Board & Master Sts. (21);
h. 2310 Pine St., Philadelphia 3, Pa.

B. Haddonfield, N.J., July 11, 1896. *Studied*: PMSch A.,
B.F.A. *Member*: Phila. WC Cl.; Assoc., AID. Lectures:
History of Furniture. *Position*: Dir., Interior Des. Dept.,
Moore Inst. A., Philadelphia, Pa.

**WALTON, MARION (Mrs. Marion Walton Putnam)—
Sculptor**
49 Irving Pl., New York 3, N.Y.

B. New Rochelle, N.Y., Nov. 19, 1899. *Studied*: ASL;
Grande Chaumiere, Paris, with Antoine Bourdelle; Bor-
glum Sch. Sculpture. *Member*: S. Gld.; AEA. *Work*:
Univ. Nebraska; WFNY, 1939. *Exhibited*: WMAA; MMA;
MModA; BM; Newark Mus.; AIC; BMA; WMA; Wash.
D.C.; SFMA; San Diego, Cal.; Lincoln, Neb.; Paris,
France; PAFA; Carnegie Inst.; Weyhe Gal. (one-man);
Dallas Mus. FA; Los A. Mus. A.; Paris, France.

WALTRIP, MILDRED—Painter, Gr., Des., I.
210 Sixth Ave., New York 14, N.Y.

B. Nebo, Ky., Oct. 4, 1911. *Studied*: AIC; Northwestern
Univ.; N.Y. Univ., Sch. Edu.; & with Moholy-Nagy,
Alexander Archipenko, Fernand Leger. *Member*: NSMP;
Intl. Soc. General Semantics. *Awards*: Raymond F., AIC,
1933. *Work*: murals, Oak Park (Ill.) Pub. Sch.; Chicago
Park Bd., Administration Bldg.; Cook County Hospital,
Chicago; Scott Field, Belleville, Ill. *Exhibited*: AIC, 1935;
Phila. A. All.; Phila. Pr. Cl., 1950; SAGA, 1951; Los
A. Mus. A. I., "Guide Book to Cairo, Illinois," 1950-58;
science textbooks, "Science for Better Living" (5 books);
"Exploring Physics," 1952, rev. 1959; "The Physical
World," 1958; "New World of Chemistry," 1955; chil-
dren's books: "The First Book of Submarines," 1957;
"The First Book of The Earth," 1958.

WALZER, MARJORIE SCHAFER—Painter, C.

18 Dogwood Lane, Westport, Conn.

B. New York, N.Y., July 3, 1912. *Studied*: ASL, with Kuniyoshi, Bouche, and others; Silvermine Gld. A., with Albert Jacobson, Julius Schmidt. *Member*: Silvermine Gld. A.; Conn. Crafts; N.Y. Soc. Ceramic A. *Exhibited*: PAFA, 1943; Montclair A. Mus., 1943; WMA, 1955; N.Y. Ceramic A., 1955; Silvermine Gld. A., 1955; Conn. Crafts, 1954; Smithsonian Inst. traveling exh., 1955-56.

WANDS, ALFRED J.—Painter, Lith., T., L.

2065 Ivanhoe St., Denver 7, Colo.

B. Cleveland, Ohio, Feb. 19, 1904. *Studied*: Cleveland Sch. A.; Julian Acad., Paris; John Huntington Inst.; Western Reserve Univ., B.S. *Member*: Denver A. Gld.; Ohio WC Soc.; Carmel AA; Chicago Galleries Assn.; AAPL. *Awards*: prizes, Paris Salon, 1936; CMA, 1923-1930; Palace Legion Honor, 1932; Denver Art Mus., 1932, 1945-1951; Med., Kansas City AI; 1934; Denver A. Gld., 1958. *Work*: BM; CMA; Palace Legion Honor; Cleveland Pub. Sch.; Denver Pub. Sch.; Denver A. Mus.; murals, Colo. Woman's Col.; Methodist Church, Sterling, Colo. *Exhibited*: Carnegie Inst., 1928; PAFA, 1924, 1926, 1928, 1932, 1934; WFNY 1939; AIC, 1934, 1954; CGA, 1935; CMA, 1923-1937, 1939, 1940; Kansas City AI, 1930-1934; Denver A. Mus., 1931-1951, 1953, 1954; Mus. FA of Houston, 1950, 1951; Denver Mus. Natural Hist., 1951 (one-man); San F. AA, 1950-1952. *Position*: Instr., Cleveland Inst. A., 1925-30; CMA, 1927-30; Colorado Women's Col., 1930-47; Fndr., T., Wands A. Sch., Estes Park, Colo., 1947- .

WANKELMAN, WILLARD F.—Educator

Bowling Green State University, Bowling Green, Ohio

Position: Chm., Art Department, Bowling Green State University.*

WANKER, MAUDE WALLING—

Painter, T., Mus. Dir., L.

P.O. Box 63, Wecoma Beach, Ore.

B. Oswego, Ore., Oct. 22, 1882. *Studied*: Univ. Oregon; AIC; Portland A. Mus. Sch. *Member*: Lincoln County A. Center, DeLake, Ore.; Portland A. Assn.; Oregon A. All.; Master WC Soc. of Oregon; Coquille Valley AA. *Awards*: Honor Roll, AAPL; Woman of Achievement, Sigma Theta Phi, 1958. *Exhibited*: 1956-58 (many others prior), one-man: Colo., Ill., Ind., Kans., Mich., Mo., Nev., Ore., Utah., Wash. Organizes and conducts Oregon circuit shows. Lectures on art throughout the Pacific Northwest. *Positions*: Fndr.-Dir., Lincoln County A. Center & Gallery; Fndr.-Dir., Oregon Coast AA, Master Watercolor Soc. of Oregon; Instr., Coquille Valley AA.

WARD, CHARLES W.—Painter, T., Gr.

Carversville, Pa.

B. Trenton, N.J., Jan. 24, 1900. *Studied*: Sch. Indst. A., Trenton, N.J.; PAFA. *Awards*: Cresson traveling scholarship, PAFA, 1930. *Work*: F.PAFA; Everhart Mus.; murals, USPO, Trenton, N.J.; Roanoke Rapids, N.C.; Playhouse Inn, New Hope, Pa.

WARD, CLARENCE—Educator, Mus. Dir., W., L., Des.

335 East College St., Oberlin, Ohio

B. Brooklyn, N.Y., Mar. 11, 1884. *Studied*: Princeton Univ., A.B., A.M., Ph.D. *Member*: Soc. Arch. Historians. Author: "Mediaeval Church Vaulting," 1915. Lectures: History of Art. *Position*: Prof. Hist. & Appreciation of A., Dir., Dudley Peter Allen Mus., Oberlin Col., Oberlin, Ohio, 1916-49, 1952-53; Visiting Prof. FA, Berea Col., Berea, Ky., 1950; Actg. Hd. Dept. FA, Johns Hopkins Univ., 1950-51; John Hay Whitney Prof. FA, Univ. of the South, Sewanee, Tenn., 1953-54, Prof. FA, 1954-55; Visiting L., Oberlin Col., 1956-57.

WARD, IRENE STEPHENSON (Mrs. H. W.)—Painter

Oakman, Ala.

B. Oakman, Ala., July 18, 1898. *Studied*: Mississippi State Col. *Member*: Birmingham AC; Ala. A. Lg.; SSAL. *Awards*: prizes, VMFA, 1938; Soc. Indp. A., 1943; Montgomery, Ala., 1938-1946. *Exhibited*: Ala. A. Lg., 1938-1946; Birmingham A. Lg., 1938-1946; VMFA, 1938; To-

ledo, Ohio, 1946; NAD, 1950; Birmingham, Ala., 1950 (one-man); Atlanta Mus. A.; Atlanta Pub. Lib.; MMA, 1957; Tuscaloosa, Ala., (one-man).

WARD, LOUISA COOKE—Painter, T.

6702 South Arlington Ave., Los Angeles 43, Cal.

B. Harwinton, Conn., Feb. 13, 1888. *Studied*: Yale Sch. FA. *Member*: Yale Women of So. California; Cal. A. Cl.; Las Artistas; Brush & Palette Gld.; Southland AA; Cal. Fed. Women's Cl. *Awards*: prizes, Los Angeles Library, 1945; Las Artistas Exh., Los A., 1946, 1948; Los A. City Hall, 1953, and others. *Work*: ports., landscapes in private coll. *Exhibited*: Bridgeport Women's A. Cl.; Los A. City Hall; Los A. Library; many women's clubs; Santa Monica Pub. Lib.; Los A. Mus. A.; Carlsbad, Cal.; Greek Theatre, Los A.; and others. *Position*: A. Chm., Los A. County Fed Women's Cl., 1946-48, 1950-52; Pres., Las Artistas, 1950-51.

WARD, LYND (KENDALL)—

Lithographer, Eng., I., W., L.

Lambs Lane, Cresskill, N.J.

B. Chicago, Ill., June 26, 1905. *Studied*: T. Col., Columbia Univ., B.S.; & in Germany. *Member*: NA; SAGA (Pres. 1953-57); SI. *Awards*: Zella de Milhau prize, 1947; LC, 1948; NAD, 1949; Caldecott medal, for "The Biggest Bear," 1953. *Work*: Lib. Cong.; Newark Mus.; MMA; Montclair A. Mus. *Exhibited*: Am. A. Cong.; WFNY, 1939; NAD; John Herron AI; Lib. Cong. Novels in woodcuts: "Madman's Drum," 1930; "Song Without Words," 1936; "Vertigo," 1937; & others. Contributor of: articles on book illustration to Horn Book; American Artist and other magazines.

WARDER, WILLIAM—Painter, W.

304 Laguayra Drive, Northeast, Albuquerque, N.M.

B. Guadalupita, N.M., July 23, 1920. *Studied*: Bisttram Sch. FA; Univ. New Mexico, B.F.A.; ASL; UCLA. *Member*: AEA; Contemp. Am. AA. *Awards*: scholarships, Bisttram Sch. FA; Univ. New Mexico; purchase award, Mus. New Mexico, 1957. *Work*: murals, Raton (N.M.) Pub. Lib.; Ford Motor Co., Albuquerque. *Exhibited*: Mus. New Mexico, Santa Fe, 1942-1946, 1948, 1949, 1954, 1955, traveling exh., 1954-58; Butler AI, 1946; New Mexico State Fair, 1954, 1955; Art: USA, 1958; one-man: Mus. New Mexico, Santa Fe, 1944, 1946, 1955. *Position*: T., Albuquerque Pub. Schs., 1948-50; Owner, Dollar Sign Co., Advertising, 1953- .

WARK, ROBERT RODGER—Museum Curator, Hist.

Henry E. Huntington Library & Art Gallery, San Marino, Cal.; h. 551 South Hill St., Pasadena, Cal.

B. Edmonton, Canada, Oct. 7, 1924. *Studied*: Univ. Alberta, B.A., M.A.; Harvard Univ., A.M., Ph.D. *Member*: CAA. Ed., "Catalogue of William Blake's Drawings and Paintings in the Huntington Library," by C. H. Collins Baker, enlarged and revised by Wark, 1957. Contributor to: Burlington Magazine; Warburg and Courtauld Journal; College Art Journal; Huntington Library Quarterly. *Positions*: Instr., FA, Harvard Univ., 1952-54; History of Art, Yale Univ., 1954-56; Cur., Art Collections, Henry E. Huntington Library & Art Gallery, San Marino, Cal., 1956- .

WARKANY, JOSEF—Etcher

3535 Biddle St., Cincinnati 20, Ohio

B. Vienna, Austria, Mar. 25, 1902. *Awards*: prizes, Am. Physician's AA, 1938-1941. *Exhibited*: Int. Etching & Engraving Exhs., 1938; Lib. Cong., 1945, 1948; SAE, 1945; Ohio Pr. M., 1938-1944, 1957; CM, 1944 (one-man); several group shows.

WARNEKE, HEINZ—Sculptor, E.

1063 31st St., N.W., Washington 7, D.C.; s. The Mowings, East Haddam, Conn.

B. Bremen, Germany, June 30, 1895. *Studied*: in Berlin, Germany. *Member*: ANA; NSS; S.Gld.; Conn. Acad. FA.; Wash. A. Gld.; Assn. Salon des Tuileries. *Awards*: prizes, St. Louis A. Gld., 1925; Salon des Tuileries, Paris, 1926, AIC, 1930; prizes, med., Wash. AA, 1943; med., PAFA, 1935. *Work*: Brookgreen Gardens, S.C.; AIC; Univ. Nebraska; AGAA; CGA; MModA; BM; reliefs, mem., groups, etc.; Masonic Temple, Ft. Scott, Kan.; Medical Soc., St. Louis, Mo.; Nat. Cathedral, Wash., D.C.; Public Accounting Bldg., Wash., D.C.; YMCA, City Hall, both in St. Louis; Office Postmaster-General, Wash., D.C.; Interior Bldg., Wash., D.C.; Fairmount Park, Phila., Pa.; etc. *Position*: Hd. S. Dept., CGA, Washington, D.C., 1942-46.

WARNER, EVERETT (LONGLEY)—
Painter, Et., T., L., W.
Westmoreland, N.H.

B. Vinton, Iowa, July 16, 1877. *Member*: NA; Soc. Wash. A.; Wash. WC Cl.; Assoc. A. Pittsburgh; AWCS; NAC. *Awards*: prizes, Wash. WC Cl., 1902; NAD, 1912, 1937; SC, 1913; Lyme AA, 1937; Assoc. A. Pittsburgh, 1940; WFNY, 1939; med., PAFA, 1908; Int. Exp., Buenos Aires, 1910; Soc. Wash. A., 1913; Pan-Pacific Exp., 1915. *Work*: Hanover Col.; Pa. Col. for Women; CGA; PAFA; BMFA; Toledo Mus. A.; Syracuse Mus. FA; CAM; AIC; N.Y. Pub. Lib.; Gibbes A. Gal., Charleston, S.C.; Oklahoma A. Lg.; Mus. City of N.Y.; N.Y. Hist. Soc.; Cayuga Mus. Hist. & A. *Exhibited*: nationally. *Position*: Assoc. Prof., Carnegie Inst., Pittsburgh, Pa., 1924-42. Contributor to Traffic Quarterly; Illuminating Engineer; Atlantic Monthly.

WARNER, HARRY B., JR.—Critic, W.
423 Summit Ave., Hagerstown, Md.

B. Chambersburg, Pa., Dec. 19, 1922. *Position*: A. Cr., Morning Herald, Hagerstown, Md., at present.

WARREN, CHARLES BRADLEY—Sculptor
233 Ridge Ave., Ben Avon, Pittsburgh 2, Pa.

B. Pittsburgh, Pa., Dec. 19, 1903. *Studied*: Carnegie Inst.; BAID. *Member*: Assoc. A., Pittsburgh; Pittsburgh Soc. S. *Awards*: prizes, Carnegie Inst., 1936, 1941. *Work*: North Carolina State Col.; Greek Catholic Seminary, Pittsburgh; Dept. Justice, Raleigh, N.C.; County Bldg., High Point, N.C.; Stevens Sch., Pittsburgh; Catholic H.S., Pittsburgh; St. Athanasius Church, West View, Pa.; St. Paul Orphanage, St. Francis Xavier, United Steelworkers Bldg., all of Pittsburgh; U.S. Steel Research Lab., Monroeville, Pa.; Mount St. Joseph, Wheeling, W. Va.; many port. reliefs; Stephen Foster Mem. Medal; St. George Activities Bldg., Pittsburgh. *Exhibited*: Assoc A. Pittsburgh, 1930-41, 1950-55; Arch. Lg., 1940-42; Soc. S. Pittsburgh, 1935-45, 1950-57; NSS, 1952.

WARREN, ELISABETH B. (Mrs. Tod Lindenmuth)—
Painter, S., I.
Aviles St., St. Augustine, Fla.; Bearskin Neck, Rockport, Mass.; h. 46 Carrera St., St. Augustine, Fla.

B. Bridgeport, Conn., Aug. 28, 1886. *Studied*: Mass. Sch. A.; Vesper George Sch. A.; & with W. H. Bicknell, Provincetown, Mass.; Charles Simpson, England. *Member*: St. Augustine AC; Rockport AA. *Awards*: prizes, Fla. Fed. A. *Exhibited*: SAE; Chicago SE; Cal. Pr. M.; Phila. Pr. Cl.; Phila. A. All.; Rockport AA, 1955 (one-man); Fla. Fed. A.; 2-man exhs., 1955-1958, with Tod Lindenmuth, St. Augustine; Tarpon Springs, Naples, Fla.; St. Petersburgh AA, 1956; Allentown (Pa.) A. Mus., 1958. I., children's books. Specializes in ports. of children in pastel.

WARREN, FERDINAND E.—Painter, C., Gr.
131 College Place, Decatur, Ga.

B. Independence, Mo., Aug. 1, 1899. *Studied*: Kansas City AI; Tiffany Fnd.; Grand Central Sch. A.; ASL. *Member*: NA; Audubon A.; SC; Am. Veterans Soc. A.; AWS. *Awards*: prizes, NAD, 1935; All. A. Am., 1939; SC, 1938, 1940, 1942, 1944, 1947; AWS, 1948; Audubon A., 1950; Southeastern AA, 1951; Butler AI, 1954; medals, Midwestern A.; AWS, 1950; Tiffany Fnd. F., 1925-26. *Work*: MMA; BM; Rochester Mem. A. Gal.; NAD; New Britain Mus. A.; Maxwell House Coll.; Univ. Georgia Mus.; Butler AI; Currier Gal. A.; Atlanta AA, and in private colls. *Exhibited*: NAD; All. A. Am.; Brooklyn Soc. A.; Randolph-Macon Woman's Col.; AIC; PAFA; CGA; VMFA; Carnegie Inst.; NAC; SC; Audubon A; BM; Berkshire A. Center; Illinois Wesleyan Univ.; Bucks County AA; Dallas AA; Walker A. Center; R. I. Sch. Des.; N.Y. Bd. Edu.; Montclair A. Mus.; John Herron AI; Am. Veterans Soc. A.; Springfield AA; Univ. Ne-

braska; Nat. Inst. A. & Let.; Toledo Mus. A.; Farnsworth Mus. A.; MMA; one-man: Kansas City, Mo.; 2-man: Milch Gal., N.Y., and many others. *Position*: Instr. A., Resident A., Univ. Georgia, 1950-51; Hd. Dept. A., Agnes Scott Col., Decatur, Ga., at present.

WARREN, JEFFERSON T.—Museum Director
John Woodman Higgins Armory, 100 Barbar Ave., Worcester, Mass.*

WARREN, L. D.—Cartoonist
Cincinnati Enquirer (1); h. 2619 Cleinview Ave., Cincinnati 20, Ohio

B. Wilmington, Del., Dec. 27, 1906. *Position*: Cart., Cincinnati Enquirer.

WARSAW, ALBERT TAYLOR—Painter, Des., Lith.
40 East 34th St., New York 16, N.Y.; h. 3532 157th St., Flushing, L.I., N.Y.

B. New York, N.Y., Oct. 6, 1899 *Studied*: NAD; ASL; BAID. *Member*: AWS. *Exhibited*: AWS; Phila. WC Cl.; PAFA; All. A. Am. *Position*: A. Des., Warsaw & Co., New York, N.Y.

WARSHAW, HOWARD—Painter
755 El Bosque Road, Santa Barbara, Cal.*

WARTHOE, CHRISTIAN—Sculptor, W.
1951 Humboldt Blvd., Chicago 47, Ill.

B. Salten, Denmark, June 15, 1892. *Studied*: Royal Acad. FA, Copenhagen, Denmark; Minneapolis Sch. A.; ASL; BAID. *Member*: NSS; Am. Veterans Soc. A. *Work*: Grand View Col., Des Moines, Iowa; Silkeborg Mus., and Bay Monument, Rudkobing, Denmark; in Germany; mem., Chicago, Ill. *Exhibited*: Am Veterans Soc. A.; NSS; NAD; S. Gld. Contributor to Danish American Press.

WARWICK, EDWARD—Painter, Eng., E., W., L.
346 Pelham Rd., Philadelphia 19, Pa.

B. Philadelphia, Pa., Dec. 10, 1881. *Studied*: Univ. Pennsylvania; PMSchIA. *Member*: Phila. A. All.; Phila. WC Cl.; Phila. Sketch Cl. *Exhibited*: PAFA, annually; Pr.Cl., WC Cl., Sketch Cl., Phila., Pa. Co-Author: "Early American Costume." Position: Instr., 1932-47, Dean, 1937-52, Dean Emeritus, 1952- , PMSchIA, Philadelphia, Pa.

WARWICK, ETHEL HERRICK (Mrs. Edward)—Painter
346 Pelham Rd., Philadelphia 19, Pa.

B. New York, N.Y. *Studied*: Moore Inst. Des.; PAFA. *Member*: Plastics Cl., A. All., WC Cl., all of Phila., Pa.; Nat. Lg. Am. Pen Women. *Awards*: F., PAFA; prizes, Phila. Plastic Cl. *Work*: Pa. State Col.; many portrait commissions. *Exhibited*: PAFA, annually; Woodmere A. Gal.; Phila. Plastic Cl.; F.PAFA; Nat. Lg. Am. Pen Women, annually.

WASEY, JANE (Mrs. Jane Wasey Mortellito)—
Sculptor
178 East 75th St., New York 21, N.Y.

B. Chicago, Ill., June 28, 1912. *Studied*: in Paris, with Paul Landowski; in New York with Simon Moselsio, John Flanagan, and in Connecticut with Heinz Warneke. *Member*: S. Gld.; NSS; Audubon A; NAWA; AEA; N.Y. Ceramic Soc. *Awards*: prizes, Lighthouse Exh., N.Y., 1951; NAWA; Gld. Hall, East Hampton, L.I., 1949-1956; Arch. Lg., 1955; Parrish Mus., Southampton. *Work*: WMAA; PAFA; Univ. Nebraska; Univ. Arizona; CAM; Univ. Colorado. *Exhibited*: WMAA; MMA; AIC; PMA; Syracuse Mus. FA; CM; CAM; Burlington Gal., London; PAFA; Nebraska AI; Univ. Colorado; Audubon A; one-man: Montross Gal., 1934; Delphic Studio, 1935; Philbrook A. Center, 1947; Contemporaries, 1954; Kraushaar Gal., 1955; Mus. Natural History, N.Y., 1958. *Position*: Instr. S., Bennington Col., 1949; V.Pres., Arch. Lg.

WASHBURN, CADWALLADER—Painter, Et., W.
1806 Oak Ave., Brunswick, Ga.

B. Minneapolis, Minn. *Studied*: MIT; ASL, and with Sorolla in Spain; Besnard in Paris; Mowbray and Chase in New York. *Member*: ANA; NAC; AFA; Wash. A. Cl.; SAGA. *Awards*: prize, Paris, France; medal, Pan-Pacific Exp. *Work*: Luxembourg Mus., Bibliotheque Nationale, Paris; Victoria & Albert Mus., London; Rijks Mus., Amsterdam; NGA; LC; MMA; N.Y. Pub. Lib.; PMA; Honolulu Acad. A.; Mus. FA of Houston. *Exhibited*: one-man: deYoung Mem. Mus., 1954; MIT, 1954; Bowdoin Col., 1954; Atlanta AA, 1956; Telfair Acad., Savannah, 1958.

WASHBURN, GORDON BAILEY—Museum Director
Department of Fine Arts, Carnegie Institute, 4400 Forbes St.; h. 420 Coventry Rd., Pittsburgh 13, Pa.
B. Wellesley Hills, Mass., Nov. 7, 1904. *Studied*: Deerfield Acad.; Williams Col., A.B.; FMA, Harvard Univ. *Member*: CAA; Assn. A. Mus. Dir.; AAMus. *Awards*: Guggenheim F., 1949-50; Chevalier, Legion of Honor, 1952; Hon. degree, M.F.A., Williams Col., 1938. Author: "Master Drawings," 1935, "Master Bronzes," 1937 both Albright Gal. A.; "Old and New England," 1945, "Isms in Art Since 1800," both R.I. Sch. Des.; "French Painting 1100-1900," 1951; "Pictures of Everyday Life-Genre Painting in Europe, 1500-1900," both Carnegie Inst. (latter, 1954). Lectures cover all periods of art history. Exhibitions arranged: Pittsburgh International (triennially); French Painting 1100-1900, Carnegie Inst.; Pictures of Everyday Life-Genre Painting in Europe, 1500-1900, Carnegie Inst. *Position*: Dir., Albright A. Gal., Buffalo, N.Y., 1931-42; Dir., Mus. A., Rhode Island Sch. Des., 1942-49; Dir., Dept. FA, Carnegie Inst., Pittsburgh, Pa., 1950- .

WASHBURN, JEANNETTE—Painter
136 West 10th St., Jacksonville 8, Fla.
B. Susquehanna, Pa., Sept. 25, 1905. *Studied*: Florida State Women's Col., A.B.; Syracuse Univ., B.F.A.; ASL, and with Kenneth Hayes Miller. *Member*: Fla. Fed. A.; St. Augustine AA; Jacksonville A. Cl. *Award*: Prize, Jacksonville A. Cl., 1951; Jacksonville A. Mus., 1957. *Work*: Univ. Alaska; Jacksonville Pub. Sch. No. 11; Fla. State Board of Health. *Exhibited*: Butler AI, 1941; PBA, 1941; Norton Gal. A.; Tampa AI; Blue Ridge, N.C., 1941; Jacksonville A. Cl., 1946, 1948-1952; Fla. Fed. A., 1948-1950, 1953, 1954; Jacksonville A. Mus., 1953-1958; St. Augustine AA, 1952-1956; Southside Branch Lib., Jacksonville, 1955; Fla. Southern Col., 1952; Manatee A. Lg., 1957; Jacksonville A. Festival, 1958. *Positions*: A. & Crafts Specialist, Am. Red Cross, assigned to Army hospitals, 1944-46; A., Fla. State Bd. of Health, Jacksonville, Fla., 1946-1957.

WASHBURN, KENNETH (LELAND)—Painter, E., S.
81 Madrona St., San Carlos, Cal.
B. Franklinville, N.Y., Jan. 23, 1904. *Studied*: Cornell Univ., B.F.A., M.F.A. *Member*: AWCS. *Awards*: prizes, Cortland County (N.Y.) State Exh., 1945; Finger Lakes Exh., Auburn, N.Y., 1944. *Work*: Springfield (Ill.) Mus. A.; Binghamton (N.Y.) Mus. A.; IBM Coll.; murals, plaque, USPO, Binghamton, N.Y.; Moravia, N.Y. *Exhibited*: Texas Centennial, 1934; WFNY 1939; NAD, 1942-1944; AWCS, 1942-1945; PAFA, 1940, 1941, 1946; Rochester Mem. A. Gal., 1943-1946; Finger Lakes Exh., 1941-1946; etc. *Position*: Instr. FA, 1928-34, Asst. Prof. FA, 1934-44, Assoc. Prof. A., 1944-50, Cornell Univ., Ithaca, N.Y.; Co-Director, Washburn-White A. Center, San Carlos, Cal., 1953- .*

WASHBURN, LOUESE B. (Mrs. Clayton)—Painter
136 West 10th St., Jacksonville 8, Fla.
B. Dimock, Pa., Jan. 17, 1875. *Studied*: PIASch.; Broadmoor A. Acad.; Colorado Springs FA Center; & with Ross Moffett, Henry Varnum Poor, & others. *Member*: Fla. Fed. A.; Jacksonville AC. *Awards*: prizes, Tampa, Fla.; 1924; Jacksonville AC, 1928; Fla. Fed. A., 1929, 1931, 1933, 1934, 1954; IBM purchase prize, 1941. *Work*: St. Luke's Hospital, Jacksonville, Fla.; Hope Haven Hospital for Crippled Children, Fla.; Thornwell Orphanage, Clinton, N.C. *Exhibited*: FAP, 1941; Argent Gal., 1939, 1940; Univ. Alaska, 1935; Blue Ridge, N.C., 1941; Tampa AI, 1941; Univ. Florida, 1930; Jacksonville Pub. Lib., 1935; Jacksonville A. Cl., 1948-1951; Jacksonville Pub. Lib., 1948-1952; Vogue A. Gal., Jacksonville, 1952; Fla. Fed. A., 1953, 1954; Springfield Branch Lib., 1953-1955; Jacksonville A. Mus., 1953-1957.

WASSERMAN, ALBERT—Painter, Des., T.
34-24 82nd St., Jackson Heights 72, N.Y.
B. New York, N.Y., Aug. 22, 1920. *Studied*: ASL, with Charles Chapman; NAD, with Sidney Dickinson. *Member*: All. A. Am.; New Jersey P. & S. Soc.; AEA; ASL; AWS. *Awards*: Pulitzer Scholarship, NAD, 1940, Obrig prize, 1941; All. A. Am., 1941, 1944; Ogunquit A. Centre, 1952. *Exhibited*: NAD, 1940-1942; All. A. Am., 1941, 1942, 1947-1958; Audubon A., 1953; AWS, 1950-1956; New Jersey P. & S. Soc., 1949-1954. *Position*: Instr., Portrait & Still Life, Jackson Heights A. Cl.; ASL.

WATERS, HERBERT (OGDEN)—Wood Engraver, T.
Mad River Road, Campton, N.H.
B. Swatow, China, Nov. 15, 1903. *Studied*: Harvard Univ.; Denison Univ., Ph.B.; AIC; PMSchA. *Member*: SAGA; Boston Pr. M.; New Hampshire AA. *Awards*: prizes, Indp. Soc. Pr. M.; 1945; New Hampshire A., 1951, 1954, 1955; SAGA, 1955; Academic A., Springfield, 1955; Denison Univ., 1956. *Work*: prints, AGAA; R.I. Sch. Des.; Univ. New Hampshire; Dartmouth Col.; Middlebury Col.; Pa. State Univ.; Boston and N.Y. Pub. Libs.; NAD; MMA; LC. Mural, Campton (N.H.) Baptist Church; Mem. bookplate, Denison Univ. Lib. *Exhibited*: Phila. Pr. Cl.; Carnegie Inst.; Boston A. Festival. Illus., "New England Year," 1939; "New England Days," 1940 (and author); "Fragments," 1941. *Position*: A.T., Holderness Sch. for Boys, Plymouth, N.H., 1946- .

WATERSTON, MRS. G. CHYCHELE. See Atkinson, Alica

WATKINS, FRANCES EMMA—Museum Curator, W., L.
533 San Marino Ave., San Marino, Cal.
B. Denver, Colo., Dec. 27, 1899. *Studied*: Univ. Denver, A.B.; Univ. Southern California, Ph.D. Author: "The Navaho," 1943; "Hopi Toys," 1946; leaflets for Southwest Mus., Los A., Cal. *Member*: Western Mus. Conference; Keith AA. Contributor to The Masterkey, California History Nugget, Quarterly of Southern California Hist. Soc., California Folklore Journal, and other publications. Lectures: Arts & Crafts of the American Indian Women; American Indian Basketry, etc. *Position*: Asst. Cur., Southwest Mus., Los Angeles, Cal., 1929-46 in absentia, 1946-56, Consultant, 1956- .

WATKINS, FRANKLIN C.—Painter, T.
2026 Spruce St., Philadelphia 3, Pa.
B. New York, N.Y., Dec. 30, 1894. *Studied*: Univ. Virginia; Univ. Pennsylvania; PAFA. *Member*: ANA; Nat. Inst. A. & Let. *Awards*: prizes, Carnegie Inst., 1931; AIC, 1938; GGE 1939; med., Paris Salon, 1937; CGA, 1938, 1939; prizes, med., PAFA, 1941, 1942, 1944. *Work*: PAFA; MMA; WMAA; PMA; MModA; CGA; PMG; Smith Col.; Courtauld Inst., London; murals, Rodin Mus., Phila. *Position*: Instr. Painting, PAFA, Philadelphia, Pa., at present.

WATKINS, LOUISE LOCHRIDGE—
Museum Director, T., L.
George Walter Vincent Smith Art Museum (5); h. 17 Garfield St., Springfield 8, Mass.
B. Springfield, Mass., July 6, 1905. *Studied*: Skidmore Col., B.S. Contributor to Springfield Republican; Springfield Union; Museum Bulletin. Lectures: Decorative Arts; History of Cloisonne; History of Enameling; Chinese Jades, etc. *Position*: Instr., 1936-38, Asst. to Dir., 1938-50, Dir., 1951- , George Walter Vincent Smith A. Mus., Springfield, Mass.*

WATKINS, WILLIAM REGINALD—
Designer, P., Lith., T.
3120 Weaver Ave., Baltimore 14, Md.
B. Manchester, England, Nov. 11, 1890. *Studied*: Maryland Inst., and with Hans Schuler, C. Y. Turner, Maxwell Miller, and others. *Member*: Balt. WC Cl.; AAPL; F. Royal Soc. A. London; Balt. A. Dir. Cl.; Nat. A. Dir.; Maryland Inst. Alum. Bd. *Awards*: prizes, PAFA, 1930; BMA; Timonium Fair, Md., 1930; Seton Hall Univ., 1958; Balt. WC Cl. *Work*: Md. Jockey Cl.; Univ. Maryland; Seton Hall Univ. *Exhibited*: PAFA, 1930; BMA, 1927-1933; Peabody Gal., 1916-1924; Mun. Mus., Balt., 1941-1946, 1951; Md. Inst. (one-man); Balt. Charcoal Cl.

(one-man); Grand Central A. Gal.; Balt. WC Cl., 1950-1952; Oklahoma A. Center; Univ. Maine; Springfield, Ill.; Izmer, Turkey; Bronxville Pub. Lib.; Hilltop, Vagabond, Center Theatres, Balt., and others. *Position*: Instr., Comm. Illus. & Life Drawing, Maryland Inst.; drawing, Univ. Maryland, Baltimore, Md.; Bd. Gov., Vice-Pres., 1954-55, Balt. WC Cl.; A. Comm., BMA, 1952-55.

WATROUS, JAMES S.—*Painter, E., C., W.*
2809 Sylvan Ave., Madison 5, Wis.

B. Winfield, Kan., Aug. 3, 1908. *Studied*: Univ. Wisconsin, B.S., M.A., Ph.D. *Member*: NSMP; CAA. *Awards*: Ford F., 1954-55. *Work*: Milwaukee AI; Univ. Wisconsin; Lawrence Col.; Kansas State Col.; murals, Wis. Union; Fed. Bldg., Park Falls, Wis.; USPO, Grand Rapids, Minn.; Democrat Printing Co., Madison, Mis.; mosaic murals, Commerce Bldg., Univ. Wisconsin (2); Chemical Eng. Bldg., Washington Univ., St. Louis; exterior arch. sculpture, State of Wisconsin Bar Assn. Bldg. Author: "The Craft of Old-Master Drawings," 1957. *Position*: Prof. 1939- , Chm. Dept. A. Hist., 1953- , Univ. Wisconsin, Madison, Wis.; Sec., Governor's Comm. on FA, 1953- .

WATSON, ALDREN AULD—*Illustrator, Des., P., Gr.*
Putney, Vt.

B. Brooklyn, N.Y., May 10, 1917. *Studied*: ASL, with George Bridgman, Charles Chapman, Robert Brackman, William Auerbach-Levy, and others. *Awards*: prize, Domesday Book Illustration Comp., 1945. *Work*: mural, S.S. President Hayes; illus. books in libraries in U.S., Canada, Europe and private colls. Contributor to Encyclopaedia Britannica; Time magazine war maps, 1941. *Exhibited*: AIGA, 1937-1956. Represented in "Fifty Color Prints," 1935. Illus., "Grimms Fairy Tales," 1940; "Shakespeare's Sonnets," 1942; "Cavalleria Rusticana," 1952; "Walden," 1942; Kipling's "Jungle Books," 1946; "Gulliver's Travels"; "Hunting of the Snark," 1954; "Red Badge of Courage," 1953; "Whose Birthday Is It?", 1954; "When is Tomorrow?" 1955; "What Does A Begin With?" 1956; "Fairy Tale Picture Book," 1957; "Arabian Nights Picture Book," 1958, as well as 60 other books including trade, juvenile, text and language books. Biographical chapter in "Forty Illustrators and How They Work."

WATSON, DUDLEY CRAFTS—*Painter, E., W., L.*
Art Institute of Chicago, Chicago, Ill.; h. 291 Marshman St., Highland Park, Ill.

B. Lake Geneva, Wis., Apr. 28, 1885. *Studied*: AIC; Beloit Col., D.F.A.; & with Alfred East, London. *Member*: Chicago AC. *Awards*: prizes, Milwaukee AI, 1923; AIC, 1926; decorated by Govt. of Ecuador, 1946. *Work*: Burlington (Iowa) Pub. Lib.; Milwaukee AI; Layton Gal. A.; IBM Coll.; Wendell Phillips H.S., Chicago. *Exhibited*: AIC, annually; Grand Central A. Gal. Author: "Nineteenth Century Painting," 1931; "Twentieth Century Painting," 1932. Lectures: Art and Travel. *Position*: L., AIC, Chicago, Ill., 1926-55; Special L., AIC, 1955- .

WATSON, JEAN—*Painter*
5029 Pulaski Ave., Philadelphia 44, Pa.

B. Philadelphia, Pa. *Studied*: PAFA, and with Earl Horter. *Member*: Phila. A. All.; NAWA; Phila. Pr. Cl.; AEA; Pen & Brush Cl.; F., PAFA; Woodmere A. Gal. *Awards*: F., PAFA; prize, PAFA, 1943, 1951; Pen & Brush Cl., 1954; medal, Phila. Plastic Cl., 1935, 1938; Phila. Sketch Cl., 1937. *Work*: Woodmere A. Gal., Phila.; mural, USPO, Madison, N.C.; Stoughton, Mass. *Exhibited*: PAFA, 1935, 1937, 1939, 1940, 1943-1946, 1950; CGA, 1937, 1939, 1941; VMFA, 1938, 1940; WFNY 1939; GGE 1939; AIC, 1940; Carnegie Inst., 1941; CM, 1939, 1941; NAD, 1938, 1941, 1945; MMA, 1942; Audubon A., 1945; Lilienfeld Gal., 1940 (one-man); Donovan Gal., Phila. 1952 (one-man); NAWA, 1952, 1955; Argent Gal., 1955 (one-man); Woodmere A. Gal., 1957.

WATSON, (JAMES) ROBERT (JR.)—*Painter*
6 Ardmore Rd., Berkeley 7, Cal.

B. Martinez, Cal., Feb. 28, 1923. *Studied*: Univ. California; Univ. Illinois; Univ. Wisconsin, with Frederick Taubes. *Awards*: prizes, Cal. State Fair, 1956; San F. A. Festival, 1958. *Work*: Toledo Mus. A.; Mills Col., Oakland, Cal.; St. Mary's Col., Orinda, Cal.; Gardena H.S.;

Costa Mesa H.S.; Vallejo H.S.; Cal. PLH. *Exhibited*: NAD, 1955; Univ. Illinois, 1955; Cal. PLH, 1952; Cal. State Fair, 1952, 1955; San F. Art Festival, 1951-1954.

WATT, WILLIAM GODFREY—*Painter*
20 North St., Suffield, Conn.

B. New York, N.Y., Apr. 2, 1885. *Studied*: with W. Lester Stevens, Aldro T. Hibbard, Roger Wolcott, Harriet Loomis. *Member*: Springfield A. Lg. *Awards*: prize, Bridgeport AA, 1945. *Exhibited*: Am. Veterans Soc. A., 1940, 1945; Chicago, Ill., 1945; San F., Cal., 1946; Springfield, Mass.; Hartford, Conn.; Westfield, Mass.

WATTS, MELVIN E.—*Museum Curator*
Currier Gallery of Art, 192 Orange St., Manchester, N.H.*

WAUGH, COULTON—*Painter, Cart., W.*
R.R. 2, Box 133, Newburgh, N.Y.

B. Cornwall, England, Mar. 10, 1896. *Studied*: ASL; & with George Bridgman, Frank DuMond. *Member*: Grand Central Gal. *Exhibited*: NAD; PAFA; Carnegie Inst., 1943, 1944, 1946; GGE 1939; Provincetown AA, 1925-1943; 7 one-man exhs., New York, 1935-55. Contributor to: Yachting, Fortune magazines; Encyclopaedia Britannica. Author, I., comic strip, "Dickie Dare," Assoc. Press, 1934-57. Author, "The Comics," 1947. *Positions*: Instr., A., Adult classes, Bethlehem A. Center, 1955- ; A.T., Cornwall (N.Y.) Central Sch., 1957- .

WAUGH, SIDNEY—*Sculptor, Des.*
101 Park Ave., New York 17, N.Y.

B. Amherst, Mass., Jan. 17, 1904. *Studied*: Amherst Col.; MIT; Ecole des Beaux-Arts, Paris; Am. Acad. in Rome. *Member*: NA; NSS; Nat. Inst. A. & Let.; N.Y. City A. Comm.; Century Assn.; NAC (hon. life). *Awards*: Hon. degree, M.A., Amherst Col., 1938; D.F.A., Univ. Massachusetts, 1953; medal, Paris Salon, 1928, 1929; Saltus award, Am. Numismatic Soc., 1954; Prix de Rome, 1929; Croix de Guerre, French Govt. (2); Bronze Star; Knight of the Crown of Italy. *Work*: MMA; Victoria & Albert Mus., London; CMA; Toledo Mus. A.; AIC; John Herron AI; monument, Richmond, Tex.; Pulaski monument, Phila., Pa.; sculptures, Corning Bldg., N.Y.; Smith Col.; Buhl Planetarium, Pittsburgh; Fed. Trade Comm. Bldg., Wash., D.C.; Dept. Justice Bldg., Wash., D.C.; Mead Art Bldg., Amherst Col.; Bethlehem Steel Co. Main Office Bldg., Fed. Courts Bldg., Wash., D.C.; Mellon Mem. fountain, Wash., D.C.; Bank of the Manhattan Co., N.Y.; Battle Monument, Florence, Italy, and others; port. statues, Johns Hopkins Univ.; USPO Bldg., Wash., D.C.; Nat. Archives Bldg., Wash., D.C.; medals by Waugh: President of Chile; Parsons Sch. Des.; Atoms for Peace award; Am. Inst. Arch.; Squibb Centennial. Work in the colls. of prominent national and international figures. Author: "The Art of Glassmaking," 1938. Pres., NSS, 1948-50; Vice-Pres., NAD, 1952-54.

WAXMAN, MRS. BASHKA PAEFF. See Paeff, Bashka

WAY, EDNA (MARTHA)—*Painter, E.*
22 North Congress St., Athens, Ohio

B. Manchester, Vt., Jan. 5, 1897. *Studied*: T. Col., Columbia Univ., B.S., M.A.; & in Paris, France. *Member*: Tri-State Creative A.; AEA; Ohio WC Soc.; Columbus A. Lg. *Awards*: prizes, Stockbridge, Mass., 1934; NAWA, 1936, 1944; Columbus A. Lg., 1939, 1943, 1946, 1955; Wash. WC Cl., 1945, 1946; Ohio WC Cl., 1952. *Work*: AGAA; Fleming Mus. A., Burlington, Vt. *Exhibited*: NAWA, 1937-1946; PAFA, 1936-1938, 1941-1944; AWCS, 1936-1939; Studio Gld., 1938-1940; Southern Vermont A.; Ohio WC Soc.; Columbus A. Lg.; Springfield A. Lg.; Butler AI; CM; Huntington (W. Va.) Gal., 1957 and prior. Lectures: Art in Everyday Life. *Position*: Prof. A., Textile Des., Interior, Fashion, Ohio Univ., Athens, Ohio, 1926- .

WEAVER, ROBERT E(DWARD)—*Painter*
482 West Main St., Peru, Ind.

B. Peru, Ind., Nov. 15, 1914. *Studied*: John Herron AI, B.F.A. *Member*: Indiana A. Cl.; Hoosier Salon; Indiana A. *Awards*: prize, NAD, 1938; Chaloner prize, 1937.

Work: Nat. Cash Register Corp.; John Herron AI; murals, Indianapolis Methodist Hospital; Alameda (Cal.) Naval Air Station; Eli Lilly Co.; Knightstown (Ind.) Soldiers and Sailors Children's Home. *Exhibited*: CGA; PAFA; GGE 1939; Hoosier Salon; Indiana A.; Indiana A. Cl.; and others. *Position*: Instr., John Herron A. Sch., Indianapolis, Ind.

WEBB, GRACE (AGNES) (PARKER)—
Painter, C., Gr., T., L.
196 South Union St., Burlington, Vt.

B. Vergennes, Vt., Aug. 24, 1888. *Studied*: ASL; PIASch.; Univ. Vermont; Univ. California; Simmons Col.; & with Barse Miller, Paul Sample, Rex Brandt, John Carlson, Charles Allen, & others. *Member*: Phila. WC Cl.; NAWA; AEA; AAPL; ASL; Lg. Vermont Writers; Northern Vermont AA; Vermont Hist. Soc. *Awards*: Vt. Fed. Women's Cl., 1954; gold medal AAPL, 1958; Nat. Lg. Am. Pen Women, 1958. *Work*: Fleming Mus. A., Burlington, Vt.; Shelburne Mus. A. *Exhibited*: PAFA, 1940-1944; NAWA, 1944, 1946, 1958; AWCS, 1943; Soc. for Sanity in Art, Boston, 1941; High Mus. A., 1944; Northern Vermont A., annually; Phila. WC Cl., 1944-46, 1958; AAPL, 1958; Nat. Lg. Am. Pen Women, 1958. Lectures: Historical & Contemporary Art. *Position*: Pres., Green Mt. Branch, Nat. Lg. Am. Pen Women, 1958-60; Vermont A. Chm., 1956, 1958.

WEBB, MARGARET ELY—*Painter, Eng., I., W., Des.*
P.O. Box 665, Santa Barbara, Cal.

B. Urbana, Ill., Mar. 27, 1877. *Studied*: ASL; CUASch.; & with Kenyon Cox, Arthur Dow, George Bridgman, John Twachtman, & others. *Member*: Boston Soc. A. & Crafts; Am. Soc. Bookplate Collectors & Des. *Awards*: prizes, Bookplate Soc., 1924, 1925; Madonna Festival, Los A., 1955. *Work*: bookplates, Am. Antiquarian Soc.; Huntington Lib.; Santa Barbara Natural Hist. Mus.; Wilshire Methodist Church, Los A.; Mount Calvary Monastery, Santa Barbara, Cal.; Liverpool (England) Pub. Lib.; British Mus., London; Solvang (Cal.) Episcopal Church; St. Mary's Church, Santa Barbara. *Exhibited*: Soc. Women P. & S.; Oakland A. Gal.; Boston AC; Copley Soc.; Madonna Festival, Los A.; Santa Paula, Cal.; Santa Barbara AA; Faulkner Mem. Gal., Santa Barbara, Cal.; Bowers Mem. Mus., Santa Ana. I., numerous books. Contributor to: Saint Nicholas, Churchman, Dutch Ex Libris Journal.

WEBB, PAUL—*Cartoonist*
Shepard Hill Rd., Newtown, Conn.

B. Towanda, Pa., Sept. 20, 1902. *Studied*: PMSchIA; PAFA. *Awards*: two traveling scholarships, 1927-28. *Member*: SI; A. & Writers Assn.; Westport AA. Author, I., "Comin' Round the Mountain," 1938; "Keep 'Em Flyin'," 1942; Creator of "The Mountain Boys."

WEBER, MAX—*Painter*
11 Hartley Rd., Great Neck, L.I., N.Y.

B. Bialystok, Russia, Apr. 18, 1881. *Studied*: PIASch.; Julian Acad., Paris; & with Jean Paul Laurens, Henri Matisse, Arthur Dow. *Member*: Nat. Inst. A. & Let. *Awards*: prizes, AIC, 1941; La Tausca Pearls Comp., 1946; Pepsi-Cola Comp., 1945, 1946; PAFA, 1956; med., AIC, 1928; CGA, 1941; PAFA, 1941; Hon. degree, D.H.L., Brandeis Univ., 1957. *Work*: MMA; WMAA; MModA; Jewish Theological Seminary of Am.; Tel-Aviv Mus.; AIC; Los A. Mus. A.; Palace Legion Honor; Santa Barbara Mus. A.; Wichita A. Mus.; Newark Mus.; Walker A. Center; Univ. Nebraska; BM; CMA; PMG; etc. *Exhibited*: nationally and internationally. Author: "Essays on Art," 1916; "Primitives," 1926.

WEBER, ROBERT—*Cartoonist*
327 Central Park West, New York 25, N.Y.

B. Los Angeles, Cal., Apr. 22, 1924. *Studied*: A. Center Sch., Los A.; PIASch.; ASL. Contributor cartoons to Sat. Eve. Post; Look; True and other national magazines.*

WEBSTER, BERNICE M.—*Painter, L.*
Northfield, Mass.; s. Ames Hill, Brattleboro, Vt.

B. Northfield, Mass., Dec. 13, 1895. *Studied*: Mass. Sch. A.; T. Col., Columbia Univ., B.S. in A., and with Henry

B. Snell, Arthur Woelffle. *Member*: Albany Inst. Hist. & A.; So. Vermont A. Center. *Exhibited*: All. A. Am., 1941; NAC, 1931-1948; Vendome Gal., 1941; "Tomorrow's Masterpieces," 1943; Springfield A. Lg., 1947; Baer Gal., 1948-1950; So. Vermont A. Center, 1954-1958; A. of the Upper Hudson, 1948-1950; one-man: Albany Inst. Hist. & A., 1948; Bedford, N.Y., 1948, 1950, 1952; Greenfield, Mass., 1948, 1957 (one-man); Pawling, N.Y., 1949; New Canaan, Conn., 1949; Ridgefield, Conn., 1950-1952; Northfield, Mass., 1950; Northfield Sch. for Girls, 1955. Lectures on Art and Travel.

WEBSTER, DAVID S.—*Assistant Museum Director*
Shelburne Museum, Shelburne, Vt.*

WEBSTER, HERMAN A.—*Etcher, P., Draughtsman*
39 Rue d'Artois, Paris, France

B. New York, N.Y., Apr. 6, 1878. *Studied*: St. Pauls' Sch.; Yale Univ., Ph.D., and in Paris with J. P. Laurens. *Member*: Royal Soc. P., Et. & Eng., London; SAGA; Societe National des Beaux-Arts, Paris; Societe des Peintures-Graveurs Francais. *Awards*: gold medal, Pan-Pacific Exp., 1915; prize, SAGA, 1932; Officer, Legion d'Honneur, France; Grand Prix de Gravure, Paris Int. Exp., 1937. *Work*: AIC; LC; FMA; N.Y. Pub. Lib.; Yale Univ.; Bibliotheque Nationale, Paris; Victoria & Albert Mus., London; AIC; Carnegie Inst.; Chalcographie du Louvre, Paris, etc. *Exhibited*: NAD; Royal Acad., London; Venice, Italy; SAGA; Salon de la Societe Nationale des Beaux-Arts, Paris; Intl. Expo. of Engraving, Yugoslavia, 1955; and in leading U.S. museums and galleries. Contributor to The Century, L'Illustration, Bulletin of the Soc. for the Preservation of Ancient Buildings, London, and other publications.

WEDDERSPOON, RICHARD G.—*Painter, E.*
125 North Main St., Yardley, Pa.

B. Red Bank, N.J., Oct. 15, 1889. *Studied*: Carnegie Inst.; Corcoran Sch. A.; PAFA. *Member*: Fla. A. Group; Chicago AC; Syracuse SA. *Awards*: European scholarship, PAFA, 1915, 1916; prizes, PAFA, 1917; Syracuse Mus. FA, 1926, 1944; AIC, 1922. *Work*: Chicago Mun. Coll.; Vanderpoel Coll.; De Pauw Univ. *Exhibited*: CGA; PAFA; Peabody Inst., Balt., Md.; AIC; Syracuse Mus. FA, 1926-1946. *Position*: Prof. Painting, Syracuse Univ., 1923-49 (retired).

WEDDIGE, EMIL—*Lithographer, P., E., Des., L.*
870 Stein Rd., Ann Arbor, Mich.

B. Ontario, Canada, Dec. 23, 1907. *Studied*: Michigan State Normal Col., B.S.; Univ. Michigan, M. Des.; ASL, with Morris Kantor, Emil Ganso. *Member*: Phila. Pr. Cl.; Am. Color Print Soc.; Michigan WC Soc.; AAUP; Acad. A., Sc. & Let. *Awards*: prizes, Detroit Inst. A.; Friends of Mod. A., Grand Rapids, Mich., 1950; LC, 1950; Am. Color Pr. Soc., 1950, 1954, 1957; South Bend AA, 1957; AFA 1957; Am. Connoisseur Selection, 1953. *Work*: Univ. Michigan; Grand Rapids Mus. A.; Detroit Inst. A.; Univ. Maine; Smithsonian Inst.; Chrysler Corp.; Parke Davis Co.; MMA; BM; CM; N.Y. Pub. Lib.; Grace Dow Mem. Lib.; Univ. Kentucky; Saginaw Mus. A.; LC; Western Canada A. Circuit; AFA; Bradford Jr. Col.; Univ. North Carolina; Edinboro T. Col.; Albion Mus. A.; murals, Mich. Consolidated Gas Co. *Exhibited*: Nationally and internationally. One-man: Contemporaries Gal., N.Y., 1953; Farnsworth Mus., 1955; NGA, 1955; Grace Dow Mem. Lib., 1955; Jackson AA, 1957; Edinboro State T. Col., 1957; Grand Rapids, 1958; Miami Univ., 1958; Univ. North Carolina, 1958; Bradford Jr. Col., 1958; South Bend A. Center, 1958; Women's City Cl., Detroit, 1956; Horace Rackham Bldg., Detroit, 1956, 1958, and many others. *Position*: Assoc. Prof., Printmaking & Des., Univ. Michigan, Ann Arbor, Mich.

WEDIN, ELOF—*Painter*
3512 James Ave., Minneapolis 12, Minn.

B. Sweden, June 28, 1901. *Studied*: AIC; Minneapolis Inst. A. *Awards*: prizes, Minnesota State Fair, 1953, 1954, 1957; Minneapolis Inst. A., 1954; Women's Cl. Minneapolis, 1956; WAC, 1958. *Work*: Minneapolis Inst. A.; Univ. Minnesota; Minneapolis Women's Cl.; Dayton Co., Minneapolis; Smith Col.; murals, USPO, Litchfield, Minn.; Mobridge, S.D. *Exhibited*: Los A. Mus. A., 1945; Texas Centennial, 1936; Minneapolis Inst. A., 1937; GGE 1939;

AFA traveling exh., 1954, 1958; Colorado Springs FA Center, 1954; St. Paul A. Gal., 1955; one-man: WAC, 1954; retrospective, Am.-Swedish Inst., Minneapolis, 1956; Bethel Col., 1957; Winona Pub. Lib., 1957; Kilbride Gal., Minneapolis, 1958.

WEEKS, LEO ROSCO—*Illustrator, P.*

Popular Mechanics Magazine, 200 East Ontario St.; h. 407 Eugenie St., Chicago 14, Ill.

B. LaCrosse, Ind., June 23, 1903. *Studied*: Am. Acad. A., Chicago, and with Glen Sheffer. *Member*: All-Illinois Soc. FA; Assn. Chicago P. & S.; Hoosier Salon; Palette & Chisel Acad., Chicago. *Awards*: prizes, Palette & Chisel Acad., 1943, 1944, 1956, 1958; Hoosier Salon, 1948; All-Illinois Soc. FA, 1946, 1952. *Work*: Pub. Schs., Cairo, Herrin, Downers Grove, Rock Island, Ill.; in private colls., U.S. & Central America. *Exhibited*: Hoosier Salon; Palette & Chisel Acad.; All-Illinois Soc. FA, and others. I., "Penny Wise," 1942 and other children's books. Illus. for Popular Mechanics Magazine.

WEEMS, KATHARINE LANE—*Sculptor*

825 Fifth Ave., New York 21, N.Y.; s. Manchester, Mass.

B. Boston, Mass., Feb. 22, 1899. *Studied*: BMFA Sch., and with Charles Grafly, Anna Hyatt Huntington, Brenda Putnam. *Member*: NA; Nat. Inst. A. & Let.; NAWA; NSS; Arch. Lg.; Pen & Brush Cl.; Gld. Boston A.; North Shore AA. *Awards*: Medal, Sesqui-Centennial Exp., Phila., 1926; Boston Tercentenary Exh., 1930; prizes, PAFA, 1927; Paris Salon, 1928; Nat. Assn. Women P. & S., 1928; Grand Central A. Gal., 1929; NAD, 1931, 1932; Arch. Lg., 1942; NAWA, 1946. *Work*: BMFA; Reading Mus.; PAFA; Brookgreen Gardens, S.C.; BMA; carvings, bronzes, doors, Inst. Biology, Harvard Univ.; S.; fountain, Boston, Mass.; medals, U.S. Legion of Merit; U.S. Medal for Merit; Fincke Mem. Medal, Groton Sch.; Goodwin Medal, MIT. *Exhibited*: NAD; Nat. Acad. A. & Let., etc.

WEESE, MYRTLE A.—*Painter*

358 North Canon Drive, Sierra Madre, Cal.

B. Roslyn, Wash., Oct. 30, 1903. *Studied*: Los Angeles County AI, and with George Flower, Ejnar Hansen. *Member*: Scandinavian-Am. Soc.; Whittier AA; Prof. A. of Los Angeles. *Awards*: prizes, Friday Morning Cl., 1955; Sierra Madre Soc. *Work*: paintings, and ports. in private collections. *Exhibited*: Bowers Mem. Mus., Santa Ana; Greek Theatre, Los A.; Sierra Madre City Hall; Los Angeles City Hall; Women's Cl. (2 one-man).

WEGER, MARIE—*Painter*

436 Nuber Ave., Mount Vernon, N.Y.

B. Murten, Switzerland, Dec. 24, 1882. *Studied*: in Munich, Germany, with Paul Nauen, Wilhelm von Dietz. *Member*: All. A. Am.; Beaux Arts Soc., Munich & Paris. *Work*: City Hall, Munich. *Exhibited*: BM; All. A. Am.; AAPL; Queensboro SA; Tricker Gal.; & extensively in Europe.*

WEHR, PAUL ADAM—*Illustrator, Comm. A.*

620 North Michigan Ave., Chicago 11, Ill.; h. 6038 Allisonville Rd., Indianapolis 2, Ind.

B. Mt. Vernon, Ind., May 16, 1914. *Studied*: John Herron AI, B.F.A. *Member*: Indiana A. Cl. *Awards*: prizes, Indiana State Fair, 1940, 1941; Indiana A., 1942, 1944, 1951, 1956; Hoosier Salon, 1943, 1944; A. Dir. Cl., Chicago, 1945. *Work*: Herron AI; covers for Popular Mechanics magazine. *Exhibited*: PAFA, 1940, 1943; Advertising A. Exh., N.Y., 1945; A. Dir. Cl. Chicago, 1945, 1954; Hoosier Salon, 1943, 1944; Indiana A., 1937, 1942, 1943; Indiana AC, 1944; Indiana State Fair, 1936, 1940, 1941. Illus., Collier's, Coronet, Red Book magazines. *Position*: Hd., Commercial A. Dept., John Herron AI, Indianapolis, Ind., 1937-45; I., Stevens, Gross Studios, Inc., Chicago, Ill. Covers for Sports Afield; Coronet; Country Gentleman magazines.

WEIDENAAR, REYNOLD H(ENRY)—*Printmaker, I., P.*

827 Giddings Ave., Southeast, Grand Rapids 6, Mich.

B. Grand Rapids, Mich., Nov. 17, 1915. *Studied*: Kansas City AI. *Member*: ANA; Phila. Pr. Cl.; Phila. WC Cl.; SAGA; Chicago, Wash., Cal. Soc. Et.; AAPL; Michigan Pr. M.; Michigan Acad. Sc., A. & Let.; North Shore AA; Springfield A. Lg., and many other organizations. *Awards*:

Guggenheim F., 1944; Tiffany Fnd. scholarship, 1948; prizes, Detroit Inst. A., 1946, 1949, 1953; Bridgeport A. Lg., 1947, 1949, 1953, 1954; George Walter Vincent Smith Mus., 1948; Conn. Acad. FA, 1948; Delgado Mus. A., 1948; Norton Gal. A., 1948; New Jersey P. & S. Soc., 1948; Fla. Fed. A., 1949-1951, 1953; SAGA, 1950; Cal. Soc. Et., 1950; Audubon A., 1950; Oakland A. Gal., 1951; Providence A. Cl., 1951; Springfield Mus. A., 1952; Chicago Soc. Et., 1951; Clearwater Mus. A., 1951, 1952; Fla. Southern Col., 1952; Brick Store Mus., 1953; Dallas Pr. Soc., 1954; NAD, 1954, and many others. *Work*: PMA; BMFA; Norfolk Mus. A. & Sc.; Brooks Mem. Mus.; L.D.M. Sweat Mem. Mus.; Nat. Gal., New South Wales; Liverpool, England, Pub. Lib.; CMA; Oklahoma A. & M. Col.; N.Y. Pub. Lib.; Carnegie Inst.; CM; DMFA; MMA; Pa. State Univ.; WMA; LC; U.S. Nat. Mus.; Detroit Inst. A.; Nelson Gal. A.; Hackley A. Gal. *Exhibited*: Bradley Univ., 1952; Oakland A. Gal., 1948-1951; SAGA, 1948-1952, 1953, 1954; PAFA; Audubon A., 1948-1952, 1954, 1955; Northwest Pr. M., 1948-1952; NAD, Mus. A., 1954; Wichita AA, 1954; New Orleans AA, 1948-1952, 1954, 1955; Wash. WC Cl., 1955; Portland 1948-1951, 1954, 1955; Detroit Inst. A., 1948-1951, 1954, 1955, 1957; Phila. Pr. Cl., 1949, 1952; Chicago Soc. Et., 1948-1952; LC, 1951; Butler Inst. Am. A., 1957, 1958; AWS, 1957; traveling exh. Am. Prints, 1951; one-man: Hamline Gal., 1948; Albany Inst. Hist. & A., 1948; Fla. Southern Col., 1950; Miami A. Center, 1950; Okla. A. & M. Col., 1950; Wustum Mus. A., 1950, 1952; Univ. British Columbia, 1951; Wesleyan Univ., 1952; and others. Contributor to Design Magazine; Art Material Trade News. *Position*: Assoc. Ed., Design magazine; Hd. Dept. Life Drawing, Kendall Sch. Des., Grand Rapids, Mich.

WEIDNER, DORIS KUNZIE—*Painter, Ser., Lith.*

R.F.D. 1, Christiana, Pa.

Studied: Barnes Fnd.; PAFA. *Awards*: prizes, PAFA, 1944, 1946; Oklahoma Lith. Exh., 1941; Pepsi-Cola, 1945. *Work*: Woodmere A. Gal., Phila.; PAFA; LC; Okla. A. Center. *Exhibited*: PAFA, 1938-1952; Audubon A.; NAD; VMFA; CGA; one-man: PAFA, 1948; Phila., Pa., 1953.

WEIDNER, ROSWELL THEODORE—*Painter, Lith., T.*

107 North Van Pelt St., Philadelphia 3, Pa.

B. Reading, Pa., Sept. 18, 1911. *Studied*: Barnes Fnd.; PAFA. *Awards*: F., PAFA; Cresson traveling scholarship, PAFA, 1936. *Work*: Reading Mus. A.; MMA; LC; PAFA; Pa. State Col.; PMA. *Exhibited*: PAFA; NAD; CGA; Pepsi-Cola; Phila. Sketch Cl.; Phila. A. All.; Kutztown State T. Col.; Woodmere A. Gal.; one-man: PAFA, 1948. *Position*: Instr., Painting & Drawing, PAFA, Philadelphia, Pa.; Pres., F., PAFA, 1957- .

WEILAND, JAMES G.—*Portrait Painter*

Beaver Brook Rd., Lyme, Conn.

B. Toledo, Ohio, Nov. 30, 1872. *Studied*: NAD; ASL; & abroad. *Work*: Conn. State Capitol; U.S. Nat. Mus.; Conn. State Lib.; Conn. Supreme Court; Court Houses at New London, Putnam, Willimantic, Bridgeport, Hartford, Conn.; Cleveland Pub. Lib.; Western Reserve Univ. *Exhibited*: NAD; All. A. Am.; Brooklyn SA; Lyme AA.

WEILL, ERNA—*Sculptor, C., T.*

886 Alpine Dr., Teaneck, N.J.

B. Germany. *Studied*: Univ. Frankfurt, Germany. *Member*: N.Y. Soc. Craftsmen; N.Y. Soc. Ceramic A.; AEA; Com. on A. Edu. *Awards*: prizes, Intl. Exh. Women's Art, 1946, 1947. *Work*: Tel-Aviv Mus., Israel; Bezalel Mus., Jerusalem; Hebrew Univ., Jerusalem; Georgia State Mus., Athens; Hyde Park Lib.; Jewish Mus., N.Y.; Birmingham Mus. A.; ports. in private colls. *Exhibited*: BM, 1951; Village A. Center, 1948-1954; Mus. Natural Hist., N.Y.; N.Y. Soc. Craftsmen; N.Y. Soc. Ceramic A.; Jewish Mus., N.Y., 1953, 1955; AEA; one-man: Carlebach Gal., N.Y., 1951; Schoeneman Gal., N.Y., 1957. Contributor to Design, School Arts magazines. Lectures: Religious Art; Ceremonial Objects. *Position*: Instr., S., Ceramics, BM, 1942-43; Forest Hills, N.Y. and Teaneck, N.J. Community Centers; and privately.

WEIN, ALBERT W.—*Sculptor, P., Des.*

454 South Oakhurst Drive, Beverly Hills, Cal.

B. New York, N.Y., July 27, 1915. *Studied*: Maryland Inst.; BAID; NAD; Grand Central Sch. A. *Member*: F.,

Am. Acad. in Rome; F., NSS; Arch. Lg.; All. A. Am.; F., Huntington Hartford Fnd. *Awards*: prizes, Prix de Rome, 1947, 1948; Tiffany Fnd. grant, 1949; Hudson Valley AA, 1948; Medallic Art Co., 1949; Ecclesiastical S. Comp., 1950; NSS, 1942, 1946; Mun. A. Comm., 1938; BAID, 1934; Arch. Lg., 1944. *Work*: Gramercy Park Mem. Chapel, N.Y.; USPO, Frankfort, N.Y.; Eugene Higgins Mem., Woodlawn Cemetery, N.Y.; Brookgreen Gardens, S.C.; medal for Soc. Medalists; medallion, Am. Inst. of Commemorative Art.; Des. for Steuben Glass Co., presentation bowl for Pres. Trujillo, Dominican Republic, among others. *Exhibited*: NAD; MMA; Arch. Lg.; WMAA; SFMA; Jewish Mus., N.Y.; Mun. A. Gal.; Argent Gal., 1951 (one-man); Cowie Gal., Los A., 1957, 1958 (one-man).

WEINBERG, ELBERT—*Sculptor*
207 Lafayette St.; h. 40 Academy St., New Haven, Conn.

B. Hartford, Conn., May 27, 1928. *Studied*: Hartford A. Sch.; R.I. Sch. Des., B.F.A., with Waldemar Raemisch; Yale Univ., M.F.A. *Awards*: Prix de Rome, 1951; Guggenheim F., 1959. *Work*: MModA; Jewish Mus., N.Y.; AGAA; Yale Univ. A. Gal.; wall, lobby of 405 Park Ave., N.Y.; Menorah Synagogue; dec., children's ward, Warm Springs (Ga.) Polio Fnd. *Exhibited*: WMAA, 1935, 1936, 1957; one-man: Providence (R.I.) A. Center, 1951, 1954; Grace Borgenicht Gal., 1958. *Positions*: Asst. Instr., R.I. Sch. Des. & Yale Univ.; S., and Des., Cooper Union A. Sch., New York, N.Y., 1956- .

WEINBERG, LOUIS—*Sculptor, E., Des.*
University of Wisconsin, Department Art Education, Madison, Wis.

B. Troy, Kans., June 19, 1918. *Studied*: Univ. Kansas, B.F.A., M.S. *Member*: AEA; AAUP; CAA; NAEA; Western AA. *Work*: Philbrook A. Center; Univ. Wisconsin, and in private colls. *Exhibited*: PAFA; Delgado Mus. A.; Syracuse Mus. FA; Denver A. Mus.; DMFA; Philbrook A. Center; SFMA; Creative Gal., N.Y.; Forum Gal., N.Y., and others. *Position*: Instr., Univ. Wisconsin, Dept. A. Edu., Madison, Wis.†

WEINDORF, ARTHUR—*Painter, I., T.*
34-25—34th St., Long Island City 6, N.Y.

B. Long Island City, N.Y., May 25, 1885. *Member*: Soc. Indp. A. *Exhibited*: Lib. Cong., 1943; NAD, 1944, 1945; Phila. Pr. Cl., 1942, 1943; Wash. WC Cl., 1942; Brooklyn SA, 1944; Oakland A. Gal., 1943; Portland SA, 1941, 1942; Bridgeport A. Lg., 1942; Irvington A. & Mus. Assn., 1943. Contributor to: builders' & designers' magazines, with architectural & design articles. Specialist in scale models.

WEINER, A(BRAHAM) S.—*Painter, Des.*
2405—3rd St., Santa Monica, Cal.

B. Vinnitza, Russia, Mar. 30, 1897. *Studied*: Univ. Michigan, B.S. in Arch.; Studio Sch. A., Chicago; & with Alexander Archipenko, John Norton. *Member*: Cal. WC Soc.; Los A. AA. *Awards*: prizes, Du Page County (Ill.) A., 1935; Glendale (Cal.) AA, 1945. *Exhibited*: Pepsi-Cola, 1949; Denver A. Mus., 1944, 1945; Univ. Illinois, 1948; Oakland A. Gal., 1944-1946; Santa Barbara Mus. A., 1944; AIC, 1931, 1934; Los A. Mus. A., 1944-1946, 1951; Santa Monica Pub. Lib.; one-man exh.: Univ. California at Los A., 1943; SFMA, 1943; Santa Barbara Mus. A., 1946; Los A. Mus. A., 1945; Cowie Gal., Los A., 1947, 1950, 1954. *Position*: Set designer, 20th-Century Fox Film Corp.

WEINER, EGON—*Sculptor, E., L.*
835 Michigan Ave., Evanston, Ill.

B. Vienna, Austria, July 24, 1906. *Studied*: Sch. A. & Crafts, Acad. FA, Vienna. *Member*: AEA; MModA.; Hon. F., Am-Scandinavian Fnd. *Awards*: prizes, Grand Prix, Paris, 1925; Blumfield award, Vienna, 1932-34; Mun. A. Lg., Chicago, 1948; Syracuse Mus. FA, 1949; AIA, 1955; Mus. Science & Indst., Chicago, 1955; Roosevelt Univ., Chicago, 1956; medals, AIC, 1949; Oakland A. Mus., 1945, 1951. *Work*: Syracuse Mus. FA; Augsburg Col., Minneapolis; Augustana Col., Rock Island, Ill.; groups, reliefs, figures, Church of St. Augustin, Vienna; Salem Church, Chicago; windows (6) Standard Cl., Chicago; figure, Concordia Col., Ft. Wayne, Ind.; Chicago Airport; Glencoe, Ill.; Amalgamated Meatcutters Union Bldg., Chicago. *Ex-*

hibited: AIC, 1940-1953; PAFA, 1941, 1947, 1949-1951; Oakland Mus. A., 1942, 1945, 1946, 1948-1951; Univ. Chicago, 1943, 1945; Syracuse Mus. FA, 1948-1951, 1958; Portland (Ore.) A. Mus., 1948; CAM, 1949; Assoc. Am. A., Chicago, 1949; MMA, 1951; A. Center, Chicago, 1954; Religious Art exh., Minneapolis, 1957; one-man: AIC; Renaissance Soc., 1947; Illinois Inst. Tech., 1949; Univ. Illinois, 1951; Lawrence Col., 1951; Palmer House, Chicago, 1955; Davenport Mun. A. Gal., 1958; Augustana Col., 1958. Contributor to American-German Review; Frontiers; Figure magazines. Lectures, U.S. and abroad. *Position*: Prof. S. and Life Drawing, AIC, Chicago, Ill. Visiting Prof. A., Augustana Col., 1956.

WEINGAERTNER, HANS—*Painter*
312 Lake Ave., Lyndhurst, N.J.

B. Kraiburg, Germany, Sept. 11, 1896. *Studied*: Royal Acad., Munich, Germany, and with Ludwig Klein, Moritz Hyman. *Member*: Assoc. A. New Jersey; Conn. Acad. FA; Audubon A.; New Jersey WC Soc.; New Haven Paint & Clay Cl. *Awards*: prizes, Montclair A. Mus., 1949, 1950; New Haven Paint & Clay Cl., 1950; Newark A. Cl., 1951. *Work*: Newark Mus. *Exhibited*: Soc. Indp. A., 1929-1940; BM, 1932; AIC; CGA; Newark Mus.; Carnegie Inst.; VMFA; New Haven Paint & Clay Cl.; Montclair A. Mus.; New Jersey State Mus.; Pa. State T. Col.; PAFA; WMAA; NAD; Conn. Acad. FA. *Position*: Instr., Newark Sch. F. & Indst. A., Newark, N.J.

WEINMAN, ROBERT ALEXANDER—*Sculptor*
333 Fourth Ave., New York 10, N.Y.; h. 40 Choate Lane, Pleasantville, N.Y.

B. New York, N.Y., Mar. 19, 1915. *Studied*: NAD. *Member*: NSS. *Awards*: prizes, NSS, 1952. *Work*: Brookgreen Gardens, S.C.; Our Lady Queen of Martyrs Church, N.Y.; U.S. Military Acad., West Point, N.Y.; bronze doors, Armstrong Lib., Waco, Tex.; medals, series of 12 for Nat. Collegiate Athletic Assn.; Am. Arbitration Assn.; Am. Chemical Soc.; Airmen's Mem., Tulsa, Okla.; figures, Mary Immaculate Seminary, Northampton, Pa.; sc. entrance, Our Lady of Perpetual Help, Richmond Hill, N.Y.; medals, Crusade for Freedom; Studebaker 100th Anniversary; Helms Athletic Fnd.; Intl. Golf Assn.; Canada Cup Medal; Immaculate Conception; Nash Conservation Award medal; trophies; Sports magazine award; Intl. Golf Low Score Trophy; sc. dec., Fed. Reserve Bank, Buffalo, N.Y., and others. *Exhibited*: NAD; PAFA; Albany Inst. Hist. & A.; NAC; NSS.

WEISGARD, LEONARD—*Illustrator, Des., L.*
Roxbury, Mass.

B. New Haven, Conn., Dec. 13, 1916. *Studied*: PIASch.; & with A. Brodovitch. *Awards*: prizes, Caldecott award, 1947. *Work*: MModA Children's Coll. *Exhibited*: MModA; MMA; AIGA, 1958; & in many libraries. Author: numerous children's books, 1936-1946; "Silly Willy Nilly," publ. in Near East. Author, I., "Treasures to See," 1957; "Mr. Peaceable Paints," 1957; I., "First Days of the World," 1959; "First People in the World," publ. in Persian, 1958. Contributor to: New Yorker, American Home, Ladies Home Journal, & other magazines. Lectures: "Primitive Art Forms in Relation to Children's Books"; "How to Illustrate a Child's Book." Des. for San Francisco Ballet Co.; children's greeting cards, United Nations. *Positions*: A. Consultant, Field Edu. Enterprises, 1958; Consultant with Boston Univ. seminar Television and the Child, 1958.

WEISMAN, JOSEPH—*Painter, Des., I., T.*
411 North Spaulding Ave., Los Angeles 36, Cal.

B. Schenectady, N.Y., Feb. 17, 1907. *Studied*: Chouinard AI; Los A. A. Center Sch.; & with Barse Miller, Millard Sheets, Clarence Hinkle, & others. *Member*: AEA. *Awards*: prizes, Cal. State Fair, 1938, 1939. *Work*: Manual Arts H.S., Metropolitan H.S., Los A., Cal. *Exhibited*: Santa Barbara Mus., A., 1944; PAFA, 1936-1937; Laguna Beach AA, 1938; Los A. Mus. A., 1930, 1931, 1933, 1937-1939; San Diego FA Soc., 1931, 1933, 1940; Oakland A. Gal., 1933, 1936-1938; Los A. AA, 1944, 1945, 1946, 1953; Santa Cruz A. Lg., 1933-1938; 1946; Cal. State Fair, 1932-1936, 1938, 1939; Los A. County Fair, 1929-1931, 1936, 1938; GGE 1939; Santa Paula, Cal., 1945; Madonna Festival, 1955. *Position*: Instr., Hollywood A. Center Sch., 1954-55; Adult Edu., Los A. Bd. Edu., 1954- .

WEISMAN, WINSTON R.—Educator, W.

Art Department, Pennsylvania State University, University Park, Pa.; h. 525 Glenn Road, State College, Pa.

B. New York, N.Y., Feb. 3, 1909. *Studied*: Ohio State Univ., B.A., Ph.D.; N.Y. Univ., Inst. FA, M.A. *Member*: CAA; Soc. Architectural Hist. *Awards*: Carnegie Fnd. Scholarship; Am. Council of Learned Soc. Research grant; Am. Philosophical Research grant (2). Many contributions to: Architectural Review; Journal of the Soc. of Arch. Hist.; Catholic Art Quarterly; College Art Journal; Journal of the Am. Inst. Arch.; American Heritage; N.Y. Times Sunday Magazine; Art Bulletin, etc.

WEISMANN, DONALD LeROY—
Educator, P., Cr., L., W.

Department of Art, University Texas (12); h. Rt. 7, Box 68W, Austin, Tex.

B. Milwaukee, Wis., Oct. 12, 1914. *Studied*: Wisconsin State Col., B.S.; Univ. Minnesota; Univ. Wisconsin, Ph.M.; St. Louis Univ.; Harvard Univ.; Ohio State Univ., Ph.D. *Member*: Am. Soc. for Aesthetics; AAUP; CAA; Com. on A. Edu., MModA; Am. Studies Assn.; Texas FA Soc. *Awards*: Carnegie FA Scholarship, Harvard Univ., 1941; prizes, Wis. P. & S., 1934, 1936; Wis. Mem. Gal., 1937; Ky.-Ind. Exh., J. B. Speed Mus. A., 1953; DMFA, 1955-1957 (purchase); Butler Inst. Am. A., 1957 (purchase); D. D. Feldman Exh., 1955, 1956, 1957, 1958 (purchase). *Work*: mural, Illinois Centennial Bldg. *Exhibited*: Nationally and internationally, 1934-1958. Contributor to College Art Journal; Midwest Review; Univ. Kansas City Review. Lectures: Aesthetics; 19th & 20th Century Painting. Assembled, catalogued exhs.: Ulfert Wilke Retrospective Exh., Univ. Kentucky FA Gal.; Victor Hammer Retrospective, Univ. Kentucky. *Position*: Asst. Prof., Illinois State Normal Univ., 1940-48; Prof., Wayne Univ., 1949-51; Prof., Hd. A. Dept., Univ. Kentucky, 1951-54; Prof., Chm., Dept., A., Univ. Texas, 1954- , Austin, Tex.

WEISS, DOROTHEA PATTERSON—Painter

McDowell Road, Mesilla Park, N.M.

B. Philadelphia, Pa.; Feb. 15, 1910. *Studied*: Moore Inst. A.; Yale Sch. FA, B.F.A. *Award*: prize, El Paso AA. *Work*: Mus. New Mexico, Santa Fe; Texas Western Univ.; Stations of the Cross, Our Lady of the Valley, Ysleta, Tex.; Christo Rey Church, Santa Fe; mural, St. Joseph's Church, El Paso. *Exhibited*: San F. AA, 1937; El Paso Sun Carnival, 1951, 1952, 1953, 1958; Mus. New Mexico Fiesta Exh., 1948-1957; Rio Grande Valley Exh., Mus. New Mexico A. Gal., 1956; New Mexico A., 1954. *Position*: Incorporator, Memb., Mesilla Design Center.

WEISSBERGER, HERBERT P.—Museum Curator

Carnegie Institute, Department of Fine Arts, 4400 Forbes St., Pitttsburgh 13, Pa.*

WEISSER, LEONIE OELKERS (Mrs. Fred W. Weisser)—
Painter

New Braunfels, Tex.

B. Guadalupe County, Tex., Oct. 5, 1890. *Studied*: with Minnie Stanford, John E. Jenkins, R. J. Onderdonk. *Member*: San Antonio A. Lg. *Awards*: prizes, Hays County, Tex., Fair, 1922-1924; Fed. Women's Cl., Lubbock, Tex., 1931. *Work*: Witte Mem. Mus. *Exhibited*: San Marcos, Tex.; Hays County, Tex.; Texas A.; SSAL; San Antonio, Tex.

WEISSMAN, POLAIRE—Museum Director

Costume Institute, Metropolitan Museum of Art, Fifth Ave. at 82nd St., New York 28, N.Y.*

WELCH, MABEL R.—Miniature Painter

171 Main St., Wilbraham, Mass.

B. New Haven, Conn. *Studied*: ASL; & with Cox, Reid; in Paris, with Garrido, Lazar, Scott, Van der Weyden. *Member*: ASMP; NAWA; Brooklyn Soc. Min. P.; Pa. Soc. Min. P. *Awards*: med., Pan-Pacific Exp., 1915; Pa. Soc. Min. P., 1920; ASMP, 1935, 1940; Cal. Soc. Min. P., 1937; prizes, Brooklyn Soc. Min. P., 1933; NAWA, 1938; PAFA; 1938. *Work*: BM; PMA; CGA.

WELDON, WALTER A.—Ceramic Craftsman, Des.

621 Edgewood St., Baltimore 29, Md.

B. Rochester, N.Y., May 4, 1890. *Studied*: Johns Hopkins Univ. *Member*: F., Am. Ceramic Soc.; Kiln Cl., Wash., D.C. *Award*: Charles Fergus Binns medal, 1953 for Ceramic art. *Exhibited*: Syracuse Mus. FA; extensively in ceramic exh. in U.S. Contributor to: Ceramic Industry; Am. Ceramic Soc. Bulletin. Lectures: The Art of the Potter. Author: "The Potter's Corner." *Position*: Memb. United Nations Tech. Assistance Admin. Mission to India, 1952, Yugoslavia, 1953.*

WELLER, ALLEN STUART—Educator, Cr., W., L.

110 Architecture Bldg., University Illinois; h. 412 West Iowa St., Urbana, Ill.

B. Chicago, Ill., Feb. 1, 1907. *Studied*: Univ. Chicago, Ph.B., Ph.D.; Princeton Univ., A.M. *Member*: CAA (Bd. Dir.); Nat. Assn. Sch. Des. (Bd. Dir.); Midwestern College A. Conf.; Soc. Arch. Historians. *Awards*: Carnegie F., 1927-28; Princeton Univ. F., 1928-29; Bureau of Univ. Travel F., 1929; Legion of Merit, 1945. Author: "Francesco di Giorgio, 1439-1501"; "Abraham Rattner," 1956. Contributor articles and reviews to art magazines. Book review Ed., College Art Journal, 1949- ; Chicago correspondent, Arts 1952-1958. *Position*: Asst. Prof., Univ. Missouri, 1929-42, Assoc. Prof., 1946-47; Hd. A. Dept. 1948-54, Dean, Col. F. & App. A., 1954- , Univ. Illinois, Urbana, Ill.; Visiting Prof. Hist. A., Univ. Minnesota, 1947, Univ. Colorado, 1949, Univ. California, 1950, 1953.

WELLER, PAUL—Painter, Lith., Des., Photog.

227 East 67th St., New York 21, N.Y.

B. Boston, Mass., Dec. 20, 1912. *Studied*: NAD. *Member*: Soc. Magazine Photographers. *Work*: MMA; Springfield Mus. A.; BM; mural, USPO, Baldwinsville, N.Y. *Exhibited*: AIC, 1936; PAFA, 1936; MModA, 1939; one-man: BM, 1952-53. *Position*: A. Dir., Infinity Magazine, 1953- .

WELLS, JAMES LESESNE—Painter, Lith., Eng.

1333 R St., Northwest, Washington 9, D.C.

B. Atlanta, Ga., Nov. 2, 1902. *Studied*: Lincoln Univ.; T. Col., Columbia Univ., B.S., M.A.; NAD, and with Frank Nankivell. *Member*: AFA; Wash. WC Cl. *Awards*: medal, 1931, prize, 1933, Harmon Fnd.; Wash. Artists, 1957. *Work*: PMG; Valentine Mus. A.; Thayer Mus. A.; Univ. Kansas; Hampton Inst.; Howard Univ.; Lincoln Univ.; IBM. *Exhibited*: CGA, 1952; Smithsonian Inst., 1947 (one-man); SAGA, 1956; BM; Phila. Pr. Cl.; Howard Univ., 1947, 1948, 1950, 1953; Plaza Theatre Gal., Wash., D.C., 1954; New-Age Gal., 1947-1950; Barnett Aden Gal., 1949; Du Pont Theatre Gal., 1949; Soc. Wash. Pr. M., 1953, 1956, 1958; Inspiration House, Wash., D.C., 1953; Wash. WC Cl., 1956; circulating exh. Wash. Artists, 1957; Artists' Mart, 1957; one-man: Barnett Aden Gal., 1950. *Position*: Assoc. Prof. A., Howard Univ., Washington, D.C.

WELTON, MRS. JAMES B. See Cavanna, Elise

WENG, SIEGFRIED R.—Museum Director, E., Gr., L.

Evansville Museum of Arts & Science, 216 Northwest Second St., Evansville 8, Ind.; h. Newburgh, Ind.

B. Oshkosh, Wis., May 20, 1904. *Studied*: Oshkosh State T. Col.; AIC; Univ. Chicago, M.A.; Fogg Mus. A., Harvard Univ. *Member*: AFA; AAMus.; Midwest Mus. Assn. *Position*: Vice-Pres., Midwest Mus. Assn. for Indiana, 1954-55; Pres., Midwest Mus. Assn., 1948; Lecture Asst. to Lorado Taft, Chicago, 1928; Dir., Dayton AI & Sch. A., 1929-50; Dir., Evansville Mus. A. & Science, Evansville, Ind., 1950- .

WENGENROTH, STOW—Lithographer

717 Main St., Greenport, N.Y.

B. Brooklyn, N.Y., July, 1906. *Studied*: ASL; Grand Central A. Sch.; & with George Pearse Ennis, John Carlson. *Member*: NA; Nat. Inst. A. & Let.; Providence WC Cl.; Conn. Acad. FA; SC; Prairie Pr. M.; Smithsonian FA Comm. *Awards*: prizes, Phila. Pr. Cl., 1937, 1939; SC, 1937; AV, 1942; Northwest Pr. M., 1943; Conn. Acad. FA, 1943, 1946; Mint Mus. A., 1944; med., Phila. WC Cl., 1933, 1943; Audubon A., 1945, 1955; A. Fellowship med., 1944. *Work*: Syracuse Mus. FA; BMA; AGAA; Lib.

Cong.; N.Y. Pub. Lib.; WMAA; Denver A. Mus.; Milwaukee AI; Los A. Mus. A.; SAM; FMA; BMFA; PAFA; MMA; Carnegie Inst.; Albany Inst. Hist. & A.; etc. *Exhibited*: nationally. Author: "Making a Lithograph," 1936.

WENGER, JOHN—Painter, Des.
252 West 76th St., New York 23, N.Y.

B. Russia, June 16, 1891. *Studied*: NAD; and in Russia. *Member*: Audubon A.; AWS; Un. Scenic A.; Nat. Soc. Painters in Casein. *Awards*: prizes, Fla. Southern Col., 1952; Tel-Aviv Mus., Israel; medal, Sesqui-Centennial Exp., Phila., Pa., 1926. *Work*: Tel-Aviv Mus.; Mus. City of New York; des. for many stage and film productions, concert settings. *Exhibited*: CGA, 1936; PAFA; NAD; AIC; AWS; Audubon A., 1945, 1953, 1954, 1956; Rochester Mem. A. Gal.; MMA, 1949; BM; MModA; Mus. City of New York; Stendahl Gal., Los A.; Nat. Soc. Painters in Casein, 1954, 1955; Grand Central A. Gal., 1956; oneman: Ferargil Gal., 1925; Montross Gal., 1931-1934; Grand Central A. Gal., 1929, 1935, 1938, 1940, 1944, 1950, 1956; Staten Island Inst., 1945.

WENLEY, ARCHIBALD GIBSON—Museum Director
4348 Garfield St., Northwest, Washington 7, D.C.

B. Ann Arbor, Mich., May 5, 1898. *Studied*: Univ. Michigan, A.B.; L'Ecole des Langues Orientales Vivantes, Institut des Hautes Etudes Chinoises, and College de France, Paris. *Member*: Am. Oriental Soc.; Smithsonian A. Comm.; Chinese A. Soc. Am.; Far Eastern Assn. *Work*: Freer Gal. A., Wash., D.C. Co-author, "China," Smithsonian Inst. War Background Studies, No. 20; Author, Freer Gal. A. Occasional Papers, No. 1: "Grand Empress Dowager Wen Ming and the Northern Wei Necropolis at Fang Shan," 1947; Co-author, 'A Descriptive and Illustrative Catalogue of Chinese Bronzes Acquired During the Administration of John Ellerton Lodge," Freer Gal. A. Oriental Studies No. 3, 1946. Contributor to Journal of Am. Oriental Soc. Lectures on Arts of China, Japan and Korea. *Position*: Dir., Freer Gal. A., Washington, D.C., 1943- ; Research Prof. Oriental A., Univ. Michigan.

WENTWORTH, HARRIET MARSHALL—Painter
New Hope, Pa.

B. New Hope, Pa., Sept. 7, 1896. *Studied*: PAFA; Grande Chaumiere, Academie Colorossi, Paris, and with Daniel Garber, William Lathrop, A. Margaretta Archambault, Cecilia Beaux, F. Luis Mora. *Member*: AEA. *Work*: PAFA; Smithsonian Inst. *Exhibited*: PAFA; Smithsonian Inst.; Ainslie Gal., N.Y. (one-man); Phillips Mill, New Hope, Pa.

WENZEL, WILLIAM MICHAEL (BILL)—Cartoonist, I.
58 Olean Blvd., Atlantic Highlands, N.J.

B. Union, N.J., Jan. 22, 1918. *Studied*: CUASch. *Member*: Nat. Cartoonists Soc. Illus., Ed., "Love Ledger," 1946; "Off Limits," 1952; "Flimsey Report," 1953. Contributor cartoons to Colliers; Sat. Eve. Post; True; Cavalier; This Week; Saga; Argosy; N.Y. Journal-American, and other national magazines and newspapers.*

WERBE, ANNA LAVICK (Mrs. David B.)—Painter, T.
1986 Oakman Blvd., Detroit, Mich.

B. Chicago, Ill. *Studied*: AIC. *Member*: Detroit FA All.; Detroit Mus. A. Founders Soc.; AIC Alum. Assn.; Detroit A. Market; Michigan WC Soc. *Awards*: medal, Michigan State Fair, 1934; prize, Detroit Inst. A., 1948; Michigan A., 1952. *Work*: Detroit Inst. A. *Exhibited*: Los A. Mus. A.; Butler AI; Detroit Inst. A.; Grand Central A. Gal.; PAFA; Flint Inst. A.; Ann Arbor Mus. A.; AIC (retrospective); one-man: Arthur Newton Gal., N.Y.*

WERLEY, BEATRICE B.—Painter, I., Comm. A.
P.O. Box 1025, Eau Gallie, Fla.

B. Pittsburgh, Pa., Mar. 28, 1906. *Studied*: Cleveland Col.; Huntington Polytechnic Inst.; & with Henry Keller, Frank Wilcox, W. Combs. *Awards*: Med., Cleveland Clinic. *Work*: Three animated medical movies for educational purposes; Am. Med. Assn. exhibits, San F., 1946, Cleveland, 1946. I., "The Extremities," 1945. Lectures: Medical Art. *Position*: Staff A., Cleveland Clinic, Cleveland, Ohio, 1935-49; Pres., Melbourne AA, 1951-53; I., Patrick Air Force Base, Fla., 1955-1956.

WERNER, CHARLES GEORGE—Cartoonist, L.
Indianapolis Star; h. 4445 Brown Rd., Devon Hills, Indianapolis, Ind.

B. Marshfield, Wis., Mar. 23, 1909. *Studied*: Oklahoma City Univ.; Northwestern Univ. *Member*: Nat. Cartoonists Soc. *Awards*: Pulitzer prize, 1938; Sigma Delta Chi, 1943; Nat. Headliners Cl., 1951; Freedom Fnd., 1951, 1952. *Work*: Huntington Lib.; LC; White House, Wash. D.C. *Exhibited*: Nat. Cartoonists Soc. Lectures: History of Cartooning. *Position*: Cart., Daily Oklahoman, 1935-41; Chicago Sun, 1941-47; Indianapolis Star, 1947- .*

WERNER, MRS. GERALDINE PINE. See Pine, Geri

WERNER, NAT—Sculptor
215 East 11th St., New York 3, N.Y.

B. New York, N.Y., Dec. 8, 1910. *Studied*: Col. City of N.Y., B.A.; ASL; & with Robert Laurent. *Member*: S. Gld. *Work*: Lyman Allyn Mus.; WMAA; James Madison H.S., N.Y.; N.Y. Engineering Soc.; USPO, Fowler, Ind. *Exhibited*: WMAA, 1936-1946; PAFA, 1942, 1943, 1945, 1946; AIC, 1942, 1943; MMA, 1941; MModA; ACA Gal., 1938, 1941, 1942, 1944, 1946, 1950, 1952, 1956 (all oneman exh.) Lectures: Contemporary Sculpture.

WERTH, KURT—Illustrator
645 West 239th St., New York 63, N.Y.

B. Leipzig, Germany, Sept. 21, 1896. *Studied*: State Acad. for Graphic Arts, Leipzig. *Work*: Museum of Art, Leipzig. *Exhibited*: one-man exhibitions, Leipzig and New York State. Illus.: "Merry Miller," 1952; "No Ducks for Dinner," 1953; "Bakers Man," 1954; "Aldos Tower," 1954; "Tailor's Trick," 1955; "One Mitten Louis," 1955; "Picnic Pony," 1956; "The Year Without a Santa Claus," 1957; "Jonathan D," 1959. Cart., I., The New York Times magazine.

WESCHLER, ANITA—Sculptor, P.
136 Waverly Place, New York 14, N.Y.

B. New York, N.Y. *Studied*: Parsons Sch. Des.; ASL, with Zorach; PAFA, with Laessle. *Member*: NAWA; Arch. Lg.; Fed. Mod. P. & S.; S. Gld.; Audubon A.; Artist-Craftsmen of N.Y. *Awards*: medal, Montclair A. Mus.; Soc. Wash. A.; prizes, Friends of Am. A., Grand Rapids, Mich.; F., McDowell Colony; prize, AFA traveling exh., 1951; NAWA, 1952; F., PAFA, 1957. *Work*: WMAA; MMA; Univ. Nebraska; Norfolk Mus. A. & Sc.; Tel-Aviv Mus.; Turkish All.; USPO, Elkin, N.C. *Exhibited*: MMA; WMAA; MModA; BM; AIC; PAFA; PMA; Carnegie Inst.; AFA traveling exh.; SFMA; S. Gld.; Am. Acad. A. & Lets.; Fed. Mod. P. & S.; Silvermine Gld. A.; New Jersey P. & S. Soc.; Audubon A.; Art: USA, 1958, and others; one-man: Assoc. Am. A.; Weyhe Gal.; Hudson Park Branch, N.Y. Pub. Lib.; Robinson Gal.; Levitt Gal.; translucent paintings in fiber glass and plastic resin, 1956.

WESCOTT, PAUL—Painter
331 West Miner St., West Chester, Pa.; Friendship, Me.

B. Milwaukee, Wis., Apr. 12, 1904. *Studied*: AIC; PAFA. *Member*: F., PAFA (life); Chester County AA (life, Dir.); Phila. A. All.; AFA; Wilmington Soc. FA. *Awards*: Cresson traveling scholarship, Toppan prize, PAFA, 1930, Lambert Fund, 1943; NAD, Ranger Fund, 1953, Obrig prize, 1954, Palmer prize, 1956; prize, Art: USA, 1958. *Work*: PAFA, NAD, etc. *Exhibited*: MMA; PAFA; NAD; PMA; BMA; CGA; AIC; Detroit Inst. A.; Toledo Mus. A.; CAM; Butler Inst. Am. A.; Farnsworth Mus. A.; Phila. A. All.; Portland Mus. A., and others. *Position*: Instr., Dir., A. & Crafts, The Hill Sch., Pottstown, Pa., 1933-52.

WESSEL, BESSIE HOOVER—Painter
2152 Alpine Pl., Cincinnati 6, Ohio

B. Brookville, Ind., Jan. 7, 1889. *Studied*: Cincinnati A. Acad.; & with Frank Duveneck. *Member*: Cincinnati Professional A.; Cincinnati Woman's AC. *Awards*: prizes, Cincinnati Woman's AC, 1937, 1939, 1940, 1948, 1950; Hoosier Salon, 1943, 1945, 1947. *Work*: Christian Col., Columbia, Mo.; NAD; Anderson House, Wash., D.C.; Am. Legion Auxiliary Hdqtrs., Indianapolis, Ind. *Exhibited*: CM, 1944; annually: Cincinnati Professional A., Woman's AC, Hoosier Salon.

WESSEL, HERMAN HENRY—*Painter, T.*
2152 Alpine Pl., Cincinnati 6, Ohio

B. Vincennes, Ind., Jan. 16, 1878. *Studied*: Cincinnati A. Acad., with Frank Duveneck. *Member*: Cincinnati AC; Cincinnati Professional A. *Work*: CM; murals, Scioto County Court House; Fed. Reserve Bank, Holmes Hospital, West Hills H.S., all in Cincinnati; Ohio State Office Bldg., Columbus; USPO, Springfield, Ohio.

WESSELS, GLENN ANTHONY—*Painter, W., L., E.*
Art Department, University of California, Berkeley 4, Cal.; h. 1601 La Vereda Road, Berkeley 9, Cal.

B. Capetown, South Africa, Dec. 15, 1895. *Studied*: Cal. Col. A. & Crafts, B.F.A.; Univ. California, B.A., M.A.; & in Paris, France; Munich, Germany. *Member*: San F. AA; AAUP. *Awards*: prize, SAM; San F. AA, 1956; Oakland A. Mus., 1957. *Work*: SFMA; Univ. California; SAM; Washington State Col.; Oakland A. Mus.; murals, Laguna Honda Home for the Aged, San F., Cal. *Exhibited*: Oakland A. Mus., 1935, 1957; San F. AA, 1935-1956; SAM; Santa Barbara Mus. A., 1946 (one-man). Author, I., Correspondence manuals in drawing & painting (Univ. California Extension Div.), 1945, 1946. Contributor to Encyclopaedia Americana, 1946. Lectures: Modern Art; Art History & Art Appreciation. *Position*: Instr., California Col. A. & Crafts, Berkeley, Cal., 1930-1940; Mills Col., Oakland, Cal., 1932; Assoc. Prof. FA, Washington State Col., Pullman, Wash., 1940-1956; Assoc. Prof. A., Univ. California, Berkeley, Cal., 1946-50, Prof. A., 1951- .

WEST, BERNICE (Mrs. Robert A. Beyers)—*Sculptor*
10008 Meadowbrook Drive, Dallas 29, Tex.

B. New York, N.Y., Apr. 26, 1906. *Studied*: with Alexander Archipenko, Edmond Amateis, Lu Duble, William Zorach, Winold Reiss. *Member*: NAWA; Pen & Brush Cl.; Conn. Acad. FA; Southern Vermont A. *Awards*: med., NAWA, 1932; SSAL, 1940; Conn. Acad. FA, 1943; Fed. A. 1955. *Work*: monument, Silver Springs, Fla.; Mead Botanical Gardens, Winter Park, Fla.; Wadsworth Atheneum; Mint. Mus. A.; High Point (N.C.) Mus.; Swarthmore Col.; mural, Charlotte (N.C.) Little Theatre; Manning House, Dallas. *Exhibited*: NAD, 1941; Conn. Acad. FA, 1941-1952; Mint Mus. A., 1940, 1941, 1945, 1946; Southern Vermont A., 1926-1958; SSAL, 1938-1941; Westport A. Market, 1932-1935; Mt. Dora (Fla.) A. Lg., 1935-1940; DMFA, 1958; one-man exh.: Contemporary A., 1931; Midtown Gal., 1932; Ferargil Gal., 1933; Mint Mus. A., 1941.

WEST, CLIFFORD BATEMAN—*Painter, T., Lith.*
225 Lone Pine Road, Bloomfield Hills, Mich.

B. Cleveland, Ohio, July 4, 1916. *Studied*: Cleveland Sch. A.; Adams State T. Col., Alamosa, Colo., B.A.; Colorado Springs FA Center; Cranbrook Acad. A., M.A.; & with Boardman Robinson, Arnold Blanch, & others. *Awards*: Prix de Rome, 1939; prize, Flint Inst A. *Work*: Massillon Mus. A.; Iowa State T. Col.; Cranbrook Mus. A.; murals, Rackham Mem. Bldg., Detroit; Alamosa (Colo.) Nat. Bank; City Bank, Detroit; Casa Contenta Hotel, Guatemala; Veterans Mem. Bldg., Detroit; Fox & Hounds Inn, Bloomfield Hills. *Exhibited*: AIC, 1937, 1939, 1943-1945; MMA (AV), 1942; Detroit Inst. A., 1937, 1938, 1940-1945, 1955; CMA, 1934, 1937; Butler AI, 1938, 1943, 1946, 1955; Massillon Mus. A., 1953, 1954; Denver A. Mus., 1937, 1939, 1943; Milwaukee AI, 1946. Lectures: Art in Education; Design in Photography; Design & Composition. *Position*: Instr. Anatomy, Cranbrook Acad. A., Bloomfield Hills, Mich., Instr., Painting & A., Hist., Kingswood School, Cranbrook; Instr., Life Drawing, Bloomfield AA.

WEST, HAROLD E.—*Painter, I., C., Des., Gr.*
601 Canyon Rd., Santa Fé, N.M.

B. Honey Grove, Tex., Oct. 16, 1902. *Exhibited*: Mus. New Mexico, Santa Fé; Fiesta Show, 1958; AIC. *Award*: Southwest Annual, 1957. I., "Broadside to the Sun," 1946; Author, I., "Cowboy Calendar," 1946 (hand-blocked prints).

WEST, LOWREN—*Painter, I.*
610 West 113th St., New York 25, N.Y.

B. New York, N.Y., Feb. 28, 1923. *Studied*: PIASch.; Hans Hofmann Sch. FA; Columbia Univ. *Exhibited*: City

Center Gal., 1955; James Gal., 1956, 1958 (2-man); Panoras Gal., 1956 (2-man); Art:USA, 1958; Rabin Kreuger Gal., Newark, N.J.; Nat. Lithographers' Exh., 1956-57. Contributor illus. to Esquire; New Yorker magazines; N.Y. Times; Fortune; Graphis.

WEST, PENNERTON—*Painter, C., S., Et.*
126 West 23rd St., New York 11, N.Y.; h. Mohegan Lake, N.Y.

B. New York, N.Y., Apr. 11, 1913. *Studied*: ASL; CUASch.; Hans Hofmann Sch. FA, and with William Hayter. *Member*: Silvermine Gld. A.; AEA. *Work*: MModA; N.Y. Pub. Lib. *Exhibited*: U.S. State Dept. traveling exh., Europe, 1953; BM, 1950; AFA traveling exh., 1951; Mus. Mod. A., Paris, 1951; Atelier 17 group exhs., 1951; Kootz Gal., 1950; Stable Gallery, 1955.

WEST, WALTER RICHARD—*Painter, T.*
Bacone College, Muskogee, Okla.

B. Darlington, Okla., Sept. 8, 1912. *Studied*: Bacone Col.; Univ. Oklahoma, B.F.A., M.F.A.; Univ. Redlands, Cal.; Tulsa Univ *Awards*: prizes, Kansas City, Mo.; Philbrook A. Center, Nat. Indian Exh., 1949, 1950, 1955. *Work*: William Rockhill Nelson Gal. A.; U.S. Dept. Interior, Wash., D.C.; Chappell A. Gal., Pasadena, Cal.; Phoenix Indian H.S.; USPO, Okemah, Okla.; Bacone Col.; James Graham & Son, N.Y.; NGA. *Exhibited*: Kansas City, Mo., 1937; Tulsa, Okla., 1938; Dept. Interior, Wash., D.C.; Chappell Gal. A., 1941; Am. Indian A. Exh., Philbrook A. Center, 1946, 1949, 1950, 1955; one-man: Univ. Redlands, 1952; Esquire Theatre Gal., Chicago; Oshkosh Pub. Mus.; Bacone Col.; Telfair Acad. A.; Philbrook A. Center, 1955; Tulsa, 1957; Eastern A. & M. Col., Wilburton, Okla., 1958. I., "The Cheyenne Way," 1941; "The Thankful People," 1950; "Tales of the Cheyennes," 1952. Lectures: "Art of the North American Indians"; "Indian Art," especially own series of religious interpretations. *Position*: Hd. A. Dept., Bacone Col., Muskogee, Okla., 1947- .

WEST, WILBUR WARNE—*Educator*
Armstrong Hall of Fine Arts, Cornell College; h. 324 South Third St., West, Mount Vernon, Iowa

B. Indiana, Mar. 10, 1912. *Studied*: Ohio State Univ., B.S., with Arthur Baggs, Edgar Littlefield; Columbia Univ., M.A.; Woodstock, N.Y. *Member*: NAEA; Western AA; Northern Indiana A.; AAUP; CAA. *Awards*: Midland Gal., 1935; Scholarship, AIA, 1946. *Exhibited*: Nat. Ceramics Exh.; Butler Inst. Am. A.; Midland Gal., South Bend; Hoosier Salon; Northern Indiana A.; Columbus A. Lg.; Indiana State Fair; Akron AI; Kent Univ. Lectures: Art & Architecture of Europe; Design Today. *Position*: Hd., A. Dept., Gallery Dir., Cornell College, Mount Vernon, Iowa.

WESTBROOK, LLOYD LEONARD—*Painter*
25693 Mill St., Olmsted Falls, Ohio

B. Olmsted Falls, Ohio, Apr. 28, 1903. *Studied*: Oberlin Col.; Cleveland Sch. A.; & with Henry Keller, Frank N. Wilcox. *Work*: CMA. *Exhibited*: Carnegie Inst., 1941; VMFA, 1946; CMA, 1946-1951.

WESTCOTT, WILLIAM CARTER—*Sculptor*
248 East 33rd St., New York, N.Y.; s. Barnstable, Devon, England

B. Atlantic City, N.J., Oct. 4, 1900. *Studied*: Sorbonne, Paris, France; ASL. *Member*: NSS; F., Royal Soc. A., London. *Awards*: Earle award for sculpture (2). *Work*: Lou Gehrig Mem. bust, Boy's Town; monuments, busts, mem., Staunton, Va.; Virginia Military Acad.; Mayfield, Pa.; St. Lo, France; Bush Terminal, Brooklyn, N.Y.; Northwestern Military and Naval Acad.; many portrait busts of prominent persons. *Exhibited*: nationally.*

WESTERMEIER, CLIFFORD PETER—*Educator, W., L., P., I.*
521 Adams St., Fayetteville, Ark.

B. Buffalo, N.Y., Mar. 4, 1910. *Studied*: Buffalo Sch. FA; PIASch; N.Y. Sch. F. & App. A.; Univ. Buffalo, B.S.; Univ. Colorado, Ph.D. *Member*: Buffalo SA. *Awards*: prizes, The Patteran, 1939, 1940. *Work*: Albright A. Gal.; many portraits. *Exhibited*: Albright A. Gal., 1937-1943;

AWCS, 1939; Syracuse Mus. FA, 1941; Boulder, Colo.; & in Paris, London; one-man: Denver, Colo., 1950; Santa Fé, N.M., 1950. Contributor to: Britannica Junior; Encyclopaedia Britannica. Author: "Man, Beast and Dust: The Story of Rodeo," 1947; Author, I., "Trailing the Cowboy," 1955; "Who Rush to Glory," 1958. *Positions*: Instr., Buffalo Sch. FA, 1935-44; Univ. Buffalo, 1935-44; Univ. Colorado, 1944-46; Asst. Prof. A., St. Louis Univ. & Maryville Col., St. Louis, Mo., 1946- ; Prof., Univ. Arkansas, Fayetteville, Ark., 1952- ; Guest L., Univ. Texas, 1954. Guest Lecturer, Univ. Colorado, 1957.

WESTON, HAROLD—*Painter*
282 Bleecker St., New York 14, N.Y.; s. St. Hubert's, N.Y.

B. Merion, Pa., Feb. 14, 1894. *Studied*: Harvard Univ., B.A. *Member*: Fed. Mod. P. & S. *Awards*: prize, GGE, 1939. *Work*: Rochester Mem. A. Gal.; PAFA; PMG; Yale Univ.; SFMA; Columbia Univ. Lib.; MModA; CGA; Smithsonian Inst.; Regional Bldg., Dept. Interior, Wash., D.C.; FMA. *Exhibited*: ten one-man exhs., New York, and others. *Position*: Pres., Fed. Mod. P. & S., 1953-55, 1955-57; U.S. Delegate, Intl. Assn. Plastic A., 1954, 1957; Liaison Officer, U.S. Comm., Intl. Assn. Plastic A., 1958; Vice-Chm., Com. on Arts & Government, 1954-58; A. Consultant in Europe for USIA, 1957.

WETHEY, HAROLD EDWIN—*Educator, L., W.*
2009 Morton Ave., Ann Arbor, Mich.

B. Port Byron, N.Y., Apr. 10, 1902. *Studied*: Cornell Univ., A.B.; Harvard Univ., M.A., Ph.D. *Member*: CAA; Hispanic Soc Am.; Soc. Arch. Historians; Acad de S. Fernando; Soc Peruana Historians. *Awards*: F., Rockefeller Fnd., 1944-1945; Sheldon F., Harvard Univ., 1932-1933; Paris Scholarship, Inst. Int. Edu., 1931, 1934; Guggenheim F., 1949; Fulbright F., to Italy, 1958-59. Author: "Gil de Siloe and His School," 1936; "Colonial Architecture and Sculpture in Peru," 1949; "Alonso Cano, Painter, Sculptor and Architect," 1955. Contributor to: Thieme-Becker's "Kunstler-Lexikon;" Art Quarterly; Art Bulletin; etc. Lectures: Spanish and Latin American Art. *Position*: Instr., Asst. Prof., Bryn Mawr Col., 1934-38; Washington Univ., St. Louis, Mo., 1938-40; Assoc. Prof., 1940-46, Prof., 1946- , Univ. Michigan, Ann Arbor, Mich.

WHEAT, JOHN POTTER—*Painter, T.*
Hollow Tree Ridge Rd., Darien, Conn.

B. New York, N.Y., Apr. 22, 1920. *Studied*: Yale Univ., B.F.A. *Member*: AWS; Conn. Acad. FA; Silvermine Gld. A. *Awards*: prizes, NAC, 1946; Abbey Mem. Sscholarship, 1946-47; NSMP, 1944; Conn. Acad. FA, 1948; NAD, 1949, 1952; Silvermine Gld. A., 1955. *Exhibited*: MMA, 1942; AIC, 1943; NAC, 1946; NAD, 1949, 1952-1954; Audubon A., 1953, 1954; All. A. Am., 1953, 1954; Conn. Acad. FA, 1953-1955; AWS, 1954; Conn. WC Soc., 1953-1955.*

WHARTON, JAMES PEARCE—*Educator, P.*
Art Department, University of Maryland; h. 106 West University Parkway, College Park 10, Md.

B. Waterloo, S.C., Apr. 18, 1893. *Studied*: Lander Col.; Wofford Col.; Duke Univ., A.B.; Univ. Guanajuato, Mexico, M.F.A.; Maryland AI, and with Wayman Adams, Leon Kroll, Robert Brackman, Maurice Davidson and others. *Member*: Balt. WC Cl.; Charcoal Cl. of Balt. *Awards*: prizes, High Mus. A.; 1937; BMA, 1944; Balt. WC Cl., 1954. *Work*: paintings, Nat. Radio Inst. of Am.; St. Mary's Col., St. Mary's, Md.; Univ. Maryland. *Exhibited*: Wash. A. Cl.; High Mus. A.; Columbus (Ga.) A. Cl.; San Miguel de Allende, Mexico; Manila, Philippines; BMA; Maryland AI; Balt. Charcoal Cl.; Balt. WC Cl. Contributor to Magazine section, Atlanta Journal; Balt. Sunday Sun; Life magazine; Army Publications; Covers for Infantry Journal. *Positions*: Hd., Manila A. Sch., 1938-40; Columbus Sch. A., 1934-38; Prof. A., Hd. A. Dept., University of Maryland, College Park, Md., 1948- .

WHEELER, CLEORA CLARK—
Designer, Illuminator, L., W.
1376 Summit Ave., St. Paul 5, Minn.

B. Austin, Minn. *Studied*: Univ. Minnesota, B.A., Ctf. Adv. Engineering Drafting; N.Y. Sch. F. & App. A. *Member*: Am. Soc. Bookplate Collectors & Des.; Nat.

Lg. Am. Pen Women. *Awards*: prizes, Minn. A. Soc., 1913; Nat. Lg. Am. Pen Women, 1942, 1950; Achievement Award, Kappa Kappa Gamma, 1952. *Work*: LC; Yale Cl., N.Y.; Minnesota State Hist. Soc.; Minneapolis Inst. A.; St. Paul Pub. Lib.; Minneapolis Pub. Lib.; Los A. Pub. Lib.; Am. Lib. in Paris; Libraries of: Brown, Columbia, Harvard, Minnesota, Princeton, Stanford, Rochester and Yale Universities; Bryn Mawr, Mills, Monmouth, Mt. Holyoke, Radcliffe, Smith, Vassar, Wellesley and Wells colleges; Pub. Lib., City of Liverpool, England; Am. Assn. Univ. Women; brass wall plaque, Minn. Chapter House Lib., Kappa Kappa Gamma. *Exhibited*: annually 1916-1925, Am. Bookplate Soc.; Avery Lib., Columbia Univ.; Grolier Cl.; Bookplate Assn. Int. Exh., 1926, 1931-1936; N.Y. Times Book Fair, 1937; Northwest States Book Fair, Minneapolis, 1940; Boston Book Fair, 1940; Nat. Lg. Am. Pen Women, 1936, 1938, 1940, 1944, 1946, 1948, 1950, 1952, 1954; U.S. Nat. Mus., 1946, 1948, 1950, 1952, 1954; Minn. State A. Soc.; St. Paul Inst.; Minneapolis Inst. A.; AAUW, St. Paul Branch, 1958. Numerous one-man exhs., including Univ. Minnesota, 1956. Author series 6 articles on bookplates, Minnesota Medicine magazine.

WHEELER, KATHLEEN (Mrs. Kathleen Wheeler Crump)
—*Sculptor*
319 Dorset Ave., Chevy Chase, Md.

B. Reading, England, Oct. 15, 1884. *Studied*: Slade Sch., London Univ., London, England. *Member*: Soc. Wash. A. *Awards*: prizes, AIC; Soc. Wash. A. *Work*: Harvey's Mus., St. John's Wood, London; Hackley A. Gal., Muskegon, Mich.; Ackermann Gal., N.Y.; W. Russell Button, Chicago; Purvell Gal., Balt., Md.*

WHEELER, ROBERT G.—*Historian, L., W.*
Sleepy Hollow Restorations, Tarrytown, N.Y.

B. Kinderhook, N.Y., Sept. 20, 1917. *Studied*: Syracuse Univ.; Columbia Univ.; N.Y. State Col. for Teachers. *Member*: AAMus.; Northeastern Conf., AAMus.; AFA. Contributor to Antiques Magazine; American Collector; New York History; N.Y. Sun; N.Y. World-Telegram & Sun. Lectures: 17th, 18th and 19th Century Arts & Crafts of the Hudson Valley. *Position*: Pres., Northeastern Conf., AAMus., 1953-54, Bd. Memb., 1954-55; Instr., Am. A. Hist., A. Appreciation, Russell Sage Col., Albany Div., 1950-1956; Asst. Dir., 1947-49, Dir., 1949-56, Albany Inst. Hist. & A., Albany, N.Y.; Dir. Research & Publ., Sleepy Hollow Restorations, Tarrytown, N.Y., 1956- .

WHEELER, ZONA LORRAINE—*Painter, Des., I.*
1501 East Douglas Ave.; h. 230 South Belmont Ave., Wichita 8, Kans.

B. Linsborg, Kans., Feb. 15, 1913. *Studied*: Bethany Col., B.F.A., with Birger Sandzen; Am. Acad. A., Chicago; Wichita A. Assn. Sch. *Member*: Wichita A. Gld.; Nat. Lg. Am. Pen Women; Wichita AA; NSMP; Altrusa Intl.; F., Int. Inst. A. & Lets. *Awards*: prizes, Prairie WC Cl., 1946, 1950; Naftzger award, 1947; Printing Industry of Am.; Direct Mail Adv. *Work*: Wichita AA; Wichita Mun. Mus.; Bethany Col.; Kansas State Col.; Women's Fed. Clubs of Kansas; Altarpiece, U.S. Veterans' Hospital, Wichita; mural-dec., Hotel Lassen, Wichita.*Exhibited*: San F. AA; Corpus Christi Caller-Times; Wash. WC Cl.; Denver A. Mus.; Springfield (Mo.) Mus. A.; Joslyn A. Mus.; Assoc. Am. A., N.Y.; Wichita AA (one-man); Wustum Mus. A. (one-man); Rutgers Univ. (one-man); Phila. Pr. Cl.; Kansas City AI; Assoc. Am. A., and in England. Contributor layouts and illus. to Sat. Eve. Post, Colliers, New Yorker, Fortune, Direct Mail Advertising, magazines. *Position*: Adv. Des., I., McCormick Armstrong Co., Wichita, Kans., 1943- .

WHEELOCK, WARREN (FRANK)—
Painter, S., C., T., W.
424 Delgado Pl., Santa Fe, N.M.

B. Sutton, Mass., Jan. 15, 1880. *Studied*: PIASch. *Member*: S. Gld.; An Am. Group. *Work*: WMAA; AIC; IBM Coll.; Mus. New Mexico; BM; AIC; Los A. Mus. A.; WMAA; PMA; Corporation of Glasgow, Scotland; Bartlett H.S., Webster, Mass. *Exhibited*: Musee du Jeu de Paume, Paris, 1938; MModA, 1939; Carnegie Inst., 1941; PMA, 1940; PAFA, 1932, 1934, 1944-1946; AIC, 1942; Denver A. Mus., 1941; WMAA, 1932-1946; BM, 1938; MMA (AV), 1942; S. Gld., annually. Contributor to: American Artist magazine. *Position*: Instr. Drawing, PIASch., Brooklyn, N.Y., 1905-10; Instr. S., CUASch., New York, N.Y., 1940-45.

WHEELWRIGHT, ELIZABETH S.—
   Teacher, Eng., P., I., C.
   The Crossroads, Route 12, Keene, N.H.

B. Boston, Mass., Oct. 11, 1915. *Studied*: Child-Walker Sch. A.; Newton Col. of the Sacred Heart, B.A.; in Italy; & with Eliot O'Hara. *Member*: New Hampshire AA; Copley Soc., Boston; Catholic AA; Sharon A. Center. *Exhibited*: Boston AC; Boston Soc. Indp. A.; Southern Pr. M.; New England Pr. Assn.; Catholic AA; Sharon A. Center; New Hampshire AA. *Position*: Instr., Newton Col. of the Sacred Heart, Newton, Mass.; Keene Jr. H.S.*

WHELAN, BLANCHE—*Painter*
   386 South Burnside Ave., Apt. 9B, Los Angeles 36, Cal.

B. Los Angeles, Cal. *Studied*: Stanford Univ., A.B.; Los A. Sch. A. & Des.; ASL. *Member*: Cal. AC; Laguna Beach AA; Women Painters of the West. *Awards*: prize, Ariz. State Fair, 1931.

WHINSTON, CHARLOTTE (Mrs. Charles N.)—
   Sculptor, P., Gr.
   2 Tudor City Place, New York 17, N.Y.

B. New York, N.Y. *Studied*: N.Y. Sch. F. & App. A.; NAD; CUASch.; ASL, and with George Luks, George Maynard and others. *Member*: NAWA; Pen & Brush Cl.; ASL; AEA; New Jersey P. & S. Soc.; Knickerbocker A.; Brooklyn Soc. A.; Nat. Soc. Painters in Casein. *Awards*: prizes, scholarship, N.Y. Sch. F. & App. A., 1915; prizes, CUASch., 1921; AAPL, 1947; Yonkers AA, 1948; New Rochelle Women's Cl., 1948, 1951; State T. Col., Indiana, Pa., 1949; Westchester Fed. Women's Cl., 1949; medals, City Col., N.Y., 1916; NAD, 1917; Pen & Brush Cl., 1948; Argent Gal., 1957; Church of the Covenant, 1958; silver medal, Seton Hall Univ., 1958; gold medal, Catholic A. Soc., 1958. *Work*: Norfolk Mus. A.; Seton Hall Univ.; exterior mural, Ave. of the Americas (44th-45th Sts.), N.Y. *Exhibited*: Paris, France; Amsterdam, Holland; Antwerp and Brussels, Belgium; Naples, Italy; Athens and Salonika, Greece; NAWA, 1946-1958; Pen & Brush Cl., 1946-1958; State T. Col., Indiana, Pa., 1947-1954; Audubon A., 1947, 1953; All. A. Am., 1950-1953; Westchester A. & Crafts Gld., 1944-1955; Yonkers AA, 1944-1951; Soc. Indp. A., 1943, 1944; Hudson Valley AA, 1948-1951; AAPL, 1947-1951; New Jersey P. & S., 1951-1956; Norlyst Gal., 1945, 1946; Contemp. A., 1945-1947; AEA, 1950-1953; WMAA, 1951; Knickerbocker A., 1955, 1958; one-man: Contemp. Cl., White Plains, N.Y., 1947; Pen & Brush Cl., 1949, 1955; Engineering Women, N.Y., 1950. *Position*: Chm., traveling WC Exhs., NAWA, 1955-57; Rec. Sec., Pen & Brush Cl., 1954-56.

WHIPPLE, ENEZ (Mrs.)—*Art Director*
   Guild Hall of East Hampton, Easthampton, N.Y.
Position: Dir., Guild Hall, Easthampton, N.Y.*

WHITAKER, FREDERIC—*Painter, W.*
   Murray St., R.R. 1, Norwalk, Conn.

B. Providence, R.I., Jan. 9, 1891. *Member*: NSMP (Hon.); NAC; SC; Providence A. Cl.; All. A. Am.; Am. Veterans Soc. A.; Cal. WC Soc.; Conn. WC Soc.; New Orleans AA; Silvermine Gld. A., and many others. *Awards*: 60 prizes throughout the U.S. *Work*: in permanent Coll. in New York, Boston, Providence, Lakeland, Fla., Pocatello, Idaho, Atchison, Kans., Terre Haute, Ind., and others. *Position*: Pres. (1949-56) AWS; Member Council (1952-55), NAD; Dir., Audubon A. (Founder, 1943, Pres., 1943-46), New York, N.Y.; U.S. Vice-Pres., Intl. Assn. Plastic A.; Contributing Ed., American Artist magazine.

WHITAKER, MRS. FREDERIC. See Monaghan, Eileen

WHITAKER, IRWIN (A.) (JR.)—*Educator, C.*
   Art Department, Michigan State University; h. 1810 Melrose Ave., East Lansing, Mich.

B. Wirt, Okla.. Oct. 19, 1919. *Studied*: San Jose State Col., B.A.; Claremont Col., M.F.A. *Member*: Am. Crafts-

men's Council; Midwest Des.-Craftsmen (Rec. Sec.). *Awards*: prizes, Cal. State Fair, 1949 (2). *Work*: Scripps Col.; Los Angeles County Fair Coll. *Exhibited*: Syracuse Mus. FA Ceramics, 1951, 1952, 1954; Wichita Dec. A. & Ceramic Exh., 1953; Los A. County Fair, 1950-1956; Miami Nat. Ceramic, 1954, 1956; Scripps Col., Intl. Ceramic, 1955 and Nat., 1952, 1956-1958; Midwest Des.-Craftsmen, 1954; Michigan Des.-Craftsmen, 1951-1956, 1958; Ravinia Festival, 1958, and others. Contributor to Craft Horizons. *Positions*: Instr., Ceramics, A. Edu., Des., Southern Oregon College, 1949-50; Michigan State Univ., East Lansing, Mich., 1950- .

WHITCOMB, JON—*Illustrator*
   8 Circle Rd., Darien, Conn.

B. Weatherford, Okla. *Studied*: Ohio Wesleyan Univ.; Ohio State Univ., A.B. Contributor to Ladies Home Journal, McCall's, Cosmopolitan, Redbook, Good Housekeeping magazines. *Position*: Faculty, Famous Artists School, Westport, Conn.*

WHITE, AGNES HOFMAN—*Painter*
   321 Fifth St., Marietta, Ohio

B. Columbus, Ohio, Jan. 8, 1897. *Studied*: Columbus A. Sch.; PAFA; Ecole des Beaux-Arts, Fontainebleau, France. *Member*: Nat. Soc. A. & Let.; Soc. Four A., Palm Beach, Fla.; Marietta A. Lg.; Nat. Soc. A. & Let. (Pres., Ohio River Valley Chptr.). *Work*: port., Marietta Col.; murals, Hobe Sound, Fla.; Airport, Stuart, Fla. *Exhibited*: AWCS, 1941; Soc. Four A., 1942-1945; Columbus Gal. FA, 1941-1946; Marietta A. Lg., 1956-1958; Ogleby Inst., 1958.

WHITE, AMBROSIA CHUSE (Mrs. John C.)—
   Painter, T., W.
   435 East Harlem Rd., Rockford, Ill.

B. Belleville, Ill., Dec. 3, 1894. *Studied*: Notre Dame Acad.; St. Louis Sch. FA; Univ. Wisconsin, B.S.; & with Frederic Taubes. *Member*: Madison A. Gld. *Exhibited*: St. Louis A. Gld., 1935; All-Illinois Soc. FA, 1936-1938; Milwaukee AI, 1938; Wis. Salon A., 1943; Madison A. Gld., 1935-1946. Author: "Holiday Story Book." *Position*: A.T., Jr. H.S., Beloit, Wis., 1945-46; A. Supv., Dane County Rural Schs., 1947-49; A. T., St. James Parochial Schs., Madison, Mis., 1949-52; Primary T., Dist. 122, Rockford, Ill., 1953-55.*

WHITE, DORIS ANNE—*Painter, C., Des., Ser.*
   2044 North 86th St., Wauwatosa 13, Wis.

B. Eau Claire, Wis., July 27, 1924. *Studied*: Univ. Berne, Switzerland; AIC. *Member*: Wisconsin P. & S. *Exhibited*: AWS, 1958; Wisconsin Salon A., 1956-1958; Kenosha A. Mus.; Cardinal Stritch College, Racine; one-man: Panoras Gal., N.Y., 1958.

WHITE, ELIZABETH—*Etcher, P., I., T.*
   421 North Main St., Sumter, S.C.

B. Sumter, S.C. *Studied*: Columbia Univ.; PAFA; and with Alfred Hutty, Wayman Adams. *Award*: prize, SSAL. *Work*: LC; Carnegie Lib., Sumter, S.C. *Member*: Tiffany Fnd.; MacDowell Colony. *Exhibited*: Florence (S.C.) Mus.; Columbus (S.C.) Mus.; one-man: Smithsonian Inst.; Chapin Mem. Lib.; Asheville Mus. A.; Univ. North Carolina; Tryon, N.C. I., "Crossin' Over," and historical pamphlets.

WHITE, ETHYLE HERMAN (Mrs. S. Roy)—
   Painter, I., W.
   P.O. Box 176, Anahuac, Tex.

B. San Antonio, Tex., Apr. 10, 1904. *Studied*: San Antonio AI; in Europe; and with Frederick Taubes, Etienne Ret, Paul Schuman, and others. *Member*: Texas FA Assn.; Artists, Composers & Authors; Nat. Lg. Am. Pen Women. *Exhibited*: Texas FA Assn.; San Antonio River A.; Delgado Mus. A.; Beaumont A. Lg.; Houston A. Lg.; FA Center of Houston; Caller-Times Exh.; one-man: Gates Lib., Port Arthur; Anahuac, Tex., 1943, 1957. Author, I., "Arabella," 1954.

WHITE, EUGENE B.—*Painter*

Manatee Art School, Bradenton, Fla.; h. 5214 David Ave., Sarasota, Fla.

B. Middle Point, Ohio, Mar. 7, 1913. *Studied*: Ft. Wayne A. Sch.; Ringling Sch. A. *Member*: Fla. A. Group; Sarasota AA; Manatee A. Lg.; Tampa AI; Long Boat Key Group. *Awards*: prizes, Sarasota AA, 1955, 1957; Ft. Wayne A. Mus., 1955; Toledo Mus. A., 1957; Knickerbocker A., 1957; Columbus, Ohio, 1957; Van Wert, Ohio, 1957, 1958; Montpelier, Ohio, 1956, 1957; Manatee A. Lg., 1958; Longboat Key, 1958; Sarasota Nat., 1955. *Work*: Ringling Sch. A.; Bradenton A. Center; Chrysler Motors, Detroit; Milwaukee County Stadium. *Exhibited*: Sarasota AA, 1950-1958; Ft. Lauderdale, Fla., 1955; Ohio Valley, 1952-1955; Fla. A. Group, 1953-1958; Ft. Wayne Mus. A., 1956, 1957; Ringling Mus. A., 1957; Columbus Gal. FA; Toledo Mus. A.; Detroit Inst. A.; Tampa AI, 1958; Univ. Ohio, 1956; Rowland's traveling exh., 1958; Ft. Wayne, 1956, 1957; one-man: Sarasota AA; Manatee A. Lg.; Long Boat Key; Van Wert, Ohio; Orlando AI; Lima, Ohio; Toledo Mus. A.; Tampa AI; Bellair A. Center; St. Petersburg AA; Pinellas Park, Fla., and others. *Position*: Instr., A. Lg. of Manatee, Bradenton, Fla.

WHITE, J(ACOB) C(AUPEL)—

Designer, P., Et., I., Comm. A.

Idlehour, Oakdale, L.I., N.Y.

B. New York, N.Y., Oct. 1, 1895. *Studied*: NAD; Julian Acad., Paris, France. *Member*: Advertising Cl., N.Y. *Awards*: F., Tiffany Fnd.; prize, Cartoon Comp., Liberty magazine. *Work*: Tiffany Fnd. *Exhibited*: NAD; Salon de Tunis; Tiffany Fnd. *Position*: A. Dir., Am. Merrilei Corp., Brooklyn, N.Y.

WHITE, J. GORDON—*Painter, T., Des.*

101 West State St., Trenton 8, N.J.

B. Granville, N.Y., Aug. 28, 1903. *Studied*: Cornell Univ., B.F.A., with Olaf Brauner, Walter K. Stone; Inst. Des., Chicago, with Moholy-Nagy; Columbia Univ., M.A. *Member*: New Jersey A. Edu. Assn.; Southern Vermont A.; Mid-Vermont A.; Morrisville-Trenton A. Group. *Awards*: Sands medal, 1926, Sampson prize, 1927, Cornell Univ. *Work*: murals, Ajax Eng. Corp., Trenton, N.J. *Exhibited*: Boston Soc. Indp. A.; Middlebury, Vt.; Mid-Vermont A., annually; Southern Vermont A., annually; Morrisville-Trenton A. Group, annually; Contemp. Cl., Trenton, 1948, 1955; State Mus., Trenton, 1954. *Position*: Instr., FA, Cornell Univ., 1927-28; Hd. A. Dept., Trenton Junior College, Sch. Indst. A., Trenton, N.J., 1952- .

WHITE, LAWRENCE EUGENE—*Educator*

George Pepperdine College, 1121 West 79th St., (44); h. 7810 Brighton Ave., Los Angeles 47, Cal.

B. Abilene, Tex., Dec. 2, 1908. *Studied*: Abilene Christian Col., B.A.; Univ. So. California, M.A. *Member*: Pacific AA; NAEA. Author: "Art for the Child," 1950. *Positions*: Instr., Abilene Christian College, 1932-36; Prof. A., George Pepperdine College, Los Angeles, Cal., at present.

WHITE, LEO (F.)—*Cartoonist*

Boston American, 5 Winthrop Square, Boston, Mass.; h. 211 Cedar St., Dedham, Mass.

B. Holliston, Mass., Apr. 8, 1918. *Studied*: Sch. Practical A., Boston; Evans Sch. Cartooning, Cleveland. Creator of "You Said It," Boroth Features, Spokane, Wash.; "Weird World of Scizzo." Creator of "Sportscramble." *Position*: Sports & Editorial Cartoonist, Boston American, Boston, Mass.

WHITE, MABLE DUNN (Mrs. Edgar R.)—*Painter*

2875 Stonemont St., Jacksonville 7, Fla.

B. Charlotte, N.C., Jan. 28, 1902. *Studied*: Greenville (S.C.) Col. for Women. *Member*: St. Augustine AA; Jacksonville AA; SSAL; AAPL; FA Lg. of the Carolinas. *Awards*: prize, Mint. Mus. A. *Exhibited*: Nat. Exh. Am. A., N.Y., 1941; SSAL, 1941, 1943; Mint Mus. A.; Gibbes A. Gal.; Blue Ridge AI; St. Augustine, Jacksonville, Fla. one-man exh.: Greenville (S.C.) Civic A. Gal., 1942; Asheville (N.C.) Civic A. Gal., 1942.

WHITE, NELSON COOKE—*Painter, W.*

Waterford, Conn.

B. Waterford, Conn., June 11, 1900. *Studied*: NAD; & with Henry Cooke White. *Member*: Conn. Acad. FA. *Exhibited*: NAD; AWCS. Author: "The Life and Art of J. Frank Currier," 1936; "Abbott H. Thayer—Painter and Naturalist," 1951. Contributor to: Art in America; Art & Archaeology. *Position*: Trustee, Lyman Allyn Mus., New London, Conn.; Wadsworth Atheneum, Hartford, Conn.*

WHITE, RALPH ERNEST, JR.—*Educator, P., Des., I.*

Department of Art, University of Texas; h. Route 7, Box 39 R, Austin 4, Tex.

B. Minneapolis, Minn., Jan. 3, 1921. *Studied*: Minneapolis Sch. A.; Univ. Minnesota; PIASch. *Awards*: Vanderlip F., Minneapolis, 1942; prizes, purchase awards: Twin Cities annual, 1942; Corpus Christi, Tex., 1948; Minnesota Centennial Exh., 1949; Texas annual, 1949; Texas FA Assn., 1955, and others; other prizes, DMFA, 1947; Austin, Texas, and others. *Work*: Minneapolis Inst. A.; Witte Mem. Mus.; Texas A. & I. College, Kingsville; Corpus Christi Mem. Mus.; D. D. Feldman Coll.; Texas FA Assn.; Laguna Gloria Mus., Austin. *Exhibited*: Nelson Gal. A., Kansas City, 1951; Denver A. Mus., 1953; Butler Inst. Am. A., 1956, 1957; D. D. Feldman Exh., 1956; AFA traveling exh., 1957; Texas annual, 1947, 1948, 1949, 1950, 1953-1957; Texas WC Soc.; Texas FA Assn., annually; Delgado Mus. A., 1957, 1958; Austin State Col., 1956; Kansas State Col., 1954. Illus., "In a Scout's Boots," 1957; "Sam Bass," 1958; "Big Foot Wallace," 1957, and others. *Positions*: Consulting A. Dir., DGB Adv. Co. (10 yrs.); Clark Printing Co., San Antonio (3 yrs.); Prof. A., Univ. Texas, Austin, Texas, at present.

WHITE, (CLARENCE) SCOTT—*Painter, I.*

97 Somerset St., Belmont 78, Mass.

B. Boston, Mass., Mar. 14, 1872. *Studied*: with Charles Herbert Woodbury. *Member*: Copley Soc., Boston; Boston Soc. WC Painters. *Exhibited*: BMFA; Boston Soc. WC Painters; one-man exhs., Northeast Harbor, Me., annually. I., "Pilgrim Trails"; "Bermuda Journey."*

WHITE, VERA—*Painter, Lith.*

114 Llanfair Rd., Ardmore, Pa.; Wind-in-the-Willows, Downingtown, Pa.

B. St. Louis, Mo. *Awards*: prize, Chester County AA. *Work*: Temple Univ.; PMA; PAFA. *Exhibited*: PAFA; WMAA; AIC; Phila. Pr. Cl.; Lib. Cong.; Chester County AA; Phila. A. All.; Edward Side Gal., McClees Gal., Carlen Gal., Phila.; Columbus Gal. FA; Honolulu Acad. A.; Reid & Lefevre Gal., London; one-man exh.: Ferargil, Marie Sterner, Durand-Ruel, Seligmann Gal., N.Y.; PAFA, 1951; Bryn Mawr A. Center, 1954; Chester County AA, 1955; Sessler Gal., Phila., Pa., 1955, 1956, 1957.

WHITE, WALTER CHARLES LOUIS—*Painter, T., L.*

119-07 Farmers Ave., St. Albans 12, L.I., N.Y.

B. Sheffield, England. *Studied*: T. Col., Columbia Univ., B.S., M.A.; PIASch.; & with Carlson, Dow, Hawthorne. *Member*: SC; Long Island Soc. Arch. (Hon.); Brooklyn Soc. A. (Pres.); A. Lg. of Nassau (Pres.); AWS (Sec.). *Awards*: prize, A. Lg. Nassau County, 1929, 1934, 1937; Mineola Fair, 1938; med., Miss. AA, 1926. *Work*: Vanderpoel Coll. *Exhibited*: WFNY 1939; Sesqui-Centennial Exp., Phila., Pa., 1926; Wash. WC. Cl.; BM; Toledo Mus. A.; AWCS, 1948-1951; AFA traveling exh.; SC, 1948-1951; Mississippi AA; A. Lg. Nassau County; Brooklyn Soc. A., 1950; NAC, 1950-1952; CM; Columbus Gal. FA; Dayton AI; AIC.

WHITEHEAD, JAMES L.—*Museum Director*

Staten Island Museum of Arts & Sciences, 75 Stuyvesant Place; h. 105 Emerson Ave., Staten Island 1, N.Y.

B. Demopolis, Ala., Feb. 21, 1913. *Studied*: Birmingham Southern College, A.B.; Vanderbilt Univ., M.A.; Univ. Pennsylvania. *Member*: AAMus.; Mus. Council of New York City. Contributor to Pennsylvania Historical Review. *Positions*: Asst. Archivist, F. D. Roosevelt Lib., Hyde Park, N.Y., 1941-43; Asst. to the Dir., Minnesota Hist. Soc., 1949-50; Dir., Staten Island Museum of A. & Sciences, Staten Island, N.Y., at present.

WHITEHEAD, PHILIP BARROWS—
Educator, W., L., Mus. Cur.
623-B College St., Beloit, Wis.

B. Janesville, Wis., Jan. 29, 1884. *Studied*: Beloit Col., B.A.; Yale Univ., Ph.D.; Am. Acad. in Rome. Contributor to: American Journal of Archaeology. Lectures: American Painting; American Architecture. (Retired.)

WHITEHILL, WALTER MUIR—*Museum Director, W., E.*
Boston Athenaeum, 10½ Beacon St.; Boston, Mass.; h. Old Berry House, North Andover, Mass.

B. Cambridge, Mass., Sept. 28, 1905. *Studied*: Harvard Univ., A.B., A.M.; Univ. London, Courtauld Inst., Ph.D.; & in Spain, France, Ireland. *Member*: Mass. Hist. Soc.; Am. Antiquarian Soc.; Hispanic Soc. Am.; CAA; Mediaeval Acad. Am.; etc. Author: "Spanish Romanesque Architecture of the Eleventh Century," 1941; "The East India Marine Society and the Peabody Museum of Salem, a Sesqui-Centennial History," 1949; "Boston Public Library, a Centennial History," 1956; & other books. Contributor to: art & educational journals & bulletins, with articles concerning mediaeval Spanish art. *Position*: Asst. Dir., 1936-46, Trustee, 1950- , Peabody Mus., Salem, Mass.; Dir. & Libn., Boston Athenaeum, Boston, Mass., 1946- ; Memb. Faculty, Peabody Mus., Harvard Univ., 1951- ; Senior Tutor, Lowell House, Harvard Univ., 1952-1956; Trustee, Boston Mus. FA, 1953- ; Editor, Am. Acad. A. & Sc., 1954-1957. Lecturer, Harvard Univ., 1956-57; Lowell Inst., 1958.

WHITENER, PAUL (AUSTIN) W(AYNE)—
Museum Director, P., L.
215 7th St., Southeast, Hickory, N.C.

B. Lincoln County, N.C., Sept. 1, 1911. *Studied*: Duke Univ.; Ringling Sch. A.; & with Wilford Conrow, Donald Blake, Frank Herring. *Member*: AAPL; North Carolina State A. Soc.; SC; Kappa Pi (hon.); Duke Univ. A. Council. *Work*: Duke Univ.; Lenoir Rhyne Col., Hickory, N.C.; Hickory Mus. A.; many portrait commissions. *Exhibited*: Mint Mus. A., 1944; Hickory Mus. A., 1943-1946; SSAL, 1942; Duke Univ., 1945 (one-man). Lectures: Art Appreciation. *Position*: Dir., Hickory Mus. A., 1943- ; Nat. Dir., AAPL Honor Roll.*

WHITESIDE, HENRYETTE STADELMAN—*Painter*
Brook Valley Rd., Greenville 7, Del.

B. Brownsville, Pa., Dec. 5, 1891. *Studied*: PAFA; in Italy, with Donati; & with Thomas Anschutz, Hugh Breckenridge, Charles Hawthorne. *Member*: Phila. WC Cl.; Phila. A. All.; Wilmington Soc. FA. *Award*: prize, Nat. Lg. Am. Pen Women. *Work*: State House, Dover, Del.; Wilmington Soc. FA. *Exhibited*: PAFA; NAD; AIC; WFNY 1939; Delaware A. Center; Ogunquit A. Center; Nat. Lg. Am. Pen Women. *Position*: Founder, Dir., Wilmington Acad. A., until merged with Delaware A. Center, 1942.*

WHITFORD, WILLIAM GARRISON—*Craftsman, E., W.*
University of Chicago, Chicago 37, Ill.; h. 20525 Hellenic Dr., Olympia Fields, Ill.

B. Nile, N.Y., Dec. 12, 1886. *Studied*: Alfred Univ., Ph.B., D.F.A.; AIC; Iowa State Col., S.M. *Member*: F., Am. Ceramic Soc.; Nat. Edu. Assn.; Western AA. Author: "Introduction to Art," 1937; Co-Author: "The Classroom Teacher," Vol I, II, III, 1933-1935; "Art Stories" Books 1, 2 & 3, 1933-1935; "High School Curriculum Reorganization," 1933, & other books on Art Education. Contributor to: School Arts, School Review, Design, & other magazines; Dictionary of Education, 1945; Encyclopaedia of the Arts, 1946. *Position*: Hd., Dept. Des. & Ceramics, Maryland Inst., 1911-13; Dir., Workshop in A. & Crafts, & T. Training, Univ. Chicago, Ill., 1913-52; Prof. Emeritus of A. Edu., Univ. Chicago, 1952- .

WHITIES-SANNER, GLENNA—*Painter*
111½ East Sandusky St., Findlay, Ohio

B. Kalida, Ohio. *Studied*: with Leon Pescheret, Mrs. Vance Whities, and others. *Member*: Ohio WC Soc.; AEA; AWS; Toledo A. Cl. *Work*: Veterans Hospital, Dayton, Ohio; Fort Recovery (Ohio) Hist. Mus. *Exhibited*: Toledo Mus. A., 1943, 1944; Taft Mus.; Ohio WC Soc. traveling exh., 1942, 1943; Findlay, Ohio, 1943; Kent State Univ.; Dayton AI; CMA; Butler AI; Columbus Gal. FA; Ohio Univ.; Canton AI; Fort Recovery Hist. Mus. Lib.,

1951 (one-man); Findlay Col., 1956 (one-man). Author, I., "The Book of Orchids"; Illus., Biology and Botany textbooks, 1956. *Position*: Instr., A. Dept., Findlay Col., Cur., Col. Mus., 1953- .

WHITING, ALMON CLARK—*Painter, Et., Des.*
c/o Salmagundi Club, 47 Fifth Ave., New York 3, N.Y.

B. Worcester, Mass., Mar. 5, 1878. *Studied*: Mass. Normal A. Sch.; Julian Acad., Paris, France. *Member*: SC; ARA Assn. *Work*: Toledo Mus. A. *Position*: Founder, Dir., Toledo Mus. A., Toledo, Ohio, 1901-03.

WHITING, GERTRUDE—*Painter*
"Green Shadows," Old Lyme, Conn.; Box 675, Woods Hole, Mass.

B. Milwaukee, Wis., July 3, 1898. *Studied*: BMFA Sch.; ASL, and with Philip Hale. *Member*: All. A. Am.; AAPL; Cape Cod AA; North Shore AA. *Award*: prize, All. A. Am.; 1950. *Work*: Univ. Georgia; Princeton Univ.; war mem., Australia; Marine Biological Laboratory, Woods Hole, Mass.; Mus. of the City of N.Y.; mem., Australia. *Exhibited*: NAD; All. of Am.; Palm Beach A. Cl.; Montclair A. Mus.; Conn. Acad. FA; Argent Gal. (one-man).

WHITING, JOHN DOWNES—*Painter, I., W.*
254 Laurence St.; h. 291 Edwards St., New Haven, Conn.

B. Ridgefield, Conn., July 20, 1884. *Studied*: Yale Sch. B.F.A.; & with Clifton S. Carbee, Lucius Hitchcock. *Member*: New Haven Paint & Clay Cl.; Conn. Acad. FA; Rockport AA; Meriden A. & Crafts Soc. *Work*: Nat. Lib. Color Slides, Wash., D.C.; Mun. Coll., New Haven, Conn. *Exhibited*: New Haven Paint & Clay Cl.; Rockport AA; Conn. Acad. FA; Conn. WC Soc.; Meriden A. & Crafts Soc.; Hartford, Conn., (one-man). Author, I., "Practical Illustration," 1920; "Light and Color for the Vacation Painter," 1958, & other books. Covers & illus. for book & magazine publishers.

WHITING, MILDRED RUTH—*Educator, P.*
Eastern Illinois State College, Charleston, Ill.; h. 1702 South 48th St., Lincoln, Neb.

B. Seattle, Wash. *Studied*: Univ. Nebraska, B.F.A., Ph.D.; Univ. Minnesota. *Member*: Eastern Illinois A. Gld.; Western AA; Nat. A. Edu. Assn.; Illinois A. Edu. Assn.; Midwestern Col. A. Conference. *Exhibited*: All-Illinois Soc. FA, 1942, 1943; Eastern Ill. A. Gld., annually; Faculty Exhs., 1949, 1951; Swope Gal. A.; Charleston (Ill.) H.S., 1950 (one-man); Wabash Valley Exh., 1948, 1949. *Position*: Instr., 1936- , Hd. A. Dept., 1939- , Eastern Illinois State Col., Charleston, Ill.; Pres. Eastern Illinois A. Gld., 1951-52.*

WHITLATCH, HOWARD J.—*Educator*
Art Department, University of Arkansas, Fayetteville, Ark.*

WHITMAN, JOHN FRANKLIN, JR.—*Illustrator, Des.*
1006 Arch St., Philadelphia 7, Pa.; h. R.D. 1, Lebanon, Pa.

B. Philadelphia, Pa., Aug. 27, 1896. *Studied*: Univ. Pennsylvania; PAFA; Ecole des Beaux-Arts, Fontainebleau, France; & with McCarter, Despujols, Carlu. *Awards*: med., A.Dir.Cl., 1928; Modern Packaging Exh., 1937. Designing and illus. for books and advertising.*

WHITMER, HELEN C.—*Painter*
Orchard House, La Grangeville, N.Y.

B. Darby, Pa., Jan. 6, 1870. *Studied*: PAFA; Phila. Sch. Des. for Women. *Member*: Assoc. A. Pittsburgh; Dutchess County AA. *Exhibited*: PAFA; Assoc. A. Pittsburgh; Dutchess County AA.

WHITMORE, COBY—*Illustrator*
Hyatt Rd., Briarcliff Manor, N.Y.
Member: SI.*

WHITMORE, ROBERT HOUSTON—
Painter, Et., Eng., C.
Rt. 1, Box 76, Yellow Springs, Ohio

B. Dayton, Ohio, Feb. 22, 1890. *Studied*: AIC; Cincinnati
A. Acad. *Member*: Dayton Soc. P. & S.; Dayton SE.
Awards: prize, AIC, 1921; Springfield AA, 1950-1952; Int.
Pr. M. Exh., Los A., Cal., 1924. *Work*: Los A. Mus. A.;
Dayton AI; Normal Sch., Dayton; Coshocton (Ohio) Pub.
Lib.; Antioch Col., Yellow Springs, Ohio; Vanderpoel Coll.
Exhibited: NAD, 1944; Lib. Cong., 1944; Phila. Pr. Cl.,
1945; Ohio Pr. traveling exh., 1935-1952; Springfield AA,
1953-1955; Dayton AI, 1936-1955; Northwest Pr. M., 1947;
Wichita, Kans., 1947; Terry AI, 1952; Butler AI, 1942;
Dayton SE, 1921-1942. *Position*: Instr. Painting, 1925-27,
Asst. Prof., 1927-32, Assoc. Prof., 1932-56, Emeritus, 1956- ,
Antioch Col., Yellow Springs, Ohio.

WHITNEY, EDGAR A.—*Painter, T., W., L.*
1970—81st St., Jackson Heights 70, N.Y.

B. New York, N.Y., Apr. 16, 1891. *Studied*: ASL; Grand
Central A. Sch.; CUASch.; NAD. *Member*: AWS; Phila.
WC Cl.; A. Lg. of Long Island; ASL (life). *Awards*:
prizes, Audubon A., 1958; Hudson Valley AA, 1958; Brick
Store Mus., 1957, 1958; A. Lg. of Long Island, 1956-1958.
Work: Farnsworth Mus.; St. Petersburg, Fla; A. Lg. of
Long Island. *Exhibited*: AWS, 1950-1958; Phila. WC Cl.,
1956-1958; Knickerbocker A., 1956; A. Lg. Long Island,
1955-1958; Brick Store Mus., 1956-1958; Audubon A., 1958;
NAD, 1957; Hudson Valley AA, 1958. Author: "Water
Color: The Hows and Whys," 1958. Contributor to Ameri-
can Artist Magazine. *Position*: Instr., Watercolor, PIASch.;
N.Y. Botanical Gardens; A. Lg. of Long Island.

WHITNEY, MARJORIE FAYE—*Educator, P., Des.*
326 Indiana St., Lawrence, Kan.

B. Salina, Kans. *Studied*: Kansas Wesleyan Univ.; Univ.
Kansas, B.F.A.; Cal. Col. A. & Crafts; & with Frank G.
Hale. *Member*: CAA; Galveston A. Cl.; Western AA;
Kansas Fed. A.; Kansas A. T. Assn. *Exhibited*: Galveston,
Tex., 1950, 1953-1958; Wichita A. Mus., 1951, 1953-1955;
Topeka, Kans., 1951, 1953-1955; Manhattan, Kans., 1952.
Position: Asst. Instr., Instr., Asst. Prof., Assoc. Prof.,
1928-46, Dir., Design Dept., 1940- , Univ. Kansas, Law-
rence, Kans.

WHITNEY, PHILIP RICHARDSON—*Painter, C.*
P.O. Box 314; h. Glenwood & Lake Aves., Moylan, Pa.

B. Council Bluffs, Iowa, Dec. 31, 1878. *Studied*: MIT,
B.S. in Arch., and with Fred Wagner. *Member*: Phila. WC
Cl.; Swarthmore Players Cl. *Exhibited*: Phila. WC Cl.;
PAFA; Swarthmore annual. *Position*: Prof., Sch. FA,
Univ. Pennsylvania, retired 1936.

WHITTEMORE, GRACE CONNER (Mrs. George A.)—
Painter
6 Morse Ave., East Orange, N.J.

B. Columbia County, Pa., Oct. 29, 1876. *Studied*: Phila.
Sch. Des. for Women; PAFA. *Member*: Essex WC Cl.; A.
Center of the Oranges. *Awards*: prizes, N.J. State Fed.
Women's Cl., 1942, 1943; Woman's Cl., Orange, N.J.
Exhibited: A. Center of the Oranges; Essex WC Cl.; Mont-
clair A. Mus.; Woman's Cl., Orange, N.J.; etc.*

WHITTEMORE, MARGARET EVELYN—*Writer, Gr., I.*
31 Martindale Rd., Short Hills, N.J.; also, Sarasota,
Fla.

B. Topeka, Kans. *Studied*: Washburn Col., A.B.; AIC.
Member: Nat. Lg. Am. Pen Women; Nat. Soc. New
England Women. I., "Bird Notes," 1932; "Adventures
in Thrift," 1946, and other books. Author, I., "Historic
Kansas," 1954.

WICKHAM, NANCY (Mrs. W. A. Boyd, Jr.)—
Craftsman
Central St., Woodstock, Vt.

B. Ardsley, N.Y., Aug. 11, 1923. *Studied*: Sacker Sch.,
Boston; Alfred Univ. Sch. Ceramics; New Sch. for Social
Research, with Schanker; BM Sch. A., with Candell.
Awards: prizes, Intl. Exh. of Ceramics, Cannes, France,
1955; Syracuse Mus. FA, 1948, 1949, 1954; Young Ameri-

cans Exh., N.Y., 1951. *Exhibited*: Syracuse Mus. FA,
1947-1949, 1954; WMA, 1955; many other major exhs.,
1949-1956. Contributor to Ceramic Age; Craft Horizons.

WICKISER, RALPH LEWANDA—
Painter, W., L., E., Gr.
State University Teachers College, New Paltz, N.Y.

B. Greenup, Ill., Mar. 20, 1910. *Studied*: AIC; Eastern
Illinois State T. Col., B.A.; Peabody Col., M.A., Ph.D.
Member: Am. Soc. for Aesthetics. *Awards*: F., Tiffany
Fnd., 1934; Ford grant, 1952-53; prizes, New Orleans, La.,
1946; Louisiana Exh., 1946. *Work*: Delgado Mus. A.;
Lehigh Univ.; Currier Gal. A.; Mint Mus. A.; Atlanta
AA; Louisiana A. Comm.; Eastern Illinois State T. Col.
Exhibited: Assoc. Am. A., 1944, 1946; PAFA, 1951;
Woodstock AA; AFA traveling exh.; CM, 1952; Univ.
Louisville (one-man); Wash. WC Cl., 1943, 1944; Lib.
Cong., 1946; SFMA, 1941-1943, 1946; WMAA, 1953;
George Binet traveling exh.; State Dept. traveling exh. to
Europe and North Africa. Contributor to Sat. Review of
Literature; College Art Journal. Author: "An Introduction
to Art Activities," 1941; "An Introduction to Art Educa-
tion," 1957. Contributing Ed., Dictionary of Fine Arts.
Position: Hd. FA Dept., Louisiana State Univ., Baton
Rouge, La., 1941-1956; Dir. Art, State Univ. T. Col., New
Paltz, N.Y., 1956- .

WIDSTROM, EDWARD FREDERICK—*Sculptor*
21 Lydale Pl., Meriden, Conn.

B. Wallingford, Conn., Nov. 1, 1903. *Studied*: ASL; &
with Arthur Lee, William Zorach. *Member*: Conn. Acad.
FA; New Haven Paint & Clay Cl.; NSS; AAPL; Meriden
A. & Crafts Assn. *Awards*: prizes, Meriden A. & Crafts
Assn., 1937, 1946. *Work*: port. relief, port. bust, St.
Stephen's Sch., Bridgeport, Conn.; Meriden A. & Crafts
Assn. *Exhibited*: NAD, 1940, 1953, 1955; PAFA, 1939,
1940; Fairmount Park, Phila., 1940; Conn. Acad. FA,
1934-1955; New Haven Paint & Clay Cl., 1939-1955; Meri-
den A. & Crafts Assn., 1936-1955; Cayuga Mus. Hist. &
Art, 1941 (one-man).

WIEGAND, GUSTAVE—*Painter*
Windward Hill, Old Chatham, N.Y.

B. Bremen, Germany, Oct. 2, 1870. *Studied*: Royal Acad.,
Berlin, Dresden, Germany; & with William M. Chase,
Eugen Bracht. *Member*: NAC; All. A. Am.; N.Y. Soc.
Painters. *Awards*: med., World's Fair, St. Louis, Mo.;
prize, NAD. *Work*: BM; NAC; Newark Mus. *Exhibited*:
extensively in U.S.*

WIEGHARDT, PAUL—*Painter, E.*
School of the Art Institute of Chicago, Chicago 3, Ill.

B. Germany, Aug. 26, 1897. *Studied*: Sch. FA, Cologne,
Germany; Bauhaus, Weimar, with Klee; Acad, FA, Dres-
den, Germany. *Work*: Albright A. Gal.; Barnes Fnd.,
Merion, Pa.; Berkshire Mus.; PC; Rosenwald Coll.; Jen-
kintown, Pa.; Smith Col. Mus., and in private colls. *Ex-
hibited*: Salon d'Automne, Salon des Tuileries, Salon des
Independants, Paris, France; AIC; PAFA; LC; Soc. Contemp. A.,
Chicago; Stanford Univ.; Univ. Illinois; Salon d'Automne,
1947-1955; one-man, 1941-58: Berkshire Mus.; Harvard
Univ.; St. Paul A. Gal.; PC; Knoedler Gal.; Springfield
Mus. FA; AIC; Illinois Inst. Tech.; Syracuse Univ.; Mil-
waukee AI; Osthaus Mus., Hagen, West Germany; Univ.
Arizona; 1020 A. Center, Chicago, and others. *Position*:
Prof., AIC, Chicago, Ill., 1946- ; Instr., Dept. Arch., Ill.
Inst. of Tech., Chicago, 1950- .

WIER, GORDON D. (DON)—*Designer, P., T., I.*
718 Fifth Ave., New York 19, N.Y.; h. Minor Ave.,
Stratford, Conn.

B. Orchard Lake, Mich., June 14, 1903. *Studied*: Univ.
Michigan, A.B.; Chicago Acad. FA; Grand Central Sch.
A., and with J. Scott Williams. *Member*: Silvermine Gld.
A.; Washington (Conn.) AA; AIGA. *Exhibited*: Balt.
WC Cl.; Decorators Cl.; Bridgeport, Conn. (one-man);
Delaware River A. I., "Adventures par la Lecture," 1932;
"The Victors," 1933. *Position*: Des., Steuben Glass, 1945-
49; Corning-Steuben Glass, 1949-50; Des., Steuben Glass,
1950-51, A. Dir., 1952- .*

WIESE, KURT—Illustrator, W.

R.D. 1, Frenchtown, N.J.

B. Minden, Germany, Apr. 22, 1887. *Studied*: abroad. *Member*: Phila. WC Cl.; Hunterdon County A. All. *Work*: Author, I., "The Chinese Ink Stick"; "Liang and Lo"; "Karoo the Kangaroo"; "Ella, The Elephant"; "The Rabbit's Revenge"; "The Parrot Dealer"; "Fish in the Air"; "The Dog, The Fox and The Fleas"; "Happy Easter"; "The Cunning Turtle," and other books. Illus. over 300 children's books.

WIESE, LUCIE—Writer, Cr., L.

130 West 57th St., New York 19, N.Y.

B. Russia. *Studied*: Simmons Col.; Portia Law Sch.; Harvard Univ.; Sorbonne, Paris, France. *Awards*: Bollingen and William Lyons Phelps awards. Editor: "Emergence of American Art"; Co-editor: "Paul Rosenfeld-Voyager in the Arts"; Editor of exhibition catalogs. *Position*: Writer & Editor on the arts; Counsel to Collectors; Editorial Counsel to Research & Development Information Offices.

WIEST, K. VAN ELMENDORF—
Painter, T., Comm. A., Des., I.

519 Camino Don Miguel; h. 924 Canyon Rd., Santa Fe, N.M.

B. Little Rock, Ark., May 24, 1915. *Studied*: Am. Acad. A., Chicago; AIC, with Louis Ritman; Royal Acad. A., London, with Middleton Todd; Ecole des Beaux-Arts, Paris, France, Marquette Univ.; Northwestern Univ.; Univ. New Mexico. *Member*: Nat. Lg. Am. Pen Women (First Pres. Corralles Branch); Santa Fe AA. *Awards*: prizes, Paris, France, 1945; Botts Mem. Gal., Albuquerque, 1953, 1956. *Work*: murals, Veterans of Foreign Wars, Albuquerque; many port. commissions U.S. and abroad. *Exhibited*: NGA, 1950-1952; Mus. New Mexico, Santa Fe, 1948-1950, 1952, 1953; Layton A. Gal., Milwaukee, 1940; Newton A. Gal., N.Y., 1946; Fishers A. Gal., N.Y.; and in Santa Fe, Albuquerque, Carlsbad, Gallup and Taos, N.M. Lectures: Portraiture. *Position*: Instr., Portraiture, Univ. New Mexico (evening course); St. Michael's H.S.; Assoc., Albuquerque Mod. Mus.; Asst. to Carl Albach, Consulting Electrical Engineer, Santa Fe; Engineering Asst. to various firms, 1942- . Illus., Des., Statistical Charting, Visual Aid and Exh. material for the New Mexico State Land Office, Dept. of Game & Fish and the Economic Development Comm.

WIGGINS, BILL—Painter, T., S., Gr.

711 West 8th St., Roswell, N.M.

B. Roswell, N.M., Sept. 24, 1917. *Studied*: Abilene Christian College; Am. Univ., Shrivenham, England. *Work*: Roswell Mus. & A. Centre. *Exhibited*: Newport, R.I., 1954; Mus. New Mexico, 1952, 1958; one-man: Roswell Mus., 1951, 1955, 1957; Odessa (Tex.) College, 1955; Midland (Tex.) Woman's Cl., 1955.

WIGGINS, GUY—Painter, T., L.

Old Lyme, Conn.

B. Brooklyn, N.Y. *Studied*: NAD; & with Carleton Wiggins. *Member*: NA; SC; Conn. Acad. FA; Lotos Cl.; NAC; Lyme AA; Kit Kat Cl.; New Haven Paint & Clay Cl. *Awards*: prizes, Conn. Acad. FA, 1916, 1918, 1926, 1931, 1933; SC, 1916, 1919; AIC, 1917; R.I. Sch. Des., 1922; New Haven Paint & Clay Cl., 1930; Lotos Cl., 1938. *Work*: MMA; NGA; Brooklyn Inst. Mus.; Hackley A. Gal., Muskegon, Mich.; AIC; Dallas AA; Lincoln (Neb.) AA; Newark Mus.; Lotos Cl., Wadsworth Atheneum, Hartford, Conn.; etc. Lectures to art museum and art club audiences nationally.

WIGHT, FREDERICK S.—Educator, Gal. Dir., W., L.

Art Galleries, University of California, (24); h. 456 North Bundy Drive, Los Angeles 49, Cal.

B. New York, N.Y., June 1, 1902. *Studied*: Academie Julian, and others, Paris, France; Univ. Virginia, B.A.; Harvard Univ., M.A. Author: Van Gogh, 1953; Goya, 1954; John Marin, 1955; Morris Graves, 1956; Verge of Glory, 1956; Hans Hofmann, 1957; Arthur G. Dove, 1958; New Art in America (co-author). Contributor to Atlantic Monthly; The Kenyon Review; Art News; Arts. Organized major traveling exhibition for Inst. Contemp. A., Boston, of the work of Louis Sullivan, Le Corbusier, Walter Gropius, and Orozco; for the UCLA Galleries: Charles Sheeler, John Marin, Morris Graves, Hans Hofmann, Arthur G. Dove, Richard Neutra, with catalogues and pub. *Positions*: Asst. Dir., Inst. Contemp. A., Boston; Dir., Art Galleries, Univ. California at Los Angeles, at present.

WILBANKS, W. H.—Art Director

Arts & Crafts Society of Portland, 2381 Northwest Flanders St., Portland, Ore.*

WILBUR, DOROTHY THORNTON—Painter, I.

18 Fourth St., Southeast, Washington 3, D.C.

B. Fincastle, Va. *Studied*: with Frederick Fursman, Julius Golz, Alice Schille. *Awards*: prize, Minnesota SA.

WILBUR, LAWRENCE NELSON—
Painter, Et., Eng., Des.

125 West 96th St., New York 25, N.Y.

B. Whitman, Mass., Dec. 21, 1897. *Studied*: Mass. Normal A. Sch.; Otis AI; Grand Central Sch. A., and with N. C. Wyeth. *Member*: SAGA; AWS; SC; Chicago Soc. Et.; All. A. Am.; Audubon A. *Awards*: prizes, AWS, 1943; medal, 1951; SC, 1941, 1943; bronze medal, All. A. Am., 1952; bronze medal, Am. Artist magazine, 1958; New Jersey P. & S. Soc. *Work*: LC; NGA; PMA. *Exhibited*: NAD; SAGA; AWS; Chicago Soc. Et.; All. A. Am.; Audubon A.; New Jersey P. & S. Soc.; SC. *Position*: Exh. Chm. Audubon A., 1953.*

WILBY, MARGARET CROWINSHIELD—Painter

1130 Parker Ave., Detroit 14, Mich.

B. Detroit, Mich., Jan. 3, 1890. *Studied*: AIC; ASL; Ontario Col. A., Ontario, Canada; & with Eliot O'Hara. *Member*: Detroit Soc. Women Painters; Mich. Acad. Sc., A. & Let. *Exhibited*: NAWA, 1932-1934, 1939, 1940; Detroit Inst. A., 1939, 1942, 1943; Detroit Women Painters, 1934-1958; Detroit WC Soc., 1946; Rockport AA, 1931; Gloucester AA, 1934; Deerfield Valley AA, 1933, 1934, 1937, 1938; Mich. Acad. Sc., A. & Let., 1947-1954; Greenfield, Mass., 1948.

WILCOCKS, EDNA MARRETT—Painter

701 West Foothill Blvd., Arcadia, Cal.; h. 1310 Boston St., Altadena, Cal.

B. Portland, Me. *Studied*: Vassar Col.; BMFA Sch.; ASL; & with Frank Benson, Edmund Tarbell, Philip Hale, & others. *Member*: Women Painters of the West; Nat. Soc. A. & Lets., Pasadena Chaptr. (Chm., A. Comm.). *Work*: Court House, Wilkes-Barre, Pa.; Bowdoin Col., Burnswick, Me.; Court House, Edmonton, Alberta, Can.; ports. in private colls. *Exhibited*: Women Painters of the West, 1933-1955; Pasadena SA, 1930-1934; Griffith Park, Los A.; Pasadena AA; Santa Barbara, Cal.; Denver, Colo. *Position*: Dir. A., Anoakia Sch., Arcadia, Cal., 1936-56.

WILCOX, FRANK NELSON—
Painter, Gr., Ser., T., W., L.

Cleveland Institute of Art; h. 1879 Page Ave., East Cleveland 12, Ohio

B. Cleveland, Ohio, Oct. 3, 1887. *Studied*: Cleveland Sch. A., and with Henry Keller. *Member*: Cleveland Soc. A.; AWS; Phila. WC Cl. *Awards*: Penton medal, Cleveland. *Work*: CMA; Toledo Mus. A.; BM; dioramas, Western Reserve Hist. Soc. Author, I., "Ohio Indian Trails." *Position*: Instr. A., Cleveland Inst. A., Cleveland, Ohio.

WILCOX, RAY—Painter, I., W.

24 Ravine Rd., Tenafly, N.J.

B. Elmira, N.Y., Dec. 9, 1883. *Studied*: Rochester Athenaeum; ASL; & in Paris, France. *Member*: AAPL. *Awards*: prizes, Kresge Gal., Newark, N.J., 1933; med., AAPL, 1935; Montclair AA, 1936; SC, 1936. *Work*: Historic murals, Fashion Park, Rochester, N.Y.; Finchley, New York, Chicago and Palm Beach; Knickerbocker Country Cl., Tenafly, N.J. *Exhibited*: National & State Exh.†

WILCOX, RUTH—*Painter, C., Comm. A.*
284 Piermont Rd., Closter, N.J.

B. New York, N.Y., Aug. 4, 1908. *Studied*: ASL; N.Y. Sch. F. & App. A.; PAFA; Julian Acad., Paris, France. *Member*: AAPL. *Awards*: prizes, NAWA, 1932, 1934; NAD, 1934; Ridgewood (N.J) AA, 1935, 1947, 1948; Wichita A. Mus., 1937; Fitzwilliam, N.H., 1938-1941; medal, Montclair A. Mus., 1936, 1939. *Work*: Maugham Sch., Tenafly, N.J.; Grammar Sch., Leonia, N.J.; Palisades Interstate Park Comm.; murals, Provident Institution for Savings, Jersey City; Colonial Life Ins. Co., East Orange, N.J.; Knickerbocker Country Club, Tenafly, N.J. *Exhibited*: NAD; PAFA; NAWA; Carnegie Inst.; Conn. Acad. FA; Montclair A. Mus., etc.

WILCOX, R. TURNER—*Painter, I., W.*
Tenafly, N.J.

B. New York, N.Y., Apr. 29, 1888. *Studied*: Julian Acad., Paris, France; & in Munich, Germany. *Exhibited*: NAWA; Wichita Mus. A.; Delgado Mus. A.; Montclair A. Mus. Author, I., "The Mode in Hats and Headdress," 1945; "The Mode in Footwear," 1948; "The Mode in Furs," 1951; "The Mode in Costume," 1942, 2nd rev. ed., 1948, 3rd rev. ed., 1958.

WILDE, JOHN—*Painter, E.*
Department of Art Education, University of Wisconsin, Madison, Wis.; also, 335 South 1st St., Evansville, Wis.

B. Milwaukee, Wis., Dec. 12, 1919. *Studied*: Univ. Wisconsin, B.S., M.S. *Work*: Milwaukee AI; PAFA; Univ. Nebraska; Marquette Univ.; Santa Barbara Mus. A.; WMAA; Wadsworth Atheneum; Milwaukee War Memorial; Detroit Inst. A. *Exhibited*: CGA, 1953; PAFA, 1940, 1946, 1947, 1950-1958; WMAA, 1952-1957; MMA, 1950, 1952, 1957; AIC, 1941, 1947, 1948, 1950-1953; VMFA, 1948; Univ. Illinois, 1948, 1952, 1953, 1955, 1957; Walker A. Center; Milwaukee AI; Denver A. Mus.; A. Festival, Spoleto, Italy; several one-man exhs. *Position*: Instr., Dept. A. Edu., 1948-50, Asst. Prof., 1950-55, Assoc. Prof., 1955- , Univ. Wisconsin, Madison, Wis.

WILDENHAIN, FRANS RUDOLF—
Ceramic Craftsman, P., S., T.
School for American Craftsmen, 65 Plymouth Ave., South, Rochester, N.Y.; h. R.D. Bushnell's Basin, Pittsford, N.Y.

B. Leipzig, Germany, June 5, 1905. *Studied*: Bauhaus, Weimar, Germany. *Awards*: prizes, Int. Exp., Paris, 1939; Exh. A., Los A., 1949 (2); Cal. State Fair, 1949 (2); Wichita AA, 1951; Rochester Mem. A. Gal., 1951 (2), 1953 (2), 1954 (2), 1955, 1956 (2), 1958; Univ. Rochester, 1953; Albright A. Gal., 1952, 1954, 1957, 1958; St. Paul A. Gal., 1955; Miami Nat., 1957, 1958; Syracuse Mus. FA, 1957; Guggenheim F., 1958. *Work*: Stedeljik Mus., Amsterdam; Boymans Mus., Rotterdam; Stoke-Upon-Trent, England; Mons, Belgium; Faenza and Milan, Italy; Portland A. Mus.; SAM; Scripps Col.; BMA; Indianapolis AA; AIC; Rochester Mem. A. Gal.; Univ. Illinois; St. Paul A. Gal.; Munson-Williams-Proctor Inst. *Exhibited*: MMA, 1929; SFMA, 1949; deYoung Mem. Mus., 1948; Portland A. Mus., 1949; San Diego A. Gal.; AIC; Walker A. Center; Des Moines A. Center; VMFA; Univ. California; Univ. California at Los A.; Dallas Mus. FA; Ft. Worth AA; Univ. Redlands; Henry Gal., Seattle; Wichita AA; BMA; Syracuse Mus. FA, 1952, 1954, 1955, 1956, 1958; Rochester Mem. A. Gal., 1951-1958; Univ. Illinois, 1953, 1955, 1956, 1957; BM, 1953; Albright A. Gal., 1954-1958; Corning Glass Center, 1954; Nebraska AA, 1955; America House, N.Y., 1955; Iowa State Univ., 1955; Cannes, France, 1955; Miami Nat., 1957, 1958; Mus. Contemp. Crafts, 1956; Brussels Fair, 1958; and many others. Contributor of ceramic designs to Arts & Architecture, House Beautiful, Crafts Horizons, Ceramic Monthly, American Artist, and other publications. *Position*: Instr., Ceramics, Sch. for Am. Craftsmen, Rochester, N.Y., at present.

WILDER, MITCHELL—*Educator*
Chouinard Art Institute, 743 South Grand View St., Los Angeles 57, Cal.

B. Colorado Springs, Colo., Aug. 19, 1913. *Studied*: McGill Univ., Montreal, Canada, A.B.; Univ. California. Ed., Santos' "Religious Folk Art of New Mexico." *Position*: Dir., Chouinard Art Inst., Los Angeles, Cal.

WILES, BERTHA HARRIS—*Educator*
5528 Hyde Park Blvd., Chicago 37, Ill.

B. Sedalia, Mo., Dec. 17, 1896. *Studied*: Univ. Illinois, B.A.; Univ. Wisconsin, M.A.; Am. Acad. in Rome; Radcliffe Col., M.A., Ph.D. *Member*: CAA. *Awards*: Carnegie F., 1927, 1928; traveling scholarship, 1929; Am. Council Learned Soc. grant, 1931; Sachs F., Harvard Univ., 1936. Author: "Fountains of Florentine Sculptors," 1933. Contributor to: art magazines & museums bulletins. Lectures: Florentine Fountains (Sculpture). *Position*: Instr. A., Radcliffe Col., 1930-35; Instr. A., 1940- , Cur., Max Epstein Archive, 1938- , A. Librarian, 1939-43, Univ. Chicago, Ill.*

WILES, GLADYS—*Painter*
Peconic, N.Y.

B. New York, N.Y. *Studied*: with Cox, Chase, Johansen, Wiles. *Member*: ANA; AAPL; All. A. Am.; Audubon A. *Awards*: med., NAWA, 1919.*

WILEY, HEDWIG—*Painter*
The Lenox, 13th & Spruce Sts., Philadelphia 7, Pa.

B. Philadelphia, Pa. *Studied*: PAFA; Univ. Pennsylvania, B.S.; Columbia Univ.; Harvard Summer School; & with William Chase, Cecilia Beaux, Henry Snell, & others. *Member*: A. All., Pr. Cl., PAFA, all of Phila., Pa. *Exhibited*: PAFA; Phila. AC.

WILEY, HUGH SHELDON—*Painter*
56 Palmer Ave., Bronxville, N.Y.

B. Auburn, Ind., Oct. 27, 1922. *Studied*: PAFA; and in Mexico City. *Member*: NSMP. *Awards*: Cresson traveling scholarship, PAFA, 1948; prize, Rome Comp., 1949. *Work*: murals in homes and office bldgs., in Mexico City; New York; Wash., D.C.; Beach Haven, N.J.; Phila., Pa.; Newark Prudential Life Ins. Co.; Ball State T. Col. *Exhibited*: PAFA, 1947, 1952-1954; Mexico City, 1952, 1953; Bertha Schaefer Gal., 1956-1958; Ball State T. Col., 1958; one-man: Bertha Schaefer Gal., 1955, 1956, 1957; Ball State T. Col., 1957; Mexico City, 1953. Contributor to Architectural Record; Design (Bombay, India); Architectural Forum. *Position*: Visiting A., Ball State T. Col., 1957; PMSchA, 1958.

WILFORD, LORAN FREDERICK—*Painter, T.*
Ringling School of Art, Sarasota, Fla.

B. Wamego, Kan., Sept. 13, 1893. *Studied*: Kansas City AI, and with Charles Wilimovsky, George Pearse Ennis. *Member*: AWS; Audubon A. *Awards*: prizes, AWS, 1929, 1932; Phila. WC Cl., 1931; SC, 1930, 1953; Audubon A., 1945; Sarasota AA, 1954; Ft. Lauderdale, Fla., 1954. *Work*: Toledo Mus. A.; N.Y. Pub. Lib.; murals, Holmes Pub. Sch., Darien, Conn. *Exhibited*: Carnegie Inst.; CGA; NAD; PAFA; GGE 1939; Audubon A.; AWS; Palm Beach, Fla.; Ft. Lauderdale, Fla. *Position*: Instr., Ringling Sch. A., Sarasota, Fla.

WILIMOVSKY, CHARLES A.—*Etcher, Eng., P., T.*
Art Center School, 5353 West 3rd St., Los Angeles, Cal.

B. Chicago, Ill., Sept. 10, 1885. *Studied*: AIC; Julian Acad., Paris, France; & with J. C. Johansen, William Chase. *Member*: Chicago SE; SAGA. *Awards*: prizes, Kansas City AI; Rosenwald, Carr, Clussman prizes, AIC; med., Univ. Oklahoma. *Work*: Kansas City AI; AIC; Springfield (Mass.) Pub. Lib.; Honolulu Acad. A.; Modern Gal., Prague. *Exhibited*: nationally; & in Paris, Brussels, Florence, Rome. *Position*: Instr., Art Center Sch., Los Angeles, Cal.*

WILKE, ULFERT S.—*Painter, E., Mus. Dir.*
Art Department, University of Louisville; h. 1417 Hepburn Ave., Louisville 4, Ky.

B. Bad Toelz, Germany, July 14, 1907. *Studied*: in Germany; Paris, France; Harvard Univ.; State Univ. Iowa, M.A. *Member*: CAA. *Awards*: Albrecht Durer prize, Germany, 1928; Delgado Mus. A., 1944; Ky.-Ind. Exh., 1951-1957; Soc. Four Arts, Palm Beach, 1944, 1946; Va. Intermont Col., 1951; medal, Army Art Comp., 1945. *Work*: Hanover Mus., Germany; Univ. Iowa; Univ. Louisville; Univ. Illinois; Stanford Univ.; Mills Col.; Univ. Kentucky; Wadsworth Atheneum; Carnegie Inst.; AGAA;

Dayton AI; Joslyn Mem. Mus., and in private colls. *Exhibited*: Berlin Acad., 1930, 1931; MMA, 1952; AIC, 1944; Guggenheim Mus., N.Y., 1954; BM, 1955, 1957; VMFA, 1958; Smithsonian Inst. traveling exh.; more than 30 one-man exhs., U.S. and Germany; one-man, Kyoto, Japan, 1958. Illus., "The Best of De Maupassant"; "Music To Be Seen," 1956; "Fragments From Nowhere," 1958. Lectures: under auspices of Assn. of Am. Colleges. *Position*: Dir., Kalamazoo Inst. A., 1940-42; Dir., Springfield (Ill.) AA, 1946; Asst. Prof., Univ. Iowa, 1947; Assoc. Prof., Univ. Louisville, 1948- ; (On sabbatical leave, Japan, 1958); Visiting Prof., A. in Res., Univ. Georgia, 1955-56.

WILKEVICH, ELEANOR (Mrs. Proto A.)—Painter, T.

3461 Ullman St., San Diego 6, Cal.

B. New York, N.Y., Aug. 2, 1910. *Studied*: Grand Central Sch. A.; ASL; & with George Pearse Ennis, Henry B. Snell, Aldro Hibbard. *Member*: San Diego A. Gld.; La Jolla A. Center; San Diego County A. Council; La Jolla A. Lib. Assn. *Awards*: prizes, San Diego FA Soc., 1943, 1946, 1952; San Diego County Fair; Carlsbad-Oceanside Gld.; Spanish Village Assn. *Work*: San Diego FA Gal.; Russell A. Mus., Great Falls, Mont.; mural, San Diego County Hospital. *Exhibited*: GGE 1939; one-man exh.: La Jolla A. Center; Laguna Beach AA; La Jolla A. Gld.; San Diego A. Gld.; Cedar City, Utah. *Position*: Instr., Painting, San Diego City Schs., Dept. Adult Edu.

WILL, BLANCA—Sculptor, P., T., Des., Gr.

Studio Cabin, U.S. 71, Rt. 2, Winslow, Ark.; Blue Hill, Me.

B. Rochester, N.Y., July 7, 1881. *Studied*: Rochester Mechanics Inst.; Hans Hofmann Sch. FA; Grande Chaumiere, Paris; in Germany; & with Castellucho, Luhring, Tryon, & others. *Awards*: prizes, Rochester Mem. A. Gal., 1932, 1933; Fairchild award, Rochester, 1934; Mus. FA, Little Rock, Ark.; New Mexico State Fair, 1938-1940. *Work*: Rochester Mem. A. Gal.; Univ. Arkansas; Cal. PLH; numerous sculptured busts, oil portraits. *Exhibited*: NAD; PAFA; traveling exh. bronzes, U.S. & Canada; Coronado, Cal.; Univ. New Mexico; Albuquerque, N.M.; Mus. New Mexico, Santa Fé (one-man); Rochester, N.Y. (one-man); Univ. Arkansas (one-man); retrospective exh., Mus. FA of Little Rock, 1958.

WILLARD, RODLOW—Cartoonist, I., Des., W.

421 West 57th St., New York 19, N.Y.

B. Rochester, N.Y., Sept. 4, 1906. *Studied*: Univ. California, B.A. *Member*: A. Gld.; Nat. Cartoonists Soc. *Exhibited*: Cartoonists' Gld. traveling exh., 1938-1940. I., "Word Magic," 1939; "Hungry Hill," 1943 (King Features Syndicated version). Contributor to: national magazines & newspaper syndicates. Creator, "Scorchy Smith," daily and Sunday syndicated adventure feature, Assoc. Press News Features 1945-54. Story Boards, "Cinerama Holiday," 1955. Creator of "Jo and Jill," "Gal Friday," "Aunt Teek," newspaper comics, 1954-56. *Position*: Staff Cart., Digest magazine, Review of Reviews, 1936-37; A. Dir., Condé Nast Business Magazines, 1938-40; Ed., Juvenile Magazines, Dell Publications, 1939-40; Staff A., King Features Syndicate, 1941-45.*

WILLE, O. LOUIS—Sculptor, T.

Aspen, Colo.

B. St. Paul, Minn., Apr. 27, 1917. *Studied*: Univ. Minnesota, B.A., M.A. *Exhibited*: Kraushaar Gal.; Sculpture Center, N.Y.; Walker A. Center; Minneapolis Inst. A.; Univ. Minnesota; Syracuse Mus. FA; Denver A. Mus. *Position*: Dir., Aspen A. Sch., Aspen, Colo.

WILLET, HENRY LEE—Craftsman, W., L.

3900 Girard Ave., Philadelphia 4, Pa.; h. Willow Wadi Farm, Ambler, Pa.

B. Pittsburgh, Pa., Dec. 7, 1899. *Studied*: Princeton Univ.; Univ. Pennsylvania, and in Europe. *Awards*: medal, Phila. A. & Crafts Gld.; Phila. A. All.; Doctor of Art, Lafayette Col., 1951. *Member*: AFA; AIA; Arch. Lg.; Stained Glass Assn. Am.; PAFA; Fairmount Park Assn.; Church Architectural Gld. *Work*: stained glass windows, Nat. Cathedral, Wash., D.C.; U.S. Cadet Chapel, West Point, N.Y.; Westminster Presbyterian Church, Detroit; Princeton Univ. Chapel; Chicago Theological Seminary; Grosse Pointe (Mich.) Mem. Church; Westwood Community Church, Los A., Cal.; Univ. Presbyterian Church, Seattle, Wash.;

Medical Center Chapel, Houston; Mich. State Univ. Chapel; St. John's Lutheran Church, Wheaton, Ill.; Bryn Mawr Presbyterian Church, Pa.; Montview Church, Denver, Colo.; Highland Park Presbyterian Church, Dallas; Robinson Sch., Puerto Rico; Westminster Church, Buffalo, N.Y.; St. Mary's Sch., Glens Falls, N.Y., and many others. *Exhibited*: in leading U.S. galleries. Exh. of Am. Stained Glass, U.S. Dept. Commerce, World Trade Fair, Poznan, Poland, 1958. Lecturer with traveling exh. "New Work in Stained Glass," at museums & colleges. "Gold" Process window illus. in Life magazine, 1955. Co-author, "Stained Glass," Encyclopaedia Americana. Contributor to Architectural Forum, Stained Glass Quarterly, Religion in Life, and other magazines. *Position*: Pres., Willet Stained Glass Co.; Past Pres., 1942-44, Chm. Edu. & Pub. Rel., Stained Glass Assn. Am.

WILLEY, EDITH M(ARING) (Mrs. N. C.)—Painter, Et., T., W., L.

1715 South Marine Drive, Bremerton, Wash.

B. Seattle, Wash. *Studied*: with C. C. Maring; Eustace Paul Ziegler, Peter Camfferman, Edgar Forner, May Marshall, Mark Tobey, and others. *Member*: Pacific Coast P. S. & W.; Nat. Lg. Am. Pen Women; Women Painters of Wash. *Work*: Law Lib., State Capitol, Olympia, Wash.; John Hay Sch., King County Court House, First Nat. Bank, Scottish Rite Temple, all of Seattle; Puget Sound Hospital, Bremerton, and in private colls. U.S. and abroad. *Exhibited*: SFMA; CM; BM; Portland (Ore.) A. Mus.; Frye Mus., A., Seattle; Sears-Roebuck Gal., Wash., D.C.; A. Lg. of Wash.; one-man: Frederick & Nelson Gal., Seattle, 1937-1942; Northwest Gal., 1933.

WILLIAMS, BEN F.—Museum Curator, P.

North Carolina Museum of Art; h. 2813 Mayview Road, Raleigh, N.C.

B. Lumberton, N.C., Dec. 24, 1925. *Studied*: Corcoran Sch. A., with Eugen Weisz; George Washington Univ., A.A.; Univ. North Carolina, A.B.; Columbia Univ., Paris Extension, Ecole du Louvre; ASL. *Member*: AAMus.; Southeastern Mus. Conf.; CAA. *Awards*: prizes, Southeastern Annual, 1947; North Carolina A., 1947; Wash. Soc. A., 1947; Wash. A. Fair, 1946; Ronsheim Mem. award, Corcoran Sch. A., 1946. *Work*: Atlanta AA; North Carolina Mus. A.; Greenville (N.C.) Civic A. Gal.; Duke Univ.; Knoll Assoc., N.Y. *Exhibited*: CGA; PC; Atlanta AA; VMFA; Jacques Seligmann Gal.; Virginia Intermont, Bristol, Va.; Weatherspoon Gal., Greensboro; Person Hall Gal., Chapel Hill, N.C.; Asheville A. Mus.; AFA traveling exhs. Contributor articles on 19th Century American Painting & Sculpture to North Carolina Museum of Art Bulletin; North Carolina Historical Review. Assisted with exhibitions "Rembrandt and His Pupils"; "E. L. Kirchner," and the collections of the North Carolina Museum of Art. In charge of Annual North Carolina Artists' Exhibition. *Position*: Cur., North Carolina Museum of Art, Raleigh, N.C.

WILLIAMS, CHESTER R.—Painter, W., L., I.

28 Yeoman's Row, London, S.W. 3, England

B. Lewiston, Idaho, Oct. 14, 1921. *Studied*: Lukits Acad. FA; Courtald Inst., London, and in Venice, Italy. *Member*: Cal. WC Soc.; Soc. Western A.; Nat. Soc. A. & Lets.; Hesketh Hubbard A. Soc. *Work*: Italian Govt. *Exhibited*: Bordighera, Italy, 1953; Cal. WC Soc., 1953; Nat. Orange Flower Show, 1955; Soc. Western A., 1955; Britain in Water-Colour, 1956-1958; one-man: Nurnberg, Germany, 1953; London, England, 1954. Contributor to Music of the West magazine.

WILLIAMS, ESTHER—Painter, Lith.

Peacham, Vt.; mail: R.F.D. West Danville, Vt.

B. Boston, Mass., Feb. 19, 1907. *Studied*: BMFA Sch.; in Paris; & with Philip Hale. *Member*: Rockport AA. *Awards*: prizes, PAFA, 1935; WMA, 1935; med., prize, AIC, 1938; Am. Acad. A. & Let. & Nat. Inst. A. & Let. grant, 1944; prize, Rockport AA, 1955. *Work*: PAFA; WMAA; WMA; BMFA; AGAA; MMA; New Britain (Conn.) A. Mus. *Exhibited*: Nationally and internationally.

WILLIAMS, GARTH MONTGOMERY—Illustrator, S., P., W., Des.

Box 1, Aspen, Colo.

B. New York, N.Y., Apr. 16, 1912. *Studied*: Westminster Sch. A.; Royal Col. A., London, England. *Awards*: Prix de Rome, 1936. *Exhibited*: British Royal Acad., 1933-1935, 1938. Des. theatre sets; Sculpture ports., and groups; advertising in press and posters. Illus.: "Stuart Little"; "Little Fur Family"; "Wait 'Til the Moon is Full"; "Charlotte's Web"; "Flossie and Bossie"; "Little House Books" (8); "Do You Know What I'll Do"; "Over and Over"; "Three Little Animals"; "The Happy Orphalines"; "The Family Under the Bridge"; "Tall Book of Make Believe"; for Golden Books: "The Friendly Book"; "Mr. Dog"; "Sailor Dog"; "Animal Friends"; "Baby Animals"; "Elves and Fairies," and others; Adult books: "In Our Town," and others. Author, I., "Benjamin Pink," 1951; "The Rabbits Wedding," 1958.

WILLIAMS, GLUYAS—Illustrator Cart., W.
Sylvan Ave., West Newton 65, Mass.

B. San Francisco, Cal., July 23, 1888. *Studied*: Harvard Univ., A.B. *Work*: Lib. Cong. *Exhibited*: BMFA, 1946. Author: "The Gluyas Williams Book," 1929; "Fellow Citizens," 1940; "The Gluyas Williams Gallery," 1957. I., "Daily Except Sunday," 1938; "People of Note," 1940; "Father of the Bride," 1949; all books by Robert C. Benchley. Contributor to: New Yorker magazine.

WILLIAMS, HELEN F.—Ceramic Craftsman, E.
Craft Building, Syracuse University; h. 225 Dale St., Syracuse 8, N.Y.

B. Syracuse, N.Y., Oct. 13, 1907. *Studied*: Syracuse Univ., B.F.A. *Member*: AAPL; Lg. Am. Pen Women. *Awards*: prizes, Assoc. A. Syracuse, 1937, 1946-1951; Nat. Lg. Am. Pen Women, 1956. *Work*: IBM Corp. Mus., Endicott, N.Y.; Syracuse Mus. FA. *Exhibited*: Syracuse Mus. FA, 1932-1941, 1946-1958; WFNY 1939; Paris Salon, 1937; BMA, 1944; Lg. Am. Pen Women, 1946, 1955; Syracuse Ceramic Gld.; Lowe Gal. A., Syracuse Univ., 1958 (one-man) and prior. *Position*: Prof., Univ. Syracuse, N.Y., at present.

WILLIAMS, HERMANN WARNER, JR.—
Museum Director, W., T., L.
Corcoran Gallery of Art, 17th St. & New York Ave.; h. 3226 Woodley Rd., Northwest, Washington 8, D.C.

B. Boston, Mass., Nov. 2, 1908. *Studied*: Harvard Col., A.B.; Harvard Univ., M.A.; Univ. London, Ph.D.; N.Y. Univ. *Member*: AAMus.; CAA; Assn. A. Mus. Dir. Co-Author: "William Sidney Mount, 1807-1868," 1944. Contributor to: Burlington Magazine; MMA Bulletin & art magazines. *Positions*: Asst. Cur., Renaissance Art, BM, 1936; Asst. Cur., Painting, MMA, 1936-46; Chief, Hist. Properties Section, War Dept., 1945-46; Asst. Dir., CGA, Washington, D.C., 1946-47, Dir., 1947- .

WILLIAMS, J. SCOTT—Painter, C., Des.
35 Heathcote Rd., Scarsdale, N.Y.

B. Liverpool, England, Aug. 18, 1887. *Studied*: AIC. *Member*: NA; AWS; NSMP; SC; Arch. Lg. *Awards*: prizes, AIC, 1924; AWS, 1925, 1927; SC, 1928. *Work*: AIC; Indiana State Lib. & Historical Bldg., Indianapolis; Johns Hopkins Univ.; USPO, Newcastle, Del. Completed 102 maps in porcelain enamel, for American Battle Monuments Commission; stained glass window to coordinate with two murals, Arsenal Tech. H.S., Indianapolis.

WILLIAMS, LEWIS W., II—Educator, Hist.
Art Department, Beloit College; h. 647 College St., Beloit, Wis.

B. Champaign, Ill., Apr. 24, 1918. *Studied*: Univ. Illinois, B.F.A., M.F.A.; Univ. Chicago, Ph.D. *Member*: CAA. Lectures: History of Art—American, Modern and Renaissance. *Position*: Prof. A., Beloit College, Beloit, Wis.

WILLIAMS, MARY FRANCES—Educator
Art Department, Randolph-Macon Woman's College; h. 239 Westmoreland St., Lynchburg, Va.

B. Providence, R.I., Apr. 26, 1905. *Studied*: Radcliffe Col., B.A., M.A., Ph.D. *Member*: CAA; Soc. Arch. Historians; Archaeological Inst. Am.; AAUW; AAUP; Lynchburg A. Cl.; Lynchburg FA Center. *Awards*: Jonathan Fay award, 1927; Caroline Wilby award, 1931. Contributor reviews of exhibitions local newspapers. In progress: Catalogue of Randolph-Macon Woman's College collection of American Painting. *Positions*: Asst. Prof. A., Hollins Col., 1936-39;

Mt. Holyoke Col.; Northwestern Univ., 1950-51; Assoc. Prof. A., State T. Col., St. Cloud, Minn.; Prof. A., Chm. Dept. Art, Randolph-Macon Woman's Col., 1952- ; Member, Va. State A. Commission, 1956- .

WILLIAMS, MAY—Painter, Des., T.
King Edward Apts., 4601 Bayard St., Pittsburgh 13, Pa.

B. Pittsburgh, Pa. *Studied*: Carnegie Col. FA; Univ. Pittsburgh FA & Crafts; N.Y. Sch. F. & App. A.; Ecole des Beaux-Arts, Fontainebleau, France. *Member*: AFA; Assoc. A. Pittsburgh; Pa. Craftsmen's Gld.; Pittsburgh A Center. *Work*: Carnegie Inst.; Pittsburgh A. Center. *Position*: Instr., A. & Crafts, Shady Side Acad., and Winchester-Thurston Schs., Pittsburgh, Pa.

WILLIAMS, MILDRED EMERSON—Painter, Lith.
565 Baldwin Court, Birmingham, Mich.

B. Detroit, Mich., Aug. 9, 1892. *Studied*: PAFA; ASL; & with Henry McCarter, Robert Henri, Charles Locke, John Sloan, George Luks, & others. *Member*: Detroit Soc. Women Painters; Birmingham Soc. Women Painters; Mich. Acad. Sc., A. & Let. *Awards*: prizes, PAFA, 1928; Detroit Inst. A., 1934, 1939, 1940. *Work*: N.Y. Pub. Lib.; PAFA; McGregor Lib., Highland Park, Mich.; Detroit Inst. A.; Children's Mus., Detroit. *Exhibited*: PAFA, 1925, 1926, 1928; AIC, 1935; CGA, 1936; AFA traveling exh.; Carnegie Inst., 1941; AIGA, 1935; Detroit Inst. A., 1956, 1957; Mich. Acad. Sciences, Arts & Letters, Ann Arbor.

WILLIAMS, (JOHN) NELSON—Painter, Des.
43 West 55th St., New York 19, N.Y.

B. Brazil, Ind., Apr. 18, 1912. *Studied*: John Herron AI; De Pauw Univ.; Corcoran Sch. A.; ASL. *Awards*: prizes, Mississippi AA, 1945, 1946; John Herron AI, 1946, 1948; Alabama WC Soc., 1948. *Exhibited*: AWS, 1945, 1950; Albany Inst. Hist. & A., 1945; SFMA, 1945; Mississippi AA, 1945, 1946; Audubon A., 1946, 1948; Alabama WC Soc., 1948-1950; Butler AI, 1946, 1947, 1950; Portland Soc. A., 1946; Phila. WC Cl., 1948-1950, 1955.*

WILLIAMS, PAULINE BLISS (Mrs. Ronald Croft)—
Painter
115 Marmion Way, Rockport, Mass.

B. Springfield, Mass., July 12, 1888. *Studied*: ASL; Henri Sch. A.; & with Frank DuMond, F. Luis Mora, George Bellows, & others. *Member*: NAWA; North Shore AA; Springfield A. Lg.; Pa. Soc. Min. P. *Awards*: prizes, Springfield, Mass., 1926, 1928; Soc. for Sanity in A., Chicago, 1941; AIC., 1941. *Exhibited*: NAWA; Pa. Soc. Min. P.; NSMP; North Shore AA; Brooklyn Soc. Min. P.; North Shore AA traveling exh., 1957-1959, etc. Lectures: History of Miniature Painting.

WILLIAMS, WARNER—Sculptor, Des., L., P., T.
Culver Military Academy, Culver, Ind.

B. Henderson, Ky., Apr. 23, 1903. *Studied*: Berea Col.; Herron AI; AIC, B.F.A. *Member*: Chicago AC; Chicago AA; Hoosier Salon. *Awards*: prizes, AIC, 1941; Herron AI, 1925; Hoosier Salon, 1928, 1930, 1931, 1932, 1937, 1942; North Shore AA, 1939; City of Chicago award, 1938. *Work*: mem., bas-reliefs, etc.; Court House, Frankfort, Ky.; Berea Col.; Indiana Univ.; City Church, Gary, Ind.; Purdue Univ.; Bradwell Sch., Chicago; Francis Parker Sch., Chicago; Univ. Pittsburgh; Ball Mem., Indiana State Col.; McCormick Mem., Northwestern Univ. Medical Sch., Chicago; Peck Recreational Area, Detroit; Hektoen Mem., Hektoen Clinic, Chicago; port., Cardinal Stritch Tomb, Chicago. *Exhibited*: AIC, 1932-1942; Century of Progress, Chicago, 1932; Hoosier Salon, 1928-1943; Milwaukee AI, 1939. Contributor to: Design magazine. *Position*: A. in Residence, Culver Military Acad., Culver, Ind., 1940- .

WILLIAMS, WHEELER—Sculptor, L., W., P.
15 West 67th St., New York 23, N.Y.; also, Madison, Conn.

B. Chicago, Ill., Nov. 3, 1897. *Studied*: Yale Univ., Ph.B.; Harvard Univ. Sch. Arch., M. Arch.; Ecole des Beaux-Arts, Paris, France. *Member*: NA; NSS; Arch.L.; FA Fed. N.Y.; Mun. A Soc., N.Y.; AAPL (Pres.); Am. Veterans Soc. A. *Awards*: prize, NAD, 1936; gold medal, NAC, 1956; AAPL, 1957; med., Paris Exp., 1937, and others.

Work: San Diego FA Soc.; Brookgreen Gardens, S.C.; Four A. Gal., Palm Beach, Fla.; Norton Gal. A., West Palm Beach, Fla.; AIC; Hackley A. Gal.; many architectural & monumental works throughout U.S., South Africa, & Canada. *Exhibited*: Salon des Artistes Francais, 1923-1927; Salon d'Automne, Paris; PAFA; AIC; WFNY, 1939; NAD; GGE, 1939; Palace Legion Honor; NSS, etc.; one-man exh.: Ferargil Gal.; Arden Gal., Guild Hall, East Hampton, L.I., N.Y.; Soc. Four A.; etc. Lectures: Garden Sculpture; Portrait Sculpture; Methods & Techniques. Author: Monograph on Sculpture, 1947.

WILLIAMSON, WILLIAM HARVEY—*Painter, Des.*
Box 591, Carmel, Cal.

B. Denver, Colo., Oct. 31, 1908. *Studied*: Chouinard AI; A. Center Sch., Los A., and with Will Foster, F. Tolles Chamberlin. *Member*: NSMP; Arch. Lg.; Carmel AA; Soc. Western A.; Oakland Mus. Assn. *Work*: Oakland A. Mus.; Douglas Aircraft Corp., and in private colls.; murals, Am. Automobile Assn. Office Bldg., San Francisco; Salinas (Cal.) Airport Terminal Bldg.; costume and mural sketches for 20th Century-Fox, Hollywood. *Exhibited*: NSMP; Arch. Lg., 1956; deYoung Mem. Mus.; Oakland A. Mus.; Stockton, Cal.; Cal. State Fair; Santa Cruz A. Lg.; Fresno A. Lg.; Laguna Beach AA; Col. of Marin; Santa Paula, Cal.; Carmel AA; Maxwell Gal., San F.; Harrison Mem. Lib., Carmel. One-man: Maxwell Gal., San F., 1958; AIA exh., Monterey, Cal., 1958. Contributor to Christian Science Monitor; Monterey Peninsula-Herald.

WILLIAMSON, WILLIAM M.—*Museum Curator*
Museum of the City of New York, Fifth Ave. at 103rd St., New York 29, N.Y.*

WILLING, JESSIE GILLESPIE. See *Gillespie, Jessie*

WILLSON, JAMES MALLORY—*Painter, Et., T.*
414 Gardenia St., West Palm Beach, Fla.

B. Kissimmee, Fla., Dec. 28, 1890. *Studied*: Acad. Colorossi, Paris; Rollins Col.; NAD; ASL; & with Henri, Bridgman, Johansen. *Member*: Chicago Soc. Et.; Fla. A. Group. *Awards*: prize, Soc. Four A., Palm Beach, Fla., 1941. *Work*: Lib. Cong. *Exhibited*: SAGA, 1940, 1945; AV, 1942; NAD, 1944-1946; Lib. Cong., 1943, 1945; Soc. Four A., 1939, 1946; Palm Beach A. Lg., 1939, 1946; Norton Gal., 1944-1945; Fla. A. Group traveling exh., 1955-56. *Position*: Instr., Drawing & Painting, Norton Sch. A., West Palm Beach, Fla., 1946- .

WILMETH, CLAIRE P.—*Painter*
400 East 52nd St., New York 22, N.Y.

B. Riverton, N.J., Sept. 24, 1900. *Studied*: ASL, with George Bridgman, Wayman Adams; and in France, Italy and South America. *Member*: All. A. Am. *Work*: Vanderpoel Coll., Chicago.*

WILMETH, HAL TURNER—*Educator, Gal. Dir., L., P.*
California College of Arts & Crafts, Oakland, Cal.; 970 Idylberry Road, Lucas Valley, San Rafael, Cal.

B. Lincoln, Neb., July 9, 1917. *Studied*: Kansas City AI, B.F.A.; Drury Col.; Univ. Nebraska; Univ. Chicago, M.A.; in Italy and with Thomas Hart Benton, Ulrich Middeldorf, Roberto Longhi. *Member*: Midwestern AA; AAUP; AFA; Italy-America Soc.; CAA. *Awards*: Vanderslice scholarship, Sch. Des. scholarship, Kansas City AI, 1937-38; Fulbright F., 1949-50, 1950-51. *Work*: Univ. Oklahoma, and in private colls. *Position*: Instr., Kansas City AI, 1938-40; Instr., 1948-51, Asst. Prof. A. Hist., 1951-54, Univ. Nebraska; Dir.; Gump's Gal., San F., 1954- ; Assoc. Prof., Dean of Students, Cal. Col. A. & Crafts, Oakland, Cal., 1955- ; Univ. California Ext. Div., 1958- .

WILNER, MARIE (SPRING)—*Painter*
1248 White Plains Road, New York 72, N.Y.

B. Paris, France, July 24, 1910. *Studied*: Hunter Col., B.A.; ASL; New Sch. for Social Research, N.Y. *Member*: NAWA; AEA; AWS; A. Lg. of Long Island; Cape Cod AA. *Awards*: prizes, Ross Exh., Newark, N.J.; Village A. Center; Seton Hall Univ. *Work*: Norfolk Mus. A.; N.Y. Univ.; Lowe Gal. A., Coral Gables, Fla.; Richmond (Ind.) AI; Evansville Mus. A.; Seton Hall Univ.; and in France. *Exhibited*: PAFA, 1957; Knickerbocker A., 1954, 1956,

1957; Chautauqua AA, 1958; Collectors of Am. A., 1955-1957; P. & S. Soc. of New Jersey, 1955-1957; NAWA, 1956, 1957; AAPL, 1956, 1957; Seton Hall Univ., 1957; Peabody Inst., Balt., Md.; Irvington A. Mus. Assn., 1952, 1953; Hudson Valley AA, 1953; Parke-Bernet Gal., 1957; Barzansky Gal., 1956; Bodley Gal., 1957; A. Lg. of Long Island Hyannis AA, 1956, and others.

WILSON, BEN—*Painter, T.*
38 West 22nd St., New York 11, N.Y.; h. 596 Broad Ave., Ridgefield, N.J.

B. Philadelphia, Pa., June 23, 1913. *Studied*: Col. City of N.Y., B.S.S.; NAD; & with Karl Anderson, Leon Kroll, George Eggers. *Member*: Soc. Indp. A.; Hetero A. Group. *Awards*: prize, Col. City of N.Y., 1933; med., NAD, 1932. *Work*: Everhart Mus., Scranton, Pa. *Exhibited*: Audubon A., 1945, 1951; PAFA, 1946, 1955; Pepsi-Cola, 1946; Norlyst Gal., 1945; Riverside Mus., 1942; Am.-British A. Center, 1943; Soc. Indp. A., 1944; Newark Mus., 1952, 1955; New Sch. Social Research, 1952; Phila. A. All., 1955; DMFA, 1955; CMA, 1955; Albright A. Gal., 1955; CGA, 1955; Montclair A. Mus., 1956; YMHA, 1957; Newark Mus. A., 1958; Art: USA, 1958; one-man: Galerie Neuf, 1946; Artists Gal., 1949; Rutgers Univ., 1949; Salpeter Gal., 1950, 1952, 1955, 1957. Lectures: Modern Art.

WILSON, CHARLES BANKS—*Painter, Lith., I., W., E.*
100 North Main St.; h. 24 A St., Northwest, Miami, Okla.

B. Miami, Okla., Aug. 6, 1918. *Studied*: AIC. *Awards*: prizes, AIC, 1939; Laguna Beach AA, 1945; NAD, 1942, 1945; Mint Mus. A., 1944; BM, 1943; Wichita AA, 1945; Joslyn A. Mus., 1954; Hendrix Col., 1946; Chicago Soc. Et., 1939; LC, 1953, 1954; Philbrook A. Center, 1945, 1952, 1954, 1955; Springfield A. Mus., 1945. *Work*: Abbott Laboratories Coll.; Taggert Coll., Glasgow, Scotland; MMA; Gilcrease Inst.; Ford Motor Co.; Teton Nat. Park, Jackson Lake Lodge, and in many private colls. *Exhibited*: 1939-1958: Oakland A. Mus.; AIC; U.S. Dept. Interior; Denver A. Mus.; Laguna Beach AA; NAD; Mint Mus. A.; BM; Texas FA Assn.; LC; SAM; SFMA; AIGA; PAFA; DMFA; Joslyn A. Mus.; Philbrook A. Center; Oklahoma A. Center; Crocker Gal. A., Sacramento; Assoc. Am. A.; Univ. Kansas; Nelson Gal. A.; CGA; CAM; Hendrix Col.; NGA; Gilcrease Inst.; Okla. A. & M. Col.; Rochester Pr. Cl.; Minneapolis Inst. A.; Colorado Springs FA Center; Cal. PLH; Carnegie Inst.; Mus. FA of Houston; Delgado Mus. A., and many others throughout U.S. One-man: Philbrook A. Center; Oklahoma A. Center; Springfield Mus. A.; Univ. Tulsa; Smithsonian Inst.; Gilcrease Inst.; Tulsa Lib.; Tri-State Fair, Amarillo, Tex., and others. Illus., State sch. text "Oklahoma, Our Home," 1955; "Whispering Wind," 1955; Author: "Indians of Eastern Oklahoma"; color film: "Indians in Paint," 1955. Other illus.: "Henry's Lincoln," 1945; "Treasure Island," 1948; "The Mustangs," 1952; "The Texas Rangers," 1957; "On the Chisholm Trail," 1958; "The History of Geronimo," 1958, and others. Contributor articles to Coronet, Colliers magazines; United Newspapers Magazine Corp.; U.S. Dept. Interior; Daily Oklahoman; regularly, watercolors to Ford Times magazine. Paintings used on Will Rogers Calendars, 1959, 1960, nationally publ. by Gerlach-Barklow Co. *Position*: Hd., Div. A., Northeastern Oklahoma A. & M. Col., Miami, Okla., 1948- .

WILSON, CHARLES J. A.—*Etcher, P., I.*
74 Brookside Ave., Newtonville, Mass.

B. Glasgow, Scotland, June 23, 1880. *Member*: Boston Soc. Pr. M. *Work*: Marine Mus., Boston; New Haven R.R.; U.S. Coast Guard Acad., New London, Conn.; Mun. Mus. of Baltimore; U.S. Naval Acad., Annapolis, Md.; Mariner's Mus., Newport News, Va.; MIT. *Exhibited*: PAFA, 1929; Int. Pr. M., 1930; Currier Gal. A., 1932; Lyman Allyn Mus., 1934; SAE, 1931; Lib.Cong., 1943, 1944; Boston Soc. Pr. M., 1948-1950.

WILSON, DELLA FORD—*Educator, C., W.*
116 East Gorham St., Madison 3, Wis.

B. Hartsell, Ala., Mar. 31, 1888. *Studied*: James Milliken Univ., B.S.; Peoples Univ., St. Louis, with Frederick Rhead; Alfred Univ., with Charles F. Binns; T. Col., Columbia Univ., M.A. *Member*: Nat. Edu. Assn.; Wisconsin T. Assn.; Western AA; Nat. Lg. Am. Pen Women; Madison AA. *Exhibited*: Wis. Salon A., 1942; Madison AA, 1941. Author, I., "Primary Industrial Arts," 1927-1935.

Position: Prof. A. Edu., 1915-54, Prof. Emeritus, 1954- , Chm., A. Edu. Dept., 1943-46, Univ. Wisconsin, Madison, Wis.

WILSON, EDWARD A.—*Illustrator, Lith., P.*
South Pamet Rd., Truro, Mass.

B. Glasgow, Scotland, Mar. 4, 1886. *Studied*: AIC; & with Howard Pyle. *Member*: SC; ANA; F.; Royal Soc. A.; Century Assn.; AIGA; SI. *Awards*: med., A.Dir.Cl., N.Y., 1926, 1930; prizes, SC, 1926, 1942; Bookplate International, Los A., Cal., 1923; Limited Editions Cl. silver medal, 1954. *Work*: Lib.Cong.; N.Y.Pub.Lib.; MMA; Princeton Pr. Cl. I., "The Hunting of the Snark," 1932; "A Shropshire Lad," 1935; "The Tempest," 1940; "Jane Eyre," 1944; "Westward Ho!" 1946; "Ivanhoe"; "Dr. Jekyll and Mr. Hyde"; "The Book of Edward A. Wilson"; "The Seven Voyages of Sinbad the Sailor"; "By These Words," 1954; "Twenty Thousand Leagues Under The Sea," 1955. *Exhibited*: one-man: SI, 1954; R.I. Sch. Des., 1953; Pratt Inst., 1954.

WILSON, EDWARD N.—*Sculptor, E., Des., I.*
Department of Art, North Carolina College; h. 517 George St., Durham, N.C.

B. Baltimore, Md., Mar. 28, 1925. *Studied*: Univ. Iowa, B.A., M.A. *Member*: CAA; AFA. *Awards*: Carnegie Grant, 1952; prizes, Yellow Cab Co. for portraiture, 1956; BMA. *Exhibited*: Art: USA, 1958; Univ. Iowa, 1951, 1954; North Carolina A., 1955; Maryland A., 1956; Duke Univ., 1956. Illus. for College and University Business, Vol. 23, 1957. *Position*: Instr. A., 1951-53, Actg. Chm., 1953-54, Chm., Dept. Art, 1955- , North Carolina College, Durham, N.C.

WILSON, ELLIS—*Painter*
123 East 18th St., New York 3, N.Y.

B. Mayfield, Ky. *Studied*: Kentucky State Col.; AIC. *Awards*: Guggenheim F., 1944-1946; prizes, Atlanta Univ., 1946; Terry AI, 1952, 1953; Ky.So. Ind. Exh., 1954. *Exhibited*: one-man: J. B. Speed Mus. A.; Murray State Col., Ky.; Mayfield Pub. Lib.; South Side A. Center, Chicago; Barnett Aden Gal.; Contemp. A. Gal., N.Y.*

WILSON, ERNEST M.—*Painter, Gr., Comm. A., I., L.*
508 South Hill St., Oceanside, Cal.; h. 701 Valley Dr., Vista, Cal.

B. Göteborg, Sweden, June 24, 1885. *Studied*: in Germany; California AI; A. Center Sch., Los A.; Univ. California, B.A., and with Carl Oscar Borg. *Member*: Santa Monica AA; Westwood Village AA; Carlsbad-Oceanside A. Lg.; Vista A. Gld. *Awards*: prizes, Montana State Fair, 1918, 1919; Göteborg, Sweden, 1920; Santa Monica AA, 1946, 1948. *Exhibited*: Sweden, 1932; Montana State Fair, 1918-1920; Pomona County Fair, 1922, 1924; Santa Monica AA, 1946-1948; Westwood Village AA, 1949; Santa Monica Lib., 1948-1950; San Diego Fair, 1955; Carlsbad Acad. Exh., 1955; Los A. Mus. A., 1925, 1930. Contributor covers to California Classroom Teacher.

WILSON, HARRIET (Mrs. William E.)—*Painter*
21 Condit Terr., West Orange, N.J.

B. New York, N.Y., 1886. *Member*: AWS; New Jersey WC Soc.; All. A. Am.; A. Center of the Oranges. *Awards*: prizes, AWS; A. Center of the Oranges, 1948-1952, 1954, 1955; Newark A. Cl., 1949, 1952; All. A. Am., 1953; New Jersey WC Soc., 1954. *Exhibited*: AWS; Newark A. Cl.; A. Center of the Oranges; New Jersey WC Soc.*

WILSON, HELEN LOUISE—*Sculptor*
68½ Morton St., New York 14, N.Y.

B. Chicago, Ill. *Studied*: Wellesley Col., B.A., and with Bourdelle, Lantchansky, in Paris, France. *Member*: S. Gld.; Audubon A.; NAWA; Arch. Lg. *Awards*: Nat. Comm. FA, Wash., D.C., 1940; NAWA, 1949, 1957; Arch. Lg.; 1952; Audubon A., 1954. *Work*: private coll. in U.S. and abroad; sc. relief, USPO, Lowville, N.Y. *Exhibited*: WFNY 1939; WMAA, 1949; NAWA, annually; S. Gld., annually; Audubon A., annually; PAFA, 1952; Salon d'Automne, Salon des Independentes, Paris; Argent Gal., 1950 (one-man); Riverside Mus., 1957.

WILSON, HILDA LOVEMAN—*Writer*
2441 Webb Ave., New York 68, N.Y.

B. Chattanooga, Tenn., Nov. 19, 1915. *Studied*: Barnard Col., Columbia Univ., A.B. Contributor to: Newsweek—weekly department containing news of art events & personalities. *Position*: A.Ed., Newsweek, 1942-47; Freelance writer, 1947- .

WILSON, JOHN WOODROW—*Painter, Lith., T.*
1204B Tremont St., Roxbury, Mass.

B. Roxbury, Mass., Apr. 14, 1922. *Studied*: BMFA Sch.; Tufts Col., B.S. in Edu.; in Paris with Fernand Leger and in Mexico. *Awards*: prizes, BMFA Sch.; Atlanta Univ., 1954, 1955; Inst. Mod. A., Boston; Pepsi-Cola, 1946; Paige traveling scholarship, BMFA Sch., 1946; John Hay Whitney F., 1950-51; International Inst. of Exchange F., for study in Mexico, 1952. *Work*: Smith Col.; MModA; Atlanta Univ.; Carnegie Inst.; Howard Univ.; Pepsi-Cola Coll.; Dept. FA, French Govt. *Exhibited*: Nat. Negro A. Exh., Atlanta Univ., 1943-1952; Carnegie Inst., 1944-1946; LC, 1945, 1953; Smith Col., 1941; Wellesley Col., 1943; Inst. Mod. A., 1943-1945; Springfield Mus. A., 1945, 1946; Boris Mirski Gal., Boston, 1944-1956; AGAA, 1946; MMA, 1950; Am. Pr. M., Paris, France; SAGA, 1953, 1955; CM, 1953; MModA, 1954; Art Wood Gal., Boston, 1954 (one-man); Exch. Exh. Am. Prints, Italy, 1955.*

WILSON, L. ALICE. See Vitacco, Alice

WILSON, NORMAN BADGLEY—*Painter, Eng.*
6612 College Ave., Indianapolis 5, Ind.

B. Arcadia, Ind., Dec. 1, 1906. *Member*: Indiana AA; Indiana Soc. Pr. M. *Awards*: prizes, South Bend AA, 1951; Ft. Wayne, AI, 1951; John Herron, AI, 1952. *Exhibited*: PAFA, 1937; John Herron AI, 1937, 1939, 1944, 1946, 1948-1952; Butler AI, 1945, 1946, 1948, 1949; Tri-State Print Exh., 1944, 1945, 1948; Milwaukee AI, 1946; South Bend AA, 1950-1952; Ft. Wayne AI, 1951; Carnegie Inst.; J. B. Speed Mem. Mus.; Phila. Pr. Cl.*

WILSON, ROWLAND—*Cartoonist*
133-08 Centerville St., North Ozone Park, N.Y.

B. Dallas, Tex., Aug. 3, 1930. *Studied*: Univ. Texas, B.F.A.; Columbia Univ. Contributor cartoons to Sat. Eve. Post; Colliers; True; Esquire; American; Ladies Home Journal; American Legion magazines.*

WILSON, SCOTT—*Industrial Designer*
54 East 58th St. (22); h. 301 East 66th St., New York 21, N.Y.

B. Vigan, P.I., Mar. 19, 1903. *Studied*: Harvard Univ., A.B. *Member*: F., IDI; Nat. Soc. for Dec. Des. Author, I., "Tommy Tomato and the Vegets," 1936; "Tommy Tomato Saves the Garden," 1937. Contributor to trade and scientific publications. *Position*: Nat. Dir., Inter-Society Color Council, 1954-56; Vice-Pres., Nat. Soc. for Decoration Design, 1955-56; Owner, Scott Wilson Designs, New York, N.Y.

WILSON, SOL—*Painter*
567 Ave. of the Americas; h. 530 West 113th St., New York 25, N.Y.

B. Vilno, Poland, Aug. 11, 1896. *Studied*: CUASch.; NAD; BAID; & with George Bellows, Robert Henri. *Member*: AEA; Cape Cod AA; Provincetown AA; Audubon A. *Awards*: prizes, Am. Red Cross, 1942; AV, 1943; Pepsi-Cola, 1944; Audubon A, 1947, 1949; CGA, 1947; Carnegie Inst., 1947; Am. Acad. A. & Let., 1950; Cape Cod AA, 1953, 1954, 1956; Nat. Soc. Painters in Casein, 1955; NAD, 1958. *Work*: Telfair Acad.; Lincoln H.S., N.Y.; Brooklyn Col.; BM; Am. Red Cross; LC; WMAA; Butler AI; BMA; Delgado Mus. A.; MMA; Newark Mus.; Univ. Minnesota; SAM; CAM; USPO, Delmar, N.Y.; Westhampton, N.Y.; Living Arts Fnd., N.Y.; Nebraska AA. *Exhibited*: NAD, 1938, 1940, 1945, 1946; PAFA, 1934, 1935, 1940, 1945; Carnegie Inst., 1943-1946; WMAA, 1945; CGA, 1935, 1945; AIC, 1935, 1943, 1945; VMFA, 1942, 1944, 1946; Critics Choice, N.Y., 1945; Nebraska AA, 1945, 1946; Lib. Cong., 1944; Univ. Iowa, 1945, 1946; CAM, 1939; Pepsi-Cola, 1944, 1945; etc.

WILT, RICHARD—*Painter, E.*

1301 Pomona Road, Ann Arbor, Mich.

B. Tyrone, Pa., June 16, 1915. *Studied*: Pa. State Univ.; Carnegie Inst.; New School for Social Research, N.Y.; Univ. Pittsburgh, M.A. *Awards*: prizes, Assoc. A. Pittsburgh, 1947-1949, 1951, 1953, 1954; Michigan A., 1949, 1951-1954, 1956; Old Northwest Terr. Exh., 1950, 1951; Butler Inst. Am. A., 1953; Michiana Exh., 1955; Mich. State Fair, 1955, 1957; Mich. Acad., 1956, 1957. *Work*: Detroit Inst. A.; Butler Inst. Am. A.; Illinois State Mus.; Indiana State T. Col.; South Bend Mus. A. *Exhibited*: One-man: A. & Crafts Center, Pittsburgh, 1950; Grand Rapids A. Mus., 1950; Inst. Contemp. A., 1951, circulated by AFA, 1952; Butler Inst. Am. A., 1951; Detroit Inst. A., 1952; Sioux City A. Center, 1952; Rackham Gal., Ann Arbor, 1955. *Position*: Assoc. Prof. A., Dept. A., College of Arch. & Des., Univ. Michigan, Ann Arbor, Mich.

WILTON, ANNA KEENER. See *Keener, Anna Wilton*

WILTZ, MRS. MADELINE E. See *Shiff, Madeline E.*

WINCHELL, ELIZABETH BURT (Mrs. John P.)— *Painter, C., Des., T.*

5 East Main St., Yarmouth, Me.

B. Brooklyn, N.Y., June 20, 1890. *Studied*: Moore Inst. Des., Phila.; PAFA; PMSchIA; & with Henry Snell, Samuel Murray, & others. *Member*: Freeport AC; Maine Craft Gld.; Portland WC Soc. *Work*: Moore Inst. Des.; Brunswick (Me.) Savings Banks; Camden (Me.) Mun. Coll. *Exhibited*: PAFA; BM; Portland SA; Freeport AC annually; Walker A. Center; Lincolnville, Me.; Providence, R.I.; Maine WC Soc.; St. Augustine, Fla.; Hooked rugs exhibited Ogunquit A. Center; Mass. House Workshop; Farnsworth Mus.; Portland A. Mus., etc.

WINEBRENNER, HARRY FIELDING—*Painter, S.*

11100 Lurline St., Chatsworth, Cal.

B. Summersville, W. Va., Jan. 4, 1885. *Studied*: Univ. Chicago; AIC; British Acad., Rome Italy; Grande Chaumiere, Academie Julian, France. *Member*: Soc. for Sanity in Art. *Exhibited*: Oakland A. Gal., 1948; Paris, France, 1950 (one-man). *Work*: Hist. Soc., Oklahoma City, Okla.; Carmel Sch., Avranches, France; Mun. A. Gal., Oklahoma City, Okla.; Oklahoma A. Mus.; murals, Northern Oklahoma Jr. College. Author, I., "Practical Art Education."

WINER, DONALD ARTHUR—*Painter, Mus. Cur., C., E.*

Brooks Memorial Art Gallery, Overton Park; h. 1683 Peach Ave., Memphis 12, Tenn.

B. St. Louis, Mo., Oct. 26, 1927. *Studied*: Univ. Missouri, B.S., M.A. *Member*: AAMus.; CAA. *Exhibited*: CAM, 1951; Springfield Annual, 1951, 1955-1957; Springfield (Ill.) 1953; Mulvane Mus. A., 1953; Nelson Gal. A., 1956; Mid-South Annual, 1958; one-man: Springfield A. Mus., 1955. Arranged exh., "American Pottery, 1690-1910," Brooks Gallery, 1957. *Positions*: Edu. Cur., Springfield A. Mus., Springfield, Mo., 1954-57; Dir. Edu., Brooks Memorial Art Gallery, Memphis, Tenn., 1957- .

WINGATE, ARLINE (Mrs. Clifford Hollander)— *Sculptor, C.*

23 East 74th St., New York 21, N.Y.

B. New York, N.Y., Oct. 18, 1906. *Studied*: Smith Col.; in Europe, and with Alexander Archipenko. *Member*: Fed. Mod. P. & S.; NAWA; S. Gld.; Arch Lg. *Awards*: prizes, NAWA, 1945; Amelia Peabody award, 1956; Easthampton Gld. Hall, 1958. *Work*: Nat. Mus., Stockholm, Sweden; Newark Mus.; Ghent Mus., Belgium. *Exhibited*: NAC; NAWA; PAFA; BM; Wadsworth Atheneum; Smith Col.; WMAA; AIC; Riverside Mus.; Midtown Gal.; SFMA; BMA; Fairmount Park, Phila.; MMA; one-man (2), Midtown Gal., N.Y.; Petit Palais, Paris, France, and in Belgium.

WINGERT, PAUL STOVER—*Educator, W., L.*

Department of Fine Arts and Archaeology, Columbia University; h. 88 Morningside Dr., New York 27, N.Y.

B. Waynesboro, Pa., Nov. 13, 1900. *Studied*: Columbia Col., A.B.; Columbia Univ., M.A., Ph.D.; Univ. London; Sorbonne, Paris, France. *Member*: CAA; Am. Ethnologi-cal Soc.; Polynesian Soc.; Am. Anthropological Assn.; F., Am. Assn. for Advancement of Science; F., Royal Anthropological Inst.; F., Italiana di Antropologiae Etnologia. *Awards*: Wenner-Gren grant to South Seas, 1952; Guggenheim F., 1955. Author: "The Sculpture of William Zorach," 1938; "An Outline Guide to the Art of the South Pacific," 1946; "American Indian Sculpture," 1949; "The Sculpture of Negro Africa," 1950; "Art of the South Pacific Islands," 1953. Co-author: "Arts of the South Seas," 1946; "History of World Art," 1949, 2nd ed. rev., 1958; "The Tsimshian: Their Arts and Music," 1951. Contributor articles and reviews to Art Bulletin; Am. Anthropologist; Transactions in New York Academy of Sciences; College Art Journal; Art Digest; Book of Knowledge; Records of the Auckland (N.Z.) Inst. & Museum; Sat. Review, and others. Exhs. on Primitive Art, organized or supervised: "Arts of the South Seas," MModA (with Ralph Linton, Rene d'Harnoncourt), 1946; "African Negro Sculpture," deYoung Mem. Mus., 1948; "Prehistoric Stone Sculpture of the Pacific Northwest," Portland (Ore.) A. Mus., 1951; "Melanesian Art," War Mem. Mus., Auckland, N.Z., 1952; "African Sculpture," BMA, 1954; "Oceanic Art," BMA, 1955-56 (with Douglas F. Fraser), and other exhs. *Position*: Cur. FA & Archaeology, 1934-42, Instr., 1942-49, Asst. Prof. FA & Archaeology, 1949-54, Assoc. Prof. FA & Archaeology, 1954-58; Prof., 1958- , Columbia Univ., New York, N.Y.

WINKEL, NINA—*Sculptor*

185-36 Galway Ave., St. Albans, L.I., N.Y.

B. Borken, Germany, May 21, 1905. *Studied*: in Germany. *Member*: S. Center; S. Gld.; NSS. *Awards*: medal, NAD, 1945; Avery award, 1958. *Work*: mem., Seward Park H.S., N.Y.; monument, Charlotte, N.C. *Exhibited*: NAD, 1953, 1957; PAFA, 1958 and prior; Nebraska AA, 1946; S. Center, 1944 (one-man); 1948-1952, 1958 (one-man); Newark Mus., 1944; Fairmount Park, Phila., Pa.; WMAA, 1954; Univ. Notre Dame, 1958 (one-man) and prior; Detroit Inst. A., 1958.

WINSEY, A. REID—*Painter, I., Cart., W., E., L.*

609 Ridge Ave., Greencastle, Ind.

B. Appleton, Wis., June 6, 1905. *Studied*: Univ. Wisconsin, B.S., M.S.; Yale Univ.; Am. Acad. A., Chicago; & with Elmer Taflinger, Thomas Hart Benton. *Member*: Hoosier Salon; Indiana AC; Indiana Fed. AC; Chicago SE. *Work*: Layton A. Gal.; Wis. General Hospital, Madison, Wis.; Central Nat. Bank, Greencastle, Ind.; A. Edu. Bldg., Madison, Wis.; Atwater Training Sch., New Haven, Conn. *Exhibited*: Wis. Salon. Author, I., "Freehand Drawing Manual"; "Drawing Simplified." Contributor to: School & Art magazines. *Position*: Hd. Dept. F. & App. A., De Pauw Univ., Greencastle, Ind., 1935- . Conducts art tours to Europe each summer, for college credit.

WINSHIP, FLORENCE SARAH—*Illustrator, W., Des.*

590 Whittier Ave., Deerfield, Ill.

B. Elkhart, Ind. *Studied*: Chicago Acad. FA; AIC. *Member*: Children's Reading Round Table, Chicago. I., 1940-1956: "ABC Picture Book"; "Sounding Rhymes"; "Counting Rhymes"; "Woofus"; "Miss Sniff"; "Sir Gruff"; "What Happened to Fluffy"; "Roosty"; "See It"; "Snowball"; "Lady, the Little Blue Mare"; "Poppyseed," and other books for children. I., 1958: "Mimi"; "The Night Before Christmas"; "Clip Clop."

WINSLOW, EARLE B.—*Illustrator, Lith., T., P., I.*

Woodstock, N.Y.

B. Northville, Mich., Feb. 21, 1884. *Studied*: Sch. FA, Detroit, Mich.; AIC; ASL. *Member*: SI; A. Gld.; Woodstock AA. *Exhibited*: Int. WC Soc., 1928-1940; CAA; SI, 1931-1945; PAFA, 1919, 1920; Macbeth Gal. (one-man); Audubon A.; Nat. Soc. Painters in Casein; A. of the Upper Hudson. I., "Robbin's Journal," 1931; "Gospel of St. Mark," 1932; "Fire Fighters," 1939; & other books. Lectures: Illustration. *Position*: Pres., A. Gld., 1940-44; Chm. Exh. Com., SI, New York, N.Y., 1940-44; Instr., PIASch., 1946-48; Cart. & Illus. Sch., New York, N.Y., 1949-51.

WINSLOW, MRS. RANDOLPH. See *Comes, Marcella*

WINSTON, MRS. FISHER. See *Atkins, Mildred Tommy*

WINTER, ALICE BEACH—*Painter, S., I., T.*
134 Mt. Pleasant Ave., East Gloucester, Mass.

B. Greenridge, Mo., Mar. 22, 1877. *Studied*: St. Louis Sch. FA; ASL, and with George de Forest Brush, Joseph De Camp. *Member*: North Shore AA; Business & Prof. Women's Cl., Gloucester. *Awards*: medal, St. Louis Sch. FA; prize, Gloucester Chamber of Commerce, 1954. *Work*: many portraits of children. *Exhibited*: NAD; PAFA; Carnegie Inst.; CAM; Los A. Mus. A.; NAWA; North Shore AA; Contemp. New England A.; Gloucester Festival A. Illustrations for stories and covers of child-life for national magazines.

WINTER, CLARK—*Sculptor*
College of Fine Arts, Carnegie Institute of Technology; h. 119 Carnegie Pl., Pittsburgh 8, Pa.

B. Cambridge, Mass., Apr. 4, 1907. *Studied*: Harvard Univ., A.B.; Indiana Univ., M.F.A.; Fontainebleau Acad. A.; Cranbrook Acad. A.; ASL. *Member*: AEA. *Awards*: prizes, Oakland A. Mus.; Mid-America A.; Wichita AA; Fla. Southern Col. *Exhibited*: MMA; PAFA; Audubon A.; John Herron AI; Sculpture Center, N.Y.; PMA; WMAA; Carnegie Inst.; Kansas City AI (one-man); SFMA. *Position*: Instr., Indiana Univ., 1947-49; Hd. Sc. Dept., Kansas City AI, 1949-53; Visiting Assoc. Prof., Univ. California, Berkeley, 1953-55; Assoc. Prof., Col. FA, Carnegie Inst., Pittsburgh, Pa., 1955- .

WINTER, LUMEN MARTIN—*Painter, Des., I., Gr., S.*
96 Fifth Ave., New York 11, N.Y.; h. 30 Evergreen Ave., New Rochelle, N.Y.

B. Ellery, Ill., Dec. 12, 1908. *Studied*: Cleveland Sch. A.; NAD; Grand Central Sch. A.; BAID. *Member*: Arch. Lg. (Vice-Pres.); NSMP; SI; N.Y. Fed. FA; AEA. *Awards*: prize, CM, 1944; New Rochelle, N.Y.; Ohio Univ. (purchase), and awards in numerous competitions. *Work*: murals, Michigan Union H.S., Grand Rapids; Fed. Bldg., Hutchison, Kans.; Friars Cl., Cincinnati; East Brooklyn Savings Bank; Holton Mus., Miami, Fla.; Founders Room, Sheraton Cadillac, Detroit; Park Sheraton Hotel, Wash., D.C.; mosaic with marble bas-relief and monument, Church of St. Paul the Apostle, N.Y.; mosaic, AFL Hdqtr. Bldg., Wash., D.C.; bronze figure, White Plains, N.Y.; mosaic and fresco, Southland Center, Dallas, Tex. *Exhibited*: CM; Grand Rapids A. Gal.; Butler AI; SAM; BM; PAFA; AIC; Detroit Inst. A.; Wilmington Mus. FA; Cincinnati A. Cl.; SAGA; Alabama WC Soc.; Salons of America; Univ. Ohio; AWS; Arch. Lg.; SC; one-man: Hackley A. Gal.; Grand Rapids Pub. Lib.; Brown Gal., Cincinnati; Bonestell Gal.; Center Gal., N.Y.; A.F.I. Gal., N.Y.; Argent Gal.; Salpeter Gal. Co-author, I., "Epics of Flight"; "Story of Leonardo da Vinci's 'Last Supper' "; I., "Family Book of Dogs," 1954, and many others.

WINTER, RUTH—*Painter*
98-50 67th Ave., Rego Park 74, N.Y.

B. New York, N.Y., Jan. 17, 1913. *Studied*: N.Y. Univ., B.S., M.A.; ASL. *Member*: Mahopac A. Lg.; NAWA. *Award*: prize, NAWA, 1957. *Exhibited*: Art: USA, 1958; Provincetown A. Festival, 1958; City Center, N.Y., 1956-1958; Argent Gal., 1957; Silvermine Gld. A., 1957, 1958; Orange, N.J., 1957; Gallery 15, 1958.

WINTERS, DENNY (Miss)—*Painter, T., I., Gr., C.*
Rockport, Me.

B. Grand Rapids, Mich., Mar. 17, 1909. *Studied*: AIC; Chicago Acad. FA. *Member*: Los A. WC Soc. *Awards*: prizes, Denver A. Mus., 1941; Guggenheim F., 1948; SFMA, 1941. *Work*: PMA; SFMA. I., "Full Fathom Five." *Exhibited*: MModA; AIC, 1936, 1937, 1945; PAFA, 1940, 1941; SFMA, 1939-1943; Carnegie Inst. 1945, 1946; Colorado Springs FA Center, 1943; Los A. Mus. A., 1939-1945 (one-man 1944); SFMA, 1943 (one-man); Perls Gal., 1942; Levitt Gal., 1945 (one-man); Rehn Gal., 1953, 1954, 1957 (all one-man); Univ. Maine, 1951 (one-man); Riverside Mus., 1954.

WINTERS, JOHN (RICHARD)—*Painter, S.*
422 Harwicke Rd., Springfield, Pa.

B. Omaha, Neb., May 12, 1904. *Studied*: Chicago Acad. FA; AIC; & with Frederick Poole, J. Allen St. John. *Work*: murals, Steinmetz H.S., Chicago; Northwest Airlines, Seattle; Cook County Hospital, Ill.; Hatch Sch., Oak

Park, Ill.; Brookfield (Ill.) Zoo; mural, USPO, Petersburg, Ill. *Exhibited*: CGA, 1934; Denver A. Mus.; Wichita AA; Kansas State Col.; Tulsa AA; Topeka A. Gld.; Salina (Kan.) AA; AIC, 1935, 1936, 1938, 1940; Springfield (Mass.) Mus.. A., 1938; Little Gal., Chicago; Carson Pirie Scott Co., Chicago; Chicago Woman's Cl., 1938; Springfield, Pa., 1955; Wallingford, Pa., 1956. Des., Christmas Cathedral, Grand Court, John Wanamaker's, Phila., Pa., 1955. *Position*: Instr., Layton Sch. A., Milwaukee, Wis., 1946-47; Kansas State Col., 1947-48; Chief Des., Display Dept., John Wanamaker's, Phila., Pa., 1949- .*

WIRES, HAZEL KITTS—*Painter*
Peru, Vt.

B. Oswego, N.Y., Feb. 16, 1903. *Studied*: Corcoran Sch. A. *Member*: AWS; Academic A., Springfield, Mass.; Londonderry A. Gld., Vt.; Miller A. Center, Springfield, Vt.; Rockport AA; Southern Vermont A. Center.

WISE, VERA—*Painter, Lith., E.*
1105 North Virginia St., El Paso, Tex.

B. Iola, Kans. *Studied*: Willamette Univ., Salem, Ore., B.A.; Chicago Acad. FA; Kansas City AI. *Member*: Cal. WC Soc.; Texas FA Assn.; Texas WC Soc. *Awards*: prizes, Ft. Worth, Tex., 1942; Abilene Mus. A., 1946, 1950, 1951; Texas WC Soc., 1951, 1957; Beaumont Mus., 1954; Chautauqua Nat., 1958; Texas FA Assn., 1953, 1955. *Work*: Idaho State Col.; Texas FA Assn.; So. Methodist Univ. *Exhibited*: AWS, 1939, 1947, 1954; NAWA, 1942, 1943, 1945; CM, 1935; Jackson (Miss.) Mus. FA, 1943, 1951; SSAL, 1943, 1945; Wash. WC Cl., 1943; Texas FA Assn., 1943, 1946, 1949-1957; West Texas Exh., 1942-1946; Texas Pr. Exh., 1945; Denver A. Mus., 1934-1937, 1943, 1944, 1949; Texas P. & S., 1949-1952; Texas WC Soc., 1950-1958; Phila. WC Cl., 1949; William Rockhill Nelson Gal. A., 1951; Cal. WC Soc., 1958; Art: USA, 1958; Beaumont Mus. A., 1958; Northwest Pr. M., 1954; Romano Gal., Biblioteca Nacional, Mexico, 1951; one-man traveling exh. Texas museums and colleges, 1955-56; Roswell Mus., 1957; El Paso Pub. Lib., 1958; Laguna Gloria Mus., Austin, 1958. *Position*: Prof., Hd. A. Dept., Texas Western Col., El Paso, Tex.

WITHERS, LORIS ALVIN—*Painter, Des., T.*
3 Overlook Dr., Port Washington, L.I., N.Y.

B. Philadelphia, Pa., Feb. 22, 1891. *Studied*: Carnegie Inst., A.B.; ASL; NAD; Grande Chaumiere, Paris, France. *Member*: SC. *Work*: Haskell Mem., Palm Beach, Fla.; Cornell Univ.; Church of the Holy Family, Columbus, Ga.; many ports.; windows, Bethesda-by-the-Sea Church, Palm Beach, Fla.; Cathedral St. John the Divine, N.Y. *Exhibited*: Arch.L.; Salon des Tuileries, Paris; SC. *Position*: Instr. A., Hunter Col., 1926-33; Brooklyn (N.Y.) Col., 1933-43. Des., Stained Glass Windows, Heinigke & Smith, New York, N.Y.; Frederick L. Leuchs, Inc., 1956-58.

WITMEYER, STANLEY H.—*Educator, Des., P., W., L.*
School of Art & Design, Rochester Institute of Technology; h. 51 Kron St., Rochester 19, N.Y.

B. Palmyra, Pa., Feb. 14, 1913. *Studied*: Rochester Inst. Tech.; N.Y. State Univ. T. Col., B.S. in Ed.; Syracuse Univ., M.F.A. *Member*: N.Y. State A. T. Assn.; Eastern AA; NAEA; Rochester A. Cl.; Rochester A. Council. *Award*: Grad. Scholarship, Syracuse Univ., 1944. *Exhibited*: Rochester Mem. A. Gal.; Olean, N.Y.; Albright A. Gal.; Harrisburg, Pa.; Honolulu Acad. A.; Bevier & Rundel Gal. Contributor to School Arts, Design, Everyday Art, Torch magazines. *Position*: Prof., Hd. Sch. of A. & Design, Rochester Inst. Tech., Rochester, N.Y.

WITTERS, NELL—*Painter, C.*
609 West 137th St., New York 31, N.Y.

B. Grand Rapids, Mich. *Studied*: AIC; PAFA; ASL; T. Col., Columbia Univ., and with Eliot O'Hara, George Elmer Browne. *Member*: Pen & Brush Cl.; Wolfe A. Cl.; ASL; York State Craftsmen; Village A. Center; 8th St. A. Assn.; Little Studio A. Gal.; Brooklyn Soc. A.; AAPL. *Awards*: prizes, Wolfe A. Cl.; AIC; Pen & Brush Cl.; Brooklyn Soc. A.

WITTKOWER, RUDOLF—*Educator, Hist., W., L.*
Columbia University; h. 400 West 118th St., New York 27, N.Y.

B. Berlin, Germany, June 22, 1901. *Studied:* Univ. Munich; Univ. Berlin, Ph.D. *Member:* Soc. Arch. Historians; Renaissance Soc. of Am.; Archaeological Inst. of Great Britain and Ireland. *Awards:* F., British Acad., 1958; Hon. F., Warburg Inst., London, 1958; Serena Medal, British Acad., 1957. Author: "British Art and the Mediterranean," 1948; "Architectural Principles in the Age of Humanism," 1949; "The Drawings of Carracci," 1952; "The Artist and the Liberal Arts," 1952; "Gian Lorenzo Bernini," 1955; "Art and Architecture in Italy, 1600-1750," 1958. Contributor to Art Bulletin; Burlington Magazine; Warburg Inst. Journal; Courtauld Inst. Journal; Archaeological Journal, etc. *Positions:* Bibliotheca Hertziana, Rome, 1934-56; Warburg Inst., Univ. London, 1949-56; Prof. Hist. A., Univ. London; Prof., Columbia Univ., New York, N.Y., 1956- .

WITTMANN, OTTO, JR.—*Museum Director*
Toledo Museum of Art (1); h. 3428 Brantford Road, Toledo 6, Ohio

B. Kansas City, Mo., Sept. 1, 1911. *Studied:* Harvard Col., A.B.; Harvard Univ. *Member:* Assn. A. Mus. Dirs.; AAMus.; CAA; Intermuseum Conservation Assn. *Award:* Knight, Order of Orange-Nassau, 1956. Contributor to Art News; Art Quarterly; College Art Journal; American Quarterly and numerous museum publications. *Positions:* Prof. A. Hist., Skidmore Col., 1938-40; Sec.-Treas., Assn. A. Mus. Dirs., 1958- ; Pres., Intermuseum Conservation Assn., 1956-57; Dir., Toledo Museum of Art, Toledo, Ohio, 1957- .

WOLCHONOK, LOUIS—*Painter, Et., Des., T., C., W.*
60 West 76th St., New York 23, N.Y.

B. New York, N.Y., Jan. 12, 1898. *Studied:* CUASch.; NAD; Col. City of N.Y., B.S.; Julian Acad., Paris, France. *Member:* N.Y. Soc. Craftsmen (1st V.Pres., 1951-53). *Work:* CMA; Univ. Nebraska; Bibliotheque Nationale, Paris. *Exhibited:* WMAA, 1934; AIC, 1930-1932; NAD; PAFA; Los A. Mus. A.; Tate Gal., London; one-man exh.: Milch Gal.; ACA Gal.; Newhouse Gal.; Ainslie Gal. Lectures: Appreciation & History of Art. Author, I., "Design for Artists and Craftsmen," 1954. *Position:* Asst. Prof., Drafting, Col. City of N.Y., 1930- ; Instr., Design, Etching, Painting, Craft Students League of the YWCA, New York, N.Y., 1932- .*

WOLCOTT ROGER AUGUSTUS—
Painter, E., Des., C., S.
"Sky Acres," Agawam, Mass.; h. 1400 South Barton St., Apt. 430, Arlington, Va.

B. Amherst, Mass., Aug. 25, 1909. *Studied:* Mass. Col. A.; Cornell Univ.; N.Y. Sch. F. & App. A.; & with Richard Andrew, Joseph Cowell, Ernest Major. *Member:* Rockport AA; Springfield A. Gld.; Am. Assn. Agricultural Col. Editors. *Work:* Springfield Mus. Natural Hist. *Position:* Instr. A., Springfield Mus. FA, Springfield, Mass., 1933-40; Indst. Des. Research, Anglar Research, Inc., Framingham, Mass., 1940-43; Des. Research, Nikor Products, Springfield, Mass., 1943-46; Indst. Des. Consultant, 1946-51; Asst. Prof. Visual Arts, Univ. Massachusetts, Amherst, Mass.; Audio-Visual Advisor, Intl. Cooperation Admin., Panama City, C.Z., 1956-1958.

WOLF, BEN—*Painter, Cr., W., I., T. L.*
4618 Pine St., Philadelphia 43, Pa.

B. Philadelphia, Pa., Oct. 17, 1914. *Studied:* with Carl H. Nordstrom, Justin Pardi, Hans Hofmann. *Member:* AEA; Phila. A. All.; Phila. Pr. Cl. *Exhibited:* PMA, 1955; one-man: Santa Barbara Mus. A., 1947; Minnesota State Fair, 1947; Mus. New Mexico, Santa Fe, 1949; Babcock Gal., 1950; Delgado Mus. A., 1950; Bijou Theatre, N.Y., Cyrano Exh., 1950; Carriage House, Phila., 1955; Phila. A. All., 1959. I., "Memoirs of C. N. Buck," 1941; "The King of the Golden River," 1945. Contributor to "Art in the Armed Forces," 1944; "G.I. Sketch Book," 1944; Life magazine, Art Digest, Child Life magazines. Author: monograph on Raymond Jonson, in "Artists of New Mexico," Univ. New Mexico Press. *Positions:* Assoc. Ed., Art Digest, 1944-47; Assoc. Ed., Picture on Exhibit, 1947; A. Cr., Santa Fe New Mexican, 1948-49; Instr., PMSchA, at present.

WOLF, HAMILTON (ACHILLE)—*Painter, E., L.*
1735 Hyde St., San Francisco, Cal.

B. New York, N.Y. *Studied:* NAD; Columbia Univ.; ASL; BAID; in Paris; & with Robert Henri, William Chase. *Member:* San F. AA. *Awards:* prizes, Seattle A. Soc., 1917; Oakland A. Gal., 1929, 1950; Cal. State Exh., 1930, 1934, 1940; SFMA; Bakersfield, Cal.; Pomona, Cal., 1938; San F. AA, 1939, 1944. *Work:* mural, Shell Laboratories, Emeryville, Cal. *Exhibited:* WFNY 1939; GGE 1939; Crocker A. Gal.; Pomona, Cal.; Western Mus. Assn.; Cal. PLH; Carnegie Inst.; de Young Mem. Mus.; San F. AA; Roerich Mus.; Riverside Mus.; Mills Col.; Oakland A. Mus.; SAM; Crocker A. Gal.; Stanford Univ.; Rotunda Gal., San F.; Fnd. Western A., Los A., Cal.; one-man: Macbeth Gal.; Delphic Studios; Rutgers Univ.; Cal. PLH; Oakland A. Mus. (retrospective); Seattle A. Soc.; Gumps Gal.; Mexico City; Instituto de Allende, Mexico. Lectures, History & Appreciation of Art. *Positions:* Prof. A., Univ. California Extension Div., 1929-38; California Col. A. & Crafts, Oakland, Cal., 1929-1952.

WOLFE, ANN (Mrs. Ann Wolfe Graubard)—
Sculptor, W., L.
4035 Lyndale Ave., South, Minneapolis 9, Minn.

B. Poland, Nov. 14, 1905. *Studied:* Hunter Col., B.A.; in Paris, with Despiau. *Member:* Soc. Minnesota S. *Awards:* prizes, Soc. Wash. A., 1945; Minn. State Fair, 1949; Minneapolis Inst. A., 1951; Minneapolis Woman's Cl., 1954. *Work:* Col. City of N.Y.; Mus. A., Jerusalem; Hamline Univ.; Colgate Univ. *Exhibited:* All. A. Am., 1936; AGAA, 1942; A. Gld. Wash., 1942-1945; Soc. Wash. A., 1944, 1945; WMA, 1940, 1946; Walker A. Center, 1948, 1953, 1956-1958; PAFA, 1951; Minneapolis Inst. A.; Sc. Center, N.Y., 1953; Minn. State Fair, 1956-1958; Rochester A. Center; Kraushaar Gal.; St. Paul Gal. A., 1956-1958; 3rd Sc. Intl., 1949; one-man: WMA, 1939; Grace Horne Gal., 1940; Whyte Gal., Wash., D.C., 1946; Hamline Univ., 1951; Minn. State Fair, 1951; Walker A. Center, 1955; World Gal., St. Paul, 1954.

WOLFE, JACK D.—*Craftsman, Des., T., L.*
62 Horatio St., New York 14, N.Y.; h. 40-04 Utopia Parkway, Flushing, L.I., N.Y.

B. New York, N.Y., Mar. 4, 1915. *Studied:* with Ruth Canfield, Maija Grotel, Alexander Couard, Peter Muller Munk. *Member:* N.Y. Soc. Ceramic A.; Long Island A. Lg. *Awards:* prize, N.Y. Soc. Ceramic A., 1948. *Exhibited:* Long Island A. Lg.; N.Y. Soc. Ceramic A. Lectures: Ceramics. *Work:* MModA, and in private colls. *Position:* Instr., Ceramics, N.Y. Univ.; Universal Sch. of Handicrafts; Henry St. Settlement; Freelance consultant and des. for factories and individuals.

WOLFE, KARL (FERDINAND)—*Painter, E.*
4308 Old Canton Rd., Jackson 6, Miss.

B. Brookhaven, Miss., Jan. 25, 1904. *Studied:* AIC, and with William M. R. French. *Member:* Mississippi AA. *Awards:* gold medal, Mississippi AA, 1932; Brooks Mem. A. Gal., 1935; prizes, SSAL, 1933, 1934, 1937; Miss. AA, 1951. *Work:* Montgomery Mus. FA; Governor's Mansion, Jackson, Miss.; USPO, Louisville, Ky.; Municipal A. Gal., Jackson; Mississippi State Col. for Women; Lib. Bldg., Mississippi A. & M. Col., Starkville, Miss., and others. *Exhibited:* CGA, 1932; PAFA, 1933; AIC, 1935; Carnegie Inst., 1941; Mississippi AA, 1932-1955; Delgado Mus. A., 1934-1942; Along the Mississippi, 1942; SSAL, 1932-1942. *Position:* Instr. A., Milsaps Col., Jackson, Miss., 1947- ; Allison's Wells A. Colony, Way, Miss.*

WOLFE, MEYER—*Painter, Lith.*
58 West 57th St., New York 19, N.Y.; h. Frenchtown, N.J.

B. Louisville, Ky., Sept. 10, 1897. *Studied:* Chicago Acad. FA; ASL, and in Paris, France. *Member:* AEA. *Work:* Univ. Minnesota. *Exhibited:* NAD, 1941, 1945; PAFA, 1935, 1941; AIC, 1938; Carnegie Inst., 1948, 1949; LC, 1944, 1948-1950; WFNY 1939.*

WOLFE, MILDRED (Mrs. Karl)—*Painter, S.*
4308 Old Canton Road, Jackson, Miss.

B. Celina, Ohio, Aug. 23, 1912. *Studied:* Athens Col.; Alabama State Col. for Women, A.B.; Colorado Springs FA Center, M.A.; AIC; ASL, and with Boardman Robinson. *Member*: Mississippi AA; Atlanta A. Lg. *Awards*: prizes, Alabama A. Lg., 1935, 1940; McDowell Gal., 1938; Jackson, Miss., 1947, 1949, 1950, 1951, 1953, 1955. *Work*: Montgomery Mus. FA; Mun. A. Gal., Jackson; Mississippi State Col.; Alabama Polytechnic Inst.; LC; murals, St. Andrew's Episcopal Day School, Jackson, Miss.; Jacksonian Highway Hotel; Stevens Dept. Store, Richton, Miss. *Exhibited*: WFNY 1939; CGA, 1939, 1949; Mississippi AA, 1945-1956; Alabama A. Lg., 1935-1940, 1952; Birmingham Mus. A., 1956. *Position*: Instr. Hist. of Art, Milsaps College, Jackson, Miss., 1957- .

WOLFE-PARKER, VIOLA—*Painter, S., Ser., C.*

1926 Penn Ave., Minneapolis 11, Minn.

B. Minneapolis, Minn., Oct. 21, 1904. *Studied*: Univ. Minnesota; Minneapolis Sch. A., and with B. J. O. Nordfeldt, Paul Burlin, Charles Burchfield. *Member*: Cal. WC Soc.; Minnesota AA; AEA; Provincetown AA. *Awards*: prizes, Minneapolis Inst. A., 1947, 1949; Minnesota State Fair, 1947, 1949; Woman's Cl., 1949. *Work*: Minneapolis Woman's Cl.; Minneapolis Chamber of Commerce; work included in Minn. Centennial Commission's film "Art in Minnesota," 1958. *Exhibited*: Riverside Mus., 1948; Grand Central A. Gal., 1948; Los A. County Fair, 1947-1949; de Young Mem. Mus., 1947; Pasadena AI, 1945-1949; Santa Barbara, Cal., 1945-1949; San Diego, Cal., 1945-1949; Seattle, Wash., 1945-1949; Joslyn A. Mus., 1948, 1950, 1951; Terry AI, 1952; numerous traveling exh., 1945-1950; Minnesota State Fair, 1940-1951, 1956, 1958; Harriet Hanley Gal., 1940; Minneapolis Inst. A., 1941-1952; Minneapolis Woman's Cl., 1942-1952, 1954, 1956; St. Paul A. Gal., 1946-1949; Walker A. Center, 1947, 1954; Minneapolis Aquatennial, 1947-1952; Five Twin City Artists, 1949; Minneapolis AA, 1949, 1955, 1956; Minn. Women A., 1950; Swedish-Am. Inst. A., 1952, 1954 (one-man), 1958; Carleton Col., 1954; Wis. State T. Col., 1954; St. Paul Carnival Exh., 1955, 1958; AEA, 1952; Centennial Expo., 1958; Minnesota AA, 1955, 1956. *Position*: Bd. Dir., Rec. Sec., Twin City Chptr., AEA, 1952-58; Member, Visual A. & Arch. Committee, Minn. Centennial Comm., 1958; Pres., Minn. AA, 1956-58; A. Chm., St. Paul Winter Carnival Art Exh., 1957-58.

WOLFF, MRS. HAROLD G. *See Bishop, Isabel*

WOLFF, ROBERT JAY—*Painter, E., Des., W., L.*

Brooklyn College, Brooklyn, N.Y.; h. New Preston, Conn.

B. Chicago, Ill., July 27, 1905. *Studied*: Yale Univ.; & in Paris, with Georges Mouveau. *Awards*: prizes, AIC, 1933, 1934. *Work*: Guggenheim Mus.; BM. *Exhibited*: Am. Abstract A., 1938-1950; one-man exh.: Quest & Kuh Gal., Chicago; Reinhardt Gal., Nierendorf Gal., Kleemann Gal., Guggenheim Mus., 1952; Saidenberg Gal., 1954, 1955, N.Y.; Borgenicht Gal., 1956, 1958; also group exh. U.S. and abroad. Author, I., "Elements of Design," 1945. Contributor to: art magazines. *Position*: Dean, Hd. Painting & S. Dept., Inst. Des., Chicago, Ill., 1939-42; Hd., Graphic Dept., U.S. Naval Training Aids Development Center, 1943-45; Prof. A., Chm. A. Dept., Brooklyn Col., Brooklyn, N.Y., 1946- ; Des., Advertising, New York, N.Y., 1945- ; Consultant, Dir. Adv. Des., Kroll Fabrics, Inc., N.Y., 1947- .

WOLFS, WILMA DIENA—*Sculptor, P., Gr., E., I., L.*

1522 Waterbury Rd., Lakewood 7, Ohio

B. Cleveland, Ohio. *Studied*: Western Reserve Univ., B.A., B.S.; Cleveland Sch. A.; Univ. Minnesota; Radcliffe Col., A.M.; Ecole des Beaux-Arts, Paris; & with Henry Keller, Rolf Stoll, & others. *Member*: Am. Assn. Univ. Women; Ohio WC Soc.; Arkansas WC Soc.; Soc. Indp. A.; New Hampshire A. & Crafts Soc. *Awards*: prizes, Mus. FA, Little Rock, Ark., 1939; med., Arkansas WC Soc., 1938; Carnegie Scholarships for study in Paris, France, & at N.Y. Univ., Harvard Univ., Univ. Pennsylvania. *Work*: Univ. Arkansas; Hendrix Col., Conway, Ark.; s. Catholic Church, Winter Park, Fla.; Research Studio, Maitland, Fla. *Exhibited*: CGA; CMA; Butler AI; Mus. FA, Little Rock, Ark.; Wichita A. Mus.; Philbrook A. Center; Studio Gld.; Univ. Arkansas; Brooks Gal., Cleveland; Akron AI; Columbus Gal. FA; Dayton AI; Massillon Mus.; Ohio Univ.; Zanesville AI; Toledo Mus. A.; & many others. *Position*: Hd. A. Dept., Hendrix Col., Conway, Ark., 1936-37; State T. Col., Keene, N.H., 1937-38; Instr. A., MacMurray Col., Jacksonville, Ill., 1938-39; Asst. Prof. A., Florida State Col. for Women, Tallahassee, Fla., 1939-40.*

WOLLE, MURIEL SIBELL (Mrs. Francis Wolle)—*Educator, W., L., P., Gr.*

Fine Arts Department, University of Colorado; h. 763 16th St., Boulder, Colo.

B. Brooklyn, N.Y., Apr. 3, 1898. *Studied*: N.Y. Sch. F. & App. A.; N.Y. Univ., B.S. in A. Edu.; Univ. Colorado, M.A. *Member*: Boulder A. Gld.; Colorado Edu. Assn.; Idaho State Hist. Soc.; The Westerners; Colo. State Hist. Soc.; Montana State Hist. Soc.; Wyoming State Hist. Soc. *Awards*: prizes, Kansas City, AI, 1932, medal, 1934; NAWA, 1934; Springfield (Mo.) AA; Norlin medal, Univ. Colorado, 1957; Laureate Key, Delta Phi Delta, 1958. *Work*: Denver A. Mus.; Springfield AA. *Exhibited*: Denver A. Mus., 1928-1944; Boulder A. Gld., 1927-1958; NAWA, 1932-1941; Kansas City AI, 1932-1938; Joslyn A. Mus., 1932-1940. Author, I., "Ghost Cities of Colorado," 1933; "Cloud Cities of Colorado," 1934; "Stampede to Timberline," 1949; "The Bonanza Trail," 1953. Contributor to The Mining Journal, The Mining World, Colorado Quarterly, The Brand Book, and other publications. Lectures: Ghost Towns of Colorado. *Position*: Instr. A., Texas State Col. for Women, 1920-23; N.Y. Sch. F. & App. A., 1923-26; Hd. Dept. A., 1928-47, Prof., Dept. FA, Univ. Colorado, Boulder, Colo., 1926- .

WOLSKY, MILTON LABAN—*Illustrator, P.*

5804 Leavenworth St, Omaha 6, Neb.

B. Omaha, Neb., Jan. 23, 1916. *Studied*: Univ. Omaha; AIC; ASL, and with Julian Levi, Hans Hofmann. *Member*: SI; AWS; Intl. Inst. A. & Lets.; Nat. Soc. A. Dirs.; Omaha Artists-Art Dirs.; Assoc. Omaha A. *Work*: Air Force Hist. Fnd.; producing, at present a series of Cities of the Northern Plains, appearing in Time magazine for the Northern Natural Gas Co.; editorial and advertising illus. in national magazines. *Exhibited*: AWS, 1947, 1948, 1950, 1953; Audubon A., 1947; Joslyn Mus. A., 1938-1942, 1955; Mid-west Exh., 1957.

WOLTER, ADOLPH G. (Adolph Gustav Wolter von Ruemelin)—*Sculptor, E., L.*

1031 Carrollton Ave.; h. 616 East 58th St., Indianapolis 20, Ind.

B. Reutlingen, Germany, Sept. 7, 1903. *Studied*: Kunstkewerbe Schule, Acad. FA, Stuttgart, Germany; John Herron AI. *Member*: Indiana A. Cl.; Alumn. Assn., John Herron, AI; the 20's. *Awards*: prizes, Herron AI, 1938; Hoosier Salon, 1946; Indiana State Fair, 1935, 1937-1940. *Work*: S., Indiana State Lib.; mem., Detroit, Mich.; American Legion Office Bldg., Wash., D.C.; Indianapolis Star, etc.; Port. busts, reliefs, Wood County Court House, Wisconsin Rapids, Wis.; Indiana Nat. Bank, Indianapolis; Indianapolis Speedway Trophy; Mem. Center & Life Science Bldg., Purdue Univ.; Tenn. State Capitol; Wabash Col.; Ball State T. Col.; De Pauw Univ.; Indiana State House. *Exhibited*: Nat. Exh. Am. A., N.Y., 1938; Indiana State Fair, 1935-1940, 1951; Herron AI, 1938, 1943, 1945; Hoosier Salon. Lectures on Art Appreciation.

WOLTMAN, NANCY COLDWELL (WINSLOW)—*Painter*

405 East 78th St., New York 21, N.Y.

B. East Lynn, Mass., Feb. 23, 1913. *Studied*: ASL; Farnsworth Sch. A.; Amagansett A. Sch. *Member*: NAWA; Copley Soc., Boston; New Jersey P. & S.; AEA; Woodstock AA. *Awards*: prizes, Michigan, 1951; NAWA, 1953. *Work*: in private colls. *Exhibited*: Audubon A., 1949; New Jersey P. & S., 1951, 1952; Sarasota, Fla., 1951; NAWA, 1952-1957; New England annual, 1949, 1950; Provincetown AA, 1948, 1949; Copley Soc., 1950, 1951; Caravan Gal., 1953-1955; Woodstock AA, 1955; Michigan, 1951; 2 one-man exhs., N.Y., 1957; one-man, Mass., 1956.

WONG, TYRUS—*Painter, Des., Et., Lith., I.*

10112 La Canada Way, Shadow Hills, Sunland, Cal.

B. Canton, China, Oct. 25, 1910. *Studied*: Otis AI. *Member*: Cal. WC Soc.; AWS; Motion Picture Set Des.; Los A. Mus. Assn.; Los A. AA; Motion Picture Illustrators. *Work*: Honolulu Acad. FA; Santa Barbara Mus. A.; Los A. AA; Los A. Mus. A. *Awards*: prizes, Los A. Mus. A., 1954, 1955. *Exhibited*: PAFA, 1948, 1952; WFNY 1939; AWS, 1947-1949, 1955; Cal. WC Soc., 1948-1955; LC, 1951, 1952; Denver A. Mus., 1948, 1954, 1955; Los A. Mus. A., 1950, 1952, 1954, 1955; Cal. State Fair, 1950-1952; Butler AI, 1955; Oakland A. Mus., 1955, and others. I., "Footprints of the Dragon," 1949; text & illus. "Watercolor Portraiture," 1949; cover illus., Los A. Times

Home Magazine, 1954, 1955. Contributor illus. to Arts & Architecture, Coronet, Western Art Review magazines. *Position*: Production Des., Walt Disney Studios, 1937-40; Production Illus., Warner Bros. Studio, 1941- ; California Artists Card Designer.*

WONSETLER, JOHN CHARLES—Painter, I., W.

Noe Ave. & Southern Blvd., Chatham, N.J.

B. Camden, N.J., Aug. 25, 1900. *Studied*: PMSchA, with Thornton Oakley. *Awards*: prize, PMSchA., 1925. *Work*: murals, Franklin & Marshall Col., Lancaster, Pa.; many hotels, churches, theatres, in Pennsylvania, New York, Maryland, Virginia, Delaware, etc. *Exhibited*: Phila. A. All.; Wanamaker Gal., Phila.; PMSchA. Co-Author, I., "Me and the General"; "Liberty for Johanny"; Author. I., "Yanks in Action"; I., "Lambs's Tales from Shakespeare"; "Our Lusty Forefathers"; "Treasure Island"; "Up the Trail from Texas"; "Rogers Rangers"; "Buffalo Bill and the Great Wild West Show." Illus. for children's books and magazines.

WOOD, EDITH LONGSTRETH (Mrs. William S.)— Painter, Lith.

34 South 17th St. (3); h. 2139 Cypress St., Philadelphia 3, Pa.

B. Philadelphia, Pa. *Studied*: Bryn Mawr Col., A.B.; PAFA, and in England and France. *Member*: Phila. A. All.; Phila. Pr. Cl.; Southern Vt. A. *Awards*: F., PAFA, medal, Phila. Plastic Cl., 1933; Cresson traveling scholarship, PAFA. *Work*: PAFA; La France Inst., Phila., Pa.; Phila. A. All. *Exhibited*: NAD; PAFA, 1932-1946; F. PAFA, 1956-1958; Southern Vermont A, 1956-1958; CGA, and others in New England, New Mexico and California.

WOOD, ELLA MIRIAM—Portrait Painter

1464 Eleonore St., New Orleans 15, La.

B. Birmingham, Ala., Feb. 18, 1888. *Studied*: Newcomb Col., Tulane Univ.; PAFA; & with Henry McCarter, Charles Hawthorne, Daniel Garber. *Member*: New Orleans AA; New Orleans A. & Crafts Cl. *Awards*: prize, Newcomb A. Sch. *Work*: mural, altarpieces, St. Augustine Church, New Orleans, La.; Port. Newcomb Col., Charity Hospital, New Orleans. *Exhibited*: Delgado Mus. A.; New Orleans A. & Crafts Cl.; Lousiana State Exh., Baton Rouge, La.

WOOD, ELOISE—Etcher, P., E.

97 St. Clair St., Geneva, N.Y.

B. Geneva, N.Y., Sept. 7, 1897. *Studied*: Albright A. Sch.; Farnsworth Sch. A.; ASL; William Smith Col., Geneva, N.Y.; T. Col., Columbia Univ. *Member*: AAUP. *Work*: MMA; altarpiece, St. John's Chapel, Hobart Col.; windows, Sampson Air Base, N.Y.; 41 Heraldic Shields, Coxe Hall, Hobart Col. *Exhibited*: Phila. SE, 1931; NAC, 1930; Brooklyn SE, 1931; Chicago SE, 1931; Cal. Pr.M., 1931; Phila. Pr. Cl., 1931; Kennedy Gal., N.Y., 1932 (one-man). *Position*: Assoc. Prof., Chm. A. Dept., Hobart & William Smith Col., Geneva, N.Y., at present.

WOOD, E. SHOTWELL—Painter, T.

341 Clay St., Nevada City, Cal.

B. San Francisco, Cal., July 30, 1887. *Studied*: Cal. Sch. FA; Ecole des Beaux-Arts, Fontainebleau, France; & with Andre L'Hote, Paul Beaudoin, Jean Despujols. *Member*: Cal. Soc. Women A.; Marin SA; Cal. Soc. Mural P. *Awards*: San F. Soc. Women A.; Marin SA; Cal. State Fair, 1939; AAUW, 1953; Nevada County Fair, 1955. *Work*: frescoes, Fontainebleau, France; San F., Cal.; San Mateo, Cal. *Exhibited*: WMAA, 1920; Independents, Paris, 1928; San F., Soc. Women A., 1934-1945, traveling exh., 1948-1952; Marin SA, 1937-1945; Nevada City AA; Kingsley A. Cl., 1952, and later; SFMA, 1948-1952; AAUW; Nevada County Fair. Lectures: Art.

WOOD, HARRY EMSLEY, JR.—Educator, L., P.

Art Department, Arizona State College, Tempe, Ariz.

B. Indianapolis, Ind., Dec. 10, 1910. *Studied*: Univ. Wisconsin, B.A., M.A.; Ohio State Univ., M.A., Ph. D.; Accademia dei Belli Arti, Florence, Italy, with Ottono Rosai; and with John Frazier, Provincetown, Mass.; Emil Bittram, Taos, N.M. *Member*: CAA; NAEA; Pacific AA; Am. Soc. for Aesthetics. *Work*: murals, Great Central Ins. Co., Peoria, Ill.; Memorial Union, Arizona State College,

Tempe. Many portraits of promiment persons. *Exhibited*: one-man: Columbus, Ohio, 1941; Peoria, Ill., 1944; Decatur, Ill., 1945; Galesburg, Ill., 1946; Beloit, Wis., 1947; Illinois State Mus., 1949; Florence, Italy, 1950; Indiana A. Retrospective, John Herron AI, 1953; Arizona A., Tucson, 1956, 1957. *Positions*: Prof. A., Illinois Wesleyan, Bloomington, 1942-44; Dean, Col. of FA, Bradley Univ., Peoria, 1944-50; Chm. A. Dept., Arizona State College, Tempe, Ariz., 1954- ; Pres., Pacific AA, 1958-60; Pres., Ariz. A. Edu. Assn., 1954-55.

WOOD, LILLIAN LEE—Portrait Painter

2702 Monument Ave., Richmond 20, Va.

B. Richmond, Va., Dec. 18, 1906. *Studied*: Sweet Briar Col., B.A.; ASL, with Kenneth Hayes Miller, Kimon Nicolaides. *Awards*: prize, Virginia Mechanics Inst., 1932. *Work*: Richmond (Va.) Armory. *Exhibited*: VMFA; Richmond Acad. A.

WOOD, MEMPHIS (Miss)—Painter, T.

Woodside Lane, Mandarin 7, Fla.; h. Rte. 6, Box 78 WA, Jacksonville 7, Fla.

B. Dacula, Ga., Jan. 29, 1902. *Studied*: Univ. Georgia, M.F.A.; Univ. Florida. *Member*: Southeastern AA; Fla. A. Group; Fla. Craftsmen; Jacksonville AA. *Work*: Univ. Georgia; Murray State T. Col.; Stetson Univ. *Exhibited*: High Mus. A., 1951-1953; Fla. A. Group, 1956, 1958; Jacksonville Mus. A., biannually; Ringling Mus. A., 1955; one-man: Gainesville (Fla.) AA, 1955; Jacksonville Mus. A., 1950; Stetson Univ. (2-man), 1956.

WOODHAM, JEAN (CARAWAY)—Sculptor

Wayfaring Rd., Norwalk, Conn.

B. Midland City, Ala., Aug. 16, 1925. *Studied*: Alabama Polytechnic Inst., B.A.; Sculpture Center, N.Y.; Univ. Illinois. *Member*: AEA; NAWA; N.Y. Soc. Ceramic A.; Silvermine Gld. A. *Awards*: F., Univ. Illinois, 1950; NAWA, 1956; New England Annual, 1956-1958; Audubon A., 1958. *Work*: Massillon Mus. A. *Exhibited*: PAFA, 1950, 1954; Audubon A., 1951; NAWA, 1951-1958; London, England, 1954; Syracuse Mus. FA, 1948, 1952; N.Y. Soc. Ceramic A., 1951-1955; Sculpture Center, N.Y., 1947-1949, 1951; John Heller Gal., 1954; BMFA; CM; High Mus. A.; Montgomery Mus. FA; New England Annual, 1956-1958; Barone Gal., N.Y.; Stuttman Gal.; one-man: Ala. Polytechnic Inst., 1950; Univ. Illinois, 1952; Silvermine Gld. A., 1955; Wesleyan Univ., Middletown, Conn. *Positions*: Instr. S., 1956-57, Bd. Managers, 1958- , Silvermine Gld. A.

WOODHOUSE, BETTY BURROUGHS—Teacher, S.

Rhode Island School of Design, Providence, R.I.; h. Little Compton, R.I.

B. Norwich, Conn., Aug. 17, 1899. *Studied*: ASL, and abroad. *Member*: CAA. Ed., "Vasari's Lives of the Painters," 1946. *Position*: Cur. Edu., Museum of Art, L., Hist. A., Instr., Adult Classes in P. & S., Rhode Island Sch. Des., Providence, R.I.

WOODROOFE, LOUISE M.—Painter, E.

1207 West Oregon St., Urbana, Ill.

B. Champaign, Ill. *Studied*: Univ. Illinois; Syracuse Univ., B.P.; & with Hugh Breckenridge. *Member*: NAWA. *Position*: Prof. A., Univ. Illinois, Urbana, Ill., at present.

WOODRUFF, HALE ASPACIO—Painter, E., L.

Art Department, School of Education, New York University; h. 22 East 8th St., New York 3, N.Y.

B. Cairo, Ill., Aug. 26, 1900. *Studied*: John Herron AI; Academie Moderne, Paris; Harvard Univ.; and in Mexico. *Member*: Com. on A. Edu., MModA. *Awards*: prizes, Harmon Fnd., 1926; Diamond Jubilee Exp., Chicago, 1940; High Mus. A., 1940. *Work*: Newark Mus.; Howard Univ.; Atlanta Univ.; murals, Talladega Col., Ala.; Golden State Mutual Life Ins. Co., Los A., Cal.; Atlanta Univ. Lib. *Exhibited*: VMFA; High Mus. A.; Assn. Georgia A.; BMFA; Los A. Mus. A.; AIC; John Herron AI; BMA; WMAA, 1954; one-man: Bertha Schaefer Gal., 1953, 1954, 1958; Univ. Southern Ill., 1956; Hampton Inst., 1957; Eastern Michigan State Col., 1956; Univ. North Carolina, 1955. Lectures, auspices of Assn. Am. Colleges. *Position*: Prof. A. Edu., N.Y. Univ.

WOODS, GURDON G.—*Educator,* S.

California School of Fine Arts, 800 Chestnut St. (11); h. 611 Wisconsin St., San Francisco, Cal.

B. Savannah, Ga., Apr. 15, 1915. *Studied*: Copley Soc., Boston; ASL. *Member*: AEA; San F. AA; Bohemian Cl., San F. *Awards*: prizes, NAD, 1949; San F. A. Festival (purchase); San F. AA, 1952; Wells Fargo award, 1954. *Work*: in private colls. Fountain, IBM Bldg., San Jose, Cal.; Masson Champagne Bldg., Los Gatos, Cal. *Exhibited*: Riverside Mus., N.Y., 1945; Sao Paulo, Brazil, 1955; San F. AA, annually; WMAA; NAD; Denver A. Mus., 1952, 1953, 1958; Erik Locke Gal., San F., 1958; Richmond & Walnut Creek, Cal., annuals, 1949-1955. *Positions*: Member, San Francisco A. Comm., 1954-55; Dir., California School of Fine Arts, San Francisco, Cal., at present.

WOODS, WILLIS FRANKLIN—*Museum Director*

Norton Gallery & School of Art, Pioneer Park; h. 255 Worth Court South, West Palm Beach, Fla.

B. Washington, D.C., July 25, 1920. *Studied*: Brown Univ., A.B.; American Univ.; Univ. Oregon. *Member*: Southern A. Mus. Dir. Assn.; Am. Assn. Mus. Dir.; Florida A. Group. *Position*: Mngr., Watkins Mem. Gal., 1946-47; Asst. Dir., CGA, 1947-49; Dir., Norton Gal. & Sch. A., West Palm Beach, Fla., 1949- ; Pres., Fla. A. Group, 1951-52; Chm., Southern A. Mus. Dir. Assn., 1954-55; Pres., Fla. Fed. A., 1954-56.

WOODWARD, ROBERT STRONG—*Painter*

Shelburne Falls, Mass.; h. Buckland, Mass.

B. Northampton, Mass., May 11, 1885. *Studied*: BMFA Sch.; & with Edmund Tarbell, Philip Hale. *Member*: SC; Boston AC; Gld. Boston A.; Springfield (Mass.) A. Lg.; Pittsfield (Mass.) A. Lg. *Awards*: prizes, NAD, 1919; Springfield A. Lg., 1927; Albany Inst. Hist. & A., 1937; med., Tercentenary Exp., Boston, 1930; Ogunquit A. Center, 1948; Boston AC. 1932. *Work*: Springfield A. Mus.; Canajoharie A. Gal.; Syracuse Mus. FA; BMFA; Williston Acad., Easthampton, Mass.; Stockridge Pub. Lib.; Yale Univ.; Pasadena AI; San Diego FA Soc.; Northfield (Mass.) Seminary; Mount Holyoke Col.; Putnam Mem. Hospital, Bennington, Vt.; etc. *Exhibited*: NAD; Carnegie Inst.; CGA; AIC; PAFA; BMFA; WFNY 1939; GGE 1939; Deerfield Valley AA; Williston Acad.; Springfield AA.*

WOODWARD, STANLEY—*Painter, Et., W., I., T.*

36 Main St., h. 27 South St., Rockport, Mass.

B. Malden, Mass., Dec. 11, 1890. *Studied*: BMFA Sch.; PAFA. *Member*: Gld. Boston A.; AWS; Wash. WC Cl.; Conn. Acad. FA; Boston Soc. WC Painters; SAGA; Audubon A.; All. A. Am.; New Haven Paint & Clay Cl.; Rockport AA; North Shore AA; SC. *Awards*: prizes, NAD, 1925; AWS, 1927; Balt. WC Cl., 1927; Springfield A. Lg., 1928; Stockbridge AA, 1931; New Haven Paint & Clay Cl.; Rockport AA, 1940, 1948, 1955; Wash. WC Cl., 1940; North Shore AA, 1941; Meriden AA, 1950; medals, Boston Tercentenary, 1930; Jordan Marsh, Boston, 1949. *Work*: BMFA; Bowdoin Col.; Converse Mem. Gal., Malden, Mass.; Ft. Worth Mus. A.; Ball State T. Col.; New Haven, Conn.; Amherst Coll.; Wheaton Col.; Washington County Mus., Hagerstown, Md.; BM; Vanderpoel Coll.; Framingham (Mass.) Lib.; Wilton (N.H.) Lib.; Wellesley Hills Lib. *Exhibited*: PAFA; CGA; AIC; BMFA; CAM; NAD; Pepsi-Cola. Author: "Adventure in Marine Painting," 1948. Illus. to Collier's and Ford Times magazines. *Position*: Instr., Woodward Outdoor Painting Sch., 1935- .

WOOLLEY, VIRGINIA—*Painter*

615 Seaview St., Laguna Beach, Cal.

B. Selma, Ala., Aug. 27, 1884. *Studied*: AIC, and in Paris, France. *Member*: Laguna Beach AA; Nat. Lg. Am. Pen Women. *Work*: High Mus. A., Atlanta.

WORCESTER, EVA—*Painter, S., T.*

80 Sunningdale Drive, Grosse Pointe Shores 36, Mich.

B. Erie, Mich., June 9, 1892. *Studied*: BMFA Sch.; and with Eliot O'Hara, Hobson Pittman, Emile Gruppe, and others. *Member*: Michigan WC Soc.; Grosse Pointe A.; Copley Soc., Boston; Chicago A. Cl.; Michigan A.; Fed. Am. A. *Awards*: prizes, Grosse Pointe A., 1955; Nat. Lg. Am. Pen Women, 1953. *Work*: War Mem. Coll., Detroit; Grosse Pointe Garden Center; Nat. Fed. Women's Cl.,

Boston; Lobby, Detroit TV-Radio Station Bldg., and in private colls. *Exhibited*: Nat. Lg. Am. Pen Women, 1953, 1954; Detroit Inst. A., annually; one-man: Copley Gal., Boston, 1952; Washington Gal., Miami Beach, 1954; Detroit War Mem., 1956; Palm Springs, Cal., 1957, 1958.

WORMLEY, EDWARD—*Industrial, Textile Designer*

450 East 52nd St., New York 22, N.Y.

B. Oswego, Ill., Dec. 31, 1907. *Studied*: AIC. *Member*: IDI; Arch. Lg.; AID. *Awards*: AID, 1950, 1951; MModA, 1950, 1951, 1952. *Exhibited*: MMoA, 1947-1954; Arch. Lg., 1947-1949; BMA, 1951; Akron AI; R.I. Sch. Des., 1948; Albright A. Gal., 1947; Dayton AI. Lectures on Furniture Design; Modern Design, Harvard Univ., John Herron AI, BMA, Parsons Sch. Des.. Visiting Consultant and Lecturer, Cornell Univ., Sch. Arch., 1955.

WORTH, PETER JOHN—*Designer, S., E.*

Department of Art, Morrill Hall, University of Nebraska; h. 1945 E St., Lincoln, Neb.

B. Ipswich, England, Mar. 16, 1917. *Studied*: Ipswich Sch. A.; Royal Col. A. *Member*: CAA; Egypt Exploration Soc., London. *Work*: Denver A. Mus.; Joslyn A. Mus. *Exhibited*: SFMA, 1950; Walker A. Center, 1951; AIC, 1951; Denver A. Mus., 1952, 1953; Nelson Gal. A., 1950, 1953, 1954. *Position*: Assoc. Prof. A., Chm. Dept. A., Univ. Nebraska, Lincoln, Neb.*

WORTHAM, C(LYDE) H(AROLD)—*Painter, E., W.*

San Opropio 4, Madrid, Spain; also, American Security & Trust Bank, Washington, D.C.

B. Shawnee, Okla., Jan. 24, 1909. *Studied*: Yard Sch. FA, Wash., D.C.; ASL; Madrid Acad. FA. *Awards*: prizes, Metropolitan A. Exh., Wash., D.C., 1936; A. Exh., Wash., D.C., 1951; Madrid Acad. FA, 1952, 1953. *Exhibited*: Wash., D.C. exhs., 1936-1949; one-man: Rosenberg Lib., Galveston, Tex., 1942, 1953; Casa Americana, Madrid, Spain, 1952, and in Madrid galleries, 1957, 1958. Contributor to Spanish periodicals. Work in private colls., Spain.

WRENN, HAROLD HOLMES—*Painter, T.*

40 Warrenton Rd.,Baltimore 10, Md.

B. Norfolk, Va., Apr. 27, 1887. *Studied*: Norfolk Acad., Norfolk, Va.; Univ. Virginia; Columbia Univ. *Member*: AFA; A. Un.; Provincetown AA; Mun. A. Soc., Balt. *Awards*: prizes, BMA, 1939; Mun. Mus., Balt., Md., 1943. *Work*: Phila.A.All.; Norfolk Mus. A. & Sc.; VMFA; BMA; Mun. Mus., Balt., Md. *Exhibited*: CGA, 1935; AFA traveling exh., 1935; WFNY 1939; MModA; VMFA; Pepsi-Cola traveling exh., 1945; BMA, annually; Phila. A. All.; Mun. Mus., Balt., Md. *Position*: Hd. A. Dept., Gilman Sch., Baltimore, Md.*

WRIGHT, ALICE MORGAN—*Sculptor, W.*

393 State St., Albany 10, N.Y.

B. Albany, N.Y., Oct. 10, 1881. *Studied*: Smith Col., A.B.; St. Agnes Sch., Albany, N.Y.; Russell Sage Col., L.H.D.; ASL; Academie Colorossi, Ecole des Beaux-Arts, Paris, France, and with Hermon MacNeil, Gutzon Borglum, James Earle Fraser. *Member*: F., NSS; NAWA. *Awards*: NAWA; NAC; NAD. *Work*: Folger Shakespeare Mus., Wash., D.C.; U.S. Nat. Mus., Wash., D.C.; Newark Mus.; Bleecker Hall, Albany, N.Y.; London Mus.; Kensington Palace; Bay Ridge H.S., Brooklyn, N.Y.; John M. Greene Hall, College Hall and Smith Col. Lib., Northampton, Mass.; Brookgreen Gardens, S.C. *Exhibited*: NAD; PAFA; AIC; Soc. Indp. A.; NAWA; Paris Salon; Salon d'Automne, Salon des Beaux-Arts, Paris. Contributor to Harper's, Bookman magazines; wrote first acting version, in the U.S. of "Sakuntala," performed at Smith Col.

WRIGHT, BARTON ALLEN—*Museum Curator, I.*

Museum of Northern Arizona; h. Box 402, Flagstaff, Ariz.

B. Bisbee, Ariz., Dec. 21, 1920. *Studied*: Univ. Arizona, B.A., M.A. *Member*: Am. Archaeological Soc.; Western Mus. Conf. I., "Ventana Cave," 1950; "Upper Pima of San Cayetano del Tumacacori," 1956; "Master of the Moving Sea," 1958; "Corridors of Time" (pamphlet); "University Indian Ruin" (Univ. Ariz. pamphlet). Contributor to Ceramic Series; Plateau; Kiva; American

Antiquities. Arranged: Junior Indian Art Show; Hopi Craftsman; Navajo Craftsman; 1956—"Southwestern Architecture"; "Navajo Sandpaintings"; "Mars Hill"; 1957— "Historic Maps"; "Tattletale Bones"; 1958—"The Southwest"; "M.R.F. Colton Paintings"; "Timber." *Positions*: State Archaeological Asst., Town Creek Indian Mound, N.C., 1949-51; Archaeologist, Amerind Fnd., Dragoon, Ariz., 1952-55; Cur. A. & Exhibits, Mus. Northern Arizona, Flagstaff, Ariz., 1955- .

WRIGHT, CATHARINE MORRIS (Mrs.)—
Painter, T., W., L.
  Fox Hill, Jamestown, R.I.
B. Philadelphia, Pa., Jan. 26, 1899. *Studied*: Moore Inst. A., and with Henry B. Snell, Leopold Seyffert. *Member*: ANA; AWS; Phila. WC Cl. (V.-Pres.); All. A. Am.; Audubon A.; Newport AA; Authors Lg. Am. *Awards*: prizes, PAFA; NAD; Newport AA; Germantown A. Lg.; Silvermine Gld. A., 1955; All. A. Am.; medal, Springside (Pa.) Sch. *Work*: PAFA; Allentown Mus.; Moore Inst. A.; New Britain AI; Woodmere A. Gal.; Univ. Pennsylvania; Pa. State Col.; PMA; NAD. *Exhibited*: PAFA, 1918-1952; CGA, 1921-1941; NAD, 1930-1952; AIC, 1921-1942; Carnegie Inst.; All.A.Am.; Audubon A.; Newport AA, 1918-1946; Woodmere A. Gal.; Phila.A.All.; one-man: Syracuse Mus. FA; New Britain AI; deCordova Mus.; PAFA; Fitchburg (Mass.) Mus. A.; Mt. Holyoke Col. Contributor to Scribners, Story Parade, Sat. Eve. Post, Atlantic Monthly magazines. *Position*: Founder, Instr., Fox Hill Sch. A., Jamestown, R.I. Author: "The Simple Nun"; "Seaweed Their Pasture"; "The Color of Life," 1957.

WRIGHT, ELVA M.—Painter
  298 Liberty St., Long Branch, N.J.
B. New Haven, Conn. *Studied*: Columbia Univ.; ASL. *Member*: NAWA; AAPL; Asbury Park Soc. FA. *Awards*: prizes, New Jersey A. Gal., Newark, 1938, 1940; Asbury Park Soc. FA, 1939, 1942-1944; AAPL, 1942, 1950, 1951, 1952, 1953; Deal, N.J., 1954, 1955. *Exhibited*: AAPL, 1937-1952; Asbury Park Soc. FA, 1935-1952; Newark Mus., 1938; WFNY 1939; ASL, 1950; State House, Trenton, N.J., 1951; Montclair A. Mus., 1953; NAC, 1954, 1955; NAWA, 1955; Old Mill Annual, Tinton Falls, N.J., 1953, 1954.*

WRIGHT, FRED WILLIAM—Portrait Painter
  7000 Beach Plaza, St. Petersburg Beach, Fla.
B. Crawfordsville, Ind., Oct. 12, 1880. *Studied*: John Herron AI; ASL; CUASch., and in France. *Work*: State Capitol and Law Sch., Albany, N.Y.; State Capitol, Annapolis, Md.; Union, Catholic, and Nat. Democratic Clubs, New York City; N.Y. County Lawyers' Assn.; Waldorf Astoria Hotel; Libby Owens Bd. Room, Toledo, Ohio; DuPont, Wilmington, Del.; Dun and Bradstreet; Univ. Delaware; Columbia Univ.; Brown Univ.; Harvard Univ.; CM; Haverstraw (N.Y.) Hospital; Col. of Surgeons, Chicago.

WRIGHT, JAMES COUPER—Painter, T., L.
  4 Lida Lane, Pasadena 3, Cal.
B. Kirkwall, Orkney Islands, Scotland, Mar. 21, 1906. *Studied*: Edinburgh Col. A., Scotland, D.A.; in Europe (scholarship). *Member*: Cal. WC Soc.; Pasadena Soc. A.; AWS. *Awards*: 42 awards for watercolors. *Work*: SFMA; Oakland A. Mus.; Santa Barbara Mus. A.; Los A. Mus. A.; Pasadena A. Mus.; San Diego FA Gal. *Exhibited*: Nationally and with numerous one-man exhibitions. *Position*: Instr., Pasadena City Schs.; summer at Los Angeles Harbor.

WRIGHT, LOUIS BOOKER—Museum Director, Hist.
  Folger Shakespeare Library, 201 East Capitol St. (3); h. 2915 Foxhall Road, Northwest, Washington 9, D.C.
B. Greenwood, S.C., Mar. 1, 1899. *Studied*: Wofford Col., A.B.; Univ. North Carolina, M.A., Ph.D. *Member*: Mod. Language Assn.; Am. Hist. Assn.; Am. Antiquarian Soc.; Am. Philosophical Soc.; Grolier Cl.; Colonial Soc. of Mass.; Mass. Hist. Soc. *Award*: Guggenheim F., 1928-29, 1930. Author: "Middle-Class Culture in Elizabethan England," 1935; "The First Gentlemen of Virginia," 1940; "Conservation of Culture on the Moving Frontier," 1953; "The Cultural Life of the American Colonies," 1957. Contributor to American Historical Review; Saturday Review,

and other learned journals. Lectures: British and American colonial history. *Positions*: Instr., Am. Hist., Bibliography, Research Methods: Univ. North Carolina, Emory Univ., Univ. Michigan, Univ. Washington, UCLA, and others; Memb. Permanent Research Group & Chm. Comm. on Fellowships, Huntington Lib., 1932-48; Dir., Folger Shakespeare Library, Washington, D.C., at present.

WRIGHT, STANLEY MARC—Painter, T., L.
  Stowe, Vt.
B. Irvington, N.J., May 24, 1911. *Studied*: PIASch.; Tiffany Fnd., and with Jerry Farnsworth. *Member*: SC; AAPL; Audubon A.; Am. Veterans Soc. A.; Newark A. Cl.; A. Center of the Oranges. *Awards*: Montclair A. Mus., 1947, 1948, 1951; Fleming Mus. A., 1950-1958; Newark Mus., 1946; Jersey City Mus. A., 1948; Spring Lake, 1947, 1948; SC, 1953; Ogunquit A. Center, 1953, 1958; Newbury A. Center, 1953-1956; Irvington A. & Mus. Assn., 1946; Millburn-Short Hills, 1947, 1948; Newark A. Cl., 1946-1948; SC, 1952. *Work*: mural, Newark Airport. *Exhibited*: MMA, 1942; NAD; Audubon A, 1949-1958; NAC, 1949, 1950; All. A. Am.; CGA; Grand Central A. Gal.; New Hope, Pa.; Provincetown, Mass.; SC; Montclair A. Mus.; Wash. Congressional Cl.; Silvermine Gld. A.; Wood A. Gal., and others. I., "Creation of Man." *Position*: Instr., Newark Sch. FA; Wright Sch. A.

WRIGLEY, VIOLA B. (Mrs. Roy F.)—Painter, Lith.
  12 Stewart Pl., White Plains, N.Y.
B. Kendallville, Ind., Dec. 27, 1892. *Studied*: Oberlin Col.; Univ. Kansas; T. Col., Columbia Univ.; & with Charles Martin. *Member*: NAWA; Hudson Valley A. Gld.; Pen & Brush Cl.; Westchester A. Gld. *Exhibited*: NAWA; Westchester A. Gld.; Toronto, Canada, 1941.*

WUERMER, CARL—Painter
  c/o Grand Central Art Galleries, The Biltmore Hotel, Vanderbilt Ave. & 43rd St., New York 17, N.Y.; h. Woodstock, N.Y.
B. Munich, Germany, Aug. 3, 1900. *Studied*: AIC; ASL; & with W. J. Reynolds. *Member*: A. Fellowship, Inc.; All. A. Am. *Awards*: prizes, AIC, 1927; NAD, 1928; Grand Central A. Gal., 1929, 1945; Springfield (Mass.) A. Lg., 1928; Buck Hill Falls(Pa.) AA, 1943; Carnegie Inst., 1949; Jasper Cropsey award, Hudson Valley AA, 1958. *Work*: Mun. Coll., Chicago; Buck Hill AA; IBM Coll.; Amherst Col.; Mun. Coll. City of Chicago; Encyclopaedia Britannica Coll. *Exhibited*: nationally; one-man exh.: Anderson Gal., Chicago, 1925, 1926; AIC, 1928; Grand Central A. Gal., 1930, 1934, 1938, 1943, 1947, 1948, 1953, 1956 (one-man); O'Brien A. Gal., Chicago, 1931. *Position*: Trustee, A. Fellowship, Inc.

WYCKOFF, SYLVIA SPENCER—Painter, E.
  Syracuse University; h. 705 East Molloy Rd., R.D. 2, Syracuse 11, N.Y.
B. Pittsburgh, Pa., Nov. 14, 1915. *Studied*: Syracuse Univ., B.F.A., M.F.A. *Member*: Nat. Lg. Am. Pen Women; AAUP; All. A. Syracuse; Daubers Cl., Syracuse; NAWA; Assoc. A. Syracuse; Eight Syracuse Watercolorists; Eastern AA. *Awards*: prizes, Assoc. A. Syracuse, 1943; Onondaga Historical Exh., 1945; Nat. Lg. Am. Pen Women, 1948. *Exhibited*: NAWA; Eight Syracuse Watercolorists, 1943-1952; Assoc. A. Syracuse; Daubers Cl.; Onondaga Hist. Exh.; Munson-Williams-Proctor Inst.; Cortland County Fair; Nat. Lg. Am. Pen Women; Lowe A. Center, Syracuse; Syracuse Mus. FA. *Position*: Assoc. Prof. A., Syracuse Univ., Syracuse, N.Y., 1942- .

WYETH, ANDREW NEWELL—Painter
  Chadds Ford, Pa.
B. Chadds Ford, Pa., July 12, 1917. *Studied*: with N.C. Wyeth. *Member*: NA; Audubon A. (Dir.); Phila. WC Cl. (Dir.); AWCS; Nat. Acad. A. & Let.; Am. Acad. A. & Let. *Awards*: prize, Wilmington (Del.) Mus. A.; Butler AI; award of merit med. & prize, Am. Acad. A. & Let., 1947; PAFA; Carnegie Inst.; medal, AWS; Hon. degree, D.F.A., Harvard Univ., 1955; Colby Col., 1955; Dickinson Col., 1958; Swarthmore Col., 1958. *Work*: MMA; BMFA; AIC; BMFA; MModA; Canajoharie A. Gal.; Univ. Nebraska; AGAA; New Britain Mus.; Butler AI; Wilmington Mus. A.; Lincoln Mus., England. *Exhibited*: AIC (one-man); MModA; Brussels Fair, 1958; PAFA, 1947; travel-

ing shows: Japan, India (AFA), 1954; Germany, Switzerland, England, 1955-56; Italy, 1958. *Position*: Memb. FA Com. for Smithsonian Inst.

WYETH, HENRIETTE (Mrs. Peter Hurd)—Painter
San Patricio, N.M.

B. Wilmington, Del., Oct. 22, 1907. *Studied*: Normal A. Sch., Boston, Mass.; PAFA, and with N. C. Wyeth. *Awards*: prizes, 4 firsts, Wilmington Soc. FA; PAFA, 1935. *Work*: Wilmington Soc. FA; Roswell Mus. A.; New Britain (Conn.) Mus. A.; Lubbock Mus., A.; Texas Tech. Col.; portraits in private collections. *Exhibited*: Carnegie Inst.; AIC; MMA; Roswell Mus. A.; New York City, and others.

WYKES, FREDERIC KIRTLAND—Painter
2670 Thornapple River Dr., Southwest, Grand Rapids 6, Mich.

B. Grand Rapids, Mich., July 23, 1905. *Studied*: John B. Stetson Univ.; Univ. Michigan, A.B.; AIC; & with Frederic Fursman, Jean Paul Slusser, & others. *Work*: IBM Coll.; Grand Rapids A. Gal.; Michigan Nat. Bank; mural, Orthopedic Sch., Grand Rapids, Mich.; work in private colls.

WYLIE, J(OHN) C.—Painter, T.
Address unknown.

B. El Paso, Tex., Aug. 18, 1918. *Studied*: Univ. Minnesota; New Mexico Highland Univ., B.A.; Cranbrook Acad. A., M.F.A., with Zoltan Sepeshy; AIC, and with Richard Neutra. *Awards*: prizes, Cranbrook Acad. A., 1949; Mus. New Mexico, 1946, 1951; Philbrook A. Center, 1947, 1952; AWS, 1952. *Work*: Cranbrook Acad. A.; Philbrook A. Center. *Exhibited*: Newport AA, 1946; DMFA, 1947; Brooks Mem. Mus., 1949; Detroit A. Gal., 1949; Cranbrook Acad. A., 1949; BM, 1951; Mus. New Mexico, 1946, 1951; Philbrook A. Center, 1952; AWS, 1952; St. Paul A. Gal., 1953; Minneapolis Inst. A., 1952, 1953; Mulvane A. Mus., 1954; Univ. Nebraska, 1954; one-man: Univ. New Mexico, 1948; Museum New Mexico, 1948; Baldwin-Kingrey, Chicago, 1949; Bressler A. Gal., Milwaukee, 1949; Harriet Hanley Gal., Minneapolis, 1953; Walker A. Center, 1953; John Heller Gal., N.Y., 1953. *Position*: Instr., Hd. Des. Dept., Memphis Acad. A., 1950-51; Hd. Des. Dept., Minneapolis Sch., 1952-54.

WYNNE, ALBERT GIVENS—Painter, E., Des.
Iowa Wesleyan College; h. 300 East Monroe St., Mt. Pleasant, Iowa

B. Colorado Springs, Colo., Jan. 3, 1922. *Studied*: Univ. Denver; Iowa Wesleyan Col., B.A.; State Univ. of Iowa, M.A., and with Boardman Robinson, John E. Thompson, James Lechay, and others. *Member*: Midwestern A. Conf.; AAUP. *Awards*: prizes, A. Exh., Anchorage, Alaska; Des Moines A. Center. *Exhibited*: Indiana, Pa., 1948; Wash. WC Cl., 1953; Virginia Intermont Col., 1953; Fur Rendezvous, Anchorage, Alaska, 1955, 1956; Alaska Contemp. A., 1956; Iowa A., 1957, 1958; Joslyn A. Mus., 1958; WAC, 1958; one-man: Iowa Wesleyan Col., 1950, 1957; Mel Kohler Des. Studio, Anchorage, Alaska, 1955. *Position*: Hd. A. Dept., Iowa Wesleyan Col., Mt. Pleasant, Iowa.

WYNNE, EVELYN B.—Printmaker, Comm. A., T.
3401 Thornapple St., Chevy Chase 15, Md.

B. New York, N.Y., Aug. 22, 1895. *Studied*: ASL; Royal Col. Engraving, London, England; Univ. Michigan; Corcoran A. Sch.; & with Malcolm Osborn, Avard Fairbanks, Eugene Weiss. *Member*: Lg. Am. Pen Women; Wash. WC Cl.; Wash. Pr. M.; Corcoran Alumni. *Awards*: prize, Corcoran A. Sch. 1942. *Exhibited*: Lib. Cong., 1943, 1949, 1952; Wash. SE, 1944-1954, 1958; Wash. Soc. Min. P., 1946; Soc. Wash. A., 1946, 1947, 1958; Smithsonian Inst.; CGA.

WYNNE, LESLIE BERNARD, JR.—Painter, C., Gr., I.
86 East Alegria Ave., Sierra Madre, Cal.

B. Indianapolis, Ind., May 13, 1920. *Studied*: Pasadena City Col.; Pasadena AI; Claremont Col., and with Ejnar Hansen, S. MacDonald-Wright, James Chapin, Norman Rockwell, Alfred Dewey, and others. *Member*: Cal. WC Soc.; A. of the Southwest. *Exhibited*: Pasadena AI; Los A. County Fair; Greek Theatre, Los A.; John Herron AI; Ebell Cl., Lafayette, La. (one-man.)

XCERON, JEAN—Painter
54 West 74th St., New York 23, N.Y.

B. Isari, Likosouras, Greece, Feb. 24, 1890. *Studied*: Corcoran Sch. A.; Ecole de Paris, France. *Member*: Am. Abstract A.; Fed. Mod. P. & S. *Awards*: prizes, Univ. Illinois. *Work*: MModA; PC; Guggenheim Mus.; Univ. Georgia; Univ. Illinois; Berkshire Mus. A.; Brandeis Univ.; Smith Col.; Washington Univ., St. Louis; Cahiers d'Art, Paris; Staatliche Kunsthalle, Karlsruhe, Germany. *Exhibited*: Indp. A., N.Y., 1921-1924; Guggenheim Mus., 1939-1952, 1954-1956; Am. Abstract A., 1941-1944, 1951-1958; NAC, 1942; Carnegie Inst., 1942-1944, 1946-1950; United Nations, San F., 1945; WMAA, 1946, 1949, 1952, 1956; Univ. Illinois, 1948-1950, 1952, 1955, 1957; WAC, 1953; Yale Univ., 1957; BM, 1957; Montreal Mus. FA, 1955; Rose Fried Gal., 1956; AFA, 1958; and in Paris, Athens, Barcelona, Brussels, Sao Paulo. One-man: Galerie de France, Paris, 1931; Galerie Percier, Paris, 1933; Galerie Pierre, Paris, 1934; Garland Gal., N.Y., 1935; Nierendorf Gal., 1938; Bennington Col., 1944; Janis Gal., 1950; Rose Fried Gal., 1955, 1957; traveling one-man: New Mexico, California, Washington, 1948-49; Newcomb Col., 1957. *Position*: A. Consultant, S. R. Guggenheim Museum, New York, N.Y.

YACOE, DONALD EDWARD—Painter, T.
1124 North Stoneman Ave., Alhambra, Cal.

B. Chicago, Ill., Nov. 22, 1923. *Studied*: AIC, B.F.A., M.F.A. *Awards*: Traveling scholarship, 1948, Logan prize, 1952, AIC; purchase prizes: Pasadena A. Mus., 1957; Cal. State Fair, 1957. *Work*: murals, Hotels Sherman and Chicagoan, Chicago, Ill.; Clock Country Cl., Whittier, Cal.; Turf Cl., Las Vegas, Nev.; Hotel Fremont, Las Vegas. *Exhibited*: AIC, 1947-1952; PAFA, 1949; BM, 1949; Rochester Mem. A. Gal., 1948; SAM, 1949; NAD, 1948; MModA, 1956; Los A. Mus. A., 1954, 1955, 1958; Denver A. Mus., 1954, 1955; SFMA, 1955, 1956; Pasadena A. Mus., 1956-1958; Santa Barbara A. Mus., 1955; Long Beach, Cal., 1957; Cal. State Fair, 1957, 1958. One-man: Babcock Gal., N.Y., 1946; Elizabeth Nelson Gal., Chicago, 1952; Palmer House Gal., Chicago, 1953; Landau Gal., Los A., 1954, 1956; Pasadena A. Mus., 1958. *Position*: Instr., Pasadena City Col., Pasadena, Cal.

YAGHJIAN, EDMUND—Painter, E., L.
1730 College St., Columbia, S.C.

B. Armenia, Feb. 16, 1904. *Studied*: R.I. Sch. Des., B.F.A.; ASL. *Member*: CAA; AFA; Southeastern AA; ASL; AAUP. *Awards*: prizes, So. Carolina State Exh., 1946, 1947, 1949; Southeastern Annual, 1947; Gld. South Carolina A., 1954, 1955; Columbia A. Gld., 1955. *Work*: N.Y. Pub. Lib.; Duke Univ.; Ossining (N.Y.) Mus.; Montpelier, Vt.; High Mus. A.; Gibbes A. Gal.; Furman Univ.; numerous H.S. and Hospitals. *Exhibited*: CGA, 1936, 1939, 1945; PAFA, 1934, 1936, 1939, 1941, 1943, 1949, 1951, 1953; NAD, 1934, 1936; MMA, 1942; Pepsi-Cola, 1944; WMAA, 1936, 1939, 1942; GGE, 1939; Carnegie Inst., 1936, 1941, 1945; Birmingham Mus. A.; Gld. South Carolina A., 1956, 1957; BMA; Butler AI; one-man: Kraushaar Gal.; Gibbes A. Gal.; Telfair Acad.; Columbia Mus. A.; Florence Mus. A.; Univ. Missouri; Univ. South Carolina; ASL; Vose Gal., Boston; Converse Col. *Position*: Hd. A. Dept., Univ. South Carolina, Columbia, S.C., 1945- .

YAMAMOTO, TARO—Painter
c/o L. P. Eisenhart, 270 Jay St., Brooklyn 1, N.Y.

B. Hollywood, Cal., Oct. 29, 1919. *Studied*: Santa Monica City Col.; ASL, with Kuniyoshi, Kantor, Browne, Vytlacil. *Awards*: Scholarships and Fellowships, Hans Hofmann Sch. FA, 1951; John Sloan Mem., ASL, 1952; McDowell traveling F., 1953; McDowell Colony, 1954, 1956-1957. *Work*: Methodist Church, Los Angeles; Walter Chrysler Coll. *Exhibited*: PAFA, 1951; Provincetown A. A., 1952, 1954-1958; Contemp. A. Gal., N.Y., 1953; Sun Gal., Gal. 256, Little Gal., all Provincetown, 1955-1957; one-man: ASL, 1955; Galerie Huit, Paris, 1953 (2); Provincetown A. Gal., 1958.

YAMMERINO, AURELIO JAMES—Painter, T.
353 Willett Ave., Port Chester, N.Y.; h. 67 River St., New Rochelle, N.Y.

B. New Rochelle, N.Y., Nov. 26, 1912. *Studied*s NAD, and with Leon Kroll, Gifford Beal, George Picken, and others. *Member*: Westchester A. & Crafts Gld.; Mamaroneck A. Gld.; SC; AAPL; Wash. Square AA. *Awards*: prizes, Hudson Valley AA, 1948; Hudson Valley Indp. A., 1949; White Plains, N.Y., 1948; Wash. Square AA, 1948-1950; Westchester A. & Crafts Gld., 1958; Women's Cl., Portchester, N.Y. *Exhibited*: NAD, 1951; AWS, 1951; Audubon A., 1951; All. A. Am., 1950; NAC, 1952; AAPL, 1949-1952; SC, annually; Creative A. Gal.; A.F.I. Gal.; Village A. Center; Hudson Valley AA; Hudson Soc. Indp. A.; Little Studio, N.Y.; Quaker Ridge Sch., Scarsdale, N.Y., 1954-1958; Westchester County Center, White Plains, N.Y., 1955; Travis Gal., N.Y., 1955; Greene Gal., New Rochelle; Sidin-Harris Gal., Hartsdale, N.Y.; Mamaroneck Lib., 1958 (one-man); Greenwich (Conn.) AA, 1958; Cos Cob, Conn., 1958. *Position*: Instr., Westchester County Workshop, White Plains, N.Y.; Jewish Community Center, Port Chester, N.Y.

YARDLEY, RALPH O.—*Cartoonist*
Rte 3, Box 60, Mesa Dr., Carmel, Cal.

B. Stockton, Cal., Sept. 2, 1878. *Studied*: Mark Hopkins AI. *Work*: Huntington Lib., San Marino, Cal. *Position*: Staff Cart., Stockton Record, Stockton, Cal. (Retired).

YARON, ALEXANDER A.—*Painter, Comm. A., I.*
112-53 Queens Blvd., Forest Hills 75, N.Y.; h. 9 Kew Gardens Rd., Apt. 203, Kew Gardens 15, N.Y.

B. Tallinn, Estonia, Aug. 1, 1910. *Studied*: with V. Podgoursky, V. Zasipkin, F. H. Hindle, in Shanghai. *Member*: Shanghai A. Cl. *Work*: mural, Presidential Palace, El Salvador; ports. in private colls. *Exhibited*: Cathay Mansions, Shanghai, 1943; Dominico-American Inst., 1950; Hotel Prado, Tegucigalpa, Honduras; San Salvador, 1951; New Orleans, La., 1952; Shelbourne Hotel, Miami, 1953. *Position*: Illus., J. C. Martin, Inc., New York, N.Y.*

YATER, GEORGE DAVID—*Painter, I., W.*
Brewster St., Provincetown, Mass.

B. Madison, Ind., Nov. 30, 1910. *Studied*: John Herron AI; Cape Sch. A., and with Henry Hensche. *Member*: Phila. WC Cl.; Provincetown AA; Indianapolis AA. *Awards*: Traveling scholarship, John Herron AI, 1932; Scholarship, Cape Sch. A.; prize, Hoosier Salon, 1931, 1946, 1954, 1956; Indiana State Fair, 1930; Indiana AA, 1936, 1953; Cape Cod AA, 1953. *Work*: Paper Mill Playhouse; Ford Motor Co.; N.Y.-New Haven & Hartford Railroad Coll. *Exhibited*: NAD; PAFA; AWS; Inst. Mod. A., Boston; Univ. Illinois; Currier Gal. A.; Provincetown AA; Indiana AA; Hoosier Salon; Indiana State Fair; Lyme AA; Butler AI; Cape Cod AA; Key West A. & Hist. Soc.; Henry Ford Mus.; Detroit Inst. A.; deCordova & Dana Mus.; Sarasota AA; Seligmann Gal.; Ringling Mus. A.; Chrysler A. Mus., Provincetown; Stuart Gal., Boston; one-man: Babcock Gal., 1936, 1939; Grace Horne Gal., Boston, 1941; Hanover Col., 1939, 1950; Provincetown AA, 1950; Madison, Ind., 1950; Key West A. & Hist. Soc., 1952, 1953, and others. Illus. for Ford Times; Lincoln-Mercury Times; New England Journeys; articles and photographs for Rudder; Motor Boating; Yachting; Popular Photography, etc. *Position*: Dir., Provincetown AA, 1947- ; Dir., Sarasota AA, 1955-1956.

YATES, RUTH—*Sculptor*
58 West 57th St., New York 19, N.Y.

G. Greenville, Ohio, Dec. 31, 1896. *Studied*: Cincinnati A. Acad.; ASL; Grand Central A. Sch.; Academie Julian, and with Jose De Creeft. *Member*: ASL; AEA; Pen & Brush Cl.; Westchester Clay & Chisel Cl. (Fndr. & Pres.); NSS. *Awards*: prizes, NAWA, 1939, 1951; Pen & Brush Cl., 1945, 1949; A. for Democratic Living award, 1951. *Work*: Norfolk Mus. A. & Sc.; Brookgreen Gardens, S.C. *Exhibited*: NAD, 1931; PAFA, 1942, 1943; NSS, 1940, 1949, 1952; MMA, 1942; Pen & Brush Cl., 1945-1949; Argent Gal., 1950-1952; NAWA, 1931, 1932, 1938-1943, 1949, 1951, 1952. *Positions*: Pres., NAWA, 1949-51, Treas., 1952- ; Rec. Sec., NSS, 1943-46, 1949-50; Dir., New York City Center Gal., 1953- *

YEOMANS, WALTER C.—*Printmaker, Comm. A., P.*
Aviles Sts., St. Augustine, Fla.; h. Star Route, Cornwall Bridge, Conn.

B. Avon, Ill., May 17, 1882. *Studied*: Univ. Illinois. *Member*: Chicago Soc. Et.; Boston Pr. M.; St. Augustine AA; Kent AA. *Awards*: Irvington A. & Mus. Assn.; Chicago Soc. Et. *Exhibited*: Chicago Soc. Et.; Boston Pr. M.; Rock-

port AA; Kent AA; Springfield A. Lg.; Albany Pr. Cl.; Buffalo Pr. Cl.; LC; SAGA; Laguna Beach AA; WFNY 1939; Victoria & Albert Mus., London.

YIP, RICHARD D.—*Painter, T., L.*
1432 East Sonora St., Stockton, Cal.

B. Canton, China, July 15, 1919. *Studied*: Cal. Col. A. & Crafts; Col. of the Pacific, B.A.; Univ. California, Berkeley, M.A. *Member*: Cal. WC Soc.; Marin Soc. A. *Awards*: prizes, San F. A. Festival, 1951; AWS, 1952; Outdoor Festival, Bloomfield Hills, Mich., 1954 (purchase); Cal. State Fair, 1955. *Work*: Marin Soc. A.; Col. of the Pacific. *Exhibited*: AWS, 1951; PAFA, 1953; Butler AI, 1954; Cal. WC Soc., 1948; Denver A. Mus., 1954; SAM, 1955. *Position*: Special A. Instr., Col. of the Pacific, Stockton, Cal., 1949- .

YOAKUM, DELMER J.—*Painter, Des., Ser.*
10200 West Pico St., Los Angeles, Cal.; h. 904 McCarthy St., El Segundo, Cal.

B. St. Joseph, Mo., Dec. 6, 1915. *Studied*: Kansas City AI; Jepson AI; Chouinard AI, and with Henry Lee McFee, Herbert Jepson, Phil Dike, Rico LeBrun, Richard Haines, and others. *Member*: AEA; Cal. WC Soc.; Los A. AA; Los A. Mus. Assn.; South Bay AA; Motion Picture Scenic A. *Awards*: prizes, Nat. G.I. Exh., Santa Monica, 1948; Newport Harbor purchase, 1954; Cal. WC Soc., 1954; Santa Monica, 1948, 1949; medal, Oakland A. Mus., 1949; purchase, Wiseburn Sch., Hawthorne, Cal., 1957; prize, Frye Mus. A., Seattle, 1958. *Work*: Newport (Cal.) H.S.; San Diego FA Soc. *Exhibited*: G.I. Exh., 1948; Butler AI, 1953, 1955, 1956, 1958; Denver A. Mus., 1953, 1954; Los A. Mus. A., 1946, 1948-1950, 1952, 1954-1958; Oakland A. Mus., 1949, 1950, 1952, 1954; Los A. AA, 1946-1949, 1951-1953; Univ. Wash., 1954; Arizona State Fair, 1948; Nat. Orange Show, 1949, 1952; Newport Harbor, 1952-1955; Assoc. Am. A., 1949; PAFA, 1957; Frye Mus. A., 1958; Cal. WC Soc., 1954, 1956-1958; Stockton, Cal., 1957; Univ. So. Cal., 1957; Pasadena A. Mus., 1957, 1958; Cal. PLH, 1958; traveling exh., Cal. WC Soc., 1954, 1957, 1958. *Position*: AEA Bd., Los A. Chptr., 1951-55.

YOCHIM, LOUISE DUNN—
Painter, S., T., W., C., Lith.
228 North La Salle St. (1); h. 9545 Drake Ave., Skokie, Ill.

B. Jitomir, Ukraine, July 18, 1909. *Studied*: AIC, M.A.E.; Univ. Chicago. *Member*: NAEA; Western Edu. Assn.; AEA; Chicago Soc. A.; Am. Jewish Cl.; Renaissance Soc. A. *Awards*: prizes, Chicago Soc. A., 1953; Am. Jewish A. Cl., 1947, 1954, 1955, 1958. *Exhibited*: AIC, 1935-1937, 1941, 1942, 1944; Detroit Inst. A., 1945; Chicago FA Gal., 1945; Univ. Chicago, 1946; Todros Geller Gal., 1947, 1951-1955; Assoc. A. Gal., 1949; Riverside Mus., 1951; Kansas City, Mo., 1948; Terry AI, 1952; Des Moines A. Center, 1955; Cromer & Quint Gal., Chicago, 1954, 1955; Werbe Gal., Detroit; Old Orchard Fair, Skokie, Ill.; Evanston A. Center; Spearfish, N.D.; Rapid City, N.D.; Mandel Bros., 1953-1955, 1957; 4 one-man exhs., Chicago, 1947, 1951, 1952, 1957. *Work*: in private colls. Author: "Building Human Relationships Through Art," 1954. Contributor articles and reviews to Sentinel magazine. *Position*: Instr. A., Chicago H.S., 1938-50; Acad. FA, Chicago, 1952; Supv. A., Dist. 6, Chicago Pub. Schs., at present; Instr., Chicago T. Col., 1953; Wright Jr. Col., 1952, 1953.

YOORS, JAN—*Craftsman, Des., P., W.*
329 East 47th St., New York 17, N.Y.

B. Antwerp, Belgium, Apr. 12, 1922. *Studied*: in Belgium; Univ. Col., London; Sch. Oriental & African Studies, London. *Member*: AFA. *Work*: mural, North Queens Medical Center. *Exhibited*: tapestries, Montclair A. Mus., 1956-57; DMFA, 1958; one-man: London, 1948; Brussels, 1949; New York, 1953-1955; Denver, 1956. Des.-Weaver specializing in modern tapestries.

YORK, ROBERT—*Cartoonist*
Louisville Times; h. 3611 Kings Highway, Louisville, Ky.

B. Minneapolis, Minn., Aug. 23, 1909. *Studied*: Cummings Sch. A.; Drake Univ.; Chicago Acad. FA. *Member*: Sigma Delta Chi (Journalistic Fraternity); Am. Assn. Editorial Cartoonists. *Awards*: Pulitzer Prize, 1956.

YOST, FRED—*Painter, Lith., T.*
931 Hardesty Blvd., Akron, Ohio

B. Berne, Switzerland, Nov. 6, 1888. *Studied*: Mt. Union Col., Alliance, Ohio; ASL, and with Homer Boss, John Sloan, Robert Henri. *Member*: Ohio WC Soc. *Awards*: prizes, Massillon Mus., 1944; Ohio WC Soc., 1944, 1948; Indianapolis, Ind., 1944; Tri-State Pr. M., 1945, 1946; Butler AI, 1946; Ohio Univ., 1950; Ethel Printz award, 1950; Fla. Southern Col., 1952; Akron AI, 1952, 1956-1958; medal, Phila. Pa., 1950. *Work*: Massillon Mus.; Youngstown Pub. Sch. Coll.; Butler AI; Akron AI; Kennedy & Co., N.Y.; Beaver Col., Beaver Falls, Pa.; Block Gal., Indianapolis; Prospect Park, N.Y.; murals, Sioux City Steak House; Sioux City A. Center; City Hall, Sioux City. *Exhibited*: MMA, 1945; AIC; Butler AI, 1947-1951; Ohio WC Soc.; PAFA, 1948-1950; Akron AI, 1947-1951, 1958; Fla. Southern Col., 1952; Ohio Univ., 1950; Columbus Gal. FA, 1947-1950; Carnegie Inst., 1946-1948; AWS, 1958. *Position*: Instr. A., Akron, AI, Akron, Ohio; Cur. Historical House of Refuge, 1955.

YOUNG, ARTHUR RAYMOND—*Painter, Gr., E.*
420 West 118th St., New York 27, N.Y.

B. New York, N.Y., July 10, 1895. *Studied*: NAD; ASL. *Work*: British Mus., London. *Exhibited*: BM; one-man exh.: Weyhe Gal.; Daniels Gal.; Pan-Hellenic Engineers Cl. Contributor to: Art Education Today. Lectures: Graphic Arts; Painting. *Position*: Prof., Painting & Graphics, T. Col., Columbia Univ., New York, N.Y., 1927- .*

YOUNG, CHARLES MORRIS—*Painter, Et.*
Hare's Lane, Radnor, Pa.; s. Drifton, Pa.

B. Gettysburg, Pa., Sept. 23, 1869. *Studied*: PAFA; Acad. Colarossi, Paris, France. *Member*: ANA; Phila. A. Cl. *Awards*: medals, St. Louis Expo., 1904; Pan-Pacific Expo., 1915; PAFA, 1921; Phila. A. Cl.; Buenos Aires Expo., 1910; Amsterdam, Holland, 1929; prizes, PAFA, 1921, 1925. *Work*: PAFA; CGA; Nat. Gal., Budapest; Albright A. Gal.; Rochester Mem. A. Gal.; Nat. Gal., Santiago, Chile; Reading Mus. A.; PMA; PAFA; Allentown A. Gal.; Boston A. Cl.; St. Louis A. Cl.; Sandhurst Military Acad., England, and in private colls.

YOUNG, CHIC—*Cartoonist*
c/o King Features, 235 East 45th St., New York, N.Y.*

YOUNG, (F.) CLIFF(ORD)—*Illustrator, W., P., L., T.*
19 West 44th St.; h. 364 West 57th St., New York 19, N.Y.

B. New Waterford, Ohio, Dec. 27, 1905. *Studied*: Pittsburgh AI, and with Charles Schroeder, Leon Kroll, Harvey Dunn, and others. *Member*: SI; SC; A. Gld.; AAPL; NSMP; Fifty Am. A.; Nat. Soc. Painters in Casein. Author, I., "Figure Drawing Without a Model," 1946; "Drawing Drapery from Head to Toe." *Work*: murals, Federal Hall, N.Y.; St. Francis Monastery, Utuado, P.R.*

YOUNG, DOROTHY O. (Mrs. Jack J. Sophir)—*Sculptor, P., T., C.*
9120 Meyer Lane, Crestwood 23, Mo.

B. St. Louis, Mo., June 22, 1903. *Studied*: St. Louis Sch. FA, Washington Univ.; ASL, and with E. Wuerpel, Leo Lentelli, George Bridgman. *Member*: St. Louis A. Gld.; County AA; Soc. Indp. A.; St. Louis; Am. A. All. *Awards*: prizes, St. Louis A. Gld., 1925, 1949; Soc. Indp. A., 1937, 1940, 1943, 1944, 1945, 1947-1949, 1950, 1952, 1953, 1955; Henry Shaw Cactus Soc., 1955; St. Louis County Fair, 1947. *Work*: Office, St. Louis Council, Boy Scouts of Am.; Rockwoods (Mo.) Mus.; Jackson Park Sch., St. Louis. *Exhibited*: St. Louis A. Gld., 1925-1952; Kansas City AI, 1928-1932, 1934; Soc. Indp. A., St. Louis, 1930-1955; Joslyn A. Mus., 1939, 1941, 1944; Springfield A. Mus., 1947; CAM, 1939-1946, 1949; William Rockhill Nelson Gal. A., 1947; St. Louis A. Gld., 1946 (one-man); Am. A. All., 1946-1955; Mo. Fed. Cl. traveling exh., 1947, 1948, 1952-1955; St. Louis A. Festival, 1950; Peoples' A. Center Assn. Fair, 1955; St. Louis A. Lg., 1924-1934.*

YOUNG, FLORENCE—*Painter, Eng., T.*
29 South Granada Ave., Alhambra, Cal.

B. Fort Dodge, Iowa, Nov. 6, 1872. *Studied*: AIC, with John Vanderpoel; ASL, with Kenyon Cox, Carol Beckwith, Frank DuMond, William M. Chase, and others. *Member*: Women Painters of the West. *Awards*: prizes, Los A. Mus. A., 1943; Greek Theatre, 1955; A. of the Southwest, 1951. *Work*: Pomona Col. *Exhibited*: GGE, 1939; Los A. Mus. A.; Los A. Pub. Lib.; Ebell Cl.; Friday Morning Cl.; City Hall, Los A.; Greek Theatre; San Diego, Santa Paula, Cal., and others. Contributor to Widening Horizons in Creative Art.*

YOUNG, FRANK HERMAN—*Designer, W., T.*
30 East Adams St., Chicago 3, Ill.

B. Nebraska City, Neb., Dec. 11, 1888. *Studied*: AIC. *Member*: SI; Chicago Gld. Free Lance A. Author: "Advertising Layout," 1928; "Modern Advertising Art," 1931; "Technique of Advertising Layout," 1935. Contributor to: trade publications. Lectures: Advertising Layout. *Position*: Founder, Pres., Young & Timmins Advertising Art Studios, Chicago, Ill.; Founder and Dir., Am. Acad. A., Chicago, Ill.

YOUNG, GLADYS G.—*Painter*
9 East 63rd St., New York 21, N.Y.

B. Vevey, Switzerland. *Studied*: ASL; & in Paris with Andre L'Hote. *Member*: Audubon A.; N.Y. Soc. Women A. *Award*: prize, NAWA, 1951, 1958. *Exhibited*: CGA, 1941; Gal. 460 Park Ave., N.Y., 1941 (one-man); Ferargil Gal., 1945 (one-man).

YOUNG, J. DONALD—*Educator*
Occidental College, Los Angeles 41, Cal.; h. 541 South Greenwood Ave., Pasadena 10, Cal.

B. New York, N.Y., May 15, 1897. *Studied*: Columbia Univ., A.B.; Princeton Univ., M.A., M.F.A.; Am. Sch. Classical Studies, Athens, Greece. *Member*: CAA; Archaeological Inst. Am.; Am. Soc. for Aesthetics. Contributor to: American Journal of Archaeology; Art Bulletin; College Art Journal. *Position*: Instr., 1923-25, Asst. Prof., 1925-36, Columbia Univ., N.Y.; Asst. Prof., 1936-38, Assoc. Prof., 1938-40, Prof., 1940- , Chm. A. Dept., 1937- , Occidental Col., Los Angeles 41, Cal.

YOUNG, JOSEPH LOUIS—
Mural Painter, S., C., Gr., E., L.
8426 Melrose Ave.; h. 7917½ West Norton Ave., Los Angeles 46, Cal.

B. Pittsburgh, Pa., Nov. 27, 1919. *Studied*: Westminster Col., New Wilmington, Pa., A.B.; BMFA Sch.; ASL; Cranbrook Acad. A.; MIT; mosaics in Rome with Gulio Giovanetti. *Member*: NSMP; F., Intl. Inst. A. & Lets.; Los A. AA. *Awards*: Guest, Am. Acad. in Rome, 1951-52; Abbey scholarship for mural painting, 1949-50; F., BMFA Sch., 1951-52; F., Huntington Hartford Fnd., 1952-53. *Work*: murals, QM Headquarters, Miami Beach, Fla.; Baptist Church, Manchester, Conn.; Courtyard Silversmiths, Boston; BMFA Sch.; Temple Emanuel, Beverly Hills, Cal.; Don Bosco Tech. H.S., San Gabriel, Cal.; cantilevered mural (mosaic) Los Angeles Police Facilities Bldg.; Southland Shopping Center, Los. A.; Texaco Bldg., Los. A. *Exhibited*: Arch. Lg., 1951; Butler AI, 1948; Nat. Army Exh., 1945; one-man: Falk-Raboff Gal., Los A., 1953. Author: "Bibliography of Mural Painting in USA," 1946; "A Plan for Mural Painting in Israel" (for Ministry of Education of the State of Israel); "A Course in Making Mosaics," 1957. Work subject of documentary film with sound and color, "The World of Mosaic." Contributor of articles to AIA Bulletin of Southern California. Lectures (with slides): The History of Architectural Mosaics; Murals for Contemporary Architecture, etc. *Position*: Dir., Pittsburgh office of Stewart Howe Alumni Service, 1941-42; Radio News Analyst, United Press Assn., N.Y., 1942-43; Special Services, AAF, 1943-46; Chm., Exhs., BMFA Sch., 1950-51; Instr., BMFA Sch., 1950-51; Dir., Mosaic Workshop, Los Angeles, Cal.

YOUNG, MAHONRI SHARP—*Museum Director*
Columbus Gallery of Fine Arts, East Broad St., Columbus 15, Ohio; h. Lancaster Rd., Granville, Ohio

B. New York, N.Y., July 23, 1911. *Studied*: Dartmouth Col., A.B.; Univ. Paris; N.Y. Univ., Inst. FA, M.A.

Member: Assn. A. Mus. Dir. Author: "Old George," 1940. Contributor to American Scholar; Art News. Exhibitions arranged, "International Masterpieces," 1956; "Sir Joshua Reynolds and His American Contemporaries," 1957, Columbus Gal. FA. *Position*: Instr., A. Dept., Sarah Lawrence Col., 1941-50; Chm. A. Dept., Sarah Lawrence Col., 1948-50; Actg. Dir., Community A. Program, Munson-Williams-Proctor Inst., Utica, N.Y., 1951-53; Dir., Columbus Gal. FA, Columbus, Ohio, 1953- .

YOUNG, MAY BELLE—*Painter*
Hotel Geneve, Mexico City, D.F.

B. Charleston, S.C., Aug. 22, 1891. *Studied*: NAD; ASL; PIASch.; Grand Central Sch. A. *Work*: Victoria (B.C.) Pub. Lib., and in private colls. *Exhibited*: NAWA; Town Hall Cl., N.Y.; Studio Gld.; Gotham Painters; Phila. WC Cl.; AWS; one-man: Thos. E. Cook Travel Bureau, N.Y.; Jacksonville A. Center, 1950; Barbizon Hotel, N.Y., 1949; St. Augustine (Fla.) AA, 1955.*

YOUNG, WEBB—*Painter*
702 Canyon Rd.; h. 540 Camino Rancheros, Santa Fe, N.M.

B. Covington, Ky., Sept. 2, 1913. *Studied*: AIC, with Gerald Cassidy; Famous Artists Schs. *Exhibited*: Mus. New Mexico, Santa Fe, regularly; traveling exhs., Taos AA, Santa Fe A. Gal. Contributor covers to New Mexico Magazine; 20 booklet covers for Nat. Park Service's Monuments; creator Air Corps 188th Fighter Squadron's symbol; New Mexico State Tourist Bureau's Vacation Map; State Game & Fish Dept.'s illus. fishing map; contributor to Ford Times. Specializing in The New Mexico scene.

YOUNG, WILLIAM THOMAS (TOM)—
Painter, Et., Lith., E.
207 West 21st St., New York 11, N.Y.

B. Huntington, W. Va., Oct. 7, 1924. *Studied*: Univ. Cincinnati; Univ. Alabama, B.F.A., M.A.; Ohio State Univ.; Univ. So. California; Columbia Univ.; John Herron AI; Chouinard AI; Hans Hofmann Sch. FA; Cincinnati Acad. A. *Member*: Comm. on A. Edu. *Awards*: prizes, Scholarship, John Herron AI, 1940; Alabama WC Soc., 1954; Staten Island Mus. Hist. & A., 1955. *Work*: Univ. Alabama; Army Air Force Base, Okla. (mural). *Exhibited*: Alabama WC Soc., 1949; PMA, 1950; BM, 1950; Canton A. Mus., 1951; Birmingham, 1953, 1954; N.Y. City Center, 1956, 1957; Wagner Col., 1957; CM, 1946; Mich. State Univ., 1947; Montgomery Mus. FA, 1950; A. Lg. of Long Island, 1954; Pietrantonio Gal., N.Y., 1956; Kauffman Gal., 1956; Tanager Gal., 1957; Davida Gal., 1957; March Gal., 1958; Marino Gal., 1958; one-man: Univ. Alabama, 1948-1950. *Positions*: Instr., A., Univ. Alabama, 1949-50; Prof. A., Alabama State Col., 1950-52; Hd. A. Dept., Wagner College, Staten Island, N.Y., 1953- .

YOUNGERMAN, JACK—*Painter*
27 Coenties Slip, New York 4, N.Y.

B. Louisville, Ky., Mar. 25, 1926. *Studied*: Univ. North Carolina; and in Paris. *Work*: Reynolds Bldg., Richmond, Va. *Exhibited*: Carnegie Inst., 1958; CGA, 1959; and group shows in Paris. One-man: Betty Parsons Gal., N.Y., 1958.

YOUNGERMAN, REYNA ULLMAN—*Painter, L., T.*
3000 Prairie Ave., Miami Beach, Fla.

B. New Haven, Conn., June 26, 1902. *Studied*: Yale Sch. FA, B.F.A.; ASL; & with Wayman Adams, Alexander Brook, Jerry Farnsworth. *Member*: Conn. Acad. FA; Blue Dome F.; Fla. A. Group; Sarasota AA; NAWA; AEA; Miami WC Soc.; Des.-Dec. Gld.; New Haven Paint & Clay Cl.; Brush & Palette Cl.; Meriden SA; Conn. WC Soc. *Awards*: F., Tiffany Fnd., 1926-1927; prizes, New Haven Paint & Clay Cl., 1942; Meriden SA, 1934, 1945, 1946; Miami A.; Blue Dome Fellowship; Pan-American portrait award; AAPL; Lowe Gal.; Conn. Acad. FA; Fla. Painters Group; medal, Beaux-Arts (4). *Work*: Tiffany Fnd.; Superior Court, New Haven, Conn. *Exhibited*: NAWA, 1932-1946; BMFA; Morgan Mem.; Avery Mus.; Yale Gal. FA; NAD; Conn. Acad. FA; New Haven Paint & Clay Cl.; Brush & Palette Cl.; Copley Soc., Boston; Norton Gal. A.; Soc. Four A.; Miami A. Center; Barzansky Gal.; Butler AI; Argent Gal.; Audubon A.; Mayo Hill Gal., Wellfleet; Provincetown A. Gal.; Sarasota AA;

Lowe Gal. A.; Rockport A. Gal.; Hartford Atheneum; Montreal, Canada; PAFA; Nationale Palazio des Artes, Cuba, and others.

YOUNGLOVE, RUTH ANN (Mrs. Benjamin Rhees Loxley)—*Painter, C., L.*
1180 Yocum St., Pasadena 3, Cal.

B. Chicago, Ill., Feb. 14, 1909. *Studied*: Univ. California at Los A., B.E.; & with Orrin White. *Member*: Cal. WC Soc.; Pasadena SA; A. Assoc.; Laguna Beach AA. *Awards*: prizes, Los A. County Fair, 1937-1941. *Exhibited*: Pasadena SA; Laguna Beach AA, 1956-1958; Los Angeles City Hall, 1957; Greek Theatre, 1957; Friday Morning Cl., 1956, 1958; Pasadena Pub. Lib., 1958; Pasadena Soc. A., 1957; Santa Paula, 1955, 1957, 1958; Sierra Cl., 1957, 1958; Newport Harbor, 1954, 1955; Pasadena, 1955 (one-man); Pasadena Folk Dance Group, 1945-1958. Lectures: Landscape Painting. *Position*: Patron Chm., Pasadena Soc. A., 1954-55, 1955-56.

YUNKERS, ADJA (Mr.)—*Painter, Lith., Eng., L., I., T.*
351 East 19th St., New York 3, N.Y.

B. Riga, Latvia, July 15, 1900. *Studied*: Leningrad, Berlin, Paris, London. *Awards*: Guggenheim F., 1949-1950, 1954-1955; prize, BM, 1952. *Work*: MMoA; MMA; N.Y. Pub. Lib.; BM; PMA; Phila. Pr. Cl.; BMA; FMA; BMFA; WMA; Springfield Mus. A.; Colorado Springs FA Center; NGA; CGA; Minneapolis Inst. A.; Bibliotheque Nationale, Paris; Bibliotheque Royale de Belgique, Brussels; Johannesburg A. Gal., South Africa; Mus. Mod. A., Sao Paulo, Brazil, and in private coll. *Exhibited*: MModA, 1949; Int. Print Exh., Paris, 1949; Contemp. Am. Gr. A., Germany, 1950-1952; Int. Print Exh., Paris, 1951-1952; Int. Print Exh., Switzerland, 1951-1952; Galeria Buchholz, Madrid, 1952; one-man: Kleeman Gal.; CGA; Smithsonian Inst.; Phila. A. All.; AIC; Colorado Springs FA Center; Pasadena AI; SFMA; Ministry of Information, Lisbon; Mus. Mod. A., Madrid, 1955; Paris, London, Basel, Florence, Rome, Berlin and New York. *Position*: Ed., Publ., "Ars-Portfolio," Stockholm, Sweden, 1942-45, and Albuquerque, N.M., 1952- ; Faculty, New Sch. for Social Research, New York, N.Y., 1947-1956; Cooper Union, New York, N.Y.

YUTZEY, MARVIN GLEN—*Designer, C.*
908 Sixth St., Moundsville, W. Va.

B. Canton, Ohio, May 25, 1912. *Studied*: Cleveland Sch. A. *Member*: IDI; Am. Ceramic Soc. *Position*: Des.-Dir., Fostoria Glass Co., Moundsville, W. Va., 1936- .

ZACCONE, FABIAN F.—*Painter, Des., Lith., T., L.*
6002 Hudson Ave., West New York, N.J.

B. Italy, Sept. 3, 1910. *Studied*: PIASch.; N.Y. Univ., M.A. *Member*: Knickerbocker A.; Associate A. New Jersey. *Awards*: prize, Montclair A. Mus., 1952; medals, Montclair A. Mus., 1934, 1936, 1939; Audubon A., 1951; Jersey City Mus., 1952; NAC, 1955; New Jersey P. & S. Soc. *Work*: mural, Pub. Lib., West New York, N.J.; stained glass windows and mosaic mural, Mother Cabrini Shrine, New York, N.Y. *Exhibited*: LC; Riverside Mus., 1944; Artists of Today, 1943, 1944 (one-man); BM; Kennedy Gal.; NAD; NAC; Sweden; Venice, Italy. I., "Behold Your King," 1946. *Position*: A. Supv., West New York, N.J., Pub. Schs.

ZAKHEIM, BERNARD BARUCH—
Painter, S., C., Des., T.
1512 19th St., San Francisco 7, Cal.; h. 9790 O'Connell Rd., Sebastopol, Cal.

B. Warsaw, Poland, Apr. 4, 1898. *Studied*: San F. Sch. FA; & in Europe. *Awards*: med., San F. AA, 1935, 1940. *Work*: SFMA; frescoes, Coit Mem. Tower, Jewish Community Center, Univ. Cal. Medical Sch., Univ. Cal. Hospital, all in San F.; murals, USPO, Mineola, Tex.; Rusk, Tex.; Alemany Health Center, San F. *Exhibited*: San Diego traveling exh., 1940; U.S. Treasury Dept., 1940; SFMA, annually; GGE, 1939; Palace Legion Honor; Wash. State Fair, 1946; Rome, Italy, 1958. *Position*: Instr., Adult Dept., San F., Pub. Sch.; Instr., Occupational Therapy, Presidio, San Francisco, Cal.

ZEIGLER, JOHN ARVIN—*Designer*

Procter & Gamble, Cincinnati 1, Ohio; h. 32 Winnebago Dr., Milford, Ohio

B. Cincinnati, Ohio, Jan. 30, 1930. *Studied*: Col. of App. A., Univ. Cincinnati, B.S. Illus., "Training for Fun and Profit," 1946. Contributor cartoons to Sat. Eve. Post. *Position*: Asst. A. Dir., Procter & Gamble Co., Cincinnati, Ohio; Vice-Pres., Cincinnati A. Dir. Cl.

ZEIL, WILLIAM FRANCIS VON—*Painter, Eng., Hist.*

115 Elfreth's Alley, Philadelphia, Pa.

B. Harrisburg, Pa., July 11, 1914. *Studied*: Villanova Col., A.B.; Webster Col., St. Louis Univ., M.A.; & with Carl Shaffer, Morris Blackburn. *Member*: Phila. Pr. Cl.; Phila. A. All.; Mediaeval Acad. Am. *Awards*: Hon. degree, LL.D., Webster Col., 1945; med., Villanova Col., 1934. *Exhibited*: Phila. Pr. Cl., 1945, 1946, 1953-1955, 1957, 1958; Phila. A. All., 1944, 1945; Phila. Sketch Cl.; 1943; Ragan Gal., 1943; C. Shaffer Gal., Phila., 1958. Author: "The Development of Christian Symbolism in Western Art," 1945. *Position*: Artist-in-Residence, Girard Col., Philadelphia, Pa.

ZEIS, JOSEPH—*Cartoonist*

601 Hillcrest Ave., Morrisville, Pa.

B. Trenton, N.J., Apr. 12, 1923. *Exhibited*: Intl. Exh., Bordighera, Italy, 1955, 1956, 1957. Contributor of cartoons to Sat. Eve. Post; Redbook; True; American Weekly and other national publications.

ZERBE, KARL—*Painter*

1807 Atapha St., Tallahassee, Fla.

B. Berlin, Germany, Sept. 16, 1903. *Studied*: in Germany and Italy; Boston Univ. (Ctf.). *Member*: AEA; CAA; SAGA. *Awards*: John Barton Paine award, Richmond, Va., 1942; Blair award, Chicago, 1944; Harris award, Chicago, 1946; Carnegie Inst., 1949; PAFA, 1947, 1949, 1951. *Work*: Nat. Inst. A. & Let.; MMA; WMAA; BM; Albright A. Gal.; AIC; Butler AI; CAM; Cranbrook Acad. A.; FMA; Harvard Univ.; Ft. Worth AA; John Herron AI; Los A. Mus. A.; MIT; Munson-Williams-Proctor Inst.; Newark Mus.; New Britain AI; PMG; R.I.Sch. Des.; San Diego FA Gal.; VMFA; Walker A. Center; Tel-Aviv Mus.; Univ. Georgia, Illinois, Iowa, Nebraska, Minnesota, Oklahoma, Rochester, Washington; IBM; Des Moines A. Center, and others. *Exhibited*: nationally; one-man: Harvard Univ., 1934; Berkshire Mus., 1943, 1947; AIC, 1945, 1946; Phila. A. All., 1949, Munson-Williams-Proctor Inst., 1950; Inst. Contemp. A., 1950; Currier Gal. A., 1951; MIT, 1952; BMA, 1952; deYoung Mem. Mus., 1952; Colorado Springs FA Center, 1952. *Position*: Hd., Dept. Painting, BMFA Sch., Boston, Mass., 1937-54; Prof. A., Fla. State Univ., Tallahassee, Fla., 1954- ; Pres., AEA, 1957-59.

ZERBO, VALERIO J., JR. (Bill)—*Designer, Comm. A.*

159 East 64th St., New York 21, N.Y.; h. "Willowmere," Riverside, Conn.

B. New York, N.Y., Nov. 18, 1905. *Studied*: ASL; N.Y. Acad. FA; and in Rome, Italy. *Member*: SI; A. & Writers.*

ZEREGA, ANDREA PIETRO—*Painter, T., L.*

2908 M. St., Northwest, Washington, D.C.

B. De Zerega, Italy, Oct. 21, 1917. *Studied*: Corcoran Sch. A., with Richard Lahey, Hobart Nichols, Mathilde Mueden Leisenring; in Italy, with Dr. Gaspare Biggio; Tiffany Fnd. *Member*: A. Gld. Wash.; Soc. Wash. A.; Wash. WC Cl.; SSAL; Landscape Cl. Wash.; Corcoran Alum. Assn.; Georgetown A. Group; Third Order Secular of St. Francis of Assisi, Mt. St. Sepulchre Fraternity. *Awards*: F., Tiffany Fnd., 1938; prizes, Wash. A. 1940; Soc. Wash. A., 1942; Times Herald Exh., 1943; Landscape Cl., 1945; BMA, 1952; medals, Soc. Wash. A., 1945; Landscape Cl., 1944, 1946, 1952, 1953; Religious Art Exh., Wash., D.C., 1958. *Work*: PMG; Barnett Aden Gal.; Tiffany Fnd.; Butler Inst. Am. A.; Toledo Mus. A., and in private colls. U.S. & abroad. *Exhibited*: CGA; PAFA; Carnegie Inst.; NAD; MMA; VMFA; Va. Acad. FA; PMG; Ferargil Gal.; Wash. A. Cl.; Univ. Kentucky; Catholic Univ. of Am.; BMA; Minn. State Fair; Richmond AA; Brooks Mem. A. Gal.; Currier Gal. A.; Vassar Col.; Muehlenberg Col.; J. B. Speed Mem. Mus.; Munson-Williams-Proctor Inst.; U.S. Nat. Mus.; Barnett Aden Gal.; Franz Bader Gal., Wash.,

D.C.; Univ. Illinois; one-man: Wash. Pub. Lib.; Catholic Univ. of Am.; Whyte Gal.; Playhouse Gal., Wash., D.C.; CGA, 1952 (retrospective). *Position*: Dir., Studio San Luca, Georgetown, D.C.; Instr. A., Marymount Col., Arlington, Va.

ZEVON, IRENE (Mrs. John Murray Barton)—*Painter, Gr.*

222 West 23rd St., New York 11, N.Y.

B. New York, N.Y., Nov. 24, 1918. *Studied*: Tschacbasov Sch. A. *Member*: NAWA; Village A. Center. *Award*: prize, NAWA, 1957. *Exhibited*: NAWA; NAD; Intl. Graphic Exh.

ZIBELLI, THOMAS A. (TOM ZIB)—*Cartoonist*

167 East Devonia Ave., Mt. Vernon, N.Y.

B. Mt. Vernon, N.Y., Oct. 28, 1916. *Studied*: Grand Central A. Sch.; Commercial Illustration Studios. *Exhibited*: OWI Exh., Am. FA Soc., N.Y., 1943, 1944; El Paso, Tex., 1945. Contributor cartoons to Best Cartoons to Best Cartoons of the Year, 1947-1956 inclusive; Best From Yank; "Honey, I'm Home"; "You've Got Me on the Hook"; "But That's Unprintable," etc. Also, cartoons to Colliers; Look; Sat. Eve. Post; Ladies Home Journal; American; This Week; Argosy and many other national magazines.

ZIEGLER, LAURA (BELLE)—*Sculptor*

via del Babuino 144, Rome, Italy; h. 1471 East Columbus St., Columbus 6, Ohio

B. Columbus, Ohio. *Studied*: Columbus A. Sch.; Ohio State Univ., B.F.A.; Cranbrook Acad. A., and in Italy. *Member*: S. Gld. *Awards*: prize, Columbus A. Lg., 1947-1949; Fulbright grant, Rome, Italy, 1950. *Work*: sc., MModA; Columbus Gal. FA, and in many private colls. 18 foot Cross, St. Stephens Episcopal Church, Columbus, Ohio. *Exhibited*: Biennale, Venice, Italy, 1956, 1958; one-man: Schneider Gal., Rome, 1955; O'Hara Gal., London, England, 1956; Duveen-Graham Gal., N.Y., 1956; Inst. Contemp. A., Boston, 1957; Columbus Gal. FA, 1957.

ZIEGLER, MARY—*Associate Museum Director*

Frye Museum of Art, 704 Terry Ave., Seattle, Wash.*

ZIEGLER, SAMUEL P.—*Painter, Gr., E.*

2908 West Lowden St., Fort Worth 9, Tex.

B. Lancaster, Pa., Jan. 4, 1882. *Studied*: PAFA; Texas Christian Univ., B.A., M.A. *Member*: AFA; AAPL; Texas FA Assn.; Ft. Worth AA; Ft. Worth City A. Comm. (1925-38). *Awards*: Cresson traveling scholarship, PAFA, 1912; med., Dallas, Tex., 1924; prize, SSAL, 1929. *Work*: Carnegie Lib., Univ. Cl., Texas Christian Univ., Mus. A., Stirling & Polytechnic H.S., all in Ft. Worth, Tex. *Exhibited*: SSAL, annually in regional & local exhs. *Position*: Hd. A. Dept., Texas Christian Univ., Ft. Worth, Tex., 1926-53; Prof. Emeritus, Advisor, 1953- .

ZIEGLER, SIEGFRIED—*Painter, Gr.*

27 West 67th St., New York 23, N.Y.

B. Munich, Germany, Mar. 23, 1894. *Studied*: Munich Acad. FA, with Angelo Jank, Hugo von Habermann. *Member*: Audubon A. *Awards*: Govt. prize, Munich, 1915; silver medal, Intl. Exh., Munich, 1921. *Work*: State Coll., Munich; Lafayette Mus., Paris, France; Kaiser Friedrich Mus., Berlin; Newcomen Soc., London; Warwick, Pa.; Annheuser-Busch Co. *Exhibited*: Audubon A., annually. Contributor to La Revue Moderne, Paris; St. Paul Pioneer Press; Die Jugend, Munich.

ZIGROSSER, CARL—*Museum Curator, W., Cr.*

Philadelphia Museum of Art, Parkway at 26th St.; h. 5535½ Pulaski Ave., Philadelphia 44, Pa.

B. Indianapolis, Ind., Sept. 28, 1891. *Studied*: Columbia Univ., A.B. *Member*: Phila. A. All.; Phila. Pr. Cl. *Awards*: Guggenheim F., 1939, 1940. Author, Ed., "Twelve Prints by Contemporary American Artists," 1919; "The Artist in America," 1942; "John B. Flannagan," 1942; "Kaethe Kollwitz," 1946; "Lithographs by Toulouse Lautrec," 1946; "The Book of Fine Prints," 1948; "Caroline Durieux," 1949; "Masterpieces of Drawing in America," 1950; "Ars Medica," 1955; "The Expressionists: A Survey of their Graphic Art," 1957, and other books. Contributor to: Print Collector's Quarterly, Print Connoisseur, Creative Art, Twice a Year, Magazine of Art, & other publications. Consultant in Graphic Art of the XVIII-XX Centuries for the Carnegie Study of the Arts of the United States. *Position*: Dir., Weyhe Gal., New York, N.Y., 1919-40; Cur., Prints & Drawings, PMA, Philadelphia, Pa., 1941- ; Trustee, Solomon R. Guggenheim Fnd., 1951- ; Vice-Dir., PMA, 1955- .

ZILVERBERG, JIM—*Cartoonist, Comm. A., W.*
2921 Lyndale Ave., South, Minneapolis, Minn.; h. 14833 Timber Hill Road, Hopkins, Minn.

B. Tripp, S.D., Aug. 23, 1918. *Studied*: Northern State T. Col., Aberdeen, S.D. *Work*: Political cartoons, Sec. of Agriculture Coll., Wash., D.C.; Nat. Red Cross Campaign. Contributor to cartoon anthologies; magazine covers and illus.; sport features and illus. to Minneapolis Star; Farm Journal; Sports Afield; Farmers Union, etc. Awarded Minnesota Outdoor Award for contribution to conservation through cartooning. Creator of new comic strip, "The Tillers" as well as "Hired Hiram." Lectures on Art and Cartooning.

ZILZER, GYULA—*Etcher, Lith., P., Des.*
27 West 96th St., New York 25, N.Y.

B. Budapest, Hungary, Feb. 3, 1898. *Studied*: Royal Acad. A., Budapest; Hans Hofmann Sch. A., Munich; Royal Polytechnic Univ., Budapest; Academie Colorossi, Paris. *Awards*: Intl. Exh., Moscow, 1927 (purchase); Intl. Exh., Bordeaux, France, 1927; Scholarship, French Govt., 1928. *Work*: Graphische Cabinet, Munich; Mus. Mod. A., Budapest; ports., U.S. District Court for the Southern Dist. of N.Y.; graphics: MMoDA; N.Y. Pub. Lib.; MMA; Los A. Mus. A.; San Diego FA Center; Luxembourg Mus., Paris; Musee de l'Art d'Occident, Moscow. *Exhibited*: In Europe, 1925-1930; AIC, 1932-1937; one-man: Galerie Billiet, Paris, 1926; Amsterdam, Holland, 1931; Bloomsbury Gal., London, 1931; Mellon Gal., Phila., 1933; New Sch. for Social Research, N.Y., 1933; Assoc. Am. A., 1937; Los A. Mus. A., 1943; deYoung Mem. Mus., San F., 1927; Art of Today Gal., N.Y., 1957. Production Des. & A. Dir., for major films, Hollywood, Cal., 1938-48; Cinerama, 1958.

ZIMMERMAN, ALICE E.—*Craftsman, T.*
"Ridgehigh," P.O. Box 564 Gatlinburg, Tenn.

B. Mount Vernon, Ind. *Studied*: DePauw Univ., B.M.; Columbia Univ., M.A.; Universal Sch. Crafts; AIC; Ringling Sch. A.; Univ. Tennessee Craft Workshop; Craft Study Tour of Scandinavia; San Miguel de Allende, Mexico; Univ. Tennessee. *Member*: NAEA; Indiana Craftsmen; Southern Highland Handcraft Gld.; AAUW; Western A.; Indiana A. Edu. Assn.; Midwest Des-Craftsmen. *Exhibited*: Am. Jewelry & Related Objects Exh., 1955, 1956, 1958; Louisville A. Center, 1955; Indianapolis Hobby Show, 1954; Southern Highlands, 1949, 1950, 1951; Hoosier Craft Gld. Fairs, 1949-1957; Tri-State Annual, 1950-1958. Contributor to School Arts magazine. Lectures with slides on various crafts. *Position*: Instr., Hanover H.S., 1928-33; Reitz H.S., 1934-58; Evansville Col., Evansville, Ind., 1947- .

ZIMMERMAN, CARL JOHN—*Painter*
Kerr Cemetery Rd., Loveland, Ohio

B. Indianapolis, Ind., Sept. 13, 1900. *Studied*: Herron AI; Chicago Acad. FA; Cincinnati A. Acad.; & with Jean Marchand in Paris. *Member*: Cincinnati AC; Professional A., Cincinnati. *Work*: murals, Cathedral of St. Monica, Cincinnati; St. Paul's Church, Marty, S.D.; SS. Peter & Paul Church, Norwood, Ohio; Cincinnati Cl. *Exhibited*: regional & local exh.*

ZIMMERMAN, ELINOR CARR—*Painter*
212 West Highland St., Lakeland, Fla.

B. St. Louis, Mo., Dec. 14, 1878. *Studied*: Washington Univ., B.S., B.Arch.; PAFA, and with A.M. Archambault; Mabel Welch, Wayman Adams, Gertrude Whiting. *Member*: Pa. Soc. Min. P.; AAPL; Phila. Plastic Cl. *Work*: PMA; many miniature commissions. *Awards*: Fla. Southern Col., 1952. *Exhibited*: PAFA, 1936, 1949; AAPL, 1945, 1948; miniature exhs., Chicago, Los Angeles, Washington, New York, and elsewhere. One-man: Asbury Park, N.J.; Kansas City; San Diego FA Gal.

ZIMMERMAN, FREDERICK A.—*Painter, Cr., T., S., L.*
20 West Colorado Blvd., Pasadena, Cal.

B. Canton, Ohio. *Studied*: Univ. Southern California; & with Victor Brenner. *Member*: Pasadena SA (life); Pasadena FA Cl.; Nat. Inst. A. & Lets. (Bd. Adv.); Pasadena AA. *Work*: John Muir Pub. Sch., Seattle, Wash.; Pasadena Pub. Lib.; Monrovia (Cal.) H.S. *Exhibited*: Pasadena SA, annually; Los A. Mus. A.; Sacramento State Fair; San Diego FA Soc.; Detroit Inst. A. *Position*: Instr., Pasadena AI, Pasadena City Col., Adult classes, Pasadena, Cal.

ZIMMERMAN, PAUL WARREN—*Painter, T.*
25 Atheneum Square, North; h. 257 Victoria Rd., Hartford, Conn.

B. Toledo, Ohio. Apr. 29, 1921. *Studied*: John Herron AI, B.F.A. *Member*: Conn. WC Soc.; Springfield A. Lg.; Indiana AA; Berkshire AA; Wadsworth Atheneum. *Awards*: prizes, Indiana AA, 1945, 1947-1949, 1951, 1955, 1957; Mary Milliken F., John Herron AI, 1946; Springfield A. Lg., 1949, 1954; Butler AI, 1950; Conn. Acad. FA, 1950; Silvermine Gld. A., 1951, 1953, 1954; Conn. WC Soc., 1952-1954; Norwich AA, 1953, 1955, 1956; NAD, 1954, 1956; Boston A. Festival, 1954; Berkshire A. Festival, 1954; Hoosier Salon, 1955; Chautauqua, N.Y., 1955; Essex AA, 1952, 1955, 1958; *Work*: Wadsworth Atheneum; de-Cordova & Dana Mus.; NAD; Mus. FA of Houston; New Britain Inst.; Springfield Mus. FA, and in private colls. *Exhibited*: PAFA, 1946, 1949-1952; CGA, 1948; NAD, 1952; Butler AI, 1947-1955; Pasadena AI, 1946; Conn. Acad FA, 1946-1952; Springfield A. Lg., 1947-1952; Univ. Illinois, 1948; Indiana AA, 1945-1955; Hoosier Salon, 1950-1954; Silvermine Gld. A., 1951, 1952; Essex AA, 1948, 1952; Conn. WC Soc., 1947-1951, and many others. One-man: Wellons Gal., 1953; Design Assoc., Hartford, 1951; deCordova & Dana Mus., 1955; Shore Gal., Boston, 1958; Jacques Seligmann Gal., 1958. *Position*: Instr., Hartford A. Sch., Hartford, Conn., 1947- .

ZINGALE, SANTOS—*Painter, E.*
3006 Waunona Way, Madison 5, Wis.

B. Milwaukee, Wis., Apr. 17, 1908. *Studied*: Milwaukee State T. Col.; Univ. Wisconsin. *Member*: Madison AA. *Awards*: prizes, Madison Salon, 1937, 1942; Madison AA, 1951; Gimbel Comp., 1949-1952; Midwest Landscape Exh., 1953; Wis. P. & S., 1937. *Work*: murals, Marquette Univ.; Henry Mitchell H.S., Racine, Wis.; Univ. Wisconsin; USPO, Sturgeon Bay, Wis. *Exhibited*: Wis. P. & S., 1931-1943, 1946, 1955; Madison Salon, 1937-1946, 1951-1955; PAFA, 1949-1950, 1952; Gimbel's Centennial Exh., Milwaukee, 1948-1951; Minnesota Centennial, 1949; Assoc. Am. A., Chicago, 1949; Walker A. Center, 1949, 1954; AIC; AFA traveling exh.; Birmingham Mus. A., 1954; BM, 1958; Butler Inst. Am. A., 1956; Wichita AA, 1957; LC, 1957. *Position*: Assoc. Prof. A., Univ. Wisconsin, Madison, Wis., 1946- .

ZIOLKOWSKI, KORCZAK—*Sculptor*
Crazy Horse, Custer, S.D.

B. Boston, Mass., Sept. 6, 1908. *Studied*: Rindge Tech. Sch. *Member*: NSS. *Awards*: prize, WFNY 1939. *Work*: mem., portrait busts, statues, figures, etc.; SFMA; Symphony Hall, Boston; Vassar Col.; WFNY 1939; granite port. of Wild Bill Hickok, Deadwood, S.D.; West Hartford, Conn. Assisted Gutzon Borglum on Mount Rushmore Nat. Mem., South Dakota; now engaged on equestrian figure of Crazy Horse, Chief of the Dakota Indians, at Custer, S.D. *Position*: Pres. Bd., Crazy Horse Mem. Fnd.*

ZIROLI, NICOLA—*Painter, C., Gr., E., L.*
623½ South Wright St., Champaign, Ill.

B. Montenero, Italy, May 8, 1908. *Studied*: AIC. *Member*: Audubon A; AAUP; New Orleans AA; Phila. WC Cl.; AWS; Nat. Soc. Painters in Casein. *Awards*: prizes, Wash. Soc. A., 1934; AIC, 1938, 1939, 1948, 1955; Springfield (Mo.) A. Mus., 1945, 1946, 1956; Decatur A. Center, 1945, 1946; Ohio Univ., 1946; Mint Mus. A., 1946; Chicago Newspaper Gld., 1946; State T. Col., Indiana, Pa., 1947, 1948; Mississippi AA, 1952; Ohio Valley, 1952, 1954; Magnificent Mile, Chicago, 1954, 1955; Springfield, Ill., 1952, 1954; Audubon A., 1953, 1955, 1956; Butler AI, 1955, 1956; AIC, 1955; medals, San F. AA, 1939; Audubon A., 1947; Nat. Soc. Painters in Casein, 1957.

Work: Springfield Mus. A.; IBM; Vanderpoel Coll.; Chicago Pub. Lib.; MMA; WMAA; Univ. Minnesota; Univ. Nebraska; Washburn Univ.; Pa. State T. Col.; Ill. State T. Col.; Ohio Univ.; Mulvane Mus.; Butler AI. *Exhibited*: Albany Inst. Hist. & A.; Albright A. Gal.; Cal. PLH; Carnegie Inst.; AIC; CM; CMA; CGA; Denver A. Mus.; Detroit Inst. A.; Los A. Mus. A.; MMA; Milwaukee AI; Mint Mus. A.; NAD; WMAA; Oakland A. Gal.; VMFA; Audubon A.; Univ. Ohio; PAFA; Toledo Mus. A.; A. Gal., Toronto; SFMA; Phila. WC Cl.; Grand Rapids A. Gal.; Terry AI; Ill. State Mus.; Mississippi AA; Witte Mem. Mus.; Kansas City AI; and many other museums and galleries.

ZISLA, HAROLD—*Painter, E., Des., L., Mus. Dir.*

South Bend Art Center; h. 1230 Dennis Drive, South Bend, Ind.

B. Cleveland, Ohio, June 28, 1925. *Studied*: Cleveland Inst. A.; Western Reserve Univ., B.S. in Ed., A.M. *Exhibited*: CMA, 1948; South Bend Michiana, 1955, 1956. *Positions*: Instr., Indiana Univ. Ext. (South Bend), 1955; South Bend A. Center, 1953- ; Dir., South Bend A. Center, 1957- .

ZOELLER, ROBERT (FREDRIC)—*Painter*

Harbor Rd., Mt. Sinai, L.I., N.Y.

B. Pittsburgh, Pa., July 19, 1894. *Studied*: Corcoran Sch. A.; Carnegie Inst.; Pittsburgh AI, and with Gordon Grant. *Member*: A. Lg. of Long Island; Am. Veterans Soc. A.; NSMP; Old Town A. & Crafts, Southold, L.I. *Awards*: prizes, A. Lg. of Long Island; Mineola Fair; St. James, L.I., 1951. *Work*: murals, Union Savings Bank, Brookhaven Town Hall, Patchogue, L.I., and in private colls. *Exhibited*: Grand Central A. Gal.; Am. Inst. Sporting A., New York and Chicago; Am. Veterans Soc. A.; A. Lg. of Long Island; Long Island A. Festival; Suffolk County Mus., Stony Brook, L.I., Parrish Mus.; St. James, and Southold, L.I.

ZOELLER, MRS. ROBERT. See Olds, Sara Whitney

ZOELLNER, RICHARD CHARLES—
Painter, Gr., I., L., T.

University of Alabama, University, Ala.; h. 21 Audubon Place, Tuscaloosa, Ala.

B. Portsmouth, Ohio, June 30, 1908. *Studied*: Cincinnati A. Acad.; Tiffany Fnd. *Member*: SSAL; Ala. A. Lg.; Birmingham A. Cl.; Am. Assn. Univ. Prof.; Southeastern Col. A. Conference; SAGA. *Awards*: prizes, Indiana Soc. Pr. M., 1944; Northwest Pr. M., 1945; Ala. A. Lg., 1945; Ala. WC Soc., 1946; Delgado Mus. A., 1950, 1955; Ala. State Fair, 1951; PAFA; BM, 1955. *Work*: LC; La. Polytechnic Inst.; SAM; Government House, V.I.; BM; Univ. Chattanooga; Univ. Mississippi; Univ. Alabama; PAFA; PMA; Birmingham A. Mus.; VMFA; murals, USPO, Portsmouth, Georgetown, Medina, Cleveland, Ohio; Mannington, W. Va. *Exhibited*: LC, 1943, 1945; PAFA; AIC, 1941, 1942; WFNY 1939; SAM, 1944; SFMA, 1944; Dayton AI, 1942, 1943; CM, 1944, 1952; Intermont Col., 1944; SSAL, 1945; Carnegie Inst.; 1949; Albany Inst. Hist. & A., 1949; High Mus. A., 1949-1951; Delgado Mus. A., 1950; SAGA, 1950-1952; BM, 1949-1952, 1955; Birmingham Mus. A., 1954 (one-man); Bradley Univ., 1955. *Position*: Prof. A., Univ. Alabama, University, Ala., at present.*

ZORACH, MARGUERITE THOMPSON—*Painter, C.*

276 Hicks St., Brooklyn 1, N.Y.

B. Santa Rosa, Cal., Sept. 25, 1887. *Studied*: in Paris, France. *Awards*: medal, Pan-Pacific Exp., 1915; Logan medal, Chicago. *Work*: MMA; WMAA; MMoDA; Newark Mus.; BM; murals, USPO, Peterborough, N.H.; Ripley, Tenn.; Monticello, Ill. *Exhibited*: Paris Salon, 1908, 1911; Armory Show, N.Y., 1913; Kraushaar Gal, 1953, 1957 (one-man); WMAA, 1952; Brummer Gal.; Downtown Gal.; Knoedler Gal; "Zorach Day," Bowdoin Col., 1958.

ZORACH, WILLIAM—*Sculptor, P., W., T., L.*

276 Hicks St., Brooklyn 1, N.Y.

B. Eurburick-Kovno, Russia, Feb. 28, 1887. *Studied*: Cleveland Sch.A.; NAD; & in Paris, France. *Awards*: med., AIC, 1931, 1932; Arch. Lg., 1958; Hon. Deg., M.F.A., Bowdoin Col., 1958; Citation, Bates Col., 1958. *Member*: S. Gld. *Work*: MMA; MMoDA; Berkshire Mus.;

Newark Mus.; Radio City Music Hall; WMAA; Wichita A. Mus.; Norton Gal. A.; Swope A. Gal.; Munson-Williams-Proctor Inst.; BMFA; BM; CMA; Los A. Mus. A.; WMAA; AIC; PMG, etc.; statue, USPO Bldg., Wash., D.C.; figs., facade, Mayo Clinic. *Exhibited*: nationally; one-man: Downtown Gal., N.Y. Contributor to: Magazine of Art, Creative Arts, National Encyclopaedia, & other publications. Lectures: "History of Sculpture from Primitive to Modern Times." Author: "Zorach Explains Sculpture." *Position*: Instr. S., ASL, New York, N.Y., 1929- ; Vice-Pres., Nat. Inst. A. & Let., New York, N.Y.

ZORNES, (JAMES) MILFORD—
Painter, I., Comm. A., T., W., L.

4244 Via Padova, Claremont, Cal.

B. Camargo, Okla., Jan. 25, 1908. *Studied*: Pomona Col.; Otis AI; and with Chamberlin, Sheets. *Member*: Cal. WC Soc.; AWS; Southern Pr. M.; San Diego FA Soc.; Western Fnd. A.; Pasadena Soc. A.; Nat. Soc. Pr. M.; Council All. A. *Awards*: Tuthill prize, 1938; prizes, MMA, 1941; Bombay, India, 1944; Pomona Col., 1931, 1946; Los Angeles County Fair, 1933, 1936; San Diego FA Soc., 1937; Arizona State Fair, 1950. *Work*: MMA; Los A. Mus. A.; San Diego FA Soc.; Butler AI; White House Coll., Wash., D.C.; Glendale H.S.; Beverly Hills H.S.; U.S. War Dept.; Los Angeles County Lib.; Newport Beach H.S.; Pomona Col.; murals, USPO, El Campo, Tex.; Claremont, Cal. *Exhibited*: MMA; Western Fnd. A.; Los A. Mus. A.; San Diego FA Soc.; AWS; CGA; AIC; Denver A. Mus.; CMA; Riverside Mus.; BM; NAD; PAFA; CM; Toledo Mus. A.; Bombay AA, India; Pomona Col.; Butler AI, and many others. Illus. "Manual of Southern California Botany," 1935; "Palomar," 1952. Contributor to Ford Times. *Position*: Instr., Pomona Col., 1946-50; A. Dir., Padua Hills, 1955- .

ZORTHIAN, JIRAYR H(AMPARZOOM)—
Painter, C., Des., L., Gr., T.

3990 North Fair Oaks Ave., Altadena, Cal.

B. Kutahia, Armenia, Apr. 14, 1912. *Studied*: Yale Sch. FA, B.F.A., and in Italy. *Member*: Pasadena AA; Pasadena Soc. A.; AEA. *Work*: murals, State Capitol, Nashville, Tenn.; United Illuminating Co., New Haven, Conn.; New Plaza Hotel, Harrisburg, Pa.; Camp Ritchie, Md.; USPO, St. Johnsville, N.Y. *Exhibited*: New Haven Paint & Clay Cl., 1936, 1938, 1941; BMA, 1943-1945; Washington County Mus. FA, 1945; Cal. State Fair; PAFA; Cal. PLH; Los A. Mus. A.; Los A. County Fair; Pasadena A. Mus., 1954 (one-man), 1955; Nat. Orange Show, 1954; Sierra Madre Lib. (one-man). *Position*: A., Pasadena Independent Star News, 1953-58; Instr. A., Tom Chandler Sch., Pasadena, Cal., 1958.

ZSISSLY. See Albright, Malvin Marr

ZUCKER, JACQUES—*Painter*

44 West 77th St., New York 24, N.Y.

B. Radom, Poland, June, 1900. *Studied*: Julian Academie, Grande Chaumiere, Paris, France. *Work*: Mus. Mod. A., Paris, France; Tel-Aviv Mus., Israel. *Exhibited*: MMA; Carnegie Inst.; PAFA; AIC; Smith Col.; Springfield Mus. A.; Inst. Mod. A., Boston; WMA; WMAA; BM; Assoc. Am. A.; Bignou Gal.; Wadsworth Atheneum; Yale Univ.; Dudensing Gal.; Ferargil Gal.; Reinhardt Gal.; Wildenstein Gal.; Tel-Aviv Mus.; 1950; Galerie Andre Weil, Paris; Milch Gal., N.Y., 1952, one-man, 1955.

ZUCKER, PAUL—*Educator, Cr., W.*

Cooper Union for the Advancement of Science and Art, Fourth Ave. at 7th St.; h. 227 East 57th St., New York 22, N.Y.

B. Berlin, Germany, Aug. 14, 1890. *Studied*: Univ. Berlin and Munich; Inst. Tech., Berlin and Munich, Ph.D. *Member*: CAA; Am. Soc. Arch. Historians; Am. Soc. for Aesthetics. *Awards*: prizes, Architectural Comp., Germany, 1933; Arnold W. Brunner Scholarship, AIA, 1953. Author: "Stage Setting at the Time of the Baroque"; "Stage Setting at the Time of the Classicism"; "Architecture in Italy at the Time of the Renaissance"; "American Bridges and Dams"; "Styles in Painting," 1950, and many other books. Ed., "The Music Lover's Almanac" (with William Hendelson); "New Architecture and City Planning, A Symposium." *Position*: Adjunct Prof., Cooper Union, New York, N.Y., 1938- ; Instr., New Sch. for Social Research, New York, N.Y.

Canadian Biographies

Canadian Abbreviations

AA Mtl—Art Association of Montreal (Museum of Fine Arts), Montreal

AG—Art Gallery

AG Tor—Art Gallery of Toronto

Alta—Alberta

ARA—Associate of the Royal Academy (England)

ARCA—Associate of the Royal Canadian Academy

BC—British Columbia

CAC—Canadian Arts Council

Can—Canada, Canadian

CAS, Mtl—Contemporary Arts Society, Montreal

CGP—Canadian Group of Painters

CNE—Canadian National Exhibition (annual), Toronto

CSGA—Canadian Society of Graphic Art

CSPEE—Canadian Society of Painter-Etchers and Engravers

CSPWC—Canadian Society of Painters in Water Colour

Dom—Dominion (of Canada)

Eng—England

FCA—Federation of Canadian Artists

Man—Manitoba

MPQ—Musée de la Province de Québec, Quebec City

Mtl—Montreal

N.B.—New Brunswick

NGC—National Gallery of Canada, Ottawa

N.S.—Nova Scotia

OCA—Ontario College of Art, Toronto

OSA—Ontario Society of Artists

P.E.I.—Prince Edward Island

P.Q.—Province of Quebec

R—Royal

RA—Royal Academy (or Academician)

RCA—Royal Canadian Academy (or Academician)

RCAF—Royal Canadian Air Force

RSBA—Royal Society of British Artists (England)

Sask.—Saskatchewan

SSC—Sculptors' Society of Canada

Tech.—Technical

Tor.—Toronto

ABBREVIATIONS FOR PRINCIPAL EXHIBITIONS

Addison 1942—Contemporary Painting in Canada, Addison Gallery, Andover, Mass., 1942.

Albany 1946—Painting in Canada, Albany Institute of History and Art, Albany, N.Y., 1946.

Coronation 1937—Artists of the British Empire Overseas Exhibition, Royal Institute Galleries, London; Walker Art Gallery, Liverpool, 1937.

DPC 1945—Development of Painting in Canada, National Gallery of Canada; Art Association of Montreal; Musée de la Province de Québec; Art Gallery of Toronto, 1945.

Paris 1927—Exposition d'Art Canadien, Musée du Jeu de Paume, Paris, 1927.

Rio 1944, '46—Exhibition of Canadian Painting, Rio de Janeiro and Sao Paulo, 1944; Artes Graficas do Canada, Rio de Janeiro and Sao Paulo, 1946.

S. Dominions 1936—Contemporary Canadian Painting arranged by the National Gallery for circulation in the Southern Dominions of the British Empire, 1936.

Tate 1938—A Century of Canadian Art, Tate Gallery, London, 1938.

UNESCO 1946—Canadian Painting, United Nations Educational and Scientific and Cultural Organizations, Musée du Trocadéro, Paris, 1946.

Wembley 1924, '25—Canadian Section, Fine Arts, British Empire Exhibition, Wembley, England, 1924 and 1925.

WFNY 1939—Canadian Art, New York World's Fair, 1939.

Yale 1944—Canadian Art 1760-1943, Yale University Art Gallery, New Haven, Conn., 1942.

A *Biographical Directory of* | Canadian
Canadian painters, sculptors,
museum directors, writers, etc. | Biographies

AIROLA, PAAVO—*Painter, E.*

Colborne, Ont.

B. Baltimore, Md., June 14, 1918. *Studied*: Isac Grune-wald & Otte Skold's A. Sch., Stockholm; Academie Libre, Stockholm, Sweden. *Member*: CSPWC; Colour & Form Soc., Toronto. *Work*: Hudiksvall A. Mus., Sweden; Ostersunds Mus. FA, Sweden. *Exhibited*: Canadian Nat. Exh., 1953-1956, 1958; RA, 1953-1957; OSA, 1953, 1954, 1956-1958; Montreal Mus. A., 1953-1957; CSPWC, 1953, 1956, 1957; NGC, 1954, 1956 (traveling); and in London, Winnipeg, Hamilton, etc. One-man: Stockholm, 1948, 1950; Hart House, Toronto, 1955; Greenwich Gal., 1957; AG Tor., 1958. *Positions*: Instr., Belleville A. & Crafts; Trenton and Coburg AA.

ALDWINCKLE, ERIC—*Designer, P., I., L.*

80 Elm Ave., Toronto, Ont.

B. Oxford, England, Jan. 22, 1909. *Member*: OSA; FCA; A. & Letters Cl., Tor. *Honours*: medal, prize, A. Dir. Cl., Tor., 1948, 1949. *Work*: NGC War Records. Commissions: Official war artist with RCAF 1943-46; Sunnybrook Hospital, Tor. *Exhibited*: CSGA 1931-35; OSA 1936-41; NGC Annual 1938; WFNY 1939; War Art, NG London 1943, 1945; War Art NGC 1945, 1946. Illus., "Canada's Tomorrow," 1953.

ANDREWS, SYBIL (MORGAN) (MRS.)—*Painter, Gr.*

R.R. #1, Willow Point, Campbell River, B.C.

B. Bury St. Edmund's, England, Apr. 19, 1898. *Studied*: Heatherley Sch. FA, London, and with Boris Heroys. *Member*: CSPEE. *Honour*: G.A. Reid award, CSPEE, 1951. *Work*: Victoria & Albert Mus., London; Leeds Mus., England; Dublin Mus.; Los A. Mus. A.; Mass. Soc. A.; Nat. Gal., South Australia. *Exhibited*: "200 Years of British Graphic Art," Prague, Bucharest, Vienna, 1936; Buenos Aires, 1954; Cal. Pr. M.; and in Great Britain, Canada, U.S.A., South Africa, Australia, China.

ALFRED, PAUL (A. E. MEISTER)—*Painter, T. I., Des.*

144 Concord St., Ottawa, Ont.

B. Hanley, Eng., Apr. 10, 1892. *Studied*: Polytechnic Sch. of A., Hanley; Chelsea Polytechnic, London. *Member*: OSA; CSPWC; CSGA. *Honours*: Hon. mention, Willingdon Competition 1927. *Work*: NGC: Edmonton Mus.; Dominion Archives, Ottawa. Commissions: Murals in officers' messes, Ottawa and Petawawa 1944. *Exhibited*: Lo Angeles; Wembley 1925; Paris 1927; S. Dominions 1936; Tate 1938. *Position*: Publicity artist, Dept. of Interior, Canada.*

ARCHAMBAULT, LOUIS—*Sculptor*

278 Sanford Ave., St. Lambert, Montreal 23, P.Q.

B. Mtl., Apr. 4, 1915. *Studied*: Col. Jean-de-Brebeuf, Mtl., B.A.; Ecole des Beaux-Arts de Montreal. *Honours*: Les Concours Artistiques de la Province de Quebec, 1948, 1950; Canadian Govt. Overseas Award, 1953-54. *Work*: Musee de Quebec; AG Tor.; NGC; Museo Internazionale della Ceramica, Faenza, Italy; Ottawa City Hall; Toronto Sun Life Bldg. *Exhibited*: Battersea Park, London, Eng., 1951; Intl. Sc. Exh., London, 1951; Venice Biennale, 1956; Milan, 1954, 1957; Brussels World's Fair, 1958; Carnegie Inst., 1958.

ARISS, HERBERT JOSHUA—*Painter, T., L.*

770 LeRoy Crescent, London, Ont.

B. Guelph, Ont., Canada, Sept. 29, 1918. *Studied*: Ontario Col. of A. *Member*: Western A. Lg. (Vice-Pres.). *Work*: AG Tor.; AG London. *Exhibited*: CGP, 1955; NGC, 1955; CSPWC, 1953-1955; OSA, 1953, 1954; Western A. Lg., 1948-1955; AG Hamilton, 1950, 1951,

1955. Illus., Educational books. *Position*: Instr., H.B. Beal Tech. & Comm. H.S., London, Ont.; Doon Sch. FA.*

ARISS, MARGOT PHILLIPS—*Painter*

770 LeRoy Crescent, London, Ont.

B. Belleville, Ont., Sept. 14, 1929. *Member*: Western A. Lg. *Exhibited*: Young Contemporaries Exh., 1953-1955; Hamilton, 1952-1955; Western A. Lg., 1951-1955; 3-man exh., 1955; traveling exhs.*

AYRE, ROBERT HUGH—*Editor, W., Cr.*

5552 Snowdon Ave.; Publ. Relations Dept., Canadian National Rys., Montreal, P.Q.

B. Napinka, Man., Apr. 3, 1900. *Honours*: Can. Drama Award 1942. Contributor: Canadian Art; various periodicals and yearbooks. Lectures and radio talks: Art in Canada; Nature of Art, etc. *Position*: Joint editor, Canadian Art, P.O. Box 384, Ottawa; A.Cr., Montreal Star.

BALDWIN, MARTIN—*Museum Director*

Thornhill, Ont.; Art Gallery of Toronto, Orange Park, Toronto 2B, Ont.

B. Tor., Aug. 31, 1891. *Studied*: Trinity Col., Port Hope, Ontario; Univ. Tor. (B.A.Sc.). *Member*: A. Mus. Directors' Assn.; Am. Assn. of Museums; Canadian Branch, Intl. Assn. A. Critic; Canadian Mus. Assn. (Pres.). *Work*: Buildings in Tor. Contributor: Museum News, Magazine of Art; R.A.I.C. Journal. *Teaching*: Univ. Tor. Organized: Great Paintings 1940; Development of Painting in Can. 1945; Emily Carr Exh. 1946, etc. *Position*: Dir., Art Gallery of Tor.; Council, Am. Assn. A. Mus.; Councillor, Ontario College of Art.

BARBEAU, MARIUS—*Writer, Mus. Wkr.*

260 MacLaren St.; National Museum of Canada, Ottawa, Ont.

B. Ste-Marie, Beauce Co., P.Q., Mar. 5, 1883. *Studied*: Univ. Laval, LL.L.; Oxford, B.A.; Univ. de Paris. *Honours*: Fellow, R. Soc. of Can. 1916; Pres., Am. Folklore Soc. 1917-18; Doctor honoris causa, Univ. Mtl. 1935; Member Washington Acad. of Sciences 1936; Hon. Fellow, Oriel Col., Oxford 1941; Gold Medal, ACFAS, Quebec 1946; D. Litt., honoris causa, Oxford Univ., 1953. Author: "Totem Poles of the Gitksan"; "Cornelius Krieghoff, Pioneer Painter of America"; "Saintes Artisanes"; "Totem Poles of Canada"; "Alaska Beckons"; "L'Arbes des Rêves"; Le Rêve de Kamalmouk"; "Le Merveilleuse Aventure de Jacques Cartier"; "Alouette"; "Québec, où survit l'ancienne France"; "Haida Myths'; "The Tree of Dreams"; "Totem Poles, I and II"; "Haida Carvers"; "Medicine Men"; "Roundelays-Dansons à la Ronde"; Trésor des Anciens Jésuites"; "I Have Seen Quebec"; "Pathfinders in the North Pacific," and many others; volumes in "Canadian Artists" series; and many books and articles on Canadian folklore, art, and anthropology. Contributor: Transactions of the R. Soc. of Can.; Canadian Art; Antiques; Art News; Art Quarterly; Gants du Ciel, etc. Lectures: Pacific Indian Art; French Can. Art, etc. *Teaching*: Univs. Ottawa, Mtl. and Laval, Quebec. Organized: French Can. exhs. at Nat. Mus. of Can.; NGC; AG Tor; AA Mtl.; Detroit Inst. of A. *Position*: Anthropologist and Folklorist, National Museum of Canada; Vice-Pres., Intl. Folk Music Council; Chm., Canadian Folk Music Soc.

BARR, ALLAN—*Portrait Painter*

2 Glen Elm Ave., Toronto 7, Ont.

B. London, Eng., Jan. 10, 1890. *Studied*: London Sch. of A. under Brangwyn, & others. *Honours*: ARCA; W. M. Chase Scholarship 1910. *Member*: Ontario Inst. Painters.

Work: Victoria & Albert Mus., London; NGC; Muskegon, Mich.; AG Tor; Brasenose Col. Oxford. *Exhibited*: Paris Salon 1912; Int. Soc. London, 1912, '14, 19; RA 1913, '16, '21; Pittsburgh Int. 1914; Buenos Aires; WFNY 1939; AA Mtl.; NGC; AG Tor.; Canadian Nat. Exh., 1953, 1955, etc.

BATES, MAXWELL—*Painter, Gr., W., Arch.*
1411 7th St., Southwest, Calgary, Alta.

B. Calgary, Alta., Dec. 14, 1906. *Studied*: Provincial Inst. Tech. & A.; BMSch., with Max Beckmann; and with Abraham Rattner. *Member*: CGP; CSPWC; CSGA; Alberta Soc. A. *Honours*: CSPWC, 1957; Minneapolis, Minn., 1958; Winnipeg A. Gal., 1957 (purchase). *Work*: NGC; AG Tor.; Winnipeg A. Gal.; Norman Mackenzie A. Gal., Regina; Calgary All. A. Centre. Other work: Bldg., and interior furnishings in marble, bronze, oak, etc., by A. W. Hodges Friba and Maxwell Bates (Archs.), St. Mary's Cathedral, Calgary, Alta., Canada. *Exhibited*: NGC, 1930, 1931, 1953, 1955, and traveling exh., 1958-1959; Intl. Biennial of Lith., Cincinnati, Ohio, 1958; Phila. Pr. Cl., 1958; Biennial Exh. A., Minneapolis, Minn., 1958; one-man: Manchester, England, 1934; London, 1938; Vancouver A. Gal., 1947; Queen's Univ., 1950; Manitoba Univ., 1956; Laurel Gal., N.Y., 1950; Montreal, 1951, and many others. Contributor to Canadian Art; Royal Architectural Institute of Canada Journal, with articles of art criticism.

BEAMENT, COMMANDER HAROLD—*Painter, Des.*
4709 The Boulevard, Westmount, P.Q.

B. Ottawa, July 23, 1898. *Studied*: Osgoode Hall, Tor.; OCA. *Member*: RCA. *Honours*: Jessie Dow Prize, AA Mtl. 1935. *Work*: War Records NGC; Dominion Archives, Ottawa; A. Gal., London, Ont.; MPQ; AA Mtl. Commissions: official war artist with R. Can. Navy 1943-46; des current 10¢ stamp (Eskimo) for Canadian Govt. *Exhibited*: RCA 1922; NGC 1926-33; Wembley 1925; Paris 1927; S. America 1929; S. Dominions 1936; Coronation 1937; Tate 1938; WFNY 1939; War art, NG London, NGC 1945, '46; OSA. *Teaching*: AA Mtl. 1936. *Position*: War Artist, Royal Canadian Navy; Hon. Treas., RCA, 1958.

BENTON, MARGARET PEAKE—
Miniature and Portrait Painter
205 Madison Ave., Toronto 5, Ont.

B. South Orange, N.J. *Studied*: OCA under Sir Wyly Grier and Archibald Barnes. *Member*: AG Tor.; Pa. Soc. Min. P.; Min. P. S. & Gravers, Wash., D.C. *Work*: portraits, Wesley Bldg., Tor.; North Tor. Collegiate Inst.; Nurmanzil Psychiatric Centre, Lucknow, India; King's Col., Halifax, N.S.; PMA; murals, St. John's Garrison Church, Tor. *Exhibited*: OSA, 1933; PAFA 1940, 1941, 1943, 1945-1951; NCFA 1943, 1945-1947, 1951-1958; RCA 1938-1940, 1942, 1948, 1949; Royal Acad. A., London, 1950.

BENY, WILFRED ROLOFF—*Painter, Et., L., Eng.*
432 13th St. South, Lethbridge, Alta.

B. Medicine Hat, Alta., Jan. 7, 1924. *Studied*: Banff Sch. FA; Univ. Tor., B.A.; State Univ. Iowa, M.A. *Honours*: F., Univ. Iowa; Guggenheim F., 1952. *Work*: St. Hilda's Col., Univ. Tor.; Univ. Iowa; FMA; MMoDA; BM; N.Y. Pub. Lib.; Yale Univ.; CM; Wesleyan Univ.; NGC; A. Gal. Toronto; Oslo Mus., Norway; Bezalel Mus., Jerusalem; Redfern Gal., London, and others. Author, Photographer, "The Thrones of Earth and Heaven," 1958. *Exhibited*: CSPWC 1942-1944; OSA 1943-1945; AA Mtl. 1945; Nat. Print Show, Wichita, Kans. 1946; Phila. Print Cl., 1946; Milan, Italy, 1952; Weyhe Gal., N.Y., 1947; Palazzo Strozzi, Florence, 1949; Knoedler Gal., 1951; Merano, Vicenza, Italy, 1951; one-man: Hart House, Univ. Tor., Eaton College, Tor.; Univ. Iowa 1946; Libraire Paul Morihien, Paris, 1952; Florence, Italy, 1949; Knoedler Gal., N.Y., 1951, 1954; A. Gal., Toronto, 1954; Robertson Gal., Ottawa, 1954; Waldorf Gal., Montreal, 1954; Contemp. Gal., N.Y., 1955; Western Canada Circuit, 1955, and in Italy and France.

BICE, CLARE—*Painter, Mus. Cur.*
1010 Wellington St.; Williams Memorial Art Gallery and Museum, London, Ont.

B. Durham, Ont., Jan. 24, 1909. *Studied*: Univ. West Ont., B.A.; ASL; Grand Central Sch. of A., N.Y. *Mem-*

ber: OSA. *Honours*: ARCA; Canadian Govt. F., 1953. *Exhibited*: OSA, 1937-58; RCA 1938-58; CNE 1938-58; WFNY 1939; Western Ont. Exh. 1940-58; NGC Can. Army Art Exh. 1944. Author: "Jory's Cove"; "Across Canada"; also I. of other children's books; Author, I., "The Great Island," 1954; "A Dog for Davie's Hill," 1956. *Position*: Cur., Williams Memorial Art Gallery, London, Ont.

BIELER, ANDRE—*Painter, E., L.*
33 Hill St.; Dept. of Art, Queen's University, Kingston, Ont.

B. Lausanne, Switzerland, Oct. 8, 1896. *Studied*: ASL; Ecole du Louvre, Paris, under Maurice Dennis; Switzerland under Ernest Biéler. *Member*: RCA; OSA, CGP, CSPWC, CSGA, FCA. *Honours*: Pres. FCA 1942-4; Vice-Pres. CGP 1943; ARCA; Forster award, OSA, 1957. *Work*: NGC; MPQ; AA Mtl.; AG Tor.; Winnipeg AG; Hart House, Univ. Tor.; Queen's Univ.; Aluminum Co. of Canada; mural, East Mem. Bldg., Ottawa; Edmonton A. Gal.; Windsor AA, 1955; Mus. FA, Montreal, 1952, and others. *Exhibited*: Intl. WC, Chicago; Brooklyn; Coronation 1937; Tate 1938; Chicago 1939; WFNY 1939; Addison 1942; Yale 1944; Rio 1944, '46; DPC 1945; UNESCO 1946; BMFA, 1946; VMFA, 1949; Contemp. Can. Art, 1950; Brazil, 1950; SFMA, 1956; One-man: Mtl. 1924; '26, '45; Paris 1936; Ottawa, 1954; Kingston, 1954, 1955; Mus. FA, Montreal, 1952, and others. Contributor: Kingston Conference Proceedings 1941; Maritime Art; Canadian Art. Lectures: Spanish, Mexican, Canadian art on tour of E. Canada; "Modern Art," Windsor and Ottawa. *Position*: Head, Dept. of A., Queen's Univ., Kingston, Ont.; Dir. Etherington Art Centre.

BINNING, BERTRAM CHARLES—
Painter, E., Mus. Cur.
2968 Mathers Crescent, West Vancouver; University of British Columbia, Vancouver, B.C.

B. Medicine Hat, Alta., 1909. *Studied*: Vancouver Sch. A.; ASL; Univ. Oregon; in London under Henry Moore, Ozenfant and Meninsky. *Member*: FCA; British Columbia Soc. FA; CSGA; CGP; ARCA. *Honours*: medal, Vancouver, 1951; Carnegie Scholarship, 1936, 1951. *Work*: NGC; AG Tor.; Hart House, Univ. Tor.; Vancouver A. Gal. *Exhibited*: British Columbia Soc. A., 1932-1945; British Columbia Soc. FA, 1935-1946; OSGA, 1941-1946; CGP, 1943, 1944; Rio 1946; BMFA, 1949, 1955; AG Tor., 1949; NGA, 1950; Canadian Biennial, 1954; Venice Biennale, 1954; Sao Paulo, Brazil, 1953; PC (3 Canadians), 1955; Valencia, Venezuela, 1955; Milan Triennial, 1957. *Position*: Assoc. Prof. A., Univ. British Columbia, and Cur. FA Gal., Univ. British Columbia.

BOBAK, BRUNO—*Painter, T.*
1191 Wellington Drive, North Vancouver, B.C.

B. Wawelowka, Poland, Dec. 28, 1923. *Studied*: Central Tech. Sch., Tor. *Member*: CSPWC; CPE; B.C. Soc. FA; CSGA. *Honours*: prize, SAM, 1955. *Work*: NGC; AG Tor.; Government House, Ottawa. Commissions: war artist with Can. Army, 1944-46. *Exhibited*: NGC 1944, 1946; AG Tor., 1956 (4-man); Victoria & Albert Mus., London, 1955. *Position*: Hd., Des. Dept., Vancouver (B.C.) Sch. A.*

BOBAK, MOLLY LAMB (Mrs.)—*Painter, T.*
1191 Wellington Drive, North Vancouver, B.C.

B. Vancouver, B.C.; Feb. 25, 1922. *Studied*: Vancouver Sch. A. *Honours*: prize, Can. Army A., 1944; French Govt. scholarship, 1950-51. *Work*: NGC; AG Tor. Commissions: war artist with Can. Army 1945-46. *Exhibited*: Can. Army Art Exh., NGC, 1944; War Art, 1945, 1946; Rio 1946, 1952; Festival of Britain, 1951; Vancouver AG, 1952. *Position*: Instr., Painting, Vancouver (B.C.) Sch. A.*

BONNYCASTLE, MURRAY CARLAW—*Painter*
356 Bloor St., East, Toronto 5, Ont.

B. Campbellford, Ont., Aug. 18, 1909. *Studied*: OCA. *Exhibited*: CSPWC; CSGA; CGP; OSA; RCA; CNE; NG traveling exhs.; Coronation 1937; WFNY 1939; Gloucester 1939; New Zealand 1948; Picture Loan Soc., Tor., 1950 (fourth one-man); Barbados, Br. Guiana, 1953. Contributor to Canadian Forum.

BORDUAS, PAUL-EMILE—*Painter*
19 rue Rousselet, Paris, France

B. St.-Hilaire, P.Q., Nov. 1, 1905. *Studied*: in Canada and France. *Honours*: medal, Beaux-Art Mtl., and French Govt. *Work*: NGC; AG Tor.; MPQ; Mus. des Beaux-Arts, Mtl.; MModA, and others. *Exhibited*: Addison 1944; Yale 1944; Rio 1944; DPC 1945; Albany 1946; UNESCO 1946; Venice, Italy, 1952, 1954; Sao Paulo, Brazil, 1953, 1955; Carnegie Inst., 1952, 1955; Smithsonian Inst., 1956, 1957; Canadian Biennial, 1957; Tooth Gal., London, 1957; Brussels World's Fair, 1958; Mexico, 1958; DMFA, 1958; one-man: Ermitage 1942; Dominion Gal., 1943; Morgan Gal., Mtl., 1946; Picture Loan Soc., Tor., 1951; Passedoit Gal., N.Y., 1954, 1955; Lefort Gal., Mtl., 1956-1958; GCA Gal., Tor., 1957; Martha Jackson Gal., N.Y., 1957; Dusseldorf, 1958. Author: "Refus Global," 1948; "Projections Liberantes," 1950.

BOUCHARD, LORNE—*Painter, Des., I., Comm. A.*
4070 Jauron St., Montreal 9, P.Q.

B. Montreal, P.Q., Mar. 19, 1913. *Studied*: in Montreal with W.M. Barnes; Ecole des Beaux-Arts, Montreal. *Member*: ARCA; A. Dir. Cl., Montreal; Pen & Pencil Cl.; Montreal A. Cl. *Work*: Provincial Mus. of Quebec; in private colls. Canada, U.S.A., Australia, Switzerland, and England. *Exhibited*: Mtl. Mus. FA; RCA traveling exh., 1957-1958; CNE exh., Toronto, 1958; OSA; Seagram's "Cities of Canada" world circuit; one-man: Montreal. *Position*: Freelance I., & Des.

BOYD, JAMES—*Printmaker, Des., T.*
479 Bank St.; 550 O'Connor St., Ottawa, Ont.

B. Ottawa, Ont., Dec. 16, 1928. *Studied*: ASL, with Will Barnet, Bernard Klonis; NAD, with Robert Phillip; Contemporaries Graphic A. Centre. *Member*: CSGA. *Work*: Toronto Telegram Coll.; murals, Canadian Tourist Bureau, Chicago; N.Y. World Trade Fair—Canadian Section, 1958. *Exhibited*: CSGA, 1955-1958; SAGA, 1956; "Winnipeg Show," 1957, 1958; Minneapolis, 1958; one-man: Loranger Gal., Ottawa, 1956; Robertson Gal., Ottawa, 1958. *Positions*: Instr., Graphic A., Ottawa Municipal A. Centre, 1957, 1958; Port. and Vignette Engraver-Bank Notes—1946-1952; Exh. Des., Canadian Section, Brussels World's Fair, 1958.

BRANDTNER, FRITZ—*Painter, C., Des., Gr.*
4840 Plamondon Ave., Montreal, P.Q.

B. Danzig, July 28, 1896. *Studied*: Danzig Acad. under F. A. Pfuhle. *Member*: CGP; CSPWC. *Honours*: prizes, AA Mtl., 1946; Canadian Olympic Comp., 1948; Comp. for des. of commemorative 5-cent piece, 1950. *Work*: Central Station, Mtl.; Bell Telephone Co., Berkeley Hotel, Trans-Canada Airlines, Mtl.; Can. Nat. Railways, Boston; Hotel Vancouver; Bishop's Col., Lennoxville, P.Q.; NGC; AG Tor.; Vancouver AG; Hart House, Univ. Tor.; Can. Nat. Railways, St. Johns, Newfoundland. *Exhibited*: S. Dominions 1936; Gloucester 1939; WFNY 1939; Addison 1942; Yale 1944; DPC 1945; Elmira, N.Y., 1946; Rio 1946; Phila. WC Cl., 1946; Vancouver AG; Winnipeg AG; CSGA; CSPWC; CGP; Sao Paulo, Brazil. Lectures, radio talks. *Positions*: A. Master, Miss Edgar's and Miss Cramp's Sch., Mtl., 1944- ; L., McGill Univ., 1948- ; Dir., Observatory A. Centre, Univ. New Brunswick Summer Sch., 1949-53.

BRIANSKY, RITA (PREZAMENT)—*Etcher, P.*
4903 West Hill Ave., Montreal 29, P.Q.

B. Grajewa, Poland, July 25, 1925. *Studied*: Montreal Mus. FA, with Jacques de Tonnancoeur, Eldon Grier; Ecole des Beaux-Arts; ASL, N.Y., with Corbino, Sternberg, Bosa and Vytlacil. *Member*: CSGA. *Honour*: prize, Montreal Mus. FA, 1949. *Exhibited*: Phila. Pr. Cl., 1949; OSA, Toronto, 1958; CSPEE, 1958; CSGA, Vancouver, Hamilton, 1957, Toronto, 1958; Montreal Spring Shows, 1945-1958; YWCA, Montreal, 1958; one-man: Montreal Mus. FA, 1958; various group shows, 1949-1958.

BRIEGER, PETER H.—*Educator, Historian*
University of Toronto; 51 Woodlawn Ave., West, Toronto 5, Ont.

Position: Prof. Hd. Dept. A. & Archaeology, Univ. Toronto, Toronto, Ont.*

BRIGDEN, FREDERICK HENRY—*Painter*
130 Duchess St., Toronto, Ont.

B. London, Eng., Apr. 9, 1871. *Studied*: Central Ont. Sch. of A. *Member*: OSA, CSPWC. *Honours*: RCA 1939; Pres. OSA 1927-37; 1st Pres. CPWC. *Work*: NGC, AG Tor., Winnipeg AG, Williams Mem. Gal., London, Ont. *Exhibited*: St. Louis 1903; *Wembley* 1925; S. Dominions 1936; Coronation 1937; Tate 1938; Gloucester 1939; WFNY 1939; DPC 1945. Author: "Canadian Landscape." Lectures: Canadian art. *Position*: Head of Brigden's Ltd., Tor.*

BRITTAIN, MILLER GORE—*Painter*
42 Princess St.; 14 Chipman Hill, Saint John, N.B.

B. West Saint John, N.B., Nov. 12, 1912. *Studied*: ASL. *Member*: CSGA. *Honours*: prizes, CSGA, 1941, 1947. *Work*: New Brunswick Mus.; Sao Paulo, Brazil; Beaverbrook Coll.; Fredericton, N.B.; murals, Convent of the Good Shepherd, Saint John; Lancaster Veterans Hospital, Saint John. *Exhibited*: CSGA 1936-1941, 1947; CNE; Maritime AA; WFNY 1939; AG Tor., 1955; NGC; Clearwater (Fla.) Mus. A., 1950; Fla. Southern Col., 1950; one-man: New Brunswick Mus., Saint John, 1948; Dayton AI 1948; Binet Gal., N.Y., 1950; J. P. Hartet, N.Y., 1953, 1955; L'Atelier, Ottawa, 1953; Macdonald Col., 1954.*

BROOKS, (FRANK) LEONARD—*Painter, T.*
28 Northmount Ave., Downsview P.O., Toronto, Ont.

B. London, England, Nov. 11, 1911. *Member*: RCA; CGP. *Work*: NGC; AG Tor.; AG London (Ont.); WMA; Dartmouth Col.; Univ. Ohio. *Exhibited*; RCA, 1936-1955; OSA, annually since 1936; Barcelona, Spain, 1934; Royal Inst., London, 1937; CSPW, from 1937; CPE; NGC, 1946; Mexico City, 1948; Los A. Cal., 1949; Dartmouth Col.; Santa Barbara Mus. A.; Kenyon Col.; Univ. Ohio; Toronto; Vancouver; San F., Cal.; San Antonio, Tex. Contributor to Canadian Art; Atlantic Monthly. Author: "Watercolor—A Challenge," 1957. *Position*: Instr., Wells Col., Aurora, N.Y., 1956; guest instr., 1951-56, Ohio Univ., Doon Sch. FA, Ontario, Univ. British Columbia, San Antonio AI.

BROOMFIELD, ADOLPHUS GEORGE—
Painter, Et., Textile Des., L.
R.R. 1, Cooksville, Ont.; 1179 King St., W., Toronto, Ont.

B. Tor., Aug. 26, 1906. *Studied*: OCA under F. S. Haines, J. W. Beatty, A. Lismer and J. E. H. MacDonald. *Member*: ARCA; CSPEE; OSA; Ont Inst. Painters. *Honours*: ARCA; prize, RCAF exh. 1944. *Work*: RCAF; Sarnia AG; Nat. Defense Col., Ottawa; Canada Wire & Cable Coll., Toronto. *Exhibited*: CSGA 1928-1938; CNE 1930-1938, 1958; OSA 1930-1945, traveling exhs., 1955-1958; CSPEE 1935-1939; RCA 1935-1945; NG London war art 1944; AG Tor.; AG Mtl.; Ottawa, Ont.; traveling exhs. of OSA, RCA.

BROWNHILL, HAROLD—*Painter, Et., Lith., Cart.*
8 Norwood St., East, Halifax, N.S.

B. Sheffield, England, July 12, 1887. *Studied*: Sheffield Col. A., with Cook, Jahn. *Member*: Nova Scotia Soc. A. *Honour*: several certifs., South Kensington Bd. Edu. *Exhibited*: Nova Scotia traveling exh., 1952; Nova Scotia Soc. A., 1933-1936, 1948-1955. Cart., Halifax Herald & Evening Mail; Yorkshire Telegraph & Star.

BRUCE, ANNIE PRISCILLA (Mrs.)—*Painter, C.*
P.O. Box 37, Shelburne, N.S.

B. Jordan Ferry, N.S., Aug. 14, 1868. *Member*: Brookline (Mass.) Soc. A.; Nova Scotia Soc. A.; Nova Scotia Craftsmen's Gld. *Exhibited*: Brookline Soc. A., 1953, 1954; "60-Plus Activities Show," Boston, 1954-1958.

BUCHANAN, DONALD WILLIAM—
Museum Assoc. Dir., W.
National Gallery of Canada; "Canadian Art," Box 384, Ottawa, Ont.; 265 Daly Ave., Ottawa, Ont.

B. Lethbridge, Alta., Apr. 9, 1908. *Studied*: Univ. Tor., B.A.; Univ. Oxford (Eng.). Author: "James Wilson Morrice," 1937; "This is Canada," 1945; "Canadian Painters," 1946; "The Growth of Canadian Painting," 1950. Contributor to Canadian Art, Studio, Univ. Toronto Quarterly, Canadian Geographical Journal, and others. *Position*: Assoc. Dir., National Gallery of Canada, Ottawa, Ont.

BUSH, JACK HAMILTON—*Painter, I., Des.*
1 Eastview Cres., Toronto, Ont.

B. Tor., Mar. 20, 1909. *Studied*: OCA; RCA classes and under A. Sheriff Scott, Mtl. *Member*: CSPWC; OSA; Painters Eleven. *Honours*: Pres. CSPWC; Rolph Clark Stone purchase prize, OSA exh., 1946; J. W. L. Forster award, OSA, 1952; CNE, 1957. *Exhibited*: RCA 1932-46; OSA 1934-46; CSPWC 1934-46; Hart House, Univ. Tor., 1945; CGP 1946; Sudbury, Ont. 1946; Roberts Gal., 1949, 1952 (one-man); Park Gal., 1958 (one-man).

CAHEN, OSCAR—*Painter, I.*
2102 Elmhurst Ave., Oakville, Ont.

B. Copenhagen, Denmark, Feb. 8, 1916. *Studied*: Dresden A. Acad., and other schools in Europe. *Member*: OSA; CSPWC; CSGA; A. Dir. Cl., Toronto. *Honours*: prizes, T.D.F. award, Toronto, 1951; Canadian Nat. Exh., 1953 (purchase); CSGA, 1955; Winnipeg, 1955; medals, Toronto A. Dir. Cl., 1950, 1951, 1953, 1955; Montreal A. Dir. Cl. 1952 and 9 merit awards, 1950-55. *Work*: NGC. Mural, Imperial Oil Bldg., Toronto. *Exhibited*: OSA, 1947-1955; RCA, 1950-1955; CSGA, 1948-1955; Sao Paulo, Brazil, 1953; Cal. WC Soc., 1955; One or two-man: AG Hamilton; AG Windsor; AG London (Ont.); Mtl. A. Gal. Contributor illus. to Creative Living; MacLean's; Canadian Home Journal; Chatelaine; Mayfair and other publications.*

CAISERMAN, GHITTA—*Painter, Lith., T.*
353 Kensington Ave., Westmount 6, Que.

B. Montreal, P.Q., Mar. 2, 1923. *Studied*: Parsons Sch. Des., A.B.; ASL, and with Moses Soyer. *Member*: ARCA; CSGA; CGP. *Honours*: Scholarship, Parsons Sch. Des.; O'Keefe Art Award, 1950; F., Institute Allende, Mexico. *Work*: NGC; Beaverbrook Coll., Fredericton; Mtl. Mus. FA; AG Hamilton; AG Tor.; Univ. Toronto; Saskatoon A. Centre; Imperial Oil Co.; Helena Rubinstein Coll.; Windsor AA Col.; AG Vancouver. *Exhibited*: LC, 1954; CSGA; CGP, 1952, 1954, 1956; RCA, 1954, 1956; Montreal; Seattle, Wash.; and others. Contributor illus. to Weekend Magazine of Montreal Daily Star. *Position*: Instr. FA, Sir George Williams College.

CARDIFF, M. KATHLEEN—*Painter, Ser., T.*
11311 58th St., Edmonton, Alta.

B. Edmonton, Alta., Apr. 6, 1913. *Studied*: Univ. Alberta, with H. G. Glyde, J. B. Taylor, D. Barry, and others. *Member*: Edmonton A. Cl.; Alberta Soc. A.; CSPEE (Assoc.). *Work*: CSPEE; Edmonton Jr. Hospital Lg.; murals in private homes. *Exhibited*: Winnipeg Show, 1956; Canadian Women Painters, 1957; CSPEE, 1955-1958; Alberta Soc. A., 1948-1958; Western Pr. M., 1957; Edmonton A. Cl., 1938-1958; Edmonton A. Gal. Teachers' Exh., 1956-1958. Contributor illus., Art Forum. *Positions*: Instr. A., Hillcrest Country Cl., Edmonton; Edmonton A. Gal.; Sec., Alberta Soc. A., 1954-1956, 1958.

CASSON, ALFRED JOSEPH—*Painter, Des.*
43 Rochester Ave., Toronto, Ont.

B. Tor., May 17, 1898. *Studied*: OCA under H. Britton. *Member*: Group of Seven, 1926-33; OSA; CGP; CSPWC. *Honours*: RCA (Pres. 1948-52); pres. OSA 1941-5. *Work*: AG Tor.; NGC; Williams Memorial Gal., London, Ont.; Hart House, Univ. Tor. *Exhibited*: OSA 1921-46; RCA 1923-46; Group of Seven 1924-31 & '36; Wembley 1924-5; Pittsburgh 1925; Paris 1927; Baltimore 1931; CGP 1931-46; S. Dominions 1936; Toledo 1936; Coronation 1937; Tate 1938; Gloucester 1939; WFNY 1939; GGE 1939; Rio 1944; Yale 1944; DPC 1945; UNESCO 1946. *Position*: V. Pres., A. Dir., Sampson-Matthews, Ltd., Toronto.*

CHALLENER, FREDERICK SPROSTON—*Mural Painter*
1 Breadalbane St., Toronto, Ont.

B. Whetstone, Eng., July 7, 1869. *Studied*: Ont. Sch. of A., and under George Reid, Tor. *Member*: OSA; hon. memb., Tor. A. & Let. Cl. *Honours*: ARCA 1891; RCA 1899; medal Buffalo 1901, St. Louis 1904. *Work*: hon. City of Toronto; Ontario Parliament Bldg.; mural dec. in theatres, hotels, houses. Commissions: Can. War Memorials, 1918. *Exhibited*: Indian and Colonial Exh., London 1886; OSA 1889-1952; RCA 1890-1941; CNE, Tor. 1890-1950; Chicago 1893; Pan-Am. Exh. Buffalo 1901; St. Louis 1904; Festival of the Empire 1910; Wembley 1924-5; NGC

Can. War Memorials 1924; Paris 1927; Tate 1938; WFNY 1939; DPC 1945. *Teaching*: Central Tech. Sch., Tor. 1921-4; OCA 1927-1952 (Retired).*

CHAMBERS, ROBERT WILLIAM—*Cartoonist*
Halifax Herald, Ltd.; 23 MacDonald St., Halifax, N.S.

B. Wolfville, N.S., Apr. 13, 1905. *Studied*: ASL, with George Bridgman, Frank DuMond; Grand Central A. Sch., with Pruett Carter. *Member*: Nova Scotia Soc. A. *Honours*: Nat. Newspaper Citation, 1950, 1952, award, 1953. *Exhibited*: Nova Scotia Soc. A. *Position*: Cart., Halifax Herald, Ltd., Halifax, N.S.

CHIARANDINI, ALBERT—*Painter*
32 Rutland St., Toronto, Ont.

B. Udine, Italy, Sept. 30, 1915. *Studied*: Ontario Col. A., with A. Beatty, F. Challener, J. Alfsen. *Honours*: Scholarship (2), Ontario Col. A. *Exhibited*: OSA, 1938; RCA, 1948; AG Hamilton, 1952, 1954, 1955; Hamilton A. Gal., 1956; Victoria, B.C., 1957; Italian Spring Festival, Toronto, 1958.

CHICOINE, RENE—*Painter, T., Cr.*
Ecole des Beaux-Arts, 3450 rue St.-Urbain, Montreal, P.Q.

B. Montreal, 1910. *Studied*: Beaux-Arts, Mtl. *Work*: Musee de Quebec; Court House, Mtl. *Exhibited*: since 1928. *Position*: Instr., Ecole des Beaux-Arts, Montreal, P.Q.; A. Cr., Le Devoir, Montreal, 1956- .

CHRYSTAL, ARTHUR—*Painter, Et., Eng.*
1424 King St., East, Hamilton, Ont.

B. Edinburgh, Scotland, Mar. 20, 1904. *Studied*: Edinburgh Col. A., D.A. *Member*: Soc. Scottish A. *Work*: Perth, Scotland A. Gal.; AG Hamilton. *Exhibited*: Royal Scottish Acad., 1938-1947; Soc. Scottish A., annually; AG Hamilton, 1954 (one-man). Guide lecture with the exh. "Some Edinburgh Painters," AG Hamilton. *Position*: Instr., Central Tech. Sch., Hamilton, Ont., 1949, 1955-56.*

CLARK, (MRS.) PARASKEVA—*Painter*
56 Roxborough Dr., E., Toronto 5, Ont.

B. St. Petersburg, Russia, Oct. 28, 1898. *Studied*: under S. Zaidenberg, V. Schoukhaeff, C. Petrov-Vodkin, and at Leningrad Acad. of Arts 1918-21. *Honours*: Hamilton, Ont., 1948; purchase prize, Winnipeg A. Gal., 1954. *Member*: CGP; CSPWC; OSA; ARCA. *Work*: NGC; AG Tor.; Napier AG, New Zealand; Dalhousie Univ. Commissions: war records of women's divisions armed forces 1945. *Exhibited*: S. Dominions 1936; Coronation 1937; Tate 1938; Great Lake Exh. 1938-9; Gloucester 1939; Int. WC, Chicago 1939; WFNY 1939; Addison 1942; Yale 1944; Hackley A. Gal., 1955; Rio 1944; DPC 1945; CGP; CSPWC; OSA; New Zealand, 1958; PAFA 1949; BMFA 1949; NGA, Wash., D.C. 1950; Sao Paulo, Brazil, 1951; Festival of Britain, 1951; WAC, 1958; AG Tor., 1953 (2-man); AA Mtl., 1955-56 (2-man); Macdonald Col. (one-man); Hart House, Univ. Toronto, 1956 (one-man).

CLOUTIER, ALBERT EDWARD—*Painter, Des., Ser.*
522 Pine Ave., West, Montreal 18, P.Q.

B. Leominster, Mass., June 12, 1902. *Studied*: Monument National, Mtl., under E. Dyonnet, E. H. Holgate, A. Y. Jackson. *Member*: RCA; CSPWC; CSGA; FCA. *Honours*: Dow prize, 1949, 1951. *Work*: NGC; Dept. External Affairs; Seagram Coll.; Pulp & Paper Assn. of Canada; murals, Queen Elizabeth Hotel, Mtl.; des. Canadian pavilion, WFNY 1939; work also in private colls. *Exhibited*: AA Mtl., 1938-1948; S. Dominions, 1936; RCA; NGC, 1945, 1946; Montreal Mus. FA, 1958 (one-man); Montreal A. Cl., 1958 (one-man). *Positions*: Chief, Gr. Dept., Canadian Govt. War Services, 1940-43; RCAF war artist, 1943-46; Des.-Consultant, freelance, 1955- ; Instr., Ecole des Beaux-Arts, 1955-57.

COLVILLE, ALEXANDER—*Painter, E.*
Mount Allison University, Sackville, N.B.

B. Toronto, Ont., Aug. 24, 1920. *Studied*: Mount Allison Univ. with Stanley Royle, B.F.A. *Work*: New Brunswick Mus.; NGC; AG Tor.; AG Hamilton; Lord Beaverbrook

Coll., and private colls. in U.S. and Canada. *Exhibited*: "Sporting Arts," AFA Olympics Exh., 1956; Walker A. Center, 1954; Nebraska AA, 1954; Valencia, Venezuela, 1955; Brussels World's Fair, 1958; one-man: Hewitt Gal., N.Y., 1953, 1955; Laing Gal., and Hart House, Toronto, 1958. *Position*: Instr., Mount Allison Univ., Sackville, N.B.

COMFORT, CHARLES FRASER—*Painter, E.*
104 South Drive, Toronto 5, Ont.

B. Edinburgh, Scotland, July 22, 1900. *Studied*: Winnipeg Sch. A.; ASL, N.Y.; Univ. Utrecht. *Member*: RCA (Pres.); CGP; OSA; CSPWC; F., RSA, London. *Honours*: prizes, Great Lakes Exh., Buffalo, 1938; Toronto 1951; Doctor of Laws, Mount Allison Univ., 1958. *Work*: NGC; AG Tor.; Hart House, Univ. Tor.; AG Winnipeg; AG Hamilton; murals, North American Life Bldg., Stock Exchange, Tor.; Hotel Vancouver, Dominion Bank Bldg., Vancouver; Central Station, Mtl. *Exhibited*: S. Dominions 1936; Tate 1938; WFNY 1939; Gloucester 1939; Addison 1942; Yale 1944; Rome, Italy; Amsterdam, Holland, 1945; Nat. Gal., London, 1944, 1945; NGC 1945; UNESCO 1946. Contributor to Canadian Art, Journal of Canadian Architectural Inst., and others. Lectures: Canadian Art; Material Techniques of Painting. *Position*: Assoc. Prof., Dept. A. & Archaeology, Univ. Toronto.

COOKE, EDWY FRANCIS—*Painter, T. L.*
Department of Art & Archaeology, University of Toronto, 86 Queen's Park (5); 190 Heward Ave., Toronto 8, Ont.

B. Toronto, Ont., Mar. 10, 1926. *Studied*: Univ. Toronto, B.A.; Univ. Iowa, M.F.A. *Member*: CSPWC. *Honour*: Canada Council grant for overseas research, 1958. *Work*: AG Tor.; London (Ont.) Mus. A. *Exhibited*: Extensively in Canada, 1944-58 with RCA; CGP; CSPWC; CSGA; Mtl. Mus. A.; NGC; OSA; Can. Nat. Exh., etc. One-man: Hart House, Univ. Toronto, 1947, 1952; London (Ont.) A. Mus., 1955. *Position*: Instr., Drawing & Painting, A. Workshop, 1951- ; AG Tor., 1951- ; Univ. Toronto, 1954- . Cur., Lee Collection, Hart House, Univ. Toronto, 1953- ; L., Hist. of Art, Univ. Toronto, 1952- .

COOMBS, EDITH GRACE (Mrs. James Sharp Lawson) —*Painter, S., Gr., L., T., I.*
58 Howitt St., Guelph, Ont.

B. Hamilton, Ont., Dec. 22, 1891. *Studied*: OCA with G. A. Reid, J. E. H. MacDonald, A. Lismer; N.Y. Sch. F. & App. A. *Member*: OSA; CSGA; WAA; Three Arts Cl., N.Y.; CAA. *Work*: Hart House, Univ. Tor.; NGC; Hamilton AG; Queen's Univ., Kingston; Machar House, Kingston; St. Joseph's Guelph; NGC. *Exhibited*: NGC; Wembley, 1925; Paris, 1927; Women's Int. Exh., Detroit; Willingdon Comp., Ottawa, 1929; CNE; OSA; AA Mtl.; CSGA; AG Tor., 1950; London (Ont.) AG 1952; Hamilton AG 1952; OSA Small Pictures Exh., 1948-1958; Ont. Agricultural Col., Guelph, 1954 (one-man) traveling exh., 1952-1956. Illus., "The Brave Little People," 1933; "E. Grace Coombs" by Lorne Pierce, 1949. *Position*: Instr., OCA, 1918-1956.

COPE, DOROTHY (Mrs. C. A.)—*Painter*
840 Evelyn Drive, West Vancouver, B.C.

B. Vancouver, B.C., Sept. 5, 1915. *Studied*: Vancouver A. Sch. *Member*: B.C. Soc. A.; CSPWC. *Honour*: Winnipeg Show, 1957 award. *Exhibited*: B.C. Annual, 1938-1958; B.C. Soc. A., 1949-1958; CSPWC, 1954-1958; Winnipeg Show, 1956-1958; OSA, 1958; Montreal Spring Show, 1958; "100 Years of British Columbia Art," 1958.

CORKUM, HILDA—*Painter*
37 Walnut St., Bridgewater, N.S.

Studied: Vesper George Sch. A.; Ogunquit Sch. Painting; Dalhousie Univ. Summer Sch. *Member*: Nova Scotia A. Soc.; South Shore A. Center, Bridgewater (Sec.). *Exhibited*: Nova Scotia Soc. A., annually; Nova Scotia traveling exhs.; 2 one-man exhs., Nova Scotia. *Positions*: Instr., Adult Edu., Yarmouth, N.S.; Nova Scotia College of Art.

COSGROVE, STANLEY—*Painter*
1507 Crescent St., Montreal, P.Q.

B. Montreal, Dec. 23, 1911. *Studied*: Beaux-Arts, Mtl.; AA Mtl., and with Orozco in Mexico. *Honours*: medal,

Beaux-Arts, Mtl.; traveling scholarship in Quebec; Govt. F., France, 1953. *Work*: NGC; Vancouver A. Gal.; Winnipeg A. Gal. *Exhibited*: Yale 1944; DPC 1945; Rio 1946; UNESCO 1946; one-man: Beaux-Arts 1939; AA Mtl., 1944; Mexico 1943; Quebec 1939; Dominion Gal., 1949.

COUGHTRY, JOHN GRAHAM—
Painter, S., Des., T.
7 Sultan St., Toronto, Ont.

B. St. Lambert, Que., June 8, 1931. *Studied*: Montreal Sch. A. & Des.; Ontario Col. A. *Honours*: Eaton traveling scholarship, Toronto, 1953; prizes, Winnipeg Nat. Exh., 1957; Montreal Mus. FA, 1958; A. Dir. Cl., Toronto, 1956-1958, medal, 1956. *Work*: Toronto A. Gal.; Winnipeg A. Gal.; NGC. Mural, Revere Electric Bldg., Toronto; sc. relief, Beth David Synagogue, Toronto. *Exhibited*: Guggenheim Mus., N.Y., 1958; Carnegie Inst., 1958; 2nd Biennial Canadian Art, 1957; WAC, 1958; major Canadian exhibitions, 1957-1958. *Positions*: Instr., drawing & painting, Ontario Col. of Art; Animated Film Des., Canadian Broadcasting Corp., 1956-1958.

COULING, GORDON—*Educator, P.*
Macdonald Institute, Ontario Agricultural College; h. 5 Simpson Way, Guelph, Ont.

B. Guelph, Ont., Nov. 21, 1913. *Studied*: Ontario Col. A., Toronto; N.Y. Univ. *Member*: Canadian Assn. Univ. T.; Western A. Lg.; Guelph Creative AA; CAA. *Work*: murals, St. Michael's Cathedral, Toronto; Metropolitan United Church, Toronto; St. John's, Elora; Trinity United Church, Kitchener, and other churches and public buildings in Ontario; Ontario Agricultural College; London A. Gal. *Exhibited*: OSA, 1947; Can. Younger A. Group, 1946, 1947; British Columbia FA Soc., 1945, 1946; AG Hamilton, 1951, 1952, 1955; Guelph Creative AA, 1948-1955; Western Ontario Fair; Kitchener A. Gal.; Five Counties A.T. traveling exh.; Western Ontario A. Lg., 1953-1958; one-man: Vancouver AG, 1946; Ontario Col. A. Lectures: "Community Art Organization"; "Art and Adult Education"; "Good Design in the Home." Assisted Ontario Dept. Edu. in founding & developing the following: Northern Ontario AA, Canadian Lakehead AA, Five Counties AA, Guelph Creative AA. *Position*: Pres., Guelph Creative A., 1948-53; Fed. Canadian A. (Nat. Exec.), 1948-49; Fed. Canadian A., Ontario Region, 1953; Asst. Prof., Dept. A. & Home Planning, Macdonald Inst., Ontario Agricultural Col., Guelph, Ont., 1949- .

COURTICE, RODY KENNY—*Painter, T.*
R.R. 1, Markham, Ont.

B. Renfrew, Ont., Aug. 30, 1895. *Studied*: OCA, Tor.; AIC; in Paris, France, and London, England. *Member*: CSGA; CSPWC; OSA; CGP; Heliconian Cl. *Work*: various public and private colls. *Exhibited*: Nationally and internationally. Lectures on Children's Art. *Position*: Instr., children's classics, AG Tor.*

COX, ELFORD B.—*Sculptor*
520 Finch Ave., East, Willowdale, Ont.

B. Botha, Alta., July 16, 1941. *Studied*: Univ. Toronto, B.A. *Member*: OSA; SSC. *Exhibited*: AG Tor.; OSA; SSC.*

CRAWFORD, CATHERINE BETTY—*Painter, Gr.*
342 Thames St., South, Ingersoll, Ont.

B. Ingersoll, Ont., Feb. 5, 1910. *Studied*: Univ. Toronto, B.A., with Gordon Payne, F. H. Varley, Carl Schaeffer and others. *Member*: CSPEE. *Work*: CSPEE; Lending Lib. Canadian Art, London, Ont. *Exhibited*: CSPEE, 1951-1958; traveling exhs., CSPEE; Retrospective show of Canadian Printmaking, Toronto, 1958; Western Ontario exhs. since 1945; 3-man show, London A. Mus., 1948, 2-man, 1953; traveling exhs., Western Ontario A., 1949, 1955, 1957. *Position*: Lib., Cur. Exhibits, Public Lib., Ingersoll, Ont.

CRAWFORD, JULIA TILLEY—*Painter, T.*
49 Canterbury St.; P.O. Box 211, Saint John, N.B.

B. Kingston, N.B., Apr. 18, 1896. *Studied*: PIASch.; Cape Sch. A., with Henry Hensche, and in Europe. *Member*: N.Y. WC Cl. (Assoc.); CSPWC. *Work*: Toronto A. Gal.; New Brunswick Mus.; IBM, and in private colls. *Exhibited*: London, England, Edinburgh, Scotland; Paris,

France; CSPWC; CSGA; OSA; Montreal AA; Elmira, N.Y.; Phila., Pa.; Western Ontario circuits; Canadian Women A. traveling exhs. for Armed Forces; annually with Canadian exhs. One-man: New Brunswick Mus., 1949, 1957; Univ. New Brunswick, 1949; Acadia Univ.; Wolfville, N.S., 1949, 1956; St. Stephens, St. Andrews, N.B., 1950, 1951; Univ. Maine, 1954; Netherwood, N.B., 1956.

CROUCH, RICHARD EDWIN—*Museum Director*
Victoria St.; Williams Mem. Library and Art Gallery, London, Ont.

B. London, Ont., Apr. 14, 1895. *Studied:* Univ. W. Ont., B.A., LL.D.; Univ. of Paris. *Member:* Am Library Assn. Contributor: Can. art and library journals. Lectures: functions of art museum, libraries. *Positions:* Dir. Workers' Educ. Assn. for W. Ont. 1922-3; Chief Librarian, London, from 1923; Dir. Art Mus. from 1940.

CRYDERMAN, MACKIE (Mrs.)—
Educator, P., Et., L., C., Des.
12 Chalmers Ave., London, Ont.

B. Dutton, Ont. *Studied:* Winnipeg Sch. A., with Franz Johnston; Ontario Col. A.; Artisans Gld., Detroit, with Arthur Neville Kirk; Gld. of All. Arts & Crafts; Soc. Arts & Crafts, with Sarkis Sarkisian, and privately with Francis de Erdely. *Member:* CSPEE (Assoc.). *Honour:* prize, Western Fair, 1955. *Work:* Medway H.S.; H. B. Beal Tech. Sch., and in private colls. Scenery and sets for London Little Theatre, Dominion Drama Festival, 1949. *Exhibited:* RCA, 1938, 1939, 1941, 1944, 1945; OSA, 1940-1943; CSPWC, 1942, 1943; Contemp. Canadian A., 1950; CSPEE, 1956-1958; Canadian Nat. Exh., 1956; Western A. Lg., 1936-1956; Hamilton A. Gal.; traveling exhs.; London (Ont.) A. Gal., 1957. *Positions:* Instr. A., summer school, Univ. Western Ontario, 1946; Dept. Edu., Ontario, 1947, 1948; Dir. A., H. B. Beal Tech. & Commercial H.S., London, Ont., 1927- .

DALY, KATHLEEN (Mrs. George Pepper)—*Painter*
441 Walmer Rd., Toronto, Ont.

B. Napanee, Ont., May 28, 1898. *Studied:* OCA; Grande Chaumiere, and with Rene Pottier in Paris, France. *Member:* ARCA; OSA; Zonta Cl.; CGP; Heliconian Cl. *Work:* AG Tor.; Canadian Embassy, Copenhagen; Women's Union, Univ. Col., Univ. of Toronto; Victoria Lib., Tor. Univ.; legislative bldg., Edmonton; London (Ont.) A. Mus. *Exhibited:* OSA from 1926; RCA 1928-1958; Buenos Aires 1930; CGP 1932-1958; S. Dominions 1936; Coronation 1937; Tate 1938; WFNY 1939; Rio 1944; CSGA; CSPEE; CNE; AA Mtl.; Vancouver AG; Pratt Lib., Baltimore, Md.; Hart House, Univ. Tor.; Banff Sch. FA, 1958. Illus., "Kingdom of the Saguenay," by M. Barbeau. Contributor articles to Globe & Mail magazine.

DAOUST, SYLVIA—*Sculptor*
237 St. Joseph St., Strathmore, P.Q.

B. Mtl., May 23, 1902. *Studied:* Beaux-Arts, Mtl. *Member:* SSC. *Honours:* 1st prize (ex-aequo) Willingdon Arts Competition 1929; Prov. of Quebec scholarship to Europe 1929; ARCA 1943; Canadian Govt. scholarship, France, 1955-56. *Work:* MPQ; Collège St.-Laurent; Mtl., Monastère St. Benoît-du-lac; Univ. Mtl.; port. busts, monuments, in several chapels and churches, Mtl.; mon., "Frère Marie-Victorin," Botanical Gardens, Mtl. Commissions: Int. Bus. Machines; Portraits for Can. Bar Assn.; and Gov't Quebec. *Exhibited:* NGC; MPQ; AG Tor.; AA Mtl.; RCA since 1930; Tate 1938; Rio 1946; Albany 1946; N.Y. 1946; Expo. Religious Art, Rome, 1950. *Position:* Instr., Ecole des Beaux-Arts, Mtl.*

DAY, MABEL K.—*Painter*
24 Chestnut St., Yarmouth, N.S.

B. Yarmouth, N.S., July 7, 1884. *Studied:* N.Y. Sch. Des. (2 scholarships); Robert Henri A. Sch., and with Henry Snell, Leopold Seyffert. *Member:* Nova Scotia AA. *Honours:* prizes, Carnegie Inst. *Exhibited:* Carnegie Inst., 1 .27; AIC; PAFA; Montreal AA; Nova Scotia AA.

DEAN, ERNEST WILFRID—*Painter, Et., Ser.*
543 Simcoe St., Collingwood, Ont.

B. London, England, Sept. 8, 1890. *Studied:* Central Tech. Sch., with Frederick Challoner. *Member:* CSPEE (Assoc.). *Honour:* prize, Canadian Nat. Exh., Toronto. *Exhibited:* CSPEE, 1953-1958; traveling exhs.

deGARTHE, WILLIAM E.—*Painter*
Peggy's Cove, Halifax County, N.S.

B. Kasko, Finland, Apr. 14, 1907. *Studied:* Mount Allison Univ.; Montreal Mus. FA; and with Stanley Woodward, Rockport, Mass.; Emil Gruppe, Gloucester, Mass.; in Europe. *Member:* Nova Scotia Mus. FA; Maritime AA; Nova Scotia Soc. A.; Moncton A. Soc. *Work:* Nova Scotia Mus. FA; Barbados Mus., Bridgetown, B.W.I. *Exhibited:* Canadian traveling exhs.; Hamilton; Maritime AA; Nova Scotia Soc. A.; one-man: Halifax, N.S.; Moncton, N.B.; Fredericton, N.B.; Barbados, B.W.I. (3 one-man). Author, I., "This Is Peggy's Cove," 1956.

de PEDERY-HUNT, DORA—*Sculptor, Des.*
112 Cumberland St., Toronto, Ont.

B. Budapest, Hungary, Nov. 16, 1913. *Studied:* Royal Sch. App. A., Budapest, M.A. *Member:* ARCA; SSC. *Work:* NGC; figures, medals, ports, reliefs, paintings, etc.: St. Joseph's Motherhouse, Hamilton and Pembroke; St. Joseph's Col., Toronto; St. Peter's H.S., Peterborough; Carpenter's Union Bldg., Toronto; Notre Dame Acad., and in private colls. U.S., Canada, South America and Europe.

DEPEW, VIOLA—*Engraver, T.*
44 Westwood Ave., Hamilton, Ont.

B. Hamilton, Ont., Sept. 10, 1894. *Studied:* Ontario Col. A.; Cleveland (Ohio) Sch. A., and with J. R. Seavey; Leonard Hutchinson. *Member:* CSPEE; CSGA; Women's A. Assn. of Canada; A. Gal. Assn., Hamilton. *Honours:* gold medal, Hamilton AA, 1938; colour print chosen by CSPEE for Honorary Members' Print, 1956. *Work:* Hamilton A. Gal.; Hamilton Pub. Lib.; London (Ont.) A. Mus.; Willistead A. Mus.; Univ. Western Ontario, London. *Exhibited:* Canadian Nat. Exh., 1937; CSGA, 1935-1938; CSPEE, 1936, 1937, 1943-1946, 1956; traveling exhs.; Hamilton AA, 1937, 1938; Women's AA of Hamilton, 1943, 1944, 1946, 1956. *Position:* Supv. A., Hamilton Elementary Schs., 1946-1955.

DE TONNANCOUR, JACQUES G.—*Painter, T.*
211 Walnut Ave., St-Lambert, P.Q.

B. Mtl., Jan. 3, 1917. *Studied:* Collège Brébeuf; Beaux-Arts Mtl.; AA Mtl. under G. Roberts. *Member:* CGP Mtl. *Honours:* Brazilian govt. scholarship to Rio de Janeiro 1945-6. *Work:* NGC; AG Tor.; etc. *Exhibited:* Addison Gal. 1942; Yale 1944; Rio 1944, '46; DPC 1945; UNESCO; one-man (5) Mtl. Lectures: Can. art. Author: "Roberts." *Position:* Instr. Beaux-Arts, Mtl.; Mtl. Sch. A. & Des.*

DES BIENS, GERARD—*Sculptor, E.*
75 Deziel St., Levis, P.Q.

B. Levis, P.Q., Feb. 11, 1925. *Studied:* Quebec City Sch. FA. *Member:* Societe des Sculpteurs du Canada. *Honour:* Concours Artistiques de la Province de Quebec, 1952. *Exhibited:* Quebec Mus., 1950; Concours Artistiques, 1952 and in Montreal, Toronto. *Position:* Prof., University Laval, Quebec City, 1946-1951.

DINGLE, ADRIAN—*Painter, I.*
Upper Middle Rd., Erindale, R.R. 1, Ont.

B. Barmouth, Wales, Feb. 4, 1911. *Studied:* Goldsmiths' Col. Sch., London, and with J. W. Beatty. *Member:* Ontario Inst. Painters; ARCA; A. & Let. Cl., Toronto. *Work:* AG London (Ont.); Huron Col.; Univ. Cl., Toronto; Ontario Cl., Toronto. *Exhibited:* RCA, 1934, 1937-1958; OSA, 1934-1958; London (England) Port. Soc.; 1936; CNE, 1938, 1939; Sydney, Australia, 1955; Nat. Gal. New South Wales. Illus., covers, MacLean's magazine; Mtl. Standard. *Positions:* A. Staff, Stillwell & Darby, London, 1935-37; A. Dir., Bell Features Publ. Co., Tor., 1944; Instr., Doon Sch. FA, summer, 1952-54; private studio classes, and community groups. Book illus., Macmillan and Ryerson Publs., fictional and educational.

EVELEIGH, HENRY—*Painter, Des., E.*
1239 Green St., Montreal, P.Q.

B. Shanghai, July 26, 1909. *Studied:* Slade Sch., London. *Member:* Contemp. A. Soc., Mtl. *Honours:* prizes. Slade Sch., 1933, 1934; Can. A. Dir. Cl.; UN Poster Comp., 1947. *Work:* AA Mtl. *Exhibited:* New English Contemp. A. Soc., London Group; Addison 1942; Yale 1944; DPC

1945; Rio 1944, 1946; Albany 1946; one-man: numerous one-man exhs., Mtl., 1944-51. *Position*: Prof., Ecole des Beaux-Arts, Montreal, P.Q., 1947- .*

FARLEY, LILIAS MARIANNE—*Painter, S., T.*
1109 Fifth Ave., Whitehorse, Yukon Terr., Canada

B. Ottawa, Ont., May 2, 1907. *Studied*: Vancouver A. Sch.; Univ. British Columbia. *Member*: Northwest Inst. Sculpture; British Columbia Soc. A.; Sculptors Soc. of Canada. *Honours*: prizes, IBM (purchase); Vancouver A. Gal. *Work*: IBM; and in private colls. Murals, Hotel Vancouver (B.C.); Federal Bldg., White Horse; color plates for Dept. Indian Affairs, Ottawa; bronze details, Hotel Vancouver; Post-office, Vancouver, B.C. *Exhibited*: RCA, 1937, 1938, 1940; Sc. Soc. of Canada, 1942-1958; Northwest Inst. Sc., 1956-1958; British Columbia Soc. A., annually; Vancouver A. Gal., 1958; one-man: Vancouver A. Gal., 1945; Univ. British Columbia, 1958.

FAUCHER, JEAN-CHARLES—*Painter, E., I.*
357 avenue de L'Epee, Outremont, Montreal, Que.

B. Montreal, May 8, 1907. *Studied*: Beaux-Arts, Mtl.; and in Paris, France. *Work*: MPQ. *Exhibited*: Yale 1944; Rio 1944; DPC 1945; Albany 1946; UNESCO 1946. Illus. children's readers, exercise books. *Position*: Prof., Ecole Normale Jacques-Cartier, Montreal, P.Q., and Ecole des Beaux-Arts, Montreal.

FENWICK, KATHLEEN M.—*Museum Curator, Ed.*
National Gallery of Canada; 218 MacLaren St., Ottawa, Ont.

B. London, England, June 17, 1901. *Studied*: Oxford Univ.; Julian Acad., Grande Chaumiere, Paris; Goldsmiths' Col.; Univ. London; Victoria & Albert Mus.; British Mus. *Work*: NGC. Contributor to many NGC publications. Organized numerous exhibitions for NGC. Lectures on prints and drawings. *Positions*: Asst. Ed., Canadian Art; Adviser, Canadian Delegation UNESCO, First A, General Conference, Paris, 1946; Adjudicator Canadian Film Awards, 1958; Cur., Prints and Drawings, National Gallery of Canada, Ottawa, Ont. Art Com., Canadian Section, Brussels World's Fair, 1958.

FERNALD, HELEN ELIZABETH—
Museum Curator, E., W., L., P.
Royal Ontario Museum; 291 Avenue Road, Toronto 7, Canada

B. Baltimore, Md., Dec. 24, 1891. *Studied*: Mount Holyoke Col., A.B.; ASL; Columbia Univ.; Bryn Mawr Col.; Courtauld Inst., Univ. London. *Member*: Am. Artists Cong.; Soc. Women Geographers; Far Eastern Ceramic Group; Assn. for Asian Studies; Chinese Art Soc. of Am.; Univ. Women's Col., Toronto, Canada. *Awards*: Citation, Mt. Holyoke Col., 1952; Mary Lyon scholar in A. & Archaeology, & Zoology, 1914. *Exhibited*: Phila. Plastic Cl.; Orlando, Fla., 1941. Author: "Chinese Paintings," (pamphlet), 1922; "Chinese Court Costumes," 1946; Co-compiler, Index to Journal of the American Oriental Soc., 1955. Contributor to: Educational & art magazines. Lectures: Chinese Art & Archaeology. Included in Anthology "A Harp With a Thousand Strings," 1944; "Chinese Pottery Figurines," Rome, 1950. *Positions*: Cur., Far Eastern Section, Univ. Pennsylvania Mus., 1921-35; Map Ed., China Unit of U.S. Army Map Service, 1943-44; Asst. Prof., Chinese Studies, Univ. Toronto, 1944-54; Acting Keeper, East Asiatic Art, Univ. Toronto, 1946- ; Cur., Far Eastern A., Royal Ontario Mus., Toronto, 1947-1958; Research Cur., 1958- .

FINLEY, FREDERICK JAMES—*Painter, T., I.*
63 Warland Ave., Toronto 6, Ont.

B. Newcastle, Australia, June 4, 1894. *Studied*: Acad. Julien, Paris; Bavarian Acad., Munich. *Member*: RCA; OSA; CSPEE. *Honours*: J. W. L. Forster award, 1956. *Work*: NGC; Nat. Gal., Sydney. *Exhibited*: Paris, London, New York, Chicago and in Canadian exhs. since 1940. *Position*: Sec.-Treas., Royal Canadian Acad. A.; Vice-Pres., Treas., Ontario Soc. A.

FISHER, ORVILLE NORMAN—*Painter, Et., Eng., T.*
509 East 20th Ave., Vancouver, B.C.

B. Vancouver, B.C., Nov. 24, 1911. *Studied*: Vancouver Sch. of A.; B.C. Col. of FA under F. H. Varley. *Work*: NGC War Records. Commissions: Murals for R.C. Church and King Edward Hotel, New Westminster; B.C. Govt.; United Church, Nanaimo; First United Church, Vancouver; B.C. pavilion, GGE 1939; Malespina Hotel, Nanaimo; official war artist with Can. Army 1943-6. *Exhibited*: Vancouver AG 1930-9; AG Tor., 1933-7; WFNY 1939; War Art 1943, '45, NG London; War Art 1945 Stedelijk Mus., Amsterdam; War Art 1945, '46, NGC. *Position*: Inst. Vancouver Sch. of A.*

FORBES, KENNETH KEITH—*Portrait Painter*
83 Alcina Ave., Toronto, Ont.

B. Toronto, July 4, 1892. *Studied*: St. John's Wood A. Schs., London; Newlyn A. Sch.; Slade Sch. of A. under H.H. Tonks; New A. Sch. under Orchardson, London. *Member*: OSA; RCA; Wm. M. Chase Scholarship; Proctor Port. Prize 1932, '40, NAD. *Work*: Walker AG, Liverpool; Columbus (Ohio) Gal. FA; AG Tor.; NGC. *Exhibited*: NAD; RA; Carnegie Intl.; RCA; Can. War Memorials, NGC 1923, '24; Tate 1938; WFNY 1939; DPC 1945.

FOX, CHARLES HAROLD—*Craftsman*
18 Caldwell Ave., Kentville, N.S.

B. Clarks Harbour, N.S., Jan. 15, 1905. *Honours*: prizes, Canadian Nat. Exh., Toronto, 1953, 1955; Nat. Exh., St. John, N.B., 1957. *Work*: Commissioned by Gov. of Nova Scotia to execute jewelry as a gift to Princess Elizabeth and the Duke of Edinburgh, 1951. *Exhibited*: Canadian Nat. Exh., 1953, 1955, 1957; New Brunswick, 1957.

FOX, WINIFRED GRACE—*Craftsman, P., I., Des.*
18 Caldwell Ave., Kentville, N.S.

B. Avondale, N.S., Nov. 26, 1909. *Studied*: Mount Allison Univ., Sch. FA; ASL, with George Bridgman. *Member*: Nova Scotia Soc. A. *Honours*: prizes, Canadian Nat. Exh., Toronto, 1951, 1953, 1955; Nat. Exh., St. John, N.B., 1957. *Work*: des. and executed gift of jewelry for Princess Elizabeth and the Duke of Edinburgh as gift of the Province of Nova Scotia, 1951. *Exhibited*: Montreal AA; Canadian Nat. Exh., 1953, 1955, 1957; New Brunswick, 1957; Nova Scotia Soc. A., annually; Maritime and Nova Scotia traveling exhs.; one-man: Zwickers A. Gal., Halifax, N.S. Illus., "We Keep a Light"; "The Flowing Summer". *Position*: Des., Dept. Handcrafts, Nova Scotia Provincial Government, 1945- .

FRANCIS, HAROLD CARLETON—*Painter, Eng.*
Kininview Drive, London, Ont.

B. Culloden, Ont., Feb. 19, 1919. *Studied*: ASL, with Robert Brackman. *Member*: CSPEE. *Exhibited*: CSPEE, 1949-1958; CSGA, 1943, 1944, 1953; Canadian Nat. Exh., 1957; Hamilton A. Gal., 1954; Western Ontario Exh., 1942-1958. Contributor articles and illus. to Canadian Forum.

FRANCK, ALBERT JACQUES—*Painter, Rest.*
90 Hazelton Ave., Toronto 5, Ont.

B. Middleburg, Holland, Apr. 2, 1899. *Member*: OSA. *Exhibited*: RCA; OSA; CSPWC; CSGA, all annually.

GAUTHIER, JOACHIM GEORGE—*Painter*
184 Ranleigh Ave.; 1189 Yonge St., Toronto, Ont.

B. North Bay, Ont., Aug. 20, 1897. Self-taught: later studied under Frank Carmichael, Tor. *Member*: CSPWC; OSA; ARCA. *Exhibited*: WFNY 1939; Gloucester 1939.

GILLING, LUCILLE—*Etcher*
178 Alfred Ave., Willowdale, Ont.

B. Hamilton, Mo., Sept. 28, 1905. *Studied*: Kansas City AI; N.Y. Sch. F. & Appl. A.; Queens Univ., Kingston, Ont.; and in Europe. *Member*: CSPEE (Assoc.). *Exhibited*: CSPEE, 1956-1958; CSGA, 1958; Canadian Nat. Exh., 1957.

GILSON, JACQUELINE—*Painter*
8 Elmsley Pl., Toronto, Ont.

B. Melun, France, June 27, 1912. *Studied*: Ateliers d'Art Sacre, Paris, under Maurice Denis, George Devallieres.

Member: Salon d'Automne, Societe Nationale des Beaux-Arts, Paris; F., Ateliers d'Art Sacre. *Honours*: medal, Int. Exh. Dec. Arts, Paris, 1937. *Work*: paintings, AG of Castres, France; AG London, Ont.; Church of Lioux-les-Monge, France; murals, Chapel of Hospital of Brevannes, Paris, France; Way of the Cross, Basilian Seminary, Tor., Ont. *Exhibited*: Salon d'Automne, Societe des Beaux-Arts, Paris, annually, 1931-52; Salon des Tuileries, 1941-1952; one-man: Krogh Gal., Paris, 1936; Hart House, Univ. Tor., 1952; AG London (Ont.) 1951; CGP 1952-1955.*

GLYDE, HENRY GEORGE—Painter, E.
   #4 University Campus, Univ. Alberta, Edmonton, Alta.

B. Luton, England, June 18, 1906. *Studied*: Hastings Sch. of A. and Science; R. Col. A., London. *Honours*: ARCA; Pres. Alta. SA. *Work*: AG Tor.; Edmonton Mus.; NGC. *Exhibited*: R. Brit. Artists, London; RA, London; RCA; OSA; CSGA, etc. Lectures: history of art. *Teaching*: Demonstrator, R. Col. of A., London, 1930; Instr. Borough Polytechnic, London; Croydon Sch. of A.; High Wycombe Sch. of A.; head of art dept., Prov. Inst. of Technology and A., Alta. *Positions*: Prof., Hd. Dept. FA, Univ. Alberta, Edmonton, Alta.

GOETZ, PETER—Painter, T.
   59 Allen St., West, Waterloo, Ont.

B. Siberia, Russia, Sept. 8, 1917. *Studied*: Waterloo Col.; Doon Sch. FA with F. H. Varley; Mtl. Mus. FA with N. Cleghorn. *Member*: Western A. Lg.; Five Counties AA. *Honours*: prizes, Western Ontario, 1955; London, 1958; Nat. Exh., 1956-1958. *Work*: Waterloo Lib.; Kitchener YMCA. *Exhibited*: CSPWC, 1956-1958; RCA, 1958; OSA, 1958; Mtl. Mus. FA, 1955-1957; Hamilton A. Gal., 1956, 1957; Winnipeg Show, 1957; NGC traveling exh., 1958; CNE, 1956; Sports Hall of Fame, CNE, 1956, 1957; Quebec Nat. Exh., 1956-1958; Western A. Lg., 1952-1958; Western Fair, 1956-1958; Victoria, B.C., 1957; Waterloo Centennial, 1957; 3-man, London, 1958. *Positions*: Pres., Five Counties AA T. Council; Pres., Kitchener-Waterloo A. Soc.; Instr., FA, Preston H.S.

GOLDBERG, ERIC—Painter
   331 Clarke Ave., Westmount, Montreal, P.Q.

B. Berlin, Germany, Oct. 28, 1890. *Studied*: Beaux-Arts and Acad. Julian, Paris. *Member*: Eastern Group. *Work*: NGC; AA Mtl.; Joliette, P.Q. Mus.; Fredericton, N.B.; CM; Jerusalem. *Exhibited*: WFNY 1939; Addison 1942; Yale 1944; Rio 1944. *Teaching*: painting, Berlin Acad.; arts & crafts, Jerusalem.*

GOLDBERG, (MRS.) REGINA SEIDEN—Painter
   331 Clarke Ave., Westmount, Montreal, P.Q.

B. Rigaud, P.Q., July 4, 1897. *Studied*: AA Mtl.; Acad. Julian, Paris. *Member*: Contemporary A. Soc.; Mtl. *Work*: NGC. *Exhibited*: Wembley 1925; Paris 1927.*

GOLDHAMER, CHARLES—Painter, T., Lith.
   Center Rd., South Cooksville, Ont.

B. Philadelphia, Pa., Aug. 21, 1903. *Studied*: OCA. *Member*: CSPWC (Past Pres.); OSA; CSGA; CSPEE; A. & Letters Cl., Tor. *Honours*: Adamson prize for life drawing, OCA. *Work*: AG Tor.; Hart House, Univ. Tor.; War Records NGC. Commissions: official war artist with RCAF 1943-6. *Exhibited*: RCA 1928-39; OSA 1930-9; CSGA 1928-39; CSPWC 1930-9; S. Dominions 1936; Coronation 1937; Tate 1938; Gloucester 1939; WFNY 1939; War Art 1946 NGC. Author: "Lithographs of Ontario" portfolio. Contributor: Canadian Art. Lectures: Lithography. *Position*: Dir. A., Central Tech. Sch., Tor. since 1928.

GOODELL, MARY ELIZABETH—Painter, L., T.
   Mahone Bay, N.S.

B. Kirkville, N.Y., Aug. 18, 1888. *Studied*: Syracuse Univ.; Columbia Univ., T. Col., B.S.; N.Y. Sch. F. & Appl. A. *Member*: Arts Council for Nova Scotia; South Shore A. Group. *Position*: A. Instr., New York City Schools, 23 years; private instruction, Mahone Bay, N.S., at present.

GRANDMAISON, NICKOLA DE—Painter
   125 Cave Ave., Banff, Alta.

B. Russia, Feb. 24, 1892. *Studied*: St. John's Wood Sch. of A., London. *Honours*: ARCA; medal, Int. Bus. Machines exh., NY 1939. *Work*: portraits, Manitoba Law Soc. *Exhibited*: RCA 1943.*

GRAY, JOHN LORIMER (JACK)—Painter
   c/o Kennedy Galleries, 785 Fifth Ave., New York, N.Y.

B. Halifax, N.S., Apr. 28, 1927. *Studied*: Nova Scotia Col. A.; Mtl. Mus. FA, with Arthur Lismer, Gooderich Roberts. *Work*: Dalhousie Univ.; Kipling Lib.; Dominion Steel & Coal Co., Montreal; Foundation Co. of Canada; Oland's Breweries, Ltd., Canada, etc. *Exhibited*: Mtl. Mus. FA, 1944-1947, 1951, 1953; Nova Scotia Soc. A., 1945-1954; Nova Scotia Dept. Edu. traveling exh.; Maritime AA, and others. I., "A Muster of Arms," 1954.*

GRAYSON, VAUGHAN—Painter, Ser., W., L., T.
   Oyama, B.C.; also Box 247, Summerland, B.C.

B. Moose Jaw, Sask., Sept. 14, 1895. *Studied*: T. Col., Regina, Sask.; Columbia Univ. T. Col., B.S. *Member*: Nat. Ser. Soc., N.Y.; CSPEE. *Work*: Royal Ontario Mus. *Exhibited*: CSPEE, 1954, 1955, 1957; Moose Jaw, Sask., 1956 (one-man); Kelona, B.C., 1956 (one-man); Vancouver A. Gal.; Calgary, Alta. Author: "Picture Appreciation-Elementary School"; "Picture Appreciation—Junior High School." Lectures: Canadian Art.

GRIFFITH, JULIUS—Painter, Gr.
   102 Hillsdale Ave., West, Toronto 7, Ont.

B. Vancouver, B.C., Apr. 21, 1912. *Studied*: Vancouver Sch. A., with MacDonald, Varley; Central Sch. A. & Crafts, London, England, with Noel Rooke, John Farleigh; Royal Col. A., London. *Member*: CSGA; CSWPC (Pres.). *Work*: British War Artists Coll.; AG Hamilton; AG Kitchener-Waterloo, Ontario; Carleton Col., Ottawa. *Exhibited*: 1st Biennial Print Show, Tokyo, 1957; CSGA, 1947, 1951-1958; CSPWC, 1956, 1957; CSPEE, 1956-1958; one-man: Picture Loan Soc., Toronto, 1954, 1956, 1958; AG Hamilton, 1958. Illus., "River For My Sidewalk," 1953; "Sainte-Marie Among the Hurons," 1953.

GROVES, NAOMI JACKSON (Mrs.)—Writer, L., P.
   Box 167, Britannia Heights, Ottawa, Ont.

B. Montreal, Canada. *Studied*: Rannows A. Sch., Copenhagen; Sir George Williams Col.; McGill Univ., B.A., M.A.; Heidelberg, Berlin and Munich Univs.; Radcliffe Col., A.M., Ph.D. *Member*: CAA; Ernst Barlach Gesellschaft; Arctic Circle. *Honours*: Gov. General's gold medal, McGill Univ., 1933; traveling F., Canadian Fed. of Univ. Women, 1936-37. *Exhibited*: RCA, 1934; one-man: Radcliffe Col., 1939; Wheaton Col., 1942; McMaster Univ., 1953; Mtl. Mus. FA; AG Hamilton. Contributor articles and illus. to: Toronto Saturday Night; FMA Bulletin; Christian Science Monitor; Geographic Quarterly; Art News and others. Lectures: "Goethe's Drawings"; "Ernst Barlach as Sculptor, As Dramatist." Arranged graphic works of Ernst Barlach at Mtl. Mus. FA, and Royal Ontario Mus., 1951; assisted in preparation of catalog for traveling exh. of Ernst Barlach, 1955-56. *Position*: L., McGill Univ., 1933-36, Wheaton Col. 1940-42, Carleton Col., 1943-45; Asst. to Dir., NGC, 1942-43; Assoc Prof. in charge of FA, McMaster Univ., 1951-1958.

HAGAN, (ROBERT) FREDERICK—Printmaker, E., P.
   296 Court St., Newmarket, Ont.

B. Tor., May 21, 1918. *Studied*: OCA; ASL; & with George Miller, N.Y. *Member*: CSGA; CSPEE. *Exhibited*: CSGA from 1938; RCA 1939-44; WFNY 1939; OSA from 1940; CSPWC, 1940, '43, '45; CGP 1941-3; CSPEE from 1941; Rio 1946; LC, 1954, 1955; CM, 1950, 1952, 1954. Teaching: Res. Artist, Pickering College, Newmarket, Ont., 1942-6. *Position*: Instr., Graphic A., OCA, Toronto, Ont.

HAGEN, ALICE M.—Painter, C., T.
   Clairmont, Box 94, Mahone Bay, N.S.

B. Halifax, N.S., May 28, 1872. *Studied*: Victoria Sch. A. & Des. *Member*: Nova Scotia Mus. FA; Nova Scotia

A. Soc.; Canadian Gld. Potters; Nova Scotia Craftsmen's Gld. *Honour*: Silver and bronze medals, Kingston, Jamaica Inst. for Ceramic Decoration and Teaching. *Work*: Provincial Mus. Citadel, Halifax. *Position*: Instr., Vocational Sch., Nova Scotia.

HAHN, SYLVIA—*Painter, I., C., S., Eng., T.*
15 Dale Ave., Toronto, Ont.

B. Tor., May 2, 1911. *Studied*: Univ. Tor.; OCA under G. Hahn, J. W. Beatty, & others. *Member*: OSA; CSPEE. *Honours*: Gov. General's Medal, OCA, 1932. Commissions: 11 murals, R. Ont. Mus., Tor.; altar-pieces, chapel of Cowley Fathers, Bracebridge, Ont.; St. Mary Magdalene, Tor., etc. *Work*: prints in R. Ont. Mus.; Hart House, Univ. Tor. *Exhibited*: OSA from 1934; CSPEE from 1934; RCA. Illus., "Carolina Quest"; "Canadians of Long Ago." *Teaching*: Instr. Univ. Tor. Occupational Therapy course 1937-45. *Position*: Instr., Metalwork, OCA, Toronto, Ont., 1950-51.*

HAINES, FREDERICK STANLEY—
Painter, E., Et., Eng.
3 Colborne St., Thornhill, Ont.

B. Meaford, Ont., Mar. 31, 1879. *Studied*: Central Sch. A., Toronto, with William Cruickshank, G.A. Reid; Acad. Royale de Beaux-Arts, Antwerp. *Member*: OSA; RCA; Soc. Hungarian P. & Et. (hon.); Printers & Gravers in Color, London, England; Chicago Soc. Et.; CSPEE; CSPWC. *Honours*: medal, Academie Royale des Beaux-Arts, 1914. *Work*: NGC; AG Tor.; Sarnia Pub. Lib.; Saskatoon A. Gal. *Exhibited*: OSA since 1910; RCA, since 1914; Wembley, 1924, '25; Southern Dominions, 1936; Tate Gal., London, 1938; WFNY 1939; AG Tor.; and in Paris, France. *Position*: Cur., AG Tor., 1927-32; Commissioner of FA, Canadian Nat. Exh., 1932-45 ; Principal, Ontario Col. A., 1932-51. Now retired.*

HALL, JOHN A.—*Painter, E., Eng., I., Des.*
10 Kilbarry Rd.; University of Toronto, Toronto, Ont.

B. Toronto, Ont., Oct. 10, 1914. *Studied*: Ontario Col. A. *Member*: CSGA; OSA. *Work*: AG Tor. *Exhibited*: CGP; CSPWC; OSA; RCA; CSGA; WFNY 1939; Yale Univ., 1944; Rio, 1944, '46. Illustrated: "Spirit of Canadian Democracy," 1945; "These English"; "The Grandmothers"; "Glooscap's Country." *Position*: Asst. Prof. in Drawing & Des., Sch. & Dept. A. & Archaeology, Univ. Toronto. Exhibition Design: Canadian Nat. Exh.; Canadian Furniture Mart., private practice. Instr., AG Tor.; Ontario Teacher's courses; Upper Can. College, Toronto; Univ. Toronto.

HANES, URSULA ANN—*Sculptor*
41 Woodlawn Ave., West, Toronto 5, Ont.

B. Toronto, Ont., Jan. 18, 1932. *Studied*: Cambridge Sch. A., England; ASL; Columbia Univ.; Univ. Toronto, and in Italy and England. *Member*: Sculptors Soc. of Canada. *Honour*: prize, New England Soc. A., 1953. *Work*: port. bust, Stratford Shakespearian Festival Theatre, Ontario; fountains, Sheridan Nurseries, Toronto; Clarke Irwin Publ. Co., Toronto; Bas-relief murals, lobby, Temple Sinai, Toronto; Cedarbrook Sch., Toronto. *Exhibited*: Royal Canadian Acad. A., 1955, 1957, 1958; Canadian Nat. Exh., 1955, 1957, 1958; Sc. Soc. of Canada, 1955, 1958; New England Soc. A., 1953; Stratford Festival Exh., 1955, 1957; Young Canadian Contemporaries, 1957; Ontario Soc. A., 1954, 1955, 1957, 1958.

HANSON, JEAN—*Painter, Des., Gr.*
1193 Sarta Road, Oakville, Ont.

B. Toronto, Ont., Sept. 27, 1933. *Studied*: Ontario Col. A., with John Martin, Carl Schaefer, R. York Wilson. *Exhibited*: CSPWC, 1955-1958; AG Hamilton, 1955, 1957, 1958; Chapellier Gal., N.Y., 1953; Smithsonian Inst., 1956; NGC traveling exh., 1955; Montreal Mus. FA, 1956; Western Exh., London, Ont., 1956-1958; Canadian Nat. Exh., 1956; Monsanto Canadian A. Comp., 1957; OSA, 1957; Royal Ontario Mus., 1958.

HARLEY, HARRY GEORGE—*Cartoonist*
185 James St., St. Catharines, Ont.

B. St. Catharines, Ont., Feb. 22, 1929. *Studied*: Ontario Col. A.; St. Catharines Collegiate Inst.; Univ. Toronto.

Contributor cartoons to: American Weekly; Goodyear Publs.; Phila. Inquirer; Medical Economics; True Detective; Argosy; True Police Cases; Toronto Star Weekly; Weekend (Montreal Standard Magazine); Montrealer; Wall Street Journal; King Features Syndicate (Laff-A-Day); A.T.&T. Publications Syndicate, and other publications. *Position*: Editorial Cart., St. Catharines Standard, 1956- .

HARRIS, LAWREN—*Painter*
4760 Belmont Ave., Vancouver, B.C.

B. Brantford, Ont., Oct. 23, 1885. *Studied*: Univ. Tor. & in Germany & France. *Member*: Group of Seven; CGP; FCA. *Honours*: Pres. FCA 1945; LL.D., Univ. B.C.; LL.D., Univ. Toronto, 1951. *Work*: NGC; AA Mtl.; AG Tor.; Detroit Inst. of A.; Williams AG, London, Ont. *Exhibited*: all important Can. Exhs.; Wembley 1925; Paris 1927; Group of Seven 1936; S. Dominions 1936; Coronation 1937; West Coast Exh. NGC 1937; Tate 1938; WFNY 1939; Addison 1942; Rio 1944; Yale 1944; DPC 1945; Albany 1946; etc. Contributor: Canadian Art; Can. Review of Music and Art. Lectures: Democracy and Art; Abstract Painting. *Position*: Trustee, NGC, 1948- .*

HARRIS, LAWREN PHILLIPS—*Painter, T.*
Mount Allison University, Sackville, N.B.

B. Toronto, Oct. 10, 1910. *Studied*: BMFA and with his father, Lawren S. Harris, Toronto. *Member*: OSA; CGP; ARCA. *Honour*: Canadian Govt. Overseas F., 1957-58. *Work*: War Records, NGC. Commissions: official war artist with Can. Army 1943-6. *Exhibited*: S. Dominions 1936; OSA from 1936; RCA from 1938; CGP from 1938; Great Lakes Exh., Buffalo 1938-9; WFNY 1939; CSGA 1939-41; War Art 1945, '46 NGC; UNESCO 1946. *Teaching*: Instr. N. Vocational Sch., Tor., 1938-40; Trinity College Sch., Port Hope, Ont., 1940-1. *Position*: Dir. Mount Allison Sch. F. & App. A., Sackville, N.B.

HAWORTH, (Mrs. Zema)—B. COGILL—
Painter, C., T.
111 Cluny Drive, Toronto, Ont.

B. Queenstown, South Africa. *Studied*: R. Col. of A., London, under Rothenstein. *Member*: ARCA; CGP; CSPWC; OSA; Ont. Gld. of Potters. *Honours*: Dow prize, Mtl. Mus. FA, 1952. *Work*: NGC; NG South Africa; AG Tor. Commissions: murals, illuminated MSS. *Exhibited*: S. Dominions 1936; Coronation 1937; Tate 1938; Gloucester 1939; WFNY 1939; Rio 1944; CGP; CSPWC; OSA; RCA, etc. Illustrated: "Kingdom of the Saguenay." *Lectures*: Ceramics. *Positions*: Instr. Ceramics, Central Tech. Sch. and Univ. Tor.; Pres., CSPWC, 1955-56.*

HAWORTH, PETER—*Painter, Stained Glass Des.*
111 Cluny Drive, Toronto, Ont.

B. Lancashire, Eng., Feb. 28, 1889. *Studied*: R. Col. of A., London, under Rothenstein, & others. *Member*: CGP; OSA; RCA; CSPWC; A. & Letters Cl., Tor. *Honours*: prize, CSPWC, 1955; Pres., CSPWC 1936-40; Pres., Ont. region FCA 1944-5. *Work*: NGC; AG Tor.; Brazil; U.S.A. Commissions: Stained Glass in many churches throughout Canada; murals in publ. bldgs. and churches. *Exhibited*: S. Dominion 1936; Coronation 1937; Tate 1938; Gloucester 1939; WFNY 1939; Rio 1944; DPC 1945; RCA; CGP; CSPWC; OSA, etc. Illustrated: "Kingdom of the Saguenay," etc. *Lectures*: Stained Glass; Decoration; History of Art. *Positions*: Pres., OSA, 1955- .*

HEBERT, JULIEN—*Sculptor, Des., E.*
1632 Sherbrooke St., West; 4211 Westhill Ave., Montreal, P.Q.

B. Rigaud, Can., Aug. 19, 1917. *Studied*: Ecole des Beaux-Arts, Mtl.; Univ. Montreal; and with Zadkine, Paris, France. *Member*: Assn. Canadian Indst. Des.; Interior Dec. Soc. of Quebec; Sculptors Soc. of Canada. *Honours*: Des. awards, Nat. Indst. Des. Council and others, 1953-1958. *Exhibited*: Milan Trienniale, 1954, Intl. and Canadian Section; Design exhs., Canada and abroad. *Teaching*: Hist A., Ecole des Beaux-Arts, Mtl.; furniture des., Inst. of Appl. A., Mtl. *Positions*: Pres., Assn. of Canadian Indst. Des., 1958-59; Pres., Nat. Com., Intl. Plastic Arts Assn, 1957-58.

HEDLEY, ROBERT WESLEY—Art Critic

11020 89th Ave., Edmonton, Alta.

B. Ontario, Oct. 18, 1871. *Studied*: Univ. Toronto, B.A. Math.; Univ. Alberta, M.A., M.Ed., LL.D.; Columbia Univ. *Member*: Alberta Soc. A.; Edmonton A. Cl.; F., Royal Soc. A., London, England. *Exhibited*: Edmonton Soc. A. Lectures: Oriental Art; Modern Art; Art History. Author: "Art for High Schools", 1939. *Positions*: A. Supv., Edmonton Schs., 1914-29; Instr., Univ. Alberta Summer Sch., 1915-37; Normal Sch., 1929-37; A. Instr., Faculty of Edu., Univ. Alberta, 1930-39; Dir., Edmonton Mus. A., 1943-50; A. Cr., Edmonton Journal, 1951-1955 (Retired).

HEWITT, MINNIE—Educator

Lunenburg, N.S.

B. Lunenburg, N.S., Aug. 22, 1868. *Studied*: Mount Allison Col.; Halifax Sch. FA, with Sir Stanley Royale; and with Chetcuti. *Member*: Nova Scotia Soc. A.; Maritime A. Soc.; Bermuda A. Soc.; South Shore A. Centre. *Exhibited*: Nova Scotia Soc. A.; Maritime A. Soc.; Bermuda A. Soc., annually from 1931; Grand Central A. Gal.; South Shore A. Centre, annually. *Teaching*: Lunenburg County Academy; Gilbert Inst., Bermuda.

HEWTON, RANDOLPH STANLEY—Painter, T.

Glen Miller, Ont.

B. Megantic, P.Q., June 12, 1888. *Studied*: Paris under J. P. Laurens, C. Delavaille; AA Mtl. under W. Brymner. *Member*: A. Cl., Mtl.; CGP. *Honours*: RCA. *Work*: NGC; MPQ; AG Tor. *Exhibited*: RCA; AA Mtl.; CGP; Wembley 1925; Paris 1927; S. Dominions 1936. *Teaching*: AA Mtl. and RCA classes, Mtl.*

HICKLING, WALTER ROBERT—Painter, T.

40 Delaware Ave., Burlington, Ont.

B. Delhi, Ont., Mar. 1, 1924. *Studied*: Ontario Col. A.; Grande Chaumiere, Paris, France. *Exhibited*: RCA, 1948; CNE, 1951; CGP, 1955, 1956; OSA, 1954, 1958; Western Ontario, 1955; AG Hamilton, 1954, 1955. One-man: AG Hamilton, 1957; Alan Gal., Hamilton, 1958.

HILTS, ALAN—Sculptor

106 McLaughlin Blvd., Oshawa, Ont.

B. Newmarket, Ont., Apr. 2, 1908. *Studied*: in Mexico; and with Frances Loring. *Member*: Sculptors Soc. Canada (Pres. 1956-1958). *Work*: War mem., Newmarket; churches in Timmins, Kirkland Lake, Newmarket; and in private colls. *Exhibited*: RCA, 1954-1956; Sculptors Soc., 1948, 1953, 1958; NGC; AG Toronto; Vancouver A. Gal.; AG Hamilton. *Teaching*: Sculpture, Pickering Col., Newmarket; Oshawa Collegiate & Vocational Sch.

HOLGATE, EDWIN HEADLEY—Painter

Morin Heights, P.Q.

B. Allandale, Ont., Aug. 19, 1892. *Studied*: AA Mtl.; Paris under Lucien Simon, & others. *Member*: Group of Seven 1931-3; CGP; FCA. *Honours*: RCA 1935. Commissions: murals, Château Laurier Hotel, Ottawa; official war artist, RCAF 1943-4. *Work*: NGC; MPQ; Sarnia AG; AA Mtl.; Le Havre, France. *Exhibited*: Wembley 1925; NGC West Coast Exh. 1927; Paris 1927; S. Dominions 1936; Group of Seven Exh. 1936; Coronation 1937; Tate 1938; WFNY 1939; Yale 1944; Rio 1944, '46; DPC 1945; NGC War Art 1945, '46; UNESCO 1946; CGP; RCA; one-man: AA Mtl. 1933; Scott Gal., Mtl. 1937; Dom. Gal., Mtl. 1946. Illustrator: "Other Days, Other Ways," etc. *Teaching*: Instr., AA, Mtl.; wood engraving, Ecole des Beaux-Arts, Montreal.

HOLMES, REGINALD—Painter, Ser., Lith., T.

3034 West 12th St., Vancouver 8, B.C.

B. Calgary, Alta., Oct. 4, 1934. *Studied*: Vancouver A. Sch., and with Jack Shadbolt. *Member*: Fed. Canadian A.; CSPEE; Western Pr. M. *Honour*: A. E. Grauer award, Vancouver, 1958. *Exhibited*: CSPEE, 1956-1958; Western Pr. M., 1957; Contemp. A., 1958; British Columbia A., 1956-1958; British Columbia Pr. M., 1956, 1957; British Columbia Centennial, 1958; Victoria A. Gal., 1958; Vancouver A. Gal., 1958; one-man: Hart House, Univ. Toronto, 1957. *Teaching*: Drawing & Painting, Vancouver A. Sch., Vancouver A. Gal., and Univ. British Columbia.

HOO, SING (Sing Hoo Yuen)—Sculptor, T.

139 Livingstone Ave., Toronto, Ont.

B. Canton, China, Feb. 2, 1909. *Studied*: OCA; Slade Sch., London. *Member*: OSA; ARCA; SSC. Commissions: exhibits of marine life of six geological periods, 1934-9. *Exhibited*: CNE 1932-40, 1956, 1957; OSA from 1932; RCA from 1938; Sculptors Soc., 1957, 1958. Lectures: Oriental and Occidental A.

HORNE, (ARTHUR EDWARD) CLEEVE—Painter, S.

181 Balmoral Ave., Toronto, Ont.

B. Jamaica, B.W.I., Jan. 9, 1912. *Studied*: in England with D. Dick; OCA; and in Europe. *Member*: RCA; A. & Let. Cl., Toronto (Pres. 1955-); OSA; SSC. *Work*: Alexander Bell mem., Brantford, Ont.; war mem., Law Soc. of Upper Canada; NGC; Shakespeare Mem., Stratford, Ont.; Ports. of persons prominent in Govt., industry, banking, edu., etc. *Exhibited*: NGC; RCA since 1928; OSA 1939; SSC since 1935; CNE since 1936. *Positions*: A. Consultant, Imperial Oil Bldg., Toronto; A. Adv., Ontario Hydroelectric Power Comm.; St. Lawrence Seaway Power House Project, 1957-1958.

HORNYANSKY, NICHOLAS—Etcher, Des., T.

44 Westmoreland Ave., Toronto 4, Ont.

B. Budapest, Hungary, Apr. 11, 1896. *Studied*: Acad., Budapest; with Porcaboeuf, in Paris. *Member*: OSA; RCA; CSPEE; A. & Letters Cl., Tor.; Am. Color Pr. Soc. *Honours*: G. A. Reid award, 1955. *Work*: NGC; Royal Ont. Mus., Tor.; Musee Plantain, Antwerp; Budapest Mus.; Mercier Mem. Hall, Malines, Belgium; Mus. New Mexico; Parliament, Budapest; LC. *Exhibited*: OSA 1933-1958; PAFA 1934; S. Dominions 1936; LC 1945-1954; RCA; CSPEE; WFNY 1939; Buenos Aires; Univ. Maine, 1952. *Position*: Instr., Printmaking, Etching, OCA, Toronto, Ont.

HOUSSER, YVONNE McKAGUE—Painter, Des., I., L.

R.R. #1, Markham, Ont.

B. Toronto, Aug. 4, 1898. *Studied*: OCA; Academies Colarossi, Grande Chaumiere and Ranson, Paris, France; in Vienna with Cizek. *Member*: CGP; OSA; AG Tor.; RCA. *Work*: NGC; AG Tor.; Hart House, Univ. Tor.; AG London (Ont.); Trinity Col.; Victoria Col., Tor.; murals, Canadian Pacific Railways; and work in many private colls. *Exhibited*: Wembley 1925; S. Dominions 1936; Coronation 1937; Great Lakes Exh., 1938; Tate 1938; WFNY 1939; Rio 1944; DPC 1945; NGC; RCA; AA Mtl.; OSA; CSGA; CGP; 2-man: Montreal Mus. FA; 3-man: AG Toronto. Illus., covers, Canadian Home Journal. Lectures: Child Art, Vision and Art. *Position*: Instr., OCA, Toronto, Ont., 25 years (now retired); Instr., Doon Sch. FA, summer sessions.

HUBBARD, ROBERT HAMILTON—Museum Curator, E.

National Gallery of Canada (4); 255 Metcalfe St., Ottawa 4, Ont.

B. Hamilton, Ont., June 17, 1916. *Studied*: McMaster Univ., B.A.; Inst. d'art et d'archéologie, Paris; Musées Royaux, Brussels; Univ. Wisconsin, M.A., Ph.D. *Member*: CAA; AAM. Contributor: Canadian Art; Art Quarterly; Architectural Review; Journal Royal Architectural Int. of Canada; Connoisseur; Oxford Companion to Art; Everyman's Encyclopaedia, and other publications. Author: "European Paintings in Canadian Collections," 1955; new catalogues of NGC Collections: Vol. 1 (Older Schools), 1957; Vol. 2 (Modern European Schools), 1958; Vol. 3 (Canadian Schools), 1959. Lectures: Canadian Art. *Teaching*: history of art, Univ. Kansas City 1942-4; McMaster Univ., 1943-4; Univ. Toronto 1945-6; Carleton Univ., Ottawa 1944-52. *Position*: Chief Cur., National Gallery of Canada.

HUGHES, EDWARD JOHN—Painter

Shawnigan Lake, B.C.

B. North Vancouver, B.C., Feb. 17, 1913. *Studied*: Vancouver Sch. A. *Member*: CGP. *Honours*: Vancouver Sch. A. scholarships; Emily Carr scholarship, 1947; Canada Council Fellowship, 1958. *Work*: NGC; AG Tor.; AG Vancouver; Dominion Gal., Mtl.; Hart House, Univ. Toronto; Brock Hall, Vancouver; Univ. New Brunswick; AG Victoria, and others. *Exhibited*: AG Vancouver; NGC.

HUME, R. M.—*Museum Curator*

Vancouver Art Gallery, West Georgia St., Vancouver, B.C.

Member: Am. Assn. Mus. Dirs.; Canadian Mus. Assn. *Position*: Cur., Vancouver A. Gallery, Vancouver, B.C.

HUMPHREY, JACK WELDON—*Painter*

10 Spruce St., Saint John, N.B.

B. Saint John, N.B., Jan. 12, 1901. *Studied*: BMFA Sch.; NAD; Cape Cod Sch. A. *Member*: CGP; CSPWC; CSGA (V.Pres. '52); Maritime A; Saint John A. Cl. *Honours*: Hon. deg., LL.D., Univ. New Brunswick, 1951; Canadian Govt. Overseas F., 1952-54; Canada Council grant, 1958. *Work*: NGC; Hart House, Univ. Tor.; AG Tor.; New Brunswick Mus.; Saint John A. Cl.; Mt. Allison Univ.; Dalhousie Univ.; Lord Beaverbrook Coll., and in many private colls. *Exhibited*: Tate 1938; Gloucester 1939; WFNY 1939; CSGA from 1939; BM 1941; Addison 1942; United Nations Print Exh., Phila., Pa., 1943; Rio 1944, 1946; Yale 1944; DPC 1945; Arnot A. Gal., 1945; CGP; CSPWC; Phila. WC Cl.; UNESCO, 1946; VMFA 1949; NGA, Wash., D.C., 1950; SFMA 1950; SAM 1950; BMFA 1949; AG Tor.; Picture Loan Soc., Tor., and many others. One-man: AA Mtl., 1943; AG Vancouver 1945; New Brunswick Mus., 1949 (retrospective), 1954; Mt. Allison Univ.; Univ. New Brunswick; Robertson Gal., Ottawa, 1954; Salon d'Art Libre, Paris, 1953; DMFA, 1958; London, England, 1955; Canadian Biennial, 1955, 1957.

HYDE, LAURENCE—*Engraver, P., W.*

83 John St., Ottawa, Ont.

B. London, England, June 6, 1914. *Studied*: Central Tech. Sch., Tor. *Member*: CSGA. *Work*: NGC; AG Vancouver; LC; AG Tor. *Exhibited*: CSGA; OSA; CSPEE; WFNY 1939; Rio 1946. Author: "Southern Cross" (novel in wood engravings, chosen as one of "Best Western Books," 1952). Author, I., "Brave Davy Coon," 1955; Des. seven stamps for Canadian Postal Dept. *Position*: A. Dir., Nat. Film Bd. of Canada.*

HYNDMAN, ROBERT STEWART—*Painter, Des., T.*

233 Metcalfe St.; 74 Acacia Ave., Ottawa, Ont.

B. Edmonton, Alta., June 28, 1915. *Studied*: Central Tech. Sch., Tor.; Central Sch. A. & Crafts, London. *Work*: I., Canadian Club booklets; weekly editorial cartoon for Ottawa Evening Journal; War Records, NGC; Government House, Ottawa. *Exhibited*: RCAF Exh., 1945, 1955; NGC; War Art, 1945, 1946; AG Mtl.; AG Vancouver; AG Hamilton; Ottawa, Ont.; Venezuela. *Position*: Instr., Eve. classes, Ottawa H.S.*

INGLIS, JOHN NOEL—*Painter*

42 Blantyre Ave., Toronto 13, Ont.

B. Toronto, Ont., Feb. 25, 1931. *Studied*: Ontario Col. A. *Member*: CSGA. *Honours*: prizes, Ontario Col. A., 1951, 1952. *Exhibited*: OSA, 1952; one-man: McKellar, Ont., 1953; Woodsworth House, Toronto, 1954; Hayter Gal., Toronto, 1958.

ISKOWITZ, GERSHON—*Painter, Et., Lith.*

59 Borden St., Toronto, Ont.

B. Warsaw, Poland, Nov. 24, 1922. *Studied*: Warsaw Acad.; Crakow Acad.; Munich Acad. FA, and with Oscar Kokoschka. *Member*: CSGA. *Honours*: Scholarship to Munich Acad. FA, 1946; traveling scholarship, 1947.

JACKSON, ALEXANDER YOUNG—*Painter*

Manotick, Ont.

B. Montreal, P.Q., Oct. 3, 1882. *Studied*: Monument National, Mtl.; AIC; Acad. Julian, Paris, under J. P. Laurens. *Member*: CGP; Group of Seven (orginal); OSA; A. & Letters Cl., Tor. *Honours*: RCA (resigned 1933); LL.D., Queen's Univ.; C.M.G. 1946. *Work*: Tate, London; Springfield (Ill.) AA; Dunedin Gal., New Zealand; NGC; AG Tor.; AA Mtl.; MPQ, etc. Commissions: official war artist with Can. Army in France 1917-18. *Exhibited*: Can. War Memorials 1923, '24; Wembley 1925; West Coast Exh., NGC 1927; Paris 1927; S. Dominions 1936; Group of Seven Exh. 1936; Coronation 1937; Tate 1938; WFNY 1939; Addison 1942; Rio 1944; Yale 1944; DPC 1945; Albany 1946; UNESCO 1946. Author and

Illustrator: "The Far North " 1928 "Banting as an Artist," 1943; "A Painter's Country," 1958. Contributor: Canadian Art magazine. *Position*: Instr., Banff Sch. of FA from 1943-49.

JANES, PHYLLIS [Mrs. H. F.]—*Painter, Lith., I.*

320 Keewatin Ave., Toronto, Ont.

B. Alliston, Ont., Feb. 15, 1905. *Studied*: Ontario Col. A.; Toronto Univ. *Member*: CSGA; OSA. *Work*: Imperial Oil, Ltd.; Toronto Telegram Coll. *Exhibited*: LC; OSA; CGP; various exhs. in Canadian galleries. One-man: Picture Loan Soc., 1952; Victoria Col., 1955; Imperial Oil Exh., 1958. I., Safety Books for Children and numerous booklets.

JONES, JACOBINE—*Sculptor*

49 Highland Crescent, York Mills, Ont.

B. London, England. *Studied*: Regent St. Polytechnic, and under H. Brownsword, London; and in Denmark. *Member*: RCA; SSC; OSA. *Honours*: gold medal, Regent St. Polytechnic, London. *Work*: Kelvin Mus., Glasgow; Confederation Life Bldg., Toronto; Trinity Col. Chapel; St. John's Convent, Willowdale, Ont.; NGC; panels, Gore Fire Insurance Bldg., Galt, Ont.; Bank of Montreal, Tor.; Bank of Canada, Ottawa; York Township Bldg.; St. Thomas Hospital; Hart House, Tor.; Bank of Nova Scotia, Tor.; figures, Our Lady of Mercy Hospital, Tor.; Archives Bldg., Tor. *Exhibited*: Liverpool 1929; RA 1930; Paris Salon 1932; RCA from 1932; AA Mtl. 1934; Tate 1938; WFNY 1939. Lectures on Sculpture.

KAHANE, ANNE—*Sculptor*

5232 Byron Ave.; 3125 Maplewood Ave., Montreal, P.Q.

B. Vienna, Austria, Mar. 1, 1924. *Studied*: CUASch., N.Y. *Member*: Sculptors Soc. of Canada. *Honours*: prizes, Concours Artistiques, Quebec, 1956; Winnipeg Show, 1955, 1956, 1957. *Work*: NGC; Provincial Mus., Quebec; AG Toronto. *Exhibited*: Canadian Pavilion, Brussels World Fair, 1958; Venice Biennale, 1958; Carnegie Inst., 1958; Winnipeg Show, 1955-1957; Canadian Nat. Exh., 1958.

KLOEZEMAN, BERT—

Painter, Des., T., Gr., Comm. A., I., L.

553 Mary St., Woodstock, Ont.

B. Ipoh, Malaya, July 16, 1921. *Studied*: Royal Acad. FA, The Hague, Holland. *Member*: ACPE. *Exhibited*: CSPEE, 1956-1958; Western A. Lg., 1954-1956; Royal Acad. FA, The Hague, 1943, 1944, 1950; The Hague Mun. Mus., 1950; one-man: Zwolle, Holland, 1942, 1945; Woodstock, Ont., 1953-1958; Ingersoll, Can., 1957; Woodstock Mun. Mus., 1957. Contributor illus. to De Wereld. *Position*: Comm. A., Holland and Canada, 1947- .

KOPMANIS, AUGUSTS A.—*Sculptor*

19 Millbrook Crescent, Toronto 6, Ont.

B. Riga, Latvia, Mar. 17, 1910. *Studied*: Acad. FA, Riga, Latvia. *Member*: Sculptors Soc. of Canada; Colour & Form A. Soc., Toronto. *Exhibited*: Montreal Mus. FA, 1954-1957; Winnipeg Show, 1956, 1957; RCA, 1958; Sculptors Soc., 1958; Open Air Exh., Montreal Parks Dept., 1958; Colour & Form Soc., 1953-1958; Western Ontario Exh., 1956, 1957; Hamilton, Ont., 1957, 1958; OSA, 1956, 1958. Illus., "Season in Latvian Folk Songs," 1956.

KRAMOLC, THEODORE MARIA—*Painter, Et., Eng.*

46 Foxden St., Don Mills, Ont.

B. Ljubljana, Yugoslavia, Mar. 27, 1922. *Studied*: in Yugoslavia; Ontario Col. A., and with Hornyansky. *Member*: CSGA, CSPEE. *Work*: AG Hamilton. *Exhibited*: CSPEE, 1950-1958; CSGA, 1951-1958; Fed. Canadian A., 1950; Canadian Nat., 1951; AG Hamilton, 1950-1953, 1955, 1957, 1958; London, Ont., 1958; Unaffiliated A., 1950-1952; Picture Loan Soc., 1952, 1955, 1958; RCA, 1954, 1955; Buenos Aires, 1954; Washington, D.C. Prints, 1955; Contemp. Canadian and European A. (Graphic), Greenwich Gal., Toronto, 1956; Stratford, Ont., 1956; CNE, 1956, 1957; Vancouver A. Gal., 1957; Eglinton Gal., Toronto, 1958; Reference Lib., Toronto, 1958; WAC, 1958; traveling exhs. One-man: Hart House,

Univ. Toronto, 1955; Upper Canada Col., 1957; Picture Loan Soc., 1957; Little Gal., Toronto, 1958 and previously in Europe.

LAW, ANTHONY—*Painter*

c/o Armdale P.O., Halifax, N.S.

B. London, England, Oct. 15, 1916. *Studied*: Univ. Ottawa, with F. Hennessy, F. Brownell, F. H. Varley and P. Tudor-Hart. *Member*: FCA; Nova Scotia Soc. A. *Honours*: Dow prize, AA Mtl., 1939, 1950. *Work*: NGC; MPQ. *Exhibited*: NG London, 1943, 1944; NGC 1945, 1946; Ottawa AA 1935, 1936; Beaux-Arts, Quebec, 1937; AA Mtl., 1938, 1939, 1950; Portland Soc. A., 1938; Royal Canadian Acad., 1948; Vancouver, B.C., 1951. *Position*: Cdr., RCN, at present.*

LAWSON, MRS. JAMES SHARP.

See Coombs, Edith Grace

LEFORT, AGNES—*Painter, I., E., Cr., L.*

1504 Sherbrooke St., West, Montreal, P.Q.

B. Saint-Remi, P.Q., Jan. 5, 1895. *Studied*: Monument National, and with J. St. Charles, Dyonnet, J. Y. Johnstone, Mtl.; Beaux-Art, Paris, with Andre L'Hote; Beaux-Arts, Mtl. *Member*: AA Mtl.; Canadian Authors Assn. *Work*: MPQ, Quebec; Mus. Seminary Joliette; College Grasset. *Exhibited*: AA Mtl., since 1923; RCA since 1923; Rio de Janeiro, 1944, 1946; DPC 1945; Sao Paulo, Brazil; MPQ 1946, 1947; Riverside Mus., N.Y., and traveling exhs. in Canada and U.S.A.; one-man: Montreal 1936, 1949. Illus., "Science sans Douleur"; "Histoire des Sciences." *Position*: Owner-Dir., Agnes Lefort Galleries, Montreal.

LEIGHTON, A. C.—*Painter, E., Des., I., L.*

134 6th Ave., Northwest, Calgary, Alta.; also P.O. Box 38, Midnapore, Alta.

B. Hastings, Eng., 1901. *Member*: Ridley A. Cl.; East Sussex A. Cl.; Imperial A. Lg.; R. Soc. Br. Artists; CSPWC. *Honours*: ARCA. *Work*: Eastborne, Hastings, Brighton, Hull, Glasgow; Vancouver AG; Edmonton Mus.; AA Mtl.; Commissions: paintings for English railways, Can. Pacific Ry., Vickers, Ltd., London. *Exhibited*: WFNY 1939; RA; RSBA; R. Soc. WC Painters; R. Inst., London; Paris Salon; Hull Municipal AG; RCA. Illustrator: "Far Horizons"; "Victoria, B.C." Contributor: Studio; Sphere, London; Revue moderne, Paris. Lectures: Art Appreciation. *Position*: Art Dir., Prov. of Alta. 1929-37; founded Banff Sch. of FA (Retired).

LEMIEUX, JEAN PAUL—*Painter*

2008 Dickson, Sillery, P.Q.

B. Quebec, Nov. 18, 1904. *Studied*: Beaux-Arts, Mtl.; Acad. Colarossi, Paris. *Honours*: prizes Quebec Provincial Painting; AA Mtl., 1934, 1951; Govt. Overseas Award, 1954-55. *Member*: ARCA. *Work*: Painting chosen for Coll. of Queen Elizabeth; AG Tor.; MPQ. *Exhibited*: AA Mtl. 1931, '34, '38, '41; RCA 1934, '40, '42; Addison Gal., 1942; Yale 1944; DPC 1945; Albany 1946; UNESCO 1946; CGP, 1951; Palais Montcalm, Quebec, 1953 (one-man); Sao Paulo, Brazil, 1957; Brussels World's Fair, 1958; Canadian Nat., 1957; Mexico City, 1958; Australian Tour of Canadian Painting, 1957; Carnegie Inst., 1958; Univ. of British Columbia, Vancouver, 1958 (one-man). Contributor: Canadian Art Magazine. Lectures: Can. Art, Blake, Gauguin. *Teaching*: Beaux-Arts, Mtl., 1933-4; Ecole du Meuble, Mtl. 1935-6. *Position*: Instr. Beaux-Arts, Quebec.

LENNIE, BEATRICE—*Painter, S., Des., I., T., L., C.*

909 Drayton Road, Vancouver North, B.C.

B. Nelson, B.C., June 16, 1906. *Studied*: Vancouver Sch. A.; Cal. Sch. FA., and with H. Tauber, Frederick Varley, Ralph Stackpole. *Member*: British Columbia Soc. A.; Sculptors Soc. of Canada; Puppeteers of Am.; Northwest Inst. of Sc.; Vancouver A. Cl. *Work*: on public buildings and in private colls. U.S. and Canada. Port. busts, plaques, fountains, panels, figs., Patullo Bridge, New Westminster, B.C.; Federal Bldg., Vancouver; Shaughnessy Military Hospital; Acad. of Medicine; Vancouver Hotel; Vancouver Labor Temple; Ryerson Mem. Centre, and others. *Exhibited*: NGC; Sculptors Soc.; RCA; Vancouver

A. Gal.; AG Toronto; Mtl. AA; Seattle, Puyallup, Wash.; San Francisco, Cal. Cartoons to Vancouver Daily Province.

LISMER, ARTHUR—*Painter, E., L.*

1485 Fort St., Montreal, P.Q.; Art Association of Montreal, 1379 Sherbrooke St., W., Montreal, P.Q.

B. Sheffield, England, June 27, 1885. *Studied*: Sheffield Col. of A.; Antwerp Acad. *Member*: OSA; FCA; CGP; CSPWC. *Honours*: ARCA 1919; hon. diploma N.S. Col. of A. 1940; LL.D., Dalhousie Univ. 1941. *Work*: NGC; Vancouver AG; AG Tor.; AA Mtl.; MPQ; Hart House, Univ. Tor., etc. *Exhibited*: Can. War Memorials, NGC 1923, '24; Wembley 1925; Paris 1927; Carnegie Int. 1935; Group of Seven, 1936; S. Dominions 1936; Coronation 1937; Tate 1938; Gloucester 1939; WFNY 1939; GGE 1939; Addison 1942; Yale 1944; Rio 1944, '46; DPC 1945; Albany 1946; UNESCO 1946. Lectures: Hist. and appreciation of art; Design; Child Art; Art Education, etc. *Teaching*: Principal, NS Col. of A. 1916-19; OCA 1919-27; Educ. Supv. AG Tor. 1926-38; taught in S. British Dominions 1938; Prov. Teachers' College, Columbia 1938-9; Educ. dir., NGC 1939-40. *Position*: Principal, Sch. of A. and Des., AA Mtl.*

LOCHHEAD, KENNETH CAMPBELL—*Educator, P.*

Regina College School of Art, Regina, Sask.

B. Ottawa, Ont., May 22, 1926. *Studied*: Queen's Univ., Kingston; PAFA; Barnes Fnd. *Honours*: Cresson traveling scholarship, PAFA; Lewis Ware scholarhip, PAFA; prize, O'Keefe award, 1950; Western Canada A. Exh., 1953; NGC Biennial, Mural Commission, Regina Branch Canadian Legion. *Position*: Dir., Sch. A., Regina Col., Regina, Sask.*

LONG, MARION—*Painter*

261 Poplar Plains Rd., Toronto, Ont.

B. Tor., Sept. 19, 1882. *Studied*: Tor. under G. A. Reid; N.Y. under Wm. Chase and R. Henri. *Member*: OSA. *Honours*: RCA 1933; OSA. *Work*: AG Tor.; Sch. of Nursing, Univ. Toronto; St. Hilda's Col., Tor.; Univ. of Sask.; Queen's Univ., Kingston. Commissions: Portraits, St. Hilda's Col., Tor.; Fed. of Medical Women of Can.; Royal Norwegian Air Force Hdqtrs., Oslo; Branksome Hall, Toronto; Academy of Medicine, Toronto; Knox Col., Toronto. *Exhibited*: OCA since 1908; Tate 1938; DPC 1945; RCA annually; Mus. A., London, Ont., 1957; Canadian Nat., 1958.

LORING, FRANCES NORMA—*Sculptor, Des.*

110 Glenrose Ave., Toronto, Ont.

B. Wardner, Idaho, Oct. 14, 1887. *Studied*: Beaux-Arts, Geneva; Munich under C. Guttner; Acad. Colarossi, Paris; BMFA; AIC; ASL. *Member*: FCA; RCA; OSA; SSC; Women's AA. *Honours*: medal, Univ. Alberta, 1955; Hon. LL.D., Univ. Toronto. *Work*: NGC; AG Tor. Commissions: war records 1918; Monuments at Galt; St. Stephen's, Osgoode Hall, Tor.; architectural sc., Parliament Bldgs., St. Michael's Hosp., Bank of Mtl., Tor.; Rainbow Bridge, Niagara Falls; panels, Bank of Montreal. *Exhibited*: Can. War Memorials NGC 1923, '24; Wembley 1925; Paris 1927; Coronation 1937; Tate 1938; WFNY 1939. Author: "Wood Carving." Lectures: sculpture, dec.; Fndr., past Pres., SSC; Fndr (one) FCA, Nat. A. Council.*

LUKE, ALEXANDRA

(Margaret Alexandra Luke McLaughlin)—*Painter*

705 Simcoe St., North, Oshawa, Ont.

B. Montreal, P.Q., May 14, 1901. *Studied*: Banff Sch. FA; Hans Hoffmann Sch. FA. *Member*: Heliconian; CGP; CSPWC; Painters Eleven, Toronto; Women's Lyceum AA, Oshawa. *Work*: Univ. Alberta; Trinity Col., Univ. Toronto; King St. H.S., Oshawa. *Exhibited*: RCA, 1954, 1955; OSA, 1950-1952; CGP, 1953, 1955, 1956; Canadian Nat. Exh., 1954-1958; Canadian Biennial, 1955; Mtl. Mus. FA, 1952; Provincetown AA, 1950; Painters Eleven, 1954, 1955, traveling exh., 1958; Riverside Mus., N.Y., 1956; DMFA, 1958; Winnipeg Show, 1957; CSPWC, 1953-1958; one-man: Picture Loan Soc., Toronto, 1952; Eglinton Gal., Toronto, 1955; Park Gal., Toronto, 1958.

LUZ, VIRGINIA—*Painter, T.*

Central Technical School; 113 Delaware Ave., Toronto 4, Ont.

B. Toronto, Ont., Oct. 15, 1911. *Studied*: Central Tech. Sch., with Peter Haworth, Charles Goldhamer, Robert Ross. *Member*: OSA. *Work*: Huron Col., London, Ont.; Canadian Dept. External Affairs; and in private colls. *Exhibited*: RCA, 1952, 1958; CGP, 1945, 1947, 1948, 1952, 1953; CSPWC, 1947, 1948, 1952, 1953, 1956-1958; CNE, 1953, 1956; Canadian Women A., 1947 (N.Y.); Canadian Tour, 1948-49; OSA, 1945, 1946, 1948, 1952-1958; AG Hamilton, 1952, 1953, 1955-1958; 2-man: Toronto, 1951, 1952; 3-man: London, 1954. *Position*: Instr., Illus., Central Tech. Sch., Toronto, Ont.

LYMAN, JOHN—*Painter, E.*

1509 Sherbrooke St., West, Montreal 25, P.Q.

B. Biddeford, Maine, Sept. 29, 1886. *Studied*: McGill Univ.; Royal Col. A., South Kensington, England; Julian Acad., and with Matisse, Paris, France. *Member*: F., Royal Soc. A., London; Humanities Assn. of Canada. *Work*: NGC; MPQ; Mtl. Mus. FA; Univ. Manitoba; McGill Univ.; Lord Beaverbrook Gal., Fredericton, N.B. *Exhibited*: Salon d'Automne; Salon des Tuileries; Salon des Independentes, Paris; Dallas 1937; Tate 1938; WFNY 1939; Addison 1942; Detroit Inst. A. 1943; SFMA 1943; Portland (Ore.) A. Mus. 1944; Univ. Vermont 1944; Yale 1944; Rio 1944, 1946; Sao Paulo, Brazil, 1945; Albany Inst. Hist. & A., 1945; Santiago, Chile, 1946; UNESCO 1946; BMFA 1949; NGA, Wash., D.C., 1950; Coronation Exh., 1953, and principal cities of Canada since 1913. Author: "Morrice." Contributor numerous articles in journals. *Position*: Assoc. Prof. FA, Former Chm. Dept., McGill Univ., Montreal, Quebec (Retired).

MACDONALD, GRANT—*Painter, I., T.*

"Tarquin," R.R. 7, Kingston, Ont.

B. Montreal, Que., June 27, 1909. *Studied*: OCA; ASL; Heatherley's A. Sch., London, Eng. *Member*: ARCA; OSA; CSGA. *Honours*: medal, A. Dir. Cl., Tor., 1952. *Work*: Redpath Lib., McGill Univ.; Univ. Toronto; AG Tor.; Queen's Univ.; Kingston Collegiate Inst.; many portraits, 1940-52. *Exhibited*: OSA 1949, 1951-1955; Canadian Nat. Exh., Tor., 1949-51; CGP 1950, 1952; CSGA 1947, 1950-1952; RCA 1949, 1951-1955; AA Mtl., 1941-1944, 1949, 1953-1955; A. Dir. Cl., Tor., 1951, 1952; AG Hamilton 1949, 1951, 1953-1955; AA Kingston 1948-1955; Vancouver A. Gal., 1952-1955. Illus., "Shakespeare for Young Players," 1942; "Haida," 1946; "Behind the Log," 1947; "Jimney Cricket," 1927; "Sunshine Sketches of a Little Town," 1948; "A Masque of Aesop," 1952; "Renown at Stratford"; "Twice Have the Trumpets Sounded," and others. *Position*: Instr., Figure Drawing, Queen's Univ., Kingston, Ont., summer school, 1948, 1952, 1953.*

MACDONALD, JAMES WILLIAMSON GALLOWAY—*Painter, Des., T.*

Ontario College of Art; 4 Maple Ave., Toronto, Ont.

B. Thurso, Scotland, May 31, 1897. Studied: Edinburgh Col. of A. *Member*: CGP; British Columbia Soc. FA (life); CSPWC; CSA; Painters Eleven. *Honours*: Canadian Govt. Overseas F., 1954. *Work*: NGC; AG Vancouver; Univ. British Columbia; Imperial Oil, Ltd., Coll., and in private colls. Commissions: murals in Hotel Vancouver. *Exhibited*: RCA 1939-36; S. Dominions 1936; Coronation 1937; Tate 1938; DPC 1945; CGP, 1945-1955, 1958; OSA, 1945-1955; CSPWC, 1945-1955; Painters Eleven, 1953-1955, 1957; Can. Nat. Traveling Exhs.; DMFA, 1958; one-man: Hart House, Univ. Toronto, 1957; Park Gal., Toronto, 1958. *Teaching*: Vancouver Sch. A., 1926-33; British Columbia Col. A., 1933-35; Provincial Inst. Tech. & A., Calgary, 1946-47; Banff Summer Sch. FA, 1940-46. *Positions*: Textile Des., Sundours Fabrics, Carlisle, England, 1922-25; Hd. A., Prov. Inst. Tech. & A., Calgary; Prof. Painting, Ontario Col. A., Toronto, 1947- .

MacDONALD, MANLY—*Painter*

4 Rosedale Rd., Toronto, Ont.

B. Point Anne, Ont., Aug. 15, 1889. *Studied*: OCA; Albright A. Sch.; BMFA. *Member*: OSA. *Honours*: RCA trav. scholarship 1920; ARC. *Work*: NGC; A. Mus. London, Ont. *Exhibited*: Can. War Memorials NGC 1923, '24; Wembley 1924; WFNY 1939; Rio 1944; RCA.*

MacDONALD, THOREAU—*Illustrator, P., Des.*

Thornhill, Ont.

B. Tor., Apr. 21, 1901. *Studied*: under his father, J. E. H. MacDonald, but largely self-taught. *Work*: NGC, AG Tor. *Exhibited*: Wembley 1925; Paris 1927; Coronation 1937; Tate 1938; WFNY 1939. Illustrator: "Maria Chapdelaine" 1938, and about 50 other books.*

MACKAY, DONALD CAMERON—*Educator, P., Et.*

Nova Scotia College of Art; 26 South Park St., Halifax, N.S.

B. Fredericton, N.B., Mar. 30, 1906. *Studied*: Nova Scotia Col. A.; Dalhousie Univ.; Academie Colorossi, Paris, and with Arthur Lismer. *Member*: Maritime AA; New Brunswick Soc. A.; CSGA; F., Royal Soc. A.; Canadian A. Council; Canadian Soc. Edu. through Art. *Honours*: bronze medal, Art of the Western Hemisphere Exh., 1940; silver medal, Royal Inst. Canadian Architects, 1955. *Work*: NGC; Nova Scotia Mus. FA; T. Col., Nova Scotia; BM; N.Y. Pub. Lib.; AIC. Murals, Halifax Mem. Lib.; port., Dalhousie Univ. *Exhibited*: RCA; CSPWC; CSPEE; CSGA; Canadian Art Exh.; Maritime AA; Nova Scotia Prov. Painters; Nova Scotia Soc. A.; Chelsea A., London, England; one and two-man exhs., Halifax, London and Toronto. Author: "Master Goldsmiths and Silversmiths of Nova Scotia," 1948; I., "Warden of the North"; "History of Nova Scotia"; "Story of Newfoundland"; "Story of Nova Scotia"; "Highlights of Nova Scotia History"; "Tales of the Sea." Contributor to Journal of Education; Dalhousie Review; Halifax Chronicle; most Canadian young people's publications. *Positions*: Special Lecturer in FA, Dalhousie Univ.; Prof. A., Nova Scotia Dept. Edu.; Principal, Nova Scotia College of Art, Halifax, N.S., 1938- .

MacNAMARA, GORDON—*Painter*

25 Severn St., Toronto, Ont.

B. Toronto, Ont., Dec. 14, 1910. *Work*: NGC. *Exhibited*: Toronto, Ont.; Montreal, Que.; in Mexico; Ottawa; Long Island, N.Y.; 20 one-man exhs., Toronto, Montreal, Ottawa, Long Island.

MADSEN, AAGE—*Sculptor*

Piedmont, P.Q.

B. Rierslev, Denmark, Nov. 4, 1898. *Member*: Sculptors Soc. of Canada. *Work*: NGC. *Exhibited*: Canadian Nat. Exh., 1956. *Honours*: prizes, Wood Carving Exh., (3). Specializes in bas-relief wood sculpture.

MANAREY, THELMA (Mrs. C. H.)—*Painter, Ser., T.*

12026 93rd St., Edmonton, Alta.

B. Edmonton, Alta., May 2, 1913. *Studied*: Univ. Alberta; Univ. Washington (summer); Banff Sch. FA. *Member*: Alberta Soc. A.; Edmonton A. Cl.; CSPEE. *Honours*: Banff Sch. FA scholarship, 1955; Banff Sch. FA purchase award, 1956. *Exhibited*: Nat. Ser. Soc., N.Y., 1956; CSPEE, Toronto, 1956-1958.

MARKELL, JOHN H.—*Painter, T.*

1474 Main St.; 9 St. John's Ave., Winnipeg, Man.

B. Winnipeg, Man., May 14, 1919. *Studied*: ASL, with Jon Corbino; with A. J. Musgrove, Winnipeg. *Member*: Winnipeg Soc. A. *Honours*: scholarship, ASL, 1940. *Work*: Winnipeg A. Gal.; NGC; Ballet paintings for Royal Winnipeg Ballet. *Exhibited*: NGC, 1955; Royal Canadian Acad., 1953-1955; Canadian Painters, London, England, 1955; Winnipeg A. Gal., 1942-1955; Western Canadian Painters, 1953, 1954; AG Tor., 1954, 1955; AG Hamilton, 1953-1956; Mtl. Mus. FA, 1946, 1947; Vancouver A. Gal., 1954-1956, etc.*

MARTIN, BERNICE FENWICK (Mrs. Langton)—*Painter*

150 Millwood Road, Toronto 7, Ont.

B. Shelburne, Ont., July 7, 1912. *Studied*: Univ. Toronto; Ontario Col. A., and with J. W. Beatty, Frank Carmichael, P.C. Sheppard. *Member*: Fed. Canadian A. *Honours*: prize, Malloney's A. Gal., 1941. *Work*: in many private colls. *Exhibited*: AG Tor., 1943; Royal Canadian Acad. A.; Mtl. Mus. FA, 1945, 1947; Quebec Mus. FA, 1947; Winnipeg A. Gal., 1947-1954; AG Hamilton, 1950, 1955; one-man: Eaton's Gal., 1943, 1952; Casa Loma A. Gal., 1943; Towne Cinema, 1950; Gld. All. A., 1951-1958; Beaches Lib., 1952, and abroad.

MARTIN, JOHN—*Painter, Des., C., Gr., I., T., L.*
    Swan St., Ayr, Ont.

B. Nuneaton, England, Aug. 1, 1904. *Studied*: Nottingham Sch. A.; Slade Sch. A., London. *Members* CSPWC; ARCA; A. & Letters Cl., Tor.; A. Dir. Cl., Tor.; CPE; OSA. *Honours*: Needham prize, England, 1916; prize, CPE, 1936; Reid prize, Tor., 1943, 1944; purchase, Mtl., 1957; purchase, AG Hamilton, 1958. *Work*: Nuneaton A. Cl.; Leicester AG; London Mus. A.; Ontario Hist. Soc.; Sarnia, Hamilton AG; Royal Ontario Mus. *Exhibited*: RCA 1935-1952; OSA 1930-1952; CPE 1934-1946; Sarnia AG 1933-1935, 1939, 1941, 1942; CSPWC 1940-1952; Vancouver AG 1950-1952; London AG 1950-1952. Lectures: Industrial and Social Design; History of Art. *Position*: Dir., Dept. Des., OCA, Toronto, Ont.; private classes, Stratford A. Soc., Tillsonburg A. Soc., at present; Instr., summer schs. at Stratford; Intr., Lakehead AA; A. Dir., Ridley Col., St. Catharines, Ont.; St. Catharines AA.

MARTIN, LANGTON—*Painter, C., Des., Et., Eng.*
    200 Sterling Tower (1); 150 Millwood Road, Toronto 7, Ont.

B. Toronto, Ont., May 15, 1903. *Studied*: Ontario Col. A.; Univ. Toronto, and with J. W. Beatty, Peter Sheppard. *Member*: Fed. Canadian A.; CSPEE. *Honours*: prizes, Canadian Nat. Exh. (Leathercraft), 1953. *Exhibited*: Canadian Nat. Exh., 1953; CSPEE traveling exhs., 1954, 1958; Toronto Pub. Lib., 1950; Royal Ontario Mus., 1954, 1958.

MASSE, GEORGES SEVERE—*Painter, T., L.*
    4823 St. Catherine St., West; 5655 Cote St-Luc Rd., Montreal, P.Q.

B. Montreal, P.Q., Aug. 10, 1918. *Studied*: Mtl. Mus. FA Sch., with Sherriff-Scott; Banff Sch. FA, with Frederic Taubes. *Honours*: prize, Mtl. FA, 1938. *Exhibited*: Mtl. Mus. FA, 1942, 1944, 1946, 1947, 1955; Royal Canadian Acad., 1948, 1958; Quebec A. Festival, 1951; AG Hamilton, 1948, 1949, 1951, 1952, 1954, 1955; Quebec Provincial Exh., 1956, 1957; Victoria A. Gal., 1957, 1958; one-man: Montreal. *Position*: Scientific Illus., Univ. Montreal, 1941; Instr., Montreal Mus. FA, 1942-43; Dir. own Art School, 1944- .

MASSON, HENRI—*Painter, T.*
    70 Spruce St., Ottawa, Ont.

B. Namur, Belgium, Jan. 10, 1907. *Studied*: Athénée Royale, Brussels; Ottawa AA. *Member*: CGP; CSPWC; CSGA. *Honours*: LL.D., Assumption Col., Windsor, Ont., 1955. *Work*: NGC; MPQ; AG Tor.; Hart House, Univ. Tor.; Vancouver AG; Winnipeg AG; etc.; Caracas (Venezuela) Mus.; Vinadelmar (Chile). *Exhibited*: WFNY 1939; Addison Gal. 1942; Intl. WC Exh., Brooklyn 1942; Yale 1944; Rio 1944, '46, DPC 1945; Phila. WC Cl., 1946; UNESCO 1946; Wash., D.C., 1951; Sao Paulo, Brazil; one-man: Toronto, Eaton Gal., 1945-6; Ottawa, Little Gal. 1944-6; Mtl., Art Français 1946; AA Mtl., 1953; Winnipeg, Ottawa, Robertson Gal., etc. *Position*: Instr., children's classes, NGC, 1948-50; Instr., Queen's Univ. Summer Sch., 1948-52; Banff Sch. FA, 1954.*

MAY, HENRIETTA MABEL—*Painter, T.*
    1495 Balfour Ave., Vancouver, B.C.

B. Montreal, P.Q. *Studied*: AA Mtl. under Wm. Brymner; Paris. *Member*: CGP; FCA; B.C. Soc. A. *Honours*: ARCA; Jessie Dow prize, AA Mtl. 1915, '18; Mtl. Women's Cl. prize 1919. *Work*: NGC; Musée de la Province de Quebec; AA Mtl.; Brandon Hospital; Regina Pub. Lib.; AG Tor.; Vancouver AG. *Exhibited*: RCA since 1913; Can. War Memorials NGC 1923, '24; Wembley 1925; Paris 1927; Buenos Aires 1930; CGP since 1933; S. Dominions 1936; Coronation 1937; Tate 1938; WFNY 1939; Rio 1944; DPC 1945; AA Mtl.; Beaver Hall Grp., Mtl. *Positions*: Supv. children's classes, National Gallery of Canada and Instr. Elmwood School, Rockcliffe, Ottawa.*

McCARTHY, DORIS JEAN—*Painter, T., C.*
    Central Technical School, Toronto, Ont.; 1 Meadowcliff Dr., Toronto 13, Ont.

B. Calgary, Alta., July 7, 1910. *Studied*: OCA; Central Sch. A. & Crafts, London, Eng. *Member*: ARCA; OSA; CSPWC. *Work*: AG Tor.; Regina AG; Victoria Col.; Pickering Col.; Huron Col. Commissions: mural, Earls-court Lib., Tor.; Creche St-Aidan's Church, Tor. *Exhibited*: with all major society exhs. in Canada since 1931. *Position*: Instr., Drawing & Painting, Central Tech. Sch., Toronto, Ont.

McCURRY, HARRY ORR—*Former Museum Director*
    Kingsmere, P.Q.

B. Ottawa, Ont., Aug. 21, 1889. *Studied*: art and art administration in U.S.A., England and Europe. *Member*: Museums Assn (England); Assn. A. Mus. Dir.; AAMus. *Honours*: (Hon.) LL.D., F., Royal Soc. A.; Officier d'Academie, France, 1948. Organized many exhibitions at and circulated by, NGC, including Wembley 1924, 1925; Paris 1927; S. Dominions 1936; Tate 1938; WFNY 1939; Rio 1944, 1946; DPC 1945 (jointly); UNESCO 1946; Design in Industry 1946 to present; Canadian Painting, BMFA 1949; Canadian Painting, NGA, Wash., D.C. 1950; Sao Paulo, Brazil, 1951; Venice Biennale 1952, and others in British Commonwealth and U.S.A.; loan exh. programme throughout Canada; lending and edu. services of NGC, including distribution of silk screen prints to armed services in Canada and overseas during the war, and to schools; NGC school broadcasts. *Positions*: Government Service, 1910; Dir., Nat. Film Inst., Pres. Ottawa Branch, 1941-43; Organizer, 1st Pres., Canadian Mus. Assn.; Chm. War Artists Com., 1942-46; Exec. Asst., 1919, Sec., 1922, Asst. Dir., 1928, Dir., 1939-55, National Gallery of Canada, Ottawa, Ont., Canada.*

McGEOCH, LILLIAN JEAN—*Painter, Des.*
    King Georges Road, Toronto 18, Ont.

B. Sundridge, Ont., Jan. 17, 1903. *Studied*: Ontario Col. A. *Member*: Nova Scotia Soc. A.; Women's A. Assn., Toronto; Hamilton AA. *Work*: Nova Scotia Soc. A.; Maritime AA; Dept. Edu., Halifax. *Exhibited*: Nova Scotia Soc. A.; Maritime AA; Women's A; one-man: Halifax, 1950; Toronto, 1957.

McINNES, GRAHAM CAMPBELL—*Writer, Cr.*
    454 Cloverdale Rd., Rockcliffe Park, Ottawa, Ont.

B. London, England, Feb. 18, 1912. *Studied*: Univ. Melbourne, Australia, M.A. Author: "A Short History of Canadian Art," 1939; "Canadian Art," 1950; "Lost Island," 1954. Contributor: "Canadian Portraits," 1941; "A Pocketful of Canada," 1946. Contributor to Canadian art publications and journals. *Position*: Hd., Commonwealth Div., Dept. External Affairs, Ottawa, Ont.*

McLAUGHLIN, MARGARET ALEXANDRIA LUKE.
    See Luke, Alexandra

MELVIN, GRACE WILSON—*Painter, Des., T., I., L.*
    6212 Balaclava St., Vancouver 13, B.C.

B. Glasgow, Scotland. *Studied*: Glasgow Sch. A. *Member*: British Columbia Soc. A.; CSGA; Canadian Fed. A. *Honours*: Traveling scholarship, Glasgow Sch. A.; prize, Winnipeg Show, 1956. *Work*: NGC; Victoria Gal. A.; Canadian Engineers "Book of Remembrance" (2 World Wars) now in St. Paul's Cathedral, London, England. Illus., "The Indian Speaks," and other books. *Exhibited*: CGP, 1954, 1958; British Columbia Centennial, 1958; British Columbia Soc. A., 1953-1958; British Columbia Soc. Graphic A., 1946-1958; Winnipeg Show, 1956, 1957; one-man: Vancouver A. Gal.; Victoria A. Gal.; Univ. British Columbia, etc. *Position*: Hd. Dept. Des., Vancouver Sch. A., 1934-52, and other teaching positions prior.

MILLER, H. McRAE—*Sculptor, Des., Comm. A., T., P.*
    R.R. #2, Range 6, Ste. Agathe des Monts, P.Q.

B. Montreal, Que., 1897. *Studied*: ASL, N.Y. under John Sloan; Beaux-Arts, Mtl., under Alfred Laliberte; and with C. W. Simpson, F. S. Coburn. *Honours*: ARCA 1944; SSC 1948; RCA, 1955. *Work*: NGC; Quebec Provincial Mus. Commissions: portrait sc., Quebec Provincial Mus. *Exhibited*: RCA 1927-1930, 1936-1951, 1955, 1958; Mtl. Mus. FA 1927-1930, 1935-1945; NGC 1950. *Position*: Pres., SSC, 1955-56.

MITCHELL, JOCELYN TAYLOR. See Taylor, Jocelyn

MITCHELL, THOMAS W.—*Painter, I., E.*
56 Drury Lane, Barrie, Ont.

B. Clarksburg, Ont., May 14, 1879. *Studied:* PAFA. *Member:* OSA. *Honours:* ARCA; Pres. CSGA 1912-14; Vice-Pres. OSA 1923-35. *Work:* NGC; Saskatoon AG; many private colls. in Canada, U.S. and Great Britain. *Exhibited:* NGC; RCA; OSA; AA Mtl.; CSPWC; one-man: Toronto, Mtl.; Winnipeg. Illustrator: Canadian Mag.; Macleans' Mag.; Toronto Star. Lectures: Can. artists. *Positions:* art dir., J. J. Gibbons Ltd., Tor. 1905-12; and Brigdens' Ltd. 1916-32; Instr., A. Cr., Barrie Collegiate Inst., Barrie, Ont.; Instr., A. Cr., Barrie A. Cl., 1938- .

MORISSET, GERARD— *Educator, W., Mus. Cur.*
1180 West rue Saint-Cyril, Quebec, P.Q.; Museum of the Province of Quebec, Quebec, P.Q.

B. Cap-Santé, P.Q., Dec. 11, 1898. *Studied:* L. en Loi, Univ. Laval; diplomé, Ecole du Louvre, Paris. *Member:* Fellow, Royal Soc. of Can.; Attaché hon. des Musées nationaux de France. *Honours:* medal, Royal Soc. of Canada, 1954. Author: "Paintres et Tableaux"; "Coup d'Oeil sur les Arts en Nouvelle-France"; "Paul Lambert"; "Vie et oeuvre du Frère Luc"; "François Ranvoysé"; etc. Contributor: Revue populaire; Monde Français, Voix du Canada (Radio). *Position:* Cur., Provincial Mus. and Dir. of Inventaire des oeuvres d'art, Province of Quebec.

MORRIS, KATHLEEN MOIR—*Painter*
Apt., 1, 3745 Coronet Rd., Montreal, P.Q.

B. Montreal, P.Q., Dec. 2, 1893. *Studied:* AA Mtl. *Member:* CGP; CSPWC. *Honours:* ARCA 1929; Willington A. Comp. *Work:* NGC; AA Mtl.; Hart House, Univ. Tor.; Mackenzie King Mus.; Canadian Legation, Paris, France. *Exhibited:* Wembley 1924, 1925; RCA since 1914; OSA 1921-1923; Paris 1927; Buenos Aires 1930; S. Dominions 1936; Coronation 1937; Tate 1938; WFNY 1939; Rio 1944; Corcoran Gal.; Brussels, Belgium; Canadian Cl., N.Y., 1950; Festival of Britain, 1951; RCA exh., Toronto and Halifax, 1957; one-man: Montreal A. Cl., 1956.

MOULD, LOLA FROWDE (Mrs. William)— *Painter, Des.*
15 Amelia St., Sydney, N.S.

B. Sydney, N.S., Dec. 3, 1908. *Studied:* Mount Allison Univ.; New England Sch. Des., Boston; N.Y. Sch. Des. *Member:* Maritime AA; Nova Scotia Soc. A.; Dept. Edu. Curriculum Research for Art. *Work:* mural, Sydney Bank of Montreal. *Exhibited:* Maritime AA; Nova Scotia Dept. Edu. traveling exhs.; Nova Scotia Soc. A.; in Sydney and Cape Breton. Lectures: Pre-Historic to Modern Art.

MOUNT, RITA—*Painter*
8005 Outremont Ave., Montreal, P.Q.

B. Mtl. *Studied:* Atelier Delécluse and Cercle Internationale des Beaux-Arts, Paris; AA Mtl.; ASL, Woodstock. *Honours:* ARCA 1938; 2 scholarships AA Mtl. 1913. *Work:* NGC; MPQ; Canadian Nat. Railways; AA Mtl. *Exhibited:* OSA; AA Mtl.; RCA; S. Dominions 1936; Coronation 1937; WFNY 1939; one-man: AA Mtl. 1934; MPQ 1943.*

MOWAT, ALEXANDER SUTHERLAND—*Educator, P.*
2 Studley Ave., Halifax, N.S.

B. Bonnybridge, Scotland, Feb. 19, 1905. *Studied:* Edinburgh Univ., M.A., B. Ed. *Member:* Nova Scotia Soc. A. (Pres.); Maritime AA (Treas.). *Exhibited:* Nova Scotia Soc. A.; Maritime AA, both regularly. *Position:* Prof. Edu., Dalhousie Univ., Halifax, N.S.

MUHLSTOCK, LOUIS—*Painter*
3414 Sainte-Famille St., Montreal, P.Q.

B. Narajow, Poland, Apr. 23, 1904. *Studied:* Mtl.; in Paris under L.-F. Biloul. *Member:* CSGA; CGP; FCA; CAS Mtl. *Work:* NGC; AG Tor.; MPQ; A. Mus., London, Ont.; Mtl. Mus. FA; Winnipeg AG; Edmonton AG; Hart House, Univ. Tor.; Victoria Col.; McGill Univ. *Exhibited:* Paris Salon 1930, 1931; S. Dominions 1936; Coronation 1937; WFNY 1939; Gloucester 1939; Am-British A. Center, N.Y., 1940; Addison 1942; Yale 1944; DPC 1945; Rio 1946; UNESCO 1946; CGP; CSGA; BMFA 1949; NGA, Wash., D.C. 1950; Intl. Gr. Exh., Lugano, 1954; Sao Paulo, Brazil, 1954; NGC, 1955;

Carnegie Inst., 1955; one-man: Mtl. Mus. FA 1951, 1954; Western Canada Circuit, 1950; numerous other one-man exhs., Montreal, Toronto and Western Canada.*

MURPHY, ROWLEY WALTER— *Painter, Stained Glass Des., I., T., W., L.*
230 Glen Rd., Toronto 5, Ont.

B. Toronto, Ont., May 28, 1891. *Studied:* OCA; PAFA under J. Pennell, Henry McCarter, Joseph Pearson, H. H. Breckenridge, and others. *Member:* OSA; ARCA; F.; PAFA; Fed. Canadian A.; AG Tor.; Great Lakes Hist. Soc., Cleveland. *Honours:* ARCA; 1st prize drawing, Tor. 1929; Lea Prize, PAFA; Cresson European scholarship, PAFA 1913-14; Victory Loan Poster prize, Ottawa 1940. *Work:* NGC War Records; PAFA; London Mus. A.; Royal Canadian Navy, London; Hamilton AG; R. Can. Yacht Cl. Commissions: official war artist with R. C. Navy 1943-4; Paintings, Can. Bank of Commerce 1946; Stained Glass, Bryn Athyn Cathedral, Pa.; Meaford, Ont.; 2 series of plates of Historic Vessels of the Great Lakes and Canadian Historical Vessels; murals, Bd. Room, Toronto Harbour Comm.; Illus. historical articles "Inland Seas," Cleveland; "The Telescope," Detroit on La Salles's Griffon; Illus. "The Griffon" by C. H. J. Snider; Historical Illus. for Toronto-Dominion Bank and Imperial Bank of Canada, etc. *Exhibited:* PAFA 1913-5; '17-8; AFA 1913; OSA from 1918; RCA from 1926; War Art 1945 NGC; 1958: Toronto, Hamilton, Montreal, Halifax, Vancouver. Author and Ill.: "Wrecks on the Island Shore" 1945; Illus.: "War Log of the Nancy"; "Toronto's Hundred Years." Contributor: Maclean's Mag.; Sat. Eve. Post; Can. Art., etc. Lectures: Navy Art. *Positions:* Instr., Hamilton and Tor. Tech. Schs.; des. of camouflage, R.C.N. 1941-2; Instr. OCA from 1927; Ontario Dept. Edu., 1931- .

NAKAMURA, KAZUO—*Painter, S.*
1201 Dufferin St., Toronto 4, Ont.

B. Vancouver, B.C., Oct. 13, 1926. *Studied:* Central Tech. Sch., Toronto. *Member:* CSGA; CSPWC; CGP. *Honours:* prize, Intl. Exh., Lugano, Switzerland, 1956. *Work:* Hart House, Univ. Toronto; Lord Beaverbrook A. Gal.; Dept. External Affairs; AG Toronto; NGC. *Exhibited:* Painters Eleven, Riverside Mus., N.Y., 1956; Intl. Exh., Switzerland, 1956; Smithsonian traveling exh. of Canadian Abstract Art, 1956-57; Canadian Art traveling exh., Australia, 1957; Mexico City, 1958; Canadian Contemp. Painting, Switzerland, 1958; DMFA, 1958; Western Canada A. Circuit, 1955-56; one-man: Hart House, Univ. Toronto, 1953; 4-man: AG Toronto, 1957; London (Ont.) A. Mus., 1958.

NEDDEAU, DONALD FREDERICK PRICE— *Painter, Des., T., L., Gr.*
21 Sherwood Ave., Toronto, Ont.

B. Toronto, Ont., Jan. 28, 1913. *Studied:* Ontario Col. A., and with J. W. Beatty, Franklin Carmichael, Archibald Barnes. *Member:* OSA; CSPWC; Canadian Gld. Potters; A. & Let. Cl., Toronto. *Honours:* scholarship, Ontario Col. A., 1935, Rous and Mann award, 1936. *Exhibited:* RCA, 1936, 1948, 1951, 1954-1958; OSA, 1942, 1944-1948, 1951-1958, traveling exhs., 1944-48, 1951-58; CSPWC, 1943, 1948-1958, traveling exhs., 1949-58; CSPWC & Cal. WC Soc. Exh., 1950-1958; CGP, 1955, 1956, 1958. *Position:* Instr. A., Central Tech. Sch., Toronto, Ont., 1948-58.

NEWCOMBE, W(ILLIAM) J(OHN) B(ERTRAM)— *Painter, Des., Comm. A.*
R.R. 2, Vast Acre Farm, Weston, Ont.

B. Victoria, B.C., July 18, 1907. *Member:* Cal. WC Soc.; CSGA; CSPWC; Canadian A. Council. *Work:* BMFA; Philbrook A. Center; Joslyn A. Mus.; Wadsworth Atheneum; Illinois State Mus.; William Rockhill Nelson A. Gal. *Exhibited:* RCA 1938, 1947, 1949; CSPWC 1948-49, 1951, 1952; CSGA 1940, 1941, 1945, 1947, 1949, 1951, 1952; AWS 1947-48; Audubon A., 1951; Contemp. Canadian A., 1950; British Columbia Soc. FA 1928-1930, 1945-1947, 1949, 1950; Ferargil Gal., N.Y., 1946; Davenport, Iowa, 1947; New Britain, Conn., 1947; Ft. Worth, Tex., 1947; Springfield, Ill., 1948; OSA 1941, 1948, 1949, 1951, 1952; Cal. WC Soc. 1947, 1948; Vancouver B.C., 1952; Hart House, 1950. *Position:* Chm., Prof. Interests Com., Canadian Arts Council, 1950-52.*

PALMER, HERBERT SIDNEY—*Painter*
170 St. Clements Ave., Toronto, Ont.

B. Tor., June 15, 1881. *Studied*: OCA. *Member*: OSA. *Honours*: RCA; Painting presented by City of Toronto to H.R.H. Princess Elizabeth and the Duke of Edinburgh, 1951. *Work*: NGC; AG Tor.; Univ. Tor.; Sarnia Publ. Lib., etc. *Exhibited*: RCA, OSA, CNE annually; Can. War Memorials NGC 1924; Wembley 1925; Paris 1927; S. Dominions 1936; DPC 1945. *Positions*: Cur. FA Dept., CNE 1926-41; Sec. OSA from 1926; Sec., RCA, 1948-51.*

PANABAKER, FRANK S.—*Painter*
Ancaster, Ont.

B. Hespeler, Ont. *Studied*: OCA; Grand Cent. Sch. of A. and ASL, N.Y. *Member*: Allied Artists of Am. *Honours*: ARCA; Jessie Dow prize, AA Mtl. 1930. *Work*: AG Tor.; A. Gal., Hamilton, A. Gal., London, Ont. *Exhibited*: NAD 1929; Allied Artists of Am.; RCA; OSA; CNE; Salmagundi Cl., N.Y.; Canadian Painting Exh., London, England, 1955.*

PAUL, GREGORY P.—*Painter*
503 Castlefield Ave., Toronto, Ont.

B. Toronto, Ont., Mar. 18, 1933. *Studied*: Northern Tech. Sch., with John Bennett, L. C. Patton. *Exhibited*: RCA, 1954; AG London (Ont.), 1955; AG Hamilton, 1955.*

PEHAP, ERICH K.—*Painter, Gr., Des., I., T., L.*
751 Carlaw Ave., Toronto 6, Ont.

B. Viljandi, Estonia, Apr. 10, 1912. *Studied*: in Europe. *Member*: CSGA; Estonian A. Cl., Toronto; Assn. Estonian A., N.Y. *Honours*: Estonian Govt. Ministry of Edu. award, 1940, 1941. *Work*: Estonian Nat. Mus.; AG Hamilton. *Exhibited*: extensively in Europe; AG Hamilton, 1950; CSPEE, 1952; CSGA, 1951-1955, 1957, 1958; Western Ontario Exh., 1950; Windsor AA, 1951, 1952; RCA, 1954; Manitoba Soc. A., 1954; OSA, 1955; Colour & Form Soc., 1952-1954; Estonian A. Exh., Montreal, 1951-1955; New Canadian A. Exh., 1951, 1952; one-man exhs., Estonia, Stockholm, Sweden, Toronto, Can., and others. Illus., A. Poldmaa "Selected Poems," 1942; "The Country Life," album of 12 linoleum engravings.

PELLAN, ALFRED—*Painter, Theatre Des., T.*
649 est, Bas Grande Côte, Ste.-Rose, Cte., Laval, P.Q.

B. Quebec, P.Q., May 16, 1906. *Studied*: Beaux-Arts, Quebec; Beaux-Arts, Paris. *Honours*: Bourse de la P.Q. to Europe 1926; premier prix d'art mural, Paris 1935; Bourse de recherche de la Societe Royale du Canada en France, 1952-53; Senior F. award, Canada Council, 1958. *Work*: Grenoble Mus.; NGC; MPQ; Montreal Mus. FA; AG Toronto; Musée Nationale d'art Modern, Paris. Commissions: Murals, Can. Embassies in Rio de Janeiro and Paris; City Centre Bldg., Montreal. *Exhibited*: Paris; Prague; London; MPQ; Mtl.; Joliette Seminary; Addison Gal. 1942; Yale 1944; Rio 1944, '46; DPC 1945; Albany 1946; UNESCO 1946; NGC, 1953; AG Tor., 1953; Mtl. Mus. FA, 1953; Bezalel Mus., Jerusalem, 1953; Paris, France (3), 1953, 1955; Venezuela, 1954; Mexico City, 1958; Brussels World's Fair, 1958; one-man: City Hall, Mtl., 1956; Denise Delrue Gal., Mtl., 1958. Author: "50 Dessins d'Alfred Pellan," 1945; illus.: "Voyage d'Arlequin" by E. de Grandmont, 1946; "Les Iles de la Nuit" by A. Grandois 1944. Contributor: illus. in Fortune, Time, Le Canada, Regards, Amérique Française, Almanach des Arts de Paris, Journal des Beaux-Arts de Paris, etc.

PEPPER, GEORGE DOUGLAS—*Painter, T.*
441 Walmer Rd.; Ontario College of Art, Toronto, Ont.

B. Ottawa, Feb. 25, 1903. *Studied*: OCA; Acad. Grande Chaumière, Paris. *Member*: OSA; CGP; A. & Letters, Tor.; CSPWC. *Honours*: RCA; Willingdon prize 1930 (shared with F. H. Varley). *Work*: NGC; AG Tor.; NG South Africa. Commissions: official war artist with Can. Army 1943-6; murals, Canadian Pacific Railways; Veterans Mem. Bldg., Ottawa. *Exhibited*: Wembley 1925; RCA 1930-42; OSA since 1930; S. Dominions 1936; Coronation 1937; Tate 1938; Great Lakes Exh., Buffalo 1938; Gloucester 1939; WFNY 1939; GGE 1939; Rio 1944; Brussels 1944; DPC 1945; War art in NG London, NGC 1945, '46; CGP; NAD. Lectures: Can. war art; Van Gogh; Spain & Morocco, 1957-58, in Banff, Montreal, Toronto. *Position*: Vice-Principal, OCA.

PEPPER, MRS. GEORGE. See Daly, Kathleen

PIERCE, ELIZABETH R. (Mrs. Vernon L.)—*Painter*
R.R. #1, Yarmouth, N.S.

B. Brooklyn, N.Y. *Studied*: Columbia Univ. Ext.; ASL, with John Steuart Curry, Richard Lahey, Anne Goldthwaite. *Member*: NAWA; Nat. Lg. Am. Pen Women; A. Lg. of Long Island; ASL. *Awards*: prizes, Douglaston A. Lg., 1946; Women's Intl. Expo., 1947; A. Lg. Long Island, 1950; Kew Forest AA, 1954 (med.), 1955. *Work*: Queensboro Pub. Lib., Jamaica Br.; P.S. 131, Brooklyn, and in private colls. *Exhibited*: BM; ASL; Jersey City Mus.; NAD; Douglaston A. Lg.; A. Lg. of Long Island; Nat. Mus., Wash., D.C.; Argent Gal.; Creative Gal.; Hudson Valley AA; NAC; Riverside Mus.; Pen & Brush Cl. *Position*: Dir., A. Lg., Long Island, 1954-57.

PINSKY, ALFRED—*Painter, Lith., T.*
353 Kensington Ave., Westmount 6, Montreal, P.Q.

B. Montreal, P.Q., Mar. 31, 1921. *Studied*: Mtl. Mus. FA, and with Anne Savage. *Member*: CSGA. *Honours*: scholarship, Mtl. Mus. FA, 1938-39. *Exhibited*: CSGA; CGP; Mtl. Mus. FA.*

PLAMONDON, MARIUS GERALD—*Sculptor, E., Des.*
1871 Sheppard Ave., Quebec 6, P.Q.

B. Quebec, P.Q., July 21, 1919. *Studied*: Ecole des Beaux-Arts, Quebec, and in France and Italy. *Member*: Sculptors Soc. of Canada; Stained Glass Assn. of Am. *Honours*: Scholarship to Europe, 1938-40; Royal Soc. F., 1955-56. *Work*: stone carvings, stained glass, for numerous churches, university buildings, hotels and hospitals. *Exhibited*: nationally and internationally. *Position*: Hd., Sculpture & Stained Glass Depts., Ecole des Beaux-Arts, Quebec.

PORTER, ANN PEARSON (Mrs.)—*Painter*
59 Claude Ave., Dorval, P.Q.

B. Halifax, N.S., Sept. 5, 1929. *Studied*: Nova Scotia Col. A.; Mount Allison Summer Sch. Painting; Dalhousie Univ. *Member*: Nova Scotia Soc. A. *Honours*: Elizabeth C. Nutt Mem. award, Nova Scotia Col. A., 1951. *Exhibited*: Nova Scotia Dept. Adult Edu. traveling exhs., 1957, 1958.

PREZAMENT, JOSEPH—*Painter, Ser.*
4903 West Hill Ave., Montreal, P.Q.

B. Winnipeg, Man., Jan. 3, 1923. *Studied*: Winnipeg Sch. A., with Lemoine Fitzgerald; Montreal Mus. FA, with Arthur Lismer; Montreal A. Sch., with Ghitta Caiserman, Alfred Pinsky. *Member*: CSGA. *Exhibited*: AG Toronto, 1950; Mtl. Mus. FA, 1954-1958; CSGA, 1957, 1958; Royal Canadian Acad., 1958.

PRICE, ART(HUR) (DONALD)—*Craftsman, S., Des.*
Box 116, R.R. #1, Cyrville (Ottawa), Ont.

B. Edmonton, Alta., May 22, 1918. *Studied*: Western Tech. Sch.; Ontario Col. A.; McDowell Fashion Sch., N.Y. *Member*: Sculptors Soc. Canada; Montreal Mus. FA. *Honours*: prizes, Canadian Handicrafts Gld. (3). *Work*: Imperial Inst., London, England; sc., metalcraft, sc. murals, Jasper Park Lodge, Alta.; Canadian Comm. Bd. Rooms, Rome, Italy; Blackburn Pub. Sch.; Canadian Pavilion, Brussels World's Fair; Royal York Hotel, Toronto; Ottawa City Hall. *Exhibited*: Montreal Mus. FA; RCA; AG London (Ont.); World Wide Shop, Ottawa, 1957; Sculptors Soc. of Canada, 1958; one-man: Stratford Festival, 1957; Gallery of the Canadian Pavilion, Brussels World's Fair, 1958; St. Helen's Island Outdoor Sculpture Show, 1957, 1958; Montreal Sculpture Exhs., etc. Des. and illus.: "Totem Poles"; "Haida Myths"; "Medicine Men"; "Alaska Beckons"; "Pathfinders on the North Pacific"; "Golden Phoenix"; "I Have Seen Quebec," and other books. Contributor to Macleans Magazine; French Reader's Digest.

RAYMOND, MAURICE—*Painter, T., I., E.*
105 Querbes Ave., Outremont, Que.

B. Mtl., July 23, 1912. *Studied*: Collège Mont-Saint-Louis, Mtl. *Member*: Assn. des Artistes Non-figuratif de Montreal. *Honours*: Teaching diploma, Beaux-Arts Mtl. *Quebec Govt. traveling scholarship to USA 1941 and Grand Prix de Peinture 1945. *Work*: MPQ; Montreal Mus. FA;

Séminaire de Joliette Mus. Commision: Mural, St. Emile, Montreal. *Exhibited*: Rio 1944, '46; DPC 1945; Albany 1946; Canadian Biennale, etc. Illustrator: "Petite Histoire de France" by R. Ristelhueber 1946. *Teaching*: Dir., Studies, Hd. Composition Dept., Ecole des Beaux-Arts, Mtl.

RANEY, SUZANNE BRYANT—*Engraver*
R.R. #7, Dunnville, Ont.
B. London, England, Oct. 7, 1918. *Studied*: Ontario College of Art. *Member*: CSPEE. *Exhibited*: major art galleries in Canada annually; RCA; OSA; Hamilton, London, etc.

ROBERTS, (WILLIAM) GOODRIDGE—*Painter*
460 Grosvenor Ave., Montreal, P.Q.
B. Barbados, B.W.I., Sept. 24, 1904. *Studied*: Beaux-Arts, Mtl.; ASL. *Member*: CGP; CSGA; CSPWC; CAS Mtl.; RCA; Eastern Group. *Honours*: prize, Quebec Provincial, 1948; Mtl. Mus. FA 1948, 1956: R. Can. Air Force 1952; Canadian Govt. Overseas F., 1953-54; Winnipeg AG, 1957. *Work*: NGC; Mtl. Mus. FA; Vancouver A. Gal.; Winnipeg A. Gal.; Bezalel Mus., Israel; MPQ; AG Tor.; Edmonton Mus.; AG Hamilton. Commissions: official war artist, RCAF 1943-45. *Exhibited*: WFNY 1939; Addison Gal. 1942; Rio 1944, 1946; War Art 1944; NG London; Yale 1944; NGC; DPC 1945; UNESCO 1946; Sao Paulo, Brazil 1951, 1953; Venice, Italy 1952; Carnegie Inst. 1952, 1955; Valencia Intl. 1955; Mexico City, 1958; Brussels, 1958; one-man: A. Cl. Mtl., 1932, 1939, 1941; Ottawa 1933, 1938; Hart House, 1933, 1938, 1951; Queen's Univ., 1934, 1935; AA Mtl. 1940, 1942; Beaux-Arts, Mtl. 1940, 1942; McGill Univ. 1942, 1945; Dominion Gal. 1943, 1945, 1948-50, 1952, 1953, 1955; Galerie Creuze, Paris, 1954; Vancouver AG 1943; College Brebeuf, Mtl., 1943; Scott Gal., Mtl. 1943, 1945; Mtl. Mus. FA, 1951.

ROBERTS, THOMAS KEITH (TOM)—*Painter*
1312 Stavebank Rd., Port Credit, Ont.
B. Toronto, Ont., Dec. 22, 1909. *Studied*: Central Tech. Sch.; Ontario Col. A. *Member*: RCA; OSA. *Honours*: Rolph, Clarke, Stone, Ltd., purchase award, 1949, Toronto. *Work*: NGC; Seagram Coll.; Canadian Bank of Commerce; Univ. Club, Toronto; AG London (Ont.); series of paintings for Rio Tinto Mining Co.; in banks, insurance companies, etc., Canada; in private colls. in U.S., Canada, England, India, etc. *Exhibited*: RCA, 1932, annually to 1958; OSA, 1929-1958; Mtl. Mus. FA, 1934-1952, 1956-1958; Canadian Nat. Exh., 1932-1958; numerous traveling exhs.; annual one-man exhs. in Toronto, Windsor, Hamilton and Winnipeg.

ROBERTS, WILLIAM GRIFFITH—*Painter*, T.
The Ontario College of Arts, The Grange, Toronto, Ont.; 29 Hardisty Drive, Rexdale, Ont.
B. Nelson, B.C., July 25, 1921. *Studied*: Ontario Col. A.; Vancouver Sch. A. *Member*: OSA; RCA (Assoc.). *Honours*: Monsanto Award, Montreal, 1958. *Work*: Calgary A. Council; AG Winnipeg; NGC. *Exhibited*: Canadian Biennial, 1957; London, England; RCA, 1952-1957; OSA, 1952-1957; CSPWC, 1953-1957; traveling exhs. to Montreal, Winnipeg, Vancouver.

ROBINSON, ALBERT HENRY—*Painter*
3475 King Edward Ave., Montreal 28, P.Q.
B. Hamilton, Ont., Jan., 1881. *Studied*: Julian Acad., Ecole des Beaux-Arts, Paris; under T. W. Marshall. *Member*: Pen & Pencil Cl., Mtl. *Honours*: RCA; medal, Phila. 1926. *Work*: Luxembourg, Paris; NGC; AG Tor.; MPQ; AA Mtl.; A. Gal., Hamilton; Musée de la Province de Quebec; Canada House, London, England. *Exhibited*: Can. War Memorials 1923, '24 NGC; Wembley 1925; Paris 1927; S. Dominions 1936; Coronation 1937; Tate 1938; WFNY 1939; Yale 1944; DPC 1945; A. Gal. Hamilton, 1955 (retrospective); NGC, 1955. Contributor article and cover reproduction, Educational Record.*

SALTMARCHE, KENNETH CHARLES—
Museum Curator, P., W.
240 Giles Blvd., West, Windsor, Ont.
B. Cardiff, Wales, Sept. 29, 1920. *Studied*: OCA; ASL, N.Y. *Position*: Curator, Willistead Art Gallery, 1946- .*

SAVAGE, ANNIE DOUGLAS—*Painter*, T.
4090 Highland Ave., Montreal, P.Q.
B. Mtl., July 27, 1896. *Studied*: AA Mtl.; Minneapolis Soc. Des. *Member*: CGP. *Honours*: Order of Scholastic Merit, Prot. Sch. Bd. Mtl., 1943. *Work*: BGC; AG Tor.; AA Mtl.; Hart House, Univ. Tor.; Canadian Embassy, Wash., D.C. *Exhibited*: Wembley 1925; West Coast Exh. NGC 1927; Paris 1927; S. Dominions 1936; Coronation 1937; Corcoran Gal.; WFNY 1939; Yale 1944; DPS 1945; AA Mtl.; NGC Trav. exhs.; CGP traveling exh.; Dept. for External Affairs. *Position*: Instr., Baron Byng High Sch., Mtl.; Supv. A., Montreal Pub. Schs. (Retired); Chm., "Child Art Council," Montreal (Retired).

SCHAEFER, CARL FELLMAN—*Painter*, T., *Lith.*
157 St. Clements Ave., Toronto, Ont.
B. Hanover, Ont., Apr. 30, 1903. *Studied*: OCA; Central Sch. of A. and Des., London. *Member*: ARCA; CGP; F., Intl. Inst. A. & Lets.; CSPWC; CSGA. *Honours*: Guggenheim Fellow 1940-1; Coronation medal Elizabeth II, 1953; Pres. CSPWC 1937-9. *Work*: Hart House, Univ. Toronto; NGC; AG Tor.; A. Gal., Hamilton; Queens Univ.; Pickering Col.; Dalhousie Univ.; Dept. External Affairs; Upper Canada College, Toronto; Univ. College. Commissions: official war artist with RCAF 1943-6; Ser. ptgs. for Canada Packers. *Exhibited*: OSA; CSGA; Group of Seven; CGP, annually; Int. Exh. of Wood Eng., Warsaw, etc., 1933, '36; S. Dominions 1936; Coronation 1937, R Scot. Soc. PWC, Edinburgh 1938-9; Tate 1938; Great Lakes Exh., Buffalo 1938-9; WFNY 1939; Gloucester 1939; 18th Intl. WC Exh. Chicago 1939; 38th Phila. WC 1940; Am. WC Soc. and N.Y. WC 1941; Phila. WC & Print 1941; 11th Int. Biennial, Brooklyn 1941; AIC 1941; Addison Gal. 1942; Senate 1942; United Nations Print Exh. Phila. 1943; Yale 1944; War Art NG London, 1944, '45; War Art NGC 1945; Art of United Nations, San Francisco 1945; N.Y. 1945; Rio 1946; UNESCO 1946; Phila. WC Cl., 1946; RCA CSPWC (all Canadian exhs. through 1958); Vancouver AG, 1956-1958; Australia & New Zealand, 1948; Queen's Univ., BMFA 1949; PAFA 1949; NGA, Wash., D.C., 1950; Sao Paulo, Brazil, 1952; Canadian Exh., London, England, 1955; New Zealand, 1955; Canadian-Am. joint traveling exh., 1955-56; First Canadian exh. painting to Asia, Ceylon, Pakistan, etc., 1955; one-man: Hart House 1951; Canadian Cl., N.Y., 1948; VMFA 1949; AG Tor., 1954 (2-man retrospective); Upper Canada Col., 1957. *Position*: Hd. Dept. Drawing & Painting, Ontario Col. A., Toronto, 1955- .

SCOTT, LLOYD (EDWARD WILLIAM)—*Illustrator*
Main St., East, Beaverton, Ont.; 52 Eccles St., North, Barrie, Ont.
B. Foam Lake, Sask., Jan. 22, 1911. *Studied*: Ontario Col. A. (Assoc. degree). *Member*: CSPEE (Assoc.). *Exhibited*: OSA, 1937; CSPEE, 1950, 1951. Illus.: "Story of Our Prairie Provinces," 1943; "Canadian Magic," 1946; "Dorothy Jane's Book," 1949; "The Great Adventure," 1950; "Dorothy Jane's Other Book," 1953; "Pirates and Pathfinders," 1954; "Toronto," 1956; "Salvador, The Horse That Joined the Mounties," 1957; "My First History of Canada," 1958; "Using Our Language" (series for six grades), 1941-1948, and other books. Contributor illus. to The Beaver, Magazine of the North.

SCOTT, CHARLES HEPBURN—*Painter*, E., Et.
6212 Balaclava St.; Vancouver School of Art, Vancouver, B.C.
B. Newmilns, Scotland, Nov. 29, 1886. *Studied*: Glasgow Sch. of A.; Brussels, etc. *Member*: CGP; CSGA; B.C. Soc. FA. *Honours*: ARCA; Fellow R. Soc. of A. *Exhibited*: Wembley 1925; NGC West Coast Exh. 1927; S. Dominions 1936; Coronation 1937; WFNY 1939; CGP; CSGA; one-man: Vancouver AG 1943. Author: "Drawings of the B.C. Coast."*

SCOTT, (Mrs.) MARIAN D.—*Painter*
451 Clarke Ave., Westmount, Montreal, P.Q.
B. Mtl., June 26, 1906. *Studied*: AA Mtl.; Beaux-Arts, Mtl.; Slade Sch., London. *Member*: CGP. *Work*: Bezalel Mus., Israel; Vancouver A. Gal.; AA Mtl.; AG Tor.; NGC; Musee de Quebec; Mtl. Mus. FA. Commissions: "Endocrinology" in McGill Univ. Medical Bldg.; mural, "Tree of Life," chapel of General Hospital, Montreal. *Exhibited*: CNE; OSA; RCA; NGC 1936; CGP from 1939;

WFNY 1939; Addison Gal. 1942; Yale 1944; Sao Paulo, Brazil, 1951, 1953; Rio 1944, '46; Grand Central Gal. 1945; DPC 1945; DMFA, 1958; one-man: Grace Horne Gal., Boston 1941; 2-man, Mtl. Mus. FA and AG Tor., 1953-1955; Queens Col., (one-man); Dominion Gal., Montreal 1956, 1958 (one-man).

SEGUIN, TUTZI HASPEL—*Painter, C., Ser., T., L.*
43 Camberwell Rd., Toronto, Ont.

B. Bucharest, Romania, Oct. 14, 1911. *Studied*: Romanian Acad. Art. *Member*: FCA; AG Tor. *Honours*: gold medal, CNE 1938. Commission: church mural, Tor. 1942. *Exhibited*: Bucharest Salon 1934-7; RCA 1938; CSPWC from 1944; CSGA 1944, '46; one-man: A. Cl., Tor., 1943, '45, '46. Specializing in enamel on copper. Demonstrations and lectures to groups and on TV.*

SHADBOLT, JACK LEONARD—*Painter, T.*
461 North Glynde St., Vancouver, B.C.

B. Shoeburyness, England, Feb. 4, 1909. *Studied*: Euston Road Group, London, England; Andre Lhote, Paris; ASL, N.Y. *Honours*: Canadian Govt. F., France, 1957; Carnegie Intl. award, 1958. *Work*: AG Tor.; NGC; Mtl. Mus. FA; SAM; Vancouver A. Gal.; Victoria A. Centre; AG Hamilton. *Exhibited*: represented frequently in Canadian traveling exhs.; Sao Paulo, Brazil, 1953; Caracas, Venezuela, 1953; Valencia, Venice, Venezuela, 1955; Carnegie Inst., 1955; one-man: Toronto, Montreal, Winnipeg, Vancouver, Canada; also, New York, Seattle, San Francisco; Brussels World's Fair, 1958; Mexico City, 1958. L., Writer, in Canada, on contemporary art problems. *Position*: Hd., Drawing & Painting Section, Vancouver Sch. A., Vancouver, B.C.

SHEPPARD, PETER CLAPHAM—*Painter, T.*
35 Northumberland St., Toronto, Ont.

B. Toronto, Ont., Oct. 21, 1882. *Studied*: OCA. *Member*: OSA. *Honours*: RCA 1929; Walker Scholarship, OCA. *Work*: NGC; AG Tor. *Exhibited*: Wembley 1925; Paris 1927; S. Dominions 1936; WFNY 1939; Grand Central Gal., 1945; Dayton AI, 1943; Halifax, N.S., 1949; Am-British A. Center, N.Y., 1951; 1955-56 exhs. in Montreal, Toronto, Hamilton, and London; traveling exh. Canada.*

SIMARD, JEAN—*Painter, E., I., W., L.*
3651, rue Durocher, Montreal, P.Q.

B. Quebec, P.Q. *Studied*: Beaux-Arts, Mtl. *Exhibited*: DPC 1945. *Position*: Prof., Beaux-Arts, Mtl.

SIMMINS, RICHARD BEAUFORT—*Lecturer, Cur.*
Norman MacKenzie Art Gallery, Regina College, Regina, Sask.

B. Ottawa, Ont., Oct. 14, 1924. *Studied*: Univ. College, Tor., B.A.; Courtauld Inst., Univ. London; Univ. Toronto, M.A. *Position*: Cur., A. Collections, Regina College, Univ. Saskatchewan, Canada.*

SMITH, GORDON—*Painter, Ser., E.*
Fine Arts Department, University of British Columbia; 4590 Keith Road, West Vancouver, B.C.

B. Brighton, England, June 18, 1919. *Studied*: Winnipeg Sch. A.; Vancouver Sch. A.; California Sch. FA; Harvard Summer Sch. *Member*: British Columbia Soc. A.; CSPEE; CGP. *Honours*: Canadian Biennial, 1956. *Work*: NGC; AG Toronto; AG Winnipeg; London (Ont.) Mus. A.; Hart House, Univ. Toronto; Univ. British Columbia; AG Vancouver; Queen's Univ., Kingston, Ont. *Exhibited*: Guggenheim Mus., N.Y., 1957; Mexico City, 1958; Canadian Biennial, 1955, 1957; one-man: Hart House, 1957; AG Vancouver, 1957. *Position*: Prof. A., Univ. British Columbia, Vancouver, B.C.

SNELGROVE, GORDON WILLIAM—*Educator, L., W.*
848 Saskatchewan Cresc. E.; Univ. of Saskatchewan, Saskatoon, Sask.

B. Millbrook, Ont., Sept. 18, 1898. *Studied*: Univ. Sask., B.A.; Univ. Chicago, M.A.; Univ. of London, Ph.D.; Columbia Univ.; Univ. Paris; Acad. Julian, Paris. *Member*: FCA; AFA. *Honours*: Sask. Govt. Paris scholarship 1927-8; Carnegie NGC travelling scholarship 1934-6. Contributor: Connoisseur. Lectures: Canadian art, modern art.

Positions: Instr. Collegiate Inst., Moose Jaw 1924-34; Prof. Regina Col. 1936-9; Prof., Hd. A. Dept., Univ. Sask. from 1939 (sabbatical leave for Europe, 1952-53); Guest Prof., Univ. Alberta Summer Sch., 1951, 1952, 1956, 1957.

SNOW, JOHN (HAROLD THOMAS)—*Lithographer*
915 18th Ave., Southwest, Calgary, Alta.

B. Vancouver, B.C., Dec. 12, 1911. *Member*: CSGA; Alberta Soc. A. *Honour*: prize, CSGA, 1957. *Exhibited*: Intl. Biennial Exh. Prints, Tokyo, 1957; Canadian Biennial, 1957; Intl. Biennial, Color Lithography, Cincinnati, 1958; Inter-Am. Biennial, Mexico City, 1958; Winnipeg Show, 1955-1957; Montreal Mus. FA, 1956-1958; New Design Gal., Vancouver, 1957; Norman Mackenzie Gal., Regina, 1958.

SOUCY, JEAN-BAPTISTE—*Educator*
37 St. Joachim, Quebec, P.Q.; 2084 Bourbonniere, Sillery, P.Q.

B. St. Antonin, P.Q., July 1, 1899. *Studied*: Collège Ste-Anne de la Pocatière, Kamouraska; Beaux-Arts, Mtl.; Ecole des Arts Decoratifs. Paris (diplome architecte). *Member*: F., Royal Arch. Inst. of Canada; Hon. member, Societe des Decorateurs-Ensemblirs du Quebec; Arch. Assn. of the P.Q.; Rotary. *Position*: Dir. and Prof., Ecole des Beaux-Arts, Quebec.*

STEVENS, DOROTHY (Mrs. Austin)—*Painter, T., Et.*
127 Park Road; 23 Prince Arthur Ave., Toronto, Ont.

B. Tor., Sept. 2, 1890. *Studied*: Slade Sch., London; Acad. Grande Chaumière, Paris; pupil of P. W. Steer, Henry Tonks, etc. *Member*: OSA; RCA. *Honours*: Scholarship in Europe 1919; silver medal for etching, San Francisco exh. *Work*: NGC; AG Tor.; Edmonton Mus.; Hart House, Univ. Tor.; A. Mus., London, Ont.; Tor. Publ. Lib. *Exhibited*: RCA & OSA from 1916; Can. War Memorials NGC 1924; Wembley 1925; Paris 1927; S. Dominions 1936; Tate 1938; WFNY 1939; DPC 1945; CSPEE. Illustrator: "Canadian Cities of Romance" and "Canadian Houses" by Katherine Hale. *Teaching*: children's classes, WAA Tor.; summer sesion, Doon Sch. FA; Portrait Class, Artist's Workshop.

SURREY, PHILIP HENRY—*Painter, W.*
478 Grosvenor Ave., Montreal, P.Q.

B. Calgary, Alta., Oct. 8, 1910. *Member*: CAS; Eastern Group; FCA; CSGA. *Honours*: prize, Montreal, 1953. *Work*: AG Tor.; Mtl. Mus. FA; Musee de Quebec; Bezalel Mus., Jerusalem; NGC; AG Hamilton. *Exhibited*: WFNY 1939; Addison Gal., 1942; Yale 1944; DPC 1945; Rio 1946; Montreal Mus. FA, 1957; one-man: Watson Gal., Montreal, 1951; Roberts Gal., Toronto, 1953; Montreal Mus. FA, 1955.

SWINTON, GEORGE—*Painter, Et., Lith., E., W.*
University of Manitoba, School of Art; 191 Yale Ave., Winnipeg 9, Man.

B. Vienna, Austria, Apr. 17, 1917. *Studied*: Univ. Vienna; McGill Univ., B.A.; Montreal Sch. A. & Des.; ASL, N.Y., with Will Barnet, Harry Sternberg, Morris Kantor. *Member*: CSGA; Canadian Soc. for Edu. through Art. *Honour*: prizes, Winnipeg Show (2). *Work*: Smith Col. Mus.; Israeli Mus. FA; NGC; Queen's Univ.; Calgary A. Centre. Murals, Women's Recreation Centre, Winnipeg; Simpson-Sears, Winnipeg. *Exhibited*: Graphic Arts Today, 1952; Boston Pub. Lib., 1952; NGC, 1955; DMFA, 1958; Canadian Biennial; CGP, and many others in U.S. and Canada. One-man: Kingston, Toronto, Vancouver, Winnipeg, Saskatoon, Victoria, Regina, etc. Contributor articles to Queen's Quarterly; Colliers Encyclopaedia; Canadian Art. Regular A. Critic for Winnipeg Tribune. Lectures: First Hundred Years of Printmaking; Contemporary Graphic Arts; Canadian Art; etc. *Position*: Cur., Saskatoon A. Centre, 1947-49; Instr., Smith Col., 1950-53; Queen's Univ., 1953-54; Univ. Manitoba, Winnipeg, Man., 1954- .

SYLVESTRE, GUY—*Editor, Cr., W., L.*
355 Wilbrod St., Ottawa, Ont.

B. Sorel, P.Q., May 17, 1918. *Studied*: College Ste-Marie, Mtl.; Univ. Ottawa, L.Ph., M.A. *Member*: FCA; Societe des ecrivains canadiens; Canadian Lib. Assn.; Royal Soc. of Canada. Editor: Gants du ciel, 1943-46; Anthologie de la poesie canadienne, 1943-1958; Co-editor, la Nouvelle Revue canadienne. Author: "Poetes Catholiques de la France contemporaine," 1944; "Sondages," 1945; "Impressions de theatre," 1950. Contributor to numerous art and educational publications. *Position*: Prof., Canadian Literature, Univ., Ottawa; Associate Parliamentary Libn., Library of Parliament, Ottawa.

TAYLOR, FREDERICK (BOURCHIER)—*Etcher, Ser., P.*
3690 Mountain St., Montreal 25, P.Q.

B. Ottawa, Ont., July 27, 1906. *Studied*: McGill Univ., B. Arch.; Byam Shaw Sch. Drawing, Painting & Des.; London, England; London County Council Central Sch. A. & Crafts; Goldsmith's Col. A., Univ. London. *Member*: Royal Canadian Acad. A. (Assoc.); CSPEE; CSGA. *Honours*: McGill Univ., Delta Upsilon Mem. Scholarship, 1930. *Work*: Prints & drawings: NGC; Dominion Archives, Ottawa; AG Hamilton; London (Ont.) A. Mus.; McGill Univ.; paintings: Beaverbrook A. Gal., Fredericton, N.B.; Bezalel Mus., Jerusalem; IBM; McGill Univ.; McCord Mus., Mtl.; Montreal Mus. FA; AG Toronto; Bomar Law Lib., Fredericton; Algoma Ore Properties; Algoma Steel Corp.; Brewing Corp. of Am.; Canadian Breweries, Ltd.; Canadian Corporations, Ltd.; Canadian Ingersoll-Rand; Canadian Railways; Distillers Corp.; Dominick Corp.; Dominion Govt. of Canada; Henry Birks & Sons; Kerr Steamships; Dow Brewery; Sun Life Assurance Co., and others. *Exhibited*: prints and drawings in all major shows in Canada since 1932; paintings, prints and drawings in Canadian exhs., since 1937; exh. widely in U.S. and abroad. *Positions*: Exec. Comm., Canadian Arts Council, 1952-53; Council Memb., RCA, 1955-57.

TAYLOR, JOCELYN (Jocelyn Taylor Mitchell)— *Painter, C., Des., T.*
275 Lippincott St., Toronto, Ont.; R.R. 1, Streetsville, Ont.

B. Toronto, Ont., May 29, 1899. *Studied*: Central Tech. Sch.; Ontario Col. A.; ASL, N.Y. *Member*: Heliconian Cl., Toronto; CSPWC. *Exhibited*: RCA; OSA; CSPWC, all from 1949 to present; ceramics, Montreal and Toronto, 1955. *Illus.* "The School Theatre," 1925; "Creative Theatre," 1929; "Pirates and Pathfinders," 1947; "Living Latin," 1950. *Position*: Asst. to Dir., 1919-21, Tech. Dir., 1925-26, Hart House Theatre, Univ. Toronto; Instr., N.Y. Univ., 1931-43; Instr. A., Central Tech. Sch., Toronto, Ont., 1946- .

THOMSON, GEORGE—*Painter*
591 Eighth St., Owen Sound, Ont.

B. Claremont, Ont., Feb. 10, 1868. *Studied*: Univ. Washington, LL.B.; ASL; Old Lyme, Conn. *Member*: OSA. *Work*: NGC; AG Tor. *Exhibited*: NAD; AIC; New Haven Paint & Clay Cl.; OSA; RCA.

THORNE, GORDON KIT— *Painter, Et., Lith., T., Comm. A., Des.*
742 Broughton St., Vancouver 5, B.C.

B. Stanway, England, Aug. 21, 1896. *Studied*: Goldsmith's Sch. A., Univ. London, England. *Member*: British Columbia Soc. A. (Assoc.); Fed. Canadian A.; CSPEE; Western A. Circle (Vice-Pres.); British Columbia A. & Hist. Assn. *Work*: Vancouver Pub. Mus. & A. Assn. Gallery. Work in many leading hotels and in private homes. *Exhibited*: CSPEE, 1952-1956; Fed. Canadian A. traveling exh., 1956-1958; Western A. Circle, and others; Vancouver A. Gal.; retrospective exh., Vancouver City Mus., 1958.

THORNE, M. ART—*Painter, T.*
606 Avenue Road, Toronto 7, Ont.

B. Devon, N.B., Nov. 15, 1909. *Studied*: Ontario Col. A., Assoc. degree, with John Alfsen, George Pepper, Gustav Hahn, Emanuel Hahn; ASL, N.Y., with Vytlacil, Marsh, Kantor. *Member*: Canadian Younger Artists; Fed. Canadian A.; ASL; Ontario Col. A. Alumni Assn. *Work*: murals, British American Oil Co., Toronto. *Exhibited*: CSGA, 1944; Canadian Younger A., 1948-1950; Nova Scotia Soc. A., 1944, 1945; Rochester Mus. A. & Sc., 1949; Royal Ontario Mus., 1948; AG Toronto, 1948.

TINNING, G. CAMPBELL—*Painter*
207/1178 Phillips Pl., Montreal 2, Que.

B. Saskatoon, Sask., Feb. 25, 1910. *Studied*: ASL; Eliot O'Hara Sch., Maine. *Member*: CSPWC; ARCA. *Honours*: Jessie Dow prize for WC, AA Mtl. 1942, 1947. *Work*: AA Mtl.; Ford Motor Co.; Bank of Commerce, Mtl.; in England, Newfoundland, Nova Scotia; War Records NGC. Commissions: official war artist with Can. Army 1943-6. *Exhibited*: Phila. WC Cl. 1938; WFNY 1939; CNE 1940; AG Tor. 1943; Vancouver AG 1943; A. Mus. London, Ont. 1943; War art NG London 1944, '45; War art at Rimini, Urbino, Amsterdam 1944; War Art NGC 1945, '46.*

TOLGYESY, VICTOR—*Craftsman, S.*
319 Queen St.; 157 Stanley Ave., Ottawa, Ont.

B. Miskolc, Hungary, Aug. 22, 1928. *Member*: Sculptors Soc. of Canada. *Honours*: Canada Council Grant, 1957. *Work*: NGC, and in private colls. *Exhibited*: Sculptors Soc., 1953; AG Toronto, 1957; Nat. Crafts Exh., Ottawa, 1957; Los A. Mus. A., 1957; Brussels World's Fair, 1958; one-man: Ottawa, 1953, 1956, 1957; Religious Art Exh., Ottawa, 1954.

TRAVERS, GWYNETH (Mrs. C. H.)—*Printmaker*
234 Albert St., Kingston, Ont.

B. Kingston, Ont., Apr. 6, 1911. *Studied*: Queen's Univ., B.A.; Queen's Summer Sch. Painting. *Honours*: prizes, Quebec Nat. Comp., 1958; Reid award, CSPEE, 1958; Expo. Provincial de Quebec, 1958. *Exhibited*: Can. Nat. Exh., 1957, 1958; Winnipeg Show, 1958; CSPEE, 1956-1958; Expo. Provincial, 1958; Kingston AA, 1948-1958; Eastern Ontario Traveling Exh., 1954, 1955; Kingston Prints & Drawings, 1958; Kingston Group, 1957.

TRENKA, STEPHEN—*Sculptor, Medalist*
Greenlane, Thornhill, Ont.

B. Budapest, Hungary, June 22, 1909. *Studied*: Royal Hungarian Sch. Indst. A.; Ontario Col. A. *Member*: Sculptors Soc. of Canada. *Work*: Canadian Commemorative 5 cent piece, 1951; Canadian Silver Dollar commemorating British Columbia's Centennial, 1958. *Exhibited*: Chicago World's Fair; Tate Gal., London, England; Sculptors Soc. of Canada, annually.

TURNER, STANLEY—*Illustrator, Et., P., Des.*
272 Redpath Ave., Toronto, Ont.

B. Aylesbury, Eng., Aug. 1, 1883. *Studied*: S. Kensington, London; OCA. *Member*: OSA. *Honours*: ARCA; medallist R. Soc. of A. & Commerce, London 1898. *Work*: Victoria & Albert Mus., London; AG Tor.; NGC; R. Ont. Mus. *Exhibited*: Buenos Aires 1930; Wembley 1925; WFNY 1939; AG Tor.; NGC. Illustrator: "The First Christmas Carol" by Middleton 1920; "Billy Topsail and Co." 1946; "Bright Paths to Adventure" 1945 by G. Sinclair; "Tambour" by Raddal 1945; "Son of the Hawk," 1950, and others; Maclean's Magazine.*

VALIUS, TELESFORAS—*Engraver, Lith.*
84 Pine Crest Road, Toronto 9, Ont.

B. Riga, Latvia, July 10, 1914. *Studied*: Sch. A., Kaunas, Lithuania, and in Paris, France. *Member*: CSGA; CSPEE; Am. Color Pr. Soc. *Honours*: prizes, CSGA, 1958; Royal Ontario Mus., 1958. *Work*: AG London (Ont.), and in museums in Lithuania. *Exhibited*: Lithuanian A. Soc., 1937-1942; in Germany, Austria, France, Belgium, Argentina, New Zealand; CSGA, 1953-1955, 1957, 1958; NGC, 1954-1956, 1958; Montreal Mus. FA, 1954, 1955, 1957; Rochester Mem. A. Gal., 1953; Chicago, 1956, 1958; New York, N.Y., 1958.

VICKERS, GEORGE STEPHEN—*Educator*
Dept. of Art & Archeology, Univ. of Tor., Toronto, Ont.; 84 Walmer Rd., Toronto, Ont.

B. St. Catharines, Ont., Dec. 19, 1913. *Studied*: McMaster Univ., B.A.; Harvard Univ., A. M. Contributor: Art Bulletin. *Honours*: Junior Fellow, Harvard, 1939-42. *Position*: Assoc. Prof., Univ. Tor.; Hon. Pres., Ontario Soc. for Edu. through Art; Council Memb., Ontario Col. Art.

WATSON, SYDNEY H.—*Painter, E., Des.*

2 Nesbitt Dr., Toronto 5, Ont.

B. Toronto, Ont., Apr. 6, 1911. *Studied*: Central Tech. Sch. *Member*: RCA; CSPWC; OSA; CGP; A. & Let. Cl., Toronto. *Work*: in public and private collections including NGC and Hart House Coll. of Canadian Art. *Exhibited*: regularly in Canada and in Canadian exhs. abroad. *Position*: Principal, Ontario Col. A., Toronto, Ont.

WEBBER, GORDON McKINLEY—*Painter, Des., T.*

1102 Elgin Terrace; McGill Univ., Montreal, P.Q.

B. Sault Ste. Marie, Ont., Mar. 12, 1909. *Studied*: OCA; ASL Tor. under A. Lismer, A. Y. Jackson, L. Harris; Sch. of Des., Chicago under Moholy-Nagy. *Member*: CGP; FCA; Faculty Cl., McGill Univ. *Honours*: fellowships OCA 1924, '27; and ASL Tor.; Carnegie Fellowship to Chicago Sch. Des. 1939-42; MOMA prize 1941. *Work*: AG Tor.; Hart House, Univ. Tor.; AA Mtl.; Guggenheim Mus., NY; NG, Auckland, N.Z. Commissions: Murals, Hart House, Univ. Tor. 1927; Can. Youth Congress 1936. *Exhibited*: OSA 1930-5; CSGA 1932; CSPWC 1934-6; CGP from 1935; S. Dominions 1936; Great Lakes Exh., Buffalo 1938; Gloucester 1939; WFNY 1939; AA Mtl. from 1942; DPC 1945. Contributor: School Arts; Canadian Art; Theatre Arts. Lectures: art history, child art, modern des. *Teaching*: child art, ptg., 3-dimensional projects AG Tor.; AA Mtl.; Sch. of Des. Chicago; colour, light, texture, Mills Col., California. *Positions*: Instr. AG Tor. 1930-6; AA Mtl. and McGill Univ., Mtl. from 1942; special designer to Nat. Film Bd. 1945-6; Dir. of adult art programme, MacDonald Col. 1943-6, Mtl.*

WEBER, GEORGE—*Printmaker, P., Des., Comm. A.*

11254 92nd St., Edmonton, Alta.

B. Munich, Germany, Mar. 31, 1907. *Studied*: Ontario Col. A.; Univ. Alberta. *Member*: Fed. Canadian A.; CSPEE. *Work*: CSPEE; A. & Let. Cl., Toronto, and in private colls. *Exhibited*: CSPEE annually since 1950; Northwest Pr. M., 1953; CSPWC, 1957, 1958; Hart House, Univ. Toronto, 1957. Lectures: Serigraphy. *Position*: Hd. A. Dept., Hamly Press, Ltd., 1942- .

WESTON, WILLIAM PERCY—*Painter, T.*

1419 Dogwood Ave., Vancouver, B.C.

B. London, Eng., Nov. 30, 1879. *Studied*: Borough Rd. Col.; Putney Sch. of A., London. *Member*: CGP; B.C. Soc. of FA. *Honours*: ARCA; Pres. B.C. Soc. FA 1931-8. *Work*: NGC; Hart House, Univ. Tor. *Exhibited*: CGP 1930; RCA from 1931; Coronation 1937; Tate 1938; WFNY 1939; DPC 1945. Lectures: Art Appreciation, Des., etc. *Positions*: Instr. Vancouver High Sch. 1909-10; Dir. of Art, Vancouver City Schs. 1910-14; Instr. Prov. Normal Sch. from 1914-46.*

WHEELER, ORSON SHOREY—*Sculptor, T., L.*

1441 Drummond St., Montreal, P.Q.

B. Barston, P.Q., Sept. 17, 1902. *Studied*: Bishop's Univ., B.A.; RCA classes, Mtl.; Cooper Union, N.Y.; NAD, N.Y.; NAD, and in Europe. *Member*: SSC; Pen & Pencil, Mtl. *Honours*: RCA. Commissions: bust, Can. Pacific Railways; Jacobs mon., Mtl.; Supreme Court, Ottawa; Morril mon., and Hackett mon., Stanstead, P.Q.; bust, Court House, Mtl.; Bishop's Univ., P.Q.; Montreal Children's Hospital; Mtl. Mus. FA; King's Col., Halifax, N.S., and in private colls, in Canada & U.S. *Exhibited*: AA Mtl., 1928 and from 1932; RCA, 1931-1958; Tate 1938; WFNY 1939; NAD 1940; SSC; Smith Col. 1945; Ottawa, 1950; Quebec City 1951, Mtl. Mus. FA, 1952-1957; has made over 100 scale models of world famous buildings to illus. history of architecture. Models exhibited Mtl. Mus. FA, 1955. T.V. Film: "Quebec Arts '58" produced by C.B.C. French version "Madones et Ab-stractions" shown at Brussels World's Fair, 1958. *Positions*: Instr., Sir George William Col. from 1931; Chm. Permanent Coll., Can. Handicrafts Gld. since 1944; Sessional Lecturer in Arch., McGill Univ., 1949- ; Treas., SSC, 1952- .

WHITEHEAD, ALFRED—*Painter, E.*

52 Havelock St., Amherst, N.S.

B. Peterborough, England, July 10, 1887. *Member*: Nova Scotia Soc. A. *Exhibited*: Montreal Spring Exhs., 1942-1947; Nova Scotia Soc. A., 1948, 1949, 1952-1958; Maritime AA, etc. One-man: Mount Allison Univ., 1951; Amherst, N.S., 1952; Netherwood Col., Rothesay, N.B., 1946, 1947. *Position*: Dean, Music, Mount Allison Univ., Sackville, N.B., 1947-53; Emeritus, 1953- .

WILSON, R. YORK—*Painter*

8 Apsely Rd., Toronto, Ont.

B. Toronto, Dec. 6, 1907. *Member*: OSA; RCA; A. & Letters Cl., Tor. *Honours*: RCA; OSA; J.W.L. Forster award, 1945, 1950, Tor. *Work*: AG Tor.; A. Mus., London, Ont.; NGC; Branksome Hall, Tor.; Imperial Oil, Ltd.; mural, Northern Publ. Co., Timmins, Ont. *Exhibited*: WFNY 1939; OSA from 1939; CGP 1939, 1945, 1946; RCA from 1941; CSPWC 1942-1944; MPQ 1944; A. Mus., London, Ont., 1945; WAA 1945; Windsor AG 1945; Eaton Gal., Tor. 1944-1946; Mexico 1949, 1951; New Zealand, 1949; Carnegie Inst., 1952; one-man: Hart House 1945; Toronto 1948, 1950; Montreal 1951; Santa Cruz, Canary Islands, 1952.*

WOOD, ELIZABETH WYN—*Sculptor*

51 Plymbridge Road, York Mills Valley, Willowdale, Ont.

B. Orillia, Ont., Oct. 8, 1903. *Studied*: Ontario Col. A. (Assoc.); ASL. *Member*: RCA; Sculptors Soc. of Canada. *Honours*: prize, Willingdon award, 1929; gold medal, Univ. Alberta, 1958; Governor General's Medal. *Work*: monuments, mural sculpture, tablets, fountains, memorials, etc: Welland-Crowland War Mem., Chippewa Park, Welland, Ont.; Navy Hall Grounds, Niagara-on-the-Lake; Rainbow Bridge Approach Plaza, Niagara Falls; Bank of Montreal; Orillia Pub. Lib.; Univ. British Columbia Lib.; Bd. Education Bldg., Toronto; (Royal Arms) Royal Box, Old Woodbine Racetrack, Toronto; Sudbury (Ont.) Mem. Hospital; Queen Elizabeth Bldg., Toronto; other work: NGC; AG Winnipeg; AG Toronto; AG Vancouver.

WOODS, REX NORMAN—*Illustrator, Comm. A., P.*

707 Eglinton Ave., West, Toronto 10, Ont.

B. Gainsborough, England, July 21, 1903. *Studied*: Gainsborough Sch. of Sc. & A.; OCA. *Member*: SI, N.Y.; Canadian Authors Assn.; Nat. Soc. A. Dir. Commissions: posters for Gen. Motors; Canadian War Savings; posters, adv. illus., MacDonald Tobacco Co.; Canadian Breweries, Ltd.; Hudson's Bay Co. Contributor to Maclean's magazine, and others. Represented in Canadian Historical Coll. of Confederation Life Assn., Toronto, 1956- .

WYLE, FLORENCE—*Sculptor*

110 Glen Rd., Toronto, Ont.

B. Trenton, Ill., 1881. *Studied*: Univ. Ill.; AIC. *Member*: Potters' Gld. Tor.; SSC; WAA. *Honours*: RCA; medal, from Queen Elizabeth II, 1953. *Work*: NGC; Winnipeg AG; AG, Tor. Commissions: Artist for Can. War Memorials 1919; Edith Cavell Monument, Tor.; fountain, Mem. Park, London, Ont.; garden sculpture, etc. *Exhibited*: RCA; SSC; OSA; Potters' Gld., Tor.; AF Tor.; Can. War Memorials 1923, '24; Wembley 1925; Paris 1927; West Coast Exh. NGC; Coronation '37; Tate 1938; WFNY; RCA; A. Gal., Hamilton. *Position*: one of Fndrs., past Pres., SSC.

Geographical Index

Abbreviations

Adv. Des.—Advertising Designer
Arch.—Architect
Arch. Des.—Architectural Designer
Arch. Hist.—Architectural Historian
Art.—Artist
Art Cent. Dir.—Art Center Director
Art E.—Art Educator
Art Ed.—Art Editor
Art Lib.—Art Librarian
Art Publ.—Art Publicist
Art Sch. Dir.—Art School Director
Art Soc. Dir.—Art Society Director

Bk. Bndr.—Bookbinder
Bkp. Des.—Bookplate Designer

C.—Craftsman
Call.—Calligrapher
Cart.—Cartoonist
Carto.—Cartographer
Cer. C.—Ceramic Craftsman
Cer. Des.—Ceramic Designer
Chief Exh. Div.—Chief Exhibits Division
Comm. A.—Commercial Artist
Cons. A. Dir.—Consulting Art Director
Cr.—Critic
Cur. Collections—Curator of Collections

Dean E.—Dean of Education
Des.—Designer
Dir.—Director
Dir. Rest.—Director of Restoration

E.—Educator
Ed.—Editor
Ed. of Publ.—Editor of Publications
Eng.—Engraver
Et.—Etcher

Fash. I.—Fashion Illustrator
Flm. Mk.—Film Maker
Form. Mus. Dir.—Former Museum Director

Gal. Dir.—Gallery Director
Gr.—Graphic Artist
Gr. Des.—Graphic Designer

Hist.—Historian

I.—Illustrator
Ill.—Illuminator

Indst. Des.—Industrial Designer
Indst. I.—Industrial Illustrator

L.—Lecturer
Lib. Dir.—Library Director
Libr.—Librarian
Lith.—Lithographer

Mar. P.—Marine Painter
Med. I.—Medical Illustrator
Min. P.—Miniature Painter
Mur. P.—Mural Painter
Mus. A.—Museum Associate
Mus. Admin.—Museum Administrator
Mus. Asst. Dir.—Museum Assistant Director
Mus. Assoc. Cur.—Museum Associate Curator
Mus. Cons.—Museum Conservator
Mus. Consult.—Museum Consultant
Mus. Cur.—Museum Curator
Mus. Des. Exh.—Museum Designer of Exhibitions
Mus. Dir.—Museum Director
Mus. L.—Museum Lecturer
Mus. Off.—Museum Officer
Mus. Prep.—Museum Preparator
Mus. Res. F.—Museum Research Fellow
Mus. Rest.—Museum Restorer
Mus. Res. & Pro. Asst.—Museum Research & Program Assistant
Mus. Sec.—Museum Secretary
Mus. Staff A.—Museum Staff Artist

P.—Painter
Pack. Des.—Package Designer
Por. P.—Portrait Painter
Pr.—Painter
Pr. M.—Printmaker

S.—Sculptor
Sc. Des.—Scenic Designer
Ser.—Serigrapher
Supv.—Supervisor

T.—Teacher
Tex. Des.—Textile Designer
Theat. Des.—Theatrical Designer
Typ.—Typographer
Typ. Des.—Typographic Designer

W.—Writer

Geographical Index

ALABAMA

Auburn

Applebee, Frank Woodberry—P., E.
James, Alfred Everett—P., S., Et., Des., T., C.
Sykes, William Maltby—P., Gr., E., L.

Birmingham

Bridges, Georges—S., Des.
Gunter, Frank Elliott—P.
Howard, Richard Foster—Mus. Dir.
Price, Rosalie Pettus (Mrs.)—P.

Florence

Tuthill, Corinne—P., C., E.

Foley

Albrizio, Conrad Alfred—P., E., Des.

Homewood

Clancy, Joe Wheeler—P., Lith., Des., T., L.

Mobile

Bush, William Broughton—P., I.
deCelle, Edmond Carl—P., Des.

Montevallo

Allen, Martha—C., S., E.
Barnes, Virginia—T., P., Ser.
Huntley, David Collins—P., E., C., Des.
Kennedy, Dawn S.—E., L., P.

Montgomery

Nix, Frances Nimmo Greene—Mus. Dir., P.
Peacock, Claude—I., Comm. A., P., T., Cart.
Stegall, Irma Matthews (Mrs.)—P., L.

Oakman

Ward, Irene Stephenson (Mrs.)—P.

Rockford

Le Bron, Warree Carmichael (Mrs.)—P.

Talladega

Driskell, David Clyde—P., E.

Tuscaloosa

Bolt, Joseph Sullivan—E., P., Art Hist.
Brough, Richard Burrell—E., P., Des., Comm. A.
Findley, Ila B. (Mrs.)—P.
Zoellner, Richard Charles—P., Gr., I., L., T.

University

Goodson, Howard—E.

ALASKA

Anchorage

Anderson, Alma—P.
Brennan, Dean—P.
Combs, Alex—C., P., T.
Conder, Jacques—P., T.
Goodale, Ellen Henne—P.
Goodale, Harvey—P.
Hamill, Mildred—P.
Kimura, William—P.
Kirschbaum, Armond—P., Adv. Des.
Kohler, Melvin Otto—Des.
Park, A. E.—P., T.
Van Housen, Beth—P., Des.

Palmer

Machetanz, Fred—Pr. M., P., L., W., Film Maker
Machetanz, Sara—Pr. M., P., L., W., Film Maker

ARIZONA

Apache Junction

Lansing, Ambrose—Mus. Cur.

Camp Verde

Dyck, Paul—P.

Duncan

Empie, Hal H.—Cart., I., P., T., W., L.

Flagstaff

Colton, Harold S.—Mus. Dir.
Colton, Mary-Russell Ferrell (Mrs.)—P., S., C.
Danson, Edward B.—Asst. Mus. Dir.
Wright, Barton Allen—Mus. Cur., I.

Oraibi

Kabotie, Fred—P., I., T., W., L.

Phoenix

Arriola, Gus—Cart.
Bastian, Rufus A.—P., Et., Lith., T., W.
Bell, Edith Marian—P., T.
Bensco, Charles J.—P.
Bergamo, Dorothy Johnson—P., Lith., T., L.
Coze, Paul Jean—P., W., I., L., T.
Datus, Jay—P., T., W.
Halseth, Odd Sigurd—Mus. Dir., E., Cr., W., L.
Hinkhouse, Forest Melick—Mus. Dir.
Keane, Bil—Cart.
Lange, Erna—P., T.
Manning, Reginald West—Cart., W., Des.

Prescott

Phillips, Claire Dooner—P., Et.

Sasabe

Schaldach, William Joseph—Et., P., W.

Scottsdale

Beaugureau, Francis Henry—P., T.
Davis, Lew E.—P.
Grosse, Garnet Davy—P., Des., W., L., Cr.
Harris, Robert George—I., Comm. A., P., L.
Jacobson, Arthur R.—P., Gr., E.
Kloster, Paula Rebecca—Mus. Cur., E., P., W.
Sanderson, Raymond Phillips—S.
Schaefer, Mathilde (Mrs.)—S.
Strobel, Oscar A.—P., Lith., I.

Sedona

Abiskhairoun, Nassan—S., Des.

Tempe

Failing, Frances Elizabeth—P., T.
Goo, Benjamin—S., Des., E.
Harter, Tom J.—E., P., Des., I.
Stevens, Lawrence Tenney—S., Gr., P., L., T.
Wood, Harry Emsley, Jr.—E., L., P.

Tucson

Andersen, Andreas Storrs—E., P.
Bain, Joan (Mrs.)—P.
Church, Robert M.—E., Mus. Dir.
Edgerly, Beatrice (Mrs.)—P., Lith., I., T., Cr., W.
Fairchild, Hurlstone—P.
Golden, Charles O.—P., Lith., S., T.
Hamlin, Edith (Mrs.)—P.
Loney, Doris Howard (Mrs.)—P., T.
Modjeska, Marylka (Mrs.)—P., Et.
Nichols, Dale William—P., Des., Lith., I., W., L., E.
Peirce, Gerry—P., Et., I., W., T., L.
Scott, James Powell—P., E., Lith., I.
Spencer, Margaret Fulton (Mrs.)—P.
Voris, Mark—E., P., Des., Eng., L.

ARKANSAS

Batesville

King, Mrs. Harry—C., Des.

Fayetteville

Durst, David—P., E., Mus. Dir.
Krueger, Lothar—E.
Okerbloom, Charles I., Jr.—P., Gr., E.
Reif, Rubin—P., Gr., Des. Comm. A., E.
Westermeier, Clifford Peter—E., W., L., P., I.
Whitlatch, Howard J.—E.

Little Rock

Graham, William Karr—Cart.
Hancock, James Carl—Et., Des., P., Comm. A.
Sorensen, John Hjelmhof—Cart.
Steadman, William E., Jr.—Mus. Dir., E., P., L.

Marianna

Govan, Francis Hawks—E., P., C., Des., L.

Pine Bluff

Gregory, Barbara Delle Simmons (Mrs.)—P.

Searcy

Mason, Elizabeth Brewer—E., P., L.

Texarkana

Acruman, Paul—Cart., I., P.

Winslow

Cockrell, Dura Brokaw (Mrs.)—E., P., W.
Will, Blanca—S., P., T., Des., Gr.

CALIFORNIA

Alhambra

Harris, Samuel Hyde—P.
Mitchell, Laura M. D. (Mrs.)—Min. P., W.
Norris, Vera Pearl—P.
Yacoe, Donald Edward—P., T.
Young, Florence—P., Eng., T.

Altadena

Acker, Herbert V. B.—Port. P.
Gammon, Estella—P., Des., T.
Goodall, Donald B.—E.
Green, David Oliver, Jr.—S., Des., Gr., E., L.
Jordan, Dorothy Foote (Mrs.)—P.
Kubacki, Raymond—P.
Monhoff, Frederick—Et., Lith., L., T., Arch.
Taggart, Richard T.—P., Des., W.
Wilcocks, Edna Marrett—P.
Zorthian, Jirayr Hamparzoom—P., C., Des., L., Gr., T.

Arcadia

Hanscom, Trude (Mrs.)—P., Et., E.
Hartmetz, Herrica H.—P.
Kushner, Dorothy Browdy—P., C., T.
Roysher, Hudson Brisbine—C., Des., E., L.

Arcata

Degenhart, Pearl C.—P., T., W.

Bakersfield

Howen, Ellis Alexander—P., T., L.
Howen, Lillian Harris (Mrs.)—P.

Belvedere

Cummings, Harold W.—C.
Ludekens, Fred—I., Des.
Strawbridge, Edward Richie—P.

Ben Lomond

Prescott, Preston L.—S., T.

Berkeley

Blos, May—I., T., P., C.
Blos, Peter W.—P., C., T.
Brezee, Evelyn—P., E.
Cornin, Jon—P., Des., E.
Davies, Elton Morrow—P., Gr., T.
Gaw, William A.—P., E., L.
Horn, Walter W.—E.
Hough, Helen Halley Brewster—Art Cur., T., L.
Lockwood, Ward—P., E., L.
Loran, Erle—P., E., W.
McKee, Katherine Louise (Mrs.)—P., S., Gr., Des., Comm. A., C.
Nelson, Lucretia—E., P.

Nicholson, Douglas Cornwall—P., I.
Paget-Fredericks, J. Rous-Marten—I., W., Des., L., E.
Park, David—P., T.
Pepper, Stephen Coburn—E., W., L., Cr.
Prestini, James—Des., S., C., E.
Ruvolo, Felix—P., E.
Ryder, Worth—P., E., L.
Shear, Fera Webber—P., L.
Swift, Florence Alstin—P., C., Des.
Taylor, Edgar—P., T.
Watson, James Robert, Jr.—P.
Wessels, Glenn Anthony—P., W., L., E.

Beverly Hills

Alvarez, Mabel—P., Lith.
Attridge, Irma Gertrude (Mrs.)—P.
Bjerregaard-Poulsen, Jacob—W.
Blair, Camille—P.
Blair, Streeter—P.
Clemens, Paul Lewis—P.
Daraio, Innocenzo—P.
Johnson, Ferd—Cart.
Johnston, Ynez—P., Et.
Karpf, Fay B.—W., T., P.
Longstreet, Stephen—P., S., T., Cr., W., L.
Wein, Albert W.—S., P., Des.

Big Sur

Bowman, Dorothy Louise (Mrs.)—Ser., P.
Bradford, Howard—Ser., P., T.

Bishop

Clunie, Robert—P.

Brookdale

Irwin, William Hyde—P., T.

Burbank

Gebhardt, Harold—S., T.
Massard, Jack Klett—Cr.
Raskin, Milton W.—P.
Saul—Et., Lith., P.
Smyth, Edmund R.—Des., P.

Burlingame

MacDonald, Katharine Heilner—Pr. M., T.
Sanford, Isobel Burgess—P., Des., Eng.

Cambria

Paradise, Phil—P., Lith., Ser., T., L.

Capistrano Beach

Leyden, Louise Hannon (Mrs.)—P., C., Des.
Partch, Virgil Franklin—Cart.

Cardiff-By-The-Sea

Baker, Lloyd Theron—Cart., Comm. A.
Louden, Orren R.—P., W., L.

Carlsbad

Hagen, Ethel Hall—P., C.
Hankins, Vina S. (Mrs.)—P., T.
Rost, Miles Ernest—P.
Selinger, Armand—P.
van de Velde, Alfred E. R.—P.

Carmel

Adriani, Bruno—W.
Anderson, Alma—E., L., P.

Aurner, Kathryn Dayton (Mrs.)—P., Gr., E., W.
Baer, Martin—P., Et.
Cunningham, John—P., T., Des.
Cunningham, Patricia—P., T., Des.
MacLennan, Eunice Cashion—P., T., Lith., I., W., Cr., L.
Mays, Paul Kirtland—P.
Moore, Frank M.—P.
Shoemaker, Vaughn—Cart.
Teague, Donald—P.
Williamson, William Harvey—P., Des.
Yardley, Ralph O.—Cart.

Carmel Valley

Ketcham, Henry King—Cart.
O'Neal, Frank E.—Cart.
Parker, Alfred—I.

Carpinteria

Tuckerman, Lilia McCauley (Mrs.)—P.

Cathedral City

Pelton, Agnes—P.

Chatsworth

Holmes, Ralph—P., T.
Maccoy, Guy—P., Ser., L.
Winebrenner, Harry Fielding—P., S.

Chico

Schneider, Elsbeth—P., E., Eng.

Claremont

Ames, Jean Goodwin—C., P., E.
Darrow, Paul Gardner—P., Gr., T., Cart.
Dike, Philip Latimer—P., Des., C.
Hueter, James W.—P., S., T.
Jurecka, Cyril—E., S.
Scott, David Winfield—P., L., T.
Sheets, Millard Owen—P., T., Des., I., C.
Skelton, Phillis Hepler—P.
Stewart, Albert T.—S.
Zornes, James Milford—P., I., Comm. A., T., W., L.

Colma

Arnautoff, Victor Michail—P., E., Gr.

Columbia

Surendorf, Charles—Eng., P., T.

Corona del Mar

Brandt, Rexford—P., I., W., L., T., Des.
d'Usseau, Leon—P., S., C.
Irving, Joan—P., C., T.
Manoir, Irving K.—P., C., Et., L., W.

Coronado

Lewis, Monty—P., Des., L., E., W.
Walcott, Anabel H. (Mrs.)—P.

Covina

Cross, Watson, Jr.—P.

Culver City

Dripps, Clara Reinicke (Mrs.)—P., C., Comm. A.

Cupertino

Johnson, J. Theodore—P., E.

Daly City

Gutmann, John—E., P., Gr.

Dana Point

Keeler, Charles Butler—Et., P.

Davis

Baird, Joseph A., Jr.—E., W., L.
Nelson, Richard L.—E., P., L.

Del Mar

Turner, Herbert B.—P., S.

Downey

Elliott, Ethel M. (Mrs.)—P.

El Segundo

Yoakum, Delmer J.—P., Des., Ser.

Encino

Doggett, Jean—P., L.
Polkinghorn, George—P.
Timmins, Harry L.—I., T.

Escondido

Hurd, Angela M.—P., T.

Fallbrook

Swope, Emma Ludwig—C., Des., T.

Fillmore

Hinckley, Lawrence Bradford—P., L., Des.

Fresno

Gale, Jane Greene—P., E.
Musselman, Darwin B.—P., E., Comm. A.
Odorfer, Adolf—C., E.
Pickford, Rollin, Jr.—P., Des., I.

Glendale

Ackerman, Frank Edward—P.
Evans, Naomi T. (Mrs.)—P., T., L.
La Com, Wayne Carl—P., Des., Comm. A., T., Ser.
Miller, Marie Clark—P., I., W., L.
Thorpe, Dorothy Carpenter—C., Des.

Glen Ellen

Degen, Ida Day—S., Des., T., L.

Goleta

Fenton, Howard C.—E.

Hermosa Beach

Fels, Catherine Phillips—P., Gr., T., C.

Hollywood

Anderson, Dorothy Visju—P., T., S., W.
Argall, Charles G.—P.
Band, Max—P., W.
Bennett, Ruth M.—C., T., P.
Biberman, Edward—P., Ser.
Finney, Betty Morris—P.
Ganine, Peter—S., Indst. Des.
Houser, Victor Carl—S., W., L.
Hulett, Charles Willard—P., T., Cart., I.
Kelsey, Richmond—Des., P., Comm. A.
Klinker, Orpha—Et., P., I., L.
Klynn, Herbert David—P., Des., Cart., Comm. A., I., L.
Lovins, Henry—Mural P., Des., W., E., L., C.

Mallon, Grace Elizabeth—I., Des., P.
Parker, Gladys—Cart.
Paval, Philip—P., S., C., L., Des.
Ret, Etienne (Mr.)—P., W., L.
Scarpitta, Nadja—S., L., W., T., P.
Scott, Benton—P., T.
Smiley, Ralph J.—Port. P.
Steere, Lora Woodhead—S.

Inglewood

Morris, Patricia M.—P.

Kentfield

Otis, George Demont—P., Et., L.

La Canada

Knight, Julia Murray—P.
Shackelford, Katharine Buzzell—P., T., C.

La Crescenta

Dickinson, Daisy Olivia—S., C., P., L.
Dickinson, Ross Edward—P., I., T.
Hulett, Ralph—P., Des., Cart., I.
Rollins, Helen Jordan (Mrs.)—P., C., I.

Lafayette

Kasten, Karl—P., E., Et.
Rackley, Mildred (Mrs.)—Ser., P., C.

Laguna Beach

Armstrong, Roger Joseph—Cart., P., I.
Blacketer, James Richard—P., Des.
Cromwell, Joane (Mrs.)—P., Comm. A.
Dunn, Marjorie Cline—Port. P., S.
Dupont, Alfred—P., Comm. A., I., W., T.
Gardner, Gertrude Gazelle—P., T.
Henry, H. Raymond—P., W., Cr.
Interlandi, Frank—Cart., P.
Iredell, Russell—P., I., S., Des.
Nofziger, Edward C.—Cart., I., W.
Patty, William A.—P., T., L.
Scheu, Leonard—P., E.
Schwankovsky, Frederick John—P., T., W., L.
Vander Velde, Henry F.—P., E.
Volkmar, Leon—Cer., P.
Woolley, Virginia—P.

La Jolla

Abbott, Edith Abigail—P., C., E., Des.
Donaldson, Elise—P., Lith.
Goodell, William Newport—P., Ser., C., T., I.
Harris, Laurence W.—Cart.
Levy, Beatrice S.—P., Gr.
Malone, Patrick Thomas—Mus. Dir.
Murphy, Harry Daniels—Cart., L.
Verhaeren, Carolus—P.

La Mesa

Porter, James Tank—S.
Swiggett, Jean (Mr.)—E., P., Ser., Des., C.

Long Beach

Barlow, Marvin K.—Cart.
Donson, Jerome Allan—Mus. Dir., S., T., Cr.
Greene, Lucille Brown (Mrs.)—P., T., W.
Hay, Velma Messick—P.
Hyde, Josephine E. (Mrs.)—P., C., T.
Messick, Benjamin Newton—P., Lith., T., L.

Los Angeles

Adams, Velma—Lith., Et., Eng., P., S.
Aldrin, Anders Gustave—P.
Aller, Gladys (Mrs.)—P.
Anderson, Web—E., P., C., Gr.
Andreson, Laura—E.
Askenazy, Mischa—P.
Ayres, Martha Oathout—S., P., T., W., L.
Barton, Loren (Mrs.)—P., Et., I.
Beck-Meyer, Richard Christian—P., T.
Belt, A. Elmer—Lib. Dir.
Beynon, William—P., Des., Cart., Comm. A.
Billington, John J.—P., T., Lith., Ser., I.
Bloch, E. Maurice—E., L., Mus. Cur., W., P.
Blower, David Harrison—P.
Blumberg, Ron—P., T.
Brice, William—P., E.
Brigante, Nicholas P.—P.
Buckley, Jean—S., P., C., Lith., T.
Burkhardt, Hans Gustav—P.
Burnham, Roger Noble—S., T., L.
Calkins, Loring Gary—Bookplate Des., Et., I.
Campbell, Isabella F. (Mrs.)—P.
Carroll, Nellie—Cart., Des.
Cavanna, Elise (Mrs.)—P., I.
Chodorow, Eugene—Ser., S., P.
Chouinard, Nelbert M. (Mrs.)—E.
Clark, Mabel Beach—P.
Cook, Alma May—E., Cr.
Cruze, Charles—Indst. Des.
Curtis, Leland—P.
Cutrow, Leonard A.—P., T., Des., Comm. A.
D'Agostino, Vincent—P.
Dedeaux, Helen—P.
de Erdely, Francis—P., E.
Delacour, Jean T.—Mus. Dir.
Deutsch, Boris—P., Et., Lith., T.
Drudis, Jose—P., L.
Duer, Ben F.—P., Des., E., I., W., L.
Elliott, Ruth Cass—P., Des., Gr.
Ellsworth, Clarence Arthur—I., P.
Ewing, Edgar—P.
Ferren, John—P., S., Des., Gr., T.
Finch, Keith—P.
Fisher, Anya—P.
Franklin, Arla (Mrs.)—P., T.
Freed, Ernest Bradfield—Et., Eng., P., E.
Gehring, C. F.—Asst. Mus. Dir.
Gibson, George—P., Des., I., L.
Gleason, Joe Duncan—P., I., W.
Gluckmann, Grigory—P.
Guenther, Pearl Harder—P.
Hammargren, Frederick—S.
Hansen, Florence Froney—P.
Helder, Z. Vanessa (Mrs.)—P., C.
Henry, Charles Trumbo—P., T., L.
Herron, Jason (Miss)—S., W., L.
Hoowij, Jan—P.
Hughes, Daisy Marguerite—P.
Jacobs, Leonebel—Port. P.
Jacoby, Ned Levering—Des., T., P.
Jones, John Paul—Et., P.
Kelly, Francis Robert, Jr.—P., Gr.
Kester, Lenard—P., Des., Gr., I., T.
Kleidman, Rose—P., Ser.
Kopenhaver, Josephine Young—P., T.
Kosa, Emil J., Jr.—P., Lith., W., L.
Krehm, William P.—P.
Kurtzworth, Harry Muir—Art. Dir., P., Des., W., E., L.
Landacre, Paul Hambleton—Eng., I., T.
Landers, Bertha—P., Libn., Et., W.
Lanfair, Harold Edward—Des., I., P.
Lanzi, Emil—P., W., L.
Laporte, Paul M.—E., Pr. M., C., W., L.
Lauritz, Paul—P., T., L.
Lebrun, Rico—P., T., L.
Leeper, John P.—P.
Lesovsky, Adolf—P., Des.
Lidow, Leza—P.

Lion, Henry—S., P.
Little, Gertrude L.—Min. P.
Lukits, Theodore N.—P., I., E., L.
Lutz, Dan—P., T.
Mallary, Robert Wenley—P., S., Gr., Des., E.
Matthews, Lester Nathan—S., P., C., Des., Gr.
Merideth, John Gray—P., Comm. A., T.
Miller, Reeva Anna (Mrs.)—P., C.
Motts, Alicia Sundt—P., W., L.
Natzler, Gertrude—Ceramic C.
Natzler, Otto—Ceramic C.
Newcombe, Warren—P., Lith.
Nicolosi, Joseph—S., L.
Nieto, Grace A.—P., C., S.
Nunes, Gordon—P., E.
Nutting, Myron C.—P., Gr., T., Cr.
Ott, Peterpaul—S., C., Gr., L., T.
Palansky, Abraham—P., S.
Park, Hazel A. Hanes—P., C.
Parsons, Claude P.—P., L.
Payne, Elsie Palmer (Mrs.)—P., T., L.
Penny, Aubrey John Robert—P.
Perret, Ferdinand—Art. Hist., P., Des., Gr., I., W., L.
Pillin, Polia—P., C.
Quinn, Noel—P., Des., E., I., Gr.
Reid, Aurelia Wheeler—P., C., S.
Robinson, Irene Bowen (Mrs.)—I., P.
Robison, Anna Dorothy—P., Et., L.
Ross, Kenneth—Mus. Dir., Cr., L.
Ruben, Richard—P., T., Ser.
Russell, Bruce Alexander—Cart.
Scott, Clyde Eugene—P., T.
Seely, Walter Fredrick—P., Cr.
Seletz, Emil—S.
Serisawa, Sueo—P., T.
Sider, Deno—P., S., C., T.
Singer, Burr (Mrs.)—P., Lith.
Singer, William Earl—P., W., L., T.
Sklar, Dorothy (Mrs.)—P., T., Des.
Smith, Walt Allen—S., Des., L., T.
Starkey, Jo-Anita (Mrs.)—P., C., Des.
Steinitz, Kate Trauman—Art Libn., P., W., L.
Swift, Dick—Pr. M., P., E.
Van Leyden, Ernst Oscar Mauritz—P., S.
Van Leyden, Karin Elizabeth—P., Des., I.
Vann, Loli (Mrs.)—P.
Van Young, Oscar—P., T., L., Lith.
Von Schneidau, Christian—P., S., W., L.
Waana-Gano, Joe—P., Des., I., W., L.
Ward, Louisa Cooke—P., T.
Weisman, Joseph—P., Des., I., T.
Whelan, Blanche—P.
White, Lawrence Eugene—E.
Wight, Frederick S.—E., Gal. Dir., W., L.
Wilder, Mitchell—E.
Wilimovsky, Charles A.—Et., Eng., P., T.
Young, Joseph Louis—Mural P., S., C., Gr., E., L.

Malibu

Brown, Dorothy Woodhead—P., E., W., L., Cr.
Rosenthal, Bernard—S.

Manhattan Beach

Baker, Doris Winchell—P.
Crown, Keith Allan, Jr.—P., E., Gr., W., I., L.

Millbrae

Nepote, Alexander—P., E., L.

Mill Valley

Bergmann, Franz W.—P., C., I., W.
Oehler, Helen Gapen (Mrs.)—P., L., T.

O'Hanlon, Richard Emmett—S., L.
Pomeroy, Elsie Lower—P., I., T.
Rasmusen, Henry N.—P., W., E.
Riegger, Hal—C., E., S.

Monrovia

Codman, Ruth (Mrs.)—P.
Stevens, Mildred Lapson—P., T., L., W., Ser., Des.

Montclair

McClellan, Douglas Eugene—P., T., L.

Monterey

Boundey, Burton Shepard—P., T., Gr.
Dedini, Eldon—Cart.
Frances, Gene (Mrs.)—P., W.
Gilbert, Arthur Hill—P.

Montrose

Leeper, Vera—P., T., L.

Nevada City

Gilberg, Robert George—P., T.
Wood, E. Shotwell—P., T.

Northridge

Dentzel, Carl Schaefer—Mus. Dir., W., L.
Earle, Eyvind—Des., P., Comm. A., I.

Oakland

Baca, Catherine Eaton—Watercolorist
Bellis, Daisy Maude—P., Des., W., L., E.
Boratko, Andre—P., S., T.
Clark, Claude—P., E., Gr.
Danysh, Joseph A.—E., P.
Defenbacher, Daniel S.—E., W., L.
Holden, James Albert—Mural Painter
Hungerland, Helmut—E.
Lagorio, Irene R.—P., Gr., Des., W., L.
Meyer, Frederick H.—E., Des.
Neumeyer, Alfred—E., Mus. Dir., W.
Partridge, Roi—Et., E.
Polos, Theodore C.—P., Lith., T.
Rice, William Seltzer—Et., T., P., Des., I., W., L.
Schoener, Jason—P., C., S., E.
Siegriest, Lundy—P., Gr., T.
Strawn, Melvin Nicholas—P., S., Des., Gr., T., Ser.

Oceanside

Baldwin, Clifford Park—I., P.
De Witt, Jessie R.—P.

Ojai

Koch, Gerd—P., S., Gr., T., Des.
Koch, Irene Skiffington—P., Gr., T.
Nimmo, Louise Everett—P., C.

Ontario

Bloodworth, Alvin Hale—Cart.
Fleck, Robert John—P., T., L.

Orinda

Neuhaus, Eugen—P., W., L., E.

Oxnard

Durfee, Mildred Lucille—E., P.

Pacific Grove

Goethe, Joseph Alexander—S., P., C., Gr.
Miller, Dorothy Elizabeth (Mrs.)—P.

Pacific Palisades

Barker, George—P., T., L.
Barker, Olive Ruth—P.
Campbell, Richard H.—P.
Longman, Lester D.—E., L., W.
Macdonald-Wright, Stanton—P., W., L.
McClelland, Amy Woller (Mrs.)—E.
Rogers, Charles B.—P., Et., Lith., T., C.
Stone, Fern Cunningham (Mrs.)—P., T., L., C.
Van Cleve, Helen (Mrs.)—P., S., W.

Palm Desert

Harding, G. Powell (Mrs.)—P., L.

Palm Springs

Cordrey, Earl Somers—I.
Richmond, Gaylord D.—P., Des., C., T.

Palo Alto

de Lemos, Pedro J.—Des., I., P., C., L., W., Mus. Dir.
Hoffman, Florice W.—P.
Mendelowitz, Daniel Marcus—P., E., W.
Norton, Elizabeth—S., Gr.

Palos Verdes Estates

Gurrey, Hartley Fletcher (Mrs.)—Lith., P., Des., T.

Pasadena

Baugh, Dorothy Geraldine—P.
Birch, Geraldine (Mrs.)—P., Et.
Block, Maurice—Dir. of Restoration
Buff, Conrad—P., Lith., I., Des.
Carmichael, Jae—P.
Chamberlin, Frank Tolles—P., S., Et., T.
Dann, Frode—P., T., C., W., L.
Doolittle, Harold L.—Et., Lith.
Dreyfuss, Henry—Des., E., W., L.
Edmondson, Leonard—P., Et., E.
Glenn, Sally (Mrs.)—P.
Hansen, Ejnar—P., Lith., S., T.
Jones, Elberta Mohler—P., W., L.
Kempster, Ruth—P.
Leavitt, Thomas Whittlesey—Mus. Dir.
Levy, Hilda—P., Ser.
Lindsay, Ruth Andrews (Mrs.)—P.
Manuel, Donaldo—Restorer, P., L.
Meador, Joshua Lawrence—P.
Norman-Wilcox, Gregor—Mus. Cur., W., L.
Scott, Jonathan—P., T.
Skeele, Anna Katharine—P., T.
Smith, Marie Vaughan—E., P., C., L., W.
Stetson, Katharine Beecher (Mrs.)—S., P.
Thurston, Jane McDuffie—P., Et.
Tompkins, Florence Lusk—P., T.
Trueworthy, Jay—P.
Wark, Robert Rodger—Mus. Cur., Hist.
Wright, James Couper—P., T., L.
Young, J. Donald—E.
Younglove, Ruth Ann (Mrs.)—P., C., L.
Zimmerman, Frederick A.—P., Cr., T., S., L.

Pebble Beach

Burgdorff, Ferdinand—P., Gr., C.
Hatlo, Jimmy—Cart.
Lewis, Jeannette Maxfield (Mrs.)—Et., Eng., P.
Ragan, Leslie—P., I.

Pescadero

Reitzel, Marques E.—P., E., Gr., L.

Piedmont

Johnson, Doris Miller (Mrs.)—P., T.
Mills, Paul Chadbourne—Mus. Dir.

Pittsburgh

Nuhfer, Olive Harriett—P., S., T., L

Point Richmond

Kees, Weldon—P., W., Cr.

Pomona

Rein, Harry—P., Ser., Des., C.

Potrero

Hendrickson, David—I.

Ramona

Gavencky, Frank J.—P., T.

Richmond

Haley, John Charles—P., E.
Salmi, Hazel Gowan—Art Center Dir.
Sussman, Richard N.—P., Gr., Des.

Sacramento

Beck, Dunbar—P., T.
Kent, Frank Ward—P., E., Gr., I.
Matthew, John Britton—E., P., L.

Salinas

Amyx, Leon Kirkman—P., E.

San Anselmo

Stoll, John Theodor Edward—Et., P.,
S.

San Bernardino

Rea, James Edward—P., S., Des., L.,
T., I.

San Carlos

Washburn, Kenneth Leland—P., E., S.

San Diego

Baranceanu, Belle—P., Eng., I., T.
Beach, Warren—Mus. Dir., P.
Ellison, J. Milford—T., P., L., Gr., C.
Hess, Sara—P.
Hord, Donal—S.
Jackson, Everett Gee—E., P., I.
Klapp, Freda Leslie—L., W.
Mitchell, Alfred R.—P., T.
O'Gorman, Jacqui (Mrs.)—P.
Rea, Pauline De Vol—P., Des., T.
Schrack, Joseph Earl—P., T., Des., I.,
L.
Sentovic, John M.—I., Comm. A.
Severance, Julia Gridley—S., Et.
Sieberns, Caroline Lenore (Mrs.)—P.,
Des.
Truax, Sarah E.—P.
Wilkevich, Eleanor (Mrs.)—P., T.

San Francisco

Adams, Mark—Des., P.
Asawa, Ruth—S.
Baldwin, Frances—P.
Baumann, Karl Herman—P., Des.,
Lith.
Beetz, Carl Hugo—Lith., P., E., W.
Bischoff, Elmer Nelson—P., T.
Bothwell, Dorr—P., Gr., Des., T.
Brannan, Sophie Marston—P., S.
Bufano, Beniamino—S.

Campbell, William Addison, Jr.—P.,
E.
Cole, Gail Shepardson—P., T.
Cook, John—Cart., I.
Cravath, Ruth (Mrs.)—S., T.
Culler, George D.—Assoc. Mus. Dir.
Davy, James Benjamin—Et., S., P.
Erik-Alt, Lenore (Mrs.)—P., Gr., S.,
T., L.
Fossum, Sydney Glenn—P., Gr., E., L.
Frankenstein, Alfred Victor—Cr., W.,
L., T.
Fried, Alexander—Cr.
Garth, John—P., W., L., Cr., T., Gr.
Gershoy, Eugenie—S., P., Gr., T., Des.
Ginno, Elizabeth de Gebele—Et., Lith.
Graziotti, Ugo Adriano—S., P., E., L.,
W.
Heil, Dr. Walter—Mus. Dir.
Howard, Robert Boardman—S., P.,
C., T.
Howe, Thomas Carr—Mus. Dir.
Jonniaux, Alfred—Port. P.
Kent, Adaline (Mrs.)—S., P.
Kirby, Glo—P., Lith.
Landau, Rom—S., E., W., L.
Lederer, Wolfgang—Des., E., Comm.
A., I.
Leighton, Thomas C.—Port. P., T.,
L.
Leong, James Chan—P.
Lindstrom, Charles Wesley—Mus.
Cur., T., L., P., Des.
Lindstrom, Miriam B. (Mrs.)—Mus.
Cur., E., W., L.
Lundy, Fred Ralph—Cart.
Milsk, Mark (Mrs.)—Et., Lith.
Morris, Alice—P., Lith.
Mundt, Ernest Karl—S., W., L., E.
Oldfield, Otis William—P., C., Des.,
Lith., T.
Oneto, Joseph A.—P.
Packard, Emmy Lou—P., C., Gr., I.
Pommer, Mildred Newell—P., Gr.,
Des., C., T.
Post, George Booth—P., E.
Puccinelli, Raymond—S., P., E., L.
Rambo, James I.—Mus. Cur.
Randall, Byron—P., Eng., T.
Rathbone, Augusta Payne—P., Et., I.
Sandona, Matteo—Port. P.
Schnier, Jacques—E., S., W.
Smith, Howard Ross—Mus. Cur.
Troche, E. Gunter—Mus. Dir.
Ulreich, Eduard Buk—P., S., Des.
van Hoesen, Beth (Mrs.)—Et., Eng.
Van Hoesen, Beth Adams (Mrs.)—Pr.
M.
Von Meyer, Michael—S., T.
Wolf, Hamilton Achille—P., E., L.
Woods, Gurdon G.—E., S.

San Gabriel

Duquette, Mae—P., S., T.

San Jose

Auvil, Kenneth William—Ser., Lith.,
Et., T., P.
French, James C.—Mus. Cur., W., L.
French, John E.—E.

San Marino

McCluskey, Grace Dickover—P., T.
Pomfret, John—Art Lib. Dir.
Rankin, Mary Kirk (Mrs.)—P.
Sandford, Frank Leslie—P., Des.
Watkins, Frances Emma—Mus. Cur.,
W., L.

San Mateo

Stephens, Richard—P., Cart., L., T.,
Comm. A.

San Pedro

Strain, Oma (Miss)—E., P.

San Rafael

Wilmeth, Hal Turner—E., Gal. Dir.,
L., P.

Santa Ana

Miller, Evylena Nunn (Mrs.)—P., I.,
L., T.
Newcomb, Rexford—W., E., L.
Shafer, Burr—Cart., L., W., Hist.

Santa Barbara

Abel, Christine Jeannette—E., P., S.,
Des., L.
Backus, Standish, Jr.—P., I., Des., Gr.
Danner, Sara Kolb (Mrs.)—P.
de Zoro—dei Cappeller, Ettore—S.
Dole, William—P., E.
Dominique, John A.—P.
Foster, James W., Jr.—Mus. Dir.
Harcoff, Lyla Marshall—P.
Hebert, Marian—P., Et., C., Des., E.
Helm, MacKinley—W.
Hinkle, Clarence—P., T.
Phelps, Edith Catlin—P.
Rich, Frances—S.
Richmond, Evelyn K.—P.
Warshaw, Howard—P.
Webb, Margaret Ely—P., Eng., I.,
W., Des.

Santa Clara

Hilpert, Josef—Mus. Dir., P., L.

Santa Cruz

Baum, Franz—P., Et., L.
Buck, Claude—P., T.
Buck, Leslie Binner (Mrs.)—P.
Rogers, Margaret Esther—P., T.

Santa Monica

Gage, Merrell—S., E., L.
Haines, Richard—P., Des., Lith., E.
Mullican, Lee—P., S., E.
Reindel, Edna—P.
Weiner, Abraham S.—P., Des.

Santa Paula

Botke, Jessie Arms—P.

Sausalito

Bowden, Harry—P., Des.
Freeman, Don—P., I., Gr.
Georgetti, Wedo—P., Gr.
Pollak, Max—Et., P.

Sebastopol

Schulz, Charles Monroe—Cart.
Zakheim, Bernard Baruch—P., S., C.,
Des., T.

Sherman Oaks

Greene, J. Barry—P., Et., T.
Haase, Madeline (Mrs.)—P., Gr., C.,
T.
Nowak, Leo—Port. P., Cart., Comm.
A., I.
Silsby, Clifford—P., Et.
Tolegian, Manuel J.—P., W., I., Des.

Sierra Madre

Christenson, John Leonard—P., C.
Reimer, Cornelia (Mrs.)—P., T.
Suman, Lawrence—P., C.
Weese, Myrtle A.—P.
Wynne, Leslie Bernard, Jr.—P., C.,
Gr., I.

Signal Hill

Nagelvoort, Betty (Mrs.)—Des., C.,
Eng.

Stanford

Farmer, Edward McNeil—E., P., Eng., L.
Faulkner, Ray Nelson—E., W., Mus. Dir.

Stockton

Dooley, Helen Bertha—E., L., P., W.
Karnes, Harley—Cart.
Parker, Margery Shale—P., T.
Reynolds, Richard Henry—E., P., Des., S., W., L., Cr.
Rowland, Earl—Mus. Dir., L., E., P.
Yip, Richard D.—P., T., L.

Studio City

Finley, Mary L. (Mrs.)—P., Gr., E., I., Des.
Reep, Edward—P., T., Lith.

Sunland

Wong, Tyrus—P., Des., Et., Lith., I.

Taft

Turman, William T.—P., E.

Temecula

Horvath, Ferdinand Huszti—I., Ceramic Des., W., Cart., C.

Vallejo

Boswell, Normen Gould—P., Des., S., I., T., W., Gr.

Valley Center

Miller, Mildred Bunting—P., T., W., L.

Van Nuys

Bernat, Martha Miligan—S.
Davis, Emma Lu—P., S., T.
James, Frances K.—P.
Kendall, Viona Ann (Mrs.)—P., T.
Landy, Arthur Charles Landmesser—P., Lith., T., C., Ser.
Van Wolf, Henry—S.

Venice

Fordham, Elwood James—P., T.

Ventura

Moser, Julon Modjeska—P.

Victorville

Turner, Jean Leavitt (Mrs.)—P., I., S., T., L.

Vista

Prunier, Arthur William—P., T., Des., Comm. A.
Wilson, Ernest M.—P., Gr., Comm. A., I., L.

Walnut Creek

Dennis, Charles H.—Cart.

Whittier

Olds, Marion (Mrs.)—P.
Vaught, Larken—P.

Woodacre

Palmer, Arthur W.—P., Et., T.

Woodland Hills

Alexander, Dora Block (Mrs.)—P.

COLORADO

Aspen

Bayer, Herbert—P., Des.
Wille, O. Louis—S., T.
Williams, Garth Montgomery—I., S., P., W., Des.

Bailey

Bancroft, Albert Stokes—P.

Boulder

Black, Wendell—E., Pr. M.
Drewelowe, Eve—P., S.
Geck, Francis Joseph—Des., P., E.
Megrew, Alden Frick—E., Hist.
Neher, Fred—Cart.
Pneuman, Mildred Young (Mrs.)—P., Gr.
Wolle, Muriel Sibell (Mrs.)—E., W., L., P., Gr.

Briggsdale

Bidwell, Watson—P., E., Cr., L.

Collins

Booth, Zadie Cory—S., P., T.

Colorado Springs

Bartlett, Fred Stewart—Mus. Dir., T., W.
Bransby, Eric James—P., I., T.
Britton, Edgar—S., P., L., C.
Cornelius, Francis duPont—Conservator, P.
Mills, George Thompson—Mus. Cur.
Musick, Archie L.—P., Lith., T., W.
Parsons, Ernestine—P.
Stewart, Esther L.—P., T., L.

Denver

Bach, Otto Karl—Mus. Dir., P., Cr., E., W., L., C.
Billmyer, John Edward—E., C., P., Gr.
Black, Oswald Ragan—I., Comm. A., Cart., L., T.
Gray, Mary Chilton—P., I.
Hansen, Frances Frakes—E., P., Des.
Kirchner, Eva Lucille—Ceramist, S., Ser., T., L.
Kirkland, Vance—E.
Miller, Marion E.—E.
Smith, Paul Kauvar—P.
Sorby, J. Richard—P., E., Des.
Traher, William Henry—P., I., L.
Verhelst, Wilbert—S., P., T., Assoc. Mus. Cur.
Wands, Alfred J.—P., Lith., T., L.

Estes Park

Byxbe, Lyman—Et.
Samuelson, Fred B.—P., T.
Stirling, Dave—P.

Evergreen

Lindneux, Robert Ottokar—P., T., L.

Fort Collins

Hatton, Clara Anna—E., C., Gr., P.

Grand Junction

Redden, Alvie Edward—E., P.

Greeley

Perry, Kenneth F.—E.

Gunnison

Julio, Pat T.—E., C., Eng.

La Veta

Staples, Clayton Henri—P., L., E.

Pagosa Springs

Harmon, Fred—I.

Pueblo

Knobbs, Harry R.—Et., P.

Silverton

Pozzatti, Rudy O.—P., Gr., I., E.

CONNECTICUT

Berlin

Benson, Hannah Nicholson (Mrs.)—P., W., L.
Freer, Howard Mortimer—P., Des., T., I.

Bethel

Farris, Joseph G.—Cart., P.
Huntington, Anna Hyatt (Mrs.)—S.
Keeler, Louis Bertrand Rolston—P.
Pascal, David—Cart.
Schmidt, Alwin E.—I.

Bethlehem

Nelson, Ralph L.—P.

Bridgeport

Christensen, Ralph A.—P., C., S., Des., I., T., L.
Florian, Gordon William—Des., P., L.

Bridgewater

Brindle, Melbourne—Comm. A., I.

Brookfield Center

Beall, Lester Thomas—Indst. Des., P., I.

Byram

Dole, Margaret Fernald—P., L.

Cannondale

Lipman, Jean—W., Editor, L.

Chester

Knollenberg, Mary Tarleton—S.
Rosenmeier, Isador—P.
Spencer, Hugh—I., L.

Cornwall Bridge

Bradford, Francis Scott—Mural P.
Gray, Cleve—P., W.
Yeomans, Walter C.—Pr. M., Comm. A., P.

Cos Cob

Green, Herbert Lewis—Cart.
Kane, Margaret Brassler—S.

Danbury

Cleland, Thomas Maitland—I., Des., P., C.
Kraus, Robert—Cart., I., W.
Riley, Kenneth—I.
Rosenbauer, Wallace—E., S., Mus. Cur.

Darien

Bostelman, Else W. von Roeder—P., C., Des., I., Comm. A., W.
Claxton, William Rockliff—Des., I., P., Cart., C., Comm. A.
Foxley, Griffith—I.
Hardin, Adlai S.—S.
Newman, Ralph Albert—Cart., W.
O'Hara, Dorothea Warren—Potter, P., W.
Ray, Ruth (Mrs.)—P., Comm. A
Wheat, John Potter—P., T.
Whitcomb, Jon—I.

Easton

Vitacco, Alice—P., I., Des.

Essex

Browne, Aldis B., II—P.
Champlain, Duane—S.
Kreis, Henry—S., T.
Mayer, Henrik Martin—P., Lith., L., E.

Fairfield

Anderson, Lyman—I.
Skilton, John Davis, Jr.—W., Former Mus. Cur.

Falls Village

Carlsen, Dines (Mr.)—P.

Farmington

Churchill, Rose—P.
Hogan, Jean Virginia—P.
Talcott, Dudley Vaill—S., I., W., P.

Gaylordsville

Maurer, Sascha—P.

Glenbrook

Arthur, Revington—P., E., Gr., L.
Rummler, Alexander J.—P.

Granby

Wadsworth, Frances L. (Mrs.)—S.

Greens Farms

Rebay, Hilla—P., W., L.
Rosenberg, Louis Conrad—Et., I., Arch.

Greenwich

Barrie, Erwin S.—P.
Bentley, Lester W.—P
Brown, William Ferdinand II—Cart.
D'Elia, Teresa Ilda—P., Gr., C., Comm. A., T.
Estin, Peter George—Cart., I., Comm. A.
Kaep, Louis J.—P.
Lionni, Leo—P., Des., E., Cr.
Ochtman, Dorothy (Mrs.)—P.
Paddock, Robert Rowe—Theatrical Des.
Vibberts, Eunice Walker (Mrs.)—P.
Walker, Mort—Cart.

Guilford

Telling, Elisabeth—P., L.

Haddam

Gleeson, Charles K.—Et., P.

Hadlyme

Gordon, Elisabeth Chandler—S.

Hamden

Barton, Catherine Graeff—S.
Keller, Deane—E., P.

Hampton

Farnum, Royal Bailey—E., W., C.

Hartford

Alvord, Muriel—P.
Anderson, Genevieve Dillaye—P., C., E.
Behl, Wolfgang—S., T.
Beverly-Haynes, Dorothy Frances—P., Des., Comm. A.
Cunningham, Charles C.—Mus. Dir., W., L.
Katzenstein, Irving—P., T., W., L.
Parke, Nathaniel Ross—P., T., Des.
Squarey, Gerry—P., T., L.
Stimpson, Helen Townsend—P.
Taylor, John C. E.—P., E.
Tompkins, Alan—P., T., I., L., Des.
Zimmerman, Paul Warren—P., T.

Higganum

Read, Ralph Miner—P.

Ivoryton

Bendig, William C.—P., T.

Kensington

Edwardson, Laurence Christie—P.

Kent

Breasted, James Henry, Jr.—L., Hist.
Howard, Len R.—C.
Nelson, George Laurence—P., Lith.

Lakeville

Blagden, Thomas P.—P., T.
Chapin, Cornelia Van Auken—S., L.
Sanford, Marion—S., I.

Lime Rock

Hubbard, Earl Wade—P., S., W.
McLellan, Ralph—P., T.

Litchfield

Caesar, Doris—S.
Landeck, Armin—Et., Eng., Lith.
Purves, Austin—Mural P., S., C., E.

Long Hill

McCurry, Charles Ray—P., I.

Lyme

Artzybasheff, Boris—I., P., Des., W.
Fehrer, Oscar—P.
Nason, Thomas W.—Eng., Et., I.
Weiland, James G.—Port. P.

Madison

Crandell, Bradshaw—Port. P.

Manchester

Klar, Walter Hughes—E., W., P., L.
Knobler, Lois Jean—P.
Knobler, Nathan—P., E., Lith.
Terenzio, Anthony—P., E.

Meriden

Bowers, Beulah Sprague—P., C., S., T., L.
Helander, Lillian Valborg Mariea—Des.
Widstrom, Edward Frederick—S.

Middlebury

Gabo, Naum—S., E., P., Eng.
Swantees, Ethel Lucile—P., Et., Lith., T.

Middletown

Bennett, Mary Elizabeth—P.
Green, Samuel M.—E., P.
Limbach, Russell T.—Lith. P., E., W.
Risley, John—S., Des., E.
Risley, Mary Kring—C., T.
Schwarz, Heinrich—Mus. Cur., W., L.

Milford

Muelke, Robert—Des., E., L., S., C., Comm. A.

Mystic

Bates, Gladys Edgerly—S.
Bates, Kenneth—P.
Boronda, Beonne—Animal S., T.
Soderberg, Yngve Edward—P., Et., T., W., Comm. A.

Naugatuck

Thompson, Ben—Cart.

New Canaan

Arcier, Joseph William—P.
Avison, George Alfred—I., P., W.
Barbarite, James Peter—P., E.
Barton, August Charles—Des., P., E., L.
Brinley, Daniel Putnam—P., I., C.
Cavalli, Dick—Cart.
Eberman, Edwin—Des., E., P.
Geerlings, Gerald K.—Indst. Des., Et., Lith., W., Arch.
Henderson, Tom—Cart., Comm. A.
Hildebrandt, Cornelia E. (Mrs.)—P., L.
Lamb, Adrian—Port. P.
Margolies, Ethel Polacheck—P., W., T., C.
Richards, Glenora—Min. P.
Saxon, Charles D.—Cart.
Seyffert, Richard L.—P.
Soby, James Thrall—W., Cr.
Symon, Gail—P., T.

New Hartford

Ballinger, Harry Russell—P., T., W., L.
Mollison, Kay (Mrs.)—P.

New Haven

Albers, Anni—Des., C., E., W., L.
Albers, Josef—P., E., Cr., W., L., Gr.
Banever, Gilbert—Des., P., I., Comm. A., T., W.
Brodeur, Clarence A.—P., W., L.
Catlin, Stanton L.—Asst. Gal. Dir.
Chase, Alice Elizabeth—E., L.
Danes, Gibson—E., L., Cr.
Gute, Herbert Jacob—P., E.
Hamilton, George Heard—Mus. Cur., E.
Kubler, George—E., W., L.
Newton, Helen F.—P., W., T.
Purdue, Christine M.—C., S., T.
Rathbone, Richard Adams—P., E., L., W.
Ritchie, Andrew C.—Mus. Dir., L., W.

Rogers, Meyric Reynold—Mus. Cur., E., W., L.
Rollins, Carl Purington—Book Des., C.
Sexton, Frederick Lester—P., T., L.
Seymour, Charles, Jr.—E., Mus. Cur., Hist., L.
Sizer, Theodore—E., C., W.
Smith, Minna Walker—P.
Weinberg, Elbert—S.
Whiting, John Downes—P., I., W.

Newington

Martin, Gail Wycoff—P., T., Gr.
Preu, John D.—T., C., P.

New London

Mayhew, Edgar De Noailles—E., Mus. Cur., L., W.
McCloy, William Ashby—E., P., Et., Mus. Cur.
Park, Rosemary—Mus. Dir.

New Milford

Ashe, Edd M., Jr.—Cart., P., I.
Cole, Jack R.—Cart.
Cowles, Russell—P.
Hunt, Stanley Lloyd—Cart.
Kappel, Philip—Et., I., W., L.
Newton, Edith—Lith., P., W.
Sloane, Eric—I., W., P., L.

New Preston

Neufeld, Woldemar—P., Eng., T.
Wolff, Robert Jay—P., E., Des., W., L.

Newtown

Irvin, Rea—P., I., Cart.
Keeler, Katherine Southwick (Mrs.) —I., W.
Keeler, R. Burton—P., Des.
Low, Joseph—Gr., Des.
Schnakenberg, Henry—P.
Webb, Paul—Cart.

Noank

Brackman, Robert—P.
Lukosius, Richard—P.
Stein, Harve—I., P., E., Gr., L.

Norfolk

Clark, Isaac Carpenter—Et.
Kelemen, Pal—W., Hist., E.

Noroton

Aymar, Gordon Christian—Port. P., Des.
Timmins, William F.—I., Des.

North Canton

Kelsey, Dorothy Storey—P.

North Haven

Sims, Florence—Min. P.

North Sterling

Holden, Raymond J.—I., P., Comm. A.

Norwalk

Broudy, Miriam L.—P.
Chappell, Warren—I., Des., Gr.
Dahler, Warren—P., S., C.
Frasconi, Antonio—P., Des., T., Gr., I.
Frismuth, Harriet W.—S.
Koch, Robert—E., W., L.

Lasker, Joseph Leon—P.
Monaghan, Eileen (Mrs.)—P.
Silvercruys, Suzanne (Mrs.)—S., W., L.
Stavenitz, Alexander Raoul—Et., Lith., Des., T.
Vassos, John—P., Des.
Whitaker, Frederic—P., W.
Woodham, Jean Caraway—S.

Norwich

Dodge, Ozias (Mrs.)—Mus. Dir.
Gualtieri, Joseph Peter—P., T.
Triplett, Margaret L.—E., P.

Norwich Town

Eastman, Charlotte Fuller (Mrs.)—P., I., E.

Old Greenwich

Amick, Robert Wesley—P., E., Comm. A., I.
Anderson, Harold N.—I.
Maynard, Richard Field—P., S., W.
Salter, Stefan—Book Des., T.
Thompson, Alan—P., I., Des.

Old Lyme

Banning, Beatrice Harper (Mrs.)—Et., P.
Bruestle, Bertram G.—P.
Burr, Harold Saxton—P., T.
Dudley, Fanny—C.
Ebert, Charles H.—P.
Ebert, Mary Roberts (Mrs.)—P., C.
Hoffman, Harry L.—P.
Ingle, Thomas Hughes—P., T., L., Cr.
Loftus, John—P.
Niles, Rosamond—P., Et.
Pattee, Elsie Dodge—P., I., T., W., L.
Rook, Edward F.—P.
Whiting, Gertrude—P.
Wiggins, Guy—P., T., L.

Orange

Chaet, Bernard R.—P., E.
Davies, Kenneth Southworth—P., Comm. A., I.
Goitein, Olga—S.
Koepf, Werner—P.

Redding

Briggs, Austin—I.
Gianninoto, Frank A.—Indst Des., L.
Ryan, Sally—S., P.

Redding Ridge

Ridabock, Raymond Budd—P., T.

Ridgefield

Andrews, Sperry—P.
Belmont, Lu—P., T.
Boulton, Joseph L.—S., T.
Fawcett, Robert—I.
Nitsche, Erik—Des., I.

Riverside

Decker, Richard—I., Cart.
McMillen, Jack—P., Des., T.
Nevell, Thomas G.—Indst. Des., W.
Thompson, James Bradbury—Des.
Zerbo, Valerio J., Jr.—Des., Comm. A.

Rowayton

Ernst, Jimmy—P.
Marinsky, Harry—S., P., Des., I.
Peterdi, Gabor—P., Et., Eng., L., T.
Rose, Carl—I.

Roxbury

Calder, Alexander—S., P., I.
Weisgard, Leonard—I., Des., L.

Salisbury

MacDermott, Stewart Sinclair—P., Et.

Sandy Hook

Angel, John—S., C., L.

Sherman

Blume, Peter—P.

Silvermine

McCullough, Lucerne (Mrs.)—P., T.

Southbury

Lafon, Gertrude Van Allen (Mrs.)—P., C.

Southington

Low, Sanford—P., E., Mus. Dir.

South Kent

Nisbet, Robert H.—P., Et., T., Eng., L.

Southport

Finn, Kathleen Macy (Mrs.)—Et., L.

Stamford

Bach, Alfons—Des., P.
Bushmiller, Ernest Paul—Cart.
Dalton, William Bower—P., W., C.
Edson, Gus—Cart.
Luhde, Ernest T.—Mus. Dir.
Ogg, Oscar—Des., W., L., T., Cr.
Sorgman, Mayo—T., P., Des., L.
Tulk, Alfred James—Mural P., P.

Storrs

Gregoropoulos, John—P., T.
Kiley, Robert L.—P., Gr., E.
Meigs, Walter—P., E.

Stratford

Weir, Gordon D.—Des., P., T., I.

Suffield

Watt, William Godfrey—P.

Thompsonville

Apostle, James—P., I.

Tolland

Hicks, Elizabeth—P.

Torrington

Abbate, Paolo S.—S., Mus. Cur., W., L.
Lenski, Lois (Mrs.)—I., W., P.

Trumbull

Wade, Jean Elizabeth (Mrs.)—P., I.

Uncasville

Cuming, Beatrice—P., E.

Washington

Talbot, William—S.

Waterbury

Anderson, Joel Randolph—Et., Lith., P., Des., T.
Birkenberger, William—P., Des., C.

Waterford

Branner, Martin M.—Cart.
Dennis, Roger Wilson—P., Lith., T., Conservator
White, Nelson Cooke—P., W.

Westbrook

Kingsland, James—P.

West Cornwall

Gannett, Ruth Chrisman—I.
Simont, Marc—I., W.

West Haven

Paier, Edward Theodore—P., T., L.

Weston

Darrow, Whitney, Jr.—Cart.

Westport

Baar, Marion (Mrs.)—P., T., W., L., Cr.
Banks, Virginia—P.
Beckhoff, Harry—I.
Besser, Leonard—P., T., Gr., I.
Blair, Preston E.—Cart., Des., P.
Cowan, Wood—Cart. L., W.
Cumming, George Burton—Editor Art Books, T., L., W.
Daugherty, James Henry—P., Lith., W., I., L.
Dohanos, Stevan—I., Gr.
Egan, Eloise—P.
Ferne, Hortense—P., Et., Lith.
Fraser, Laura Gardin (Mrs.)—S.
Fuller, Arthur D.—I., P.
Gibbons, Margarita (Mrs.)—P.
Gramatky, Hardie—I., P., W.
Heath, Howard—P., Gr., Des., I., T.
Holden, Lephe Kingsley (Mrs.)—E., P.
Lambdin, Robert L.—P., I., Des.
Lichtenauer, Joseph Mortimer—P., S.
Lovell, Tom—I.
McCullough, Suzanne (Mrs.)—P.
Olsen, Herbert Vincent—P., W., L.
Pellew, John C.—P.
Price, Garrett—I.
Nebel, Berthold—S.
Niswonger, Ilse (Mrs.)—S., C.
Rabut, Paul—I., Des., P.
Rand, Paul—Des., P., W., I., T., Cr.
Reindorf, Samuel—P., Eng., Lith., I.
Rosendale, Harriet—P.
Sargent, Mary F. (Mrs.)—Et., C.
Sewell, Amos—I.
Skemp, Robert Oliver—P., Comm. A., I.
Tate, Sally—Port. P., I.
Viviano, Emmanuel Gerald—S., T.
Von Schmidt, Harold—I., P., L.
Walzer, Marjorie Schafer—P., C.

Wethersfield

Smith, Bissell Phelps—P., T., Gr., I., W., L.

Willimantic

Cohen, Esther Sima—Ceramist, E.

Wilton

Abell, Margaret Noel—S., C., P.
Bastrup, Leonard Hollis—Des., P.
Birmingham, Lloyd Paul—I., Cart., P.
Browne, Dik—Cart.

Chadbourn, Alfred Cheney—P.
Connelly, Brian—P.
d'Aulaire, Edgar Parin—P., Et., Lith.
d'Aulaire, Ingri Mortenson Parin—W., I., Lith., P.
Fleming, Frank—P., Des., I.
Pont, Charles E.—Pr. M., P., I., L., C., W.
Prins, Benjamin Kimberly—I.
Putnam, Brenda—S., W., T.
Ross, Alex—I., P.
Schmitt, Carl—P., W., T.

Woodbridge

Crosby, Sumner McKnight—E.

Woodbury

Leighton, Clare—Pr. M.
Sage, Kay Tanguy—P.
Savage, Eugene Francis—P., T., S.

DELAWARE

Frederica

Leach, Ethel Pennewill Brown—P., Gr.

Greenville

Whiteside, Henryette Stadelman—P.

Milford

Kuhlmann, Edward—W., P.

Millsboro

Peets, Orville Houghton—P., Gr.

Newark

Gowans, Alan—E., W.
Plunguian, Gina—P., S., T., L.
Prosser, Margaret (Mrs.)—E., P.

Seaford

Lockwood, Douglas—P., T.

Wilmington

Balch, Gertrude Howland—P., T., Et.
Bryson, Robert Alexander—P.
Coll, Francis A.—Artist-Craftsman
Grant, Edward Lynam—Des., P., T.
Hoskins, Gayle Porter—P., I., Des.
MacLellan, Charles Archibald—P., T.
Moore, Constance—Former Mus. Dir.
Pyle, Margery Kathleen—P.
St. John, Bruce—Mus. Dir.
Sala, Jeanne—P., T.
Stan, Walter P.—I., Des., Cart., P.
Vinson, Charles Nicholas—P.

Winterthur

Montgomery, Charles Franklin—Mus. Dir.

DISTRICT OF COLUMBIA

Washington, D. C.

Abbott, Anne Fuller (Mrs.)—P.
Acheson, Alice (Mrs.)—P., I.
Aden, Alonzo J.—Mus. Dir.
Anderson, Gwen—P., T., Cr., L.
Atkyns, Lee—P., T., Gr., S., L., I.
Breitenbach, Edgar—Chief, Pr. Div.
Bache, Martha Moffett (Mrs.)—P., T., W.
Baker, Sarah M.—E., P.
Baruch, Anne Barbara—P.
Bell, Philip Fletcher—P.
Berryman, Florence Seville—Cr., W., L.

Berryman, James Thomas—Cart., I., W.
Bittinger, Charles—P.
Bolton, Mimi Dubois—P., L.
Bookatz, Samuel—P.
Brown, Gertrude G.—P., C., E.
Buckner, Melvin D.—P., Des., T., Comm. A.
Campbell, William P.—Mus. Cur.
Carter, Albert Joseph—Mus. Cur., T.
Coleman, Laurence Vail—W., Mus. Dir.
Comes, Marcella (Mrs.)—P., W.
Cooke, Hereward Lester, Jr.—Mus. Cur. W., P.
Cott, Perry Blythe—Mus. Cur.
Cox, Theodosia—Editor and Libn.
Crowder, Conrad William—S., L., E.
Custis, Eleanor Parke—P., Et., I.
Deak-Ebner, Ilona—E., P., L.
Demonet, Inez Michon—P., Medical I., Et.
Der Nersessian, Sirarpie—E., W., L.
de Rosen, John Henry—P., E.
de Weldon, Felix Weihs—S., P., T., L.
Dorra, Henri—Asst. Mus. Dir.
Douglas Lester—Des., W., L.
Eckert, Evelyn E.—Comm. A., P.
Egbert, Lyn (Mrs.)—Des., C., Gr., E., W.
Ettinghausen, Richard—Mus. Cur., W., L., Hist.
Evans, Rudulph—S.
Ferry, Frances—P.
Finley, David E.—Former Mus. Dir.
Fontanini, Clare—E., S., Des., I., W., L.
Foster, Ethel Elizabeth—P.
Fowler, Alfred—W., Cr.
Gernand, John—P.
Greene, Francina—Mus. Cur.
Groce, George C.—Art Hist., W., Cr., L.
Haden, Eunice Barnard—P., I.
Harlan, Roma Christine—Port. P.
Herring, James Vernon—E., L., C., P.
Holland, Janice—I., P.
Hollerith, Lucia Beverly—P.
Holt, Naomi (Mrs.)—Port. P.
Howland, Richard Hubbard—E.
Hoyt, Edith—P., I.
Jones, Lois Mailou (Mrs.)—P., Des., E., Comm. A.
Jones, Thomas Hudson—S.
Kagy, Sheffield Harold—P., Gr., E., S.
Kainen, Jacob—Mus. Cur., Et., Lith., P.
Kane, Theodora—P., T.
Kelpe, Paul—P., E., Lith.
Kimberly, Cara Draper—P.
Kormendi, Elizabeth (Mrs.)—P., S.
Kormendi, Eugene—S.
Lane, Marian U. M.—Bookbinder, Illuminator
Lazzari, Pietro—P., S., T.
Lyon, Rowland—P., Gr., T., C., Cart.
Mason, John Russell—Cur. & Libn.
Milligan, Gladys—P., W., Hist.
Millsaps, Daniel Webster, III—P., Des., Gr., I., T.
Mongan, Elizabeth—Mus. Cur.
Moore, Benson Bond—P., Et., T.
Moore, E. Bruce—S.
Noyes, Bertha—P.
O'Hara, Eliot—P., Gr., W., L., T.
Olson, Henry W.—P., E.
Perlmutter, Jack—Lith., P., T.
Peters, Francis Charles—P.
Phillips, Duncan—Mus. Dir., W., L., Cr., P.
Phillips, Marjorie—Assoc. Mus. Dir., P.
Pope, Annemarie H. (Mrs.)—Chief, Traveling Exhibition Service
Pope, John Alexander—Asst. Mus. Dir.
Porter, James A.—P., W., E.

Porter, Leslie Judd (Mrs.)—Cr., W.
Quandt, Russell Jerome—Mus. Art Restorer
Rathbun, Seward Hume—P., T., W.
Raul, Harry Lewis—S., Former Mus. Administrator, L., Des.
Rennie, Helen Sewell—P., Des.
Richman, Robert M.—Mus. Dir., W., Cr., E.
Safford, Ruth Perkins—P.
Sauer, Margarita—P.
Schlaikjer, Jes Wilhelm—Port. P., I., T.
Shapley, Fern Rusk (Mrs.)—Mus. Cur., W.
Sickman, Jessalee Bane—P., T.
Silverman, Miles M.—P., Gr., I., E.
Sivard, Robert Paul—P., Des., Lith.
Snow, Mary Ruth (Mrs.)—P.
Stambaugh, Dean—P., T.
Summerford, Ben L.—Mus. Dir.
Summy, Katherine Strong—P., T.
Tabary, Celine Marie—P., Des., T.
Tasev, Atanas—P.
Thacher, John Seymour—Mus. Dir.
Todd, Frances Carroll—P.
Tolman, Nelly McKenzie (Mrs.)—Min. P.
Tolman, Ruel Pardee—Mus. Dir., P., Et., W.
Ulman, Elinor—T., P.
Vance, Mae H.—P., Des., I.
Walker, John—Mus. Dir.
Warneke, Heinz—S., E.
Walter, William F.—P., T.
Wells, James Lesesne—P., Lith., Eng.
Wenley, Archibald Gibson—Mus. Dir.
Wilbur, Dorothy Thornton—P., I.
Williams, Hermann Warner, Jr.—Mus. Dir., W., T., L.
Wright, Louis Booker—Mus. Dir., Hist.
Zerega, Andrea Pietro—P., T., L.

FLORIDA

Belleair

Boudreau, James Clayton—E., Lith., L., W.

Boca Grande

Stults, Elwin Martin, Jr.—P., Des.

Clearwater

Savage-Jones, James—S., P., C.
Savage-Jones, Trudi (Mrs.)—Port S., T.
Tucker, Peri (Mrs.)—W., Comm. A.

Cocoa

Brockdorff, Hermann—S., P., T.

Coconut Grove

Barker, Virgil—W., Cr., L.
Davis, Elizabeth Upham (Mrs.)—P., E., L., C.
Farkas, George B.—Indst. Des., Arch.
Merrick, Richard L.—P., Gr., E.

Coral Gables

Aldridge, C. Clay—Mus. Dir.
Bollin, Leone Cobbum (Mrs.)—P., T.
Clephane, Rosebud (Mrs.)—P.
Corrington, Veronica E. (Mrs.)—P.
Hunter, Edmund Robert—Mus. Dir., L.
May, Elizabeth M.—P., C., Ser.
McIntyre, Oliver Franklyn—P., Cart., I.

Daytona Beach

Skiles, Charles—Cart.

Deland

Freund, Elsie Marie—C., P., Lith., T.
Freund, Harry Louis—P., E., I.
Harvey, Sara Edith—E., P.

Delray Beach

Enright, Walter J.—W., Cart., I.
Raveson, Sherman Harold—P., Des., Typographer, A. Dir.

Dunedin

Neal, Grace Pruden (Mrs.)—S., P.

Eau Gallie

De Graff, Stanley Conrad—Pr. M., P., C., T.
Werley, Beatrice B.—P., I., Comm. A.

Edgewater

Knapp, Walter Howard—I., Comm. A., Des., P.

Ellenton

Davidson, Lillian Margaret (Mrs.)—P.

Englewood

Bernd-Cohen, Max—P., E., W., L., Cr.
Norton, Foster B.—P.
Tracy, Lois Bartlett—P.

Fort Lauderdale

Brown, Anne R. (Mrs.)—P., C.
Hamilton, Hildegard—P.
Jonas, Schubert Emerson—Mus. Dir., Hist., T., L.
Koch, Lizette J.—I., Comm. A., P., T.
Luchtemeyer, Edward A.—P., Des., Comm. A.

Ft. Pierce

Clear, Charles Val—Mus. Consultant, E., Des., Cr., P., L., W.

Gainesville

Adams, Clinton—P., Lith., E., Cr.
Buchholz, Emmaline Hardy (Mrs.)—P., I., T.
Craven, Roy C., Jr.—P., E., Des.
Holbrook, Hollis Howard—E., P., Des., I., L.
Holbrook, Vivian Nicholas—P.
Purser, Mary May—P., Des., E., I., C.
Purser, Stuart R.—P., E.

Hollywood

Toran, Alfonso T.—P.

Hobe Sound

Jacobs, Jay Wesley—Port. P.

Homestead

Basso, Tony—Cart.

Jacksonville

Adams, Lee—P., I., L.
Barnett, Bion—P., L.
Hicken, Russell Bradford—Mus. Dir., T., L.
Quan, Mun S.—P.
Washburn, Jeannette—P.
Washburn, Louese B. (Mrs.)—P.
White, Mable Dunn (Mrs.)—P.
Wood, Memphis (Miss)—P., T.

Key West

Di Negro, Paul Gwynn—P., Et., C.
Leake, Gerald—P., T.

Lakeland

Stoddard, Donna Melissa—E., W., L., P.
Zimmerman, Elinor Carr—P.

Lake Worth

Stoll, Rolf—Port. P.

Leesburg

Smith, Irwin Elwood—P.

Maitland

Smith, Andre—P., Arch., Et., S., W.

Melbourne

Rowell, Samuel Torrigrossa—P., Cart., T.
Walters, Doris Lawrence (Mrs.)—P., Comm. A.

Miami

Amoroso, Louis—P.
Bacon, Irving R.—P., S., W.
Bergling, Virginia G.—W.
Bradford, Myrtle Taylor—P., W., L., T.
Charles, Clayton Henry—S., E., P., L.
Creekmore, Raymond L.—I., Lith., Et., T.
Davis, Robert Tyler—E.
Draper, Robert Sargent—P., L., W.
Fisher, Ethel—P., Et., Lith.
Humes, Ralph Hamilton—S.
Kennedy, Janet Robson (Mrs.)—P.
Kostka, Richard Louis—Indst. Des.
Laessle, Paul—P., I.
Lefranc, Margaret (Mrs.)—P., Des., I., C., L., T., Gr.
Massin, Eugene Max—P., T.
Powell, Violet Louise (Mrs.)—P.
Quistgaard, Harold Ivar de Rehling—P.
Randolph, Gladys Conrad (Mrs.)—P., W.
Sahlin, Carl Folke—P., Comm. A., I.
Sansone, Leonard—Des., Cart.
Schenck, Marie Pfeifer (Mrs.)—Art Dir., S.
Schlazer, Michael—P., I., T.
Sherman, F. Taylor—P.
Soned, Warren—P., Des., S., T., L.
Spencer, Edna Isbester—S., P., T., Comm. A.
Spicer-Simson, Theodore—S.
Storm, La Rue—P., Et., Lith.

Miami Beach

Hoff, Syd—Cart.
Schein, Eugenie—P., T.
Youngerman, Reyna Ullman—P., L., T.

Miami Shores

Thorndike, Charles Jesse—Cart., Comm. A., W., L., T.

Marathon

Tingler, Chester J.—P.

Naples

Dorey, Elsie (Mrs.)—P.

Orange City

Allen, Anna Elizabeth—P., I.

Orange Park

Hunt, Julian Courtenay—P.

Orlando

Bagley, Ralph Leon—P., E., L.
Crane, Royston Campbell—Cart., W.
Fraser, Mary Aldrich—S.

Ormond Beach

Marsh, Fred Dana—Mural P., S., P., Gr., T., C.

Palm Beach

Bevelacqua, Salvatore—Indst. Des., Arch.
Dietsch, C. Percival—S., P.
Plimpton, Russell—Mus. Dir.
Shepherd, J. Clinton—P., S., L.

Palmetto

Kellogg, Janet Reid—P.
McKelvey, Helen F. (Mrs.)—Mus. Dir.

Pensacola

Hirsch, Richard—Mus. Dir., T., Gr.

Pompano Beach

Allenbrook, Charles Theadore—P., L.

St. Augustine

Lawton, Alice—C., W.
Lindenmuth, Tod—P., Gr.
Pfeiffer, Heinrich—P.
Meurer, Albert John Theodore—Gr., Des., I., P., L.
Muller-Uri, Hildegarde—P., T.
Warren, Elisabeth B. (Mrs.)—P., S., I.

St. Petersburg

Anshutz, Elsa Martin—P., T.
Clinedinst, May Spear—P., T.
Fulton, Ellen M.—W.
Hill, George Snow—P.
Hill, Polly Knipp (Mrs.)—Et., P., I.
Matthews, Lou (Mrs.)—P., T.
Merkel, Walter M.—Cr., W., L., P., I.
Sprague, Robert Burkitt—P., Des., T., Comm. A., W., L., Cr.
Terry, Marion E.—P., E.
Wright, Fred William—Port. P.

Sarasota

Allen, Colin—Cart., I.
Andrews, Edna Rozina—Art E., I., P., Et., Comm. A.
Cameron-Menk, Hazel—P., S., W.
Clement, Shirley—P., T.
Coler, Stella C. (Mrs.)—P., T., L.
Dame, Lawrence—Cr., W.
Donahue, Kenneth—Mus. Dir.
Farnsworth, Jerry—P., T.
Floethe, Richard—I., Des., Gr.
Gee, John—I., Lith., T., W.
Kelsey, Muriel Chamberlin—S.
Kimbrough, Verman—E.
Leech, Dorothy Sherman—P.
Leech, Hilton—P., T.
May, John—C.
Murray, Marian—W., Former Mus. Pub. Relations
Parton, Nike—P., T., S.
Posey, Leslie Thomas—S., C., T., L.
Remsen, Helen Q.—S., T.
Ridgeway, Frank Edward, Jr.—Cart.
Roddy, Edith Jeannette—P., Et.
Rowland, Elden—P., T.
Sanders, Andrew—P., T.
Saunders, Guy Howard—P., Des.
Sawyer, Helen (Mrs.)—P., Lith., T., W.

Stuart

Mosley, Zack T.—I., Cart.
Schmidt, Stephen—Mus. Dir.

Tallahassee

Ferguson, Van Hood—P.
Johnson, Ivan Earl—E., C.
Kawa, Florence Kathryn—P., T.
Mooty, Mary Elizabeth—E.
Zerbe, Karl—P.

Tampa

Bignell, James F.—E.
Borchardt, Norman—E., I., P., Et., L.
Coe, Theodore Demerest—Landscape P.
Giles, Charles—P., S., C., L., E.

Tarpon Springs

Banta, Ethel Zabriskie Smith—P., T.
Covey, Arthur—P., Lith.
Donnelly, Mary E.—P.
Smith, Oliver—C., P.

Valparaiso

Holzhauer, Emil Eugen—P.

Vero Beach

Herold, Don—Cart., W., Des.

West Palm Beach

Barrett, Oliver O'Connor—S., I., E., W.
Bean, Caroline Van H.—P., Et.
Keyes, Emilie (Mrs.)—W., Cr.
Lundgren, Eric—P., Gr., I., T., L.
Norton, Ann—S.
Willson, James Mallory—P., Et., T.
Woods, Willis Franklin—Mus. Dir.

Winter Park

Clark, Virginia Keep (Mrs.)—P., I.
Genius, Jeannette M. (Mrs.)—P.
King, Frank O.—Cart.
McComb, Marie Louise—P.
McKean, Hugh Ferguson—P., L., E.
Ortmayer, Constance—S., E.
Peck, Glenna Hughes—P., Des.
Polasek, Albin—S.
Silins, Janis (Mr.)—E., Gal. Dir., P., W., L., Hist.

GEORGIA

Athens

Blackshear, Annie Laura Eve—P., T., W.
Dodd, Lamar—P., E., L.
Flanigen, Jean Nevitt—P., I.
Holbrook, Alfred H.—Mus. Dir., P., W., L.
Thomas, Howard—E., P., Eng., Lith.
Thomas, Mary Alice Leath—P., E.

Atlanta

Brumbaugh, Thomas B.—E., L.
Brunell, Richard H.—E.
Edwards, Kate Flournoy—Port. P.
Gregg, Lewis C.—Port. P.
Harris, Julian Hoke—S., E., W., L.
Hutchinson, Mary Elizabeth—P., T., L.
Katz, Leo—P., Gr., E., W., L.

Solomon, Syd—P., T., Lith.
Stahl, Benjamin Albert—P., I., L., T., Lith.
Sweney, Fredric—I., Comm. A., W., T.
White, Eugene B.—P.
Wilford, Loran Frederick—P., T.

Mack, Frank—P.
Nesbitt, Jackson Lee—P., Et., I.
Poland, Reginald—Mus. Dir., W., L., T., Cr.
Rogers, Robert Stockton—P., T., L.
Shute, Ben E.—P., T., Comm. A.
Shute, Nell Choate—P.
Snowden, William Etsel, Jr.—Des., I., Gr., W.

Augusta

Jones, David Taylor Swatling—Mus. Dir., P., C., Gr., S.

Brunswick

Washburn, Cadwallader—P., Et., W.

Columbus

Shorter, Edward Swift—Mus. Dir., P., E., Cr., W., L.

Decatur

Warren, Ferdinand E.—P., C., Gr.

Lithonia

Alexander, Frances B. (Mrs.)—P., L., T.

Macon

Morrison, Monte B.—P., E., Gr., L.

Mt. Airy

Anderson, Martha Fort (Mrs.)—P., C., L.

Rising Fawn

Dudley, Virginia Evelyn—Enamelist, P., S., Gr., T., L., C.

Rome

Marshall, MacLean—S.

Sandy Springs

Dodd, Edward Benton—Cart.

Savannah

Cabaniss, Lila Marguerite—T., P.
Hampton, Phillip Jewel—P., E., Lith.
Murphy, Christopher, Jr.—P., Et., Lith., Des., T.
Nash, Anne Taylor (Mrs.)—Port. P.
Reese, David Mosley—Mus. Dir., P., T.
Rivers, Cornelia McIntire—P., T.

Waverly Hall

Baker, Lamar—Et., Lith., P., I.

Wildwood

Cash, Harold—S.

HAWAII

Honolulu

Charlot, Jean—P., Gr., E., I., W., L.
Cox, J. Halley—P., E.
Ecke, Gustave—Mus. Cur.
Emerson, Arthur Webster—P., Gr., W.
Griffing, Robert Perkins, Jr.—Mus. Dir., L.
Hart, Marvell Allison—Mus. Cur.
Karawina, Erica (Mrs.)—C., P., Des., Gr., L.
Kelly, John Melville—C., Et.

Downers Grove

Benson, Ben Albert—Eng., Des., I., Comm. A.
Benson, Tressa Emerson (Mrs.)—P., T.

Edwardsville

Dressel, Frannie—Pr. M., Des., C., Comm. A.

Elgin

Chipman, C. Dean—Mus. Dir., E.
Rovelstad, Trygve—S.

Elmhurst

Carey, Charles Christopher—Et., P.
King, Eleanor (Mrs.)—P., W., L., T., Cr.

Elmwood Park

Mazeski, Walter Adolph—Des., P., I., Cart., L.

Elsah

Green, James Leahan—P., T.

Evanston

Adams, Walter Burt—P., Cart.
Algoren, Lionel C.—Des.
Berglund, Amanda—P.
Bjorncrantz, Carl G.—Indst. Des.
Folds, Thomas McKey—E., L., Des.
McNear, Everett C.—P., Des.
Mink, David D. C.—Comm. A., I., P.
Myers, Charles Stowe—Indst. Des., E., L.
Thomas, Howard Ormsby—P., Gr., Des., C.
Weiner, Egon—S., E., L.

Freeport

Blackwood, Gladys Rourke—I., Port. P.
Perkins, Stella Mary (Mrs.)—P., W., L.

Geneva

Huntley, Victoria Hutson—Lith., P., L.

Glen Ellyn

Thompson, Floyd Leslie—Et., P., Des., Comm. A., T., L.

Glenview

Colmorgan, Paul—Des., P., T.

Highland Park

Lazard, Alice A.—P.
Watson, Dudley Crafts—P., E., W., L.

Kenilworth

Barrett, Neil (Mrs.)—P.
Dunn, Calvin E.—P., Cart., Comm. A.

Lake Bluff

MacAlister, Paul R.—Des., C., W., L.
Parker, Helen Mary—L.
Ropp, Hubert—P., E.

Lake Forest

Judson, Sylvia Shaw—S., C.
Lockhart, James Leland—I., P., W.
Schulze, Franz—P., Des., E., Cr.

Libertyville

Holland, Daniel E.—Cart.

Lombard

Ubaldi, Mario Carmelo—S., Des.

Macomb

Loomer, Gifford C.—P., E., S.

Mt. Prospect

Ozmun, Pauline Graff (Mrs.)—P.

Monee

Meyer, Alvin William Carl—S.

Monmouth

Gholson, Samuel Creed—P., T., S.
Hamilton, Thomas H.—E., W., Cr.

Normal

Hoover, F. Louis—E., Editor

Northbrook

Eitel, Cliffe D.—Des., P., I., Gr.
Melchert, Ernest Albert—Et., Eng., Ser., L., P.

Northfield

Glass, Henry Peter—Des., T.
Johnson, M. Martin—Des.

Oak Park

Gentile, Edward—Des., P.
Junge, Carl Stephen—Des., P., I.

Olney

Sterchi, Eda—P.

Olympia Fields

Whitford, William Garrison—C., E., W.

Palos Heights

Ball, Leroy—Cart.

Park Forest

Beck, Jay—I., S., C., P., L.
Himmel, Kalman Edward—P., E.

Park Ridge

Iannelli, Alfonso—S., Des., C., L., E., P.
Steinfels, Melville P.—P., Des., I., E.

Peoria

Annear, Roger—P., T.
Correll, Grace Van Norman (Mrs.)—Des., P.
Fromberg, Gerald—P., E.
Fromberg, Laverne Ray—P., T., Gr.
Nicholson, Edward—Port. P., T.

Rockford

Barloga, Viola H.—P., T.
Paulin, Richard Calkins—Mus. Dir., T.
Pearman, Katharine K.—P., L., T.
Sibley, Marguerite (Mrs.)—S.
Swenson, Howard William—S., Des., Gr.
White, Ambrosia Chuse (Mrs.)—P., T., W.

Roselle

Martyl—P., Lith.

Springfield

Cantrall, Harriet M.—E., P.
Deuel, Thorne—Mus. Dir.
Ridgely, Frances Summers (Mrs.)—Mus. Cur., W., L., P.

Skokie

Ed, Carl—Cart.
Yochim, Louise Dunn—P., S., T., W., C., Lith.

Urbana

Bailey, La Force—P., T.
Bradshaw, Glenn Raymond—E., P.
Britsky, Nicholas—P., E.
Chesney, Lee R., Jr.—Gr., Pr. M., P., E.
Creese, Walter Littlefield—E.
Donovan, Cecil Vincent—E., P.
Doolittle, Warren Ford, Jr.—E., P.
Schultz, Harold A.—P., L., E.
Weller, Allen Stuart—E., Cr., W., L.
Woodroofe, Louise M.—P., E.

Villa Park

Ekdahl, Anne Anderson (Mrs.)—Et., P.

Warrenville

Albright, Malvin Marr—S.
Marzolo, Leo Aurelio—P.

Waukegan

Misunas, Everett P.—E., Eng., Des.

Western Springs

Gage, Jane (Mrs.)—P.

Wilmette

Huntley, George Haydn—E.
Schrom, Archie Mark—Des., Gr.
Selleck, Margaret—P., I., L.

Winfield

Himmelfarb, Samuel—P., Des., L.

Winnetka

Burnham, Anita Willets—P., W., L., T., Et.
Burnham, Carol-Lou—P., T., I., L.
Hahn, Nancy Coonsman—S., T.
Parrish, Joseph Lee—Cart.
Pattison, Abbott—S., P.
Philbrick, Allen Erskine—P., Et., Eng., E.
Treiman, Joyce Wahl—P.

Woodstock

Knoche, Lucille Morley—Des., S., P.

INDIANA

Anderson

Byrum, Ruthven Holmes—E., P., W., L.

Bloomington

Alford, John—E., W., L., P.
Engel, Harry—P., E., L.
Gilbert, Creighton—Art Hist., E.
Hope, Henry Radford—E.

Brazil

Bott, Earle Wayne—P., Des., Lith., Eng., I., Cart., L., Comm., Gr.
Bott, Mabel Siegelin (Mrs.)—T., C., P., Des.
James, Evalyn Gertrude—P., I., W., E

Brownsburg

Davis, Harry Allen—P., T.

Butler

Ashby, Paul W.—Gr., T., P., L.

Carmel

Trissel, Lawrence E.—P., Des., I., Comm. A.

Cherokee

Frankforter, W. D.—Mus. Dir.

Columbus

Voris, Millie Roesgen—P., W., L., T.

Crawfordsville

Gerard, David Charles—Cart.

Culver

Williams, Warner—S., Des., L., P., T.

Dunkirk

Harshman, Arthur L.—Des., P., S., Gr.

Evansville

Fricke, Della Emelia—E.
Keve, Florence—E., P., C.
Knecht, Karl Kae—Cart., W.
Osborne, Robert Lee—P., T.
Simpson, Herbert William—Des.
Singer, George Frederic—P., Comm. A.
Stevens, Bernice A.—C., T.

Fort Wayne

Bonsib, Louis William—P.
Dickerson, Grace Leslie—P., S., C., T.
McBride, James J.—P., Comm. A., I.
Stark, Forrest F.—Port. P., S., T.

Franklin

Grepp, John—E.
Sevin, Whitney—E., P., S.

Gary

Fenerty, Agnes Lawson—P.
Huber, Helen Ruth—T., W., L., P., Cr.
Nichols, Jeannettie D.—P., E., Des.

Greencastle

Winsey, A. Reid—P., I., Cart., W., E., L.

Indianapolis

Anderson, Ruth Bernice—P., Et., T.
Antreasian, Garo Zareh—P., Lith., T., L.
Blasingham, Katherine Groh (Mrs.)—P., T., L.
Bobbs, Ruth Pratt (Mrs.)—Port. P.
Boyce, Gerald Gladwin—E., P., C.
Brucker, Edmund—P., T.
Denney, Gladys A.—P., C., T., Des.
Gaskins, Letha Heckman (Mrs.)—P.
Goth, Marie—Port. P.

Grow, Lottie Lyons (Mrs.)—P., Et., W., L.
Hart, Drennan Wilson—Adv. Des.
Hasselman, Anna—Mus. Cur., P., E.
Kaeser, William Frederick—P., Des.
Mattison, Donald Magnus—P., E.
Mess, Evelynne B. (Mrs.)—Et., Lith., P., I., T.
Mess, George Jo—Et., Lith., P., Des., L., T.
Mess, Gordon Benjamin—P., Des., T., L.
Peat, Wilbur David—Mus. Dir., W., L.
Richey, Oakley E.—P., E., L.
Riffle, Elba Louisa (Mrs.)—I., Comm. A., P.
Rubins, David Kresz—S., Lith., T.
Shover, Edna Mann—P., Des., I., W., T.
Spiegel, Dorothy A.—P.
Tschaegle, Robert—L., W., Mus. Cur., S., Cr.
Wehr, Paul Adam—I., Comm. A.
Werner, Charles George—Cart., L.
Wilson, Norman Badgley—P., Eng.
Wolter, Adolph G.—S., E., L.

Kokomo

Scott, Geraldine Armstrong—P., L., T.

Lafayette

Calkin, Carleton Ivers—E., P.
Schantz-Hansen, Laurentza—E., L.

Lawrenceburg

Pribble, Easton—P., L.

Martinsville

Mosier, Martha Hinkle—P., T.

Michigan City

Harbart, Gertrude F. (Mrs.)—P., T.

Muncie

Brown, Francis F.—E., P.
Nichols, Alice Welty—E., P., Gal. Dir., Des.
Sharp, Hill—P., Lith., T.

Nashville

Bessire, Dale Philip—P.
Bohm, C. Curry—P., T.
Cariani, Varaldo J.—P.
La Chance, Georges—P.
Shulz, Adolph Robert—P.
Shulz, Alberta Rehm—P.
Stoddard, Musette Osler—P., C., T., L.

Newburgh

Weng, Siegfried R.—Mus. Dir., E., Gr., L.

New Castle

Shafer, Elizabeth Dodds (Mrs.)—P.

Noblesville

Hopper, Floyd D.—P., Lith., T.

North Manchester

Allen, Max I.—E.

Notre Dame

Lauck, Anthony (Rev.)—S., E., W., L.

Peru

Weaver, Robert Edward—P.

Pine Village

Currey, Ruth Dunlop—C., Des., P., T.

Richmond

Bernhardt, Barbara—P., Et., Cart., L.
Bond, Byron L.—Des., P., Gr., I., Comm. A., Cart.
Kelly, Gordon Ray—P., T.
Kempton, Elmira—P., E.
McConaha, Lawrence—P.
Neidigh, Pansy Mills (Mrs.)—P., C., T., L.
Nusbaum, Esther Commons—P., T.

St. Mary-of-the-Woods

Esther, Sister—E., P., L., W.

Schererville

Bielecky, Stanley—P., T.

South Bend

Cloetingh, James H.—P., Des.
Mestrovic, Ivan—S.
Sessler, Stanley Sascha—P., E., Et., L.
Zisla, Harold—P., E., Des., L., Mus. Dir.

Terre Haute

Albert, Allen D.—Mus. Dir.
Foster, Betty Elizabeth Jane—T., Des., L., P.
Porter, Elmer Johnson—C., P., E., L.
Reynerson, June—E.

Vincennes

Patterson, Marion Lois—E., P., L.

Warsaw

Gerard, Allee Whittenberger (Mrs.)—P., T.

Whiting

Manchak, Albert—P., T.

IOWA

Ames

Adams, Bertrand R.—I., C., P.
Camprubi, Leontine (Mrs.)—P.
Davis, Alice—E., P.
Garfield, Marjorie S.—P., Des., E., Gr., W., L.
Hansen, Joanne Margarethe—E., L., Des., C.
Rayness, Velma Wallace—P., I.

Burlington

Hohlen, May Marjorie—E., P., C., Ser.

Cedar Falls

Campbell, Marjorie Dunn—E., P.
Guillaume, Harry George—E., C.
Nuhn, Marjorie Ann—P.

Cedar Rapids

Bruns, Edwin John—P., I., Comm. A.
Cone, Marvin—P., E.

Davenport

Geiken, Elizabeth Moeller (Mrs.)—Mus. Dir., P., E.
Herold, Donald G.—Mus. Dir.

Des Moines

Cumming, Alice McKee (Mrs.)—P., L., E.
Fairbanks, Richard—C., T.
Good, Leonard—E., P., Cr., L., W.
Kirsch, Dwight—Art Consultant, P., E., W., L.
Laskoski, Pearl—P.
Marquis, Gulielma Dorothea Tomlinson—P., Indst. Des.
Mattern, Karl—P., E., L., Gr.
Miller, Elizabeth Slaughter—P., T.
Myers, Denys Peter—Mus. Dir.
Robertson, Persis W. (Mrs.)—Lith.
Stacey, Dorothy Howe-Layman—P., Des., W., Comm. A.
Stacey, Lynn Nelson—P., Des., I., Comm. A.

Dubuque

Engel, George Leslie—P., I., C.
Glasell, Criss—P., C., L.

Fort Dodge

Halm, Robert J.—Mus. Dir., P., Gr., E.

Fort Madison

Bunn, William Edward Lewis—P., Des., C., W., T.

Grinnell

Sternfeld, Edith A.—P., E.

Iowa City

Albrizio, Humbert—S.
Burke, William Lozier Munro—Hist.
Cuttler, Charles David—Hist., P.
Edie, Stuart Carson—P., E.
Hickey, Rose Van Vranken—S., Et., Lith.
Lasansky, Mauricio—P., Gr.
Lechay, James—P., E.
Mason, Doris Belle Eaton (Mrs.)—S., L., T., C.

Keokuk

Ebersole, Mabel Helen—P.

Lacona

Ford, Edwin Joseph—I., Des., P.

Le Mars

Johnson, Evert A.—E., P., C.

Melrose

Talbot, Sophia Davis—P.

Mt. Pleasant

Fracassini, Silvio Carl—P., E., Des.
Wynne, Albert Givens—P., E., Des.

Mount Vernon

West, Wilbur Warne—E.

Sioux City

Dailey, Joseph Charles—P., Des., Ser., C., Mus. Asst. Dir.
Ishikawa, Joseph—Mus. Dir.
Thiel, Richard G.—C., S., T.

Waterloo

Bradbury, Edith M.—E., P.
Held, Alma M.—P., T.

KANSAS

Atchison

Schreiber, Isabel—P.

Beloit

Eresch, Josie—Lith., Et., P., W., I., L., C.

Chanute

Junod, Ila M.—Port. P., I.

Emporia

Eppink, Helen B. (Mrs.)—P., Des.
Eppink, Norman R.—P., Gr., L., E.

Hays

Moss, Joel, Dr.—P., C., S., E.

Hutchinson

Ely, Wolcott—P.

Independence

Burdette, Dorothy May—P.

Lawrence

Berger, Klaus—E., W.
Bloch, Albert—P., W., L., E., Gr., Cr.
Carey, James Sheldon—E., C.
Eastwood, Raymond J.—P., E.
Green, Robert Berkeley—P., E.
Maser, Edward Andrew—Mus. Dir., E.
Musgrave, Shirley D. Hudson—P., Gr., T.
Sudlow, Robert Newton—P., E.
Whitney, Marjorie Faye—E., P., Des.

Lindsborg

Bashor, John William—E., P.
Pearson, Anton—C., P., S.
Sandzen, Margaret (Mrs.)—P., L., T.
Spear, Lloyd—E.

Manhattan

Barfoot, Dorothy—E., P., C., Des., L.
Helm, John F., Jr.—E., Gr., P.

Mission

Kelleher, Patrick J.—Mus. Cur., Hist.

Olathe

Tabor, Robert Byron—P.

Ottawa

Scott, Catherine—P.

Salina

Logan, Herschel C.—Eng., Des., I., W., Comm. A.
Stiles, Joseph Edwin—E., P., Lith.

Topeka

Hunt, Robert James—P., Gr., T.
Huntoon, Mary (Mrs.)—P., S., Gr., W., L., E.
Tillotson, Alexander—P., Mus. Dir., E.

Wichita

Bernard, David Edwin—Lith., P., E.
Bosin, F. Blackbear—P.
Capps, Charles Merrick—Et., Lith.
Dickerson, William J.—P., Lith., T.
Grove, Richard George—Mus. Dir., W.
Simoni, John Peter—E., P., C., S., W., L., Gal. Dir.
Wheeler, Zona Lorraine—P., Des., I.

Winfield

Raymond, Grace Russell—P., L., T.

KENTUCKY

Anchorage

Bier, Justus—E., W., Cr., L.
Bier, Senta Dietzel (Mrs.)—E., W., Cr.
Bright, Barney—S., T., Des.

Barbourville

Hitchcock, Howard Gilbert—E., S.

Berea

Delavan, Nelson B., Jr.—P., C., T.
Long, Frank Weathers—P., Eng., C., L.
Pross, Lester Fred—E., P.

Burlington

Hentschel, William Ernst—P., T., Des., C.
Stratton, Alza (Mrs.)—P., Des., T., Comm. A.

Danville

Kellam, Jack Burnett—P., E.

Disputanta

Mullins, Bert Ruebin—P.

Egypt

Faulkner, Henry Lawrence—P., T.

Frankfort

Collins, Harold Dean—P., I., Des., Comm. A.
Scott, Bertha—Port. P., W.

Harrods Creek

Shallenberger, Martin—P., L.

Hebron

Helwig, Arthur Louis—P., Gr., T.

Lexington

Amyx, Clifford—E., P., W.
Freeman, Richard B.—E., Mus. Cur.
Hammer, Victor Karl—P., C., S., Des., E., Gr., W.
Rannells, Edward Warder—W., E., L., P.

Louisville

Block, Lou—P., T., I., W., L.
Covi, Dario A.—Mus. Cur., E.
Fischer, William Lee—P.
Fitzpatrick, Joseph Lloveras—P., Des., W.
Hadley, Mary Alice—Des.
Harris, Paul Stewart—Mus. Dir., L., W.
Kohlhepp, Dorothy Irene—P.

Kohlhepp, Norman—P., Lith.
Leake, Eugene Walter, Jr.—P., T., L.
Nay, Mary Spencer (Mrs.)—P., Gr., T.
Peterson, Daniel Roy—C.
Peterson, Nelle Freeman—T., C.
Wilke, Ulfert S.—P., E., Mus. Dir.
York, Robert—Cart.

Morehead

Claypool, Naomi—E.

Mt. Sterling

Bush, Lucile Elizabeth—E., P.

Murray

Boaz, William G.—T., S., P.
Eagle, Clara M.—E.

Owensboro

Houser, James Cowing, Jr.—E., P.

Richmond

Giles, Frederic Parker—E., C., P., L.

LOUISIANA

Barksdale Air Force Base

MacSparran, Terry—P.

Baton Rouge

Bosch, Gulnar Kheirallah—E.
Brent, Adalie Margules—T., Comm. A., I., Des., P.
Durieux, Caroline (Mrs.)—Lith., P., E.
Guaccero, I. Vincent—E., Des., Gr., C., P., S.
Rutt, Anna Hong—W., L., P., E.

Covington

Cramer, Carl—S., L., T.

Lafayette

Allen, Margo (Mrs.)—S., P., L., W.
Shaw, Harry Hutchison—P., E., L.

Monroe

James, Bess B. (Mrs.)—P.

Natchitoches

Hanchey, Orville James—P., C., Des., E.

New Orleans

Burkenroad, Flora Salinger—P.
Feitel, Arthur Henry—Former Mus. Pres.
Gregory, Angela—S., P., L.
Lansford, Alonzo—P., I., W., Cr., L.
Lugano, Ines Somenzini (Mrs.)—Min. and Port. P.
McCrady, John—P., I., Lith., T.
Millet, Clarence—P., Et.
O'Brien, Nell Pomeroy (Mrs.)—P., S., L.
Parker, John Clay—P.
Rickey, George Warren—S., P., E.
Rieker, Albert George—S.
Sarre, Carmen G.—P., L., T.
Seidenberg, Jacob Jean—P., S., Des., T.
Stanton, Gideon Townsend—P.
Steg, James Louis—E., Pr. M.
Struppeck, Julius—S., E., W.
Thompson, Georgette R.—P., Des., I., C., T.

Thurman, Sue (Mrs.)—Mus. Dir.
Trivigno, Pat—P., E., L.
Wood, Ella Miriam—Port. P.

Pineville

Llort, Martha—E., P., Comm. A.
Nichols, Raymond D.—E., P.

Ruston

Bethea, F. Elizabeth—E., P.

Shreveport

Du Val, Flora (Mrs.)—P.
Friedenberg, Elizabeth Z.—P., Gr., T., L.
Morgan, Arthur C.—S., E., W., L.
Morgan, Gladys B. (Mrs.)—P., L., T.
Sicard, Louis G.—P.
Stone, Ruth Andress—P., C., Gr., W.

MAINE

Addison

Thompson, Susie Wass—Watercolorist

Augusta

Rockwell, Frederick F.—P., S.

Bar Harbor

Dacey, William—P., W., T., L.

Biddeford

Crisp, Arthur—Mural P.

Boothbay Harbor

Eames, John Heagan—Et., P.
Sisson, Laurence Philip—P.

Brunswick

Beam, Philip Conway—Mus. Dir., E.
Hammond, Ruth Evelyn (Mrs.)—P., T., W.

Cape Neddick

Laurent, Robert—S., E.

Cape Rosier

McCloskey, Robert—I., W.

Damariscotta

Melville, Grevis Whitaker—P., Lith.
Mountfort, Julia Ann—P., I., W.

East Boothbay

Brigham, Gertrude Richardson—Art School Dir.

Eastport

Craig, Robert—P., Et., Lith.
Schildknecht, Edmund G.—P., Et., T.

Fryeburg

Bradley, Anne Cary—P.

Kennebunk Beach

Perkins, Edna—P.

Kennebunkport

Deering, Roger L.—P., L., T.
Fisher, William—P., L., T., S.

Lamoine

Cochran, Gifford Alexander—P.

Monhegan

Fuller, Alfred—P., T., Lith.
Hudson, Jacqueline—Lith., P.
Meissner, Leo—Eng., P.

Newcastle

Eberhard, Robert Georges—E., S., L., C., Mus. Cur.

North Bridgton

Hamlin, James Betts—C., Des., T.

Ogunquit

Asherman, David G.—P., L., W., T., Des., Lith.
Fisher, Stowell Le Cain (Mrs.)—P.
Hensel, Hopkins—P.
Mattei, Antonio—P., C., L.
Ritter, Chris—P.
Strater, Henry—P., Mus. Dir.

Orono

Hartgen, Vincent Andrew—P., E., Des., Mus. Cur.

Port Clyde

Thon, William—P.

Portland

Brown, Bradford—Mus. Dir., P., T.
La Mendola, George Dole—Cart., I., P.
Muench, John—P., Gr., T.
Trefethen, Jessie Bryan—P., E., Et., L.

Robinhood

Ipcar, Dahlov (Mrs.)—P., I., W.

Rockland

Hadlock, Wendell Stanwood—Mus. Dir., E., W., L.

Rockport

Sherry, William Grant—P., T.
Winters, Denny (Miss)—P., T., I., Gr., C.

Searsmont

Merritt, Francis Sumner—P., T., Lith., Des., L., W.

Searsport

Peirce, Waldo—P., I., W.

Skowhegan

Cummings, Willard Warren—P., T.

South Harpswell

Etnier, Stephen Morgan—P.

Southport

Tenggren, Gustaf Adolf—I., P., Des., Lith.

South Portland

Dow, William James—P., Des., T.
Gill, Berniece Cram (Mrs.)—W., Cr.
Libby, Francis O.—P.
Shaw, Alice Harmon (Mrs.)—P., Et.

Stonington

Muir, Emily—P.
Muir, William Horace—S., L., P.

Tenants' Harbor

Logan, Robert Fulton—P., Et., E., L., Des.

Thomaston

Langlais, Bernard—P.

Waterville

Carpenter, James M.—E., Mus. Cur.

Winter Harbor

Browne, Syd—P., Lith., Et., T.
James, Sandra—P.

Wiscasset

Burrage, Mildred Giddings—P., Mus. Dir.
Shelton, Alphonse Joseph—P.

Yarmouth

Winchell, Elizabeth Burt (Mrs.)—P., C., Des., T.

MARYLAND

Baltimore

Austrian, Florence Hochschild (Mrs.) —P.
Beadenkopf, Anne—P.
Berge, Edward Henry—S.
Borum, Linwood Clarke—Marine P.
Breeskin, Adelyn Dohme (Mrs.)—Mus. Dir.
Burroughs, Louise (Mrs.)—W.
Coplan, Kate M.—Lib. Exhibits Div.
Crummer, Mary Worthington—P., C., Et.
Davis, Ranice (Mrs.)—Medical I., E.
Di Crispino, Mary Reina—P.
Forman, Henry Chandlee—E., W., L., P.
Foster, James W.—Mus. Dir.
Gale, Walter Rasin—E., P., I.
Glace, Margaret F. S.—E.
Glushakow, Jacob—P.
Goldstein, Gladys—P.
Grandy, Julia Selden—P.
Gray, Christopher—E.
Hill, Dorothy Kent—Mus. Cur.
Hoffman, Harry Zee—P., T., Comm. A., I., Cart.
Hunter, Wilbur Harvey, Jr.—Mus. Dir., E.
Ingle, Eliza—C., Gr.
Ireland, Richard Wilson—P., T., I., Gr.
Jones, Thomas Benedict—P., Lith., Ser.
Katzenellenbogen, Adolf—E.
Kilpatrick, Mary Grace—P., W.
King, Edward S.—Mus. Dir., E.
Kramer, Reuben Robert—S., T.
Kurtz, Benjamin Turner—S., E., W., L.
Mackall, Robert McGill—P., E., Des.
Maril, Herman—P., T.
Martin, Keith Morrow—P.
Martinet, Marjorie D.—P., T.
Maurice, Alfred Paul—E., Des., Gr.
Miner, Dorothy—Mus. Cur., L., W.
Oppenheimer, Selma L.—P.
Pagon, Katharine D.—P.
Philpot, S. H.—P., T., I.
Poole, Lynn D. (Mr.)—E.
Rembski, Stanislav—P., W., T., L.
Roche, M. Paul—P., Et., Lith., S., L.
Rollins, Warren Eliphalet—P., T.
Rosenfeld, Edward—P.
Rosenthal, Gertrude—Mus. Cur., E.
Shackelford, Shelby—P., E., W., I., Gr.
Sommer, A. Evelyn—P., Gr., T., Des., W., L.

Sopher, Aaron—P., Cart., I.
Spencer, Eleanor Patterson—E.
Streett, Tylden Westcott—S.
Swann, Samuel Donovan—Eng.
Turnbull, Grace Hill—S., P., W.
Walter, Valerie Harrisse—S.
Watkins, William Reginald—Des., P., Lith., T.
Weldon, Walter A.—Ceramic C., Des.
Wrenn, Harold Holmes—P., T.

Bethesda

Jackson, Vaughn Lyle—Comm. A., Des., I., P.
Scheirer, George A.—Hand Bookbinder

Bozman

Starr, Lorraine Webster (Mrs.)—P., I., L., T.

Butler

Clarke, Carl Dame—Medical I., E., W., L.
Hebb, Mathilde M. Mylander—S.

Catonsville

Carothers, Sarah Pace (Mrs.)—Et., P., T.
Dew, Henrietta (Mrs.)—C., T.

Cheverly

Mansfield, Richard Harvey—Cart., L., T.

Chevy Chase

Asher, Lila Oliver—P., Des., T., S.
Baer, John M.—Cart., Des., W., Comm. A.
Carrington, Omar Raymond—P., Gr., I., E.
Lee, Ruth Hudson—P.
Rakeman, Carl—P., I.
Wheeler, Kathleen (Mrs.)—S.
Wynne, Evelyn B.—Pr. M., Comm. A., T.

College Park

Wharton, James Pearce—E., P.

Easton

Dodge, Frances Farrand (Mrs.)—P., Et., L.
Lawrie, Lee—S.

Elkridge

Bahr, Florence Riefle (Mrs.)—P., I.
Bahr, Leonard Marion—P., T., I., L.

Frederick

Davis, Jack C.—P., E.
Smith, Helen Leona—P., C.
Urner, Joseph Walker—S., P., Et.

Garrett Park

Stites, Raymond Somers—E., Hist., W., L.

Greenbelt

Abramowitz, Benjamin—P., Lith., T., L.

Hagerstown

Chrissinger, Mary Helen—P.
Etchison, Bruce—Mus. Dir., P., T., Gr.
Warner, Harry B., Jr.—Cr., W.

Hyattsville

Hoke, Robert A.—I., Port. P.
Rawls, James—I., P., Comm. A.

Kensington

Genders, Richard Atherstone—P.
Houston, Russell A.—S., W., P.

Lanham

Christensen, Erwin Ottomar—Mus. Cur., E., W., L.

Linthicum Heights

Paul, Bernard H.—C.

North Beach

Burrus, Garland—P., Et., T.

Pikesville

Schwartz, Alvin Howard—P., Des.

Reisterstown

Tunis, Edwin—W., I., P., Des.

Rockville

Wagner, S. Peter—P., Et., T.

Royal Oak

Starin, Arthur Newman—P.

Ruxton

Hawks, Rachel Marshall—S.
Huey, Florence Greene (Mrs.)—P.

Silver Spring

Cuneo, George Humbert—E., P.
Karaberi, Marianthe—S., P.

Westminster

James, Macgill—Mus. Cur., W.
MacDonald, William Allan—Asst. Mus. Dir., E.

MASSACHUSETTS

Amherst

Coe, Roland—Cart.
Coulter, Mary J. (Mrs.)—Et., P., L., W.
Matheson, Donald Roy—Pr. M., P., E., Former Mus. Dir.
Morgan, Charles Hill—E., Mus. Dir.
Norton, Paul F.—E., Hist.

Andover

Atkinson, Alica (Mrs.)—P., T.
Dalton, Frances L.—P., T.
Goriansky, Lev Vladimir—P., Des., T., W.
Hayes, Bartlett Harding, Jr.—Mus. Dir., E., L., W.
Whitehill, Walter Muir—Mus. Dir., W., E.

Arlington

Parke, Jessie Burns—P.
Richert, Charles H.—P., T.
Rosenberg, Jakob—Mus. Cur., E.

Attleboro

Cannard, Ruth E. Hintz—E., L., Mus. Dir.

Bedford

Minty, John—P., C.

Belmont

Koehler, Wilhelm R. W.—E.
Reynolds, Joseph G., Jr.—Des., C., L., W.
White, Clarence Scott—P., I.

Berkshire

Blake, Leo B.—P., T., L., I.

Beverly

Broudo, Joseph David—E., C., P., L.

Blandford

Arms, Winifred Lefferts—P., Des.
Taylor, Richard Lippincott Denison—Cart., P.

Boston

Adlow, Dorothy (Mrs.)—Cr., L., E.
Allen, Greta (Mrs.)—Port. P.
Bahm, Henry—P.
Barbarossa, Theodore Cotillo—S.
Beatty, Richard R.—Lith., T.
Berger, Jason—P.
Binder, Jacob—Port. P.
Bjareby, Alfred Gunnar—P., S., I., C.
Bloom, Hyman—P.
Bogart, Stella Marshall (Mrs.)—P.
Bourne, Gertrude B. (Mrs.)—P.
Browne, Margaret Fitzhugh—P., T.
Butera, Joseph Charles—E., L., Restorer
Cabot, Hugh, III—P.
Carson, Frank—P., T., Cr., W.
Coletti, Joseph Arthur—S., L., W.
Cormier, Robert John—P.
Cox, John William Smith—P., T.
Crite, Allan Rohan—P., I., L., W., C.
Cumming, Robert Homer—P., Mus. Dir., E., W.
Davis, Marguerite—I., P.
Dunbar, Daphne French—Lith., Des., P., T.
Gammell, Robert Hale Ives—P., W.
Halberstadt, Ernst—P., S.
Hopkinson, Charles—P.
Hunter, Robert Douglas—P., I., T., L.
Huse, Marion (Mrs.)—P., Gr.
Inglis, Antoinette (Mrs.)—P.
Jacobson, Nathaniel Judah—P., T.
Kubinyi, Kalman Matyas Bela—Enamelist, C., Et., P., I.
MacDonald, Geneva A.—Gr.
MacFadden, Priscilla Sophia—Art Libn.
Mason, William N.—Asst. Mus. Dir.
Messer, Thomas M.—Mus. Dir., Cr., W., L., Hist.
Minna—Des., C., T.
Nelson, Carl Gustaf—P., Gr., T.
Nyme, Joseph—P., C.
Peabody, Amelia—S.
Perkins, Harley—P.
Pleadwell, Amy Margaret—P.
Quincy, Edmund—P.
Randall, Eleanor Elizabeth—P., E.
Rotenberg, Harold—P., T.
Rudd, Tracy Porter—Des., C., I.
Searles, Stephen—S., T.
Sherman, Jessie Gordan—P., Des.
Stout, George Leslie—Mus. Dir.
Stratton, Grace Hall—C., Des.
Sundin, Adelaide Althin Toombs (Mrs.)—Ceramic S., C., L., T.
Thal, Samuel—Et., S., P., L.
Thayer, Polly (Mrs.)—P.
Tolford, Irina Poroshina (Mrs.)—P.
Tolford, Joshua—P., I.
Trefonides, Steven—P., Photog.

Boylston

Gray, Robert W.—E., C.
Gray, Verdelle (Mrs.)—C.

Bradford

Wade, Robert—P., T.

Brookline

Aarons, George—S.
Barron, Harris—S., Arch. Des.
Barron, Ros—S., Des.
Brown, Grace Evelyn—P., W., L., T.
Bruce, Marjorie Mackenzie—Des., C.
Carmack, Paul R.—Cart.
Eastman, Alvan Clark—Orientalist, W., Mus. Dir.
Fuller, Andrew Daniel, Jr.—E., L., W., Cr., Des., P.
Hibel, Edna—P.
Jackson, Annie H.—P.
Lourie, Herbert S.—P., E.
Pineda, Marianna Packard Tovish—S.
Smith, Russell Train—E., Des., L.
Tovish, Harold—S.
Van Cleve, Kate—C., T., Des.

Buckland

Woodward, Robert Strong—P.

Cambridge

Burnett, Calvin—Gr. A., P., T.
Chiu, Alfred Kaiming—Libn., Mus. Consultant
Constable, William George—Mus. Advisor, A. Hist.
Coolidge, John Phillips—Mus. Dir.
Cox, Gardner—P.
Dooley, William Germain—E., Cr.
Feininger, T. Lux—P., T.
Forbes, Edward Waldo—Mus. Dir., E., L.
Fulton, W. Joseph—Mus. Dir., E., W.
Goodridge, Elinor—P.
Hofer, Philip—Mus. Sec., Des., W., L., T.
James, William—P.
Kepes, Gyorgy—P., Des., E., W.
Kuhn, Charles L.—Mus. Cur.
Merrill, Hiram Campbell—P., Eng.
Mongan, Agnes—Mus. Cur., W., Cr., L.
Noble, Verrill Ruth—W., Des., L.
Opdycke, Leonard—E.
Paeff, Bashka (Mrs.)—S., L.
Palmer, Mildred Trumbull—Bookbinder
Pancoast, Morris Hall—P., I., Cart.
Pintner, Dora—P., C., Des.
Plaut, James S.—Former Mus. Dir.
Preusser, Robert Ormerod—P., T., L.
Rathbone, Perry Townsend—Mus. Dir.
Rowland, Benjamin, Jr.—E., W., P., L.
Saarinen, Lily—S.
Sachs, Paul Joseph—E., W., L., Cr.
Saunderson, Laura Howland Dudley (Mrs.)—Mus. Cur., W., L.
Schroeder, Eric—Mus. Cur., P.
Siple, Ella Simons (Mrs.)—W., L., Mus. Cur., E., C.
Steele, Marian Williams (Mrs.)—P.
Swarzenski, Hanns—E., Mus. Cur., W.
Wadsworth, Charles E.—P.

Cape Cod

Musgrave, Arthur Franklyn—P.
Myers, Ethel (Mrs.)—S., L., T.

Centerville

Coleman, Vernon Herbert—E., P., Des., I., Cart., Comm. A.

Chatham

Orr, Elliot—P.

Chestnut Hill

Cook, Gretchen—T., P.
Saltonstall, Elizabeth—Lith., P.

Conway

Stevens, W. Lester—P.

Danvers

Dodge, Ernest Stanley—Mus. Dir., W., L.

Dedham

Eaton, Sidney Lovett—P., T.
Homburger, Freddy (Dr.)—P., W.
Pratt, Katharine—C.
White, Leo F.—Cart.

Deerfield

Maniatty, Stephen G.—P., T., C., Et., I., L.

Dorchester

MacNutt, Glenn Gordon—P., I.

East Colrain

Greason, Donald Carlisle—P., E., Cr., L., Des., Comm. A.

East Weymouth

Cain, Theron Irving—P., E., Des., W., L.

Falmouth

Littlefield, William Horace—P.
Sisson, Frederick R.—P., Cr., T.

Fitchburg

Harris, Mrs. Mason Dix—Mus. Dir.

Framingham

Fuller, Meta Vaux Warrick—S., T., L.
Walser, Floyd N.—Et., P.

Gloucester

Anderson, Beatrice M.—C., Textile Des.
Anderson, Emily Delia—P., Comm. A.
Anderson, Viola—C., Textile Des.
Andrus, Vera—P., Lith., W., T., L., I.
Davis, Helen S.—S.
Gage, Harry Lawrence—Typog. Des., W., P., L., Gr.
Gruppe, Emile Albert—P., T.
Hall, Doris (Mrs.)—Enamelist, P.
Hammond, John Hays—Mus. Dir.
Hancock, Walker Kirtland—S., T.
Winter, Alice Beach—P., S., I., T.

Great Barrington

Story, Ala—Former Mus. Dir.

Greenbush

Goodnow, Catherine Spencer—Port. P.

Groveland

Baldwin, Barbara—S., P., W.

Harvard

Abbott, Agnes Anne—P., E.

Hingham

Smith, Frank Vining—Marine P., W.

Holden

Levenson, Minnie G. (Mrs.)—E.

Hopkinton

Amendola, Robert—S.

Housatonic

Ramsdell, M. Louise—P.

Hudson

Braga, Alfred Maynard—P., T., Indst. Des.

Huntington

Nagler, Edith Kroger—P., I., T., W.

Hyannis

Reed, Florence (Mrs.)—P., Gr., T., L.

Jamaica Plain

Rines, Frank M.—P., T.
Tyng, Griswold—P., I., Des., E., L.

Lenox

Epping, Franc Dorothy—S., T.

Leominster

Field, Beatrice (Mrs.)—P., L., T.

Lexington

Berry, Ruth Linnell—P., T.
Ciampa, Emilius Rogers—S.
Ripley, Aiden Lassell—P., Et.

Lincoln

Walkey, Frederick P.—Mus. Dir.

Longmeadow

Catok, Lottie Meyer—P.
Robinson, Frederick Bruce—Mus. Dir., E., L.

Lynnfield Centre

Lambert, George E., Jr.—Des.

Manchester

Pezzati, Pietro—Port. P.

Marblehead

Chamberlain, Samuel—Et., Lith., W., E., L.
Creighton, Bessy—P., W.
Heintzelman, Arthur William—Et., Mus. Cur., W., L.
Morse, Sadie May—E., Des., C., P.
Turner, Hamlin—P.

Martha's Vineyard

Brehm, George—I., P.

Mattapoisett

Kelsey, Philip H.—E., Comm. A.

Medford

Perrin, Charles Robert—P., Des., Cart., I., L.

Melrose

Bengtz, Eric Algot Ture—P., Et., Lith., T., Des., L.
Saulnier, James Philippe—Port. P., Des., I., Comm. A.

Melrose Highlands

Burnham, Wilbur Herbert—C., Des., P.

Milton

Jones, Theodore Stephen—E.

Montague

Kamys, Walter—P., T.

Monterey

Montague, Ruth DuBarry (Mrs.)—W., L., T., P.
Prickett, Roland Pierson—P., W., T., I.

Nantucket

Greene, Elmer Westley—P.
Sutton, Ruth Haviland—Port. P., Lith.

Natick

Kupferman, Lawrence—P., E.

Needham

Castano, Giovanni—P.
Dennis, Charles Warren—P., I.

New Bedford

Currier, Allen Dale—P., E., L., Comm. A.
Haggett, Hiram Rockwell—E., Des., Comm. A., L.

Newbury

Ahl, Henry Curtis—P., I., W.

Newburyport

Douglas, Chester—Des., P., T., I., Comm. A.

Newton

Bang, Eleonore E.—C., E., W.
Hicken, Philip Burnham—P., Ser., T.
Morenon, Ernest E.—S., T.
Siporin, Mitchell—P., E.

Newton Center

Brodney, Edward—P.
Orr, Eleanor Mason—Min. P.
Shepler, Dwight Clark—P., I., W., S.
Thompson, Leslie P.—P., T.

Newtonville

Bonnar, James King—P., Des.
Skinner, Orin Ensign—Des., L., W., C.
Wilson, Charles J. A.—Et., P., I.

Norfolk

Orr, Forrest Walker—P., I., Comm. A., Des., C.

Northampton

Baskin, Leonard—S., Gr.
Cohen, H. George—P., E., L., Des., I.
Hitchcock, Henry-Russell—E., Hist., Cr., Mus. Dir.
Jules, Mervin—P., Gr., I., L., E.
Kennedy, Clarence—E.
Kennedy, Ruth Wedgwood—E., L.
Larkin, Oliver—E., W., Cr., L.
Parks, Robert Owens—Mus. Dir.
Van Der Poel, Priscilla Paine (Mrs.)— E., P., Cart., L.

Northfield

Webster, Bernice M.—P., L.

Orleans

Smith, Vernon B.—P., C.

Pepperill

Cooney, Barbara (Mrs.)—I.

Petersham

Eaton, Dorothy—P.

Pittsfield

Henry, Stuart Compton—Mus. Dir., P., Des.

Plymouth

Alden, Katharine L.—C., Des., E.

Provincetown

Burlingame, Sheila Ellsworth—S., P., Des.
Euler, Reeves—P., S.
Freborg, Stanley—P.
Gregory, Dorothy Lake (Mrs.)—P., L., I.
Gregory, John Worthington—Lith., W., L., Photog.
Hensche, Henry—P., L., T.
Kaeselau, Charles Anton—P., T.
Knaths, Otto Karl—P., L., T.
Malicoat, Philip C.—P.
Moffett, Ross E.—P.
Pfeiffer, Fritz—P., T.
Pfeiffer, Hope Voorhees (Mrs.)—P., T.
Rayner, Ada (Mrs.)—P.
Yater, George David—P., I., W.

Quincy

Reardon, Mary A.—P., Et., Lith., I.

Raynham

Vaughan, Lester Howard—C.

Rockport

Allen, Frank Leonard—E., P., Gr., W., L.
Bate, Rutledge—P., T.
Beatty, Hetty Burlingame—S., Des., I., C., W.
Callahan, Jack—Port. P.
Chetcuti, John—P., T.
Colman, Blanche Emily—P., Et., Des.
Cook, Otis—P.
Corbino, Jon—P., T.
Crane, Alan Horton—P., Lith., I., W.
Denghausen, Franz H.—S.
Dinckel, George William—P., T., L.
Gellman, Beatrice McNulty (Mrs.)— P., S., T., W., L.
Greenleaf, Jacob I.—P., Des., T.
Hibbard, Aldro Thompson—P., T.
Hirota, Susumu—P.
Holberg, Ruth Langland (Mrs.)—W.
Howell, Felicie (Mrs.)—P.
Jeswald, Joseph—P.
Jones, Mildred C.—P.
Jones, Prescott M.—P., Et., T.
Knauth, Arnold Whitman, II—P.
Longley, Evelyn Louise—P., I., Comm A., T., L.
Marston, Charles Gordon—P.
Martin, Roger H., Jr.—P., Gr., T., I., W.
Murphy, Gladys Wilkins (Mrs.)—P., C., Des., Pr. M.
Murphy, Herbert A.—P., C., Des.
Oliver, Frederick W.—P.
Parsons, Kitty (Mrs.)—P., W.
Pearson, Marguerite S.—P., T.
Preston, Harriet Brown—P., T., Cr.
Recchia, Richard Henry—S.
Regester, Charlotte—P., S., C., Des., T.

Ricci, Jerri—P.
Williams, Pauline Bliss (Mrs.)—P.
Woodward, Stanley—P., Et., W., I., T.

Roxbury

Wilson, John Woodrow—P., Lith., T.

Salem

Brewington, Marion Vernon—Mus. Cur., W.
Merrill, Walter McIntosh—Mus. Dir., E., L., P.

Sandwich

French, Hazel Blake—C.

Scituate

Bissell, Charles Philip—Cart., I.
Furlong, Charles Wellington—W., E., L., I., P.

Segreganset

Macomber, Allison R.—S.

Sheffield

Frame, Walter Keith—Pr. M., P., Comm. A., Gr., I.

Sherborn

Pickhardt, Carl E., Jr.—P., Et., Lith., T., L.

Shrewsbury

Graziani, Sante—P., Des., T.

South Dartmouth

Rapoza, Francisco—P., T., L.

South Egremont

Haupt, Erik Guide—Port. P.

South Hadley

Cogswell, Dorothy McIntosh—E., P., L., I.
Corbett, Edward M.—E., P.
Foss, Florence Winslow—S., E.
Hayes, Marian—E., L.
Rox, Henry—S., E., I., Comm. A.

South Hamilton

Sawyer, Dantan Winslow—P., Arch. Des.

Springfield

Chaffetz, Asa—Eng., I.
Ellis, Harriet A.—P., Ser.
Foote, David S.—Asst. Mus. Dir.
Knox, Helen Estelle—P.
Sturtevant, Wallis Hall—P., I.
Watkins, Louise Lochridge—Mus. Dir., T., L.

State Line

Lane, Harry—P.

Stockbridge

Cresson, Margaret French—S., W.
Rockwell, Norman—I.

Sudbury

Aronson, David—P.
Coleman, Loring Wilkins, Jr.—P., T.
Hosmer, Florence Armes—P., T., L.

Swampscott

Cooper, Edward J. W.—P., T., Cr., L.

Truro

Allen, Courtney—I., S., C., Gr.
L'Engle, Lucy—P., C.
Wilson, Edward A.—I., Lith., P.

Vineyard Haven

Berresford, Virginia—P.
Thompson, Helen Lathrop (Mrs.)—P.

Waban

Reynolds, Gordon L.—E., L., C., P.
Spear, Arthur P.—P.

Wakefield

Bradshaw, Alexandra Christine (Mrs.) —P., E., Lith., L.

Walpole

Goss, John—I., P., Lith. T.

Waltham

Keyes, Bernard M.—Port. P.
Stevens, Vera (Mrs.)—P., T.

Watertown

Coolidge, Rosamond—Port. P.
Novak, Louis—Pr. M., P., T.

Wellesley

Aiken, John Dary—P., E., L., Des.
Charles, Sam—P.
McAndrew, John—Mus. Dir., E., Hist., W., L.
Unwin, Nora Spicer—Eng., I., W.

Wellesley Hills

Aiken, Charles Avery—P., Gr.
Huntington, Elizabeth Hamilton Thayer (Mrs.)—P.
Paramino, John F.—S., W.

Wellfleet

Parsons, Walter Edward—P.

West Newbury

Craver, Margaret—C.

West Newton

Williams, Gluyas—I., Cart., W.

Weston

Fiske, Gertrude—P.
Kaler, Gladys R. (Mrs.)—C., Des., P.

Westwood

Philbrick, Margaret Elder (Mrs.)— Et., P.
Philbrick, Otis—P., Lith., E.

Weymouth

Bill, Carroll M.—P., I.

Wilbraham

Welch, Mabel R.—Min. P.

Williamstown

Faison, S. Lane, Jr.—E., W., L., Cr.
Guille, Peter—Mus. Dir.

Winchester

Lobingier, Elizabeth Miller (Mrs.)— P., W., E.

Woburn

Ayer, Ralph Dwight—P., T.

Wollaston

Smongeski, Joseph L.—Book Des., P., Lith., Ser., T.

Worcester

Brown, William Joseph—C., Des., T.
Dresser, Louisa—Mus. Cur., L., W.
Hovsepian, Leon—P., Gr., L., T.
Kurwacz, William—C.
La Rocco, Anthony—C.
Rich, Daniel Catton—Mus. Dir., W., L.
Scott, Stella Bradford (Mrs.)—P., Lith.
Waite, Emily Burling (Mrs.)—P., Et., L.
Warren, Jefferson T.—Mus. Dir.

Wrentham

Cowell, Joseph Goss—P., E., S., L., W.

MICHIGAN

Ada

Collins, Kreigh—I.

Adrian

Helene, Sister—C., S., P., Gr., W.

Albion

Bobbitt, Vernon L.—P., T.
Fowler, Constance—E.
Leach, Richard—E.

Ann Arbor

Bradfield, Margaret Jewell (Mrs.)— P., I., L., W.
Brown, May Morgan (Mrs.)—P.
Cassara, Frank—P., Pr. M.
Daniels, Elmer Harland—S., Indst. Des.
Gooch, Donald B.—Des., I., E.
Gores, Walter W. J.—Des., C., W., L., E.
Hall, Helen Benedict—Mus. Cur.
Iglehart, Robert L.—E.
Irvin, Virginia Hendrickson—Min. P.
Kamrowski, Gerome—E., P.
La More, Chet Harmon—P., Gr., T.
Lopez, Rhoda LeBlanc—C., T., Medical I.
Makielski, Leon A.—Port. P., T.
McClure, Thomas F.—S., E.
Porter, Doris (Mrs.)—P., L., T.
Prendergast, James Donald—P., E., L., Lith., W.
Reider, David H.—Des., E. Photog.
Sawyer, Charles Henry—E., Mus. Dir.
Shaw, Wilfred B.—P., Et., I., W., Hist.
Slusser, Jean Paul—Mus. Dir., P., W., E.
Vidar, Frede—P., E.
Weddidge, Emil—Lith., P., E., Des., L.
Wethey, Harold Edwin—E., L., W.
Wilt, Richard—P., E.

Birmingham

Fredericks, Marshall M.—S.
Thom, Robert Alan—I., P.
Williams, Mildred Emerson—P., Lith.

Bloomfield Hills

Coppin, John Stephens—P., Comm. A., W.
Grotell, Maija—C., T.
Mitchell, Wallace MacMahon—P., T.
Pasternacki, Vetold Henry—P.
Sepeshy, Zoltan—P., T.
West, Clifford Bateman—P., T., Lith.

Dearborn

Baeb, Henry R.—Cart., Comm. A.
Culver, Charles—P.
Nelson, Hans Peter—Indst. Des., E., I., C.
Rogers, Gertrude (Mrs.)—P.
Smith, Jerome Irving—Mus. Cur., W.

Detroit

Barnes, Ernest Harrison—P., T.
Bernstein, Henry—P.
Bigler, Mary Jane White—E., P.
Bland, Garnet William—Des., P., I., Comm. A., Cart.
Bostick, William Allison—P., C., Cart., I., Lith., L., E., W.
Broner, Robert—Et., Eng., P., T., Cr.
Calder, James John—P.
Claxton, Wayne L.—E.
Crathern, Helen Goodwin—T., P., L.
Dioda, Adolph—S.
Gamble, Roy C.—P.
Grigaut, Paul L.—Mus. Cur.
Page, Addison Franklin—Mus. Cur., T.
Papsdorf, Frederick—P., Et.
Richardson, Constance Coleman (Mrs.)—P.
Richardson, Edgar Preston—Mus. Dir., W., L.
Sarkisian, Sarkis—E., P.
Sparks, Joseph—P., Lith., L.
Werbe, Anna Lavick (Mrs.)—P., T.
Wilby, Margaret Crowinshield—P.

East Lansing

Brainard, Owen D.—E., P., Ser.
Brauner, Erling B.—E., P.
Church, C. Howard—E., P., Lith.
Gamble, William Sylvester—P., E., Gr., Comm. A., I.
Henricksen, Ralf Christian—P., E.
Hodge, Stuart—E., P., Et.
Hurtig, Martin—P., Et., Lith., E.
Jungwirth, Irene Gayas (Mrs.)—P., E., L., C.
Jungwirth, Leonard D.—S., E., L.
Soria, Martin Sebastian—E., W., L., Mus. Consultant
Whitaker, Irwin A., Jr.—E., C.

Eaton Rapids

Knopf, Nellie Augusta—P., T., L.

Fenton

Gath, Ethel Robertson—P.

Grand Rapids

Ford, Dale Vinton—Des., E.
Galbraith—Cart., I.
Kirkpatrick, Marie (Mrs.)—Indst. Des.
Mast, Gerald—P., E.
McBride, Walter H.—Mus. Dir., T., C., P.
McMullen, E. Ormond—P., I., Gr.
Weidenaar, Reynold Henry—Pr. M., I., P.
Wykes, Frederic Kirtland—P.

Grosse Pointe Farms

Firth, Karl W.—P., Des., Cart.
Miller, Iris Andrews—Port. P.
Scanes, Ernest William—P., Des.

Grosse Pointe Shores

Worcester, Eva—P., S., T.

Hart

Kuhne, Hedvig Harriett B.—P., C., S., T., E.

Highland Park

Midener, Walter—S., C., T.

Huntington Woods

Packman, Frank G.—P., T., Des., I., L.

Kalamazoo

Cornish, Ned A.—Mus. Dir.
Kemper, John Garner—E., P., Des., L., W.
Siedschlag, Lydia—E., Des.
Spencer, Marion Dickinson (Mrs.)—P., E.
Stevenson, Elaine Louise—C., E.

Lansing

Alexander, Robert Seymour—Ind. Des., P., T.
Leepa, Allen—P., E., W.

Laurium

Steck, Alden L.—P., T.

Livonia

Beerbohm, Marvin—P.
Rousseau, Angeline Marie—P.

Lowell

Godfrey, Rob. W.—P., Lith., Des.

Manistee

Trevitts, Joseph—P., T.

Marquette

Harrison, Cleobelle—E.

Mount Morris

Ferguson, Edward R., Jr.—P., Gr.

Okemos

Jones, Murray—P., E., Gr.
Pollock, Charles Cecil—P., T.

Owosso

Schlag, Felix Oscar—S.

Richland

Walker, James Adams—T., P., W.

Romeo

Newberry, John S.—Mus. Cur.

Royal Oak

Serth, Arthur—P., C.

Saginaw

Faletti, Vincent—Cart.
Roecker, Julia (Mrs.)—Mus. Dir.

Saugatuck

Taylor, Cora Bliss—P., L., T.

Temperance

Harbauer, Hazel Jacoby—P., Gr., C., L.

Traverse City

Hoffmaster, Maud Miller—P., Pr. M., W., L., T., I.
Jewett, Eleanor (Mrs.)—Cr., W., L.

Watersmeet

Freund, William F.—P., C., E.

Watervliet

Elias, Harold John—P., C., Des., T., L.

MINNESOTA

Anoka

Follrath, Darwin—P., C., T.

Excelsior

Nash, Katherine (Mrs.)—S., T., Gal. Dir., C., L.

Hopkins

Bryan, Wilhelmus B.—E.
Le Sueur, Mac—P., L., T.
Zilverberg, Jim—Cart., Comm. A., W.

Mankato

Koch, Berthe Couch—P., E., S., Gr., W., L.
Koch, M. Robert—C., E., Gr., L.

Marine-on-St. Croix

Dunn, Montfort—Gal. Dir.

Minneapolis

Amberg, H. George—W., E., L.
Arnason, H. Harvard—E., Mus. Dir., Art Historian, W., L.
Booth, Cameron—P., T.
Brock, Emma L.—W., I.
Darr, Harold Winfred—Des., C., Et., E., L.
Davis, Richard S.—Mus. Dir.
Friedman, Martin L.—Mus. Cur.
Greenman, Frances Cranmer—P., Cr., W., L., T.
Justus, Roy Braxton—Cart.
Krollmann, Gustav Wilhelm—P., T.
Lawrence, Ruth (Mrs.)—Mus. Dir., E., L., W., S., C.
Long, Scott—Cart.
Myers, Malcolm Haynie—P., Et., Eng.
Preuss, Roger Emil—P., I., Des., W.
Quirt, Walter—P., E.
Ranney, Glen Allison—P., T.
Raymond, Leone Evelyn—S., L., T.
Rollins, Josephine Lutz—P., E.
Rood, John—S., P., W., L., E.
Sherman, John Kurtz—Cr.
Socha, John Martin—P., T.
Sohner, Theodore—P., L.
Torbert, Meg (Mrs.)—Mus. Cur., Des.
Wedin, Elof—P.
Wolfe, Ann (Mrs.)—S., W., L.
Wolfe-Parker, Viola—P., S., Ser., C.

Northfield

Hyslop, Alfred John—E., P.

Rochester

Saltzman, William—P., Mus. Dir., T., L.

St. Cloud
Chase, Marion Crouze (Mrs.)—P., Gr.
Reiff, Robert Frank—P., E.

St. Paul
Bobleter, Lowell Stanley—P., E., Gr., L., W.
Brewer, Floyd E.—Mural Tapestry Des., P., T., L.
Caponi, Anthony—E., S.
Duncan, Jean—P., T., L.
Gayne, Clifton Alexander, Jr.—E.
Harrison, Robert Rice—E., P., W.
Haupers, Clement Bernard—P., Gr., S., L., T.
Hauser, Alonzo—S.
Jemne, Elsa Laubach (Mrs.)—P., I.
Kolb, Delmar M.—Mus. Cur., C., T.
Lein, Malcolm E.—Mus. Dir., E.
Lupori, Peter—S., E.
Mairs, Clara Gardner—P., Ser.
Millis, Charlotte Melissa—S.
Mosman, Warren T.—S., T.
Oja, Alexander—P., Lith., E.
Rahja, Virginia Helga—E., P., S., C., Gal. Dir.
Swanson, Bennet A.—P., Lith., T.
Tsclos, Dimitri Theodore—E., L.
Uptegrove, Sister M. Irena—E., Des., P., I., S.
Wheeler, Cleora Clark—Des., Illuminator, L., W.

Stillwater
Old, Bertrand E.—P., T.

Wayzata
Hunter, Sam—Mus. Cur., W., L.

Winona
Murray, Floretta—E., P., S.

MISSISSIPPI

Biloxi
Duckett, Albert—Cart., P.

Clinton
Gore, Samuel M.—E.

Columbus
Dice, Elizabeth Jane—E., C., P.
Hudson, Ralph M.—E., Des., P., W., L., Comm. A.
Robinson, Virginia Carolyn—P., Hist., I.
Stringer, Mary Evelyn—E., P.

Greenwood
Lewis, Lalla Walker—P., Comm. A., Eng.

Hattiesburg
Ambrose, Charles Edward—P., E., S.

Holly Springs
Clark, Freeman—P.

Jackson
Green, Myra (Mrs.)—P., L., T.
Howard, Ann Ammons—T., P., C.
Hull, Marie Atkinson (Mrs.)—P., T.
Lotterhos, Helen Jay—P., T.
Mason, Ella May—P., E.
Wolfe, Karl Ferdinand—P., E.
Wolfe, Mildred (Mrs.)—P., S.

Laurel
Davis, Nell—Art Libn.

Meridian
Casteel, Homer, Jr.—P.

Ocean Springs
Richards, William Coolidge—P.
Steene, William—Port. P.

Oxford
Hamblett, Theora—P.
Rowland, Mrs. Herron—Mus. Dir.

Summit
Atkinson, Ruth M. (Mrs.)—P.
Barnes, Halcyone—P.
Dawson, Bess Phipps—P.

University
Brandt, Warren—E., P.

Vicksburg
Bradfield, Edward Orr—P., Eng.
Bucci, Andrew A.—P., Gr.
Compton, Caroline Russell—P.

Yazoo City
Summer, Emily Eugenia—P., T.

MISSOURI

Affton
Bauer, William—P., Comm. A., I., Gr.

Cape Girardeau
Bedford, Helen de Wilton—E.

Carthage
Spencer, Bertha Augusta—C., Et., E., W., L.

Cedar Hill
Vogel, Valentine—P., T.

Clayton
Nuderscher, Frank Bernard—P., Des.

Columbia
Beresford, Helen Elizabeth—E., L., Des.
Green, Russell—E.
Hansen, Douglas Reid—P., E.
McKinin, Lawrence—E., P., C., Des.
Shane, Frederick E.—P., Lith., E.

Crestwood
Young, Dorothy O. (Mrs.)—S., P., T., C.

Forsyth
Ganser, Ivan Laurence—S., C.

Gashland
Ray, Silvey Jackson—Cart.

Glendale
Goetsch, Gustav F.—P., E.

Independence
Howe, Robert Munson—E., Eng., Et., S.
Tindall, Robert Elton—P., T., C.

Jefferson City
Parks, James Dallas—P., Lith., E.

Kansas City
Becker, Joseph Hubert—Cart., W., P., Des., C.
Benton, Thomas Hart—P., T., W.
Bohan, Ruth H.—P., Et., Lith.
Braught, Ross—P., Lith., T.
Bruton, David Thomas—P., Lith., T.
Campanella, Vincent Richard—P., E., L.
Carstenson, Cecil C.—S., T.
Deines, Ernest Hubert—Eng., Des.
Hammond, Mildred Welsh—P., T.
Havlena, Jari (Miss)—P., T., L.
Henry, Coah—P., T.
James, Frederic—P., I., Des.
Kucharyson, Paul—Et., Eng., C., Des., I., S.
McKim, William Wind—Lith., P., T.
Moulton, Mary Elisabeth—L., T.
Neufeld, Paula—P., T.
Peck, Verna Johnston (Mrs.)—P., T.
Peet, Margot—P.
Roberts, Dwight V.—Port. P.
Roth, James Buford—P., Conservator
Sapp, Kitt George (Mr.)—P.
Scott, Henry Edwards, Jr.—P., Des., L., E., Mus. Cur., W.
Sickman, Laurence C. S.—Mus. Dir., L.
Townsend, Marvin—Cart., Comm. A.
Walker, Marian—C., P., Des., L.

Kirkwood
Arnold, Newell Hillis—S., C., T.
Reinhardt, Siegfried Gerhard—P., Des., T., L.

Manchester
Thalinger, E. Oscar—P., E.

Marshall
Heuermann, Magda—P., W., L., T., Des.

Maryville
De Luce, Olive S.—E., P.

Richmond Heights
Walsh, Noemi M.—C., T.

St. Joseph
Hartley, Harrison Smith—P., Des., Cart., L., I., Comm. A.

St. Louis
Becker, Fred—E., Pr. M.
Calvert, Melvina—P., Gr.
Carpenter, Fred Green—P., T., C.
Carpenter, Mildred Bailey (Mrs.)—P., W., I., T., L.
Charpiot, Donald—P., S., T., L.
Conway, Fred—P., E., L.
Drewes, Werner—P., Gr., E.
Duhme, H. Richard, Jr.—S., E.
Edsall, Mabel Meeker—P., T., Cart.
Eisendrath, William Nathan, Jr.—Asst. Mus. Dir., Hist.
Eppensteiner, John Joseph—P., I.
Fitzpatrick, Daniel R.—Cart.
Funsch, Edyth (Mrs.)—I., Des., P.
Hoopes, Thomas Temple—Mus. Cur., L.
Horwitz, Louise McMahan—P., Des.
Hudson, Kenneth Eugene—E., P.
MacNutt, J. Scott—Port. P.
Mauldin, Bill—Cart.
Milovich, Tanasko—P., C., Des., T.
Morgenthaler, Charles Albert—I., P., Des., C., T.

Mose, Carl C.—S., L.
Nagel, Charles—Mus. Dir., L.
Neuman, Dorothy B. (Mrs.)—Libn.
Palmer, Lucie Mackay—P., L.
Pflager, Dorothy Holloway (Mrs.)—P.
Quest, Charles F.—P., Gr., E.
Quest, Dorothy Johnson (Mrs.)—Port.
  P., E., L.
Schnittman, Sacha S.—S., W., L., E.
Schweig, Aimee (Mrs.)—P., T.
Skelly, Gladys Gertrude—C.
Smith, Helen M. (Mrs.)—E., P., Des.
Thoele, Lillian Caroline Anne—P., I.,
  Comm. A., Des.

Springfield

Corbett, Oliver J.—P.
Kennon, Ethelyn M.—C., T.
Kennon, Raymond Kenneth—P., C.,
  Des.
Shuck, Kenneth Menaugh—Mus. Dir.,
  P.

University City

Mylonas, George Emmanuel—E., W.,
  L.
Spaulding, Warren—P., E.

Warrensburg

Ellis, Edwin Charles—E., Gr.

Washington

Richter, Louise C. (Mrs.)—Des., E.

Webster Groves

Boccia, Edward Eugene—P.
Cooper, Leone—P., E., L., Gr., I.
Rickly, Jessie Beard—P., Gr., L., Cart.

MONTANA

Billings

Bailey, Earl Clifford—T., P.
Dietrich, John Franklin—E., C., Des.,
  P.
Greene, LeRoy E.—P.
Ralston, James Kenneth—P., I.

Butte

Lochrie, Elizabeth—P., S., L.

Great Falls

Stevenson, Branson Graves—Gr., C.,
  P., L.

Missoula

Casterton, Eda Nemoede (Mrs.)—P.
Hook, Walter—E., P.

NEBRASKA

Chadron

Artis, William Ellisworth—E., C., S.,
  Lith., L.

Fremont

Hopkins, Lin (Mr.)—P., Et.
Hopkins, Ruth Joy (Mrs.)—Port. P.

Kearney

Ahrendts, Harold L.—E.
Aspen, Phyllis Campbell (Mrs.)—E.,
  S., L.

Lincoln

Butt, Gail Hammond, Jr.—P., E.
Geske, Norman Albert—Mus. Dir., E.,
  L.

Keiler, Manfred L.—P., E.
Laging, Duard Walter—E.
Lux, Gladys Marie—P., E., Ser., C.
Mills, Loren Sturdevant—S., Des., C.
Ross, Barbara Ellis (Mrs.)—P.
Seyler, David Woods—S., P., I., Des.,
  E.
Whiting, Mildred Ruth—E., P.
Worth, Peter John—Des., S., E.

Omaha

Dunbier, Augustus William—P., L.
Hammon, Bill J.—P., C., S., Des., T.,
  Gr., I., L.
Kingman, Eugene—Mus. Dir., P.,
  Lith.
Martin, Francis Thomas Beckett—P.
Swan, Walter Buckingham—P., W.,
  L.
Thiessen Charles Leonard—Des., P.,
  Gr., C., S., L., T.
Wolsky, Milton Laban—I., P.

Peru

Diddel, Norma L.—E., P., Gr.

Shelby

Duren, Terence Romaine—P., I.

Wayne

Lesh, Richard D.—E., P.

NEVADA

Gardnerville

Lawrence, James A.—P., T., Comm.
Photog.

Reno

Edmundson, Carolyn—P., Des., I.,
  Comm. A., T.

Virginia City

Andrus, Zoray—P., I., Des., T., S.

NEW HAMPSHIRE

Campton

Drerup, Karl—C., P., E., Gr.
Waters, Herbert Ogden—Wood Eng.,
  T.

Concord

Chandler, John William—E.
Hoffmann, Lilly E.—C., Des., T.
Luneau, Omer Joachim—P., T., L.

Dover

Burdoin, Juliet Howson—P.
Huffer, Cornelia Cunningham—P., I.,
  T.
Tonkin, John Carter—C.

Dublin

Carlsson, Oscar T.—P., Gr., C.
Meryman, Richard S.—P., T.

Durham

Scheier, Edwin—Ceramist, E., S., P.
Scheier, Mary—Ceramist, Des., C., E.,
  P.
Thomas, George R.—E., Ser., L.

Exeter

Krause, Glen Adolph—Mus. Dir., P.,
  T.
Squier, Donald Gordon—P., Comm.
  A.

Hampton

Johnson, Arthur Clark—Port. P.

Hanover

Lathrop, Churchill Pierce—E., Gal.
  Dir.
Nash, Ray—W., E., L.
Stearns, John Barker—E.

Hopkinton

Heino, Otto—C., E.
Heino, Vivika—C., Des., E.

Keene

Faulkner, Barry—P., T.
Wheelwright, Elizabeth S.—T., Eng.,
  P., I., C.

Manchester

Buckley, Charles E.—Mus. Dir.
Graubart, Z. Peter—E.
Lassonde, Omer Thomas—P.
Ledoux, Eva M. B.—P., T., Des.
Watts, Melvin E.—Mus. Cur.

Mason

Anderson, Clarence William—Et., I.,
  Lith., W.
Jones, Elizabeth Orton—I., W., P.,
  Gr.

Merrimack

Carlson, Oscar A.—P., Des., Et., Eng.,
  C., Lith.

New London

Fussiner, Howard Robert—P., T., W.

Ossipee

Butler, John Davidson—C., T., Gr.,
  P., L.

Plainfield

Boyd, Fiske—P., Gr.

Portsmouth

Harding, Dorothy Sturgis (Mrs.)—
  Des.
Harlow, Harry Merrick Sutton—P.,
  Des., Gr., L.

Sutton

Salo, George K.—C.

Webster

Tudor, Tasha (Mrs.)—I., W., Des.,
  Comm. A.

West Andover

Eaves, Winslow Bryan—S., C., Des.

Westmoreland Depot

Warner, Everett Longley—P., Et., T.,
  L., W.

Whitefield

Vogelgesang, Shepard—Des.

NEW JERSEY

Asbury Park

Dengrove, Ida Leibovitz—P., Gr., T.

Atlantic Highlands
Helfond, Riva (Mrs.)—Lith., Ser., P.
Wenzel, William Michael—Cart., I.

Bayonne
Abramson, Maurice—P., L., T.
Gorman, William D.—P., I.
Grasso, Doris Elsie—P., C., Des., Et., I., T.

Bedminster
Meyers, Robert William—I.

Belleville
Ahneman, Leonard J.—P., Des., E.

Belmar
Doane, Pelagie (Mrs.)—I., W.

Bergenfield
Drake, William A.—Et., Lith., P., C., T.

Berkeley Heights
Mills, Hugh Lauren—P., Et., Lith.

Bloomfield
Jones, Doris Jardine—P., Comm. A.
Swanson, George Alan—P., I.

Bound Brook
Gregory, Waylande—S., Des., W., L., P.

Brielle
Marron, Eugenie Marie—P., S., W.

Butler
Law, Pauline—P.

Caldwell
Lenney, Annie (Mrs.)—P., T., L.

Camden
Cannon, Florence V.—P., Gr., E., L.
Reiter, Freda Leibovitz (Mrs.)—P., Gr., I.

Cape May
Gilmore, Ethel (Mrs.)—P., Gr., T.
Romans, Charles John—P., T., C.

Cape May Courthouse
Nunn, Frederic—P.

Cape May Point
Bailey, William J.—Cart., I., Des.

Chatham
Angela, Emilio—S.
Goff, Harry Sharp, Jr.—Cart., I.
Hill, Homer—I., Comm. A., Des., P.
Stea, Cesare—S., P., T.
Wonsetler, John Charles—P., I., W.

Clifton
Rossi, Joseph—P., Des., T., L.
Scheffel, Herbert H.—P., Comm. A.

Closter
Belskie, Abram—S.
Wilcox, Ruth—P., C., Comm. A.

Collingswood
Howe, Winifred Eva—W., Hist.

Colonia
Lella, Carl—P.

Cranford
Hoe, Mable Kent—P., S.
Thurston, Gerald Edwin—Indst. Des.

Cream Ridge
Steig, William—Cart., S.

Cresskill
Lamb, Katharine (Mrs.)—Des., P., C.
Smyth, Craig Hugh—E.
Ward, Lynd Kendall—Lith., Eng., I., W., L.

Dover
Johnson, Avery F.—P., I., T.

Dumont
Silvan, Rita—P., T., L.
von Riegen, William—Cart., I., P., T.

Dunellen
Silkotch, Mary Ellen—P., T.

Elberon
Stamaty, Stanley—Cart., Comm. A., I.

Elizabeth
Guntrum, Emilie Ida—P.

Englewood
Baumgartner, Warren W.—I., P.
Breger, Dave—Cart.
Dawes, Dexter B.—P.
Grushkin, Philip—Des., T., Calligrapher
Romano, Clare Ross—Lith., Eng., P.
Ross, John—Eng., Lith., T.
Spiegel, Doris—Et., Eng., I., W.

Fair Haven
Smith, Paul—Des., I., W.

Fanwood
Arnold, Howard Weston—I., Des., P., C., E., Comm. A., L.
Cooper, Fred G.—Cart., Des.
Kauffman, G. Francis—Cart., Comm. A.

Flemington
Hewitt, Donald C.—I., Comm. A.

Franklin Lakes
Brockhurst, Gerald L.—P.

Frenchtown
Saalburg, Allen Russell—P., Des., Comm. A., I., Ser.
Strauss, Charles Earl—Cart., Comm. A., T.
Wiese, Kurt—I., W.
Wolfe, Meyer—P., Lith.

Gladstone
Duvoisin, Roger A.—I., W.

Glen Ridge
Kato, Kay—Cart., I., P., L.
Macdonald, Herbert Evans—P.
Townsend, Ethel Hore (Mrs.)—P.

Hackensack
Anthony, Elisabeth Mary—P., Des., T.
Dorsey, Thomas—Des., I., L., Comm. A.

Hackettstown
Goodwin, Gilberta D. (Mrs.)—E., P.
Niese, Henry Ernst—P., T.

Hammonton
Baker, Mary Hofstetter—P., Des.
Baker, Raymond Nelson—Des., P., Gr.

Hanover
Schwacha, George—P., T., L.

Harvey Cedars
Kelly, Leon—P.

Hasbrouck Heights
Perham, Roy Gates—P., L.

Hawthorne
Calcia, Lillian Acton—E.

Hazlet
Temes, Mort—Cart., Comm. A.

Herbertsville
Stroud, Clara—P., C., Des., W.

Highland Park
Buros, Luella (Mrs.)—P., Des.
Herrmann, E. Adele—P., T.

Highlands
Pratt, Inga—P., Comm. A., I.

Hillside
Schweitzer, Gertrude—P.

Hoboken
Korn, Elizabeth P.—P., E., I.

Irvington
Grabach, John R.—P., S.
Rosser, Alvin Raymon—P., T.

Jersey City
McCormick, Daniel S., Jr.—Cart.
Mount, Pauline Ward—P., S., E., L.
Skinas, John Constantine—P.
Smith, Robert Harmer—P., Arch. Delineator
Stevens, Edward John, Jr.—P., Et.

Kingston
Cook, Peter Geoffrey—P.

Kresson
Cortese, Edward Fortunato—I., Des., Comm. A.

Lambertville
Abbott, Emily (Mrs.)—P.
Davenport, Ethel (Mrs.)—C., Des., W.

Gatch, Harry Lee—P.
Stone, Louis K.—P.

Leonia

Boyer, Helen King—Eng., Des., P., Et., C.
Boyer, Louise Rive-King Miller—Eng., P., Des., L., T., C.
Chapman, Charles Shepard—P., Lith., L., T.
Hawkins, Arthur, Jr.—Des., Consulting A. Dir., P.
Johnson, Selina Tetzlaff (Mrs.)—Mus. Dir., E., I.
Jones, Paul Haller—P., T.
Reynard, Grant Tyson—P., Et., Lith., L.

Lincoln Park

Gillooly, Wilhelmina R.—Des., P.

Linden

Smith, Dorothy Oldach—T., P., W., L.

Long Branch

Wright, Elva M.—P.

Lyndhurst

Weingaertner, Hans—P.

Mahwah

Chapman, Frederick T.—I.
Foord, (Fritz) Frederick A.—Indst. Des.

Mantua

Barnes, Catherine J.—I., Des.

Maplewood

Feldman, Hilda (Mrs.)—P., T.
Joffe, Bertha—Tex. Des.
Oliver, Jane—P., Comm. A., I.
Pease, Lucius Curtis—Cart.

Mendham

Giusti, George—Adv. Des.
Hobbie, Lucille—P., Lith., T.

Metuchen

Stoffa, Michael—P., T., Cr., L.

Middletown

Gulick, Henry T.—P.

Middle Valley

Ciampaglia, Carlo—Mural P., T.

Milford

Carter, Clarence Holbrook—P., E., L., Des.
Taskey, Harry LeRoy—P., Et., Lith., I.
Wahl, Theodore—Lith.

Millington

Keskulla, Carolyn Windeler—Lith., P., T.

Milltown

Bradshaw, Robert George—E., P.

Montclair

Askin, Jules—P., Des., T., L., W., Cr., Restorer

Coes, Kent Day—P., Des., I.
Dane, William Jerald—Art Libn.
Gamble, Kathryn Elizabeth—Mus. Dir.
Lahee, Arnold Warburton—P., E.
Maurice, Eleanore Ingersoll (Mrs.)—P., T.
Voute, Kathleen—P., Des., I.

Moorestown

Hagert, Henry—Indst. Des.
Howard, Lucile (Mrs.)—P., T., L.
Nelson, D. Earle—Indst. Des., P., Gr.

Morristown

Howell, John S.—P., T.
Jones, Joseph John—P., Lith.

Mountain Lakes

Craven, Edgar Malin—P.
Fitz-Gerald, Boylan—P., W., L., T., Lith.

Mountainside

Devlin, Harry Arthur—Cart., I., Port. P.
Domareki, Joseph T.—P., S.
Souder, Bertha Klandrud—P.

Mt. Freedom

Schainen, Herman Jack—S., Des.

Mt. Tremper

Garel, Leo—P., Cart., I.

Newark

Baker, Mildred (Mrs.)—Assoc. Mus. Dir.
Baretski, Charles Allan—Art Libn., Archivist
Cicero, Carmen Louis—P.
Coffey, Katherine—Mus. Dir.
Cohen, Nessa—S., P.
Crawford, William H.—Cart., S., I.
Frebault, Marcelle—Art Libn.
Garbely, Edward—P.
Jannelli, Vincent—P., T.
Konrad, Adolf Ferdinand—P., T.
Nugent, Arthur William—Cart., I., W.
Sabine, Julia—Art Libn.

New Brunswick

Cantor, Robert Lloyd—E., Des., C., Cr., W., L.
Fulton, Dorothy—P., S., C., T., L.
Hunt, Kari (Mrs.)—S., L., C.
Noe, Sydney Philip—Mus. Cur., W.
Von Erffa, Helmut—E., P., W., L.

Nixon

Onton, Sophie Wall (Mrs.)—P., Comm. A., T.

North Arlington

Herz, Nora Evelyn—S., C., T., W.

North Bergen

Bell, Enid (Mrs.)—S., C., T., I., W., L.
Botto, Otto—P., I., T., L.
Herric, Prudence C.—I.
Makarenko, Zachary Philip—P., S.

North Haledon

Heusser, Eleanore Elizabeth—P.

Nutley

Armstrong, Estelle—E., P.
Carlin, James—P., T.

Cole, Ann—P., C., S., Des., T., L.
Lenson, Michael—P., E., L., W., Cr.
Sergeant, Edgar—P.

Oranges, The

Anderson, C. Stephen—Des., P.
Barber, Muriel V. (Mrs.)—P., C., S., T., Cr.
Canter, Albert M.—P., T.
Crocker, Dick—P.
Gasser, Henry Martin—P., Des., T., W., L.
Hunter, Graham—Cart., W.
Krebs, Columba (Mrs.)—P., W., I.
Lozowick, Louis—Pr. M., P., W., I., L.
Luffman, Charles E.—P.
Magrath, Edmund—Port. P.
Mueller, George Ludwig—P.
Sozio, Armando—P., T., Eng.
Thorward, Clara—P., C., Et., T.
Trowbridge, Gail—P., Lith., T.
Whittemore, Grace Conner (Mrs.)—P.
Wilson, Harriet (Mrs.)—P.

Passaic

Bonar, Henry—Des.
Cowdrey, Mary Bartlett—Hist., W., Cr., Mus. Dir., Archivist

Paterson

Benz, Otto Charles—Des., P., L.
di Benedetto, Angelo—P., C.
Dodds, Peggy—P., W., L.
Tiffany, Marguerite Bristol—P., E., C., L.

Peapack

Alain, D. A.—Cart., W., I.

Pitman

Crowther, Robert W.—I.

Pittstown

Marsh, Anne Steele (Mrs.)—P., Gr., T., C.

Plainfield

De Leeuw, Cateau—W., L., P., I.
Garrett, Adams Wirt—P.
Hoyt, Robert Townsend—Cart., Comm. A., W.
Reiber, Cora Sarah (Mrs.)—P., Des.
Simpson-Middleman—P., T.
Taylor, Rosemary—C.

Pompton Lakes

Seckar, Alvena Vajda—P., W.

Princeton

Brown, Joseph—S., E.
Davis, James Edward—Film-Maker, S., P., E.
Delarue, Allison—W.
de Tolnay, Charles—E., W.
De Wald, Ernest Theodore—Mus. Dir., E.
Ettl, Alex J.—S., Des.
Garnsey, Julian Ellsworth—P.
Green, Rosalie B.—Hist., E.
Greenbaum, Dorothea S.—S.
Harlow, Robert Elsing, Jr.—P., Ser., C., W.
Homer, William Innes—E., Mus. Cur., W.
Jones, Frances Follin—Asst. to Mus. Dir., Cur.
Lee, Rensselaer Wright—E., L.
Meiss, Millard—E., W.
Morris, Dudley Henry, Jr.—P., Lith., I., W., T.

Patterson, Howard Ashman—P., Lith., Des., T.
Seitz, William Chapin—P., W., E., L.
Thompson, Dorothy Burr (Mrs.)—Arch., W., L.
Tribble, Dagmar Haggstrom—P.

Rahway

Davis, Elisabeth Logan (Mrs.)—P., W., L.

Ramsey

De Baun, Etta V.—P.

Red Bank

Brzostoski—P., Gr., T., L., Mus. Consultant
Gray, William J.—Comm. A., T., W., Des.
Jones, Arthur Sidney H.—P.
Murray, Alexander—P., I.
Pohl, Lavera Ann (Mrs.)—P., W., L.

Ridgefield

Wilson, Ben—P., T.

Riverton

Anderson, Claude J. K.—P., W.

River Vale

Collier, Nathan Leo—Cart., W.

Roosevelt

Prestopino, Gregorio—P., T.
Shahn, Ben—P., I., Ser., L.

Rutherford

Mitchell, George Bertrand—P., W., L., I.

Saddle River

Gaugler, Joseph P.—P., Des., T., W., L.
Quanchi, Leo—P.

Scotch Plains

Simpson, Maxwell Stewart—P.

Ship Bottom

Blain, Julia—T., P., C., L.

Short Hills

Cushing, George—Indst. Des., L., T.
Greenleaf, Esther (Mrs.)—P., C., T.
Shirley, Alfaretta Donkersloat—C., S., T.
Whittemore, Margaret Evelyn—W., Gr., I.

Shrewsbury

Morris, George Ford—P., W., S., I., Gr.

Sparta

Giacomantonio, A. A.—S.

Stockton

Davison, Austin L.—Decorative Des., I., T.
Laszlo, George—Et., Lith., P., L.

Stone Harbor

Gabriele, Gabrielle (Mrs.)—P., C.

Summit

Bugbird, Mary Bayne (Mrs.)—P., T.
Crawford, Lesley—P., Lith.
Davis, Gerald Vivian—P., E.
Stromsted, Alf Jorgen—P., T.

Sussex

Greenbowe, Frederick Douglas—P.

Teaneck

Borzemsky, Bohdan—P.
Cafarelli, Michele A.—P.
Condit, Eleanor Louise (Mrs.)—Mus. Supervisor
Girona, Julio—P.
Rosen, Esther Yovits—P.
Weill, Erna—S., C., T.

Tenafly

Price, George—Cart.
Versen, Kurt—Des.
Wilcox, R. Turner—P., I., W.

Trenton

Bradshaw, George A.—Et., P., T.
Dey, Maurice Robert—Pr. M., C., S., P.
Fell, Amy Watson Wells—P., Des., L., T., Gr.
Greywacz, Kathryn Burch—Mus. Dir.
Holmes, Frank Graham, Jr.—P.
Jamieson, Bernice Evelyn—Mus. Asst. Cur., Des., Eng., Ser., I., L., P.
Remlinger, Joseph J.—P.
Von Erdberg, Joan Prentice—Mus. Cur.

Upper Montclair

Melville, Marguerite Louise—P.
Newhall, Adelaide—P.

Ventnor

de Hellebranth, Bertha—S., P.
de Hellebranth, Elena Maria—P., T., L., W., Cr.

Waldwick

Kerr, James Wilfrid—P., L.

Washington

MacLeary, Bonnie—S.

Wayne

Notaro, Anthony—S.

Wenonah

Van Dyke, Ella Tuthill—P., E., L.

West Englewood

Bressler, Harry S.—P., L.

Westfield

Allen, Josephine L. (Mrs.)—Former Mus. Cur.
Budell, Ada—P., I.
Budell, Emily Hortense—P.
de Camp, Harold Sydney—P., C.
Finck, Hazel (Mrs.)—P.
Hall, Edith E. (Mrs.)—P.
Hanan, Harry—Cart.

West New York

Zaccone, Fabian F.—P., Des., Lith., T., L.

Westwood

Burns, Paul Callan—P., Des., I., Comm. A.
Saslow, Herbert—P.

Woodbury

Adams, Florence Bowman—E., P., L.

Wyckoff

Greene, Vernon Van Atta—Cart., L., T.

NEW MEXICO

Abiquiu

O'Keeffe, Georgia—P.

Alamogordo

Shoesmith, Mark—S.

Albuquerque

Abbey, Rita Deanin—P.
Adams, Kenneth Miller—P., Lith., E.
Douglass, Ralph Waddell—E., P., Gr., Des., Cart.
Garver, Jack—P., T.
Goldman, Herbert—S., C., T.
Haas, Lez L.—P., E.
Jonson, Raymond—P., Gal. Dir.
Kercheville, Christina (Mrs.)—P., C., T.
Murphey, Mimi—S., C.
O'Hara, James Frederick—Gr., P., E., L.
Pearce, Helen S. (Mrs.)—P., Des., I., T.
Smith, Sam—P., E., C., Des., I.
Sowers, Miriam R. (Mrs.)—P.
Tatschl, John—C., S., E., Gr.
Theis, Gladys Huling—S.
Von Auw, Emilie—P., S., C., Des., W., L.
Warder, William—P., W.

Alcalde

Hall, Arthur William—Et., P.
Hall, Norma Bassett—P., Eng.

Carlsbad

Mead, Roderick—Et., Eng., P., T.

Clovis

Cervantez, Pedro L.—P., Comm. A.

Espanola

Tedford, Elsie Mae (Mrs.)—P.

Gallup

O'Connor, John Gerard—P., Lith., Mus. Dir., Des.

Las Cruces

Barrick, Kenneth Roberts—P., E., I.
Shannon, Aileen Phillips (Mrs.)—P.

Las Vegas

Payant, Felix—W., L., E.

Mesilla Park

Weiss, Dorothea Patterson—P.

Montezuma

Schooley, Elmer Wayne—Lith., P., E.
Du Jardin, Gussie—P., S., Gr.

Ranchos de Taos

Cook, Howard—P., Gr., E., S., L.
Dasburg, Andrew Michael—P., T.
Latham, Barbara—P., Gr., I.
Rogoway, Alfred—P.

Roswell

Gebhard, David—Mus. Dir., E.
Nickson, Lia (Mrs.)—P., Ser., T.
Wiggins, Bill—P., T., S., Gr.

Sandoval P.O., Corrales

Black, Frederick Edward—P., Lith.

San Patricio

Gardner, Paul—Mus. Dir.
Hurd, Peter—P., W.
Meigs, John Liggett—P.
Wyeth, Henriette (Mrs.)—P.

Santa Fe

Bacigalupa, Andrea—P., C.
Bakos, Jozef G.—E., P.
Bakos, Teresa—P.
Baldridge, Cyrus Leroy—I., W., P.,
  Des., Gr.
Baumann, Gustave—Eng., P., C., W.
Boyd, E. (Miss)—W., Mus. Cur., P.,
  L.
Cassidy, Ina Sizer (Mrs.)—W., C., S.,
  T., L.
Chapman, Kenneth Milton—E., W., I.,
  L., P.
Davey, Randall—P., Et., Lith., E.
de Ghize, Eleanor—P.
Dutton, Bertha P.—Mus. Cur., E.,
  W., L.
Ellis, Fremont F.—P.
Ferdon, Edwin Nelson, Jr.—Assoc.
  Mus. Dir.
Fisher, Reginald—Mus. Dir., W., L.,
  E., Des.
Foster, Kenneth E.—Mus. Dir.
Goldman, Albert Martin—P.
Harvey, Laura Cornell (Mrs.)—P.
Hullenkremer, Odon—P., T.
Hurford, Miriam Story (Mrs.)—P.,
  Comm. A., I.
Jones, Hester—Mus. Cur.
Keener, Anna Elizabeth—P., Gr., E.
Larsson, Karl—P., S., Eng., I., T.
Lippincott, Janet—P.
Longley, Bernique—P., C.
Lumpkins, William Thomas—Des., P.,
  C., S.
Mauzy, Wayne L.—Mus. Dir.
Montoya, Geronima Cruz—P., T.
Morang, Dorothy Alden Clark—P.,
  Mus. Cur., C., Cr., W.
Naumer, Helmuth—P.
Nedwill, Rose—P., Et., I., T.
Newberry, Clare Turlay—W., I.
Parrott, Allen—Mus. Cur.
Rush, Olive—P.
Schlater, Katharine—P., I., Lith., Des.,
  L.
Schleeter, Howard Behling—P., C.,
  E., L.
Shonnard, Eugenie F.—S., C.
Shuster, Will—P., Gr., S.
Sims, Agnes—P., S.
Skolle, John—P., T., I., L.
Spencer, Mary Jones—P., Des., L.
Springer, Eva—P., Gr.
Stubbs, Stanley A.—Mus. Cur.
Tait, Agnes (Mrs.)—P., Lith., I.
Van Soelen, Theodore—P., Lith., W.
West, Harold E.—P., I., C., Des., Gr.
Wheelock, Warren Frank—P., S., C.,
  T., W.
Wiest, K. Van Elmendorf—P., T.,
  Comm. A., Des., I.
Young, Webb—P.

Silver City

Bittinger, Ross Thomas (Dr.)—E., C.

State College

Mannen, Paul William—P., E., L.

Taos

Bisttram, Emil—P., Des., L., T.
Blumenschein, Ernest Leonard—P., I.
Blumenschein, Helen Greene—P., I.
Boyer, Jack K.—Mus. Dir., Cur.
Brett, Dorothy Eugenie—P., W.
Dolmith, Rex—P., T., L.
Egri, Ted—S., P., L.
Fleck, Joseph Amadeus—P., Lith.
Gibberd, Eric Waters—P., T., L.
Heaton, William—P., S.
Hennings, E. Martin—P.
Hoffman, Frank B.—P., S., I.
Kaminsky, Dora (Mrs.)—Ser., P.,
  Des., C., L.
Kloss, Gene—Et., P.
Mandelman, Beatrice—P., Ser.
McAfee, Ila (Mrs.)—P., I.
Ray, Robert Donald—P., Gr.
Rednick, Hermen—P., Lith.
Reynolds, Charles Henry—P.
Ribak, Louis—P., T.
Spohn, Clay Edgar—P., T.

NEW YORK

Albany

Brooks, Erica May—L., P., C., Gr.,
  E.
Lathrop, Dorothy Pulis—I., W., Eng.,
  P.
Lathrop, Gertrude K.—S.
MacFarlane, Janet R.—Mus. Dir.,
  Hist., P.
Rosen, Hyman Joseph—Cart.
Rothstein, Elizabeth L.—P., T., Des.,
  L.
Schafer, Alice Pauline—Et., Eng.
Wright, Alice Morgan—S., W.

Alfred

Cushing, Val Murat—C., T.
Ekdahl, Kurt—E., C.
Harder, Charles Mabry—C., Des., E.
Klitzke, Theodore E.—E.
Randall, Theodore A.—Cr., E., S.
Rhodes, Daniel—E., C.
Rhodes, Lillyan (Mrs.)—S.
Turner, Robert C.—Ceramic C.

Allaben

Swenson, Valerie—P.

Almond

Phelan, Linn Lovejoy—C., Des., T.

Altamont

Cowley, Edward P.—E., P.

Annandale-on-Hudson

Hirsch, Stefan—E., P., Gr., L.

Auburn

Long, Walter Kinscella—Mus. Dir.,
  P., S., Des., T.

Aurora

Rusk, William Sener—E.

Ausable Forks

Kent, Rockwell—Eng., Lith., P., I.,
  W., L.

Batavia

Mason, Roy Martell—P., I.

Bearsville

Burke, E. Ainslie—P.
Klitgaard, Georgina—P.
Siegel, Adrian—P., Photog.
Varian, Dorothy—P.

Bedford Hills

Johnson, Tom Loftin—P., Des., E.,
  Arch.

Blauvelt

Gorsline, Douglas Warner—P., I., Gr.,
  T.
Hoyt, Whitney Ford—P.
Leber, Roberta McVeigh—C., T.
Orb, Ovan John Carbone—S., P., L.,
  T., C.

Blue Mountain Lake

Inverarity, Robert Bruce—
  Des., Mus. Dir.

Bolton Landing

Smith, David—S., Eng.

Boston

Bradley, Charles B.—E., W., L., C.,
  P.

Boston Corners

Helck, C. Peter—I., P., Gr., T.

Brewster

Amateis, Edmond—S., E., W.
Karasz, Mariska—C., Des., W.
Varga, Margit—W., P.

Briarcliff Manor

Whitmore, Coby—I.

Bronxville

Angelo, Valenti—I., Eng., Des., P., S.,
  W.
Arnheim, Rudolf—E., W.
Brown, Elmore J.—P., I.
Craig, Nancy Ellen—P.
Mawicke, Tran—I., P.
McKean, Robert—Indst. Des.
Neuwirth, Morris—Des., Comm. A.,
  P.
Nichols, Hobart—P.
Phoenix, Lauros Monroe—P., E.,
  Des., L.
Poucher, Elizabeth Morris—S., Lith.
Price, Alice Hendee (Mrs.)—P.
Price, Chester B.—I., Et.
Rojankovsky, Feodor Stepanovich—I.
Seckler, Dorothy Gees—Cr., T., L.
Sterrett, Cliff—Cart.
Wiley, Hugh Sheldon—P.

Brooklyn

Albert, Calvin—S., E.
Alpert, Alexander—P.
Ames, Lee J.—I.
Annus, Augustus—P., E., Des.
Aunio, Irene (Mrs.)—P.
Baumbach, Harold—P.
Beerman, Herbert—P., L.
Blass, Charlotte L.—P.
Blatt, Louis—P., T.
Boog, Carle Michel—P., I.
Bove, Richard John—P., Et., E.
Bower, Helen Lane—P., Des.
Casarella, Edmond—E., Pr. M.
Castellon, Federico—P., Gr., I., T., L.
Chanase, Dane—P., Eng.
Childs, George Henshaw—C., P.,
  Cart., W.

Christ-Janer, Albert William—E., W., P.
Comito, Nicholas U.—P., Lith., T.
Cosgrove, John O'Hara, II—I., P., Gr., W.
Cramer, Abraham—Cart., Comm. A., P.
Crichlow, Ernest—I., P., Lith., T.
Crossgrove, Roger Lynn—P., E.
Csoka, Stephen—Et., P., E.
d'Andrea, Albert Philip—E., S., Eng.
De'Prey, Juan—P., Muralist
Dubin, Ralph—P., Gr., T.
Ericson, Eric—Cart.
Felix, Franz—Port. P.
Fessenden, DeWitt Harvey—Et., P., Des., W., Cr.
Fife, Mary E. (Mrs.)—P., T.
Fjelde, Paul—S., E.
Flory, Gaylord—P., T.
Frederick, Carroll Glenn—Cart.
Freilicher, Hy—S., C., T.
Geltman, Lily—P.
Gerberg, Morris—Cart., P.
Gordon, John—Mus. Cur.
Grebanier, Joseph Philip—C., T.
Griswold, Virginia—P.
Guerin, Joseph—P.
Gurr, Lena—P., Ser., Lith.
Hahn, Joseph Frederic—P.
Hoyer, Frans—P.
Jackson, Ella F. (Mrs.)—P., Gr., T.
Johnson, Una E.—Mus. Cur., W.
Jones, Nell Choate—P.
Kallweit, Helmut G.—P., S., Des.
Kamen, Samuel—P.
Kathe, Betty Kathryn Bernstein—P., Lith., L.
Kaz, Nathaniel—S., T.
Keck, Sheldon—Conservator
Kellner, Mary—S.
Khouri, Alfred—P., L., T.
Kienzle, George Vincent—Comm. A.
Kish, Maurice—P.
Klein, Frank Anthony—S., C.
Kupferman, Murray—P., C., T.
Lawrence, Jacob—P., I.
Leff, Rita—P., Pr. M.
Lerner, Abe—Book Des., A. Dir.
Leventhal, Ethel S.—P., Lith.
Levinson, Fred—Cart., Comm. A.
Lieber, Hugh Gray—E., P., I., W.
Lubin, Jack—P., T.
Lush, Vivian—S.
MacDonald, Robert H.—Des., Comm. A., I.
Macsoud, Nicholas S.—P.
Marans, Moissaye (Mr.)—S., L., T.
Mayhew, Richard—P., I.
McEntee, Dorothy Layng—E., I., P., Des.
Megargee, Lawrence A.—Animal I.
Menken, Marie—P., C.
Mitnitzky, Herman—P.
Morse, Jennie Greene (Mrs.)—E., Des., P., C.
Moscon, Hannah—P.
Nichols, Edith L.—P., W., C., T.
Peck, Augustus—E.
Pickering, Simeon Horace—P., I., L., Comm. A., Hist.
Pierotti, John—Cart.
Ranson, Nancy Sussman (Mrs.)—P., Ser.
Reinman, Paul—P., I., Cart., Comm. A.
Richmond, Agnes M.—P.
Rose, Dorothy—P.
Rosenson, Olga—P., Et.
Rothbort, Samuel—P., S., W., L.
Rothman, Joseph—P.
Sanders, Adam A.—S., W., T., P.
Scharff, Constance Kramer—P., Pr. M.
Schenck, Edgar C.—Mus. Dir.
Schucker, Charles—P., T.
Schwartz, Marvin David—Mus. Cur.
Shuff, Lily (Mrs.)—P., Eng.
Spencer, Leontine G.—P., T.
Stackel, Alle—S., P., T.
Starkweather, William Edward Bloomfield—P., W., L., T.

Stevenson, Beulah—P., Lith.
Stone, Stanford Byron—P., Des., I.
Svoboda, Vincent A.—P., Cart.
Taylor, Ruth P.—P., Gr., E.
Tinkelman, Murray Herbert—P.
Tooker, George—P.
Trommer, Marie—W., Cr., P., T.
Trunk, Herman, Jr.—P.
Turney, Winthrop Duthie—P.
Viesulas, Romas—P., Et., Lith.
Volovich, Iakov—P., T.
Von Wicht, John—P., Gr., Des.
Wahl, Bernhard O.—P.
Walkowitz, Abraham—P., Gr., I.
Yamamoto, Taro—P.
Zorach, Marguerite Thompson—P., C.
Zorach, William—S., P., W., T., L.

Buffalo

Anderson, John K.—S., P., Arch., Des.
Cuthbert, Virginia (Mrs.)—P., T., Cr., Comm. A.
Doub, Janet Ann (Mrs.)—Tex. Des., Gr., P., E.
Elliott, Philip Clarkson—P., E.
Friedman, William—Des., E., Mus. Cur.
Henrich, Mrs. Jean MacKay—S., T., L., P.
Hoffman, Ruth Erb (Mrs.)—P., S., E.
Howe, Beatrice—Asst. Mus. Dir.
Johnt, Ethel (Mrs.)—P., T.
Knapp, Frank De Villo—Indst. I., Des., P.
Langenbach, Clara Emma—P.
O'Callahan, Kevin B.—Des., Gr., C.
Richter, Julius—P., Eng., L., Et.
Roche, Leo Joseph—Cart.
Sawyer, Esther Hoyt (Mrs.)—P., Gr.
Shanks, Bruce McKinley—Editorial Cart.
Smith, Gordon Mackintosh—Mus. Dir.
Szabo, Laszlo—Port. P., T., L.

Camillus

Trimm, George Lee—P., I.

Canaan

Jacobsson, Edward Gustave—P., T., Des.

Carmel

Kainz, Martin—P., Lith.
Lee, Robert J.—P., Des., Cart., I., T., Comm. A.

Cazenovia

Bailey, Merrill A.—P., T.
Jenney, Priscilla Burg—P., E., W.

Chappaqua

Aucello, Salvatore L.—P., S., C., Des.
Fagg, Kenneth S.—I., P., Comm. A.
Reibel, Bertram—Wood Engraver, Gr., S.

Chatham

Trimm, H. Wayne—I.

Chazy

Dossert, Norma Barton (Mrs.)—Des., C., P.
Lefevre, Lawrence E.—P.

Clinton

Palmer, William C.—P., L., E.
Penney, James—P.
Sauter, Willard J.—E., P., Des., Comm. A., L.

Cold Spring

Nordmark, Olof E.—P., Gr., W., T.

Cooperstown

Oudin, Dorothy Savage—P.
Rath, Frederick L., Jr.—Hist., Mus. Dir., L., W.

Corning

Brown, James M., III—Mus. Dir.
Buechner, Thomas S.—Mus. Dir.
Perrot, Paul N.—Asst. Mus. Dir.
Von Manikowski, Boles—P., Des., S.

Cortland

Olcott, Lillia Morwick—P., W., E., Des., L.

Cragsmoor

Buttrick, Sue Kingsland (Mrs.)—C., L., Des.

Craryville

Bate, Stanley—P., Gr.

Crestwood

Eaton, Allen Hendershott—W., E., L.

Cross River

Smith, Lawrence Beall—P., I., Lith., Comm. A.

Croton Falls

Pratt, Dudley—S.

Croton-on-Hudson

Biddle, George—P., S., Gr., W., Cr., L.
Birnbaum, Abe—P., Cart., I.
Dehner, Dorothy (Mrs.)—P., Pr. M.
Gropper, William—P., Lith., I., W.
Harari, Hananiah—P., I., Ser.
Sardeau, Helene (Mrs.)—S.

Delmar

Christensen, Ethel Madill (Mrs.)—P., T.

Dobbs Ferry

Borgatta, Isabel Case—S.
Borgatta, Robert E.—P., E.
Butler, Joseph Thomas—Mus. Cur., W.
Rothschild, Lincoln—S., P., W., E., L.
Lissim, Simon—P., Des., E., I., L.

Eagle Bridge

Moses, Anna Mary Robertson—P.

East Aurora

Jennings, Rixford—P., Adv. Des., Et., T.
Price, Margaret Evans—I., W., P.
Rohrbach, Charles—Comm. A., Des., P., C.
Stewart, Marion Louise—P.

East Chatham

Carroll, John—P.

Eastchester

Halper, Estelle L. (Mrs.)—C., Des., S., E., L.

Ebenezer

Gundlach, Helen Fuchs (Mrs.)—P., C., S.

Elmira

Anderson, Ernfred—S., Mus. Dir., E., L., P.
Bjorvand, Helen H. (Mrs.)—T., I.
Bridaham, Lester B.—Mus. Dir., W., E., L., P., Eng.
Fox, Roy C.—Et., Eng., P.
Nordgren, Oke Gustaf—P.

Elmsford

Kidd, Steven R.—P., I., W.

Endicott

Lindsay, Kenneth C.—E., W., L.

Fairport

Havens, James Dexter—Gr., P.
Peters, Carl W.—P.

Fishkill

Grossmann, Edwin Booth—P.
Mayer, Louis—S., P., T., Cr., W., L.

Fort Edward

Porter, Laura Schaefer (Mrs.)—P., E.

Fredonia

De Vinney, Laura Laurett—E., P., C., Gr., L.

Gardenville

Burchfield, Charles E.—P.

Garrison

Locke, Charles Wheeler—P., Gr., Cart., I.

Geneva

Wood, Eloise—Et., P., E., L.

Glens Falls

Dodge, Joseph Jeffers—P., Mus. Cur., Cr., W., L., T.

Grand Island

Dyczkowski, Eugene M.—P., Des., Cart., I., T.

Grandview-on-Hudson

Dalton, Peter—S.
Hader, Elmer Stanley—I., W.

Groton

Colby, Victor—E., S.

Hamburg

Valentine, Francis B.—P., T., Comm. A., L., I.

Harmon

Schus, Adolph—Cart.

Harpursville

Hamlin, Genevieve Karr—S., T., C., L.

Harrison

Roberts, Morton—P., I., T.

Hartsdale

Miller, Marshall Dawson—I.

Hastings-on-Hudson

Begg, John Alfred—S., P., Des.
Bohnert, Henry—P., I., Comm. A., T.
Bohnert, Herbert—Port. P., T.
Bohnert, Rosetta (Mrs.)—P., W., T.
Freedman, Maurice—P.
Howe, Gertrude Herrick—I., P.
Kammerer, Herbert Lewis—S.
Kipp, Lyman E., Jr.—S.
Moser, Frank H.—P., Cart., I., T.
Riesenberg, Sidney—P., I., T.

Haverstraw

Taubes, Frederic—P., Et., Lith., W., L., E., Cr.

Holland

Blair, Robert N.—P., S., Gr., E., I.

Hopewell Junction

Attardi, Thomas—P., T.
Schnitzler, Max—P.

Houghton

Ortlip, Aimee E. (Mrs.)—P., E.
Ortlip, H. Willard—P., E.

Hyde Park

Pearson, Edwin—S., P., C., Des., T.

Irvington-on-Hudson

Adams, Walter Langley—P., L., E.
Sheeler, Charles—P.

Ithaca

Abbe, Elfriede Martha—S., Gr., I.
Daly, Norman David—P., E.
Finlayson, Donald Lord—E.
Hartell, John Anthony—P., T.
Mahoney, James Owen—P., E.
Solomon, Alan Robert—Mus. Dir., E.
Squier, Jack—E., S.
True, Virginia—E., P.
Waage, Frederick O.—E.

Jamestown

Trimm, Adon—P.

Katonah

Abrahams, Joseph B.—Des., Gr., I., W.
Baur, John I. H.—Assoc. Mus. Dir., L., W.
Park, Madeleine F.—S.
Roesch, Kurt Ferdinand—P., Et., Eng., T., I.

Kenmore

Czurles, Stanley A.—E., P., W., L., Des., Et.

Kingsbridge

Kughler, William Francis Vandeveer—P.

Kingston

Berardinelli, Dennis—P., T., Eng., I.

Lackawanna

Dlugosz, Louis Frank—S.

La Grangeville

Whitmer, Helen C.—P.

Lake Mahopac

Meltzer, Anna Elkan—P., T.

Larchmont

Allen, James E.—Et., Lith., P.
Fitzgerald, Edmond James—P.
Richard, Betti—S.
Schwarm, Wesley A.—P.

Lewiston

Gay, Ruth A. (Mrs.)—S., P., T.

LONG ISLAND

Amagansett

Prohaska, Ray—I., P.

Amityville

Dillon, John Knox—P.

Astoria

Mommer, Peter Paul—P.

Babylon

Mohn, Sigvard M.—P., Et.

Bayside

Goldstein, Milton—Et., P., T., L.

Beechhurst

Altvater, Cathy (Mrs.)—P.

Belle Harbor

Blackman, Leonard—P., Des., T., L.

Bethpage

Vagis, Polygnotos—S.

Brookhaven

Quastler, Gertrude (Mrs.)—Pr. M., P.
Rea, Gardner—Cart.

Centerport

Fasbender, Walter—Mus. Exec. Dir.

Cold Spring Harbor

Davenport, Jane (Mrs.)—P., S., T., C., I.

Douglaston

Altson, Louise—Port. P.
Farndon, Walter—P.
Preston, H. Malcolm—P., E.

East Hampton

De Pauw, Victor—P., C., Lith., W.
Johnson, Buffie—P.
Little, John—P.
Moran, Edward—Et., P.
Schoch, Pearl—P.
Whipple, Enez (Mrs.)—A. Dir.

East Marion

Stamos, Theodoros—P., T., I., Des.

East Meadow

Terken, John Raymond—S., T., L.

East Norwich

Netter, Frank H.—Medical I.

East Williston

Lewis, Cyril Arthur—P., Des., L.

Elmhurst

Elskus, Albinas—P., Des., C.
Recca, George—P., Comm. A.

Elmont

Rogers, John—P., I., T., L.

Flushing

Baranik, Rudolf—P.
Bergere, Richard—P., Des., W.
Cheney, Warren—S., W., L., E., Cr.
Cooper, Brother Etienne—S., P., T.
Hirsch, David W.—Cart.
Hoffmann, Arnold, Jr.—P., Des., I.,
    Comm. A.
Lees, Harry Hanson—I.
Muniak, Helen—P.
O'Meara, Mae—P., T., S., L.
Ornstein, Jacob Arthur—P., W., L.,
    E.
Reiss, Lee (Mrs.)—P.
Sievan, Maurice—P., T.
Stevens, May—P.
Warsaw, Albert Taylor—P., Des.,
    Lith.
Wolfe, Jack D.—C., Des., T., L.

Forest Hills

Catan-Rose, Richard—P., T., Et., S.,
    Lith., L., I.
Clark, G. Fletcher—S.
Freeman, A. Albert—Des., E., W., L.
Hasselriis, Malthe C. M.—P., I.,
    Comm. A.
Langton, Berenice (Mrs.)—S.
Lombardo, Josef Vincent—E., P., W.,
    L.
Noback, Gustave Joseph—S., E., L.
Ostrowsky, Abbo—P., Et., T.
Rostand, Michel—P.
Sharp, William—P., Et., Lith., I.
Sterinbach, Natalie—P.
Vermes, Madelaine—C.
Walker, Hudson D.—Art Specialist

Freeport

Lariar, Lawrence—Cart., I., W.,
    Editor, S.
Rowan, Frances—P., Gr., T.
Sparling, John Edmond—I., Cart., P.,
    S.

Fresh Meadows

Shapiro, Frank D.—P.

Garden City

Kelley, Albert S.—E.

Glen Cove

Bastian, Rufus A.—P., Et., Lith., T.,
    W.
Sternberg, Harry—P., Gr., T., L., Des.

Great Neck

Auchmoody, Elaine Plishker—P., L.
Blair, Lee E.—P., Des.
Bodkin, Sally Grosz—S.
Filmus, Tully (Mr.)—P., L., T.
Harvey, Jacqueline—P.
Hermansader, John B.—P., Des.
Marein, Edmund—Des., T.
Miller, Martha Weinberg—P., C., T.
Roston, Arnold—Des., P., E., W.
Sarnoff, Arthur—I., Comm. A.
Seeman, James—P., Des., Ser.
Seide, Charles—P., T., L., W.
Seidler, Doris—P., Et., Eng.
Van Buren, Raeburn—I., Cart., L.
Weber, Max—P.

Greenport

Hubbard, Whitney Myron—P., T.
Wengenroth, Stow—Lith.

Hampton Bays

Burliuk, David—P., L., W.

Hempstead

Hornung, Clarence Pearson—Des., I.,
    W.

Hollis

Harris, Alexandrina Robertson—Min.
    P.
Mayer, Fred A.—I.
Olsen, Harry Emil—P., I.

Huntington

Boardman, Rosina Cox—Min. P.
Callery, Mary—S.
Engel, Michael Martin, II—P., Des.,
    Lith., W.
Glarner, Fritz—P.
Grudin, Shim—P.
Smith, Albert Delmont—P.

Jackson Heights

Berdanier, Paul F., Sr.—Cart., P., Et.
Bettelheim, Jolan Gross—P., Et., Lith.
Chamberlin, Helen—I., P.
De Pol, John—Pr. M., I., Des.
Dolbin, B. F.—P., I., W., Cart., Cr.
Fliegel, Leslie—P., T., L.
Kappel, R. Rose (Mrs.)—P., Des., I.,
    Et., T., Lith., Comm. A.
Morpurgo, Vilna Jorgen—P., S., T.,
    W.
Neafie, Edith S.—P., T.
Reilly, Mildred A.—P.
Schmeidler, Blanche J.—P., Gr., Des.
Sennhauser, John—P., T.
Suozzi, Constantin N.—Cart.
Tishler, Harold—Des., C.
Wasserman, Albert—P., Des., T.
Whitney, Edgar A.—P., T., W., L.

Jamaica

Donato, Louis Nicholas—P., Des., T.
Eliasoph, Paula—P., Gr., C., W., L.,
    T.
Freigang, Paul—C.
Jonynas, Vytautas K.—P., Des., Gr.,
    T.
Liberts, Ludolfs—P., Des., E.
Rannit, Aleksis—E., Hist., Cr., W.
Shannon, Howard J.—I., W., P.
Tschamber, Hellmuth George—P., T.,
    Comm. A.

Kew Gardens

Englander, Gertrud—C., T.
Schultheiss, Carl Max—Et., Eng., I.,
    P.
Yaron, Alexander A.—P., Comm. A.,
    I.

Kings Point

d'Andrea, Bernard L.—I., Comm. A.
Fox, Lorraine D'Andrea—
    Comm. A., I.
Frankle, Philip—P., I., T., L.

Lattingtown Harbor

Lippold, Richard—S., E., Des.

Laurelton

Hoerger, D. Adelbert—Des., P.

Lawrence

Lichtenberg, Manes—P., T.

Levittown

Hoehn, Harry—P., Des., Gr.

Locust Valley

Gates, John Monteith—Arch. Des.
Rogalski, Walter—Pr. M., C., T.

Long Island City

Allen, Charles—T., Comm. A., Cart.
de Gerenday, Laci—S.
Klein, Isidore—Cart., P.
Quattrochi, Edmondo—S.
Schwarzburg, Nathaniel—P., L., T.
Sitton, John Melza—P., Gr., Des.,
    W., L., E.
Soriano, Esteban—P., C., Des., Cart.,
    Comm. A., I.
Sowinski, Jan—S., P.
Stone, Allen—P., T., L.
Weindorf, Arthur—P., I., T.

Lynbrook

Madsen, Viggo Holm—P., T., Lith.
Phillips, Melville A.—P., T., Comm.
    A., I.
Saxe, Carolyn N.—P., T., L., Des.

Malverne

Rebajes, Francisco—C., Des., T.

Manhasset

Fogarty, Frank Joseph—
    Cart., Des., P.
Petersen, Eugen H.—E., P., Des.,
    Comm. A., I., L.
Spierer, William McK.—
    Des., T., P., L.

Maspeth

Schor, Rhea Iress—P., S., W.

Massapequa

Celentano, Daniel Ralph—P., Des.
Pepi, Vincent—Des., P.

Montauk

Greene, Balcomb—P., E.

Mount Sinai

Olds, Sara Whitney (Mrs.)—
    Port P., T.
Zoeller, Robert Fredric—P.

New Hyde Park

Goldberg, Robert I.—Indst. Des., E.,
    W., L.
Kramer, Shirley—T., P., L., Des., C.

Northport

Baumhofer, Walter M.—I., P.,
    Comm. A.
Floherty, John J., Jr.—I., Comm. A.,
    Des., Cart., P.
Lewicki, James—I., P., Des., T.
Twardowicz, Stanley—P., T.

Oakdale

White, Jacob Caupel—Des., P., Et.,
    I., Comm. A.

Oakland Gardens

Wade, Claire E. (Mrs.)—P., T.

Orient

Davis, William Steeple—P., Gr.

Oyster Bay

Golinkin, Joseph Webster—P., Lith.

Ozone Park

Shepard, Gilbert C.—P.
Wilson, Rowland—Cart.

Peconic

Wiles, Gladys—P.

Plainview

Liberi, Dante—P., I.

Plandome Manor

Miller, Barse—P., E.
Mullin, Willard—Cart.

Port Washington

Cooper, Mario—P., S., E., I.
Kleinholz, Frank—P., T.
Kubach, Allen Edward—
    P., Lith., Des., T.
Mayer, Peter Bela—P.
Ronay, Stephen R.—P., Comm. A., I.
Taggart, George Henry—Port. P.
Withers, Loris Alvin—P., Des., T.

Queens Village

Allston, George Alcorn—P., Et.
Henkel, August—Ser., Cart., P.

Rego Park

Aronson, Irene—Des., P., Gr., T.
Tobias, Abraham Joel—
    P., S., Lith., W., L.
Winter, Ruth—P.

Riverhead

Fanning, Ralph—E., W., L., P.

Rockaway Beach

Kochmeister, Samuel—P.
Lorne, Naomi—P., W., L.

Rockville Centre

Day, Robert James—Cart.
Merrylen—Cart.

Roslyn

Fredman, Harry Homer—
    Comm. A., I.
Glannon, Edward J.—P., T.

Roslyn Heights

Orling, Anne—P.

Sag Harbor

Brook, Alexander—P.
Knee, Gina (Mrs.)—P.

Saint Albans

Coppolino, Joseph—S., Des.
White, Walter Charles Louis—
    P., T., L.
Winkel, Nina—S.

Setauket

Beckwith, James—P., Des.
Bishop, Marjorie Cutler—P., T.
Koch, John—P.

Shelter Island

Mosca, August—P.

Shoreham

Dennis, Burt Morgan—
    Et., I., W., L., P.

Smithtown Branch

Burr, Frances—Port. P., I.

South Farmingdale

Elias, Leopold—Cart., I., T.

Sunnyside

Beach, Sara Berman—P., Lith.
Dahlin, Ed—Cart.
Mankowski, Bruno—S., P., C.

Syosset

Griscom, Lloyd C.—P.
Talbot, Grace Helen—S.

Valley Stream

Trifon, Harriette—P., T.

Wading River

Wallace, Lucy (Mrs.)—
    P., C., Des., T.

Westbury

Cronbach, Robert M.—S., E., L.
Howell, Douglass Morse—
    C., P., Et., Eng., Hist., W., L.
Murray, Harold Paul—P., T.

Whitestone

Burchess, Arnold—P., T., Comm. A.
De Cesare, Sam—P., S., C., T.

Woodhaven

Rupprecht, George—I., Des.

Woodside

Amoroso, Anthony—P., T.
Barrer, Gertrude Russell—P., C.
De Filippo, Antonio—S.
Fax, Elton Clay—I.
Russell, Frank John—
    P., C., Comm. A.

Wyandanch

Springweiler, Erwin Frederick—S., C.

NEW YORK STATE
(Contd.)

Mamaroneck

Berni, Alan—Indst. Des.
Connery, Ruth McGrath—P., T., L.
Kent, Norman—Eng., P., W., L.,
    Des.
Samstag, Gordon—P., I., T., L.
Sloan, Robert Smullyan—P.

Manlius

Beck, George Anthony—Indst. Des.

Mechanicsville

Quinn, Robert Hayes—
    I., Gr., W., Comm. A.

Middletown

Ericson, Beatrice—P.
Parker, Roy D.—P.
Walling, Anna M.—
    C., P., Des., T., L.

Mohegan Lake

West, Pennerton—P., C., S., Et.

Montgomery

Seredy, Kate—W., I.

Mount Kisco

Bonn, Marion—S., C., T.
Burton, Netta M.—
    P., C., T., Des., Gr.
Haas, Clara (Mrs.)—P.
Hocker, Trew—P., Des., Gr.
Jones, Amy—P., I., T., L.
Kenyon, Norman—P., I., Comm. A.
Liebman, Aline Meyer (Mrs.)—P.

Mount Vernon

Brown, Aaron I.—P.
Caplane, Felice—P.
D'Amico, Victor E.—E., W., L.
Fenton, John Nathaniel—P.
Gilchrist, Agnes Addison (Mrs.)—
    Arch. Hist., W., L.
Horne, Laura Trevitte—P., Des.
Kleinbardt, Ernest—P., L.
Lewis, Ruth—P.
Seliger, Charles—P., Des., T.
Van Hook, Nell—P., S., C.
Weger, Marie—P.
Zibelli, Thomas A.—Cart.

Newburgh

Desmond, Alice Curtis (Mrs.)—
    W., P.
Jackson, Hazel Brill—S., Eng.
Waugh, Coulton—P., Cart., W.

New City

Caniff, Milton A.—Cart., I., W., L.
Corcos, Lucille—P., I., Des., Cart.
Simon, Sidney—P., T., S.

New Paltz

Bolotowsky, Ilya—P., T.
Wickiser, Ralph Lewanda—
    P., W., L., E., Gr.

New Rochelle

Beall, Cecil Calvert—
    I., P., S., Des., Comm. A., W., L.
Beling, Helen (Mrs.)—S., T., L.
Conant, Howard S.—E., W., L., P.
Dodds, Robert E.—P., T., W., L.
Fleischmann, Glen—I.
Herman, Vic—Cart., Des., I., W.
Humphrey, Walter Beach—I., P., T.
Kinghan, Charles R.—
    P., Comm. A., I., T.
Lantz, Michael—S.
Samerjan, George E.—Des., P., T., L.,
    S.
Schaeffler, Lizbeth—
    S., P., T., Comm. A.
Spencer, Jean—P.
Spidell, Enid Jean—P., E.
Thompson, Ernest Thorne—
    Et., Lith., P., E.
Winter, Lumen Martin—
    P., Des., I., Gr., S.
Yammerino, Aurelio James—P., T.

New York City

Abadi, Fritzie—P., Gr.
Abbot, Edith R.—E., L., P., W.

Abracheff, Ivan—E., L., P.
Abracheff, Nicolai—E., W., L., P.
Abrams, Ruth—P.
Adams, Harriet Dyer—I., L.
Addams, Charles—Cart.
Ades, Hal—P., I., Comm. A., E.
Adler, Samuel M.—P., E., L.
Agha, Mehemed Fehmy—Des., W., L.
Ahlskog, Sirkka—C., T., S.
Alajalov, Constantin—I., P.
Alber, Rose—P., T., Des.
Albrecht, Frederick E.—P., I.
Alegre, A. Villamor—P., I.
Alexander, Christine—Mus. Cur., W., L.
Allen, Junius—P.
Allen, Patricia—P., S., T., Gr., W.
Alston, Charles Henry—P., S., T.
Ambellan, Harold—S., Indst. Des.
Amen, Irving—Eng. P., S.
Amino, Leo—S., Des., T.
Amore, John—S., E.
Andrus, Vincent D.—Mus. Cur.
Angel, Rifka—P.
Angelo, Nicholas Joseph—P., Comm. A.
Ansbacher, Jessie—P., T.
Appel, Jack—S.
Archipenko, Alexander—S., T., L.
Arens, Egmont—Indust. Des., E., W., L.
Arnest, Bernard Patrick—P.
Arno, Peter—Cart.
Aronson, Boris—P., Des., Gr., I., W.
Aronson, Joseph—Des. W., L.
Asch, Stan—Cart., L.
Ascher, Mary G. (Mrs.)—P.
Atkin, Mildred Tommy (Mrs.)—P.
Atkins, David—P., Lith., L.
Austin, Darrel—P.
Avery, Frances—P., T.
Avery, Milton—P.
Avery, Myrtilla—Museum Dir., E.
Avlon-Daphnis, Helen—P., T.
Ayer, Margaret—I.
Babcock, Elizabeth Jones (Mrs.)—P.
Bach, Richard Franz—Edu. Dir., T., L., W.
Bachrach, Gladys Wertheim—P.
Bacon, Peggy Brook—P., Gr., I., W., Cart.
Baehr, Francine (Mrs.)—P.
Baer, Howard—P., I., Cart.
Bageris, John—P., T.
Bahnc, Salcia—P., Lith., I., T.
Baizerman, Saul—P.
Baker, Bryant—S.
Baker, Charles Edwin—Editor, W.
Baldwin, Muriel Frances—Former Art Libn.
Ballinger, Maxil—Pr. M., P., W.
Bama, James E.—I.
Bancel, Henry A.—P.
Barber, George Rodgers—P., T.
Bare, Arnold Edwin—I., P., Des.
Barile, Xavier J.—P., T., L., Et., W., L.
Barnet, Will—P., T., Gr.
Barney, Maginel Wright (Mrs.)—C., I.
Barr, Alfred Hamilton, Jr.—Dir. of Mus. Collections, W.
Barrett, Robert D.—P., C., E.
Barron, Grace—P., T.
Barry, Edith Cleaves—P., S., Des.
Bartlett, Ivan—Des., P., Lith., Ser., I.
Barto, Emily (Mrs.)—P., I., Cr., W.
Barton, Ethel Rose—P., Des.
Barton, John Murray—P., Gr., L.
Barzun, Jacques—W., T., Hist., Cr., L.
Baskerville, Charles—P.
Bassford, Wallace—P., Des.
Batchelor, C. D.—Cart.
Bauer, Elias—Cart.
Baum, Mark—P.
Baziotes, William A.—P.
Bearden, Romare—P.
Becker, Charlotte—I., P., W.
Becker, Maurice—P., I.
Beline, George—P., S.
Bell, Clara Louise (Mrs.)—P.

Bellin, Milton Rockwell—P.
Belmont, Ira Jean—P., W.
Bemelmans, Ludwig—P., Gr., W., I.
Beneker, Katharine—Des. Mus. Exhs., P.
Benisovich, Michel N.—W., T.
Benjamin, Gershon—P.
Benn, Ben—P., T.
Benney, Robert—P., I., W., L.
Benno, Benjamin Greenstein—P.
Bensing, Frank C.—Port P., I., Des.
Ben-Zion—P., Gr., T.
Bergier, Arnold Henry—S., Des., C., L.
Berkman, Aaron—P., T., L., W.
Berkman-Hunter, Bernece—P., Gr., Des.
Berkoff, Blanche—I., Des., Comm. A., T.
Bernhard, Lucian—Des., P.
Bernstein, Theresa F. (Mrs.)—P., Et., Lith., T., W.
Bessemer, Auriel—P., E., I., W., L.
Bianco, Pamela (Mrs.)—I., P., Lith., W.
Biebel, Franklin Matthews—Mus. Dir.
Bigelow, Olive (Mrs.)—P.
Billings, Henry—P., Des., I., W.
Binder, Joseph—Des.
Bing, Alexander—P.
Birnbaum, Martin—W., Cr., L.
Bischoff, Ilse Martha—I., P., Gr.
Bishop, Isabel (Mrs.)—P., Et.
Blackstone, Rozsika B.—C., P., Des.
Blaine, Nell—P., Gr., Des., Comm. A., T.
Blaisdell, Elinore—I., T., W.
Blanc, Peter—P., E., W.
Blatas, Arbit—P.
Blattner, Rose—P., T., Des., W.
Blaustein, Alfred—P., Gr.
Bliss, Alma Hirsig (Mrs.)—P.
Block, Adolph—S.
Block, Dorothy—P., Lith.
Bloom, Hyman—Painter
Blumberg, Yuli—P., Lith., I.
Blumenthal, Margaret M.—Des., T.
Boardman, Nell—P.
Bock, Vera—I., Des.
Bodin, Paul—P.
Bogdanovich, Borislav—P., W., L.
Boime, Albert I.—Cart., Comm. A.
Bok, Hannes Vajn—P., I., Lith.
Bolton, Theodore—W., Art Hist.
Bomar, Bill—P.
Bond, Gwendoline Maplesden (Mrs.)—Et., P., T., W., L., S.
Borghi, Guido Rinaldo—P., S., T.
Botkin, Henry—P., Cr., W., L.
Botts, Hugh—Pr. M., P., Des., S., C., I., W.
Bouche, Louis—P., T.
Bourgeois, Louise—S., Eng.
Bradish, Ethelwyn—P., W., L.
Brall, Ruth—S., T.
Bransom, John Paul—P., I., Et.
Brecher, Samuel—P., T.
Breinin, Raymond—P., S., T.
Brenson, Theodore—P., Gr., E., L., W.
Bridge, Evelyn—Et., W., P., I., Gr.
Briggs, Berta N. (Mrs.)—P., W., L.
Briggs, Judson Reynolds—P., Eng., T., L.
Brindesi, Olympio—S., T.
Brogden, Robert B.—Cart.
Brooks, Howard Griggs—P., Des., C., T.
Brooks, James—P., T.
Brossard, Raymond—P.
Brown, Arthur William—I.
Browne, Byron—P.
Browning, Colleen—P., I.
Brumme, Carl Ludwig—S., P., W., Cr.
Brussel-Smith, Bernard—Pr. M.
Bry, Edith—P., Lith.
Buchholz, Frederick—P.
Buholz, Frances—P., I., T.
Buller, Cecil (Mrs.)—Wood Eng., P.
Bull-Teilman, Gunvor (Mrs.)—P., S., I., W., L., C.

Buongiorno, Nick—P., Et., Lith.
Burgess, Joseph E.—P., I.
Burlin, Paul—P., Lith.
Burnett, E. K.—Mus. Dir.
Burnett, Louis Anthony—P., T.
Butterworth, Rod—Adv. Des.
Buzzelli, Joseph Anthony—P., Lith., Ser., C., T., L., Enamelist
Byrnes, Eugene—Cart., W., I.
Cadmus, Paul—P., Et.
Cadoret, Michel de l'Epineguen—P., Gr., I.
Cady, Harrison—I., Et., P.
Cajori, Charles—P., T.
Calapai, Letterio—P., Eng., Et., L.
Califano, Michael—Port. P.
Calnek, Louis Hermann—Comm. A., Cart.
Campbell, Orland—Port. P.
Campbell, Sara Wendell (Mrs.)—I., Des., Comm. A.
Candell, Victor—P., T.
Cantarella, Maria Boveri—P.
Caparn, Rhys (Mrs.)—S.
Capp, Al—Cart.
Carewe, Sylvia—P., Pr. M., Tapestry Des.
Carlson, Mrs. Valerie Klee—P.
Carter, Betty M.—P., Des., T.
Carter, Esther Flint (Mrs.)—P., C., L., T.
Carter, Helene—I.
Carter, Marcellus—P., S., Cart., C., Des., T., Comm. A.
Carvallo, Suzanne (Mrs.)—P.
Carver, Mabel Macdonald (Mrs.)—P., Gr.
Caseau, Charles Henry—Des., P.
Cassel, John Harmon—Cart., I.
Casson, Mel—Cart.
Castaldo, Amaylia (Mrs.)—Port. P.
Cavallito, Albino—S.
Cecere, Ada Rasario—P., T.
Cecere, Gaetano—S., E., L.
Chace, Lester Merton, Jr.—Port. P.
Chaliapin, Boris—P.
Chamalian, Lillian—I.
Chamberlain, Wynn—P.
Chambers, Robert L.—I.
Chen, Chi—P.
Cherner, Norman—Des., T., L., I., W.
Cherney, Marvin—P.
Cherry, Herman—P., T.
Chinn, Yuen Yuey—P., Gr.
Choate, Nathaniel—S., C.
Christensen, Gardell Dano—Des., S., I., P.
Church, Frederic E.—P.
Cikovsky, Nicolai—P., Lith., T.
Cimotti, Gustave—P.
Citron, Minna Wright—P., Gr., T., W., L.
Clad, Jean Davies—P.
Clapp, Frederick Mortimer—Former Mus. Dir., L., Cr., W.
Clapp, Marcia—Port. S., L.
Clark, Benton Henderson—P., I.
Clark, Eliot Candee—P., W., L., E., Cr.
Clawson, Rex Martin—P.
Clendenin, Eve—P., C.
Cobham, Ethel Rundquist—I., Comm. A.
Cohen, Hy—P.
Cohn, Max Arthur—P., Ser., W.
Cole, Alphaeus P.—P., I., T., Des., W.
Cole, Thomas Casilear—P., L.
Comfort, Barbara—P., I.
Constant, George—P.
Cook, Gladys Emerson—I., P., Et., W., L.
Cook, Walter W. S.—E.
Cootes, Frank Graham—Port. P., Comm. A.
Copeland, Lila—P.
Copelin, Jeannette Knowles—P., T.
Cornwell, Dean—Mural P., I.
Cortlandt, Lyn—P., Lith., Ser.
Cortor, Eldzier—P., Lith., Eng.
Cotsworth, Staats—P., I.

Cotton, Lillian—P.
Cowan, Mary Elizabeth (Mrs.)—C., Des., S., W., L., P.
Cox, Allyn—P., T., L., W.
Cox, Warren Earle—C., P., Des., W., L., T., Cr.
Cozzens, Evangeline Chapman—P.
Craig, Martin—S., T., Des.
Crane, Roy—Cart.
Crawford, Ralston—P., Lith., Photog., I., T., L.
Crespi, Pachita—P., I., Des., L., W.
Cresson, Cornelia (Mrs.)—S., Eng.
Crimi, Alfred Di Giorgio—P., T., I.
Criss, H. Francis—P.
Croft, Lewis Scott—P.
Cross, Louise—S., W.
Cummings, Mary Barrett (Mrs.)—C., Des., T.
Curtis, Constance—Port. P.
Custer, Bernadine—P., I., W.
Cusumano, Stefano—P., T.
Dabo, Leon—P.
da Costa, Antonio—S.
Daingerfield, Marjorie (Mrs.)—S., T., L.
d'Alessio, Gregory—Cart., P., I.
Dante, Giglio, Raphael—P., S.
Daphnis, Nassos—P.
D'Arista, Robert—P.
Darnault, Florence Malcolm—S.
Datz, A. Mark—P., Et., S.
Davidson, Marshall Bowman—Editor of Publications, W., L.
Davis, George—Cart., I.
Davis, Gladys Rockmore—P., W.
Davis, Hubert—P., Lith., Et., I., W.
Davis, Stuart—P., Gr., W., L.
Dean, Abner—Cart., I.
de Carmel, Anne Gutman—C.
deCreeft, Jose—S.
de Diego, Julio—P., Gr., I., C., T.
de Francisci, Anthony—S., T.
de Groot, Adelaide Milton—P.
d'Harnoncourt, Rene—Mus. Dir.
Dehn, Adolf Arthur—P., Lith.
de Kooning, Elaine Marie Catherine—P.
Delbos, Julius—P., T.
Del Mar, Frances—P., L., W., Et.
De Lue, Donald—S.
De Luna, Francis P.—S.
de Marco, Jean—S., C., Gr., T.
De Martelly, John Stockton—P., Gr., E., I., Cart.
De Martini, Joseph—P.
Denslow, Dorothea Henrietta—S., T.
de Rivera, Jose—S.
Derujinsky, Gleb W.—S., C.
Deskey, Donald—Indst. Des.
De Vitis, Themis—P., Des., T., Cr.
Devree, Howard—Cr.
de Witt, Cornelius Hugh—I., Gr., P.
Dickinson, Edwin—P., T.
Dickinson, Sidney E.—P.
Dienes, Sari—P., Gr., Des., T.
di Gioia, Frank—P.
Diller, Mary Black—P., I., W., Des., T.
Dimand, Maurice S.—Mus. Cur., W.
Dirk, Nathaniel—P., T., W., L.
Dirnfeld, Frederick Arnold—P., Et.
Dixon, Francis Stilwell—P.
Dobkin, Alexander—P., I., W., L., Gr., T.
Dockstader, Frederick J.—Asst. Mus. Dir., C.
Dombek, Blanche—S.
Donahue, William Howard—P.
Donnell, Edna B.—Mus. Cur., W.
Dora—I., T.
Dorne, Albert—P., I., T., W., L.
Douglass, Robert W.—P., I.
Dowden, Raymond Baxter—E., Des., P.
Dows, Olin—P., Lith., Eng., W., L.
Dralle, Elizabeth M.—Indst. Des., Comm. A., I.
Draper, William Fanklin—P.
Drew, Dorothy Hart—P.
Dryfoos, Nancy Proskauer—S.

Duble, Lu—S.
Duffy, Edmund—Cart.
Dulac, Margarita Walker (Mrs.)—P., S., Comm. A., I., W., T.
Duncalfe, W. Douglas—P., T.
Dunn, Alan Cantwell—Cart., I., W., P.
Dunn, Robert—P.
Dunwiddie, Charlotte—S.
Du Pre, Grace Annette—Port. P.
Earle, Robert Maxwell—Des., P., C., T.
Earley, Mary—P.
Eaton, Myrwyn L.—E., P., L., W.
Ede-Else—P.
Ehrenreich, Emma—P., Wood Eng.
Eisner, Anne—P., L., W.
Eisner, Dorothy (Mrs.)—P.
Elias, Arthur Louis—P., T.
Eliot, Lucy—P.
Elise—P., Gr., I., Des.
Elliott, Ronnie—P.
Ellsworth, Cheryl Lawther—S.
Ely, Fanny G.—P.
Engel, Michael M., Sr.—Art Publicist, W., L., I.
England, Paul—P., S., Ser., Cr., W.
Ente, Lily (Mrs.)—S., Et., T.
Enters, Angna—W., P., I., Gr., S., Cart.
Ericson, Ernest—I., Des., P., E.
Erlanger, Elizabeth N.—P., Lith., T.
Ernst, James—P., E., L.
Esman, Betty—P.
Ets, Marie Hall (Mrs.)—I., W.
Ettenberg, Eugene M.—Book & Adv. Des., T., W., L., Cr.
Evergood, Philip—P., Gr., W., L., Des., I.
Fabri, Ralph—P., Et., W., Cr., E.
Facci, Domenico Aurelio—S., C., Des.
Falls, Charles Buckles—I., P., Des., Gr.
Farr, Dorathy—P., C., T.
Farr, Fred White—S., C., T.
Farruggio, Remo Michael—P.
Fasano, Clara—S., T.
Feigin, Dorothy Lubell (Mrs.)—P., Et., Lith., T.
Feldman, George (Dr.)—P., C.
Ferber, Herbert—S., P., C.
Feron, Louis—C., S., Des., E.
Ferriss, Dorothy—P.
Fields, Mitchell—S.
Fiene, Alicia—P.
Fiene, Ernest—P., Et., Lith., T.
Fiero, Emilie Louise—S.
Filtzer, Hyman—S.
Fine, Perle—P., T., Gr., L., W.
Fingesten, Peter—S., E., W., L.
Finkle, Melik—S., C., Des.
Flanagan, Albert E.—Et., Arch.
Fleischmann, Adolf Richard—P.
Fleri, Joseph C.—S.
Flexner, James Thomas—W., Cr., L.
Floch, Joseph—P.
Follett, Jean Frances—P., S.
Forst, Miles—P.
Forsyth, William H.—Mus. Assoc. Cur., W.
Fosburgh, James Whitney—P., T., W., L.
Foster, Judith—P., Gr.
Foster, Robert—Gr. Des.
Franck, Frederick S. (Dr.)—P., I., Des., W.
Frank, Bena Virginia (Mrs.)—P., T.
Frank, Emily S.—P., Des.
Frank, Helen—P., Des., I.
Frankenthaler, Helen—P.
Franks, Seymour—P., Des.
Freed, William—P.
Freeman, Jane—P., T.
Freeman, Margaret B.—Mus. Cur.
Freeman, Mark—Lith., T., Comm. A., P.
Freeman, Paul K.—P., C., Des., Comm. A., I.
French, Jared—S., P., Et.
Frenkel, Nora—P.

Frick, John Lawrence—Cart., Comm. A.
Fried, Theodore—P.
Friedensohn, Elias—P., T.
Friedlander, Isac—Eng., Et.
Friedman, Mark—S., C., T.
Friedman, Martin—P.
Friend, David—P.
Fuller, Sue—P., S., Gr., E., W., L.
Gabriel, Ada V.—P., Lith., Des.
Gage, George W.—P., T.
Gahman, Floyd—P., Et., L., C., Gr., E.
Galos, Ben—P., T., I.
Gannam, John—I.
Gasparo, Oronzo Vito—P., Des., C.
Gee, Yun—P., T.
Geissbuhler, Arnold—S., T.
Geissmann, Robert—I., Des., P.
Gelb, Jan—P., Et., T.
Genauer, Emily—Cr., W., L.
Gentry, Helen—Book Des.
Geoghegan, Walter B.—Art. Dir., Des.
Gerardia, Helen—P., Gr.
Gerbino, Rosario Urbino—P.
Gervasi, Frank—P.
Getz, Ilse—P.
Geyer, Harold Carl—Et., W., L.
Gikow, Ruth—P., I., Ser.
Gilbert, Michel G.—P., I., L.
Gillespie, Jessie (Miss)—Des., I., W., Comm. A.
Gilman, Esther Morganstern—P., Lith., I.
Ginsburg, Abraham—P., T.
Glickman, Maurice—S., P., T., W.
Glinsky, Vincent—S., Et., Lith., P., T.
Goetz, Esther Becker—P., I.
Goetz, Oswald H.—L., W.
Goff, Lloyd Lozes—P., I., Gr., W., E.
Goff, Sudduth—Port. P.
Golbin, Andree (Mrs.)—P.
Goldberg, Rube—Cart., I.
Goldman, Julia—P., L., T., Des.
Goldring, Milton—P.
Goldwater, Robert—Mus. Dir., E., W., Cr., L.
Gomberg, Stan—Cart., Des.
Gonzalez, Xavier—P., S.
Goodelman, Aaron J.—S., T., L.
Goodenow, Earle—P., I.
Goodman, Bertram—P., Gr.
Goodrich, Gertrude—Comm. A., Des., P.
Goodrich, Lloyd—Mus. Dir., W., L.
Gordin, Sidney—S.
Gordon, Maxwell—P.
Gottlieb, Adolph—P.
Gottlieb, Harry—P., Ser.
Goulet, Lorrie (Mrs.)—S., P.
Goya-Lukich, Jorge—P., Lith.
Graham, Laura Margaret—P.
Granowitter, Jules—I., P., Des., Cart., Comm. A.
Grant, Gordon Hope—P., Et., Lith.
Graves, Maitland—P., T., W.
Graves, Morris—P.
Greenberg, Clement—W., Cr., P.
Greenwood, Marion—P., Lith., I., T., L.
Grier, Harry Dobson Miller—Asst. Mus. Dir.
Grillo, John—P.
Grimes, Frances—S.
Grippe, Florence—C., P., S., Des.
Grippe, Peter—S., Gr., P.
Grippi, Salvatore William—P., Gr., T.
Gross, Chaim—S., T.
Gross, Sidney—P.
Groth, John—P., I., Gr., T., L., Cart., W.
Gruppe, Karl H.—S.
Guck, Edna—P., S.
Guerrero, Jose—P.
Guggenheimer, Richard H.—P., T., W., L.
Guimard, Adeline O.—P.
Guion, Molly—Port. P.
Gunkel, Virginia P.—P., T.
Gunther, Floyd Theodore—Comm. A., I.

Gurdus, Luba (Mrs.)—P., I., Hist.
Gussow, Bernard—P., Lith., T.
Gusten, Theodore J. H.—Art Dir.
Guston, Philip—P., T.
Gwathmey, Robert—P., Ser., T.
Haas, Helen (Mrs.)—S.
Haenigsen, Harry—I., Cart., Comm. A., W.
Hafner, Charles Andrew—S., T., P.
Hale, Robert Beverly—Mus. Cur., E., W., L.
Halpert, A.—Cart.
Hamar, Irene—P., S.
Hamlin, Talbot—E., W., L., Cr.
Hannah, Muriel—P., I., Gr.
Hare, Channing Weir—P.
Harkavy, Minna—S.
Harmon, Lily—P., Lith.
Harris, Caryl—P.
Harris, Louis—P., T.
Harris, Margo Liebes—S.
Harrison, Dorothy—P., T.
Harriton, Abraham—P., T.
Hartman, Bertram—P.
Hartman, Gertrude—C.
Hartmann, Georg T.—P., Et.
Hartwig, Cleo—S., T.
Harvey, James V.—P.
Haseltine, Herbert—S.
Hathaway, Calvin S.—Mus. Dir.
Hawley, Margaret Foote—P.
Hayes, William Christopher—Assoc. Cur.
Hayter, Stanley William—P., Gr., T., W., L.
Hayward, Mildred (Mrs.)—P., W.
Hazelet, Sally Potter—P.
Hebald, Milton Elting—S., C., T.
Hechenbleikner, Louis—T., Gr.
Hecht, Zoltan—P., E.
Heilemann, Charles Otto—Comm. A., I., Des., P., T.
Heiloms, May—P., T., L.
Heine, Marc K.—P., I., Des., T., Comm. A.
Heller, Maxwell L.—T., P., W., L.
Hendricks, Geoffrey—E., P., Gr.
Henoch, Hanley—P., Des.
Hering, Harry—P., Gr., C.
Hess, Emil John—P., S.
Hiler, Hilaire—P., C., Des.
Hillsmith, Fannie—P., Et., Eng.
Hios, Theodore—P., Gr.
Hirsch, Joseph—P., Lith.
Hirschfeld, Albert—Caricaturist, I., W., Gr.
Hirschfield, Harry—I.
Hobson, Katherine Thayer—S.
Hoeckner, Carl—P., Gr.
Hoening, Margaret (Mrs.)—P., Et.
Hoffman, Irwin D.—Port. P., Lith., Et.
Hoffman, Malvina—S.
Hoffmann, Arnold—P., T., L.
Hofmann, Hans—P., S., E.
Hogner, Nils—P., Et., T., L., I.
Holder, Charles Albert—P., T.
Hollerbach, Serge—P., I.
Hollister, Paul—P.
Holme, Siv Muse—P., Gr.
Holmgren, R. John—I.
Holton, Leonard T.—I.
Holty, Carl Robert—P., L., T.
Hood, Ethel P.—S.
Hopper, Jo N. (Mrs.)—P.
Hopper, Edward—P.
Horch, Nettie S. (Mrs.)—Mus. Dir.
Hovannes, John—S., T.
Hovell, Joseph—S., T.
Howard, Loretta (Mrs.)—P.
Howell, Hannah Johnson (Mrs.)—Art Libn.
Hoyt, Dorothy King—P., Et., Eng.
Hultberg, John Phillip—P.
Hurst, Earl Oliver—I., W., Des.
Husted-Andersen, Adda—C., Des., T.
Imler, Edgar—P., Et., Eng., W.
Inman, Pauline Winchester (Mrs.)—Eng., I.
Ippolito, Angelo—P.
Irvine, Rosalind—Mus. Cur.

Isaacs, Betty Lewis—S.
Iselin, Lewis—S.
Isenburger, Eric—P.
Jackson, Beatrice Humphreys—P.
Jackson, Harlan—P.
Jackson, Lee—P.
Jacobs, Ted Seth—P., Des.
Janowsky, Bela—S.
Jauss, Anne Marie—P., I., Des.
Ject-Key, David Wu—P.
Ject-Key, Elsie—P.
Jelinek, Hans—Gr., Wood Eng., E.
Jennewein, C. Paul—S.
Jochimsen, Marion—P., T.
Johansen, John C.—Port. P.
Johns, Erik—P.
Jones, Edward Powis—P., Et.
Jones, Eugene A.—Et.
Jones, Ralston—Cart.
Jones, Tom Douglas—Mus. Dir.
Judd, Don—P., Lith., T.
Junker, Leo Helmholz—P., Et.
Kahan, Sol B.—S.
Kahn, Ely Jacques—E., Arch., P.
Kahn, Olivia—P.
Kahn, Wolf—P.
Kainz, Luise—Et., Eng., T., W.
Kaish, Luise—S.
Kajiwara, Takuma—P.
Kallem, Henry—P., Gr.
Kallman, Kermah—S.
Kantor, Morris—P., T.
Kaplan, Joseph—P.
Karfunkle, David—P., T.
Karoly, Andrew B.—P., Et.
Karoly, Fredric—P.
Karpick, John J.—P., Des., Lith.
Kassoy, Bernard—P., T., Cart.
Kastor, Hugo—P.
Katz, A. Raymond—P., Des., W., L.
Katz, Ethel—P., T., Lith.
Katz, Hilda—P., Gr.
Katzman, Herbert—P.
Katzman, Lawrence—Des., Cart.
Kaufman, Enit—P.
Kaufman, Joe—I.
Kaufmann, Arthur—P., E.
Kaufmann, Edgar, Jr.—T., Cr., W., L., Des.
Kayser, Stephen S.—E., W., L.
Keen, Helen B.—P.
Kelly, Ellsworth—S., P.
Kendall, Beatrice—P., C., Des., T., L.
Kennedy, Sybil—S.
Key-Oberg, Ellen Burke—S., T.
Key-Oberg, Rolf—C., T.
Keyser, Robert—P.
Kienbusch, William Austin—P., S.
Kiesler, Frederick John—Arch., S., P., Des.
Kimball, Yeffe—P., Des., I., W.
King, Jane Spear—P.
King, William Dickey—S.
Kingman, Dong—P., T.
Kinigstein, Jonah—P., Des., Comm. A.
Kinstler, Everett Raymond—Port. P., I.
Kirk, Frank C.—P.
Kirschenbaum, Jules—P.
Kirstein, Lincoln Edward—Cr., W., L.
Kiselewski, Joseph—S.
Klett, Walter Charles—I., P., Des.
Kline, Franz Josef—P.
Klonis, Stewart—P., T., L.
Klous, Rose (Mrs.)—P., Et.
Knight, Frederic Charles—P., E.
Knight, Hilary—P.
Knox, Susan Ricker—P.
Kocherthaler, Mina—P.
Kocsis, Ann—P.
Koehler, Henry—I., Des.
Koerner, Daniel—P., Cart., Comm. A., T.
Koffler, Mary Mintz—P.
Kogan, Belle—Indst. Des.
Kolin, Sacha—P., S.
Koni, Nicolaus—S., P., C., T.
Konzal, Joseph—S.
Kootz, Samuel M.—W., Gal. Dir.
Kopman, Benjamin—P., Gr., I.
Koppelman, Chaim—Et., T.

Koslowsky, Nota—P., Des., Eng., I., W., T., Cart.
Kotin, Albert—P., E., L.
Kozlow, Sigmund—P.
Kramer, Helen Kroll—C.
Kramer, Hilton—Cr., W., T., L.
Krebs, Rose K.—Ceramic Sculptor, P.
Kredel, Fritz—I., Cart.
Kreindler, Doris Barsky—P., Et., T.
Kremp, Marie Ada—P., Et., T., S., L.
Kriensky, Morris E.—P.
Kroll, Leon—P., Lith., L.
Kronberg, Louis—P.
Kroth, Richard—P., L., T.
Kruger, Louise—S., Des., Gr.
Kruse, Alexander Zerdin—P., Et., Lith., W., Cr., L., T.
Kuehne, Max—P., C., Gr.
Kup, Karl—Libn., Cur., T., L., Cr.
Kuper, Rose—P.
Kusanobu, Murray—P.
Kwong Hui Ka—C.
La Gambina, Vincent—P., T., Gr.
Lamont, Frances (Mrs.)—S.
Landis, Lily—S.
Laning, Edward—P., T.
Lansing, Winifred Justine—S.
Lansner, Fay Gross—P., Des., Cr.
Larsen, Erik—E., Cr., W., L.
Lassaw, Ibram—S., T., W., L.
Lasswell, Fred—Cart.
Laufman, Sidney—P., T.
Laurent, John Louis—P., T., Gr.
Laurer, Robert—Asst. Mus. Dir.
Lavalle, John—P.
Lawrence, Marion—E., Hist.
Lax, David—P., E., L.
Layton, Gloria (Mrs.)—P.
Leaycraft, Julia Searing—P., T., W., Cr., Lith.
Lebedev, Vladimir—P.
Lee, George Joseph—Mus. Cur.
Lehman, Harold—P., S., T., Des.
Lehman, Irving G.—P., Eng., Des., T.
Lekberg, Barbara Hult—S.
Lenssen, Heidi Ruth (Mrs.)—P., I., W., T.
Lerman, Leo—W., E., L., Des.
Levering, Robert K.—I.
Levi, Julian Clarence—P., Arch., Et.
Levi, Julian E.—P., T.
Levine, Jack—P.
Levit, Herschel—P., I., E.
Levitan, Israel—S., T.
Levitt, Alfred—P., Lith., L., W.
Lev-Landau—P.
Lewis, Martin—Pr. M., P.
Lewis, Norman—P.
Liberte, L. Jean—P., T., C., L.
Lieberman, William S.—Mus. Cur.
Liebes, Dorothy (Mrs.)—Tex. Des., C., L., W., T.
Lindner, Richard—P., I., T.
Lindquist, Ronald Edward—Cart., Comm. A.
Link, Carl—P.
Linton—S.
Lipinsky de Orlov, Lino Sigismondo—P., Et., S., Conservator, Des.
Lipman-Wulf, Peter—S., Pr. M., T.
Lipton, Seymour—S.
Liszt, Maria—P.
Livingston, Sidnee—P., Pr. M.
Lober, Georg John—S.
Loederer, Richard A.—P., Et., Des., I., Cart., Comm. A., W.
Loew, Michael—P., T., W.
Logan, Elizabeth Dulaney (Mrs.)—I., Cart., Comm. A.
Lohse, Willis R.—Des., I.
Lo Medico, Thomas G.—S.
Lonergan, John—Lith., Ser., P., C., W., T.
Lopez-Rey, Jose—E., W., L.
Lovet-Lorski, Boris—S.
Lowe, Emily (Mrs.)—P.
Luban, Boris—Port. P.
Luck, Robert Henry—Art Administrator
Ludins, Ryah (Miss)—P., I., W., Gr., Des., T., L.

Lund, David Nathan—P.
Lundean, Louis—I., P., W., L., T.
Lux, Gwen—S.
Lynch, Irene Deroche—P.
Lynch, James O'Connor—Cr., P., E.
MacAgy, Douglas—E., W.
MacKendrick, Lilian—P.
MacLane, Jean—P.
MacNicol, Roy Vincent—P., Des., T., W., L.
MacRae, Emma Fordyce (Mrs.)—P.
Maldarelli, Oronzio—S., E.
Malloy, Susan Rabinowitz (Mrs.)—P.
Maloney, Daniel—P.
Malten, Charlotte—C., Des., T.
Manca, Albino—S.
Mangravite, Peppino—P., E., W., L.
Manship, Paul—S., L., T.
Manso, Leo—P., Des., T.
Manville, Elsie—P.
Marantz, Irving—P.
Marder, Dorie—P., Ser.
Margo, Boris—P., Gr., E., L.
Margon, Lester—Des., W.
Margoulies, Berta (Mrs.)—S., T.
Margules, DeHirsh—P., L.
Margulies, Joseph—P., T.
Markell, Isabella Banks—Gr., P., S.
Markow, Jack—P., Lith., Cart.
Marsh, Lucile Patterson—I., Gr.
Marshall, Jonathan—W., Cr., Program Associate
Marsicano, Nicholas—P.
Martin, Benjamin C.—Cart.
Martin, Charles E.—Cart., P., Des.
Martin, Christine—P.
Martinelli, Ezio—S., P., Gr.
Mason, Alice Trumbull—P., Gr.
Matulka, Jan—P., Lith.
Maunsbach, George Eric—P., S., T.
Mayen, Paul—Des.
Mayer, Grace M.—Former Mus. Cur., W.
Mayer, Ralph—P., W., T., L.
Mayers, Myron—P.
Mayor, Alpheus Hyatt—Mus. Cur., W., L.
McArdle, Jim—I., Cart.
McBride, Henry—C., W.
McCall, Robert Theador—P., Des., Comm. A., I.
McCausland, Elizabeth—W., Cr., L., T.
McNulty, William Charles—P., Et., E., Comm. A., I.
Means, Elliott—P., I., S.
Meiere, Hildreth—Mural P.
Melcarth, Edward—P., T., I., L.
Melcher, Betsy Flagg—Min. P.
Melicov, Dina—S.
Melik, Soss Efrem—P.
Mellon, Eleanor M.—S.
Meltzer, Doris—Pr. M., P., A. Dir.
Menkes, Sigmund—P.
Mermin, Mildred Shire (Mrs.)—P.
Mesibov, Hugh—P., T., Ser., C.
Metz, Frank R.—P.
Metzl, Ervine—I., Cart., Des., T., W.
Meyerowitz, William—Et., P.
Michelson, Leo—P., I., E.
Michnick, David—S.
Middleton, Samuel M.—P., C.
Mielziner, Jo—Stage Des.
Milcinovic, Desha A.—P., Ser., Des., Lith., T.
Miles, Jeanne Patterson—P.
Miller, Dorothy Canning—Mus. Cur., W.
Miller, Jane—I., W.
Minewski, Alex—P.
Mirsky, Samuel—Port. P.
Mitchell, Glen—P., I., T.
Mittleman, Ann—P.
Mocharniuk, Nicholas—S., C., Des.
Mock, Gladys P.—Eng.
Model, Elisabeth—S., Gr.
Moir, Robert—S., P., T.
Moller, Hans—P., Des., Lith., T.
Molzahn, Johannes—P., Des., E., W., L.

Montana, Bob—Cart.
Montana, Pietro—S., P., T.
Moore, Bruce—P., Des., T.
Moore, Martha E. (Mrs.)—P., T.
Morley, Grace L. McCann—Asst. Mus. Dir.
Morris, George L. K.—P., S., W., L., T.
Morris, Kyle Randolph—P.
Morrison, George—P.
Morrison, Mark—S.
Morse, John D.—W., Editor, T.
Morson, Lidia (Mrs.)—P.
Moskowitz, Ira—Et., Lith., P.
Motherwell, Robert—P., T.
Moy, Seong—P., Gr., T., L.
Moyer, Roy—P., Asst. Dir. A. Fed., T.
Mull, Jane Addams—Hist.
Mullen, Buell (Mrs.)—P., C.
Murch, Walter Tandy—P., I.
Murphy, Alice Harold—P., Et., Lith., T.
Murray, Albert K.—Port. P.
Myer, John Walden—Mus. Dir.
Myers, John—P.
Myrhl, Sarah—P.
Nagel, Stina (Mrs.)—P.
Nagler, Fred—P., S.
Nash, James Harley—Indst. Des., Comm. A.
Nason, Gertrude—P.
Neale, Mrs. Sidnee—I., Comm. A.
Neilson, Raymond Perry Rodgers—P.
Neumark, Anne—P.
Nevelson, Louise—S.
Newman, Barnett—P.
Newman, Elias—P., L., T., W.
Newman, Irene Hodes—P.
Newman, Joseph—P.
Newton, Marion Cleever Whiteside—P., I., Des.
Nickford, Juan—S.
Nisbet, Mary Jacquetta—Des., C., P., I., S., T.
Nordhausen, August Henry—P., T., L.
Norment, John Murray—Cart.
O'Connor, Henry M.—P., Et.
Oenslager, Donald Mitchell—Scenic Des.
Offin, Charles Z.—Cr., Et.
Offner, Richard—E.
O'Keeffe, Neil—I., Comm. A.
Olds, Elizabeth—P., I., W., L.
Oley, Moses—P., Gr.
Olinsky, Ivan G.—P., T.
Olsen, Earle—P.
Olshan, Bernard—P., Des.
Oppenheim, S. Edmund—Port. P.
Orfuss, Elsie—P., Des.
Osborne, Lue—P., Eng.
Paddock, Josephine—P., T., L., W.
Panchak, William—P.
Pandolfini, Joseph Paul—P., C., I., T.
Paris, Dorothy—P.
Parish, Betty Waldo (Mrs.)—P., Pr. M.
Pascal, Theo—P., C., Des., I., Pub. Rel.
Patterson, Charles Allen—P.
Paullin, Ethel Parsons (Mrs.)—P., Eng., Indst. Des.
Paxson, Ethel (Mrs.)—P., T., W., L.
Payor, Eugene—P., Des., I., Comm. A.
Pearlstein, Philip—P.
Pels, Albert—P., T.
Penny, Carlton P.—P.
Pereira, I. Rice—P., T., L.
Perlin, Bernard—P., I.
Perry, Bart—P., T.
Perry, Raymond—P., I., Des., L.
Persons, Simmons—P.
Peters, Eric A.—P., Gr., Cart., Comm. A.
Peterson, Jane—P.
Philipp, Robert—P.
Phillips, Anne Cole (Mrs.)—P.
Phillips, John Goldsmith—Mus. Cur.
Phillips, Margaret McDonald—P., T., W., L.
Picken, George—P., Et., Lith., T., L.

Pine, Geri (Mrs.)—P.
Pittman, Kitty Butner (Mrs.)—P., T., S.
Pizzitola, Vincent—P., T.
Platt, Eleanor—Port. Sculptor
Platt, Mary Cheney—P., Des., T.
Pleissner, Ogden—P.
Pollet, Joseph—P., Gr., W., L., T.
Polony, Elemer—P., T.
Ponce De Leon, Michael—Pr. M., P., T.
Poor, Henry Varnum—P., C., S., E., W.
Porter, Priscilla Manning—C., T., W., L.
Powell, Leslie J.—P.
Powers, Mary Swift—P.
Pratt, Elizabeth Southwick (Mrs.)—P., Lith.
Pratt, Frances (Mrs.)—P.
Prehn, Hans Ernst—S., P., C.
Presser, Josef—P., E., L.
Pressoir, Esther—P., C., I.
Prezzi, Wilma Maria—P., S., T.
Price, Frederic Newlin—Mus. Dir., W., L.
Pride, Joy—P., C., Des., T., L.
Priest, Alan—Mus. Cur.
Prior, Harris King—Art Administrator, E.
Puzinas, Paul—P., E.
Pytlak, Leonard—Ser., Lith., P., T.
Quintanilla, Luis—P., Gr., L.
Quistgaard, Johann Waldemar de Rehling—P.
Racz, Andre—P., Gr., E., W., L.
Radulovic, Savo—P., C., Gr., T., L.
Raskin, Joseph—P., Et.
Raskin, Saul—Et., Lith., P., I., W., L.
Rasko, Maximilian Aurel Reinitz—Port. P., T., L.
Ratkai, George—P., I., Lith.
Ratkai, Helen—P.
Rattner, Abraham—P.
Ratzka, Arthur L.—Port. P.
Redein, Alex—P., T.
Reder, Bernard—S., Et., Eng., Lith.
Redka, Eugenia—P., T., Gr., Des.
Reeves, Ruth—Des., C., P., W., L., T.
Rehberger, Gustav—P., Des., Comm. A., I.
Reilly, Frank Joseph—P., T., L., W., I.
Reinhardt, Ad F.—P., E., L.
Reisman, Philip—P., I., Et., T.
Reiss, Henriette—P., Des., L., T., W.
Reiss, Lionel S.—P., Lith., I., Et., Des.
Renier, Joseph Emile—S.
Rensie, Florine (Mrs.)—P.
Rethi, Lili—Indst. A., I., Lith.
Reva—P., Comm. A., I., Des.
Rewald, John—W.
Rey, Hans Augusto—I., W., Lith., Cart., L., Comm. A.
Reynal, Jeanne Sills—C.
Rhoden, John W.—S.
Ricci, Ulysses Anthony—S.
Richardson, Gretchen (Mrs.)—S.
Riley, Bill—Cart., I.
Rittenberg, Henry R.—P., T.
Robbins, Frank—Cart., P., I.
Robbins, Hulda Dornblatt—Ser., P., T.
Roberts, Colette Jacqueline—Cr., L., P., Gal. Dir.
Robertson, Paul Chandler—P., Des.
Robins, Seymour—I., P.
Robinson, Mary Turlay—P., L.
Robinson, Maude—C.
Robus, Hugo—S., T.
Roir, Irving—Cart.
Roland, Jay—P.
Rollo, Joseph—P.
Romano, Emanuel Glicen—P., I., T.
Romano, Umberto—P., Lith., S., T., L.
Rondell, Lester—Des., P.
Rorimer, James J.—Mus. Dir. & Cur., W., L.
Rose, Herman—P., T.
Rose, Iver—P.

Ziegler, Siegfried—P., Gr.
Zilzer, Gyula—Et., Lith., P., Des.
Zucker, Jacques—P.
Zucker, Paul—E., Cr., W.

Niagara Falls

Langs, Mary Metcalf—S.

North Salem

Hammond, Natalie Hays—P., W., Mus. Dir.

North Tarrytown

Cater, Harold Dean—Mus. Dir., W.

Nyack

Borne, Mortimer—Et., P., S., E., W., L.
Bruckner, William—P., Des., Comm. A., T.
Chace, Dorothea (Mrs.)—P., T.
Dahlberg, Edwin Lennart—I., P.
Forbes-Oliver, Harriette—P., S., L.
Howard, John Langley—P., I., T.
Lynch, Donald Cornelius—I., P., T.
Phillips, Blanche Howard—S.

Oceanside

Rose, William F.—I.

Old Chatham

Coates, Robert M.—W., Cr.
Wiegand, Gustave—P.

Orangeburg

Costigan, John Edward—P., Et.
Der Harootian, Koren—S., P.

Ossining

Auerbach-Levy, William—Et., I., L., P., T.
Eliscu, Frank—S.
Hess, Lowell Francis—Des., Comm. A., I.

Oswego

Saunders, Aulus Ward—E., P.
Shoenfelt, Joseph Franklin—P., C., E.

Palatine Bridge

Biggs, Geoffrey—I.

Pawling

Belle, Cecile (Mrs.)—P.

Pelham

Boal, Sara Metzner—P., T.
de Leon, Amanda—P.
Heim, Nara—P., S.

Penn Yann

Gazzetta, Mary A.—P., T.

Piermont

Bindrum, John I.—P., T., L.
Davidson, Morris—P., W., L., T.
Savage, Whitney Lee—P., Des.

Pittsford

Wildenhain, Frans Rudolf—Ceramic C., P., S., T.

Pleasantville

Cawein, Kathrin—Et., Eng., Lith.
Handville, Robert Tompkins—P., Comm. A., I.
Hawkins, Benjamin F.—S.
Johnson, Grace Mott—S., P., W.
Menconi, Ralph Joseph—S.
Themal, Joachim Hans—P., T.
Weinman, Robert Alexander—S.

Port Chester

Blattner, Robert Henry—Des., I., T., P., W., L.

Portland

Anderson, Brad J.—Cart.

Poughkeepsie

Acker, Geraldine D. N. (Mrs.)—Port. P.
Chatterton, Clarence K.—P., E.
Rubenstein, Lewis W.—P., E., Gr.
Smith, Eunice Hatfield—Port. P.
Walters, Emile—P., T.

Poughquag

Lidov, Arthur—P., Des., Gr., S., I.

Pound Ridge

Walleen, Hans Axel—P., I.

Putnam Valley

Beach, Beata (Mrs.)—P., Des., Et., I.
Porter, Vernon Carroll—Dir., P., Des.

Rhinebeck

Fairchild, Elizabeth Nelson—P.
Fairchild, May (Mrs.)—P.

Riverdale

See New York City

Rochester

Alexander, Jon H.—S., I., P.
Altschule, Hilda (Mrs.)—P., S.
Avery, Ralph H.—P., Comm. A.
Barschel, Hans Joachim—Advertising Des.
Bate, Norman Arthur—Et., I., W., T.
Boardman, E. T.—Asst. Mus. Dir.
Christensen, Hans Jorgen—C., Des., T.
Copeland, Lawrence G.—C., Des., E.
Ehrich, William E.—E., S., C.
Gurney, Edith B.—Art Libn.
Herdle, Isabel C.—Assoc. Mus. Dir.
Hersey, Carl Kenneth—E.
Holm, Milton W.—P.
Menihan, John C.—P., Lith., Ser., T., L., Des.
Moore, Gertrude Herdle—Mus. Dir., E.
Newhall, Beaumont—Mus. Dir.
Raschen, Carl Martin—P., I., Et., T.
Witmeyer, Stanley H.—E., Des., P., W., L.

Rock City Falls

Davidson, Robert—S., E.

Rye

Block, Julian—I., P.
Blum, Alex A.—Et., P.
Boccini, Manuel Fiorito—P., S., Et., Lith.
Morgan, Frances Mallory—S.
Schmid, Elsa—P., C.

Saratoga Springs

Baruzzi, Peter B.—P., C., Gr., T.
Pease, Marion Dietz—E., C.

Saugerties

Fite, Harvey—S., E., L., W.

Scarborough

Dinneen, Alice (Mrs.)—P., Des.

Scarsdale

Arbeit, Arnold A.—Des., P., E., Cr., L.
Barber, H. Waddell—P., T., I., L.
Brody, Philip Morton—Des., Gr., P., L.
Durlacher, Ruth (Mrs.)—P.
Fox, Milton S.—P., Lith., T., W., L.
Greacen, Nan (Mrs.)—P.
Kizer, Charlotte E.—C., P., T.
Lippincott, J. Gordon—Des., W., L.
Roth, Ben—Cart.
Schutz, Anton—Et., Editor
Williams, J. Scott—P., C., Des.

Schenectady

Batzell, Edgar A.—Comm. A., P., T.

Scottsville

Meyer, Frederick Robert—P., T., S.

Selkirk

Sprinchorn, Carl—P.

Seneca Falls

Schabbehar, Ann Brennan—I., Comm. A., T.

Shady

Taylor, John Williams—P., Pr. M.

Snyder

Andersen, Niels Yde—Des., Et., P., E.
Davis, Faith Howard—P., S., T.

South Salem

Horn, Axel—Des., P., S.
Underwood, Elisabeth Kendall—S., P.

Springfield Center

Salvatore, Victor—S.

Spring Valley

Brule, Elmo A.—P., T., Comm. A., I.
Purdy, Maud H.—I., P.

Staten Island

Bell, Cecil Crosley—P.
Bernstein, Gerald—Mus. Cur., P., T., L.
Betsberg, Ernestine (Mrs.)—P.
Davis, Richard Allen—Mus. Cur., Gr., T.
Leason, Percy Alexander—P., E., L., W.
Lorenzani, Arthur E.—S.
Noble, John Alexander—Marine P., Lith.
Osver, Arthur—P.
Salerno, Charles—S., T.
Whitehead, James L.—Mus. Dir.

Stephentown

Harsanyi, Charles—P.

Syracuse

Addison, Wilfred John—P., Lith., Des., I., Comm. A.
Apgar, Nicolas Adam—P.
Berman, Anni Radin—P., S.
Bischof, Severin—P., C.
Charman, Frederick Montague—E., P., Des., L., W.
Coye, Lee Brown—S., P., C., Eng., I.
Dillenback, L. C.—E.
Horle, Edith Louisa—Et., Eng., P., T., C.
Hull, William—Mus. Dir.
Kerfoot, Margaret (Mrs.)—E., P.
Kimak, George—P., Gr., T., L.
Kline, Hibberd Van Buren—P., I.
Mundy, Ethel Frances—S.
Olmsted, Anna Wetherill—Mus. Dir., W., L., Cr.
Randall, Ruth Hunie (Mrs.)—E., C., W.
Saunders, Albert Frederic—Des., W., L.
Schmeckebier, Laurence E.—E., L., Cr., W., S.
Scott, Dorothy Carnine (Mrs.)—P., Pr. M., L.
Trimm, Lee S.—P.
Williams, Helen F.—Ceramic C., E.
Wyckoff, Sylvia Spencer—P., E.

Tarrytown

Brown, Ozni (Mr.)—P., E.
Davis, Robert Allen—P., I., Gr., C., E., L.
Hatch, Emily Nichols—P., Gr., W., L., T.
Jorgulesco, Jonel—Des.
Wheeler, Robert G.—Hist., L., W.

Troy

Healey, Ruth Leyden—E.
Holloway, H. Maxson—Mus. Dir., Hist., W., L.

Tuckahoe

Campbell, Helena Eastman Ogden (Mrs.)—P., T.
Cristina, S. Alfio—Gr., Pr. M., P., S., Des., T.
Emmerich, Irene Hillebrand—P., Comm. A.
Enser, George—Des., T., L., I.
Hintermeister, Henry—Comm. A., I., P.
Hubert, Harry—P., Comm. A.
Rosenblatt, Alice—C., P., Des., T.

Tuxedo

Prescott, William Linzee—P.

Upper Jay

Conwell, Averil Courtney (Mrs.)—P.

Utica

De Spirito, Henry—S.
Huntington, A. Montgomery—Des., P., Mus. Publ. Rel. Dir.
McLanathan, Richard Barton Kennedy —Mus. Dir.
Moshier, Elizabeth Alice—E., Des., P., C.

Valhalla

Donnelly, Thomas—P., T.
Pousette-Dart, Nathaniel—P., Des., Et., T., W., L.

Valley Cottage

Greene, Stephen—P., E.
Heaton, Maurice—C.
Scheffler, Rudolf—P.

Watertown

Arnold, Grant—P., Lith., T., W.
Morley, Mary Cecilia—P., T.

Webster

Brennan, Harold James—E., C., L., W.

Wells

Shoudy, Theodore—P., T.

Wellsville

Shea, Aileen Ortlip (Mrs.)—P., T.

West Nyack

Higgins, Cardwell S.—I., Des., P.
Olsen, Chris E.—P., C., S., Mus. Preparator, L.

White Plains

Broemel, Carl W.—P.
Buell, Alice Standish—Et.
Friedlander, Leo—S.
Greenfield, Maccabi—P., Gr., T.
Kimmey, Zara B. (Mrs.)—E.
Nickerson, Ruth—S.
Von Der Lancken, Giulia—P., T.
Wrigley, Viola B. (Mrs.)—P., Lith.

Whitesboro

Christiana, Edward I.—P., T.

Williamsville

Bissell, Dorothy Pendennis (Mrs.)— S., P., Des.

Woodstock

Alan, Jay—Cart.
Appel, Marianne (Mrs.)—P., I.
Arndt, Paul Wesley—P.
Beck, Rosemarie Phelps—P., T.
Blanch, Arnold—P., Gr., I., W., T., L., Des.
Bolton, Clarence—Lith., P., Des.
Champanier, Abram August—P., Des., T., L.
Chase, Edward Leigh—P., W.
Chavez, Edward Arcenio—P., Lith., T.
Cramer, Florence Ballin—P., C.
Cramer, Konrad—P., Gr., Des., I., L., C.
Crane, Stanley William—P., Des.
Crist, Richard—P., I., W.
Edwards, Eleanor—P.
Edwards, Emmet—P.
Faggi, Alfeo—S., L.
Fischer, Anton Otto—I.
Fisher, Orr Cleveland—P., Cart., W.
Fortess, Karl Eugene—P., Lith., T.
Foster, Holland—P., S., T.
Gardner, Beatrice Sturtevant—P., T., L.
Hart, Agnes—P., T.
Heermann, Norbert Leo—P., W., L., Cr.
Higgins, Mollie Smith (Mrs.)—P., W., T.
Johnson, Benjamin Franklin—P.
Lee, Doris—P., Gr., I.
Loomis, Lillian Anderson—Des., P.
Ludins, Eugene—P.
Magafan, Ethel—P.
Mandel, Howard—P., S., I.
Martin, Fletcher—P., Lith., T., L.
Mattson, Henry Elis—P.
Millman, Edward—P., E., L.
Pachner, William—P., Lith., T.
Petersham, Maud Fuller—I., W.
Petersham, Miska—I., W.
Pike, John—P., I.
Refregier, Anton—P.

Ruellan, Andree—P., Lith., Et.
Seaton, Walter Wallace—I.
Schrader, Gustave—P.
Schuster, Carl—W.
Shiff, E. Madeline (Mrs.)—P., C.
Shotwell, Helen Harvey—P., Pictorial Photog.
Small, Hannah Ludins—S.
Smith, Judson—P., T., L.
Summers, Dudley Gloyne—I., P.
Vukovic, Marko—P.,
Winslow, Earle B.—I., Lith., T., P.
Wuermer, Carl—P.

Yonkers

Bernstein, Sylvia—P.
Clarke, Rene—P., Des.
Eichenberg, Fritz—Pr. M., Eng., Lith., I., T., W.
Heliker, John Edward—P., T.
Laune, Paul—I., Port. P., Des., S.
Miller, Ralph Rillman—Asst. Mus. Dir., P., Des.
Voter, Thomas W.—Mus. Dir.

Yorktown Heights

Putnam, Wallace B.—P., W., I.
Schwebel, Celia—P.

NORTH CAROLINA

Asheville

Cunningham, Theodore Saint-Amant— P.
Harrison, William Sherman, Jr.—Cart.
Lee, Cuthbert—Port. P.
Stonier, Lucille Holderness (Mrs.)— P., C., Comm. A.

Blowing Rock

Price, Irene—Port. P.

Chapel Hill

Allcott, John Volney—Mus. Dir., E., L.
Ness, Albert Kenneth—P., E., Des.
Sloane, Joseph Curtis—E., Hist., Mus. Dir.

Charlotte

Bartlett, Paul—P., T.
Gebhardt, Ann Stellhorn (Mrs.)—P., E.
Kortheuer, Dayrell—Port. P., T., W.
Schlageter, Robert—Mus. Dir.
Steadman, L. Alice Tuttle (Mrs.)—S., P., T.
Tucker, Charles Clement—Port. P.

Cherokee

Crowe, Amanda Maria—S., C., T.

Durham

Hall, Louise—E.
Lankes, Julius J.—Eng., I.
Patrick, Ransom R.—E., P., Hist.
Sunderland, Elizabeth Read—E.
Wilson, Edward N.—S., E., Des., I.

Franklin

McDowell, Helen (Mrs.)—P.

Greensboro

Rood, Henry, Jr.—P., I., T.

Campbell, Harriet (Mrs.)—P., Des.
Canzani, Joseph V.—E.
Evatt, Harriet Torrey (Mrs.)—
    P., I., W.
Frey, Erwin F.—S., E., W.
Gatrell, Marion Thompson—
    P., Gr., E.
Gatrell, Robert M.—P., Gr., E.
Hewett, Edward Wilson—P., T.
Kirkpatrick, Harriet—P.
Rannells, Will—I.
Reeder, Flora MacLean (Mrs.)—
    P., T.
Nicodemus, Chester R.—S., C., T.
Ziegler, Laura—S.

Cozaddale

Luderowski, Theodore Edward—
    E., Indst. Des., P.

Cuyahoga Falls

Flint, Leroy W.—
    Mus. Dir., T., P., Et.
Grathwol, Ray Anthony—P.

Dayton

Burroughs, Edward R.—
    P., E., Des., Gr.
Busch, Elizabeth W. (Mrs.)—
    P., Lith., Ser.
Colt, Priscilla C.—
    Mus. Research & Program Asst.
Colt, Thomas C., Jr.—Mus. Dir.
Eberle, Merab (Miss)—Cr.
Gadbury, Harry Lee—P., Et., T.
King, John M.—Port. P., T.
Koepnick, Robert Charles—S., T.
Pinkney, Helen Louise—
    Mus. Cur., Libn.
Raffel, Alvin R.—P., T.
Sauer, Leroy D.—Des., Comm. A.,
    C., L.
Schauer, Martha K.—T., P., L.
Thompson, Lewis Eugene—
    P., E., Cr., W., L.

Delaware

Engle, Robert—E.
Humphreys, Sallie Thomson—
    Des., P., L., E.
Stewart, Jarvis Anthony—E., P.
Swisher, Amy Margaret—C., Et., E.
Vickers, Robert—E.

East Cleveland

Jeffery, Charles Bartley—C., T.
Wilcox, Frank Nelson—
    P., Gr., Ser., T., W., L.

East Liverpool

Broomhall, Vincent—C., Des.
Schreckengost, Don—S., P., C., E.

East Palestine

McCloskey, Martha Linwood—P.

Elida

Beiler, Ida Zoe—P., T., L.

Euclid

Bates, Kenneth Francis—C., T., L.

Findlay

Whities-Sanner, Glenna—P.

Gambier

Rahming, Norris—P., E., Et., L.

Gates Mills

Francis, Henry Sayles—Mus. Cur.
van Gent, Cock—P.

Granville

King, Horace—E., Des., P., L.
Young, Mahonri Sharp—Mus. Dir.

Kent

Novotny, Elmer Ladislaw—P., E.
Reynolds, Douglas Wolcott—P., E.

Lakewood

Deike, Clara L.—P., W., L., T.
Prasse, Leona E.—Mus. Assoc. Cur.
Wolfs, Wilma Diena—
    S., P., Gr., E., I., L.

Loveland

Zimmerman, Carl John—P.

Lyndhurst

Cass, Katherine Dorn (Mrs.)—
    T., P., L.

Mansfield

Brown, Howard Scott—Cart.

Marietta

White, Agnes Hofman—P.

Massillon

Hise, Albert E.—Mus. Cur.
Townsend, Armine (Mrs.)—P.

Mechanicsburg

Hopkins, James R.—E., P.

Milford

Zeigler, John Arvin—Des.

Newark

Eckert, William Dean—E., P., Gr.

North Canton

Rainey, Robert E. L.—
    P., Ser., Des., T.

North Lima

Greenamyer, Leah J.—
    P., C., Des., L., W., T., Et.

North Olmsted

Kuekes, Edward D.—Cart.

Oberlin

Arnold, Paul B.—E., P., Gr.
Bongiorno, Laurine Mack (Mrs.)—E.
Buck, Richard David—Mus. Cur., L.
Parkhurst, Charles Percy—
    Mus. Dir., E., Hist.
Schauffler, Margaret Reynolds—
    P., E., C.
Stechow, Wolfgang—E.
Ward, Clarence—E., Mus. Dir., W.,
    L., Des.

Olmsted Falls

Westbrook, Lloyd Leonard—P.

Oxford

Fulwider, Edwin L.—P., E., Gr., Des.
Hodgin, Marston Dean—E., P.
Stewart, Marie H.—
    P., Des., C., T., W.

Painesville

McGee, Winston Eugene—E., P.

Piqua

Condon, Grattan—P., E.

Poland

Butler, Joseph G.—Mus. Dir., E., P.

Roseville

Cope, Leslie—P., Et., Des.

Rossmoyne

Schlapp, Charles W. L.—
    P., Lith., T.

Sandusky

Brown, Daniel Quilter—Cart.
Chaudhry, Aloys Sacksteder—
    Ceramist, E.

Shaker Heights

Bauer, Sol A.—S., T.
Colman, Charles C.—
    Des., Et., I., W.
Lange, Katharine Gruener (Mrs.)—S.
Miller, Leon Gordon—Des., P., Gr.
Stone, Iva Goldhamer—P., T.

Springfield

McKnight, Robert J.—
    S., Indst. Des., P.
Morgan, Helen Bosart (Mrs.)—S., T.
Thompson, Ralston—P., E.

Sylvania

Godwin, Blake-More—Mus. Dir.
Sinclair, Ellen Chisholm—P., Gr.

Toledo

Abramofsky, Israel—P., Cr.
Bruner, Louise (Mrs.)—Cr.
Gregg, Richard Nelson—
    Mus. Cur., Des., W., L., E.
Jensen, George—P., T., Comm. A.
Lawson, Edward Pitt—E.
MacLean, J. Arthur—
    W., L., C., E., Gr.
Saunders, John Allen—Cart., W., L.
Thorne, Anna Louise—P.
Wittmann, Otto, Jr.—Mus. Dir.

Troy

Allen, Mary Coleman—P.

University Heights

Sinz, Walter A.—S., T., L.

West Carrollton

Banker, William Edwin—Des., I.

Whitehouse

Dehner, Walter Leonard—P.

Willoughby

Eschmann, Jean Charles—C.

Willowick

Gebhart, Paul—Adv. Des.

Worthington

Frasch, Miriam R.—P.
Littlefield, Edgar—C., E.
Russell, Mark—P., Des., I.
Severino, D. Alexander—E., L., P.

West Milton

Osborne, Roland D.—P.

Yellow Springs

Metcalf, Robert Marion—
  Stained Glass Des., P., E., L.
Velsey, Seth M.—S., P., T., Des.
Whitmore, Robert Houston—
  P., Et., Eng., C.

Youngstown

Singer, Clyde J.—P., T.
Vaccaro, Patrick Frank—Ser., T.

Zanesville

Dietz, Charles—Mus. Dir.

OKLAHOMA

Ada

Hoover, Ida L.—E.

Bartlesville

Patterson, George W. Patrick—
  Mus. Dir., P.

Durant

Baker, Minnie Mitchell—E., P., S., L.

Enid

Randolph, John W.—E., P., Lith.

Miami

Wilson, Charles Banks—
  P., Lith., I., W., E.

Muskogee

West, Walter Richard—P., T.

Norman

Bavinger, Eugene A.—
  Mus. Dir., T., Des., P.
de Borhegyi, Stephan—Mus. Dir., E.
Jacobson, Oscar Brousse—
  P., E., W., L.
O'Neil, John—P., E.
Sutton, George Miksch—
  P., I., W., L., Mus. Cur.

Oklahoma City

Abbott, Edward Roydon—P.
Joslyn, Florence Brown—P., Des., I.
McChristy, Quentin L.—
  P., Des., T., Gr., I.
Moore, Loraine Elizabeth—Et., P.
Patterson, Patty (Mrs.)—
  P., C., T., L., W.
Sheets, Nan (Mrs.)—
  Mus. Dir., Cr., P., L.
Stevenson, Edna Bradley—P., E., L.

Shawnee

Bond, Leroy—E.
Gyermek, Stephen A.—
  Mus. Dir., P., E., C.

Stillwater

Berry, Camelia (Mrs.)—P., I.
Jack, Ella—E., P.
McVicker, J. Jay—P., S., Gr., E.
Reed, Doel—Et., P., E., L.
Schwarz, Felix Conrad—
  P., E., W., L.
Schwarz, Myrtle Cooper—E., C., W.
Stevens, Dwight Elton—Des., P., E.

Texhoma

Burrows, Pearl (Mrs.)—P., L.

Tulsa

Albin, Edgar A.—E., P., Eng.
Allen, Clarence Canning—
  P., Des., Cart., I., W., L.
Broadd, Harry Andrew—
  E., P., L., A. Hist.
Carrothers, Grace Neville (Mrs.)—
  P., E., Lith., T.
Forrest, James Taylor—
  Mus. Dir., W., Hist.
Frazier, Bernard—S., L., C.
Hogue, Alexandre—P., Lith., W., T.
Montgomery, Claude—P.
Packer, Clair Lange (Mr.)—
  P., Comm. A., Des., Cart., I.
Proctor, Charles—Mus. Cur.
Shultz, George Leonard—Port. P., L.
Slack, Erle B.—Cart., I.
Snodgrass, Jeanne Owen (Mrs.)—
  Mus. Cur., Comm. A., L.
Steinke, Bettina Blair—P., Comm. A.

OREGON

Ashland

Ady, Marion—E.

Corvallis

Gilkey, Gordon Waverly—
  Et., Eng., E., W., L.
Gunn, Paul James—E., P., Gr.
Huck, Robert E.—E., P., Gr.
Jameson, Demetrios George—
  E., P., Gr.
Levine, Shepard—P., E., Lith., L.
Rock, John Henry—E., P., Lith.
Sandgren, Ernest Nelson—
  E., P., Lith.
Tayson, Wayne Pendleton—S., E.

Eugene

Baldinger, Wallace Spencer—
  Mus. Dir., E., Cr., W., L.
Colley, James F.—Mus. Cur., P., T.
Kerns, Maude Irvine—P., Gr., E.
Kutka, Anne (Mrs.)—P.
McCosh, David John—P., E.
Vincent, Andrew McDuffie—P., E.

Gearhart

Klep, Rolf—I., Comm. A., Des.

McMinnville

Emerson, Sybil Davis—
  P., I., E., W., Des., C.

Monmouth

Heath, Pearl B.—E.

Nehalem

Runquist, Arthur—P., Et., Lith., T.

Oswego

Bunce, Louis—P., Gr., T.
Haseltine, James—P., Gr.
Haseltine, Margaret Wilson Maury—
  P., C., T.

Portland

Cameron, Josephine Elaine—P., Eng.
Dowling, Colista (Mrs.)—P., I.
Geiser, Bernard—P.
Gerlach, Albert A.—
  Des., C., P., L., Cr.
Givler, William Hubert—
  P., Et., Lith., T.
Haley, Sally (Mrs.)—P., T.
Hall, Lindsley Foote—
  Mus. Research Fellow

Halvorsen, Ruth Elise—E., P.
Heidel, Frederick H.—P., E.
Hill, Hedley—Assoc. Mus. Dir.
Hinshaw, Bernard—E.
Kennedy, Leta M.—
  C., Des., Gr., L., E.
Krause, La Verne (Mrs.)—
  P., Gr., Des.
McLarty, William James—
  P., T., Lith.
Morris, Carl—P.
Morris, Hilda (Mrs.)—S.
Newton, Francis John—Mus. Cur.
Sullivan, Max William—
  Mus. Dir., E.
Wilbanks, W. H.—A. Dir.

Salem

Hall, Carl A.—P., Gr., Cr., T.

Troutdale

Jones, Catherine (Mrs.)—W., Cr.

Wecoma Beach

Wanker, Maude Walling—
  P., T., Mus. Dir., L.

PENNSYLVANIA

Abington

McGarvey, Elsie Siratz (Mrs.)—
  Mus. Cur., T.

Aldan-Clifton Heights

Foulke, Viola—P., L.

Allentown

Cantieni, Margaret Balzer (Mrs.)—P.
Dreisbach, Clarence Ira—P., Des., T.
Lucas, Blanche Wingert—
  P., T., W., L.
Swallow, William Weldon—
  S., P., T.

Altoona

Counsel, Frederick Alan—P., T.
La Grange, Jacques—P., T., Gr.

Ambler

Lee, Manning de Villeneuve—P., I.
Willet, Henry Lee—C., W., L.

Arcola

Mitchell, Henry Weber—S.

Ardmore

McCall, Virginia Armitage—
  P., Med. I., Gr., W., L.
White, Vera—P., Lith.

Barto

Bertoia, Harry—S., Des., P., C.

Bedminster

Solowey, Ben—P., S.

Berwyn

Mason, John Alden—
  Former Mus. Cur., W.

Bethel Park

Bassett, Charles Preston—
  Des., P., Lith., S., T., L., C.
Bassett, Margaret Giffen (Mrs.)—
  P., T., Des., L., C.

Bethlehem

Goodman, Ann Taube—P.
Quirk, Francis J.—P., E., L., Cr.

Birchrunville

Hopkins, Kendal Coles—P., T.

Boyertown

Martin, Basil E.—P.

Bridgeport

Garrett, Priscilla Longshore—P., L.

Bryn Athyn

Ewald, Louis—P., Des.
Pendleton, Constance—P., T.

Bryn Mawr

Bernheimer, Richard—E., L., W.
Borgstedt, Douglas—Cart., W.
Davis, Emma Earlenbaugh (Mrs.)—
    P., I.
Pittman, Hobson—P., L.
Tuttle, Helen Norris—P., E.

Buck Hills Falls

Monaghan, Gertrude—
    Mural P., Arch. Des.

Buckingham

Bye, Ranulph de Bayeux—P.

Camp Hill

Michener, Edward C.—P., I., Des.

Carnegie

Long, Robert Dickson—P., C., L.

Carversville

Hargens, Charles W., Jr.—I.
Ward, Charles W.—P., T., Gr.

Chadds Ford

McCoy, John W., II—P., T.
Wyeth, Andrew Newell—P.

Chambersburg

Biehl, Godfrey F.—P., Gr., C., E., L.
Harris, Josephine Marie—E.

Cheltenham

Day, Laurence James—P., Gr., T.
Goldman, Robert Douglas—
    P., E., L., W.

Christiana

Weidner, Doris Kunzie—
    P., Ser., Lith.

Coopersburg

Riu, Victor—S.

Coraopolis

Olshanska, Stephanie (Mrs.)—
    P., E., L.

Davids

Terry, Duncan Niles—C., Des.

Dayton

Lias, Thomas R.—P., S., E., Gr.

Devon

Barrett, Lisbeth S. (Mrs.)—Min. P.

Doylestown

Crooks, Forrest C.—
    Des., C., P., Comm. A.
Speight, Francis—P., T.

Drexel Hill

Campbell, C. Isabel—P.
Corasick, William W.—P., T.
Hudson, Kenton Warne—
    P., Comm. A., Des., I.
Robinson, Ruth M.—P., Des., T.
Sklar, George—Animal P., E., L., Des.

Easton

Collins, Mary Susan—P., C., T.
Sturtevant, Edith Louise—P., E.

Edinboro

Doucette, Aime Henri—E., C.
Stapp, Ray V.—
    E., C., P., S., Comm. A.

Elkins Park

Berenstain, Stanley—Cart., W.
Scalella, Jules—P., Des., T.

Erie

Lord, Don W.—P.
Plavcan, Catharine Burns (Mrs.)—
    Cr., T., P., L.
Plavcan, Joseph Michael—P., T., L.

Erwinna

Adler, Elmer—Typog., E., L., W.

Germantown

Denis, Leonard—Comm. A., W., Cr.
Ferguson, Nancy Maybin—P.

Gettysburg

Peck, Clara Elsene—I., P., Et.

Gibsonia

de Coux, Janet—S.

Glenside

Brehme, Claire—P., I., L., T., W.
Marshall, Margaret Jane— P., I., W.

Greensburg

Chew, Paul Albert—Mus. Dir.
Irvin, Sister Mary Francis—
    P., E., Gr.

Gwynedd Valley

Stuempfig, Walter—P.

Harrisburg

Roderick, John M.—P.

Hartsville

Maxwell, John Raymond—P.

Hatboro

Eltonhead, Frank—Art Editor, E.

Havertown

Cooke, Donald Ewin—
    W., I., Des., L.

Gasparro, Frank—S., T.
Jayne, De Witt Whistler—I.

Hazleton

Meyer, William C.—P.

Hellerstown

Albee, Percy F.—P., Gr.

Holicong

Bye, Arthur Edwin—C., P., W., L.
Sotter, Alice Bennett (Mrs.)—
    C., P., Des.

Honesdale

Stegner, Nicholas—P., C.

Huntingdon Valley

Meltzer, Arthur—P., C., L.
Saint, Lawrence—P., W., L., C.
Van Roekens, Paulette (Mrs.)—
    P., T.

Indiana

Biamonte, Grace Houston—T., P., L.
Kipp, Orval—P., E., Gr., I., L.
Reynolds, Ralph William—E., P.

Jenkintown

Brown, Bo (Robert Franklin)—Cart.
Brown, Mary Chalmers—Des., E.
Coleman, Ralph Pallen—P., I.

Johnstown

Lohr, Kathryn Lavina—P., T.
Price, Helen F.—P., W., L.

Kempton

Hesketh—S.

Kutztown

de Francesco, Italo L.—E., P.

Lahaska

Blondheim, Adolphe Wiener—
    P., Et., Lith., T.
Teller, Jane Simon—S.

Lancaster

Book, Harry Martin—P.
Kermes, Constantine John—P.

Lansdale

Stuart, Kenneth James—I.

Lansdowne

Kennedy, William D.—P., Et.

Latrobe

Frola, Joseph R.—P.
Himler, Mary Martha—
    P., Ser., T., L., Cr.

Lebanon

Whitman, John Franklin, Jr.—
    I., Des.

Lock Haven

Bottorf, Edna Annabelle—
    E., P., W., L.
Gummo, Blanchard Stanley—
    P., E., L., Gr., W.

Malvern

Doyle, Jerry—Cart., T.

McKeesport

Ulm, John Louis—I., Cart.

Mechanicsburg

Newton, Earle Williams—
Mus. Dir., Hist., E.

Media

Adams, Marjorie Nickles (Mrs.)—
P., C.
Berd, Morris—P., T.
Blank, John Philip—Des., P., Cart.
Cooke, Edna (Mrs.)—I.
Hildebrandt, William Albert, Jr.—
P., S., E., I.
Shuler, Clyde—Des., E.

Melrose Park

Flory, Arthur L.—Gr., P., T., I.
Sabatini, Raphael—P., S., E., Gr., L.

Merion

Barber, John—P., Et., I., L.
Fritz, Henry Eugene—
E., W., L., P., I., Gr.
Ligget, Jane Stewart—S.
Muller, Helen Chance (Mrs.)—P.
Robb, David M.—E.
Sankowsky, Itzhak—P., Eng., T.
Trump, Rachel Bulley (Mrs.)—
Port. P.

Mill Hall

Bossert, Edythe Hoy—P., T.

Milton

Mitchell, Bruce Handiside—
P., E., L.

Minisink Hills

Harriton, David M.—
Des., C., P., S., L.

Monroeville

Libby, William Charles—
P., Pr. M., I.

Morrisville

Donelson, Earl Tomlinson—P., Lith.
White, J. Gordon—P., T., Des.
Zeis, Joseph—Cart.

Mount Pocono

Staehle, Albert—I., Des.

Moylan

Brown, William Norman—E., W., L.
Whitney, Philip Richardson—P., C.

New Hope

Badura, Bernard—P., C.
Chapman, William McKissack—Con-
sultant on Art Films, W., L., Editor
Charry, John—S., T.
Cheney, Sheldon—W., Cr.
Folinsbee, John Fulton—P., T.
Froelich, Paul—
P., Des., Gr., Comm. A., I.
Godwin, Frank—P., I., Cart., Et.,
Des.
Harbeson, Georgiana Brown (Mrs.)—
P., Des., C., W., L.

Leith-Ross, Harry—
P., Comm. A., T., W., Cr., L.
McKie, Roy—Cart., Comm. A.
Pershing, Louise—P., L.
Price, M. Elizabeth—P., L., T.
Redfield, Edward W.—P.
Rosin, Harry—S., T.
Swengel, Faye (Mrs.)—P.
Wentworth, Harriet Marshall—P.

Newtown

Fry, Guy Edgar—Des., I., E.

Newtown Square

Lindborg, Alice Whitten (Mrs.)—
P., W.
Lindborg, Carl—P., S., W., I., T.
Serwazi, Albert B.—P., Des., I.

New Wilmington

Sheridan, Joseph Marsh—
P., Gr., S., I., L., E.

Norristown

Stallman, Emma S.—C.

Nottingham

Rist, Louis G.—Pr. M.

Orwigsburg

Egas, Camilo—P., S., Et., Lith., T.

Ottsville

Glasco, Joseph—P., S.
Rudy, Charles—S., E.

Paoli

Esherick, Wharton—S., Des., C., Gr.

Penn Wynne

Angelo, Emidio—Cart., P., L.
Martino, Giovanni—P.

Perkasie

Falter, John—I.
Meierhans, Joseph—P.

Philadelphia

Acker, Edna Leonhardt—
Des., E., P., L.
Alexander, Franklin O.—Cart.
Allen, Agnes—P.
Anderson, Arnold Nelson—Et., Des.
Anthes, Rudolf—Mus. Cur., E.
Armstrong, Carolyn Faught (Mrs.)—
P., T.
Arnett, Eleanor—P.
Ashton, Ethel V.—P., Gr.
Ballinger, Louise Bowen (Mrs.)—E.
Bard, Sara Foresman—P., T.
Barnett, William—P.
Battaglia, Pasquale Michael—P., T.
Bendiner, Alfred—Arch., P., Gr.,
Cart., W.
Benson, Emanuel—E., W., Cr., L.
Benson, Gertrude A.—
Cr., Feature Writer
Berman, Elliott Walter—P., Eng.
Bistline, Edna Marian (Mrs.)—P.
Blackburn, Morris—
P., Et., Eng., Lith., Ser., T.
Blai, Boris—S., E.
Bloch, Julia (Mrs.)—
Pr. M., I., P., W.
Bloch, Julius T.—P.
Bonelli, James P.—P., Des., T.
Bookbinder, Jack—
P., Lith., T., L., W.
Bortin, Dora (Mrs.)—P., T.

Bowling, Jack Frank—
Eng., Lith., C., I.
Bradway, Florence Dell—P., T.
Bregler, Charles—P., W.
Buzek, Irene M.—P., Indst. I.
Camero, Blanche Gonzalez—
P., Et., T.
Campbell, Cora A.—
P., Et., C., T., I., L.
Capolino, John Joseph—P., E.
Cariss, Marguerite (Mrs.)—P.
Carson, Sol Kent—P., E.
Christaldi, Angeline A.—P.
Cohee, Marion M.—P., T.
Condit, Walter D.—P., T., Comm. A.
Converse, Lily S.—Lith., P.
Cooley, Ruth Patton—P.
Crawford, Barbara (Mrs.)—W., P., E.
de Angeli, Marguerite Lofft—I., W.
Dellaripa, Filomena Joan—
P., Lith., T.
de Merlier, Franz—P., T., W., L.
Denney, Irene—P.
Dillon, Mildred Murphy (Mrs.)—
Pr. M., Et., Ser.
Donovan, Ellen (Mrs.)—
P., T., L., Lith.
Drabkin, Stella (Mrs.)—
P., Mosaicist, Gr., Des.
Drucker, Boris—Cart., Comm. A.,
Des.
Eiseley, Mabel L.—Asst. Mus. Dir.
Emerson, Edith—P., I., L., W.,
Mus. Cur., T.
Entenmann, Raymond Taylor—
Mus. Cur., E., L.
Etting, Emlen—P., Des., I., E., W., L.
Feinstein, Samuel Lawrence—
P., T., Cr., Gr., I., W., L.
Fenton, Beatrice—S.
Ferris, Edythe (Mrs.)—
P., C., Gr., T., W., L.
Fine, Stanley M.—Cart.
Francksen, Jean Eda—P., E., Des.
Fraser, Joseph T., Jr.—
Mus. Dir., Arch.
Frudakis, Evangelos William—S.
Gardner, Walter Henry—P.
Gest, Margaret—P.
Gill, Frederick James—
P., T., L., Lith.
Gold, Albert—P., Gr., I., T., W., L.
Grafly, Dorothy (Mrs.)—W., Cr., L.
Greenberg, Joseph J., Jr.—S.
Groff, June—Des., P., Ser.
Grossman, Joseph B.—P.
Heitland, W. Emerton—
P., I., T., L.
Henderson, Leslie (Mr.)—P., Et., T.
Hoeflich, Sherman Clark—Des., T., P.
Hood, Thomas Richard—Gr., Des., E.
Howard, Humbert L.—P.
Hutton, Dorothy Wackerman—
Et., Lith., P.
Hutton, Hugh M.—Cart.
Jennings, Francis A.—P., S., T.
Jones, Susan Alice—P., Comm. A.
Kapustin, Razel—P.
Kidder, Alfred—Asst. Mus. Dir.
Kirkbride, Earle Rosslyn—Et.
Kramrisch, Stella, (Dr.)—
Mus. Cur., E., Cr., L.
Lichten, Frances—
W., Des., Et., I., Mus. Cur.
Mackey, William Erno—P., Des., Gr.,
Cart., Comm. A., T., W.
Marceau, Henri—Mus. Dir.
Margolis, Nathan—P., Des., Lith., Ser.
Martino, Antonio—P.
McBey, James—P., Et.
McCormick, Katharine H.—P., Gr.
McCouch, Gordon Mallet—P., Gr.
McIlhenny, Henry P.—Mus. Cur.
Merrick, James Kirk—
P., T., I., W., L.
Mesibov, Harold Allan—P.
Milhous, Katherine—
Author, Artist, Des.
Miller, Isabelle Lazarus—P., C., E.
Molind, A.—P.

Montgomery, Loran A. D. (Mr.)—
P., T.
Mullineux, Mary—Pr. M., P., T.
Myers, Willard—Et., I., W.
Nelson, Leonard L.—P., T., Gr., S.
Norris, S. Walter—P., W.
Nuse, Oliver—P., T.
Oakley, Violet—
P., S., Des., I., W., L.
Oshiver, Harry J.—P., Des., Typog.
Page, Elizabeth Amie—
P., Lith., Des.
Paravicini, Lizette—P., C., T.
Peoples, Augusta H. (Mrs.)—P., T.
Peri, Eve—Tex. Des., C.
Perkins, G. Holmes—E.
Pretsch, John Edward—
Cart., Comm. A., P.
Price, John M.—Cart., A. Dir., Des.
Pullinger, Herbert—Pr. M., P., I., T.
Reece, Dora—P.
Reinsel, Walter—Des., P., Et.
Riggs, Robert—Pr. M.
Robin, Fanny—P.
Rothman, Henry L.—
P., Des., Et., Lith.
Salko, Samuel—P.
Satterthwaite, Linton—Mus. Cur.
Schell, Susan Gertrude—P., T.
Schuenemann, Mary B.—P., T.
Scull, Nina Woloshukova—P., L., T.
Shatalow, Vladimir—P.
Simon, Grant Miles—
P., Arch., Lith., L.
Smiley, Helen A.—C., T., W.
Smith, Miriam Tindall—P., C.
Smith, Wuanita—P., Gr., I., W.
Southworth, Helen McCorkle (Mrs.)
—P.
Spruance, Benton Murdoch—
Lith., P., E.
Stahl, Louise Zimmerman (Mrs.)—
P., T., I., L.
Stoddard, Alice Kent Pearson—P.
Taylor, Ralph—P., T., Gr.
Thomas, Emma Warfield—P., T., W.
Thrash, Dox—P., Et., Lith., W., L.,
Des., S.
Troth, Celeste Heckscher—P.
Turner, Matilda Hutchinson—Min. P.
Van Loan, Dorothy Leffingwell—
P., Lith.
Van Sciver, Pearl Aiman—P., T.
Wallace, David Harold—
Hist., Mus. Cur.
Walton, Edward Austin—E., Des., P.
Warwick, Edward—
P., Eng., E., W., L.
Warwick, Ethel Herrick (Mrs.)—P.
Watkins, Franklin C.—P., T.
Watson, Jean—P.
Weidner, Roswell Theodore—
P., Lith., T.
Wiley, Hedwig—P.
Wolf, Ben—P., Cr., W., I., T., L.
Wood, Edith Longstreth (Mrs.)—
P., Lith.
Zeil, William Francis Von—
P., Eng., Hist.
Zigrosser, Carl—Mus. Cur., W., Cr.

Phoenixville

Crowell, Lucius—P.

Pineville

Smith, William Arthur—
P., Lith., I., L.

Pittsburgh

Arkus, Leon Anthony—Asst. Mus. Dir.
Clifford, Lois Irene—C., T.
Cornelius, Marty (Miss)—
P., Des., T., I., W., L.
Crawford, Earl—P.
Gabriel, Robert A,—C., S., T.
Haggart, Winifred Watkins—E., P.
Hanna, Boyd—I., Eng.

Hilton, Roy—P., E.
Hovey, Walter Read—E.
Jensen, Margaret Edmonds (Mrs.)—
P., Ser.
Johnstone, B. Kenneth—Arch., E.
Koerner, Henry—P.
Le Clair, Charles George—P., E., L.
Lee, Musier Taintor (Mrs.)—P.
Lepper, Robert Lewis—P., Des., E.
McCready, Carolin (Mrs.)—P., T.
Muller-Munk, Peter—Des.
Readio, Wilfred A.—P., Lith., E.
Reiber, Richard H.—
P., Et., S., Des., L., T.
Rice, Norman Lewis—E., Gr., P.
Rosenberg, Samuel—P., E.
Scheuch, Harry William—P.
Smith, David Loeffler—E., P., L.
Sturges, Lillian—I., P., W.
Sutton, Rachel McClelland (Mrs.)—
P.
Thoburn, Jean—P., T., W., I.
Thomas, Estelle L.—P.
Twiggs, Russell Gould—P., Ser.
von Fuehrer, Ottmar F.—P., I., L.
Warren, Charles Bradley—S.
Washburn, Gordon Bailey—Mus. Dir.
Weissberger, Herbert P.—Mus. Cur.
Williams, May—P., Des., T.
Winter, Clark—S.

Plymouth Meeting

Moskowitz, Shirley (Mrs.)—P., T., L.
Pitz, Henry C.—I., E., W., P.
Pitz, Molly Wood (Mrs.)—P., T.

Quakertown

Louden, Adelaide Bolton—W., I.
Louden, Norman P.—Des., L.
Papashvily, George—S.

Radnor

Clifford, Henry—Mus. Cur.
Edrop, Arthur—I., Comm. A., W.,
L., P., Cart.
Young, Charles Morris—P., Et.

Reading

Dunkelberger, Ralph D.—P., T., I.
Penfield, Florence Bentz (Mrs.)—
P., T.
Poole, Earl Lincoln—Former Mus.
Dir., I., Gr., S., P., E.
Reichert, Oscar Alfred—
P., Des., Arch.
Waldron, James M. K.—
Mus. Cur., P., T.

Ridgway

McCloskey, Eunice LonCoske—
P., W., L.

Rosemont

Chrystie, Margaret H.—P., Lith., T.

Rushland

Nuse, Roy Cleveland—P., W., L., T.

Scalp Level

Harris, Margie Coleman—
P., E., S., Et., W., L., Cr., Gr., C.

Scranton

Shalkop, Robert L.—Mus. Dir.

Sharon

Dunn, Nate—P., T.
Smolen, Francis Frank—
P., I., Des., S., C., T.

Shiremanstown

Colt, Martha Cox—P., S., Mus. Asst.

Souderton

Hallman, H. Theodore, Jr.—C., T.

Springfield

House, James Charles, Jr.—
S., E., Cart.
Winters, John Richard—P., S.

Springtown

Albee, Grace (Mrs.)—Eng., L.

State College

Case, Andrew—P., Comm. A., E., W.
Dickson, Harold Edward—E., W.
Ferguson, Thomas Reed, Jr.—E., P.
Hyslop, Francis Edwin, Jr.—E.
Lederer, Lucy Christine Kemmerer—
P., Ser., L., Des.
Lowenfeld, Viktor—E., W., L.
Weisman, Winston R.—E., W.

Swarthmore

Walker, Robert Miller—E.

Telford

Freelon, Allan Randall—Pr. M., P.

Titusville

Herpst, Martha Jane—Port. P.

Uniontown

Sochor, Bozena (Miss)—P.

Upper Darby

Kline, Edith L. Bollinger (Mrs.)—
P., T.
Roberts, Gilroy—Eng., S.

Valley Forge

Rainey, Froelich—
Mus. Dir., E., W., L.

Villanova

Domville, Paul—E., P.

Wallingford

Holt, Justin Gordon—Cart.
Jayne, Horace H. F.—Mus. Vice-Dir.

Warren

Walker, Gene Alden—P.

Washington

Parcell, Malcolm Stephens—P.

Wayne

Borst, George H.—S.
Brodhead, Quita (Mrs.)—P., T.
Hoffman, Edward Fenno, III—S.
Key, Ted—Cart., W.
Smith, Dorothy Alden—Book Des., I.

West Chester

Jamison, Philip—P., T.
Smith, Howard E.—P.
Spencer, Howard Bonnell—P., T.
Wescott, Paul—P.

Westtown

Connelly, George L.—I.

Wilkes-Barre

Cortiglia, Niccolo—P., T.

Wyncote

Nelke, Dora K. (Mrs.)—P.
Thompson, F. Raymond—
   Cart., Comm. A.

Wynnewood

Gill, Sue May (Mrs.)—P., S., T.
Harding, George—P.
Rice, Harold R.—E., Cr., W., Gr., L.
Sweeny, Barbara—Assoc. Mus. Cur.

Yardley

Wedderspoon, Richard G.—P., E.

Yeadon

Smalley, Janet—I.

York

Lewis, Margaret Sarah—
   T., P., Gr., Des., C., L.

Zionsville

Stark, Melville F.—P., E., L.

RHODE ISLAND

Bristol

Knowlton, Daniel Gibson—
   C., Des., T.

Cranston

Leif, Florence (Mrs.)—P.
Peers, Gordon Franklin—P., T.

Coventry Center

Mays, Maxwell—I., W., P., Des.

Edgewood

Haun, Robert Charles—P., Des.

Gaspee Plateau

Doley, Peter—T., Des., P.

Jamestown

Wright, Catherine Morris (Mrs.)—
   P., T., W., L.

Johnson

Duphiney, Wilfred I.—P., T., L.

Kingston

Cain, Joseph Lambert—P., E., Lith.
Loring, Paule Stetson—
   Watercolorist, Des., Cart., I.
Rachotes, Matene (Mrs.)—
   P., T., Lith.

Little Compton

Buller, Audrey (Mrs.)—P., Des.
Burroughs, Betty (Mrs.)—T., S.
Luce, Molly (Mrs.)—P.
Medary, Amie Hampton—
   P., W., L., Des.
Parsons, Lloyd Holman—P., Des.

Middletown

Murray, Martin J.—P., T.

Newport

Carry, Marion Katherine—P., T., Lith.
Drury, Hope Curtis (Mrs.)—P.
Drury, William H.—P., Et.
Holt, Dorothy M. (Mrs.)—P., I., T.
Price, Edith Ballinger—I., P., W.
Sturtevant, Louisa Clark—
   Des., P., T.

Providence

Breul, Harold G.—Des., Cart., I., P.
Brigham, William Edgar—C., T., Des.
Brown, William Alden—P.
Casciano, August—P.
Casey, Elizabeth T.—Mus. Cur.
Cianfarani, Aristide Berto—S., Des.
Cirino, Antonio—P., C., W., T., Des.
Congdon, William—P.
Conti, Gino Emilio—P., S., T., C., L.
Davidson, Bernice—Mus. Cur.
Day, Martha B. Willson—
   P., Miniaturist
Downing, George Elliott—E., P.
Ducasse, Mabel Lisle—P.
Feldman, Walter—P., E., Gr.
Frazier, John Robinson—E., P.
Herbert, James Drummond—T., P., S.
Hershey, Samuel F.—E., Des., P.
Holton, Grace M.—
   E., P., Des., C., W., L.
Howell, Marie W. (Mrs.)—
   Des., T., C.
Keith, D. G.—Mus. Cur.
Nalbandian, Karnig—P., Et.
Neilson, Katharine Bishop—
   E., L., W.
Nesbitt, Alexander John—
   Des., E., W., L.

Saylesville

Harris, Charles Gordon—P.

Wakefield

Smith, Sibley—P.

Warwick

Verrecchia, Alfeo—Lith., P., Des.

West Barrington

Jones, Nancy (Mrs.)—P., T.
Love, George Paterson—P., T.

Westerly

Day, Chon (Chauncey Addison)—
   Cart.
Killam, Walt—P., Gr., T., C.
Tillinghast, Archie Chapman—
   P., Des., T.

SOUTH CAROLINA

Charleston

Halsey, William Melton—P., T., I.
Hirsch, Willard—S., L.
McCallum, Corrie (Mrs.)—
   P., I., T., C.
McCormack, Helen Gardner—
   Mus. Dir.
Mikell, Minnie Robertson (Mrs.)—
   P., Comm. A., Des., T.
Verner, Elizabeth O'Neill—
   Et., P., W., L.

Clemson

Fernow, Bernice Pauahi Andrews
   (Mrs.)—P., T.

Clinton

Anderson, Loulie—P., T., C.

Columbia

Coles, Ann Cadwallader—P.
Craft, John Richard—Mus. Dir.
Petroff, Gilmer—P., Des., E.
Yaghjian, Edmund—P., E., L.

Greenville

Bopp, Emery—E., P.
Havens, Murray P.—Des., T.
Gustafson, Dwight Leonard—E.

Hartsville

Brumbaugh, R. Nickey—E., P., Des.

McConnels

Settlemyre, Julius Lee, Jr.—
   P., L., T., Mus. Dir.

Meggett

Dick, John Henry—P.

Ridgeland

Sheridan, Mark—Des., P.

Rock Hill

Grant, Vernon—I., W., Des., L.

Spartanburg

Cook, August—E., P., Eng.

Sumter

White, Elizabeth—Et., P., I., T.

Winnsboro

Douglas, Laura Glenn—P., L., T.

SOUTH DAKOTA

Aberdeen

Holaday, William H.—E., P., C., Gr.

Brookings

Ritz, Madeline Gateka—E.

Custer

Ziolkowski, Korczak—S.

Sioux Falls

Eide, Palmer—E., Des., C., S.

Spearfish

Cocking, Gretta—P., E., W., L.

Vermillion

Stilwell, Wilber Moore—
   E., P., Des., Gr., L., I., W.

Yankton

Janssen, Hans—E., Mus. Cur., L.
Liepe, Wolfgang—E., Mus. Cur., W.

TENNESSEE

Copperhill

Mitchell, Sue Lavinia—P.

Gatlinburg

Zimmerman, Alice E.—C., T.

Knoxville

Chumley, John Wesley—P.
Ewing, Charles Kermit—
E., P., C., Lith.
Sivyer, Henrietta R.—E.

Maryville

Beard, Richard Elliott—E., P.

Memphis

Ackerman, Marie Featherston (Mrs.)
—Asst. Mus. Dir.
Bush, Ruth C. (Mrs.)—Mus. Dir.
Callicott, Burton Harry—
P., E., Calligrapher
Clark, Louise Bennett (Mrs.)—
Mus. Dir., L.
Cloar, Carroll—P., Lith.
Lehman, Louise Brasell (Mrs.)—P.
McIntyre, Florence M.—E., W., L.
McNett, Elizabeth Vardell (Mrs.)—
P., Med. I., T., Gr.
McNett, William Brown—I., Lith., P.
Rust, Edwin C.—S., E.
Schwartz, Marjorie Watson (Mrs.)—
P., C., T.
Searcy, Elisabeth—P., Et., T., W., L.
Winer, Donald Arthur—
P., Mus. Cur., C., E.

Nashville

Bachmura, Barbara Lee (Mrs.)—P.,
E., C., Gr.
Dutch, George Sheldon—E., W.
Freundlich, August L.—E., P.
Junkin, Marion Montague (Mr.)—
P., E.
Partee, McCullough—S., I., T., Des.

Old Hickory

Donelson, Mary Hooper (Mrs.)—
S., P.

Sewanee

Fieschi, Giannetto—E., P., Gr.

Signal Mountain

Cress, George Ayres—P., E.

White Haven

Fyfe, John Hamilton—P., Cart., I.

TEXAS

Abilene

Lacy, Margaret Luella—E., P., C.
Perini, Maxine Walker—P., L., T.
Smith, John Bertie—P., E., W.

Amarillo

Garnsey, Clarke Henderson—
P., Et., C., E., L.

Anahuac

White, Ethyle Herman (Mrs.)—
P., I., W.

Arlington

Joyner, Howard Warren—
E., P., L., Des.

Austin

Adams, Margaret Boroughs (Mrs.)—
P., Lith., C., I.
Coulter, Doris Mary—Des., C., E.
Davis, Marian B.—E.
Fearing, Kelly—P., Et., E.
Fogel, Seymour—P., Muralist, W., L.
Forsyth, Constance—Et., Lith., P., E.

Guerin, John William—P., E.
Hatgil, Paul Peter—E., C.
Lester, William Lewis—P., T., Lith.
Mozley, Loren Norman—
P., Gr., L., W.
Spruce, Everett Franklin—P., E.
Stevens, Kelly Haygood—P., C., T.
Umlauf, Charles—S.
Weismann, Donald LeRoy—
E., P., Cr., L., W.
White, Ralph Ernest, Jr.—
E., P., Des., I.

Bay City

Bess, Forrest Clemenger—P., L.

Beaumont

Boughton, Cleta Olmstead Robbins—
W.
Boughton, William Harrison—
P., T.
Coe, Matchett Herring—S.
David, Lorene—P., E., Gr., L.

Belton

Hanna, Edith Margaret—E., C., P., S.

Canyon

Robinson, Virginia Isabel—
E., P., C., Gr.

Clarendon

Bugbee, Harold Dow—I., P.

Corpus Christi

Cain, Joseph A.—P., T., Cr.
Locke, Lucie Harris (Mrs.)—
P., W., I., T., S., Cr.
Thomson, Adele Underwood (Mrs.)
—P., T., Cr.

Corsicana

Noble, Mamie Jones (Mrs.)—
P., C., W., L., T.

Dallas

Bearden, Edward Carpenter—
E., P., Des., I., Comm. A., Lith.
Brunet, Adele Laure—
P., T., Des., Cr., L., I.
Buchanan, Laura—P.
Bywaters, Jerry—
Mus. Dir., E., W., P., L.
Culwell, Bennie Lee—P.
Davis, Jessie Freemont Snow—
P., S., T.
Dowling, Jacques MacCuiston (Mrs.)
—S., P., L., T.
Dozier, Otis—P., Lith.
Eisenlohr, Edward G.—P., Lith., L.
Elder, Inez Staub—P., T., L.
Huseby, Arleen Meister—P., C.
La Mond, Stella Lodge—
C., Lith., Ser., E., L.
Mauzey, Merritt—Lith., W., P., I., L.
McClung, Florence—
P., Lith., C., E., L.
Medellin, Octavio—S.
Palmer, Jessie (Mrs.)—P., S., T.
Polvogt, Carl William, Jr.—
Cart., Comm. A., Des.
Scruggs-Carruth, Margaret Ann
(Mrs.)—Et., T., I., W., L., C.
Smith, Robin Artine—P., Comm. A.
Speed, Rosalie—P., Des., Comm. A.
Tennant, Allie Victoria—S.
Travis, Kathryne Hail—P., T.
Travis, Olin Herman—P., Lith., L., E.
Walmsley, Elizabeth (Mrs.)—
E., Lith., Ser.
West, Bernice (Mrs.)—S.

Denton

Brisac, Edith Mae—
E., Des., P., C., Comm. A., L.
Jamison, Celia (Mrs.)—P., T., C.
Loomis, Kenneth Bradley—E., P.
Spellman, Coreen Mary—
Lith., P., Des., I., T., L.
Wahlert, Ernst Henry—S., P., T.

El Paso

Ball, Kate Kraus (Mrs.)—P.
deBruyn, Erich C.—
Comm. A., Des., T., P.
Emeree, Berla Ione (Mrs.)—
P., T., C., L.
Lanier, Fanita McClean (Mrs.)—
I., P., Des.
Lea, Tom—P., I., W.
Wise, Vera—P., Lith., E.

Enterprise

Langford, Ruth Betty—P., Gr., T.

Fort Worth

Bullock, Mary Jane McLean (Mrs.)
—P., C., T.
Caldwell, Henry Bryan—Mus. Dir.
East, Pattie Richardson (Mrs.)—
P., C.
Francis, Muriel Wilkins—
T., P., C., Comm. A.
McVeigh, Blanche—Et.
Richards, Karl Frederick—E., P., W.
Smith, Emily Guthrie (Mrs.)—P., T.
Ziegler, Samuel P.—P., Gr., E.

Galveston

Newman, George W.—
P., Med. I., Gr.

Georgetown

Callcott, Frank—E., P., Gr.

Greenville

McGough, Charles E.—
E., Ser., P., Des.

Harlingen

Knight, Normah Alcott (Mrs.)—P.

Holland

Mewhinney, Ella K.—P.

Houston

Biggers, John Thomas—
P., S., Lith., I., E.
Boynton, James W.—P.
Chillman, James, Jr.—E., L.
Collins, Lowell Daunt—P., E., L., Gr.
John, Grace Spaulding—P., S., W.
MacAgy, Jermayne—Mus. Dir.
Malone, Lee H. B.—Mus. Dir., T., L.
Schiwetz, Edward M.—Des., P., L.
Skinner, Frances Johnson—P., T.
Snowden, Chester Dixon—
P., I., T., W.
Swain, Jerre (Mrs.)—P., T.
Truitt, Una B. (Mrs.)—P., W., L., T.
Uhler, Ruth Pershing—P., E., L.

Huntsville

Geeslin, Lee Gaddis—P., Gr., E.

Kingsville

Bailey, Ben P., Jr.—E., P., S., L., I.

Lubbock

Hubbard, Bess Bigham (Mrs.)—
S., Lith., Eng., C.
Kleinschmidt, Florian Arthur—E., L.
Tippit, Jack D.—Cart., Comm. A.

Nacogdoches

Schlicher, Karl Theodore—E., P., W.
Turner, Janet Elizabeth—
P., Gr., E., L.

New Braunfels

Weisser, Leonie Oelkers (Mrs.)—P.

Ovalo

Landers, Della A.—P., T., Gr., L.

Richardson

Collison, Marjory (Mrs.)—
I., P., Lith., Des., Comm. A.

Robstown

Rutland, Emily (Mrs.)—P.

San Angelo

Heddins, Tincie Hughs (Mrs.)—
P., Lith., T.

San Antonio

Achning, Estellyn Allday (Mrs.)—
P., Lith., I.
Adams, John Squire—
T., P., Comm. A.
Bennett, Bertha (Mrs.)—P., Et., Lith.
Casebier, Cecil Lang—P.
Dugosh, Ruby Evelyn—
T., P., L., Des., I.
Franklin, Ione—S., E., C.
Free, Mary Arnold (Mrs.)—
E., P., Lith.
Green, Rena (Mrs.)—P.
Kent, Jack Wellington—Cart.
Lee, Amy Freeman—
P., Cr., L., W., T.
Leeper, John Palmer—Mus. Dir.
Naylor, Alice (Mrs.)—P., Lith., T.
Pace, Margaret (Mrs.)—P., C., T.
Pohl, Hugo David—P., Et., T.
Quillin, Ellen S. (Mrs.)—Mus. Dir.
Reed, Robert K.—P.
Robinson, Adah Matilda—
P., Des., L., E.
Schoolfield, Garcie M.—P., C., Ser.
Shook, Janet (Mrs.)—P., T., C.
Steinbomer, Dorothy H. (Mrs.)—
Des., C., L.
Tauch, Waldine—S., P., T.
Teichmueller, M. (Mrs.)—P.
Tharsilla, Sister M.—E., P.

San Diego

Garcia, Antonio E.—P., T.

Sweetwater

Shaw, Lois Hogue (Mrs.)—P.

Victoria

Thurmond, Ethel Dora—P., T.

Waco

Kilian, Austin Farland—
E., P., Des., L.

UTAH

Kaysville

Stewart, LeConte—P., Gr., E., L.

Logan

Fletcher, Calvin—E., P.
Lindstrom, Gaell—P., C., E.
Reynolds, Harry Reuben—P., C., E.
Thorpe, Everett Clark—
P., Des., E., I., L.

Provo

Andrus, J. Roman—E., Lith.
de Jong, Gerrit, Jr.—E., W.
Larsen, Bent Franklin—P., E.

Salt Lake City

Atwater, Mary Meigs—
Des., T., W., L.
Birrell, Verla Leone—
P., L., E., W., Des., C.
Fairbanks, Avard Tennyson—
S., E., Des., L.
Fausett, Lynn—P., Ser.
Frazer, Mabel Pearl—E., P., L.

VERMONT

Arlington

Schwarz, William Tefft—P., I.

Barton

Baker, Anna P.—P., Gr.

Bennington

Barret, Richard Carter—
Mus. Dir., Cur., W., L., E.
Burt, Marie Haines (Mrs.)—P., C.
Moselsio, Herta—Ceramist, S., T.
Moselsio, Simon—S., P., T., Gr.
Santo, Pasquale—P.
Shapiro, Daniel—P., Gr., E., Des.

Bondville

Landon, Edward—Ser., S., W.

Bristol

Mould, Ruth Greene (Mrs.)—
P., C., T.

Burlington

Coburn, Ruth Winona—E.
Coburn, Francis Peabody—P., L.
Webb, Grace Agnes Parker—
P., C., Gr., T., L.

Charlotte

Aschenbach, Paul—S.

Danby

Lillie, Ella Fillmore (Mrs.)—
Lith., P., Ser.

Derby Line

Earle, Edwin—P., Eng., T., I.

Dorset

Bley, Elsa W.—P., T.
Calfee, William H.—S.
Dern, Claude—P., T.
Fausett, William Dean—
P., Et., Lith.
Humphreys, David—P.
Meyer, Herbert—P.

Fairlee

MacGinnis, Henry Ryan—P., T.

Grafton

Stewart, David—P., T.

Halifax

Markham, Kyra (Mrs.)—
P., Et., Lith., C.

Jeffersonville

Bryan, Alden—P.
Bryan, Mary Taylor Lewis—P.

Johnston

Balch, Georgia W. (Mrs.)—P., C.

Londonderry

Shokler, Harry—
Pr. M., P., L., W., T.

Manchester

McCoy, Dorothy H. (Mrs.)—P.
McCoy, Lawrence R.—P.

Manchester Depot

Lucioni, Luigi—P., Et.

Middlebury

Burrage, Jane B. (Mrs.)—
Mus. Dir., W., L.
Healy, Arthur Kelly David—
P., Arch., W., L.

Newfane

Halladay, Milton Rawson—Cart.

Norwich

Cochran, Dewees (Mrs.)—
P., C., Des., S., T.
Sample, Paul—P.

Pawlet

Connaway, Jay Hall—P., T., L.

Peru

Wires, Hazel Kitts—P.

Pittsford

Belcher, Hilda—P.

Poultney

Vargish, Andrew—
P., Indst. Des., E., L.

Pownal

Chiu, Teng H.—P., Des., Lith.

Putney

Gerassi, Fernando—P.
Watson, Aldren Auld—
I., Des., P., Gr.

St. Johnsbury

Finck, Furman J.—P., T.

Salisbury

Berry, Helen Murrin (Mrs.)—P., C.
Shanes, Harry B.—P., C.

Shelburne

Emerson, Sterling Deal—Mus. Dir.
Webster, David S.—Asst. Mus. Dir.

South Newbury
Boyd, Moreon Beurnere—P., W.

Stowe
Blodgett, Edmund Walton—P.
Wright, Stanley Marc—P., T., L.

West Danville
Williams, Esther—P., Lith.

Westminster West
Inglis, Kate Peters—C.

Wilmington
Bayard, Clifford Adams—P., Et., Lith., T., L.
de Laittre, Eleanor (Mrs.)—S., P.

Windsor
Parrish, Maxfield—P., I.

Woodstock
Gyra, Francis Joseph, Jr.—P., I., T., L.
Thomas, Byron—P., Lith.
Wickham, Nancy (Mrs.)—C.

VIRGINIA

Alexandria
Adams, Katharine Langhorne (Mrs.)—P., L.
Bailey, Worth—Mus. Cur., E., Des.
Berkman, Jack—P.
Chapman, Howard Eugene—Cart., Comm. A., P.
Crandall, Norris Ingersoll—E., Arch.
Day, Worden (Miss)—P., Gr.
Dougherty, Bertha Hurlbut—Pr. M., E., P., I., L.
Harper, Edwin Laurence—Cart., Des., P., I., T., W.
Richards, Jeanne Herron—Et., Eng., Lith.
Rose, Ruth Starr—P., Lith., Ser., L., T.
Sanborn, Herbert J.—Lith., L.

Appomatox
Shouse, Helen Bigoney (Mrs.)—C., P., Des., E.

Arlington
Bier, Elmira—Asst. to Mus. Dir.
Bryans, John Armond—P., T.
Coe, Helen Stotesbury (Mrs.)—P., T.
Fenical, Marlin Edward—P., Comm. A., I.
Herrin, M. H.—P., W.
Jex, Garnet W.—P., I., Des.
Leich, Chester—Et., P.
Payne, George Kimpton—Des., P., Gr., S., C., I.
Peacock, Jean Eleanor (Mrs.)—P., Gr., T.
Richardson, Gerard—P., Des.
Taylor, Prentiss—P., Lith., T., L., I., W.
Wolcott, Roger Augustus—P., E., Des., C., S.

Blacksburg
Carter, Dean—S.

Bremo Bluff
Cousins, Clara Lea (Mrs.)—S., P., T., L.

Bristol
Cooke, C. Ernest—E., W., Cr., L., P.
Sella, Alvin Conrad—P., E.

Charlottesville
Barritt, Robert Carlyle—Port. P., T.
Hale, Lilian Westcott—P.
Makielski, Bronislaw Alexander—P., I., E., L.
O'Neal, William Bainter—E., Mus. Cur., W.
Priest, Hartwell Wyse—Et., Lith., P.
Smith, Charles William—P., Gr., E.

Danville
Davenport, Carson S.—P., Gr.

Falls Church
Bruskin, Kathleen Spencer (Mrs.)—P.
Foster, Francis—P., S., Gr.
Jamieson, Mitchell—P., T.

Farmville
Bedford, Virginia—E.

Fredericksburg
Van Winckel, Dorothy D. (Mrs.)—E., Lith., Eng.

Gloucester
de Leslie, Alexandre—Port. P.

Hampton
Holt, Julia Samuel Travis—P.
Jones, Allan D., Jr.—P., E., L., Cr.

Hollins College
Ballator, John R.—P., E., Lith.

Lively
Simonson, Marion—P.

Lynchburg
Diuguid, Mary Sampson—P.
Williams, Mary Frances—E.

Madison Heights
Roller, Samuel K.—P., E.

Martinsville
Shumate, Jessamine W.—P., Ser.

McLean
Beggs, Thomas Montague—Mus. Dir., P.
Bose, Norma—P., T.
Gates, Margaret Casey (Mrs.)—P.

Newport News
Sniffen, Harold S.—Asst. Mus. Dir.
Sylvester, E. W.—Mus. Dir.

Norfolk
Durham, Isaiah Davis—T., P.
Hatch, John Davis, Jr.—Mus. Dir., E.
Matson, Elina—C.
Matson, Greta—P., Lith., T.
Sibley, Charles Kenneth—P., E.
Sloane, E. K.—Mus. Dir.
Taylor, Bertha Fanning—P., L., Mus. Cur., W., T., Cr.

Powhatan
Binford, Julian—P., S.

Richmond
Archer, Edmund Minor—P., E.
Barksdale, George Edward—P.
Begien, Jeanne (Mrs.)—P., E.
Bolling, Leslie Garland—S.
Campbell, Jewett—P.
Cheek, Leslie, Jr.—Mus. Dir.
Davis, Edward Morris, III—Mus. Dir.
Fauntleroy, Martha Lorimer—P.
Glasser, Hannelore—Mus. Cur.
Hattorf, Alvin—P.
Johnson, George H. Ben—P., Cart., I.
Jones, James Pope—P.
King, Helen A. Hattorf—P., C., T.
Lorraine, Helen Louise—Medical I.
Pollak, Theresa—E., P., L.
Seibel, Frederick Otto—Cart.
Sievers, Frederick William—S., C.
Von Jost, Alexander—P., Et.
Wood, Lillian Lee—Port. P.

Salem
Biggs, Walter—P., I.

Staunton
Day, Horace Talmage—P., E.

Suffolk
Krize, Emilie Mary—P., Medical I.

Sweet Briar
Barton, Eleanor Dodge—E.
Bernheimer, Franz Karl—E., P., S., Cr.

Vienna
Gonzales, Carlotta (Mrs.)—P., S., T., I.
Kumm, Marguerite Elizabeth—P., Eng., Et.
Lahey, Richard Francis—P., Gr., E., L.

Warrenton
Cheney, Philip—Lith., P.

White Post
Bowmann, Jean—P., I.

Williamsburg
Graham, John Meredith, II—Dir. & Cur. of Collections
Roseberg, Carl Anderson—S., Eng., E.
Thorne, Thomas—P., E., L.

WASHINGTON

Bellevue
Carter, Dudley C.—S., T.
Isaacs, Walter—E., P., W., L.
Reed, Truman Gervais—Asst. Mus. Dir., T.

Bellingham
Loggie, Helen A.—Et.

Bremerton
Willey, Edith Maring (Mrs.)—P., Et., T., W., L.

Ellensburg
Bach, Emanuel Frank—E., S., Art Film Producer
Hogue, Herbert Glenn—E., C.
Spurgeon, Sarah Edna M.—E., P.

Kent

Pierce, Danny—P., Et., Eng.

Kirkland

Sawyer, Edmund J.—P., I., W., L., Des., C.

Langley

Camfferman, Margaret Gove (Mrs.)— P.

Maryhill

Dolph, Clifford R.—Mus. Dir.

Mercer Island

Horder, Jocelyn Clise—Eng., Lith.

Pullman

Griffin, Worth Dickman—P., E., L.
Hansen, Gaylen Capener—P., I., T.
Laisner, George Alois—S., C., P., E., L., Gr.
Monaghan, Keith—E., P.

Seattle

Alps, Glen—E.
Brazeau, Wendell Phillips—P., Gr., T.
Burnley, John Edwin—E., P., Des., Comm. A., I.
Callahan, Kenneth—P., W.
Du Pen, Everett George—S., E.
Elshin, Jacob Alexander—P., I., T.
Everett, Elizabeth Rinehart—P., C., S., L.
Fuller, Richard Eugene—Mus. Dir.
Gilbert, Louise Lewis (Mrs.)—P., Et.
Gonzales, Boyer—P., E.
Greathouse, Walser S.—Mus. Dir.
Horder, Nellie P. (Mrs.)—P.
Humber, Yvonne Twining—P., T.
Immel, Paul—E., P., C., Des., Comm. A.
Kirsten, Richard Charles—P., Gr., S.
Murton, Clarence C.—Comm. A., L., E., P.
Norling, Ernest Ralph—P., I., W., C.
Norling, Josephine Stearns—W.
Patterson, Ambrose—P., E.
Patterson, Viola—P.
Peck, James Edward—P., Des., I.
Portmann, Frieda Bertha Anne—P., T., Gr., C., Des., W., L., S.
Pries, Lionel H.—E., P., Et., L.
Raymond, Eugenia—Art Libn., E.
Rising, Dorothy Milne—P., T., L., W.
Rogers, Millard Buxton—Assoc. Mus. Dir., Hist.
Simms, Theodore Freeland—Indst. Des., Gr., P., C.
Thomas, Edward B.—Edu. Dir., E., L., Ser., P.
Walkinshaw, Jeanie Walter (Mrs.)— P., I.
Ziegler, Mary—Assoc. Mus. Dir.

Spokane

Ballou, Bertha—P., L., T., S.
Fleckenstein, Opal (Mrs.)—P., T., C.
McCoy, Wirth Vaughan—P., E., L.

Tacoma

Alcorn, Rowena Lung (Mrs.)—E., P., W.
Chubb, Frances Fullerton—E., P., S., Gr.

Vancouver

Hansen, James Lee—S.

Yakima

Cook, Blanche McLane (Mrs.)—P., T.

WEST VIRGINIA

Buckhannon

Messersmith, Fred Lawrence—E., P.

Charleston

Hosterman, Naomi S. (Mrs.)—P., I.
Keane, Lucina Mabel—E., P., S., I., L.
Taylor, Grace Martin—P., Gr., E., L.

Clarksburg

Howes, Alfred Loomis—P., Des.

Huntington

Dugan, Irvin—Cart., I., P.
Jablonski, Joseph S.—E., Et., P., C.
Triplett, Fred J.—Mus. Dir.

Moundsville

Evans, Virginia Bargar—Des., P., T.
Yutzey, Marvin Glen—Des., C.

Wheeling

Scott, Charlotte T. (Mrs.)—P.
Steckel, Edwin M.—Mus. Dir.

White Sulphur Springs

Tuke, Gladys—S., C., T.

WISCONSIN

Appleton

Brooks, Charles M., Jr.—E.
Dietrich, Thomas Mueller—P., E.

Ashland

Eckels, Robert Jevert—P., C., Gr., T.

Beloit

Boggs, Franklin—P., I., Des., E.
Grauel, Anton C.—S.
Popinsky, Arnold Dave—S., E., Gr.
Shaffer, Owen Vernon—Mus. Dir., E., P.
Whitehead, Philip Barrows—E., W., L., Mus. Cur.
Williams, Lewis W., II—E., Hist.

Brookfield

Anders, Willi—P.
Stoltenberg, Hans John—P., T.

Cedarburg

Gehr, James L.—S., Des.

Chippewa Falls

Baesemann, Margaret Maassen—Des., P., E.

Delavan

Kinzinger, Edmund D.—P., S., C., Gr.

Green Bay

Burcaw, G. Ellis—Mus. Dir.
Dury, Loraine Lucille—P., T.
Juhre, William H.—Mus. Cur.
Neuman, Vincent Howard— Comm. A., Des., P.

Hartland

Stonebarger, Virginia—T., P.

Kenosha

Faulkner, Kady B.—P., Et., Lith. Ser., E.
Roeder, Norbert—Mus. Dir.

Madison

Anderson, Donald M.—E., P., Des.
Annen, Helen Wann (Mrs.)— E., P., L., I., W.
Blair, Lawrence Edson—T., I., W.
Bohrod, Aaron—P.
Butts, Porter Freeman—Mus. Dir., E., W., L.
Byrd, Decatur Gibson—P., T.
Colescott, Warrington—P., Ser., E., Et.
Doudna, William L.—Cr.
Engel, Wilhelmina (Mrs.)—P., T.
Ingraham, Katherine Ely—Et.
Knipschild, Robert—P., T.
Krentzin, Earl—C., S., E.
Logan, Frederick M.—P., E., L., W.
Meeker, Dean Jackson—Pr. M., Muralist
Schinneller, James Arthur—E.
Sessler, Alfred—P., E., Gr., L.
Starks, Elliott Roland—E., A. Dir.
Stebbins, Roland Stewart—P., E., L.
Steppat, Leo Ludwig—S., E.
Tomlinson, Florence K. (Mrs.)— P., Eng., I., T.
Watrous, James S.—P., E., C., W.
Weinberg, Louis—S., E., Des.
Wilde, John—P., E.
Wilson, Della Ford—E., C., W.
Zingale, Santos—P., E.

Manitowoc

Brixius, Dorothy Ann—Des., P., I.
Lozar, Rajko—Mus. Dir.

Mazomanie

Utpatel, Frank Albert Bernhardt —Eng.

McFarland

Marx, Robert Ernst—P., Gr.

Milwaukee

Allen, Hazel Leigh—S., P., C.
Biehn, Irving Lew—P.
Boerner, Edward A.—P., E., S.
Chase, Joseph Cummings— Port. P., W., L.
Copp, Gertrude M.—C., P., T., Des.
Dietrich, George Adams—S., P., Des., L., E.
Dwight, Edward H.—Mus. Dir.
Faber, Eugene James—P., Des., C., W., L., T.
Faulkner, Paul W.—P.
Fischer, Hulda Rotier—P., Gr., T., L.
Gebhardt, C. Keith—P., S., Des., L., W., I.
Green, Dorinne Traulsen—E., P., Gr., C.
Green, Edward Anthony—P., Des., Gr., E.
Green, George Alan—Des., Gr., C., P., E.
Groom, Emily Parker—P., T.
Grotenrath, Ruth (Mrs.)—P., Ser., Eng., C.
Johann, Helen L.—Pr. M., T.
Lewandowski, Edmund D.—P., T.
Lewis, Ross A.—Cart.
Lichtner, Schomer—P., C., Des., Ser., T.
Lueloff, Marjorie Kaltenback— P., Des., L.
Meredith, Dorothy Laverne—P., C., E.
Miller, Donna (Mrs.)—Lith., P.
Moynihan, Helen S.—P.

Canadian Index

Shelburne

Bruce, Annie Priscilla (Mrs.)—P., C.

Sydney

Mould, Lola Frowde (Mrs.)—P., Des.

Yarmouth

Day, Mabel K.—P.
Pierce, Elizabeth R. (Mrs.)—P.

ONTARIO

Ancaster

Panabaker, Frank S.—P.

Ayr

Martin, John—P., Des., C., Gr., I., T., L.

Barrie

Mitchell, Thomas W.—P., I., E.
Scott, Lloyd Edward William—I.

Burlington

Hickling, Walter Robert—P., T.

Colborne

Airola, Paavo—P., E.

Collingwood

Dean, Ernest Wilfrid—P., Et., Ser.

Cooksville

Goldhamer, Charles—P., T., Lith.

Cyrville

Price, Arthur Donald—C., S., Des.

Don Mills

Kramolc, Theodore Maria—P., Et., Eng.

Dunnville

Raney, Suzanne Bryant—Eng.

Erindale

Dingle, Adrian—P., I.

Glen Miller

Hewton, Randolph Stanley—P., T.

Guelph

Coomb, Edith Grace (Mrs.)—P., S., Gr., L., T., I.
Couling, Gordon—E., P.

Hamilton

Chrystal, Arthur—P., Et., Eng.
Depew, Viola—Eng., T.

Ingersoll

Crawford, Catherine Betty—P., Gr.

Kingston

Biéler, André—P., E., L.
Macdonald, Grant—P., I., T.
Travers, Gwyneth (Mrs.)—Pr. M.

London

Ariss, Herbert Joshua—P., T., L.
Ariss, Margot Phillips—P.

Bice

Bice, Clare—P., Mus. Cur.
Crouch, Richard Edwin—Mus. Dir.
Cryderman, Mackie (Mrs.)—E., P., Et., L., C., Des.
Francis, Harold Carleton—P., Eng.

Manotick

Jackson, Alexander Young—P.

Markham

Courtice, Rody Kenny—P., T.
Housser, Yvonne McKague—P., Des., I., L.

Newmarket

Hagan, Robert Frederick—Pr. M., E., P.

Oakville

Cahen, Oscar—P., I.
Hanson, Jean—P., Des., Gr.

Oshawa

Hilts, Alan—S.
Luke, Alexandra—P.

Ottawa

Alfred, Paul—P., T., I., Des.
Barbeau, Marius—W., Mus. Wkr.
Boyd, James—Pr. M., Des., T.
Buchanan, Donald William—Mus. Assoc. Dir., W.
Fenwick, Kathleen M.—Mus. Cur., Ed.
Groves, Naomi Jackson (Mrs.)—W., L., P.
Hubbard, Robert Hamilton—Mus. Cur., E.
Hyde, Laurence—Eng., P., W.
Hyndman, Robert Stewart—P., Des., T.
Masson, Henri—P., T.
McInnes, Graham Campbell—W., Cr.
Sylvestre, Guy—Ed., Cr., W., L.
Tolgyesy, Victor—C., S.

Owen Sound

Thomson, George—P.

Port Credit

Roberts, Thomas Keith—P.

Rexdale

Roberts, William Griffith—P., T.

St. Catherines

Harley, Harry George—Cart.

Streetsville

Taylor, Jocelyn—P., C., Des., T.

Thornhill

Haines, Frederick Stanley—P., E., Et., Eng.
MacDonald, Thoreau—I., P., Des.
Trenka, Stephen—S., Medalist

Toronto

Aldwinckle, Eric—Des., P., I., L.
Baldwin, Martin—Mus. Dir.
Barr, Allan—Port. P.
Benton, Margaret Peake—Min. and Port. P.
Bonnycastle, Murray Carlaw—P.
Brieger, Peter H.—E., Hist.
Brigden, Frederick Henry—P.
Brooks, Frank Leonard—P., T.

Broomfield, Adolphus George—P., Et., Tex. Des., L.
Bush, Jack Hamilton—P., I., Des.
Casson, Alfred Joseph—P., Des.
Challener, Frederick Sproston—Mural P.
Chiarandini, Albert—P.
Clark, Paraskeva (Mrs.)—P.
Comfort, Charles Fraser—P., E.
Cooke, Edwy Francis—P., T., L.
Coughtry, John Graham—P., S., Des., T.
Daly, Kathleen (Mrs.)—P.
de Pedery-Hunt, Dora—S., Des.
Fernald, Helen Elizabeth—Mus. Cur., E., W., L., P.
Finley, Frederick James—P., T., I.
Forbes, Kenneth Keith—Port. P
Franck, Albert Jacques—P., Rest.
Gauthier, Joachim George—P.
Gilson, Jacqueline—P.
Griffith, Julius—P., Gr.
Hahn, Sylvia—P., I., C., S., Eng., T.
Hall, John A.—P., E., Eng., I., Des.
Hanes, Ursula Ann—S.
Haworth, B. Cogill (Mrs.)—P., C., T.
Haworth, Peter—P., Stained Glass Des.
Hoo, Sing—S., T.
Horne, Arthur Edward Cleeve—P., S.
Hornyansky, Nicholas—Et., Des., T.
Inglis, John Noel—P.
Iskowitz, Gershon—P., Et., Lith.
Janes, Phyllis (Mrs.)—P., Lith., I.
Kopmanis, Augusts A.—S.
Long, Marion—P.
Loring, Frances Norma—S., Des.
Luz, Virginia—P., T.
MacDonald, James Williamson Galloway—P., Des., T.
MacDonald, Manly—P.
MacNamara, Gordon—P.
Martin, Bernice Fenwick (Mrs.)—P.
Martin, Langton—P., C., Des., Et., Eng.
McCarthy, Doris Jean—P., T., C.
McGeoch, Lillian Jean—P., Des.
Murphy, Rowley Walter—P., Des., I., T., W., L.
Nakamura, Kazuo—P., S.
Neddeau, Donald Frederick Price—P., Des., T., L., Gr.
Palmer, Herbert Sidney—P.
Paul, Gregory P.—P.
Pehap, Erich K.—P., Gr., Des., I., T., L.
Pepper, George Douglas—P., T.
Schaefer, Carl Fellman—P., T., Lith.
Seguin, Tutzi Haspel—P., C., Ser., T., L.
Sheppard, Peter Clapham—P., T.
Stevens, Dorothy (Mrs.)—P., T., Et.
Thorne, M. Art—P., T.
Turner, Stanley—Et., I., P., Des.
Valius, Telesforas—Eng., Lith.
Vickers, George Stephen—E.
Watson, Sydney H.—P., E., Des.
Wilson, R. York—P.
Woods, Rex Norman—I., Comm. A., P.
Wyle, Florence—S.

Waterloo

Goetz, Peter—P., T.

Weston

Newcombe, William John Bertram—P., Des., Comm. A.

Willowdale

Cox, Elford B.—S.
Gilling, Lucille—Et.
Wood, Elizabeth Wyn—S.

Windsor

Saltmarche, Kenneth Charles—Mus. Cur., P., W.

Woodstock

Kloezeman, Bert—P., Des., T., Gr., Comm. A., I., L.

York Mills

Jones, Jacobine—S.

QUEBEC

Dorval

Porter, Ann Pearson (Mrs.)—P.

Kingsmere

McCurry, Harry Orr—
Former Mus. Dir.

Laval

Pellan, Alfred—P., Des., T.

Levis

Des Biens, Gerard—S., E.

Montreal

Archambault, Louis—S.
Ayre, Robert Hugh—Editor, W., Cr.
Bouchard, Lorne—
   P., Des., I., Comm. A.
Brandtner, Fritz—P., C., Des., Gr.
Briansky, Rita Prezament—Et., P.
Chicoine, Rene—P., T., Cr.
Cloutier, Albert Edward—P., Des., Ser.
Cosgrove, Stanley—P.
Eveleigh, Henry—P., Des., E.

Faucher, Jean-Charles—P., E., I.
Goldberg, Eric—P.
Goldberg, Regina Seiden (Mrs.)—P.
Hebert, Julien—S., Des., E.
Kahane, Anne—S.
Lefort, Agnes—P., I., E., Cr., L.
Lismer, Arthur—P., E., L.
Lyman, John—P., E.
Masse, Georges Severe—P., T., L.
Morris, Kathleen Moir—P.
Mount, Rita—P.
Muhlstock, Louis—P.
Pinsky, Alfred —P., Lith., T.
Prezament, Joseph—P., Ser.
Roberts, William Goodridge—P.
Robinson, Albert Henry—P.
Savage, Annie Douglas—P., T.
Scott, Marian D. (Mrs.)—P.
Simard, Jean—P., E., I., W., L.
Surrey, Philip Henry—P., W.
Taylor, Frederick Bourchier—
   Et., Ser., P.
Tinning, G. Campbell—P.
Webber, Gordon McKinley—P., Des., T.
Wheeler, Orson Shorey—S., T., L.

Morin Heights

Holgate, Edwin Headley—P.

Outremont

Raymond, Maurice—P., T., I., E.

Piedmont

Madsen, Aage—S.

Ste. Agathe des Monts

Miller, H. McRae—
   S., Des., Comm. A., T., P.

Saint-Lambert

De Tonnancour, Jacques G.—P., T.

Sillery

Lemieux, Jean Paul—P.
Soucy, Jean-Baptiste—E.

Quebec

Morisset, Gerard—E., W., Mus. Cur.
Plamondon, Marius Gerald—S., E., Des.

Strathmore

Daoust, Sylvia—S.

Westmount

Beament, Commander Harold—
   P., Des.
Caiserman, Ghitta—P., Lith., T.

SASKATCHEWAN

Regina

Lochhead, Kenneth Campbell—E., P.
Simmins, Richard Beaufort—L., Cur.

Saskatoon

Snelgrove, Gordon William—E., L., W.

YUKON TERRITORY

Whitehorse

Farley, Lilias Marianne—P., S., T.

Foreign Index

AUSTRIA

Vienna

Benesch, Otto—Hist., W., L.

BAHAMAS

Man-o-War Cay

Johnston, Randolph W.—S., I., W., C.

BERMUDA

Harrington Sound

Ronnebeck, Louise Emerson—P., L., T.

BRITISH WEST INDIES

Jamaica

Barthe, Richmond—S.

CUBA

Havana

Serra, Daniel—P., E., W., Gr.

ENGLAND

Essex

Howard, Charles—P.

London

Williams, Chester R.—P., W., L., I.

Manchester

Cunliffe, Mitzi—S., Des., L.

ETHIOPIA

Addis Ababa

Van Hook, Katrina (Mrs.)—T., L.

FRANCE

Aix-en-Provence

Ozier, Kenneth H.—P., Et., Lith., Des., W.

Cannes

Ozenfant, Amedee J.—P., W., E., L.

Paris

Barr, Roger Terry—P., E., Gr.
Borduas, Paul-Emile—P.
Ford, Charles Henri—P., W.

Pollack, Reginald Murray—P., S., Gr.
Stillman, Ary—P.
Webster, Herman A.—
   Et., P., Draughtsman

HOLLAND

The Hague

Canfield, Lillian Caroline—Mus. Cur.

ITALY

Naples

Petrina, Charlotte Kennedy—P., I., Gr., T.

Rome

Berman, Eugene—P., Des., Scenic Des., Gr.
Brown, Carlyle—P.
Lentelli, Leo—S.
Poidimani, Gino—S., T.
Richter, Gisela Marie Augusta—
   Mus. Cur., W., L., C.

JAPAN

Okayama City

Blair, Dorothy Lillian—Mus. Cur., T., W., L.

Obituaries

Obituaries

ABBREVIATIONS

d.—died.

WWAA—Who's Who in American Art (followed by volume year). For other abbreviations, see list preceding main body of this volume, page x-xi.

Note: Where information of demise was obtained from postal or other sources impossible to check, N.D. is used to denote no date available.

ABELL, WALTER HALSEY—Educator; d. Feb. 28, 1956, age 59. See WWAA 1956.

ADAMS, WAYMAN—Portrait Painter; d. Apr. 8, 1959, age 74, in Austin, Tex. See WWAA 1956.

AJOOTIAN, KHOSROV—Educator; d. Nov. 27, 1958, age 67.

ALBRIGHT, ADAM EMORY—Painter; d. Sept. 13, 1957, age 95. See WWAA 1956.

ALMY, FRANK ATWOOD—Museum Director; d. 1956, N.D. See WWAA 1956.

AMBERSON, GRACE D. (Mrs. William R.)—Painter; d. Dec. 28, 1957, age 63. See WWAA 1956.

AUSUBEL, SHEVA—Painter; d. May 13, 1957, in New York City, age 61. See WWAA 1956.

AYLWARD, WILLIAM J.—Painter; d. N.D. See WWAA 1956.

BALLIN, HUGO—Painter; d. Nov. 27, 1956. See WWAA 1956.

BARTLETT, DANA—Painter; d. July, 1957, age 75. See WWAA 1956.

BATES, CAROL—Painter; d. N.D. See WWAA 1956.

BEL GEDDES, NORMAN—Designer; d. May 8, 1958, age 65, in New York City. See WWAA 1956.

BERNARDINI, ORESTES—Designer; d. Nov., 1957, in Astoria, L.I., N.Y., age 77. See WWAA 1956.

BERNSTEIN, MRS. EVA—Painter; d. May 14, 1958, age 87, in New York City.

BLANCHFIELD, HOWARD JAMES—Painter; d. Sept., 1957, in Schenectady, N.Y., age 61. See WWAA 1956.

BLANDING, DON—Author; d. June 9, 1957.

BLODGETT, GEORGE WINSLOW—Sculptor; d. N.D. See WWAA 1956.

BLUMENSCHEIN, MARY GREENE (Mrs.)—Painter; d. May 24, 1958, in Taos, N.M. See WWAA 1956.

BODINE, HELEN—Miniature Painter; d. N.D. See WWAA 1956.

BOHLAND, GUSTAV—Sculptor; d. Apr. 22, 1959, age 62, in Miami, Fla. See WWAA 1956.

BOOGAR, WILLIAM F.—Sculptor; d. July 20, 1958, in Provincetown, Mass., age 65. See WWAA 1956.

BOOTH, NINA MASON—Painter; d. N.D. See WWAA 1956.

BRITTON, HARRY—Painter; d. July 23, 1958, in Toronto, Canada, age 79.

BROWN, BRIAN—Art Director; d. Nov. 13, 1958, in his home at Alexandria, Va., age 47.

BROWN, PAUL—Illustrator; d. Dec. 25, 1958, in Mineola, L.I., age 65.

BROWN, ROY—Painter; d. 1956, age 77. See WWAA 1956.

BUCKLEY, JOHN MICHAEL—Painter; d. Feb. 4, 1958, in Pigeon Cove, Mass., age 67. See WWAA 1956.

BURNEY, MINNA—Educator; d. Apr. 21, 1958, in Rome, Ga., age 67. See WWAA 1956.

CAMFFERMAN, PETER MARIENUS—Painter; d. Nov. 15, 1957, in Langley, Wash., age 67. See WWAA 1956.

CARTER, AUGUSTUS D. (AD)—Cartoonist; d. June 25, 1957, age 62, at his home in Mamaroneck, N.Y.

CHAPIN, MYRON BUTMAN—Painter; d. Feb., 1958, age 71. See WWAA 1956.

CHASE, FRANK SWIFT—Painter; d. July 27, 1958, in Woodstock, N.Y., age 72. See WWAA 1956.

CHASE, SIDNEY M.—Painter; d. June 12, 1957, age 80. See WWAA 1956.

CLARK, MABEL BEATRICE SMITH—Miniature Painter; d. May, 1957, in Hollywood, Cal. See WWAA 1956.

CLARK, ROLAND—Painter; d. April, 1957, age 83, in Norwalk, Conn.

CLIME, WINFIELD SCOTT—Painter; d. Mar. 13, 1958, in Old Lyme, Conn., age 77. See WWAA 1956.

COFFMAN, HAL—Cartoonist; d. Aug. 31, 1958, in Fort Worth, Tex., age 75.

COLLES, GERTRUDE—Painter; d. Sept. 24, 1957, age 88. See WWAA 1956.

CONROW, WILFORD SEYMOUR—Portrait Painter; d. N.D. See WWAA 1956.

COOLEY, DIXIE (Mrs. John L.)—Painter; d. N.D. See WWAA 1956.

COPPINI, POMPEO LUIGI—Sculptor; d. Sept. 26, 1957, in San Antonio, Tex., age 87. See WWAA 1956.

COTTON, WILLIAM HENRY—Painter; d. 1958, age 78. See WWAA 1956.

DAVENPORT, EDITH FAIRFAX—Painter; d. Nov. 1, 1957, in Winter Park, Fla., age 77. See WWAA 1956.

DAVISSON, HOMER G.—Painter; d. N.D. See WWAA 1956.

DOBSON, DAVID IRVING (DIAMONDSTEIN)—Painter; d. Nov. 3, 1957, age 74. See WWAA 1956.

DODGE, HAZEL (Mrs. Wm. T. Turman)—Museum Curator; d. Apr. 5, 1957, age 54. See WWAA 1956.

DORNER, ALEXANDER—Historian; d. N.D. See WWAA 1956.

DOUGLAS, FREDERIC HUNTINGTON—Museum Curator; d. N.D. See WWAA 1956.

DROGKAMP, CHARLES—Painter; d. June 1, 1958, in Los Angeles, Cal. See WWAA 1956.

DU BOIS, GUY PENE—Painter; d. July 18, 1958, in Boston, Mass., age 74. See WWAA 1956.

DUFNER, EDWARD—Painter; d. 1957, age 86. See WWAA 1956.

DWIGGINS, CLARE—Cartoonist; d. Oct. 26, 1958, in North Hollywood, Cal., age 84.

DWIGGINS, WILLIAM ADDISON—Book and Type Designer; d. Dec. 25, 1956, in Hingham, Mass., age 76. See WWAA 1956.

EGGERS, GEORGE WILLIAM—Educator; d. Sept. 25, 1958, in New York City, age 75. See WWAA 1956.

ELLERHUSEN, ULRIC H.—Sculptor; d. 1957, age 78. See WWAA 1956.

ENFIELD, HARRY—Illustrator; d. Sept. 13, 1958, age 52.

FARLOW, HARRY—Portrait Painter; d. 1956, in West Hartford, Conn., age 74. See WWAA 1956.

FARMER, MABEL McKIBBIN—Engraver; d. N.D., in Stanford, Cal. See WWAA 1956.

FAY, WILBUR M.—Designer; d. Feb. 2, 1959, age 55. See WWAA 1956.

FINTA, ALEXANDER—Sculptor; d. N.D. See WWAA 1956.

FISH, DOROTHY S.—Ceramist; d. Jan. 2, 1958, age 52, at her home in Larchmont, N.Y. See WWAA 1956.

FRANKL, PAUL THEODORE—Designer; d. Mar. 21, 1958, in Palos Verdes Estates, Cal., age 72. See WWAA 1956.

FREDENTHAL, DAVID—Painter; d. in Rome, Italy, age 44. See WWAA 1956.

FROUCHTBEN, BERNARD—Painter; d. Jan. 31, 1956, in New York City, age 84. See WWAA 1956.

GARBER, DANIEL—Painter; d. July 6, 1958, age 78. See WWAA 1956.

GARRISON, JESSE JANES—Educator; d. N.D. See WWAA 1956.

GLAMAN, EUGENIE FISH—Etcher; d. 1956, in Chicago, Ill. See WWAA 1956.

GREENE, GERTRUDE (Mrs. Balcomb Greene)—Painter; d. Nov. 25, 1956, age 52. See WWAA 1956.

GREGORY, JOHN—Sculptor; d. 1958, age 79. See WWAA 1956.

GRIFFITH, LOUIS OSCAR—Painter; d. Nov. 13, 1956, age 81. See WWAA 1956.

GROSZ, GEORGE—Painter; d. July 6, 1959, age 66, in West Berlin, Germany. See WWAA 1956.

GUGLIELMI, LOUIS O.—Painter; d. Sept. 3, 1956, age 50, in Amagansett, N.Y. See WWAA 1956.

HAHN, EMANUEL OTTO—Sculptor; d. Feb. 14, 1957, age 76. See WWAA 1956—Canadian Section.

HALEY, ROBERT D.—Portrait Painter; d. June 25, 1959, in Trumbull, Conn., age 66.

HAMM, BETH CREEVY—Painter; d. Nov. 21, 1958, in New York City, age 73. See WWAA 1956.

HANSEN, ARMIN CARL—Painter; d. 1957, age 71. See WWAA 1956.

HARRIS, BEN JORJ—Illustrator; d. Dec. 19, 1957, in New Rochelle, N.Y., age 53. See WWAA 1956.

HAZELL, FRANK—Painter; N.D. See WWAA 1956.

HEBER, CARL A.—Sculptor; d. 1956, age 71. See WWAA 1956.

HELD, JOHN, JR.—Cartoonist; d. Mar. 2, 1958, age 69, in Belmar, N.J.

HIGGINS, EUGENE—Painter; d. Feb. 18, 1958, age 83. See WWAA 1956.

HILDEBRANDT, HOWARD LOGAN—Painter; d. Nov. 11, 1958, age 84. See WWAA 1956.

HOWARD, CECIL—Sculptor; d. 1956, age 68. See WWAA 1956.

HOWE, KATHARINE L. MALLETT—Painter; d. Sept. 23, 1957, at her home in New York City. See WWAA 1956.

HOWITT, JOHN NEWTON—Illustrator; d. Jan. 24, 1958, age 73. See WWAA 1956.

HUNTER, FRANCIS TIPTON—Illustrator; d. N.D. See WWAA 1956.

HUNTINGTON, MARGARET WENDELL—Painter; d. Apr. 18, 1958, age 91, in New York City.

IORIO, ADRIAN J.—Illustrator; d. May 15, 1957, in Randolph, Mass., age 78. See WWAA 1956.

IRVING, ANNA DUER—Painter; d. Nov. 11, 1957, age 84, in The Bronx; N.Y. See WWAA 1956.

JACKSON, ANN (Mrs.)—Painter; d. Mar. 12, 1956. See WWAA 1956.

JACKSON, LESLEY (Miss)—Painter; d. Jan. 19, 1958, age 92. See WWAA 1956.

JACOBS, MICHEL—Painter; d. Feb. 4, 1958, in Rumson, N.J., age 81. See WWAA 1956.

JOHNSON, JEANNE PAYNE (Mrs. Louis C.)—Painter; d. Oct. 11, 1958. See WWAA 1956.

JONES, ALBERTUS EUGENE—Painter; d. Mar. 1, 1957, in South Windsor, Conn., age 75. See WWAA 1956.

JORNS, BYRON CHARLES—Painter; d. July 7, 1958, in Mt. Horeb, Wis., age 60. See WWAA 1956.

JOSSET, RAOUL—Sculptor; d. 1957, age 57. See WWAA 1956.

KACHINSKY, ALEXANDER—Painter; d. Jan. 22, 1958, in White Plains, N.Y., age 70. See WWAA 1956.

KAHILL, JOSEPH B.—Portrait Painter; d. June 29, 1957, in Portland, Me., age 75. See WWAA 1956.

KAUFMANN, ROBERT—Painter; d. Apr. 18, 1959, age 45, at his home in Key West, Fla.

KIBBEY, ILAH MARIAN—Painter; d. Aug. 10, 1958, age 75. See WWAA 1956.

KIHN, WILLIAM LANGDON—Painter; d. Dec. 12, 1957, age 59. See WWAA 1956.

KILENYI, JULIO—Sculptor; d. Jan. 29, 1959, in New York City, age 73. See WWAA 1956.

KLEY, ALFRED JULIUS—Craftsman; d. June 26, 1957, in Los Angeles, Cal., age 62. See WWAA 1956.

KLINE, GEORGE T.—Medical Illustrator; d. May 24, 1956, age 82. See WWAA 1956.

KLONIS, BERNARD—Painter; d. June 21, 1957, age 51, in New York City. See WWAA 1956.

KNOWLTON, MAUDE BRIGGS (Mrs.)—Painter; d. July 15, 1956, age 80. See WWAA 1956.

KOLDE, FREDERICK WILLIAM—Painter; d. N.D. See WWAA 1956.

KOPLOWITZ, BENJAMIN (BEN KOPEL)—Marine Painter; d. N.D. See WWAA 1956.

LAHEY, MARGUERITE DUPREZ—Rare Book Binder; d. Oct., 1958, in The American Hospital, Paris, France, age 78.

LAUTERER, ARCH—Theatrical Designer; d. N.D. See WWAA 1956.

LAW, MARGARET—Painter; d. N.D. See WWAA 1956.

LAWSON, ROBERT—Illustrator; d. May 26, 1957, age 65, at his home in Westport, Conn. See WWAA 1956.

LAZZELL, BLANCHE—Painter; d. June 1, 1956, in Morgantown, W. Va. See WWAA 1956.

LEACH, LOUIS LAWRENCE—Sculptor; d. Feb. 10, 1957, age 72. See WWAA 1956.

LEAR, GEORGE—Engraver; d. May 5, 1956, age 77. See WWAA 1956.

L'ENGLE, WILLIAM JOHNSON—Painter; d. Nov. 24, 1957, in Truro, Mass., age 73. See WWAA 1956.

LEVER, R. HAYLEY—Painter; d. Dec. 6, 1958, in Mt. Vernon, N.Y., age 82. See WWAA 1956.

LEWIS, ALLEN—Etcher; d. 1957, age 84. See WWAA 1956.

LORD, MISS HARRIET—Painter; d. July 24, 1958, age 79, at Nantucket, Mass.

LOWELL, ORSON BYRON—Illustrator; d. 1956, in New Rochelle, N.Y., age 85. See WWAA 1956.

LOWENGRUND, MARGARET—Painter; d. Nov. 1957, age 52. See WWAA 1956.

MACKY, SPENCER—Educator; d. May 5, 1958, in San Francisco, Cal., age 78. See WWAA 1956.

MALMAN, CHRISTINA—Magazine Cover Artist; d. Jan. 14, 1958, in New York City, age 46.

MALVERN, CORINNE—Illustrator; d. Oct., 1956, in Norwalk, Conn. See WWAA 1956.

MARINO-MERLO JOSEPH—Painter; d. Aug. 1., 1956, age 50. See WWAA 1956.

MASON, MAUDE M.—Painter; d. Aug. 28, 1956, age 89. See WWAA 1956.

McCREERY, FRANC ROOT (Mrs.)—Painter; d. Oct. 31, 1957, in Buffalo, N.Y. See WWAA 1956.

McMANUS, JAMES—Painter; d. Sept. 15, 1958, in Old Lyme, Conn., age 76.

McMILLAN, MARY—Painter; d. N.D. See WWAA 1956.

MILLER, BURR—Sculptor; d. Oct. 10, 1958, in Brattleboro, Vt., age 54. See WWAA 1956.

MILLER, HELEN PENDLETON—Etcher; d. June 24, 1957, age 69, in Port Washington, L.I., N.Y. See WWAA 1956.

MOCK, GEORGE ANDREW—Painter; d. N.D. See WWAA 1956.

MORANG, ALFRED GWYNNE—Painter; d. N.D. See WWAA 1956.

MORROW, BENJAMIN FRANCIS (Dr.)—Painter; d. Oct. 27, 1958, in West Palm Beach, Fla., age 67. See WWAA 1956.

MULLER, GEORGE F.—Painter; d. Aug. 4, 1958, age 92, in Orange, Conn.

MURRAY, FRANK WALDO—Portrait Painter; d. Sept. 3, 1956, in Cambridge, Mass., age 72. See WWAA 1956.

MYERS, FRANK HARMON—Painter; d. Mar. 7, 1956, age 57. See WWAA 1956.

MYERS, GEORGE HEWITT—Museum President; d. Dec., 1957, age 82. See WWAA 1956.

NEANDROSS, SIGURD—Sculptor; d. Dec. 15, 1958, in Ridgefield, N.J., age 89.

NEWTON, MRS. GRACE HAMILTON (Mrs. Arthur Newton)—Painter; d. Aug. 4, 1958, in Kingston, N.Y.

NORDELL, EMMA PARKER (POLLY)—Painter; d. N.D. See WWAA 1956.

OBERHARDT, WILLIAM—Illustrator; d. July 22, 1958, age 76. See WWAA 1956.

ORLOFF, LILY—Painter; d. Aug. 6, 1957, in New York City. See WWAA 1956.

PACH, WALTER—Writer; d. Nov. 27, 1958, in New York City, age 75. See WWAA 1956.

PACKER, FRANCIS H.—Sculptor; d. July 13, 1957, age 84, in Long Island City, N.Y.

PACKER, FRED L.—Editorial Cartoonist; d. N.D.

PADDOCK, WILLARD DRYDEN—Painter; d. Nov. 25, 1956, age 83. See WWAA 1956.

PAGE, GROVER—Cartoonist; d. Aug. 5, 1958, age 65. See WWAA 1956.

PAPASIAN, JACK—Sculptor; d. 1957.

PARKER, GEORGE WALLER—Painter; d. 1957. See WWAA 1956.

PARSHALL, DeWITT—Painter; d. 1956, age 92. See WWAA 1956.

PARSONS, EDITH BARRETTO—Sculptor; d. 1956, age 78.

PEARSON, RALPH M.—Etcher; d. Apr. 27, 1958, age 75. See WWAA 1956.

PEEBLES, ROY B.—Painter; d. Nov. 17, 1957, in Adams, Mass., age 58. See WWAA 1956.

PENNOYER, A. SHELDON—Painter; d. Aug. 17, 1957, age 69, in auto accident in Madrid, Spain. See WWAA 1956.

PERARD, VICTOR S.—Etcher; d. July 1957, age 90. See WWAA 1956.

PETERSON, PERRY—Illustrator; d. Nov. 28, 1958, in New York City, age 50.

POLLEY, FREDERICK—Painter; d. N.D. See WWAA 1956.

POPE, MARION HOLDEN—Painter; d. Aug. 21, 1958. See WWAA 1956.

PORSMAN, FRANK O.—Painter; d. N.D. See WWAA 1956.

PRESTON, ALICE BOLAM (Mrs. Frank I.)—Illustrator; d. Aug. 12, 1958, in Beverly Farms, Mass., age 69. See WWAA 1956.

PRICE, MINNIE—Painter; d. Dec. 15, 1957, in Las Vegas, Nev., age 80. See WWAA 1956.

RANN, VOLLIAN BURR—Painter; d. Jan. 23, 1956, in Provincetown, Mass., age 59. See WWAA 1956.

RAYMOND, ALEXANDER—Cartoonist; d. Sept. 6, 1956, age 47, in Connecticut. See WWAA 1956.

READE, ROMA (MABEL KELLEY AUBREY)—Painter; d. Sept. 24, 1958, in Pasadena, Cal., age 81. See WWAA 1956.

REILLY, ELVIRA—Painter; d. May 19, 1958, age 59, in Oak Ridge, N.J. See WWAA 1956.

REMMEY, PAUL B.—Illustrator; N.D. See WWAA 1956.

ROBERTS, MRS. VIOLET KENT—Painter; d. N.D. See WWAA 1956.

ROGERS, BRUCE—Book Designer; d. May 19, 1957, in Danbury, Conn., age 87. See WWAA 1956.

ROOT, EDWARD WALES—Art Authority & Collector; d. Dec. 5, 1956, age 72, in New York City.

ST. GAUDENS, HOMER—Educator; d. Dec. 8, 1958, in Miami, Fla., age 79. See WWAA 1956.

SCHNIEWIND, CARL O.—Museum Curator; d. Aug. 30, 1957, age 57, in Florence, Italy. See WWAA 1956.

SCHOEN, EUGENE—Designer; d. Aug. 16, 1957, in New York City, age 77. See WWAA 1956.

SEWELL, HELEN MOORE—Illustrator; d. 1957, age 60, in New York City. See WWAA 1956.

SHERWOOD, SHERRY—Designer; d. N.D. See WWAA 1956.

SIMPSON, MARSHALL—Painter; d. Nov. 29, 1958, age 58. See WWAA 1956.

SMEDLEY, WILL LARYMORE—Painter; d. N.D. See WWAA 1956.

SMITH, JACOB GETLAR—Painter; d. Oct. 28, 1958, age 60. See WWAA 1956.

SOLON, HARRY—Portrait Painter; d. Aug. 5, 1958, age 85, in New York City.

STAGG, MRS. JESSIE—Sculptor; d. 1958.

STAPLES, ROY HARVARD—Painter; d. Aug. 20, 1958.

STAUFFER, EDNA PENNYPACKER—Painter; d. 1956, in New York City, age 69. See WWAA 1956.

STERNE, MAURICE—Painter; d. July 23, 1957, age 79, at Mt. Kisco. N.Y. See WWAA 1956.

STROTHMANN, FRED—Illustrator; d. May, 1958, age 78. See WWAA 1956.

SWARZENSKI, GEORG—Research Fellow; d. June 14, 1957, in Brookline, Mass., age 81. See WWAA 1956.

TAYLOR, ANNA HEYWARD—Painter; d. 1956, age 77. See WWAA 1956.

TAYLOR, FRANCIS HENRY—Museum Director; d. Nov. 22, 1957, age 54, in Worcester, Mass. See WWAA 1956.

THOMPSON, FREDERICK—Painter; d. June 26, 1956, age 52, in Hollis, N.Y. See WWAA 1956.

THOMPSON, JULIET H.—Painter; d. Dec. 4, 1956, in New York City.

TRAPIER, PIERRE PINCKNEY ALSTON—Painter; d. Apr. 9, 1957, age 60. See WWAA 1956.

TUBBY, JOSIAH THOMAS—Painter; d. July 5, 1958, in Portland, Me. See WWAA 1956.

ULP, CLIFFORD McCORMICK—Painter; d. Jan. 22, 1957, in Rochester, N.Y., age 72. See WWAA 1956.

USHER, RUBY WALKER—Painter; d. 1957, age 68. See WWAA 1956.

VALENTINER, WILLIAM REINHOLD—Museum Director; d. Sept. 6, 1958, age 78. See WWAA 1956. 1956.

VAN DOREN, HAROLD LIVINGSTON—Designer; d. Feb. 3, 1957, in Byrn Mawr, Pa., age 61. See WWAA

WAGNER, BLANCHE COLLET—Lecturer; d. N.D. See WWAA 1956.

WALKER, LYDIA LE BARON—Designer; d. Apr. 27, 1958, age 89. See WWAA 1956.

WALL, MISS MARGARET V.—Museum Director; d. July 5, 1958, age 63, at Stony Brook, L.I., N.Y.

WALLACE, FREDERICK E.—Portrait Painter; d. May 9, 1958, in Norfolk, Va., age 65. See WWAA 1956.

WEBER, FREDERICK THEODORE—Painter; d. Jan. 1, 1956, age 73. See WWAA 1956.

WEBER, SYBILLA MITTELL—Painter; d. July 31, 1957, in New York City. See WWAA 1956.

WEINBERG, LOUIS—Sculptor; d. N.D. See WWAA 1956.

WELLS, CADY—Painter; d. N.D. in Santa Fe, N.M. See WWAA 1956.

WHARTON, CAROL FORBES (Mrs. James P.)—Miniature Painter; d. June 30, 1958, in Baltimore, Md., age 51. See WWAA 1956.

WHITTEMORE, HELEN SIMPSON—Painter; d. N.D. See WWAA 1956.

WHORF, JOHN—Painter; d. Feb. 13, 1959, age 56, in Provincetown, Mass. See WWAA 1956.

WIGGINS, MYRA ALBERT—Painter; d. Jan. 14, 1956, in Seattle, Wash., age 87. See WWAA 1956.

WILCOX, RUTH—Art Librarian; d. Jan. 12, 1958, in Cleveland, Ohio, age 69. See WWAA 1956.

WILLARD, FRANK—Cartoonist; d. Jan. 1958.

WILLETT, JACQUES—Painter; d. May 19, 1958, age 76, in New York City.

WILLIAMS, FREDERIC ALLEN—Sculptor; d. Dec. 6, 1958, in New York City, age 60. See WWAA 1956.

WILLIAMS, FREDERICK BALLARD—Painter; d. 1956, age 85. See WWAA 1956.

WILLIAMSON, ADA C.—Painter; d. Oct. 31, 1958, in Ogunquit, Me., age 75. See WWAA 1956.

WINTER, ANDREW—Painter; d. Oct. 27, 1958, in Brookline, Mass., age 66. See WWAA 1956.

WITTMACK, EDGAR FRANKLIN—Illustrator; d. Apr. 26, 1956, in New York City, age 62. See WWAA 1956.

WORTMAN, DENYS—Cartoonist; d. Sept. 20, 1958, in Vineyard Haven, Mass., age 71. See WWAA 1956.

WRIGHT, ROBERT A.—Newspaper Cartoonist; d. Aug. 13, 1958, age 58.

WUERPEL, EDMUND HENRY—Painter; d. Feb. 24, 1958, age 92. See WWAA 1956.

YOUNG, MAHONRI M.—Sculptor; d. Nov. 2, 1957, age 80, in Norwalk, Conn. See WWAA 1956.

Open Exhibitions

Open Exhibitions
National and Regional

These exhibitions are open to all artists unless otherwise noted. Asterisk(*) denotes no answer received to questionnaire.

CALIFORNIA

CALIFORNIA SOCIETY OF ETCHERS, San Francisco. Annual: prints—November. Fee $2 for non-members. Awards. *For further information write California Society of Etchers, 1814 Pacific Ave., San Francisco 9, Cal.**

CALIFORNIA WATER COLOR SOCIETY, Los Angeles. Annual: water color—November-December; jury, awards. Entry fee $10 annual dues of CWCS, $9 refunded if work not accepted. Entry due Sept. *For further information write Elsa Warner, Sec., 332 S. Serrano St., Los Angeles 5, Cal.*

NORTHERN CALIFORNIA ARTS, GRAPHIC AND DECORATIVE ARTS EXHIBITION, Sacramento, Cal. Annual: prints, drawings, sculpture, pottery, weaving, mosaic, metal work—March. Open to artists of Northern California. No fee. Jury, awards. Entry due February. *For further information write Alicia Hook, Prints Librarian, California State Library, Sacramento 9, Cal.*

OAKLAND ART MUSEUM. CALIFORNIA SCULPTORS' EXHIBITION—November. Open to artists residing in California; all media including mobiles, welded metal, ceramics, reliefs, etc. Mosaic panels not eligible. No fee; one-man jury; approx. $500 purchase awards. Entries due Oct.

BAY PRINTMAKERS' SOCIETY NATIONAL PRINT EXHIBITION. Open to artists residing in the United States—November. Original prints in any medium, except monotypes, photographs, or prints colored or retouched subsequent to printing; one-man jury, $500 purchase awards. Fee, $2 for 1 or 2 entries. Entries limited to 2 per person. Entry due Oct. 15.

CALIFORNIA PAINTERS—Annual: Jan. Open to artists residing in California—all painting media. No fee; three-man jury; approx. $1000 awards. Entry due Dec. *For further information on these three exhibitions write Oakland Art Museum, 1000 Fallon St., Oakland 7, Cal.*

SAN FRANCISCO ART ASSOCIATION. Annuals: drawings and prints—winter (December); painting and sculpture—spring. Open to all artists. No fee. Jury awards. *For further information write San Francisco Museum of Art, Civic Center, San Francisco, Cal.*

SANTA CRUZ ART LEAGUE. Annual: Oil only—March. Open to all residents of California. Fee $1 each entry, two may be submitted but only one hung if passed by jury. Jury, awards announced on entry blanks. *For further information write Gladys Howland, Exhibition Chm., 116 Market St., Santa Cruz, Cal.*

COLORADO

DENVER ART MUSEUM. Annuals: all media—June. Open to artists of Illinois, Wisconsin, and all states west of the Mississippi. Jury, purchase awards; fee $2. Artists of Metropolitan Denver—all media—November. Jury, purchase award.

OWN YOUR OWN—Annual Sales Exhibition of works of artists in the Rocky Mountain Empire. All media. (Artists not heretofore exhibited are requested to send photos or slides)—March. *For further information write Denver Art Museum, 1343 Acoma St., Denver, Colo.*

CONNECTICUT

CONNECTICUT ACADEMY OF FINE ARTS, Hartford. Annual: oil, tempera, sculpture, etchings, drypoint, lithographs, woodblocks—March-April. Open to all artists. Fee $5 for one or more, $4 for black and whites. *For further information write Louis J. Fusari, Sec., P.O. Box 204, Hartford 1, Conn.*

NEW HAVEN PAINT AND CLAY CLUB. Annual: oil, watercolor, black and white, sculpture—March. Open to all artists. Jury, awards; fee $3 for each non-member entry. Entry due February. *For further information write Mrs. Herman Levy, Sec., 29 Old Hartford Turnpike, Hamden, Conn.*

SILVERMINE GUILD OF ARTISTS, Silvermine, Norwalk, Conn. NEW ENGLAND EXHIBITION—Annual: oil, water color, casein, pastel, sculpture, ceramic sculpture—June. Jury, awards. Open to artists born in New England or resident therein for a minimum of 2 months a year. Fee $4. *For further information write Revington Arthur, Silvermine Guild of Artists, Norwalk, Conn.* NEW ENGLAND EXHIBITION OF PRINTS AND DRAWINGS—Annual: all print media except monotypes—all drawing media—March. Jury, awards; fee $2 for print or drawing, $1 for each additional print or drawing. *For further information write Revington Arthur, Silvermine Guild of Artists, Norwalk, Conn.**

DISTRICT OF COLUMBIA

CORCORAN GALLERY OF ART, Washington, D.C. ANNUAL AREA EXHIBITION. Annual: paintings, watercolor, prints, drawings, sculpture, ceramics, textiles, silver, stained glass—November-December. Open to artists and craftsmen living within 50 miles of Washington, D.C. Jury, awards; fee varies $.50 to $2. Entry due October. *For further information write Area Exhibition, Corcoran Gallery of Art, Washington 6, D.C.*

BIENNIAL EXHIBITION OF CONTEMPORARY AMERICAN PAINTING. Oil—January 17-March 8. Open to any professional painter living in the United States or its possessions. No fee. Jury, awards. Entry due November. *For further information write Biennial Secretary, Corcoran Gallery of Art, Washington 6, D.C.*

LIBRARY OF CONGRESS, PRINTS AND PHOTOGRAPHS DIVISION, Washington 25, D.C. NATIONAL EXHIBITION OF PRINTS—Annual: all fine print media—May-August. Open to print-makers of U.S.A., Canada, Cuba and Mexico. Original prints in all media, black and white or color, exclusive of monotypes, drawings, photographs or prints colored after printing. No fee. Jury, purchases for the J. & E. R. Pennell Collection. Entries due Feb. *For further information write Prints and Photographs Division, Library of Congress, Washington 25, D.C.*

MINIATURE PAINTERS, SCULPTORS & GRAVERS SOCIETY OF WASHINGTON, D.C. Annual: all media—April-May. Open to all miniature artists (International Show). Jury, awards; fee $2 for local entries; $3 for out-of-town entries plus postage for return of work. Entry due April, send to National Collection of Fine Arts, 10th and Constitution Ave., N.W., Washington 25, D.C. *For further information write Miss Eleanor Cox, Sec., 4411 Fairfax Road, Route #1, Box 98, McLean, Va.*

SOCIETY OF WASHINGTON ARTISTS, Washington, D.C. Annual: oil, sculpture—November-December. Open to artists in Washington and area. Jury, awards; fee $1 per entry. *For further information write Mrs. Joyce Field, 3362 N. Dickerson St., Arlington 7, Va.**

SOCIETY OF WASHINGTON PRINTMAKERS, D.C. Annual: all graphic media except drawing. Jury, purchase award for presentation to Library of Congress collection. Fee $1. Date not finally decided but approx. January. *For further information write Mrs. W. H. Walker, Sec. 5315 Massachusetts Ave., N.W., Washington 16, D.C.**

WASHINGTON WATERCOLOR CLUB. Annual: water color, pastel, graphic media—June. Jury, awards. Fee $2 to non-members, handling fees for out of town entrants. *For further information write Mrs. William F. Foshag, 5202 Westwood Drive, Washington 16, D.C.**

FLORIDA

SARASOTA ART ASSOCIATION NATIONAL EXHIBITION. Annual: all media—March. Open to all artists. Fee $5, non-resident membership. Jury, awards. Entry due Jan. *For further information write Pat Scott, Sarasota Art Association, Sarasota, Fla.*

GEORGIA

ATLANTA UNIVERSITY. Annual: oil, gouache, watercolor, pastel, sculpture, tempera, lithograph, wood or linoleum block, etchings, pen or pencil drawings—April. Open to Negro artists. No fee. Jury, awards. *For further information write Chairman of Art Exhibition Committee, Atlanta University, Atlanta 14, Ga.*

SOUTHEASTERN EXHIBITION, Atlanta, Ga. Annual: oil, watercolor—September-October. Open to artists living in Virginia, North and South Carolina, Florida, Alabama, Mississippi, Tennessee, Louisiana, Georgia. Fee $4 per entry; jury, awards. Entry due September. *For further information write George Rhoads, Exec. Sec., Atlanta Art Assn., 1280 Peachtree St., Northeast, Atlanta, Ga.*

ILLINOIS

ART INSTITUTE OF CHICAGO. Annual: painting, sculpture, prints, drawings—May-June. Open to artists living within 100 miles of the Chicago Loop within the state of Illinois. Jury, awards; fee none. *For further information write Frederick A. Sweet, The Art Institute of Chicago, Chicago 3, Ill.*

DECATUR ART CENTER. Annual: oil, watercolor—February-March. Open to artists within 150 miles of Decatur. No fee. Jury, awards. Entry due January. *For further information write Decatur Art Center, Decatur, Ill.*

INDIANA

JOHN HERRON ART INSTITUTE, Indianapolis. Annual: oil, watercolor, sculpture—May. Open to artists of Indiana and former residents. Jury (for out-of-state artists), awards; fee $3. Entry due April. *For further information write John Herron Art Institute, 110 East 16th St., Indianapolis 2, Ind.*

HOOSIER SALON, Indianapolis. Annual: all media—January-February. Open to Indiana artists, native or by residence in the state for one year minimum. Fee $7.50; jury, awards $4,000—$5,000. Entry due January. *For further information write Mrs. Leonidas F. Smith, Exec. Chm., Hoosier Salon Patrons Assn., 610 State Life Bldg., Indianapolis 4, Ind.*

MICHIANA LOCAL ART EXHIBITION, South Bend, Ind. Biennial: oil, watercolor, drawings, prints—March. Open to artists within 100 miles radius. Jury, awards; fee $2 (limited to 2 entries). Entry due February.

REGIONAL CERAMICS EXHIBITION. Annual: ceramics, ceramic sculpture, enamels—May. Open to artists of Michigan and Indiana. Jury, awards; fee $2. Entry due April-May. *For further information on these two exhibitions, write Lorraine Paluzzi, 620 W. Washington St., South Bend 16, Ind.*

IOWA

SIOUX CITY ART CENTER. Annual: (The May Show) oil only—May. One-man jury, awards; no fee. Open to residents of Iowa, Nebraska, Minnesota, South Dakota. *For further information write Director, Sioux City Art Center, Commerce Bldg., Sioux City, Iowa.**

KANSAS

WICHITA ART ASSOCIATION. Annual: Graphic & Drawing Exhibition—January. Open to all American artists. Block prints, wood engravings, original drawings, lithographs, etchings, aquatints, mezzotints, silk screen prints, either black and white or in color. Drawings in any media. Jury, purchase awards; fee $1. Entry due December.

NATIONAL DECORATIVE ARTS — CERAMIC EXHIBITION. Annual:—April-May. Open to American craftsmen. Textiles, silversmithing, jewelry, metal, ceramic or wood sculpture, garden sculpture, enamel, mosaic, glass. Jury, awards; fee $3. Entry due February. *For further information on these two. exhibitions, write Mrs. Maude G. Schollenberger, Pres., 401 N. Belmont Ave., Wichita, Kans.*

LOUISIANA

NEW ORLEANS ART ASSOCIATION. Annual: oil, water color, sculpture, prints, drawings, crafts—March. Open to members. Jury, awards. *For further information write Exhibition, Delgado Museum of Art, City Park, Lelong Ave., New Orleans 19, La.**

MAINE

OGUNQUIT ART ASSOCIATION. Annual: all media—July-August. Open to members. Jury (for new members). Fee, annual membership $15. Entry due June. *For further information write Ogunquit Art Association, Ogunquit, Maine.*

PORTLAND SOCIETY OF ART. Annual: oil, water color, pastels—March. Jury. Fee $3. *For further information write Portland Society of Art, 111 High St., Portland, Me.**

MARYLAND

BALTIMORE MUSEUM OF ART. MARYLAND REGIONAL EXHIBITION—Feb. Open to artists of Maryland, Delaware, District of Columbia; media—painting, sculpture, graphic arts; jury, awards. Fee $1 per entry, due Jan. *For further information write Mr. Allan MacDonald, Ass't. Dir., Baltimore Museum of Art, Baltimore 18, Md.*

WASHINGTON COUNTY MUSEUM OF FINE ARTS, Hagerstown. CUMBERLAND VALLEY ARTISTS. Annual: oil tempera, gouache, watercolor, sculpture, graphics—April. Open to artists resident or former residents of Cumberland Valley area. No fee; jury, awards. Entry due March.

CUMBERLAND VALLEY PHOTOGRAPHIC SALON. Annual: 16 x 20 inches, mounted black and white or colored prints; 35mm color slides—November. Jury, awards (3 each class). Open to residents and former residents. Entry due October. *For further information write Washington County Museum of Fine Arts, Box 423, Hagerstown, Md.*

MASSACHUSETTS

SPRINGFIELD ART LEAGUE. Annual: oil, watercolor, casein, pastel, gouache, sculpture, prints. (Members Fall Show; Annual Jury Show). Open to members. Jury, awards; fee $4 (students $2). *For further information write Harriet Richard, 109 Caseland St., Springfield, Mass.*

MINNESOTA

WALKER ART CENTER, Minneapolis. Biennial: painting, graphics, sculpture—Spring of alternate years, next in 1960. Open to artists of Minnesota, Wisconsin, Iowa, Nebraska, North and South Dakota, Ontario, Manitoba and Saskatchewan, Canada. No fee; jury and awards. *For further information write Biennial of Painting, Prints & Sculpture, Walker Art Center, 1710 Lyndale South, Minneapolis 3, Minn.*

NEBRASKA

JOSLYN ART MUSEUM, Omaha. MIDWEST DESIGNER-CRAFTSMEN. Textiles, ceramics (not to include ceramic sculpture), enamel, metal work (including silversmithing and jewelry). Open to Designer-Craftsmen of the Mississippi basin. Jury, awards; fee $3. *For further information write Joslyn Art Museum, 2218 Dodge St., Omaha, Neb.*

NEW JERSEY

MONTCLAIR ART MUSEUM, NEW JERSEY STATE EXHIBITION. Annual: oil, watercolor, pastel, prints, drawing, sculpture—November. Open to artists now living in New Jersey, or who were born in the state. Jury, awards. Entry due October; fee, $1 per entry insurance and handling charge. *For further information write Kathryn E. Gamble, Director, Montclair Art Museum, South Mountain & Bloomfield Aves., Montclair, N.J.*

NEW JERSEY WATERCOLOR SOCIETY. Annual: watercolor, casein, tempera, pastel—October. Open to all present or former residents of New Jersey. Fee $3 for non-members for 1 or 2 entries. 3-man jury, awards. *For further information write Arthur Barbour, Sec., 116 Park Ave., Paterson, N.J.*

PAINTERS AND SCULPTORS SOCIETY OF NEW JERSEY, Jersey City. Annual: oil, watercolor, casein, pastels, graphics, sculpture—March. Open to all artists of U.S. and Canada. Jury, awards (cash and medals); fee $5. ($2 refunded if not accepted). Entry due February at Jersey City Museum. *For further information write Frances Hulmes, Sec., 15 Park Ave., Rutherford, N.J.*

NEW MEXICO

MUSEUM OF NEW MEXICO, Santa Fe. Annual: all media in painting, sculpture. Open to New Mexico artists—June. Jury, awards. 30 works selected for traveling exhibition. *For further information write Dorothy Morang, Cur., Traveling Exhibitions, Museum of New Mexico, Santa Fe, N.M.**

THE FIESTA SHOW: annual: all media in painting, printmaking and sculpture—August. Open to painters, sculptors, graphic artists of New Mexico. *For further information write Dorothy Morang, Cur., Traveling Exhibitions, Museum of New Mexico, Santa Fe, N.M.**

GRAPHIC ARTS IN NEW MEXICO. Annual: drawings, prints, photographs—January. Open to graphic artists and photographers of New Mexico. Jury, awards; works selected for traveling exhibition. *For further information write Dorothy Morang, Cur., Traveling Exhibitions, Museum of New Mexico, Santa Fe, N.M.**

NEW YORK

ALLIED ARTISTS OF AMERICA, New York City. Annual: oil, watercolor, gouache, pastel, sculpture—October. Jury, awards; fee $4 (no refunds). Entry due early October. For further information write *Secretary, Allied Artists of America, c/o National Academy of Design, 1083 Fifth Ave., New York 28, N.Y.*

AMERICAN WATERCOLOR SOCIETY, New York City. Annual: watercolor, pastel, casein—April. Jury, awards; fee $5. Entry due March. Open to all artists. *For further information write Cyril A. Lewis, Cor. Sec., 175 Fifth Ave., New York 10, N.Y.*

ART DIRECTORS CLUB, New York City. Annual Exhibition of Advertising and Editorial Art and Design. Open to advertising or editorial material. Fee $1 per proof, $5 each TV film. March-April. Entries due December; jury, medals and certificates. *For further information write The Art Directors Club, 115 East 40th St., New York 16, N.Y.*

ARTISTS OF THE UPPER HUDSON, Albany, N.Y. Annual: watercolor, oil, sculpture, pastel—April-May. Open to all artists living within 100 miles of Albany. Jury, purchase prize plus cash awards; fee $1 for maximum of 2 entries in any one medium. Entry due April. *For further information write Miss Janet R. MacFarlane, Dir., Albany Institute of History & Art, Albany, N.Y.*

AUDUBON ARTISTS, New York City. Annual: oil, watercolor, graphics, sculpture—January-February. Open to all artists. Jury, awards ($3,000 and medals); fee $5 for non-members. Entry due December. *For further information write Miss Margery Ryerson, Cor. Sec., 1083 Fifth Ave., New York 28, N.Y.*

BRONX ARTISTS GUILD, New York City. Annual: all media—April. Jury. Fee $1 per entry, limit 2. *For further information write Mrs. Edna Mead, Sec., Bronx Artists Guild, 3060 Decatur Ave., Bronx 67, N.Y.**

EMILY LOWE AWARD, New York City. Annual: oil, watercolors, gouache, casein—October. Open to artists 25 years of age or over. No fee; jury, prizes. Entry due September. *For further information write Ward Eggleston, Dir., Eggleston Galleries, 969 Madison Ave., New York 21, N.Y.*

KNICKERBOCKER ARTISTS, New York City. Annual: oil, casein, watercolor, graphics, sculpture—March-April. Open to all artists. Fee $5; jury, awards. Entry due March. *For further information write Elsie Ject-Key, 49 East 9th St., New York 3, N.Y.*

NATIONAL ACADEMY OF DESIGN, New York City. Annual: oil, sculpture, members and non-members; watercolor, graphics, members only—February-March. Jury for oil and sculpture, non-members, awards; no fee. Entry due February. *For further information write National Academy of Design, 1083 Fifth Ave., New York 28, N.Y.*

NATIONAL ASSOCIATION OF WOMEN ARTISTS, New York City. Annual: Graphics, oils, watercolors, miniature, sculpture—April-May. Jury, awards; no fee. Entry due April. *For further information write National Association of Women Artists, 236 East 60th St., New York 22, N.Y.*

NATIONAL SERIGRAPH SOCIETY, New York City. Annual: Original serigraphs (no photographic stencils)—March. Open to all artists. No fee; jury for non-members; 5 or more cash awards. *For further information write Herdis Bull Teilman, Registrar, National Serigraph Society, 38 West 57th St., New York 19, N.Y.*

SOCIETY OF AMERICAN GRAPHIC ARTISTS, New York City. Annual: Prints in Intaglio, Relief, and Planographic media; Miniature Prints—February. Jury, awards. *For further information write Cor. Sec., Society of American Graphic Artists, 1083 Fifth Ave., New York 28, N.Y.**

SYRACUSE MUSEUM OF FINE ARTS, Syracuse, N.Y. Biennial: Ceramics—November-December. Open to potters, sculptors, enamelists, architects. Jury (6 regional, 1 final), awards, and also 1 for architectural sculpture. Fee $3. *For further information write Syracuse Museum of Fine Arts, Syracuse, N.Y.**

HUDSON RIVER MUSEUM, Yonkers, N.Y. MILE OF PAINTING. All media—May. Open to all artists. Fee $1. Entry due May. *For further information write Hudson River Museum, Trevor Park, Yonkers, N.Y.*

OHIO

BUTLER INSTITUTE OF AMERICAN ART, Youngstown. Annual. (Midyear Show): oil, watercolor—June-September. Open to artists of the United States. Jury, awards (over $5,000.); fee $2. Entry due May. *For further information write Secretary, The Butler Institute of American Art, Youngstown 2, Ohio.*

CANTON ART INSTITUTE. Annual: oil, watercolor, prints—September. Open to artists of Northeast Ohio. Jury, awards; fee $1 per media. *For further information write Canton Art Institute, 1717 Market Ave., No., Canton, Ohio.**

OHIO VALLEY OIL AND WATER COLOR EXHIBITION, Athens, Ohio. Annual: oil, watercolor—July. Open to artists of Ohio, Kentucky, Pennsylvania, West Virginia, Indiana and Illinois. Fee $2.50. Jury, awards. Entry due May-June. *For further information write Dr. Frederick D. Leach, School of Painting & Allied Arts, Ohio University, Athens, Ohio.*

OHIO WATERCOLOR SOCIETY. Annual Circuit: Watercolor, gouache, pastel. Open to Ohio residents; also native Ohioians out of state. Jury, awards. Fee $3.50. *For further information write Miss Margaret Riggs Mellen, Pres., P.O. Box 3513, Cleveland Heights 18, Ohio.**

PENNSYLVANIA

AMERICAN COLOR PRINT SOCIETY, Philadelphia, Pa. Annual: all print media in color—March. Open to all printmakers working in color. Fee $2.50; jury, awards. Entry due February. *For further information write Katharine H. McCormick, Treas., 300 W. Upsal St., Philadelphia 19, Pa.*

PENNSYLVANIA ACADEMY OF THE FINE ARTS, Philadelphia. Annual: oil, sculpture—January-April. Open to American artists. No fee. Jury, awards. *For further information write The Pennsylvania Academy of Fine Arts, Broad & Cherry Sts., Philadelphia 2, Pa.*

PRINT CLUB, Philadelphia, Pa. Annual: lithography—January. Open to all artists. Lithographs made in 1959. Jury, awards; fee $1.75 non-members. Entry due December.

WOOD ENGRAVING, BLOCK PRINTS. Annual: wood engraving, woodcuts, lino. prints—February. Open to all artists. Jury, awards; fee $1.75 non-members. Entry due January.

ETCHING EXHIBITION. Annual: prints. Open to all artists. Jury, awards; fee $1.75 non-members. Entry due March. *For further information on these three exhibitions, write Bertha von Moschzisker, Dir., The Print Club, 1614 Latimer St., Philadelphia 3, Pa.*

RHODE ISLAND

ART ASSOCIATION OF NEWPORT. Annual: oil, watercolor, prints, small sculpture—July. Open to all American artists. Jury, awards; fee $2. Entry due June. *For further information write Mrs. Paul C. Rogers, Art Association of Newport, 76 Bellevue Ave., Newport, R.I.*

PROVIDENCE ART CLUB. Annual: oil, watercolor, drawing, etching, lithography, prints, sculpture—January. Open to all artists; jury. Entry due January. *For further information write Mrs. Fowler Wooley, Providence Art Club, 11 Thomas St., Providence 3, R.I.*

TENNESSEE

BROOKS MEMORIAL ART GALLERY, Memphis, Tenn. Biennial: oil, watercolor, prints, sculpture—December. Open to artists born in or residents of Arkansas, Mississippi, Tennessee. Jury, awards. *For further information write Memphis Biennial Assn., Brooks Memorial Art Gallery, Memphis 12, Tenn.**

TEXAS

TEXAS ANNUAL OF PAINTING AND SCULPTURE. Annual: October-November, then on circuit. Open to Texas artists. No fee; jury, awards. Entry due September.

DALLAS COUNTY PAINTING, SCULPTURE, DRAWING. Annual: May-June; oil, pastel, sculpture, drawing. Open to artists of Dallas County. Jury, awards; no fee. Entry due April.

SOUTHWESTERN EXHIBITION, Dallas. Annual: prints, drawings—January-February. Open to residents of Texas, Oklahoma, Louisiana, New Mexico, Colorado, Arizona. Jury, awards. Entry due December. No fee.

TEXAS CRAFTS EXHIBITION. Annual: textile, ceramics, metal, wood, bookbinding—November-December. Open to Texas craftsmen; jury, awards. Fee $3. Entry due November. *For further information on these four exhibitions write Charlotte Stephens, Dallas Museum of Fine Arts, Dallas 26, Texas.*

VERMONT

MID-VERMONT ARTISTS, Rutland, Vt. Annual: summer exhibition: oil, watercolor, small sculpture, black and white—June. Open to artists living in Vermont or within 50 miles of Rutland, Vt. Fee $2. *For further information write Katherine King Johnson, 40 Piedmont Parkway, Rutland, Vt.**

VIRGINIA

INTERMONT REGIONAL, Bristol, Va. Annual: oils, watercolors, drawings, graphics—May. Jury, awards. Open to artists of Virginia, West Virginia, Kentucky, Tennessee, Ohio, North Carolina, Georgia, Alabama, and District of Columbia. Fee $2 for oils, $1 for other media. Entry due April. *For further information write Prof. C. Ernest Cooke, Virginia Intermont College, Bristol, Va.*

VIRGINIA MUSEUM OF FINE ARTS, Richmond. Biennial: painting, sculpture, graphic arts, crafts—March. Open to artists living in or born in Virginia or having residence in Virginia for 4 years. Jury, awards (purchase). Fee $3 for three entries. *For further information write Mrs. Muriel B. Christison, Assoc. Dir., Gallery Division, Virginia Museum of Fine Arts, Richmond, Va.**

WEST VIRGINIA

PARKERSBURG FINE ARTS CENTER. Annual: oil, watercolor—April. Open to artists now or formerly residing in West Virginia, Ohio, Virginia, Pennsylvania, Kentucky, District of Columbia. *Address: 317 Ninth St., Parkersburg, W. Va.**

WISCONSIN

WISCONSIN PAINTERS AND SCULPTORS. Annual: oil, watercolor, pastel, sculpture, etc. (no prints or drawings) May-June. Open to all artists of Wisconsin 18 years of age and over. Fee $1.50; no fee for members or members of Milwaukee Art Center; jury, awards.

WISCONSIN DESIGNER-CRAFTSMEN. Annual: Open to all craftsmen of Wisconsin—November. Jury, award. Fee $1.50 to non-members of Milwaukee Art Center and Wisconsin Designer-Craftsmen. Entry due Sept. *For further information on these two exhibitions write Mrs. Laurence V. Donovan, Admin. Ass't., Milwaukee Art Center, 750 N. Lincoln Memorial Drive, Milwaukee 2, Wis.*

WISCONSIN SALON OF ART. Annual: oil, tempera, watercolor, pastel, graphics, sculpture—November-December. No fee; jury, awards. Open to Wisconsin artists with 3 years residence in Wisconsin including past year; ten years residence in Wisconsin if now living outside the state; currently a student or faculty member of a Wisconsin art school. Entry due November. *For further information write Elliott Starks, Art Director, Wisconsin Union, Madison 10, Wis.*

Index
of Advertisers